*ANDERSON'S*

# 2011-2 OHIO CRIMINAL LAW HANDBOOK

**Containing Title 29, the Ohio Criminal Code, as amended by the Ohio General Assembly and filed with the Secretary of State through October 1, 2011**

**Also including:**

**Miscellaneous Related Statutes through October 1, 2011**
**United States Constitution**
**Ohio Constitution (Selected Provisions)**
**Table of Penalties and Index of Offenses**
**Elements of Offenses**
**Time Table in Criminal Cases**
**Ohio Criminal, Evidence, Juvenile and Traffic Rules through July 1, 2011**
**Selected Rules of Superintendence for the Courts of Ohio**

LexisNexis®

## QUESTIONS ABOUT THIS PUBLICATION?

For CUSTOMER SERVICE ASSISTANCE concerning replacement pages, shipments, billing, reprint permission, or other matters,

please call Customer Service Department at 800-833-9844
email *customer.support@lexisnexis.com*
or visit our interactive customer service website at *www.lexisnexis.com/printcdsc*

For EDITORIAL **content questions** concerning this publication,

please email: *LEpublications@lexisnexis.com*

For **information on other LEXISNEXIS MATTHEW BENDER publications,**

please call us at 877-461-8801
or visit our online bookstore at *www.lexisnexis.com/bookstore*

---

ISBN: 978-1-4224-9004-4



® LexisNexis®

Matthew Bender & Company, Inc.
Editorial Offices
701 E. Water Street
Charlottesville, VA 22902
800-446-3410
www.lexisnexis.com

Product Number 3302127

(Pub. 33020)

# TABLE OF CONTENTS



# ABBREVIATIONS

App. R. — Ohio Rules of Appellate Procedure
Civ. R. — Ohio Rules of Civil Procedure
Crim. R. — Ohio Rules of Criminal Procedure
Evid. R. — Ohio Rules of Evidence
Juv. R. — Ohio Rules of Juvenile Procedure
OCP&P — Ohio Criminal Practice & Procedure
Sup. R. — Rules of Superintendence of the Supreme Court of Ohio
Traf. R. — Ohio Traffic Rules

# PREFACE

This book collects in a compact format statutes, rules, and special features for the use of judges, attorneys, law enforcement officers, students, and others involved in the Ohio criminal justice process. It is designed to be a basic guide to Ohio criminal law. More detailed treatment of criminal law issues can be found in Ohio Criminal Practice and Procedure.

# SECTIONS AFFECTED BY 2011 LEGISLATION, FILES 1 THROUGH 47

| Section | Action | Effective Date | File | Bill No. | Sec. No. |
|---|---|---|---|---|---|
| 1.01 | Amended | 6-29-11 | 9 | HB 9 | 1 |
| 1.60 | Amended | 2-18-11 | 1 | HB 1 | 1 |
| 109.33 | Amended | 7-1-11 | 10 | SB 5 | 1 |
| 109.36 | Amended | 9-29-11 | 28 | HB 153 | 101.01 |
| 109.42 | Amended | 9-30-11 | 29 | HB 86 | 1 |
| 109.43 | Amended | 9-29-11 | 28 | HB 153 | 101.01 |
| 109.57 | Amended | 5-20-11 | 19 | HB 93 | 1 |
| 109.57 | Amended | 9-29-11 | 28 | HB 153 | 101.01 |
| 109.572 | Amended | 7-1-11 | 28 | HB 153 | 101.01 |
| 109.64 | Amended | 9-29-11 | 28 | HB 153 | 101.01 |
| 109.71 | Amended | 9-29-11 | 28 | HB 153 | 101.01 |
| 109.801 | Amended | 9-29-11 | 28 | HB 153 | 101.01 |
| 109.90 | Enacted | 5-20-11 | 19 | HB 93 | 1 |
| 109.91 | Amended | 6-30-11 | 39 | SB 171 | 1 |
| 120.40 | Amended | 9-29-11 | 28 | HB 153 | 101.01 |
| 124.34 | Amended | 7-1-11 | 10 | SB 5 | 1 |
| 124.34 | Amended | 9-29-11 | 28 | HB 153 | 101.01 |
| 149.43 | Amended | 9-29-11 | 28 | HB 153 | 101.01 |
| 149.43 | Amended | 10-17-11 | 43 | HB 64 | 1 |
| 306.35 | Amended | 6-30-11 | 28 | HB 153 | 101.01 |
| 309.09 | Amended | 9-30-11 | 33 | SB 120 | 1 |
| 309.18 | Amended | 9-30-11 | 29 | HB 86 | 1 |
| 311.29 | Amended | 9-29-11 | 28 | HB 153 | 101.01 |
| 311.31 | Amended | 9-29-11 | 28 | HB 153 | 101.01 |
| 313.212 | Enacted | 5-20-11 | 19 | HB 93 | 1 |
| 341.12 | Amended | 9-30-11 | 29 | HB 86 | 1 |
| 341.192 | Amended | 9-29-11 | 28 | HB 153 | 101.01 |
| 503.41 | Amended | 9-29-11 | 28 | HB 153 | 101.01 |
| 505.105 | Amended | 9-29-11 | 28 | HB 153 | 101.01 |
| 505.106 | Amended | 9-29-11 | 28 | HB 153 | 101.01 |
| 505.107 | Amended | 9-29-11 | 28 | HB 153 | 101.01 |
| 505.108 | Amended | 9-29-11 | 28 | HB 153 | 101.01 |
| 505.109 | Amended | 9-29-11 | 28 | HB 153 | 101.01 |
| 505.17 | Amended | 9-29-11 | 28 | HB 153 | 101.01 |
| 505.373 | Amended | 6-30-11 | 28 | HB 153 | 101.01 |
| 505.48 | Amended | 9-29-11 | 28 | HB 153 | 101.01 |
| 505.482 | Amended | 9-29-11 | 28 | HB 153 | 101.01 |
| 505.483 | Enacted | 9-29-11 | 28 | HB 153 | 101.01 |
| 505.484 | Enacted | 9-29-11 | 28 | HB 153 | 101.01 |
| 505.49 | Amended | 7-1-11 | 10 | SB 5 | 1 |
| 505.49 | Amended | 9-29-11 | 28 | HB 153 | 101.01 |
| 505.491 | Amended | 9-29-11 | 28 | HB 153 | 101.01 |
| 505.492 | Amended | 9-29-11 | 28 | HB 153 | 101.01 |
| 505.493 | Amended | 9-29-11 | 28 | HB 153 | 101.01 |
| 505.494 | Amended | 9-29-11 | 28 | HB 153 | 101.01 |
| 505.495 | Amended | 9-29-11 | 28 | HB 153 | 101.01 |
| 505.50 | Amended | 9-29-11 | 28 | HB 153 | 101.01 |
| 505.51 | Amended | 9-29-11 | 28 | HB 153 | 101.01 |
| 505.511 | Amended | 9-29-11 | 28 | HB 153 | 101.01 |
| 505.52 | Amended | 9-29-11 | 28 | HB 153 | 101.01 |
| 505.53 | Amended | 9-29-11 | 28 | HB 153 | 101.01 |
| 505.54 | Amended | 9-29-11 | 28 | HB 153 | 101.01 |
| 505.541 | Amended | 9-29-11 | 28 | HB 153 | 101.01 |

| Section | Action | Effective Date | File | Bill No. | Sec. No. |
|---|---|---|---|---|---|
| 505.55 | Amended | 9-29-11 | 28 | HB 153 | 101.01 |
| 505.551 | Enacted | 9-29-11 | 28 | HB 153 | 101.01 |
| 505.73 | Amended | 9-29-11 | 28 | HB 153 | 101.01 |
| 509.15 | Amended | 9-29-11 | 28 | HB 153 | 101.01 |
| 737.022 | Amended | 9-29-11 | 28 | HB 153 | 101.01 |
| 737.04 | Amended | 9-29-11 | 28 | HB 153 | 101.01 |
| 737.041 | Amended | 9-29-11 | 28 | HB 153 | 101.01 |
| 737.32 | Amended | 9-29-11 | 28 | HB 153 | 101.01 |
| 951.01 | Repealed | 9-23-11 | 26 | HB 22 | 2 |
| 951.02 | Amended | 9-23-11 | 26 | HB 22 | 1 |
| 951.99 | Amended | 9-23-11 | 26 | HB 22 | 1 |
| 955.012 | Amended | 9-29-11 | 28 | HB 153 | 101.01 |
| 959.14 | Amended | 10-17-11 | 42 | HB 229 | 1 |
| 1333.99 | Amended | 9-30-11 | 29 | HB 86 | 1 |
| 1547.01 | Amended | 9-29-11 | 28 | HB 153 | 101.01 |
| 2151.011 | Amended | 9-29-11 | 28 | HB 153 | 101.01 |
| 2151.23 | Amended | 9-30-11 | 29 | HB 86 | 1 |
| 2151.282 | Repealed | 6-30-11 | 39 | SB 171 | 2 |
| 2151.312 | Amended | 6-30-11 | 38 | SB 122 | 1 |
| 2151.354 | Amended | 6-30-11 | 38 | SB 122 | 1 |
| 2151.3515 | Amended | 9-29-11 | 28 | HB 153 | 101.01 |
| 2151.412 | Amended | 9-29-11 | 28 | HB 153 | 101.01 |
| 2151.421 | Amended | 9-29-11 | 28 | HB 153 | 101.01 |
| 2151.424 | Amended | 9-29-11 | 28 | HB 153 | 101.01 |
| 2151.429 | Enacted | 9-29-11 | 28 | HB 153 | 101.01 |
| 2151.541 | Amended | 9-29-11 | 28 | HB 153 | 101.01 |
| 2151.56 | Repealed and Reenacted | 6-30-11 | 38 | SB 122 | 1 |
| 2151.57 | Repealed and Reenacted | 6-30-11 | 38 | SB 122 | 1 |
| 2151.58 | Repealed and Reenacted | 6-30-11 | 38 | SB 122 | 1 |
| 2151.59 | Repealed and Reenacted | 6-30-11 | 38 | SB 122 | 1 |
| 2151.60 | Repealed | 6-30-11 | 38 | SB 122 | 2 |
| 2151.61 | Repealed | 6-30-11 | 38 | SB 122 | 2 |
| 2152.02 | Amended | 9-30-11 | 29 | HB 86 | 1 |
| 2152.021 | Amended | 9-30-11 | 29 | HB 86 | 1 |
| 2152.12 | Amended | 9-30-11 | 29 | HB 86 | 1 |
| 2152.121 | Enacted | 9-30-11 | 29 | HB 86 | 1 |
| 2152.13 | Amended | 9-30-11 | 29 | HB 86 | 1 |
| 2152.14 | Amended | 9-30-11 | 29 | HB 86 | 1 |
| 2152.17 | Amended | 9-30-11 | 29 | HB 86 | 1 |
| 2152.22 | Amended | 9-30-11 | 29 | HB 86 | 1 |
| 2152.26 | Amended | 6-30-11 | 38 | SB 122 | 1 |
| 2152.51 | Enacted | 9-30-11 | 29 | HB 86 | 1 |
| 2152.52 | Enacted | 9-30-11 | 29 | HB 86 | 1 |
| 2152.53 | Enacted | 9-30-11 | 29 | HB 86 | 1 |
| 2152.54 | Enacted | 9-30-11 | 29 | HB 86 | 1 |
| 2152.55 | Enacted | 9-30-11 | 29 | HB 86 | 1 |
| 2152.56 | Enacted | 9-30-11 | 29 | HB 86 | 1 |
| 2152.57 | Enacted | 9-30-11 | 29 | HB 86 | 1 |
| 2152.58 | Enacted | 9-30-11 | 29 | HB 86 | 1 |
| 2152.59 | Enacted | 9-30-11 | 29 | HB 86 | 1 |
| 2152.72 | Amended | 9-29-11 | 28 | HB 153 | 101.01 |
| 2301.27 | Amended | 9-30-11 | 29 | HB 86 | 1 |
| 2301.271 | Enacted | 9-30-11 | 29 | HB 86 | 1 |
| 2301.30 | Amended | 9-30-11 | 29 | HB 86 | 1 |
| 2307.52 | Amended | 10-20-11 | 45 | HB 78 | 1 |

| Section | Action | Effective Date | File | Bill No. | Sec. No. |
|---|---|---|---|---|---|
| 2317.02 | Amended | 7-1-11 | 28 | HB 153 | 101.01 |
| 2317.422 | Amended | 7-1-11 | 28 | HB 153 | 101.01 |
| 2335.061 | Enacted | 9-29-11 | 28 | HB 153 | 101.01 |
| 2901.01 | Amended | 9-29-11 | 28 | HB 153 | 101.01 |
| 2901.02 | Amended | 9-23-11 | 25 | HB 5 | 1 |
| 2901.08 | Amended | 9-30-11 | 29 | HB 86 | 1 |
| 2903.01 | Amended | 9-30-11 | 29 | HB 86 | 1 |
| 2903.11 | Amended | 9-30-11 | 29 | HB 86 | 1 |
| 2903.12 | Amended | 9-30-11 | 29 | HB 86 | 1 |
| 2903.13 | Amended | 9-30-11 | 29 | HB 86 | 1 |
| 2903.33 | Amended | 7-1-11 | 28 | HB 153 | 101.01 |
| 2905.01 | Amended | 9-30-11 | 29 | HB 86 | 1 |
| 2905.02 | Amended | 9-30-11 | 29 | HB 86 | 1 |
| 2907.21 | Amended | 9-30-11 | 29 | HB 86 | 1 |
| 2907.22 | Amended | 9-30-11 | 29 | HB 86 | 1 |
| 2907.323 | Amended | 9-30-11 | 29 | HB 86 | 1 |
| 2909.03 | Amended | 9-30-11 | 29 | HB 86 | 1 |
| 2909.05 | Amended | 9-30-11 | 29 | HB 86 | 1 |
| 2909.11 | Amended | 9-30-11 | 29 | HB 86 | 1 |
| 2911.12 | Amended | 9-30-11 | 29 | HB 86 | 1 |
| 2913.01 | Amended | 9-30-11 | 29 | HB 86 | 1 |
| 2913.02 | Amended | 9-30-11 | 29 | HB 86 | 1 |
| 2913.03 | Amended | 9-30-11 | 29 | HB 86 | 1 |
| 2913.04 | Amended | 9-30-11 | 29 | HB 86 | 1 |
| 2913.11 | Amended | 9-30-11 | 29 | HB 86 | 1 |
| 2913.21 | Amended | 9-30-11 | 29 | HB 86 | 1 |
| 2913.31 | Amended | 9-30-11 | 29 | HB 86 | 1 |
| 2913.32 | Amended | 9-30-11 | 29 | HB 86 | 1 |
| 2913.34 | Amended | 9-30-11 | 29 | HB 86 | 1 |
| 2913.40 | Amended | 9-30-11 | 29 | HB 86 | 1 |
| 2913.401 | Enacted | 9-30-11 | 29 | HB 86 | 1 |
| 2913.42 | Amended | 9-30-11 | 29 | HB 86 | 1 |
| 2913.421 | Amended | 9-30-11 | 29 | HB 86 | 1 |
| 2913.43 | Amended | 9-30-11 | 29 | HB 86 | 1 |
| 2913.45 | Amended | 9-30-11 | 29 | HB 86 | 1 |
| 2913.46 | Amended | 9-30-11 | 29 | HB 86 | 1 |
| 2913.47 | Amended | 9-30-11 | 29 | HB 86 | 1 |
| 2913.48 | Amended | 9-30-11 | 29 | HB 86 | 1 |
| 2913.49 | Amended | 9-30-11 | 29 | HB 86 | 1 |
| 2913.51 | Amended | 9-30-11 | 29 | HB 86 | 1 |
| 2913.61 | Amended | 9-30-11 | 29 | HB 86 | 1 |
| 2915.01 | Amended | 10-17-11 | 44 | HB 277 | 1 |
| 2915.05 | Amended | 9-30-11 | 29 | HB 86 | 1 |
| 2917.21 | Amended | 9-30-11 | 29 | HB 86 | 1 |
| 2917.31 | Amended | 9-30-11 | 29 | HB 86 | 1 |
| 2917.32 | Amended | 9-30-11 | 29 | HB 86 | 1 |
| 2917.40 | Amended | 9-29-11 | 28 | HB 153 | 101.01 |
| 2919.16 | Amended | 10-20-11 | 45 | HB 78 | 1 |
| 2919.17 | Enacted | 10-20-11 | 45 | HB 78 | 1 |
| 2919.17 | Repealed | 10-20-11 | 45 | HB 78 | 2 |
| 2919.171 | Enacted | 10-20-11 | 45 | HB 78 | 1 |
| 2919.18 | Enacted | 10-20-11 | 45 | HB 78 | 1 |
| 2919.18 | Repealed | 10-20-11 | 45 | HB 78 | 2 |
| 2919.21 | Amended | 9-30-11 | 29 | HB 86 | 1 |
| 2919.22 | Amended | 9-30-11 | 29 | HB 86 | 1 |
| 2919.271 | Amended | 9-29-11 | 28 | HB 153 | 101.01 |
| 2921.01 | Amended | 2-18-11 | 1 | HB 1 | 1 |
| 2921.13 | Amended | 9-30-11 | 29 | HB 86 | 1 |
| 2921.34 | Amended | 9-30-11 | 29 | HB 86 | 1 |

| Section | Action | Effective Date | File | Bill No. | Sec. No. |
|---|---|---|---|---|---|
| 2921.41 | Amended | 9-30-11 | 29 | HB 86 | 1 |
| 2923.01 | Amended | 9-30-11 | 29 | HB 86 | 1 |
| 2923.121 | Amended | 9-30-11 | 34 | SB 17 | 1 |
| 2923.125 | Amended | 9-30-11 | 34 | SB 17 | 1 |
| 2923.128 | Amended | 9-30-11 | 34 | SB 17 | 1 |
| 2923.13 | Amended | 9-30-11 | 30 | HB 54 | 1 |
| 2923.14 | Amended | 9-30-11 | 30 | HB 54 | 1 |
| 2923.16 | Amended | 9-30-11 | 34 | SB 17 | 1 |
| 2923.17 | Amended | 6-29-11 | 9 | HB 9 | 1 |
| 2923.31 | Amended | 9-30-11 | 29 | HB 86 | 1 |
| 2923.32 | Amended | 9-30-11 | 29 | HB 86 | 1 |
| 2925.01 | Amended | 9-30-11 | 29 | HB 86 | 1 |
| 2925.02 | Amended | 9-30-11 | 29 | HB 86 | 1 |
| 2925.02 | Amended | 10-17-11 | 43 | HB 64 | 1 |
| 2925.03 | Amended | 9-30-11 | 29 | HB 86 | 1 |
| 2925.03 | Amended | 10-17-11 | 43 | HB 64 | 1 |
| 2925.04 | Amended | 9-30-11 | 29 | HB 86 | 1 |
| 2925.041 | Amended | 9-30-11 | 29 | HB 86 | 1 |
| 2925.05 | Amended | 9-30-11 | 29 | HB 86 | 1 |
| 2925.11 | Amended | 9-30-11 | 29 | HB 86 | 1 |
| 2925.11 | Amended | 10-17-11 | 43 | HB 64 | 1 |
| 2925.36 | Amended | 9-30-11 | 29 | HB 86 | 1 |
| 2929.01 | Amended | 9-30-11 | 29 | HB 86 | 1 |
| 2929.11 | Amended | 9-30-11 | 29 | HB 86 | 1 |
| 2929.13 | Amended | 9-30-11 | 29 | HB 86 | 1 |
| 2929.14 | Amended | 9-30-11 | 29 | HB 86 | 1 |
| 2929.143 | Enacted | 9-30-11 | 29 | HB 86 | 1 |
| 2929.15 | Amended | 9-30-11 | 29 | HB 86 | 1 |
| 2929.18 | Amended | 9-23-11 | 25 | HB 5 | 1 |
| 2929.19 | Amended | 9-30-11 | 29 | HB 86 | 1 |
| 2929.191 | Amended | 9-30-11 | 29 | HB 86 | 1 |
| 2929.192 | Amended | 7-29-11 | 16 | HB 123 | 101 |
| 2929.193 | Enacted | 7-29-11 | 16 | HB 123 | 101 |
| 2929.20 | Amended | 9-30-11 | 29 | HB 86 | 1 |
| 2929.24 | Amended | 9-23-11 | 25 | HB 5 | 1 |
| 2929.25 | Amended | 9-23-11 | 25 | HB 5 | 1 |
| 2929.26 | Amended | 9-30-11 | 29 | HB 86 | 1 |
| 2929.27 | Amended | 9-23-11 | 25 | HB 5 | 1 |
| 2929.28 | Amended | 9-23-11 | 25 | HB 5 | 1 |
| 2929.34 | Amended | 9-30-11 | 29 | HB 86 | 1 |
| 2929.41 | Amended | 9-30-11 | 29 | HB 86 | 1 |
| 2929.71 | Amended | 9-29-11 | 28 | HB 153 | 101.01 |
| 2930.12 | Amended | 9-30-11 | 29 | HB 86 | 1 |
| 2930.16 | Amended | 9-30-11 | 29 | HB 86 | 1 |
| 2930.17 | Amended | 9-30-11 | 29 | HB 86 | 1 |
| 2935.01 | Amended | 9-29-11 | 28 | HB 153 | 101.01 |
| 2935.03 | Amended | 9-29-11 | 28 | HB 153 | 101.01 |
| 2935.041 | Amended | 9-30-11 | 29 | HB 86 | 1 |
| 2937.36 | Amended | 9-30-11 | 29 | HB 86 | 1 |
| 2941.141 | Amended | 9-30-11 | 29 | HB 86 | 1 |
| 2941.142 | Amended | 9-30-11 | 29 | HB 86 | 1 |
| 2941.143 | Amended | 9-30-11 | 29 | HB 86 | 1 |
| 2941.144 | Amended | 9-30-11 | 29 | HB 86 | 1 |
| 2941.145 | Amended | 9-30-11 | 29 | HB 86 | 1 |
| 2941.146 | Amended | 9-30-11 | 29 | HB 86 | 1 |
| 2941.1411 | Amended | 9-30-11 | 29 | HB 86 | 1 |
| 2941.1412 | Amended | 9-30-11 | 29 | HB 86 | 1 |
| 2941.1414 | Amended | 9-30-11 | 29 | HB 86 | 1 |
| 2941.1415 | Amended | 9-30-11 | 29 | HB 86 | 1 |

| Section | Action | Effective Date | File | Bill No. | Sec. No. |
|---|---|---|---|---|---|
| 2941.1421 | Amended | 9-30-11 | 29 | HB 86 | 1 |
| 2941.1422 | Amended | 9-30-11 | 29 | HB 86 | 1 |
| 2941.1423 | Amended | 9-30-11 | 29 | HB 86 | 1 |
| 2945.371 | Amended | 9-29-11 | 28 | HB 153 | 101.01 |
| 2945.38 | Amended | 9-29-11 | 28 | HB 153 | 101.01 |
| 2945.39 | Amended | 9-29-11 | 28 | HB 153 | 101.01 |
| 2945.40 | Amended | 9-29-11 | 28 | HB 153 | 101.01 |
| 2945.401 | Amended | 9-29-11 | 28 | HB 153 | 101.01 |
| 2945.402 | Amended | 9-29-11 | 28 | HB 153 | 101.01 |
| 2949.14 | Amended | 9-29-11 | 28 | HB 153 | 101.01 |
| 2950.17 | Enacted | 9-30-11 | 29 | HB 86 | 1 |
| 2950.99 | Amended | 9-30-11 | 29 | HB 86 | 1 |
| 2951.02 | Amended | 9-23-11 | 25 | HB 5 | 1 |
| 2951.022 | Enacted | 9-30-11 | 29 | HB 86 | 1 |
| 2951.041 | Amended | 9-30-11 | 29 | HB 86 | 1 |
| 2951.08 | Amended | 9-30-11 | 29 | HB 86 | 1 |
| 2953.08 | Amended | 9-30-11 | 29 | HB 86 | 1 |
| 2953.321 | Amended | 9-30-11 | 34 | SB 17 | 1 |
| 2953.33 | Amended | 9-30-11 | 34 | SB 17 | 1 |
| 2953.35 | Amended | 9-30-11 | 34 | SB 17 | 1 |
| 2953.37 | Enacted | 9-30-11 | 34 | SB 17 | 1 |
| 2961.21 | Enacted | 9-30-11 | 29 | HB 86 | 1 |
| 2961.22 | Enacted | 9-30-11 | 29 | HB 86 | 1 |
| 2961.23 | Enacted | 9-30-11 | 29 | HB 86 | 1 |
| 2961.24 | Enacted | 9-30-11 | 29 | HB 86 | 1 |
| 2967.14 | Amended | 9-30-11 | 29 | HB 86 | 1 |
| 2967.19 | Enacted | 9-30-11 | 29 | HB 86 | 1 |
| 2967.193 | Amended | 9-30-11 | 29 | HB 86 | 1 |
| 2967.28 | Amended | 9-30-11 | 29 | HB 86 | 1 |
| 2971.03 | Amended | 9-30-11 | 29 | HB 86 | 1 |
| 2981.01 | Amended | 6-29-11 | 9 | HB 9 | 1 |
| 2981.07 | Amended | 9-30-11 | 29 | HB 86 | 1 |
| 2981.11 | Amended | 9-29-11 | 28 | HB 153 | 101.01 |
| 2981.12 | Amended | 9-29-11 | 28 | HB 153 | 101.01 |
| 2981.13 | Amended | 9-29-11 | 28 | HB 153 | 101.01 |
| 3113.06 | Amended | 10-1-11 | 28 | HB 153 | 101.01 |
| 3345.34 | Amended | 4-29-11 | 18 | HB 139 | 1 |
| 3599.03 | Amended | 9-30-11 | 40 | HB 194 | 1 |
| 3599.07 | Amended | 9-30-11 | 40 | HB 194 | 1 |
| 3599.17 | Amended | 9-30-11 | 40 | HB 194 | 1 |
| 3599.19 | Amended | 9-30-11 | 40 | HB 194 | 1 |
| 3599.30 | Enacted | 9-30-11 | 40 | HB 194 | 1 |
| 3599.31 | Amended | 9-30-11 | 40 | HB 194 | 1 |
| 3719.01 | Amended | 10-17-11 | 43 | HB 64 | 1 |
| 3719.013 | Enacted | 10-17-11 | 43 | HB 64 | 1 |
| 3719.031 | Enacted | 5-20-11 | 19 | HB 93 | 1 |
| 3719.08 | Amended | 5-20-11 | 19 | HB 93 | 1 |
| 3719.14 | Amended | 6-29-11 | 9 | HB 9 | 1 |
| 3719.141 | Amended | 9-29-11 | 28 | HB 153 | 101.01 |
| 3719.41 | Amended | 9-29-11 | 28 | HB 153 | 101.01 |
| 3719.41 | Amended | 10-17-11 | 43 | HB 64 | 1 |
| 3722.151 | Amended | 7-1-11 | 28 | HB 153 | 101.01 |
| 3719.99 | Amended | 9-30-11 | 29 | HB 86 | 1 |
| 3737.73 | Amended | 9-29-11 | 28 | HB 153 | 101.01 |
| 3737.88 | Amended | 9-29-11 | 28 | HB 153 | 101.01 |
| 3737.88 | Amended | 6-30-11 | 39 | SB 171 | 1 |
| 3743.64 | Amended | 9-29-11 | 28 | HB 153 | 101.01 |
| 3743.75 | Amended | 9-23-11 | 27 | HB 128 | 1 |
| 3767.29 | Amended | 6-29-11 | 9 | HB 9 | 1 |

| Section | Action | Effective Date | File | Bill No. | Sec. No. |
|---|---|---|---|---|---|
| 3767.32 | Amended | 9-29-11 | 28 | HB 153 | 101.01 |
| 4117.10 | Amended | 7-1-11 | 10 | SB 5 | 1 |
| 4163.07 | Amended | 6-29-11 | 7 | HB 114 | 101.01 |
| 4301.62 | Amended | 9-29-11 | 7 | HB 114 | 101.01 |
| 4301.62 | Amended | 6-30-11 | 28 | HB 153 | 101.01 |
| 4501.01 | Amended | 6-29-11 | 7 | HB 114 | 101.01 |
| 4503.235 | Amended | 9-29-11 | 28 | HB 153 | 101.01 |
| 4506.08 | Amended | 6-29-11 | 7 | HB 114 | 101.01 |
| 4507.02 | Amended | 9-23-11 | 25 | HB 5 | 1 |
| 4507.05 | Amended | 6-29-11 | 7 | HB 114 | 101.01 |
| 4507.111 | Amended | 9-29-11 | 28 | HB 153 | 101.01 |
| 4507.1612 | Amended | 6-29-11 | 7 | HB 114 | 101.01 |
| 4507.164 | Amended | 9-23-11 | 25 | HB 5 | 1 |
| 4507.164 | Amended | 9-29-11 | 28 | HB 153 | 101.01 |
| 4507.23 | Amended | 6-29-11 | 7 | HB 114 | 101.01 |
| 4507.35 | Amended | 9-23-11 | 25 | HB 5 | 1 |
| 4507.45 | Amended | 6-29-11 | 7 | HB 114 | 101.01 |
| 4507.51 | Amended | 9-30-11 | 29 | HB 86 | 1 |
| 4509.101 | Amended | 6-29-11 | 7 | HB 114 | 101.01 |
| 4509.81 | Amended | 6-29-11 | 7 | HB 114 | 101.01 |
| 4510.036 | Amended | 9-23-11 | 25 | HB 5 | 1 |
| 4510.037 | Amended | 9-23-11 | 25 | HB 5 | 1 |
| 4510.10 | Amended | 6-29-11 | 7 | HB 114 | 101.01 |
| 4510.11 | Amended | 9-23-11 | 25 | HB 5 | 1 |
| 4510.111 | Enacted | 9-23-11 | 25 | HB 5 | 1 |
| 4510.12 | Amended | 9-23-11 | 25 | HB 5 | 1 |
| 4510.14 | Amended | 9-23-11 | 25 | HB 5 | 1 |
| 4510.16 | Amended | 9-23-11 | 25 | HB 5 | 1 |
| 4510.161 | Amended | 9-23-11 | 25 | HB 5 | 1 |
| 4510.21 | Amended | 9-23-11 | 25 | HB 5 | 1 |
| 4510.22 | Amended | 6-29-11 | 7 | HB 114 | 101.01 |
| 4510.22 | Amended | 9-23-11 | 25 | HB 5 | 1 |
| 4510.41 | Amended | 9-23-11 | 25 | HB 5 | 1 |
| 4510.43 | Amended | 6-29-11 | 7 | HB 114 | 101.01 |
| 4510.72 | Amended | 6-29-11 | 7 | HB 114 | 101.01 |
| 4511.091 | Amended | 9-30-11 | 29 | HB 86 | 1 |
| 4511.108 | Amended | 6-29-11 | 7 | HB 114 | 101.01 |
| 4511.19 | Amended | 9-23-11 | 25 | HB 5 | 1 |
| 4511.191 | Amended | 6-29-11 | 7 | HB 114 | 101.01 |
| 4511.191 | Amended | 6-30-11 | 28 | HB 153 | 101.01 |
| 4511.193 | Amended | 9-29-11 | 28 | HB 153 | 101.01 |
| 4511.203 | Amended | 9-23-11 | 25 | HB 5 | 1 |
| 4511.53 | Amended | 6-29-11 | 7 | HB 114 | 101.01 |
| 4511.69 | Amended | 6-29-11 | 7 | HB 114 | 101.01 |
| 4513.24 | Amended | 6-29-11 | 7 | HB 114 | 101.01 |
| 4513.263 | Amended | 6-29-11 | 7 | HB 114 | 101.01 |
| 4513.39 | Amended | 9-29-11 | 28 | HB 153 | 101.01 |
| 4513.60 | Amended | 9-29-11 | 28 | HB 153 | 101.01 |
| 4513.61 | Amended | 6-29-11 | 7 | HB 114 | 101.01 |
| 4513.61 | Amended | 6-30-11 | 28 | HB 153 | 101.01 |
| 4513.62 | Amended | 9-29-11 | 28 | HB 153 | 101.01 |
| 4513.63 | Amended | 9-29-11 | 28 | HB 153 | 101.01 |
| 4513.64 | Amended | 9-29-11 | 28 | HB 153 | 101.01 |
| 4513.66 | Amended | 9-29-11 | 28 | HB 153 | 101.01 |
| 4549.02 | Amended | 9-23-11 | 25 | HB 5 | 1 |
| 4549.021 | Amended | 9-23-11 | 25 | HB 5 | 1 |
| 4549.03 | Amended | 9-23-11 | 25 | HB 5 | 1 |
| 4549.17 | Amended | 9-29-11 | 28 | HB 153 | 101.01 |
| 4729.01 | Amended | 5-20-11 | 19 | HB 93 | 1 |

| Section | Action | Effective Date | File | Bill No. | Sec. No. |
|---|---|---|---|---|---|
| 4729.162 | Enacted | 5-20-11 | 19 | HB 93 | 1 |
| 4729.29 | Amended | 5-20-11 | 19 | HB 93 | 1 |
| 4729.51 | Amended | 6-29-11 | 9 | HB 9 | 1 |
| 4729.51 | Amended | 5-20-11 | 19 | HB 93 | 1 |
| 4729.52 | Amended | 9-29-11 | 28 | HB 153 | 101.01 |
| 4729.54 | Amended | 5-20-11 | 19 | HB 93 | 1 |
| 4729.541 | Amended | 5-20-11 | 19 | HB 93 | 1 |
| 4729.55 | Amended | 5-20-11 | 19 | HB 93 | 1 |
| 4729.552 | Enacted | 5-20-11 | 19 | HB 93 | 1 |
| 4729.552 | Amended | 9-29-11 | 28 | HB 153 | 101.01 |
| 4729.571 | Enacted | 5-20-11 | 19 | HB 93 | 1 |
| 4729.69 | Enacted | 5-20-11 | 19 | HB 93 | 1 |
| 4729.75 | Amended | 5-20-11 | 19 | HB 93 | 1 |
| 4729.77 | Amended | 5-20-11 | 19 | HB 93 | 1 |
| 4729.78 | Amended | 5-20-11 | 19 | HB 93 | 1 |
| 4729.79 | Amended | 5-20-11 | 19 | HB 93 | 1 |
| 4729.80 | Amended | 5-20-11 | 19 | HB 93 | 1 |
| 4729.81 | Enacted | 5-20-11 | 19 | HB 93 | 1 |
| 4729.82 | Enacted | 5-20-11 | 19 | HB 93 | 1 |
| 4729.83 | Enacted | 5-20-11 | 19 | HB 93 | 1 |
| 4729.84 | Enacted | 5-20-11 | 19 | HB 93 | 1 |
| 4729.85 | Amended | 5-20-11 | 19 | HB 93 | 1 |
| 4729.86 | Enacted | 5-20-11 | 19 | HB 93 | 1 |
| 4729.99 | Amended | 5-20-11 | 19 | HB 93 | 1 |
| 4729.99 | Amended | 9-30-11 | 29 | HB 86 | 1 |
| 5101.61 | Amended | 7-1-11 | 28 | HB 153 | 101.01 |
| 5104.012 | Amended | 9-29-11 | 28 | HB 153 | 101.01 |
| 5104.013 | Amended | 9-29-11 | 28 | HB 153 | 101.01 |
| 5119.85 | Amended | 7-1-11 | 28 | HB 153 | 101.01 |
| 5120.031 | Amended | 9-30-11 | 29 | HB 86 | 1 |
| 5120.036 | Enacted | 9-30-11 | 29 | HB 86 | 1 |
| 5120.07 | Amended | 9-30-11 | 29 | HB 86 | 1 |
| 5120.092 | Enacted | 6-30-11 | 28 | HB 153 | 101.01 |
| 5120.111 | Amended | 9-30-11 | 29 | HB 86 | 1 |
| 5120.113 | Enacted | 9-30-11 | 29 | HB 86 | 1 |
| 5120.114 | Enacted | 9-30-11 | 29 | HB 86 | 1 |
| 5120.115 | Enacted | 9-30-11 | 29 | HB 86 | 1 |
| 5120.12 | Repealed | 9-30-11 | 35 | HB 133 | 2 |
| 5120.135 | Amended | 9-29-11 | 28 | HB 153 | 101.01 |
| 5120.16 | Amended | 9-30-11 | 29 | HB 86 | 1 |
| 5120.17 | Amended | 9-29-11 | 28 | HB 153 | 101.01 |
| 5120.22 | Amended | 9-29-11 | 28 | HB 153 | 101.01 |
| 5120.28 | Amended | 9-29-11 | 28 | HB 153 | 101.01 |
| 5120.29 | Amended | 9-29-11 | 28 | HB 153 | 101.01 |
| 5120.331 | Amended | 9-30-11 | 29 | HB 86 | 1 |
| 5120.48 | Amended | 9-30-11 | 29 | HB 86 | 1 |
| 5120.59 | Amended | 9-30-11 | 29 | HB 86 | 1 |
| 5120.60 | Amended | 9-30-11 | 29 | HB 86 | 1 |
| 5120.66 | Amended | 9-30-11 | 29 | HB 86 | 1 |
| 5122.01 | Amended | 9-29-11 | 28 | HB 153 | 101.01 |
| 5122.01 | Amended | 10-1-12 | 28 | HB 153 | 120.20 |
| 5122.02 | Amended | 10-1-12 | 28 | HB 153 | 120.20 |
| 5122.15 | Amended | 7-1-11 | 28 | HB 153 | 101.01 |
| 5122.21 | Amended | 9-29-11 | 28 | HB 153 | 101.01 |
| 5122.31 | Amended | 9-29-11 | 28 | HB 153 | 101.01 |
| 5122.31 | Amended | 10-1-12 | 28 | HB 153 | 120.20 |
| 5122.32 | Amended | 10-1-12 | 28 | HB 153 | 120.20 |
| 5123.01 | Amended | 9-29-11 | 28 | HB 153 | 101.01 |
| 5123.51 | Amended | 7-1-11 | 10 | SB 5 | 1 |

| Section | Action | Effective Date | File | Bill No. | Sec. No. |
|---|---|---|---|---|---|
| 5123.61 | Amended | 10-1-12 | 28 | HB 153 | 120.20 |
| 5123.701 | Amended | 10-1-12 | 28 | HB 153 | 120.20 |
| 5123.99 | Amended | 10-1-12 | 28 | HB 153 | 120.20 |
| 5502.61 | Amended | 9-29-11 | 28 | HB 153 | 101.01 |
| 5502.68 | Amended | 9-29-11 | 28 | HB 153 | 101.01 |
| 5503.02 | Amended | 6-29-11 | 7 | HB 114 | 101.01 |
| 5503.03 | Amended | 7-1-11 | 10 | SB 5 | 1 |
| 5705.19 | Amended | 9-29-11 | 28 | HB 153 | 101.01 |

# TABLE OF PENALTIES

(Including legislation passed and filed with the Secretary of State through October 1, 2011)

## SPECIAL FELONIES (SpecF)

(2929.02—2929.04)

| Classification | Confinement | Maximum Fine | Organizational Fine (2929.31) |
|---|---|---|---|
| **AGGRAVATED MURDER** (2903.01) | | | |
| —death specifications | Death, life imprisonment without parole, life with parole after 20 years, life with parole after 25 years, or life with parole after 30 years | $25,000 | $100,000 |
| —no death specification | Life with parole after 20 years | | |
| **MURDER** (2903.02) | 15 years to life, or 30 years to life if victim was under 13 and the defendant had a sexual motivation (see §2929.02); in addition, may be fined up to $15,000 | $15,000 | $ 50,000 |

## FELONIES (F)

(2929.14)

| Classification | Confinement[1] | Maximum Fine | Organizational Fine (2929.31) |
|---|---|---|---|
| **FELONY 1 (F1)** | 3, 4, 5, 6, 7, 8, 9, 10, or 11 years (Additional 1 to 10 years for certain offenses)[2] | $20,000 | $25,000 |
| **FELONY 2 (F2)** | 2, 3, 4, 5, 6, 7, or 8 years (Additional 1 to 10 years for certain offenses)[2] | $15,000 | $20,000 |
| **FELONY 3 (F3)** | 9, 12, 18, 24, 30, or 36 months[3] | $10,000 | $15,000 |
| **FELONY 4 (F4)** | 6, 7, 8, 9, 10, 11, 12, 13, 14, 15, 16, 17, or 18 months | $ 5,000 | $10,000 |
| **FELONY 5 (F5)** | 6, 7, 8, 9, 10, 11, or 12 months | $ 2,500 | $ 7,500 |

**ENHANCEMENTS**

A. Additional penalties for use or possession of a firearm (2929.14(D)(1)(a)).
1. Possession of an automatic or muffled firearm—6 additional years.
2. Displaying, brandishing, or using firearm—3 additional years.
3. Firearm not factor in committing the crime—1 additional year.
4. Drive-by shooting—5 additional years plus penalty for use or possession of gun as above plus penalty for the underlying offense.
5. Discharging firearm at peace or corrections office—7 additional years (2929.14(D)(1)(f))[4]
6. The additional prison terms imposed under this section may not be reduced by §§ 2929.20, 2967.193, or any other provision of Chapters 2967. or 5120.

B. Additional penalties for repeat violent offenders (2929.14(D)(2)).
- Where there is no physical harm or disfigurement, the offender shall be sentenced to any prison term specified in the range of prison terms for the specific offense.
- Where there is physical harm with a substantial risk of death or permanent disfigurement, the offender shall be sentenced to the longest prison term specified in the range of prison terms for the specific offense.
- If the prison terms specified for the specific offense are inadequate to punish the offender and protect the public from future crime because the offender is likely to commit future crimes and the terms are demeaning to the seriousness of the offense because the offender's conduct is more serious than normal (2929.12), the offender shall be sentenced to an additional term of 1 to 10 years.

The additional prison term imposed under this section may not be reduced by §§ 2929.20, 2967.193, or any other provision of Chapters 2967. or 5120.

C. Additional penalties for major drug offenders, corrupt activity, attempted forcible rape and attempted felonious sexual penetration when victim is under 13 years of age (2929.13(F), 2929.14(D)(3)).
- Where a mandatory 10 year sentence is required and a finding is made that the term is inadequate to punish the offender and protect the public from future crimes because the offender is likely to commit future crimes and the term is demeaning to the seriousness of the offense because the offender's conduct is more serious than normal (2929.12), the offender shall be sentenced to an additional term of 1 to 10 years.

---

[1] The overriding purposes of felony sentencing are (1) to protect the public from future crime by the offender and others, and (2) to punish the offender. To achieve these purposes the court is required to consider the need for incapacitating the offender, deterring the offender and others from future crime, rehabilitating the offender, and making restitution to the victim of the offense, the public, or both. A sentence imposed for a felony must be reasonably calculated to achieve the above-stated purposes, commensurate with and not demeaning to the seriousness of the offender's conduct and its impact upon the victim, and consistent with sentences imposed for similar crimes committed by other offenders with similar characteristics. (2929.11) If the offender is eligible to be sentenced to community control sanctions, the court shall consider the appropriateness of imposing a financial sanction pursuant to § 2929.18 or a sanction of community service pursuant to § 2929.17 as the sole sanction for the offense. If the court is required to impose a mandatory prison term for the offense for which sentence is being imposed, the court may also impose a financial sanction pursuant to § 2929.18 but may not impose any additional sanction or combination of sanctions under §§ 2929.16 or 2929.17 (2929.13). The offender may also be ordered to pay all or part of the cost of purchasing and using an immobilizing or disabling device, including a certified ignition interlock device, or a remote alcohol monitoring device that a court orders an offender to use under section 4510.13 of the Revised Code.

[2] Repeat violent offenders (2929.14(D)(2)), and major drug offenders (2929.14(D)(3)).

[3] If a violation of section 2903.06, 2903.08, 2907.03, 2907.04, or 2907.05 of the Revised Code or that is a violation of section 2911.02 or 2911.12 of the Revised Code if the offender previously has been convicted of or pleaded guilty in two or more separate proceedings to two or more violations of section 2911.01, 2911.02, 2911.11, or 2911.12 of the Revised Code, prison term shall be 12, 18, 24, 30, 36, 42, 48, 54, or 60 months.

[4] Additional 7-year term cannot be imposed unless indictment or information states specification (2941.14.12).

The additional prison term imposed under this section may not be reduced by §§ 2929.20, 2967.193, or any other provision of Chapters 2967. or 5120.

D. Additional prison term of 2 years for offenders convicted of aggravated murder, murder, or a felony of the first, second or third degree that is an offense of violence and is also convicted of a section 2941.143 specification that charges the offender with having committed the offense in a school safety zone or towards a person in a school safety zone (2929.14(J)).

E. Additional penalty for kidnapping victim under 13 years of age and offender also is convicted of or pleads guilty to a sexual motivation specification that was included in the indictment, count in the indictment, or information charging the offense, sentence of 15 years to life (or 10 years to life if victim was released unharmed in a safe place). (2905.01)

F. If an offender is convicted of or pleads guilty to a felony violation of section 2907.22, 2907.24, 2907.241, or 2907.25 of the Revised Code and to a specification of the type described in section 2941.1421 of the Revised Code and if the court imposes a prison term on the offender for the felony violation, the court may impose upon the offender an additional prison term as follows:

(i) Subject to division (J)(2)(a)(ii) of this section, an additional prison term of one, two, three, four, five, or six months;

(ii) If the offender previously has been convicted of or pleaded guilty to one or more felony or misdemeanor violations of section 2907.22, 2907.23, 2907.24, 2907.241, or 2907.25 of the Revised Code and also was convicted of or pleaded guilty to a specification of the type described in section 2941.1421 of the Revised Code regarding one or more of those violations, an additional prison term of one, two, three, four, five, six, seven, eight, nine, ten, eleven, or twelve months.

In lieu of imposing this additional term, the court may directly impose on the offender a sanction that requires the offender to wear a real-time processing, continual tracking electronic monitoring device during the period of time specified by the court. The period of time specified by the court shall equal the duration of an additional prison term that the court could have imposed upon the offender. The offender shall pay all costs associated with a sanction imposed under this division, including the cost of the use of the monitoring device. (§ 2929.14(J)(2))

G. Additional prison term of one, two, three, four, five, or six months under division (J)(2)(a)(i) of section 2929.14 of the Revised Code, an additional prison term of one, two, three, four, five, six, seven, eight, nine, ten, eleven, or twelve months under division (J)(2)(a)(ii) of section 2929.14 of the Revised Code, an additional definite jail term of not more than sixty days under division (F)(1)(a) of section 2929.24 of the Revised Code, or an additional definite jail term of not more than one hundred twenty days under division (F)(1)(b) of section 2929.24 of the Revised Code is precluded unless the indictment, count in the indictment, or information charging a felony violation of section 2907.22, 2907.24, 2907.241, or 2907.25 of the Revised Code or a misdemeanor violation of section 2907.23, 2907.24, 2907.241, or 2907.25 of the Revised Code, whichever is applicable, specifies that the violation was committed in proximity to a school. (§ 2941.1421)

H. If an offender is convicted of or pleads guilty to a felony violation of section 2905.01, 2905.02, 2907.21, 2907.22, or 2923.32, division (A)(1) or (2) of section 2907.323, or division (B)(1), (2), (3), (4), or (5) of section 2919.22 of the Revised Code and also is convicted of or pleads guilty to a specification of the type described in section 2941.1422 [2941.14.22] of the Revised Code that charges that the offender knowingly committed the offense in furtherance of human trafficking, the court shall impose on the offender a mandatory prison term that is one of the following:

(i) If the offense is a felony of the first degree, a definite prison term of not less than five years and not greater than ten years;

(ii) If the offense is a felony of the second or third degree, a definite prison term of not less than three years and not greater than the maximum prison term allowed for the offense by division (A) of section 2929.14 of the Revised Code;

(iii) If the offense is a felony of the fourth or fifth degree, a definite prison term that is the maximum prison term allowed for the offense by division (A) of section 2929.14 of the Revised.

I. If an offender is convicted of or pleads guilty to a felony violation of section 2903.11, 2903.12, or 2903.13 of the Revised Code and also is convicted of or pleads guilty to a specification of the type described in section 2941.1423 of the Revised Code that charges that the victim of the violation was a woman whom the offender knew was pregnant at the time of the violation, the court shall impose on the offender a mandatory prison term that is either a definite prison term of six months or one of the prison terms prescribed for felonies of the same degree as the violation.

## MISDEMEANORS (M)

(2929.24, 2929.28)[5]

| Classification | Confinement[6] | Maximum Fine[7] | Organizational Fine (2929.31) |
|---|---|---|---|
| **MISDEMEANOR 1 (M1)** | Maximum sentence of 180 days | $ 1,000 | $ 5,000 |
| **MISDEMEANOR 2 (M2)** | Maximum sentence of 90 days | $ 750 | $ 4,000 |
| **MISDEMEANOR 3 (M3)** | Maximum sentence of 60 days | $ 500 | $ 3,000 |
| **MISDEMEANOR 4 (M4)** | Maximum sentence of 30 days | $ 250 | $ 2,000 |
| **MINOR MISDEMEANOR (MM)** | None | $ 150 | $ 1,000 |

A. If an offender is convicted of or pleads guilty to a misdemeanor violation of section 2907.23, 2907.24, 2907.241, or 2907.25 of the Revised Code and to a specification of the type described in section 2941.1421 of the Revised Code and if the court imposes a jail term on the offender for the misdemeanor violation, the court may impose upon the offender an additional definite jail term as follows:

(a) Subject to division (F)(1)(b) of this section, an additional definite jail term of not more than sixty days;

(b) If the offender previously has been convicted of or pleaded guilty to one or more misdemeanor or felony violations of section 2907.22, 2907.23, 2907.24, 2907.241, or 2907.25 of the Revised Code and also was convicted of or pleaded guilty to a specification of the type described in section 2941.1421 of the Revised Code regarding one or more of those violations, an additional definite jail term of not more than one hundred twenty days.

In lieu of imposing an additional definite jail term, the court may directly impose on the offender a sanction that requires the offender to wear a real-time processing, continual tracking electronic monitoring device during the period of time specified by the court. The period of time specified by the court shall equal the duration of an additional jail term that the court could have imposed upon the offender.

B. If an offender is convicted of or pleads guilty to a misdemeanor violation of section 2903.13 of the Revised Code and also is convicted of or pleads guilty to a specification of the type described in section 2941.1423 of the Revised Code that charges that the victim of the violation was a woman whom the offender knew was pregnant at the time of the violation, the court shall impose on the offender a mandatory jail term that is a definite term of at least thirty days.

---

[5] Committed on or after 1/1/04, restitution may also be required, R.C. § 2929.28(A). *See also* R.C. §§ 2929.21-2929.24 (misdemeanor sentencing).

[6] *See also* R.C. § 2967.193 regarding days of credit.
Maximum reductions are set forth following this Table of Penalties.

[7] Offender required to pay towing and storage fees if convicted of theft offense involving motor vehicle or major part thereof. *See* R.C. § 2913.82.

## DAYS OF CREDIT

Revised Code § 2967.193 allows persons confined to state correctional institutions to earn one day of credit as a deduction from the person's stated prison term for each full month during which the person productively participates in an education program, vocational training, employment in prison industries, treatment for substance abuse, treatment as a sex offender, or any other constructive program developed by the Department with specific standards for performance by prisoners. At the end of each calendar month in which a prisoner productively participates in such a program or activity, the Department of Rehabilitation and Correction shall deduct one day from the date on which the prisoner's stated prison term will expire. If the prisoner violates prison rules, the Department may deny the prisoner a credit that otherwise would have been awarded or may withdraw one or more credits previously earned by the prisoner. If a prisoner is released early by reason of credit under Revised Code § 2967.193, the Department shall retain control of the prisoner by means of an appropriate post-release control sanction imposed by the parole board until the end of the prisoner's stated term if the parole board imposes a post-release control sanction pursuant to section 2967.28 of the Revised Code. If the parole board is not required to impose a post-release control sanction under section 2967.28 of the Revised Code, the parole board may elect not to impose a post-release control sanction on the prisoner. No person who is serving a sentence of life imprisonment without parole imposed under Revised Code § 2929.03 or 2929.06 or who is serving a prison term or a term of life imprisonment without parole imposed pursuant to Revised Code § 2971.03 shall be awarded any days of credit.

## BAD TIME

Revised Code § 2967.11 authorizes the Parole Board to punish a violation committed by the prisoner by extending the prisoner's stated prison term for a period of 15, 30, 60, or 90 days, but no stated prison term could be extended for a period longer than one-half of the stated prison term's duration for all violations occurring during the course of the prisoner's stated prison term, including violations occurring while the offender is serving extended time under this section or serving a prison term imposed for a failure to meet the conditions of a post-release control sanction imposed under section 2967.28 of the Revised Code. The extension period is referred to as "bad time."

# INDEX OF OFFENSES

*References are to the Revised Code and to penalty classifications abbreviated as follows: F—Felony; M—Misdemeanor; MM—Minor Misdemeanor; 1, 2, 3, 4, 5—First, Second, Third, Fourth, or Fifth Degree.*

*For the specific penalty of a given offense, consult the Table of Penalties, page A-1, preceding this Index. The General Index is located at the end of this book.*

**ARSON**
defraud, to (2909.03), F4
hire, for (2909.03), F3
public buildings (2909.03), F4
public parks (2909.03), F4
without owner's consent (2903.03)
harm or property under $500 (2909.03), M1
harm or property more than $500 (2909.03), F4

**ARSON, AGGRAVATED** (2909.02), F2, F1

**ASSAULT** (2903.13), M1, F5, F4, F3

**ASSAULT, AGGRAVATED** (2903.12), F4
victim is peace officer (2903.12), F3

**ASSAULT, FELONIOUS** (2903.11), F2
victim is peace officer or an investigator of the bureau of criminal identification and investigation (2903.11), F1

**ASSAULTING OR HARASSING POLICE DOG OR HORSE OR HANDICAPPED ASSISTANCE DOG** (2921.32.1), M2, M1, F5, F4

**ASSAULT, NEGLIGENT** (2903.14), M3

**ATTEMPT** (2923.02), 1 degree less than substantive crime murder, to commit, F1, F2, F3, F4, F5, M1, M4

**BAD CHECKS, PASSING**—*see* CHECKS

**BARBITURATES**—*see* DRUG ABUSE

**BEER**—*see also* INTOXICATING LIQUOR
keeping place where sold or furnished illegally (4399.09), $100-500 fine

**BIGAMY** (2919.01), M1

**BINGO**
failure to maintain records (2915.10), M1
illegal conduct of a raffle (2915.092), M1, F5
illegal instant bingo conduct (2915.091, 2915.094), M1, F5
illegally conducting (2915.09), F4, M1, MM
illegally operating as distributor (2915.081), M1, F5
illegally operating as manufacturer (2915.082), M1, F5
inspection of, interfering with (2915.10), M1
operator under 18 (2915.11), M3
operator with prior offense (2915.11), M1
without license (2915.07), F4

**BLACKMAIL**—*see* COERCION; EXTORTION

**BLOCK PARENT SYMBOL, UNAUTHORIZED USE OF** (2917.46), MM

**BLOOD, CONTAMINATED, SELLING OR DONATING** (2927.13), F4

**BREAKING AND ENTERING** (2911.13), F5

**BRIBERY** (2921.02), F3

**CHILD ENDANGERING** (2919.22)
abuse or neglect, M1
prior conviction, F4
resulting in serious physical harm, F3, F2
administering extreme and cruel abuse or discipline, F3
prior conviction or resulting in serious physical harm, F2
operate motor vehicle in violation of 4511.19(A) with child under 18 in vehicle (2919.22), M1
prior conviction or resulting in serious physical harm, F5, F4
permitting/encouraging child to act/participate in pornography (2919.22), F2

**CHILDREN, IMPROPER SOLICITATION OF CONTRIBUTIONS FOR MISSING** (2901.32), M3

**CIGARETTES, TOBACCO PRODUCTS**
permitting children to use (2927.02), M4
prior conviction, M3
sale or distribution to minors prohibited (2927.02), M4
prior conviction, M3

**CIVIL RIGHTS, INTERFERING WITH** (2921.45), M1

**COCAINE**—*see* DRUG ABUSE

**COERCION** (2905.12), M2

**COIN MACHINES, TAMPERING WITH**—*see* TAMPERING WITH COIN MACHINES

**COMPELLING PROSTITUTION**—*see* PROSTITUTION

**COMPLICITY** (2923.03), same as substantive offense

**COMPOUNDING CRIME**—*see* CRIME, COMPOUNDING

**COMPUTER, CABLE OR TELECOMMUNICATIONS PROPERTY, UNAUTHORIZED USE OF** (2913.04), F5

**COMPUTER, UNAUTHORIZED ACCESS OF** (2913.421), F3, F4

**CONSPIRACY** (2923.01), 1 degree less than substantive offense
aggravated murder or murder, to commit (2923.01), F1

**CONTAMINATING SUBSTANCE FOR HUMAN CONSUMPTION OR USE** (2927.24), F1
amount sufficient to cause death, F1 with life imprisonment with parole eligibility after 15 years
resulting in serious physical harm, F1 with life imprisonment with parole eligibility after 15 years

**CONTAMINATION WITH A HAZARDOUS CHEMICAL, BIOLOGICAL, OR RADIOACTIVE SUBSTANCE** (2927.24), F1
amount sufficient to cause death (2927.24), F1 with life imprisonment with parole eligibility after 15 years
resulting in serious physical harm (2927.24), F1 with life imprisonment with parole eligibility after 15 years

**CONTRABAND**
possession, concealment, transportation, receipt, purchase, sale, lease, ent, transfer (2933.42)

**CONTRIBUTING TO UNRULINESS/DELINQUENCY OF A CHILD**—*see* CHILD, CONTRIBUTING TO UNRULINESS/DELINQUENCY OF

**CONTROLLED SUBSTANCES**—*see* DRUG ABUSE

**CRIMINAL SIMULATION** (2913.32), M1
value between $1,000 and $7,500, F5
value between $7,500 and $150,000, F4
value more than $150,000, F3

**CRIMINAL TOOLS, POSSESSING** (2923.24), M1, F5

**CRIMINAL TRESPASS** (2911.21), M4
place of public amusement (2911.23), M1

**CROPS, DAMAGING** (901.51), M4

**CROWD SAFETY, ENDANGERING** (2917.40), M1

**CUSTODY, INTERFERENCE WITH** (2919.23), M3, M1, F5, F4

**DANGEROUS ORDNANCE**—*see* WEAPONS OFFENSES

**DEATH, FAILURE TO REPORT** (2921.22), M4

**DECEPTION TO SECURE WRITINGS**
value under $1,000 (2913.43), M1
value of $1,000 but under $7,500 (2913.43), F5
value of $7,500 but under $150,000 (2913.43), F4
value of $150,000 or more (2913.43), F3
victim elderly person or disabled adult—
  less than $1,000 (2913.43), F5
  $1,000 or more and less than $7,500 (2913.43), F4
  $7,500 or more and less than $37,500 (2913.43), F3
  $37,500 or more (2913.43), F2

**DEFRAUDING CREDITORS** (2913.45), M1
value of $1,000 but under $7,500, F5
value of $7,500 but under $150,000, F4
value of $150,000 or more, F3

**DERELICTION OF DUTY** (2921.44), M2

**DESECRATION** (2927.11), M2, F5, F4, F3

**DISCLOSURE OF CONFIDENTIAL INFORMATION** (2921.24), M4

**DISORDERLY CONDUCT** (2917.11), MM—*see also* RIOT
in presence of law enforcement officer, firefighter, rescuer, medical person, emergency medical service person, or other authorized person at the scene of a fire, accident, disaster, riot, or emergency (2917.11), M4
persist after request to desist (2917.11), M4
school, near (2917.11), M4

**DISRUPTING PUBLIC SERVICES** (2909.04), F4

**DISTURBING LAWFUL MEETING** (2917.12), M4

**DIVULGING CONFIDENTIAL INFORMATION**
sealed record of conviction (2953.35), M4

**DOMESTIC VIOLENCE** (2919.25), M1

prior conviction (2919.25), F4

**DOWNBLOUSING**—*see* VOYEURISM

**DRIVER'S LICENSE**—*see* MOTOR VEHICLES/TRAFFIC LAWS

**DRIVING UNDER THE INFLUENCE**—*see* MOTOR VEHICLES/TRAFFIC LAWS *at* D.U.I.

**DRUG ABUSE**

- anabolic steroids, illegal administration or distribution of (2925.06), F4
- conveyance of drug of abuse onto the grounds of detention, etc., facility (2921.36), F3
- corrupting another with drugs —
  - marihuana (2925.02), F4
    - near school premises (2925.02), F3
  - schedule I or II substance (except marihuana) (2925.02), F2
    - near school premises (2925.02), F1
  - schedule III, IV, or V (2925.02), F2
    - near school premises (2925.02), F2
- counterfeit controlled substances—
  - aggravated trafficking (2925.37), F4
  - fraudulent advertising (2925.37), F5
    - offense committed in the vicinity of school or juvenile (2925.37), F4
  - possession (2925.37), M1
  - promoting drug abuse (2925.37), F5
    - offense committed in the vicinity of school or juvenile, F4
  - trafficking (2925.37), F5
    - offense committed in the vicinity of school or juvenile (2925.37), F4
- cultivation of marihuana, illegal (2925.04), MM, M4, F5, F3, F2
- deception to obtain dangerous drugs (2925.22)
    - schedule I or II substance (except marihuana) (2925.22), F4
    - schedule III, IV or V substance or marihuana (2925.22), F5
- driving under the influence—*see* MOTOR VEHICLES/TRAFFIC LAWS at D.U.I.
- drug documents, illegal processing of (2925.23)
  - dangerous drug, schedule III, IV, or V substance, or marihuana (2925.23), F5
  - schedule I or II substance (except marihuana) (2925.23), F4
- drug samples, illegal dispensing of (2925.36)
  - dangerous drug, schedule III, IV, or V substance, or marihuana (2925.36), M2
    - offense committed in the vicinity of school or juvenile, M1
  - schedule I or II substance (except marihuana) (2925.23), F5
    - offense committed in the vicinity of school or juvenile, F4
- harmful intoxicants, abusing (2925.31), M1
  - prior conviction (2925.31), F5
- illegal assembly or possession of chemicals for the manufacture of drugs (2925.04.1), F3
- knowingly obtain, possess, or use a controlled substance—
  - cocaine (2925.11), F5, F4, F3, F2, F1
  - hashish (2925.11), MM, M4, F5, F3, F2
  - heroin (2925.11), F5, F4, F3, F2, F1
  - LSD (2925.11), F5, F4, F3, F2, F1
  - marihuana (2925.11), MM, M4, F5, F3, F2
  - schedule I or II substance (except marihuana, cocaine, LSD, heroin, and hashish) (2925.11), F5, F3, F2, F1
  - schedule III, IV or V substance (2925.11), M3, M2, F4, F3, F2
- livestock, offenses involving (2925.09), F5, F4
- manufacture of drugs, illegal (2925.04), F3, F2
- marihuana trafficking, funding of (2925.05), F3
- methamphetamine, illegal manufacture (2925.04), F1
- nitrous oxide—
  - improperly dispensing or distributing (2925.32), M4
  - possessing in motor vehicle (2925.33), M4
- paraphernalia, (2925.14), M4, M2, M1

**FALSE ALARMS** (2917.32), M1
violation pertains to purported, threatened or actual use of a weapon of mass destruction (2917.32), F3
violation resulting in economic harm of $1,000 or more but less than $7,500, F5
violation resulting in economic harm of $7,500 or more but less than $150,000, F4
violation resulting in economic harm of $150,000 or more, F3

**FALSE ALLEGATION OF PEACE OFFICER MISCONDUCT** (2921.15), M1

**FALSIFICATION** (2921.13), M1

**FALSIFICATION IN A THEFT OFFENSE**
value under $1,000 (2921.13), M1
value of $1,000 but under $7,500 (2921.13), F5
value of $7,500 but under $150,000 (2921.13), F4
value of $150,000 or more, (2921.13), F3

**FALSIFICATION TO OBTAIN A CONCEALED HANDGUN LICENSE,** F4

**FALSIFICATION TO PURCHASE FIREARM** (2921.13), F5

**FAMILY DAY-CARE HOME, FAILURE TO DISCLOSE DEATH OR SERIOUS INJURY OF CHILD** (2919.22.5), M4

**FAX MACHINE**—*see* FACSIMILE DEVICE, TRANSMITTING ADVERTISING TO

**FELONIOUS ASSAULT**—*see* ASSAULT, FELONIOUS

**FETICIDE, PARTIAL BIRTH** (2919.15.1), F2

**FIREARMS, DANGEROUS ORDNANCE**—*see* WEAPONS OFFENSES

**FLEEING OR ELUDING OFFICER** (2921.33.1), M1, F4, F3

**FOOD ADULTERATED** (3716.11), M1

**FOOD STAMPS OR COUPONS**
illegal use (2913.46)—
  value under $1,000, F5
  value of $1,000 but less than $7,500, F4
  value $7,500 but less than $150,000, F3
  value $150,000 or more, F2

**FORGERY** (2913.31[A]), F5—*see also* CHECKS
  loss value between $7,500 and $150,000, F4
  loss value over $150,000, F3
identification cards, offenses involving (2913.31[B]), M1
victim elderly person or disabled adult—
  less than $1,000 (2913.31), F5
  $1,000 or more and less than $7,500 (2913.31), F4
  $7,500 or more and less than $37,500 (2913.31), F3
  $37,500 or more (2913.31), F2

**FRAUDS**—*see* specific topics

**FUNCTIONALLY IMPAIRED PERSON, FAILING TO PROVIDE FOR** (2903.16), M1, M2, F4

**GAMBLING** (2915.02), M1—*see* also BINGO; CHEATING; CORRUPTING SPORTS prior conviction (2915.02), F5

**GAMBLING HOUSE, OPERATING** (2915.03), M1
prior conviction (2915.03), F5

**GAMING, PUBLIC** (2915.04), MM
prior conviction (2915.04), M4

**GANGS, PARTICIPATING IN CRIMINAL** (2923.42), F2

**GARBAGE, OFFENSES INVOLVING** (3767.32, 3767.99), M3

**GRAND THEFT**—*see* THEFT

**GROSS SEXUAL IMPOSITION**—*see* SEXUAL IMPOSITION, GROSS

**GUNSHOT WOUND, STAB WOUND, BURN VIOLENTLY INFLICTED, FAILURE TO REPORT** (2921.22), M2, MM

**HALLUCINOGENS**—*see* DRUG ABUSE

**HANDICAPPED PERSON**—*see* FUNCTIONALLY IMPAIRED PERSON, FAILING TO PROVIDE FOR

**HARASSMENT WITH BODILY SUBSTANCE** (2921.38), F5, F3

**HARASSMENT, TELEPHONE**—*see* TELECOMMUNICATIONS HARASSMENT

**HARBORING CRIMINAL**—*see* OBSTRUCTING JUSTICE

**HAZING** (2903.31), M4

**HEROIN**—*see* DRUG ABUSE

**HIT & RUN**—*see* MOTOR VEHICLES/TRAFFIC LAWS *at* accident, failure to stop after

**HOAX WEAPON OF MASS DESTRUCTION, UNLAWFUL POSSESSION OR USE** (2917.33), F4

**HOMICIDE**—*see* ABORTION MANSLAUGHTER; MANSLAUGHTER, INVOLUNTARY; MANSLAUGHTER, VOLUNTARY; MURDER; NEGLIGENT HOMICIDE; VEHICULAR HOMICIDE

**HOUSING RIGHTS, INTERFERENCE WITH** (2927.03), M1

**IDENTIFICATION CARDS, FORGED** (2913.31), M1

**IDENTITY FRAUD**
elderly or disabled victim (2913.49), F5, F3, F2, F1
value $1,000 or more but less than $7,500 (2913.49), F4
value $7,500 or more but less than $150,000 (2913.49), F3
value less than $1,000 (2913.49), M1
value more than $150,000 (2913.49), F2

**ILLEGAL BAIL BOND AGENT PRACTICES** (2927.27), M1, F3

**MOTOR VEHICLES/TRAFFIC LAWS**

accident, failure to stop after (4549.02), M1
  injury to person or property, when (4549.02.1), M1, F5
  injury to real property, when (4549.03), M1
air bag, improper placement (4549.20), M1
  subsequent offenses (4549.20), F5
assured clear distance, (4511.21), MM
  previous convictions, M4, M3
bumpers (4513.02.1), MM
  subsequent offense (4513.02.1), M3
certificate of registration, failure to display on commercial car (4549.18), MM
child restraint device required (4511.81), MM, M4
commercial vehicle—
  driving with impaired alertness (4511.79), MM
    subsequent offense (4511.79), M4
  electronic clearance devices, unauthorized use (4549.081), M4
    subsequent offenses (4549.081), M3
  noncompliance at scale locations (4511.121), MM
    second offense (4511.121), M4
    subsequent offenses (4511.121), M3
directional signals required (4513.26.1), MM
drag racing (4511.25.1), M1
driver's (operator's) license—
  driving under specified lifetime suspension (4510.18), F3
  driving under suspension (4510.11), M, M1
  operating without a valid license (4510.12), M, MM, M1
D.U.I. (driving under the influence of alcohol or drug of abuse or both) (4511.19), M1, F4, F3
  no prior D.U.I. nor vehicular homicide involving D.U.I. within 6 years (4511.19)
  one prior D.U.I. or vehicular homicide with D.U.I. within 6 years (4511.19)
  two prior D.U.I.'s or vehicular homicide with D.U.I. within 6 years (4511.19)
  three or more prior D.U.I.'s or vehicular homicide with D.U.I. within 5 years (4511.19)
  vehicular homicide while—*see* VEHICULAR HOMICIDE
earphones, wearing (4511.84), MM, M4, M3
financial responsibility act, failure to comply with (4509.10.1,4509.78), $500 maximum and/or 90 days maximum. See text of 4509.101 for possible civil penalties
firearms re—*see* WEAPONS OFFENSES
grand theft—*see* THEFT
hit & run—*see* accident, failing to stop after, this entry
junk vehicle—
  abandoning (4513.64), MM
  noncompliance with order to remove (4513.65), MM
license plates—
  foreign, when resident of this state (4549.12), MM
    subsequent offense (4549.12), M4
  invalid plate or identification mark (4549.08), M4
    subsequent offense (4549.08), M3
  operation without (4549.10), MM
  previous registration, driving with (4549.11), MM
    subsequent offense (4549.11), M4
motorized bicycle without license or safety equipment (4511.52.1), MM
odometer tampering (4549.42), F5
  subsequent offense (4549.42), F4
operating a motor vehicle after under-age alcohol consumption (4511.19), M4, M3
order, failure to comply with (2921.33.1), M1
O.V.I. *see* D.U.I.
O.V.U.C. *see* operating a motor vehicle after under-age consumption
parking on posted private property (4511.68.1), MM
  use of unlicensed tow truck by property owner (4513.60), MM
physical control of a vehicle while under the influence (4511.19.4), M1
points (4510.03.6)
resisting traffic officer (4513.36) MM

causing serious physical harm to victim (2907.02), F1 with life imprisonment without parole
previous conviction or guilty plea to rape or substantially similar law (2907.02), F1 with life imprisonment without parole
victim's ability to resist or consent is substantially impaired because of mental or physical condition or advanced age and offender knows, or has reasonable cause to believe the victim's ability to resist or consent is substantially impaired by such condition or advanced age (2907.02), F1
force or threat, by (2907.02), F1
victim under 13 years of age, life imprisonment, unless defendant under 16 years of age and victim 10 years of age or older and no serious physical harm caused and no prior conviction (2907.02), F1
force or threat, by (2907.02), F1 with life imprisonment
victim under 10 years of age (2907.02), F1 with life imprisonment

**RECEIVING STOLEN PROPERTY**
value less than $1,000 (2913.51), M1
value of $1,000 or more but less than $7,500, or special property of R.C. § 2913.71 (2913.51), F5
value of $7,500 or more but less than $150,000; or motor vehicle; or dangerous drug; or firearm or dangerous ordnance (2913.51), F4
value of $150,000 or more, F3

**RECKLESS HOMICIDE** (2903.04.1), F3

**RECOGNIZANCE, FAILURE TO APPEAR**
original charge, felony (2937.29, 2937.99), F4
original charge, misdemeanor (2937.29, 2937.99), M1

**RECORDS, TAMPERING WITH**—*see* TAMPERING WITH RECORDS

**RESIDENTS OF CARE FACILITIES**—*see* PATIENTS

**RESISTANCE TO LAWFUL AUTHORITY**—*see* ESCAPE

**RESISTING ARREST** (2921.33), M2, M1, F4

**RESTRAINT, UNLAWFUL**—*see* UNLAWFUL RESTRAINT

**RETALIATION** (2921.05), F3

**RICO**—*see* CORRUPT ACTIVITY, PATTERN OF

**RIOT** (2917.03), M1—*see also* DISORDERLY CONDUCT
failure to disperse (2917.04). MM, M4
inciting to violence (2917.01), M1, F3
inmate, by (2917.02), F4, F3

**RIOT, AGGRAVATED** (2917.02), F5, F4, F3

**ROBBERY** (2911.02), F3, F2

**ROBBERY, AGGRAVATED** (2911.01), F1

**SAFECRACKING** (2911.31), F4

**SCHOOL BUSES**—*see* MOTOR VEHICLES/TRAFFIC LAWS

**SEARCH**
conducting unauthorized (2933.32), M1
failure to prepare proper report, M4

violation resulting in economic harm of $150,000 or more, F3

**TELECOMMUNICATIONS PROPERTY, UNAUTHORIZED USE OF** (2913.04), F5

**TELEPHONE NUMBER**
recording when check presented (1349.17, 1349.99)

**TERMINATING OR ATTEMPTING TO TERMINATE HUMAN PREGNANCY AFTER VIABILITY** (2919.17), F4

**TERRORISM** (2909.24), 1 degree higher than the most serious underlying specified offense
making a terroristic threat (2909.23), F3
soliciting or providing support for an act of terrorism (2909.22), F3

**THEFT**
drugs, dangerous—
  no prior felony drug abuse conviction (2913.02), F4
  prior felony drug abuse conviction (2913.02), F3
firearm (2913.02), F3
firearm from dealer (2913.02), F1
from an elderly person or disabled adult—
  less than $1,000 (2913.02), F5
  $1,000 or more, less than $7,500 (2913.02), F4
  $7,500 or more, less than $37,500 (2913.02), F3
  $37,500 or more, less than $150,000 (2913.02), F2
  $150,000 or more (2913.02), F1
gasoline (2913.02), driver's license sanction for "gas and go" retail offense
motion picture piracy, (2913.07), M1, F5
motor vehicle (2913.02), F4
ordnance, dangerous (2913.02), F3
value—
  less than $1,000 (2913.02), M1
  $1,000 or more, less than $7,500 (2913.02), F5
  $7,500 or more, less than $150,000 (2913.02), F4
  $150,000 or more, less than $750,000 (2913.02), F3
  $750,000 or more, less than $1,500,000 (2913.02), F2
  $1,500,000 or more (2913.02), F1

**THEFT IN OFFICE** (2921.41), F5, F4, F3

**THREATS**—*see* COERCION; EXTORTION

**TOBACCO PRODUCTS, ILLEGAL DISTRIBUTION OF** (2927.02), M4
prior conviction (2927.02), M3

**TRADEMARK COUNTERFEITING** (2913.34), M1, F5, F4, F3

**TRAFFIC CONTROL DEVICES**
Possession or Sale (4511.18), M3
Tampering (4511.17), MM, M4, M3
Unauthorized (4511.16), MM, M4, M3

**TRAFFIC OFFENSES**—*see* MOTOR VEHICLES/TRAFFIC LAWS

**TRASH, OFFENSES INVOLVING** (3767.32, 3767.99), M3

**TREES, DAMAGING** (901.51, 901.99), M4

**TRESPASS**—*see* CRIMINAL TRESPASS

**VIEWING BOOTHS DEPICTING SEXUAL CONDUCT, UNLAWFUL OPERATION** (2907.38), M1

**VIOLENCE, INCITING TO**—*see* RIOT

**VOLUNTARY MANSLAUGHTER**—*see* MANSLAUGHTER, VOLUNTARY

**VOYEURISM**
to photograph the other person in a state of nudity (2907.08), M2
if the other person is minor (2907.08), M1
if the other person is minor and (2907.08), F5
the offender is the minor's natural or adoptive parent, stepparent, guardian, or custodian, or person in loco parentis to the minor
*(or)*
the minor is in the custody of law or is a patient in a hospital or other institution, and the offender has supervisory or disciplinary authority over the minor
*(or)*
the offender is a teacher, administrator, coach, or other person in authority employed by or serving in a school for which the state board of education prescribes minimum standards pursuant to RC § 3301.07(D), the minor is enrolled in or attends that school, and the offender is not enrolled in and does not attend that school
*(or)*
the offender is a teacher, administrator, coach, or other person in authority employed by or serving in an institution of higher education, and the minor is enrolled in or attends that institution
*(or)*
the offender is a caregiver, administrator, or other person in authority employed by or serving in a child day-care center, Type A family day-care home, or Type B family day-care home, and the minor is enrolled in or attends that center or home
*(or)*
the offender is the minor's athletic or other type of coach, is the minor's instructor, is the leader of the scouting troop or which the minor is a member, provided babysitting care for the minor, or is a person with temporary or occasional disciplinary control over the minor
to secretly or surreptitiously videotape, film, photograph, or otherwise record another under/through clothing in order to view body/undergarments (2907.08), M1
to spy or eavesdrop on another (2907.08), M3

**WEAPONS OFFENSES**—*see also* CARRYING CONCEALED WEAPONS
conveyance into detention facility or institution (2921.36), F4
dangerous ordnance, failure to secure (2923.19), M2
dangerous ordnance, unlawful possession (2923.17), F5
discharge of a firearm on or near prohibited premises (2923.16.2), M4, M1
drug dependent person/chronic alcoholic, use of weapon by (2923.13), F3
drug of abuse, using weapon while under influence of (2923.15), M1
firearms in motor vehicle,
knowingly discharge (2923.16), F4
loaded (2923.16), F5
unloaded (2923.16), M4
firearms, defacing identification marks (2923.201), F4, M1
firearms, improperly discharging at or into habitation or in a school safety zone, (2923.16.1), F2
firearms, improperly furnishing to minor (2923.21), F5
handgun, failure to disclose licensed carrying (2923.12), M1
handgun, failure to keep hands in plain sight (2923.12), M1, F5
handgun, removing or grasping (2923.12), F5
handgun, failure to comply with lawful order (2923.12), M1, F5
having while under disability (2923.13), F3
intoxicated, using while (2923.15), M1
liquor permit premises, possession of firearm in (2923.12.1), F5
possessing criminal tools (2923.24), M1, F5
possession of a deadly weapon while under detention (2923.13.1), M1, F5, F4, F3, F2, F1
possession of an object indistinguishable from a firearm on school premises (2923.12.2), M1, F5

# ELEMENTS OF OFFENSES



### Explanatory Note

In this division of the Handbook, the elements of each offense in Title 29 of the Ohio Revised Code, plus other selected offenses, are set forth. Venue is included under each offense. Venue must be proved in every case, although technically it is not an element. *State v. Draggo,* 65 Ohio St. 2d 88, 19 Ohio Op. 3d 294, 418 N.E. 2d 1343 (1981). For a complete discussion, *see* Chapter 15, Anderson's Ohio Criminal Practice and Procedure.

The headings consist of the name of the offense, the statute in which it is defined, and the classification and degree of the offense. Felony is abbreviated **F,** misdemeanor is **M,** and minor misdemeanor is **MM.** Numbers following the abbreviations indicate the degree of the offense. Thus, **F3** denotes a felony of the third degree. Multiple classifications indicate that the offense may fall under more than one classification, depending on the circumstances of the offense or on the offender's past record. This is explained in the Penalty section under each offense.

The date on which an offense was committed may affect the prosecution of the offense. *See* R.C. § 2929.61.

## MISSING CHILDREN

***IMPROPER SOLICITATION OF CONTRIBUTIONS FOR MISSING CHILDREN,* R.C. § 2901.32 [M3]**

Division (A):
(1) Being an organization
(2) Solicit contributions
(3) For purpose of distributing materials containing information relating to missing children
(4) Unless
  (a) For period of two years prior to time of such solicitation
    (i) Incorporated under R.C. Chapter 1702. or nonprofit corporation law of another state
    *(and)*
    (ii) Exempt from federal income taxation under I.R.C. § 501(a) and described in I.R.C. § 501(c)(3), 501(c)(4), 501(c)(8), 501(c)(10) or 501(c)(19)
    (and)
  (b) Does not use fund-raising counsel, professional solicitors, commercial co-venturers, or other charitable organizations as defined in R.C. § 1716.01 to solicit such contributions
(5) Venue

Division (B):
(1) Being an organization
(2) Solicit contributions for purpose of distributing materials containing information relating to missing children
(3) Expressly stating or implying in any way that it is affiliated with or soliciting contributions on behalf of an organization established to assist in the location of missing children

(4) Without the express written consent of that organization
(5) Venue
*Penalty:* A misdemeanor of the third degree (2929.21-2929.31)

## HOMICIDES AND ASSAULTS

***AGGRAVATED MURDER*, R.C. § 2903.01 [F]**

Division (A):
(1) Purposely
(2) With prior calculation and design
(3) (a) Cause another's death
*(or)*
(b) The unlawful termination of another's pregnancy
(4) Venue

Division (B):
(1) Purposely
(2) (a) Cause another's death
*(or)*
(b) The unlawful termination of another's pregnancy
(3) While committing, attempting to commit, fleeing immediately after committing or attempting to commit
(4) Kidnapping, rape, aggravated arson, arson, aggravated robbery, robbery, aggravated burglary, burglary, trespass in a habitation when a person is present or likely to be present, terrorism, or escape
(5) Venue

Division (C):
(1) Purposely
(2) Cause the death
(3) Of another who is under 13 at the time of the commission of the offense
(4) Venue

Division (D):
(1) Being a person
(a) Who is under detention as a result of having been found guilty of or having pleaded guilty to a felony
*(or)*
(b) Who breaks such detention
(2) Purposely
(3) Cause the death
(4) Of another
(5) Venue

Division (E):
(1) Purposely
(2) Cause the death
(3) Of a law enforcement officer
(4) Whom the offender knows or has reasonable cause to know is a law enforcement officer
(5) When
(a) The victim, at the time of the commission of the offense, is engaged in the victim's duties
*(or)*
(b) It is the offender's specific purpose to kill a law enforcement officer
(6) Venue
*Penalty:* Death, life imprisonment without parole, life with parole after 20 years, life with parole after 25 years, or life with parole after 30 years according to R.C. §§ 2929.02, 2929.022, 2929.03 and 2929.04 and up to $25,000, except that persons who were not 18 years of age or older at the time of commission of the offense shall not suffer death. Indictment or count in indictment must contain one or more specifications of aggravating circumstances listed in R.C. § 2929.04(A) for capital offense, R.C. § 2901.02(B)
Organization: Up to $100,000
*Notes:* In addition to any other sanctions, if the offender used a motor vehicle as the means to commit the violation, the court shall order a class two suspension of the offender's driver's license, commercial driver's license, temporary instruction permit, probationary license, or nonresident operating privilege

***MURDER*, R.C. § 2903.02 [F]**

Division (A):
(1) Purposely
(2) (a) Cause another's death
*(or)*

(b) The unlawful termination of another's pregnancy
(3) Venue

Division (B):
(1) Cause
(2) Another's death
(3) As a proximate result of the offender's committing or attempting to commit
(4) An offense of violence that is a felony of the first or second degree and that is not a violation of 2903.03 or 2903.04
*Penalty:* Indefinite term of 15 years to life or 30 years to life if victim under 13 years of age and offender had a sexual motivation (see Section 2929.02). In addition, the offender may be fined not more than $15,000. Organization: Up to $50,000
*Notes:* Division (B) does not apply to an offense that becomes a felony of the first or second degree only if the offender previously has been convicted of that offense or another specified offense

***VOLUNTARY MANSLAUGHTER,* R.C. § 2903.03 [F1]**

(1) Knowingly
(2) (a) Cause another's death
*(or)*
(b) Cause the unlawful termination of another's pregnancy
(3) While under the influence of sudden passion or in a sudden fit of rage
(4) Brought on by serious provocation occasioned by the victim
(5) Reasonably sufficient to incite the offender
(6) To use deadly force
(7) Venue
*Penalty:* A felony of the first degree (2929.11-2929.18, 2929.31)

***INVOLUNTARY MANSLAUGHTER,* R.C. § 2903.04 [F1, F3]**

Division (A): **[F1]**
(1) (a) Cause another's death
*(or)*
(b) Cause the unlawful termination of another's pregnancy
(2) As proximate result of committing or attempting to commit a felony
(3) Venue
*Penalty:* A felony of the first degree (2929.11-2929.18, 2929.31)

Division (B): **[F3]**
(1) (a) Cause another's death
*(or)*
(b) Cause the unlawful termination of another's pregnancy
(2) As proximate result of committing or attempting to commit a misdemeanor of any degree, a regulatory offense, or a minor misdemeanor other than a violation of any section contained in Title XLV of the Revised Code that is a minor misdemeanor and other than a violation of an ordinance or a municipal corporation that, regardless of the penalty set by ordinance for the violation, is substantially equivalent to any section contained in Title XLV of the Revised Code that is a minor misdemeanor
(3) Venue
*Penalty:* A felony of the third degree (2929.11-2929.18, 2929.31)
*Notes:* If offense that proximately resulted in death of victim or the unlawful termination of another's pregnancy and that is basis of violation was a violation of division (A) or (B) of R.C. § 4511.19 or of a substantially equivalent municipal ordinance or included as an element the offender's operation or participation in the operation of a snowmobile, locomotive, watercraft, or aircraft while under the influence of alcohol, drug of abuse, both of the following should apply. The Court shall impose a class one suspension of the offender's driver's or commercial driver's license or permit or nonresident operating privilege and the court shall impose a mandatory prison term from the range of prison terms authorized for the level of the offense under R.C. § 2929.14

***RECKLESS HOMICIDE,* R.C. § 2903.041 [F3]**

(1) Recklessly
(2) (a) Cause another's death
*(or)*
(b) Cause the unlawful termination of another's pregnancy
(3) Venue
*Penalty:* A felony of the third degree (2929.11-2929.18, 2929.31)

***NEGLIGENT HOMICIDE,* R.C. § 2903.05 [M1]**

(1) Negligently
(2) (a) Cause another's death
*(or)*

(b) Cause the unlawful termination of another's pregnancy
(3) By means of a deadly weapon or dangerous ordnance
(4) Venue
*Penalty:* A misdemeanor of the first degree (2929.21-2929.31)
*Definitions:* "Deadly weapon," "dangerous ordnance," R.C. § 2923.11

***AGGRAVATED VEHICULAR HOMICIDE; VEHICULAR HOMICIDE*, R.C. § 2903.06 [M2, M1, F4, F3, F2, F1]**

Division (A)(1) (aggravated vehicular homicide):
(1) As the proximate result of committing a violation of R.C. § 4511.19(A), R.C. § 1547.11(A), R.C. § 4561.15(A)(3) or of a substantially equivalent municipal ordinance
(2) (a) Cause another's death
*(or)*
(b) Cause the unlawful termination of another's pregnancy
(3) While operating or participating in operation of
(4) Motor vehicle, motorcycle, snowmobile, locomotive, watercraft, or aircraft
(5) Venue
*Penalty:* A felony of the second degree (2929.11-2929.18, 2929.31)
If, at the time of the offense, the offender was driving under a suspension or cancellation imposed under Chapter 4510. or any other provision of the Revised Code or was operating a motor vehicle or motorcycle, did not have a valid driver's license, commercial driver's license, temporary instruction permit, probationary license, or nonresident operating privilege, and was not eligible for renewal of the offender's driver's license or commercial driver's license without examination under section 4507.10 of the Revised Code or if the offender previously has been convicted of or pleaded guilty to a violation of this section or any traffic-related homicide, manslaughter, or assault offense
*Penalty:* A felony of the second degree (2929.11-2929.18, 2929.31)
*Notes:* In addition to any other sanction imposed, the court shall impose a class one suspension of the offender's driver's license, commercial driver's license, temporary instruction permit, probationary license or nonresident operating privilege pursuant to R.C. § 4510.02

Division (A)(2) (aggravated vehicular homicide):
(1) (a) Recklessly
*(or)*
(b) As the proximate result of committing, while operating or participating in the operation of a motor vehicle or motorcycle in a construction zone, a reckless operation offense, provided that this division applies only if the person whose death is caused or whose pregnancy is unlawfully terminated is in the construction zone at the time of the offender's commission of the reckless operation offense in the construction zone and does not apply as described in division (F) of this section.
(2) (a) Cause another's death
*(or)*
(b) Cause the unlawful termination of another's pregnancy
(3) While operating or participating in operation of
(4) Motor vehicle, motorcycle, snowmobile, locomotive, watercraft, or aircraft
(5) Venue
*Penalty:* A felony of the third degree (2929.11-2929.18, 2929.31)
If, at the time of the offense, the offender was driving under a suspension or cancellation imposed under Chapter 4510. or any other provision of the Revised Code or was operating a motor vehicle or motorcycle, did not have a valid driver's license, commercial driver's license, temporary instruction permit, probationary license, or nonresident operating privilege, and was not eligible for renewal of the offender's driver's license or commercial driver's license without examination under section 4507.10 of the Revised Code or if the offender previously has been convicted of or pleaded guilty to a violation of this section or any traffic-related homicide, manslaughter, or assault offense
*Penalty:* A felony of the second degree (2929.11-2929.18, 2929.31)
*Notes:* In addition to any other sanction imposed, the court shall impose a class two suspension of the offender's driver's license, commercial driver's license, temporary instruction permit, probationary license or nonresident operating privilege pursuant to R.C. § 4510.02

Division (A)(3) (vehicular homicide):
(1) (a) Negligently
*(or)*
(b) As the proximate result of committing, while operating or participating in the operation of a motor vehicle or motorcycle in a construction zone, a speeding offense, provided that this division applies only if the person whose death is caused or whose pregnancy is unlawfully terminated is in the construction zone at the time of the offender's commission of the speeding offense in the construction zone and does not apply as described in division (F) of this section.
(2) (a) Cause another's death
*(or)*
(b) Cause the unlawful termination of another's pregnancy
(3) While operating or participating in operation of
(4) Motor vehicle, motorcycle, snowmobile, locomotive, watercraft, or aircraft

(5) Venue
*Penalty:* A misdemeanor of the first degree (2929.21-2929.31)
If, at the time of the offense, the offender was driving under a suspension or cancellation imposed under Chapter 4510. or any other provision of the Revised Code or was operating a motor vehicle or motorcycle, did not have a valid driver's license, commercial driver's license, temporary instruction permit, probationary license, or nonresident operating privilege, and was not eligible for renewal of the offender's driver's license or commercial driver's license without examination under section 4507.10 of the Revised Code or if the offender previously has been convicted of or pleaded guilty to a violation of this section or any traffic-related homicide, manslaughter, or assault offense
*Penalty:* A felony of the fourth degree (2929.11-2929.18, 2929.31)
*Notes:* In addition to any other sanction imposed, the court shall impose a class four suspension of the offender's driver's license, commercial driver's license, temporary instruction permit, probationary license or nonresident operating privilege pursuant to R.C. § 4510.02 or, if the offender previously has been convicted of or pleaded guilty to a violation of this section or any traffic-related homicide, manslaughter, or assault offense, a class three suspension

Division (A)(4) (vehicular homicide):
(1) As the proximate result of committing a violation of any provision of any section contained in Tide 45 of the Revised Code that is a minor misdemeanor or of a municipal ordinance that, regardless of the penalty set by ordinance for the violation, is substantially equivalent to any provision contained in any section of Title 45 of the Revised Code that is a minor misdemeanor
(2) (a) Cause another's death
*(or)*
(b) Cause the unlawful termination of another's pregnancy
(3) While operating or participating in operation of
(4) Motor vehicle, motorcycle, snowmobile, locomotive, watercraft, or aircraft
(5) Venue
*Penalty:* A misdemeanor of the second degree (2929.21-2929.31)
If at the time of the offense, the offender was driving under a suspension imposed under Chapter 4510 or if the offender previously has been convicted of or pleaded guilty to a violation of this section, any traffic-related homicide, manslaughter, or assault offense
*Penalty:* A misdemeanor of the first degree (2929.21-2929.31)
*Notes:* In addition to any other sanction imposed, the court shall impose a class six suspension of the offender's driver's license, commercial driver's license, temporary instruction permit, probationary license or nonresident operating privilege or, if the offender previously has been convicted of or pleaded guilty to a violation of this section or any traffic-related homicide, manslaughter, or assault offense, a class four suspension
The court shall impose a mandatory prison term on an offender who is convicted of or pleads guilty to a violation of division (A)(1), (A)(2), or (A)(3) of this section if either of the following applies:
(1) The offender previously has been convicted of or pleaded guilty to a violation of this section or section 2903.08
(2) At the time of the offense, the offender was driving under suspension under Chapter 4510
(3) The offender has three or more prior violations of § 4511.19, § 1547.11(A), § 4561.15(A)(3), § 2903.06(A)(1), § 2903.08(A)(1), § 2903.04 (when Division (D) of that section applied) or any combination thereof within the previous six years
(4) The offender has two or more prior felony violations of § 4511.19(A)

***AGGRAVATED VEHICULAR ASSAULT; VEHICULAR ASSAULT,* R.C. § 2903.08 [F4, F3, F2, M1]**

Division (A)(1) (aggravated vehicular assault):
(1) As the proximate result of committing a violation of R.C. § 4511.19(A), R.C. § 1547.11(A), R.C. § 4561.15(A)(3) or of a substantially equivalent municipal ordinance
(2) (a) While operating
*(or)*
(b) While participating in the operation of
(3) A motor vehicle, motorcycle, snowmobile, locomotive, watercraft, or aircraft
(4) Cause
(5) Serious physical harm
(6) (a) To another person
*(or)*
(b) Another's unborn
(7) Venue
*Penalty:* A felony of the third degree (2929.11-2929.18, 2929.31)
If at the time of the offense, the offender was driving under a suspension imposed under Chapter 4510 or any other provision of the Revised Code or if the offender previously has been convicted of or pleaded guilty to a violation of this section, any traffic-related homicide, manslaughter, or assault offense; three or more prior violations of R.C. § 4511.19, R.C. § 1547.11(A), R.C. § 4561.15(A)(3), or violations of any combination of the offenses listed in R.C. § 2903.08 (B)(1)(d), (e), or (f) or of a substantially equivalent municipal ordinance within the previous 6 years; or a second or subsequent felony violation of R.C. § 4511.19(A)
*Penalty:* A felony of the second degree (2929.11-2929.18, 2929.31)

*Notes:* In addition to any other sanction imposed, the court shall impose a class three suspension of the offender's driver's license, commercial driver's license, temporary instruction permit, probationary license or nonresident operating privilege pursuant to R.C. § 4510.02 or, if the offender previously has been convicted of or pleaded guilty to a violation of this section or any traffic-related homicide, manslaughter, or assault offense, a class two suspension

The court shall impose a mandatory prison term on an offender who is convicted of or pleads guilty to a violation of this division

Division (A)(2) (vehicular assault):

(1) (a) As the proximate result of committing, while operating or participating in the operation of a motor vehicle or motorcycle in a construction zone, a reckless operation offense, provided that this division applies only if the person to whom the serious physical harm is caused or to whose unborn the serious physical harm is caused is in the construction zone at the time of the offender's commission of the reckless operation offense in the construction zone and does not apply as described in division (E) of this section

*(or)*

(b) Recklessly.

(2) (a) While operating

*(or)*

(b) While participating in the operation of

(3) A motor vehicle, motorcycle, snowmobile, locomotive, watercraft, or aircraft

(4) Cause

(5) Serious physical harm

(6) (a) To another person

*(or)*

(b) Another's unborn

(7) Venue

*Penalty:* A felony of the fourth degree (2929.11-2929.18, 2929.31)

If at the time of the offense, the offender was driving under a suspension imposed under Chapter 4510 or any other provision of the Revised Code or if the offender previously has been convicted of or pleaded guilty to a violation of this section, any traffic-related homicide, manslaughter, or assault offense

*Penalty:* A felony of the third degree (2929.11-2929.18, 2929.31)

*Notes:* In addition to any other sanction imposed, the court shall impose a class four suspension of the offender's driver's license, commercial diver's license, temporary instruction permit, probationary license or nonresident operating privilege pursuant to R.C. § 4510.02 or, if the offender previously has been convicted of or pleaded guilty to a violation of this section or any traffic-related homicide, manslaughter, or assault offense, a class three suspension

The court shall impose a mandatory prison term on an offender who is convicted of or pleads guilty to a violation of this division if either of the following applies:

(1) The offender previously has been convicted of or pleaded guilty to a violation of this section or section 2903.06

(2) At the time of the offense, the offender was driving under suspension under Chapter 4510 or any other provision of the Revised Code

Division (A)(3) (vehicular assault):

(1) As the proximate result of committing, while operating or participating in the operation of a motor vehicle or motorcycle in a construction zone, a speeding offense, provided that this division applies only if the person to whom the serious physical harm is caused or to whose unborn the serious physical harm is caused is in the construction zone at the time of the offender's commission of the speeding offense in the construction zone and does not apply as described in division (E) of this section.

(2) (a) While operating

*(or)*

(b) While participating in the operation of

(3) A motor vehicle, motorcycle, snowmobile, locomotive, watercraft, or aircraft

(4) Cause

(5) Serious physical harm

(6) (a) To another person

*(or)*

(b) Another's unborn

(7) Venue

*Penalty:* A misdemeanor of the first degree (2929.21, 2929.31)

Vehicular assault committed in violation of division (A)(3) of this section is a felony of the fourth degree (2929.11-2929.18, 2929.31) if, at the time of the offense, the offender was driving under a suspension imposed under Chapter 4510. or any other provision of the Revised Code or if the offender previously has been convicted of or pleaded guilty to a violation of this section or any traffic-related homicide, manslaughter, or assault offense

*Notes:* In addition to any other sanctions imposed, the court shall impose upon the offender a class four suspension of the offender's driver's license, commercial driver's license, temporary instruction permit, probationary license, or nonresident operating privilege from the range specified in division (A)(4) of section 4510.02 of the Revised Code or, if the offender previously has been convicted of or pleaded guilty to a violation of this section

or any traffic-related homicide, manslaughter, or assault offense, a class three suspension of the offender's driver's license, commercial driver's license, temporary instruction permit, probationary license, or nonresident operating privilege from the range specified in division (A)(3) of section 4510.02 of the Revised Code
The court shall impose a mandatory prison term on an offender who is convicted of or pleads guilty to a violation of division (A)(2) of this section or a felony violation of division (A)(3) of this section if either of the following applies:
(a) The offender previously has been convicted of or pleaded guilty to a violation of this section or section 2903.06 of the Revised Code
(b) At the time of the offense, the offender was driving under suspension under Chapter 4510. or any other provision of the Revised Code
The court shall impose a mandatory jail term of at least seven days on an offender who is convicted of or pleads guilty to a misdemeanor violation of division (A)(3) of this section and may impose upon the offender a longer jail term as authorized pursuant to section 2929.24 of the Revised Code
Divisions (A)(2)(a) and (3) of this section do not apply in a particular construction zone unless signs of the type described in section 2903.081 [2903.08.1] of the Revised Code are erected in that construction zone in accordance with the guidelines and design specifications established by the director of transportation under section 5501.27 of the Revised Code. The failure to erect signs of the type described in section 2903.081 [2903.08.1] of the Revised Code in a particular construction zone in accordance with those guidelines and design specifications does not limit or affect the application of division (A)(1) or (2)(b) of this section in that construction zone or the prosecution of any person who violates either of those divisions in that construction zone

***FELONIOUS ASSAULT,* R.C. § 2903.11 [F2, F1]**

Division (A):
(1) Knowingly
(2) (a) Cause serious physical harm to another or to another's unborn
*(or)*
(b) Cause or attempt to cause physical harm to another or to another's unborn by use of deadly weapon/ dangerous ordnance
(3) Venue

Division (B):
(1) Knowing that the person has tested positive as a carrier of a virus that causes AIDS
(2) (a) Engage in sexual conduct with another person without disclosing that knowledge to the other person prior to engaging in the sexual conduct
*(or)*
(b) Engage in sexual conduct with another person whom the offender knows or has reasonable cause to believe lacks the mental capacity to appreciate the significance of the knowledge that the offender has tested positive as a carrier of a virus that causes AIDS
*(or)*
(c) Engage in sexual conduct with a person under 18 years of age who is not the spouse of the offender
(3) Venue
*Penalty:* A felony of the second degree (2929.11-2929.18, 2929.31)
If victim is a peace officer
*Penalty:* A felony of the first degree (2929.11-2929.18, 2929.31)
If victim is a peace officer or an investigator of the bureau of criminal identification and investigation and if the victim suffered serious physical harm as a result of the commission of the offense
*Penalty:* A felony of the fourth degree (2929.11-2929.18, 2929.31) and the court shall impose a mandatory prison term from one of the prison terms prescribed by 2929.13 for a felony of the fourth degree
*Definitions:* "Deadly weapon," "dangerous ordnance," R.C. § 2923.11
"Physical harm to persons," R.C. § 2901.01(A)(3)
"Serious physical harm to persons," R.C. § 2901.01(A)(5)
"Firearm," R.C. § 2923.11(B)
"Peace officer," R.C. § 2935.01(B)
"Investigator of the bureau of criminal identification and investigation," R.C. § 2903.11(E)
"Investigator," R.C. § 2903.11(E)
*Notes:* In addition to any other sanctions, if a deadly weapon used is a motor vehicle, the court shall order a class two suspension of the offender's driver's license, commercial driver's license, temporary instruction permit, probationary license, or nonresident operating privilege
Mandatory prison term if the offender knew the victim was pregnant

***AGGRAVATED ASSAULT,* R.C. § 2903.12 [F4, F3]**

(1) While under
(a) the influence of sudden passion or in a sudden fit of rage
*(or)*
(b) extreme emotional stress
(2) Brought on by serious provocation occasioned by the victim reasonably sufficient to incite him to use deadly force

(3) Knowingly
(a) Cause serious physical harm to another or to another's unborn
*(or)*
(b) Cause or attempt to cause physical harm to another or to another's unborn by means of deadly weapon or dangerous ordnance
(4) Venue
*Penalty:* A felony of the fourth degree (2929.11-2929.18, 2929.31)
If the victim is a peace officer or an investigator of the bureau of criminal identification and investigation
*Penalty:* A felony of the third degree (2929.11-2929.18, 2929.31)
If victim is a peace officer or an investigator of the bureau of criminal identification and investigation and if the victim suffered serious physical harm as a result of the commission of the offense
*Penalty:* A felony of the third degree (2929.11-2929.18. 2929.31) and the court shall impose a mandatory prison term from one of the prison terms prescribed by 2929.13 for a felony of the third degree
*Definitions:* "Deadly weapon," "dangerous ordnance," "firearm," R.C. § 2923.11
"Investigator of the bureau of criminal identification and investigation," R.C. § 2903.11(E)
"Peace officer," R.C. § 2935.01
*Notes:* Mandatory prison term if the offender knew the victim was pregnant

**_ASSAULT_, R.C. § 2903.13 [M1, F5, F4, F3]**

Division (A):
(1) Knowingly
(2) Cause or attempt to cause
(3) Physical harm to another or to another's unborn
(4) Venue

Division (B):
(1) Recklessly
(2) Cause serious physical harm to another or to another's unborn
(3) Venue
*Penalty:* A misdemeanor of the first degree (2929.21-2929.31)
If committed by a caretaker against a functionally impaired person under the caretaker's care
*Penalty:* A felony of the fourth degree (2929.11-2929.18, 2929.31)
If committed by a caretaker against a functionally impaired person under the caretaker's care, and if the offender has been previously convicted under R.C. § 2903.11, 2903.13, or 2903.16, and if the previous offense was against a functionally impaired person under the care of the offender, who was acting as a caretaker
*Penalty:* A felony of the third degree (2929.11-2929.18, 2929.31)
If committed (a) in or on the grounds of a state correctional institution or an institution of the Department of Youth Services, the victim is an employee of the Department of Rehabilitation and Correction, the Department of Youth Services, or a probation department or is on the premises of the particular institution for business purposes or as a visitor, and the offense is committed by a person incarcerated in the state correctional institution, by a person institutionalized in the Department of Youth Services institution pursuant to a commitment to the Department of Youth Services, by a parolee, by an offender under transitional control, under a community control sanction, or on an escorted visit, by a person under post-release control, or by an offender under any other type of supervision by a government agency; or (b) in or on the grounds of a local correctional facility, the victim is an employee of the local correctional facility or a probation department or is on the premises of the facility for business purposes or as a visitor, and the offense is committed by a person who is under custody in the facility subsequent to the person's arrest for any crime or delinquent act, subsequent to the person being charged with or convicted of any crime, or subsequent to the person being alleged to be or adjudicated a delinquent child; or (c) off the grounds of a state correctional institution and off the grounds of an institution of the Department of Youth Services, the victim is an employee of the Department of Rehabilitation and Correction, the Department of Youth Services, or a probation department, the offense occurs during the employee's official work hours and while the employee is engaged in official work responsibilities, and the offense is committed by a person incarcerated in a state correctional institution or institutionalized in the Department of Youth Services who temporarily is outside of the institution for any purpose, by a parolee, by an offender under transitional control, under a community control sanction, or on an escorted visit, by a person under post-release control, or by an offender under any other type of supervision by a government agency; or (d) off the grounds of a local correctional facility, the victim is an employee of the local correctional facility or probation department, the offense occurs during the employee's official work hours and while the employee is engaged in official work responsibilities, and the offense is committed by a person who is under custody in the facility subsequent to the person's arrest for any crime or delinquent act, subsequent to the person being charged with or convicted of any crime, or subsequent to the person being alleged to be or adjudicated a delinquent child and who temporarily is outside of the facility for any purpose or by a parolee, by an offender under transitional control, under a community control sanction, or on an escorted visit, by a person under post-release control, or by an offender under any other type of supervision by a government agency; or (e) in a school, on school premises, in a school building, on a school bus, or while the victim is outside of school premises or a school bus and is engaged in duties or official responsibilities associated with victim's employment or position as a school teacher or administrator or a school bus operator, including, but not limited to, driving, accompanying, or chaperoning students at or on class or field trips, athletic events or other school extracurricular activities or functions outside school premises

*Penalty:* A felony of the fifth degree (2929.11-2929.18, 2929.31)
If the victim of the offense is a peace officer or an investigator of the bureau of criminal identification and investigation, a firefighter, or person performing emergency medical service, while in the performance of their official duties
*Penalty:* A felony of the fourth degree (2929.11-2929.18, 2929.31)
If victim is a peace officer or an investigator of the bureau of criminal identification and investigation and if the victim suffered serious physical harm as a result of the commission of the offense
*Penalty:* A felony of the fourth degree (2929.11-2929.18, 2929.31) and the court shall impose a mandatory prison term from one of the prison terms prescribed by 2929.13 for a felony of the fourth degree
*Definitions:* "Caretaker," "functionally impaired person," R.C. § 2903.10
"Peace officer," R.C. § 2935.01(B)
"School," "school building," "school premises," R.C. § 2925.01
"School bus," R.C. § 4511.01
"Investigator of the bureau of criminal identification and investigation," R.C. § 2903.11(E)
*Notes:* Mandatory prison term if the offender knew the victim was pregnant

***NEGLIGENT ASSAULT,* R.C. § 2903.14 [M3]**

(1) Negligently
(2) By means of a deadly weapon or dangerous ordnance
(3) Cause physical harm to another or to another's unborn
(4) Venue
*Penalty:* A misdemeanor of the third degree (2929.21-2929.31)
*Definitions:* "Deadly weapon," "dangerous ordnance," R.C. § 2923.11

***PERMITTING CHILD ABUSE,* R.C. § 2903.15 [F1, F3]**

(1) Being a parent, guardian, custodian, or person having custody of a child under 18 or of a mentally or physically handicapped child under 21
(2) Cause serious physical harm or death to such child
(3) As a proximate result of permitting the child to be
(a) Abused
*(or)*
(b) Tortured
*(or)*
(c) Administered corporal punishment or other physical disciplinary measure
*(or)*
(d) Physically restrained in a cruel manner or for a prolonged period
(4) Venue
*Penalty:* If the violation causes serious physical harm to the child, a felony of the third degree (2929.11-2929.18, 2929.31)
If the violation causes the death of the child
*Penalty:* A felony of the first degree (2929.11-2929.18, 2929.31)
*Notes:* It is an affirmative defense that the defendant did not have readily available a means to prevent the harm or death and that the defendant took timely and reasonable steps to summon aid

***FAILING TO PROVIDE FOR A FUNCTIONALLY IMPAIRED PERSON,* R.C. § 2903.16 [M1, M2, F4]**

Division (A): Knowingly Failing to Provide for a Functionally Impaired Person
(1) Being a caretaker
(2) Knowingly
(3) Fail to provide
(4) To a functionally impaired person under the caretaker's care
(5) Any treatment, care, goods, or service
(6) Necessary to maintain the health or safety of the functionally impaired person
(7) When the failure results in physical harm or serious physical harm to the functionally impaired person
(8) Venue
*Penalty:* A misdemeanor of the first degree (2929.21-2929.31)
If the functionally impaired person under the offender's care suffers serious physical harm as a result of the violation
*Penalty:* A felony of the fourth degree (2929.11-2929.18, 2929.31)

Division (B): Recklessly Failing to Provide for a Functionally Impaired Person
(1) Being a caretaker
(2) Recklessly
(3) Fail to provide
(4) To a functionally impaired person under the caretaker's care
(5) Any treatment, care, goods, or service
(6) Necessary to maintain the health or safety of the functionally impaired person
(7) When the failure results in serious physical harm to the functionally impaired person
(8) Venue

*Penalty:* A misdemeanor of the second degree (2929.21-2929.31)
If the functionally impaired person under the offender's care suffers serious physical harm as a result of the violation
*Penalty:* A felony of the fourth degree (2929.11-2929.18, 2929.31)
*Note: See* R.C. § 2903.34 for similar offenses involving residents or patients of care facilities
*Definitions:* "Caretaker," "Functionally impaired person," R.C. § 2903.10

**_AGGRAVATED MENACING,_ R.C. § 2903.21 [M1, F4]**

(1) Knowingly
(2) Cause another to believe
(3) That the offender will cause serious physical harm to the person or property of such other person, such other person's unborn, or member of the other person's immediate family
(4) Venue

*Penalty:* A misdemeanor of the first degree (2929.21-2929.31)
*Penalty:* a felony of the fourth degree (2929.11-2929.18, 2929.31)
If the victim of the offense is an officer or employee of a public children services agency or a private child placing agency and the offense relates to the officer's or employee's performance or anticipated performance of official responsibilities or duties, aggravated menacing is a felony of the fifth degree or, if the offender previously has been convicted of or pleaded guilty to an offense of violence, the victim of that prior offense was an officer or employee of a public children services agency or private child placing agency, and that prior offense related to the officer's or employee's performance or anticipated performance of official responsibilities or duties

**_MENACING BY STALKING,_ R.C. § 2903.211 [M1, F4, F5]**

Division (A)(1):
(1) By engaging in a pattern of conduct
(2) Knowingly
(3) (a) Cause another person to believe that the offender will cause physical harm to the other person
*(or)*
(b) Cause mental distress to the other person
(4) Venue

Division (A)(2):
(1) Through the use of any electronic method of remotely transferring information, including, but not limited to, any computer, computer network, computer program, or computer system
(2) Post a message
(3) With purpose
(4) To urge or incite another
(5) To commit a violation of RC § 2903.211(A)(1)

Division (A)(3):
(1) Violating (A)(1) or (A)(2) of this section
(2) With a sexual motivation.

*Penalty:* A misdemeanor of the first degree. Penalties for menacing by stalking are increased if the offender acted with a sexual motivation. (2929.21-2929.31)
If
(1) the offender has previously been convicted of or pleaded guilty to a violation of this section or 2911.211;
(2) in committing the offense the offender (1) made a threat of physical harm to or against the victim, or as a result of an offense committed under R.C. § 2903.21.l(A)(2), a third person induced by the offender's posted message made a threat of physical harm to or against the victim, (2) trespassed on the land or premises where the victim lives, is employed or attends school, or as a result of an offense committed under R.C. § 2903.211(A)(2), a third person induced by the offender's posted message trespassed on the land or premises where the victim lives, is employed, or attends school;
(3) the victim is a minor;
(4) the offender has a history of violence toward the victim or any other person or a history of other violent acts toward the victim or another person;
(5) while committing the offense the offender had a deadly weapon or about his person or under his control;
(6) at the time of the commission of the offense the offender was the subject of a protection order issued under 2903.213 or 2903.214, regardless of whether the person to be protected under the order is the victim of the offense or another person;
(7) in committing the offense the offender caused serious physical harm to the premises at which the victim resides, to the real property on which that premises is located, or to any personal property located on that premises, or as a result of an offense committed under R.C. § 2903.211(A)(2), a third person induced by the offender's posted message caused serious physical harm to that premises, that real property, or any personal property on that premises; or,
(8) prior to committing the offense, the offender had been determined to represent a substantial risk of physical harm to others as manifested by evidence of then-recent homicidal or other violent behavior, evidence of then-recent threats that placed another in reasonable fear of violent behavior and serious physical harm, or other evidence of then-present dangerousness.

or if
(1) the offender previously has been convicted of or pleaded guilty to an offense of violence;
(2) the victim of that prior offense was an officer or employee of a public children services agency or private child placing agency; and
(3) that prior offense related to the officer's or employee's performance or anticipated performance of official responsibilities or duties.

*Penalty:* A felony of the fourth degree. Penalties for menacing by stalking are increased if the offender acted with a sexual motivation. (2929.11-2929.18. 2929.31)

If
(1) the offender has previously been convicted of or pleaded guilty to a violation of this section or Section 2911.211;
(2) in committing the offense the offender (1) made a threat of physical harm to or against the victim, or as a result of an offense committed under division (A)(2) or (3) of this section, a third person induced by the offender's posted message made a threat of physical harm to or against the victim; (2) trespassed on the land or premises where the victim lives, is employed or attends school; or as a result of an offense committed under division (A)(2) or (3) of this section, a third person induced by the offender's posted message trespassed on the land or premises where the victim lives, is employed, or attends school;
(3) the victim is a minor;
(4) the offender has a history of violence toward the victim or any other person or a history of other violent acts toward the victim or another person;
(5) while committing the offense the offender had a deadly weapon or about his person or under his control;
(6) at the time of the commission of the offense the offender was the subject of a protection order issued under Section 2903.213 or 2903.214 regardless of whether the person to be protected under the order is the victim of the offense or another person;
(7) in committing the offense the offender caused serious physical harm to the premises at which the victim resides, to the real property on which that premises is located, or to any personal property located on that premises; or as a result of an offense committed under division (A)(2) or an offense committed under (A)(3) based on a violation of division (A)(2) of this section, a third person induced by the offender's posted message caused serious physical harm to that premises, that real property, or any personal property on that premises; or,
(8) prior to committing the offense, the offender had been determined to represent a substantial risk of physical harm to others as manifested by evidence of then-recent homicidal or other violent behavior, evidence of then-recent threats that placed another in reasonable fear of violent behavior and serious physical harm, or other evidence of then-present dangerousness.

*Penalty:* A felony of the fifth degree. Penalties for menacing by stalking are increased if the offender acted with a sexual motivation. (2929.11-2929.18, 2929.31)

*Notes:* Section 2919.271 of the Revised Code applies in relation to a defendant charged with a violation of this section
*See* R.C. § 2903.212 for special provisions concerning repeat offenders and offenders violating prior orders
*See* R.C. § 2903.212 for special provisions concerning bail
*See* R.C. § 2903.214 for special provisions concerning petition for protection order to protect victim of menacing by stalking
*See* R.C. §§ 2903.213 and 2919.26 for special provisions concerning protection orders
*See* R.C. § 2925.03 for special provisions concerning arrest and detention

*Definitions:* "Pattern of conduct" means two or more actions or incidents closely related in time, whether or not there has been a prior conviction based on any of those actions or incidents. Actions or incidents that prevent, obstruct, or delay the performance by a public official, firefighter, rescuer, emergency medical services person, or emergency facility person of any authorized act within the public official's, firefighter's, rescuer s, emergency medical services person's, or emergency facility person's official capacity or the posting of messages or receipt of information or data through the use of an electronic method of remotely transferring information, including, but not limited to, a computer, computer network, computer program, computer system, or telecommunications device may constitute a "pattern of conduct." R.C. § 2903.211

"Mental distress" means any mental illness or condition that involves some temporary substantial incapacity or mental illness or condition that would normally require psychiatric treatment, psychological treatment, or other mental health services, whether or not any person requested or received psychiatric treatment, psychological treatment, or other mental health services. R.C. § 2903.211

"Emergency medical services person" is the singular of "emergency medical services personnel" as defined in section 2133.21 of the Revised Code. R.C. § 2903.211

"Emergency facility person" is the singular of "emergency facility personnel" as defined in section 2909.04 of the Revised Code. R.C. § 2903.211

"Public official" has the same meaning as in R.C. § 2921.01

"Computer," "computer network," "computer program, computer system," and "telecommunications device" have the same meanings as in R.C. § 2913.01

"Post a message" means transferring, sending, posting, publishing, disseminating, or otherwise communicating, or attempting to transfer, send, post, publish, disseminate, or otherwise communicate, any message or information, whether truthful or untruthful, about an individual, and whether done under one's own name, under the name of another, or while impersonating another

"Third person" means, in relation to conduct as described in R.C. § 2903.211(A)(2), an individual who is neither the offender nor the victim of the conduct

***MENACING*, R.C. § 2903.22 [M4]**

(1) Knowingly
(2) Cause another to believe
(3) That the offender will cause physical harm to the person or property of such other person, such other person's unborn, or member of the other person's immediate family
(4) Venue
*Penalty:* A misdemeanor of the fourth degree (2929.21-2929.31)

***HAZING*, R.C. § 2903.31 [M4]**

Division (B)(1):
(1) Recklessly
(2) Participate in hazing
(3) Another
(4) Venue

Division (B)(2):
(1) Being an administrator, employee, or faculty member
(2) Of a public or private primary, secondary, post-secondary school, or other educational institution
(3) Recklessly
(4) Permit hazing
(5) Any person
(6) Venue
*Penalty:* A misdemeanor of the fourth degree (2929.21-2929.31)
*Notes:* Hazing is defined as doing any act or coercing another, including the victim, to do any act of initiation into any student or other organization that causes or creates a substantial risk of causing mental or physical harm to any person. R.C. § 2903.31(A)
See R.C. § 2307.44 for provisions regarding civil liability

***PATIENT ABUSE; NEGLECT*, R.C. § 2903.34 [M1, M2, F3, F4, F5]**

A. PATIENT ABUSE **[F4, F3]**

(1) While owning, operating, administering, or an agent or employee of a care facility
(2) (a) Knowingly cause physical harm
*(or)*
(b) Recklessly cause serious physical harm
(3) To a resident or patient of the facility
(4) (a) By physical contact with the person
*(or)*
(b) By the inappropriate use of physical or chemical restraint, medication, or isolation on the person (i.e., use as punishment, for staff convenience, excessively, as substitute for treatment, or in quantities which preclude habilitation or treatment)
(5) Venue
If no prior offense under this section
*Penalty:* A felony of the fourth degree (2929.11-2929.18, 2929.31)
If prior offense under this section
*Penalty:* A felony of the third degree (2929.11-2929.18, 2929.31)

B. GROSS PATIENT NEGLECT **[M1, F5]**

(1) While owning, operating, administering, or an agent or employee of a care facility
(2) Knowingly
(3) Fail to provide
(4) To a resident or patient of the facility
(5) Any treatment, care, goods, or service
(6) Necessary to maintain the health or safety of the person
(7) When the failure results in physical harm or serious physical harm to the person
(8) Venue
If no prior offense under this section
*Penalty:* A misdemeanor of the first degree (2929.21-2929.31)
If prior offense under this section
*Penalty:* A felony of the fifth degree (2929.11-2929.18, 2929.31)

C. PATIENT NEGLECT **[M2, F5]**

(1) While owning, operating, administering, or an agent or employee of a care facility
(2) Recklessly
(3) Fail to provide
(4) To a resident or patient of the facility

(5) Any treatment, care, goods, or service
(6) Necessary to maintain the health or safety of the person
(7) When the failure results in serious physical harm to the person
(8) Venue
If no prior offense under this section
*Penalty:* A misdemeanor of the second degree (2929.21-2929.31)
If prior offense under this section
*Penalty:* A felony of the fifth degree (2929.11-2929.18, 2929.31)
*Notes:* Any individual convicted of felony violation of this statute who is required to be licensed under Ohio law shall have license revoked. R.C. § 2903.37
Affirmative defense to charge of neglect or gross neglect that conduct in good faith solely because ordered by person with supervisory authority. *See* R.C. § 2903.34(B)(2)
Person who relies on treatment by spiritual means through prayer alone under tenets of recognized denomination not to be considered neglected under (C) above for that reason alone. *See* R.C. § 2903.34(B)(1)
Discharge, discrimination, and retaliation for filing complaint, etc., prohibited, *see* R.C. § 2903.36
Filing false complaint, *see* R.C. § 2903.35
Attorney General to investigate, refer, and (when appropriate) prosecute violations, *see* R.C. § 109.86
Local officials — proceedings hereunder, *see* R.C. § 109.86
*See also* R.C. §§ 2903.11, 2903.13, 2903.16 for similar offenses involving functionally impaired persons
*Definitions:* "Care facility," "abuse," "gross neglect," "neglect," "inappropriate use of a physical or chemical restraint, medication, or isolation," R.C. § 2903.33

**_PATIENT ENDANGERMENT,_ R.C. § 2903.341 (M1, F3, F4)**

Division (B):
(1) MR/DD caretaker
(2) Create a substantial risk
(3) To the health or safety of a
(4) Mentally retarded person or a developmentally disabled person.
(5) Venue

Division (C):
(1) (a) No person who owns, operates, or administers a care facility
*(or)*
(b) Who is an agent of a care facility
(2) (a) Condone
*(or)*
(b) Knowingly permit
(3) Any conduct by an MR/DD caretaker who is employed by or under the control of the owner, operator, administrator, or agent that is in violation of division (B) of this section
(4) Involving a mentally retarded person or a developmentally disabled person who is under the care of the owner, operator, administrator, or agent.
(5) Venue
*Penalties:* A misdemeanor of the first degree. (2929.21-2929.31)
*(or)*
If the offender previously has been convicted of, or pleaded guilty to, a violation of this section, patient endangerment is a felony of the fourth degree. (2929.11-2929.18, 2929.31)
*(or)*
If the violation results in serious physical harm to the person with mental retardation or a developmental disability, patient endangerment is a felony of the third degree. (2929.11-2929.18, 2929.31)

**_FILING A FALSE PATIENT ABUSE OR NEGLECT COMPLAINT,_ R.C. § 2903.35 [M1]**

(1) Knowingly
(2) (a) Make a false statement
*(or)*
(b) Swear or affirm the truth of a false statement previously made
(3) Alleging a violation of R.C. § 2903.34
(4) When statement made with purpose to incriminate another
(5) Venue
*Penalty:* A misdemeanor of the first degree (2929.21-2929.31)

## KIDNAPPING AND EXTORTION

**_KIDNAPPING,_ R.C. § 2905.01 [F1, F2]**

Division (A):

(1) (a) By force, threat, or deception
*(or)*
(b) By any means where victim is under 13 or mentally incompetent
(2) (a) Remove person from the place the other person is found
*(or)*
(b) Restrain another person of the other person's liberty
(3) With a purpose to:
(a) Hold for ransom, or as a shield or hostage
(b) Facilitate commission of any felony or flight thereafter
(c) Terrorize or inflict serious physical harm on the victim or another
(d) Engage in sexual activity (R.C. § 2907.01) with the victim against the victim's will
(e) Hinder, impede, or obstruct a function of government, or to force any action or concession on the part of governmental authority
(f) Hold in a condition of involuntary servitude
(4) Venue

Division (B):
(1) (a) By force, threat, or deception
*(or)*
(b) By any means where victim is under 13 or mentally incompetent
(2) Knowingly
(3) Under circumstances creating a substantial risk of serious physical harm to the victim or, in the case of a minor victim, under circumstances that either create a substantial risk of serious physical harm to the victim or cause physical harm to the victim
(4) (a) Remove another from the place the other person is found
*(or)*
(b) Restrain another of the other person's liberty
(5) Venue
*Penalty:* A felony of the first degree (2929.11-2929.18, 2929.31)
If victim released in a safe place unharmed
*Penalty:* A felony of the second degree (2929.11-2929.18, 2929.31)
*Penalty:* Felony of the first degree. If the victim is released in a safe place, unharmed, a felony of the second degree. If the victim is under 13 years of age, mandatory minimum 15 years imprisonment (or 10 years if the victim is released in a safe place). (2971.03)

**_ABDUCTION_, R.C. § 2905.02 [F3]**

(1) Knowingly
(2) (a) Remove another by force or threat from the place where the other person is found
*(or)*
(b) Restrain the liberty of another person by force or threat under circumstances creating a risk of physical harm to the victim or by placing the other person in fear
*(or)*
(c) Hold another in a condition of involuntary servitude
(3) Without privilege to do so
(4) Venue
*Penalty:* A felony of the third degree (2929.11-2929.18, 2929.31). If violate Division (A)(3) or violate division (B) involving conduct of the type described in division (A)(3)
*Penalty:* A felony of the second degree (2929.11-2929.18, 2929.31)

**_UNLAWFUL RESTRAINT_, R.C. § 2905.03 [M3]**

Division (A)
(1) Knowingly
(2) Restrain another of his liberty
(3) Without privilege to do so
(4) Venue
Division (B)
(1) Without privilege to do so and
(2) With a sexual motivation,
(3) Knowingly
(4) Restrain another of his liberty.
*Penalty:* A misdemeanor of the third degree (2929.21-2929.31)

**_CRIMINAL CHILD ENTICEMENT_, R.C. § 2905.05 [M1, F5]**

Division (A)
(1) Knowingly
(2) By any means
(3) Without privilege to do so

(4) Solicit, coax, entice, or lure
(5) Any child under 14 years of age (regardless of actor's ignorance of child's age)
(6) To accompany the person in any manner, including entering into any vehicle or onto any vessel
(7) If actor does not have express or implied consent of child's parent, guardian, or other legal custodian
(8) (a) Where actor is not either of the following
(i) A law enforcement officer, medic, firefighter, or other person regularly providing emergency services
*(or)*
(ii) An employee or agent of, or volunteer acting under the direction of, any board of education
*(or)*
(b) Where actor is a person described in (a)(i) or (ii) who at the time is not acting within the scope of the actor's lawful duties in that capacity
(9) Venue
Division (B)
(1) Violating Division (A) of this section
(2) With a sexual motivation.
*Penalty:* A misdemeanor of the first degree (2929.21-2929.31). If the offender has previously been convicted of an offense under Sections 2905.05, 2907.02, 2907.03, former 2907.12, 2905.01 or 2907.05 when the victim was under 17, then a felony of the fifth degree (2929.11-2929.18, 2929.31)
*Note:* It is an affirmative defense that the actor undertook the activity in response to a bona fide emergency situation, or in a reasonable belief that it was necessary to preserve the health, safety, or welfare of the child

**_EXTORTION_, R.C. § 2905.11 [F3]**

(1) With a purpose to:
(a) Obtain anything of value or valuable benefit
*(or)*
(b) To induce another to do any unlawful act
(2) (a) Threaten to commit a felony
*(or)*
(b) Threaten to commit an offense of violence
*(or)*
(c) Violate R.C. § 2903.21 or 2903.22
*(or)*
(d) Utter or threaten any calumny against any person
*(or)*
(e) Expose or threaten to expose any matter that tends to:
(i) Subject any person to hatred, contempt, or ridicule
*(or)*
(ii) Damage any person's personal or business reputation
*(or)*
(iii) Impair any person's credit
(3) Venue
*Penalty:* A felony of the third degree (2929.11-2929.18, 2929.31)
*Note:* Threat includes direct threat and threat by innuendo

**_COERCION_, R.C. § 2905.12 [M2]**

(1) With purpose to coerce another into taking or refraining from action concerning which the other person has a legal freedom of choice
(2) (a) Threaten to commit any offense
*(or)*
(b) Utter or threaten any calumny against any person
*(or)*
(c) Expose or threaten to expose any matter tending to:
(i) Subject any person to hatred, contempt, or ridicule
*(or)*
(ii) Damage any person's personal or business repute
*(or)*
(iii) Impair any person's credit
*(or)*
(d) Institute or threaten criminal proceedings against any person
*(or)*
(e) Take or withhold, or threaten to take or to withhold official action, or cause or threaten to cause official action to be taken or withheld
(3) Venue
*Penalty:* A misdemeanor of the second degree (2929.21-2929.31)
*Notes:* Threat includes direct threat and threat by innuendo
Affirmative defenses are set forth in the statute

***EXTORTIONATE EXTENSION OF CREDIT; CRIMINAL USURY,* R.C. § 2905.22 [F4, M1]**

Division (A)(1) or (2): **[F4]**
(1) Knowingly
(2) Make or participate in an extortionate extension of credit
*(or)*
(3) Engage in criminal usury
(4) Venue
*Penalty:* A felony of the fourth degree (2929.11-2929.18, 2929.31)

Division (A)(3): **[M1]**
(1) Possess
(2) Any writing, paper, instrument or article used to record criminally usurious transactions
(3) Knowing that the contents record a criminally usurious transaction
(4) Venue
*Penalty:* A misdemeanor of the first degree (2929.21-2929.31)
*Notes: See* R.C. § 2905.23 for standard of proof that an extension of credit is extortionate
See R.C. § 2905.24 for evidence admissible to prove an implicit threat as means of collection
*Definitions:* "To extend credit," "collect an extension of credit," "extortionate extension of credit," "extortionate means, criminal usury," R.C. § 2905.21

***COMPULSION TO INVOLUNTARY SERVITUDE,* R.C. § 2905.32**

(1) Knowingly
(2) recruiting, luring, enticing, isolating, harboring, transporting, providing, obtaining, or maintaining, or attempting to recruit, lure, entice, isolate, harbor, transport, provide, obtain, or maintain, another person
(3) knowing that the person will be subjected to involuntary servitude or be compelled to engage in sexual activity for hire, engage in a performance that is obscene, sexually oriented, or nudity oriented, or be a model or participant in the production of material that is obscene, sexually oriented, or nudity oriented
(4) Venue
*Penalty:* A felony of the second degree. (2929.11-2929.18, 2929.31)

***UNLAWFUL CONDUCT WITH RESPECT TO DOCUMENTS,* R.C. § 2905.33**

(1) Without privilege to do so,
(2) knowingly
(3) destroying, concealing, removing, confiscating, or possesing any actual or purported government identification document or passport of another person
(4) in the course of a violation of, with intent to violate, or with intent to facilitate a violation of §§ 2905.01, 2905.02, 2905.32, 2907.21, 2907.22, 2907.32, 2907.321, 2907.322, or 2907.32
(5) Venue
*Penalty:* A felony of the third degree. (2929.11-2929.18, 2929.31)

---

## SEX OFFENSES

***RAPE,* R.C. § 2907.02 [F1]**

(1) Engage in sexual conduct
(2) (a) With another by purposely compelling submission by force or threat of force
*(or)*
(b) With another not offender's spouse or with offender's spouse if living separate and apart, if:
(i) For purpose of preventing resistance, offender substantially impairs victim's judgment or control by administering any drug, intoxicant, or controlled substance surreptitiously or by force, threat of force, or deception
*(or)*
(ii) Victim under 13, regardless of offender's knowledge of age
*(or)*
(iii) Victim's ability to resist or consent is substantially impaired because of a mental or physical condition or because of advanced age and the offender knows or has reasonable cause to believe that the victim's ability to resist or consent is substantially impaired by such condition or advanced age
(3) Venue
*Penalty:* A felony of the first degree (2929.11-2929.18, 2929.31)
If the offender under division 2(b)(i) substantially impairs the other persons judgment or control by administering any controlled substance described in 3719.41 to the other person surreptitiously or by force, threat of force, or deception, the prison term imposed upon the offender shall be one of the prison terms prescribed for a felony of the first degree in 2929.14 that is not less than 5 years
If both elements 2(a) and 2(b)(ii) apply
*Penalty:* Life imprisonment, without parole if

(1) the victim was under 10 years old, regardless of use or threat of force
*(or)*
(2) the offender has a previous conviction of a similar offense
*(or)*
(3) the offender caused serious physical harm to the victim

*Penalty:* Life imprisonment if the victim was under 13 years of age, unless the victim was at least 10 years of age, the offender was under 16 years of age and had no prior convictions, and no serious physical harm was caused, in which case, felony of the first degree

*Notes:* Victim need not prove physical resistance

A peace officer, prosecutor, or other public official shall not ask or require a victim of an alleged sex offense to submit to a polygraph examination as a condition for proceeding with the investigation of the alleged sex offense. The refusal of the victim of an alleged sex offense to submit to a polygraph examination shall not prevent the investigation of the alleged sex offense, the filing of criminal charges with respect to the alleged sex offense, or the prosecution of the alleged perpetrator of the alleged sex offense. (§ 2907.10)

*See* R.C. § 2907.02(D)-(F) for provisions re evidence of prior sexual activity of victim/offender, admissibility of evidence, and victim's right to counsel in proceeding to determine admissibility

*See* R.C. § 2907.27 for provisions regarding mandatory medical tests for persons charged under this statute

***SEXUAL BATTERY*, R.C. § 2907.03 [F3]**

(1) Engage in sexual conduct
(2) With a person not the spouse of the offender when:
  (a) The offender knowingly coerced the other person to submit by any means that would prevent resistance by a person of ordinary resolution
  *(or)*
  (b) The offender knows that the other's ability to appraise the nature of or control the other person's own conduct is substantially impaired
  *(or)*
  (c) The offender knows the other person submits because the other person is unaware that the act is being committed
  *(or)*
  (d) The offender knows the other person submits because the other person mistakenly identifies the offender as the other person's spouse
  *(or)*
  (e) The offender is the other person's natural/adoptive parent, stepparent, guardian, custodian, or person in loco parentis
  *(or)*
  (f) The offender has supervisory or disciplinary authority over the other person and such person is in legal custody or a patient in a hospital or other institution
  *(or)*
  (g) The offender is a teacher, administrator, coach, or other person in authority in a school for which the state board of education prescribes minimum standards in which the other person is enrolled or attends that school and the offender is not enrolled and does not attend that school
  *(or)*
  (h) The other person is a minor, the offender is a teacher, administrator, coach, or other person in authority employed by or serving in an institution of higher education and the other person is enrolled in that institution
  *(or)*
  (i) The other person is a minor, and the offender is the other person's athletic or other type of coach, is the other person's instructor, is the leader of a scouting troop of which the other person is a member, or is a person with temporary or occasional disciplinary control over the other person
  *(or)*
  (j) The offender is a mental health professional, the other person is a mental health client or patient of the offender, and the offender induces the other person to submit by falsely representing to the other person that the sexual conduct is necessary for mental health treatment purposes.
  (k) The other person is confined in a detention facility, and the offender is an employee of that detention facility.
  (l) The other person is a minor, the offender is a cleric, and the other person is a member of, or attends, the church or congregation served by the cleric.
  (m) The other person is a minor, the offender is a peace officer, and the officer is more than two years older than the minor.
(3) Venue

*Penalty:* A felony of the third degree (2929.11-2929.18, 2929.31)

If the other person is less than thirteen years of age, sexual battery is a felony of the second degree, and the court shall impose upon the offender a mandatory prison term equal to one of the prison terms prescribed in section 2929.14 of the Revised Code for a felony of the second degree (2929.11-2929.18, 2929.31)

*Notes:* A peace officer, prosecutor, or other public official shall not ask or require a victim of an alleged sex offense to submit to a polygraph examination as a condition for proceeding with the investigation of the alleged sex offense. The refusal of the victim of an alleged sex offense to submit to a polygraph examination shall not

prevent the investigation of the alleged sex offense, the filing of criminal charges with respect to the alleged sex offense, or the prosecution of the alleged perpetrator of the alleged sex offense. (§ 2907.10)
*See* R.C. § 2907.27 for provisions regarding mandatory medical tests for persons charged under this statute
*Definitions:* "Mental health client," "mental health professional," R.C. 2305.51

***UNLAWFUL SEXUAL CONDUCT WITH A MINOR,*** **R.C. § 2907.04 [F4, M1, F3, F2]**

(1) Being 18 or older
(2) Engage in sexual conduct
(3) With another who is not the offender's spouse when:
  (a) Offender knows the other person is 13 years of age or older, but less than 16 years of age
  *(or)*
  (b) Offender is reckless in this regard
(4) Venue

*Penalty:* A felony of the fourth degree (2929.11-2929.18, 2929.31)
If offender is less than 4 years older than the victim
*Penalty:* A misdemeanor of the first degree (2929.21-2929.31)
If offender is ten or more years older than the victim
*Penalty:* A felony of the third degree (2929.11-2929.18, 2929.31)
If offender has previously been convicted of a violation of R.C. § 2907.02, 2907.03, 2907.04, or former 2907.12
*Penalty:* A felony of the second degree (2929.11-2929.18, 2929.31)
*Notes:* A peace officer, prosecutor, or other public official shall not ask or require a victim of an alleged sex offense to submit to a polygraph examination as a condition for proceeding with the investigation of the alleged sex offense. The refusal of the victim of an alleged sex offense to submit to a polygraph examination shall not prevent the investigation of the alleged sex offense, the filing of criminal charges with respect to the alleged sex offense, or the prosecution of the alleged perpetrator of the alleged sex offense. (§ 2907.10)
*See* R.C. § 2907.27 for provisions regarding mandatory medical tests for persons charged under this statute

***GROSS SEXUAL IMPOSITION,*** **R.C. § 2907.05 [F4, F3]**

Division (A)
(1) (a) Have sexual contact with another, not the spouse of the offender
  *(or)*
  (b) Cause another, not the spouse of the offender, to have sexual contact with the offender
  *(or)*
  (c) Cause two or more other persons to have sexual contact
(2) (a) By purposely compelling the other, or one of the others, to submit by force or threat of force
  *(or)*
  (b) For the purpose of preventing resistance, the offender substantially impairs the judgment or control of the other person or of one of the other persons by administering any drug, intoxicant, or controlled substance to the other person, surreptitiously or by force, threat of force, or deception
  *(or)*
  (c) The offender knows that the judgment or control of the other person, or of one of the other persons is substantially impaired as a result of the influence of any drug or intoxicant administered to the other person with the other person's consent for the purpose of any kind of medical or dental examination, treatment, or surgery
  *(or)*
  (d) The other person, or one of the other persons, is less than thirteen years of age whether or not the offender knows the age of that person
  *(or)*
  (e) The ability of the other person to resist or consent or the ability of one of the other persons to resist or consent is substantially impaired because of a mental or physical condition or because of advanced age, and the offender knows or has reasonable cause to believe that the ability to resist or consent of the other person or one of the other persons is substantially impaired because of a mental or physical condition or because of advanced age
(3) Venue

Division (B)[F3]
(1) Knowingly
(2) Touching the genitalia of a person under twelve years of age (whether or not the offender knows the age of that person)
(3) When the touching is not through clothing and
(4) Is done with an intent to abuse, humiliate, harass, degrade, or arouse or gratify the sexual desire of any person.
(5) Venue

*Penalty:* Gross sexual imposition committed in violation of division (2)(a), (b), (c), or (e) of this section is a felony of the fourth degree (2929.11-2929.18, 2929.31)
If the offender under division (2)(b) of this section substantially impairs the judgment or control of the other person or one of the other persons by administering any controlled substance described in section 3719.41 of the Revised

Code to the person surreptitiously or by force, threat of force, or deception, gross sexual imposition committed in violation of division (2)(b) of this section is a felony of the third degree (2929.11-2929.18, 2929.31)
Gross sexual imposition committed in violation of division (2)(d) of this section is a felony of the third degree (2929.11-2929.18, 2929.31). Except as otherwise provided in this division, for gross sexual imposition committed in violation of division (2)(d) of this section there is a presumption that a prison term shall be imposed for the offense. The court shall impose on an offender convicted of gross sexual imposition in violation of division (2)(d) of this section a mandatory prison term equal to one of the prison terms prescribed in section 2929.14 of the Revised Code for a felony of the third degree (2929.11-2929.18, 2929.31) if either of the following applies:
(a) Evidence other than the testimony of the victim was admitted in the case corroborating the violation;
(b) The offender previously was convicted of or pleaded guilty to a violation of this section, rape, the former offense of felonious sexual penetration, or sexual battery, and the victim of the previous offense was under thirteen years of age

*Penalty:* Felony of the third degree. Except as otherwise provided in this division, there is a presumption that a prison term shall be imposed for the offense. The court shall impose a mandatory prison term equal to one of the prison terms prescribed in section 2929.14 of the Revised Code for a felony of the third degree if either of the following applies:
(a) Evidence other than the testimony of the victim was admitted in the case corroborating the violation;
(b) The offender previously was convicted of or pleaded guilty to a violation of this section, rape, the former offense of felonious sexual penetration, or sexual battery, and the victim of the previous offense was under thirteen years of age.

*Notes:* Victim need not prove physical resistance
A peace officer, prosecutor, or other public official shall not ask or require a victim of an alleged sex offense to submit to a polygraph examination as a condition for proceeding with the investigation of the alleged sex offense. The refusal of the victim of an alleged sex offense to submit to a polygraph examination shall not prevent the investigation of the alleged sex offense, the filing of criminal charges with respect to the alleged sex offense, or the prosecution of the alleged perpetrator of the alleged sex offense. (§ 2907.10)
*See* R.C. § 2907.05(D)-(F) for provisions re evidence of prior sexual activity of victim/offender, admissibility of evidence, and victim's right to counsel in proceeding to determine admissibility

## *SEXUAL IMPOSITION*, R.C. § 2907.06 [M3, M1]

(1) (a) Have sexual contact with another, not the spouse of the offender
*(or)*
(b) Cause another, not the spouse of the offender, to have sexual contact with the offender
*(or)*
(c) Cause two or more other persons to have sexual contact
(2) (a) The offender knows that the sexual contact is offensive to the other person, or one of the other persons, or is reckless in that regard
*(or)*
(b) The offender knows that the other person's, or one of the other persons', ability to appraise the nature of or control the offender's or the touching person's conduct is substantially impaired
*(or)*
(c) The offender knows that the other person, or one of the other persons, submits because of being unaware of the sexual contact
*(or)*
(d) The other person, or one of the other persons, is 13 years of age or older, but less than 16 years of age, regardless of the offender's knowledge of this, and the offender is at least 18 and 4 or more years older than such other person.
*(or)*
(e) The offender is a mental health professional, the other person or one of the other persons is a mental health client or patient of the offender, and the offender induces the other person who is the client or patient to submit by falsely representing to the other person who is the client or patient that the sexual conduct is necessary for mental health treatment purposes.
(3) Venue

*Penalty:* A misdemeanor of the third degree (2929.21-2929.31)
If prior conviction under this section or R.C. §§ 2907.02, 2907.03, 2907.04, 2907.05, or former 2907.12
*Penalty:* A misdemeanor of the first degree (2929.21-2929.31)
*Notes:* A person may not be convicted of sexual imposition without evidence corroborating victim's testimony
A peace officer, prosecutor, or other public official shall not ask or require a victim of an alleged sex offense to submit to a polygraph examination as a condition for proceeding with the investigation of the alleged sex offense. The refusal of the victim of an alleged sex offense to submit to a polygraph examination shall not prevent the investigation of the alleged sex offense, the filing of criminal charges with respect to the alleged sex offense, or the prosecution of the alleged perpetrator of the alleged sex offense. (§ 2907.10)
*Definitions:* "Mental health client," "mental health professional," R.C. 2305.51

## *IMPORTUNING*, R.C. § 2907.07 [M1, F5, F4, F3]

Division (A): **[F3, F2]**
(1) Solicit a person who is less than 13

(2) To engage in sexual activity with the offender
(3) Whether or not offender knows age of such person
(4) Venue

*Penalty:* A felony of the third degree on the first offense and a felony of the second degree on each subsequent offense

Division (B): **[F5, F4]**
(1) Solicit another person, not the spouse of offender
(2) To engage in sexual conduct with the offender
(3) When offender is 18 or older and 4 or more years older than other person, and other person is 13 years or older but less than 16 years
(4) Whether or not offender knows age of such person
(5) Venue

*Penalty:* A felony of the fifth degree on the first offense and a felony of the fourth degree on each subsequent offense (2929.11-2929.18, 2929.31)

Division (C): **[F3, F2]**
(1) Solicit another
(2) By means of a telecommunications device (defined in Section 2913.01)
(3) To engage in sexual activity with the offender
(4) When the offender is 18 or older and either of the following applies:
  (a) The other person is less than 13, and the offender knows that the other person is less than 13 or is reckless in that regard
  *(or)*
  (b) The other person is a law enforcement officer posing as a person who is less than 13, and the offender believes that the other person is less than 13 or is reckless in that regard
(5) Venue

*Penalty:* A felony of the third degree on the first offense and a felony of the second degree on each subsequent offense

Division (D): **[F5, F4]**
(1) Solicit another
(2) By means of a telecommunications device (defined in Section 2913.02)
(3) To engage in sexual activity with the offender
(4) When the offender is 18 or older and either of the following applies:
  (a) The other person is 13 or older but less than 16, and the offender knows that the other person is 13 or older but less than 16 or is reckless in that regard and the offender is 4 or more years older than the victim
  *(or)*
  (b) The other person is a law enforcement officer posing as a person 13 or older but less than 16, and the offender believes that the other person is 13 or older but less than 16 or is reckless in that regard and the offender is 4 or more years older than the age assumed by the law enforcement officer
(5) Venue

*Penalty:* A felony of the fifth degree on a first offense and a felony of the fourth degree on each subsequent offense (2929.11-2929.18, 2929.31)

*Notes:* Divisions (C) and (D) of this section apply to any solicitation that is contained in a transmission via telecommunications device that either originates in this state or is received in this state
A peace officer, prosecutor, or other public official shall not ask or require a victim of an alleged sex offense to submit to a polygraph examination as a condition for proceeding with the investigation of the alleged sex offense. The refusal of the victim of an alleged sex offense to submit to a polygraph examination shall not prevent the investigation of the alleged sex offense, the filing of criminal charges with respect to the alleged sex offense, or the prosecution of the alleged perpetrator of the alleged sex offense. (§ 2907.10)

***VOYEURISM*, R.C. § 2907.08 [M3, M2, M1, F5]**

Division (A): **[M3]**
(1) Trespass or otherwise surreptitiously invade privacy of another
(2) To spy or eavesdrop upon another
(3) With purpose of sexually arousing or gratifying self
(4) Venue

*Penalty:* A misdemeanor of the third degree (2929.21-2929.31)

Division (B): **[M2]**
(1) Trespass or otherwise surreptitiously invade the privacy of another
(2) To videotape, film, photograph, or otherwise record the other person in a state of nudity
(3) With the purpose of sexually arousing or gratifying self
(4) Venue

*Penalty:* A misdemeanor of the second degree (2929.21-2929.31)

Division (C): **[M1]**
(1) Trespass or otherwise surreptitiously invade the privacy of another
(2) To videotape, film, photograph, or otherwise record the other person in a state of nudity if the other person is a minor

(3) With the purpose of sexually arousing or gratifying self
(4) Venue
*Penalty:* A misdemeanor of the first degree (2929.21-2929.31)

Division (D): **[F5]**
(1) Trespass or otherwise surreptitiously invade the privacy of another
(2) To videotape, film, photograph, or otherwise record the other person in a state of nudity if the other person is a minor and
  (a) The offender is the minor's natural or adoptive parent, stepparent, guardian, or custodian, or person in loco parentis to the minor
  *(or)*
  (b) The minor is in the custody of law or is a patient in a hospital or other institution, and the offender has supervisory or disciplinary authority over the minor
  *(or)*
  (c) The offender is a teacher, administrator, coach, or other person in authority employed by or serving in a school for which the state board of education prescribes minimum standards pursuant to R.C. § 3301.07(D), the minor is enrolled in or attends that school, and the offender is not enrolled in and does not attend that school
  *(or)*
  (d) The offender is a teacher, administrator, coach, or other person in authority employed by or serving in an institution of higher education, and the minor is enrolled in or attends that institution
  *(or)*
  (e) The offender is a caregiver, administrator, or other person in authority employed by or serving in a child day-care center, Type A family day-care home, or Type B family daycare home, and the minor is enrolled in or attends that center or home
  *(or)*
  (f) The offender is the minor's athletic or other type of coach, is the minor's instructor, is the leader of the scouting troop or which the minor is a member, provided babysitting care for the minor, or is a person with temporary or occasional disciplinary control over the minor
(3) With the purpose of sexually arousing or gratifying self
(4) Venue
*Penalty:* A felony of the fifth degree (2929.11-2929.18, 2929.31)

Division (E): **[M1]**
(1) Secretly or surreptitiously
(2) Videotape, film, photograph, or otherwise record another
(3) Under or through that person's clothing
(4) For purpose of viewing body of or undergarments worn by that person
(5) Venue
*Penalty:* A misdemeanor of the first degree (2929.21-2929.31)

***PUBLIC INDECENCY*, R.C. § 2907.09 [F5, M4, M3, M2, M1]**

Division (A): **[M4, M3, M2, M1]**
(1) Recklessly
(2) Under circumstances in which the person's conduct is likely to be viewed by and affront others who are in the person's physical proximity and who are not members of the person's household
(3) (a) Expose his or her private parts;
  *(or)*
  (b) Engage in sexual conduct or masturbation;
  *(or)*
  (c) Engage in conduct that to an ordinary observer would appear to be sexual conduct or masturbation
(4) Venue

Division (B): **[F5, M2, M1]**
(1) Knowingly
(2) Under circumstances in which the person's conduct is likely to be viewed by and affront another person who is a minor, who is not the spouse of the offender, and who resides in the person's household
(3) (a) Engage in masturbation;
  *(or)*
  (b) Engage in sexual conduct;
  *(or)*
  (c) Engage in conduct that to an ordinary observer would appear to be sexual conduct or masturbation;
  *(or)*
  (d) Expose the person's private parts with the purpose of personal sexual arousal or gratification or to lure the minor into sexual activity
(4) Venue
*Penalty:* Except as otherwise provided, a violation of division (A)(3)(a) of this section is a misdemeanor of the fourth degree

*Penalty:* If the offender previously has been convicted of or pleaded guilty to one violation of this section, a violation of division (A)(3)(a) of this section is a misdemeanor of the third degree, or a misdemeanor of the second degree if any person who was likely to view and be affronted by the offender's conduct was a minor

*Penalty:* If the offender previously has been convicted of or pleaded guilty to two violations of this section, a violation of division (A)(3)(a) of this section is a misdemeanor of the second degree, or a misdemeanor of the first degree if any person who was likely to view and be affronted by the offender's conduct was a minor

*Penalty:* If the offender previously has been convicted of or pleaded guilty to three or more violations of this section, a violation of division (A)(3)(a) of this section is a misdemeanor of the first degree, or a felony of the fifth degree if any person who was likely to view and be affronted by the offender's conduct was a minor

*Penalty:* Except as otherwise provided, a violation of division (A)(3)(b) or (A)(3)(c) of this section is a misdemeanor of the third degree

*Penalty:* If the offender previously has been convicted of or pleaded guilty to one violation of this section, a violation of division (A)(3)(b) or (A)(3)(c) of this section is a misdemeanor of the second degree, or a misdemeanor of the first degree if any person who was likely to view and be affronted by the offender's conduct was a minor

*Penalty:* If the offender previously has been convicted of or pleaded guilty to two or more violations of this section, a violation of division (A)(3)(b) or (A)(3)(c) of this section is a misdemeanor of the first degree, or a felony of the fifth degree if any person who was likely to view and be affronted by the offender's conduct was a minor

*Penalty:* Except as otherwise provided, a violation of division (B)(3)(a), (b), or (c) of this section is a misdemeanor of the second degree

*Penalty:* If the offender previously has been convicted of or pleaded guilty to one violation of this section, a violation of division (B)(3)(a), (b), or (c) of this section is a misdemeanor of the first degree

*Penalty:* If the offender previously has been convicted of or pleaded guilty to two or more violations of this section, a violation of division (B)(3)(a), (b), or (c) of this section is a felony of the fifth degree

*Penalty:* Except as otherwise provided, a violation of division (B)(3)(d) of this section is a misdemeanor of the first degree

*Penalty:* If the offender previously has been convicted of or pleaded guilty to any violation of this section, a violation of division (B)(3)(d) of this section is a felony of the fifth degree

### ***COMPELLING PROSTITUTION,*** **R.C. § 2907.21 [F3, F2]**

(1) Knowingly

(2) (a) Compel another to engage in sexual activity for hire
*(or)*

(b) Induce, procure, encourage, solicit, request, or otherwise facilitate a minor or a person the offender believes to be a minor to engage in sexual activity for hire, whether or not there is actual knowledge as to minor's age
*(or)*

(c) Pay or agree to pay a minor or a person the offender believes to be a minor, directly or through the minor's or person's agent, so that the minor or person will engage in sexual activity, whether or not there is actual knowledge of the minor's age
*(or)*

(d) Pay a minor or a person the offender believes to be a minor, directly or through the minor's or person's agent, for the minor or the person having engaged in sexual activity pursuant to a prior agreement, whether or not there is actual knowledge of the minor's age
*(or)*

(e) Allow a minor or a person the offender believes to be a minor to engage in sexual activity for hire if the person allowing the minor or person to engage in sexual activity for hire is the parent, guardian, custodian, person having custody or control, or person in loco parentis of the minor or person

(3) Venue

*Penalty:* A felony of the third degree (2929.11-2929.18, 2929.31)

If offender commits a violation of Division (2)(a) and the person compelled to engage in sexual activity for hire is at least 16 but less than 18

*Penalty:* A felony of the second degree (2929.11-2929.18, 2929.31)

If offender commits a violation of Division (2)(a) and the person compelled to engage in sexual activity for hire is less than 16

*Penalty:* A felony of the first degree (2929.11-2929.18, 2929.31)

*Notes: See* R.C. § 2907.26 for rules of evidence in prostitution cases
Sentences of imprisonment for violations under 2(b), (c), and (d) above are to be served consecutively to any other sentence of imprisonment, R.C. § 2929.41

*Definitions:* "Minor" means a person under the age of eighteen, R.C. § 2907.01
"Sexual activity," R.C. § 2907.01

### ***PROMOTING PROSTITUTION,*** **R.C. § 2907.22 [F4, F3]**

(1) Knowingly

(2) (a) Establish, maintain, operate, manage, supervise, control, or have an interest in a brothel
*(or)*

(b) Supervise, manage or control activities of a prostitute in engaging in sexual activity for hire
*(or)*

(c) (i) Transport, or cause another to be transported
(ii) Across the boundary of Ohio or any county in Ohio
(iii) To facilitate the other person's engaging in sexual activity for hire
*(or)*
(d) (i) Induce or procure another to engage in sexual activity for hire
(ii) For the purpose of violating or facilitating a violation of this section
(3) Venue
*Penalty:* A felony of the fourth degree (2929.11-2929.18, 2929.31)
If the prostitute or the person transported, induced, or procured to engage in sexual activity for hire is a minor, regardless of whether the offender knows the age
*Penalty:* A felony of the third degree (2929.11-2929.18, 2929.31)
*Notes: See* R.C. § 2907.26 for rules of evidence in prostitution cases
Any sentence of imprisonment imposed for an F3 conviction is to be served consecutively to any other term of imprisonment
*Definitions:* "Minor" means a person under the age of eighteen, R.C. § 2907.01
"Sexual activity," R.C. § 2907.01

***PROCURING*, R.C. § 2907.23 [M1]**

Division (A):
(1) Knowingly
(2) For gain
(3) (a) Entice or solicit another to patronize a prostitute or brothel
*(or)*
(b) Procure a prostitute for another to patronize
*(or)*
(c) Take or direct another person to place for the purpose of patronizing a prostitute as requested by such other person
(4) Venue

Division (B):
(1) While having authority/responsibility over premises
(2) Knowingly
(3) Permit the premises to be used
(4) For the purpose of engaging in sexual activity for hire
(5) Venue
*Penalty:* A misdemeanor of the first degree (2929.21-2929.31)
*Note: See* R.C. § 2907.26 for rules of evidence in prostitution cases

***SOLICITING; AFTER POSITIVE HIV TEST*, R.C. § 2907.24 [M3, F3]**

Division (A): **[M3]**
(1) Solicit another
(2) To engage in sexual activity for hire
(3) Venue
*Penalty:* A misdemeanor of the third degree (2929.21-2929.31)

Division (B): **[F3]**
(1) Engage in conduct in violation of Division A
(2) With knowledge that he or she has tested positive as a carrier of a virus that causes AIDS
(3) Venue
*Penalty:* A felony of the third degree (2929.11-2929.18, 2929.31)
*Notes:* See R.C. § 2907.26 for rules of evidence in prostitution cases
*See* R.C. § 2907.27 for provisions regarding mandatory medical tests for persons charged under this statute
In addition to or independent of all other penalties, class six suspension of the offender's driver's license, if the person, in committing or attempting to commit the violation, was in, was on, or used a motor vehicle

***LOITERING TO ENGAGE IN SOLICITATION; SOLICITATION AFTER A POSITIVE HIV TEST*, R.C. § 2907.241 [M3, F5]**

Division (A): **[M3]**
(1) (a) Beckon to, stop, or attempt to stop another
*(or)*
(b) Engage, or attempt to engage another in conversation
*(or)*
(c) Stop or attempt to stop the operator of a vehicle or approach a stationary vehicle
*(or)*
(d) If the offender is the operator of or a passenger in a vehicle, stop, attempt to stop, beckon to, attempt to beckon to, or entice another to approach or enter the vehicle of which the offender is the operator or

passenger
*(or)*
(e) Interfere with the passage of another
(2) While in or near a public place
(3) With purpose to solicit another to engage in sexual activity for hire
(4) Venue
*Penalty:* A misdemeanor of the third degree (2929.21-2929.31)

Division (B): **[F5]**
(1) Engage in conduct in violation of Division (A)
(2) With knowledge that he or she has tested positive as a carrier of a virus that causes AIDS
(3) Venue
*Penalty:* A felony of the fifth degree (2929.11-2929.18, 2929.31)

***PROSTITUTION; AFTER POSITIVE HIV TEST,* R.C. § 2907.25 [M3, F3]**

Division (A): **[M3]**
(1) Engage in sexual activity
(2) For hire
(3) Venue
*Penalty:* A misdemeanor of the third degree (2929.21-2929.31)

Division (B): **[F3]**
(1) Engage in sexual activity
(2) For hire
(3) With knowledge that he or she has tested positive as a carrier of a virus that causes AIDS
(4) Venue
*Penalty:* A felony of the third degree (2929.11-2929.18, 2929.31)
*Notes: See* R.C. § 2907.26 for rules of evidence in prostitution cases
*See* R.C. § 2907.27 for provisions regarding mandatory medical tests for persons charged under this statute

***DISSEMINATING MATTER HARMFUL TO JUVENILES,* R.C. § 2907.31 [M1, F5, F4]**

(1) Recklessly
(2) With knowledge of its character or content
(3) (a) Directly sell, deliver, furnish, disseminate, provide, exhibit, rent, or present to a juvenile, a group of juveniles, a law enforcement officer posing as a juvenile, or a group of law enforcement officers posing as juveniles, any material or performance that is obscene or harmful to juveniles
*(or)*
(b) Directly offer or agree to sell, deliver, furnish, disseminate, provide, exhibit, rent, or present to a juvenile, a group of juveniles, a law enforcement officer posing as a juvenile, or a group of law enforcement officers posing as juveniles, any material or performance that is obscene or harmful to juveniles
*(or)*
(c) While in the physical proximity of the juvenile or law enforcement officer posing as a juvenile, allow any juvenile or law enforcement officer posing as a juvenile to review or peruse any material or view any live performance that is harmful to juveniles
(4) Venue
If the material or performance is harmful to juveniles but not obscene
*Penalty:* A misdemeanor of the first degree (2929.21-2929.31)
If the material or performance is obscene and the juvenile is thirteen years of age or older
*Penalty:* A felony of the fifth degree (2929.11-2929.18, 2929.31)
If the material or performance is obscene and the juvenile is under thirteen years of age
*Penalty:* A felony of the fourth degree (2929.11-2929.18, 2929.31)
*Note: See* R.C. §§ 2907.31 and 2907.35 for affirmative defenses
*Definitions:* "Juvenile' means an unmarried person under the age of eighteen, R.C. § 2907.01
"Harmful to juveniles," "material," "obscene," "performance," R.C. § 2907.01

***DISPLAYING MATTER HARMFUL TO JUVENILES,* R.C. § 2907.311 [M1]**

(1) Having custody, control, or supervision of a commercial establishment
(2) With knowledge of the character or content of the material involved
(3) Display at the establishment
(4) Any material that is
(a) Harmful to juveniles
*(and)*
(b) Open to view by juveniles as part of the invited general public
(5) Venue
*Penalty:* A misdemeanor of the first degree (2929.21-2929.31)
*Notes:* Each day of violation is a separate offense
*See* R.C. § 2907.311 for provisions regarding 'blinder racks,' placing material behind counter, etc.
*See* R.C. § 2907.35 for affirmative defense

*Definitions:* "Juvenile" means an unmarried person under the age of eighteen, R.C. § 2907.01
"Harmful to juveniles," "material," "obscene," R.C. § 2907.01

***PANDERING OBSCENITY,* R.C. § 2907.32 [F5, F4]**

(1) Knowing the character of the material or performance involved
(2) (a) (i) Create, reproduce or publish obscene material
(ii) Knowing that the material is to be used for commercial exploitation or will be publicly disseminated or displayed, or is reckless in that regard
*(or)*
(b) (i) Promote or advertise for sale, delivery, or dissemination, or sell, deliver, or publicly disseminate, display, exhibit, present, rent, provide, or offer to do any of the foregoing
(ii) Obscene material
*(or)*
(c) (i) Create, direct or produce
(ii) An obscene performance
(iii) Knowing it is to be commercially exploited or publicly presented, or being reckless in that regard
*(or)*
(d) (i) Advertise or promote an obscene performance for presentation
(ii) Present or participate in an obscene performance
(iii) Which is presented publicly, or when admission is charged
*(or)*
(e) (i) Buy, procure, possess or control obscene material
(ii) With purpose to violate (2) (b) or (2) (d) above
(3) Venue
*Penalty:* A felony of the fifth degree (2929.11-2929.18, 2929.31)
Where there is a prior conviction under this section or R.C. § 2907.31
*Penalty:* A felony of the fourth degree (2929.11-2929.18, 2929.31)
*Note: See* R.C. § 2907.32 for affirmative defenses
*Definitions:* "Harmful to juveniles," "material," "obscene," "performance," R.C. § 2907.01

***PANDERING OBSCENITY INVOLVING A MINOR,* R.C. § 2907.321 [F2, F3, F4]**

(1) With knowledge of the character of the material or performance
(2) (a) Create, reproduce, or publish
(i) Any obscene material
(ii) That has a minor as one of its participants or portrayed observers
(iii) When the offender knows that it will be used for commercial exploitation or will be publicly disseminated or displayed, or is reckless in that regard
*(or)*
(b) Promote or advertise for sale or dissemination, sell, deliver, or disseminate, display, exhibit, present, rent, or provide, or offer to do any of the foregoing
(i) Any obscene material
(ii) That has a minor as one of its participants or portrayed observers
*(or)*
(c) Create, direct, or produce
(i) An obscene performance
(ii) That has a minor as one of its participants
(iii) When the offender knows that it will be used for commercial exploitation or will be publicly presented, or is reckless in that regard
*(or)*
(d) Advertise or promote for presentation, present, or participate in presenting
(i) An obscene performance
(ii) That has a minor as one of its participants
(iii) When the performance is presented publicly or admission is charged
*(or)*
(e) Buy, procure. possess, or control
(i) Any obscene material
(ii) That has a minor as one of its participants
(f) Bring or cause to be brought into this state
(i) Any obscene material
(ii) That has a minor as one of its participants or portrayed observers
(3) Venue
Violation of any provision but (e)
*Penalty:* A felony of the second degree (2929.11-2929.18, 2929.31)
Violation of (e)
*Penalty:* A felony of the fourth degree (2929.11-2929.18, 2929.31)
If prior conviction under R.C. §§ 2907.321-2907.323
*Penalty:* A felony of the third degree (2929.11-2929.18, 2929.31)

*Notes:* This section does not apply to any material or performance that is sold, disseminated, displayed, possessed, controlled, brought or caused to be brought into this state, or presented for a bona fide medical, scientific, educational, religious, governmental, judicial, or other proper purpose, by or to a physician, psychologist, sociologist, scientist, teacher, person pursuing bona fide studies or research, librarian, clergyman, prosecutor, judge, or other person having a proper interest in the material or performance
Mistake of age is not a defense
*See* R.C. § 2907.321 for provisions regarding permissible inferences of age by the trier of fact. A sentence of imprisonment is to be served consecutively to any other sentence of imprisonment, R.C. § 2929.41
*Definitions:* "Minor" means a person under the age of eighteen, R.C. § 2907.01
"Material," "obscene," "performance," R.C. § 2907.01

***PANDERING SEXUALLY ORIENTED MATTER INVOLVING A MINOR*, R.C. § 2907.322 [F4, F3, F2]**

(1) With knowledge of the character of the material or performance involved
(2) (a) Create, record, photograph, film, develop, reproduce, or publish any material
*(or)*
(b) Advertise for sale or dissemination, sell, distribute, transport, disseminate, exhibit, or display any material that shows
*(or)*
(c) Create, direct, or produce a performance that shows
*(or)*
(d) Advertise for presentation, present, or participate in presenting a performance that shows
*(or)*
(e) Knowingly solicit, receive, purchase, exchange, possess or control any material that shows
*(or)*
(f) Bring or cause to be brought into this state any material that shows
*(or)*
(g) Bring, cause to be brought, or finance the bringing of a minor into or across this state, with the intent that
*(or)*
(h) Bring, cause to be brought, or finance the bringing of a minor into or across this state, for the purpose of producing material containing a visual representation depicting
(3) A minor
(4) Participating or engaging in sexual activity, masturbation, or bestiality
(5) Venue
*Penalty:* A felony of the second degree (2929.11-2929.18, 2929.31)
Offense under 2(e), above
*Penalty:* A felony of the fourth degree (2929.11-2929.18, 2929.31)
Offense under 2(e) above, and prior conviction under R.C. §§ 2907.321-2907.323
*Penalty:* A felony of the third degree (2929.11-2929.18, 2929.31)
*Notes:* This section does not apply to materials or performances used for a proper purpose by persons having a proper interest therein. Proper purposes include bona fide medical, scientific, educational, religious, governmental, judicial, and other proper purposes; persons having a proper interest include physicians, psychologists, sociologists, scientists, teachers, persons pursuing bona fide studies or research, librarians, clergymen, prosecutors, judges, or other persons having a proper interest in the material or performance
Mistake of age is not a defense
*See* R.C. § 2907.322 for provisions regarding permissible inferences of age by the trier of fact
A sentence of imprisonment is to be served consecutively to any other sentence of imprisonment
*Definitions:* "Minor" means a person under the age of eighteen, R.C. § 2907.01
"Material," "performance," "sexual activity," R.C. § 2907.01

***ILLEGAL USE OF MINOR IN NUDITY-ORIENTED MATERIAL OR PERFORMANCE*, R.C. § 2907.323 [F5, F4, F2]**

[A](1) (a) Photograph
*(or)*
(b) Create, direct, produce, or transfer any material or performance showing
(2) A minor who is not the actor's child or ward
(3) In a state of nudity
(4) Unless
(a) The material or performance is or is to be sold, disseminated, displayed, possessed, controlled, brought or caused to be brought into this state
(i) For a proper purpose
(ii) By or to a person having a proper interest
*(and)*
(b) The minor's parents, guardian, or custodian consents in writing to the photographing of the minor, to the use of the minor in the material or performance, or to the transfer of the material and to the specific manner in which the material or performance is to be used
(5) Venue

[B](1) (a) Photograph
*(or)*
(b) Consent to
(i) Photographing of
*(or)*
(ii) Use in any material or performance of
*(or)*
(c) Use or transfer of any material or performance using
(2) The actor's minor child or ward
(3) In a state of nudity
(4) Unless the material or performance is sold, disseminated, displayed, possessed, controlled, brought or caused to be brought into this state
(i) For a proper purpose
(ii) By or to a person having a proper interest
(5) Venue
[C](1) (a) Possess
*(or)*
(b) View
(2) Any material or performance showing
(3) A minor who is not the actor's child or ward
(4) In a state of nudity
(5) Unless
(a) The material or performance is sold, disseminated, displayed, possessed, controlled, brought or caused to be brought into this state
(i) For a proper purpose
(ii) By or to a person having a proper interest
*(or)*
(b) The actor knows that the child's parents, guardian, or custodian has consented in writing to the photographing or use of the minor in a state of nudity, and to the manner in which the material or performance is used or transferred
(6) Venue
*Penalty:* A felony of the second degree (2929.11-2929.18, 2929.31)
Offense under [C], above
*Penalty:* A felony of the fifth degree (2929.11-2929.18, 2929.31)
Offense under [C], above, plus prior conviction under R.C. §§ 2907.321-2907.323
*Penalty:* A felony of the fourth degree (2929.11-2929.18, 2929.31)
*Note:* Under this section, a proper purpose is a bona fide artistic, medical, scientific, educational, religious, governmental, judicial, or other proper purpose; a person having a proper interest includes a physician, psychologist, sociologist, scientist, teacher, persons pursuing bona fide studies or research, librarian, clergyman, prosecutor, judge, or other person having a proper interest in the material or performance
*Definitions:* "Minor" means a person under the age of eighteen, R.C. § 2907.01
"Material," "nudity," "performance," R.C. § 2907.01

### *DECEPTION TO OBTAIN MATTER HARMFUL TO JUVENILES,* R.C. § 2907.33 [M2]

Division (A):
(1) With purpose to enable a juvenile to obtain material, or gain admission to a performance, harmful to juveniles
(2) (a) Falsely represent that he is the juvenile's parent, guardian, or spouse
*(or)*
(b) Furnish the juvenile with identification or documents purporting to show the juvenile is 18 or over, or married
(3) Venue

Division (B):
(1) Being a juvenile
(2) For purpose of obtaining material, or gaining admission to a performance, harmful to juveniles
(3) (a) Falsely represent the juvenile is 18 or over or married
*(or)*
(b) Exhibit identification or documents purporting to show the juvenile is 18 or over or married
(4) Venue
*Penalty:* A misdemeanor of the second degree (2929.21-2929.31)
*Note: See* "unruly child," R.C. § 2151.022
*Definitions:* "Juvenile" means an unmarried person under the age of eighteen, R.C. § 2907.01
"Harmful to juveniles," "material," "performance," R.C. § 2907.01

### *COMPELLING ACCEPTANCE OF OBJECTIONABLE MATERIALS,* R.C. § 2907.34 [F5]

Division (A):
(1) As a precondition to the sale, allocation, consignment, or delivery of any material or goods

(2) Over objections of the purchaser/consignee
(3) Require such purchaser/consignee
(4) To accept other material reasonably believed to be obscene, or which, if furnished/presented to a juvenile, would violate R.C. § 2907.31
(5) Venue

Division (B):
(1) (a) Deny or threaten to deny any franchise to
*(or)*
(b) Impose or threaten to impose any financial penalty upon
(2) Any purchaser or consignee
(3) (a) Because the purchaser or consignee failed or refused to accept any material reasonably believed to be obscene as a condition to the sale, allocation, consignment, or delivery of any other material or goods
*(or)*
(b) Because purchaser or consignee returned any material believed to be obscene which the purchaser or consignee initially accepted
(4) Venue
*Penalty:* A felony of the fifth degree (2929.11-2929.18, 2929.31)
*Definitions:* "Material," "obscene," R.C. § 2907.01

***PERMITTING UNLAWFUL OPERATION OF VIEWING BOOTHS DEPICTING SEXUAL CONDUCT,* R.C. § 2907.38 [M1]**
(1) Knowingly
(2) (2) In custody, control, or supervision of a commercial establishment
(3) With knowledge of the character of the visual material or performance involved
(4) Permit the use of, or offer the use of
(5) Viewing booths, stalls, or partitioned portions of a room located in the commercial establishment
(6) for the purpose of viewing visual materials or performances depicting sexual conduct
(7) Venue
*Penalty:* A misdemeanor of the first degree (2929.21-2929.31).
*Note:* See text of statute for two prerequisites for lawful operation of viewing booths
See also text of statute for affirmative defenses to charges brought under the new law

***PERMITTING JUVENILE ON PREMISES OF ADULT ENTERTAINMENT ESTABLISHMENT; USE BY JUVENILE OF FALSE INFORMATION TO ENTER ADULT ENTERTAINMENT ESTABLISHMENT,* R.C. § 2907.39 [M4, M1]**
Division (B):
(1) Knowingly
(2) Allow
(3) An individual, including, but not limited to, a patron, customer, or employee, who is under eighteen years of age
(4) On the premises of an adult entertainment establishment.
(5) Venue
*Penalty:*A misdemeanor of the first degree (2929.21-2929.31). Each day a person violates this division constitutes a separate offense.
Division (C):
(1) Under eighteen years of age
(2) Knowingly
(3) Show or give
(4) False information concerning the individual's name or age, or other false identification
(5) For the purpose of gaining entrance to an adult entertainment establishment
(6) Venue
*Penalty:* A delinquent act that would be a misdemeanor of the fourth degree (2929.21-2929.31) if committed by an adult

***ILLEGALLY OPERATING SEXUALLY ORIENTED BUSINESS,* R.C. § 2907.40(B) [M1]**
(1) A sexually oriented business
(2) Being or remaining open for business
(3) Between 12:00 midnight and 6:00 a.m. on any day,
(4) Except that a sexually oriented business that holds a liquor permit pursuant to Chapter 4303. of the Revised Code may remain open until the hour specified in that permit if it does not conduct, offer, or allow sexually oriented entertainment activity in which the performers appear nude.
*Penalty:* A misdemeanor of the first degree (2929.21-2929.31).

***ILLEGAL SEXUALLY ORIENTED ACTIVITY IN SEXUALLY ORIENTED BUSINESS,* R.C. § 2907.40(C) [M4, M1]**
Division (C)(1)
(1) A patron who is not a member of the employee's immediate family
(2) Knowingly
(3) Touching any employee or the clothing of any employee

(4) While that employee is nude or seminude;
Division (C)(2)
(1) An employee who regularly appears nude or seminude on the premises of a sexually oriented business,
(2) While on the premises of the business and nude or seminude,
(3) Knowingly
(4) Touching a patron or another employee, or the clothing of a patron or another employee, who is not a member of the employee's immediate family.
*Penalty:* If the offender touches a specified anatomical area (including human genitals, pubic region, and buttocks and the human female breast below a point immediately above the top of the areola) of the patron or employee, or the clothing covering a specified anatomical area, misdemeanor of the first degree. Otherwise, a misdemeanor of the fourth degree. (2929.21-2929.28)

---

## ARSON AND RELATED OFFENSES

### *AGGRAVATED ARSON*, R.C. § 2909.02 [F2, F1]

(1) Knowingly
(2) (a) Create substantial risk of serious physical harm to any person other than the offender
*(or)*
(b) Cause physical harm to an occupied structure
*(or)*
(c) Create, through the offer or acceptance of an agreement for hire or other consideration, a substantial risk of physical harm to any occupied structure
(3) By means of fire or explosion
(4) Venue
Violation of Division (2)(a) or (c)
*Penalty:* A felony of the first degree (2929.11-2929.18, 2929.31)
Violation of Division (2)(b)
*Penalty:* A felony of the second degree (2929.11-2929.18, 2929.31)
*Notes:* R.C. § 2929.28 sets forth requirements for hearings on reimbursement to agencies
*Definitions:* "Create a substantial risk of serious physical harm to any person" includes the creation of a substantial risk of serious physical harm to any emergency personnel,. R.C. § 2909.01
"Emergency personnel," R.C. § 2909.01
"Occupied structure," R.C. § 2909.01
"Political subdivision," R.C. § 2909.01
"State," R.C. § 2909.01

### *ARSON*, R.C. § 2909.03 [F4, F3, M1]

(1) Knowingly
(2) (a) Cause or create substantial risk of physical harm to any property of another without the other person's consent
*(or)*
(b) Cause or create substantial risk of physical harm to any property of the offender or another, with purpose to defraud
*(or)*
(c) Cause or create substantial risk of physical harm to statehouse, courthouse, school building, or other building or structure owned or controlled by state or any political subdivision, or any department, agency, instrumentality of either the state or a political subdivision, and used for public purpose
*(or)*
(d) Cause, or create a substantial risk of, physical harm, through the offer or the acceptance of an agreement for hire or other consideration, to any property of another without the other person's consent or to any property of the offender or another with purpose to defraud
(e) Cause, or create a substantial risk of, physical harm to any park, preserve, wildlands, brush-covered land, cut-over land, forest, timberland, greenlands, woods, or similar real property that is owned or controlled by another person, the state, or a political subdivision without the consent of the other person, the state, or the political subdivision;
*(or)*
(f) With purpose to defraud, cause, or create a substantial risk of, physical harm to any park, preserve, wildlands, brush-covered land, cut-over land, forest, timberland, greenlands, woods, or similar real property that is owned or controlled by the offender, another person, the state, or a political subdivision
(3) By means of fire or explosion
(4) Venue
Violation of (2)(a) above, value of property or amount of physical harm less than $1,000
*Penalty:* A misdemeanor of the first degree (2929.21-2929.31)
Violation of (2)(a) above, value of property or amount of physical harm $1,000 or more
*Penalty:* A felony of the fourth degree (2929.11-2929.18, 2929.31)

Violation of (2)(b), (c), (e), or (f)
*Penalty:* A felony of the fourth degree (2929.11-2929.18, 2929.31)
Violation of (2)(d)
*Penalty:* A felony of the third degree (2929.11-2929.18, 2929.31)
*Notes:* R.C. § 2909.11 sets forth requirements for findings concerning property value damage and amount of physical harm
R.C. § 2929.28 sets forth requirements for hearings on reimbursement to agencies
*Definitions:* "Political subdivision," R.C. § 2909.01
"State," R.C. § 2909.01

***DISRUPTING PUBLIC SERVICES*, R.C. § 2909.04 [F4]**

Division (A):
(1) (a) Purposely by any means
*(or)*
(b) Knowingly, by damaging or tampering with property
(2) (a) Interrupt or impair
(i) TV, radio, telephone, telegraph, or other mass communications service
*(or)*
(ii) Police, fire, other public service communications
*(or)*
(iii) Radar, loran, radio, other electronic aids to air or marine navigation or communications
*(or)*
(iv) Amateur or citizens band radio communications being used for public service or emergency communications
*(or)*
(v) Public transportation, including school bus transportation, water supply, gas, power, other utility service to public
*(or)*
(b) Substantially impair
(i) Ability of law enforcement officers, firefighters, rescue personnel, emergency medical services personnel, or emergency facility personnel to respond to emergency or to protect and preserve any person or property from serious physical harm
(3) Venue

Division (B):
(1) Knowingly use
(2) Any computer, computer system, computer network, telecommunications device, or other electronic device or system or the internet
(3) So as to disrupt, interrupt, or impair
(4) The functions of any police, fire, educational, commercial, or governmental operations.
(5) Venue
*Penalty:* Felony of the fourth degree. (2929.11-2929.18, 2929.31)

***VANDALISM*, R.C. § 2909.05 [F5, F4, F3]**

Division (A):
(1) Knowingly cause serious physical harm to
(2) Occupied structure or any of its contents
(3) Venue

Division (B)(1):
(1) Knowingly cause physical harm to
(2) Property owned or possessed by another and which is
(a) Used by its owner or possessor in the owner or possessor's profession, business, trade, occupation, and value of property or physical harm is $1,000 or more
*(or)*
(b) Such property or equivalent necessary for its owner or possessor to engage in profession, business, trade, occupation
(3) Venue

Division (B)(2):
(1) Knowingly cause serious physical harm to
(2) Property owned, leased, or controlled by a government entity
(3) Venue

Division (C):
(1) Knowingly, and without privilege to do so, cause serious physical harm to
(2) (a) Any tomb, monument, gravestone, or other similar structure used as a memorial for the dead
*(or)*

(b) Any fence, railing, curb, or other property used to protect, enclose, or ornament any cemetery
*(or)*
(c) A cemetery
(3) Venue

Division (D):
Knowingly, and without privilege to do so, cause physical harm to
(2) A place of burial
(3) By breaking and entering into a tomb, crypt, casket, or other structure that is used as a memorial for the dead or as an enclosure for the dead
(4) Venue
Value of property or amount of physical harm less than $7,500
*Penalty:* A felony of the fifth degree (2929.11-.2929.18, 2929.31) with possible additional fine of up to $2,500
Value of property or amount of physical harm more than $7,500 but less than $150,000
*Penalty:* A felony of the fourth degree (2929.11-2929.18, 2929.31)
Value of property or amount of physical harm more than $150,000
*Penalty:* A felony of the third degree (2929.11-2929.18, 2929.31)
*Notes: See* R.C. § 2307.70 regarding civil actions
*See* R.C. § 2909.05 for examples of "government entities"
R.C. § 2909.11 sets forth requirements for findings concerning property value damage and amount of physical harm
*Definitions:* "Occupied structure," R.C. § 2909.01

***CRIMINAL DAMAGING OR ENDANGERING*, R.C. § 2909.06 [M2, M1, F5, F4]**

(1) Cause or create substantial risk of physical harm to property of another without consent
(2) (a) Knowingly, by any means
*(or)*
(b) Recklessly, by fire, explosion, flood, poison gas, poison, radioactive material, caustic or corrosive material, other inherently dangerous agency or substance
(3) Venue
*Penalty:* A misdemeanor of the second degree (2929.21-2929.31)
If violation creates risk of physical harm to a person
*Penalty:* A misdemeanor of the first degree (2929.21-2929.31)
If the property involved in a violation of this section is an aircraft, an aircraft engine, propeller, appliance, spare part, or any other equipment or implement used or intended to le used in the operation of an aircraft and if the violation creates a risk of physical harm to any person
*Penalty:* A felony of the fifth degree (2929.11-2929.18, 2929.31)
If the property involved in a violation is an aircraft, an aircraft engine, propeller, appliance, spare part, or any other equipment or implement used or intended to be used in the operation of the aircraft and if the violation creates a substantial risk of physical harm to any person or if the property involved is an occupied aircraft
*Penalty:* A felony of the fourth degree (2929.11-2929.18, 2929.31)

***CRIMINAL MISCHIEF*, R.C. § 2909.07 [M3, M1, F5, F4]**

(1) Without privilege knowingly move, deface, damage, destroy, or otherwise improperly tamper with property of another
*(or)*
(2) With purpose to interfere with use or enjoyment of property of another, employ tear gas device, stink bomb, smoke generator, or other device, releasing a substance harmful or offensive to persons exposed, or that tends to cause public alarm
*(or)*
(3) Without privilege to do so, knowingly move, deface, damage, destroy, or otherwise improperly tamper with bench mark, triangulation station, boundary marker, other survey station, monument, or marker
*(or)*
(4) Without privilege to do so, knowingly move, deface, damage, destroy, or otherwise improperly tamper with any safety device, property of another or the offender, when required or placed for safety of others, so as to destroy or diminish its effectiveness or availability for intended purpose
*(or)*
(5) With purpose to interfere with the use or enjoyment of the property of another, set a fire on the land of another or place personal property that has been set on fire on the land of another, which fire or personal property is outside and apart from any building, other structure, or personal property that is on that land
(6) Without privilege to do so, and with intent to impair the functioning of any computer, computer system, computer network, computer software, or computer program, knowingly do any of the following:
(a) In any manner or by any means, including, but not limited to, computer hacking, alter, damage, destroy, or modify a computer, computer system, computer network, computer software, or computer program or data contained in a computer, computer system, computer network, computer software, or computer program;
*(or)*

(b) Introduce a computer contaminant into a computer, computer system, computer network, computer software, or computer program.

(7) Venue

*Penalty:* A misdemeanor of the third degree (2929.21-2929.31) unless a risk of physical harm to any person, then a misdemeanor of the first degree (2929.21-2929.31). If the property involved in violation of this section is an aircraft, an aircraft engine, propeller, appliance, spare part, fuel, lubricant, hydraulic fluid, any other equipment, implement, or material used or intended to be used in the operation of an aircraft, or any cargo carried or intended to be carried in an aircraft and if the violation creates a risk of physical harm to any person, then a felony of the fifth degree (2929.11-2929.18, 2929.31). If the property involved in a violation is an aircraft, an aircraft engine, propeller, appliance, spare part, or any other equipment or implement used or intended to be used in the operation of an aircraft and if the violation causes substantial risk of physical harm to any person or if the property involved is an occupied aircraft, a felony of the fourth degree (2929.11-2929.18, 2929.31)

Criminal mischief committed in violation of (6) is a misdemeanor of the first degree (2929.21-2929.31). Except as otherwise provided in this division, if the value of the computer, computer system, computer network, computer software, computer program, or data involved in the violation of (6) or the loss to the victim resulting from the violation is one thousand dollars or more and less than ten thousand dollars, or if the computer, computer system, computer network, computer software, computer program, or data involved in the violation of (6) is used or intended to be used in the operation of an aircraft and the violation creates a risk of physical harm to any person, criminal mischief committed in violation of (6) is a felony of the fifth degree (2929.11-2929.18, 2929.31). If the value of the computer, computer system, computer network, computer software, computer program, or data involved in the violation (6) or the loss to the victim resulting from the violation is ten thousand dollars or more, or if the computer, computer system, computer network, computer software, computer program, or data involved in the violation of (6) is used or intended to be used in the operation of an aircraft and the violation creates a substantial risk of physical harm to any person or the aircraft in question is an occupied aircraft, criminal mischief committed in violation of division (6) is a felony of the fourth degree (2929.11-2929.18, 2929.31)

***ENDANGERING AIRCRAFT OR AIRPORT OPERATIONS*, R.C. § 2909.08 [M2, MI, F5, F4]**

[A](1) Knowingly

(2) (a) (i) Throw an object at or drop an object upon

(ii) Any moving aircraft

*(or)*

(b) (i) Shoot with a bow and arrow or discharge a firearm, air gun, or spring-operated gun

(ii) At or toward any aircraft

(3) Venue

[B](1) Knowingly or recklessly

(2) Shoot with a bow and arrow or discharge a firearm, air gun, or spring-operated gun

(3) Upon or over any airport operational surface

(4) Venue

Offense under Division [A] above [endangering aircraft]

*Penalty:* A misdemeanor of the first degree (2929.21-2929.31)

If violation creates risk of physical harm

*Penalty:* A felony of the fifth degree (2929.11-2929.18, 2929.31)

If violation creates a substantial risk of physical harm to any person or if the aircraft is occupied

*Penalty:* A felony of the fourth degree (2929.11-2929.18, 2929.31)

Offense under Division [B] above [endangering airport operations]

*Penalty:* A misdemeanor of the second degree (2929.21-2929.31)

If violation creates risk of physical harm

*Penalty:* A felony of the fifth degree (2929.11-2929.18, 2929.31)

If the violation creates a substantial risk of physical harm to any person

*Penalty:* A felony of the fourth degree (2929.11-2929.18, 2929.31)

*Notes:* Division [B] above does not apply to any federal or Ohio or other state officer, agent, or employee, or any law enforcement officer, who is authorized to discharge firearms and is acting within the scope of the officer's, agent's, or employee's duties; or to any person who, with the consent of the owner or operator of the airport operational surface or the authorized agent of either, is lawfully engaging in any hunting or sporting activity or is otherwise lawfully discharging a firearm. See R.C. § 2909.08(C)

R.C. § 2909.08(F) provides that any bow and arrow, air gun, spring-operated gun, or firearm used in a felony violation of this section shall be seized and forfeited, and disposed of pursuant to R.C. § 2933.41

In addition to any other penalty or section imposed for a violation of Division [B], the hunting license or permit of the offender shall be suspended or revoked

*Definitions:* "Air gun," "firearm," "spring-operated gun," and "airport operational surface," R.C. § 2909.08

***INTERFERING WITH OPERATION OF AIRCRAFT WITH LASER*, R.C. § 2909.081 [F2]**

(1) Knowingly

(2) Discharge

(3) A laser or other device that creates visible light

(4) Into the cockpit of an aircraft

(5) In the process of taking off or landing or is in flight.
(6) Venue
*Penalty:* A felony of the second degree (2929.11-2929.18, 2929.31)

***VEHICULAR VANDALISM,* R.C. § 2909.09 [M1, F4, F3, F2]**

(1) Knowingly
(2) Drop or throw
(3) Any object
(4) (a) At
*(or)*
(b) Onto
*(or)*
(c) Into the path of
(5) (a) Any vehicle, streetcar, or trackless trolley on a highway
*(or)*
(b) Any boat or vessel on any waters in this state
(6) Venue
*Penalty:* A misdemeanor of the first degree (2929.11-2929.18, 2929.31)
If the violation creates a substantial risk of physical harm to any person or causes serious physical harm to property
*Penalty:* A felony of the fourth degree (2929.11-2929.18, 2929.31)
If the violation causes physical harm to any person
*Penalty:* A felony of the third degree (2929.11-2929.18, 2929.31)
If the violation causes serious physical harm to any person
*Penalty:* A felony of the second degree (2929.11-2929.18, 2929.31)

***RAILROAD VANDALISM, TRESPASS, INTERFERENCE,* R.C. § 2909.10 [M1, F4, F3, F2]**

Division A: Railroad Vandalism
(1) Knowingly
(2) Drop or throw
(3) Any object
(4) (a) At
*(or)*
(b) Onto
*(or)*
(c) Into the path of
(5) (a) Any railroad rail or railroad track
*(or)*
(b) (i) Any locomotive, engine, railroad car, or other vehicle of a railroad company
(ii) While such vehicle is on a railroad track
(6) Venue
*Penalty:* A misdemeanor of the first degree (2929.11-2929.18, 2929.31)
If the violation creates a substantial risk of physical harm to any person or causes serious physical harm to property
*Penalty:* A felony of the fourth degree (2929.11-2929.18, 2929.31)
If the violation causes physical harm to any person
*Penalty* : A felony of the third degree (2929.11-2929.18, 2929.31)
If the violation causes serious physical harm to any person
*Penalty:* A felony of the second degree (2929.11-2929.18, 2929.31)

Division B: Criminal Trespass on a Railroad Vehicle
(1) Without privilege to do so
(2) Climb upon or into
(3) Any locomotive, engine, railroad car, or other vehicle of a railroad company
(4) While such vehicle is on a railroad track
(5) Venue
*Penalty:* A misdemeanor of the first degree (2929.11-2929.18, 2929.31)
If the violation creates a substantial risk of physical harm to any person or causes serious physical harm to property
*Penalty:* A felony of the fourth degree (2929.11-2929.18, 2929.31)
If the violation causes physical harm to any person
*Penalty:* A felony of the third degree (2929.11-2929.18, 2929.31)
If the violation causes serious physical harm to any person
*Penalty:* A felony of the second degree (2929.11-2929.18, 2929.31)

Division C: Interference with Operation of a Train
(1) Without privilege to do so
(2) (a) Disrupt
*(or)*
(b) Delay
*(or)*

(c) Prevent the operation of
(3) Any train or other vehicle of a railroad company
(4) While such vehicle is on a railroad track
(5) Venue
*Penalty:* A misdemeanor of the first degree (2929.11-2929.18, 2929.31)
If the violation creates a substantial risk of physical harm to any person or causes serious physical harm to property
*Penalty:* A felony of the fourth degree (2929.11-2929.18, 2929.31)
If the violation causes physical harm to any person
*Penalty:* A felony of the third degree (2929.11-2929.18, 2929.31)
If the violation causes serious physical harm to any person
*Penalty:* A felony of the second degree (2929.11-2929.18, 2929.31)

Division D: Criminal Trespass on the Land or Premises of a Railroad Company
(1) Without privilege to do so
(2) Knowingly
(3) (a) Enter
*(or)*
(b) Remain on
(4) The land or premises of
(5) A Railroad Company
(6) Venue
*Penalty:* A misdemeanor of the fourth degree (2929.11-2929.18, 2929.31)

***RAILROAD GRADE CROSSING DEVICE VANDALISM,* R.C. § 2909.101 [M1, F4, F3, F2]**

(1) Knowingly
(2) (a) Deface
*(or)*
(b) Damage
*(or)*
(c) Obstruct
*(or)*
(d) Remove
*(or)*
(e) Otherwise impair the operation of
(3) (a) Any railroad grade crossing warning signal
*(or)*
(b) Other protective device (e.g., any gate, bell, light, crossbuck, stop sign, yield sign, advance warning sign, or advance pavement marking)
(4) Venue
*Penalty:* A misdemeanor of the first degree (2929.11-2929.18, 2929.31)
If the violation creates a substantial risk of physical harm to any person or causes serious physical harm to property
*Penalty:* A felony of the fourth degree (2929.11-2929.18, 2929.31)
If the violation causes physical harm to any person
*Penalty:* A felony of the third degree (2929.11-2929.18, 2929.31)
If the violation causes serious physical harm to any person
*Penalty:* A felony of the second degree (2929.11-2929.18, 2929.31)

***SOLICITING OR PROVIDING SUPPORT TO AN ACT OF TERRORISM,* R.C. § 2909.22 [F3]**

(1) Raise, solicit, collect, donate, or provide
(2) Any material support or resources
(3) With the purpose that such support/resources will be used in whole or in part to
(4) (a) Plan
*(or)*
(b) Prepare
*(or)*
(c) Carry out
*(or)*
(d) Aid in
(5) (a) An act of terrorism
*(or)*
(b) The concealment of or an escape from an act of terrorism
(6) Venue
*Penalty:* A felony of the third degree (2929.11-2929.18, 2929.31)
R.C. § 2909.25, authorizing a sentencing court to order an offender to pay government agencies reasonably incurred costs of investigating and prosecuting the violation, as well as actual response costs incurred, applies to persons convicted under this section

*Definitions:* "Act of terrorism," R.C. § 2909.21(A)
"Material support or resources," R.C. § 2909.21(B)

***MAKING A TERRORISTIC THREAT,* R.C. § 2909.23 [F3]**

(1) (a) Threaten to commit
*(or)*
(b) Threaten to cause to be committed
(2) A "specified offense"
(3) Where
(a) The person makes the threat with purpose to
(i) Intimidate or coerce a civilian population
*(or)*
(ii) Influence the policy of any government by intimidation or coercion
*(or)*
(iii) Affect the conduct of any government by the threat or by the specified offense
*(and)*
(b) As a result of the threat, the person causes a reasonable expectation or fear of the imminent commission of the specified offense
(4) Venue

*Penalty:* A felony of the third degree (2929.11-2929.18, 2929.31)
R.C. § 2909.25, authorizing a sentencing court to order an offender to pay government agencies reasonably incurred costs of investigating and prosecuting the violation, as well as actual response costs incurred, applies to persons convicted under this section

*Note:* "Specified offense" means any of the following: (1) A felony offense of violence, a violation of R.C. § 2909.04 or 2927.24, or a felony of the first degree that is not a violation of any provision in R.C. Chapter 2925. or 3719.; (2) An attempt to commit, complicity in committing, or a conspiracy to commit an offense listed in (1)

***TERRORISM,* R.C. § 2909.24 [one degree higher than most serious underlying specified offense]**

(1) Commit a "specified offense"
(2) With purpose to
(a) Intimidate or coerce a civilian population
*(or)*
(b) Influence the policy of any government by intimidation or coercion
*(or)*
(c) Affect the conduct of any government by the specified offense
(3) Venue

*Penalty:* If the most serious underlying specified offense the defendant committed is a felony of the first degree or murder, the offender shall be sentenced to life imprisonment without parole. If the most serious underlying specified offense the defendant committed is aggravated murder, the offender shall be sentenced to life imprisonment without parole or death pursuant to R.C. §§ 2929.02 to 2929.06. (2909.24(B))

*Note:* "Specified offense" means any of the following: (1) A felony offense of violence, a violation of R.C. § 2909.04 or 2927.24, or a felony of the first degree that is not a violation of any provision in R.C. Chapter 2925. or 3719.; (2) An attempt to commit, complicity in committing, or a conspiracy to commit an offense listed in (1)

***CRIMINAL POSSESSION OF CHEMICAL WEAPON, BIOLOGICAL WEAPON, RADIOLOGICAL OR NUCLEAR WEAPON, OR EXPLOSIVE DEVICE,* R.C. § 2909.26 [F3, F2]**

Division (A) [F3]:
(1) Knowingly
(2) Possess
(3) (a) Any chemical weapon
*(or)*
(b) Biological weapon
*(or)*
(c) Radiological or nuclear weapon
*(or)*
(d) Explosive device
(4) With the intent to use it to cause serious physical harm or death to another person
(5) Venue

Division (B) [F2]:
(1) Knowingly
(2) Possess
(3) (a) Any chemical weapon
*(or)*
(b) Biological weapon
*(or)*

(c) Radiological or nuclear weapon
*(or)*
(d) Explosive device
(4) With the intent to use the weapon to do any of the following:
(a) Intimidate or coerce a civilian population
*(or)*
(b) Influence the policy of any government by intimidation or coercion
*(or)*
(c) Affect the conduct of any government by murder, assassination, or kidnapping.
(5) Venue
*Penalty:* A violation of division (A) of this section is a felony of the third degree (2929.11-2929.18, 2929.31)
*Penalty:* A violation of division (B) of this section is a felony of the second degree (2929.11-2929.18, 2929.31)

***CRIMINAL USE OF CHEMICAL WEAPON, BIOLOGICAL WEAPON, RADIOLOGICAL OR NUCLEAR WEAPON, OR EXPLOSIVE DEVICE, R.C. § 2909.27 [F2, F1]***

Division (A) [F2]:
(1) Recklessly
(2) Use, deploy, release, or cause to be used, deployed, or released
(3) (a) Any chemical weapon
*(or)*
(b) Biological weapon
*(or)*
(c) Radiological or nuclear weapon
*(or)*
(d) Explosive device
(4) That creates a risk of death or serious physical harm to another person not a participant in the offense
(5) Venue

Division (B) [F1]:
(1) Knowingly
(2) Use, deploy, release, or cause to be used, deployed, or released
(3) (a) Any chemical weapon
*(or)*
(b) Biological weapon
*(or)*
(c) Radiological or nuclear weapon
*(or)*
(d) Explosive device
(4) With the intent to
(a) Intimidate or coerce a civilian population
*(or)*
(b) Influence the policy of any government by intimidation or coercion
*(or)*
(c) Affect the conduct of any government by murder, assassination, or kidnapping
*(or)*
(d) Cause physical harm to, or the death of, any person who is not a participant in the offense
(5) Venue
*Penalty:* A violation of division (A) of this section is a felony of the second degree (2929.11-2929.18, 2929.31)
*Penalty:* A violation of division (B) of this section is a felony of the first degree (2929.11-2929.18, 2929.31)

***ILLEGAL ASSEMBLY OR POSSESSION OF CHEMICALS OR SUBSTANCES FOR THE MANUFACTURE OF CHEMICAL WEAPON, BIOLOGICAL WEAPON, RADIOLOGICAL OR NUCLEAR WEAPON, OR EXPLOSIVE DEVICE, R.C. § 2909.28 [F4]***

(1) Knowingly
(2) With the intent to manufacture a chemical weapon, biological weapon, radiological or nuclear weapon, or explosive device
(3) Assemble or possess
(4) One or more toxins, toxic chemicals, precursors of toxic chemicals, vectors, biological agents, or hazardous radioactive substances, including, but not limited to, those listed in rules the director of public safety adopts, that may be used to manufacture a chemical weapon, biological weapon, radiological or nuclear weapon, or explosive device
(5) Venue
*Penalty:* A felony of the fourth degree (2929.11-2929.18, 2929.31)

***MONEY LAUNDERING IN SUPPORT OF TERRORISM, R.C. § 2909.29 [M1, F5, F4, F3, F2]***

(1) Knowing that property is the proceeds of an act of terrorism or a monetary instrument given, received, or intended to be used in support of an act of terrorism

(2) Conduct or attempt to conduct
(3) (a) Any transaction involving that property
*(or)*
(b) Transport, transmit or transfer that monetary instrument with the intent to do any of the following
(i) Commit or further the commission of criminal activity
*(or)*
(ii) Conceal or disguise the nature, location, source, ownership, or control of either the proceeds of an act of terrorism or a monetary instrument given, received, or intended to be used to support an act of terrorism
*(or)*
(iii) Conceal or disguise the intent to avoid a transaction reporting requirement under section 1315.53 of the Revised Code or federal law
(4) Venue
*Penalty:* A misdemeanor of the first degree (2929.21-2929.31), except as otherwise provided in this division
*Penalty:* A violation of this section is a felony of the fifth degree (2929.11-2929.18, 2929.31) if the total value of the property or monetary instrument involved in the transaction equals or exceeds one thousand dollars and is less than five thousand dollars
*Penalty:* A violation of this section is a felony of the fourth degree (2929.11-2929.18, 2929.31) if the total value of the property or monetary instrument involved in the transaction equals or exceeds five thousand dollars and is less than twenty-five thousand dollars
*Penalty:* A violation of this section is a felony of the third degree (2929.11-2929.18, 2929.31) if the total value of the property or monetary instrument involved in the transaction equals or exceeds twenty-five thousand dollars and is less than seventy-five thousand dollars
*Penalty:* A violation of this section is a felony of the second degree (2929.11-2929.18, 2929.31) if the total value of the property or monetary instrument involved in the transaction equals or exceeds seventy-five thousand dollars

---

## ROBBERY, BURGLARY, TRESPASS

### *AGGRAVATED ROBBERY,* R.C. § 2911.01 [F1]

Division (A):
(1) (a) Attempt or commit theft offense
*(or)*
(b) Flee immediately after the theft or attempt
(2) While
(a) Having a deadly weapon on or about the offender's person or under the offender's control and either display the weapon, brandish it, indicate that the offender possesses it, or use it
*(or)*
(b) Having a dangerous ordnance on or about the offender's person or under the offender's control
*(or)*
(c) Inflicting or attempting to inflict serious physical harm on another
(3) Venue

Division (B):
(1) (a) Knowingly remove or attempt to remove
*(or)*
(b) Knowingly deprive or attempt to deprive
(2) From the person of a law enforcement officer
(3) A deadly weapon
(4) When
(a) The law enforcement officer, at the time of the removal, attempted removal, deprivation, or attempted deprivation is acting within the course and scope of the officer's duties
*(or)*
(b) The offender knows or has reason to know that the law enforcement officer is a law enforcement officer
(5) Venue
*Penalty:* A felony of the first degree (2929.11-2929.18, 2929.31)

### *ROBBERY,* R.C. § 2911.02 [F3, F2]

(1) (a) Attempt or commit theft offense
*(or)*
(b) Flee immediately after the attempt or offense
(2) While
(a) Having a deadly weapon on or about the offender's person or under the offender's control
*(or)*
(b) Inflicting, or attempting to inflict, or threatening to inflict physical harm on another
*(or)*

(c) Use or threaten the immediate use of force against another
Violation of division (2)(a) or (b)
*Penalty:* A felony of the second degree (2929.11-2929.18, 2929.31)
Violation of division (2)(c)
*Penalty:* A felony of the third degree (2929.11-2929.18, 2929.31)

***AGGRAVATED BURGLARY*, R.C. § 2911.11 [F1]**

(1) Trespass in
  (a) Occupied structure
    *(or)*
  (b) A separately secured or separately occupied portion of an occupied structure
(2) By force, stealth, or deception
(3) When another person other than an accomplice of the offender is present
(4) With purpose to commit in the structure or in the separately secured or separately occupied portion of the structure any criminal offense
(5) If any of the following apply:
  (a) The offender inflicts, attempts or threatens to inflict physical harm on another
    *(or)*
  (b) The offender has a deadly weapon or dangerous ordnance on or about the offender's person or under the offender's control
(6) Venue
*Penalty:* A felony of the first degree (2929.11-2929.18, 2929.31)
*Definitions:* "Occupied structure," R.C. § 2909.11
"Weapons/ordnance," R.C. § 2923.11

***BURGLARY*, R.C. § 2911.12(A) [F2, F3]**

**Elements:**
(1) By means of force, stealth, or deception
(2) Trespass
(3) (a) In an occupied structure or in a separately secured or separately occupied portion of an occupied structure when another person other than an accomplice of the offender is present, with purpose to commit in the structure or in the separately secured or separately occupied portion of the structure any criminal offense
    *(or)*
  (b) In an occupied structure or in a separately secured or separately occupied portion of an occupied structure that is a permanent or temporary habitation of any person when any person other than an accomplice of the offender is present or likely to be present, with purpose to commit in the habitation any criminal offense
    *(or)*
  (c) In an occupied structure or in a separately secured or separately occupied portion of an occupied structure, with purpose to commit in the structure or separately occupied portion of the structure any criminal offense
  (4) Venue
Offense under (3)(a) or (3)(b)
*Penalty:* A felony of the second degree (2929.11-2929.18, 2929.31)
Offense under (3)(c)
*Penalty:* A felony of the third degree (2929.11-2929.18, 2929.31)

***TREPASS IN A HABITATION WHEN A PERSON IS PRESENT OR LIKELY TO BE PRESENT*, R.C. § 2911.12(B) [F4]**

**Elements:**
(1) By means of force, stealth, or deception
(2) Trespass in a permanent or temporary habitation of any person
(3) When any person other than an accomplice of the offender is present or likely to be present
(4) Venue
*Penalty:* A felony of the fourth degree (2929.11-2929.18, 2929.31)

***BREAKING AND ENTERING*, R.C. § 2911.13 [F5]**

Division (A):
(1) With purpose to commit a theft offense or any felony therein
(2) Trespass in unoccupied structure
(3) By force, stealth, or deception
(4) Venue

Division (B):
(1) With purpose to commit a felony
(2) Trespass on land or premises of another
(3) Venue
*Penalty:* A felony of the fifth degree (2929.11-2929.18, 2929.31)

***CRIMINAL TRESPASS*, R.C. § 2911.21 [M4]**

(1) Without privilege to do so
(2) (a) Knowingly enter or remain on land or premises of another
*(or)*
(b) (i) Knowingly enter or remain on land or premises of another, use of which is lawfully restricted to certain persons, purposes, modes, or hours
(ii) When the offender knows he is violating such restrictions or is reckless in that regard
*(or)*
(c) Recklessly enter or remain on the land or premises of another, as to which notice against unauthorized access or presence is given
(i) By actual communication to the offender
*(or)*
(ii) In a manner prescribed by law
*(or)*
(iii) By posting in a manner reasonably calculated to come to the attention of potential intruders
*(or)*
(iv) By fencing or other enclosure manifestly designed to restrict access
*(or)*
(d) (i) Being on the land or premises of another
(ii) Negligently failing or refusing to leave
(iii) Upon being notified to do so by signage posted in a conspicuous place or otherwise being notified to do so by the owner or occupant, or the agent or servant of either
(3) Venue

*Penalty:* A misdemeanor of the fourth degree (2929.21-2929.31)
If the person, in committing the violation of this section, used a snowmobile, off-highway motorcycle, or all-purpose vehicle, the court shall impose a fine of two times the usual amount imposed for the violation.

*Note:* It is no defense to this charge that the premises were owned or controlled by a public agency, or that there was authority to enter when such authorization was obtained by deception
If an offender previously has been convicted of or pleaded guilty to two or more violations of this section or a substantially equivalent municipal ordinance, and the offender, in committing each violation, used a snowmobile, off-highway motorcycle, or all-purpose vehicle, the court, in addition to or independent of all other penalties imposed for the violation, may impound the certificate of registration of that snowmobile or off-highway motorcycle or the certificate of registration and license plate of that all-purpose vehicle for not less than sixty days

*Definitions:* "Land or premises," as used in this section, includes any land, building structure, or place belonging to, controlled by, or in custody of another, and any separate enclosure or room, or portion thereof, R.C. § 2911.21

***AGGRAVATED TRESPASS*, R.C. § 2911.211 [M1]**

(1) (a) Enter
*(or)*
(b) Remain
(2) On the land or premises of another
(3) With purpose to commit
(4) On that land or those premises
(5) A misdemeanor the elements of which involve
(6) (a) Causing physical harm to another person
*(or)*
(b) Causing another person to believe that the offender will cause physical harm to him
(7) Venue

*Penalty:* A misdemeanor of the first degree (2929.21-2929.31)

*Notes: See* R.C. § 2919.251 for special provisions concerning repeat offenders and offenders violating prior protection orders or consent orders
*See* R.C. § 2919.251 for special provisions concerning bail
*See* R.C. § 2919.26 for special provisions concerning protection orders
*See* R.C. § 2925.03 for special provisions concerning arrest and detention

***CRIMINAL TRESSPASS ON PLACE OF PUBLIC AMUSEMENT*, R.C. § 2911.23 [M1]**

(1) Knowingly
(2) Without privilege to do so
(3) Enter or remain on
(4) Any restricted portion of a place of public amusement
(5) Interrupt or cause the delay
(6) Of the live performance, sporting event, or other activity taking place at the place of public amusement
(7) After a printed written notice has been given as provided in division (D)(1) of this section that the general public is restricted from access to that restricted portion of the place of public amusement.
(8) Venue

*Penalty:* A misdemeanor of the first degree (2929.21-2929.31)
*Note:* See text of statute for detailed written notice provisions

***SAFECRACKING*, R.C. § 2911.31 [F4]**

(1) With purpose to commit an offense
(2) Knowingly enter, force entry into or tamper with a vault, safe or strongbox
(3) Venue
*Penalty:* A felony of the fourth degree (2929.11-2929.18, 2929.31)

***TAMPERING WITH COIN MACHINES*, R.C. § 2911.32 [M1, F5]**

(1) With purpose to commit a theft or to defraud
(2) Knowingly
(3) Enter, force entrance into, tamper with or insert any part of an instrument into
(4) A coin machine
(5) Venue
*Penalty:* A misdemeanor of the first degree (2929.21-2929.31)
If a prior conviction under this section or of a theft offense
*Penalty:* A felony of the fifth degree (2929.11-2929.18, 2929.31)

---

## THEFTS AND FRAUDS

***THEFT*, R.C. § 2913.02 [M1, F5, F4, F3, F2, F1]**

(1) Knowingly
(2) Obtain or exert control over property or services
(3) With purpose to deprive the owner thereof
(4) (a) Without consent of owner or person authorized to consent
*(or)*
(b) Beyond the scope of the express or implied consent of owner or person authorized to consent
*(or)*
(c) By deception
*(or)*
(d) By threat
*(or)*
(e) By intimidation
(5) Venue

PETTY THEFT:

*Penalty:* A misdemeanor of the first degree (2929.21-2929.31)

THEFT:

If value is $1,000 or more and is less than $7,500 or if object is one of the following listed in R.C. § 2913.71: credit card/printed form for check or other negotiable instrument which identifies the drawer, maker, or account, etc./motor vehicle license plate/temporary license placard or sticker/blank certificate of title, or manufacturer's or importer's certificate to a motor vehicle/blank form for any license listed in R.C. § 4507.01
*Penalty:* A felony of the fifth degree (2929.11-2929.18, 2929.31)
If the offender committed the violation by causing a motor vehicle to leave the premises of an establishment at which gasoline is offered for retail sale without the offender making full payment for gasoline that was dispensed into the fuel tank of the motor vehicle or into another container, the court may do one of the following:
(a) Unless division (B)(7)(b) of this section applies, suspend for not more than six months the offender's driver's license, probationary driver's license, commercial driver's license, temporary instruction permit, or nonresident operating privilege;
(b) If the offender's driver's license, probationary driver's license, commercial driver's license, temporary instruction permit, or nonresident operating privilege has previously been suspended pursuant to division (B)(7)(a) of this section, impose a class seven suspension of the offender's license, permit, or privilege from the range specified in division (A)(7) of section 4510.02 of the Revised Code, provided that the suspension shall be for at least six months.
If the offender commits theft by stealing rented property or rental services, the court may order that the offender make restitution, including, but not limited to, the cost of repairing or replacing the stolen property, or the cost of repairing the stolen property and any loss of revenue resulting from deprivation of the property due to theft of rental services that is less than or equal to the actual value of the property at the time it was rented.

GRAND THEFT:

If value is $7,500 or more and less than $150,000 or the property stolen is a firearm or dangerous ordnance, or the property stolen is a motor vehicle

*Penalty:* A felony of the fourth degree (2929.11-2929.18, 2929.31), except that where property stolen is a firearm or dangerous ordnance, a felony in the third degree or felony of the first degree when stolen from a federally licensed firearms dealer
*Definitions:* "Federally licensed firearms dealer," R.C. § 5502.63

AGGRAVATED THEFT:

If value is $150,000 or more and less than $750,000
*Penalty:* A felony of the third degree (2929.11-2929.18, 2929.31)
If the value of the property or services stolen is $750,000 or more and less than $1,500,000
*Penalty:* A felony of the second degree (2929.11-2929.18, 2929.31)
If the value of the property or services stolen is $1,500,000 or more
*Penalty:* A felony of the first degree (2929.11-2929.18, 2929.31)

THEFT FROM AN ELDERLY PERSON OR DISABLED ADULT:

If the victim of the offense is an elderly person or a disabled adult
*Penalty:* A felony of the fifth degree (2929.11-2929.18, 2929.31)
If the value of the property or services stolen is $1,000 or more and less than $7,500
*Penalty:* A felony of the fourth degree (2929.11-2929.18, 2929.31)
If the value of the property or services stolen is $7,500 or more and less than $37,500
*Penalty:* A felony of the third degree (2929.11-2929.18, 2929.31)
If the value of the property or services stolen is $37,500 or more and is less than $150,000
*Penalty:* A felony of the second degree (2929.11-2929.18, 2929.31)
If the value of the property or services stolen is $150,000 or more
*Penalty:* A felony of the first degree (2929.11-2929.18, 2929.31)

THEFT OF DRUGS:

If property stolen is any dangerous drug and no prior felony drug abuse conviction
*Penalty:* A felony of the fourth degree (2929.11-2929.18, 2929.31)
If property stolen is any dangerous drug and prior felony drug abuse conviction
*Penalty:* A felony of the third degree (2929.11-2929.18, 2929.31)

THEFT OF POLICE DOG OR HORSE OR SERVICE DOG:

If the property stolen is a police dog or horse or an assistance dog and the offender knows or should know that the property stolen is a police dog or horse or an assistance dog
*Penalty:* A felony of the third degree (2929.11-2929.18, 2929.31)

THEFT OF ANHYDROUS AMMONIA:

*Penalty:* A felony of the third degree (2929.11-2929.18, 2929.31)

***UNAUTHORIZED USE OF VEHICLE*, R.C. § 2913.03 [M1, F5, F4, F3, F2]**

Division (A): **[M1, F5, F4, F3, F2]**
(1) Knowingly
(2) Use or operate
(3) Aircraft, motor vehicle, motorboat, other motor propelled vehicle
(4) Without consent of owner or person authorized to give consent
(5) Venue
*Penalty:* A misdemeanor of the first degree (2929.21-2929.31)
If the victim of the offense is an elderly person or disabled adult and if the victim incurs a loss as a result of the violation
*Penalty:* A felony of the fifth degree (2929.11-2929.18, 2929.31)
If the loss to the victim is $1,000 or more and is less than $7,500
*Penalty:* A felony of the fourth degree (2929.11-2929.18, 2929.31)
If the loss to the victim is $7,500 or more and is less than $37,500
*Penalty:* A felony of the third degree (2929.11-2929.18, 2929.31)
If the loss to the victim is $37,500 or more
*Penalty:* A felony of the second degree (2929.11-2929.18, 2929.31)

Division (B): **[F5, F4, F3, F2]**
(1) Knowingly
(2) Use or operate
(3) Aircraft, motor vehicle, motorcycle, motorboat, other motor propelled vehicle
(4) Without consent of owner or person authorized to give consent
(5) Remove from Ohio, or keep possession more than 48 hours
(6) Venue
*Penalty:* A felony of the fifth degree (2929.11-2929.18, 2929.31)
If the victim of the offense is an elderly person or disabled adult and if the victim incurs a loss as a result of the violation
*Penalty:* A felony of the fifth degree (2929.11-2929.18, 2929.31)

If the loss to the victim is $1,000 or more and is less than $7,500
*Penalty:* A felony of the fourth degree (2929.11-2929.18, 2929.31)
If the loss to the victim is $7,500 or more and is less than $37,500
*Penalty:* A felony of the third degree (2929.11-2929.18, 2929.31)
If the loss to the victim is $37,500 or more
*Penalty:* A felony of the second degree (2929.11-2929.18, 2929.31)

***UNAUTHORIZED USE OF PROPERTY; COMPUTER, CABLE OR TELECOMMUNICATION PROPERTY; LAW ENFORCEMENT AUTOMATED DATABASE,* R.C. § 2913.04 [M4, M1, F5, F4, F3, F2]**

Division (A):
(1) Knowingly
(2) Use or operate
(3) Property of another
(4) Without owner's consent or consent of authorized person
(5) Venue

Division (B):
(1) In any manner and by any means, including, but not limited to, computer hacking
(2) Knowingly
(3) Gain access to or cause access to be gained to
(4) Any computer, computer system, computer network, cable service, cable system, telecommunications device, telecommunications service, or information service
(5) Without the consent of, or beyond the scope of the express or implied consent of,
(6) The owner of the computer, computer system, computer network, telecommunications device, telecommunications service, or information service or other person authorized to give consent
(7) Venue

Division (C):
(1) Knowingly
(2) Gain access to, attempt to gain access to, cause access to be granted to, or disseminate information gained from access to
(3) Law enforcement automated database created pursuant to Section 5503.10 of the revised code
(4) Without the consent of or beyond the scope of the express or implied consent of
(5) The chair of the law enforcement automated data system steering committee
(6) Venue

Division (D)
(1) Knowingly
(2) Gain access to, attempt to gain access to, cause access to be granted to, or disseminate information gained from access to
(3) The Ohio Law Enforcement Gateway established and operated pursuant to § 109.57(C)(1)
(4) Without the consent of, or beyond the scope of the express or implied consent of
(5) The Superintendent of the Bureau of Criminal Identification and Investigation
(6) Venue
*Penalty:* (A) A misdemeanor of the fourth degree (2929.21-2929.31)
If committed for the purpose of devising or executing a scheme to defraud or to obtain property or services and the value of the property or services or the loss to the victim is less than $1,000, a misdemeanor of the first degree (2929.21-2929.31)
If the value of the property or services or the loss to the victim is $1,000 or more and is less than $7,500, a felony of the fifth degree (2929.11-2929.18, 2929.31)
If the value of the property or services or the loss to the victim is $7,500 or more and less than $150,000, a felony of the fourth degree (2929.11-2929.18, 2929.31)
If the value of the property or services or the loss to the victim is $150,000 or more, a felony of the third degree (2929.11-2929.18, 2929.31)
If the victim of the offense is an elderly person or disabled adult, a felony of the fifth degree (2929.11-2929.18, 2929.31)
If the value of the property or services or the loss to the victim is $1,000 or more and is less than $7,500, a felony of the fourth degree (2929.11-2929.18, 2929.31)
If the value of the property or services or the loss to the victim is $7,500 or more and is less than $37,500, a felony of the third degree (2929.11-2929.18, 2929.31). If the value of the property or services or the loss to the victim is $37,500 or more, a felony of the second degree (2929.11-2929.18, 2929.31)
(B) A felony of the fifth degree (2929.11-2929.18, 2929.31)
If unauthorized use of computer, cable, or telecommunication property is committed for the purpose of devising or executing a scheme to defraud or to obtain property or services, for obtaining money, property, or services by false or fraudulent pretenses, or for committing any other criminal offense, unauthorized use of computer, cable, or telecommunication property is whichever of the following is applicable:
If the value of the property or services involved or the loss to the victim is $7,500 or more and less than $150,000, a felony of the fourth degree (2929.11-2929.18, 2929.31);

If the value of the property or services involved or the loss to the victim is $150,000 or more, a felony of the third degree (2929.11-2929.18, 2929.31)
If the victim of the offense is an elderly person or disabled adult, unauthorized use of computer, cable, or telecommunication property is whichever of the following is applicable:
(a) Except as otherwise provided in division (b), (c), or (d), a felony of the fifth degree (2929.11-2929.18, 2929.31);
(b) If the value of the property or services or loss to the victim is $1,000 or more and is less than $7,500, a felony of the fourth degree (2929.11-2929.18, 2929.31);
(c) If the value of the property or services or loss to the victim is $7,500 or more and is less than $37,500, a felony of the third degree (2929.11-2929.18, 2929.31);
(d) If the value of the property or services or loss to the victim is $37,500 or more, a felony of the second degree (2929.11-2929.18, 2929.31)
(C) A felony of the fifth degree (2929.11-2929.18, 2929.31)
(D) A felony of the fifth degree (2929.11-2929.18, 2929.31)

***POSSESSION OR SALE OF UNAUTHORIZED CABLE TELEVISION DEVICE*, R.C. § 2913.041 [F5, F4]**

Division (A): **[F5]**
(1) Knowingly
(2) Possess any device, including any instrument, apparatus, computer chip, equipment, decoder, descrambler, converter, software, or other device specially adapted, modified, or remanufactured for gaining access to cable television service
(3) Without securing authorization from or paying the required compensation to the owner or operator of the system that provides the cable television service
(4) Venue
*Penalty:* A felony of the fifth degree (2929.11-2929.18, 2929.31)

Division (B): **[F4]**
(1) Knowingly
(2) Sell, distribute or manufacture any device, including any instrument, apparatus, computer chip, equipment, decoder, descrambler, converter, software, or other device specially adapted, modified, or remanufactured for gaining access to cable television service
(3) Without securing authorization from or paying the required compensation to the owner or operator of the system that provides the cable television service
(4) Venue
*Penalty:* A felony of the fourth degree (2929.11-2929.18, 2929.31)

***TELECOMMUNICATIONS FRAUD*, R.C. § 2913.05 [F5, F4, F3]**

(1) Having devised a scheme to defraud
(2) Knowingly
(3) (a) Disseminate
*(or)*
(b) Transmit
*(or)*
(c) Cause to be disseminated or transmitted
(4) By means of a
(a) Wire
*(or)*
(b) Radio
*(or)*
(c) Satellite
*(or)*
(d) Telecommunication
*(or)*
(e) Telecommunications device
*(or)*
(f) Telecommunication service
(5) Any
(a) Writing
*(or)*
(b) Data
*(or)*
(c) Sign
*(or)*
(d) Signal
*(or)*
(e) Picture
*(or)*

(f) Sound
*(or)*
(g) Image
(6) With purpose to execute or otherwise further the scheme to defraud
(7) Venue
*Penalty:* A felony of the fifth degree (2929.11-2929.18, 2929.31)
If the value of the benefit obtained by the offender or of the detriment to the victim of the fraud is $5,000 or more but less than $100,000
*Penalty:* A felony of the fourth degree (2929.11-2929.18, 2929.31)
If the value of the benefit obtained by the offender or of the detriment to the victim of the fraud is $100,000 or more
*Penalty:* A felony of the third degree (2929.11-2929.18, 2929.31)

**_UNLAWFUL USE OF A TELECOMMUNICATION DEVICE,_ R.C. § 2913.06 [F5]**

Division (A):
(1) Knowingly
(2) (a) Manufacture
*(or)*
(b) Possess
*(or)*
(c) Deliver
*(or)*
(d) Offer to deliver
*(or)*
(e) Advertise
(3) A counterfeit telecommunications device
(4) With purpose to use it criminally

Division (B):
(1) Knowingly
(2) (a) Manufacture
*(or)*
(b) Possess
*(or)*
(c) Deliver
*(or)*
(d) Offer to deliver
*(or)*
(e) Advertise
(3) A counterfeit telecommunications device
(4) (a) With purpose to use that device or to allow that device to be used to
*(or)*
(b) Knowing or having reason to know that another person may use that device to
(5) (a) Obtain or attempt to obtain telecommunications service or information service with purpose to avoid a lawful charge for that service or aid or cause another person to obtain or attempt to obtain telecommunications service or information service with purpose to avoid a lawful charge for that service
*(or)*
(b) Conceal the existence, place of origin, or destination of a telecommunications service or information service
(6) Venue
*Penalty:* A felony of the fifth degree (2929.11-2929.18. 2929.31)

**_MOTION PICTURE PIRACY,_ R.C. § 2913.07 [M1, F5]**

(1) Without the written consent of
(a) the owner or lessee of the facility
*(and)*
(b) of the licensor of the motion picture
(2) Knowingly operate
(3) An audiovisual recording function of a device
(4) In a facility in which a motion picture is being shown
(5) Venue
*Penalty:* A misdemeanor of the first degree on the first offense and a felony of the fifth degree on each subsequent offense (2929.11-2929.18, 2929.21-2929.31)

**_PASSING BAD CHECKS,_ R.C. § 2913.11 [M1, F5, F4, F3]**

(1) Issue, transfer or cause to be issued or transferred
(2) Check or other negotiable instrument
(3) (a) Knowing it will be dishonored
*(or)*

(b) Knowing that a person has ordered or will order stop payment on the check or other negotiable instrument
(4) With purpose to defraud
(5) Venue
*Penalty:* A misdemeanor of first degree (2929.21-2929.31)
If the check or checks or other negotiable instrument or instruments are issued or transferred to a single vendor or single other person for the payment of $1,000 or more but less than $7,500 or if the check or checks or other negotiable instrument or instruments are issued or transferred to multiple vendors or persons for the payment of $1,000 or more but less than $7,500
*Penalty:* A felony of the fifth degree (2929.11-2929.18, 2929.31)
If the check or checks or other negotiable instrument or instruments are for the payment of $7,500 or more but less than $150,000
*Penalty:* A felony of the fourth degree (2929.11-2929.18, 2929.31)
If the check or checks or other negotiable instrument or instruments are for the payment of $150,000 or more
*Penalty:* A felony of the third degree (2929.11-2929.18, 2929.31)
*Note:* In determining the value of the payment for purposes of penalty provisions, the court may aggregate all checks and other negotiable instruments that the offender issued or transferred or caused to be issued or transferred in violation of this section within a period of one hundred eighty consecutive days

***MISUSE OF CREDIT CARDS*, R.C. § 2913.21 [M1, F5, F4, F3, F2]**

Division (A):
(1) Procure the issuance of a credit card by deception which is relied upon
*(or)*
(2) Knowingly buy or sell a credit card from or to a person other than the issuer
(3) Venue

Division (B): With a purpose to defraud
(1) Obtain control of a credit card to secure a debt
*(or)*
(2) Obtain property or services by use of a credit card, in one or more transactions, knowing or having reasonable cause to believe the card was expired, revoked, or was obtained, retained, or being used illegally
*(or)*
(3) Furnish property or services on the presentation of a credit card, knowing the card is being used illegally
*(or)*
(4) Representing or causing it to be represented to the issuer of a credit card that property/services were furnished, knowing the representation to be false
(5) Venue

Division (C):
(1) With a purpose to violate this section
(2) Receive, possess, control or dispose of a credit card
(3) Venue

If violation of (A), (B)(1) or (C) **[M1]**
If violation of (B)(2), (3), or (4) and cumulative retail value of property and services involved in one or more violations is $1,000 or less and the violations involve one or more credit card accounts and occur within a period of 90 consecutive days commencing on the date of the first violation
*Penalty:* A misdemeanor of the first degree (2929.21-2929.31)
If violation of (B)(2), (3), or (4) and cumulative retail value of property and services involved in one or more violations is $1,000 or more and less than $7,500 and the violations involve one or more credit card accounts and occur within a period of 90 consecutive days commencing on the date of the first violation
*Penalty:* A felony of the fifth degree (2929.11-2929.18, 2929.31)
If violation of (B)(2), (3), or (4) and cumulative retail value of property and services involved in one or more violations is $7,500 or more and less than $150,000 and the violations involve one or more credit card accounts and occur within a period of 90 consecutive days commencing on the date of the first violation
*Penalty:* A felony of the fourth degree (2929.11-2929.18, 2929.31)
If violation of (B)(2), (3), or (4) and cumulative retail value of property and services in one or more violations is $150,000 or more and violations involve one or more accounts and occur within period of 90 consecutive days commencing on date of first violation
*Penalty:* A felony of the third degree (2929.11-2929.18, 2929.31)

VICTIM ELDERLY PERSON OR DISABLED ADULT:

If the victim of the offense is an elderly person or disabled adult and the offense involves a violation of Division (B)(1) or (2)
*Penalty:* A felony of the fifth degree (2929.11-2929.18, 2929.31)
If the debt for which the card is held as security or the cumulative retail value of the property or services involved is $1,000 or more and is less than $7,500
*Penalty:* A felony of the fourth degree (2929.11-2929.18, 2929.31)

If the debt for which the card is held as security or the cumulative retail value of the property or services involved is $7,500 or more and is less than $37,500
*Penalty:* A felony of the third degree (2929.11-2929.18, 2929.31)
If the debt for which the card is held as security or the cumulative retail value of the property or services involved is $37,500 or more
*Penalty:* A felony of the second degree (2929.11-2929.18, 2929.31)

***FORGERY,* R.C. § 2913.31(A) [F5, F4, F3, F2]**

(1) With a purpose to defraud or knowing the person is facilitating a fraud
 (a) Forge another's writing without the other person's authority
 *(or)*
 (b) Forge a writing so that it
 (i) Appears to be genuine when it actually is spurious
 *(or)*
 (ii) Purports to be the act of another though actually unauthorized
 *(or)*
 (iii) Purports to have been executed at a time or place or with different terms from what in fact was the case
 *(or)*
 (iv) Purports to be a copy of an original when no such original existed
 *(or)*
 (c) Utter, or possess with purpose to utter, any writing known to have been forged
(2) Venue
*Penalty:* A felony of the fifth degree (2929.11-2929.18, 2929.31)
If property or services are involved or the victim suffers a loss and if the value of the property or services or the loss to the victim is $7,500 or more and less than $150,000
*Penalty:* A felony of the fourth degree (2929.11-2929.18, 2929.31)
If property or services are involved or the victim suffers a loss and if the value of the property or services or the loss to the victim is $150,000 or more
*Penalty:* A felony of the third degree (2929.11-2929.18, 2929.31)

VICTIM ELDERLY PERSON OR DISABLED ADULT:

If the victim of the offense is an elderly person or disabled adult
*Penalty:* A felony of the fifth degree (2929.11-2929.18, 2929.31)
If the value of the property or services or the loss to the victim is $1,000 or more and is less than $7,500
*Penalty:* A felony of the fourth degree (2929.11-2929.18. 2929.31)
If the value of the property or services or the loss to the victim is $7,500 or more and is less than $37,500
*Penalty:* A felony of the third degree (2929.11-2929.18, 2929.31)
If the value of the property or services or the loss to the victim is $37,500 or more
*Penalty:* A felony of the second degree (2929.11-2929.18, 2929.31)

***FORGING IDENTIFICATION CARDS***
***SELLING FORGED IDENTIFICATION CARDS***
***DISTRIBUTING FORGED IDENTIFICATION CARDS,* R.C. § 2913.31(B) [M1]**

(1) Knowingly
(2) (a) Forge an identification card
 *(or)*
 (b) Sell or otherwise distribute a card that purports to be an identification card, knowing it to have been forged.
(3) Venue
*Penalty:* A misdemeanor of the first degree (2929.21-2929.31)
If prior conviction under this subsection
*Penalty:* A misdemeanor of the first degree (2929.21-2929.31)
Mandatory Minimum Fine: $250
*Definitions:* "Identification card," R.C. § 2913.31(B)
*Note: See also* R.C. § 4301.636 for offenses involving false official identification cards

***CRIMINAL SIMULATION,* R.C. § 2913.32 [M1, F5, F4, F3]**

(1) With a purpose to defraud or knowing the person is facilitating a fraud
(2) (a) Make or alter any object so that it appears to have value due to antiquity, rarity, curiosity, source, authorship but which it does not in fact possess
 *(or)*
 (b) Practice deception in making, retouching, editing or reproducing a photograph, movie film, video tape, phonograph record, recording tape
 *(or)*
 (c) Falsely or fraudulently make, simulate, forge, alter, or counterfeit any wrapper, label, stamp, cork, or cap prescribed by the Liquor Control Commission under Chapters 4301. and 4303., falsely or fraudulently cause

to be made, simulated, forged, altered, or counterfeited any wrapper, label, stamp, cork, or cap prescribed by the Liquor Control Commission under Chapters 4301. and 4303., or use more than once any wrapper, label, stamp, cork, or cap prescribed by the Liquor Control Commission under Chapters 4301. and 4303.
*(or)*
(d) Utter, or possess with a purpose to utter, any object known to have been simulated as above
(3) Venue
*Penalty:* A misdemeanor of the first degree (2929.21-2929.31)
If the loss to the victim is $1,000 or more and less than $7,500
*Penalty:* A felony of the fifth degree (2929.11-2929.18, 2929.31)
If the loss to the victim is $7,500 or more and less than $150,000
*Penalty:* A felony of the fourth degree (2929.11-2929.18, 2929.31)
If the loss to the victim is more than $150,000
*Penalty:* A felony of the third degree (2929.11-2929.18, 2929.31)

***MAKING OR USING SLUGS,* R.C. § 2913.33 [M2]**

(1) (a) With purpose to defraud, insert or deposit a slug in a coin machine
*(or)*
(b) With purpose of enabling another to defraud by inserting or depositing in coin machine, make, possess or dispose of a slug
(2) Venue
*Penalty:* A misdemeanor of the second degree (2929.21-2929.31)

***TRADEMARK COUNTERFEITING,* R.C. § 2913.34 [M1, F5, F4, F3]**

Division (A)(1): **[F5, F4, F3]**
(1) Knowingly
(2) Attach, affix, or otherwise use
(3) A counterfeit mark
(4) In connection with the manufacture of goods or services
(5) Whether or not the goods or services are intended for sale or resale
*Penalty:* A felony of the fifth degree (2929.11-2929.18, 2929.31)
If the cumulative sales price of the goods or services to which or in connection with which the counterfeit mark is attached, affixed, or otherwise used in the offense is $7,500 or more but less than $150,000 or if the number of units of goods to which or in connection with which the counterfeit mark is attached, affixed, or otherwise used in the offense is more than 100 units but less than 1,000 units
*Penalty:* A felony of the fourth degree (2929.11-2929.18, 2929.31)
If the cumulative sales price of the goods or services to which or in connection with which the counterfeit mark is attached, affixed, or otherwise used in the offense is $150,000 or more or if the number of units of goods to which or in connection with which the counterfeit mark is attached, affixed, or otherwise used in the offense is 1,000 units or more
*Penalty:* A felony of the third degree (2929.11-2929.18, 2929.31)

Division (A)(2): **[M1, F5]**
(1) Knowingly
(2) Possess, sell, or offer for sale
(3) Tools, machines, instruments, materials, articles, or other items of personal property
(4) Knowing that they are designed for the production or reproduction of counterfeit marks
*Penalty:* A misdemeanor of the first degree (2929.21-2929.31)
If the circumstances of the violation indicate that the tools, machines, instruments, materials, articles, or other items of personal property involved were intended for use in the commission of a felony
*Penalty:* A felony of the fifth degree (2929.11-2929.18, 2929.31)

Division (A)(3): **[M1, F5, F4, F3]**
(1) Knowingly
(2) Purchase or otherwise acquire goods
(3) Keep or otherwise have the goods in the person's possession
(4) Knowing that a counterfeit mark is attached to, affixed to, or otherwise used in connection with the goods
(5) With the intent to sell or otherwise dispose of the goods
*Penalty:* A misdemeanor of the first degree (2929.21-2929.31)
If the cumulative sales price of the goods or services to which or in connection with which the counterfeit mark is attached, affixed, or otherwise used is $1,000 or more but less than $7,500
*Penalty:* A felony of the fifth degree (2929.11-2929.18, 2929.31)
If the cumulative sales price of the goods or services to which or in connection with which the counterfeit mark is attached, affixed, or otherwise used is $7,500 or more but less than $150,000 or if the number of units of goods to which the counterfeit mark is attached, affixed, or otherwise used is more than 100 units but less than 1,000 units
*Penalty:* A felony of the fourth degree (2929.11-2929.18, 2929.31)
If the cumulative sales price of the goods or services to which or in connection with which the counterfeit mark is attached, affixed, or otherwise used is $150,000 or more or if the number of units of goods to which or in connection with which the counterfeit mark is attached, affixed, or otherwise used is 1,000 units or more

*Penalty:* A felony of the third degree (2929.11-2929.18, 2929.31)

Division (A)(4): **[M1, F5, F4, F3]**
(1) Knowingly
(2) Sell, offer for sale, or otherwise dispose of goods in the person's possession
(3) Knowing that a counterfeit mark is attached to, affixed to, or otherwise used in connection with the goods
*Penalty:* A misdemeanor of the first degree (2929.21-2929.31)
If the cumulative sales price of the goods or services to which or in connection with which the counterfeit mark is attached, affixed, or otherwise used is $1,000 or more but less than $7,500
*Penalty:* A felony of the fifth degree (2929.11-2929.18, 2929.31)
If the cumulative sales price of the goods or services to which or in connection with which the counterfeit mark is attached, affixed, or otherwise used is $7,500 or more but less than $150,000 or if the number of units of goods to which the counterfeit mark is attached, affixed, or otherwise used is more than 100 units but less than 1,000 units
*Penalty:* A felony of the fourth degree (2929.11-2929.18, 2929.31)
If the cumulative sales price of the goods or services to which or in connection with which the counterfeit mark is attached, affixed, or otherwise used is $150,000 or more or if the number of units of goods to which or in connection with which the counterfeit mark is attached, affixed, or otherwise used is 1,000 units or more
*Penalty:* A felony of the third degree (2929.11-2929.18, 2929.31)

Division (A)(5): **[M1, F5, F4, F3]**
(1) Knowingly
(2) Sell, offer for sale, or otherwise provide services
(3) Knowing that a counterfeit mark is used in connection with that sale, offer for sale, or other provision of services
*Penalty:* A misdemeanor of the first degree (2929.21-2929.31)
If the cumulative sales price of the goods or services to which or in connection with which the counterfeit mark is attached, affixed, or otherwise used is $1,000 or more but less than $7,500
*Penalty:* A felony of the fifth degree (2929.11-2929.18, 2929.31)
If the cumulative sales price of the goods or services to which or in connection with which the counterfeit mark is attached, affixed, or otherwise used is $7,500 or more but less than $150,000 or if the number of units of goods to which the counterfeit mark is attached, affixed, or otherwise used is more than 100 units but less than 1,000 units
*Penalty:* A felony of the fourth degree (2929.11-2929.18, 2929.31)
If the cumulative sales price of the goods or services to which or in connection with which the counterfeit mark is attached, affixed, or otherwise used is $150,000 or more or if the number of units of goods to which or in connection with which the counterfeit mark is attached, affixed, or otherwise used is 1,000 units or more
*Penalty:* A felony of the third degree (2929.11-2929.18, 2929.31)

***MEDICAID FRAUD*, R.C. § 2913.40 [M1, F5, F4, F3]**

Division (B):
(1) Knowingly
(2) Make or cause to be made
(3) False or misleading statement or representation
(4) For use in obtaining reimbursement from the Medical Assistance Program
(5) Venue

Division (C)(1):
(1) (a) With purpose to commit fraud
*(or)*
(b) knowing that the person is facilitating a fraud
(2) Contrary to the terms of the person's provider agreement
(3) Charge, solicit, accept, or receive
(4) For goods or services that the person provides under the medical assistance program
(5) Any property, money, or other consideration in addition to the amount of reimbursement under the medical assistance program and the person's provider agreement
(6) For the goods or services and any deductibles or co-payments authorized by section 5111.0112 [5111.01.12] of the Revised Code or rules adopted pursuant to section 5111.01, 5111.011 [5111.01.1], or 5111.02 of the Revised Code.
(7) Venue

Division (C)(2):
(1) (a) With purpose to commit fraud
*(or)*
(b) knowing that the person is facilitating a fraud
(2) Solicit, offer, or receive
(3) Any remuneration, other than any deductibles or co-payments authorized by section 5111.0112 [5111.01.12] of the Revised Code or rules adopted under section 5111.01, 5111.011 [5111.01.1], or 5111.02 of the Revised Code, in cash or in kind, including, but not limited to, a kickback or rebate,
(4) In connection with the furnishing of goods or services for which whole or partial reimbursement is or may be made under the medical assistance program.

(5) Venue

Division (D):
(1) Having submitted a claim for or provided goods or services under the Medical Assistance Program
(2) Knowingly
(3) Alter, falsify, destroy, conceal, or remove
(4) Any records that are necessary to fully disclose
(5) (a) Nature of all goods or services for which the claim was submitted, or for which reimbursement was received, by the person
*(or)*
(b) All income and expenditures upon which rates of reimbursements were based for the person
(6) For a period of six years after a reimbursement pursuant to that claim or a reimbursement for those goods or services is received under the Medical Assistance Program
(7) Venue
*Penalty:* A misdemeanor of the first degree (2929.21-2929.31)
If the value of property, services, or funds is more than $500 and less than $5,000
*Penalty:* A felony of the fifth degree (2929.11-2929.18, 2929.31)
If the value of property, services or funds is more than $5,000 and less than $100,000
*Penalty:* A felony of the fourth degree (2929.11-2929.18, 2929.31)
If the value of property, services or funds is $100,000 or more
*Penalty:* A felony of the third degree (2929.11-2929.18, 2929.31)
*Note:* Provisions of this section not intended to be exclusive remedies

**_MEDICAID ELIGIBILITY FRAUD_, R.C. § 2913.401 [M1, F5, F4, F3]**

(1) Knowingly
(2) In an application for medicaid benefits or in a document that requires a disclosure of assets for the purpose of determining eligibility to receive medicaid benefits
(3) (a) Make or cause to be made a false or misleading statement;
*(or)*
(b) Conceal an interest in property;
*(or)*
(c) (i) Fail to disclose a transfer of property that occurred during the period beginning thirty-six months before submission of the application or document and ending on the date the application or document was submitted;
*(or)*
(ii) Fail to disclose a transfer of property that occurred during the period beginning sixty months before submission of the application or document and ending on the date the application or document was submitted and that was made to an irrevocable trust a portion of which is not distributable to the applicant for medicaid benefits or the recipient of medicaid benefits or to a revocable trust.
(3) Venue
*Penalty:* A misdemeanor of the first degree
*Penalty:* If the value of the medicaid benefits paid as a result of the violation is $1,000 or more and is less than $7,500, a violation of this section is a felony of the fifth degree
*Penalty:* If the value of the medicaid benefits paid as a result of the violation is $7,500 or more and is less than $150,000, a violation of this section is a felony of the fourth degree
*Penalty:* If the value of the medicaid benefits paid as a result of the violation is $150,000 or more, a violation of this section is a felony of the third degree

**_TAMPERING WITH RECORDS_, R.C. § 2913.42 [M1, F5, F4, F3]**

(1) (a) Falsify, destroy, remove, conceal, alter, deface, or mutilate any writing, computer software, data, computer data, or record
*(or)*
(b) Utter any writing or record knowing it has been tampered with as above
(2) Knowing the person has no privilege to do so and with a purpose to defraud or knowingly to facilitate a fraud
(3) Venue
Offense not involving data or computer software, and writing or record is not unrevoked will
*Penalty:* A misdemeanor of the first degree (2929.21-2929.31)
Offense not involving data or computer software, and writing or record is unrevoked will
*Penalty:* A felony of the fifth degree (2929.11-2929.18, 2929.31)
Offense involving data or computer software and the value of the data or computer software involved or the loss to the victim is less than $1,000
*Penalty:* A misdemeanor of the first degree (2929.21-2929.31)
Offense involving data or computer software and the value of the data or computer software involved or the loss to the victim is $1,000 or more and is less than $7,500
*Penalty:* A felony of the fifth degree (2929.11-2929.18, 2929.31)
Offense involving data or computer software and the value of the data or Computer software involved or the loss to the victim is $7,500 or more and is less than $150,000

*Penalty:* A felony of the fourth degree (2929.11-2929.18, 2929.31)
Offense involving data or computer software and the value of the data or computer software involved or the loss to the victim is $150,000 or more or if the offense is committed for the purpose of devising or executing a scheme to defraud or to obtain property or services and the value of the property or services or the loss to the victim is $7,500 or more
*Penalty:* A felony of the third degree (2929.11-2929.18, 2929.31)
If the writing, data, computer software, or record is kept by or belongs to a local, state, or federal governmental entity
*Penalty:* A felony of the third degree (2929.11-2929.18, 2929.31)

***ILLEGALLY TRANSMITTING MULTIPLE COMMERCIAL ELECTRONIC MAIL MESSAGES; UNAUTHORIZED ACCESS OF COMPUTER,* R.C. § 2913.421 [F5, F4, F3]**

Division (B):
(1) Knowingly
(2) With regard to commercial electronic mail messages sent from or to a computer in this state
(3) (a) Use a computer to relay or retransmit multiple commercial electronic mail messages, with the intent to deceive or mislead recipients or any electronic mail service provider, as to the origin of those messages;
*(or)*
(b) Materially falsify header information in multiple commercial electronic mail messages and purposely initiate the transmission of those messages;
*(or)*
(c) Register, using information that materially falsifies the identity of the actual registrant, for five or more electronic mail accounts or online user accounts or two or more domain names and purposely initiate the transmission of multiple commercial electronic mail messages from one, or any combination, of those accounts or domain names;
*(or)*
(d) Falsely represent the right to use five or more internet protocol addresses, and purposely initiate the transmission of multiple commercial electronic mail messages from those addresses.
(4) Venue

Division (D):
(1) Knowingly
(2) With regard to commercial electronic mail messages sent from or to a computer in this state
(3) Access a computer without authorization and purposely initiate the transmission of multiple commercial electronic mail messages from or through the computer.
(4) Venue
*Penalty:*
Division (B):
A felony of the fifth degree (2929.11-2929.18, 2929.31)
A felony of fourth degree (2929.11-2929.18, 2929.31) if regarding a violation of division (B)(3) of this section, the offender, using information that materially falsifies the identity of the actual registrant, knowingly registers for twenty or more electronic mail accounts or online user accounts or ten or more domain names, and purposely initiates, or conspires to initiate, the transmission of multiple commercial electronic mail messages from the accounts or domain names
A felony of the fourth degree (2929.11-2929.18, 2929.31) if regarding any violation of division (B) of this section, the volume of commercial electronic mail messages the offender transmitted in committing the violation exceeds two hundred and fifty during any twenty-four-hour period, two thousand five hundred during any thirty-day period, or twenty-five thousand during any one-year period
A felony of the fourth degree (2929.11-2929.18, 2929.31) if regarding any violation of division (B) of this section, during any one-year period the aggregate loss to the victim or victims of the violation is $1,000 or more, or during any one-year period the aggregate value of the property or services obtained by any offender as a result of the violation is $1,000 or more
A felony of the fourth degree (2929.11-2929.18, 2929.31) if regarding any violation of division (B) of this section, the offender committed the violation with three or more other persons with respect to whom the offender was the organizer or leader of the activity that resulted in the violation
A felony of the fourth degree (2929.11-2929.18, 2929.31) if regarding any violation of division (B) of this section, the offender knowingly assisted in the violation through the provision or selection of electronic mail addresses to which the commercial electronic mail message was transmitted, if that offender knew that the electronic mail addresses of the recipients were obtained using an automated means from an internet web site or proprietary online service operated by another person, and that web site or online service included, at the time the electronic mail addresses were obtained, a notice stating that the operator of that web site or online service will not transfer addresses maintained by that web site or online service to any other party for the purposes of initiating the transmission of, or enabling others to initiate the transmission of, electronic mail messages
A felony of the fourth degree (2929.11-2929.18, 2929.31) if regarding any violation of division (B) of this section, the offender knowingly assisted in the violation through the provision or selection of electronic mail addresses of the recipients obtained using an automated means that generates possible electronic mail addresses by combining names, letters, or numbers into numerous permutations

A felony of the third degree (2929.11-2929.18, 2929.31) if the offender previously has been convicted of a violation of this section, or a violation of a law of another state or the United States regarding the transmission of electronic mail messages or unauthorized access to a computer, or if the offender committed the violation of this section in the furtherance of a felony
Division (D):
A felony of the fourth degree (2929.11-2929.18, 2929.31)
A felony of the third degree (2929.11-2929.18, 2929.31) if the offender previously has been convicted of a violation of this section, or a violation of a law of another state or the United States regarding the transmission of electronic mail messages or unauthorized access to a computer, or if the offender committed the violation of this section in the furtherance of a felony

***SECURING WRITINGS BY DECEPTION*, R.C. § 2913.43 [M1, F5, F4, F3, F2]**

(1) By deception
(2) Cause another to execute a writing disposing of or encumbering property or creating pecuniary obligation
(3) Venue
*Penalty:* A misdemeanor of the first degree (2929.21-2929.31)
If property or obligation value is $1,000 or more and less than $7,500
*Penalty:* A felony of the fifth degree (2929.11-2929.18, 2929.31)
If property or obligation value is $7,500 or more but less than $150,000
*Penalty:* A felony of the fourth degree (2929.11-2929.18, 2929.31)
If property or obligation value is $150,000 or more
*Penalty:* A felony of the third degree (2929.11-2929.18, 2929.31)

VICTIM ELDERLY PERSON OR DISABLED ADULT:

If the victim of the offense is an elderly person or disabled adult
*Penalty:* A felony of the fifth degree (2929.11-2929.18, 2929.31)
If the value of the property or obligation involved is $1,000 or more and is less than $7,500
*Penalty:* A felony of the fourth degree (2929.11-2929.18, 2929.31)
If the value of the property or obligation involved is $7,500 or more and is less than $37,500
*Penalty:* A felony of the third degree (2929.11-2929.18, 2929.31)
If the value of the property or obligation involved is $37,500 or more
*Penalty:* A felony of the second degree (2929.11-2929.18, 2929.31)

***PERSONATING AN OFFICER*, R.C. § 2913.44 [M1]**

(1) (a) With purpose to defraud or knowingly to facilitate a fraud
*(or)*
(b) With purpose to induce another to buy property or services
(2) Personate a law enforcement officer, inspector, investigator or agent of any governmental agency
(3) Venue
*Penalty:* A misdemeanor of the first degree (2929.21-2929.31)

***ILLEGAL DISPLAY OF LAW ENFORCEMENT EMBLEM*, R.C. § 2913.441 [MM]**

(1) Knowingly display on a motor vehicle
(2) Emblem of a law enforcement agency or an organization of law enforcement officers
(3) By a person who is not entitled to do so
(4) Venue
*Penalty:* A minor misdemeanor (2929.21-2929.31)

***DEFRAUDING CREDITORS*, R.C. § 2913.45 [M1, F5, F4, F3]**

(1) (a) Remove, conceal, destroy, encumber, convey, or otherwise deal with any of the person's property
*(or)*
(b) Misrepresent or refuse to disclose to fiduciary appointed to administer or manage the person's affairs or estate, the existence, amount, location of any of the person's property, or any other information regarding such property which the person is legally required to furnish fiduciary
(2) With purpose to defraud a creditor
(3) Venue
*Penalty:* A misdemeanor of the first degree (2929.21-2929.31)
If the value of the property involved is $1,000 or more and less than $7,500
*Penalty:* A felony of the fifth degree (2929.11-2929.18, 2929.31)
If the value of the property involved is $7,500 or more and less than $150,000
*Penalty:* A felony of the fourth degree (2929.11-2929.18, 2929.31)
If the value of the property involved is $150,000 or more
*Penalty:* A felony of the third degree (2929.11-2929.18, 2929.31)

***ILLEGAL USE OF SUPPLEMENTAL NUTRITION ASSISTANCE PROGRAM BENEFITS OR WIC PROGRAM BENEFITS*, R.C. § 2913.46 [F5, F4, F3, F2]**

Division (B):
(1) Individual
(2) Knowingly
(3) Possess, buy, sell, use, alter, accept, or transfer
(4) Supplemental nutrition assistance program benefits, WIC program benefits or any electronically transferred benefits
(5) In manner not authorized by the Food and Nutrition Act of 2008 or the Child Nutrition Act of 1966
(6) Venue

Division (C)(1):
(1) Organization
(2) Knowingly
(3) Allow an employee
(4) To sell, transfer, or trade items or services the purchase of which is prohibited by the Food and Nutrition Act of 2008 or the Child Nutrition Act of 1966
(5) In exchange for supplemental nutrition assistance program benefits, WIC program benefits or any electronically transferred benefits
(6) Venue

Division (C)(2):
(1) Organization
(2) Negligently
(3) Allow an employee
(4) To sell, transfer, or exchange supplemental nutrition assistance program benefits, WIC program benefits or any electronically transferred benefits
(5) For anything of value
(6) Venue
If value is less than $1,000
*Penalty:* A felony of the fifth degree (2929.11-2929.18, 2929.31)
If value is $1,000 and less than $7,500
*Penalty:* A felony of the fourth degree (2929.11-2929.18, 2929.31)
If the value is $7,500 or more and is less than $150,000
*Penalty:* A felony of the third degree (2929.11-2929.18, 2929.31)
If the value is $150,000 or more
*Penalty:* A felony of the second degree (2929.11-2929.18, 2929.31)

***INSURANCE FRAUD*, R.C. § 2913.47 [M1, F5, F4, F3]**

(1) (a) With purpose to defraud
*(or)*
(b) Knowing that the person is facilitating a fraud
(2) (a) Present to or cause to be presented to an insurer any written or oral statement
*(or)*
(b) Assist, aid, abet, solicit, procure, or conspire with another to prepare or make any written or oral statement that is intended to be presented to an insurer
(3) If the statement is part of, or in support of
(4) (a) An application for insurance
*(or)*
(b) A claim for payment pursuant to a policy
*(or)*
(c) A claim for any other benefit pursuant to a policy
(5) Knowing that the statement or any part of the statement is false or deceptive
(6) Venue
*Penalty:* A misdemeanor of the first degree (2929.21-2929.31)
If the amount of the application or claim is $1,000 or more, but less than $7,500
*Penalty:* A felony of the fifth degree (2929.11-2929.18, 2929.31)
If the amount of the application or claim is $7,500 or more, but less than $150,000
*Penalty:* A felony of the fourth degree (2929.11-2929.18, 2929.31)
If the amount of the application or claim is $150,000 or more
*Penalty:* A felony of the third degree (2929.11-2929.18, 2929.31)
*Note:* This statute does not abrogate, waive, or modify, R.C. § 2317.02(A), concerning the attorney-client privilege
*Definitions:* "Data," "deceptive," "insurer," "policy," "statement," R.C. § 2913.47

***WORKERS' COMPENSATION FRAUD*, R.C. § 2913.48 [M1, F5, F4, F3]**

(1) (a) With purpose to defraud
*(or)*

(b) Knowing that the person is facilitating a fraud
(2) (a) Receive workers' compensation benefits to which the person is not entitled
*(or)*
(b) Make or present or cause to be made or presented a false or misleading statement with the purpose to secure payment for goods or services rendered under R.C. Ch. 4121., 4123., 4127., or 4131. or to secure workers' compensation benefits
*(or)*
(c) Alter, falsify, destroy, conceal, or remove any record or document that
(i) is necessary to fully establish the validity of any claim filed with the bureau of workers' compensation or a self-insuring employer
*(or)*
(ii) is necessary to establish the nature of goods and services for which reimbursement or payment was received or is requested from, the bureau of workers' compensation or a self-insuring employer
*(or)*
(d) Enter into an agreement or conspiracy to defraud the bureau or a self-insuring employer by making or presenting or causing to be made or presented a false claim for workers' compensation benefits
(e) Make or present or cause to be made or presented a false statement concerning manual codes, classification of employees, payroll, paid compensation, or number of personnel, when information of that nature is necessary to determine the actual workers' compensation premium or assessment owed to the bureau by an employer;
(f) Alter, forge, or create a workers' compensation certificate to falsely show current or correct workers' compensation coverage;
(g) Fail to secure or maintain workers' compensation coverage as required by Chapter 4123. of the Revised Code with the intent to defraud the bureau of workers' compensation.
(3) Venue
If the value of the goods, services, property, or money stolen is less than $1,000
*Penalty:* A misdemeanor of the first degree (2929.21-2929.31)
If the value of premiums and assessments unpaid pursuant to actions described in division (1)(e), (f), or (g) of this section, or of goods, services, property, or money stolen is $1,000 or more and is less than $7,500
*Penalty:* A felony of the fifth degree (2929.11-2929.18, 2929.31)
If the value of premiums and assessments unpaid pursuant to actions described in division (1)(e), (f), or (g) of this section, or of goods, services, property, or money stolen is $7,500 or more and is less than $150,000
*Penalty:* A felony of the fourth degree (2929.11-2929.18, 2929.31)
If the value of premiums and assessments unpaid pursuant to actions described in division (1)(e), (f), or (g) of this section, or of goods, services, property, or money stolen is $150,000 or more
*Penalty:* A felony of the third degree (2929.11-2929.18, 2929.31)

***IDENTITY FRAUD*, R.C. § 2913.49 [M1, F5, F4, F3, F2, F1]**

[B](1) Without the express or implied consent of the other person
(2) (a) Use
*(or)*
(b) Obtain
*(or)*
(c) Possess
(3) Any personal identifying information of another person
(4) With intent to
(5) (a) Hold the person out to be the other person
*(or)*
(b) Represent the other person's personal identifying information as the person's own personal identifying information
(6) Venue
[C](1) (a) Create
*(or)*
(b) Obtain
*(or)*
(c) Possess
*(or)*
(d) Use
(2) The personal identifying information of another person
(3) With the intent to aid or abet another person
(4) In violating division B of this section
(5) Venue
[D](1) With intent to defraud
(2) Permit another person
(3) To use the person's own personal identifying information.
(4) Venue
[E](1) Having obtained permission as described in division D of this section

(2) (a) Use
*(or)*
(b) Obtain
*(or)*
(c) Possess
(3) Another person's personal identifying information
(4) With intent to defraud any person
(5) By doing any act identified in division B of this section
(6) Venue
*Penalty:* A misdemeanor of the first degree (2929.21-2929.31)
If the value of the credit, property, services, debt, or other legal obligation involved in the violation or course of conduct is $1,000 or more but less than $7,500
*Penalty:* A felony of the fourth degree (2929.11-2929.18, 2929.31)
If the value of the credit, property, services, debt, or other legal obligation involved in the violation or course of conduct is $7,500 or more but less than $150,000
*Penalty:* A felony of the third degree (2929.11-2929.18, 2929.31)
If the value of the credit, property, services, debt, or other legal obligation involved in the violation or course of conduct is $150,000 or more
*Penalty:* A felony of the second degree (2929.11-2929.18, 2929.31)

***RECEIVING STOLEN PROPERTY,*** **R.C. § 2913.51 [M1, F5, F4, F3]**

(1) Receive, retain or dispose of property of another
(2) (a) Knowing
*(or)*
(b) Having reasonable cause to believe
(3) Such property has been obtained through commission of theft offense
(4) Venue
*Penalty:* A misdemeanor of the first degree (2929.21-2929.31)
If the victim of the offense is an elderly person or disabled adult
*Penalty:* A felony of the fifth degree (2929.11-2929.18, 2929.31)
If the value of the credit, property, services, debt, or other legal obligation involved in the violation or course of conduct is $1,000 or more but less than $7,500
*Penalty:* A felony of the fourth degree (2929.11-2929.18, 2929.31)
If the value of the credit, property, services, debt, or other legal obligation involved in the violation or course of conduct is $7,500 or more but less than $150,000, or if the victim of the offense is an elderly person or disabled adult and the value of the credit, property, services, debt, or other legal obligation involved in the violation or course of conduct is $1,000 or more but less than $7,500
*Penalty:* A felony of the third degree (2929.11-2929.18, 2929.31)
If the value of the credit, property, services, debt, or other legal obligation involved in the violation or course of conduct is $150,000 or more, or if the victim of the offense is an elderly person or disabled adult and the value of the credit, property, services, debt, or other legal obligation involved in the violation or course of conduct is $7,500 or more but less than $150,000
*Penalty:* A felony of the second degree (2929.11-2929.18, 2929.31)
If the victim of the offense is an elderly person or disabled adult and the value of the credit, property, services, debt, or other legal obligation involved in the violation or course of conduct is $150,000 or more
*Penalty:* A felony of the first degree. (2929.11-2929.18, 2929.31)
*Note:* It is not a defense that the property was obtained by means other than through the commission of a theft offense if the property was explicitly represented to the accused person as being obtained through the commission of a theft offense

---

## GAMBLING

***GAMBLING,*** **R.C. § 2915.02 [M1, F5]**

(1) (a) Engage in bookmaking
*(or)*
(b) (i) Knowingly
(ii) Engage in conduct that facilitates bookmaking (i.e., aid an illegal bookmaking operation, including without limitation placing a bet with a person engaged in or facilitating illegal bookmaking)
*(or)*
(c) (i) Establish, promote, or operate
(ii) Any game of chance conducted for profit or any scheme of chance
*(or)*
(d) (i) Knowingly
(ii) Engage in conduct that facilitates any scheme or game of chance conducted for profit (i.e., in any way knowingly and in the conduct or operation of any such scheme or game, including without limitation

playing the scheme or game)
*(or)*
(e) (i) Knowingly
(ii) Procure, transmit, exchange or engage in conduct that facilitates the procurement, transmission, or exchange of
(iii) Information for use in establishing odds or determining winners in connection with
(iv) Bookmaking or any scheme or game of chance conducted for profit
*(or)*
(f) (i) Engage in betting or in playing any scheme or game of chance, except a charitable bingo game
(ii) As a substantial source of income or livelihood
*(or)*
(g) (i) With purpose to violate this section as set forth above
(ii) Acquire, possess, control, or operate
(iii) Any gambling device
*(or)*
(h) (i) Receive
(ii) Any commission, wage, salary, tip, reward, donation, gratuity, or other form of compensation
(iii) Directly or indirectly
(iv) For operating or assisting in the operation of
(v) Any scheme or game of chance
(2) Venue
*Penalty:* A misdemeanor of the first degree (2929.21-2929.31)
If prior gambling conviction
*Penalty:* A felony of the fifth degree (2929.11-2929.18, 292931)
*Note:* This section does not prohibit conduct in connection with gambling expressly permitted by law.

***OPERATING GAMBLING HOUSE*, R.C. § 2915.03 [MI, F5]**

(1) Being an owner, lessee, or person having control/supervision of premises
(2) (a) Use or occupy premises for gambling in violation of R.C. § 2915.02
*(or)*
(b) Recklessly permit premises to be used or occupied for gambling as above
(3) Venue
*Penalty:* A misdemeanor of the first degree (2929.21-2929.31)
If prior gambling conviction
*Penalty:* A felony of the fifth degree (2929.11-2929.18, 2929.31)

***PUBLIC GAMING*, R.C. § 2915.04 [MM, M4]**

Division (A):
(1) While at a hotel, restaurant, tavern, store, arena, hall, or other place of public accommodation, business, amusement or resort
(2) Make a bet or play a game of chance or scheme of chance
(3) Venue

Division (B):
(1) Being an owner, lessee, or person having control/supervision of:
(a) Premises as listed in Division (A)(1)(a) above
(2) Recklessly permit such premises to be used or occupied for purpose of making a bet or playing a game of chance
(3) Venue
*Penalty:* A minor misdemeanor (2929.21-2929.31)
If prior conviction of gambling offense
*Penalty:* A misdemeanor of the fourth degree (2929.21-2929.31)

***CHEATING; CORRUPTING SPORTS*, R.C. § 2915.05 [M1, F5, F4]**

Division (A): **[M1, F5]**
(1) With purpose to defraud or to facilitate a fraud
(2) Engage in conduct designed to corrupt the outcome of
(3) (a) A bet
*(or)*
(b) A contest of knowledge, skill, or endurance that is not an athletic or sporting event
*(or)*
(c) A scheme or game of chance
(d) Bingo
(4) Venue
*Penalty:* A misdemeanor of the first degree (2929.21-2929.31)
If prior theft offense or gambling conviction, or the potential gain is $1,000 or more
*Penalty:* A felony of the fifth degree (2929.11-2929.18, 2929.31)

Division (B): **[F5, F4]**
(1) Knowingly
(2) (a) Offer, give, solicit, or accept anything of value to corrupt the outcome of an athletic or sporting event
*(or)*
(b) Engage in conduct designed to corrupt the outcome of an athletic or sporting event
(3) Venue
*Penalty:* A felony of the fifth degree (2929.11-2929.18, 2929.31)
If prior conviction of a gambling or theft offense
*Penalty:* A felony of the fourth degree (2929.11-2929.18, 2929.31)

### *CONDUCTING BINGO,* R.C. § 2915.07 [F4]

(1) Conduct or advertise
(2) Bingo
(3) Without having obtained a license pursuant to R.C. § 2915.08
(4) Venue
*Penalty:* A felony of the fourth degree (2929.11-2929.18, 2929.31)
*Notes:* This section does not apply to bingo games conducted for amusement only. R.C. § 2915.12. *See* R.C. § 173.121 for special provisions concerning bingo games involving only persons sixty or older and conducted at certain senior centers

### *ILLEGALLY OPERATING AS A BINGO DISTRIBUTOR,* R.C. § 2915.081 [M1, F5]

Division (A):
(1) Being a bingo distributor
(2) (a) Sell
*(or)*
(b) Offer to sell
*(or)*
(c) Otherwise provide
*(or)*
(d) Offer to provide
*(or)*
(e) Modify, convert, add to, or remove parts from bingo supplies to further their promotion or sale
(3) Bingo supplies
(4) To another person
(5) For use in this state
(6) Not having obtained a license from the attorney general
(7) Venue

Division (E)(1)[a]:
(1) Being a bingo distributor
(2) (a) Sell
*(or)*
(b) Offer to sell
*(or)*
(c) Otherwise provide
*(or)*
(d) Offer to provide
*(or)*
(e) Modify, convert, add to, or remove parts from bingo supplies to further their promotion or sale
(3) Bingo supplies
(4) To another person not either
(5) (a) A charitable organization issued a license under R.C. § 2915.08
*(or)*
(b) Another distributor issued a license under R.C. § 2915.081
(6) For use in this state
(7) Venue

Division (E)(1)[b]:
(1) Being a bingo distributor
(2) Accept payment
(3) For the sale or other provision of bingo supplies
(4) Other than by check or electronic fund transfer
(5) Venue

Division (E)(2):
(1) Being a bingo distributor
(2) (a) Donate
*(or)*

(b) Give
*(or)*
(c) Loan
*(or)*
(d) Lease
*(or)*
(e) Otherwise provide
(3) (a) Any bingo supplies or equipment
*(or)*
(b) Modify, convert, add to, or remove parts from bingo supplies to further their promotion or sale
(4) To a charitable organization
(5) For use in a bingo session
(6) Conditioned on or in consideration for
(7) An exclusive right to provide bingo supplies to the charitable organization
(8) Venue

Division (E)(3)[a]:
(1) Being a bingo distributor
(2) Purchase bingo supplies
(3) From any person not either
(4) (a) A manufacturer issued a license under R.C. § 2915.082
*(or)*
(b) Another distributor issued a license under R.C. § 2915.082
(5) For use in this state
(6) Venue

Division (E)(3)[b]:
(1) Being a bingo distributor
(2) Pay for purchased bingo supplies
(3) Other than by check or electronic fund transfer
(4) Venue

Division (E)(4):
(1) Being a bingo distributor
(2) (a) (i) Participate in the conduct of bingo
(ii) On behalf of a charitable organization
*(or)*
(b) (i) Have any direct or indirect ownership interest
(ii) In a premises used for the conduct of bingo
(3) Venue

Division (E)(5):
(1) Being a bingo distributor
(2) Knowingly
(3) (a) Solicit
*(or)*
(b) Offer
*(or)*
(c) Pay
*(or)*
(d) Receive
(4) Any kickback, bribe, or undocumented rebate
(5) Directly or indirectly
(6) Overtly or covertly
(7) In cash or in kind
(8) In return for
(9) Providing bingo supplies
(10) To any person in this state
(11) Venue

*Penalty:* A misdemeanor of the first degree (2929.21-2929.31). If the offender previously has been convicted of a violation, a felony of the fifth degree (2929.11-2929.18, 2929.31)

***ILLEGALLY OPERATING AS A BINGO MANUFACTURER,*** **R.C. § 2915.082 [M1, F5]**

Division (A):
(1) Being a bingo manufacturer
(2) (a) Sell
*(or)*
(b) Offer to sell
*(or)*

(c) Otherwise provide
*(or)*
(d) Offer to provide
(3) Bingo supplies
(4) For use in this state
(5) Not having obtained a license from the attorney general under R.C. § 2915.082
(6) Venue

Division (D)(1)[a]:
(1) Being a bingo manufacturer
(2) (a) Sell
*(or)*
(b) Offer to sell
*(or)*
(c) Otherwise provide
*(or)*
(d) Offer to provide
(3) Bingo supplies
(4) For use in this state
(5) To any person not a distributor issued a license under R.C. § 2915.081

Division (D)(1)[b]:
(1) Being a bingo manufacturer
(2) Accept payment
(3) For the sale of bingo supplies
(4) Other than by check or electronic fund transfer
(5) Venue

Division (D)(2):
(1) Being a bingo manufacturer
(2) Knowingly
(3) (a) Solicit
*(or)*
(b) Offer
*(or)*
(c) Pay
*(or)*
(d) Receive
(4) Any kickback, bribe, or undocumented rebate
(5) Directly or indirectly
(6) Overtly or covertly
(7) In cash or in kind
(8) In return for
(9) Providing bingo supplies
(10) To any person in this state
(11) Venue

*Penalty:* A misdemeanor of the first degree (2929.21-2929.3 1). If the offender previously has been convicted of a violation, a felony of the fifth degree (2929.11-2929.18, 2929.31)

***ILLEGALLY CONDUCTING BINGO*, R.C. § 2915.09 [MM, M1, F4]**

Division (A)(1):
(1) Being a charitable organization
(2) Conduct bingo without
(a) Owning all equipment used to conduct bingo
*(or)*
(b) Leasing such equipment from a licensed charitable organization at a customary and reasonable rental rate
(3) Venue

Division (A)(2):
(1) Being a charitable organization
(2) Conduct bingo
(3) (a) Without using all gross receipts for paying prizes
*(or)*
(b) Using an amount of the receipts above the amount reasonably and customarily spent for similar purchases, leases, hiring or advertising for
(i) Reimbursement of expenses for or for purchasing, or leasing bingo supplies used in conducting bingo
*(or)*
(ii) Reimbursement of expenses for or for hiring security personnel
*(or)*

(iii) Reimbursement of expenses for or for advertising bingo
*(or)*
(iv) Reimbursement of expenses for or for renting premises in which to conduct the bingo game
*(or)*
(v) Reimbursement of other expenses or for other expenses listed in division (LL) of section 2915.01 of the Revised Code
*(or)*
(c) For each bingo session, deducting from the gross receipts a sum in excess of the lesser of $600 or 45% of the gross receipts as consideration for the use of the premises owned by the charitable organization conducting the game
(4) Venue

Division (A)(3):
(1) Being a charitable organization
(2) (a) Use, give, donate, or otherwise transfer
(b) Any of the net profit derived from bingo
(c) Other than for a charitable purpose listed in its license application and described in R.C. § 2915.01(Z)
*(or)*
(3) (a) Distribute
(b) Any of the net profit derived from instant bingo
(c) Other than as stated in its license application and described in R.C. § 2915.101
(4) Venue

Divisions (B)(1)-(3):
(1) Being a charitable organization
(2) Conduct bingo
(3) On premises not
(a) Owned by charitable organization
*(or)*
(b) Leased from another charitable organization at a rate not exceeding $600 per session or 45% of the gross receipts (*Note:* A charitable organization shall not lease premises that it owns to more than one other charitable organization per calendar week for the purpose of conducting bingo on the premises.)
*(or)*
(c) Leased from a person other than a charitable organization at a rental rate that is more than is customary and reasonable for premises similar in location, size, and quality, but not exceeding $450 per session. (*Note:* Lessor other than charitable organization shall lease premises only and shall not provide special personnel, services or equipment.)
*(or)*
(d) Subleased from another charitable organization that leases from a person other than a charitable organization at a rate not exceeding $450 per session
*(or)*
(4) Fail to display its bingo license conspicuously at the location where the bingo game is conducted
*(or)*
(5) Fail to conduct the bingo in accordance with definition in R.C. § 2915.01(S)(1)
(6) Venue

Division (C)(1)-(12):
(1) Being a charitable organization
(2) Conduct a bingo game and
(3) (a) (i) Pay compensation to a bingo game operator for operating a bingo game or for preparing, selling or serving food or beverages at the site of the bingo game
*(or)*
(ii) Permit any auxiliary unit or society of the charitable organization to pay compensation to any bingo game operator who prepares, sells or serves food or beverages at a bingo session
*(or)*
(iii) Permit any auxiliary unit or society of the charitable organization to prepare, sell or serve beverages at a bingo session if the auxiliary unit or society pays compensation to the bingo game operators who prepare, sell or serve the food or beverages
*(or)*
(b) Pay consulting fees to any person for any services performed in relation to the bingo game
*(or)*
(c) Pay concession fees to any person who provides refreshments to participants in the bingo game
*(or)*
(d) Conduct more than three bingo sessions on any premises in any calendar week except that a volunteer firefighter's organization or a volunteer rescue service organization that conducts not more than five bingo sessions in a calendar year may conduct more than three bingo sessions in a seven-day period after notifying the attorney general when it will conduct the sessions.
*(or)*

(e) Pay out more than $6,500 in prizes during any bingo session
*(or)*
(f) (i) Do so at any time during the 10 hour period between midnight and 10 a.m.
*(or)*
(ii) Do so at any time during, or within 10 hours of, a bingo game conducted for amusement only pursuant to R.C. § 2915.12
*(or)*
(iii) Do so at any location, on any day of the week, or during any time period not specified on its bingo license
*(or)*
(g) Permit any person whom the charitable organization knows, or should have known, is under the age of 18 to work as a bingo game operator
(h) Permit any person whom the charitable organization knows, or should have known, has been convicted of a felony or gambling offense to be a bingo game operator
(i) Permit the lessor of the premises on which bingo is conducted, if the lessor is not a charitable organization, to provide the charitable organization with bingo game operators, security personnel, concessions, bingo equipment, or any other type of service
(j) Purchase or lease bingo supplies from any person except a distributor issued a license under R.C. § 2915.081
(k) Use or permit the use of electronic bingo aids except as permitted under R.C. § 2915.09(C)(11)
(l) Permit any person the charitable organization knows, or should have known, to be under eighteen years of age to play bingo
(4) Venue

Division (D):
(1) (a) Being a bingo game operator
(b) Receive or accept
*(or)*
(2) (a) Being a charitable organization
(b) Provide to a bingo game operator
(3) Directly or indirectly, regardless of the source
(4) Any commission, wage, salary, reward, tip, donation, gratuity or other form of compensation
(5) (a) For operating a bingo game
*(or)*
(b) For providing other work or labor at the site of the bingo game
(6) Venue
*Penalty:* Violation of (A)(2) is a felony of the fourth degree (2929.11-2929.18, 2929.31)
Violation of (A)(1), (3), (4), (5), (B) or (C) is a minor misdemeanor (2929.21-2929.31). If prior conviction for violation of (A)(1), (3), (4), (5), (B), or (C) violation of (A)(1), (3), (4), (5), (B), or (C) is a misdemeanor of the first degree (2929.21-2929.31)
For a violation of Division C(3)(l), a misdemeanor of the first degree (2929.21-2929.31); if prior conviction, a felony of the fourth degree (2929.11-2929.18, 2929.31)

***ILLEGAL INSTANT BINGO CONDUCT [by charitable organization],* R.C. § 2915.091 [M1, F5]**

Division (A)(1)
(1) Being a charitable organization that conducts instant bingo
(2) Fail to comply with the requirements of R.C. § 2915.09(A)(1), (2), & (3)
(3) Venue

Division (A)(2)
(1) Being a charitable organization
(2) Conduct instant bingo unless either it
(3) (a) (i) Is and has received an IRS determination letter stating that it is exempt from federal income taxation under I.R.C. § 501(a)
(ii) Is described in I.R.C. § 501(c)(3)
(iii) Is a charitable organization as defined in R.C. § 2915.01
(iv) Is in good standing pursuant to R.C. § 2915.08
(v) Is in compliance R.C. Ch 1716
*(or)*
(b) (i) Is and has received an IRS determination letter stating that it is exempt from federal income taxation under I.R.C. § 501(a)
(ii) Is described in I.R.C. § 501(c)(7), 501(c)(8), 501(c)(10), or 501(c)(19) or is a veteran's organization described in I.R.C. § 501(c)(4)
(iii) Conducts instant bingo under R.C. § 2915.13
(4) Venue

Division (A)(3)
(1) Being a charitable organization
(2) Conduct instant bingo

(3) (a) On any day
*(or)*
(b) At any time
*(or)*
(c) At any premises
(4) Not specified on the organization's license issued pursuant to R.C. § 2915.08
(5) Venue

Division (A)(4)
(1) Being a charitable organization
(2) Permit any person
(3) Whom the organization knows or should have known
(4) Has been convicted of a felony or gambling offense in any jurisdiction
(5) To be a bingo game operator
(6) In the conduct of instant bingo
(7) Venue

Division (A)(5)
(1) Being a charitable organization
(2) Purchase or lease supplies
(3) Used to conduct instant bingo or punch board games
(4) From any person not a distributor licensed under R.C. § 2915.081
(5) Venue

Division (A)(6)
(1) Being a charitable organization
(2) (a) Sell
*(or)*
(b) Provide
(3) Any instant bingo ticket or card
(4) For a price different from the price printed on it by the manufacturer on either the instant bingo ticket or the game flare
(5) Venue

Division (A)(7)
(1) Being a charitable organization
(2) Sell
(3) An instant bingo ticket or card
(4) To a person under eighteen years of age
(5) Venue

Division (A)(8)
(1) Being a charitable organization
(2) Fail to keep
(3) Unsold instant bingo tickets or cards
(4) For less than three years
(5) Venue

Division (A)(9)[a]
(1) Being a charitable organization
(2) Pay any compensation
(3) To a bingo game operator
(4) (a) For conducting instant bingo that is conducted by the organization
*(or)*
(b) For preparing, selling, or serving food or beverages at the site of the instant bingo game
(5) Venue

Division (A)(9)[b]
(1) Being a charitable organization
(2) Permit any auxiliary unit or society of the organization
(3) (a) To pay compensation to any bingo game operator who prepares, sells, or serves food or beverages at an instant bingo game conducted by the organization
*(or)*
(b) To prepare, sell, or serve food or beverages at an instant bingo game conducted by the organization if the auxiliary unit or society pays any compensation to the bingo game operators who prepare, sell, or serve the food or beverages
(4) Venue

Division (A)(10)
(1) Being a charitable organization

(2) Pay fees to any person
(3) For any services performed
(4) In relation to an instant bingo game
(5) Venue

Division (A)(11)
(1) Being a charitable organization
(2) Pay fees to any person
(3) Who provides refreshments
(4) To the participants in an instant bingo game
(5) Venue

Division (A)(12)
(1) Being a charitable organization
(2) Allow
(3) Instant bingo tickets or cards
(4) To be sold
(5) (a) To bingo game operators at a premises at which the organization sells instant bingo tickets
*(or)*
(b) To employees of a D permit holder who are working at a premises at which instant bingo tickets or cards are sold
(6) Venue

Division (A)(13)
(1) Being a charitable organization
(2) Fail to display
(3) (a) Its bingo license
*(or)*
(b) The serial numbers of the deal of instant bingo tickets or cards to be sold
(4) Conspicuously
(5) At each premises at which it sells instant bingo tickets or cards
(6) Venue

Division (A)(14)
(1) Being a charitable organization
(2) Possess
(3) A deal of instant bingo tickets or cards
(4) (a) That was not purchased from a distributor licensed under R.C. § 2915.081
(b) As reflected on an invoice issued by the distributor that contains all of the information required by R.C. § 2915.10(E)
(5) Venue

Division (A)(15)
(1) Being a charitable organization
(2) Fail, once it opens a deal of instant bingo tickets or cards
(3) To continue to sell the tickets or cards in that deal until the tickets or cards with the top two highest tiers of prizes in that deal are sold
(4) Venue

Division (A)(16)
(1) Being a charitable organization
(2) Possess
(3) Bingo supplies
(4) That were not obtained in accordance with R.C. §§ 2915.01 to 2915.13
(5) Venue

Division (B)
(1) Being a charitable organization
(2) Conduct instant bingo
(3) Other than at a bingo session
(4) At more than five separate locations
(5) Venue

*Penalty:* A misdemeanor of the first degree (2929.21-2929.31). If the offender previously has been convicted of a violation, a felony of the fifth degree (2929.11-2929.18, 2929.31)
*Note:* A charitable organization may purchase, lease, or use instant bingo ticket dispensers to sell instant bingo tickets or cards.

**_ILLEGAL CONDUCT OF A RAFFLE_, R.C. § 2915.092 [M1, F5]**

(1) Conduct

(2) Raffle drawing
(3) (a) For profit
*(or)*
(3) (b) Not for profit
(4) Venue

*Penalty:* A misdemeanor of the first degree (2929.21-2929.31). If the offender previously has been convicted of a violation, a felony of the fifth degree (2929.11-2929.18, 2929.31)

*Notes:* A charitable organization, a public school, a chartered nonpublic school, a community school, or a veteran's organization, fraternal organization, or sporting organization that is exempt from federal income taxation under subsection 501(a) and is described in subsection 501(c)(3), 501(c)(4), 501(c)(7), 501(c)(8), 501(c)(10), or 501(c)(19) of the Internal Revenue Code may conduct a raffle to raise money for the organization or school and does not need a license to conduct bingo in order to conduct a raffle drawing that is not for profit

If a charitable organization that is described in the preceding paragraph, but that is not also described in subsection 501(c)(3) of the Internal Revenue Code, conducts a raffle, the charitable organization shall distribute at least fifty per cent of the net profit from the raffle to a charitable purpose described in division (Z) of section 2915.01 of the Revised Code or to a department or agency of the federal government, the state, or any political subdivision

**_ILLEGAL INSTANT BINGO CONDUCT_ [by owner/lessor of premises], R.C. § 2915.094 [M1, F5]**

Division (C)
(1) Being an owner or lessor of a location
(2) That enters into a written contract as prescribed in R.C. § 2915.094(A)
(3) (a) Violate
*(or)*
(b) Permit, aid, or abet any other person in violating
(4) Any provision of R.C. Ch. 2915
(5) Venue

Division (D)
(1) Being an owner or lessor of a location
(2) That enters into a written contract as prescribed in R.C. § 2915.094(A)
(3) Violate the terms of the contract
(4) Venue

*Penalty:* A misdemeanor of the first degree (2929.21-2929.31). If the offender previously has been convicted of a violation, a felony of the fifth degree (2929.11-2929.18, 2929.31)

**_FAILURE TO MAINTAIN RECORDS OF BINGO SESSION OR SCHEME OR GAME OF CHANCE FOR THREE YEARS_, R.C. § 2915.10(A) [M1]**

(1) Being a charitable organization
(2) Conduct bingo or game of chance
(3) Fail to maintain the following records for at least three years from the date on which the bingo session or scheme or game of chance is conducted
(a) An itemized list of the gross receipts of each bingo session, each game of instant bingo by serial number, each raffle, each punch board game, and each game of chance and an itemized list of the gross profits of each game of instant bingo by serial number
(b) An itemized list of all expenses other than prizes that are incurred in conducting bingo or instant bingo, the name of each person to whom the expenses are paid, and a receipt for all of the expenses
(c) A list of all prizes awarded during each bingo session, each raffle, each punch board game, and each game of chance conducted by the charitable organization, the total prizes awarded from each game of instant bingo by serial number, and the name, address, and social security number of all persons who are winners of prizes of $600 or more in value
(d) An itemized list of the recipients of the net profit of the bingo or game of chance, including the name and address of each recipient to whom the money is distributed, and if the organization uses the net profits of bingo or the money or assets received from a scheme or game of chance for any charitable or other purpose set forth in R.C. § 2915.01(Z), R.C. § 2915.02(D) or § 2915.101, a list of each purpose and an itemized list of each expenditure for each purpose
(e) The number of persons who participate in any bingo session or game of chance that is conducted by the charitable organization
(f) A list of receipts from the sale of food and beverages by the charitable organization or one of its auxiliary units or societies, if the receipts are excluded from gross receipts under R.C. § 2915.01(X)
(g) An itemized list of all expenses incurred at each bingo session, each raffle, each punch board game, or each game of instant bingo conducted by the charitable organization in the sale of food or beverages by the charitable organization or by an auxiliary unit or society of the charitable organization, the name of each person to whom the expenses are paid, and a receipt for all of the expenses
(4) Venue

*Penalty:* A misdemeanor of the first degree (2929.21-2929.31)

*Notes:* R.C. § 2915.10(B) provides attorney general or local law enforcement may inspect and investigate charitable organization, its officers and accounts, games in session and premises where held

This section does not apply to bingo games conducted for amusement only. R.C. § 2915.12
*See* R.C. § 173.121 for special provisions concerning bingo games involving only persons sixty or older and conducted at certain senior centers

***ILLEGAL ACTS RE INSPECTION OF BINGO GAME OR GAME OF CHANCE,* R.C. § 2915.10(C) [M1]**

(1) (a) Destroy, alter, conceal, withhold, or deny access to any accounts or records of a charitable organization that have been requested for examination
*(or)*
(b) Obstruct, impede, or interfere with any inspection, audit, or observation of
(i) bingo or game of chance
*(or)*
(ii) premises where bingo or game of chance is conducted
*(or)*
(c) Refuse to comply with any reasonable request of, or obstruct, impede, or interfere with any other reasonable action undertaken by the attorney general or a law enforcement agency pursuant to R.C. § 2915.10(H)
(2) Venue
*Penalty:* A misdemeanor of the first degree (2929.21-2929.31)
*Notes:* This section does not apply to bingo games conducted for amusement only
*See* R.C. § 173.121 for special provisions concerning bingo games involving only persons sixty or older and conducted at certain senior centers

***OPERATION OF BINGO GAME BY MINOR,* R.C. § 2915.11(A) [M3]**

(1) Being under the age of 18
(2) Operate a bingo game
(3) Venue
*Penalty:* A misdemeanor of the third degree (2929.21-2929.31)
*Notes:* This section does not apply to bingo games conducted for amusement only
*See* R.C. § 173.121 for special provisions concerning bingo games involving only persons sixty or older and conducted at certain senior centers

***OPERATION OF BINGO GAME BY FORMER OFFENDER,* R.C. § 2915.11(B) [M1]**

(1) Being a person who has been convicted in any jurisdiction of
(a) felony
*(or)*
(b) gambling offense
(2) Operate a bingo game
(3) Venue
*Penalty:* A misdemeanor of the first degree (2929.21-2929.31)
*Notes:* This section does not apply to bingo games conducted for amusement only
*See* R.C. § 173.121 for special provisions concerning bingo games involving only persons sixty or older and conducted at certain senior centers

---

## OFFENSES AGAINST THE PUBLIC PEACE

***INCITING TO VIOLENCE,* R.C. § 2917.01 [M1, F3]**

(1) Knowingly
(2) Engage in conduct designed to urge or incite another to commit an offense of violence
(3) Under circumstances where
(a) The conduct creates clear and present danger that an offense of violence will result
*(or)*
(b) The conduct proximately results in an offense of violence
(4) Venue
If the offense of violence that the other person is being urged or incited to commit is a misdemeanor
*Penalty:* A misdemeanor of the first degree (2929.21-2929.31)
If the offense of violence that the other person is being urged or incited to commit is a felony
*Penalty:* A felony of the third degree (2929.11-2929.18, 2929.31)

***AGGRAVATED RIOT,* R.C. § 2917.02 [F5, F4, F3]**

Division (A):
(1) Participate with 4 or more others
(2) In a course of disorderly conduct contrary to R.C. § 2917.11
(3) (a) With a purpose to commit or facilitate a felony
*(or)*

(b) With purpose to commit or facilitate an offense of violence
*(or)*
(c) While the offender, or any participant to the knowledge of the offender, has a deadly weapon or dangerous ordnance on or about the offender's or participant's person or under his control, uses, or intends to use same
(4) Venue

Division (B):
(1) Being an inmate of a detention facility
(2) Violate division (A)(3)(a) or (c)
*(or)*
(3) Violate division (A)(3)(b) or R.C. § 2917.03
(4) Venue
A violation of division (A)(3)(a) or (c)
*Penalty:* A felony of the fifth degree (2929.11-2929.18, 2929.31)
A violation of division (A)(3)(b) or (B)(2)
*Penalty:* A felony of the fourth degree (2929.11-2929.18, 2929.31)
A violation of division (B)(3)
*Penalty:* A felony of the third degree (2929.11-2929.18, 2929.31)
*Definitions:* "Deadly weapon," "dangerous ordnance," RC. § 2923.11

***RIOT*, R.C. § 2917.03 [M1]**

Division (A):
(1) Participate with 4 or more others
(2) In a course of disorderly conduct contrary to R.C. § 2917.11
(3) (a) With purpose to commit or facilitate a misdemeanor other than disorderly conduct
*(or)*
(b) With purpose to intimidate a public official or employee into taking or refraining from taking official action
*(or)*
(c) With a purpose to hinder, impede, obstruct function of government
*(or)*
(d) With a purpose to hinder, impede or obstruct the orderly administration of or instruction at an educational institution, or interfere with or disrupt its activities
(4) Venue

Division (B):
(1) Participate with 4 or more others
(2) With purpose to do an act with unlawful force or violence
(3) Although such act would otherwise be lawful
(4) Venue
*Penalty:* A misdemeanor of the first degree (2929.21-2929.31)

***FAILURE TO DISPERSE*, R.C. § 2917.04 [MM, M4]**

(1) When five or more persons are participating in disorderly conduct in violation of R.C. § 2917.11
(2) With other persons in vicinity and whose presence creates:
(a) A likelihood of physical harm to persons/property
*(or)*
(b) Serious public inconvenience, annoyance, or alarm
(3) And a law enforcement officer or other public official orders all of above to disperse
(4) Knowingly fail to obey such order
(5) Venue
*Penalty:* A minor misdemeanor unless the failure to obey the order creates the likelihood of physical harm to persons or is committed at the scene of a fire, accident, disaster, riot, or emergency of any kind, then misdemeanor of the fourth degree is the offense classification (2929.21-2929.31)

***DISORDERLY CONDUCT*, R.C. § 2917.11 [MM, M4]**

Division (A):
(1) Recklessly
(2) Cause inconvenience, annoyance or alarm to another by means of
(a) Fighting/threatening harm to persons or property/violent or turbulent behavior
*(or)*
(b) Making unreasonable noise/offensively coarse utterances/gestures, displays, or communicating unwarranted and grossly abusive language to others
*(or)*
(c) Insulting/taunting/challenging another under circumstances in which such conduct is likely to provoke a violent response
*(or)*

(d) Hindering or preventing movement of persons upon a public street/road/highway/rightof-way, or to or from public/private property, so as to interfere with rights of others by acts that serve no lawful/reasonable purpose
*(or)*
(e) Creating a physically offensive condition or one that presents a risk of physical harm to persons/property by acts serving no lawful reasonable purpose
(3) Venue

Division (B):
(1) While voluntarily intoxicated
(2) (a) In a public place or in the presence of 2 or more persons
(i) Engage in conduct likely to be offensive
*(or)*
(ii) Cause inconvenience, annoyance, or alarm to persons of ordinary sensibilities, which conduct the offender, if the offender were not intoxicated, should know is likely to have that effect on others
*(or)*
(b) Engage in conduct or create a condition that presents a risk of physical harm to the offender or another, or the property of another
(3) Venue
*Penalty:* A minor misdemeanor (2929.21-2929.31)
If the offender persists after a reasonable warning or request to desist, or if the offense is committed in the vicinity of a school or in a school safety zone, or if the offense is committed in the presence of any law enforcement officer, firefighter, rescuer, medical person, emergency medical services person, or other authorized person who is engaged in the person's duties at the scene of a fire, accident, disaster, riot, or emergency of any kind, or if the offense is committed in the presence of any emergency facility person who is engaged in the person's duties in an emergency facility
*Penalty:* A misdemeanor of the fourth degree (2929.21-2929.31)
*Note:* The violation of a statute or ordinance in which an element is operating motor vehicle, locomotive, watercraft, aircraft, or other vehicle under the influence of alcohol or drugs of abuse, is not a violation of Division (B)
*Definitions:* "School," "school premises," "school building," R.C. §§ 2917.11, 2925.01
"Emergency medical services person," "emergency facility person," "emergency facility," R.C. §§ 2133.21, 2909.04

### *DISTURBING A LAWFUL MEETING,* R.C. § 2917.12 [M4]

(1) With a purpose to prevent or disrupt
(2) (a) Do anything which obstructs or interferes with the conduct of a meeting, procession, or gathering
*(or)*
(b) Make utterances, gestures, or displays which outrage the sensibilities of group
(3) Venue
*Penalty:* A misdemeanor of the fourth degree (2929.21-2929.31)

### *MISCONDUCT AT AN EMERGENCY,* R.C. § 2917.13 [M4, M1]

(1) Knowingly
(a) Hamper lawful operations of any law enforcement officer, firefighter, rescuer, medical person, emergency medical services person or other authorized person, engaged in duties at a fire, accident, disaster, riot, or emergency
*(or)*
(b) Hamper the lawful activities of any emergency facility person who is engaged in the person's duties in an emergency facility;
*(or)*
(c) Fail to obey a lawful order of any law enforcement officer engaged in duties at the scene or in connection with a fire, accident, disaster, riot, or emergency
(2) Venue
*Penalty:* A misdemeanor of the first degree (2929.21-2929.31)
If a violation results in physical harm to another
*Penalty:* A felony of the fourth degree (2929.11-2929.18, 2929.31)
If violation results in economic harm of $500 or more but less than $5,000
*Penalty:* A felony of the fifth degree (2929.11-2929.18, 2929.31)
If violation results in economic harm of $5,000 or more but less than $100,000
*Penalty:* A felony of the fourth degree (2929.11-2929.18, 2929.31)
If violation results in economic harm of $100,000 or more
*Penalty:* A felony of the third degree (2929.11-2929.18, 2929.31)
If the violation pertains to a purported, threatened, or actual use of a "weapon of mass destruction"
*Penalty:* A felony of the fourth degree (2929.11-2929.18, 2929.31)
If such violation results in physical harm to any person
*Penalty:* A felony of the third degree (2929.11-2929.18, 2929.31)
If such violation results in economic harm of $100,000 or more

*Penalty:* A felony of the third degree (2929.11-2929.18, 2929.31)
If the public place involved in a violation of (3)(a) is a school or institution of higher learning
*Penalty:* A felony of the second degree (2929.11-2929.18, 2929.31)
*Note:* Nothing in this section shall be construed to limit access or deny information to any news media representative in the lawful exercise of the person's duties
*Definitions:* "Emergency medical services person," "emergency facility person," "emergency facility," R.C. §§ 2133.21, 2909.04

***TELECOMMUNICATIONS HARASSMENT,* R.C. § 2917.21 [M1, F5]**

Division (A):
(1) Knowingly
(2) (a) Make a telecommunication
*(or)*
(b) Cause a telecommunication to be made
*(or)*
(c) Permit a telecommunication to be made from a telecommunications device under the offender's control
(3) To another
(4) If the caller does any of the following:
(a) Fails to identify the caller to the recipient of the telecommunication and makes the telecommunication with purpose to harass or abuse any person at the premises to which the telecommunication is made, whether or not actual communication takes place between the caller and the recipient
*(or)*
(b) Describes, suggests, requests, or proposes that the caller, the recipient of the telecommunication, or any other person engage in, sexual activity, and the recipient, or another person at the premises to which the telecommunication is made, has requested, in a previous telecommunication or in the immediate telecommunication, that the caller not make a telecommunication to the recipient of the telecommunication or to the premises to which the telecommunication is made
*(or)*
(c) During the telecommunication, violates section 2903.21 of the Revised Code
*(or)*
(d) Knowingly states to the recipient of the telecommunication that the caller intends to cause damage to or destroy public or private property, and the recipient, any member of the recipient's family, or any other person who resides at the premises to which the telecommunication is made owns, leases, resides, or works in, will at the time of the destruction or damaging be near or in, has the responsibility of protecting, or insures the property that will be destroyed or damaged
*(or)*
(e) Knowingly makes the telecommunication to the recipient of the telecommunication, to another person at the premises to which the telecommunication is made, or to those premises, and the recipient, or another person at those premises, previously has told the caller not to make a telecommunication to those premises or to any persons at those premises
(5) Venue

Division (B):
(1) (a) Make a telecommunication
*(or)*
(b) Cause a telecommunication to be made
*(or)*
(c) Permit a telecommunication to be made from a telecommunications device under the offender's control
(2) With purpose to
(a) Abuse
*(or)*
(b) Threaten
*(or)*
(c) Harass
(3) Another person
(4) Venue
Violation of division (A)(4)(a), (b), (c), (e), or (B):
*Penalty:* A misdemeanor of the first degree (2929.21-2929.31)
If prior conviction under this section
*Penalty:* A felony of the fifth degree (2929.11-2929.18, 2929.31)
Violation of division (A)(4)(d):
*Penalty:* A misdemeanor of the first degree (2929.21-2929.31)
If prior conviction under this section
*Penalty:* A felony of the fifth degree (2929.11-2929.18, 2929.31)
If violation results in economic harm of $1,000 or more but less than $7,500
*Penalty:* A felony of the fifth degree (2929.11-2929.18, 2929.31)
If violation results in economic harm of $7,500 or more but less than $150,000

*Penalty:* A felony of the fourth degree (2929.11-2929.18, 2929.31)
If violation results in economic harm of $150,000 or more
*Penalty:* A felony of the third degree (2929.11-2929.18, 2929.31)

***INDUCING PANIC*, R.C. § 2917.31 [M1, F5, F4, F3, F2]**

(1) Cause
(2) The evacuation of a public place or serious public inconvenience or alarm
(3) By means of
  (a) Initiating or circulating a report or warning of alleged or impending fire, explosion, crime or other catastrophe, knowing such to be false
  *(or)*
  (b) Threatening to commit any offense of violence
  *(or)*
  (c) Committing any offense with reckless disregard of the likelihood that it will cause serious public inconvenience or alarm
(4) Venue
*Penalty:* Penalties for inducing panic range from a misdemeanor of the first degree to a felony of the fourth, third, or second degree. The more serious penalties are incurred when there is physical or economic harm, when the public place involved is a school or institution of higher learning, or when a weapon of mass destruction is involved. The dollar amount of economic harm can raise the degree of the offense.

***MAKING FALSE ALARMS*, R.C. § 2917.32 [M1]**

(1) (a) Initiate or circulate a report/warning of alleged or impending fire, explosion, crime, or other catastrophe
  (b) Knowing it to be both false and likely to cause public inconvenience/alarm
  *(or)*
(2) (a) Knowingly cause
  (b) A false alarm of fire or other emergency
  (c) To be transmitted to or within
  (d) A public or private organization dealing with emergencies which involve a risk of physical harm to persons/property
  *(or)*
(3) (a) Report to any law enforcement agency
  (b) Alleged offense or other incident
  (c) Knowing such did not occur
(4) Venue
*Penalty:* A misdemeanor of the first degree (2929.21-2929.31)
If violation results in economic harm of $1,000 or more but less than $7,500
*Penalty:* A felony of the fifth degree (2929.11-2929.18, 2929.31)
If violation results in economic harm of $7,500 or more but less than $150,000
*Penalty:* A felony of the fourth degree (2929.11-2929.18, 2929.31)
If violation results in economic harm of $150,000 or more
*Penalty:* A felony of the third degree (2929.11-2929.18, 2929.31)
If the violation pertains to a purported, threatened, or actual use of a "weapon of mass destruction"
*Penalty:* A felony of the third degree (2929.11-2929.18, 2929.31)
*Note:* This section does not apply to any person conducting an authorized fire emergency drill

***UNLAWFUL POSSESSION OR USE OF "WEAPON OF MASS DESTRUCTION,"* R.C. § 2917.33 [F4]**

(1) Without privilege to do so
(2) (a) Manufacture
  *(or)*
  (b) Possess
  *(or)*
  (c) Sell
  *(or)*
  (d) Deliver
  *(or)*
  (e) Display
  *(or)*
  (f) Use
  *(or)*
  (g) Threaten to use
  *(or)*
  (h) Attempt to use
  *(or)*
  (i) Conspire to use
  *(or)*

(j) Make readily accessible to others
(3) A "hoax weapon of mass destruction"
(4) With intent to deceive or mislead one or more persons
(5) Into believing that such weapon will cause
(6) (a) Terror
*(or)*
(b) Bodily harm
*(or)*
(c) Property damage
(7) Venue
*Penalty:* A felony of the fourth degree (2929.11-2929.18, 2929.31)
*Definitions:* "Hoax weapon of mass destruction," R.C. § 2917.33(E)

***CROWD SAFETY*, R.C. § 2917.40 [M1]**

Division (B)(1):
(1) (a) Sell
*(or)*
(b) Offer to sell
*(or)*
(c) Offer in return for a donation
(2) Ticket that is not numbered and that does not correspond to a specific seat for admission to
(3) (a) A live entertainment performance that is not exempted under R.C. § 2917.40(D), that is held in a restricted entertainment area, and for which more than eight thousand tickets are offered to the public
*(or)*
(b) A concert that is not exempted under R.C. § 2917.40(D) and for which more than three thousand tickets are offered to the public
(4) Venue

Division (B)(2):
(1) Advertise
(2) A live entertainment performance that is not exempted under R.C. § 2917.40(D) that is held in a restricted entertainment area, and for which more then eight thousand tickets are offered to the public
(3) Without including the words "reserved seats only"
(4) Venue

Division (C):
(1) (a) Being the owner of a restricted entertainment area
*(or)*
(b) Being the operator of a restricted entertainment area
(2) Fail to open, maintain and properly staff
(3) Number of entrances designated by R.C. § 2917.40(E)
(4) For a minimum of 90 minutes prior to the start of alive entertainment performance
(5) Held in a restricted entertainment area
(6) For which more than 3,000 tickets are
(a) Sold
*(or)*
(b) Offered for sale
*(or)*
(c) Offered in return for a donation
(7) Venue

Division (F):
(1) Enter into contract
(2) For a live entertainment performance
(3) That does not
(a) Require
*(or)*
(b) Permit
(4) Compliance with R.C. § 2917.40
*Penalty:* A misdemeanor of the first degree (2929.21-2929.31)
*Notes:* If any individual suffers physical harm to his person as a result of a violation of this section, the sentencing court shall consider this factor in favor of imposing a term of imprisonment upon the offender
Exempted performances, *see* R.C. § 2917.40(D)
Responsibility for designating number of open, staffed entrances, *see* R.C. § 2917.40(E)
Performances outside the scope of R.C. § 2917.40, *see* R.C. § 2917.40(G)
Municipalities may impose additional requirements, *see* § 2917.40(H)

***MISCONDUCT INVOLVING A PUBLIC TRANSPORTATION SYSTEM,* R.C. § 2917.41 [M4, M3]**

Division (A): **[M4}**
(1) Evade payment
(2) Of known fares
(3) Of a public transportation system
(4) Venue

Division (B): **[M4]**
(1) Alter any transfer, pass, ticket, or token
(2) Of a public transportation system
(3) With purpose of evading the payment of fares or of defrauding the system
(4) Venue

Division (C): **[MM, M4]**
(1) (a) Play sound equipment without proper use of a private earphone
*(or)*
(b) (i) Smoke, eat, or drink
(ii) In any area where such activity is clearly marked as being prohibited
*(or)*
(c) Expectorate upon a facility or vehicle
(2) While in any facility or vehicle
(3) Of a public transportation system
(4) Venue

Division (D): **[M3]**
(1) Write, deface, draw, or otherwise mark
(2) On any facility or vehicle
(3) Of a public transportation system
(4) Venue

Division (E): **[M4]**
(1) Fail to comply with a lawful order
*(and)*
(2) Resist, obstruct, or abuse
(3) A public transportation system police officer in the performance of the officer's duties
(4) Venue
Offense under Division (A), (B), or (E)
*Penalty:* A misdemeanor of the fourth degree (2929.21-2929.31)
Offense under Division (C)
*Penalty:* A minor misdemeanor; a misdemeanor of the fourth degree on a second offense (2929.21-2929.31)
Offense under Division (D)
*Penalty:* A misdemeanor of the third degree (2929.21-2929.31)
*Definition:* "Public transportation system," R.C. § 2917.41(G)

***UNAUTHORIZED USE OF BLOCK PARENT SYMBOL,* R.C. § 2917.46 [MM]**

(1) With intent to identify a building as a block parent home or building
(2) (a) Display the block parent symbol, unless authorized
*(and)*
(b) Display a symbol that falsely gives the appearance of being the block parent symbol
(3) Venue
*Penalty:* A minor misdemeanor (2929.21-2929.31)
*Note: See* R.C. §§ 3301.076, 3313.206 regarding adoption and use of block parent symbols

***IMPROPERLY HANDLING INFECTIOUS AGENTS,* R.C. § 2917.47 [F2]**

(1) Knowingly
(2) Possess, send, receive, or cause to be sent or received
(3) An isolate or derivative of an isolate of an infectious agent
*Penalty:* A felony of the second degree (2929.11-2929.18, 2929.31)
*Note:* A person may possess, send, receive, or cause to be sent or received an isolate or derivative of an isolate of an infectious agent as permitted by state or federal law, including for purposes of biomedical or biotechnical research or production, provision of health care services, or investigation of disease by public health agencies

---

## OFFENSES AGAINST THE FAMILY

***BIGAMY,* R.C. § 2919.01 [M1]**

(1) Being married

(2) (a) Marry another
*(or)*
(b) Continue to cohabit with another in this state
(3) Venue
*Penalty:* A misdemeanor of the first degree (2929.21-2929.31)
*Note:* It is an affirmative defense that the spouse was continuously absent for five years and was not known by the actor to be alive, R.C. § 2919.01(B)

***UNLAWFUL ABORTION,* R.C. § 2919.12 [M1, F4, F5]**

(1) Perform or induce abortion without informed consent of pregnant woman
*(or)*
(2) Knowingly perform or induce abortion upon woman who is pregnant, unmarried, under eighteen, and unemancipated unless:
(a) Person performing has given 24 hours actual notice to one parent, guardian, or custodian
*(or)*
(b) Woman has requested to notify one of certain specified relatives in lieu of parents, guardian, or custodian, affidavits containing specified information have been filed in juvenile court, the court has notified the person performing of the filing of the affidavits, the juvenile court has been given name and address of person performing, and the person performing has given 24 hours actual notice to the specified relative
*(or)*
(c) One parent, guardian, or custodian has given written consent
*(or)*
(d) Juvenile court has authorized woman to consent without notification pursuant to R.C. § 2151.85
*(or)*
(e) Juvenile court or court of appeals by inaction has constructively authorized woman to consent without notification pursuant to R.C. § 2151.85 or § 2505.073
*(or)*
(f) Parent, guardian, custodian, or specified relative notified in accordance with statute clearly and unequivocably expresses he or she does not wish to consult with the woman
*(or)*
(g) Reasonable efforts to give actual notice to appropriate person have failed, and 48 hours constructive notice has been given in manner specified in statute
(3) Venue
*Penalty:* A misdemeanor of the first degree (2929.21-2929.31)
Subsequent offenses under division (1)
*Penalty:* A felony of the fourth degree (2929.11-2929.18, 2929.31)
Subsequent offenses under division (2)
*Penalty:* A felony of the fifth degree (2929.11-2929.18, 2929.31)
*Notes:* Affirmative defense that woman provided false, misleading, or incorrect information on specified matters and person had no reasonable cause to disbelieve such information
Affirmative defense that compliance not possible because immediate threat of serious risk to life or health of woman created emergency necessitating immediate performance or inducement of abortion
Offender also liable for civil compensatory and exemplary damages
*Definitions:* "Unemancipated," R.C. § 2919.12(F)

***UNLAWFUL ABORTION,* R.C. § 2919.121 [M1, F4]**

(1) Knowingly
(2) (a) Perform
*(or)*
(b) Induce
(3) An abortion
(4) Upon a pregnant minor
(5) Unless
(a) The attending physician has secured the informed written consent of the minor and one parent, guardian, or custodian
*(or)*
(b) The minor is emancipated and the attending physician has received her written informed consent
*(or)*
(c) The minor has been authorized to consent to the abortion by a court order issued pursuant to division (C) of this section, and the attending physician has received her informed written consent
*(or)*
(d) The court has given its consent in accordance with division (C) of this section and the minor is having the abortion willingly
(6) Venue
*Penalty:* A misdemeanor of the first degree (2929.21-2929.31)
If the offender previously has been convicted of or pleaded guilty to a violation of this section
*Penalty:* A felony of the fourth degree (2929.11-2929.18, 2929.31)

*Notes:* A minor shall be considered "emancipated" if the minor has married, entered the armed services of the United States, become employed and self-subsisting, or has otherwise become independent from the care and control of her parent, guardian, or custodian

It is an affirmative defense to any civil, criminal, or professional disciplinary claim brought under this section that compliance with the requirements of this section was not possible because an immediate threat of serious risk to the life or physical health of the minor from the continuation of her pregnancy created an emergency necessitating the immediate performance or inducement of an abortion

Whoever violates this section is liable to the pregnant minor and her parents, guardian, or custodian for civil, compensatory, and exemplary damages

***UNLAWFUL DISTRIBUTION OF ABORTION-INDUCING DRUG,* R.C. § 2919.123 [F4, F3]**

Division (A):
(1) Not being a physician
(2) Knowingly
(3) Give, sell, dispense, administer, otherwise provide, or prescribe
(4) RU-486 (mifepristone) to another
(5) For the purpose of inducing an abortion in any person or enabling the other person to induce an abortion in any person
(6) Venue
*(or)*
(1) Being a physician
(2) Give, sell, dispense, administer, or otherwise provide or prescribe the RU-486 (mifepristone)
(3) Did not satisfy all the criteria established by federal law that a physician must satisfy in order to provide RU-486 (mifepristone) for inducing abortions
(4) Fails to provide the RU-486 (mifepristone) to the other person for the purpose of inducing an abortion in accordance with all provisions of federal law that govern the use of RU-486 (mifepristone) for inducing abortions.
(5) Venue

Division (B):
(1) Being a physician
(2) Provides RU-486 (mifepristone) to another for the purpose of inducing an abortion as authorized under division (A) of this section
(3) Knowingly
(4) Fail to comply with the applicable requirements of any federal law that pertain to follow-up examinations or care for persons to whom or for whom RU-486 (mifepristone) is provided for the purpose of inducing an abortion.
(5) Venue

Division (C):
(1) Being a physician
(2) Provides RU-486 (mifepristone) to another for the purpose of inducing an abortion
(3) Knows that the person who uses the RU-486 (mifepristone) for the purpose of inducing an abortion experienced during or after the use an incomplete abortion, severe bleeding, or an adverse reaction to the RU-486 (mifepristone) or is hospitalized, received a transfusion, or experienced any other serious event
(4) Knowingly
(5) Fail to promptly provide a written report of the incomplete abortion, severe bleeding, adverse reaction, hospitalization, transfusion, or serious event to the state medical board.
(6) Venue

*Penalty:* A misdemeanor felony of the fourth degree (2929.11-2929.18, 2929.31). If the offender previously has been convicted of or pleaded guilty to a violation of this section or of section 2919.12, 2919.121 [2919.12.1], 2919.13, 2919.14, 2919.151 [2919.15.1], 2919.17, or 2919.18 of the Revised Code, a felony of the third degree (2929.11-2929.18, 2929.31)

*Note:* Division (A) of this section does not apply to any of the following to a pregnant woman who obtains or possesses RU-486 (mifepristone) for the purpose of inducing an abortion to terminate her own pregnancy; the legal transport of RU-486 (mifepristone) by any person or entity and the legal delivery of the RU-486 (mifepristone) by any person to the recipient, provided that this division does not apply regarding any conduct related to the RU-486 (mifepristone) other than its transport and delivery to the recipient; and the distribution, provision, or sale of RU-486 (mifepristone) by any legal manufacturer or distributor of RU-486 (mifepristone), provided the manufacturer or distributor made a good faith effort to comply with any applicable requirements of federal law regarding the distribution, provision, or sale

If the offender is a professionally licensed person, in addition to any other sanction imposed by law for the offense, the offender is subject to sanctioning as provided by law by the regulatory or licensing board or agency that has the administrative authority to suspend or revoke the offender's professional license, including the sanctioning provided in section 4731.22 of the Revised Code for offenders who have a certificate to practice or certificate of registration issued under that chapter

***ABORTION MANSLAUGHTER,* R.C. § 2919.13 [F1]**

Division (A):
(1) Purposely
(2) Take the life of a child
  (a) Born by attempted abortion
  (b) Alive when removed from the uterus of the pregnant woman
(3) Venue

Division (B):
(1) Being a person performing an abortion
(2) Fail to take measures required by the exercise of medical judgment in light of the attending circumstances to preserve the life of a child who is alive when removed from the uterus of a pregnant woman
(3) Venue
*Penalty:* A felony of the first degree (2929.11-2929.18, 2929.31)

***ABORTION TRAFFICKING,* R.C. § 2919.14 [MI]**

(1) (a) Experiment upon
  *(or)*
  (b) Sell
(2) The aborted product of human conception
(3) Venue
*Penalty:* A misdemeanor of the first degree (2929.21-2929.31)
*Note:* "Experiment" does not include autopsies pursuant to R.C. §§ 313.13, 2108.50

***PARTIAL BIRTH FETICIDE,* R.C. § 2919.151 [F2]**

Division (B):
(1) Knowingly
(2) Perform
(3) A partial birth feticide
(4) On a pregnant woman, when the fetus that is the subject of the procedure is viable and when the procedure is not necessary, in reasonable medical judgment, to preserve the life or health of the mother as a result of the mother's life or health being endangered by a serious risk of the substantial and irreversible impairment of a major bodily function
(5) Venue

Division (C):
(1) Knowingly
(2) Perform
(3) A partial birth feticide
(4) On a pregnant woman, when the fetus that is the subject of the procedure is not viable and when the procedure is not necessary, in reasonable medical judgment, to preserve the life or health of the mother as a result of the mother's life or health being endangered by a serious risk of the substantial and irreversible impairment of a major bodily function
(5) Venue
*Penalty:* A felony of the second degree (2929.11-2929.18, 2929.31)
*Notes:* A pregnant woman upon whom a partial birth procedure is performed in violation of this section is not guilty of committing, attempting to commit, complicity in the commission of, or conspiracy in the commission of a violation of this section
This section does not prohibit the suction curettage procedure of abortion, the suction aspiration procedure of abortion, or the dilation and evacuation procedure of abortion
This section does not apply to any person who performs or attempts to perform a legal abortion if the act that causes the death of the fetus is performed prior to the fetus being partially born even though the death of the fetus occurs after it is partially born

***TERMINATING OR ATTEMPTING TO TERMINATE HUMAN PREGNANCY AFTER VIABILITY,* R.C. § 2919.17 [F4]**

Division (A):
(1) Purposely
(2) (a) Perform or induce
  *(or)*
  (b) Attempt to perform or induce
(3) An abortion
(4) Upon a pregnant woman
(5) If the unborn human is viable unless the abortion is performed or induced or attempted to be performed or induced by a physician and that physician determines, in good faith and in the exercise of reasonable medical judgment,

(a) that the abortion is necessary to prevent the death of the pregnant woman or a serious risk of the substantial and irreversible impairment of a major bodily function of the pregnant woman
*(or)*
(b) after making a determination relative of the viability of the unborn human in conformity with Division (A) of R.C. § 2919.18 that the unborn human is not viable
(6) Venue

Division (B):
(1) Physician
(2) Purposely
(3) (a) Perform or induce
*(or)*
(b) Attempt to perform or induce
(4) An abortion
(5) Upon a pregnant woman when the unborn human is viable and when the physician has determined, in good faith and reasonable medical judgment, that the abortion is necessary to prevent the death of the pregnant woman or a serious risk of the substantial and irreversible impairment of a major bodily function of the pregnant woman, unless each of the following is satisfied:
(a) the physician certifies in writing that he has determined, in good faith and the exercise of reasonable medical judgment, that the abortion is necessary to prevent the death of the pregnant woman or a serious risk of the substantial and irreversible impairment of a major bodily function of the pregnant woman
*(and)*
(b) the determination referred to in (5)(a) is concurred in by at least one other physician who certifies in writing that the concurring physician has determined, in good faith and the exercise of reasonable medical judgment, and following a review of the available medical records of and any available test results pertaining to the pregnant woman, that the abortion is necessary to prevent the death of the pregnant woman or a serious risk of the substantial and irreversible impairment of a major bodily function of the pregnant woman
*(and)*
(c) the abortion is performed or induced or attempted to be performed or induced in a health care facility that has or has access to appropriate neonatal services for premature infants
*(and)*
(d) the physician who performs or induces or attempts to perform or induce the abortion terminates or attempts to terminate the pregnancy in the manner that provides the best opportunity for the unborn human to survive, unless that physician determines, in good faith and in the exercise of reasonable medical judgment, that the termination of the pregnancy in that manner poses a significantly greater risk of the death of the pregnant woman or a serious risk of the substantial and irreversible impairment of a major bodily function of the pregnant woman than would other available methods of abortion
*(and)*
(e) the physician who performs or induces or attempts to perform or induce the abortion has arranged for the attendance in the same room in which the abortion is to be performed or induced or attempted to be performed or induced of at least one other physician who is to take control of, provide immediate medical care for, and take all reasonable steps necessary to preserve the life and health of the unborn human immediately upon the unborn human's complete expulsion or extraction from the pregnant woman
(6) Venue

*Penalty:* A felony of the fourth degree (2929.11-2929.18, 2929.31)

*Notes:* Division (B) does not prohibit the performance or inducement or attempted performance or inducement of an abortion without prior satisfaction of each of the conditions described in Division (B)(5)(a)-(e) if the physician in good faith and reasonable medical judgment believes that a medical emergency exists that prevents compliance with one or more of those conditions

### *FAILURE TO PERFORM VIABILITY TESTING,* R.C. § 2919.18 [M4]

Division (A)(1):
(1) Physician
(2) (a) Perform or induce
*(or)*
(b) Attempt to perform or induce
(3) An abortion
(4) Upon a pregnant woman after the beginning of her twenty-second week of pregnancy unless the physician determines in good faith and in the exercise of reasonable medical judgment, that the unborn human is not viable, and the physician makes that determination after performing a medical examination and after performing or causing the performance of gestational age, weight, lung maturity, or other tests of the unborn human that a reasonable physician making a determination as to whether an unborn human is or is not viable would perform or cause to be performed
(5) Venue

Division (A)(2):
(1) Physician

(2) (a) Perform or induce
*(or)*
(b) Attempt to perform or induce
(3) An abortion
(4) Upon a pregnant woman after the beginning of her twenty-second week of pregnancy without first entering the determination described in Division (A)(1) and the associated findings of the medical examination and tests in the medical record of the woman
(5) Venue
*Penalty:* A misdemeanor of the fourth degree (2929.21-2929.31)
*Notes:* Divisions (A)(1) and (2) do not prohibit a physician from performing or inducing or attempting to perform or induce an abortion on a pregnant woman after the beginning of her twenty-second week of pregnancy if a medical emergency exists

***NONSUPPORT OR CONTRIBUTING TO NONSUPPORT OF DEPENDENTS,* R.C. § 2919.21 [M1, F5, F4]**

Division (A): **[M1, F5, F4]**
(1) Abandon or fail to support adequately according to law
(2) (a) A spouse
*(or)*
(b) A child under 18, or a mentally or physically handicapped child under 21
*(or)*
(c) An aged/infirm parent or adoptive parent who is unable to provide adequately the parent's own support
(3) Venue

Division (B): **[MI, F5, F4]**
(1) Abandon or fail to provide support as established by a court order to
(2) Another person
(3) Whom by court order or decree,
(4) The person is legally obligated to support
(5) Venue
*Penalty:* A misdemeanor of the first degree (2929.21-2929.31)
If previously convicted under (A)(2)(b) or (B), above, or if the offender has failed to provide support under (A)(2)(b) or (B), above for 26 of 104 weeks
*Penalty:* A felony of the fifth degree (2929.11-2929.18, 2929.31)
If previously convicted of a felony violation of (A)(2)(b) or (B) of this section
*Penalty:* A felony of the fourth degree (2929.11-2929.18, 2929.31)

Division (C): **[M1]**
(1) Aid, abet, induce, cause, encourage, or contribute to
(2) (a) Child
*(or)*
(b) Ward of juvenile court
(3) (a) Becoming a dependent child as defined in R.C. § 2151.04
*(or)*
(b) Becoming a neglected child as defined in R.C. § 2151.03
(4) Venue
*Penalty:* A misdemeanor of the first degree (2929.21-2929.31)
*Notes:* It is an affirmative defense to a charge under this section that the accused was unable to provide adequate support or the established support, and provided such support as was within his ability and means. In addition, it is an affirmative defense to a charge under (A)(2)(c) above, that the parent abandoned, or failed to support the accused as required by law, while the accused was under age 18, or was mentally or physically handicapped and under age 21
It is not a defense to a charge under division (B) that the person whom a court has ordered the accused to support is being adequately supported by someone other than the accused
Court costs and the attorney fees of adverse parties are to be assessed for a violation of a support order issued on or after 4-15-85
Each day of violation of Division (C) is a separate offense

***ENDANGERING CHILDREN,* R.C. § 2919.22 [M1, F5, F4, F3, F2]**

Division (A):
(1) Being a parent, guardian, custodian, person with custody or control, or a person in loco parentis
(2) Create a substantial risk to the health or safety of
(3) A child under 18 or a mentally or physically handicapped person under 21
(4) By violating a duty of care, protection, or support
(5) Venue

Division (B):
(1) (a) Abuse a child
*(or)*

(b) Torture/cruelly abuse a child
*(or)*

(c) Administer corporal punishment or use other physical disciplinary measures, or physically restrain a child in a cruel manner or for prolonged periods in a manner excessive under the circumstances and which creates substantial risk of serious physical harm
*(or)*

(d) Repeatedly administer unwarranted disciplinary measures to a child involving substantial risk that such conduct, if continued, will seriously impair or retard mental health/development if continued
*(or)*

(e) Entice, coerce, permit, encourage, compel, employ, hire, use, or allow the child to act, model, or in any other way participate in, or be photographed for, the production, presentation, dissemination, or advertisement of any material or performance that he knows or reasonably should know is obscene, as defined in R.C. § 2907.01, or any material or performance that is a sexually- or nudity-oriented matter
*(or)*

(f) Allow the child to be on the same parcel of real property and within one hundred feet of, or, in the case of more than one housing unit on the same parcel of real property, in the same housing unit and within one hundred feet of, any act in violation of section 2925.04 or 2925.041 [2925.04.1] of the Revised Code when the person knows that the act is occurring, whether or not any person is prosecuted for or convicted of the violation of section 2925.04 or 2925.041 [2925.04.1] of the Revised Code that is the basis of the violation of this division.

(2) When such child is under 18 or is a mentally or physically handicapped child under 21
(3) Venue

Division (C):
(1) Operate a vehicle, streetcar, or trackless trolley
(2) Within this state
(3) In violation of Division (A) of R.C. § 4511.19
(4) When one or more children under 18 are in the vehicle, streetcar, or trackless trolley
(5) Venue

*Penalty:* A violation of Division (A) or (B)(1)(a), a misdemeanor of the first degree (2929.21-2929.31). Where offender has previously been convicted under this section or of any offense involving neglect, abandonment, contributing to the delinquency of, or physical abuse of a child, a felony of the fourth degree (2929.11-2929.18, 2929.31)

Where offender violates Division (A) and serious physical harm results to child, a felony of the third degree (2929.11-2929.18, 2929.31). Where offender violates Division (B)(1) and serious physical harm results to a child, a felony of the second degree (2929.11-2929.18, 2929.31)

A violation of Division (B)(1)(b), (c), (d), or (f) a felony of the third degree (2929.11-2929.18, 2929.31) unless serious physical harm to the child, or there has been a previous conviction under R.C. § 2919.22, or an offense involving neglect, abandonment, contributing to the delinquency of, or physical abuse of a child, then a felony of the second degree (2929.11-2929.18, 2929.31)

A violation of Division (B)(1)(e), a felony of the second degree (2929.11-2929.18, 2929.31)

A violation of Division (C) with no violation of (E)(5)(b) or (c), a misdemeanor of the first degree (2929.21-2929.31).

A violation of Division (C) with no violation of (E)(5)(c) and serious harm results to the child or the offender has been previously convicted of an offense under this section or any offense involving neglect, abandonment, contributing to the delinquency of, or physical abuse of a child, a felony of the fifth degree (2929.11-2929.18, 2929.31). A violation of Division (C) resulting in serious physical harm to the child involved and the offender has been previously convicted of a violation of Division (C) of this section, R.C. § 2903.06, or 2903.08, or 2903.07 as it existed prior to March 23, 2000, or R.C. § 2903.04 in a case in which the offender was subject to the sanctions described in Division (D) of that section, a felony of the fourth degree (2929.11-2929.18, 2929.31)

Where offender violates division (B)(2), (3), (4), or (6) of this section, except as otherwise provided in this division, endangering children is a felony of the third degree (2929.11-2929.18, 2929.31). If the violation results in serious physical harm to the child involved, or if the offender previously has been convicted of an offense under this section or of any offense involving neglect, abandonment, contributing to the delinquency of, or physical abuse of a child, endangering children is a felony of the second degree (2929.11-2929.18, 2929.31). If the offender violates division (B)(6) of this section and the drug involved is methamphetamine, the court shall impose a mandatory prison term on the offender as follows:

(a) If the violation is a violation of division (B)(6) of this section that is a felony of the third degree (2929.11-2929.18, 2929.31) under division (E)(3) of this section and the drug involved is methamphetamine, except as otherwise provided in this division, the court shall impose as a mandatory prison term one of the prison terms prescribed for a felony of the third degree (2929.11-2929.18, 2929.31) that is not less than two years. If the violation is a violation of division (B)(6) of this section that is a felony of the third degree (2929.11-2929.18, 2929.31) under division (E)(3) of this section, if the drug involved is methamphetamine, and if the offender previously has been convicted of or pleaded guilty to a violation of division (B) (6) of this section, a violation of division (A) of section 2925.04 of the Revised Code, or a violation of division (A) of section 2925.041 [2925.04.1] of the Revised Code, the court shall impose as a mandatory prison term one of the prison terms prescribed for a felony of the third degree (2929.11-2929.18, 2929.31) that is not less than five years

(b) If the violation is a violation of division (B)(6) of this section that is a felony of the second degree (2929.11-2929.18, 2929.31) under division (E)(3) of this section and the drug involved is methamphetamine, except as otherwise provided in this division, the court shall impose as a mandatory prison term one of the prison terms prescribed for a felony of the second degree (2929.11-2929.18, 2929.31) that is not less than three years. If the violation is a violation of division (B)(6) of this section that is a felony of the second degree (2929.11-2929.18, 2929.31) under division (E)(3) of this section, if the drug involved is methamphetamine, and if the offender previously has been convicted of or pleaded guilty to a violation of division (B)(6) of this section, a violation of division (A) of section 2925.04 of the Revised Code, or a violation of division (A) of section 2925.041 [2925.04.1] of the Revised Code, the court shall impose as a mandatory prison term one of the prison terms prescribed for a felony of the second degree (2929.11-2929.18, 2929.31) that is not less than five years

Where the offender violates division (B)(5) of this section, endangering children is a felony of the second degree (2929.11-2929.18, 2929.31)

*Notes:* It is not a violation of a duty of care, protection or support under Division (A) when the parent, guardian, custodian, or person having custody or control of a child treats the physical or mental illness or defect of such child by spiritual means—through prayer alone, in accordance with the tenets of a recognized religious body

Division (B) of this section does not apply to any material or performance that is produced, presented, or disseminated for a bona fide medical, scientific, educational, religious, governmental, judicial, or other proper purpose, by or to a physician, psychologist, sociologist, scientist, teacher, person pursuing bona fide studies or research, librarian, member of the clergy, prosecutor, judge, or other person having a proper interest in the material or performance

Mistake of age is not a defense under (B)(1)(e) above

As used in Division (B)(1)(e) of this section:

(a) "Material," "performance," and "sexual activity" have the same meanings as in section 2907.01 of the Revised Code

(b) "Nudity-oriented matter" means any material or performance that shows a minor in a state of nudity and that, taken as a whole by the average person applying contemporary community standards, appeals to prurient interest

(c) "Sexually oriented matter" means any material or performance that shows a minor participating or engaging in sexual activity, masturbation, or bestiality

Any sentence of imprisonment imposed under (B)(1)(e) above is to be served consecutively to any other sentence of imprisonment

Revised Code § 2933.16 provides that if an offender is convicted of or pleads guilty to a violation of R.C. § 2919.22(B), the court may suspend execution of sentence and place the offender on probation conditioned upon the participation of the offender, to the satisfaction of the court, in a program of clinically appropriate psychiatric or psychological treatment

### *PARENTAL EDUCATION NEGLECT,* R.C. § 2919.222 [M4]

(1) Fail to attend a parental education or training program
(2) The person is required to attend pursuant to a policy adopted under R.C. § 3313.663
(3) Venue

*Penalty:* A misdemeanor of the fourth degree (2929.21-2929.31)

### *MISREPRESENTATION BY CHILD CARE PROVIDER,* R.C. § 2919.224 [M1]

(1) Being a child care provider
(2) Knowingly
(3) Misrepresent
(4) To
    (a) A parent, guardian, custodian, or other person responsible for the care of a child in the provider's facility or receiving child care from the provider
    *(or)*
    (b) A parent, guardian, custodian, or other person responsible for the care of a child who is considering the provider as a child care provider for the child
    *(or)*
    (c) A public official responsible for issuing the provider a license or certificate to provide child care
    *(or)*
    (d) A public official investigating or inquiring about the provision of child care by the provider
    (or)
    (e) A peace officer.
(5) Any factor or condition that relates to the provision of child care that substantially affects the health or safety of any child or children in that provider's facility or receiving child care from that provider
(6) Venue

*Note:* For the purposes of this section, "any factor or condition that relates to the provision of child care" includes, but is not limited to, the following: (1) The person or persons who will provide child care to the child of the parent, guardian, custodian, or other person responsible for the care of the child, or to the children in general; (2) The qualifications to provide child care of the child care provider, of a person employed by the provider, or of a person who provides child care as a volunteer; (3) The number of children to whom child care is provided at one time or the number of children receiving child care in the child care facility at one time; (4) The conditions or safety features of the child care facility; (5) The area of the child care facility in which child day-care is provided

*Penalty:* A misdemeanor of the first degree (2929.21-2929.31)

***FAILURE OF A TYPE A OR TYPE B FAMILY DAY-CARE HOME TO DISCLOSE DEATH OR SERIOUS INJURY OF CHILD*, R.C. § 2919.225 [M4]**

Division (A)

(1) Being an owner, provider, or administrator of a type A family day-care home or type B family day-care home

(2) Knowing

(a) A child died while under the care of the home or while receiving child care from the owner, provider, or administrator or died as a result of injuries suffered while under the care of the home or while receiving child care from the owner, provider, or administrator.

*(or)*

(b) Within the preceding ten years, a child suffered injuries while under the care of the home or while receiving child care from the owner, provider, or administrator, and those injuries led to the child being hospitalized for more than twenty-four hours.

(3) Accept a child into that home without first disclosing such incidents to the parent, guardian, custodian, or other person responsible for the care of that child

(4) Venue

Division (B):

(1) Being an owner, provider, or administrator of a type A family day-care home or type B family day-care home

(2) Fail to provide notice in accordance with division (B)(3) of this section *[see first Note below]* of

(a) A child who is under the care of the home or is receiving child care from the owner, provider, or administrator dies while under the care of the home or while receiving child care from the owner, provider, or administrator or dies as a result of injuries suffered while under the care of the home or while receiving child day-care from the owner, provider, or administrator.

*(or)*

(b) A child who is under the care of the home or is receiving child care from the owner, provider, or administrator is hospitalized for more than twenty-four hours as a result of injuries suffered while under the care of the home or while receiving child care from the owner, provider, or administrator.

(3) To

(a) For each child who, at the time of the injury or death for which the notice is required, is receiving or is enrolled to receive child care at the home or from the owner, provider, or administrator, to the parent, guardian, custodian, or other person responsible for the care of the child;

*(or)*

(b) If the notice is required as the result of the death of a child as described in division (B)(2)(a), to the public children services agency of the county in which the home is located or the child care was given, a municipal or county peace officer in the county in which the child resides or in which the home is located or the child care was given, and the child fatality review board appointed under section 307.621 of the Revised Code that serves the county in which the home is located or the child care was given.

(4) Venue

*Note:* Division (B)(3) provides:

An owner, provider, or administrator of a home shall provide the notices required by divisions (B)(1) and (2) of this section not later than forty-eight hours after the child dies or, regarding a child who is hospitalized for more than twenty-four hours as a result of injuries suffered while under the care of the home, not later than forty-eight hours after the child suffers the injuries. If a child is hospitalized for more than twenty-four hours as a result of injuries suffered while under the care of the home, and the child subsequently dies as a result of those injuries, the owner, provider, or administrator shall provide separate notices under divisions (B)(1) and (2) of this section regarding both the injuries and the death. All notices provided under divisions (B)(1) and (2) of this section shall state that the death or injury occurred

Limitation on notice requirements as set out in Division (C):

Division (A) of this section does not require more than one person to make disclosures to the same parent, guardian, custodian, or other person responsible for the care of a child regarding any single injury or death for which disclosure is required under that division. Division (B) of this section does not require more than one person to give notices to the same parent, guardian, custodian, other person responsible for the care of the child, public children services agency, peace officer, or child fatality review board regarding any single injury or death for which disclosure is required under division (B)(1) of this section

*Penalty:* A misdemeanor of the fourth degree (2929.21-2929.31)

***FAILURE OF CHILD CARE CENTER TO DISCLOSE DEATH OR SERIOUS INJURY OF A CHILD*, R.C. § 2919.227 [M4]**

Division (A)(1):

(1) Being a child care center licensee

(2) Accept a child into that center without first providing

(3) Upon request
(4) To the parent, guardian, custodian, or other person responsible for the care of that child the following information
(5) (a) The types of injuries to children, as reported in accordance with rules adopted under section 5104.011 of the Revised Code, that occurred at the center on or after April 1, 2003, or the date that is two years before the date the information is requested, whichever date is more recent;
*(or)*
(b) The number of each type of injury to children that occurred at the center during that period.
(6) Venue

Division (A)(2):
(1) If
(a) A child died while under the care of the center or while receiving child care from the owner, provider, or administrator of the center
*(or)*
(b) A child died as a result of injuries suffered while under the care of the center or while receiving child care from the owner, provider, or administrator of the center.
(2) During the fifteen-year period immediately preceding the date that the parent, guardian, custodian, or other person responsible for the care of a child seeks to enroll that child
(3) Being a child care center licensee
(4) Accept that child into that center without first providing to the parent, guardian, custodian, or other person responsible for the care of that child a notice that states that the death occurred.
(5) Venue

Division (B):
(1) Being a child care center licensee
(2) Fail to provide notice in accordance with division (B)(3) of this section *[see Note below]*
(3) To
(a) The parent, guardian, custodian, or other person responsible for the care of each child who, at the time of the death for which notice is required, is receiving or is enrolled to receive child care from the center
*(or)*
(b) The public children services agency of the county in which the center is located or the child care was given
*(or)*
(c) A municipal or county peace officer in the county in which the child resides or in which the center is located or the child care was given
*(or)*
(d) The child fatality review board appointed under section 307.621 of the Revised Code that serves the county in which the center is located or the child care was given.
(4) If a child who is under the care of the center or is receiving child care from the owner, provider, or administrator of the center dies while under the care of the center or while receiving child care from the owner, provider, or administrator or dies as a result of injuries suffered while under the care of the center or while receiving child care from the owner, provider, or administrator.
(5) Venue

*Note:* Subdivision (B)(3) provides:
A child care center licensee shall provide the notice required by Division (B) not later than forty-eight hours after the child dies. The notice shall state that the death occurred.
*Penalty:* A misdemeanor of the fourth degree (2929.21-2929.31)

***INTERFERENCE WITH CUSTODY*, R.C. § 2919.23 [M3, M1, F5, F4]**

Division (A):
(1) (a) Knowing the person is without privilege to do so
*(or)*
(b) Being reckless in that regard
(2) Entice, take, keep or harbor from parent, guardian or custodian
(3) (a) A child under 18 or mentally/physically handicapped child under 21
*(or)*
(b) A person committed by laws to an institution for delinquent, unruly, neglected, abused, or dependent children
*(or)*
(c) A person committed by laws to an institution for the mentally ill/mentally retarded
(4) Venue

Division (B):
(1) Aid, abet, induce, cause, or encourage
(2) (a) Child
*(or)*
(b) Ward of the juvenile court

(3) Who has been committed to the custody of any person, department, or public or private institution
(4) To leave the custody of that person, department, or institution
(5) Without legal consent
(6) Venue

Division (A)(3)(a)
*Penalty:* A misdemeanor of the first degree (2929.21-2929.31)
If the child is removed from the state or if the offender previously has been convicted of an offense under this section
*Penalty:* A felony of the fifth degree (2929.11-2929.18, 2929.31)
If the child suffers physical harm as a result of the violation
*Penalty:* A felony of the fourth degree (2929.11-2929.18, 2929.31)

Division (A)(3)(b) or (c)
*Penalty:* A misdemeanor of the third degree (2929.21-2929.31)

Division (B)
*Penalty:* A misdemeanor of the first degree (2929.21-2929.31)
*Notes:* It is an affirmative defense to a charge of enticing or taking, under Division (A)(3)(a), above, that the actor reasonably believed that his conduct was necessary to preserve the child's health or safety. It is an affirmative defense to a charge of keeping or harboring under this section, that the actor in good faith gave notice to law enforcement or judicial authorities within a reasonable time after the child or committed person came under his shelter, protection or influence
Each day of violation of Division (B) is a separate offense

***INTERFERING WITH ACTION TO ISSUE OR MODIFY SUPPORT ORDER,* R.C. § 2919.231 [M1, F5]**

(1) By using physical harassment or threats of violence against another person
(2) (a) Interfere with the other person's initiation or continuance of
*(or)*
(b) Attempt to prevent the other person from initiating or continuing an action to issue or modify
(3) A support order under Chapter 3115., or under R.C. §§ 2151.23, 2151.231, 2151.232, 2151.33, 2151.36, 2151.361, 2151.49, 3105.18, 3105.21, 3109.05, 3109.19, 3111.13, 3113.04, 3113.07, or 3113.31
(4) Venue
*Penalty:* A misdemeanor of the first degree (2929.21-2929.31)
If prior conviction under this section or R.C. § 3111.19
*Penalty:* A felony of the fifth degree (2929.11-2929.18, 2929.31)

***CONTRIBUTING TO THE UNRULINESS OR DELINQUENCY OF A CHILD,* R.C. § 2919.24 [M1]**

(1) (a) Aid, abet, induce, cause, encourage, or contribute to
*(or)*
(b) Act in a way tending to cause
(2) (a) Child
*(or)*
(b) Ward of the juvenile court
(3) (a) Becoming (to become) an unruly child, as defined in R.C. § 2151.022
*(or)*
(b) Becoming (to become) a delinquent child, as defined in R.C. § 2152.02
(4) Venue
*Penalty:* A misdemeanor of the first degree (2929.21-292931)
*Note:* It is also a violation of this Section for a parent, guardian, or custodian of a child, who is not emancipated, and who has duties under Chapters 2152. and 2950. to register, to register a new residence address, and to periodically verify a residence address and, if applicable send a notice of intent to reside, to fail to ensure that the child complies with those duties. Each day of violation is a separate offense

***DOMESTIC VIOLENCE,* R.C. § 2919.25 [M4, M3, M1, F5]**

Division (A):
(1) Knowingly
(2) Cause or attempt to cause
(3) Physical harm
(4) To a family or household member
(5) Venue

Division (B):
(1) Recklessly
(2) Cause
(3) Serious physical harm
(4) To a family or household member
(5) Venue

Division (C):
(1) Knowingly
(2) By force or threat of force
(3) Cause
(4) A family or household member to believe
(5) The offender will cause imminent physical harm
(6) To the family or household member
(7) Venue

Division (A) or (B), no previous conviction under this section or conviction under R.C. §§ 2903.11, 2903.12, 2903.13, 2903.14, 2903.21, 2903.211, 2903.22, 2911.211, or 2919.22 involving person who was family or household member at time of violation or a violation of a law of the United States or another state or a municipal ordinance that is substantially similar to one of those sections involving person who was family or household member at time of violation
*Penalty:* A misdemeanor of the first degree (2929.21-2929.31)
If the offender knew the victim to be pregnant, felony of the fifth degree.
Division (A) or (B), previous conviction of domestic violence, of a violation of municipal ordinance that is substantially similar to domestic violence, of a violation of R.C. §§ 2903.11, 2903.12, 2903.13, 2903.14, 2903.21, 2903.211, 2903.22, 2911.211, or 2919.22 involving person who was family or household member at time of violation or of a violation of a law of the United States or another state or a municipal ordinance that is substantially similar to one of those sections involving a person who was a family or household member at the time of the violation
*Penalty:* A felony of the fifth degree (2929.11-2929.18, 2929.31)
Division (C), no previous conviction under this section or conviction under R.C. §§ 2903.11, 2903.12, 2903.13, 2903.14, 2903.21, 2903.211, 2903.22, 2911.211, or 2919.22 involving person who was family or household member at time of violation or of a violation of a law of the United States or another state or a municipal ordinance that is substantially similar to one of those sections involving a person who was a family or household member at the time of the violation
*Penalty:* A misdemeanor of the fourth degree (2929.21-2929.31)
Division (C), previous conviction of domestic violence, of a violation of law of the United States or another state or a municipal ordinance that is substantially similar to domestic violence, of a violation of R.C. §§ 2903.11, 2903.12, 2903.13, 2903.14, 2903.21, 2903.211, 2903.22, 2911.211, or 2919.22 involving person who was family or household member at time of violation or a violation of a law of the United States or another state or a municipal ordinance that is substantially similar to one of those sections involving person who was family or household member at time of violation
*Penalty:* A misdemeanor of the third degree (2929.21-2929.31)
*Notes:* R.C. § 2933.16 provides that if an offender is convicted of or pleads guilty to a violation of R.C. § 2919.25, the court may suspend execution of sentence and place the offender on probation conditioned upon the participation of the offender, to the satisfaction of the court, in a program of clinically appropriate psychiatric or psychological treatment
For bail considerations for prior offenders or persons subject to protection order or consent agreement, *see* R.C. § 2919.251
*Definitions:* "Family or household member," "person living as a spouse," R.C. § 2919.25(E)
"Motion for temporary protection order," R.C. § 2919.26

### *VIOLATING PROTECTION ORDER OR CONSENT AGREEMENT,* R.C. § 2919.27 [M1, F5]

(1) Recklessly
(2) Violate any terms
(3) Of protection order issued or consent agreement approved pursuant to § 3113.31
*(or)*
(4) Of a protection order issued pursuant to R.C. §§ 2151.34, 2903.213 or 2903.214
(5) Of protection order issued by a court of another state
(6) Venue
*Penalty:* A misdemeanor of the first degree (2929.21-2929.31)
Violation of (3)
*Penalty:* A misdemeanor of the first degree (2929.21-2929.31)
If previously convicted of, pleaded guilty to, or adjudicated a delinquent child for a violation of a protection order issued pursuant to R.C. §§ 2151.34, 2903.213 or 2903.214, two or more violations of R.C. §§ 2903.21, 2903.211, 2903.22, or 2911.211 that involved the same person who is the subject of the protection order or consent agreement, or one or more violations of this section
*Penalty:* A felony of the fifth degree (2929.11-2929.18, 2929.31)
Violation of (4)
*Penalty:* A misdemeanor of the first degree (2929.21-2929.31)
If previously convicted of, pleaded guilty to, or adjudicated a delinquent child for a violation of a protection order issued pursuant to R.C. §§ 2151.34, 2903.213 or 2903.214, two or more violations of R.C. §§ 2903.21, 2903.211, 2903.22, or 2911.211 that involved the same person who is the subject of the protection order or consent agreement, or one or more violations of this section
*Penalty:* A felony of the fifth degree (2929.11-2929.18, 2929.31)
*Notes: See* R.C. §§ 2919.271, 2937.23, concerning mental examination of defendants

If in a hearing for a protection order the court finds upon clear and convincing evidence that the petitioner reasonably believed that the respondent's conduct at any time preceding the filing of the petition endangered the health, welfare, or safety of the person to be protected and that the respondent presents a continuing danger to the person to be protected, the court may order that the respondent be electronically monitored, in addition to any other relief granted. If the court orders electronic monitoring of the respondent under this section, the court shall direct the sheriff's office or any other appropriate law enforcement agency to install the electronic monitoring device and to monitor the respondent. Unless the court determines that the respondent is indigent, the court shall order the respondent to pay the cost of the installation and monitoring of the electronic monitoring device. (R.C. § 2903.214) If an offender violates a protection order requiring electronic monitoring, in addition to any other sentence the court may require that the offender be electronically monitored for a period not exceeding five years by a law enforcement agency

## OFFENSES AGAINST JUSTICE AND PUBLIC ADMINISTRATION

### *BRIBERY*, R.C. § 2921.02 [F3]

Division (A):
(1) With purpose to corrupt or improperly influence
(2) A public servant or party official whether before or after attaining office
(3) With respect to the discharge of his duty
(4) Promise, offer or give any valuable thing or benefit
(5) Venue

Division (B):
(1) Knowingly solicit/accept any valuable thing or benefit for himself or another person
(2) As a public servant/party official
(3) To corrupt or improperly influence him or another public servant or party official
(4) With respect to the discharge of his or the other servant's or official's duty
(5) Before or after attaining office
(6) Venue

Division (C):
(1) With purpose to corrupt a witness or improperly influence his testimony in an official proceeding
(2) Promise, offer or give any valuable thing or benefit to said witness or another person
(3) Either before or after he is subpoenaed or sworn
(4) Venue

Division (D):
(1) Knowingly solicit or accept a valuable thing or benefit for himself or another person
(2) To corrupt or improperly influence acceptor's testimony in an official proceeding
(3) Venue

*Penalty:* A felony of the third degree (2929.11-2929.18, 2929.31)
*Note:* If public servant or party official is convicted, he is forever disqualified from holding public office, employment, or position of trust in state

### *INTIMIDATION*, R.C. § 2921.03 [F3]

(1) Knowingly
(2) By force, unlawful threat of harm, or by filing, recording, or otherwise using a materially false or fraudulent writing with malicious purpose, in bad faith, or in a wanton and reckless manner
(3) Attempt to influence, intimidate or hinder a public servant, party official, an attorney, or witness involved in a civil action or proceeding
(4) In the discharge of the duties of the public servant, party official, attorney, or witness
(5) Venue

*Penalty:* A felony of the third degree (2929.11-2929.18, 2929.31)

### *INTIMIDATION OF ATTORNEY, VICTIM OR WITNESS IN CRIMINAL CASE*, R.C. § 2921.04 [M1, F3]

Division (A): **[M1]**
(1) Knowingly
(2) Attempt to
(3) (a) Intimidate
*(or)*
(b) Hinder
(4) (a) A victim of crime
(i) In filing of criminal charges
*(or)*
(ii) In prosecution of criminal charges
*(or)*

(b) A witness involved in a criminal action or proceeding in the discharge of the duties of the witness
(5) Venue
*Penalty:* A misdemeanor of the first degree (2929.21-2929.31)
*Note:* Division (A) above does not apply to any person who, either prior or subsequent to the filing of the complaint, indictment, information, is either attempting to resolve a dispute pertaining to the alleged commission of a criminal offense, or is attempting to arbitrate, mediate, compromise, settle, or assist in the conciliation of that dispute pursuant to an authorization for arbitration, mediation, compromise, settlement, or conciliation of a dispute of that nature. *See* R.C. § 2921.04(C)

Division (B): **[F3]**
(1) Knowingly
(2) (a) By force
*(or)*
(b) By unlawful threat of harm to any person or property
(3) Attempt to
(4) (a) Influence
*(or)*
(b) Intimidate
*(or)*
(c) Hinder
(5) (a) A victim of crime
(i) In filing of criminal charges
*(or)*
(ii) In prosecution of criminal charges
*(or)*
(b) An attorney or witness involved in a criminal action or proceeding in the discharge of the duties of the attorney or witness
(6) Venue
*Penalty:* A felony of the third degree (2929.11-2929.18, 2929.31)

***RETALIATION*, R.C. § 2921.05 [F3]**

Division (A):
(1) Purposely
(2) (a) By force
*(or)*
(b) By unlawful threat of harm to any person or property
(3) Retaliate against a public servant, a party official, or an attorney or witness who was involved in a civil or criminal action or proceeding
(4) Because the public servant, party official, or attorney or witness discharged the duties of the public servant, party official, attorney, or witness
(5) Venue

Division (B):
(1) Purposely
(2) (a) By force
*(or)*
(b) By unlawful threat of harm to any person or property
(3) Retaliate against the victim of a crime
(4) Because the victim filed or prosecuted criminal charges
(5) Venue
*Penalty:* A felony of the third degree (2929.11-2929.18, 2929.31)

***PERJURY*, R.C. § 2921.11 [F3]**

(1) Knowingly
(2) (a) Make a false statement under oath or affirmation
*(or)*
(b) Swear or affirm the truth of a false statement previously made
(3) In an official proceeding
(4) When either statement is material to such proceeding
(5) Venue
*Penalty:* A felony of the third degree (2929.11-2929.18, 2929.31)
*Notes:* No conviction may be had under this section where proof of falsity rests solely upon contradictory testimony of one person, other than defendant. However, where contradictory statements relating to the same material fact are made by the offender under oath or affirmation and within the period of the statute of limitations for perjury, it is not necessary for the prosecution to prove which statement was false, but only that one or the other was false
A falsification is material, regardless of its admissibility in evidence, if it can affect the course or outcome of the

proceeding. It is no defense to a charge under this section that the offender mistakenly believed a falsification to be immaterial

**_TAMPERING WITH EVIDENCE,_ R.C. § 2921.12 [F3]**

(1) Knowing an official proceeding or investigation is in progress, or is about to be or is likely to be instituted
(2) (a) (i) Alter, destroy, conceal, or remove any record, document, or thing
(ii) With purpose to impair its value or availability as evidence in such proceeding or investigation
*(or)*
(b) (i) Make, present, or use any record, document or thing
(ii) Knowing it to be false
(iii) With purpose to mislead a public official who is or may be engaged in a proceeding or investigation or with a purpose to corrupt the outcome of any proceeding or investigation
(3) Venue
*Penalty:* A felony of the third degree (2929.11-2929.18, 2929.31)

**_FALSIFICATION; IN THEFT OFFENSE; TO PURCHASE FIREARM,_ R.C. § 2921.13 [M1, F5, F4, F3]**

Division (A):
(1) Knowingly
(a) Make a false statement
*(or)*
(b) Swear or affirm the truth of a previous false statement
(2) When such is:
(a) Made in official proceeding
*(or)*
(b) Made with purpose to incriminate another
*(or)*
(c) Made with purpose to mislead public official in performing his official function
*(or)*
(d) Made with a purpose to secure payment of unemployment compensation; Ohio Works First; prevention, retention, and contingency benefits and services; disability assistance; retirement benefits; economic development assistance as defined in § 9.66 of the Revised Code; or other benefits administered by governmental agency or paid out of public treasury
*(or)*
(e) Made with a purpose to secure issuance by governmental agency of license, permit, authorization, certificate, registration, release, or provider agreement
*(or)*
(f) Sworn or affirmed before notary public or other person empowered to administer oath
*(or)*
(g) In writing on or in connection with a report or return that is required or authorized by law
*(or)*
(h) In writing, and made with purpose to induce another to extend credit, employ offender; confer any degree, diploma, certificate of attainment, award of excellence, honor on offender; extend or bestow on offender any other valuable benefit or distinction when person to whom statement directed relies upon it to that person's detriment
*(or)*
(i) Made with purpose to commit or facilitate commission of theft offense
*(or)*
(j) Made to a probate court in connection with any action, proceeding, or other matter within its jurisdiction, either orally or in a written document, including but not limited to, an application, petition, complaint, or other pleading, or an inventory, account, or report
*(or)*
(k) Made on an account, record, stamp, or other writing that is required by law.
*(or)*
(l) Made in connection with the purchase of a firearm, as defined in R.C. § 2923.11, and in conjunction with the furnishing to the seller of the firearm of a fictitious or altered driver's or commercial driver's license or permit, a fictitious or altered identification card, or any other document that contains false information about the purchaser's identity
*(or)*
(m) Made in a document or instrument of writing that purports to be a judgment, lien, or claim of indebtedness and is filed or recorded with the secretary of state, a county recorder, or the clerk of a court of record
*(or)*
(n) Made in an application filed with a county sheriff pursuant to R.C. § 2923.125 in order to obtain or renew a license to carry a concealed handgun
*(or)*
(o) Required under R.C. § 5743.71 in connection with the person's purchase of cigarettes or tobacco products in a delivery sale.
(3) Venue

Division (B):
(1) In connection with the purchase of a firearm
(2) Knowingly furnish to the seller of the firearm a fictitious or altered driver's or commercial driver's license or permit, a fictitious or altered identification card, or any other document that contains false information about the purchaser's identity
(3) Venue

Division (C):
(1) In an attempt to obtain a license to carry a concealed handgun under R.C. § 2923.125
(2) Shall knowingly present
(3) To a sheriff
  (a) A fictitious
  *(or)*
  (b) Altered document
(4) That purports to be certification of the person's competence in handling a handgun as described in division (B)(3) of R.C. § 2923.125
(5) Venue
Violation of (A)(2)(a)(b)(c)(d)(e)(f)(g)(h)(j)(k)(m)
*Penalty:* A misdemeanor of the first degree (2929.21-2929.31)
Violation of (A)(2)(i) (falsification in a theft offense)
*Penalty:* A misdemeanor of the first degree (2929.21-2929.31)
If the value of the property or services stolen is $1,000 or more and is less than $7,500
*Penalty:* A felony of the fifth degree (2929.11-2929.18, 2929.31)
If the value of the property or services stolen is $7,500 or more and less than $150,000
*Penalty:* A felony of the fourth degree (2929.11-2929.18, 2929.31)
If the value of the property or services stolen is $150,000 or more
*Penalty:* A felony of the third degree (2929.11-2929.18, 2929.31)
Violation of (A)(2)(l) or (B)
*Penalty:* A felony of the fifth degree (2929.11-2929.18, 2929.31)
Violation of (A)(2)(n) or (C) (Falsification to obtain a concealed handgun license)
*Penalty:* A felony of the fourth degree (2929.11-2929.18, 2929.31)

***FALSE REPORT OF CHILD ABUSE OR NEGLECT*, R.C. § 2921.14 [M1]**

(1) Knowingly
(2) (a) Make
  *(or)*
  (b) Cause another person to make
(3) A false report under R.C. § 2151.421(B) that any person has committed an act or omission that resulted in a child being
  (a) An abused child as defined in R.C. § 2151.031
  *(or)*
  (b) A neglected child as defined in R.C. § 2151.03
(4) Venue
*Penalty:* A misdemeanor of the first degree (2929.21-2929.31)

***FALSE ALLEGATION OF PEACE OFFICER MISCONDUCT*, R.C. § 2921.15 [M1)**

(1) Knowingly
(2) File
(3) A complaint against a peace officer [as defined in R.C. § 2935.01] that alleges misconduct in the performance of the officer's duties
(4) Knowing the allegation is false
*Penalty:* A misdemeanor of the first degree (2929.21-2929.31)

***COMPOUNDING A CRIME*, R.C. § 2921.21 [M1]**

(1) Knowingly
(2) Demand, accept, or agree to accept
(3) Anything of value
(4) In consideration for abandoning or agreeing to abandon a pending prosecution
(5) Venue
*Penalty:* A misdemeanor of the first degree (2929.21-2929.31)
*Note:* There is no violation if pending prosecution is for a violation of R.C. §§ 2913.02 (theft), 2913.11 (bad checks), 2913.21(B)(2) (credit cards), or 2913.47 (insurance fraud), the actor under this section is the victim, and the thing of value received did not exceed amount which actor reasonably believed due him as restitution for loss caused by offense

**_FAILURE TO REPORT A CRIME OR KNOWLEDGE OF A DEATH, OR BURN INJURY,_ R.C. § 2921.22 [M4, M2, MM]**

Division (A): **[M4]** Failure to report a crime (Felony)
(1) While having knowledge that a felony has been or is being committed
(2) Knowingly
(3) Fail to report
(4) To law enforcement authorities
(5) That a felony has been or is being committed
*Penalty:* A misdemeanor of the fourth degree (2929.21-2929.31)

Division (B): **[M2]** Failure to report a crime (Injury from offense of violence)
(1) While a physician, limited practitioner, nurse, or other person giving aid to a sick or injured person
(2) Negligently
(3) Fail to report
(4) To law enforcement authorities
(5) (a) Any gunshot wound treated or observed by the physician, limited practitioner, nurse, or person
*(or)*
(b) Any stab wound treated or observed by the physician, limited practitioner, nurse, or person
*(or)*
(c) Any serious physical harm to persons that the physician, limited practitioner, nurse, or person knows or has reasonable cause to believe resulted from an offense of violence
*Penalty:* A misdemeanor of the second degree (2929.21-2929.31)

Division (C): **[M4]** Failure to report knowledge of a death
(1) (a) Having discovered the body of a person
*(or)*
(b) Having acquired the first knowledge of the death of a person
(2) Fail to report the death immediately to
(3) (a) Any physician known to be treating the deceased for a condition from which death at such time would not be unexpected
*(or)*
(b) A law enforcement officer
*(or)*
(c) An ambulance service
*(or)*
(d) An emergency squad
*(or)*
(e) The coroner in a political subdivision in which the body is discovered, the death is believed to have occurred, or knowledge concerning the death is obtained
*Penalty:* A misdemeanor of the fourth degree (2929.21-2929.31)

Division (D): **[M4]** Failure to report knowledge of a death (Facts bearing on investigation of death)
(1) Fail to provide
(2) (a) Upon request of the person to whom a report under (C) above was made
*(or)*
(b) To any law enforcement officer who has reasonable cause to assert the authority to investigate the circumstances surrounding the death
(3) Any facts within the person's knowledge that may have a bearing on the facts of the death
*Penalty:* A misdemeanor of the fourth degree (2929.21-2929.31)

Division (E): **[M2, MM]** Failure to report a burn injury
(1) (a) While a physician, nurse, or limited practitioner outside a hospital, sanitarium, or other medical facility who attends or treats a person who has sustained a
*(or)*
(b) While a manager, superintendent, or other person in charge of a hospital, sanitarium, or other medical facility in which a person is attended or treated for any
(2) Burn injury
(3) (a) Inflicted by an explosion or other incendiary device
*(or)*
(b) That shows evidence of having been inflicted in a violent, malicious, or criminal manner
(4) (a) Fail to report the bum injury immediately to the local arson or fire and explosion investigation bureau if there is one in the jurisdiction in which the person is attended or treated or otherwise to local law enforcement authorities
*(or)*
(b) Fail to file within three working days after attending or treating the victim, a written report, on a form to be provided by the state fire marshal, with the state fire marshal
Negligent violation of (E)
*Penalty:* A minor misdemeanor (2929.21-2929.31)

Knowing violation of (E)
*Penalty:* A misdemeanor of the second degree (2929.21-2929.31)
*Note:* Division (A) or (D) does not apply in privileged relationships listed in R.C. § 2921.22(F); R.C. § 2921.22(G) disallows liability for breach of privilege in disclosures under R.C. § 2921.22.
*Definition:* "Burn injury" means any second or third degree burns, burns to the upper respiratory tract or laryngeal edema due to the inhalation of superheated air, or any burn injury or wound that may result in death, or any physical harm to persons caused by or as the result of the use of fireworks, novelties and trick noisemakers, and wire sparklers, as defined by R.C. § 3743.01. R.C. § 2921.22(E)

### *FAILURE TO AID LAW ENFORCEMENT OFFICER,* R.C. § 2921.23 [MM]

(1) When called upon to assist law enforcement officer in preventing/halting commission of offense, or in apprehension or detention of an offender
(2) Negligently fail or refuse to render aid
(3) When such aid can be given without substantial risk of physical harm to person called upon
(4) Venue
*Penalty:* A minor misdemeanor (2929.21-2929.31)

### *DISCLOSURE OF CONFIDENTIAL INFORMATION,* R.C. § 2921.24 [M4]

(1) Being an officer or employee
(2) (a) Of a law enforcement agency or court
*(or)*
(b) Of the office of the clerk of any court
(3) Disclose
(4) During the pendency of any criminal case
(5) The home address of any peace officer as defined in R.C. § 2935.01
(6) Who is a witness or arresting officer in the case
(7) Venue
*Penalty:* A misdemeanor of the fourth degree (2929.21-2929.31)
*Notes:* The court in which any criminal case is pending may order the disclosure of the home address of any peace officer in the case pursuant to a written request and for good cause shown. *See* R.C. § 2921.24(C)
This section does not prohibit a peace officer from disclosing his own address, and does not apply to any person who discloses such address pursuant to a court order. *See* R.C. § 2921.24(B)

### *FAILURE TO DISCLOSE ONE'S PERSONAL INFORMATION,* R.C. § 2921.29 [M4]

(1) In a public place
(2) Refuse to disclose
(3) (a) name
*(or)*
(b) address
*(or)*
(c) date of birth
(4) When requested by a law enforcement officer
(5) Who reasonably suspects
(a) the person is committing, has committed, or is about to commit a criminal offense
*(or)*
(b) The person witnessed any of the following:
(i) An offense of violence that would constitute a felony under the laws of this state
*(or)*
(ii) A felony offense that causes or results in, or creates a substantial risk of, serious physical harm to another person or to property
*(or)*
(iii) Any attempt or conspiracy to commit, or complicity in committing, any offense identified in division (A)(2)(a) or (b) of this section
*(or)*
(iv) Any conduct reasonably indicating that any offense identified in division (5)(b)(i) or (ii) of this section or any attempt, conspiracy, or complicity described in division (5)(b)(iii) of this section has been, is being, or is about to be committed
(6) Venue
*Penalty:* A misdemeanor of the fourth degree (2929.21-2929.31)

### *OBSTRUCTING OFFICIAL BUSINESS,* R.C. § 2921.31 [M2, F5]

(1) Perform any act that hampers/impedes a public official in the performance of the public official's lawful duties
(2) With a purpose to prevent, obstruct, or delay performance by a public official of the public official's authorized acts
(3) Without having a privilege to do so
(4) Venue

*Penalty:* A misdemeanor of the second degree (2929.21-2929.31)
If violation creates a risk of physical harm to any person
*Penalty:* A felony of the fifth degree (2929.11-2929.18, 2929.31)

**_OBSTRUCTING JUSTICE_, R.C. § 2921.32 [MM, M4, M3, M2, M1, F5, F3]**

(1) With a purpose
  (a) To hinder the discovery, apprehension, prosecution, conviction, or punishment of another for crime or to assist another to benefit from the commission of a crime
  *(or)*
  (b) To hinder the discovery, apprehension, prosecution, adjudication as a delinquent child, or disposition of a child for an act that if committed by an adult would be a crime or to assist a child to benefit from the commission of an act that if committed by an adult would be a crime
(2) (a) Harbor or conceal the other person or child
  *(or)*
  (b) Provide the other person or child with money, transportation, a weapon, disguise or other means of avoiding discovery or apprehension
  *(or)*
  (c) Warn the other person or child of impending discovery or apprehension
  *(or)*
  (d) Destroy or conceal physical evidence of a crime or act
  *(or)*
  (e) Induce anyone to withhold testimony or information, or elude legal process summoning the other person to testify or supply evidence
  *(or)*
  (f) Communicate false information to anyone
  *(or)*
  (g) Prevent or obstruct any person, by means of force, intimidation, or deception, from performing any act to aid in the discovery, apprehension, or prosecution of the other person or child
(3) Venue

If the crime committed by the person aided is a misdemeanor or if the act committed by the child aided would be a misdemeanor if committed by an adult, a misdemeanor of the same degree as the crime committed by the person aided or a misdemeanor of the same degree that the act committed by the child aided would be if committed by an adult **[MM, M4, M3, M2, M1]**
If the crime committed by the person aided is a felony or if the act committed by the child aided would be a felony if committed by an adult
*Penalty:* A felony of the fifth degree (2929.11-2929.18, 2929.31)
If the crime committed by the person aided is aggravated murder, murder, or a felony of the first or second degree or if the act committed by the child aided would be one of those offenses if committed by an adult and if the offender knows or has reason to believe that the crime committed by the person aided is one of those offenses or that the act committed by the child aided would be one of those offenses if committed by an adult
*Penalty:* A felony of the third degree (2929.11-2929.18, 2929.31)
A person may be prosecuted for, and may be convicted of or adjudicated a delinquent child for committing, a violation of this section regardless of whether the person or child aided ultimately is apprehended for, is charged with, is convicted of, pleads guilty to, or is adjudicated a delinquent child for committing the crime or act the person or child aided committed. The crime or act the person or child aided committed shall be used in determining the penalty for the violation of this section, regardless of whether the person or child aided ultimately is apprehended for, is charged with, is convicted of, pleads guilty to, or is adjudicated a delinquent child for committing the crime or act the person or child aided committed
If the crime or act committed by the person or child aided is an act of terrorism
*Penalty:* A felony of the second degree (2929.11-2929.18, 2929.31)
If the act of terrorism resulted in the death of a person who was not a participant in the act of terrorism
*Penalty:* A felony of the first degree (2929.11-2929.18, 2929.31)

**_ASSAULTING OR HARASSING A POLICE DOG OR HORSE OR SERVICE DOG_, R.C. § 2921.321 [M2, M1, F4, F3]**

Division (A):
(1) Knowingly
(2) Cause or attempt to cause
(3) Physical harm
(4) To a police dog or horse
(5) In either of the following circumstances:
  (i) the police dog or horse is assisting a law enforcement officer in the performance of the officer's official duties at the time the physical harm is caused or attempted
  *(or)*
  (ii) the police dog or horse is not assisting a law enforcement officer in the performance of the officer's official duties at the time the physical harm is caused or attempted, but the offender has actual knowledge that the dog or horse is a police dog or horse

(6) Venue

Division (B):
(1) Recklessly
(2) Taunt, torment, or strike a police dog or horse
*(or)*
(3) Throw an object or substance at a police dog or horse
*(or)*
(4) Interfere with or obstruct a police dog or horse or interfere with or obstruct a law enforcement officer who is being assisted by a police dog or horse in a manner that does any of the following:
(i) inhibits or restricts the law enforcement officer's control of the police dog or horse;
(ii) deprives the law enforcement officer of control of the police dog or horse;
(iii) releases the police dog or horse from its area of control;
(iv) enters the area of control of the police dog or horse without consent of the law enforcement officer, including placing food or any other object or substance into that area
(v) inhibits or restricts the ability of the police dog or horse to assist a law enforcement officer
*(or)*
(5) Engage in any conduct that is likely to cause serious physical injury or death to a police dog or horse
*(or)*
(6) If the person is the owner, keeper, or harborer of a dog, fail to reasonably restrain the dog from taunting, tormenting, chasing, approaching in a menacing fashion or apparent attitude of attack, or attempting to bite or otherwise endanger a police dog or horse that at the time of the conduct is assisting a law enforcement officer in the performance of the officer's duties or that the person knows is a police dog or horse
(7) Venue

Division (C):
(1) Knowingly
(2) Cause or attempt to cause
(3) Physical harm
(4) To a service dog
(5) In either of the following circumstances:
(i) the service dog is assisting or serving a blind, deaf, or mobility impaired person or person with a seizure disorder at the time the physical harm is attempted or caused
*(or)*
(ii) the service dog is not assisting a blind, deaf, or mobility impaired person or person with seizure disorder at the time the physical harm is caused or attempted, but the offender has actual knowledge that the dog is a service dog
(6) Venue

Division (D):
(1) Recklessly do any of the following:
(2) Taunt, torment, or strike a service dog
*(or)*
(3) Throw an object or substance at a service dog
*(or)*
(4) Interfere with or obstruct a service dog, or interfere with or obstruct a blind, deaf, or mobility impaired person or person with a seizure disorder who is being assisted or served by a service dog, in a manner that does any of the following:
(i) inhibits or restricts the assisted or served person's control of the service dog;
(ii) deprives the assisted or served person of control of the service dog;
(iii) releases the service dog from its area of control;
(iv) enters the area of control of the service dog without the consent of the assisted or served person, including placing food or any other object or substance into that area;
(v) inhibits or restricts the ability of the service dog to assist the assisted or served person.
*(or)*
(5) Engage in any conduct that is likely to cause serious physical injury or death to a service dog;
*(or)*
(6) If the person is the owner, keeper, or harborer of a dog, fail to reasonably restrain the dog from taunting, tormenting, chasing, approaching in a menacing fashion or apparent attitude of attack, or attempting to bite or otherwise endanger a service dog that at the time of the conduct is assisting or serving a blind, deaf, or mobility impaired person or person with a seizure disorder or that the person knows is a service dog.
(7) Venue

*Penalty:*

Division (A):
A misdemeanor of the second degree (2929.21-2929.31). If the violation results in the death of the police dog or horse, assaulting a police dog or horse is a felony of the third degree (2929.11-2929.18, 2929.31). If the violation results in serious physical harm to the police dog or horse other than its death, assaulting a police dog or horse is a felony of the

fourth degree (2929.11-2929.18, 2929.31). If the violation results in physical harm to the police dog or horse other than death or serious physical harm, assaulting a police dog or horse is a misdemeanor of the first degree (2929.21-2929.31)

Division (B):
A misdemeanor of the second degree (2929.21-2929.31). If the violation results in the death of the police dog or horse, harassing a police dog or horse is a felony of the third degree (2929.11-2929.18, 2929.31). If the violation results in serious physical harm to the police dog or horse but does not result in its death, harassing a police dog or horse is a felony of the fourth degree (2929.11-2929.18, 2929.31). If the violation results in physical harm to the police dog or horse but does not result in its death or in serious physical harm to it, harassing a police dog or horse is a misdemeanor of the first degree (2929.21-2929.31)

Division (C):
A misdemeanor of the second degree (2929.21-2929.31). If the violation results in the death of the service dog, assaulting a service dog is a felony of the third degree (2929.11-2929.18, 2929.31). If the violation results in serious physical harm to the service dog other than its death, assaulting a service dog is a felony of the fourth degree (2929.11-2929.18, 2929.31). If the violation results in physical harm to the service dog other than death or serious physical harm, assaulting a service dog is a misdemeanor of the first degree (2929.21-2929.31)

Division (D):
A misdemeanor of the second degree (2929.21-2929.31). If the violation results in the death of the service dog, harassing a service dog is a felony of the third degree (2929.11-2929.18, 2929.31). If the violation results in serious physical harm to the service dog but does not result in its death, harassing a service dog is a felony of the fourth degree (2929.11-2929.18, 2929.31). If the violation results in physical harm to the service dog but does not result in its death or in serious physical harm to it, harassing a service dog is a misdemeanor of the first degree (2929.21-2929.31)

*Note:* In addition to any other sanction or penalty imposed for the offense under this section, Chapter 2929., or any other provision of the Revised Code, whoever violates division (A), (B), (C), or (D) of this section is responsible for the payment of all of the following:
- (a) Any veterinary bill or bill for medication incurred as a result of the violation by the police department regarding a violation of division (A) or (B) of this section or by the blind, deaf, or mobility impaired person or person with a seizure disorder assisted or served by the service dog regarding a violation of division (C) or (D) of this section;
- (b) The cost of any damaged equipment that results from the violation;
- (c) If the violation did not result in the death of the police dog or horse or the service dog that was the subject of the violation and if, as a result of that dog or horse being the subject of the violation, the dog or horse needs further training or retraining to be able to continue in the capacity of a police dog or horse or a service dog, the cost of any further training or retraining of that dog or horse by a law enforcement officer or by the blind, deaf, or mobility impaired person or person with a seizure disorder assisted or served by the service dog;
- (d) If the violation resulted in the death of the police dog or horse or the service dog that was the subject of the violation or resulted in serious physical harm to that dog or horse to the extent that the dog or horse needs to be replaced on either a temporary or a permanent basis, the cost of replacing that dog or horse and of any further training of a new police dog or horse or a new service dog by a law enforcement officer or by the blind, deaf, or mobility impaired person or person with a seizure disorder assisted or served by the service dog, which replacement or training is required because of the death of or the serious physical harm to the dog or horse that was the subject of the violation

***RESISTING ARREST*, R.C. § 2921.33 [M2, M1, F4]**

Division (A): **[M2]**
(1) Recklessly or by means of force
(2) Resist/interfere with lawful arrest
(3) Of the person or another
(4) Venue
*Penalty:* A misdemeanor of the second degree (2929.21-2929.31)

Division (B): **[M1]**
(1) Recklessly or by means of force
(2) Resist/interfere with a lawful arrest
(3) During the course of or as a result of the resistance or interference, cause physical harm to a law enforcement officer
(4) Venue
*Penalty:* A misdemeanor of the first degree (2929.21-2929.31)

Division (C): **[F4]**
(1) Recklessly or by means of force
(2) Resist/interfere with a lawful arrest if
- (a) the offender, during the course of or as a result of the resistance or interference, recklessly causes physical harm to a law enforcement officer by means of a deadly weapon
  *(or)*

(b) the offender, during the course of the resistance or interference, brandishes a deadly weapon
(3) Venue
*Penalty:* A felony of the fourth degree (2929.11-2929.18, 2929.31)

***FAILURE TO COMPLY WITH ORDER OR SIGNAL OF POLICE OFFICER,* R.C. § 2921.331 [M1, F4, F3]**

Division (A): **[M1]**
(1) Fail to comply
(2) With any lawful order or direction
(3) Of any police officer invested with authority to direct, control, or regulate traffic
(4) Venue
*Penalty:* A misdemeanor of the first degree (2929.21-2929.31)

Division (B): **[M1, F4, F3]**
(1) Operate a motor vehicle
(2) So as willfully to elude or flee
(3) A police officer
(4) After receiving a visible or audible signal
(5) From a police officer
(6) To bring the person's motor vehicle to a stop
(7) Venue
*Penalty:* A misdemeanor of the first degree (2929.21-2929.31)
If the trier of fact finds beyond a reasonable doubt that the offense (a violation of Division (B)) was committed while the offender was fleeing immediately after committing a felony
*Penalty:* A felony of the fourth degree (2929.11-2929.18, 2929.31)
If the trier of fact finds beyond a reasonable doubt that in violating Division (B), (1) the operation of the motor vehicle by the offender was a proximate cause of serious physical harm to persons or property or (2) the operation of the motor vehicle by the offender caused a substantial risk of serious physical harm to persons or property
*Penalty:* A felony of the third degree (2929.11-2929.18, 2929.31)
*Note:* The court may impose a class one or class two suspension in addition to any other penalty
*Definitions:* "Police officer," R.C. §§ 2921.331(D), 4511.01

***ESCAPE,* R.C. § 2921.34 [M1, F5, F3, F2]**

Division (A)(1):
(1) Knowing oneself to be under detention or being reckless in that regard
(2) (a) Purposely break or attempt to break that detention
*(or)*
(b) Purposely fail to return to detention, either following a temporary leave granted for a specific purpose or limited period, or at the time required when serving a sentence in intermittent confinement
(3) Venue

Division (A)(2):
(1) No person who is adjudicated a sexually violent predator and is sentenced to a prison term pursuant to division (A)(3) or (B) of section 2971.03 of the Revised Code for the sexually violent offense whose sentence has been modified and is restricted to a geographic area
(2) Knowing that the person is under a geographic restriction or being reckless in that regard
(3) (a) Purposely leave the geographic area to which the restriction applies
*(or)*
(b) Purposely fail to return to that geographic area following a temporary leave granted for a specific purpose or for a specific period of time
(4) Venue

Division (A)(3):
(1) No person, knowing the person is under supervised release detention or being reckless in that regard,
(2) Shall purposely break or attempt to break the supervised release detention or purposely fail to return to the supervised release detention,
(3) Either following temporary leave granted for a specific purpose or limited period, or at the time required when serving a sentence in intermittent confinement.

If the offender, at the time of the commission of the offense, was under detention as an alleged or adjudicated delinquent or unruly child, if the act for which the offender was under detention would not be a felony if committed by an adult
*Penalty:* A misdemeanor of the first degree (2929.21-2929.31)
If the offender, at the time of the commission of the offense, was under detention in any other manner or was a sexually violent predator for whom the requirement that the entire prison term imposed pursuant to R.C. § 2971.03(A)(3) or (B) be served in a state correctional institution has been modified pursuant to R.C. § 2971.05, when the most serious offense for which the offender was under detention or adjudicated a sexually violent predator is aggravated murder, murder, or a felony of the first or second degree or, if the person was under detention as an alleged or adjudicated delinquent child, when the most serious act for which the person was under detention would be aggravated murder, murder, or a felony of the first or second degree if committed by an adult

*Penalty:* A felony of the second degree (2929.11-2929.18, 2929.31)
If the offender, at the time of the commission of the offense, was under detention in any other manner or was a sexually violent predator for whom the requirement that the entire prison term imposed pursuant to R.C. § 2971.03(A)(3) or (B) be served in a state correctional institution has been modified pursuant to R.C. § 2971.05, or the offender is a person who was convicted or pleaded guilty to committing a violation of R.C. § 2907.02(A)(1)(b) for whom the requirement that the entire prison term imposed upon the person pursuant to R.C. 2971.03(B)(1)(a), (b), or (c) be served in a state correctional institution has been modified pursuant to R.C. § 2971.05, or the offender is a person who was convicted of or pleaded guilty to committing attempted rape, who also was convicted of or pleaded guilty to a specification of the type described in R.C. § 2941.1418, § 2941.1419, or § 2941.1420, who was sentenced pursuant to R.C. § 2971.03(B)(2)(a), (b), or (c) and for whom the requirement that the entire prison term imposed pursuant to that division be served in a state correctional institution has been modified pursuant to R.C. § 2971.05, when the most serious offense for which the offender was under detention or sentenced to a prison term under R.C. § 2971.03(A)(3), (B)(1)(a), (b), or (c) or (B)(2)(a), (b), or (c) is aggravated murder, murder, or a felony of the first or second degree or, if the person was under detention as an alleged or adjudicated delinquent child, when the most serious act for which the person was under detention
*Penalty:* A felony of the third degree (2929.11-2929.18, 2929.31)
If the offender, at the time of the commission of the offense, was under detention in any other manner or was a sexually violent predator for whom the requirement that the entire prison term imposed pursuant to R.C. § 2971.03(A)(3) or (B) be served in a state correctional institution has been modified pursuant to R.C. § 2971.05, or the offender is a person who was convicted or pleaded guilty to committing a violation of R.C. § 2907.02(A)(1)(b) for whom the requirement that the entire prison term imposed upon the person pursuant to R.C. 2971.03(B)(1)(a), (b), or (c) be served in a state correctional institution has been modified pursuant to R.C. § 2971.05, or the offender is a person who was convicted of or pleaded guilty to committing attempted rape, who also was convicted of or pleaded guilty to a specification of the type described in R.C. § 2941.1418, § 2941.1419, or § 2941.1420, who was sentenced pursuant to R.C. § 2971.03(B)(2)(a), (b), or (c) and for whom the requirement that the entire prison term imposed pursuant to that division be served in a state correctional institution has been modified pursuant to R.C. § 2971.05, when the most serious offense for which the offender was under detention or sentenced to a prison term under R.C. § 2971.03(A)(3), (B)(1)(a), (b), or (c) or (B)(2)(a), (b), or (c) is a felony of the third, fourth, or fifth degree or an unclassified felony or, if the person was under detention as an alleged or adjudicated delinquent child, when the most serious act for which the person was under detention would be a third, fourth, or fifth degree or an unclassified felony if committed by an adult
*Penalty:* A felony of the fifth degree (2929.11-2929.18, 2929.31)
If the offender at the time of the commission of the offense, was under detention in any other manner, when the person was found not guilty by reason of insanity and the person's detention consisted of hospitalization, institutionalization, or confinement in a facility under an order made pursuant to R.C. § 2945.40, 2945.401, or 2945.402
*Penalty:* A felony of the fifth degree (2929.11-2929.18, 2929.31)
If the offender at the time of the commission of the offense, was under detention in any other manner, when the most serious offense for which the offender was under detention is a misdemeanor and when the person fails to return to the detention at a specified time following temporary leave granted for a specific purpose or limited period or at the time required when serving a sentence in intermittent confinement
*Penalty:* A misdemeanor of the first degree (2929.21-2929.31)
*Penalty:* A felony of the fifth degree. If at the time of the commission of the offense, the most serious offense for which the offender was under supervised release detention was aggravated murder, murder, any other offense for which a sentence of life imprisonment was imposed, or a felony of the first or second degree, a felony of the fourth degree
*Definitions:* "Detention," "detention facility," R.C. § 2921.01

### *AIDING ESCAPE OR RESISTANCE TO AUTHORITY,* R.C. § 2921.35 [F4]

Division (A):
(1) With a purpose to promote or facilitate an escape or resistance to lawful authority
(2) (a) Convey into a detention facility
*(or)*
(b) Provide to anyone confined therein instruments or things which may be used to escape or resist authority
(3) Venue

Division (B):
(1) Being confined in a detention facility
(2) Make, procure, conceal, unlawfully possess or give to another inmate
(3) Any instrument or thing which may be used for such purposes
(4) With a purpose to promote or facilitate escape or resistance to lawful authority
(5) Venue
*Penalty:* A felony of the fourth degree (2929.11-2929.18, 2929.31)

### *ILLEGAL CONVEYANCE OF WEAPONS OR PROHIBITED ITEMS ONTO DETENTION FACILITY OR INSTITUTION,* R.C. § 2921.36 [F3, F4, F5, M1, M2]

(1) Knowingly

(a) Convey or attempt to convey onto the grounds of
*(or)*
(b) Deliver or attempt to deliver to any person who is confined in
(2) (a) A detention facility
*(or)*
(b) An institution under the control of the Department of Mental Health or the Department of Developmental Disabilities
(3) (a) Any deadly weapon or dangerous ordnance as defined in R.C. § 2923.11
*(or)*
(b) Any part of or ammunition for use in such deadly weapon or dangerous ordnance
*(or)*
(4) Any drug of abuse as defined in R.C. § 3719.011
*(or)*
(5) Any intoxicating liquor as defined in R.C. § 4301.01
*(or)*
(6) Cash
*(or)*
(7) A cellular telephone, two-way radio, or other electronic communications device
(8) Venue

***CASH*** **[F5, M1]**

If offender has not been previously convicted under division (D) of this section
*Penalty:* A misdemeanor of the first degree (2929.21-2929.31)
If offender has previously been convicted under division (D) of this section
*Penalty:* A felony of the fifth degree (2929.11-2929.18, 2929.31)

***DEADLY WEAPON/DANGEROUS ORDNANCE*** **[F4]**

*Penalty:* A felony of the fourth degree (2929.11-2929.18, 2929.31)
If the offender is an officer or employee of the Department of Rehabilitation and Correction or of the Department of Youth Services, the court shall impose a mandatory prison term

***DRUG OF ABUSE*** **[F3]**

*Penalty:* A felony of the third degree (2929.11-2929.18, 2929.31)
If the offender is an officer or employee of the Department of Rehabilitation and Correction or of the Department of Youth Services, the court shall impose a mandatory prison term

***INTOXICATING LIQUOR*** **[M2]**

*Penalty:* A misdemeanor of the second degree (2929.21-2929.31)

***ELECTRONIC COMMUNICATIONS DEVICE*** **[M1, F5]**

*Penalty:* A misdemeanor of the first degree. If the offender previously has been convicted under this subsection, a felony of the fifth degree (2929.21-2929.31)
*Notes:* For exceptions to (1)(a), above, when person has written authorization, *see* R.C. § 2921.36(B)
For affirmative defenses to charge involving (1)(b), above, *see* R.C. § 2921.36(D). *See also* R.C. § 2921.37, for arrest powers of person in charge of detention facility re violation of R.C. § 2921.36
*Definitions:* "Deadly weapon," "dangerous ordnance," R.C. § 2923.11
"Drug abuse," R.C. § 3719.011
"Intoxicating liquor," R.C. § 4301.01
"Institution under the control of the department of mental health and mental retardation," R.C § 5123.11

***HARASSMENT WITH BODILY SUBSTANCE,*** **R.C. § 2921.38 [F5, F3]**

Division (A): **[F5]**
(1) Being a person confined in a detention facility
(2) Cause or attempt to cause another person to come into contact with blood, semen, urine, feces, or another bodily substance
(a) by throwing the bodily substance at the other person
*(or)*
(b) by expelling the bodily substance upon the other person
*(or)*
(c) in any other manner
(3) With intent to harass, annoy, threaten, or alarm the other person
(4) Venue
*Penalty:* A felony of the fifth degree (2929.11-2929.18, 2929.31)

Division (B): **[F5]**

(1) Cause or attempt to cause a law enforcement officer to come into contact with blood, semen, urine, feces, or another bodily substance
  (a) by throwing the bodily substance at the law enforcement officer
    *(or)*
  (b) by expelling the bodily substance upon the law enforcement officer
    *(or)*
  (c) in any other manner
(3) With intent to harass, annoy, threaten, or alarm the law enforcement officer.
(4) Venue.
*Penalty:* Felony of the fifth degree. (2929.11-2929.18, 2929.31)

Division (C): **[F3]**
(1) With knowledge that the person is
  (a) a carrier of the virus that causes AIDS
    *(or)*
  (b) a carrier of a hepatitis virus
    *(or)*
  (c) infected with tuberculosis
(2) Cause or attempt to cause another person to come into contact with blood, semen, urine, feces, or another bodily substance
  (a) by throwing the bodily substance at the other person
    *(or)*
  (b) by expelling the bodily substance upon the other person
    *(or)*
  (c) in any other manner
(3) With intent to harass, annoy, threaten, or alarm the other person
(4) Venue
*Penalty:* A felony of the third degree (2929.11-2929.18, 2929.31)
*Notes:* This section does not apply to a person who is hospitalized, institutionalized, or confined in a facility operated by the Department of Mental Health or the Department of Developmental Disabilities

### *THEFT IN OFFICE*, R.C. § 2921.41 [F5, F4, F3]

(1) Being a public official/party official
(2) Commit a theft offense:
  (a) Using the offender's office or permitting its use or assenting to its use in aid of such offense
    *(or)*
  (b) Involving property or service owned by this or any state, the United States, a county, municipal corporation, or township, or any political subdivision, department, or agency thereof or by a political party, or which is part of a political campaign fund
(3) Venue
*Penalty:* A felony of the fifth degree (2929.11-2929.18, 2929.31)
If the value of the property or services stolen is $1,000 or more and is less than $7,500
*Penalty:* A felony of the fourth degree (2929.11-2929.18, 2929.31)
If the value of the property or services stolen is $7,500 or more
*Penalty:* A felony of the third degree (2929.11-2929.18, 2929.31)
*Note:* A person convicted or pleading guilty hereunder is forever barred from office of public trust. In addition to any imprisonment or fine, the court shall require restitution [R.C. § 2921.41(C)(2)]. State retirement and deferred compensation benefits may be withheld to effect restitution, and the prosecutor must notify the retirement and deferred compensation systems of the filing of charges

### *HAVING UNLAWFUL INTEREST IN A PUBLIC CONTRACT*, R.C. § 2921.42 [F4, M1]

Division (A): **[F4]**
(1) Being a public official
(2) Knowingly authorize or employ the authority or influence of his office
  (a) To secure authorization of a public contract in which he, his family, or business associate has an interest
    *(or)*
  (b) To secure the investment of public funds in any share, bond, mortgage or other security which such public official, his family member or business associate has an interest, or is an underwriter, or receives any brokerage, origination or servicing fees
(3) Venue
*Penalty:* A felony of the fourth degree (2929.11-2929.18, 2929.31)

Division (B): **[M1]**
(1) (a) Being or having been a public official, during his term or within one year thereafter occupy a position of profit in the prosecution of a public contract authorized by him or by a legislative body, commission or board of which he was a member at the time of authorization, and which was not let by competitive bidding, or if let by competitive bidding, in which his is not the lowest and best bid
    *(or)*

(b) Have an interest in profits or benefits of a public contract:
(i) Entered into by, or for the use of a political subdivision/governmental agency/instrumentality with which he is connected
*(or)*
(ii) Involving more than $150, not let by competitive bidding when so required by law
(2) Venue
*Penalty:* A misdemeanor of the first degree (2929.21-2929.31)
*Notes:* Defenses to this violation are set forth in R.C. § 2921.42(B) and (C)
It is not a violation of this section for a prosecuting attorney to appoint assistants and employees in accordance with R.C. § 309.06 or for a chief legal officer of a municipal corporation or an official designated as prosecutor in a municipal corporation to appoint assistants and employees in accordance with R.C. § 733.621
*Definitions:* "Public contract," "chief legal officer," R.C. § 2921.42

## *SOLICITING OR RECEIVING IMPROPER COMPENSATION*, R.C. § 2921.43 [M1]

Division (A):
(1) (a) Knowingly promise or give to a public servant
*(or)*
(b) Being a public servant, knowingly solicit or accept
(2) (a) Any compensation other than as allowed by law
(i) To perform the public servant's official duties
*(or)*
(ii) To perform any other act in the public servant's public capacity
*(or)*
(iii) For the general performance of the duties of the public servant's public office or public employment
*(or)*
(iv) As a supplement to the public servant's public compensation
*(or)*
(b) Additional or greater fees or costs than allowed by law to perform the public servant's official duties
(3) Venue

Division (B):
(1) (a) For one's own personal or business use (whether a public servant or not)
*(or)*
(b) For the personal or business use of a public servant or party official
(2) Solicit or accept anything of value in consideration of:
(a) Appointing/securing/maintaining/renewing the appointment of anyone to public office, employment or agency
*(or)*
(b) Preferring/maintaining the status of any public employee with respect to compensation, duties, placement, location, promotion or other material aspects of employment
(3) Venue

Division (C):
(1) Coerce a contribution
(2) For the benefit of a political party, campaign committee, legislative campaign fund, political action committee, or political contributing entity
(3) In consideration of:
(a) Appointing/securing/maintaining/renewing the appointment of anyone to public office, employment, or agency
*(or)*
(b) Preferring/maintaining the status of any public employee with respect to compensation, duties, placement, location, promotion or other material aspects of employment
(4) Venue
*Penalty:* A misdemeanor of the first degree (2929.21-2929.31)
*Note:* A public servant convicted hereunder is barred from public office, employment, or position of trust for 7 years
*Definitions:* R.C. § 2921.01

## *DERELICTION OF DUTY*, R.C. § 2921.44 [M2]

Division (A):
(1) Being a law enforcement officer
(2) Negligently fail
(3) (a) To serve a warrant without delay
*(or)*
(b) To prevent/halt the commission of an offense, or to apprehend an offender, when it is in the law enforcement officer's power to do so alone or with available assistance
(4) Venue

Division (B):
(1) Being a law enforcement, ministerial or judicial officer
(2) Negligently fail
(3) To perform one's duty in a criminal proceeding
(4) Venue

Division (C):
(1) Being an officer in charge of a detention facility
(2) Negligently
(3) (a) Allow the facility to become littered or unsanitary
*(or)*
(b) Fail to provide prisoners with adequate food, clothing, bedding, shelter or medical attention
*(or)*
(c) Fail to control an unruly prisoner or prevent intimidation of or physical harm to a prisoner
*(or)*
(d) Allow a prisoner to escape
*(or)*
(e) Fail to observe all lawful and reasonable regulations for the management of the facility
(4) Venue

Division (D):
(1) Being a public official of the state
(2) Recklessly
(3) (a) Create a deficiency
*(or)*
(b) Incur a liability
*(or)*
(c) Expend a greater sum than appropriated by general assembly for one year's use by the department, agency or institution with which the public official is connected
(4) Venue

Division (E):
(1) Being a public servant
(2) Recklessly
(3) (a) Fail to perform a duty imposed by law
*(or)*
(b) Do any act forbidden by law with respect to the public servant's office
(4) Venue
*Penalty:* A misdemeanor of the second degree (2929.21-2929.31)

***INTERFERING WITH CIVIL RIGHTS*, R.C. § 2921.45 [M1]**

(1) Being a public servant
(2) Under color of one's office, employment or authority
(3) Knowingly
(4) Deprive, or conspire or attempt to deprive another
(5) Of a constitutional or statutory right
(6) Venue
*Penalty:* A misdemeanor of the first degree (2929.21-2929.31)

***IMPERSONATING PEACE OFFICER OR PRIVATE POLICEMAN*, R.C. § 2921.51 [M4, M1, F4, F3]**

Division (B): **[M4]**
(1) Impersonate
(2) (a) Peace officer
*(or)*
(b) Private police officer or a federal law enforcement officer
(3) Venue
*Penalty:* A misdemeanor of the fourth degree (2929.21-2929.31)

Division (C): **[M1]**
(1) By impersonation of
(2) (a) Peace officer
*(or)*
(b) Private police officer or a federal law enforcement officer
(3) (a) Arrest or detain any person
*(or)*
(b) Search any person
*(or)*
(c) Search the property of any person

(4) Venue
*Penalty:* A misdemeanor of the first degree (2929.21-2929.31)

Division (D): **[M1, F4]**
(1) Impersonate
(2) (a) Peace officer
*(or)*
(b) Private police officer or a federal law enforcement officer
*(or)*
(c) An officer, agent or employee of the state
(3) With purpose to facilitate the commission of an offense
(4) Venue
*Penalty:* A misdemeanor of the first degree (2929.21-2929.31)
If the purpose of violation of Division (D) is to commit or facilitate the commission of a felony
*Penalty:* A felony of the fourth degree (2929.11-2929.18, 2929.31)

Division (E): **[F3]**
(1) While impersonating
(2) (a) Peace officer
*(or)*
(b) Private police officer or a federal law enforcement officer
*(or)*
(c) An officer, agent or employee of the state
(3) Commit a felony
(4) Venue
*Penalty:* A felony of the third degree (2929.11-2929.18, 2929.31)
*Note:* It is an affirmative defense to a charge under Division (B) that the impersonation of the peace officer was for a lawful purpose
*Definitions:* "Peace officer," "private police officer," "impersonate," R.C. § 2921.51(A)

***USING SHAM LEGAL PROCESS*, R.C. § 2921.52 [M4, M1, F4, F3]**

(1) Knowingly
(2) (a) Issue, display, deliver, distribute, or otherwise use sham legal process
*(or)*
(b) Use sham legal process to arrest, detain, search, or seize any person or the property of another
*(or)*
(c) Commit or facilitate the commission of an offense, using sham legal process
*(or)*
(d) Commit a felony by using sham legal process
(3) Venue

Division (2)(a) **[M4]**
*Penalty:* A misdemeanor of the fourth degree (2929.21-2929.31)

Division (2)(b) or (c) **[M1, F4]**
*Penalty:* A misdemeanor of the first degree (2929.21-2929.31)
If the purpose of the violation of Division (2)(c) is to commit or facilitate the commission of a felony
*Penalty:* A felony of the fourth degree (2929.11-2929.18, 2929.31)

Division (2)(d) **[F3]**
*Penalty:* A felony of the third degree (2929.11-2929.18, 2929.31)

---

## WEAPONS/ORDNANCE/CONSPIRACY/ATTEMPT

***CONSPIRACY*, R.C. § 2923.01 [F1, M1)**

(1) With purpose
(2) To commit, promote or facilitate the commission of (a) aggravated murder or murder, (b) kidnapping, (c) abduction, (d) compelling or promoting prostitution, (e) trafficking in persons, (f) aggravated burglary, burglary, or trespass in a habitation when a person is present or likely to be present, or (g) aggravated robbery or robbery, (h) aggravated burglary or burglary, or (i) engaging in a pattern of corrupt activity, or (j) corrupting another with drugs, a felony drug trafficking, manufacturing, processing, or possession offense, theft of drugs, or illegal possessing of drug documents, or (k) felony offense of unauthorized use of vehicle or (l) violation of R.C. Chapter 3734, relating to hazardous wastes, other than R.C. § 3734.18
(3) (a) Plan or aid in planning with another person or persons the commission of any of the specified offenses
*(or)*

(b) Agree with another person or persons that one or more will engage in conduct which facilitates commission of any of the specified offenses

(4) The offender, or one of his co-conspirators

(a) Subsequent to the offender's entrance into the conspiracy

(b) Does an overt act

(c) Which is in furtherance of the conspiracy, and is of a character that manifests a purpose on the part of the actor that the object of the conspiracy be completed

(5) Venue

If principal offense is aggravated murder, murder, or an offense for which the maximum penalty is imprisonment for life

*Penalty:* A felony of the first degree (2929.11-2929.18, 2929.31)

If element 2(g) applies

*Penalty:* Above, plus fine of 3 times gross value gained/loss caused, court costs, costs of investigation/prosecution, criminal forfeiture of real and personal property. *See* R.C. § 2923.32

A conspiracy to commit a first, second, third, or fourth degree felony is a felony of the next lesser degree

A conspiracy relating to hazardous waste provisions is a felony punishable by a fine of not more than $25,000 or imprisonment for not more than 18 months, or both

A conspiracy to commit a fifth degree felony

*Penalty:* A misdemeanor of the first degree (2929.21-2929.31)

*Notes:* When the offender knows or has reasonable cause to believe that a person with whom he conspires has also conspired or is conspiring with another to commit the same offense, then the offender is guilty of conspiracy with such other person, even though his identity may be unknown to the offender

It is no defense to a charge of conspiracy that, in retrospect, commission of the offense which was the object of the conspiracy was impossible under the circumstances

A conspiracy terminates when the offense or offenses which are its objects are committed, or when it is abandoned by all conspirators. In the absence of abandonment, it is no defense to a charge of conspiracy that no offense which was the object of the conspiracy was committed

A person who conspires to commit more than one offense is guilty of only one conspiracy, when such offenses are the object of the same agreement or continuous conspiratorial relationship

When a person is convicted of committing or attempting to commit a specific offense or a complicity in the commission of or attempt to commit such offense, he shall not be convicted of conspiracy involving the same offense

The testimony of a co-conspirator alone is not enough to convict of conspiracy, unless the conspiracy results in an attempt to commit an offense or in the commission of an offense

Affirmative defenses, *see* R.C. § 2923.01(I)

**_ATTEMPT_, R.C. § 2923.02 [F1, F2, F3, F4, F5, M1, M4]**

(1) Purposely or knowingly (when purpose or knowledge is sufficient culpability)

(2) Engage in conduct that, if successful, would result in an offense

(3) Venue

Where offense attempted is aggravated murder, murder, or an offense for which the maximum penalty is imprisonment for life

*Penalty:* Attempted rape when the offender also is convicted of or pleads guilty to a specification of the type described in R.C. § 2941.1418, § 2941.1419, or § 2941.1420, is punishable by a prison term or term of life imprisonment pursuant to R.C. § 2971.03

*Penalty:* A felony of the first degree (2929.11-2929.18, 2929.31)

An attempt to commit a drug abuse offense for which the penalty is determined by the amount or number of unit doses of the controlled substance involved in the drug abuse offense is an offense of the same degree as the drug abuse offense attempted would be if that drug abuse offense had been committed and had involved an amount or number of unit doses of the controlled substance that is within the next lower range of controlled substance amounts than was involved in the attempt

An attempt to violate hazardous waste provisions, R.C. Chapter 3734., other than R.C. § 3734.18, is a felony punishable by a fine up to $25,000 or imprisonment up to 18 months, or both

Other attempts are offenses of the next lesser degree than the offenses attempted

An attempt to commit a felony offense not specifically classified

*Penalty:* A misdemeanor of the first degree (2929.21-2929.31)

An attempt to commit a misdemeanor offense not specifically classified

*Penalty:* A misdemeanor of the fourth degree (2929.21-2929.31)

Attempt to commit minor misdemeanor, or to engage in conspiracy, is no offense

*Notes:* A person may not be convicted of attempt if he is convicted of committing the attempted offense, of complicity in the commission of an offense, or of conspiracy to commit an offense

It is no defense to a charge of attempt that, in retrospect, commission of the offense which was the object of the attempt was either factually or legally impossible under the attendant circumstances, if that offense could have been committed had the attendant circumstances been as the actor believed them to be

It is an affirmative defense that the actor abandoned his effort to commit the offense or otherwise prevented its commission, under circumstances manifesting a complete and voluntary renunciation of his criminal purpose

In a prosecution for aggravated attempted murder or attempted murder, in addition to any other sanctions, if the offender used a motor vehicle as the means to attempt the offense, the court shall order a class two suspension of the offender's driver's license, commercial driver's license, temporary instruction permit, probationary license, or nonresident operating privilege

***COMPLICITY*, R.C. § 2923.03 [Same as principal offense]**

(1) Acting with the culpability required in the principal offense
(2) (a) Solicit or procure another to commit the offense
*(or)*
(b) Aid or abet another to commit the offense
*(or)*
(c) Conspire with another to commit the offense in violation of R.C. § 2923.01
*(or)*
(d) Cause an innocent or irresponsible person to commit the offense
(3) Venue

*Penalty:* Same as that for principal offense

*Notes:* Complicity may be charged in terms of this section or terms of the principal offense

No person shall be convicted of complicity under this section unless an offense is actually committed, but a person may be convicted of complicity in an attempt to commit an offense in violation of R.C. § 2923.02. It is an affirmative defense to a charge of complicity that, prior to the commission of or attempt to commit the offense, the actor terminated his complicity, under circumstances manifesting a complete and voluntary renunciation of his criminal purpose. It is no defense, however, to a charge of complicity that no person with whom the accused was in complicity has been convicted as a principal offender

***CARRYING CONCEALED WEAPONS*, R.C. § 2923.12 [MM, M1, F4, F3]**

Division (A): **[MM, M1, F4, F3]**

(1) Knowingly
(2) Carry or have
(3) (a) Concealed on the person's person
*(or)*
(b) Concealed ready at hand
(4) (a) A deadly weapon other than a handgun;
*(or)*
(b) A handgun other than a dangerous ordnance;
*(or)*
(c) A dangerous ordnance.
(5) Venue

Division (B): **[F5, M1]**

(1) Issued a license or temporary emergency license to carry a concealed handgun under section 2923.125 [2923.12.5] or 2923.1213 [2923.12.13] of the Revised Code or a license to carry a concealed handgun that was issued by another state with which the attorney general has entered into a reciprocity agreement under section 109.69 of the Revised Code
(2) Stopped for a law enforcement purpose
(3) Who is carrying a concealed handgun
(4) (a) Fail to promptly inform any law enforcement officer who approaches the person after the person has been stopped that the person has been issued a license or temporary emergency license to carry a concealed handgun and that the person then is carrying a concealed handgun
*(or)*
(b) Knowingly fail to keep the person's hands in plain sight at any time after any law enforcement officer begins approaching the person while stopped and before the law enforcement officer leaves, unless the failure is pursuant to and in accordance with directions given by a law enforcement officer.
*(or)*
(c) Knowingly remove or attempt to remove the loaded handgun from the holster, pocket, or other place in which the person is carrying it, knowingly grasp or hold the loaded handgun, or knowingly have contact with the loaded handgun by touching it with the person's hands or fingers at any time after the law enforcement officer begins approaching and before the law enforcement officer leaves, unless acting in accordance with directions given by the law enforcement officer.
*(or)*
(d) Knowingly disregard or fail to comply with any lawful order of any law enforcement officer given while the person is stopped, including, but not limited to, a specific order to the person to keep the person's hands in plain sight.

Division (A):

*Penalty:* A misdemeanor of the first degree. (2929.21-2929.31)

Where the offender previously has been convicted of a violation of this section or of any offense of violence, if the weapon involved is a firearm that is either loaded or for which the offender has ammunition ready at hand, or if the weapon involved is dangerous ordnance

*Penalty:* A felony of the fourth degree (2929.11-2929.18, 2929.31)
Where the offense is committed aboard an aircraft, or with purpose to carry a concealed weapon aboard an aircraft, regardless of the weapon involved

*Penalty:* A felony of the third degree (2929.11-2929.18, 2929.31)
Mitigation of Division (A) violation where weapon is handgun other than a deadly ordinance: See Subdivision (G)(2) of this section
Section does not apply to transportation or storage of a firearm (other than a firearm described in divisions (G) to (M) of R.C. § 2923.11) in a motor vehicle for any lawful purpose if the firearm is not on the actor's person or in the actor's own home for any lawful purpose.

Division (B):

*Penalty:* If the offender violates division (B)(4)(a) of this section, a misdemeanor of the first degree. In addition to any other penalty, the offender's license or temporary emergency license to carry a concealed handgun shall be suspended
If the offender violates division (B)(4)(b) or (d) of this section, a misdemeanor of the first degree, or a felony of the fifth degree if previously convicted or pleaded guilty. In addition to any other penalty, the offender's license or temporary emergency license to carry a concealed handgun shall be suspended
If the offender violates division (B)(4)(c) of this section, felony of the fifth degree
However, if, at the time of the stop of the offender for a law enforcement purpose that was the basis of the violation, any law enforcement officer involved with the stop had actual knowledge that the offender has been issued a license or temporary emergency license to carry a concealed handgun, carrying concealed weapons in violation of division (B)(1) of this section is a minor misdemeanor, and the offender's license or temporary emergency license to carry a concealed handgun shall not be suspended.

***ILLEGAL POSSESSION OF FIREARM IN LIQUOR PERMIT PREMISES*, R.C. § 2923.121 [F5]**

(1) Possess
(2) Firearm
(3) In any room in which any person is consuming beer or intoxicating liquor
(4) (a) In premises for which a D permit issued under R.C. Chapter 4303.
(b) Or in an open air arena for which a permit of that nature has been issued
(5) Venue
*Penalty:* A felony of the fifth degree (2929.11-2929.18, 2929.31) or, if knowingly carrying or having the firearm concealed on the offender's person or concealed ready at hand, felony of the third degree.
Defenses: *See* R.C. § 2923.121
*Note:* Does not apply to the permit holder for the establishment, if that permit holder also has a concealed carry license and is not consuming liquor

***ILLEGAL CONVEYANCE OR POSSESSION OF A DEADLY WEAPON OR DANGEROUS ORDNANCE OR ILLEGAL POSSESSION OF AN OBJECT INDISTINGUISHABLE FROM A FIREARM IN SCHOOL SAFETY ZONE*, R.C. § 2923.122 [M1, F5, F4]**

Division (A) — Conveyance:
(1) Knowingly
(2) (a) Convey
*(or)*
(b) Attempt to convey
(3) (a) Deadly weapon
*(or)*
(b) Dangerous ordnance
(4) Into a school safety zone
(5) Venue

Division (B) — Possession:
(1) Knowingly
(2) Possess
(3) (a) Deadly weapon
*(or)*
(b) Dangerous ordnance
(4) In a school safety zone
(5) Venue
No previous conviction under this section
*Penalty:* A felony of the fifth degree (2929.11-2929.18, 2929.31)
Previous conviction under this section
*Penalty:* A felony of the fourth degree (2929.11-2929.18, 2929.31)

Division (C):
(1) Knowingly
(2) Possess

(3) An object
(a) that is indistinguishable from a firearm, whether or not capable of being fired
*(and)*
(b) the person indicates that the person possesses the object and that it is a firearm, or the person knowingly displays or brandishes the object and indicates that it is a firearm
(4) In a school safety zone
(5) Venue

*Penalty:* A misdemeanor of the first degree (2929.21-2929.31)

*Notes:* This section does not apply to officers, agents, or employees of Ohio or any other state or the United States or to law enforcement officers authorized to carry deadly weapons or dangerous ordnance and acting within the scope of their duties, to any on-duty security officer employed by the board or governing authorization to convey or possess deadly weapons or dangerous ordnance. R.C. § 2923.122

In addition to the penalties listed, the driver's license, permit or nonresident operating privilege of any person who is under 19 shall be subject to a class four suspension.

This section does not apply to a holder of a concealed carry permit in a motor vehicle while immediately in the process of picking up or dropping off a child.

*Definitions:* "Deadly weapon," "dangerous ordnance," R.C. § 2923.11

### *ILLEGAL CONVEYANCE OF DEADLY WEAPON OR DANGEROUS ORDNANCE INTO COURTHOUSE; ILLEGAL POSSESSION OR CONTROL IN COURTHOUSE,* R.C. § 2923.12.3 [F5, F4]

Division (A):
(1) Knowingly
(2) Convey or attempt to convey
(3) Deadly weapon or dangerous ordnance
(4) Into a
(a) Courthouse
*(or)*
(b) Other building or structure in which a courtroom is located
(5) Venue

*Penalty:* A felony of the fifth degree (2929.11-2929.18, 2929.31)

If the offender previously has been convicted of a violation of Division (A) or (B) of this section

*Penalty:* A felony of the fourth degree (2929.11-2929.18, 2929.31)

Division (B):
(1) Knowingly
(2) (a) Possess
*(or)*
(b) Have under the person's control
(3) Deadly weapon or dangerous ordnance
(4) In a
(a) Courthouse
*(or)*
(b) Other building or structure in which a courtroom is located
(5) Venue

*Penalty:* A felony of the fifth degree (2929.11-2929.18, 2929.31)

If the offender previously has been convicted of a violation of Division (A) or (B) of this section

*Penalty:* A felony of the fourth degree (2929.11-2929.18, 2929.31)

### *ILLEGAL RELEASE OF CONFIDENTIAL CONCEALED HANDGUN LICENSE RECORDS,* R.C. § 2923.129 [F5]

(1) Release or otherwise disseminate
(2) Records that are confidential under Division (A) of this section
(3) Unless required to do so pursuant to court order

*Penalty:* A felony of the fifth degree (2929.11-2929.18, 2929.31)

### *FALSIFICATION OF CONCEALED HANDGUN LICENSE OR POSSESSING REVOKED OR SUSPENDED LICENSE,* R.C. § 2923.1211 [F5, M3]

Division (A) — Falsification **[F5]**
(1) Alter
(2) License or temporary emergency license to carry a concealed handgun
(3) Issued pursuant to section 2923.125 [2923.12.5] or 2923.1213 [2923.12.13] of the Revised Code
(4) Venue
*(or)*
(1) Create
(2) Fictitious document that purports to be a license of that nature.
(3) Venue

*Penalty:* A felony of the fifth degree (2929.11-2929.18, 2929.31)

Division (B) — Possession **[M3]**
(1) Except in the performance of official duties
(2) Possess
(3) (a) Concealed handgun license that was issued and has been revoked or suspended pursuant to section 2923.128 [2923.12.8] of the Revised Code
*(or)*
(b) Temporary emergency license to carry concealed handgun that was issued and has been revoked pursuant to section 2923.1213 [2923.12.13] of the Revised Code.
(4) Venue
*Penalty:* A misdemeanor of the third degree (2929.21-2929.31)

***HAVING WEAPONS WHILE UNDER DISABILITY,* R.C. § 2923.13 [F3]**

Division (A): **[F5]**
(1) Knowingly
(2) Acquire, have, carry, or use
(3) Firearm/dangerous ordnance
(4) While
(a) A fugitive from justice
*(or)*
(b) Under indictment, or convicted of any felony offense of violence, or adjudicated a delinquent child for the commission of an offense that, if committed by an adult, would have been an offense of violence
*(or)*
(c) Under indictment, or previously convicted of felony offenses involving illegal possession, use, sale, administration, distribution, trafficking in drugs of abuse, or adjudicated a delinquent child for commission of such offense
*(or)*
(d) Drug dependent person/in danger of becoming drug dependent or a chronic alcoholic
*(or)*
(e) Adjudicated mentally incompetent, has been adjudicated as a mental defective, has been committed to a mental institution, has been found by a court to be a mentally ill person subject to hospitalization by court order, or is an involuntary patient other than one who is a patient only for purposes of observation.
(5) Unless relieved of above disabilities under R.C. § 2923.14
(6) Venue
*Penalty:* A felony of the third degree (2929.11-2929.18, 2929.31)
*Definitions:* "Dangerous ordnance," "deadly weapon," R.C. § 2923.11
"Drug dependent/in danger of becoming drug dependent," R.C. § 3719.50
"Mentally ill person subject to hospitalization by court order" and "patient", R.C. § 5122.01

***POSSESSION OF DEADLY WEAPON WHILE UNDER DETENTION,* R.C. § 2923.131 [M1, F5, F4, F3, F2, F1]**

(1) Possess
(2) Deadly weapon
(3) While under detention at a detention facility
(4) Venue
If the offender, at the time of the commission of the offense, was under detention as an alleged or adjudicated delinquent child or unruly child and if at the time the offender commits the act for which the offender was under detention it would not be a felony if committed by an adult **[M1]**
*Penalty:* A misdemeanor of the first degree (2929.21-2929.31)
If the offender, at the time of the commission of the offense, was under detention in any other manner:
When the most serious offense for which the person was under detention is aggravated murder or murder and regardless of when the aggravated murder or murder occurred, or if the person was under detention as an alleged or adjudicated delinquent child, when the most serious act for which the person was under detention would be aggravated murder or murder if committed by an adult and regardless of when that occurred **[F1]**
*Penalty:* A felony of the first degree (2929.11-2929.18, 2929.31)
When the most serious offense for which the person was under detention is a felony of the first degree committed on or after July 1, 1996, or an aggravated felony of the first degree committed prior to July 1, 1996 **[F2]**
*Penalty:* A felony of the second degree (2929.11-2929.18, 2929.31)
If the person was under detention as an alleged or adjudicated delinquent child, the most serious act for which the person was under detention was committed on or after July 1, 1996, and would be a felony of the first degree if committed by an adult, or was committed prior to July 1, 1996, and would have been an aggravated felony of the first degree if committed by an adult **[F2]**
*Penalty:* A felony of the second degree (2929.11-2929.18, 2929.31)
When the most serious offense for which the person was under detention is a felony of the second degree committed on or after July 1, 1996, or an aggravated felony of the second degree or a felony of the first degree committed prior to July 1, 1996 **[F3]**
*Penalty:* A felony of the third degree (2929.11-2929.18, 2929.31)

If the person was under detention as an alleged or adjudicated delinquent child, the most serious act for which the person was under detention was committed on or after July 1, 1996, and would be a felony of the second degree if committed by an adult, or was committed prior to July 1, 1996, and would have been an aggravated felony of the second degree or a felony of the first degree if committed by an adult **[F3]**
*Penalty:* A felony of the third degree (2929.11-2929.18, 2929.31)
When the most serious offense for which the person was under detention is a felony of the third degree committed on or after July 1, 1996, or an aggravated felony of the third degree or a felony of the second degree committed prior to July 1, 1996, or is a felony of the third degree committed prior to July 1, 1996, that, if it had been committed on or after July 1, 1996, also would be a felony of the third degree **[F4]**
*Penalty:* A felony of the fourth degree (2929.11-2929.18, 2929.31)
If the person was under detention as an alleged or adjudicated delinquent child, the most serious act for which the person was under detention was committed on or after July 1, 1996, and would be a felony of the third degree if committed by an adult, or was committed prior to July 1, 1996, and would have been an aggravated felony of the third degree or a felony of the second degree if committed by an adult, or was committed prior to July 1, 1996, would have been a felony of the third degree if committed by an adult, and, if it had been committed on or after July 1, 1996 also would be a felony of the third degree if committed by an adult **[F4]**
*Penalty:* A felony of the fourth degree (2929.11-2929.18, 2929.31)
When the most serious offense for which the person was under detention is a felony of the fourth or fifth degree committed on or after July 1, 1996, is a felony of the third degree committed prior to July 1, 1996, that, if committed on or after July 1, 1996, would be a felony of the fourth degree, is a felony of the fourth degree committed prior to July 1, 1996, or is an unclassified felony or misdemeanor regardless of when the unclassified felony or misdemeanor is committed **[F5]**
*Penalty:* A felony of the fifth degree (2929.11-2929.18, 2929.31)
If the person was under detention as an alleged or adjudicated delinquent child, the most serious act for which the person was under detention was committed on or after July 1, 1996, and would be a felony of the fourth or fifth degree if committed by an adult, was committed prior to July 1, 1996, and would have been a felony of the third degree if committed by an adult, and, if it had been committed on or after July 1, 1996, would be a felony of the fourth degree if committed by an adult, was committed prior to July 1, 1996, and would have been a felony of the fourth degree if committed by an adult, and, or would be an unclassified felony if committed by an adult regardless of when the act is committed **[F5]**
*Penalty:* A felony of the fifth degree (2929.11-2929.18, 2929.31)

### ***USING WEAPONS WHILE INTOXICATED,*** **R.C. § 2923.15 [M1]**

(1) Use or carry
(2) Any firearm/dangerous ordnance
(3) While under influence of alcohol or drug of abuse
(4) Venue
*Penalty:* A misdemeanor of the first degree (2929.21-2929.31)
*Definitions:* "Deadly weapon," "dangerous ordnance," R.C. § 2923.11

### ***IMPROPERLY HANDLING FIREARMS IN A MOTOR VEHICLE,*** **R.C. § 2923.16 [M1, M4, F4, F5]**

Division (A): **[F4]**
(1) While in or on a motor vehicle
(2) Knowingly discharge a firearm
(3) Venue

Division (B): **[M1, F4]**
(1) Knowingly
(2) Transport or have a loaded firearm
(3) In a motor vehicle
(4) So that firearm is accessible to operator or passenger without leaving the vehicle
(5) Venue
*Penalty:* A misdemeanor of the first degree or felony of the fourth degree (2929.21-2929.31) (2929.11-2929.18, 2929.31)

Division (C): **[M4]**
(1) Knowingly
(2) Transport or have firearm
(3) In motor vehicle
(4) Unless lawfully possessed under federal or state law and
(5) Unloaded and carried:
  (a) In closed package, box, or case
  *(or)*
  (b) In compartment accessible only by leaving vehicle
  *(or)*
  (c) In plain sight and secured in rack or holder made for that purpose
  *(or)*

(d) If the firearm is at least twenty-four inches in overall length as measured from the muzzle to the part of the stock furthest from the muzzle and if the barrel is at least eighteen inches in length, either in plain sight with the action open or the weapon stripped, or, if the firearm is of a type on which the action will not stay open or which cannot easily be stripped, in plain sight

(6) Venue

*Penalty:* A misdemeanor of the fourth degree (2929.21-2929.31)

*Note:* As used here, "unloaded" means:

- no ammunition is in the firearm, and no ammunition is loaded into a magazine or speed loader that may be used with the firearm is located anywhere within the vehicle (ammunition held in stripper-clips or in en-bloc clips is not considered ammunition that is loaded into a magazine or speed loader), *or*
- with respect to a firearm employing a percussion cap, flintlock, or other obsolete ignition system, the weapon is uncapped or the priming charge is removed from the pan.

Division (D): **[F5]**

(1) Knowingly

(2) Transport or have a loaded handgun

(3) In a motor vehicle if, at the time of that transportation or possession, any of the following applies:

(4) (a) The person is under the influence of alcohol, a drug of abuse, or a combination of them.

*(or)*

(b) The person's whole blood, blood serum or plasma, breath, or urine contains a concentration of alcohol, a listed controlled substance, or a listed metabolite of a controlled substance prohibited for persons operating a vehicle, as specified in division (A) of section 4511.19 of the Revised Code, regardless of whether the person at the time of the transportation or possession as described in this division is the operator of or a passenger in the motor vehicle.

(5) Venue

*Penalty:* A felony of the fifth degree, or a felony of the fourth degree if the handgun is concealed upon the offender's person (2929.11-2929.18, 2929.21-2929.31)

Division (E)(1): **[MM, M1]**

(1) Driver or an occupant of a vehicle

(2) Who has been issued a license or temporary emergency license under section 2923.125 or section 2923.1213 of the Revised Code to carry a concealed handgun or a license to carry a concealed handgun that was issued to the person by another state with which the attorney general has entered into a reciprocity agreement under section 109.69 of the Revised Code

(3) Failing to promptly inform any law enforcement officer who approaches the vehicle while stopped that the person has been issued a license or temporary emergency license to carry a concealed handgun and that the person then possesses or has a loaded handgun in the motor vehicle;

Division (E)(2): **[MM, M1]**

(1) Driver or an occupant of a vehicle

(2) Who has been issued a license or temporary emergency license under section 2923.125 or section 2923.1213 of the Revised Code to carry a concealed handgun or a license to carry a concealed handgun that was issued to the person by another state with which the attorney general has entered into a reciprocity agreement under section 109.69 of the Revised Code

(3) Failing to promptly inform the employee of the unit who approaches the vehicle while stopped that the person has been issued a license or temporary emergency license to carry a concealed handgun and that the person then possesses or has a loaded handgun in the commercial motor vehicle.

Division (E)(3): **[M1, F5]**

(1) Driver or an occupant of a vehicle

(2) Who has been issued a license or temporary emergency license under section 2923.125 or section 2923.1213 of the Revised Code to carry a concealed handgun or a license to carry a concealed handgun that was issued to the person by another state with which the attorney general has entered into a reciprocity agreement under section 109.69 of the Revised Code

(3) Knowingly failing to remain in the motor vehicle while stopped or knowingly fail to keep the person's hands in plain sight at any time after any law enforcement officer begins approaching the person while stopped and before the law enforcement officer leaves, unless the failure is pursuant to and in accordance with directions given by a law enforcement officer;

Division (E)(4): **[F5]**

(1) Driver or an occupant of a vehicle

(2) Who has been issued a license or temporary emergency license under section 2923.125 or section 2923.1213 of the Revised Code to carry a concealed handgun or a license to carry a concealed handgun that was issued to the person by another state with which the attorney general has entered into a reciprocity agreement under section 109.69 of the Revised Code

(3) Knowingly having contact with the loaded handgun by touching it with the person's hands or fingers in the motor vehicle at any time after the law enforcement officer begins approaching and before the law enforcement officer leaves, unless the person removes, attempts to remove, grasps, holds, or has contact with the loaded handgun pursuant to and in accordance with directions given by the law enforcement officer;

Division (E)(5): **[M1, F5]**
(1) Driver or an occupant of a vehicle
(2) Who has been issued a license or temporary emergency license under section 2923.125 or section 2923.1213 of the Revised Code to carry a concealed handgun or a license to carry a concealed handgun that was issued to the person by another state with which the attorney general has entered into a reciprocity agreement under section 109.69 of the Revised Code
(3) Knowingly disregarding or failing to comply with any lawful order of any law enforcement officer given while the motor vehicle is stopped, including, but not limited to, a specific order to the person to keep the person's hands in plain sight.

*Penalties:* A violation of division (E)(1) or (2) of this section is a misdemeanor of the first degree, and, in addition to any other penalty or sanction imposed for the violation, the offender's license or temporary emergency license to carry a concealed handgun shall be suspended pursuant to division (A)(2) of section 2923.128 of the Revised Code. If at the time of the stop of the offender for a traffic stop, for another law enforcement purpose, or for a purpose defined in section 5503.34 of the Revised Code that was the basis of the violation any law enforcement officer involved with the stop or the employee of the motor carrier enforcement unit who made the stop had actual knowledge of the offender's status as a licensee, a violation of division (E)(1) or (2) of this section is a minor misdemeanor, and the offender's license or temporary emergency license to carry a concealed handgun shall not be suspended pursuant to division (A)(2) of section 2923.128 of the Revised Code. A violation of division (E)(4) of this section is a felony of the fifth degree. A violation of division (E)(3) or (5) of this section is a misdemeanor of the first degree or, if the offender previously has been convicted of or pleaded guilty to a violation of division (E)(3) or (5) of this section, a felony of the fifth degree. In addition to any other penalty or sanction imposed for a misdemeanor violation of division (E)(3) or (5) of this section, the offender's license or temporary emergency license to carry a concealed handgun shall be suspended pursuant to division (A)(2) of section 2923.128 of the Revised Code.

***IMPROPERLY DISCHARGING A FIREARM AT OR INTO A HABITATION OR IN A SCHOOL SAFETY ZONE,* R.C. § 2923.161 [F2]**

(1) Without privilege to do so
(2) Knowingly
(3) Discharge a firearm
(4) (a) At or into an occupied structure that is a permanent or temporary habitation of any individual
*(or)*
(b) At, in, or into a school safety zone
*(or)*
(c) Within one thousand feet of any school building or of the boundaries of any school premises with the intent to
(i) Cause physical harm to another who is in the school, in the school building, or at a function or activity associated with the school
*(or)*
(ii) Cause panic or fear of physical harm to another who is in the school, in the school building, or at a function or activity associated with the school
*(or)*
(iii) Cause the evacuation of the school, the school building, or a function or activity associated with the school
(5) Venue

*Penalty:* A felony of the second degree (2929.11-2929.18, 2929.31)
*Notes:* This section does not apply to any officer, agent, or employee of Ohio, any other state, or the United States, or to any law enforcement officer who discharges the firearm while acting within the scope of the officer's, agent's, or employee's duties
*Definitions:* "Occupied structure," R.C. § 2901.01

***DISCHARGE OF FIREARM ON OR NEAR PROHIBITED PREMISES,* R.C. § 2923.162 [M4, M1, F4, F3, F1]**

Division (A)(1):
(1) Being one not on his own land
(2) Without permission from the proper officials
(3) Discharge
(4) A firearm
(5) (a) Upon or over a cemetery
*(or)*
(b) Within one hundred yards of a cemetery

*Penalty:* A misdemeanor of the fourth degree (2929.21-2929.31)

Division (A)(2):
(1) Being a person who owns any type of property described in (A)(2)(4) and who, while on the person's own enclosure
(2) Discharge
(3) A firearm

(4) On a lawn, park, pleasure ground, orchard, or other ground appurtenant to a schoolhouse, church, or inhabited dwelling, the property of another, or a charitable institution
*Penalty:* A misdemeanor of the fourth degree (2929.21-2929.31)

Division (A)(3):
(1) Discharge
(2) A firearm
(3) (a) Upon
*(or)*
(b) Over
(4) A public road or highway
*Penalty:* A misdemeanor of the first degree (2929.21-2929.31)
If the violation created a substantial risk of physical harm to any person or caused serious physical harm to property, a felony of the third degree (2929.11-2929.18, 2929.31)
If the violation caused physical harm to any person, a violation of division (A)(3), a felony of the second degree (2929.11-2929.18, 2929.31)
If the violation caused serious physical harm to any person, a felony of the first degree (2929.11-2929.18, 2929.31)

***UNLAWFUL POSSESSION OF DANGEROUS ORDNANCE; ILLEGALLY MANUFACTURING OR PROCESSING EXPLOSIVES,* R.C. § 2923.17 [F5, F2]**

Division (A): **[F5]**
(1) Knowingly
(2) Acquire, have, carry or use
(3) Dangerous ordnance
(4) Venue
*Penalty:* A felony of the fifth degree (2929.11-2929.18, 2929.31)

Division (B): **[F2]**
(1) Manufacture or process an explosive
(2) At any location in this state
(3) Unless the person first has been issued a license, certificate of registration, or permit to do so from a fire official of a political subdivision of the state or from the fire marshal
(4) Venue
*Penalty:* A felony of the second degree (2929.11-2929.18, 2929.31)
*Note:* Division (A) does not apply to, among others listed in R.C. § 2923.17, the holders of a license or temporary permit issued and in effect pursuant to R.C. § 2923.18, with respect to dangerous ordnance lawfully acquired, possessed, carried, or used for the purposes and in the manner specified in such license or permit
*Definitions:* "Dangerous ordnance," R.C. § 2923.11

***FAILURE TO SECURE DANGEROUS ORDNANCE,* R.C. § 2923.19 [M2]**

(1) Negligently
(2) Fail to take proper precautions to
(3) (a) Secure against theft, acquisition or use by unauthorized or incompetent person
*(or)*
(b) Insure safety of persons and property
(4) In acquiring, possessing, carrying or using
(5) Dangerous ordnance
(6) Venue
*Penalty:* A misdemeanor of the second degree (2929.21-2929.31)
*Definitions:* "Dangerous ordnance," R.C. § 2923.11

***UNLAWFUL TRANSACTIONS IN WEAPONS,* R.C. § 2923.20 [F4, M2, M4]**

A. (1) Recklessly
(2) Sell, lend, give or furnish
(3) Firearm
(4) To any person prohibited under R.C. §§ 2923.13 (Having weapons while under disability), 2923.15 (Using weapons while intoxicated)
(5) Venue **[F4]**
*(or)*
B. (1) Recklessly
(2) Sell, lend, give or furnish
(3) Dangerous ordnance
(4) To any person prohibited under R.C. §§ 2923.13 (Having weapons while under disability), 2923.15 (Using weapons while intoxicated), 2923.17 (Unlawful possession of dangerous ordnance)
(5) Venue **[F4]**
*(or)*

C. (1) Possess
(2) Firearm/dangerous ordnance
(3) With purpose to dispose of it in violation of A or B above
(4) Venue **[F4]**
*(or)*

D. (1) Manufacture, possess for sale, sell or furnish
(2) To any person (other than law enforcement agency for use in police work)
(3) Brass knuckles, cestus, billy, blackjack, sandbag, switch-blade knife, springblade knife, gravity knife or similar weapon
(4) Venue **[M2]**
*(or)*

E. (1) When transferring dangerous ordnance to another
(2) Negligently
(3) Fail to require transferee to exhibit identification, license, permit, showing him authorized to acquire dangerous ordnance under R.C. § 2923.17 (unlawful possession of dangerous ordnance)
(4) Venue **[M2]**
*(or)*

F. (1) When transferring dangerous ordnance to another
(2) Negligently
(3) Fail to take a complete record of the transaction and forthwith forward the record of the transaction to the sheriff of the county or the safety director or police chief of the municipality where the transaction takes place
(4) Venue **[M2]**
*(or)*

G. (1) Knowingly
(2) Fail to report to law enforcement authority
(3) Forthwith
(4) Loss or theft
(5) Firearm or dangerous ordnance under person's control
(6) Venue **[M4]**

*Penalty:* A felony of the fourth degree (2929.11-2929.18, 2929.31)
D, E, and F: A misdemeanor of the second degree (2929.21-2929.31)
G: A misdemeanor of the fourth degree (2929.21-2929.31)

*Definitions:* "Firearm," "dangerous ordnance," R.C. § 2923.11

### *DEFACING IDENTIFICATION MARKS OF FIREARM*, R.C. § 2923.201 [F4, M1]

Division (A)(1):
(1) Change, alter, remove, or obliterate
(2) Name of the manufacturer, model, manufacturer's serial number, or other mark of identification
(3) On a firearm
(4) Venue

*Penalty:* A misdemeanor of the first degree (2929.11-2929.18, 2929.31). If the offender previously has been convicted of or pleaded guilty to a violation of division (A)(1) of this section, defacing identification marks of a firearm is a felony of the fourth degree (2929.11-2929.18, 2929.31)

Division (A)(2):
(1) Possess
(2) Firearm
(3) Knowing or having reasonable cause to believe
(4) Name of the manufacturer, model, manufacturer's serial number, or other mark of identification on the firearm
(5) Has been changed, altered, removed, or obliterated
(6) Venue

*Penalty:* A misdemeanor of the first degree (2929.11-2929.18, 2929.31). If the offender previously has been convicted of or pleaded guilty to a violation of division (A)(2) of this section, possessing a defaced firearm is a felony of the fourth degree (2929.11-2929.18, 2929.31)

### *IMPROPERLY FURNISHING FIREARMS TO MINOR*, R.C. § 2923.21 [F5]

(1) Sell a firearm to person under 18
*(or)*
(2) Subject to Division (B) of this section, sell a handgun to person under 21
*(or)*
(3) Furnish firearm to a person under 18 or subject to Division (B) of the section, any handgun to a person under 21, except for purpose of lawful hunting/instruction in firearms safety, care, handling or marksmanship under direct supervision or control of responsible adult
*(or)*
(4) Sell or furnish a firearm to a person 18 or older if the seller or furnisher knows, or has reason to know, that the person is purchasing or receiving the firearm for the purpose of selling or furnishing the firearm to a person

under 18
*(or)*
(5) Sell or furnish a handgun to a person 21 or older if the seller or furnisher knows, or has reason to know, that the person is purchasing or receiving the handgun for the purpose of selling or furnishing the handgun to a person under 21
*(or)*
(6) Purchase or attempt to purchase any firearm with the intent to sell or furnish the handgun to a person under 18
*(or)*
(7) Purchase or attempt to purchase any handgun with the intent to sell or furnish the handgun to a person under 21
(8) Venue
*Penalty:* A felony of the fifth degree (2929.11-2929.18, 2929.31)
*Definitions:* "Handgun," "firearm," "deadly weapon," R.C. § 2923.11
*Note:* Divisions (A)(1) and (2) of this section do not apply to the sale or furnishing of a handgun to a person 18 or older and under 21 if the person is a law enforcement officer who is properly appointed or employed as a law enforcement officer and has received firearms training approved by the Ohio Peace Officer Training Council or equivalent firearms training

***UNDERAGE PURCHASE OF FIREARM OR HANDGUN*, R.C. § 2923.211 [M2]**

(A)(1) No person under 18
(2) Shall purchase or attempt to purchase
(3) A firearm
*Penalty:* Whoever violates division (A) of this section is guilty of underage purchase of a firearm, a delinquent act that would be a felony of the fourth degree if it could be committed by an adult
(B)(1) No person under 21
(2) Shall purchase or attempt to purchase
(3) A handgun
*Penalty:* A misdemeanor of the second degree (2929.21-2929.31)
*Note:* Division (B) of this section does not apply to the purchase or attempted purchase of a handgun by a person 18 or older and under 21 if the person is a law enforcement officer who is properly appointed or employed as a law enforcement officer and has received firearms training approved by the Ohio Peace Officer Training Council or equivalent firearms training

***POSSESSING CRIMINAL TOOLS*, R.C. § 2923.24 [F5, M1]**

(1) Have possession or control of
(2) Any substance, device, instrument, or article
(3) With purpose to use it criminally
(4) Venue
*Penalty:* A misdemeanor of the first degree (2929.21-2929.31)
If the circumstances indicate that the substance, device, instrument, or article involved in the offense was intended for use in the commission of a felony
*Penalty:* A felony of the fifth degree (2929.11-2929.18, 2929.31)

***ENGAGING IN PATTERN OF CORRUPT ACTIVITY*, R.C. § 2923.32 [F1, F2]**

[A](1) Being employed by or associated with any enterprise
(2) Conduct or participate in affairs of enterprise
(3) Directly or indirectly
(4) (a) Through pattern of corrupt activity
*(or)*
(b) Through collection of unlawful debt (5) Venue
*(or)*
[B](1) (a) Through pattern of corrupt activity
*(or)*
(b) Through collection of unlawful debt
(2) Acquire or maintain
(3) Directly or indirectly
(4) Interest in or control of
(5) Any enterprise or real property
(6) Venue
*(or)*
[C](1) Knowingly having received
(2) Any proceeds
(3) Derived
(4) Directly or indirectly
(5) (a) From pattern of corrupt activity
*(or)*

(b) From collection of any unlawful debt
(6) Use or invest
(7) Directly or indirectly
(8) (a) Any part of those proceeds
*(or)*
(b) Any proceeds derived from use/investment of those proceeds
(9) (a) In acquisition of any title to, right, interest, or equity in real property
*(or)*
(b) In establishment or operation of any enterprise
(10) Venue

*Penalty:* A felony of the second degree (2929.11-2929.18, 2929.31)
Also, fine of 3 times gross value gained/loss caused, court costs, costs of investigation/prosecution, criminal forfeiture of real and personal property
If at least one of the incidents of corrupt activity is a felony of the first, second, or third degree, aggravated murder, or murder, if at least one of the incidents of corrupt activity was a felony under the laws of this state that was committed prior to the effective date of this amendment and that would constitute a felony of the first, second, or third degree, aggravated murder, or murder, if committed on or after the effective date of this amendment, or if at least one of the incidents of corrupt activity is a felony under the laws of the United States or of another state that, if committed in this state on or after the effective date of this amendment, would constitute a felony of the first, second, or third degree, aggravated murder, or murder under the laws of this state
*Penalty:* A felony of the first degree (2929.11-2929.18, 2929.31)
Also, fine of 3 times gross value gained/loss caused, court costs, costs of investigation/prosecution, criminal forfeiture of real and personal property
*Definitions:* Generally, R.C. § 2923.31
*Notes:* For preserving reachability of property, R.C. § 2923.33
For provisions regarding civil proceedings, R.C. § 2923.34
For provisions regarding corrupt activity liens, R.C. § 2923.36
For provisions regarding disposition of property forfeited, fines, and civil penalties, R.C. § 2923.35
Regarding purchase of securities on open market without intent to control issuer, R.C. § 2923.32(A)(3)

***PARTICIPATING IN CRIMINAL GANG*, R.C. § 2923.42 [F2]**

(1) Being a person who actively participates in a criminal gang
(2) With knowledge that the criminal gang engages in or has engaged in a pattern of criminal gang activity
(3) (a) Purposely promote, further or assist any criminal conduct
*(or)*
(b) Purposely commit or engage in any act that constitutes criminal conduct

*Penalty:* A felony of the second degree (2929.11-2929.18, 2929.31)
*Notes:* A prosecution for a violation of this section does not preclude a prosecution of a violation of any other section of the Revised Code, one or more acts, a series of acts, or a course of behavior that can be prosecuted under this section or any other section of the Revised Code may be prosecuted under this section, the other section, or both
*Definitions:* "Criminal conduct," R.C. § 2923.41(C)

---

## DRUG ABUSE OFFENSES

***CORRUPTING ANOTHER WITH DRUGS*, R.C. § 2925.02 [F1, F2, F3, F4]**

Division (A)(1):
(1) Knowingly
(2) By force, threat, or deception
(3) Administer to another or induce or cause another to use
(4) A controlled substance
(5) Venue

Division (A)(2):
(1) Knowingly
(2) By any means
(3) Administer or furnish to another or induce or cause another to use
(4) A controlled substance
(5) With purpose to cause serious physical harm to the other person, or with purpose to cause the other person to become drug dependent
(6) Venue

Division (A)(3):
(1) Knowingly
(2) By any means

(3) Administer or furnish to another or induce or cause another to use
(4) A controlled substance
(5) And thereby cause serious physical harm to the other person, or cause the other person to become drug dependent
(6) Venue

Division (A)(4)(a-c):
(1) Knowingly
(2) By any means
(3) (a) Administer or furnish a controlled substance to a juvenile who is at least two years the offender's junior *(or)*
(b) Induce or cause a juvenile who is at least two years the offender's junior to use a controlled substance *(or)*
(c) Induce or cause a juvenile who is at least two years the offender's junior to commit a felony drug abuse offense
(4) When the offender knows the age of the juvenile or is reckless in that regard
(5) Venue

Division (A)(4)(d):
(1) Use a juvenile
(2) To perform any surveillance activity that is intended to prevent
(3) (a) The detection of the offender or any other person in the commission of *(or)*
(b) The arrest of the offender or any other person for the commission of
(4) A felony drug abuse offense
(5) Whether or not the offender knows the age of the juvenile
(6) Venue

Where drug involved is schedule I or II substance (except marihuana or synthetic cannabinoids) **[F2]**
*Penalty:* Mandatory prison term of 2, 3, 4, 5, 6, 7, or 8 years and up to $15,000
Mandatory minimum fine: $7,500
Organization: Up to $20,000
Where drug involved is a schedule I or II substance (except marihuana) and the offense was committed in the vicinity of a school **[F1]**
*Penalty:* Mandatory prison term of 3, 4, 5, 6, 7, 8, 9, or 10 years and up to $20,000
Mandatory minimum fine: $10,000
Organization: Up to $25,000
If the violation involves the sale, offer to sell, or possession of a schedule I or II controlled substance (except marihuana), and if the court imposing sentence on the offender finds that the offender, as a result of the violation, is a major drug offender and is guilty of a specification of the type described in R.C. § 2941.1410, the court, in lieu of the prison term that is authorized or required, shall impose upon the offender the mandatory ten-year prison term under R.C. § 2929.14(D)(3)(a)
Where drug involved is schedule III, IV, or V substance **[F2]**
*Penalty:* Presumption of a prison term of 2, 3, 4, 5, 6, 7, or 8 years and up to $15,000
Mandatory minimum fine: $7,500
Organization: Up to $20,000
Where drug involved is a schedule III, IV, or V substance and the offense was committed in the vicinity of a school **[F2]**
*Penalty:* Mandatory prison term of 2, 3, 4, 5, 6, 7, or 8 years and up to $15,000
Mandatory minimum fine: $7,500
Organization: Up to $20,000
Where drug involved is marihuana **[F4]**
*Penalty:* R.C. § 2929.13(C) applies in determining whether to impose a prison term of 6, 7, 8, 9, 10, 11, 12, 13, 14, 15, 16, 17, or 18 months on the offender and up to $5,000
Organization: Up to $10,000
Where drug involved is marihuana and the offense was committed in the vicinity of a school **[F3]**
*Penalty:* R.C. § 2929.13(C) applies in determining whether to impose a prison term of 9, 12, 18, 24, 30, or 36 months and up to $10,000
Mandatory minimum fine: $5,000
Organization: Up to $15,000
*Notes:* Laboratory report as prima-facie evidence in drug abuse cases; rights of accused in re, R.C. § 2925.51
Manufacturers, licensed health professionals authorized to prescribe drugs, pharmacists, owners of pharmacies, and others are excepted from A., C., and D. under R.C. § 2925.02(B)
*See* statute for special provisions concerning attorneys and professionally licensed persons convicted under this statute
*See* statute for provisions exempting indigents from mandatory fines
*See* statute for provisions allowing revocation or suspension of driver's and commercial driver's licenses
*Definitions:* "Drug dependent person," R.C. § 3719.011
"Felony drug abuse offense," R.C. § 2925.01

"Juvenile," R.C. § 2925.01
"Professionally licensed person," R.C. § 2925.01
"School," "school building," "school premises," R.C. § 2925.01

***TRAFFICKING IN DRUGS*, R.C. § 2925.03 [MM, M3, F5, F4, F3, F2, F1]**

(1) Knowingly
(2) Sell or offer to sell
(3) A controlled substance
(4) Venue
*(or)*
(1) Knowingly
(2) Prepare for shipment, ship, transport, deliver, prepare for distribution or distribute
(3) A controlled substance
(4) When the offender knows or has reasonable cause to believe that the controlled substance is intended for sale or resale by the offender or another person

AGGRAVATED TRAFFICKING IN DRUGS

If the drug involved in the violation is any compound, mixture, preparation or substance included in schedule I or II (except marijuana, synthetic cannabinoids, cocaine, L.S.D., heroin, and hashish) **[F4]**
*Penalty:* R.C. § 2929.13(C) applies in determining whether to impose a prison term of 6, 7, 8, 9, 10, 11, 12, 13, 14, 15, 16, 17, or 18 months and up to $5,000
Organization: Up to $10,000
If the offense was committed in the vicinity of a school, or in the vicinity of a juvenile **[F3]**
*Penalty:* R.C. § 2929.13(C) applies in determining whether to impose a prison term of 1, 2, 3, 4, or 5 years and up to $10,000
Mandatory minimum fine: $5,000
Organization: Up to $15,000
If the amount of the drug involved equals or exceeds the bulk amount but is less than five times the bulk amount **[F3]**
*Penalty:* Mandatory prison term of 1, 2, 3, 4, or 5 years and up to $10,000
Mandatory minimum fine: $5,000
Organization: Up to $15,000
If the amount of the drug involved equals or exceeds the bulk amount but is less than five times the bulk amount and the offense was committed in the vicinity of a school, or in the vicinity of a juvenile **[F2]**
*Penalty:* Mandatory prison term of 2, 3, 4, 5, 6, 7, or 8 years and up to $15,000
Mandatory minimum fine: $7,500
Organization: Up to $20,000
If the amount of the drug involved equals or exceeds five times the bulk amount but is less than fifty times the bulk amount **[F2]**
*Penalty:* Mandatory prison term of 2, 3, 4, 5, 6, 7, or 8 years and up to $15,000
Mandatory minimum fine: $7,500
Organization: Up to $20,000
If the amount of the drug involved equals or exceeds five times the bulk amount but is less than fifty times the bulk amount and the offense was committed in the vicinity of a school, or in the vicinity of a juvenile **[F1]**
*Penalty:* Mandatory prison term of 3, 4, 5, 6, 7, 8, 9, or 10 years and up to $20,000
Mandatory minimum fine: $10,000
Organization: Up to $25,000
If the amount of the drug involved equals or exceeds fifty times the bulk amount but is less than one hundred times the bulk amount and regardless of whether the offense was committed in the vicinity of a school or in the vicinity of a juvenile **[F1]**
*Penalty:* Mandatory prison term of 3, 4, 5, 6, 7, 8, 9, or 10 years and up to $20,000
Mandatory minimum fine: $10,000
Organization: Up to $25,000
If the amount of the drug involved equals or exceeds one hundred times the bulk amount and regardless of whether the offense was committed in the vicinity of a school or in the vicinity of a juvenile, the offender is a major drug offender **[F1]**
*Penalty:* Mandatory prison term of 10 years and up to $20,000 and may impose an additional prison term under R.C. § 2929.14(D)(3)(b) of 1, 2, 3, 4, 5, 6, 7, 8, 9, or 10 years
Mandatory minimum fine: $10,000
Organization: Up to $25,000

TRAFFICKING IN DRUGS

If the drug involved in the violation is any compound, mixture, preparation or substance included in schedule III, IV, or V **[F5]**
*Penalty:* R.C. § 2929.13(C) applies in determining whether to impose a prison term of 6, 7, 8, 9, 10, 11, or 12 months and up to $2,500
Organization: Up to $7,500

If the offense was committed in the vicinity of a school, or in the vicinity of a juvenile **[F4]**
*Penalty:* R.C. § 2929.13(C) applies in determining whether to impose a prison term of 6, 7, 8, 9, 10, 11, 12, 13, 14, 15, 16, 17, or 18 months and up to $5,000
Organization: Up to $10,000
If the amount of the drug involved equals or exceeds the bulk amount but is less than five times the bulk amount **[F4]**
*Penalty:* Presumption of prison term of 6, 7, 8, 9, 10, 11, 12, 13, 14, 15, 16, 17, or 18 months and up to $5,000
Organization: Up to $10,000
If the amount of the drug involved equals or exceeds the bulk amount but is less than five times the bulk amount and the offense was committed in the vicinity of a school, or in the vicinity of a juvenile **[F3]**
*Penalty:* Presumption of prison term of 1, 2, 3, 4, or 5 years and up to $10,000
Mandatory minimum fine: $5,000
Organization: Up to $15,000
If the amount of the drug involved equals or exceeds five times the bulk amount but is less than fifty times the bulk amount **[F3]**
*Penalty:* Presumption of prison term of 1, 2, 3, 4, or 5 years and up to $10,000
Mandatory minimum fine: $5,000
Organization: Up to $15,000
If the amount of the drug involved equals or exceeds five times the bulk amount but is less than fifty times the bulk amount and the offense was committed in the vicinity of a juvenile **[F2]**
*Penalty:* Presumption of prison term of 2, 3, 4, 5, 6, 7, or 8 years and up to $15,000
Mandatory minimum fine: $7,500
Organization: Up to $25,000
If the amount of the drug involved equals or exceeds fifty times the bulk amount **[F2]**
*Penalty:* Mandatory prison term of 2, 3, 4, 5, 6, 7, or 8 years and up to $15,000
Mandatory minimum fine: $7,500
Organization: Up to $20,000
If the amount of the drug involved equals or exceeds fifty times the bulk amount and the offense was committed in the vicinity of a school, or in the vicinity of a juvenile **[F1]**
*Penalty:* Mandatory prison term of 3, 4, 5, 6, 7, 8, 9, or 10 years and up to $20,000
Mandatory minimum fine: $10,000
Organization: Up to $25,000

TRAFFICKING IN MARIHUANA

If the drug involved in the violation is marihuana or a compound, mixture, preparation, or substance containing marihuana other than hashish **[F5]**
*Penalty:* R.C. § 2929.13(C) applies in determining whether to impose a prison term of 6, 7, 8, 9, 10, 11, or 12 months and up to $2,500
Organization: Up to $7,500
If the offense was committed in the vicinity of a school, or in the vicinity of a juvenile **[F4]**
*Penalty:* R.C. § 2929.13(C) applies in determining whether to impose a prison term of 6, 7, 8, 9, 10, 11, 12, 13, 14, 15, 16, 17, or 18 months and up to $5,000
Organization: Up to $10,000
If the amount of the drug involved equals or exceeds 200 grams but is less than 1,000 grams **[F4]**
*Penalty:* R.C. § 2929.13(C) applies in determining whether to impose a prison term of 6, 7, 8, 9, 10, 11, 12, 13, 14, 15, 16, 17, or 18 months and up to $5,000
Organization: Up to $10,000
If the amount of the drug involved equals or exceeds 200 grams but is less than 1,000 grams and the offense was committed in the vicinity of a school, or in the vicinity of a juvenile **[F3]**
*Penalty:* R.C. § 2929.13(C) applies in determining whether to impose a prison term of 1, 2, 3, 4, or 5 years and up to $10,000
Mandatory minimum fine: $5,000
Organization: Up to $15,000
If the amount of the drug involved equals or exceeds 1,000 grams but is less than 5,000 grams **[F3]**
*Penalty:* R.C. § 2929.13(C) applies in determining whether to impose a prison term of 1, 2, 3, 4, or 5 years and up to $10,000
Mandatory minimum fine: $5,000
Organization: Up to $15,000
If the amount of the drug involved equals or exceeds 1,000 grams but is less than 5,000 grams and the offense was committed in the vicinity of a school, or in the vicinity of a juvenile **[F2]**
*Penalty:* Presumption of prison term of 2, 3, 4, 5, 6, 7, or 8 years and up to $15,000
Mandatory minimum fine: $7,500
Organization: Up to $25,000
If the amount of the drug involved equals or exceeds 5,000 grams but is less than 20,000 grams **[F3]**
*Penalty:* Presumption of prison term of 1, 2, 3, 4, or 5 years and up to $10,000
Mandatory minimum fine: $5,000
Organization: Up to $15,000

If the amount of the drug involved equals or exceeds 5,000 grams but is less than 20,000 grams and the offense was committed in the vicinity of a school, or in the vicinity of a juvenile **[F2]**
*Penalty:* Presumption of prison term of 2, 3, 4, 5, 6, 7, or 8 years and up to $15,000
Mandatory minimum fine: $7,500
Organization: Up to $25,000
If the amount of the drug involved equals or exceeds 20,000 grams but is less than 40,000 grams **[F2]**
*Penalty:* Mandatory prison term of 5, 6, 7, or 8 years and up to $15,000
Mandatory minimum fine: $7,500
Organization: $20,000
If the amount of the drug involved equals or exceeds 20,000 grams and the offense was committed in the vicinity of a school, or in the vicinity of a juvenile **[F1]**
*Penalty:* Mandatory prison term of 10 years and up to $20,000
Mandatory minimum fine: $10,000
Organization: $25,000
If the amount of the drug involved equals or exceeds 40,000 grams **[F2]**
*Penalty:* Mandatory prison term of 8 years and up to $15,000
Mandatory minimum fine: $7,500
Organization: $20,000
If the amount of the drug involved equals or exceeds 40,000 grams and the offense was committed in the vicinity of a school, or in the vicinity of a juvenile **[F1]**
*Penalty:* Mandatory prison term of 10 years and up to $20,000
Mandatory minimum fine: $10,000
Organization: $25,000
If the offense involves a gift of 20 grams or less and is a first offense **[MM]**
*Penalty:* No prison term and up to $100
Organization: Up to $1,000
If the offense involves a gift of 20 grams or less and there is a prior offense **[M3]**
*Penalty:* Up to 60 days or up to $500 or both
Organization: Up to $3,000
If the offense involves a gift of 20 grams or less and the offense was committed in the vicinity of a school, or in the vicinity of a juvenile **[M3]**
*Penalty:* Up to 60 days or up to $500 or both
Organization: Up to $3,000

TRAFFICKING IN COCAINE

If the drug involved in the violation is cocaine or a compound, mixture, preparation, or substance containing cocaine **[F5]**
*Penalty:* R.C. § 2929.13(C) applies in determining whether to impose a prison term
Organization: $7,500
If the offense was committed in the vicinity of a school, or in the vicinity of a juvenile **[F4]**
*Penalty:* R.C. § 2929.13(C) applies in determining whether to impose a prison term
Organization: $10,000
If the amount of the drug involved equals or exceeds five grams but is less than ten grams **[F4]**
*Penalty:* R.C. § 2929.13(B) applies in determining whether to impose a prison term
Organization: $10,000
If the amount of the drug involved equals or exceeds five grams but is less than ten grams and the offense was committed in the vicinity of a school, or in the vicinity of a juvenile **[F3]**
*Penalty:* Presumption of a prison term
Mandatory minimum fine: $5,000
Organization: $15,000
If the amount of the drug involved equals or exceeds ten grams but is less than twenty grams **[F3]**
*Penalty:* Mandatory prison term of 9, 12, 18, 24, 30, or 36 months and up to $10,000
Mandatory minimum fine: $5,000
Organization: $15,000
If the amount of the drug involved equals or exceeds ten grams but is less than twenty grams and the offense was committed in the vicinity of a school, or in the vicinity of a juvenile **[F2]**
*Penalty:* Mandatory prison term of 2, 3, 4, 5, 6, 7, or 8 years and up to $15,000
Mandatory minimum fine: $7,500
Organization: $20,000
If the amount of the drug involved equals or exceeds five grams but is less than ten grams and the offense was committed in the vicinity of a school, or in the vicinity of a juvenile **[F3]**
*Penalty:* Presumption of a prison term
Mandatory minimum fine: $5,000
Organization: $15,000
If the amount of the drug involved equals or exceeds twenty grams but is less than twenty-seven grams **[F2]**
*Penalty:* Mandatory prison term one of the prison terms prescribed for a felony of the second degree
Mandatory minimum fine: $5,000
Organization: $20,000

If the amount of the drug involved equals or exceeds twenty grams but is less than twenty-seven grams and the offense was committed in the vicinity of a school, or in the vicinity of a juvenile **[F1]**
*Penalty:* Mandatory prison term one of the prison terms prescribed for a felony of the first degree
Mandatory minimum fine: $5,000
If the amount of the drug involved equals or exceeds twenty-seven grams but is less than one hundred grams **[F1]**
*Penalty:* Mandatory prison term one of the prison terms prescribed for a felony of the first degree
Mandatory minimum fine: $5,000
Organization: $25,000
If the amount of the drug involved equals or exceeds one hundred grams **[F1]**
*Penalty:* The offender is a offender is a major drug offender and court shall impose a mandatory prison term one of the prison terms prescribed for a felony of the first degree
Mandatory minimum fine: $5,000
Organization: $25,000

TRAFFICKING IN L.S.D.

If the drug involved in the violation is L.S.D. or a compound, mixture, preparation, or substance containing L.S.D. **[F5]**
*Penalty:* R.C. § 2929.13(C) applies in determining whether to impose a prison term and up to $2,500
Organization: $7,500
If the offense was committed in the vicinity of a school, or in the vicinity of a juvenile **[F4]**
*Penalty:* R.C. § 2929.13(C) applies in determining whether to impose a prison term and up to $5,000
Organization: $10,000
If the amount of the drug involved equals or exceeds ten unit doses but is less than fifty unit doses of L.S.D. in a solid form or equals or exceeds one gram but is less than five grams of L.S.D. in a liquid concentrate, liquid extract, or liquid distillate form **[F4]**
*Penalty:* Presumption of prison term of 6, 7, 8, 9, 10, 11, 12, 13, 14, 15, 16, 17, or 18 months and up to $5,000
Organization: $10,000
If the amount of the drug involved equals or exceeds ten unit doses but is less than fifty unit doses of L.S.D. in a solid form or equals or exceeds one gram but is less than five grams of L.S.D. in a liquid concentrate, liquid extract, or liquid distillate form, and the offense was committed in the vicinity of a school, or in the vicinity of a juvenile **[F3]**
*Penalty:* Presumption of prison term of 9, 12, 18, 24, 30, or 36 months and up to $10,000
Mandatory minimum fine: $5,000
Organization: $15,000
If the amount of the drug involved equals or exceeds fifty unit doses but is less than two hundred fifty unit doses of L.S.D. in a solid form or equals or exceeds five grams but is less than twenty-five grams of L.S.D. in a liquid concentrate, liquid extract, or liquid distillate form **[F3]**
*Penalty:* Presumption of (or, if third or subsequent offense, mandatory) prison term of 9, 12, 18, 24, 30, or 36 months and up to $10,000
Mandatory minimum fine: $5,000
Organization: $15,000
If the amount of the drug involved equals or exceeds fifty unit doses but is less than two hundred fifty unit doses of L.S.D. in a solid form or equals or exceeds five grams but is less than twenty-five grams of L.S.D. in a liquid concentrate, liquid extract, or liquid distillate form, and the offense was committed in the vicinity of a school, or in the vicinity of a juvenile **[F2]**
*Penalty:* Mandatory prison term of 2, 3, 4, 5, 6, 7, or 8 years and up to $15,000
Mandatory minimum fine: $7,500
Organization: $20,000
If the amount of the drug involved equals or exceeds two hundred fifty unit doses but is less than one thousand unit doses of L.S.D. in a solid form or equals or exceeds twenty-five grams but is less than one hundred grams of L.S.D. in a liquid concentrate, liquid extract, or liquid distillate form **[F2]**
*Penalty:* Mandatory prison term of 2, 3, 4, 5, 6, 7, or 8 years and up to $15,000
Mandatory minimum fine: $7,500
Organization: $20,000
If the amount of the drug involved equals or exceeds two hundred fifty unit doses but is less than one thousand unit doses of L.S.D. in a solid form or equals or exceeds twenty-five grams but is less than one hundred grams of L.S.D. in a liquid concentrate, liquid extract, or liquid distillate form, and the offense was committed in the vicinity of a school, or in the vicinity of a juvenile **[F1]**
*Penalty:* Mandatory prison term of 3, 4, 5, 6, 7, 8, 9, or 10 years and up to $20,000
Mandatory minimum fine: $10,000
Organization: $25,000
If the amount of the drug involved equals or exceeds one thousand unit doses but is less than five thousand unit doses of L.S.D. in a solid form or equals or exceeds one hundred grams but is less than five hundred grams of L.S.D. in a liquid concentrate, liquid extract, or liquid distillate form, and regardless of whether the offense was committed in the vicinity of a school, or in the vicinity of a juvenile **[F1]**
*Penalty:* Mandatory prison term of 3, 4, 5, 6, 7, 8, 9, or 10 years and up to $20,000
Mandatory minimum fine: $10,000
Organization: $25,000

If the amount of the drug involved equals or exceeds five thousand unit doses of L.S.D. in a solid form or equals or exceeds five hundred grams of L.S.D. in a liquid concentrate, liquid extract, or liquid distillate form, and regardless of whether the offense was committed in the vicinity of a school, or in the vicinity of a juvenile, the offender is a major drug offender **[F1]**
*Penalty:* Mandatory prison term of 10 years and up to $20,000
Mandatory minimum fine: $10,000
Organization: $25,000

TRAFFICKING IN HEROIN

If the drug involved in the violation is heroin or a compound, mixture, preparation, or substance containing heroin **[F5]**
*Penalty:* R.C. § 2929.13(C) applies in determining whether to impose a prison term and up to $2,500
Organization: $7,500
If the offense was committed in the vicinity of a school, or in the vicinity of a juvenile **[F4]**
*Penalty:* R.C. § 2929.13(C) applies in determining whether to impose a prison term and up to $5,000
Organization: $10,000
If the amount of the drug involved equals or exceeds ten unit doses but is less than fifty unit doses or equals or exceeds one gram but is less than five grams **[F4]**
*Penalty:* R.C. § 2929.13 applies in determining whether to impose a prison term and up to $5,000
Organization: $10,000
If the amount of the drug involved equals or exceeds ten unit doses but is less than fifty unit doses or equals or exceeds one gram but is less than five grams and the offense was committed in the vicinity of a school, or in the vicinity of a juvenile **[F3]**
*Penalty:* Presumption of prison term of 1, 2, 3, 4, or 5 years and up to $10,000
Mandatory minimum fine: $5,000
Organization: $15,000
If the amount of the drug involved equals or exceeds fifty unit doses but is less than one hundred unit doses or equals or exceeds five grams but is less than ten grams **[F3]**
*Penalty:* Presumption of prison term of 9, 12, 18, 24, 30, or 36 months and up to $10,000
Mandatory minimum fine: $5,000
Organization: $15,000
If the amount of the drug involved equals or exceeds fifty unit doses but is less than one hundred unit doses or equals or exceeds five grams but is less than ten grams and the offense was committed in the vicinity of a school, or in the vicinity of a juvenile **[F2]**
*Penalty:* Presumption of prison term of 2, 3, 4, 5, 6, 7, or 8 years and up to $15,000
Mandatory minimum fine: $7,500
Organization: $2,000
If the amount of the drug involved equals or exceeds one hundred unit doses but is less than five hundred unit doses or equals or exceeds ten grams but is less than fifty grams **[F2]**
*Penalty:* Mandatory prison term of 2, 3, 4, 5, 6, 7, or 8 years and up to $15,000
Mandatory minimum fine: $7,500
Organization: $20,000
If the amount of the drug involved equals or exceeds one hundred unit doses but is less than five hundred unit doses or equals or exceeds ten grams but is less than fifty grams and the offense was committed in the vicinity of a school, or in the vicinity of a juvenile **[F1]**
*Penalty:* Mandatory prison term of 3, 4, 5, 6, 7, 8, 9, or 10 years and up to $20,000
Mandatory minimum fine: $10,000
Organization: $25,000
If the amount of the drug involved equals or exceeds five hundred unit doses but is less than two thousand five hundred unit doses or equals or exceeds fifty grams but is less than two hundred fifty grams and regardless of whether the offense was committed in the vicinity of a school, or in the vicinity of a juvenile **[F1]**
*Penalty:* Mandatory prison term of 3, 4, 5, 6, 7, 8, 9, 10, or 11 years and up to $20,000
Mandatory minimum fine: $10,000
Organization: $25,000
If the amount of the drug involved equals or exceeds two thousand five hundred unit doses or equals or exceeds two hundred fifty grams and regardless of whether the offense was committed in the vicinity of a school, or in the vicinity of a juvenile, the offender is a major drug offender **[F1]**
*Penalty:* Mandatory prison term of 10 years and up to $20,000
Mandatory minimum fine: $10,000
Organization: $25,000

TRAFFICKING IN HASHISH

If the drug involved in the violation is hashish or a compound, mixture, preparation or substance containing hashish **[F5]**
*Penalty:* R.C. § 2929.13(C) applies in determining whether to impose a prison term of 6, 7, 8, 9, 10, 11, or 12 months and up to $2,500
Organization: $7,500

If the offense was committed in the vicinity of a school, or in the vicinity of a juvenile **[F4]**
*Penalty:* R.C. § 2929.13(B) applies in determining whether to impose a prison term and up to $5,000
Organization: $10,000
If the amount of the drug involved equals or exceeds ten grams but is less than fifty grams of hashish in a solid form or equals or exceeds two grams but is less than ten grams of hashish in a liquid concentration, liquid extract, or liquid distillate form **[F4]**
*Penalty:* R.C. § 2929.13(B) applies in determining whether to impose a prison term and up to $5,000
Organization: $10,000
If the amount of the drug involved equals or exceeds ten grams but is less than fifty grams of hashish in a solid form or equals or exceeds two grams but is less than ten grams of hashish in a liquid concentration, liquid extract, or liquid distillate form and the offense was committed in the vicinity of a school, or in the vicinity of a juvenile **[F3]**
*Penalty:* R.C. § 2929.13(C) applies in determining whether to impose a prison term of 1, 2, 3, 4, or 5 years and up to $10,000
Mandatory minimum fine: $5,000
Organization: $10,000
If the amount of the drug involved equals or exceeds fifty grams but is less than two hundred fifty grams of hashish in a solid form or equals or exceeds ten grams but is less than fifty grams of hashish in a liquid concentration, liquid extract, or liquid distillate form **[F3]**
*Penalty:* R.C. § 2929.13(C) applies in determining whether to impose a prison term of 9, 12, 18, 24, 30, or 36 months and up to $10,000
Mandatory minimum fine: $5,000
Organization: $15,000
If the amount of the drug involved equals or exceeds fifty grams but is less than two hundred fifty grams of hashish in a solid form or equals or exceeds ten grams but is less than fifty grams of hashish in a liquid concentration, liquid extract, or liquid distillate form and the offense was committed in the vicinity of a school, or in the vicinity of a juvenile **[F2]**
*Penalty:* Presumption of prison term of 2, 3, 4, 5, 6, 7, or 8 years and up to $15,000
Mandatory minimum fine: $7,500
Organization: $20,000
If the amount of the drug involved equals or exceeds two hundred fifty grams but is less than one thousand grams of hashish in a solid form or equals or exceeds fifty grams but is less than two hundred grams of hashish in a liquid concentration, liquid extract, or liquid distillate form **[F3]**
*Penalty:* Presumption of prison term of 9, 12, 18, 24, 30, or 36 months and up to $10,000
Mandatory minimum fine: $5,000
Organization: $15,000
If the amount of the drug involved equals or exceeds two hundred fifty grams but is less than one thousand grams of hashish in a solid form or equals or exceeds fifty grams but is less than two hundred grams of hashish in a liquid concentration, liquid extract, or liquid distillate form and the offense was committed in the vicinity of a school, or in the vicinity of a juvenile **[F2]**
*Penalty:* Presumption of prison term of 2, 3, 4, 5, 6, 7, or 8 years and up to $15,000
Mandatory minimum fine: $7,500
Organization: $20,000
If the amount of the drug involved equals or exceeds equals or exceeds one thousand grams but is less than two thousand grams of hashish in a solid form or equals or exceeds two hundred grams but is less than four hundred grams of hashish in a liquid concentrate, liquid extract, or liquid distillate form **[F2]**
*Penalty:* Mandatory prison term of 6, 7, or 8 years and up to $15,000
Mandatory minimum fine: $7,500
Organization: $20,000
If the amount of the drug involved equals or exceeds equals or exceeds one thousand grams but is less than two thousand grams of hashish in a solid form or equals or exceeds two hundred grams but is less than four hundred grams of hashish in a liquid concentrate, liquid extract, or liquid distillate form and the offense was committed in the vicinity of a school, or in the vicinity of a juvenile **[F1]**
*Penalty:* Mandatory prison term of 3, 4, 5, 6, 7, 8, 9, 10, or 11 years and up to $20,000
Mandatory minimum fine: $10,000
Organization: $25,000
If the amount of the drug involved equals or exceeds two thousand grams of hashish in a solid form or equals or exceeds four hundred grams of hashish in a liquid concentrate, liquid extract, or liquid distillate form **[F2]**
*Penalty:* Mandatory prison term of 2, 3, 4, 5, 6, 7, or 8 years and up to $15,000
Mandatory minimum fine: $10,000
Organization: $20,000
If the amount of the drug involved equals or exceeds two thousand grams of hashish in a solid form or equals or exceeds four hundred grams of hashish in a liquid concentrate, liquid extract, or liquid distillate form and the offense was committed in the vicinity of a school, or in the vicinity of a juvenile **[F1]**
*Penalty:* Mandatory prison term of 3, 4, 5, 6, 7, 8, 9, 10, or 11 years and up to $20,000
Mandatory minimum fine: $10,000
Organization: $25,000

***ILLEGAL MANUFACTURE OF DRUGS OR CULTIVATION OF MARIHUANA*, R.C. § 2925.04 [MM, M4, F5, F3, F2, F1]**

(1) Knowingly
(2) Cultivate
(3) Marihuana
(4) Venue
*(or)*
(1) Knowingly
(2) Manufacture or otherwise engage in
(3) Any part of the production of a controlled substance
(4) Venue

*Penalty:*

If the drug involved in the violation of division (A) of this section is any compound, mixture, preparation, or substance included in schedule I or II, with the exception of methamphetamine or marihuana, illegal manufacture of drugs is a felony of the second degree (2929.11-2929.18, 2929.31), and, subject to division (E) [Major Drug Offender penalty enhancement] of this section, the court shall impose as a mandatory prison term one of the prison terms prescribed for a felony of the second degree (2929.11-2929.18, 2929.31)

If the drug involved in the violation is any compound, mixture, preparation, or substance included in schedule I or II, with the exception of marihuana, and if the offense was committed in the vicinity of a juvenile or in the vicinity of a school, illegal manufacture of drugs is a felony of the first degree (2929.11-2929.18, 2929.31), and, subject to division (E) [Major Drug Offender penalty enhancement] of this section, the court shall impose as a mandatory prison term one of the prison terms prescribed for a felony of the first degree (2929.11-2929.18, 2929.31)

If the drug involved in the violation of division (A) of this section is methamphetamine, the penalty for the violation shall be determined as follows:

(a) Except as otherwise provided in subsection (b) immediately below, if the drug involved in the violation is methamphetamine, illegal manufacture of drugs is a felony of the second degree (2929.11-2929.18, 2929.31), and, subject to division (E) [Major Drug Offender penalty enhancement] of this section, the court shall impose a mandatory prison term on the offender determined in accordance with this division. Except as otherwise provided in this division, the court shall impose as a mandatory prison term one of the prison terms prescribed for a felony of the second degree (2929.11-2929.18, 2929.31) that is not less than three years. If the offender previously has been convicted of or pleaded guilty to a violation of division (A) of this section, a violation of division (B)(6) of section 2919.22 of the Revised Code, or a violation of division (A) of section 2925.041 of the Revised Code, the court shall impose as a mandatory prison term one of the prison terms prescribed for a felony of the second degree (2929.11-2929.18, 2929.31) that is not less than five years

(b) If the drug involved in the violation is methamphetamine and if the offense was committed in the vicinity of a juvenile, in the vicinity of a school, or on public premises, illegal manufacture of drugs is a felony of the first degree (2929.11-2929.18, 2929.31), and, subject to division (E) [Major Drug Offender penalty enhancement] of this section, the court shall impose a mandatory prison term on the offender determined in accordance with this division. Except as otherwise provided in this division, the court shall impose as a mandatory prison term one of the prison terms prescribed for a felony of the first degree (2929.11-2929.18, 2929.31) that is not less than four years. If the offender previously has been convicted of or pleaded guilty to a violation of division (A) of this section, a violation of division (B)(6) of section 2919.22 of the Revised Code, or a violation of division (A) of section 2925.041 of the Revised Code, the court shall impose as a mandatory prison term one of the prison terms prescribed for a felony of the first degree (2929.11-2929.18, 2929.31) that is not less than five years

If the drug involved in the violation of division (A) of this section is any compound, mixture, preparation, or substance included in schedule III, IV, or V, illegal manufacture of drugs is a felony of the third degree (2929.11-2929.18, 2929.31) or, if the offense was committed in the vicinity of a school or in the vicinity of a juvenile, a felony of the second degree (2929.11-2929.18, 2929.31), and there is a presumption for a prison term for the offense If the drug involved in the violation is marihuana, the penalty for the offense shall be determined as follows:

(a) Except as otherwise provided in subsections (b), (c), (d), (e), or (f) immediately below, illegal cultivation of marihuana is a minor misdemeanor or, if the offense was committed in the vicinity of a school or in the vicinity of a juvenile, a misdemeanor of the fourth degree (2929.21-2929.31)

(b) If the amount of marihuana involved equals or exceeds one hundred grams but is less than two hundred grams, illegal cultivation of marihuana is a misdemeanor of the fourth degree (2929.21-2929.31) or, if the offense was committed in the vicinity of a school or in the vicinity of a juvenile, a misdemeanor of the third degree (2929.21-2929.31)

(c) If the amount of marihuana involved equals or exceeds two hundred grams but is less than one thousand grams, illegal cultivation of marihuana is a felony of the fifth degree (2929.11-2929.18, 2929.31) or, if the offense was committed in the vicinity of a school or in the vicinity of a juvenile, a felony of the fourth degree (2929.11-2929.18, 2929.31), and division (B) of section 2929.13 of the Revised Code applies in determining whether to impose a prison term on the offender

(d) If the amount of marihuana involved equals or exceeds one thousand grams but is less than five thousand grams, illegal cultivation of marihuana is a felony of the third degree (2929.11-2929.18, 2929.31) or, if the offense was committed in the vicinity of a school or in the vicinity of a juvenile, a felony of the second degree (2929.11-2929.18, 2929.31), and division (C) of section 2929.13 of the Revised Code applies in determining whether to impose a prison term on the offender

(e) If the amount of marihuana involved equals or exceeds five thousand grams but is less than twenty thousand grams, illegal cultivation of marihuana is a felony of the third degree (2929.11-2929.18, 2929.31) or, if the offense was committed in the vicinity of a school or in the vicinity of a juvenile, a felony of the second degree (2929.11-2929.18, 2929.31), and there is a presumption for a prison term for the offense

(f) Except as otherwise provided in this division, if the amount of marihuana involved equals or exceeds twenty thousand grams, illegal cultivation of marihuana is a felony of the second degree (2929.11-2929.18, 2929.31, and the court shall impose as a mandatory prison term the maximum prison term prescribed for a felony of the second degree (2929.11-2929.18, 2929.31). If the amount of the drug involved equals or exceeds twenty thousand grams and if the offense was committed in the vicinity of a school or in the vicinity of a juvenile, illegal cultivation of marihuana is a felony of the first degree (2929.11-2929.18, 2929.31), and the court shall impose as a mandatory prison term the maximum prison term prescribed for a felony of the first degree (2929.11-2929.18, 2929.31)

***ILLEGAL ASSEMBLY OR POSSESSION OF CHEMICALS FOR THE MANUFACTURE OF DRUGS,* R.C. § 2925.041 [F3, F2]**

Elements:
(1) Knowingly
(2) Assemble
*(or)*
Possess
(3) One or more chemicals to manufacture a controlled substance in schedule I or II
(4) Intending
(5) To manufacture a controlled substance in schedule I or II
(6) Violating R.C. § 2925.04

*Penalty:*
Whoever violates this section is guilty of illegal assembly or possession of chemicals for the manufacture of drugs. Except as otherwise provided in this division, illegal assembly or possession of chemicals for the manufacture of drugs is a felony of the third degree, and, except as otherwise provided in division (C)(1) or (2) of this section, division (C) of section 2929.13 of the Revised Code applies in determining whether to impose a prison term on the offender. If the offense was committed in the vicinity of a juvenile or in the vicinity of a school, illegal assembly or possession of chemicals for the manufacture of drugs is a felony of the second degree, and, except as otherwise provided in division (C)(1) or (2) of this section, division (C) of section 2929.13 of the Revised Code applies in determining whether to impose a prison term on the offender. If the violation of division (A) of this section is a felony of the third degree under this division and if the chemical or chemicals assembled or possessed in violation of division (A) of this section may be used to manufacture methamphetamine, there either is a presumption for a prison term for the offense or the court shall impose a mandatory prison term on the offender, determined as follows:

(1) Except as otherwise provided in this division, there is a presumption for a prison term for the offense. If the offender two or more times previously has been convicted of or pleaded guilty to a felony drug abuse offense, except as otherwise provided in this division, the court shall impose as a mandatory prison term one of the prison terms prescribed for a felony of the third degree that is not less than two years. If the offender two or more times previously has been convicted of or pleaded guilty to a felony drug abuse offense and if at least one of those previous convictions or guilty pleas was to a violation of division (A) of this section, a violation of division (B)(6) of section 2919.22 of the Revised Code, or a violation of division (A) of section 2925.04 of the Revised Code, the court shall impose as a mandatory prison term one of the prison terms prescribed for a felony of the third degree that is not less than five years.

(2) If the violation of division (A) of this section is a felony of the second degree under division (C) of this section and the chemical or chemicals assembled or possessed in committing the violation may be used to manufacture methamphetamine, the court shall impose as a mandatory prison term one of the prison terms prescribed for a felony of the second degree that is not less than three years. If the violation of division (A) of this section is a felony of the second degree under division (C) of this section, if the chemical or chemicals assembled or possessed in committing the violation may be used to manufacture methamphetamine, and if the offender previously has been convicted of or pleaded guilty to a violation of division (A) of this section, a violation of division (B)(6) of section 2919.22 of the Revised Code, or a violation of division (A) of section 2925.04 of the Revised Code, the court shall impose as a mandatory prison term one of the prison terms prescribed for a felony of the second degree that is not less than five years.

***FUNDING OF DRUG OR MARIHUANA TRAFFICKING,* R.C. § 2925.05 [F3, F2, F1]**

(1) Knowingly
(2) Provide
(3) Money
*(or)*
Other items of value
(4) To another person
(5) With the purpose that the recipient of the money or items of value use them to obtain any controlled substance
(6) (a) For the purpose of violating R.C. § 2925.04
*(or)*
(b) for the purpose of selling or offering to sell the controlled substance in the following amount:

(1) if the drug to be sold or offered for sale is any compound, mixture, preparation, or substance included in schedule I or II, with the exception of marihuana, cocaine, L.S.D., heroin, and hashish, or schedule III, IV, or V, an amount of the drug that equals or exceeds the bulk amount of the drug;
(2) if the drug to be sold or offered for sale is marihuana or a compound, mixture, preparation, or substance other than hashish containing marihuana, an amount of the marihuana that equals or exceeds two hundred grams;
(3) if the drug to be sold or offered for sale is cocaine or a compound, mixture, preparation, or substance containing cocaine, an amount of the cocaine that equals or exceeds five grams;
(4) if the drug to be sold or offered for sale is L.S.D. or a compound, mixture, preparation, or substance containing L.S.D., an amount of the L.S.D. that equals or exceeds ten unit doses if the L.S.D. is in a solid form or equals or exceeds one gram if the L.S.D. is in a liquid concentrate, liquid extract, or liquid distillate form;
(5) if the drug to be sold or offered for sale is heroin or a compound, mixture, preparation, or substance containing heroin, an amount of the heroin that equals or exceeds ten unit doses or equals or exceeds one gram;
(6) if the drug to be sold or offered for sale is hashish or a compound, mixture, preparation, or substance containing hashish, an amount of the hashish that equals or exceeds ten grams if the hashish is in a solid form or equals or exceeds two grams if the hashish is in a liquid concentrate, liquid extract, or liquid distillate form;
(7) Venue

AGGRAVATED FUNDING OF DRUG TRAFFICKING

If the drug involved is any compound, mixture, preparation, or substance included in schedule I or II (except marihuana) **[F1]**
*Penalty:* Mandatory prison term of 3, 4, 5, 6, 7, 8, 9, or 10 years and up to $20,000
Mandatory minimum fine: $10,000
Organization: Up to $25,000
If the above violation involves the sale, offer to sell or possession of a schedule I or II controlled substance (except marijuana) and if the offender, as a result of the violation, is a major drug offender
*Penalty:* Mandatory prison term of 10 years, up to $20,000 and may impose under R.C. § 2929.14(D)(3)(b) an additional 1 to 10 years
Mandatory minimum fine: $10,000
Organization: Up to $25,000

FUNDING OF DRUG TRAFFICKING

If the drug involved is any compound, mixture, preparation, or substance included in schedule III, IV, or V **[F2]**
*Penalty:* Mandatory prison term of 2, 3, 4, 5, 6, 7, or 8 years and up to $15,000
Mandatory minimum fine: $7,500
Organization: Up to $20,000

FUNDING OF MARIHUANA TRAFFICKING

If the drug involved is marihuana **[F3]**
*Penalty:* Presumption of prison term and up to $10,000
Mandatory minimum fine: $5,000
Organization: Up to $15,000
If the drug involved is marihuana and if the offender two or more times previously has been convicted of or pleaded guilty to a felony drug abuse offense **[F3]**
*Penalty:* Mandatory 9, 12, 18, 24, 30, or 36 months imprisonment and up to $10,000
Mandatory minimum fine: $5,000
Organization: Up to $15,000

***ILLEGAL ADMINISTRATION OR DISTRIBUTION OF ANABOLIC STEROIDS*, R.C. § 2925.06 [F4]**

(1) Knowingly
(2) Administer to
*(or)*
Prescribe to
*(or)*
Dispense for administration to
(3) A human being
(4) Any anabolic steroid not approved by the FDA for administration to human beings
(5) Venue

*Penalty:* R.C. § 2929.13(C) applies in determining whether to impose a prison term of 6, 7, 8, 9, 10, 11, 12, 13, 14, 15, 16, 17, or 18 months and up to $5,000
Organization: Up to $10,000

***OFFENSES INVOLVING UNAPPROVED DRUGS; DANGEROUS DRUG OFFENSES INVOLVING LIVESTOCK*, R.C. § 2925.09 [F5, F4]**

Division (A):
(1) Administer, dispense, distribute, manufacture, possess, sell, or use
(2) Any drug, other than a controlled substance, that is not approved by the United States Food and Drug Administration, or the United States Department of Agriculture, unless one of the following applies
  (a) The United States Food and Drug Administration has approved an application for investigational use in accordance with the "Federal Food, Drug, and Cosmetic Act," 52 Stat. 1040 (1938), 21 U.S.C.A. 301, as amended, and the drug is used only for the approved investigational use
  *(or)*
  (b) The United States Department of Agriculture has approved an application for investigational use in accordance with the federal "Virus Serum-Toxin Act," 37 Stat. 832 (1913), 21 U.S.C.A. 151, as amended, and the drug is used only for the approved investigational use
  *(or)*
  (c) A licensed health professional authorized to prescribe drugs, other than a veterinarian, prescribes or combines two or more drugs as a single product for medical purposes
  *(or)*
  (d) A pharmacist, pursuant to a prescription, compounds and dispenses two or more drugs as a single product for medical purposes
(3) Venue

Division (B)(2):
(1) Administer, dispense, distribute, manufacture, possess, sell, or use
(2) Any dangerous drug to or for livestock or any animal that is generally used for food or in the production of food, unless the drug is prescribed by a licensed veterinarian by prescription or other written order and the drug is used in accordance with the veterinarian's order or direction
(3) Venue
*Penalty:* A felony of the fifth degree (2929.11-2929.18, 2929.31)
Subsequent offenses **[F4]**
*Penalty:* A felony of the fourth degree (2929.11-2929.18, 2929.31)
*Notes:* Division (B)(2) of this section does not apply to a registered wholesale distributor of dangerous drugs, a licensed terminal distributor of dangerous drugs, or a person who possesses, possesses for sale, or sells, at retail, a drug in accordance with Chapters 3719., 4729., or 4741. of the Revised Code

***POSSESSION OF DRUGS*, R.C. § 2925.11 [MM, M4, M3, F5, F4, F3, F2, F1]**

(1) Knowingly
(2) Obtain, possess or use
(3) Controlled substance
(4) Venue

AGGRAVATED POSSESSION OF DRUGS

If the drug involved is a compound, mixture, preparation, or substance included in schedule I or II (except marihuana, cocaine, L.S.D., heroin, and hashish) **[F5]**
*Penalty:* R.C. § 2929.13(B) applies in determining whether to impose a prison term of 6, 7, 8, 9, 10, 11, or 12 months and up to $2,500
Organization: Up to $7,500
If the amount of the drug involved equals or exceeds the bulk amount but is less than five times the bulk amount **[F3]**
*Penalty:* Presumption of a prison term of 1, 2, 3, 4, or 5 years and up to $10,000
Mandatory minimum fine: $5,000
Organization: Up to $15,000
If the amount of the drug involved equals or exceeds five times the bulk amount but is less than fifty times the bulk amount **[F2]**
*Penalty:* Mandatory prison term of 2, 3, 4, 5, 6, 7, or 8 years and up to $15,000
Mandatory minimum fine: $7,500
Organization: Up to $20,000
If the amount of the drug involved equals or exceeds fifty times the bulk amount but is less than one hundred times the bulk amount **[F1]**
*Penalty:* Mandatory prison term of 3, 4, 5, 6, 7, 8, 9, or 10 years and up to $20,000
Mandatory minimum fine: $10,000
Organization: Up to $25,000
If the amount of the drug involved equals or exceeds one hundred times the bulk amount, the offender is a major drug offender **[F1]**
*Penalty:* Mandatory prison term of 10 years and up to $20,000
Mandatory minimum fine: $10,000
Organization: Up to $25,000

POSSESSION OF DRUGS

If the drug involved is a compound, mixture, preparation, or substance included in schedule III, IV, or V **[M3]**
*Penalty:* A misdemeanor of the first degree (2929.21-2929.31)
If the offender above has previously been convicted of a drug abuse offense **[M2]**
*Penalty:* A felony of the fifth degree (2929.21-2929.31)
If the drug involved is an anabolic steroid included in schedule III and the offense is a M3, the court may place the offender under a community control sanction that requires the offender to perform supervised community service work
If the amount of the drug involved equals or exceeds the bulk amount but is less than five times the bulk amount **[F4]**
*Penalty:* R.C. § 2929.13(C) applies in determining whether to impose a prison term of 6, 7, 8, 9, 10, 11, 12, 13, 14, 15, 16, 17, or 18 months and up to $5,000
Organization: Up to $10,000
If the amount of the drug involved equals or exceeds five times the bulk amount but is less than fifty times the bulk amount **[F3]**
*Penalty:* Presumption of a prison term of 1, 2, 3, 4, or 5 years and up to $10,000
Mandatory minimum fine: $5,000
Organization: Up to $15,000
If the amount of the drug involved equals or exceeds fifty times the bulk amount **[F2]**
*Penalty:* Mandatory prison term of 2, 3, 4, 5, 6, 7, or 8 years and up to $15,000
Mandatory minimum fine: $7,500
Organization: Up to $20,000

POSSESSION OF MARIHUANA

If the drug involved in the violation is marihuana or a compound, mixture, preparation, or substance containing marihuana other than hashish **[MM]**
*Penalty:* A minor misdemeanor (2929.21-2929.31)
If the amount of the drug involved equals or exceeds one hundred grams but is less than two hundred grams **[M4]**
*Penalty:* A misdemeanor of the fourth degree (2929.21-2929.31)
If the amount of the drug involved equals or exceeds two hundred grams but is less than one thousand grams **[F5]**
*Penalty:* R.C. § 2929.13(B) applies in determining whether to impose a prison term of 6, 7, 8, 9, 10, 11, or 12 months and up to $2,500
Organization: Up to $7,500
If the amount of the drug involved equals or exceeds one thousand grams but is less than five thousand grams **[F3]**
*Penalty:* R.C. § 2929.13(C) applies in determining whether to impose a prison term of 1, 2, 3, 4, or 5 years and up to $10,000
Mandatory minimum fine: $5,000
Organization: Up to $15,000
If the amount of the drug involved equals or exceeds five thousand grams but is less than twenty thousand grams **[F3]**
*Penalty:* Presumption of a prison term of 1, 2, 3, 4, or 5 years and up to $10,000
Mandatory minimum fine: $5,000
Organization: Up to $15,000
If the amount of the drug involved equals or exceeds twenty thousand grams but is less than forty thousand grams **[F2]**
*Penalty:* Mandatory prison term of 5, 6, 7, or 8 years and up to $15,000
Mandatory minimum fine: $7,500
Organization: Up to $20,000
If the amount of the drug involved equals or exceeds forty thousand grams **[F2]**
*Penalty:* Mandatory prison term of 2, 3, 4, 5, 6, 7, or 8 years and up to $15,000
Mandatory minimum fine: $7,500
Organization: Up to $20,000

POSSESSION OF COCAINE

If the drug involved in the violation is cocaine or a compound, mixture, preparation, or substance containing cocaine **[F5]**
*Penalty:* R.C. § 2929.13(B) applies in determining whether to impose a prison term of 6, 7, 8, 9, 10, 11, or 12 months and up to $2,500
Organization: Up to $7,500
If the amount of the drug involved equals or exceeds five grams but is less than ten grams of cocaine **[F4]**
*Penalty:* Section 2929.13(B) applies in determining whether to impose a prison term and up to $5,000
Organization: Up to $10,000
If the amount of the drug involved equals or exceeds ten grams but is less than twenty grams of cocaine **[F3]**
*Penalty:* Presumption of (or, if third or subsequent offense, mandatory) prison term of 9, 12, 18, 24, 30, or 36 months and up to $10,000
Mandatory minimum fine: $5,000
Organization: Up to $15,000
If the amount of the drug involved equals or exceeds twenty grams but is less than twenty-seven grams of cocaine **[F2]**

*Penalty:* Mandatory prison term of 2, 3, 4, 5, 6, 7, or 8 years and up to $15,000
Mandatory minimum fine: $7,500
Organization: Up to $20,000
If the amount of the drug involved equals or exceeds twenty-seven grams but is less than one hundred grams of cocaine **[F1]**
*Penalty:* Mandatory prison term of 3, 4, 5, 6, 7, 8, 9, 10, or 11 years and up to $20,000
Mandatory minimum fine: $10,000
Organization: Up to $25,000
If the amount of the drug involved equals or exceeds one hundred grams **[F1]**
*Penalty:* Mandatory prison term of 10 years and up to $20,000
Mandatory minimum fine: $10,000
Organization: Up to $25,000

POSSESSION OF L.S.D.

If the drug involved is L.S.D. or a compound, mixture, preparation, or substance containing L.S.D. **[F5]**
*Penalty:* R.C. § 2929.13(B) applies in determining whether to impose a prison term of 6, 7, 8, 9, 10, 11, or 12 months and up to $2,500
Organization: Up to $7,500
If the amount of L.S.D. involved equals or exceeds ten unit doses but is less than fifty unit doses of L.S.D. in a solid form or equals or exceeds one gram but is less than five grams of L.S.D. in a liquid concentrate, liquid extract, or liquid distillate form **[F4]**
*Penalty:* R.C. § 2929.13(C) applies in determining whether to impose a prison term of 6, 7, 8, 9, 10, 11, 12, 13, 14, 15, 16, 17, or 18 months and up to $5,000
Organization: Up to $10,000
If the amount of L.S.D. involved equals or exceeds fifty unit doses but is less than two hundred fifty unit doses of L.S.D. in a solid form or equals or exceeds five grams but is less than twenty-five grams of L.S.D. in a liquid concentrate, liquid extract, or liquid distillate form **[F3]**
*Penalty:* Presumption of a prison term of 1, 2, 3, 4, or 5 years and up to $10,000
Mandatory minimum fine: $5,000
Organization: Up to $15,000
If the amount of L.S.D. involved equals or exceeds two hundred fifty unit doses but is less than one thousand unit doses of L.S.D. in a solid form or equals or exceeds twenty-five grams but is less than one hundred grams of L.S.D. in a liquid concentrate, liquid extract, or liquid distillate form **[F2]**
*Penalty:* Mandatory prison term of 2, 3, 4, 5, 6, 7, or 8 years and up to $15,000
Mandatory minimum fine: $7,500
Organization: Up to $20,000
If the amount of L.S.D. involved equals or exceeds one thousand unit doses but is less than five thousand unit doses of L.S.D. in a solid form or equals or exceeds one hundred grams but is less than five hundred grams of L.S.D. in a liquid concentrate, liquid extract, or liquid distillate form **[F1]**
*Penalty:* Mandatory prison term of 3, 4, 5, 6, 7, 8, 9, or 10 years and up to $20,000
Mandatory minimum fine: $10,000
Organization: Up to $25,000
If the amount of L.S.D. involved equals or exceeds five thousand unit doses of L.S.D. in a solid form or equals or exceeds five hundred grams of L.S.D. in a liquid concentrate, liquid extract, or liquid distillate form the offender is a major drug offender **[F1]**
*Penalty:* Mandatory prison term of 10 years and up to $20,000
Mandatory minimum fine: $10,000
Organization: Up to $25,000

POSSESSION OF HEROIN

If the drug involved in the violation is heroin or a compound, mixture, preparation, or substance containing heroin **[F5]**
*Penalty:* R.C. § 2929.13(B) applies in determining whether to impose a prison term of 6, 7, 8, 9, 10, 11, or 12 months and up to $2,500
Organization: Up to $7,500
If the amount of the drug involved equals or exceeds ten unit doses but is less than fifty unit doses or equals or exceeds one gram but is less than five grams **[F4]**
*Penalty:* R.C. § 2929.13(C) applies in determining whether to impose a prison term of 6, 7, 8, 9, 10, 11, 12, 13, 14, 15, 16, 17, or 18 months and up to $5,000
Organization: Up to $10,000
If the amount of the drug involved equals or exceeds fifty unit doses but is less than one hundred unit doses or equals or exceeds five grams but is less than ten grams **[F3]**
*Penalty:* Presumption of a prison term of 1, 2, 3, 4, or 5 years and up to $10,000
Mandatory minimum fine: $5,000
Organization: Up to $15,000
If the amount of the drug involved equals or exceeds one hundred unit doses but is less than five hundred unit doses or equals or exceeds ten grams but is less than fifty grams **[F2]**

*Penalty:* Mandatory prison term of 2, 3, 4, 5, 6, 7, or 8 years and up to $15,000
Mandatory minimum fine: $7,500
Organization: Up to $20,000
If the amount of the drug involved equals or exceeds five hundred unit doses but is less than two thousand five hundred unit doses or equals or exceeds fifty grams but is less than two hundred fifty grams **[F1]**
*Penalty:* Mandatory prison term of 3, 4, 5, 6, 7, 8, 9, or 10 years and up to $20,000
Mandatory minimum fine: $10,000
Organization: Up to $25,000
If the amount of the drug involved equals or exceeds two thousand five hundred unit doses or equals or exceeds two hundred fifty grams, the offender is a major drug offender **[F1]**
*Penalty:* Mandatory prison term of 10 years and up to $20,000
Mandatory minimum fine: $10,000
Organization: Up to $25,000

POSSESSION OF HASHISH

If the drug involved in the violation is hashish or a compound, mixture, preparation, or substance containing hashish **[MM]**
*Penalty:* A minor misdemeanor (2929.21-2929.31)
If the amount of the drug involved equals or exceeds five grams but is less than ten grams of hashish in a solid form or equals or exceeds one gram but is less than two grams of hashish in a liquid concentrate, liquid extract, or liquid distillate form **[M4]**
*Penalty:* A misdemeanor of the fourth degree (2929.21-2929.31)
If the amount of the drug involved equals or exceeds ten grams but is less than fifty grams of hashish in a solid form or equals or exceeds two grams but is less than ten grams of hashish in a liquid concentrate, liquid extract, or liquid distillate form **[F5]**
*Penalty:* R.C. § 2929.13(B) applies in determining whether to impose a prison term of 6, 7, 8, 9, 10, 11, or 12 months and up to $2,500
Organization: Up to $7,500
If the amount of the drug involved equals or exceeds fifty grams but is less than two hundred fifty grams of hashish in a solid form or equals or exceeds ten grams but is less than fifty grams of hashish in a liquid concentrate, liquid extract, or liquid distillate form **[F3]**
*Penalty:* R.C. § 2929.13(B) applies in determining whether to impose a prison term of 1, 2, 3, 4, or 5 years and up to $10,000
Mandatory minimum fine: $5,000
Organization: Up to $15,000
If the amount of the drug involved equals or exceeds two hundred fifty grams but is less than one thousand grams of hashish in a solid form or equals or exceeds fifty grams but is less than two hundred grams of hashish in a liquid concentrate, liquid extract, or liquid distillate form **[F3]**
*Penalty:* Presumption of a prison term of 2, 3, 4, 5, 6, 7, or 8 years and up to $15,000
Mandatory minimum fine: $5,000
Organization: Up to $15,000
If the amount of the drug involved equals or exceeds one thousand grams but is less than two thousand grams of hashish in a solid form or equals or exceeds two hundred grams but is less than four hundred grams of hashish in a liquid concentrate, liquid extract, or liquid distillate form **[F2]**
*Penalty:* Mandatory prison term of 5, 6, 7, or 8 years and up to $15,000
Mandatory minimum fine: $7,500
Organization: Up to $20,000
If the amount of the drug involved equals or exceeds two thousand grams of hashish in a solid form or equals or exceeds four hundred grams of hashish in a liquid concentrate, liquid extract, or liquid distillate form **[F2]**
*Penalty:* Mandatory prison term of 2, 3, 4, 5, 6, 7, or 8 years and up to $15,000
Mandatory minimum fine: $7,500
Organization: Up to $20,000
*Notes: See* statute for provisions exempting some pates from provisions concerning anabolic steroids
*See* statute for special provisions concerning attorneys and professionally licensed persons convicted under this statute
*See* statute for provisions exempting indigents from mandatory fines
*See* statute for provisions allowing revocation or suspension of driver's and commercial driver's licenses
*See* statute for special provisions concerning probation, treatment, and counseling
*See* statute for special provisions concerning pregnant offenders
Arrest or conviction for a minor misdemeanor violation of this section does not constitute a criminal record. R.C. § 2925.11(D)
Laboratory report as prima-facie evidence in drug abuse cases; rights of accused in re, R.C. § 2925.51
*Definitions:* "Controlled substance," R.C. § 3719.01(D)
"Marihuana," R.C. § 3719.01(Q)
"Possess," R.C. § 2925.01
"Professionally licensed person," R.C. § 2925.01

***POSSESSING DRUG ABUSE INSTRUMENTS*, R.C. § 2925.12 [M2, M1]**

(1) Knowingly
(2) Make, obtain, possess, or use
(3) Any instrument, article, or thing the customary and primary purpose of which is for the administration or use of a dangerous drug, other than marihuana
(4) When the instrument involved is a hypodermic or syringe, whether or not of crude or extemporized manufacture or assembly
*(and)*
(5) The instrument, article or thing involved has been used by the offender
(a) To unlawfully administer or use a dangerous drug, other than marihuana,
*(or)*
(b) To prepare a dangerous drug, other than marihuana, for unlawful administration or use
(6) Venue

*Penalty:* A misdemeanor of the second degree (2929.21-2929.31)
Where previously convicted of drug abuse offense **[M1]**
*Penalty:* A misdemeanor of the first degree (2929.21-2929.31)
*Notes:* This section does not apply to manufacturers, licensed health professionals authorized to prescribe drugs, pharmacists, owners of pharmacies, and other persons whose conduct was in accordance with Chapters 3719., 4715., 4723., 4729., 4730., 4731., and 4741. of the Revised Code
*See* statute for special provisions concerning attorneys and professionally licensed persons convicted under this statute
*See* statute for provisions allowing suspension of driver's and commercial driver's licenses
*Definitions:* "Dangerous drugs," R.C. § 4729.01(F)
"Hypodermic," R.C. § 3719.01(M)
"Professionally licensed person," R.C. § 2925.01

***POSSESSION, SALE, AND DISPOSAL OF HYPODERMICS*, R.C. § 3719.172 [F4, F3, M3, M1]**

Division (B): **[M3]**
(1) (a) Being a manufacturer, distributor, or dealer in hypodermics or medication packaged in hypodermics, or their authorized agents or employees or terminal distributor of dangerous drugs
(b) Display any hypodermic for sale
*(or)*
(2) (a) Being authorized to possess a hypodermic under division (A)
(i) Negligently fail to take reasonable precautions to prevent any hypodermic in his possession from theft or acquisition by any unauthorized person
(3) Venue

*Penalty:* A misdemeanor of the third degree (2929.21-2929.31)
Where previously convicted **[M1]**
*Penalty:* A misdemeanor of the first degree (2929.21-2929.31)

Division (C): **[F4]**
(1) Not being a manufacturer, distributor, dealer in hypodermics or medication packaged in hypodermics, or their authorized agents or employees, terminal distributor of dangerous drugs, person under the direct supervision of a pharmacist or licensed health professional authorized to prescribe drugs
(2) Sell or furnish a hypodermic to another
(3) Venue

*Penalty:* A felony of the fourth degree (2929.11-2929.18, 2929.31)
Where previously convicted **[F3]**
*Penalty:* A felony of the third degree (2929.11-2929.18, 2929.31)

Division (D): **[F4]**
(1) Sell or furnish a hypodermic
(2) To another whom he knows or has reasonable cause to believe
(3) Is not authorized by division (A) to possess a hypodermic
(4) Venue

*Penalty:* A felony of the fourth degree (2929.11-2929.18, 2929.31)

***PERMITTING DRUG ABUSE*, R.C. § 2925.13 [M1, F5]**

Division (A):
(1) Being the owner, operator, or person in charge of a locomotive, watercraft, aircraft, or other vehicle as defined in R.C. § 4501.01(A)
(2) Knowingly
(3) Permit such vehicle to be used for commission of felony drug abuse offense
(4) Venue

Division (B):
(1) Being the owner, lessee, or occupant, or having custody, control, or supervision of premises, or real estate, including vacant land
(2) Knowingly
(3) Permit premises, or real estate, including vacant land, to be used for commission of a felony drug abuse offense
(4) By another person
(5) Venue
*Penalty:* A misdemeanor of the first degree (2929.21-2929.31)
If the felony drug offense in question involves corrupting another with drugs (R.C. § 2925.02), or the sale of a controlled substance [violation of R.C. § 2925.03] **[F5]**
*Penalty:* A felony of the fifth degree (2929.11-2929.18, 2929.31)
If the violation of Division (A) involves the sale, offer to sell, or possession of schedule I or II controlled substance (except marihuana) and if the offender as a result of the violation is a major drug offender, the court in lieu of the prison term otherwise authorized or required, shall impose upon the offender a mandatory 10 year prison term and may impose an additional prison term of 1 to 10 years pursuant to R.C. § 2929.14(D)(3)
*Notes:* Any premises or real estate that is permitted to be used in violation of division (B) of this section constitutes a nuisance subject to abatement pursuant to Chapter 3767. of the Revised Code
*See* statute for special provisions concerning attorneys and professionally licensed persons convicted under this statute
*See* statute for provisions allowing suspension of driver's and commercial driver's licenses
Laboratory report as prima-facie evidence in drug abuse cases; rights of accused in re, R.C. § 2925.51
*Definitions:* "Felony drug abuse offense," R.C. § 2925.01

### ***DRUG PARAPHERNALIA,* R.C. § 2925.14 [M4, M2, M1]**

Illegal Use or Possession of Drug Paraphernalia [Division (C)(1)] **[M4]**
(1) Knowingly
(2) (a) Use
*(or)*
(b) Possess with purpose to use
(3) Drug paraphernalia
(4) Venue
*Penalty:* A misdemeanor of the fourth degree (2929.21-2929.31)
Dealing in Drug Paraphernalia [Division (C)(2)] **[M2]**
(1) Knowingly
(2) (a) Sell
*(or)*
(b) Possess with purpose to sell
*(or)*
(c) Manufacture with purpose to sell
(3) Drug paraphernalia
(4) If the person knows or reasonably should know the equipment, product, or material will be used as drug paraphernalia
(5) Venue
*Penalty:* A misdemeanor of the second degree (2929.21-2929.31)
Selling Drug Paraphernalia to Juveniles [Divisions (Q(2), (F)(3)] **[M1]**
(1) Knowingly
(2) (a) Sell
*(or)*
(b) Possess with purpose to sell
*(or)*
(c) Manufacture with purpose to sell
(3) Drug paraphernalia
(4) To a juvenile
(5) Venue
*Penalty:* A misdemeanor of the first degree (2929.21-2929.31)
Illegal Advertising of Drug Paraphernalia [Division (C)(3)] **[M2]**
(1) Place an advertisement
(2) In any newspaper, magazine, handbill, or other publication that is published and printed, circulates primarily within this state
(3) Knowing that the purpose of the advertisement is to promote the illegal sale in this state of the equipment, product, or material that the offender intended or designed for use as drug paraphernalia
(4) Venue
*Penalty:* A misdemeanor of the second degree (2929.21-2929.31)
*Notes:* See R.C. § 2925.14 for special provisions regarding seizure and disposal
*See* statute for special provisions concerning attorneys and professionally licensed persons convicted under this statute
*See* statute for provisions allowing suspension of driver's and commercial driver's licenses
This statute does not apply to manufacturers, licensed health professionals authorized to prescribe drugs,

pharmacists, owners of pharmacies, and other persons whose conduct is in accordance with Chapter 3719., 4715., 4723., 4729., 4730., 4731., or 4741. of the Revised Code

This statute is not to be construed to prohibit the possession or use of a hypodermic as authorized by section 3719.172 of the Revised Code

*Definitions:* "Drug paraphernalia," R.C. § 2925.14

### *DECEPTION TO OBTAIN DANGEROUS DRUG,* R.C. § 2925.22 [F5, F4]

(1) By deception as defined in R.C. § 2913.01

(2) (a) Procure the administration of, a prescription for, or the dispensing of, a dangerous drug

*(or)*

(b) Possess an uncompleted preprinted prescription blank used for writing a prescription for a dangerous drug

(3) Venue

If the person possesses an uncompleted preprinted prescription blank used for writing a prescription for a dangerous drug or if the drug involved is a dangerous drug, except as otherwise provided below **[F5]**

If the offender previously has been convicted of or pleaded guilty to a drug abuse offense **[F4]**

*Penalty:* R.C. § 2929.13(C) applies in determining whether to impose a prison term of 6, 7, 8, 9, 10, 11, 12, 13, 14, 15, 16, 17, or 18 months and up to $5,000

If the drug involved is a compound, mixture, preparation, or substance included in schedule I or II (except marihuana) **[F4]**

*Penalty:* R.C. § 2929.13(C) applies in determining whether to impose a prison term of 6, 7, 8, 9, 10, 11, 12, 13, 14, 15, 16, 17, or 18 months and up to $5,000

Organization: Up to $10,000

If the drug involved is a compound, mixture, preparation, or substance included in schedule I or II (except marihuana)and the amount of the drug involved equals or exceeds the bulk amount but is less than five times the bulk amount, or if the amount of the drug involved that could be obtained pursuant to the prescription would equal or exceed the bulk amount but would be less than five times the bulk amount **[F3]**

If the drug involved is a compound, mixture, preparation, or substance included in schedule I or II (except marihuana)and the amount of the drug involved equals or exceeds five times the bulk amount but is less than fifty times the bulk amount, or if the amount of the drug involved that could be obtained pursuant to the prescription would equal or exceed five times the bulk amount but would be less than fifty times the bulk amount **[F2]**

If the drug involved is a compound, mixture, preparation, or substance included in schedule I or II (except marihuana)and the amount of the drug involved equals or exceeds fifty times the bulk amount, or if the amount of the drug involved that could be obtained pursuant to the prescription would equal or exceed fifty times the bulk amount **[F1]**

If the drug involved is a compound, mixture, preparation, or substance included in schedule III, IV, or V or is marihuana **[F5]**

*Penalty:* R.C. § 2929.13(C) applies in determining whether to impose a prison term of 6, 7, 8, 9, 10, 11, or 12 months and up to $2,500

Organization: Up to $7,500

If the drug involved is a compound, mixture, preparation, or substance included in schedule III, IV, or V or is marihuana and the amount of the drug involved equals or exceeds the bulk amount but is less than five times the bulk amount, or if the amount of the drug involved that could be obtained pursuant to the prescription would equal or exceed the bulk amount but would be less than five times the bulk amount **[F4]**

If the drug involved is a compound, mixture, preparation, or substance included in schedule III, IV, or V or is marihuana and the amount of the drug involved equals or exceeds five times the bulk amount but is less than fifty times the bulk amount, or if the amount of the drug involved that could be obtained pursuant to the prescription would equal or exceed five times the bulk amount but would be less than fifty times the bulk amount **[F3]**

If the drug involved is a compound, mixture, preparation, or substance included in schedule III, IV, or V or is marihuana and the amount of the drug involved equals or exceeds fifty times the bulk amount, or if the amount of the drug involved that could be obtained pursuant to the prescription would equal or exceed fifty times the bulk amount **[F2]**

*Notes:* Laboratory report as prima-facie evidence in drug abuse cases; rights of accused in re, R.C. § 2925.51

*See* statute for special provisions concerning attorneys and professionally licensed persons convicted under this statute

*See* statute for provisions allowing suspension of driver's and commercial driver's licenses

*Definitions:* "Prescription," R.C. § 3719.01(CC)

### *ILLEGAL PROCESSING OF DRUG DOCUMENTS,* R.C. § 2925.23 [F5, F4]

Division (A):

(1) Knowingly

(2) Make a false statement in any prescription, order, report, or record required by R.C. Chapter 3719. or 4729.

(3) Venue

Division (B):

(1) (a) Intentionally make, utter, or sell

*(or)*

(b) Knowingly possess

(2) A false or forged
  (a) Prescription
    *(or)*
  (b) Uncompleted preprinted prescription blank used for writing a prescription
    *(or)*
  (c) Official written order
    *(or)*
  (d) License for a terminal distributor of dangerous drugs as required in R.C. § 4729.60
    *(or)*
  (e) Registration certificate for a wholesale distributor of dangerous drugs as required in R.C. § 4729.60
(3) Venue

Division (C):
(1) By theft, as defined in R.C. § 2913.02
(2) Acquire
(3) (a) A prescription
    *(or)*
  (b) An uncompleted preprinted prescription blank used for writing a prescription
    *(or)*
  (c) An official written order
    *(or)*
  (d) A blank official written order
    *(or)*
  (e) A license or blank license for a terminal distributor of dangerous drugs as required in R.C. § 4729.60
    *(or)*
  (f) A registration certificate or blank registration certificate for a wholesale distributor of dangerous drugs as required in R.C. § 4729.60
(4) Venue

Division (D):
(1) Knowingly
(2) Make or affix
(3) Any false or forged label
(4) To a package or receptacle containing any dangerous drug
(5) Venue

If the offender violates division (A), (B)(2)(b), (d), or (e) or division (C)(3)(b), (d), (e), or (f)
*Penalty:* A felony of the fifth degree (2929.11-2929.18, 2929.31)
If the offender violates division (A), (B)(2)(a) or (c), division (C)(3)(a) or (c), or division (D) and if the drug involved is a compound, mixture, preparation, or substance included in schedule I or II (except marihuana) **[F4]**
*Penalty:* R.C. § 2929.13(C) applies in determining whether to impose a prison term of 6, 7, 8, 9, 10, 11, 12, 13, 14, 15, 16, 17, or 18 months and up to $5,000
  Organization: Up to $10,000
If the offender violates division (A), (B)(2)(a) or (c), division (C)(3)(a) or (c), or division (D) and if the drug involved is a dangerous drug or a compound, mixture, preparation, or substance included in schedule III, IV, or V or is marihuana **[F5]**
*Penalty:* R.C. § 2929.13(C) applies in determining whether to impose a prison term of 6, 7, 8, 9, 10, 11, or 12 months and up to $2,500
  Organization: Up to $7,500
*Notes:* Divisions (A) and (D) do not apply to manufacturers, licensed health professionals authorized to prescribe drugs, pharmacists, owners of pharmacies, and other persons whose conduct is in accordance with R.C. Chapters 3719., 4715., 4723., 4729., 4730., 4731., and 4741. of the Revised Code
  *See* statute for special provisions concerning attorneys and professionally licensed persons convicted under this statute
  *See* statute for provisions allowing suspension of driver's and commercial driver's licenses
*Definitions:* "Felony drug abuse offense," R.C. § 2925.01
  "Official written order," R.C. § 3719.01(U)
  "Prescription," R.C. § 3719.01(CC)

### *TAMPERING WITH DRUGS*, R.C. § 2925.24 [F3, F2]

Division (A):
(1) Knowingly
(2) (a) Adulterate or alter any dangerous drug (or)
  (b) Substitute any dangerous drug with another substance
(3) Venue

Division (B):
(1) Knowingly
(2) (a) Adulterate or alter any package or receptacle containing any dangerous drug (or)

(b) Substitute any package or receptacle containing any dangerous drug with another package or receptacle
(3) Venue
*Penalty:* A felony of the third degree (2929.11-2929.18, 2929.31)
If the violation results in physical harm to any person **[F2]**
*Penalty:* A felony of the second degree (2929.11-2929.18, 2929.31)
*Notes:* This section does not apply to manufacturers, practitioners, pharmacists, owners of pharmacies, nurses, and other persons, when the conduct of the manufacturer, practitioner, pharmacist, owner of a pharmacy, nurse, or other person is in accordance with Chapters 3719., 4715., 4723., 4729., 4731., and 4741. of the Revised Code
It is an affirmative defense to a charge under this section alleging that a person altered a dangerous drug that the dangerous drug the person allegedly altered was lawfully prescribed for the person's personal use and that the person did not sell or transfer or intend to sell or transfer the dangerous drug to another person

### *ABUSING HARMFUL INTOXICANTS*, R.C. § 2925.31 [M1, F5]

(1) Except for lawful research, clinical, medical, dental, or veterinary purposes
(2) Obtain, possess, or use
(3) A harmful intoxicant
(4) With purpose to induce intoxication or similar physiological effects
(5) Venue
*Penalty:* A misdemeanor of the first degree (2929.21-2929.31)
Where previously convicted of drug abuse offense **[F5]**
*Penalty:* A felony of the fifth degree (2929.11-2929.18, 2929.31)
*Notes:* Laboratory report as prima-facie evidence in drug abuse cases; rights of accused in re, R.C. § 2925.51
*See* statute for special provisions concerning attorneys and professionally licensed persons convicted under this statute
*See* statute for provisions allowing suspension of driver's and commercial driver's licenses
*Definitions:* "Drug abuse offense," R.C. § 2925.01
"Harmful intoxicant," R.C. § 2925.01

### *TRAFFICKING IN HARMFUL INTOXICANTS; IMPROPERLY DISPENSING OR DISTRIBUTING NITROUS OXIDE*, R.C. § 2925.32 [M4, F5, F4]

Division (A)(1): **[F5, F4]**
(1) Knowingly
(2) Dispense or distribute
(3) A harmful intoxicant (excluding nitrous oxide)
(4) To a person age 18 or older
(5) Believing or having reason to believe that the harmful intoxicant will be used in violation of R.C. § 2925.31
(6) Venue

Division (A)(2): **[F5, F4]**
(1) Knowingly
(2) Dispense or distribute
(3) A harmful intoxicant (excluding nitrous oxide)
(4) To a person under age 18
(5) Believing or having reason to believe that the harmful intoxicant will be used in violation of R.C. § 2925.31
(6) Venue

Division (B)(1): **[F5, F4]**
(1) Knowingly
(2) Dispense or distribute
(3) Nitrous oxide
(4) To a person age 21 or older
(5) Knowing or having reason to believe that the nitrous oxide will be used in violation of R.C. § 2925.31
(6) Venue

Division (B)(2): **[F5, F4]**
(1) Knowingly
(2) Dispense or distribute
(3) Nitrous oxide
(4) To a person under 21
(5) Except for lawful medical, dental or clinical purposes
(6) Venue

Division (B)(3): **[F5, F4]**
(1) Sell
(2) Device that allows the purchaser to inhale nitrous oxide from cartridges or to hold nitrous oxide released from cartridges for purposes of inhalation
(3) At the time a cartridge of nitrous oxide is sold to another person
(4) Venue

*Penalty:* A felony of the fifth degree (2929.11-2929.18, 2929.31)
If the offender previously has been convicted of a drug abuse offense **[F4]**
*Penalty:* A felony of the fourth degree (2929.11-2929.18, 2929.31)

Division (B)(4): **[M4]**
(1) Being a person who dispenses or distributes nitrous oxide in cartridges
(2) Fail to comply with
(3) (a) The record-keeping requirements established under Division (F) of this section
*(or)*
(b) The labeling and transaction identification requirements established under Division (F) of this section
(4) Venue
*Penalty:* A misdemeanor of the fourth degree (2929.21-2929.31)
*Notes:* Division (A)(2) of this section does not prohibit dispensing or distributing a harmful intoxicant to a person under 18 if a written order from the juvenile's parent or guardian is provided to the dispenser or distributor or dispensing or distributing gasoline or diesel fuel to a person under 18 if the dispenser or distributor does not know or have reason to believe the product will be used in violation of R.C. § 2925.31. A person is not required to obtain a written order from the parent or guardian of a person under age 18 in order to distribute or dispense gasoline or diesel fuel to the person
The sale of such a device as described in Division (B)(3) constitutes a rebuttable presumption that the person knew or had reason to believe that the purchaser intended to abuse the nitrous oxide
This section does not apply to products used in making, fabricating, assembling, transporting, or constructing a product or structure by manual labor or machinery for sale or lease to another person, or to the mining, refining, or processing of natural deposits
In addition to any other sanction imposed for trafficking in harmful intoxicants, the court shall suspend for not less than six months or more than five years the driver's or commercial driver's license or permit of any person who is convicted of or has pleaded guilty to trafficking in harmful intoxicants. If the offender is a professionally licensed person or a person who has been admitted to the bar by order of the supreme court, in addition to any other sanction imposed, the court forthwith shall comply with R.C. § 2925.38

***POSSESSING NITROUS OXIDE IN MOTOR VEHICLE,* R.C. § 2925.33 [M4]**

(1) Possess
(2) An open cartridge of nitrous oxide
(3) (a) While operating or being a passenger in or on a motor vehicle on a street, highway, or other public or private property open to the public for purposes of vehicular traffic or parking
*(or)*
(b) While being in or on a stationary motor vehicle on a street, highway, or other public or private property open to the public for purposes of vehicular traffic or parking
(4) Unless authorized under Chapter 3719., 4715., 4729., 4731., 4741., or 4765.
(5) Venue
*Penalty:* A misdemeanor of the fourth degree (2929.21-2929.31)

***ILLEGAL DISPENSING OF DRUG SAMPLES,* R.C. § 2925.36 [M2, M1, F5, F4]**

(1) Knowingly
(2) Furnish
(3) Another
(4) A sample drug
(5) Venue
If the drug involved is a compound, mixture, preparation, or substance included in schedule I or II (except marihuana) **[F5]**
*Penalty:* R.C. § 2929.13(C) applies in determining whether to impose a prison term of 6, 7, 8, 9, 10, 11, or 12 months and up to $2,500
Organization: Up to $7,500
If the offense was committed in the vicinity of a school or in the vicinity of a juvenile **[F4]**
*Penalty:* R.C. § 2929.13(C) applies in determining whether to impose a prison term of 6, 7, 8, 9, 10, 11, 12, 13, 14, 15, 16, 17, or 18 months and up to $5,000
Organization: Up to $10,000
If the drug involved is a dangerous drug or a compound, mixture, preparation, or substance included in schedule III, IV, or V or is marihuana **[M2]**
*Penalty:* A misdemeanor of the second degree (2929.21-2929.31)
If the offense was committed in the vicinity of a school or in the vicinity of a juvenile **[M1]**
*Penalty:* A misdemeanor of the first degree (2929.21-2929.31)
*Notes:* *See* statute for special provisions concerning attorneys and professionally licensed persons convicted under this statute
*See* statute for provisions allowing suspension of driver's and commercial driver's licenses
Laboratory report as prima-facie evidence in drug abuse cases; rights of accused in re, R.C. § 2925.51
*Definitions:* "Dispense," R.C. § 3719.01(F)
"Drug abuse offense," R.C. § 2925.01
"Sample drug," R.C. § 2925.01

***OFFENSES INVOLVING COUNTERFEIT CONTROLLED SUBSTANCES*, R.C. § 2925.37 [M1, F5, F4]**

Division (A):
(1) Knowingly
(2) Possess
(3) Any counterfeit controlled substance
(4) Venue

Division (B):
(1) Knowingly
(2) Make, sell, offer to sell, or deliver
(3) Any substance
(4) Knowing it is a counterfeit controlled substance
(5) Venue

Division (C):

(1) Make, possess, sell, offer to sell, or deliver
(2) Any punch, die, plate, stone, or other device
(3) Knowing or having a reason to know
(4) That it will be used to print or reproduce a trademark, trade name or other identifying mark
(5) Upon a counterfeit controlled substance
(6) Venue

Division (D):
(1) Sell, offer to sell, give, or deliver
(2) Any counterfeit controlled substance
(3) To a juvenile
(4) Venue

Division (E):
(1) Directly or indirectly represent
(2) A counterfeit controlled substance
(3) As a controlled substance
(4) By describing its effects
(5) As the physical or psychological effects associated with the use of controlled substances
(6) Venue

Division (F):
(1) Directly or indirectly falsely represent or advertise
(2) A counterfeit controlled substance
(3) As a controlled substance
(4) Venue

Division (A) Possession of counterfeit controlled substances **[M1]**
*Penalty:* A misdemeanor of the first degree (2929.21-2929.31)

Divisions (B) or (C) Trafficking in counterfeit controlled substances **[F5]**
*Penalty:* R.C. § 2929.13(C) applies in determining whether to impose a prison term of 6, 7, 8, 9, 10, 11, or 12 months and up to $2,500
Organization: Up to $7,500
If the offense was committed in the vicinity of a school or in the vicinity of a juvenile **[F4]**
*Penalty:* R.C. § 2929.13(C) applies in determining whether to impose a prison term of 6, 7, 8, 9, 10, 11, 12, 13, 14, 15, 16, 17, or 18 months and up to $5,000
Organization: Up to $10,000

Division (D) Aggravated trafficking in counterfeit controlled substances **[F4]**
*Penalty:* R.C. § 2929.13(C) applies in determining whether to impose a prison term of 6, 7, 8, 9, 10, 11, 12, 13, 14, 15, 16, 17, or 18 months and up to $5,000
Organization: Up to $10,000

Division (E) Promoting and encouraging drug abuse **[F5]**

*Penalty:* R.C. § 2929.13(C) applies in determining whether to impose a prison term of 6, 7, 8, 9, 10, 11, or 12 months and up to $2,500
Organization: Up to $7,500
If the offense was committed in the vicinity of a school or in the vicinity of a juvenile **[F4]**
*Penalty:* R.C. § 2929.13(C) applies in determining whether to impose a prison term of 6, 7, 8, 9, 10, 11, 12, 13, 14, 15, 16, 17, or 18 months and up to $5,000
Organization: Up to $10,000

Division (F) Fraudulent drug advertising **[F5]**

*Penalty:* R.C. § 2929.13(C) applies in determining whether to impose a prison term of 6, 7, 8, 9, 10, 11, or 12 months and up to $2,500
Organization: Up to $7,500
If the offense was committed in the vicinity of a school or in the vicinity of a juvenile **[F4]**
*Penalty:* R.C. § 2929.13(C) applies in determining whether to impose a prison term of 6, 7, 8, 9, 10, 11, 12, 13, 14, 15, 16, 17, or 18 months and up to $5,000
Organization: Up to $10,000
*Notes: See* statute for special provisions concerning attorneys and professionally licensed persons convicted under this statute
*See* statute for provisions allowing suspension of driver's and commercial driver's licenses
*Definitions:* "Advertise," R.C. § 2925.37
"Advertisement," R.C. § 3715.01

***PROHIBITIONS CONCERNING PURCHASING PSEUDOEPHEDRINE PRODUCTS,* R.C. § 2925.55 [M4, M1]**

Division (B):
(1) Knowingly
(2) Purchase, receive, or otherwise acquire
(3) More than nine grams of any pseudoephedrine product
(4) Within a period of thirty consecutive days,
(5) Venue

Division (C):
(1) Individual under eighteen years of age
(2) Knowingly
(3) Purchase, receive, or otherwise acquire
(4) A pseudoephedrine product
(5) Venue

Division (D):
(1) Individual under eighteen years of age
(2) Knowingly
(3) Show or give
(4) False information concerning the individual's name, age, or other identification
(5) For the purpose of purchasing, receiving, or otherwise acquiring a pseudoephedrine product.
(6) Venue

Division (E):
(1) Knowingly
(2) Fail to comply with
(3) The requirements of division (C)(3) [As purchaser of pseudoephedrine product, sign and print the purchaser's name and address in the retailer's log book and provide a government-issued identification card to the retailer or terminal distributor of dangerous drugs to verify the purchaser's identity] of section 3715.05 of the Revised Code.
(4) Venue

*Notes:*
General exception clause for Divisions (B) and (C):
Unless the pseudoephedrine product is dispensed by a pharmacist pursuant to a valid prescription issued by a licensed health professional authorized to prescribe drugs and the conduct of the pharmacist and the licensed health professional authorized to prescribe drugs is in accordance with Chapter 3719., 4715., 4723., 4729., 4731., or 4741. of the Revised Code.
Specific exception clause for Division (B):
It is not a violation of Division (B) of this section for an individual to receive or accept more than nine grams of any pseudoephedrine product within a period of thirty consecutive days if the individual is an employee of a retailer or terminal distributor of dangerous drugs, and the employee receives or accepts from the retailer or terminal distributor of dangerous drugs the pseudoephedrine product in a sealed container in connection with manufacturing, warehousing, placement, stocking, bagging, loading, or unloading of the product.
Specific inapplicability clause for Division (C):
Division (C) of this section does not apply to an individual under eighteen years of age who purchases, receives, or otherwise acquires a pseudoephedrine product from any of the following:
(a) A licensed health professional authorized to prescribe drugs or pharmacist who dispenses, sells, or otherwise provides the pseudoephedrine product to that individual and whose conduct is in accordance with Chapter 3719., 4715., 4723., 4729., 4731., or 4741. of the Revised Code;
(b) A parent or guardian of that individual who provides the pseudoephedrine product to the individual;
(c) A person, as authorized by that individual's parent or guardian, who dispenses, sells, or otherwise provides the pseudoephedrine product to the individual;

(d) A retailer or terminal distributor of dangerous drugs who provides the pseudoephedrine product to that individual if the individual is an employee of the retailer or terminal distributor of dangerous drugs and the individual receives or accepts from the retailer or terminal distributor of dangerous drugs the pseudoephedrine product in a sealed container in connection with manufacturing, warehousing, placement, stocking, bagging, loading, or unloading of the product.

*Penalty:*
Division (B): a misdemeanor of the first degree (2929.21-2929.31)
Division (C): a delinquent act that would be a misdemeanor of the fourth degree (2929.21-2929.31) if it could be committed by an adult
Division (D): a delinquent act that would be a misdemeanor of the first degree (2929.21-2929.31) if it could be committed by an adult
Division (E): a misdemeanor of the fourth degree (2929.21-2929.31)

***UNLAWFUL OR IMPROPER SALES OF PSEUDOEPHEDRINE PRODUCTS*, R.C. § 2925.56 [M4, M2, M1]**

Division (A):
(1) (a) Retailer
*(or)*
(b) Terminal distributor
*(or)*
(c) Employee of a retailer
*(or)*
(d) Employee of a terminal distributor
(2) Of dangerous drugs
(3) Knowingly
(4) Sell, offer to sell, hold for sale, deliver, or otherwise provide
(5) To any individual
(6) Within a period of thirty consecutive days
(7) An amount of pseudoephedrine product that is greater than nine grams
(8) Venue

Division (B):
(1) (a) Retailer
*(or)*
(b) Terminal distributor
*(or)*
(c) Employee of a retailer
*(or)*
(d) Employee of a terminal distributor
(2) Of dangerous drugs
(3) Knowingly
(4) Sell, offer to sell, hold for sale, deliver, or otherwise provide
(5) A pseudoephedrine product
(6) To an individual
(7) Who is under eighteen years of age
(8) Venue

Division (C):
(1) (a) Retailer
*(or)*
(b) Terminal distributor
(2) Of dangerous drugs
(3) Fail to comply with
(4) The requirements of division (C)(2) [extensive requirements for maintenance of pseudoephedrine product sales logbook] of section 3715.05 of the Revised Code.
(5) Venue

*Notes:*
Inapplicability and exception provisions for Division (A):

Division (A) of this section does not apply to any quantity of pseudoephedrine product dispensed by a pharmacist pursuant to a valid prescription issued by a licensed health professional authorized to prescribe drugs if the conduct of the pharmacist and the licensed health professional authorized to prescribe drugs is in accordance with Chapter 3719., 4715., 4723., 4729., 4731., or 4741. of the Revised Code.

It is not a violation of division (A) of this section for a retailer, terminal distributor of dangerous drugs, or employee of either to provide to an individual more than nine grams of any pseudoephedrine product within a period of thirty consecutive days if the individual is an employee of the retailer or terminal distributor of dangerous drugs, and the employee receives or accepts from the retailer, terminal distributor of dangerous drugs, or employee the pseudoephedrine product in a sealed container in connection with manufacturing, warehousing, placement, stocking, bagging, loading, or unloading of the product.

Inapplicability provisions for Division (B):

Division (B) of this section does not apply to any of the following:
(a) A licensed health professional authorized to prescribe drugs or pharmacist who dispenses, sells, or otherwise provides a pseudoephedrine product to an individual under eighteen years of age and whose conduct is in accordance with Chapter 3719., 4715., 4723., 4729., 4731., or 4741. of the Revised Code;
(b) A parent or guardian of an individual under eighteen years of age who provides a pseudoephedrine product to the individual;
(c) A person who, as authorized by the individual's parent or guardian, dispenses, sells, or otherwise provides a pseudoephedrine product to an individual under eighteen years of age;
(d) The provision by a retailer, terminal distributor of dangerous drugs, or employee of either of a pseudoephedrine product in a sealed container to an employee of the retailer or terminal distributor of dangerous drugs who is under eighteen years of age in connection with manufacturing, warehousing, placement, stocking, bagging, loading, or unloading of the product.

*Penalty:* Division (A): a misdemeanor of the first degree (2929.21-2929.31)
Division (B): a misdemeanor of the fourth degree (2929.21-2929.31)
Division (C): a misdemeanor of the second degree (2929.21-2929.31)

## MISCELLANEOUS OFFENSES

### *ABUSE OF CORPSE*, R.C. § 2927.01(A) [M2]

(1) Without authority of law
(2) Treat a human corpse
(3) In a manner which the offender knows would outrage reasonable family sensibilities
(4) Venue

*Penalty:* A misdemeanor of the second degree (2929.21-2929.31)

### *GROSS ABUSE OF A CORPSE*, R.C. § 2927.01(B) [F5]

(1) Without authority of law
(2) Treat a human corpse
(3) In a manner that would outrage reasonable community sensibilities
(4) Venue

*Penalty:* A felony of the fifth degree (2929.11-2929.18, 2929.31)

### *ILLEGAL DISTRIBUTION OF CIGARETTES OR OTHER TOBACCO PRODUCTS*, R.C. § 2927.02 [M4, M3]

Division (B):
(1) (a) Being a manufacturer, producer, distributor, wholesaler, or retailer of cigarettes, other tobacco products, or papers used to roll cigarettes
*(or)*
(b) Being an agent, employee, or representative of any of the above, and no other person
(2) (a) (i) Give, sell, or otherwise distribute
(ii) Cigarettes, other tobacco products, or papers used to roll cigarettes
(iii) To any child
*(or)*
(b) (i) Give away, sell, or distribute
(ii) Cigarettes, other tobacco products, or papers used to roll cigarettes
(iii) In any place that does not have posted in a conspicuous place
(iv) A sign staling that giving, selling, or otherwise distributing cigarettes, other tobacco products, or papers used to roll cigarettes to a person under 18 years of age is against the law
*(or)*
(c) (i) Knowingly furnish
(ii) Information regarding the name, age, or other identification
(iii) Of any child
(iv) With purpose to obtain cigarettes, other tobacco products, or papers used to roll cigarettes for that child
*(or)*
(d) (i) Manufacture, sell, or distribute in this state
(ii) Any pack or other container of cigarettes
(iii) Containing fewer than 20 cigarettes
*(or)*
(e) (i) Manufacture, sell, or distribute in this state
(ii) Any package of roll-your-own tobacco
(iii) Containing less than 0.6 ounce of tobacco
*(or)*
(f) (i) Sell cigarettes
(ii) In a smaller quantity

(iii) Than that placed in the pack or other container by the manufacturer
(3) Venue

Division (C):
(1) (a) Sell
*(or)*
(b) Offer to sell
(2) Cigarettes or other tobacco products
(3) From a vending machine which is not
(a) In an area within a factory, business, office, or other place open to the general public
*(or)*
(b) An area to which children are generally permitted access
*(or)*
(c) Any other place identified in (3)(a) or (b) above, where the vending machine is
(i) Located within the immediate vicinity, plain view, and control of the person who owns or operates the place, or an employee of that person, so that all cigarettes and other tobacco product purchases from the vending machine will be readily observed by the person who owns or operates the place or an employee of that person
*(and)*
(ii) Inaccessible to the public when the place is closed
(4) Venue

*Penalty:* A misdemeanor of the fourth degree, if prior conviction under this section, a misdemeanor of the third degree (2929.21-2929.31)

*Note:* For purposes of this section, a vending machine located in any unmonitored area, including an unmonitored coatroom, restroom, hallway, or outer waiting area, shall not be considered located within the immediate vicinity, plain view, and control of the person who owns or operates the place, or an employee of that person. The following are affirmative defenses to a charge under division (B)(1) of this section:
(1) the child was accompanied by a parent, spouse who is eighteen years of age or older, or legal guardian of the child
(2) the person who gave, sold, or distributed cigarettes, other tobacco products, or papers used to roll cigarettes to a child under division (B)(1) of this section is a parent, spouse who is eighteen years of age or older, or legal guardian of the child

*Definitions:* "Child" has the same meaning as in section 2151.011 of the Revised Code
"Cigarette" includes clove cigarettes and hand-rolled cigarettes
"Distribute" means to furnish, give, or provide cigarettes, other tobacco products, or papers used to roll cigarettes to the ultimate consumer of the cigarettes, other tobacco products, or papers used to roll cigarettes
"Proof of age" means a driver's license, a commercial driver's license, a military identification card, a passport, or an identification card issued under sections 4507.50 to 4507.52 of the Revised Code that shows that a person is eighteen years of age or older
"Tobacco product" means any product that is made from tobacco, including, but not limited to, a cigarette, a cigar, pipe tobacco, chewing tobacco, or snuff
"Vending machine" has the same meaning as "coin machine" in section 2913.01 of the Revised Code

## *INTERFERENCE WITH FAIR HOUSING RIGHTS*, R.C. § 2927.03 [M1]

(1) Whether or not acting under color of law
(2) (a) By force
*(or)*
(b) By threat of force
(3) Willfully
(4) (a) Injure, intimidate, or interfere with
*(or)*
(b) Attempt to injure, intimidate or interfere with
(5) Any person
(6) (a) (i) Because of race, color, religion, sex, familial status, national origin, disability, or ancestry
*(and)*
(ii) Because that person is or has been
(A) Selling, purchasing, renting, financing, occupying, or contracting for any housing accommodations
*(or)*
(B) Negotiating for the sale, purchase, rental, financing, or occupation of any housing accommodations
*(or)*
(C) Applying for or participating in any service, organization, or facility relating to the business of selling or renting housing accommodations
*(or)*
(b) (i) (A) Because that person is or has been
*(or)*

(B) In order to intimidate that person or any other person or class of persons from
(ii) (A) Participating, without discrimination on account of race, color, religion, sex, familial status, national origin, disability, or ancestry, in any of the activities, services, organizations, or facilities described in 6(a)(ii), above
*(or)*
(B) Affording another person or class of persons opportunity to participate, without discrimination on account of race, color, religion, sex, familial status, national origin, disability, or ancestry, in any of the activities, services, organizations, or facilities described in 6(a)(ii), above
*(or)*
(c) (i) (A) Because that person is or has been
*(or)*
(B) In order to discourage that person or any other person from
(ii) (A) Lawfully aiding or encouraging other persons to participate, without discrimination on account of race, color, religion, sex, familial status, national origin, disability, or ancestry, in any of the activities, services, organizations, or facilities described in 6(a)(ii) above
*(or)*
(B) Participating lawfully in speech or peaceful assembly opposing any denial of the opportunity to participate, without discrimination on account of race, color, religion, sex, familial status, national origin, disability, or ancestry, in any of the activities, services, organizations, or facilities described in 6(a)(ii), above
(7) Venue
*Penalty:* A misdemeanor of the first degree (2929.21-2929.31)
*Definitions:* "Familial status," "handicap," R.C. § 4112.01

***DESECRATION*, R.C. § 2927.11 [M2, F5, F4, F3]**

(1) Purposely
(2) Deface, damage, pollute or physically mistreat
(3) (a) The United States flag or the flag of Ohio
*(or)*
(b) A public monument
*(or)*
(c) A historical or commemorative marker, or any structure, Indian mound or earthwork, cemetery, thing, or site of great historical or archaeological interest
*(or)*
(d) A place of worship or its furnishings, or religious artifacts or sacred texts within the place of worship
*(or)*
(e) A work of art or museum piece
(f) Any object of reverence or devotion
(4) Without privilege to do so
(5) Venue
*Penalty:* A misdemeanor of the second degree (2929.21-2929.31)
If violation of 3(d), above **[F5]**
*Penalty:* A felony of the fifth degree (2929.11-2929.18, 2929.31)
If the value of the property or the amount of physical harm involved in a violation of (3)(d) is $5,000 or more but less than $100,000
*Penalty:* A felony of the fourth degree (2929.11-2929.18, 2929.31)
If the value of the property or the amount of physical harm involved in a violation of (3)(d) is $100,000 or more
*Penalty:* A felony of the third degree (2929.11-2929.18, 2929.31)
*Note: See* R.C. § 2307.70 regarding civil damages

***ETHNIC INTIMIDATION*, R.C. § 2927.12**

(1) Violate R.C. § 2903.21, 2903.22, 2909.06, 2909.07, or 2917.21(A)(3), (4), or (5)
(2) By reason of the race, color, religion, or national origin
(3) Of another person or group of persons
(4) Venue
*Penalty:* Next higher degree than offense which is a necessary element
*Note:* See R.C. § 2307.70 regarding civil damages

***SELLING OR DONATING CONTAMINATED BLOOD*, R.C. § 2927.13 [F4]**

(1) With knowledge that the person is a carrier of a virus that causes Acquired Immune Deficiency Syndrome
(2) (a) Sell
*(or)*
(b) Donate
(3) (a) The person's blood
*(or)*
(b) The person's plasma
*(or)*

(c) A product of the person's blood
(4) If the person knows or should know that it is being accepted for the purpose of transfusion to another individual
(5) Venue
*Penalty:* A felony of the fourth degree (2929.11-2929.18, 2929.31)

**_UNLAWFUL COLLECTION OF A BODILY SUBSTANCE,_ R.C. § 2927.15 [M1, F5]**

Division (A):
(1) Knowingly
(2) Collect any blood, urine, tissue, or other bodily substance of another person
(3) Without privilege or consent to do so
(4) Venue
*Penalty:* A misdemeanor of the first degree (2929.21-2929.31)
If previously convicted of or pleaded guilty to, a violation of Division (A),
*Penalty:* A felony of the fifth degree (2929.11-2929.18, 2929.31)
*Note:* Division (A) of this section does not apply to any of the following:
(a) The collection of any bodily substance of a person by a law enforcement officer, or by another person pursuant to the direction or advice of a law enforcement officer, for purposes of a chemical test or tests of the substance under division (A)(1) of section 1547.111 or division (A)(2) of section 4511.191 of the Revised Code to determine the alcohol, drug, controlled substance, metabolite of a controlled substance, or combination content of the bodily substance;
(b) The collection of any bodily substance of a person by a peace officer, or by another person pursuant to the direction or advice of a peace officer, for purposes of a test or tests of the substance as provided in division (A) of section 4506.17 of the Revised Code to determine the person's alcohol concentration or the presence of any controlled substance or metabolite of a controlled substance.

**_DUTY TO REPORT ESCAPE OF ANIMAL,_ R.C. § 2927.21 [M1]**

(1) Being the owner or keeper of animal
(a) not indigenous to Ohio
*(or)*
(b) presenting risk of serious physical harm to persons or property
(2) Fail to report the animal's escape to appropriate law enforcement officer and to clerk of council or fiscal officer within one hour after one discovers the escape or reasonably should have discovered it
(3) Venue
*Penalty:* A misdemeanor of the first degree (2929.21-2929.31)
*Note:* If the office of the clerk of a legislative authority or township clerk is closed to the public at the time a report is required by this section, then it is sufficient compliance with this section if the owner or keeper makes the report within one hour after the office is next open to the public

**_CONTAMINATING SUBSTANCE FOR HUMAN CONSUMPTION OR USE; CONTAMINATION WITH HAZARDOUS CHEMICAL, BIOLOGICAL, OR RADIOACTIVE SUBSTANCE,_ R.C. § 2927.24 [F1]**

[B][l] (1) (a) Knowingly
(b) Mingle a poison, hazardous chemical, biological, or radioactive substance, or other harmful substance with
(c) (i) food
*(or)*
(ii) drink
*(or)*
(iii) nonprescription drug
*(or)*
(iv) prescription drug
*(or)*
(v) pharmaceutical product
*(or)*
(2) (a) Knowingly
(b) Place a poison, hazardous chemical, biological, or radioactive substance, or other harmful substance in a
(c) (i) spring
*(or)*
(ii) well
*(or)*
(iii) reservoir
*(or)*
(iv) public water supply
(3) If the person knows or has reason to know that
(4) (a) The food
*(or)*

(b) drink
*(or)*
(c) nonprescription drug
*(or)*
(d) prescription drug
*(or)*
(e) pharmaceutical product
*(or)*
(f) water
(5) May be ingested or used by another person
(6) Venue

*Penalty:* A felony of the first degree (2929.11-2929.18, 2929.31)
If the offense involved an amount of the harmful substance sufficient to cause death if ingested or used, or if the offense resulted in serious physical harm to another person, the offender shall be imprisoned for life with parole eligibility after serving 15 years imprisonment
*Definitions:* "Hazardous chemical, biological, or radioactive substance," R.C. § 2927.24(A)

[B][2] (1) Knowingly
(2) (a) Release into the air
*(or)*
(b) Leave in any public place
*(or)*
(c) Expose one or more persons to
(3) Any hazardous chemical, biological, or radioactive substance
(4) With the intent to cause, or create a risk of
(5) Death or serious physical harm to any person
(6) Venue

*Penalty:* A felony of the first degree (2929.11-2929.18, 2929.31)
If the offense involved an amount of the harmful substance sufficient to cause death to persons exposed to it, or if the offense resulted in serious physical harm to another person, the offender shall be imprisoned for life with parole eligibility after serving 15 years imprisonment
*Definitions:* "Hazardous chemical, biological, or radioactive substance," R.C. § 2927.24(A)

***SPREADING FALSE REPORT OF CONTAMINATION,* R.C. § 2927.24 [F4]**

[C][1] (1) Inform another person
(2) That a poison, hazardous chemical, biological, or radioactive substance, or other harmful substance
(3) Has been or will be placed in
(4) (a) A food
*(or)*
(b) Drink
*(or)*
(c) Nonprescription drug
*(or)*
(d) Prescription drug
*(or)*
(e) Other pharmaceutical product
*(or)*
(f) Spring
*(or)*
(g) Well
*(or)*
(h) Reservoir
*(or)*
(i) Public water supply
(5) If the placement of the poison, hazardous chemical, biological, or radioactive substance, or other harmful substance would be a violation of division (B) of this section
(6) The person knows that the information is
(a) False
*(and)*
(b) Will likely be disseminated to the public
(7) Venue

*Penalty:* A felony of the fourth degree (2929.11-2929.18, 2929.31)
*Definitions:* "Poison," R.C. § 3719.01
"Drug," R.C. § 4729.01
"Hazardous chemical, biological, or radioactive substance," R.C. § 2927.24(A)

[C][2] (1) Inform another person
(2) That a poison, hazardous chemical, biological, or radioactive substance, or other harmful substance

(3) Has been or will be
(a) Released into the air
*(or)*
(b) Left in a public place
(4) If the release or leaving of the substance would violate [B][2] (above)
(5) The person knows that the information
(a) Is false
*(and)*
(b) Will likely be disseminated to the public
(6) Venue
*Penalty:* A felony of the fourth degree (2929.11-2929.18, 2929.31)
*Definitions:* "Hazardous chemical, biological, or radioactive substance," R.C. § 2927.24(A)

[C][3] (1) Inform another person
(2) That one or more persons
(3) Has been or will be exposed
(4) To a hazardous chemical, biological, or radioactive substance, or other harmful substance
(5) If the exposure of the substance would violate [B][2] (above)
(6) The person knows that the information
(a) Is false
*(and)*
(b) Will likely be disseminated to the public
(7) Venue
*Penalty:* A felony of the fourth degree (2929.11-2929.18, 2929.31)
*Definitions:* "Hazardous chemical, biological, or radioactive substance," R.C. § 2927.24(A)

### *ILLEGAL BAIL BOND AGENT PRACTICES,* R.C. § 2927.27 [M1, F3]

Division (A):
(1) No person, other than a law enforcement officer, shall
(2) Apprehend
*(or)*
(3) Detain
*(or)*
(4) Arrest
(5) A principal on bond, unless that person meets all of the following criteria:
(a) The person is any of the following:
(i) Qualified, licensed, and appointed as a surety bail bond agent under sections 3905.83 to 3905.95
(ii) Licensed as a surety bail bond agent by the state where the bond was written
(iii) Licensed as a private investigator under Chapter 4749
(iv) Licensed as a private investigator by the state where the bond was written
(v) An off-duty police officer, as defined in section 2921.51
(b) The person, prior to apprehending, detaining, or arresting the principal, has entered into a written contract with the surety or with a licensed surety bail bond agent appointed by the surety, which contract sets forth the name of the principal who is to be apprehended, detained, or arrested
(c) The person, prior to apprehending, detaining, or arresting the principal, has notified the local law enforcement agency having jurisdiction over the area in which such activities will be performed and has provided any form of identification or other information requested by the law enforcement agency
*Penalty:* A misdemeanor of the first degree, or with two or more violations of this division a felony of the third degree

Division (B):
(1) No person shall
(2) Represent
(3) The person's self to be
(4) Bail enforcement agent
*(or)*
(5) Bounty hunter
*(or)*
(6) Claim any similar title
*Penalty:* A misdemeanor of the first degree (2929.21-2929.31), or with two or more violations of this division a felony of the third degree (2929.11-2929.18. 2929.31)
*Note:* For purposes of Division (A)(2) of this section, "surety" has the same meaning as in section 3905.83

### *CONDUCTING UNAUTHORIZED BODY CAVITY OR STRIP SEARCH; FAILURE TO PREPARE PROPER REPORT,* R.C. § 2933.32 [M4, M1]

[A] (Conducting unauthorized body cavity or strip search) **[M1]**
(1) Being a law enforcement officer, other employee of a law enforcement agency, registered nurse, or licensed practical nurse
(2) Conduct or cause to be conducted

(3) (a) A body cavity search
*(or)*
(b) A strip search
(4) Where any of the following requirements is not met
(a) (i) (A) A law enforcement officer or employee of a law enforcement agency
(B) Has probable cause to believe, based upon the nature of the offense with which the person is charged, the circumstances of his arrest, and his prior conviction record (if known)
(C) That the person is concealing evidence of the commission of a criminal offense, including fruits or tools of a crime, contraband, or a deadly weapon as defined in R.C. § 2923.11
(D) That could not otherwise be discovered
*(or)*
(ii) The search is conducted for a legitimate medical or hygienic reason
*(and)*
(b) The search is conducted
(i) Following issuance of a search warrant authorizing the search (unless there is a legitimate medical reason or medical emergency justifying the warrantless search)
*(and)*
(ii) Under sanitary conditions
*(and)*
(iii) By a physician or registered nurse or licensed practical nurse registered or licensed to practice in this state
*(and)*
(iv) After a law enforcement officer or employee of a law enforcement agency obtains written authorization therefor from the person in command of the agency or from his specific designee (unless there is a legitimate medical reason or medical emergency making obtaining such authorization impracticable)
*(and)*
(v) By a person or persons of the same sex as the person being searched
*(and)*
(vi) In a manner and in a location that permits only the person(s) conducting the search and the person being searched to observe it.
(5) Venue
[B] (Failure to prepare proper report) **[M4]**
(1) Following completion of a body cavity search or strip search
(2) Being the person(s) conducting the search
(3) Fail to prepare a written report containing all of the following
(a) The written authorization for the search by the person in command of the law enforcement agency (if required)
*(and)*
(b) The name of the person searched
*(and)*
(c) The name of the person(s) conducting the search, and the time and date of and place at which the search was conducted
*(and)*
(d) A list of items recovered during the search (if any)
*(and)*
(e) The facts upon which the law enforcement agency officer or employee based his probable cause for the search, including his review of the nature of the offense with which the person is charged, the circumstances of his arrest, and his prior conviction record (if known)
*(and)*
(f) If the search was conducted without issuance of a search warrant or without the granting of a written authorization, the legitimate medical reason or emergency that justified the warrantless search or made obtaining written authorization impracticable
(4) Venue

Division [A] [Unauthorized body cavity or strip search] **[MI]**
*Penalty:* A misdemeanor of the first degree (2929.21-2929.31)

Division [B] [Failure to prepare proper search report] **[M4]**
*Penalty:* A misdemeanor of the fourth degree (2929.21-2929.31)
*Note:* R.C. § 2933.32(C)(2) provides that a copy of the required body cavity or strip search report is to be kept on file in the law enforcement agency, and that another copy is to be given to the person searched. This section does not apply to searches of persons sentenced to and serving a term in a detention facility, as defined in R.C. § 2921.01, R.C. § 2933.32(D)
*Definitions:* "Body cavity search" and "strip search," R.C. § 2933.32(A)

**_CONTRABAND_, R.C. § 2933.42 [F4]**

(1) (a) Possess
*(or)*

(b) Conceal
*(or)*
(c) Transport
*(or)*
(d) Receive
*(or)*
(e) Purchase
*(or)*
(f) Sell
*(or)*
(g) Lease
*(or)*
(h) Rent
*(or)*
(i) Otherwise transfer
(2) Any contraband
(3) Venue
*Penalty:* Seizure and forfeiture under certain conditions-see R.C. §§ 2933.42 and 2933.43
*Notes:* R.C. § 2933.43 contains procedural requirements regarding seizure, custody, and disposition of contraband
*See* statute for provisions concerning forfeiture of contraband possessed or owned by persons under eighteen
*Definition:* "Contraband," R.C. §§ 2901.01, 2933.42

***INTERCEPTION OF WIRE, ORAL OR ELECTRONIC COMMUNICATION*, R.C. § 2933.52 [F4]**

(1) (a) Purposely
(b) (i) Intercept
*(or)*
(ii) Attempt to intercept
*(or)*
(iii) Procure any other person to intercept or attempt to intercept
(c) (i) Any wire communication
*(or)*
(ii) Any oral communication
*(or)*
(iii) any electronic communication
(d) Venue
*(or)*
(2) (a) Purposely
(b) (i) Use
*(or)*
(ii) Attempt to use
*(or)*
(iii) Procure any other person to use or attempt to use
(c) Any interception device which
(i) Is affixed to, or otherwise transmits a signal through a wire, cable, satellite, microwave or other similar method of connection used in wire communications
*(or)*
(ii) Transmits communications by radio, or interferes with the transmission of communication by radio
(d) To intercept any wire, oral, or electronic communication
(e) Venue
*(or)*
(3) (a) Purposely
(b) (i) Use
*(or)*
(ii) Attempt to use The contents of (c)
(d) Any wire, oral or electronic communication
(e) Knowing or having reason to know
(f) That the contents were obtained
(g) Through the interception of wire, oral, or electronic communication in violation of R.C. §§ 2933.51 to 2933.66
(h) Venue
*Penalty:* A felony of the fourth degree (2929.11-2929.18, 2929.31)
*Notes:* For exclusions, see R.C. § 2933.52
For provisions concerning interception warrants, see R.C. §§ 2933.53-2933.61, 2933.66
For provisions regarding evidentiary issues, see R.C. §§ 2933.59, 2933.62, 2933.63
For provisions concerning civil cause of action, see R.C. § 2933.65
For other provisions regarding telephone offenses, see R.C. Chapter 4931., Miscellaneous Statutory Provisions
*Definitions:* Generally, R.C. § 2933.51

***PRESENTING ALTERED RECORD OF INTERCEPTED COMMUNICATION,* R.C. § 2933.59(C) [F3]**

(1) With intent to present the altered recording or resume
(2) (a) In any judicial proceeding
*(or)*
(b) In any proceeding under oath or affirmation
(3) Purposefully
(a) Edit
*(or)*
(b) Alter
*(or)*
(c) Tamper with
*(or)*
(d) Attempt to alter, edit, or tamper with
(4) Any recording or resume of any intercepted wire or oral communication
(5) Present or permit presentation of any altered recording or resume
(6) (a) In any judicial proceeding
*(or)*
(b) In any proceeding under oath or affirmation
(7) Without fully indicating the nature of the changes made
(8) Venue

*Penalty:* A felony of the third degree (2929.11-2929.18, 2929.31)

***ADULTERATED FOOD,* R.C. § 3716.11 [M1]**

(1) With knowledge, or having reasonable cause to believe, another may suffer physical harm or be seriously inconvenienced or annoyed:
(a) Place a pin, needle, razor blade, glass, laxative, drug of abuse, or other harmful/hazardous object/substance in food or confections
*(or)*
(b) Furnish to another food or confections adulterated in violation of (a) above
(2) Venue

*Penalty:* A misdemeanor of the first degree (2929.21-2929.31)

***REGULATING THE SALE OF POISONS,* R.C. § 3719.32 [MM]**

(1) Knowingly
(2) Sell or deliver
(3) (a) To any person other than in the manner prescribed by law
*(or)*
(b) To a minor under 16 in the manner prescribed by law but without written order of an adult
(4) (a) Any of the substances listed in this section [includes many scheduled drugs]
*(or)*
(b) Any poisonous compounds, combinations, or preparations thereof
(5) Venue

*Penalty:* A minor misdemeanor (2929.21-2929.31)

***OPENED CONTAINER,* R.C. § 4301.62 [MM]**

(1) Have in one's possession
(2) An opened container of beer or intoxicating liquor
(3) (a) In a state liquor store
*(or)*
(b) On the premises of the holder of any permit issued by the department of liquor control
*(or)*
(c) In any other public place
*(or)*
(d) While operating or being a passenger in or on a motor vehicle on any street, highway, or other public or private property open to the public for purposes of vehicular travel or parking
*(or)*
(e) While being in or on a stationary motor vehicle on any street, highway, or other public or private property open to the public for purposes of vehicular travel or parking
(4) Venue

*Penalty:* A minor misdemeanor (2929.21-2929.31)

*Notes:* The statute specifies exceptions for beer or intoxicating liquor which has been lawfully bought for consumption on certain permit premises or convention premises

A person may have in the person's possession an opened or unopened container of beer or intoxicating liquor at an outdoor location at which the person is attending an orchestral performance if the person with supervision and control over the performance grants permission for the possession and consumption of beer or intoxicating liquor in certain predesignated areas of that outdoor location.

***MOTOR VEHICLES, DRIVING UNDER AN OVI SUSPENSION UNDER* R.C. § 4510.14**

(1) driver's or commercial driver's license or permit or nonresident operating privilege
(2) suspended under R.C. § 4511.19, 4511.191, or 4511.196 or 4510.07 for a conviction of a violation of a municipal OVI ordinance
(3) operate any motor vehicle
(4) upon the public roads or highways within this state
(5) during the period of the suspension

If no conviction within six years of the offense under this section or an equivalent offense **[M1]**

*Penalty:* Mandatory jail term: 3 consecutive days
Mandatory fine: $250 to $1,000
Class seven suspension
Vehicle immobilization and license plate impoundment

If, within six years of the offense, the offender previously has been convicted of or pleaded guilty to one violation of this section or one equivalent offense **[MI]**

*Penalty:* Mandatory jail term: 10 consecutive days
Mandatory fine: $500 to $2,500
Class seven suspension
Vehicle immobilization and license plate impoundment

If, within six years of the offense, the offender previously has been convicted of or pleaded guilty to two or more violations of this section or two or more equivalent offenses **[M]**

*Penalty:* Mandatory jail term: 30 consecutive days
Mandatory fine: $500 to $2,500
Class seven suspension
Criminal forfeiture of vehicle

***MOTOR VEHICLES, OPERATING WHILE UNDER THE INFLUENCE,* R.C. § 4511.19 [M1, F4, F3]**

Division (A)(1):
(1) Operate any vehicle, streetcar, or trackless trolley
(2) Within this state
(3) At the time of operation:
  (a) While under the influence of alcohol, a drug of abuse, or combination thereof
  *(or)*
  (b) While having a concentration of .08 of 1% or more but less than .17 of 1% by weight per unit volume of alcohol in the person's whole blood
  *(or)*
  (c) While having a concentration of .096 of 1% or more but less than .204 of 1% by weight per unit volume of alcohol in the person's blood serum or plasma
  *(or)*
  (d) While having a concentration of .08 of 1 gram or more but less than .17 of I gram by weight of alcohol per 210 liters of breath
  *(or)*
  (e) While having a concentration of .11 of 1 gram or more but less than .238 of 1 gram by weight of alcohol per 100 milliliters of urine
  *(or)*
  (f) While having a concentration of .17 of 1% or more by weight per unit volume of alcohol in the person's whole blood
  *(or)*
  (g) While having a concentration of .204 if 1% or more by weight per unit volume of alcohol in the person's blood serum or plasma
  *(or)*
  (h) While having a concentration of .17 of 1 gram or more by weight of alcohol per 210 liters of breath
  *(or)*
  (i) While having a concentration of .238 of I gram or more by weight of alcohol per 100 milliliters of urine
  (j) Except as provided in division (K) of this section, the person has a concentration of any of the following controlled substances or metabolites of a controlled substance in the person's whole blood, blood serum or plasma, or urine that equals or exceeds any of the following:
    (i) The person has a concentration of amphetamine in the person's urine of at least five hundred nanograms of amphetamine per milliliter of the person's urine or has a concentration of amphetamine in the person's whole blood or blood serum or plasma of at least one hundred nanograms of amphetamine per milliliter of the person's whole blood or blood serum or plasma.
    (ii) The person has a concentration of cocaine in the person's urine of at least one hundred fifty nanograms of cocaine per milliliter of the person's urine or has a concentration of cocaine in the person's whole blood or blood serum or plasma of at least fifty nanograms of cocaine per milliliter of the person's whole blood or blood serum or plasma.
    (iii) The person has a concentration of cocaine metabolite in the person's urine of at least one hundred fifty nanograms of cocaine metabolite per milliliter of the person's urine or has a concentration of cocaine

metabolite in the person's whole blood or blood serum or plasma of at least fifty nanograms of cocaine metabolite per milliliter of the person's whole blood or blood serum or plasma.

(iv) The person has a concentration of heroin in the person's urine of at least two thousand nanograms of heroin per milliliter of the person's urine or has a concentration of heroin in the person's whole blood or blood serum or plasma of at least fifty nanograms of heroin per milliliter of the person's whole blood or blood serum or plasma.

(v) The person has a concentration of heroin metabolite (6-monoacetyl morphine) in the person's urine of at least ten nanograms of heroin metabolite (6-monoacetyl morphine) per milliliter of the person's urine or has a concentration of heroin metabolite (6-monoacetyl morphine) in the person's whole blood or blood serum or plasma of at least ten nanograms of heroin metabolite (6-monoacetyl morphine) per milliliter of the person's whole blood or blood serum or plasma.

(vi) The person has a concentration of L.S.D. in the person's urine of at least twenty-five nanograms of L.S.D. per milliliter of the person's urine or a concentration of L.S.D. in the person's whole blood or blood serum or plasma of at least ten nanograms of L.S.D. per milliliter of the person's whole blood or blood serum or plasma.

(vii) The person has a concentration of marihuana in the person's urine of at least ten nanograms of marihuana per milliliter of the person's urine or has a concentration of marihuana in the person's whole blood or blood serum or plasma of at least two nanograms of marihuana per milliliter of the person's whole blood or blood serum or plasma.

(viii) Either of the following applies:

(I) The person is under the influence of alcohol, a drug of abuse, or a combination of them, and, as measured by gas chromatography mass spectrometry, the person has a concentration of marihuana metabolite in the person's urine of at least fifteen nanograms of marihuana metabolite per milliliter of the person's urine or has a concentration of marihuana metabolite in the person's whole blood or blood serum or plasma of at least five nanograms of marihuana metabolite per milliliter of the person's whole blood or blood serum or plasma.

(II) As measured by gas chromatography mass spectrometry, the person has a concentration of marihuana metabolite in the person's urine of at least thirty-five nanograms of marihuana metabolite per milliliter of the person's urine or has a concentration of marihuana metabolite in the person's whole blood or blood serum or plasma of at least fifty nanograms of marihuana metabolite per milliliter of the person's whole blood or blood serum or plasma.

(ix) The person has a concentration of methamphetamine in the person's urine of at least five hundred nanograms of methamphetamine per milliliter of the person's urine or has a concentration of methamphetamine in the person's whole blood or blood serum or plasma of at least one hundred nanograms of methamphetamine per milliliter of the person's whole blood or blood serum or plasma.

(x) The person has a concentration of phencyclidine in the person's urine of at least twenty-five nanograms of phencyclidine per milliliter of the person's urine or has a concentration of phencyclidine in the person's whole blood or blood serum or plasma of at least ten nanograms of phencyclidine per milliliter of the person's whole blood or blood serum or plasma.

(xi) The person has a concentration of salvia divinorum or salvinorin A in the person's urine, whole blood, or blood serum or plasma of at least the amount prohibited by rule by the State Board of Pharmacy.

Division (A) (2):

(1) Within twenty years of the conduct described in paragraph (2), previously having been convicted of or pleaded guilty to a violation of this division, division (A)(1) or (B) of this section, or a municipal OVI offense

(2) Operate any vehicle, streetcar, or trackless trolley within this state while under the influence of alcohol, a drug of abuse, or a combination of them;

(3) Subsequent to being arrested for operating the vehicle, streetcar, or trackless trolley as described in paragraph (2) of this section, being asked by a law enforcement officer to submit to a chemical test or tests under section 4511.191 [4511.19.1] of the Revised Code, and being advised by the officer in accordance with section 4511.192 [4511.19.2] of the Revised Code of the consequences of the person's refusal or submission to the test or tests, refuse to submit to the test or tests.

Division (B)(1), (2) or (3):

Operating a Vehicle After Underage Alcohol Consumption:

(1) Being under 21 years of age

(2) Operate any vehicle, streetcar, or trackless trolley

(3) Within this state

(4) At the time of operation

(5) While having a concentration of at least

(A) .02 of 1% but less than .08 of 1% by weight per unit volume of alcohol in the person's whole blood

*(or)*

(B) .03 of 1% but less than .12 of 1% by weight per unit volume of alcohol in the person's blood serum or plasma

*(or)*

(C) .02 of 1 gram but less than .08 of 1 gram by weight of alcohol per 210 liters of breath

*(or)*

(D) .028 of 1 gram but less than .11 of 1 gram by weight of alcohol per 100 milliliters of the urine

*Penalty:*

(1) Whoever violates any provision of divisions (A)(1)(a) to (i) or (A)(2) of this section is guilty of operating a vehicle under the influence of alcohol, a drug of abuse, or a combination of them. Whoever violates division (A)(1)(j) of this section is guilty of operating a vehicle while under the influence of a listed controlled substance or a listed metabolite of a controlled substance. The court shall sentence the offender for either offense under Chapter 2929 of the Revised Code, except as otherwise authorized or required by divisions (G)(1)(a) to (e) of this section:

(a) Except as otherwise provided in division (G)(1)(b), (c), (d), or (e) of this section, the offender is guilty of a misdemeanor of the first degree, and the court shall sentence the offender to all of the following:

(i) If the sentence is being imposed for a violation of division (A)(1)(a), (b), (c), (d), (e), or (j) of this section, a mandatory jail term of three consecutive days. As used in this division, three consecutive days means seventy-two consecutive hours. The court may sentence an offender to both an intervention program and a jail term. The court may impose a jail term in addition to the three-day mandatory jail term or intervention program. However, in no case shall the cumulative jail term imposed for the offense exceed six months.

The court may suspend the execution of the three-day jail term under this division if the court, in lieu of that suspended term, places the offender under a community control sanction pursuant to section 2929.25 of the Revised Code and requires the offender to attend, for three consecutive days, a drivers' intervention program certified under section 3793.10 of the Revised Code. The court also may suspend the execution of any part of the three-day jail term under this division if it places the offender under a community control sanction pursuant to section 2929.25 of the Revised Code for part of the three days, requires the offender to attend for the suspended part of the term a drivers' intervention program so certified, and sentences the offender to a jail term equal to the remainder of the three consecutive days that the offender does not spend attending the program. The court may require the offender, as a condition of community control and in addition to the required attendance at a drivers' intervention program, to attend and satisfactorily complete any treatment or education programs that comply with the minimum standards adopted pursuant to Chapter 3793 of the Revised Code by the director of alcohol and drug addiction services that the operators of the drivers' intervention program determine that the offender should attend and to report periodically to the court on the offender's progress in the programs. The court also may impose on the offender any other conditions of community control that it considers necessary.

(ii) If the sentence is being imposed for a violation of division (A)(1)(f), (g), (h), or (i) or division (A)(2) of this section, except as otherwise provided in this division, a mandatory jail term of at least three consecutive days and a requirement that the offender attend, for three consecutive days, a drivers' intervention program that is certified pursuant to section 3793.10 of the Revised Code. As used in this division, three consecutive days means seventy-two consecutive hours. If the court determines that the offender is not conducive to treatment in a drivers' intervention program, if the offender refuses to attend a drivers' intervention program, or if the jail at which the offender is to serve the jail term imposed can provide a driver's intervention program, the court shall sentence the offender to a mandatory jail term of at least six consecutive days.

The court may require the offender, under a community control sanction imposed under section 2929.25 of the Revised Code, to attend and satisfactorily complete any treatment or education programs that comply with the minimum standards adopted pursuant to Chapter 3793 of the Revised Code by the director of alcohol and drug addiction services, in addition to the required attendance at drivers' intervention program, that the operators of the drivers' intervention program determine that the offender should attend and to report periodically to the court on the offender's progress in the programs. The court also may impose any other conditions of community control on the offender that it considers necessary.

(iii) In all cases, a fine of not less than three hundred seventy-five and not more than one thousand seventy-five dollars;

(iv) In all cases, a class five license suspension of the offender's driver's or commercial driver's license or permit or nonresident operating privilege from the range specified in division (A)(5) of section 4510.02 of the Revised Code. The court may grant limited driving privileges relative to the suspension under sections 4510.021 and 4510.13 of the Revised Code.

(b) Except as otherwise provided in division (G)(1)(e) of this section, an offender who, within six years of the offense, previously has been convicted of or pleaded guilty to one violation of division (A) or (B) of this section or one other equivalent offense is guilty of a misdemeanor of the first degree. The court shall sentence the offender to all of the following:

(i) If the sentence is being imposed for a violation of division (A)(1)(a), (b), (c), (d), (e), or (j) of this section, a mandatory jail term of ten consecutive days. The court shall impose the ten-day mandatory jail term under this division unless, subject to division (G)(3) of this section, it instead imposes a sentence under that division consisting of both a jail term and a term of house arrest with electronic monitoring, with continuous alcohol monitoring, or with both electronic monitoring and continuous alcohol monitoring. The court may impose a jail term in addition to the ten-day mandatory jail term. The cumulative jail term imposed for the offense shall not exceed six months.

In addition to the jail term or the term of house arrest with electronic monitoring or continuous alcohol monitoring or both types of monitoring and jail term, the court shall require the offender to be assessed by an alcohol and drug treatment program that is authorized by section 3793.02 of the Revised Code, subject to division (I) of this section, and shall order the offender to follow the treatment recommendations of the program. The purpose of the assessment is to determine the degree of the offender's alcohol usage and to determine whether or not treatment is warranted. Upon the request of the court, the program shall submit the results of the assessment to the court, including all treatment recommendations and clinical diagnoses related to alcohol use.

(ii) If the sentence is being imposed for a violation of division (A)(1)(f), (g), (h), or (i) or division (A)(2) of this section, except as otherwise provided in this division, a mandatory jail term of twenty consecutive days. The court shall impose the twenty-day mandatory jail term under this division unless, subject to division (G)(3) of this section, it instead imposes a sentence under that division consisting of both a jail term and a term of house arrest with electronic monitoring, with continuous alcohol monitoring, or with both electronic monitoring and continuous alcohol monitoring. The court may impose a jail term in addition to the twenty-day mandatory jail term. The cumulative jail term imposed for the offense shall not exceed six months.

In addition to the jail term or the term of house arrest with electronic monitoring or continuous alcohol monitoring or both types of monitoring and jail term, the court shall require the offender to be assessed by an alcohol and drug treatment program that is authorized by section 3793.02 of the Revised Code, subject to division (I) of this section, and shall order the offender to follow the treatment recommendations of the program. The purpose of the assessment is to determine the degree of the offender's alcohol usage and to determine whether or not treatment is warranted. Upon the request of the court, the program shall submit the results of the assessment to the court, including all treatment recommendations and clinical diagnoses related to alcohol use.

(iii) In all cases, notwithstanding the fines set forth in Chapter 2929 of the Revised Code, a fine of not less than five hundred twenty-five and not more than one thousand six hundred twenty-five dollars;

(iv) In all cases, a class four license suspension of the offender's driver's license, commercial driver's license, temporary instruction permit, probationary license, or nonresident operating privilege from the range specified in division (A)(4) of section 4510.02 of the Revised Code. The court may grant limited driving privileges relative to the suspension under sections 4510.021 and 4510.13 of the Revised Code.

(v) In all cases, if the vehicle is registered in the offender's name, immobilization of the vehicle involved in the offense for ninety days in accordance with section 4503.233 of the Revised Code and impoundment of the license plates of that vehicle for ninety days.

(c) Except as otherwise provided in division (G)(1)(e) of this section, an offender who, within six years of the offense, previously has been convicted of or pleaded guilty to two violations of division (A) or (B) of this section or other equivalent offenses is guilty of a misdemeanor. The court shall sentence the offender to all of the following:

(i) If the sentence is being imposed for a violation of division (A)(1)(a), (b), (c), (d), (e), or (j) of this section, a mandatory jail term of thirty consecutive days. The court shall impose the thirty-day mandatory jail term under this division unless, subject to division (G)(3) of this section, it instead imposes a sentence under that division consisting of both a jail term and a term of house arrest with electronic monitoring, with continuous alcohol monitoring, or with both electronic monitoring and continuous alcohol monitoring. The court may impose a jail term in addition to the thirty-day mandatory jail term. Notwithstanding the jail terms set forth in sections 2929.21 to 2929.28 of the Revised Code, the additional jail term shall not exceed one year, and the cumulative jail term imposed for the offense shall not exceed one year.

(ii) If the sentence is being imposed for a violation of division (A)(1)(f), (g), (h), or (i) or division (A)(2) of this section, a mandatory jail term of sixty consecutive days. The court shall impose the sixty-day mandatory jail term under this division unless, subject to division (G)(3) of this section, it instead imposes a sentence under that division consisting of both a jail term and a term of house arrest with electronic monitoring, with continuous alcohol monitoring, or with both electronic monitoring and continuous alcohol monitoring. The court may impose a jail term in addition to the sixty-day mandatory jail term. Notwithstanding the jail terms set forth in sections 2929.21 to 2929.28 of the Revised Code, the additional jail term shall not exceed one year, and the cumulative jail term imposed for the offense shall not exceed one year.

(iii) In all cases, notwithstanding the fines set forth in Chapter 2929. of the Revised Code, a fine of not less than eight hundred fifty and not more than two thousand seven hundred fifty dollars;

(iv) In all cases, a class three license suspension of the offender's driver's license, commercial driver's license, temporary instruction permit, probationary license, or nonresident operating privilege from the range specified in division (A)(3) of section 4510.02 of the Revised Code. The court may grant limited driving privileges relative to the suspension under sections 4510.021 and 4510.13 of the Revised Code.

(v) In all cases, if the vehicle is registered in the offender's name, criminal forfeiture of the vehicle involved in the offense in accordance with section 4503.234 of the Revised Code. Division (G)(6) of this section applies regarding any vehicle that is subject to an order of criminal forfeiture under this division.

(vi) In all cases, the court shall order the offender to participate in an alcohol and drug addiction program authorized by section 3793.02 of the Revised Code, subject to division (I) of this section, and shall order the offender to follow the treatment recommendations of the program. The operator of the program shall determine and assess the degree of the offender's alcohol dependency and shall make recommendations for treatment. Upon the request of the court, the program shall submit the results of the assessment to the court, including all treatment recommendations and clinical diagnoses related to alcohol use.

(d) Except as otherwise provided in division (G)(1)(e) of this section, an offender who, within six years of the offense, previously has been convicted of or pleaded guilty to three or four violations of division (A) or (B) of this section or other equivalent offenses or an offender who, within twenty years of the offense, previously has been convicted of or pleaded guilty to five or more violations of that nature is guilty of a felony of the fourth degree. The court shall sentence the offender to all of the following:

(i) If the sentence is being imposed for a violation of division (A)(1)(a), (b), (c), (d), (e), or (j) of this section, a mandatory prison term of one, two, three, four, or five years as required by and in accordance with division (G)(2) of section 2929.13 of the Revised Code if the offender also is convicted of or also pleads guilty to a specification of the type described in section 2941.1413 of the Revised Code or, in the discretion of the court, either a mandatory term of local incarceration of sixty consecutive days in accordance with division (G)(1) of section 2929.13 of the Revised Code or a mandatory prison term of sixty consecutive days in accordance with division (G)(2) of that section if the offender is not convicted of and does not plead guilty to a specification of that type. If the court imposes a mandatory term of local incarceration, it may impose a jail term in addition to the sixty-day mandatory term, the cumulative total of the mandatory term and the jail term for the offense shall not exceed one year, and, except as provided in division (A)(1) of section 2929.13 of the Revised Code, no prison term is authorized for the offense. If the court imposes a mandatory prison term, notwithstanding division (A)(4) of section 2929.14 of the Revised Code, it also may sentence the offender to a definite prison term that shall be not less than six months and not more than thirty months and the prison terms shall be imposed as described in division (G)(2) of section 2929.13 of the Revised Code. If the court imposes a mandatory prison term or mandatory prison term and additional prison term, in addition to the term or terms so imposed, the court also may sentence the offender to a community control sanction for the offense, but the offender shall serve all of the prison terms so imposed prior to serving the community control sanction.

(ii) If the sentence is being imposed for a violation of division (A)(1)(f), (g), (h), or (i) or division (A)(2) of this section, a mandatory prison term of one, two, three, four, or five years as required by and in accordance with division (G)(2) of section 2929.13 of the Revised Code if the offender also is convicted of or also pleads guilty to a specification of the type described in section 2941.1413 of the Revised Code or, in the discretion of the court, either a mandatory term of local incarceration of one hundred twenty consecutive days in accordance with division (G)(1) of section 2929.13 of the Revised Code or a mandatory prison term of one hundred twenty consecutive days in accordance with division (G)(2) of that section if the offender is not convicted of and does not plead guilty to a specification of that type. If the court imposes a mandatory term of local incarceration, it may impose a jail term in addition to the one hundred twenty-day mandatory term, the cumulative total of the mandatory term and the jail term for the offense shall not exceed one year, and, except as provided in division (A)(1) of section 2929.13 of the Revised Code, no prison term is authorized for the offense. If the court imposes a mandatory prison term, notwithstanding division (A)(4) of section 2929.14 of the Revised Code, it also may sentence the offender to a definite prison term that shall be not less than six months and not more than thirty months and the prison terms shall be imposed as described in division (G)(2) of section 2929.13 of the Revised Code. If the court imposes a mandatory prison term or mandatory prison term and additional prison term, in addition to the term or terms so imposed, the court also may sentence the offender to a community control sanction for the offense, but the offender shall serve all of the prison terms so imposed prior to serving the community control sanction.

(iii) In all cases, notwithstanding section 2929.18 of the Revised Code, a fine of not less than one thousand three hundred fifty nor more than ten thousand five hundred dollars;

(iv) In all cases, a class two license suspension of the offender's driver's license, commercial driver's license, temporary instruction permit, probationary license, or nonresident operating privilege from the range specified in division (A)(2) of section 4510.02 of the Revised Code. The court may grant limited driving privileges relative to the suspension under sections 4510.021 and 4510.13 of the Revised Code.

(v) In all cases, if the vehicle is registered in the offender's name, criminal forfeiture of the vehicle involved in the offense in accordance with section 4503.234 of the Revised Code. Division (G)(6) of this section applies regarding any vehicle that is subject to an order of criminal forfeiture under this division.

(vi) In all cases, the court shall order the offender to participate in an alcohol and drug addiction program authorized by section 3793.02 of the Revised Code, subject to division (I) of this section, and shall order the offender to follow the treatment recommendations of the program. The operator of the program shall determine and assess the degree of the offender's alcohol dependency and shall make recommendations for treatment. Upon the request of the court, the program shall submit the results of the assessment to the court, including all treatment recommendations and clinical diagnoses related to alcohol use.

(vii) In all cases, if the court sentences the offender to a mandatory term of local incarceration, in addition to the mandatory term, the court, pursuant to section 2929.17 of the Revised Code, may impose a term of house arrest with electronic monitoring. The term shall not commence until after the offender has served the mandatory term of local incarceration.

(e) An offender who previously has been convicted of or pleaded guilty to a violation of division (A) of this section that was a felony, regardless of when the violation and the conviction or guilty plea occurred, is guilty of a felony of the third degree. The court shall sentence the offender to all of the following:

(i) If the offender is being sentenced for a violation of division (A)(1)(a), (b), (c), (d), (e), or (j) of this section, a mandatory prison term of one, two, three, four, or five years as required by and in accordance with division (G)(2) of section 2929.13 of the Revised Code if the offender also is convicted of or also pleads guilty to a specification of the type described in section 2941.1413 of the Revised Code or a mandatory prison term of sixty consecutive days in accordance with division (G)(2) of section 2929.13 of the Revised Code if the offender is not convicted of and does not plead guilty to a specification of that type. The court may impose a prison term in addition to the mandatory prison term. The cumulative total of a sixty-day mandatory prison term and the additional prison term for the offense shall not exceed five years. In addition to the mandatory prison term or mandatory prison term and additional prison term the court imposes, the court also may sentence the offender to a community control sanction for the offense, but the offender shall serve all of the prison terms so imposed prior to serving the community control sanction.

(ii) If the sentence is being imposed for a violation of division (A)(1)(f), (g), (h), or (i) or division (A)(2) of this section, a mandatory prison term of one, two, three, four, or five years as required by and in accordance with division (G)(2) of section 2929.13 of the Revised Code if the offender also is convicted of or also pleads guilty to a specification of the type described in section 2941.1413 of the Revised Code or a mandatory prison term of one hundred twenty consecutive days in accordance with division (G)(2) of section 2929.13 of the Revised Code if the offender is not convicted of and does not plead guilty to a specification of that type. The court may impose a prison term in addition to the mandatory prison term. The cumulative total of a one hundred twenty-day mandatory prison term and the additional prison term for the offense shall not exceed five years. In addition to the mandatory prison term or mandatory prison term and additional prison term the court imposes, the court also may sentence the offender to a

community control sanction for the offense, but the offender shall serve all of the prison terms so imposed prior to serving the community control sanction.
(iii) In all cases, notwithstanding section 2929.18 of the Revised Code, a fine of not less than one thousand three hundred fifty nor more than ten thousand five hundred dollars;
(iv) In all cases, a class two license suspension of the offender's driver's license, commercial driver's license, temporary instruction permit, probationary license, or nonresident operating privilege from the range specified in division (A)(2) of section 4510.02 of the Revised Code. The court may grant limited driving privileges relative to the suspension under sections 4510.021 and 4510.13 of the Revised Code.
(v) In all cases, if the vehicle is registered in the offender's name, criminal forfeiture of the vehicle involved in the offense in accordance with section 4503.234 of the Revised Code. Division (G)(6) of this section applies regarding any vehicle that is subject to an order of criminal forfeiture under this division.
(vi) In all cases, the court shall order the offender to participate in an alcohol and drug addiction program authorized by section 3793.02 of the Revised Code, subject to division (I) of this section, and shall order the offender to follow the treatment recommendations of the program. The operator of the program shall determine and assess the degree of the offender's alcohol dependency and shall make recommendations for treatment. Upon the request of the court, the program shall submit the results of the assessment to the court, including all treatment recommendations and clinical diagnoses related to alcohol use.
(2) An offender who is convicted of or pleads guilty to a violation of division (A) of this section and who subsequently seeks reinstatement of the driver's or occupational driver's license or permit or nonresident operating privilege suspended under this section as a result of the conviction or guilty plea shall pay a reinstatement fee as provided in division (F)(2) of section 4511.191 of the Revised Code.
(3) If an offender is sentenced to a jail term under division (G)(1)(b)(i) or (ii) or (G)(1)(c)(i) or (ii) of this section and if, within sixty days of sentencing of the offender, the court issues a written finding on the record that, due to the unavailability of space at the jail where the offender is required to serve the term, the offender will not be able to begin serving that term within the sixty-day period following the date of sentencing, the court may impose an alternative sentence under this division that includes a term of house arrest with electronic monitoring, with continuous alcohol monitoring, or with both electronic monitoring and continuous alcohol monitoring.
As an alternative to a mandatory jail term of ten consecutive days required by division (G)(1)(b)(i) of this section, the court, under this division, may sentence the offender to five consecutive days in jail and not less than eighteen consecutive days of house arrest with electronic monitoring, with continuous alcohol monitoring, or with both electronic monitoring and continuous alcohol monitoring. The cumulative total of the five consecutive days in jail and the period of house arrest with electronic monitoring, continuous alcohol monitoring, or both types of monitoring shall not exceed six months. The five consecutive days in jail do not have to be served prior to or consecutively to the period of house arrest.
As an alternative to the mandatory jail term of twenty consecutive days required by division (G)(1)(b)(ii) of this section, the court, under this division, may sentence the offender to ten consecutive days in jail and not less than thirty-six consecutive days of house arrest with electronic monitoring, with continuous alcohol monitoring, or with both electronic monitoring and continuous alcohol monitoring. The cumulative total of the ten consecutive days in jail and the period of house arrest with electronic monitoring, continuous alcohol monitoring, or both types of monitoring shall not exceed six months. The ten consecutive days in jail do not have to be served prior to or consecutively to the period of house arrest.
As an alternative to a mandatory jail term of thirty consecutive days required by division (G)(1)(c)(i) of this section, the court, under this division, may sentence the offender to fifteen consecutive days in jail and not less than fifty-five consecutive days of house arrest with electronic monitoring, with continuous alcohol monitoring, or with both electronic monitoring and continuous alcohol monitoring. The cumulative total of the fifteen consecutive days in jail and the period of house arrest with electronic monitoring, continuous alcohol monitoring, or both types of monitoring shall not exceed one year. The fifteen consecutive days in jail do not have to be served prior to or consecutively to the period of house arrest.
As an alternative to the mandatory jail term of sixty consecutive days required by division (G)(1)(c)(ii) of this section, the court, under this division, may sentence the offender to thirty consecutive days in jail and not less than one hundred ten consecutive days of house arrest with electronic monitoring, with continuous alcohol monitoring, or with both electronic monitoring and continuous alcohol monitoring. The cumulative total of the thirty consecutive days in jail and the period of house arrest with electronic monitoring, continuous alcohol monitoring, or both types of monitoring shall not exceed one year. The thirty consecutive days in jail do not have to be served prior to or consecutively to the period of house arrest.
(4) If an offender's driver's or occupational driver's license or permit or nonresident operating privilege is suspended under division (G) of this section and if section 4510.13 of the Revised Code permits the court to grant limited driving privileges, the court may grant the limited driving privileges in accordance with that section. If division (A)(7) of that section requires that the court impose as a condition of the privileges that the offender must display on the vehicle that is driven subject to the privileges restricted license plates that are issued under section 4503.231 of the Revised Code, except as provided in division (B) of that section, the court shall impose that condition as one of the conditions of the limited driving privileges granted to the offender, except as provided in division (B) of section 4503.231 of the Revised Code.
(5) Fines imposed under this section for a violation of division (A) of this section shall be distributed as follows:
(a) Twenty-five dollars of the fine imposed under division (G)(1)(a)(iii), thirty-five dollars of the fine imposed under division (G)(1)(b)(iii), one hundred twenty-three dollars of the fine imposed under division (G)(1)(c)(iii), and two hundred ten dollars of the fine imposed under division (G)(1)(d)(iii) or (e)(iii) of this section shall be paid to an

enforcement and education fund established by the legislative authority of the law enforcement agency in this state that primarily was responsible for the arrest of the offender, as determined by the court that imposes the fine. The agency shall use this share to pay only those costs it incurs in enforcing this section or a municipal OVI ordinance and in informing the public of the laws governing the operation of a vehicle while under the influence of alcohol, the dangers of the operation of a vehicle under the influence of alcohol, and other information relating to the operation of a vehicle under the influence of alcohol and the consumption of alcoholic beverages.

(b) Fifty dollars of the fine imposed under division (G)(1)(a)(iii) of this section shall be paid to the political subdivision that pays the cost of housing the offender during the offender's term of incarceration. If the offender is being sentenced for a violation of division (A)(1)(a), (b), (c), (d), (e), or (j) of this section and was confined as a result of the offense prior to being sentenced for the offense but is not sentenced to a term of incarceration, the fifty dollars shall be paid to the political subdivision that paid the cost of housing the offender during that period of confinement. The political subdivision shall use the share under this division to pay or reimburse incarceration or treatment costs it incurs in housing or providing drug and alcohol treatment to persons who violate this section or a municipal OVI ordinance, costs of any immobilizing or disabling device used on the offender's vehicle, and costs of electronic house arrest equipment needed for persons who violate this section.

(c) Twenty-five dollars of the fine imposed under division (G)(1)(a)(iii) and fifty dollars of the fine imposed under division (G)(1)(b)(iii) of this section shall be deposited into the county or municipal indigent drivers' alcohol treatment fund under the control of that court, as created by the county or municipal corporation under division (F) of section 4511.191 of the Revised Code.

(d) One hundred fifteen dollars of the fine imposed under division (G)(1)(b)(iii), two hundred seventy-seven dollars of the fine imposed under division (G)(1)(c)(iii), and four hundred forty dollars of the fine imposed under division (G)(1)(d)(iii) or (e)(iii) of this section shall be paid to the political subdivision that pays the cost of housing the offender during the offender's term of incarceration. The political subdivision shall use this share to pay or reimburse incarceration or treatment costs it incurs in housing or providing drug and alcohol treatment to persons who violate this section or a municipal OVI ordinance, costs for any immobilizing or disabling device used on the offender's vehicle, and costs of electronic house arrest equipment needed for persons who violate this section.

(e) Fifty dollars of the fine imposed under (G)(1)(a)(iii), (G)(1)(b)(iii), (G)(1)(c)(iii), (G)(1)(d)(iii), and (G)(1)(e)(iii) of this section shall be deposited into the special projects fund of the court in which the offender was convicted and that is established under division (E)(1) of section 2303.201 or division (B)(1) of section 1901.26 of the Revised Code, to be used exclusively to cover the cost of immobilizing or disabling devices, including certified ignition interlock devices, and remote alcohol monitoring devices for indigent offenders who are required by a judge to use either of these devices. If the county or municipal corporation in which the offender was convicted does not have a special projects fund that is established under division (E)(1) of section 2303.201 or division (B)(1) of section 1901.26 of the Revised Code, the fifty dollars shall be deposited into the indigent drivers interlock and alcohol monitoring fund under division (I) of section 4511.191 of the Revised Code.

(f) Seventy-five dollars of the fine imposed under division (G)(1)(a)(iii), one hundred twenty-five dollars of the fine imposed under division (G)(1)(b)(iii), two hundred fifty dollars of the fine imposed under division (G)(1)(c)(iii), and five hundred dollars of the fine imposed under division (G)(1)(d)(iii) or (e)(iii) of this section shall be transmitted to the treasurer of state for deposit into the indigent defense support fund established under section 120.08 of the Revised Code.

(g) The balance of the fine imposed under division (G)(1)(a)(iii), (b)(iii), (c)(iii), (d)(iii), or (e)(iii) of this section shall be disbursed as otherwise provided by law.

## *MOTOR VEHICLES, RECKLESS DRIVING,* R.C. §§ 4511.20, 4511.201 [MM, M4, M3]

(a) Operate a motor vehicle, trackless trolley, or streetcar
(b) On any street or highway
(c) In willful or wanton disregard of the safety of persons or property
(d) Venue

*(or)*

(a) Operate a motor vehicle, trackless trolley, or streetcar
(b) On public or private property other than streets or highways
(c) In willful or wanton disregard of the safety of persons or property
(d) Venue

*Penalty:* [First offense]: A minor misdemeanor (2929.21-2929.31)
*Penalty:* [Second offense within 1 year of first]: A misdemeanor of the fourth degree (2929.21-2929.31)
*Penalty:* [Third and further offenses within 1 year of first]: A misdemeanor of the third degree (2929.21-2929.31)
*Note:* Competition among vehicles with consent of property owner is excepted under R.C. § 4511.201

## *MOTOR VEHICLES, OPERATING WITHOUT REASONABLE CONTROL,* R.C. § 4511.202 [MM]

(1) Operate a motor vehicle, trackless trolley, or streetcar
(2) On any street, highway, or property open to the public for vehicular traffic
(3) Without being in reasonable control
(4) Of the vehicle, trackless trolley, or streetcar
(5) Venue

*Penalty:* A minor misdemeanor (2929.21-2929.31)

***MOTOR VEHICLES, SPEED LIMITS/ASSURED CLEAR DISTANCE,* R.C. § 4511.21 [MM, M4, M3]**

Speed Limits:
(1) Operate a motor vehicle, trackless trolley, or streetcar
(2) At a speed greater or less than is reasonable or proper, having due regard to the traffic, surface, and width of the street or highway and any other conditions
*(or)*
(1) Operate a motor vehicle, trackless trolley, or streetcar upon a street or highway
(2) (a) At a speed exceeding fifty-five miles per hour, except upon a freeway as provided in division (B)(13) of this section
*(or)*
(b) At a speed exceeding sixty-five miles per hour upon a freeway as provided in division (B)(13) of this section except as otherwise provided in division (D)(3) of this section
*(or)*
(c) If a motor vehicle weighing in excess of eight thousand pounds empty weight or a noncommercial bus as prescribed in division (B)(11) of this section, at a speed exceeding fifty-five miles per hour upon a freeway as provided in that division
*(or)*
(d) At a speed exceeding the posted speed limit upon a freeway for which the director has determined and declared a speed limit of not more than sixty-five miles per hour pursuant to division (L)(2) or (M) of this section
*(or)*
(e) At a speed exceeding sixty-five miles per hour upon a freeway for which such a speed limit has been established through the operation of division (L)(3) of this section
*(or)*
(f) At a speed exceeding the posted speed limit upon a freeway for which the director has determined and declared a speed limit pursuant to division (I)(2) of this section

Assured Clear Distance
(1) Drive any motor vehicle, trackless trolley, or streetcar
(2) In and upon any street or highway
(3) At a greater speed than will permit him to bring it to a stop within the assured clear distance ahead

First offense **[MM]**
*Penalty:* A minor misdemeanor (2929.21-2929.31)
Second offense within one year of the first **[M4]**
*Penalty:* A misdemeanor of the fourth degree (2929.21-2929.31)
Subsequent offenses within one year of the first **[M3]**
*Penalty:* A misdemeanor of the third degree (2929.21-2929.31)
If the offender has not previously been convicted of or pleaded guilty to a violation of any provision of this section or of any provision of a municipal ordinance that is substantially similar to this section and operated a motor vehicle faster than thirty-five miles an hour in a business district of a municipal corporation, faster than fifty miles an hour in other portions of a municipal corporation, or faster than thirty-five miles an hour in a school zone during recess or while children are going to or leaving school during the school's opening or closing hours
*Penalty:* A misdemeanor of the fourth degree (2929.11-2929.18, 2929.31)
*Note: See* statute for speeds considered prima-facie lawful in absence of lower limits declared by director of transportation or local authorities
No person shall be arrested, charged, or convicted of a violation of any provision of divisions (B) to (O) of section 4511.21 or section 4511.211 of the Revised Code or a substantially similar municipal ordinance based on a peace officer's unaided visual estimation of the speed of a motor vehicle, trackless trolley, or streetcar. This division does not do any of the following:
(a) Preclude the use by a peace officer of a stopwatch, radar, laser, or other electrical, mechanical, or digital device to determine the speed of a motor vehicle;
(b) Apply regarding any violation other than a violation of divisions (B) to (O) of section 4511.21 or section 4511.211 of the Revised Code or a substantially similar municipal ordinance;
(c) Preclude a peace officer from testifying that the speed of operation of a motor vehicle, trackless trolley, or streetcar was at a speed greater or less than a speed described in division (A) of section 4511.21 of the Revised Code, the admission into evidence of such testimony, or preclude a conviction of a violation of that division based in whole or in part on such testimony.

***MOTOR VEHICLES, MASTER CAR KEYS,* R.C. § 4549.042 [F5, F4]**

(1) Sell or dispose of
(2) Master key for more than one motor vehicle
(3) Knowing or having reasonable cause to believe key will be used to commit offense
(4) Venue
*(or)*
(1) Buy, receive or possess
(2) Master key for more than one motor vehicle
(3) With purpose to use it to commit a crime

(4) Venue
*Penalty:* [First offense]: A felony of the fifth degree (2929.11-2929.18, 2929.31)

# TITLE XXIX [29]

# CRIMES — PROCEDURE

# CHAPTER 2901: GENERAL PROVISIONS

*For text of the Ohio Rules of Criminal Procedure, see page 1629*

Section



## [IN GENERAL]

### § 2901.01 Definitions.

(A) As used in the Revised Code:

(1) "Force" means any violence, compulsion, or constraint physically exerted by any means upon or against a person or thing.

(2) "Deadly force" means any force that carries a substantial risk that it will proximately result in the death of any person.

(3) "Physical harm to persons" means any injury, illness, or other physiological impairment, regardless of its gravity or duration.

(4) "Physical harm to property" means any tangible or intangible damage to property that, in any degree, results in loss to its value or interferes with its use or enjoyment. "Physical harm to property" does not include wear and tear occasioned by normal use.

(5) "Serious physical harm to persons" means any of the following:

(a) Any mental illness or condition of such gravity as would normally require hospitalization or prolonged psychiatric treatment;

(b) Any physical harm that carries a substantial risk of death;

(c) Any physical harm that involves some permanent incapacity, whether partial or total, or that involves some temporary, substantial incapacity;

(d) Any physical harm that involves some permanent disfigurement or that involves some temporary, serious disfigurement;

(e) Any physical harm that involves acute pain of such duration as to result in substantial suffering or that involves any degree of prolonged or intractable pain.

(6) "Serious physical harm to property" means any physical harm to property that does either of the following:

(a) Results in substantial loss to the value of the property or requires a substantial amount of time, effort, or money to repair or replace;

(b) Temporarily prevents the use or enjoyment of the property or substantially interferes with its use or enjoyment for an extended period of time.

(7) "Risk" means a significant possibility, as contrasted with a remote possibility, that a certain result may occur or that certain circumstances may exist.

(8) "Substantial risk" means a strong possibility, as contrasted with a remote or significant possibility, that a certain result may occur or that certain circumstances may exist.

(9) "Offense of violence" means any of the following:

(a) A violation of section 2903.01, 2903.02, 2903.03, 2903.04, 2903.11, 2903.12, 2903.13, 2903.15, 2903.21, 2903.211, 2903.22, 2905.01, 2905.02, 2905.11, 2905.32, 2907.02, 2907.03, 2907.05, 2909.02, 2909.03, 2909.24, 2911.01, 2911.02, 2911.11, 2917.01, 2917.02, 2917.03, 2917.31, 2919.25, 2921.03, 2921.04, 2921.34, or 2923.161, of division (A)(1), (2), or (3) of section 2911.12, or of division (B)(1), (2), (3), or (4) of section 2919.22 of the Revised Code or felonious sexual penetration in violation of former section 2907.12 of the Revised Code;

(b) A violation of an existing or former municipal ordinance or law of this or any other state or the United States, substantially equivalent to any section, division, or offense listed in division (A)(9)(a) of this section;

(c) An offense, other than a traffic offense, under an existing or former municipal ordinance or law of this or any other state or the United States, committed purposely or knowingly, and involving physical harm to persons or a risk of serious physical harm to persons;

(d) A conspiracy or attempt to commit, or complicity in committing, any offense under division (A)(9)(a), (b), or (c) of this section.

(10)(a) "Property" means any property, real or personal, tangible or intangible, and any interest or license in that property. "Property" includes, but is not limited to, cable television service, other telecommunications service, telecommunications devices, information service, computers, data, computer software, financial instruments associated with computers, other documents associated with computers, or copies of the documents, whether in machine or human readable form, trade secrets, trademarks, copyrights, patents, and property protected by a trademark, copyright, or patent. "Financial instruments associated with computers" include, but are not limited to, checks, drafts, warrants, money orders, notes of indebtedness, certificates of deposit, letters of credit, bills of credit or debit cards, financial transaction authorization mechanisms, marketable securities, or any computer system representations of any of them.

(b) As used in division (A)(10) of this section, "trade secret" has the same meaning as in section 1333.61 of the Revised Code, and "telecommunications service" and "information service" have the same meanings as in section 2913.01 of the Revised Code.

(c) As used in divisions (A)(10) and (13) of this section, "cable television service," "computer," "computer software," "computer system," "computer network," "data," and "telecommunications device" have the same meanings as in section 2913.01 of the Revised Code.

(11) "Law enforcement officer" means any of the following:

(a) A sheriff, deputy sheriff, constable, police officer of a township or joint police district, marshal, deputy marshal, municipal police officer, member of a police force employed by a metropolitan housing authority under division (D) of section 3735.31 of the Revised Code, or state highway patrol trooper;

(b) An officer, agent, or employee of the state or any of its agencies, instrumentalities, or political subdivisions, upon whom, by statute, a duty to conserve the peace or to enforce all or certain laws is imposed and the authority to arrest violators is conferred, within the limits of that statutory duty and authority;

(c) A mayor, in the mayor's capacity as chief conservator of the peace within the mayor's municipal corporation;

(d) A member of an auxiliary police force organized by county, township, or municipal law enforcement authorities, within the scope of the member's appointment or commission;

(e) A person lawfully called pursuant to section 311.07 of the Revised Code to aid a sheriff in keeping the peace, for the purposes and during the time when the person is called;

(f) A person appointed by a mayor pursuant to section 737.01 of the Revised Code as a special patrolling officer during riot or emergency, for the purposes and during the time when the person is appointed;

(g) A member of the organized militia of this state or the armed forces of the United States, lawfully called to duty to aid civil authorities in keeping the peace or protect against domestic violence;

(h) A prosecuting attorney, assistant prosecuting attorney, secret service officer, or municipal prosecutor;

(i) A veterans' home police officer appointed under section 5907.02 of the Revised Code;

(j) A member of a police force employed by a regional transit authority under division (Y) of section 306.35 of the Revised Code;

(k) A special police officer employed by a port authority under section 4582.04 or 4582.28 of the Revised Code;

(l) The house of representatives sergeant at arms if the house of representatives sergeant at arms has arrest authority pursuant to division (E)(1) of section 101.311 of the Revised Code and an assistant house of representatives sergeant at arms;

(m) A special police officer employed by a municipal corporation at a municipal airport, or other municipal air navigation facility, that has scheduled operations, as defined in section 119.3 of Title 14 of the Code of Federal Regulations, 14 C.F.R. 119.3, as amended, and that is required to be under a security program and is governed by aviation security rules of the transportation security administration of the United States department of transportation as provided in Parts 1542. and 1544. of Title 49 of the Code of Federal Regulations, as amended.

(12) "Privilege" means an immunity, license, or right conferred by law, bestowed by express or implied grant, arising out of status, position, office, or relationship, or growing out of necessity.

(13) "Contraband" means any property that is illegal for a person to acquire or possess under a statute, ordinance, or rule, or that a trier of fact lawfully determines to be illegal to possess by reason of the property's involvement in an offense. "Contraband" includes, but is not limited to, all of the following:

(a) Any controlled substance, as defined in section 3719.01 of the Revised Code, or any device or paraphernalia;

(b) Any unlawful gambling device or paraphernalia;

(c) Any dangerous ordnance or obscene material.

(14) A person is "not guilty by reason of insanity" relative to a charge of an offense only if the person proves, in the manner specified in section 2901.05 of the Revised Code, that at the time of the commission of the offense, the person did not know, as a result of a severe mental disease or defect, the wrongfulness of the person's acts.

(B)(1)(a) Subject to division (B)(2) of this section, as used in any section contained in Title XXIX of the Revised Code that sets forth a criminal offense, "person" includes all of the following:

(i) An individual, corporation, business trust, estate, trust, partnership, and association;

(ii) An unborn human who is viable.

(b) As used in any section contained in Title XXIX of the Revised Code that does not set forth a criminal offense, "person" includes an individual, corporation, business trust, estate, trust, partnership, and association.

(c) As used in division (B)(1)(a) of this section:

(i) "Unborn human" means an individual organism of the species Homo sapiens from fertilization until live birth.

(ii) "Viable" means the stage of development of a human fetus at which there is a realistic possibility of maintaining and nourishing of a life outside the womb with or without temporary artificial life-sustaining support.

(2) Notwithstanding division (B)(1)(a) of this section, in no case shall the portion of the definition of the term "person" that is set forth in division (B)(1)(a)(ii) of this

section be applied or construed in any section contained in Title XXIX of the Revised Code that sets forth a criminal offense in any of the following manners:

(a) Except as otherwise provided in division (B)(2)(a) of this section, in a manner so that the offense prohibits or is construed as prohibiting any pregnant woman or her physician from performing an abortion with the consent of the pregnant woman, with the consent of the pregnant woman implied by law in a medical emergency, or with the approval of one otherwise authorized by law to consent to medical treatment on behalf of the pregnant woman. An abortion that violates the conditions described in the immediately preceding sentence may be punished as a violation of section 2903.01, 2903.02, 2903.03, 2903.04, 2903.05, 2903.06, 2903.08, 2903.11, 2903.12, 2903.13, 2903.14, 2903.21, or 2903.22 of the Revised Code, as applicable. An abortion that does not violate the conditions described in the second immediately preceding sentence, but that does violate section 2919.12, division (B) of section 2919.13, or section 2919.151, 2919.17, or 2919.18 of the Revised Code, may be punished as a violation of section 2919.12, division (B) of section 2919.13, or section 2919.151, 2919.17, or 2919.18 of the Revised Code, as applicable. Consent is sufficient under this division if it is of the type otherwise adequate to permit medical treatment to the pregnant woman, even if it does not comply with section 2919.12 of the Revised Code.

(b) In a manner so that the offense is applied or is construed as applying to a woman based on an act or omission of the woman that occurs while she is or was pregnant and that results in any of the following:

(i) Her delivery of a stillborn baby;

(ii) Her causing, in any other manner, the death in utero of a viable, unborn human that she is carrying;

(iii) Her causing the death of her child who is born alive but who dies from one or more injuries that are sustained while the child is a viable, unborn human;

(iv) Her causing her child who is born alive to sustain one or more injuries while the child is a viable, unborn human;

(v) Her causing, threatening to cause, or attempting to cause, in any other manner, an injury, illness, or other physiological impairment, regardless of its duration or gravity, or a mental illness or condition, regardless of its duration or gravity, to a viable, unborn human that she is carrying.

(C) As used in Title XXIX of the Revised Code:

(1) "School safety zone" consists of a school, school building, school premises, school activity, and school bus.

(2) "School," "school building," and "school premises" have the same meanings as in section 2925.01 of the Revised Code.

(3) "School activity" means any activity held under the auspices of a board of education of a city, local, exempted village, joint vocational, or cooperative education school district; a governing authority of a community school established under Chapter 3314. of the Revised Code; a governing board of an educational service center, or the governing body of a school for which the state board of education prescribes minimum standards under section 3301.07 of the Revised Code.

(4) "School bus" has the same meaning as in section 4511.01 of the Revised Code.

**HISTORY: 142 v H 708 (Eff 4-19-88); 143 v S 24 (Eff 7-24-90); 144 v H 77 (Eff 9-17-91); 144 v S 144 (Eff 8-8-91); 146 v S 2 (Eff 7-1-96); 146 v S 269 (Eff 7-1-96); 146 v H 445 (Eff 9-3-96); 146 v S 239 (Eff 9-6-96); 146 v S 277 (Eff 3-31-97); 147 v H 565 (Eff 3-30-99); 148 v S 1 (Eff 8-6-99); 148 v H 162 (Eff 8-25-99); 148 v S 107 (Eff 3-23-2000); 148 v S 137 (Eff 5-17-2000); 148 v H 351 (Eff 8-18-2000); 148 v S 317 (Eff 3-22-2001); 149 v S 184 (Eff 5-15-2002); 149 v H 675 (Eff 3-14-2003); 149 v H 545 (Eff 3-19-2003); 149 v H 364. Eff 4-8-2003; 151 v H 241, § 1, eff. 7-1-07; 153 v S 235, § 1, eff. 3-24-11; 2011 HB 153, § 101.01, eff. Sept. 29, 2011.**

The provisions of § 3(A) of 151 v H 241 read as follows:

SECTION 3. (A) Section 2901.01 of the Revised Code is presented in this act as a composite of the section as amended by Sub. H.B. 364, Sub. H.B. 545, and H.B. 675 of the 124th General Assembly. The General Assembly, applying the principle stated in division (B) of section 1.52 of the Revised Code that amendments are to be harmonized if reasonably capable of simultaneous operation, finds that the composites are the resulting versions of the sections in effect prior to the effective date of the sections as presented in this act.

The provisions of § 4 of 151 v H 241 read as follows:

SECTION 4. Sections 1, 2, and 3 of this act shall take effect on July 1, 2007. If a criminal or civil forfeiture action relating to misconduct under Title XXIX of the Revised Code was or is commenced before July 1, 2007, and is still pending on that date, the court in which the case is pending shall, to the extent practical, apply the provisions of Chapter 2981. of the Revised Code in the case.

**Analogous to former RC § 2901.01 (134 v H 511; 139 v H 437; 139 v S 199; 140 v S 183; 140 v H 632; 140 v H 129, §§ 1, 3; 141 v H 49, §§ 1, 3; 141 v S 69, §§ 1, 3; 141 v H 428; 142 v H 231; 142 v H 261), repealed 142 v H 708, § 2, eff 12-31-87.**

**Not analogous to former RC § 2901.01 (RS § 6808; S&C 401; 33 v 33; 93 v 223; GC §§ 12399, 12400; 118 v 288; 120 v 413; Bureau of Code Revision, 10-1-53), repealed 134 v H 511, § 2, eff 1-1-74.**

## § 2901.02 Classification of offenses.

As used in the Revised Code:

(A) Offenses include aggravated murder, murder, felonies of the first, second, third, fourth, and fifth degree, misdemeanors of the first, second, third, and fourth degree, minor misdemeanors, and offenses not specifically classified.

(B) Aggravated murder when the indictment or the count in the indictment charging aggravated murder contains one or more specifications of aggravating circumstances listed in division (A) of section 2929.04 of Revised Code, and any other offense for which death may be imposed as a penalty, is a capital offense.

(C) Aggravated murder and murder are felonies.

(D) Regardless of the penalty that may be imposed, any offense specifically classified as a felony is a felony, and any offense specifically classified as a misdemeanor is a misdemeanor.

(E) Any offense not specifically classified is a felony if imprisonment for more than one year may be imposed as a penalty.

(F) Any offense not specifically classified is a misdemeanor if imprisonment for not more than one year may be imposed as a penalty.

(G) Any offense not specifically classified is a minor misdemeanor if the only penalty that may be imposed is one of the following:

(1) For an offense committed prior to January 1, 2004, a fine not exceeding one hundred dollars;

(2) For an offense committed on or after January 1, 2004, a fine not exceeding one hundred fifty dollars, community service under division (D) of section 2929.27 of the Revised Code, or a financial sanction other than a fine under section 2929.28 of the Revised Code.

**HISTORY: 134 v H 511 (Eff 1-1-74); 139 v S 199 (Eff 7-1-83); 140 v H 380 (Eff 4-3-84); 146 v S 2. Eff 7-1-96; 149 v H 490, § 1, eff. 1-1-04; 2011 HB 5, § 1, eff. Sept. 23, 2011.**

The effective date is set by section 4 of HB 490.

**Not analogous to former RC § 2901.02 (RS §§ 6808, 6809; S&S 268; S&C 401; 33 v 33; 60 v 17; 93 v 223; GC § 12401; Bureau of Code Revision, 10-1-53), repealed 134 v H 511, § 2, eff 1-1-74.**

## § 2901.03 Common law offenses abrogated.

(A) No conduct constitutes a criminal offense against the state unless it is defined as an offense in the Revised Code.

(B) An offense is defined when one or more sections of the Revised Code state a positive prohibition or enjoin a specific duty, and provide a penalty for violation of such prohibition or failure to meet such duty.

(C) This section does not affect any power of the general assembly under section 8 of Article II, Ohio Constitution, nor does it affect the power of a court to punish for contempt or to employ any sanction authorized by law to enforce an order, civil judgment, or decree.

**HISTORY: 134 v H 511. Eff 1-1-74.**

**Not analogous to former RC § 2901.03 (RS § 7388-52; 98 v 180; GC § 12402; Bureau of Code Revision, 10-1-53; 126 v 575), repealed 134 v H 511, § 2, eff 1-1-74.**

The effective date is set by section 4 of HB 511.

## § 2901.04 Rules of construction; references to previous conviction; interpretation of statutory references that define or specify a criminal offense.

(A) Except as otherwise provided in division (C) or (D) of this section, sections of the Revised Code defining offenses or penalties shall be strictly construed against the state, and liberally construed in favor of the accused.

(B) Rules of criminal procedure and sections of the Revised Code providing for criminal procedure shall be construed so as to effect the fair, impartial, speedy, and sure administration of justice.

(C) Any provision of a section of the Revised Code that refers to a previous conviction of or plea of guilty to a violation of a section of the Revised Code or of a division of a section of the Revised Code shall be construed to also refer to a previous conviction of or plea of guilty to a substantially equivalent offense under an existing or former law of this state, another state, or the United States or under an existing or former municipal ordinance.

(D) Any provision of the Revised Code that refers to a section, or to a division of a section, of the Revised Code that defines or specifies a criminal offense shall be construed to also refer to an existing or former law of this state, another state, or the United States, to an existing or former municipal ordinance, or to an existing or former division of any such existing or former law or ordinance that defines or specifies, or that defined or specified, a substantially equivalent offense.

**HISTORY: 134 v H 511 (Eff 1-1-74); 148 v S 107. Eff 3-23-2000; 150 v S 146, § 1, eff. 9-23-04.**

**Not analogous to former RC § 2901.04 (GC § 12402-1; 109 v 545; 111 v 77; Bureau of Code Revision, 10-1-53), repealed 134 v H 511, § 2, eff 1-1-74.**

## § 2901.05 Burden and degree of proof; presumption concerning self-defense or defense of another; jury instructions concerning reasonable doubt.

(A) Every person accused of an offense is presumed innocent until proven guilty beyond a reasonable doubt, and the burden of proof for all elements of the offense is upon the prosecution. The burden of going forward with the evidence of an affirmative defense, and the burden of proof, by a preponderance of the evidence, for an affirmative defense, is upon the accused.

(B)(1) Subject to division (B)(2) of this section, a person is presumed to have acted in self defense or defense of another when using defensive force that is intended or likely to cause death or great bodily harm to another if the person against whom the defensive force is used is in the process of unlawfully and without privilege to do so entering, or has unlawfully and without privilege to do so entered, the residence or vehicle occupied by the person using the defensive force.

(2)(a) The presumption set forth in division (B)(1) of this section does not apply if the person against whom the defensive force is used has a right to be in, or is a lawful resident of, the residence or vehicle.

(b) The presumption set forth in division (B)(1) of this section does not apply if the person who uses the defensive force uses it while in a residence or vehicle and the person is unlawfully, and without privilege to be, in that residence or vehicle.

(3) The presumption set forth in division (B)(1) of this section is a rebuttable presumption and may be rebutted by a preponderance of the evidence.

(C) As part of its charge to the jury in a criminal case, the court shall read the definitions of "reasonable doubt" and "proof beyond a reasonable doubt," contained in division (D) of this section.

(D) As used in this section:

(1) An "affirmative defense" is either of the following:

(a) A defense expressly designated as affirmative;

(b) A defense involving an excuse or justification peculiarly within the knowledge of the accused, on which the accused can fairly be required to adduce supporting evidence.

(2) "Dwelling" means a building or conveyance of any kind that has a roof over it and that is designed to be occupied by people lodging in the building or conveyance at night, regardless of whether the building or conveyance is temporary or permanent or is mobile or immobile. As used in this division, a building or conveyance includes, but is not limited to, an attached porch, and a building or conveyance with a roof over it includes, but is not limited to, a tent.

(3) "Residence" means a dwelling in which a person resides either temporarily or permanently or is visiting as a guest.

(4) "Vehicle" means a conveyance of any kind, whether or not motorized, that is designed to transport people or property.

(E) "Reasonable doubt" is present when the jurors, after they have carefully considered and compared all the evidence, cannot say they are firmly convinced of the truth of the charge. It is a doubt based on reason and common sense. Reasonable doubt is not mere possible doubt, because everything relating to human affairs or depending on moral evidence is open to some possible or imaginary doubt. "Proof beyond a reasonable doubt" is proof of such character that an ordinary person would be willing to rely and act upon it in the most important of the person's own affairs.

**HISTORY: 134 v H 511 (Eff 1-1-74); 137 v H 1168. Eff 11-1-78; 152 v S 184, § 1, eff. 9-9-08.**

**Not analogous to former RC § 2901.05 (RS § 6810; S&C 402; 33 v 33; GC § 12403; 124 v 14; Bureau of Code Revision, eff 10-1-53), repealed 134 v H 511, § 2, eff 1-1-74.**

## § 2901.06 Battered woman syndrome testimony as evidence relevant to claim of self-defense.

(A) The general assembly hereby declares that it recognizes both of the following, in relation to the "battered woman syndrome:"

(1) That the syndrome currently is a matter of commonly accepted scientific knowledge;

(2) That the subject matter and details of the syndrome are not within the general understanding or experience of a person who is a member of the general populace and are not within the field of common knowledge.

(B) If a person is charged with an offense involving the use of force against another and the person, as a defense to the offense charged, raises the affirmative defense of self-defense, the person may introduce expert testimony of the "battered woman syndrome" and expert testimony that the person suffered from that syndrome as evidence to establish the requisite belief of an imminent danger of death or great bodily harm that is necessary, as an element of the affirmative defense, to justify the person's use of the force in question. The introduction of any expert testimony under this division shall be in accordance with the Ohio Rules of Evidence.

**HISTORY: 143 v H 484. Eff 11-5-90.**

**Not analogous to former RC § 2901.06 (RS § 6811; S&C 403; 33 v 33; GC § 12404; 116 v 205; Bureau of Code Revision, 10-1-53), repealed, 134 v H 511, § 2, eff 1-1-74.**

## § 2901.07 Collection of DNA specimen from adult arrested for felony offense; collection of DNA specimen from felony offenders and certain misdemeanor offenders.

(A) As used in this section:

(1) "DNA analysis" and "DNA specimen" have the same meanings as in section 109.573 [109.57.3] of the Revised Code.

(2) "Jail" and "community-based correctional facility" have the same meanings as in section 2929.01 of the Revised Code.

(3) "Post-release control" has the same meaning as in section 2967.01 of the Revised Code.

(4) "Head of the arresting law enforcement agency" means whichever of the following is applicable regarding the arrest in question:

(a) If the arrest was made by a sheriff or a deputy sheriff, the sheriff who made the arrest or who employs the deputy sheriff who made the arrest;

(b) If the arrest was made by a law enforcement officer of a law enforcement agency of a municipal corporation, the chief of police, marshal, or other chief law enforcement officer of the agency that employs the officer who made the arrest;

(c) If the arrest was made by a constable or a law enforcement officer of a township police department or police district police force, the constable who made the arrest or the chief law enforcement officer of the department or agency that employs the officer who made the arrest;

(d) If the arrest was made by the superintendent or a trooper of the state highway patrol, the superintendent of the state highway patrol;

(e) If the arrest was made by a law enforcement officer not identified in division (A)(4)(a), (b), (c), or (d) of this section, the chief law enforcement officer of the law enforcement agency that employs the officer who made the arrest.

(B)(1) On and after July 1, 2011, a person who is eighteen years of age or older and who is arrested on or after July 1, 2011, for a felony offense shall submit to a DNA specimen collection procedure administered by the head of the arresting law enforcement agency. The head of the arresting law enforcement agency shall cause the DNA specimen to be collected from the person during the intake process at the jail, community-based correctional facility, detention facility, or law enforcement agency office or station to which the arrested person is taken after the arrest. The head of the arresting law enforcement agency shall cause the DNA specimen to be collected in accordance with division (C) of this section.

(2) Regardless of when the conviction occurred or the guilty plea was entered, a person who has been convicted of, is convicted of, has pleaded guilty to, or pleads guilty to a felony, who is sentenced to a prison term or to a community residential sanction in a jail or community-based correctional facility for that offense pursuant to section 2929.16 of the Revised Code, and who does not provide a DNA specimen pursuant to division (B)(1) of this section, and a person who has been convicted of, is convicted of, has pleaded guilty to, or pleads guilty to a misdemeanor offense listed in division (D) of this section, who is sentenced to a term of imprisonment for that offense, and who does not provide a DNA specimen pursuant to division (B)(1) of this section, shall submit to a DNA specimen collection procedure administered by the director of rehabilitation and correction or the chief administrative officer of the jail or other detention facility in which the person is serving the term of imprisonment. If the person serves the prison term in a state correctional institution, the director of rehabilitation and correction shall cause the DNA specimen to be collected from the person during the intake process at the reception facility designated by the director. If the person serves the community residential sanction or term of imprisonment in a jail, a community-based correctional facility, or another county, multicounty, municipal, municipal-county, or multicounty-municipal detention facility, the chief administrative officer of the jail, community-based correctional facility, or detention facility shall cause the DNA specimen to be collected from the person during the intake process at the jail, community-based correctional facility, or detention facility. The DNA specimen shall be collected in accordance with division (C) of this section.

(3) Regardless of when the conviction occurred or the guilty plea was entered, if a person has been convicted of, is convicted of, has pleaded guilty to, or pleads guilty to a felony offense or a misdemeanor offense listed in division (D) of this section, is serving a prison term, community residential sanction, or term of imprisonment for that offense, and does not provide a DNA specimen pursuant to division (B)(1) or (2) of this section, prior to the person's release from the prison term, community residential sanc-

tion, or imprisonment, the person shall submit to, and the director of rehabilitation and correction or the chief administrative officer of the jail, community-based correctional facility, or detention facility in which the person is serving the prison term, community residential sanction, or term of imprisonment shall administer, a DNA specimen collection procedure at the state correctional institution, jail, community-based correctional facility, or detention facility in which the person is serving the prison term, community residential sanction, or term of imprisonment. The DNA specimen shall be collected in accordance with division (C) of this section.

(4)(a) Regardless of when the conviction occurred or the guilty plea was entered, if a person has been convicted of, is convicted of, has pleaded guilty to, or pleads guilty to a felony offense or a misdemeanor offense listed in division (D) of this section and the person is on probation, released on parole, under transitional control, on community control, on post-release control, or under any other type of supervised release under the supervision of a probation department or the adult parole authority for that offense, and did not provide a DNA specimen pursuant to division (B)(1), (2), or (3) of this section, the person shall submit to a DNA specimen collection procedure administered by the chief administrative officer of the probation department or the adult parole authority. The DNA specimen shall be collected in accordance with division (C) of this section. If the person refuses to submit to a DNA specimen collection procedure as provided in this division, the person may be subject to the provisions of section 2967.15 of the Revised Code.

(b) If a person to whom division (B)(4)(a) of this section applies is sent to jail or is returned to a jail, community-based correctional facility, or state correctional institution for a violation of the terms and conditions of the probation, parole, transitional control, other release, or post-release control, if the person was or will be serving a term of imprisonment, prison term, or community residential sanction for committing a felony offense or for committing a misdemeanor offense listed in division (D) of this section, and if the person did not provide a DNA specimen pursuant to division (B)(1), (2), (3), or (4)(a) of this section, the person shall submit to, and the director of rehabilitation and correction or the chief administrative officer of the jail or community-based correctional facility shall administer, a DNA specimen collection procedure at the jail, community-based correctional facility, or state correctional institution in which the person is serving the term of imprisonment, prison term, or community residential sanction. The DNA specimen shall be collected from the person in accordance with division (C) of this section.

(5) Regardless of when the conviction occurred or the guilty plea was entered, if a person has been convicted of, is convicted of, has pleaded guilty to, or pleads guilty to a felony offense or a misdemeanor offense listed in division (D) of this section, the person is not sentenced to a prison term, a community residential sanction in a jail or community-based correctional facility, a term of imprisonment, or any type of supervised release under the supervision of a probation department or the adult parole authority, and the person does not provide a DNA specimen pursuant to division (B)(1), (2), (3), (4)(a), or (4)(b) of this section, the sentencing court shall order the person to report to the county probation department immediately after sentencing to submit to a DNA specimen collection procedure administered by the chief administrative officer of the county probation office. If the person is incarcerated at the time of sentencing, the person shall submit to a DNA specimen collection procedure administered by the director of rehabilitation and correction or the chief administrative officer of the jail or other detention facility in which the person is incarcerated. The DNA specimen shall be collected in accordance with division (C) of this section.

(C) If the DNA specimen is collected by withdrawing blood from the person or a similarly invasive procedure, a physician, registered nurse, licensed practical nurse, duly licensed clinical laboratory technician, or other qualified medical practitioner shall collect in a medically approved manner the DNA specimen required to be collected pursuant to division (B) of this section. If the DNA specimen is collected by swabbing for buccal cells or a similarly noninvasive procedure, this section does not require that the DNA specimen be collected by a qualified medical practitioner of that nature. No later than fifteen days after the date of the collection of the DNA specimen, the head of the arresting law enforcement agency regarding a DNA specimen taken pursuant to division (B)(1) of this section, the director of rehabilitation and correction or the chief administrative officer of the jail, community-based correctional facility, or other county, multicounty, municipal, municipal-county, or multicounty-municipal detention facility, in which the person is serving the prison term, community residential sanction, or term of imprisonment regarding a DNA specimen taken pursuant to division (B)(2), (3), or (4)(b) of this section, the chief administrative officer of the probation department or the adult parole authority regarding a DNA specimen taken pursuant to division (B)(4)(a) of this section, or the chief administrative officer of the county probation office, the director of rehabilitation and correction, or the chief administrative officer of the jail or other detention facility in which the person is incarcerated regarding a DNA specimen taken pursuant to division (B)(5) of this section, whichever is applicable, shall cause the DNA specimen to be forwarded to the bureau of criminal identification and investigation in accordance with procedures established by the superintendent of the bureau under division (H) of section 109.573 [109.57.3] of the Revised Code. The bureau shall provide the specimen vials, mailing tubes, labels, postage, and instructions needed for the collection and forwarding of the DNA specimen to the bureau.

(D) The DNA specimen collection duty set forth in division (B)(1) of this section applies to any person who is eighteen years of age or older and who is arrested on or after July 1, 2011, for any felony offense. The DNA specimen collection duties set forth in divisions (B)(2), (3), (4)(a), (4)(b), and (5) of this section apply to any person who has been convicted of, is convicted of, has pleaded guilty to, or pleads guilty to any felony offense or any of the following misdemeanor offenses:

(1) A misdemeanor violation, an attempt to commit a misdemeanor violation, or complicity in committing a misdemeanor violation of section 2907.04 of the Revised Code;

(2) A misdemeanor violation of any law that arose out of the same facts and circumstances and same act as did a charge against the person of a violation of section 2903.01, 2903.02, 2905.01, 2907.02, 2907.03, 2907.04, 2907.05, or 2911.11 of the Revised Code that previously was dismissed or amended or as did a charge against the person of a violation of section 2907.12 of the Revised Code as it existed prior to September 3, 1996, that previously was dismissed or amended;

(3) A misdemeanor violation of section 2919.23 of the Revised Code that would have been a violation of section 2905.04 of the Revised Code as it existed prior to July 1, 1996, had it been committed prior to that date;

(4) A sexually oriented offense or a child-victim oriented offense, both as defined in section 2950.01 of the Revised Code, that is a misdemeanor, if, in relation to that offense, the offender is a tier III sex offender/child-victim offender, as defined in section 2950.01 of the Revised Code.

(E) The director of rehabilitation and correction may prescribe rules in accordance with Chapter 119. of the Revised Code to collect a DNA specimen, as provided in this section, from an offender whose supervision is transferred from another state to this state in accordance with the interstate compact for adult offender supervision described in section 5149.21 of the Revised Code.

**HISTORY: 146 v H 5 (Eff 8-30-95); 146 v S 269 (Eff 7-1-96); 146 v H 180 (Eff 1-1-97); 146 v H 124 (Eff 3-31-97); 147 v S 111 (Eff 3-17-98); 147 v H 526 (Eff 9-1-98); 149 v H 427. Eff 8-29-2002; 150 v S 5, § 1, Eff 7-31-03; 150 v H 525, § 1, eff. 5-18-05; 151 v H 66, § 101.01, eff. 6-30-05†; 151 v S 262, § 1, eff. 7-11-06; 152 v S 10, § 1, eff. 1-1-08; 153 v S 77, § 1, eff. 7-6-10.**

The effective date is set by § 3 of 152 v S 10.

The provisions of § 3 of 151 v S 262 read as follows:

SECTION 3. (A) The General Assembly hereby declares that its purpose in amending section 2901.07 of the Revised Code in Sections 1 and 2 of this act is to reaffirm that it is the General Assembly's intent that, under that section as it existed prior to the effective date of this act, a person who is in any of the categories of offenders described in division (B)(1), (2), (3), or (4) of that section in relation to a conviction of or plea of guilty to a felony offense or a misdemeanor offense listed in division (D) of that section is subject to the DNA specimen collection provisions of divisions (B) and (C) of that section regardless of when the conviction of or plea of guilty to the felony offense or the misdemeanor offense occurs or is entered.

(B) The General Assembly declares that it believes that the amendments to section 2901.07 of the Revised Code made in Sections 1 and 2 of this act are not substantive in nature and merely clarify that divisions (B)(1), (2), (3), and (4) and (C) of that section operate as described in division (A) of this Section, and that the amendments to section 2901.07 of the Revised Code made in Sections 1 and 2 of this act thus are remedial in nature. The General Assembly declares that it intends that the clarifying, remedial amendments to section 2901.07 of the Revised Code made in Sections 1 and 2 of this act apply to all convicted offenders described in division (A) of this Section, regardless of when they were convicted of or pleaded guilty to the felony or the specified misdemeanor or are convicted of or plead guilty to the felony or the specified misdemeanor.

(C) In compliance with the Ohio Supreme Court decision in *Van Fossen v. Babcock & Wilcox Co.* (1988), 36 Ohio St.3d 100, and with section 1.48 of the Revised Code, the General Assembly expressly states its intent that the amendments to section 2901.07 of the Revised Code made in Sections 1 and 2 of this act shall apply retrospectively.

The provisions of § 4 of 151 v S 262 read as follows:

SECTION 4. This act is hereby declared to be an emergency measure necessary for the immediate preservation of the public peace, health, and safety. The reason for such necessity is that the amendments made in Sections 1 and 2 of this act to section 2901.07 of the Revised Code are crucially needed to protect the residents of this state from the consequences that might result if crimes go unsolved because the DNA specimen collection provisions of that section are not applied to all persons who have been convicted of or pleaded guilty to a felony offense or a misdemeanor offense listed in division (D) of that section and are in any of the categories of offenders described in division (B)(1), (2), (3), or (4) of that section. Therefore, this act shall go into immediate effect.

151 v S 262, effective July 11, 2006, rewrote the section.

The effective date is set by § 612.12 of 151 v H 66.

**Not analogous to former RC § 2901.07 (GC § 12401-1; 124 v 177; Bureau of Code Revision, 10-1-53), repealed 134 v H 511, § 2, Eff 1-1-74.**

**Comment, Legislative Service Commission**

† Section 2901.07 of the Revised Code is amended by Am. Sub. H.B. 66 of the 126th General Assembly and Sub. H.B. 525 of the 125th General Assembly. H.B. 525 prevails, making the amendment by H.B. 66 ineffective. The amendment by H.B. 525 in effect repealed the section H.B. 66 attempted to amend.

## § 2901.08 Status of juvenile adjudication as prior conviction.

(A) If a person is alleged to have committed an offense and if the person previously has been adjudicated a delinquent child or juvenile traffic offender for a violation of a law or ordinance, except as provided in division (B) of this section, the adjudication as a delinquent child or as a juvenile traffic offender is a conviction for a violation of the law or ordinance for purposes of determining the offense with which the person should be charged and, if the person is convicted of or pleads guilty to an offense, the sentence to be imposed upon the person relative to the conviction or guilty plea.

(B) A previous adjudication of a person as a delinquent child or juvenile traffic offender for a violation of a law or ordinance is not a conviction for a violation of the law or ordinance for purposes of determining whether the person is a repeat violent offender, as defined in section 2929.01 of the Revised Code, or whether the person should be sentenced as a repeat violent offender under division (B)(2) of section 2929.14 and section 2941.149 of the Revised Code.

**HISTORY: 146 v H 1. Eff 1-1-96; 151 v H 95, § 1, eff. 8-3-06; 2011 HB 86, § 1, eff. Sept. 30, 2011.**

**Not analogous to former RC § 2901.08 (GC § 12405; RS § 6812; S&S 266; S&C 415; 58 v 65, § 34; Bureau of Code Revision, 10-1-53), repealed 134 v H 511, § 2, Eff 1-1-74.**

The effective date is set by section 6 of HB 1.

## § 2901.09 When there is no duty to retreat before using force in self-defense, defense of another, or defense of residence.

(A) As used in this section, "residence" and "vehicle" have the same meanings as in section 2901.05 of the Revised Code.

(B) For purposes of any section of the Revised Code that sets forth a criminal offense, a person who lawfully is in that person's residence has no duty to retreat before using force in self-defense, defense of another, or defense of that person's residence, and a person who lawfully is an occupant of that person's vehicle or who lawfully is an occupant in a vehicle owned by an immediate family member of the person has no duty to retreat before using force in self-defense or defense of another.

**HISTORY: 152 v S 184, § 1, eff. 9-9-08.**

**Not analogous to former RC § 2901.09 (RS §§ 6812—6812-2; S&C 415; S&S 266; 58 v 65; 95 v 276; GC §§ 12405—12407; 124 v 177; Bureau of Code Revision, 10-1-53), repealed 134 v H 511, § 2, eff 1-1-74, concerning malicious injury, poisoning, and taking the life of a president or governor.**

## § 2901.10 Repealed, 134 v H 511, § 2 [RS §§ 6812—6812-2; S&C 415; S&S 266; 58 v 65; 95 v 276;

GC §§ 12405—12407; 124 v 177; Bureau of Code Revision, 10-1-53]. Eff 1-1-74.

This section concerned malicious injury, poisoning, and taking the life of president or governor.

## [JURISDICTION, VENUE, AND LIMITATION OF PROSECUTIONS]

### § 2901.11 Criminal law jurisdiction.

(A) A person is subject to criminal prosecution and punishment in this state if any of the following occur:

(1) The person commits an offense under the laws of this state, any element of which takes place in this state.

(2) While in this state, the person attempts to commit, or is guilty of complicity in the commission of, an offense in another jurisdiction, which offense is an offense under both the laws of this state and the other jurisdiction, or, while in this state, the person conspires to commit an offense in another jurisdiction, which offense is an offense under both the laws of this state and the other jurisdiction, and a substantial overt act in furtherance of the conspiracy is undertaken in this state by the person or another person involved in the conspiracy, subsequent to the person's entrance into the conspiracy. In any case in which a person attempts to commit, is guilty of complicity in the commission of, or conspires to commit an offense in another jurisdiction as described in this division, the person is subject to criminal prosecution and punishment in this state for the attempt, complicity, or conspiracy, and for any resulting offense that is committed or completed in the other jurisdiction.

(3) While out of this state, the person conspires or attempts to commit, or is guilty of complicity in the commission of, an offense in this state.

(4) While out of this state, the person omits to perform a legal duty imposed by the laws of this state, which omission affects a legitimate interest of the state in protecting, governing, or regulating any person, property, thing, transaction, or activity in this state.

(5) While out of this state, the person unlawfully takes or retains property and subsequently brings any of the unlawfully taken or retained property into this state.

(6) While out of this state, the person unlawfully takes or entices another and subsequently brings the other person into this state.

(7) The person, by means of a computer, computer system, computer network, telecommunication, telecommunications device, telecommunications service, or information service, causes or knowingly permits any writing, data, image, or other telecommunication to be disseminated or transmitted into this state in violation of the law of this state.

(B) In homicide, the element referred to in division (A)(1) of this section includes the act that causes death, the physical contact that causes death, the death itself, or any other element that is set forth in the offense in question. If any part of the body of a homicide victim is found in this state, the death is presumed to have occurred within this state.

(C)(1) This state includes the land and water within its boundaries and the air space above that land and water, with respect to which this state has either exclusive or concurrent legislative jurisdiction. Where the boundary between this state and another state or foreign country is disputed, the disputed territory is conclusively presumed to be within this state for purposes of this section.

(2) The courts of common pleas of Adams, Athens, Belmont, Brown, Clermont, Columbiana, Gallia, Hamilton, Jefferson, Lawrence, Meigs, Monroe, Scioto, and Washington counties have jurisdiction beyond the north or northwest shore of the Ohio river extending to the opposite shore line, between the extended boundary lines of any adjacent counties or adjacent state. Each of those courts of common pleas has concurrent jurisdiction on the Ohio river with any adjacent court of common pleas that borders on that river and with any court of Kentucky or of West Virginia that borders on the Ohio river and that has jurisdiction on the Ohio river under the law of Kentucky or the law of West Virginia, whichever is applicable, or under federal law.

(D) When an offense is committed under the laws of this state, and it appears beyond a reasonable doubt that the offense or any element of the offense took place either in this state or in another jurisdiction or jurisdictions, but it cannot reasonably be determined in which it took place, the offense or element is conclusively presumed to have taken place in this state for purposes of this section.

(E) When a person is subject to criminal prosecution and punishment in this state for an offense committed or completed outside of this state, the person is subject to all specifications for that offense that would be applicable if the offense had been committed within this state.

(F) Any act, conduct, or element that is a basis of a person being subject under this section to criminal prosecution and punishment in this state need not be committed personally by the person as long as it is committed by another person who is in complicity or conspiracy with the person.

(G) This section shall be liberally construed, consistent with constitutional limitations, to allow this state the broadest possible jurisdiction over offenses and persons committing offenses in, or affecting, this state.

(H) For purposes of division (A)(2) of this section, an overt act is substantial when it is of a character that manifests a purpose on the part of the actor that the object of the conspiracy should be completed.

(I) As used in this section, "computer," "computer system," "computer network," "information service," "telecommunication," "telecommunications device," "telecommunications service," "data," and "writing" have the same meanings as in section 2913.01 of the Revised Code.

**HISTORY: 134 v H 511 (Eff 1-1-74); 144 v S 371 (Eff 1-17-93); 147 v H 565. Eff 3-30-99; 151 v S 20, § 1, eff. 7-13-05.**

The provisions of § 3 of 151 v S 20 read as follows:

SECTION 3. The General Assembly hereby declares that it intends by the amendments made by Sections 1 and 2 of this act to prospectively overrule the decision of the Ohio Supreme Court in *State v. Yarbrough* (2004), 104 Ohio St. 3d 1.

**Not analogous to former RC § 2901.11 (RS § 7388-52; 98 v 180; GC § 12408; Bureau of Code Revision, 10-1-53; 125 v H 88; 132 v H 65; 133 v H 1), repealed 134 v H 511, § 2, Eff 1-1-74.**

### § 2901.12 Venue.

(A) The trial of a criminal case in this state shall be held in a court having jurisdiction of the subject matter, and in the territory of which the offense or any element of the offense was committed.

(B) When the offense or any element of the offense was committed in an aircraft, motor vehicle, train, watercraft, or other vehicle, in transit, and it cannot reasonably be determined in which jurisdiction the offense was committed, the offender may be tried in any jurisdiction through which the aircraft, motor vehicle, train, watercraft, or other vehicle passed.

(C) When the offense involved the unlawful taking or receiving of property or the unlawful taking or enticing of another, the offender may be tried in any jurisdiction from which or into which the property or victim was taken, received, or enticed.

(D) When the offense is conspiracy, attempt, or complicity cognizable under division (A)(2) of section 2901.11 of the Revised Code, the offender may be tried in any jurisdiction in which the conspiracy, attempt, complicity, or any of its elements occurred. If an offense resulted outside this state from the conspiracy, attempt, or complicity, that resulting offense also may be tried in any jurisdiction in which the conspiracy, attempt, complicity, or any of the elements of the conspiracy, attempt, or complicity occurred.

(E) When the offense is conspiracy or attempt cognizable under division (A)(3) of section 2901.11 of the Revised Code, the offender may be tried in any jurisdiction in which the offense that was the object of the conspiracy or attempt, or any element of that offense, was intended to or could have taken place. When the offense is complicity cognizable under division (A)(3) of section 2901.11 of the Revised Code, the offender may be tried in any jurisdiction in which the principal offender may be tried.

(F) When an offense is considered to have been committed in this state while the offender was out of this state, and the jurisdiction in this state in which the offense or any material element of the offense was committed is not reasonably ascertainable, the offender may be tried in any jurisdiction in which the offense or element reasonably could have been committed.

(G) When it appears beyond a reasonable doubt that an offense or any element of an offense was committed in any of two or more jurisdictions, but it cannot reasonably be determined in which jurisdiction the offense or element was committed, the offender may be tried in any of those jurisdictions.

(H) When an offender, as part of a course of criminal conduct, commits offenses in different jurisdictions, the offender may be tried for all of those offenses in any jurisdiction in which one of those offenses or any element of one of those offenses occurred. Without limitation on the evidence that may be used to establish the course of criminal conduct, any of the following is prima-facie evidence of a course of criminal conduct:

(1) The offenses involved the same victim, or victims of the same type or from the same group.

(2) The offenses were committed by the offender in the offender's same employment, or capacity, or relationship to another.

(3) The offenses were committed as part of the same transaction or chain of events, or in furtherance of the same purpose or objective.

(4) The offenses were committed in furtherance of the same conspiracy.

(5) The offenses involved the same or a similar modus operandi.

(6) The offenses were committed along the offender's line of travel in this state, regardless of the offender's point of origin or destination.

(I)(1) When the offense involves a computer, computer system, computer network, telecommunication, telecommunications device, telecommunications service, or information service, the offender may be tried in any jurisdiction containing any location of the computer, computer system, or computer network of the victim of the offense, in any jurisdiction from which or into which, as part of the offense, any writing, data, or image is disseminated or transmitted by means of a computer, computer system, computer network, telecommunication, telecommunications device, telecommunications service, or information service, or in any jurisdiction in which the alleged offender commits any activity that is an essential part of the offense.

(2) As used in this section, "computer," "computer system," "computer network," "information service," "telecommunication," "telecommunications device," "telecommunications service," "data," and "writing" have the same meanings as in section 2913.01 of the Revised Code.

(J) When the offense involves the death of a person, and it cannot reasonably be determined in which jurisdiction the offense was committed, the offender may be tried in the jurisdiction in which the dead person's body or any part of the dead person's body was found.

(K) Notwithstanding any other requirement for the place of trial, venue may be changed, upon motion of the prosecution, the defense, or the court, to any court having jurisdiction of the subject matter outside the county in which trial otherwise would be held, when it appears that a fair and impartial trial cannot be held in the jurisdiction in which trial otherwise would be held, or when it appears that trial should be held in another jurisdiction for the convenience of the parties and in the interests of justice.

**HISTORY: 134 v H 511 (Eff 1-1-74); 141 v H 49 (Eff 6-26-86); 143 v S 64 (Eff 10-26-89); 147 v H 565. Eff 3-30-99; 151 v S 20, § 1, eff. 7-13-05.**

See provisions of § 3 of 151 v S 20 following RC § 2901.11.

**Not analogous to former RC § 2901.12 (RS § 6818; S&C 406; 33 v 33; 80 v 38; GC § 12432; 109 v 612; 118 v 611; Bureau of Code Revision, 10-1-53; 129 v 1704), repealed 134 v H 511, § 2, eff 1-1-74.**

## § 2901.13 Limitation of criminal prosecutions.

(A)(1) Except as provided in division (A)(2) or (3) of this section or as otherwise provided in this section, a prosecution shall be barred unless it is commenced within the following periods after an offense is committed:

(a) For a felony, six years;

(b) For a misdemeanor other than a minor misdemeanor, two years;

(c) For a minor misdemeanor, six months.

(2) There is no period of limitation for the prosecution of a violation of section 2903.01 or 2903.02 of the Revised Code.

(3) Except as otherwise provided in divisions (B) to (H) of this section, a prosecution of any of the following offenses shall be barred unless it is commenced within twenty years after the offense is committed:

(a) A violation of section 2903.03, 2903.04, 2905.01, 2907.02, 2907.03, 2907.04, 2907.05, 2907.21, 2909.02, 2909.22, 2909.23, 2909.24, 2909.26, 2909.27, 2909.28, 2909.29, 2911.01, 2911.02, 2911.11, 2911.12, or 2917.02 of the Revised Code, a violation of section 2903.11 or 2903.12 of the Revised Code if the victim is a peace officer, a violation of section 2903.13 of the Revised Code that is a felony, or a violation of former section 2907.12 of the Revised Code;

(b) A conspiracy to commit, attempt to commit, or complicity in committing a violation set forth in division (A)(3)(a) of this section.

(B)(1) Except as otherwise provided in division (B)(2) of this section, if the period of limitation provided in division (A)(1) or (3) of this section has expired, prosecution shall be commenced for an offense of which an element is fraud or breach of a fiduciary duty, within one year after discovery of the offense either by an aggrieved person, or by the aggrieved person's legal representative who is not a party to the offense.

(2) If the period of limitation provided in division (A)(1) or (3) of this section has expired, prosecution for a violation of section 2913.49 of the Revised Code shall be commenced within five years after discovery of the offense either by an aggrieved person or the aggrieved person's legal representative who is not a party to the offense.

(C)(1) If the period of limitation provided in division (A)(1) or (3) of this section has expired, prosecution shall be commenced for the following offenses during the following specified periods of time:

(a) For an offense involving misconduct in office by a public servant, at any time while the accused remains a public servant, or within two years thereafter;

(b) For an offense by a person who is not a public servant but whose offense is directly related to the misconduct in office of a public servant, at any time while that public servant remains a public servant, or within two years thereafter.

(2) As used in this division:

(a) An "offense is directly related to the misconduct in office of a public servant" includes, but is not limited to, a violation of section 101.71, 101.91, 121.61 or 2921.13, division (F) or (H) of section 102.03, division (A) of section 2921.02, division (A) or (B) of section 2921.43, or division (F) or (G) of section 3517.13 of the Revised Code, that is directly related to an offense involving misconduct in office of a public servant.

(b) "Public servant" has the same meaning as in section 2921.01 of the Revised Code.

(D) An offense is committed when every element of the offense occurs. In the case of an offense of which an element is a continuing course of conduct, the period of limitation does not begin to run until such course of conduct or the accused's accountability for it terminates, whichever occurs first.

(E) A prosecution is commenced on the date an indictment is returned or an information filed, or on the date a lawful arrest without a warrant is made, or on the date a warrant, summons, citation, or other process is issued, whichever occurs first. A prosecution is not commenced by the return of an indictment or the filing of an information unless reasonable diligence is exercised to issue and execute process on the same. A prosecution is not commenced upon issuance of a warrant, summons, citation, or other process, unless reasonable diligence is exercised to execute the same.

(F) The period of limitation shall not run during any time when the corpus delicti remains undiscovered.

(G) The period of limitation shall not run during any time when the accused purposely avoids prosecution. Proof that the accused departed this state or concealed the accused's identity or whereabouts is prima-facie evidence of the accused's purpose to avoid prosecution.

(H) The period of limitation shall not run during any time a prosecution against the accused based on the same conduct is pending in this state, even though the indictment, information, or process that commenced the prosecution is quashed or the proceedings on the indictment, information, or process are set aside or reversed on appeal.

(I) The period of limitation for a violation of any provision of Title XXIX of the Revised Code that involves a physical or mental wound, injury, disability, or condition of a nature that reasonably indicates abuse or neglect of a child under eighteen years of age or of a mentally retarded, developmentally disabled, or physically impaired child under twenty-one years of age shall not begin to run until either of the following occurs:

(1) The victim of the offense reaches the age of majority.

(2) A public children services agency, or a municipal or county peace officer that is not the parent or guardian of the child, in the county in which the child resides or in which the abuse or neglect is occurring or has occurred has been notified that abuse or neglect is known, suspected, or believed to have occurred.

(J) As used in this section, "peace officer" has the same meaning as in section 2935.01 of the Revised Code.

**HISTORY: 134 v H 511 (Eff 1-1-74); 147 v H 49. Eff 3-9-99; 151 v S 9, § 1, eff. 4-14-06; 151 v S 17, § 1, eff. 8-3-06; 152 v S 219, § 1, eff. 7-21-08; 152 v H 46, § 1, eff. 9-1-08.**

The effective date is set by § 3 of 152 v H 46.

The provisions of § 3 of 152 v S 219 read as follows:

SECTION 3. In amending section 2901.13 of the Revised Code, it is the intent of the General Assembly to supersede the effect of the holding of the Ohio Supreme Court in *State v. Climaco, Climaco, Seminatore, Lefkowitz & Garofoli Co., L.P.A.* (1999), 85 Ohio St.3d 582, with respect to the running of the criminal statute of limitations for certain offenses having a direct relation to certain public servants, whether or not the discovery of the corpus delicti of those offenses occurs within or outside of the otherwise generally applicable period of limitation for criminal prosecution under section 2901.13 of the Revised Code.

**Not analogous to former RC § 2901.13 (GC § 12432-1; 118 v 611; Bureau of Code Revision, 10-1-53; 134 v H 143), repealed 134 v H 511, § 2, eff 1-1-74.**

The provisions of § 3 of HB 49 (147 v —) read as follows:

SECTION 3. Section 2901.13 of the Revised Code, as amended by this act, applies to an offense committed on and after the effective date of this act and applies to an offense committed prior to the effective date of this act if prosecution for that offense was not barred under section 2901.13 of the Revised Code as it existed on the day prior to the effective date of this act.

**Comment, Legislative Service Commission**

Section 2901.13 of the Revised Code is amended by Sub. H.B. 46 and S.B. 219 of the 127th General Assembly. Comparison of these amendments in pursuance of section 1.52 of the Revised Code discloses that they are not irreconcilable so that they are required by that section to be harmonized to give effect to each amendment.

**§ 2901.14** Repealed, 134 v H 511, § 2 [RS §§ 6813—6815; S&C 440; S&S 272; 32 v 20, §§ 1, 3, 4; 64 v 135, § 2; GC §§ 12410—12412; Bureau of Code Revision, 10-1-53]. Eff 1-1-74.

This section concerned administering medicine while intoxicated.

**§ 2901.15** Repealed, 134 v H 511, § 2 [RS §§ 6813—6815; S&C 440; S&S 272; 32 v 20, §§ 1, 3, 4; 64

v 135, § 2; GC §§ 12410—12412; Bureau of Code Revision, 10-1-53]. Eff 1-1-74.

This section concerned prescribing secret medicine.

## § 2901.16 Repealed, 134 v H 511, § 2 [RS §§ 6813—6815; S&C 440; S&S 272; 32 v 20, §§ 1, 3, 4; 64 v 135, § 2; GC §§ 12410—12412; Bureau of Code Revision, 10-1-53]. Eff 1-1-74.

This section concerned abortion.

## § 2901.17 Repealed, 134 v H 511, § 2 [RS §§ 6819, 6984a; S&C 411; 33 v 33, § 23; 78 v 43; 81 v 184; 83 v 27; 95 v 273 (646); GC §§ 12412-1, 12416, 12428; 101 v 210; Bureau of Code Revision, 10-1-53; 131 v 670]. Eff 1-1-74.

This section concerned abortion, torture, and maiming.

## § 2901.18 Repealed, 134 v H 511, § 2 [RS §§ 6819, 6984a; S&C 411; 33 v 33, § 23; 78 v 43; 81 v 184; 83 v 27; 95 v 273 (646); GC §§ 12412-1, 12416, 12428; 101 v 210; Bureau of Code Revision, 10-1-53; 131 v 670]. Eff 1-1-74.

This section concerned abortion, torture, and maiming.

## § 2901.19 Repealed, 134 v H 511, § 2 [RS §§ 6819, 6984a; S&C 411; 33 v 33, § 23; 78 v 43; 81 v 184; 83 v 27; 95 v 273 (646); GC §§ 12412-1, 12416, 12428; 101 v 210; Bureau of Code Revision, 10-1-53; 131 v 670]. Eff 1-1-74.

This section concerned abortion, torture, and maiming.

## § 2901.20 Repealed, 134 v H 511, § 2 [RS § 6819-1; 90 v 353; 98 v 124; GC § 12417; Bureau of Code Revision, 10-1-53]. Eff 1-1-74.

This section concerned hazing.

[CRIMINAL LIABILITY]

## § 2901.21 Requirements for criminal liability.

(A) Except as provided in division (B) of this section, a person is not guilty of an offense unless both of the following apply:

(1) The person's liability is based on conduct that includes either a voluntary act, or an omission to perform an act or duty that the person is capable of performing;

(2) The person has the requisite degree of culpability for each element as to which a culpable mental state is specified by the section defining the offense.

(B) When the section defining an offense does not specify any degree of culpability, and plainly indicates a purpose to impose strict criminal liability for the conduct described in the section, then culpability is not required for a person to be guilty of the offense. When the section neither specifies culpability nor plainly indicates a purpose to impose strict liability, recklessness is sufficient culpability to commit the offense.

(C) Voluntary intoxication may not be taken into consideration in determining the existence of a mental state that is an element of a criminal offense. Voluntary intoxication does not relieve a person of a duty to act if failure to act constitutes a criminal offense. Evidence that a person was voluntarily intoxicated may be admissible to show whether or not the person was physically capable of performing the act with which the person is charged.

(D) As used in this section:

(1) Possession is a voluntary act if the possessor knowingly procured or received the thing possessed, or was aware of the possessor's control of the thing possessed for a sufficient time to have ended possession.

(2) Reflexes, convulsions, body movements during unconsciousness or sleep, and body movements that are not otherwise a product of the actor's volition, are involuntary acts.

(3) "Culpability" means purpose, knowledge, recklessness, or negligence, as defined in section 2901.22 of the Revised Code.

(4) "Intoxication" includes, but is not limited to, intoxication resulting from the ingestion of alcohol, a drug, or alcohol and a drug.

**HISTORY: 134 v H 511 (Eff 1-1-74); 148 v H 318. Eff 10-27-2000.**

**Not analogous to former RC § 2901.21 (RS § 6819-1a; 98 v 124; GC § 12418; Bureau of Code Revision, 10-1-53), repealed 134 v H 511, § 2, eff 1-1-74.**

## § 2901.22 Culpable mental states.

(A) A person acts purposely when it is his specific intention to cause a certain result, or, when the gist of the offense is a prohibition against conduct of a certain nature, regardless of what the offender intends to accomplish thereby, it is his specific intention to engage in conduct of that nature.

(B) A person acts knowingly, regardless of his purpose, when he is aware that his conduct will probably cause a certain result or will probably be of a certain nature. A person has knowledge of circumstances when he is aware that such circumstances probably exist.

(C) A person acts recklessly when, with heedless indifference to the consequences, he perversely disregards a known risk that his conduct is likely to cause a certain result or is likely to be of a certain nature. A person is reckless with respect to circumstances when, with heedless indifference to the consequences, he perversely disregards a known risk that such circumstances are likely to exist.

(D) A person acts negligently when, because of a substantial lapse from due care, he fails to perceive or avoid a risk that his conduct may cause a certain result or may be of a certain nature. A person is negligent with respect to circumstances when, because of a substantial lapse from due care, he fails to perceive or avoid a risk that such circumstances may exist.

(E) When the section defining an offense provides that negligence suffices to establish an element thereof, then recklessness, knowledge, or purpose is also sufficient culpability for such element. When recklessness suffices to establish an element of an offense, then knowledge or purpose is also sufficient culpability for such element. When knowledge suffices to establish an element of an offense, then purpose is also sufficient culpability for such element.

**HISTORY: 134 v H 511. Eff 1-1-74.**

**Not analogous to former RC § 2901.22 (RS § 6819-2; 90 v 353; GC § 12419; Bureau of Code Revision, 10-1-53), repealed 134 v H 511, § 2, eff 1-1-74.**

The effective date is set by section 4 of HB 511.

## § 2901.23 Organizational criminal liability.

(A) An organization may be convicted of an offense under any of the following circumstances:

(1) The offense is a minor misdemeanor committed by an officer, agent, or employee of the organization acting in its behalf and within the scope of his office or employment, except that if the section defining the offense designates the officers, agents, or employees for whose conduct the organization is accountable or the circumstances under which it is accountable, such provisions shall apply.

(2) A purpose to impose organizational liability plainly appears in the section defining the offense, and the offense is committed by an officer, agent, or employee of the organization acting in its behalf and within the scope of his office or employment, except that if the section defining the offense designates the officers, agents, or employees for whose conduct the organization is accountable or the circumstances under which it is accountable, such provisions shall apply.

(3) The offense consists of an omission to discharge a specific duty imposed by law on the organization.

(4) If, acting with the kind of culpability otherwise required for the commission of the offense, its commission was authorized, requested, commanded, tolerated, or performed by the board of directors, trustees, partners, or by a high managerial officer, agent, or employee acting in behalf of the organization and within the scope of his office or employment.

(B) When strict liability is imposed for the commission of an offense, a purpose to impose organizational liability shall be presumed, unless the contrary plainly appears.

(C) In a prosecution of an organization for an offense other than one for which strict liability is imposed, it is a defense that the high managerial officer, agent, or employee having supervisory responsibility over the subject matter of the offense exercised due diligence to prevent its commission. This defense is not available if it plainly appears inconsistent with the purpose of the section defining the offense.

(D) As used in this section, "organization" means a corporation for profit or not for profit, partnership, limited partnership, joint venture, unincorporated association, estate, trust, or other commercial or legal entity. "Organization" does not include an entity organized as or by a governmental agency for the execution of a governmental program.

**HISTORY: 134 v H 511. Eff 1-1-74.**

**Not analogous to former RC § 2901.23 (RS § 6820; S&S 265; S&C 411; 64 v 43; GC § 12420; Bureau of Code Revision, 10-1-53), repealed 134 v H 511, § 2, eff 1-1-74.**

The effective date is set by section 4 of HB 511.

## § 2901.24 Personal accountability for organizational conduct.

(A) An officer, agent, or employee of an organization as defined in section 2901.23 of the Revised Code may be prosecuted for an offense committed by such organization, if he acts with the kind of culpability required for the commission of the offense, and any of the following apply:

(1) In the name of the organization or in its behalf, he engages in conduct constituting the offense, or causes another to engage in such conduct, or tolerates such conduct when it is of a type for which he has direct responsibility;

(2) He has primary responsibility to discharge a duty imposed on the organization by law, and such duty is not discharged.

(B) When a person is convicted of an offense by reason of this section, he is subject to the same penalty as if he had acted in his own behalf.

**HISTORY: 134 v H 511. Eff 1-1-74.**

**Not analogous to former RC § 2901.24 (RS § 6821; S&S 262; S&C 407; 62 v 77; 95 v 344; GC § 12421; Bureau of Code Revision, 10-1-53; 129 v 1704), repealed 134 v H 511, § 2, eff 1-1-74.**

The effective date is set by section 4 of HB 511.

## § 2901.241 Repealed, 134 v H 511, § 2 [128 v 560]. Eff 1-1-74.

This section concerned assault with a dangerous or deadly weapon.

## § 2901.25 Repealed, 134 v H 511, § 2 [RS § 6823; S&S 276; 64 v 21; GC § 12423; Bureau of Code Revision, 10-1-53]. Eff 1-1-74.

This section concerned assault and battery, and menacing threats.

## § 2901.251 Repealed, 134 v H 511, § 2 [131 v 670; 132 v H 996]. Eff 1-1-74.

This section concerned throwing at or towards a person.

## § 2901.252 Repealed, 134 v H 511, § 2 [131 v 670; 132 v H 996]. Eff 1-1-74.

This section concerned assault and battery upon law enforcement officers and firemen.

## § 2901.26 Repealed, 134 v H 511, § 2 [RS §§ 6824, 6830-1, 6830-2; S&S 275; 65 v 87; 79 v 132; 95 v 100; 95 v 648, § 2; GC §§ 12424, 12427, 13386; 101 v 263; 115 v PtII, 73, 90; 117 v 485; Bureau of Code Revision, 10-1-53]. Eff 1-1-74.

This section concerned kidnapping.

## § 2901.27 Repealed, 134 v H 511, § 2 [RS §§ 6824, 6830-1, 6830-2; S&S 275; 65 v 87; 79 v 132; 95 v 100; 95 v 648, § 2; GC §§ 12424, 12427, 13386; 101 v 263; 115 v PtII, 73, 90; 117 v 485; Bureau of Code Revision, 10-1-53]. Eff 1-1-74.

This section concerned kidnapping.

## § 2901.28 Repealed, 134 v H 511, § 2 [RS §§ 6824, 6830-1, 6830-2; S&S 275; 65 v 87; 79 v 132; 95

v 100; 95 v 648, § 2; GC §§ 12424, 12427, 13386; 101 v 263; 115 v PtII, 73, 90; 117 v 485; Bureau of Code Revision, 10-1-53]. Eff 1-1-74.

This section concerned kidnapping.

**§ 2901.29** Repealed, 134 v H 511, § 2 [GC § 13386-1; 115 v PtII, 90; Bureau of Code Revision, 10-1-53]. Eff 1-1-74.

This section concerned kidnapping.

## [MISSING CHILDREN]

### § 2901.30 Missing child report; notice to child's school; notice of return.

(A) As used in sections 2901.30 to 2901.32 of the Revised Code:

(1) "Information" means information that can be integrated into the computer system and that relates to the physical or mental description of a minor including, but not limited to, height, weight, color of hair and eyes, use of eyeglasses or contact lenses, skin coloring, physical or mental handicaps, special medical conditions or needs, abnormalities, problems, scars and marks, and distinguishing characteristics, and other information that could assist in identifying a minor including, but not limited to, full name and nickname, date and place of birth, age, names and addresses of parents and other relatives, fingerprints, dental records, photographs, social security number, driver's license number, credit card numbers, bank account numbers, and clothing.

(2) "Minor" means a person under eighteen years of age.

(3) "Missing children" or "missing child" means either of the following:

(a) A minor who has run away from or who otherwise is missing from the home of, or the care, custody, and control of, the minor's parents, parent who is the residential parent and legal custodian, guardian, legal custodian, or other person having responsibility for the care of the minor;

(b) A minor who is missing and about whom there is reason to believe the minor could be the victim of a violation of section 2905.01, 2905.02, 2905.03, or 2919.23 of the Revised Code or of a violation of section 2905.04 of the Revised Code as it existed prior to July 1, 1996.

(B) When a law enforcement agency in this state that has jurisdiction in the matter is informed that a minor is or may be a missing child and that the person providing the information wishes to file a missing child report, the law enforcement agency shall take that report. Upon taking the report, the law enforcement agency shall take prompt action upon it, including, but not limited to, concerted efforts to locate the missing child. No law enforcement agency in this state shall have a rule or policy that prohibits or discourages the filing of or the taking of action upon a missing child report, within a specified period following the discovery or formulation of a belief that a minor is or could be a missing child.

(C) If a missing child report is made to a law enforcement agency in this state that has jurisdiction in the matter, the law enforcement agency shall gather readily available information about the missing child and integrate it into the national crime information center computer immediately following the making of the report. The law enforcement agency shall make reasonable efforts to acquire additional information about the missing child following the transmittal of the initially available information, and promptly integrate any additional information acquired into such computer systems.

Whenever a law enforcement agency integrates information about a missing child into the national crime information center computer, the law enforcement agency promptly shall notify the missing child's parents, parent who is the residential parent and legal custodian, guardian, or legal custodian, or any other person responsible for the care of the missing child, that it has so integrated the information.

The parents, parent who is the residential parent and legal custodian, guardian, legal custodian, or other person responsible for the care of the missing child shall provide available information upon request, and may provide information voluntarily, to the law enforcement agency during the information gathering process. The law enforcement agency also may obtain available information about the missing child from other persons, subject to constitutional and statutory limitations.

(D) Upon the filing of a missing child report, the law enforcement agency involved may notify the public or nonpublic school in which the missing child is or was most recently enrolled, as ascertained by the agency, that the child is the subject of a missing child report and that the child's school records are to be marked in accordance with section 3313.672 [3313.67.2] of the Revised Code.

(E) Upon the filing of a missing child report, the law enforcement agency involved promptly shall make a reasonable attempt to notify other law enforcement agencies within its county and, if the agency has jurisdiction in a municipal corporation or township that borders another county, to notify the law enforcement agency for the municipal corporation or township in the other county with which it shares the border, that it has taken a missing child report and may be requesting assistance or cooperation in the case, and provide relevant information to the other law enforcement agencies. The agency may notify additional law enforcement agencies, appropriate public children services agencies, about the case, request their assistance or cooperation in the case, and provide them with relevant information.

Upon request from a law enforcement agency, a public children services agency shall grant the law enforcement agency access to all information concerning a missing child that the agency possesses that may be relevant to the law enforcement agency in investigating a missing child report concerning that child. The information obtained by the law enforcement agency shall be used only to further the investigation to locate the missing child.

(F) Upon request, law enforcement agencies in this state shall provide assistance to, and cooperate with, other law enforcement agencies in their investigation of missing child cases. The assistance and cooperation under this paragraph shall be pursuant to any terms agreed upon by the law enforcement agencies, which may include the provision of law enforcement services or the use of law enforcement equipment or the interchange of services and equipment among the cooperating law enforcement agencies. Chapter 2744. of the Revised Code, insofar as it applies to the operation of law enforcement agencies, shall apply to the cooperating political subdivisions and to the law enforcement agency employees when they are rendering services pursuant to this paragraph outside the territory of the political subdivision by which they are employed. Law enforcement agency employees rendering services outside the territory of the political subdivision in which they are employed, pursuant to this paragraph, shall be entitled to participate in any indemnity fund established by their employer to the same extent as if they were rendering service within the territory of their employing political subdivision. Those law enforcement agency employees also shall be entitled to all the rights and benefits of Chapter 4123. of the Revised Code to the same extent as if rendering services within the territory of their employing political subdivision.

The information in any missing child report made to a law enforcement agency shall be made available, upon request, to law enforcement personnel of this state, other states, and the federal government when the law enforcement personnel indicate that the request is to aid in identifying or locating a missing child or the possible identification of a deceased minor who, upon discovery, cannot be identified.

(G) When a missing child has not been located within thirty days after the date on which the missing child report pertaining to the child was filed with a law enforcement agency, that law enforcement agency shall request the missing child's parents, parent who is the residential parent and legal custodian, guardian, or legal custodian, or any other person responsible for the care of the missing child, to provide written consent for the law enforcement agency to contact the missing child's dentist and request the missing child's dental records. Upon receipt of such written consent, the dentist shall release a copy of the missing child's dental records to the law enforcement agency and shall provide and encode the records in such form as requested by the law enforcement agency. The law enforcement agency then shall integrate information in the records into the national crime information center computer in order to compare the records to those of unidentified deceased persons. This division does not prevent a law enforcement agency from seeking consent to obtain copies of a missing child's dental records, or prevent a missing child's parents, parent who is the residential parent and legal custodian, guardian, or legal custodian, or any other person responsible for the care of the missing child, from granting consent for the release of copies of the missing child's dental records to a law enforcement agency, at any time.

(H) A missing child's parents, parent who is the residential parent and legal custodian, guardian, or legal custodian, or any other persons responsible for the care of a missing child, immediately shall notify the law enforcement agency with which they filed the missing child report whenever the child has returned to their home or to their care, custody, and control, has been released if the missing child was the victim of an offense listed in division (A)(3)(b) of this section, or otherwise has been located. Upon such notification or upon otherwise learning that a missing child has returned to the home of, or to the care, custody, and control of the missing child's parents, parent who is the residential parent and legal custodian, guardian, legal custodian, or other person responsible for the missing child's care, has been released if the missing child was the victim of an offense listed in division (A)(3)(b) of this section, or otherwise has been located, the law enforcement agency involved promptly shall integrate the fact that the minor no longer is a missing child into the national crime information center computer and shall inform any school that was notified under division (D) of this section that the minor is no longer a missing child.

(I) Nothing contained in this section shall be construed to impair the confidentiality of services provided to runaway minors by shelters for runaway minors pursuant to sections 5119.64 to 5119.68 of the Revised Code.

**HISTORY: 140 v S 321 (Eff 4-9-85); 143 v S 3 (Eff 4-11-91); 146 v S 2 (Eff 7-1-96); 147 v H 408. Eff 10-1-97; 152 v S 87, § 1, eff. 6-20-08; 152 v H 181, § 1, eff. 9-12-08.**

**Not analogous to former RC § 2901.30 (GC § 13386-2; 115 v PtII, 90, § 3; Bureau of Code Revision, 10-1-53), repealed 134 v H 511, § 2, eff 1-1-74.**

The effective date is set by section 26 of HB 408.

## § 2901.31 Cooperation in locating missing children.

Law enforcement agencies in this state shall cooperate fully with the United States attorney general in the collection of information that would assist in the identification of unidentified deceased persons and information that would assist in the location of missing persons under the "Federal Missing Children Act of 1982," 96 Stat. 1259, 28 U.S.C. 534, as amended.

Law enforcement agencies in this state that are investigating missing children cases shall utilize the records and information compiled by the United States attorney general pursuant to that act when the circumstances of an investigation indicate that the records and information may be of assistance and when the act authorizes it.

**HISTORY: 140 v S 321. Eff 4-9-85.**

**Not analogous to former RC § 2901.31 (GC § 13386-3; 115 v PtII, 90, § 4; Bureau of Code Revision, 10-1-53), repealed 134 v H 511, § 2, eff 1-1-74.**

## § 2901.32 Improper solicitation of contributions for missing children.

(A) No organization shall solicit contributions for the purpose of distributing materials containing information relating to missing children unless it complies with all of the following requirements:

(1) It has been incorporated under Chapter 1702. of the Revised Code or the nonprofit corporation law of another state for a period of two years prior to the time of the solicitation of contributions.

(2) It has been exempt from federal income taxation under subsection 501(a) and described in subsection 501(c)(3), 501(c)(4), 501(c)(8), 501(c)(10), or 501(c)(19) of the Internal Revenue Code of 1954, 68A Stat. 3, 26 U.S.C. 1, as now or hereafter amended, for a period of two years prior to the time of the solicitation of contributions.

(3) It does not use fund-raising counsel, professional solicitors, commercial co-venturers, or other charitable organizations, as these terms are defined in section 1716.01 of the Revised Code, to solicit such contributions.

(B) No organization that solicits contributions for the purpose of distributing materials containing information relating to missing children shall expressly state or imply in any way that it is affiliated with, or is soliciting contributions on behalf of, an organization established to assist in the location of missing children without the express written consent of that organization.

(C) Whoever violates division (A) or (B) of this section is guilty of improper solicitation of contributions for missing children, a misdemeanor of the third degree.

**HISTORY: 140 v S 321 (Eff 4-9-85); 143 v H 486. Eff 11-7-90.**

**Not analogous to former RC § 2901.32 (GC § 13386-4; 115 v PtII, 90, § 5; Bureau of Code Revision, 10-1-53), repealed 134 v H 511, § 2, eff 1-1-74.**

## [REPEALED]

**§ 2901.33** Repealed, 134 v H 511, § 2 [RS §§ 4426-1, 4426-2, 6825; S&C 457; 73 v 207; 81 v 15, 90; 91 v 17; GC §§ 12425, 12940, 12941, 13386-5; 115 v PtII, 90; 117 v 274; Bureau of Code Revision, 10-1-53]. Eff 1-1-74.

This section concerned kidnapping and discrimination.

**§ 2901.34** Repealed, 134 v H 511, § 2 [RS §§ 4426-1, 4426-2, 6825; S&C 457; 73 v 207; 81 v 15, 90; 91 v 17; GC §§ 12425, 12940, 12941, 13386-5; 115 v PtII, 90; 117 v 274; Bureau of Code Revision, 10-1-53]. Eff 1-1-74.

This section concerned kidnapping and discrimination.

**§ 2901.35** Repealed, 134 v H 511, § 2 [RS §§ 4426-1, 4426-2, 6825; S&C 457; 73 v 207; 81 v 15, 90; 91 v 17; GC §§ 12425, 12940, 12941, 13386-5; 115 v PtII, 90; 117 v 274; Bureau of Code Revision, 10-1-53]. Eff 1-1-74.

This section concerned kidnapping and discrimination.

**§ 2901.36** Repealed, 134 v H 511, § 2 [RS §§ 4426-2, 6828, 6830; S&S 279; S&C 431; 64 v 69; 76 v 167; 79 v 84; 81 v 15, 90; 91 v 17; GC §§ 12942, 13383, 13384; 116 v 373; Bureau of Code Revision, 10-1-53; 126 v 575]. Eff 1-1-74.

This section referred to prosecution, libel and blackmail.

**§ 2901.37** Repealed, 134 v H 511, § 2 [RS §§ 4426-2, 6828, 6830; S&S 279; S&C 431; 64 v 69; 76 v 167; 79 v 84; 81 v 15, 90; 91 v 17; GC §§ 12942, 13383, 13384; 116 v 373; Bureau of Code Revision, 10-1-53; 126 v 575]. Eff 1-1-74.

This section referred to prosecution, libel and blackmail.

**§ 2901.38** Repealed, 134 v H 511, § 2 [RS §§ 4426-2, 6828, 6830; S&S 279; S&C 431; 64 v 69; 76 v 167; 79 v 84; 81 v 15, 90; 91 v 17; GC §§ 12942, 13383, 13384; 116 v 373; Bureau of Code Revision, 10-1-53; 126 v 575]. Eff 1-1-74.

This section referred to prosecution, libel and blackmail.

**§ 2901.39** Repealed, 134 v H 511, § 2 [RS §§ 6829, 7017-3; S&C 430; 29 v 144; 93 v 114; 98 v 98; GC §§ 12429, 12430, 13385; 111 v 85; 115 v 144; Bureau of Code Revision, 10-1-53; 126 v 429]. Eff 1-1-74.

This section prohibited threatening letters and provided for destitute, infirm, or aged parents.

**§ 2901.40** Repealed, 134 v H 511, § 2 [RS §§ 6829, 7017-3; S&C 430; 29 v 144; 93 v 114; 98 v 98; GC §§ 12429, 12430, 13385; 111 v 85; 115 v 144; Bureau of Code Revision, 10-1-53; 126 v 429]. Eff 1-1-74.

This section prohibited threatening letters and provided for destitute, infirm, or aged parents.

## [MISSING PERSONS]

### § 2901.41 Best practices protocol for missing person reports; law enforcement agency to adopt written policy.

(A) As used in this section and section 2901.42 of the Revised Code, "missing person" means an individual who is eighteen years of age or older, whose temporary or permanent residence is in Ohio, and who meets one of the following characteristics:

(1) The individual has a physical or mental disability.

(2) The individual is missing under circumstances indicating that the individual's safety may be in danger.

(3) The individual is missing under circumstances indicating that the individual's disappearance was not voluntary.

(B) The attorney general shall publish and distribute to all law enforcement agencies in this state a best practices protocol for addressing reports of missing persons. Upon receipt of the best practices protocol from the attorney general, each law enforcement agency in this state shall develop and adopt a written policy establishing reasonable procedures to be followed by the law enforcement agency when the agency is informed that a person is or may be a missing person.

(C) After a law enforcement agency adopts a written policy as required by division (B) of this section, the peace officers that are employed by that agency shall make a good faith effort to follow the procedures contained in the policy.

(D) The requirements of this section do not create a private cause of action for damages against the state or any law enforcement agency, political subdivision, peace officer, or other person who fails to comply with the requirements of this section.

**HISTORY: 151 v H 571, § 1, eff. 4-5-07.**

**Not analogous to former RC § 2901.41 (RS §§ 6829, 7017-3; S&C 430; 29 v 144; 93 v 114; 98 v 98; GC §§ 12429, 12430, 13385; 111 v 85; 115 v 144; Bureau of Code Revision, 10-1-53; 126 v 429), repealed 134 v H 511, § 2, eff 1-1-74.**

### § 2901.42 Missing person information made available through national crime information center.

(A) If a law enforcement agency receives an initial report or receives additional information for the report that a person who is at least eighteen but less than twenty-one years of age is missing, the law enforcement agency shall make available through the national crime information center all information contained in the report immediately after the law enforcement agency receives the report or additional information.

(B)(1) If a law enforcement agency receives a report that a person who is twenty-one years of age or older is missing and if there is evidence that the person was a victim of foul play at the time the victim is reported missing, the law enforcement agency shall make available through the national crime information center all information contained in the report not later than seven days after the law enforcement agency receives the report. If there is no evidence that the person was a victim of foul play, and no evidence to the contrary is received, the law enforcement agency shall make the information available through the national crime information center not later than thirty days after receiving the report that the person is missing.

(2) If a law enforcement agency receives a report that a person who is twenty-one years of age or older is missing and there is no evidence of foul play at the time the agency receives the report and if the agency discovers after the law enforcement agency receives the report but before the end of the seven-day period under division (B)(1) of this section evidence that the person who is missing was a victim of foul play, the law enforcement agency shall make available through the national crime information center all information contained in the report by the end of that seven-day period. If a law enforcement agency receives a report that a person who is twenty-one years of age or older is missing and there is no evidence of foul play at the time the agency receives the report and if the agency discovers after the end of the seven-day period under division (B)(1) of this section evidence that the person who is missing was a victim of foul play, the law enforcement agency shall make available through the national crime information center all information contained in the report not later than forty-eight hours after discovering the evidence that the person was a victim of foul play.

(C) If a law enforcement agency pursuant to divisions (A) and (B) of this section made available through the national crime information center information contained in a report that a person is missing and the missing person is found, the agency shall promptly remove that information from the law enforcement automated data system.

(D) As used in this section, indicators that a person was a victim of "foul play" include, but are not limited to, evidence that the person's home or car is in disarray, evidence of a struggle between the person and another person, or evidence a law enforcement agency determines to be foul play through the written policy the law enforcement agency develops and adopts pursuant to division (B) of section 2901.41 of the Revised Code.

**HISTORY: 151 v H 571, § 1, eff. 4-5-07; 152 v S 87, § 1, eff. 6-20-08.**

**Not analogous to former RC § 2901.42 (RS § 7017-3; 93 v 114; 98 v 98; GC § 12431; Bureau of Code Revision, 10-1-53; 131 v 670, 671), repealed 134 v H 511, § 2, eff 1-1-74.**

## § 2901.43 Prosecutor's notice to public retirement system.

(A)(1) As used in this section:

(a) "Public retirement system," "alternative retirement plan," and "prosecutor" have the same meanings as in section 2907.15 of the Revised Code.

(b) "Position of honor, trust, or profit" has the same meaning as in section 2929.192 [2929.19.2] of the Revised Code.

(2) For purposes of divisions (B) and (C) of this section, a violation of section 2923.32 of the Revised Code or any other violation or offense that includes as an element a course of conduct or the occurrence of multiple acts is "committed on or after the effective date of this section" if the course of conduct continues, one or more of the multiple acts occurs, or the subject person's accountability for the course of conduct or for one or more of the multiple acts continues, on or after the effective date of this section.

(B) Upon the filing of charges against a person alleging that the person committed on or after the effective date of this section any violation or offense specified in division (C) of this section, if the person allegedly committed the violation or offense while serving in a position of honor, trust, or profit and if the person is an electing employee participating in an alternative retirement plan or a member of a public retirement system, the prosecutor who is assigned the case shall send written notice that those charges have been filed against that person to the alternative retirement plan in which the person is a participant or the public retirement system in which the person is a member, whichever is applicable. The written notice shall specifically identify the person charged.

(C) Division (B) of this section applies when a person is charged with committing on or after the effective date of this section any offense or violation listed or described in divisions (D)(1) to (3) of section 2929.192 [2929.19.2] of the Revised Code that is a felony, in the circumstances specified in the particular division.

**HISTORY: 152 v S 3, § 1, eff. 5-15-08.**

**Not analogous to former RC § 2901.43 (RS § 7017-3; 93 v 114; 98 v 98; GC § 12431; Bureau of Code Revision, 10-1-53; 131 v 670, 671), repealed 134 v H 511, § 2, eff 1-1-74.**

## § 2901.44 Repealed, 134 v H 511, § 2 [RS § 7017-3; 93 v 114; 98 v 98; GC § 12431; Bureau of Code Revision, 10-1-53; 131 v 670, 671]. Eff 1-1-74.

This section concerned duty to support destitute parent, deprivation of equal protection of law, and threats to destroy buildings or property.

## § 2901.45 Repealed, 135 v H 716, § 2 [134 v S 538]. Eff 1-1-74.

This section concerned adulterating candy or food.

# CHAPTER 2903: HOMICIDE AND ASSAULT



[HOMICIDE]

## § 2903.01 Aggravated murder.

(A) No person shall purposely, and with prior calculation and design, cause the death of another or the unlawful termination of another's pregnancy.

(B) No person shall purposely cause the death of another or the unlawful termination of another's pregnancy while committing or attempting to commit, or while fleeing immediately after committing or attempting to commit, kidnapping, rape, aggravated arson, arson, aggravated robbery, robbery, aggravated burglary, burglary, trespass in a habitation when a person is present or likely to be present, terrorism, or escape.

(C) No person shall purposely cause the death of another who is under thirteen years of age at the time of the commission of the offense.

(D) No person who is under detention as a result of having been found guilty of or having pleaded guilty to a felony or who breaks that detention shall purposely cause the death of another.

(E) No person shall purposely cause the death of a law enforcement officer whom the offender knows or has reasonable cause to know is a law enforcement officer when either of the following applies:

(1) The victim, at the time of the commission of the offense, is engaged in the victim's duties.

(2) It is the offender's specific purpose to kill a law enforcement officer.

(F) Whoever violates this section is guilty of aggravated murder, and shall be punished as provided in section 2929.02 of the Revised Code.

(G) As used in this section:

(1) "Detention" has the same meaning as in section 2921.01 of the Revised Code.

(2) "Law enforcement officer" has the same meaning as in section 2911.01 of the Revised Code.

**HISTORY: 134 v H 511 (Eff 1-1-74); 139 v S 1 (Eff 10-19-81); 146 v S 239 (Eff 9-6-96); 147 v S 32 (Eff 8-6-97); 147 v H 5 (Eff 6-30-98); 147 v S 193 (Eff 12-29-98); 149 v S 184. Eff 5-15-2002; 2011 HB 86, § 1, eff. Sept. 30, 2011.**

**Not analogous to former RC § 2903.01 (GC § 12423-1; 109 v 45; 121 v 557 (572); Bureau of Code Revision, 10-1-53; 126 v 114), repealed 134 v H 511, § 2, eff 1-1-74.**

## § 2903.02 Murder.

(A) No person shall purposely cause the death of another or the unlawful termination of another's pregnancy.

(B) No person shall cause the death of another as a proximate result of the offender's committing or attempting to commit an offense of violence that is a felony of the first or second degree and that is not a violation of section 2903.03 or 2903.04 of the Revised Code.

(C) Division (B) of this section does not apply to an offense that becomes a felony of the first or second degree only if the offender previously has been convicted of that offense or another specified offense.

(D) Whoever violates this section is guilty of murder, and shall be punished as provided in section 2929.02 of the Revised Code.

**HISTORY: 134 v H 511 (Eff 1-1-74); 146 v S 239 (Eff 9-6-96); 147 v H 5. Eff 6-30-98.**

**Not analogous to former RC § 2903.02 (RS § 6998; S&S 377; 59 v 65; 83 v 202; GC §§ 12962, 12963; Bureau of Code Revision, 10-1-53; 131 v 671), repealed 134 v H 511, § 2, eff 1-1-74.**

## § 2903.03 Voluntary manslaughter.

(A) No person, while under the influence of sudden passion or in a sudden fit of rage, either of which is brought on by serious provocation occasioned by the victim that is reasonably sufficient to incite the person into using deadly force, shall knowingly cause the death of another or the unlawful termination of another's pregnancy.

(B) Whoever violates this section is guilty of voluntary manslaughter, a felony of the first degree.

**HISTORY: 134 v H 511 (Eff 1-1-74); 139 v H 103 (Eff 5-19-82); 139 v S 199 (Eff 1-5-83); 146 v S 2 (Eff 7-1-96); 146 v S 239. Eff 9-6-96.**

**Not analogous to former RC § 2903.03 (RS § 6937; S&C 667; 54 v 196; GC § 12964; 103 v 864; Bureau of Code Revision, 10-1-53), repealed 134 v H 511, § 2, eff 1-1-74.**

## § 2903.04 Involuntary manslaughter.

(A) No person shall cause the death of another or the unlawful termination of another's pregnancy as a proximate result of the offender's committing or attempting to commit a felony.

(B) No person shall cause the death of another or the unlawful termination of another's pregnancy as a proximate result of the offender's committing or attempting to commit a misdemeanor of any degree, a regulatory offense, or a minor misdemeanor other than a violation of any section contained in Title XLV of the Revised Code that is a minor misdemeanor and other than a violation of an ordinance of a municipal corporation that, regardless of the penalty set by ordinance for the violation, is substantially equivalent to any section contained in Title XLV of the Revised Code that is a minor misdemeanor.

(C) Whoever violates this section is guilty of involuntary manslaughter. Violation of division (A) of this section is a felony of the first degree. Violation of division (B) of this section is a felony of the third degree.

(D) If an offender is convicted of or pleads guilty to a violation of division (A) or (B) of this section and if the felony, misdemeanor, or regulatory offense that the offender committed or attempted to commit, that proximately resulted in the death of the other person or the unlawful termination of another's pregnancy, and that is the basis of the offender's violation of division (A) or (B) of this section was a violation of division (A) or (B) of section 4511.19 of the Revised Code or of a substantially equivalent municipal ordinance or included, as an element of that felony, misdemeanor, or regulatory offense, the offender's operation or participation in the operation of a snowmobile, locomotive, watercraft, or aircraft while the offender was under the influence of alcohol, a drug of abuse, or alcohol and a drug of abuse, both of the following apply:

(1) The court shall impose a class one suspension of the offender's driver's or commercial driver's license or permit or nonresident operating privilege as specified in division (A)(1) of section 4510.02 of the Revised Code.

(2) The court shall impose a mandatory prison term for the violation of division (A) or (B) of this section from the range of prison terms authorized for the level of the offense under section 2929.14 of the Revised Code.

**HISTORY: 134 v H 511 (Eff 1-1-74); 139 v S 199 (Eff 7-1-83); 144 v S 275 (Eff 7-1-93)†; 145 v H 236 (Eff 9-29-94); 146 v S 2 (Eff 7-1-96); 146 v S 269 (Eff 7-1-96); 146 v S 239 (Eff 9-6-96); 148 v S 107. Eff 3-23-2000; 149 v S 123, § 1, eff. 1-1-04.**

The provisions of § 5 of S.B. 123 (149 v —), as amended by § 3 of H.B. 163 (150 v —), read as follows:

SECTION 5. (A) Notwithstanding division (B) of section 1.58 of the Revised Code, the provisions of the Revised Code amended or enacted in Sections 1 and 2 of Am. Sub. S.B. 123 of the 124th General Assembly shall apply only in relation to conduct and offenses committed on or after January 1, 2004. Conduct and offenses committed prior to January 1, 2004, shall be governed by the law in effect on the date the conduct or offense was committed.

° ° °

The effective date is set by section 4 of S.B. 123.

**Not analogous to former RC § 2903.04 (RS §§ 4364-38, 4364-39; 90 v 235; 91 v 311; 92 v 71; GC § 12965; 101 v 133; Bureau of Code Revision, 10-1-53), repealed 134 v H 511, § 2, eff 1-1-74.**

† The provisions of §§ 4, 5 of SB 62 (145 v —) read as follows:

SECTION 4. That Section 3 of Sub. S.B. 275 of the 119th General Assembly be amended to read as follows:

"Sec. 3. Sections 1 and 2 of this act shall take effect September 1, 1993."

SECTION 5. That existing Section 3 of Sub. S.B. 275 of the 119th General Assembly is hereby repealed.

## § 2903.041 Reckless homicide.

(A) No person shall recklessly cause the death of another or the unlawful termination of another's pregnancy.

(B) Whoever violates this section is guilty of reckless homicide, a felony of the third degree.

**HISTORY: 148 v H 37. Eff 9-29-99.**

## § 2903.05 Negligent homicide.

(A) No person shall negligently cause the death of another or the unlawful termination of another's pregnancy by means of a deadly weapon or dangerous ordnance as defined in section 2923.11 of the Revised Code.

(B) Whoever violates this section is guilty of negligent homicide, a misdemeanor of the first degree.

**HISTORY: 134 v H 511 (Eff 1-1-74); 146 v S 239. Eff 9-6-96.**

**Not analogous to former RC § 2903.05 (RS § 6986b; 80 v 222; GC § 12966; 103 v 864; Bureau of Code Revision, 10-1-53), repealed 134 v H 511, § 2, eff 1-1-74.**

## § 2903.06 Aggravated vehicular homicide; vehicular homicide; vehicular manslaughter.

(A) No person, while operating or participating in the operation of a motor vehicle, motorcycle, snowmobile, locomotive, watercraft, or aircraft, shall cause the death of another or the unlawful termination of another's pregnancy in any of the following ways:

(1)(a) As the proximate result of committing a violation of division (A) of section 4511.19 of the Revised Code or of a substantially equivalent municipal ordinance;

(b) As the proximate result of committing a violation of division (A) of section 1547.11 of the Revised Code or of a substantially equivalent municipal ordinance;

(c) As the proximate result of committing a violation of division (A)(3) of section 4561.15 of the Revised Code or of a substantially equivalent municipal ordinance.

(2) In one of the following ways:

(a) Recklessly;

(b) As the proximate result of committing, while operating or participating in the operation of a motor vehicle or motorcycle in a construction zone, a reckless operation offense, provided that this division applies only if the person whose death is caused or whose pregnancy is unlawfully terminated is in the construction zone at the time of the offender's commission of the reckless operation offense in the construction zone and does not apply as described in division (F) of this section.

(3) In one of the following ways:

(a) Negligently;

(b) As the proximate result of committing, while operating or participating in the operation of a motor vehicle or motorcycle in a construction zone, a speeding offense, provided that this division applies only if the person whose death is caused or whose pregnancy is unlawfully terminated is in the construction zone at the time of the offender's commission of the speeding offense in the construction zone and does not apply as described in division (F) of this section.

(4) As the proximate result of committing a violation of any provision of any section contained in Title XLV of the Revised Code that is a minor misdemeanor or of a municipal ordinance that, regardless of the penalty set by ordinance for the violation, is substantially equivalent to any provision of any section contained in Title XLV of the Revised Code that is a minor misdemeanor.

(B)(1) Whoever violates division (A)(1) or (2) of this section is guilty of aggravated vehicular homicide and shall be punished as provided in divisions (B)(2) and (3) of this section.

(2)(a) Except as otherwise provided in division (B)(2)(b) or (c) of this section, aggravated vehicular homicide committed in violation of division (A)(1) of this section is a felony of the second degree and the court shall impose a mandatory prison term on the offender as described in division (E) of this section.

(b) Except as otherwise provided in division (B)(2)(c) of this section, aggravated vehicular homicide committed in violation of division (A)(1) of this section is a felony of the first degree, and the court shall impose a mandatory prison term on the offender as described in division (E) of this section, if any of the following apply:

(i) At the time of the offense, the offender was driving under a suspension or cancellation imposed under Chapter 4510. or any other provision of the Revised Code or was operating a motor vehicle or motorcycle, did not have a valid driver's license, commercial driver's license, temporary instruction permit, probationary license, or nonresident operating privilege, and was not eligible for renewal of the offender's driver's license or commercial driver's license without examination under section 4507.10 of the Revised Code.

(ii) The offender previously has been convicted of or pleaded guilty to a violation of this section.

(iii) The offender previously has been convicted of or pleaded guilty to any traffic-related homicide, manslaughter, or assault offense.

(c) Aggravated vehicular homicide committed in violation of division (A)(1) of this section is a felony of the first degree, and the court shall sentence the offender to a mandatory prison term as provided in section 2929.142 [2929.14.2] of the Revised Code and described in division (E) of this section if any of the following apply:

(i) The offender previously has been convicted of or pleaded guilty to three or more prior violations of section 4511.19 of the Revised Code or of a substantially equivalent municipal ordinance within the previous six years.

(ii) The offender previously has been convicted of or pleaded guilty to three or more prior violations of division (A) of section 1547.11 of the Revised Code or of a substantially equivalent municipal ordinance within the previous six years.

(iii) The offender previously has been convicted of or pleaded guilty to three or more prior violations of division (A)(3) of section 4561.15 of the Revised Code or of a substantially equivalent municipal ordinance within the previous six years.

(iv) The offender previously has been convicted of or pleaded guilty to three or more prior violations of division (A)(1) of this section within the previous six years.

(v) The offender previously has been convicted of or pleaded guilty to three or more prior violations of division (A)(1) of section 2903.08 of the Revised Code within the previous six years.

(vi) The offender previously has been convicted of or pleaded guilty to three or more prior violations of section 2903.04 of the Revised Code within the previous six years in circumstances in which division (D) of that section applied regarding the violations.

(vii) The offender previously has been convicted of or pleaded guilty to three or more violations of any combination of the offenses listed in division (B)(2)(c)(i), (ii), (iii), (iv), (v), or (vi) of this section within the previous six years.

(viii) The offender previously has been convicted of or pleaded guilty to a second or subsequent felony violation of division (A) of section 4511.19 of the Revised Code.

(d) In addition to any other sanctions imposed pursuant to division (B)(2)(a), (b), or (c) of this section for aggravated vehicular homicide committed in violation of division (A)(1) of this section, the court shall impose upon the offender a class one suspension of the offender's driver's license, commercial driver's license, temporary instruction permit, probationary license, or nonresident operating privilege as specified in division (A)(1) of section 4510.02 of the Revised Code.

(3) Except as otherwise provided in this division, aggravated vehicular homicide committed in violation of division (A)(2) of this section is a felony of the third degree. Aggravated vehicular homicide committed in violation of division (A)(2) of this section is a felony of the second degree if, at the time of the offense, the offender was driving under a suspension or cancellation imposed under Chapter 4510. or any other provision of the Revised Code or was operating a motor vehicle or motorcycle, did not have a valid driver's license, commercial driver's license, temporary instruction permit, probationary license, or nonresident operating privilege, and was not eligible for renewal of the offender's driver's license or commercial driver's license without examination under section 4507.10 of the Revised Code or if the offender previously has been convicted of or pleaded guilty to a violation of this section or any traffic-related homicide, manslaughter, or assault offense. The court shall impose a mandatory prison term on the offender when required by division (E) of this section.

In addition to any other sanctions imposed pursuant to this division for a violation of division (A)(2) of this section, the court shall impose upon the offender a class two suspension of the offender's driver's license, commercial driver's license, temporary instruction permit, probationary license, or nonresident operating privilege from the range specified in division (A)(2) of section 4510.02 of the Revised Code or, if the offender previously has been convicted of or pleaded guilty to a traffic-related murder, felonious assault, or attempted murder offense, a class one suspension of the offender's driver's license, commercial driver's license, temporary instruction permit, probationary license, or nonresident operating privilege as specified in division (A)(1) of that section.

(C) Whoever violates division (A)(3) of this section is guilty of vehicular homicide. Except as otherwise provided in this division, vehicular homicide is a misdemeanor of the first degree. Vehicular homicide committed in violation of division (A)(3) of this section is a felony of the fourth degree if, at the time of the offense, the offender was driving under a suspension or cancellation imposed under Chapter 4510. or any other provision of the Revised Code or was operating a motor vehicle or motorcycle, did not have a valid driver's license, commercial driver's license, temporary instruction permit, probationary license, or nonresident operating privilege, and was not eligible for renewal of the offender's driver's license or commercial driver's license without examination under section 4507.10 of the Revised Code or if the offender previously has been convicted of or pleaded guilty to a violation of this section or any traffic-related homicide, manslaughter, or assault offense. The court shall impose a mandatory jail term or a mandatory prison term on the offender when required by division (E) of this section.

In addition to any other sanctions imposed pursuant to this division, the court shall impose upon the offender a class four suspension of the offender's driver's license, commercial driver's license, temporary instruction permit, probationary license, or nonresident operating privilege from the range specified in division (A)(4) of section 4510.02 of the Revised Code, or, if the offender previously has been convicted of or pleaded guilty to a violation of this section or any traffic-related homicide, manslaughter, or assault offense, a class three suspension of the offender's driver's license, commercial driver's license, temporary instruction permit, probationary license, or nonresident operating privilege from the range specified in division (A)(3) of that section, or, if the offender previously has been convicted of or pleaded guilty to a traffic-related murder, felonious assault, or attempted murder offense, a class two suspension of the offender's driver's license, commercial driver's license, temporary instruction permit, probationary license, or nonresident operating privilege as specified in division (A)(2) of that section.

(D) Whoever violates division (A)(4) of this section is guilty of vehicular manslaughter. Except as otherwise provided in this division, vehicular manslaughter is a misdemeanor of the second degree. Vehicular manslaughter is a misdemeanor of the first degree if, at the time of the offense, the offender was driving under a suspension or cancellation imposed under Chapter 4510. or any other provision of the Revised Code or was operating a motor vehicle or motorcycle, did not have a valid driver's license, commercial driver's license, temporary instruction permit, probationary license, or nonresident operating privilege, and was not eligible for renewal of the offender's driver's license or commercial driver's license without examination under section 4507.10 of the Revised Code or if the offender previously has been convicted of or pleaded guilty to a violation of this section or any traffic-related homicide, manslaughter, or assault offense.

In addition to any other sanctions imposed pursuant to this division, the court shall impose upon the offender a class six suspension of the offender's driver's license, commercial driver's license, temporary instruction permit, probationary license, or nonresident operating privilege from the range specified in division (A)(6) of section 4510.02 of the Revised Code or, if the offender previously has been convicted of or pleaded guilty to a violation of this section, any traffic-related homicide, manslaughter, or assault offense, or a traffic-related murder, felonious assault, or attempted murder offense, a class four suspension of the offender's driver's license, commercial driver's license, temporary instruction permit, probationary license, or nonresident operating privilege from the range specified in division (A)(4) of that section.

(E) The court shall impose a mandatory prison term on an offender who is convicted of or pleads guilty to a violation of division (A)(1) of this section. If division (B)(2)(c)(i), (ii), (iii), (iv), (v), (vi), (vii), or (viii) of this section applies to an offender who is convicted of or pleads guilty to the violation of division (A)(1) of this section, the court shall impose the mandatory prison term pursuant to section 2929.142 [2929.14.2] of the Revised Code. The court shall impose a mandatory jail term of at least fifteen days on an offender who is convicted of or pleads guilty to a misdemeanor violation of division (A)(3)(b) of this section and may impose upon the offender a longer jail term as authorized pursuant to section 2929.24 of the Revised Code. The court shall impose a mandatory prison term on an offender who is convicted of or pleads guilty to a violation of division (A)(2) or (3)(a) of this section or a felony violation of division (A)(3)(b) of this section if either of the following applies:

(1) The offender previously has been convicted of or pleaded guilty to a violation of this section or section 2903.08 of the Revised Code.

(2) At the time of the offense, the offender was driving under suspension or cancellation under Chapter 4510. or any other provision of the Revised Code or was operating a motor vehicle or motorcycle, did not have a valid driver's license, commercial driver's license, temporary instruction permit, probationary license, or nonresident operating privilege, and was not eligible for renewal of the offender's driver's license or commercial driver's license without examination under section 4507.10 of the Revised Code.

(F) Divisions (A)(2)(b) and (3)(b) of this section do not apply in a particular construction zone unless signs of the type described in section 2903.081 [2903.08.1] of the Revised Code are erected in that construction zone in accordance with the guidelines and design specifications established by the director of transportation under section 5501.27 of the Revised Code. The failure to erect signs of the type described in section 2903.081 [2903.08.1] of the Revised Code in a particular construction zone in accordance with those guidelines and design specifications does not limit or affect the application of division (A)(1), (A)(2)(a), (A)(3)(a), or (A)(4) of this section in that construction zone or the prosecution of any person who violates any of those divisions in that construction zone.

(G)(1) As used in this section:

(a) "Mandatory prison term" and "mandatory jail term" have the same meanings as in section 2929.01 of the Revised Code.

(b) "Traffic-related homicide, manslaughter, or assault offense" means a violation of section 2903.04 of the Revised Code in circumstances in which division (D) of that section applies, a violation of section 2903.06 or 2903.08 of the Revised Code, or a violation of section 2903.06, 2903.07, or 2903.08 of the Revised Code as they existed prior to March 23, 2000.

(c) "Construction zone" has the same meaning as in section 5501.27 of the Revised Code.

(d) "Reckless operation offense" means a violation of section 4511.20 of the Revised Code or a municipal ordinance substantially equivalent to section 4511.20 of the Revised Code.

(e) "Speeding offense" means a violation of section 4511.21 of the Revised Code or a municipal ordinance pertaining to speed.

(f) "Traffic-related murder, felonious assault, or attempted murder offense" means a violation of section 2903.01 or 2903.02 of the Revised Code in circumstances in which the offender used a motor vehicle as the means to commit the violation, a violation of division (A)(2) of section 2903.11 of the Revised Code in circumstances in which the deadly weapon used in the commission of the violation is a motor vehicle, or an attempt to commit aggravated murder or murder in violation of section 2923.02 of the Revised Code in circumstances in which the offender used a motor vehicle as the means to attempt to commit the aggravated murder or murder.

(g) "Motor vehicle" has the same meaning as in section 4501.01 of the Revised Code.

(2) For the purposes of this section, when a penalty or suspension is enhanced because of a prior or current violation of a specified law or a prior or current specified offense, the reference to the violation of the specified law or the specified offense includes any violation of any substantially equivalent municipal ordinance, former law of this state, or current or former law of another state or the United States.

**HISTORY: 134 v H 511 (Eff 1-1-74); 135 v H 716 (Eff 1-1-74); 139 v S 432 (Eff 3-16-83); 141 v H 265 (Eff 7-24-86); 141 v S 356 (Eff 9-24-86); 141 v S 262 (Eff 3-20-87); 141 v H 428 (Eff 12-23-86); 143 v H 381 (Eff 7-1-89); 143 v S 49 (Eff 11-3-89); 143 v S 131 (Eff 7-25-90); 144 v S 275 (Eff 7-1-93) †; 146 v S 2 (Eff 7-1-96); 146 v S 269 (Eff 7-1-96); 146 v S 239 (Eff 9-6-96); 148 v S 107. Eff 3-23-2000; 149 v S 123, § 1, eff. 1-1-04; 150 v H 50, § 1, eff. 10-21-03; 150 v H 50, § 4, eff. 1-1-04; 150 v H 52, § 1, eff. 6-1-04; 151 v H 461, § 1, eff. 4-4-07; 152 v H 215, § 1, eff. 4-7-09.**

The effective date is set by section 6 of H.B. 50.

See provisions, § 5 of S.B. 123 (149 v —), following RC § 2903.04.

**Not analogous to former RC § 2903.06 (RS § 6986a; 77 v 79; GC § 12967; 103 v 864; Bureau of Code Revision, 10-1-53), repealed 134 v H 511, § 2, eff 1-1-74.**

**For current analogous provision to former RC § 2903.06 see RC § 2923.21.**

† See provisions, §§ 4, 5 of SB 62 (145 v —) following RC § 2903.04.

## § 2903.07 Repealed, 148 v S 107, § 2 [134 v H 511; 135 v H 716; 139 v S 432; 141 v H 265; 141 v S 356; 141 v S 262; 141 v H 428; 143 v H 381; 143 v S 131; 144 v S 275; 146 v S 2; 146 v S 269; 146 v S 239; 148 v H 61]. Eff 3-23-2000.

This section concerned vehicular homicide. See now RC § 2903.06.

## § 2903.08 Aggravated vehicular assault; vehicular assault.

(A) No person, while operating or participating in the operation of a motor vehicle, motorcycle, snowmobile, locomotive, watercraft, or aircraft, shall cause serious physical harm to another person or another's unborn in any of the following ways:

(1)(a) As the proximate result of committing a violation of division (A) of section 4511.19 of the Revised Code or of a substantially equivalent municipal ordinance;

(b) As the proximate result of committing a violation of division (A) of section 1547.11 of the Revised Code or of a substantially equivalent municipal ordinance;

(c) As the proximate result of committing a violation of division (A)(3) of section 4561.15 of the Revised Code or of a substantially equivalent municipal ordinance.

(2) In one of the following ways:

(a) As the proximate result of committing, while operating or participating in the operation of a motor vehicle or motorcycle in a construction zone, a reckless operation offense, provided that this division applies only if the person to whom the serious physical harm is caused or to whose unborn the serious physical harm is caused is in the construction zone at the time of the offender's commission of the reckless operation offense in the construction zone and does not apply as described in division (E) of this section;

(b) Recklessly.

(3) As the proximate result of committing, while operating or participating in the operation of a motor vehicle or motorcycle in a construction zone, a speeding offense, provided that this division applies only if the person to whom the serious physical harm is caused or to whose unborn the serious physical harm is caused is in the construction zone at the time of the offender's commission of the speeding offense in the construction zone and does not apply as described in division (E) of this section.

(B)(1) Whoever violates division (A)(1) of this section is guilty of aggravated vehicular assault. Except as otherwise provided in this division, aggravated vehicular assault is a felony of the third degree. Aggravated vehicular assault is a felony of the second degree if any of the following apply:

(a) At the time of the offense, the offender was driving under a suspension imposed under Chapter 4510. or any other provision of the Revised Code.

(b) The offender previously has been convicted of or pleaded guilty to a violation of this section.

(c) The offender previously has been convicted of or pleaded guilty to any traffic-related homicide, manslaughter, or assault offense.

(d) The offender previously has been convicted of or pleaded guilty to three or more prior violations of section 4511.19 of the Revised Code or a substantially equivalent municipal ordinance within the previous six years.

(e) The offender previously has been convicted of or pleaded guilty to three or more prior violations of division (A) of section 1547.11 of the Revised Code or of a substantially equivalent municipal ordinance within the previous six years.

(f) The offender previously has been convicted of or pleaded guilty to three or more prior violations of division (A)(3) of section 4561.15 of the Revised Code or of a substantially equivalent municipal ordinance within the previous six years.

(g) The offender previously has been convicted of or pleaded guilty to three or more prior violations of any combination of the offenses listed in division (B)(1)(d), (e), or (f) of this section.

(h) The offender previously has been convicted of or pleaded guilty to a second or subsequent felony violation of division (A) of section 4511.19 of the Revised Code.

(2) In addition to any other sanctions imposed pursuant to division (B)(1) of this section, except as otherwise provided in this division, the court shall impose upon the offender a class three suspension of the offender's driver's license, commercial driver's license, temporary instruction permit, probationary license, or nonresident operating

privilege from the range specified in division (A)(3) of section 4510.02 of the Revised Code. If the offender previously has been convicted of or pleaded guilty to a violation of this section, any traffic-related homicide, manslaughter, or assault offense, or any traffic-related murder, felonious assault, or attempted murder offense, the court shall impose either a class two suspension of the offender's driver's license, commercial driver's license, temporary instruction permit, probationary license, or nonresident operating privilege from the range specified in division (A)(2) of that section or a class one suspension as specified in division (A)(1) of that section.

(C)(1) Whoever violates division (A)(2) or (3) of this section is guilty of vehicular assault and shall be punished as provided in divisions (C)(2) and (3) of this section.

(2) Except as otherwise provided in this division, vehicular assault committed in violation of division (A)(2) of this section is a felony of the fourth degree. Vehicular assault committed in violation of division (A)(2) of this section is a felony of the third degree if, at the time of the offense, the offender was driving under a suspension imposed under Chapter 4510. or any other provision of the Revised Code, if the offender previously has been convicted of or pleaded guilty to a violation of this section or any traffic-related homicide, manslaughter, or assault offense, or if, in the same course of conduct that resulted in the violation of division (A)(2) of this section, the offender also violated section 4549.02, 4549.021 [4549.02.1], or 4549.03 of the Revised Code.

In addition to any other sanctions imposed, the court shall impose upon the offender a class four suspension of the offender's driver's license, commercial driver's license, temporary instruction permit, probationary license, or nonresident operating privilege from the range specified in division (A)(4) of section 4510.02 of the Revised Code or, if the offender previously has been convicted of or pleaded guilty to a violation of this section, any traffic-related homicide, manslaughter, or assault offense, or any traffic-related murder, felonious assault, or attempted murder offense, a class three suspension of the offender's driver's license, commercial driver's license, temporary instruction permit, probationary license, or nonresident operating privilege from the range specified in division (A)(3) of that section.

(3) Except as otherwise provided in this division, vehicular assault committed in violation of division (A)(3) of this section is a misdemeanor of the first degree. Vehicular assault committed in violation of division (A)(3) of this section is a felony of the fourth degree if, at the time of the offense, the offender was driving under a suspension imposed under Chapter 4510. or any other provision of the Revised Code or if the offender previously has been convicted of or pleaded guilty to a violation of this section or any traffic-related homicide, manslaughter, or assault offense.

In addition to any other sanctions imposed, the court shall impose upon the offender a class four suspension of the offender's driver's license, commercial driver's license, temporary instruction permit, probationary license, or nonresident operating privilege from the range specified in division (A)(4) of section 4510.02 of the Revised Code or, if the offender previously has been convicted of or pleaded guilty to a violation of this section, any traffic-related homicide, manslaughter, or assault offense, or any traffic-related murder, felonious assault, or attempted murder offense, a class three suspension of the offender's driver's license, commercial driver's license, temporary instruction permit, probationary license, or nonresident operating privilege from the range specified in division (A)(3) of section 4510.02 of the Revised Code.

(D)(1) The court shall impose a mandatory prison term on an offender who is convicted of or pleads guilty to a violation of division (A)(1) of this section.

(2) The court shall impose a mandatory prison term on an offender who is convicted of or pleads guilty to a violation of division (A)(2) of this section or a felony violation of division (A)(3) of this section if either of the following applies:

(a) The offender previously has been convicted of or pleaded guilty to a violation of this section or section 2903.06 of the Revised Code.

(b) At the time of the offense, the offender was driving under suspension under Chapter 4510. or any other provision of the Revised Code.

(3) The court shall impose a mandatory jail term of at least seven days on an offender who is convicted of or pleads guilty to a misdemeanor violation of division (A)(3) of this section and may impose upon the offender a longer jail term as authorized pursuant to section 2929.24 of the Revised Code.

(E) Divisions (A)(2)(a) and (3) of this section do not apply in a particular construction zone unless signs of the type described in section 2903.081 [2903.08.1] of the Revised Code are erected in that construction zone in accordance with the guidelines and design specifications established by the director of transportation under section 5501.27 of the Revised Code. The failure to erect signs of the type described in section 2903.081 [2903.08.1] of the Revised Code in a particular construction zone in accordance with those guidelines and design specifications does not limit or affect the application of division (A)(1) or (2)(b) of this section in that construction zone or the prosecution of any person who violates either of those divisions in that construction zone.

(F) As used in this section:

(1) "Mandatory prison term" and "mandatory jail term" have the same meanings as in section 2929.01 of the Revised Code.

(2) "Traffic-related homicide, manslaughter, or assault offense" and "traffic-related murder, felonious assault, or attempted murder offense" have the same meanings as in section 2903.06 of the Revised Code.

(3) "Construction zone" has the same meaning as in section 5501.27 of the Revised Code.

(4) "Reckless operation offense" and "speeding offense" have the same meanings as in section 2903.06 of the Revised Code.

(G) For the purposes of this section, when a penalty or suspension is enhanced because of a prior or current violation of a specified law or a prior or current specified offense, the reference to the violation of the specified law or the specified offense includes any violation of any substantially equivalent municipal ordinance, former law of this state, or current or former law of another state or the United States.

**HISTORY: 143 v S 131 (Eff 7-25-90); 144 v S 275 (Eff 7-1-93) †; 145 v H 236 (Eff 9-29-94); 146 v S 2 (Eff 7-1-96); 146 v S 269 (Eff 7-1-96); 146 v S 239 (Eff 9-6-96); 148 v S 107. Eff 3-23-2000; 149 v S 123, § 1, eff. 1-1-04; 150 v H 50, § 1, eff. 10-21-03; 150 v H 50, § 4, eff. 1-1-04; 150 v H 52, § 1, eff. 6-1-04; 150 v H 163, § 1, eff. 9-23-04; 151 v H 461, § 1, eff. 4-4-07.**

The provisions of § 5(A) of 151 v H 461 read as follows:

SECTION 5. (A) Section 2903.08 of the Revised Code is

presented in this act as a composite of the section as amended by both Sub. H.B. 52 and Am. Sub. H.B. 163 of the 125th General Assembly. The General Assembly, applying the principle stated in division (B) of section 1.52 of the Revised Code that amendments are to be harmonized if reasonably capable of simultaneous operation, finds that the composite is the resulting version of the section in effect prior to the effective date of the section as presented in this act.

The effective date is set by section 4 of S.B. 123.

See provisions, § 5 of S.B. 123 (149 v —), following RC § 2903.04.

**Not analogous to former RC § 2903.08 (RS §§ 6984a, 6985; 73 v 219, §§ 1-6; 81 v 181, 184; 83 v 27; 95 v 273; GC §§ 12970, 12971; Bureau of Code Revision, 10-1-53; 132 v S 65), repealed 134 v H 511, § 2, eff 1-1-74.**

† See provisions, §§ 4, 5 of SB 62 (145 v —) following RC § 2903.04.

## § 2903.081 Signs in construction zones concerning vehicular homicide and assault offenses.

(A) As used in this section:

(1) "Construction zone" has the same meaning as in section 5501.27 of the Revised Code.

(2) "Reckless operation offense" and "speeding offense" have the same meanings as in section 2903.06 of the Revised Code.

(B) The director of transportation, board of county commissioners, or board of township trustees shall cause signs to be erected in construction zones notifying motorists of the prohibitions set forth in sections 2903.06 and 2903.08 of the Revised Code regarding the death of or injury to any person in the construction zone as a proximate result of a reckless operation offense or speeding offense in the construction zone. The prohibitions set forth in divisions (A)(2)(b) and (3)(b) of section 2903.06 and divisions (A)(2)(a) and (3) of section 2903.08 of the Revised Code apply to persons who commit a reckless operation offense or speeding offense in a particular construction zone only when signs of that nature are erected in that construction zone in accordance with the guidelines and design specifications established by the director under section 5501.27 of the Revised Code. The failure to erect signs of that nature in a particular construction zone in accordance with those guidelines and design specifications does not limit or affect the application of division (A)(1), (A)(2)(a), (A)(3)(a), or (A)(4) of section 2903.06 or division (A)(1) or (2)(b) of section 2903.08 of the Revised Code in that construction zone or the prosecution of any person who violates either of those divisions in that construction zone.

**HISTORY: 150 v H 52, § 1, eff. 6-1-04.**

## § 2903.09 Legal abortions and acts or omissions of pregnant woman excepted from liability.

As used in sections 2903.01 to 2903.08, 2903.11 to 2903.14, 2903.21, and 2903.22 of the Revised Code:

(A) "Unlawful termination of another's pregnancy" means causing the death of an unborn member of the species homo sapiens, who is or was carried in the womb of another, as a result of injuries inflicted during the period that begins with fertilization and that continues unless and until live birth occurs.

(B) "Another's unborn" or "such other person's unborn" means a member of the species homo sapiens, who is or was carried in the womb of another, during a period that begins with fertilization and that continues unless and until live birth occurs.

(C) Notwithstanding divisions (A) and (B) of this section, in no case shall the definitions of the terms "unlawful termination of another's pregnancy," "another's unborn," and "such other person's unborn" that are set forth in division (A) of this section be applied or construed in any of the following manners:

(1) Except as otherwise provided in division (C)(1) of this section, in a manner so that the offense prohibits or is construed as prohibiting any pregnant woman or her physician from performing an abortion with the actual consent of the pregnant woman, with the consent of the pregnant woman implied by law in a medical emergency, or with the approval of one otherwise authorized by law to consent to medical treatment on behalf of the pregnant woman. An abortion that violates the conditions described in the immediately preceding sentence may be punished as a violation of section 2903.01, 2903.02, 2903.03, 2903.04, 2903.05, 2903.06, 2903.08, 2903.11, 2903.12, 2903.13, 2903.14, 2903.21, or 2903.22 of the Revised Code, as applicable. An abortion that does not violate the conditions described in the second immediately preceding sentence, but that does violate section 2919.12, division (B) of section 2919.13, or section 2919.151 [2919.15.1], 2919.17, or 2919.18 of the Revised Code, may be punished as a violation of section 2919.12, division (B) of section 2919.13, or section 2919.151 [2919.15.1], 2919.17, or 2919.18 of the Revised Code, as applicable.

(2) In a manner so that the offense is applied or is construed as applying to a woman based on an act or omission of the woman that occurs while she is or was pregnant and that results in any of the following:

(a) Her delivery of a stillborn baby;

(b) Her causing, in any other manner, the death in utero of an unborn that she is carrying;

(c) Her causing the death of her child who is born alive but who dies from one or more injuries that are sustained while the child is an unborn;

(d) Her causing her child who is born alive to sustain one or more injuries while the child is an unborn;

(e) Her causing, threatening to cause, or attempting to cause, in any other manner, an injury, illness, or other physiological impairment, regardless of its duration or gravity, or a mental illness or condition, regardless of its duration or gravity, to an unborn that she is carrying.

**HISTORY: 146 v S 239 (Eff 9-6-96); 148 v S 107 (Eff 3-23-2000); 148 v H 351. Eff 8-18-2000.**

**Not analogous to former RC § 2903.09 (GC §§ 12970-1, 12970-2; 101 v 233; 103 v 864 (907); 113 v 281; Bureau of Code Revision; 10-1-53; 132 v S 65; 133 v H 1), repealed 134 v H 511, § 2, eff 1-1-74.**

## § 2903.10 Definitions: functionally impaired person; caretaker.

As used in sections 2903.13 and 2903.16 of the Revised Code:

(A) "Functionally impaired person" means any person who has a physical or mental impairment that prevents him from providing for his own care or protection or whose infirmities caused by aging prevent him from providing for his own care or protection.

(B) "Caretaker" means a person who assumes the duty to provide for the care and protection of a functionally impaired person on a voluntary basis, by contract, through receipt of payment for care and protection, as a result of a family relationship, or by order of a court of competent jurisdiction. "Caretaker" does not include a person who owns, operates, or administers, or who is an agent or employee of, a care facility, as defined in section 2903.33 of the Revised Code.

**HISTORY: 142 v H 642. Eff 3-17-89.**

**Not analogous to former RC § 2903.10 (126 v 1039; 130 v 658; 130 v PtII, 143), repealed 134 v H 511, § 2, eff 1-1-74.**

[ASSAULT]

## § 2903.11 Felonious assault.

(A) No person shall knowingly do either of the following:

(1) Cause serious physical harm to another or to another's unborn;

(2) Cause or attempt to cause physical harm to another or to another's unborn by means of a deadly weapon or dangerous ordnance.

(B) No person, with knowledge that the person has tested positive as a carrier of a virus that causes acquired immunodeficiency syndrome, shall knowingly do any of the following:

(1) Engage in sexual conduct with another person without disclosing that knowledge to the other person prior to engaging in the sexual conduct;

(2) Engage in sexual conduct with a person whom the offender knows or has reasonable cause to believe lacks the mental capacity to appreciate the significance of the knowledge that the offender has tested positive as a carrier of a virus that causes acquired immunodeficiency syndrome;

(3) Engage in sexual conduct with a person under eighteen years of age who is not the spouse of the offender.

(C) The prosecution of a person under this section does not preclude prosecution of that person under section 2907.02 of the Revised Code.

(D)(1)(a) Whoever violates this section is guilty of felonious assault. Except as otherwise provided in this division or division (D)(1)(b) of this section, felonious assault is a felony of the second degree. If the victim of a violation of division (A) of this section is a peace officer or an investigator of the bureau of criminal identification and investigation, felonious assault is a felony of the first degree.

(b) Regardless of whether the felonious assault is a felony of the first or second degree under division (D)(1)(a) of this section, if the offender also is convicted of or pleads guilty to a specification as described in section 2941.1423 of the Revised Code that was included in the indictment, count in the indictment, or information charging the offense, except as otherwise provided in this division or unless a longer prison term is required under any other provision of law, the court shall sentence the offender to a mandatory prison term as provided in division (B)(8) of section 2929.14 of the Revised Code. If the victim of the offense is a peace officer or an investigator of the bureau of criminal identification and investigation, and if the victim suffered serious physical harm as a result of the commission of the offense, felonious assault is a felony of the first degree, and the court, pursuant to division (F) of section 2929.13 of the Revised Code, shall impose as a mandatory prison term one of the prison terms prescribed for a felony of the first degree.

(2) In addition to any other sanctions imposed pursuant to division (D)(1) of this section for felonious assault committed in violation of division (A)(2) of this section, if the deadly weapon used in the commission of the violation is a motor vehicle, the court shall impose upon the offender a class two suspension of the offender's driver's license, commercial driver's license, temporary instruction permit, probationary license, or nonresident operating privilege as specified in division (A)(2) of section 4510.02 of the Revised Code.

(E) As used in this section:

(1) "Deadly weapon" and "dangerous ordnance" have the same meanings as in section 2923.11 of the Revised Code.

(2) "Motor vehicle" has the same meaning as in section 4501.01 of the Revised Code.

(3) "Peace officer" has the same meaning as in section 2935.01 of the Revised Code.

(4) "Sexual conduct" has the same meaning as in section 2907.01 of the Revised Code, except that, as used in this section, it does not include the insertion of an instrument, apparatus, or other object that is not a part of the body into the vaginal or anal opening of another, unless the offender knew at the time of the insertion that the instrument, apparatus, or other object carried the offender's bodily fluid.

(5) "Investigator of the bureau of criminal identification and investigation" means an investigator of the bureau of criminal identification and investigation who is commissioned by the superintendent of the bureau as a special agent for the purpose of assisting law enforcement officers or providing emergency assistance to peace officers pursuant to authority granted under section 109.541 of the Revised Code.

(6) "Investigator" has the same meaning as in section 109.541 of the Revised Code.

**HISTORY: 134 v H 511 (Eff 1-1-74); 139 v S 199 (Eff 7-1-83); 139 v H 269 (Eff 7-1-83); 140 v S 210 (Eff 7-1-83); 146 v S 2 (Eff 7-1-96); 146 v S 239 (Eff 9-6-96); 148 v S 142 (Eff 2-3-2000); 148 v H 100. Eff 3-23-2000; 151 v H 95, § 1, eff. 8-3-06; 151 v H 347, § 1, eff. 3-14-07; 151 v H 461, § 1, eff. 4-4-07; 152 v H 280, § 1, eff. 4-7-09; 2011 HB 86, § 1, eff. Sept. 30, 2011.**

The provisions of § 5 of 152 v H 280 read in part as follows:

SECTION 5. * * * Section 2903.11 of the Revised Code is presented in this act as a composite of the section as amended by both Sub. H.B. 347 and Am. Sub. H.B. 461 of the 126th General Assembly. The General Assembly, applying the principle stated in division (B) of section 1.52 of the Revised Code that amendments are to be harmonized if reasonably capable of simultaneous operation, finds that the composite is the resulting version of the section in effect prior to the effective date of the section as presented in this act.

Governor Taft's veto of HB 347 was overridden by the Ohio General Assembly.

**Not analogous to former RC § 2903.11 (126 v 1039; 130 v 658), repealed 133 v H 84, § 2, eff 9-15-70.**

## § 2903.12 Aggravated assault.

(A) No person, while under the influence of sudden passion or in a sudden fit of rage, either of which is brought on by serious provocation occasioned by the victim that is reasonably sufficient to incite the person into using deadly force, shall knowingly:

(1) Cause serious physical harm to another or to another's unborn;

(2) Cause or attempt to cause physical harm to another or to another's unborn by means of a deadly weapon or dangerous ordnance, as defined in section 2923.11 of the Revised Code.

(B) Whoever violates this section is guilty of aggravated assault. Except as otherwise provided in this division, aggravated assault is a felony of the fourth degree. If the victim of the offense is a peace officer or an investigator of the bureau of criminal identification and investigation, aggravated assault is a felony of the third degree. Regardless of whether the offense is a felony of the third or fourth degree under this division, if the offender also is convicted of or pleads guilty to a specification as described in section 2941.1423 of the Revised Code that was included in the indictment, count in the indictment, or information charging the offense, except as otherwise provided in this division, the court shall sentence the offender to a mandatory prison term as provided in division (B)(8) of section 2929.14 of the Revised Code. If the victim of the offense is a peace officer or an investigator of the bureau of criminal identification and investigation, and if the victim suffered serious physical harm as a result of the commission of the offense, aggravated assault is a felony of the third degree, and the court, pursuant to division (F) of section 2929.13 of the Revised Code, shall impose as a mandatory prison term one of the prison terms prescribed for a felony of the third degree.

(C) As used in this section:

(1) "Investigator of the bureau of criminal identification and investigation" has the same meaning as in section 2903.11 of the Revised Code.

(2) "Peace officer" has the same meaning as in section 2935.01 of the Revised Code.

**HISTORY: 134 v H 511 (Eff 1-1-74); 139 v H 103 (Eff 5-19-82); 139 v S 199 (Eff 7-1-83); 139 v H 269 (Eff 7-1-83); 140 v S 210 (Eff 7-1-83); 140 v H 37 (Eff 6-22-84); 146 v S 239 (Eff 9-6-96); 148 v S 142. Eff 2-3-2000; 151 v H 347, § 1, eff. 3-14-07; 152 v H 280, § 1, eff. 4-7-09; 2011 HB 86, § 1, eff. Sept. 30, 2011.**

Governor Taft's veto of HB 347 was overridden by the Ohio General Assembly.

**Not analogous to former RC § 2903.12 (130 v 659), repealed 134 v H 511, § 2, eff 1-1-74.**

**Analogous to former RC § 2901.18 (RS § 6984a; 81 v 184; 83 v 27; 95 v 273; GC § 12428; Bureau of Code Revision, 10-1-53; 131 v 670), repealed 134 v H 511, § 2, eff 1-1-74.**

**Publisher's Note:**

Three subsequent amendments to the section in 1983, S 199, H 269, S 210 picked up the original "extreme emotional stress" wording of division (A). The Legislative Service Commission advises that comparison of H 103 with S 199, H 269, and S 210 pursuant to section 1.52 of the Revised Code discloses that they are not irreconcilable, so that they are required by that section to be harmonized to give effect to each amendment.

The most recent amendment to subdivision (A) is H 37, an act which harmonizes "multiple prior amendments" and corrects "nonsubstantive errors." This amendment uses the "sudden passion" language.

See Publisher's Note re H 511 Committee Comment following RC § 2903.03.

## § 2903.13 Assault.

(A) No person shall knowingly cause or attempt to cause physical harm to another or to another's unborn.

(B) No person shall recklessly cause serious physical harm to another or to another's unborn.

(C) Whoever violates this section is guilty of assault, and the court shall sentence the offender as provided in this division and divisions (C)(1), (2), (3), (4), (5), and (6) of this section. Except as otherwise provided in division (C)(1), (2), (3), (4), or (5) of this section, assault is a misdemeanor of the first degree.

(1) Except as otherwise provided in this division, if the offense is committed by a caretaker against a functionally impaired person under the caretaker's care, assault is a felony of the fourth degree. If the offense is committed by a caretaker against a functionally impaired person under the caretaker's care, if the offender previously has been convicted of or pleaded guilty to a violation of this section or section 2903.11 or 2903.16 of the Revised Code, and if in relation to the previous conviction the offender was a caretaker and the victim was a functionally impaired person under the offender's care, assault is a felony of the third degree.

(2) If the offense is committed in any of the following circumstances, assault is a felony of the fifth degree:

(a) The offense occurs in or on the grounds of a state correctional institution or an institution of the department of youth services, the victim of the offense is an employee of the department of rehabilitation and correction, the department of youth services, or a probation department or is on the premises of the particular institution for business purposes or as a visitor, and the offense is committed by a person incarcerated in the state correctional institution, by a person institutionalized in the department of youth services institution pursuant to a commitment to the department of youth services, by a parolee, by an offender under transitional control, under a community control sanction, or on an escorted visit, by a person under post-release control, or by an offender under any other type of supervision by a government agency.

(b) The offense occurs in or on the grounds of a local correctional facility, the victim of the offense is an employee of the local correctional facility or a probation department or is on the premises of the facility for business purposes or as a visitor, and the offense is committed by a person who is under custody in the facility subsequent to the person's arrest for any crime or delinquent act, subsequent to the person's being charged with or convicted of any crime, or subsequent to the person's being alleged to be or adjudicated a delinquent child.

(c) The offense occurs off the grounds of a state correctional institution and off the grounds of an institution of the department of youth services, the victim of the offense is an employee of the department of rehabilitation and correction, the department of youth services, or a probation department, the offense occurs during the employee's official work hours and while the employee is engaged in official work responsibilities, and the offense is committed by a person incarcerated in a state correctional institution or institutionalized in the department of youth services who temporarily is outside of the institution for any purpose, by a parolee, by an offender under transitional control, under a community control sanction, or on an escorted visit, by a person under post-release control, or by an offender under any other type of supervision by a government agency.

(d) The offense occurs off the grounds of a local correctional facility, the victim of the offense is an employee of the local correctional facility or a probation department, the offense occurs during the employee's official work hours and while the employee is engaged in official work responsibilities, and the offense is committed by a person who is under custody in the facility subsequent to the person's arrest for any crime or delinquent act, subsequent to the person being charged with or convicted of any crime, or subsequent to the person being alleged to be or adjudicated a delinquent child and who temporarily is outside of the facility for any purpose or by a parolee, by an offender under transitional control, under a community control sanction, or on an escorted visit, by a person under post-release control, or by an offender under any other type of supervision by a government agency.

(e) The victim of the offense is a school teacher or administrator or a school bus operator, and the offense occurs in a school, on school premises, in a school building, on a school bus, or while the victim is outside of school premises or a school bus and is engaged in duties or official responsibilities associated with the victim's employment or position as a school teacher or administrator or a school bus operator, including, but not limited to, driving, accompanying, or chaperoning students at or on class or field trips, athletic events, or other school extracurricular activities or functions outside of school premises.

(3) If the victim of the offense is a peace officer or an investigator of the bureau of criminal identification and investigation, a firefighter, or a person performing emergency medical service, while in the performance of their official duties, assault is a felony of the fourth degree.

(4) If the victim of the offense is a peace officer or an investigator of the bureau of criminal identification and investigation and if the victim suffered serious physical harm as a result of the commission of the offense, assault is a felony of the fourth degree, and the court, pursuant to division (F) of section 2929.13 of the Revised Code, shall impose as a mandatory prison term one of the prison terms prescribed for a felony of the fourth degree that is at least twelve months in duration.

(5) If the victim of the offense is an officer or employee of a public children services agency or a private child placing agency and the offense relates to the officer's or employee's performance or anticipated performance of official responsibilities or duties, assault is either a felony of the fifth degree or, if the offender previously has been convicted of or pleaded guilty to an offense of violence, the victim of that prior offense was an officer or employee of a public children services agency or private child placing agency, and that prior offense related to the officer's or employee's performance or anticipated performance of official responsibilities or duties, a felony of the fourth degree.

(6) If an offender who is convicted of or pleads guilty to assault when it is a misdemeanor also is convicted of or pleads guilty to a specification as described in section 2941.1423 of the Revised Code that was included in the indictment, count in the indictment, or information charging the offense, the court shall sentence the offender to a mandatory jail term as provided in division (G) of section 2929.24 of the Revised Code.

If an offender who is convicted of or pleads guilty to assault when it is a felony also is convicted of or pleads guilty to a specification as described in section 2941.1423 of the Revised Code that was included in the indictment, count in the indictment, or information charging the offense, except as otherwise provided in division (C)(4) of this section, the court shall sentence the offender to a mandatory prison term as provided in division (B)(8) of section 2929.14 of the Revised Code.

(D) As used in this section:

(1) "Peace officer" has the same meaning as in section 2935.01 of the Revised Code.

(2) "Firefighter" has the same meaning as in section 3937.41 of the Revised Code.

(3) "Emergency medical service" has the same meaning as in section 4765.01 of the Revised Code.

(4) "Local correctional facility" means a county, multicounty, municipal, municipal-county, or multicounty-municipal jail or workhouse, a minimum security jail established under section 341.23 or 753.21 of the Revised Code, or another county, multicounty, municipal, municipal-county, or multicounty-municipal facility used for the custody of persons arrested for any crime or delinquent act, persons charged with or convicted of any crime, or persons alleged to be or adjudicated a delinquent child.

(5) "Employee of a local correctional facility" means a person who is an employee of the political subdivision or of one or more of the affiliated political subdivisions that operates the local correctional facility and who operates or assists in the operation of the facility.

(6) "School teacher or administrator" means either of the following:

(a) A person who is employed in the public schools of the state under a contract described in section 3319.08 of the Revised Code in a position in which the person is required to have a certificate issued pursuant to sections 3319.22 to 3319.311 of the Revised Code.

(b) A person who is employed by a nonpublic school for which the state board of education prescribes minimum standards under section 3301.07 of the Revised Code and who is certificated in accordance with section 3301.071 of the Revised Code.

(7) "Community control sanction" has the same meaning as in section 2929.01 of the Revised Code.

(8) "Escorted visit" means an escorted visit granted under section 2967.27 of the Revised Code.

(9) "Post-release control" and "transitional control" have the same meanings as in section 2967.01 of the Revised Code.

(10) "Investigator of the bureau of criminal identification and investigation" has the same meaning as in section 2903.11 of the Revised Code.

**HISTORY: 134 v H 511 (Eff 1-1-74); 142 v H 642 (Eff 3-17-89); 144 v H 561 (Eff 4-9-93); 145 v S 116 (Eff 9-29-94); 145 v H 571 (Eff 10-6-94); 146 v H 614 (Eff 6-16-96); 146 v S 2 (Eff 7-1-96); 146 v S 239 (Eff 9-6-96); 146 v H 480 (Eff 10-16-96); 147 v H 106 (Eff 11-21-97); 147 v S 111 (Eff 3-17-98); 148 v S 1 (Eff 8-6-99); 148 v S 142 (Eff 2-3-2000); 148 v H 412. Eff 4-10-2001; 149 v H 490, § 1, eff. 1-1-04; 151 v H 347, § 1, eff. 3-14-07; 152 v H 280, § 1, eff. 4-7-09; 2011 HB 86, § 1, eff. Sept. 30, 2011.**

Governor Taft's veto of HB 347 was overridden by the Ohio General Assembly.

The effective date is set by section 4 of HB 490.

**Not analogous to former RC § 2903.13 (133 v H 84), repealed 134 v H 511, § 2, eff 1-1-74.**

## § 2903.14 Negligent assault.

(A) No person shall negligently, by means of a deadly weapon or dangerous ordnance as defined in section 2923.11 of the Revised Code, cause physical harm to another or to another's unborn.

(B) Whoever violates this section is guilty of negligent assault, a misdemeanor of the third degree.

HISTORY: 134 v H 511 (Eff 1-1-74); 146 v S 239. Eff 9-6-96.

Not analogous to former RC § 2903.14 (133 v H 84), repealed 134 v H 511, § 2, eff 1-1-74.

## § 2903.15 Permitting child abuse.

(A) No parent, guardian, custodian, or person having custody of a child under eighteen years of age or of a mentally or physically handicapped child under twenty-one years of age shall cause serious physical harm to the child, or the death of the child, as a proximate result of permitting the child to be abused, to be tortured, to be administered corporal punishment or other physical disciplinary measure, or to be physically restrained in a cruel manner or for a prolonged period.

(B) It is an affirmative defense to a charge under this section that the defendant did not have readily available a means to prevent the harm to the child or the death of the child and that the defendant took timely and reasonable steps to summon aid.

(C) Whoever violates this section is guilty of permitting child abuse. If the violation of this section causes serious physical harm to the child, permitting child abuse is a felony of the third degree. If the violation of this section causes the death of the child, permitting child abuse is a felony of the first degree.

HISTORY: 148 v H 162. Eff 8-25-99.

Not analogous to former RC § 2903.15 (133 v H 84; 135 v S 62), repealed 134 v H 511, § 2, eff 1-1-74.

## § 2903.16 Failing to provide for a functionally impaired person.

(A) No caretaker shall knowingly fail to provide a functionally impaired person under the caretaker's care with any treatment, care, goods, or service that is necessary to maintain the health or safety of the functionally impaired person when this failure results in physical harm or serious physical harm to the functionally impaired person.

(B) No caretaker shall recklessly fail to provide a functionally impaired person under the caretaker's care with any treatment, care, goods, or service that is necessary to maintain the health or safety of the functionally impaired person when this failure results in serious physical harm to the functionally impaired person.

(C)(1) Whoever violates division (A) of this section is guilty of knowingly failing to provide for a functionally impaired person, a misdemeanor of the first degree. If the functionally impaired person under the offender's care suffers serious physical harm as a result of the violation of this section, a violation of division (A) of this section is a felony of the fourth degree.

(2) Whoever violates division (B) of this section is guilty of recklessly failing to provide for a functionally impaired person, a misdemeanor of the second degree. If the functionally impaired person under the offender's care suffers serious physical harm as a result of the violation of this section, a violation of division (B) of this section is a felony of the fourth degree.

HISTORY: 142 v H 642 (Eff 3-17-89); 146 v S 2. Eff 7-1-96.

Not analogous to former RC § 2903.16 (133 v H 84), repealed 134 v H 511, § 2, eff 1-1-74.

The effective date is set by section 6 of SB 2.

[MENACING]

## § 2903.21 Aggravated menacing.

(A) No person shall knowingly cause another to believe that the offender will cause serious physical harm to the person or property of the other person, the other person's unborn, or a member of the other person's immediate family.

(B) Whoever violates this section is guilty of aggravated menacing. Except as otherwise provided in this division, aggravated menacing is a misdemeanor of the first degree. If the victim of the offense is an officer or employee of a public children services agency or a private child placing agency and the offense relates to the officer's or employee's performance or anticipated performance of official responsibilities or duties, aggravated menacing is a felony of the fifth degree or, if the offender previously has been convicted of or pleaded guilty to an offense of violence, the victim of that prior offense was an officer or employee of a public children services agency or private child placing agency, and that prior offense related to the officer's or employee's performance or anticipated performance of official responsibilities or duties, a felony of the fourth degree.

HISTORY: 134 v H 511 (Eff 1-1-74); 146 v S 239 (Eff 9-6-96); 148 v H 412. Eff 4-10-2001.

[STALKING]

## § 2903.211 Menacing by stalking.

(A)(1) No person by engaging in a pattern of conduct shall knowingly cause another person to believe that the offender will cause physical harm to the other person or cause mental distress to the other person.

(2) No person, through the use of any electronic method of remotely transferring information, including, but not limited to, any computer, computer network, computer program, or computer system, shall post a message with purpose to urge or incite another to commit a violation of division (A)(1) of this section.

(3) No person, with a sexual motivation, shall violate division (A)(1) or (2) of this section.

(B) Whoever violates this section is guilty of menacing by stalking.

(1) Except as otherwise provided in divisions (B)(2) and (3) of this section, menacing by stalking is a misdemeanor of the first degree.

(2) Menacing by stalking is a felony of the fourth degree if any of the following applies:

(a) The offender previously has been convicted of or pleaded guilty to a violation of this section or a violation of section 2911.211 of the Revised Code.

(b) In committing the offense under division (A)(1), (2), or (3) of this section, the offender made a threat of physical harm to or against the victim, or as a result of an offense committed under division (A)(2) or (3) of this section, a third person induced by the offender's posted message made a threat of physical harm to or against the victim.

(c) In committing the offense under division (A)(1), (2), or (3) of this section, the offender trespassed on the land or premises where the victim lives, is employed, or attends school, or as a result of an offense committed under division (A)(2) or (3) of this section, a third person induced by the offender's posted message trespassed on the land or premises where the victim lives, is employed, or attends school.

(d) The victim of the offense is a minor.

(e) The offender has a history of violence toward the victim or any other person or a history of other violent acts toward the victim or any other person.

(f) While committing the offense under division (A)(1) of this section or a violation of division (A)(3) of this section based on conduct in violation of division (A)(1) of this section, the offender had a deadly weapon on or about the offender's person or under the offender's control. Division (B)(2)(f) of this section does not apply in determining the penalty for a violation of division (A)(2) of this section or a violation of division (A)(3) of this section based on conduct in violation of division (A)(2) of this section.

(g) At the time of the commission of the offense, the offender was the subject of a protection order issued under section 2903.213 or 2903.214 of the Revised Code, regardless of whether the person to be protected under the order is the victim of the offense or another person.

(h) In committing the offense under division (A)(1), (2), or (3) of this section, the offender caused serious physical harm to the premises at which the victim resides, to the real property on which that premises is located, or to any personal property located on that premises, or as a result of an offense committed under division (A)(2) of this section or an offense committed under division (A)(3) of this section based on a violation of division (A)(2) of this section, a third person induced by the offender's posted message caused serious physical harm to that premises, that real property, or any personal property on that premises.

(i) Prior to committing the offense, the offender had been determined to represent a substantial risk of physical harm to others as manifested by evidence of then-recent homicidal or other violent behavior, evidence of then-recent threats that placed another in reasonable fear of violent behavior and serious physical harm, or other evidence of then-present dangerousness.

(3) If the victim of the offense is an officer or employee of a public children services agency or a private child placing agency and the offense relates to the officer's or employee's performance or anticipated performance of official responsibilities or duties, menacing by stalking is either a felony of the fifth degree or, if the offender previously has been convicted of or pleaded guilty to an offense of violence, the victim of that prior offense was an officer or employee of a public children services agency or private child placing agency, and that prior offense related to the officer's or employee's performance or anticipated performance of official responsibilities or duties, a felony of the fourth degree.

(C) Section 2919.271 of the Revised Code applies in relation to a defendant charged with a violation of this section.

(D) As used in this section:

(1) "Pattern of conduct" means two or more actions or incidents closely related in time, whether or not there has been a prior conviction based on any of those actions or incidents. Actions or incidents that prevent, obstruct, or delay the performance by a public official, firefighter, rescuer, emergency medical services person, or emergency facility person of any authorized act within the public official's, firefighter's, rescuer's, emergency medical services person's, or emergency facility person's official capacity, or the posting of messages or receipt of information or data through the use of an electronic method of remotely transferring information, including, but not limited to, a computer, computer network, computer program, computer system, or telecommunications device, may constitute a "pattern of conduct."

(2) "Mental distress" means any of the following:

(a) Any mental illness or condition that involves some temporary substantial incapacity;

(b) Any mental illness or condition that would normally require psychiatric treatment, psychological treatment, or other mental health services, whether or not any person requested or received psychiatric treatment, psychological treatment, or other mental health services.

(3) "Emergency medical services person" is the singular of "emergency medical services personnel" as defined in section 2133.21 of the Revised Code.

(4) "Emergency facility person" is the singular of "emergency facility personnel" as defined in section 2909.04 of the Revised Code.

(5) "Public official" has the same meaning as in section 2921.01 of the Revised Code.

(6) "Computer," "computer network," "computer program," "computer system," and "telecommunications device" have the same meanings as in section 2913.01 of the Revised Code.

(7) "Post a message" means transferring, sending, posting, publishing, disseminating, or otherwise communicating, or attempting to transfer, send, post, publish, disseminate, or otherwise communicate, any message or information, whether truthful or untruthful, about an individual, and whether done under one's own name, under the name of another, or while impersonating another.

(8) "Third person" means, in relation to conduct as described in division (A)(2) of this section, an individual who is neither the offender nor the victim of the conduct.

(9) "Sexual motivation" has the same meaning as in section 2971.01 of the Revised Code.

(E) The state does not need to prove in a prosecution under this section that a person requested or received psychiatric treatment, psychological treatment, or other mental health services in order to show that the person was caused mental distress as described in division (D)(2)(b) of this section.

(F)(1) This section does not apply to a person solely because the person provided access or connection to or from an electronic method of remotely transferring information not under that person's control, including having provided capabilities that are incidental to providing access or connection to or from the electronic method of remotely transferring the information, and that do not include the creation of the content of the material that is the subject of the access or connection. In addition, any person providing access or connection to or from an electronic method of remotely transferring information not under that person's control shall not be liable for any action voluntarily taken in good faith to block the receipt or transmission through its service of any information that it believes is, or will be sent, in violation of this section.

(2) Division (F)(1) of this section does not create an affirmative duty for any person providing access or connection to or from an electronic method of remotely transferring information not under that person's control to block the receipt or transmission through its service of any information that it believes is, or will be sent, in violation of this section except as otherwise provided by law.

(3) Division (F)(1) of this section does not apply to a person who conspires with a person actively involved in the creation or knowing distribution of material in violation of this section or who knowingly advertises the availability of material of that nature.

**HISTORY: 144 v H 536 (Eff 11-5-92); 146 v S 2 (Eff 7-1-96); 147 v S 215 (Eff 3-30-99); 148 v H 137 (Eff 3-10-2000); 148 v H 202, § 3 (Eff 3-10-2000); 148 v H 412 (Eff 4-10-2001); 149 v S 40. Eff 1-25-2002; 150 v S 8, § 1, eff. 8-29-03; 150 v S 47, § 1, eff. 8-29-03; 152 v S 10, § 1, eff. 1-1-08.**

The effective date is set by § 3 of 152 v S 10.

## § 2903.212 Considerations in setting amount and conditions of bail for certain offenses.

(A) Except when the complaint involves a person who is a family or household member as defined in section 2919.25 of the Revised Code, if a person is charged with a violation of section 2903.21, 2903.211 [2903.21.1], 2903.22, or 2911.211 [2911.21.1] of the Revised Code, a violation of a municipal ordinance that is substantially similar to one of those sections, or a sexually oriented offense and if the person, at the time of the alleged violation, was subject to the terms of any order issued pursuant to section 2903.213 [2903.21.3], 2933.08, or 2945.04 of the Revised Code or previously had been convicted of or pleaded guilty to a violation of section 2903.21, 2903.211 [2903.21.1], 2903.22, or 2911.211 [2911.21.1] of the Revised Code that involves the same complainant, a violation of a municipal ordinance that is substantially similar to one of those sections and that involves the same complainant, or a sexually oriented offense that involves the same complainant, the court shall consider all of the following, in addition to any other circumstances considered by the court and notwithstanding any provisions to the contrary contained in Criminal Rule 46, before setting the amount and conditions of the bail for the person:

(1) Whether the person has a history of violence toward the complainant or a history of other violent acts;

(2) The mental health of the person;

(3) Whether the person has a history of violating the orders of any court or governmental entity;

(4) Whether the person is potentially a threat to any other person;

(5) Whether setting bail at a high level will interfere with any treatment or counseling that the person is undergoing.

(B) Any court that has jurisdiction over violations of section 2903.21, 2903.211 [2903.21.1], 2903.22, or 2911.211 [2911.21.1] of the Revised Code, violations of a municipal ordinance that is substantially similar to one of those sections, or sexually oriented offenses may set a schedule for bail to be used in cases involving those violations. The schedule shall require that a judge consider all of the factors listed in division (A) of this section and may require judges to set bail at a certain level or impose other reasonable conditions related to a release on bail or on recognizance if the history of the alleged offender or the circumstances of the alleged offense meet certain criteria in the schedule.

(C) As used in this section, "sexually oriented offense" has the same meaning as in section 2950.01 of the Revised Code.

**HISTORY: 144 v H 536. Eff 11-5-92; 151 v S 260, § 1, eff. 1-2-07.**

## § 2903.213 Motion for protection order as pretrial condition of release.

(A) Except when the complaint involves a person who is a family or household member as defined in section 2919.25 of the Revised Code, upon the filing of a complaint that alleges a violation of section 2903.11, 2903.12, 2903.13, 2903.21, 2903.211 [2903.21.1], 2903.22, or 2911.211 [2911.21.1] of the Revised Code, a violation of a municipal ordinance substantially similar to section 2903.13, 2903.21, 2903.211 [2903.21.1], 2903.22, or 2911.211 [2911.21.1] of the Revised Code, or the commission of a sexually oriented offense, the complainant, the alleged victim, or a family or household member of an alleged victim may file a motion that requests the issuance of a protection order as a pretrial condition of release of the alleged offender, in addition to any bail set under Criminal Rule 46. The motion shall be filed with the clerk of the court that has jurisdiction of the case at any time after the filing of the complaint. If the complaint involves a person who is a family or household member, the complainant, the alleged victim, or the family or household member may file a motion for a temporary protection order pursuant to section 2919.26 of the Revised Code.

(B) A motion for a protection order under this section shall be prepared on a form that is provided by the clerk of the court, and the form shall be substantially as follows:

"Motion for Protection Order

......................

Name and address of court

State of Ohio

v. No .....

......................................

Name of Defendant

..............................................

Name of Defendant

(Name of person), moves the court to issue a protection order containing terms designed to ensure the safety and protection of the complainant or the alleged victim in the above-captioned case, in relation to the named defendant, pursuant to its authority to issue a protection order under section 2903.213 [2903.21.3] of the Revised Code.

A complaint, a copy of which has been attached to this motion, has been filed in this court charging the named defendant with a violation of section 2903.11, 2903.12, 2903.13, 2903.21, 2903.211 [2903.21.1], 2903.22, or 2911.211 [2911.21.1] of the Revised Code, a violation of a municipal ordinance substantially similar to section 2903.13, 2903.21, 2903.211 [2903.21.1], 2903.22, or 2911.211 [2911.21.1] of the Revised Code, or the commission of a sexually oriented offense.

I understand that I must appear before the court, at a time set by the court not later than the next day that the court is in session after the filing of this motion, for a hearing on the motion, and that any protection order granted pursuant to this motion is a pretrial condition of release and is effective only until the disposition of the criminal proceeding arising out of the attached complaint or until the issuance under section 2903.214 [2903.21.4] of the Revised Code of a protection order arising out of the same activities as those that were the basis of the attached complaint.

..............................................

Signature of person

..............................................

Address of person"

(C)(1) As soon as possible after the filing of a motion that requests the issuance of a protection order under this section, but not later than the next day that the court is in session after the filing of the motion, the court shall conduct a hearing to determine whether to issue the order. The person who requested the order shall appear before the court and provide the court with the information that it requests concerning the basis of the motion. If the court finds that the safety and protection of the complainant or the alleged victim may be impaired by the continued presence of the alleged offender, the court may issue a protection order under this section, as a pretrial condition of release, that contains terms designed to ensure the safety and protection of the complainant or the alleged victim, including a requirement that the alleged offender refrain from entering the residence, school, business, or place of employment of the complainant or the alleged victim.

(2)(a) If the court issues a protection order under this section that includes a requirement that the alleged offender refrain from entering the residence, school, business, or place of employment of the complainant or the alleged victim, the order shall clearly state that the order cannot be waived or nullified by an invitation to the alleged offender from the complainant, the alleged victim, or a family or household member to enter the residence, school, business, or place of employment or by the alleged offender's entry into one of those places otherwise upon the consent of the complainant, the alleged victim, or a family or household member.

(b) Division (C)(2)(a) of this section does not limit any discretion of a court to determine that an alleged offender charged with a violation of section 2919.27 of the Revised Code, with a violation of a municipal ordinance substantially equivalent to that section, or with contempt of court, which charge is based on an alleged violation of a protection order issued under this section, did not commit the violation or was not in contempt of court.

(D)(1) Except when the complaint involves a person who is a family or household member as defined in section 2919.25 of the Revised Code, upon the filing of a complaint that alleges a violation specified in division (A) of this section, the court, upon its own motion, may issue a protection order under this section as a pretrial condition of release of the alleged offender if it finds that the safety and protection of the complainant or the alleged victim may be impaired by the continued presence of the alleged offender.

(2) If the court issues a protection order under this section as an ex parte order, it shall conduct, as soon as possible after the issuance of the order but not later than the next day that the court is in session after its issuance, a hearing to determine whether the order should remain in effect, be modified, or be revoked. The hearing shall be conducted under the standards set forth in division (C) of this section.

(3) If a municipal court or a county court issues a protection order under this section and if, subsequent to the issuance of the order, the alleged offender who is the subject of the order is bound over to the court of common pleas for prosecution of a felony arising out of the same activities as those that were the basis of the complaint upon which the order is based, notwithstanding the fact that the order was issued by a municipal court or county court, the order shall remain in effect, as though it were an order of the court of common pleas, while the charges against the alleged offender are pending in the court of common pleas, for the period of time described in division (E)(2) of this section, and the court of common pleas has exclusive jurisdiction to modify the order issued by the municipal court or county court. This division applies when the alleged offender is bound over to the court of common pleas as a result of the person waiving a preliminary hearing on the felony charge, as a result of the municipal court or county court having determined at a preliminary hearing that there is probable cause to believe that the felony has been committed and that the alleged offender committed it, as a result of the alleged offender having been indicted for the felony, or in any other manner.

(E) A protection order that is issued as a pretrial condition of release under this section:

(1) Is in addition to, but shall not be construed as a part of, any bail set under Criminal Rule 46;

(2) Is effective only until the disposition, by the court that issued the order or, in the circumstances described in division (D)(3) of this section, by the court of common pleas to which the alleged offender is bound over for prosecution, of the criminal proceeding arising out of the complaint upon which the order is based or until the issuance under section 2903.214 [2903.21.4] of the Revised Code of a protection order arising out of the same activities as those that were the basis of the complaint filed under this section;

(3) Shall not be construed as a finding that the alleged offender committed the alleged offense and shall not be introduced as evidence of the commission of the offense at the trial of the alleged offender on the complaint upon which the order is based.

(F) A person who meets the criteria for bail under Criminal Rule 46 and who, if required to do so pursuant to that rule, executes or posts bond or deposits cash or securities as bail, shall not be held in custody pending a hearing before the court on a motion requesting a protection order under this section.

(G)(1) A copy of a protection order that is issued under this section shall be issued by the court to the complainant, to the alleged victim, to the person who requested the order, to the defendant, and to all law enforcement agencies that have jurisdiction to enforce the order. The court shall direct that a copy of the order be delivered to the defendant on the same day that the order is entered. If a municipal court or a county court issues a protection order under this section and if, subsequent to the issuance of the order, the defendant who is the subject of the order is bound over to the court of common pleas for prosecution as described in division (D)(3) of this section, the municipal court or county court shall direct that a copy of the order be delivered to the court of common pleas to which the defendant is bound over.

(2) All law enforcement agencies shall establish and maintain an index for the protection orders delivered to the agencies pursuant to division (G)(1) of this section. With respect to each order delivered, each agency shall note on the index the date and time of the agency's receipt of the order.

(3) Regardless of whether the petitioner has registered the protection order in the county in which the officer's agency has jurisdiction, any officer of a law enforcement agency shall enforce a protection order issued pursuant to this section in accordance with the provisions of the order.

(H) Upon a violation of a protection order issued pursuant to this section, the court may issue another protection order under this section, as a pretrial condition of release, that modifies the terms of the order that was violated.

(I) Notwithstanding any provision of law to the contrary and regardless of whether a protection order is issued or a consent agreement is approved by a court of another county or by a court of another state, no court or unit of state or local government shall charge any fee, cost, deposit, or money in connection with the filing of a motion pursuant to this section, in connection with the filing, issuance, registration, or service of a protection order or consent agreement, or for obtaining certified copies of a protection order or consent agreement.

(J) As used in this section, "sexually oriented offense" has the same meaning as in section 2950.01 of the Revised Code.

**HISTORY: 144 v H 536 (Eff 11-5-92); 145 v S 31 (Eff 9-27-93); 147 v H 93 (Eff 12-31-97); 147 v S 98 (Eff 3-17-98); 147 v H 302 (Eff 7-29-98); 148 v H 137 (Eff 3-10-2000); 149 v H 548. Eff 3-31-2003; 151 v S 260, § 1, eff. 1-2-07; 152 v H 562, § 101.01, eff. 6-24-08; 153 v H 238, § 1, eff. 9-8-10.**

The effective date is set by § 812.20 of 152 v H 562.

## § 2903.214 Petition for protection order to protect victim of menacing by stalking or sexually oriented offense.

(A) As used in this section:

(1) "Court" means the court of common pleas of the county in which the person to be protected by the protection order resides.

(2) "Victim advocate" means a person who provides support and assistance for a person who files a petition under this section.

(3) "Family or household member" has the same meaning as in section 3113.31 of the Revised Code.

(4) "Protection order issued by a court of another state" has the same meaning as in section 2919.27 of the Revised Code.

(5) "Sexually oriented offense" has the same meaning as in section 2950.01 of the Revised Code.

(6) "Electronic monitoring" has the same meaning as in section 2929.01 of the Revised Code.

(B) The court has jurisdiction over all proceedings under this section.

(C) A person may seek relief under this section for the person, or any parent or adult household member may seek relief under this section on behalf of any other family or household member, by filing a petition with the court. The petition shall contain or state all of the following:

(1) An allegation that the respondent is eighteen years of age or older and engaged in a violation of section 2903.211 [2903.21.1] of the Revised Code against the person to be protected by the protection order or committed a sexually oriented offense against the person to be protected by the protection order, including a description of the nature and extent of the violation;

(2) If the petitioner seeks relief in the form of electronic monitoring of the respondent, an allegation that at any time preceding the filing of the petition the respondent engaged in conduct that would cause a reasonable person to believe that the health, welfare, or safety of the person to be protected was at risk, a description of the nature and extent of that conduct, and an allegation that the respondent presents a continuing danger to the person to be protected;

(3) A request for relief under this section.

(D)(1) If a person who files a petition pursuant to this section requests an ex parte order, the court shall hold an ex parte hearing as soon as possible after the petition is filed, but not later than the next day that the court is in session after the petition is filed. The court, for good cause shown at the ex parte hearing, may enter any temporary orders, with or without bond, that the court finds necessary for the safety and protection of the person to be protected by the order. Immediate and present danger to the person to be protected by the protection order constitutes good cause for purposes of this section. Immediate and present danger includes, but is not limited to, situations in which the respondent has threatened the person to be protected by the protection order with bodily harm or in which the respondent previously has been convicted of or pleaded guilty to a violation of section 2903.211 [2903.21.1] of the Revised Code or a sexually oriented offense against the person to be protected by the protection order.

(2)(a) If the court, after an ex parte hearing, issues a protection order described in division (E) of this section, the court shall schedule a full hearing for a date that is within ten court days after the ex parte hearing. The court shall give the respondent notice of, and an opportunity to be heard at, the full hearing. The court shall hold the full hearing on the date scheduled under this division unless the court grants a continuance of the hearing in accordance with this division. Under any of the following circumstances or for any of the following reasons, the court may grant a continuance of the full hearing to a reasonable time determined by the court:

(i) Prior to the date scheduled for the full hearing under this division, the respondent has not been served with the petition filed pursuant to this section and notice of the full hearing.

(ii) The parties consent to the continuance.

(iii) The continuance is needed to allow a party to obtain counsel.

(iv) The continuance is needed for other good cause.

(b) An ex parte order issued under this section does not expire because of a failure to serve notice of the full hearing upon the respondent before the date set for the full hearing under division (D)(2)(a) of this section or because the court grants a continuance under that division.

(3) If a person who files a petition pursuant to this section does not request an ex parte order, or if a person requests an ex parte order but the court does not issue an ex parte order after an ex parte hearing, the court shall proceed as in a normal civil action and grant a full hearing on the matter.

(E)(1)(a) After an ex parte or full hearing, the court may issue any protection order, with or without bond, that contains terms designed to ensure the safety and protection of the person to be protected by the protection order, including, but not limited to, a requirement that the respondent refrain from entering the residence, school, business, or place of employment of the petitioner or family or household member. If the court includes a requirement that the respondent refrain from entering the residence, school, business, or place of employment of the petitioner or family or household member in the order, it also shall include in the order provisions of the type described in division (E)(5) of this section.

(b) After a full hearing, if the court considering a petition that includes an allegation of the type described in division (C)(2) of this section, or the court upon its own motion, finds upon clear and convincing evidence that the petitioner reasonably believed that the respondent's conduct at any time preceding the filing of the petition endangered the health, welfare, or safety of the person to be protected and that the respondent presents a continuing danger to the person to be protected, the court may order that the respondent be electronically monitored for a period of time and under the terms and conditions that the court determines are appropriate. Electronic monitoring shall be in addition to any other relief granted to the petitioner.

(2)(a) Any protection order issued pursuant to this section shall be valid until a date certain but not later than five years from the date of its issuance.

(b) Any protection order issued pursuant to this section may be renewed in the same manner as the original order was issued.

(3) A court may not issue a protection order that requires a petitioner to do or to refrain from doing an act that the court may require a respondent to do or to refrain from doing under division (E)(1) of this section unless all of the following apply:

(a) The respondent files a separate petition for a protection order in accordance with this section.

(b) The petitioner is served with notice of the respondent's petition at least forty-eight hours before the court holds a hearing with respect to the respondent's petition, or the petitioner waives the right to receive this notice.

(c) If the petitioner has requested an ex parte order pursuant to division (D) of this section, the court does not delay any hearing required by that division beyond the time specified in that division in order to consolidate the hearing with a hearing on the petition filed by the respondent.

(d) After a full hearing at which the respondent presents evidence in support of the request for a protection order and the petitioner is afforded an opportunity to defend against that evidence, the court determines that the petitioner has committed a violation of section 2903.211 [2903.21.1] of the Revised Code against the person to be protected by the protection order issued pursuant to division (E)(3) of this section, has committed a sexually oriented offense against the person to be protected by the protection order issued pursuant to division (E)(3) of this section, or has violated a protection order issued pursuant to section 2903.213 [2903.21.3] of the Revised Code relative to the person to be protected by the protection order issued pursuant to division (E)(3) of this section.

(4) No protection order issued pursuant to this section shall in any manner affect title to any real property.

(5)(a) If the court issues a protection order under this section that includes a requirement that the alleged offender refrain from entering the residence, school, business, or place of employment of the petitioner or a family or household member, the order shall clearly state that the order cannot be waived or nullified by an invitation to the alleged offender from the complainant to enter the residence, school, business, or place of employment or by the alleged offender's entry into one of those places otherwise upon the consent of the petitioner or family or household member.

(b) Division (E)(5)(a) of this section does not limit any discretion of a court to determine that an alleged offender charged with a violation of section 2919.27 of the Revised Code, with a violation of a municipal ordinance substantially equivalent to that section, or with contempt of court, which charge is based on an alleged violation of a protection order issued under this section, did not commit the violation or was not in contempt of court.

(F)(1) The court shall cause the delivery of a copy of any protection order that is issued under this section to the petitioner, to the respondent, and to all law enforcement agencies that have jurisdiction to enforce the order. The court shall direct that a copy of the order be delivered to the respondent on the same day that the order is entered.

(2) Upon the issuance of a protection order under this section, the court shall provide the parties to the order with the following notice orally or by form:

"NOTICE

As a result of this order, it may be unlawful for you to possess or purchase a firearm, including a rifle, pistol, or revolver, or ammunition pursuant to federal law under 18 U.S.C. 922(g)(8). If you have any questions whether this law makes it illegal for you to possess or purchase a firearm or ammunition, you should consult an attorney."

(3) All law enforcement agencies shall establish and maintain an index for the protection orders delivered to the agencies pursuant to division (F)(1) of this section. With respect to each order delivered, each agency shall note on the index the date and time that it received the order.

(4) Regardless of whether the petitioner has registered the protection order in the county in which the officer's agency has jurisdiction pursuant to division (M) of this section, any officer of a law enforcement agency shall enforce a protection order issued pursuant to this section by any court in this state in accordance with the provisions of the order, including removing the respondent from the premises, if appropriate.

(G) Any proceeding under this section shall be conducted in accordance with the Rules of Civil Procedure, except that a protection order may be obtained under this section with or without bond. An order issued under this section, other than an ex parte order, that grants a protection order, or that refuses to grant a protection order, is a final, appealable order. The remedies and procedures provided in this section are in addition to, and not in lieu of, any other available civil or criminal remedies.

(H) The filing of proceedings under this section does not excuse a person from filing any report or giving any notice required by section 2151.421 [2151.42.1] of the Revised Code or by any other law.

(I) Any law enforcement agency that investigates an alleged violation of section 2903.211 [2903.21.1] of the Revised Code or an alleged commission of a sexually oriented offense shall provide information to the victim and the family or household members of the victim regarding the relief available under this section and section 2903.213 [2903.21.3] of the Revised Code.

(J) Notwithstanding any provision of law to the contrary and regardless of whether a protection order is issued or a consent agreement is approved by a court of another county or by a court of another state, no court or unit of state or local government shall charge any fee, cost, deposit, or money in connection with the filing of a petition pursuant to this section, in connection with the filing, issuance, registration, or service of a protection order or consent agreement, or for obtaining a certified copy of a protection order or consent agreement.

(K)(1) A person who violates a protection order issued under this section is subject to the following sanctions:

(a) Criminal prosecution for a violation of section 2919.27 of the Revised Code, if the violation of the protection order constitutes a violation of that section;

(b) Punishment for contempt of court.

(2) The punishment of a person for contempt of court for violation of a protection order issued under this section does not bar criminal prosecution of the person for a violation of section 2919.27 of the Revised Code. However, a person punished for contempt of court is entitled to credit for the punishment imposed upon conviction of a violation of that section, and a person convicted of a violation of that section shall not subsequently be punished for contempt of court arising out of the same activity.

(L) In all stages of a proceeding under this section, a petitioner may be accompanied by a victim advocate.

(M)(1) A petitioner who obtains a protection order under this section or a protection order under section 2903.213 [2903.21.3] of the Revised Code may provide notice of the issuance or approval of the order to the judicial and law enforcement officials in any county other than the county in which the order is issued by registering that order in the other county pursuant to division (M)(2) of this section and filing a copy of the registered order with a law enforcement agency in the other county in accordance with that division. A person who obtains a protection order issued by a court of another state may provide notice of the issuance of the order to the judicial and law enforcement officials in any county of this state by registering the order in that county pursuant to section 2919.272 [2919.27.2] of the Revised Code and filing a copy of the registered order with a law enforcement agency in that county.

(2) A petitioner may register a protection order issued pursuant to this section or section 2903.213 [2903.21.3] of the Revised Code in a county other than the county in which the court that issued the order is located in the following manner:

(a) The petitioner shall obtain a certified copy of the order from the clerk of the court that issued the order and present that certified copy to the clerk of the court of common pleas or the clerk of a municipal court or county court in the county in which the order is to be registered.

(b) Upon accepting the certified copy of the order for registration, the clerk of the court of common pleas, municipal court, or county court shall place an endorsement of registration on the order and give the petitioner a copy of the order that bears that proof of registration.

(3) The clerk of each court of common pleas, municipal court, or county court shall maintain a registry of certified copies of protection orders that have been issued by courts in other counties pursuant to this section or section 2903.213 [2903.21.3] of the Revised Code and that have been registered with the clerk.

(N)(1) If the court orders electronic monitoring of the respondent under this section, the court shall direct the sheriff's office or any other appropriate law enforcement agency to install the electronic monitoring device and to monitor the respondent. Unless the court determines that the respondent is indigent, the court shall order the respondent to pay the cost of the installation and monitoring of the electronic monitoring device. If the court determines that the respondent is indigent and subject to the maximum amount allowable to be paid in any year from the fund and the rules promulgated by the attorney general under division (N)(2) of this section, the cost of the installation and monitoring of the electronic monitoring device may be paid out of funds from the reparations fund created pursuant to section 2743.191 [2743.19.1] of the Revised Code. The total amount of costs for the installation and monitoring of electronic monitoring devices paid pursuant to this division and sections 2151.34 and 2919.27 of the Revised Code from the reparations fund shall not exceed three hundred thousand dollars per year.

(2) The attorney general may promulgate rules pursuant to section 111.15 of the Revised Code to govern payments made from the reparations fund pursuant to this division and sections 2151.34 and 2919.27 of the Revised Code. The rules may include reasonable limits on the total cost paid pursuant to this division and sections 2151.34 and 2919.27 of the Revised Code per respondent, the amount of the three hundred thousand dollars allocated to each county, and how invoices may be submitted by a county, court, or other entity.

**HISTORY: 147 v H 302 (Eff 7-29-98); 149 v H 548. Eff 3-31-2003; 151 v S 260, § 1, eff. 1-2-07; 152 v H 562, § 101.01, eff. 6-24-08; 152 v H 471, § 1, eff. 4-7-09; 153 v H 1, § 101.01, eff. 10-16-09; 153 v H 10, § 1, eff. 6-17-10.**

The provisions of § 3 of 153 v H 10 read as follows:

SECTION 3. Sections 2151.23, 2151.358, 2152.02, 2743.191, 2903.214, 2919.25, 2919.27, 3113.31, and 3113.33 of the Revised Code, as amended by this act, and section 2151.34 of the Revised Code, as enacted by this act, shall be named the "Shynerra Grant Law."

The effective date is set by § 812.10 of 153 v H 1.

The effective date is set by § 812.20 of 152 v H 562.

**Not analogous to former RC § 2903.21.4 (144 v H 536), repealed 146 v S 2, § 2, eff 7-1-96.**

## § 2903.215 Repealed, 146 v S 2, § 2 [144 v H 536]. Eff 7-1-96.

This section concerned evaluation of mental condition of defendant charged with such a violation.

The effective date is set by section 6 of SB 2.

## § 2903.22 Menacing.

(A) No person shall knowingly cause another to believe that the offender will cause physical harm to the person or property of the other person, the other person's unborn, or a member of the other person's immediate family.

(B) Whoever violates this section is guilty of menacing. Except as otherwise provided in this division, menacing is a misdemeanor of the fourth degree. If the victim of the offense is an officer or employee of a public children services agency or a private child placing agency and the offense relates to the officer's or employee's performance or anticipated performance of official responsibilities or duties, menacing is a misdemeanor of the first degree or, if the offender previously has been convicted of or pleaded guilty to an offense of violence, the victim of that prior offense was an officer or employee of a public children services agency or private child placing agency, and that prior offense related to the officer's or employee's performance or anticipated performance of official responsibilities or duties, a felony of the fourth degree.

**HISTORY: 134 v H 511 (Eff 1-1-74); 146 v S 239 (Eff 9-6-96); 148 v H 412. Eff 4-10-2001.**

## § 2903.31 Hazing.

(A) As used in this section, "hazing" means doing any act or coercing another, including the victim, to do any act of initiation into any student or other organization that causes or creates a substantial risk of causing mental or physical harm to any person.

(B)(1) No person shall recklessly participate in the hazing of another.

(2) No administrator, employee, or faculty member of any primary, secondary, or post-secondary school or of any other educational institution, public or private, shall recklessly permit the hazing of any person.

(C) Whoever violates this section is guilty of hazing, a misdemeanor of the fourth degree.

**HISTORY: 139 v H 444. Eff 3-3-83.**

## [PATIENT ABUSE AND NEGLECT IN CARE FACILITIES]

### § 2903.33 Definitions.

As used in sections 2903.33 to 2903.36 of the Revised Code:

(A) "Care facility" means any of the following:

(1) Any "home" as defined in section 3721.10 or 5111.20 of the Revised Code;

(2) Any "residential facility" as defined in section 5123.19 of the Revised Code;

(3) Any institution or facility operated or provided by the department of mental health or by the department of developmental disabilities pursuant to sections 5119.02 and 5123.03 of the Revised Code;

(4) Any "residential facility" as defined in section 5119.22 of the Revised Code;

(5) Any unit of any hospital, as defined in section 3701.01 of the Revised Code, that provides the same services as a nursing home, as defined in section 3721.01 of the Revised Code;

(6) Any institution, residence, or facility that provides, for a period of more than twenty-four hours, whether for a consideration or not, accommodations to one individual or two unrelated individuals who are dependent upon the services of others;

(7) Any "adult care facility" as defined in section 5119.70 of the Revised Code;

(8) Any adult foster home certified under section 5119.692 of the Revised Code.

(B) "Abuse" means knowingly causing physical harm or recklessly causing serious physical harm to a person by physical contact with the person or by the inappropriate use of a physical or chemical restraint, medication, or isolation on the person.

(C)(1) "Gross neglect" means knowingly failing to provide a person with any treatment, care, goods, or service that is necessary to maintain the health or safety of the person when the failure results in physical harm or serious physical harm to the person.

(2) "Neglect" means recklessly failing to provide a person with any treatment, care, goods, or service that is necessary to maintain the health or safety of the person when the failure results in serious physical harm to the person.

(D) "Inappropriate use of a physical or chemical restraint, medication, or isolation" means the use of physical or chemical restraint, medication, or isolation as punishment, for staff convenience, excessively, as a substitute for treatment, or in quantities that preclude habilitation and treatment.

**HISTORY: 141 v H 566 (Eff 9-17-86); 142 v S 156 (Eff 7-1-88); 143 v S 2 (Eff 11-1-89); 143 v H 253 (Eff 11-15-90); 145 v H 152 (Eff 7-1-93); 145 v S 21 (Eff 10-29-93); 146 v S 2. Eff 7-1-96; 153 v S 79, § 1, eff. 10-6-09; 153 v H 1, § 101.01, eff. 10-16-09; 2011 HB 153, § 101.01, eff. July 1, 2011.**

Acts 2011, HB 153, § 815.20 provides: "The General Assembly, applying the principle stated in division (B) of section 1.52 of the Revised Code that amendments are to be harmonized if reasonably capable of simultaneous operation, finds that the following sections, presented in this act as composites of the sections as amended by the acts indicated, are the resulting versions of the sections in effect prior to the effective date of the sections as presented in this act:

"Section 2903.33 of the Revised Code as amended by Am. Sub. H.B. 1 and Sub. S.B. 79 of the 128th General Assembly."

The effective date is set by § 812.10 of 153 v H 1.

The effective date is set by section 6 of SB 2.

The provisions of § 7 of SB 2 (146 v —) read as follows:

SECTION 7. * * * Section 2903.33 of the Revised Code is presented in this act as a composite of the section as amended by both Am. Sub. H.B. 152 and Am. Sub. S.B. 21 of the 120th General Assembly, with the new language of neither of the acts shown in capital letters. * * * This is in recognition of the principle stated in division (B) of section 1.52 of the Revised Code that such amendments are to be harmonized where not substantively irreconcilable and constitutes a legislative finding that such is the resulting version in effect prior to the effective date of this act.

**Comment, Legislative Service Commission**

Section 2903.33 of the Revised Code is amended by Am. Sub. H.B. 1 and Sub. S.B. 79 of the 128th General Assembly. Comparison of these amendments in pursuance of section 1.52 of the Revised Code discloses that they are not irreconcilable so that they are required by that section to be harmonized to give effect to each amendment.

### § 2903.34 Patient abuse; neglect.

(A) No person who owns, operates, or administers, or who is an agent or employee of, a care facility shall do any of the following:

(1) Commit abuse against a resident or patient of the facility;

(2) Commit gross neglect against a resident or patient of the facility;

(3) Commit neglect against a resident or patient of the facility.

(B)(1) A person who relies upon treatment by spiritual means through prayer alone, in accordance with the tenets of a recognized religious denomination, shall not be considered neglected under division (A)(3) of this section for that reason alone.

(2) It is an affirmative defense to a charge of gross neglect or neglect under this section that the actor's conduct was committed in good faith solely because the actor was ordered to commit the conduct by a person with supervisory authority over the actor.

(C) Whoever violates division (A)(1) of this section is guilty of patient abuse, a felony of the fourth degree. If the offender previously has been convicted of, or pleaded guilty to, any violation of this section, patient abuse is a felony of the third degree.

(D) Whoever violates division (A)(2) of this section is guilty of gross patient neglect, a misdemeanor of the first degree. If the offender previously has been convicted of, or pleaded guilty to, any violation of this section, gross patient neglect is a felony of the fifth degree.

(E) Whoever violates division (A)(3) of this section is guilty of patient neglect, a misdemeanor of the second degree. If the offender previously has been convicted of or pleaded guilty to any violation of this section, patient neglect is a felony of the fifth degree.

**HISTORY: 141 v H 566 (Eff 9-17-86); 146 v S 2. Eff 7-1-96.**

The effective date is set by section 6 of SB 2.

## § 2903.341 Patient endangerment.

(A) As used in this section:

(1) "MR/DD caretaker" means any MR/DD employee or any person who assumes the duty to provide for the care and protection of a mentally retarded person or a developmentally disabled person on a voluntary basis, by contract, through receipt of payment for care and protection, as a result of a family relationship, or by order of a court of competent jurisdiction. "MR/DD caretaker" includes a person who is an employee of a care facility and a person who is an employee of an entity under contract with a provider. "MR/DD caretaker" does not include a person who owns, operates, or administers a care facility or who is an agent of a care facility unless that person also personally provides care to persons with mental retardation or a developmental disability.

(2) "Mentally retarded person" and "developmentally disabled person" have the same meanings as in section 5123.01 of the Revised Code.

(3) "MR/DD employee" has the same meaning as in section 5123.50 of the Revised Code.

(B) No MR/DD caretaker shall create a substantial risk to the health or safety of a mentally retarded person or a developmentally disabled person. An MR/DD caretaker does not create a substantial risk to the health or safety of a mentally retarded person or a developmentally disabled person under this division when the MR/DD caretaker treats a physical or mental illness or defect of the mentally retarded person or developmentally disabled person by spiritual means through prayer alone, in accordance with the tenets of a recognized religious body.

(C) No person who owns, operates, or administers a care facility or who is an agent of a care facility shall condone, or knowingly permit, any conduct by an MR/DD caretaker who is employed by or under the control of the owner, operator, administrator, or agent that is in violation of division (B) of this section and that involves a mentally retarded person or a developmentally disabled person who is under the care of the owner, operator, administrator, or agent. A person who relies upon treatment by spiritual means through prayer alone, in accordance with the tenets of a recognized religious denomination, shall not be considered endangered under this division for that reason alone.

(D)(1) It is an affirmative defense to a charge of a violation of division (B) or (C) of this section that the actor's conduct was committed in good faith solely because the actor was ordered to commit the conduct by a person to whom one of the following applies:

(a) The person has supervisory authority over the actor.

(b) The person has authority over the actor's conduct pursuant to a contract for the provision of services.

(2) It is an affirmative defense to a charge of a violation of division (C) of this section that the person who owns, operates, or administers a care facility or who is an agent of a care facility and who is charged with the violation is following the individual service plan for the involved mentally retarded person or a developmentally disabled person or that the admission, discharge, and transfer rule set forth in the Administrative Code is being followed.

(3) It is an affirmative defense to a charge of a violation of division (C) of this section that the actor did not have readily available a means to prevent either the harm to the person with mental retardation or a developmental disability or the death of such a person and the actor took reasonable steps to summon aid.

(E)(1) Except as provided in division (E)(2) or (E)(3) of this section, whoever violates division (B) or (C) of this section is guilty of patient endangerment, a misdemeanor of the first degree.

(2) If the offender previously has been convicted of, or pleaded guilty to, a violation of this section, patient endangerment is a felony of the fourth degree.

(3) If the violation results in serious physical harm to the person with mental retardation or a developmental disability, patient endangerment is a felony of the third degree.

**HISTORY: 150 v S 178, § 1, eff. 1-30-04.**

## § 2903.35 Filing false patient abuse or neglect complaints.

(A) No person shall knowingly make a false statement, or knowingly swear or affirm the truth of a false statement previously made, alleging a violation of section 2903.34 of the Revised Code, when the statement is made with purpose to incriminate another.

(B) Whoever violates this section is guilty of filing a false patient abuse or neglect complaint, a misdemeanor of the first degree.

**HISTORY: 141 v H 566. Eff 9-17-86.**

## § 2903.36 Discrimination, retaliation prohibited.

No care facility shall discharge or in any manner discriminate or retaliate against any person solely because such person, in good faith, filed a complaint, affidavit, or other document alleging a violation of section 2903.34 of the Revised Code.

**HISTORY: 141 v H 566. Eff 9-17-86.**

## § 2903.37 License revocation.

Any individual, who owns, operates, or administers, or who is an agent or employee of, a care facility, who is convicted of a felony violation of section 2903.34 of the Revised Code, and who is required to be licensed under any law of this state, shall have his license revoked in accordance with Chapter 119. of the Revised Code.

**HISTORY: 141 v H 566. Eff 9-17-86.**

# CHAPTER 2905: KIDNAPPING AND EXTORTION



## [KIDNAPPING AND RELATED OFFENSES]

### § 2905.01 Kidnapping.

(A) No person, by force, threat, or deception, or, in the case of a victim under the age of thirteen or mentally incompetent, by any means, shall remove another from the place where the other person is found or restrain the liberty of the other person, for any of the following purposes:

(1) To hold for ransom, or as a shield or hostage;

(2) To facilitate the commission of any felony or flight thereafter;

(3) To terrorize, or to inflict serious physical harm on the victim or another;

(4) To engage in sexual activity, as defined in section 2907.01 of the Revised Code, with the victim against the victim's will;

(5) To hinder, impede, or obstruct a function of government, or to force any action or concession on the part of governmental authority;

(6) To hold in a condition of involuntary servitude.

(B) No person, by force, threat, or deception, or, in the case of a victim under the age of thirteen or mentally incompetent, by any means, shall knowingly do any of the following, under circumstances that create a substantial risk of serious physical harm to the victim or, in the case of a minor victim, under circumstances that either create a substantial risk of serious physical harm to the victim or cause physical harm to the victim:

(1) Remove another from the place where the other person is found;

(2) Restrain another of the other person's liberty.

(C)(1) Whoever violates this section is guilty of kidnapping. Except as otherwise provided in this division or division (C)(2) or (3) of this section, kidnapping is a felony of the first degree. Except as otherwise provided in this division or division (C)(2) or (3) of this section, if an offender who violates division (A)(1) to (5), (B)(1), or (B)(2) of this section releases the victim in a safe place unharmed, kidnapping is a felony of the second degree.

(2) If the offender in any case also is convicted of or pleads guilty to a specification as described in section 2941.1422 of the Revised Code that was included in the indictment, count in the indictment, or information charging the offense, the court shall order the offender to make restitution as provided in division (B)(8) of section 2929.18 of the Revised Code and, except as otherwise provided in division (C)(3) of this section, shall sentence the offender to a mandatory prison term as provided in division (B)(7) of section 2929.14 of the Revised Code.

(3) If the victim of the offense is less than thirteen years of age and if the offender also is convicted of or pleads guilty to a sexual motivation specification that was included in the indictment, count in the indictment, or information charging the offense, kidnapping is a felony of the first degree, and, notwithstanding the definite sentence provided for a felony of the first degree in section 2929.14 of the Revised Code, the offender shall be sentenced pursuant to section 2971.03 of the Revised Code as follows:

(a) Except as otherwise provided in division (C)(3)(b) of this section, the offender shall be sentenced pursuant to that section to an indefinite prison term consisting of a minimum term of fifteen years and a maximum term of life imprisonment.

(b) If the offender releases the victim in a safe place unharmed, the offender shall be sentenced pursuant to that section to an indefinite term consisting of a minimum term of ten years and a maximum term of life imprisonment.

(D) As used in this section:

(1) "Involuntary servitude" has the same meaning as in section 2905.31 of the Revised Code.

(2) "Sexual motivation specification" has the same meaning as in section 2971.01 of the Revised Code.

**HISTORY: 134 v H 511 (Eff 1-1-74); 139 v S 199 (Eff 1-5-83); 146 v S 2. Eff 7-1-96; 152 v S 10, § 1, eff. 1-1-08; 152 v H 280, § 1, eff. 4-7-09; 153 v S 235, § 1, eff. 3-24-11; 2011 HB 86, § 1, eff. Sept. 30, 2011.**

The effective date is set by § 3 of 152 v S 10.

**Not analogous to former RC § 2905.01 (Bureau of Code Revision, 10-1-53), repealed 134 v H 511, § 2, eff 1-1-74.**

The effective date is set by section 6 of SB 2.

### § 2905.02 Abduction.

(A) No person, without privilege to do so, shall knowingly do any of the following:

(1) By force or threat, remove another from the place where the other person is found;

(2) By force or threat, restrain the liberty of another person under circumstances that create a risk of physical harm to the victim or place the other person in fear;

(3) Hold another in a condition of involuntary servitude.

(B) No person, with a sexual motivation, shall violate division (A) of this section.

(C) Whoever violates this section is guilty of abduction. A violation of division (A)(1) or (2) of this section or a violation of division (B) of this section involving conduct of the type described in division (A)(1) or (2) of this section is a felony of the third degree. A violation of division (A)(3) of this section or a violation of division (B) of this section involving conduct of the type described in division (A)(3) of this section is a felony of the second degree. If the offender in any case also is convicted of or pleads guilty to a specification as described in section 2941.1422 of the Revised Code that was included in the indictment, count in the indictment, or information charging the offense, the court shall sentence the offender to a mandatory prison term as provided in division (B)(7) of section 2929.14 of the Revised Code and shall order the offender to make restitution as provided in division (B)(8) of section 2929.18 of the Revised Code.

(D) As used in this section:

(1) "Involuntary servitude" has the same meaning as in section 2905.31 of the Revised Code.

(2) "Sexual motivation" has the same meaning as in section 2971.01 of the Revised Code.

**HISTORY: 134 v H 511 (Eff 1-1-74); 139 v S 199 (Eff 7-1-83); 146 v S 2. Eff 7-1-96; 152 v S 10, § 1, eff. 1-1-08; 152 v H 280, § 1, eff. 4-7-09; 153 v S 235, § 1, eff. 3-24-11; 2011 HB 86, § 1, eff. Sept. 30, 2011.**

The effective date is set by § 3 of 152 v S 10.

**Not analogous to former RC § 2905.02 (RS §§ 6816, 6817; S&C 404; 72 v 93; 84 v 65; 91 v 61; 92 v 54; 95 v 344; GC § 12413; Bureau of Code Revision, 10-1-53), repealed 134 v H 511, § 2, eff 1-1-74.**

The effective date is set by section 6 of SB 2.

## § 2905.03 Unlawful restraint.

(A) No person, without privilege to do so, shall knowingly restrain another of the other person's liberty.

(B) No person, without privilege to do so and with a sexual motivation, shall knowingly restrain another of the other person's liberty.

(C) Whoever violates this section is guilty of unlawful restraint, a misdemeanor of the third degree.

(D) As used in this section, "sexual motivation" has the same meaning as in section 2971.01 of the Revised Code.

**HISTORY: 134 v H 511. Eff 1-1-74; 152 v S 10, § 1, eff. 1-1-08.**

The effective date is set by § 3 of 152 v S 10.

**Not analogous to former RC § 2905.03 (RS §§ 6816, 6817; S&C 404; 72 v 93; 84 v 65; 91 v 61; 92 v 54; 95 v 344; GC § 12414; Bureau of Code Revision, 10-1-53), repealed 134 v H 511, § 2, eff 1-1-74.**

**Analogous to former RC § 2921.08 (RS § 6826; 69 v 189; 73 v 249; 95 v 69; 97 v 306; GC § 12426; Bureau of Code Revision, 10-1-53), repealed 134 v H 511, § 2, eff 1-1-74.**

The effective date is set by section 4 of HB 511.

## § 2905.031 Repealed, 134 v H 511, § 2 [129 v 998]. Eff 1-1-74.

This section concerned rape of a person under fourteen.

## § 2905.04 Repealed, 146 v S 2, § 2 [134 v H 511; 140 v S 321]. Eff 7-1-96.

This section defined child stealing. See provisions of RC § 2905.01.

The effective date is set by section 6 of SB 2.

## § 2905.041 Repealed, 134 v H 511, § 2 [129 v 998]. Eff 1-1-74.

This section concerned attempted rape of a person under fourteen.

## § 2905.05 Criminal child enticement.

(A) No person, by any means and without privilege to do so, shall knowingly solicit, coax, entice, or lure any child under fourteen years of age to accompany the person in any manner, including entering into any vehicle or onto any vessel, whether or not the offender knows the age of the child, if both of the following apply:

(1) The actor does not have the express or implied permission of the parent, guardian, or other legal custodian of the child in undertaking the activity.

(2) The actor is not a law enforcement officer, medic, firefighter, or other person who regularly provides emergency services, and is not an employee or agent of, or a volunteer acting under the direction of, any board of education, or the actor is any of such persons, but, at the time the actor undertakes the activity, the actor is not acting within the scope of the actor's lawful duties in that capacity.

(B) No person, with a sexual motivation, shall violate division (A) of this section.

(C) It is an affirmative defense to a charge under division (A) of this section that the actor undertook the activity in response to a bona fide emergency situation or that the actor undertook the activity in a reasonable belief that it was necessary to preserve the health, safety, or welfare of the child.

(D) Whoever violates this section is guilty of criminal child enticement, a misdemeanor of the first degree. If the offender previously has been convicted of a violation of this section, section 2907.02 or 2907.03 or former section 2907.12 of the Revised Code, or section 2905.01 or 2907.05 of the Revised Code when the victim of that prior offense was under seventeen years of age at the time of the offense, criminal child enticement is a felony of the fifth degree.

(E) As used in this section:

(1) "Sexual motivation" has the same meaning as in section 2971.01 of the Revised Code.

(2) "Vehicle" has the same meaning as in section 4501.01 of the Revised Code.

(3) "Vessel" has the same meaning as in section 1547.01 of the Revised Code.

**HISTORY: 140 v S 321 (Eff 4-9-85); 146 v S 2 (Eff 7-1-96); 148 v S 312. Eff 4-9-2001; 150 v S 160, § 1, eff. 4-11-05; 152 v S 10, § 1, eff. 1-1-08.**

The effective date is set by § 3 of 152 v S 10.

**Not analogous to former RC § 2905.05 (GC § 13444-24; 113 v 123(191), ch 23, § 24; Bureau of Code Revision, 10-1-53), repealed 134 v H 511, § 2, eff 1-1-74.**

The effective date is set by section 6 of SB 2.

## § 2905.06 Repealed, 134 v H 511, § 2 [RS §§ 7019—7021; S&C 404, 405, 430, 431; 29 v 144; 33 v

33; GC §§ 13023—13025; Bureau of Code Revision, 10-1-53]. Eff 1-1-74.

This section concerned carnal knowledge.

**§ 2905.07** Repealed, 134 v H 511, § 2 [RS §§ 7019—7021; S&C 404, 405, 430, 431; 29 v 144; 33 v 33; GC §§ 13023—13025; Bureau of Code Revision, 10-1-53]. Eff 1-1-74.

This section concerned incest.

**§ 2905.08** Repealed, 134 v H 511, § 2 [RS §§ 7019—7021; S&C 404, 405, 430, 431; 29 v 144; 33 v 33; GC §§ 13023—13025; Bureau of Code Revision, 10-1-53]. Eff 1-1-74.

This section concerned adultery.

**§ 2905.09** Repealed, 134 v H 511, § 2 [RS §§ 7022, 7023; S&S 273; S&C 452; 56 v 158; 65 v 204; 82 v 209; 84 v 43; 92 v 207; GC §§ 13026, 13027; Bureau of Code Revision, 10-1-53; 126 v 575]. Eff 1-1-74.

This section dealt with seduction under promise to marry.

**§ 2905.10** Repealed, 134 v H 511, § 2 [RS §§ 7022, 7023; S&S 273; S&C 452; 56 v 158; 65 v 204; 82 v 209; 84 v 43; 92 v 207; GC §§ 13026, 13027; Bureau of Code Revision, 10-1-53; 126 v 575]. Eff 1-1-74.

This section dealt with inducing or permitting illicit intercourse.

## [EXTORTION]

### § 2905.11 Extortion.

(A) No person, with purpose to obtain any valuable thing or valuable benefit or to induce another to do an unlawful act, shall do any of the following:

(1) Threaten to commit any felony;

(2) Threaten to commit any offense of violence;

(3) Violate section 2903.21 or 2903.22 of the Revised Code;

(4) Utter or threaten any calumny against any person;

(5) Expose or threaten to expose any matter tending to subject any person to hatred, contempt, or ridicule, or to damage any person's personal or business repute, or to impair any person's credit.

(B) Whoever violates this section is guilty of extortion, a felony of the third degree.

(C) As used in this section, "threat" includes a direct threat and a threat by innuendo.

**HISTORY: 134 v H 511 (Eff 1-1-74); 139 v S 199 (Eff 7-1-83); 146 v S 2. Eff 7-1-96.**

**Not analogous to former RC § 2905.11 (RS § 7023a; 82 v 209; GC § 13028; Bureau of Code Revision, 10-1-53), repealed 134 v H 511, § 2, eff 1-1-74.**

The effective date is set by section 6 of SB 2.

### § 2905.12 Coercion.

(A) No person, with purpose to coerce another into taking or refraining from action concerning which the other person has a legal freedom of choice, shall do any of the following:

(1) Threaten to commit any offense;

(2) Utter or threaten any calumny against any person;

(3) Expose or threaten to expose any matter tending to subject any person to hatred, contempt, or ridicule, to damage any person's personal or business repute, or to impair any person's credit;

(4) Institute or threaten criminal proceedings against any person;

(5) Take, withhold, or threaten to take or withhold official action, or cause or threaten to cause official action to be taken or withheld.

(B) Divisions (A)(4) and (5) of this section shall not be construed to prohibit a prosecutor or court from doing any of the following in good faith and in the interests of justice:

(1) Offering or agreeing to grant, or granting immunity from prosecution pursuant to section 2945.44 of the Revised Code;

(2) In return for a plea of guilty to one or more offenses charged or to one or more other or lesser offenses, or in return for the testimony of the accused in a case to which the accused is not a party, offering or agreeing to dismiss, or dismissing one or more charges pending against an accused, or offering or agreeing to impose, or imposing a certain sentence or modification of sentence;

(3) Imposing a community control sanction on certain conditions, including without limitation requiring the offender to make restitution or redress to the victim of the offense.

(C) It is an affirmative defense to a charge under division (A)(3), (4), or (5) of this section that the actor's conduct was a reasonable response to the circumstances that occasioned it, and that the actor's purpose was limited to any of the following:

(1) Compelling another to refrain from misconduct or to desist from further misconduct;

(2) Preventing or redressing a wrong or injustice;

(3) Preventing another from taking action for which the actor reasonably believed the other person to be disqualified;

(4) Compelling another to take action that the actor reasonably believed the other person to be under a duty to take.

(D) Whoever violates this section is guilty of coercion, a misdemeanor of the second degree.

(E) As used in this section:

(1) "Threat" includes a direct threat and a threat by innuendo.

(2) "Community control sanction" has the same meaning as in section 2929.01 of the Revised Code.

**HISTORY: 134 v H 511. Eff 1-1-74; 149 v H 490, § 1, eff. 1-1-04.**

The effective date is set by section 4 of HB 490.

**Not analogous to former RC § 2905.12 (RS § 6824; S&S 275; 65 v 87; 79 v 132; 95 v 100; GC § 13029; Bureau of Code Revision, 10-1-53), repealed 134 v H 511, § 2, eff 1-1-74.**

**§ 2905.13** Repealed, 134 v H 511, § 2 [RS §§ 7024, 7025; S&C 879; 53 v 140; 75 v 142; 83 v 92; 85 v 137; 92 v 398; GC §§ 13030—13031-1; 101 v 50; 103 v 188; Bureau of Code Revision, 10-1-53]. Eff 1-1-74.

This section concerned intercourse with female pupil and prostitution.

**§ 2905.14** Repealed, 134 v H 511, § 2 [RS §§ 7024, 7025; S&C 879; 53 v 140; 75 v 142; 83 v 92; 85 v 137; 92 v 398; GC §§ 13030—13031-1; 101 v 50; 103 v 188; Bureau of Code Revision, 10-1-53]. Eff 1-1-74.

This section concerned intercourse with female pupil and prostitution.

**§ 2905.15** Repealed, 134 v H 511, § 2 [RS §§ 7024, 7025; S&C 879; 53 v 140; 75 v 142; 83 v 92; 85 v 137; 92 v 398; GC §§ 13030—13031-1; 101 v 50; 103 v 188; Bureau of Code Revision, 10-1-53]. Eff 1-1-74.

This section concerned intercourse with female pupil and prostitution.

**§ 2905.16** Repealed, 134 v H 511, § 2 [GC §§ 13031-2, 13031-3, 13031-9; 101 v 50; 103 v 188; Bureau of Code Revision, 10-1-53]. Eff 1-1-74.

This section concerned prostitution.

**§ 2905.17** Repealed, 134 v H 511, § 2 [GC §§ 13031-2, 13031-3, 13031-9; 101 v 50; 103 v 188; Bureau of Code Revision, 10-1-53]. Eff 1-1-74.

This section concerned prostitution.

**§ 2905.18** Repealed, 134 v H 511, § 2 [GC §§ 13031-2, 13031-3, 13031-9; 101 v 50; 103 v 188; Bureau of Code Revision, 10-1-53]. Eff 1-1-74.

This section concerned prostitution.

**§ 2905.19** Repealed, 134 v H 511, § 2 [GC §§ 13031-4, 13031-5; 101 v 50; 103 v 188; Bureau of Code Revision, 10-1-53]. Eff 1-1-74.

This section concerned prostitution.

**§ 2905.20** Repealed, 134 v H 511, § 2 [GC §§ 13031-4, 13031-5; 101 v 50; 103 v 188; Bureau of Code Revision, 10-1-53]. Eff 1-1-74.

This section concerned prostitution.

## [EXTORTIONATE EXTENSION OF CREDIT; CRIMINAL USURY]

### § 2905.21 Definitions.

As used in sections 2905.21 to 2905.24 of the Revised Code:

(A) "To extend credit" means to make or renew any loan, or to enter into any agreement, express or implied, for the repayment or satisfaction of any debt or claim, regardless of whether the extension of credit is acknowledged or disputed, valid or invalid, and however arising.

(B) "Creditor" means any person who extends credit, or any person claiming by, under, or through such a person.

(C) "Debtor" means any person who receives an extension of credit, any person who guarantees the repayment of an extension of credit, or any person who in any manner undertakes to indemnify the creditor against loss resulting from the failure of any recipient to repay an extension of credit.

(D) "Repayment" of an extension of credit means the repayment, satisfaction, or discharge in whole or in part of any debt or claim, acknowledged or disputed, valid or invalid, resulting from or in connection with that extension of credit.

(E) "Collect an extension of credit" means an attempt to collect from a debtor all or part of an amount due from the extension of credit.

(F) "Extortionate extension of credit" means any extension of credit with respect to which it is the understanding of the creditor and the debtor at the time it is made that delay in making repayment or failure to make repayment will result in the use of an extortionate means or if the debtor at a later time learns that failure to make repayment will result in the use of extortionate means.

(G) "Extortionate means" is any means that involves the use, or an express or implicit threat of use, of violence or other criminal means to cause harm to the person or property of the debtor or any member of his family.

(H) "Criminal usury" means illegally charging, taking, or receiving any money or other property as interest on an extension of credit at a rate exceeding twenty-five per cent per annum or the equivalent rate for a longer or shorter period, unless either:

(1) The rate of interest is otherwise authorized by law;

(2) The creditor and the debtor, or all the creditors and all the debtors are members of the same immediate family.

(I) "Immediate family" means a person's spouse residing in the person's household, brothers and sisters of the whole or of the half blood, and children, including adopted children.

**HISTORY: 137 v H 88. Eff 10-9-78.**

**Not analogous to former RC § 2905.21 (GC § 13031-6; 101 v 50, § 6; 103 v 188; Bureau of Code Revision, 10-1-53), repealed 134 v H 511, § 2, eff 1-1-74.**

### § 2905.22 Extortionate extension of credit; criminal usury.

(A) No person shall:

(1) Knowingly make or participate in an extortionate extension of credit;

(2) Knowingly engage in criminal usury;

(3) Possess any writing, paper, instrument, or article used to record criminally usurious transactions, knowing that the contents record a criminally usurious transaction.

(B) Whoever violates division (A)(1) or (2) of this section is guilty of a felony of the fourth degree. Whoever violates division (A)(3) of this section is guilty of a misdemeanor of the first degree.

**HISTORY: 137 v H 88 (Eff 10-9-78); 146 v S 2. Eff 7-1-96.**

**Not analogous to former RC § 2905.22 (GC § 13031-7; 101 v 50; Bureau of Code Revision, 10-1-53), repealed 134 v H 511, § 2, eff 1-1-74.**

The effective date is set by section 6 of SB 2.

### § 2905.23 Probable cause to believe that extension of credit was extortionate.

In any prosecution under sections 2905.21 to 2905.24 of the Revised Code, if it is shown that any of the following factors were present in connection with the extension of credit, there is probable cause to believe that the extension of credit was extortionate:

(A) The extension of credit was made at a rate of interest in excess of that established for criminal usury;

(B) At the time credit was extended, the debtor reasonably believed that:

(1) One or more extensions of credit by the creditor were collected or attempted to be collected by extortionate means, or the nonrepayment thereof was punished by extortionate means;

(2) The creditor had a reputation for the use of extortionate means to collect extensions of credit or punish the nonrepayment thereof.

**HISTORY: 137 v H 88. Eff 10-9-78.**

**Not analogous to former RC § 2905.23 (GC § 13031-10; 103 v 188; Bureau of Code Revision, 10-1-53), repealed 134 v H 511, § 2, eff 1-1-74.**

## § 2905.24 Evidence of implicit threat as means of collection.

In any prosecution under sections 2905.21 to 2905.24 of the Revised Code, for the purpose of showing an implicit threat as a means of collection, evidence may be introduced tending to show that one or more extensions of credit by the creditor were, to the knowledge of the person against whom the implicit threat is alleged to have been made, collected, or attempted to be collected by extortionate means or that the nonrepayment thereof was punished by extortionate means.

**HISTORY: 137 v H 88. Eff 10-9-78.**

**Not analogous to former RC § 2905.24 (GC § 13031-8; 101 v 50; Bureau of Code Revision, 10-1-53), repealed 134 v H 511, § 2, eff 1-1-74.**

## § 2905.25 Repealed, 134 v H 511, § 2 [GC §§ 13031-11, 13031-13, 13031-14; 103 v 188; 108 v PtI, 730; Bureau of Code Revision, 10-1-53; 130 v PtII, 143, 144]. Eff 1-1-74.

This section concerned prostitution.

## § 2905.26 Repealed, 134 v H 511, § 2 [GC §§ 13031-11, 13031-13, 13031-14; 103 v 188; 108 v PtI, 730; Bureau of Code Revision, 10-1-53; 130 v PtII, 143, 144]. Eff 1-1-74.

This section concerned prostitution.

## § 2905.27 Repealed, 134 v H 511, § 2 [GC §§ 13031-11, 13031-13, 13031-14; 103 v 188; 108 v PtI, 730; Bureau of Code Revision, 10-1-53; 130 v PtII, 143, 144]. Eff 1-1-74.

This section concerned prostitution.

## § 2905.28 Repealed, 134 v H 511, § 2 [RS § 7026; S&S 289; 59 v 32; 89 v 127; GC §§ 13031-15, 13031-17, 13032; 108 v PtI, 730; 118 v 301, 121 v 557; Bureau of Code Revision, 10-1-53; 129 v 1670; 130 v PtII, 143, 144, 659; 131 v 672]. Eff 1-1-74.

This section concerned prostitution, indecent exposure, and obscene language.

## § 2905.29 Repealed, 134 v H 511, § 2 [RS § 7026; S&S 289; 59 v 32; 89 v 127; GC §§ 13031-15, 13031-17, 13032; 108 v PtI, 730; 118 v 301, 121 v 557; Bureau of Code Revision, 10-1-53; 129 v 1670; 130 v PtII, 143, 144, 659; 131 v 672]. Eff 1-1-74.

This section concerned prostitution, indecent exposure, and obscene language.

## § 2905.30 Repealed, 134 v H 511, § 2 [RS § 7026; S&S 289; 59 v 32; 89 v 127; GC §§ 13031-15, 13031-17, 13032; 108 v PtI, 730; 118 v 301, 121 v 557; Bureau of Code Revision, 10-1-53; 129 v 1670; 130 v PtII, 143, 144, 659; 131 v 672]. Eff 1-1-74.

This section concerned prostitution, indecent exposure, and obscene language.

## § 2905.301 Repealed, 134 v H 511, § 2 [130 v 659]. Eff 1-1-74.

This section concerned obscene language.

[INVOLUNTARY SERVITUDE]

## § 2905.31 Involuntary servitude.

As used in sections 2905.31 to 2905.33 of the Revised Code:

(A) "Involuntary servitude" means being compelled to perform labor or services for another against one's will.

(B) "Material that is obscene, sexually oriented, or nudity oriented" and "performance that is obscene, sexually oriented, or nudity oriented" have the same meanings as in section 2929.01 of the Revised Code.

**HISTORY: 153 v S 235, § 1, eff. 3-24-11.**

**Not analogous to former RC § 2905.31 (RS §§ 7029, 7030; S&S 272; 64 v 202; GC §§ 13032-1, 13033, 13034; 118 v 428; 121 v 557(573); Bureau of Code Revision, 10-1-53), repealed 134 v H 511, § 2, eff 1-1-74.**

## § 2905.32 Compulsion to involuntary servitude.

(A) No person shall knowingly recruit, lure, entice, isolate, harbor, transport, provide, obtain, or maintain, or knowingly attempt to recruit, lure, entice, isolate, harbor, transport, provide, obtain, or maintain, another person knowing that the person will be subjected to involuntary servitude or be compelled to engage in sexual activity for hire, engage in a performance that is obscene, sexually oriented, or nudity oriented, or be a model or participant in the production of material that is obscene, sexually oriented, or nudity oriented.

(B) For a prosecution under this section, the element "compelled" does not require that the compulsion be openly displayed or physically exerted. The element "compelled" has been established if the state proves that the victim's will was overcome by force, fear, duress, or intimidation.

(C) In a prosecution under this section, proof that the defendant engaged in sexual activity with any person, or solicited sexual activity with any person, whether or not for hire, without more, does not constitute a violation of this section.

(D) A prosecution for a violation of this section does not preclude a prosecution of a violation of any other section of the Revised Code. One or more acts, a series of acts, or a course of behavior that can be prosecuted under this section or any other section of the Revised Code may be prosecuted under this section, the other section of the Revised Code, or both sections. However, if an offender is convicted of or pleads guilty to a violation of this section and also is convicted of or pleads guilty to any other offense based on the same conduct involving the same victim that was the basis of the violation of this section, the two offenses are allied offenses of similar import under section 2941.25 of the Revised Code.

(E) Whoever violates this section is guilty of trafficking in persons, a felony of the second degree.

**HISTORY: 153 v S 235, § 1, eff. 3-24-11.**

**Not analogous to former RC § 2905.32 (RS §§ 7029, 7030; S&S 272; 64 v 202; GC §§ 13032-1, 13033, 13034; 118 v 428; 121 v 557(573); Bureau of Code Revision, 10-1-53), repealed 134 v H 511, § 2, eff 1-1-74.**

## § 2905.33 Unlawful conduct with respect to documents.

(A) No person, without privilege to do so, shall knowingly destroy, conceal, remove, confiscate, or possess any actual or purported government identification document or passport of another person in the course of a violation of, with intent to violate, or with intent to facilitate a violation of section 2905.01, 2905.02, 2905.32, 2907.21, 2907.22, 2907.32, 2907.321 [2907.32.1], 2907.322 [2907.32.2], or 2907.323 [2907.32.3] of the Revised Code.

(B) Whoever violates this section is guilty of unlawful conduct with respect to documents, a felony of the third degree.

**HISTORY: 153 v S 235, § 1, eff. 3-24-11.**

**Not analogous to former RC § 2905.32 (RS §§ 7029, 7030; S&S 272; 64 v 202; GC §§ 13032-1, 13033, 13034; 118 v 428; 121 v 557(573); Bureau of Code Revision, 10-1-53), repealed 134 v H 511, § 2, eff 1-1-74.**

## § 2905.34 Repealed, 134 v H 511, § 2 [RS § 7027; 73 v 158; 82 v 184; 91 v 330; GC § 13035; 118 v 420; 120 v 230; Bureau of Code Revision, 10-1-53; 131 v 672; 133 v H 84]. Eff 1-1-74.

This section prohibited the selling, exhibiting, and possessing of obscene literature or drugs for criminal purposes.

## § 2905.341 Repealed, 133 v H 84, § 2 [126 v 1039]. Eff 9-15-70.

This section prohibited conditional sales of obscene magazines, exhibition of films, and depicting public disorder.

## § 2905.342 Repealed, 133 v H 84, § 2 [126 v 1039]. Eff 9-15-70.

This section prohibited conditional sales of obscene magazines, exhibition of films, and depicting public disorder.

## § 2905.343 Repealed, 133 v H 84, § 2 [126 v 1039]. Eff 9-15-70.

This section prohibited conditional sales of obscene magazines, exhibition of films, and depicting public disorder.

## § 2905.35 Repealed, 134 v H 511, § 2 [133 v H 84]. Eff 1-1-74.

This section concerned obscene material.

## § 2905.36 Repealed, 134 v H 511, § 2 [133 v H 84]. Eff 1-1-74.

This section concerned obscene material.

## § 2905.37 Repealed, 134 v H 511, § 2 [133 v H 84]. Eff 1-1-74.

This section concerned obscene material.

## § 2905.371 Repealed, 133 v H 84, § 2 [129 v 1400]. Eff 9-15-70.

This section provided immunity from the provisions of former RC §§ 2905.34 to 2905.37 and RC § 2933.21.

## § 2905.38 Repealed, 134 v H 511, § 2 [133 v H 84; 135 v S 62, eff 10-31-73]. Eff 1-1-74.

This section concerned obscene matter.

## § 2905.39 Repealed, 133 v H 84, § 2 [RS §§ 7027-1—7027-3; 86 v 320; 98 v 303; GC §§ 13039—13041; 100 v 91; Bureau of Code Revision, 10-1-53]. Eff 9-15-70.

This section concerned lewd pictures and exhibitions.

## § 2905.40 Repealed, 133 v H 84, § 2 [RS §§ 7027-1—7027-3; 86 v 320; 98 v 303; GC §§ 13039—13041; 100 v 91; Bureau of Code Revision, 10-1-53]. Eff 9-15-70.

This section concerned lewd pictures and exhibitions.

## § 2905.41 Repealed, 133 v H 84, § 2 [RS §§ 7027-1—7027-3; 86 v 320; 98 v 303; GC §§ 13039—13041; 100 v 91; Bureau of Code Revision, 10-1-53]. Eff 9-15-70.

This section concerned lewd pictures and exhibitions.

## § 2905.42 Repealed, 134 v H 511, § 2 [RS §§ 6989, 7018, 7021-1; S&C 404, 1396; 9 v 115; 33 v 33;

82 v 241; 86 v 251; GC §§ 13022, 13042, 13043; 121 v 417; Bureau of Code Revision, 10-1-53; 129 v 252]. Eff 1-1-74.

This section concerned enticing to abandon marriage, bigamy, and sodomy.

**§ 2905.43** Repealed, 134 v H 511, § 2 [RS §§ 6989, 7018, 7021-1; S&C 404, 1396; 9 v 115; 33 v 33; 82 v 241; 86 v 251; GC §§ 13022, 13042, 13043; 121 v 417; Bureau of Code Revision, 10-1-53; 129 v 252]. Eff 1-1-74.

This section concerned enticing to abandon marriage, bigamy, and sodomy.

**§ 2905.44** Repealed, 134 v H 511, § 2 [RS §§ 6989, 7018, 7021-1; S&C 404, 1396; 9 v 115; 33 v 33; 82 v 241; 86 v 251; GC §§ 13022, 13042, 13043; 121 v 417; Bureau of Code Revision, 10-1-53; 129 v 252]. Eff 1-1-74.

This section concerned enticing to abandon marriage, bigamy, and sodomy.

# CHAPTER 2907: SEX OFFENSES



[IN GENERAL]

## § 2907.01 Definitions.

As used in sections 2907.01 to 2907.38 of the Revised Code:

(A) "Sexual conduct" means vaginal intercourse between a male and female; anal intercourse, fellatio, and cunnilingus between persons regardless of sex; and, without privilege to do so, the insertion, however slight, of any part of the body or any instrument, apparatus, or other object into the vaginal or anal opening of another. Penetration, however slight, is sufficient to complete vaginal or anal intercourse.

(B) "Sexual contact" means any touching of an erogenous zone of another, including without limitation the thigh, genitals, buttock, pubic region, or, if the person is a female, a breast, for the purpose of sexually arousing or gratifying either person.

(C) "Sexual activity" means sexual conduct or sexual contact, or both.

(D) "Prostitute" means a male or female who promiscuously engages in sexual activity for hire, regardless of whether the hire is paid to the prostitute or to another.

(E) "Harmful to juveniles" means that quality of any material or performance describing or representing nudity, sexual conduct, sexual excitement, or sado-masochistic abuse in any form to which all of the following apply:

(1) The material or performance, when considered as a whole, appeals to the prurient interest of juveniles in sex.

(2) The material or performance is patently offensive to prevailing standards in the adult community as a whole with respect to what is suitable for juveniles.

(3) The material or performance, when considered as a whole, lacks serious literary, artistic, political, and scientific value for juveniles.

(F) When considered as a whole, and judged with reference to ordinary adults or, if it is designed for sexual deviates or other specially susceptible group, judged with reference to that group, any material or performance is "obscene" if any of the following apply:

(1) Its dominant appeal is to prurient interest;

(2) Its dominant tendency is to arouse lust by displaying or depicting sexual activity, masturbation, sexual excitement, or nudity in a way that tends to represent human beings as mere objects of sexual appetite;

(3) Its dominant tendency is to arouse lust by displaying or depicting bestiality or extreme or bizarre violence, cruelty, or brutality;

(4) Its dominant tendency is to appeal to scatological interest by displaying or depicting human bodily functions of elimination in a way that inspires disgust or revulsion in persons with ordinary sensibilities, without serving any genuine scientific, educational, sociological, moral, or artistic purpose;

(5) It contains a series of displays or descriptions of sexual activity, masturbation, sexual excitement, nudity, bestiality, extreme or bizarre violence, cruelty, or brutality, or human bodily functions of elimination, the cumulative effect of which is a dominant tendency to appeal to prurient or scatological interest, when the appeal to such an interest is primarily for its own sake or for commercial exploitation, rather than primarily for a genuine scientific, educational, sociological, moral, or artistic purpose.

(G) "Sexual excitement" means the condition of human male or female genitals when in a state of sexual stimulation or arousal.

(H) "Nudity" means the showing, representation, or depiction of human male or female genitals, pubic area, or buttocks with less than a full, opaque covering, or of a female breast with less than a full, opaque covering of any portion thereof below the top of the nipple, or of covered male genitals in a discernibly turgid state.

(I) "Juvenile" means an unmarried person under the age of eighteen.

(J) "Material" means any book, magazine, newspaper, pamphlet, poster, print, picture, figure, image, description, motion picture film, phonographic record, or tape, or other tangible thing capable of arousing interest through sight, sound, or touch and includes an image or text appearing on a computer monitor, television screen, liquid crystal display, or similar display device or an image or text recorded on a computer hard disk, computer floppy disk, compact disk, magnetic tape, or similar data storage device.

(K) "Performance" means any motion picture, preview, trailer, play, show, skit, dance, or other exhibition performed before an audience.

(L) "Spouse" means a person married to an offender at the time of an alleged offense, except that such person shall not be considered the spouse when any of the following apply:

(1) When the parties have entered into a written separation agreement authorized by section 3103.06 of the Revised Code;

(2) During the pendency of an action between the parties for annulment, divorce, dissolution of marriage, or legal separation;

(3) In the case of an action for legal separation, after the effective date of the judgment for legal separation.

(M) "Minor" means a person under the age of eighteen.

(N) "Mental health client or patient" has the same meaning as in section 2305.51 of the Revised Code.

(O) "Mental health professional" has the same meaning as in section 2305.115 [2305.11.5] of the Revised Code.

(P) "Sado-masochistic abuse" means flagellation or torture by or upon a person or the condition of being fettered, bound, or otherwise physically restrained.

**HISTORY: 134 v H 511 (Eff 1-1-74); 136 v S 144 (Eff 8-27-75); 142 v H 51 (Eff 3-17-89); 143 v H 514 (Eff 1-1-91); 146 v H 445 (Eff 9-3-96); 147 v H 32 (Eff 3-10-98); 149 v S 9 (Eff 5-14-2002); 149 v H 8. Eff 8-5-2002; 149 v H 490, § 1, eff. 1-1-04; 151 v H 95, § 1, eff. 8-3-06; 151 v H 23, § 1, eff. 8-17-06; 152 v S 10, § 1, eff. 1-1-08.**

The effective date is set by § 3 of 152 v S 10.

The provisions of § 6 of 152 v S 10 read as follows:

SECTION 6. Section 2907.01 of the Revised Code is presented in this act as a composite of the section as amended by both Am. Sub. H.B. 23 and Am. Sub. H.B. 95 of the 126th General Assembly. * * * The General Assembly, applying the principle stated in division (B) of section 1.52 of the Revised Code that amendments are to be harmonized if reasonably capable of simultaneous operation, finds that the composites are the resulting versions of the sections in effect prior to the effective date of the sections as presented in this act.

The effective date is set by section 4 of HB 490.

The provisions of § 5 of HB 490 (149 v —) read as follows:

SECTION 5. Section 2907.01 of the Revised Code is presented in this act as a composite of the section as amended by both Sub. H.B. 8 and Am. Sub. S.B. 9 of the 124th General Assembly. The General Assembly, applying the principle stated in division (B) of section 1.52 of the Revised Code that amendments are to be harmonized if reasonably capable of simultaneous operation, finds that the specified composite is the resulting version of the specified sections in effect prior to the effective date of the section as presented in this act.

**Not analogous to former RC § 2907.01 (RS § 6830-3; 95 v 649; GC § 13387; Bureau of Code Revision, 10-1-53), repealed 134 v H 511, § 2, eff 1-1-74.**

## [SEXUAL ASSAULTS]

## § 2907.02 Rape.

(A)(1) No person shall engage in sexual conduct with another who is not the spouse of the offender or who is the spouse of the offender but is living separate and apart from the offender, when any of the following applies:

(a) For the purpose of preventing resistance, the offender substantially impairs the other person's judgment or control by administering any drug, intoxicant, or controlled substance to the other person surreptitiously or by force, threat of force, or deception.

(b) The other person is less than thirteen years of age, whether or not the offender knows the age of the other person.

(c) The other person's ability to resist or consent is substantially impaired because of a mental or physical condition or because of advanced age, and the offender knows or has reasonable cause to believe that the other person's ability to resist or consent is substantially impaired because of a mental or physical condition or because of advanced age.

(2) No person shall engage in sexual conduct with another when the offender purposely compels the other person to submit by force or threat of force.

(B) Whoever violates this section is guilty of rape, a felony of the first degree. If the offender under division (A)(1)(a) of this section substantially impairs the other person's judgment or control by administering any controlled substance described in section 3719.41 of the Revised Code to the other person surreptitiously or by force, threat of force, or deception, the prison term imposed upon the offender shall be one of the prison terms prescribed for a felony of the first degree in section 2929.14 of the Revised Code that is not less than five years. Except as otherwise provided in this division, notwithstanding sections 2929.11 to 2929.14 of the Revised Code, an offender under division (A)(1)(b) of this section shall be sentenced to a prison term or term of life imprisonment pursuant to section 2971.03 of the Revised Code. If an offender is convicted of or pleads guilty to a violation of division (A)(1)(b) of this section, if the offender was less than sixteen years of age at the time the offender committed the violation of that division, and if the offender during or immediately after the commission of the offense did not cause serious physical harm to the victim, the victim was ten years of age or older at the time of the commission of the violation, and the offender has not previously been convicted of or pleaded guilty to a violation of this section or a substantially similar existing or former law of this state, another state, or the United States, the court shall not sentence the offender to a prison term or term of life imprisonment pursuant to section 2971.03 of the Revised Code, and instead the court shall sentence the offender as otherwise provided in this division. If an offender under division (A)(1)(b) of this section previously has been convicted of or pleaded guilty to violating division (A)(1)(b) of this section or to violating an existing or former law of this state, another state, or the United States that is substantially similar to division (A)(1)(b) of this section, if the offender during or immediately after the commission of the offense caused serious physical harm to the victim, or if the victim under division (A)(1)(b) of this section is less than ten years of age, in lieu of sentencing the offender to a prison term or term of life imprisonment pursuant to section 2971.03 of the Revised Code, the court may impose upon the offender a term of life without parole. If the court imposes a term of life without parole pursuant to this division, division (F) of section 2971.03 of the Revised Code applies, and the offender automatically is classified a tier III sex offender/child-victim offender, as described in that division.

(C) A victim need not prove physical resistance to the offender in prosecutions under this section.

(D) Evidence of specific instances of the victim's sexual activity, opinion evidence of the victim's sexual activity, and reputation evidence of the victim's sexual activity shall not be admitted under this section unless it involves evidence of the origin of semen, pregnancy, or disease, or the victim's past sexual activity with the offender, and only to the extent that the court finds that the evidence is material to a fact at issue in the case and that its inflammatory or prejudicial nature does not outweigh its probative value.

Evidence of specific instances of the defendant's sexual activity, opinion evidence of the defendant's sexual activity, and reputation evidence of the defendant's sexual activity shall not be admitted under this section unless it involves evidence of the origin of semen, pregnancy, or disease, the defendant's past sexual activity with the victim, or is admissible against the defendant under section 2945.59 of the Revised Code, and only to the extent that the court finds that the evidence is material to a fact at issue in the case and that its inflammatory or prejudicial nature does not outweigh its probative value.

(E) Prior to taking testimony or receiving evidence of any sexual activity of the victim or the defendant in a proceeding under this section, the court shall resolve the admissibility of the proposed evidence in a hearing in chambers, which shall be held at or before preliminary hearing and not less than three days before trial, or for good cause shown during the trial.

(F) Upon approval by the court, the victim may be represented by counsel in any hearing in chambers or other proceeding to resolve the admissibility of evidence. If the victim is indigent or otherwise is unable to obtain the services of counsel, the court, upon request, may appoint counsel to represent the victim without cost to the victim.

(G) It is not a defense to a charge under division (A)(2) of this section that the offender and the victim were married or were cohabiting at the time of the commission of the offense.

**HISTORY: 134 v H 511 (Eff 1-1-74); 136 v S 144 (Eff 8-27-75); 139 v S 199 (Eff 7-1-83); 141 v H 475 (Eff 3-7-86); 145 v S 31 (Eff 9-27-93); 146 v S 2 (Eff 7-1-96); 147 v H 32 (Eff 3-10-98); 149 v H 485. Eff 6-13-2002; 151 v S 260, § 1, eff. 1-2-07; 152 v S 10, § 1, eff. 1-1-08.**

The effective date is set by § 3 of 152 v S 10.

The provisions of § 4 of 151 v S 260 read as follows:

SECTION 4. It is the intent of the General Assembly that the offense of child rape described in division (A)(1)(b) of section 2907.02 of the Revised Code, as enacted by this act, prevails over the offense of sexual battery committed against a person who is under the age of thirteen as described in section 2907.03 of the Revised Code in circumstances when a person violates the prohibitions of both offenses.

**Not analogous to former RC § 2907.02 (RS § 6831; S&C 406; S&S 267, 268; 33 v 33; 60 v 85; 66 v 122; 83 v 81; 86 v 3; GC § 12433; 113 v 541; Bureau of Code Revision, 10-1-53; 131 v 673), repealed 134 v H 511, § 2, eff 1-1-74.**

## § 2907.021 Repealed, 134 v H 511, § 2 [132 v H 179; 133 v H 1]. Eff 1-1-74.

This section concerned prohibition of manufacture, distribution or possession of fire bombs.

## § 2907.03 Sexual battery.

(A) No person shall engage in sexual conduct with another, not the spouse of the offender, when any of the following apply:

(1) The offender knowingly coerces the other person to submit by any means that would prevent resistance by a person of ordinary resolution.

(2) The offender knows that the other person's ability to appraise the nature of or control the other person's own conduct is substantially impaired.

(3) The offender knows that the other person submits because the other person is unaware that the act is being committed.

(4) The offender knows that the other person submits because the other person mistakenly identifies the offender as the other person's spouse.

(5) The offender is the other person's natural or adoptive parent, or a stepparent, or guardian, custodian, or person in loco parentis of the other person.

(6) The other person is in custody of law or a patient in a hospital or other institution, and the offender has supervisory or disciplinary authority over the other person.

(7) The offender is a teacher, administrator, coach, or other person in authority employed by or serving in a school for which the state board of education prescribes minimum standards pursuant to division (D) of section 3301.07 of the Revised Code, the other person is enrolled in or attends that school, and the offender is not enrolled in and does not attend that school.

(8) The other person is a minor, the offender is a teacher, administrator, coach, or other person in authority employed by or serving in an institution of higher education, and the other person is enrolled in or attends that institution.

(9) The other person is a minor, and the offender is the other person's athletic or other type of coach, is the other person's instructor, is the leader of a scouting troop of which the other person is a member, or is a person with

temporary or occasional disciplinary control over the other person.

(10) The offender is a mental health professional, the other person is a mental health client or patient of the offender, and the offender induces the other person to submit by falsely representing to the other person that the sexual conduct is necessary for mental health treatment purposes.

(11) The other person is confined in a detention facility, and the offender is an employee of that detention facility.

(12) The other person is a minor, the offender is a cleric, and the other person is a member of, or attends, the church or congregation served by the cleric.

(13) The other person is a minor, the offender is a peace officer, and the offender is more than two years older than the other person.

(B) Whoever violates this section is guilty of sexual battery. Except as otherwise provided in this division, sexual battery is a felony of the third degree. If the other person is less than thirteen years of age, sexual battery is a felony of the second degree, and the court shall impose upon the offender a mandatory prison term equal to one of the prison terms prescribed in section 2929.14 of the Revised Code for a felony of the second degree.

(C) As used in this section:

(1) "Cleric" has the same meaning as in section 2317.02 of the Revised Code.

(2) "Detention facility" has the same meaning as in section 2921.01 of the Revised Code.

(3) "Institution of higher education" means a state institution of higher education defined in section 3345.011 [3345.01.1] of the Revised Code, a private nonprofit college or university located in this state that possesses a certificate of authorization issued by the Ohio board of regents pursuant to Chapter 1713. of the Revised Code, or a school certified under Chapter 3332. of the Revised Code.

(4) "Peace officer" has the same meaning as in section 2935.01 of the Revised Code.

**HISTORY: 134 v H 511 (Eff 1-1-74); 145 v H 454 (Eff 7-19-94); 146 v S 2 (Eff 7-1-96); 147 v S 6 (Eff 6-20-97); 147 v H 32 (Eff 3-10-98); 149 v S 9 (Eff 5-14-2002); 149 v H 510. Eff 3-31-2003; 151 v S 17, § 1, eff. 8-3-06; 151 v H 95, § 1, eff. 8-3-06; 152 v H 209, § 1, eff. 4-7-09.**

The provisions of § 3 of 152 v H 209 read as follows:

SECTION 3. Section 2907.03 of the Revised Code is presented in this act as a composite of the section as amended by both Am. Sub. H.B. 95 and Am. Sub. S.B. 17 of the 126th General Assembly. The General Assembly, applying the principle stated in division (B) of section 1.52 of the Revised Code that amendments are to be harmonized if reasonably capable of simultaneous operation, finds that the composite is the resulting version of the section in effect prior to the effective date of the section as presented in this act.

See provisions of § 4 of 151 v S 260 following RC § 2907.02.

**Not analogous to former RC § 2907.03 (GC § 12433-1; 113 v 541; Bureau of Code Revision, 10-1-53), repealed 134 v H 511, § 2, eff 1-1-74.**

## § 2907.04 Unlawful sexual conduct with minor.

(A) No person who is eighteen years of age or older shall engage in sexual conduct with another, who is not the spouse of the offender, when the offender knows the other person is thirteen years of age or older but less than sixteen years of age, or the offender is reckless in that regard.

(B) Whoever violates this section is guilty of unlawful sexual conduct with a minor.

(1) Except as otherwise provided in divisions (B)(2), (3), and (4) of this section, unlawful sexual conduct with a minor is a felony of the fourth degree.

(2) Except as otherwise provided in division (B)(4) of this section, if the offender is less than four years older than the other person, unlawful sexual conduct with a minor is a misdemeanor of the first degree.

(3) Except as otherwise provided in division (B)(4) of this section, if the offender is ten or more years older than the other person, unlawful sexual conduct with a minor is a felony of the third degree.

(4) If the offender previously has been convicted of or pleaded guilty to a violation of section 2907.02, 2907.03, or 2907.04 of the Revised Code or a violation of former section 2907.12 of the Revised Code, unlawful sexual conduct with a minor is a felony of the second degree.

**HISTORY: 134 v H 511 (Eff 1-1-74); 143 v H 44 (Eff 7-24-90); 146 v S 2 (Eff 7-1-96); 148 v H 442. Eff 10-17-2000.**

**Not analogous to former RC § 2907.04 (RS § 6832; S&C 457a, 457b; 57 v 49; GC § 12434; 113 v 541; Bureau of Code Revision, 10-1-53), repealed 134 v H 511, § 2, eff 1-1-74.**

## § 2907.05 Gross sexual imposition.

(A) No person shall have sexual contact with another, not the spouse of the offender; cause another, not the spouse of the offender, to have sexual contact with the offender; or cause two or more other persons to have sexual contact when any of the following applies:

(1) The offender purposely compels the other person, or one of the other persons, to submit by force or threat of force.

(2) For the purpose of preventing resistance, the offender substantially impairs the judgment or control of the other person or of one of the other persons by administering any drug, intoxicant, or controlled substance to the other person surreptitiously or by force, threat of force, or deception.

(3) The offender knows that the judgment or control of the other person or of one of the other persons is substantially impaired as a result of the influence of any drug or intoxicant administered to the other person with the other person's consent for the purpose of any kind of medical or dental examination, treatment, or surgery.

(4) The other person, or one of the other persons, is less than thirteen years of age, whether or not the offender knows the age of that person.

(5) The ability of the other person to resist or consent or the ability of one of the other persons to resist or consent is substantially impaired because of a mental or physical condition or because of advanced age, and the offender knows or has reasonable cause to believe that the ability to resist or consent of the other person or of one of the other persons is substantially impaired because of a mental or physical condition or because of advanced age.

(B) No person shall knowingly touch the genitalia of another, when the touching is not through clothing, the other person is less than twelve years of age, whether or not the offender knows the age of that person, and the touching is done with an intent to abuse, humiliate, harass, degrade, or arouse or gratify the sexual desire of any person.

(C) Whoever violates this section is guilty of gross sexual imposition.

(1) Except as otherwise provided in this section, gross sexual imposition committed in violation of division (A)(1), (2), (3), or (5) of this section is a felony of the fourth degree. If the offender under division (A)(2) of this section substantially impairs the judgment or control of the other person or one of the other persons by administering any controlled substance described in section 3719.41 of the Revised Code to the person surreptitiously or by force, threat of force, or deception, gross sexual imposition committed in violation of division (A)(2) of this section is a felony of the third degree.

(2) Gross sexual imposition committed in violation of division (A)(4) or (B) of this section is a felony of the third degree. Except as otherwise provided in this division, for gross sexual imposition committed in violation of division (A)(4) or (B) of this section there is a presumption that a prison term shall be imposed for the offense. The court shall impose on an offender convicted of gross sexual imposition in violation of division (A)(4) or (B) of this section a mandatory prison term equal to one of the prison terms prescribed in section 2929.14 of the Revised Code for a felony of the third degree if either of the following applies:

(a) Evidence other than the testimony of the victim was admitted in the case corroborating the violation;

(b) The offender previously was convicted of or pleaded guilty to a violation of this section, rape, the former offense of felonious sexual penetration, or sexual battery, and the victim of the previous offense was less than thirteen years of age.

(D) A victim need not prove physical resistance to the offender in prosecutions under this section.

(E) Evidence of specific instances of the victim's sexual activity, opinion evidence of the victim's sexual activity, and reputation evidence of the victim's sexual activity shall not be admitted under this section unless it involves evidence of the origin of semen, pregnancy, or disease, or the victim's past sexual activity with the offender, and only to the extent that the court finds that the evidence is material to a fact at issue in the case and that its inflammatory or prejudicial nature does not outweigh its probative value.

Evidence of specific instances of the defendant's sexual activity, opinion evidence of the defendant's sexual activity, and reputation evidence of the defendant's sexual activity shall not be admitted under this section unless it involves evidence of the origin of semen, pregnancy, or disease, the defendant's past sexual activity with the victim, or is admissible against the defendant under section 2945.59 of the Revised Code, and only to the extent that the court finds that the evidence is material to a fact at issue in the case and that its inflammatory or prejudicial nature does not outweigh its probative value.

(F) Prior to taking testimony or receiving evidence of any sexual activity of the victim or the defendant in a proceeding under this section, the court shall resolve the admissibility of the proposed evidence in a hearing in chambers, which shall be held at or before preliminary hearing and not less than three days before trial, or for good cause shown during the trial.

(G) Upon approval by the court, the victim may be represented by counsel in any hearing in chambers or other proceeding to resolve the admissibility of evidence. If the victim is indigent or otherwise is unable to obtain the services of counsel, the court, upon request, may appoint counsel to represent the victim without cost to the victim.

**HISTORY: 134 v H 511 (Eff 1-1-74); 136 v S 144 (Eff 8-27-75); 137 v H 134 (Eff 8-8-77); 143 v H 208 (Eff 4-11-90); 145 v S 31 (Eff 9-27-93); 147 v H 32. Eff 3-10-98; 151 v H 95, § 1, eff. 8-3-06; 152 v S 10, § 1, eff. 1-1-08.**

The effective date is set by § 3 of 152 v S 10.

**Not analogous to former RC § 2907.05 (RS § 6833; S&C 425; 54 v 162; GC § 12435; 113 v 541; Bureau of Code Revision, 10-1-53), repealed 134 v H 511, § 2, eff 1-1-74.**

## § 2907.06 Sexual imposition.

(A) No person shall have sexual contact with another, not the spouse of the offender; cause another, not the spouse of the offender, to have sexual contact with the offender; or cause two or more other persons to have sexual contact when any of the following applies:

(1) The offender knows that the sexual contact is offensive to the other person, or one of the other persons, or is reckless in that regard.

(2) The offender knows that the other person's, or one of the other person's, ability to appraise the nature of or control the offender's or touching person's conduct is substantially impaired.

(3) The offender knows that the other person, or one of the other persons, submits because of being unaware of the sexual contact.

(4) The other person, or one of the other persons, is thirteen years of age or older but less than sixteen years of age, whether or not the offender knows the age of such person, and the offender is at least eighteen years of age and four or more years older than such other person.

(5) The offender is a mental health professional, the other person or one of the other persons is a mental health client or patient of the offender, and the offender induces the other person who is the client or patient to submit by falsely representing to the other person who is the client or patient that the sexual contact is necessary for mental health treatment purposes.

(B) No person shall be convicted of a violation of this section solely upon the victim's testimony unsupported by other evidence.

(C) Whoever violates this section is guilty of sexual imposition, a misdemeanor of the third degree. If the offender previously has been convicted of a violation of this section or of section 2907.02, 2907.03, 2907.04, 2907.05, or 2907.12† of the Revised Code, a violation of this section is a misdemeanor of the first degree.

**HISTORY: 134 v H 511 (Eff 1-1-74); 137 v H 134 (Eff 8-8-77); 143 v H 44 (Eff 7-24-90); 146 v S 2 (Eff 7-1-96); 149 v S 9. Eff 5-14-2002.**

† RC § 2907.12, repealed by 146 v H 445, § 2, effective 9-3-96. See now section 2907.01(A).

**Not analogous to former RC § 2907.06 (GC § 12435-1; 113 v 541; Bureau of Code Revision, 10-1-53), repealed 134 v H 511, § 2, eff 1-1-74.**

## § 2907.07 Importuning.

(A) No person shall solicit a person who is less than thirteen years of age to engage in sexual activity with the offender, whether or not the offender knows the age of such person.

(B) No person shall solicit another, not the spouse of the offender, to engage in sexual conduct with the offender, when the offender is eighteen years of age or older and four or more years older than the other person, and the other person is thirteen years of age or older but less than sixteen years of age, whether or not the offender knows the age of the other person.

(C) No person shall solicit another by means of a telecommunications device, as defined in section 2913.01 of the Revised Code, to engage in sexual activity with the offender when the offender is eighteen years of age or older and either of the following applies:

(1) The other person is less than thirteen years of age, and the offender knows that the other person is less than thirteen years of age or is reckless in that regard.

(2) The other person is a law enforcement officer posing as a person who is less than thirteen years of age, and the offender believes that the other person is less than thirteen years of age or is reckless in that regard.

(D) No person shall solicit another by means of a telecommunications device, as defined in section 2913.01 of the Revised Code, to engage in sexual activity with the offender when the offender is eighteen years of age or older and either of the following applies:

(1) The other person is thirteen years of age or older but less than sixteen years of age, the offender knows that the other person is thirteen years of age or older but less than sixteen years of age or is reckless in that regard, and the offender is four or more years older than the other person.

(2) The other person is a law enforcement officer posing as a person who is thirteen years of age or older but less than sixteen years of age, the offender believes that the other person is thirteen years of age or older but less than sixteen years of age or is reckless in that regard, and the offender is four or more years older than the age the law enforcement officer assumes in posing as the person who is thirteen years of age or older but less than sixteen years of age.

(E) Divisions (C) and (D) of this section apply to any solicitation that is contained in a transmission via a telecommunications device that either originates in this state or is received in this state.

(F)(1) Whoever violates this section is guilty of importuning.

(2) Except as otherwise provided in this division, a violation of division (A) or (C) of this section is a felony of the third degree on a first offense, and, notwithstanding division (C) of section 2929.13 of the Revised Code, there is a presumption that a prison term shall be imposed as described in division (D) of section 2929.13 of the Revised Code. If the offender previously has been convicted of a sexually oriented offense or a child-victim oriented offense, a violation of division (A) or (C) of this section is a felony of the second degree, and the court shall impose upon the offender as a mandatory prison term one of the prison terms prescribed in section 2929.14 of the Revised Code for a felony of the second degree.

(3) A violation of division (B) or (D) of this section is a felony of the fifth degree on a first offense, and, notwithstanding division (B) of section 2929.13 of the Revised Code, there is a presumption that a prison term shall be imposed as described in division (D) of section 2929.13 of the Revised Code. If the offender previously has been convicted of a sexually oriented offense or a child-victim oriented offense, a violation of division (B) or (D) of this section is a felony of the fourth degree, and the court shall impose upon the offender as a mandatory prison term one of the prison terms prescribed in section 2929.14 of the Revised Code for a felony of the fourth degree that is not less than twelve months in duration.

**HISTORY: 134 v H 511 (Eff 1-1-74); 148 v H 724 (Eff 3-22-2001); 149 v S 175. Eff 5-7-2002; 150 v S 5, § 1, eff. 7-31-03; 151 v S 260, § 1, eff. 1-2-07; 152 v S 183, § 1, eff. 9-11-08.**

**Not analogous to former RC § 2907.07 (RS § 6834; S&C 432; 72 v 149; GC § 12436; Bureau of Code Revision, 10-1-53), repealed 134 v H 511, § 2, eff 1-1-74.**

**Analogous to former RC § 2905.30 (RS § 7026; S&S 289; 59 v 32; 89 v 127; GC § 13032; 121 v 557(573); Bureau of Code Revision, 10-1-53; 129 v 1670; 130 v 659; 131 v 672), repealed 134 v H 511, § 2, eff 1-1-74.**

## § 2907.08 Voyeurism.

(A) No person, for the purpose of sexually arousing or gratifying the person's self, shall commit trespass or otherwise surreptitiously invade the privacy of another, to spy or eavesdrop upon another.

(B) No person, for the purpose of sexually arousing or gratifying the person's self, shall commit trespass or otherwise surreptitiously invade the privacy of another to videotape, film, photograph, or otherwise record the other person in a state of nudity.

(C) No person, for the purpose of sexually arousing or gratifying the person's self, shall commit trespass or otherwise surreptitiously invade the privacy of another to videotape, film, photograph, otherwise record, or spy or eavesdrop upon the other person in a state of nudity if the other person is a minor.

(D) No person shall secretly or surreptitiously videotape, film, photograph, or otherwise record another person under or through the clothing being worn by that other person for the purpose of viewing the body of, or the undergarments worn by, that other person.

(E)(1) Whoever violates this section is guilty of voyeurism.

(2) A violation of division (A) of this section is a misdemeanor of the third degree.

(3) A violation of division (B) of this section is a misdemeanor of the second degree.

(4) A violation of division (D) of this section is a misdemeanor of the first degree.

(5) A violation of division (C) of this section is a felony of the fifth degree.

**HISTORY: 134 v H 511 (Eff 1-1-74); 147 v S 82 (Eff 1-30-98); 148 v H 448 (Eff 10-5-2000); 148 v H 504 (Eff 10-10-2000); 148 v H 332. Eff 1-1-2001; 151 v H 310, § 1, eff. 6-15-06; 152 v H 74, § 1, eff. 4-7-09.**

The provisions of § 3 of 151 v H 310 read as follows:

SECTION 3. The General Assembly hereby declares that its purpose in amending divisions (B), (C), and (D) of section 2907.08 of the Revised Code in Section 1 of this act is to clarify the meaning of the term "photograph" as used in those divisions. The General Assembly declares that it believes that the term "photograph," as used in those divisions as they existed prior to the effective date of this act, included within its scope all types of the recording of an image, including, but not limited to, videotaping, filming, photographing, or otherwise recording an image; that it is not its intent in amending those divisions to declare or otherwise give the impression that, prior to the effective date of this act, the term "photograph" as used in those divisions did not include within its scope videotaping, filming, or other recording of an image; and that it believes that the amendments to those divisions are not substantive in nature and merely clarify the fact that the term "photograph" as used in those divisions includes within its scope all types of the recording of an image, including, but not limited to, videotaping, filming, photographing, or otherwise recording an image. Further, the General Assembly hereby declares that the amendments to those divisions do not invalidate, and shall not be construed as invalidating, any prior convictions for violating a prohibition contained in any of those divisions prior to the effective date of this act based on conduct that involved videotaping, filming, or other recording of an image.

The provisions of § 4 of 151 v H 310 read as follows:

SECTION 4. Section 2907.08 of the Revised Code is presented in this act as a composite of the section as amended by Sub. H.B. 332, Sub. H.B. 448, and Sub. H.B. 504 of the 123rd General Assembly. The General Assembly, applying the principle stated in division (B) of section 1.52 of the Revised Code that amendments are to be harmonized if reasonably capable of simultaneous operation, finds that the composite is the resulting version of the section in effect prior to the effective date of the section as presented in this act.

**Not analogous to former RC § 2907.08 (Bureau of Code Revision, 10-1-53; 132 v H 996), repealed 134 v H 511, § 2, eff 1-1-74.**

The effective date is set by section 5 of HB 332.

## § 2907.081 Repealed, 134 v H 511, § 2 [129 v 562; 131 v 674]. Eff 1-1-74.

This section concerned penalty and intentional injury or damage to public or private property.

## § 2907.082 Repealed, 134 v H 511, § 2 [129 v 562; 131 v 674]. Eff 1-1-74.

This section concerned penalty and intentional injury or damage to public or private property.

## § 2907.09 Public indecency.

(A) No person shall recklessly do any of the following, under circumstances in which the person's conduct is likely to be viewed by and affront others who are in the person's physical proximity and who are not members of the person's household:

(1) Expose the person's private parts;

(2) Engage in sexual conduct or masturbation;

(3) Engage in conduct that to an ordinary observer would appear to be sexual conduct or masturbation.

(B) No person shall knowingly do any of the following, under circumstances in which the person's conduct is likely to be viewed by and affront another person who is a minor, who is not the spouse of the offender, and who resides in the person's household:

(1) Engage in masturbation;

(2) Engage in sexual conduct;

(3) Engage in conduct that to an ordinary observer would appear to be sexual conduct or masturbation;

(4) Expose the person's private parts with the purpose of personal sexual arousal or gratification or to lure the minor into sexual activity.

(C)(1) Whoever violates this section is guilty of public indecency and shall be punished as provided in divisions (C)(2), (3), (4), and (5) of this section.

(2) Except as otherwise provided in division (C)(2) of this section, a violation of division (A)(1) of this section is a misdemeanor of the fourth degree. If the offender previously has been convicted of or pleaded guilty to one violation of this section, a violation of division (A)(1) of this section is a misdemeanor of the third degree or, if any person who was likely to view and be affronted by the offender's conduct was a minor, a misdemeanor of the second degree. If the offender previously has been convicted of or pleaded guilty to two violations of this section, a violation of division (A)(1) of this section is a misdemeanor of the second degree or, if any person who was likely to view and be affronted by the offender's conduct was a minor, a misdemeanor of the first degree. If the offender previously has been convicted of or pleaded guilty to three or more violations of this section, a violation of division (A)(1) of this section is a misdemeanor of the first degree or, if any person who was likely to view and be affronted by the offender's conduct was a minor, a felony of the fifth degree.

(3) Except as otherwise provided in division (C)(3) of this section, a violation of division (A)(2) or (3) of this section is a misdemeanor of the third degree. If the offender previously has been convicted of or pleaded guilty to one violation of this section, a violation of division (A)(2) or (3) of this section is a misdemeanor of the second degree or, if any person who was likely to view and be affronted by the offender's conduct was a minor, a misdemeanor of the first degree. If the offender previously has been convicted of or pleaded guilty to two or more violations of this section, a violation of division (A)(2) or (3) of this section is a misdemeanor of the first degree or, if any person who was likely to view and be affronted by the offender's conduct was a minor, a felony of the fifth degree.

(4) Except as otherwise provided in division (C)(4) of this section, a violation of division (B)(1), (2), or (3) of this section is a misdemeanor of the second degree. If the offender previously has been convicted of or pleaded guilty to one violation of this section, a violation of division (B)(1), (2), or (3) of this section is a misdemeanor of the first degree. If the offender previously has been convicted of or pleaded guilty to two or more violations of this section, a violation of division (B)(1), (2), or (3) of this section is a felony of the fifth degree.

(5) Except as otherwise provided in division (C)(5) of this section, a violation of division (B)(4) of this section is a misdemeanor of the first degree. If the offender previously has been convicted of or pleaded guilty to any violation of this section, a violation of division (B)(4) of this section is a felony of the fifth degree.

**HISTORY: 134 v H 511 (Eff 1-1-74); 143 v H 214 (Eff 4-13-90); 146 v S 2. Eff 7-1-96; 151 v H 50, § 1, eff. 9-26-05; 151 v S 245, § 1, eff. 4-4-07.**

**Not analogous to former RC § 2907.09 (RS § 6835; 69 v 10; 82 v 161; 95 v 561; 96 v 14; 98 v 3; GC § 12437; 100 v 5; 101 v 128; Bureau of Code Revision, 10-1-53; 129 v 1426), repealed 134 v H 511, § 2, eff 1-1-74.**

The effective date is set by section 6 of SB 2.

## § 2907.10 Polygraph examination of victim of alleged sex offense.

(A)(1) A peace officer, prosecutor, or other public official shall not ask or require a victim of an alleged sex offense to submit to a polygraph examination as a condition for proceeding with the investigation of the alleged sex offense.

(2) The refusal of the victim of an alleged sex offense to submit to a polygraph examination shall not prevent the investigation of the alleged sex offense, the filing of criminal charges with respect to the alleged sex offense, or the prosecution of the alleged perpetrator of the alleged sex offense.

(B) As used in this section:

(1) "Peace officer" has the same meaning as in section 2921.51 of the Revised Code.

(2) "Polygraph examination" means any mechanical or electrical instrument or device of any type used or allegedly used to examine, test, or question an individual for the purpose of determining the individual's truthfulness.

(3) "Prosecution" means the prosecution of criminal charges in a criminal prosecution or the prosecution of a delinquent child complaint in a delinquency proceeding.

(4) "Prosecutor" has the same meaning as in section 2935.01 of the Revised Code.

(5) "Public official" has the same meaning as in section 117.01 of the Revised Code.

(6) "Sex offense" means a violation of any provision of sections 2907.02 to 2907.09 of the Revised Code.

**HISTORY: 152 v H 562, § 101.01, eff. 6-24-08.**

**Not analogous to former RC § 2907.10 (136 v S 144; 137 v H 565; 138 v H 900), repealed 139 v S 199, § 2, eff 7-1-83.**

The effective date is set by § 812.20 of 152 v H 562.

## § 2907.11 Victim or offender may request temporary suppression of information.

Upon the request of the victim or offender in a prosecution under any provision of sections 2907.02 to 2907.07 of the Revised Code, the judge before whom any person is brought on a charge of having committed an offense under a provision of one of those sections shall order that the names of the victim and offender and the details of the alleged offense as obtained by any law enforcement officer be suppressed until the preliminary hearing, the accused is arraigned in the court of common pleas, the charge is dismissed, or the case is otherwise concluded, whichever occurs first. Nothing in this section shall be construed to deny to either party in the case the name and address of the other party or the details of the alleged offense.

**HISTORY: 136 v S 144 (Eff 8-27-75); 146 v H 445. Eff 9-3-96.**

**Not analogous to former RC § 2907.11 (RS § 6835; 69 v 10; 82 v 161; 95 v 561; 96 v 14; 98 v 3; GC § 12439; 100 v 5; Bureau of Code Revision, 10-1-53), repealed 134 v H 511, § 2, eff 1-1-74.**

## § 2907.12 Repealed, 146 v H 445, § 2 [136 v S 144; 139 v S 199; 141 v H 475; 143 v S 94; 145 v S 31; 146 v S 2]. Eff 9-3-96.

This section defined felonious sexual penetration. See now RC § 2907.01(A).

The provisions of § 3(A)-(J) of HB 445 (146 v —) read as follows:

SECTION 3. (A) When a complaint is filed alleging that a child is a delinquent child for committing felonious sexual penetration in violation of former section 2907.12 of the Revised Code and the arresting authority, a court, or a probation officer discovers that the child or a person whom the child caused to engage in sexual activity has a communicable disease, the arresting authority, court, or probation officer shall notify the victim of the delinquent act of the nature of the disease in accordance with division (C) of section 2151.14 of the Revised Code.

As used in division (A) of Section 3 of this act:

(1) "Child" has the same meaning as in section 2151.011 of the Revised Code.

(2) "Delinquent child" has the same meaning as in section 2151.02 of the Revised Code.

(3) "Sexual activity" has the same meaning as in section 2907.01 of the Revised Code.

(B) If a child is adjudicated a delinquent child for violating any provision of former section 2907.12 of the Revised Code other than division (A)(1)(b) of that section when the insertion involved was consensual and when the victim of the violation of division (A)(1)(b) of that section was older than the delinquent child, was the same age as the delinquent child, or was less that three years younger than the delinquent child, the juvenile court with jurisdiction over the child may commit the child to the legal custody of the department of youth services pursuant to division (A)(5)(a) of section 2151.355 of the Revised Code, as amended by this act, and all provisions of the Revised Code that apply to a disposition otherwise imposed pursuant to division (A)(5)(a) of section 2151.355 of the Revised Code, as amended by this act, apply to a disposition imposed in accordance with division (B) of Section 3 of this act.

As used in division (B) of Section 3 of this act:

(1) "Child" and "legal custody" have the same meanings as in section 2151.011 of the Revised Code.

(2) "Delinquent child" has the same meaning as in section 2151.02 of the Revised Code.

(C) Section 2151.3511 of the Revised Code, as amended by this act, applies to a proceeding in juvenile court involving a complaint in which a child is charged with committing an act that if committed by an adult would be felonious sexual penetration in violation of former section 2907.12 of the Revised Code and in which an alleged victim of the act was a child who was under eleven years of age when the complaint was filed.

As used in division (C) of Section 3 of this act, "child" has the same meaning as in section 2151.011 of the Revised Code.

(D) Division (E) of section 2743.62 of the Revised Code applies to a claim for an award of reparations arising out of the commission of felonious sexual penetration in violation of former section 2907.12 of the Revised Code.

(E) Section 2907.11 of the Revised Code, as amended by this act, applies to a prosecution for felonious sexual penetration committed in violation of former section 2907.12 of the Revised Code.

(F) Division (A) of section 2907.28 and sections 2907.29 and 2907.30 of the Revised Code, as amended by this act, apply to a victim of felonious sexual penetration committed in violation of former section 2907.12 of the Revised Code.

(G) Sections 2907.41 and 2945.49 of the Revised Code, as amended by this act, apply to a trial or other proceeding involving a charges of felonious sexual penetration in violation of former section 2907.12 of the Revised Code in which an alleged victim of the offense was a child who was under eleven years of age when the complaint, indictment, or information was filed relative to the trial or other proceeding.

(H) Divisions (B) and (C) of section 2937.11 of the Revised Code, as amended by this act, apply to a case involving an alleged commission of the offense of felonious sexual penetration in violation of former section 2907.12 of the Revised Code.

(I) Notwithstanding section 2967.13 of the Revised Code, as amended by this act, a prisoner serving a term of imprisonment for life for committing the offense of felonious sexual penetration in violation of former section 2907.12 of the Revised Code becomes eligible for parole after serving a term of ten full years' imprisonment.

(J) Notwithstanding section 2967.18 of the Revised Code, as amended by this act, no reduction of sentence pursuant to division (B)(1) of section 2967.18 of the Revised Code shall be given to a person who is serving a term of imprisonment for the commission of felonious sexual penetration in violation of former section 2907.12 of the Revised Code.

## § 2907.121 Repealed, 134 v H 511, § 2 [132 v H 656]. Eff 1-1-74.

This section concerned forcing entry into coin-receiving device.

## § 2907.13 Repealed, 134 v H 511, § 2 [RS § 6836; S&C 407, 426; 33 v 33; 78 v 28; GC § 12441; 113

v 502; Bureau of Code Revision, 10-1-53; 129 v 1812; 129 v 1426; 130 v 660]. Eff 1-1-74.

This section concerned malicious entry and definition of financial institution.

**§ 2907.14** Repealed, 134 v H 511, § 2 [RS § 6836; S&C 407, 426; 33 v 33; 78 v 28; GC § 12441; 113 v 502; Bureau of Code Revision, 10-1-53; 129 v 1812; 129 v 1426; 130 v 660]. Eff 1-1-74.

This section concerned malicious entry and definition of financial institution.

**§ 2907.141** Repealed, 134 v H 511, § 2 [129 v 1812]. Eff 1-1-74.

This section concerned unlawful entry of financial institution.

**§ 2907.142** Repealed, 134 v H 511, § 2 [129 v 1812]. Eff 1-1-74.

This section concerned unlawful entry of financial institution.

**§ 2907.143** Repealed, 134 v H 511, § 2 [129 v 1812]. Eff 1-1-74.

This section concerned unlawful entry of financial institution.

**§ 2907.144** Repealed, 134 v H 511, § 2 [129 v 1812]. Eff 1-1-74.

This section concerned unlawful entry of financial institution.

**§ 2907.145** Repealed, 134 v H 511, § 2 [129 v 1812]. Eff 1-1-74.

This section concerned unlawful entry of financial institution.

### § 2907.15 Motion for withholding of restitution needed from government deferred compensation or public retirement system payment.

(A) As used in this section:

(1) "Public retirement system" means the public employees retirement system, state teachers retirement system, school employees retirement system, Ohio police and fire pension fund, state highway patrol retirement system, or a municipal retirement system of a municipal corporation of this state.

(2) "Government deferred compensation program" means such a program offered by the Ohio public employees deferred compensation board; a municipal corporation; or a governmental unit, as defined in section 148.06 of the Revised Code.

(3) "Deferred compensation program participant" means a "participating employee" or "continuing member," as defined in section 148.01 of the Revised Code, or any other public employee who has funds in a government deferred compensation program.

(4) "Alternative retirement plan" means an alternative retirement plan provided pursuant to Chapter 3305. of the Revised Code.

(5) "Prosecutor" has the same meaning as in section 2935.01 of the Revised Code.

In any case in which a sentencing court orders restitution to the victim under section 2929.18 or 2929.28 of the Revised Code for a violation of section 2907.02, 2907.03, 2907.04, or 2907.05 of the Revised Code and in which the offender is a government deferred compensation program participant, is an electing employee, as defined in section 3305.01 of the Revised Code, or is a member of, or receiving a pension, benefit, or allowance, other than a survivorship benefit, from, a public retirement system and committed the offense against a child, student, patient, or other person with whom the offender had contact in the context of the offender's public employment, at the request of the victim the prosecutor shall file a motion with the sentencing court specifying the government deferred compensation program, alternative retirement plan, or public retirement system and requesting that the court issue an order requiring the government deferred compensation program, alternative retirement plan, or public retirement system to withhold the amount required as restitution from one or more of the following: any payment to be made from a government deferred compensation program, any payment or benefit under an alternative retirement plan, or under a pension, annuity, allowance, or any other benefit, other than a survivorship benefit, that has been or is in the future granted to the offender; from any payment of accumulated employee contributions standing to the offender's credit with the government deferred compensation program, alternative retirement plan, or public retirement system; or from any payment of any other amounts to be paid to the offender pursuant to Chapter 145., 148., 742., 3307., 3309., or 5505. of the Revised Code on withdrawal of contributions. The motion may be filed at any time subsequent to the conviction of the offender or entry of a guilty plea. On the filing of the motion, the clerk of the court in which the motion is filed shall notify the offender and the government deferred compensation program, alternative retirement plan, or public retirement system, in writing, of all of the following: that the motion was filed; that the offender will be granted a hearing on the issuance of the requested order if the offender files a written request for a hearing with the clerk prior to the expiration of thirty days after the offender receives the notice; that, if a hearing is requested, the court will schedule a hearing as soon as possible and notify the offender and the government deferred compensation program, alternative retirement plan, or public retirement system of the date, time, and place of the hearing; that, if a hearing is conducted, it will be limited to a consideration of whether the offender can show good cause why the order should not be issued; that, if a hearing is conducted, the court will not issue the order if the court determines, based on evidence presented at the hearing by the offender, that there is good cause for the order not to be issued; that the court will issue the order if a hearing is not requested or if a hearing is conducted but the court does not determine, based on evidence presented at the hearing by the offender, that there is good cause for the order not to be issued; and that, if the order is issued, the government deferred compensation program, alternative retirement plan, or public retirement system specified in the motion will be required to withhold the amount required as restitution from payments to the offender.

(B) In any case in which a motion requesting the issuance of a withholding order as described in division (A) of this section is filed, the offender may receive a hearing on the motion by delivering a written request for a hearing to the court prior to the expiration of thirty days after the offender's receipt of the notice provided pursuant to division (A) of this section. If the offender requests a hearing within the prescribed time, the court shall schedule a hearing as soon as possible after the request is made and notify the offender and the government deferred compensation program, alternative retirement plan, or public retirement system of the date, time, and place of the hearing. A hearing scheduled under this division shall be limited to a consideration of whether there is good cause, based on evidence presented by the offender, for the requested order not to be issued. If the court determines, based on evidence presented by the offender, that there is good cause for the order not to be issued, the court shall deny the motion and shall not issue the order. Good cause for not issuing the order includes a determination by the court that the order would severely impact the offender's ability to support the offender's dependents.

If the offender does not request a hearing within the prescribed time or the court conducts a hearing but does not determine, based on evidence presented by the offender, that there is good cause for the order not to be issued, the court shall order the government deferred compensation program, alternative retirement plan, or public retirement system to withhold the amount required as restitution from one or more of the following: any payments to be made from a government deferred compensation program, any payment or benefit under an alternative retirement plan, or under a pension, annuity, allowance, or under any other benefit, other than a survivorship benefit, that has been or is in the future granted to the offender; from any payment of accumulated employee contributions standing to the offender's credit with the government deferred compensation program, alternative retirement plan, or public retirement system; or from any payment of any other amounts to be paid to the offender upon withdrawal of contributions pursuant to Chapter 145., 148., 742., 3307., 3309., or 5505. of the Revised Code and to continue the withholding for that purpose, in accordance with the order, out of each payment to be made on or after the date of issuance of the order, until further order of the court. On receipt of an order issued under this division, the government deferred compensation program, alternative retirement plan, or public retirement system shall withhold the amount required as restitution, in accordance with the order, from any such payments and immediately forward the amount withheld to the clerk of the court in which the order was issued for payment to the person to whom restitution is to be made. The order shall not apply to any portion of payments made from a government deferred compensation program, alternative retirement plan, or public retirement system to a person other than the offender pursuant to a previously issued domestic court order.

(C) Service of a notice required by division (A) or (B) of this section shall be effected in the same manner as provided in the Rules of Civil Procedure for the service of process.

(D) Upon the filing of charges under section 2907.02, 2907.03, 2907.04, or 2907.05 of the Revised Code against a person who is a deferred compensation program participant, an electing employee participating in an alternative retirement plan, or a member of, or receiving a pension benefit, or allowance, other than a survivorship benefit, from a public retirement system for an offense against a child, student, patient, or other person with whom the offender had contact in the context of the offender's public employment, the prosecutor shall send written notice that charges have been filed against that person to the appropriate government deferred compensation program, alternative retirement plan, or public retirement system. The notice shall specifically identify the person charged.

**HISTORY: 146 v H 668 (Eff 12-6-96); 148 v H 222 (Eff 11-2-99); 148 v H 628 (Eff 9-21-2000); 148 v H 535. Eff 4-1-2001; 149 v H 490, § 1, eff. 1-1-04.**

The effective date is set by section 4 of HB 490.

**Not analogous to former RC § 2907.15 (RS § 6837; S & C 435; 52 v 28; 88 v 432; GC § 12442; 109 v 53; Bureau of Code Revision, 10-1-53; 129 v 1426), repealed 134 v H 511, § 2, eff 1-1-74.**

## § 2907.16 Repealed, 134 v H 511, § 2 [RS § 6838; S&C 426; 29 v 144, § 1; GC § 12443; Bureau of Code Revision, 10-1-53]. Eff 1-1-74.

This section concerned entry in the night season and committing personal violence.

## [NOTICE OF SEXUAL MISCONDUCT BY MENTAL HEALTH PROFESSIONAL]

## § 2907.17 Notice to administrative entity regulating mental health professional.

If a mental health professional is indicted or charged and bound over to the court of common pleas for trial for an alleged violation of division (A)(10) of section 2907.03 or division (A)(5) of section 2907.06 of the Revised Code, the prosecuting attorney handling the case shall send written notice of the indictment or the charge and bind over to the regulatory or licensing board or agency, if any, that has the administrative authority to suspend or revoke the mental health professional's professional license, certification, registration, or authorization.

**HISTORY: 149 v S 9. Eff 5-14-2002.**

**Not analogous to former RC § 2907.17 (RS § 6839; S&C 427; 29 v 144, § 2; GC § 12444; Bureau of Code Revision, 10-1-53; 129 v 1426(1428), § 1; 130 v 660, § 1), repealed 134 v H 511, § 2, eff 1-1-74.**

## § 2907.171 Effect of prosecutor's failure to give notice.

The failure of the prosecuting attorney to give the notice required by section 2907.17 of the Revised Code does not give rise to a claim for damages against the prosecuting attorney or the county. The failure of the prosecuting attorney to give the notice does not constitute grounds for declaring a mistrial or new trial, for setting aside a conviction or sentence, or for granting postconviction relief to a defendant.

**HISTORY: 149 v S 9. Eff 5-14-2002.**

## § 2907.18 Notice of conviction of mental health professional.

If a mental health professional is convicted of or pleads guilty to a violation of division (A)(10) of section 2907.03 or division (A)(5) of section 2907.06 of the Revised Code, the court shall transmit a certified copy of the judgment entry of conviction to the regulatory or licensing board or agency, if any, that has the administrative authority to suspend or revoke the mental health professional's professional license, certification, registration, or authorization.

**HISTORY: 149 v S 9. Eff 5-14-2002.**

**Not analogous to former RC § 2907.18 (RS § 6840; S&S 279; 60 v 5, § 1; GC § 12445; Bureau of Code Revision, 10-1-53), repealed 134 v H 511, § 2, eff 1-1-74.**

## § 2907.19 Repealed, 134 v H 511, § 2 [RS §§ 3107, 6856; S&C 408, 439, 1632; S&S 263, 457; 47 v 21; 60 v 20; 63 v 70; 66 v 341; 68 v 87; 69 v 67; GC §§ 12446—12447; 124 v 466; Bureau of Code Revision, 10-1-53; 132 v H 996; 133 v H 49]. Eff 1-1-74.

This section prohibited breaking and entering and theft.

## § 2907.20 Repealed, 134 v H 511, § 2 [RS §§ 3107, 6856; S&C 408, 439, 1632; S&S 263, 457; 47 v 21; 60 v 20; 63 v 70; 66 v 341; 68 v 87; 69 v 67; GC §§ 12446—12447; 124 v 466; Bureau of Code Revision, 10-1-53; 132 v H 996; 133 v H 49]. Eff 1-1-74.

This section prohibited breaking and entering and theft.

## § 2907.201 Repealed, 134 v H 511, § 2 [133 v S 346; 134 v S 302]. Eff 1-1-74.

This section concerned credit card theft and fraud.

[PROSTITUTION]

## § 2907.21 Compelling prostitution.

(A) No person shall knowingly do any of the following:
(1) Compel another to engage in sexual activity for hire;
(2) Induce, procure, encourage, solicit, request, or otherwise facilitate either of the following:
(a) A minor to engage in sexual activity for hire, whether or not the offender knows the age of the minor;
(b) A person the offender believes to be a minor to engage in sexual activity for hire, whether or not the person is a minor.
(3)(a) Pay or agree to pay a minor, either directly or through the minor's agent, so that the minor will engage in sexual activity, whether or not the offender knows the age of the minor;
(b) Pay or agree to pay a person the offender believes to be a minor, either directly or through the person's agent, so that the person will engage in sexual activity, whether or not the person is a minor.
(4)(a) Pay a minor, either directly or through the minor's agent, for the minor having engaged in sexual activity pursuant to a prior agreement, whether or not the offender knows the age of the minor;
(b) Pay a person the offender believes to be a minor, either directly or through the person's agent, for the person having engaged in sexual activity pursuant to a prior agreement, whether or not the person is a minor.
(5)(a) Allow a minor to engage in sexual activity for hire if the person allowing the child to engage in sexual activity for hire is the parent, guardian, custodian, person having custody or control, or person in loco parentis of the minor;
(b) Allow a person the offender believes to be a minor to engage in sexual activity for hire if the person allowing the person to engage in sexual activity for hire is the parent, guardian, custodian, person having custody or control, or person in loco parentis of the person the offender believes to be a minor, whether or not the person is a minor.

(B) For a prosecution under division (A)(1) of this section, the element "compel" does not require that the compulsion be openly displayed or physically exerted. The element "compel" has been established if the state proves that the victim's will was overcome by force, fear, duress, or intimidation.

(C) Whoever violates this section is guilty of compelling prostitution. Except as otherwise provided in this division, compelling prostitution is a felony of the third degree. If the offender commits a violation of division (A)(1) of this section and the person compelled to engage in sexual activity for hire in violation of that division is sixteen years of age or older but less than eighteen years of age, compelling prostitution is a felony of the second degree. If the offender commits a violation of division (A)(1) of this section and the person compelled to engage in sexual activity for hire in violation of that division is less than sixteen years of age, compelling prostitution is a felony of the first degree. If the offender in any case also is convicted of or pleads guilty to a specification as described in section 2941.1422 of the Revised Code that was included in the indictment, count in the indictment, or information charging the offense, the court shall sentence the offender to a mandatory prison term as provided in division (B)(7) of section 2929.14 of the Revised Code and shall order the offender to make restitution as provided in division (B)(8) of section 2929.18 of the Revised Code.

**HISTORY: 134 v H 511 (Eff 1-1-74); 142 v H 51 (Eff 3-17-89); 146 v S 2. Eff 7-1-96; 152 v S 183, § 1, eff. 9-11-08; 152 v H 280, § 1, eff. 4-7-09; 153 v S 235, § 1, eff. 3-24-11; 2011 HB 86, § 1, eff. Sept. 30, 2011.**

**Not analogous to former RC § 2907.21 (GC § 12447-1; 120 v 444; 124 v 466; Bureau of Code Revision, 10-1-53; 129 v 340; 130 v 660; 133 v S 346), repealed 134 v H 511, § 2, eff 1-1-74.**

The effective date is set by section 6 of SB 2.

## § 2907.22 Promoting prostitution.

(A) No person shall knowingly:
(1) Establish, maintain, operate, manage, supervise, control, or have an interest in a brothel;
(2) Supervise, manage, or control the activities of a prostitute in engaging in sexual activity for hire;
(3) Transport another, or cause another to be transported across the boundary of this state or of any county in this state, in order to facilitate the other person's engaging in sexual activity for hire;
(4) For the purpose of violating or facilitating a violation of this section, induce or procure another to engage in sexual activity for hire.

(B) Whoever violates this section is guilty of promoting prostitution. Except as otherwise provided in this division, promoting prostitution is a felony of the fourth degree. If any prostitute in the brothel involved in the offense, or the prostitute whose activities are supervised, managed, or controlled by the offender, or the person transported, induced, or procured by the offender to engage in sexual activity for hire, is a minor, whether or not the offender knows the age of the minor, then promoting prostitution is a felony of the third degree. If the offender in any case also is convicted of or pleads guilty to a specification as described in section 2941.1422 of the Revised Code that was included in the indictment, count in the indictment, or information charging the offense, the court shall sentence the offender to a mandatory prison term as provided in division (B)(7) of section 2929.14 of the Revised Code and shall order the offender to make restitution as provided in division (B)(8) of section 2929.18 of the Revised Code.

**HISTORY: 134 v H 511 (Eff 1-1-74); 142 v H 51 (Eff 3-17-89); 146 v S 2. Eff 7-1-96; 152 v H 280, § 1, eff. 4-7-09; 2011 HB 86, § 1, eff. Sept. 30, 2011.**

**Not analogous to former RC § 2907.22 (RS § 6857; S&C 412; 33 v 33; GC § 12448; 107 v 558; 110 v 58; Bureau of Code Revision, 10-1-53), repealed 134 v H 511, § 2, eff 1-1-74.**

The effective date is set by section 6 of SB 2.

## § 2907.23 Procuring.

(A) No person, knowingly and for gain, shall do either of the following:

(1) Entice or solicit another to patronize a prostitute or brothel;

(2) Procure a prostitute for another to patronize, or take or direct another at his or her request to any place for the purpose of patronizing a prostitute.

(B) No person, having authority or responsibility over the use of premises, shall knowingly permit such premises to be used for the purpose of engaging in sexual activity for hire.

(C) Whoever violates this section is guilty of procuring, a misdemeanor of the first degree.

**HISTORY: 134 v H 511. Eff 1-1-74.**

**Not analogous to former RC § 2907.23 (GC § 12448-1; 117 v 821; Bureau of Code Revision, 10-1-53), repealed 134 v H 511, § 2, eff 1-1-74.**

The effective date is set by section 4 of HB 511.

## § 2907.24 Soliciting; after positive HIV test; driver's license suspension.

(A) No person shall solicit another to engage with such other person in sexual activity for hire.

(B) No person, with knowledge that the person has tested positive as a carrier of a virus that causes acquired immunodeficiency syndrome, shall engage in conduct in violation of division (A) of this section.

(C)(1) Whoever violates division (A) of this section is guilty of soliciting, a misdemeanor of the third degree.

(2) Whoever violates division (B) of this section is guilty of engaging in solicitation after a positive HIV test. If the offender commits the violation prior to July 1, 1996, engaging in solicitation after a positive HIV test is a felony of the second degree. If the offender commits the violation on or after July 1, 1996, engaging in solicitation after a positive HIV test is a felony of the third degree.

(D) If a person is convicted of or pleads guilty to a violation of any provision of this section, an attempt to commit a violation of any provision of this section, or a violation of or an attempt to commit a violation of a municipal ordinance that is substantially equivalent to any provision of this section and if the person, in committing or attempting to commit the violation, was in, was on, or used a motor vehicle, the court, in addition to or independent of all other penalties imposed for the violation, shall impose upon the offender a class six suspension of the person's driver's license, commercial driver's license, temporary instruction permit, probationary license, or nonresident operating privilege from the range specified in division (A)(6) of section 4510.02 of the Revised Code.

**HISTORY: 134 v H 511 (Eff 1-1-74); 146 v H 40. Eff 5-30-96; 149 v S 123, § 1, eff. 1-1-04.**

The effective date is set by section 4 of S.B. 123.

The provisions of § 5 of S.B. 123 (149 v —), as amended by § 3 of H.B. 163 (150 v —), read as follows:

SECTION 5. (A) Notwithstanding division (B) of section 1.58 of the Revised Code, the provisions of the Revised Code amended or enacted in Sections 1 and 2 of Am. Sub. S.B. 123 of the 124th General Assembly shall apply only in relation to conduct and offenses committed on or after January 1, 2004. Conduct and offenses committed prior to January 1, 2004, shall be governed by the law in effect on the date the conduct or offense was committed.

° ° °

**Not analogous to former RC § 2907.24 (GC § 12448-2; 117 v 821; Bureau of Code Revision, 10-1-53), repealed 134 v H 511, § 2, eff 1-1-74.**

**Analogous to former RC § 2905.27 (GC § 13031-13; 108 v PtI, 730; Bureau of Code Revision, 10-1-53; 130 v PtII, 143), repealed 134 v H 511, § 2, eff 1-1-74.**

## § 2907.241 Loitering to engage in solicitation; solicitation after positive HIV test.

(A) No person, with purpose to solicit another to engage in sexual activity for hire and while in or near a public place, shall do any of the following:

(1) Beckon to, stop, or attempt to stop another;

(2) Engage or attempt to engage another in conversation;

(3) Stop or attempt to stop the operator of a vehicle or approach a stationary vehicle;

(4) If the offender is the operator of or a passenger in a vehicle, stop, attempt to stop, beckon to, attempt to beckon to, or entice another to approach or enter the vehicle of which the offender is the operator or in which the offender is the passenger;

(5) Interfere with the free passage of another.

(B) No person, with knowledge that the person has tested positive as a carrier of a virus that causes acquired immunodeficiency syndrome, shall engage in conduct in violation of division (A) of this section.

(C) As used in this section:

(1) "Vehicle" has the same meaning as in section 4501.01 of the Revised Code.

(2) "Public place" means any of the following:

(a) A street, road, highway, thoroughfare, bikeway, walkway, sidewalk, bridge, alley, alleyway, plaza, park, driveway, parking lot, or transportation facility;

(b) A doorway or entrance way to a building that fronts on a place described in division (C)(2)(a) of this section;

(c) A place not described in division (C)(2)(a) or (b) of this section that is open to the public.

(D)(1) Whoever violates division (A) of this section is guilty of loitering to engage in solicitation, a misdemeanor of the third degree.

(2) Whoever violates division (B) of this section is guilty of loitering to engage in solicitation after a positive HIV test. If the offender commits the violation prior to July 1, 1996, loitering to engage in solicitation after a positive HIV test is a felony of the fourth degree. If the offender

commits the violation on or after July 1, 1996, loitering to engage in solicitation after a positive HIV test is a felony of the fifth degree.

**HISTORY: 146 v H 40. Eff 5-30-96.**

## § 2907.25 Prostitution; after positive HIV test.

(A) No person shall engage in sexual activity for hire.

(B) No person, with knowledge that the person has tested positive as a carrier of a virus that causes acquired immunodeficiency syndrome, shall engage in sexual activity for hire.

(C)(1) Whoever violates division (A) of this section is guilty of prostitution, a misdemeanor of the third degree.

(2) Whoever violates division (B) of this section is guilty of engaging in prostitution after a positive HIV test. If the offender commits the violation prior to July 1, 1996, engaging in prostitution after a positive HIV test is a felony of the second degree. If the offender commits the violation on or after July 1, 1996, engaging in prostitution after a positive HIV test is a felony of the third degree.

**HISTORY: 134 v H 511 (Eff 1-1-74); 146 v H 40. Eff 5-30-96.**

**Not analogous to former RC § 2907.25 (GC § 12448-3; 117 v 821; Bureau of Code Revision, 10-1-53), repealed 134 v H 511, § 2, eff 1-1-74.**

**Analogous to former RC § 2905.27 (GC § 13031-13; 108 v PtI, 730; Bureau of Code Revision, 10-1-53; 130 v PtII, 143), repealed 134 v H 511, § 2, eff 1-1-74.**

## § 2907.26 Rules of evidence in prostitution cases.

(A) In any case in which it is necessary to prove that a place is a brothel, evidence as to the reputation of such place and as to the reputation of the persons who inhabit or frequent it, is admissible on the question of whether such place is or is not a brothel.

(B) In any case in which it is necessary to prove that a person is a prostitute, evidence as to the reputation of such person is admissible on the question of whether such person is or is not a prostitute.

(C) In any prosecution for a violation of sections 2907.21 to 2907.25 of the Revised Code, proof of a prior conviction of the accused of any such offense or substantially equivalent offense is admissible in support of the charge.

(D) The prohibition contained in division (D) of section 2317.02 of the Revised Code against testimony by a husband or wife concerning communications between them does not apply, and the accused's spouse may testify concerning any such communication, in any of the following cases:

(1) When the husband or wife is charged with a violation of section 2907.21 of the Revised Code, and the spouse testifying was the victim of the offense;

(2) When the husband or wife is charged with a violation of section 2907.22 of the Revised Code, and the spouse testifying was the prostitute involved in the offense, or the person transported, induced, or procured by the offender to engage in sexual activity for hire;

(3) When the husband or wife is charged with a violation of section 2907.23 of the Revised Code, and the spouse testifying was the prostitute involved in the offense or the person who used the offender's premises to engage in sexual activity for hire;

(4) When the husband or wife is charged with a violation of section 2907.24 or 2907.25 of the Revised Code.

**HISTORY: 134 v H 511 (Eff 1-1-74); 137 v H 1. Eff 8-26-77.**

**Not analogous to former RC § 2907.26 (GC § 12448-4; 117 v 821; 119 v 554; Bureau of Code Revision, 10-1-53), repealed 134 v H 511, § 2, eff 1-1-74.**

## § 2907.27 Testing of accused for venereal diseases and HIV.

(A)(1) If a person is charged with a violation of section 2907.02, 2907.03, 2907.04, 2907.24, 2907.241 [2907.24.1], or 2907.25 of the Revised Code or with a violation of a municipal ordinance that is substantially equivalent to any of those sections, the arresting authorities or a court, upon the request of the prosecutor in the case or upon the request of the victim, shall cause the accused to submit to one or more appropriate tests to determine if the accused is suffering from a venereal disease.

(2) If the accused is found to be suffering from a venereal disease in an infectious stage, the accused shall be required to submit to medical treatment for that disease. The cost of the medical treatment shall be charged to and paid by the accused who undergoes the treatment. If the accused is indigent, the court shall order the accused to report to a facility operated by a city health district or a general health district for treatment. If the accused is convicted of or pleads guilty to the offense with which the accused is charged and is placed under a community control sanction, a condition of community control shall be that the offender submit to and faithfully follow a course of medical treatment for the venereal disease. If the offender does not seek the required medical treatment, the court may revoke the offender's community control and order the offender to undergo medical treatment during the period of the offender's incarceration and to pay the cost of that treatment.

(B)(1)(a) If a person is charged with a violation of division (B) of section 2903.11 or of section 2907.02, 2907.03, 2907.04, 2907.05, 2907.12, 2907.24, 2907.241 [2907.24.1], or 2907.25 of the Revised Code or with a violation of a municipal ordinance that is substantially equivalent to that division or any of those sections, the court, upon the request of the prosecutor in the case, upon the request of the victim, or upon the request of any other person whom the court reasonably believes had contact with the accused in circumstances related to the violation that could have resulted in the transmission to that person the human immunodeficiency virus, shall cause the accused to submit to one or more tests designated by the director of health under section 3701.241 [3701.24.1] of the Revised Code to determine if the accused is infected with HIV. The court, upon the request of the prosecutor in the case, upon the request of the victim with the agreement of the prosecutor, or upon the request of any other person with the agreement of the prosecutor, may cause an accused who is charged with a violation of any other section of the Revised Code or with a violation of any other municipal ordinance to submit to one or more tests so designated by the director of health if the circumstances of the violation indicate probable cause to believe that the accused, if the accused is infected with HIV, might have transmitted HIV to any of the following persons in committing the violation:

(i) In relation to a request made by the prosecuting attorney, to the victim or to any other person;

(ii) In relation to a request made by the victim, to the victim making the request;

(iii) In relation to a request made by any other person, to the person making the request.

(b) The results of a test performed under division (B)(1)(a) of this section shall be communicated in confidence to the court, and the court shall inform the accused of the result. The court shall inform the victim that the test was performed and that the victim has a right to receive the results on request. If the test was performed upon the request of a person other than the prosecutor in the case and other than the victim, the court shall inform the person who made the request that the test was performed and that the person has a right to receive the results upon request. Additionally, regardless of who made the request that was the basis of the test being performed, if the court reasonably believes that, in circumstances related to the violation, a person other than the victim had contact with the accused that could have resulted in the transmission of HIV to that person, the court may inform that person that the test was performed and that the person has a right to receive the results of the test on request. If the accused tests positive for HIV, the test results shall be reported to the department of health in accordance with section 3701.24 of the Revised Code and to the sheriff, head of the state correctional institution, or other person in charge of any jail or prison in which the accused is incarcerated. If the accused tests positive for HIV and the accused was charged with, and was convicted of or pleaded guilty to, a violation of section 2907.24, 2907.241 [2907.24.1], or 2907.25 of the Revised Code or a violation of a municipal ordinance that is substantially equivalent to any of those sections, the test results also shall be reported to the law enforcement agency that arrested the accused, and the law enforcement agency may use the test results as the basis for any future charge of a violation of division (B) of any of those sections or a violation of a municipal ordinance that is substantially equivalent to division (B) of any of those sections. No other disclosure of the test results or the fact that a test was performed shall be made, other than as evidence in a grand jury proceeding or as evidence in a judicial proceeding in accordance with the Rules of Evidence. If the test result is negative, and the charge has not been dismissed or if the accused has been convicted of the charge or a different offense arising out of the same circumstances as the offense charged, the court shall order that the test be repeated not earlier than three months nor later than six months after the original test.

(2) If an accused who is free on bond refuses to submit to a test ordered by the court pursuant to division (B)(1) of this section, the court may order that the accused's bond be revoked and that the accused be incarcerated until the test is performed. If an accused who is incarcerated refuses to submit to a test ordered by the court pursuant to division (B)(1) of this section, the court shall order the person in charge of the jail or prison in which the accused is incarcerated to take any action necessary to facilitate the performance of the test, including the forcible restraint of the accused for the purpose of drawing blood to be used in the test.

(3) A state agency, a political subdivision of the state, or an employee of a state agency or of a political subdivision of the state is immune from liability in a civil action to recover damages for injury, death, or loss to person or property allegedly caused by any act or omission in connection with the performance of the duties required under division (B)(2) of this section unless the acts or omissions are with malicious purpose, in bad faith, or in a wanton or reckless manner.

(C) As used in this section:

(1) "Community control sanction" has the same meaning as in section 2929.01 of the Revised Code.

(2) "HIV" means the human immunodeficiency virus.

**HISTORY: 134 v H 511 (Eff 1-1-74); 143 v S 94 (Eff 9-27-89); 143 v S 2 (Eff 11-1-89); 145 v H 571 (Eff 10-6-94); 146 v H 40 (Eff 5-30-96); 148 v H 100. Eff 3-23-2000; 149 v H 490, § 1, eff. 1-1-04; 153 v H 1, § 101.01, eff. 10-16-09.**

The effective date is set by § 812.10 of 153 v H 1.

The effective date is set by section 4 of HB 490.

**Not analogous to former RC § 2907.27 (GC § 12448-5; 117 v 821; Bureau of Code Revision, 10-1-53), repealed 134 v H 511, § 2, eff 1-1-74.**

**Analogous to former RC § 2905.28 (GC § 13031-17; 108 v PtI, 730; 118 v 301; Bureau of Code Revision, 10-1-53; 130 v PtII, 144), repealed 134 v H 511, § 2, eff 1-1-74.**

## [MEDICAL ASSISTANCE FOR VICTIMS]

### § 2907.28 Payment of cost of medical examination and test of victim or accused.

(A) Any cost incurred by a hospital or emergency medical facility in conducting a medical examination of a victim of an offense under any provision of sections 2907.02 to 2907.06 of the Revised Code for the purpose of gathering physical evidence for a possible prosecution, including the cost of any antibiotics administered as part of the examination, shall be paid out of the reparations fund established pursuant to section 2743.191 [2743.19.1] of the Revised Code, subject to the following conditions:

(1) The hospital or emergency facility shall follow a protocol for conducting such medical examinations that is identified by the attorney general in rule adopted in accordance with Chapter 119. of the Revised Code.

(2) The hospital or emergency facility shall submit requests for payment to the attorney general on a monthly basis, through a procedure determined by the attorney general and on forms approved by the attorney general. The requests shall identify the number of sexual assault examinations performed and shall verify that all required protocols were met for each examination form submitted for payment in the request.

(3) The attorney general shall review all requests for payment that are submitted under division (A)(2) of this section and shall submit for payment as described in division (A)(5) of this section all requests that meet the requirements of this section.

(4) The hospital or emergency facility shall accept a flat fee payment for conducting each examination in the amount determined by the attorney general pursuant to Chapter 119. of the Revised Code as payment in full for any cost incurred in conducting a medical examination and test of a victim of an offense under any provision of sections 2907.02 to 2907.06 of the Revised Code for the purpose of gathering physical evidence for a possible prosecution of a person. The attorney general shall determine a flat fee payment amount to be paid under this division that is reasonable.

(5) In approving a payment under this section, the attorney general shall order the payment against the state. The payment shall be accomplished only through the following procedure, and the procedure may be enforced through a mandamus action and a writ of mandamus directed to the appropriate official:

(a) The attorney general shall provide for payment in the amount set forth in the order.

(b) The expense of the payment of the amount described in this section shall be charged against all available unencumbered moneys in the reparations fund.

(B) No costs incurred by a hospital or emergency facility in conducting a medical examination and test of any victim of an offense under any provision of sections 2907.02 to 2907.06 of the Revised Code for the purpose of gathering physical evidence for a possible prosecution of a person shall be billed or charged directly or indirectly to the victim or the victim's insurer.

(C) Any cost incurred by a hospital or emergency medical facility in conducting a medical examination and test of any person who is charged with a violation of division (B) of section 2903.11 or of section 2907.02, 2907.03, 2907.04, 2907.05, 2907.24, 2907.241 [2907.24.1], or 2907.25 of the Revised Code or with a violation of a municipal ordinance that is substantially equivalent to that division or any of those sections, pursuant to division (B) of section 2907.27 of the Revised Code, shall be charged to and paid by the accused who undergoes the examination and test, unless the court determines that the accused is unable to pay, in which case the cost shall be charged to and paid by the municipal corporation in which the offense allegedly was committed, or charged to and paid by the county if the offense allegedly was committed within an unincorporated area. If separate counts of an alleged offense or alleged separate offenses under section 2907.02, 2907.03, 2907.04, 2907.05, 2907.24, 2907.241 [2907.24.1], or 2907.25 of the Revised Code or under a municipal ordinance that is substantially equivalent to any of those sections took place in more than one municipal corporation or more than one unincorporated area, or both, the local governments shall share the cost of the examination and test. If a hospital or other emergency medical facility has submitted charges for the cost of a medical examination and test to an accused and has been unable to collect payment for the charges after making good faith attempts to collect for a period of six months or more, the cost shall be charged to and paid by the appropriate municipal corporation or county as specified in division (C) of this section.

**HISTORY: 136 v S 144 (Eff 8-27-75); 143 v S 2 (Eff 11-1-89); 146 v H 40 (Eff 5-30-96); 146 v H 445 (Eff 9-3-96); 148 v H 100 (Eff 3-23-2000); 148 v S 153. Eff 7-1-2000.**

**Not analogous to former RC § 2907.28 (GC § 12448-6; 117 v 821; Bureau of Code Revision, 10-1-53), repealed 134 v H 511, § 2, eff 1-1-74.**

The effective date is set by section 4 of SB 153.

## § 2907.29 Hospital emergency services for victims.

Every hospital of this state that offers organized emergency services shall provide that a physician, a physician assistant, a clinical nurse specialist, a certified nurse practitioner, or a certified nurse-midwife is available on call twenty-four hours each day for the examination of persons reported to any law enforcement agency to be victims of sexual offenses cognizable as violations of any provision of sections 2907.02 to 2907.06 of the Revised Code. The physician, physician assistant, clinical nurse specialist, certified nurse practitioner, or certified nurse-midwife, upon the request of any peace officer or prosecuting attorney and with the consent of the reported victim or upon the request of the reported victim, shall examine the person for the purposes of gathering physical evidence and shall complete any written documentation of the physical examination. The public health council shall establish procedures for gathering evidence under this section.

Each reported victim shall be informed of available venereal disease, pregnancy, medical, and psychiatric services.

Notwithstanding any other provision of law, a minor may consent to examination under this section. The consent is not subject to disaffirmance because of minority, and consent of the parent, parents, or guardian of the minor is not required for an examination under this section. However, the hospital shall give written notice to the parent, parents, or guardian of a minor that an examination under this section has taken place. The parent, parents, or guardian of a minor giving consent under this section are not liable for payment for any services provided under this section without their consent.

**HISTORY: 136 v S 144 (Eff 8-27-75); 146 v H 445 (Eff 9-3-96); 149 v S 245. Eff 3-31-2003.**

**Not analogous to former RC § 2907.29 (RS § 6818; S&C 406; 33 v 33; 80 v 38; GC § 12449; Bureau of Code Revision, 10-1-53), repealed 134 v H 511, § 2, eff 1-1-74.**

## § 2907.30 Victim to be interviewed by crisis intervention trained officer.

(A) A victim of a sexual offense cognizable as a violation of section 2907.02 of the Revised Code who is interviewed by a law enforcement agency shall be interviewed by a peace officer employed by the agency who has had crisis intervention training, if any of the peace officers employed by the agency who have had crisis intervention training is reasonably available.

(B) When a person is charged with a violation of section 2907.02, 2907.03, 2907.04, 2907.05, or 2907.06 of the Revised Code and the law enforcement agency that arrested the person or a court discovers that the person arrested or a person whom the person arrested caused to engage in sexual activity has a communicable disease, the law enforcement agency that arrested the person or the court immediately shall notify the victim of the nature of the disease.

(C) As used in this section, "crisis intervention training" has the same meaning as in section 109.71 of the Revised Code.

**HISTORY: 140 v H 435 (Eff 4-4-85); 141 v H 468 (Eff 9-17-86); 146 v H 445. Eff 9-3-96.**

**Not analogous to former RC § 2907.30 (RS § 6858; S&C 408, 412, 426, 439, 451; GC § 12450; 33 v 33, §§ 20, 26; 34 v 10; 37 v 74; 56 v 26; 69 v 68; 124 v 466; Bureau of Code Revision, 10-1-53), repealed 134 v H 511, § 2, eff 1-1-74.**

[OBSCENITY]

## § 2907.31 Disseminating matter harmful to juveniles.

(A) No person, with knowledge of its character or content, shall recklessly do any of the following:

(1) Directly sell, deliver, furnish, disseminate, provide, exhibit, rent, or present to a juvenile, a group of juveniles, a law enforcement officer posing as a juvenile, or a group of law enforcement officers posing as juveniles any material or performance that is obscene or harmful to juveniles;

(2) Directly offer or agree to sell, deliver, furnish, disseminate, provide, exhibit, rent, or present to a juvenile, a group of juveniles, a law enforcement officer posing as a juvenile, or a group of law enforcement officers posing as juveniles any material or performance that is obscene or harmful to juveniles;

(3) While in the physical proximity of the juvenile or law enforcement officer posing as a juvenile, allow any juvenile or law enforcement officer posing as a juvenile to review or peruse any material or view any live performance that is harmful to juveniles.

(B) The following are affirmative defenses to a charge under this section that involves material or a performance that is harmful to juveniles but not obscene:

(1) The defendant is the parent, guardian, or spouse of the juvenile involved.

(2) The juvenile involved, at the time of the conduct in question, was accompanied by the juvenile's parent or guardian who, with knowledge of its character, consented to the material or performance being furnished or presented to the juvenile.

(3) The juvenile exhibited to the defendant or to the defendant's agent or employee a draft card, driver's license, birth record, marriage license, or other official or apparently official document purporting to show that the juvenile was eighteen years of age or over or married, and the person to whom that document was exhibited did not otherwise have reasonable cause to believe that the juvenile was under the age of eighteen and unmarried.

(C)(1) It is an affirmative defense to a charge under this section, involving material or a performance that is obscene or harmful to juveniles, that the material or performance was furnished or presented for a bona fide medical, scientific, educational, governmental, judicial, or other proper purpose, by a physician, psychologist, sociologist, scientist, teacher, librarian, clergyman, prosecutor, judge, or other proper person.

(2) Except as provided in division (B)(3) of this section, mistake of age is not a defense to a charge under this section.

(D)(1) A person directly sells, delivers, furnishes, disseminates, provides, exhibits, rents, or presents or directly offers or agrees to sell, deliver, furnish, disseminate, provide, exhibit, rent, or present material or a performance to a juvenile, a group of juveniles, a law enforcement officer posing as a juvenile, or a group of law enforcement officers posing as juveniles in violation of this section by means of an electronic method of remotely transmitting information if the person knows or has reason to believe that the person receiving the information is a juvenile or the group of persons receiving the information are juveniles.

(2) A person remotely transmitting information by means of a method of mass distribution does not directly sell, deliver, furnish, disseminate, provide, exhibit, rent, or present or directly offer or agree to sell, deliver, furnish, disseminate, provide, exhibit, rent, or present the material or performance in question to a juvenile, a group of juveniles, a law enforcement officer posing as a juvenile, or a group of law enforcement officers posing as juveniles in violation of this section if either of the following applies:

(a) The person has inadequate information to know or have reason to believe that a particular recipient of the information or offer is a juvenile.

(b) The method of mass distribution does not provide the person the ability to prevent a particular recipient from receiving the information.

(E) If any provision of this section, or the application of any provision of this section to any person or circumstance, is held invalid, the invalidity does not affect other provisions or applications of this section or related sections that can be given effect without the invalid provision or application. To this end, the provisions are severable.

(F) Whoever violates this section is guilty of disseminating matter harmful to juveniles. If the material or performance involved is harmful to juveniles, except as otherwise provided in this division, a violation of this section is a misdemeanor of the first degree. If the material or performance involved is obscene, except as otherwise provided in this division, a violation of this section is a felony of the fifth degree. If the material or performance involved is obscene and the juvenile to whom it is sold, delivered, furnished, disseminated, provided, exhibited, rented, or presented, the juvenile to whom the offer is made or who is the subject of the agreement, or the juvenile who is allowed to review, peruse, or view it is under thirteen years of age, violation of this section is a felony of the fourth degree.

**HISTORY: 134 v H 511 (Eff 1-1-74); 142 v H 51 (Eff 3-17-89); 142 v H 790 (Eff 3-16-89); 146 v S 2. Eff 7-1-96; 149 v H 490, § 1, eff. 1-1-04.**

The effective date is set by section 4 of HB 490.

**Not analogous to former RC § 2907.31 (RS § 6859; S&C 1632; 47 v 21; GC § 12451; Bureau of Code Revision, 10-1-53), repealed 134 v H 511, § 2, eff 1-1-74.**

The provisions of § 7 of SB 2 (146 v —) read as follows:

SECTION 7. * * * Section 2907.31 of the Revised Code is presented in this act as a composite of the section as amended by both Sub. H.B. 51 and Am. Sub. H.B. 790 of the 117th General Assembly, with the new language of neither of the acts shown in capital letters. * * * This is in recognition of the principle stated in division (B) of section 1.52 of the Revised Code that such amendments are to be harmonized where not substantively irreconcilable and constitutes a legislative finding that such is the resulting version in effect prior to the effective date of this act.

## § 2907.311 Displaying matter harmful to juveniles.

(A) No person who has custody, control, or supervision of a commercial establishment, with knowledge of the character or content of the material involved, shall display at the establishment any material that is harmful to juveniles and that is open to view by juveniles as part of the invited general public.

(B) It is not a violation of division (A) of this section if the material in question is displayed by placing it behind "blinder racks" or similar devices that cover at least the lower two-thirds of the material, if the material in question is wrapped or placed behind the counter, or if the material in question otherwise is covered or located so that the portion that is harmful to juveniles is not open to the view of juveniles.

(C) Whoever violates this section is guilty of displaying matter harmful to juveniles, a misdemeanor of the first degree. Each day during which the offender is in violation of this section constitutes a separate offense.

**HISTORY: 142 v H 51. Eff 3-17-89.**

## § 2907.32 Pandering obscenity.

(A) No person, with knowledge of the character of the material or performance involved, shall do any of the following:

(1) Create, reproduce, or publish any obscene material, when the offender knows that the material is to be used for commercial exploitation or will be publicly disseminated or displayed, or when the offender is reckless in that regard;

(2) Promote or advertise for sale, delivery, or dissemination; sell, deliver, publicly disseminate, publicly display, exhibit, present, rent, or provide; or offer or agree to sell, deliver, publicly disseminate, publicly display, exhibit, present, rent, or provide, any obscene material;

(3) Create, direct, or produce an obscene performance, when the offender knows that it is to be used for commercial exploitation or will be publicly presented, or when the offender is reckless in that regard;

(4) Advertise or promote an obscene performance for presentation, or present or participate in presenting an obscene performance, when the performance is presented publicly, or when admission is charged;

(5) Buy, procure, possess, or control any obscene material with purpose to violate division (A)(2) or (4) of this section.

(B) It is an affirmative defense to a charge under this section, that the material or performance involved was disseminated or presented for a bona fide medical, scientific, educational, religious, governmental, judicial, or other proper purpose, by or to a physician, psychologist, sociologist, scientist, teacher, person pursuing bona fide studies or research, librarian, clergyman, prosecutor, judge, or other person having a proper interest in the material or performance.

(C) Whoever violates this section is guilty of pandering obscenity, a felony of the fifth degree. If the offender previously has been convicted of a violation of this section or of section 2907.31 of the Revised Code, then pandering obscenity is a felony of the fourth degree.

**HISTORY: 134 v H 511 (Eff 1-1-74); 142 v H 51 (Eff 3-17-89); 146 v S 2. Eff 7-1-96.**

**Not analogous to former RC § 2907.32 (RS § 6860; S&C 351; 56 v 79; 90 v 232; GC § 12452; Bureau of Code Revision, 10-1-53), repealed 134 v H 511, § 2, eff 1-1-74.**

**Analogous to former RC § 2905.35 (133 v H 84), repealed 134 v H 511, § 2, eff 1-1-74.**

The effective date is set by section 6 of SB 2.

## § 2907.321 Pandering obscenity involving a minor.

(A) No person, with knowledge of the character of the material or performance involved, shall do any of the following:

(1) Create, reproduce, or publish any obscene material that has a minor as one of its participants or portrayed observers;

(2) Promote or advertise for sale or dissemination; sell, deliver, disseminate, display, exhibit, present, rent, or provide; or offer or agree to sell, deliver, disseminate, display, exhibit, present, rent, or provide, any obscene material that has a minor as one of its participants or portrayed observers;

(3) Create, direct, or produce an obscene performance that has a minor as one of its participants;

(4) Advertise or promote for presentation, present, or participate in presenting an obscene performance that has a minor as one of its participants;

(5) Buy, procure, possess, or control any obscene material, that has a minor as one of its participants;

(6) Bring or cause to be brought into this state any obscene material that has a minor as one of its participants or portrayed observers.

(B)(1) This section does not apply to any material or performance that is sold, disseminated, displayed, possessed, controlled, brought or caused to be brought into this state, or presented for a bona fide medical, scientific, educational, religious, governmental, judicial, or other proper purpose, by or to a physician, psychologist, sociologist, scientist, teacher, person pursuing bona fide studies or research, librarian, clergyman, prosecutor, judge, or other person having a proper interest in the material or performance.

(2) Mistake of age is not a defense to a charge under this section.

(3) In a prosecution under this section, the trier of fact may infer that a person in the material or performance involved is a minor if the material or performance, through its title, text, visual representation, or otherwise, represents or depicts the person as a minor.

(C) Whoever violates this section is guilty of pandering obscenity involving a minor. Violation of division (A)(1), (2), (3), (4), or (6) of this section is a felony of the second degree. Violation of division (A)(5) of this section is a felony of the fourth degree. If the offender previously has been convicted of or pleaded guilty to a violation of this section or section 2907.322 [2907.32.2] or 2907.323 [2907.32.3] of the Revised Code, pandering obscenity involving a minor in violation of division (A)(5) of this section is a felony of the third degree.

**HISTORY: 137 v S 243 (Eff 11-17-77); 140 v H 44 (Eff 9-27-84); 142 v H 51. Eff 3-17-89.**

## § 2907.322 Pandering sexually oriented matter involving a minor.

(A) No person, with knowledge of the character of the material or performance involved, shall do any of the following:

(1) Create, record, photograph, film, develop, reproduce, or publish any material that shows a minor participating or engaging in sexual activity, masturbation, or bestiality;

(2) Advertise for sale or dissemination, sell, distribute, transport, disseminate, exhibit, or display any material that shows a minor participating or engaging in sexual activity, masturbation, or bestiality;

(3) Create, direct, or produce a performance that shows a minor participating or engaging in sexual activity, masturbation, or bestiality;

(4) Advertise for presentation, present, or participate in presenting a performance that shows a minor participating or engaging in sexual activity, masturbation, or bestiality;

(5) Knowingly solicit, receive, purchase, exchange, possess, or control any material that shows a minor participating or engaging in sexual activity, masturbation, or bestiality;

(6) Bring or cause to be brought into this state any material that shows a minor participating or engaging in sexual activity, masturbation, or bestiality, or bring, cause to be brought, or finance the bringing of any minor into or across this state with the intent that the minor engage in

sexual activity, masturbation, or bestiality in a performance or for the purpose of producing material containing a visual representation depicting the minor engaged in sexual activity, masturbation, or bestiality.

(B)(1) This section does not apply to any material or performance that is sold, disseminated, displayed, possessed, controlled, brought or caused to be brought into this state, or presented for a bona fide medical, scientific, educational, religious, governmental, judicial, or other proper purpose, by or to a physician, psychologist, sociologist, scientist, teacher, person pursuing bona fide studies or research, librarian, clergyman, prosecutor, judge, or other person having a proper interest in the material or performance.

(2) Mistake of age is not a defense to a charge under this section.

(3) In a prosecution under this section, the trier of fact may infer that a person in the material or performance involved is a minor if the material or performance, through its title, text, visual representation, or otherwise, represents or depicts the person as a minor.

(C) Whoever violates this section is guilty of pandering sexually oriented matter involving a minor. Violation of division (A)(1), (2), (3), (4), or (6) of this section is a felony of the second degree. Violation of division (A)(5) of this section is a felony of the fourth degree. If the offender previously has been convicted of or pleaded guilty to a violation of this section or section 2907.321 [2907.32.1] or 2907.323 [2907.32.3] of the Revised Code, pandering sexually oriented matter involving a minor in violation of division (A)(5) of this section is a felony of the third degree.

**HISTORY: 140 v H 44 (Eff 9-27-84); 142 v H 51 (Eff 3-17-89); 146 v S 2 (Eff 7-1-96); 148 v H 724. Eff 3-22-2001.**

## § 2907.323 Illegal use of minor in nudity-oriented material or performance.

(A) No person shall do any of the following:

(1) Photograph any minor who is not the person's child or ward in a state of nudity, or create, direct, produce, or transfer any material or performance that shows the minor in a state of nudity, unless both of the following apply:

(a) The material or performance is, or is to be, sold, disseminated, displayed, possessed, controlled, brought or caused to be brought into this state, or presented for a bona fide artistic, medical, scientific, educational, religious, governmental, judicial, or other proper purpose, by or to a physician, psychologist, sociologist, scientist, teacher, person pursuing bona fide studies or research, librarian, member of the clergy, prosecutor, judge, or other person having a proper interest in the material or performance;

(b) The minor's parents, guardian, or custodian consents in writing to the photographing of the minor, to the use of the minor in the material or performance, or to the transfer of the material and to the specific manner in which the material or performance is to be used.

(2) Consent to the photographing of the person's minor child or ward, or photograph the person's minor child or ward, in a state of nudity or consent to the use of the person's minor child or ward in a state of nudity in any material or performance, or use or transfer a material or performance of that nature, unless the material or performance is sold, disseminated, displayed, possessed, controlled, brought or caused to be brought into this state, or presented for a bona fide artistic, medical, scientific, educational, religious, governmental, judicial, or other proper purpose, by or to a physician, psychologist, sociologist, scientist, teacher, person pursuing bona fide studies or research, librarian, member of the clergy, prosecutor, judge, or other person having a proper interest in the material or performance;

(3) Possess or view any material or performance that shows a minor who is not the person's child or ward in a state of nudity, unless one of the following applies:

(a) The material or performance is sold, disseminated, displayed, possessed, controlled, brought or caused to be brought into this state, or presented for a bona fide artistic, medical, scientific, educational, religious, governmental, judicial, or other proper purpose, by or to a physician, psychologist, sociologist, scientist, teacher, person pursuing bona fide studies or research, librarian, member of the clergy, prosecutor, judge, or other person having a proper interest in the material or performance.

(b) The person knows that the parents, guardian, or custodian has consented in writing to the photographing or use of the minor in a state of nudity and to the manner in which the material or performance is used or transferred.

(B) Whoever violates this section is guilty of illegal use of a minor in a nudity-oriented material or performance. Whoever violates division (A)(1) or (2) of this section is guilty of a felony of the second degree. Except as otherwise provided in this division, whoever violates division (A)(3) of this section is guilty of a felony of the fifth degree. If the offender previously has been convicted of or pleaded guilty to a violation of this section or section 2907.321 or 2907.322 of the Revised Code, illegal use of a minor in a nudity-oriented material or performance in violation of division (A)(3) of this section is a felony of the fourth degree. If the offender who violates division (A)(1) or (2) of this section also is convicted of or pleads guilty to a specification as described in section 2941.1422 of the Revised Code that was included in the indictment, count in the indictment, or information charging the offense, the court shall sentence the offender to a mandatory prison term as provided in division (B)(7) of section 2929.14 of the Revised Code and shall order the offender to make restitution as provided in division (B)(8) of section 2929.18 of the Revised Code.

**HISTORY: 140 v H 44 (Eff 9-27-84); 140 v S 321 (Eff 4-9-85); 142 v H 51 (Eff 3-17-89); 146 v S 2. Eff 7-1-96; 152 v H 280, § 1, eff. 4-7-09; 2011 HB 86, § 1, eff. Sept. 30, 2011.**

The effective date is set by section 6 of SB 2.

## § 2907.33 Deception to obtain matter harmful to juveniles.

(A) No person, for the purpose of enabling a juvenile to obtain any material or gain admission to any performance which is harmful to juveniles, shall do either of the following:

(1) Falsely represent that he is the parent, guardian, or spouse of such juvenile;

(2) Furnish such juvenile with any identification or document purporting to show that such juvenile is eighteen years of age or over or married.

(B) No juvenile, for the purpose of obtaining any material or gaining admission to any performance which is harmful to juveniles, shall do either of the following:

(1) Falsely represent that he is eighteen years of age or over or married;

(2) Exhibit any identification or document purporting to show that he is eighteen years of age or over or married.

(C) Whoever violates this section is guilty of deception to obtain matter harmful to juveniles, a misdemeanor of the second degree. A juvenile who violates division (B) of this section shall be adjudged an unruly child, with such disposition of the case as may be appropriate under Chapter 2151. of the Revised Code.

**HISTORY: 134 v H 511. Eff 1-1-74.**

**Not analogous to former RC § 2907.33 (RS § 7071; S&C 351; 56 v 79; GC § 13127; Bureau of Code Revision, 10-1-53), repealed 134 v H 511, § 2, eff 1-1-74.**

**Analogous to former RC § 2903.16 (133 v H 84; 135 v S 62), repealed 134 v H 511, § 2, eff 1-1-74.**

The effective date is set by section 4 of HB 511.

## § 2907.34 Compelling acceptance of objectionable materials.

(A) No person, as a condition to the sale, allocation, consignment, or delivery of any material or goods of any kind, shall require the purchaser or consignee to accept any other material reasonably believed to be obscene, or which if furnished or presented to a juvenile would be in violation of section 2907.31 of the Revised Code.

(B) No person shall deny or threaten to deny any franchise or impose or threaten to impose any financial or other penalty upon any purchaser or consignee because the purchaser or consignee failed or refused to accept any material reasonably believed to be obscene as a condition to the sale, allocation, consignment, or delivery of any other material or goods or because the purchaser or consignee returned any material believed to be obscene that the purchaser or consignee initially accepted.

(C) Whoever violates this section is guilty of compelling acceptance of objectionable materials, a felony of the fifth degree.

**HISTORY: 134 v H 511 (Eff 1-1-74); 142 v H 51 (Eff 3-17-89); 146 v S 2. Eff 7-1-96.**

**Not analogous to former RC § 2907.34 (RS § 6842; S&C 240, 426; 55 v 84; 66 v 29; 73 v 31; 73 v 86; 78 v 186; 82 v 140; 83 v 23; 95 v 303; 97 v 67; GC § 12467; 111 v 101; 124 v 466; Bureau of Code Revision, 10-1-53), repealed 134 v H 511, § 2, eff 1-1-74.**

**Analogous to former RC § 2905.36 (133 v H 84), repealed 134 v H 511, § 2, eff 1-1-74.**

The effective date is set by section 6 of SB 2.

## § 2907.35 Presumptions; notice.

(A) An owner or manager, or agent or employee of an owner or manager, of a bookstore, newsstand, theater, or other commercial establishment engaged in selling materials or exhibiting performances, who, in the course of business:

(1) Possesses five or more identical or substantially similar obscene articles, having knowledge of their character, is presumed to possess them in violation of division (A)(5) of section 2907.32 of the Revised Code;

(2) Does any of the acts prohibited by section 2907.31 or 2907.32 of the Revised Code, is presumed to have knowledge of the character of the material or performance involved, if the owner, manager, or agent or employee of the owner or manager has actual notice of the nature of such material or performance, whether or not the owner, manager, or agent or employee of the owner or manager has precise knowledge of its contents.

(B) Without limitation on the manner in which such notice may be given, actual notice of the character of material or a performance may be given in writing by the chief legal officer of the jurisdiction in which the person to whom the notice is directed does business. Such notice, regardless of the manner in which it is given, shall identify the sender, identify the material or performance involved, state whether it is obscene or harmful to juveniles, and bear the date of such notice.

(C) Sections 2907.31 and 2907.32 of the Revised Code do not apply to a motion picture operator or projectionist acting within the scope of employment as an employee of the owner or manager of a theater or other place for the showing of motion pictures to the general public, and having no managerial responsibility or financial interest in the operator's or projectionist's place of employment, other than wages.

(D)(1) Sections 2907.31, 2907.311 [2907.31.1], 2907.32, 2907.321 [2907.32.1], 2907.322 [2907.32.2], 2907.323 [2907.32.3], and 2907.34 and division (A) of section 2907.33 of the Revised Code do not apply to a person solely because the person provided access or connection to or from an electronic method of remotely transferring information not under that person's control, including having provided capabilities that are incidental to providing access or connection to or from the electronic method of remotely transferring the information, and that do not include the creation of the content of the material that is the subject of the access or connection.

(2) Division (D)(1) of this section does not apply to a person who conspires with an entity actively involved in the creation or knowing distribution of material in violation of section 2907.31, 2907.311 [2907.31.1], 2907.32, 2907.321 [2907.32.1], 2907.322 [2907.32.2], 2907.323 [2907.32.3], 2907.33, or 2907.34 of the Revised Code or who knowingly advertises the availability of material of that nature.

(3) Division (D)(1) of this section does not apply to a person who provides access or connection to an electronic method of remotely transferring information that is engaged in the violation of section 2907.31, 2907.311 [2907.31.1], 2907.32, 2907.321 [2907.32.1], 2907.322 [2907.32.2], 2907.323 [2907.32.3], 2907.33, or 2907.34 of the Revised Code and that contains content that person has selected and introduced into the electronic method of remotely transferring information or content over which that person exercises editorial control.

(E) An employer is not guilty of a violation of section 2907.31, 2907.311 [2907.31.1], 2907.32, 2907.321 [2907.32.1], 2907.322 [2907.32.2], 2907.323 [2907.32.3], 2907.33, or 2907.34 of the Revised Code based on the actions of an employee or agent of the employer unless the employee's or agent's conduct is within the scope of employee's or agent's employment or agency, and the employer does either of the following:

(1) With knowledge of the employee's or agent's conduct, the employer authorizes or ratifies the conduct.

(2) The employer recklessly disregards the employee's or agent's conduct.

(F) It is an affirmative defense to a charge under section 2907.31 or 2907.311 [2907.31.1] of the Revised Code as the section applies to an image transmitted through the internet or another electronic method of remotely transmitting information that the person charged with violating the section has taken, in good faith, reasonable, effective, and appropriate actions under the circumstances to restrict or prevent access by juveniles to material that is harmful to juveniles, including any method that is feasible under available technology.

(G) If any provision of this section, or the application of any provision of this section to any person or circumstance, is held invalid, the invalidity does not affect other provisions or applications of this section or related sections that can be given effect without the invalid provision or application. To this end, the provisions are severable.

**HISTORY: 134 v H 511 (Eff 1-1-74); 135 v S 62 (Eff 1-1-74); 149 v H 8. Eff 8-5-2002; 149 v H 490, § 1, eff. 1-1-04.**

The effective date is set by section 4 of HB 490.

**Not analogous to former RC § 2907.35 (RS § 6843; S&C 426; 37 v 74; GC § 12468; Bureau of Code Revision, 10-1-53), repealed 134 v H 511, § 2, eff 1-1-74.**

## § 2907.36 Declaratory judgment.

(A) Without limitation on the persons otherwise entitled to bring an action for a declaratory judgment pursuant to Chapter 2721. of the Revised Code, involving the same issue, the following persons have standing to bring a declaratory judgment action to determine whether particular materials or performances are obscene or harmful to juveniles:

(1) The chief legal officer of the jurisdiction in which there is reasonable cause to believe that section 2907.31 or 2907.32 of the Revised Code is being or is about to be violated;

(2) Any person who, pursuant to division (B) of section 2907.35 of the Revised Code, has received notice in writing from a chief legal officer stating that particular materials or performances are obscene or harmful to juveniles.

(B) Any party to an action for a declaratory judgment pursuant to division (A) of this section is entitled, upon the party's request, to trial on the merits within five days after joinder of the issues, and the court shall render judgment within five days after trial is concluded.

(C) An action for a declaratory judgment pursuant to division (A) of this section shall not be brought during the pendency of any civil action or criminal prosecution, when the character of the particular materials or performances involved is at issue in the pending case, and either of the following applies:

(1) Either of the parties to the action for a declaratory judgment is a party to the pending case.

(2) A judgment in the pending case will necessarily constitute res judicata as to the character of the materials or performances involved.

(D) A civil action or criminal prosecution in which the character of particular materials or performances is at issue, brought during the pendency of an action for a declaratory judgment involving the same issue, shall be stayed during the pendency of the action for a declaratory judgment.

(E) The fact that a violation of section 2907.31 or 2907.32 of the Revised Code occurs prior to a judicial determination of the character of the material or performance involved in the violation does not relieve the offender of criminal liability for the violation, even though prosecution may be stayed pending the judicial determination.

**HISTORY: 134 v H 511 (Eff 1-1-74); 148 v H 58. Eff 9-24-99.**

**Not analogous to former RC § 2907.36 (RS § 6844; S&C 426, 1425; 37 v 74; 57 v 15; 72 v 20; GC § 12469; 124 v 466; Bureau of Code Revision, 10-1-53), repealed 134 v H 511, § 2, eff 1-1-74.**

**Analogous to former RC § 2905.38 (133 v H 84), repealed 134 v H 511, § 2, eff 1-1-74.**

## § 2907.37 Injunction.

(A) Where it appears that section 2907.31 or 2907.32 of the Revised Code is being or is about to be violated, the chief legal officer of the jurisdiction in which the violation is taking place or is about to take place may bring an action to enjoin the violation. The defendant, upon his request, is entitled to trial on the merits within five days after joinder of the issues, and the court shall render judgment within five days after trial is concluded.

(B) Premises used or occupied for repeated violations of section 2907.31 or 2907.32 of the Revised Code constitute a nuisance subject to abatement pursuant to sections 3767.01 to 3767.99 of the Revised Code.

**HISTORY: 134 v H 511. Eff 1-1-74.**

**Not analogous to former RC § 2907.37 (RS § 6845; S&C 421, 423; 42 v 49; 50 v 132; 71 v 66; 78 v 15; GC § 12470; Bureau of Code Revision, 10-1-53), repealed 134 v H 511, § 2, eff 1-1-74.**

**Analogous to former RC § 2905.37 (133 v H 84), repealed 134 v H 511, § 2, eff 1-1-74.**

The effective date is set by section 4 of HB 511.

## § 2907.38 Permitting unlawful operation of viewing booths depicting sexual conduct.

(A) As used in this section:

(1) "Commercial establishment" means an entity that is open to the public and to which either of the following applies:

(a) It has a substantial or significant portion of its stock in trade of the sale, rental, or viewing of visual materials or performances depicting sexual conduct.

(b) It has as a principal business purpose the sale, rental, or viewing of visual materials or performances depicting sexual conduct.

(2) "Visual materials or performances" means films, videos, CD-ROM discs, streaming video, or other motion pictures.

(B) No person who has custody, control, or supervision of a commercial establishment, with knowledge of the character of the visual material or performance involved, shall knowingly permit the use of, or offer the use of, viewing booths, stalls, or partitioned portions of a room located in the commercial establishment for the purpose of viewing visual materials or performances depicting sexual conduct unless both of the following apply:

(1) The inside of each booth, stall, or partitioned room is visible from, and at least one side of each booth, stall, or partitioned room is open to, a continuous and contiguous main aisle or hallway that is open to the public areas of the commercial establishment and is not obscured by any curtain, door, or other covering or enclosure.

(2) No booth, stall, or partitioned room is designed, constructed, pandered, or allowed to be used for the purpose of encouraging or facilitating nudity or sexual activity on the part of or between patrons or members of the public, and no booth, stall, or partitioned room has any aperture, hole, or opening for the purpose of encouraging or facilitating nudity or sexual activity.

(C) It is an affirmative defense to a charge under this section that either of the following applies to the involved visual materials or performances:

(1) The visual materials or performances depicting sexual conduct are disseminated or presented for a bona fide medical, scientific, educational, religious, governmental, judicial, or other proper purpose and by or to a physician, psychologist, sociologist, scientist, teacher, person pursuing bona fide studies or research, librarian, member of the clergy, prosecutor, judge, or other person having a proper interest in the visual materials or performances.

(2) The visual materials or performances depicting sexual conduct, taken as a whole, would be found by a reasonable person to have serious literary, artistic, political, or scientific value or are presented or disseminated in good faith for a serious literary, artistic, political, or scientific purpose and are not pandered for their prurient appeal.

(D) Whoever violates this section is guilty of permitting unlawful operation of viewing booths depicting sexual conduct, a misdemeanor of the first degree.

**HISTORY: 151 v H 23, § 1, eff. 8-17-06.**

**Not analogous to former RC § 2907.38 (RS § 6849a; 82 v 247; 99 v 460; GC §§ 12471, 12475, 12475-1; 124 v 360; 124 v 466; Bureau of Code Revision, 10-1-53), repealed 134 v H 511, § 2, eff 1-1-74.**

The provisions of § 3 of 151 v H 23 read as follows:

SECTION 3. In enacting new sections 503.51 and 503.52 and sections 2907.38 and 2907.39 of the Revised Code, the General Assembly makes the following statement of intent and findings:

(A)(1) Adult entertainment establishments require special supervision from the public safety agencies of this state in order to protect and preserve the health, safety, morals, and welfare of the patrons and employees of the businesses as well as the citizens of this state.

(2) The General Assembly finds that adult entertainment establishments are frequently used for unlawful sexual activities, including prostitution and sexual liaisons of a casual nature.

(3) The concern over sexually transmitted diseases is a legitimate health concern of this state that demands reasonable regulation of adult entertainment establishments by the state in the specified manner, and expanded authority for reasonable regulation of adult entertainment establishments by local governments, in order to protect the health and well-being of the citizens.

(4) Minimal regulations enacted by local governments or the state are a legitimate and reasonable means of accountability to ensure that operators of adult entertainment establishments comply with reasonable regulations and to ensure that operators do not knowingly allow their establishments to be used as places of illegal sexual activity or solicitation.

(5) There is convincing documented evidence that adult entertainment establishments, because of their very nature, have a deleterious effect on both the existing businesses around them and the surrounding residential areas adjacent to them and cause increased crime, particularly in the overnight hours, and the downgrading of property values.

(6) The General Assembly desires to minimize and control these adverse effects by regulating adult entertainment establishments in the specified manner and by expanding the authority of local governments to regulate adult entertainment establishments and, by minimizing and controlling these adverse effects, to protect the health, safety, and welfare of the citizenry; protect the citizens from increased crime; preserve the quality of life; preserve the property values and character of surrounding neighborhoods; and deter the spread of urban blight.

(7) The General Assembly has determined that current local zoning and other locational criteria do not adequately protect the health, safety, and general welfare of the people of this state and that expanded local government authority to regulate adult entertainment establishments is necessary.

(8) It is not the intent of the General Assembly in enacting this act to suppress, or authorize the suppression of, any speech activities protected by the First Amendment but to enact content-neutral statutes that expand local government authority to address the secondary effects of adult entertainment establishments.

(9) It is not the intent of the General Assembly to condone or legitimize the distribution of obscene material, and the General Assembly recognizes that state and federal law prohibits the distribution of obscene materials and expects and encourages state law enforcement officials to enforce state obscenity statutes against any such illegal activities in this state.

(B) It is the intent of the General Assembly in enacting new sections 503.51 and 503.52 and sections 2907.38 and 2907.39 of the Revised Code to regulate in the specified manner, and to expand the authority of local governments to regulate, adult entertainment establishments in order to promote the health, safety, morals, and general welfare of the citizens of this state and establish reasonable regulations to prevent the deleterious secondary effects of adult entertainment establishments within this state. The provisions of new sections 503.51 and 503.52 and sections 2907.38 and 2907.39 of the Revised Code have neither the purpose nor effect of imposing a limitation or restriction on the content of any communicative materials, including sexually oriented materials. Similarly, it is not the intent nor effect of the General Assembly in enacting new sections 503.51 and 503.52 and sections 2907.38 and 2907.39 of the Revised Code to restrict or deny, or authorize the restriction or denial of, access by adults to sexually oriented materials protected by the First Amendment, or to deny, or authorize the denial of, access by the distributors and exhibitors of adult entertainment and adult materials to their intended market. Neither is it the intent nor effect of the General Assembly in enacting new sections 503.51 and 503.52 and sections 2907.38 and 2907.39 of the Revised Code to condone or legitimize the distribution or exhibition of obscene material.

(C) Based on evidence concerning the adverse secondary effects of adult uses on communities presented in hearings and in reports made available to the legislature and on findings incorporated in the cases of *City of Littleton, Colorado v. Z.J. Gifts D-4, L.L.C. (2004), 541 U.S. 774, City of Erie v. Pap's A.M.* (2000), 529 U.S. 277; *Barnes v. Glen Theatre, Inc.* (1991), 501 U.S. 560; *City of Renton v. Playtime Theatres, Inc.* (1986), 475 U.S. 41; *Young v. American Mini Theatres* (1976), 426 U.S. 50; *California v. LaRue* (1972), 409 U.S. 109; *DLS, Inc. v. City of Chattanooga* (6th Cir. 1997) 107 F.3d 403; *East Brooks Books, Inc. v. City of Memphis,* (6th Cir. 1995), 48 F.3d 220; *Harris v. Fitchville Township Trustees* (N.D. Ohio 2000), 99 F. Supp.2d 837; *Bamon Corp. v. City of Dayton* (S.D. Ohio 1990), 730 F. Supp. 90, *aff'd* (6th Cir. 1991), 923 F.2d 470; *Broadway Books v. Roberts* (E.D. Tenn. 1986), 642 F. Supp. 486; *Bright Lights, Inc. v. City of Newport* (E.D. Ky. 1993), 830 F. Supp. 378; *Richland Bookmart v. Nichols* (6th Cir. 1998), 137 F.3d 435; *Deja Vu v. Metro Government* (6th Cir. 1999), 1999 U.S. App. LEXIS 535; *Threesome Entertainment v. Strittmather* (N.D. Ohio 1998), 4 F.Supp.2d 710; *J.L. Spoons, Inc. v. City of Brunswick* (N.D. Ohio 1999), 49 F. Supp.2d 1032; *Triplett Grille, Inc. v. City of Akron* (6th Cir. 1994) 40 F.3d 129; *Nightclubs, Inc. v. City of Paducah* (6th Cir. 2000), 202 F.3d 884; *O'Connor v. City and County of Denver* (10th Cir. 1990), 894 F.2d 1210; *Deja Vu of Nashville, Inc., et al. v. Metropolitan Government of Nashville and Davidson County* (6th Cir. 2001), 2001 U.S. App. LEXIS 26007; *State of Ohio ex rel. Rothal v. Smith* (Ohio C.P. 2002), Summit C.P. No. CV 01094594; *Z.J. Gifts D-2, L.L.C. v. City of Aurora* (10th Cir. 1998), 136 F.3d 683; *Connection Distrib. Co. v. Reno* (6th Cir. 1998), 154 F.3d 281; *Sundance Assocs. v. Reno* (10th Cir. 1998), 139 F.3d 804; *American Library Association v. Reno* (D.C. Cir. 1994), 33 F.3d 78; *American Target Advertising, Inc. v. Giani* (10th Cir. 2000), 199 F.3d 1241; and other cases and on reports of secondary effects occurring in and around adult entertainment establishments in Phoenix, Arizona (1984); Minneapolis, Minnesota (1980); Houston, Texas (1983); Indianapolis, Indiana (1984); Amarillo, Texas (1977); Garden Grove, California (1991); Los Angeles, California (1977); Whittier, California (1978); Austin, Texas (1986); Seattle, Washington (1989); Oklahoma City, Oklahoma (1986); Cleveland, Ohio (1977); Dallas, Texas (1997); St. Croix County, Wisconsin (1993); Bellevue, Washington (1998); Newport News, Virginia (1996); Tucson, Arizona (1990); St. Paul, Minnesota (1988); Oklahoma City, Oklahoma (1986 and 1992); Beaumont, Texas (1982); New York, New York (1994); Ellicottville,

New York (1998); Des Moines, Iowa (1984); Islip, New York (1980); Adams County, Colorado (1987); Manatee County, Florida (1987); New Hanover County, North Carolina (1989); Las Vegas, Nevada (1978); Cattaraugas County, New York (1998); Cleburne, Texas (1997); Dallas, Texas (1997); El Paso, Texas (1986); New York Times Square study (1994); Report to ACLJ on the Secondary Impacts of Sex Oriented Businesses (1996); the findings from the Report of the Attorney General's Working Group On The Regulation Of Sexually Oriented Businesses (June 6, 1989, State of Minnesota); and on testimony to Congress in 136 Cong. Rec. S. 8987; 135 Cong. Rec. S. 14519; 135 Cong. Rec. S. 5636, 134 Cong. Rec. E. 3750; and also on findings from the paper entitled "Stripclubs According to Strippers: Exposing Workplace Sexual Violence," by Kelly Holsopple, Program Director, Freedom and Justice Center for Prostitution Resources, Minneapolis, Minnesota; and from "Sexually Oriented Businesses: An Insider's View," by David Sherman, presented to the Michigan House Committee on Ethics and Constitutional Law, Jan. 12, 2000; and from various other police reports, testimony, newspaper reports, and other documentary evidence, the General Assembly finds:

(1) Adult entertainment establishments lend themselves to ancillary unlawful and unhealthy activities that are presently uncontrolled by the operators of the establishments. Further, there is presently no statewide mechanism, and no general or comprehensive grant of authority enabling local governments, to make the owners of these establishments responsible for the activities that occur on their premises.

(2) Certain employees of adult entertainment establishments, as defined in section 2907.39 of the Revised Code as adult theaters and cabarets, engage in a higher incidence of certain types of illicit sexual behavior than employees of other establishments.

(3) Sexual acts, including masturbation and oral and anal sex, occur at adult entertainment establishments, especially those that provide private or semiprivate booths or cubicles for viewing films, videos, or live sex shows. The "couch dances" or "lap dances" that frequently occur in adult entertainment establishments featuring live nude or seminude dancers constitute or may constitute the offense of "engaging in prostitution" under section 2907.25 of the Revised Code.

(4) Offering and providing such space encourages such activities, which creates unhealthy conditions.

(5) Persons frequent certain adult theaters, adult arcades, and other adult entertainment establishments for the purpose of engaging in sexual activity within the premises of those adult entertainment establishments.

(6) Numerous communicable diseases may be spread by activities occurring in sexually oriented businesses, including, but not limited to, syphilis, gonorrhea, human immunodeficiency virus infection (HIV-AIDS), genital herpes, hepatitis salmonella, campylobacter and shigella infections, chlamydial, myoplasmal and ureoplasmal infections, trichomoniasis, and chancroid.

(7) Since 1981 and to the present, there has been an increasing cumulative number of reported cases of AIDS caused by the human immunodeficiency virus (HIV) in the United States: 600 in 1982, 2,200 in 1983, 4,600 in 1984, 8,555 in 1985, and 253,448 through December 31, 1992.

(8) A total of 10,255 AIDS cases had been reported in Ohio as of January 1999. Ohio has required HIV case reporting since 1990, and the reported information shows 7,969 people living with (HIV) (4,213) and (AIDS) (3,756) in the state.

(9) Since 1981 and to the present, there have been an increasing cumulative number of persons testing positive for the HIV antibody test in Ohio.

(10) The number of cases of early (less than one year) syphilis in the Unites States reported annually has risen. 33,613 cases were reported in 1982, and 45,200 cases were reported through November 1990.

(11) The number of cases of gonorrhea in the United States reported annually remains at a high level, with over one-half million cases being reported in 1990.

(12) The Surgeon General of the United States in his report of October 22, 1986, has advised the American public that AIDS and HIV infection may be transmitted through sexual contact, intravenous drug abuse, and exposure to infected blood and blood components, and from an infected mother to her newborn.

(13) According to the best scientific evidence, AIDS and HIV infection, as well as syphilis and gonorrhea, are principally transmitted by sexual acts.

(14) Sanitary conditions in some adult entertainment establishments are unhealthy, in part, because the activities conducted there are unhealthy, and, in part, because of the unregulated nature of the activities and the failure of the owners and the operators of the facilities to self-regulate those activities and maintain those facilities.

(15) The findings noted in divisions (C)(1) to (14) of this section raise substantial governmental concerns.

(16) Adult entertainment establishments have operational characteristics that should subject them to reasonable government regulation in order to protect those substantial governmental concerns.

(17) The enactment of new sections 503.51 and 503.52 and sections 2907.38 and 2907.39 of the Revised Code will promote the general welfare, health, morals, and safety of the citizens of this state.

## § 2907.39 Permitting juvenile on premises of adult entertainment establishment; use by juvenile of false information to enter adult entertainment establishment.

(A) As used in this section:

(1) "Adult arcade" means any place to which the public is permitted or invited in which coin-operated, slug-operated, or electronically, electrically, or mechanically controlled still or motion picture machines, projectors, or other image-producing devices are regularly maintained to show images to five or fewer persons per machine at any one time, and in which the images so displayed are distinguished or characterized by their emphasis upon matter exhibiting or describing specified sexual activities or specified anatomical areas.

(2)(a) "Adult bookstore," "adult novelty store," or "adult video store" means a commercial establishment that, for any form of consideration, has as a significant or substantial portion of its stock-in-trade in, derives a significant or substantial portion of its revenues from, devotes a significant or substantial portion of its interior business or advertising to, or maintains a substantial section of its sales or display space for the sale or rental of any of the following:

(i) Books, magazines, periodicals, or other printed matter, or photographs, films, motion pictures, video cassettes, compact discs, slides, or other visual representations, that are characterized by their emphasis upon the exhibition or description of specified sexual activities or specified anatomical areas;

(ii) Instruments, devices, or paraphernalia that are designed for use or marketed primarily for stimulation of human genital organs or for sadomasochistic use or abuse of self or others.

(b) "Adult bookstore," "adult novelty store," or "adult video store" includes a commercial establishment as defined in section 2907.38 of the Revised Code. An establishment may have other principal business purposes that do not involve the offering for sale, rental, or viewing of materials exhibiting or describing specified sexual activities or specified anatomical areas and still be categorized as an adult bookstore, adult novelty store, or adult video store. The existence of other principal business purposes does not exempt an establishment from being categorized as an adult bookstore, adult novelty store, or adult video store so long as one of its principal business purposes is offering for sale or rental, for some form of consideration, such materials that exhibit or describe specified sexual activities or specified anatomical areas.

(3) "Adult cabaret" means a nightclub, bar, juice bar, restaurant, bottle club, or similar commercial establishment, whether or not alcoholic beverages are served, that regularly features any of the following:

(a) Persons who appear in a state of nudity or seminudity;

(b) Live performances that are characterized by the exposure of specified anatomical areas or specified sexual activities;

(c) Films, motion pictures, video cassettes, slides, or other photographic reproductions that are distinguished or characterized by their emphasis upon the exhibition or description of specified sexual activities or specified anatomical areas.

(4) "Adult entertainment" means the sale, rental, or exhibition, for any form of consideration, of books, films, video cassettes, magazines, periodicals, or live performances that are characterized by an emphasis on the exposure or display of specified anatomical areas or specified sexual activity.

(5) "Adult entertainment establishment" means an adult arcade, adult bookstore, adult novelty store, adult video store, adult cabaret, adult motion picture theater, adult theater, nude or seminude model studio, or sexual encounter establishment. An establishment in which a medical practitioner, psychologist, psychiatrist, or similar professional person licensed by the state engages in medically approved and recognized therapy, including, but not limited to, massage therapy, as regulated pursuant to section 4731.15 of the Revised Code, is not an "adult entertainment establishment."

(6) "Adult motion picture theater" means a commercial establishment where films, motion pictures, video cassettes, slides, or similar photographic reproductions that are distinguished or characterized by their emphasis upon the exhibition or description of specified sexual activities or specified anatomical areas are regularly shown for any form of consideration.

(7) "Adult theater" means a theater, concert hall, auditorium, or similar commercial establishment that, for any form of consideration, regularly features persons who appear in a state of nudity or seminudity or live performances that are characterized by their emphasis upon the exposure of specified anatomical areas or specified sexual activities.

(8) "Distinguished or characterized by their emphasis upon" means the dominant or principal character and theme of the object described by this phrase. For instance, when the phrase refers to films "that are distinguished or characterized by their emphasis upon the exhibition or description of specified sexual activities or specified anatomical areas," the films so described are those whose dominant or principal character and theme are the exhibition or description of specified sexual activities or specified anatomical areas.

(9)(a) "Nude or seminude model studio" means any place where a person, who regularly appears in a state of nudity or seminudity, is provided for money or any other form of consideration to be observed, sketched, drawn, painted, sculptured, photographed, or similarly depicted by other persons.

(b) A modeling class or studio is not a nude or seminude model studio and is not subject to this chapter if it is operated in any of the following ways:

(i) By a college or university supported entirely or partly by taxation;

(ii) By a private college or university that maintains and operates educational programs, the credits for which are transferable to a college or university supported entirely or partly by taxation;

(iii) In a structure that has no sign visible from the exterior of the structure and no other advertising indicating that a person appearing in a state of nudity or seminudity is available for viewing, if in order to participate in a class in the structure, a student must enroll at least three days in advance of the class and if not more than one nude or seminude model is on the premises at any one time.

(10) "Nudity," "nude," or "state of nudity" means the showing of the human male or female genitals, pubic area, vulva, anus, anal cleft, or cleavage with less than a fully opaque covering; or the showing of the female breasts with less than a fully opaque covering of any part of the nipple.

(11) "Regularly features" or "regularly shown" means a consistent or substantial course of conduct, such that the films or performances exhibited constitute a substantial portion of the films or performances offered as a part of the ongoing business of the adult entertainment establishment.

(12) "Seminude" or "state of seminudity" means a state of dress in which opaque clothing covers not more than the genitals, pubic region, and nipple of the female breast, as well as portions of the body covered by supporting straps or devices.

(13)(a) "Sexual encounter establishment" means a business or commercial establishment that, as one of its principal business purposes, offers for any form of consideration a place where either of the following occur:

(i) Two or more persons may congregate, associate, or consort for the purpose of engaging in specified sexual activities.

(ii) Two or more persons appear nude or seminude for the purpose of displaying their nude or seminude bodies for their receipt of consideration or compensation in any type or form.

(b) An establishment where a medical practitioner, psychologist, psychiatrist, or similar professional person licensed by the state engages in medically approved and recognized therapy, including, but not limited to, massage therapy, as regulated pursuant to section 4731.15 of the Revised Code, is not a "sexual encounter establishment."

(14) "Specified anatomical areas" means the cleft of the buttocks, anus, male or female genitals, or the female breast.

(15) "Specified sexual activity" means any of the following:

(a) Sex acts, normal or perverted, or actual or simulated, including intercourse, oral copulation, masturbation, or sodomy;

(b) Excretory functions as a part of or in connection with any of the activities described in division (A)(15)(a) of this section.

(B) No person knowingly shall allow an individual, including, but not limited to, a patron, customer, or employee, who is under eighteen years of age on the premises of an adult entertainment establishment.

(C) No individual who is under eighteen years of age knowingly shall show or give false information concerning the individual's name or age, or other false identification, for the purpose of gaining entrance to an adult entertainment establishment.

(D) A person shall not be found guilty of a violation of division (B) of this section if the person raises as an affirmative defense and if the jury or, in a nonjury trial, the court finds the person has established by a preponderance of the evidence, all of the following:

(1) The individual gaining entrance to the adult entertainment establishment exhibited to an operator, employee, agent, or independent contractor of the adult entertainment establishment a driver's or commercial driver's license or an identification card issued under sections 4507.50 and 4507.52 of the Revised Code showing that the individual was then at least eighteen years of age.

(2) The operator, employee, agent, or independent contractor made a bona fide effort to ascertain the true age of the individual gaining entrance to the adult entertainment establishment by checking the identification presented, at the time of entrance, to ascertain that the description on the identification compared with the appearance of the individual and that the identification had not been altered in any way.

(3) The operator, employee, agent, or independent contractor had reason to believe that the individual gaining entrance to the adult entertainment establishment was at least eighteen years of age.

(E) In any criminal action in which the affirmative defense described in division (D) of this section is raised, the registrar of motor vehicles or the deputy registrar who issued a driver's or commercial driver's license or an identification card under sections 4507.50 and 4507.52 of the Revised Code shall be permitted to submit certified copies of the records, in the registrar's or deputy registrar's possession, of the issuance of the license or identification card in question, in lieu of the testimony of the personnel of the bureau of motor vehicles in the action.

(F)(1) Whoever violates division (B) of this section is guilty of permitting a juvenile on the premises of an adult entertainment establishment, a misdemeanor of the first degree. Each day a person violates this division constitutes a separate offense.

(2) Whoever violates division (C) of this section is guilty of use by a juvenile of false information to enter an adult entertainment establishment, a delinquent act that would be a misdemeanor of the fourth degree if committed by an adult.

**HISTORY: 151 v H 23, § 1, eff. 8-17-06.**

**Not analogous to former RC § 2907.39 (RS § 6849a; 82 v 247; 99 v 460; GC §§ 12471, 12475, 12475-1; 124 v 360; 124 v 466; Bureau of Code Revision, 10-1-53), repealed 134 v H 511, § 2, eff 1-1-74.**

See provisions of § 3 of 151 v H 23 following RC § 2907.38.

## § 2907.40 Illegally operating sexually oriented business; illegal sexually oriented activity in sexually oriented business.

(A) As used in this section:

(1) "Adult bookstore" or "adult video store" means a commercial establishment that has as a significant or substantial portion of its stock in trade or inventory in, derives a significant or substantial portion of its revenues from, devotes a significant or substantial portion of its interior business or advertising to, or maintains a substantial section of its sales or display space for the sale or rental, for any form of consideration, of books, magazines, periodicals, or other printed matter, or photographs, films, motion pictures, video cassettes, compact discs, slides, or other visual representations, that are characterized by their emphasis upon the exhibition or description of specified sexual activities or specified anatomical areas.

(2) "Adult cabaret" has the same meaning as in section 2907.39 of the Revised Code.

(3) "Adult motion picture theater" means a commercial establishment where films, motion pictures, videocassettes, slides, or similar photographic reproductions that are characterized by their emphasis upon the display of specified sexual activities or specified anatomical areas are regularly shown to more than five individuals for any form of consideration.

(4) "Characterized by" means describing the essential character or quality of an item.

(5) "Employee" means any individual who performs any service on the premises of a sexually oriented business on a full-time, part-time, or contract basis, regardless of whether the individual is denominated an employee, independent contractor, agent, or otherwise, but does not include an individual exclusively on the premises for repair or maintenance of the premises or for the delivery of goods to the premises.

(6) "Nudity," "nude," or "state of nudity" has the same meaning as in section 2907.39 of the Revised Code.

(7) "Operator" means any individual on the premises of a sexually oriented business who causes the business to function or who puts or keeps in operation the business or who is authorized to manage the business or exercise overall operational control of the business premises.

(8) "Patron" means any individual on the premises of a sexually oriented business except for any of the following:

(a) An operator or an employee of the sexually oriented business;

(b) An individual who is on the premises exclusively for repair or maintenance of the premises or for the delivery of goods to the premises;

(c) A public employee or a volunteer firefighter emergency medical services worker acting within the scope of the public employee's or volunteer's duties as a public employee or volunteer.

(9) "Premises" means the real property on which the sexually oriented business is located and all appurtenances to the real property, including, but not limited, to the sexually oriented business, the grounds, private walkways, and parking lots or parking garages adjacent to the real property under the ownership, control, or supervision of the owner or operator of the sexually oriented business.

(10) "Regularly" means consistently or repeatedly.

(11) "Seminude" or "state of seminudity" has the same meaning as in section 2907.39 of the Revised Code.

(12) "Sexual device" means any three-dimensional object designed and marketed for stimulation of the male or female human genitals or anus or female breasts or for sadomasochistic use or abuse of oneself or others, including, but not limited to, dildos, vibrators, penis pumps, and physical representations of the human genital organs, but not including devices primarily intended for protection against sexually transmitted diseases or for preventing pregnancy.

(13) "Sexual device shop" means a commercial establishment that regularly features sexual devices, but not including any pharmacy, drug store, medical clinic, or establishment primarily dedicated to providing medical or healthcare products or services, and not including any commercial establishment that does not restrict access to its premises by reason of age.

(14) "Sexual encounter center" means a business or commercial enterprise that, as one of its principal business purposes, purports to offer for any form of consideration physical contact in the form of wrestling or tumbling between individuals of the opposite sex when one or more of the individuals is nude or seminude.

(15) "Sexually oriented business" means an adult bookstore, adult video store, adult cabaret, adult motion picture theater, sexual device shop, or sexual encounter center, but does not include a business solely by reason of its showing, selling, or renting materials that may depict sex.

(16) "Specified anatomical areas" includes human genitals, pubic region, and buttocks and the human female breast below a point immediately above the top of the areola.

(17) "Specified sexual activity" means sexual intercourse, oral copulation, masturbation, or sodomy, or excretory functions as a part of or in connection with any of these activities.

(B) No sexually oriented business shall be or remain open for business between 12:00 midnight and 6:00 a.m. on any day, except that a sexually oriented business that holds a liquor permit pursuant to Chapter 4303. of the Revised Code may remain open until the hour specified in that permit if it does not conduct, offer, or allow sexually oriented entertainment activity in which the performers appear nude.

(C)(1) No patron who is not a member of the employee's immediate family shall knowingly touch any employee while that employee is nude or seminude or touch the clothing of any employee while that employee is nude or seminude.

(2) No employee who regularly appears nude or seminude on the premises of a sexually oriented business, while on the premises of that sexually oriented business and while nude or seminude, shall knowingly touch a patron who is not a member of the employee's immediate family or another employee who is not a member of the employee's immediate family or the clothing of a patron who is not a member of the employee's immediate family or another employee who is not a member of the employee's immediate family or allow a patron who is not a member of the employee's immediate family or another employee who is not a member of the employee's immediate family to touch the employee or the clothing of the employee.

(D) Whoever violates division (B) of this section is guilty of illegally operating a sexually oriented business, a misdemeanor of the first degree.

(E) Whoever violates division (C) of this section is guilty of illegal sexually oriented activity in a sexually oriented business. If the offender touches a specified anatomical area of the patron or employee, or the clothing covering a specified anatomical area, a violation of division (C) of this section is a misdemeanor of the first degree. If the offender does not touch a specified anatomical area of the patron or employee, or the clothing covering a specified anatomical area, a violation of division (C) of this section is a misdemeanor of the fourth degree.

**HISTORY: 152 v S 16, § 1, eff. 9-4-07; 152 v S 97, § 1, eff. 9-4-07; 152 v S 183, § 1, eff. 9-11-08.**

The provisions of § 3 of 152 v S 97 read as follows:

SECTION 3. * * * The amendment to section 2907.40 of the Revised Code that is made by Sections 1 and 2 of this act takes effect the same day section 2907.40 of the Revised Code as enacted in Sub. S.B. 16 of the 127th General Assembly takes effect.

**Not analogous to former RC § 2907.40 (RS § 6849a; 82 v 247; 99 v 460; GC §§ 12471, 12475, 12475-1; 124 v 360; 124 v 466; Bureau of Code Revision, 10-1-53), repealed 134 v H 511, § 2, eff 1-1-74.**

## § 2907.41 Mandatory court appearance for setting bail for person charged with sexually oriented offense or public indecency who has prior conviction.

(A) Subject to division (D) of this section, a person who is charged with the commission of any sexually oriented offense or with a violation of section 2907.09 of the Revised Code shall appear before the court for the setting of bail if the person charged previously was convicted of or pleaded guilty to a sexually oriented offense, a violation of section 2907.09 of the Revised Code, or a violation of an existing or former municipal ordinance or law of this or any other state or the United States that is substantially similar to section 2907.09 of the Revised Code.

(B) To the extent that information about any of the following is available to the court, the court, in addition to any other circumstances considered by the court and notwithstanding any provisions to the contrary contained in Criminal Rule 46, shall consider all of the following before setting bail for a person who appears before the court pursuant to division (A) of this section:

(1) Whether the person previously has been adjudicated a sexual predator or child-victim predator pursuant to Chapter 2950. of the Revised Code, previously has been determined to be a habitual sex offender or habitual child-victim offender pursuant to that Chapter, has a history of committing sexually oriented offenses or child-victim oriented offenses, or has a history of committing violations of section 2907.09 of the Revised Code or violations of an existing or former municipal ordinance or law of this or any other state or the United States that is substantially similar to that section;

(2) The mental health of the person;

(3) Whether the person has a history of violating the orders of any court or governmental entity;

(4) Whether the person is potentially a threat to any other person;

(5) Whether the person has access to deadly weapons or a history of using deadly weapons;

(6) Whether the person has a history of abusing alcohol or any controlled substance;

(7) The severity of the alleged conduct of the person that is the basis of the offense, including but not limited to, the duration of the alleged conduct, and whether the alleged conduct involved physical injury, assault, violence, or forcible entry to gain access to an alleged victim;

(8) Whether the person has exhibited obsessive or controlling behaviors toward another person, including, but not limited to, stalking, surveillance, or isolation of another person;

(9) Whether the person has expressed suicidal or homicidal ideations;

(10) Any information contained in the complaint and any police reports, affidavits, or other documents accompanying the complaint.

(C) Any court that has jurisdiction over charges alleging the commission of a sexually oriented offense or a violation of section 2907.09 of the Revised Code, in circumstances in which the person charged previously was convicted of or pleaded guilty to any of the offenses or violations described in division (A) of this section, may set a schedule for bail to be used in cases involving those offenses and violations. The schedule shall require that a judge consider all of the factors listed in division (B) of this section and may require judges to set bail at a certain level if the history of the alleged offender or the circumstances of the alleged offense meet certain criteria in the schedule.

(D)(1) Upon the court's own motion or the motion of a party and upon any terms that the court may direct, a court may permit a person who is required to appear before it by division (A) of this section to appear by video conferencing equipment.

(2) If, in the opinion of the court, the appearance in person or by video conferencing equipment of a person who is charged with a misdemeanor and who is required to appear before the court by division (A) of this section is not practicable, the court may waive the appearance and release the person on bail in accordance with the court's schedule for bail set under division (C) of this section or, if the court has not set a schedule for bail under that division, on one or both of the following types of bail in an amount set by the court:

(a) A bail bond secured by a deposit of ten per cent of the amount of the bond in cash;

(b) A surety bond, a bond secured by real estate or securities as allowed by law, or the deposit of cash, at the option of the person.

(3) Division (A) of this section does not create a right in a person to appear before the court for the setting of bail or prohibit a court from requiring any person charged with a sexually oriented offense or a violation of section 2907.09 of the Revised Code who is not described in that division from appearing before the court for the setting of bail.

(E) As used in this section, "child-victim oriented offense," "child-victim predator," "habitual child-victim offender," "habitual sex offender," "sexually oriented offense," and "sexual predator" have the same meanings as in section 2950.01 of the Revised Code.

**HISTORY: 151 v S 245, § 1, eff. 4-4-07.**

**Not analogous to former RC § 2907.41, amended and renumbered to RC § 2945.481 by 147 v S 53, eff 10-14-97.**

## § 2907.42 Repealed, 134 v H 511, § 2 [RS §§ 1280, 1281, 6880; S&C 432, 1612; S&S 284; 29 v 144, 470; 56 v 72; 62 v 139; 66 v 287; 69 v 67; GC §§ 12465, 12466, 12476-2, 12490; 112 v 420; 117 v 430; Bureau of Code Revision, 10-1-53]. Eff 1-1-74.

This section concerned conversion of personal property and destroying trees.

## § 2907.43 Repealed, 134 v H 511, § 2 [RS §§ 1280, 1281, 6880; S&C 432, 1612; S&S 284; 29 v 144, 470; 56 v 72; 62 v 139; 66 v 287; 69 v 67; GC §§ 12465, 12466, 12476-2, 12490; 112 v 420; 117 v 430; Bureau of Code Revision, 10-1-53]. Eff 1-1-74.

This section concerned conversion of personal property and destroying trees.

## § 2907.44 Repealed, 134 v H 511, § 2 [RS §§ 1280, 1281, 6880; S&C 432, 1612; S&S 284; 29 v 144, 470; 56 v 72; 62 v 139; 66 v 287; 69 v 67; GC §§ 12465, 12466, 12476-2, 12490; 112 v 420; 117 v 430; Bureau of Code Revision, 10-1-53]. Eff 1-1-74.

This section concerned conversion of personal property and destroying trees.

## § 2907.45 Repealed, 134 v H 511, § 2 [125 v H 457, 131 v 674]. Eff 1-1-74.

This section concerned conversion of personal property and removal of name or serial number.

## § 2907.46 Repealed, 134 v H 511, § 2 [125 v H 457, 131 v 674]. Eff 1-1-74.

This section concerned conversion of personal property and removal of name or serial number.

## § 2907.47 Repealed, 134 v H 511, § 2 [125 v H 457, 131 v 674]. Eff 1-1-74.

This section concerned conversion of personal property and removal of name or serial number.

## § 2907.48 Repealed, 134 v H 511, § 2 [133 v H 49]. Eff 1-1-74.

This section prohibited shoplifting.

# CHAPTER 2909: ARSON AND RELATED OFFENSES



## § 2909.01 Definitions.

As used in sections 2909.01 to 2909.07 of the Revised Code:

(A) To "create a substantial risk of serious physical harm to any person" includes the creation of a substantial risk of serious physical harm to any emergency personnel.

(B) "Emergency personnel" means any of the following persons:

(1) A peace officer, as defined in section 2935.01 of the Revised Code;

(2) A member of a fire department or other firefighting agency of a municipal corporation, township, township fire district, joint fire district, other political subdivision, or combination of political subdivisions;

(3) A member of a private fire company, as defined in section 9.60 of the Revised Code, or a volunteer firefighter;

(4) A member of a joint ambulance district or joint emergency medical services district;

(5) An emergency medical technician-basic, emergency medical technician-intermediate, emergency medical technician-paramedic, ambulance operator, or other member of an emergency medical service that is owned or operated by a political subdivision or a private entity;

(6) The state fire marshal, the chief deputy state fire marshal, or an assistant state fire marshal;

(7) A fire prevention officer of a political subdivision or an arson, fire, or similar investigator of a political subdivision.

(C) "Occupied structure" means any house, building, outbuilding, watercraft, aircraft, railroad car, truck, trailer, tent, or other structure, vehicle, or shelter, or any portion thereof, to which any of the following applies:

(1) It is maintained as a permanent or temporary dwelling, even though it is temporarily unoccupied and whether or not any person is actually present.

(2) At the time, it is occupied as the permanent or temporary habitation of any person, whether or not any person is actually present.

(3) At the time, it is specially adapted for the overnight accommodation of any person, whether or not any person is actually present.

(4) At the time, any person is present or likely to be present in it.

(D) "Political subdivision" and "state" have the same meanings as in section 2744.01 of the Revised Code.

(E) "Computer," "computer hacking," "computer network," "computer program," "computer software," "computer system," "data," and "telecommunications device" have the same meanings as in section 2913.01 of the Revised Code.

(F) "Computer contaminant" means a computer program that is designed to modify, damage, destroy, disable, deny or degrade access to, allow unauthorized access to, functionally impair, record, or transmit information within a computer, computer system, or computer network without the express or implied consent of the owner or other person authorized to give consent and that is of a type or kind described in divisions (F)(1) to (4) of this section or of a type or kind similar to a type or kind described in divisions (F)(1) to (4) of this section:

(1) A group of computer programs commonly known as "viruses" and "worms" that are self-replicating or self-propagating and that are designed to contaminate other computer programs, compromise computer security, consume computer resources, modify, destroy, record, or transmit data, or disrupt the normal operation of the computer, computer system, or computer network;

(2) A group of computer programs commonly known as "Trojans" or "Trojan horses" that are not self-replicating or self-propagating and that are designed to compromise computer security, consume computer resources, modify, destroy, record, or transmit data, or disrupt the normal operation of the computer, computer system, or computer network;

(3) A group of computer programs commonly known as "zombies" that are designed to use a computer without the knowledge and consent of the owner, or other person authorized to give consent, and that are designed to send large quantities of data to a targeted computer network for the purpose of degrading the targeted computer's or network's performance, or denying access through the network to the targeted computer or network, resulting in

what is commonly known as "Denial of Service" or "Distributed Denial of Service" attacks;

(4) A group of computer programs commonly know as "trap doors," "back doors," or "root kits" that are designed to bypass standard authentication software and that are designed to allow access to or use of a computer without the knowledge or consent of the owner, or other person authorized to give consent.

(G) "Internet" has the same meaning as in section 341.42 of the Revised Code.

**HISTORY: 134 v H 511 (Eff 1-1-74); 144 v H 675 (Eff 3-19-93); 146 v S 150 (Eff 11-24-95); 147 v S 30 (Eff 5-6-98); 149 v S 115. Eff 3-19-2003; 150 v S 146, § 1, eff. 9-23-04.**

**Not analogous to former RC § 2909.01 (RS § 6863; S&S 56, 155, 162, 263, 284, 736; S&C 419, 420, 429, 430, 445, 446; 29 v 144; 43 v 92; 54 v 36; 54 v 99; 59 v 57; 60 v 20; 62 v 8; 62 v 72; 64 v 74; 64 v 128; 66 v 122; 66 v 341; 68 v 42; 68 v 87; 69 v 82; 70 v 215; 73 v 64; 73 v 94; 73 v 180; GC § 12477; Bureau of Code Revision, 10-1-53), repealed 134 v H 511, § 2, eff 1-1-74.**

## § 2909.02 Aggravated arson.

(A) No person, by means of fire or explosion, shall knowingly do any of the following:

(1) Create a substantial risk of serious physical harm to any person other than the offender;

(2) Cause physical harm to any occupied structure;

(3) Create, through the offer or acceptance of an agreement for hire or other consideration, a substantial risk of physical harm to any occupied structure.

(B)(1) Whoever violates this section is guilty of aggravated arson.

(2) A violation of division (A)(1) or (3) of this section is a felony of the first degree.

(3) A violation of division (A)(2) of this section is a felony of the second degree.

**HISTORY: 134 v H 511 (Eff 1-1-74); 136 v S 282 (Eff 5-21-76); 139 v S 199 (Eff 1-5-83); 146 v S 2 (Eff 7-1-96); 146 v S 269. Eff 7-1-96.**

**Not analogous to former RC § 2909.02 (RS § 6864; S&C 433, 437, 438, 1612; S&S 282—284; 29 v 470; 29 v 144; 59 v 27; 59 v 79; 62 v 139; 69 v 67; GC § 12478; 124 v 466; Bureau of Code Revision, 10-1-53), repealed 134 v H 511, § 2, eff 1-1-74.**

The effective date is set by section 5 of SB 269.

## § 2909.03 Arson.

(A) No person, by means of fire or explosion, shall knowingly do any of the following:

(1) Cause, or create a substantial risk of, physical harm to any property of another without the other person's consent;

(2) Cause, or create a substantial risk of, physical harm to any property of the offender or another, with purpose to defraud;

(3) Cause, or create a substantial risk of, physical harm to the statehouse or a courthouse, school building, or other building or structure that is owned or controlled by the state, any political subdivision, or any department, agency, or instrumentality of the state or a political subdivision, and that is used for public purposes;

(4) Cause, or create a substantial risk of, physical harm, through the offer or the acceptance of an agreement for hire or other consideration, to any property of another without the other person's consent or to any property of the offender or another with purpose to defraud;

(5) Cause, or create a substantial risk of, physical harm to any park, preserve, wildlands, brush-covered land, cut-over land, forest, timberland, greenlands, woods, or similar real property that is owned or controlled by another person, the state, or a political subdivision without the consent of the other person, the state, or the political subdivision;

(6) With purpose to defraud, cause, or create a substantial risk of, physical harm to any park, preserve, wildlands, brush-covered land, cut-over land, forest, timberland, greenlands, woods, or similar real property that is owned or controlled by the offender, another person, the state, or a political subdivision.

(B)(1) Whoever violates this section is guilty of arson.

(2) A violation of division (A)(1) of this section is one of the following:

(a) Except as otherwise provided in division (B)(2)(b) of this section, a misdemeanor of the first degree;

(b) If the value of the property or the amount of the physical harm involved is one thousand dollars or more, a felony of the fourth degree.

(3) A violation of division (A)(2), (3), (5), or (6) of this section is a felony of the fourth degree.

(4) A violation of division (A)(4) of this section is a felony of the third degree.

**HISTORY: 134 v H 511 (Eff 1-1-74); 136 v S 282 (Eff 5-21-76); 139 v S 199 (Eff 1-1-83); 144 v H 675 (Eff 3-19-93); 146 v S 2. Eff 7-1-96; 2011 HB 86, § 1, eff. Sept. 30, 2011.**

The provisions of § 4 of HB 86 read as follows:

"SECTION 4. The amendments to sections 926.99, 1333.99, 1707.99, 1716.99, 2909.03, 2909.05, 2909.11, 2913.02, 2913.03, 2913.04, 2913.11, 2913.21, 2913.31, 2913.32, 2913.34, 2913.40, 2913.401, 2913.42, 2913.421, 2913.43, 2913.45, 2913.46, 2913.47, 2913.48, 2913.49, 2913.51, 2913.61, 2915.05, 2917.21, 2917.31, 2917.32, 2921.13, 2921.41, 2923.31, and 2981.07, division (B) of section 2929.13, and division (A) of section 2929.14 of the Revised Code that are made in this act apply to a person who commits an offense specified or penalized under those sections on or after the effective date of this section and to a person to whom division (B) of section 1.58 of the Revised Code makes the amendments applicable.

"The provisions of sections 926.99, 1333.99, 1707.99, 1716.99, 2909.03, 2909.05, 2909.11, 2913.02, 2913.03, 2913.04, 2913.11, 2913.21, 2913.31, 2913.32, 2913.34, 2913.40, 2913.401, 2913.42, 2913.421, 2913.43, 2913.45, 2913.46, 2913.47, 2913.48, 2913.49, 2913.51, 2913.61, 2915.05, 2917.21, 2917.31, 2917.32, 2921.13, 2921.41, 2923.31, and 2981.07 of the Revised Code in existence prior to the effective date of this section shall apply to a person upon whom a court imposed sentence prior to the effective date of this section for an offense specified or penalized under those sections. The amendments to sections 926.99, 1333.99, 1707.99, 1716.99, 2909.03, 2909.05, 2909.11, 2913.02, 2913.03, 2913.04, 2913.11, 2913.21, 2913.31, 2913.32, 2913.34, 2913.40, 2913.401, 2913.42, 2913.421, 2913.43, 2913.45, 2913.46, 2913.47, 2913.48, 2913.49, 2913.51, 2913.61, 2915.05, 2917.21, 2917.31, 2917.32, 2921.13, 2921.41, 2923.31, and 2981.07 of the Revised Code that are made in this act do not apply to a person who upon whom a court imposed sentence prior to the effective date of this section for an offense specified or penalized under those sections."

**Not analogous to former RC § 2909.03 (GC § 12478-1; 106 v 104; Bureau of Code Revision, 10-1-53), repealed 134 v H 511, § 2, eff 1-1-74.**

The effective date is set by section 6 of SB 2.

## § 2909.04 Disrupting public services.

(A) No person, purposely by any means or knowingly by damaging or tampering with any property, shall do any of the following:

(1) Interrupt or impair television, radio, telephone, telegraph, or other mass communications service; police, fire, or other public service communications; radar, loran, radio, or other electronic aids to air or marine navigation or communications; or amateur or citizens band radio communications being used for public service or emergency communications;

(2) Interrupt or impair public transportation, including without limitation school bus transportation, or water supply, gas, power, or other utility service to the public;

(3) Substantially impair the ability of law enforcement officers, firefighters, rescue personnel, emergency medical services personnel, or emergency facility personnel to respond to an emergency or to protect and preserve any person or property from serious physical harm.

(B) No person shall knowingly use any computer, computer system, computer network, telecommunications device, or other electronic device or system or the internet so as to disrupt, interrupt, or impair the functions of any police, fire, educational, commercial, or governmental operations.

(C) Whoever violates this section is guilty of disrupting public services, a felony of the fourth degree.

(D) As used in this section:

(1) "Emergency medical services personnel" has the same meaning as in section 2133.21 of the Revised Code.

(2) "Emergency facility personnel" means any of the following:

(a) Any of the following individuals who perform services in the ordinary course of their professions in an emergency facility:

(i) Physicians authorized under Chapter 4731. of the Revised Code to practice medicine and surgery or osteopathic medicine and surgery;

(ii) Registered nurses and licensed practical nurses licensed under Chapter 4723. of the Revised Code;

(iii) Physician assistants authorized to practice under Chapter 4730. of the Revised Code;

(iv) Health care workers;

(v) Clerical staffs.

(b) Any individual who is a security officer performing security services in an emergency facility;

(c) Any individual who is present in an emergency facility, who was summoned to the facility by an individual identified in division (D)(2)(a) or (b) of this section.

(3) "Emergency facility" means a hospital emergency department or any other facility that provides emergency medical services.

(4) "Hospital" has the same meaning as in section 3727.01 of the Revised Code.

(5) "Health care worker" means an individual, other than an individual specified in division (D)(2)(a), (b), or (c) of this section, who provides medical or other health-related care or treatment in an emergency facility, including medical technicians, medical assistants, orderlies, aides, or individuals acting in similar capacities.

**HISTORY: 134 v H 511 (Eff 1-1-74); 146 v S 2 (Eff 7-1-96); 148 v H 137 (Eff 3-10-2000); 149 v S 40. Eff 1-25-2002; 150 v S 146, § 1, eff. 9-23-04.**

**Not analogous to former RC § 2909.04 (GC § 12479; 99 v 526; Bureau of Code Revision, 10-1-53), repealed 134 v H 511, § 2, eff 1-1-74.**

## § 2909.05 Vandalism.

(A) No person shall knowingly cause serious physical harm to an occupied structure or any of its contents.

(B)(1) No person shall knowingly cause physical harm to property that is owned or possessed by another, when either of the following applies:

(a) The property is used by its owner or possessor in the owner's or possessor's profession, business, trade, or occupation, and the value of the property or the amount of physical harm involved is one thousand dollars or more;

(b) Regardless of the value of the property or the amount of damage done, the property or its equivalent is necessary in order for its owner or possessor to engage in the owner's or possessor's profession, business, trade, or occupation.

(2) No person shall knowingly cause serious physical harm to property that is owned, leased, or controlled by a governmental entity. A governmental entity includes, but is not limited to, the state or a political subdivision of the state, a school district, the board of trustees of a public library or public university, or any other body corporate and politic responsible for governmental activities only in geographical areas smaller than that of the state.

(C) No person, without privilege to do so, shall knowingly cause serious physical harm to any tomb, monument, gravestone, or other similar structure that is used as a memorial for the dead; to any fence, railing, curb, or other property that is used to protect, enclose, or ornament any cemetery; or to a cemetery.

(D) No person, without privilege to do so, shall knowingly cause physical harm to a place of burial by breaking and entering into a tomb, crypt, casket, or other structure that is used as a memorial for the dead or as an enclosure for the dead.

(E) Whoever violates this section is guilty of vandalism. Except as otherwise provided in this division, vandalism is a felony of the fifth degree that is punishable by a fine of up to two thousand five hundred dollars in addition to the penalties specified for a felony of the fifth degree in sections 2929.11 to 2929.18 of the Revised Code. If the value of the property or the amount of physical harm involved is seven thousand five hundred dollars or more but less than one hundred fifty thousand dollars, vandalism is a felony of the fourth degree. If the value of the property or the amount of physical harm involved is one hundred fifty thousand dollars or more, vandalism is a felony of the third degree.

(F) For purposes of this section:

(1) "Cemetery" means any place of burial and includes burial sites that contain American Indian burial objects placed with or containing American Indian human remains.

(2) "Serious physical harm" means physical harm to property that results in loss to the value of the property of one thousand dollars or more.

**HISTORY: 134 v H 511 (Eff 1-1-74); 137 v H 741 (Eff 10-9-78); 138 v H 618 (Eff 7-31-80); 139 v S 199 (Eff 1-5-83); 139 v H 269 (Eff 1-5-83); 141 v S 316 (Eff 3-19-87); 144 v H 675 (Eff 3-19-93); 146 v S 2 (Eff 7-1-96); 147 v H 429. Eff 9-30-98; 2011 HB 86, § 1, eff. Sept. 30, 2011.**

The provisions of § 4 of HB 86 read as follows:

"SECTION 4. The amendments to sections 926.99, 1333.99, 1707.99, 1716.99, 2909.03, 2909.05, 2909.11, 2913.02, 2913.03, 2913.04, 2913.11, 2913.21, 2913.31, 2913.32, 2913.34, 2913.40, 2913.401, 2913.42, 2913.421, 2913.43, 2913.45, 2913.46, 2913.47, 2913.48, 2913.49, 2913.51, 2913.61, 2915.05, 2917.21, 2917.31, 2917.32, 2921.13, 2921.41, 2923.31, and 2981.07, division (B) of section 2929.13, and division (A) of section 2929.14 of the Revised Code that are made in this act apply to a person who commits an offense specified or penalized under those sections on or after the effective date of this section and to a person to whom division (B) of section 1.58 of the Revised Code makes the amendments applicable.

"The provisions of sections 926.99, 1333.99, 1707.99, 1716.99, 2909.03, 2909.05, 2909.11, 2913.02, 2913.03, 2913.04, 2913.11, 2913.21, 2913.31, 2913.32, 2913.34, 2913.40, 2913.401, 2913.42, 2913.421, 2913.43, 2913.45, 2913.46, 2913.47, 2913.48, 2913.49, 2913.51, 2913.61, 2915.05, 2917.21, 2917.31, 2917.32, 2921.13, 2921.41, 2923.31, and 2981.07 of the Revised Code in existence prior to the effective date of this section shall apply to a person upon whom a court imposed sentence prior to the effective date of this section for an offense specified or penalized under those sections. The amendments to sections 926.99, 1333.99, 1707.99, 1716.99, 2909.03, 2909.05, 2909.11, 2913.02, 2913.03, 2913.04, 2913.11, 2913.21, 2913.31, 2913.32, 2913.34, 2913.40, 2913.401, 2913.42, 2913.421, 2913.43, 2913.45, 2913.46, 2913.47, 2913.48, 2913.49, 2913.51, 2913.61, 2915.05, 2917.21, 2917.31, 2917.32, 2921.13, 2921.41, 2923.31, and 2981.07 of the Revised Code that are made in this act do not apply to a person who upon whom a court imposed sentence prior to the effective date of this section for an offense specified or penalized under those sections."

**Not analogous to former RC § 2909.05 (RS § 6865; S&C 429; 29 v 144; 75 v 130; GC § 12480; Bureau of Code Revision, 10-1-53), repealed 134 v H 511, § 2, eff 1-1-74.**

## § 2909.06 Criminal damaging or endangering.

(A) No person shall cause, or create a substantial risk of physical harm to any property of another without the other person's consent:

(1) Knowingly, by any means;

(2) Recklessly, by means of fire, explosion, flood, poison gas, poison, radioactive material, caustic or corrosive material, or other inherently dangerous agency or substance.

(B) Whoever violates this section is guilty of criminal damaging or endangering, a misdemeanor of the second degree. If a violation of this section creates a risk of physical harm to any person, criminal damaging or endangering is a misdemeanor of the first degree. If the property involved in a violation of this section is an aircraft, an aircraft engine, propeller, appliance, spare part, or any other equipment or implement used or intended to be used in the operation of an aircraft and if the violation creates a risk of physical harm to any person, criminal damaging or endangering is a felony of the fifth degree. If the property involved in a violation of this section is an aircraft, an aircraft engine, propeller, appliance, spare part, or any other equipment or implement used or intended to be used in the operation of an aircraft and if the violation creates a substantial risk of physical harm to any person or if the property involved in a violation of this section is an occupied aircraft, criminal damaging or endangering is a felony of the fourth degree.

**HISTORY: 134 v H 511 (Eff 1-1-74); 140 v H 570 (Eff 3-28-85); 146 v S 2. Eff 7-1-96.**

**Not analogous to former RC § 2909.06 (GC § 12480-1; 102 v 297; Bureau of Code Revision, 10-1-53), repealed 134 v H 511, § 2, eff 1-1-74.**

The effective date is set by section 6 of SB 2.

## § 2909.07 Criminal mischief.

(A) No person shall:

(1) Without privilege to do so, knowingly move, deface, damage, destroy, or otherwise improperly tamper with the property of another;

(2) With purpose to interfere with the use or enjoyment of property of another, employ a tear gas device, stink bomb, smoke generator, or other device releasing a substance that is harmful or offensive to persons exposed or that tends to cause public alarm;

(3) Without privilege to do so, knowingly move, deface, damage, destroy, or otherwise improperly tamper with a bench mark, triangulation station, boundary marker, or other survey station, monument, or marker;

(4) Without privilege to do so, knowingly move, deface, damage, destroy, or otherwise improperly tamper with any safety device, the property of another, or the property of the offender when required or placed for the safety of others, so as to destroy or diminish its effectiveness or availability for its intended purpose;

(5) With purpose to interfere with the use or enjoyment of the property of another, set a fire on the land of another or place personal property that has been set on fire on the land of another, which fire or personal property is outside and apart from any building, other structure, or personal property that is on that land;

(6) Without privilege to do so, and with intent to impair the functioning of any computer, computer system, computer network, computer software, or computer program, knowingly do any of the following:

(a) In any manner or by any means, including, but not limited to, computer hacking, alter, damage, destroy, or modify a computer, computer system, computer network, computer software, or computer program or data contained in a computer, computer system, computer network, computer software, or computer program;

(b) Introduce a computer contaminant into a computer, computer system, computer network, computer software, or computer program.

(B) As used in this section, "safety device" means any fire extinguisher, fire hose, or fire axe, or any fire escape, emergency exit, or emergency escape equipment, or any life line, life-saving ring, life preserver, or life boat or raft, or any alarm, light, flare, signal, sign, or notice intended to warn of danger or emergency, or intended for other safety purposes, or any guard railing or safety barricade, or any traffic sign or signal, or any railroad grade crossing sign, signal, or gate, or any first aid or survival equipment, or any other device, apparatus, or equipment intended for protecting or preserving the safety of persons or property.

(C)(1) Whoever violates this section is guilty of criminal mischief, and shall be punished as provided in division (C)(2) or (3) of this section.

(2) Except as otherwise provided in this division, criminal mischief committed in violation of division (A)(1), (2), (3), (4), or (5) of this section is a misdemeanor of the third degree. Except as otherwise provided in this division, if the violation of division (A)(1), (2), (3), (4), or (5) of this section creates a risk of physical harm to any person, criminal mischief committed in violation of division (A)(1), (2), (3), (4), or (5) of this section is a misdemeanor of the first degree. If the property involved in the violation of division (A)(1), (2), (3), (4), or (5) of this section is an aircraft, an aircraft engine, propeller, appliance, spare part, fuel, lubricant, hydraulic fluid, any other equipment, implement, or material used or intended to be used in the operation of an aircraft, or any cargo carried or intended to be carried in an aircraft, criminal mischief committed in violation of division (A)(1), (2), (3), (4), or (5) of this section is one of the following:

(a) If the violation creates a risk of physical harm to any person, except as otherwise provided in division (C)(2)(b) of this section, criminal mischief committed in violation of division (A)(1), (2), (3), (4), or (5) of this section is a felony of the fifth degree.

(b) If the violation creates a substantial risk of physical harm to any person or if the property involved in a violation of this section is an occupied aircraft, criminal mischief committed in violation of division (A)(1), (2), (3), (4), or (5) of this section is a felony of the fourth degree.

(3) Except as otherwise provided in this division, criminal mischief committed in violation of division (A)(6) of this section is a misdemeanor of the first degree. Except as otherwise provided in this division, if the value of the computer, computer system, computer network, computer software, computer program, or data involved in the violation of division (A)(6) of this section or the loss to the victim resulting from the violation is one thousand dollars or more and less than ten thousand dollars, or if the computer, computer system, computer network, computer software, computer program, or data involved in the violation of division (A)(6) of this section is used or intended to be used in the operation of an aircraft and the violation creates a risk of physical harm to any person, criminal mischief committed in violation of division (A)(6) of this section is a felony of the fifth degree. If the value of the computer, computer system, computer network, computer software, computer program, or data involved in the violation of division (A)(6) of this section or the loss to the victim resulting from the violation is ten thousand dollars or more, or if the computer, computer system, computer network, computer software, computer program, or data involved in the violation of division (A)(6) of this section is used or intended to be used in the operation of an aircraft and the violation creates a substantial risk of physical harm to any person or the aircraft in question is an occupied aircraft, criminal mischief committed in violation of division (A)(6) of this section is a felony of the fourth degree.

**HISTORY: 134 v H 511 (Eff 1-1-74); 135 v H 89 (Eff 1-1-74); 140 v H 570 (Eff 3-28-85); 141 v S 316 (Eff 3-19-87); 146 v S 2. Eff 7-1-96; 150 v S 146, § 1, eff. 9-23-04.**

**Analogous to former RC § 2909.07 (RS § 6866; 69 v 81; GC § 12481; Bureau of Code Revision, 10-1-53), repealed 134 v H 511, § 2, eff 1-1-74.**

The effective date is set by section 6 of SB 2.

## § 2909.08 Endangering aircraft or airport operations.

(A) As used in this section:

(1) "Air gun" means a hand pistol or rifle that propels its projectile by means of releasing compressed air, carbon dioxide, or other gas.

(2) "Firearm" has the same meaning as in section 2923.11 of the Revised Code.

(3) "Spring-operated gun" means a hand pistol or rifle that propels a projectile not less than four or more than five millimeters in diameter by means of a spring.

(4) "Airport operational surface" means any surface of land or water that is developed, posted, or marked so as to give an observer reasonable notice that the surface is designed and developed for the purpose of storing, parking, taxiing, or operating aircraft, or any surface of land or water that is actually being used for any of those purposes.

(B) No person shall do either of the following:

(1) Knowingly throw an object at, or drop an object upon, any moving aircraft;

(2) Knowingly shoot with a bow and arrow, or knowingly discharge a firearm, air gun, or spring-operated gun, at or toward any aircraft.

(C) No person shall knowingly or recklessly shoot with a bow and arrow, or shall knowingly or recklessly discharge a firearm, air gun, or spring-operated gun, upon or over any airport operational surface. This division does not apply to the following:

(1) An officer, agent, or employee of this or any other state or the United States, or a law enforcement officer, authorized to discharge firearms and acting within the scope of the officer's, agent's, or employee's duties;

(2) A person who, with the consent of the owner or operator of the airport operational surface or the authorized agent of either, is lawfully engaged in any hunting or sporting activity or is otherwise lawfully discharging a firearm.

(D) Whoever violates division (B) of this section is guilty of endangering aircraft, a misdemeanor of the first degree. If the violation creates a risk of physical harm to any person, endangering aircraft is a felony of the fifth degree. If the violation creates a substantial risk of physical harm to any person or if the aircraft that is the subject of the violation is occupied, endangering aircraft is a felony of the fourth degree.

(E) Whoever violates division (C) of this section is guilty of endangering airport operations, a misdemeanor of the second degree. If the violation creates a risk of physical harm to any person, endangering airport operations is a felony of the fifth degree. If the violation creates a substantial risk of physical harm to any person, endangering airport operations is a felony of the fourth degree. In addition to any other penalty or sanction imposed for the violation, the hunting license or permit of a person who violates division (C) of this section while hunting shall be suspended or revoked pursuant to section 1533.68 of the Revised Code.

(F) Any bow and arrow, air gun, spring-operated gun, or firearm that has been used in a felony violation of this section shall be seized or forfeited, and shall be disposed of pursuant to Chapter 2981. of the Revised Code.

**HISTORY: 140 v H 570 (Eff 3-28-85); 146 v S 2. Eff 7-1-96; 151 v H 241, § 1, eff. 7-1-07.**

See provisions of § 4 of 151 v H 241 following RC § 2901.01.

**Not analogous to former RC § 2909.08 (RS § 6868; S&S 285; S&C 436; 60 v 85; GC § 12483; Bureau of Code Revision, 10-1-53; 131 v 674), repealed 134 v H 511, § 2, eff 1-1-74.**

The effective date is set by section 6 of SB 2.

## § 2909.081 Interfering with operation of aircraft with laser.

(A) No person shall knowingly discharge a laser or other device that creates visible light into the cockpit of an aircraft that is in the process of taking off or landing or is in flight.

(B) Whoever violates this section is guilty of interfering with the operation of an aircraft with a laser, a felony of the second degree.

(C) As used in this section, "laser" means both of the following:

(1) Any device that utilizes the natural oscillations of atoms or molecules between energy levels for generating coherent electromagnetic radiation in the ultraviolet, visible, or infrared region of the spectrum and when discharged exceeds one milliwatt continuous wave;

(2) Any device designed or used to amplify electromagnetic radiation by simulated emission that is visible to the human eye.

**HISTORY: 151 v H 231, § 1, eff. 7-20-06.**

## § 2909.09 Vehicular vandalism.

(A) As used in this section:

(1) "Highway" means any highway as defined in section 4511.01 of the Revised Code or any lane, road, street, alley, bridge, or overpass.

(2) "Alley," "street," "streetcar," "trackless trolley," and "vehicle" have the same meanings as in section 4511.01 of the Revised Code.

(3) "Vessel" and "waters in this state" have the same meanings as in section 1547.01 of the Revised Code.

(B) No person shall knowingly, and by any means, drop or throw any object at, onto, or in the path of any of the following:

(1) Any vehicle, streetcar, or trackless trolley on a highway;

(2) Any boat or vessel on any of the waters in this state.

(C) Whoever violates this section is guilty of vehicular vandalism. Except as otherwise provided in this division, vehicular vandalism is a misdemeanor of the first degree. Except as otherwise provided in this division, if the violation of this section creates a substantial risk of physical harm to any person or the violation of this section causes serious physical harm to property, vehicular vandalism is a felony of the fourth degree. Except as otherwise provided in this division, if the violation of this section causes physical harm to any person, vehicular vandalism is a felony of the third degree. If the violation of this section causes serious physical harm to any person, vehicular vandalism is a felony of the second degree.

**HISTORY: 149 v S 163. Eff 4-9-2003.**

**Not analogous to former RC § 2909.09 (RS § 6877; S&C 457b; S&S 280; 63 v 175, § 1; 70 v 216, § 73; GC § 12487; Bureau of Code Revision, 10-1-53; 131 v 674), repealed 134 v H 511, § 2, eff 1-1-74.**

## § 2909.10 Railroad vandalism or criminal trespass; interference with operation of train.

(A) No person shall knowingly, and by any means, drop or throw any object at, onto, or in the path of, any railroad rail, railroad track, locomotive, engine, railroad car, or other vehicle of a railroad company while such vehicle is on a railroad track.

(B) No person, without privilege to do so, shall climb upon or into any locomotive, engine, railroad car, or other vehicle of a railroad company when it is on a railroad track.

(C) No person, without privilege to do so, shall disrupt, delay, or prevent the operation of any train or other vehicle of a railroad company while such vehicle is on a railroad track.

(D) No person, without privilege to do so, shall knowingly enter or remain on the land or premises of a railroad company.

(E) Whoever violates division (A) of this section is guilty of railroad vandalism. Whoever violates division (B) of this section is guilty of criminal trespass on a locomotive, engine, railroad car, or other railroad vehicle. Whoever violates division (C) of this section is guilty of interference with the operation of a train.

Except as otherwise provided in this division, railroad vandalism; criminal trespass on a locomotive, engine, railroad car, or other railroad vehicle; and interference with the operation of a train each is a misdemeanor of the first degree. Except as otherwise provided in this division, if the violation of division (A), (B), or (C) of this section causes serious physical harm to property or creates a substantial risk of physical harm to any person, the violation is a felony of the fourth degree. Except as otherwise provided in this division, if the violation of division (A), (B), or (C) of this section causes physical harm to any person, the violation is a felony of the third degree. If the violation of division (A), (B), or (C) of this section causes serious physical harm to any person, the violation is a felony of the second degree.

(F) Whoever violates division (D) of this section is guilty of criminal trespass on the land or premises of a railroad company, a misdemeanor of the fourth degree.

**HISTORY: 149 v S 163. Eff 4-9-2003.**

**Not analogous to former RC § 2909.10 (RS § 6878; S&S 285; 63 v 8, § 1; GC § 12488; 123 v 468, § 1; Bureau of Code Revision, 10-1-53), repealed 134 v H 511, § 2, eff 1-1-74.**

## § 2909.101 Railroad grade crossing device vandalism.

(A) No person shall knowingly deface, damage, obstruct, remove, or otherwise impair the operation of any railroad grade crossing warning signal or other protective device, including any gate, bell, light, crossbuck, stop sign, yield sign, advance warning sign, or advance pavement marking.

(B) Whoever violates this section is guilty of railroad grade crossing device vandalism. Except as otherwise provided in this division, railroad grade crossing device vandalism is a misdemeanor of the first degree. Except as otherwise provided in this division, if the violation of this section causes serious physical harm to property or creates a substantial risk of physical harm to any person, railroad grade crossing device vandalism is a felony of the fourth degree. Except as otherwise provided in this division, if the violation of this section causes physical harm to any person, railroad grade crossing device vandalism is a felony of the third degree. If the violation of this section causes serious physical harm to any person, railroad grade crossing device vandalism is a felony of the second degree.

**HISTORY: 149 v S 163. Eff 4-9-2003.**

## § 2909.11 Determining property value or amount of physical harm.

(A) When a person is charged with a violation of division (A)(1) of section 2909.03 of the Revised Code involving property value or an amount of physical harm of one thousand dollars or more or with a violation of section 2909.05 of the Revised Code involving property value or an amount of physical harm of one thousand dollars or more, the jury or court trying the accused shall determine the value of the property or amount of physical harm and, if a guilty verdict is returned, shall return the finding as part of the verdict. In any such case, it is unnecessary to find or return the exact value or amount of physical harm, section 2945.75 of the Revised Code applies, and it is sufficient if either of the following applies, as appropriate, relative to the finding and return of the value or amount of physical harm:

(1) If the finding and return relate to a violation of division (A)(1) of section 2909.03 of the Revised Code and are that the value or amount of the physical harm was one

thousand dollars or more, the finding and return shall include a statement that the value or amount was one thousand dollars or more.

(2) If the finding and return relate to a violation of section 2909.05 of the Revised Code and are that the value or amount of the physical harm was in any of the following categories, the finding and return shall include one of the following statements, as appropriate:

(a) If the finding and return are that the value or amount was one hundred fifty thousand dollars or more, a statement that the value or amount was one hundred fifty thousand dollars or more;

(b) If the finding and return are that the value or amount was seven thousand five hundred dollars or more but less than one hundred fifty thousand dollars a statement that the value or amount was seven thousand five hundred dollars or more but less than one hundred fifty thousand dollars;

(c) If the finding and return are that the value or amount was one thousand dollars or more but less than seven thousand five hundred dollars, a statement that the value or amount was one thousand dollars or more but less than seven thousand five hundred dollars.

(B) The following criteria shall be used in determining the value of property or amount of physical harm involved in a violation of division (A)(1) of section 2909.03 or section 2909.05 of the Revised Code:

(1) If the property is an heirloom, memento, collector's item, antique, museum piece, manuscript, document, record, or other thing that is either irreplaceable or is replaceable only on the expenditure of substantial time, effort, or money, the value of the property or the amount of physical harm involved is the amount that would compensate the owner for its loss.

(2) If the property is not covered under division (B)(1) of this section and the physical harm is such that the property can be restored substantially to its former condition, the amount of physical harm involved is the reasonable cost of restoring the property.

(3) If the property is not covered under division (B)(1) of this section and the physical harm is such that the property cannot be restored substantially to its former condition, the value of the property, in the case of personal property, is the cost of replacing the property with new property of like kind and quality, and, in the case of real property or real property fixtures, is the difference in the fair market value of the property immediately before and immediately after the offense.

(C) As used in this section, "fair market value" has the same meaning as in section 2913.61 of the Revised Code.

(D) Prima-facie evidence of the value of property, as provided in division (E) of section 2913.61 of the Revised Code, may be used to establish the value of property pursuant to this section.

**HISTORY: 134 v H 511 (Eff 1-1-74); 137 v H 741 (Eff 10-9-78); 138 v H 618 (Eff 7-31-80); 139 v S 199 (Eff 1-5-83); 139 v H 269 (Eff 1-5-83); 144 v H 675 (Eff 3-19-93); 146 v S 2. Eff 7-1-96; 2011 HB 86, § 1, eff. Sept. 30, 2011.**

The provisions of § 4 of HB 86 read as follows:

"SECTION 4. The amendments to sections 926.99, 1333.99, 1707.99, 1716.99, 2909.03, 2909.05, 2909.11, 2913.02, 2913.03, 2913.04, 2913.11, 2913.21, 2913.31, 2913.32, 2913.34, 2913.40, 2913.401, 2913.42, 2913.421, 2913.43, 2913.45, 2913.46, 2913.47, 2913.48, 2913.49, 2913.51, 2913.61, 2915.05, 2917.21, 2917.31, 2917.32, 2921.13, 2921.41, 2923.31, and 2981.07, division (B) of section 2929.13, and division (A) of section 2929.14 of the Revised Code that are made in this act apply to a person who commits an offense specified or penalized under those sections on or after the effective date of this section and to a person to whom division (B) of section 1.58 of the Revised Code makes the amendments applicable.

"The provisions of sections 926.99, 1333.99, 1707.99, 1716.99, 2909.03, 2909.05, 2909.11, 2913.02, 2913.03, 2913.04, 2913.11, 2913.21, 2913.31, 2913.32, 2913.34, 2913.40, 2913.401, 2913.42, 2913.421, 2913.43, 2913.45, 2913.46, 2913.47, 2913.48, 2913.49, 2913.51, 2913.61, 2915.05, 2917.21, 2917.31, 2917.32, 2921.13, 2921.41, 2923.31, and 2981.07 of the Revised Code in existence prior to the effective date of this section shall apply to a person upon whom a court imposed sentence prior to the effective date of this section for an offense specified or penalized under those sections. The amendments to sections 926.99, 1333.99, 1707.99, 1716.99, 2909.03, 2909.05, 2909.11, 2913.02, 2913.03, 2913.04, 2913.11, 2913.21, 2913.31, 2913.32, 2913.34, 2913.40, 2913.401, 2913.42, 2913.421, 2913.43, 2913.45, 2913.46, 2913.47, 2913.48, 2913.49, 2913.51, 2913.61, 2915.05, 2917.21, 2917.31, 2917.32, 2921.13, 2921.41, 2923.31, and 2981.07 of the Revised Code that are made in this act do not apply to a person who upon whom a court imposed sentence prior to the effective date of this section for an offense specified or penalized under those sections."

**Not analogous to former RC § 2909.11 (RS § 6879; S&C 336, 433, 1313; S&S 665; 29 v 144; 36 v 104; 65 v 14; GC § 12489; Bureau of Code Revision, 10-1-53), repealed 134 v H 511, § 2, eff 1-1-74.**

The effective date is set by section 6 of SB 2.

## § 2909.12 Repealed, 134 v H 511, § 2 [RS §§ 6862, 6883, 6885; S&S 9, 281; 64 v 127, 254; 76 v 11; 81 v 125; 84 v 81; Bureau of Code Revision, 10-1-53; 126 v 575; 131 v 675]. Eff 1-1-74.

This section concerned offenses against property.

## § 2909.13 Repealed, 134 v H 511, § 2 [RS §§ 6862, 6883, 6885; S&S 9, 281; 64 v 127, 254; 76 v 11; 81 v 125; 84 v 81; Bureau of Code Revision, 10-1-53; 126 v 575; 131 v 675]. Eff 1-1-74.

This section concerned offenses against property.

## § 2909.14 Repealed, 134 v H 511, § 2 [RS §§ 6862, 6883, 6885; S&S 9, 281; 64 v 127, 254; 76 v 11; 81 v 125; 84 v 81; Bureau of Code Revision, 10-1-53; 126 v 575; 131 v 675]. Eff 1-1-74.

This section concerned offenses against property.

## § 2909.15 Repealed, 134 v H 511, § 2 [RS §§ 6854a—6854c; 90 v 329; GC §§ 12514—12516; Bureau of Code Revision, 10-1-53]. Eff 1-1-74.

This section concerned offenses against property.

## § 2909.16 Repealed, 134 v H 511, § 2 [RS §§ 6854a—6854c; 90 v 329; GC §§ 12514—12516; Bureau of Code Revision, 10-1-53]. Eff 1-1-74.

This section concerned offenses against property.

## § 2909.17 Repealed, 134 v H 511, § 2 [RS §§ 6854a—6854c; 90 v 329; GC §§ 12514—12516; Bureau of Code Revision, 10-1-53]. Eff 1-1-74.

This section concerned offenses against property.

## § 2909.18 Repealed, 134 v H 511, § 2 [RS §§ 3713-7—3713-9; 82 v 208; 86 v 302; 92 v 157; 95 v 241; GC §§ 12518—12520; Bureau of Code Revision, 10-1-53; 129 v 582(746)]. Eff 1-1-74.

This section concerned offenses against property.

## § 2909.19 Repealed, 134 v H 511, § 2 [RS §§ 3713-7—3713-9; 82 v 208; 86 v 302; 92 v 157; 95 v 241; GC §§ 12518—12520; Bureau of Code Revision, 10-1-53; 129 v 582(746)]. Eff 1-1-74.

This section concerned offenses against property.

## § 2909.20 Repealed, 134 v H 511, § 2 [RS §§ 3713-7—3713-9; 82 v 208; 86 v 302; 92 v 157; 95 v 241; GC §§ 12518—12520; Bureau of Code Revision, 10-1-53; 129 v 582(746)]. Eff 1-1-74.

This section concerned offenses against property.

# [TERRORISM]

## § 2909.21 Definitions.

As used in sections 2909.21 to 2909.34 of the Revised Code:

(A) "Act of terrorism" means an act that is committed within or outside the territorial jurisdiction of this state or the United States, that constitutes a specified offense if committed in this state or constitutes an offense in any jurisdiction within or outside the territorial jurisdiction of the United States containing all of the essential elements of a specified offense, and that is intended to do one or more of the following:

(1) Intimidate or coerce a civilian population;

(2) Influence the policy of any government by intimidation or coercion;

(3) Affect the conduct of any government by the act that constitutes the offense.

(B) "Biological agent," "delivery system," "toxin," and "vector" have the same meanings as in section 2917.33 of the Revised Code.

(C) "Biological weapon" means any biological agent, toxin, vector, or delivery system or combination of any biological agent or agents, any toxin or toxins, any vector or vectors, and any delivery system or systems.

(D) "Chemical weapon" means any one or more of the following:

(1) Any toxic chemical or precursor of a toxic chemical that is listed in Schedule 1, Schedule 2, or Schedule 3 of the international "Convention on the Prohibition of the Development, Production, Stockpiling and Use of Chemical Weapons and on their Destruction (CWC)," as entered into force on April 29, 1997;

(2) A device specifically designed to cause death or other harm through the toxic properties of a toxic chemical or precursor identified in division (D)(1) of this section that would be created or released as a result of the employment of that device;

(3) Any equipment specifically designed for use directly in connection with the employment of devices identified in division (D)(2) of this section.

(E) "Radiological or nuclear weapon" means any device that is designed to create or release radiation or radioactivity at a level that is dangerous to human life or in order to cause serious physical harm to persons as a result of the radiation or radioactivity created or released.

(F) "Explosive device" has the same meaning as in section 2923.11 of the Revised Code.

(G) "Key component of a binary or multicomponent chemical system" means the precursor that plays the most important role in determining the toxic properties of the final product and reacts rapidly with other chemicals in the binary or multicomponent chemical system.

(H) "Material assistance" means any of the following:

(1) Membership in an organization on the United States department of state terrorist exclusion list;

(2) Use of the person's position of prominence within any country to persuade others to support an organization on the United States department of state terrorist exclusion list;

(3) Knowingly soliciting funds or other things of value for an organization on the United States department of state terrorist exclusion list;

(4) Solicitation of any individual for membership in an organization on the United States department of state terrorist exclusion list;

(5) Commission of an act that the person knows, or reasonably should have known, affords material support or resources to an organization on the United States department of state terrorist exclusion list;

(6) Hiring or compensating a person known by the person hiring or providing the compensation to be a member of an organization on the United States department of state terrorist exclusion list or a person known by the person hiring or providing the compensation to be engaged in planning, assisting, or carrying out an act of terrorism.

(I) "Material support or resources" means currency, payment instruments, other financial securities, funds, transfer of funds, financial services, communications, lodging, training, safe houses, false documentation or identification, communications equipment, facilities, weapons, lethal substances, explosives, personnel, transportation, and other physical assets, except medicine or religious materials.

(J) "Payment instrument" means a check, draft, money order, traveler's check, cashier's check, teller's check, or other instrument or order for the transmission or payment of money, regardless of whether the item in question is negotiable.

(K) "Peace officer" and "prosecutor" have the same meanings as in section 2935.01 of the Revised Code.

(L) "Precursor" means any chemical reactant that takes part at any stage in the production by whatever method of a toxic chemical, including any key component of a binary or multicomponent chemical system.

(M) "Response costs" means all costs a political subdivision incurs as a result of, or in making any response to, a threat of a specified offense made as described in section 2909.23 of the Revised Code or a specified offense committed as described in section 2909.24 of the Revised Code, including, but not limited to, all costs so incurred by any law enforcement officers, firefighters, rescue personnel, or emergency medical services personnel of the political subdivision and all costs so incurred by the political subdivision that relate to laboratory testing or hazardous material cleanup.

(N) "Specified offense" means any of the following:

(1) A felony offense of violence, a violation of section 2909.04, 2909.081 [2909.08.1], 2909.22, 2909.23, 2909.24, 2909.26, 2909.27, 2909.28, 2909.29, or 2927.24 of the Revised Code, a felony of the first degree that is not a violation of any provision in Chapter 2925. or 3719. of the Revised Code;

(2) An attempt to commit, complicity in committing, or a conspiracy to commit an offense listed in division (N)(1) of this section.

(O) "Toxic chemical" means any chemical that through its chemical action on life processes can cause death or serious physical harm to persons or animals, regardless of its origin or of its method of production and regardless of whether it is produced in facilities, in munitions, or elsewhere.

(P) "United States department of state terrorist exclusion list" and "terrorist exclusion list" means the list compiled by the United States secretary of state, in consultation with or upon the request of the United States attorney general, that designates terrorist organizations for immigration purposes. "United States department of state terrorist exclusion list" and "terrorist exclusion list" also mean the list of terrorist organizations the director of public safety prepares pursuant to rules adopted in accordance with Chapter 119. of the Revised Code, that is comprised of lists of organizations officials of the United States government designate as terrorist, including the "terrorist exclusion list" described in this division, the list of "foreign terrorist organizations" the Unites States secretary of state prepares in consultation with the United States attorney general and the United States secretary of the treasury, and the list of charities that support terrorist activities, known as "designated charities," that the United States department of treasury compiles.

(Q) "Hazardous radioactive substance" means any substance or item that releases or is designed to release radiation or radioactivity at a level dangerous to human life.

**HISTORY: 149 v S 184. Eff 5-15-2002; 151 v S 9, § 1, eff. 4-14-06; 151 v H 231, § 1, eff. 7-20-06.**

151 v H 231, effective July 20, 2006, rewrote (P); and corrected internal references.

**Not analogous to former RC § 2909.21 (RS § 6880e; 91 v 224; GC § 12522; Bureau of Code Revision, 10-1-53), repealed 134 v H 511, § 2, eff 1-1-74.**

## § 2909.22 Soliciting or providing support for act of terrorism.

(A) No person shall raise, solicit, collect, donate, or provide any material support or resources, with purpose that the material support or resources will be used in whole or in part to plan, prepare, carry out, or aid in either an act of terrorism or the concealment of, or an escape from, an act of terrorism.

(B) Whoever violates this section is guilty of soliciting or providing support for an act of terrorism, a felony of the third degree. Section 2909.25 of the Revised Code applies regarding an offender who is convicted of or pleads guilty to a violation of this section.

(C) A prosecution for a violation of this section does not preclude a prosecution for a violation of any other section of the Revised Code. One or more acts, a series of acts, or a course of behavior that can be prosecuted under this section or any other section of the Revised Code may be prosecuted under this section, the other section, or both sections.

**HISTORY: 149 v S 184. Eff 5-15-2002.**

**Not analogous to former RC § 2909.22 (RS § 6881-1; 82 v 166; GC § 12530; 102 v 88; Bureau of Code Revision, 10-1-53), repealed 134 v H 511, § 2, eff 1-1-74.**

## § 2909.23 Making terroristic threat.

(A) No person shall threaten to commit or threaten to cause to be committed a specified offense when both of the following apply:

(1) The person makes the threat with purpose to do any of the following:

(a) Intimidate or coerce a civilian population;

(b) Influence the policy of any government by intimidation or coercion;

(c) Affect the conduct of any government by the threat or by the specified offense.

(2) As a result of the threat, the person causes a reasonable expectation or fear of the imminent commission of the specified offense.

(B) It is not a defense to a charge of a violation of this section that the defendant did not have the intent or capability to commit the threatened specified offense or that the threat was not made to a person who was a subject of the threatened specified offense.

(C) Whoever violates this section is guilty of making a terroristic threat, a felony of the third degree. Section 2909.25 of the Revised Code applies regarding an offender who is convicted of or pleads guilty to a violation of this section.

**HISTORY: 149 v S 184. Eff 5-15-2002.**

**Not analogous to former RC § 2909.23 (RS § 4905; 73 v 117; Bureau of Code Revision, 10-1-53), repealed 134 v H 511, § 2, eff 1-1-74.**

## § 2909.24 Terrorism.

(A) No person shall commit a specified offense with purpose to do any of the following:

(1) Intimidate or coerce a civilian population;

(2) Influence the policy of any government by intimidation or coercion;

(3) Affect the conduct of any government by the specified offense.

(B)(1) Whoever violates this section is guilty of terrorism.

(2) Except as otherwise provided in divisions (B)(3) and (4) of this section, terrorism is an offense one degree higher than the most serious underlying specified offense the defendant committed.

(3) If the most serious underlying specified offense the defendant committed is a felony of the first degree or murder, the person shall be sentenced to life imprisonment without parole.

(4) If the most serious underlying specified offense the defendant committed is aggravated murder, the offender shall be sentenced to life imprisonment without parole or death pursuant to sections 2929.02 to 2929.06 of the Revised Code.

(5) Section 2909.25 of the Revised Code applies regarding an offender who is convicted of or pleads guilty to a violation of this section.

**HISTORY: 149 v S 184. Eff 5-15-2002.**

**Not analogous to former RC § 2909.24 (127 v 810), repealed 134 v H 511, § 2, eff 1-1-74.**

## § 2909.25 Reimbursement of investigation, prosecution, and response costs concerning act of terrorism.

(A) In addition to the financial sanctions authorized under section 2929.18 of the Revised Code, the court imposing sentence upon an offender who is convicted of or pleads guilty to a violation of section 2909.22, 2909.23, or 2909.24 of the Revised Code or to a violation of section 2921.32 of the Revised Code when the offense or act committed by the person aided or to be aided as described in that section is an act of terrorism may order the offender to pay to the state, municipal, or county law enforcement agencies that handled the investigation and prosecution all of the costs that the state, municipal corporation, or county reasonably incurred in the investigation and prosecution of the violation. The court shall hold a hearing to determine the amount of costs to be imposed under this section. The court may hold the hearing as part of the sentencing hearing for the offender.

(B) If a person is convicted of or pleads guilty to a violation of section 2909.23 or 2909.24 of the Revised Code and if any political subdivision incurred any response costs as a result of, or in making any response to, the threat of the specified offense involved in the violation of section 2909.23 of the Revised Code or the actual specified offense involved in the violation of section 2909.24 of the Revised Code, in addition to the financial sanctions authorized under section 2929.18 of the Revised Code, the court imposing sentence upon the offender for the violation may order the offender to reimburse the involved political subdivision for the response costs it so incurred.

**HISTORY: 149 v S 184. Eff 5-15-2002.**

**Not analogous to former RC § 2909.25 (128 v 467), repealed 134 v H 511, § 2, eff 1-1-74.**

## § 2909.26 Criminal possession of chemical weapon, biological weapon, radiological or nuclear weapon, or explosive device.

(A) No person shall knowingly possess any chemical weapon, biological weapon, radiological or nuclear weapon, or explosive device with the intent to use it to cause serious physical harm or death to another person.

(B) No person shall knowingly possess any chemical weapon, biological weapon, radiological or nuclear weapon, or explosive device with intent to use the weapon to do any of the following:

(1) Intimidate or coerce a civilian population;

(2) Influence the policy of any government by intimidation or coercion;

(3) Affect the conduct of any government by murder, assassination, or kidnapping.

(C) Whoever violates this section is guilty of criminal possession of a chemical weapon, biological weapon, radiological or nuclear weapon, or explosive device. A violation of division (A) of this section is a felony of the third degree. A violation of division (B) of this section is a felony of the second degree.

(D) This section does not apply when the items described in division (A) of this section are possessed for a purpose related to the performance of official duties related to any military purpose of the United States and any law enforcement purpose, including any domestic riot control purpose.

**HISTORY: 151 v S 9, § 1, eff. 4-14-06.**

**Not analogous to former RC § 2909.26 (132 v H 996), repealed 134 v H 511, § 2, eff 1-1-74.**

This section prohibited unauthorized trespass upon premises damaged during a public emergency natural disaster.

## § 2909.27 Criminal use of chemical weapon, biological weapon, radiological or nuclear weapon, or explosive device.

(A) No person shall recklessly use, deploy, release, or cause to be used, deployed, or released any chemical weapon, biological weapon, radiological or nuclear weapon, or explosive device that creates a risk of death or serious physical harm to another person not a participant in the offense.

(B) No person shall knowingly use, deploy, release, or cause to be used, deployed, or released any chemical weapon, biological weapon, radiological or nuclear weapon, or explosive device with the intent to do any of the following:

(1) Intimidate or coerce a civilian population;

(2) Influence the policy of any government by intimidation or coercion;

(3) Affect the conduct of any government by murder, assassination, or kidnapping;

(4) Cause physical harm to, or the death of, any person who is not a participant in the offense.

(C) Whoever violates this section is guilty of criminal use of a chemical weapon, biological weapon, radiological or nuclear weapon, or explosive device. A violation of division (A) of this section is a felony of the second degree. A violation of division (B) of this section is a felony of the first degree.

(D)(1) Division (A) of this section does not apply to any person who uses any of the following:

(a) Any household product that is generally available for sale to consumers in this state in the quantity and concentration available for sale to those consumers;

(b) A self-defense spray;

(c) A biological agent, toxin, or delivery system the person possesses solely for protective, bona fide research, or other peaceful purposes;

(d) A chemical weapon that the person possesses solely for a purpose not prohibited under this section if the type and quantity is consistent with that purpose.

(2) For purposes of this division, "a purpose not prohibited under this section" means any of the following:

(a) Any peaceful purpose related to an industrial, agricultural, research, medical, or pharmaceutical activity or other peaceful activity;

(b) Any purpose directly related to protection against toxic chemicals and to protection against chemical weapons;

(c) Any military purpose of the United States that is not connected with the use of a chemical weapon or that is not dependent on the use of the toxic or poisonous properties of the chemical weapon to cause death or other harm, when related to the performance of official duties;

(d) Any law enforcement purpose, including any domestic riot control purpose, when related to the performance of official duties.

**HISTORY: 151 v S 9, § 1, eff. 4-14-06.**

## § 2909.28 Illegal assembly or possession of chemicals or substances for the manufacture of chemical weapon, biological weapon, radiological or nuclear weapon, or explosive device.

(A) No person, with the intent to manufacture a chemical weapon, biological weapon, radiological or nuclear weapon, or explosive device, shall knowingly assemble or possess one or more toxins, toxic chemicals, precursors of toxic chemicals, vectors, biological agents, or hazardous radioactive substances, including, but not limited to, those listed in rules the director of public safety adopts, that may be used to manufacture a chemical weapon, biological weapon, radiological or nuclear weapon, or explosive device.

(B) In a prosecution under this section, it is not necessary to allege or prove that the offender assembled or possessed all chemicals or substances necessary to manufacture a chemical weapon, biological weapon, radiological or nuclear weapon, or explosive device. The assembly or possession of a single chemical or substance, with the intent to use that chemical or substance in the manufacture of a chemical weapon, biological weapon, radiological or nuclear weapon, or explosive device, is sufficient to violate this section.

(C) Whoever violates this section is guilty of illegal assembly or possession of chemicals or substances for the manufacture of a chemical weapon, biological weapon, radiological or nuclear weapon, or explosive device, which is a felony of the fourth degree.

(D) This section does not apply when the items described in division (A) of this section are assembled or possessed for a purpose related to the performance of official duties related to any military purpose of the United States and any law enforcement purpose, including any domestic riot control purpose.

**HISTORY: 151 v S 9, § 1, eff. 4-14-06.**

## § 2909.29 Money laundering in support of terrorism.

(A) No person, knowing that property is the proceeds of an act of terrorism or a monetary instrument given, received, or intended to be used in support of an act of terrorism, shall conduct or attempt to conduct any transaction involving that property or transport, transmit or transfer that monetary instrument with the intent to do any of the following:

(1) Commit or further the commission of criminal activity;

(2) Conceal or disguise the nature, location, source, ownership, or control of either the proceeds of an act of terrorism or a monetary instrument given, received, or intended to be used to support an act of terrorism;

(3) Conceal or disguise the intent to avoid a transaction reporting requirement under section 1315.53 of the Revised Code or federal law.

(B)(1) Whoever violates this section is guilty of money laundering in support of terrorism, which is a misdemeanor of the first degree, except as otherwise provided in this division.

(2) A violation of division (A) of this section is a felony of the fifth degree if the total value of the property or monetary instrument involved in the transaction equals or exceeds one thousand dollars and is less than five thousand dollars.

(3) Money laundering in support of terrorism is a felony of the fourth degree if the total value of the property or monetary instrument involved in the transaction equals or exceeds five thousand dollars and is less than twenty-five thousand dollars.

(4) Money laundering in support of terrorism is a felony of the third degree if the total value of the property or monetary instrument involved in the transaction equals or exceeds twenty-five thousand dollars and is less than seventy-five thousand dollars.

(5) Money laundering in support of terrorism is a felony of the second degree if the total value of the property or monetary instrument involved in the transaction equals or exceeds seventy-five thousand dollars.

**HISTORY: 151 v S 9, § 1, eff. 4-14-06.**

## § 2909.30 Suspected alien convicted of or pleading guilty to felony, or serving prison term.

(A) A judge of a court of record shall direct the clerk of that court to notify the immigration and customs enforcement section of the United States department of homeland security when a suspected alien has been convicted of or pleaded guilty to a felony.

(B) The department of rehabilitation and correction monthly shall compile a list of suspected aliens who are serving a prison term. The list shall include the earliest possible date of release of the offender, whether through expiration of prison term, parole, or other means. The department shall provide a copy of the list to the immigration and customs enforcement section of the United States department of homeland security for the section to determine whether it wishes custody of the suspected alien. If the immigration and customs enforcement section indicates it wishes custody, the department of rehabilitation and correction is responsible for the suspected alien until the section takes custody.

(C) The department of rehabilitation and correction, pursuant to a valid detainer lodged against an alien who is not legally present in the United States and who has been convicted of or pleaded guilty to a felony, shall transfer that alien to the custody of the immigration and enforcement section of the United States department of homeland security upon completion of the alien's prison term.

(D) As used in this section, "alien" means an individual who is not a citizen of the United States.

**HISTORY: 151 v S 9, § 1, eff. 4-14-06.**

## § 2909.31 Identification when entering critical transportation infrastructure site.

(A) No person entering an airport, train station, port, or other similar critical transportation infrastructure site shall refuse to show identification when requested by a law enforcement officer when there is a threat to security and the law enforcement officer is requiring identification of all persons entering the site.

(B) A law enforcement officer may prevent any person who refuses to show identification when asked under the circumstances described in division (A) of this section from entering the critical transportation infrastructure site.

**HISTORY: 151 v S 9, § 1, eff. 4-14-06.**

**§ 2909.32 Identification of licenses for which holder with terrorist connections presents potential risk; declaration of material assistance/nonassistance; denial or revocation of license.**

(A)(1) The director of public safety shall adopt rules in accordance with Chapter 119. of the Revised Code to identify licenses the state issues for which a holder with a connection to a terrorist organization would present a potential risk to the residents of this state. The rules shall not identify a renewable driver's license or permit as a license of this nature if the applicant is a resident of this state.

(2)(a) The director shall prepare a document to serve as a declaration of material assistance/nonassistance for agencies to use to identify whether an applicant for a license or the renewal of a license has provided material assistance to an organization listed in the United States department of state terrorist exclusion list. The declaration shall be substantially in the form and of the same content as set forth in division (A)(2)(b) of this section. The director shall make the declaration available to each issuing agency of a license the director identifies pursuant to division (A)(1) of this section, along with a then-current copy of the United States department of state terrorist exclusion list. The director may adopt rules governing the preparation of the declaration and the distribution of the declaration and the list.

(b) The declaration of material assistance/nonassistance this section requires shall be substantially as follows and shall include the following questions and the associated spaces for answering the questions:

"DECLARATION REGARDING MATERIAL ASSISTANCE/NONASSISTANCE TO TERRORIST ORGANIZATION

(1) Are you a member of an organization on the U.S. Department of State Terrorist Exclusion List? Yes ..... ; No .....

(2) Have you used any position of prominence you have within any country to persuade others to support an organization on the U.S. Department of State Terrorist Exclusion List? Yes ..... ; No .....

(3) Have you knowingly solicited funds or other things of value for an organization on the U.S. Department of State Terrorist Exclusion List? Yes ..... ; No .....

(4) Have you solicited any individual for membership in an organization on the U.S. Department of State Terrorist Exclusion List? Yes ..... ; No .....

(5) Have you committed an act that you know, or reasonably should have known, affords "material support or resources" (see below) to an organization on the U.S. Department of State Terrorist Exclusion List? Yes ..... ; No .....

(6) Have you hired or compensated a person you knew to be a member of an organization on the U.S. Department of State Terrorist Exclusion List or a person you knew to be engaged in planning, assisting, or carrying out an act of terrorism? Yes ..... ; No .....

For purposes of this declaration of material assistance/nonassistance, "material support or resources" means currency, payment instruments, other financial securities, funds, transfer of funds, and financial services that are in excess of one hundred dollars, as well as communications, lodging, training, safe houses, false documentation or identification, communications equipment, facilities, weapons, lethal substances, explosives, personnel, transportation, and other physical assets, except medicine or religious materials."

(B)(1) Any agency that issues a license the director identifies pursuant to division (A)(1) of this section shall include with the agency's application form a copy of the declaration of material assistance/nonassistance the director prepares pursuant to this section and a then-current copy of the terrorist exclusion list. The agency shall inform applicants that they must truthfully answer each question.

(2) Any person provided a declaration of material assistance/nonassistance pursuant to this section shall answer each question and attach the completed declaration to the application for the license or the license renewal.

(C)(1) Any answer of "yes" to any question, or the failure to answer "no" to any question, on a declaration of material assistance/nonassistance an agency provides pursuant to this section shall serve for purposes of this section as a disclosure that the applicant has provided material assistance to an organization listed on the terrorist exclusion list.

(2) Any person who discloses the provision of material assistance to any organization on the terrorist exclusion list shall be denied the license or the renewal of the license unless the department of public safety reinstates the application pursuant to division (D) of this section.

(3) Any licensing entity that denies a license or a renewal of a license pursuant to this division shall send written notice of that denial to the applicant within three business days of the decision to deny. The notice shall inform the applicant of the right to have the department of public safety review the denial if the applicant requests a review within sixty days after the mailing date of the notice. The licensing entity shall provide the department of public safety with a copy of any notice that it sends to an applicant pursuant to this division.

(D) The department of public safety shall review any decision to deny an application within thirty days of receiving an applicant's request for a review. The department shall reinstate the license application for good cause if it determines all of the following pursuant to guidelines the director adopts by rule:

(1) That the provision of material assistance to an organization on the terrorist exclusion list was made more than ten years prior to the time of the application, or the applicant provided material assistance during the ten years prior to the application and the date of the review, but at the time of the assistance, the organization was either not on the list or was not involved in any activity or conduct that would have merited inclusion on the list had it existed at the time, or at the time of the assistance it was not reasonable to know of the organization's activities that would have merited its inclusion on the list.

(2) That the applicant is unlikely in the future to provide material assistance to any organization on the terrorist exclusion list;

(3) That the applicant does not pose a risk to the residents of this state.

(E) The failure of an applicant for a license to complete and attach a declaration of material assistance/nonassistance as this section requires, the failure to disclose material assistance to an organization on the terrorist exclusion list, or the making of false statements regarding material assistance to an organization the applicant knew or should have known was on the terrorist exclusion list, shall result in the denial of the application and in the revocation of the license.

(F) The failure of an applicant for a license to disclose, as this section requires, the provision of material assistance to an organization on the terrorist exclusion list or knowingly making false statements regarding material assistance to an organization on that list is a felony of the fifth degree.

(G) An issuing agency shall notify the department of public safety if it denies an application for a license or the renewal of a license because the applicant disclosed the provision of material assistance to an organization listed on the terrorist exclusion list.

(H) An agency may revoke a license issued to any person who, after providing a declaration of material assistance/nonassistance pursuant to this section, takes an action that would result in "yes" being the correct answer to any question on the declaration, had the declaration been readministered after taking that action. The agency shall conduct a hearing pursuant to Chapter 119. of the Revised Code prior to revoking any license pursuant to this division.

(I) This section does not apply to a license issued to either of the following:

(1) A federally insured depository institution that is subject to anti-money laundering and antiterrorism requirements under federal law, any subsidiary of such a depository institution, or an officer or employee of such a depository institution or subsidiary when that license is related to the person's duties as an officer or employee;

(2) Any affiliate of a depository institution described in division (I)(1) of this section, other than an affiliate that is a subsidiary of a depository institution, when that affiliate is subject to anti-money laundering and antiterrorism requirements under federal law, or an officer or employee of such an affiliate when that license is related to the person's duties as an officer or employee.

**HISTORY: 151 v S 9, § 1, eff. 4-14-06; 151 v H 461, § 1, eff. 4-4-07.**

## § 2909.33 Declaration of material assistance/nonassistance to organization on terrorist exclusion list; restrictions on governmental contracts and funding.

(A)(1) The director of public safety shall prepare a document to serve as a declaration of material assistance/nonassistance by which any person, company, affiliated group, or organization, or person who holds, owns, or otherwise has a controlling interest in a company, affiliated group, or organization, when required by this section, shall certify any provision of material assistance to an organization listed on the United States department of state terrorist exclusion list. The declaration shall be substantially in the same format and of the same content as set forth in division (A)(2)(b) of section 2909.32 of the Revised Code.

(2) The director of public safety and the director of budget and management shall make available on their respective department web sites and by any other means the director of public safety deems appropriate, the declaration of material assistance/nonassistance and a then-current copy of the terrorist exclusion list. The director of public safety, in consultation with the director of budget and management, may adopt rules that govern the preparation of the declaration and the distribution of the declaration and terrorist exclusion list.

(3)(a) Prior to entering into a contract to conduct business with or receive funding from any state agency, instrumentality, or political subdivision of the state any person, company, affiliated group, or organization, or person who holds, owns, or otherwise has a controlling interest in a company, affiliated group, or organization, may precertify that it has not provided material assistance to an organization on the terrorist exclusion list. The precertification this division describes shall be granted to any person, company, affiliated group, or organization that submits to the director of budget and management a completed copy of the declaration prepared pursuant to this section, with an answer of "no" to all questions. No person shall require any person, company, affiliated group, or organization that is precertified to complete any additional declarations prior to the expiration of a precertification. All precertifications expire the thirtieth day of June of the second year of each state biennium period. To be precertified during the two years subsequent to that expiration date, an entity shall submit a new declaration to the director of budget and management pursuant to rules the director adopts.

(b) Any person, company, affiliated group, or organization that is precertified pursuant to this division and that takes any action or learns of anything that would result in an answer of "yes" to any question on the declaration of material assistance/nonassistance this division requires, shall cease to represent that it is precertified and, within thirty days of taking that action or learning the new information, shall notify the director of budget and management to request its precertification be rescinded.

(c) When applying for a contract, falsely representing precertification, or representing precertification when that precertification has been rescinded or should have been rescinded pursuant to this division, is a felony of the fifth degree.

(B) Any person who submits a declaration of material assistance/nonassistance pursuant to this section shall complete the entire declaration. Any answer of "yes" to any question, or the failure to answer "no" to any question, on the declaration shall serve for purposes of this section as a disclosure of the provision of material assistance to an organization that is listed on the terrorist exclusion list.

(C)(1) Except as otherwise provided in divisions (C)(2) and (H) of this section, prior to entering into a contract with any state agency, instrumentality, or political subdivision to conduct business or receive funding, any person, company, affiliated group, or organization, and any person who holds, owns, or otherwise has a controlling interest in a company, affiliated group, or organization shall certify that it does not provide material assistance to any organization on the United States department of state terrorist exclusion list. The certification shall be made by completing and submitting the declaration of material assistance/nonassistance as described in division (A) of this section.

(2) Certification pursuant to this division shall not be required unless the entity entering into a contract for business or funding has received, or will have received as a result of the pending contract, an aggregate amount greater than one hundred thousand dollars in business or funding, excluding the amount of any personal benefit, from the state, instrumentalities, and political subdivisions during the current fiscal year, measured from the first day of July until the thirtieth day of June.

(D)(1) No state agency, instrumentality, or political subdivision shall conduct business with or provide any funding to any person, company, affiliated group or organization, or any person who has a controlling interest in a company, affiliated group, or organization unless that person, company, affiliated group, or organization is certified as this section requires.

(2) No person, company, affiliated group or organization, or any person who holds, owns, or otherwise has a controlling interest in a company, affiliated group, or organization shall enter into a contract to conduct business with or receive funding from the state, an agency or instrumentality of the state, or a political subdivision of the state unless it is certified as this section requires.

(E) For the purposes of this section, the office of budget and management shall be the repository for all declarations received pursuant to division (A)(3)(a) of this section and the director of budget and management shall maintain a centralized database of all such declarations received. If a person, company, affiliated group, or organization discloses the provision of material assistance to an organization listed on the terrorist exclusion list, within three business days of that disclosure, the director shall send the declarant a written notice of prohibition against doing business or receiving funding. The notice shall inform the declarant of the right to a review of the prohibition by the department of public safety if the declarant requests that review within sixty days after the notice of prohibition was mailed. The director shall send copy of any notice sent pursuant to this division to the department of public safety.

The department of public safety shall review any prohibition within thirty days of the receipt of a request for a review and determine whether the prohibitions against doing business or receiving funding set forth in divisions (D)(1) and (D)(2) of this section should apply. The department of public safety shall order that the prohibitions do not apply if it determines all of the following pursuant to guidelines the director adopts by rule:

(1) That the provision of material assistance to an organization on the terrorist exclusion list was made more than ten years prior to the time the declaration of material assistance/nonassistance was filled out, or the material assistance was provided during the ten years prior to the application and the date of the review, but at the time of the assistance, the organization was either not on the list or would not have merited inclusion had it existed at the time, or at the time of the assistance it was not reasonable to know of the organization's activities that would have merited its inclusion on the list.

(2) That it is unlikely in the future that the person, company, affiliated group, or organization will provide material assistance to any organization on the terrorist exclusion list;

(3) The person, company, affiliated group, or organization does not pose a risk to the residents of this state.

(F) Any person, company, affiliated group, or organization that had not provided material assistance at the time a declaration of material assistance/nonassistance was answered, but starts providing material assistance to an organization on the terrorist exclusion list during the course of doing business with or receiving funding from the state, an agency or instrumentality of the state, or a subdivision of the state, is prohibited from entering into additional contracts to do business with or receive funding from the state, any agency or instrumentality, or any subdivision for a period of ten years after the provision of material assistance is discovered.

(G)(1) Any person, company, affiliated group, or organization that knowingly provides a false certification pursuant to this section is permanently banned from conducting business with or receiving funding from the state, an agency or instrumentality of the state, or a political subdivision of the state is guilty of a felony of the fifth degree.

(2) Any person, company, affiliated group, or organization that fails to certify as this section requires is subject to a fine of one thousand dollars for each day of doing business or receiving funding, except that any person, company, affiliated group, or organization that first reaches the threshold of one hundred thousand dollars in business or funding, due to the contract that it is entering into, shall not be subject to the fine for the first thirty days after entering into that contract, after which it shall be subject to the fine for each day that it is not certified.

(H) This section does not apply to the following types of transactions:

(1) An investment in a company that is publicly traded in any United States market;

(2) An investment that is traded on a foreign market where United States investors regularly make investments;

(3) An investment that is made through an agent or investment manager who has a fiduciary responsibility to the investor;

(4) An investment in public agency debt;

(5) An investment in derivatives that are regulated by a government agency;

(6) Financial services provided by or through either of the following:

(a) A federally insured depository institution that is subject to anti-money laundering and antiterrorism requirements under federal law or any subsidiary of such a depository institution;

(b) An affiliate of a depository institution described in division (H)(6)(a) of this section, other than an affiliate that is a subsidiary of the depository institution, when the affiliate is subject to anti-money laundering and antiterrorism requirements under federal law.

"Financial services" include, but are not limited to, services related to currency, payment instruments, other financial securities, funds, and transfer of funds;

(7) Any contract to conduct business or receive funding between state agencies, instrumentalities, or political subdivisions of the state;

(8) Any person, company, affiliated group, or organization providing necessary, nonelective healthcare services.

(I) As used in this section, "personal benefit" means all of the following:

(1) Pensions and disability and survivor benefits;

(2) Money, goods, services, or other things of value provided by the United States, the state, or a political subdivision of the state to which the recipient is entitled by reason of age, medical condition, or a financial need that is established pursuant to an act of congress or the general assembly;

(3) Salary or compensation a person receives as an employee of the state or a political subdivision of the state.

**HISTORY: 151 v S 9, § 1, eff. 4-14-06; 151 v H 461, § 1, eff. 4-4-07.**

## § 2909.34 Public employment of person with ties to terrorist organization prohibited.

(A)(1) The director of public safety shall prepare a document to serve as a declaration of material assistance/nonassistance for the state, instrumentalities of the state, and political subdivisions of the state to use to determine whether any person who is under final consideration for employment has provided material assistance to an organization listed on the United States department of state terrorist exclusion list. The declaration shall be substantially in the same format and of the same content as set forth in division (A)(2)(b) of section 2909.32 of the Revised Code.

(2) The director shall make the declaration of material assistance/nonassistance available to the state, instrumentalities of the state, and political subdivisions of the state, along with a then-current copy of the terrorist exclusion list. The director may adopt rules that govern the preparation and distribution of the declaration and the terrorist exclusion list.

(3) The director may adopt rules that establish categories of employment that are exempt from the disclosure requirements of this section.

(B) Any person under final consideration for employment who is provided a declaration of material assistance/nonassistance pursuant to this section shall complete the declaration prior to being employed. Any answer of "yes" to any question, or the failure to answer "no" to any question, shall serve for purposes of this section as a disclosure of the provision of material assistance to an organization that is listed on the terrorist exclusion list.

(C)(1) The state, a state instrumentality, or a political subdivision of the state shall provide each person who is under final consideration for a category of employment for which this section requires disclosure with a copy of the declaration of material assistance/nonassistance and a then-current copy of the terrorist exclusion list. The state, instrumentality, or subdivision shall not employ any person who discloses the provision of material assistance to an organization that is listed on the terrorist exclusion list.

(2) The state, or any instrumentality or political subdivision of the state that denies employment pursuant to this section, shall send written notice of that denial to the applicant within three business days of the decision to deny, along with notice of the applicant's right to a review of the denial by the department of public safety if the applicant requests a review within sixty days of the mailing date of the notice. An entity that denies employment pursuant to this section shall send a copy of any notice of denial of employment to the department of public safety.

(D) The department of public safety, upon receiving a request for a review from any person who has been denied employment under division (C) of this section, shall review the request within thirty days to determine if the denial of employment should be voided. The department shall void that denial if it determines all of the following pursuant to guidelines the director adopts by rule:

(1) That the provision of material assistance to an organization on the terrorist exclusion list was made more than ten years prior to the time the declaration of material assistance/nonassistance was filled out, or the material assistance was provided during the ten years prior to the application and the date of the review, but at the time of the assistance, the organization was either not on the list or would not have merited inclusion on the list had it existed at the time, or at the time of the assistance it was not reasonable to know of the organization's activities that would have merited its inclusion on the list.

(2) That it is unlikely in the future that the person will provide material assistance to any organization on the terrorist exclusion list;

(3) The person does not pose a risk to the residents of the state.

(E) The failure of an applicant for employment to disclose, as this section requires, the provision of material assistance to an organization on the terrorist exclusion list, or knowingly making false statements regarding material assistance to an organization on that list, is a felony of the fifth degree.

(F)(1) The state, or any instrumentality or political subdivision of the state, may terminate any employee who, after providing a declaration of material assistance/nonassistance pursuant to this section, takes an action that would result in "yes" being the correct answer to any question on the declaration, had the declaration been readministered after taking that action.

(2) No employer shall terminate an employee pursuant to this division unless the employer complies with one of the following hearing procedures:

(a) If the employee is entitled to termination proceedings under a collective bargaining agreement, the employer shall comply with those procedures.

(b) If the employee is entitled to termination proceedings pursuant to division (C) of section 124.34 of the Revised Code, the employer shall comply with those procedures.

(c) If the employee does not qualify for the termination proceedings described in division (F)(2)(a) or (b) of this section, the employer shall comply with the procedures set forth in division (B) of section 124.34 of the Revised Code.

**HISTORY: 151 v S 9, § 1, eff. 4-14-06; 151 v H 461, § 1, eff. 4-4-07.**

# CHAPTER 2911: ROBBERY, BURGLARY, TRESPASS AND SAFECRACKING



[ROBBERY]

## § 2911.01 Aggravated robbery.

(A) No person, in attempting or committing a theft offense, as defined in section 2913.01 of the Revised Code, or in fleeing immediately after the attempt or offense, shall do any of the following:

(1) Have a deadly weapon on or about the offender's person or under the offender's control and either display the weapon, brandish it, indicate that the offender possesses it, or use it;

(2) Have a dangerous ordnance on or about the offender's person or under the offender's control;

(3) Inflict, or attempt to inflict, serious physical harm on another.

(B) No person, without privilege to do so, shall knowingly remove or attempt to remove a deadly weapon from the person of a law enforcement officer, or shall knowingly deprive or attempt to deprive a law enforcement officer of a deadly weapon, when both of the following apply:

(1) The law enforcement officer, at the time of the removal, attempted removal, deprivation, or attempted deprivation, is acting within the course and scope of the officer's duties;

(2) The offender knows or has reasonable cause to know that the law enforcement officer is a law enforcement officer.

(C) Whoever violates this section is guilty of aggravated robbery, a felony of the first degree.

(D) As used in this section:

(1) "Deadly weapon" and "dangerous ordnance" have the same meanings as in section 2923.11 of the Revised Code.

(2) "Law enforcement officer" has the same meaning as in section 2901.01 of the Revised Code and also includes employees of the department of rehabilitation and correction who are authorized to carry weapons within the course and scope of their duties.

**HISTORY: 134 v H 511 (Eff 1-1-74); 139 v S 199 (Eff 1-5-83); 140 v S 210 (Eff 7-1-83); 146 v S 2 (Eff 7-1-96); 147 v H 151. Eff 9-16-97.**

**Not analogous to former RC § 2911.01 (RS § 7076; 70 v 39; 73 v 20; 74 v 41; GC § 13104; 124 v 466; Bureau of Code Revision, 10-1-53; 129 v 344), repealed 134 v H 511, § 2, eff 1-1-74.**

## § 2911.02 Robbery.

(A) No person, in attempting or committing a theft offense or in fleeing immediately after the attempt or offense, shall do any of the following:

(1) Have a deadly weapon on or about the offender's person or under the offender's control;

(2) Inflict, attempt to inflict, or threaten to inflict physical harm on another;

(3) Use or threaten the immediate use of force against another.

(B) Whoever violates this section is guilty of robbery. A violation of division (A)(1) or (2) of this section is a felony of the second degree. A violation of division (A)(3) of this section is a felony of the third degree.

(C) As used in this section:

(1) "Deadly weapon" has the same meaning as in section 2923.11 of the Revised Code.

(2) "Theft offense" has the same meaning as in section 2913.01 of the Revised Code.

**HISTORY: 134 v H 511 (Eff 1-1-74); 139 v S 199 (Eff 7-1-83); 146 v S 2 (Eff 7-1-96); 146 v S 269. Eff 7-1-96.**

**Not analogous to former RC § 2911.02 (RS § 7075; 59 v 193; 102 v 114; GC § 13105; 124 v 466; Bureau of Code Revision, 10-1-53), repealed 134 v H 511, § 2, eff 1-1-74.**

The effective date is set by section 5 of SB 269.

**§ 2911.03** Repealed, 134 v H 511, § 2 [GC §§ 13105-1, 13108, 13108-1; 111 v 257, 258; 124 v 466; Bureau of Code Revision, 10-1-53; 126 v 575]. Eff 1-1-74.

This section concerned false statements and stock brokers.

**§ 2911.04** Repealed, 134 v H 511, § 2 [GC §§ 13105-1, 13108, 13108-1; 111 v 257, 258; 124 v 466; Bureau of Code Revision, 10-1-53; 126 v 575]. Eff 1-1-74.

This section concerned false statements and stock brokers.

**§ 2911.05** Repealed, 134 v H 511, § 2 [GC §§ 13105-1, 13108, 13108-1; 111 v 257, 258; 124 v 466; Bureau of Code Revision, 10-1-53; 126 v 575]. Eff 1-1-74.

This section concerned false statements and stock brokers.

**§ 2911.06** Repealed, 134 v H 511, § 2 [GC §§ 13108-2—13108-4; 111 v 258; Bureau of Code Revision, 10-1-53; 126 v 575]. Eff 1-1-74.

This section concerned false statements and stock brokers.

## § 2911.07 Repealed, 134 v H 511, § 2 [GC §§ 13108-2—13108-4; 111 v 258; Bureau of Code Revision, 10-1-53; 126 v 575]. Eff 1-1-74.

This section concerned false statements and stock brokers.

## § 2911.08 Repealed, 134 v H 511, § 2 [GC §§ 13108-2—13108-4; 111 v 258; Bureau of Code Revision, 10-1-53; 126 v 575]. Eff 1-1-74.

This section concerned false statements and stock brokers.

## § 2911.09 Repealed, 134 v H 511, § 2 [GC §§ 13108-5, 13108-6; 111 v 258, 259; Bureau of Code Revision, 10-1-53]. Eff 1-1-74.

This section concerned false statements and stock brokers.

## § 2911.10 Element of trespass clarified.

As used in sections 2911.11 to 2911.13 of the Revised Code, the element of trespass refers to a violation of section 2911.21 of the Revised Code.

**HISTORY: 151 v H 96, § 1, eff. 8-3-06.**

**Not analogous to former RC § 2911.10 (GC §§ 13108-5, 13108-6; 111 v 258, 259; Bureau of Code Revision, 10-1-53), repealed 134 v H 511, § 2, eff 1-1-74.**

[BURGLARY]

## § 2911.11 Aggravated burglary.

(A) No person, by force, stealth, or deception, shall trespass in an occupied structure or in a separately secured or separately occupied portion of an occupied structure, when another person other than an accomplice of the offender is present, with purpose to commit in the structure or in the separately secured or separately occupied portion of the structure any criminal offense, if any of the following apply:

(1) The offender inflicts, or attempts or threatens to inflict physical harm on another;

(2) The offender has a deadly weapon or dangerous ordnance on or about the offender's person or under the offender's control.

(B) Whoever violates this section is guilty of aggravated burglary, a felony of the first degree.

(C) As used in this section:

(1) "Occupied structure" has the same meaning as in section 2909.01 of the Revised Code.

(2) "Deadly weapon" and "dangerous ordnance" have the same meanings as in section 2923.11 of the Revised Code.

**HISTORY: 134 v H 511 (Eff 1-1-74); 139 v S 199 (Eff 1-5-83); 140 v S 210 (Eff 7-1-83); 146 v S 2 (Eff 7-1-96); 146 v S 269. Eff 7-1-96.**

**Not analogous to former RC § 2911.11 (RS § 7085; S&C 422; 50 v 132; 57 v 56; GC § 13115; Bureau of Code Revision, 10-1-53), repealed 134 v H 511, § 2, eff 1-1-74.**

The effective date is set by section 5 of SB 269.

## § 2911.111 Repealed, 134 v H 511, § 2 [132 v S 97]. Eff 1-1-74.

This section concerned checks drawn on insufficient funds.

## § 2911.12 Burglary.

(A) No person, by force, stealth, or deception, shall do any of the following:

(1) Trespass in an occupied structure or in a separately secured or separately occupied portion of an occupied structure, when another person other than an accomplice of the offender is present, with purpose to commit in the structure or in the separately secured or separately occupied portion of the structure any criminal offense;

(2) Trespass in an occupied structure or in a separately secured or separately occupied portion of an occupied structure that is a permanent or temporary habitation of any person when any person other than an accomplice of the offender is present or likely to be present, with purpose to commit in the habitation any criminal offense;

(3) Trespass in an occupied structure or in a separately secured or separately occupied portion of an occupied structure, with purpose to commit in the structure or separately secured or separately occupied portion of the structure any criminal offense.

(B) No person, by force, stealth, or deception, shall trespass in a permanent or temporary habitation of any person when any person other than an accomplice of the offender is present or likely to be present.

(C) As used in this section, "occupied structure" has the same meaning as in section 2909.01 of the Revised Code.

(D) Whoever violates division (A) of this section is guilty of burglary. A violation of division (A)(1) or (2) of this section is a felony of the second degree. A violation of division (A)(3) of this section is a felony of the third degree.

(E) Whoever violates division (B) of this section is guilty of trespass in a habitation when a person is present or likely to be present, a felony of the fourth degree.

**HISTORY: 134 v H 511 (Eff 1-1-74); 139 v S 199 (Eff 7-1-83); 143 v H 837 (Eff 7-3-90); 146 v S 2 (Eff 7-1-96); 146 v S 269. Eff 7-1-96; 2011 HB 86, § 1, eff. Sept. 30, 2011.**

**Not analogous to former RC § 2911.12 (RS § 7080; S&C 703; 70 v 40; GC § 13126; Bureau of Code Revision, 10-1-53), repealed 134 v H 511, § 2, eff 1-1-74.**

The effective date is set by section 5 of SB 269.

## § 2911.13 Breaking and entering.

(A) No person by force, stealth, or deception, shall trespass in an unoccupied structure, with purpose to commit therein any theft offense, as defined in section 2913.01 of the Revised Code, or any felony.

(B) No person shall trespass on the land or premises of another, with purpose to commit a felony.

(C) Whoever violates this section is guilty of breaking and entering, a felony of the fifth degree.

**HISTORY: 134 v H 511 (Eff 1-1-74); 146 v S 2. Eff 7-1-96.**

**Not analogous to former RC § 2911.13 (RS §§ 7076-4—7076-6; 95 v 306; GC § 13130; 123 v 700; Bureau of Code Revision, 10-1-53), repealed 134 v H 511, § 2, eff 1-1-74.**

The effective date is set by section 6 of SB 2.

## § 2911.131 Repealed, 134 v H 511, § 2 [133 v H 192]. Eff 1-1-74.

This section concerned false motor vehicle repair estimates and fraudulent charges.

**§ 2911.14** Repealed, 134 v H 511, § 2 [RS §§ 7017-4, 7017-5, 7076a—7076c, 7087; S&C 422; 44 v 34; 83 v 138; 94 v 20, 363; 99 v 115, 116; GC §§ 13131, 13143, 13145; 110 v 29; Bureau of Code Revision, 10-1-53]. Eff 1-1-74.

This section concerned miscellaneous frauds.

**§ 2911.15** Repealed, 134 v H 511, § 2 [RS §§ 7017-4, 7017-5, 7076a—7076c, 7087; S&C 422; 44 v 34; 83 v 138; 94 v 20, 363; 99 v 115, 116; GC §§ 13131, 13143, 13145; 110 v 29; Bureau of Code Revision, 10-1-53]. Eff 1-1-74.

This section concerned miscellaneous frauds.

**§ 2911.16** Repealed, 134 v H 511, § 2 [RS §§ 7017-4, 7017-5, 7076a—7076c, 7087; S&C 422; 44 v 34; 83 v 138; 94 v 20, 363; 99 v 115, 116; GC §§ 13131, 13143, 13145; 110 v 29; Bureau of Code Revision, 10-1-53]. Eff 1-1-74.

This section concerned miscellaneous frauds.

**§ 2911.17** Repealed, 134 v H 511, § 2 [RS § 7017-6; 95 v 68; GC § 13148; Bureau of Code Revision, 10-1-53]. Eff 1-1-74.

This section prohibited the performance of dramatic compositions without consent of owner.

**§ 2911.18** Repealed, 129 v 13 (182), § 2 [RS § 6993; 66 v 93; GC § 13149; Bureau of Code Revision, 10-1-53]. Eff 7-1-62.

This section concerned taking or selling note for patent right.

**§ 2911.19** Repealed, 134 v H 511, § 2 [RS §§ 7076-3, 7105-1; 88 v 64; 90 v 131; GC §§ 13146, 13158; Bureau of Code Revision, 10-1-53]. Eff 1-1-74.

This section concerned misrepresentation by married man, and furnishing false pedigree.

**§ 2911.20** Repealed, 134 v H 511, § 2 [RS §§ 7076-3, 7105-1; 88 v 64; 90 v 131; GC §§ 13146, 13158; Bureau of Code Revision, 10-1-53]. Eff 1-1-74.

This section concerned misrepresentation by married man, and furnishing false pedigree.

## [TRESPASS]

### § 2911.21 Criminal trespass.

(A) No person, without privilege to do so, shall do any of the following:

(1) Knowingly enter or remain on the land or premises of another;

(2) Knowingly enter or remain on the land or premises of another, the use of which is lawfully restricted to certain persons, purposes, modes, or hours, when the offender knows the offender is in violation of any such restriction or is reckless in that regard;

(3) Recklessly enter or remain on the land or premises of another, as to which notice against unauthorized access or presence is given by actual communication to the offender, or in a manner prescribed by law, or by posting in a manner reasonably calculated to come to the attention of potential intruders, or by fencing or other enclosure manifestly designed to restrict access;

(4) Being on the land or premises of another, negligently fail or refuse to leave upon being notified by signage posted in a conspicuous place or otherwise being notified to do so by the owner or occupant, or the agent or servant of either.

(B) It is no defense to a charge under this section that the land or premises involved was owned, controlled, or in custody of a public agency.

(C) It is no defense to a charge under this section that the offender was authorized to enter or remain on the land or premises involved, when such authorization was secured by deception.

(D)(1) Whoever violates this section is guilty of criminal trespass, a misdemeanor of the fourth degree.

(2) Notwithstanding section 2929.28 of the Revised Code, if the person, in committing the violation of this section, used a snowmobile, off-highway motorcycle, or all-purpose vehicle, the court shall impose a fine of two times the usual amount imposed for the violation.

(3) If an offender previously has been convicted of or pleaded guilty to two or more violations of this section or a substantially equivalent municipal ordinance, and the offender, in committing each violation, used a snowmobile, off-highway motorcycle, or all-purpose vehicle, the court, in addition to or independent of all other penalties imposed for the violation, may impound the certificate of registration of that snowmobile or off-highway motorcycle or the certificate of registration and license plate of that all-purpose vehicle for not less than sixty days. In such a case, section 4519.47 of the Revised Code applies.

(E) Notwithstanding any provision of the Revised Code, if the offender, in committing the violation of this section, used an all-purpose vehicle, the clerk of the court shall pay the fine imposed pursuant to this section to the state recreational vehicle fund created by section 4519.11 of the Revised Code.

(F) As used in this section:

(1) "All-purpose vehicle," "off-highway motorcycle," and "snowmobile" have the same meanings as in section 4519.01 of the Revised Code.

(2) "Land or premises" includes any land, building, structure, or place belonging to, controlled by, or in custody of another, and any separate enclosure or room, or portion thereof.

**HISTORY: 134 v H 511. Eff 1-1-74; 150 v H 12, § 1, eff. 4-8-04; 153 v H 2, § 101.01, eff. 7-1-09; 153 v H 1, § 101.01, eff. 10-16-09.**

The effective date is set by § 812.10 of 153 v H 1.
The effective date is set by § 812.10 of 153 v H 2.
The provisions of § 6, H.B. 12 (150 v —), read as follows:
SECTION 6. In amending sections 1547.69, 2911.21, 2921.13, 2923.12, 2923.121, 2923.123, 2923.13, 2923.16, 2953.32, and 4749.10 of the Revised Code and in enacting sections 109.69,

109.731, 311.41, 311.42, and 2923.124 to 2923.1213 of the Revised Code in this act, the General Assembly hereby declares its intent to recognize both of the following:

(A) The inalienable and fundamental right of an individual to defend the individual's person and the members of the individual's family;

(B) The fact that the right described in division (A) of this section predates the adoption of the United States Constitution, the adoption of the Ohio Constitution, and the enactment of all statutory laws by the General Assembly and may not be infringed by any enactment of the General Assembly.

The provisions of § 7, H.B. 12 (150 v —), read as follows:

SECTION 7. In enacting sections 109.69, 109.731, 311.41, 311.42, and 2923.124 to 2923.1213 of the Revised Code in this act and in amending sections 1547.69, 2911.21, 2921.13, 2923.12, 2923.121, 2923.123, 2923.13, 2923.16, 2953.32, and 4749.10 of the Revised Code in this act relative to licenses to carry a concealed handgun, the General Assembly hereby declares that it is not its intent to declare or otherwise give the impression that, prior to the effective date of this act, an individual did not have an inalienable and fundamental right, or a right under the Ohio Constitution or the United States Constitution, to carry a concealed handgun or other firearm for the defense of the individual's person or a member of the individual's family while engaged in lawful activity. Further, the General Assembly declares that it is not its intent to invalidate any prior convictions for violating any section of the Revised Code or a municipal ordinance prior to the effective date of this act or to prevent the prosecution of any violation committed prior to the effective date of this act.

The provisions of § 9, H.B. 12 (150 v —), read as follows:

SECTION 9. The General Assembly finds that licenses to carry concealed handguns are a matter of statewide concern and wishes to ensure uniformity throughout the state regarding the qualifications for a person to hold a license to carry a concealed handgun and the authority granted to a person holding a license of that nature. It is the intent of the General Assembly in amending sections 1547.69, 2911.21, 2921.13, 2923.12, 2923.121, 2923.123, 2923.16, 2953.32, and 4749.10 and enacting sections 109.69, 109.731, 311.41, 311.42, and 2923.124 to 2923.1213 of the Revised Code to enact laws of a general nature, and, by enacting those laws of a general nature, the state occupies and preempts the field of issuing licenses to carry a concealed handgun and the validity of licenses of that nature. No municipal corporation may adopt or continue in existence any ordinance, and no township may adopt or continue in existence any resolution, that is in conflict with those sections, including, but not limited to, any ordinance or resolution that attempts to restrict the places where a person possessing a valid license to carry a concealed handgun may carry a handgun concealed.

The provisions of § 10, H.B. 12 (150 v —), read as follows:

SECTION 10. If any provision of sections 1547.69, 2911.21, 2913.02, 2921.13, 2923.12, 2923.121, 2923.123, 2923.16, 2929.14, 2953.32, and 4749.10 of the Revised Code, as amended by this act, any provision of sections 109.69, 109.731, 311.41, 311.42, 2923.124, 2923.125, 2923.126, 2923.127, 2923.128, 2923.129, 2923.1210, 2923.1211, 2923.1212, and 2923.1213 of the Revised Code, as enacted by this act, or the application of any provision of those sections to any person or circumstance is held invalid, the invalidity does not affect other provisions or applications of the particular section or related sections that can be given effect without the invalid provision or application, and to this end the provisions of the particular section are severable.

**Not analogous to former RC § 2911.21 (RS §§ 7076-1, 7076-2; 84 v 213; GC § 13162; 109 v 406; Bureau of Code Revision, 10-1-53; 126 v 575), repealed 134 v H 511, § 2, eff 1-1-74.**

## § 2911.211 Aggravated trespass.

(A) No person shall enter or remain on the land or premises of another with purpose to commit on that land or those premises a misdemeanor, the elements of which involve causing physical harm to another person or causing another person to believe that the offender will cause physical harm to him.

(B) Whoever violates this section is guilty of aggravated trespass, a misdemeanor of the first degree.

**HISTORY: 144 v H 536. Eff 11-5-92.**

## § 2911.22 Repealed, 134 v H 511, § 2 [RS §§ 4355a, 7069-5; 78 v 242; 83 v 162; GC §§ 13129, 13147, 13162-1; 109 v 406; Bureau of Code Revision, 10-1-53]. Eff 1-1-74.

This section concerned unlawful entries; sales of seed, tobacco, and wool.

## § 2911.23 Criminal trespass on place of public amusement.

(A) As used in this section, "place of public amusement" means a stadium, theater, or other facility, whether licensed or not, at which a live performance, sporting event, or other activity takes place for entertainment of the public and to which access is made available to the public, regardless of whether admission is charged.

(B) No person, without privilege to do so, shall knowingly enter or remain on any restricted portion of a place of public amusement and, as a result of that conduct, interrupt or cause the delay of the live performance, sporting event, or other activity taking place at the place of public amusement after a printed written notice has been given as provided in division (D)(1) of this section that the general public is restricted from access to that restricted portion of the place of public amusement. A restricted portion of a place of public amusement may include, but is not limited to, a playing field, an athletic surface, or a stage located at the place of public amusement.

(C) An owner or lessee of a place of public amusement, an agent of the owner or lessee, or a performer or participant at a place of public amusement may use reasonable force to restrain and remove a person from a restricted portion of the place of public amusement if the person enters or remains on the restricted portion of the place of public amusement and, as a result of that conduct, interrupts or causes the delay of the live performance, sporting event, or other activity taking place at the place of public amusement. This division does not provide immunity from criminal liability for any use of force beyond reasonable force by an owner or lessee of a place of public amusement, an agent of either the owner or lessee, or a performer or participant at a place of public amusement.

(D)(1) Notice has been given that the general public is restricted from access to a portion of a place of public amusement if a printed written notice of the restricted access has been conspicuously posted or exhibited at the entrance to that portion of the place of public amusement. If a printed written notice is posted or exhibited as described in this division regarding a portion of a place of public amusement, in addition to that posting or exhibition, notice that the general public is restricted from access to that portion of the place of public amusement also may be given, but is not required to be given, by either of the following means:

(a) By notifying the person personally, either orally or in writing, that access to that portion of the place of public amusement is restricted;

(b) By broadcasting over the public address system of the place of public amusement an oral warning that access to that portion of the place of public amusement is restricted.

(2) If notice that the general public is restricted from access to a portion of a place of public amusement is provided by the posting or exhibition of a printed written notice as described in division (D)(1) of this section, the state, in a criminal prosecution for a violation of division (B) of this section, is not required to prove that the defendant received actual notice that the general public is restricted from access to a portion of a place of public amusement.

(E)(1) Whoever violates division (B) of this section is guilty of criminal trespass on a place of public amusement, a misdemeanor of the first degree.

(2) In addition to any jail term, fine, or other sentence, penalty, or sanction it imposes upon the offender pursuant to division (E)(1) of this section, a court may require an offender who violates this section to perform not less than thirty and not more than one hundred twenty hours of supervised community service work.

**HISTORY: 151 v H 96, § 1, eff. 8-3-06.**

**Not analogous to former RC § 2911.23 (RS §§ 4355a, 7069-5; 78 v 242; 83 v 162; GC §§ 13129, 13147, 13162-1; 109 v 406; Bureau of Code Revision, 10-1-53), repealed 134 v H 511, § 2, eff 1-1-74.**

## § 2911.24 Repealed, 134 v H 511, § 2 [RS §§ 4355a, 7069-5; 78 v 242; 83 v 162; GC §§ 13129, 13147, 13162-1; 109 v 406; Bureau of Code Revision, 10-1-53]. Eff 1-1-74.

This section concerned unlawful entries; sales of seed, tobacco, and wool.

## § 2911.25 Repealed, 134 v H 511, § 2 [RS §§ 7069-3, 7069-4, 7088-2; 85 v 285; 86 v 5; 99 v 114; GC §§ 13114, 13163, 13164; 109 v 228; Bureau of Code Revision, 10-1-53; 131 v 675]. Eff 1-1-74.

This section concerned unlawful sales of wool; insignia or badge.

## § 2911.26 Repealed, 134 v H 511, § 2 [RS §§ 7069-3, 7069-4, 7088-2; 85 v 285; 86 v 5; 99 v 114; GC §§ 13114, 13163, 13164; 109 v 228; Bureau of Code Revision, 10-1-53; 131 v 675]. Eff 1-1-74.

This section concerned unlawful sales of wool; insignia or badge.

## § 2911.27 Repealed, 134 v H 511, § 2 [RS §§ 7069-3, 7069-4, 7088-2; 85 v 285; 86 v 5; 99 v 114; GC §§ 13114, 13163, 13164; 109 v 228; Bureau of Code Revision, 10-1-53; 131 v 675]. Eff 1-1-74.

This section concerned unlawful sales of wool; insignia or badge.

## § 2911.28 Repealed, 134 v H 511, § 2 [99 v 336; GC §§ 13163-1, 13175, 14867-21, 14867-22; 108 v PtI, 64; 109 v 312; Bureau of Code Revision, 10-1-53; 129 v 582(746)]. Eff 1-1-74.

This section concerned unlawful wearing of insignia or badge; prospectus.

## § 2911.29 Repealed, 134 v H 511, § 2 [99 v 336; GC §§ 13163-1, 13175, 14867-21, 14867-22; 108 v PtI, 64; 109 v 312; Bureau of Code Revision, 10-1-53; 129 v 582(746)]. Eff 1-1-74.

This section concerned unlawful wearing of insignia or badge; prospectus.

## § 2911.30 Repealed, 134 v H 511, § 2 [99 v 336; GC §§ 13163-1, 13175, 14867-21, 14867-22; 108 v PtI, 64; 109 v 312; Bureau of Code Revision, 10-1-53; 129 v 582(746)]. Eff 1-1-74.

This section concerned unlawful wearing of insignia or badge; prospectus.

# [SAFECRACKING]

## § 2911.31 Safecracking.

(A) No person, with purpose to commit an offense, shall knowingly enter, force an entrance into, or tamper with any vault, safe, or strongbox.

(B) Whoever violates this section is guilty of safecracking, a felony of the fourth degree.

**HISTORY: 134 v H 511 (Eff 1-1-74); 146 v S 2. Eff 7-1-96.**

**Not analogous to former RC § 2911.31 (RS § 3184c; 86 v 374; 95 v 210; 97 v 499; GC § 13180; Bureau of Code Revision, 10-1-53), repealed 134 v H 511, § 2, eff 1-1-74.**

**Analogous to former RC § 2907.12 (RS § 6835-1; 95 v 122; GC § 12440; Bureau of Code Revision, 10-1-53), repealed 134 v H 511, § 2, eff 1-1-74.**

The effective date is set by section 6 of SB 2.

## § 2911.32 Tampering with coin machines.

(A) No person, with purpose to commit theft or to defraud, shall knowingly enter, force an entrance into, tamper with, or insert any part of an instrument into any coin machine.

(B) Whoever violates this section is guilty of tampering with coin machines, a misdemeanor of the first degree. If the offender previously has been convicted of a violation of this section or of any theft offense as defined in section 2913.01 of the Revised Code, tampering with coin machines is a felony of the fifth degree.

**HISTORY: 134 v H 511 (Eff 1-1-74); 146 v S 2. Eff 7-1-96.**

**Not analogous to former RC § 2911.32 (RS § 3231-5; 86 v 121; GC § 13181; 107 v 181; Bureau of Code Revision, 10-1-53), repealed 134 v H 511, § 2, eff 1-1-74.**

**Analogous to former RC § 2907.12.1 (132 v H 656), repealed 134 v H 511, § 2, eff 1-1-74.**

The effective date is set by section 6 of SB 2.

## § 2911.33 Repealed, 134 v H 511, § 2 [RS §§ 7088, 7090-1; 73 v 19; 93 v 168, 313; GC §§ 13144, 13152, 13183; 114 v 118; Bureau of Code Revision, 10-1-53]. Eff 1-1-74.

This section concerned crockery; mails; coins; slugs.

## § 2911.34 Repealed, 134 v H 511, § 2 [RS §§ 7088, 7090-1; 73 v 19; 93 v 168, 313; GC §§ 13144,

13152, 13183; 114 v 118; Bureau of Code Revision, 10-1-53]. Eff 1-1-74.

This section concerned crockery; mails; coins; slugs.

**§ 2911.35** Repealed, 134 v H 511, § 2 [RS §§ 7088, 7090-1; 73 v 19; 93 v 168, 313; GC §§ 13144, 13152, 13183; 114 v 118; Bureau of Code Revision, 10-1-53]. Eff 1-1-74.

This section concerned crockery; mails; coins; slugs.

**§ 2911.36** Repealed, 134 v H 511, § 2 [GC §§ 13184, 13184-1, 13187; 114 v 118; 115 v 247; 119 v 312; Bureau of Code Revision, 10-1-53]. Eff 1-1-74.

This section concerned coins; slugs; batteries.

**§ 2911.37** Repealed, 134 v H 511, § 2 [GC §§ 13184, 13184-1, 13187; 114 v 118; 115 v 247; 119 v 312; Bureau of Code Revision, 10-1-53]. Eff 1-1-74.

This section concerned coins; slugs; batteries.

**§ 2911.38** Repealed, 134 v H 511, § 2 [GC §§ 13184, 13184-1, 13187; 114 v 118; 115 v 247; 119 v 312; Bureau of Code Revision, 10-1-53]. Eff 1-1-74.

This section concerned coins; slugs; batteries.

**§ 2911.39** Repealed, 134 v H 511, § 2 [GC §§ 13187-1, 13193-2, 13194-1; 103 v 43; 115 v 248; 121 v 72, 590; Bureau of Code Revision, 10-1-53; 127 v 461; 129 v 1305]. Eff 1-1-74.

This section concerned batteries; advertising.

**§ 2911.40** Repealed, 134 v H 511, § 2 [GC §§ 13187-1, 13193-2, 13194-1; 103 v 43; 115 v 248; 121 v 72, 590; Bureau of Code Revision, 10-1-53; 127 v 461; 129 v 1305]. Eff 1-1-74.

This section concerned batteries; advertising.

**§ 2911.41** Repealed, 134 v H 511, § 2 [GC §§ 13187-1, 13193-2, 13194-1; 103 v 43; 115 v 248; 121 v 72, 590; Bureau of Code Revision, 10-1-53; 127 v 461; 129 v 1305]. Eff 1-1-74.

This section concerned batteries; advertising.

**§ 2911.42** Repealed, 134 v H 511, § 2 [GC § 13193-3; 121 v 590; Bureau of Code Revision, 10-1-53; 129 v 13 (179)]. Eff 1-1-74.

This section concerned fraudulent advertising; bills of lading.

**§ 2911.43** Repealed, 134 v H 511, § 2 [GC § 13193-3; 121 v 590; Bureau of Code Revision, 10-1-53; 129 v 13 (179)]. Eff 1-1-74.

This section concerned fraudulent advertising; bills of lading.

**§ 2911.44** Repealed, 134 v H 511, § 2 [GC § 13193-3; 121 v 590; Bureau of Code Revision, 10-1-53; 129 v 13 (179)]. Eff 1-1-74.

This section concerned fraudulent advertising; bills of lading.

**§ 2911.45** Repealed, 134 v H 511, § 2 [129 v 13 (179)]. Eff 1-1-74.

This section concerned bills of lading.

**§ 2911.46** Repealed, 134 v H 511, § 2 [129 v 13 (179)]. Eff 1-1-74.

This section concerned bills of lading.

**§ 2911.47** Repealed, 134 v H 511, § 2 [129 v 13 (179)]. Eff 1-1-74.

This section concerned bills of lading.

**§ 2911.48** Repealed, 134 v H 511, § 2 [129 v 13 (179)]. Eff 1-1-74.

This section concerned bills of lading.

**§ 2911.49** Repealed, 134 v H 511, § 2 [129 v 13 (179)]. Eff 1-1-74.

This section concerned bills of lading.

**§ 2911.71** Repealed, 134 v H 511, § 2 [129 v 1023; 133 v S 6]. Eff 1-1-74.

This section concerned frauds involving electronic picture tubes, and medical fraud and misrepresentations.

**§ 2911.72** Repealed, 134 v H 511, § 2 [129 v 1023; 133 v S 6]. Eff 1-1-74.

This section concerned frauds involving electronic picture tubes, and medical fraud and misrepresentations.

**§ 2911.73** Repealed, 134 v H 511, § 2 [129 v 1023; 133 v S 6]. Eff 1-1-74.

This section concerned frauds involving electronic picture tubes, and medical fraud and misrepresentations.

# CHAPTER 2913: THEFT AND FRAUD



## [IN GENERAL]

### § 2913.01 Definitions.

As used in this chapter, unless the context requires that a term be given a different meaning:

(A) "Deception" means knowingly deceiving another or causing another to be deceived by any false or misleading representation, by withholding information, by preventing another from acquiring information, or by any other conduct, act, or omission that creates, confirms, or perpetuates a false impression in another, including a false impression as to law, value, state of mind, or other objective or subjective fact.

(B) "Defraud" means to knowingly obtain, by deception, some benefit for oneself or another, or to knowingly cause, by deception, some detriment to another.

(C) "Deprive" means to do any of the following:

(1) Withhold property of another permanently, or for a period that appropriates a substantial portion of its value or use, or with purpose to restore it only upon payment of a reward or other consideration;

(2) Dispose of property so as to make it unlikely that the owner will recover it;

(3) Accept, use, or appropriate money, property, or services, with purpose not to give proper consideration in return for the money, property, or services, and without reasonable justification or excuse for not giving proper consideration.

(D) "Owner" means, unless the context requires a different meaning, any person, other than the actor, who is the owner of, who has possession or control of, or who has any license or interest in property or services, even though the ownership, possession, control, license, or interest is unlawful.

(E) "Services" include labor, personal services, professional services, rental services, public utility services including wireless service as defined in division (F)(1) of section 4931.40 of the Revised Code, common carrier services, and food, drink, transportation, entertainment, and cable television services and, for purposes of section 2913.04 of the Revised Code, include cable services as defined in that section.

(F) "Writing" means any computer software, document, letter, memorandum, note, paper, plate, data, film, or other thing having in or upon it any written, typewritten, or printed matter, and any token, stamp, seal, credit card, badge, trademark, label, or other symbol of value, right, privilege, license, or identification.

(G) "Forge" means to fabricate or create, in whole or in part and by any means, any spurious writing, or to make, execute, alter, complete, reproduce, or otherwise purport to authenticate any writing, when the writing in fact is not authenticated by that conduct.

(H) "Utter" means to issue, publish, transfer, use, put or send into circulation, deliver, or display.

(I) "Coin machine" means any mechanical or electronic device designed to do both of the following:

(1) Receive a coin, bill, or token made for that purpose;

(2) In return for the insertion or deposit of a coin, bill, or token, automatically dispense property, provide a service, or grant a license.

(J) "Slug" means an object that, by virtue of its size, shape, composition, or other quality, is capable of being inserted or deposited in a coin machine as an improper substitute for a genuine coin, bill, or token made for that purpose.

(K) "Theft offense" means any of the following:

(1) A violation of section 2911.01, 2911.02, 2911.11, 2911.12, 2911.13, 2911.31, 2911.32, 2913.02, 2913.03, 2913.04, 2913.041, 2913.05, 2913.06, 2913.11, 2913.21, 2913.31, 2913.32, 2913.33, 2913.34, 2913.40, 2913.42, 2913.43, 2913.44, 2913.45, 2913.47, 2913.48, former section 2913.47 or 2913.48, or section 2913.51, 2915.05, or 2921.41 of the Revised Code;

(2) A violation of an existing or former municipal ordinance or law of this or any other state, or of the United States, substantially equivalent to any section listed in division (K)(1) of this section or a violation of section 2913.41, 2913.81, or 2915.06 of the Revised Code as it existed prior to July 1, 1996;

(3) An offense under an existing or former municipal ordinance or law of this or any other state, or of the United States, involving robbery, burglary, breaking and entering, theft, embezzlement, wrongful conversion, forgery, counterfeiting, deceit, or fraud;

(4) A conspiracy or attempt to commit, or complicity in committing, any offense under division (K)(1), (2), or (3) of this section.

(L) "Computer services" includes, but is not limited to, the use of a computer system, computer network, computer program, data that is prepared for computer use, or data that is contained within a computer system or computer network.

(M) "Computer" means an electronic device that performs logical, arithmetic, and memory functions by the manipulation of electronic or magnetic impulses. "Computer" includes, but is not limited to, all input, output, processing, storage, computer program, or communication facilities that are connected, or related, in a computer system or network to an electronic device of that nature.

(N) "Computer system" means a computer and related devices, whether connected or unconnected, including, but not limited to, data input, output, and storage devices, data communications links, and computer programs and data that make the system capable of performing specified special purpose data processing tasks.

(O) "Computer network" means a set of related and remotely connected computers and communication facilities that includes more than one computer system that has the capability to transmit among the connected computers and communication facilities through the use of computer facilities.

(P) "Computer program" means an ordered set of data representing coded instructions or statements that, when executed by a computer, cause the computer to process data.

(Q) "Computer software" means computer programs, procedures, and other documentation associated with the operation of a computer system.

(R) "Data" means a representation of information, knowledge, facts, concepts, or instructions that are being or have been prepared in a formalized manner and that are intended for use in a computer, computer system, or computer network. For purposes of section 2913.47 of the Revised Code, "data" has the additional meaning set forth in division (A) of that section.

(S) "Cable television service" means any services provided by or through the facilities of any cable television system or other similar closed circuit coaxial cable communications system, or any microwave or similar transmission service used in connection with any cable television system or other similar closed circuit coaxial cable communications system.

(T) "Gain access" means to approach, instruct, communicate with, store data in, retrieve data from, or otherwise make use of any resources of a computer, computer system, or computer network, or any cable service or cable system both as defined in section 2913.04 of the Revised Code.

(U) "Credit card" includes, but is not limited to, a card, code, device, or other means of access to a customer's account for the purpose of obtaining money, property, labor, or services on credit, or for initiating an electronic fund transfer at a point-of-sale terminal, an automated teller machine, or a cash dispensing machine. It also includes a county procurement card issued under section 301.29 of the Revised Code.

(V) "Electronic fund transfer" has the same meaning as in 92 Stat. 3728, 15 U.S.C.A. 1693a, as amended.

(W) "Rented property" means personal property in which the right of possession and use of the property is for a short and possibly indeterminate term in return for consideration; the rentee generally controls the duration of possession of the property, within any applicable minimum or maximum term; and the amount of consideration generally is determined by the duration of possession of the property.

(X) "Telecommunication" means the origination, emission, dissemination, transmission, or reception of data, images, signals, sounds, or other intelligence or equivalence of intelligence of any nature over any communications system by any method, including, but not limited to, a fiber optic, electronic, magnetic, optical, digital, or analog method.

(Y) "Telecommunications device" means any instrument, equipment, machine, or other device that facilitates telecommunication, including, but not limited to, a computer, computer network, computer chip, computer circuit, scanner, telephone, cellular telephone, pager, personal communications device, transponder, receiver, radio, modem, or device that enables the use of a modem.

(Z) "Telecommunications service" means the providing, allowing, facilitating, or generating of any form of telecommunication through the use of a telecommunications device over a telecommunications system.

(AA) "Counterfeit telecommunications device" means a telecommunications device that, alone or with another telecommunications device, has been altered, constructed, manufactured, or programmed to acquire, intercept, receive, or otherwise facilitate the use of a telecommunications service or information service without the authority or consent of the provider of the telecommunications service or information service. "Counterfeit telecommunications device" includes, but is not limited to, a clone telephone, clone microchip, tumbler telephone, or tumbler microchip; a wireless scanning device capable of acquiring, intercepting, receiving, or otherwise facilitating the use of telecommunications service or information service without immediate detection; or a device, equipment, hardware, or software designed for, or capable of, altering or changing the electronic serial number in a wireless telephone.

(BB)(1) "Information service" means, subject to division (BB)(2) of this section, the offering of a capability for generating, acquiring, storing, transforming, processing, retrieving, utilizing, or making available information via telecommunications, including, but not limited to, electronic publishing.

(2) "Information service" does not include any use of a capability of a type described in division (BB)(1) of this section for the management, control, or operation of a telecommunications system or the management of a telecommunications service.

(CC) "Elderly person" means a person who is sixty-five years of age or older.

(DD) "Disabled adult" means a person who is eighteen years of age or older and has some impairment of body or mind that makes the person unable to work at any substantially remunerative employment that the person otherwise would be able to perform and that will, with reasonable probability, continue for a period of at least twelve months without any present indication of recovery from the impairment, or who is eighteen years of age or older and has been certified as permanently and totally disabled by an agency of this state or the United States that has the function of so classifying persons.

(EE) "Firearm" and "dangerous ordnance" have the same meanings as in section 2923.11 of the Revised Code.

(FF) "Motor vehicle" has the same meaning as in section 4501.01 of the Revised Code.

(GG) "Dangerous drug" has the same meaning as in section 4729.01 of the Revised Code.

(HH) "Drug abuse offense" has the same meaning as in section 2925.01 of the Revised Code.

(II)(1) "Computer hacking" means any of the following:

(a) Gaining access or attempting to gain access to all or part of a computer, computer system, or a computer network without express or implied authorization with the intent to defraud or with intent to commit a crime;

(b) Misusing computer or network services including, but not limited to, mail transfer programs, file transfer programs, proxy servers, and web servers by performing functions not authorized by the owner of the computer, computer system, or computer network or other person authorized to give consent. As used in this division, "misuse of computer and network services" includes, but is not limited to, the unauthorized use of any of the following:

(i) Mail transfer programs to send mail to persons other than the authorized users of that computer or computer network;

(ii) File transfer program proxy services or proxy servers to access other computers, computer systems, or computer networks;

(iii) Web servers to redirect users to other web pages or web servers.

(c)(i) Subject to division (II)(1)(c)(ii) of this section, using a group of computer programs commonly known as "port scanners" or "probes" to intentionally access any computer, computer system, or computer network without the permission of the owner of the computer, computer system, or computer network or other person authorized to give consent. The group of computer programs referred to in this division includes, but is not limited to, those computer programs that use a computer network to access a computer, computer system, or another computer network to determine any of the following: the presence or types of computers or computer systems on a network; the computer network's facilities and capabilities; the availability of computer or network services; the presence or versions of computer software including, but not limited to, operating systems, computer services, or computer contaminants; the presence of a known computer software deficiency that can be used to gain unauthorized access to a computer, computer system, or computer network; or any other information about a computer, computer system, or computer network not necessary for the normal and lawful operation of the computer initiating the access.

(ii) The group of computer programs referred to in division (II)(1)(c)(i) of this section does not include standard computer software used for the normal operation, administration, management, and test of a computer, computer system, or computer network including, but not limited to, domain name services, mail transfer services, and other operating system services, computer programs commonly called "ping," "tcpdump," and "traceroute" and other network monitoring and management computer software, and computer programs commonly known as "nslookup" and "whois" and other systems administration computer software.

(d) The intentional use of a computer, computer system, or a computer network in a manner that exceeds any right or permission granted by the owner of the computer, computer system, or computer network or other person authorized to give consent.

(2) "Computer hacking" does not include the introduction of a computer contaminant, as defined in section 2909.01 of the Revised Code, into a computer, computer system, computer program, or computer network.

(JJ) "Police dog or horse" has the same meaning as in section 2921.321 of the Revised Code.

(KK) "Anhydrous ammonia" is a compound formed by the combination of two gaseous elements, nitrogen and hydrogen, in the manner described in this division. Anhydrous ammonia is one part nitrogen to three parts hydrogen (NH3). Anhydrous ammonia by weight is fourteen parts nitrogen to three parts hydrogen, which is approximately eighty-two per cent nitrogen to eighteen per cent hydrogen.

(LL) "Assistance dog" has the same meaning as in section 955.011 of the Revised Code.

(MM) "Federally licensed firearms dealer" has the same meaning as in section 5502.63 of the Revised Code.

**HISTORY: 134 v H 511 (Eff 1-1-74); 139 v H 437 (Eff 7-21-82); 140 v H 97 (Eff 3-20-84); 140 v S 183 (Eff 9-26-84); 141 v H 340 (Eff 5-20-86); 141 v H 49 (Eff 6-26-86); 142 v H 182 (Eff 7-7-87); 143 v H 347 (Eff 7-18-90); 146 v S 2 (Eff 7-1-96); 146 v S 277 (Eff 3-31-97); 147 v H 565 (Eff 3-30-99); 148 v H 2 (Eff 11-10-99); 149 v H 327. Eff 7-8-2002; 150 v S 82, § 1, eff. 2-12-04; 150 v S 146, § 1, eff. 9-23-04; 150 v H 369, § 1, eff. 11-26-04; 150 v H 536, § 1, eff. 4-15-05; 150 v H 361, § 1, eff. 5-6-05; 151 v H 530, § 101.01, eff. 6-30-06; 151 v H 347, § 1, eff. 3-14-07; 152 v S 320, § 1, eff. 4-7-09; 2011 HB 86, § 1, eff. Sept. 30, 2011.**

The provisions of § 4 of HB 86 read as follows:

SECTION 4. The amendments to sections 926.99, 1333.99, 1707.99, 1716.99, 2909.03, 2909.05, 2909.11, 2913.02, 2913.03, 2913.04, 2913.11, 2913.21, 2913.31, 2913.32, 2913.34, 2913.40, 2913.401, 2913.42, 2913.421, 2913.43, 2913.45, 2913.46, 2913.47, 2913.48, 2913.49, 2913.51, 2913.61, 2915.05, 2917.21, 2917.31, 2917.32, 2921.13, 2921.41, 2923.31, and 2981.07, division (B) of section 2929.13, and division (A) of section 2929.14 of the Revised Code that are made in this act apply to a person who commits an offense specified or penalized under those sections on or after the effective date of this section and to a person to whom division (B) of section 1.58 of the Revised Code makes the amendments applicable.

The provisions of sections 926.99, 1333.99, 1707.99, 1716.99, 2909.03, 2909.05, 2909.11, 2913.02, 2913.03, 2913.04, 2913.11, 2913.21, 2913.31, 2913.32, 2913.34, 2913.40, 2913.401, 2913.42, 2913.421, 2913.43, 2913.45, 2913.46, 2913.47, 2913.48, 2913.49, 2913.51, 2913.61, 2915.05, 2917.21, 2917.31, 2917.32, 2921.13,

2921.41, 2923.31, and 2981.07 of the Revised Code in existence prior to the effective date of this section shall apply to a person upon whom a court imposed sentence prior to the effective date of this section for an offense specified or penalized under those sections. The amendments to sections 926.99, 1333.99, 1707.99, 1716.99, 2909.03, 2909.05, 2909.11, 2913.02, 2913.03, 2913.04, 2913.11, 2913.21, 2913.31, 2913.32, 2913.34, 2913.40, 2913.401, 2913.42, 2913.421, 2913.43, 2913.45, 2913.46, 2913.47, 2913.48, 2913.49, 2913.51, 2913.61, 2915.05, 2917.21, 2917.31, 2917.32, 2921.13, 2921.41, 2923.31, and 2981.07 of the Revised Code that are made in this act do not apply to a person who upon whom a court imposed sentence prior to the effective date of this section for an offense specified or penalized under those sections.

Governor Taft's veto of HB 347 was overridden by the Ohio General Assembly.

The effective date is set by § 812.03 of 151 v H 530.

The provisions of § 831.03 of 151 v H 530 read in part as follows:

SECTION 831.03. The General Assembly, applying the principle stated in division (B) of section 1.52 of the Revised Code that amendments are to be harmonized if reasonably capable of simultaneous operation, finds that the following sections, presented in this act as composites of the sections as amended by the acts indicated, are the resulting versions of the sections in effect prior to the effective date of the sections as presented in this act:

° ° °

Section 2913.01 of the Revised Code as amended by Am. Sub. H.B. 361, Am. Sub. H.B. 369, Sub. H.B. 536, and Am. Sub. S.B. 146, all of the 125th General Assembly.

° ° °

The finding in this section takes effect at the same time as the section referenced in the finding takes effect.

The provisions of § 3 of H.B. 536 (150 v —) read as follows:

SECTION 3. Section 2913.01 of the Revised Code is presented in this act as a composite of the section as amended by both Am. Sub. H.B. 369 and Am. Sub. S.B. 146 of the 125th General Assembly. The General Assembly, applying the principle stated in division (B) of section 1.52 of the Revised Code that amendments are to be harmonized if reasonably capable of simultaneous operation, finds that the composite is the resulting version of the section in effect prior to the effective date of the section as presented in this act.

**Not analogous to former RC § 2913.01 (RS § 7091; S&S 264; S&C 409; 73 v 59; GC § 13083; 101 v 206; Bureau of Code Revision, 10-1-53), repealed 134 v H 511, § 2, eff 1-1-74.**

## [THEFT]

## § 2913.02 Theft.

(A) No person, with purpose to deprive the owner of property or services, shall knowingly obtain or exert control over either the property or services in any of the following ways:

(1) Without the consent of the owner or person authorized to give consent;

(2) Beyond the scope of the express or implied consent of the owner or person authorized to give consent;

(3) By deception;

(4) By threat;

(5) By intimidation.

(B)(1) Whoever violates this section is guilty of theft.

(2) Except as otherwise provided in this division or division (B)(3), (4), (5), (6), (7), or (8) of this section, a violation of this section is petty theft, a misdemeanor of the first degree. If the value of the property or services stolen is one thousand dollars or more and is less than seven thousand five hundred dollars or if the property stolen is any of the property listed in section 2913.71 of the Revised Code, a violation of this section is theft, a felony of the fifth degree. If the value of the property or services stolen is seven thousand five hundred dollars or more and is less than one hundred fifty thousand dollars, a violation of this section is grand theft, a felony of the fourth degree. If the value of the property or services stolen is one hundred fifty thousand dollars or more and is less than seven hundred fifty thousand dollars, a violation of this section is aggravated theft, a felony of the third degree. If the value of the property or services is seven hundred fifty thousand dollars or more and is less than one million five hundred thousand dollars, a violation of this section is aggravated theft, a felony of the second degree. If the value of the property or services stolen is one million five hundred thousand dollars or more, a violation of this section is aggravated theft of one million five hundred thousand dollars or more, a felony of the first degree.

(3) Except as otherwise provided in division (B)(4), (5), (6), (7), or (8) of this section, if the victim of the offense is an elderly person or disabled adult, a violation of this section is theft from an elderly person or disabled adult, and division (B)(3) of this section applies. Except as otherwise provided in this division, theft from an elderly person or disabled adult is a felony of the fifth degree. If the value of the property or services stolen is one thousand dollars or more and is less than seven thousand five hundred dollars, theft from an elderly person or disabled adult is a felony of the fourth degree. If the value of the property or services stolen is seven thousand five hundred dollars or more and is less than thirty-seven thousand five hundred dollars, theft from an elderly person or disabled adult is a felony of the third degree. If the value of the property or services stolen is thirty-seven thousand five hundred dollars or more and is less than one hundred fifty thousand dollars, theft from an elderly person or disabled adult is a felony of the second degree. If the value of the property or services stolen is one hundred fifty thousand dollars or more, theft from an elderly person or disabled adult is a felony of the first degree.

(4) If the property stolen is a firearm or dangerous ordnance, a violation of this section is grand theft. Except as otherwise provided in this division, grand theft when the property stolen is a firearm or dangerous ordnance is a felony of the third degree, and there is a presumption in favor of the court imposing a prison term for the offense. If the firearm or dangerous ordnance was stolen from a federally licensed firearms dealer, grand theft when the property stolen is a firearm or dangerous ordnance is a felony of the first degree. The offender shall serve a prison term imposed for grand theft when the property stolen is a firearm or dangerous ordnance consecutively to any other prison term or mandatory prison term previously or subsequently imposed upon the offender.

(5) If the property stolen is a motor vehicle, a violation of this section is grand theft of a motor vehicle, a felony of the fourth degree.

(6) If the property stolen is any dangerous drug, a violation of this section is theft of drugs, a felony of the fourth degree, or, if the offender previously has been convicted of a felony drug abuse offense, a felony of the third degree.

(7) If the property stolen is a police dog or horse or an assistance dog and the offender knows or should know that the property stolen is a police dog or horse or an assistance dog, a violation of this section is theft of a police dog or horse or an assistance dog, a felony of the third degree.

(8) If the property stolen is anhydrous ammonia, a violation of this section is theft of anhydrous ammonia, a felony of the third degree.

(9) In addition to the penalties described in division (B)(2) of this section, if the offender committed the violation by causing a motor vehicle to leave the premises of an establishment at which gasoline is offered for retail sale without the offender making full payment for gasoline that was dispensed into the fuel tank of the motor vehicle or into another container, the court may do one of the following:

(a) Unless division (B)(9)(b) of this section applies, suspend for not more than six months the offender's driver's license, probationary driver's license, commercial driver's license, temporary instruction permit, or nonresident operating privilege;

(b) If the offender's driver's license, probationary driver's license, commercial driver's license, temporary instruction permit, or nonresident operating privilege has previously been suspended pursuant to division (B)(9)(a) of this section, impose a class seven suspension of the offender's license, permit, or privilege from the range specified in division (A)(7) of section 4510.02 of the Revised Code, provided that the suspension shall be for at least six months.

(10) In addition to the penalties described in division (B)(2) of this section, if the offender committed the violation by stealing rented property or rental services, the court may order that the offender make restitution pursuant to section 2929.18 or 2929.28 of the Revised Code. Restitution may include, but is not limited to, the cost of repairing or replacing the stolen property, or the cost of repairing the stolen property and any loss of revenue resulting from deprivation of the property due to theft of rental services that is less than or equal to the actual value of the property at the time it was rented. Evidence of intent to commit theft of rented property or rental services shall be determined pursuant to the provisions of section 2913.72 of the Revised Code.

(C) The sentencing court that suspends an offender's license, permit, or nonresident operating privilege under division (B)(9) of this section may grant the offender limited driving privileges during the period of the suspension in accordance with Chapter 4510. of the Revised Code.

**HISTORY: 134 v H 511 (Eff 1-1-74); 138 v S 191 (Eff 6-20-80); 139 v S 199 (Eff 1-1-83); 140 v H 632 (Eff 3-28-85); 141 v H 49 (Eff 6-26-86); 143 v H 347 (Eff 7-18-90); 143 v S 258 (Eff 11-20-90); 146 v H 4 (Eff 11-9-95); 146 v S 2 (Eff 7-1-96); 147 v S 66 (Eff 7-22-98); 148 v H 2. Eff 11-10-99; 150 v H 7, § 1, eff. 9-16-03; 150 v H 179, § 1, eff. 3-9-04; 150 v H 12, § 1, eff. 4-8-04; 150 v H 369, § 1, eff. 11-26-04; 150 v H 536, § 1, eff. 4-15-05; 151 v H 530, § 101.01, eff. 6-30-06; 151 v H 347, § 1, eff. 3-14-07; 152 v S 320, § 1, eff. 4-7-09; 2011 HB 86, § 1, eff. Sept. 30, 2011.**

The provisions of § 4 of HB 86 read as follows:

"SECTION 4. The amendments to sections 926.99, 1333.99, 1707.99, 1716.99, 2909.03, 2909.05, 2909.11, 2913.02, 2913.03, 2913.04, 2913.11, 2913.21, 2913.31, 2913.32, 2913.34, 2913.40, 2913.401, 2913.42, 2913.421, 2913.43, 2913.45, 2913.46, 2913.47, 2913.48, 2913.49, 2913.51, 2913.61, 2915.05, 2917.21, 2917.31, 2917.32, 2921.13, 2921.41, 2923.31, and 2981.07, division (B) of section 2929.13, and division (A) of section 2929.14 of the Revised Code that are made in this act apply to a person who commits an offense specified or penalized under those sections on or after the effective date of this section and to a person to whom division (B) of section 1.58 of the Revised Code makes the amendments applicable.

"The provisions of sections 926.99, 1333.99, 1707.99, 1716.99, 2909.03, 2909.05, 2909.11, 2913.02, 2913.03, 2913.04, 2913.11, 2913.21, 2913.31, 2913.32, 2913.34, 2913.40, 2913.401, 2913.42, 2913.421, 2913.43, 2913.45, 2913.46, 2913.47, 2913.48, 2913.49, 2913.51, 2913.61, 2915.05, 2917.21, 2917.31, 2917.32, 2921.13, 2921.41, 2923.31, and 2981.07 of the Revised Code in existence prior to the effective date of this section shall apply to a person upon whom a court imposed sentence prior to the effective date of this section for an offense specified or penalized under those sections. The amendments to sections 926.99, 1333.99, 1707.99, 1716.99, 2909.03, 2909.05, 2909.11, 2913.02, 2913.03, 2913.04, 2913.11, 2913.21, 2913.31, 2913.32, 2913.34, 2913.40, 2913.401, 2913.42, 2913.421, 2913.43, 2913.45, 2913.46, 2913.47, 2913.48, 2913.49, 2913.51, 2913.61, 2915.05, 2917.21, 2917.31, 2917.32, 2921.13, 2921.41, 2923.31, and 2981.07 of the Revised Code that are made in this act do not apply to a person who upon whom a court imposed sentence prior to the effective date of this section for an offense specified or penalized under those sections."

Governor Taft's veto of HB 347 was overridden by the Ohio General Assembly.

The effective date is set by § 812.03 of 151 v H 530.

The provisions of § 3 of H.B. 369 (150 v —) read as follows:

SECTION 3. Section 2913.02 of the Revised Code is presented in this act as a composite of the section as amended by Am. Sub. H.B. 7, Am. Sub. H.B. 12, and Sub. H.B. 179, all of the 125th General Assembly. The General Assembly, applying the principle stated in division (B) of section 1.52 of the Revised Code that amendments are to be harmonized if reasonably capable of simultaneous operation, finds that the composite is the resulting version of the section in effect prior to the effective date of the section as presented in this act.

The provisions of § 10, H.B. 12 (150 v —), read as follows:

SECTION 10. If any provision of sections 1547.69, 2911.21, 2913.02, 2921.13, 2923.12, 2923.121, 2923.123, 2923.16, 2929.14, 2953.32, and 4749.10 of the Revised Code, as amended by this act, any provision of sections 109.69, 109.731, 311.41, 311.42, 2923.124, 2923.125, 2923.126, 2923.127, 2923.128, 2923.129, 2923.1210, 2923.1211, 2923.1212, and 2923.1213 of the Revised Code, as enacted by this act, or the application of any provision of those sections to any person or circumstance is held invalid, the invalidity does not affect other provisions or applications of the particular section or related sections that can be given effect without the invalid provision or application, and to this end the provisions of the particular section are severable.

The provisions of § 3, H.B. 179 (150 v —), read as follows:

SECTION 3. The General Assembly declares that the sections of the Revised Code that regulate persons who leave the premises of establishments at which gasoline is offered for retail sale without the person making full payment for gasoline that was dispensed at that establishment, including section 2913.02 of the Revised Code, are general laws that completely fill the field of regulation of that nature. Any municipal ordinance that prohibits establishments at which gasoline is offered for retail sale from requiring the prepayment of gasoline is in conflict with those general laws.

**Not analogous to former RC § 2913.02 (RS § 7092; 71 v 3; GC § 13084; Bureau of Code Revision, 10-1-53), repealed 134 v H 511, § 2, eff 1-1-74.**

## § 2913.03 Unauthorized use of a vehicle.

(A) No person shall knowingly use or operate an aircraft, motor vehicle, motorcycle, motorboat, or other motor-propelled vehicle without the consent of the owner or person authorized to give consent.

(B) No person shall knowingly use or operate an aircraft, motor vehicle, motorboat, or other motor-propelled vehicle without the consent of the owner or person authorized to give consent, and either remove it from this state or keep possession of it for more than forty-eight hours.

(C) The following are affirmative defenses to a charge under this section:

(1) At the time of the alleged offense, the actor, though mistaken, reasonably believed that the actor was authorized to use or operate the property.

(2) At the time of the alleged offense, the actor reasonably believed that the owner or person empowered to give

consent would authorize the actor to use or operate the property.

(D)(1) Whoever violates this section is guilty of unauthorized use of a vehicle.

(2) Except as otherwise provided in division (D)(4) of this section, a violation of division (A) of this section is a misdemeanor of the first degree.

(3) Except as otherwise provided in division (D)(4) of this section, a violation of division (B) of this section is a felony of the fifth degree.

(4) If the victim of the offense is an elderly person or disabled adult and if the victim incurs a loss as a result of the violation, a violation of division (A) or (B) of this section is whichever of the following is applicable:

(a) Except as otherwise provided in division (D)(4)(b), (c), or (d) of this section, a felony of the fifth degree;

(b) If the loss to the victim is one thousand dollars or more and is less than seven thousand five hundred dollars, a felony of the fourth degree;

(c) If the loss to the victim is seven thousand five hundred dollars or more and is less than thirty-seven thousand five hundred dollars, a felony of the third degree;

(d) If the loss to the victim is thirty-seven thousand five hundred dollars or more, a felony of the second degree.

**HISTORY: 134 v H 511 (Eff 1-1-74); 146 v S 2 (Eff 7-1-96); 148 v H 2. Eff 11-10-99; 2011 HB 86, § 1, eff. Sept. 30, 2011.**

† So in enrolled bill, division (D)(4)(a). There is no division (D)(4)(e).

The provisions of § 4 of HB 86 read as follows:

"SECTION 4. The amendments to sections 926.99, 1333.99, 1707.99, 1716.99, 2909.03, 2909.05, 2909.11, 2913.02, 2913.03, 2913.04, 2913.11, 2913.21, 2913.31, 2913.32, 2913.34, 2913.40, 2913.401, 2913.42, 2913.421, 2913.43, 2913.45, 2913.46, 2913.47, 2913.48, 2913.49, 2913.51, 2913.61, 2915.05, 2917.21, 2917.31, 2917.32, 2921.13, 2921.41, 2923.31, and 2981.07, division (B) of section 2929.13, and division (A) of section 2929.14 of the Revised Code that are made in this act apply to a person who commits an offense specified or penalized under those sections on or after the effective date of this section and to a person to whom division (B) of section 1.58 of the Revised Code makes the amendments applicable.

"The provisions of sections 926.99, 1333.99, 1707.99, 1716.99, 2909.03, 2909.05, 2909.11, 2913.02, 2913.03, 2913.04, 2913.11, 2913.21, 2913.31, 2913.32, 2913.34, 2913.40, 2913.401, 2913.42, 2913.421, 2913.43, 2913.45, 2913.46, 2913.47, 2913.48, 2913.49, 2913.51, 2913.61, 2915.05, 2917.21, 2917.31, 2917.32, 2921.13, 2921.41, 2923.31, and 2981.07 of the Revised Code in existence prior to the effective date of this section shall apply to a person upon whom a court imposed sentence prior to the effective date of this section for an offense specified or penalized under those sections. The amendments to sections 926.99, 1333.99, 1707.99, 1716.99, 2909.03, 2909.05, 2909.11, 2913.02, 2913.03, 2913.04, 2913.11, 2913.21, 2913.31, 2913.32, 2913.34, 2913.40, 2913.401, 2913.42, 2913.421, 2913.43, 2913.45, 2913.46, 2913.47, 2913.48, 2913.49, 2913.51, 2913.61, 2915.05, 2917.21, 2917.31, 2917.32, 2921.13, 2921.41, 2923.31, and 2981.07 of the Revised Code that are made in this act do not apply to a person who upon whom a court imposed sentence prior to the effective date of this section for an offense specified or penalized under those sections."

**Not analogous to former RC § 2913.03 (RS § 7092a; 81 v 165; GC § 13085; Bureau of Code Revision, 10-1-53), repealed 134 v H 511, § 2, eff 1-1-74.**

## § 2913.04 Unauthorized use of property; computer, cable, or telecommunication property or service; Ohio law enforcement gateway.

(A) No person shall knowingly use or operate the property of another without the consent of the owner or person authorized to give consent.

(B) No person, in any manner and by any means, including, but not limited to, computer hacking, shall knowingly gain access to, attempt to gain access to, or cause access to be gained to any computer, computer system, computer network, cable service, cable system, telecommunications device, telecommunications service, or information service without the consent of, or beyond the scope of the express or implied consent of, the owner of the computer, computer system, computer network, cable service, cable system, telecommunications device, telecommunications service, or information service or other person authorized to give consent.

(C) No person shall knowingly gain access to, attempt to gain access to, cause access to be granted to, or disseminate information gained from access to the law enforcement automated database system created pursuant to section 5503.10 of the Revised Code without the consent of, or beyond the scope of the express or implied consent of, the chair of the law enforcement automated data system steering committee.

(D) No person shall knowingly gain access to, attempt to gain access to, cause access to be granted to, or disseminate information gained from access to the Ohio law enforcement gateway established and operated pursuant to division (C)(1) of section 109.57 of the Revised Code without the consent of, or beyond the scope of the express or implied consent of, the superintendent of the bureau of criminal identification and investigation.

(E) The affirmative defenses contained in division (C) of section 2913.03 of the Revised Code are affirmative defenses to a charge under this section.

(F)(1) Whoever violates division (A) of this section is guilty of unauthorized use of property.

(2) Except as otherwise provided in division (F)(3) or (4) of this section, unauthorized use of property is a misdemeanor of the fourth degree.

(3) Except as otherwise provided in division (F)(4) of this section, if unauthorized use of property is committed for the purpose of devising or executing a scheme to defraud or to obtain property or services, unauthorized use of property is whichever of the following is applicable:

(a) Except as otherwise provided in division (F)(3)(b), (c), or (d) of this section, a misdemeanor of the first degree.

(b) If the value of the property or services or the loss to the victim is one thousand dollars or more and is less than seven thousand five hundred dollars, a felony of the fifth degree.

(c) If the value of the property or services or the loss to the victim is seven thousand five hundred dollars or more and is less than one hundred fifty thousand dollars, a felony of the fourth degree.

(d) If the value of the property or services or the loss to the victim is one hundred fifty thousand dollars or more, a felony of the third degree.

(4) If the victim of the offense is an elderly person or disabled adult, unauthorized use of property is whichever of the following is applicable:

(a) Except as otherwise provided in division (F)(4)(b), (c), or (d) of this section, a felony of the fifth degree;

(b) If the value of the property or services or loss to the victim is one thousand dollars or more and is less than seven thousand five hundred dollars, a felony of the fourth degree;

(c) If the value of the property or services or loss to the victim is seven thousand five hundred dollars or more and is less than thirty-seven thousand five hundred dollars, a felony of the third degree;

(d) If the value of the property or services or loss to the victim is thirty-seven thousand five hundred dollars or more, a felony of the second degree.

(G)(1) Whoever violates division (B) of this section is guilty of unauthorized use of computer, cable, or telecommunication property, and shall be punished as provided in division (G)(2), (3), or (4) of this section.

(2) Except as otherwise provided in division (G)(3) or (4) of this section, unauthorized use of computer, cable, or telecommunication property is a felony of the fifth degree.

(3) Except as otherwise provided in division (G)(4) of this section, if unauthorized use of computer, cable, or telecommunication property is committed for the purpose of devising or executing a scheme to defraud or to obtain property or services, for obtaining money, property, or services by false or fraudulent pretenses, or for committing any other criminal offense, unauthorized use of computer, cable, or telecommunication property is whichever of the following is applicable:

(a) Except as otherwise provided in division (G)(3)(b) of this section, if the value of the property or services involved or the loss to the victim is seven thousand five hundred dollars or more and less than one hundred fifty thousand dollars, a felony of the fourth degree;

(b) If the value of the property or services involved or the loss to the victim is one hundred fifty thousand dollars or more, a felony of the third degree.

(4) If the victim of the offense is an elderly person or disabled adult, unauthorized use of computer, cable, or telecommunication property is whichever of the following is applicable:

(a) Except as otherwise provided in division (G)(4)(b), (c), or (d) of this section, a felony of the fifth degree;

(b) If the value of the property or services or loss to the victim is one thousand dollars or more and is less than seven thousand five hundred dollars, a felony of the fourth degree;

(c) If the value of the property or services or loss to the victim is seven thousand five hundred dollars or more and is less than thirty-seven thousand five hundred dollars, a felony of the third degree;

(d) If the value of the property or services or loss to the victim is thirty-seven thousand five hundred dollars or more, a felony of the second degree.

(H) Whoever violates division (C) of this section is guilty of unauthorized use of the law enforcement automated database system, a felony of the fifth degree.

(I) Whoever violates division (D) of this section is guilty of unauthorized use of the Ohio law enforcement gateway, a felony of the fifth degree.

(J) As used in this section:

(1) "Cable operator" means any person or group of persons that does either of the following:

(a) Provides cable service over a cable system and directly or through one or more affiliates owns a significant interest in that cable system;

(b) Otherwise controls or is responsible for, through any arrangement, the management and operation of a cable system.

(2) "Cable service" means any of the following:

(a) The one-way transmission to subscribers of video programming or of information that a cable operator makes available to all subscribers generally;

(b) Subscriber interaction, if any, that is required for the selection or use of video programming or of information that a cable operator makes available to all subscribers generally, both as described in division (J)(2)(a) of this section;

(c) Any cable television service.

(3) "Cable system" means any facility, consisting of a set of closed transmission paths and associated signal generation, reception, and control equipment that is designed to provide cable service that includes video programming and that is provided to multiple subscribers within a community. "Cable system" does not include any of the following:

(a) Any facility that serves only to retransmit the television signals of one or more television broadcast stations;

(b) Any facility that serves subscribers without using any public right-of-way;

(c) Any facility of a common carrier that, under 47 U.S.C.A. 522(7)(c), is excluded from the term "cable system" as defined in 47 U.S.C.A. 522(7);

(d) Any open video system that complies with 47 U.S.C.A. 573;

(e) Any facility of any electric utility used solely for operating its electric utility system.

**HISTORY: 134 v H 511 (Eff 1-1-74); 141 v H 49 (Eff 6-26-86); 146 v S 2 (Eff 7-1-96); 146 v S 269 (Eff 7-1-96); 147 v H 565 (Eff 3-30-99); 148 v H 2 (Eff 11-10-99); 149 v H 327. Eff 7-8-2002; 150 v H 12, § 1, eff. 4-8-04; 150 v S 146, § 1, eff. 9-23-04; 153 v H 10, § 1, eff. 6-17-10; 2011 HB 86, § 1, eff. Sept. 30, 2011.**

The provisions of § 4 of HB 86 read as follows:

"SECTION 4. The amendments to sections 926.99, 1333.99, 1707.99, 1716.99, 2909.03, 2909.05, 2909.11, 2913.02, 2913.03, 2913.04, 2913.11, 2913.21, 2913.31, 2913.32, 2913.34, 2913.40, 2913.401, 2913.42, 2913.421, 2913.43, 2913.45, 2913.46, 2913.47, 2913.48, 2913.49, 2913.51, 2913.61, 2915.05, 2917.21, 2917.31, 2917.32, 2921.13, 2921.41, 2923.31, and 2981.07, division (B) of section 2929.13, and division (A) of section 2929.14 of the Revised Code that are made in this act apply to a person who commits an offense specified or penalized under those sections on or after the effective date of this section and to a person to whom division (B) of section 1.58 of the Revised Code makes the amendments applicable.

"The provisions of sections 926.99, 1333.99, 1707.99, 1716.99, 2909.03, 2909.05, 2909.11, 2913.02, 2913.03, 2913.04, 2913.11, 2913.21, 2913.31, 2913.32, 2913.34, 2913.40, 2913.401, 2913.42, 2913.421, 2913.43, 2913.45, 2913.46, 2913.47, 2913.48, 2913.49, 2913.51, 2913.61, 2915.05, 2917.21, 2917.31, 2917.32, 2921.13, 2921.41, 2923.31, and 2981.07 of the Revised Code in existence prior to the effective date of this section shall apply to a person upon whom a court imposed sentence prior to the effective date of this section for an offense specified or penalized under those sections. The amendments to sections 926.99, 1333.99, 1707.99, 1716.99, 2909.03, 2909.05, 2909.11, 2913.02, 2913.03, 2913.04, 2913.11, 2913.21, 2913.31, 2913.32, 2913.34, 2913.40, 2913.401, 2913.42, 2913.421, 2913.43, 2913.45, 2913.46, 2913.47, 2913.48, 2913.49, 2913.51, 2913.61, 2915.05, 2917.21, 2917.31, 2917.32, 2921.13, 2921.41, 2923.31, and 2981.07 of the Revised Code that are made in this act do not apply to a person who upon whom a court imposed sentence prior to the effective date of this section for an offense specified or penalized under those sections."

**Not analogous to former RC § 2913.04 (RS § 7093; S&S 57; 64 v 128; 66 v 99; 70 v 156; GC § 13086; Bureau of Code Revision, 10-1-53; 129 v 1594), repealed 134 v H 511, § 2, eff 1-1-74.**

## § 2913.041 Possession or sale of unauthorized cable television device.

(A) No person shall knowingly possess any device, including any instrument, apparatus, computer chip, equipment, decoder, descrambler, converter, software, or other device specially adapted, modified, or remanufactured for gaining access to cable television service, without securing authorization from or paying the required compensation to the owner or operator of the system that provides the cable television service.

(B) No person shall knowingly sell, distribute, or manufacture any device, including any instrument, apparatus, computer chip, equipment, decoder, descrambler, converter, software, or other device specially adapted, modified, or remanufactured for gaining access to cable television service, without securing authorization from or paying the required compensation to the owner or operator of the system that provides the cable television service.

(C) Whoever violates division (A) of this section is guilty of possession of an unauthorized device, a felony of the fifth degree. Whoever violates division (B) of this section is guilty of sale of an unauthorized device, a felony of the fourth degree.

(D) A person commits a separate violation of this section with regard to each device that is sold, distributed, manufactured, or possessed in violation of division (A) or (B) of this section.

**HISTORY: 146 v S 2. Eff 7-1-96.**

The effective date is set by section 6 of SB 2.

## § 2913.05 Telecommunications fraud.

(A) No person, having devised a scheme to defraud, shall knowingly disseminate, transmit, or cause to be disseminated or transmitted by means of a wire, radio, satellite, telecommunication, telecommunications device, or telecommunications service any writing, data, sign, signal, picture, sound, or image with purpose to execute or otherwise further the scheme to defraud.

(B) Whoever violates this section is guilty of telecommunications fraud. Except as otherwise provided in this division, telecommunications fraud is a felony of the fifth degree. If the value of the benefit obtained by the offender or of the detriment to the victim of the fraud is five thousand dollars or more but less than one hundred thousand dollars, telecommunications fraud is a felony of the fourth degree. If the value of the benefit obtained by the offender or of the detriment to the victim of the fraud is one hundred thousand dollars or more, telecommunications fraud is a felony of the third degree.

**HISTORY: 147 v H 565. Eff 3-30-99.**

**Not analogous to former RC § 2913.05 (RS § 7094; S & S 57; 64 v 128, §§ 7, 8; 66 v 99, § 1; 70 v 156, § 2; GC § 13087; 114 v 119, § 1; Bureau of Code Revision, 10-1-53; 129 v 1594, § 1), repealed 134 v H 511, § 2, eff 1-1-74.**

## § 2913.06 Unlawful use of telecommunications device.

(A) No person shall knowingly manufacture, possess, deliver, offer to deliver, or advertise a counterfeit telecommunications device with purpose to use it criminally.

(B) No person shall knowingly manufacture, possess, deliver, offer to deliver, or advertise a counterfeit telecommunications device with purpose to use that device or to allow that device to be used, or knowing or having reason to know that another person may use that device, to do any of the following:

(1) Obtain or attempt to obtain telecommunications service or information service with purpose to avoid a lawful charge for that service or aid or cause another person to obtain or attempt to obtain telecommunications service or information service with purpose to avoid a lawful charge for that service;

(2) Conceal the existence, place of origin, or destination of a telecommunications service or information service.

(C) Whoever violates this section is guilty of unlawful use of a telecommunications device, a felony of the fifth degree.

(D) This section does not prohibit or restrict a person who holds an amateur service license issued by the federal communications commission from possessing a radio receiver or transceiver that is intended primarily or exclusively for use in the amateur radio service and is used for lawful purposes.

(E) This section does not preclude a person from disputing charges imposed for telecommunications service or information service by the provider of that service.

**HISTORY: 147 v H 565. Eff 3-30-99.**

**Not analogous to former RC § 2913.06 (RS § 7095; 67 v 17, § 1; GC § 13088; Bureau of Code Revision, 10-1-53; 127 v 1039 (1095), § 1), repealed 134 v H 511, § 2, eff 1-1-74.**

## § 2913.07 Motion picture piracy.

(A) As used in this section:

(1) "Audiovisual recording function" means the capability of a device to record or transmit a motion picture or any part of a motion picture by means of any technology existing on, or developed after, the effective date of this section.

(2) "Facility" means a movie theater.

(B) No person, without the written consent of the owner or lessee of the facility and of the licensor of the motion picture, shall knowingly operate an audiovisual recording function of a device in a facility in which a motion picture is being shown.

(C) Whoever violates division (B) of this section is guilty of motion picture piracy, a misdemeanor of the first degree on the first offense and a felony of the fifth degree on each subsequent offense.

(D) This section does not prohibit or restrict a lawfully authorized investigative, law enforcement, protective, or intelligence gathering employee or agent of the government of this state or a political subdivision of this state, or of the federal government, when acting in an official capacity, from operating an audiovisual recording function of a device in any facility in which a motion picture is being shown.

(E) Division (B) of this section does not limit or affect the application of any other prohibition in the Revised Code. Any act that is a violation of both division (B) of this section and another provision of the Revised Code may be prosecuted under this section, under the other provision of the Revised Code, or under both this section and the other provision of the Revised Code.

**HISTORY: 150 v H 179, § 1, eff. 3-9-04; 150 v S 57, § 1, eff. 3-9-04.**

**Not analogous to former RC § 2913.07 (RS §§ 7094—7096; S&C 454; S&S 57, 286; 56 v 86; 62 v 179; 64 v 128; 66 v 99; 67 v 17; 70 v 156; GC §§ 13087—13089; 114 v 119; Bureau of Code Revision, 10-1-53; 127 v 1039(1095); 129 v 1594), repealed, 134 v H 511, eff. 1-1-74.**

The provisions of § 3, H.B. 57 (150 v —), read as follows:

SECTION 3. The amendment by this act of section 2913.07 of the Revised Code is contingent upon Sub. H.B. 179 of the 125th

General Assembly becoming law in the same form as it passed the Senate and was concurred in by the House of Representatives.

**§ 2913.08** Repealed, 134 v H 511, § 2 [RS §§ 7098—7101; S&C 413, 455; S&S 269; 33 v 33; 56 v 86; 61 v 79; GC §§ 13091, 13094, 13096; Bureau of Code Revision, 10-1-53; 126 v 575]. Eff 1-1-74.

This section concerned forgery and counterfeiting.

**§ 2913.09** Repealed, 134 v H 511, § 2 [RS §§ 7098—7101; S&C 413, 455; S&S 269; 33 v 33; 56 v 86; 61 v 79; GC §§ 13091, 13094, 13096; Bureau of Code Revision, 10-1-53; 126 v 575]. Eff 1-1-74.

This section concerned forgery and counterfeiting.

**§ 2913.10** Repealed, 134 v H 511, § 2 [RS §§ 7098—7101; S&C 413, 455; S&S 269; 33 v 33; 56 v 86; 61 v 79; GC §§ 13091, 13094, 13096; Bureau of Code Revision, 10-1-53; 126 v 575]. Eff 1-1-74.

This section concerned forgery and counterfeiting.

## [PASSING BAD CHECKS]

### § 2913.11 Passing bad checks.

(A) As used in this section:

(1) "Check" includes any form of debit from a demand deposit account, including, but not limited to any of the following:

(a) A check, bill of exchange, draft, order of withdrawal, or similar negotiable or non-negotiable instrument;

(b) An electronic check, electronic transaction, debit card transaction, check card transaction, substitute check, web check, or any form of automated clearing house transaction.

(2) "Issue a check" means causing any form of debit from a demand deposit account.

(B) No person, with purpose to defraud, shall issue or transfer or cause to be issued or transferred a check or other negotiable instrument, knowing that it will be dishonored or knowing that a person has ordered or will order stop payment on the check or other negotiable instrument.

(C) For purposes of this section, a person who issues or transfers a check or other negotiable instrument is presumed to know that it will be dishonored if either of the following occurs:

(1) The drawer had no account with the drawee at the time of issue or the stated date, whichever is later;

(2) The check or other negotiable instrument was properly refused payment for insufficient funds upon presentment within thirty days after issue or the stated date, whichever is later, and the liability of the drawer, indorser, or any party who may be liable thereon is not discharged by payment or satisfaction within ten days after receiving notice of dishonor.

(D) For purposes of this section, a person who issues or transfers a check, bill of exchange, or other draft is presumed to have the purpose to defraud if the drawer fails to comply with section 1349.16 of the Revised Code by doing any of the following when opening a checking account intended for personal, family, or household purposes at a financial institution:

(1) Falsely stating that the drawer has not been issued a valid driver's or commercial driver's license or identification card issued under section 4507.50 of the Revised Code;

(2) Furnishing such license or card, or another identification document that contains false information;

(3) Making a false statement with respect to the drawer's current address or any additional relevant information reasonably required by the financial institution.

(E) In determining the value of the payment for purposes of division (F) of this section, the court may aggregate all checks and other negotiable instruments that the offender issued or transferred or caused to be issued or transferred in violation of division (A) of this section within a period of one hundred eighty consecutive days.

(F) Whoever violates this section is guilty of passing bad checks. Except as otherwise provided in this division, passing bad checks is a misdemeanor of the first degree. If the check or checks or other negotiable instrument or instruments are issued or transferred to a single vendor or single other person for the payment of one thousand dollars or more but less than seven thousand five hundred dollars or if the check or checks or other negotiable instrument or instruments are issued or transferred to multiple vendors or persons for the payment of one thousand five hundred dollars or more but less than seven thousand five hundred dollars, passing bad checks is a felony of the fifth degree. If the check or checks or other negotiable instrument or instruments are for the payment of seven thousand five hundred dollars or more but less than one hundred fifty thousand dollars, passing bad checks is a felony of the fourth degree. If the check or checks or other negotiable instrument or instruments are for the payment of one hundred fifty thousand dollars or more, passing bad checks is a felony of the third degree.

**HISTORY: 134 v H 511 (Eff 1-1-74); 139 v S 199 (Eff 1-5-83); 139 v H 269 (Eff 1-5-83); 141 v H 49 (Eff 6-26-86); 143 v H 711 (Eff 10-16-90); 146 v S 2. Eff 7-1-96; 150 v H 401, § 1, eff. 5-18-05; 2011 HB 86, § 1, eff. Sept. 30, 2011.**

The provisions of § 4 of HB 86 read as follows:

"SECTION 4. The amendments to sections 926.99, 1333.99, 1707.99, 1716.99, 2909.03, 2909.05, 2909.11, 2913.02, 2913.03, 2913.04, 2913.11, 2913.21, 2913.31, 2913.32, 2913.34, 2913.40, 2913.401, 2913.42, 2913.421, 2913.43, 2913.45, 2913.46, 2913.47, 2913.48, 2913.49, 2913.51, 2913.61, 2915.05, 2917.21, 2917.31, 2917.32, 2921.13, 2921.41, 2923.31, and 2981.07, division (B) of section 2929.13, and division (A) of section 2929.14 of the Revised Code that are made in this act apply to a person who commits an offense specified or penalized under those sections on or after the effective date of this section and to a person to whom division (B) of section 1.58 of the Revised Code makes the amendments applicable.

"The provisions of sections 926.99, 1333.99, 1707.99, 1716.99, 2909.03, 2909.05, 2909.11, 2913.02, 2913.03, 2913.04, 2913.11, 2913.21, 2913.31, 2913.32, 2913.34, 2913.40, 2913.401, 2913.42, 2913.421, 2913.43, 2913.45, 2913.46, 2913.47, 2913.48, 2913.49, 2913.51, 2913.61, 2915.05, 2917.21, 2917.31, 2917.32, 2921.13, 2921.41, 2923.31, and 2981.07 of the Revised Code in existence prior to the effective date of this section shall apply to a person upon whom a court imposed sentence prior to the effective date of this section for an offense specified or penalized under those sections. The amendments to sections 926.99, 1333.99, 1707.99, 1716.99, 2909.03, 2909.05, 2909.11, 2913.02, 2913.03, 2913.04, 2913.11, 2913.21, 2913.31, 2913.32, 2913.34, 2913.40, 2913.401, 2913.42, 2913.421, 2913.43, 2913.45, 2913.46, 2913.47, 2913.48, 2913.49, 2913.51, 2913.61, 2915.05, 2917.21, 2917.31, 2917.32, 2921.13, 2921.41, 2923.31, and 2981.07 of the Revised Code that are made in this act do not apply to a person who upon whom a court imposed sentence prior to the effective date of this section for an offense specified or penalized under those sections."

**Not analogous to former RC § 2913.11 (GC § 13097-1; 115 v 46; Bureau of Code Revision, 10-1-53), repealed 134 v H 511, § 2, eff 1-1-74.**

**Analogous to former RC § 2911.11.1 (132 v S 97), repealed 134 v H 511, § 2, eff 1-1-74.**

The effective date is set by section 6 of SB 2.

**§ 2913.12** Repealed, 134 v H 511, § 2 [RS §§ 7102, 7103; S&C 415; S&S 270; 33 v 33; 61 v 79; GC §§ 13097-2, 13098, 13099; 115 v 226; Bureau of Code Revision, 10-1-53; 126 v 575]. Eff 1-1-74.

This section concerned counterfeiting.

**§ 2913.13** Repealed, 134 v H 511, § 2 [RS §§ 7102, 7103; S&C 415; S&S 270; 33 v 33; 61 v 79; GC §§ 13097-2, 13098, 13099; 115 v 226; Bureau of Code Revision, 10-1-53; 126 v 575]. Eff 1-1-74.

This section concerned counterfeiting.

**§ 2913.14** Repealed, 134 v H 511, § 2 [RS §§ 7102, 7103; S&C 415; S&S 270; 33 v 33; 61 v 79; GC §§ 13097-2, 13098, 13099; 115 v 226; Bureau of Code Revision, 10-1-53; 126 v 575]. Eff 1-1-74.

This section concerned counterfeiting.

**§ 2913.15** Repealed, 134 v H 511, § 2 [RS §§ 3031, 7104, 7105; S&C 413, 415, 425; S&S 267, 450; 33 v 33; 55 v 149; 58 v 5; 63 v 70; GC §§ 13093, 13100, 13101; Bureau of Code Revision, 10-1-53]. Eff 1-1-74.

This section concerned counterfeiting.

**§ 2913.16** Repealed, 134 v H 511, § 2 [RS §§ 3031, 7104, 7105; S&C 413, 415, 425; S&S 267, 450; 33 v 33; 55 v 149; 58 v 5; 63 v 70; GC §§ 13093, 13100, 13101; Bureau of Code Revision, 10-1-53]. Eff 1-1-74.

This section concerned counterfeiting.

**§ 2913.17** Repealed, 134 v H 511, § 2 [RS §§ 3031, 7104, 7105; S&C 413, 415, 425; S&S 267, 450; 33 v 33; 55 v 149; 58 v 5; 63 v 70; GC §§ 13093, 13100, 13101; Bureau of Code Revision, 10-1-53]. Eff 1-1-74.

This section concerned counterfeiting.

## [MISUSE OF CREDIT CARDS]

### § 2913.21 Misuse of credit cards.

(A) No person shall do any of the following:

(1) Practice deception for the purpose of procuring the issuance of a credit card, when a credit card is issued in actual reliance thereon;

(2) Knowingly buy or sell a credit card from or to a person other than the issuer.

(B) No person, with purpose to defraud, shall do any of the following:

(1) Obtain control over a credit card as security for a debt;

(2) Obtain property or services by the use of a credit card, in one or more transactions, knowing or having reasonable cause to believe that the card has expired or been revoked, or was obtained, is retained, or is being used in violation of law;

(3) Furnish property or services upon presentation of a credit card, knowing that the card is being used in violation of law;

(4) Represent or cause to be represented to the issuer of a credit card that property or services have been furnished, knowing that the representation is false.

(C) No person, with purpose to violate this section, shall receive, possess, control, or dispose of a credit card.

(D)(1) Whoever violates this section is guilty of misuse of credit cards.

(2) Except as otherwise provided in division (D)(4) of this section, a violation of division (A), (B)(1), or (C) of this section is a misdemeanor of the first degree.

(3) Except as otherwise provided in this division or division (D)(4) of this section, a violation of division (B)(2), (3), or (4) of this section is a misdemeanor of the first degree. If the cumulative retail value of the property and services involved in one or more violations of division (B)(2), (3), or (4) of this section, which violations involve one or more credit card accounts and occur within a period of ninety consecutive days commencing on the date of the first violation, is one thousand dollars or more and is less than seven thousand five hundred dollars, misuse of credit cards in violation of any of those divisions is a felony of the fifth degree. If the cumulative retail value of the property and services involved in one or more violations of division (B)(2), (3), or (4) of this section, which violations involve one or more credit card accounts and occur within a period of ninety consecutive days commencing on the date of the first violation, is seven thousand five hundred dollars or more and is less than one hundred fifty thousand dollars, misuse of credit cards in violation of any of those divisions is a felony of the fourth degree. If the cumulative retail value of the property and services involved in one or more violations of division (B)(2), (3), or (4) of this section, which violations involve one or more credit card accounts and occur within a period of ninety consecutive days commencing on the date of the first violation, is one hundred fifty thousand dollars or more, misuse of credit cards in violation of any of those divisions is a felony of the third degree.

(4) If the victim of the offense is an elderly person or disabled adult, and if the offense involves a violation of division (B)(1) or (2) of this section, division (D)(4) of this section applies. Except as otherwise provided in division (D)(4) of this section, a violation of division (B)(1) or (2) of this section is a felony of the fifth degree. If the debt for which the card is held as security or the cumulative retail value of the property or services involved in the violation is one thousand dollars or more and is less than seven thousand five hundred dollars, a violation of either of those divisions is a felony of the fourth degree. If the debt for which the card is held as security or the cumulative retail value of the property or services involved in the violation is seven thousand five hundred dollars or more and is less than thirty-seven thousand five hundred dollars,

a violation of either of those divisions is a felony of the third degree. If the debt for which the card is held as security or the cumulative retail value of the property or services involved in the violation is thirty-seven thousand five hundred dollars or more, a violation of either of those divisions is a felony of the second degree.

**HISTORY: 134 v H 511 (Eff 1-1-74); 137 v S 289 (Eff 5-23-78); 139 v S 199 (Eff 1-5-83); 139 v H 269 (Eff 1-5-83); 140 v S 210 (Eff 7-1-83); 141 v H 49 (Eff 6-26-86); 146 v S 2 (Eff 7-1-96); 148 v H 2. Eff 11-10-99; 2011 HB 86, § 1, eff. Sept. 30, 2011.**

The provisions of § 4 of HB 86 read as follows:

"SECTION 4. The amendments to sections 926.99, 1333.99, 1707.99, 1716.99, 2909.03, 2909.05, 2909.11, 2913.02, 2913.03, 2913.04, 2913.11, 2913.21, 2913.31, 2913.32, 2913.34, 2913.40, 2913.401, 2913.42, 2913.421, 2913.43, 2913.45, 2913.46, 2913.47, 2913.48, 2913.49, 2913.51, 2913.61, 2915.05, 2917.21, 2917.31, 2917.32, 2921.13, 2921.41, 2923.31, and 2981.07, division (B) of section 2929.13, and division (A) of section 2929.14 of the Revised Code that are made in this act apply to a person who commits an offense specified or penalized under those sections on or after the effective date of this section and to a person to whom division (B) of section 1.58 of the Revised Code makes the amendments applicable.

"The provisions of sections 926.99, 1333.99, 1707.99, 1716.99, 2909.03, 2909.05, 2909.11, 2913.02, 2913.03, 2913.04, 2913.11, 2913.21, 2913.31, 2913.32, 2913.34, 2913.40, 2913.401, 2913.42, 2913.421, 2913.43, 2913.45, 2913.46, 2913.47, 2913.48, 2913.49, 2913.51, 2913.61, 2915.05, 2917.21, 2917.31, 2917.32, 2921.13, 2921.41, 2923.31, and 2981.07 of the Revised Code in existence prior to the effective date of this section shall apply to a person upon whom a court imposed sentence prior to the effective date of this section for an offense specified or penalized under those sections. The amendments to sections 926.99, 1333.99, 1707.99, 1716.99, 2909.03, 2909.05, 2909.11, 2913.02, 2913.03, 2913.04, 2913.11, 2913.21, 2913.31, 2913.32, 2913.34, 2913.40, 2913.401, 2913.42, 2913.421, 2913.43, 2913.45, 2913.46, 2913.47, 2913.48, 2913.49, 2913.51, 2913.61, 2915.05, 2917.21, 2917.31, 2917.32, 2921.13, 2921.41, 2923.31, and 2981.07 of the Revised Code that are made in this act do not apply to a person who upon whom a court imposed sentence prior to the effective date of this section for an offense specified or penalized under those sections."

**Analogous to former RC § 2907.20.1 (133 v S 346; 134 v S 302), repealed 134 v H 511, § 2, eff 1-1-74.**

## [FORGERY]

### § 2913.31 Forgery; identification card offenses.

(A) No person, with purpose to defraud, or knowing that the person is facilitating a fraud, shall do any of the following:

(1) Forge any writing of another without the other person's authority;

(2) Forge any writing so that it purports to be genuine when it actually is spurious, or to be the act of another who did not authorize that act, or to have been executed at a time or place or with terms different from what in fact was the case, or to be a copy of an original when no such original existed;

(3) Utter, or possess with purpose to utter, any writing that the person knows to have been forged.

(B) No person shall knowingly do either of the following:

(1) Forge an identification card;

(2) Sell or otherwise distribute a card that purports to be an identification card, knowing it to have been forged.

As used in this division, "identification card" means a card that includes personal information or characteristics of an individual, a purpose of which is to establish the identity of the bearer described on the card, whether the words "identity," "identification," "identification card," or other similar words appear on the card.

(C)(1)(a) Whoever violates division (A) of this section is guilty of forgery.

(b) Except as otherwise provided in this division or division (C)(1)(c) of this section, forgery is a felony of the fifth degree. If property or services are involved in the offense or the victim suffers a loss, forgery is one of the following:

(i) If the value of the property or services or the loss to the victim is seven thousand five hundred dollars or more and is less than one hundred fifty thousand dollars, a felony of the fourth degree;

(ii) If the value of the property or services or the loss to the victim is one hundred fifty thousand dollars or more, a felony of the third degree.

(c) If the victim of the offense is an elderly person or disabled adult, division (C)(1)(c) of this section applies to the forgery. Except as otherwise provided in division (C)(1)(c) of this section, forgery is a felony of the fifth degree. If property or services are involved in the offense or if the victim suffers a loss, forgery is one of the following:

(i) If the value of the property or services or the loss to the victim is one thousand dollars or more and is less than seven thousand five hundred dollars, a felony of the fourth degree;

(ii) If the value of the property or services or the loss to the victim is seven thousand five hundred dollars or more and is less than thirty-seven thousand five hundred dollars, a felony of the third degree;

(iii) If the value of the property or services or the loss to the victim is thirty-seven thousand five hundred dollars or more, a felony of the second degree.

(2) Whoever violates division (B) of this section is guilty of forging identification cards or selling or distributing forged identification cards. Except as otherwise provided in this division, forging identification cards or selling or distributing forged identification cards is a misdemeanor of the first degree. If the offender previously has been convicted of a violation of division (B) of this section, forging identification cards or selling or distributing forged identification cards is a misdemeanor of the first degree and, in addition, the court shall impose upon the offender a fine of not less than two hundred fifty dollars.

**HISTORY: 134 v H 511 (Eff 1-1-74); 144 v H 162 (Eff 11-11-91); 146 v S 2 (Eff 7-1-96); 148 v H 2. Eff 11-10-99; 2011 HB 86, § 1, eff. Sept. 30, 2011.**

The provisions of § 4 of HB 86 read as follows:

"SECTION 4. The amendments to sections 926.99, 1333.99, 1707.99, 1716.99, 2909.03, 2909.05, 2909.11, 2913.02, 2913.03, 2913.04, 2913.11, 2913.21, 2913.31, 2913.32, 2913.34, 2913.40, 2913.401, 2913.42, 2913.421, 2913.43, 2913.45, 2913.46, 2913.47, 2913.48, 2913.49, 2913.51, 2913.61, 2915.05, 2917.21, 2917.31, 2917.32, 2921.13, 2921.41, 2923.31, and 2981.07, division (B) of section 2929.13, and division (A) of section 2929.14 of the Revised Code that are made in this act apply to a person who commits an offense specified or penalized under those sections on or after the effective date of this section and to a person to whom division (B) of section 1.58 of the Revised Code makes the amendments applicable.

"The provisions of sections 926.99, 1333.99, 1707.99, 1716.99, 2909.03, 2909.05, 2909.11, 2913.02, 2913.03, 2913.04, 2913.11, 2913.21, 2913.31, 2913.32, 2913.34, 2913.40, 2913.401, 2913.42, 2913.421, 2913.43, 2913.45, 2913.46, 2913.47, 2913.48, 2913.49,

2913.51, 2913.61, 2915.05, 2917.21, 2917.31, 2917.32, 2921.13, 2921.41, 2923.31, and 2981.07 of the Revised Code in existence prior to the effective date of this section shall apply to a person upon whom a court imposed sentence prior to the effective date of this section for an offense specified or penalized under those sections. The amendments to sections 926.99, 1333.99, 1707.99, 1716.99, 2909.03, 2909.05, 2909.11, 2913.02, 2913.03, 2913.04, 2913.11, 2913.21, 2913.31, 2913.32, 2913.34, 2913.40, 2913.401, 2913.42, 2913.421, 2913.43, 2913.45, 2913.46, 2913.47, 2913.48, 2913.49, 2913.51, 2913.61, 2915.05, 2917.21, 2917.31, 2917.32, 2921.13, 2921.41, 2923.31, and 2981.07 of the Revised Code that are made in this act do not apply to a person who upon whom a court imposed sentence prior to the effective date of this section for an offense specified or penalized under those sections."

## § 2913.32 Criminal simulation.

(A) No person, with purpose to defraud, or knowing that the person is facilitating a fraud, shall do any of the following:

(1) Make or alter any object so that it appears to have value because of antiquity, rarity, curiosity, source, or authorship, which it does not in fact possess;

(2) Practice deception in making, retouching, editing, or reproducing any photograph, movie film, video tape, phonograph record, or recording tape;

(3) Falsely or fraudulently make, simulate, forge, alter, or counterfeit any wrapper, label, stamp, cork, or cap prescribed by the liquor control commission under Chapters 4301. and 4303. of the Revised Code, falsely or fraudulently cause to be made, simulated, forged, altered, or counterfeited any wrapper, label, stamp, cork, or cap prescribed by the liquor control commission under Chapters 4301. and 4303. of the Revised Code, or use more than once any wrapper, label, stamp, cork, or cap prescribed by the liquor control commission under Chapters 4301. and 4303. of the Revised Code.

(4) Utter, or possess with purpose to utter, any object that the person knows to have been simulated as provided in division (A)(1), (2), or (3) of this section.

(B) Whoever violates this section is guilty of criminal simulation. Except as otherwise provided in this division, criminal simulation is a misdemeanor of the first degree. If the loss to the victim is one thousand dollars or more and is less than seven thousand five hundred dollars, criminal simulation is a felony of the fifth degree. If the loss to the victim is seven thousand five hundred dollars or more and is less than one hundred fifty thousand dollars, criminal simulation is a felony of the fourth degree. If the loss to the victim is one hundred fifty thousand dollars or more, criminal simulation is a felony of the third degree.

**HISTORY: 134 v H 511 (Eff 1-1-74); 146 v S 2. Eff 7-1-96; 2011 HB 86, § 1, eff. Sept. 30, 2011.**

The provisions of § 4 of HB 86 read as follows:

"SECTION 4. The amendments to sections 926.99, 1333.99, 1707.99, 1716.99, 2909.03, 2909.05, 2909.11, 2913.02, 2913.03, 2913.04, 2913.11, 2913.21, 2913.31, 2913.32, 2913.34, 2913.40, 2913.401, 2913.42, 2913.421, 2913.43, 2913.45, 2913.46, 2913.47, 2913.48, 2913.49, 2913.51, 2913.61, 2915.05, 2917.21, 2917.31, 2917.32, 2921.13, 2921.41, 2923.31, and 2981.07, division (B) of section 2929.13, and division (A) of section 2929.14 of the Revised Code that are made in this act apply to a person who commits an offense specified or penalized under those sections on or after the effective date of this section and to a person to whom division (B) of section 1.58 of the Revised Code makes the amendments applicable.

"The provisions of sections 926.99, 1333.99, 1707.99, 1716.99, 2909.03, 2909.05, 2909.11, 2913.02, 2913.03, 2913.04, 2913.11, 2913.21, 2913.31, 2913.32, 2913.34, 2913.40, 2913.401, 2913.42, 2913.421, 2913.43, 2913.45, 2913.46, 2913.47, 2913.48, 2913.49, 2913.51, 2913.61, 2915.05, 2917.21, 2917.31, 2917.32, 2921.13, 2921.41, 2923.31, and 2981.07 of the Revised Code in existence prior to the effective date of this section shall apply to a person upon whom a court imposed sentence prior to the effective date of this section for an offense specified or penalized under those sections. The amendments to sections 926.99, 1333.99, 1707.99, 1716.99, 2909.03, 2909.05, 2909.11, 2913.02, 2913.03, 2913.04, 2913.11, 2913.21, 2913.31, 2913.32, 2913.34, 2913.40, 2913.401, 2913.42, 2913.421, 2913.43, 2913.45, 2913.46, 2913.47, 2913.48, 2913.49, 2913.51, 2913.61, 2915.05, 2917.21, 2917.31, 2917.32, 2921.13, 2921.41, 2923.31, and 2981.07 of the Revised Code that are made in this act do not apply to a person who upon whom a court imposed sentence prior to the effective date of this section for an offense specified or penalized under those sections."

The effective date is set by section 6 of SB 2.

## § 2913.33 Making or using slugs.

(A) No person shall do any of the following:

(1) Insert or deposit a slug in a coin machine, with purpose to defraud;

(2) Make, possess, or dispose of a slug, with purpose of enabling another to defraud by inserting or depositing it in a coin machine.

(B) Whoever violates this section is guilty of making or using slugs, a misdemeanor of the second degree.

**HISTORY: 134 v H 511. Eff 1-1-74.**

## § 2913.34 Trademark counterfeiting.

(A) No person shall knowingly do any of the following:

(1) Attach, affix, or otherwise use a counterfeit mark in connection with the manufacture of goods or services, whether or not the goods or services are intended for sale or resale;

(2) Possess, sell, or offer for sale tools, machines, instruments, materials, articles, or other items of personal property with the knowledge that they are designed for the production or reproduction of counterfeit marks;

(3) Purchase or otherwise acquire goods, and keep or otherwise have the goods in the person's possession, with the knowledge that a counterfeit mark is attached to, affixed to, or otherwise used in connection with the goods and with the intent to sell or otherwise dispose of the goods;

(4) Sell, offer for sale, or otherwise dispose of goods with the knowledge that a counterfeit mark is attached to, affixed to, or otherwise used in connection with the goods;

(5) Sell, offer for sale, or otherwise provide services with the knowledge that a counterfeit mark is used in connection with that sale, offer for sale, or other provision of the services.

(B)(1) Whoever violates this section is guilty of trademark counterfeiting.

(2) Except as otherwise provided in this division, a violation of division (A)(1) of this section is a felony of the fifth degree. Except as otherwise provided in this division, if the cumulative sales price of the goods or services to which or in connection with which the counterfeit mark is attached, affixed, or otherwise used in the offense is five thousand dollars or more but less than one hundred thousand dollars or if the number of units of goods to which or in connection with which the counterfeit mark is attached, affixed, or otherwise used in the offense is more than one hundred units but less than one thousand units, a violation of division (A)(1) of this section is a felony of the fourth degree. If the cumulative sales price of the

goods or services to which or in connection with which the counterfeit mark is attached, affixed, or otherwise used in the offense is one hundred thousand dollars or more or if the number of units of goods to which or in connection with which the counterfeit mark is attached, affixed, or otherwise used in the offense is one thousand units or more, a violation of division (A)(1) of this section is a felony of the third degree.

(3) Except as otherwise provided in this division, a violation of division (A)(2) of this section is a misdemeanor of the first degree. If the circumstances of the violation indicate that the tools, machines, instruments, materials, articles, or other items of personal property involved in the violation were intended for use in the commission of a felony, a violation of division (A)(2) of this section is a felony of the fifth degree.

(4) Except as otherwise provided in this division, a violation of division (A)(3), (4), or (5) of this section is a misdemeanor of the first degree. Except as otherwise provided in this division, if the cumulative sales price of the goods or services to which or in connection with which the counterfeit mark is attached, affixed, or otherwise used in the offense is one thousand dollars or more but less than seven thousand five hundred dollars, a violation of division (A)(3), (4), or (5) of this section is a felony of the fifth degree. Except as otherwise provided in this division, if the cumulative sales price of the goods or services to which or in connection with which the counterfeit mark is attached, affixed, or otherwise used in the offense is seven thousand five hundred dollars or more but less than one hundred fifty thousand dollars or if the number of units of goods to which or in connection with which the counterfeit mark is attached, affixed, or otherwise used in the offense is more than one hundred units but less than one thousand units, a violation of division (A)(3), (4), or (5) of this section is a felony of the fourth degree. If the cumulative sales price of the goods or services to which or in connection with which the counterfeit mark is attached, affixed, or otherwise used in the offense is one hundred fifty thousand dollars or more or if the number of units of goods to which or in connection with which the counterfeit mark is attached, affixed, or otherwise used in the offense is one thousand units or more, a violation of division (A)(3), (4), or (5) of this section is a felony of the third degree.

(C) A defendant may assert as an affirmative defense to a charge of a violation of this section defenses, affirmative defenses, and limitations on remedies that would be available in a civil, criminal, or administrative action or proceeding under the "Lanham Act," 60 Stat. 427-443 (1946), 15 U.S.C. 1051-1127, as amended, "The Trademark Counterfeiting Act of 1984," 98 Stat. 2178, 18 U.S.C. 2320, as amended, Chapter 1329. or another section of the Revised Code, or common law.

(D)(1) Law enforcement officers may seize pursuant to Criminal Rule 41 or Chapter 2933. or 2981. of the Revised Code either of the following:

(a) Goods to which or in connection with which a person attached, affixed, otherwise used, or intended to attach, affix, or otherwise use a counterfeit mark in violation of this section;

(b) Tools, machines, instruments, materials, articles, vehicles, or other items of personal property that are possessed, sold, offered for sale, or used in a violation of this section or in an attempt to commit or complicity in the commission of a violation of this section.

(2) Notwithstanding any contrary provision of Chapter 2981. of the Revised Code, if a person is convicted of or pleads guilty to a violation of this section, an attempt to violate this section, or complicity in a violation of this section, the court involved shall declare that the goods described in division (D)(1)(a) of this section and the personal property described in division (D)(1)(b) of this section are contraband and are forfeited. Prior to the court's entry of judgment under Criminal Rule 32, the owner of a registered trademark or service mark that is the subject of the counterfeit mark may recommend a manner in which the forfeited goods and forfeited personal property should be disposed of. If that owner makes a timely recommendation of a manner of disposition, the court is not bound by the recommendation. If that owner makes a timely recommendation of a manner of disposition, the court may include in its entry of judgment an order that requires appropriate persons to dispose of the forfeited goods and forfeited personal property in the recommended manner. If that owner fails to make a timely recommendation of a manner of disposition or if that owner makes a timely recommendation of the manner of disposition but the court determines to not follow the recommendation, the court shall include in its entry of judgment an order that requires the law enforcement agency that employs the law enforcement officer who seized the forfeited goods or the forfeited personal property to destroy them or cause their destruction.

(E) This section does not affect the rights of an owner of a trademark or a service mark, or the enforcement in a civil action or in administrative proceedings of the rights of an owner of a trademark or a service mark, under the "Lanham Act," 60 Stat. 427-443 (1946), 15 U.S.C. 1051-1127, as amended, "The Trademark Counterfeiting Act of 1984," 92 Stat. 2178, 18 U.S.C. 2320, as amended, Chapter 1329. or another section of the Revised Code, or common law.

(F) As used in this section:

(1)(a) Except as provided in division (F)(1)(b) of this section, "counterfeit mark" means a spurious trademark or a spurious service mark that satisfies both of the following:

(i) It is identical with or substantially indistinguishable from a mark that is registered on the principal register in the United States patent and trademark office for the same goods or services as the goods or services to which or in connection with which the spurious trademark or spurious service mark is attached, affixed, or otherwise used or from a mark that is registered with the secretary of state pursuant to sections 1329.54 to 1329.67 of the Revised Code for the same goods or services as the goods or services to which or in connection with which the spurious trademark or spurious service mark is attached, affixed, or otherwise used, and the owner of the registration uses the registered mark, whether or not the offender knows that the mark is registered in a manner described in division (F)(1)(a)(i) of this section.

(ii) Its use is likely to cause confusion or mistake or to deceive other persons.

(b) "Counterfeit mark" does not include a mark or other designation that is attached to, affixed to, or otherwise used in connection with goods or services if the holder of the right to use the mark or other designation authorizes the manufacturer, producer, or vendor of those goods or services to attach, affix, or otherwise use the mark or other designation in connection with those goods or services at the time of their manufacture, production, or sale.

(2) "Cumulative sales price" means the product of the lowest single unit sales price charged or sought to be charged by an offender for goods to which or in connection with which a counterfeit mark is attached, affixed, or otherwise used or of the lowest single service transaction price charged or sought to be charged by an offender for services in connection with which a counterfeit mark is used, multiplied by the total number of those goods or services, whether or not units of goods are sold or are in an offender's possession, custody, or control.

(3) "Registered trademark or service mark" means a trademark or service mark that is registered in a manner described in division (F)(1) of this section.

(4) "Trademark" and "service mark" have the same meanings as in section 1329.54 of the Revised Code.

**HISTORY: 146 v S 277. Eff 3-31-97; 151 v H 241, § 1, eff. 7-1-07; 2011 HB 86, § 1, eff. Sept. 30, 2011.**

The provisions of § 4 of HB 86 read as follows:

"SECTION 4. The amendments to sections 926.99, 1333.99, 1707.99, 1716.99, 2909.03, 2909.05, 2909.11, 2913.02, 2913.03, 2913.04, 2913.11, 2913.21, 2913.31, 2913.32, 2913.34, 2913.40, 2913.401, 2913.42, 2913.421, 2913.43, 2913.45, 2913.46, 2913.47, 2913.48, 2913.49, 2913.51, 2913.61, 2915.05, 2917.21, 2917.31, 2917.32, 2921.13, 2921.41, 2923.31, and 2981.07, division (B) of section 2929.13, and division (A) of section 2929.14 of the Revised Code that are made in this act apply to a person who commits an offense specified or penalized under those sections on or after the effective date of this section and to a person to whom division (B) of section 1.58 of the Revised Code makes the amendments applicable.

"The provisions of sections 926.99, 1333.99, 1707.99, 1716.99, 2909.03, 2909.05, 2909.11, 2913.02, 2913.03, 2913.04, 2913.11, 2913.21, 2913.31, 2913.32, 2913.34, 2913.40, 2913.401, 2913.42, 2913.421, 2913.43, 2913.45, 2913.46, 2913.47, 2913.48, 2913.49, 2913.51, 2913.61, 2915.05, 2917.21, 2917.31, 2917.32, 2921.13, 2921.41, 2923.31, and 2981.07 of the Revised Code in existence prior to the effective date of this section shall apply to a person upon whom a court imposed sentence prior to the effective date of this section for an offense specified or penalized under those sections. The amendments to sections 926.99, 1333.99, 1707.99, 1716.99, 2909.03, 2909.05, 2909.11, 2913.02, 2913.03, 2913.04, 2913.11, 2913.21, 2913.31, 2913.32, 2913.34, 2913.40, 2913.401, 2913.42, 2913.421, 2913.43, 2913.45, 2913.46, 2913.47, 2913.48, 2913.49, 2913.51, 2913.61, 2915.05, 2917.21, 2917.31, 2917.32, 2921.13, 2921.41, 2923.31, and 2981.07 of the Revised Code that are made in this act do not apply to a person who upon whom a court imposed sentence prior to the effective date of this section for an offense specified or penalized under those sections."

See provisions of § 4 of 151 v H 241 following RC § 2901.01.

[FRAUDS]

## § 2913.40 Medicaid fraud.

(A) As used in this section:

(1) "Statement or representation" means any oral, written, electronic, electronic impulse, or magnetic communication that is used to identify an item of goods or a service for which reimbursement may be made under the medical assistance program or that states income and expense and is or may be used to determine a rate of reimbursement under the medical assistance program.

(2) "Medical assistance program" means the program established by the department of job and family services to provide medical assistance under section 5111.01 of the Revised Code and the medicaid program of Title XIX of the "Social Security Act," 49 Stat. 620 (1935), 42 U.S.C. 301, as amended.

(3) "Provider" means any person who has signed a provider agreement with the department of job and family services to provide goods or services pursuant to the medical assistance program or any person who has signed an agreement with a party to such a provider agreement under which the person agrees to provide goods or services that are reimbursable under the medical assistance program.

(4) "Provider agreement" means an oral or written agreement between the department of job and family services and a person in which the person agrees to provide goods or services under the medical assistance program.

(5) "Recipient" means any individual who receives goods or services from a provider under the medical assistance program.

(6) "Records" means any medical, professional, financial, or business records relating to the treatment or care of any recipient, to goods or services provided to any recipient, or to rates paid for goods or services provided to any recipient and any records that are required by the rules of the director of job and family services to be kept for the medical assistance program.

(B) No person shall knowingly make or cause to be made a false or misleading statement or representation for use in obtaining reimbursement from the medical assistance program.

(C) No person, with purpose to commit fraud or knowing that the person is facilitating a fraud, shall do either of the following:

(1) Contrary to the terms of the person's provider agreement, charge, solicit, accept, or receive for goods or services that the person provides under the medical assistance program any property, money, or other consideration in addition to the amount of reimbursement under the medical assistance program and the person's provider agreement for the goods or services and any cost-sharing expenses authorized by section 5111.0112 of the Revised Code or rules adopted pursuant to section 5111.01, 5111.011, or 5111.02 of the Revised Code.

(2) Solicit, offer, or receive any remuneration, other than any cost-sharing expenses authorized by section 5111.0112 of the Revised Code or rules adopted under section 5111.01, 5111.011, or 5111.02 of the Revised Code, in cash or in kind, including, but not limited to, a kickback or rebate, in connection with the furnishing of goods or services for which whole or partial reimbursement is or may be made under the medical assistance program.

(D) No person, having submitted a claim for or provided goods or services under the medical assistance program, shall do either of the following for a period of at least six years after a reimbursement pursuant to that claim, or a reimbursement for those goods or services, is received under the medical assistance program:

(1) Knowingly alter, falsify, destroy, conceal, or remove any records that are necessary to fully disclose the nature of all goods or services for which the claim was submitted, or for which reimbursement was received, by the person;

(2) Knowingly alter, falsify, destroy, conceal, or remove any records that are necessary to disclose fully all income and expenditures upon which rates of reimbursements were based for the person.

(E) Whoever violates this section is guilty of medicaid fraud. Except as otherwise provided in this division, medicaid fraud is a misdemeanor of the first degree. If the value of property, services, or funds obtained in violation of this section is one thousand dollars or more and is less than seven thousand five hundred dollars, medicaid fraud is a felony of the fifth degree. If the value of property, services, or funds obtained in violation of this section is seven thousand five hundred dollars or more and is less than one hundred fifty thousand dollars, medicaid fraud is a felony of the fourth degree. If the value of the property, services, or funds obtained in violation of this section is one hundred fifty thousand dollars or more, medicaid fraud is a felony of the third degree.

(F) Upon application of the governmental agency, office, or other entity that conducted the investigation and prosecution in a case under this section, the court shall order any person who is convicted of a violation of this section for receiving any reimbursement for furnishing goods or services under the medical assistance program to which the person is not entitled to pay to the applicant its cost of investigating and prosecuting the case. The costs of investigation and prosecution that a defendant is ordered to pay pursuant to this division shall be in addition to any other penalties for the receipt of that reimbursement that are provided in this section, section 5111.03 of the Revised Code, or any other provision of law.

(G) The provisions of this section are not intended to be exclusive remedies and do not preclude the use of any other criminal or civil remedy for any act that is in violation of this section.

**HISTORY: 141 v H 340 (Eff 5-20-86); 143 v H 672 (Eff 11-14-89); 146 v S 2 (Eff 7-1-96); 148 v H 471 (Eff 7-1-2000); 149 v S 261. Eff 6-5-2002; 151 v H 66, § 101.01, eff. 9-29-05; 152 v H 119, § 101.01, eff. 9-29-07; 2011 HB 86, § 1, eff. Sept. 30, 2011.**

The provisions of § 4 of HB 86 read as follows:

"SECTION 4. The amendments to sections 926.99, 1333.99, 1707.99, 1716.99, 2909.03, 2909.05, 2909.11, 2913.02, 2913.03, 2913.04, 2913.11, 2913.21, 2913.31, 2913.32, 2913.34, 2913.40, 2913.401, 2913.42, 2913.421, 2913.43, 2913.45, 2913.46, 2913.47, 2913.48, 2913.49, 2913.51, 2913.61, 2915.05, 2917.21, 2917.31, 2917.32, 2921.13, 2921.41, 2923.31, and 2981.07, division (B) of section 2929.13, and division (A) of section 2929.14 of the Revised Code that are made in this act apply to a person who commits an offense specified or penalized under those sections on or after the effective date of this section and to a person to whom division (B) of section 1.58 of the Revised Code makes the amendments applicable.

"The provisions of sections 926.99, 1333.99, 1707.99, 1716.99, 2909.03, 2909.05, 2909.11, 2913.02, 2913.03, 2913.04, 2913.11, 2913.21, 2913.31, 2913.32, 2913.34, 2913.40, 2913.401, 2913.42, 2913.421, 2913.43, 2913.45, 2913.46, 2913.47, 2913.48, 2913.49, 2913.51, 2913.61, 2915.05, 2917.21, 2917.31, 2917.32, 2921.13, 2921.41, 2923.31, and 2981.07 of the Revised Code in existence prior to the effective date of this section shall apply to a person upon whom a court imposed sentence prior to the effective date of this section for an offense specified or penalized under those sections. The amendments to sections 926.99, 1333.99, 1707.99, 1716.99, 2909.03, 2909.05, 2909.11, 2913.02, 2913.03, 2913.04, 2913.11, 2913.21, 2913.31, 2913.32, 2913.34, 2913.40, 2913.401, 2913.42, 2913.421, 2913.43, 2913.45, 2913.46, 2913.47, 2913.48, 2913.49, 2913.51, 2913.61, 2915.05, 2917.21, 2917.31, 2917.32, 2921.13, 2921.41, 2923.31, and 2981.07 of the Revised Code that are made in this act do not apply to a person who upon whom a court imposed sentence prior to the effective date of this section for an offense specified or penalized under those sections."

The effective date is set by § 812.03 of 152 v H 119.

The effective date is set by § 612.03 of 151 v H 66.

The effective date is set by section 37 of SB 261.

## § 2913.401 Medicaid eligibility fraud.

(A) As used in this section:

(1) "Medicaid benefits" means benefits under the medical assistance program established under Chapter 5111. of the Revised Code.

(2) "Property" means any real or personal property or other asset in which a person has any legal title or interest.

(B) No person shall knowingly do any of the following in an application for medicaid benefits or in a document that requires a disclosure of assets for the purpose of determining eligibility to receive medicaid benefits:

(1) Make or cause to be made a false or misleading statement;

(2) Conceal an interest in property;

(3)(a) Except as provided in division (B)(3)(b) of this section, fail to disclose a transfer of property that occurred during the period beginning thirty-six months before submission of the application or document and ending on the date the application or document was submitted;

(b) Fail to disclose a transfer of property that occurred during the period beginning sixty months before submission of the application or document and ending on the date the application or document was submitted and that was made to an irrevocable trust a portion of which is not distributable to the applicant for medicaid benefits or the recipient of medicaid benefits or to a revocable trust.

(C)(1) Whoever violates this section is guilty of medicaid eligibility fraud. Except as otherwise provided in this division, a violation of this section is a misdemeanor of the first degree. If the value of the medicaid benefits paid as a result of the violation is one thousand dollars or more and is less than seven thousand five hundred dollars, a violation of this section is a felony of the fifth degree. If the value of the medicaid benefits paid as a result of the violation is seven thousand five hundred dollars or more and is less than one hundred fifty thousand dollars, a violation of this section is a felony of the fourth degree. If the value of the medicaid benefits paid as a result of the violation is one hundred fifty thousand dollars or more, a violation of this section is a felony of the third degree.

(2) In addition to imposing a sentence under division (C)(1) of this section, the court shall order that a person who is guilty of medicaid eligibility fraud make restitution in the full amount of any medicaid benefits paid on behalf of an applicant for or recipient of medicaid benefits for which the applicant or recipient was not eligible, plus interest at the rate applicable to judgments on unreimbursed amounts from the date on which the benefits were paid to the date on which restitution is made.

(3) The remedies and penalties provided in this section are not exclusive and do not preclude the use of any other criminal or civil remedy for any act that is in violation of this section.

(D) This section does not apply to a person who fully disclosed in an application for medicaid benefits or in a document that requires a disclosure of assets for the purpose of determining eligibility to receive medicaid benefits all of the interests in property of the applicant for or recipient of medicaid benefits, all transfers of property by the applicant for or recipient of medicaid benefits, and the circumstances of all those transfers.

(E) Any amounts of medicaid benefits recovered as restitution under this section and any interest on those amounts shall be credited to the general revenue fund, and any applicable federal share shall be returned to the appropriate agency or department of the United States.

**HISTORY: 151 v H 66, § 101.01, eff. 9-29-05; 2011 HB 86, § 1, eff. Sept. 30, 2011.**

The provisions of § 4 of HB 86 read as follows:

"SECTION 4. The amendments to sections 926.99, 1333.99, 1707.99, 1716.99, 2909.03, 2909.05, 2909.11, 2913.02, 2913.03, 2913.04, 2913.11, 2913.21, 2913.31, 2913.32, 2913.34, 2913.40, 2913.401, 2913.42, 2913.421, 2913.43, 2913.45, 2913.46, 2913.47, 2913.48, 2913.49, 2913.51, 2913.61, 2915.05, 2917.21, 2917.31, 2917.32, 2921.13, 2921.41, 2923.31, and 2981.07, division (B) of section 2929.13, and division (A) of section 2929.14 of the Revised Code that are made in this act apply to a person who commits an offense specified or penalized under those sections on or after the effective date of this section and to a person to whom division (B) of section 1.58 of the Revised Code makes the amendments applicable.

"The provisions of sections 926.99, 1333.99, 1707.99, 1716.99, 2909.03, 2909.05, 2909.11, 2913.02, 2913.03, 2913.04, 2913.11, 2913.21, 2913.31, 2913.32, 2913.34, 2913.40, 2913.401, 2913.42, 2913.421, 2913.43, 2913.45, 2913.46, 2913.47, 2913.48, 2913.49, 2913.51, 2913.61, 2915.05, 2917.21, 2917.31, 2917.32, 2921.13, 2921.41, 2923.31, and 2981.07 of the Revised Code in existence prior to the effective date of this section shall apply to a person upon whom a court imposed sentence prior to the effective date of this section for an offense specified or penalized under those sections. The amendments to sections 926.99, 1333.99, 1707.99, 1716.99, 2909.03, 2909.05, 2909.11, 2913.02, 2913.03, 2913.04, 2913.11, 2913.21, 2913.31, 2913.32, 2913.34, 2913.40, 2913.401, 2913.42, 2913.421, 2913.43, 2913.45, 2913.46, 2913.47, 2913.48, 2913.49, 2913.51, 2913.61, 2915.05, 2917.21, 2917.31, 2917.32, 2921.13, 2921.41, 2923.31, and 2981.07 of the Revised Code that are made in this act do not apply to a person who upon whom a court imposed sentence prior to the effective date of this section for an offense specified or penalized under those sections."

The effective date is set by § 612.03 of 151 v H 66.

## § 2913.41 Defrauding a livery or hostelry.

In a prosecution of a person for a theft offense that alleges that the person, with purpose to defraud or knowing that the person was facilitating a fraud, hired or rented an aircraft, motor vehicle, motorcycle, motorboat, sailboat, camper, trailer, horse, buggy, or other property or equipment, kept or operated any of the same that has been hired or rented, or engaged accommodations at a hotel, motel, inn, campground, or other hostelry, it is prima-facie evidence of purpose to defraud if the person did any of the following:

(A) Used deception to induce the rental agency to furnish the person with the aircraft, motor vehicle, motorcycle, motorboat, sailboat, camper, trailer, horse, buggy, or other property or equipment, or used deception to induce the hostelry to furnish the person with accommodations;

(B) Hired or rented any aircraft, motor vehicle, motorcycle, motorboat, sailboat, camper, trailer, horse, buggy, or other property or equipment, or engaged accommodations, knowing the person was without sufficient means to pay the hire or rental;

(C) Absconded without paying the hire or rental;

(D) Knowingly failed to pay the hire or rental as required by the contract of hire or rental, without reasonable excuse for such failure;

(E) Knowingly failed to return hired or rented property as required by the contract of hire or rental, without reasonable excuse for the failure.

**HISTORY: 134 v H 511 (Eff 1-1-74); 146 v S 2 (Eff 7-1-96); 148 v H 263. Eff 4-10-2001.**

## § 2913.42 Tampering with records.

(A) No person, knowing the person has no privilege to do so, and with purpose to defraud or knowing that the person is facilitating a fraud, shall do any of the following:

(1) Falsify, destroy, remove, conceal, alter, deface, or mutilate any writing, computer software, data, or record;

(2) Utter any writing or record, knowing it to have been tampered with as provided in division (A)(1) of this section.

(B)(1) Whoever violates this section is guilty of tampering with records.

(2) Except as provided in division (B)(4) of this section, if the offense does not involve data or computer software, tampering with records is whichever of the following is applicable:

(a) If division (B)(2)(b) of this section does not apply, a misdemeanor of the first degree;

(b) If the writing or record is a will unrevoked at the time of the offense, a felony of the fifth degree.

(3) Except as provided in division (B)(4) of this section, if the offense involves a violation of division (A) of this section involving data or computer software, tampering with records is whichever of the following is applicable:

(a) Except as otherwise provided in division (B)(3)(b), (c), or (d) of this section, a misdemeanor of the first degree;

(b) If the value of the data or computer software involved in the offense or the loss to the victim is one thousand dollars or more and is less than seven thousand five hundred dollars, a felony of the fifth degree;

(c) If the value of the data or computer software involved in the offense or the loss to the victim is seven thousand five hundred dollars or more and is less than one hundred fifty thousand dollars, a felony of the fourth degree;

(d) If the value of the data or computer software involved in the offense or the loss to the victim is one hundred fifty thousand dollars or more or if the offense is committed for the purpose of devising or executing a scheme to defraud or to obtain property or services and the value of the property or services or the loss to the victim is seven thousand five hundred dollars or more, a felony of the third degree.

(4) If the writing, data, computer software, or record is kept by or belongs to a local, state, or federal governmental entity, a felony of the third degree.

**HISTORY: 134 v H 511 (Eff 1-1-74); 141 v H 49 (Eff 6-26-86); 141 v H 428 (Eff 12-23-86); 146 v S 2 (Eff 7-1-96); 147 v H 565. Eff 3-30-99; 2011 HB 86, § 1, eff. Sept. 30, 2011.**

The provisions of § 4 of HB 86 read as follows:

"SECTION 4. The amendments to sections 926.99, 1333.99, 1707.99, 1716.99, 2909.03, 2909.05, 2909.11, 2913.02, 2913.03, 2913.04, 2913.11, 2913.21, 2913.31, 2913.32, 2913.34, 2913.40, 2913.401, 2913.42, 2913.421, 2913.43, 2913.45, 2913.46, 2913.47, 2913.48, 2913.49, 2913.51, 2913.61, 2915.05, 2917.21, 2917.31, 2917.32, 2921.13, 2921.41, 2923.31, and 2981.07, division (B) of section 2929.13, and division (A) of section 2929.14 of the Revised Code that are made in this act apply to a person who commits an offense specified or penalized under those sections on or after the effective date of this section and to a person to whom division (B) of section 1.58 of the Revised Code makes the amendments applicable.

"The provisions of sections 926.99, 1333.99, 1707.99, 1716.99, 2909.03, 2909.05, 2909.11, 2913.02, 2913.03, 2913.04, 2913.11, 2913.21, 2913.31, 2913.32, 2913.34, 2913.40, 2913.401, 2913.42, 2913.421, 2913.43, 2913.45, 2913.46, 2913.47, 2913.48, 2913.49, 2913.51, 2913.61, 2915.05, 2917.21, 2917.31, 2917.32, 2921.13, 2921.41, 2923.31, and 2981.07 of the Revised Code in existence prior to the effective date of this section shall apply to a person upon whom a court imposed sentence prior to the effective date of this section for an offense specified or penalized under those sections. The amendments to sections 926.99, 1333.99, 1707.99,

1716.99, 2909.03, 2909.05, 2909.11, 2913.02, 2913.03, 2913.04, 2913.11, 2913.21, 2913.31, 2913.32, 2913.34, 2913.40, 2913.401, 2913.42, 2913.421, 2913.43, 2913.45, 2913.46, 2913.47, 2913.48, 2913.49, 2913.51, 2913.61, 2915.05, 2917.21, 2917.31, 2917.32, 2921.13, 2921.41, 2923.31, and 2981.07 of the Revised Code that are made in this act do not apply to a person who upon whom a court imposed sentence prior to the effective date of this section for an offense specified or penalized under those sections."

## § 2913.421 Illegally transmitting multiple commercial electronic mail messages; unauthorized access of computer.

(A) As used in this section:

(1) "Computer," "computer network," and "computer system" have the same meanings as in section 2913.01 of the Revised Code.

(2) "Commercial electronic mail message" means any electronic mail message the primary purpose of which is the commercial advertisement or promotion of a commercial product or service, including content on an internet web site operated for a commercial purpose, but does not include a transactional or relationship message. The inclusion of a reference to a commercial entity or a link to the web site of a commercial entity does not, by itself, cause that message to be treated as a commercial electronic mail message for the purpose of this section, if the contents or circumstances of the message indicate a primary purpose other than commercial advertisement or promotion of a commercial product or service.

(3) "Domain name" means any alphanumeric designation that is registered with or assigned by any domain name registrar, domain name registry, or other domain name registration authority as part of an electronic address on the internet.

(4) "Electronic mail," "originating address," and "receiving address" have the same meanings as in section 2307.64 of the Revised Code.

(5) "Electronic mail message" means each electronic mail addressed to a discrete addressee.

(6) "Electronic mail service provider" means any person, including an internet service provider, that is an intermediary in sending and receiving electronic mail and that provides to the public electronic mail accounts or online user accounts from which electronic mail may be sent.

(7) "Header information" means the source, destination, and routing information attached to an electronic mail message, including the originating domain name, the originating address, and technical information that authenticates the sender of an electronic mail message for computer network security or computer network management purposes.

(8) "Initiate the transmission" or "initiated" means to originate or transmit a commercial electronic mail message or to procure the origination or transmission of that message, regardless of whether the message reaches its intended recipients, but does not include actions that constitute routine conveyance of such message.

(9) "Internet" has the same meaning as in section 341.42 of the Revised Code.

(10) "Internet protocol address" means the string of numbers by which locations on the internet are identified by routers or other computers connected to the internet.

(11) "Materially falsify" means to alter or conceal in a manner that would impair the ability of a recipient of an electronic mail message, an electronic mail service provider processing an electronic mail message on behalf of a recipient, a person alleging a violation of this section, or a law enforcement agency to identify, locate, or respond to the person that initiated the electronic mail message or to investigate an alleged violation of this section.

(12) "Multiple" means more than ten commercial electronic mail messages during a twenty-four-hour period, more than one hundred commercial electronic mail messages during a thirty-day period, or more than one thousand commercial electronic mail messages during a one-year period.

(13) "Recipient" means a person who receives a commercial electronic mail message at any one of the following receiving addresses:

(a) A receiving address furnished by an electronic mail service provider that bills for furnishing and maintaining that receiving address to a mailing address within this state;

(b) A receiving address ordinarily accessed from a computer located within this state or by a person domiciled within this state;

(c) Any other receiving address with respect to which this section can be imposed consistent with the United States Constitution.

(14) "Routine conveyance" means the transmission, routing, relaying, handling, or storing, through an automated technical process, of an electronic mail message for which another person has identified the recipients or provided the recipient addresses.

(15) "Transactional or relationship message" means an electronic mail message the primary purpose of which is to do any of the following:

(a) Facilitate, complete, or confirm a commercial transaction that the recipient has previously agreed to enter into with the sender;

(b) Provide warranty information, product recall information, or safety or security information with respect to a commercial product or service used or purchased by the recipient;

(c) Provide notification concerning a change in the terms or features of; a change in the recipient's standing or status with respect to; or, at regular periodic intervals, account balance information or other type of account statement with respect to, a subscription, membership, account, loan, or comparable ongoing commercial relationship involving the ongoing purchase or use by the recipient of products or services offered by the sender;

(d) Provide information directly related to an employment relationship or related benefit plan in which the recipient is currently involved, participating, or enrolled;

(e) Deliver goods or services, including product updates or upgrades, that the recipient is entitled to receive under the terms of a transaction that the recipient has previously agreed to enter into with the sender.

(B) No person, with regard to commercial electronic mail messages sent from or to a computer in this state, shall do any of the following:

(1) Knowingly use a computer to relay or retransmit multiple commercial electronic mail messages, with the intent to deceive or mislead recipients or any electronic mail service provider, as to the origin of those messages;

(2) Knowingly and materially falsify header information in multiple commercial electronic mail messages and purposely initiate the transmission of those messages;

(3) Knowingly register, using information that materially falsifies the identity of the actual registrant, for five or more electronic mail accounts or online user accounts or

two or more domain names and purposely initiate the transmission of multiple commercial electronic mail messages from one, or any combination, of those accounts or domain names;

(4) Knowingly falsely represent the right to use five or more internet protocol addresses, and purposely initiate the transmission of multiple commercial electronic mail messages from those addresses.

(C)(1) Whoever violates division (B) of this section is guilty of illegally transmitting multiple commercial electronic mail messages. Except as otherwise provided in division (C)(2) or (E) of this section, illegally transmitting multiple commercial electronic mail messages is a felony of the fifth degree.

(2) Illegally transmitting multiple commercial electronic mail messages is a felony of the fourth degree if any of the following apply:

(a) Regarding a violation of division (B)(3) of this section, the offender, using information that materially falsifies the identity of the actual registrant, knowingly registers for twenty or more electronic mail accounts or online user accounts or ten or more domain names, and purposely initiates, or conspires to initiate, the transmission of multiple commercial electronic mail messages from the accounts or domain names.

(b) Regarding any violation of division (B) of this section, the volume of commercial electronic mail messages the offender transmitted in committing the violation exceeds two hundred and fifty during any twenty-four-hour period, two thousand five hundred during any thirty-day period, or twenty-five thousand during any one-year period.

(c) Regarding any violation of division (B) of this section, during any one-year period the aggregate loss to the victim or victims of the violation is one thousand dollars or more, or during any one-year period the aggregate value of the property or services obtained by any offender as a result of the violation is one thousand dollars or more.

(d) Regarding any violation of division (B) of this section, the offender committed the violation with three or more other persons with respect to whom the offender was the organizer or leader of the activity that resulted in the violation.

(e) Regarding any violation of division (B) of this section, the offender knowingly assisted in the violation through the provision or selection of electronic mail addresses to which the commercial electronic mail message was transmitted, if that offender knew that the electronic mail addresses of the recipients were obtained using an automated means from an internet web site or proprietary online service operated by another person, and that web site or online service included, at the time the electronic mail addresses were obtained, a notice stating that the operator of that web site or online service will not transfer addresses maintained by that web site or online service to any other party for the purposes of initiating the transmission of, or enabling others to initiate the transmission of, electronic mail messages.

(f) Regarding any violation of division (B) of this section, the offender knowingly assisted in the violation through the provision or selection of electronic mail addresses of the recipients obtained using an automated means that generates possible electronic mail addresses by combining names, letters, or numbers into numerous permutations.

(D)(1) No person, with regard to commercial electronic mail messages sent from or to a computer in this state, shall knowingly access a computer without authorization and purposely initiate the transmission of multiple commercial electronic mail messages from or through the computer.

(2) Except as otherwise provided in division (E) of this section, whoever violates division (D)(1) of this section is guilty of unauthorized access of a computer, a felony of the fourth degree.

(E) Illegally transmitting multiple commercial electronic mail messages and unauthorized access of a computer in violation of this section are felonies of the third degree if the offender previously has been convicted of a violation of this section, or a violation of a law of another state or the United States regarding the transmission of electronic mail messages or unauthorized access to a computer, or if the offender committed the violation of this section in the furtherance of a felony.

(F)(1) The attorney general or an electronic mail service provider that is injured by a violation of this section may bring a civil action in an appropriate court of common pleas of this state seeking relief from any person whose conduct violated this section. The civil action may be commenced at any time within one year of the date after the act that is the basis of the civil action.

(2) In a civil action brought by the attorney general pursuant to division (F)(1) of this section for a violation of this section, the court may award temporary, preliminary, or permanent injunctive relief. The court also may impose a civil penalty against the offender, as the court considers just, in an amount that is the lesser of: (a) twenty-five thousand dollars for each day a violation occurs, or (b) not less than two dollars but not more than eight dollars for each commercial electronic mail message initiated in violation of this section.

(3) In a civil action brought by an electronic mail service provider pursuant to division (F)(1) of this section for a violation of this section, the court may award temporary, preliminary, or permanent injunctive relief, and also may award damages in an amount equal to the greater of the following:

(a) The sum of the actual damages incurred by the electronic mail service provider as a result of a violation of this section, plus any receipts of the offender that are attributable to a violation of this section and that were not taken into account in computing actual damages;

(b) Statutory damages, as the court considers just, in an amount that is the lesser of: (i) twenty-five thousand dollars for each day a violation occurs, or (ii) not less than two dollars but not more than eight dollars for each commercial electronic mail message initiated in violation of this section.

(4) In assessing damages awarded under division (F)(3) of this section, the court may consider whether the offender has established and implemented, with due care, commercially reasonable practices and procedures designed to effectively prevent the violation, or the violation occurred despite commercially reasonable efforts to maintain the practices and procedures established.

(G) Any equipment, software, or other technology of a person who violates this section that is used or intended to be used in the commission of a violation of this section, and any real or personal property that constitutes or is traceable to the gross proceeds obtained from the commission of a violation of this section, is contraband and is subject to seizure and forfeiture pursuant to Chapter 2981. of the Revised Code.

(H) The attorney general may bring a civil action, pursuant to the "CAN-SPAM Act of 2003," Pub. L. No. 108-187, 117 Stat. 2699, 15 U.S.C. 7701 et seq., on behalf of the residents of the state in a district court of the United States that has jurisdiction for a violation of the CAN-SPAM Act of 2003, but the attorney general shall not bring a civil action under both this division and division (F) of this section. If a federal court dismisses a civil action brought under this division for reasons other than upon the merits, a civil action may be brought under division (F) of this section in the appropriate court of common pleas of this state.

(I) Nothing in this section shall be construed:

(1) To require an electronic mail service provider to block, transmit, route, relay, handle, or store certain types of electronic mail messages;

(2) To prevent or limit, in any way, an electronic mail service provider from adopting a policy regarding electronic mail, including a policy of declining to transmit certain types of electronic mail messages, or from enforcing such policy through technical means, through contract, or pursuant to any remedy available under any other federal, state, or local criminal or civil law;

(3) To render lawful any policy adopted under division (I)(2) of this section that is unlawful under any other law.

**HISTORY: 150 v H 383, § 1, eff. 5-6-05; 151 v H 241, § 1, eff. 7-1-07; 2011 HB 86, § 1, eff. Sept. 30, 2011.**

The provisions of § 4 of HB 86 read as follows:

"SECTION 4. The amendments to sections 926.99, 1333.99, 1707.99, 1716.99, 2909.03, 2909.05, 2909.11, 2913.02, 2913.03, 2913.04, 2913.11, 2913.21, 2913.31, 2913.32, 2913.34, 2913.40, 2913.401, 2913.42, 2913.421, 2913.43, 2913.45, 2913.46, 2913.47, 2913.48, 2913.49, 2913.51, 2913.61, 2915.05, 2917.21, 2917.31, 2917.32, 2921.13, 2921.41, 2923.31, and 2981.07, division (B) of section 2929.13, and division (A) of section 2929.14 of the Revised Code that are made in this act apply to a person who commits an offense specified or penalized under those sections on or after the effective date of this section and to a person to whom division (B) of section 1.58 of the Revised Code makes the amendments applicable.

"The provisions of sections 926.99, 1333.99, 1707.99, 1716.99, 2909.03, 2909.05, 2909.11, 2913.02, 2913.03, 2913.04, 2913.11, 2913.21, 2913.31, 2913.32, 2913.34, 2913.40, 2913.401, 2913.42, 2913.421, 2913.43, 2913.45, 2913.46, 2913.47, 2913.48, 2913.49, 2913.51, 2913.61, 2915.05, 2917.21, 2917.31, 2917.32, 2921.13, 2921.41, 2923.31, and 2981.07 of the Revised Code in existence prior to the effective date of this section shall apply to a person upon whom a court imposed sentence prior to the effective date of this section for an offense specified or penalized under those sections. The amendments to sections 926.99, 1333.99, 1707.99, 1716.99, 2909.03, 2909.05, 2909.11, 2913.02, 2913.03, 2913.04, 2913.11, 2913.21, 2913.31, 2913.32, 2913.34, 2913.40, 2913.401, 2913.42, 2913.421, 2913.43, 2913.45, 2913.46, 2913.47, 2913.48, 2913.49, 2913.51, 2913.61, 2915.05, 2917.21, 2917.31, 2917.32, 2921.13, 2921.41, 2923.31, and 2981.07 of the Revised Code that are made in this act do not apply to a person who upon whom a court imposed sentence prior to the effective date of this section for an offense specified or penalized under those sections."

See provisions of § 4 of 151 v H 241 following RC § 2901.01.

## § 2913.43 Securing writings by deception.

(A) No person, by deception, shall cause another to execute any writing that disposes of or encumbers property, or by which a pecuniary obligation is incurred.

(B)(1) Whoever violates this section is guilty of securing writings by deception.

(2) Except as otherwise provided in this division or division (B)(3) of this section, securing writings by deception is a misdemeanor of the first degree. If the value of the property or the obligation involved is one thousand dollars or more and less than seven thousand five hundred dollars, securing writings by deception is a felony of the fifth degree. If the value of the property or the obligation involved is seven thousand five hundred dollars or more and is less than one hundred fifty thousand dollars, securing writings by deception is a felony of the fourth degree. If the value of the property or the obligation involved is one hundred fifty thousand dollars or more, securing writings by deception is a felony of the third degree.

(3) If the victim of the offense is an elderly person or disabled adult, division (B)(3) of this section applies. Except as otherwise provided in division (B)(3) of this section, securing writings by deception is a felony of the fifth degree. If the value of the property or obligation involved is one thousand dollars or more and is less than seven thousand five hundred dollars, securing writings by deception is a felony of the fourth degree. If the value of the property or obligation involved is seven thousand five hundred dollars or more and is less than thirty-seven thousand five hundred dollars, securing writings by deception is a felony of the third degree. If the value of the property or obligation involved is thirty-seven thousand five hundred dollars or more, securing writings by deception is a felony of the second degree.

**HISTORY: 134 v H 511 (Eff 1-1-74); 139 v S 199 (Eff 1-5-83); 139 v H 269 (Eff 1-5-83); 141 v H 49 (Eff 6-26-86); 146 v S 2 (Eff 7-1-96); 148 v H 2. Eff 11-10-99; 2011 HB 86, § 1, eff. Sept. 30, 2011.**

The provisions of § 4 of HB 86 read as follows:

"SECTION 4. The amendments to sections 926.99, 1333.99, 1707.99, 1716.99, 2909.03, 2909.05, 2909.11, 2913.02, 2913.03, 2913.04, 2913.11, 2913.21, 2913.31, 2913.32, 2913.34, 2913.40, 2913.401, 2913.42, 2913.421, 2913.43, 2913.45, 2913.46, 2913.47, 2913.48, 2913.49, 2913.51, 2913.61, 2915.05, 2917.21, 2917.31, 2917.32, 2921.13, 2921.41, 2923.31, and 2981.07, division (B) of section 2929.13, and division (A) of section 2929.14 of the Revised Code that are made in this act apply to a person who commits an offense specified or penalized under those sections on or after the effective date of this section and to a person to whom division (B) of section 1.58 of the Revised Code makes the amendments applicable.

"The provisions of sections 926.99, 1333.99, 1707.99, 1716.99, 2909.03, 2909.05, 2909.11, 2913.02, 2913.03, 2913.04, 2913.11, 2913.21, 2913.31, 2913.32, 2913.34, 2913.40, 2913.401, 2913.42, 2913.421, 2913.43, 2913.45, 2913.46, 2913.47, 2913.48, 2913.49, 2913.51, 2913.61, 2915.05, 2917.21, 2917.31, 2917.32, 2921.13, 2921.41, 2923.31, and 2981.07 of the Revised Code in existence prior to the effective date of this section shall apply to a person upon whom a court imposed sentence prior to the effective date of this section for an offense specified or penalized under those sections. The amendments to sections 926.99, 1333.99, 1707.99, 1716.99, 2909.03, 2909.05, 2909.11, 2913.02, 2913.03, 2913.04, 2913.11, 2913.21, 2913.31, 2913.32, 2913.34, 2913.40, 2913.401, 2913.42, 2913.421, 2913.43, 2913.45, 2913.46, 2913.47, 2913.48, 2913.49, 2913.51, 2913.61, 2915.05, 2917.21, 2917.31, 2917.32, 2921.13, 2921.41, 2923.31, and 2981.07 of the Revised Code that are made in this act do not apply to a person who upon whom a court imposed sentence prior to the effective date of this section for an offense specified or penalized under those sections."

**Analogous to former RC § 2911.01 (RS § 7076; 70 v 39; 73 v 20; 74 v 41; GC § 13104; 124 v 466; Bureau of Code Revision, 10-1-53; 129 v 344), repealed 134 v H 511, § 2, eff 1-1-74.**

## § 2913.44 Personating an officer.

(A) No person, with purpose to defraud or knowing that he is facilitating a fraud, or with purpose to induce another to purchase property or services, shall personate a law enforcement officer, or an inspector, investigator, or agent of any governmental agency.

(B) Whoever violates this section is guilty of personating an officer, a misdemeanor of the first degree.

**HISTORY: 134 v H 511. Eff 1-1-74.**

## § 2913.441 Law enforcement emblem display.

(A) No person who is not entitled to do so shall knowingly display on a motor vehicle the emblem of a law enforcement agency or an organization of law enforcement officers.

(B) Whoever violates this section is guilty of the unlawful display of the emblem of a law enforcement agency or an organization of law enforcement officers, a minor misdemeanor.

**HISTORY: 136 v H 1363. Eff 1-11-77.**

## § 2913.45 Defrauding creditors.

(A) No person, with purpose to defraud one or more of the person's creditors, shall do any of the following:

(1) Remove, conceal, destroy, encumber, convey, or otherwise deal with any of the person's property;

(2) Misrepresent or refuse to disclose to a fiduciary appointed to administer or manage the person's affairs or estate, the existence, amount, or location of any of the person's property, or any other information regarding such property that the person is legally required to furnish to the fiduciary.

(B) Whoever violates this section is guilty of defrauding creditors. Except as otherwise provided in this division, defrauding creditors is a misdemeanor of the first degree. If the value of the property involved is one thousand dollars or more and is less than seven thousand five hundred dollars, defrauding creditors is a felony of the fifth degree. If the value of the property involved is seven thousand five hundred dollars or more and is less than one hundred fifty thousand dollars, defrauding creditors is a felony of the fourth degree. If the value of the property involved is one hundred fifty thousand dollars or more, defrauding creditors is a felony of the third degree.

**HISTORY: 134 v H 511 (Eff 1-1-74); 146 v S 2. Eff 7-1-96; 2011 HB 86, § 1, eff. Sept. 30, 2011.**

The provisions of § 4 of HB 86 read as follows:

"SECTION 4. The amendments to sections 926.99, 1333.99, 1707.99, 1716.99, 2909.03, 2909.05, 2909.11, 2913.02, 2913.03, 2913.04, 2913.11, 2913.21, 2913.31, 2913.32, 2913.34, 2913.40, 2913.401, 2913.42, 2913.421, 2913.43, 2913.45, 2913.46, 2913.47, 2913.48, 2913.49, 2913.51, 2913.61, 2915.05, 2917.21, 2917.31, 2917.32, 2921.13, 2921.41, 2923.31, and 2981.07, division (B) of section 2929.13, and division (A) of section 2929.14 of the Revised Code that are made in this act apply to a person who commits an offense specified or penalized under those sections on or after the effective date of this section and to a person to whom division (B) of section 1.58 of the Revised Code makes the amendments applicable.

"The provisions of sections 926.99, 1333.99, 1707.99, 1716.99, 2909.03, 2909.05, 2909.11, 2913.02, 2913.03, 2913.04, 2913.11, 2913.21, 2913.31, 2913.32, 2913.34, 2913.40, 2913.401, 2913.42, 2913.421, 2913.43, 2913.45, 2913.46, 2913.47, 2913.48, 2913.49, 2913.51, 2913.61, 2915.05, 2917.21, 2917.31, 2917.32, 2921.13, 2921.41, 2923.31, and 2981.07 of the Revised Code in existence prior to the effective date of this section shall apply to a person upon whom a court imposed sentence prior to the effective date of this section for an offense specified or penalized under those sections. The amendments to sections 926.99, 1333.99, 1707.99, 1716.99, 2909.03, 2909.05, 2909.11, 2913.02, 2913.03, 2913.04, 2913.11, 2913.21, 2913.31, 2913.32, 2913.34, 2913.40, 2913.401, 2913.42, 2913.421, 2913.43, 2913.45, 2913.46, 2913.47, 2913.48, 2913.49, 2913.51, 2913.61, 2915.05, 2917.21, 2917.31, 2917.32, 2921.13, 2921.41, 2923.31, and 2981.07 of the Revised Code that are made in this act do not apply to a person who upon whom a court imposed sentence prior to the effective date of this section for an offense specified or penalized under those sections."

The effective date is set by section 6 of SB 2.

## § 2913.46 Illegal use of supplemental nutrition or WIC program benefits.

(A)(1) As used in this section:

(a) "Electronically transferred benefit" means the transfer of supplemental nutrition assistance program benefits or WIC program benefits through the use of an access device.

(b) "WIC program benefits" includes money, coupons, delivery verification receipts, other documents, food, or other property received directly or indirectly pursuant to section 17 of the "Child Nutrition Act of 1966," 80 Stat. 885, 42 U.S.C.A. 1786, as amended.

(c) "Access device" means any card, plate, code, account number, or other means of access that can be used, alone or in conjunction with another access device, to obtain payments, allotments, benefits, money, goods, or other things of value or that can be used to initiate a transfer of funds pursuant to section 5101.33 of the Revised Code and the Food and Nutrition Act of 2008 (7 U.S.C. 2011 et seq.), or any supplemental food program administered by any department of this state or any county or local agency pursuant to section 17 of the "Child Nutrition Act of 1966," 80 Stat. 885, 42 U.S.C.A. 1786, as amended. An "access device" may include any electronic debit card or other means authorized by section 5101.33 of the Revised Code.

(d) "Aggregate value of supplemental nutrition assistance program benefits, WIC program benefits, and electronically transferred benefits involved in the violation" means the total face value of any supplemental nutrition assistance program benefits, plus the total face value of WIC program coupons or delivery verification receipts, plus the total value of other WIC program benefits, plus the total value of any electronically transferred benefit or other access device, involved in the violation.

(e) "Total value of any electronically transferred benefit or other access device" means the total value of the payments, allotments, benefits, money, goods, or other things of value that may be obtained, or the total value of funds that may be transferred, by use of any electronically transferred benefit or other access device at the time of violation.

(2) If supplemental nutrition assistance program benefits, WIC program benefits, or electronically transferred benefits or other access devices of various values are used, transferred, bought, acquired, altered, purchased, possessed, presented for redemption, or transported in violation of this section over a period of twelve months, the course of conduct may be charged as one offense and the values of supplemental nutrition assistance program benefits, WIC program benefits, or any electronically transferred benefits or other access devices may be aggregated in determining the degree of the offense.

(B) No individual shall knowingly possess, buy, sell, use, alter, accept, or transfer supplemental nutrition assistance program benefits, WIC program benefits, or any electronically transferred benefit in any manner not authorized by the Food and Nutrition Act of 2008 (7 U.S.C. 2011 et seq.) or section 17 of the "Child Nutrition Act of 1966," 80 Stat. 885, 42 U.S.C. 1786, as amended.

(C) No organization, as defined in division (D) of section 2901.23 of the Revised Code, shall do either of the following:

(1) Knowingly allow an employee or agent to sell, transfer, or trade items or services, the purchase of which is prohibited by the Food and Nutrition Act of 2008 (7 U.S.C. 2011 et seq. or section 17 of the "Child Nutrition Act of 1966," 80 Stat. 885, 42 U.S.C. 1786, as amended, in exchange for supplemental nutrition assistance program benefits, WIC program benefits, or any electronically transferred benefit;

(2) Negligently allow an employee or agent to sell, transfer, or exchange supplemental nutrition assistance program benefits, WIC program benefits, or any electronically transferred benefit for anything of value.

(D) Whoever violates this section is guilty of illegal use of supplemental nutrition assistance program benefits or WIC program benefits. Except as otherwise provided in this division, illegal use of supplemental nutrition assistance program benefits or WIC program benefits is a felony of the fifth degree. If the aggregate value of the supplemental nutrition assistance program benefits, WIC program benefits, and electronically transferred benefits involved in the violation is one thousand dollars or more and is less than seven thousand five hundred dollars, illegal use of supplemental nutrition assistance program benefits or WIC program benefits is a felony of the fourth degree. If the aggregate value of the supplemental nutrition assistance program benefits, WIC program benefits, and electronically transferred benefits involved in the violation is seven thousand five hundred dollars or more and is less than one hundred fifty thousand dollars, illegal use of supplemental nutrition assistance program benefits or WIC program benefits is a felony of the third degree. If the aggregate value of the supplemental nutrition assistance program benefits, WIC program benefits, and electronically transferred benefits involved in the violation is one hundred fifty thousand dollars or more, illegal use of supplemental nutrition assistance program benefits or WIC program benefits is a felony of the second degree.

**HISTORY: 140 v H 291 (Eff 7-1-83); 146 v S 162 (Eff 10-29-95); 146 v H 239 (Eff 11-24-95); 146 v S 107 (Eff 5-8-96); 146 v S 2 (Eff 7-1-96); 146 v S 269 (Eff 7-1-96); 146 v S 293. Eff 9-26-96; 153 v H 1, § 101.01, eff. 10-16-09; 2011 HB 86, § 1, eff. Sept. 30, 2011.**

The provisions of § 4 of HB 86 read as follows:

"SECTION 4. The amendments to sections 926.99, 1333.99, 1707.99, 1716.99, 2909.03, 2909.05, 2909.11, 2913.02, 2913.03, 2913.04, 2913.11, 2913.21, 2913.31, 2913.32, 2913.34, 2913.40, 2913.401, 2913.42, 2913.421, 2913.43, 2913.45, 2913.46, 2913.47, 2913.48, 2913.49, 2913.51, 2913.61, 2915.05, 2917.21, 2917.31, 2917.32, 2921.13, 2921.41, 2923.31, and 2981.07, division (B) of section 2929.13, and division (A) of section 2929.14 of the Revised Code that are made in this act apply to a person who commits an offense specified or penalized under those sections on or after the effective date of this section and to a person to whom division (B) of section 1.58 of the Revised Code makes the amendments applicable.

"The provisions of sections 926.99, 1333.99, 1707.99, 1716.99, 2909.03, 2909.05, 2909.11, 2913.02, 2913.03, 2913.04, 2913.11, 2913.21, 2913.31, 2913.32, 2913.34, 2913.40, 2913.401, 2913.42, 2913.421, 2913.43, 2913.45, 2913.46, 2913.47, 2913.48, 2913.49, 2913.51, 2913.61, 2915.05, 2917.21, 2917.31, 2917.32, 2921.13, 2921.41, 2923.31, and 2981.07 of the Revised Code in existence prior to the effective date of this section shall apply to a person upon whom a court imposed sentence prior to the effective date of this section for an offense specified or penalized under those sections. The amendments to sections 926.99, 1333.99, 1707.99, 1716.99, 2909.03, 2909.05, 2909.11, 2913.02, 2913.03, 2913.04, 2913.11, 2913.21, 2913.31, 2913.32, 2913.34, 2913.40, 2913.401, 2913.42, 2913.421, 2913.43, 2913.45, 2913.46, 2913.47, 2913.48, 2913.49, 2913.51, 2913.61, 2915.05, 2917.21, 2917.31, 2917.32, 2921.13, 2921.41, 2923.31, and 2981.07 of the Revised Code that are made in this act do not apply to a person who upon whom a court imposed sentence prior to the effective date of this section for an offense specified or penalized under those sections."

The effective date is set by § 812.10 of 153 v H 1.

The provisions of 815.10 of 153 v H 1 read as follows:

SECTION 815.10. The General Assembly, applying the principle stated in division (B) of section 1.52 of the Revised Code that amendments are to be harmonized if reasonably capable of simultaneous operation, finds that the following sections, presented in this act as composites of the sections as amended by the acts indicated, are the resulting versions of the sections in effect prior to the effective date of the sections as presented in this act:

* * *

Section 2913.46 of the Revised Code as amended by Am. Sub. S.B. 107, Am. Sub. S.B. 269, and Am. Sub. S.B. 293, all of the 121st General Assembly.

* * *

## § 2913.47 Insurance fraud.

(A) As used in this section:

(1) "Data" has the same meaning as in section 2913.01 of the Revised Code and additionally includes any other representation of information, knowledge, facts, concepts, or instructions that are being or have been prepared in a formalized manner.

(2) "Deceptive" means that a statement, in whole or in part, would cause another to be deceived because it contains a misleading representation, withholds information, prevents the acquisition of information, or by any other conduct, act, or omission creates, confirms, or perpetuates a false impression, including, but not limited to, a false impression as to law, value, state of mind, or other objective or subjective fact.

(3) "Insurer" means any person that is authorized to engage in the business of insurance in this state under Title XXXIX of the Revised Code, the Ohio fair plan underwriting association created under section 3929.43 of the Revised Code, any health insuring corporation, and any legal entity that is self-insured and provides benefits to its employees or members.

(4) "Policy" means a policy, certificate, contract, or plan that is issued by an insurer.

(5) "Statement" includes, but is not limited to, any notice, letter, or memorandum; proof of loss; bill of lading; receipt for payment; invoice, account, or other financial statement; estimate of property damage; bill for services; diagnosis or prognosis; prescription; hospital, medical, or dental chart or other record; x-ray, photograph, videotape, or movie film; test result; other evidence of loss, injury, or expense; computer-generated document; and data in any form.

(B) No person, with purpose to defraud or knowing that the person is facilitating a fraud, shall do either of the following:

(1) Present to, or cause to be presented to, an insurer any written or oral statement that is part of, or in support of, an application for insurance, a claim for payment pursuant to a policy, or a claim for any other benefit pursuant to a policy, knowing that the statement, or any part of the statement, is false or deceptive;

(2) Assist, aid, abet, solicit, procure, or conspire with another to prepare or make any written or oral statement that is intended to be presented to an insurer as part of, or in support of, an application for insurance, a claim for payment pursuant to a policy, or a claim for any other benefit pursuant to a policy, knowing that the statement, or any part of the statement, is false or deceptive.

(C) Whoever violates this section is guilty of insurance fraud. Except as otherwise provided in this division, insurance fraud is a misdemeanor of the first degree. If the amount of the claim that is false or deceptive is one thousand dollars or more and is less than seven thousand five hundred dollars, insurance fraud is a felony of the fifth degree. If the amount of the claim that is false or deceptive is seven thousand five hundred dollars or more and is less than one hundred fifty thousand dollars, insurance fraud is a felony of the fourth degree. If the amount of the claim that is false or deceptive is one hundred fifty thousand dollars or more, insurance fraud is a felony of the third degree.

(D) This section shall not be construed to abrogate, waive, or modify division (A) of section 2317.02 of the Revised Code.

**HISTORY: 143 v H 347 (Eff 7-18-90); 146 v S 2 (Eff 7-1-96); 146 v S 269 (Eff 7-1-96); 147 v S 67. Eff 6-4-97; 2011 HB 86, § 1, eff. Sept. 30, 2011.**

The provisions of § 4 of HB 86 read as follows:

"SECTION 4. The amendments to sections 926.99, 1333.99, 1707.99, 1716.99, 2909.03, 2909.05, 2909.11, 2913.02, 2913.03, 2913.04, 2913.11, 2913.21, 2913.31, 2913.32, 2913.34, 2913.40, 2913.401, 2913.42, 2913.421, 2913.43, 2913.45, 2913.46, 2913.47, 2913.48, 2913.49, 2913.51, 2913.61, 2915.05, 2917.21, 2917.31, 2917.32, 2921.13, 2921.41, 2923.31, and 2981.07, division (B) of section 2929.13, and division (A) of section 2929.14 of the Revised Code that are made in this act apply to a person who commits an offense specified or penalized under those sections on or after the effective date of this section and to a person to whom division (B) of section 1.58 of the Revised Code makes the amendments applicable.

"The provisions of sections 926.99, 1333.99, 1707.99, 1716.99, 2909.03, 2909.05, 2909.11, 2913.02, 2913.03, 2913.04, 2913.11, 2913.21, 2913.31, 2913.32, 2913.34, 2913.40, 2913.401, 2913.42, 2913.421, 2913.43, 2913.45, 2913.46, 2913.47, 2913.48, 2913.49, 2913.51, 2913.61, 2915.05, 2917.21, 2917.31, 2917.32, 2921.13, 2921.41, 2923.31, and 2981.07 of the Revised Code in existence prior to the effective date of this section shall apply to a person upon whom a court imposed sentence prior to the effective date of this section for an offense specified or penalized under those sections. The amendments to sections 926.99, 1333.99, 1707.99, 1716.99, 2909.03, 2909.05, 2909.11, 2913.02, 2913.03, 2913.04, 2913.11, 2913.21, 2913.31, 2913.32, 2913.34, 2913.40, 2913.401, 2913.42, 2913.421, 2913.43, 2913.45, 2913.46, 2913.47, 2913.48, 2913.49, 2913.51, 2913.61, 2915.05, 2917.21, 2917.31, 2917.32, 2921.13, 2921.41, 2923.31, and 2981.07 of the Revised Code that are made in this act do not apply to a person who upon whom a court imposed sentence prior to the effective date of this section for an offense specified or penalized under those sections."

**Not analogous to former RC § 2913.47 (140 v H 97), repealed 140 v H 632, § 2, eff 3-28-85.**

## § 2913.48 Workers' compensation fraud.

(A) No person, with purpose to defraud or knowing that the person is facilitating a fraud, shall do any of the following:

(1) Receive workers' compensation benefits to which the person is not entitled;

(2) Make or present or cause to be made or presented a false or misleading statement with the purpose to secure payment for goods or services rendered under Chapter 4121., 4123., 4127., or 4131. of the Revised Code or to secure workers' compensation benefits;

(3) Alter, falsify, destroy, conceal, or remove any record or document that is necessary to fully establish the validity of any claim filed with, or necessary to establish the nature and validity of all goods and services for which reimbursement or payment was received or is requested from, the bureau of workers' compensation, or a self-insuring employer under Chapter 4121., 4123., 4127., or 4131. of the Revised Code;

(4) Enter into an agreement or conspiracy to defraud the bureau or a self-insuring employer by making or presenting or causing to be made or presented a false claim for workers' compensation benefits;

(5) Make or present or cause to be made or presented a false statement concerning manual codes, classification of employees, payroll, paid compensation, or number of personnel, when information of that nature is necessary to determine the actual workers' compensation premium or assessment owed to the bureau by an employer;

(6) Alter, forge, or create a workers' compensation certificate to falsely show current or correct workers' compensation coverage;

(7) Fail to secure or maintain workers' compensation coverage as required by Chapter 4123. of the Revised Code with the intent to defraud the bureau of workers' compensation.

(B) Whoever violates this section is guilty of workers' compensation fraud. Except as otherwise provided in this division, a violation of this section is a misdemeanor of the first degree. If the value of premiums and assessments unpaid pursuant to actions described in division (A)(5), (6), or (7) of this section, or of goods, services, property, or money stolen is one thousand dollars or more and is less than seven thousand five hundred dollars, a violation of this section is a felony of the fifth degree. If the value of premiums and assessments unpaid pursuant to actions described in division (A)(5), (6), or (7) of this section, or of goods, services, property, or money stolen is seven thousand five hundred dollars or more and is less than one hundred fifty thousand dollars, a violation of this section is a felony of the fourth degree. If the value of premiums and assessments unpaid pursuant to actions described in division (A)(5), (6), or (7) of this section, or of goods, services, property, or money stolen is one hundred fifty thousand dollars or more, a violation of this section is a felony of the third degree.

(C) Upon application of the governmental body that conducted the investigation and prosecution of a violation of this section, the court shall order the person who is convicted of the violation to pay the governmental body its costs of investigating and prosecuting the case. These costs are in addition to any other costs or penalty provided in the Revised Code or any other section of law.

(D) The remedies and penalties provided in this section are not exclusive remedies and penalties and do not preclude the use of any other criminal or civil remedy or penalty for any act that is in violation of this section.

(E) As used in this section:

(1) "False" means wholly or partially untrue or deceptive.

(2) "Goods" includes, but is not limited to, medical supplies, appliances, rehabilitative equipment, and any other apparatus or furnishing provided or used in the care, treatment, or rehabilitation of a claimant for workers' compensation benefits.

(3) "Services" includes, but is not limited to, any service provided by any health care provider to a claimant for workers' compensation benefits and any and all services provided by the bureau as part of workers' compensation insurance coverage.

(4) "Claim" means any attempt to cause the bureau, an independent third party with whom the administrator or an employer contracts under section 4121.44 of the Revised Code, or a self-insuring employer to make payment or reimbursement for workers' compensation benefits.

(5) "Employment" means participating in any trade, occupation, business, service, or profession for substantial gainful remuneration.

(6) "Employer," "employee," and "self-insuring employer" have the same meanings as in section 4123.01 of the Revised Code.

(7) "Remuneration" includes, but is not limited to, wages, commissions, rebates, and any other reward or consideration.

(8) "Statement" includes, but is not limited to, any oral, written, electronic, electronic impulse, or magnetic communication notice, letter, memorandum, receipt for payment, invoice, account, financial statement, or bill for services; a diagnosis, prognosis, prescription, hospital, medical, or dental chart or other record; and a computer generated document.

(9) "Records" means any medical, professional, financial, or business record relating to the treatment or care of any person, to goods or services provided to any person, or to rates paid for goods or services provided to any person, or any record that the administrator of workers' compensation requires pursuant to rule.

(10) "Workers' compensation benefits" means any compensation or benefits payable under Chapter 4121., 4123., 4127., or 4131. of the Revised Code.

**HISTORY: 145 v H 107 (Eff 10-20-93); 146 v S 2 (Eff 7-1-96); 147 v S 45 †; 151 v S 7, § 1, eff. 6-30-06; 2011 HB 86, § 1, eff. Sept. 30, 2011.**

† The amendments made by SB 45 (147 v —) were rejected by the 11-4-97 referendum vote on Issue 2.

The provisions of § 4 of HB 86 read as follows:

"SECTION 4. The amendments to sections 926.99, 1333.99, 1707.99, 1716.99, 2909.03, 2909.05, 2909.11, 2913.02, 2913.03, 2913.04, 2913.11, 2913.21, 2913.31, 2913.32, 2913.34, 2913.40, 2913.401, 2913.42, 2913.421, 2913.43, 2913.45, 2913.46, 2913.47, 2913.48, 2913.49, 2913.51, 2913.61, 2915.05, 2917.21, 2917.31, 2917.32, 2921.13, 2921.41, 2923.31, and 2981.07, division (B) of section 2929.13, and division (A) of section 2929.14 of the Revised Code that are made in this act apply to a person who commits an offense specified or penalized under those sections on or after the effective date of this section and to a person to whom division (B) of section 1.58 of the Revised Code makes the amendments applicable.

"The provisions of sections 926.99, 1333.99, 1707.99, 1716.99, 2909.03, 2909.05, 2909.11, 2913.02, 2913.03, 2913.04, 2913.11, 2913.21, 2913.31, 2913.32, 2913.34, 2913.40, 2913.401, 2913.42, 2913.421, 2913.43, 2913.45, 2913.46, 2913.47, 2913.48, 2913.49, 2913.51, 2913.61, 2915.05, 2917.21, 2917.31, 2917.32, 2921.13, 2921.41, 2923.31, and 2981.07 of the Revised Code in existence prior to the effective date of this section shall apply to a person upon whom a court imposed sentence prior to the effective date of this section for an offense specified or penalized under those sections. The amendments to sections 926.99, 1333.99, 1707.99, 1716.99, 2909.03, 2909.05, 2909.11, 2913.02, 2913.03, 2913.04, 2913.11, 2913.21, 2913.31, 2913.32, 2913.34, 2913.40, 2913.401, 2913.42, 2913.421, 2913.43, 2913.45, 2913.46, 2913.47, 2913.48, 2913.49, 2913.51, 2913.61, 2915.05, 2917.21, 2917.31, 2917.32, 2921.13, 2921.41, 2923.31, and 2981.07 of the Revised Code that are made in this act do not apply to a person who upon whom a court imposed sentence prior to the effective date of this section for an offense specified or penalized under those sections."

The provisions of § 3 of 151 v S 7 read as follows:

SECTION 3. This act applies to all claims pursuant to Chapters 4121., 4123., 4127., and 4131. of the Revised Code arising on and after the effective date of this act, except that division (H) of section 4123.512 as amended by this act also applies to claims that are pending on the effective date of this act.

**Not analogous to former RC § 2913.48 (140 v H 97), repealed 140 v H 632, § 2, eff 3-28-85.**

## § 2913.49 Identity fraud.

(A) As used in this section, "personal identifying information" includes, but is not limited to, the following: the name, address, telephone number, driver's license, driver's license number, commercial driver's license, commercial driver's license number, state identification card, state identification card number, social security card, social security number, birth certificate, place of employment, employee identification number, mother's maiden name, demand deposit account number, savings account number, money market account number, mutual fund account number, other financial account number, personal identification number, password, or credit card number of a living or dead individual.

(B) No person, without the express or implied consent of the other person, shall use, obtain, or possess any personal identifying information of another person with intent to do either of the following:

(1) Hold the person out to be the other person;

(2) Represent the other person's personal identifying information as the person's own personal identifying information.

(C) No person shall create, obtain, possess, or use the personal identifying information of any person with the intent to aid or abet another person in violating division (B) of this section.

(D) No person, with intent to defraud, shall permit another person to use the person's own personal identifying information.

(E) No person who is permitted to use another person's personal identifying information as described in division (D) of this section shall use, obtain, or possess the other person's personal identifying information with intent to defraud any person by doing any act identified in division (B)(1) or (2) of this section.

(F)(1) It is an affirmative defense to a charge under division (B) of this section that the person using the personal identifying information is acting in accordance with a legally recognized guardianship or conservatorship or as a trustee or fiduciary.

(2) It is an affirmative defense to a charge under division (B), (C), (D), or (E) of this section that either of the following applies:

(a) The person or entity using, obtaining, possessing, or creating the personal identifying information or permitting it to be used is a law enforcement agency, authorized fraud personnel, or a representative of or attorney for a law enforcement agency or authorized fraud personnel and is using, obtaining, possessing, or creating the personal identifying information or permitting it to be used, with prior consent given as specified in this division, in a bona fide investigation, an information security evaluation, a pretext calling evaluation, or a similar matter. The prior consent required under this division shall be given by the person whose personal identifying information is being used, obtained, possessed, or created or is being permitted to be used or, if the person whose personal identifying information is being used, obtained, possessed, or created or is being permitted to be used is deceased, by that deceased person's executor, or a member of that deceased person's family, or that deceased person's attorney. The prior consent required under this division may be given orally or in writing by the person whose personal identifying information is being used, obtained, possessed, or created or is being permitted to be used or that person's executor, or family member, or attorney.

(b) The personal identifying information was obtained, possessed, used, created, or permitted to be used for a lawful purpose, provided that division (F)(2)(b) of this section does not apply if the person or entity using, obtaining, possessing, or creating the personal identifying information or permitting it to be used is a law enforcement agency, authorized fraud personnel, or a representative of or attorney for a law enforcement agency or authorized fraud personnel that is using, obtaining, possessing, or creating the personal identifying information or permitting it to be used in an investigation, an information security evaluation, a pretext calling evaluation, or similar matter.

(G) It is not a defense to a charge under this section that the person whose personal identifying information was obtained, possessed, used, created, or permitted to be used was deceased at the time of the offense.

(H)(1) If an offender commits a violation of division (B), (D), or (E) of this section and the violation occurs as part of a course of conduct involving other violations of division (B), (D), or (E) of this section or violations of, attempts to violate, conspiracies to violate, or complicity in violations of division (C) of this section or section 2913.02, 2913.04, 2913.11, 2913.21, 2913.31, 2913.42, 2913.43, or 2921.13 of the Revised Code, the court, in determining the degree of the offense pursuant to division (I) of this section, may aggregate all credit, property, or services obtained or sought to be obtained by the offender and all debts or other legal obligations avoided or sought to be avoided by the offender in the violations involved in that course of conduct. The course of conduct may involve one victim or more than one victim.

(2) If an offender commits a violation of division (C) of this section and the violation occurs as part of a course of conduct involving other violations of division (C) of this section or violations of, attempts to violate, conspiracies to violate, or complicity in violations of division (B), (D), or (E) of this section or section 2913.02, 2913.04, 2913.11, 2913.21, 2913.31, 2913.42, 2913.43, or 2921.13 of the Revised Code, the court, in determining the degree of the offense pursuant to division (I) of this section, may aggregate all credit, property, or services obtained or sought to be obtained by the person aided or abetted and all debts or other legal obligations avoided or sought to be avoided by the person aided or abetted in the violations involved in that course of conduct. The course of conduct may involve one victim or more than one victim.

(I)(1) Whoever violates this section is guilty of identity fraud.

(2) Except as otherwise provided in this division or division (I)(3) of this section, identity fraud is a felony of the fifth degree. If the value of the credit, property, services, debt, or other legal obligation involved in the violation or course of conduct is one thousand dollars or more and is less than seven thousand five hundred dollars, except as otherwise provided in division (I)(3) of this section, identity fraud is a felony of the fourth degree. If the value of the credit, property, services, debt, or other legal obligation involved in the violation or course of conduct is seven thousand five hundred dollars or more and is less than one hundred fifty thousand dollars, except as otherwise provided in division (I)(3) of this section, identity fraud is a felony of the third degree. If the value of the credit, property, services, debt, or other legal obligation involved in the violation or course of conduct is one hundred fifty thousand dollars or more, except as otherwise provided in division (I)(3) of this section, identity fraud is a felony of the second degree.

(3) If the victim of the offense is an elderly person or disabled adult, a violation of this section is identity fraud against an elderly person or disabled adult. Except as otherwise provided in this division, identity fraud against an elderly person or disabled adult is a felony of the fifth degree. If the value of the credit, property, services, debt, or other legal obligation involved in the violation or course of conduct is one thousand dollars or more and is less than seven thousand five hundred dollars, identity fraud against an elderly person or disabled adult is a felony of the third degree. If the value of the credit, property, services, debt, or other legal obligation involved in the violation or course of conduct is seven thousand five hundred dollars or more and is less than one hundred fifty thousand dollars, identity fraud against an elderly person or disabled adult is a felony of the second degree. If the value of the credit, property, services, debt, or other legal obligation involved in the violation or course of conduct is one hundred fifty thousand dollars or more, identity fraud against an elderly person or disabled adult is a felony of the first degree.

**HISTORY: 148 v S 7 (Eff 8-25-99); 149 v H 309. Eff 9-27-2002; 151 v H 48, § 1, eff. 9-16-05; 2011 HB 86, § 1, eff. Sept. 30, 2011.**

The provisions of § 4 of HB 86 read as follows:

"SECTION 4. The amendments to sections 926.99, 1333.99, 1707.99, 1716.99, 2909.03, 2909.05, 2909.11, 2913.02, 2913.03, 2913.04, 2913.11, 2913.21, 2913.31, 2913.32, 2913.34, 2913.40, 2913.401, 2913.42, 2913.421, 2913.43, 2913.45, 2913.46, 2913.47, 2913.48, 2913.49, 2913.51, 2913.61, 2915.05, 2917.21, 2917.31, 2917.32, 2921.13, 2921.41, 2923.31, and 2981.07, division (B) of section 2929.13, and division (A) of section 2929.14 of the Revised Code that are made in this act apply to a person who commits an offense specified or penalized under those sections on or after the effective date of this section and to a person to whom division (B) of section 1.58 of the Revised Code makes the amendments applicable.

"The provisions of sections 926.99, 1333.99, 1707.99, 1716.99, 2909.03, 2909.05, 2909.11, 2913.02, 2913.03, 2913.04, 2913.11, 2913.21, 2913.31, 2913.32, 2913.34, 2913.40, 2913.401, 2913.42, 2913.421, 2913.43, 2913.45, 2913.46, 2913.47, 2913.48, 2913.49, 2913.51, 2913.61, 2915.05, 2917.21, 2917.31, 2917.32, 2921.13, 2921.41, 2923.31, and 2981.07 of the Revised Code in existence prior to the effective date of this section shall apply to a person upon whom a court imposed sentence prior to the effective date of this section for an offense specified or penalized under those sections. The amendments to sections 926.99, 1333.99, 1707.99, 1716.99, 2909.03, 2909.05, 2909.11, 2913.02, 2913.03, 2913.04, 2913.11, 2913.21, 2913.31, 2913.32, 2913.34, 2913.40, 2913.401, 2913.42, 2913.421, 2913.43, 2913.45, 2913.46, 2913.47, 2913.48, 2913.49, 2913.51, 2913.61, 2915.05, 2917.21, 2917.31, 2917.32, 2921.13, 2921.41, 2923.31, and 2981.07 of the Revised Code that are made in this act do not apply to a person who upon whom a court imposed sentence prior to the effective date of this section for an offense specified or penalized under those sections."

## [RECEIVING]

### § 2913.51 Receiving stolen property.

(A) No person shall receive, retain, or dispose of property of another knowing or having reasonable cause to believe that the property has been obtained through commission of a theft offense.

(B) It is not a defense to a charge of receiving stolen property in violation of this section that the property was obtained by means other than through the commission of a theft offense if the property was explicitly represented to the accused person as being obtained through the commission of a theft offense.

(C) Whoever violates this section is guilty of receiving stolen property. Except as otherwise provided in this division, receiving stolen property is a misdemeanor of the first degree. If the value of the property involved is one thousand dollars or more and is less than seven thousand five hundred dollars, if the property involved is any of the property listed in section 2913.71 of the Revised Code, receiving stolen property is a felony of the fifth degree. If the property involved is a motor vehicle, as defined in section 4501.01 of the Revised Code, if the property involved is a dangerous drug, as defined in section 4729.01 of the Revised Code, if the value of the property involved is seven thousand five hundred dollars or more and is less than one hundred fifty thousand dollars, or if the property involved is a firearm or dangerous ordnance, as defined in section 2923.11 of the Revised Code, receiving stolen property is a felony of the fourth degree. If the value of the property involved is one hundred fifty thousand dollars or more, receiving stolen property is a felony of the third degree.

**HISTORY: 134 v H 511 (Eff 1-1-74); 138 v S 191 (Eff 6-20-80); 139 v S 199 (Eff 1-5-83); 139 v H 269 (Eff 1-5-83); 140 v S 210 (Eff 7-1-83); 141 v H 49 (Eff 6-26-86); 146 v H 4 (Eff 11-9-95); 146 v S 2 (Eff 7-1-96); 147 v S 66 (Eff 7-22-98); 148 v S 64. Eff 10-29-99; 2011 HB 86, § 1, eff. Sept. 30, 2011.**

The provisions of § 4 of HB 86 read as follows:

"SECTION 4. The amendments to sections 926.99, 1333.99, 1707.99, 1716.99, 2909.03, 2909.05, 2909.11, 2913.02, 2913.03, 2913.04, 2913.11, 2913.21, 2913.31, 2913.32, 2913.34, 2913.40, 2913.401, 2913.42, 2913.421, 2913.43, 2913.45, 2913.46, 2913.47, 2913.48, 2913.49, 2913.51, 2913.61, 2915.05, 2917.21, 2917.31, 2917.32, 2921.13, 2921.41, 2923.31, and 2981.07, division (B) of section 2929.13, and division (A) of section 2929.14 of the Revised Code that are made in this act apply to a person who commits an offense specified or penalized under those sections on or after the effective date of this section and to a person to whom division (B) of section 1.58 of the Revised Code makes the amendments applicable.

"The provisions of sections 926.99, 1333.99, 1707.99, 1716.99, 2909.03, 2909.05, 2909.11, 2913.02, 2913.03, 2913.04, 2913.11, 2913.21, 2913.31, 2913.32, 2913.34, 2913.40, 2913.401, 2913.42, 2913.421, 2913.43, 2913.45, 2913.46, 2913.47, 2913.48, 2913.49, 2913.51, 2913.61, 2915.05, 2917.21, 2917.31, 2917.32, 2921.13, 2921.41, 2923.31, and 2981.07 of the Revised Code in existence prior to the effective date of this section shall apply to a person upon whom a court imposed sentence prior to the effective date of this section for an offense specified or penalized under those sections. The amendments to sections 926.99, 1333.99, 1707.99, 1716.99, 2909.03, 2909.05, 2909.11, 2913.02, 2913.03, 2913.04, 2913.11, 2913.21, 2913.31, 2913.32, 2913.34, 2913.40, 2913.401, 2913.42, 2913.421, 2913.43, 2913.45, 2913.46, 2913.47, 2913.48, 2913.49, 2913.51, 2913.61, 2915.05, 2917.21, 2917.31, 2917.32, 2921.13, 2921.41, 2923.31, and 2981.07 of the Revised Code that are made in this act do not apply to a person who upon whom a court imposed sentence prior to the effective date of this section for an offense specified or penalized under those sections."

[VALUE]

## § 2913.61 Value of stolen property.

(A) When a person is charged with a theft offense, or with a violation of division (A)(1) of section 1716.14 of the Revised Code involving a victim who is an elderly person or disabled adult that involves property or services valued at one thousand dollars or more, property or services valued at one thousand dollars or more and less than seven thousand five hundred dollars, property or services valued at one thousand five hundred dollars or more and less than seven thousand five hundred dollars, property or services valued at seven thousand five hundred dollars or more and less than thirty-seven thousand five hundred dollars, property or services valued at seven thousand five hundred dollars or more and less than one hundred fifty thousand dollars, property or services valued at thirty-seven thousand five hundred dollars or more and less than one hundred fifty thousand dollars, property or services valued at thirty-seven thousand five hundred dollars or more, property or services valued at one hundred fifty thousand dollars or more, property or services valued at one hundred fifty thousand dollars or more and less than seven hundred fifty thousand dollars, property or services valued at seven hundred fifty thousand dollars or more and less than one million five hundred thousand dollars, or property or services valued at one million five hundred thousand dollars or more, the jury or court trying the accused shall determine the value of the property or services as of the time of the offense and, if a guilty verdict is returned, shall return the finding of value as part of the verdict. In any case in which the jury or court determines that the value of the property or services at the time of the offense was one thousand dollars or more, it is unnecessary to find and return the exact value, and it is sufficient if the finding and return is to the effect that the value of the property or services involved was one thousand dollars or more and less than seven thousand five hundred dollars, was one thousand dollars or more and less than seven thousand five hundred dollars, was seven thousand five hundred dollars or more and less than thirty-seven thousand five hundred dollars, was seven thousand five hundred dollars or more and less than thirty-seven thousand five hundred dollars, was seven thousand five hundred dollars or more and less than one hundred fifty thousand dollars, was thirty-seven thousand five hundred dollars or more and less than one hundred fifty thousand dollars, was thirty-seven thousand five hundred dollars or more and less than one hundred fifty thousand dollars, was one hundred fifty thousand dollars or more, was one hundred fifty thousand dollars or more and less than seven hundred fifty thousand dollars, was seven hundred fifty thousand dollars or more and less than one million five hundred thousand dollars, or was one million five hundred thousand dollars or more, whichever is relevant regarding the offense.

(B) If more than one item of property or services is involved in a theft offense or in a violation of division (A)(1) of section 1716.14 of the Revised Code involving a victim who is an elderly person or disabled adult, the value of the property or services involved for the purpose of determining the value as required by division (A) of this section is the aggregate value of all property or services involved in the offense.

(C)(1) When a series of offenses under section 2913.02 of the Revised Code, or a series of violations of, attempts to commit a violation of, conspiracies to violate, or complicity in violations of division (A)(1) of section 1716.14, section 2913.02, 2913.03, or 2913.04, division (B)(1) or (2) of section 2913.21, or section 2913.31 or 2913.43 of the Revised Code involving a victim who is an elderly person or disabled adult, is committed by the offender in the offender's same employment, capacity, or relationship to another, all of those offenses shall be tried as a single offense. The value of the property or services involved in the series of offenses for the purpose of determining the value as required by division (A) of this section is the aggregate value of all property and services involved in all offenses in the series.

(2) If an offender commits a series of offenses under section 2913.02 of the Revised Code that involves a common course of conduct to defraud multiple victims, all of the offenses may be tried as a single offense. If an offender is being tried for the commission of a series of violations of, attempts to commit a violation of, conspiracies to violate, or complicity in violations of division (A)(1) of section 1716.14, section 2913.02, 2913.03, or 2913.04, division (B)(1) or (2) of section 2913.21, or section 2913.31 or 2913.43 of the Revised Code, whether committed against one victim or more than one victim, involving a victim who is an elderly person or disabled adult, pursuant to a scheme or course of conduct, all of those offenses may be tried as a single offense. If the offenses are tried as a single offense, the value of the property or services involved for the purpose of determining the value as required by division (A) of this section is the aggregate value of all property and services involved in all of the offenses in the course of conduct.

(3) When a series of two or more offenses under section 2913.40, 2913.48, or 2921.41 of the Revised Code is committed by the offender in the offender's same employment, capacity, or relationship to another, all of those offenses may be tried as a single offense. If the offenses are tried as a single offense, the value of the property or services involved for the purpose of determining the value as required by division (A) of this section is the aggregate value of all property and services involved in all of the offenses in the series of two or more offenses.

(4) In prosecuting a single offense under division (C)(1), (2), or (3) of this section, it is not necessary to separately allege and prove each offense in the series. Rather, it is sufficient to allege and prove that the offender, within a given span of time, committed one or more theft offenses or violations of section 2913.40, 2913.48, or 2921.41 of the Revised Code in the offender's same employment, capacity, or relationship to another as described in division (C)(1) or (3) of this section, or committed one or more theft offenses that involve a common course of conduct to defraud multiple victims or a scheme or course of conduct as described in division (C)(2) of this section. While it is not necessary to separately allege and prove each offense in the series in order to prosecute a single offense under division (C)(1), (2), or (3) of this section, it remains necessary in prosecuting them as a single offense to prove the aggregate value of the property or services in order to meet the requisite statutory offense level sought by the prosecution.

(D) The following criteria shall be used in determining the value of property or services involved in a theft offense:

(1) The value of an heirloom, memento, collector's item, antique, museum piece, manuscript, document, record, or other thing that has intrinsic worth to its owner and that either is irreplaceable or is replaceable only on the expenditure of substantial time, effort, or money, is the amount that would compensate the owner for its loss.

(2) The value of personal effects and household goods, and of materials, supplies, equipment, and fixtures used in the profession, business, trade, occupation, or avocation of its owner, which property is not covered under division (D)(1) of this section and which retains substantial utility for its purpose regardless of its age or condition, is the cost of replacing the property with new property of like kind and quality.

(3) The value of any real or personal property that is not covered under division (D)(1) or (2) of this section, and the value of services, is the fair market value of the property or services. As used in this section, "fair market value" is the money consideration that a buyer would give and a seller would accept for property or services, assuming that the buyer is willing to buy and the seller is willing to sell, that both are fully informed as to all facts material to the transaction, and that neither is under any compulsion to act.

(E) Without limitation on the evidence that may be used to establish the value of property or services involved in a theft offense:

(1) When the property involved is personal property held for sale at wholesale or retail, the price at which the property was held for sale is prima-facie evidence of its value.

(2) When the property involved is a security or commodity traded on an exchange, the closing price or, if there is no closing price, the asked price, given in the latest market quotation prior to the offense is prima-facie evidence of the value of the security or commodity.

(3) When the property involved is livestock, poultry, or raw agricultural products for which a local market price is available, the latest local market price prior to the offense is prima-facie evidence of the value of the livestock, poultry, or products.

(4) When the property involved is a negotiable instrument, the face value is prima-facie evidence of the value of the instrument.

(5) When the property involved is a warehouse receipt, bill of lading, pawn ticket, claim check, or other instrument entitling the holder or bearer to receive property, the face value or, if there is no face value, the value of the property covered by the instrument less any payment necessary to receive the property is prima-facie evidence of the value of the instrument.

(6) When the property involved is a ticket of admission, ticket for transportation, coupon, token, or other instrument entitling the holder or bearer to receive property or services, the face value or, if there is no face value, the value of the property or services that may be received by the instrument is prima-facie evidence of the value of the instrument.

(7) When the services involved are gas, electricity, water, telephone, transportation, shipping, or other services for which the rate is established by law, the duly established rate is prima-facie evidence of the value of the services.

(8) When the services involved are services for which the rate is not established by law, and the offender has been notified prior to the offense of the rate for the services, either in writing, orally, or by posting in a manner reasonably calculated to come to the attention of potential offenders, the rate contained in the notice is prima-facie evidence of the value of the services.

**HISTORY: 134 v H 511 (Eff 1-1-74); 139 v S 199 (Eff 1-5-83); 139 v H 269 (Eff 1-5-83); 146 v S 2 (Eff 7-1-96); 147 v H 565 (Eff 3-30-99); 148 v H 2 (Eff 11-10-99); 148 v S 2, § 3 (Eff 11-22-99); 148 v H 364. Eff 9-14-2000; 2011 HB 86, § 1, eff. Sept. 30, 2011.**

The provisions of § 4 of HB 86 read as follows:

"SECTION 4. The amendments to sections 926.99, 1333.99,

1707.99, 1716.99, 2909.03, 2909.05, 2909.11, 2913.02, 2913.03, 2913.04, 2913.11, 2913.21, 2913.31, 2913.32, 2913.34, 2913.40, 2913.401, 2913.42, 2913.421, 2913.43, 2913.45, 2913.46, 2913.47, 2913.48, 2913.49, 2913.51, 2913.61, 2915.05, 2917.21, 2917.31, 2917.32, 2921.13, 2921.41, 2923.31, and 2981.07, division (B) of section 2929.13, and division (A) of section 2929.14 of the Revised Code that are made in this act apply to a person who commits an offense specified or penalized under those sections on or after the effective date of this section and to a person to whom division (B) of section 1.58 of the Revised Code makes the amendments applicable.

"The provisions of sections 926.99, 1333.99, 1707.99, 1716.99, 2909.03, 2909.05, 2909.11, 2913.02, 2913.03, 2913.04, 2913.11, 2913.21, 2913.31, 2913.32, 2913.34, 2913.40, 2913.401, 2913.42, 2913.421, 2913.43, 2913.45, 2913.46, 2913.47, 2913.48, 2913.49, 2913.51, 2913.61, 2915.05, 2917.21, 2917.31, 2917.32, 2921.13, 2921.41, 2923.31, and 2981.07 of the Revised Code in existence prior to the effective date of this section shall apply to a person upon whom a court imposed sentence prior to the effective date of this section for an offense specified or penalized under those sections. The amendments to sections 926.99, 1333.99, 1707.99, 1716.99, 2909.03, 2909.05, 2909.11, 2913.02, 2913.03, 2913.04, 2913.11, 2913.21, 2913.31, 2913.32, 2913.34, 2913.40, 2913.401, 2913.42, 2913.421, 2913.43, 2913.45, 2913.46, 2913.47, 2913.48, 2913.49, 2913.51, 2913.61, 2915.05, 2917.21, 2917.31, 2917.32, 2921.13, 2921.41, 2923.31, and 2981.07 of the Revised Code that are made in this act do not apply to a person who upon whom a court imposed sentence prior to the effective date of this section for an offense specified or penalized under those sections."

## [AGGRAVATING CIRCUMSTANCES]

### § 2913.71 Degree of offense when certain property involved.

Regardless of the value of the property involved and regardless of whether the offender previously has been convicted of a theft offense, a violation of section 2913.02 or 2913.51 of the Revised Code is a felony of the fifth degree if the property involved is any of the following:

(A) A credit card;

(B) A printed form for a check or other negotiable instrument, that on its face identifies the drawer or maker for whose use it is designed or identifies the account on which it is to be drawn, and that has not been executed by the drawer or maker or on which the amount is blank;

(C) A motor vehicle identification license plate as prescribed by section 4503.22 of the Revised Code, a temporary license placard or windshield sticker as prescribed by section 4503.182 [4503.18.2] of the Revised Code, or any comparable license plate, placard, or sticker as prescribed by the applicable law of another state or the United States;†

(D) A blank form for a certificate of title or a manufacturer's or importer's certificate to a motor vehicle, as prescribed by section 4505.07 of the Revised Code;

(E) A blank form for any license listed in section 4507.01 of the Revised Code.

**HISTORY: 134 v H 511 (Eff 1-1-74); 137 v H 1 (Eff 8-26-77); 138 v S 191 (Eff 6-20-80); 140 v H 632 (Eff 3-28-85); 146 v H 4 (Eff 11-9-95); 146 v S 2. Eff 7-1-96.**

† The provision in former RC § 2913.71(C) concerning a firearm or dangerous ordnance was moved to RC § 2913.02(B) in HB 4 (146 v —).

The effective date is set by section 6 of SB 2.

**Comment, Legislative Service Commission**

Section 2913.71 of the Revised Code is amended by this act [Sub. H.B. 4] and also by Am. Sub. S.B. 2 of the 121st General Assembly (effective July 1, 1996). Comparison of these amendments in pursuance of section 1.52 of the Revised Code discloses that they are not irreconcilable so that they are required by that section to be harmonized to give effect to each amendment.

### § 2913.72 Evidence of intent to commit theft of rental property or services.

(A) Each of the following shall be considered evidence of an intent to commit theft of rented property or rental services:

(1) At the time of entering into the rental contract, the rentee presented the renter with identification that was materially false, fictitious, or not current with respect to name, address, place of employment, or other relevant information.

(2) After receiving a notice demanding the return of rented property as provided in division (B) of this section, the rentee neither returned the rented property nor made arrangements acceptable with the renter to return the rented property.

(B) To establish that a rentee has an intent to commit theft of rented property or rental services under division (A)(2) of this section, a renter may issue a notice to a rentee demanding the return of rented property. The renter shall mail the notice by certified mail, return receipt requested, to the rentee at the address the rentee gave when the rental contract was executed, or to the rentee at the last address the rentee or the rentee's agent furnished in writing to the renter.

(C) A demand for the return of rented property is not a prerequisite for the prosecution of a rentee for theft of rented property or rental services. The evidence specified in division (A) of this section does not constitute the only evidence that may be considered as evidence of intent to commit theft of rented property or rental services.

(D) As used in this section:

(1) "Renter" means a person who owns rented property.

(2) "Rentee" means a person who pays consideration to a renter for the use of rented property.

**HISTORY: 146 v S 2. Eff 7-1-96; 152 v S 320, § 1, eff. 4-7-09.**

The effective date is set by section 6 of SB 2.

### § 2913.73 Evidence of victim's lack of capacity to give consent.

In a prosecution for any alleged violation of a provision of this chapter, if the lack of consent of the victim is an element of the provision that allegedly was violated, evidence that, at the time of the alleged violation, the victim lacked the capacity to give consent is admissible to show that the victim did not give consent.

As used in this section, "lacks the capacity to consent" means being impaired for any reason to the extent that the person lacks sufficient understanding or capacity to make and carry out reasonable decisions concerning the person or the person's resources.

**HISTORY: 148 v H 2. Eff 11-10-99.**

## [MISCELLANEOUS OFFENSES]

### § 2913.81 Repealed, 146 v S 2, § 2 [141 v H 49]. Eff 7-1-96.

This section concerned denying access to a computer system or services.

The effective date is set by section 6 of SB 2.

## § 2913.82 Motor vehicle theft offender to pay towing or storage costs.

If a person is convicted of a theft offense that involves a motor vehicle, as defined in section 4501.01 of the Revised Code, or any major part of a motor vehicle, and if a local authority, as defined in section 4511.01 of the Revised Code, the owner of the vehicle or major part, or a person, acting on behalf of the owner, was required to pay any towing or storage fees prior to recovering possession of the motor vehicle or major part, the court that sentences the offender, as a part of its sentence, shall require the offender to repay the fees to the local authority, the owner, or the person who paid the fees on behalf of the owner.

As used in this section, "major part" has the same meaning as in the "Motor Vehicle Theft Law Enforcement Act of 1984," 98 Stat. 2754, 15 U.S.C. 2021(7), as amended.

**HISTORY: 141 v H 546. Eff 3-25-87.**

# CHAPTER 2915: GAMBLING



## § 2915.01 Definitions.

As used in this chapter:

(A) "Bookmaking" means the business of receiving or paying off bets.

(B) "Bet" means the hazarding of anything of value upon the result of an event, undertaking, or contingency, but does not include a bona fide business risk.

(C) "Scheme of chance" means a slot machine, lottery, numbers game, pool conducted for profit, or other scheme in which a participant gives a valuable consideration for a chance to win a prize, but does not include bingo, a skill-based amusement machine, or a pool not conducted for profit.

(D) "Game of chance" means poker, craps, roulette, or other game in which a player gives anything of value in the hope of gain, the outcome of which is determined largely by chance, but does not include bingo.

(E) "Game of chance conducted for profit" means any game of chance designed to produce income for the person who conducts or operates the game of chance, but does not include bingo.

(F) "Gambling device" means any of the following:

(1) A book, totalizer, or other equipment for recording bets;

(2) A ticket, token, or other device representing a chance, share, or interest in a scheme of chance or evidencing a bet;

(3) A deck of cards, dice, gaming table, roulette wheel, slot machine, or other apparatus designed for use in connection with a game of chance;

(4) Any equipment, device, apparatus, or paraphernalia specially designed for gambling purposes;

(5) Bingo supplies sold or otherwise provided, or used, in violation of this chapter.

(G) "Gambling offense" means any of the following:

(1) A violation of section 2915.02, 2915.03, 2915.04, 2915.05, 2915.06, 2915.07, 2915.08, 2915.081, 2915.082, 2915.09, 2915.091, 2915.092, 2915.10, or 2915.11 of the Revised Code;

(2) A violation of an existing or former municipal ordinance or law of this or any other state or the United States substantially equivalent to any section listed in division (G)(1) of this section or a violation of section 2915.06 of the Revised Code as it existed prior to July 1, 1996;

(3) An offense under an existing or former municipal ordinance or law of this or any other state or the United States, of which gambling is an element;

(4) A conspiracy or attempt to commit, or complicity in committing, any offense under division (G)(1), (2), or (3) of this section.

(H) Except as otherwise provided in this chapter, "charitable organization" means any tax exempt religious, educational, veteran's, fraternal, sporting, service, nonprofit medical, volunteer rescue service, volunteer firefighter's, senior citizen's, historic railroad educational, youth athletic, amateur athletic, or youth athletic park organization. An organization is tax exempt if the organization is, and has received from the internal revenue service a determination letter that currently is in effect stating that the organization is, exempt from federal income taxation under subsection 501(a) and described in subsection 501(c)(3), 501(c)(4), 501(c)(8), 501(c)(10), or 501(c)(19) of the Internal Revenue Code, or if the organization is a sporting organization that is exempt from federal income taxation under subsection 501(a) and is described in subsection 501(c)(7) of the Internal Revenue Code. To qualify as a charitable organization, an organization, except a volunteer rescue service or volunteer firefighter's organization, shall have been in continuous existence as such in this state for a period of two years immediately preceding either the making of an application for a bingo license under section 2915.08 of the Revised Code or the conducting of any game of chance as provided in division (D) of section 2915.02 of the Revised Code. A charitable organization that is exempt from federal income taxation under subsection 501(a) and described in subsection 501(c)(3) of the Internal Revenue Code and that is created by a veteran's organization, a fraternal organization, or a sporting organization does not have to have been in continuous existence as such in this state for a period of two years immediately preceding either the making of an application for a bingo license under section 2915.08 of the Revised Code or the conducting of any game of chance as provided in division (D) of section 2915.02 of the Revised Code.

(I) "Religious organization" means any church, body of communicants, or group that is not organized or operated for profit and that gathers in common membership for regular worship and religious observances.

(J) "Educational organization" means any organization within this state that is not organized for profit, the primary purpose of which is to educate and develop the capabilities of individuals through instruction by means of operating or contributing to the support of a school, academy, college, or university.

(K) "Veteran's organization" means any individual post or state headquarters of a national veteran's association or an auxiliary unit of any individual post of a national veteran's association, which post, state headquarters, or auxiliary unit is incorporated as a nonprofit corporation and either has received a letter from the state headquarters of the national veteran's association indicating that the individual post or auxiliary unit is in good standing with the national veteran's association or has received a letter from the national veteran's association indicating that the state headquarters is in good standing with the national veteran's association. As used in this division, "national veteran's association" means any veteran's association that has been in continuous existence as such for a period of at least five years and either is incorporated by an act of the United States congress or has a national dues-paying membership of at least five thousand persons.

(L) "Volunteer firefighter's organization" means any organization of volunteer firefighters, as defined in section 146.01 of the Revised Code, that is organized and operated exclusively to provide financial support for a volunteer fire department or a volunteer fire company and that is recognized or ratified by a county, municipal corporation, or township.

(M) "Fraternal organization" means any society, order, state headquarters, or association within this state, except a college or high school fraternity, that is not organized for profit, that is a branch, lodge, or chapter of a national or state organization, that exists exclusively for the common business or sodality of its members.

(N) "Volunteer rescue service organization" means any organization of volunteers organized to function as an emergency medical service organization, as defined in section 4765.01 of the Revised Code.

(O) "Service organization" means either of the following:

(1) Any organization, not organized for profit, that is organized and operated exclusively to provide, or to contribute to the support of organizations or institutions organized and operated exclusively to provide, medical and therapeutic services for persons who are crippled, born with birth defects, or have any other mental or physical defect or those organized and operated exclusively to protect, or to contribute to the support of organizations or institutions organized and operated exclusively to protect, animals from inhumane treatment or provide immediate shelter to victims of domestic violence;

(2) Any organization that is described in subsection 509(a)(1), 509(a)(2), or 509(a)(3) of the Internal Revenue Code and is either a governmental unit or an organization that is tax exempt under subsection 501(a) and described in subsection 501(c)(3) of the Internal Revenue Code and that is an organization, not organized for profit, that is organized and operated primarily to provide, or to contribute to the support of organizations or institutions organized and operated primarily to provide, medical and therapeutic services for persons who are crippled, born with birth defects, or have any other mental or physical defect.

(P) "Nonprofit medical organization" means either of the following:

(1) Any organization that has been incorporated as a nonprofit corporation for at least five years and that has continuously operated and will be operated exclusively to provide, or to contribute to the support of organizations or institutions organized and operated exclusively to provide, hospital, medical, research, or therapeutic services for the public;

(2) Any organization that is described and qualified under subsection 501(c)(3) of the Internal Revenue Code, that has been incorporated as a nonprofit corporation for at least five years, and that has continuously operated and will be operated primarily to provide, or to contribute to the support of organizations or institutions organized and operated primarily to provide, hospital, medical, research, or therapeutic services for the public.

(Q) "Senior citizen's organization" means any private organization, not organized for profit, that is organized and operated exclusively to provide recreational or social services for persons who are fifty-five years of age or older and that is described and qualified under subsection 501(c)(3) of the Internal Revenue Code.

(R) "Charitable bingo game" means any bingo game described in division (S)(1) or (2) of this section that is conducted by a charitable organization that has obtained a license pursuant to section 2915.08 of the Revised Code and the proceeds of which are used for a charitable purpose.

(S) "Bingo" means either of the following:

(1) A game with all of the following characteristics:

(a) The participants use bingo cards or sheets, including paper formats and electronic representation or image formats, that are divided into twenty-five spaces arranged in five horizontal and five vertical rows of spaces, with each space, except the central space, being designated by a combination of a letter and a number and with the central space being designated as a free space.

(b) The participants cover the spaces on the bingo cards or sheets that correspond to combinations of letters and numbers that are announced by a bingo game operator.

(c) A bingo game operator announces combinations of letters and numbers that appear on objects that a bingo game operator selects by chance, either manually or mechanically, from a receptacle that contains seventy-five objects at the beginning of each game, each object marked by a different combination of a letter and a number that corresponds to one of the seventy-five possible combinations of a letter and a number that can appear on the bingo cards or sheets.

(d) The winner of the bingo game includes any participant who properly announces during the interval between the announcements of letters and numbers as described in division (S)(1)(c) of this section, that a predetermined and preannounced pattern of spaces has been covered on a bingo card or sheet being used by the participant.

(2) Instant bingo, punch boards, and raffles.

(T) "Conduct" means to back, promote, organize, manage, carry on, sponsor, or prepare for the operation of bingo or a game of chance.

(U) "Bingo game operator" means any person, except security personnel, who performs work or labor at the site of bingo, including, but not limited to, collecting money from participants, handing out bingo cards or sheets or objects to cover spaces on bingo cards or sheets, selecting from a receptacle the objects that contain the combination of letters and numbers that appear on bingo cards or sheets, calling out the combinations of letters and numbers, distributing prizes, selling or redeeming instant bingo tickets or cards, supervising the operation of a punch board, selling raffle tickets, selecting raffle tickets from a receptacle and announcing the winning numbers in a raffle, and preparing, selling, and serving food or beverages.

(V) "Participant" means any person who plays bingo.

(W) "Bingo session" means a period that includes both of the following:

(1) Not to exceed five continuous hours for the conduct of one or more games described in division (S)(1) of this section, instant bingo, and seal cards;

(2) A period for the conduct of instant bingo and seal cards for not more than two hours before and not more than two hours after the period described in division (W)(1) of this section.

(X) "Gross receipts" means all money or assets, including admission fees, that a person receives from bingo without the deduction of any amounts for prizes paid out or for the expenses of conducting bingo. "Gross receipts" does not include any money directly taken in from the sale of food or beverages by a charitable organization conducting bingo, or by a bona fide auxiliary unit or society of a charitable organization conducting bingo, provided all of the following apply:

(1) The auxiliary unit or society has been in existence as a bona fide auxiliary unit or society of the charitable organization for at least two years prior to conducting bingo.

(2) The person who purchases the food or beverage receives nothing of value except the food or beverage and items customarily received with the purchase of that food or beverage.

(3) The food and beverages are sold at customary and reasonable prices.

(Y) "Security personnel" includes any person who either is a sheriff, deputy sheriff, marshal, deputy marshal, township constable, or member of an organized police department of a municipal corporation or has successfully completed a peace officer's training course pursuant to sections 109.71 to 109.79 of the Revised Code and who is hired to provide security for the premises on which bingo is conducted.

(Z) "Charitable purpose" means that the net profit of bingo, other than instant bingo, is used by, or is given, donated, or otherwise transferred to, any of the following:

(1) Any organization that is described in subsection 509(a)(1), 509(a)(2), or 509(a)(3) of the Internal Revenue Code and is either a governmental unit or an organization that is tax exempt under subsection 501(a) and described in subsection 501(c)(3) of the Internal Revenue Code;

(2) A veteran's organization that is a post, chapter, or organization of veterans, or an auxiliary unit or society of, or a trust or foundation for, any such post, chapter, or organization organized in the United States or any of its possessions, at least seventy-five per cent of the members of which are veterans and substantially all of the other members of which are individuals who are spouses, widows, or widowers of veterans, or such individuals, provided that no part of the net earnings of such post, chapter, or organization inures to the benefit of any private shareholder or individual, and further provided that the net profit is used by the post, chapter, or organization for the charitable purposes set forth in division (B)(12) of section 5739.02 of the Revised Code, is used for awarding scholarships to or for attendance at an institution mentioned in division (B)(12) of section 5739.02 of the Revised Code, is donated to a governmental agency, or is used for nonprofit youth activities, the purchase of United States or Ohio flags that are donated to schools, youth groups, or other bona fide nonprofit organizations, promotion of patriotism, or disaster relief;

(3) A fraternal organization that has been in continuous existence in this state for fifteen years and that uses the net profit exclusively for religious, charitable, scientific, literary, or educational purposes, or for the prevention of cruelty to children or animals, if contributions for such use would qualify as a deductible charitable contribution under subsection 170 of the Internal Revenue Code;

(4) A volunteer firefighter's organization that uses the net profit for the purposes set forth in division (L) of this section.

(AA) "Internal Revenue Code" means the "Internal Revenue Code of 1986," 100 Stat. 2085, 26 U.S.C. 1, as now or hereafter amended.

(BB) "Youth athletic organization" means any organization, not organized for profit, that is organized and operated exclusively to provide financial support to, or to operate, athletic activities for persons who are twenty-one years of age or younger by means of sponsoring, organizing, operating, or contributing to the support of an athletic team, club, league, or association.

(CC) "Youth athletic park organization" means any organization, not organized for profit, that satisfies both of the following:

(1) It owns, operates, and maintains playing fields that satisfy both of the following:

(a) The playing fields are used at least one hundred days per year for athletic activities by one or more organizations, not organized for profit, each of which is organized and operated exclusively to provide financial support to, or to operate, athletic activities for persons who are eighteen years of age or younger by means of sponsoring, organizing, operating, or contributing to the support of an athletic team, club, league, or association.

(b) The playing fields are not used for any profit-making activity at any time during the year.

(2) It uses the proceeds of bingo it conducts exclusively for the operation, maintenance, and improvement of its playing fields of the type described in division (CC)(1) of this section.

(DD) "Amateur athletic organization" means any organization, not organized for profit, that is organized and operated exclusively to provide financial support to, or to operate, athletic activities for persons who are training for amateur athletic competition that is sanctioned by a national governing body as defined in the "Amateur Sports Act of 1978," 90 Stat. 3045, 36 U.S.C.A. 373.

(EE) "Bingo supplies" means bingo cards or sheets; instant bingo tickets or cards; electronic bingo aids; raffle tickets; punch boards; seal cards; instant bingo ticket dispensers; and devices for selecting or displaying the combination of bingo letters and numbers or raffle tickets. Items that are "bingo supplies" are not gambling devices if sold or otherwise provided, and used, in accordance with this chapter. For purposes of this chapter, "bingo supplies" are not to be considered equipment used to conduct a bingo game.

(FF) "Instant bingo" means a form of bingo that uses folded or banded tickets or paper cards with perforated break-open tabs, a face of which is covered or otherwise hidden from view to conceal a number, letter, or symbol, or set of numbers, letters, or symbols, some of which have been designated in advance as prize winners. "Instant bingo" includes seal cards. "Instant bingo" does not include any device that is activated by the insertion of a coin, currency, token, or an equivalent, and that contains as one of its components a video display monitor that is capable of displaying numbers, letters, symbols, or characters in winning or losing combinations.

(GG) "Seal card" means a form of instant bingo that uses instant bingo tickets in conjunction with a board or placard that contains one or more seals that, when removed or opened, reveal predesignated winning numbers, letters, or symbols.

(HH) "Raffle" means a form of bingo in which the one or more prizes are won by one or more persons who have purchased a raffle ticket. The one or more winners of the raffle are determined by drawing a ticket stub or other detachable section from a receptacle containing ticket stubs or detachable sections corresponding to all tickets sold for the raffle. "Raffle" does not include the drawing of a ticket stub or other detachable section of a ticket purchased to attend a professional sporting event if both of the following apply:

(1) The ticket stub or other detachable section is used to select the winner of a free prize given away at the professional sporting event; and

(2) The cost of the ticket is the same as the cost of a ticket to the professional sporting event on days when no free prize is given away.

(II) "Punch board" means a board containing a number of holes or receptacles of uniform size in which are placed, mechanically and randomly, serially numbered slips of paper that may be punched or drawn from the hole or receptacle when used in conjunction with instant bingo. A player may punch or draw the numbered slips of paper from the holes or receptacles and obtain the prize established for the game if the number drawn corresponds to a winning number or, if the punch board includes the use of a seal card, a potential winning number.

(JJ) "Gross profit" means gross receipts minus the amount actually expended for the payment of prize awards.

(KK) "Net profit" means gross profit minus expenses.

(LL) "Expenses" means the reasonable amount of gross profit actually expended for all of the following:

(1) The purchase or lease of bingo supplies;

(2) The annual license fee required under section 2915.08 of the Revised Code;

(3) Bank fees and service charges for a bingo session or game account described in section 2915.10 of the Revised Code;

(4) Audits and accounting services;

(5) Safes;

(6) Cash registers;

(7) Hiring security personnel;

(8) Advertising bingo;

(9) Renting premises in which to conduct a bingo session;

(10) Tables and chairs;

(11) Expenses for maintaining and operating a charitable organization's facilities, including, but not limited to, a post home, club house, lounge, tavern, or canteen and any grounds attached to the post home, club house, lounge, tavern, or canteen;

(12) Payment of real property taxes and assessments that are levied on a premises on which bingo is conducted;

(13) Any other product or service directly related to the conduct of bingo that is authorized in rules adopted by the attorney general under division (B)(1) of section 2915.08 of the Revised Code.

(MM) "Person" has the same meaning as in section 1.59 of the Revised Code and includes any firm or any other legal entity, however organized.

(NN) "Revoke" means to void permanently all rights and privileges of the holder of a license issued under section 2915.08, 2915.081, or 2915.082 of the Revised Code or a charitable gaming license issued by another jurisdiction.

(OO) "Suspend" means to interrupt temporarily all rights and privileges of the holder of a license issued under section 2915.08, 2915.081, or 2915.082 of the Revised Code or a charitable gaming license issued by another jurisdiction.

(PP) "Distributor" means any person who purchases or obtains bingo supplies and who does either of the following:

(1) Sells, offers for sale, or otherwise provides or offers to provide the bingo supplies to another person for use in this state;

(2) Modifies, converts, adds to, or removes parts from the bingo supplies to further their promotion or sale for use in this state.

(QQ) "Manufacturer" means any person who assembles completed bingo supplies from raw materials, other items, or subparts or who modifies, converts, adds to, or removes parts from bingo supplies to further their promotion or sale.

(RR) "Gross annual revenues" means the annual gross receipts derived from the conduct of bingo described in division (S)(1) of this section plus the annual net profit derived from the conduct of bingo described in division (S)(2) of this section.

(SS) "Instant bingo ticket dispenser" means a mechanical device that dispenses an instant bingo ticket or card as the sole item of value dispensed and that has the following characteristics:

(1) It is activated upon the insertion of United States currency.

(2) It performs no gaming functions.

(3) It does not contain a video display monitor or generate noise.

(4) It is not capable of displaying any numbers, letters, symbols, or characters in winning or losing combinations.

(5) It does not simulate or display rolling or spinning reels.

(6) It is incapable of determining whether a dispensed bingo ticket or card is a winning or nonwinning ticket or card and requires a winning ticket or card to be paid by a bingo game operator.

(7) It may provide accounting and security features to aid in accounting for the instant bingo tickets or cards it dispenses.

(8) It is not part of an electronic network and is not interactive.

(TT)(1) "Electronic bingo aid" means an electronic device used by a participant to monitor bingo cards or sheets purchased at the time and place of a bingo session and that does all of the following:

(a) It provides a means for a participant to input numbers and letters announced by a bingo caller.

(b) It compares the numbers and letters entered by the participant to the bingo faces previously stored in the memory of the device.

(c) It identifies a winning bingo pattern.

(2) "Electronic bingo aid" does not include any device into which a coin, currency, token, or an equivalent is inserted to activate play.

(UU) "Deal of instant bingo tickets" means a single game of instant bingo tickets all with the same serial number.

(VV)(1) "Slot machine" means either of the following:

(a) Any mechanical, electronic, video, or digital device that is capable of accepting anything of value, directly or indirectly, from or on behalf of a player who gives the thing of value in the hope of gain;

(b) Any mechanical, electronic, video, or digital device that is capable of accepting anything of value, directly or indirectly, from or on behalf of a player to conduct bingo or a scheme or game of chance.

(2) "Slot machine" does not include a skill-based amusement machine or an instant bingo ticket dispenser.

(WW) "Net profit from the proceeds of the sale of instant bingo" means gross profit minus the ordinary, necessary, and reasonable expense expended for the purchase of instant bingo supplies.

(XX) "Charitable instant bingo organization" means an organization that is exempt from federal income taxation under subsection 501(a) and described in subsection 501(c)(3) of the Internal Revenue Code and is a charitable organization as defined in this section. A "charitable instant bingo organization" does not include a charitable organization that is exempt from federal income taxation under subsection 501(a) and described in subsection 501(c)(3) of the Internal Revenue Code and that is created by a veteran's organization, a fraternal organization, or a sporting organization in regards to bingo conducted or assisted by a veteran's organization, a fraternal organization, or a sporting organization pursuant to section 2915.13 of the Revised Code.

(YY) "Game flare" means the board or placard that accompanies each deal of instant bingo tickets and that has printed on or affixed to it the following information for the game:

(1) The name of the game;

(2) The manufacturer's name or distinctive logo;

(3) The form number;

(4) The ticket count;

(5) The prize structure, including the number of winning instant bingo tickets by denomination and the respective winning symbol or number combinations for the winning instant bingo tickets;

(6) The cost per play;

(7) The serial number of the game.

(ZZ) "Historic railroad educational organization" means an organization that is exempt from federal income taxation under subsection 501(a) and described in subsection 501(c)(3) of the Internal Revenue Code, that owns in fee simple the tracks and the right — of — way of a historic railroad that the organization restores or maintains and on which the organization provides excursions as part of a program to promote tourism and educate visitors regarding the role of railroad transportation in Ohio history, and that received as donations from a charitable organization that holds a license to conduct bingo under this chapter an amount equal to at least fifty per cent of that licensed charitable organization's net proceeds from the conduct of bingo during each of the five years preceding June 30, 2003. "Historic railroad" means all or a portion of the tracks and right-of-way of a railroad that was owned and operated by a for-profit common carrier in this state at any time prior to January 1, 1950.

(AAA)(1) "Skill-based amusement machine" means a mechanical, video, digital, or electronic device that rewards the player or players, if at all, only with merchandise prizes or with redeemable vouchers redeemable only for merchandise prizes, provided that with respect to rewards for playing the game all of the following apply:

(a) The wholesale value of a merchandise prize awarded as a result of the single play of a machine does not exceed ten dollars;

(b) Redeemable vouchers awarded for any single play of a machine are not redeemable for a merchandise prize with a wholesale value of more than ten dollars;

(c) Redeemable vouchers are not redeemable for a merchandise prize that has a wholesale value of more than ten dollars times the fewest number of single plays necessary to accrue the redeemable vouchers required to obtain that prize; and

(d) Any redeemable vouchers or merchandise prizes are distributed at the site of the skill-based amusement machine at the time of play.

A card for the purchase of gasoline is a redeemable voucher for purposes of division (AAA)(1) of this section even if the skill-based amusement machine for the play of which the card is awarded is located at a place where gasoline may not be legally distributed to the public or the card is not redeemable at the location of, or at the time of playing, the skill-based amusement machine.

(2) A device shall not be considered a skill-based amusement machine and shall be considered a slot machine if it pays cash or one or more of the following apply:

(a) The ability of a player to succeed at the game is impacted by the number or ratio of prior wins to prior losses of players playing the game.

(b) Any reward of redeemable vouchers is not based solely on the player achieving the object of the game or the player's score;

(c) The outcome of the game, or the value of the redeemable voucher or merchandise prize awarded for winning the game, can be controlled by a source other than any player playing the game.

(d) The success of any player is or may be determined by a chance event that cannot be altered by player actions.

(e) The ability of any player to succeed at the game is determined by game features not visible or known to the player.

(f) The ability of the player to succeed at the game is impacted by the exercise of a skill that no reasonable player could exercise.

(3) All of the following apply to any machine that is operated as described in division (AAA)(1) of this section:

(a) As used in this section, "game" and "play" mean one event from the initial activation of the machine until the results of play are determined without payment of additional consideration. An individual utilizing a machine that involves a single game, play, contest, competition, or tournament may be awarded redeemable vouchers or merchandise prizes based on the results of play.

(b) Advance play for a single game, play, contest, competition, or tournament participation may be purchased. The cost of the contest, competition, or tournament participation may be greater than a single noncontest, competition, or tournament play.

(c) To the extent that the machine is used in a contest, competition, or tournament, that contest, competition, or tournament has a defined starting and ending date and is open to participants in competition for scoring and ranking results toward the awarding of redeemable vouchers or merchandise prizes that are stated prior to the start of the contest, competition, or tournament.

(4) For purposes of division (AAA)(1) of this section, the mere presence of a device, such as a pin-setting, ball-releasing, or scoring mechanism, that does not contribute to or affect the outcome of the play of the game

does not make the device a skill-based amusement machine.

(BBB) "Merchandise prize" means any item of value, but shall not include any of the following:

(1) Cash, gift cards, or any equivalent thereof;

(2) Plays on games of chance, state lottery tickets, bingo, or instant bingo;

(3) Firearms, tobacco, or alcoholic beverages; or

(4) A redeemable voucher that is redeemable for any of the items listed in division (BBB)(1), (2), or (3) of this section.

(CCC) "Redeemable voucher" means any ticket, token, coupon, receipt, or other noncash representation of value.

(DDD) "Pool not conducted for profit" means a scheme in which a participant gives a valuable consideration for a chance to win a prize and the total amount of consideration wagered is distributed to a participant or participants.

(EEE) "Sporting organization" means a hunting, fishing, or trapping organization, other than a college or high school fraternity or sorority, that is not organized for profit, that is affiliated with a state or national sporting organization, including but not limited to, the Ohio league of sportsmen, and that has been in continuous existence in this state for a period of three years.

(FFF) "Community action agency" has the same meaning as in section 122.66 of the Revised Code.

**HISTORY: 134 v H 511 (Eff 1-1-74); 136 v H 1 (Eff 6-13-75); 136 v S 398 (Eff 5-26-76); 136 v H 1547 (Eff 12-6-76); 137 v H 72 (Eff 12-15-77); 139 v S 91 (Eff 10-20-81); 143 v H 573 (Eff 4-10-91); 144 v S 98 (Eff 11-12-92); 146 v S 2, § 1 (Eff 7-1-96); 146 v H 143, § 1 (Eff 5-15-96); 146 v H 143, § 3 (Eff 7-1-96); 149 v H 512. Eff 4-3-2003; 150 v H 95, § 1, eff. 7-1-03; 150 v S 37, § 1, eff. 10-21-03; 150 v S 146, § 1, eff. 9-23-04; 150 v H 325, § 1, eff. 9-30-04; 152 v H 177, § 1, eff. 10-25-07; 153 v H 1, § 101.01, eff. 10-16-09; 153 v H 519, § 1, eff. 9-10-10; 2011 HB 277, § 1, eff. Oct. 17, 2011.**

Acts 2011, HB 277, § 5 provides: "The items of law contained in this act, and their applications, are severable. If any item of law contained in this act, or if any application of any item of law contained in this act, is held invalid, the invalidity does not affect other items of law contained in this act and their applications that can be given effect without the invalid item of law or application."

The effective date is set by § 812.10 of 153 v H 1.

The provisions of § 4, H.B. 325 (150 v —), read as follows:

SECTION 4. Section 2915.01 of the Revised Code is presented in this act as a composite of the section as amended by both Am. Sub. H.B. 95 and Am. Sub. S.B. 37 of the 125th General Assembly. The General Assembly, applying the principle stated in division (B) of section 1.52 of the Revised Code that amendments are to be harmonized if reasonably capable of simultaneous operation, finds that the composite is the resulting version of the section in effect prior to the effective date of the section as presented in this act.

The provisions of § 3, S.B. 146 (150 v —), read as follows:

SECTION 3. The versions of sections 2915.01 and 2915.092 of the Revised Code presented in this act prevail over the versions of those sections presented in Sub. H.B. 325 of the 125th General Assembly.

**Not analogous to former RC § 2915.01 (RS § 6932; S&C 662; 54 v 196; GC § 13054; Bureau of Code Revision, 10-1-53), repealed 134 v H 511, § 2, eff 1-1-74.**

**Analogous to former RC § 2915.16 (GC § 13066-1; 124 v 838; Bureau of Code Revision, 10-1-53), repealed 134 v H 511, § 2, eff 1-1-74.**

**Publisher's Note:**

The amendment of RC § 2915.01 by 153 v H 1 was disapproved in part by the Governor.

## § 2915.02 Gambling.

(A) No person shall do any of the following:

(1) Engage in bookmaking, or knowingly engage in conduct that facilitates bookmaking;

(2) Establish, promote, or operate or knowingly engage in conduct that facilitates any game of chance conducted for profit or any scheme of chance;

(3) Knowingly procure, transmit, exchange, or engage in conduct that facilitates the procurement, transmission, or exchange of information for use in establishing odds or determining winners in connection with bookmaking or with any game of chance conducted for profit or any scheme of chance;

(4) Engage in betting or in playing any scheme or game of chance as a substantial source of income or livelihood;

(5) With purpose to violate division (A)(1), (2), (3), or (4) of this section, acquire, possess, control, or operate any gambling device.

(B) For purposes of division (A)(1) of this section, a person facilitates bookmaking if the person in any way knowingly aids an illegal bookmaking operation, including, without limitation, placing a bet with a person engaged in or facilitating illegal bookmaking. For purposes of division (A)(2) of this section, a person facilitates a game of chance conducted for profit or a scheme of chance if the person in any way knowingly aids in the conduct or operation of any such game or scheme, including, without limitation, playing any such game or scheme.

(C) This section does not prohibit conduct in connection with gambling expressly permitted by law.

(D) This section does not apply to any of the following:

(1) Games of chance, if all of the following apply:

(a) The games of chance are not craps for money or roulette for money.

(b) The games of chance are conducted by a charitable organization that is, and has received from the internal revenue service a determination letter that is currently in effect, stating that the organization is, exempt from federal income taxation under subsection 501(a) and described in subsection 501(c)(3) of the Internal Revenue Code.

(c) The games of chance are conducted at festivals of the charitable organization that are conducted either for a period of four consecutive days or less and not more than twice a year or for a period of five consecutive days not more than once a year, and are conducted on premises owned by the charitable organization for a period of no less than one year immediately preceding the conducting of the games of chance, on premises leased from a governmental unit, or on premises that are leased from a veteran's or fraternal organization and that have been owned by the lessor veteran's or fraternal organization for a period of no less than one year immediately preceding the conducting of the games of chance.

A charitable organization shall not lease premises from a veteran's or fraternal organization to conduct a festival described in division (D)(1)(c) of this section if the veteran's or fraternal organization already has leased the premises twelve times during the preceding year to charitable organizations for that purpose. If a charitable organization leases premises from a veteran's or fraternal organization to conduct a festival described in division (D)(1)(c) of this section, the charitable organization shall not pay a rental rate for the premises per day of the festival that exceeds the rental rate per bingo session that a charitable organization may pay under division (B)(1) of section 2915.09 of the Revised Code when it leases premises from another charitable organization to conduct bingo games.

(d) All of the money or assets received from the games of chance after deduction only of prizes paid out during the conduct of the games of chance are used by, or given, donated, or otherwise transferred to, any organization that is described in subsection 509(a)(1), 509(a)(2), or 509(a)(3) of the Internal Revenue Code and is either a governmental unit or an organization that is tax exempt under subsection 501(a) and described in subsection 501(c)(3) of the Internal Revenue Code;

(e) The games of chance are not conducted during, or within ten hours of, a bingo game conducted for amusement purposes only pursuant to section 2915.12 of the Revised Code.

No person shall receive any commission, wage, salary, reward, tip, donation, gratuity, or other form of compensation, directly or indirectly, for operating or assisting in the operation of any game of chance.

(2) Any tag fishing tournament operated under a permit issued under section 1533.92 of the Revised Code, as "tag fishing tournament" is defined in section 1531.01 of the Revised Code;

(3) Bingo conducted by a charitable organization that holds a license issued under section 2915.08 of the Revised Code.

(E) Division (D) of this section shall not be construed to authorize the sale, lease, or other temporary or permanent transfer of the right to conduct games of chance, as granted by that division, by any charitable organization that is granted that right.

(F) Whoever violates this section is guilty of gambling, a misdemeanor of the first degree. If the offender previously has been convicted of any gambling offense, gambling is a felony of the fifth degree.

**HISTORY: 134 v H 511 (Eff 1-1-74); 136 v S 398 (Eff 5-26-76); 136 v H 1547 (Eff 12-6-76); 137 v H 72 (Eff 12-15-77); 142 v H 514 (Eff 2-11-88); 143 v H 550 (Eff 5-3-90); 143 v H 573 (Eff 4-10-91); 145 v H 104 (Eff 10-7-93); 145 v H 336 (Eff 10-29-93); 146 v S 2 (Eff 7-1-96); 147 v S 37 (Eff 7-26-97); 149 v H 512. Eff 4-3-2003; 150 v H 95, § 1, eff. 7-1-03; 153 v H 519, § 1, eff. 9-10-10.**

The effective date is set by section 182 of H.B. 95 (150 v —).

**Not analogous to former RC § 2915.02 (GC § 13054-1; Bureau of Code Revision, 10-1-53; 125 v 544), repealed 134 v H 511, § 2, eff 1-1-74.**

## § 2915.03 Operating a gambling house.

(A) No person, being the owner or lessee, or having custody, control, or supervision of premises, shall:

(1) Use or occupy such premises for gambling in violation of section 2915.02 of the Revised Code;

(2) Recklessly permit such premises to be used or occupied for gambling in violation of section 2915.02 of the Revised Code.

(B) Whoever violates this section is guilty of operating a gambling house, a misdemeanor of the first degree. If the offender previously has been convicted of a gambling offense, operating a gambling house is a felony of the fifth degree.

(C) Premises used or occupied in violation of this section constitute a nuisance subject to abatement pursuant to sections 3767.01 to 3767.99 of the Revised Code.

**HISTORY: 134 v H 511 (Eff 1-1-74); 146 v S 2. Eff 7-1-96.**

**Not analogous to former RC § 2915.03 (GC § 13054-2; 124 v 544; Bureau of Code Revision, 10-1-53), repealed 134 v H 511, § 2, eff 1-1-74.**

The effective date is set by section 6 of SB 2.

## § 2915.04 Public gaming.

(A) No person, while at a hotel, restaurant, tavern, store, arena, hall, or other place of public accommodation, business, amusement, or resort shall make a bet or play any game of chance or scheme of chance.

(B) No person, being the owner or lessee, or having custody, control, or supervision, of a hotel, restaurant, tavern, store, arena, hall, or other place of public accommodation, business, amusement, or resort shall recklessly permit those premises to be used or occupied in violation of division (A) of this section.

(C) Divisions (A) and (B) of this section do not prohibit conduct in connection with gambling expressly permitted by law.

(D) Whoever violates this section is guilty of public gaming. Except as otherwise provided in this division, public gaming is a minor misdemeanor. If the offender previously has been convicted of any gambling offense, public gaming is a misdemeanor of the fourth degree.

(E) Premises used or occupied in violation of division (B) of this section constitute a nuisance subject to abatement under Chapter 3767. of the Revised Code.

**HISTORY: 134 v H 511 (Eff 1-1-74); 149 v H 512. Eff 4-3-2003.**

**Not analogous to former RC § 2915.04 (RS § 6933; S&C 666; 29 v 442; GC § 13056; Bureau of Code Revision, 10-1-53), repealed 134 v H 511, § 2, eff 1-1-74.**

## § 2915.05 Cheating, corrupting sports.

(A) No person, with purpose to defraud or knowing that the person is facilitating a fraud, shall engage in conduct designed to corrupt the outcome of any of the following:

(1) The subject of a bet;

(2) A contest of knowledge, skill, or endurance that is not an athletic or sporting event;

(3) A scheme or game of chance;

(4) Bingo.

(B) No person shall knowingly do any of the following:

(1) Offer, give, solicit, or accept anything of value to corrupt the outcome of an athletic or sporting event;

(2) Engage in conduct designed to corrupt the outcome of an athletic or sporting event.

(C)(1) Whoever violates division (A) of this section is guilty of cheating. Except as otherwise provided in this division, cheating is a misdemeanor of the first degree. If the potential gain from the cheating is one thousand dollars or more or if the offender previously has been convicted of any gambling offense or of any theft offense, as defined in section 2913.01 of the Revised Code, cheating is a felony of the fifth degree.

(2) Whoever violates division (B) of this section is guilty of corrupting sports. Corrupting sports is a felony of the fifth degree on a first offense and a felony of the fourth degree on each subsequent offense.

**HISTORY: 134 v H 511 (Eff 1-1-74); 139 v S 199 (Eff 1-1-83); 146 v S 2 (Eff 7-1-96); 149 v H 512. Eff 4-3-2003; 2011 HB 86, § 1, eff. Sept. 30, 2011.**

The provisions of § 4 of HB 86 read as follows:

"SECTION 4. The amendments to sections 926.99, 1333.99, 1707.99, 1716.99, 2909.03, 2909.05, 2909.11, 2913.02, 2913.03, 2913.04, 2913.11, 2913.21, 2913.31, 2913.32, 2913.34, 2913.40, 2913.401, 2913.42, 2913.421, 2913.43, 2913.45, 2913.46, 2913.47, 2913.48, 2913.49, 2913.51, 2913.61, 2915.05, 2917.21, 2917.31, 2917.32, 2921.13, 2921.41, 2923.31, and 2981.07, division (B) of section 2929.13, and division (A) of section 2929.14 of the Revised Code that are made in this act apply to a person who commits an offense specified or penalized under those sections on or after the effective date of this section and to a person to whom division (B) of section 1.58 of the Revised Code makes the amendments applicable.

"The provisions of sections 926.99, 1333.99, 1707.99, 1716.99, 2909.03, 2909.05, 2909.11, 2913.02, 2913.03, 2913.04, 2913.11, 2913.21, 2913.31, 2913.32, 2913.34, 2913.40, 2913.401, 2913.42, 2913.421, 2913.43, 2913.45, 2913.46, 2913.47, 2913.48, 2913.49, 2913.51, 2913.61, 2915.05, 2917.21, 2917.31, 2917.32, 2921.13, 2921.41, 2923.31, and 2981.07 of the Revised Code in existence prior to the effective date of this section shall apply to a person upon whom a court imposed sentence prior to the effective date of this section for an offense specified or penalized under those sections. The amendments to sections 926.99, 1333.99, 1707.99, 1716.99, 2909.03, 2909.05, 2909.11, 2913.02, 2913.03, 2913.04, 2913.11, 2913.21, 2913.31, 2913.32, 2913.34, 2913.40, 2913.401, 2913.42, 2913.421, 2913.43, 2913.45, 2913.46, 2913.47, 2913.48, 2913.49, 2913.51, 2913.61, 2915.05, 2917.21, 2917.31, 2917.32, 2921.13, 2921.41, 2923.31, and 2981.07 of the Revised Code that are made in this act do not apply to a person who upon whom a court imposed sentence prior to the effective date of this section for an offense specified or penalized under those sections."

**Not analogous to former RC § 2915.05 (RS § 6935; S&C 666; 29 v 442; GC § 13057; Bureau of Code Revision, 10-1-53), repealed 134 v H 511, § 2, eff 1-1-74.**

## § 2915.06 Skill-based amusement machine prohibited conduct.

(A) No person shall give to another person any item described in division (BBB) (1), (2), (3), or (4) of section 2915.01 of the Revised Code in exchange for a noncash prize, toy, or novelty received as a reward for playing or operating a skill-based amusement machine or for a free or reduced-price game won on a skill-based amusement machine.

(B) Whoever violates division (A) of this section is guilty of skill-based amusement machine prohibited conduct. A violation of division (A) of this section is a misdemeanor of the first degree for each redemption of a prize that is involved in the violation. If the offender previously has been convicted of a violation of division (A) of this section, a violation of that division is a felony of the fifth degree for each redemption of a prize that is involved in the violation. The maximum fine authorized to be imposed for a felony of the fifth degree shall be imposed upon the offender.

**HISTORY: 152 v H 177, § 1, eff. 10-25-07.**

**Not analogous to former RC § 2915.06 (134 v H 511), repealed 146 v S 2, § 2, eff 7-1-96.**

## § 2915.061 Regulation of skill-based amusement machines.

Any regulation of skill-based amusement machines shall be governed by this chapter and not by Chapter 1345. of the Revised Code.

**HISTORY: 152 v H 177, § 1, eff. 10-25-07.**

[BINGO]

## § 2915.07 Conducting illegal bingo.

(A) No person, except a charitable organization that has obtained a license pursuant to section 2915.08 of the Revised Code, shall conduct or advertise bingo. This division does not apply to a raffle that a charitable organization conducts or advertises.

(B) Whoever violates this section is guilty of conducting illegal bingo, a felony of the fourth degree.

**HISTORY: 136 v S 398 (Eff 5-26-76); 146 v S 2 (Eff 7-1-96); 149 v H 512. Eff 4-3-2003.**

**Not analogous to former RC § 2915.07 (RS § 6936; S&C 665; 29 v 442; GC § 13058; Bureau of Code Revision, 10-1-53), repealed 134 v H 511, § 2, eff 1-1-74.**

The effective date is set by section 6 of SB 2.

## § 2915.08 Application for license.

(A)(1) Annually before the first day of January, a charitable organization that desires to conduct bingo, instant bingo at a bingo session, or instant bingo other than at a bingo session shall make out, upon a form to be furnished by the attorney general for that purpose, an application for a license to conduct bingo, instant bingo at a bingo session, or instant bingo other than at a bingo session and deliver that application to the attorney general together with a license fee as follows:

(a) Except as otherwise provided in this division, for a license for the conduct of bingo, two hundred dollars;

(b) For a license for the conduct of instant bingo at a bingo session or instant bingo other than at a bingo session for a charitable organization that previously has not been licensed under this chapter to conduct instant bingo at a bingo session or instant bingo other than at a bingo session, a license fee of five hundred dollars, and for any other charitable organization, a license fee that is based upon the gross profits received by the charitable organization from the operation of instant bingo at a bingo session or instant bingo other than at a bingo session, during the one-year period ending on the thirty-first day of October of the year immediately preceding the year for which the license is sought, and that is one of the following:

(i) Five hundred dollars, if the total is fifty thousand dollars or less;

(ii) One thousand two hundred fifty dollars plus one-fourth per cent of the gross profit, if the total is more than fifty thousand dollars but less than two hundred fifty thousand one dollars;

(iii) Two thousand two hundred fifty dollars plus one-half per cent of the gross profit, if the total is more than two hundred fifty thousand dollars but less than five hundred thousand one dollars;

(iv) Three thousand five hundred dollars plus one per cent of the gross profit, if the total is more than five hundred thousand dollars but less than one million one dollars;

(v) Five thousand dollars plus one per cent of the gross profit, if the total is one million one dollars or more;

(c) A reduced license fee established by the attorney general pursuant to division (G) of this section.

(d) For a license to conduct bingo for a charitable organization that prior to the effective date of this amendment has not been licensed under this chapter to conduct bingo, instant bingo at a bingo session, or instant bingo other than at a bingo session, a license fee established by rule by the attorney general in accordance with division (H) of this section.

(2) The application shall be in the form prescribed by the attorney general, shall be signed and sworn to by the applicant, and shall contain all of the following:

(a) The name and post-office address of the applicant;

(b) A statement that the applicant is a charitable organization and that it has been in continuous existence as a charitable organization in this state for two years immediately preceding the making of the application or for five years in the case of a fraternal organization or a nonprofit medical organization;

(c) The location at which the organization will conduct bingo, which location shall be within the county in which the principal place of business of the applicant is located, the days of the week and the times on each of those days when bingo will be conducted, whether the organization owns, leases, or subleases the premises, and a copy of the rental agreement if it leases or subleases the premises;

(d) A statement of the applicant's previous history, record, and association that is sufficient to establish that the applicant is a charitable organization, and a copy of a determination letter that is issued by the Internal Revenue Service and states that the organization is tax exempt under subsection 501(a) and described in subsection 501(c)(3), 501(c)(4), 501(c)(7), 501(c)(8), 501(c)(10), or 501(c)(19) of the Internal Revenue Code;

(e) A statement as to whether the applicant has ever had any previous application refused, whether it previously has had a license revoked or suspended, and the reason stated by the attorney general for the refusal, revocation, or suspension;

(f) A statement of the charitable purposes for which the net profit derived from bingo, other than instant bingo, will be used, and a statement of how the net profit derived from instant bingo will be distributed in accordance with section 2915.101 [2915.10.1] of the Revised Code;

(g) Other necessary and reasonable information that the attorney general may require by rule adopted pursuant to section 111.15 of the Revised Code;

(h) If the applicant is a charitable trust as defined in section 109.23 of the Revised Code, a statement as to whether it has registered with the attorney general pursuant to section 109.26 of the Revised Code or filed annual reports pursuant to section 109.31 of the Revised Code, and, if it is not required to do either, the exemption in section 109.26 or 109.31 of the Revised Code that applies to it;

(i) If the applicant is a charitable organization as defined in section 1716.01 of the Revised Code, a statement as to whether it has filed with the attorney general a registration statement pursuant to section 1716.02 of the Revised Code and a financial report pursuant to section 1716.04 of the Revised Code, and, if it is not required to do both, the exemption in section 1716.03 of the Revised Code that applies to it;

(j) In the case of an applicant seeking to qualify as a youth athletic park organization, a statement issued by a board or body vested with authority under Chapter 755. of the Revised Code for the supervision and maintenance of recreation facilities in the territory in which the organization is located, certifying that the playing fields owned by the organization were used for at least one hundred days during the year in which the statement is issued, and were open for use to all residents of that territory, regardless of race, color, creed, religion, sex, or national origin, for athletic activities by youth athletic organizations that do not discriminate on the basis of race, color, creed, religion, sex, or national origin, and that the fields were not used for any profit-making activity at any time during the year. That type of board or body is authorized to issue the statement upon request and shall issue the statement if it finds that the applicant's playing fields were so used.

(3) The attorney general, within thirty days after receiving a timely filed application from a charitable organization that has been issued a license under this section that has not expired and has not been revoked or suspended, shall send a temporary permit to the applicant specifying the date on which the application was filed with the attorney general and stating that, pursuant to section 119.06 of the Revised Code, the applicant may continue to conduct bingo until a new license is granted or, if the application is rejected, until fifteen days after notice of the rejection is mailed to the applicant. The temporary permit does not affect the validity of the applicant's application and does not grant any rights to the applicant except those rights specifically granted in section 119.06 of the Revised Code. The issuance of a temporary permit by the attorney general pursuant to this division does not prohibit the attorney general from rejecting the applicant's application because of acts that the applicant committed, or actions that the applicant failed to take, before or after the issuance of the temporary permit.

(4) Within thirty days after receiving an initial license application from a charitable organization to conduct bingo, instant bingo at a bingo session, or instant bingo other than at a bingo session, the attorney general shall conduct a preliminary review of the application and notify the applicant regarding any deficiencies. Once an application is deemed complete, or beginning on the thirtieth day after the application is filed, if the attorney general failed to notify the applicant of any deficiencies, the attorney general shall have an additional sixty days to conduct an investigation and either grant or deny the application based on findings established and communicated in accordance with divisions (B) and (E) of this section. As an option to granting or denying an initial license application, the attorney general may grant a temporary license and request additional time to conduct the investigation if the attorney general has cause to believe that additional time is necessary to complete the investigation and has notified the applicant in writing about the specific concerns raised during the investigation.

(B)(1) The attorney general shall adopt rules to enforce sections 2915.01, 2915.02, and 2915.07 to 2915.13 of the Revised Code to ensure that bingo or instant bingo is conducted in accordance with those sections and to maintain proper control over the conduct of bingo or instant bingo. The rules, except rules adopted pursuant to divisions (A)(2)(g) and (G) of this section, shall be adopted pursuant to Chapter 119. of the Revised Code. The attorney general shall license charitable organizations to conduct bingo, instant bingo at a bingo session, or instant bingo other than at a bingo session in conformance with this chapter and with the licensing provisions of Chapter 119. of the Revised Code.

(2) The attorney general may refuse to grant a license to any organization, or revoke or suspend the license of any organization, that does any of the following or to which any of the following applies:

(a) Fails or has failed at any time to meet any requirement of section 109.26, 109.31, or 1716.02, or sections 2915.07 to 2915.11 of the Revised Code, or violates or has violated any provision of sections 2915.02 or 2915.07 to 2915.13 of the Revised Code or any rule adopted by the attorney general pursuant to this section;

(b) Makes or has made an incorrect or false statement that is material to the granting of the license in an application filed pursuant to division (A) of this section;

(c) Submits or has submitted any incorrect or false information relating to an application if the information is material to the granting of the license;

(d) Maintains or has maintained any incorrect or false information that is material to the granting of the license in the records required to be kept pursuant to divisions (A) and (C) of section 2915.10 of the Revised Code, if applicable;

(e) The attorney general has good cause to believe that the organization will not conduct bingo, instant bingo at a bingo session, or instant bingo other than at a bingo session in accordance with sections 2915.07 to 2915.13 of the Revised Code or with any rule adopted by the attorney general pursuant to this section.

(3) For the purposes of division (B) of this section, any action of an officer, trustee, agent, representative, or bingo game operator of an organization is an action of the organization.

(C) The attorney general may grant licenses to charitable organizations that are branches, lodges, or chapters of national charitable organizations.

(D) The attorney general shall send notice in writing to the prosecuting attorney and sheriff of the county in which the organization will conduct bingo, instant bingo at a bingo session, or instant bingo other than at a bingo session, as stated in its application for a license or amended license, and to any other law enforcement agency in that county that so requests, of all of the following:

(1) The issuance of the license;

(2) The issuance of the amended license;

(3) The rejection of an application for and refusal to grant a license;

(4) The revocation of any license previously issued;

(5) The suspension of any license previously issued.

(E) A license issued by the attorney general shall set forth the information contained on the application of the charitable organization that the attorney general determines is relevant, including, but not limited to, the location at which the organization will conduct bingo, instant bingo at a bingo session, or instant bingo other than at a bingo session and the days of the week and the times on each of those days when bingo will be conducted. If the attorney general refuses to grant or revokes or suspends a license, the attorney general shall notify the applicant in writing and specifically identify the reason for the refusal, revocation, or suspension in narrative form and, if applicable, by identifying the section of the Revised Code violated. The failure of the attorney general to give the written notice of the reasons for the refusal, revocation, or suspension or a mistake in the written notice does not affect the validity of the attorney general's refusal to grant, or the revocation or suspension of, a license. If the attorney general fails to give the written notice or if there is a mistake in the written notice, the applicant may bring an action to compel the attorney general to comply with this division or to correct the mistake, but the attorney general's order refusing to grant, or revoking or suspending, a license shall not be enjoined during the pendency of the action.

(F) A charitable organization that has been issued a license pursuant to division (B) of this section but that cannot conduct bingo or instant bingo at the location, or on the day of the week or at the time, specified on the license due to circumstances that make it impractical to do so may apply in writing, together with an application fee of two hundred fifty dollars, to the attorney general, at least thirty days prior to a change in location, day of the week, or time, and request an amended license. The application shall describe the causes making it impractical for the organization to conduct bingo or instant bingo in conformity with its license and shall indicate the location, days of the week, and times on each of those days when it desires to conduct bingo or instant bingo. Except as otherwise provided in this division, the attorney general shall issue the amended license in accordance with division (E) of this section, and the organization shall surrender its original license to the attorney general. The attorney general may refuse to grant an amended license according to the terms of division (B) of this section.

(G) The attorney general, by rule adopted pursuant to section 111.15 of the Revised Code, shall establish a schedule of reduced license fees for charitable organizations that desire to conduct bingo or instant bingo during fewer than twenty-six weeks in any calendar year.

(H) The attorney general, by rule adopted pursuant to section 111.15 of the Revised Code, shall establish license fees for the conduct of bingo, instant bingo at a bingo session, or instant bingo other than at a bingo session for charitable organizations that prior to the effective date of this amendment have not been licensed to conduct bingo, instant bingo at a bingo session, or instant bingo other than at a bingo session under this chapter.

(I) The attorney general may enter into a written contract with any other state agency to delegate to that state agency the powers prescribed to the attorney general under Chapter 2915. of the Revised Code.

(J) The attorney general, by rule adopted pursuant to section 111.15 of the Revised Code, may adopt rules to determine the requirements for a charitable organization that is exempt from federal income taxation under subsection 501(a) and described in subsection 501(c)(3) of the Internal Revenue Code to be in good standing in the state.

**HISTORY: 136 v S 398 (Eff 5-26-76); 136 v H 1547 (Eff 12-6-76); 137 v H 72 (Eff 12-15-77); 139 v S 91 (Eff 10-20-81); 139 v S 550 (Eff 11-26-82); 140 v H 291 (Eff 7-1-83); 145 v H 104 (Eff 10-7-93); 148 v S 333 (Eff 4-10-2001); 149 v H 512. Eff 4-3-2003; 150 v H 95, § 1, eff. 7-1-03.**

The provisions of § 134.05, H.B. 95 (150 v —), read as follows:

SECTION 134.05. Division (A)(4) of section 2915.08 of the Revised Code shall not be applied until January 31, 2004.

The effective date is set by section 182 of H.B. 95 (150 v —).

**Not analogous to former RC § 2915.08 (RS § 6939; S&C 446; 75 v 57; GC §§ 13060, 13061; Bureau of Code Revision, 10-1-53), repealed 134 v H 511, § 2, eff 1-1-74.**

The provisions of §§ 3, 7 of H.B. 512 (149 v —), as amended by § 134.05 of H.B. 95 (150 v —), read as follows:

SECTION 3. The annual license fees prescribed by division (A)(1) of section 2915.08 of the Revised Code, as amended by this act, shall not be applied until one year after the effective date of this act. During that one-year period after the effective date of this act, the attorney general may, by rule adopted pursuant to section 111.15 of the Revised Code establish the license fees for the conduct of bingo, instant bingo at a bingo session, and instant bingo other than at a bingo session.

SECTION 7. Division (A)(4) of section 2915.08 of the Revised Code shall not be applied until January 31, 2004.

## § 2915.081 Distributor license for bingo supplies.

(A) No distributor shall sell, offer to sell, or otherwise provide or offer to provide bingo supplies to another person, or modify, convert, add to, or remove parts from bingo supplies to further their promotion or sale, for use in this state without having obtained a license from the attorney general under this section.

(B) The attorney general may issue a distributor license to any person that meets the requirements of this section. The application for the license shall be on a form prescribed by the attorney general and be accompanied by the annual fee prescribed by this section. The license is valid for a period of one year, and the annual fee for the license is five thousand dollars.

(C) The attorney general may refuse to issue a distributor license to any person to which any of the following applies, or to any person that has an officer, partner, or other person who has an ownership interest of ten per cent or more and to whom any of the following applies:

(1) The person, officer, or partner has been convicted of a felony under the laws of this state, another state, or the United States.

(2) The person, officer, or partner has been convicted of any gambling offense.

(3) The person, officer, or partner has made an incorrect or false statement that is material to the granting of a license in an application submitted to the attorney general under this section or in a similar application submitted to a gambling licensing authority in another jurisdiction if the statement resulted in license revocation through administrative action in the other jurisdiction.

(4) The person, officer, or partner has submitted any incorrect or false information relating to the application to the attorney general under this section, if the information is material to the granting of the license.

(5) The person, officer, or partner has failed to correct any incorrect or false information that is material to the granting of the license in the records required to be maintained under division (E) of section 2915.10 of the Revised Code.

(6) The person, officer, or partner has had a license related to gambling revoked or suspended under the laws of this state, another state, or the United States.

(D) The attorney general shall not issue a distributor license to any person that is involved in the conduct of bingo on behalf of a charitable organization or that is a lessor of premises used for the conduct of bingo. This division does not prohibit a distributor from advising charitable organizations on the use and benefit of specific bingo supplies or prohibit a distributor from advising a customer on operational methods to improve bingo profitability.

(E)(1) No distributor shall sell, offer to sell, or otherwise provide or offer to provide bingo supplies to any person, or modify, convert, add to, or remove parts from bingo supplies to further their promotion or sale, for use in this state except to or for the use of a charitable organization that has been issued a license under section 2915.08 of the Revised Code or to another distributor that has been issued a license under this section. No distributor shall accept payment for the sale or other provision of bingo supplies other than by check or electronic fund transfer.

(2) No distributor may donate, give, loan, lease, or otherwise provide any bingo supplies or equipment, or modify, convert, add to, or remove parts from bingo supplies to further their promotion or sale, to or for the use of a charitable organization for use in a bingo session conditioned on or in consideration for an exclusive right to provide bingo supplies to the charitable organization. A distributor may provide a licensed charitable organization with free samples of the distributor's products to be used as prizes or to be used for the purpose of sampling.

(3) No distributor shall purchase bingo supplies for use in this state from any person except from a manufacturer issued a license under section 2915.082 [2915.08.2] of the Revised Code or from another distributor issued a license under this section. Subject to division (D) of section 2915.082 [2915.08.2] of the Revised Code, no distributor shall pay for purchased bingo supplies other than by check or electronic fund transfer.

(4) No distributor shall participate in the conduct of bingo on behalf of a charitable organization or have any direct or indirect ownership interest in a premises used for the conduct of bingo.

(5) No distributor shall knowingly solicit, offer, pay, or receive any kickback, bribe, or undocumented rebate, directly or indirectly, overtly or covertly, in cash or in kind, in return for providing bingo supplies to any person in this state.

(F) The attorney general may suspend or revoke a distributor license for any of the reasons for which the attorney general may refuse to issue a distributor license specified in division (C) of this section or if the distributor holding the license violates any provision of this chapter or any rule adopted by the attorney general under this chapter.

(G) Whoever violates division (A) or (E) of this section is guilty of illegally operating as a distributor. Except as otherwise provided in this division, illegally operating as a distributor is a misdemeanor of the first degree. If the offender previously has been convicted of a violation of division (A) or (E) of this section, illegally operating as a distributor is a felony of the fifth degree.

**HISTORY: 149 v H 512. Eff 4-3-2003; 150 v H 95, § 1, eff. 7-1-03; 150 v H 325, § 1, eff. 9-30-04; 153 v H 519, § 1, eff. 9-10-10.**

## § 2915.082 Manufacturer of bingo supplies license.

(A) No manufacturer shall sell, offer to sell, or otherwise provide or offer to provide bingo supplies for use in this state without having obtained a license from the attorney general under this section.

(B) The attorney general may issue a manufacturer license to any person that meets the requirements of this section. The application for the license shall be on a form prescribed by the attorney general and be accompanied by the annual fee prescribed by this section. The license is valid for a period of one year, and the annual fee for the license is five thousand dollars.

(C) The attorney general may refuse to issue a manufacturer license to any person to which any of the following applies, or to any person that has an officer, partner, or other person who has an ownership interest of ten per cent or more and to whom any of the following applies:

(1) The person, officer, or partner has been convicted of a felony under the laws of this state, another state, or the United States.

(2) The person, officer, or partner has been convicted of any gambling offense.

(3) The person, officer, or partner has made an incorrect or false statement that is material to the granting of a license in an application submitted to the attorney general under this section or in a similar application submitted to a gambling licensing authority in another jurisdiction if the

statement resulted in license revocation through administrative action in the other jurisdiction.

(4) The person, officer, or partner has submitted any incorrect or false information relating to the application to the attorney general under this section, if the information is material to the granting of the license.

(5) The person, officer, or partner has failed to correct any incorrect or false information that is material to the granting of the license in the records required to be maintained under division (F) of section 2915.10 of the Revised Code.

(6) The person, officer, or partner has had a license related to gambling revoked or suspended under the laws of this state, another state, or the United States.

(D)(1) No manufacturer shall sell, offer to sell, or otherwise provide or offer to provide bingo supplies to any person for use in this state except to a distributor that has been issued a license under section 2915.081 [2915.08.1] of the Revised Code. No manufacturer shall accept payment for the sale of bingo supplies other than by check or electronic fund transfer.

(2) No manufacturer shall knowingly solicit, offer, pay, or receive any kickback, bribe, or undocumented rebate, directly or indirectly, overtly or covertly, in cash or in kind, in return for providing bingo supplies to any person in this state.

(E)(1) The attorney general may suspend or revoke a manufacturer license for any of the reasons for which the attorney general may refuse to issue a manufacturer license specified in division (C) of this section or if the manufacturer holding the license violates any provision of this chapter or any rule adopted by the attorney general under this chapter.

(2) The attorney general may perform an onsite inspection of a manufacturer of bingo supplies that is selling, offering to sell, or otherwise providing or offering to provide bingo supplies or that is applying for a license to sell, offer to sell, or otherwise provide or offer to provide bingo supplies in this state.

(F) Whoever violates division (A) or (D) of this section is guilty of illegally operating as a manufacturer. Except as otherwise provided in this division, illegally operating as a manufacturer is a misdemeanor of the first degree. If the offender previously has been convicted of a violation of division (A) or (D) of this section, illegally operating as a manufacturer is a felony of the fifth degree.

**HISTORY: 149 v H 512. Eff 4-2-2003; 150 v H 95, § 1, eff. 7-1-03; 153 v H 519, § 1, eff. 9-10-10.**

The effective date is set by section 182 of H.B. 95 (150 v —).

## § 2915.09 Rules for conducting bingo.

(A) No charitable organization that conducts bingo shall fail to do any of the following:

(1) Own all of the equipment used to conduct bingo or lease that equipment from a charitable organization that is licensed to conduct bingo, or from the landlord of a premises where bingo is conducted, for a rental rate that is not more than is customary and reasonable for that equipment;

(2) Except as otherwise provided in division (A)(3) of this section, use all of the gross receipts from bingo for paying prizes, for reimbursement of expenses for or for renting premises in which to conduct a bingo session, for reimbursement of expenses for or for purchasing or leasing bingo supplies used in conducting bingo, for reimbursement of expenses for or for hiring security personnel, for reimbursement of expenses for or for advertising bingo, or for reimbursement of other expenses or for other expenses listed in division (LL) of section 2915.01 of the Revised Code, provided that the amount of the receipts so spent is not more than is customary and reasonable for a similar purchase, lease, hiring, advertising, or expense. If the building in which bingo is conducted is owned by the charitable organization conducting bingo and the bingo conducted includes a form of bingo described in division (S)(1) of section 2915.01 of the Revised Code, the charitable organization may deduct from the total amount of the gross receipts from each session a sum equal to the lesser of six hundred dollars or forty-five per cent of the gross receipts from the bingo described in that division as consideration for the use of the premises.

(3) Use, or give, donate, or otherwise transfer, all of the net profit derived from bingo, other than instant bingo, for a charitable purpose listed in its license application and described in division (Z) of section 2915.01 of the Revised Code, or distribute all of the net profit from the proceeds of the sale of instant bingo as stated in its license application and in accordance with section 2915.101 [2915.10.1] of the Revised Code.

(B) No charitable organization that conducts a bingo game described in division (S)(1) of section 2915.01 of the Revised Code shall fail to do any of the following:

(1) Conduct the bingo game on premises that are owned by the charitable organization, on premises that are owned by another charitable organization and leased from that charitable organization for a rental rate not in excess of the lesser of six hundred dollars per bingo session or forty-five per cent of the gross receipts of the bingo session, on premises that are leased from a person other than a charitable organization for a rental rate that is not more than is customary and reasonable for premises that are similar in location, size, and quality but not in excess of four hundred fifty dollars per bingo session, or on premises that are owned by a person other than a charitable organization, that are leased from that person by another charitable organization, and that are subleased from that other charitable organization by the charitable organization for a rental rate not in excess of four hundred fifty dollars per bingo session. If the charitable organization leases from a person other than a charitable organization the premises on which it conducts bingo sessions, the lessor of the premises shall provide the premises to the organization and shall not provide the organization with bingo game operators, security personnel, concessions or concession operators, bingo supplies, or any other type of service. A charitable organization shall not lease or sublease premises that it owns or leases to more than one other charitable organization per calendar week for the purpose of conducting bingo sessions on the premises. A person that is not a charitable organization shall not lease premises that it owns, leases, or otherwise is empowered to lease to more than three charitable organizations per calendar week for conducting bingo sessions on the premises. In no case shall more than nine bingo sessions be conducted on any premises in any calendar week.

(2) Display its license conspicuously at the premises where the bingo session is conducted;

(3) Conduct the bingo session in accordance with the definition of bingo set forth in division (S)(1) of section 2915.01 of the Revised Code.

(C) No charitable organization that conducts a bingo game described in division (S)(1) of section 2915.01 of the Revised Code shall do any of the following:

(1) Pay any compensation to a bingo game operator for operating a bingo session that is conducted by the charitable organization or for preparing, selling, or serving food or beverages at the site of the bingo session, permit any auxiliary unit or society of the charitable organization to pay compensation to any bingo game operator who prepares, sells, or serves food or beverages at a bingo session conducted by the charitable organization, or permit any auxiliary unit or society of the charitable organization to prepare, sell, or serve food or beverages at a bingo session conducted by the charitable organization, if the auxiliary unit or society pays any compensation to the bingo game operators who prepare, sell, or serve the food or beverages;

(2) Pay consulting fees to any person for any services performed in relation to the bingo session;

(3) Pay concession fees to any person who provides refreshments to the participants in the bingo session;

(4) Except as otherwise provided in division (C)(4) of this section, conduct more than three bingo sessions in any seven-day period. A volunteer firefighter's organization or a volunteer rescue service organization that conducts not more than five bingo sessions in a calendar year may conduct more than three bingo sessions in a seven-day period after notifying the attorney general when it will conduct the sessions.

(5) Pay out more than six thousand dollars in prizes for bingo games described in division (S)(1) of section 2915.01 of the Revised Code during any bingo session that is conducted by the charitable organization. "Prizes" does not include awards from the conduct of instant bingo.

(6) Conduct a bingo session at any time during the ten-hour period between midnight and ten a.m., at any time during, or within ten hours of, a bingo game conducted for amusement only pursuant to section 2915.12 of the Revised Code, at any premises not specified on its license, or on any day of the week or during any time period not specified on its license. Division (A)(6) of this section does not prohibit the sale of instant bingo tickets beginning at nine a.m. for a bingo session that begins at ten a.m. If circumstances make it impractical for the charitable organization to conduct a bingo session at the premises, or on the day of the week or at the time, specified on its license or if a charitable organization wants to conduct bingo sessions on a day of the week or at a time other than the day or time specified on its license, the charitable organization may apply in writing to the attorney general for an amended license pursuant to division (F) of section 2915.08 of the Revised Code. A charitable organization may apply twice in each calendar year for an amended license to conduct bingo sessions on a day of the week or at a time other than the day or time specified on its license. If the amended license is granted, the organization may conduct bingo sessions at the premises, on the day of the week, and at the time specified on its amended license.

(7) Permit any person whom the charitable organization knows, or should have known, is under the age of eighteen to work as a bingo game operator;

(8) Permit any person whom the charitable organization knows, or should have known, has been convicted of a felony or gambling offense in any jurisdiction to be a bingo game operator;

(9) Permit the lessor of the premises on which the bingo session is conducted, if the lessor is not a charitable organization, to provide the charitable organization with bingo game operators, security personnel, concessions, bingo supplies, or any other type of service;

(10) Purchase or lease bingo supplies from any person except a distributor issued a license under section 2915.081 [2915.08.1] of the Revised Code;

(11)(a) Use or permit the use of electronic bingo aids except under the following circumstances:

(i) For any single participant, not more than ninety bingo faces can be played using an electronic bingo aid or aids.

(ii) The charitable organization shall provide a participant using an electronic bingo aid with corresponding paper bingo cards or sheets.

(iii) The total price of bingo faces played with an electronic bingo aid shall be equal to the total price of the same number of bingo faces played with a paper bingo card or sheet sold at the same bingo session but without an electronic bingo aid.

(iv) An electronic bingo aid cannot be part of an electronic network other than a network that includes only bingo aids and devices that are located on the premises at which the bingo is being conducted or be interactive with any device not located on the premises at which the bingo is being conducted.

(v) An electronic bingo aid cannot be used to participate in bingo that is conducted at a location other than the location at which the bingo session is conducted and at which the electronic bingo aid is used.

(vi) An electronic bingo aid cannot be used to provide for the input of numbers and letters announced by a bingo caller other than the bingo caller who physically calls the numbers and letters at the location at which the bingo session is conducted and at which the electronic bingo aid is used.

(b) The attorney general may adopt rules in accordance with Chapter 119. of the Revised Code that govern the use of electronic bingo aids. The rules may include a requirement that an electronic bingo aid be capable of being audited by the attorney general to verify the number of bingo cards or sheets played during each bingo session.

(12) Permit any person the charitable organization knows, or should have known, to be under eighteen years of age to play bingo described in division (S)(1) of section 2915.01 of the Revised Code.

(D)(1) Except as otherwise provided in division (D)(3) of this section, no charitable organization shall provide to a bingo game operator, and no bingo game operator shall receive or accept, any commission, wage, salary, reward, tip, donation, gratuity, or other form of compensation, directly or indirectly, regardless of the source, for conducting bingo or providing other work or labor at the site of bingo during a bingo session.

(2) Except as otherwise provided in division (D)(3) of this section, no charitable organization shall provide to a bingo game operator any commission, wage, salary, reward, tip, donation, gratuity, or other form of compensation, directly or indirectly, regardless of the source, for conducting instant bingo other than at a bingo session at the site of instant bingo other than at a bingo session.

(3) Nothing in division (D) of this section prohibits an employee of a fraternal organization, veteran's organization, or sporting organization from selling instant bingo tickets or cards to the organization's members or invited

guests, as long as no portion of the employee's compensation is paid from any receipts of bingo.

(E) Notwithstanding division (B)(1) of this section, a charitable organization that, prior to December 6, 1977, has entered into written agreements for the lease of premises it owns to another charitable organization or other charitable organizations for the conducting of bingo sessions so that more than two bingo sessions are conducted per calendar week on the premises, and a person that is not a charitable organization and that, prior to December 6, 1977, has entered into written agreements for the lease of premises it owns to charitable organizations for the conducting of more than two bingo sessions per calendar week on the premises, may continue to lease the premises to those charitable organizations, provided that no more than four sessions are conducted per calendar week, that the lessor organization or person has notified the attorney general in writing of the organizations that will conduct the sessions and the days of the week and the times of the day on which the sessions will be conducted, that the initial lease entered into with each organization that will conduct the sessions was filed with the attorney general prior to December 6, 1977, and that each organization that will conduct the sessions was issued a license to conduct bingo games by the attorney general prior to December 6, 1977.

(F) This section does not prohibit a bingo licensed charitable organization or a game operator from giving any person an instant bingo ticket as a prize.

(G) Whoever violates division (A)(2) of this section is guilty of illegally conducting a bingo game, a felony of the fourth degree. Except as otherwise provided in this division, whoever violates division (A)(1) or (3), (B)(1), (2), or (3), (C)(1) to (12), or (D) of this section is guilty of a minor misdemeanor. If the offender previously has been convicted of a violation of division (A)(1) or (3), (B)(1), (2), or (3), (C)(1) to (11), or, (D) of this section, a violation of division (A)(1) or (3), (B)(1), (2), or (3), (C), or (D) of this section is a misdemeanor of the first degree. Whoever violates division (C)(12) of this section is guilty of a misdemeanor of the first degree, if the offender previously has been convicted of a violation of division (C)(12) of this section, a felony of the fourth degree.

**HISTORY: 136 v S 398 (Eff 5-26-76); 136 v H 1547 (Eff 12-6-76); 137 v H 72 (Eff 12-15-77); 139 v S 91 (Eff 10-20-81); 143 v H 573 (Eff 4-10-91); 145 v H 104 (Eff 10-7-93); 146 v S 70 (Eff 3-5-96); 146 v S 2 (Eff 7-1-96); 149 v H 512. Eff 4-3-2003; 150 v H 95, § 1, eff. 7-1-03; 150 v H 325, § 1, eff. 9-30-04; 153 v H 519, § 1, eff. 9-10-10.**

The effective date is set by section 182 of H.B. 95 (150 v —).

**Not analogous to former RC § 2915.09 (RS § 6939a; 78 v 11; GC § 13062; Bureau of Code Revision, 10-1-53; 129 v 1513), repealed 134 v H 511, § 2, eff 1-1-74.**

The provisions of § 9 of HB 512 (149 v —) read as follows:

SECTION 9. Section 2915.09 of the Revised Code is presented in this act as a composite of the section as amended by both Am. Sub. S.B. 70 and Am. Sub. S.B. 2 of the 121st General Assembly. The General Assembly, applying the principle stated in division (B) of section 1.52 of the Revised Code that amendments are to be harmonized if reasonably capable of simultaneous operation, finds that the composite is the resulting version of the section in effect prior to the effective date of the section as presented in this act.

## § 2915.091 Rules for conducting instant bingo.

(A) No charitable organization that conducts instant bingo shall do any of the following:

(1) Fail to comply with the requirements of divisions (A)(1), (2), and (3) of section 2915.09 of the Revised Code;

(2) Conduct instant bingo unless either of the following applies:

(a) That organization is, and has received from the internal revenue service a determination letter that is currently in effect stating that the organization is, exempt from federal income taxation under subsection 501(a), is described in subsection 501(c)(3) of the Internal Revenue Code, is a charitable organization as defined in section 2915.01 of the Revised Code, is in good standing in the state pursuant to section 2915.08 of the Revised Code, and is in compliance with Chapter 1716. of the Revised Code;

(b) That organization is, and has received from the internal revenue service a determination letter that is currently in effect stating that the organization is, exempt from federal income taxation under subsection 501(a), is described in subsection 501(c)(7), 501(c)(8), 501(c)(10), or 501(c)(19) or is a veteran's organization described in subsection 501(c)(4) of the Internal Revenue Code, and conducts instant bingo under section 2915.13 of the Revised Code.

(3) Conduct instant bingo on any day, at any time, or at any premises not specified on the organization's license issued pursuant to section 2915.08 of the Revised Code;

(4) Permit any person whom the organization knows or should have known has been convicted of a felony or gambling offense in any jurisdiction to be a bingo game operator in the conduct of instant bingo;

(5) Purchase or lease supplies used to conduct instant bingo or punch board games from any person except a distributor licensed under section 2915.081 of the Revised Code;

(6) Sell or provide any instant bingo ticket or card for a price different from the price printed on it by the manufacturer on either the instant bingo ticket or card or on the game flare;

(7) Sell an instant bingo ticket or card to a person under eighteen years of age;

(8) Fail to keep unsold instant bingo tickets or cards for less than three years;

(9) Pay any compensation to a bingo game operator for conducting instant bingo that is conducted by the organization or for preparing, selling, or serving food or beverages at the site of the instant bingo game, permit any auxiliary unit or society of the organization to pay compensation to any bingo game operator who prepares, sells, or serves food or beverages at an instant bingo game conducted by the organization, or permit any auxiliary unit or society of the organization to prepare, sell, or serve food or beverages at an instant bingo game conducted by the organization, if the auxiliary unit or society pays any compensation to the bingo game operators who prepare, sell, or serve the food or beverages;

(10) Pay fees to any person for any services performed in relation to an instant bingo game;

(11) Pay fees to any person who provides refreshments to the participants in an instant bingo game;

(12)(a) Allow instant bingo tickets or cards to be sold to bingo game operators at a premises at which the organization sells instant bingo tickets or cards or to be sold to employees of a D permit holder who are working at a premises at which instant bingo tickets or cards are sold;

(b) Division (A)(12)(a) of this section does not prohibit a licensed charitable organization or a bingo game operator from giving any person an instant bingo ticket as a prize in place of a cash prize won by a participant in an instant bingo game. In no case shall an instant bingo ticket or card be sold or provided for a price different from the price printed on it by the manufacturer on either the instant bingo ticket or card or on the game flare.

(13) Fail to display its bingo license, and the serial numbers of the deal of instant bingo tickets or cards to be sold, conspicuously at each premises at which it sells instant bingo tickets or cards;

(14) Possess a deal of instant bingo tickets or cards that was not purchased from a distributor licensed under section 2915.081 of the Revised Code as reflected on an invoice issued by the distributor that contains all of the information required by division (E) of section 2915.10 of the Revised Code;

(15) Fail, once it opens a deal of instant bingo tickets or cards, to continue to sell the tickets or cards in that deal until the tickets or cards with the top two highest tiers of prizes in that deal are sold;

(16) Possess bingo supplies that were not obtained in accordance with sections 2915.01 to 2915.13 of the Revised Code.

(B)(1) A charitable organization may conduct instant bingo other than at a bingo session at not more than five separate locations. A charitable organization that is exempt from federal taxation under subsection 501(a) and described in subsection 501(c)(3) of the Internal Revenue Code and that is created by a veteran's organization or a fraternal organization is not limited in the number of separate locations the charitable organization may conduct instant bingo other than at a bingo session.

(2) A charitable organization may purchase, lease, or use instant bingo ticket dispensers to sell instant bingo tickets or cards.

(C) The attorney general may adopt rules in accordance with Chapter 119. of the Revised Code that govern the conduct of instant bingo by charitable organizations. Before those rules are adopted, the attorney general shall reference the recommended standards for opacity, randomization, minimum information, winner protection, color, and cutting for instant bingo tickets or cards, seal cards, and punch boards established by the North American gaming regulators association.

(D) Whoever violates division (A) of this section or a rule adopted under division (C) of this section is guilty of illegal instant bingo conduct. Except as otherwise provided in this division, illegal instant bingo conduct is a misdemeanor of the first degree. If the offender previously has been convicted of a violation of division (A) of this section or of such a rule, illegal instant bingo conduct is a felony of the fifth degree.

**HISTORY: 149 v H 512. Eff 4-3-2003; 150 v H 95, § 1, eff. 7-1-03; 153 v H 519, § 1, eff. 9-10-10.**

The effective date is set by section 182 of H.B. 95 (150 v —).

## § 2915.092 Raffles.

(A)(1) Subject to division (A)(2) of this section, a charitable organization, a public school, a chartered nonpublic school, a community school, or a veteran's organization, fraternal organization, or sporting organization that is exempt from federal income taxation under subsection 501(a) and is described in subsection 501(c)(3), 501(c)(4), 501(c)(7), 501(c)(8), 501(c)(10), or 501(c)(19) of the Internal Revenue Code may conduct a raffle to raise money for the organization or school and does not need a license to conduct bingo in order to conduct a raffle drawing that is not for profit.

(2) If a charitable organization that is described in division (A)(1) of this section, but that is not also described in subsection 501(c)(3) of the Internal Revenue Code, conducts a raffle, the charitable organization shall distribute at least fifty per cent of the net profit from the raffle to a charitable purpose described in division (Z) of section 2915.01 of the Revised Code or to a department or agency of the federal government, the state, or any political subdivision.

(B) Except as provided in division (A) or (B) of this section, no person shall conduct a raffle drawing that is for profit or a raffle drawing that is not for profit.

(C) Whoever violates division (B) of this section is guilty of illegal conduct of a raffle. Except as otherwise provided in this division, illegal conduct of a raffle is a misdemeanor of the first degree. If the offender previously has been convicted of a violation of division (B) of this section, illegal conduct of a raffle is a felony of the fifth degree.

**HISTORY: 149 v H 512. Eff 4-3-2003; 150 v H 95, § 1, eff. 7-1-03; 150 v S 146, § 1, eff. 9-23-04; 150 v H 325, § 1, eff. 9-30-04.**

The provisions of § 3, S.B. 146 (150 v —), read as follows:

SECTION 3. The versions of sections 2915.01 and 2915.092 of the Revised Code presented in this act prevail over the versions of those sections presented in Sub. H.B. 325 of the 125th General Assembly.

The effective date is set by section 182 of H.B. 95 (150 v —).

## § 2915.093 Conducting instant bingo other than at bingo session.

(A) As used in this section, "retail income from all commercial activity" means the income that a person receives from the provision of goods, services, or activities that are provided at the location where instant bingo other than at a bingo session is conducted, including the sale of instant bingo tickets. A religious organization that is exempt from federal income taxation under subsection 501(a) and described in subsection 501(c)(3) of the Internal Revenue Code, at not more than one location at which it conducts its charitable programs, may include donations from its members and guests as retail income.

(B) A charitable instant bingo organization may conduct instant bingo other than at a bingo session at not more than five separate locations.

(C)(1) If a charitable instant bingo organization conducts instant bingo other than at a bingo session, the charitable instant bingo organization shall enter into a written contract with the owner or lessor of the location at which the instant bingo is conducted to allow the owner or lessor to assist in the conduct of instant bingo other than at a bingo session, identify each location where the instant bingo other than at a bingo session is being conducted, and identify the owner or lessor of each location.

(2) A charitable instant bingo organization that conducts instant bingo other than at a bingo session is not required to enter into a written contract with the owner or lessor of the location at which the instant bingo is conducted provided that the owner or lessor is not assisting in the conduct of the instant bingo other than at a bingo session and provided that the conduct of the instant bingo other than at a bingo session at that location is not more than five days per calendar year and not more than ten hours per day.

(D) Except as provided in division (G) of this section, no charitable instant bingo organization shall conduct instant bingo other than at a bingo session at a location where the primary source of retail income from all commercial activity at that location is the sale of instant bingo tickets.

(E) The owner or lessor of a location that enters into a contract pursuant to division (C) of this section shall pay the full gross profit to the charitable instant bingo organization, in return for the deal of instant bingo tickets. The owner or lessor may retain the money that the owner or lessor receives for selling the instant bingo tickets, provided, however, that after the deal has been sold, the owner or lessor shall pay to the charitable instant bingo organization the value of any unredeemed instant bingo prizes remaining in the deal of instant bingo tickets.

As used in this division, "full gross profit" means the amount by which the total receipts of all instant bingo tickets, if the deal had been sold in full, exceeds the amount that would be paid out if all prizes were redeemed.

(F) A charitable instant bingo organization shall provide the attorney general with all of the following information:

(1) That the charitable instant bingo organization has terminated a contract entered into pursuant to division (C) of this section with an owner or lessor of a location;

(2) That the charitable instant bingo organization has entered into a written contract pursuant to division (C) of this section with a new owner or lessor of a location;

(3) That the charitable instant bingo organization is aware of conduct by the owner or lessor of a location at which instant bingo is conducted that is in violation of this chapter.

(G) Division (D) of this section does not apply to a volunteer firefighter's organization that is exempt from federal income taxation under subsection 501(a) and described in subsection 501(c)(3) of the Internal Revenue Code, that conducts instant bingo other than at a bingo session on the premises where the organization conducts firefighter training, that has conducted instant bingo continuously for at least five years prior to July 1, 2003, and that, during each of those five years, had gross receipts of at least one million five hundred thousand dollars.

**HISTORY: 149 v H 512. Eff 4-3-2003; 150 v H 95, § 1, eff. 7-1-03; 150 v H 325, § 1, eff. 9-30-04.**

The effective date is set by section 182 of H.B. 95 (150 v —).

## § 2915.094 Owner or lessor of location for conducting instant bingo other than at bingo session.

(A) No owner or lessor of a location shall assist a charitable instant bingo organization in the conduct of instant bingo other than at a bingo session at that location unless the owner or lessor has entered into a written contract, as described in division (C) of section 2915.093 [2915.09.3] of the Revised Code, with the charitable instant bingo organization to assist in the conduct of instant bingo other than at a bingo session.

(B) The location of the lessor or owner shall be designated as a location where the charitable instant bingo organization conducts instant bingo other than at a bingo session.

(C) No owner or lessor of a location that enters into a written contract as prescribed in division (A) of this section shall violate any provision of Chapter 2915. of the Revised Code, or permit, aid, or abet any other person in violating any provision of Chapter 2915. of the Revised Code.

(D) No owner or lessor of a location that enters into a written contract as prescribed in division (A) of this section shall violate the terms of the contract.

(E)(1) Whoever violates division (C) or (D) of this section is guilty of illegal instant bingo conduct. Except as otherwise provided in this division, illegal instant bingo conduct is a misdemeanor of the first degree. If the offender previously has been convicted of a violation of division (C) or (D) of this section, illegal instant bingo conduct is a felony of the fifth degree.

(2) If an owner or lessor of a location knowingly, intentionally, or recklessly violates division (C) or (D) of this section, any license that the owner or lessor holds for the retail sale of any goods on the owner's or lessor's premises that is issued by the state or a political subdivision is subject to suspension, revocation, or payment of a monetary penalty at the request of the attorney general.

**HISTORY: 149 v H 512. Eff 4-3-2003.**

## § 2915.095 Standard contract.

The attorney general, by rule adopted pursuant to section 111.15 of the Revised Code, shall establish a standard contract to be used by a charitable instant bingo organization, a veteran's organization, a fraternal organization, or a sporting organization for the conduct of instant bingo other than at a bingo session. The terms of the contract shall be limited to the provisions in Chapter 2915. of the Revised Code.

**HISTORY: 149 v H 512. Eff 4-3-2003; 150 v H 95, § 1, eff. 7-1-03.**

The effective date is set by section 182 of H.B. 95 (150 v —).

## § 2915.10 Records to be kept for three years.

(A) No charitable organization that conducts bingo or a game of chance pursuant to division (D) of section 2915.02 of the Revised Code shall fail to maintain the following records for at least three years from the date on which the bingo or game of chance is conducted:

(1) An itemized list of the gross receipts of each bingo session, each game of instant bingo by serial number, each raffle, each punch board game, and each game of chance, and an itemized list of the gross profits of each game of instant bingo by serial number;

(2) An itemized list of all expenses, other than prizes, that are incurred in conducting bingo or instant bingo, the name of each person to whom the expenses are paid, and a receipt for all of the expenses;

(3) A list of all prizes awarded during each bingo session, each raffle, each punch board game, and each game of chance conducted by the charitable organization, the total prizes awarded from each game of instant bingo by serial number, and the name, address, and social security number of all persons who are winners of prizes of six hundred dollars or more in value;

(4) An itemized list of the recipients of the net profit of the bingo or game of chance, including the name and address of each recipient to whom the money is distributed, and if the organization uses the net profit of bingo, or the money or assets received from a game of chance, for any charitable or other purpose set forth in division (Z) of

section 2915.01, division (D) of section 2915.02, or section 2915.101 of the Revised Code, a list of each purpose and an itemized list of each expenditure for each purpose;

(5) The number of persons who participate in any bingo session or game of chance that is conducted by the charitable organization;

(6) A list of receipts from the sale of food and beverages by the charitable organization or one of its auxiliary units or societies, if the receipts were excluded from gross receipts under division (X) of section 2915.01 of the Revised Code;

(7) An itemized list of all expenses incurred at each bingo session, each raffle, each punch board game, or each game of instant bingo conducted by the charitable organization in the sale of food and beverages by the charitable organization or by an auxiliary unit or society of the charitable organization, the name of each person to whom the expenses are paid, and a receipt for all of the expenses.

(B) A charitable organization shall keep the records that it is required to maintain pursuant to division (A) of this section at its principal place of business in this state or at its headquarters in this state and shall notify the attorney general of the location at which those records are kept.

(C) The gross profit from each bingo session or game described in division (S)(1) or (2) of section 2915.01 of the Revised Code shall be deposited into a checking account devoted exclusively to the bingo session or game. Payments for allowable expenses incurred in conducting the bingo session or game and payments to recipients of some or all of the net profit of the bingo session or game shall be made only by checks drawn on the bingo session or game account.

(D) Each charitable organization shall conduct and record an inventory of all of its bingo supplies as of the first day of November of each year.

(E) The attorney general may adopt rules in accordance with Chapter 119. of the Revised Code that establish standards of accounting, record keeping, and reporting to ensure that gross receipts from bingo or games of chance are properly accounted for.

(F) A distributor shall maintain, for a period of three years after the date of its sale or other provision, a record of each instance of its selling or otherwise providing to another person bingo supplies for use in this state. The record shall include all of the following for each instance:

(1) The name of the manufacturer from which the distributor purchased the bingo supplies and the date of the purchase;

(2) The name and address of the charitable organization or other distributor to which the bingo supplies were sold or otherwise provided;

(3) A description that clearly identifies the bingo supplies;

(4) Invoices that include the nonrepeating serial numbers of all paper bingo cards and sheets and all instant bingo deals sold or otherwise provided to each charitable organization.

(G) A manufacturer shall maintain, for a period of three years after the date of its sale or other provision, a record of each instance of its selling or otherwise providing bingo supplies for use in this state. The record shall include all of the following for each instance:

(1) The name and address of the distributor to whom the bingo supplies were sold or otherwise provided;

(2) A description that clearly identifies the bingo supplies, including serial numbers;

(3) Invoices that include the nonrepeating serial numbers of all paper bingo cards and sheets and all instant bingo deals sold or otherwise provided to each distributor.

(H) The attorney general or any law enforcement agency may do all of the following:

(1) Investigate any charitable organization or any officer, agent, trustee, member, or employee of the organization;

(2) Examine the accounts and records of the organization;

(3) Conduct inspections, audits, and observations of bingo or games of chance;

(4) Conduct inspections of the premises where bingo or games of chance are conducted;

(5) Take any other necessary and reasonable action to determine if a violation of any provision of sections 2915.01 to 2915.13 of the Revised Code has occurred and to determine whether section 2915.11 of the Revised Code has been complied with.

If any law enforcement agency has reasonable grounds to believe that a charitable organization or an officer, agent, trustee, member, or employee of the organization has violated any provision of this chapter, the law enforcement agency may proceed by action in the proper court to enforce this chapter, provided that the law enforcement agency shall give written notice to the attorney general when commencing an action as described in this division.

(I) No person shall destroy, alter, conceal, withhold, or deny access to any accounts or records of a charitable organization that have been requested for examination, or obstruct, impede, or interfere with any inspection, audit, or observation of bingo or a game of chance or premises where bingo or a game of chance is conducted, or refuse to comply with any reasonable request of, or obstruct, impede, or interfere with any other reasonable action undertaken by, the attorney general or a law enforcement agency pursuant to division (H) of this section.

(J) Whoever violates division (A) or (I) of this section is guilty of a misdemeanor of the first degree.

**HISTORY: 136 v S 398 (Eff 5-26-76); 136 v H 1547 (Eff 12-6-76); 137 v H 72 (Eff 12-15-77); 139 v S 91 (Eff 10-20-81); 146 v S 2 (Eff 7-1-96); 149 v H 512. Eff 4-3-2003; 150 v H 95, § 1, eff. 7-1-03.**

The effective date is set by section 182 of H.B. 95 (150 v —).

**Not analogous to former RC § 2915.10 (RS § 6930; S&S 287; 59 v 10; GC § 13063; 120 v 663; Bureau of Code Revision, 10-1-53; 129 v 1513), repealed 134 v H 511, § 2, eff 1-1-74.**

## § 2915.101 Distribution of net profit from instant bingo.

Except as otherwise provided by law, a charitable organization that conducts instant bingo shall distribute the net profit from the proceeds of the sale of instant bingo as follows:

(A)(1) If a veteran's organization, a fraternal organization, or a sporting organization conducted the instant bingo, the organization shall distribute the net profit from the proceeds of the sale of instant bingo, as follows:

(a) For the first two hundred fifty thousand dollars, or a greater amount prescribed by the attorney general to adjust for changes in prices as measured by the consumer price index as defined in section 325.18 of the Revised Code and other factors affecting the organization's expenses as defined in division (LL) of section 2915.01 of the

Revised Code, or less of net profit from the proceeds of the sale of instant bingo generated in a calendar year:

(i) At least twenty-five per cent shall be distributed to an organization described in division (Z)(1) of section 2915.01 of the Revised Code or to a department or agency of the federal government, the state, or any political subdivision.

(ii) Not more than seventy-five per cent may be deducted and retained by the organization for reimbursement of or for the organization's expenses, as defined in division (LL) of section 2915.01 of the Revised Code, in conducting the instant bingo game.

(b) For any net profit from the proceeds of the sale of instant bingo of more than two hundred fifty thousand dollars or an adjusted amount generated in a calendar year:

(i) A minimum of fifty per cent shall be distributed to an organization described in division (Z)(1) of section 2915.01 of the Revised Code or to a department or agency of the federal government, the state, or any political subdivision.

(ii) Five per cent may be distributed for the organization's own charitable purposes or to a community action agency.

(iii) Forty-five per cent may be deducted and retained by the organization for reimbursement of or for the organization's expenses, as defined in division (LL) of section 2915.01 of the Revised Code, in conducting the instant bingo game.

(2) If a veteran's organization, a fraternal organization, or a sporting organization does not distribute the full percentages specified in divisions (A)(1)(a) and (b) of this section for the purposes specified in those divisions, the organization shall distribute the balance of the net profit from the proceeds of the sale of instant bingo not distributed or retained for those purposes to an organization described in division (Z)(1) of section 2915.01 of the Revised Code.

(B) If a charitable organization other than a veteran's organization, a fraternal organization, or a sporting organization conducted the instant bingo, the organization shall distribute one hundred per cent of the net profit from the proceeds of the sale of instant bingo to an organization described in division (Z)(1) of section 2915.01 of the Revised Code or to a department or agency of the federal government, the state, or any political subdivision.

(C) Nothing in this section prohibits a veteran's organization, a fraternal organization, or a sporting organization from distributing any net profit from the proceeds of the sale of instant bingo to an organization that is described in subsection 501(c)(3) of the Internal Revenue Code when the organization that is described in subsection 501(c)(3) of the Internal Revenue Code is one that makes donations to other organizations and permits donors to advise or direct such donations so long as the donations comply with requirements established in or pursuant to subsection 501(c)(3) of the Internal Revenue Code.

**HISTORY: 149 v H 512. Eff 4-3-2003; 150 v H 95, § 1, eff. 7-1-03; 150 v H 325, § 1, eff. 9-30-04; 152 v H 562, § 101.01, eff. 9-23-08; 153 v H 519, § 1, eff. 9-10-10.**

The effective date is set by § 812.10 of 152 v H 562.
The effective date is set by section 182 of H.B. 95 (150 v —).

## § 2915.11 Persons prohibited from being bingo game operators.

(A) No person shall be a bingo game operator unless he is eighteen years of age or older.

(B) No person who has been convicted of a felony or a gambling offense in any jurisdiction shall be a bingo game operator.

(C) Whoever violates division (A) of this section is guilty of a misdemeanor of the third degree.

(D) Whoever violates division (B) of this section is guilty of a misdemeanor of the first degree.

**HISTORY: 136 v S 398 (Eff 5-26-76); 137 v H 72. Eff 12-15-77.**

**Not analogous to former RC § 2915.11 (GC § 13063-1; 120 v 663; Bureau of Code Revision, 10-1-53; 129 v 1409), repealed 134 v H 511, § 2, eff 1-1-74.**

## § 2915.111 Repealed, 134 v H 511, § 2 [129 v 1409]. Eff 1-1-74.

This section concerned possession of "numbers game" ticket.

## § 2915.12 Bingo for amusement only.

(A) Sections 2915.07 to 2915.11 of the Revised Code do not apply to bingo games that are conducted for the purpose of amusement only. A bingo game is conducted for the purpose of amusement only if it complies with all of the requirements specified in either division (A)(1) or (2) of this section:

(1)(a) The participants do not pay any money or any other thing of value including an admission fee, or any fee for bingo cards or sheets, objects to cover the spaces, or other devices used in playing bingo, for the privilege of participating in the bingo game, or to defray any costs of the game, or pay tips or make donations during or immediately before or after the bingo game.

(b) All prizes awarded during the course of the game are nonmonetary, and in the form of merchandise, goods, or entitlements to goods or services only, and the total value of all prizes awarded during the game is less than one hundred dollars.

(c) No commission, wages, salary, reward, tip, donation, gratuity, or other form of compensation, either directly or indirectly, and regardless of the source, is paid to any bingo game operator for work or labor performed at the site of the bingo game.

(d) The bingo game is not conducted either during or within ten hours of any of the following:

(i) A bingo session during which a charitable bingo game is conducted pursuant to sections 2915.07 to 2915.11 of the Revised Code;

(ii) A scheme or game of chance, or bingo described in division (S)(2) of section 2915.01 of the Revised Code.

(e) The number of players participating in the bingo game does not exceed fifty.

(2)(a) The participants do not pay money or any other thing of value as an admission fee, and no participant is charged more than twenty-five cents to purchase a bingo card or sheet, objects to cover the spaces, or other devices used in playing bingo.

(b) The total amount of money paid by all of the participants for bingo cards or sheets, objects to cover the spaces, or other devices used in playing bingo does not exceed one hundred dollars.

(c) All of the money paid for bingo cards or sheets, objects to cover spaces, or other devices used in playing bingo is used only to pay winners monetary and nonmonetary prizes and to provide refreshments.

(d) The total value of all prizes awarded during the game does not exceed one hundred dollars.

(e) No commission, wages, salary, reward, tip, donation, gratuity, or other form of compensation, either directly or indirectly, and regardless of the source, is paid to any bingo game operator for work or labor performed at the site of the bingo game.

(f) The bingo game is not conducted during or within ten hours of either of the following:

(i) A bingo session during which a charitable bingo game is conducted pursuant to sections 2915.07 to 2915.11 of the Revised Code;

(ii) A scheme of chance or game of chance, or bingo described in division (S)(2) of section 2915.01 of the Revised Code.

(g) All of the participants reside at the premises where the bingo game is conducted.

(h) The bingo games are conducted on different days of the week and not more than twice in a calendar week.

(B) The attorney general or any local law enforcement agency may investigate the conduct of a bingo game that purportedly is conducted for purposes of amusement only if there is reason to believe that the purported amusement bingo game does not comply with the requirements of either division (A)(1) or (2) of this section. A local law enforcement agency may proceed by action in the proper court to enforce this section if the local law enforcement agency gives written notice to the attorney general when commencing the action.

**HISTORY: 136 v S 398 (Eff 5-26-76); 137 v H 72 (Eff 12-15-77); 143 v H 573 (Eff 4-10-91); 146 v S 2 (Eff 7-1-96); 149 v H 512. Eff 4-3-2003.**

**Not analogous to former RC § 2915.12 (RS § 6931; S&S 287; 59 v 10; 70 v 123; GC § 13064; 120 v 663; Bureau of Code Revision, 10-1-53; 129 v 1409), repealed 134 v H 511, § 2, eff 1-1-74.**

## § 2915.121 Repealed, 134 v H 511, § 2 [129 v 1408]. Eff 1-1-74.

This section concerned schemes of chance.

## § 2915.122 Repealed, 134 v H 511, § 2 [129 v 1408]. Eff 1-1-74.

This section concerned possessing odds ticket on athletic events.

## § 2915.13 Veteran's, fraternal, or sporting organization conducting instant bingo.

(A) A veteran's organization, a fraternal organization, or a sporting organization authorized to conduct a bingo session pursuant to sections 2915.01 to 2915.12 of the Revised Code may conduct instant bingo other than at a bingo session if all of the following apply:

(1) The veteran's organization, fraternal organization, or sporting organization limits the sale of instant bingo to twelve hours during any day, provided that the sale does not begin earlier than ten a.m. and ends not later than two a.m.

(2) The veteran's organization, fraternal organization, or sporting organization limits the sale of instant bingo to its own premises and to its own members and invited guests.

(3) The veteran's organization, fraternal organization, or sporting organization is raising money for an organization that is described in subsection 509(a)(1), 509(a)(2), or 509(a)(3) of the Internal Revenue Code and is either a governmental unit or an organization that maintains its principal place of business in this state, that is exempt from federal income taxation under subsection 501(a) and described in subsection 501(c)(3) of the Internal Revenue Code, and that is in good standing in this state and executes a written contract with that organization as required in division (B) of this section.

(B) If a veteran's organization, fraternal organization, or sporting organization authorized to conduct instant bingo pursuant to division (A) of this section is raising money for another organization that is described in subsection 509(a)(1), 509(a)(2), or 509(a)(3) of the Internal Revenue Code and is either a governmental unit or an organization that maintains its principal place of business in this state, that is exempt from federal income taxation under subsection 501(a) and described in subsection 501(c)(3) of the Internal Revenue Code, and that is in good standing in this state, the veteran's organization, fraternal organization, or sporting organization shall execute a written contract with the organization that is described in subsection 509(a)(1), 509(a)(2), or 509(a)(3) of the Internal Revenue Code and is either a governmental unit or an organization that maintains its principal place of business in this state, that is exempt from federal income taxation under subsection 501(a) and described in subsection 501(c)(3) of the Internal Revenue Code, and that is in good standing in this state in order to conduct instant bingo. That contract shall include a statement of the percentage of the net proceeds that the veteran's, fraternal, or sporting organization will be distributing to the organization that is described in subsection 509(a)(1), 509(a)(2), or 509(a)(3) of the Internal Revenue Code and is either a governmental unit or an organization that maintains its principal place of business in this state, that is exempt from federal income taxation under subsection 501(a) and described in subsection 501(c)(3) of the Internal Revenue Code, and that is in good standing in this state.

(C)(1) If a veteran's organization, fraternal organization, or sporting organization authorized to conduct instant bingo pursuant to division (A) of this section has been issued a liquor permit under Chapter 4303. of the Revised Code, that permit may be subject to suspension, revocation, or cancellation if the veteran's organization, fraternal organization, or sporting organization violates a provision of this chapter.

(2) No veteran's organization, fraternal organization, or sporting organization that enters into a written contract pursuant to division (B) of this section shall violate any provision of this chapter or permit, aid, or abet any other person in violating any provision of this chapter.

(D) A veteran's organization, fraternal organization, or sporting organization shall give all required proceeds earned from the conduct of instant bingo to the organization with which the veteran's organization, fraternal organization, or sporting organization has entered into a written contract.

(E) Whoever violates this section is guilty of illegal instant bingo conduct. Except as otherwise provided in this division, illegal instant bingo conduct is a misdemeanor of the first degree. If the offender previously has been convicted of a violation of this section, illegal instant bingo conduct is a felony of the fifth degree.

**HISTORY: 149 v H 512. Eff 4-3-2003; 150 v H 95, § 1, eff. 7-1-03; 150 v H 325, § 1, eff. 9-30-04.**

The effective date is set by section 182 of H.B. 95 (150 v —).

**Not analogous to former RC § 2915.13 (GC § 13064-1; 120 v 663(664), § 1; Bureau of Code Revision, 10-1-53; 129 v 1409), repealed 134 v H 511, § 2, eff 1-1-74.**

**§ 2915.14** Repealed, 134 v H 511, § 2 [RS § 6934; S&C 662, 665; S&S 377; 54 v 196; 73 v 249; GC §§ 13065, 13066; 124 v 838; Bureau of Code Revision, 10-1-53]. Eff 1-1-74.

This section concerned gambling as a profession.

**§ 2915.15** Repealed, 134 v H 511, § 2 [RS § 6934; S&C 662, 665; S&S 377; 54 v 196; 73 v 249; GC §§ 13065, 13066; 124 v 838; Bureau of Code Revision, 10-1-53]. Eff 1-1-74.

This section concerned gambling devices.

**§ 2915.16** Repealed, 134 v H 511, § 2 [GC §§ 13066-1—13066-3; 124 v 838; Bureau of Code Revision, 10-1-53]. Eff 1-1-74.

This section concerned gambling devices.

**§ 2915.17** Repealed, 134 v H 511, § 2 [GC §§ 13066-1—13066-3; 124 v 838; Bureau of Code Revision, 10-1-53]. Eff 1-1-74.

This section concerned gambling devices.

**§ 2915.18** Repealed, 134 v H 511, § 2 [GC §§ 13066-1—13066-3; 124 v 838; Bureau of Code Revision, 10-1-53]. Eff 1-1-74.

This section concerned gambling devices.

**§ 2915.19** Repealed, 134 v H 511, § 2 [RS §§ 6929, 6934a; S&C 435; 49 v 105; 79 v 118; 83 v 195; GC §§ 13067-13070]. Eff 1-1-74.

This section concerned advertising lotteries.

**§ 2915.20** Repealed, 134 v H 511, § 2 [RS §§ 6929, 6934a; S&C 435; 49 v 105; 79 v 118; 83 v 195; GC §§ 13067-13070]. Eff 1-1-74.

This section concerned contracts for options on commodities.

**§ 2915.21** Repealed, 134 v H 511, § 2 [RS §§ 6929, 6934a; S&C 435; 49 v 105; 79 v 118; 83 v 195; GC §§ 13067-13070]. Eff 1-1-74.

This section concerned advertising lotteries and contracts for options on commodities.

**§ 2915.31** Repealed, 134 v H 511, § 2 [RS §§ 6934a-1, 6934a-4; 86 v 12; GC §§ 13071-13074, 13079, 13080; 102 v 317; Bureau of Code Revision, 10-1-53]. Eff 1-1-74.

This section concerned bucket shops.

**§ 2915.32** Repealed, 134 v H 511, § 2 [RS §§ 6934a-1, 6934a-4; 86 v 12; GC §§ 13071-13074, 13079, 13080; 102 v 317; Bureau of Code Revision, 10-1-53]. Eff 1-1-74.

This section concerned bucket shops.

**§ 2915.33** Repealed, 134 v H 511, § 2 [RS §§ 6934a-1, 6934a-4; 86 v 12; GC §§ 13071-13074, 13079, 13080; 102 v 317; Bureau of Code Revision, 10-1-53]. Eff 1-1-74.

This section concerned bucket shops.

**§ 2915.34** Repealed, 134 v H 511, § 2 [RS §§ 6934a-2, 6934a-3; 86 v 13, 14; GC §§ 13075-13077; 102 v 317; Bureau of Code Revision, 10-1-53]. Eff 1-1-74.

This section concerned bucket shops.

**§ 2915.35** Repealed, 134 v H 511, § 2 [RS §§ 6934a-2, 6934a-3; 86 v 13, 14; GC §§ 13075-13077; 102 v 317; Bureau of Code Revision, 10-1-53]. Eff 1-1-74.

This section concerned bucket shops.

**§ 2915.36** Repealed, 134 v H 511, § 2 [RS §§ 6934a-2, 6934a-3; 86 v 13, 14; GC §§ 13075-13077; 102 v 317; Bureau of Code Revision, 10-1-53]. Eff 1-1-74.

This section concerned bucket shops.

**§ 2915.37** Repealed, 134 v H 511, § 2 [RS § 6934a-5; 86 v 14; GC § 13081; Bureau of Code Revision, 10-1-53]. Eff 1-1-74.

This section concerned bucket shops.

**§ 2915.40** Repealed, 134 v H 511, § 2 [133 v S 284]. Eff 1-1-74.

This section concerned coerced establishment of give-away games and penalty.

# CHAPTER 2917: OFFENSES AGAINST THE PUBLIC PEACE



## [INCITING, RIOT, AND RELATED OFFENSES]

### § 2917.01 Inciting to violence.

(A) No person shall knowingly engage in conduct designed to urge or incite another to commit any offense of violence, when either of the following apply:

(1) The conduct takes place under circumstances that create a clear and present danger that any offense of violence will be committed;

(2) The conduct proximately results in the commission of any offense of violence.

(B) Whoever violates this section is guilty of inciting to violence. If the offense of violence that the other person is being urged or incited to commit is a misdemeanor, inciting to violence is a misdemeanor of the first degree. If the offense of violence that the other person is being urged or incited to commit is a felony, inciting to violence is a felony of the third degree.

**HISTORY: 134 v H 511 (Eff 1-1-74); 146 v S 2. Eff 7-1-96.**

**Not analogous to former RC § 2917.01 (RS § 6900; S&C 432, 457, 457a; 29 v 144; 57 v 47; 70 v 155; GC §§ 12823, 12824; 102 v 129; Bureau of Code Revision, 10-1-53), repealed 134 v H 511, § 2, eff 1-1-74.**

The effective date is set by section 6 of SB 2.

### § 2917.02 Aggravated riot.

(A) No person shall participate with four or more others in a course of disorderly conduct in violation of section 2917.11 of the Revised Code:

(1) With purpose to commit or facilitate the commission of a felony;

(2) With purpose to commit or facilitate the commission of any offense of violence;

(3) When the offender or any participant to the knowledge of the offender has on or about the offender's or participant's person or under the offender's or participant's control, uses, or intends to use a deadly weapon or dangerous ordnance, as defined in section 2923.11 of the Revised Code.

(B)(1) No person, being an inmate in a detention facility, shall violate division (A)(1) or (3) of this section.

(2) No person, being an inmate in a detention facility, shall violate division (A)(2) of this section or section 2917.03 of the Revised Code.

(C) Whoever violates this section is guilty of aggravated riot. A violation of division (A)(1) or (3) of this section is a felony of the fifth degree. A violation of division (A)(2) or (B)(1) of this section is a felony of the fourth degree. A violation of division (B)(2) of this section is a felony of the third degree.

(D) As used in this section, "detention facility" has the same meaning as in section 2921.01 of the Revised Code.

**HISTORY: 134 v H 511 (Eff 1-1-74); 139 v S 199 (Eff 1-5-83); 140 v S 210 (Eff 7-1-83); 146 v S 2. Eff 7-1-96.**

**Not analogous to former RC § 2917.02 (GC § 12823-1; 122 v 130; Bureau of Code Revision, 10-1-53), repealed 134 v H 511, § 2, eff 1-1-74.**

The effective date is set by section 6 of SB 2.

### § 2917.03 Riot.

(A) No person shall participate with four or more others in a course of disorderly conduct in violation of section 2917.11 of the Revised Code:

(1) With purpose to commit or facilitate the commission of a misdemeanor, other than disorderly conduct;

(2) With purpose to intimidate a public official or employee into taking or refraining from official action, or with purpose to hinder, impede, or obstruct a function of government;

(3) With purpose to hinder, impede, or obstruct the orderly process of administration or instruction at an educational institution, or to interfere with or disrupt lawful activities carried on at such institution.

(B) No person shall participate with four or more others with purpose to do an act with unlawful force or violence, even though such act might otherwise be lawful.

(C) Whoever violates this section is guilty of riot, a misdemeanor of the first degree.

**HISTORY: 134 v H 511. Eff 1-1-74.**

**Not analogous to former RC § 2917.03 (RS § 6899; S&C 431, 432; 29 v 144; 95 v 300; GC § 12825; Bureau of Code Revision, 10-1-53), repealed 134 v H 511, § 2, eff 1-1-74.**

## § 2917.031 Proof of express agreement with four or more others not required.

For the purposes of prosecuting violations of sections 2917.02 and 2917.03 of the Revised Code, the state is not required to allege or prove that the offender expressly agreed with four or more others to commit any act that constitutes a violation of either section prior to or while committing those acts.

**HISTORY: 150 v S 57, § 1, eff. 3-22-04.**

The effective date is set by section 4 of S.B. 57

## § 2917.04 Failure to disperse.

(A) Where five or more persons are participating in a course of disorderly conduct in violation of section 2917.11 of the Revised Code, and there are other persons in the vicinity whose presence creates the likelihood of physical harm to persons or property or of serious public inconvenience, annoyance, or alarm, a law enforcement officer or other public official may order the participants and such other persons to disperse. No person shall knowingly fail to obey such order.

(B) Nothing in this section requires persons to disperse who are peaceably assembled for a lawful purpose.

(C)(1) Whoever violates this section is guilty of failure to disperse.

(2) Except as otherwise provided in division (C)(3) of this section, failure to disperse is a minor misdemeanor.

(3) Failure to disperse is a misdemeanor of the fourth degree if the failure to obey the order described in division (A) of this section creates the likelihood of physical harm to persons or is committed at the scene of a fire, accident, disaster, riot, or emergency of any kind.

**HISTORY: 134 v H 511. Eff 1-1-74; 150 v S 57, § 1, eff. 3-22-04.**

The effective date is set by section 4 of S.B. 57 (150 v —).

**Not analogous to former RC § 2917.04 (GC § 12824-1; 101 v 100; Bureau of Code Revision, 10-1-53), repealed 134 v H 511, § 2, eff 1-1-74.**

Analogous to former RC § 2923.51 (132 v H 996), repealed 134 v H 511, § 2, eff 1-1-74.

## § 2917.05 Justifiable use of force to suppress riot.

A law enforcement officer or fireman, engaged in suppressing riot or in protecting persons or property during riot:

(A) Is justified in using force, other than deadly force, when and to the extent he has probable cause to believe such force is necessary to disperse or apprehend rioters;

(B) Is justified in using force, including deadly force, when and to the extent he has probable cause to believe such force is necessary to disperse or apprehend rioters whose conduct is creating a substantial risk of serious physical harm to persons.

**HISTORY: 134 v H 511. Eff 1-1-74.**

**Not analogous to former RC § 2917.05 (RS § 6899a; 95 v 300; GC § 12826; Bureau of Code Revision, 10-1-53), repealed 134 v H 511, § 2, eff 1-1-74.**

**Analogous to former RC § 2923.55 (132 v H 996), repealed 134 v H 511, § 2, eff 1-1-74.**

## § 2917.06 Repealed, 134 v H 511, § 2 [RS §§ 6899b, 6907, 6918a; S&C 258; 32 v 17; 86 v 127; 97 v 281; GC §§ 12827, 12828, 12866; 124 v 62; Bureau of Code Revision, 10-1-53; 129 v 582(746)]. Eff 1-1-74.

This section concerned bribery.

## § 2917.07 Repealed, 134 v H 511, § 2 [RS §§ 6899b, 6907, 6918a; S&C 258; 32 v 17; 86 v 127; 97 v 281; GC §§ 12827, 12828, 12866; 124 v 62; Bureau of Code Revision, 10-1-53; 129 v 582(746)]. Eff 1-1-74.

This section concerned bribery.

## § 2917.08 Repealed, 134 v H 511, § 2 [RS §§ 6899b, 6907, 6918a; S&C 258; 32 v 17; 86 v 127; 97 v 281; GC §§ 12827, 12828, 12866; 124 v 62; Bureau of Code Revision, 10-1-53; 129 v 582(746)]. Eff 1-1-74.

This section concerned bribery.

## § 2917.09 Repealed, 134 v H 511, § 2 [RS §§ 6903, 6908-1; S&C 431; 29 v 144; 93 v 411; GC §§ 12831, 12832; Bureau of Code Revision, 10-1-53]. Eff 1-1-74.

This section concerned lynching and escape of prisoner.

## § 2917.10 Repealed, 134 v H 511, § 2 [RS §§ 6903, 6908-1; S&C 431; 29 v 144; 93 v 411; GC §§ 12831, 12832; Bureau of Code Revision, 10-1-53]. Eff 1-1-74.

This section concerned escape of prisoner.

### [DISORDERLY CONDUCT]

## § 2917.11 Disorderly conduct.

(A) No person shall recklessly cause inconvenience, annoyance, or alarm to another by doing any of the following:

(1) Engaging in fighting, in threatening harm to persons or property, or in violent or turbulent behavior;

(2) Making unreasonable noise or an offensively coarse utterance, gesture, or display or communicating unwarranted and grossly abusive language to any person;

(3) Insulting, taunting, or challenging another, under circumstances in which that conduct is likely to provoke a violent response;

(4) Hindering or preventing the movement of persons on a public street, road, highway, or right-of-way, or to, from, within, or upon public or private property, so as to interfere with the rights of others, and by any act that serves no lawful and reasonable purpose of the offender;

(5) Creating a condition that is physically offensive to persons or that presents a risk of physical harm to persons or property, by any act that serves no lawful and reasonable purpose of the offender.

(B) No person, while voluntarily intoxicated, shall do either of the following:

(1) In a public place or in the presence of two or more persons, engage in conduct likely to be offensive or to cause inconvenience, annoyance, or alarm to persons of

ordinary sensibilities, which conduct the offender, if the offender were not intoxicated, should know is likely to have that effect on others;

(2) Engage in conduct or create a condition that presents a risk of physical harm to the offender or another, or to the property of another.

(C) Violation of any statute or ordinance of which an element is operating a motor vehicle, locomotive, watercraft, aircraft, or other vehicle while under the influence of alcohol or any drug of abuse, is not a violation of division (B) of this section.

(D) If a person appears to an ordinary observer to be intoxicated, it is probable cause to believe that person is voluntarily intoxicated for purposes of division (B) of this section.

(E)(1) Whoever violates this section is guilty of disorderly conduct.

(2) Except as otherwise provided in division (E)(3) of this section, disorderly conduct is a minor misdemeanor.

(3) Disorderly conduct is a misdemeanor of the fourth degree if any of the following applies:

(a) The offender persists in disorderly conduct after reasonable warning or request to desist.

(b) The offense is committed in the vicinity of a school or in a school safety zone.

(c) The offense is committed in the presence of any law enforcement officer, firefighter, rescuer, medical person, emergency medical services person, or other authorized person who is engaged in the person's duties at the scene of a fire, accident, disaster, riot, or emergency of any kind.

(d) The offense is committed in the presence of any emergency facility person who is engaged in the person's duties in an emergency facility.

(F) As used in this section:

(1) "Emergency medical services person" is the singular of "emergency medical services personnel" as defined in section 2133.21 of the Revised Code.

(2) "Emergency facility person" is the singular of "emergency facility personnel" as defined in section 2909.04 of the Revised Code.

(3) "Emergency facility" has the same meaning as in section 2909.04 of the Revised Code.

(4) "Committed in the vicinity of a school" has the same meaning as in section 2925.01 of the Revised Code.

**HISTORY: 134 v H 511 (Eff 1-1-74); 143 v H 51 (Eff 11-8-90); 146 v S 2 (Eff 7-1-96); 148 v S 1 (Eff 8-6-99); 148 v H 137 (Eff 3-10-2000); 149 v S 40. Eff 1-25-2002.**

**Not analogous to former RC § 2917.11 (RS § 6904; S&C 415, 431, 911; 29 v 144; 68 v 9; GC § 12833, Bureau of Code Revision, 10-1-53), repealed 134 v H 511, § 2, eff 1-1-74.**

## § 2917.12 Disturbing a lawful meeting.

(A) No person, with purpose to prevent or disrupt a lawful meeting, procession, or gathering, shall do either of the following:

(1) Do any act which obstructs or interferes with the due conduct of such meeting, procession, or gathering;

(2) Make any utterance, gesture, or display which outrages the sensibilities of the group.

(B) Whoever violates this section is guilty of disturbing a lawful meeting, a misdemeanor of the fourth degree.

**HISTORY: 134 v H 511. Eff 1-1-74.**

**Not analogous to former RC § 2917.12 (RS § 6904; S&C 415, 431, 911; 29 v 144; 68 v 9; GC § 12833; Bureau of Code Revision, 10-1-53), repealed 134 v H 511, § 2, eff 1-1-74.**

## § 2917.13 Misconduct at emergency.

(A) No person shall knowingly do any of the following:

(1) Hamper the lawful operations of any law enforcement officer, firefighter, rescuer, medical person, emergency medical services person, or other authorized person, engaged in the person's duties at the scene of a fire, accident, disaster, riot, or emergency of any kind;

(2) Hamper the lawful activities of any emergency facility person who is engaged in the person's duties in an emergency facility;

(3) Fail to obey the lawful order of any law enforcement officer engaged in the law enforcement officer's duties at the scene of or in connection with a fire, accident, disaster, riot, or emergency of any kind.

(B) Nothing in this section shall be construed to limit access or deny information to any news media representative in the lawful exercise of the news media representative's duties.

(C) Whoever violates this section is guilty of misconduct at an emergency. Except as otherwise provided in this division, misconduct at an emergency is a misdemeanor of the fourth degree. If a violation of this section creates a risk of physical harm to persons or property, misconduct at an emergency is a misdemeanor of the first degree.

(D) As used in this section:

(1) "Emergency medical services person" is the singular of "emergency medical services personnel" as defined in section 2133.21 of the Revised Code.

(2) "Emergency facility person" is the singular of "emergency facility personnel" as defined in section 2909.04 of the Revised Code.

(3) "Emergency facility" has the same meaning as in section 2909.04 of the Revised Code.

**HISTORY: 134 v H 511 (Eff 1-1-74); 135 v H 716 (Eff 1-1-74); 148 v H 137 (Eff 3-10-2000); 149 v S 40. Eff 1-25-2002; 150 v S 57, § 1, eff. 3-22-04.**

The effective date is set by section 4 of S.B. 57 (150 v —).

**Not analogous to former RC § 2917.13 (RS § 6905; S&C 432; 29 v 144; GC § 12834; Bureau of Code Revision, 10-1-53), repealed 134 v H 511, § 2, eff 1-1-74.**

**Analogous to former RC § 2923.43 (132 v H 332), repealed 134 v H 511, § 2, eff 1-1-74.**

## § 2917.14 Repealed, 134 v H 511, § 2 [RS § 6902; S&S 287; 62 v 109; 68 v 9; 84 v 91; 97 v 120; GC §§ 12835, 12837; 123 v 223; Bureau of Code Revision, 10-1-53; 125 v H 88]. Eff 1-1-74.

This section concerned conveying articles to prisoners.

## § 2917.15 Repealed, 134 v H 511, § 2 [RS § 6902; S&S 287; 62 v 109; 68 v 9; 84 v 91; 97 v 120; GC §§ 12835, 12837; 123 v 223; Bureau of Code Revision, 10-1-53; 125 v H 88]. Eff 1-1-74.

This section concerned conveying articles to prisoners.

## § 2917.16 Repealed, 134 v H 511, § 2 [RS § 6902; S&S 287; 62 v 109; 68 v 9; 84 v 91; 97 v 120; GC §§ 12835, 12837; 123 v 223; Bureau of Code Revision, 10-1-53; 125 v H 88]. Eff 1-1-74.

This section concerned conveying articles to prisoners.

**§ 2917.17** Repealed, 134 v H 511, § 2 [RS §§ 6827, 6902, 6947; S&C 750; S&S 287; 54 v 127; 62 v 109; 68 v 9; 73 v 249; 84 v 91; 95 v 69; 97 v 120, 307; GC §§ 12836, 12838, 12846; Bureau of Code Revision, 10-1-53; 128 v 1040; 130 v 662; 130 v PtII, 145; 134 v H 494]. Eff 1-1-74.

This section concerned conveying articles to prisoners; escapes.

**§ 2917.18** Repealed, 134 v H 511, § 2 [RS §§ 6827, 6902, 6947; S&C 750; S&S 287; 54 v 127; 62 v 109; 68 v 9; 73 v 249; 84 v 91; 95 v 69; 97 v 120, 307; GC §§ 12836, 12838, 12846; Bureau of Code Revision, 10-1-53; 128 v 1040; 130 v 662; 130 v PtII, 145; 134 v H 494]. Eff 1-1-74.

This section concerned conveying articles to prisoners; escapes.

**§ 2917.19** Repealed, 134 v H 511, § 2 [RS §§ 6827, 6902, 6947; S&C 750; S&S 287; 54 v 127; 62 v 109; 68 v 9; 73 v 249; 84 v 91; 95 v 69; 97 v 120, 307; GC §§ 12836, 12838, 12846; Bureau of Code Revision, 10-1-53; 128 v 1040; 130 v 662; 130 v PtII, 145; 134 v H 494]. Eff 1-1-74.

This section concerned conveying articles to prisoners; escapes.

**§ 2917.191** Repealed, 134 v H 511, § 2 [130 v 662]. Eff 1-1-74.

This section concerned attempting to persuade inmates to escape.

**§ 2917.20** Repealed, 134 v H 511, § 2 [GC § 12838-1; 103 v 93; Bureau of Code Revision, 10-1-53]. Eff 1-1-74.

This section concerned soliciting money from persons confined.

### [HARASSMENT]

### § 2917.21 Telecommunications harassment.

(A) No person shall knowingly make or cause to be made a telecommunication, or knowingly permit a telecommunication to be made from a telecommunications device under the person's control, to another, if the caller does any of the following:

(1) Fails to identify the caller to the recipient of the telecommunication and makes the telecommunication with purpose to harass or abuse any person at the premises to which the telecommunication is made, whether or not actual communication takes place between the caller and a recipient;

(2) Describes, suggests, requests, or proposes that the caller, the recipient of the telecommunication, or any other person engage in sexual activity, and the recipient or another person at the premises to which the telecommunication is made has requested, in a previous telecommunication or in the immediate telecommunication, that the caller not make a telecommunication to the recipient or to the premises to which the telecommunication is made;

(3) During the telecommunication, violates section 2903.21 of the Revised Code;

(4) Knowingly states to the recipient of the telecommunication that the caller intends to cause damage to or destroy public or private property, and the recipient, any member of the recipient's family, or any other person who resides at the premises to which the telecommunication is made owns, leases, resides, or works in, will at the time of the destruction or damaging be near or in, has the responsibility of protecting, or insures the property that will be destroyed or damaged;

(5) Knowingly makes the telecommunication to the recipient of the telecommunication, to another person at the premises to which the telecommunication is made, or to those premises, and the recipient or another person at those premises previously has told the caller not to make a telecommunication to those premises or to any persons at those premises.

(B) No person shall make or cause to be made a telecommunication, or permit a telecommunication to be made from a telecommunications device under the person's control, with purpose to abuse, threaten, or harass another person.

(C)(1) Whoever violates this section is guilty of telecommunications harassment.

(2) A violation of division (A)(1), (2), (3), or (5) or (B) of this section is a misdemeanor of the first degree on a first offense and a felony of the fifth degree on each subsequent offense.

(3) Except as otherwise provided in division (C)(3) of this section, a violation of division (A)(4) of this section is a misdemeanor of the first degree on a first offense and a felony of the fifth degree on each subsequent offense. If a violation of division (A)(4) of this section results in economic harm of one thousand dollars or more but less than seven thousand five hundred dollars, telecommunications harassment is a felony of the fifth degree. If a violation of division (A)(4) of this section results in economic harm of seven thousand five hundred dollars or more but less than one hundred fifty thousand dollars, telecommunications harassment is a felony of the fourth degree. If a violation of division (A)(4) of this section results in economic harm of one hundred fifty thousand dollars or more, telecommunications harassment is a felony of the third degree.

(D) No cause of action may be asserted in any court of this state against any provider of a telecommunications service or information service, or against any officer, employee, or agent of a telecommunication service or information service, for any injury, death, or loss to person or property that allegedly arises out of the provider's, officer's, employee's, or agent's provision of information, facilities, or assistance in accordance with the terms of a court order that is issued in relation to the investigation or prosecution of an alleged violation of this section. A provider of a telecommunications service or information service, or an officer, employee, or agent of a telecommunications service or information service, is immune from any civil or criminal liability for injury, death, or loss to person or property that allegedly arises out of the provider's, officer's, employee's, or agent's provision of information, facilities, or assistance in accordance with the terms of a court order that is issued in relation to the investigation or prosecution of an alleged violation of this section.

(E) As used in this section:

(1) "Economic harm" means all direct, incidental, and consequential pecuniary harm suffered by a victim as a result of criminal conduct. "Economic harm" includes, but is not limited to, all of the following:

(a) All wages, salaries, or other compensation lost as a result of the criminal conduct;

(b) The cost of all wages, salaries, or other compensation paid to employees for time those employees are prevented from working as a result of the criminal conduct;

(c) The overhead costs incurred for the time that a business is shut down as a result of the criminal conduct;

(d) The loss of value to tangible or intangible property that was damaged as a result of the criminal conduct.

(2) "Caller" means the person described in division (A) of this section who makes or causes to be made a telecommunication or who permits a telecommunication to be made from a telecommunications device under that person's control.

(3) "Telecommunication" and "telecommunications device" have the same meanings as in section 2913.01 of the Revised Code.

(4) "Sexual activity" has the same meaning as in section 2907.01 of the Revised Code.

(F) Nothing in this section prohibits a person from making a telecommunication to a debtor that is in compliance with the "Fair Debt Collection Practices Act," 91 Stat. 874 (1977), 15 U.S.C. 1692, as amended, or the "Telephone Consumer Protection Act," 105 Stat. 2395 (1991), 47 U.S.C. 227, as amended.

**HISTORY: 134 v H 511 (Eff 1-1-74); 138 v H 164 (Eff 4-9-81); 146 v S 2 (Eff 7-1-96); 147 v H 182 (Eff 10-1-97); 147 v S 215 (Eff 3-30-99); 147 v H 565. Eff 3-30-99; 153 v S 162, § 1, eff. 9-13-10; 2011 HB 86, § 1, eff. Sept. 30, 2011.**

The provisions of § 4 of HB 86 read as follows:

"SECTION 4. The amendments to sections 926.99, 1333.99, 1707.99, 1716.99, 2909.03, 2909.05, 2909.11, 2913.02, 2913.03, 2913.04, 2913.11, 2913.21, 2913.31, 2913.32, 2913.34, 2913.40, 2913.401, 2913.42, 2913.421, 2913.43, 2913.45, 2913.46, 2913.47, 2913.48, 2913.49, 2913.51, 2913.61, 2915.05, 2917.21, 2917.31, 2917.32, 2921.13, 2921.41, 2923.31, and 2981.07, division (B) of section 2929.13, and division (A) of section 2929.14 of the Revised Code that are made in this act apply to a person who commits an offense specified or penalized under those sections on or after the effective date of this section and to a person to whom division (B) of section 1.58 of the Revised Code makes the amendments applicable.

"The provisions of sections 926.99, 1333.99, 1707.99, 1716.99, 2909.03, 2909.05, 2909.11, 2913.02, 2913.03, 2913.04, 2913.11, 2913.21, 2913.31, 2913.32, 2913.34, 2913.40, 2913.401, 2913.42, 2913.421, 2913.43, 2913.45, 2913.46, 2913.47, 2913.48, 2913.49, 2913.51, 2913.61, 2915.05, 2917.21, 2917.31, 2917.32, 2921.13, 2921.41, 2923.31, and 2981.07 of the Revised Code in existence prior to the effective date of this section shall apply to a person upon whom a court imposed sentence prior to the effective date of this section for an offense specified or penalized under those sections. The amendments to sections 926.99, 1333.99, 1707.99, 1716.99, 2909.03, 2909.05, 2909.11, 2913.02, 2913.03, 2913.04, 2913.11, 2913.21, 2913.31, 2913.32, 2913.34, 2913.40, 2913.401, 2913.42, 2913.421, 2913.43, 2913.45, 2913.46, 2913.47, 2913.48, 2913.49, 2913.51, 2913.61, 2915.05, 2917.21, 2917.31, 2917.32, 2921.13, 2921.41, 2923.31, and 2981.07 of the Revised Code that are made in this act do not apply to a person who upon whom a court imposed sentence prior to the effective date of this section for an offense specified or penalized under those sections."

The provisions of § 7 of 153 v S 162 read in part as follows:

SECTION 7. Section 2917.21 of the Revised Code is presented in this act as a composite of the section as amended by both H.B. 565 and S.B. 215 of the 122nd General Assembly. * * * The General Assembly, applying the principle stated in division (B) of section 1.52 of the Revised Code that amendments are to be harmonized if reasonably capable of simultaneous operation, finds that the composites are the resulting versions of those sections in effect prior to the effective date of those sections as presented in this act.

**Not analogous to former RC § 2917.21 (RS § 6827a; 90 v 33; 95 v 69; 97 v 307; GC § 12839; Bureau of Code Revision, 10-1-53), repealed 134 v H 511, § 2, eff 1-1-74.**

## § 2917.211 Repealed, 134 v H 511, § 2 [131 v 675]. Eff 1-1-74.

This section concerned prohibition against trespassing on school grounds and penalty.

## § 2917.22 Repealed, 134 v H 511, § 2 [RS §§ 2103, 6979; S&C 412; Bates, § 1536-374; 33 v 33; 66 v 196; GC §§ 12840, 12840-1, 12841; 110 v 261; 113 v 476; Bureau of Code Revision, 10-1-53; 133 v S 460]. Eff 1-1-74.

This section concerned harboring felons and escape from a workhouse.

## § 2917.23 Repealed, 134 v H 511, § 2 [RS §§ 2103, 6979; S&C 412; Bates, § 1536-374; 33 v 33; 66 v 196; GC §§ 12840, 12840-1, 12841; 110 v 261; 113 v 476; Bureau of Code Revision, 10-1-53; 133 v S 460]. Eff 1-1-74.

This section concerned harboring felons and escape from a workhouse.

## § 2917.24 Repealed, 134 v H 511, § 2 [RS §§ 2103, 6979; S&C 412; Bates, § 1536-374; 33 v 33; 66 v 196; GC §§ 12840, 12840-1, 12841; 110 v 261; 113 v 476; Bureau of Code Revision, 10-1-53; 133 v S 460]. Eff 1-1-74.

This section concerned harboring felons and escape from a workhouse.

## § 2917.25 Repealed, 134 v H 511, § 2 [RS §§ 6897, 6906; S&C 405, 432, 546, 547, 607, 1171; 29 v 144; 33 v 33; 38 v 146; 39 v 13; 52 v 27; 54 v 83; 59 v 91; 68 v 27; 69 v 62; 73 v 58; GC §§ 12842—12844; 104 v 7; 112 v 177; Bureau of Code Revision, 10-1-53]. Eff 1-1-74.

This section concerned misconduct of witnesses.

## § 2917.26 Repealed, 134 v H 511, § 2 [RS §§ 6897, 6906; S&C 405, 432, 546, 547, 607, 1171; 29 v 144; 33 v 33; 38 v 146; 39 v 13; 52 v 27; 54 v 83; 59 v 91; 68 v 27; 69 v 62; 73 v 58; GC §§ 12842—12844; 104 v 7; 112 v 177; Bureau of Code Revision, 10-1-53]. Eff 1-1-74.

This section concerned misconduct of witnesses.

## § 2917.27 Repealed, 134 v H 511, § 2 [RS §§ 6897, 6906; S&C 405, 432, 546, 547, 607, 1171; 29 v 144; 33 v 33; 38 v 146; 39 v 13; 52 v 27; 54 v 83; 59 v 91;

68 v 27; 69 v 62; 73 v 58; GC §§ 12842—12844; 104 v 7; 112 v 177; Bureau of Code Revision, 10-1-53]. Eff 1-1-74.

This section concerned misconduct of witnesses.

**§ 2917.28** Repealed, 134 v H 511, § 2 [RS §§ 6916, 6917; S&C 433, 434, 1398, 1401; 20 v 144; 29 v 112, 144; GC §§ 12849, 12850]. Eff 1-1-74.

This section concerned misconduct of officers.

**§ 2917.29** Repealed, 134 v H 511, § 2 [RS §§ 6916, 6917; S&C 433, 434, 1398, 1401; 20 v 144; 29 v 112, 144; GC §§ 12849, 12850]. Eff 1-1-74.

This section concerned misconduct of officers.

**§ 2917.30** Repealed, 134 v H 511, § 2 [RS §§ 6916, 6917; S&C 433, 434, 1398, 1401; 20 v 144; 29 v 112, 144; GC §§ 12849, 12850]. Eff 1-1-74.

This section concerned misconduct of officers.

## [FALSE ALARMS]

### § 2917.31 Inducing panic.

(A) No person shall cause the evacuation of any public place, or otherwise cause serious public inconvenience or alarm, by doing any of the following:

(1) Initiating or circulating a report or warning of an alleged or impending fire, explosion, crime, or other catastrophe, knowing that such report or warning is false;

(2) Threatening to commit any offense of violence;

(3) Committing any offense, with reckless disregard of the likelihood that its commission will cause serious public inconvenience or alarm.

(B) Division (A)(1) of this section does not apply to any person conducting an authorized fire or emergency drill.

(C)(1) Whoever violates this section is guilty of inducing panic.

(2) Except as otherwise provided in division (C)(3), (4), (5), (6), (7), or (8) of this section, inducing panic is a misdemeanor of the first degree.

(3) Except as otherwise provided in division (C)(4), (5), (6), (7), or (8) of this section, if a violation of this section results in physical harm to any person, inducing panic is a felony of the fourth degree.

(4) Except as otherwise provided in division (C)(5), (6), (7), or (8) of this section, if a violation of this section results in economic harm, the penalty shall be determined as follows:

(a) If the violation results in economic harm of one thousand dollars or more but less than seven thousand five hundred dollars and if division (C)(3) of this section does not apply, inducing panic is a felony of the fifth degree.

(b) If the violation results in economic harm of seven thousand five hundred dollars or more but less than one hundred fifty thousand dollars, inducing panic is a felony of the fourth degree.

(c) If the violation results in economic harm of one hundred fifty thousand dollars or more, inducing panic is a felony of the third degree.

(5) If the public place involved in a violation of division (A)(1) of this section is a school or an institution of higher education, inducing panic is a felony of the second degree.

(6) If the violation pertains to a purported, threatened, or actual use of a weapon of mass destruction, and except as otherwise provided in division (C)(5), (7), or (8) of this section, inducing panic is a felony of the fourth degree.

(7) If the violation pertains to a purported, threatened, or actual use of a weapon of mass destruction, and except as otherwise provided in division (C)(5) of this section, if a violation of this section results in physical harm to any person, inducing panic is a felony of the third degree.

(8) If the violation pertains to a purported, threatened, or actual use of a weapon of mass destruction, and except as otherwise provided in division (C)(5) of this section, if a violation of this section results in economic harm of one hundred thousand dollars or more, inducing panic is a felony of the third degree.

(D)(1) It is not a defense to a charge under this section that pertains to a purported or threatened use of a weapon of mass destruction that the offender did not possess or have the ability to use a weapon of mass destruction or that what was represented to be a weapon of mass destruction was not a weapon of mass destruction.

(2) Any act that is a violation of this section and any other section of the Revised Code may be prosecuted under this section, the other section, or both sections.

(E) As used in this section:

(1) "Economic harm" means any of the following:

(a) All direct, incidental, and consequential pecuniary harm suffered by a victim as a result of criminal conduct. "Economic harm" as described in this division includes, but is not limited to, all of the following:

(i) All wages, salaries, or other compensation lost as a result of the criminal conduct;

(ii) The cost of all wages, salaries, or other compensation paid to employees for time those employees are prevented from working as a result of the criminal conduct;

(iii) The overhead costs incurred for the time that a business is shut down as a result of the criminal conduct;

(iv) The loss of value to tangible or intangible property that was damaged as a result of the criminal conduct.

(b) All costs incurred by the state or any political subdivision as a result of, or in making any response to, the criminal conduct that constituted the violation of this section or section 2917.32 of the Revised Code, including, but not limited to, all costs so incurred by any law enforcement officers, firefighters, rescue personnel, or emergency medical services personnel of the state or the political subdivision.

(2) "School" means any school operated by a board of education or any school for which the state board of education prescribes minimum standards under section 3301.07 of the Revised Code, whether or not any instruction, extracurricular activities, or training provided by the school is being conducted at the time a violation of this section is committed.

(3) "Weapon of mass destruction" means any of the following:

(a) Any weapon that is designed or intended to cause death or serious physical harm through the release, dissemination, or impact of toxic or poisonous chemicals, or their precursors;

(b) Any weapon involving a disease organism or biological agent;

(c) Any weapon that is designed to release radiation or radioactivity at a level dangerous to human life;

(d) Any of the following, except to the extent that the item or device in question is expressly excepted from the definition of "destructive device" pursuant to 18 U.S.C. 921(a)(4) and regulations issued under that section:

(i) Any explosive, incendiary, or poison gas bomb, grenade, rocket having a propellant charge of more than four ounces, missile having an explosive or incendiary charge of more than one-quarter ounce, mine, or similar device;

(ii) Any combination of parts either designed or intended for use in converting any item or device into any item or device described in division (E)(3)(d)(i) of this section and from which an item or device described in that division may be readily assembled.

(4) "Biological agent" has the same meaning as in section 2917.33 of the Revised Code.

(5) "Emergency medical services personnel" has the same meaning as in section 2133.21 of the Revised Code.

(6) "Institution of higher education" means any of the following:

(a) A state university or college as defined in division (A)(1) of section 3345.12 of the Revised Code, community college, state community college, university branch, or technical college;

(b) A private, nonprofit college, university or other post-secondary institution located in this state that possesses a certificate of authorization issued by the Ohio board of regents pursuant to Chapter 1713. of the Revised Code;

(c) A post-secondary institution with a certificate of registration issued by the state board of career colleges and schools under Chapter 3332. of the Revised Code.

**HISTORY: 134 v H 511 (Eff 1-1-74); 147 v H 182 (Eff 10-1-97); 147 v H 382 (Eff 7-22-98); 149 v H 411. Eff 9-27-2002; 152 v H 142, § 1, eff. 3-24-08; 2011 HB 86, § 1, eff. Sept. 30, 2011.**

The provisions of § 4 of HB 86 read as follows:

"SECTION 4. The amendments to sections 926.99, 1333.99, 1707.99, 1716.99, 2909.03, 2909.05, 2909.11, 2913.02, 2913.03, 2913.04, 2913.11, 2913.21, 2913.31, 2913.32, 2913.34, 2913.40, 2913.401, 2913.42, 2913.421, 2913.43, 2913.45, 2913.46, 2913.47, 2913.48, 2913.49, 2913.51, 2913.61, 2915.05, 2917.21, 2917.31, 2917.32, 2921.13, 2921.41, 2923.31, and 2981.07, division (B) of section 2929.13, and division (A) of section 2929.14 of the Revised Code that are made in this act apply to a person who commits an offense specified or penalized under those sections on or after the effective date of this section and to a person to whom division (B) of section 1.58 of the Revised Code makes the amendments applicable.

"The provisions of sections 926.99, 1333.99, 1707.99, 1716.99, 2909.03, 2909.05, 2909.11, 2913.02, 2913.03, 2913.04, 2913.11, 2913.21, 2913.31, 2913.32, 2913.34, 2913.40, 2913.401, 2913.42, 2913.421, 2913.43, 2913.45, 2913.46, 2913.47, 2913.48, 2913.49, 2913.51, 2913.61, 2915.05, 2917.21, 2917.31, 2917.32, 2921.13, 2921.41, 2923.31, and 2981.07 of the Revised Code in existence prior to the effective date of this section shall apply to a person upon whom a court imposed sentence prior to the effective date of this section for an offense specified or penalized under those sections. The amendments to sections 926.99, 1333.99, 1707.99, 1716.99, 2909.03, 2909.05, 2909.11, 2913.02, 2913.03, 2913.04, 2913.11, 2913.21, 2913.31, 2913.32, 2913.34, 2913.40, 2913.401, 2913.42, 2913.421, 2913.43, 2913.45, 2913.46, 2913.47, 2913.48, 2913.49, 2913.51, 2913.61, 2915.05, 2917.21, 2917.31, 2917.32, 2921.13, 2921.41, 2923.31, and 2981.07 of the Revised Code that are made in this act do not apply to a person who upon whom a court imposed sentence prior to the effective date of this section for an offense specified or penalized under those sections."

**Not analogous to former RC § 2917.31 (RS § 6917; S&C 434, 1398, 1401; 29 v 144; 29 v 112; GC § 12851; Bureau of Code Revision, 10-1-53), repealed 134 v H 511, § 2, eff 1-1-74.**

## § 2917.32 Making false alarms.

(A) No person shall do any of the following:

(1) Initiate or circulate a report or warning of an alleged or impending fire, explosion, crime, or other catastrophe, knowing that the report or warning is false and likely to cause public inconvenience or alarm;

(2) Knowingly cause a false alarm of fire or other emergency to be transmitted to or within any organization, public or private, for dealing with emergencies involving a risk of physical harm to persons or property;

(3) Report to any law enforcement agency an alleged offense or other incident within its concern, knowing that such offense did not occur.

(B) This section does not apply to any person conducting an authorized fire or emergency drill.

(C)(1) Whoever violates this section is guilty of making false alarms.

(2) Except as otherwise provided in division (C)(3), (4), (5), or (6) of this section, making false alarms is a misdemeanor of the first degree.

(3) Except as otherwise provided in division (C)(4) of this section, if a violation of this section results in economic harm of one thousand dollars or more but less than seven thousand five hundred dollars, making false alarms is a felony of the fifth degree.

(4) If a violation of this section pertains to a purported, threatened, or actual use of a weapon of mass destruction, making false alarms is a felony of the third degree.

(5) If a violation of this section results in economic harm of seven thousand five hundred dollars or more but less than one hundred fifty thousand dollars and if division (C)(4) of this section does not apply, making false alarms is a felony of the fourth degree.

(6) If a violation of this section results in economic harm of one hundred fifty thousand dollars or more, making false alarms is a felony of the third degree.

(D)(1) It is not a defense to a charge under this section that pertains to a purported or threatened use of a weapon of mass destruction that the offender did not possess or have the ability to use a weapon of mass destruction or that what was represented to be a weapon of mass destruction was not a weapon of mass destruction.

(2) Any act that is a violation of this section and any other section of the Revised Code may be prosecuted under this section, the other section, or both sections.

(E) As used in this section, "economic harm" and "weapon of mass destruction" have the same meanings as in section 2917.31 of the Revised Code.

**HISTORY: 134 v H 511 (Eff 1-1-74); 147 v H 182 (Eff 10-1-97); 149 v H 411. Eff 9-27-2002; 2011 HB 86, § 1, eff. Sept. 30, 2011.**

The provisions of § 4 of HB 86 read as follows:

"SECTION 4. The amendments to sections 926.99, 1333.99, 1707.99, 1716.99, 2909.03, 2909.05, 2909.11, 2913.02, 2913.03, 2913.04, 2913.11, 2913.21, 2913.31, 2913.32, 2913.34, 2913.40, 2913.401, 2913.42, 2913.421, 2913.43, 2913.45, 2913.46, 2913.47, 2913.48, 2913.49, 2913.51, 2913.61, 2915.05, 2917.21, 2917.31, 2917.32, 2921.13, 2921.41, 2923.31, and 2981.07, division (B) of section 2929.13, and division (A) of section 2929.14 of the Revised Code that are made in this act apply to a person who commits an offense specified or penalized under those sections on or after the effective date of this section and to a person to whom division (B) of section 1.58 of the Revised Code makes the amendments applicable.

"The provisions of sections 926.99, 1333.99, 1707.99, 1716.99, 2909.03, 2909.05, 2909.11, 2913.02, 2913.03, 2913.04, 2913.11, 2913.21, 2913.31, 2913.32, 2913.34, 2913.40, 2913.401, 2913.42, 2913.421, 2913.43, 2913.45, 2913.46, 2913.47, 2913.48, 2913.49, 2913.51, 2913.61, 2915.05, 2917.21, 2917.31, 2917.32, 2921.13, 2921.41, 2923.31, and 2981.07 of the Revised Code in existence prior to the effective date of this section shall apply to a person upon whom a court imposed sentence prior to the effective date of this section for an offense specified or penalized under those sections. The amendments to sections 926.99, 1333.99, 1707.99, 1716.99, 2909.03, 2909.05, 2909.11, 2913.02, 2913.03, 2913.04, 2913.11, 2913.21, 2913.31, 2913.32, 2913.34, 2913.40, 2913.401, 2913.42, 2913.421, 2913.43, 2913.45, 2913.46, 2913.47, 2913.48, 2913.49, 2913.51, 2913.61, 2915.05, 2917.21, 2917.31, 2917.32, 2921.13, 2921.41, 2923.31, and 2981.07 of the Revised Code that are made in this act do not apply to a person who upon whom a court imposed sentence prior to the effective date of this section for an offense specified or penalized under those sections."

**Not analogous to former RC § 2917.32 (RS § 6918; S&C 430; 29 v 144; GC § 12857; Bureau of Code Revision, 10-1-53), repealed 134 v H 511, § 2, eff 1-1-74.**

## § 2917.33 Unlawful possession or use of a hoax weapon of mass destruction.

(A) No person, without privilege to do so, shall manufacture, possess, sell, deliver, display, use, threaten to use, attempt to use, conspire to use, or make readily accessible to others a hoax weapon of mass destruction with the intent to deceive or otherwise mislead one or more persons into believing that the hoax weapon of mass destruction will cause terror, bodily harm, or property damage.

(B) This section does not apply to any member or employee of the armed forces of the United States, a governmental agency of this state, another state, or the United States, or a private entity, to whom all of the following apply:

(1) The member or employee otherwise is engaged in lawful activity within the scope of the member's or employee's duties or employment.

(2) The member or employee otherwise is duly authorized or licensed to manufacture, possess, sell, deliver, display, or otherwise engage in activity as described in division (A) of this section.

(3) The member or employee is in compliance with applicable federal and state law.

(C) Whoever violates this section is guilty of unlawful possession or use of a hoax weapon of mass destruction, a felony of the fourth degree.

(D) Any act that is a violation of this section and any other section of the Revised Code may be prosecuted under this section, the other section, or both sections.

(E) As used in this section:

(1) "Hoax weapon of mass destruction" means any device or object that by its design, construction, content, or characteristics appears to be, appears to constitute, or appears to contain, or is represented as being, constituting, or containing, a weapon of mass destruction and to which either of the following applies:

(a) It is, in fact, an inoperative facsimile, imitation, counterfeit, or representation of a weapon of mass destruction that does not meet the definition of a weapon of mass destruction.

(b) It does not actually contain or constitute a weapon, biological agent, toxin, vector, or delivery system.

(2) "Biological agent" means any microorganism, virus, infectious substance, or biological product that may be engineered through biotechnology, or any naturally occurring or bioengineered component of any microorganism, virus, infectious substance, or biological product that may be engineered through biotechnology, capable of causing any of the following:

(a) Death, disease, or other biological malfunction in a human, an animal, a plant, or another living organism;

(b) Deterioration of food, water, equipment, supplies, or material of any kind;

(c) Deleterious alteration of the environment.

(3) "Toxin" means the toxic material of plants, animals, microorganisms, viruses, fungi, or infectious substances or a recombinant molecule, whatever its origin or method of reproduction, including, but not limited to, any of the following:

(a) Any poisonous substance or biological product that may be engineered through biotechnology and that is produced by a living organism;

(b) Any poisonous isomer or biological product, homolog, or derivative of any substance or product described in division (D)(3)(a) of this section.

(4) "Delivery system" means any of the following:

(a) Any apparatus, equipment, device, or means of delivery specifically designed to deliver or disseminate a biological agent, toxin, or vector;

(b) Any vector.

(5) "Vector" means a living organism or molecule, including a recombinant molecule or biological product that may be engineered through biotechnology, capable of carrying a biological agent or toxin to a host.

(6) "Weapon of mass destruction" has the same meaning as in section 2917.31 of the Revised Code.

**HISTORY: 149 v H 411. Eff 9-27-2002.**

**Not analogous to former RC § 2917.33 (RS § 6908; S&C 427, 428; 29 v 144, §§ 7, 9; GC § 12858; Bureau of Code Revision, 10-1-53; 127 v 1039), repealed 134 v H 511, § 2, eff 1-1-74.**

## § 2917.34 Repealed, 134 v H 511, § 2 [RS §§ 6898, 6913a; S&C 409; 33 v 33; 97 v 319; GC §§ 12859, 12860; Bureau of Code Revision, 10-1-53; 129 v 582(746)]. Eff 1-1-74.

This section concerned resisting or impersonating an officer.

## § 2917.35 Repealed, 134 v H 511, § 2 [RS §§ 6898, 6913a; S&C 409; 33 v 33; 97 v 319; GC §§ 12859, 12860; Bureau of Code Revision, 10-1-53; 129 v 582(746)]. Eff 1-1-74.

This section concerned resisting or impersonating an officer.

## § 2917.36 Repealed, 134 v H 511, § 2 [RS §§ 6901, 7014; 75 v 517; 76 v 23; 79 v 30; 81 v 101; 91 v 361; GC §§ 12861—12863; 102 v 114; Bureau of Code Revision, 10-1-53]. Eff 1-1-74.

This section concerned compounding felonies and assignment of debt for collection outside state.

## § 2917.37 Repealed, 134 v H 511, § 2 [RS §§ 6901, 7014; 75 v 517; 76 v 23; 79 v 30; 81 v 101; 91 v

361; GC §§ 12861—12863; 102 v 114; Bureau of Code Revision, 10-1-53]. Eff 1-1-74.

This section concerned compounding felonies and assignment of debt for collection outside state.

**§ 2917.38** Repealed, 134 v H 511, § 2 [RS §§ 6901, 7014; 75 v 517; 76 v 23; 79 v 30; 81 v 101; 91 v 361; GC §§ 12861—12863; 102 v 114; Bureau of Code Revision, 10-1-53]. Eff 1-1-74.

This section concerned compounding felonies and assignment of debt for collection outside state.

**§ 2917.39** Repealed, 134 v H 511, § 2 [RS § 7014; 75 v 517; 79 v 30; 91 v 361; GC § 12864; Bureau of Code Revision, 10-1-53]. Eff 1-1-74.

This section concerned assignment of debt for collection outside state.

## [CROWD SAFETY]

### § 2917.40 Required crowd safety measures at live entertainment performances.

(A) As used in this section:

(1) "Live entertainment performance" means any live speech; any live musical performance, including a concert; any live dramatic performance; any live variety show; and any other live performance with respect to which the primary intent of the audience can be construed to be viewing the performers. A "live entertainment performance" does not include any form of entertainment with respect to which the person purchasing a ticket routinely participates in amusements as well as views performers.

(2) "Restricted entertainment area" means any wholly or partially enclosed area, whether indoors or outdoors, that has limited access through established entrances, or established turnstiles or similar devices.

(3) "Concert" means a musical performance of which the primary component is a presentation by persons singing or playing musical instruments, that is intended by its sponsors mainly, but not necessarily exclusively, for the listening enjoyment of the audience, and that is held in a facility. A "concert" does not include any performance in which music is a part of the presentation and the primary component of which is acting, dancing, a motion picture, a demonstration of skills or talent other than singing or playing an instrument, an athletic event, an exhibition, or a speech.

(4) "Facility" means any structure that has a roof or partial roof and that has walls that wholly surround the area on all sides, including, but not limited to, a stadium, hall, arena, armory, auditorium, ballroom, exhibition hall, convention center, or music hall.

(5) "Person" includes, in addition to an individual or entity specified in division (C) of section 1.59 of the Revised Code, any governmental entity.

(B)(1) No person shall sell, offer to sell, or offer in return for a donation any ticket that is not numbered and that does not correspond to a specific seat for admission to either of the following:

(a) A live entertainment performance that is not exempted under division (D) of this section, that is held in a restricted entertainment area, and for which more than eight thousand tickets are offered to the public;

(b) A concert that is not exempted under division (D) of this section and for which more than three thousand tickets are offered to the public.

(2) No person shall advertise any live entertainment performance as described in division (B)(1)(a) of this section or any concert as described in division (B)(1)(b) of this section, unless the advertisement contains the words "Reserved Seats Only."

(C) Unless exempted by division (D)(1) of this section, no person who owns or operates any restricted entertainment area shall fail to open, maintain, and properly staff at least the number of entrances designated under division (E) of this section for a minimum of ninety minutes prior to the scheduled start of any live entertainment performance that is held in the restricted entertainment area and for which more than three thousand tickets are sold, offered for sale, or offered in return for a donation.

(D)(1) A live entertainment performance, other than a concert, is exempted from the provisions of divisions (B) and (C) of this section if both of the following apply:

(a) The restricted entertainment area in which the performance is held has at least eight entrances or, if both entrances and separate admission turnstiles or similar devices are used, has at least eight turnstiles or similar devices;

(b) The eight entrances or, if applicable, the eight turnstiles or similar devices are opened, maintained, and properly staffed at least one hour prior to the scheduled start of the performance.

(2)(a) The chief of the police department of a township police district or joint police district in the case of a facility located within the district, the officer responsible for public safety within a municipal corporation in the case of a facility located within the municipal corporation, or the county sheriff in the case of a facility located outside the boundaries of a township or joint police district or municipal corporation may, upon application of the sponsor of a concert covered by division (B) of this section, exempt the concert from the provisions of that division if the official finds that the health, safety, and welfare of the participants and spectators would not be substantially affected by failure to comply with the provisions of that division.

In determining whether to grant an exemption, the official shall consider the following factors:

(i) The size and design of the facility in which the concert is scheduled;

(ii) The size, age, and anticipated conduct of the crowd expected to attend the concert;

(iii) The ability of the sponsor to manage and control the expected crowd.

If the sponsor of any concert desires to obtain an exemption under this division, the sponsor shall apply to the appropriate official on a form prescribed by that official. The official shall issue an order that grants or denies the exemption within five days after receipt of the application. The sponsor may appeal any order that denies an exemption to the court of common pleas of the county in which the facility is located.

(b) If an official grants an exemption under division (D)(2)(a) of this section, the official shall designate an on-duty law enforcement officer to be present at the concert. The designated officer has authority to issue orders to all security personnel at the concert to protect the health, safety, and welfare of the participants and spectators.

(3) Notwithstanding division (D)(2) of this section, in the case of a concert held in a facility located on the campus of an educational institution covered by section 3345.04 of the Revised Code, a state university law enforcement officer appointed pursuant to sections 3345.04 and 3345.21 of the Revised Code shall do both of the following:

(a) Exercise the authority to grant exemptions provided by division (D)(2)(a) of this section in lieu of an official designated in that division;

(b) If the officer grants an exemption under division (D)(3)(a) of this section, designate an on-duty state university law enforcement officer to be present at the concert. The designated officer has authority to issue orders to all security personnel at the concert to protect the health, safety, and welfare of the participants and spectators.

(E)(1) Unless a live entertainment performance is exempted by division (D)(1) of this section, the chief of the police department of a township police district or joint police district in the case of a restricted entertainment area located within the district, the officer responsible for public safety within a municipal corporation in the case of a restricted entertainment area located within the municipal corporation, or the county sheriff in the case of a restricted entertainment area located outside the boundaries of a township or joint police district or municipal corporation shall designate, for purposes of division (C) of this section, the minimum number of entrances required to be opened, maintained, and staffed at each live entertainment performance so as to permit crowd control and reduce congestion at the entrances. The designation shall be based on such factors as the size and nature of the crowd expected to attend the live entertainment performance, the length of time prior to the live entertainment performance that crowds are expected to congregate at the entrances, and the amount of security provided at the restricted entertainment area.

(2) Notwithstanding division (E)(1) of this section, a state university law enforcement officer appointed pursuant to sections 3345.04 and 3345.21 of the Revised Code shall designate the number of entrances required to be opened, maintained, and staffed in the case of a live entertainment performance that is held at a restricted entertainment area located on the campus of an educational institution covered by section 3345.04 of the Revised Code.

(F) No person shall enter into any contract for a live entertainment performance, that does not permit or require compliance with this section.

(G)(1) This section does not apply to a live entertainment performance held in a restricted entertainment area if one admission ticket entitles the holder to view or participate in three or more different games, rides, activities, or live entertainment performances occurring simultaneously at different sites within the restricted entertainment area and if the initial admittance entrance to the restricted entertainment area, for which the ticket is required, is separate from the entrance to any specific live entertainment performance and an additional ticket is not required for admission to the particular live entertainment performance.

(2) This section does not apply to a symphony orchestra performance, a ballet performance, horse races, dances, or fairs.

(H) This section does not prohibit the legislative authority of any municipal corporation from imposing additional requirements, not in conflict with this section, for the promotion or holding of live entertainment performances.

(I) Whoever violates division (B), (C), or (F) of this section is guilty of a misdemeanor of the first degree. If any individual suffers physical harm to the individual's person as a result of a violation of this section, the sentencing court shall consider this factor in favor of imposing a term of imprisonment upon the offender.

**HISTORY: 138 v S 320. Eff 3-23-81; 2011 HB 153, § 101.01, eff. Sept. 29, 2011.**

† In division (A)(2) and (D)(1)(a) and (b), so in enrolled bill. Apparently, "turnstiles" was intended.

**Not analogous to former RC § 2917.40 (RS § 7014; 75 v 517; 79 v 30; 91 v 361; GC § 12865; Bureau of Code Revision, 10-1-53), repealed 134 v H 511, § 2, eff 1-1-74.**

## § 2917.41 Misconduct involving public transportation system.

(A) No person shall evade the payment of the known fares of a public transportation system.

(B) No person shall alter any transfer, pass, ticket, or token of a public transportation system with the purpose of evading the payment of fares or of defrauding the system.

(C) No person shall do any of the following while in any facility or on any vehicle of a public transportation system:

(1) Play sound equipment without the proper use of a private earphone;

(2) Smoke, eat, or drink in any area where the activity is clearly marked as being prohibited;

(3) Expectorate upon a person, facility, or vehicle.

(D) No person shall write, deface, draw, or otherwise mark on any facility or vehicle of a public transportation system.

(E) No person shall fail to comply with a lawful order of a public transportation system police officer, and no person shall resist, obstruct, or abuse a public transportation police officer in the performance of the officer's duties.

(F) Whoever violates this section is guilty of misconduct involving a public transportation system.

(1) Violation of division (A), (B), or (E) of this section is a misdemeanor of the fourth degree.

(2) Violation of division (C) of this section is a minor misdemeanor on a first offense. If a person previously has been convicted of or pleaded guilty to a violation of any division of this section or of a municipal ordinance that is substantially similar to any division of this section, violation of division (C) of this section is a misdemeanor of the fourth degree.

(3) Violation of division (D) of this section is a misdemeanor of the third degree.

(G) Notwithstanding any other provision of law, seventy-five per cent of each fine paid to satisfy a sentence imposed for a violation of this section shall be deposited into the treasury of the county in which the violation occurred and twenty-five per cent shall be deposited with the county transit board, regional transit authority, or regional transit commission that operates the public transportation system involved in the violation, unless the board of county commissioners operates the public transportation system, in which case one hundred per cent of each fine shall be deposited into the treasury of the county.

(H) As used in this section, "public transportation system" means a county transit system operated in accordance with sections 306.01 to 306.13 of the Revised Code, a regional transit authority operated in accordance with sections 306.30 to 306.71 of the Revised Code, or a regional transit commission operated in accordance with sections 306.80 to 306.90 of the Revised Code.

**HISTORY: 140 v S 86 (Eff 9-20-84); 141 v H 813 (Eff 9-17-86); 146 v H 61 (Eff 10-25-95); 146 v S 2. Eff 7-1-96; 150 v H 95, § 1, eff. 9-26-03.**

The effective date is set by section 179 of H.B. 95 (150 v —).

The provisions of § 223 of H.B. 95 (150 v —) read as follows: SECTION 223. Section 2917.41 of the Revised Code is presented in this act as a composite of the section as amended by both Am. Sub. H.B. 61 and Am. Sub. S.B. 2 of the 121st General Assembly. The General Assembly, applying the principle stated in division (B) of section 152 of the Revised Code that amendments are to be harmonized if reasonably capable of simultaneous operation, finds that the composite is the resulting version of the section in effect prior to the effective date of the section as presented in this act.

**Not analogous to former RC** § 2917.41 **(RS** § **7034a; GC** § **12869; 81 v 92; Bureau of Code Revision, 10-1-53), repealed 134 v H 511,** § **2, eff 1-1-74.**

## § 2917.42 Repealed, 134 v H 511, § 2 [RS §§ 6911, 6986-1; S&C 429; 29 v 144; 98 v 99; GC §§ 12845, 12847; Bureau of Code Revision, 10-1-53; 127 v 1039; 129 v 1034; 130 v 662]. Eff 1-1-74.

This section concerned suppression of evidence, refusal to testify, encouraging lawsuits, and reporting gunshot wounds.

## § 2917.43 Repealed, 134 v H 511, § 2 [RS §§ 6911, 6986-1; S&C 429; 29 v 144; 98 v 99; GC §§ 12845, 12847; Bureau of Code Revision, 10-1-53; 127 v 1039; 129 v 1034; 130 v 662]. Eff 1-1-74.

This section concerned suppression of evidence, refusal to testify, encouraging lawsuits, and reporting gunshot wounds.

## § 2917.44 Repealed, 134 v H 511, § 2 [RS §§ 6911, 6986-1; S&C 429; 29 v 144; 98 v 99; GC §§ 12845, 12847; Bureau of Code Revision, 10-1-53; 127 v 1039; 129 v 1034; 130 v 662]. Eff 1-1-74.

This section concerned suppression of evidence, refusal to testify, encouraging lawsuits, and reporting gunshot wounds.

## § 2917.45 Repealed, 134 v H 511, § 2 [131 v 676]. Eff 1-1-74.

This section concerned disguise.

## § 2917.46 Unauthorized use of block parent or mcgruff house symbol.

(A) No person shall, with intent to identify a building as a block parent home or building, display the block parent symbol adopted by the state board of education pursuant to former section 3301.076 [3301.07.6] of the Revised Code prior to its repeal on the effective date of this amendment.

(B) No person shall, with intent to identify a building as a block parent home or building, display a symbol that falsely gives the appearance of being the block parent symbol adopted by the state board of education pursuant to former section 3301.076 [3301.07.6] of the Revised Code prior to its repeal on the effective date of this amendment.

(C) No person, with intent to identify a home or building as a mcgruff house program home or building, shall display the mcgruff house symbol adopted by the division of criminal justice services in the state department of public safety pursuant to section 5502.62 of the Revised Code unless authorized in accordance with that section, any rule adopted pursuant to that section, or section 3313.206 [3313.20.6] of the Revised Code.

(D) No person, with intent to identify a home or building as a mcgruff house program home or building, shall display a symbol that falsely gives the appearance of being the mcgruff house symbol adopted by the division of criminal justice services in the state department of public safety pursuant to section 5502.62 of the Revised Code or any rule adopted pursuant to that section.

(E)(1) Whoever violates division (A) or (B) of this section is guilty of unauthorized use of a block parent symbol, a minor misdemeanor.

(2) Whoever violates division (C) or (D) of this section is guilty of unauthorized use of a mcgruff house symbol, a minor misdemeanor.

**HISTORY: 141 v H 112 (Eff 10-17-85); 142 v H 708. Eff 4-19-88; 151 v H 374, § 1, eff. 7-1-07.**

The effective date is set by § 3(A) of 151 v H 374.

## § 2917.47 Improperly handling infectious agents.

As used in this section, "infectious agent" means a microorganism such as a virus, bacterium, or similar agent that causes disease or death in human beings.

(A) No person shall knowingly possess, send, receive, or cause to be sent or received an isolate or derivative of an isolate of an infectious agent, except as permitted by division (B) of this section.

(B) A person may possess, send, receive, or cause to be sent or received an isolate or derivative of an isolate of an infectious agent as permitted by state or federal law, including for purposes of biomedical or biotechnical research or production, provision of health care services, or investigation of disease by public health agencies.

(C) Whoever violates this section is guilty of improperly handling infectious agents, a felony of the second degree.

**HISTORY: 146 v H 456. Eff 9-10-96.**

# CHAPTER 2919: OFFENSES AGAINST THE FAMILY



**Publisher's Note:**

The Committee Comments dealing with former abortion statutes as affected by HB 511 are no longer applicable.

The Ohio Legislature, in HB 989, effective 9-16-74, repealed and re-enacted RC §§ 2919.11 and 2919.12 (134 v H 511, eff. 1-1-74), following the U.S. Supreme Court's decision in Roe v. Wade, 410 US 113, 35 LEd2d 147, 93 SCt 705 (1973).

Under the new law, abortion is no longer prohibited if performed with the consent of the pregnant woman (or with the consent of her parent or guardian if she is an unmarried minor).

Two new sections dealing with abortion were also added by HB 989: RC § 2919.13, dealing with the preservation of the life of a child born alive as the result of an abortion; and RC § 2919.14, prohibiting unauthorized experimentation on or sale of the aborted product of human conception.

## [BIGAMY]

### § 2919.01 Bigamy.

(A) No married person shall marry another or continue to cohabit with such other person in this state.

(B) It is an affirmative defense to a charge under this section that the actor's spouse was continuously absent for five years immediately preceding the purported subsequent marriage, and was not known by the actor to be alive within that time.

(C) Whoever violates this section is guilty of bigamy, a misdemeanor of the first degree.

**HISTORY: 134 v H 511. Eff 1-1-74.**

**Not analogous to former RC § 2919.01 (RS § 6841; S&C 1610; 55 v 44; 80 v 43; 91 v 338; GC §§ 12873, 12874; Bureau of Code Revision, 10-1-53; 127 v 847), repealed 134 v H 511, § 2, eff 1-1-74.**

### § 2919.02 Repealed, 134 v H 511, § 2 [RS §§ 6841—6843; S&C 240, 426; 37 v 74; 55 v 44; 66 v 29; 73 v 31, 86; 78 v 186; 80 v 43; 82 v 140; 83 v 23; 91 v 338; 95 v 303; 97 v 67; GC §§ 12875—12877; 106 v 550; 124 v 466; Bureau of Code Revision, 10-1-53]. Eff 1-1-74.

This section concerned embezzlement.

### § 2919.03 Repealed, 134 v H 511, § 2 [RS §§ 6841—6843; S&C 240, 426; 37 v 74; 55 v 44; 66 v 29; 73 v 31, 86; 78 v 186; 80 v 43; 82 v 140; 83 v 23; 91 v 338; 95 v 303; 97 v 67; GC §§ 12875—12877; 106 v 550; 124 v 466; Bureau of Code Revision, 10-1-53]. Eff 1-1-74.

This section concerned embezzlement.

### § 2919.04 Repealed, 134 v H 511, § 2 [RS §§ 6841—6843; S&C 240, 426; 37 v 74; 55 v 44; 66 v 29; 73 v 31, 86; 78 v 186; 80 v 43; 82 v 140; 83 v 23; 91 v 338; 95 v 303; 97 v 67; GC §§ 12875—12877; 106 v 550; 124 v 466; Bureau of Code Revision, 10-1-53]. Eff 1-1-74.

This section concerned embezzlement.

### § 2919.05 Repealed, 134 v H 511, § 2 [RS §§ 6846, 6847, 7373; S&C 748; 41 v 74; 66 v 263; 69 v 193; 73 v 116; GC §§ 12878—12881, 12886; Bureau of Code Revision, 10-1-53]. Eff 1-1-74.

This section concerned embezzlement and conflict of interest by public officials.

### § 2919.06 Repealed, 134 v H 511, § 2 [RS §§ 6846, 6847, 7373; S&C 748; 41 v 74; 66 v 263; 69 v 193;

73 v 116; GC §§ 12878—12881, 12886; Bureau of Code Revision, 10-1-53]. Eff 1-1-74.

This section concerned embezzlement and conflict of interest by public officials.

## § 2919.07 Repealed, 134 v H 511, § 2 [RS §§ 6846, 6847, 7373; S&C 748; 41 v 74; 66 v 263; 69 v 193; 73 v 116; GC §§ 12878—12881, 12886; Bureau of Code Revision, 10-1-53]. Eff 1-1-74.

This section concerned embezzlement and conflict of interest by public officials.

## § 2919.08 Repealed, 134 v H 511, § 2 [RS §§ 6969, 6976; 66 v 164; 73 v 31, 43, 86; 90 v 29; 94 v 391, 406; GC §§ 12910—12912; 101 v 145; Bureau of Code Revision, 10-1-53]. Eff 1-1-74.

This section concerned conflict of interest by public officials.

## § 2919.09 Repealed, 134 v H 511, § 2 [RS §§ 6969, 6976; 66 v 164; 73 v 31, 43, 86; 90 v 29; 94 v 391, 406; GC §§ 12910—12912; 101 v 145; Bureau of Code Revision, 10-1-53]. Eff 1-1-74.

This section concerned conflict of interest by public officials.

## § 2919.10 Repealed, 134 v H 511, § 2 [RS §§ 6969, 6976; 66 v 164; 73 v 31, 43, 86; 90 v 29; 94 v 391, 406; GC §§ 12910—12912; 101 v 145; Bureau of Code Revision, 10-1-53]. Eff 1-1-74.

This section concerned conflict of interest by public officials.

# [ABORTION]

## § 2919.11 Definition of abortion.

As used in the Revised Code, "abortion" means the purposeful termination of a human pregnancy by any person, including the pregnant woman herself, with an intention other than to produce a live birth or to remove a dead fetus or embryo. Abortion is the practice of medicine or surgery for the purposes of section 4731.41 of the Revised Code.

**HISTORY: 135 v H 989. Eff 9-16-74.**

**Not analogous to former RC § 2919.11 (134 v H 511 entitled "Criminal abortion."), repealed by 135 v H 989; and not analogous to former RC § 2919.11 (GC § 12912-1; 118 v 677; Bureau of Code Revision, 10-1-53), repealed 134 v H 511, § 2, eff 1-1-74.**

## § 2919.12 Unlawful abortion.

(A) No person shall perform or induce an abortion without the informed consent of the pregnant woman.

(B)(1)(a) No person shall knowingly perform or induce an abortion upon a woman who is pregnant, unmarried, under eighteen years of age, and unemancipated unless at least one of the following applies:

(i) Subject to division (B)(2) of this section, the person has given at least twenty-four hours actual notice, in person or by telephone, to one of the woman's parents, her guardian, or her custodian as to the intention to perform or induce the abortion, provided that if the woman has requested, in accordance with division (B)(1)(b) of this section, that notice be given to a specified brother or sister of the woman who is twenty-one years of age or older or to a specified stepparent or grandparent of the woman instead of to one of her parents, her guardian, or her custodian, and if the person is notified by a juvenile court that affidavits of the type described in that division have been filed with that court, the twenty-four hours actual notice described in this division as to the intention to perform or induce the abortion shall be given, in person or by telephone, to the specified brother, sister, stepparent, or grandparent instead of to the parent, guardian, or custodian;

(ii) One of the woman's parents, her guardian, or her custodian has consented in writing to the performance or inducement of the abortion;

(iii) A juvenile court pursuant to section 2151.85 of the Revised Code issues an order authorizing the woman to consent to the abortion without notification of one of her parents, her guardian, or her custodian;

(iv) A juvenile court or a court of appeals, by its inaction, constructively has authorized the woman to consent to the abortion without notification of one of her parents, her guardian, or her custodian under division (B)(1) of section 2151.85 or division (A) of section 2505.073 [2505.07.3] of the Revised Code.

(b) If a woman who is pregnant, unmarried, under eighteen years of age, and unemancipated desires notification as to a person's intention to perform or induce an abortion on the woman to be given to a specified brother or sister of the woman who is twenty-one years of age or older or to a specified stepparent or grandparent of the woman instead of to one of her parents, her guardian, or her custodian, the person who intends to perform or induce the abortion shall notify the specified brother, sister, stepparent, or grandparent instead of the parent, guardian, or custodian for purposes of division (B)(1)(a)(i) of this section if all of the following apply:

(i) The woman has requested the person to provide the notification to the specified brother, sister, stepparent, or grandparent, clearly has identified the specified brother, sister, stepparent, or grandparent and her relation to that person, and, if the specified relative is a brother or sister, has indicated the age of the brother or sister;

(ii) The woman has executed an affidavit stating that she is in fear of physical, sexual, or severe emotional abuse from the parent, guardian, or custodian who otherwise would be notified under division (B)(1)(a)(i) of this section, and that the fear is based on a pattern of physical, sexual, or severe emotional abuse of her exhibited by that parent, guardian, or custodian, has filed the affidavit with the juvenile court of the county in which the woman has a residence or legal settlement, the juvenile court of any county that borders to any extent the county in which she has a residence or legal settlement, or the juvenile court of the county in which the hospital, clinic, or other facility in which the abortion would be performed or induced is located, and has given the court written notice of the name and address of the person who intends to perform or induce the abortion;

(iii) The specified brother, sister, stepparent, or grandparent has executed an affidavit stating that the woman has reason to fear physical, sexual, or severe emotional abuse from the parent, guardian, or custodian who otherwise would be notified under division (B)(1)(a)(i) of this section, based on a pattern of physical, sexual, or severe emotional abuse of her by that parent, guardian, or custodian, and the woman or the specified brother, sister, stepparent, or grandparent has filed the affidavit with the juvenile court in which the affidavit described in division (B)(1)(b)(ii) of this section was filed;

(iv) The juvenile court in which the affidavits described in divisions (B)(1)(b)(ii) and (iii) of this section were filed has notified the person that both of those affidavits have been filed with the court.

(c) If an affidavit of the type described in division (B)(1)(b)(ii) of this section and an affidavit of the type described in division (B)(1)(b)(iii) of this section are filed with a juvenile court and the court has been provided with written notice of the name and address of the person who intends to perform or induce an abortion upon the woman to whom the affidavits pertain, the court promptly shall notify the person who intends to perform or induce the abortion that the affidavits have been filed. If possible, the notice to the person shall be given in person or by telephone.

(2) If division (B)(1)(a)(ii), (iii), or (iv) of this section does not apply, and if no parent, guardian, or custodian can be reached for purposes of division (B)(1)(a)(i) of this section after a reasonable effort, or if notification is to be given to a specified brother, sister, stepparent, or grandparent under that division and the specified brother, sister, stepparent, or grandparent cannot be reached for purposes of that division after a reasonable effort, no person shall perform or induce such an abortion without giving at least forty-eight hours constructive notice to one of the woman's parents, her guardian, or her custodian, by both certified and ordinary mail sent to the last known address of the parent, guardian, or custodian, or if notification for purposes of division (B)(1)(a)(i) of this section is to be given to a specified brother, sister, stepparent, or grandparent, without giving at least forty-eight hours constructive notice to that specified brother, sister, stepparent, or grandparent by both certified and ordinary mail sent to the last known address of that specified brother, sister, stepparent, or grandparent. The forty-eight-hour period under this division begins when the certified mail notice is mailed. If a parent, guardian, or custodian of the woman, or if notification under division (B)(1)(a)(i) of this section is to be given to a specified brother, sister, stepparent, or grandparent, the specified brother, sister, stepparent, or grandparent, is not reached within the forty-eight-hour period, the abortion may proceed even if the certified mail notice is not received.

(3) If a parent, guardian, custodian, or specified brother, sister, stepparent, or grandparent who has been notified in accordance with division (B)(1) or (2) of this section clearly and unequivocally expresses that he or she does not wish to consult with a pregnant woman prior to her abortion, then the abortion may proceed without any further waiting period.

(4) For purposes of prosecutions for a violation of division (B)(1) or (2) of this section, it shall be a rebuttable presumption that a woman who is unmarried and under eighteen years of age is unemancipated.

(C)(1) It is an affirmative defense to a charge under division (B)(1) or (2) of this section that the pregnant woman provided the person who performed or induced the abortion with false, misleading, or incorrect information about her age, marital status, or emancipation, about the age of a brother or sister to whom she requested notice be given as a specified relative instead of to one of her parents, her guardian, or her custodian, or about the last known address of either of her parents, her guardian, her custodian, or a specified brother, sister, stepparent, or grandparent to whom she requested notice be given and the person who performed or induced the abortion did not otherwise have reasonable cause to believe the pregnant woman was under eighteen years of age, unmarried, or unemancipated, to believe that the age of a brother or sister to whom she requested notice be given as a specified relative instead of to one of her parents, her guardian, or her custodian was not twenty-one years of age, or to believe that the last known address of either of her parents, her guardian, her custodian, or a specified brother, sister, stepparent, or grandparent to whom she requested notice be given was incorrect.

(2) It is an affirmative defense to a charge under this section that compliance with the requirements of this section was not possible because an immediate threat of serious risk to the life or physical health of the pregnant woman from the continuation of her pregnancy created an emergency necessitating the immediate performance or inducement of an abortion.

(D) Whoever violates this section is guilty of unlawful abortion. A violation of division (A) of this section is a misdemeanor of the first degree on the first offense and a felony of the fourth degree on each subsequent offense. A violation of division (B) of this section is a misdemeanor of the first degree on a first offense and a felony of the fifth degree on each subsequent offense.

(E) Whoever violates this section is liable to the pregnant woman and her parents, guardian, or custodian for civil compensatory and exemplary damages.

(F) As used in this section "unemancipated" means that a woman who is unmarried and under eighteen years of age has not entered the armed services of the United States, has not become employed and self-subsisting, or has not otherwise become independent from the care and control of her parent, guardian, or custodian.

**HISTORY: 135 v H 989 (Eff 9-16-74); 141 v H 319 (Eff 3-24-86); 146 v S 2. Eff 7-1-96.**

**Not analogous to former RC § 2919.12 (134 v H 511 entitled "Promoting abortion."), repealed by 135 v H 989; and not analogous to former RC § 2919.12 (RS § 6910; S&C 429; 29 v 144; GC § 12915; Bureau of Code Revision, 10-1-53), repealed 134 v H 511, § 2, eff 1-1-74.**

The effective date is set by section 6 of SB 2.

## § 2919.121 Performing or inducing unlawful abortion upon minor.

(A) For the purpose of this section, a minor shall be considered "emancipated" if the minor has married, entered the armed services of the United States, become employed and self-subsisting, or has otherwise become independent from the care and control of her parent, guardian, or custodian.

(B) No person shall knowingly perform or induce an abortion upon a pregnant minor unless one of the following is the case:

(1) The attending physician has secured the informed written consent of the minor and one parent, guardian, or custodian;

(2) The minor is emancipated and the attending physician has received her written informed consent;

(3) The minor has been authorized to consent to the abortion by a court order issued pursuant to division (C) of this section, and the attending physician has received her informed written consent;

(4) The court has given its consent in accordance with division (C) of this section and the minor is having the abortion willingly.

(C) The right of a minor to consent to an abortion under division (B)(3) of this section or judicial consent to obtain an abortion under division (B)(4) of this section may be granted by a court order pursuant to the following procedures:

(1) The minor or next friend shall make an application to the juvenile court of the county in which the minor has a residence or legal settlement, the juvenile court of any county that borders the county in which she has a residence or legal settlement, or the juvenile court of the county in which the facility in which the abortion would be performed or induced is located. The juvenile court shall assist the minor or next friend in preparing the petition and notices required by this section. The minor or next friend shall thereafter file a petition setting forth all of the following: the initials of the minor; her age; the names and addresses of each parent, guardian, custodian, or, if the minor's parents are deceased and no guardian has been appointed, any other person standing in loco parentis of the minor; that the minor has been fully informed of the risks and consequences of the abortion; that the minor is of sound mind and has sufficient intellectual capacity to consent to the abortion; that the minor has not previously filed a petition under this section concerning the same pregnancy that was denied on the merits; that, if the court does not authorize the minor to consent to the abortion, the court should find that the abortion is in the best interests of the minor and give judicial consent to the abortion; that the court should appoint a guardian ad litem; and if the minor does not have private counsel, that the court should appoint counsel. The petition shall be signed by the minor or the next friend.

(2) A hearing on the merits shall be held on the record as soon as possible within five days of filing the petition. If the minor has not retained counsel, the court shall appoint counsel at least twenty-four hours prior to the hearing. The court shall appoint a guardian ad litem to protect the interests of the minor at the hearing. If the guardian ad litem is an attorney admitted to the practice of law in this state, the court may appoint the guardian ad litem to serve as the minor's counsel. At the hearing, the court shall hear evidence relating to the emotional development, maturity, intellect, and understanding of the minor; the nature, possible consequences, and alternatives to the abortion; and any other evidence that the court may find useful in determining whether the minor should be granted the right to consent to the abortion or whether the abortion is in the best interests of the minor. If the minor or her counsel fail to appear for a scheduled hearing, jurisdiction shall remain with the judge who would have presided at the hearing.

(3) If the court finds that the minor is sufficiently mature and well enough informed to decide intelligently whether to have an abortion, the court shall grant the petition and permit the minor to consent to the abortion.

If the court finds that the abortion is in the best interests of the minor, the court shall give judicial consent to the abortion, setting forth the grounds for its finding.

If the court does not make either of the findings specified in division (C)(3) of this section, the court shall deny the petition, setting forth the grounds on which the petition is denied.

The court shall issue its order not later than twenty-four hours after the end of the hearing.

(4) No juvenile court shall have jurisdiction to rehear a petition concerning the same pregnancy once a juvenile court has granted or denied the petition.

(5) If the petition is granted, the informed consent of the minor, pursuant to a court order authorizing the minor to consent to the abortion, or judicial consent to the abortion, shall bar an action by the parents, guardian, or custodian of the minor for battery of the minor against any person performing or inducing the abortion. The immunity granted shall only extend to the performance or inducement of the abortion in accordance with this section and to any accompanying services that are performed in a competent manner.

(6) An appeal from an order issued under this section may be taken to the court of appeals by the minor. The record on appeal shall be completed and the appeal perfected within four days from the filing of the notice of appeal. Because the abortion may need to be performed in a timely manner, the supreme court shall, by rule, provide for expedited appellate review of cases appealed under this section.

(7) All proceedings under this section shall be conducted in a confidential manner and shall be given such precedence over other pending matters as will ensure that the court will reach a decision promptly and without delay.

The petition and all other papers and records that pertain to an action commenced under this section shall be kept confidential and are not public records under section 149.43 of the Revised Code.

(8) No filing fee shall be required of or court costs assessed against a person filing a petition under this section or appealing an order issued under this section.

(D) It is an affirmative defense to any civil, criminal, or professional disciplinary claim brought under this section that compliance with the requirements of this section was not possible because an immediate threat of serious risk to the life or physical health of the minor from the continuation of her pregnancy created an emergency necessitating the immediate performance or inducement of an abortion.

(E) Whoever violates division (B) of this section is guilty of unlawful abortion, a misdemeanor of the first degree. If the offender previously has been convicted of or pleaded guilty to a violation of this section, unlawful abortion is a felony of the fourth degree.

(F) Whoever violates division (B) of this section is liable to the pregnant minor and her parents, guardian, or custodian for civil, compensatory, and exemplary damages.

**HISTORY: 147 v H 421. Eff 5-6-98.**

The provisions of § 3 of HB 421 (147 v —) read as follows:

SECTION 3. It is the intention of the General Assembly that section 2919.121 of the Revised Code be interpreted and applied in accordance with the decisions in Planned Parenthood v. Ashcroft, 655 F.2d 848 (8th Cir., 1981), and Planned Parenthood v. Ashcroft, 103 S. Ct. 2517 (1983), which interpreted and upheld the Missouri statute upon which section 2919.121 of the Revised Code is based.

## § 2919.122 Application of unlawful abortion law; defenses.

Section 2919.121 [2919.12.1] of the Revised Code applies in lieu of division (B) of section 2919.12 of the Revised Code whenever its operation is not enjoined. If section 2919.121 [2919.12.1] of the Revised Code is enjoined, division (B) of section 2919.12 of the Revised Code applies.

If a person complies with the requirements of division (B) of section 2919.12 of the Revised Code under the good faith belief that the application or enforcement of section 2919.121 [2919.12.1] of the Revised Code is subject to a restraining order or injunction, good faith compliance shall constitute a complete defense to any civil, criminal, or professional disciplinary action brought under section 2919.121 [2919.12.1] of the Revised Code.

If a person complies with the requirements of section 2919.121 [2919.12.1] of the Revised Code under the good faith belief that it is not subject to a restraining order or injunction, good faith compliance shall constitute a complete defense to any criminal, civil, or professional disciplinary action for failure to comply with the requirements of division (B) of section 2919.12 of the Revised Code.

**HISTORY: 147 v H 421. Eff 5-6-98.**

## § 2919.123 Unlawful distribution of abortion-inducing drug.

(A) No person shall knowingly give, sell, dispense, administer, otherwise provide, or prescribe RU-486 (mifepristone) to another for the purpose of inducing an abortion in any person or enabling the other person to induce an abortion in any person, unless the person who gives, sells, dispenses, administers, or otherwise provides or prescribes the RU-486 (mifepristone) is a physician, the physician satisfies all the criteria established by federal law that a physician must satisfy in order to provide RU-486 (mifepristone) for inducing abortions, and the physician provides the RU-486 (mifepristone) to the other person for the purpose of inducing an abortion in accordance with all provisions of federal law that govern the use of RU-486 (mifepristone) for inducing abortions. A person who gives, sells, dispenses, administers, otherwise provides, or prescribes RU-486 (mifepristone) to another as described in division (A) of this section shall not be prosecuted based on a violation of the criteria contained in this division unless the person knows that the person is not a physician, that the person did not satisfy all the specified criteria established by federal law, or that the person did not provide the RU-486 (mifepristone) in accordance with the specified provisions of federal law, whichever is applicable.

(B) No physician who provides RU-486 (mifepristone) to another for the purpose of inducing an abortion as authorized under division (A) of this section shall knowingly fail to comply with the applicable requirements of any federal law that pertain to follow-up examinations or care for persons to whom or for whom RU-486 (mifepristone) is provided for the purpose of inducing an abortion.

(C)(1) If a physician provides RU-486 (mifepristone) to another for the purpose of inducing an abortion as authorized under division (A) of this section and if the physician knows that the person who uses the RU-486 (mifepristone) for the purpose of inducing an abortion experiences during or after the use an incomplete abortion, severe bleeding, or an adverse reaction to the RU-486 (mifepristone) or is hospitalized, receives a transfusion, or experiences any other serious event, the physician promptly must provide a written report of the incomplete abortion, severe bleeding, adverse reaction, hospitalization, transfusion, or serious event to the state medical board. The board shall compile and retain all reports it receives under this division. Except as otherwise provided in this division, all reports the board receives under this division are public records open to inspection under section 149.43 of the Revised Code. In no case shall the board release to any person the name or any other personal identifying information regarding a person who uses RU-486 (mifepristone) for the purpose of inducing an abortion and who is the subject of a report the board receives under this division.

(2) No physician who provides RU-486 (mifepristone) to another for the purpose of inducing an abortion as authorized under division (A) of this section shall knowingly fail to file a report required under division (C)(1) of this section.

(D) Division (A) of this section does not apply to any of the following:

(1) A pregnant woman who obtains or possesses RU-486 (mifepristone) for the purpose of inducing an abortion to terminate her own pregnancy;

(2) The legal transport of RU-486 (mifepristone) by any person or entity and the legal delivery of the RU-486 (mifepristone) by any person to the recipient, provided that this division does not apply regarding any conduct related to the RU-486 (mifepristone) other than its transport and delivery to the recipient;

(3) The distribution, provision, or sale of RU-486 (mifepristone) by any legal manufacturer or distributor of RU-486 (mifepristone), provided the manufacturer or distributor made a good faith effort to comply with any applicable requirements of federal law regarding the distribution, provision, or sale.

(E) Whoever violates this section is guilty of unlawful distribution of an abortion-inducing drug, a felony of the fourth degree. If the offender previously has been convicted of or pleaded guilty to a violation of this section or of section 2919.12, 2919.121 [2919.12.1], 2919.13, 2919.14, 2919.151 [2919.15.1], 2919.17, or 2919.18 of the Revised Code, unlawful distribution of an abortion-inducing drug is a felony of the third degree.

If the offender is a professionally licensed person, in addition to any other sanction imposed by law for the offense, the offender is subject to sanctioning as provided by law by the regulatory or licensing board or agency that has the administrative authority to suspend or revoke the offender's professional license, including the sanctioning provided in section 4731.22 of the Revised Code for offenders who have a certificate to practice or certificate of registration issued under that chapter.

(F) As used in this section:

(1) "Federal law" means any law, rule, or regulation of the United States or any drug approval letter of the food and drug administration of the United States that governs or regulates the use of RU-486 (mifepristone) for the purpose of inducing abortions.

(2) "Personal identifying information" has the same meaning as in section 2913.49 of the Revised Code.

(3) "Physician" has the same meaning as in section 2305.113 [2305.11.3] of the Revised Code.

(4) "Professionally licensed person" has the same meaning as in section 2925.01 of the Revised Code.

**HISTORY: 150 v H 126, § 1, eff. 9-23-04.**

## § 2919.13 Abortion manslaughter.

(A) No person shall purposely take the life of a child born by attempted abortion who is alive when removed from the uterus of the pregnant woman.

(B) No person who performs an abortion shall fail to take the measures required by the exercise of medical judgment in light of the attending circumstances to preserve the life of a child who is alive when removed from the uterus of the pregnant woman.

(C) Whoever violates this section is guilty of abortion manslaughter, a felony of the first degree.

**HISTORY: 135 v H 989. Eff 9-16-74.**

**Not analogous to former RC § 2919.13 (RS § 6909; S&C 428; 29 v 144; 70 v 61; GC §§ 12916, 12917; Bureau of Code Revision, 10-1-53), repealed 134 v H 511, § 2, eff 1-1-74.**

## § 2919.14 Abortion trafficking.

(A) No person shall experiment upon or sell the product of human conception which is aborted. Experiment does not include autopsies pursuant to sections 313.13 and 2108.50 of the Revised Code.

(B) Whoever violates this section is guilty of abortion trafficking, a misdemeanor of the first degree.

**HISTORY: 135 v H 989. Eff 9-16-74.**

**Not analogous to former RC § 2919.14 (RS § 6970; S&S 640; 66 v 57; 70 v 105; GC § 12918; 101 v 131; Bureau of Code Revision, 10-1-53), repealed 134 v H 511, § 2, eff 1-1-74.**

## § 2919.15 Repealed, 148 v H 351, § 2 [146 v H 135]. Eff 8-18-2000.

This section concerned dilation and extraction. See now RC § 2919.15.1.

## § 2919.151 Partial birth feticide.

(A) As used in this section:

(1) "Dilation and evacuation procedure of abortion" does not include the dilation and extraction procedure of abortion.

(2) "From the body of the mother" means that the portion of the fetus' body in question is beyond the mother's vaginal introitus in a vaginal delivery.

(3) "Partial birth procedure" means the medical procedure that includes all of the following elements in sequence:

(a) Intentional dilation of the cervix of a pregnant woman, usually over a sequence of days;

(b) In a breech presentation, intentional extraction of at least the lower torso to the navel, but not the entire body, of an intact fetus from the body of the mother, or in a cephalic presentation, intentional extraction of at least the complete head, but not the entire body, of an intact fetus from the body of the mother;

(c) Intentional partial evacuation of the intracranial contents of the fetus, which procedure the person performing the procedure knows will cause the death of the fetus, intentional compression of the head of the fetus, which procedure the person performing the procedure knows will cause the death of the fetus, or performance of another intentional act that the person performing the procedure knows will cause the death of the fetus;

(d) Completion of the vaginal delivery of the fetus.

(4) "Partially born" means that the portion of the body of an intact fetus described in division (A)(3)(b) of this section has been intentionally extracted from the body of the mother.

(5) "Serious risk of the substantial and irreversible impairment of a major bodily function" means any medically diagnosed condition that so complicates the pregnancy of the woman as to directly or indirectly cause the substantial and irreversible impairment of a major bodily function.

(6) "Viable" has the same meaning as in section 2901.01 of the Revised Code.

(B) When the fetus that is the subject of the procedure is viable, no person shall knowingly perform a partial birth procedure on a pregnant woman when the procedure is not necessary, in reasonable medical judgment, to preserve the life or health of the mother as a result of the mother's life or health being endangered by a serious risk of the substantial and irreversible impairment of a major bodily function.

(C) When the fetus that is the subject of the procedure is not viable, no person shall knowingly perform a partial birth procedure on a pregnant woman when the procedure is not necessary, in reasonable medical judgment, to preserve the life or health of the mother as a result of the mother's life or health being endangered by a serious risk of the substantial and irreversible impairment of a major bodily function.

(D) Whoever violates division (B) or (C) of this section is guilty of partial birth feticide, a felony of the second degree.

(E) A pregnant woman upon whom a partial birth procedure is performed in violation of division (B) or (C) of this section is not guilty of committing, attempting to commit, complicity in the commission of, or conspiracy in the commission of a violation of those divisions.

(F) This section does not prohibit the suction curettage procedure of abortion, the suction aspiration procedure of abortion, or the dilation and evacuation procedure of abortion.

(G) This section does not apply to any person who performs or attempts to perform a legal abortion if the act that causes the death of the fetus is performed prior to the fetus being partially born even though the death of the fetus occurs after it is partially born.

**HISTORY: 148 v H 351. Eff 8-18-2000.**

The provisions of § 3 of HB 351 (148 v —) read as follows:

SECTION 3. The General Assembly declares all of the following:

(A) In enacting sections 2307.53 and 2919.151 of the Revised Code, its intent is to prevent the unnecessary death of fetuses when they are substantially outside the body of the mother.

(B) This intent is based in part on a state interest in maintaining a strong public policy against infanticide, regardless of the life expectancy or state of development of the child.

(C) The right to abortion established in Roe v. Wade (1973), 410 U.S. 113, was never intended to legitimize infanticide or to deprive the state of all ability to protect fetuses who are substantially outside the body of the mother.

(D) The act also furthers the state interest in preventing unnecessary cruelty. This interest is not necessarily based solely on the ability of the fetus or child to experience pain. The indignity of being partly delivered before being deliberately killed is also a form of cruelty that should not be unnecessarily inflicted upon any being of human origin. Therefore, there are legitimate reasons for deterring the unnecessary use of the partial birth procedure, even though other abortion procedures that may cause pain remain available.

### [POST-VIABILITY ABORTION]

## § 2919.16 Definitions.

As used in sections 2919.16 to 2919.18 of the Revised Code:

(A) "Fertilization" means the fusion of a human spermatozoon with a human ovum.

(B) "Gestational age" or "gestation" means the age of an unborn child as calculated from the first day of the last menstrual period of a pregnant woman.

(C) "Health care facility" means a hospital, clinic, ambulatory surgical treatment center, other center, medical school, office of a physician, infirmary, dispensary, medical training institution, or other institution or location in or at which medical care, treatment, or diagnosis is provided to a person.

(D) "Hospital" has the same meanings as in sections 3701.01, 3727.01, and 5122.01 of the Revised Code.

(E) "Live birth" has the same meaning as in division (A) of section 3705.01 of the Revised Code.

(F) "Medical emergency" means a condition that in the physician's good faith medical judgment, based upon the facts known to the physician at that time, so complicates the woman's pregnancy as to necessitate the immediate performance or inducement of an abortion in order to prevent the death of the pregnant woman or to avoid a serious risk of the substantial and irreversible impairment of a major bodily function of the pregnant woman that delay in the performance or inducement of the abortion would create.

(G) "Physician" has the same meaning as in section 2305.113 of the Revised Code.

(H) "Pregnant" means the human female reproductive condition, that commences with fertilization, of having a developing fetus.

(I) "Pregnancy" means the condition of being pregnant.

(J) "Premature infant" means a human whose live birth occurs prior to thirty-eight weeks of gestational age.

(K) "Serious risk of the substantial and irreversible impairment of a major bodily function" means any medically diagnosed condition that so complicates the pregnancy of the woman as to directly or indirectly cause the substantial and irreversible impairment of a major bodily function.

A medically diagnosed condition that constitutes a "serious risk of the substantial and irreversible impairment of a major bodily function" includes pre-eclampsia, inevitable abortion, and premature rupture of the membranes, may include, but is not limited to, diabetes and multiple sclerosis, and does not include a condition related to the woman's mental health.

(L) "Unborn child" means an individual organism of the species homo sapiens from fertilization until live birth.

(M) "Viable" means the stage of development of a human fetus at which in the determination of a physician, based on the particular facts of a woman's pregnancy that are known to the physician and in light of medical technology and information reasonably available to the physician, there is a realistic possibility of the maintaining and nourishing of a life outside of the womb with or without temporary artificial life-sustaining support.

**HISTORY: 146 v H 135 (Eff 11-15-95); 149 v S 281. Eff 4-11-2003; 152 v H 529, § 1, eff. 4-7-09; 2011 HB 78, § 1, eff. Oct. 20, 2011.**

**Not analogous to former RC § 2919.16 (RS § 2739a; 83 v 80; GC § 12924; Bureau of Code Revision, 10-1-53), repealed 134 v H 511, § 2, eff 1-1-74.**

The provisions of § 6 of SB 281 (149 v —) read as follows:

SECTION 6. (A) Sections 1751.67, 2117.06, 2305.11, 2305.15, 2305.234, 2317.02, 2317.54, 2323.56, 2711.21, 2711.22, 2711.23, 2711.24, 2743.02, 2743.43, 2919.16, 3923.63, 3923.64, 3929.71, and 5111.018 of the Revised Code, as amended by this act, and sections 2303.23, 2305.113, 2323.41, 2323.42, 2323.43, and 2323.55 of the Revised Code, as enacted by this act, apply to civil actions upon a medical claim, dental claim, optometric claim, or chiropractic claim in which the act or omission that constitutes the alleged basis of the claim occurs on or after the effective date of this act.

(B) As used in this section, "medical claim," "dental claim," "optometric claim," and "chiropractic claim" have the same meanings as in section 2305.113 of the Revised Code.

## § 2919.17 Performance of abortion after viability prohibited.

(A) No person shall purposely perform or induce or attempt to perform or induce an abortion on a pregnant woman when the unborn child is viable.

(B)(1) It is an affirmative defense to a charge under division (A) of this section that the abortion was performed or induced or attempted to be performed or induced by a physician and that the physician determined, in the physician's good faith medical judgment, based on the facts known to the physician at that time, that either of the following applied:

(a) The unborn child was not viable.

(b) The abortion was necessary to prevent the death of the pregnant woman or a serious risk of the substantial and irreversible impairment of a major bodily function of the pregnant woman.

(2) No abortion shall be considered necessary under division (B)(1)(b) of this section on the basis of a claim or diagnosis that the pregnant woman will engage in conduct that would result in the pregnant woman's death or a substantial and irreversible impairment of a major bodily function of the pregnant woman or based on any reason related to the woman's mental health.

(C) Except when a medical emergency exists that prevents compliance with section 2919.18 of the Revised Code, the affirmative defense set forth in division (B)(1)(a) of this section does not apply unless the physician who performs or induces or attempts to perform or induce the abortion performs the viability testing required by division (A) of section 2919.18 of the Revised Code and certifies in writing, based on the results of the tests performed, that in the physician's good faith medical judgment the unborn child is not viable.

(D) Except when a medical emergency exists that prevents compliance with one or more of the following conditions, the affirmative defense set forth in division (B)(1)(b) of this section does not apply unless the physician who performs or induces or attempts to perform or induce the abortion complies with all of the following conditions:

(1) The physician who performs or induces or attempts to perform or induce the abortion certifies in writing that, in the physician's good faith medical judgment, based on the facts known to the physician at that time, the abortion is necessary to prevent the death of the pregnant woman or a serious risk of the substantial and irreversible impairment of a major bodily function of the pregnant woman.

(2) Another physician who is not professionally related to the physician who intends to perform or induce the abortion certifies in writing that, in that physician's good faith medical judgment, based on the facts known to that physician at that time, the abortion is necessary to prevent the death of the pregnant woman or a serious risk of the substantial and irreversible impairment of a major bodily function of the pregnant woman.

(3) The physician performs or induces or attempts to perform or induce the abortion in a hospital or other health care facility that has appropriate neonatal services for premature infants.

(4) The physician who performs or induces or attempts to perform or induce the abortion terminates or attempts to terminate the pregnancy in the manner that provides the best opportunity for the unborn child to survive, unless that physician determines, in the physician's good faith medical judgment, based on the facts known to the physician at that time, that the termination of the pregnancy in that manner poses a greater risk of the death of the pregnant woman or a greater risk of the substantial and irreversible impairment of a major bodily function of the pregnant woman than would other available methods of abortion.

(5) The physician certifies in writing the available method or techniques considered and the reasons for choosing the method or technique employed.

(6) The physician who performs or induces or attempts to perform or induce the abortion has arranged for the attendance in the same room in which the abortion is to be performed or induced or attempted to be performed or induced at least one other physician who is to take control of, provide immediate medical care for, and take all reasonable steps necessary to preserve the life and health of the unborn child immediately upon the child's complete expulsion or extraction from the pregnant woman.

(E) For purposes of this section, there is a rebuttable presumption that an unborn child of at least twenty-four weeks gestational age is viable.

(F) Whoever violates this section is guilty of terminating or attempting to terminate a human pregnancy after viability, a felony of the fourth degree.

(G) The state medical board shall revoke a physician's license to practice medicine in this state if the physician violates this section.

(H) Any physician who performs or induces an abortion or attempts to perform or induce an abortion with actual knowledge that neither of the affirmative defenses set forth in division (B)(1) of this section applies, or with a heedless indifference as to whether either affirmative defense applies, is liable in a civil action for compensatory and exemplary damages and reasonable attorney's fees to any person, or the representative of the estate of any person, who sustains injury, death, or loss to person or property as the result of the performance or inducement or the attempted performance or inducement of the abortion. In any action under this division, the court also may award any injunctive or other equitable relief that the court considers appropriate.

(I) A pregnant woman on whom an abortion is performed or induced or attempted to be performed or induced in violation of division (A) of this section is not guilty of violating division (A) of this section or of attempting to commit, conspiring to commit, or complicity in committing a violation of division (A) of this section.

**HISTORY: 2011 HB 78, § 1, eff. Oct. 20, 2011.**

Former RC 2919.17 was repealed by 2011 HB 78, § 2, effective October 20, 2011.

**Not analogous to former RC § 2919.17 (RS § 6913; S & C 429; 29 v 144, § 13; GC § 12925; Bureau of Code Revision, 10-1-53), repealed 134 v H 511, § 2, eff 1-1-74.**

## § 2919.171 Physicians who perform abortions required to submit report; department of health statistics report.

(A) A physician who performs or induces or attempts to perform or induce an abortion on a pregnant woman shall submit a report to the department of health in accordance with the forms, rules, and regulations adopted by the department that includes all of the information the physician is required to certify in writing or determine under sections 2919.17 and 2919.18 of the Revised Code:

(B) By September 30 of each year, the department of health shall issue a public report that provides statistics for the previous calendar year compiled from all of the reports covering that calendar year submitted to the department in accordance with this section for each of the items listed in division (A) of this section. The report shall also provide the statistics for each previous calendar year in which a report was filed with the department pursuant to this section, adjusted to reflect any additional information that a physician provides to the department in a late or corrected report. The department shall ensure that none of the information included in the report could reasonably lead to the identification of any pregnant woman upon whom an abortion is performed.

(C)(1) The physician shall submit the report described in division (A) of this section to the department of health within fifteen days after the woman is discharged. If the physician fails to submit the report more than thirty days after that fifteen-day deadline, the physician shall be subject to a late fee of five hundred dollars for each additional thirty-day period or portion of a thirty-day period the report is overdue. A physician who is required to submit to the department of health a report under division (A) of this section and who has not submitted a report or has submitted an incomplete report more than one year following the fifteen-day deadline may, in an action brought by the department of health, be directed by a court of competent jurisdiction to submit a complete report to the department of health within a period of time stated in a court order or be subject to contempt of court.

(2) If a physician fails to comply with the requirements of this section, other than filing a late report with the department of health, or fails to submit a complete report to the department of health in accordance with a court order, the physician is subject to division (B)(41) of section 4731.22 of the Revised Code.

(3) No person shall falsify any report required under this section. Whoever violates this division is guilty of abortion report falsification, a misdemeanor of the first degree.

(D) Within ninety days of the effective date of this section, the department of health shall adopt rules pursuant to section 111.15 of the Revised Code to assist in compliance with this section.

**HISTORY: 2011 HB 78, § 1, eff. Oct. 20, 2011.**

## § 2919.18 Performance of abortion after the twentieth week of gestation prohibited; exceptions; viability testing.

(A) Except in a medical emergency that prevents compliance with this division, no physician shall perform or induce or attempt to perform or induce an abortion on a pregnant woman after the beginning of the twentieth week of gestation unless, prior to the performance or inducement of the abortion or the attempt to perform or induce the abortion, the physician determines, in the physician's good faith medical judgment, that the unborn child is not viable, and the physician makes that determination after performing a medical examination of the pregnant woman and after performing or causing to be performed those tests for assessing gestational age, weight, lung maturity, or other tests that the physician, in that physician's good faith medical judgment, believes are necessary to determine whether an unborn child is viable.

(B) Except in a medical emergency that prevents compliance with this division, no physician shall perform or induce or attempt to perform or induce an abortion on a pregnant woman after the beginning of the twentieth week of gestation without first entering the determination made in division (A) of this section and the associated findings of the medical examination and tests in the medical record of the pregnant woman.

(C) Whoever violates this section is guilty of failure to perform viability testing, a misdemeanor of the fourth degree.

(D) The state medical board shall suspend a physician's license to practice medicine in this state for a period of not less than six months if the physician violates this section.

**HISTORY: 2011 HB 78, § 1, eff. Oct. 20, 2011.**

Former RC 2919.18 was repealed by 2011 HB 78, § 2, effective October 20, 2011.

**Not analogous to former RC § 2919.18 (RS § 633-14; 92 v 212, § 4; GC § 12933; Bureau of Code Revision, 10-1-53), repealed 134 v H 511, § 2, eff 1-1-74).**

## § 2919.19 Repealed, 134 v H 511, § 2 [RS §§ 181-6, 3107-48, 3107-49; 55 v 99; 85 v 149; 92 v 50; 94 v 157; GC §§ 12893, 12934; Bureau of Code Revision, 10-1-53]. Eff 1-1-74.

This section concerned hindering examination of state treasury and failure to prefer soldiers for appointments.

## § 2919.20 Repealed, 134 v H 511, § 2 [RS §§ 181-6, 3107-48, 3107-49; 55 v 99; 85 v 149; 92 v 50; 94 v 157; GC §§ 12893, 12934; Bureau of Code Revision, 10-1-53]. Eff 1-1-74.

This section concerned hindering examination of state treasury and failure to prefer soldiers for appointments.

[NONSUPPORT AND RELATED OFFENSES]

## § 2919.21 Nonsupport or contributing to nonsupport of dependents.

(A) No person shall abandon, or fail to provide adequate support to:

(1) The person's spouse, as required by law;

(2) The person's child who is under age eighteen, or mentally or physically handicapped child who is under age twenty-one;

(3) The person's aged or infirm parent or adoptive parent, who from lack of ability and means is unable to provide adequately for the parent's own support.

(B) No person shall abandon, or fail to provide support as established by a court order to, another person whom, by court order or decree, the person is legally obligated to support.

(C) No person shall aid, abet, induce, cause, encourage, or contribute to a child or a ward of the juvenile court becoming a dependent child, as defined in section 2151.04 of the Revised Code, or a neglected child, as defined in section 2151.03 of the Revised Code.

(D) It is an affirmative defense to a charge of failure to provide adequate support under division (A) of this section or a charge of failure to provide support established by a court order under division (B) of this section that the accused was unable to provide adequate support or the established support but did provide the support that was within the accused's ability and means.

(E) It is an affirmative defense to a charge under division (A)(3) of this section that the parent abandoned the accused or failed to support the accused as required by law, while the accused was under age eighteen, or was mentally or physically handicapped and under age twenty-one.

(F) It is not a defense to a charge under division (B) of this section that the person whom a court has ordered the accused to support is being adequately supported by someone other than the accused.

(G)(1) Except as otherwise provided in this division, whoever violates division (A) or (B) of this section is guilty of nonsupport of dependents, a misdemeanor of the first degree. If the offender previously has been convicted of or pleaded guilty to a violation of division (A)(2) or (B) of this section or if the offender has failed to provide support under division (A)(2) or (B) of this section for a total accumulated period of twenty-six weeks out of one hundred four consecutive weeks, whether or not the twenty-six weeks were consecutive, then a violation of division (A)(2) or (B) of this section is a felony of the fifth degree. If the offender previously has been convicted of or pleaded guilty to a felony violation of this section, a violation of division (A)(2) or (B) of this section is a felony of the fourth degree.

If the violation of division (A) or (B) of this section is a felony, all of the following apply to the sentencing of the offender:

(a) Except as otherwise provided in division (G)(1)(b) of this section, the court in imposing sentence on the offender shall first consider placing the offender on one or more community control sanctions under section 2929.16, 2929.17, or 2929.18 of the Revised Code, with an emphasis under the sanctions on intervention for nonsupport, obtaining or maintaining employment, or another related condition.

(b) The preference for placement on community control sanctions described in division (G)(1)(a) of this section does not apply to any offender to whom one or more of the following applies:

(i) The court determines that the imposition of a prison term on the offender is consistent with the purposes and principles of sentencing set forth in section 2929.11 of the Revised Code.

(ii) The offender previously was convicted of or pleaded guilty to a violation of this section that was a felony, and the offender was sentenced to a prison term for that violation.

(iii) The offender previously was convicted of or pleaded guilty to a violation of this section that was a felony, the offender was sentenced to one or more community control sanctions of a type described in division (G)(1)(a) of this section for that violation, and the offender failed to comply with the conditions of any of those community control sanctions.

(2) If the offender is guilty of nonsupport of dependents by reason of failing to provide support to the offender's child as required by a child support order issued on or after April 15, 1985, pursuant to section 2151.23, 2151.231, 2151.232, 2151.33, 3105.21, 3109.05, 3111.13, 3113.04, 3113.31, or 3115.31 of the Revised Code, the court, in addition to any other sentence imposed, shall assess all court costs arising out of the charge against the person and require the person to pay any reasonable attorney's fees of any adverse party other than the state, as determined by the court, that arose in relation to the charge.

(3) Whoever violates division (C) of this section is guilty of contributing to the nonsupport of dependents, a misdemeanor of the first degree. Each day of violation of division (C) of this section is a separate offense.

**HISTORY: 134 v H 511 (Eff 1-1-74); 140 v H 614 (Eff 4-10-85); 141 v H 349 (Eff 3-6-86); 141 v S 136 (Eff 9-24-86); 146 v S 2 (Eff 7-1-96); 146 v S 269 (Eff 7-1-96); 146 v H 274, §§ 1, 4 (Eff 8-8-96); 147 v H 352. Eff 1-1-98; 2011 HB 86, § 1, eff. Sept. 30, 2011.**

**Not analogous to former RC § 2919.21 (RS § 3107-48; 85 v 149; 92 v 50; 94 v 157; GC § 12894; Bureau of Code Revision, 10-1-53), repealed 134 v H 511, § 2, eff 1-1-74.**

The effective date is set by section 4 of HB 352.

## § 2919.22 Endangering children.

(A) No person, who is the parent, guardian, custodian, person having custody or control, or person in loco parentis of a child under eighteen years of age or a mentally or physically handicapped child under twenty-one years of age, shall create a substantial risk to the health or safety of the child, by violating a duty of care, protection, or support. It is not a violation of a duty of care, protection, or support under this division when the parent, guardian, custodian, or person having custody or control of a child treats the physical or mental illness or defect of the child by spiritual means through prayer alone, in accordance with the tenets of a recognized religious body.

(B) No person shall do any of the following to a child under eighteen years of age or a mentally or physically handicapped child under twenty-one years of age:

(1) Abuse the child;

(2) Torture or cruelly abuse the child;

(3) Administer corporal punishment or other physical disciplinary measure, or physically restrain the child in a cruel manner or for a prolonged period, which punishment, discipline, or restraint is excessive under the circumstances and creates a substantial risk of serious physical harm to the child;

(4) Repeatedly administer unwarranted disciplinary measures to the child, when there is a substantial risk that such conduct, if continued, will seriously impair or retard the child's mental health or development;

(5) Entice, coerce, permit, encourage, compel, hire, employ, use, or allow the child to act, model, or in any other way participate in, or be photographed for, the production, presentation, dissemination, or advertisement of any material or performance that the offender knows or reasonably should know is obscene, is sexually oriented matter, or is nudity-oriented matter;

(6) Allow the child to be on the same parcel of real property and within one hundred feet of, or, in the case of more than one housing unit on the same parcel of real property, in the same housing unit and within one hundred feet of, any act in violation of section 2925.04 or 2925.041 of the Revised Code when the person knows that the act is occurring, whether or not any person is prosecuted for or convicted of the violation of section 2925.04 or 2925.041 of the Revised Code that is the basis of the violation of this division.

(C)(1) No person shall operate a vehicle, streetcar, or trackless trolley within this state in violation of division (A) of section 4511.19 of the Revised Code when one or more children under eighteen years of age are in the vehicle, streetcar, or trackless trolley. Notwithstanding any other provision of law, a person may be convicted at the same trial or proceeding of a violation of this division and a violation of division (A) of section 4511.19 of the Revised Code that constitutes the basis of the charge of the violation of this division. For purposes of sections 4511.191 to 4511.197 of the Revised Code and all related provisions of law, a person arrested for a violation of this division shall be considered to be under arrest for operating a vehicle while under the influence of alcohol, a drug of abuse, or a combination of them or for operating a vehicle with a prohibited concentration of alcohol, a controlled substance, or a metabolite of a controlled substance in the whole blood, blood serum or plasma, breath, or urine.

(2) As used in division (C)(1) of this section:

(a) "Controlled substance" has the same meaning as in section 3719.01 of the Revised Code.

(b) "Vehicle," "streetcar," and "trackless trolley" have the same meanings as in section 4511.01 of the Revised Code.

(D)(1) Division (B)(5) of this section does not apply to any material or performance that is produced, presented, or disseminated for a bona fide medical, scientific, educational, religious, governmental, judicial, or other proper purpose, by or to a physician, psychologist, sociologist, scientist, teacher, person pursuing bona fide studies or research, librarian, member of the clergy, prosecutor, judge, or other person having a proper interest in the material or performance.

(2) Mistake of age is not a defense to a charge under division (B)(5) of this section.

(3) In a prosecution under division (B)(5) of this section, the trier of fact may infer that an actor, model, or participant in the material or performance involved is a juvenile if the material or performance, through its title, text, visual representation, or otherwise, represents or depicts the actor, model, or participant as a juvenile.

(4) As used in this division and division (B)(5) of this section:

(a) "Material," "performance," "obscene," and "sexual activity" have the same meanings as in section 2907.01 of the Revised Code.

(b) "Nudity-oriented matter" means any material or performance that shows a minor in a state of nudity and that, taken as a whole by the average person applying contemporary community standards, appeals to prurient interest.

(c) "Sexually oriented matter" means any material or performance that shows a minor participating or engaging in sexual activity, masturbation, or bestiality.

(E)(1) Whoever violates this section is guilty of endangering children.

(2) If the offender violates division (A) or (B)(1) of this section, endangering children is one of the following, and, in the circumstances described in division (E)(2)(e) of this section, that division applies:

(a) Except as otherwise provided in division (E)(2)(b), (c), or (d) of this section, a misdemeanor of the first degree;

(b) If the offender previously has been convicted of an offense under this section or of any offense involving neglect, abandonment, contributing to the delinquency of, or physical abuse of a child, except as otherwise provided in division (E)(2)(c) or (d) of this section, a felony of the fourth degree;

(c) If the violation is a violation of division (A) of this section and results in serious physical harm to the child involved, a felony of the third degree;

(d) If the violation is a violation of division (B)(1) of this section and results in serious physical harm to the child involved, a felony of the second degree.

(e) If the violation is a felony violation of division (B)(1) of this section and the offender also is convicted of or pleads guilty to a specification as described in section 2941.1422 of the Revised Code that was included in the indictment, count in the indictment, or information charging the offense, the court shall sentence the offender to a mandatory prison term as provided in division (B)(7) of section 2929.14 of the Revised Code and shall order the offender to make restitution as provided in division (B)(8) of section 2929.18 of the Revised Code.

(3) If the offender violates division (B)(2), (3), (4), or (6) of this section, except as otherwise provided in this division, endangering children is a felony of the third degree. If the violation results in serious physical harm to the child involved, or if the offender previously has been convicted of an offense under this section or of any offense involving neglect, abandonment, contributing to the delinquency of, or physical abuse of a child, endangering children is a felony of the second degree. If the offender violates division (B)(2), (3), or (4) of this section and the offender also is convicted of or pleads guilty to a specification as described in section 2941.1422 of the Revised Code that was included in the indictment, count in the indictment, or information charging the offense, the court shall sentence the offender to a mandatory prison term as provided in division (B)(7) of section 2929.14 of the Revised Code and shall order the offender to make restitution as provided in division (B)(8) of section 2929.18 of the Revised Code. If the offender violates division (B)(6) of this section and the drug involved is methamphetamine, the court shall impose a mandatory prison term on the offender as follows:

(a) If the violation is a violation of division (B)(6) of this section that is a felony of the third degree under division (E)(3) of this section and the drug involved is methamphetamine, except as otherwise provided in this division, the court shall impose as a mandatory prison term one of the prison terms prescribed for a felony of the third degree that is not less than two years. If the violation is a violation of division (B)(6) of this section that is a felony of the third degree under division (E)(3) of this section, if the drug involved is methamphetamine, and if the offender previously has been convicted of or pleaded guilty to a violation of division (B)(6) of this section, a violation of division (A) of section 2925.04 of the Revised Code, or a violation of division (A) of section 2925.041 of the Revised Code, the court shall impose as a mandatory prison term one of the prison terms prescribed for a felony of the third degree that is not less than five years.

(b) If the violation is a violation of division (B)(6) of this section that is a felony of the second degree under division (E)(3) of this section and the drug involved is methamphetamine, except as otherwise provided in this division, the court shall impose as a mandatory prison term one of the prison terms prescribed for a felony of the second degree that is not less than three years. If the violation is a violation of division (B)(6) of this section that is a felony of the second degree under division (E)(3) of this section, if the drug involved is methamphetamine, and if the offender previously has been convicted of or pleaded guilty to a violation of division (B)(6) of this section, a violation of division (A) of section 2925.04 of the Revised Code, or a violation of division (A) of section 2925.041 of the Revised Code, the court shall impose as a mandatory prison term one of the prison terms prescribed for a felony of the second degree that is not less than five years.

(4) If the offender violates division (B)(5) of this section, endangering children is a felony of the second degree. If the offender also is convicted of or pleads guilty to a specification as described in section 2941.1422 of the Revised Code that was included in the indictment, count in the indictment, or information charging the offense, the court shall sentence the offender to a mandatory prison term as provided in division (B)(7) of section 2929.14 of the Revised Code and shall order the offender to make restitution as provided in division (B)(8) of section 2929.18 of the Revised Code.

(5) If the offender violates division (C) of this section, the offender shall be punished as follows:

(a) Except as otherwise provided in division (E)(5)(b) or (c) of this section, endangering children in violation of division (C) of this section is a misdemeanor of the first degree.

(b) If the violation results in serious physical harm to the child involved or the offender previously has been convicted of an offense under this section or any offense involving neglect, abandonment, contributing to the delinquency of, or physical abuse of a child, except as otherwise provided in division (E)(5)(c) of this section, endangering children in violation of division (C) of this section is a felony of the fifth degree.

(c) If the violation results in serious physical harm to the child involved and if the offender previously has been convicted of a violation of division (C) of this section, section 2903.06 or 2903.08 of the Revised Code, section 2903.07 of the Revised Code as it existed prior to March 23, 2000, or section 2903.04 of the Revised Code in a case in which the offender was subject to the sanctions described in division (D) of that section, endangering children in violation of division (C) of this section is a felony of the fourth degree.

(d) In addition to any term of imprisonment, fine, or other sentence, penalty, or sanction it imposes upon the offender pursuant to division (E)(5)(a), (b), or (c) of this section or pursuant to any other provision of law and in addition to any suspension of the offender's driver's or commercial driver's license or permit or nonresident operating privilege under Chapter 4506., 4509., 4510., or

4511. of the Revised Code or under any other provision of law, the court also may impose upon the offender a class seven suspension of the offender's driver's or commercial driver's license or permit or nonresident operating privilege from the range specified in division (A)(7) of section 4510.02 of the Revised Code.

(e) In addition to any term of imprisonment, fine, or other sentence, penalty, or sanction imposed upon the offender pursuant to division (E)(5)(a), (b), (c), or (d) of this section or pursuant to any other provision of law for the violation of division (C) of this section, if as part of the same trial or proceeding the offender also is convicted of or pleads guilty to a separate charge charging the violation of division (A) of section 4511.19 of the Revised Code that was the basis of the charge of the violation of division (C) of this section, the offender also shall be sentenced in accordance with section 4511.19 of the Revised Code for that violation of division (A) of section 4511.19 of the Revised Code.

(F)(1)(a) A court may require an offender to perform not more than two hundred hours of supervised community service work under the authority of an agency, subdivision, or charitable organization. The requirement shall be part of the community control sanction or sentence of the offender, and the court shall impose the community service in accordance with and subject to divisions (F)(1)(a) and (b) of this section. The court may require an offender whom it requires to perform supervised community service work as part of the offender's community control sanction or sentence to pay the court a reasonable fee to cover the costs of the offender's participation in the work, including, but not limited to, the costs of procuring a policy or policies of liability insurance to cover the period during which the offender will perform the work. If the court requires the offender to perform supervised community service work as part of the offender's community control sanction or sentence, the court shall do so in accordance with the following limitations and criteria:

(i) The court shall require that the community service work be performed after completion of the term of imprisonment or jail term imposed upon the offender for the violation of division (C) of this section, if applicable.

(ii) The supervised community service work shall be subject to the limitations set forth in divisions (B)(1), (2), and (3) of section 2951.02 of the Revised Code.

(iii) The community service work shall be supervised in the manner described in division (B)(4) of section 2951.02 of the Revised Code by an official or person with the qualifications described in that division. The official or person periodically shall report in writing to the court concerning the conduct of the offender in performing the work.

(iv) The court shall inform the offender in writing that if the offender does not adequately perform, as determined by the court, all of the required community service work, the court may order that the offender be committed to a jail or workhouse for a period of time that does not exceed the term of imprisonment that the court could have imposed upon the offender for the violation of division (C) of this section, reduced by the total amount of time that the offender actually was imprisoned under the sentence or term that was imposed upon the offender for that violation and by the total amount of time that the offender was confined for any reason arising out of the offense for which the offender was convicted and sentenced as described in sections 2949.08 and 2967.191 of the Revised Code, and that, if the court orders that the offender be so committed, the court is authorized, but not required, to grant the offender credit upon the period of the commitment for the community service work that the offender adequately performed.

(b) If a court, pursuant to division (F)(1)(a) of this section, orders an offender to perform community service work as part of the offender's community control sanction or sentence and if the offender does not adequately perform all of the required community service work, as determined by the court, the court may order that the offender be committed to a jail or workhouse for a period of time that does not exceed the term of imprisonment that the court could have imposed upon the offender for the violation of division (C) of this section, reduced by the total amount of time that the offender actually was imprisoned under the sentence or term that was imposed upon the offender for that violation and by the total amount of time that the offender was confined for any reason arising out of the offense for which the offender was convicted and sentenced as described in sections 2949.08 and 2967.191 of the Revised Code. The court may order that a person committed pursuant to this division shall receive hour-for-hour credit upon the period of the commitment for the community service work that the offender adequately performed. No commitment pursuant to this division shall exceed the period of the term of imprisonment that the sentencing court could have imposed upon the offender for the violation of division (C) of this section, reduced by the total amount of time that the offender actually was imprisoned under that sentence or term and by the total amount of time that the offender was confined for any reason arising out of the offense for which the offender was convicted and sentenced as described in sections 2949.08 and 2967.191 of the Revised Code.

(2) Division (F)(1) of this section does not limit or affect the authority of the court to suspend the sentence imposed upon a misdemeanor offender and place the offender under a community control sanction pursuant to section 2929.25 of the Revised Code, to require a misdemeanor or felony offender to perform supervised community service work in accordance with division (B) of section 2951.02 of the Revised Code, or to place a felony offender under a community control sanction.

(G)(1) If a court suspends an offender's driver's or commercial driver's license or permit or nonresident operating privilege under division (E)(5)(d) of this section, the period of the suspension shall be consecutive to, and commence after, the period of suspension of the offender's driver's or commercial driver's license or permit or nonresident operating privilege that is imposed under Chapter 4506., 4509., 4510., or 4511. of the Revised Code or under any other provision of law in relation to the violation of division (C) of this section that is the basis of the suspension under division (E)(5)(d) of this section or in relation to the violation of division (A) of section 4511.19 of the Revised Code that is the basis for that violation of division (C) of this section.

(2) An offender is not entitled to request, and the court shall not grant to the offender, limited driving privileges if the offender's license, permit, or privilege has been suspended under division (E)(5)(d) of this section and the offender, within the preceding six years, has been convicted of or pleaded guilty to three or more violations of one or more of the following:

(a) Division (C) of this section;

(b) Any equivalent offense, as defined in section 4511.181 of the Revised Code.

(H)(1) If a person violates division (C) of this section and if, at the time of the violation, there were two or more children under eighteen years of age in the motor vehicle involved in the violation, the offender may be convicted of a violation of division (C) of this section for each of the children, but the court may sentence the offender for only one of the violations.

(2)(a) If a person is convicted of or pleads guilty to a violation of division (C) of this section but the person is not also convicted of and does not also plead guilty to a separate charge charging the violation of division (A) of section 4511.19 of the Revised Code that was the basis of the charge of the violation of division (C) of this section, both of the following apply:

(i) For purposes of the provisions of section 4511.19 of the Revised Code that set forth the penalties and sanctions for a violation of division (A) of section 4511.19 of the Revised Code, the conviction of or plea of guilty to the violation of division (C) of this section shall not constitute a violation of division (A) of section 4511.19 of the Revised Code;

(ii) For purposes of any provision of law that refers to a conviction of or plea of guilty to a violation of division (A) of section 4511.19 of the Revised Code and that is not described in division (H)(2)(a)(i) of this section, the conviction of or plea of guilty to the violation of division (C) of this section shall constitute a conviction of or plea of guilty to a violation of division (A) of section 4511.19 of the Revised Code.

(b) If a person is convicted of or pleads guilty to a violation of division (C) of this section and the person also is convicted of or pleads guilty to a separate charge charging the violation of division (A) of section 4511.19 of the Revised Code that was the basis of the charge of the violation of division (C) of this section, the conviction of or plea of guilty to the violation of division (C) of this section shall not constitute, for purposes of any provision of law that refers to a conviction of or plea of guilty to a violation of division (A) of section 4511.19 of the Revised Code, a conviction of or plea of guilty to a violation of division (A) of section 4511.19 of the Revised Code.

(I) As used in this section:

(1) "Community control sanction" has the same meaning as in section 2929.01 of the Revised Code;

(2) "Limited driving privileges" has the same meaning as in section 4501.01 of the Revised Code;

(3) "Methamphetamine" has the same meaning as in section 2925.01 of the Revised Code.

**HISTORY: 134 v H 511 (Eff 1-1-74); 137 v S 243 (Eff 11-17-77); 140 v H 44 (Eff 9-27-84); 140 v S 321 (Eff 4-9-85); 141 v H 349 (Eff 3-6-86); 142 v H 51 (Eff 3-17-89); 145 v H 236 (Eff 9-29-94); 146 v S 2 (Eff 7-1-96); 146 v S 269, § 1 (Eff 7-1-96); 146 v H 353, § 1 (Eff 9-17-96); 146 v H 167 (Eff 5-15-97); 146 v S 269, § 8 (Eff 5-15-97); 146 v H 353, § 4 (Eff 5-15-97); 147 v S 60 (Eff 10-21-97); 148 v H 162 (Eff 8-25-99); 148 v S 107 (Eff 3-23-2000); 148 v S 180. Eff 3-22-2001; 149 v H 490, § 1, eff. 1-1-04; 149 v S 123, § 1, eff. 1-1-04; 150 v S 58, § 1, eff. 8-11-04; 151 v S 53, § 1, eff. 5-17-06; 151 v S 8, § 1, eff. 8-17-06; 152 v H 280, § 1, eff. 4-7-09; 2011 HB 86, § 1, eff. Sept. 30, 2011.**

The effective date is set by section 4 of H.B. 490.

The provisions of § 5 of S.B. 123 (149 v —), as amended by § 3 of H.B. 163 (150 v —), read as follows:

SECTION 5. (A) Notwithstanding division (B) of section 1.58 of the Revised Code, the provisions of the Revised Code amended or enacted in Sections 1 and 2 of Am. Sub. S.B. 123 of the 124th General Assembly shall apply only in relation to conduct and offenses committed on or after January 1, 2004. Conduct and offenses committed prior to January 1, 2004, shall be governed by the law in effect on the date the conduct or offense was committed.

° ° °

**Not analogous to former RC § 2919.22 (RS § 1296-14; 98 v 90; GC § 12935; Bureau of Code Revision, 10-1-53), repealed 134 v H 511, § 2, eff 1-1-74.**

## § 2919.222 Parental education neglect.

No person required to attend a parental education or training program pursuant to a policy adopted under division (A) or (B) of section 3313.663 [3313.66.3] of the Revised Code shall fail to attend the program. Whoever violates this section is guilty of parental education neglect, a misdemeanor of the fourth degree.

**HISTORY: 146 v H 601. Eff 10-29-96.**

### [CHILD CARE PROVIDERS AND FACILITIES]

## § 2919.223 Definitions.

As used in sections 2919.223 [2919.22.3] to 2919.227 [2919.22.7] of the Revised Code:

(A) "Child care," "child day-care center," "in-home aide," "type A family day-care home," and "type B family day-care home" have the same meanings as in section 5104.01 of the Revised Code.

(B) "Child care center licensee" means the owner of a child day-care center licensed pursuant to Chapter 5104. of the Revised Code who is responsible for ensuring the center's compliance with Chapter 5104. of the Revised Code and rules adopted pursuant to that chapter.

(C) "Child care facility" means a child day-care center, a type A family day-care home, or a type B family day-care home.

(D) "Child care provider" means any of the following:

(1) An owner, provider, administrator, or employee of, or volunteer at, a child care facility;

(2) An in-home aide;

(3) A person who represents that the person provides child care.

(E) "Peace officer" has the same meaning as in section 2935.01 of the Revised Code.

**HISTORY: 150 v H 11, § 1, eff. 5-18-05.**

## § 2919.224 Misrepresentation by child care provider.

(A) No child care provider shall knowingly misrepresent any factor or condition that relates to the provision of child care and that substantially affects the health or safety of any child or children in that provider's facility or receiving child care from that provider to any of the following:

(1) A parent, guardian, custodian, or other person responsible for the care of a child in the provider's facility or receiving child care from the provider;

(2) A parent, guardian, custodian, or other person responsible for the care of a child who is considering the provider as a child care provider for the child;

(3) A public official responsible for issuing the provider a license or certificate to provide child care;

(4) A public official investigating or inquiring about the provision of child care by the provider;

(5) A peace officer.

(B) For the purposes of this section, "any factor or condition that relates to the provision of child care" includes, but is not limited to, the following:

(1) The person or persons who will provide child care to the child of the parent, guardian, custodian, or other person responsible for the care of the child, or to the children in general;

(2) The qualifications to provide child care of the child care provider, of a person employed by the provider, or of a person who provides child care as a volunteer;

(3) The number of children to whom child care is provided at one time or the number of children receiving child care in the child care facility at one time;

(4) The conditions or safety features of the child care facility;

(5) The area of the child care facility in which child day-care is provided.

(C) Whoever violates division (A) of this section is guilty of misrepresentation by a child care provider, a misdemeanor of the first degree.

**HISTORY: 150 v H 11, § 1, eff. 5-18-05.**

## § 2919.225 Failure of a type A or type B family day-care home to disclose death or serious injury of a child.

(A) Subject to division (C) of this section, no owner, provider, or administrator of a type A family day-care home or type B family day-care home, knowing that the event described in division (A)(1) or (2) of this section has occurred, shall accept a child into that home without first disclosing to the parent, guardian, custodian, or other person responsible for the care of that child any of the following that has occurred:

(1) A child died while under the care of the home or while receiving child care from the owner, provider, or administrator or died as a result of injuries suffered while under the care of the home or while receiving child care from the owner, provider, or administrator.

(2) Within the preceding ten years, a child suffered injuries while under the care of the home or while receiving child care from the owner, provider, or administrator, and those injuries led to the child being hospitalized for more than twenty-four hours.

(B)(1) Subject to division (C) of this section, no owner, provider, or administrator of a type A family day-care home or type B family day-care home shall fail to provide notice in accordance with division (B)(3) of this section to the persons and entities specified in division (B)(2) of this section, of any of the following that occurs:

(a) A child who is under the care of the home or is receiving child care from the owner, provider, or administrator dies while under the care of the home or while receiving child care from the owner, provider, or administrator or dies as a result of injuries suffered while under the care of the home or while receiving child day-care from the owner, provider, or administrator.

(b) A child who is under the care of the home or is receiving child care from the owner, provider, or administrator is hospitalized for more than twenty-four hours as a result of injuries suffered while under the care of the home or while receiving child care from the owner, provider, or administrator.

(2) An owner, provider, or administrator of a home shall provide the notices required under division (B)(1) of this section to each of the following:

(a) For each child who, at the time of the injury or death for which the notice is required, is receiving or is enrolled to receive child care at the home or from the owner, provider, or administrator, to the parent, guardian, custodian, or other person responsible for the care of the child;

(b) If the notice is required as the result of the death of a child as described in division (B)(1)(a) of this section, to the public children services agency of the county in which the home is located or the child care was given, a municipal or county peace officer in the county in which the child resides or in which the home is located or the child care was given, and the child fatality review board appointed under section 307.621 [307.62.1] of the Revised Code that serves the county in which the home is located or the child care was given.

(3) An owner, provider, or administrator of a home shall provide the notices required by divisions (B)(1) and (2) of this section not later than forty-eight hours after the child dies or, regarding a child who is hospitalized for more than twenty-four hours as a result of injuries suffered while under the care of the home, not later than forty-eight hours after the child suffers the injuries. If a child is hospitalized for more than twenty-four hours as a result of injuries suffered while under the care of the home, and the child subsequently dies as a result of those injuries, the owner, provider, or administrator shall provide separate notices under divisions (B)(1) and (2) of this section regarding both the injuries and the death. All notices provided under divisions (B)(1) and (2) of this section shall state that the death or injury occurred.

(C) Division (A) of this section does not require more than one person to make disclosures to the same parent, guardian, custodian, or other person responsible for the care of a child regarding any single injury or death for which disclosure is required under that division. Division (B) of this section does not require more than one person to give notices to the same parent, guardian, custodian, other person responsible for the care of the child, public children services agency, peace officer, or child fatality review board regarding any single injury or death for which disclosure is required under division (B)(1) of this section.

(D) An owner, provider, or administrator of a type A family day-care home or type B family day-care home is not subject to civil liability solely for making a disclosure required by this section.

(E) Whoever violates division (A) or (B) of this section is guilty of failure of a type A or type B family day-care home to disclose the death or serious injury of a child, a misdemeanor of the fourth degree.

**HISTORY: 150 v H 11, § 1, eff. 5-18-05.**

## § 2919.226 Child care disclosure form.

(A) If a child care provider accurately answers the questions on a child care disclosure form that is in substantially the form set forth in division (B) of this section, presents the form to a person identified in division (A)(1) or (2) of section 2919.224 [2919.22.4] of the Revised Code, and obtains the person's signature on the acknowledgement in the form, to the extent that the information set forth on the form is accurate, the provider who presents the form is not subject to prosecution under division (A) of section 2919.224 [2919.22.4] of the Revised Code regarding presentation of that information to that person.

An owner, provider, or administrator of a type A family day-care home or a type B family day-care home may comply with division (A) of section 2919.225 [2919.22.5] of the Revised Code by accurately answering the questions on a child care disclosure form that is in substantially the form set forth in division (B) of this section, providing a copy of the form to the parent, guardian, custodian, or other person responsible for the care of a child and to whom disclosure is to be made under division (A) of section 2919.225 [2919.22.5] of the Revised Code, and obtaining the person's signature on the acknowledgement in the form.

The use of the form set forth in division (B) of this section is discretionary and is not required to comply with any disclosure requirement contained in section 2919.225 [2919.22.5] of the Revised Code or for any purpose related to section 2919.224 [2919.22.4] of the Revised Code.

(B) To be sufficient for the purposes described in division (A) of this section, a child care disclosure form shall be in substantially the following form:

"CHILD CARE DISCLOSURE FORM

Please Note: This form contains information that is accurate only at the time the form is given to you. The information provided in this form is likely to change over time. It is the duty of the person responsible for the care of the child to monitor the status of child care services to ensure that those services remain satisfactory. If a question on this form is left unanswered, the child care provider makes no assertion regarding the question. Choosing appropriate child care for a child is a serious responsibility, and the person responsible for the care of the child is encouraged to make all appropriate inquiries. Also, in acknowledging receipt of this form, the person responsible for the care of the child acknowledges that in selecting the child care provider the person is not relying on any representations other than those provided in this form unless the child care provider has acknowledged the other representations in writing.

1. What are the names and qualifications to provide child care of: (a) the child care provider, (b) the employee who will provide child care to the applicant child, (c) the volunteer who will provide child care to the applicant child, and (d) any other employees or volunteers of the child care provider? (attach additional sheets if necessary):

..........................................................

..........................................................

..........................................................

..........................................................

2. What is the maximum number of children to whom you provide child care at one time? (If children are divided into groups or classes, please describe the maximum number of children in each group or class and indicate the group or class in which the applicant child will be placed.):

..........................................................

..........................................................

..........................................................

3. Where in the home will you provide child care to the applicant child?:

..........................................................

..........................................................

..........................................................

4. Has a child died while in the care of, or receiving child care from, the child care provider? (Yes/No)

Description/explanation (attach additional sheets if necessary)

..........................................................

..........................................................

..........................................................

5. Has a child died as a result of injuries suffered while under the care of, or receiving child care from, the child day-care provider? (Yes/No)

Description/explanation (attach additional sheets if necessary)

..........................................................

..........................................................

..........................................................

6. Within the preceding ten years, has a child suffered injuries while under the care of, or receiving child care from, the child care provider that led to the child being hospitalized for more than 24 hours? (Yes/No)

Description/explanation (attach additional sheets if necessary)

..........................................................

..........................................................

..........................................................

........................ .........
Signature of person completing form Date

..........................................................
Name of person completing form
(Typed or printed)

..........................................................
Title of person completing form
(Typed or printed)

Acknowledgement:

I hereby acknowledge that I have been given a copy of the preceding document and have read and understood its contents. I further acknowledge that I am not relying on any other representations in selecting the child care provider unless the child care provider has acknowledged the other representations in writing.

........................ .........
Person receiving the form Date"

(C) If a child care provider accurately answers the questions on a disclosure form that is substantially similar to the form described in division (B) of this section, presents the form to a person identified in division (A)(1) or (2) of section 2919.224 [2919.22.4] of the Revised Code, and obtains the person's signature on the acknowledgement in the form, to the extent that the information set forth on the form is accurate, the form is sufficient for the purposes described in division (A) of this section.

An owner, provider, or administrator of a type A family day-care home or a type B family day-care home who accurately answers the questions on a disclosure form that is substantially similar to the form described in division (B) of this section, provides a copy of the completed form to the parent, guardian, custodian, or other person who is responsible for the care of a child and to whom disclosure is to be made under division (A) of section 2919.225 [2919.22.5] of the Revised Code, and obtains the person's signature on the acknowledgement in the form complies with the requirements of that division. If the owner, provider, or administrator uses the disclosure form, leaving a portion of the disclosure form blank does not constitute a misrepresentation for the purposes of section 2919.224 [2919.22.4] of the Revised Code but may constitute a violation of section 2919.225 [2919.22.5] of the Revised Code. The owner, provider, or administrator of a type A family day-care home or type B family day-care home who completes the disclosure form and provides a copy of the form to any person described in section 2919.224 [2919.22.4] or 2919.225 [2919.22.5] of the Revised Code may retain a copy of the completed form.

**HISTORY: 150 v H 11, § 1, eff. 5-18-05.**

## § 2919.227 Failure of child care center to disclose death or serious injury of a child.

(A)(1) No child care center licensee shall accept a child into that center without first providing to the parent, guardian, custodian, or other person responsible for the care of that child the following information, if the parent, guardian, custodian, or other person responsible for the care of the child requests the information:

(a) The types of injuries to children, as reported in accordance with rules adopted under section 5104.011 [5104.01.1] of the Revised Code, that occurred at the center on or after April 1, 2003, or the date that is two years before the date the information is requested, whichever date is more recent;

(b) The number of each type of injury to children that occurred at the center during that period.

(2) If a death described in division (A)(2)(a) or (A)(2)(b) of this section occurred during the fifteen-year period immediately preceding the date that the parent, guardian, custodian, or other person responsible for the care of a child seeks to enroll that child, no child care center licensee shall accept that child into that center without first providing to the parent, guardian, custodian, or other person responsible for the care of that child a notice that states that the death occurred.

(a) A child died while under the care of the center or while receiving child care from the owner, provider, or administrator of the center;

(b) A child died as a result of injuries suffered while under the care of the center or while receiving child care from the owner, provider, or administrator of the center.

(3) Each child care center licensee shall keep on file at the center a copy of the information provided under this division for at least three years after providing the information.

(B)(1) No child care center licensee shall fail to provide notice in accordance with division (B)(3) of this section to the persons and entities specified in division (B)(2) of this section if a child who is under the care of the center or is receiving child care from the owner, provider, or administrator of the center dies while under the care of the center or while receiving child care from the owner, provider, or administrator or dies as a result of injuries suffered while under the care of the center or while receiving child care from the owner, provider, or administrator.

(2) A child care center licensee shall provide the notice required under division (B)(1) of this section to all of the following:

(a) The parent, guardian, custodian, or other person responsible for the care of each child who, at the time of the death for which notice is required, is receiving or is enrolled to receive child care from the center;

(b) The public children services agency of the county in which the center is located or the child care was given;

(c) A municipal or county peace officer in the county in which the child resides or in which the center is located or the child care was given;

(d) The child fatality review board appointed under section 307.621 [307.62.1] of the Revised Code that serves the county in which the center is located or the child care was given.

(3) A child care center licensee shall provide the notice required by division (B)(1) of this section not later than forty-eight hours after the child dies. The notice shall state that the death occurred.

(C) Whoever violates division (A) or (B) of this section is guilty of failure of a child care center to disclose the death or serious injury of a child, a misdemeanor of the fourth degree.

**HISTORY: 150 v H 11, § 1, eff. 5-18-05.**

## § 2919.23 Interference with custody.

(A) No person, knowing the person is without privilege to do so or being reckless in that regard, shall entice, take, keep, or harbor a person identified in division (A)(1), (2), or (3) of this section from the parent, guardian, or custodian of the person identified in division (A)(1), (2), or (3) of this section:

(1) A child under the age of eighteen, or a mentally or physically handicapped child under the age of twenty-one;

(2) A person committed by law to an institution for delinquent, unruly, neglected, abused, or dependent children;

(3) A person committed by law to an institution for the mentally ill or mentally retarded.

(B) No person shall aid, abet, induce, cause, or encourage a child or a ward of the juvenile court who has been committed to the custody of any person, department, or public or private institution to leave the custody of that person, department, or institution without legal consent.

(C) It is an affirmative defense to a charge of enticing or taking under division (A)(1) of this section, that the actor reasonably believed that the actor's conduct was necessary to preserve the child's health or safety. It is an affirmative defense to a charge of keeping or harboring under division (A) of this section, that the actor in good faith gave notice to law enforcement or judicial authorities within a reasonable time after the child or committed person came under the actor's shelter, protection, or influence.

(D)(1) Whoever violates this section is guilty of interference with custody.

(2) Except as otherwise provided in this division, a violation of division (A)(1) of this section is a misdemeanor of the first degree. If the child who is the subject of a violation of division (A)(1) of this section is removed from the state or if the offender previously has been convicted of an offense under this section, a violation of division (A)(1) of this section is a felony of the fifth degree. If the child who is the subject of a violation of division (A)(1) of this section suffers physical harm as a result of the violation, a violation of division (A)(1) of this section is a felony of the fourth degree.

(3) A violation of division (A)(2) or (3) of this section is a misdemeanor of the third degree.

(4) A violation of division (B) of this section is a misdemeanor of the first degree. Each day of violation of division (B) of this section is a separate offense.

**HISTORY: 134 v H 511 (Eff 1-1-74); 136 v H 85 (Eff 11-28-75); 141 v H 349 (Eff 3-6-86); 143 v S 3 (Eff 4-11-91); 146 v S 2. Eff 7-1-96.**

**Not analogous to former RC § 2919.23 (RS § 294; 71 v 21; 81 v 153, 156; 99 v 108; GC § 12936; Bureau of Code Revision, 10-1-53), repealed 134 v H 511, § 2, eff 1-1-74.**

The effective date is set by section 6 of SB 2.

## § 2919.231 Interfering with action to issue or modify support order.

(A) No person, by using physical harassment or threats of violence against another person, shall interfere with the other person's initiation or continuance of, or attempt to prevent the other person from initiating or continuing, an action to issue or modify a support order under Chapter 3115. or under section 2151.23, 2151.231 [2151.23.1], 2151.232 [2151.23.2], 2151.33, 2151.36, 2151.361 [2151.36.1], 2151.49, 3105.18, 3105.21, 3109.05, 3109.19, 3111.13, 3113.04, 3113.07, or 3113.31 of the Revised Code.

(B) Whoever violates this section is guilty of interfering with an action to issue or modify a support order, a misdemeanor of the first degree. If the offender previously has been convicted of or pleaded guilty to a violation of this section or of section 3111.19 of the Revised Code, interfering with an action to issue or modify a support order is a felony of the fifth degree.

**HISTORY: 144 v S 10 (Eff 7-15-92); 146 v H 167 (Eff 11-15-95); 146 v S 269 (Eff 7-1-96); 146 v H 274 (Eff 8-8-96); 147 v H 352 (Eff 1-1-98); 148 v S 180 (Eff 3-22-2001); 149 v S 27. Eff 3-15-2002.**

## § 2919.24 Contributing to unruliness or delinquency of a child.

(A) No person, including a parent, guardian, or other custodian of a child, shall do any of the following:

(1) Aid, abet, induce, cause, encourage, or contribute to a child or a ward of the juvenile court becoming an unruly child, as defined in section 2151.022 of the Revised Code, or a delinquent child, as defined in section 2152.02 of the Revised Code;

(2) Act in a way tending to cause a child or a ward of the juvenile court to become an unruly child, as defined in section 2151.022 of the Revised Code, or a delinquent child, as defined in section 2152.02 of the Revised Code;

(3) If the person is the parent, guardian, or custodian of a child who has the duties under Chapters 2152. and 2950. of the Revised Code to register, register a new residence address, and periodically verify a residence address, and, if applicable, to send a notice of intent to reside, and if the child is not emancipated, as defined in section 2919.121 of the Revised Code, fail to ensure that the child complies with those duties under Chapters 2152. and 2950. of the Revised Code.

(B) Whoever violates this section is guilty of contributing to the unruliness or delinquency of a child, a misdemeanor of the first degree. Each day of violation of this section is a separate offense.

**HISTORY: 141 v H 349 (Eff 3-6-86); 148 v S 179, § 3 (Eff 1-1-2002); 149 v S 3. Eff 1-1-2002; 150 v S 5, § 1, eff. 7-31-03.**

The provisions of § 7 of S.B. 5 (150 v —) read as follows:

SECTION 7. (A) Section 2919.24 of the Revised Code is presented in Section 1 of this act as a composite of the section as amended by Am. Sub. S.B. 3 of the 124th General Assembly and Am. Sub. S.B. 179 of the 123rd General Assembly. The General Assembly, applying the principle stated in division (B) of section 1.52 of the Revised Code that amendments are to be harmonized if reasonably capable of simultaneous operation, finds that the composites are the resulting versions of the sections in effect prior to the effective date of the sections as presented in Section 1 of this act.

### [DOMESTIC VIOLENCE]

## § 2919.25 Domestic violence.

(A) No person shall knowingly cause or attempt to cause physical harm to a family or household member.

(B) No person shall recklessly cause serious physical harm to a family or household member.

(C) No person, by threat of force, shall knowingly cause a family or household member to believe that the offender will cause imminent physical harm to the family or household member.

(D)(1) Whoever violates this section is guilty of domestic violence, and the court shall sentence the offender as provided in divisions (D)(2) to (6) of this section.

(2) Except as otherwise provided in divisions (D)(3) to (5) of this section, a violation of division (C) of this section is a misdemeanor of the fourth degree, and a violation of division (A) or (B) of this section is a misdemeanor of the first degree.

(3) Except as otherwise provided in division (D)(4) of this section, if the offender previously has pleaded guilty to or been convicted of domestic violence, a violation of an existing or former municipal ordinance or law of this or any other state or the United States that is substantially similar to domestic violence, a violation of section 2903.14, 2909.06, 2909.07, 2911.12, 2911.211 [2911.21.1], or 2919.22 of the Revised Code if the victim of the violation was a family or household member at the time of the violation, a violation of an existing or former municipal ordinance or law of this or any other state or the United States that is substantially similar to any of those sections if the victim of the violation was a family or household member at the time of the commission of the violation, or any offense of violence if the victim of the offense was a family or household member at the time of the commission of the offense, a violation of division (A) or (B) of this section is a felony of the fourth degree, and, if the offender knew that the victim of the violation was pregnant at the time of the violation, the court shall impose a mandatory prison term on the offender pursuant to division (D)(6) of this section, and a violation of division (C) of this section is a misdemeanor of the second degree.

(4) If the offender previously has pleaded guilty to or been convicted of two or more offenses of domestic violence or two or more violations or offenses of the type described in division (D)(3) of this section involving a person who was a family or household member at the time of the violations or offenses, a violation of division (A) or (B) of this section is a felony of the third degree, and, if the offender knew that the victim of the violation was pregnant at the time of the violation, the court shall impose a mandatory prison term on the offender pursuant to division (D)(6) of this section, and a violation of division (C) of this section is a misdemeanor of the first degree.

(5) Except as otherwise provided in division (D)(3) or (4) of this section, if the offender knew that the victim of the violation was pregnant at the time of the violation, a violation of division (A) or (B) of this section is a felony of the fifth degree, and the court shall impose a mandatory prison term on the offender pursuant to division (D)(6) of this section, and a violation of division (C) of this section is a misdemeanor of the third degree.

(6) If division (D)(3), (4), or (5) of this section requires the court that sentences an offender for a violation of division (A) or (B) of this section to impose a mandatory

prison term on the offender pursuant to this division, the court shall impose the mandatory prison term as follows:

(a) If the violation of division (A) or (B) of this section is a felony of the fourth or fifth degree, except as otherwise provided in division (D)(6)(b) or (c) of this section, the court shall impose a mandatory prison term on the offender of at least six months.

(b) If the violation of division (A) or (B) of this section is a felony of the fifth degree and the offender, in committing the violation, caused serious physical harm to the pregnant woman's unborn or caused the termination of the pregnant woman's pregnancy, the court shall impose a mandatory prison term on the offender of twelve months.

(c) If the violation of division (A) or (B) of this section is a felony of the fourth degree and the offender, in committing the violation, caused serious physical harm to the pregnant woman's unborn or caused the termination of the pregnant woman's pregnancy, the court shall impose a mandatory prison term on the offender of at least twelve months.

(d) If the violation of division (A) or (B) of this section is a felony of the third degree, except as otherwise provided in division (D)(6)(e) of this section and notwithstanding the range of prison terms prescribed in section 2929.14 of the Revised Code for a felony of the third degree, the court shall impose a mandatory prison term on the offender of either a definite term of six months or one of the prison terms prescribed in section 2929.14 of the Revised Code for felonies of the third degree.

(e) If the violation of division (A) or (B) of this section is a felony of the third degree and the offender, in committing the violation, caused serious physical harm to the pregnant woman's unborn or caused the termination of the pregnant woman's pregnancy, notwithstanding the range of prison terms prescribed in section 2929.14 of the Revised Code for a felony of the third degree, the court shall impose a mandatory prison term on the offender of either a definite term of one year or one of the prison terms prescribed in section 2929.14 of the Revised Code for felonies of the third degree.

(E) Notwithstanding any provision of law to the contrary, no court or unit of state or local government shall charge any fee, cost, deposit, or money in connection with the filing of charges against a person alleging that the person violated this section or a municipal ordinance substantially similar to this section or in connection with the prosecution of any charges so filed.

(F) As used in this section and sections 2919.251 [2919.25.1] and 2919.26 of the Revised Code:

(1) "Family or household member" means any of the following:

(a) Any of the following who is residing or has resided with the offender:

(i) A spouse, a person living as a spouse, or a former spouse of the offender;

(ii) A parent, a foster parent, or a child of the offender, or another person related by consanguinity or affinity to the offender;

(iii) A parent or a child of a spouse, person living as a spouse, or former spouse of the offender, or another person related by consanguinity or affinity to a spouse, person living as a spouse, or former spouse of the offender.

(b) The natural parent of any child of whom the offender is the other natural parent or is the putative other natural parent.

(2) "Person living as a spouse" means a person who is living or has lived with the offender in a common law marital relationship, who otherwise is cohabiting with the offender, or who otherwise has cohabited with the offender within five years prior to the date of the alleged commission of the act in question.

(3) "Pregnant woman's unborn" has the same meaning as "such other person's unborn," as set forth in section 2903.09 of the Revised Code, as it relates to the pregnant woman. Division (C) of that section applies regarding the use of the term in this section, except that the second and third sentences of division (C)(1) of that section shall be construed for purposes of this section as if they included a reference to this section in the listing of Revised Code sections they contain.

(4) "Termination of the pregnant woman's pregnancy" has the same meaning as "unlawful termination of another's pregnancy," as set forth in section 2903.09 of the Revised Code, as it relates to the pregnant woman. Division (C) of that section applies regarding the use of the term in this section, except that the second and third sentences of division (C)(1) of that section shall be construed for purposes of this section as if they included a reference to this section in the listing of Revised Code sections they contain.

**HISTORY: 137 v H 835 (Eff 3-27-79); 138 v H 920 (Eff 4-9-81); 140 v H 587 (Eff 9-25-84); 142 v S 6 (Eff 6-10-87); 142 v H 172 (Eff 3-17-89); 143 v S 3 (Eff 4-11-91); 144 v H 536 (Eff 11-5-92); 145 v H 335 (Eff 12-9-94); 146 v S 2 (Eff 7-1-96); 147 v S 1 (Eff 10-21-97); 147 v H 238 (Eff 11-5-97); 149 v H 327 (Eff 7-8-2002); 149 v H 548. Eff 3-31-2003; 150 v S 50, § 1, eff. 1-8-04; 152 v H 280, § 1, eff. 4-7-09; 153 v H 10, § 1, eff. 6-17-10; 153 v S 58, § 1, eff. 9-17-10.**

See provisions of § 3 of 153 v H 10 following RC § 2903.214.

## § 2919.251 Considerations in setting bail in domestic violence cases; schedule; appearance by video conferencing equipment.

(A) Subject to division (D) of this section, a person who is charged with the commission of any offense of violence shall appear before the court for the setting of bail if the alleged victim of the offense charged was a family or household member at the time of the offense and if any of the following applies:

(1) The person charged, at the time of the alleged offense, was subject to the terms of a protection order issued or consent agreement approved pursuant to section 2919.26 or 3113.31 of the Revised Code or previously was convicted of or pleaded guilty to a violation of section 2919.25 of the Revised Code or a violation of section 2919.27 of the Revised Code involving a protection order or consent agreement of that type, a violation of an existing or former municipal ordinance or law of this or any other state or the United States that is substantially similar to either section, a violation of section 2909.06, 2909.07, 2911.12, or 2911.211 [2911.21.1] of the Revised Code if the victim of the violation was a family or household member at the time of the violation a violation of an existing or former municipal ordinance or law of this or any other state or the United States that is substantially similar to any of those sections if the victim of the violation was a family or household member at the time of the commission of the violation, or any offense of violence if the victim of the offense was a family or household member at the time of the offense;

(2) The arresting officer indicates in a police report or other document accompanying the complaint any of the following:

(a) That the arresting officer observed on the alleged victim objective manifestations of physical harm that the arresting officer reasonably believes are a result of the alleged offense;

(b) That the arresting officer reasonably believes that the person had on the person's person at the time of the alleged offense a deadly weapon or dangerous ordnance;

(c) That the arresting officer reasonably believes that the person presents a credible threat of serious physical harm to the alleged victim or to any other person if released on bail before trial.

(B) To the extent that information about any of the following is available to the court, the court shall consider all of the following, in addition to any other circumstances considered by the court and notwithstanding any provisions to the contrary contained in Criminal Rule 46, before setting bail for a person who appears before the court pursuant to division (A) of this section:

(1) Whether the person has a history of domestic violence or a history of other violent acts;

(2) The mental health of the person;

(3) Whether the person has a history of violating the orders of any court or governmental entity;

(4) Whether the person is potentially a threat to any other person;

(5) Whether the person has access to deadly weapons or a history of using deadly weapons;

(6) Whether the person has a history of abusing alcohol or any controlled substance;

(7) The severity of the alleged violence that is the basis of the offense, including but not limited to, the duration of the alleged violent incident, and whether the alleged violent incident involved serious physical injury, sexual assault, strangulation, abuse during the alleged victim's pregnancy, abuse of pets, or forcible entry to gain access to the alleged victim;

(8) Whether a separation of the person from the alleged victim or a termination of the relationship between the person and the alleged victim has recently occurred or is pending;

(9) Whether the person has exhibited obsessive or controlling behaviors toward the alleged victim, including but not limited to, stalking, surveillance, or isolation of the alleged victim;

(10) Whether the person has expressed suicidal or homicidal ideations;

(11) Any information contained in the complaint and any police reports, affidavits, or other documents accompanying the complaint.

(C) Any court that has jurisdiction over charges alleging the commission of an offense of violence in circumstances in which the alleged victim of the offense was a family or household member at the time of the offense may set a schedule for bail to be used in cases involving those offenses. The schedule shall require that a judge consider all of the factors listed in division (B) of this section and may require judges to set bail at a certain level if the history of the alleged offender or the circumstances of the alleged offense meet certain criteria in the schedule.

(D)(1) Upon the court's own motion or the motion of a party and upon any terms that the court may direct, a court may permit a person who is required to appear before it by division (A) of this section to appear by video conferencing equipment.

(2) If in the opinion of the court the appearance in person or by video conferencing equipment of a person who is charged with a misdemeanor and who is required to appear before the court by division (A) of this section is not practicable, the court may waive the appearance and release the person on bail in accordance with the court's schedule for bail set under division (C) of this section or, if the court has not set a schedule for bail under that division, on one or both of the following types of bail in an amount set by the court:

(a) A bail bond secured by a deposit of ten per cent of the amount of the bond in cash;

(b) A surety bond, a bond secured by real estate or securities as allowed by law, or the deposit of cash, at the option of the person.

(3) Division (A) of this section does not create a right in a person to appear before the court for the setting of bail or prohibit a court from requiring any person charged with an offense of violence who is not described in that division from appearing before the court for the setting of bail.

(E) As used in this section:

(1) "Controlled substance" has the same meaning as in section 3719.01 of the Revised Code.

(2) "Dangerous ordnance" and "deadly weapon" have the same meanings as in section 2923.11 of the Revised Code.

**HISTORY: 141 v H 475 (Eff 3-7-86); 143 v S 3 (Eff 4-11-91); 144 v H 536 (Eff 11-5-92); 146 v S 2. Eff 7-1-96; 150 v S 50, § 1, eff. 1-8-04; 151 v H 29, § 1, eff. 8-26-05.**

The provisions of § 3 of 151 v H 29 read as follows:

SECTION 3. The General Assembly acknowledges the Supreme Court's authority to prescribe rules governing practice and procedure in the courts of this state, as provided by Section 5 of Article IV of the Ohio Constitution. Recognizing the dangers posed to victims of domestic violence and other crimes of violence when the alleged perpetrators are not physically restrained, even though they may be under bond or subject to orders of protection, the General Assembly respectfully urges the Supreme Court to amend the existing Rules of Civil and Criminal Procedure, or to adopt new rules, to acknowledge the exigency of, give priority to, and otherwise encourage the speedy resolution of cases involving domestic violence.

The effective date is set by section 6 of SB 2.

## § 2919.26 Motion for temporary protection order; form.

(A)(1) Upon the filing of a complaint that alleges a violation of section 2909.06, 2909.07, 2911.12, or 2911.211 [2911.21.1] of the Revised Code if the alleged victim of the violation was a family or household member at the time of the violation, a violation of a municipal ordinance that is substantially similar to any of those sections if the alleged victim of the violation was a family or household member at the time of the violation, any offense of violence if the alleged victim of the offense was a family or household member at the time of the commission of the offense, or any sexually oriented offense if the alleged victim of the offense was a family or household member at the time of the commission of the offense, the complainant, the alleged victim, or a family or household member of an alleged victim may file, or, if in an emergency the alleged victim is unable to file, a person who made an arrest for the alleged violation or offense under section 2935.03 of the Revised Code may file on behalf of the alleged victim, a motion that requests the issuance of a temporary protection order as a pretrial condition of release of the alleged offender, in addition to any bail set under Criminal Rule 46. The motion shall be filed with the clerk of the court that has jurisdiction of the case at any time after the filing of the complaint.

(2) For purposes of section 2930.09 of the Revised Code, all stages of a proceeding arising out of a complaint alleging the commission of a violation, offense of violence, or sexually oriented offense described in division (A)(1) of this section, including all proceedings on a motion for a temporary protection order, are critical stages of the case, and a victim may be accompanied by a victim advocate or another person to provide support to the victim as provided in that section.

(B) The motion shall be prepared on a form that is provided by the clerk of the court, which form shall be substantially as follows:

"MOTION FOR TEMPORARY PROTECTION ORDER

........................ Court

Name and address of court

State of Ohio

v. No. .......

..................................................

Name of Defendant

(name of person), moves the court to issue a temporary protection order containing terms designed to ensure the safety and protection of the complainant, alleged victim, and other family or household members, in relation to the named defendant, pursuant to its authority to issue such an order under section 2919.26 of the Revised Code.

A complaint, a copy of which has been attached to this motion, has been filed in this court charging the named defendant with ......................... (name of the specified violation, the offense of violence, or sexually oriented offense charged) in circumstances in which the victim was a family or household member in violation of (section of the Revised Code designating the specified violation, offense of violence, or sexually oriented offense charged), or charging the named defendant with a violation of a municipal ordinance that is substantially similar to ....................... (section of the Revised Code designating the specified violation, offense of violence, or sexually oriented offense charged) involving a family or household member.

I understand that I must appear before the court, at a time set by the court within twenty-four hours after the filing of this motion, for a hearing on the motion or that, if I am unable to appear because of hospitalization or a medical condition resulting from the offense alleged in the complaint, a person who can provide information about my need for a temporary protection order must appear before the court in lieu of my appearing in court. I understand that any temporary protection order granted pursuant to this motion is a pretrial condition of release and is effective only until the disposition of the criminal proceeding arising out of the attached complaint, or the issuance of a civil protection order or the approval of a consent agreement, arising out of the same activities as those that were the basis of the complaint, under section 3113.31 of the Revised Code.

......................................

Signature of person

(or signature of the arresting officer who filed the motion on behalf of the alleged victim)

......................................

Address of person (or office address of the arresting officer who filed the motion on behalf of the alleged victim)"

(C)(1) As soon as possible after the filing of a motion that requests the issuance of a temporary protection order, but not later than twenty-four hours after the filing of the motion, the court shall conduct a hearing to determine whether to issue the order. The person who requested the order shall appear before the court and provide the court with the information that it requests concerning the basis of the motion. If the person who requested the order is unable to appear and if the court finds that the failure to appear is because of the person's hospitalization or medical condition resulting from the offense alleged in the complaint, another person who is able to provide the court with the information it requests may appear in lieu of the person who requested the order. If the court finds that the safety and protection of the complainant, alleged victim, or any other family or household member of the alleged victim may be impaired by the continued presence of the alleged offender, the court may issue a temporary protection order, as a pretrial condition of release, that contains terms designed to ensure the safety and protection of the complainant, alleged victim, or the family or household member, including a requirement that the alleged offender refrain from entering the residence, school, business, or place of employment of the complainant, alleged victim, or the family or household member.

(2)(a) If the court issues a temporary protection order that includes a requirement that the alleged offender refrain from entering the residence, school, business, or place of employment of the complainant, the alleged victim, or the family or household member, the order shall state clearly that the order cannot be waived or nullified by an invitation to the alleged offender from the complainant, alleged victim, or family or household member to enter the residence, school, business, or place of employment or by the alleged offender's entry into one of those places otherwise upon the consent of the complainant, alleged victim, or family or household member.

(b) Division (C)(2)(a) of this section does not limit any discretion of a court to determine that an alleged offender charged with a violation of section 2919.27 of the Revised Code, with a violation of a municipal ordinance substantially equivalent to that section, or with contempt of court, which charge is based on an alleged violation of a temporary protection order issued under this section, did not commit the violation or was not in contempt of court.

(D)(1) Upon the filing of a complaint that alleges a violation of section 2909.06, 2909.07, 2911.12, or 2911.211 [2911.21.1] of the Revised Code if the alleged victim of the violation was a family or household member at the time of the violation, a violation of a municipal ordinance that is substantially similar to any of those sections if the alleged victim of the violation was a family or household member at the time of the violation, any offense of violence if the alleged victim of the offense was a family or household member at the time of the commission of the offense, or any sexually oriented offense if the alleged victim of the offense was a family or household member at the time of the commission of the offense, the court, upon its own motion, may issue a temporary protection order as a pretrial condition of release if it finds that the safety and protection of the complainant, alleged victim, or other family or household member of the alleged offender may be impaired by the continued presence of the alleged offender.

(2) If the court issues a temporary protection order under this section as an ex parte order, it shall conduct, as soon as possible after the issuance of the order, a hearing in the presence of the alleged offender not later than the next day on which the court is scheduled to conduct business after the day on which the alleged offender was

arrested or at the time of the appearance of the alleged offender pursuant to summons to determine whether the order should remain in effect, be modified, or be revoked. The hearing shall be conducted under the standards set forth in division (C) of this section.

(3) An order issued under this section shall contain only those terms authorized in orders issued under division (C) of this section.

(4) If a municipal court or a county court issues a temporary protection order under this section and if, subsequent to the issuance of the order, the alleged offender who is the subject of the order is bound over to the court of common pleas for prosecution of a felony arising out of the same activities as those that were the basis of the complaint upon which the order is based, notwithstanding the fact that the order was issued by a municipal court or county court, the order shall remain in effect, as though it were an order of the court of common pleas, while the charges against the alleged offender are pending in the court of common pleas, for the period of time described in division (E)(2) of this section, and the court of common pleas has exclusive jurisdiction to modify the order issued by the municipal court or county court. This division applies when the alleged offender is bound over to the court of common pleas as a result of the person waiving a preliminary hearing on the felony charge, as a result of the municipal court or county court having determined at a preliminary hearing that there is probable cause to believe that the felony has been committed and that the alleged offender committed it, as a result of the alleged offender having been indicted for the felony, or in any other manner.

(E) A temporary protection order that is issued as a pretrial condition of release under this section:

(1) Is in addition to, but shall not be construed as a part of, any bail set under Criminal Rule 46;

(2) Is effective only until the occurrence of either of the following:

(a) The disposition, by the court that issued the order or, in the circumstances described in division (D)(4) of this section, by the court of common pleas to which the alleged offender is bound over for prosecution, of the criminal proceeding arising out of the complaint upon which the order is based;

(b) The issuance of a protection order or the approval of a consent agreement, arising out of the same activities as those that were the basis of the complaint upon which the order is based, under section 3113.31 of the Revised Code;

(3) Shall not be construed as a finding that the alleged offender committed the alleged offense, and shall not be introduced as evidence of the commission of the offense at the trial of the alleged offender on the complaint upon which the order is based.

(F) A person who meets the criteria for bail under Criminal Rule 46 and who, if required to do so pursuant to that rule, executes or posts bond or deposits cash or securities as bail, shall not be held in custody pending a hearing before the court on a motion requesting a temporary protection order.

(G)(1) A copy of any temporary protection order that is issued under this section shall be issued by the court to the complainant, to the alleged victim, to the person who requested the order, to the defendant, and to all law enforcement agencies that have jurisdiction to enforce the order. The court shall direct that a copy of the order be delivered to the defendant on the same day that the order is entered. If a municipal court or a county court issues a temporary protection order under this section and if, subsequent to the issuance of the order, the defendant who is the subject of the order is bound over to the court of common pleas for prosecution as described in division (D)(4) of this section, the municipal court or county court shall direct that a copy of the order be delivered to the court of common pleas to which the defendant is bound over.

(2) Upon the issuance of a protection order under this section, the court shall provide the parties to the order with the following notice orally or by form:

"NOTICE

As a result of this protection order, it may be unlawful for you to possess or purchase a firearm, including a rifle, pistol, or revolver, or ammunition pursuant to federal law under 18 U.S.C. 922(g)(8). If you have any questions whether this law makes it illegal for you to possess or purchase a firearm or ammunition, you should consult an attorney."

(3) All law enforcement agencies shall establish and maintain an index for the temporary protection orders delivered to the agencies pursuant to division (G)(1) of this section. With respect to each order delivered, each agency shall note on the index, the date and time of the receipt of the order by the agency.

(4) A complainant, alleged victim, or other person who obtains a temporary protection order under this section may provide notice of the issuance of the temporary protection order to the judicial and law enforcement officials in any county other than the county in which the order is issued by registering that order in the other county in accordance with division (N) of section 3113.31 of the Revised Code and filing a copy of the registered protection order with a law enforcement agency in the other county in accordance with that division.

(5) Any officer of a law enforcement agency shall enforce a temporary protection order issued by any court in this state in accordance with the provisions of the order, including removing the defendant from the premises, regardless of whether the order is registered in the county in which the officer's agency has jurisdiction as authorized by division (G)(4) of this section.

(H) Upon a violation of a temporary protection order, the court may issue another temporary protection order, as a pretrial condition of release, that modifies the terms of the order that was violated.

(I)(1) As used in divisions (I)(1) and (2) of this section, "defendant" means a person who is alleged in a complaint to have committed a violation, offense of violence, or sexually oriented offense of the type described in division (A) of this section.

(2) If a complaint is filed that alleges that a person committed a violation, offense of violence, or sexually oriented offense of the type described in division (A) of this section, the court may not issue a temporary protection order under this section that requires the complainant, the alleged victim, or another family or household member of the defendant to do or refrain from doing an act that the court may require the defendant to do or refrain from doing under a temporary protection order unless both of the following apply:

(a) The defendant has filed a separate complaint that alleges that the complainant, alleged victim, or other family or household member in question who would be required under the order to do or refrain from doing the act committed a violation or offense of violence of the type described in division (A) of this section.

(b) The court determines that both the complainant, alleged victim, or other family or household member in question who would be required under the order to do or refrain from doing the act and the defendant acted primarily as aggressors, that neither the complainant, alleged victim, or other family or household member in question who would be required under the order to do or refrain from doing the act nor the defendant acted primarily in self-defense, and, in accordance with the standards and criteria of this section as applied in relation to the separate complaint filed by the defendant, that it should issue the order to require the complainant, alleged victim, or other family or household member in question to do or refrain from doing the act.

(J) Notwithstanding any provision of law to the contrary and regardless of whether a protection order is issued or a consent agreement is approved by a court of another county or a court of another state, no court or unit of state or local government shall charge any fee, cost, deposit, or money in connection with the filing of a motion pursuant to this section, in connection with the filing, issuance, registration, or service of a protection order or consent agreement, or for obtaining a certified copy of a protection order or consent agreement.

(K) As used in this section:

(1) "Sexually oriented offense" has the same meaning as in section 2950.01 of the Revised Code.

(2) "Victim advocate" means a person who provides support and assistance for a victim of an offense during court proceedings.

**HISTORY: 137 v H 835 (Eff 3-27-79); 138 v H 920 (Eff 4-9-81); 140 v H 587 (Eff 9-25-84); 143 v S 3 (Eff 4-11-91); 144 v H 536 (Eff 11-5-92); 145 v H 335 (Eff 12-9-94); 147 v S 1 (Eff 10-21-97); 147 v S 98 (Eff 3-17-98); 148 v H 137 (Eff 3-10-2000); 149 v H 548. Eff 3-31-2003; 150 v S 50, § 1, eff. 1-8-04; 151 v S 17, § 1, eff. 8-3-06; 151 v H 95, § 1, eff. 8-3-06; 151 v S 260, § 1, eff. 1-2-07; 152 v H 562, § 101.01, eff. 6-24-08; 153 v H 238, § 1, eff. 9-8-10.**

The effective date is set by § 812.20 of 152 v H 562.

**Comment, Legislative Service Commission**

Section 2919.26 of the Revised Code is amended by Am. Sub. S.B. 17 and Am. Sub. H.B. 95 of the 126th General Assembly. Comparison of these amendments in pursuance of section 1.52 of the Revised Code discloses that they are identical, and that S.B. 17 is the later amendment concurred by the General Assembly.

## § 2919.27 Violating protection order.

(A) No person shall recklessly violate the terms of any of the following:

(1) A protection order issued or consent agreement approved pursuant to section 2919.26 or 3113.31 of the Revised Code;

(2) A protection order issued pursuant to section 2151.34, 2903.213 [2903.21.3], or 2903.214 [2903.21.4] of the Revised Code;

(3) A protection order issued by a court of another state.

(B)(1) Whoever violates this section is guilty of violating a protection order.

(2) Except as otherwise provided in division (B)(3) or (4) of this section, violating a protection order is a misdemeanor of the first degree.

(3) If the offender previously has been convicted of, pleaded guilty to, or been adjudicated a delinquent child for a violation of a protection order issued pursuant to section 2151.34, 2903.213 [2903.21.3], or 2903.214 [2903.21.4] of the Revised Code, two or more violations of section 2903.21, 2903.211 [2903.21.1], 2903.22, or 2911.211 [2911.21.1] of the Revised Code that involved the same person who is the subject of the protection order or consent agreement, or one or more violations of this section, violating a protection order is a felony of the fifth degree.

(4) If the offender violates a protection order or consent agreement while committing a felony offense, violating a protection order is a felony of the third degree.

(5) If the protection order violated by the offender was an order issued pursuant to section 2151.34 or 2903.214 [2903.21.4] of the Revised Code that required electronic monitoring of the offender pursuant to that section, the court may require in addition to any other sentence imposed upon the offender that the offender be electronically monitored for a period not exceeding five years by a law enforcement agency designated by the court. If the court requires under this division that the offender be electronically monitored, unless the court determines that the offender is indigent, the court shall order that the offender pay the costs of the installation of the electronic monitoring device and the cost of monitoring the electronic monitoring device. If the court determines that the offender is indigent and subject to the maximum amount allowable and the rules promulgated by the attorney general under section 2903.214 [2903.21.4] of the Revised Code, the costs of the installation of the electronic monitoring device and the cost of monitoring the electronic monitoring device may be paid out of funds from the reparations fund created pursuant to section 2743.191 [2743.19.1] of the Revised Code. The total amount paid from the reparations fund created pursuant to section 2743.191 [2743.19.1] of the Revised Code for electronic monitoring under this section and sections 2151.34 and 2903.214 [2903.21.4] of the Revised Code shall not exceed three hundred thousand dollars per year.

(C) It is an affirmative defense to a charge under division (A)(3) of this section that the protection order issued by a court of another state does not comply with the requirements specified in 18 U.S.C. 2265(b) for a protection order that must be accorded full faith and credit by a court of this state or that it is not entitled to full faith and credit under 18 U.S.C. 2265(c).

(D) As used in this section, "protection order issued by a court of another state" means an injunction or another order issued by a criminal court of another state for the purpose of preventing violent or threatening acts or harassment against, contact or communication with, or physical proximity to another person, including a temporary order, and means an injunction or order of that nature issued by a civil court of another state, including a temporary order and a final order issued in an independent action or as a pendente lite order in a proceeding for other relief, if the court issued it in response to a complaint, petition, or motion filed by or on behalf of a person seeking protection. "Protection order issued by a court of another state" does not include an order for support or for custody of a child issued pursuant to the divorce and child custody laws of another state, except to the extent that the order for support or for custody of a child is entitled to full faith and credit under the laws of the United States.

**HISTORY: 140 v H 587 (Eff 9-25-84); 141 v H 475 (Eff 3-7-86); 144 v H 536 (Eff 11-5-92); 145 v H 335 (Eff 12-9-94); 146 v S 2 (Eff 7-1-96); 147 v S 1 (Eff 10-21-97); 147 v H 302 (Eff 7-29-98); 149 v H 548. Eff 3-31-2003; 150 v S 50, § 1, eff. 1-8-04; 152 v H 471, § 1, eff. 4-7-09; 153 v H 10, § 1, eff. 6-17-10.**

See provisions of § 3 of 153 v H 10 following RC § 2903.214.

## § 2919.271 Evaluation of defendant's mental condition.

(A)(1)(a) If a defendant is charged with a violation of section 2919.27 of the Revised Code or of a municipal ordinance that is substantially similar to that section, the court may order an evaluation of the mental condition of the defendant if the court determines that either of the following criteria apply:

(i) If the alleged violation is a violation of a protection order issued or consent agreement approved pursuant to section 2919.26 or 3113.31 of the Revised Code, that the violation allegedly involves conduct by the defendant that caused physical harm to the person or property of a family or household member covered by the order or agreement, or conduct by the defendant that caused a family or household member to believe that the defendant would cause physical harm to that member or that member's property.

(ii) If the alleged violation is a violation of a protection order issued pursuant to section 2903.213 or 2903.214 of the Revised Code or a protection order issued by a court of another state, that the violation allegedly involves conduct by the defendant that caused physical harm to the person or property of the person covered by the order, or conduct by the defendant that caused the person covered by the order to believe that the defendant would cause physical harm to that person or that person's property.

(b) If a defendant is charged with a violation of section 2903.211 of the Revised Code or of a municipal ordinance that is substantially similar to that section, the court may order an evaluation of the mental condition of the defendant.

(2) An evaluation ordered under division (A)(1) of this section shall be completed no later than thirty days from the date the order is entered pursuant to that division. In that order, the court shall do either of the following:

(a) Order that the evaluation of the mental condition of the defendant be preceded by an examination conducted either by a forensic center that is designated by the department of mental health to conduct examinations and make evaluations of defendants charged with violations of section 2903.211 or 2919.27 of the Revised Code or of substantially similar municipal ordinances in the area in which the court is located, or by any other program or facility that is designated by the department of mental health or the department of developmental disabilities to conduct examinations and make evaluations of defendants charged with violations of section 2903.211 or 2919.27 of the Revised Code or of substantially similar municipal ordinances, and that is operated by either department or is certified by either department as being in compliance with the standards established under division (H) of section 5119.01 of the Revised Code or division (C) of section 5123.04 of the Revised Code.

(b) Designate a center, program, or facility other than one designated by the department of mental health or the department of developmental disabilities, as described in division (A)(2)(a) of this section, to conduct the evaluation and preceding examination of the mental condition of the defendant.

Whether the court acts pursuant to division (A)(2)(a) or (b) of this section, the court may designate examiners other than the personnel of the center, program, facility, or department involved to make the evaluation and preceding examination of the mental condition of the defendant.

(B) If the court considers that additional evaluations of the mental condition of a defendant are necessary following the evaluation authorized by division (A) of this section, the court may order up to two additional similar evaluations. These evaluations shall be completed no later than thirty days from the date the applicable court order is entered. If more than one evaluation of the mental condition of the defendant is ordered under this division, the prosecutor and the defendant may recommend to the court an examiner whom each prefers to perform one of the evaluations and preceding examinations.

(C)(1) The court may order a defendant who has been released on bail to submit to an examination under division (A) or (B) of this section. The examination shall be conducted either at the detention facility in which the defendant would have been confined if the defendant had not been released on bail, or, if so specified by the center, program, facility, or examiners involved, at the premises of the center, program, or facility. Additionally, the examination shall be conducted at the times established by the examiners involved. If such a defendant refuses to submit to an examination or a complete examination as required by the court or the center, program, facility, or examiners involved, the court may amend the conditions of the bail of the defendant and order the sheriff to take the defendant into custody and deliver the defendant to the detention facility in which the defendant would have been confined if the defendant had not been released on bail, or, if so specified by the center, program, facility, or examiners involved, to the premises of the center, program, or facility, for purposes of the examination.

(2) A defendant who has not been released on bail shall be examined at the detention facility in which the defendant is confined or, if so specified by the center, program, facility, or examiners involved, at the premises of the center, program, or facility.

(D) The examiner of the mental condition of a defendant under division (A) or (B) of this section shall file a written report with the court within thirty days after the entry of an order for the evaluation of the mental condition of the defendant. The report shall contain the findings of the examiner; the facts in reasonable detail on which the findings are based; the opinion of the examiner as to the mental condition of the defendant; the opinion of the examiner as to whether the defendant represents a substantial risk of physical harm to other persons as manifested by evidence of recent homicidal or other violent behavior, evidence of recent threats that placed other persons in reasonable fear of violent behavior and serious physical harm, or evidence of present dangerousness; and the opinion of the examiner as to the types of treatment or counseling that the defendant needs. The court shall provide copies of the report to the prosecutor and defense counsel.

(E) The costs of any evaluation and preceding examination of a defendant that is ordered pursuant to division (A) or (B) of this section shall be taxed as court costs in the criminal case.

(F) If the examiner considers it necessary in order to make an accurate evaluation of the mental condition of a defendant, an examiner under division (A) or (B) of this section may request any family or household member of the defendant to provide the examiner with information. A family or household member may, but is not required to, provide information to the examiner upon receipt of the request.

(G) As used in this section:

(1) "Bail" includes a recognizance.

(2) "Examiner" means a psychiatrist, a licensed independent social worker who is employed by a forensic center that is certified as being in compliance with the standards established under division (H) of section 5119.01 or division (C) of section 5123.04 of the Revised Code, a licensed professional clinical counselor who is employed at a forensic center that is certified as being in compliance with such standards, or a licensed clinical psychologist, except that in order to be an examiner, a licensed clinical psychologist shall meet the criteria of division (I)(1) of section 5122.01 of the Revised Code or be employed to conduct examinations by the department of mental health or by a forensic center certified as being in compliance with the standards established under division (H) of section 5119.01 or division (C) of section 5123.04 of the Revised Code that is designated by the department of mental health.

(3) "Family or household member" has the same meaning as in section 2919.25 of the Revised Code.

(4) "Prosecutor" has the same meaning as in section 2935.01 of the Revised Code.

(5) "Psychiatrist" and "licensed clinical psychologist" have the same meanings as in section 5122.01 of the Revised Code.

(6) "Protection order issued by a court of another state" has the same meaning as in section 2919.27 of the Revised Code.

**HISTORY: 141 v H 475 (Eff 3-7-86); 146 v S 2 (Eff 7-1-96); 146 v S 223 (Eff 3-18-97); 147 v S 1 (Eff 10-21-97); 147 v H 302 (Eff 7-29-98); 148 v H 202 (Eff 2-9-2000); 149 v H 94. Eff 9-5-2001; 153 v S 79, § 1, eff. 10-6-09; 2011 HB 153, § 101.01, eff. Sept. 29, 2011.**

The effective date is set by section 204 of HB 94.

## § 2919.272 Registration and filing of out-of-state protection order.

(A) As used in this section, "protection order issued by a court of another state" has the same meaning as in section 2919.27 of the Revised Code.

(B) A person who has obtained a protection order issued by a court of another state may provide notice of the issuance of the order to judicial and law enforcement officials in any county of this state by registering the order in that county and filing a copy of the registered order with a law enforcement agency in that county. To register the order, the person shall obtain a certified copy of the order from the clerk of the court that issued the order and present that certified copy to the clerk of the court of common pleas or the clerk of a municipal court or county court in the county in which the order is to be registered. Upon accepting the certified copy of the order for registration, the clerk shall place an endorsement of registration on the order and give the person a copy of the order that bears proof of registration. The person then may file with a law enforcement agency in that county a copy of the order that bears proof of registration.

(C) The clerk of each court of common pleas and the clerk of each municipal court and county court shall maintain a registry of certified copies of protection orders issued by courts of another state that have been registered with the clerk. Each law enforcement agency shall establish and maintain a registry for protection orders delivered to the agency pursuant to this section. The agency shall note in the registry the date and time that the agency received an order.

(D) An officer of a law enforcement agency shall enforce a protection order issued by a court of another state in accordance with the provisions of the order, including removing the person allegedly violating the order from the premises, regardless of whether the order is registered as authorized by division (B) of this section in the county in which the officer's agency has jurisdiction.

(E) Notwithstanding any provision of law to the contrary and regardless of whether a protection order is issued or a consent agreement is approved by a court of another county or a court of another state, no court or unit of state or local government shall charge any fee, cost, deposit, or money in connection with the filing, issuance, registration, or service of a protection order or consent agreement or for obtaining a certified copy of a protection order or consent agreement, including a protection order issued by a court of another state.

**HISTORY: 147 v S 1 (Eff 10-21-97); 149 v H 548. Eff 3-31-2003.**

# CHAPTER 2921: OFFENSES AGAINST JUSTICE AND PUBLIC ADMINISTRATION



[IN GENERAL]

## § 2921.01 Definitions.

As used in sections 2921.01 to 2921.45 of the Revised Code:

(A) "Public official" means any elected or appointed officer, or employee, or agent of the state or any political subdivision, whether in a temporary or permanent capacity, and includes, but is not limited to, legislators, judges, and law enforcement officers. "Public official" does not include an employee, officer, or governor-appointed member of the board of directors of the nonprofit corporation formed under section 187.01 of the Revised Code.

(B) "Public servant" means any of the following:

(1) Any public official;

(2) Any person performing ad hoc a governmental function, including, but not limited to, a juror, member of a temporary commission, master, arbitrator, advisor, or consultant;

(3) A person who is a candidate for public office, whether or not the person is elected or appointed to the office for which the person is a candidate. A person is a candidate for purposes of this division if the person has been nominated according to law for election or appointment to public office, or if the person has filed a petition or petitions as required by law to have the person's name placed on the ballot in a primary, general, or special election, or if the person campaigns as a write-in candidate in any primary, general, or special election.

"Public servant" does not include an employee, officer, or governor-appointed member of the board of directors of the nonprofit corporation formed under section 187.01 of the Revised Code.

(C) "Party official" means any person who holds an elective or appointive post in a political party in the United States or this state, by virtue of which the person directs, conducts, or participates in directing or conducting party affairs at any level of responsibility.

(D) "Official proceeding" means any proceeding before a legislative, judicial, administrative, or other governmental agency or official authorized to take evidence under oath, and includes any proceeding before a referee, hearing examiner, commissioner, notary, or other person taking testimony or a deposition in connection with an official proceeding.

(E) "Detention" means arrest; confinement in any vehicle subsequent to an arrest; confinement in any public or private facility for custody of persons charged with or convicted of crime in this state or another state or under the laws of the United States or alleged or found to be a delinquent child or unruly child in this state or another state or under the laws of the United States; hospitalization, institutionalization, or confinement in any public or private facility that is ordered pursuant to or under the authority of section 2945.37, 2945.371 [2945.37.1], 2945.38, 2945.39, 2945.40, 2945.401 [2945.40.1], or 2945.402 [2945.40.2] of the Revised Code; confinement in any vehicle for transportation to or from any facility of any of those natures; detention for extradition or deportation; except as provided in this division, supervision by any employee of any facility of any of those natures that is incidental to hospitalization, institutionalization, or confinement in the facility but that occurs outside the facility; supervision by an employee of the department of rehabilitation and correction of a person on any type of release from a state correctional institution; or confinement in any vehicle, airplane, or place while being returned from outside of this state into this state by a private person or entity pursuant to a contract entered into under division (E) of section 311.29 of the Revised Code or division (B) of section 5149.03 of the Revised Code. For a person confined in a county jail who participates in a county jail industry program pursuant to section 5147.30 of the Revised Code, "detention" includes time spent at an assigned work site and going to and from the work site.

(F) "Detention facility" means any public or private place used for the confinement of a person charged with or convicted of any crime in this state or another state or under the laws of the United States or alleged or found to be a delinquent child or unruly child in this state or another state or under the laws of the United States.

(G) "Valuable thing or valuable benefit" includes, but is not limited to, a contribution. This inclusion does not indicate or imply that a contribution was not included in those terms before September 17, 1986.

(H) "Campaign committee," "contribution," "political action committee," "legislative campaign fund," "political party," and "political contributing entity" have the same meanings as in section 3517.01 of the Revised Code.

(I) "Provider agreement" and "medical assistance program" have the same meanings as in section 2913.40 of the Revised Code.

**HISTORY: 134 v H 511 (Eff 1-1-74); 141 v H 340 (Eff 5-20-86); 141 v H 300 (Eff 9-17-86); 141 v H 428 (Eff 12-23-86); 142 v H 708 (Eff 4-19-88); 143 v H 51 (Eff 11-8-90); 144 v S 37 (Eff 7-31-92); 145 v H 42 (Eff 2-9-94); 145 v H 571 (Eff 10-6-94); 146 v S 8 (Eff 8-23-95); 146 v S 2 (Eff 7-1-96); 146 v H 154 (Eff 10-4-96); 146 v S 285 (Eff 7-1-97); 147 v H 293 (Eff 3-17-98); 147 v S 134 (Eff 7-13-98); 148 v H 661. Eff 3-15-2001; 150 v H 1, § 1, eff. 3-31-05; 151 v S 115, § 1, eff. 4-26-05; 2011 HB 1, § 1, eff. Feb. 18, 2011.**

The provisions of § 3 of 2011 HB 1 read as follows:

SECTION 3. The Supreme Court of Ohio shall have exclusive, original jurisdiction over any claim asserting that any one or more sections of the Revised Code amended or enacted by this act, or any portion of one or more of those sections, or any rule adopted under one or more of those sections, violates any provision of the Ohio Constitution; and over any claim asserting that any action taken pursuant to those sections by the Governor or the nonprofit corporation formed under section 187.01 of the Revised Code violates any provision of the Ohio Constitution or any provision of the Revised Code. Any such claim shall be filed as otherwise required by the Court's rules of practice not later than the sixtieth day after the effective date of this act. If any claim over which the Supreme Court is granted exclusive, original jurisdiction by this section is filed in any lower court, the claim shall be dismissed by the court on the ground that the court lacks jurisdiction to review it.

The provisions of § 3 of 151 v S 115 read as follows:

SECTION 3. This act is hereby declared to be an emergency measure necessary for the immediate preservation of the public peace, health, and safety. The reason for the necessity is that the Court of Common Pleas of Franklin County has issued a preliminary injunction prohibiting the enforcement of section 3599.03 of the Revised Code, as enacted by Am. Sub. H.B. 1 of the 125th General Assembly, Special Session, in *United Auto Workers Local Union 1112 v. Blackwell* (March 30, 2005), Case No. O5CVH-03-2553. Therefore, this act shall go into immediate effect.

## [BRIBERY AND INTIMIDATION]

## § 2921.02 Bribery.

(A) No person, with purpose to corrupt a public servant or party official, or improperly to influence him with respect to the discharge of his duty, whether before or after he is elected, appointed, qualified, employed, summoned, or sworn, shall promise, offer, or give any valuable thing or valuable benefit.

(B) No person, either before or after he is elected, appointed, qualified, employed, summoned, or sworn as a public servant or party official, shall knowingly solicit or accept for himself or another person any valuable thing or valuable benefit to corrupt or improperly influence him or another public servant or party official with respect to the discharge of his or the other public servant's or party official's duty.

(C) No person, with purpose to corrupt a witness or improperly to influence him with respect to his testimony in an official proceeding, either before or after he is subpoenaed or sworn, shall promise, offer, or give him or another person any valuable thing or valuable benefit.

(D) No person, either before or after he is subpoenaed or sworn as a witness, shall knowingly solicit or accept for himself or another person any valuable thing or valuable benefit to corrupt or improperly influence him with respect to his testimony in an official proceeding.

(E) Whoever violates this section is guilty of bribery, a felony of the third degree.

(F) A public servant or party official who is convicted of bribery is forever disqualified from holding any public office, employment, or position of trust in this state.

**HISTORY: 134 v H 511 (Eff 1-1-74); 141 v H 300. Eff 9-17-86.**

**Not analogous to former RC § 2921.02 (RS § 6807; S&S 261; 58 v 110; GC § 12393; Bureau of Code Revision, 10-1-53), repealed 134 v H 511, § 2, eff 1-1-74.**

## § 2921.03 Intimidation.

(A) No person, knowingly and by force, by unlawful threat of harm to any person or property, or by filing, recording, or otherwise using a materially false or fraudulent writing with malicious purpose, in bad faith, or in a wanton or reckless manner, shall attempt to influence, intimidate, or hinder a public servant†, party official, or witness in the discharge of the person's duty.

(B) Whoever violates this section is guilty of intimidation, a felony of the third degree.

(C) A person who violates this section is liable in a civil action to any person harmed by the violation for injury, death, or loss to person or property incurred as a result of the commission of the offense and for reasonable attorney's fees, court costs, and other expenses incurred as a result of prosecuting the civil action commenced under this division. A civil action under this division is not the exclusive remedy of a person who incurs injury, death, or loss to person or property as a result of a violation of this section.

**HISTORY: 134 v H 511 (Eff 1-1-74); 140 v S 172 (Eff 9-26-84); 146 v H 88 (Eff 9-3-96); 146 v H 644. Eff 11-6-96.**

† The first paragraph as amended by HB 88 (146 v —) reads as follows:

"... a party official, or an attorney or witness involved in a civil action or proceeding in the discharge of the duties of the public servant, party official, attorney, or witness."

**Not analogous to former RC § 2921.03 (RS § 6886; S&S 262; 58 v 110; GC § 12394; Bureau of Code Revision, 10-1-53), repealed 134 v H 511, § 2, eff 1-1-74.**

Division (C) was added by HB 644 (146 v —).

## § 2921.04 Intimidation of attorney, victim or witness in criminal case.

(A) No person shall knowingly attempt to intimidate or hinder the victim of a crime in the filing or prosecution of criminal charges or a witness involved in a criminal action or proceeding in the discharge of the duties of the witness.

(B) No person, knowingly and by force or by unlawful threat of harm to any person or property, shall attempt to influence, intimidate, or hinder the victim of a crime in the filing or prosecution of criminal charges or an attorney or witness involved in a criminal action or proceeding in the discharge of the duties of the attorney or witness.

(C) Division (A) of this section does not apply to any person who is attempting to resolve a dispute pertaining to the alleged commission of a criminal offense, either prior to or subsequent to the filing of a complaint, indictment, or information, by participating in the arbitration, mediation, compromise, settlement, or conciliation of that dispute pursuant to an authorization for arbitration, mediation, compromise, settlement, or conciliation of a dispute of that nature that is conferred by any of the following:

(1) A section of the Revised Code;

(2) The Rules of Criminal Procedure, the Rules of Superintendence for Municipal Courts and County Courts, the Rules of Superintendence for Courts of Common Pleas, or another rule adopted by the supreme court in accordance with Section 5 of Article IV, Ohio Constitution;

(3) A local rule of court, including, but not limited to, a local rule of court that relates to alternative dispute resolution or other case management programs and that authorizes the referral of disputes pertaining to the alleged commission of certain types of criminal offenses to appropriate and available arbitration, mediation, compromise, settlement, or other conciliation programs;

(4) The order of a judge of a municipal court, county court, or court of common pleas.

(D) Whoever violates this section is guilty of intimidation of an attorney, victim, or witness in a criminal case. A violation of division (A) of this section is a misdemeanor of the first degree. A violation of division (B) of this section is a felony of the third degree.

**HISTORY: 140 v S 172 (Eff 9-26-84); 146 v H 88. Eff 9-3-96.**

**Not analogous to former RC § 2921.04 (RS §§ 803-1, 803-2; GC § 12395; 92 v 89, §§ 1, 2; 106 v 341; Bureau of Code Revision, 10-1-53), repealed 134 v H 511, § 2, eff 1-1-74.**

## § 2921.05 Retaliation.

(A) No person, purposely and by force or by unlawful threat of harm to any person or property, shall retaliate against a public servant, a party official, or an attorney or witness who was involved in a civil or criminal action or proceeding because the public servant, party official, attorney, or witness discharged the duties of the public servant, party official, attorney, or witness.

(B) No person, purposely and by force or by unlawful threat of harm to any person or property, shall retaliate against the victim of a crime because the victim filed or prosecuted criminal charges.

(C) Whoever violates this section is guilty of retaliation, a felony of the third degree.

**HISTORY: 146 v H 88. Eff 9-3-96.**

**Not analogous to former RC § 2921.05 (RS §§ 7017-7, 7017-8; 95 v 305; GC §§ 12396, 12397; Bureau of Code Revision, 10-1-53; 132 v H 664), repealed 134 v H 511, § 2, eff 1-1-74.**

## § 2921.06 Repealed, 134 v H 511, § 2 [RS § 7017-9; 95 v 305; GC §§ 12398—12398-2; 108 v PtI, 57; Bureau of Code Revision, 10-1-53]. Eff 1-1-74.

This section concerned offenses against the state.

## § 2921.07 Repealed, 134 v H 511, § 2 [RS § 7017-9; 95 v 305; GC §§ 12398—12398-2; 108 v PtI, 57; Bureau of Code Revision, 10-1-53]. Eff 1-1-74.

This section concerned offenses against the state.

## § 2921.08 Repealed, 134 v H 511, § 2 [RS §§ 218-217, 218-218, 6826; 69 v 189; 73 v 249; 76 v 187, 188; 95 v 69; 97 v 306; GC §§ 12426, 12461, 12462; Bureau of Code Revision, 10-1-53]. Eff 1-1-74.

This section concerned offenses against the state.

## § 2921.09 Repealed, 134 v H 511, § 2 [RS §§ 218-217, 218-218, 6826; 69 v 189; 73 v 249; 76 v 187, 188; 95 v 69; 97 v 306; GC §§ 12426, 12461, 12462; Bureau of Code Revision, 10-1-53]. Eff 1-1-74.

This section concerned offenses against the state.

## § 2921.10 Repealed, 134 v H 511, § 2 [RS §§ 218-217, 218-218, 6826; 69 v 189; 73 v 249; 76 v 187, 188; 95 v 69; 97 v 306; GC §§ 12426, 12461, 12462; Bureau of Code Revision, 10-1-53]. Eff 1-1-74.

This section concerned offenses against the state.

### [PERJURY]

## § 2921.11 Perjury.

(A) No person, in any official proceeding, shall knowingly make a false statement under oath or affirmation, or knowingly swear or affirm the truth of a false statement previously made, when either statement is material.

(B) A falsification is material, regardless of its admissibility in evidence, if it can affect the course or outcome of the proceeding. It is no defense to a charge under this section that the offender mistakenly believed a falsification to be immaterial.

(C) It is no defense to a charge under this section that the oath or affirmation was administered or taken in an irregular manner.

(D) Where contradictory statements relating to the same material fact are made by the offender under oath or affirmation and within the period of the statute of limitations for perjury, it is not necessary for the prosecution to prove which statement was false, but only that one or the other was false.

(E) No person shall be convicted of a violation of this section where proof of falsity rests solely upon contradiction by testimony of one person other than the defendant.

(F) Whoever violates this section is guilty of perjury, a felony of the third degree.

**HISTORY: 134 v H 511. Eff 1-1-74.**

**Not analogous to former RC § 2921.11 (RS §§ 674-13, 6827b; 89 v 40; 97 v 307; GC § 12463; Bureau of Code Revision, 10-1-53), repealed 134 v H 511, § 2, eff 1-1-74.**

## § 2921.12 Tampering with evidence.

(A) No person, knowing that an official proceeding or investigation is in progress, or is about to be or likely to be instituted, shall do any of the following:

(1) Alter, destroy, conceal, or remove any record, document, or thing, with purpose to impair its value or availability as evidence in such proceeding or investigation;

(2) Make, present, or use any record, document, or thing, knowing it to be false and with purpose to mislead a public official who is or may be engaged in such proceeding or investigation, or with purpose to corrupt the outcome of any such proceeding or investigation.

(B) Whoever violates this section is guilty of tampering with evidence, a felony of the third degree.

**HISTORY: 134 v H 511. Eff 1-1-74.**

**Not analogous to former RC § 2921.12 (RS § 6882; S&S 57; S&C 192, 449; 29 v 372; 64 v 128; GC § 12491; Bureau of Code Revision, 10-1-53), repealed 134 v H 511, § 2, eff 1-1-74.**

## § 2921.13 Falsification; in theft offense; to purchase firearm; to obtain concealed handgun license.

(A) No person shall knowingly make a false statement, or knowingly swear or affirm the truth of a false statement previously made, when any of the following applies:

(1) The statement is made in any official proceeding.

(2) The statement is made with purpose to incriminate another.

(3) The statement is made with purpose to mislead a public official in performing the public official's official function.

(4) The statement is made with purpose to secure the payment of unemployment compensation; Ohio works first; prevention, retention, and contingency benefits and services; disability financial assistance; retirement benefits; economic development assistance, as defined in section 9.66 of the Revised Code; or other benefits administered by a governmental agency or paid out of a public treasury.

(5) The statement is made with purpose to secure the issuance by a governmental agency of a license, permit, authorization, certificate, registration, release, or provider agreement.

(6) The statement is sworn or affirmed before a notary public or another person empowered to administer oaths.

(7) The statement is in writing on or in connection with a report or return that is required or authorized by law.

(8) The statement is in writing and is made with purpose to induce another to extend credit to or employ the offender, to confer any degree, diploma, certificate of attainment, award of excellence, or honor on the offender, or to extend to or bestow upon the offender any other valuable benefit or distinction, when the person to whom the statement is directed relies upon it to that person's detriment.

(9) The statement is made with purpose to commit or facilitate the commission of a theft offense.

(10) The statement is knowingly made to a probate court in connection with any action, proceeding, or other matter within its jurisdiction, either orally or in a written document, including, but not limited to, an application, petition, complaint, or other pleading, or an inventory, account, or report.

(11) The statement is made on an account, form, record, stamp, label, or other writing that is required by law.

(12) The statement is made in connection with the purchase of a firearm, as defined in section 2923.11 of the Revised Code, and in conjunction with the furnishing to the seller of the firearm of a fictitious or altered driver's or commercial driver's license or permit, a fictitious or altered identification card, or any other document that contains false information about the purchaser's identity.

(13) The statement is made in a document or instrument of writing that purports to be a judgment, lien, or claim of indebtedness and is filed or recorded with the secretary of state, a county recorder, or the clerk of a court of record.

(14) The statement is made in an application filed with a county sheriff pursuant to section 2923.125 of the Revised Code in order to obtain or renew a license to carry a concealed handgun or is made in an affidavit submitted to a county sheriff to obtain a temporary emergency license to carry a concealed handgun under section 2923.1213 of the Revised Code.

(15) The statement is required under section 5743.71 of the Revised Code in connection with the person's purchase of cigarettes or tobacco products in a delivery sale.

(B) No person, in connection with the purchase of a firearm, as defined in section 2923.11 of the Revised Code, shall knowingly furnish to the seller of the firearm a fictitious or altered driver's or commercial driver's license or permit, a fictitious or altered identification card, or any other document that contains false information about the purchaser's identity.

(C) No person, in an attempt to obtain a license to carry a concealed handgun under section 2923.125 of the Revised Code, shall knowingly present to a sheriff a fictitious or altered document that purports to be certification of the person's competence in handling a handgun as described in division (B)(3) of section 2923.125 of the Revised Code.

(D) It is no defense to a charge under division (A)(6) of this section that the oath or affirmation was administered or taken in an irregular manner.

(E) If contradictory statements relating to the same fact are made by the offender within the period of the statute of limitations for falsification, it is not necessary for the prosecution to prove which statement was false but only that one or the other was false.

(F)(1) Whoever violates division (A)(1), (2), (3), (4), (5), (6), (7), (8), (10), (11), (13), or (15) of this section is guilty of falsification, a misdemeanor of the first degree.

(2) Whoever violates division (A)(9) of this section is guilty of falsification in a theft offense. Except as otherwise provided in this division, falsification in a theft offense is a misdemeanor of the first degree. If the value of the property or services stolen is one thousand dollars or more and is less than seven thousand five hundred dollars, falsification in a theft offense is a felony of the fifth degree. If the value of the property or services stolen is seven thousand five hundred dollars or more and is less than one hundred fifty thousand dollars, falsification in a theft offense is a felony of the fourth degree. If the value of the property or services stolen is one hundred fifty thousand dollars or more, falsification in a theft offense is a felony of the third degree.

(3) Whoever violates division (A)(12) or (B) of this section is guilty of falsification to purchase a firearm, a felony of the fifth degree.

(4) Whoever violates division (A)(14) or (C) of this section is guilty of falsification to obtain a concealed handgun license, a felony of the fourth degree.

(G) A person who violates this section is liable in a civil action to any person harmed by the violation for injury, death, or loss to person or property incurred as a result of the commission of the offense and for reasonable attorney's fees, court costs, and other expenses incurred as a result of prosecuting the civil action commenced under this division. A civil action under this division is not the exclusive remedy of a person who incurs injury, death, or loss to person or property as a result of a violation of this section.

**HISTORY: 134 v H 511 (Eff 1-1-74); 136 v S 545 (Eff 1-17-77); 140 v H 632 (Eff 3-28-85); 141 v H 340 (Eff 5-20-86); 142 v H 708 (Eff 4-19-88); 143 v S 46 (Eff 1-1-90); 143 v H 347 (Eff 7-18-90); 143 v S 3 (Eff 4-11-91); 144 v H 298 (Eff 7-26-91); 145 v H 152 (Eff 7-1-93); 145 v H 107 (Eff 10-20-93); 146 v H 249 (Eff 7-17-95); 146 v H 4 (Eff 11-9-95); 146 v S 46 (Eff 11-15-95); 146 v S 2 (Eff 7-1-96); 146 v S 269 (Eff 7-1-96); 146 v H 644 (Eff 11-6-96); 147 v H 408 (Eff 10-1-97); 149 v H 94. Eff 9-5-2001; 150 v H 95, § 1, eff. 6-26-03; 150 v H 311, § 1, eff. 12-18-03; 150 v H 12, § 1, eff. 4-8-04; 151 v H 66, § 101.01, eff. 6-30-05; 151 v H 468, § 1, eff. 4-6-07; 151 v H 468, § 4, eff. 7-1-07; 152 v H 562, § 101.01, eff. 6-24-08; 153 v H 1, § 101.01, eff. 7-17-09; 2011 HB 86, § 1, eff. Sept. 30, 2011.**

The provisions of § 4 of HB 86 read as follows:

"SECTION 4. The amendments to sections 926.99, 1333.99, 1707.99, 1716.99, 2909.03, 2909.05, 2909.11, 2913.02, 2913.03, 2913.04, 2913.11, 2913.21, 2913.31, 2913.32, 2913.34, 2913.40, 2913.401, 2913.42, 2913.421, 2913.43, 2913.45, 2913.46, 2913.47, 2913.48, 2913.49, 2913.51, 2913.61, 2915.05, 2917.21, 2917.31, 2917.32, 2921.13, 2921.41, 2923.31, and 2981.07, division (B) of section 2929.13, and division (A) of section 2929.14 of the Revised Code that are made in this act apply to a person who commits an offense specified or penalized under those sections on or after the effective date of this section and to a person to whom division (B) of section 1.58 of the Revised Code makes the amendments applicable.

"The provisions of sections 926.99, 1333.99, 1707.99, 1716.99, 2909.03, 2909.05, 2909.11, 2913.02, 2913.03, 2913.04, 2913.11, 2913.21, 2913.31, 2913.32, 2913.34, 2913.40, 2913.401, 2913.42, 2913.421, 2913.43, 2913.45, 2913.46, 2913.47, 2913.48, 2913.49, 2913.51, 2913.61, 2915.05, 2917.21, 2917.31, 2917.32, 2921.13, 2921.41, 2923.31, and 2981.07 of the Revised Code in existence prior to the effective date of this section shall apply to a person upon whom a court imposed sentence prior to the effective date of this section for an offense specified or penalized under those sections. The amendments to sections 926.99, 1333.99, 1707.99, 1716.99, 2909.03, 2909.05, 2909.11, 2913.02, 2913.03, 2913.04, 2913.11, 2913.21, 2913.31, 2913.32, 2913.34, 2913.40, 2913.401, 2913.42, 2913.421, 2913.43, 2913.45, 2913.46, 2913.47, 2913.48, 2913.49, 2913.51, 2913.61, 2915.05, 2917.21, 2917.31, 2917.32, 2921.13, 2921.41, 2923.31, and 2981.07 of the Revised Code that are made in this act do not apply to a person who upon whom a court imposed sentence prior to the effective date of this section for an offense specified or penalized under those sections."

The effective date is set by § 812.20 of 153 v H 1.

The effective date is set by § 812.30 of 152 v H 562.

The effective date is set by § 612.21 of 151 v H 66.

151 v H 66, effective June 30, 2005, added (A)(16); corrected internal references in (F); and made minor stylistic changes.

See provisions of H.B. 12 (150 v —) following RC § 2911.21.

**Comment, Legislative Service Commission**

Section 2921.13 of the Revised Code is amended by Am. Sub. H.B. 311, Am. Sub. H.B. 12, and Am. Sub. H.B. 95 of the 125th General Assembly. Comparison of these amendments in pursuance of section 1.52 of the Revised Code discloses that they are not irreconcilable so that they are required by that section to be harmonized to give effect to each amendment.

## § 2921.14 Making or causing false report of child abuse or neglect.

(A) No person shall knowingly make or cause another person to make a false report under division (B) of section 2151.421 [2151.42.1] of the Revised Code alleging that any person has committed an act or omission that resulted in a child being an abused child as defined in section 2151.031 [2151.03.1] of the Revised Code or a neglected child as defined in section 2151.03 of the Revised Code.

(B) Whoever violates this section is guilty of making or causing a false report of child abuse or child neglect, a misdemeanor of the first degree.

**HISTORY: 143 v S 3. Eff 4-11-91.**

**Not analogous to former RC § 2921.14 (GC § 13116-1; 118 v 501; Bureau of Code Revision, 10-1-53; 126 v 575), repealed, 134 v H 511, § 2, eff 1-1-74.**

## § 2921.15 Making false allegation of peace officer misconduct.

(A) As used in this section, "peace officer" has the same meaning as in section 2935.01 of the Revised Code.

(B) No person shall knowingly file a complaint against a peace officer that alleges that the peace officer engaged in misconduct in the performance of the officer's duties if the person knows that the allegation is false.

(C) Whoever violates division (B) of this section is guilty of making a false allegation of peace officer misconduct, a misdemeanor of the first degree.

**HISTORY: 148 v S 317. Eff 3-22-2001.**

**Not analogous to former RC § 2921.15 (GC § 13116-2; 118 v 501, § 2), repealed 134 v H 511, § 2, eff 1-1-74.**

## § 2921.16 Repealed, 134 v H 511, § 2 [82 v 221; GC §§ 12506, 13116-3; 118 v 501; Bureau of Code Revision, 10-1-53; 130 v 663; 132 v H 65; 133 v H 1; 134 v H 494]. Eff 1-1-74.

This section concerned offenses against the state and the United States; compensation of jurors; and imprisonment.

## § 2921.17 Repealed, 134 v H 511, § 2 [82 v 221; GC §§ 12506, 13116-3; 118 v 501; Bureau of Code Revision, 10-1-53; 130 v 663; 132 v H 65; 133 v H 1; 134 v H 494]. Eff 1-1-74.

This section concerned offenses against the state and the United States; compensation of jurors; and imprisonment.

## § 2921.18 Repealed, 134 v H 511, § 2 [82 v 221; GC §§ 12506, 13116-3; 118 v 501; Bureau of Code Revision, 10-1-53; 130 v 663; 132 v H 65; 133 v H 1; 134 v H 494]. Eff 1-1-74.

This section concerned offenses against the state and the United States; compensation of jurors; and imprisonment.

### [COMPOUNDING]

## § 2921.21 Compounding a crime.

(A) No person shall knowingly demand, accept, or agree to accept anything of value in consideration of abandoning or agreeing to abandon a pending criminal prosecution.

(B) It is an affirmative defense to a charge under this section when both of the following apply:

(1) The pending prosecution involved is for a violation of section 2913.02 or 2913.11, division (B)(2) of section 2913.21, or section 2913.47 of the Revised Code, of which the actor under this section was the victim.

(2) The thing of value demanded, accepted, or agreed to be accepted, in consideration of abandoning or agreeing to abandon the prosecution, did not exceed an amount that the actor reasonably believed due him as restitution for the loss caused him by the offense.

(C) When a prosecuting witness abandons or agrees to abandon a prosecution under division (B) of this section, the abandonment or agreement in no way binds the state to abandoning the prosecution.

(D) Whoever violates this section is guilty of compounding a crime, a misdemeanor of the first degree.

**HISTORY: 134 v H 511 (Eff 1-1-74); 135 v H 716 (Eff 1-1-74); 143 v H 347. Eff 7-18-90.**

**Not analogous to former RC § 2921.21 (125 v H 308), repealed 134 v H 511, § 2, eff 1-1-74.**

**Analogous to former RC § 2917.36 (RS § 6901; 76 v 23; 81 v 101; GC § 12861; Bureau of Code Revision, 10-1-53), repealed 134 v H 511, § 2, eff 1-1-74.**

## § 2921.22 Failure to report a crime or knowledge of a death or burn injury.

(A)(1) Except as provided in division (A)(2) of this section, no person, knowing that a felony has been or is being committed, shall knowingly fail to report such information to law enforcement authorities.

(2) No person, knowing that a violation of division (B) of section 2913.04 of the Revised Code has been, or is being committed or that the person has received information derived from such a violation, shall knowingly fail to report the violation to law enforcement authorities.

(B) Except for conditions that are within the scope of division (E) of this section, no physician, limited practitioner, nurse, or other person giving aid to a sick or injured person shall negligently fail to report to law enforcement authorities any gunshot or stab wound treated or observed by the physician, limited practitioner, nurse, or person, or any serious physical harm to persons that the physician, limited practitioner, nurse, or person knows or has reasonable cause to believe resulted from an offense of violence.

(C) No person who discovers the body or acquires the first knowledge of the death of a person shall fail to report the death immediately to a physician whom the person knows to be treating the deceased for a condition from which death at such time would not be unexpected, or to a law enforcement officer, an ambulance service, an emergency squad, or the coroner in a political subdivision in which the body is discovered, the death is believed to have occurred, or knowledge concerning the death is obtained.

(D) No person shall fail to provide upon request of the person to whom a report required by division (C) of this section was made, or to any law enforcement officer who has reasonable cause to assert the authority to investigate the circumstances surrounding the death, any facts within the person's knowledge that may have a bearing on the investigation of the death.

(E)(1) As used in this division, "burn injury" means any of the following:

(a) Second or third degree burns;

(b) Any burns to the upper respiratory tract or laryngeal edema due to the inhalation of superheated air;

(c) Any burn injury or wound that may result in death;

(d) Any physical harm to persons caused by or as the result of the use of fireworks, novelties and trick noisemakers, and wire sparklers, as each is defined by section 3743.01 of the Revised Code.

(2) No physician, nurse, or limited practitioner who, outside a hospital, sanitarium, or other medical facility, attends or treats a person who has sustained a burn injury that is inflicted by an explosion or other incendiary device or that shows evidence of having been inflicted in a violent, malicious, or criminal manner shall fail to report the burn injury immediately to the local arson, or fire and explosion investigation, bureau, if there is a bureau of this type in the jurisdiction in which the person is attended or treated, or otherwise to local law enforcement authorities.

(3) No manager, superintendent, or other person in charge of a hospital, sanitarium, or other medical facility in which a person is attended or treated for any burn injury that is inflicted by an explosion or other incendiary device or that shows evidence of having been inflicted in a violent, malicious, or criminal manner shall fail to report the burn injury immediately to the local arson, or fire and explosion investigation, bureau, if there is a bureau of this type in the jurisdiction in which the person is attended or treated, or otherwise to local law enforcement authorities.

(4) No person who is required to report any burn injury under division (E)(2) or (3) of this section shall fail to file, within three working days after attending or treating the victim, a written report of the burn injury with the office of the state fire marshal. The report shall comply with the uniform standard developed by the state fire marshal pursuant to division (A)(15) of section 3737.22 of the Revised Code.

(5) Anyone participating in the making of reports under division (E) of this section or anyone participating in a judicial proceeding resulting from the reports is immune from any civil or criminal liability that otherwise might be incurred or imposed as a result of such actions. Notwithstanding section 4731.22 of the Revised Code, the physi-

cian-patient relationship is not a ground for excluding evidence regarding a person's burn injury or the cause of the burn injury in any judicial proceeding resulting from a report submitted under division (E) of this section.

(F)(1) Any doctor of medicine or osteopathic medicine, hospital intern or resident, registered or licensed practical nurse, psychologist, social worker, independent social worker, social work assistant, professional clinical counselor, or professional counselor who knows or has reasonable cause to believe that a patient or client has been the victim of domestic violence, as defined in section 3113.31 of the Revised Code, shall note that knowledge or belief and the basis for it in the patient's or client's records.

(2) Notwithstanding section 4731.22 of the Revised Code, the doctor-patient privilege shall not be a ground for excluding any information regarding the report containing the knowledge or belief noted under division (F)(1) of this section, and the information may be admitted as evidence in accordance with the Rules of Evidence.

(G) Divisions (A) and (D) of this section do not require disclosure of information, when any of the following applies:

(1) The information is privileged by reason of the relationship between attorney and client; doctor and patient; licensed psychologist or licensed school psychologist and client; member of the clergy, rabbi, minister, or priest and any person communicating information confidentially to the member of the clergy, rabbi, minister, or priest for a religious counseling purpose of a professional character; husband and wife; or a communications assistant and those who are a party to a telecommunications relay service call.

(2) The information would tend to incriminate a member of the actor's immediate family.

(3) Disclosure of the information would amount to revealing a news source, privileged under section 2739.04 or 2739.12 of the Revised Code.

(4) Disclosure of the information would amount to disclosure by a member of the ordained clergy of an organized religious body of a confidential communication made to that member of the clergy in that member's capacity as a member of the clergy by a person seeking the aid or counsel of that member of the clergy.

(5) Disclosure would amount to revealing information acquired by the actor in the course of the actor's duties in connection with a bona fide program of treatment or services for drug dependent persons or persons in danger of drug dependence, which program is maintained or conducted by a hospital, clinic, person, agency, or organization certified pursuant to section 3793.06 of the Revised Code.

(6) Disclosure would amount to revealing information acquired by the actor in the course of the actor's duties in connection with a bona fide program for providing counseling services to victims of crimes that are violations of section 2907.02 or 2907.05 of the Revised Code or to victims of felonious sexual penetration in violation of former section 2907.12 of the Revised Code. As used in this division, "counseling services" include services provided in an informal setting by a person who, by education or experience, is competent to provide those services.

(H) No disclosure of information pursuant to this section gives rise to any liability or recrimination for a breach of privilege or confidence.

(I) Whoever violates division (A) or (B) of this section is guilty of failure to report a crime. Violation of division (A)(1) of this section is a misdemeanor of the fourth degree. Violation of division (A)(2) or (B) of this section is a misdemeanor of the second degree.

(J) Whoever violates division (C) or (D) of this section is guilty of failure to report knowledge of a death, a misdemeanor of the fourth degree.

(K)(1) Whoever negligently violates division (E) of this section is guilty of a minor misdemeanor.

(2) Whoever knowingly violates division (E) of this section is guilty of a misdemeanor of the second degree.

**HISTORY: 134 v H 511 (Eff 1-1-74); 136 v H 750 (Eff 8-26-75); 136 v S 283 (Eff 11-26-75); 137 v H 1 (Eff 8-26-77); 137 v S 203 (Eff 1-13-78); 138 v H 284 (Eff 10-22-80); 142 v H 273 (Eff 9-10-87); 143 v H 317 (Eff 10-10-89); 144 v S 343 (Eff 3-24-93); 145 v H 335 (Eff 12-9-94); 146 v H 445 (Eff 9-3-96); 146 v S 223 (Eff 3-18-97); 149 v S 115. Eff 3-19-2003; 152 v S 248, § 1, eff. 4-7-09.**

**Not analogous to former RC § 2921.22 (125 v H 308), repealed 134 v H 511, § 2, eff 1-1-74.**

The provisions of § 4 of SB 115 (149 v —) read as follows:

SECTION 4. Section 2921.22 of the Revised Code is presented in this act as a composite of the section as amended by both Am. Sub. H.B. 445 and Sub. S.B. 223 of the 121st General Assembly. The General Assembly, applying the principle stated in division (B) of section 1.52 of the Revised Code that amendments are to be harmonized if reasonably capable of simultaneous operation, finds that the composite is the resulting version of the section in effect prior to the effective date of the section as presented in this act.

## § 2921.23 Failure to aid a law enforcement officer.

(A) No person shall negligently fail or refuse to aid a law enforcement officer, when called upon for assistance in preventing or halting the commission of an offense, or in apprehending or detaining an offender, when such aid can be given without a substantial risk of physical harm to the person giving it.

(B) Whoever violates this section is guilty of failure to aid a law enforcement officer, a minor misdemeanor.

**HISTORY: 134 v H 511. Eff 1-1-74.**

**Not analogous to former RC § 2921.23 (125 v H 308), repealed 134 v H 511, § 2, eff 1-1-74.**

**Analogous to former RC § 2917.32 (RS § 6918; S&C 430; 29 v 144; GC § 12857; Bureau of Code Revision, 10-1-53), repealed 134 v H 511, § 2, eff 1-1-74.**

## § 2921.24 Disclosure of confidential information.

(A) No officer or employee of a law enforcement agency or court, or of the office of the clerk of any court, shall disclose during the pendency of any criminal case the home address of any peace officer, parole officer, prosecuting attorney, assistant prosecuting attorney, correctional employee, or youth services employee who is a witness or arresting officer in the case.

(B) Division (A) of this section does not prohibit a peace officer, parole officer, prosecuting attorney, assistant prosecuting attorney, correctional employee, or youth services employee from disclosing the peace officer's, parole officer's, prosecuting attorney's, assistant prosecuting attorney's, correctional employee's, or youth services employee's own home address, and does not apply to any person who discloses the home address of a peace officer, parole officer, prosecuting attorney, assistant prosecuting attorney, correctional employee, or youth services employee pursuant to a court-ordered disclosure under division (C) of this section.

(C) The court in which any criminal case is pending may order the disclosure of the home address of any peace officer, parole officer, prosecuting attorney, assistant prosecuting attorney, correctional employee, or youth services employee who is a witness or arresting officer in the case, if the court determines after a written request for the disclosure that good cause exists for disclosing the home address of the peace officer, parole officer, prosecuting attorney, assistant prosecuting attorney, correctional employee, or youth services employee.

(D) Whoever violates division (A) of this section is guilty of disclosure of confidential information, a misdemeanor of the fourth degree.

(E) As used in this section:

(1) "Peace officer" has the same meaning as in section 2935.01 of the Revised Code.

(2) "Correctional employee" and "youth services employee" have the same meanings as in section 149.43 of the Revised Code.

**HISTORY: 140 v H 403. Eff 9-26-84; 151 v H 141, § 1, eff. 3-30-07.**

**Not analogous to former RC § 2921.24 (125 v H 308), repealed 134 v H 511, § 2, eff 1-1-74.**

## § 2921.25 Disclosure of home addresses of certain public officials and employees.

(A) No judge of a court of record, or mayor presiding over a mayor's court, shall order a peace officer, parole officer, prosecuting attorney, assistant prosecuting attorney, correctional employee, or youth services employee who is a witness in a criminal case, to disclose the peace officer's, parole officer's, prosecuting attorney's, assistant prosecuting attorney's, correctional employee's, or youth services employee's home address during the peace officer's, parole officer's, prosecuting attorney's, assistant prosecuting attorney's, correctional employee's, or youth services employee's examination in the case, unless the judge or mayor determines that the defendant has a right to the disclosure.

(B) As used in this section:

(1) "Peace officer" has the same meaning as in section 2935.01 of the Revised Code.

(2) "Correctional employee" and "youth services employee" have the same meanings as in section 149.43 of the Revised Code.

**HISTORY: 140 v H 403. Eff 9-26-84; 151 v H 141, § 1, eff. 3-30-07.**

**Not analogous to former RC § 2921.25 (125 v H 308; 130 v 663), repealed 134 v H 511, § 2, eff 1-1-74.**

## § 2921.26 Repealed, 134 v H 511, § 2 [125 v H 308]. Eff 1-1-74.

This section concerned charges to grand jury and records not to be public.

## § 2921.27 Repealed, 134 v H 511, § 2 [125 v H 308]. Eff 1-1-74.

This section concerned charges to grand jury and records not to be public.

## § 2921.29 Failure to disclose one's personal information.

(A) No person who is in a public place shall refuse to disclose the person's name, address, or date of birth, when requested by a law enforcement officer who reasonably suspects either of the following:

(1) The person is committing, has committed, or is about to commit a criminal offense.

(2) The person witnessed any of the following:

(a) An offense of violence that would constitute a felony under the laws of this state;

(b) A felony offense that causes or results in, or creates a substantial risk of, serious physical harm to another person or to property;

(c) Any attempt or conspiracy to commit, or complicity in committing, any offense identified in division (A)(2)(a) or (b) of this section;

(d) Any conduct reasonably indicating that any offense identified in division (A)(2)(a) or (b) of this section or any attempt, conspiracy, or complicity described in division (A)(2)(c) of this section has been, is being, or is about to be committed.

(B) Whoever violates this section is guilty of failure to disclose one's personal information, a misdemeanor of the fourth degree.

(C) Nothing in this section requires a person to answer any questions beyond that person's name, address, or date of birth. Nothing in this section authorizes a law enforcement officer to arrest a person for not providing any information beyond that person's name, address, or date of birth or for refusing to describe the offense observed.

(D) It is not a violation of this section to refuse to answer a question that would reveal a person's age or date of birth if age is an element of the crime that the person is suspected of committing.

**HISTORY: 151 v S 9, § 1, eff. 4-14-06.**

### [OBSTRUCTING AND ESCAPE]

## § 2921.31 Obstructing official business.

(A) No person, without privilege to do so and with purpose to prevent, obstruct, or delay the performance by a public official of any authorized act within the public official's official capacity, shall do any act that hampers or impedes a public official in the performance of the public official's lawful duties.

(B) Whoever violates this section is guilty of obstructing official business. Except as otherwise provided in this division, obstructing official business is a misdemeanor of the second degree. If a violation of this section creates a risk of physical harm to any person, obstructing official business is a felony of the fifth degree.

**HISTORY: 134 v H 511 (Eff 1-1-74); 148 v H 137. Eff 3-10-2000.**

## § 2921.32 Obstructing justice.

(A) No person, with purpose to hinder the discovery, apprehension, prosecution, conviction, or punishment of another for crime or to assist another to benefit from the commission of a crime, and no person, with purpose to hinder the discovery, apprehension, prosecution, adjudication as a delinquent child, or disposition of a child for an act that if committed by an adult would be a crime or to assist a child to benefit from the commission of an act that if committed by an adult would be a crime, shall do any of the following:

(1) Harbor or conceal the other person or child;

(2) Provide the other person or child with money, transportation, a weapon, a disguise, or other means of avoiding discovery or apprehension;

(3) Warn the other person or child of impending discovery or apprehension;

(4) Destroy or conceal physical evidence of the crime or act, or induce any person to withhold testimony or information or to elude legal process summoning the person to testify or supply evidence;

(5) Communicate false information to any person;

(6) Prevent or obstruct any person, by means of force, intimidation, or deception, from performing any act to aid in the discovery, apprehension, or prosecution of the other person or child.

(B) A person may be prosecuted for, and may be convicted of or adjudicated a delinquent child for committing, a violation of division (A) of this section regardless of whether the person or child aided ultimately is apprehended for, is charged with, is convicted of, pleads guilty to, or is adjudicated a delinquent child for committing the crime or act the person or child aided committed. The crime or act the person or child aided committed shall be used under division (C) of this section in determining the penalty for the violation of division (A) of this section, regardless of whether the person or child aided ultimately is apprehended for, is charged with, is convicted of, pleads guilty to, or is adjudicated a delinquent child for committing the crime or act the person or child aided committed.

(C)(1) Whoever violates this section is guilty of obstructing justice.

(2) If the crime committed by the person aided is a misdemeanor or if the act committed by the child aided would be a misdemeanor if committed by an adult, obstructing justice is a misdemeanor of the same degree as the crime committed by the person aided or a misdemeanor of the same degree that the act committed by the child aided would be if committed by an adult.

(3) Except as otherwise provided in divisions (C)(4) and (5) of this section, if the crime committed by the person aided is a felony or if the act committed by the child aided would be a felony if committed by an adult, obstructing justice is a felony of the fifth degree.

(4) If the crime committed by the person aided is aggravated murder, murder, or a felony of the first or second degree or if the act committed by the child aided would be one of those offenses if committed by an adult and if the offender knows or has reason to believe that the crime committed by the person aided is one of those offenses or that the act committed by the child aided would be one of those offenses if committed by an adult, obstructing justice is a felony of the third degree.

(5) If the crime or act committed by the person or child aided is an act of terrorism, obstructing justice is one of the following:

(a) Except as provided in division (C)(5)(b) of this section, a felony of the second degree;

(b) If the act of terrorism resulted in the death of a person who was not a participant in the act of terrorism, a felony of the first degree.

(D) As used in this section:

(1) "Adult" and "child" have the same meanings as in section 2151.011 [2151.01.1] of the Revised Code.

(2) "Delinquent child" has the same meaning as in section 2152.02 of the Revised Code.

(3) "Act of terrorism" has the same meaning as in section 2909.21 of the Revised Code.

**HISTORY: 134 v H 511 (Eff 1-1-74); 146 v S 2 (Eff 7-1-96); 147 v H 161 (Eff 12-31-97); 148 v S 179, § 3 (Eff 1-1-2002); 149 v S 184. Eff 5-15-2002.**

## § 2921.321 Assaulting or harassing police dog or horse or assistance dog.

(A) No person shall knowingly cause, or attempt to cause, physical harm to a police dog or horse in either of the following circumstances:

(1) The police dog or horse is assisting a law enforcement officer in the performance of the officer's official duties at the time the physical harm is caused or attempted.

(2) The police dog or horse is not assisting a law enforcement officer in the performance of the officer's official duties at the time the physical harm is caused or attempted, but the offender has actual knowledge that the dog or horse is a police dog or horse.

(B) No person shall recklessly do any of the following:

(1) Taunt, torment, or strike a police dog or horse;

(2) Throw an object or substance at a police dog or horse;

(3) Interfere with or obstruct a police dog or horse, or interfere with or obstruct a law enforcement officer who is being assisted by a police dog or horse, in a manner that does any of the following:

(a) Inhibits or restricts the law enforcement officer's control of the police dog or horse;

(b) Deprives the law enforcement officer of control of the police dog or horse;

(c) Releases the police dog or horse from its area of control;

(d) Enters the area of control of the police dog or horse without the consent of the law enforcement officer, including placing food or any other object or substance into that area;

(e) Inhibits or restricts the ability of the police dog or horse to assist a law enforcement officer.

(4) Engage in any conduct that is likely to cause serious physical injury or death to a police dog or horse;

(5) If the person is the owner, keeper, or harborer of a dog, fail to reasonably restrain the dog from taunting, tormenting, chasing, approaching in a menacing fashion or apparent attitude of attack, or attempting to bite or otherwise endanger a police dog or horse that at the time of the conduct is assisting a law enforcement officer in the performance of the officer's duties or that the person knows is a police dog or horse.

(C) No person shall knowingly cause, or attempt to cause, physical harm to an assistance dog in either of the following circumstances:

(1) The dog is assisting or serving a blind, deaf or hearing impaired, or mobility impaired person at the time the physical harm is caused or attempted.

(2) The dog is not assisting or serving a blind, deaf or hearing impaired, or mobility impaired person at the time the physical harm is caused or attempted, but the offender has actual knowledge that the dog is an assistance dog.

(D) No person shall recklessly do any of the following:

(1) Taunt, torment, or strike an assistance dog;

(2) Throw an object or substance at an assistance dog;

(3) Interfere with or obstruct an assistance dog, or interfere with or obstruct a blind, deaf or hearing impaired, or mobility impaired person who is being assisted or served by an assistance dog, in a manner that does any of the following:

(a) Inhibits or restricts the assisted or served person's control of the dog;

(b) Deprives the assisted or served person of control of the dog;

(c) Releases the dog from its area of control;

(d) Enters the area of control of the dog without the consent of the assisted or served person, including placing food or any other object or substance into that area;

(e) Inhibits or restricts the ability of the dog to assist the assisted or served person.

(4) Engage in any conduct that is likely to cause serious physical injury or death to an assistance dog;

(5) If the person is the owner, keeper, or harborer of a dog, fail to reasonably restrain the dog from taunting, tormenting, chasing, approaching in a menacing fashion or apparent attitude of attack, or attempting to bite or otherwise endanger an assistance dog that at the time of the conduct is assisting or serving a blind, deaf or hearing impaired, or mobility impaired person or that the person knows is an assistance dog.

(E)(1) Whoever violates division (A) of this section is guilty of assaulting a police dog or horse. Except as otherwise provided in this division, assaulting a police dog or horse is a misdemeanor of the second degree. If the violation results in the death of the police dog or horse, assaulting a police dog or horse is a felony of the third degree. If the violation results in serious physical harm to the police dog or horse other than its death, assaulting a police dog or horse is a felony of the fourth degree. If the violation results in physical harm to the police dog or horse other than death or serious physical harm, assaulting a police dog or horse is a misdemeanor of the first degree.

(2) Whoever violates division (B) of this section is guilty of harassing a police dog or horse. Except as otherwise provided in this division, harassing a police dog or horse is a misdemeanor of the second degree. If the violation results in the death of the police dog or horse, harassing a police dog or horse is a felony of the third degree. If the violation results in serious physical harm to the police dog or horse, but does not result in its death, harassing a police dog or horse, is a felony of the fourth degree. If the violation results in physical harm to the police dog or horse, but does not result in its death or in serious physical harm to it, harassing a police dog or horse is a misdemeanor of the first degree.

(3) Whoever violates division (C) of this section is guilty of assaulting an assistance dog. Except as otherwise provided in this division, assaulting an assistance dog is a misdemeanor of the second degree. If the violation results in the death of the assistance dog, assaulting an assistance dog is a felony of the third degree. If the violation results in serious physical harm to the assistance dog other than its death, assaulting an assistance dog is a felony of the fourth degree. If the violation results in physical harm to the assistance dog other than death or serious physical harm, assaulting an assistance dog is a misdemeanor of the first degree.

(4) Whoever violates division (D) of this section is guilty of harassing an assistance dog. Except as otherwise provided in this division, harassing an assistance dog is a misdemeanor of the second degree. If the violation results in the death of the assistance dog, harassing an assistance dog is a felony of the third degree. If the violation results in serious physical harm to the assistance dog, but does not result in its death, harassing an assistance dog is a felony of the fourth degree. If the violation results in physical harm to the assistance dog, but does not result in its death or in serious physical harm to it, harassing an assistance dog is a misdemeanor of the first degree.

(5) In addition to any other sanction or penalty imposed for the offense under this section, Chapter 2929., or any other provision of the Revised Code, whoever violates division (A), (B), (C), or (D) of this section is responsible for the payment of all of the following:

(a) Any veterinary bill or bill for medication incurred as a result of the violation by the police department regarding a violation of division (A) or (B) of this section or by the blind, deaf or hearing impaired, or mobility impaired person assisted or served by the assistance dog regarding a violation of division (C) or (D) of this section;

(b) The cost of any damaged equipment that results from the violation;

(c) If the violation did not result in the death of the police dog or horse or the assistance dog that was the subject of the violation and if, as a result of that dog or horse being the subject of the violation, the dog or horse needs further training or retraining to be able to continue in the capacity of a police dog or horse or an assistance dog, the cost of any further training or retraining of that dog or horse by a law enforcement officer or by the blind, deaf or hearing impaired, or mobility impaired person assisted or served by the assistance dog;

(d) If the violation resulted in the death of the police dog or horse or the assistance dog that was the subject of the violation or resulted in serious physical harm to that dog or horse to the extent that the dog or horse needs to be replaced on either a temporary or a permanent basis, the cost of replacing that dog or horse and of any further training of a new police dog or horse or a new assistance dog by a law enforcement officer or by the blind, deaf or hearing impaired, or mobility impaired person assisted or served by the assistance dog, which replacement or training is required because of the death of or the serious physical harm to the dog or horse that was the subject of the violation.

(F) This section does not apply to a licensed veterinarian whose conduct is in accordance with Chapter 4741. of the Revised Code.

(G) This section only applies to an offender who knows or should know at the time of the violation that the police dog or horse or assistance dog that is the subject of a violation under this section is a police dog or horse or an assistance dog.

(H) As used in this section:

(1) "Physical harm" means any injury, illness, or other physiological impairment, regardless of its gravity or duration.

(2) "Police dog or horse" means a dog or horse that has been trained, and may be used, to assist law enforcement officers in the performance of their official duties.

(3) "Serious physical harm" means any of the following:

(a) Any physical harm that carries a substantial risk of death;

(b) Any physical harm that causes permanent maiming or that involves some temporary, substantial maiming;

(c) Any physical harm that causes acute pain of a duration that results in substantial suffering.

(4) "Assistance dog," "blind," and "mobility impaired person" have the same meanings as in section 955.011 [955.01.1] of the Revised Code.

**HISTORY: 145 v S 116 (Eff 9-29-94); 146 v S 2 (Eff 7-1-96); 148 v H 701. Eff 4-9-2001; 150 v H 369, § 1, eff. 11-26-04; 151 v H 530, § 101.01, eff. 6-30-06.**

The effective date is set by § 812.03 of 151 v H 530.

## § 2921.33 Resisting arrest.

(A) No person, recklessly or by force, shall resist or interfere with a lawful arrest of the person or another.

(B) No person, recklessly or by force, shall resist or interfere with a lawful arrest of the person or another person and, during the course of or as a result of the resistance or interference, cause physical harm to a law enforcement officer.

(C) No person, recklessly or by force, shall resist or interfere with a lawful arrest of the person or another person if either of the following applies:

(1) The offender, during the course of or as a result of the resistance or interference, recklessly causes physical harm to a law enforcement officer by means of a deadly weapon;

(2) The offender, during the course of the resistance or interference, brandishes a deadly weapon.

(D) Whoever violates this section is guilty of resisting arrest. A violation of division (A) of this section is a misdemeanor of the second degree. A violation of division (B) of this section is a misdemeanor of the first degree. A violation of division (C) of this section is a felony of the fourth degree.

(E) As used in this section, "deadly weapon" has the same meaning as in section 2923.11 of the Revised Code.

**HISTORY: 134 v H 511 (Eff 1-1-74); 146 v S 2 (Eff 7-1-96); 147 v H 151. Eff 9-16-97.**

## § 2921.331 Failure to comply with order or signal of police officer.

(A) No person shall fail to comply with any lawful order or direction of any police officer invested with authority to direct, control, or regulate traffic.

(B) No person shall operate a motor vehicle so as willfully to elude or flee a police officer after receiving a visible or audible signal from a police officer to bring the person's motor vehicle to a stop.

(C)(1) Whoever violates this section is guilty of failure to comply with an order or signal of a police officer.

(2) A violation of division (A) of this section is a misdemeanor of the first degree.

(3) Except as provided in divisions (C) (4) and (5) of this section, a violation of division (B) of this section is a misdemeanor of the first degree.

(4) Except as provided in division (C) (5) of this section, a violation of division (B) of this section is a felony of the fourth degree if the jury or judge as trier of fact finds by proof beyond a reasonable doubt that, in committing the offense, the offender was fleeing immediately after the commission of a felony.

(5)(a) A violation of division (B) of this section is a felony of the third degree if the jury or judge as trier of fact finds any of the following by proof beyond a reasonable doubt:

(i) The operation of the motor vehicle by the offender was a proximate cause of serious physical harm to persons or property.

(ii) The operation of the motor vehicle by the offender caused a substantial risk of serious physical harm to persons or property.

(b) If a police officer pursues an offender who is violating division (B) of this section and division (C) (5) (a) of this section applies, the sentencing court, in determining the seriousness of an offender's conduct for purposes of sentencing the offender for a violation of division (B) of this section, shall consider, along with the factors set forth in sections 2929.12 and 2929.13 of the Revised Code that are required to be considered, all of the following:

(i) The duration of the pursuit;

(ii) The distance of the pursuit;

(iii) The rate of speed at which the offender operated the motor vehicle during the pursuit;

(iv) Whether the offender failed to stop for traffic lights or stop signs during the pursuit;

(v) The number of traffic lights or stop signs for which the offender failed to stop during the pursuit;

(vi) Whether the offender operated the motor vehicle during the pursuit without lighted lights during a time when lighted lights are required;

(vii) Whether the offender committed a moving violation during the pursuit;

(viii) The number of moving violations the offender committed during the pursuit;

(ix) Any other relevant factors indicating that the offender's conduct is more serious than conduct normally constituting the offense.

(D) If an offender is sentenced pursuant to division (C) (4) or (5) of this section for a violation of division (B) of this section, and if the offender is sentenced to a prison term for that violation, the offender shall serve the prison term consecutively to any other prison term or mandatory prison term imposed upon the offender.

(E) In addition to any other sanction imposed for a violation of this section, the court shall impose a class two suspension from the range specified in division (A)(2) of section 4510.02 of the Revised Code. If the offender previously has been found guilty of an offense under this section, the court shall impose a class one suspension as described in division (A)(1) of that section. The court shall not grant limited driving privileges to the offender. No judge shall suspend the first three years of suspension under a class two suspension of an offender's license, permit, or privilege required by this division on any portion of the suspension under a class one suspension of an offender's license, permit, or privilege required by this division.

(F) As used in this section:

(1) "Moving violation" has the same meaning as in section 2743.70 of the Revised Code.

(2) "Police officer" has the same meaning as in section 4511.01 of the Revised Code.

**HISTORY: GC § 6307-3; 119 v 766, § 3; Bureau of Code Revision, RC § 4511.02, 10-1-53; 132 v H 380 (Eff 1-1-68); 137 v S 381 (Eff 10-19-78); RC § 2921.33.1, 143 v S 49 (Eff 11-3-89); 148 v H 29. Eff 10-29-99; 149 v S 123, § 1, eff. 1-1-04.**

The effective date is set by section 4 of S.B. 123.

The provisions of § 5 of S.B. 123 (149 v —), as amended by § 3 of H.B. 163 (150 v —), read as follows:

SECTION 5. (A) Notwithstanding division (B) of section 1.58 of the Revised Code, the provisions of the Revised Code amended or enacted in Sections 1 and 2 of Am. Sub. S.B. 123 of the 124th General Assembly shall apply only in relation to conduct and offenses committed on or after January 1, 2004. Conduct and offenses committed prior to January 1, 2004, shall be governed by the law in effect on the date the conduct or offense was committed.

° ° °

## § 2921.34 Escape.

(A)(1) No person, knowing the person is under detention, other than supervised release detention, or being reckless in that regard, shall purposely break or attempt to break the detention, or purposely fail to return to detention, either following temporary leave granted for a specific purpose or limited period, or at the time required when serving a sentence in intermittent confinement.

(2)(a) Division (A)(2)(b) of this section applies to any person who is sentenced to a prison term pursuant to division (A)(3) or (B) of section 2971.03 of the Revised Code.

(b) No person to whom this division applies, for whom the requirement that the entire prison term imposed upon the person pursuant to division (A)(3) or (B) of section 2971.03 of the Revised Code be served in a state correctional institution has been modified pursuant to section 2971.05 of the Revised Code, and who, pursuant to that modification, is restricted to a geographic area, knowing that the person is under a geographic restriction or being reckless in that regard, shall purposely leave the geographic area to which the restriction applies or purposely fail to return to that geographic area following a temporary leave granted for a specific purpose or for a limited period of time.

(3) No person, knowing the person is under supervised release detention or being reckless in that regard, shall purposely break or attempt to break the supervised release detention or purposely fail to return to the supervised release detention, either following temporary leave granted for a specific purpose or limited period, or at the time required when serving a sentence in intermittent confinement.

(B) Irregularity in bringing about or maintaining detention, or lack of jurisdiction of the committing or detaining authority, is not a defense to a charge under this section if the detention is pursuant to judicial order or in a detention facility. In the case of any other detention, irregularity or lack of jurisdiction is an affirmative defense only if either of the following occurs:

(1) The escape involved no substantial risk of harm to the person or property of another.

(2) The detaining authority knew or should have known there was no legal basis or authority for the detention.

(C) Whoever violates this section is guilty of escape.

(1) If the offender violates division (A)(1) or (2) of this section, if the offender, at the time of the commission of the offense, was under detention as an alleged or adjudicated delinquent child or unruly child, and if the act for which the offender was under detention would not be a felony if committed by an adult, escape is a misdemeanor of the first degree.

(2) If the offender violates division (A)(1) or (2) of this section and if either the offender, at the time of the commission of the offense, was under detention in any other manner or the offender is a person for whom the requirement that the entire prison term imposed upon the person pursuant to division (A)(3) or (B) of section 2971.03 of the Revised Code be served in a state correctional institution has been modified pursuant to section 2971.05 of the Revised Code, escape is one of the following:

(a) A felony of the second degree, when the most serious offense for which the person was under detention or for which the person had been sentenced to the prison term under division (A)(3), (B)(1)(a), (b), or (c), (B)(2)(a), (b), or (c), or (B)(3)(a), (b), (c), or (d) of section 2971.03 of the Revised Code is aggravated murder, murder, or a felony of the first or second degree or, if the person was under detention as an alleged or adjudicated delinquent child, when the most serious act for which the person was under detention would be aggravated murder, murder, or a felony of the first or second degree if committed by an adult;

(b) A felony of the third degree, when the most serious offense for which the person was under detention or for which the person had been sentenced to the prison term under division (A)(3), (B)(1)(a), (b), or (c), (B)(2)(a), (b), or (c), or (B)(3)(a), (b), (c), or (d) of section 2971.03 of the Revised Code is a felony of the third, fourth, or fifth degree or an unclassified felony or, if the person was under detention as an alleged or adjudicated delinquent child, when the most serious act for which the person was under detention would be a felony of the third, fourth, or fifth degree or an unclassified felony if committed by an adult;

(c) A felony of the fifth degree, when any of the following applies:

(i) The most serious offense for which the person was under detention is a misdemeanor.

(ii) The person was found not guilty by reason of insanity, and the person's detention consisted of hospitalization, institutionalization, or confinement in a facility under an order made pursuant to or under authority of section 2945.40, 2945.401, or 2945.402 of the Revised Code.

(d) A misdemeanor of the first degree, when the most serious offense for which the person was under detention is a misdemeanor and when the person fails to return to detention at a specified time following temporary leave granted for a specific purpose or limited period or at the time required when serving a sentence in intermittent confinement.

(3) If the offender violates division (A)(3) of this section, except as otherwise provided in this division, escape is a felony of the fifth degree. If the offender violates division (A)(3) of this section and if, at the time of the commission of the offense, the most serious offense for which the offender was under supervised release detention was aggravated murder, murder, any other offense for which a sentence of life imprisonment was imposed, or a felony of the first or second degree, escape is a felony of the fourth degree.

(D) As used in this section, "supervised release detention" means detention that is supervision of a person by an employee of the department of rehabilitation and correction while the person is on any type of release from a state correctional institution, other than transitional control under section 2967.26 of the Revised Code or placement in a community-based correctional facility by the parole board under section 2967.28 of the Revised Code.

**HISTORY: 134 v H 511 (Eff 1-1-74); 144 v H 298 (Eff 7-26-91); 144 v S 37 (Eff 7-31-92); 144 v H 725 (Eff 4-16-93); 145 v H 42 (Eff 2-9-94); 146 v S 2 (Eff 7-1-96); 146 v H 180 (Eff 1-1-97); 146 v S 285. Eff 7-1-97; 150 v H 473, § 1, eff. 4-29-05; 151 v S 260, § 1, eff. 1-2-07; 152 v S 10, § 1, eff. 1-1-08; 2011 HB 86, § 1, eff. Sept. 30, 2011.**

The effective date is set by § 3 of 152 v S 10.

The provisions of § 3 of H.B. 473 (150 v —) read as follows:

SECTION 3. Section 2921.34 of the Revised Code is presented in this act as a composite of the section as amended by both Am. Sub. H.B. 180 and Am. Sub. S.B. 285 of the 121st General Assembly. * * * The General Assembly, applying the principle stated in division (B) of section 1.52 of the Revised Code that amendments are to be harmonized if reasonably capable of simultaneous operation, finds that the composites are the resulting versions of the sections in effect prior to the effective date of the sections as presented in this act.

The effective date is set by section 4 of SB 285.

## § 2921.35 Aiding escape or resistance to lawful authority.

(A) No person, with purpose to promote or facilitate an escape or resistance to lawful authority, shall convey into a detention facility, or provide anyone confined therein with any instrument or thing which may be used for such purposes.

(B) No person who is confined in a detention facility, and with purpose to promote or facilitate an escape or resistance to lawful authority, shall make, procure, conceal, unlawfully possess, or give to another inmate, any instrument or thing which may be used for such purposes.

(C) Whoever violates this section is guilty of aiding escape or resistance to lawful authority, a felony of the fourth degree.

**HISTORY: 134 v H 511 (Eff 1-1-74); 146 v S 2. Eff 7-1-96.**

The effective date is set by section 6 of SB 2.

## § 2921.36 Illegal conveyance of weapons or prohibited items onto grounds of specified governmental facility.

(A) No person shall knowingly convey, or attempt to convey, onto the grounds of a detention facility or of an institution, office building, or other place that is under the control of the department of mental health, the department of developmental disabilities, the department of youth services, or the department of rehabilitation and correction any of the following items:

(1) Any deadly weapon or dangerous ordnance, as defined in section 2923.11 of the Revised Code, or any part of or ammunition for use in such a deadly weapon or dangerous ordnance;

(2) Any drug of abuse, as defined in section 3719.011 [3719.01.1] of the Revised Code;

(3) Any intoxicating liquor, as defined in section 4301.01 of the Revised Code.

(B) Division (A) of this section does not apply to any person who conveys or attempts to convey an item onto the grounds of a detention facility or of an institution, office building, or other place under the control of the department of mental health, the department of developmental disabilities, the department of youth services, or the department of rehabilitation and correction pursuant to the written authorization of the person in charge of the detention facility or the institution, office building, or other place and in accordance with the written rules of the detention facility or the institution, office building, or other place.

(C) No person shall knowingly deliver, or attempt to deliver, to any person who is confined in a detention facility, to a child confined in a youth services facility, to a prisoner who is temporarily released from confinement for a work assignment, or to any patient in an institution under the control of the department of mental health or the department of developmental disabilities, any item listed in division (A)(1), (2), or (3) of this section.

(D) No person shall knowingly deliver, or attempt to deliver, cash to any person who is confined in a detention facility, to a child confined in a youth services facility, or to a prisoner who is temporarily released from confinement for a work assignment.

(E) No person shall knowingly deliver, or attempt to deliver, to any person who is confined in a detention facility, to a child confined in a youth services facility, or to a prisoner who is temporarily released from confinement for a work assignment a cellular telephone, two-way radio, or other electronic communications device.

(F)(1) It is an affirmative defense to a charge under division (A)(1) of this section that the weapon or dangerous ordnance in question was being transported in a motor vehicle for any lawful purpose, that it was not on the actor's person, and, if the weapon or dangerous ordnance in question was a firearm, that it was unloaded and was being carried in a closed package, box, or case or in a compartment that can be reached only by leaving the vehicle.

(2) It is an affirmative defense to a charge under division (C) of this section that the actor was not otherwise prohibited by law from delivering the item to the confined person, the child, the prisoner, or the patient and that either of the following applies:

(a) The actor was permitted by the written rules of the detention facility or the institution, office building, or other place to deliver the item to the confined person or the patient.

(b) The actor was given written authorization by the person in charge of the detention facility or the institution, office building, or other place to deliver the item to the confined person or the patient.

(G)(1) Whoever violates division (A)(1) of this section or commits a violation of division (C) of this section involving an item listed in division (A)(1) of this section is guilty of illegal conveyance of weapons onto the grounds of a specified governmental facility, a felony of the third degree. If the offender is an officer or employee of the department of rehabilitation and correction, the court shall impose a mandatory prison term.

(2) Whoever violates division (A)(2) of this section or commits a violation of division (C) of this section involving any drug of abuse is guilty of illegal conveyance of drugs of abuse onto the grounds of a specified governmental facility, a felony of the third degree. If the offender is an officer or employee of the department of rehabilitation and correction or of the department of youth services, the court shall impose a mandatory prison term.

(3) Whoever violates division (A)(3) of this section or commits a violation of division (C) of this section involving any intoxicating liquor is guilty of illegal conveyance of intoxicating liquor onto the grounds of a specified governmental facility, a misdemeanor of the second degree.

(4) Whoever violates division (D) of this section is guilty of illegal conveyance of cash onto the grounds of a detention facility, a misdemeanor of the first degree. If the offender previously has been convicted of or pleaded guilty to a violation of division (D) of this section, illegal conveyance of cash onto the grounds of a detention facility is a felony of the fifth degree.

(5) Whoever violates division (E) of this section is guilty of illegal conveyance of a communications device onto the grounds of a specified governmental facility, a misdemeanor of the first degree, or if the offender previously has been convicted of or pleaded guilty to a violation of division (E) of this section, a felony of the fifth degree.

**HISTORY: 137 v H 630 (Eff 5-23-78); 138 v H 900 (Eff 7-1-80); 143 v S 258 (Eff 11-20-90); 145 v H 571 (Eff 10-6-94); 146 v S 2 (Eff 7-1-96); 147 v S 111 (Eff 3-17-98); 148 v H 357 (Eff 8-10-2000); 149 v H 510. Eff 3-31-2003; 152 v H 130, § 1, eff. 4-7-09; 153 v S 79, § 1, eff. 10-6-09.**

## § 2921.37 Arrest powers of detention facility chief.

The person in charge of a detention facility shall, on the grounds of the detention facility, have the same power as a peace officer, as defined in section 2935.01 of the Revised Code, to arrest a person who violates section 2921.36 of the Revised Code.

**HISTORY: 137 v H 630. Eff 5-23-78.**

## § 2921.38 Harassment with bodily substance.

(A) No person who is confined in a detention facility, with intent to harass, annoy, threaten, or alarm another person, shall cause or attempt to cause the other person to come into contact with blood, semen, urine, feces, or another bodily substance by throwing the bodily substance at the other person, by expelling the bodily substance upon the other person, or in any other manner.

(B) No person, with intent to harass, annoy, threaten, or alarm a law enforcement officer, shall cause or attempt to cause the law enforcement officer to come into contact with blood, semen, urine, feces, or another bodily substance by throwing the bodily substance at the law enforcement officer, by expelling the bodily substance upon the law enforcement officer, or in any other manner.

(C) No person, with knowledge that the person is a carrier of the virus that causes acquired immunodeficiency syndrome, is a carrier of a hepatitis virus, or is infected with tuberculosis and with intent to harass, annoy, threaten, or alarm another person, shall cause or attempt to cause the other person to come into contact with blood, semen, urine, feces, or another bodily substance by throwing the bodily substance at the other person, by expelling the bodily substance upon the other person, or in any other manner.

(D) Whoever violates this section is guilty of harassment with a bodily substance. A violation of division (A) or (B) of this section is a felony of the fifth degree. A violation of division (C) of this section is a felony of the third degree.

(E)(1) The court, on request of the prosecutor, or the law enforcement authority responsible for the investigation of the violation, shall cause a person who allegedly has committed a violation of this section to submit to one or more appropriate tests to determine if the person is a carrier of the virus that causes acquired immunodeficiency syndrome, is a carrier of a hepatitis virus, or is infected with tuberculosis.

(2) The court shall charge the offender with the costs of the test or tests ordered under division (E)(1) of this section unless the court determines that the accused is unable to pay, in which case the costs shall be charged to the entity that operates the detention facility in which the alleged offense occurred.

(F) This section does not apply to a person who is hospitalized, institutionalized, or confined in a facility operated by the department of mental health or the department of developmental disabilities.

**HISTORY: 147 v H 37. Eff 6-11-97; 151 v H 259, § 1, eff. 4-4-07; 153 v S 79, § 1, eff. 10-6-09.**

### [PECULATION AND DERELICTION]

## § 2921.41 Theft in office; restitution; withholding of retirement benefits.

(A) No public official or party official shall commit any theft offense, as defined in division (K) of section 2913.01 of the Revised Code, when either of the following applies:

(1) The offender uses the offender's office in aid of committing the offense or permits or assents to its use in aid of committing the offense;

(2) The property or service involved is owned by this state, any other state, the United States, a county, a municipal corporation, a township, or any political subdivision, department, or agency of any of them, is owned by a political party, or is part of a political campaign fund.

(B) Whoever violates this section is guilty of theft in office. Except as otherwise provided in this division, theft in office is a felony of the fifth degree. If the value of property or services stolen is one thousand dollars or more and is less than seven thousand five hundred dollars, theft in office is a felony of the fourth degree. If the value of property or services stolen is seven thousand five hundred dollars or more, theft in office is a felony of the third degree.

(C)(1) A public official or party official who pleads guilty to theft in office and whose plea is accepted by the court or a public official or party official against whom a verdict or finding of guilt for committing theft in office is returned is forever disqualified from holding any public office, employment, or position of trust in this state.

(2)(a) A court that imposes sentence for a violation of this section based on conduct described in division (A)(2) of this section shall require the public official or party official who is convicted of or pleads guilty to the offense to make restitution for all of the property or the service that is the subject of the offense, in addition to the term of imprisonment and any fine imposed. A court that imposes sentence for a violation of this section based on conduct described in division (A)(1) of this section and that determines at trial that this state or a political subdivision of this state if the offender is a public official, or a political party in the United States or this state if the offender is a party official, suffered actual loss as a result of the offense shall require the offender to make restitution to the state, political subdivision, or political party for all of the actual loss experienced, in addition to the term of imprisonment and any fine imposed.

(b)(i) In any case in which a sentencing court is required to order restitution under division (C)(2)(a) of this section and in which the offender, at the time of the commission of the offense or at any other time, was a member of the public employees retirement system, the Ohio police and fire pension fund, the state teachers retirement system, the school employees retirement system, or the state highway patrol retirement system; was an electing employee, as defined in section 3305.01 of the Revised Code, participating in an alternative retirement plan provided pursuant to Chapter 3305. of the Revised Code; was a participating employee or continuing member, as defined in section 148.01 of the Revised Code, in a deferred compensation program offered by the Ohio public employees deferred compensation board; was an officer or employee of a municipal corporation who was a participant in a deferred compensation program offered by that municipal corporation; was an officer or employee of a government unit, as defined in section 148.06 of the Revised Code, who was a participant in a deferred compensation program offered by that government unit, or was a participating employee, continuing member, or participant in any deferred compensation program described in this division and a member of a retirement system specified in this division or a retirement system of a municipal corporation, the entity to which restitution is to be made may file a motion with the sentencing court specifying any retirement system, any provider as defined in section 3305.01 of the Revised Code, and any deferred compensation program of which the offender was a member, electing employee, participating employee, continuing member, or participant and requesting the court to issue an order requiring the specified retirement system, the specified provider under the alternative retirement plan, or the specified deferred compensation program, or, if more than one is specified in the motion, the applicable combination of these, to withhold the amount required as restitution from any payment that is to be made under a pension, annuity, or allowance, under an option in the alternative retirement plan, under a participant account, as defined in section 148.01 of the Revised Code, or under any other type of benefit, other than a survivorship benefit, that has been or is in the future granted to the offender, from any payment of accumulated employee contributions standing to the offender's credit with that retirement system, that provider of the option under the alternative retirement plan, or that deferred compensation program, or, if more than one is specified in the motion, the applicable combination of these, and from any payment of any other amounts to be paid to the offender upon the offender's withdrawal of the offender's contributions pursuant to Chapter 145., 148., 742., 3307., 3309., or 5505. of the Revised Code. A motion described in this division may be filed at any time subsequent to the conviction of the offender or entry of a guilty plea. Upon the filing of the motion, the clerk of the court in which the motion is filed shall notify the offender, the specified retirement system, the specified provider under the alternative retirement plan, or the specified deferred compensation program, or, if more than one is specified in the motion, the applicable combination of these, in writing, of all of the following: that the motion was filed; that the offender will be granted a hearing on the issuance of the requested order if the offender files a written request for a hearing with the clerk prior to the expiration of thirty days after the offender receives the notice; that, if a hearing is requested, the court will schedule a hearing as soon as possible and notify the offender, any specified retirement system, any specified provider under an alternative retirement plan, and any specified deferred compensation program of the date, time, and place of the hearing; that, if a hearing is conducted, it will be limited only to a consideration of whether the offender can show good cause why the requested order should not be issued; that, if a hearing is conducted, the court will not issue the requested order if the court determines, based on evidence presented at the hearing by the offender, that there is good cause for the requested order not to be issued; that the court will issue the requested order if a hearing is not requested or if a hearing is conducted but the court does not determine, based on evidence presented at the hearing by the offender, that there is good cause for the requested order not to be issued; and that, if the requested order is issued, any retirement system, any provider under an alternative retirement plan, and any deferred compensation program specified in the motion will be required to withhold the amount required as restitution from payments to the offender.

(ii) In any case in which a sentencing court is required to order restitution under division (C)(2)(a) of this section and in which a motion requesting the issuance of a withholding order as described in division (C)(2)(b)(i) of this section is filed, the offender may receive a hearing on the motion by delivering a written request for a hearing to the court prior to the expiration of thirty days after the offender's receipt of the notice provided pursuant to division (C)(2)(b)(i) of this section. If a request for a hearing is made by the offender within the prescribed time, the court shall schedule a hearing as soon as possible after the request is made and shall notify the offender, the specified retirement system, the specified provider under the alternative retirement plan, or the specified deferred compensation program, or, if more than one is specified in the motion, the applicable combination of these, of the date, time, and place of the hearing. A hearing scheduled under this division shall be limited to a consideration of whether there is good cause, based on evidence presented by the offender, for the requested order not to be issued. If the court determines, based on evidence presented by the offender, that there is good cause for the order not to be issued, the court shall deny the motion and shall not issue the requested order. If the offender does not request a hearing within the prescribed time or if the court conducts a hearing but does not determine, based on evidence presented by the offender, that there is good cause for the order not to be issued, the court shall order the specified retirement system, the specified provider under the alternative retirement plan, or the specified deferred compensation program, or, if more than one is specified in the motion, the applicable combination of these, to withhold the amount required as restitution under division (C)(2)(a) of this section from any payments to be made under a pension, annuity, or allowance, under a participant account, as defined in section 148.01 of the Revised Code, under an option in the alternative retirement plan, or under any other type of benefit, other than a survivorship benefit, that has been or is in the future granted to the offender, from any payment of accumulated employee contributions standing to the offender's credit with that retirement system, that provider under the alternative retirement plan, or that deferred compensation program, or, if more than one is specified in the motion, the applicable combination of these, and from any payment of any other amounts to be paid to the offender upon the offender's withdrawal of the offender's contributions pursuant to Chapter 145., 148., 742., 3307., 3309., or 5505. of the Revised Code, and to continue the withholding for that purpose, in accordance with the order, out of each payment to be made on or after the date of issuance of the order, until further order of the court. Upon receipt of an order issued under this division, the public employees retirement system, the Ohio police and fire pension fund, the state teachers retirement system, the school employees retirement system, the state highway patrol retirement system, a municipal corporation retirement system, the provider under the alternative retirement plan, and the deferred compensation program offered by the Ohio public employees deferred compensation board, a municipal corporation, or a government unit, as defined in section 148.06 of the Revised Code, whichever are applicable, shall withhold the amount required as restitution, in accordance with the order, from any such payments and immediately shall forward the amount withheld to the clerk of the court in which the order was issued for payment to the entity to which restitution is to be made.

(iii) Service of a notice required by division (C)(2)(b)(i) or (ii) of this section shall be effected in the same manner as provided in the Rules of Civil Procedure for the service of process.

(D) Upon the filing of charges against a person under this section, the prosecutor, as defined in section 2935.01 of the Revised Code, who is assigned the case shall send written notice that charges have been filed against that person to the public employees retirement system, the Ohio police and fire pension fund, the state teachers retirement system, the school employees retirement system, the state highway patrol retirement system, the provider under an alternative retirement plan, any municipal corporation retirement system in this state, and the deferred compensation program offered by the Ohio public employees deferred compensation board, a municipal corporation, or a government unit, as defined in section 148.06 of the Revised Code. The written notice shall specifically identify the person charged.

**HISTORY: 134 v H 511 (Eff 1-1-74); 140 v H 265 (Eff 9-20-84); 144 v S 300 (Eff 11-5-92); 146 v S 2 (Eff 7-1-96); 146 v H 586 (Eff 3-31-97); 148 v H 222 (Eff 11-2-99); 148 v H 628 (Eff 9-21-2000); 148 v H 535. Eff 4-1-2001; 152 v H 195, § 1, eff. 9-30-08; 2011 HB 86, § 1, eff. Sept. 30, 2011.**

The provisions of § 4 of HB 86 read as follows:

"SECTION 4. The amendments to sections 926.99, 1333.99, 1707.99, 1716.99, 2909.03, 2909.05, 2909.11, 2913.02, 2913.03, 2913.04, 2913.11, 2913.21, 2913.31, 2913.32, 2913.34, 2913.40, 2913.401, 2913.42, 2913.421, 2913.43, 2913.45, 2913.46, 2913.47, 2913.48, 2913.49, 2913.51, 2913.61, 2915.05, 2917.21, 2917.31, 2917.32, 2921.13, 2921.41, 2923.31, and 2981.07, division (B) of section 2929.13, and division (A) of section 2929.14 of the Revised Code that are made in this act apply to a person who commits an offense specified or penalized under those sections on or after the effective date of this section and to a person to whom division (B) of section 1.58 of the Revised Code makes the amendments applicable.

"The provisions of sections 926.99, 1333.99, 1707.99, 1716.99, 2909.03, 2909.05, 2909.11, 2913.02, 2913.03, 2913.04, 2913.11, 2913.21, 2913.31, 2913.32, 2913.34, 2913.40, 2913.401, 2913.42, 2913.421, 2913.43, 2913.45, 2913.46, 2913.47, 2913.48, 2913.49, 2913.51, 2913.61, 2915.05, 2917.21, 2917.31, 2917.32, 2921.13, 2921.41, 2923.31, and 2981.07 of the Revised Code in existence prior to the effective date of this section shall apply to a person upon whom a court imposed sentence prior to the effective date of this section for an offense specified or penalized under those sections. The amendments to sections 926.99, 1333.99, 1707.99, 1716.99, 2909.03, 2909.05, 2909.11, 2913.02, 2913.03, 2913.04, 2913.11, 2913.21, 2913.31, 2913.32, 2913.34, 2913.40, 2913.401, 2913.42, 2913.421, 2913.43, 2913.45, 2913.46, 2913.47, 2913.48, 2913.49, 2913.51, 2913.61, 2915.05, 2917.21, 2917.31, 2917.32, 2921.13, 2921.41, 2923.31, and 2981.07 of the Revised Code that are made in this act do not apply to a person who upon whom a court imposed sentence prior to the effective date of this section for an offense specified or penalized under those sections."

The effective date is set by section 13(A) of HB 535.

## § 2921.42 Having an unlawful interest in a public contract.

(A) No public official shall knowingly do any of the following:

(1) Authorize, or employ the authority or influence of the public official's office to secure authorization of any public contract in which the public official, a member of the public official's family, or any of the public official's business associates has an interest;

(2) Authorize, or employ the authority or influence of the public official's office to secure the investment of public funds in any share, bond, mortgage, or other security, with respect to which the public official, a member of the public official's family, or any of the public official's business associates either has an interest, is an underwriter, or receives any brokerage, origination, or servicing fees;

(3) During the public official's term of office or within one year thereafter, occupy any position of profit in the prosecution of a public contract authorized by the public official or by a legislative body, commission, or board of which the public official was a member at the time of authorization, unless the contract was let by competitive bidding to the lowest and best bidder;

(4) Have an interest in the profits or benefits of a public contract entered into by or for the use of the political subdivision or governmental agency or instrumentality with which the public official is connected;

(5) Have an interest in the profits or benefits of a public contract that is not let by competitive bidding if required by law and that involves more than one hundred fifty dollars.

(B) In the absence of bribery or a purpose to defraud, a public official, member of a public official's family, or any of a public official's business associates shall not be considered as having an interest in a public contract or the investment of public funds, if all of the following apply:

(1) The interest of that person is limited to owning or controlling shares of the corporation, or being a creditor of the corporation or other organization, that is the contractor on the public contract involved, or that is the issuer of the security in which public funds are invested;

(2) The shares owned or controlled by that person do not exceed five per cent of the outstanding shares of the corporation, and the amount due that person as creditor does not exceed five per cent of the total indebtedness of the corporation or other organization;

(3) That person, prior to the time the public contract is entered into, files with the political subdivision or governmental agency or instrumentality involved, an affidavit giving that person's exact status in connection with the corporation or other organization.

(C) This section does not apply to a public contract in which a public official, member of a public official's family, or one of a public official's business associates has an interest, when all of the following apply:

(1) The subject of the public contract is necessary supplies or services for the political subdivision or governmental agency or instrumentality involved;

(2) The supplies or services are unobtainable elsewhere for the same or lower cost, or are being furnished to the political subdivision or governmental agency or instrumentality as part of a continuing course of dealing established prior to the public official's becoming associated with the political subdivision or governmental agency or instrumentality involved;

(3) The treatment accorded the political subdivision or governmental agency or instrumentality is either preferential to or the same as that accorded other customers or clients in similar transactions;

(4) The entire transaction is conducted at arm's length, with full knowledge by the political subdivision or governmental agency or instrumentality involved, of the interest of the public official, member of the public official's family, or business associate, and the public official takes no part in the deliberations or decision of the political subdivision or governmental agency or instrumentality with respect to the public contract.

(D) Division (A)(4) of this section does not prohibit participation by a public employee in any housing program funded by public moneys if the public employee otherwise qualifies for the program and does not use the authority or influence of the public employee's office or employment to secure benefits from the program and if the moneys are to be used on the primary residence of the public employee. Such participation does not constitute an unlawful interest in a public contract in violation of this section.

(E) Whoever violates this section is guilty of having an unlawful interest in a public contract. Violation of division (A)(1) or (2) of this section is a felony of the fourth degree. Violation of division (A)(3), (4), or (5) of this section is a misdemeanor of the first degree.

(F) It is not a violation of this section for a prosecuting attorney to appoint assistants and employees in accordance with sections 309.06 and 2921.421 [2921.42.1] of the Revised Code, for a chief legal officer of a municipal corporation or an official designated as prosecutor in a municipal corporation to appoint assistants and employees in accordance with sections 733.621 [733.62.1] and 2921.421 [2921.42.1] of the Revised Code, or for a township law director appointed under section 504.15 of the Revised Code to appoint assistants and employees in accordance with sections 504.151 [504.15.1] and 2921.421 [2921.42.1] of the Revised Code.

(G) This section does not apply to a public contract in which a township trustee in a township with a population of five thousand or less in its unincorporated area, a member of the township trustee's family, or one of the township trustee's business associates has an interest, if all of the following apply:

(1) The subject of the public contract is necessary supplies or services for the township and the amount of the contract is less than five thousand dollars per year.

(2) The supplies or services are being furnished to the township as part of a continuing course of dealing established before the township trustee held that office with the township;

(3) The treatment accorded the township is either preferential to or the same as that accorded other customers or clients in similar transactions;

(4) The entire transaction is conducted with full knowledge by the township of the interest of the township trustee, member of the township trustee's family, or the township trustee's business associate.

(H) Any public contract in which a public official, a member of the public official's family, or any of the public official's business associates has an interest in violation of this section is void and unenforceable. Any contract securing the investment of public funds in which a public official, a member of the public official's family, or any of the public official's business associates has an interest, is an underwriter, or receives any brokerage, origination, or servicing fees and that was entered into in violation of this section is void and unenforceable.

(I) As used in this section:

(1) "Public contract" means any of the following:

(a) The purchase or acquisition, or a contract for the purchase or acquisition, of property or services by or for the use of the state, any of its political subdivisions, or any agency or instrumentality of either, including the employment of an individual by the state, any of its political subdivisions, or any agency or instrumentality of either;

(b) A contract for the design, construction, alteration, repair, or maintenance of any public property.

(2) "Chief legal officer" has the same meaning as in section 733.621 [733.62.1] of the Revised Code.

**HISTORY: 134 v H 511 (Eff 1-1-74); 144 v S 359 (Eff 12-22-92); 145 v H 152 (Eff 7-1-93); 145 v H 285 (Eff 3-2-94); 145 v H 150. Eff 6-23-94; 152 v H 119, § 101.01, eff. 9-29-07.**

The effective date is set by § 812.03 of 152 v H 119.

The provisions of § 824.03 of 152 v H 119 read in part as follows:

SECTION 824.03. The General Assembly, applying the principle stated in division (B) of section 1.52 of the Revised Code that amendments are to be harmonized if reasonably capable of simultaneous operation, finds that the following sections, presented in this act as composites of the sections as amended by the acts indicated, are the resulting versions of the sections in effect prior to the effective date of the sections as presented in this act:

* * *

Section 2921.42 of the Revised Code as amended by both Sub. H.B. 150 and Am. Sub. H.B. 285 of the 120th General Assembly.

* * *

The finding in this section takes effect at the same time as the section referenced in the finding takes effect.

## § 2921.421 Conditions for prosecuting attorney's appointment of assistants and employees who are associated in the private practice of law.

(A) As used in this section:

(1) "Chief legal officer" has the same meaning as in section 733.621 [733.62.1] of the Revised Code.

(2) "Political subdivision" means a county, a municipal corporation, or a township that adopts a limited home rule government under Chapter 504. of the Revised Code.

(B) A prosecuting attorney may appoint assistants and employees, except a member of the family of the prosecuting attorney, in accordance with division (B) of section 309.06 of the Revised Code, a chief legal officer of a municipal corporation or an official designated as prosecutor in a municipal corporation may appoint assistants and employees, except a member of the family of the chief legal officer or official designated as prosecutor, in accordance with section 733.621 [733.62.1] of the Revised Code, and a township law director appointed under section 504.15 of the Revised Code may appoint assistants and employees, except a member of the family of the township law director, in accordance with section 504.151 [504.15.1] of the Revised Code, if all of the following apply:

(1) The services to be furnished by the appointee or employee are necessary services for the political subdivision or are authorized by the legislative authority, governing board, or other contracting authority of the political subdivision.

(2) The treatment accorded the political subdivision is either preferential to or the same as that accorded other clients or customers of the appointee or employee in similar transactions, or the legislative authority, governing board, or other contracting authority of the political subdivision, in its sole discretion, determines that the compensation and other terms of appointment or employ-

ment of the appointee or employee are fair and reasonable to the political subdivision.

(3) The appointment or employment is made after prior written disclosure to the legislative authority, governing board, or other contracting authority of the political subdivision of the business relationship between the prosecuting attorney, the chief legal officer or official designated as prosecutor in a municipal corporation, or the township law director and the appointee or employee thereof. In the case of a municipal corporation, the disclosure may be made or evidenced in an ordinance, resolution, or other document that does either or both of the following:

(a) Authorizes the furnishing of services as required under division (B)(1) of this section;

(b) Determines that the compensation and other terms of appointment or employment of the appointee or employee are fair and reasonable to the political subdivision as required under division (B)(2) of this section.

(4) The prosecuting attorney, the elected chief legal officer, or the township law director does not receive any distributive share or other portion, in whole or in part, of the earnings of the business associate, partner, or employee paid by the political subdivision to the business associate, partner, or employee for services rendered for the political subdivision.

(C) It is not a violation of this section or of section 102.03 or 2921.42 of the Revised Code for the legislative authority, the governing board, or other contracting authority of a political subdivision to engage the services of any firm that practices the profession of law upon the terms approved by the legislative authority, the governing board, or the contracting authority, or to designate any partner, officer, or employee of that firm as a nonelected public official or employee of the political subdivision, whether the public office or position of employment is created by statute, charter, ordinance, resolution, or other legislative or administrative action.

**HISTORY: 145 v H 285 (Eff 3-2-94); 148 v H 187. Eff 9-20-99.**

## § 2921.43 Soliciting or receiving improper compensation.

(A) No public servant shall knowingly solicit or accept, and no person shall knowingly promise or give to a public servant, either of the following:

(1) Any compensation, other than as allowed by divisions (G), (H), and (I) of section 102.03 of the Revised Code or other provisions of law, to perform the public servant's official duties, to perform any other act or service in the public servant's public capacity, for the general performance of the duties of the public servant's public office or public employment, or as a supplement to the public servant's public compensation;

(2) Additional or greater fees or costs than are allowed by law to perform the public servant's official duties.

(B) No public servant for the public servant's own personal or business use, and no person for the person's own personal or business use or for the personal or business use of a public servant or party official, shall solicit or accept anything of value in consideration of either of the following:

(1) Appointing or securing, maintaining, or renewing the appointment of any person to any public office, employment, or agency;

(2) Preferring, or maintaining the status of, any public employee with respect to compensation, duties, placement, location, promotion, or other material aspects of employment.

(C) No person for the benefit of a political party, campaign committee, legislative campaign fund, political action committee, or political contributing entity shall coerce any contribution in consideration of either of the following:

(1) Appointing or securing, maintaining, or renewing the appointment of any person to any public office, employment, or agency;

(2) Preferring, or maintaining the status of, any public employee with respect to compensation, duties, placement, location, promotion, or other material aspects of employment.

(D) Whoever violates this section is guilty of soliciting improper compensation, a misdemeanor of the first degree.

(E) A public servant who is convicted of a violation of this section is disqualified from holding any public office, employment, or position of trust in this state for a period of seven years from the date of conviction.

(F) Divisions (A), (B), and (C) of this section do not prohibit a person from making voluntary contributions to a political party, campaign committee, legislative campaign fund, political action committee, or political contributing entity or prohibit a political party, campaign committee, legislative campaign fund, political action committee, or political contributing entity from accepting voluntary contributions.

**HISTORY: 134 v H 511 (Eff 1-1-74); 135 v S 46 (Eff 7-23-74); 141 v H 300 (Eff 9-17-86); 146 v S 8 (Eff 8-23-95); 147 v S 134. Eff 7-13-98; 150 v H 1, § 1, eff. 3-31-05; 151 v S 115, § 1, eff. 4-26-05.**

See provisions of § 3 of 151 v S 115 following RC § 2921.01.

## § 2921.431 Repealed, 146 v S 8, § 2 [136 v H 784]. Eff 8-23-95.

This section concerned solicitation of improper contributions by county officers. See now RC § 3517.09.2.

## § 2921.44 Dereliction of duty.

(A) No law enforcement officer shall negligently do any of the following:

(1) Fail to serve a lawful warrant without delay;

(2) Fail to prevent or halt the commission of an offense or to apprehend an offender, when it is in the law enforcement officer's power to do so alone or with available assistance.

(B) No law enforcement, ministerial, or judicial officer shall negligently fail to perform a lawful duty in a criminal case or proceeding.

(C) No officer, having charge of a detention facility, shall negligently do any of the following:

(1) Allow the detention facility to become littered or unsanitary;

(2) Fail to provide persons confined in the detention facility with adequate food, clothing, bedding, shelter, and medical attention;

(3) Fail to control an unruly prisoner, or to prevent intimidation of or physical harm to a prisoner by another;

(4) Allow a prisoner to escape;

(5) Fail to observe any lawful and reasonable regulation for the management of the detention facility.

(D) No public official of the state shall recklessly create a deficiency, incur a liability, or expend a greater sum than is appropriated by the general assembly for the use in any one year of the department, agency, or institution of the state with which the public official is connected.

(E) No public servant shall recklessly fail to perform a duty expressly imposed by law with respect to the public servant's office, or recklessly do any act expressly forbidden by law with respect to the public servant's office.

(F) Whoever violates this section is guilty of dereliction of duty, a misdemeanor of the second degree.

(G) As used in this section, "public servant" includes an officer or employee of a contractor as defined in section 9.08 of the Revised Code.

**HISTORY: 134 v H 511 (Eff 1-1-74); 148 v S 12. Eff 6-8-2000.**

## § 2921.45 Interfering with civil rights.

(A) No public servant, under color of his office, employment, or authority, shall knowingly deprive, or conspire or attempt to deprive any person of a constitutional or statutory right.

(B) Whoever violates this section is guilty of interfering with civil rights, a misdemeanor of the first degree.

**HISTORY: 134 v H 511. Eff 1-1-74.**

[IMPERSONATING PEACE OFFICER]

## § 2921.51 Impersonating peace officer, private police officer, investigator of the bureau of criminal identification and investigation, or federal law enforcement officer.

(A) As used in this section:

(1) "Peace officer" means a sheriff, deputy sheriff, marshal, deputy marshal, member of the organized police department of a municipal corporation, or township constable, who is employed by a political subdivision of this state; a member of a police force employed by a metropolitan housing authority under division (D) of section 3735.31 of the Revised Code; a member of a police force employed by a regional transit authority under division (Y) of section 306.35 of the Revised Code; a state university law enforcement officer appointed under section 3345.04 of the Revised Code; a veterans' home police officer appointed under section 5907.02 of the Revised Code; a special police officer employed by a port authority under section 4582.04 or 4582.28 of the Revised Code; an officer, agent, or employee of the state or any of its agencies, instrumentalities, or political subdivisions, upon whom, by statute, a duty to conserve the peace or to enforce all or certain laws is imposed and the authority to arrest violators is conferred, within limits of that statutory duty and authority; or a state highway patrol trooper whose primary duties are to preserve the peace, to protect life and property, and to enforce the laws, ordinances, or rules of the state or any of its political subdivisions.

(2) "Private police officer" means any security guard, special police officer, private detective, or other person who is privately employed in a police capacity.

(3) "Federal law enforcement officer" means an employee of the United States who serves in a position the duties of which are primarily the investigation, apprehension, or detention of individuals suspected or convicted of offenses under the criminal laws of the United States.

(4) "Impersonate" means to act the part of, assume the identity of, wear the uniform or any part of the uniform of, or display the identification of a particular person or of a member of a class of persons with purpose to make another person believe that the actor is that particular person or is a member of that class of persons.

(5) "Investigator of the bureau of criminal identification and investigation" has the same meaning as in section 2903.11 of the Revised Code.

(B) No person shall impersonate a peace officer, private police officer, federal law enforcement officer, or investigator of the bureau of criminal identification and investigation.

(C) No person, by impersonating a peace officer, private police officer, federal law enforcement officer, or investigator of the bureau of criminal identification and investigation, shall arrest or detain any person, search any person, or search the property of any person.

(D) No person, with purpose to commit or facilitate the commission of an offense, shall impersonate a peace officer, private police officer, federal law enforcement officer, officer, agent, or employee of the state, or investigator of the bureau of criminal identification and investigation.

(E) No person shall commit a felony while impersonating a peace officer, private police officer, federal law enforcement officer, officer, agent, or employee of the state, or investigator of the bureau of criminal identification and investigation.

(F) It is an affirmative defense to a charge under division (B) of this section that the impersonation of the peace officer, private police officer, or investigator of the bureau of criminal identification and investigation was for a lawful purpose.

(G) Whoever violates division (B) of this section is guilty of a misdemeanor of the fourth degree. Whoever violates division (C) or (D) of this section is guilty of a misdemeanor of the first degree. If the purpose of a violation of division (D) of this section is to commit or facilitate the commission of a felony, a violation of division (D) is a felony of the fourth degree. Whoever violates division (E) of this section is guilty of a felony of the third degree.

**HISTORY: 142 v H 708 (Eff 4-19-88); 144 v S 144 (Eff 8-8-91); 146 v S 2 (Eff 7-1-96); 148 v S 137 (Eff 5-17-2000); 149 v H 675. Eff 3-14-2003; 151 v S 281, § 1, eff. 1-4-07; 151 v H 259, § 1, eff. 4-4-07; 153 v H 1, § 101.01, eff. 10-16-09.**

The effective date is set by § 812.10 of 153 v H 1.

The provisions of 815.10 of 153 v H 1 read as follows:

SECTION 815.10. The General Assembly, applying the principle stated in division (B) of section 1.52 of the Revised Code that amendments are to be harmonized if reasonably capable of simultaneous operation, finds that the following sections, presented in this act as composites of the sections as amended by the acts indicated, are the resulting versions of the sections in effect prior to the effective date of the sections as presented in this act:

° ° °

Section 2921.51 of the Revised Code as amended by Sub. H.B. 259 and Sub. S.B. 281, both of the 126th General Assembly.

° ° °

**Analogous to former RC § 2921.51 (136 v H 1144; 137 v H 588; 140 v H 129; 142 v H 231; 142 v H 261), repealed 142 v H 708, § 2, eff 4-19-88.**

## § 2921.52 Using sham legal process.

(A) As used in this section:

(1) "Lawfully issued" means adopted, issued, or rendered in accordance with the United States constitution, the constitution of a state, and the applicable statutes, rules, regulations, and ordinances of the United States, a state, and the political subdivisions of a state.

(2) "State" means a state of the United States, including without limitation, the state legislature, the highest court of the state that has statewide jurisdiction, the offices of all elected state officers, and all departments, boards, offices, commissions, agencies, institutions, and other instrumentalities of the state. "State" does not include the political subdivisions of the state.

(3) "Political subdivisions" means municipal corporations, townships, counties, school districts, and all other bodies corporate and politic that are organized under state law and are responsible for governmental activities only in geographical areas smaller than that of a state.

(4) "Sham legal process" means an instrument that meets all of the following conditions:

(a) It is not lawfully issued.

(b) It purports to do any of the following:

(i) To be a summons, subpoena, judgment, or order of a court, a law enforcement officer, or a legislative, executive, or administrative body.

(ii) To assert jurisdiction over or determine the legal or equitable status, rights, duties, powers, or privileges of any person or property.

(iii) To require or authorize the search, seizure, indictment, arrest, trial, or sentencing of any person or property.

(c) It is designed to make another person believe that it is lawfully issued.

(B) No person shall, knowing the sham legal process to be sham legal process, do any of the following:

(1) Knowingly issue, display, deliver, distribute, or otherwise use sham legal process;

(2) Knowingly use sham legal process to arrest, detain, search, or seize any person or the property of another person;

(3) Knowingly commit or facilitate the commission of an offense, using sham legal process;

(4) Knowingly commit a felony by using sham legal process.

(C) It is an affirmative defense to a charge under division (B)(1) or (2) of this section that the use of sham legal process was for a lawful purpose.

(D) Whoever violates this section is guilty of using sham legal process. A violation of division (B)(1) of this section is a misdemeanor of the fourth degree. A violation of division (B)(2) or (3) of this section is a misdemeanor of the first degree, except that, if the purpose of a violation of division (B)(3) of this section is to commit or facilitate the commission of a felony, a violation of division (B)(3) of this section is a felony of the fourth degree. A violation of division (B)(4) of this section is a felony of the third degree.

(E) A person who violates this section is liable in a civil action to any person harmed by the violation for injury, death, or loss to person or property incurred as a result of the commission of the offense and for reasonable attorney's fees, court costs, and other expenses incurred as a result of prosecuting the civil action commenced under this division. A civil action under this division is not the exclusive remedy of a person who incurs injury, death, or loss to person or property as a result of a violation of this section.

**HISTORY: 146 v H 644. Eff 11-6-96.**

# CHAPTER 2923: CONSPIRACY, ATTEMPT, AND COMPLICITY; WEAPONS CONTROL; CORRUPT ACTIVITY



## [CONSPIRACY, ATTEMPT, AND COMPLICITY]

### § 2923.01 Conspiracy.

(A) No person, with purpose to commit or to promote or facilitate the commission of aggravated murder, murder, kidnapping, abduction, compelling prostitution, promoting prostitution, trafficking in persons, aggravated arson, arson, aggravated robbery, robbery, aggravated burglary, burglary, trespassing in a habitation when a person is present or likely to be present, engaging in a pattern of corrupt activity, corrupting another with drugs, a felony drug trafficking, manufacturing, processing, or possession offense, theft of drugs, or illegal processing of drug documents, the commission of a felony offense of unauthorized use of a vehicle, illegally transmitting multiple commercial electronic mail messages or unauthorized access of a computer in violation of section 2923.421 of the Revised Code, or the commission of a violation of any provision of Chapter 3734. of the Revised Code, other than section 3734.18 of the Revised Code, that relates to hazardous wastes, shall do either of the following:

(1) With another person or persons, plan or aid in planning the commission of any of the specified offenses;

(2) Agree with another person or persons that one or more of them will engage in conduct that facilitates the commission of any of the specified offenses.

(B) No person shall be convicted of conspiracy unless a substantial overt act in furtherance of the conspiracy is alleged and proved to have been done by the accused or a person with whom the accused conspired, subsequent to the accused's entrance into the conspiracy. For purposes of this section, an overt act is substantial when it is of a character that manifests a purpose on the part of the actor that the object of the conspiracy should be completed.

(C) When the offender knows or has reasonable cause to believe that a person with whom the offender conspires also has conspired or is conspiring with another to commit the same offense, the offender is guilty of conspiring with that other person, even though the other person's identity may be unknown to the offender.

(D) It is no defense to a charge under this section that, in retrospect, commission of the offense that was the object of the conspiracy was impossible under the circumstances.

(E) A conspiracy terminates when the offense or offenses that are its objects are committed or when it is abandoned by all conspirators. In the absence of abandonment, it is no defense to a charge under this section that no offense that was the object of the conspiracy was committed.

(F) A person who conspires to commit more than one offense is guilty of only one conspiracy, when the offenses are the object of the same agreement or continuous conspiratorial relationship.

(G) When a person is convicted of committing or attempting to commit a specific offense or of complicity in the commission of or attempt to commit the specific offense, the person shall not be convicted of conspiracy involving the same offense.

(H)(1) No person shall be convicted of conspiracy upon the testimony of a person with whom the defendant conspired, unsupported by other evidence.

(2) If a person with whom the defendant allegedly has conspired testifies against the defendant in a case in which the defendant is charged with conspiracy and if the testimony is supported by other evidence, the court, when it charges the jury, shall state substantially the following:

"The testimony of an accomplice that is supported by other evidence does not become inadmissible because of the accomplice's complicity, moral turpitude, or self-interest, but the admitted or claimed complicity of a witness may affect the witness' credibility and make the witness' testimony subject to grave suspicion, and require that it be weighed with great caution.

It is for you, as jurors, in the light of all the facts presented to you from the witness stand, to evaluate such testimony and to determine its quality and worth or its lack of quality and worth."

(3) "Conspiracy," as used in division (H)(1) of this section, does not include any conspiracy that results in an attempt to commit an offense or in the commission of an offense.

(I) The following are affirmative defenses to a charge of conspiracy:

(1) After conspiring to commit an offense, the actor thwarted the success of the conspiracy under circumstances manifesting a complete and voluntary renunciation of the actor's criminal purpose.

(2) After conspiring to commit an offense, the actor abandoned the conspiracy prior to the commission of or attempt to commit any offense that was the object of the conspiracy, either by advising all other conspirators of the actor's abandonment, or by informing any law enforcement authority of the existence of the conspiracy and of the actor's participation in the conspiracy.

(J) Whoever violates this section is guilty of conspiracy, which is one of the following:

(1) A felony of the first degree, when one of the objects of the conspiracy is aggravated murder, murder, or an offense for which the maximum penalty is imprisonment for life;

(2) A felony of the next lesser degree than the most serious offense that is the object of the conspiracy, when the most serious offense that is the object of the conspiracy is a felony of the first, second, third, or fourth degree;

(3) A felony punishable by a fine of not more than twenty-five thousand dollars or imprisonment for not more than eighteen months, or both, when the offense that is the object of the conspiracy is a violation of any provision of Chapter 3734. of the Revised Code, other than section 3734.18 of the Revised Code, that relates to hazardous wastes;

(4) A misdemeanor of the first degree, when the most serious offense that is the object of the conspiracy is a felony of the fifth degree.

(K) This section does not define a separate conspiracy offense or penalty where conspiracy is defined as an offense by one or more sections of the Revised Code, other than this section. In such a case, however:

(1) With respect to the offense specified as the object of the conspiracy in the other section or sections, division (A) of this section defines the voluntary act or acts and culpable mental state necessary to constitute the conspiracy;

(2) Divisions (B) to (I) of this section are incorporated by reference in the conspiracy offense defined by the other section or sections of the Revised Code.

(L)(1) In addition to the penalties that otherwise are imposed for conspiracy, a person who is found guilty of conspiracy to engage in a pattern of corrupt activity is subject to divisions (B)(2) and (3) of section 2923.32, division (A) of section 2981.04, and division (D) of section 2981.06 of the Revised Code.

(2) If a person is convicted of or pleads guilty to conspiracy and if the most serious offense that is the object of the conspiracy is a felony drug trafficking, manufacturing, processing, or possession offense, in addition to the penalties or sanctions that may be imposed for the conspiracy under division (J)(2) or (4) of this section and Chapter 2929. of the Revised Code, both of the following apply:

(a) The provisions of divisions (D), (F), and (G) of section 2925.03, division (D) of section 2925.04, division (D) of section 2925.05, division (D) of section 2925.06, and division (E) of section 2925.11 of the Revised Code that pertain to mandatory and additional fines, driver's or commercial driver's license or permit suspensions, and professionally licensed persons and that would apply under the appropriate provisions of those divisions to a person who is convicted of or pleads guilty to the felony drug trafficking, manufacturing, processing, or possession offense that is the most serious offense that is the basis of the conspiracy shall apply to the person who is convicted of or pleads guilty to the conspiracy as if the person had been convicted of or pleaded guilty to the felony drug trafficking, manufacturing, processing, or possession offense that is the most serious offense that is the basis of the conspiracy.

(b) The court that imposes sentence upon the person who is convicted of or pleads guilty to the conspiracy shall comply with the provisions identified as being applicable under division (L)(2) of this section, in addition to any other penalty or sanction that it imposes for the conspiracy under division (J)(2) or (4) of this section and Chapter 2929. of the Revised Code.

(M) As used in this section:

(1) "Felony drug trafficking, manufacturing, processing, or possession offense" means any of the following that is a felony:

(a) A violation of section 2925.03, 2925.04, 2925.05, or 2925.06 of the Revised Code;

(b) A violation of section 2925.11 of the Revised Code that is not a minor drug possession offense.

(2) "Minor drug possession offense" has the same meaning as in section 2925.01 of the Revised Code.

**HISTORY: 134 v H 511 (Eff 1-1-74); 136 v H 300 (Eff 7-1-76); 139 v H 108 (Eff 6-23-82); 139 v S 199 (Eff 7-1-83); 140 v S 210 (Eff 7-1-83); 140 v H 651 (Eff 10-1-84); 141 v H 5 (Eff 1-1-86); 141 v H 338 (Eff 9-17-86); 141 v H 428 (Eff 12-23-86); 146 v S 2 (Eff 7-1-96); 146 v H 125 (Eff 7-1-96); 146 v S 269. Eff 7-1-96; 149 v S 123, § 1, eff. 1-1-04; 150 v H 383, § 1, eff. 5-6-05; 151 v H 241, § 1, eff. 7-1-07; 153 v S 235, § 1, eff. 3-24-11; 2011 HB 86, § 1, eff. Sept. 30, 2011.**

See provisions of § 4 of 151 v H 241 following RC § 2901.01. The effective date is set by section 4 of S.B. 123.

The provisions of § 5 of S.B. 123 (149 v —), as amended by § 3 of H.B. 163 (150 v —), read as follows:

SECTION 5. (A) Notwithstanding division (B) of section 1.58 of the Revised Code, the provisions of the Revised Code amended or enacted in Sections 1 and 2 of Am. Sub. S.B. 123 of the 124th General Assembly shall apply only in relation to conduct and offenses committed on or after January 1, 2004. Conduct and offenses committed prior to January 1, 2004, shall be governed by the law in effect on the date the conduct or offense was committed. * * *

The provisions of § 8 of S.B. 123 read as follows:

SECTION 8. Section 2923.01 of the Revised Code is presented in this act as a composite of the section as amended by both Sub. H.B. 125 and Am. Sub. S.B. 269 of the 121st General Assembly. The General Assembly, applying the principle stated in division (B) of section 1.52 of the Revised Code that amendments are to be harmonized if reasonably capable of simultaneous operation, finds that the composites are the resulting versions of the sections in effect prior to the effective date of the sections as presented in this act.

## § 2923.011 Repealed, 134 v H 511, § 2 [131 v 676; 132 v H 1; 133 v H 288]. Eff 1-1-74.

This section concerned carrying firearms, explosives and other concealed weapons.

## § 2923.012 Repealed, 134 v H 511, § 2 [131 v 676; 132 v H 1; 133 v H 288]. Eff 1-1-74.

This section concerned carrying firearms, explosives and other concealed weapons.

## § 2923.02 Attempt.

(A) No person, purposely or knowingly, and when purpose or knowledge is sufficient culpability for the commission of an offense, shall engage in conduct that, if successful, would constitute or result in the offense.

(B) It is no defense to a charge under this section that, in retrospect, commission of the offense that was the object of the attempt was either factually or legally impossible under the attendant circumstances, if that offense could have been committed had the attendant circumstances been as the actor believed them to be.

(C) No person who is convicted of committing a specific offense, of complicity in the commission of an offense, or of conspiracy to commit an offense shall be convicted of an attempt to commit the same offense in violation of this section.

(D) It is an affirmative defense to a charge under this section that the actor abandoned the actor's effort to commit the offense or otherwise prevented its commission, under circumstances manifesting a complete and voluntary renunciation of the actor's criminal purpose.

(E)(1) Whoever violates this section is guilty of an attempt to commit an offense. An attempt to commit aggravated murder, murder, or an offense for which the maximum penalty is imprisonment for life is a felony of the first degree. An attempt to commit a drug abuse offense for which the penalty is determined by the amount or number of unit doses of the controlled substance involved in the drug abuse offense is an offense of the same degree as the drug abuse offense attempted would be if that drug abuse offense had been committed and had involved an amount or number of unit doses of the controlled substance that is within the next lower range of controlled substance amounts than was involved in the attempt. An attempt to commit any other offense is an offense of the next lesser degree than the offense attempted. In the case of an attempt to commit an offense other than a violation of Chapter 3734. of the Revised Code that is not specifically classified, an attempt is a misdemeanor of the first degree if the offense attempted is a felony, and a misdemeanor of the fourth degree if the offense attempted is a misdemeanor. In the case of an attempt to commit a violation of any provision of Chapter 3734. of the Revised Code, other than section 3734.18 of the Revised Code, that relates to hazardous wastes, an attempt is a felony punishable by a fine of not more than twenty-five thousand dollars or imprisonment for not more than eighteen months, or both. An attempt to commit a minor misdemeanor, or to engage in conspiracy, is not an offense under this section.

(2) If a person is convicted of or pleads guilty to attempted rape and also is convicted of or pleads guilty to a specification of the type described in section 2941.1418 [2941.14.18], 2941.1419 [2941.14.19], or 2941.1420 [2941.14.20] of the Revised Code, the offender shall be sentenced to a prison term or term of life imprisonment pursuant to section 2971.03 of the Revised Code.

(3) In addition to any other sanctions imposed pursuant to division (E)(1) of this section for an attempt to commit aggravated murder or murder in violation of division (A) of this section, if the offender used a motor vehicle as the means to attempt to commit the offense, the court shall impose upon the offender a class two suspension of the offender's driver's license, commercial driver's license, temporary instruction permit, probationary license, or nonresident operating privilege as specified in division (A)(2) of section 4510.02 of the Revised Code.

(F) As used in this section:

(1) "Drug abuse offense" has the same meaning as in section 2925.01 of the Revised Code.

(2) "Motor vehicle" has the same meaning as in section 4501.01 of the Revised Code.

**HISTORY: 134 v H 511 (Eff 1-1-74); 140 v S 210 (Eff 7-1-83); 140 v H 651 (Eff 10-1-84); 144 v H 225 (Eff 10-23-91); 146 v S 2 (Eff 7-1-96); 148 v S 107. Eff 3-23-2000; 151 v S 260, § 1, eff. 1-2-07; 151 v H 461, § 1, eff. 4-4-07.**

**Not analogous to former RC § 2923.02 (GC §§ 12819-1, 12819-2; 102 v 124; Bureau of Code Revision, 10-1-53), repealed 134 v H 511, § 2, eff 1-1-74.**

**Comment, Legislative Service Commission**

Section 2923.02 of the Revised Code is amended by Am. Sub. S.B. 260 and Am. Sub. H.B. 461 of the 126th General Assembly. Comparison of these amendments in pursuance of section 1.52 of the Revised Code discloses that they are not irreconcilable so that they are required by that section to be harmonized to give effect to each amendment. Division lettering adjusted to give effect to the manifest intent of each amendment pursuant to RC § 1.52(B).

## § 2923.021 Repealed, 134 v H 511, § 2 [125 v S 62(125)]. Eff 1-1-74.

This section concerned sale or possession of switch or spring knife.

## § 2923.03 Complicity.

(A) No person, acting with the kind of culpability required for the commission of an offense, shall do any of the following:

(1) Solicit or procure another to commit the offense;

(2) Aid or abet another in committing the offense;

(3) Conspire with another to commit the offense in violation of section 2923.01 of the Revised Code;

(4) Cause an innocent or irresponsible person to commit the offense.

(B) It is no defense to a charge under this section that no person with whom the accused was in complicity has been convicted as a principal offender.

(C) No person shall be convicted of complicity under this section unless an offense is actually committed, but a person may be convicted of complicity in an attempt to commit an offense in violation of section 2923.02 of the Revised Code.

(D) If an alleged accomplice of the defendant testifies against the defendant in a case in which the defendant is charged with complicity in the commission of or an attempt to commit an offense, an attempt to commit an offense, or an offense, the court, when it charges the jury, shall state substantially the following:

"The testimony of an accomplice does not become inadmissible because of his complicity, moral turpitude, or self-interest, but the admitted or claimed complicity of a witness may affect his credibility and make his testimony subject to grave suspicion, and require that it be weighed with great caution.

It is for you, as jurors, in the light of all the facts presented to you from the witness stand, to evaluate such testimony and to determine its quality and worth or its lack of quality and worth."

(E) It is an affirmative defense to a charge under this section that, prior to the commission of or attempt to commit the offense, the actor terminated his complicity, under circumstances manifesting a complete and voluntary renunciation of his criminal purpose.

(F) Whoever violates this section is guilty of complicity in the commission of an offense, and shall be prosecuted and punished as if he were a principal offender. A charge of complicity may be stated in terms of this section, or in terms of the principal offense.

**HISTORY: 134 v H 511 (Eff 1-1-74); 141 v H 338. Eff 9-17-86.**

**Not analogous to former RC § 2923.03 (GC § 12819-3; 115 v 189; Bureau of Code Revision, 10-1-53; 129 v 420), repealed 134 v H 511, § 2, eff 1-1-74.**

## § 2923.04 Repealed, 141 v H 5, § 2 [134 v H 511; 135 v H 716]. Eff 1-1-86.

This section concerned engaging in organized crime. See now RC § 2923.31 et seq.

## § 2923.05 Repealed, 134 v H 511, § 2 [RS § 7034; S&C 437; GC §§ 12819-6, 12819-7, 13391; 44 v 77; 67 v 25; 77 v 85; 115 v 190; Bureau of Code Revision, 10-1-53; 132 v H 45]. Eff 1-1-74.

This section concerned offenses regarding sale of firearms, war trophies and grave robbing.

## § 2923.06 Repealed, 134 v H 511, § 2 [RS § 7034; S&C 437; GC §§ 12819-6, 12819-7, 13391; 44 v 77; 67 v 25; 77 v 85; 115 v 190; Bureau of Code Revision, 10-1-53; 132 v H 45]. Eff 1-1-74.

This section concerned offenses regarding sale of firearms, war trophies and grave robbing.

## § 2923.07 Repealed, 134 v H 511, § 2 [RS § 7034; S&C 437; GC §§ 12819-6, 12819-7, 13391; 44 v 77; 67 v 25; 77 v 85; 115 v 190; Bureau of Code Revision, 10-1-53; 132 v H 45]. Eff 1-1-74.

This section concerned offenses regarding sale of firearms, war trophies and grave robbing.

## § 2923.08 Repealed, 134 v H 511, § 2 [RS §§ 1470, 7034; S&C 228, 437; GC §§ 12684, 13391-1, 13392; 44 v 77; 54 v 187, § 5; 67 v 25; 77 v 85; 120 v 111; Bureau of Code Revision, 10-1-53; 126 v 575; 129 v H 1]. Eff 1-1-74.

This section concerned offenses regarding corpses.

## § 2923.09 Repealed, 134 v H 511, § 2 [RS §§ 1470, 7034; S&C 228, 437; GC §§ 12684, 13391-1, 13392; 44 v 77; 54 v 187, § 5; 67 v 25; 77 v 85; 120 v 111; Bureau of Code Revision, 10-1-53; 126 v 575; 129 v H 1]. Eff 1-1-74.

This section concerned offenses regarding corpses.

## § 2923.10 Repealed, 134 v H 511, § 2 [RS §§ 1470, 7034; S&C 228, 437; GC §§ 12684, 13391-1, 13392; 44 v 77; 54 v 187, § 5; 67 v 25; 77 v 85; 120 v 111; Bureau of Code Revision, 10-1-53; 126 v 575; 129 v H 1]. Eff 1-1-74.

This section concerned offenses regarding corpses.

### [WEAPONS CONTROL]

## § 2923.11 Definitions.

As used in sections 2923.11 to 2923.24 of the Revised Code:

(A) "Deadly weapon" means any instrument, device, or thing capable of inflicting death, and designed or specially adapted for use as a weapon, or possessed, carried, or used as a weapon.

(B)(1) "Firearm" means any deadly weapon capable of expelling or propelling one or more projectiles by the action of an explosive or combustible propellant. "Firearm" includes an unloaded firearm, and any firearm that is inoperable but that can readily be rendered operable.

(2) When determining whether a firearm is capable of expelling or propelling one or more projectiles by the action of an explosive or combustible propellant, the trier

of fact may rely upon circumstantial evidence, including, but not limited to, the representations and actions of the individual exercising control over the firearm.

(C) "Handgun" means any of the following:

(1) Any firearm that has a short stock and is designed to be held and fired by the use of a single hand;

(2) Any combination of parts from which a firearm of a type described in division (C)(1) of this section can be assembled.

(D) "Semi-automatic firearm" means any firearm designed or specially adapted to fire a single cartridge and automatically chamber a succeeding cartridge ready to fire, with a single function of the trigger.

(E) "Automatic firearm" means any firearm designed or specially adapted to fire a succession of cartridges with a single function of the trigger. "Automatic firearm" also means any semi-automatic firearm designed or specially adapted to fire more than thirty-one cartridges without reloading, other than a firearm chambering only .22 caliber short, long, or long-rifle cartridges.

(F) "Sawed-off firearm" means a shotgun with a barrel less than eighteen inches long, or a rifle with a barrel less than sixteen inches long, or a shotgun or rifle less than twenty-six inches long overall.

(G) "Zip-gun" means any of the following:

(1) Any firearm of crude and extemporized manufacture;

(2) Any device, including without limitation a starter's pistol, that is not designed as a firearm, but that is specially adapted for use as a firearm;

(3) Any industrial tool, signalling device, or safety device, that is not designed as a firearm, but that as designed is capable of use as such, when possessed, carried, or used as a firearm.

(H) "Explosive device" means any device designed or specially adapted to cause physical harm to persons or property by means of an explosion, and consisting of an explosive substance or agency and a means to detonate it. "Explosive device" includes without limitation any bomb, any explosive demolition device, any blasting cap or detonator containing an explosive charge, and any pressure vessel that has been knowingly tampered with or arranged so as to explode.

(I) "Incendiary device" means any firebomb, and any device designed or specially adapted to cause physical harm to persons or property by means of fire, and consisting of an incendiary substance or agency and a means to ignite it.

(J) "Ballistic knife" means a knife with a detachable blade that is propelled by a spring-operated mechanism.

(K) "Dangerous ordnance" means any of the following, except as provided in division (L) of this section:

(1) Any automatic or sawed-off firearm, zip-gun, or ballistic knife;

(2) Any explosive device or incendiary device;

(3) Nitroglycerin, nitrocellulose, nitrostarch, PETN, cyclonite, TNT, picric acid, and other high explosives; amatol, tritonal, tetrytol, pentolite, pecretol, cyclotol, and other high explosive compositions; plastic explosives; dynamite, blasting gelatin, gelatin dynamite, sensitized ammonium nitrate, liquid-oxygen blasting explosives, blasting powder, and other blasting agents; and any other explosive substance having sufficient brisance or power to be particularly suitable for use as a military explosive, or for use in mining, quarrying, excavating, or demolitions;

(4) Any firearm, rocket launcher, mortar, artillery piece, grenade, mine, bomb, torpedo, or similar weapon, designed and manufactured for military purposes, and the ammunition for that weapon;

(5) Any firearm muffler or silencer;

(6) Any combination of parts that is intended by the owner for use in converting any firearm or other device into a dangerous ordnance.

(L) "Dangerous ordnance" does not include any of the following:

(1) Any firearm, including a military weapon and the ammunition for that weapon, and regardless of its actual age, that employs a percussion cap or other obsolete ignition system, or that is designed and safe for use only with black powder;

(2) Any pistol, rifle, or shotgun, designed or suitable for sporting purposes, including a military weapon as issued or as modified, and the ammunition for that weapon, unless the firearm is an automatic or sawed-off firearm;

(3) Any cannon or other artillery piece that, regardless of its actual age, is of a type in accepted use prior to 1887, has no mechanical, hydraulic, pneumatic, or other system for absorbing recoil and returning the tube into battery without displacing the carriage, and is designed and safe for use only with black powder;

(4) Black powder, priming quills, and percussion caps possessed and lawfully used to fire a cannon of a type defined in division (L)(3) of this section during displays, celebrations, organized matches or shoots, and target practice, and smokeless and black powder, primers, and percussion caps possessed and lawfully used as a propellant or ignition device in small-arms or small-arms ammunition;

(5) Dangerous ordnance that is inoperable or inert and cannot readily be rendered operable or activated, and that is kept as a trophy, souvenir, curio, or museum piece.

(6) Any device that is expressly excepted from the definition of a destructive device pursuant to the "Gun Control Act of 1968," 82 Stat. 1213, 18 U.S.C. 921(a)(4), as amended, and regulations issued under that act.

(M) "Explosive" means any chemical compound, mixture, or device, the primary or common purpose of which is to function by explosion. "Explosive" includes all materials that have been classified as division 1.1, division 1.2, division 1.3, or division 1.4 explosives by the United States department of transportation in its regulations and includes, but is not limited to, dynamite, black powder, pellet powders, initiating explosives, blasting caps, electric blasting caps, safety fuses, fuse igniters, squibs, cordeau detonant fuses, instantaneous fuses, and igniter cords and igniters. "Explosive" does not include "fireworks," as defined in section 3743.01 of the Revised Code, or any substance or material otherwise meeting the definition of explosive set forth in this section that is manufactured, sold, possessed, transported, stored, or used in any activity described in section 3743.80 of the Revised Code, provided the activity is conducted in accordance with all applicable laws, rules, and regulations, including, but not limited to, the provisions of section 3743.80 of the Revised Code and the rules of the fire marshal adopted pursuant to section 3737.82 of the Revised Code.

**HISTORY: 134 v H 511 (Eff 1-1-74); 137 v H 728 (Eff 8-22-78); 141 v H 51 (Eff 7-30-86); 142 v H 24 (Eff 7-31-87); 143 v S 96 (Eff 6-13-90); 146 v S 2. Eff 7-1-96; 150 v H 12, § 1, eff. 4-8-04; 152 v H 562, § 101.01, eff. 9-23-08.**

The effective date is set by § 812.10 of 152 v H 562.

**Not analogous to former RC § 2923.11 (RS § 7035; 67 v 25; 78 v 131; GC § 12693; Bureau of Code Revision, 10-1-53), repealed 134 v H 511, § 2, eff 1-1-74.**

The effective date is set by section 6 of SB 2.

## § 2923.12 Carrying concealed weapons.

(A) No person shall knowingly carry or have, concealed on the person's person or concealed ready at hand, any of the following:

(1) A deadly weapon other than a handgun;

(2) A handgun other than a dangerous ordnance;

(3) A dangerous ordnance.

(B) No person who has been issued a license or temporary emergency license to carry a concealed handgun under section 2923.125 [2923.12.5] or 2923.1213 [2923.12.13] of the Revised Code or a license to carry a concealed handgun that was issued by another state with which the attorney general has entered into a reciprocity agreement under section 109.69 of the Revised Code shall do any of the following:

(1) If the person is stopped for a law enforcement purpose and is carrying a concealed handgun, fail to promptly inform any law enforcement officer who approaches the person after the person has been stopped that the person has been issued a license or temporary emergency license to carry a concealed handgun and that the person then is carrying a concealed handgun;

(2) If the person is stopped for a law enforcement purpose and if the person is carrying a concealed handgun, knowingly fail to keep the person's hands in plain sight at any time after any law enforcement officer begins approaching the person while stopped and before the law enforcement officer leaves, unless the failure is pursuant to and in accordance with directions given by a law enforcement officer;

(3) If the person is stopped for a law enforcement purpose, if the person is carrying a concealed handgun, and if the person is approached by any law enforcement officer while stopped, knowingly remove or attempt to remove the loaded handgun from the holster, pocket, or other place in which the person is carrying it, knowingly grasp or hold the loaded handgun, or knowingly have contact with the loaded handgun by touching it with the person's hands or fingers at any time after the law enforcement officer begins approaching and before the law enforcement officer leaves, unless the person removes, attempts to remove, grasps, holds, or has contact with the loaded handgun pursuant to and in accordance with directions given by the law enforcement officer;

(4) If the person is stopped for a law enforcement purpose and if the person is carrying a concealed handgun, knowingly disregard or fail to comply with any lawful order of any law enforcement officer given while the person is stopped, including, but not limited to, a specific order to the person to keep the person's hands in plain sight.

(C)(1) This section does not apply to any of the following:

(a) An officer, agent, or employee of this or any other state or the United States, or to a law enforcement officer, who is authorized to carry concealed weapons or dangerous ordnance or is authorized to carry handguns and is acting within the scope of the officer's, agent's, or employee's duties;

(b) Any person who is employed in this state, who is authorized to carry concealed weapons or dangerous ordnance or is authorized to carry handguns, and who is subject to and in compliance with the requirements of section 109.801 [109.80.1] of the Revised Code, unless the appointing authority of the person has expressly specified that the exemption provided in division (C)(1)(b) of this section does not apply to the person;

(c) A person's transportation or storage of a firearm, other than a firearm described in divisions (G) to (M) of section 2923.11 of the Revised Code, in a motor vehicle for any lawful purpose if the firearm is not on the actor's person;

(d) A person's storage or possession of a firearm, other than a firearm described in divisions (G) to (M) of section 2923.11 of the Revised Code, in the actor's own home for any lawful purpose.

(2) Division (A)(2) of this section does not apply to any person who, at the time of the alleged carrying or possession of a handgun, is carrying a valid license or temporary emergency license to carry a concealed handgun issued to the person under section 2923.125 [2023.12.5] or 2923.1213 [2923.12.13] of the Revised Code or a license to carry a concealed handgun that was issued by another state with which the attorney general has entered into a reciprocity agreement under section 109.69 of the Revised Code, unless the person knowingly is in a place described in division (B) of section 2923.126 [2923.12.6] of the Revised Code.

(D) It is an affirmative defense to a charge under division (A)(1) of this section of carrying or having control of a weapon other than a handgun and other than a dangerous ordnance that the actor was not otherwise prohibited by law from having the weapon and that any of the following applies:

(1) The weapon was carried or kept ready at hand by the actor for defensive purposes while the actor was engaged in or was going to or from the actor's lawful business or occupation, which business or occupation was of a character or was necessarily carried on in a manner or at a time or place as to render the actor particularly susceptible to criminal attack, such as would justify a prudent person in going armed.

(2) The weapon was carried or kept ready at hand by the actor for defensive purposes while the actor was engaged in a lawful activity and had reasonable cause to fear a criminal attack upon the actor, a member of the actor's family, or the actor's home, such as would justify a prudent person in going armed.

(3) The weapon was carried or kept ready at hand by the actor for any lawful purpose and while in the actor's own home.

(E) No person who is charged with a violation of this section shall be required to obtain a license or temporary emergency license to carry a concealed handgun under section 2923.125 [2923.12.5] or 2923.1213 [2923.12.13] of the Revised Code as a condition for the dismissal of the charge.

(F)(1) Whoever violates this section is guilty of carrying concealed weapons. Except as otherwise provided in this division or division (F)(2) of this section, carrying concealed weapons in violation of division (A) of this section is a misdemeanor of the first degree. Except as otherwise provided in this division or division (F)(2) of this section, if the offender previously has been convicted of a violation of this section or of any offense of violence, if the weapon involved is a firearm that is either loaded or for which the offender has ammunition ready at hand, or if the weapon involved is dangerous ordnance, carrying concealed weapons in violation of division (A) of this section is a felony of the fourth degree. Except as otherwise provided in division (F)(2) of this section, if the offense is committed aboard an aircraft, or with purpose to carry a concealed weapon aboard an aircraft, regardless of the weapon involved, carrying concealed weapons in violation of division (A) of this section is a felony of the third degree.

(2) If a person being arrested for a violation of division (A)(2) of this section promptly produces a valid license or temporary emergency license to carry a concealed handgun issued under section 2923.125 [2923.12.5] or 2923.1213 [2923.12.13] of the Revised Code or a license to carry a concealed handgun that was issued by another state with which the attorney general has entered into a reciprocity agreement under section 109.69 of the Revised Code, and if at the time of the violation the person was not knowingly in a place described in division (B) of section 2923.126 [2923.12.6] of the Revised Code, the officer shall not arrest the person for a violation of that division. If the person is not able to promptly produce any of those types of license and if the person is not in a place described in that section, the officer may arrest the person for a violation of that division, and the offender shall be punished as follows:

(a) The offender shall be guilty of a minor misdemeanor if both of the following apply:

(i) Within ten days after the arrest, the offender presents a license or temporary emergency license to carry a concealed handgun issued under section 2923.125 [2923.12.5] or 2923.1213 [2923.12.13] of the Revised Code or a license to carry a concealed handgun that was issued by another state with which the attorney general has entered into a reciprocity agreement under section 109.69 of the Revised Code, which license was valid at the time of the arrest to the law enforcement agency that employs the arresting officer.

(ii) At the time of the arrest, the offender was not knowingly in a place described in division (B) of section 2923.126 [2923.12.6] of the Revised Code.

(b) The offender shall be guilty of a misdemeanor and shall be fined five hundred dollars if all of the following apply:

(i) The offender previously had been issued a license to carry a concealed handgun under section 2923.125 [2923.12.5] of the Revised Code or a license to carry a concealed handgun that was issued by another state with which the attorney general has entered into a reciprocity agreement under section 109.69 of the Revised Code and that was similar in nature to a license issued under section 2923.125 [2923.12.5] of the Revised Code, and that license expired within the two years immediately preceding the arrest.

(ii) Within forty-five days after the arrest, the offender presents any type of license identified in division (F)(2)(a)(i) of this section to the law enforcement agency that employed the arresting officer, and the offender waives in writing the offender's right to a speedy trial on the charge of the violation that is provided in section 2945.71 of the Revised Code.

(iii) At the time of the commission of the offense, the offender was not knowingly in a place described in division (B) of section 2923.126 [2923.12.6] of the Revised Code.

(c) If neither division (F)(2)(a) nor (b) of this section applies, the offender shall be punished under division (F)(1) of this section.

(3) Except as otherwise provided in this division, carrying concealed weapons in violation of division (B)(1) of this section is a misdemeanor of the first degree, and, in addition to any other penalty or sanction imposed for a violation of division (B)(1) of this section, the offender's license or temporary emergency license to carry a concealed handgun shall be suspended pursuant to division (A)(2) of section 2923.128 [2923.12.8] of the Revised Code. If, at the time of the stop of the offender for a law enforcement purpose that was the basis of the violation, any law enforcement officer involved with the stop had actual knowledge that the offender has been issued a license or temporary emergency license to carry a concealed handgun, carrying concealed weapons in violation of division (B)(1) of this section is a minor misdemeanor, and the offender's license or temporary emergency license to carry a concealed handgun shall not be suspended pursuant to division (A)(2) of section 2923.128 [2923.12.8] of the Revised Code.

(4) Carrying concealed weapons in violation of division (B)(2) or (4) of this section is a misdemeanor of the first degree or, if the offender previously has been convicted of or pleaded guilty to a violation of division (B)(2) or (4) of this section, a felony of the fifth degree. In addition to any other penalty or sanction imposed for a misdemeanor violation of division (B)(2) or (4) of this section, the offender's license or temporary emergency license to carry a concealed handgun shall be suspended pursuant to division (A)(2) of section 2923.128 [2923.12.8] of the Revised Code.

(5) Carrying concealed weapons in violation of division (B)(3) of this section is a felony of the fifth degree.

(G) If a law enforcement officer stops a person to question the person regarding a possible violation of this section, for a traffic stop, or for any other law enforcement purpose, if the person surrenders a firearm to the officer, either voluntarily or pursuant to a request or demand of the officer, and if the officer does not charge the person with a violation of this section or arrest the person for any offense, the person is not otherwise prohibited by law from possessing the firearm, and the firearm is not contraband, the officer shall return the firearm to the person at the termination of the stop. If a court orders a law enforcement officer to return a firearm to a person pursuant to the requirement set forth in this division, division (B) of section 2923.163 [2923.16.3] of the Revised Code applies.

**HISTORY: 134 v H 511 (Eff 1-1-74); 135 v H 716 (Eff 1-1-74); 141 v H 51 (Eff 7-30-86); 146 v S 2. Eff 7-1-96; 150 v H 12, § 1, eff. 4-8-04; 151 v H 347, § 1, eff. 3-14-07; 152 v S 184, § 1, eff. 9-9-08.**

Governor Taft's veto of HB 347 was overridden by the Ohio General Assembly.

The provisions of § 6, H.B. 12 (150 v —), read as follows:

SECTION 6. In amending sections 1547.69, 2911.21, 2921.13, 2923.12, 2923.121, 2923.123, 2923.13, 2923.16, 2953.32, and 4749.10 of the Revised Code and in enacting sections 109.69, 109.731, 311.41, 311.42, and 2923.124 to 2923.1213 of the Revised Code in this act, the General Assembly hereby declares its intent to recognize both of the following:

(A) The inalienable and fundamental right of an individual to defend the individual's person and the members of the individual's family;

(B) The fact that the right described in division (A) of this section predates the adoption of the United States Constitution, the adoption of the Ohio Constitution, and the enactment of all statutory laws by the General Assembly and may not be infringed by any enactment of the General Assembly.

The provisions of § 7, H.B. 12 (150 v —), read as follows:

SECTION 7. In enacting sections 109.69, 109.731, 311.41, 311.42, and 2923.124 to 2923.1213 of the Revised Code in this act and in amending sections 1547.69, 2911.21, 2921.13, 2923.12, 2923.121, 2923.123, 2923.13, 2923.16, 2953.32, and 4749.10 of the Revised Code in this act relative to licenses to carry a concealed handgun, the General Assembly hereby declares that it is not its intent to declare or otherwise give the impression that, prior to the effective date of this act, an individual did not have an inalienable and fundamental right, or a right under the Ohio Constitution or the United States Constitution, to carry a concealed handgun or other firearm for the defense of the individual's person or a member of the individual's family while engaged in lawful activity. Further, the General Assembly declares that it is not its intent to invalidate any prior convictions for violating any section of the Revised Code or a municipal ordinance prior to the effective date of this act or to prevent the prosecution of any violation committed prior to the effective date of this act.

The provisions of § 9, H.B. 12 (150 v —), read as follows:

SECTION 9. The General Assembly finds that licenses to carry concealed handguns are a matter of statewide concern and wishes to ensure uniformity throughout the state regarding the qualifications for a person to hold a license to carry a concealed handgun and the authority granted to a person holding a license of that nature. It is the intent of the General Assembly in amending sections 1547.69, 2911.21, 2921.13, 2923.12, 2923.121, 2923.123, 2923.16, 2953.32, and 4749.10 and enacting sections 109.69, 109.731, 311.41, 311.42, and 2923.124 to 2923.1213 of the Revised Code to enact laws of a general nature, and, by enacting those laws of a general nature, the state occupies and preempts the field of issuing licenses to carry a concealed handgun and the validity of licenses of that nature. No municipal corporation may adopt or continue in existence any ordinance, and no township may adopt or continue in existence any resolution, that is in conflict with those sections, including, but not limited to, any ordinance or resolution that attempts to restrict the places where a person possessing a valid license to carry a concealed handgun may carry a handgun concealed.

The provisions of § 10, H.B. 12 (150 v —), read as follows:

SECTION 10. If any provision of sections 1547.69, 2911.21, 2913.02, 2921.13, 2923.12, 2923.121, 2923.123, 2923.16, 2929.14, 2953.32, and 4749.10 of the Revised Code, as amended by this act, any provision of sections 109.69, 109.731, 311.41, 311.42, 2923.124, 2923.125, 2923.126, 2923.127, 2923.128, 2923.129, 2923.1210, 2923.1211, 2923.1212, and 2923.1213 of the Revised Code, as enacted by this act, or the application of any provision of those sections to any person or circumstance is held invalid, the invalidity does not affect other provisions or applications of the particular section or related sections that can be given effect without the invalid provision or application, and to this end the provisions of the particular section are severable.

**Not analogous to former RC § 2923.12 (GC § 13421-23; 108 v PtI, 189; Bureau of Code Revision, 10-1-53), repealed 134 v H 511, § 2, eff 1-1-74.**

The effective date is set by section 6 of SB 2.

## § 2923.121 Illegal possession of firearm in liquor permit premises.

(A) No person shall possess a firearm in any room in which any person is consuming beer or intoxicating liquor in a premises for which a D permit has been issued under Chapter 4303. of the Revised Code or in an open air arena for which a permit of that nature has been issued.

(B)(1) This section does not apply to any of the following:

(a) An officer, agent, or employee of this or any other state or the United States, or to a law enforcement officer, who is authorized to carry firearms and is acting within the scope of the officer's, agent's, or employee's duties;

(b) Any person who is employed in this state, who is authorized to carry firearms, and who is subject to and in compliance with the requirements of section 109.801 of the Revised Code, unless the appointing authority of the person has expressly specified that the exemption provided in division (B)(1)(b) of this section does not apply to the person;

(c) Any room used for the accommodation of guests of a hotel, as defined in section 4301.01 of the Revised Code;

(d) The principal holder of a D permit issued for a premises or an open air arena under Chapter 4303. of the Revised Code while in the premises or open air arena for which the permit was issued if the principal holder of the D permit also possesses a valid license or temporary emergency license to carry a concealed handgun issued to the principal holder under section 2923.125 or 2923.1213 of the Revised Code or a license to carry a concealed handgun that was issued to the principal holder by another state with which the attorney general has entered into a reciprocity agreement under section 109.69 of the Revised Code and as long as the principal holder is not consuming beer or intoxicating liquor or under the influence of alcohol or a drug of abuse, or any agent or employee of that holder who also is a peace officer, as defined in section 2151.3515 of the Revised Code, who is off duty, and who otherwise is authorized to carry firearms while in the course of the officer's official duties and while in the premises or open air arena for which the permit was issued and as long as the agent or employee of that holder is not consuming beer or intoxicating liquor or under the influence of alcohol or a drug of abuse.

(e) Any person who is carrying a valid license or temporary emergency license to carry a concealed handgun issued to the person under section 2923.125 or 2923.1213 of the Revised Code or a license to carry a concealed handgun that was issued to the person by another state with which the attorney general has entered into a reciprocity agreement under section 109.69 of the Revised Code , as long as the person is not consuming beer or intoxicating liquor or under the influence of alcohol or a drug of abuse.

(2) This section does not prohibit any person who is a member of a veteran's organization, as defined in section 2915.01 of the Revised Code, from possessing a rifle in any room in any premises owned, leased, or otherwise under the control of the veteran's organization, if the rifle is not loaded with live ammunition and if the person otherwise is not prohibited by law from having the rifle.

(3) This section does not apply to any person possessing or displaying firearms in any room used to exhibit unloaded firearms for sale or trade in a soldiers' memorial established pursuant to Chapter 345. of the Revised Code, in a convention center, or in any other public meeting place, if the person is an exhibitor, trader, purchaser, or seller of firearms and is not otherwise prohibited by law from possessing, trading, purchasing, or selling the firearms.

(C) It is an affirmative defense to a charge under this section of illegal possession of a firearm in a liquor permit premises that involves the possession of a firearm other than a handgun, that the actor was not otherwise prohibited by law from having the firearm, and that any of the following apply:

(1) The firearm was carried or kept ready at hand by the actor for defensive purposes, while the actor was engaged in or was going to or from the actor's lawful business or occupation, which business or occupation was of such character or was necessarily carried on in such manner or at such a time or place as to render the actor particularly susceptible to criminal attack, such as would justify a prudent person in going armed.

(2) The firearm was carried or kept ready at hand by the actor for defensive purposes, while the actor was engaged in a lawful activity, and had reasonable cause to fear a criminal attack upon the actor or a member of the

actor's family, or upon the actor's home, such as would justify a prudent person in going armed.

(D) No person who is charged with a violation of this section shall be required to obtain a license or temporary emergency license to carry a concealed handgun under section 2923.125 or 2923.1213 of the Revised Code as a condition for the dismissal of the charge.

(E) Whoever violates this section is guilty of illegal possession of a firearm in a liquor permit premises. Except as otherwise provided in this division, illegal possession of a firearm in a liquor permit premises is a felony of the fifth degree. If the offender commits the violation of this section by knowingly carrying or having the firearm concealed on the offender's person or concealed ready at hand, illegal possession of a firearm in a liquor permit premises is a felony of the third degree.

(F) As used in this section, "beer" and "intoxicating liquor" have the same meanings as in section 4301.01 of the Revised Code.

**HISTORY: 141 v H 51 (Eff 7-30-86); 141 v H 39 (Eff 2-21-87); 146 v S 2. Eff 7-1-96; 150 v H 12, § 1, eff. 4-8-04; 151 v H 347, § 1, eff. 3-14-07; 152 v S 184, § 1, eff. 9-9-08; 2011 SB 17, § 1, eff. Sept. 30, 2011.**

Governor Taft's veto of HB 347 was overridden by the Ohio General Assembly.

See the provisions of §§ 6, 7, 9, and 10 of H.B. 12 (150 v —) following RC § 2923.12.

The effective date is set by section 6 of SB 2.

## § 2923.122 Illegal conveyance or possession of deadly weapon or dangerous ordnance or illegal possession of object indistinguishable from firearm in school safety zone.

(A) No person shall knowingly convey, or attempt to convey, a deadly weapon or dangerous ordnance into a school safety zone.

(B) No person shall knowingly possess a deadly weapon or dangerous ordnance in a school safety zone.

(C) No person shall knowingly possess an object in a school safety zone if both of the following apply:

(1) The object is indistinguishable from a firearm, whether or not the object is capable of being fired.

(2) The person indicates that the person possesses the object and that it is a firearm, or the person knowingly displays or brandishes the object and indicates that it is a firearm.

(D)(1) This section does not apply to any of the following:

(a) An officer, agent, or employee of this or any other state or the United States, or a law enforcement officer, who is authorized to carry deadly weapons or dangerous ordnance and is acting within the scope of the officer's, agent's, or employee's duties, a security officer employed by a board of education or governing body of a school during the time that the security officer is on duty pursuant to that contract of employment, or any other person who has written authorization from the board of education or governing body of a school to convey deadly weapons or dangerous ordnance into a school safety zone or to possess a deadly weapon or dangerous ordnance in a school safety zone and who conveys or possesses the deadly weapon or dangerous ordnance in accordance with that authorization;

(b) Any person who is employed in this state, who is authorized to carry deadly weapons or dangerous ordnance, and who is subject to and in compliance with the requirements of section 109.801 [109.80.1] of the Revised Code, unless the appointing authority of the person has expressly specified that the exemption provided in division (D)(1)(b) of this section does not apply to the person.

(2) Division (C) of this section does not apply to premises upon which home schooling is conducted. Division (C) of this section also does not apply to a school administrator, teacher, or employee who possesses an object that is indistinguishable from a firearm for legitimate school purposes during the course of employment, a student who uses an object that is indistinguishable from a firearm under the direction of a school administrator, teacher, or employee, or any other person who with the express prior approval of a school administrator possesses an object that is indistinguishable from a firearm for a legitimate purpose, including the use of the object in a ceremonial activity, a play, reenactment, or other dramatic presentation, or a ROTC activity or another similar use of the object.

(3) This section does not apply to a person who conveys or attempts to convey a handgun into, or possesses a handgun in, a school safety zone if, at the time of that conveyance, attempted conveyance, or possession of the handgun, all of the following apply:

(a) The person does not enter into a school building or onto school premises and is not at a school activity.

(b) The person is carrying a valid license to carry a concealed handgun issued to the person under section 2923.125 [2923.12.5] of the Revised Code or a license to carry a concealed handgun that was issued by another state with which the attorney general has entered into a reciprocity agreement under section 109.69 of the Revised Code.

(c) The person is in the school safety zone in accordance with 18 U.S.C. 922(q)(2)(B).

(d) The person is not knowingly in a place described in division (B)(1) or (B)(3) to (10) of section 2923.126 [2923.12.6] of the Revised Code.

(4) This section does not apply to a person who conveys or attempts to convey a handgun into, or possesses a handgun in, a school safety zone if at the time of that conveyance, attempted conveyance, or possession of the handgun all of the following apply:

(a) The person is carrying a valid license or temporary emergency license to carry a concealed handgun issued to the person under section 2923.125 [2923.12.5] or 2923.1213 [2923.12.13] of the Revised Code or a license to carry a concealed handgun that was issued by another state with which the attorney general has entered into a reciprocity agreement under section 109.69 of the Revised Code.

(b) The person is the driver or passenger in a motor vehicle and is in the school safety zone while immediately in the process of picking up or dropping off a child.

(c) The person is not in violation of section 2923.16 of the Revised Code.

(E)(1) Whoever violates division (A) or (B) of this section is guilty of illegal conveyance or possession of a deadly weapon or dangerous ordnance in a school safety zone. Except as otherwise provided in this division, illegal conveyance or possession of a deadly weapon or dangerous ordnance in a school safety zone is a felony of the fifth degree. If the offender previously has been convicted of a violation of this section, illegal conveyance or possession of a deadly weapon or dangerous ordnance in a school safety zone is a felony of the fourth degree.

(2) Whoever violates division (C) of this section is guilty of illegal possession of an object indistinguishable from a firearm in a school safety zone. Except as otherwise provided in this division, illegal possession of an object indistinguishable from a firearm in a school safety zone is a misdemeanor of the first degree. If the offender previously has been convicted of a violation of this section, illegal possession of an object indistinguishable from a firearm in a school safety zone is a felony of the fifth degree.

(F)(1) In addition to any other penalty imposed upon a person who is convicted of or pleads guilty to a violation of this section and subject to division (F)(2) of this section, if the offender has not attained nineteen years of age, regardless of whether the offender is attending or is enrolled in a school operated by a board of education or for which the state board of education prescribes minimum standards under section 3301.07 of the Revised Code, the court shall impose upon the offender a class four suspension of the offender's probationary driver's license, restricted license, driver's license, commercial driver's license, temporary instruction permit, or probationary commercial driver's license that then is in effect from the range specified in division (A)(4) of section 4510.02 of the Revised Code and shall deny the offender the issuance of any permit or license of that type during the period of the suspension.

If the offender is not a resident of this state, the court shall impose a class four suspension of the nonresident operating privilege of the offender from the range specified in division (A)(4) of section 4510.02 of the Revised Code.

(2) If the offender shows good cause why the court should not suspend one of the types of licenses, permits, or privileges specified in division (F)(1) of this section or deny the issuance of one of the temporary instruction permits specified in that division, the court in its discretion may choose not to impose the suspension, revocation, or denial required in that division.

(G) As used in this section, "object that is indistinguishable from a firearm" means an object made, constructed, or altered so that, to a reasonable person without specialized training in firearms, the object appears to be a firearm.

**HISTORY: 144 v H 154 (Eff 7-31-92); 146 v S 2 (Eff 7-1-96); 146 v H 72 (Eff 3-18-97); 146 v H 124 (Eff 9-30-97); 148 v S 1. Eff 8-6-99; 149 v S 123, § 1, eff. 1-1-04; 150 v H 12, §§ 1, 3, eff. 4-8-04†; 151 v H 347, § 1, eff. 3-14-07; 152 v S 184, § 1, eff. 9-9-08.**

Governor Taft's veto of HB 347 was overridden by the Ohio General Assembly.

See provisions, § 5 of S.B. 123 (149 v —), following RC § 2923.01.

The provisions of § 3 of SB 1 (148 v —) read as follows:

SECTION 3. Section 2923.122 of the Revised Code is presented in this act as a composite of the section as amended by both Am. Sub. H.B. 72 and Am. Sub. H.B. 124 of the 121st General Assembly, with the new language of neither of the acts shown in capital letters. This is in recognition of the principle stated in division (B) of section 1.52 of the Revised Code that such amendments are to be harmonized where not substantively irreconcilable and constitutes a legislative finding that such is the resulting version in effect prior to the effective date of this act.

† Section 3, H.B. 12, Acts 2004, purported to amend the version of RC § 2923.122 as amended by S.B. 123 (149 v —), which took effect on January 1, 2004. However, H.B. 12, Acts 2004 was approved January 8, 2004, and became effective April 8, 2004.

## § 2923.123 Illegal conveyance of deadly weapon or dangerous ordnance into courthouse; illegal possession or control in courthouse.

(A) No person shall knowingly convey or attempt to convey a deadly weapon or dangerous ordnance into a courthouse or into another building or structure in which a courtroom is located.

(B) No person shall knowingly possess or have under the person's control a deadly weapon or dangerous ordnance in a courthouse or in another building or structure in which a courtroom is located.

(C) This section does not apply to any of the following:

(1) Except as provided in division (E) of this section, a judge of a court of record of this state or a magistrate;

(2) A peace officer, officer of a law enforcement agency, or person who is in either of the following categories:

(a) Except as provided in division (E) of this section, a peace officer, or an officer of a law enforcement agency of another state, a political subdivision of another state, or the United States, who is authorized to carry a deadly weapon or dangerous ordnance, who possesses or has under that individual's control a deadly weapon or dangerous ordnance as a requirement of that individual's duties, and who is acting within the scope of that individual's duties at the time of that possession or control;

(b) Except as provided in division (E) of this section, a person who is employed in this state, who is authorized to carry a deadly weapon or dangerous ordnance, who possesses or has under that individual's control a deadly weapon or dangerous ordnance as a requirement of that person's duties, and who is subject to and in compliance with the requirements of section 109.801 [109.80.1] of the Revised Code, unless the appointing authority of the person has expressly specified that the exemption provided in division (C)(2)(b) of this section does not apply to the person.

(3) A person who conveys, attempts to convey, possesses, or has under the person's control a deadly weapon or dangerous ordnance that is to be used as evidence in a pending criminal or civil action or proceeding;

(4) Except as provided in division (E) of this section, a bailiff or deputy bailiff of a court of record of this state who is authorized to carry a firearm pursuant to section 109.77 of the Revised Code, who possesses or has under that individual's control a firearm as a requirement of that individual's duties, and who is acting within the scope of that individual's duties at the time of that possession or control;

(5) Except as provided in division (E) of this section, a prosecutor, or a secret service officer appointed by a county prosecuting attorney, who is authorized to carry a deadly weapon or dangerous ordnance in the performance of the individual's duties, who possesses or has under that individual's control a deadly weapon or dangerous ordnance as a requirement of that individual's duties, and who is acting within the scope of that individual's duties at the time of that possession or control;

(6) Except as provided in division (E) of this section, a person who conveys or attempts to convey a handgun into a courthouse or into another building or structure in which a courtroom is located, who, at the time of the conveyance or attempt, is carrying a valid license or temporary emergency license to carry a concealed handgun issued to the person under section 2923.125 [2923.12.5] or 2923.1213 [2923.12.13] of the Revised Code or a license to carry a concealed handgun that was issued by another state

with which the attorney general has entered into a reciprocity agreement under section 109.69 of the Revised Code, and who transfers possession of the handgun to the officer or officer's designee who has charge of the courthouse or building. The officer shall secure the handgun until the licensee is prepared to leave the premises. The exemption described in this division applies only if the officer who has charge of the courthouse or building provides services of the nature described in this division. An officer who has charge of the courthouse or building is not required to offer services of the nature described in this division.

(D)(1) Whoever violates division (A) of this section is guilty of illegal conveyance of a deadly weapon or dangerous ordnance into a courthouse. Except as otherwise provided in this division, illegal conveyance of a deadly weapon or dangerous ordnance into a courthouse is a felony of the fifth degree. If the offender previously has been convicted of a violation of division (A) or (B) of this section, illegal conveyance of a deadly weapon or dangerous ordnance into a courthouse is a felony of the fourth degree.

(2) Whoever violates division (B) of this section is guilty of illegal possession or control of a deadly weapon or dangerous ordnance in a courthouse. Except as otherwise provided in this division, illegal possession or control of a deadly weapon or dangerous ordnance in a courthouse is a felony of the fifth degree. If the offender previously has been convicted of a violation of division (A) or (B) of this section, illegal possession or control of a deadly weapon or dangerous ordnance in a courthouse is a felony of the fourth degree.

(E) The exemptions described in divisions (C)(1), (2)(a), (2)(b), (4), (5), and (6) of this section do not apply to any judge, magistrate, peace officer, officer of a law enforcement agency, bailiff, deputy bailiff, prosecutor, secret service officer, or other person described in any of those divisions if a rule of superintendence or another type of rule adopted by the supreme court pursuant to Article IV, Ohio Constitution, or an applicable local rule of court prohibits all persons from conveying or attempting to convey a deadly weapon or dangerous ordnance into a courthouse or into another building or structure in which a courtroom is located or from possessing or having under one's control a deadly weapon or dangerous ordnance in a courthouse or in another building or structure in which a courtroom is located.

(F) As used in this section:

(1) "Magistrate" means an individual who is appointed by a court of record of this state and who has the powers and may perform the functions specified in Civil Rule 53, Criminal Rule 19, or Juvenile Rule 40.

(2) "Peace officer" and "prosecutor" have the same meanings as in section 2935.01 of the Revised Code.

**HISTORY: 146 v H 88 (Eff 9-3-96); 147 v H 151. Eff 9-16-97; 150 v H 12, § 1, eff. 4-8-04; 151 v H 347, § 1, eff. 3-14-07.**

Governor Taft's veto of HB 347 was overridden by the Ohio General Assembly.

See the provisions of §§ 6, 7, 9, and 10 of H.B. 12 (150 v —) following RC § 2923.12.

## [CONCEALED HANDGUN LICENSES]

## § 2923.124 Definitions.

As used in sections 2923.124 [2923.12.4] to 2923.1213 [2923.12.13] of the Revised Code:

(A) "Application form" means the application form prescribed pursuant to division (A)(1) of section 109.731 [109.73.1] of the Revised Code and includes a copy of that form.

(B) "Competency certification" and "competency certificate" mean a document of the type described in division (B)(3) of section 2923.125 [2923.12.5] of the Revised Code.

(C) "Detention facility" has the same meaning as in section 2921.01 of the Revised Code.

(D) "Licensee" means a person to whom a license to carry a concealed handgun has been issued under section 2923.125 [2923.12.5] of the Revised Code and, except when the context clearly indicates otherwise, includes a person to whom a temporary emergency license to carry a concealed handgun has been issued under section 2923.1213 [2923.12.13] of the Revised Code.

(E) "License fee" or "license renewal fee" means the fee for a license to carry a concealed handgun or the fee to renew that license that is prescribed pursuant to division (C) of section 109.731 [109.73.1] of the Revised Code and that is to be paid by an applicant for a license of that type.

(F) "Peace officer" has the same meaning as in section 2935.01 of the Revised Code.

(G) "State correctional institution" has the same meaning as in section 2967.01 of the Revised Code.

(H) "Valid license" means a license or temporary emergency license to carry a concealed handgun that has been issued under section 2923.125 [2923.12.5] or 2923.1213 [2923.12.13] of the Revised Code, that is currently valid, that is not under a suspension under division (A)(1) of section 2923.128 [2923.12.8] or under section 2923.1213 [2923.12.13] of the Revised Code, and that has not been revoked under division (B)(1) of section 2923.128 [2923.12.8] or under section 2923.1213 [2923.12.13] of the Revised Code.

(I) "Civil protection order" means a protection order issued, or consent agreement approved, under section 2903.214 [2903.21.4] or 3113.31 of the Revised Code.

(J) "Temporary protection order" means a protection order issued under section 2903.213 [2903.21.3] or 2919.26 of the Revised Code.

(K) "Protection order issued by a court of another state" has the same meaning as in section 2919.27 of the Revised Code.

(L) "Child day-care center," "type A family day-care home" and "type B family day-care home" have the same meanings as in section 5104.01 of the Revised Code.

(M) "Type C family day-care home" means a family day-care home authorized to provide child care by Sub. H.B. 62 of the 121st general assembly, as amended by Am. Sub. S.B. 160 of the 121st general assembly and Sub. H.B. 407 of the 123rd general assembly.

(N) "Foreign air transportation," "interstate air transportation," and "intrastate air transportation" have the same meanings as in 49 U.S.C. 40102, as now or hereafter amended.

(O) "Commercial motor vehicle" has the same meaning as in division (A) of section 4506.25 of the Revised Code.

(P) "Motor carrier enforcement unit" has the same meaning as in section 2923.16 of the Revised Code.

**HISTORY: 150 v H 12, § 1, eff. 4-8-04; 150 v H 11, § 1, eff. 5-18-05; 151 v H 347, § 1, eff. 3-14-07.**

Governor Taft's veto of HB 347 was overridden by the Ohio General Assembly.

See the provisions of §§ 6, 7, 9, and 10 of H.B. 12 (150 v —) following RC § 2923.12.

## § 2923.125 Application for license to carry concealed handgun; issuance, renewal.

(A) Upon the request of a person who wishes to obtain a license to carry a concealed handgun or to renew a license to carry a concealed handgun, a sheriff, as provided in division (I) of this section, shall provide to the person free of charge an application form and the web site address at which the pamphlet described in division (B) of section 109.731 of the Revised Code may be found. A sheriff shall accept a completed application form and the fee, items, materials, and information specified in divisions (B)(1) to (5) of this section at the times and in the manners described in division (I) of this section.

(B) An applicant for a license to carry a concealed handgun shall submit a completed application form and all of the following to the sheriff of the county in which the applicant resides or to the sheriff of any county adjacent to the county in which the applicant resides:

(1)(a) A nonrefundable license fee as described in either of the following:

(i) For an applicant who has been a resident of this state for five or more years, a fee of sixty-seven dollars;

(ii) For an applicant who has been a resident of this state for less than five years, a fee of sixty-seven dollars plus the actual cost of having a background check performed by the federal bureau of investigation.

(b) No sheriff shall require an applicant to pay for the cost of a background check performed by the bureau of criminal identification and investigation.

(c) A sheriff shall waive the payment of the license fee described in division (B)(1)(a) of this section in connection with an initial or renewal application for a license that is submitted by an applicant who is a retired peace officer, a retired person described in division (B)(1)(b) of section 109.77 of the Revised Code, or a retired federal law enforcement officer who, prior to retirement, was authorized under federal law to carry a firearm in the course of duty, unless the retired peace officer, person, or federal law enforcement officer retired as the result of a mental disability.

(d) The sheriff shall deposit all fees paid by an applicant under division (B)(1)(a) of this section into the sheriff's concealed handgun license issuance fund established pursuant to section 311.42 of the Revised Code. The county shall distribute the fees in accordance with section 311.42 of the Revised Code.

(2) A color photograph of the applicant that was taken within thirty days prior to the date of the application;

(3) One or more of the following competency certifications, each of which shall reflect that, regarding a certification described in division (B)(3)(a), (b), (c), (e), or (f) of this section, within the three years immediately preceding the application the applicant has performed that to which the competency certification relates and that, regarding a certification described in division (B)(3)(d) of this section, the applicant currently is an active or reserve member of the armed forces of the United States or within the six years immediately preceding the application the honorable discharge or retirement to which the competency certification relates occurred:

(a) An original or photocopy of a certificate of completion of a firearms safety, training, or requalification or firearms safety instructor course, class, or program that was offered by or under the auspices of the national rifle association and that complies with the requirements set forth in division (G) of this section;

(b) An original or photocopy of a certificate of completion of a firearms safety, training, or requalification or firearms safety instructor course, class, or program that satisfies all of the following criteria:

(i) It was open to members of the general public.

(ii) It utilized qualified instructors who were certified by the national rifle association, the executive director of the Ohio peace officer training commission pursuant to section 109.75 or 109.78 of the Revised Code, or a governmental official or entity of another state.

(iii) It was offered by or under the auspices of a law enforcement agency of this or another state or the United States, a public or private college, university, or other similar postsecondary educational institution located in this or another state, a firearms training school located in this or another state, or another type of public or private entity or organization located in this or another state.

(iv) It complies with the requirements set forth in division (G) of this section.

(c) An original or photocopy of a certificate of completion of a state, county, municipal, or department of natural resources peace officer training school that is approved by the executive director of the Ohio peace officer training commission pursuant to section 109.75 of the Revised Code and that complies with the requirements set forth in division (G) of this section, or the applicant has satisfactorily completed and been issued a certificate of completion of a basic firearms training program, a firearms requalification training program, or another basic training program described in section 109.78 or 109.801 of the Revised Code that complies with the requirements set forth in division (G) of this section;

(d) A document that evidences both of the following:

(i) That the applicant is an active or reserve member of the armed forces of the United States, was honorably discharged from military service in the active or reserve armed forces of the United States, is a retired trooper of the state highway patrol, or is a retired peace officer or federal law enforcement officer described in division (B)(1) of this section or a retired person described in division (B)(1)(b) of section 109.77 of the Revised Code and division (B)(1) of this section;

(ii) That, through participation in the military service or through the former employment described in division (B)(3)(d)(i) of this section, the applicant acquired experience with handling handguns or other firearms, and the experience so acquired was equivalent to training that the applicant could have acquired in a course, class, or program described in division (B)(3)(a), (b), or (c) of this section.

(e) A certificate or another similar document that evidences satisfactory completion of a firearms training, safety, or requalification or firearms safety instructor course, class, or program that is not otherwise described in division (B)(3)(a), (b), (c), or (d) of this section, that was conducted by an instructor who was certified by an official or entity of the government of this or another state or the United States or by the national rifle association, and that complies with the requirements set forth in division (G) of this section;

(f) An affidavit that attests to the applicant's satisfactory completion of a course, class, or program described in division (B)(3)(a), (b), (c), or (e) of this section and that is subscribed by the applicant's instructor or an authorized representative of the entity that offered the course, class, or program or under whose auspices the course, class, or program was offered.

(4) A certification by the applicant that the applicant has read the pamphlet prepared by the Ohio peace officer training commission pursuant to section 109.731 of the Revised Code that reviews firearms, dispute resolution, and use of deadly force matters.

(5) A set of fingerprints of the applicant provided as described in section 311.41 of the Revised Code through use of an electronic fingerprint reading device or, if the sheriff to whom the application is submitted does not possess and does not have ready access to the use of such a reading device, on a standard impression sheet prescribed pursuant to division (C)(2) of section 109.572 of the Revised Code.

(C) Upon receipt of an applicant's completed application form, supporting documentation, and, if not waived, license fee, a sheriff, in the manner specified in section 311.41 of the Revised Code, shall conduct or cause to be conducted the criminal records check and the incompetency records check described in section 311.41 of the Revised Code.

(D)(1) Except as provided in division (D)(3) or (4) of this section, within forty-five days after a sheriff's receipt of an applicant's completed application form for a license to carry a concealed handgun, the supporting documentation, and, if not waived, the license fee, the sheriff shall make available through the law enforcement automated data system in accordance with division (H) of this section the information described in that division and, upon making the information available through the system, shall issue to the applicant a license to carry a concealed handgun that shall expire as described in division (D)(2)(a) of this section if all of the following apply:

(a) The applicant is legally living in the United States, has been a resident of this state for at least forty-five days, and has been a resident of the county in which the person seeks the license or a county adjacent to the county in which the person seeks the license for at least thirty days. For purposes of division (D)(1)(a) of this section:

(i) If a person is absent from the United States, from this state, or from a particular county in this state in compliance with military or naval orders as an active or reserve member of the armed forces of the United States and if prior to leaving this state in compliance with those orders the person was legally living in the United States and was a resident of this state, the person, solely by reason of that absence, shall not be considered to have lost the person's status as living in the United States or the person's residence in this state or in the county in which the person was a resident prior to leaving this state in compliance with those orders, without regard to whether or not the person intends to return to this state or to that county, shall not be considered to have acquired a residence in any other state, and shall not be considered to have become a resident of any other state.

(ii) If a person is present in this state in compliance with military or naval orders as an active or reserve member of the armed forces of the United States for at least forty-five days, the person shall be considered to have been a resident of this state for that period of at least forty-five days, and, if a person is present in a county of this state in compliance with military or naval orders as an active or reserve member of the armed forces of the United States for at least thirty days, the person shall be considered to have been a resident of that county for that period of at least thirty days.

(b) The applicant is at least twenty-one years of age.

(c) The applicant is not a fugitive from justice.

(d) The applicant is not under indictment for or otherwise charged with a felony; an offense under Chapter 2925., 3719., or 4729. of the Revised Code that involves the illegal possession, use, sale, administration, or distribution of or trafficking in a drug of abuse; a misdemeanor offense of violence; or a violation of section 2903.14 or 2923.1211 of the Revised Code.

(e) Except as otherwise provided in division (D)(5) of this section, the applicant has not been convicted of or pleaded guilty to a felony or an offense under Chapter 2925., 3719., or 4729. of the Revised Code that involves the illegal possession, use, sale, administration, or distribution of or trafficking in a drug of abuse; has not been adjudicated a delinquent child for committing an act that if committed by an adult would be a felony or would be an offense under Chapter 2925., 3719., or 4729. of the Revised Code that involves the illegal possession, use, sale, administration, or distribution of or trafficking in a drug of abuse; and has not been convicted of, pleaded guilty to, or adjudicated a delinquent child for committing a violation of section 2903.13 of the Revised Code when the victim of the violation is a peace officer, regardless of whether the applicant was sentenced under division (C)(3) of that section.

(f) Except as otherwise provided in division (D)(5) of this section, the applicant, within three years of the date of the application, has not been convicted of or pleaded guilty to a misdemeanor offense of violence other than a misdemeanor violation of section 2921.33 of the Revised Code or a violation of section 2903.13 of the Revised Code when the victim of the violation is a peace officer, or a misdemeanor violation of section 2923.1211 of the Revised Code; and has not been adjudicated a delinquent child for committing an act that if committed by an adult would be a misdemeanor offense of violence other than a misdemeanor violation of section 2921.33 of the Revised Code or a violation of section 2903.13 of the Revised Code when the victim of the violation is a peace officer or for committing an act that if committed by an adult would be a misdemeanor violation of section 2923.1211 of the Revised Code.

(g) Except as otherwise provided in division (D)(1)(e) of this section, the applicant, within five years of the date of the application, has not been convicted of, pleaded guilty to, or adjudicated a delinquent child for committing two or more violations of section 2903.13 or 2903.14 of the Revised Code.

(h) Except as otherwise provided in division (D)(5) of this section, the applicant, within ten years of the date of the application, has not been convicted of, pleaded guilty to, or adjudicated a delinquent child for committing a violation of section 2921.33 of the Revised Code.

(i) The applicant has not been adjudicated as a mental defective, has not been committed to any mental institution, is not under adjudication of mental incompetence, has not been found by a court to be a mentally ill person subject to hospitalization by court order, and is not an involuntary patient other than one who is a patient only for purposes of observation. As used in this division, "mentally ill person subject to hospitalization by court order" and "patient" have the same meanings as in section 5122.01 of the Revised Code.

(j) The applicant is not currently subject to a civil protection order, a temporary protection order, or a protection order issued by a court of another state.

(k) The applicant certifies that the applicant desires a legal means to carry a concealed handgun for defense of the applicant or a member of the applicant's family while engaged in lawful activity.

(l) The applicant submits a competency certification of the type described in division (B)(3) of this section and submits a certification of the type described in division (B)(4) of this section regarding the applicant's reading of the pamphlet prepared by the Ohio peace officer training commission pursuant to section 109.731 of the Revised Code.

(m) The applicant currently is not subject to a suspension imposed under division (A)(2) of section 2923.128 of the Revised Code of a license to carry a concealed handgun, or a temporary emergency license to carry a concealed handgun, that previously was issued to the applicant under this section or section 2923.1213 of the Revised Code.

(2)(a) A license to carry a concealed handgun that a sheriff issues under division (D)(1) of this section on or after March 14, 2007, shall expire five years after the date of issuance. A license to carry a concealed handgun that a sheriff issued under division (D)(1) of this section prior to March 14, 2007, shall expire four years after the date of issuance.

If a sheriff issues a license under this section, the sheriff shall place on the license a unique combination of letters and numbers identifying the license in accordance with the procedure prescribed by the Ohio peace officer training commission pursuant to section 109.731 of the Revised Code.

(b) If a sheriff denies an application under this section because the applicant does not satisfy the criteria described in division (D)(1) of this section, the sheriff shall specify the grounds for the denial in a written notice to the applicant. The applicant may appeal the denial pursuant to section 119.12 of the Revised Code in the county served by the sheriff who denied the application. If the denial was as a result of the criminal records check conducted pursuant to section 311.41 of the Revised Code and if, pursuant to section 2923.127 of the Revised Code, the applicant challenges the criminal records check results using the appropriate challenge and review procedure specified in that section, the time for filing the appeal pursuant to section 119.12 of the Revised Code and this division is tolled during the pendency of the request or the challenge and review. If the court in an appeal under section 119.12 of the Revised Code and this division enters a judgment sustaining the sheriff's refusal to grant to the applicant a license to carry a concealed handgun, the applicant may file a new application beginning one year after the judgment is entered. If the court enters a judgment in favor of the applicant, that judgment shall not restrict the authority of a sheriff to suspend or revoke the license pursuant to section 2923.128 or 2923.1213 of the Revised Code or to refuse to renew the license for any proper cause that may occur after the date the judgment is entered. In the appeal, the court shall have full power to dispose of all costs.

(3) If the sheriff with whom an application for a license to carry a concealed handgun was filed under this section becomes aware that the applicant has been arrested for or otherwise charged with an offense that would disqualify the applicant from holding the license, the sheriff shall suspend the processing of the application until the disposition of the case arising from the arrest or charge.

(4) If the sheriff determines that the applicant is legally living in the United States and is a resident of the county in which the applicant seeks the license or of an adjacent county but does not yet meet the residency requirements described in division (D)(1)(a) of this section, the sheriff shall not deny the license because of the residency requirements but shall not issue the license until the applicant meets those residency requirements.

(5) If an applicant has been convicted of or pleaded guilty to an offense identified in division (D)(1)(e), (f), or (h) of this section or has been adjudicated a delinquent child for committing an act or violation identified in any of those divisions, and if a court has ordered the sealing or expungement of the records of that conviction, guilty plea, or adjudication pursuant to sections 2151.355 to 2151.358, sections 2953.31 to 2953.36, or section 2953.37 of the Revised Code or a court has granted the applicant relief pursuant to section 2923.14 of the Revised Code from the disability imposed pursuant to section 2923.13 of the Revised Code relative to that conviction, guilty plea, or adjudication, the sheriff with whom the application was submitted shall not consider the conviction, guilty plea, or adjudication in making a determination under division (D)(1) or (F) of this section or, in relation to an application for a temporary emergency license to carry a concealed handgun submitted under section 2923.1213 of the Revised Code, in making a determination under division (B)(2) of that section.

(E) If a license to carry a concealed handgun issued under this section is lost or is destroyed, the licensee may obtain from the sheriff who issued that license a duplicate license upon the payment of a fee of fifteen dollars and the submission of an affidavit attesting to the loss or destruction of the license. The sheriff, in accordance with the procedures prescribed in section 109.731 of the Revised Code, shall place on the replacement license a combination of identifying numbers different from the combination on the license that is being replaced.

(F)(1) A licensee who wishes to renew a license to carry a concealed handgun issued under this section shall do so not earlier than ninety days before the expiration date of the license or at any time after the expiration date of the license by filing with the sheriff of the county in which the applicant resides or with the sheriff of an adjacent county an application for renewal of the license obtained pursuant to division (D) of this section, a certification by the applicant that, subsequent to the issuance of the license, the applicant has reread the pamphlet prepared by the Ohio peace officer training commission pursuant to section 109.731 of the Revised Code that reviews firearms, dispute resolution, and use of deadly force matters, a nonrefundable license renewal fee in an amount determined pursuant to division (F)(4) of this section unless the fee is waived, and one of the following:

(a) If the licensee previously has not renewed a license to carry a concealed handgun issued under this section, proof that the licensee at one time had a competency certification of the type described in division (B)(3) of this section. A valid license, expired license, or any other previously issued license that has not been revoked is prima-facie evidence that the licensee at one time had a competency certification of the type described in division (B)(3) of this section.

(b) If the licensee previously has renewed a license to carry a concealed handgun issued under this section, a renewed competency certification of the type described in division (G)(4) of this section.

(2) A sheriff shall accept a completed renewal application, the license renewal fee, and information specified in division (F)(1) of this section at the times and in the

manners described in division (I) of this section. Upon receipt of a completed renewal application, of certification that the applicant has reread the specified pamphlet prepared by the Ohio peace officer training commission, of proof of a prior competency certification for an initial renewal or of a renewed competency certification for a second or subsequent renewal, and of a license renewal fee unless the fee is waived, a sheriff, in the manner specified in section 311.41 of the Revised Code shall conduct or cause to be conducted the criminal records check and the incompetency records check described in section 311.41 of the Revised Code. The sheriff shall renew the license if the sheriff determines that the applicant continues to satisfy the requirements described in division (D)(1) of this section, except that the applicant is not required to meet the requirements of division (D)(1)(l) of this section. A renewed license that is renewed on or after March 14, 2007, shall expire five years after the date of issuance, and a renewed license that is renewed prior to March 14, 2007, shall expire four years after the date of issuance. A renewed license is subject to division (E) of this section and sections 2923.126 and 2923.128 of the Revised Code. A sheriff shall comply with divisions (D)(2) to (4) of this section when the circumstances described in those divisions apply to a requested license renewal. If a sheriff denies the renewal of a license to carry a concealed handgun, the applicant may appeal the denial, or challenge the criminal record check results that were the basis of the denial if applicable, in the same manner as specified in division (D)(2)(b) of this section and in section 2923.127 of the Revised Code, regarding the denial of a license under this section.

(3) A renewal application submitted pursuant to division (F) of this section shall only require the licensee to list on the application form information and matters occurring since the date of the licensee's last application for a license pursuant to division (B) or (F) of this section. A sheriff conducting the criminal records check and the incompetency records check described in section 311.41 of the Revised Code shall conduct the check only from the date of the licensee's last application for a license pursuant to division (B) or (F) of this section through the date of the renewal application submitted pursuant to division (F) of this section.

(4) An applicant for a renewal license to carry a concealed handgun shall submit to the sheriff of the county in which the applicant resides or to the sheriff of any county adjacent to the county in which the applicant resides a nonrefundable license fee as described in either of the following:

(a) For an applicant who has been a resident of this state for five or more years, a fee of fifty dollars;

(b) For an applicant who has been a resident of this state for less than five years, a fee of fifty dollars plus the actual cost of having a background check performed by the federal bureau of investigation.

(G)(1) Each course, class, or program described in division (B)(3)(a), (b), (c), or (e) of this section shall provide to each person who takes the course, class, or program the web site address at which the pamphlet prepared by the Ohio peace officer training commission pursuant to section 109.731 of the Revised Code that reviews firearms, dispute resolution, and use of deadly force matters may be found. Each such course, class, or program described in one of those divisions shall include at least twelve hours of training in the safe handling and use of a firearm that shall include all of the following:

(a) At least ten hours of training on the following matters:

(i) The ability to name, explain, and demonstrate the rules for safe handling of a handgun and proper storage practices for handguns and ammunition;

(ii) The ability to demonstrate and explain how to handle ammunition in a safe manner;

(iii) The ability to demonstrate the knowledge, skills, and attitude necessary to shoot a handgun in a safe manner;

(iv) Gun handling training.

(b) At least two hours of training that consists of range time and live-fire training.

(2) To satisfactorily complete the course, class, or program described in division (B)(3)(a), (b), (c), or (e) of this section, the applicant shall pass a competency examination that shall include both of the following:

(a) A written section on the ability to name and explain the rules for the safe handling of a handgun and proper storage practices for handguns and ammunition;

(b) A physical demonstration of competence in the use of a handgun and in the rules for safe handling and storage of a handgun and a physical demonstration of the attitude necessary to shoot a handgun in a safe manner.

(3) The competency certification described in division (B)(3)(a), (b), (c), or (e) of this section shall be dated and shall attest that the course, class, or program the applicant successfully completed met the requirements described in division (G)(1) of this section and that the applicant passed the competency examination described in division (G)(2) of this section.

(4) A person who previously has received a competency certification as described in division (B)(3) of this section, or who previously has received a renewed competency certification as described in this division, may obtain a renewed competency certification pursuant to this division. If the person previously has received a competency certification or previously has received a renewed competency certification, the person may obtain a renewed competency certification from an entity that offers a course, class, or program described in division (B)(3)(a), (b), (c), or (e) of this section by passing a test that demonstrates that the person is range competent. In these circumstances, the person is not required to attend the course, class, or program or to take the competency examination described in division (G)(2) of this section for the renewed competency certification in order to be eligible to receive a renewed competency certification. A renewed competency certification issued under this division shall be dated and shall attest that the person has demonstrated range competency.

(H) Upon deciding to issue a license, deciding to issue a replacement license, or deciding to renew a license to carry a concealed handgun pursuant to this section, and before actually issuing or renewing the license, the sheriff shall make available through the law enforcement automated data system all information contained on the license. If the license subsequently is suspended under division (A)(1) or (2) of section 2923.128 of the Revised Code, revoked pursuant to division (B)(1) of section 2923.128 of the Revised Code, or lost or destroyed, the sheriff also shall make available through the law enforcement automated data system a notation of that fact. The superintendent of the state highway patrol shall ensure that the law enforcement automated data system is so configured as to permit the transmission through the system of the information specified in this division.

(I) A sheriff shall accept a completed application form or renewal application, and the fee, items, materials, and information specified in divisions (B)(1) to (5) or division (F) of this section, whichever is applicable, and shall provide an application form or renewal application to any person during at least fifteen hours a week and shall provide the web site address at which the pamphlet described in division (B) of section 109.731 of the Revised Code may be found at any time, upon request. The sheriff shall post notice of the hours during which the sheriff is available to accept or provide the information described in this division.

**HISTORY: 150 v H 12, § 1, eff. 4-8-04; 151 v H 347, § 1, eff. 3-14-07; 152 v S 184, § 1, eff. 9-9-08; 152 v H 450, § 1, eff. 4-7-09; 153 v H 1, § 101.01, eff. 10-16-09; 2011 SB 17, § 1, eff. Sept. 30, 2011.**

The effective date is set by § 812.10 of 153 v H 1.

Governor Taft's veto of HB 347 was overridden by the Ohio General Assembly.

See the provisions of § 10 of H.B. 12 (150 v —) following RC § 2923.12.

## § 2923.126 Expiration of license; carrying of license and identification; notice of change of residence; motor vehicle and law enforcement stops; prohibited places; retired peace officers.

(A) A license to carry a concealed handgun that is issued under section 2923.125 [2923.12.5] of the Revised Code on or after March 14, 2007, shall expire five years after the date of issuance, and a license that is so issued prior to March 14, 2007, shall expire four years after the date of issuance. A licensee who has been issued a license under that section shall be granted a grace period of thirty days after the licensee's license expires during which the licensee's license remains valid. Except as provided in divisions (B) and (C) of this section, a licensee who has been issued a license under section 2923.125 [2923.12.5] or 2923.1213 [2923.12.13] of the Revised Code may carry a concealed handgun anywhere in this state if the licensee also carries a valid license and valid identification when the licensee is in actual possession of a concealed handgun. The licensee shall give notice of any change in the licensee's residence address to the sheriff who issued the license within forty-five days after that change.

If a licensee is the driver or an occupant of a motor vehicle that is stopped as the result of a traffic stop or a stop for another law enforcement purpose and if the licensee is transporting or has a loaded handgun in the motor vehicle at that time, the licensee shall promptly inform any law enforcement officer who approaches the vehicle while stopped that the licensee has been issued a license or temporary emergency license to carry a concealed handgun and that the licensee currently possesses or has a loaded handgun; the licensee shall not knowingly diregard or fail to comply with lawful orders of a law enforcement officer given while the motor vehicle is stopped, knowingly fail to remain in the motor vehicle while stopped, or knowingly fail to keep the licensee's hands in plain sight after any law enforcement officer begins approaching the licensee while stopped and before the officer leaves, unless directed otherwise by a law enforcement officer; and the licensee shall not knowingly remove, attempt to remove, grasp, or hold the loaded handgun or knowingly have contact with the loaded handgun by touching it with the licensee's hands or fingers, in any manner in violation of division (E) of section 2923.16 of the Revised Code, after any law enforcement officer begins approaching the licensee while stopped and before the officer leaves. Additionally, if a licensee is the driver or an occupant of a commercial motor vehicle that is stopped by an employee of the motor carrier enforcement unit for the purposes defined in section 5503.04 of the Revised Code and if the licensee is transporting or has a loaded handgun in the commercial motor vehicle at that time, the licensee shall promptly inform the employee of the unit who approaches the vehicle while stopped that the licensee has been issued a license or temporary emergency license to carry a concealed handgun and that the licensee currently possesses or has a loaded handgun.

If a licensee is stopped for a law enforcement purpose and if the licensee is carrying a concealed handgun at the time the officer approaches, the licensee shall promptly inform any law enforcement officer who approaches the licensee while stopped that the licensee has been issued a license or temporary emergency license to carry a concealed handgun and that the licensee currently is carrying a concealed handgun; the licensee shall not knowingly disregard or fail to comply with lawful orders of a law enforcement officer given while the licensee is stopped or knowingly fail to keep the licensee's hands in plain sight after any law enforcement officer begins approaching the licensee while stopped and before the officer leaves, unless directed otherwise by a law enforcement officer; and the licensee shall not knowingly remove, attempt to remove, grasp, or hold the loaded handgun or knowingly have contact with the loaded handgun by touching it with the licensee's hands or fingers, in any manner in violation of division (B) of section 2923.12 of the Revised Code, after any law enforcement officer begins approaching the licensee while stopped and before the officer leaves.

(B) A valid license issued under section 2923.125 [2923.12.5] or 2923.1213 [2923.12.13] of the Revised Code does not authorize the licensee to carry a concealed handgun in any manner prohibited under division (B) of section 2923.12 of the Revised Code or in any manner prohibited under section 2923.16 of the Revised Code. A valid license does not authorize the licensee to carry a concealed handgun into any of the following places:

(1) A police station, sheriff's office, or state highway patrol station, premises controlled by the bureau of criminal identification and investigation, a state correctional institution, jail, workhouse, or other detention facility, an airport passenger terminal, or an institution that is maintained, operated, managed, and governed pursuant to division (A) of section 5119.02 of the Revised Code or division (A)(1) of section 5123.03 of the Revised Code;

(2) A school safety zone, if the licensee's carrying the concealed handgun is in violation of section 2923.122 [2923.12.2] of the Revised Code;

(3) A courthouse or another building or structure in which a courtroom is located, in violation of section 2923.123 [2923.12.3] of the Revised Code;

(4) Any premises or open air arena for which a D permit has been issued under Chapter 4303. of the Revised Code if the licensee's carrying the concealed handgun is in violation of section 2923.121 [2923.12.1] of the Revised Code;

(5) Any premises owned or leased by any public or private college, university, or other institution of higher education, unless the handgun is in a locked motor vehicle

or the licensee is in the immediate process of placing the handgun in a locked motor vehicle;

(6) Any church, synagogue, mosque, or other place of worship, unless the church, synagogue, mosque, or other place of worship posts or permits otherwise;

(7) A child day-care center, a type A family day-care home, a type B family day-care home, or a type C family day-care home, except that this division does not prohibit a licensee who resides in a type A family day-care home, a type B family day-care home, or a type C family day-care home from carrying a concealed handgun at any time in any part of the home that is not dedicated or used for day-care purposes, or from carrying a concealed handgun in a part of the home that is dedicated or used for day-care purposes at any time during which no children, other than children of that licensee, are in the home;

(8) An aircraft that is in, or intended for operation in, foreign air transportation, interstate air transportation, intrastate air transportation, or the transportation of mail by aircraft;

(9) Any building that is a government facility of this state or a political subdivision of this state and that is not a building that is used primarily as a shelter, restroom, parking facility for motor vehicles, or rest facility and is not a courthouse or other building or structure in which a courtroom is located that is subject to division (B)(3) of this section;

(10) A place in which federal law prohibits the carrying of handguns.

(C)(1) Nothing in this section shall negate or restrict a rule, policy, or practice of a private employer that is not a private college, university, or other institution of higher education concerning or prohibiting the presence of firearms on the private employer's premises or property, including motor vehicles owned by the private employer. Nothing in this section shall require a private employer of that nature to adopt a rule, policy, or practice concerning or prohibiting the presence of firearms on the private employer's premises or property, including motor vehicles owned by the private employer.

(2)(a) A private employer shall be immune from liability in a civil action for any injury, death, or loss to person or property that allegedly was caused by or related to a licensee bringing a handgun onto the premises or property of the private employer, including motor vehicles owned by the private employer, unless the private employer acted with malicious purpose. A private employer is immune from liability in a civil action for any injury, death, or loss to person or property that allegedly was caused by or related to the private employer's decision to permit a licensee to bring, or prohibit a licensee from bringing, a handgun onto the premises or property of the private employer. As used in this division, "private employer" includes a private college, university, or other institution of higher education.

(b) A political subdivision shall be immune from liability in a civil action, to the extent and in the manner provided in Chapter 2744. of the Revised Code, for any injury, death, or loss to person or property that allegedly was caused by or related to a licensee bringing a handgun onto any premises or property owned, leased, or otherwise under the control of the political subdivision. As used in this division, "political subdivision" has the same meaning as in section 2744.01 of the Revised Code.

(3)(a) Except as provided in division (C)(3)(b) of this section, the owner or person in control of private land or premises, and a private person or entity leasing land or premises owned by the state, the United States, or a political subdivision of the state or the United States, may post a sign in a conspicuous location on that land or on those premises prohibiting persons from carrying firearms or concealed firearms on or onto that land or those premises. Except as otherwise provided in this division, a person who knowingly violates a posted prohibition of that nature is guilty of criminal trespass in violation of division (A)(4) of section 2911.21 of the Revised Code and is guilty of a misdemeanor of the fourth degree. If a person knowingly violates a posted prohibition of that nature and the posted land or premises primarily was a parking lot or other parking facility, the person is not guilty of criminal trespass in violation of division (A)(4) of section 2911.21 of the Revised Code and instead is subject only to a civil cause of action for trespass based on the violation.

(b) A landlord may not prohibit or restrict a tenant who is a licensee and who on or after the effective date of this amendment enters into a rental agreement with the landlord for the use of residential premises, and the tenant's guest while the tenant is present, from lawfully carrying or possessing a handgun on those residential premises.

(c) As used in division (C)(3) of this section:

(i) "Residential premises" has the same meaning as in section 5321.01 of the Revised Code, except "residential premises" does not include a dwelling unit that is owned or operated by a college or university.

(ii) "Landlord," "tenant," and "rental agreement" have the same meanings as in section 5321.01 of the Revised Code.

(D) A person who holds a license to carry a concealed handgun that was issued pursuant to the law of another state that is recognized by the attorney general pursuant to a reciprocity agreement entered into pursuant to section 109.69 of the Revised Code has the same right to carry a concealed handgun in this state as a person who was issued a license to carry a concealed handgun under section 2923.125 [2923.12.5] of the Revised Code and is subject to the same restrictions that apply to a person who carries a license issued under that section.

(E) A peace officer has the same right to carry a concealed handgun in this state as a person who was issued a license to carry a concealed handgun under section 2923.125 [2923.12.5] of the Revised Code. For purposes of reciprocity with other states, a peace officer shall be considered to be a licensee in this state.

(F)(1) A qualified retired peace officer who possesses a retired peace officer identification card issued pursuant to division (F)(2) of this section and a valid firearms requalification certification issued pursuant to division (F)(3) of this section has the same right to carry a concealed handgun in this state as a person who was issued a license to carry a concealed handgun under section 2923.125 [2923.12.5] of the Revised Code and is subject to the same restrictions that apply to a person who carries a license issued under that section. For purposes of reciprocity with other states, a qualified retired peace officer who possesses a retired peace officer identification card issued pursuant to division (F)(2) of this section and a valid firearms requalification certification issued pursuant to division (F)(3) of this section shall be considered to be a licensee in this state.

(2)(a) Each public agency of this state or of a political subdivision of this state that is served by one or more peace officers shall issue a retired peace officer identification card to any person who retired from service as a peace officer with that agency, if the issuance is in accordance with the agency's policies and procedures and if the person, with respect to the person's service with that agency, satisfies all of the following:

(i) The person retired in good standing from service as a peace officer with the public agency, and the retirement was not for reasons of mental instability.

(ii) Before retiring from service as a peace officer with that agency, the person was authorized to engage in or supervise the prevention, detection, investigation, or prosecution of, or the incarceration of any person for, any violation of law and the person had statutory powers of arrest.

(iii) At the time of the person's retirement as a peace officer with that agency, the person was trained and qualified to carry firearms in the performance of the peace officer's duties.

(iv) Before retiring from service as a peace officer with that agency, the person was regularly employed as a peace officer for an aggregate of fifteen years or more, or, in the alternative, the person retired from service as a peace officer with that agency, after completing any applicable probationary period of that service, due to a service-connected disability, as determined by the agency.

(b) A retired peace officer identification card issued to a person under division (F)(2)(a) of this section shall identify the person by name, contain a photograph of the person, identify the public agency of this state or of the political subdivision of this state from which the person retired as a peace officer and that is issuing the identification card, and specify that the person retired in good standing from service as a peace officer with the issuing public agency and satisfies the criteria set forth in divisions (F)(2)(a)(i) to (iv) of this section. In addition to the required content specified in this division, a retired peace officer identification card issued to a person under division (F)(2)(a) of this section may include the firearms requalification certification described in division (F)(3) of this section, and if the identification card includes that certification, the identification card shall serve as the firearms requalification certification for the retired peace officer. If the issuing public agency issues credentials to active law enforcement officers who serve the agency, the agency may comply with division (F)(2)(a) of this section by issuing the same credentials to persons who retired from service as a peace officer with the agency and who satisfy the criteria set forth in divisions (F)(2)(a)(i) to (iv) of this section, provided that the credentials so issued to retired peace officers are stamped with the word "RETIRED."

(c) A public agency of this state or of a political subdivision of this state may charge persons who retired from service as a peace officer with the agency a reasonable fee for issuing to the person a retired peace officer identification card pursuant to division (F)(2)(a) of this section.

(3) If a person retired from service as a peace officer with a public agency of this state or of a political subdivision of this state and the person satisfies the criteria set forth in divisions (F)(2)(a)(i) to (iv) of this section, the public agency may provide the retired peace officer with the opportunity to attend a firearms requalification program that is approved for purposes of firearms requalification required under section 109.801 [109.80.1] of the Revised Code. The retired peace officer may be required to pay the cost of the course.

If a retired peace officer who satisfies the criteria set forth in divisions (F)(2)(a)(i) to (iv) of this section attends a firearms requalification program that is approved for purposes of firearms requalification required under section 109.801 [109.80.1] of the Revised Code, the retired peace officer's successful completion of the firearms requalification program requalifies the retired peace officer for purposes of division (F) of this section for five years from the date on which the program was successfully completed, and the requalification is valid during that five-year period. If a retired peace officer who satisfies the criteria set forth in divisions (F)(2)(a)(i) to (iv) of this section satisfactorily completes such a firearms requalification program, the retired peace officer shall be issued a firearms requalification certification that identifies the retired peace officer by name, identifies the entity that taught the program, specifies that the retired peace officer successfully completed the program, specifies the date on which the course was successfully completed, and specifies that the requalification is valid for five years from that date of successful completion. The firearms requalification certification for a retired peace officer may be included in the retired peace officer identification card issued to the retired peace officer under division (F)(2) of this section.

A retired peace officer who attends a firearms requalification program that is approved for purposes of firearms requalification required under section 109.801 [109.80.1] of the Revised Code may be required to pay the cost of the program.

(G) As used in this section:

(1) "Qualified retired peace officer" means a person who satisfies all of the following:

(a) The person satisfies the criteria set forth in divisions (F)(2)(a)(i) to (v) of this section.

(b) The person is not under the influence of alcohol or another intoxicating or hallucinatory drug or substance.

(c) The person is not prohibited by federal law from receiving firearms.

(2) "Retired peace officer identification card" means an identification card that is issued pursuant to division (F)(2) of this section to a person who is a retired peace officer.

(3) "Government facility of this state or a political subdivision of this state" means any of the following:

(a) A building or part of a building that is owned or leased by the government of this state or a political subdivision of this state and where employees of the government of this state or the political subdivision regularly are present for the purpose of performing their official duties as employees of the state or political subdivision;

(b) The office of a deputy registrar serving pursuant to Chapter 4503. of the Revised Code that is used to perform deputy registrar functions.

**HISTORY: 150 v H 12, § 1, eff. 4-8-04; 151 v H 347, § 1, eff. 3-14-07; 152 v S 184, § 1, eff. 9-9-08.**

Governor Taft's veto of HB 347 was overridden by the Ohio General Assembly.

See the provisions of § 10 of H.B. 12 (150 v —) following RC § 2923.12.

## § 2923.127 Challenge of criminal records check.

(A) If a sheriff denies an application for a license to carry a concealed handgun, denies the renewal of a license to carry a concealed handgun, or denies an application for a temporary emergency license to carry a concealed handgun as a result of the criminal records check conducted pursuant to section 311.41 of the Revised Code and if the applicant believes the denial was based on incorrect information reported by the source the sheriff used in conducting the criminal records check, the applicant may challenge the criminal records check results using whichever of the following is applicable:

(1) If the bureau of criminal identification and investigation performed the criminal records check, by using the bureau's existing challenge and review procedures;

(2) If division (A)(1) of this section does not apply, by using the existing challenge and review procedure of the sheriff who denied the application or, if the sheriff does not have a challenge and review procedure, by using the challenge and review procedure prescribed by the bureau of criminal identification and investigation pursuant to division (B) of this section.

(B) The bureau of criminal identification and investigation shall prescribe a challenge and review procedure for applicants to use to challenge criminal records checks under division (A)(2) of this section in counties in which the sheriff with whom the application for a license to carry a concealed handgun or for the renewal of a license to carry a concealed handgun was filed or with whom the application for a temporary emergency license to carry a concealed handgun was submitted does not have an existing challenge and review procedure.

**HISTORY: 150 v H 12, § 1, eff. 4-8-04; 151 v H 347, § 1, eff. 3-14-07.**

Governor Taft's veto of HB 347 was overridden by the Ohio General Assembly.

See the provisions of § 10 of H.B. 12 (150 v —) following RC § 2923.12.

## § 2923.128 Suspension or revocation of license.

(A)(1)(a) If a licensee holding a valid license issued under section 2923.125 or 2923.1213 of the Revised Code is arrested for or otherwise charged with an offense described in division (D)(1)(d) of section 2923.125 of the Revised Code or with a violation of section 2923.15 of the Revised Code or becomes subject to a temporary protection order or to a protection order issued by a court of another state that is substantially equivalent to a temporary protection order, the sheriff who issued the license or temporary emergency license shall suspend it and shall comply with division (A)(3) of this section upon becoming aware of the arrest, charge, or protection order. Upon suspending the license or temporary emergency license, the sheriff also shall comply with division (H) of section 2923.125 of the Revised Code.

(b) A suspension under division (A)(1)(a) of this section shall be considered as beginning on the date that the licensee is arrested for or otherwise charged with an offense described in that division or on the date the appropriate court issued the protection order described in that division, irrespective of when the sheriff notifies the licensee under division (A)(3) of this section. The suspension shall end on the date on which the charges are dismissed or the licensee is found not guilty of the offense described in division (A)(1)(a) of this section or, subject to division (B) of this section, on the date the appropriate court terminates the protection order described in that division. If the suspension so ends, the sheriff shall return the license or temporary emergency license to the licensee.

(2)(a) If a licensee holding a valid license issued under section 2923.125 or 2923.1213 of the Revised Code is convicted of or pleads guilty to a misdemeanor violation of division (B)(1), (2), or (4) of section 2923.12 of the Revised Code or of division (E)(1), (2), (3), or (5) of section 2923.16 of the Revised Code, except as provided in division (A)(2)(c) of this section and subject to division (C) of this section, the sheriff who issued the license or temporary emergency license shall suspend it and shall comply with division (A)(3) of this section upon becoming aware of the conviction or guilty plea. Upon suspending the license or temporary emergency license, the sheriff also shall comply with division (H) of section 2923.125 of the Revised Code.

(b) A suspension under division (A)(2)(a) of this section shall be considered as beginning on the date that the licensee is convicted of or pleads guilty to the offense described in that division, irrespective of when the sheriff notifies the licensee under division (A)(3) of this section. If the suspension is imposed for a misdemeanor violation of division (B)(1) or (2) of section 2923.12 of the Revised Code or of division (E)(1), (2), or (3) of section 2923.16 of the Revised Code, it shall end on the date that is one year after the date that the licensee is convicted of or pleads guilty to that violation. If the suspension is imposed for a misdemeanor violation of division (B)(4) of section 2923.12 of the Revised Code or of division (E)(5) of section 2923.16 of the Revised Code, it shall end on the date that is two years after the date that the licensee is convicted of or pleads guilty to that violation. If the licensee's license was issued under section 2923.125 of the Revised Code and the license remains valid after the suspension ends as described in this division, when the suspension ends, the sheriff shall return the license to the licensee. If the licensee's license was issued under section 2923.125 of the Revised Code and the license expires before the suspension ends as described in this division, or if the licensee's license was issued under section 2923.1213 of the Revised Code, the licensee is not eligible to apply for a new license under section 2923.125 or 2923.1213 of the Revised Code or to renew the license under section 2923.125 of the Revised Code until after the suspension ends as described in this division.

(c) The license of a licensee who is convicted of or pleads guilty to a violation of division (B)(1) of section 2923.12 or division (E)(1) or (2) of section 2923.16 of the Revised Code shall not be suspended pursuant to division (A)(2)(a) of this section if, at the time of the stop of the licensee for a law enforcement purpose, for a traffic stop, or for a purpose defined in section 5503.34 of the Revised Code that was the basis of the violation, any law enforcement officer involved with the stop or the employee of the motor carrier enforcement unit who made the stop had actual knowledge of the licensee's status as a licensee.

(3) Upon becoming aware of an arrest, charge, or protection order described in division (A)(1)(a) of this section with respect to a licensee who was issued a license under section 2923.125 or 2923.1213 of the Revised Code, or a conviction of or plea of guilty to a misdemeanor offense described in division (A)(2)(a) of this section with respect to a licensee who was issued a license under either section and with respect to which division (A)(2)(c) of this section does not apply, subject to division (C) of this section, the sheriff who issued the licensee's license or temporary emergency license to carry a concealed handgun shall notify the licensee, by certified mail, return receipt requested, at the licensee's last known residence

address that the license or temporary emergency license has been suspended and that the licensee is required to surrender the license or temporary emergency license at the sheriff's office within ten days of the date on which the notice was mailed. If the suspension is pursuant to division (A)(2) of this section, the notice shall identify the date on which the suspension ends.

(B)(1) A sheriff who issues a license or temporary emergency license to carry a concealed handgun to a licensee under section 2923.125 or 2923.1213 of the Revised Code shall revoke the license or temporary emergency license in accordance with division (B)(2) of this section upon becoming aware that the licensee satisfies any of the following:

(a) The licensee is under twenty-one years of age.

(b) Subject to division (C) of this section, at the time of the issuance of the license or temporary emergency license, the licensee did not satisfy the eligibility requirements of division (D)(1)(c), (d), (e), (f), (g), or (h) of section 2923.125 of the Revised Code.

(c) Subject to division (C) of this section, on or after the date on which the license or temporary emergency license was issued, the licensee is convicted of or pleads guilty to a violation of section 2923.15 of the Revised Code or an offense described in division (D)(1)(e), (f), (g), or (h) of section 2923.125 of the Revised Code.

(d) On or after the date on which the license or temporary emergency license was issued, the licensee becomes subject to a civil protection order or to a protection order issued by a court of another state that is substantially equivalent to a civil protection order.

(e) The licensee knowingly carries a concealed handgun into a place that the licensee knows is an unauthorized place specified in division (B) of section 2923.126 of the Revised Code.

(f) On or after the date on which the license or temporary emergency license was issued, the licensee is adjudicated as a mental defective or is committed to a mental institution.

(g) At the time of the issuance of the license or temporary emergency license, the licensee did not meet the residency requirements described in division (D)(1) of section 2923.125 of the Revised Code and currently does not meet the residency requirements described in that division.

(h) Regarding a license issued under section 2923.125 of the Revised Code, the competency certificate the licensee submitted was forged or otherwise was fraudulent.

(2) Upon becoming aware of any circumstance listed in division (B)(1) of this section that applies to a particular licensee who was issued a license under section 2923.125 or 2923.1213 of the Revised Code, subject to division (C) of this section, the sheriff who issued the license or temporary emergency license to carry a concealed handgun to the licensee shall notify the licensee, by certified mail, return receipt requested, at the licensee's last known residence address that the license or temporary emergency license is subject to revocation and that the licensee may come to the sheriff's office and contest the sheriff's proposed revocation within fourteen days of the date on which the notice was mailed. After the fourteen-day period and after consideration of any information that the licensee provides during that period, if the sheriff determines on the basis of the information of which the sheriff is aware that the licensee is described in division (B)(1) of this section and no longer satisfies the requirements described in division (D)(1) of section 2923.125 of the Revised Code that are applicable to the licensee's type of license, the sheriff shall revoke the license or temporary emergency license, notify the licensee of that fact, and require the licensee to surrender the license or temporary emergency license. Upon revoking the license or temporary emergency license, the sheriff also shall comply with division (H) of section 2923.125 of the Revised Code.

(C) If a sheriff who issues a license or temporary emergency license to carry a concealed handgun to a licensee under section 2923.125 or 2923.1213 of the Revised Code becomes aware that at the time of the issuance of the license or temporary emergency license the licensee had been convicted of or pleaded guilty to an offense identified in division (D)(1)(e), (f), or (h) of section 2923.125 of the Revised Code or had been adjudicated a delinquent child for committing an act or violation identified in any of those divisions or becomes aware that on or after the date on which the license or temporary emergency license was issued the licensee has been convicted of or pleaded guilty to an offense identified in division (A)(2)(a) or (B)(1)(c) of this section, the sheriff shall not consider that conviction, guilty plea, or adjudication as having occurred for purposes of divisions (A)(2), (A)(3), (B)(1), and (B)(2) of this section if a court has ordered the sealing or expungement of the records of that conviction, guilty plea, or adjudication pursuant to sections 2151.355 to 2151.358 or sections 2953.31 to 2953.36 of the Revised Code or a court has granted the licensee relief pursuant to section 2923.14 of the Revised Code from the disability imposed pursuant to section 2923.13 of the Revised Code relative to that conviction, guilty plea, or adjudication.

(D) As used in this section, "motor carrier enforcement unit" has the same meaning as in section 2923.16 of the Revised Code.

**HISTORY: 150 v H 12, § 1, eff. 4-8-04; 151 v H 347, § 1, eff. 3-14-07; 152 v S 184, § 1, eff. 9-9-08; 2011 SB 17, § 1, eff. Sept. 30, 2011.**

Governor Taft's veto of HB 347 was overridden by the Ohio General Assembly.

See the provisions of § 10 of H.B. 12 (150 v —) following RC § 2923.12.

## § 2923.129 Immunity; confidentiality of records; journalist may request disclosure of information; report by sheriff.

(A)(1) If a sheriff, the superintendent of the bureau of criminal identification and investigation, the employees of the bureau, the Ohio peace officer training commission, or the employees of the commission make a good faith effort in performing the duties imposed upon the sheriff, the superintendent, the bureau's employees, the commission, or the commission's employees by sections 109.731 [109.73.1], 311.41, and 2923.124 [2923.12.4] to 2923.1213 [2923.12.13] of the Revised Code, in addition to the personal immunity provided by section 9.86 of the Revised Code or division (A)(6) of section 2744.03 of the Revised Code and the governmental immunity of sections 2744.02 and 2744.03 of the Revised Code and in addition to any other immunity possessed by the bureau, the commission, and their employees, the sheriff, the sheriff's office, the county in which the sheriff has jurisdiction, the bureau, the superintendent of the bureau, the bureau's employees, the commission, and the commission's employees are immune from liability in a civil action for injury, death, or loss to person or property that allegedly was caused by or related to any of the following:

(a) The issuance, renewal, suspension, or revocation of a license to carry a concealed handgun or the issuance, suspension, or revocation of a temporary emergency license to carry a concealed handgun;

(b) The failure to issue, renew, suspend, or revoke a license to carry a concealed handgun or the failure to issue, suspend, or revoke a temporary emergency license to carry a concealed handgun;

(c) Any action or misconduct with a handgun committed by a licensee.

(2) Any action of a sheriff relating to the issuance, renewal, suspension, or revocation of a license to carry a concealed handgun or the issuance, suspension, or revocation of a temporary emergency license to carry a concealed handgun shall be considered to be a governmental function for purposes of Chapter 2744. of the Revised Code.

(3) An entity that or instructor who provides a competency certification of a type described in division (B)(3) of section 2923.125 [2923.12.5] of the Revised Code is immune from civil liability that might otherwise be incurred or imposed for any death or any injury or loss to person or property that is caused by or related to a person to whom the entity or instructor has issued the competency certificate if all of the following apply:

(a) The alleged liability of the entity or instructor relates to the training provided in the course, class, or program covered by the competency certificate.

(b) The entity or instructor makes a good faith effort in determining whether the person has satisfactorily completed the course, class, or program and makes a good faith effort in assessing the person in the competency examination conducted pursuant to division (G)(2) of section 2923.125 [2923.12.5] of the Revised Code.

(c) The entity or instructor did not issue the competency certificate with malicious purpose, in bad faith, or in a wanton or reckless manner.

(4) An entity that or instructor who provides a renewed competency certification of a type described in division (G)(4) of section 2923.125 [2923.12.5] of the Revised Code is immune from civil liability that might otherwise be incurred or imposed for any death or any injury or loss to person or property that is caused by or related to a person to whom the entity or instructor has issued the renewed competency certificate if all of the following apply:

(a) The entity or instructor makes a good faith effort in assessing the person in the physical demonstrations or the competency examination conducted pursuant to division (G)(4) of section 2923.125 [2923.12.5] of the Revised Code.

(b) The entity or instructor did not issue the renewed competency certificate with malicious purpose, in bad faith, or in a wanton or reckless manner.

(5) A law enforcement agency that employs a peace officer is immune from liability in a civil action to recover damages for injury, death, or loss to person or property allegedly caused by any act of that peace officer if the act occurred while the peace officer carried a concealed handgun and was off duty and if the act allegedly involved the peace officer's use of the concealed handgun. Sections 9.86 and 9.87, and Chapter 2744., of the Revised Code apply to any civil action involving a peace officer's use of a concealed handgun in the performance of the peace officer's official duties while the peace officer is off duty.

(B)(1) Notwithstanding section 149.43 of the Revised Code, except as provided in division (B)(2) of this section, the records that a sheriff keeps relative to the issuance, renewal, suspension, or revocation of a license to carry a concealed handgun or the issuance, suspension, or revocation of a temporary emergency license to carry a concealed handgun, including, but not limited to, completed applications for the issuance or renewal of a license, completed affidavits submitted regarding an application for a temporary emergency license, reports of criminal records checks and incompetency records checks under section 311.41 of the Revised Code, and applicants' social security numbers and fingerprints that are obtained under division (A) of section 311.41 of the Revised Code, are confidential and are not public records. Except as provided in division (B)(2) of this section, no person shall release or otherwise disseminate records that are confidential under this division unless required to do so pursuant to a court order.

(2)(a) A journalist, on or after April 8, 2004, may submit to a sheriff a signed, written request to view the name, county of residence, and date of birth of each person to whom the sheriff has issued a license or replacement license to carry a concealed handgun, renewed a license to carry a concealed handgun, or issued a temporary emergency license or replacement temporary emergency license to carry a concealed handgun under section 2923.125 [2923.12.5] or 2923.1213 [2923.12.13] of the Revised Code, or a signed, written request to view the name, county of residence, and date of birth of each person for whom the sheriff has suspended or revoked a license to carry a concealed handgun or a temporary emergency license to carry a concealed handgun under section 2923.128 [2923.12.8] of the Revised Code. The request shall include the journalist's name and title, shall include the name and address of the journalist's employer, and shall state that disclosure of the information sought would be in the public interest. If a journalist submits a signed, written request to the sheriff to view the information described in this division, the sheriff shall grant the journalist's request. The journalist shall not copy the name, county of residence, or date of birth of each person to or for whom the sheriff has issued, suspended, or revoked a license described in this division.

(b) As used in division (B)(2) of this section, "journalist" means a person engaged in, connected with, or employed by any news medium, including a newspaper, magazine, press association, news agency, or wire service, a radio or television station, or a similar medium, for the purpose of gathering, processing, transmitting, compiling, editing, or disseminating information for the general public.

(C) Each sheriff shall report to the Ohio peace officer training commission the number of licenses to carry a concealed handgun that the sheriff issued, renewed, suspended, revoked, or denied during the previous quarter of the calendar year, the number of applications for those licenses for which processing was suspended in accordance with division (D)(3) of section 2923.125 [2923.12.5] of the Revised Code during the previous quarter of the calendar year, and the number of temporary emergency licenses to carry a concealed handgun that the sheriff issued, suspended, revoked, or denied during the previous quarter of the calendar year. The sheriff shall not include in the report the name or any other identifying information of an applicant or licensee. The sheriff shall report that information in a manner that permits the commission to maintain the statistics described in division (D) of section 109.731 [109.73.1] of the Revised Code and to timely prepare the statistical report described in that division. The information that is received by the commission under this division is a public record kept by the commission for the purposes of section 149.43 of the Revised Code.

(D) Law enforcement agencies may use the information a sheriff makes available through the use of the law enforcement automated data system pursuant to division (H) of section 2923.125 [2923.12.5] or division (B)(2) or (D) of section 2923.1213 [2923.12.13] of the Revised Code for law enforcement purposes only. The information is confidential and is not a public record. A person who releases or otherwise disseminates this information obtained through the law enforcement automated data system in a manner not described in this division is guilty of a violation of section 2913.04 of the Revised Code.

(E) Whoever violates division (B) of this section is guilty of illegal release of confidential concealed handgun license records, a felony of the fifth degree. In addition to any penalties imposed under Chapter 2929. of the Revised Code for a violation of division (B) of this section or a violation of section 2913.04 of the Revised Code described in division (D) of this section, if the offender is a sheriff, an employee of a sheriff, or any other public officer or employee, and if the violation was willful and deliberate, the offender shall be subject to a civil fine of one thousand dollars. Any person who is harmed by a violation of division (B) or (C) of this section or a violation of section 2913.04 of the Revised Code described in division (D) of this section has a private cause of action against the offender for any injury, death, or loss to person or property that is a proximate result of the violation and may recover court costs and attorney's fees related to the action.

**HISTORY: 150 v H 12, § 1, eff. 4-8-04; 151 v H 9, § 1, eff. 9-29-07; 152 v S 184, § 1, eff. 9-9-08.**

The effective date is set by § 5 of 151 v H 9.

See the provisions of § 10 of H.B. 12 (150 v —) following RC § 2923.12.

## § 2923.1210 Forms for application and application to renew.

The application for a license to carry a concealed handgun or for the renewal of a license of that nature that is to be used under section 2923.125 [2923.12.5] of the Revised Code shall conform substantially to the following forms:

"Ohio Peace Officer Training Commission

APPLICATION FOR A LICENSE TO CARRY A CONCEALED HANDGUN

Please Type or Print in Ink

SECTION I.

This application will not be processed unless all applicable questions have been answered and until all required supporting documents as described in division (B) or (F) of section 2923.125 [2923.12.5] of the Ohio Revised Code and, unless waived, a cashier's check, certified check, or money order in the amount of the applicable license fee or license renewal fee have been submitted. FEES ARE NONREFUNDABLE.

SECTION II.

Name:

| Last | First | Middle |
|---|---|---|
| ........ | ........ | ... |

Social Security Number: ..............

Current Residence:

| Street | City | State | County | Zip |
|---|---|---|---|---|
| ........ | ........ | ........ | ........ | ........ |

Mailing Address (If Different From Above):

| Street | City | State | Zip |
|---|---|---|---|
| ........ | ........ | ........ | ........ |

| Date of Birth | Place of Birth | Sex | Race | Residence Telephone |
|---|---|---|---|---|
| .../.../... | .......... | .... | .... | (...)...... |

SECTION III. THE FOLLOWING QUESTIONS ARE TO BE ANSWERED YES OR NO

(1)(a) Are you legally living in the United States? ... YES ... NO

(b) Have you been a resident of Ohio for at least forty-five days and have you been a resident for thirty days of the county with whose sheriff you are filing this application or of a county adjacent to that county? ... YES ... NO

(2) Are you at least twenty-one years of age? ... YES ... NO

(3) Are you a fugitive from justice? ... YES ... NO

(4) Are you under indictment for a felony, or, except for a conviction or guilty plea the records of which a court has ordered sealed or expunged or relative to which a court has granted relief from disability pursuant to section 2923.14 of the Revised Code, have you ever been convicted of or pleaded guilty to a felony, or, except for a delinquent child adjudication the records of which a court has ordered sealed or expunged or relative to which a court has granted relief from disability pursuant to section 2923.14 of the Revised Code, have you ever been adjudicated a delinquent child for committing an act that would be a felony if committed by an adult? ... YES ... NO

(5) Are you under indictment for or otherwise charged with, or, except for a conviction or guilty plea the records of which a court has ordered sealed or expunged or relative to which a court has granted relief from disability pursuant to section 2923.14 of the Revised Code, have you ever been convicted of or pleaded guilty to, an offense under Chapter 2925., 3719., or 4729. of the Ohio Revised Code that involves the illegal possession, use, sale, administration, or distribution of or, except for a delinquent child adjudication the records of which a court has ordered sealed or expunged or relative to which a court has granted relief from disability pursuant to section 2923.14 of the Revised Code, trafficking in a drug of abuse, or have you ever been adjudicated a delinquent child for committing an act that would be an offense of that nature if committed by an adult? ... YES ... NO

(6) Are you under indictment for or otherwise charged with, or, except for a conviction or guilty plea the records of which a court has ordered sealed or expunged or relative to which a court has granted relief from disability pursuant to section 2923.14 of the Revised Code, have you been convicted of or pleaded guilty to within three years of the date of this application, a misdemeanor that is an offense of violence or the offense of possessing a revoked or suspended concealed handgun license, or, except for a delinquent child adjudication the records of which a court has ordered sealed or expunged or relative to which a court has granted relief from disability pursuant to section 2923.14 of the Revised Code, have you been adjudicated a delinquent child within three years of the date of this application for committing an act that would be a misdemeanor of that nature if committed by an adult? ... YES ... NO

(7) Are you under indictment for or otherwise charged with, or, except for a conviction or guilty plea the records of which a court has ordered sealed or expunged or relative to which a court has granted relief from disability pursuant to section 2923.14 of the Revised Code, have you been convicted of or pleaded guilty to within ten years of the date of this application, resisting arrest, or, except for a delinquent child adjudication the records of which a court has ordered sealed or expunged or relative to which a court has granted relief from disability pursuant to section 2923.14 of the Revised Code, have you been adjudicated a delinquent child for committing, within ten years of the date of this application an act that if committed by an adult would be the offense of resisting arrest? ... YES ... NO

(8)(a) Are you under indictment for or otherwise charged with assault or negligent assault? ... YES ... NO

(b) Have you been convicted of, pleaded guilty to, or adjudicated a delinquent child two or more times for committing assault or negligent assault within five years of the date of this application? ... YES ... NO

(c) Except for a conviction, guilty plea, or delinquent child adjudication the records of which a court has ordered sealed or expunged or relative to which a court has granted relief from disability pursuant to section 2923.14 of the Revised Code, have you ever been convicted of, pleaded guilty to, or adjudicated a delinquent child for assaulting a peace officer? ... YES ... NO

(9)(a) Have you ever been adjudicated as a mental defective? ... YES ... NO

(b) Have you ever been committed to a mental institution? ... YES ... NO

(10) Are you currently subject to a civil protection order, a temporary protection order, or a protection order issued by a court of another state? ... YES ... NO

(11) Are you currently subject to a suspension imposed under division (A)(2) of section 2923.128 [2923.12.8] of the Revised Code of a license to carry a concealed handgun, or a temporary emergency license to carry a concealed handgun, that previously was issued to you? ... YES ... NO

SECTION IV. YOU MUST COMPLETE THIS SECTION OF THE APPLICATION BY PROVIDING, TO THE BEST OF YOUR KNOWLEDGE, THE ADDRESS OF EACH PLACE OF RESIDENCE AT WHICH YOU RESIDED AT ANY TIME AFTER YOU ATTAINED EIGHTEEN YEARS OF AGE AND UNTIL YOU COMMENCED YOUR RESIDENCE AT THE LOCATION IDENTIFIED IN SECTION II OF THIS FORM, AND THE DATES OF RESIDENCE AT EACH OF THOSE ADDRESSES. IF YOU NEED MORE SPACE, COMPLETE AN ADDITIONAL SHEET WITH THE RELEVANT INFORMATION, ATTACH IT TO THE APPLICATION, AND NOTE THE ATTACHMENT AT THE END OF THIS SECTION.

Residence 1:

| Street | City | State | County | Zip |
|---|---|---|---|---|
| ........ | ........ | ........ | ........ | ........ |

Dates of residence at this address ..................

Residence 2:

| Street | City | State | County | Zip |
|---|---|---|---|---|
| ........ | ........ | ........ | ........ | ........ |

Dates of residence at this address ..................

Residence 3:

| Street | City | State | County | Zip |
|---|---|---|---|---|
| ........ | ........ | ........ | ........ | ........ |

Dates of residence at this address ..................

Residence 4:

| Street | City | State | County | Zip |
|---|---|---|---|---|
| ........ | ........ | ........ | ........ | ........ |

Dates of residence at this address ..................

SECTION V.

YOU MUST COMPLETE THIS SECTION OF THE APPLICATION BY ANSWERING THE QUESTION POSED IN PART (1) AND, IF THE ANSWER TO THE QUESTION IS "YES," BY PROVIDING IN PART (2) THE INFORMATION SPECIFIED. IF YOU NEED MORE SPACE, COMPLETE AN ADDITIONAL SHEET WITH THE RELEVANT INFORMATION, ATTACH IT TO THE APPLICATION, AND NOTE THE ATTACHMENT AT THE END OF THIS SECTION.

(1) Have you previously applied in any county in Ohio or in any other state for a license to carry a concealed handgun or a temporary emergency license to carry a concealed handgun? ... YES ... NO

(2) If your answer to the question in part (1) of this section of the application is "yes," you must complete this part by listing each county in Ohio, and each other state, in which you previously applied for either type of license and, to the best of your knowledge, the date on which you made the application.

Previous application made in ......... (insert name of Ohio county or other state) on ......... (insert date of application.)

Previous application made in ......... (insert name of Ohio county or other state) on ......... (insert date of application.)

Previous application made in ......... (insert name of Ohio county or other state) on ......... (insert date of application.)

Previous application made in ......... (insert name of Ohio county or other state) on ......... (insert date of application.)

SECTION VI.

AN APPLICANT WHO KNOWINGLY GIVES A FALSE ANSWER TO ANY QUESTION OR SUBMITS FALSE INFORMATION ON, OR A FALSE DOCUMENT WITH THE APPLICATION MAY BE PROSECUTED FOR FALSIFICATION TO OBTAIN A CONCEALED HANDGUN LICENSE, A FELONY OF THE FOURTH DEGREE, IN VIOLATION OF SECTION 2921.13 OF THE OHIO REVISED CODE.

(1) I have read the pamphlet that explains the Ohio firearms laws, that provides instruction in dispute resolution and explains the Ohio laws related to that matter, and that provides information regarding all aspects of the use of deadly force with a firearm, and I am knowledgeable of the provisions of those laws and of the information on those matters.

(2) I desire a legal means to carry a concealed handgun for defense of myself or a member of my family while engaged in lawful activity.

(3) I have never been convicted of or pleaded guilty to a crime of violence in the state of Ohio or elsewhere (if you have been convicted of or pleaded guilty to such a crime, but the records of that conviction or guilty plea have been sealed or expunged by court order or a court has granted relief pursuant to section 2923.14 of the Revised Code from the disability imposed pursuant to section 2923.13 of the Revised Code relative to that conviction or guilty plea,

you may treat the conviction or guilty plea for purposes of this paragraph as if it never had occurred). I am of sound mind. I hereby certify that the statements contained herein are true and correct to the best of my knowledge and belief. I understand that if I knowingly make any false statements herein I am subject to penalties prescribed by law. I authorize the sheriff or the sheriff's designee to inspect only those records or documents relevant to information required for this application.

(4) The information contained in this application and all attached documents are true and correct to the best of my knowledge.

............................
Signature of Applicant"

"Ohio Peace Officer Training Commission

APPLICATION TO RENEW A LICENSE TO CARRY A CONCEALED HANDGUN

Please Type or Print in Ink

SECTION I.

This application will not be processed unless all applicable questions have been answered and until all required supporting documents as described in division (B) or (F) of section 2923.125 [2923.12.5] of the Ohio Revised Code and, unless waived, a cashier's check, certified check, or money order in the amount of the applicable license fee or license renewal fee have been submitted. FEES ARE NONREFUNDABLE.

SECTION II.

Name:

| Last | First | Middle |
|---|---|---|
| ........ | ........ | ... |

Social Security Number: ...............

Current Residence:

| Street | City | State | County | Zip |
|---|---|---|---|---|
| ........ | ........ | ........ | ........ | ........ |

Mailing Address (If Different From Above):

| Street | City | State | Zip |
|---|---|---|---|
| ........ | ........ | ........ | ........ |

| Date of Birth | Place of Birth | Sex | Race | Residence Telephone |
|---|---|---|---|---|
| .../.../... | .......... | .... | ..... | (...)...... |

SECTION III. THE FOLLOWING QUESTIONS ARE TO BE ANSWERED YES OR NO

(1)(a) Are you legally living in the United States? ... YES ... NO

(b) Have you been a resident of Ohio for at least forty-five days and have you been a resident for thirty days of the county with whose sheriff you are filing this application or of a county adjacent to that county? ... YES ... NO

(2) Are you at least twenty-one years of age? ... YES ... NO

(3) Are you a fugitive from justice? ... YES ... NO

(4) Are you under indictment for a felony, or, except for a conviction or guilty plea the records of which a court has ordered sealed or expunged or relative to which a court has granted relief from disability pursuant to section 2923.14 of the Revised Code, have you ever been convicted of or pleaded guilty to a felony, or, except for a delinquent child adjudication the records of which a court has ordered sealed or expunged or relative to which a court has granted relief from disability pursuant to section 2923.14 of the Revised Code, have you ever been adjudicated a delinquent child for committing an act that would be a felony if committed by an adult? ... YES ... NO

(5) Are you under indictment for or otherwise charged with, or, except for a conviction or guilty plea the records of which a court has ordered sealed or expunged or relative to which a court has granted relief from disability pursuant to section 2923.14 of the Revised Code, have you ever been convicted of or pleaded guilty to, an offense under Chapter 2925., 3719., or 4729. of the Ohio Revised Code that involves the illegal possession, use, sale, administration, or distribution of or trafficking in a drug of abuse, or, except for a delinquent child adjudication the records of which a court has ordered sealed or expunged or relative to which a court has granted relief from disability pursuant to section 2923.14 of the Revised Code, have you ever been adjudicated a delinquent child for committing an act that would be an offense of that nature if committed by an adult? ... YES ... NO

(6) Are you under indictment for or otherwise charged with, or, except for a conviction or guilty plea the records of which a court has ordered sealed or expunged or relative to which a court has granted relief from disability pursuant to section 2923.14 of the Revised Code, have you been convicted of or pleaded guilty to within three years of the date of this application, a misdemeanor that is an offense of violence or the offense of possessing a revoked or suspended concealed handgun license, or, except for a delinquent child adjudication the records of which a court has ordered sealed or expunged or relative to which a court has granted relief from disability pursuant to section 2923.14 of the Revised Code, have you been adjudicated a delinquent child within three years of the date of this application for committing an act that would be a misdemeanor of that nature if committed by an adult? ... YES ... NO

(7) Are you under indictment for or otherwise charged with, or, except for a conviction or guilty plea the records of which a court has ordered sealed or expunged or relative to which a court has granted relief from disability pursuant to section 2923.14 of the Revised Code, have you been convicted of or pleaded guilty to within ten years of the date of this application, resisting arrest, or, except for a delinquent child adjudication the records of which a court has ordered sealed or expunged or relative to which a court has granted relief from disability pursuant to section 2923.14 of the Revised Code, have you been adjudicated a delinquent child for committing, within ten years of the date of this application an act that if committed by an adult would be the offense of resisting arrest? ... YES ... NO

(8)(a) Are you under indictment for or otherwise charged with assault or negligent assault? ... YES ... NO

(b) Have you been convicted of, pleaded guilty to, or adjudicated a delinquent child two or more times for committing assault or negligent assault within five years of the date of this application? ... YES ... NO

(c) Except for a conviction, guilty plea, or delinquent child adjudication the records of which a court has ordered sealed or expunged or relative to which a court has granted relief from disability pursuant to section 2923.14 of the Revised Code, have you ever been convicted of, pleaded guilty to, or adjudicated a delinquent child for assaulting a peace officer? ... YES ... NO

(9)(a) Have you ever been adjudicated as a mental defective? ... YES ... NO

(b) Have you ever been committed to a mental institution? ... YES ... NO

(10) Are you currently subject to a civil protection order, a temporary protection order, or a protection order issued by a court of another state? ... YES ... NO

(11) Are you currently subject to a suspension imposed under division (A)(2) of section 2923.128 [2923.12.8] of the Revised Code of a license to carry a concealed handgun, or a temporary emergency license to carry a concealed handgun, that previously was issued to you? ... YES ... NO

SECTION IV. YOU MUST COMPLETE THIS SECTION OF THE APPLICATION BY PROVIDING, TO THE BEST OF YOUR KNOWLEDGE, THE ADDRESS OF EACH PLACE OF RESIDENCE AT WHICH YOU RESIDED AT ANY TIME AFTER YOU LAST APPLIED FOR AN OHIO CONCEALED HANDGUN LICENSE THROUGH THE TIME YOU COMMENCED YOUR RESIDENCE AT THE LOCATION IDENTIFIED IN SECTION II OF THIS FORM, AND THE DATES OF RESIDENCE AT EACH OF THOSE ADDRESSES. IF YOU NEED MORE SPACE, COMPLETE AN ADDITIONAL SHEET WITH THE RELEVANT INFORMATION, ATTACH IT TO THE APPLICATION, AND NOTE THE ATTACHMENT AT THE END OF THIS SECTION.

Residence 1:

| Street | City | State | County | Zip |
|---|---|---|---|---|
| ........ | ........ | ........ | ........ | ........ |

Dates of residence at this address ..................

Residence 2:

| Street | City | State | County | Zip |
|---|---|---|---|---|
| ........ | ........ | ........ | ........ | ........ |

Dates of residence at this address ..................

Residence 3:

| Street | City | State | County | Zip |
|---|---|---|---|---|
| ........ | ........ | ........ | ........ | ........ |

Dates of residence at this address ..................

Residence 4:

| Street | City | State | County | Zip |
|---|---|---|---|---|
| ........ | ........ | ........ | ........ | ........ |

Dates of residence at this address ..................

SECTION V.

YOU MUST COMPLETE THIS SECTION OF THE APPLICATION BY ANSWERING THE QUESTION POSED IN PART (1) AND, IF THE ANSWER TO THE QUESTION IS "YES," BY PROVIDING IN PART (2) THE INFORMATION SPECIFIED. IF YOU NEED MORE SPACE, COMPLETE AN ADDITIONAL SHEET WITH THE RELEVANT INFORMATION, ATTACH IT TO THE APPLICATION, AND NOTE THE ATTACHMENT AT THE END OF THIS SECTION.

(1) Have you previously applied in any county in Ohio or in any other state for a license to carry a concealed handgun or a temporary emergency license to carry a concealed handgun? ... YES ... NO

(2) If your answer to the question in part (1) of this section of the application is "yes," you must complete this part by listing each county in Ohio, and each other state, in which you previously applied for either type of license and, to the best of your knowledge, the date on which you made the application.

Previous application made in ......... (insert name of Ohio county or other state) on ......... (insert date of application.)

Previous application made in ......... (insert name of Ohio county or other state) on ......... (insert date of application.)

Previous application made in ......... (insert name of Ohio county or other state) on ......... (insert date of application.)

Previous application made in ......... (insert name of Ohio county or other state) on ......... (insert date of application.)

SECTION VI.

AN APPLICANT WHO KNOWINGLY GIVES A FALSE ANSWER TO ANY QUESTION OR SUBMITS FALSE INFORMATION ON, OR A FALSE DOCUMENT WITH THE APPLICATION MAY BE PROSECUTED FOR FALSIFICATION TO OBTAIN A CONCEALED HANDGUN LICENSE, A FELONY OF THE FOURTH DEGREE, IN VIOLATION OF SECTION 2921.13 OF THE OHIO REVISED CODE.

(1) I have read the pamphlet that explains the Ohio firearms laws, that provides instruction in dispute resolution and explains the Ohio laws related to that matter, and that provides information regarding all aspects of the use of deadly force with a firearm, and I am knowledgeable of the provisions of those laws and of the information on those matters.

(2) I desire a legal means to carry a concealed handgun for defense of myself or a member of my family while engaged in lawful activity.

(3) I have never been convicted of or pleaded guilty to a crime of violence in the state of Ohio or elsewhere (if you have been convicted of or pleaded guilty to such a crime, but the records of that conviction or guilty plea have been sealed or expunged by court order or a court has granted relief pursuant to section 2923.14 of the Revised Code from the disability imposed pursuant to section 2923.13 of the Revised Code relative to that conviction or guilty plea, you may treat the conviction or guilty plea for purposes of this paragraph as if it never had occurred). I am of sound mind. I hereby certify that the statements contained herein are true and correct to the best of my knowledge and belief. I understand that if I knowingly make any false statements herein I am subject to penalties prescribed by law. I authorize the sheriff or the sheriff's designee to inspect only those records or documents relevant to information required for this application.

(4) The information contained in this application and all attached documents are true and correct to the best of my knowledge.

..............................
Signature of Applicant"

**HISTORY: 150 v H 12, § 1, eff. 4-8-04; 151 v H 347, § 1, eff. 3-14-07; 152 v S 184, § 1, eff. 9-9-08; 153 v H 1, § 101.01, eff. 10-16-09.**

The effective date is set by § 812.10 of 153 v H 1.

Governor Taft's veto of HB 347 was overridden by the Ohio General Assembly.

See the provisions of § 10 of H.B. 12 (150 v —) following RC § 2923.12.

## § 2923.1211 Falsification of concealed handgun license or possessing revoked or suspended license.

(A) No person shall alter a license or temporary emergency license to carry a concealed handgun that was issued pursuant to section 2923.125 [2923.12.5] or 2923.1213 [2923.12.13] of the Revised Code or create a fictitious document that purports to be a license of that nature.

(B) No person, except in the performance of official duties, shall possess a license to carry a concealed handgun that was issued and that has been revoked or suspended pursuant to section 2923.128 [2923.12.8] of the Revised Code or a temporary emergency license to carry a concealed handgun that was issued and that has been revoked pursuant to section 2923.1213 [2923.12.13] of the Revised Code.

(C) Whoever violates division (A) of this section is guilty of falsification of a concealed handgun license, a felony of the fifth degree. Whoever violates division (B) of this section is guilty of possessing a revoked or suspended concealed handgun license, a misdemeanor of the third degree.

**HISTORY: 150 v H 12, § 1, eff. 4-8-04.**

See the provisions of § 10 of H.B. 12 (150 v —) following RC § 2923.12.

## § 2923.1212 Posting of signs prohibiting deadly weapon or dangerous ordnance.

(A) The following persons, boards, and entities, or designees, shall post in the following locations a sign that contains a statement in substantially the following form: "Unless otherwise authorized by law, pursuant to the Ohio Revised Code, no person shall knowingly possess, have under the person's control, convey, or attempt to convey a deadly weapon or dangerous ordnance onto these premises.":

(1) The director of public safety or the person or board charged with the erection, maintenance, or repair of police stations, municipal jails, and the municipal courthouse and courtrooms in a conspicuous location at all police stations, municipal jails, and municipal courthouses and courtrooms;

(2) The sheriff or sheriff's designee who has charge of the sheriff's office in a conspicuous location in that office;

(3) The superintendent of the state highway patrol or the superintendent's designee in a conspicuous location at all state highway patrol stations;

(4) Each sheriff, chief of police, or person in charge of every county, multicounty, municipal, municipal-county, or multicounty-municipal jail or workhouse, community-based correctional facility, halfway house, alternative residential facility, or other local or state correctional institution or detention facility within the state, or that person's designee, in a conspicuous location at that facility under that person's charge;

(5) The board of trustees of a regional airport authority, chief administrative officer of an airport facility, or other person in charge of an airport facility in a conspicuous location at each airport facility under that person's control;

(6) The officer or officer's designee who has charge of a courthouse or the building or structure in which a courtroom is located in a conspicuous location in that building or structure;

(7) The superintendent of the bureau of criminal identification and investigation or the superintendent's designee in a conspicuous location in all premises controlled by that bureau;

(8) The owner, administrator, or operator of a child day-care center, a type A family day-care home, a type B family day-care home, or a type C family day-care home;

(9) The officer of this state or of a political subdivision of this state, or the officer's designee, who has charge of a building that is a government facility of this state or the political subdivision of this state, as defined in section 2923.126 [2923.12.6] of the Revised Code, and that is not a building that is used primarily as a shelter, restroom, parking facility for motor vehicles, or rest facility and is not a courthouse or other building or structure in which a courtroom is located that is subject to division (B)(3) of that section.

(B) The following boards, bodies, and persons, or designees, shall post in the following locations a sign that contains a statement in substantially the following form: "Unless otherwise authorized by law, pursuant to Ohio Revised Code section 2923.122 [2923.12.2], no person shall knowingly possess, have under the person's control, convey, or attempt to convey a deadly weapon or dangerous ordnance into a school safety zone.":

(1) A board of education of a city, local, exempted village, or joint vocational school district or that board's designee in a conspicuous location in each building and on each parcel of real property owned or controlled by the board;

(2) A governing body of a school for which the state board of education prescribes minimum standards under section 3301.07 of the Revised Code or that body's designee in a conspicuous location in each building and on each parcel of real property owned or controlled by the school;

(3) The principal or chief administrative officer of a nonpublic school in a conspicuous location on property owned or controlled by that nonpublic school.

**HISTORY: 150 v H 12, § 1, eff. 4-8-04; 152 v S 184, § 1, eff. 9-9-08.**

See the provisions of § 10 of H.B. 12 (150 v —) following RC § 2923.12.

## § 2923.1213 Temporary emergency license to carry concealed handgun.

(A) As used in this section:

(1) "Evidence of imminent danger" means any of the following:

(a) A statement sworn by the person seeking to carry a concealed handgun that is made under threat of perjury and that states that the person has reasonable cause to fear a criminal attack upon the person or a member of the person's family, such as would justify a prudent person in going armed;

(b) A written document prepared by a governmental entity or public official describing the facts that give the person seeking to carry a concealed handgun reasonable cause to fear a criminal attack upon the person or a member of the person's family, such as would justify a prudent person in going armed. Written documents of this nature include, but are not limited to, any temporary protection order, civil protection order, protection order issued by another state, or other court order, any court report, and any report filed with or made by a law enforcement agency or prosecutor.

(2) "Prosecutor" has the same meaning as in section 2935.01 of the Revised Code.

(B)(1) A person seeking a temporary emergency license to carry a concealed handgun shall submit to the sheriff of the county in which the person resides all of the following:

(a) Evidence of imminent danger to the person or a member of the person's family;

(b) A sworn affidavit that contains all of the information required to be on the license and attesting that the person is legally living in the United States; is at least twenty-one years of age; is not a fugitive from justice; is not under indictment for or otherwise charged with an offense identified in division (D)(1)(d) of section 2923.125 [2923.12.5] of the Revised Code; has not been convicted of or pleaded guilty to an offense, and has not been adjudicated a delinquent child for committing an act, identified in division (D)(1)(e) of that section and to which division (B)(3) of this section does not apply; within three years of the date of the submission, has not been convicted of or pleaded guilty to an offense, and has not been adjudicated a delinquent child for committing an act, identified in division (D)(1)(f) of that section and to which division (B)(3) of this section does not apply; within five years of the date of the submission, has not been convicted of, pleaded guilty, or adjudicated a delinquent child for committing two or more violations identified in division (D)(1)(g) of that section; within ten years of the date of the submission, has not been convicted of, pleaded guilty, or adjudicated a delinquent child for committing a violation identified in division (D)(1)(h) of that section and to which division (B)(3) of this section does not apply; has not been adjudicated as a mental defective, has not been committed to any mental institution, is not under adjudication of mental incompetence, has not been found by a court to be a mentally ill person subject to hospitalization by court order, and is not an involuntary patient other than one who is a patient only for purposes of observation, as described in division (D)(1)(i) of that section; is not currently subject to a civil protection order, a temporary protection order, or a protection order issued by a court of another state, as described in division (D)(1)(j) of that section; and is not currently subject to a suspension imposed under division (A)(2) of section 2923.128 [2923.12.8] of the Revised Code of a license to carry a concealed handgun, or a temporary emergency license to carry a concealed handgun, that previously was issued to the person;

(c) A nonrefundable temporary emergency license fee as described in either of the following:

(i) For an applicant who has been a resident of this state for five or more years, a fee of fifteen dollars plus the actual cost of having a background check performed by the bureau of criminal identification and investigation pursuant to section 311.41 of the Revised Code;

(ii) For an applicant who has been a resident of this state for less than five years, a fee of fifteen dollars plus the actual cost of having background checks performed by the federal bureau of investigation and the bureau of criminal identification and investigation pursuant to section 311.41 of the Revised Code.

(d) A set of fingerprints of the applicant provided as described in section 311.41 of the Revised Code through use of an electronic fingerprint reading device or, if the sheriff to whom the application is submitted does not possess and does not have ready access to the use of an electronic fingerprint reading device, on a standard impression sheet prescribed pursuant to division (C)(2) of section 109.572 [109.57.2] of the Revised Code. If the fingerprints are provided on a standard impression sheet, the person also shall provide the person's social security number to the sheriff.

(2) A sheriff shall accept the evidence of imminent danger, the sworn affidavit, the fee, and the set of fingerprints required under division (B)(1) of this section at the times and in the manners described in division (I) of this section. Upon receipt of the evidence of imminent danger, the sworn affidavit, the fee, and the set of fingerprints required under division (B)(1) of this section, the sheriff, in the manner specified in section 311.41 of the Revised Code, immediately shall conduct or cause to be conducted the criminal records check and the incompetency records check described in section 311.41 of the Revised Code. Immediately upon receipt of the results of the records checks, the sheriff shall review the information and shall determine whether the criteria set forth in divisions (D)(1)(a) to (j) and (m) of section 2923.125 [2923.12.5] of the Revised Code apply regarding the person. If the sheriff determines that all of criteria set forth in divisions (D)(1)(a) to (j) and (m) of section 2923.125 [2923.12.5] of the Revised Code apply regarding the person, the sheriff shall immediately make available through the law enforcement automated data system all information that will be contained on the temporary emergency license for the person if one is issued, and the superintendent of the state highway patrol shall ensure that the system is so configured as to permit the transmission through the system of that information. Upon making that information available through the law enforcement automated data system, the sheriff shall immediately issue to the person a temporary emergency license to carry a concealed handgun.

If the sheriff denies the issuance of a temporary emergency license to the person, the sheriff shall specify the grounds for the denial in a written notice to the person. The person may appeal the denial, or challenge criminal records check results that were the basis of the denial if applicable, in the same manners specified in division (D)(2) of section 2923.125 [2923.12.5] and in section 2923.127 [2923.12.7] of the Revised Code, regarding the denial of an application for a license to carry a concealed handgun under that section.

The temporary emergency license under this division shall be in the form, and shall include all of the information, described in divisions (A)(2) and (5) of section 109.731 [109.73.1] of the Revised Code, and also shall include a unique combination of identifying letters and numbers in accordance with division (A)(4) of that section.

The temporary emergency license issued under this division is valid for ninety days and may not be renewed. A person who has been issued a temporary emergency license under this division shall not be issued another temporary emergency license unless at least four years has expired since the issuance of the prior temporary emergency license.

(3) If a person seeking a temporary emergency license to carry a concealed handgun has been convicted of or pleaded guilty to an offense identified in division (D)(1)(e), (f), or (h) of section 2923.125 [2923.12.5] of the Revised Code or has been adjudicated a delinquent child for committing an act or violation identified in any of those divisions, and if a court has ordered the sealing or expungement of the records of that conviction, guilty plea, or adjudication pursuant to sections 2151.355 [2151.35.5] to 2151.358 [2151.35.8] or sections 2953.31 to 2953.36 of the Revised Code or a court has granted the applicant relief pursuant to section 2923.14 of the Revised Code from the disability imposed pursuant to section 2923.13 of the Revised Code relative to that conviction, guilty plea, or adjudication, the conviction, guilty plea, or adjudication shall not be relevant for purposes of the sworn affidavit described in division (B)(1)(b) of this section, and the person may complete, and swear to the truth of, the affidavit as if the conviction, guilty plea, or adjudication never had occurred.

(4) The sheriff shall waive the payment pursuant to division (B)(1)(c) of this section of the license fee in

connection with an application that is submitted by an applicant who is a retired peace officer, a retired person described in division (B)(1)(b) of section 109.77 of the Revised Code, or a retired federal law enforcement officer who, prior to retirement, was authorized under federal law to carry a firearm in the course of duty, unless the retired peace officer, person, or federal law enforcement officer retired as the result of a mental disability.

The sheriff shall deposit all fees paid by an applicant under division (B)(1)(c) of this section into the sheriff's concealed handgun license issuance fund established pursuant to section 311.42 of the Revised Code.

(C) A person who holds a temporary emergency license to carry a concealed handgun has the same right to carry a concealed handgun as a person who was issued a license to carry a concealed handgun under section 2923.125 [2923.12.5] of the Revised Code, and any exceptions to the prohibitions contained in section 1547.69 and sections 2923.12 to 2923.16 of the Revised Code for a licensee under section 2923.125 [2923.12.5] of the Revised Code apply to a licensee under this section. The person is subject to the same restrictions, and to all other procedures, duties, and sanctions, that apply to a person who carries a license issued under section 2923.125 [2923.12.5] of the Revised Code, other than the license renewal procedures set forth in that section.

(D) A sheriff who issues a temporary emergency license to carry a concealed handgun under this section shall not require a person seeking to carry a concealed handgun in accordance with this section to submit a competency certificate as a prerequisite for issuing the license and shall comply with division (H) of section 2923.125 [2923.12.5] of the Revised Code in regards to the license. The sheriff shall suspend or revoke the license in accordance with section 2923.128 [2923.12.8] of the Revised Code. In addition to the suspension or revocation procedures set forth in section 2923.128 [2923.12.8] of the Revised Code, the sheriff may revoke the license upon receiving information, verifiable by public documents, that the person is not eligible to possess a firearm under either the laws of this state or of the United States or that the person committed perjury in obtaining the license; if the sheriff revokes a license under this additional authority, the sheriff shall notify the person, by certified mail, return receipt requested, at the person's last known residence address that the license has been revoked and that the person is required to surrender the license at the sheriff's office within ten days of the date on which the notice was mailed. Division (H) of section 2923.125 [2923.12.5] of the Revised Code applies regarding any suspension or revocation of a temporary emergency license to carry a concealed handgun.

(E) A sheriff who issues a temporary emergency license to carry a concealed handgun under this section shall retain, for the entire period during which the temporary emergency license is in effect, the evidence of imminent danger that the person submitted to the sheriff and that was the basis for the license, or a copy of that evidence, as appropriate.

(F) If a temporary emergency license to carry a concealed handgun issued under this section is lost or is destroyed, the licensee may obtain from the sheriff who issued that license a duplicate license upon the payment of a fee of fifteen dollars and the submission of an affidavit attesting to the loss or destruction of the license. The sheriff, in accordance with the procedures prescribed in section 109.731 [109.73.1] of the Revised Code, shall place on the replacement license a combination of identifying numbers different from the combination on the license that is being replaced.

(G) The Ohio peace officer training commission shall prescribe, and shall make available to sheriffs, a standard form to be used under division (B) of this section by a person who applies for a temporary emergency license to carry a concealed handgun on the basis of imminent danger of a type described in division (A)(1)(a) of this section.

(H) A sheriff who receives any fees paid by a person under this section shall deposit all fees so paid into the sheriff's concealed handgun license issuance expense fund established under section 311.42 of the Revised Code.

(I) A sheriff shall accept evidence of imminent danger, a sworn affidavit, the fee, and the set of fingerprints specified in division (B)(1) of this section at any time during normal business hours. In no case shall a sheriff require an appointment, or designate a specific period of time, for the submission or acceptance of evidence of imminent danger, a sworn affidavit, the fee, and the set of fingerprints specified in division (B)(1) of this section, or for the provision to any person of a standard form to be used for a person to apply for a temporary emergency license to carry a concealed handgun.

**HISTORY: 150 v H 12, § 1, eff. 4-8-04; 151 v H 347, § 1, eff. 3-14-07; 152 v S 184, § 1, eff. 9-9-08; 153 v H 1, § 101.01, eff. 10-16-09.**

The effective date is set by § 812.10 of 153 v H 1.

Governor Taft's veto of HB 347 was overridden by the Ohio General Assembly.

See the provisions of § 10 of H.B. 12 (150 v —) following RC § 2923.12.

## [MISCELLANEOUS]

## § 2923.13 Having weapons while under disability.

(A) Unless relieved from disability as provided in section 2923.14 of the Revised Code, no person shall knowingly acquire, have, carry, or use any firearm or dangerous ordnance, if any of the following apply:

(1) The person is a fugitive from justice.

(2) The person is under indictment for or has been convicted of any felony offense of violence or has been adjudicated a delinquent child for the commission of an offense that, if committed by an adult, would have been a felony offense of violence.

(3) The person is under indictment for or has been convicted of any felony offense involving the illegal possession, use, sale, administration, distribution, or trafficking in any drug of abuse or has been adjudicated a delinquent child for the commission of an offense that, if committed by an adult, would have been a felony offense involving the illegal possession, use, sale, administration, distribution, or trafficking in any drug of abuse.

(4) The person is drug dependent, in danger of drug dependence, or a chronic alcoholic.

(5) The person is under adjudication of mental incompetence, has been adjudicated as a mental defective, has been committed to a mental institution, has been found by a court to be a mentally ill person subject to hospitalization by court order, or is an involuntary patient other than one who is a patient only for purposes of observation. As used

in this division, "mentally ill person subject to hospitalization by court order" and "patient" have the same meanings as in section 5122.01 of the Revised Code.

(B) Whoever violates this section is guilty of having weapons while under disability, a felony of the third degree.

**HISTORY: 134 v H 511 (Eff 1-1-74); 146 v S 2. Eff 7-1-96; 150 v H 12, § 1, eff. 4-8-04; 2011 HB 54, § 1, eff. Sept. 30, 2011.**

See the provisions of §§ 6 and 7 of H.B. 12 (150 v —) following RC § 2923.12.

**Not analogous to former RC § 2923.13 (GC § 13421-24; 108 v PtI, 189; Bureau of Code Revision, 10-1-53; 126 v 575), repealed 134 v H 511, § 2, eff 1-1-74.**

**Analogous to former RC § 2923.56 (133 v H 484), repealed 134 v H 511, § 2, eff 1-1-74.**

The effective date is set by section 6 of SB 2.

## § 2923.131 Possession of deadly weapon while under detention.

(A) "Detention" and "detention facility" have the same meanings as in section 2921.01 of the Revised Code.

(B) No person under detention at a detention facility shall possess a deadly weapon.

(C) Whoever violates this section is guilty of possession of a deadly weapon while under detention.

(1) If the offender, at the time of the commission of the offense, was under detention as an alleged or adjudicated delinquent child or unruly child and if at the time the offender commits the act for which the offender was under detention it would not be a felony if committed by an adult, possession of a deadly weapon while under detention is a misdemeanor of the first degree.

(2) If the offender, at the time of the commission of the offense, was under detention in any other manner, possession of a deadly weapon while under detention is one of the following:

(a) A felony of the first degree, when the most serious offense for which the person was under detention is aggravated murder or murder and regardless of when the aggravated murder or murder occurred or, if the person was under detention as an alleged or adjudicated delinquent child, when the most serious act for which the person was under detention would be aggravated murder or murder if committed by an adult and regardless of when that act occurred;

(b) A felony of the second degree if any of the following applies:

(i) The most serious offense for which the person was under detention is a felony of the first degree committed on or after July 1, 1996, or an aggravated felony of the first degree committed prior to July 1, 1996.

(ii) If the person was under detention as an alleged or adjudicated delinquent child, the most serious act for which the person was under detention was committed on or after July 1, 1996, and would be a felony of the first degree if committed by an adult, or was committed prior to July 1, 1996, and would have been an aggravated felony of the first degree if committed by an adult.

(c) A felony of the third degree if any of the following applies:

(i) The most serious offense for which the person was under detention is a felony of the second degree committed on or after July 1, 1996, or is an aggravated felony of the second degree or a felony of the first degree committed prior to July 1, 1996.

(ii) If the person was under detention as an alleged or adjudicated delinquent child, the most serious act for which the person was under detention was committed on or after July 1, 1996, and would be a felony of the second degree if committed by an adult, or was committed prior to July 1, 1996, and would have been an aggravated felony of the second degree or a felony of the first degree if committed by an adult.

(d) A felony of the fourth degree if any of the following applies:

(i) The most serious offense for which the person was under detention is a felony of the third degree committed on or after July 1, 1996, is an aggravated felony of the third degree or a felony of the second degree committed prior to July 1, 1996, or is a felony of the third degree committed prior to July 1, 1996, that, if it had been committed on or after July 1, 1996, also would be a felony of the third degree.

(ii) If the person was under detention as an alleged or adjudicated delinquent child, the most serious act for which the person was under detention was committed on or after July 1, 1996, and would be a felony of the third degree if committed by an adult, was committed prior to July 1, 1996, and would have been an aggravated felony of the third degree or a felony of the second degree if committed by an adult, or was committed prior to July 1, 1996, would have been a felony of the third degree if committed by an adult, and, if it had been committed on or after July 1, 1996, also would be a felony of the third degree if committed by an adult.

(e) A felony of the fifth degree if any of the following applies:

(i) The most serious offense for which the person was under detention is a felony of the fourth or fifth degree committed on or after July 1, 1996, is a felony of the third degree committed prior to July 1, 1996, that, if committed on or after July 1, 1996, would be a felony of the fourth degree, is a felony of the fourth degree committed prior to July 1, 1996, or is an unclassified felony or a misdemeanor regardless of when the unclassified felony or misdemeanor is committed.

(ii) If the person was under detention as an alleged or adjudicated delinquent child, the most serious act for which the person was under detention was committed on or after July 1, 1996, and would be a felony of the fourth or fifth degree if committed by an adult, was committed prior to July 1, 1996, would have been a felony of the third degree if committed by an adult, and, if it had been committed on or after July 1, 1996, would be a felony of the fourth degree if committed by an adult, was committed prior to July 1, 1996, and would have been a felony of the fourth degree if committed by an adult, or would be an unclassified felony if committed by an adult regardless of when the act is committed.

**HISTORY: 146 v H 154. Eff 10-4-96.**

## § 2923.14 Relief from disability.

(A) Any person who is prohibited from acquiring, having, carrying, or using firearms may apply to the court of common pleas in the county in which the person resides for relief from such prohibition.

(B) The application shall recite the following:

(1) All indictments, convictions, or adjudications upon which the applicant's disability is based, the sentence imposed and served, and any release granted under a community control sanction, post-release control sanction,

or parole, any partial or conditional pardon granted, or other disposition of each case, or, if the disability is based upon a factor other than an indictment, a conviction, or an adjudication, the factor upon which the disability is based and all details related to that factor;

(2) Facts showing the applicant to be a fit subject for relief under this section.

(C) A copy of the application shall be served on the county prosecutor. The county prosecutor shall cause the matter to be investigated and shall raise before the court any objections to granting relief that the investigation reveals.

(D) Upon hearing, the court may grant the applicant relief pursuant to this section, if all of the following apply:

(1) One of the following applies:

(a) If the disability is based upon an indictment, a conviction, or an adjudication, the applicant has been fully discharged from imprisonment, community control, post-release control, and parole, or, if the applicant is under indictment, has been released on bail or recognizance.

(b) If the disability is based upon a factor other than an indictment, a conviction, or an adjudication, that factor no longer is applicable to the applicant.

(2) The applicant has led a law-abiding life since discharge or release, and appears likely to continue to do so.

(3) The applicant is not otherwise prohibited by law from acquiring, having, or using firearms.

(E) Costs of the proceeding shall be charged as in other civil cases, and taxed to the applicant.

(F) Relief from disability granted pursuant to this section restores the applicant to all civil firearm rights to the full extent enjoyed by any citizen, and is subject to the following conditions :

(1) Applies only with respect to indictments, convictions, or adjudications, or to the other factor, recited in the application as the basis for the applicant's disability;

(2) Applies only with respect to firearms lawfully acquired, possessed, carried, or used by the applicant;

(3) May be revoked by the court at any time for good cause shown and upon notice to the applicant;

(4) Is automatically void upon commission by the applicant of any offense set forth in division (A)(2) or (3) of section 2923.13 of the Revised Code, or upon the applicant's becoming one of the class of persons named in division (A)(1), (4), or (5) of that section.

(G) As used in this section:

(1) "Community control sanction" has the same meaning as in section 2929.01 of the Revised Code.

(2) "Post-release control" and "post-release control sanction" have the same meanings as in section 2967.01 of the Revised Code.

**HISTORY: 134 v H 511. Eff 1-1-74; 149 v H 490, § 1, eff. 1-1-04; 2011 HB 54, § 1, eff. Sept. 30, 2011.**

Acts 2011, HB 0054, § 3 provides: "It is the intent of the General Assembly in amending section 2923.14 of the Revised Code to apply the amendments to that section retroactively to any restoration of rights granted previously to any applicant under section 2923.14 of the Revised Code or under any previous version of that section. The General Assembly is explicitly making this amendment to clarify that relief from a weapons disability granted under section 2923.14 of the Revised Code restores a person's civil firearm rights to such an extent that the uniform federal ban on possessing any firearms at all, 18 U.S.C. 922(g)(1), does not apply to that person, in correlation with the U.S. Supreme Court's interpretation of 18 U.S.C. 921(a)(20) in Caron v. U.S. (1998), 524 U.S. 308."

The effective date is set by section 4 of HB 490.

**Not analogous to former RC § 2923.14 (GC § 13421-25; 108 v PtI, 189; Bureau of Code Revision, 10-1-53; 126 v 575), repealed 134 v H 511, § 2, eff 1-1-74.**

**Analogous to former RC § 2923.56 (133 v H 484), repealed 134 v H 511, § 2, eff 1-1-74.**

## § 2923.15 Using weapons while intoxicated.

(A) No person, while under the influence of alcohol or any drug of abuse, shall carry or use any firearm or dangerous ordnance.

(B) Whoever violates this section is guilty of using weapons while intoxicated, a misdemeanor of the first degree.

**HISTORY: 134 v H 511. Eff 1-1-74.**

**Not analogous to former RC § 2923.15 (GC § 13421-26; 108 v PtI, 189; Bureau of Code Revision, 10-1-53), repealed 134 v H 511, § 2, eff 1-1-74.**

## § 2923.16 Improperly handling firearms in a motor vehicle.

(A) No person shall knowingly discharge a firearm while in or on a motor vehicle.

(B) No person shall knowingly transport or have a loaded firearm in a motor vehicle in such a manner that the firearm is accessible to the operator or any passenger without leaving the vehicle.

(C) No person shall knowingly transport or have a firearm in a motor vehicle, unless the person may lawfully possess that firearm under applicable law of this state or the United States, the firearm is unloaded, and the firearm is carried in one of the following ways:

(1) In a closed package, box, or case;

(2) In a compartment that can be reached only by leaving the vehicle;

(3) In plain sight and secured in a rack or holder made for the purpose;

(4) If the firearm is at least twenty-four inches in overall length as measured from the muzzle to the part of the stock furthest from the muzzle and if the barrel is at least eighteen inches in length, either in plain sight with the action open or the weapon stripped, or, if the firearm is of a type on which the action will not stay open or which cannot easily be stripped, in plain sight.

(D) No person shall knowingly transport or have a loaded handgun in a motor vehicle if, at the time of that transportation or possession, any of the following applies:

(1) The person is under the influence of alcohol, a drug of abuse, or a combination of them.

(2) The person's whole blood, blood serum or plasma, breath, or urine contains a concentration of alcohol, a listed controlled substance, or a listed metabolite of a controlled substance prohibited for persons operating a vehicle, as specified in division (A) of section 4511.19 of the Revised Code, regardless of whether the person at the time of the transportation or possession as described in this division is the operator of or a passenger in the motor vehicle.

(E) No person who has been issued a license or temporary emergency license to carry a concealed handgun under section 2923.125 or 2923.1213 of the Revised Code or a license to carry a concealed handgun that was issued to the person by another state with which the attorney general has entered into a reciprocity agreement under section 109.69 of the Revised Code, who is the driver or an occupant of a motor vehicle that is stopped as a result of a traffic stop or a stop for another law enforcement purpose or is the driver or an occupant of a commercial motor vehicle that is stopped by an employee of the motor carrier enforcement unit for the purposes defined in section 5503.34 of the Revised Code, and who is transporting or has a loaded handgun in the motor vehicle or commercial motor vehicle in any manner, shall do any of the following:

(1) Fail to promptly inform any law enforcement officer who approaches the vehicle while stopped that the person has been issued a license or temporary emergency license to carry a concealed handgun and that the person then possesses or has a loaded handgun in the motor vehicle;

(2) Fail to promptly inform the employee of the unit who approaches the vehicle while stopped that the person has been issued a license or temporary emergency license to carry a concealed handgun and that the person then possesses or has a loaded handgun in the commercial motor vehicle;

(3) Knowingly fail to remain in the motor vehicle while stopped or knowingly fail to keep the person's hands in plain sight at any time after any law enforcement officer begins approaching the person while stopped and before the law enforcement officer leaves, unless the failure is pursuant to and in accordance with directions given by a law enforcement officer;

(4) Knowingly have contact with the loaded handgun by touching it with the person's hands or fingers in the motor vehicle at any time after the law enforcement officer begins approaching and before the law enforcement officer leaves, unless the person removes, attempts to remove, grasps, holds, or has contact with the loaded handgun pursuant to and in accordance with directions given by the law enforcement officer;

(5) Knowingly disregard or fail to comply with any lawful order of any law enforcement officer given while the motor vehicle is stopped, including, but not limited to, a specific order to the person to keep the person's hands in plain sight.

(F)(1) Divisions (A), (B), (C), and (E) of this section do not apply to any of the following:

(a) An officer, agent, or employee of this or any other state or the United States, or a law enforcement officer, when authorized to carry or have loaded or accessible firearms in motor vehicles and acting within the scope of the officer's, agent's, or employee's duties;

(b) Any person who is employed in this state, who is authorized to carry or have loaded or accessible firearms in motor vehicles, and who is subject to and in compliance with the requirements of section 109.801 of the Revised Code, unless the appointing authority of the person has expressly specified that the exemption provided in division (F)(1)(b) of this section does not apply to the person.

(2) Division (A) of this section does not apply to a person if all of the following circumstances apply:

(a) The person discharges a firearm from a motor vehicle at a coyote or groundhog, the discharge is not during the deer gun hunting season as set by the chief of the division of wildlife of the department of natural resources, and the discharge at the coyote or groundhog, but for the operation of this section, is lawful.

(b) The motor vehicle from which the person discharges the firearm is on real property that is located in an unincorporated area of a township and that either is zoned for agriculture or is used for agriculture.

(c) The person owns the real property described in division (F)(2)(b) of this section, is the spouse or a child of another person who owns that real property, is a tenant of another person who owns that real property, or is the spouse or a child of a tenant of another person who owns that real property.

(d) The person does not discharge the firearm in any of the following manners:

(i) While under the influence of alcohol, a drug of abuse, or alcohol and a drug of abuse;

(ii) In the direction of a street, highway, or other public or private property used by the public for vehicular traffic or parking;

(iii) At or into an occupied structure that is a permanent or temporary habitation;

(iv) In the commission of any violation of law, including, but not limited to, a felony that includes, as an essential element, purposely or knowingly causing or attempting to cause the death of or physical harm to another and that was committed by discharging a firearm from a motor vehicle.

(3) Division (A) of this section does not apply to a person if all of the following apply:

(a) The person possesses a valid electric-powered all-purpose vehicle permit issued under section 1533.103 of the Revised Code by the chief of the division of wildlife.

(b) The person discharges a firearm at a wild quadruped or game bird as defined in section 1531.01 of the Revised Code during the open hunting season for the applicable wild quadruped or game bird.

(c) The person discharges a firearm from a stationary electric-powered all-purpose vehicle as defined in section 1531.01 of the Revised Code or a motor vehicle that is parked on a road that is owned or administered by the division of wildlife, provided that the road is identified by an electric-powered all-purpose vehicle sign.

(d) The person does not discharge the firearm in any of the following manners:

(i) While under the influence of alcohol, a drug of abuse, or alcohol and a drug of abuse;

(ii) In the direction of a street, a highway, or other public or private property that is used by the public for vehicular traffic or parking;

(iii) At or into an occupied structure that is a permanent or temporary habitation;

(iv) In the commission of any violation of law, including, but not limited to, a felony that includes, as an essential element, purposely or knowingly causing or attempting to cause the death of or physical harm to another and that was committed by discharging a firearm from a motor vehicle.

(4) Divisions (B) and (C) of this section do not apply to a person if all of the following circumstances apply:

(a) At the time of the alleged violation of either of those divisions, the person is the operator of or a passenger in a motor vehicle.

(b) The motor vehicle is on real property that is located in an unincorporated area of a township and that either is zoned for agriculture or is used for agriculture.

(c) The person owns the real property described in division (D)(4)(b) of this section, is the spouse or a child of another person who owns that real property, is a tenant of another person who owns that real property, or is the spouse or a child of a tenant of another person who owns that real property.

(d) The person, prior to arriving at the real property described in division (D)(4)(b) of this section, did not transport or possess a firearm in the motor vehicle in a manner prohibited by division (B) or (C) of this section while the motor vehicle was being operated on a street, highway, or other public or private property used by the public for vehicular traffic or parking.

(5) Divisions (B) and (C) of this section do not apply to a person who transports or possesses a handgun in a motor vehicle if, at the time of that transportation or possession, both of the following apply:

(a) The person transporting or possessing the handgun is carrying a valid license or temporary emergency license to carry a concealed handgun issued to the person under section 2923.125 or 2923.1213 of the Revised Code or a license to carry a concealed handgun that was issued by another state with which the attorney general has entered into a reciprocity agreement under section 109.69 of the Revised Code.

(b) The person transporting or possessing the handgun is not knowingly in a place described in division (B) of section 2923.126 of the Revised Code.

(6) Divisions (B) and (C) of this section do not apply to a person if all of the following apply:

(a) The person possesses a valid electric-powered all-purpose vehicle permit issued under section 1533.103 of the Revised Code by the chief of the division of wildlife.

(b) The person is on or in an electric-powered all-purpose vehicle as defined in section 1531.01 of the Revised Code or a motor vehicle during the open hunting season for a wild quadruped or game bird.

(c) The person is on or in an electric-powered all-purpose vehicle as defined in section 1531.01 of the Revised Code or a motor vehicle that is parked on a road that is owned or administered by the division of wildlife, provided that the road is identified by an electric-powered all-purpose vehicle sign.

(G)(1) The affirmative defenses authorized in divisions (D)(1) and (2) of section 2923.12 of the Revised Code are affirmative defenses to a charge under division (B) or (C) of this section that involves a firearm other than a handgun.

(2) It is an affirmative defense to a charge under division (B) or (C) of this section of improperly handling firearms in a motor vehicle that the actor transported or had the firearm in the motor vehicle for any lawful purpose and while the motor vehicle was on the actor's own property, provided that this affirmative defense is not available unless the person, immediately prior to arriving at the actor's own property, did not transport or possess the firearm in a motor vehicle in a manner prohibited by division (B) or (C) of this section while the motor vehicle was being operated on a street, highway, or other public or private property used by the public for vehicular traffic.

(H)(1) No person who is charged with a violation of division (B), (C), or (D) of this section shall be required to obtain a license or temporary emergency license to carry a concealed handgun under section 2923.125 or 2923.1213 of the Revised Code as a condition for the dismissal of the charge.

(2)(a) If a person is convicted of, was convicted of, pleads guilty to, or has pleaded guilty to a violation of division (E) of this section as it existed prior to the effective date of this amendment and if the conduct that was the basis of the violation no longer would be a violation of division (E) of this section on or after the effective date of this amendment, the person may file an application under section 2953.37 of the Revised Code requesting the expungement of the record of conviction.

If a person is convicted of, was convicted of, pleads guilty to, or has pleaded guilty to a violation of division (B) or (C) of this section as the division existed prior to the effective date of this amendment and if the conduct that was the basis of the violation no longer would be a violation of division (B) or (C) of this section on or after the effective date of this amendment due to the application of division (F)(5) of this section as it exists on and after the effective date of this amendment, the person may file an application under section 2953.37 of the Revised Code requesting the expungement of the record of conviction.

(b) The attorney general shall develop a public media advisory that summarizes the expungement procedure established under section 2953.37 of the Revised Code and the offenders identified in division (H)(2)(a) of this section who are authorized to apply for the expungement. Within thirty days after the effective date of this amendment, the attorney general shall provide a copy of the advisory to each daily newspaper published in this state and each television station that broadcasts in this state. The attorney general may provide the advisory in a tangible form, an electronic form, or in both tangible and electronic forms.

(I) Whoever violates this section is guilty of improperly handling firearms in a motor vehicle. Violation of division (A) of this section is a felony of the fourth degree. Violation of division (C) of this section is a misdemeanor of the fourth degree. A violation of division (D) of this section is a felony of the fifth degree or, if the loaded handgun is concealed on the person's person, a felony of the fourth degree. Except as otherwise provided in this division, a violation of division (E)(1) or (2) of this section is a misdemeanor of the first degree, and, in addition to any other penalty or sanction imposed for the violation, the offender's license or temporary emergency license to carry a concealed handgun shall be suspended pursuant to division (A)(2) of section 2923.128 of the Revised Code. If at the time of the stop of the offender for a traffic stop, for another law enforcement purpose, or for a purpose defined in section 5503.34 of the Revised Code that was the basis of the violation any law enforcement officer involved with the stop or the employee of the motor carrier enforcement unit who made the stop had actual knowledge of the offender's status as a licensee, a violation of division (E)(1) or (2) of this section is a minor misdemeanor, and the offender's license or temporary emergency license to carry a concealed handgun shall not be suspended pursuant to division (A)(2) of section 2923.128 of the Revised Code. A violation of division (E)(4) of this section is a felony of the fifth degree. A violation of division (E)(3) or (5) of this section is a misdemeanor of the first degree or, if the offender previously has been convicted of or pleaded guilty to a violation of division (E)(3) or (5) of this section, a felony of the fifth degree. In addition to any other penalty or sanction imposed for a misdemeanor violation of division (E)(3) or (5) of this section, the offender's license or temporary emergency license to carry a concealed handgun shall be suspended pursuant to division (A)(2) of section 2923.128 of the Revised Code. A violation of division (B) of this section is a felony of the fourth degree.

(J) If a law enforcement officer stops a motor vehicle for a traffic stop or any other purpose, if any person in the motor vehicle surrenders a firearm to the officer, either voluntarily or pursuant to a request or demand of the officer, and if the officer does not charge the person with a violation of this section or arrest the person for any offense, the person is not otherwise prohibited by law from possessing the firearm, and the firearm is not contraband, the officer shall return the firearm to the person at the termination of the stop. If a court orders a law enforcement officer to return a firearm to a person pursuant to the requirement set forth in this division, division (B) of section 2923.163 of the Revised Code applies.

(K) As used in this section:

(1) "Motor vehicle," "street," and "highway" have the same meanings as in section 4511.01 of the Revised Code.

(2) "Occupied structure" has the same meaning as in section 2909.01 of the Revised Code.

(3) "Agriculture" has the same meaning as in section 519.01 of the Revised Code.

(4) "Tenant" has the same meaning as in section 1531.01 of the Revised Code.

(5) "Unloaded" means any of the following:

(a) No ammunition is in the firearm in question, and no ammunition is loaded into a magazine or speed loader that may be used with the firearm in question and that is located anywhere within the vehicle in question, without regard to where ammunition otherwise is located within the vehicle in question. For the purposes of division (K)(5)(a) of this section, ammunition held in stripper-clips or in en-bloc clips is not considered ammunition that is loaded into a magazine or speed loader.

(b) With respect to a firearm employing a percussion cap, flintlock, or other obsolete ignition system, when the weapon is uncapped or when the priming charge is removed from the pan.

(6) "Commercial motor vehicle" has the same meaning as in division (A) of section 4506.25 of the Revised Code.

(7) "Motor carrier enforcement unit" means the motor carrier enforcement unit in the department of public safety, division of state highway patrol, that is created by section 5503.34 of the Revised Code.

**HISTORY: 134 v H 511 (Eff 1-1-74); 135 v H 716 (Eff 1-1-74); 147 v H 275. Eff 12-31-97; 150 v H 12, § 1, eff. 4-8-04; 151 v H 347, § 1, eff. 3-14-07; 152 v S 209, § 1, eff. 6-25-08; 152 v S 184, § 1, eff. 9-9-08; 153 v H 1, § 101.01, eff. 10-16-09; 2011 SB 17, § 1, eff. Sept. 30, 2011.**

The effective date is set by § 812.10 of 153 v H 1.

The provisions of 815.10 of 153 v H 1 read as follows:

SECTION 815.10. The General Assembly, applying the principle stated in division (B) of section 1.52 of the Revised Code that amendments are to be harmonized if reasonably capable of simultaneous operation, finds that the following sections, presented in this act as composites of the sections as amended by the acts indicated, are the resulting versions of the sections in effect prior to the effective date of the sections as presented in this act:

* * *

Section 2923.16 of the Revised Code as amended by Sub. S.B. 184 and Sub. S.B. 209, both of the 127th General Assembly.

* * *

The effective date is set by § 7 of 152 v S 209.

Governor Taft's veto of HB 347 was overridden by the Ohio General Assembly.

See the provisions of §§ 6, 7, 9, and 10 of H.B. 12 (150 v —) following RC § 2923.12.

**Not analogous to former RC § 2923.16 (RS § 7031; S&C 448, 449; 29 v 161; GC § 13390; Bureau of Code Revision, 10-1-53), repealed 134 v H 511, § 2, eff 1-1-74.**

## § 2923.161 Improperly discharging firearm at or into habitation; school-related offenses.

(A) No person, without privilege to do so, shall knowingly do any of the following:

(1) Discharge a firearm at or into an occupied structure that is a permanent or temporary habitation of any individual;

(2) Discharge a firearm at, in, or into a school safety zone;

(3) Discharge a firearm within one thousand feet of any school building or of the boundaries of any school premises, with the intent to do any of the following:

(a) Cause physical harm to another who is in the school, in the school building, or at a function or activity associated with the school;

(b) Cause panic or fear of physical harm to another who is in the school, in the school building, or at a function or activity associated with the school;

(c) Cause the evacuation of the school, the school building, or a function or activity associated with the school.

(B) This section does not apply to any officer, agent, or employee of this or any other state or the United States, or to any law enforcement officer, who discharges the firearm while acting within the scope of the officer's, agent's, or employee's duties.

(C) Whoever violates this section is guilty of improperly discharging a firearm at or into a habitation, in a school safety zone, or with the intent to cause harm or panic to persons in a school, in a school building, or at a school function or the evacuation of a school function, a felony of the second degree.

(D) As used in this section, "occupied structure" has the same meaning as in section 2909.01 of the Revised Code.

**HISTORY: 143 v S 258 (Eff 11-20-90); 146 v S 2 (Eff 7-1-96); 147 v H 5 (Eff 6-30-98); 148 v S 1 (Eff 8-6-99); 149 v H 442. Eff 10-11-2002.**

## § 2923.162 Discharge of firearm on or near prohibited premises.

(A) No person shall do any of the following:

(1) Without permission from the proper officials and subject to division (B)(1) of this section, discharge a firearm upon or over a cemetery or within one hundred yards of a cemetery;

(2) Subject to division (B)(2) of this section, discharge a firearm on a lawn, park, pleasure ground, orchard, or other ground appurtenant to a schoolhouse, church, or inhabited dwelling, the property of another, or a charitable institution;

(3) Discharge a firearm upon or over a public road or highway.

(B)(1) Division (A)(1) of this section does not apply to a person who, while on the person's own land, discharges a firearm.

(2) Division (A)(2) of this section does not apply to a person who owns any type of property described in that division and who, while on the person's own enclosure, discharges a firearm.

(C) Whoever violates this section is guilty of discharge of a firearm on or near prohibited premises. A violation of division (A)(1) or (2) of this section is a misdemeanor of the fourth degree. A violation of division (A)(3) of this section shall be punished as follows:

(1) Except as otherwise provided in division (C)(2), (3), or (4) of this section, a violation of division (A)(3) of this section is a misdemeanor of the first degree.

(2) Except as otherwise provided in division (C)(3) or (4) of this section, if the violation created a substantial risk of physical harm to any person or caused serious physical harm to property, a violation of division (A)(3) of this section is a felony of the third degree.

(3) Except as otherwise provided in division (C)(4) of this section, if the violation caused physical harm to any person, a violation of division (A)(3) of this section is a felony of the second degree.

(4) If the violation caused serious physical harm to any person, a violation of division (A)(3) of this section is a felony of the first degree.

**HISTORY: 148 v S 107. Eff 3-23-2000; 150 v H 52, § 1, eff. 6-1-04.**

## § 2923.163 Procedure for storing and returning surrendered firearms.

If a law enforcement officer stops a person for any law enforcement purpose and the person voluntarily or pursuant to a request or demand of the officer surrenders a firearm to the officer, if a law enforcement officer stops a motor vehicle for any purpose and a person in the motor vehicle voluntarily or pursuant to a request or demand of the officer surrenders a firearm to the officer, or if a law enforcement officer otherwise seizes a firearm from a person, all of the following apply:

(A) If the law enforcement officer does not return the firearm to the person at the termination of the stop or otherwise promptly return the firearm to the person after the seizure of the firearm, the officer or other personnel at the officer's law enforcement agency shall maintain the integrity and identity of the firearm in such a manner so that if the firearm subsequently is to be returned to the person it can be identified and returned to the person in the same condition it was in when it was seized.

(B) If the law enforcement officer does not return the firearm to the person at the termination of the stop or otherwise promptly return the firearm to the person after the seizure of the firearm, if a court finds that a law enforcement officer failed to return the firearm to the person after the person has demanded the return of the firearm from the officer, and if the court orders a law enforcement officer to return the firearm to the person, in addition to any other relief ordered, the court also shall award reasonable costs and attorney's fees to the person who sought the order to return the firearm.

**HISTORY: 152 v S 184, § 1, eff. 9-9-08.**

## § 2923.17 Unlawful possession of dangerous ordnance; illegally manufacturing or processing explosives.

(A) No person shall knowingly acquire, have, carry, or use any dangerous ordnance.

(B) No person shall manufacture or process an explosive at any location in this state unless the person first has been issued a license, certificate of registration, or permit to do so from a fire official of a political subdivision of this state or from the office of the fire marshal.

(C) Division (A) of this section does not apply to:

(1) Officers, agents, or employees of this or any other state or the United States, members of the armed forces of the United States or the organized militia of this or any other state, and law enforcement officers, to the extent that any such person is authorized to acquire, have, carry, or use dangerous ordnance and is acting within the scope of the person's duties;

(2) Importers, manufacturers, dealers, and users of explosives, having a license or user permit issued and in effect pursuant to the "Organized Crime Control Act of 1970," 84 Stat. 952, 18 U.S.C. 843, and any amendments or additions thereto or reenactments thereof, with respect to explosives and explosive devices lawfully acquired, possessed, carried, or used under the laws of this state and applicable federal law;

(3) Importers, manufacturers, and dealers having a license to deal in destructive devices or their ammunition, issued and in effect pursuant to the "Gun Control Act of 1968," 82 Stat. 1213, 18 U.S.C. 923, and any amendments or additions thereto or reenactments thereof, with respect to dangerous ordnance lawfully acquired, possessed, carried, or used under the laws of this state and applicable federal law;

(4) Persons to whom surplus ordnance has been sold, loaned, or given by the secretary of the army pursuant to 70A Stat. 262 and 263, 10 U.S.C. 4684, 4685, and 4686, and any amendments or additions thereto or reenactments thereof, with respect to dangerous ordnance when lawfully possessed and used for the purposes specified in such section;

(5) Owners of dangerous ordnance registered in the national firearms registration and transfer record pursuant to the act of October 22, 1968, 82 Stat. 1229, 26 U.S.C. 5841, and any amendments or additions thereto or reenactments thereof, and regulations issued thereunder.

(6) Carriers, warehouses, and others engaged in the business of transporting or storing goods for hire, with respect to dangerous ordnance lawfully transported or stored in the usual course of their business and in compliance with the laws of this state and applicable federal law;

(7) The holders of a license or temporary permit issued and in effect pursuant to section 2923.18 of the Revised Code, with respect to dangerous ordnance lawfully acquired, possessed, carried, or used for the purposes and in the manner specified in such license or permit.

(D) Whoever violates division (A) of this section is guilty of unlawful possession of dangerous ordnance, a felony of the fifth degree.

(E) Whoever violates division (B) of this section is guilty of illegally manufacturing or processing explosives, a felony of the second degree.

**HISTORY: 134 v H 511 (Eff 1-1-74); 137 v H 728 (Eff 8-22-78); 146 v S 2. Eff 7-1-96; 2011 HB 9, § 1, eff. June 29, 2011.**

Acts 2011, HB 9, § 3 provides: "This act applies to transactions entered into on or after the effective date of this act."

**Not analogous to former RC § 2923.17 (RS § 6990; 73 v 154; GC § 12678; Bureau of Code Revision, 10-1-53), repealed 134 v H 511, § 2, eff 1-1-74.**

**Analogous to former RC § 2923.04 (GC §§ 12819-4, 12819-5; 115 v 189; Bureau of Code Revision, 10-1-53; 132 v H 43), repealed 134 v H 511, § 2, eff 1-1-74.**

The effective date is set by section 6 of SB 2.

## § 2923.18 License or permit to possess dangerous ordnance.

(A) Upon application to the sheriff of the county or safety director or police chief of the municipality where the applicant resides or has his principal place of business, and upon payment of the fee specified in division (B) of this section, a license or temporary permit shall be issued to qualified applicants to acquire, possess, carry, or use dangerous ordnance, for the following purposes:

(1) Contractors, wreckers, quarrymen, mine operators, and other persons regularly employing explosives in the

course of a legitimate business, with respect to explosives and explosive devices acquired, possessed, carried, or used in the course of such business;

(2) Farmers, with respect to explosives and explosive devices acquired, possessed, carried, or used for agricultural purposes on lands farmed by them;

(3) Scientists, engineers, and instructors, with respect to dangerous ordnance acquired, possessed, carried, or used in the course of bona fide research or instruction;

(4) Financial institution and armored car company guards, with respect to automatic firearms lawfully acquired, possessed, carried, or used by any such person while acting within the scope of his duties;

(5) In the discretion of the issuing authority, any responsible person, with respect to dangerous ordnance lawfully acquired, possessed, carried, or used for a legitimate research, scientific, educational, industrial, or other proper purpose.

(B) Application for a license or temporary permit under this section shall be in writing under oath to the sheriff of the county or safety director or police chief of the municipality where the applicant resides or has his principal place of business. The application shall be accompanied by an application fee of fifty dollars when the application is for a license, and an application fee of five dollars when the application is for a temporary permit. The fees shall be paid into the general revenue fund of the county or municipality. The application shall contain the following information:

(1) The name, age, address, occupation, and business address of the applicant, if he is a natural person, or the name, address, and principal place of business of the applicant, if the applicant is a corporation;

(2) A description of the dangerous ordnance for which a permit is requested;

(3) A description of the place or places where and the manner in which the dangerous ordnance is to be kept, carried, and used;

(4) A statement of the purposes for which the dangerous ordnance is to be acquired, possessed, carried, or used;

(5) Such other information as the issuing authority may require in giving effect to this section.

(C) Upon investigation, the issuing authority shall issue a license or temporary permit only if all of the following apply:

(1) The applicant is not otherwise prohibited by law from acquiring, having, carrying or using dangerous ordnance;

(2) The applicant is age twenty-one or over, if he is a natural person;

(3) It appears that the applicant has sufficient competence to safely acquire, possess, carry, or use the dangerous ordnance, and that proper precautions will be taken to protect the security of the dangerous ordnance and ensure the safety of persons and property;

(4) It appears that the dangerous ordnance will be lawfully acquired, possessed, carried, and used by the applicant for a legitimate purpose.

(D) The license or temporary permit shall identify the person to whom it is issued, identify the dangerous ordnance involved and state the purposes for which the license or temporary permit is issued, state the expiration date, if any, and list such restrictions on the acquisition, possession, carriage, or use of the dangerous ordnance as the issuing authority considers advisable to protect the security of the dangerous ordnance and ensure the safety of persons and property.

(E) A temporary permit shall be issued for the casual use of explosives and explosive devices, and other consumable dangerous ordnance, and shall expire within thirty days of its issuance. A license shall be issued for the regular use of consumable dangerous ordnance, or for any nonconsumable dangerous ordnance, which license need not specify an expiration date, but the issuing authority may specify such expiration date, not earlier than one year from the date of issuance, as it considers advisable in view of the nature of the dangerous ordnance and the purposes for which the license is issued.

(F) The dangerous ordnance specified in a license or temporary permit may be obtained by the holder anywhere in the state. The holder of a license may use such dangerous ordnance anywhere in the state. The holder of a temporary permit may use such dangerous ordnance only within the territorial jurisdiction of the issuing authority.

(G) The issuing authority shall forward to the state fire marshal a copy of each license or temporary permit issued pursuant to this section, and a copy of each record of a transaction in dangerous ordnance and of each report of lost or stolen dangerous ordnance, given to the local law enforcement authority as required by divisions (A)(4) and (5) of section 2923.20 of the Revised Code. The state fire marshal shall keep a permanent file of all licenses and temporary permits issued pursuant to this section, and of all records of transactions in, and losses or thefts of dangerous ordnance forwarded by local law enforcement authorities pursuant to this section.

**HISTORY: 134 v H 511 (Eff 1-1-74); 137 v H 590. Eff 7-1-79.**

**Not analogous to former RC § 2923.18 (RS § 2127; Bates § 1536-740; 66 v 202; 95 v 428; GC §§ 12785, 12786; 108 v PtI, 236; Bureau of Code Revision, 10-1-53), repealed 134 v H 511, § 2, eff 1-1-74.**

**Analogous to former RC § 2923.04 (GC §§ 12819-4, 12819-5; 115 v 189, 190; Bureau of Code Revision, 10-1-53; 132 v H 43), repealed 134 v H 511, § 2, eff 1-1-74.**

The effective date is set by section 3 of HB 590.

## § 2923.19 Failure to secure dangerous ordnance.

(A) No person, in acquiring, possessing, carrying, or using any dangerous ordnance, shall negligently fail to take proper precautions:

(1) To secure the dangerous ordnance against theft, or against its acquisition or use by any unauthorized or incompetent person;

(2) To insure the safety of persons and property.

(B) Whoever violates this section is guilty of failure to secure dangerous ordnance, a misdemeanor of the second degree.

**HISTORY: 134 v H 511. Eff 1-1-74.**

**Not analogous to former RC § 2923.19 (RS § 6875; S&S 487; 62 v 67; 71 v 34; 73 v 63; GC § 12637; Bureau of Code Revision, 10-1-53), repealed 134 v H 511, § 2, eff 1-1-74.**

## § 2923.20 Unlawful transaction in weapons.

(A) No person shall:

(1) Recklessly sell, lend, give, or furnish any firearm to any person prohibited by section 2923.13 or 2923.15 of the

Revised Code from acquiring or using any firearm, or recklessly sell, lend, give, or furnish any dangerous ordnance to any person prohibited by section 2923.13, 2923.15, or 2923.17 of the Revised Code from acquiring or using any dangerous ordnance;

(2) Possess any firearm or dangerous ordnance with purpose to dispose of it in violation of division (A) of this section;

(3) Manufacture, possess for sale, sell, or furnish to any person other than a law enforcement agency for authorized use in police work, any brass knuckles, cestus, billy, blackjack, sandbag, switchblade knife, springblade knife, gravity knife, or similar weapon;

(4) When transferring any dangerous ordnance to another, negligently fail to require the transferee to exhibit such identification, license, or permit showing him to be authorized to acquire dangerous ordnance pursuant to section 2923.17 of the Revised Code, or negligently fail to take a complete record of the transaction and forthwith forward a copy of that record to the sheriff of the county or safety director or police chief of the municipality where the transaction takes place;

(5) Knowingly fail to report to law enforcement authorities forthwith the loss or theft of any firearm or dangerous ordnance in the person's possession or under the person's control.

(B) Whoever violates this section is guilty of unlawful transactions in weapons. A violation of division (A)(1) or (2) of this section is a felony of the fourth degree. A violation of division (A)(3) or (4) of this section is a misdemeanor of the second degree. A violation of division (A)(5) of this section is a misdemeanor of the fourth degree.

**HISTORY: 134 v H 511 (Eff 1-1-74); 137 v H 728 (Eff 8-22-78); 146 v S 2. Eff 7-1-96.**

**Not analogous to former RC § 2923.20 (RS § 6875; S&S 487; 62 v 67; 71 v 34; 73 v 63; GC § 12637; Bureau of Code Revision, 10-1-53), repealed 134 v H 511, § 2, eff 1-1-74.**

The effective date is set by section 6 of SB 2.

## § 2923.201 Defacing identification marks of firearm.

(A) No person shall do either of the following:

(1) Change, alter, remove, or obliterate the name of the manufacturer, model, manufacturer's serial number, or other mark of identification on a firearm.

(2) Possess a firearm knowing or having reasonable cause to believe that the name of the manufacturer, model, manufacturer's serial number, or other mark of identification on the firearm has been changed, altered, removed, or obliterated.

(B)(1) Whoever violates division (A)(1) of this section is guilty of defacing identification marks of a firearm. Except as otherwise provided in this division, defacing identification marks of a firearm is a misdemeanor of the first degree. If the offender previously has been convicted of or pleaded guilty to a violation of division (A)(1) of this section, defacing identification marks of a firearm is a felony of the fourth degree.

(2) Whoever violates division (A)(2) of this section is guilty of possessing a defaced firearm. Except as otherwise provided in this division, possessing a defaced firearm is a misdemeanor of the first degree. If the offender previously has been convicted of or pleaded guilty to a violation of division (A)(2) of this section, possessing a defaced firearm is a felony of the fourth degree.

(C) Division (A) of this section does not apply to any firearm on which no manufacturer's serial number was inscribed at the time of its manufacture.

**HISTORY: 151 v H 279, § 1, eff. 9-28-06.**

## § 2923.21 Improperly furnishing firearms to a minor.

(A) No person shall do any of the following:

(1) Sell any firearm to a person who is under eighteen years of age;

(2) Subject to division (B) of this section, sell any handgun to a person who is under twenty-one years of age;

(3) Furnish any firearm to a person who is under eighteen years of age or, subject to division (B) of this section, furnish any handgun to a person who is under twenty-one years of age, except for lawful hunting, sporting, or educational purposes, including, but not limited to, instruction in firearms or handgun safety, care, handling, or marksmanship under the supervision or control of a responsible adult;

(4) Sell or furnish a firearm to a person who is eighteen years of age or older if the seller or furnisher knows, or has reason to know, that the person is purchasing or receiving the firearm for the purpose of selling the firearm in violation of division (A)(1) of this section to a person who is under eighteen years of age or for the purpose of furnishing the firearm in violation of division (A)(3) of this section to a person who is under eighteen years of age;

(5) Sell or furnish a handgun to a person who is twenty-one years of age or older if the seller or furnisher knows, or has reason to know, that the person is purchasing or receiving the handgun for the purpose of selling the handgun in violation of division (A)(2) of this section to a person who is under twenty-one years of age or for the purpose of furnishing the handgun in violation of division (A)(3) of this section to a person who is under twenty-one years of age;

(6) Purchase or attempt to purchase any firearm with the intent to sell the firearm in violation of division (A)(1) of this section to a person who is under eighteen years of age or with the intent to furnish the firearm in violation of division (A)(3) of this section to a person who is under eighteen years of age;

(7) Purchase or attempt to purchase any handgun with the intent to sell the handgun in violation of division (A)(2) of this section to a person who is under twenty-one years of age or with the intent to furnish the handgun in violation of division (A)(3) of this section to a person who is under twenty-one years of age.

(B) Divisions (A)(1) and (2) of this section do not apply to the sale or furnishing of a handgun to a person eighteen years of age or older and under twenty-one years of age if the person eighteen years of age or older and under twenty-one years of age is a law enforcement officer who is properly appointed or employed as a law enforcement officer and has received firearms training approved by the Ohio peace officer training council or equivalent firearms training.

(C) Whoever violates this section is guilty of improperly furnishing firearms to a minor, a felony of the fifth degree.

**HISTORY: 134 v H 511 (Eff 1-1-74); 146 v H 4 (Eff 11-9-95); 146 v S 269 (Eff 7-1-96); 146 v H 124. Eff 3-31-97.**

**Not analogous to former RC § 2923.21 (RS § 6876; S&C 1642; 37 v 17; GC § 12638; Bureau of Code Revision, 10-1-53; 126 v 575), repealed 134 v H 511, § 2, eff 1-1-74.**

## § 2923.211 Underage purchase of firearm or handgun.

(A) No person under eighteen years of age shall purchase or attempt to purchase a firearm.

(B) No person under twenty-one years of age shall purchase or attempt to purchase a handgun, provided that this division does not apply to the purchase or attempted purchase of a handgun by a person eighteen years of age or older and under twenty-one years of age if either of the following apply:

(B)(1) The person is a law enforcement officer who is properly appointed or employed as a law enforcement officer and has received firearms training approved by the Ohio peace officer training council or equivalent firearms training.

(2) The person is an active or reserve member of the armed services of the United States or the Ohio national guard, or was honorably discharged from military service in the active or reserve armed services of the United States or the Ohio national guard, and the person has received firearms training from the armed services or the national guard or equivalent firearms training.

(C) Whoever violates division (A) of this section is guilty of underage purchase of a firearm, a delinquent act that would be a felony of the fourth degree if it could be committed by an adult. Whoever violates division (B) of this section is guilty of underage purchase of a handgun, a misdemeanor of the second degree.

**HISTORY: 146 v H 4 (Eff 11-9-95); 146 v H 124 (Eff 3-31-97); 148 v S 179, § 3. Eff 1-1-2002; 152 v H 450, § 1, eff. 4-7-09.**

The effective date is set by section 5 of SB 179.

## § 2923.22 Permitted interstate transactions in firearms.

(A) Any resident of Ohio age eighteen or over, and not prohibited by section 2923.13 or 2923.15 of the Revised Code or any applicable law of another state or the United States from acquiring or using firearms, may purchase or obtain a rifle, shotgun, or ammunition therefor in Indiana, Kentucky, Michigan, Pennsylvania, or West Virginia.

(B) Any resident of Indiana, Kentucky, Michigan, Pennsylvania, or West Virginia, age eighteen or over, and not prohibited by section 2923.13 or 2923.15 of the Revised Code or the laws of his domicile or the United States from acquiring or using firearms, may purchase or obtain a rifle, shotgun, or ammunition therefor in Ohio.

(C) Any purchase and sale pursuant to this section shall be for such purposes and under such circumstances and upon such conditions as are prescribed by the "Gun Control Act of 1968," 82 Stat. 1213, 18 U.S.C. 922(b)(3), and any amendments or additions thereto or reenactments thereof.

**HISTORY: 134 v H 511. Eff 1-1-74.**

**Not analogous to former RC § 2923.22 (RS § 6884; S&S 694; 71 v 105; 77 v 145; 79 v 131; 89 v 234; GC § 12639; Bureau of Code Revision, 10-1-53), repealed 134 v H 511, § 2, eff 1-1-74.**

**Analogous to former RC § 2923.57 (133 v H 484), repealed 134 v H 511, § 2, eff 1-1-74.**

## § 2923.23 Immunity from prosecution.

(A) No person who acquires, possesses, or carries a firearm or dangerous ordnance in violation of section 2923.13 or 2923.17 of the Revised Code shall be prosecuted for such violation, if he reports his possession of firearms or dangerous ordnance to any law enforcement authority, describes the firearms of [or] dangerous ordnance in his possession and where they may be found, and voluntarily surrenders the firearms or dangerous ordnance to the law enforcement authority. A surrender is not voluntary if it occurs when the person is taken into custody or during a pursuit or attempt to take the person into custody under circumstances indicating that the surrender is made under threat of force.

(B) No person in violation of section 2923.13 of the Revised Code solely by reason of his being under indictment shall be prosecuted for such violation if, within ten days after service of the indictment, he voluntarily surrenders the firearms and dangerous ordnance in his possession to any law enforcement authority pursuant to division (A) of this section, for safekeeping pending disposition of the indictment or of an application for relief under section 2923.14 of the Revised Code.

(C) Evidence obtained from or by reason of an application or proceeding under section 2923.14 of the Revised Code for relief from disability, shall not be used in a prosecution of the applicant for any violation of section 2923.13 of the Revised Code.

(D) Evidence obtained from or by reason of an application under section 2923.18 of the Revised Code for a permit to possess dangerous ordnance, shall not be used in a prosecution of the applicant for any violation of section 2923.13 or 2923.17 of the Revised Code.

**HISTORY: 134 v H 511. Eff 1-1-74.**

**Not analogous to former RC § 2923.23 (GC § 12642, repealed in 113 v 685; 115 v 70; Bureau of Code Revision, 10-1-53), repealed 134 v H 511, § 2, eff 1-1-74.**

## § 2923.24 Possessing criminal tools.

(A) No person shall possess or have under the person's control any substance, device, instrument, or article, with purpose to use it criminally.

(B) Each of the following constitutes prima-facie evidence of criminal purpose:

(1) Possession or control of any dangerous ordnance, or the materials or parts for making dangerous ordnance, in the absence of circumstances indicating the dangerous ordnance, materials, or parts are intended for legitimate use;

(2) Possession or control of any substance, device, instrument, or article designed or specially adapted for criminal use;

(3) Possession or control of any substance, device, instrument, or article commonly used for criminal purposes, under circumstances indicating the item is intended for criminal use.

(C) Whoever violates this section is guilty of possessing criminal tools. Except as otherwise provided in this division, possessing criminal tools is a misdemeanor of the first degree. If the circumstances indicate that the substance, device, instrument, or article involved in the offense was intended for use in the commission of a felony, possessing criminal tools is a felony of the fifth degree.

**HISTORY: 134 v H 511 (Eff 1-1-74); 146 v S 2. Eff 7-1-96.**

**Not analogous to former RC § 2923.24 (RS § 6928-1; 92 v 97; GC § 12779; Bureau of Code Revision, 10-1-53), repealed 134 v H 511, § 2, eff 1-1-74.**

The effective date is set by section 6 of SB 2.

## § 2923.25 Federally licensed firearms dealers to offer locking device to purchaser.

Each federally licensed firearms dealer who sells any firearm, at the time of the sale of the firearm, shall offer for sale to the purchaser of the firearm a trigger lock, gun lock, or gun locking device that is appropriate for that firearm. Each federally licensed firearms dealer shall post in a conspicuous location in the dealer's place of business the poster furnished to the dealer pursuant to section 5502.63 of the Revised Code and shall make available to all purchasers of firearms from the dealer the brochure furnished to the dealer pursuant to that section.

As used in this section, "federally licensed firearms dealer" has the same meaning as in section 5502.63 of the Revised Code.

**HISTORY: 150 v H 12, § 1, eff. 4-8-04; 151 v H 66, § 101.01, eff. 6-30-05.**

The effective date is set by § 612.12 of 151 v H 66.

**Not analogous to former RC § 2923.25, repealed, 134 v H 511, § 2 [GC § 12798-6; 108 v PtI, 419; Bureau of Code Revision, 10-1-53]. Eff 1-1-74.**

## § 2923.251 Repealed, 134 v H 511, § 2 [127 v 459; 129 v 582]. Eff 1-1-74.

This section concerned unvented gas heaters.

## § 2923.26 Repealed, 134 v H 511, § 2 [RS §§ 6884-2, 6995; GC §§ 13396, 13397, 13408; 76 v 191; 92 v 88; 99 v 86; 120 v 133; Bureau of Code Revision, 10-1-53; 129 v H 1]. Eff 1-1-74.

This section concerned offenses regarding false alarms, camping on public lands and tramps.

## § 2923.27 Repealed, 134 v H 511, § 2 [RS §§ 6884-2, 6995; GC §§ 13396, 13397, 13408; 76 v 191; 92 v 88; 99 v 86; 120 v 133; Bureau of Code Revision, 10-1-53; 129 v H 1]. Eff 1-1-74.

This section concerned offenses regarding false alarms, camping on public lands and tramps.

## § 2923.28 Repealed, 134 v H 511, § 2 [RS §§ 6884-2, 6995; GC §§ 13396, 13397, 13408; 76 v 191; 92 v 88; 99 v 86; 120 v 133; Bureau of Code Revision, 10-1-53; 129 v H 1]. Eff 1-1-74.

This section concerned offenses regarding false alarms, camping on public lands and tramps.

## § 2923.29 Repealed, 134 v H 511, § 2 [GC §§ 13383-1, 13410; 99 v 20; 101 v 263; 103 v 469; 115 v 334; Bureau of Code Revision, 10-1-53; 126 v 575]. Eff 1-1-74.

This section concerned improper use of transcripts and fraud.

## § 2923.30 Repealed, 134 v H 511, § 2 [GC §§ 13383-1, 13410; 99 v 20; 101 v 263; 103 v 469; 115 v 334; Bureau of Code Revision, 10-1-53; 126 v 575]. Eff 1-1-74.

This section concerned improper use of transcripts and fraud.

# [CORRUPT ACTIVITY]

## § 2923.31 Definitions.

As used in sections 2923.31 to 2923.36 of the Revised Code:

(A) "Beneficial interest" means any of the following:

(1) The interest of a person as a beneficiary under a trust in which the trustee holds title to personal or real property;

(2) The interest of a person as a beneficiary under any other trust arrangement under which any other person holds title to personal or real property for the benefit of such person;

(3) The interest of a person under any other form of express fiduciary arrangement under which any other person holds title to personal or real property for the benefit of such person.

"Beneficial interest" does not include the interest of a stockholder in a corporation or the interest of a partner in either a general or limited partnership.

(B) "Costs of investigation and prosecution" and "costs of investigation and litigation" mean all of the costs incurred by the state or a county or municipal corporation under sections 2923.31 to 2923.36 of the Revised Code in the prosecution and investigation of any criminal action or in the litigation and investigation of any civil action, and includes, but is not limited to, the costs of resources and personnel.

(C) "Enterprise" includes any individual, sole proprietorship, partnership, limited partnership, corporation, trust, union, government agency, or other legal entity, or any organization, association, or group of persons associated in fact although not a legal entity. "Enterprise" includes illicit as well as licit enterprises.

(D) "Innocent person" includes any bona fide purchaser of property that is allegedly involved in a violation of section 2923.32 of the Revised Code, including any person who establishes a valid claim to or interest in the property in accordance with division (E) of section 2981.04 of the Revised Code, and any victim of an alleged violation of that section or of any underlying offense involved in an alleged violation of that section.

(E) "Pattern of corrupt activity" means two or more incidents of corrupt activity, whether or not there has been a prior conviction, that are related to the affairs of the same enterprise, are not isolated, and are not so closely related to each other and connected in time and place that they constitute a single event.

At least one of the incidents forming the pattern shall occur on or after January 1, 1986. Unless any incident was an aggravated murder or murder, the last of the incidents forming the pattern shall occur within six years after the commission of any prior incident forming the pattern, excluding any period of imprisonment served by any person engaging in the corrupt activity.

For the purposes of the criminal penalties that may be imposed pursuant to section 2923.32 of the Revised Code, at least one of the incidents forming the pattern shall constitute a felony under the laws of this state in existence at the time it was committed or, if committed in violation of the laws of the United States or of any other state, shall constitute a felony under the law of the United States or the other state and would be a criminal offense under the law of this state if committed in this state.

(F) "Pecuniary value" means money, a negotiable instrument, a commercial interest, or anything of value, as defined in section 1.03 of the Revised Code, or any other property or service that has a value in excess of one hundred dollars.

(G) "Person" means any person, as defined in section 1.59 of the Revised Code, and any governmental officer, employee, or entity.

(H) "Personal property" means any personal property, any interest in personal property, or any right, including, but not limited to, bank accounts, debts, corporate stocks, patents, or copyrights. Personal property and any beneficial interest in personal property are deemed to be located where the trustee of the property, the personal property, or the instrument evidencing the right is located.

(I) "Corrupt activity" means engaging in, attempting to engage in, conspiring to engage in, or soliciting, coercing, or intimidating another person to engage in any of the following:

(1) Conduct defined as "racketeering activity" under the "Organized Crime Control Act of 1970," 84 Stat. 941, 18 U.S.C. 1961(1)(B), (1)(C), (1)(D), and (1)(E), as amended;

(2) Conduct constituting any of the following:

(a) A violation of section 1315.55, 1322.02, 2903.01, 2903.02, 2903.03, 2903.04, 2903.11, 2903.12, 2905.01, 2905.02, 2905.11, 2905.22, 2907.321, 2907.322, 2907.323, 2909.02, 2909.03, 2909.22, 2909.23, 2909.24, 2909.26, 2909.27, 2909.28, 2909.29, 2911.01, 2911.02, 2911.11, 2911.12, 2911.13, 2911.31, 2913.05, 2913.06, 2921.02, 2921.03, 2921.04, 2921.11, 2921.12, 2921.32, 2921.41, 2921.42, 2921.43, 2923.12, or 2923.17; division (F)(1)(a), (b), or (c) of section 1315.53; division (A)(1) or (2) of section 1707.042; division (B), (C)(4), (D), (E), or (F) of section 1707.44; division (A)(1) or (2) of section 2923.20; division (J)(1) of section 4712.02; section 4719.02, 4719.05, or 4719.06; division (C), (D), or (E) of section 4719.07; section 4719.08; or division (A) of section 4719.09 of the Revised Code.

(b) Any violation of section 3769.11, 3769.15, 3769.16, or 3769.19 of the Revised Code as it existed prior to July 1, 1996, any violation of section 2915.02 of the Revised Code that occurs on or after July 1, 1996, and that, had it occurred prior to that date, would have been a violation of section 3769.11 of the Revised Code as it existed prior to that date, or any violation of section 2915.05 of the Revised Code that occurs on or after July 1, 1996, and that, had it occurred prior to that date, would have been a violation of section 3769.15, 3769.16, or 3769.19 of the Revised Code as it existed prior to that date.

(c) Any violation of section 2907.21, 2907.22, 2907.31, 2913.02, 2913.11, 2913.21, 2913.31, 2913.32, 2913.34, 2913.42, 2913.47, 2913.51, 2915.03, 2925.03, 2925.04, 2925.05, or 2925.37 of the Revised Code, any violation of section 2925.11 of the Revised Code that is a felony of the first, second, third, or fourth degree and that occurs on or after July 1, 1996, any violation of section 2915.02 of the Revised Code that occurred prior to July 1, 1996, any violation of section 2915.02 of the Revised Code that occurs on or after July 1, 1996, and that, had it occurred prior to that date, would not have been a violation of section 3769.11 of the Revised Code as it existed prior to that date, any violation of section 2915.06 of the Revised Code as it existed prior to July 1, 1996, or any violation of division (B) of section 2915.05 of the Revised Code as it exists on and after July 1, 1996, when the proceeds of the violation, the payments made in the violation, the amount of a claim for payment or for any other benefit that is false or deceptive and that is involved in the violation, or the value of the contraband or other property illegally possessed, sold, or purchased in the violation exceeds one thousand dollars, or any combination of violations described in division (I)(2)(c) of this section when the total proceeds of the combination of violations, payments made in the combination of violations, amount of the claims for payment or for other benefits that is false or deceptive and that is involved in the combination of violations, or value of the contraband or other property illegally possessed, sold, or purchased in the combination of violations exceeds one thousand dollars;

(d) Any violation of section 5743.112 of the Revised Code when the amount of unpaid tax exceeds one hundred dollars;

(e) Any violation or combination of violations of section 2907.32 of the Revised Code involving any material or performance containing a display of bestiality or of sexual conduct, as defined in section 2907.01 of the Revised Code, that is explicit and depicted with clearly visible penetration of the genitals or clearly visible penetration by the penis of any orifice when the total proceeds of the violation or combination of violations, the payments made in the violation or combination of violations, or the value of the contraband or other property illegally possessed, sold, or purchased in the violation or combination of violations exceeds one thousand dollars;

(f) Any combination of violations described in division (I)(2)(c) of this section and violations of section 2907.32 of the Revised Code involving any material or performance containing a display of bestiality or of sexual conduct, as defined in section 2907.01 of the Revised Code, that is explicit and depicted with clearly visible penetration of the genitals or clearly visible penetration by the penis of any orifice when the total proceeds of the combination of violations, payments made in the combination of violations, amount of the claims for payment or for other benefits that is false or deceptive and that is involved in the combination of violations, or value of the contraband or other property illegally possessed, sold, or purchased in the combination of violations exceeds one thousand dollars;

(g) Any violation of section 2905.32 of the Revised Code to the extent the violation is not based solely on the same conduct that constitutes corrupt activity pursuant to division (I)(2)(c) of this section due to the conduct being in violation of section 2907.21 of the Revised Code.

(3) Conduct constituting a violation of any law of any state other than this state that is substantially similar to the conduct described in division (I)(2) of this section, provided the defendant was convicted of the conduct in a criminal proceeding in the other state;

(4) Animal or ecological terrorism;

(5)(a) Conduct constituting any of the following:

(i) Organized retail theft;

(ii) Conduct that constitutes one or more violations of any law of any state other than this state, that is substantially similar to organized retail theft, and that if committed in this state would be organized retail theft, if the defendant was convicted of or pleaded guilty to the conduct in a criminal proceeding in the other state.

(b) By enacting division (I)(5)(a) of this section, it is the intent of the general assembly to add organized retail theft and the conduct described in division (I)(5)(a)(ii) of this section as conduct constituting corrupt activity. The enactment of division (I)(5)(a) of this section and the addition by division (I)(5)(a) of this section of organized retail theft and the conduct described in division (I)(5)(a)(ii) of this section as conduct constituting corrupt activity does not limit or preclude, and shall not be construed as limiting or precluding, any prosecution for a violation of section 2923.32 of the Revised Code that is based on one or more violations of section 2913.02 or 2913.51 of the Revised Code, one or more similar offenses under the laws of this state or any other state, or any combination of any of those violations or similar offenses, even though the conduct constituting the basis for those violations or offenses could be construed as also constituting organized retail theft or conduct of the type described in division (I)(5)(a)(ii) of this section.

(J) "Real property" means any real property or any interest in real property, including, but not limited to, any lease of, or mortgage upon, real property. Real property and any beneficial interest in it is deemed to be located where the real property is located.

(K) "Trustee" means any of the following:

(1) Any person acting as trustee under a trust in which the trustee holds title to personal or real property;

(2) Any person who holds title to personal or real property for which any other person has a beneficial interest;

(3) Any successor trustee.

"Trustee" does not include an assignee or trustee for an insolvent debtor or an executor, administrator, administrator with the will annexed, testamentary trustee, guardian, or committee, appointed by, under the control of, or accountable to a court.

(L) "Unlawful debt" means any money or other thing of value constituting principal or interest of a debt that is legally unenforceable in this state in whole or in part because the debt was incurred or contracted in violation of any federal or state law relating to the business of gambling activity or relating to the business of lending money at an usurious rate unless the creditor proves, by a preponderance of the evidence, that the usurious rate was not intentionally set and that it resulted from a good faith error by the creditor, notwithstanding the maintenance of procedures that were adopted by the creditor to avoid an error of that nature.

(M) "Animal activity" means any activity that involves the use of animals or animal parts, including, but not limited to, hunting, fishing, trapping, traveling, camping, the production, preparation, or processing of food or food products, clothing or garment manufacturing, medical research, other research, entertainment, recreation, agriculture, biotechnology, or service activity that involves the use of animals or animal parts.

(N) "Animal facility" means a vehicle, building, structure, nature preserve, or other premises in which an animal is lawfully kept, handled, housed, exhibited, bred, or offered for sale, including, but not limited to, a zoo, rodeo, circus, amusement park, hunting preserve, or premises in which a horse or dog event is held.

(O) "Animal or ecological terrorism" means the commission of any felony that involves causing or creating a substantial risk of physical harm to any property of another, the use of a deadly weapon or dangerous ordnance, or purposely, knowingly, or recklessly causing serious physical harm to property and that involves an intent to obstruct, impede, or deter any person from participating in a lawful animal activity, from mining, foresting, harvesting, gathering, or processing natural resources, or from being lawfully present in or on an animal facility or research facility.

(P) "Research facility" means a place, laboratory, institution, medical care facility, government facility, or public or private educational institution in which a scientific test, experiment, or investigation involving the use of animals or other living organisms is lawfully carried out, conducted, or attempted.

(Q) "Organized retail theft" means the theft of retail property with a retail value of one thousand dollars or more from one or more retail establishments with the intent to sell, deliver, or transfer that property to a retail property fence.

(R) "Retail property" means any tangible personal property displayed, held, stored, or offered for sale in or by a retail establishment.

(S) "Retail property fence" means a person who possesses, procures, receives, or conceals retail property that was represented to the person as being stolen or that the person knows or believes to be stolen.

(T) "Retail value" means the full retail value of the retail property. In determining whether the retail value of retail property equals or exceeds one thousand dollars, the value of all retail property stolen from the retail establishment or retail establishments by the same person or persons within any one-hundred-eighty-day period shall be aggregated.

**HISTORY: 141 v H 5 (Eff 1-1-86); 141 v S 74 (Eff 9-3-86); 142 v H 708 (Eff 4-19-88); 142 v H 624 (Eff 3-17-89); 143 v H 347 (Eff 7-18-90); 144 v S 323 (Eff 4-16-93); 146 v S 2 (Eff 7-1-96); 146 v S 269 (Eff 7-1-96); 146 v H 333 (Eff 9-19-96); 146 v S 214, § 1 (Eff 12-5-96); 146 v S 214, § 3 (Eff 12-5-96); 146 v S 277 (Eff 3-31-97); 147 v H 565 (Eff 3-30-99); 149 v S 184. Eff 5-15-2002; 151 v S 9, § 1, eff. 4-14-06; 151 v H 241, § 1, eff. 7-1-07; 152 v S 320, § 1, eff. 4-7-09; 153 v S 235, § 1, eff. 3-24-11; 2011 HB 86, § 1, eff. Sept. 30, 2011.**

The provisions of § 4 of HB 86 read as follows:

"SECTION 4. The amendments to sections 926.99, 1333.99, 1707.99, 1716.99, 2909.03, 2909.05, 2909.11, 2913.02, 2913.03, 2913.04, 2913.11, 2913.21, 2913.31, 2913.32, 2913.34, 2913.40, 2913.401, 2913.42, 2913.421, 2913.43, 2913.45, 2913.46, 2913.47, 2913.48, 2913.49, 2913.51, 2913.61, 2915.05, 2917.21, 2917.31, 2917.32, 2921.13, 2921.41, 2923.31, and 2981.07, division (B) of section 2929.13, and division (A) of section 2929.14 of the Revised Code that are made in this act apply to a person who commits an offense specified or penalized under those sections on or after the effective date of this section and to a person to whom division (B) of section 1.58 of the Revised Code makes the amendments applicable.

"The provisions of sections 926.99, 1333.99, 1707.99, 1716.99, 2909.03, 2909.05, 2909.11, 2913.02, 2913.03, 2913.04, 2913.11, 2913.21, 2913.31, 2913.32, 2913.34, 2913.40, 2913.401, 2913.42, 2913.421, 2913.43, 2913.45, 2913.46, 2913.47, 2913.48, 2913.49, 2913.51, 2913.61, 2915.05, 2917.21, 2917.31, 2917.32, 2921.13, 2921.41, 2923.31, and 2981.07 of the Revised Code in existence prior to the effective date of this section shall apply to a person upon whom a court imposed sentence prior to the effective date of this section for an offense specified or penalized under those sections. The amendments to sections 926.99, 1333.99, 1707.99, 1716.99, 2909.03, 2909.05, 2909.11, 2913.02, 2913.03, 2913.04, 2913.11, 2913.21, 2913.31, 2913.32, 2913.34, 2913.40, 2913.401,

2913.42, 2913.421, 2913.43, 2913.45, 2913.46, 2913.47, 2913.48, 2913.49, 2913.51, 2913.61, 2915.05, 2917.21, 2917.31, 2917.32, 2921.13, 2921.41, 2923.31, and 2981.07 of the Revised Code that are made in this act do not apply to a person who upon whom a court imposed sentence prior to the effective date of this section for an offense specified or penalized under those sections."

See provisions of § 4 of 151 v H 241 following RC § 2901.01.

**Not analogous to former RC § 2923.31 (RS § 6983-1; 92 v 122; GC § 13411; Bureau of Code Revision, 10-1-53), repealed 134 v H 511, § 2, eff 1-1-74.**

## § 2923.32 Engaging in pattern of corrupt activity; forfeiture.

(A)(1) No person employed by, or associated with, any enterprise shall conduct or participate in, directly or indirectly, the affairs of the enterprise through a pattern of corrupt activity or the collection of an unlawful debt.

(2) No person, through a pattern of corrupt activity or the collection of an unlawful debt, shall acquire or maintain, directly or indirectly, any interest in, or control of, any enterprise or real property.

(3) No person, who knowingly has received any proceeds derived, directly or indirectly, from a pattern of corrupt activity or the collection of any unlawful debt, shall use or invest, directly or indirectly, any part of those proceeds, or any proceeds derived from the use or investment of any of those proceeds, in the acquisition of any title to, or any right, interest, or equity in, real property or in the establishment or operation of any enterprise.

A purchase of securities on the open market with intent to make an investment, without intent to control or participate in the control of the issuer, and without intent to assist another to do so is not a violation of this division, if the securities of the issuer held after the purchase by the purchaser, the members of the purchaser's immediate family, and the purchaser's or the immediate family members' accomplices in any pattern of corrupt activity or the collection of an unlawful debt do not aggregate one per cent of the outstanding securities of any one class of the issuer and do not confer, in law or in fact, the power to elect one or more directors of the issuer.

(B)(1) Whoever violates this section is guilty of engaging in a pattern of corrupt activity. Except as otherwise provided in this division, engaging in corrupt activity is a felony of the second degree. Except as otherwise provided in this division, if at least one of the incidents of corrupt activity is a felony of the first, second, or third degree, aggravated murder, or murder, if at least one of the incidents was a felony under the law of this state that was committed prior to July 1, 1996, and that would constitute a felony of the first, second, or third degree, aggravated murder, or murder if committed on or after July 1, 1996, or if at least one of the incidents of corrupt activity is a felony under the law of the United States or of another state that, if committed in this state on or after July 1, 1996, would constitute a felony of the first, second, or third degree, aggravated murder, or murder under the law of this state, engaging in a pattern of corrupt activity is a felony of the first degree. If the offender also is convicted of or pleads guilty to a specification as described in section 2941.1422 of the Revised Code that was included in the indictment, count in the indictment, or information charging the offense, engaging in a pattern of corrupt activity is a felony of the first degree, and the court shall sentence the offender to a mandatory prison term as provided in division (B)(7) of section 2929.14 of the Revised Code and shall order the offender to make restitution as provided in division (B)(8) of section 2929.18 of the Revised Code. Notwithstanding any other provision of law, a person may be convicted of violating the provisions of this section as well as of a conspiracy to violate one or more of those provisions under section 2923.01 of the Revised Code.

(2) Notwithstanding the financial sanctions authorized by section 2929.18 of the Revised Code, the court may do all of the following with respect to any person who derives pecuniary value or causes property damage, personal injury other than pain and suffering, or other loss through or by the violation of this section:

(a) In lieu of the fine authorized by that section, impose a fine not exceeding the greater of three times the gross value gained or three times the gross loss caused and order the clerk of the court to pay the fine into the state treasury to the credit of the corrupt activity investigation and prosecution fund, which is hereby created;

(b) In addition to the fine described in division (B)(2)(a) of this section and the financial sanctions authorized by section 2929.18 of the Revised Code, order the person to pay court costs;

(c) In addition to the fine described in division (B)(2)(a) of this section and the financial sanctions authorized by section 2929.18 of the Revised Code, order the person to pay to the state, municipal, or county law enforcement agencies that handled the investigation and prosecution the costs of investigation and prosecution that are reasonably incurred.

The court shall hold a hearing to determine the amount of fine, court costs, and other costs to be imposed under this division.

(3) In addition to any other penalty or disposition authorized or required by law, the court shall order any person who is convicted of or pleads guilty to a violation of this section or who is adjudicated delinquent by reason of a violation of this section to criminally forfeit to the state under Chapter 2981. of the Revised Code any personal or real property in which the person has an interest and that was used in the course of or intended for use in the course of a violation of this section, or that was derived from or realized through conduct in violation of this section, including any property constituting an interest in, means of control over, or influence over the enterprise involved in the violation and any property constituting proceeds derived from the violation, including all of the following:

(a) Any position, office, appointment, tenure, commission, or employment contract of any kind acquired or maintained by the person in violation of this section, through which the person, in violation of this section, conducted or participated in the conduct of an enterprise, or that afforded the person a source of influence or control over an enterprise that the person exercised in violation of this section;

(b) Any compensation, right, or benefit derived from a position, office, appointment, tenure, commission, or employment contract described in division (B)(3)(a) of this section that accrued to the person in violation of this section during the period of the pattern of corrupt activity;

(c) Any interest in, security of, claim against, or property or contractual right affording the person a source of influence or control over the affairs of an enterprise that the person exercised in violation of this section;

(d) Any amount payable or paid under any contract for goods or services that was awarded or performed in violation of this section.

**HISTORY: 141 v H 5 (Eff 1-1-86); 141 v S 74 (Eff 9-3-86); 142 v H 708 (Eff 4-19-88); 143 v H 215 (Eff 4-11-90); 143 v H 266 (Eff 9-6-90); 146 v S 2 (Eff 7-1-96); 147 v S 164 (Eff 1-15-98); 148 v S 179, § 3. Eff 1-1-2002; 151 v H 241, § 1, eff. 7-1-07; 152 v H 280, § 1, eff. 4-7-09; 2011 HB 86, § 1, eff. Sept. 30, 2011.**

See provisions of § 4 of 151 v H 241 following RC § 2901.01.

**Not analogous to former RC § 2923.32 (GC § 12674; 114 v 143; Bureau of Code Revision, 10-1-53), repealed 134 v H 511, § 2, eff 1-1-74.**

The effective date is set by section 5 of SB 179.

## § 2923.33 Repealed, 151 v H 241, § 2 [141 v H 5 (Eff 1-1-86); 143 v H 266 (Eff 9-6-90); 148 v S 179, § 3. Eff 1-1-2002]. Eff 7-1-07.

See provisions of § 4 of 151 v H 241 following RC § 2901.01.

This section concerned motion and order to preserve reachability of property subject to forfeit. See now RC § 2981.01 et seq.

## § 2923.34 Civil proceedings for relief from violation; civil penalty.

(A) Any person who is injured or threatened with injury by a violation of section 2923.32 of the Revised Code may institute a civil proceeding in an appropriate court seeking relief from any person whose conduct violated or allegedly violated section 2923.32 of the Revised Code or who conspired or allegedly conspired to violate that section, except that the pattern of corrupt activity alleged by an injured person or person threatened with injury shall include at least one incident other than a violation of division (A)(1) or (2) of section 1707.042 [1707.04.2] or division (B), (C)(4), (D), (E), or (F) of section 1707.44 of the Revised Code, of 18 U.S.C. 1341, 18 U.S.C. 1343, 18 U.S.C. 2314, or any other offense involving fraud in the sale of securities.

(B) If the plaintiff in a civil action instituted pursuant to this section proves the violation by a preponderance of the evidence, the court, after making due provision for the rights of innocent persons, may grant relief by entering any appropriate orders to ensure that the violation will not continue or be repeated. The orders may include, but are not limited to, orders that:

(1) Require the divestiture of the defendant's interest in any enterprise or in any real property;

(2) Impose reasonable restrictions upon the future activities or investments of any defendant in the action, including, but not limited to, restrictions that prohibit the defendant from engaging in the same type of endeavor as the enterprise in which the defendant was engaged in violation of section 2923.32 of the Revised Code;

(3) Order the dissolution or reorganization of any enterprise;

(4) Order the suspension or revocation of a license, permit, or prior approval granted to any enterprise by any department or agency of the state;

(5) Order the dissolution of a corporation organized under the laws of this state, or the revocation of the authorization of a foreign corporation to conduct business within this state, upon a finding that the board of directors or an agent acting on behalf of the corporation, in conducting the affairs of the corporation, has authorized or engaged in conduct in violation of section 2923.32 of the Revised Code, and that, for the prevention of future criminal conduct, the public interest requires the corporation to be dissolved or its license revoked.

(C) Relief pursuant to division (B)(3), (4), or (5) of this section shall not be granted in any civil proceeding instituted by an injured person unless the attorney general intervenes in the civil action pursuant to this division.

Upon the filing of a civil proceeding for relief under division (B)(3), (4), or (5) of this section by an allegedly injured person other than a prosecuting attorney, the allegedly injured person immediately shall notify the attorney general of the filing. The attorney general, upon timely application, may intervene in any civil proceeding for relief under division (B)(3), (4), or (5) if the attorney general certifies that, in the attorney general's opinion, the proceeding is of general public interest. In any proceeding brought by an injured person under division (B)(3), (4), or (5) of this section, the attorney general is entitled to the same relief as if the attorney general instituted the proceeding.

(D) In a civil proceeding under division (B) of this section, the court may grant injunctive relief without a showing of special or irreparable injury.

Pending final determination of a civil proceeding initiated under this section, the court may issue a temporary restraining order or a preliminary injunction upon a showing of immediate danger or significant injury to the plaintiff, including the possibility that any judgment for money damages might be difficult to execute, and, in a proceeding initiated by an aggrieved person, upon the execution of proper bond against injury for an improvidently granted injunction.

(E) In a civil proceeding under division (A) of this section, any person directly or indirectly injured by conduct in violation of section 2923.32 of the Revised Code or a conspiracy to violate that section, other than a violator of that section or a conspirator to violate that section, in addition to relief under division (B) of this section, shall have a cause of action for triple the actual damages the person sustained. To recover triple damages, the plaintiff shall prove the violation or conspiracy to violate that section and actual damages by clear and convincing evidence. Damages under this division may include, but are not limited to, competitive injury and injury distinct from the injury inflicted by corrupt activity.

(F) In a civil action in which the plaintiff prevails under division (B) or (E) of this section, the plaintiff shall recover reasonable attorney fees in the trial and appellate courts, and the court shall order the defendant to pay to the state, municipal, or county law enforcement agencies that handled the investigation and litigation the costs of investigation and litigation that reasonably are incurred and that are not ordered to be paid pursuant to division (B)(2) of section 2923.32 of the Revised Code or division (H) of this section.

(G) Upon application, based on the evidence presented in the case by the plaintiff, as the interests of justice may require, the trial court may grant a defendant who prevails in a civil action brought pursuant to this section all or part of the defendant's costs, including the costs of investigation and litigation reasonably incurred, and all or part of the defendant's reasonable attorney fees, unless the court finds that special circumstances, including the relative economic position of the parties, make an award unjust.

(H) If a person, other than an individual, is not convicted of a violation of section 2923.32 of the Revised Code, the prosecuting attorney may institute proceedings against the person to recover a civil penalty for conduct that the prosecuting attorney proves by clear and convincing evidence is in violation of section 2923.32 of the Revised Code. The civil penalty shall not exceed one hundred thousand dollars and shall be paid into the state treasury to the credit of the corrupt activity investigation and prosecution fund created in section 2923.32 of the Revised Code. If a civil penalty is ordered pursuant to this division, the court shall order the defendant to pay to the state, municipal, or county law enforcement agencies that handled the investigation and litigation the costs of investigation and litigation that are reasonably incurred and that are not ordered to be paid pursuant to this section.

(I) A final judgment, decree, or delinquency adjudication rendered against the defendant or the adjudicated delinquent child in a civil action under this section or in a criminal or delinquency action or proceeding for a violation of section 2923.32 of the Revised Code shall estop the defendant or the adjudicated delinquent child in any subsequent civil proceeding or action brought by any person as to all matters as to which the judgment, decree, or adjudication would be an estoppel as between the parties to the civil, criminal, or delinquency proceeding or action.

(J) Notwithstanding any other provision of law providing a shorter period of limitations, a civil proceeding or action under this section may be commenced at any time within five years after the unlawful conduct terminates or the cause of action accrues or within any longer statutory period of limitations that may be applicable. If a criminal proceeding, delinquency proceeding, civil action, or other proceeding is brought or intervened in by the state to punish, prevent, or restrain any activity that is unlawful under section 2923.32 of the Revised Code, the running of the period of limitations prescribed by this division with respect to any civil action brought under this section by a person who is injured by a violation or threatened violation of section 2923.32 of the Revised Code, based in whole or in part upon any matter complained of in the state prosecution, action, or proceeding, shall be suspended during the pendency of the state prosecution, action, or proceeding and for two years following its termination.

(K) Personal service of any process in a proceeding under this section may be made upon any person outside this state if the person was involved in any conduct constituting a violation of section 2923.32 of the Revised Code in this state. The person is deemed by the person's conduct in violation of section 2923.32 of the Revised Code to have submitted to the jurisdiction of the courts of this state for the purposes of this section.

(L) The application of any civil remedy under this section shall not preclude the application of any criminal remedy or criminal forfeiture under section 2923.32 of the Revised Code or any other provision of law, or the application of any delinquency disposition under Chapter 2152. of the Revised Code or any other provision of law.

(M)(1) Any person who prevails in a civil action pursuant to this section has a right to any property, or the proceeds of any property, criminally forfeited to the state pursuant to section 2981.04 of the Revised Code or against which any fine under section 2923.32 of the Revised Code or civil penalty under division (H) of this section may be imposed.

The right of any person who prevails in a civil action pursuant to this section, other than a prosecuting attorney performing official duties under that section, to forfeited property, property against which fines and civil penalties may be imposed, and the proceeds of that property is superior to any right of the state, a municipal corporation, or a county to the property or the proceeds of the property, if the civil action is brought within one hundred eighty days after the entry of a sentence of forfeiture or a fine pursuant to sections 2923.32 and 2981.04 of the Revised Code or the entry of a civil penalty pursuant to division (H) of this section.

The right is limited to the total value of the treble damages, civil penalties, attorney's fees, and costs awarded to the prevailing party in an action pursuant to this section, less any restitution received by the person.

(2) If the aggregate amount of claims of persons who have prevailed in a civil action pursuant to this section against any one defendant is greater than the total value of the treble fines, civil penalties, and forfeited property paid by the person against whom the actions were brought, all of the persons who brought their actions within one hundred eighty days after the entry of a sentence or disposition of forfeiture or a fine pursuant to section 2923.32 of the Revised Code or the entry of a civil penalty pursuant to division (H) of this section, first shall receive a pro rata share of the total amount of the fines, civil penalties, and forfeited property. After the persons who brought their actions within the specified one-hundred-eighty-day period have satisfied their claims out of the fines, civil penalties, and forfeited property, all other persons who prevailed in civil actions pursuant to this section shall receive a pro rata share of the total amount of the fines, civil penalties, and forfeited property that remains in the custody of the law enforcement agency or in the corrupt activity investigation and prosecution fund.

(N) As used in this section, "law enforcement agency" includes, but is not limited to, the state board of pharmacy.

**HISTORY: 141 v H 5 (Eff 1-1-86); 141 v H 428 (Eff 12-23-86); 143 v H 266 (Eff 9-6-90); 148 v S 179, § 3. Eff 1-1-2002; 151 v H 241, § 1, eff. 7-1-07.**

See provisions of § 4 of 151 v H 241 following RC § 2901.01.

**Not analogous to former RC § 2923.34 (GC § 12674-2; 114 v 143, § 3; Bureau of Code Revision, 10-1-53), repealed 134 v H 511, § 2, eff 1-1-74.**

The effective date is set by section 5 of SB 179.

## § 2923.35 Repealed, 151 v H 241, § 2 [141 v H 5 (Eff 1-1-86); 141 v S 74 (Eff 9-3-86); 143 v H 215 (Eff 4-11-90); 143 v H 261 (Eff 7-18-90); 143 v H 266 (Eff 9-6-90); 143 v S 258 (Eff 11-20-90); 144 v S 174 (Eff 7-31-92); 145 v H 152 (Eff 7-1-93); 146 v H 1 (Eff 1-1-96); 146 v H 670 (Eff 12-2-96); 147 v S 164. Eff 1-15-98; 150 v H 95, § 1, eff. 6-26-03; 151 v H 66, § 101.01, eff. 9-29-05]. Eff 7-1-07.

See provisions of § 4 of 151 v H 241 following RC § 2901.01.

This section concerned disposition of forfeited property, fine or civil penalty. See now RC § 2981.01 et seq.

## § 2923.36 Filing of corrupt activity lien notice; lis pendens.

(A) Upon the institution of any criminal proceeding charging a violation of section 2923.32 of the Revised Code, the filing of any complaint, indictment, or information in juvenile court alleging a violation of that section as a delinquent act, or the institution of any civil proceeding under section 2923.34 or 2981.05 of the Revised Code, the state, at any time during the pendency of the proceeding, may file a corrupt activity lien notice with the county recorder of any county in which property subject to forfeiture may be located. No fee shall be required for filing the notice. The recorder immediately shall record the notice pursuant to section 317.08 of the Revised Code.

(B) A corrupt activity lien notice shall be signed by the prosecuting attorney who files the lien. The notice shall set forth all of the following information:

(1) The name of the person against whom the proceeding has been brought. The prosecuting attorney may specify in the notice any aliases, names, or fictitious names under which the person may be known. The prosecuting attorney also may specify any corporation, partnership, or other entity in which the person has an interest subject to forfeiture under Chapter 2981. of the Revised Code and shall describe in the notice the person's interest in the corporation, partnership, or other entity.

(2) If known to the prosecuting attorney, the present residence and business addresses of the person or names set forth in the notice;

(3) A statement that a criminal or delinquency proceeding for a violation of section 2923.32 of the Revised Code or a civil proceeding under section 2923.34 or 2981.05 of the Revised Code has been brought against the person named in the notice, the name of the county in which the proceeding has been brought, and the case number of the proceeding;

(4) A statement that the notice is being filed pursuant to this section;

(5) The name and address of the prosecuting attorney filing the notice;

(6) A description of the real or personal property subject to the notice and of the interest in that property of the person named in the notice, to the extent the property and the interest of the person in it reasonably is known at the time the proceeding is instituted or at the time the notice is filed.

(C) A corrupt activity lien notice shall apply only to one person and, to the extent applicable, any aliases, fictitious names, or other names, including names of corporations, partnerships, or other entities, to the extent permitted in this section. A separate corrupt activity lien notice is required to be filed for any other person.

(D) Within seven days after the filing of each corrupt activity lien notice, the prosecuting attorney who files the notice shall furnish to the person named in the notice by certified mail, return receipt requested, to the last known business or residential address of the person, a copy of the recorded notice with a notation on it of any county in which the notice has been recorded. The failure of the prosecuting attorney to furnish a copy of the notice under this section shall not invalidate or otherwise affect the corrupt activity lien notice when the prosecuting attorney did not know and could not reasonably ascertain the address of the person entitled to notice.

After receipt of a copy of the notice under this division, the person named in the notice may petition the court to authorize the person to post a surety bond in lieu of the lien or to otherwise modify the lien as the interests of justice may require. The bond shall be in an amount equal to the value of the property reasonably known to be subject to the notice and conditioned on the payment of any judgment and costs ordered in an action pursuant to Chapter 2981. of the Revised Code up to the value of the bond.

(E) From the date of filing of a corrupt activity lien notice, the notice creates a lien in favor of the state on any personal or real property or any beneficial interest in the property located in the county in which the notice is filed that then or subsequently is owned by the person named in the notice or under any of the names set forth in the notice.

The lien created in favor of the state is superior and prior to the interest of any other person in the personal or real property or beneficial interest in the property, if the interest is acquired subsequent to the filing of the notice.

(F)(1) Notwithstanding any law or rule to the contrary, in conjunction with any civil proceeding brought pursuant to section 2981.05 of the Revised Code, the prosecuting attorney may file in any county, without prior court order, a lis pendens pursuant to sections 2703.26 and 2703.27 of the Revised Code. In such a case, any person acquiring an interest in the subject property or beneficial interest in the property, if the property interest is acquired subsequent to the filing of the lis pendens, shall take the property or interest subject to the civil proceeding and any subsequent judgment.

(2) If a corrupt activity lien notice has been filed, the prosecuting attorney may name as a defendant in the lis pendens, in addition to the person named in the notice, any person acquiring an interest in the personal or real property or beneficial interest in the property subsequent to the filing of the notice. If a judgment of forfeiture is entered in the criminal or delinquency proceeding pursuant to section 2981.04 of the Revised Code in favor of the state, the interest of any person in the property that was acquired subsequent to the filing of the notice shall be subject to the notice and judgment of forfeiture.

(G) Upon a final judgment of forfeiture in favor of the state pursuant to Chapter 2981. of the Revised Code, title of the state to the forfeited property shall do either of the following:

(1) In the case of real property, or a beneficial interest in it, relate back to the date of filing of the corrupt activity lien notice in the county where the property or interest is located. If no corrupt activity lien notice was filed, title of the state relates back to the date of the filing of any lis pendens under division (F) of this section in the records of the county recorder of the county in which the real property or beneficial interest is located. If no corrupt activity lien notice or lis pendens was filed, title of the state relates back to the date of the recording of the final judgment of forfeiture in the records of the county recorder of the county in which the real property or beneficial interest is located.

(2) In the case of personal property or a beneficial interest in it, relate back to the date on which the property or interest was seized by the state, or the date of filing of a corrupt activity lien notice in the county in which the property or beneficial interest is located. If the property was not seized and no corrupt activity lien notice was filed, title of the state relates back to the date of the recording of the final judgment of forfeiture in the county in which the personal property or beneficial interest is located.

(H) If personal or real property, or a beneficial interest in it, that is subject to forfeiture pursuant to section 2923.32 of the Revised Code is conveyed, alienated, disposed of, or otherwise rendered unavailable for forfeiture after the filing of either a corrupt activity lien notice, or a criminal or delinquency proceeding for a violation of section 2923.32 or a civil proceeding under section 2981.05 of the Revised Code, whichever is earlier, the state may bring an action in any court of common pleas against the person named in the corrupt activity lien notice or the defendant in the criminal, delinquency, or civil proceeding to recover the value of the property or interest. The court shall enter final judgment against the person named in the notice or the defendant for an amount equal to the value of the property or interest together with investigative costs and attorney's fees incurred by the state in the action. If a civil proceeding is pending, an action pursuant to this section shall be filed in the court in which the proceeding is pending.

(I) If personal or real property, or a beneficial interest in it, that is subject to forfeiture pursuant to Chapter 2981. of the Revised Code is alienated or otherwise transferred or disposed of after either the filing of a corrupt activity lien notice, or the filing of a criminal or delinquency proceeding for a violation of section 2923.32 or a civil proceeding under section 2981.05 of the Revised Code, whichever is earlier, the transfer or disposal is fraudulent as to the state and the state shall have all the rights granted a creditor under Chapter 1336. of the Revised Code.

(J) No trustee, who acquires actual knowledge that a corrupt activity lien notice, a criminal or delinquency proceeding for a violation of section 2923.32 or a civil proceeding under section 2981.05 of the Revised Code has been filed against any person for whom the trustee holds legal or record title to personal or real property, shall recklessly fail to furnish promptly to the prosecuting attorney all of the following:

(1) The name and address of the person, as known to the trustee;

(2) The name and address, as known to the trustee, of all other persons for whose benefit the trustee holds title to the property;

(3) If requested by the prosecuting attorney, a copy of the trust agreement or other instrument under which the trustee holds title to the property.

Any trustee who fails to comply with this division is guilty of failure to provide corrupt activity lien information, a misdemeanor of the first degree.

(K) If a trustee transfers title to personal or real property after a corrupt activity lien notice is filed against the property, the lien is filed in the county in which the property is located, and the lien names a person who holds a beneficial interest in the property, the trustee, if the trustee has actual notice of the notice, shall be liable to the state for the greater of the following:

(1) The proceeds received directly by the person named in the notice as a result of the transfer;

(2) The proceeds received by the trustee as a result of the transfer and distributed to the person named in the notice;

(3) The fair market value of the interest of the person named in the notice in the property transferred.

However, if the trustee transfers property for at least its fair market value and holds the proceeds that otherwise would be paid or distributed to the beneficiary, or at the direction of the beneficiary or the beneficiary's designee, the liability of the trustee shall not exceed the amount of the proceeds held by the trustee.

(L) The filing of a corrupt activity lien notice does not constitute a lien on the record title to personal or real property owned by the trustee, except to the extent the trustee is named in the notice.

The prosecuting attorney for the county may bring a civil action in any court of common pleas to recover from the trustee the amounts set forth in division (H) of this section. The county may recover investigative costs and attorney's fees incurred by the prosecuting attorney.

(M)(1) This section does not apply to any transfer by a trustee under a court order, unless the order is entered in an action between the trustee and the beneficiary.

(2) Unless the trustee has actual knowledge that a person owning a beneficial interest in the trust is named in a corrupt activity lien notice or otherwise is a defendant in a civil proceeding brought pursuant to section 2923.34 or 2981.05 of the Revised Code, this section does not apply to either of the following:

(a) Any transfer by a trustee required under the terms of any trust agreement, if the agreement is a matter of public record before the filing of any corrupt activity lien notice;

(b) Any transfer by a trustee to all of the persons who own a beneficial interest in the trust.

(N) The filing of a corrupt activity lien notice does not affect the use to which personal or real property, or a beneficial interest in it, that is owned by the person named in the notice may be put or the right of the person to receive any proceeds resulting from the use and ownership, but not the sale, of the property, until a judgment of forfeiture is entered.

(O) The term of a corrupt activity lien notice is five years from the date the notice is filed, unless a renewal notice has been filed by the prosecuting attorney of the county in which the property or interest is located. The term of any renewal of a corrupt activity lien notice granted by the court is five years from the date of its filing. A corrupt activity lien notice may be renewed any number of times while a criminal or civil proceeding under section 2923.34, 2981.04, or 2981.05 of the Revised Code, or an appeal from either type of proceeding, is pending.

(P) The prosecuting attorney who files the corrupt activity lien notice may terminate, in whole or part, any corrupt activity lien notice or release any personal or real property or beneficial interest in the property upon any terms that the prosecuting attorney determines are appropriate. Any termination or release shall be filed by the prosecuting attorney with each county recorder with whom the notice was filed. No fee shall be imposed for the filing.

(Q)(1) If no civil proceeding has been brought by the prosecuting attorney pursuant to section 2923.34 of the Revised Code against the person named in the corrupt activity lien notice, the acquittal in a criminal or delinquency proceeding for a violation of section 2923.32 of the Revised Code of the person named in the notice or the dismissal of a criminal or delinquency proceeding for such a violation against the person named in the notice terminates the notice. In such a case, the filing of the notice has no effect.

(2) If a civil proceeding has been brought pursuant to section 2923.34 or 2981.05 of the Revised Code with respect to any property that is the subject of a corrupt activity lien notice and if the criminal or delinquency proceeding brought against the person named in the notice for a violation of section 2923.32 of the Revised Code has been dismissed or the person named in the notice has been acquitted in the criminal or delinquency proceeding for such a violation, the notice shall continue for the duration of the civil proceeding and any appeals from the civil proceeding, except that it shall not continue any longer than the term of the notice as determined pursuant to division (O) of this section.

(3) If no civil proceeding brought pursuant to section 2981.05 of the Revised Code then is pending against the person named in a corrupt activity lien notice, any person

so named may bring an action against the prosecuting attorney who filed the notice, in the county where it was filed, seeking a release of the property subject to the notice or termination of the notice. In such a case, the court of common pleas promptly shall set a date for hearing, which shall be not less than five nor more than ten days after the action is filed. The order and a copy of the complaint shall be served on the prosecuting attorney within three days after the action is filed. At the hearing, the court shall take evidence as to whether any personal or real property, or beneficial interest in it, that is owned by the person bringing the action is covered by the notice or otherwise is subject to forfeiture. If the person bringing the action shows by a preponderance of the evidence that the notice does not apply to the person or that any personal or real property, or beneficial interest in it, that is owned by the person is not subject to forfeiture, the court shall enter a judgment terminating the notice or releasing the personal or real property or beneficial interest from the notice.

At a hearing, the court may release from the notice any property or beneficial interest upon the posting of security, by the person against whom the notice was filed, in an amount equal to the value of the property or beneficial interest owned by the person.

(4) The court promptly shall enter an order terminating a corrupt activity lien notice or releasing any personal or real property or beneficial interest in the property, if a sale of the property or beneficial interest is pending and the filing of the notice prevents the sale. However, the proceeds of the sale shall be deposited with the clerk of the court, subject to the further order of the court.

(R) Notwithstanding any provision of this section, any person who has perfected a security interest in personal or real property or a beneficial interest in the property for the payment of an enforceable debt or other similar obligation prior to the filing of a corrupt activity lien notice or a lis pendens in reference to the property or interest may foreclose on the property or interest as otherwise provided by law. The foreclosure, insofar as practical, shall be made so that it otherwise will not interfere with a forfeiture under Chapter 2981. of the Revised Code.

**HISTORY: 141 v H 5 (Eff 1-1-86); 143 v H 190 (Eff 9-25-89); 143 v H 266 (Eff 9-6-90); 143 v H 506 (Eff 9-28-90); 148 v S 179, § 3. Eff 1-1-2002; 151 v H 241, § 1, eff. 7-1-07.**

See provisions of § 4 of 151 v H 241 following RC § 2901.01. The effective date is set by section 5 of SB 179.

The provisions of § 11 of SB 179 (148 v —) read, in part, as follows:

SECTION 11. * * * Section 2923.36 of the Revised Code is presented in this act as a composite of the section as amended by both Sub. H.B. 266 and Sub. H.B. 506 of the 118th General Assembly, with the new language of neither of the acts shown in capital letters. Section 2929.01 of the Revised Code is presented in this act as a composite of the section as amended by Am. Sub. H.B. 349, Am. S.B. 9, Am. Sub. S.B. 22, and Am. Sub. S.B. 107 of the 123rd General Assembly, with the new language of none of the acts shown in capital letters. Section 2929.12 of the Revised Code is presented in this act as a composite of the section as amended by both Am. S.B. 9 and Am. Sub. S.B. 107 of the 123rd General Assembly, with the new language of neither of the acts shown in capital letters. * * * This is in recognition of the principle stated in division (B) of section 1.52 of the Revised Code that such amendments are to be harmonized where not substantively irreconcilable and constitutes a legislative finding that such is the resulting version in effect prior to the effective date of this act.

## [CRIMINAL GANGS]

### § 2923.41 Definitions.

As used in sections 2923.41 to 2923.44 of the Revised Code:

(A) "Criminal gang" means an ongoing formal or informal organization, association, or group of three or more persons to which all of the following apply:

(1) It has as one of its primary activities the commission of one or more of the offenses listed in division (B) of this section.

(2) It has a common name or one or more common, identifying signs, symbols, or colors.

(3) The persons in the organization, association, or group individually or collectively engage in or have engaged in a pattern of criminal gang activity.

(B)(1) "Pattern of criminal gang activity" means, subject to division (B)(2) of this section, that persons in the criminal gang have committed, attempted to commit, conspired to commit, been complicitors in the commission of, or solicited, coerced, or intimidated another to commit, attempt to commit, conspire to commit, or be in complicity in the commission of two or more of any of the following offenses:

(a) A felony or an act committed by a juvenile that would be a felony if committed by an adult;

(b) An offense of violence or an act committed by a juvenile that would be an offense of violence if committed by an adult;

(c) A violation of section 2907.04, 2909.06, 2911.211 [2911.21.1], 2917.04, 2919.23, or 2919.24 of the Revised Code, section 2921.04 or 2923.16 of the Revised Code, section 2925.03 of the Revised Code if the offense is trafficking in marihuana, or section 2927.12 of the Revised Code.

(2) There is a "pattern of criminal gang activity" if all of the following apply with respect to the offenses that are listed in division (B)(1)(a), (b), or (c) of this section and that persons in the criminal gang committed, attempted to commit, conspired to commit, were in complicity in committing, or solicited, coerced, or intimidated another to commit, attempt to commit, conspire to commit, or be in complicity in committing:

(a) At least one of the two or more offenses is a felony.

(b) At least one of those two or more offenses occurs on or after January 1, 1999.

(c) The last of those two or more offenses occurs within five years after at least one of those offenses.

(d) The two or more offenses are committed on separate occasions or by two or more persons.

(C) "Criminal conduct" means the commission of, an attempt to commit, a conspiracy to commit, complicity in the commission of, or solicitation, coercion, or intimidation of another to commit, attempt to commit, conspire to commit, or be in complicity in the commission of an offense listed in division (B)(1)(a), (b), or (c) of this section or an act that is committed by a juvenile and that would be an offense, an attempt to commit an offense, a conspiracy to commit an offense, complicity in the commission of, or solicitation, coercion, or intimidation of another to commit, attempt to commit, conspire to commit, or be in complicity in the commission of an offense listed in division (B)(1)(a), (b), or (c) of this section if committed by an adult.

(D) "Juvenile" means a person who is under eighteen years of age.

(E) "Law enforcement agency" includes, but is not limited to, the state board of pharmacy and the office of a prosecutor.

(F) "Prosecutor" has the same meaning as in section 2935.01 of the Revised Code.

**HISTORY: 147 v H 2. Eff 1-1-99; 151 v H 241, § 1, eff. 7-1-07.**

See provisions of § 4 of 151 v H 241 following RC § 2901.01.

**Not analogous to former RC § 2923.41 (125 v S 28 (211); 134 v H 344), repealed 134 v H 511, § 2, eff 1-1-74.**

The effective date is set by section 4 of HB 2.

The provisions of § 3 of HB 2 (147 v —) read as follows:

SECTION 3. (A) The General Assembly finds that it is the right of every individual, regardless of race, color, creed, religion, national origin, sex, age, sexual orientation, or handicap, to be secure and protected from fear, intimidation, and physical harm caused by the activities of violent groups and individuals. It is not the intent of this act to interfere with the exercise of the constitutionally protected rights of freedom of expression and association. The General Assembly recognizes the constitutional right of every citizen to harbor and express beliefs on any lawful subject whatsoever, to lawfully associate with others who share similar beliefs, to petition lawfully constituted authority for a redress of grievances, and to participate in the electoral process.

(B) The General Assembly finds, however, that the state of Ohio is facing a mounting crisis caused by criminal gangs whose members threaten and terrorize peaceful citizens and commit a multitude of crimes. These activities, both individually and collectively, present a clear and present danger to public order and safety and are not constitutionally protected.

(C) It is the intent of the General Assembly to eradicate the terror created by criminal gangs by providing enhanced penalties and by eliminating the patterns, profits, proceeds, and instrumentalities of criminal gang activity.

## § 2923.42 Participating in criminal gang.

(A) No person who actively participates in a criminal gang, with knowledge that the criminal gang engages in or has engaged in a pattern of criminal gang activity, shall purposely promote, further, or assist any criminal conduct, as defined in division (C) of section 2923.41 of the Revised Code, or shall purposely commit or engage in any act that constitutes criminal conduct, as defined in division (C) of section 2923.41 of the Revised Code.

(B) Whoever violates this section is guilty of participating in a criminal gang, a felony of the second degree.

(C)(1) Notwithstanding any contrary provision of any section of the Revised Code, the clerk of the court shall pay any fine imposed for a violation of this section pursuant to division (A) of section 2929.18 of the Revised Code to the county, township, municipal corporation, park district, as created pursuant to section 511.18 or 1545.04 of the Revised Code, or state law enforcement agencies in this state that primarily were responsible for or involved in making the arrest of, and in prosecuting, the offender. However, the clerk shall not pay a fine so imposed to a law enforcement agency unless the agency has adopted a written internal control policy under division (C)(2) of this section that addresses the use of the fine moneys that it receives. Each agency shall use the fines so paid in accordance with the written internal control policy adopted by the recipient agency under division (C)(2) of this section to subsidize the agency's law enforcement efforts that pertain to criminal gangs.

(2)(a) Prior to receiving any fine moneys under division (C)(1) of this section or division (B) of section 2923.44 of the Revised Code, a law enforcement agency shall adopt a written internal control policy that addresses the agency's use and disposition of all fine moneys so received and that provides for the keeping of detailed financial records of the receipts of those fine moneys, the general types of expenditures made out of those fine moneys, and the specific amount of each general type of expenditure. The policy shall not provide for or permit the identification of any specific expenditure that is made in an ongoing investigation. All financial records of the receipts of those fine moneys, the general types of expenditures made out of those fine moneys, and the specific amount of each general type of expenditure by an agency are public records open for inspection under section 149.43 of the Revised Code. Additionally, a written internal control policy adopted under division (C)(2)(a) of this section is a public record open for inspection under section 149.43 of the Revised Code, and the agency that adopted the policy shall comply with it.

(b) Each law enforcement agency that receives in any calendar year any fine moneys under division (C)(1) of this section or division (B) of section 2923.44 of the Revised Code shall prepare a report covering the calendar year that cumulates all of the information contained in all of the public financial records kept by the agency pursuant to division (C)(2)(a) of this section for that calendar year and shall send a copy of the cumulative report, no later than the first day of March in the calendar year following the calendar year covered by the report, to the attorney general. Each report received by the attorney general is a public record open for inspection under section 149.43 of the Revised Code. Not later than the fifteenth day of April in the calendar year in which the reports are received, the attorney general shall send the president of the senate and the speaker of the house of representatives a written notice that does all of the following:

(i) Indicates that the attorney general has received from law enforcement agencies reports of the type described in division (C)(2)(b) of this section that cover the previous calendar year and indicates that the reports were received under division (C)(2)(b) of this section;

(ii) Indicates that the reports are open for inspection under section 149.43 of the Revised Code;

(iii) Indicates that the attorney general will provide a copy of any or all reports to the president of the senate or the speaker of the house upon request.

(D) A prosecution for a violation of this section does not preclude a prosecution of a violation of any other section of the Revised Code. One or more acts, a series of acts, or a course of behavior that can be prosecuted under this section or any other section of the Revised Code may be prosecuted under this section, the other section of the Revised Code, or both sections.

**HISTORY: 147 v H 2. Eff 1-1-99; 151 v H 241, § 1, eff. 7-1-07.**

See provisions of § 4 of 151 v H 241 following RC § 2901.01.

**Not analogous to former RC § 2923.42 (128 v 623; 129 v 376; 129 v 582 (748)), repealed 134 v H 511, § 2, eff 1-1-74.**

The effective date is set by section 4 of HB 2.

See provisions, § 3 of HB 2 (147 v —), following RC § 2923.41.

## § 2923.43 Criminal gang premises constitute nuisance.

Any building, premises, or real estate, including vacant land, that is used or occupied by a criminal gang on more than two occasions within a one-year period to engage in a pattern of criminal gang activity constitutes a nuisance subject to abatement pursuant to sections 3767.01 to 3767.11 of the Revised Code.

**HISTORY: 147 v H 2. Eff 1-1-99.**

**Not analogous to former RC § 2923.43 (132 v H 332), repealed 134 v H 511, § 2, eff 1-1-74.**
The effective date is set by section 4 of HB 2.
See provisions, § 3 of HB 2 (147 v —), following RC § 2923.41.

## § 2923.44 Fines.

(A) If a person is convicted of or pleads guilty to a violation of section 2923.42 of the Revised Code, or a juvenile is found by a juvenile court to be a delinquent child for an act that is a violation of section 2923.42 of the Revised Code, and derives profits or other proceeds from the offense or act, the court that imposes sentence or an order of disposition upon the offender or delinquent child, in lieu of any fine that the court is otherwise authorized or required to impose, may impose upon the offender or delinquent child a fine of not more than twice the gross profits or other proceeds so derived.

(B) Notwithstanding any contrary provision of the Revised Code, the clerk of the court shall pay all fines imposed pursuant to this section to the county, municipal corporation, township, park district created pursuant to section 511.18 or 1545.01 of the Revised Code, or state law enforcement agencies in this state that were primarily responsible for or involved in making the arrest of, and in prosecuting, the offender. However, the clerk shall not pay a fine so imposed to a law enforcement agency unless the agency has adopted a written internal control policy pursuant to division (C)(2) of section 2923.42 of the Revised Code that addresses the use of the fine moneys that it receives under this section and division (C)(1) of section 2923.42 of the Revised Code. The law enforcement agencies shall use the fines imposed and paid pursuant to this section to subsidize their efforts pertaining to criminal gangs, in accordance with the written internal control policy adopted by the recipient agency pursuant to division (C)(2) of section 2923.42 of the Revised Code.

**HISTORY: 147 v H 2 (Eff 1-1-99); 148 v S 179, § 3. Eff 1-1-2002; 151 v H 241, § 1, eff. 7-1-07.**

See provisions of § 4 of 151 v H 241 following RC § 2901.01.
The effective date is set by section 5 of SB 179.

## § 2923.45 Repealed, 151 v H 241, § 2 [147 v H 2 (Eff 1-1-99); 148 v S 179, § 3. Eff 1-1-2002]. Eff 7-1-07.

See provisions of § 4 of 151 v H 241 following RC § 2901.01. This section concerned property subject to civil forfeiture and seizure. See now RC § 2981.01 et seq.

## § 2923.46 Repealed, 151 v H 241, § 2 [147 v H 2. Eff 1-1-99; 151 v H 66, § 101.01, eff. 9-29-05; 151 v H 530, § 101.01, eff. 3-30-06]. Eff 7-1-07.

See provisions of § 4 of 151 v H 241 following RC § 2901.01. This section concerned options of head of law enforcement agency as to seized property; disposition; application of general forfeiture provision. See now RC § 2981.01 et seq.

## § 2923.47 Repealed, 151 v H 241, § 2 [147 v H 2. Eff 1-1-99]. Eff 7-1-07.

See provisions of § 4 of 151 v H 241 following RC § 2901.01. This section concerned motion for return of seized property. See now RC § 2981.01 et seq.

## § 2923.51 Repealed, 134 v H 511, § 2 [132 v H 996]. Eff 1-1-74.

This section concerned riot control.

## § 2923.52 Repealed, 134 v H 511, § 2 [132 v H 996]. Eff 1-1-74.

This section concerned riot control.

## § 2923.53 Repealed, 134 v H 511, § 2 [132 v H 996]. Eff 1-1-74.

This section concerned riot control.

## § 2923.54 Repealed, 134 v H 511, § 2 [132 v H 996]. Eff 1-1-74.

This section concerned riot control.

## § 2923.55 Repealed, 134 v H 511, § 2 [132 v H 996]. Eff 1-1-74.

This section concerned riot control.

## § 2923.56 Repealed, 134 v H 511, § 2 [133 v H 484]. Eff 1-1-74.

This section concerned rules and transactions regarding firearms.

## § 2923.57 Repealed, 134 v H 511, § 2 [133 v H 484]. Eff 1-1-74.

This section concerned rules and transactions regarding firearms.

## § 2923.61 Repealed, 134 v H 511, § 2 [133 v H 1219]. Eff 1-1-74.

This section concerned disrupting college activities.

## § 2923.99 Repealed, 129 v 582(990), § 2 [127 v 459]. Eff 1-10-61.

This section provided a penalty for former RC § 2923.25.1 concerning unvented gas heaters.

# CHAPTER 2925: DRUG OFFENSES



## § 2925.01 Definitions.

As used in this chapter:

(A) "Administer," "controlled substance," "dispense," "distribute," "hypodermic," "manufacturer," "official written order," "person," "pharmacist," "pharmacy," "sale," "schedule I," "schedule II," "schedule III," "schedule IV," "schedule V," and "wholesaler" have the same meanings as in section 3719.01 of the Revised Code.

(B) "Drug dependent person" and "drug of abuse" have the same meanings as in section 3719.011 of the Revised Code.

(C) "Drug," "dangerous drug," "licensed health professional authorized to prescribe drugs," and "prescription" have the same meanings as in section 4729.01 of the Revised Code.

(D) "Bulk amount" of a controlled substance means any of the following:

(1) For any compound, mixture, preparation, or substance included in schedule I, schedule II, or schedule III, with the exception of marihuana, cocaine, L.S.D., heroin, and hashish and except as provided in division (D)(2) or (5) of this section, whichever of the following is applicable:

(a) An amount equal to or exceeding ten grams or twenty-five unit doses of a compound, mixture, preparation, or substance that is or contains any amount of a schedule I opiate or opium derivative;

(b) An amount equal to or exceeding ten grams of a compound, mixture, preparation, or substance that is or contains any amount of raw or gum opium;

(c) An amount equal to or exceeding thirty grams or ten unit doses of a compound, mixture, preparation, or substance that is or contains any amount of a schedule I hallucinogen other than tetrahydrocannabinol or lysergic acid amide, or a schedule I stimulant or depressant;

(d) An amount equal to or exceeding twenty grams or five times the maximum daily dose in the usual dose range specified in a standard pharmaceutical reference manual of a compound, mixture, preparation, or substance that is or contains any amount of a schedule II opiate or opium derivative;

(e) An amount equal to or exceeding five grams or ten unit doses of a compound, mixture, preparation, or substance that is or contains any amount of phencyclidine;

(f) An amount equal to or exceeding one hundred twenty grams or thirty times the maximum daily dose in the usual dose range specified in a standard pharmaceutical reference manual of a compound, mixture, preparation, or substance that is or contains any amount of a schedule II stimulant that is in a final dosage form manufactured by a person authorized by the "Federal Food, Drug, and Cosmetic Act," 52 Stat. 1040 (1938), 21 U.S.C.A. 301, as amended, and the federal drug abuse control laws, as defined in section 3719.01 of the Revised Code, that is or contains any amount of a schedule II depressant substance or a schedule II hallucinogenic substance;

(g) An amount equal to or exceeding three grams of a compound, mixture, preparation, or substance that is or contains any amount of a schedule II stimulant, or any of its salts or isomers, that is not in a final dosage form manufactured by a person authorized by the Federal Food, Drug, and Cosmetic Act and the federal drug abuse control laws.

(2) An amount equal to or exceeding one hundred twenty grams or thirty times the maximum daily dose in the usual dose range specified in a standard pharmaceutical reference manual of a compound, mixture, preparation, or substance that is or contains any amount of a schedule III or IV substance other than an anabolic steroid or a schedule III opiate or opium derivative;

(3) An amount equal to or exceeding twenty grams or five times the maximum daily dose in the usual dose range specified in a standard pharmaceutical reference manual of a compound, mixture, preparation, or substance that is or contains any amount of a schedule III opiate or opium derivative;

(4) An amount equal to or exceeding two hundred fifty milliliters or two hundred fifty grams of a compound, mixture, preparation, or substance that is or contains any amount of a schedule V substance;

(5) An amount equal to or exceeding two hundred solid dosage units, sixteen grams, or sixteen milliliters of a compound, mixture, preparation, or substance that is or contains any amount of a schedule III anabolic steroid.

(E) "Unit dose" means an amount or unit of a compound, mixture, or preparation containing a controlled substance that is separately identifiable and in a form that indicates that it is the amount or unit by which the controlled substance is separately administered to or taken by an individual.

(F) "Cultivate" includes planting, watering, fertilizing, or tilling.

(G) "Drug abuse offense" means any of the following:

(1) A violation of division (A) of section 2913.02 that constitutes theft of drugs, or a violation of section 2925.02, 2925.03, 2925.04, 2925.041, 2925.05, 2925.06, 2925.11, 2925.12, 2925.13, 2925.22, 2925.23, 2925.24, 2925.31, 2925.32, 2925.36, or 2925.37 of the Revised Code;

(2) A violation of an existing or former law of this or any other state or of the United States that is substantially equivalent to any section listed in division (G)(1) of this section;

(3) An offense under an existing or former law of this or any other state, or of the United States, of which planting, cultivating, harvesting, processing, making, manufacturing, producing, shipping, transporting, delivering, acquiring, possessing, storing, distributing, dispensing, selling, inducing another to use, administering to another, using, or otherwise dealing with a controlled substance is an element;

(4) A conspiracy to commit, attempt to commit, or complicity in committing or attempting to commit any offense under division (G)(1), (2), or (3) of this section.

(H) "Felony drug abuse offense" means any drug abuse offense that would constitute a felony under the laws of this state, any other state, or the United States.

(I) "Harmful intoxicant" does not include beer or intoxicating liquor but means any of the following:

(1) Any compound, mixture, preparation, or substance the gas, fumes, or vapor of which when inhaled can induce intoxication, excitement, giddiness, irrational behavior, depression, stupefaction, paralysis, unconsciousness, asphyxiation, or other harmful physiological effects, and includes, but is not limited to, any of the following:

(a) Any volatile organic solvent, plastic cement, model cement, fingernail polish remover, lacquer thinner, cleaning fluid, gasoline, or other preparation containing a volatile organic solvent;

(b) Any aerosol propellant;

(c) Any fluorocarbon refrigerant;

(d) Any anesthetic gas.

(2) Gamma Butyrolactone;

(3) 1,4 Butanediol.

(J) "Manufacture" means to plant, cultivate, harvest, process, make, prepare, or otherwise engage in any part of the production of a drug, by propagation, extraction, chemical synthesis, or compounding, or any combination of the same, and includes packaging, repackaging, labeling, and other activities incident to production.

(K) "Possess" or "possession" means having control over a thing or substance, but may not be inferred solely from mere access to the thing or substance through ownership or occupation of the premises upon which the thing or substance is found.

(L) "Sample drug" means a drug or pharmaceutical preparation that would be hazardous to health or safety if used without the supervision of a licensed health professional authorized to prescribe drugs, or a drug of abuse, and that, at one time, had been placed in a container plainly marked as a sample by a manufacturer.

(M) "Standard pharmaceutical reference manual" means the current edition, with cumulative changes if any, of any of the following reference works:

(1) "The National Formulary";

(2) "The United States Pharmacopeia," prepared by authority of the United States Pharmacopeial Convention, Inc.;

(3) Other standard references that are approved by the state board of pharmacy.

(N) "Juvenile" means a person under eighteen years of age.

(O) "Counterfeit controlled substance" means any of the following:

(1) Any drug that bears, or whose container or label bears, a trademark, trade name, or other identifying mark used without authorization of the owner of rights to that trademark, trade name, or identifying mark;

(2) Any unmarked or unlabeled substance that is represented to be a controlled substance manufactured, processed, packed, or distributed by a person other than the person that manufactured, processed, packed, or distributed it;

(3) Any substance that is represented to be a controlled substance but is not a controlled substance or is a different controlled substance;

(4) Any substance other than a controlled substance that a reasonable person would believe to be a controlled substance because of its similarity in shape, size, and color, or its markings, labeling, packaging, distribution, or the price for which it is sold or offered for sale.

(P) An offense is "committed in the vicinity of a school" if the offender commits the offense on school premises, in a school building, or within one thousand feet of the boundaries of any school premises, regardless of whether the offender knows the offense is being committed on school premises, in a school building, or within one thousand feet of the boundaries of any school premises.

(Q) "School" means any school operated by a board of education, any community school established under Chapter 3314. of the Revised Code, or any nonpublic school for which the state board of education prescribes minimum standards under section 3301.07 of the Revised Code, whether or not any instruction, extracurricular activities, or training provided by the school is being conducted at the time a criminal offense is committed.

(R) "School premises" means either of the following:

(1) The parcel of real property on which any school is situated, whether or not any instruction, extracurricular activities, or training provided by the school is being conducted on the premises at the time a criminal offense is committed;

(2) Any other parcel of real property that is owned or leased by a board of education of a school, the governing authority of a community school established under Chapter 3314. of the Revised Code, or the governing body of a nonpublic school for which the state board of education prescribes minimum standards under section 3301.07 of the Revised Code and on which some of the instruction, extracurricular activities, or training of the school is conducted, whether or not any instruction, extracurricular activities, or training provided by the school is being conducted on the parcel of real property at the time a criminal offense is committed.

(S) "School building" means any building in which any of the instruction, extracurricular activities, or training provided by a school is conducted, whether or not any instruction, extracurricular activities, or training provided by the school is being conducted in the school building at the time a criminal offense is committed.

(T) "Disciplinary counsel" means the disciplinary counsel appointed by the board of commissioners on grievances and discipline of the supreme court under the Rules for the Government of the Bar of Ohio.

(U) "Certified grievance committee" means a duly constituted and organized committee of the Ohio state bar association or of one or more local bar associations of the state of Ohio that complies with the criteria set forth in Rule V, section 6 of the Rules for the Government of the Bar of Ohio.

(V) "Professional license" means any license, permit, certificate, registration, qualification, admission, temporary license, temporary permit, temporary certificate, or temporary registration that is described in divisions (W)(1) to (36) of this section and that qualifies a person as a professionally licensed person.

(W) "Professionally licensed person" means any of the following:

(1) A person who has obtained a license as a manufacturer of controlled substances or a wholesaler of controlled substances under Chapter 3719. of the Revised Code;

(2) A person who has received a certificate or temporary certificate as a certified public accountant or who has registered as a public accountant under Chapter 4701. of the Revised Code and who holds an Ohio permit issued under that chapter;

(3) A person who holds a certificate of qualification to practice architecture issued or renewed and registered under Chapter 4703. of the Revised Code;

(4) A person who is registered as a landscape architect under Chapter 4703. of the Revised Code or who holds a permit as a landscape architect issued under that chapter;

(5) A person licensed under Chapter 4707. of the Revised Code;

(6) A person who has been issued a certificate of registration as a registered barber under Chapter 4709. of the Revised Code;

(7) A person licensed and regulated to engage in the business of a debt pooling company by a legislative authority, under authority of Chapter 4710. of the Revised Code;

(8) A person who has been issued a cosmetologist's license, hair designer's license, manicurist's license, esthetician's license, natural hair stylist's license, managing cosmetologist's license, managing hair designer's license, managing manicurist's license, managing esthetician's license, managing natural hair stylist's license, cosmetology instructor's license, hair design instructor's license, manicurist instructor's license, esthetics instructor's license, natural hair style instructor's license, independent contractor's license, or tanning facility permit under Chapter 4713. of the Revised Code;

(9) A person who has been issued a license to practice dentistry, a general anesthesia permit, a conscious intravenous sedation permit, a limited resident's license, a limited teaching license, a dental hygienist's license, or a dental hygienist's teacher's certificate under Chapter 4715. of the Revised Code;

(10) A person who has been issued an embalmer's license, a funeral director's license, a funeral home license, or a crematory license, or who has been registered for an embalmer's or funeral director's apprenticeship under Chapter 4717. of the Revised Code;

(11) A person who has been licensed as a registered nurse or practical nurse, or who has been issued a certificate for the practice of nurse-midwifery under Chapter 4723. of the Revised Code;

(12) A person who has been licensed to practice optometry or to engage in optical dispensing under Chapter 4725. of the Revised Code;

(13) A person licensed to act as a pawnbroker under Chapter 4727. of the Revised Code;

(14) A person licensed to act as a precious metals dealer under Chapter 4728. of the Revised Code;

(15) A person licensed as a pharmacist, a pharmacy intern, a wholesale distributor of dangerous drugs, or a terminal distributor of dangerous drugs under Chapter 4729. of the Revised Code;

(16) A person who is authorized to practice as a physician assistant under Chapter 4730. of the Revised Code;

(17) A person who has been issued a certificate to practice medicine and surgery, osteopathic medicine and surgery, a limited branch of medicine, or podiatry under Chapter 4731. of the Revised Code;

(18) A person licensed as a psychologist or school psychologist under Chapter 4732. of the Revised Code;

(19) A person registered to practice the profession of engineering or surveying under Chapter 4733. of the Revised Code;

(20) A person who has been issued a license to practice chiropractic under Chapter 4734. of the Revised Code;

(21) A person licensed to act as a real estate broker or real estate salesperson under Chapter 4735. of the Revised Code;

(22) A person registered as a registered sanitarian under Chapter 4736. of the Revised Code;

(23) A person licensed to operate or maintain a junkyard under Chapter 4737. of the Revised Code;

(24) A person who has been issued a motor vehicle salvage dealer's license under Chapter 4738. of the Revised Code;

(25) A person who has been licensed to act as a steam engineer under Chapter 4739. of the Revised Code;

(26) A person who has been issued a license or temporary permit to practice veterinary medicine or any of its branches, or who is registered as a graduate animal technician under Chapter 4741. of the Revised Code;

(27) A person who has been issued a hearing aid dealer's or fitter's license or trainee permit under Chapter 4747. of the Revised Code;

(28) A person who has been issued a class A, class B, or class C license or who has been registered as an investigator or security guard employee under Chapter 4749. of the Revised Code;

(29) A person licensed and registered to practice as a nursing home administrator under Chapter 4751. of the Revised Code;

(30) A person licensed to practice as a speech-language pathologist or audiologist under Chapter 4753. of the Revised Code;

(31) A person issued a license as an occupational therapist or physical therapist under Chapter 4755. of the Revised Code;

(32) A person who is licensed as a professional clinical counselor or professional counselor, licensed as a social worker or independent social worker, or registered as a social work assistant under Chapter 4757. of the Revised Code;

(33) A person issued a license to practice dietetics under Chapter 4759. of the Revised Code;

(34) A person who has been issued a license or limited permit to practice respiratory therapy under Chapter 4761. of the Revised Code;

(35) A person who has been issued a real estate appraiser certificate under Chapter 4763. of the Revised Code;

(36) A person who has been admitted to the bar by order of the supreme court in compliance with its prescribed and published rules.

(X) "Cocaine" means any of the following:

(1) A cocaine salt, isomer, or derivative, a salt of a cocaine isomer or derivative, or the base form of cocaine;

(2) Coca leaves or a salt, compound, derivative, or preparation of coca leaves, including ecgonine, a salt, isomer, or derivative of ecgonine, or a salt of an isomer or derivative of ecgonine;

(3) A salt, compound, derivative, or preparation of a substance identified in division (X)(1) or (2) of this section that is chemically equivalent to or identical with any of those substances, except that the substances shall not include decocainized coca leaves or extraction of coca leaves if the extractions do not contain cocaine or ecgonine.

(Y) "L.S.D." means lysergic acid diethylamide.

(Z) "Hashish" means the resin or a preparation of the resin contained in marihuana, whether in solid form or in a liquid concentrate, liquid extract, or liquid distillate form.

(AA) "Marihuana" has the same meaning as in section 3719.01 of the Revised Code, except that it does not include hashish.

(BB) An offense is "committed in the vicinity of a juvenile" if the offender commits the offense within one hundred feet of a juvenile or within the view of a juvenile, regardless of whether the offender knows the age of the juvenile, whether the offender knows the offense is being committed within one hundred feet of or within view of the juvenile, or whether the juvenile actually views the commission of the offense.

(CC) "Presumption for a prison term" or "presumption that a prison term shall be imposed" means a presumption, as described in division (D) of section 2929.13 of the Revised Code, that a prison term is a necessary sanction for a felony in order to comply with the purposes and principles of sentencing under section 2929.11 of the Revised Code.

(DD) "Major drug offender" has the same meaning as in section 2929.01 of the Revised Code.

(EE) "Minor drug possession offense" means either of the following:

(1) A violation of section 2925.11 of the Revised Code as it existed prior to July 1, 1996;

(2) A violation of section 2925.11 of the Revised Code as it exists on and after July 1, 1996, that is a misdemeanor or a felony of the fifth degree.

(FF) "Mandatory prison term" has the same meaning as in section 2929.01 of the Revised Code.

(GG) "Adulterate" means to cause a drug to be adulterated as described in section 3715.63 of the Revised Code.

(HH) "Public premises" means any hotel, restaurant, tavern, store, arena, hall, or other place of public accommodation, business, amusement, or resort.

(II) "Methamphetamine" means methamphetamine, any salt, isomer, or salt of an isomer of methamphetamine, or any compound, mixture, preparation, or substance containing methamphetamine or any salt, isomer, or salt of an isomer of methamphetamine.

(JJ) "Lawful prescription" means a prescription that is issued for a legitimate medical purpose by a licensed health professional authorized to prescribe drugs, that is not altered or forged, and that was not obtained by means of deception or by the commission of any theft offense.

(KK) "Deception" and "theft offense" have the same meanings as in section 2913.01 of the Revised Code.

**HISTORY: 136 v H 300 (Eff 7-1-76); 136 v S 414 (Eff 9-22-76); 137 v H 565 (Eff 11-1-78); 138 v H 900 (Eff 7-1-80); 138 v S 378 (Eff 3-23-81); 139 v H 535 (Eff 8-20-82); 139 v S 199 (Eff 7-1-83); 141 v H 281 (Eff 7-18-85); 143 v H 215 (Eff 4-11-90); 143 v S 258 (Eff 11-20-90); 144 v H 62 (Eff 5-21-91); 144 v H 322 (Eff 3-2-92); 145 v H 156 (Eff 5-19-93); 146 v S 143, § 1 (Eff 3-5-96); 146 v S 2 (Eff 7-1-96); 146 v S 143, § 5 (Eff 7-1-96); 146 v H 125 (Eff 7-1-96); 146 v S 269 (Eff 7-1-96); 146 v S 223 (Eff 3-18-97); 147 v S 66 (Eff 7-22-98); 147 v S 117 (Eff 8-5-98); 147 v H 606 (Eff 3-9-99); 147 v S 200 (Eff 3-30-99); 148 v H 18 (Eff 10-20-99); 148 v H 202 (Eff 2-9-2000); 149 v H 7 (Eff 8-7-2001); 149 v H 273 (Eff 7-23-2002); 149 v H 415 (4-7-2003); 149 v H 364, § 1, eff. 4-8-2003; 149 v H 364, § 8, eff. 1-1-04; 149 v S 123, § 1, eff. 1-1-04; 150 v H 163, § 1, eff. 9-23-04; 150 v S 209, § 1, eff. 5-6-05; 151 v S 53, § 1, eff. 5-17-06; 152 v H 195, § 1, eff. 9-30-08; 2011 HB 86, § 1, eff. Sept. 30, 2011.**

The provisions of § 3 of HB 86 read as follows:

"SECTION 3. The amendments to sections 2925.01, 2925.03, 2925.05, and 2925.11 of the Revised Code, and to division (W) of section 2929.01 of the Revised Code, that are made in this act apply to a person who commits an offense involving marihuana, cocaine, or hashish on or after the effective date of this act and to a person to whom division (B) of section 1.58 of the Revised Code makes the amendments applicable.

"The provisions of sections 2925.01, 2925.03, 2925.05, and 2925.11 of the Revised Code, and of division (W) of section 2929.01 of the Revised Code, in existence prior to the effective date of this act shall apply to a person upon whom a court imposed sentence prior to the effective date of this act for an offense involving marihuana, cocaine, or hashish. The amendments to sections 2925.01, 2925.03, 2925.05, and 2925.11 of the Revised Code, and to division (W) of section 2929.01 of the Revised Code, that are made in this act do not apply to a person upon whom a court imposed sentence prior to the effective date of this act for an offense involving marihuana, cocaine, or hashish."

The provisions of § 5, H.B. 163 (150 v —), read as follows:

SECTION 5. (A) Section 2925.01 of the Revised Code is presented in this act as a composite of the section as amended by both Sub. H.B. 364 and Am. Sub. H.B. 415 of the 124th General Assembly. The General Assembly, applying the principle stated in division (B) of section 1.52 of the Revised Code that amendments are to be harmonized if reasonably capable of simultaneous operation, finds that the composite is the resulting version of the section in effect prior to the effective date of the section as presented in this act. * * *

The effective date is set by section 4 of S.B. 123.

The provisions of § 5 of S.B. 123 (149 v —), as amended by § 3 of H.B. 163 (150 v —), read as follows:

SECTION 5. Notwithstanding division (B) of section 1.58 of the Revised Code, the provisions of the Revised Code amended or enacted in Sections 1 and 2 of this act shall apply only in relation to conduct and offenses committed on or after January 1, 2004. Conduct and offenses committed prior to January 1, 2004, shall be governed by the law in effect on the date the conduct or offense was committed.

**Publisher's Note:**

The amendments made by HB 415 (149 v —) and HB 364, § 1 (149 v —) have been combined. See provisions of RC § 1.52.

## [CORRUPTING; TRAFFICKING]

### § 2925.02 Corrupting another with drugs.

(A) No person shall knowingly do any of the following:

(1) By force, threat, or deception, administer to another or induce or cause another to use a controlled substance;

(2) By any means, administer or furnish to another or induce or cause another to use a controlled substance with purpose to cause serious physical harm to the other person, or with purpose to cause the other person to become drug dependent;

(3) By any means, administer or furnish to another or induce or cause another to use a controlled substance, and thereby cause serious physical harm to the other person, or cause the other person to become drug dependent;

(4) By any means, do any of the following:

(a) Furnish or administer a controlled substance to a juvenile who is at least two years the offender's junior, when the offender knows the age of the juvenile or is reckless in that regard;

(b) Induce or cause a juvenile who is at least two years the offender's junior to use a controlled substance, when the offender knows the age of the juvenile or is reckless in that regard;

(c) Induce or cause a juvenile who is at least two years the offender's junior to commit a felony drug abuse offense, when the offender knows the age of the juvenile or is reckless in that regard;

(d) Use a juvenile, whether or not the offender knows the age of the juvenile, to perform any surveillance activity that is intended to prevent the detection of the offender or any other person in the commission of a felony drug abuse offense or to prevent the arrest of the offender or any other person for the commission of a felony drug abuse offense.

(B) Division (A)(1), (3), or (4) of this section does not apply to manufacturers, wholesalers, licensed health professionals authorized to prescribe drugs, pharmacists, owners of pharmacies, and other persons whose conduct is in accordance with Chapters 3719., 4715., 4723., 4729., 4730., 4731., and 4741. of the Revised Code.

(C) Whoever violates this section is guilty of corrupting another with drugs. The penalty for the offense shall be determined as follows:

(1) Except as otherwise provided in this division, if the drug involved is any compound, mixture, preparation, or substance included in schedule I or II, with the exception of marihuana, 1-Pentyl-3-(1-naphthoyl)indole, 1-Butyl-3-(1-naphthoyl)indole, 1-[2-(4-morpholinyl)ethyl]-3-(1-naphthoyl)indole, 5-(1,1-dimethylheptyl)-2-[(1R,3S)-3-hydroxycyclohexyl]-phenol, and 5-(1,1-dimethyloctyl)-2-[(1R,3S)-3-hydroxycyclohexyl]-phenol, corrupting another with drugs is a felony of the second degree, and, subject to division (E) of this section, the court shall impose as a mandatory prison term one of the prison terms prescribed for a felony of the second degree. If the drug involved is any compound, mixture, preparation, or substance included in schedule I or II, with the exception of marihuana, 1-Pentyl-3-(1-naphthoyl)indole, 1-Butyl-3-(1-naphthoyl)indole, 1-[2-(4-morpholinyl)ethyl]-3-(1-naphthoyl)indole, 5-(1,1-dimethylheptyl)-2-[(1R,3S)-3-hydroxycyclohexyl]-phenol, or 5-(1,1-dimethyloctyl)-2-[(1R,3S)-3-hydroxycyclohexyl]-phenol, and if the offense was committed in the vicinity of a school, corrupting another with drugs is a felony of the first degree, and, subject to division (E) of this section, the court shall impose as a mandatory prison term one of the prison terms prescribed for a felony of the first degree.

(2) Except as otherwise provided in this division, if the drug involved is any compound, mixture, preparation, or substance included in schedule III, IV, or V, corrupting another with drugs is a felony of the second degree, and there is a presumption for a prison term for the offense. If the drug involved is any compound, mixture, preparation, or substance included in schedule III, IV, or V and if the offense was committed in the vicinity of a school, corrupting another with drugs is a felony of the second degree, and the court shall impose as a mandatory prison term one of the prison terms prescribed for a felony of the second degree.

(3) Except as otherwise provided in this division, if the drug involved is marihuana, 1-Pentyl-3-(1-naphthoyl)indole, 1-Butyl-3-(1-naphthoyl)indole, 1-[2-(4-morpholinyl)ethyl]-3-(1-naphthoyl)indole, 5-(1,1-dimethylheptyl)-2-[(1R,3S)-3-hydroxycyclohexyl]-phenol, or 5-(1,1-dimethyloctyl)-2-[(1R,3S)-3-hydroxycyclohexyl]-phenol, corrupting another with drugs is a felony of the fourth degree, and division (C) of section 2929.13 of the Revised Code applies in determining whether to impose a prison term on the offender. If the drug involved is marihuana, 1-Pentyl-3-(1-naphthoyl)indole, 1-Butyl-3-(1-naphthoyl)indole, 1-[2-(4-morpholinyl)ethyl]-3-(1-naphthoyl)indole, 5-(1,1-dimethylheptyl)-2-[(1R,3S)-3-hydroxycyclohexyl]-phenol, or 5-(1,1-dimethyloctyl)-2-[(1R,3S)-3-hydroxycyclohexyl]-phenol, and if the offense was committed in the vicinity of a school, corrupting another with drugs is a felony of the third degree, and division (C) of section 2929.13 of the Revised Code applies in determining whether to impose a prison term on the offender.

(D) In addition to any prison term authorized or required by division (C) or (E) of this section and sections 2929.13 and 2929.14 of the Revised Code and in addition to any other sanction imposed for the offense under this section or sections 2929.11 to 2929.18 of the Revised Code, the court that sentences an offender who is convicted of or pleads guilty to a violation of division (A) of this section or the clerk of that court shall do all of the following that are applicable regarding the offender:

(1)(a) If the violation is a felony of the first, second, or third degree, the court shall impose upon the offender the mandatory fine specified for the offense under division (B)(1) of section 2929.18 of the Revised Code unless, as specified in that division, the court determines that the offender is indigent.

(b) Notwithstanding any contrary provision of section 3719.21 of the Revised Code, any mandatory fine imposed pursuant to division (D)(1)(a) of this section and any fine imposed for a violation of this section pursuant to division (A) of section 2929.18 of the Revised Code shall be paid by the clerk of the court in accordance with and subject to the requirements of, and shall be used as specified in, division (F) of section 2925.03 of the Revised Code.

(c) If a person is charged with any violation of this section that is a felony of the first, second, or third degree, posts bail, and forfeits the bail, the forfeited bail shall be paid by the clerk of the court pursuant to division (D)(1)(b) of this section as if it were a fine imposed for a violation of this section.

(2) The court shall suspend for not less than six months nor more than five years the offender's driver's or commercial driver's license or permit. If an offender's driver's or commercial driver's license or permit is suspended pursuant to this division, the offender, at any time after the expiration of two years from the day on which the offender's sentence was imposed or from the day on which the offender finally was released from a prison term under the sentence, whichever is later, may file a motion with the sentencing court requesting termination of the suspension. Upon the filing of the motion and the court's finding of good cause for the termination, the court may terminate the suspension.

(3) If the offender is a professionally licensed person, in addition to any other sanction imposed for a violation of this section, the court immediately shall comply with section 2925.38 of the Revised Code.

(E) Notwithstanding the prison term otherwise authorized or required for the offense under division (C) of this section and sections 2929.13 and 2929.14 of the Revised Code, if the violation of division (A) of this section involves the sale, offer to sell, or possession of a schedule I or II controlled substance, with the exception of marihuana, 1-Pentyl-3-(1-naphthoyl)indole, 1-Butyl-3-(1-naphthoyl)indole, 1-[2-(4-morpholinyl)ethyl]-3-(1-naphthoyl)indole, 5-(1,1-dimethylheptyl)-2-[(1R,3S)-3-hydroxycyclohexyl]-phenol, and 5-(1,1-dimethyloctyl)-2-[(1R,3S)-3-hydroxycyclohexyl]-phenol, and if the court imposing sentence upon the offender finds that the offender as a result of the violation is a major drug offender and is guilty of a specification of the type described in section 2941.1410 of the Revised Code, the court, in lieu of the prison term that otherwise is authorized or required, shall impose upon the offender the mandatory prison term specified in division (B)(3)(a) of section 2929.14 of the Revised Code.

**HISTORY: 136 v H 300 (Eff 7-1-76); 143 v H 215 (Eff 4-11-90); 143 v S 258 (Eff 11-20-90); 144 v H 591 (Eff 11-2-92); 145 v H 377 (Eff 9-30-93); 145 v H 391 (Eff 7-21-94); 146 v S 2 (Eff 7-1-96); 146 v S 269 (Eff 7-1-96); 147 v S 66 (Eff 7-22-98); 148 v S 107 (Eff 3-23-2000); 148 v H 241. Eff 5-17-2000; 149 v S 123, § 1, eff. 1-1-04; 151 v S 154, § 1, eff. 5-17-06; 2011 HB 86, § 1, eff. Sept. 30, 2011; 2011 HB 64, § 1, eff. Oct. 17, 2011.**

The effective date is set by section 4 of S.B. 123.

See provisions of § 5 of S.B. 123 (149 v —) following RC § 2925.01.

## § 2925.03 Trafficking in drugs.

(A) No person shall knowingly do any of the following:

(1) Sell or offer to sell a controlled substance;

(2) Prepare for shipment, ship, transport, deliver, prepare for distribution, or distribute a controlled substance, when the offender knows or has reasonable cause to believe that the controlled substance is intended for sale or resale by the offender or another person.

(B) This section does not apply to any of the following:

(1) Manufacturers, licensed health professionals authorized to prescribe drugs, pharmacists, owners of pharmacies, and other persons whose conduct is in accordance with Chapters 3719., 4715., 4723., 4729., 4730., 4731., and 4741. of the Revised Code;

(2) If the offense involves an anabolic steroid, any person who is conducting or participating in a research project involving the use of an anabolic steroid if the project has been approved by the United States food and drug administration;

(3) Any person who sells, offers for sale, prescribes, dispenses, or administers for livestock or other nonhuman species an anabolic steroid that is expressly intended for administration through implants to livestock or other nonhuman species and approved for that purpose under the "Federal Food, Drug, and Cosmetic Act," 52 Stat. 1040 (1938), 21 U.S.C.A. 301, as amended, and is sold, offered for sale, prescribed, dispensed, or administered for that purpose in accordance with that act.

(C) Whoever violates division (A) of this section is guilty of one of the following:

(1) If the drug involved in the violation is any compound, mixture, preparation, or substance included in schedule I or schedule II, with the exception of marihuana, 1-Pentyl-3-(1-naphthoyl)indole, 1-Butyl-3-(1-naphthoyl)indole, 1-[2-(4-morpholinyl)ethyl]-3-(1-naphthoyl)indole, 5-(1,1-dimethylheptyl)-2-[(1R,3S)-3-hydroxycyclohexyl]-phenol, 5-(1,1-dimethyloctyl)-2-[(1R,3S)-3-hydroxycyclohexyl]-phenol, cocaine, L.S.D., heroin, and hashish, whoever violates division (A) of this section is guilty of aggravated trafficking in drugs. The penalty for the offense shall be determined as follows:

(a) Except as otherwise provided in division (C)(1)(b), (c), (d), (e), or (f) of this section, aggravated trafficking in drugs is a felony of the fourth degree, and division (C) of section 2929.13 of the Revised Code applies in determining whether to impose a prison term on the offender.

(b) Except as otherwise provided in division (C)(1)(c), (d), (e), or (f) of this section, if the offense was committed in the vicinity of a school or in the vicinity of a juvenile, aggravated trafficking in drugs is a felony of the third degree, and division (C) of section 2929.13 of the Revised Code applies in determining whether to impose a prison term on the offender.

(c) Except as otherwise provided in this division, if the amount of the drug involved equals or exceeds the bulk amount but is less than five times the bulk amount, aggravated trafficking in drugs is a felony of the third degree, and, except as otherwise provided in this division, there is a presumption for a prison term for the offense. If aggravated trafficking in drugs is a felony of the third degree under this division and if the offender two or more times previously has been convicted of or pleaded guilty to a felony drug abuse offense, the court shall impose as a mandatory prison term one of the prison terms prescribed for a felony of the third degree. If the amount of the drug involved is within that range and if the offense was committed in the vicinity of a school or in the vicinity of a juvenile, aggravated trafficking in drugs is a felony of the second degree, and the court shall impose as a mandatory prison term one of the prison terms prescribed for a felony of the second degree.

(d) Except as otherwise provided in this division, if the amount of the drug involved equals or exceeds five times the bulk amount but is less than fifty times the bulk amount, aggravated trafficking in drugs is a felony of the second degree, and the court shall impose as a mandatory prison term one of the prison terms prescribed for a felony of the second degree. If the amount of the drug involved is within that range and if the offense was committed in the vicinity of a school or in the vicinity of a juvenile, aggravated trafficking in drugs is a felony of the first degree, and the court shall impose as a mandatory prison term one of the prison terms prescribed for a felony of the first degree.

(e) If the amount of the drug involved equals or exceeds fifty times the bulk amount but is less than one hundred times the bulk amount and regardless of whether the offense was committed in the vicinity of a school or in the vicinity of a juvenile, aggravated trafficking in drugs is a felony of the first degree, and the court shall impose as a mandatory prison term one of the prison terms prescribed for a felony of the first degree.

(f) If the amount of the drug involved equals or exceeds one hundred times the bulk amount and regardless of whether the offense was committed in the vicinity of a school or in the vicinity of a juvenile, aggravated trafficking in drugs is a felony of the first degree, the offender is a major drug offender, and the court shall impose as a mandatory prison term the maximum prison term prescribed for a felony of the first degree.

(2) If the drug involved in the violation is any compound, mixture, preparation, or substance included in schedule III, IV, or V, whoever violates division (A) of this section is guilty of trafficking in drugs. The penalty for the offense shall be determined as follows:

(a) Except as otherwise provided in division (C)(2)(b), (c), (d), or (e) of this section, trafficking in drugs is a felony of the fifth degree, and division (C) of section 2929.13 of the Revised Code applies in determining whether to impose a prison term on the offender.

(b) Except as otherwise provided in division (C)(2)(c), (d), or (e) of this section, if the offense was committed in the vicinity of a school or in the vicinity of a juvenile, trafficking in drugs is a felony of the fourth degree, and division (C) of section 2929.13 of the Revised Code applies in determining whether to impose a prison term on the offender.

(c) Except as otherwise provided in this division, if the amount of the drug involved equals or exceeds the bulk amount but is less than five times the bulk amount, trafficking in drugs is a felony of the fourth degree, and division (B) of section 2929.13 of the Revised Code applies in determining whether to impose a prison term for the offense. If the amount of the drug involved is within that range and if the offense was committed in the vicinity of a school or in the vicinity of a juvenile, trafficking in drugs is a felony of the third degree, and there is a presumption for a prison term for the offense.

(d) Except as otherwise provided in this division, if the amount of the drug involved equals or exceeds five times the bulk amount but is less than fifty times the bulk amount, trafficking in drugs is a felony of the third degree, and there is a presumption for a prison term for the offense. If the amount of the drug involved is within that range and if the offense was committed in the vicinity of a school or in the vicinity of a juvenile, trafficking in drugs is a felony of the second degree, and there is a presumption for a prison term for the offense.

(e) Except as otherwise provided in this division, if the amount of the drug involved equals or exceeds fifty times the bulk amount, trafficking in drugs is a felony of the second degree, and the court shall impose as a mandatory prison term one of the prison terms prescribed for a felony of the second degree. If the amount of the drug involved equals or exceeds fifty times the bulk amount and if the offense was committed in the vicinity of a school or in the vicinity of a juvenile, trafficking in drugs is a felony of the first degree, and the court shall impose as a mandatory prison term one of the prison terms prescribed for a felony of the first degree.

(3) If the drug involved in the violation is marihuana or a compound, mixture, preparation, or substance containing marihuana other than hashish, whoever violates division (A) of this section is guilty of trafficking in marihuana. The penalty for the offense shall be determined as follows:

(a) Except as otherwise provided in division (C)(3)(b), (c), (d), (e), (f), (g), or (h) of this section, trafficking in marihuana is a felony of the fifth degree, and division (B) of section 2929.13 of the Revised Code applies in determining whether to impose a prison term on the offender.

(b) Except as otherwise provided in division (C)(3)(c), (d), (e), (f), (g), or (h) of this section, if the offense was committed in the vicinity of a school or in the vicinity of a juvenile, trafficking in marihuana is a felony of the fourth degree, and division (B) of section 2929.13 of the Revised Code applies in determining whether to impose a prison term on the offender.

(c) Except as otherwise provided in this division, if the amount of the drug involved equals or exceeds two hundred grams but is less than one thousand grams, trafficking in marihuana is a felony of the fourth degree, and division (B) of section 2929.13 of the Revised Code applies in determining whether to impose a prison term on the offender. If the amount of the drug involved is within that range and if the offense was committed in the vicinity of a school or in the vicinity of a juvenile, trafficking in marihuana is a felony of the third degree, and division (C) of section 2929.13 of the Revised Code applies in determining whether to impose a prison term on the offender.

(d) Except as otherwise provided in this division, if the amount of the drug involved equals or exceeds one thousand grams but is less than five thousand grams, trafficking in marihuana is a felony of the third degree, and division (C) of section 2929.13 of the Revised Code applies in determining whether to impose a prison term on the offender. If the amount of the drug involved is within that range and if the offense was committed in the vicinity of a school or in the vicinity of a juvenile, trafficking in marihuana is a felony of the second degree, and there is a presumption that a prison term shall be imposed for the offense.

(e) Except as otherwise provided in this division, if the amount of the drug involved equals or exceeds five thousand grams but is less than twenty thousand grams, trafficking in marihuana is a felony of the third degree, and there is a presumption that a prison term shall be imposed for the offense. If the amount of the drug involved is within that range and if the offense was committed in the vicinity of a school or in the vicinity of a juvenile, trafficking in marihuana is a felony of the second degree, and there is a presumption that a prison term shall be imposed for the offense.

(f) Except as otherwise provided in this division, if the amount of the drug involved equals or exceeds twenty thousand grams but is less than forty thousand grams, trafficking in marihuana is a felony of the second degree, and the court shall impose a mandatory prison term of five, six, seven, or eight years. If the amount of the drug involved is within that range and if the offense was committed in the vicinity of a school or in the vicinity of a juvenile, trafficking in marihuana is a felony of the first degree, and the court shall impose as a mandatory prison term the maximum prison term prescribed for a felony of the first degree.

(g) Except as otherwise provided in this division, if the amount of the drug involved equals or exceeds forty thousand grams, trafficking in marihuana is a felony of the second degree, and the court shall impose as a mandatory prison term the maximum prison term prescribed for a felony of the second degree. If the amount of the drug involved equals or exceeds forty thousand grams and if the offense was committed in the vicinity of a school or in the vicinity of a juvenile, trafficking in marihuana is a felony of the first degree, and the court shall impose as a mandatory prison term the maximum prison term prescribed for a felony of the first degree.

(h) Except as otherwise provided in this division, if the offense involves a gift of twenty grams or less of marihuana, trafficking in marihuana is a minor misdemeanor upon a first offense and a misdemeanor of the third degree upon a subsequent offense. If the offense involves a gift of twenty grams or less of marihuana and if the offense was committed in the vicinity of a school or in the vicinity of a juvenile, trafficking in marihuana is a misdemeanor of the third degree.

(4) If the drug involved in the violation is cocaine or a compound, mixture, preparation, or substance containing cocaine, whoever violates division (A) of this section is guilty of trafficking in cocaine. The penalty for the offense shall be determined as follows:

(a) Except as otherwise provided in division (C)(4)(b), (c), (d), (e), (f), or (g) of this section, trafficking in cocaine is a felony of the fifth degree, and division (C) of section 2929.13 of the Revised Code applies in determining whether to impose a prison term on the offender.

(b) Except as otherwise provided in division (C)(4)(c), (d), (e), (f), or (g) of this section, if the offense was committed in the vicinity of a school or in the vicinity of a juvenile, trafficking in cocaine is a felony of the fourth degree, and division (C) of section 2929.13 of the Revised Code applies in determining whether to impose a prison term on the offender.

(c) Except as otherwise provided in this division, if the amount of the drug involved equals or exceeds five grams but is less than ten grams of cocaine, trafficking in cocaine is a felony of the fourth degree, and division (B) of section 2929.13 of the Revised Code applies in determining whether to impose a prison term for the offense. If the amount of the drug involved is within that range and if the offense was committed in the vicinity of a school or in the vicinity of a juvenile, trafficking in cocaine is a felony of the third degree, and there is a presumption for a prison term for the offense.

(d) Except as otherwise provided in this division, if the amount of the drug involved equals or exceeds ten grams but is less than twenty grams of cocaine, trafficking in cocaine is a felony of the third degree, and, except as otherwise provided in this division, there is a presumption for a prison term for the offense. If trafficking in cocaine is a felony of the third degree under this division and if the offender two or more times previously has been convicted of or pleaded guilty to a felony drug abuse offense, the court shall impose as a mandatory prison term one of the prison terms prescribed for a felony of the third degree. If the amount of the drug involved is within that range and if the offense was committed in the vicinity of a school or in the vicinity of a juvenile, trafficking in cocaine is a felony of the second degree, and the court shall impose as a mandatory prison term one of the prison terms prescribed for a felony of the second degree.

(e) Except as otherwise provided in this division, if the amount of the drug involved equals or exceeds twenty grams but is less than twenty-seven grams of cocaine, trafficking in cocaine is a felony of the second degree, and the court shall impose as a mandatory prison term one of the prison terms prescribed for a felony of the second degree. If the amount of the drug involved is within that range and if the offense was committed in the vicinity of a school or in the vicinity of a juvenile, trafficking in cocaine is a felony of the first degree, and the court shall impose as a mandatory prison term one of the prison terms prescribed for a felony of the first degree.

(f) If the amount of the drug involved equals or exceeds twenty-seven grams but is less than one hundred grams of cocaine and regardless of whether the offense was committed in the vicinity of a school or in the vicinity of a juvenile, trafficking in cocaine is a felony of the first degree, and the court shall impose as a mandatory prison term one of the prison terms prescribed for a felony of the first degree.

(g) If the amount of the drug involved equals or exceeds one hundred grams of cocaine and regardless of whether the offense was committed in the vicinity of a school or in the vicinity of a juvenile, trafficking in cocaine is a felony of the first degree, the offender is a major drug offender, and the court shall impose as a mandatory prison term the maximum prison term prescribed for a felony of the first degree.

(5) If the drug involved in the violation is L.S.D. or a compound, mixture, preparation, or substance containing L.S.D., whoever violates division (A) of this section is guilty of trafficking in L.S.D. The penalty for the offense shall be determined as follows:

(a) Except as otherwise provided in division (C)(5)(b), (c), (d), (e), (f), or (g) of this section, trafficking in L.S.D. is a felony of the fifth degree, and division (C) of section 2929.13 of the Revised Code applies in determining whether to impose a prison term on the offender.

(b) Except as otherwise provided in division (C)(5)(c), (d), (e), (f), or (g) of this section, if the offense was committed in the vicinity of a school or in the vicinity of a juvenile, trafficking in L.S.D. is a felony of the fourth degree, and division (C) of section 2929.13 of the Revised Code applies in determining whether to impose a prison term on the offender.

(c) Except as otherwise provided in this division, if the amount of the drug involved equals or exceeds ten unit doses but is less than fifty unit doses of L.S.D. in a solid form or equals or exceeds one gram but is less than five grams of L.S.D. in a liquid concentrate, liquid extract, or liquid distillate form, trafficking in L.S.D. is a felony of the fourth degree, and division (B) of section 2929.13 of the Revised Code applies in determining whether to impose a prison term for the offense. If the amount of the drug involved is within that range and if the offense was committed in the vicinity of a school or in the vicinity of a juvenile, trafficking in L.S.D. is a felony of the third degree, and there is a presumption for a prison term for the offense.

(d) Except as otherwise provided in this division, if the amount of the drug involved equals or exceeds fifty unit doses but is less than two hundred fifty unit doses of L.S.D. in a solid form or equals or exceeds five grams but is less than twenty-five grams of L.S.D. in a liquid concentrate, liquid extract, or liquid distillate form, trafficking in L.S.D. is a felony of the third degree, and, except as otherwise provided in this division, there is a presumption for a prison term for the offense. If trafficking in L.S.D. is a felony of the third degree under this division and if the offender two or more times previously has been convicted of or pleaded guilty to a felony drug abuse offense, the court shall impose as a mandatory prison term one of the prison terms prescribed for a felony of the third degree. If the amount of the drug involved is within that range and if the offense was committed in the vicinity of a school or in the vicinity of a juvenile, trafficking in L.S.D. is a felony of the second degree, and the court shall impose as a mandatory prison term one of the prison terms prescribed for a felony of the second degree.

(e) Except as otherwise provided in this division, if the amount of the drug involved equals or exceeds two hundred fifty unit doses but is less than one thousand unit doses of L.S.D. in a solid form or equals or exceeds twenty-five grams but is less than one hundred grams of L.S.D. in a liquid concentrate, liquid extract, or liquid distillate form, trafficking in L.S.D. is a felony of the second degree, and the court shall impose as a mandatory prison term one of the prison terms prescribed for a felony of the second degree. If the amount of the drug involved is within that range and if the offense was committed in the vicinity of a school or in the vicinity of a juvenile, trafficking in L.S.D. is a felony of the first degree, and the court shall impose as a mandatory prison term one of the prison terms prescribed for a felony of the first degree.

(f) If the amount of the drug involved equals or exceeds one thousand unit doses but is less than five thousand unit doses of L.S.D. in a solid form or equals or exceeds one hundred grams but is less than five hundred grams of L.S.D. in a liquid concentrate, liquid extract, or liquid distillate form and regardless of whether the offense was committed in the vicinity of a school or in the vicinity of a juvenile, trafficking in L.S.D. is a felony of the first degree, and the court shall impose as a mandatory prison term one of the prison terms prescribed for a felony of the first degree.

(g) If the amount of the drug involved equals or exceeds five thousand unit doses of L.S.D. in a solid form or equals or exceeds five hundred grams of L.S.D. in a liquid concentrate, liquid extract, or liquid distillate form and regardless of whether the offense was committed in the vicinity of a school or in the vicinity of a juvenile, trafficking in L.S.D. is a felony of the first degree, the offender is a major drug offender, and the court shall impose as a mandatory prison term the maximum prison term prescribed for a felony of the first degree.

(6) If the drug involved in the violation is heroin or a compound, mixture, preparation, or substance containing heroin, whoever violates division (A) of this section is guilty of trafficking in heroin. The penalty for the offense shall be determined as follows:

(a) Except as otherwise provided in division (C)(6)(b), (c), (d), (e), (f), or (g) of this section, trafficking in heroin is a felony of the fifth degree, and division (C) of section 2929.13 of the Revised Code applies in determining whether to impose a prison term on the offender.

(b) Except as otherwise provided in division (C)(6)(c), (d), (e), (f), or (g) of this section, if the offense was committed in the vicinity of a school or in the vicinity of a juvenile, trafficking in heroin is a felony of the fourth degree, and division (C) of section 2929.13 of the Revised Code applies in determining whether to impose a prison term on the offender.

(c) Except as otherwise provided in this division, if the amount of the drug involved equals or exceeds ten unit doses but is less than fifty unit doses or equals or exceeds one gram but is less than five grams, trafficking in heroin is a felony of the fourth degree, and division (B) of section 2929.13 of the Revised Code applies in determining whether to impose a prison term for the offense. If the amount of the drug involved is within that range and if the offense was committed in the vicinity of a school or in the vicinity of a juvenile, trafficking in heroin is a felony of the third degree, and there is a presumption for a prison term for the offense.

(d) Except as otherwise provided in this division, if the amount of the drug involved equals or exceeds fifty unit doses but is less than one hundred unit doses or equals or exceeds five grams but is less than ten grams, trafficking in heroin is a felony of the third degree, and there is a presumption for a prison term for the offense. If the amount of the drug involved is within that range and if the offense was committed in the vicinity of a school or in the vicinity of a juvenile, trafficking in heroin is a felony of the second degree, and there is a presumption for a prison term for the offense.

(e) Except as otherwise provided in this division, if the amount of the drug involved equals or exceeds one hundred unit doses but is less than five hundred unit doses or equals or exceeds ten grams but is less than fifty grams, trafficking in heroin is a felony of the second degree, and the court shall impose as a mandatory prison term one of the prison terms prescribed for a felony of the second degree. If the amount of the drug involved is within that range and if the offense was committed in the vicinity of a school or in the vicinity of a juvenile, trafficking in heroin is a felony of the first degree, and the court shall impose as a mandatory prison term one of the prison terms prescribed for a felony of the first degree.

(f) If the amount of the drug involved equals or exceeds five hundred unit doses but is less than two thousand five hundred unit doses or equals or exceeds fifty grams but is less than two hundred fifty grams and regardless of whether the offense was committed in the vicinity of a school or in the vicinity of a juvenile, trafficking in heroin is a felony of the first degree, and the court shall impose as a mandatory prison term one of the prison terms prescribed for a felony of the first degree.

(g) If the amount of the drug involved equals or exceeds two thousand five hundred unit doses or equals or exceeds two hundred fifty grams and regardless of whether the offense was committed in the vicinity of a school or in the vicinity of a juvenile, trafficking in heroin is a felony of the first degree, the offender is a major drug offender, and the court shall impose as a mandatory prison term the maximum prison term prescribed for a felony of the first degree.

(7) If the drug involved in the violation is hashish or a compound, mixture, preparation, or substance containing hashish, whoever violates division (A) of this section is

guilty of trafficking in hashish. The penalty for the offense shall be determined as follows:

(a) Except as otherwise provided in division (C)(7)(b), (c), (d), (e), (f), or (g) of this section, trafficking in hashish is a felony of the fifth degree, and division (B) of section 2929.13 of the Revised Code applies in determining whether to impose a prison term on the offender.

(b) Except as otherwise provided in division (C)(7)(c), (d), (e), (f), or (g) of this section, if the offense was committed in the vicinity of a school or in the vicinity of a juvenile, trafficking in hashish is a felony of the fourth degree, and division (B) of section 2929.13 of the Revised Code applies in determining whether to impose a prison term on the offender.

(c) Except as otherwise provided in this division, if the amount of the drug involved equals or exceeds ten grams but is less than fifty grams of hashish in a solid form or equals or exceeds two grams but is less than ten grams of hashish in a liquid concentrate, liquid extract, or liquid distillate form, trafficking in hashish is a felony of the fourth degree, and division (B) of section 2929.13 of the Revised Code applies in determining whether to impose a prison term on the offender. If the amount of the drug involved is within that range and if the offense was committed in the vicinity of a school or in the vicinity of a juvenile, trafficking in hashish is a felony of the third degree, and division (C) of section 2929.13 of the Revised Code applies in determining whether to impose a prison term on the offender.

(d) Except as otherwise provided in this division, if the amount of the drug involved equals or exceeds fifty grams but is less than two hundred fifty grams of hashish in a solid form or equals or exceeds ten grams but is less than fifty grams of hashish in a liquid concentrate, liquid extract, or liquid distillate form, trafficking in hashish is a felony of the third degree, and division (C) of section 2929.13 of the Revised Code applies in determining whether to impose a prison term on the offender. If the amount of the drug involved is within that range and if the offense was committed in the vicinity of a school or in the vicinity of a juvenile, trafficking in hashish is a felony of the second degree, and there is a presumption that a prison term shall be imposed for the offense.

(e) Except as otherwise provided in this division, if the amount of the drug involved equals or exceeds two hundred fifty grams but is less than one thousand grams of hashish in a solid form or equals or exceeds fifty grams but is less than two hundred grams of hashish in a liquid concentrate, liquid extract, or liquid distillate form, trafficking in hashish is a felony of the third degree, and there is a presumption that a prison term shall be imposed for the offense. If the amount of the drug involved is within that range and if the offense was committed in the vicinity of a school or in the vicinity of a juvenile, trafficking in hashish is a felony of the second degree, and there is a presumption that a prison term shall be imposed for the offense.

(f) Except as otherwise provided in this division, if the amount of the drug involved equals or exceeds one thousand grams but is less than two thousand grams of hashish in a solid form or equals or exceeds two hundred grams but is less than four hundred grams of hashish in a liquid concentrate, liquid extract, or liquid distillate form trafficking in hashish is a felony of the second degree, and the court shall impose a mandatory prison term of five, six, seven, or eight years. If the amount of the drug involved is within that range and if the offense was committed in the vicinity of a school or in the vicinity of a juvenile, trafficking in hashish is a felony of the first degree, and the court shall impose as a mandatory prison term the maximum prison term prescribed for a felony of the first degree.

(g) Except as otherwise provided in this division, if the amount of the drug involved equals or exceeds two thousand grams of hashish in a solid form or equals or exceeds four hundred grams of hashish in a liquid concentrate, liquid extract, or liquid distillate form, trafficking in hashish is a felony of the second degree, and the court shall impose as a mandatory prison term the maximum prison term prescribed for a felony of the second degree. If the amount of the drug involved equals or exceeds two thousand grams of hashish in a solid form or equals or exceeds four hundred grams of hashish in a liquid concentrate, liquid extract, or liquid distillate form and if the offense was committed in the vicinity of a school or in the vicinity of a juvenile, trafficking in hashish is a felony of the first degree, and the court shall impose as a mandatory prison term the maximum prison term prescribed for a felony of the first degree.

(8) If the drug involved in the violation is 1-Pentyl-3-(1-naphthoyl)indole, 1-Butyl-3-(1-naphthoyl)indole, 1-[2-(4-morpholinyl)ethyl]-3-(1-naphthoyl)indole, 5-(1,1-dimethylheptyl)-2-[(1R,3S)-3-hydroxycyclohexyl]-phenol, or 5-(1,1-dimethyloctyl)-2-[(1R,3S)-3-hydroxycyclohexyl]-phenol or a compound, mixture, preparation, or substance containing 1-Pentyl-3-(1-naphthoyl)indole, 1-Butyl-3-(1-naphthoyl)indole, 1-[2-(4-morpholinyl)ethyl]-3-(1-naphthoyl)indole, 5-(1,1-dimethylheptyl)-2-[(1R,3S)-3-hydroxycyclohexyl]-phenol, or 5-(1,1-dimethyloctyl)-2-[(1R,3S)-3-hydroxycyclohexyl]-phenol, whoever violates division (A) of this section is guilty of trafficking in spice. The penalty for the offense shall be determined as follows:

(a) Except as otherwise provided in division (C)(8)(b) of this section, trafficking in spice is a felony of the fifth degree, and division (C) of section 2929.13 of the Revised Code applies in determining whether to impose a prison term on the offender.

(b) If the offense was committed in the vicinity of a school or in the vicinity of a juvenile, trafficking in spice is a felony of the fourth degree, and division (C) of section 2929.13 of the Revised Code applies in determining whether to impose a prison term on the offender.

(D) In addition to any prison term authorized or required by division (C) of this section and sections 2929.13 and 2929.14 of the Revised Code, and in addition to any other sanction imposed for the offense under this section or sections 2929.11 to 2929.18 of the Revised Code, the court that sentences an offender who is convicted of or pleads guilty to a violation of division (A) of this section shall do all of the following that are applicable regarding the offender:

(1) If the violation of division (A) of this section is a felony of the first, second, or third degree, the court shall impose upon the offender the mandatory fine specified for the offense under division (B)(1) of section 2929.18 of the Revised Code unless, as specified in that division, the court determines that the offender is indigent. Except as otherwise provided in division (H)(1) of this section, a mandatory fine or any other fine imposed for a violation of this section is subject to division (F) of this section. If a person is charged with a violation of this section that is a felony of the first, second, or third degree, posts bail, and forfeits the bail, the clerk of the court shall pay the forfeited bail pursuant to divisions (D)(1) and (F) of this

section, as if the forfeited bail was a fine imposed for a violation of this section. If any amount of the forfeited bail remains after that payment and if a fine is imposed under division (H)(1) of this section, the clerk of the court shall pay the remaining amount of the forfeited bail pursuant to divisions (H)(2) and (3) of this section, as if that remaining amount was a fine imposed under division (H)(1) of this section.

(2) The court shall suspend the driver's or commercial driver's license or permit of the offender in accordance with division (G) of this section.

(3) If the offender is a professionally licensed person, the court immediately shall comply with section 2925.38 of the Revised Code.

(E) When a person is charged with the sale of or offer to sell a bulk amount or a multiple of a bulk amount of a controlled substance, the jury, or the court trying the accused, shall determine the amount of the controlled substance involved at the time of the offense and, if a guilty verdict is returned, shall return the findings as part of the verdict. In any such case, it is unnecessary to find and return the exact amount of the controlled substance involved, and it is sufficient if the finding and return is to the effect that the amount of the controlled substance involved is the requisite amount, or that the amount of the controlled substance involved is less than the requisite amount.

(F)(1) Notwithstanding any contrary provision of section 3719.21 of the Revised Code and except as provided in division (H) of this section, the clerk of the court shall pay any mandatory fine imposed pursuant to division (D)(1) of this section and any fine other than a mandatory fine that is imposed for a violation of this section pursuant to division (A) or (B)(5) of section 2929.18 of the Revised Code to the county, township, municipal corporation, park district, as created pursuant to section 511.18 or 1545.04 of the Revised Code, or state law enforcement agencies in this state that primarily were responsible for or involved in making the arrest of, and in prosecuting, the offender. However, the clerk shall not pay a mandatory fine so imposed to a law enforcement agency unless the agency has adopted a written internal control policy under division (F)(2) of this section that addresses the use of the fine moneys that it receives. Each agency shall use the mandatory fines so paid to subsidize the agency's law enforcement efforts that pertain to drug offenses, in accordance with the written internal control policy adopted by the recipient agency under division (F)(2) of this section.

(2)(a) Prior to receiving any fine moneys under division (F)(1) of this section or division (B) of section 2925.42 of the Revised Code, a law enforcement agency shall adopt a written internal control policy that addresses the agency's use and disposition of all fine moneys so received and that provides for the keeping of detailed financial records of the receipts of those fine moneys, the general types of expenditures made out of those fine moneys, and the specific amount of each general type of expenditure. The policy shall not provide for or permit the identification of any specific expenditure that is made in an ongoing investigation. All financial records of the receipts of those fine moneys, the general types of expenditures made out of those fine moneys, and the specific amount of each general type of expenditure by an agency are public records open for inspection under section 149.43 of the Revised Code. Additionally, a written internal control policy adopted under this division is such a public record, and the agency that adopted it shall comply with it.

(b) Each law enforcement agency that receives in any calendar year any fine moneys under division (F)(1) of this section or division (B) of section 2925.42 of the Revised Code shall prepare a report covering the calendar year that cumulates all of the information contained in all of the public financial records kept by the agency pursuant to division (F)(2)(a) of this section for that calendar year, and shall send a copy of the cumulative report, no later than the first day of March in the calendar year following the calendar year covered by the report, to the attorney general. Each report received by the attorney general is a public record open for inspection under section 149.43 of the Revised Code. Not later than the fifteenth day of April in the calendar year in which the reports are received, the attorney general shall send to the president of the senate and the speaker of the house of representatives a written notification that does all of the following:

(i) Indicates that the attorney general has received from law enforcement agencies reports of the type described in this division that cover the previous calendar year and indicates that the reports were received under this division;

(ii) Indicates that the reports are open for inspection under section 149.43 of the Revised Code;

(iii) Indicates that the attorney general will provide a copy of any or all of the reports to the president of the senate or the speaker of the house of representatives upon request.

(3) As used in division (F) of this section:

(a) "Law enforcement agencies" includes, but is not limited to, the state board of pharmacy and the office of a prosecutor.

(b) "Prosecutor" has the same meaning as in section 2935.01 of the Revised Code.

(G) When required under division (D)(2) of this section or any other provision of this chapter, the court shall suspend for not less than six months or more than five years the driver's or commercial driver's license or permit of any person who is convicted of or pleads guilty to any violation of this section or any other specified provision of this chapter. If an offender's driver's or commercial driver's license or permit is suspended pursuant to this division, the offender, at any time after the expiration of two years from the day on which the offender's sentence was imposed or from the day on which the offender finally was released from a prison term under the sentence, whichever is later, may file a motion with the sentencing court requesting termination of the suspension; upon the filing of such a motion and the court's finding of good cause for the termination, the court may terminate the suspension.

(H)(1) In addition to any prison term authorized or required by division (C) of this section and sections 2929.13 and 2929.14 of the Revised Code, in addition to any other penalty or sanction imposed for the offense under this section or sections 2929.11 to 2929.18 of the Revised Code, and in addition to the forfeiture of property in connection with the offense as prescribed in Chapter 2981. of the Revised Code, the court that sentences an offender who is convicted of or pleads guilty to a violation of division (A) of this section may impose upon the offender an additional fine specified for the offense in division (B)(4) of section 2929.18 of the Revised Code. A fine imposed under division (H)(1) of this section is not subject to division (F) of this section and shall be used solely for the support of one or more eligible alcohol and drug addiction programs in accordance with divisions (H)(2) and (3) of this section.

(2) The court that imposes a fine under division (H)(1) of this section shall specify in the judgment that imposes the fine one or more eligible alcohol and drug addiction programs for the support of which the fine money is to be used. No alcohol and drug addiction program shall receive or use money paid or collected in satisfaction of a fine imposed under division (H)(1) of this section unless the program is specified in the judgment that imposes the fine. No alcohol and drug addiction program shall be specified in the judgment unless the program is an eligible alcohol and drug addiction program and, except as otherwise provided in division (H)(2) of this section, unless the program is located in the county in which the court that imposes the fine is located or in a county that is immediately contiguous to the county in which that court is located. If no eligible alcohol and drug addiction program is located in any of those counties, the judgment may specify an eligible alcohol and drug addiction program that is located anywhere within this state.

(3) Notwithstanding any contrary provision of section 3719.21 of the Revised Code, the clerk of the court shall pay any fine imposed under division (H)(1) of this section to the eligible alcohol and drug addiction program specified pursuant to division (H)(2) of this section in the judgment. The eligible alcohol and drug addiction program that receives the fine moneys shall use the moneys only for the alcohol and drug addiction services identified in the application for certification under section 3793.06 of the Revised Code or in the application for a license under section 3793.11 of the Revised Code filed with the department of alcohol and drug addiction services by the alcohol and drug addiction program specified in the judgment.

(4) Each alcohol and drug addiction program that receives in a calendar year any fine moneys under division (H)(3) of this section shall file an annual report covering that calendar year with the court of common pleas and the board of county commissioners of the county in which the program is located, with the court of common pleas and the board of county commissioners of each county from which the program received the moneys if that county is different from the county in which the program is located, and with the attorney general. The alcohol and drug addiction program shall file the report no later than the first day of March in the calendar year following the calendar year in which the program received the fine moneys. The report shall include statistics on the number of persons served by the alcohol and drug addiction program, identify the types of alcohol and drug addiction services provided to those persons, and include a specific accounting of the purposes for which the fine moneys received were used. No information contained in the report shall identify, or enable a person to determine the identity of, any person served by the alcohol and drug addiction program. Each report received by a court of common pleas, a board of county commissioners, or the attorney general is a public record open for inspection under section 149.43 of the Revised Code.

(5) As used in divisions (H)(1) to (5) of this section:

(a) "Alcohol and drug addiction program" and "alcohol and drug addiction services" have the same meanings as in section 3793.01 of the Revised Code.

(b) "Eligible alcohol and drug addiction program" means an alcohol and drug addiction program that is certified under section 3793.06 of the Revised Code or licensed under section 3793.11 of the Revised Code by the department of alcohol and drug addiction services.

(I) As used in this section, "drug" includes any substance that is represented to be a drug.

**HISTORY: 136 v H 300 (Eff 7-1-76); 141 v S 67 (Eff 8-29-86); 143 v H 215 (Eff 4-11-90); 143 v H 261 (Eff 7-18-90); 143 v H 266 (Eff 9-6-90); 143 v S 258 (Eff 11-20-90); 144 v H 62 (Eff 5-21-91); 144 v S 174 (Eff 7-31-92); 144 v H 591 (Eff 11-2-92); 145 v H 377 (Eff 9-30-93); 145 v H 391 (Eff 7-21-94); 146 v S 2 (Eff 7-1-96); 146 v S 269 (Eff 7-1-96); 146 v S 166 (Eff 10-17-96); 147 v S 164 (Eff 1-15-98); 147 v S 66 (Eff 7-22-98); 148 v S 107 (Eff 3-23-2000); 148 v H 241 (Eff 5-17-2000); 148 v H 528. Eff 2-13-2001; 149 v S 123, § 1, eff. 1-1-04; 151 v S 154, § 1, eff. 5-17-06; 151 v H 241, § 1, eff. 7-1-07; 152 v H 195, § 1, eff. 9-30-08; 2011 HB 86, § 1, eff. Sept. 30, 2011; 2011 HB 64, § 1, eff. Oct. 17, 2011.**

Acts 2011, HB 86, § 3 provides: "The amendments to sections 2925.01, 2925.03, 2925.05, and 2925.11 of the Revised Code, and to division (W) of section 2929.01 of the Revised Code, that are made in this act apply to a person who commits an offense involving marihuana, cocaine, or hashish on or after the effective date of this act and to a person to whom division (B) of section 1.58 of the Revised Code makes the amendments applicable.

"The provisions of sections 2925.01, 2925.03, 2925.05, and 2925.11 of the Revised Code, and of division (W) of section 2929.01 of the Revised Code, in existence prior to the effective date of this act shall apply to a person upon whom a court imposed sentence prior to the effective date of this act for an offense involving marihuana, cocaine, or hashish. The amendments to sections 2925.01, 2925.03, 2925.05, and 2925.11 of the Revised Code, and to division (W) of section 2929.01 of the Revised Code, that are made in this act do not apply to a person upon whom a court imposed sentence prior to the effective date of this act for an offense involving marihuana, cocaine, or hashish."

See provisions of § 4 of 151 v H 241 following RC § 2901.01.

The effective date is set by section 4 of S.B. 123.

See provisions of § 5 of S.B. 123 (149 v —) following RC § 2925.01.

The provisions of § 8 of S.B. 123 read as follows:

SECTION 8. Section 2925.03 of the Revised Code is presented in this act as a composite of the section as amended by both Am. H.B. 528 and Am. Sub. S.B. 107 of the 123rd General Assembly. The General Assembly, applying the principle stated in division (B) of section 1.52 of the Revised Code that amendments are to be harmonized if reasonably capable of simultaneous operation, finds that the composites are the resulting versions of the sections in effect prior to the effective date of the sections as presented in this act.

## [DRUG ABUSE]

### § 2925.04 Illegal manufacture of drugs or cultivation of marihuana.

(A) No person shall knowingly cultivate marihuana or knowingly manufacture or otherwise engage in any part of the production of a controlled substance.

(B) This section does not apply to any person listed in division (B)(1), (2), or (3) of section 2925.03 of the Revised Code to the extent and under the circumstances described in those divisions.

(C)(1) Whoever commits a violation of division (A) of this section that involves any drug other than marihuana is guilty of illegal manufacture of drugs, and whoever commits a violation of division (A) of this section that involves marihuana is guilty of illegal cultivation of marihuana.

(2) Except as otherwise provided in this division, if the drug involved in the violation of division (A) of this section is any compound, mixture, preparation, or substance included in schedule I or II, with the exception of methamphetamine or marihuana, illegal manufacture of

drugs is a felony of the second degree, and, subject to division (E) of this section, the court shall impose as a mandatory prison term one of the prison terms prescribed for a felony of the second degree.

If the drug involved in the violation is any compound, mixture, preparation, or substance included in schedule I or II, with the exception of methamphetamine or marihuana, and if the offense was committed in the vicinity of a juvenile or in the vicinity of a school, illegal manufacture of drugs is a felony of the first degree, and, subject to division (E) of this section, the court shall impose as a mandatory prison term one of the prison terms prescribed for a felony of the first degree.

(3) If the drug involved in the violation of division (A) of this section is methamphetamine, the penalty for the violation shall be determined as follows:

(a) Except as otherwise provided in division (C)(3)(b) of this section, if the drug involved in the violation is methamphetamine, illegal manufacture of drugs is a felony of the second degree, and, subject to division (E) of this section, the court shall impose a mandatory prison term on the offender determined in accordance with this division. Except as otherwise provided in this division, the court shall impose as a mandatory prison term one of the prison terms prescribed for a felony of the second degree that is not less than three years. If the offender previously has been convicted of or pleaded guilty to a violation of division (A) of this section, a violation of division (B)(6) of section 2919.22 of the Revised Code, or a violation of division (A) of section 2925.041 of the Revised Code, the court shall impose as a mandatory prison term one of the prison terms prescribed for a felony of the second degree that is not less than five years.

(b) If the drug involved in the violation is methamphetamine and if the offense was committed in the vicinity of a juvenile, in the vicinity of a school, or on public premises, illegal manufacture of drugs is a felony of the first degree, and, subject to division (E) of this section, the court shall impose a mandatory prison term on the offender determined in accordance with this division. Except as otherwise provided in this division, the court shall impose as a mandatory prison term one of the prison terms prescribed for a felony of the first degree that is not less than four years. If the offender previously has been convicted of or pleaded guilty to a violation of division (A) of this section, a violation of division (B)(6) of section 2919.22 of the Revised Code, or a violation of division (A) of section 2925.041 of the Revised Code, the court shall impose as a mandatory prison term one of the prison terms prescribed for a felony of the first degree that is not less than five years.

(4) If the drug involved in the violation of division (A) of this section is any compound, mixture, preparation, or substance included in schedule III, IV, or V, illegal manufacture of drugs is a felony of the third degree or, if the offense was committed in the vicinity of a school or in the vicinity of a juvenile, a felony of the second degree, and there is a presumption for a prison term for the offense.

(5) If the drug involved in the violation is marihuana, the penalty for the offense shall be determined as follows:

(a) Except as otherwise provided in division (C)(5)(b), (c), (d), (e), or (f) of this section, illegal cultivation of marihuana is a minor misdemeanor or, if the offense was committed in the vicinity of a school or in the vicinity of a juvenile, a misdemeanor of the fourth degree.

(b) If the amount of marihuana involved equals or exceeds one hundred grams but is less than two hundred grams, illegal cultivation of marihuana is a misdemeanor of the fourth degree or, if the offense was committed in the vicinity of a school or in the vicinity of a juvenile, a misdemeanor of the third degree.

(c) If the amount of marihuana involved equals or exceeds two hundred grams but is less than one thousand grams, illegal cultivation of marihuana is a felony of the fifth degree or, if the offense was committed in the vicinity of a school or in the vicinity of a juvenile, a felony of the fourth degree, and division (B) of section 2929.13 of the Revised Code applies in determining whether to impose a prison term on the offender.

(d) If the amount of marihuana involved equals or exceeds one thousand grams but is less than five thousand grams, illegal cultivation of marihuana is a felony of the third degree or, if the offense was committed in the vicinity of a school or in the vicinity of a juvenile, a felony of the second degree, and division (C) of section 2929.13 of the Revised Code applies in determining whether to impose a prison term on the offender.

(e) If the amount of marihuana involved equals or exceeds five thousand grams but is less than twenty thousand grams, illegal cultivation of marihuana is a felony of the third degree or, if the offense was committed in the vicinity of a school or in the vicinity of a juvenile, a felony of the second degree, and there is a presumption for a prison term for the offense.

(f) Except as otherwise provided in this division, if the amount of marihuana involved equals or exceeds twenty thousand grams, illegal cultivation of marihuana is a felony of the second degree, and the court shall impose as a mandatory prison term the maximum prison term prescribed for a felony of the second degree. If the amount of the drug involved equals or exceeds twenty thousand grams and if the offense was committed in the vicinity of a school or in the vicinity of a juvenile, illegal cultivation of marihuana is a felony of the first degree, and the court shall impose as a mandatory prison term the maximum prison term prescribed for a felony of the first degree.

(D) In addition to any prison term authorized or required by division (C) or (E) of this section and sections 2929.13 and 2929.14 of the Revised Code and in addition to any other sanction imposed for the offense under this section or sections 2929.11 to 2929.18 of the Revised Code, the court that sentences an offender who is convicted of or pleads guilty to a violation of division (A) of this section shall do all of the following that are applicable regarding the offender:

(1) If the violation of division (A) of this section is a felony of the first, second, or third degree, the court shall impose upon the offender the mandatory fine specified for the offense under division (B)(1) of section 2929.18 of the Revised Code unless, as specified in that division, the court determines that the offender is indigent. The clerk of the court shall pay a mandatory fine or other fine imposed for a violation of this section pursuant to division (A) of section 2929.18 of the Revised Code in accordance with and subject to the requirements of division (F) of section 2925.03 of the Revised Code. The agency that receives the fine shall use the fine as specified in division (F) of section 2925.03 of the Revised Code. If a person is charged with a violation of this section that is a felony of the first, second, or third degree, posts bail, and forfeits the bail, the clerk shall pay the forfeited bail as if the

forfeited bail were a fine imposed for a violation of this section.

(2) The court shall suspend the offender's driver's or commercial driver's license or permit in accordance with division (G) of section 2925.03 of the Revised Code. If an offender's driver's or commercial driver's license or permit is suspended in accordance with that division, the offender may request termination of, and the court may terminate, the suspension in accordance with that division.

(3) If the offender is a professionally licensed person, the court immediately shall comply with section 2925.38 of the Revised Code.

(E) Notwithstanding the prison term otherwise authorized or required for the offense under division (C) of this section and sections 2929.13 and 2929.14 of the Revised Code, if the violation of division (A) of this section involves the sale, offer to sell, or possession of a schedule I or II controlled substance, with the exception of marihuana, and if the court imposing sentence upon the offender finds that the offender as a result of the violation is a major drug offender and is guilty of a specification of the type described in section 2941.1410 of the Revised Code, the court, in lieu of the prison term otherwise authorized or required, shall impose upon the offender the mandatory prison term specified in division (B)(3)(a) of section 2929.14 of the Revised Code.

(F) It is an affirmative defense, as provided in section 2901.05 of the Revised Code, to a charge under this section for a fifth degree felony violation of illegal cultivation of marihuana that the marihuana that gave rise to the charge is in an amount, is in a form, is prepared, compounded, or mixed with substances that are not controlled substances in a manner, or is possessed or cultivated under any other circumstances that indicate that the marihuana was solely for personal use.

Notwithstanding any contrary provision of division (F) of this section, if, in accordance with section 2901.05 of the Revised Code, a person who is charged with a violation of illegal cultivation of marihuana that is a felony of the fifth degree sustains the burden of going forward with evidence of and establishes by a preponderance of the evidence the affirmative defense described in this division, the person may be prosecuted for and may be convicted of or plead guilty to a misdemeanor violation of illegal cultivation of marihuana.

(G) Arrest or conviction for a minor misdemeanor violation of this section does not constitute a criminal record and need not be reported by the person so arrested or convicted in response to any inquiries about the person's criminal record, including any inquiries contained in an application for employment, a license, or any other right or privilege or made in connection with the person's appearance as a witness.

**HISTORY: 146 v S 2 (Eff 7-1-96); 146 v S 269 (Eff 7-1-96); 148 v S 107 (Eff 3-23-2000); 149 v H 7. Eff 8-7-2001; 149 v S 123, § 1, eff. 1-1-04; 150 v S 58, § 1, eff. 8-11-04; 151 v S 53, § 1, eff. 5-17-06; 2011 HB 86, § 1, eff. Sept. 30, 2011.**

The effective date is set by section 4 of S.B. 123.

See provisions of § 5 of S.B. 123 (149 v —) following RC § 2925.01.

## § 2925.041 Illegal assembly or possession of chemicals for the manufacture of drugs.

(A) No person shall knowingly assemble or possess one or more chemicals that may be used to manufacture a controlled substance in schedule I or II with the intent to manufacture a controlled substance in schedule I or II in violation of section 2925.04 of the Revised Code.

(B) In a prosecution under this section, it is not necessary to allege or prove that the offender assembled or possessed all chemicals necessary to manufacture a controlled substance in schedule I or II. The assembly or possession of a single chemical that may be used in the manufacture of a controlled substance in schedule I or II, with the intent to manufacture a controlled substance in either schedule, is sufficient to violate this section.

(C) Whoever violates this section is guilty of illegal assembly or possession of chemicals for the manufacture of drugs. Except as otherwise provided in this division, illegal assembly or possession of chemicals for the manufacture of drugs is a felony of the third degree, and, except as otherwise provided in division (C)(1) or (2) of this section, division (C) of section 2929.13 of the Revised Code applies in determining whether to impose a prison term on the offender. If the offense was committed in the vicinity of a juvenile or in the vicinity of a school, illegal assembly or possession of chemicals for the manufacture of drugs is a felony of the second degree, and, except as otherwise provided in division (C)(1) or (2) of this section, division (C) of section 2929.13 of the Revised Code applies in determining whether to impose a prison term on the offender. If the violation of division (A) of this section is a felony of the third degree under this division and if the chemical or chemicals assembled or possessed in violation of division (A) of this section may be used to manufacture methamphetamine, there either is a presumption for a prison term for the offense or the court shall impose a mandatory prison term on the offender, determined as follows:

(1) Except as otherwise provided in this division, there is a presumption for a prison term for the offense. If the offender two or more times previously has been convicted of or pleaded guilty to a felony drug abuse offense, except as otherwise provided in this division, the court shall impose as a mandatory prison term one of the prison terms prescribed for a felony of the third degree that is not less than two years. If the offender two or more times previously has been convicted of or pleaded guilty to a felony drug abuse offense and if at least one of those previous convictions or guilty pleas was to a violation of division (A) of this section, a violation of division (B)(6) of section 2919.22 of the Revised Code, or a violation of division (A) of section 2925.04 of the Revised Code, the court shall impose as a mandatory prison term one of the prison terms prescribed for a felony of the third degree that is not less than five years.

(2) If the violation of division (A) of this section is a felony of the second degree under division (C) of this section and the chemical or chemicals assembled or possessed in committing the violation may be used to manufacture methamphetamine, the court shall impose as a mandatory prison term one of the prison terms prescribed for a felony of the second degree that is not less than three years. If the violation of division (A) of this section is a felony of the second degree under division (C) of this section, if the chemical or chemicals assembled or possessed in committing the violation may be used to manufacture methamphetamine, and if the offender previously has been convicted of or pleaded guilty to a violation of division (A) of this section, a violation of division (B)(6) of section 2919.22 of the Revised Code, or a violation of division (A) of section 2925.04 of the Revised Code, the court shall impose as a mandatory prison term

one of the prison terms prescribed for a felony of the second degree that is not less than five years.

(D) In addition to any prison term authorized by division (C) of this section and sections 2929.13 and 2929.14 of the Revised Code and in addition to any other sanction imposed for the offense under this section or sections 2929.11 to 2929.18 of the Revised Code, the court that sentences an offender who is convicted of or pleads guilty to a violation of this section shall do all of the following that are applicable regarding the offender:

(1) The court shall impose upon the offender the mandatory fine specified for the offense under division (B)(1) of section 2929.18 of the Revised Code unless, as specified in that division, the court determines that the offender is indigent. The clerk of the court shall pay a mandatory fine or other fine imposed for a violation of this section under division (A) of section 2929.18 of the Revised Code in accordance with and subject to the requirements of division (F) of section 2925.03 of the Revised Code. The agency that receives the fine shall use the fine as specified in division (F) of section 2925.03 of the Revised Code. If a person charged with a violation of this section posts bail and forfeits the bail, the clerk shall pay the forfeited bail as if the forfeited bail were a fine imposed for a violation of this section.

(2) The court shall revoke or suspend the offender's driver's or commercial driver's license or permit in accordance with division (G) of section 2925.03 of the Revised Code. If an offender's driver's or commercial driver's license or permit is revoked in accordance with that division, the offender may request termination of, and the court may terminate, the revocation in accordance with that division.

(3) If the offender is a professionally licensed person or a person who has been admitted to the bar by order of the supreme court in compliance with its prescribed and published rules, the court shall comply with section 2925.38 of the Revised Code.

**HISTORY: 149 v H 7. Eff 8-7-2001; 150 v S 58, § 1, eff. 8-11-04; 151 v S 53, § 1, eff. 5-17-06; 2011 HB 86, § 1, eff. Sept. 30, 2011.**

## § 2925.05 Funding of drug or marihuana trafficking.

(A) No person shall knowingly provide money or other items of value to another person with the purpose that the recipient of the money or items of value use them to obtain any controlled substance for the purpose of violating section 2925.04 of the Revised Code or for the purpose of selling or offering to sell the controlled substance in the following amount:

(1) If the drug to be sold or offered for sale is any compound, mixture, preparation, or substance included in schedule I or II, with the exception of marihuana, cocaine, L.S.D., heroin, and hashish, or schedule III, IV, or V, an amount of the drug that equals or exceeds the bulk amount of the drug;

(2) If the drug to be sold or offered for sale is marihuana or a compound, mixture, preparation, or substance other than hashish containing marihuana, an amount of the marihuana that equals or exceeds two hundred grams;

(3) If the drug to be sold or offered for sale is cocaine or a compound, mixture, preparation, or substance containing cocaine, an amount of the cocaine that equals or exceeds five grams;

(4) If the drug to be sold or offered for sale is L.S.D. or a compound, mixture, preparation, or substance containing L.S.D., an amount of the L.S.D. that equals or exceeds ten unit doses if the L.S.D. is in a solid form or equals or exceeds one gram if the L.S.D. is in a liquid concentrate, liquid extract, or liquid distillate form;

(5) If the drug to be sold or offered for sale is heroin or a compound, mixture, preparation, or substance containing heroin, an amount of the heroin that equals or exceeds ten unit doses or equals or exceeds one gram;

(6) If the drug to be sold or offered for sale is hashish or a compound, mixture, preparation, or substance containing hashish, an amount of the hashish that equals or exceeds ten grams if the hashish is in a solid form or equals or exceeds two grams if the hashish is in a liquid concentrate, liquid extract, or liquid distillate form.

(B) This section does not apply to any person listed in division (B)(1), (2), or (3) of section 2925.03 of the Revised Code to the extent and under the circumstances described in those divisions.

(C)(1) If the drug involved in the violation is any compound, mixture, preparation, or substance included in schedule I or II, with the exception of marihuana, whoever violates division (A) of this section is guilty of aggravated funding of drug trafficking, a felony of the first degree, and, subject to division (E) of this section, the court shall impose as a mandatory prison term one of the prison terms prescribed for a felony of the first degree.

(2) If the drug involved in the violation is any compound, mixture, preparation, or substance included in schedule III, IV, or V, whoever violates division (A) of this section is guilty of funding of drug trafficking, a felony of the second degree, and the court shall impose as a mandatory prison term one of the prison terms prescribed for a felony of the second degree.

(3) If the drug involved in the violation is marihuana, whoever violates division (A) of this section is guilty of funding of marihuana trafficking, a felony of the third degree, and, except as otherwise provided in this division, there is a presumption for a prison term for the offense. If funding of marihuana trafficking is a felony of the third degree under this division and if the offender two or more times previously has been convicted of or pleaded guilty to a felony drug abuse offense, the court shall impose as a mandatory prison term one of the prison terms prescribed for a felony of the third degree.

(D) In addition to any prison term authorized or required by division (C) or (E) of this section and sections 2929.13 and 2929.14 of the Revised Code and in addition to any other sanction imposed for the offense under this section or sections 2929.11 to 2929.18 of the Revised Code, the court that sentences an offender who is convicted of or pleads guilty to a violation of division (A) of this section shall do all of the following that are applicable regarding the offender:

(1) The court shall impose the mandatory fine specified for the offense under division (B)(1) of section 2929.18 of the Revised Code unless, as specified in that division, the court determines that the offender is indigent. The clerk of the court shall pay a mandatory fine or other fine imposed for a violation of this section pursuant to division (A) of section 2929.18 of the Revised Code in accordance with and subject to the requirements of division (F) of section 2925.03 of the Revised Code. The agency that receives the fine shall use the fine in accordance with division (F) of section 2925.03 of the Revised Code. If a person is charged with a violation of this section, posts bail,

and forfeits the bail, the forfeited bail shall be paid as if the forfeited bail were a fine imposed for a violation of this section.

(2) The court shall suspend the offender's driver's or commercial driver's license or permit in accordance with division (G) of section 2925.03 of the Revised Code. If an offender's driver's or commercial driver's license or permit is suspended in accordance with that division, the offender may request termination of, and the court may terminate, the suspension in accordance with that division.

(3) If the offender is a professionally licensed person, the court immediately shall comply with section 2925.38 of the Revised Code.

(E) Notwithstanding the prison term otherwise authorized or required for the offense under division (C) of this section and sections 2929.13 and 2929.14 of the Revised Code, if the violation of division (A) of this section involves the sale, offer to sell, or possession of a schedule I or II controlled substance, with the exception of marihuana, and if the court imposing sentence upon the offender finds that the offender as a result of the violation is a major drug offender and is guilty of a specification of the type described in section 2941.1410 of the Revised Code, the court, in lieu of the prison term otherwise authorized or required, shall impose upon the offender the mandatory prison term specified in division (B)(3) of section 2929.14 of the Revised Code.

**HISTORY: 146 v S 2 (Eff 7-1-96); 146 v S 269 (Eff 7-1-96); 148 v S 107. Eff 3-23-2000; 149 v S 123, § 1, eff. 1-1-04; 2011 HB 86, § 1, eff. Sept. 30, 2011.**

The provisions of § 3 of HB 86 read as follows:

"SECTION 3. The amendments to sections 2925.01, 2925.03, 2925.05, and 2925.11 of the Revised Code, and to division (W) of section 2929.01 of the Revised Code, that are made in this act apply to a person who commits an offense involving marihuana, cocaine, or hashish on or after the effective date of this act and to a person to whom division (B) of section 1.58 of the Revised Code makes the amendments applicable.

"The provisions of sections 2925.01, 2925.03, 2925.05, and 2925.11 of the Revised Code, and of division (W) of section 2929.01 of the Revised Code, in existence prior to the effective date of this act shall apply to a person upon whom a court imposed sentence prior to the effective date of this act for an offense involving marihuana, cocaine, or hashish. The amendments to sections 2925.01, 2925.03, 2925.05, and 2925.11 of the Revised Code, and to division (W) of section 2929.01 of the Revised Code, that are made in this act do not apply to a person upon whom a court imposed sentence prior to the effective date of this act for an offense involving marihuana, cocaine, or hashish."

The effective date is set by section 4 of S.B. 123.

See provisions of § 5 of S.B. 123 (149 v —) following RC § 2925.01.

## § 2925.06 Illegal administration or distribution of anabolic steroids.

(A) No person shall knowingly administer to a human being, or prescribe or dispense for administration to a human being, any anabolic steroid not approved by the United States food and drug administration for administration to human beings.

(B) This section does not apply to any person listed in division (B) (1), (2), or (3) of section 2925.03 of the Revised Code to the extent and under the circumstances described in those divisions.

(C) Whoever violates division (A) of this section is guilty of illegal administration or distribution of anabolic steroids, a felony of the fourth degree, and division (C) of section 2929.13 of the Revised Code applies in determining whether to impose a prison term on the offender.

(D) In addition to any prison term authorized or required by division (C) of this section and sections 2929.13 and 2929.14 of the Revised Code and in addition to any other sanction imposed for the offense under this section or sections 2929.11 to 2929.18 of the Revised Code, the court that sentences an offender who is convicted of or pleads guilty to a violation of division (A) of this section shall do both of the following:

(1) The court shall suspend the offender's driver's or commercial driver's license or permit in accordance with division (G) of section 2925.03 of the Revised Code. If an offender's driver's or commercial driver's license or permit is suspended in accordance with that division, the offender may request termination of, and the court may terminate, the suspension in accordance with that division.

(2) If the offender is a professionally licensed person, the court immediately shall comply with section 2925.38 of the Revised Code.

(E) If a person commits any act that constitutes a violation of division (A) of this section and that also constitutes a violation of any other provision of the Revised Code, the prosecutor, as defined in section 2935.01 of the Revised Code, using customary prosecutorial discretion, may prosecute the person for a violation of the appropriate provision of the Revised Code.

**HISTORY: 146 v S 2 (Eff 7-1-96); 146 v S 269. Eff 7-1-96; 149 v S 123, § 1, eff. 1-1-04.**

The effective date is set by section 4 of S.B. 123.

See provisions of § 5 of S.B. 123 (149 v —) following RC § 2925.01.

## § 2925.07 Repealed, 148 v H 528, § 2 [147 v H 122]. Eff 2-13-2001.

This section concerned preparation of drugs for sale. See now RC § 2925.03 (A)(1), (2).

## § 2925.09 Offenses involving unapproved drugs; dangerous drug offenses involving livestock.

(A) No person shall administer, dispense, distribute, manufacture, possess, sell, or use any drug, other than a controlled substance, that is not approved by the United States food and drug administration, or the United States department of agriculture, unless one of the following applies:

(1) The United States food and drug administration has approved an application for investigational use in accordance with the "Federal Food, Drug, and Cosmetic Act," 52 Stat. 1040 (1938), 21 U.S.C.A. 301, as amended, and the drug is used only for the approved investigational use;

(2) The United States department of agriculture has approved an application for investigational use in accordance with the federal "Virus-Serum-Toxin Act," 37 Stat. 832 (1913), 21 U.S.C.A. 151, as amended, and the drug is used only for the approved investigational use;

(3) A licensed health professional authorized to prescribe drugs, other than a veterinarian, prescribes or combines two or more drugs as a single product for medical purposes;

(4) A pharmacist, pursuant to a prescription, compounds and dispenses two or more drugs as a single product for medical purposes.

(B)(1) As used in this division, "dangerous drug," "prescription," "sale at retail," "wholesale distributor of dangerous drugs," and "terminal distributor of dangerous drugs," have the same meanings as in section 4729.01 of the Revised Code.

(2) Except as provided in division (B)(3) of this section, no person shall administer, dispense, distribute, manufacture, possess, sell, or use any dangerous drug to or for livestock or any animal that is generally used for food or in the production of food, unless the drug is prescribed by a licensed veterinarian by prescription or other written order and the drug is used in accordance with the veterinarian's order or direction.

(3) Division (B)(2) of this section does not apply to a registered wholesale distributor of dangerous drugs, a licensed terminal distributor of dangerous drugs, or a person who possesses, possesses for sale, or sells, at retail, a drug in accordance with Chapters 3719., 4729., or 4741. of the Revised Code.

(C) Whoever violates division (A) or (B)(2) of this section is guilty of a felony of the fifth degree on a first offense and of a felony of the fourth degree on each subsequent offense.

**HISTORY: RC § 2925.04, 146 v H 202 (Eff 6-14-95); RC § 2925.09, 146 v S 269 (Eff 7-1-96); 147 v S 66. Eff 7-22-98.**

**Publisher's Note:**

Two sections numbered RC § 2925.04 were enacted in the 121st General Assembly in HB 202 and SB 2. The HB 202 section was renumbered to RC § 2925.09 by SB 269.

## § 2925.11 Possession of drugs.

(A) No person shall knowingly obtain, possess, or use a controlled substance.

(B) This section does not apply to any of the following:

(1) Manufacturers, licensed health professionals authorized to prescribe drugs, pharmacists, owners of pharmacies, and other persons whose conduct was in accordance with Chapters 3719., 4715., 4723., 4729., 4730., 4731., and 4741. of the Revised Code;

(2) If the offense involves an anabolic steroid, any person who is conducting or participating in a research project involving the use of an anabolic steroid if the project has been approved by the United States food and drug administration;

(3) Any person who sells, offers for sale, prescribes, dispenses, or administers for livestock or other nonhuman species an anabolic steroid that is expressly intended for administration through implants to livestock or other nonhuman species and approved for that purpose under the "Federal Food, Drug, and Cosmetic Act," 52 Stat. 1040 (1938), 21 U.S.C.A. 301, as amended, and is sold, offered for sale, prescribed, dispensed, or administered for that purpose in accordance with that act;

(4) Any person who obtained the controlled substance pursuant to a lawful prescription issued by a licensed health professional authorized to prescribe drugs.

(C) Whoever violates division (A) of this section is guilty of one of the following:

(1) If the drug involved in the violation is a compound, mixture, preparation, or substance included in schedule I or II, with the exception of marihuana, 1-Pentyl-3-(1-naphthoyl)indole, 1-Butyl-3-(1-naphthoyl)indole, 1-[2-(4-morpholinyl)ethyl]-3-(1-naphthoyl)indole, 5-(1,1-dimethylheptyl)-2-[(1R,3S)-3-hydroxycyclohexyl]-phenol, 5-(1,1-dimethyloctyl)-2-[(1R,3S)-3-hydroxycyclohexyl]-phenol, cocaine, L.S.D., heroin, and hashish, whoever violates division (A) of this section is guilty of aggravated possession of drugs. The penalty for the offense shall be determined as follows:

(a) Except as otherwise provided in division (C)(1)(b), (c), (d), or (e) of this section, aggravated possession of drugs is a felony of the fifth degree, and division (B) of section 2929.13 of the Revised Code applies in determining whether to impose a prison term on the offender.

(b) If the amount of the drug involved equals or exceeds the bulk amount but is less than five times the bulk amount, aggravated possession of drugs is a felony of the third degree, and there is a presumption for a prison term for the offense.

(c) If the amount of the drug involved equals or exceeds five times the bulk amount but is less than fifty times the bulk amount, aggravated possession of drugs is a felony of the second degree, and the court shall impose as a mandatory prison term one of the prison terms prescribed for a felony of the second degree.

(d) If the amount of the drug involved equals or exceeds fifty times the bulk amount but is less than one hundred times the bulk amount, aggravated possession of drugs is a felony of the first degree, and the court shall impose as a mandatory prison term one of the prison terms prescribed for a felony of the first degree.

(e) If the amount of the drug involved equals or exceeds one hundred times the bulk amount, aggravated possession of drugs is a felony of the first degree, the offender is a major drug offender, and the court shall impose as a mandatory prison term the maximum prison term prescribed for a felony of the first degree.

(2) If the drug involved in the violation is a compound, mixture, preparation, or substance included in schedule III, IV, or V, whoever violates division (A) of this section is guilty of possession of drugs. The penalty for the offense shall be determined as follows:

(a) Except as otherwise provided in division (C)(2)(b), (c), or (d) of this section, possession of drugs is a misdemeanor of the first degree or, if the offender previously has been convicted of a drug abuse offense, a felony of the fifth degree.

(b) If the amount of the drug involved equals or exceeds the bulk amount but is less than five times the bulk amount, possession of drugs is a felony of the fourth degree, and division (C) of section 2929.13 of the Revised Code applies in determining whether to impose a prison term on the offender.

(c) If the amount of the drug involved equals or exceeds five times the bulk amount but is less than fifty times the bulk amount, possession of drugs is a felony of the third degree, and there is a presumption for a prison term for the offense.

(d) If the amount of the drug involved equals or exceeds fifty times the bulk amount, possession of drugs is a felony of the second degree, and the court shall impose upon the offender as a mandatory prison term one of the prison terms prescribed for a felony of the second degree.

(3) If the drug involved in the violation is marihuana or a compound, mixture, preparation, or substance containing marihuana other than hashish, whoever violates division (A) of this section is guilty of possession of marihuana. The penalty for the offense shall be determined as follows:

(a) Except as otherwise provided in division (C)(3)(b), (c), (d), (e), (f), or (g) of this section, possession of marihuana is a minor misdemeanor.

(b) If the amount of the drug involved equals or exceeds one hundred grams but is less than two hundred grams, possession of marihuana is a misdemeanor of the fourth degree.

(c) If the amount of the drug involved equals or exceeds two hundred grams but is less than one thousand grams, possession of marihuana is a felony of the fifth degree, and division (B) of section 2929.13 of the Revised Code applies in determining whether to impose a prison term on the offender.

(d) If the amount of the drug involved equals or exceeds one thousand grams but is less than five thousand grams, possession of marihuana is a felony of the third degree, and division (C) of section 2929.13 of the Revised Code applies in determining whether to impose a prison term on the offender.

(e) If the amount of the drug involved equals or exceeds five thousand grams but is less than twenty thousand grams, possession of marihuana is a felony of the third degree, and there is a presumption that a prison term shall be imposed for the offense.

(f) If the amount of the drug involved equals or exceeds twenty thousand grams but is less than forty thousand grams, possession of marihuana is a felony of the second degree, and the court shall impose a mandatory prison term of five, six, seven, or eight years.

(g) If the amount of the drug involved equals or exceeds forty thousand grams, possession of marihuana is a felony of the second degree, and the court shall impose as a mandatory prison term the maximum prison term prescribed for a felony of the second degree.

(4) If the drug involved in the violation is cocaine or a compound, mixture, preparation, or substance containing cocaine, whoever violates division (A) of this section is guilty of possession of cocaine. The penalty for the offense shall be determined as follows:

(a) Except as otherwise provided in division (C)(4)(b), (c), (d), (e), or (f) of this section, possession of cocaine is a felony of the fifth degree, and division (B) of section 2929.13 of the Revised Code applies in determining whether to impose a prison term on the offender.

(b) If the amount of the drug involved equals or exceeds five grams but is less than ten grams of cocaine, possession of cocaine is a felony of the fourth degree, and division (B) of section 2929.13 of the Revised Code applies in determining whether to impose a prison term on the offender.

(c) If the amount of the drug involved equals or exceeds ten grams but is less than twenty grams of cocaine, possession of cocaine is a felony of the third degree, and, except as otherwise provided in this division, there is a presumption for a prison term for the offense. If possession of cocaine is a felony of the third degree under this division and if the offender two or more times previously has been convicted of or pleaded guilty to a felony drug abuse offense, the court shall impose as a mandatory prison term one of the prison terms prescribed for a felony of the third degree.

(d) If the amount of the drug involved equals or exceeds twenty grams but is less than twenty-seven grams of cocaine, possession of cocaine is a felony of the second degree, and the court shall impose as a mandatory prison term one of the prison terms prescribed for a felony of the second degree.

(e) If the amount of the drug involved equals or exceeds twenty-seven grams but is less than one hundred grams of cocaine, possession of cocaine is a felony of the first degree, and the court shall impose as a mandatory prison term one of the prison terms prescribed for a felony of the first degree.

(f) If the amount of the drug involved equals or exceeds one hundred grams of cocaine, possession of cocaine is a felony of the first degree, the offender is a major drug offender, and the court shall impose as a mandatory prison term the maximum prison term prescribed for a felony of the first degree.

(5) If the drug involved in the violation is L.S.D., whoever violates division (A) of this section is guilty of possession of L.S.D. The penalty for the offense shall be determined as follows:

(a) Except as otherwise provided in division (C)(5)(b), (c), (d), (e), or (f) of this section, possession of L.S.D. is a felony of the fifth degree, and division (B) of section 2929.13 of the Revised Code applies in determining whether to impose a prison term on the offender.

(b) If the amount of L.S.D. involved equals or exceeds ten unit doses but is less than fifty unit doses of L.S.D. in a solid form or equals or exceeds one gram but is less than five grams of L.S.D. in a liquid concentrate, liquid extract, or liquid distillate form, possession of L.S.D. is a felony of the fourth degree, and division (C) of section 2929.13 of the Revised Code applies in determining whether to impose a prison term on the offender.

(c) If the amount of L.S.D. involved equals or exceeds fifty unit doses, but is less than two hundred fifty unit doses of L.S.D. in a solid form or equals or exceeds five grams but is less than twenty-five grams of L.S.D. in a liquid concentrate, liquid extract, or liquid distillate form, possession of L.S.D. is a felony of the third degree, and there is a presumption for a prison term for the offense.

(d) If the amount of L.S.D. involved equals or exceeds two hundred fifty unit doses but is less than one thousand unit doses of L.S.D. in a solid form or equals or exceeds twenty-five grams but is less than one hundred grams of L.S.D. in a liquid concentrate, liquid extract, or liquid distillate form, possession of L.S.D. is a felony of the second degree, and the court shall impose as a mandatory prison term one of the prison terms prescribed for a felony of the second degree.

(e) If the amount of L.S.D. involved equals or exceeds one thousand unit doses but is less than five thousand unit doses of L.S.D. in a solid form or equals or exceeds one hundred grams but is less than five hundred grams of L.S.D. in a liquid concentrate, liquid extract, or liquid distillate form, possession of L.S.D. is a felony of the first degree, and the court shall impose as a mandatory prison term one of the prison terms prescribed for a felony of the first degree.

(f) If the amount of L.S.D. involved equals or exceeds five thousand unit doses of L.S.D. in a solid form or equals or exceeds five hundred grams of L.S.D. in a liquid concentrate, liquid extract, or liquid distillate form, possession of L.S.D. is a felony of the first degree, the offender is a major drug offender, and the court shall impose as a mandatory prison term the maximum prison term prescribed for a felony of the first degree.

(6) If the drug involved in the violation is heroin or a compound, mixture, preparation, or substance containing heroin, whoever violates division (A) of this section is guilty of possession of heroin. The penalty for the offense shall be determined as follows:

(a) Except as otherwise provided in division (C)(6)(b), (c), (d), (e), or (f) of this section, possession of heroin is a felony of the fifth degree, and division (B) of section

2929.13 of the Revised Code applies in determining whether to impose a prison term on the offender.

(b) If the amount of the drug involved equals or exceeds ten unit doses but is less than fifty unit doses or equals or exceeds one gram but is less than five grams, possession of heroin is a felony of the fourth degree, and division (C) of section 2929.13 of the Revised Code applies in determining whether to impose a prison term on the offender.

(c) If the amount of the drug involved equals or exceeds fifty unit doses but is less than one hundred unit doses or equals or exceeds five grams but is less than ten grams, possession of heroin is a felony of the third degree, and there is a presumption for a prison term for the offense.

(d) If the amount of the drug involved equals or exceeds one hundred unit doses but is less than five hundred unit doses or equals or exceeds ten grams but is less than fifty grams, possession of heroin is a felony of the second degree, and the court shall impose as a mandatory prison term one of the prison terms prescribed for a felony of the second degree.

(e) If the amount of the drug involved equals or exceeds five hundred unit doses but is less than two thousand five hundred unit doses or equals or exceeds fifty grams but is less than two hundred fifty grams, possession of heroin is a felony of the first degree, and the court shall impose as a mandatory prison term one of the prison terms prescribed for a felony of the first degree.

(f) If the amount of the drug involved equals or exceeds two thousand five hundred unit doses or equals or exceeds two hundred fifty grams, possession of heroin is a felony of the first degree, the offender is a major drug offender, and the court shall impose as a mandatory prison term the maximum prison term prescribed for a felony of the first degree.

(7) If the drug involved in the violation is hashish or a compound, mixture, preparation, or substance containing hashish, whoever violates division (A) of this section is guilty of possession of hashish. The penalty for the offense shall be determined as follows:

(a) Except as otherwise provided in division (C)(7)(b), (c), (d), (e), (f), or (g) of this section, possession of hashish is a minor misdemeanor.

(b) If the amount of the drug involved equals or exceeds five grams but is less than ten grams of hashish in a solid form or equals or exceeds one gram but is less than two grams of hashish in a liquid concentrate, liquid extract, or liquid distillate form, possession of hashish is a misdemeanor of the fourth degree.

(c) If the amount of the drug involved equals or exceeds ten grams but is less than fifty grams of hashish in a solid form or equals or exceeds two grams but is less than ten grams of hashish in a liquid concentrate, liquid extract, or liquid distillate form, possession of hashish is a felony of the fifth degree, and division (B) of section 2929.13 of the Revised Code applies in determining whether to impose a prison term on the offender.

(d) If the amount of the drug involved equals or exceeds fifty grams but is less than two hundred fifty grams of hashish in a solid form or equals or exceeds ten grams but is less than fifty grams of hashish in a liquid concentrate, liquid extract, or liquid distillate form, possession of hashish is a felony of the third degree, and division (C) of section 2929.13 of the Revised Code applies in determining whether to impose a prison term on the offender.

(e) If the amount of the drug involved equals or exceeds two hundred fifty grams but is less than one thousand grams of hashish in a solid form or equals or exceeds fifty grams but is less than two hundred grams of hashish in a liquid concentrate, liquid extract, or liquid distillate form, possession of hashish is a felony of the third degree, and there is a presumption that a prison term shall be imposed for the offense.

(f) If the amount of the drug involved equals or exceeds one thousand grams but is less than two thousand grams of hashish in a solid form or equals or exceeds two hundred grams but is less than four hundred grams of hashish in a liquid concentrate, liquid extract, or liquid distillate form, possession of hashish is a felony of the second degree, and the court shall impose a mandatory prison term of five, six, seven, or eight years.

(g) If the amount of the drug involved equals or exceeds two thousand grams of hashish in a solid form or equals or exceeds four hundred grams of hashish in a liquid concentrate, liquid extract, or liquid distillate form, possession of hashish is a felony of the second degree, and the court shall impose as a mandatory prison term the maximum prison term prescribed for a felony of the second degree.

(8) If the drug involved is 1-Pentyl-3-(1-naphthoyl)indole, 1-Butyl-3-(1-naphthoyl)indole, 1-[2-(4-morpholinyl)ethyl]-3-(1-naphthoyl)indole, 5-(1,1-dimethylheptyl)-2-[(1R,3S)-3-hydroxycyclohexyl]-phenol, or 5-(1,1-dimethyloctyl)-2-[(1R,3S)-3-hydroxycyclohexyl]-phenol or a compound, mixture, preparation, or substance containing 1-Pentyl-3-(1-naphthoyl)indole, 1-Butyl-3-(1-naphthoyl)indole, 1-[2-(4-morpholinyl)ethyl]-3-(1-naphthoyl)indole, 5-(1,1-dimethylheptyl)-2-[(1R,3S)-3-hydroxycyclohexyl]-phenol, or 5-(1,1-dimethyloctyl)-2-[(1R,3S)-3-hydroxycyclohexyl]-phenol, whoever violates division (A) of this section is guilty of possession of spice, a minor misdemeanor.

(D) Arrest or conviction for a minor misdemeanor violation of this section does not constitute a criminal record and need not be reported by the person so arrested or convicted in response to any inquiries about the person's criminal record, including any inquiries contained in any application for employment, license, or other right or privilege, or made in connection with the person's appearance as a witness.

(E) In addition to any prison term or jail term authorized or required by division (C) of this section and sections 2929.13, 2929.14, 2929.22, 2929.24, and 2929.25 of the Revised Code and in addition to any other sanction that is imposed for the offense under this section, sections 2929.11 to 2929.18, or sections 2929.21 to 2929.28 of the Revised Code, the court that sentences an offender who is convicted of or pleads guilty to a violation of division (A) of this section shall do all of the following that are applicable regarding the offender:

(1)(a) If the violation is a felony of the first, second, or third degree, the court shall impose upon the offender the mandatory fine specified for the offense under division (B)(1) of section 2929.18 of the Revised Code unless, as specified in that division, the court determines that the offender is indigent.

(b) Notwithstanding any contrary provision of section 3719.21 of the Revised Code, the clerk of the court shall pay a mandatory fine or other fine imposed for a violation of this section pursuant to division (A) of section 2929.18 of the Revised Code in accordance with and subject to the requirements of division (F) of section 2925.03 of the

Revised Code. The agency that receives the fine shall use the fine as specified in division (F) of section 2925.03 of the Revised Code.

(c) If a person is charged with a violation of this section that is a felony of the first, second, or third degree, posts bail, and forfeits the bail, the clerk shall pay the forfeited bail pursuant to division (E)(1)(b) of this section as if it were a mandatory fine imposed under division (E)(1)(a) of this section.

(2) The court shall suspend for not less than six months or more than five years the offender's driver's or commercial driver's license or permit.

(3) If the offender is a professionally licensed person, in addition to any other sanction imposed for a violation of this section, the court immediately shall comply with section 2925.38 of the Revised Code.

(F) It is an affirmative defense, as provided in section 2901.05 of the Revised Code, to a charge of a fourth degree felony violation under this section that the controlled substance that gave rise to the charge is in an amount, is in a form, is prepared, compounded, or mixed with substances that are not controlled substances in a manner, or is possessed under any other circumstances, that indicate that the substance was possessed solely for personal use. Notwithstanding any contrary provision of this section, if, in accordance with section 2901.05 of the Revised Code, an accused who is charged with a fourth degree felony violation of division (C)(2), (4), (5), or (6) of this section sustains the burden of going forward with evidence of and establishes by a preponderance of the evidence the affirmative defense described in this division, the accused may be prosecuted for and may plead guilty to or be convicted of a misdemeanor violation of division (C)(2) of this section or a fifth degree felony violation of division (C)(4), (5), or (6) of this section respectively.

(G) When a person is charged with possessing a bulk amount or multiple of a bulk amount, division (E) of section 2925.03 of the Revised Code applies regarding the determination of the amount of the controlled substance involved at the time of the offense.

**HISTORY: 138 v S 184, § 5 (Eff 6-20-84); 143 v S 258 (Eff 11-20-90); 144 v H 62 (Eff 5-21-91); 144 v H 298 (Eff 7-26-91); 145 v H 377 (Eff 9-30-93); 145 v H 391 (Eff 7-21-94); 146 v H 249 (Eff 7-17-95); 146 v S 2 (Eff 7-1-96); 146 v S 269 (Eff 7-1-96); 147 v S 2 (Eff 6-20-97); 147 v S 66 (Eff 7-22-98); 148 v S 107 (Eff 3-23-2000); 148 v H 241. Eff 5-17-2000; 149 v H 490, § 1, eff. 1-1-04; 149 v S 123, § 1, eff. 1-1-04; 151 v S 154, § 1, eff. 5-17-06; 152 v H 195, § 1, eff. 9-30-08; 2011 HB 86, § 1, eff. Sept. 30, 2011; 2011 HB 64, § 1, eff. Oct. 17, 2011.**

The effective date is set by section 4 of H.B. 490.

See provisions of § 5 of S.B. 123 (149 v —) following RC § 2925.01.

**Analogous to former RC § 2925.11 (136 v H 300; 138 v S 184), repealed 138 v S 184, § 4, eff 6-20-84.**

Acts 2011, HB 86, § 3 provides: "The amendments to sections 2925.01, 2925.03, 2925.05, and 2925.11 of the Revised Code, and to division (W) of section 2929.01 of the Revised Code, that are made in this act apply to a person who commits an offense involving marihuana, cocaine, or hashish on or after the effective date of this act and to a person to whom division (B) of section 1.58 of the Revised Code makes the amendments applicable.

"The provisions of sections 2925.01, 2925.03, 2925.05, and 2925.11 of the Revised Code, and of division (W) of section 2929.01 of the Revised Code, in existence prior to the effective date of this act shall apply to a person upon whom a court imposed sentence prior to the effective date of this act for an offense involving marihuana, cocaine, or hashish. The amendments to sections 2925.01, 2925.03, 2925.05, and 2925.11 of the Revised Code, and to division (W) of section 2929.01 of the Revised Code, that are made in this act do not apply to a person upon whom a court imposed sentence prior to the effective date of this act for an offense involving marihuana, cocaine, or hashish."

## § 2925.12 Possessing drug abuse instruments.

(A) No person shall knowingly make, obtain, possess, or use any instrument, article, or thing the customary and primary purpose of which is for the administration or use of a dangerous drug, other than marihuana, when the instrument involved is a hypodermic or syringe, whether or not of crude or extemporized manufacture or assembly, and the instrument, article, or thing involved has been used by the offender to unlawfully administer or use a dangerous drug, other than marihuana, or to prepare a dangerous drug, other than marihuana, for unlawful administration or use.

(B) This section does not apply to manufacturers, licensed health professionals authorized to prescribe drugs, pharmacists, owners of pharmacies, and other persons whose conduct was in accordance with Chapters 3719., 4715., 4723., 4729., 4730., 4731., and 4741. of the Revised Code.

(C) Whoever violates this section is guilty of possessing drug abuse instruments, a misdemeanor of the second degree. If the offender previously has been convicted of a drug abuse offense, a violation of this section is a misdemeanor of the first degree.

(D) In addition to any other sanction imposed upon an offender for a violation of this section, the court shall suspend for not less than six months or more than five years the offender's driver's or commercial driver's license or permit. If the offender is a professionally licensed person, in addition to any other sanction imposed for a violation of this section, the court immediately shall comply with section 2925.38 of the Revised Code.

**HISTORY: 136 v H 300 (Eff 7-1-76); 143 v S 258 (Eff 11-20-90); 145 v H 377 (Eff 9-30-93); 145 v H 391 (Eff 7-21-94); 146 v S 2 (Eff 7-1-96); 146 v S 269 (Eff 7-1-96); 147 v S 66 (Eff 7-22-98); 148 v H 241. Eff 5-17-2000; 149 v S 123, § 1, eff. 1-1-04; 151 v S 154, § 1, eff. 5-17-06.**

The effective date is set by section 4 of S.B. 123.

See provisions of § 5 of S.B. 123 (149 v —) following RC § 2925.01.

## § 2925.13 Permitting drug abuse.

(A) No person who is the owner, operator, or person in charge of a locomotive, watercraft, aircraft, or other vehicle, as defined in division (A) of section 4501.01 of the Revised Code, shall knowingly permit the vehicle to be used for the commission of a felony drug abuse offense.

(B) No person who is the owner, lessee, or occupant, or who has custody, control, or supervision, of premises or real estate, including vacant land, shall knowingly permit the premises or real estate, including vacant land, to be used for the commission of a felony drug abuse offense by another person.

(C)(1) Whoever violates this section is guilty of permitting drug abuse.

(2) Except as provided in division (C) (3) of this section, permitting drug abuse is a misdemeanor of the first degree.

(3) Permitting drug abuse is a felony of the fifth degree, and division (C) of section 2929.13 of the Revised Code

applies in determining whether to impose a prison term on the offender, if the felony drug abuse offense in question is a violation of section 2925.02 or 2925.03 of the Revised Code.

(D) In addition to any prison term authorized or required by division (C) of this section and sections 2929.13 and 2929.14 of the Revised Code and in addition to any other sanction imposed for the offense under this section or sections 2929.11 to 2929.18 of the Revised Code, the court that sentences a person who is convicted of or pleads guilty to a violation of division (A) of this section shall do all of the following that are applicable regarding the offender:

(1) The court shall suspend for not less than six months or more than five years the offender's driver's or commercial driver's license or permit.

(2) If the offender is a professionally licensed person, in addition to any other sanction imposed for a violation of this section, the court immediately shall comply with section 2925.38 of the Revised Code.

(E) Notwithstanding any contrary provision of section 3719.21 of the Revised Code, the clerk of the court shall pay a fine imposed for a violation of this section pursuant to division (A) of section 2929.18 of the Revised Code in accordance with and subject to the requirements of division (F) of section 2925.03 of the Revised Code. The agency that receives the fine shall use the fine as specified in division (F) of section 2925.03 of the Revised Code.

(F) Any premises or real estate that is permitted to be used in violation of division (B) of this section constitutes a nuisance subject to abatement pursuant to Chapter 3767. of the Revised Code.

**HISTORY: 136 v H 300 (Eff 7-1-76); 143 v H 215 (Eff 4-11-90); 143 v S 258 (Eff 11-20-90); 144 v H 591 (Eff 11-2-92); 145 v H 377 (Eff 9-30-93); 146 v S 2 (Eff 7-1-96); 146 v S 269 (Eff 7-1-96); 148 v S 107. Eff 3-23-2000; 149 v S 123, § 1, eff. 1-1-04.**

The effective date is set by section 4 of S.B. 123.

See provisions of § 5 of S.B. 123 (149 v —) following RC § 2925.01.

## § 2925.14 Drug paraphernalia offenses.

(A) As used in this section, "drug paraphernalia" means any equipment, product, or material of any kind that is used by the offender, intended by the offender for use, or designed for use, in propagating, cultivating, growing, harvesting, manufacturing, compounding, converting, producing, processing, preparing, testing, analyzing, packaging, repackaging, storing, containing, concealing, injecting, ingesting, inhaling, or otherwise introducing into the human body, a controlled substance in violation of this chapter. "Drug paraphernalia" includes, but is not limited to, any of the following equipment, products, or materials that are used by the offender, intended by the offender for use, or designed by the offender for use, in any of the following manners:

(1) A kit for propagating, cultivating, growing, or harvesting any species of a plant that is a controlled substance or from which a controlled substance can be derived;

(2) A kit for manufacturing, compounding, converting, producing, processing, or preparing a controlled substance;

(3) Any object, instrument, or device for manufacturing, compounding, converting, producing, processing, or preparing methamphetamine;

(4) An isomerization device for increasing the potency of any species of a plant that is a controlled substance;

(5) Testing equipment for identifying, or analyzing the strength, effectiveness, or purity of, a controlled substance;

(6) A scale or balance for weighing or measuring a controlled substance;

(7) A diluent or adulterant, such as quinine hydrochloride, mannitol, mannite, dextrose, or lactose, for cutting a controlled substance;

(8) A separation gin or sifter for removing twigs and seeds from, or otherwise cleaning or refining, marihuana;

(9) A blender, bowl, container, spoon, or mixing device for compounding a controlled substance;

(10) A capsule, balloon, envelope, or container for packaging small quantities of a controlled substance;

(11) A container or device for storing or concealing a controlled substance;

(12) A hypodermic syringe, needle, or instrument for parenterally injecting a controlled substance into the human body;

(13) An object, instrument, or device for ingesting, inhaling, or otherwise introducing into the human body, marihuana, cocaine, hashish, or hashish oil, such as a metal, wooden, acrylic, glass, stone, plastic, or ceramic pipe, with or without a screen, permanent screen, hashish head, or punctured metal bowl; water pipe; carburetion tube or device; smoking or carburetion mask; roach clip or similar object used to hold burning material, such as a marihuana cigarette, that has become too small or too short to be held in the hand; miniature cocaine spoon, or cocaine vial; chamber pipe; carburetor pipe; electric pipe; air driver pipe; chillum; bong; or ice pipe or chiller.

(B) In determining if any equipment, product, or material is drug paraphernalia, a court or law enforcement officer shall consider, in addition to other relevant factors, the following:

(1) Any statement by the owner, or by anyone in control, of the equipment, product, or material, concerning its use;

(2) The proximity in time or space of the equipment, product, or material, or of the act relating to the equipment, product, or material, to a violation of any provision of this chapter;

(3) The proximity of the equipment, product, or material to any controlled substance;

(4) The existence of any residue of a controlled substance on the equipment, product, or material;

(5) Direct or circumstantial evidence of the intent of the owner, or of anyone in control, of the equipment, product, or material, to deliver it to any person whom the owner or person in control of the equipment, product, or material knows intends to use the object to facilitate a violation of any provision of this chapter. A finding that the owner, or anyone in control, of the equipment, product, or material, is not guilty of a violation of any other provision of this chapter does not prevent a finding that the equipment, product, or material was intended or designed by the offender for use as drug paraphernalia.

(6) Any oral or written instruction provided with the equipment, product, or material concerning its use;

(7) Any descriptive material accompanying the equipment, product, or material and explaining or depicting its use;

(8) National or local advertising concerning the use of the equipment, product, or material;

(9) The manner and circumstances in which the equipment, product, or material is displayed for sale;

(10) Direct or circumstantial evidence of the ratio of the sales of the equipment, product, or material to the total sales of the business enterprise;

(11) The existence and scope of legitimate uses of the equipment, product, or material in the community;

(12) Expert testimony concerning the use of the equipment, product, or material.

(C)(1) No person shall knowingly use, or possess with purpose to use, drug paraphernalia.

(2) No person shall knowingly sell, or possess or manufacture with purpose to sell, drug paraphernalia, if the person knows or reasonably should know that the equipment, product, or material will be used as drug paraphernalia.

(3) No person shall place an advertisement in any newspaper, magazine, handbill, or other publication that is published and printed and circulates primarily within this state, if the person knows that the purpose of the advertisement is to promote the illegal sale in this state of the equipment, product, or material that the offender intended or designed for use as drug paraphernalia.

(D) This section does not apply to manufacturers, licensed health professionals authorized to prescribe drugs, pharmacists, owners of pharmacies, and other persons whose conduct is in accordance with Chapters 3719., 4715., 4723., 4729., 4730., 4731., and 4741. of the Revised Code. This section shall not be construed to prohibit the possession or use of a hypodermic as authorized by section 3719.172 [3719.17.2] of the Revised Code.

(E) Notwithstanding Chapter 2981. of the Revised Code, any drug paraphernalia that was used, possessed, sold, or manufactured in a violation of this section shall be seized, after a conviction for that violation shall be forfeited, and upon forfeiture shall be disposed of pursuant to division (B) of section 2981.12 of the Revised Code.

(F)(1) Whoever violates division (C)(1) of this section is guilty of illegal use or possession of drug paraphernalia, a misdemeanor of the fourth degree.

(2) Except as provided in division (F)(3) of this section, whoever violates division (C)(2) of this section is guilty of dealing in drug paraphernalia, a misdemeanor of the second degree.

(3) Whoever violates division (C)(2) of this section by selling drug paraphernalia to a juvenile is guilty of selling drug paraphernalia to juveniles, a misdemeanor of the first degree.

(4) Whoever violates division (C)(3) of this section is guilty of illegal advertising of drug paraphernalia, a misdemeanor of the second degree.

(G) In addition to any other sanction imposed upon an offender for a violation of this section, the court shall suspend for not less than six months or more than five years the offender's driver's or commercial driver's license or permit. If the offender is a professionally licensed person, in addition to any other sanction imposed for a violation of this section, the court immediately shall comply with section 2925.38 of the Revised Code.

**HISTORY: 143 v H 182 (Eff 11-2-89); 143 v S 258 (Eff 11-20-90); 145 v H 377 (Eff 9-30-93); 145 v H 391 (Eff 7-21-94); 146 v S 2 (Eff 7-1-96); 146 v S 269 (Eff 7-1-96); 147 v S 66 (Eff 7-22-98); 148 v H 241 (Eff 5-17-2000); 149 v H 7. Eff 8-7-2001; 149 v S 123, § 1, eff. 1-1-04; 151 v S 53, § 1, eff. 5-17-06; 151 v S 154, § 1, eff. 5-17-06; 151 v H 241, § 1, eff. 7-1-07.**

The provisions of § 3(B) of 151 v H 241 read as follows:

SECTION 3. * * * (B) Section 2925.14 of the Revised Code is presented in this act as a composite of the section as amended by both Am. Sub. S.B. 53 and Sub. S.B. 154 of the 126th General Assembly. The General Assembly, applying the principle stated in division (B) of section 1.52 of the Revised Code that amendments are to be harmonized if reasonably capable of simultaneous operation, finds that the composite is the resulting version of the section in effect prior to the effective date of the section as presented in this act.

See provisions of § 4 of 151 v H 241 following RC § 2901.01.

The effective date is set by section 4 of S.B. 123.

See provisions of § 5 of S.B. 123 (149 v —) following RC § 2925.01.

**Analogous in part to former RC § 2925.14 (138 v S 378; 142 v H 790), repealed, 143 v H 182, § 2, eff 11-2-89.**

## [DRUG THEFT]

**§ 2925.21** Repealed, 143 v S 258, § 2 [136 v H 300]. Eff 11-20-90.

This section concerned theft of drugs.

The effective date is set by section 15 of SB 258.

## § 2925.22 Deception to obtain a dangerous drug.

(A) No person, by deception, shall procure the administration of, a prescription for, or the dispensing of, a dangerous drug or shall possess an uncompleted preprinted prescription blank used for writing a prescription for a dangerous drug.

(B) Whoever violates this section is guilty of deception to obtain a dangerous drug. The penalty for the offense shall be determined as follows:

(1) If the person possesses an uncompleted preprinted prescription blank used for writing a prescription for a dangerous drug or if the drug involved is a dangerous drug, except as otherwise provided in division (B)(2) or (3) of this section, deception to obtain a dangerous drug is a felony of the fifth degree or, if the offender previously has been convicted of or pleaded guilty to a drug abuse offense, a felony of the fourth degree. Division (C) of section 2929.13 of the Revised Code applies in determining whether to impose a prison term on the offender pursuant to this division.

(2) If the drug involved is a compound, mixture, preparation, or substance included in schedule I or II, with the exception of marihuana, the penalty for deception to obtain drugs is one of the following:

(a) Except as otherwise provided in division (B)(2)(b), (c), or (d) of this section, it is a felony of the fourth degree, and division (C) of section 2929.13 of the Revised Code applies in determining whether to impose a prison term on the offender.

(b) If the amount of the drug involved equals or exceeds the bulk amount but is less than five times the bulk amount, or if the amount of the drug involved that could be obtained pursuant to the prescription would equal or exceed the bulk amount but would be less than five times the bulk amount, it is a felony of the third degree, and there is a presumption for a prison term for the offense.

(c) If the amount of the drug involved equals or exceeds five times the bulk amount but is less than fifty times the bulk amount, or if the amount of the drug involved that could be obtained pursuant to the prescription would equal or exceed five times the bulk amount but would be less than fifty times the bulk amount, it is a felony of the second degree, and there is a presumption for a prison term for the offense.

(d) If the amount of the drug involved equals or exceeds fifty times the bulk amount, or if the amount of the drug involved that could be obtained pursuant to the prescription would equal or exceed fifty times the bulk amount, it is a felony of the first degree, and there is a presumption for a prison term for the offense.

(3) If the drug involved is a compound, mixture, preparation, or substance included in schedule III, IV, or V or is marihuana, the penalty for deception to obtain a dangerous drug is one of the following:

(a) Except as otherwise provided in division (B)(3)(b), (c), or (d) of this section it is a felony of the fifth degree, and division (C) of section 2929.13 of the Revised Code applies in determining whether to impose a prison term on the offender.

(b) If the amount of the drug involved equals or exceeds the bulk amount but is less than five times the bulk amount, or if the amount of the drug involved that could be obtained pursuant to the prescription would equal or exceed the bulk amount but would be less than five times the bulk amount, it is a felony of the fourth degree, and division (C) of section 2929.13 of the Revised Code applies in determining whether to impose a prison term on the offender.

(c) If the amount of the drug involved equals or exceeds five times the bulk amount but is less than fifty times the bulk amount, or if the amount of the drug involved that could be obtained pursuant to the prescription would equal or exceed five times the bulk amount but would be less than fifty times the bulk amount, it is a felony of the third degree, and there is a presumption for a prison term for the offense.

(d) If the amount of the drug involved equals or exceeds fifty times the bulk amount, or if the amount of the drug involved that could be obtained pursuant to the prescription would equal or exceed fifty times the bulk amount, it is a felony of the second degree, and there is a presumption for a prison term for the offense.

(C) In addition to any prison term authorized or required by division (B) of this section and sections 2929.13 and 2929.14 of the Revised Code and in addition to any other sanction imposed for the offense under this section or sections 2929.11 to 2929.18 of the Revised Code, the court that sentences an offender who is convicted of or pleads guilty to a violation of division (A) of this section shall do both of the following:

(1) The court shall suspend for not less than six months or more than five years the offender's driver's or commercial driver's license or permit.

(2) If the offender is a professionally licensed person, in addition to any other sanction imposed for a violation of this section, the court immediately shall comply with section 2925.38 of the Revised Code.

(D) Notwithstanding any contrary provision of section 3719.21 of the Revised Code, the clerk of the court shall pay a fine imposed for a violation of this section pursuant to division (A) of section 2929.18 of the Revised Code in accordance with and subject to the requirements of division (F) of section 2925.03 of the Revised Code. The agency that receives the fine shall use the fine as specified in division (F) of section 2925.03 of the Revised Code.

**HISTORY: 136 v H 300 (Eff 7-1-76); 143 v S 258 (Eff 11-20-90); 143 v H 615 (Eff 3-27-91); 145 v H 377 (Eff 9-30-93); 146 v S 2 (Eff 7-1-96); 146 v S 269. Eff 7-1-96; 149 v S 123, § 1, eff. 1-1-04; 152 v H 195, § 1, eff. 9-30-08.**

The effective date is set by section 4 of S.B. 123.

See provisions of § 5 of S.B. 123 (149 v —) following RC § 2925.01.

## § 2925.23 Illegal processing of drug documents.

(A) No person shall knowingly make a false statement in any prescription, order, report, or record required by Chapter 3719. or 4729. of the Revised Code.

(B) No person shall intentionally make, utter, or sell, or knowingly possess any of the following that is a false or forged:

(1) Prescription;

(2) Uncompleted preprinted prescription blank used for writing a prescription;

(3) Official written order;

(4) License for a terminal distributor of dangerous drugs as required in section 4729.60 of the Revised Code;

(5) Registration certificate for a wholesale distributor of dangerous drugs as required in section 4729.60 of the Revised Code.

(C) No person, by theft as defined in section 2913.02 of the Revised Code, shall acquire any of the following:

(1) A prescription;

(2) An uncompleted preprinted prescription blank used for writing a prescription;

(3) An official written order;

(4) A blank official written order;

(5) A license or blank license for a terminal distributor of dangerous drugs as required in section 4729.60 of the Revised Code;

(6) A registration certificate or blank registration certificate for a wholesale distributor of dangerous drugs as required in section 4729.60 of the Revised Code.

(D) No person shall knowingly make or affix any false or forged label to a package or receptacle containing any dangerous drugs.

(E) Divisions (A) and (D) of this section do not apply to licensed health professionals authorized to prescribe drugs, pharmacists, owners of pharmacies, and other persons whose conduct is in accordance with Chapters 3719., 4715., 4723., 4725., 4729., 4730., 4731., and 4741. of the Revised Code.

(F) Whoever violates this section is guilty of illegal processing of drug documents. If the offender violates division (B)(2), (4), or (5) or division (C)(2), (4), (5), or (6) of this section, illegal processing of drug documents is a felony of the fifth degree. If the offender violates division (A), division (B)(1) or (3), division (C)(1) or (3), or division (D) of this section, the penalty for illegal processing of drug documents shall be determined as follows:

(1) If the drug involved is a compound, mixture, preparation, or substance included in schedule I or II, with the exception of marihuana, illegal processing of drug documents is a felony of the fourth degree, and division (C) of section 2929.13 of the Revised Code applies in determining whether to impose a prison term on the offender.

(2) If the drug involved is a dangerous drug or a compound, mixture, preparation, or substance included in schedule III, IV, or V or is marihuana, illegal processing of drug documents is a felony of the fifth degree, and division (C) of section 2929.13 of the Revised Code applies in

determining whether to impose a prison term on the offender.

(G) In addition to any prison term authorized or required by division (F) of this section and sections 2929.13 and 2929.14 of the Revised Code and in addition to any other sanction imposed for the offense under this section or sections 2929.11 to 2929.18 of the Revised Code, the court that sentences an offender who is convicted of or pleads guilty to any violation of divisions (A) to (D) of this section shall do both of the following:

(1) The court shall suspend for not less than six months or more than five years the offender's driver's or commercial driver's license or permit.

(2) If the offender is a professionally licensed person, in addition to any other sanction imposed for a violation of this section, the court immediately shall comply with section 2925.38 of the Revised Code.

(H) Notwithstanding any contrary provision of section 3719.21 of the Revised Code, the clerk of court shall pay a fine imposed for a violation of this section pursuant to division (A) of section 2929.18 of the Revised Code in accordance with and subject to the requirements of division (F) of section 2925.03 of the Revised Code. The agency that receives the fine shall use the fine as specified in division (F) of section 2925.03 of the Revised Code.

**HISTORY: 136 v H 300 (Eff 7-1-76); 143 v S 258 (Eff 11-20-90); 144 v S 110 (Eff 5-19-92); 145 v H 377 (Eff 9-30-93); 145 v H 391 (7-21-94); 146 v S 2 (Eff 7-1-96); 146 v S 269 (Eff 7-1-96); 147 v S 66 (Eff 7-22-98); 148 v S 107 (Eff 3-23-2000); 148 v H 241 (Eff 5-17-2000); 149 v H 327. Eff 7-8-2002; 149 v S 123, § 1, eff. 1-1-04; 151 v S 154, § 1, eff. 5-17-06.**

The effective date is set by section 4 of S.B. 123.

See provisions of § 5 of S.B. 123 (149 v —) following RC § 2925.01.

## § 2925.24 Tampering with drugs.

(A) No person shall knowingly adulterate or alter any dangerous drug or substitute any dangerous drug with another substance.

(B) No person shall knowingly adulterate or alter any package or receptacle containing any dangerous drug or substitute any package or receptacle containing any dangerous drug with another package or receptacle.

(C) Divisions (A) and (B) of this section do not apply to manufacturers, practitioners, pharmacists, owners of pharmacies, nurses, and other persons, when the conduct of the manufacturer, practitioner, pharmacist, owner of a pharmacy, nurse, or other person is in accordance with Chapters 3719., 4715., 4723., 4729., 4731., and 4741. of the Revised Code.

(D) It is an affirmative defense to a charge under this section alleging that a person altered a dangerous drug that the dangerous drug the person allegedly altered was lawfully prescribed for the person's personal use and that the person did not sell or transfer or intend to sell or transfer the dangerous drug to another person.

(E) Whoever violates this section is guilty of tampering with drugs, a felony of the third degree. If the violation results in physical harm to any person, tampering with drugs is a felony of the second degree.

**HISTORY: 148 v H 202. Eff 2-9-2000.**

[HARMFUL INTOXICANTS]

## § 2925.31 Abusing harmful intoxicants.

(A) Except for lawful research, clinical, medical, dental, or veterinary purposes, no person, with purpose to induce intoxication or similar physiological effects, shall obtain, possess, or use a harmful intoxicant.

(B) Whoever violates this section is guilty of abusing harmful intoxicants, a misdemeanor of the first degree. If the offender previously has been convicted of a drug abuse offense, abusing harmful intoxicants is a felony of the fifth degree.

(C) In addition to any other sanction imposed upon an offender for a violation of this section, the court shall suspend for not less than six months or more than five years the offender's driver's or commercial driver's license or permit. If the offender is a professionally licensed person, in addition to any other sanction imposed for a violation of this section, the court IMMEDIATELY shall comply with section 2925.38 of the Revised Code.

**HISTORY: 136 v H 300 (Eff 7-1-76); 143 v S 258 (Eff 11-20-90); 145 v H 377 (Eff 9-30-93); 146 v S 2 (Eff 7-1-96); 146 v H 162. Eff 1-1-97; 149 v S 123, § 1, eff. 1-1-04.**

The effective date is set by section 4 of S.B. 123.

See provisions of § 5 of S.B. 123 (149 v —) following RC § 2925.01.

## § 2925.32 Trafficking in harmful intoxicants; improperly dispensing or distributing nitrous oxide.

(A) Divisions (A) (1) and (2) of this section do not apply to the dispensing or distributing of nitrous oxide.

(1) No person shall knowingly dispense or distribute a harmful intoxicant to a person age eighteen or older if the person who dispenses or distributes it knows or has reason to believe that the harmful intoxicant will be used in violation of section 2925.31 of the Revised Code.

(2) No person shall knowingly dispense or distribute a harmful intoxicant to a person under age eighteen if the person who dispenses or distributes it knows or has reason to believe that the harmful intoxicant will be used in violation of section 2925.31 of the Revised Code. Division (A) (2) of this section does not prohibit either of the following:

(a) Dispensing or distributing a harmful intoxicant to a person under age eighteen if a written order from the juvenile's parent or guardian is provided to the dispenser or distributor;

(b) Dispensing or distributing gasoline or diesel fuel to a person under age eighteen if the dispenser or distributor does not know or have reason to believe the product will be used in violation of section 2925.31 of the Revised Code. Division (A) (2) (a) of this section does not require a person to obtain a written order from the parent or guardian of a person under age eighteen in order to distribute or dispense gasoline or diesel fuel to the person.

(B)(1) No person shall knowingly dispense or distribute nitrous oxide to a person age twenty-one or older if the person who dispenses or distributes it knows or has reason to believe the nitrous oxide will be used in violation of section 2925.31 of the Revised Code.

(2) Except for lawful medical, dental, or clinical purposes, no person shall knowingly dispense or distribute nitrous oxide to a person under age twenty-one.

(3) No person, at the time a cartridge of nitrous oxide is sold to another person, shall sell a device that allows the purchaser to inhale nitrous oxide from cartridges or to hold nitrous oxide released from cartridges for purposes of inhalation. The sale of any such device constitutes a rebuttable presumption that the person knew or had reason to believe that the purchaser intended to abuse the nitrous oxide.

(4) No person who dispenses or distributes nitrous oxide in cartridges shall fail to comply with either of the following:

(a) The record-keeping requirements established under division (F) of this section;

(b) The labeling and transaction identification requirements established under division (G) of this section.

(C) This section does not apply to products used in making, fabricating, assembling, transporting, or constructing a product or structure by manual labor or machinery for sale or lease to another person, or to the mining, refining, or processing of natural deposits.

(D)(1) Whoever violates division (A) (1) or (2) or division (B) (1), (2), or (3) of this section is guilty of trafficking in harmful intoxicants, a felony of the fifth degree. If the offender previously has been convicted of a drug abuse offense, trafficking in harmful intoxicants is a felony of the fourth degree. In addition to any other sanction imposed upon an offender for trafficking in harmful intoxicants, the court shall suspend for not less than six months or more than five years the offender's driver's or commercial driver's license or permit. If the offender is a professionally licensed person, in addition to any other sanction imposed for trafficking in harmful intoxicants, the court immediately shall comply with section 2925.38 of the Revised Code.

(2) Whoever violates division (B) (4) (a) or (b) of this section is guilty of improperly dispensing or distributing nitrous oxide, a misdemeanor of the fourth degree.

(E) It is an affirmative defense to a charge of a violation of division (A) (2) or (B) (2) of this section that:

(1) An individual exhibited to the defendant or an officer or employee of the defendant, for purposes of establishing the individual's age, a driver's license or permit issued by this state, a commercial driver's license or permit issued by this state, an identification card issued pursuant to section 4507.50 of the Revised Code, for† another document that purports to be a license, permit, or identification card described in this division;

(2) The document exhibited appeared to be a genuine, unaltered document, to pertain to the individual, and to establish the individual's age;

(3) The defendant or the officer or employee of the defendant otherwise did not have reasonable cause to believe that the individual was under the age represented.

(F) Beginning July 1, 2001, a person who dispenses or distributes nitrous oxide shall record each transaction involving the dispensing or distributing of the nitrous oxide on a separate card. The person shall require the purchaser to sign the card and provide a complete residence address. The person dispensing or distributing the nitrous oxide shall sign and date the card. The person shall retain the card recording a transaction for one year from the date of the transaction. The person shall maintain the cards at the person's business address and make them available during normal business hours for inspection and copying by officers or employees of the state board of pharmacy or of other law enforcement agencies of this state or the United States that are authorized to investigate violations of Chapter 2925., 3719., or 4729. of the Revised Code or the federal drug abuse control laws.

The cards used to record each transaction shall inform the purchaser of the following:

(1) That nitrous oxide cartridges are to be used only for purposes of preparing food;

(2) That inhalation of nitrous oxide can have dangerous health effects;

(3) That it is a violation of state law to distribute or dispense cartridges of nitrous oxide to any person under age twenty-one, punishable as a felony of the fifth degree.

(G)(1) Each cartridge of nitrous oxide dispensed or distributed in this state shall bear the following printed warning:

"Nitrous oxide cartridges are to be used only for purposes of preparing food. Nitrous oxide cartridges may not be sold to persons under age twenty-one. Do not inhale contents. Misuse can be dangerous to your health."

(2) Each time a person dispenses or distributes one or more cartridges of nitrous oxide, the person shall mark the packaging containing the cartridges with a label or other device that identifies the person who dispensed or distributed the nitrous oxide and the person's business address.

**HISTORY: 136 v S 414 (Eff 9-22-76); 143 v S 258 (Eff 11-20-90); 145 v H 377 (Eff 9-30-93); 146 v S 2 (Eff 7-1-96); 146 v H 162 (Eff 1-1-97); 147 v H 122 (Eff 7-29-98); 148 v S 55 (Eff 10-26-99); 148 v H 331. Eff 10-10-2000; 149 v S 123, § 1, eff. 1-1-04.**

† The word "for" appears in the enactment of division (E)(1) by HB 162 (146 v —).

The effective date is set by section 4 of S.B. 123.

See provisions of § 5 of S.B. 123 (149 v —) following RC § 2925.01.

In amending sections 1547.69, 2911.21, 2921.13, 2923.12, 2923.121, 2923.123, 2923.13, 2923.16, 2953.32, and 4749.10 of the Revised Code and in enacting sections 109.69, 109.731, 311.41, 311.42, and 2923.124 to 2923.1212 of the Revised Code in this act, the General Assembly hereby declares its intent to recognize both of the following:

The inalienable and fundamental right of an individual to defend the individual's person and the members of the individual's family;

The fact that the right described in division (A) of this section predates the adoption of the United States Constitution, the adoption of the Ohio Constitution, and the enactment of all statutory laws by the General Assembly and may not be infringed by any enactment of the General Assembly.

## § 2925.33 Possessing nitrous oxide in motor vehicle.

(A) As used in this section, "motor vehicle," "street," and "highway" have the same meanings as in section 4511.01 of the Revised Code.

(B) Unless authorized under Chapter 3719., 4715., 4729., 4731., 4741., or 4765. of the Revised Code, no person shall possess an open cartridge of nitrous oxide in either of the following circumstances:

(1) While operating or being a passenger in or on a motor vehicle on a street, highway, or other public or private property open to the public for purposes of vehicular traffic or parking;

(2) While being in or on a stationary motor vehicle on a street, highway, or other public or private property open to the public for purposes of vehicular traffic or parking.

(C) Whoever violates this section is guilty of possessing nitrous oxide in a motor vehicle, a misdemeanor of the fourth degree.

**HISTORY: 146 v H 162. Eff 1-1-97.**

The effective date is set by section 3 of HB 162.

[DRUG SAMPLES]

### § 2925.36 Illegal dispensing of drug samples.

(A) No person shall knowingly furnish another a sample drug.

(B) Division (A) of this section does not apply to manufacturers, wholesalers, pharmacists, owners of pharmacies, licensed health professionals authorized to prescribe drugs, and other persons whose conduct is in accordance with Chapters 3719., 4715., 4723., 4725., 4729., 4730., 4731., and 4741. of the Revised Code.

(C)(1) Whoever violates this section is guilty of illegal dispensing of drug samples.

(2) If the drug involved in the offense is a compound, mixture, preparation, or substance included in schedule I or II, with the exception of marihuana, the penalty for the offense shall be determined as follows:

(a) Except as otherwise provided in division (C)(2)(b) of this section, illegal dispensing of drug samples is a felony of the fifth degree, and, subject to division (E) of this section, division (C) of section 2929.13 of the Revised Code applies in determining whether to impose a prison term on the offender.

(b) If the offense was committed in the vicinity of a school or in the vicinity of a juvenile, illegal dispensing of drug samples is a felony of the fourth degree, and, subject to division (E) of this section, division (C) of section 2929.13 of the Revised Code applies in determining whether to impose a prison term on the offender.

(3) If the drug involved in the offense is a dangerous drug or a compound, mixture, preparation, or substance included in schedule III, IV, or V, or is marihuana, the penalty for the offense shall be determined as follows:

(a) Except as otherwise provided in division (C)(3)(b) of this section, illegal dispensing of drug samples is a misdemeanor of the second degree.

(b) If the offense was committed in the vicinity of a school or in the vicinity of a juvenile, illegal dispensing of drug samples is a misdemeanor of the first degree.

(D) In addition to any prison term authorized or required by division (C) or (E) of this section and sections 2929.13 and 2929.14 of the Revised Code and in addition to any other sanction imposed for the offense under this section or sections 2929.11 to 2929.18 of the Revised Code, the court that sentences an offender who is convicted of or pleads guilty to a violation of division (A) of this section shall do both of the following:

(1) The court shall suspend for not less than six months or more than five years the offender's driver's or commercial driver's license or permit.

(2) If the offender is a professionally licensed person, in addition to any other sanction imposed for a violation of this section, the court immediately shall comply with section 2925.38 of the Revised Code.

(E) Notwithstanding the prison term authorized or required by division (C) of this section and sections 2929.13 and 2929.14 of the Revised Code, if the violation of division (A) of this section involves the sale, offer to sell, or possession of a schedule I or II controlled substance, with the exception of marihuana, and if the court imposing sentence upon the offender finds that the offender as a result of the violation is a major drug offender and is guilty of a specification of the type described in section 2941.1410 of the Revised Code, the court, in lieu of the prison term otherwise authorized or required, shall impose upon the offender the mandatory prison term specified in division (B)(3)(a) of section 2929.14 of the Revised Code.

(F) Notwithstanding any contrary provision of section 3719.21 of the Revised Code, the clerk of the court shall pay a fine imposed for a violation of this section pursuant to division (A) of section 2929.18 of the Revised Code in accordance with and subject to the requirements of division (F) of section 2925.03 of the Revised Code. The agency that receives the fine shall use the fine as specified in division (F) of section 2925.03 of the Revised Code.

**HISTORY: 136 v H 300 (Eff 7-1-76); 143 v H 215 (Eff 4-11-90); 143 v S 258 (Eff 11-20-90); 144 v S 110 (Eff 5-19-92); 144 v H 591 (Eff 11-2-92); 145 v H 377 (Eff 9-30-93); 145 v H 391 (Eff 7-21-94); 146 v S 2 (Eff 7-1-96); 146 v S 269 (Eff 7-1-96); 148 v S 107 (Eff 3-23-2000); 148 v H 241. Eff 5-17-2000; 149 v S 123, § 1, eff. 1-1-04; 151 v S 154, § 1, eff. 5-17-06; 2011 HB 86, § 1, eff. Sept. 30, 2011.**

The effective date is set by section 4 of S.B. 123.

See provisions of § 5 of S.B. 123 (149 v —) following RC § 2925.01.

### § 2925.37 Offenses involving counterfeit controlled substances.

(A) No person shall knowingly possess any counterfeit controlled substance.

(B) No person shall knowingly make, sell, offer to sell, or deliver any substance that the person knows is a counterfeit controlled substance.

(C) No person shall make, possess, sell, offer to sell, or deliver any punch, die, plate, stone, or other device knowing or having reason to know that it will be used to print or reproduce a trademark, trade name, or other identifying mark upon a counterfeit controlled substance.

(D) No person shall sell, offer to sell, give, or deliver any counterfeit controlled substance to a juvenile.

(E) No person shall directly or indirectly represent a counterfeit controlled substance as a controlled substance by describing its effects as the physical or psychological effects associated with use of a controlled substance.

(F) No person shall directly or indirectly falsely represent or advertise a counterfeit controlled substance as a controlled substance. As used in this division, "advertise" means engaging in "advertisement, " as defined in section 3715.01 of the Revised Code.

(G) Whoever violates division (A) of this section is guilty of possession of counterfeit controlled substances, a misdemeanor of the first degree.

(H) Whoever violates division (B) or (C) of this section is guilty of trafficking in counterfeit controlled substances. Except as otherwise provided in this division, trafficking in counterfeit controlled substances is a felony of the fifth degree, and division (C) of section 2929.13 of the Revised Code applies in determining whether to impose a prison term on the offender. If the offense was committed in the vicinity of a school or in the vicinity of a juvenile, trafficking in counterfeit controlled substances is a felony of the fourth degree, and division (C) of section 2929.13 of the Revised Code applies in determining whether to impose a prison term on the offender.

(I) Whoever violates division (D) of this section is guilty of aggravated trafficking in counterfeit controlled substances. Except as otherwise provided in this division, aggravated trafficking in counterfeit controlled substances is a felony of the fourth degree, and division (C) of section 2929.13 of the Revised Code applies in determining whether to impose a prison term on the offender.

(J) Whoever violates division (E) of this section is guilty of promoting and encouraging drug abuse. Except as otherwise provided in this division, promoting and encouraging drug abuse is a felony of the fifth degree, and division (C) of section 2929.13 of the Revised Code applies in determining whether to impose a prison term on the offender. If the offense was committed in the vicinity of a school or in the vicinity of a juvenile, promoting and encouraging drug abuse is a felony of the fourth degree, and division (C) of section 2929.13 of the Revised Code applies in determining whether to impose a prison term on the offender.

(K) Whoever violates division (F) of this section is guilty of fraudulent drug advertising. Except as otherwise provided in this division, fraudulent drug advertising is a felony of the fifth degree, and division (C) of section 2929.13 of the Revised Code applies in determining whether to impose a prison term on the offender. If the offense was committed in the vicinity of a school or in the vicinity of a juvenile, fraudulent drug advertising is a felony of the fourth degree, and division (C) of section 2929.13 of the Revised Code applies in determining whether to impose a prison term on the offender.

(L) In addition to any prison term authorized or required by divisions (H) to (K) of this section and sections 2929.13 and 2929.14 of the Revised Code and in addition to any other sanction imposed for the offense under this section or sections 2929.11 to 2929.18 of the Revised Code, the court that sentences an offender who is convicted of or pleads guilty to a violation of division (B), (C), (D), (E), or (F) of this section shall do both of the following:

(1) The court shall suspend for not less than six months or more than five years the offender's driver's or commercial driver's license or permit.

(2) If the offender is a professionally licensed person, in addition to any other sanction imposed for a violation of this section, the court immediately shall comply with section 2925.38 of the Revised Code.

(M) Notwithstanding any contrary provision of section 3719.21 of the Revised Code, the clerk of the court shall pay a fine imposed for a violation of this section pursuant to division (A) of section 2929.18 of the Revised Code in accordance with and subject to the requirements of division (F) of section 2925.03 of the Revised Code. The agency that receives the fine shall use the fine as specified in division (F) of section 2925.03 of the Revised Code.

**HISTORY: 139 v H 535 (Eff 8-20-82); 143 v S 258 (Eff 11-20-90); 145 v H 377 (Eff 9-30-93); 146 v S 2 (Eff 7-1-96); 146 v S 269. Eff 7-1-96; 149 v S 123, § 1, eff. 1-1-04.**

The effective date is set by section 4 of S.B. 123.

See provisions of § 5 of S.B. 123 (149 v —) following RC § 2925.01.

## § 2925.38 Convictions to be reported to professional licensing authorities.

If a person who is convicted of or pleads guilty to a violation of section 2925.02, 2925.03, 2925.04, 2925.041, 2925.05, 2925.06, 2925.11, 2925.12, 2925.13, 2925.14, 2925.22, 2925.23, 2925.31, 2925.32, 2925.36, or 2925.37 of the Revised Code is a professionally licensed person, in addition to any other sanctions imposed for the violation, the court, except as otherwise provided in this section, immediately shall transmit a certified copy of the judgment entry of conviction to the regulatory or licensing board or agency that has the administrative authority to suspend or revoke the offender's professional license. If the professionally licensed person who is convicted of or pleads guilty to a violation of any section listed in this section is a person who has been admitted to the bar by order of the supreme court in compliance with its prescribed and published rules, in addition to any other sanctions imposed for the violation, the court immediately shall transmit a certified copy of the judgment entry of conviction to the secretary of the board of commissioners on grievances and discipline of the supreme court and to either the disciplinary counsel or the president, secretary, and chairperson of each certified grievance committee.

**HISTORY: 143 v S 258 (Eff 11-20-90); 146 v S 2 (Eff 7-1-96); 149 v H 7. Eff 8-7-2001; 149 v S 123, § 1, eff. 1-1-04.**

The effective date is set by section 4 of S.B. 123.

See provisions of § 5 of S.B. 123 (149 v —) following RC § 2925.01.

### [FORFEITURE OF PROPERTY RELATING TO FELONY DRUG ABUSE OFFENSE]

## § 2925.41 Repealed, 151 v H 241, § 2 [143 v S 258. Eff 11-20-90]. Eff 7-1-07.

See provisions of § 4 of 151 v H 241 following RC § 2901.01.

This section concerned definitions. See now RC § 2981.01 et seq.

## § 2925.42 Fines.

(A) If a person is convicted of or pleads guilty to a felony drug abuse offense, or a juvenile is found by a juvenile court to be a delinquent child for an act that, if committed by an adult, would be a felony drug abuse offense, and derives profits or other proceeds from the offense or act, the court that imposes sentence or an order of disposition upon the offender or delinquent child, in lieu of any fine that the court is otherwise authorized or required to impose, may impose upon the offender or delinquent child a fine of not more than twice the gross profits or other proceeds so derived.

(B) Notwithstanding any contrary provision of section 3719.21 of the Revised Code, all fines imposed pursuant to this section shall be paid by the clerk of the court to the county, municipal corporation, township, park district, as created pursuant to section 511.18 or 1545.01 of the Revised Code, or state law enforcement agencies in this state that were primarily responsible for or involved in making the arrest of, and in prosecuting, the offender. However, no fine so imposed shall be paid to a law enforcement agency unless the agency has adopted a written internal control policy under division (F)(2) of section 2925.03 of the Revised Code that addresses the use of the fine moneys that it receives under this division and division (F)(1) of section 2925.03 of the Revised Code. The fines imposed and paid pursuant to this division shall be used by the law enforcement agencies to subsidize their efforts pertaining to drug offenses, in accordance with the written internal control policy adopted by the recipient agency under division (F)(2) of section 2925.03 of the Revised Code.

(C) As used in this section:

(1) "Law enforcement agencies" includes, but is not limited to, the state board of pharmacy and the office of a prosecutor.

(2) "Prosecutor" has the same meaning as in section 2935.01 of the Revised Code.

**HISTORY: 143 v S 258 (Eff 11-20-90); 144 v S 174 (Eff 7-31-92); 146 v S 2 (Eff 7-1-96); 148 v S 179, § 3. Eff 1-1-2002; 151 v H 241, § 1, eff. 7-1-07.**

See provisions of § 4 of 151 v H 241 following RC § 2901.01. The effective date is set by section 5 of SB 179.

## § 2925.43 Repealed, 151 v H 241, § 2 [143 v S 258 (Eff 11-20-90); 148 v S 179, § 3. Eff 1-1-2002]. Eff 7-1-07.

See provisions of § 4 of 151 v H 241 following RC § 2901.01. This section concerned civil forfeiture action prior to prosecution. See now RC § 2981.01 et seq.

## § 2925.44 Repealed, 151 v H 241, § 2 [143 v S 258 (Eff 11-20-90); 144 v S 218 (Eff 10-11-91); 144 v S 174 (Eff 7-31-92); 146 v H 107 (Eff 6-30-95); 146 v H 1 (Eff 1-1-96); 147 v H 210 (Eff 6-30-97); 148 v H 163. Eff 6-30-99; 150 v H 95, § 1, eff. 6-26-03; 151 v H 66, § 101.01, eff. 9-29-05; 151 v H 530, § 101.01, eff. 3-30-06]. Eff 7-1-07.

See provisions of § 4 of 151 v H 241 following RC § 2901.01. This section concerned rights of law enforcement agency seizing property; disposition of forfeited property. See now RC § 2981.01 et seq.

## § 2925.45 Repealed, 151 v H 241, § 2 [143 v S 258. Eff 11-20-90]. Eff 7-1-07.

See provisions of § 4 of 151 v H 241 following RC § 2901.01. This section concerned motion alleging seizure was unlawful; return of property. See now RC § 2981.01 et seq.

### [FEDERAL NARCOTIC LAWS]

## § 2925.50 Effect of federal prosecution.

If a violation of this chapter is a violation of the federal drug abuse control laws, as defined in section 3719.01 of the Revised Code, a conviction or acquittal under the federal drug abuse control laws for the same act is a bar to prosecution in this state.

**HISTORY: 136 v H 300 (Eff 7-1-76); 147 v S 66. Eff 7-22-98.**

### [LABORATORY EVIDENCE]

## § 2925.51 Laboratory report as evidence; requirements; violation.

(A) In any criminal prosecution for a violation of this chapter or Chapter 3719. of the Revised Code, a laboratory report from the bureau of criminal identification and investigation, a laboratory operated by another law enforcement agency, or a laboratory established by or under the authority of an institution of higher education that has its main campus in this state and that is accredited by the association of American universities or the north central association of colleges and secondary schools, primarily for the purpose of providing scientific services to law enforcement agencies and signed by the person performing the analysis, stating that the substance that is the basis of the alleged offense has been weighed and analyzed and stating the findings as to the content, weight, and identity of the substance and that it contains any amount of a controlled substance and the number and description of unit dosages, is prima-facie evidence of the content, identity, and weight or the existence and number of unit dosages of the substance. In any criminal prosecution for a violation of section 2925.041 [2925.04.1] of the Revised Code or a violation of this chapter or Chapter 3719. of the Revised Code that is based on the possession of chemicals sufficient to produce a compound, mixture, preparation, or substance included in schedule I, II, III, IV, or V, a laboratory report from the bureau or from any laboratory that is operated or established as described in this division that is signed by the person performing the analysis, stating that the substances that are the basis of the alleged offense have been weighed and analyzed and stating the findings as to the content, weight, and identity of each of the substances, is prima-facie evidence of the content, identity, and weight of the substances.

Attached to that report shall be a copy of a notarized statement by the signer of the report giving the name of the signer and stating that the signer is an employee of the laboratory issuing the report and that performing the analysis is a part of the signer's regular duties, and giving an outline of the signer's education, training, and experience for performing an analysis of materials included under this section. The signer shall attest that scientifically accepted tests were performed with due caution, and that the evidence was handled in accordance with established and accepted procedures while in the custody of the laboratory.

(B) The prosecuting attorney shall serve a copy of the report on the attorney of record for the accused, or on the accused if the accused has no attorney, prior to any proceeding in which the report is to be used against the accused other than at a preliminary hearing or grand jury proceeding where the report may be used without having been previously served upon the accused.

(C) The report shall not be prima-facie evidence of the contents, identity, and weight or the existence and number of unit dosages of the substance if the accused or the accused's attorney demands the testimony of the person signing the report, by serving the demand upon the prosecuting attorney within seven days from the accused or the accused's attorney's receipt of the report. The time may be extended by a trial judge in the interests of justice.

(D) Any report issued for use under this section shall contain notice of the right of the accused to demand, and the manner in which the accused shall demand, the testimony of the person signing the report.

(E) Any person who is accused of a violation of this chapter or of Chapter 3719. of the Revised Code is entitled, upon written request made to the prosecuting attorney, to have a portion of the substance that is, or of each of the substances that are, the basis of the alleged violation preserved for the benefit of independent analysis performed by a laboratory analyst employed by the accused person, or, if the accused is indigent, by a qualified laboratory analyst appointed by the court. Such portion shall be a representative sample of the entire substance that is, or of each of the substances that are, the basis of the alleged violation and shall be of sufficient size, in the opinion of the court, to permit the accused's analyst to make a thorough scientific analysis concerning the identity of the substance or substances. The prosecuting attorney shall provide the accused's analyst with the sample portion at least fourteen days prior to trial, unless the trial is to be held in a court not of record or unless the accused person is charged with a minor misdemeanor, in which case the prosecuting attorney shall provide the accused's analyst with the sample portion at least three days prior to trial. If the prosecuting attorney determines that such a sample portion cannot be preserved and given to the accused's analyst, the prosecuting attorney shall so inform the accused person or his attorney. In such a circumstance, the accused person is entitled, upon written request made to the prosecuting attorney, to have the accused's privately employed or court appointed analyst present at an analysis of the substance that is, or the substances that are, the basis of the alleged violation, and, upon further written request, to receive copies of all recorded scientific data that result from the analysis and that can be used by an analyst in arriving at conclusions, findings, or opinions concerning the identity of the substance or substances subject to the analysis.

(F) In addition to the rights provided under division (E) of this section, any person who is accused of a violation of this chapter or of Chapter 3719. of the Revised Code that involves a bulk amount of a controlled substance, or any multiple thereof, or who is accused of a violation of section 2925.11 of the Revised Code, other than a minor misdemeanor violation, that involves marihuana, is entitled, upon written request made to the prosecuting attorney, to have a laboratory analyst of the accused's choice, or, if the accused is indigent, a qualified laboratory analyst appointed by the court present at a measurement or weighing of the substance that is the basis of the alleged violation. Also, the accused person is entitled, upon further written request, to receive copies of all recorded scientific data that result from the measurement or weighing and that can be used by an analyst in arriving at conclusions, findings, or opinions concerning the weight, volume, or number of unit doses of the substance subject to the measurement or weighing.

**HISTORY: 136 v H 300 (Eff 7-1-76); 136 v S 541 (Eff 6-28-76); 137 v S 201 (Eff 11-16-77); 149 v H 7. Eff 8-7-2001.**

## § 2925.511 Reimbursement of costs of drug tests confirming that substance contained controlled substance.

In addition to the financial sanctions authorized or required under sections 2929.18 and 2929.28 of the Revised Code and to any costs otherwise authorized or required under any provision of law, the court imposing sentence upon an offender who is convicted of or pleads guilty to a drug abuse offense may order the offender to pay to the state, municipal, or county law enforcement agencies that handled the investigation and prosecution all of the costs that the state, municipal corporation, or county reasonably incurred in having tests performed under section 2925.51 of the Revised Code or in any other manner on any substance that was the basis of, or involved in, the offense to determine whether the substance contained any amount of a controlled substance if the results of the tests indicate that the substance tested contained any controlled substance. No court shall order an offender under this section to pay the costs of tests performed on a substance if the results of the tests do not indicate that the substance tested contained any controlled substance.

The court shall hold a hearing to determine the amount of costs to be imposed under this section. The court may hold the hearing as part of the sentencing hearing for the offender.

**HISTORY: 151 v H 163, § 1, eff. 10-12-06.**

## § 2925.52 Motion for destruction of chemicals sufficient to produce methamphetamine.

(A) If a person is charged with a violation of section 2925.041 [2925.04.1] of the Revised Code or with any violation of this chapter or Chapter 3719. of the Revised Code that is based on the possession of chemicals sufficient to produce methamphetamine, the law enforcement agency that has custody of the chemicals may file a motion with the court in which the charges are pending requesting the court to order the chemicals destroyed in accordance with this division. If a law enforcement agency files a motion of that type with a court, the court may issue an order that requires the containers in which the chemicals are contained be photographed, orders the chemicals forfeited, and requires that the chemicals be destroyed.

(B) If the court issues an order under division (A) of this section, the court may include in the order a requirement that the chemicals be sampled prior to their destruction and that the samples be preserved.

**HISTORY: 149 v H 7. Eff 8-7-2001; 151 v S 53, § 1, eff. 5-17-06.**

### [PSEUDOEPHEDRINE SALES]

## § 2925.55 Definitions; prohibitions concerning purchasing pseudoephedrine products.

(A) As used in sections 2925.55 to 2925.58 of the Revised Code:

(1) "Consumer product" means any food or drink that is consumed or used by humans and any drug, including a drug that may be provided legally only pursuant to a prescription, that is intended to be consumed or used by humans.

(2) "Terminal distributor of dangerous drugs" has the same meaning as in section 4729.01 of the Revised Code.

(3) "Pseudoephedrine" means any material, compound, mixture, or preparation that contains any quantity of pseudoephedrine, any of its salts, optical isomers, or salts of optical isomers.

(4) "Pseudoephedrine product" means a consumer product consisting of a single-ingredient preparation of pseudoephedrine in which pseudoephedrine is the active ingredient. "Pseudoephedrine product" does not include either of the following:

(a) A consumer product containing pseudoephedrine that is in a liquid, liquid capsule, or gel capsule form;

(b) A consumer product primarily intended for administration to children under twelve years of age, according to the label instructions, in solid dosage form, including chewable tablets, when individual dosage units do not exceed fifteen milligrams of pseudoephedrine.

(5) "Retailer" means a place of business that offers consumer products for sale to the general public.

(6) "Single-ingredient preparation" means a compound, mixture, preparation, or substance that contains a single active ingredient.

(B)(1) No individual shall knowingly purchase, receive, or otherwise acquire more than nine grams of any pseudoephedrine product within a period of thirty consecutive days, unless the pseudoephedrine product is dispensed by a pharmacist pursuant to a valid prescription issued by a licensed health professional authorized to prescribe drugs and the conduct of the pharmacist and the licensed health professional authorized to prescribe drugs is in accordance with Chapter 3719., 4715., 4723., 4729., 4731., or 4741. of the Revised Code.

(2) It is not a violation of division (B)(1) of this section for an individual to receive or accept more than nine grams of any pseudoephedrine product within a period of thirty consecutive days if the individual is an employee of a retailer or terminal distributor of dangerous drugs, and the employee receives or accepts from the retailer or terminal distributor of dangerous drugs the pseudoephedrine product in a sealed container in connection with manufacturing, warehousing, placement, stocking, bagging, loading, or unloading of the product.

(C)(1) No individual under eighteen years of age shall knowingly purchase, receive, or otherwise acquire a pseudoephedrine product, unless the pseudoephedrine product is dispensed by a pharmacist pursuant to a valid prescription issued by a licensed health professional authorized to prescribe drugs and the conduct of the pharmacist and the licensed health professional authorized to prescribe drugs is in accordance with Chapter 3719., 4715., 4723., 4729., 4731., or 4741. of the Revised Code.

(2) Division (C)(1) of this section does not apply to an individual under eighteen years of age who purchases, receives, or otherwise acquires a pseudoephedrine product from any of the following:

(a) A licensed health professional authorized to prescribe drugs or pharmacist who dispenses, sells, or otherwise provides the pseudoephedrine product to that individual and whose conduct is in accordance with Chapter 3719., 4715., 4723., 4729., 4731., or 4741. of the Revised Code;

(b) A parent or guardian of that individual who provides the pseudoephedrine product to the individual;

(c) A person, as authorized by that individual's parent or guardian, who dispenses, sells, or otherwise provides the pseudoephedrine product to the individual;

(d) A retailer or terminal distributor of dangerous drugs who provides the pseudoephedrine product to that individual if the individual is an employee of the retailer or terminal distributor of dangerous drugs and the individual receives or accepts from the retailer or terminal distributor of dangerous drugs the pseudoephedrine product in a sealed container in connection with manufacturing, warehousing, placement, stocking, bagging, loading, or unloading of the product.

(D) No individual under eighteen years of age shall knowingly show or give false information concerning the individual's name, age, or other identification for the purpose of purchasing, receiving, or otherwise acquiring a pseudoephedrine product.

(E) No individual shall knowingly fail to comply with the requirements of division (C)(3) of section 3715.05 of the Revised Code.

(F) Whoever violates division (B)(1) of this section is guilty of unlawful purchase of a pseudoephedrine product, a misdemeanor of the first degree.

(G) Whoever violates division (C)(1) of this section is guilty of underage purchase of a pseudoephedrine product, a delinquent act that would be a misdemeanor of the fourth degree if it could be committed by an adult.

(H) Whoever violates division (D) of this section is guilty of using false information to purchase a pseudoephedrine product, a delinquent act that would be a misdemeanor of the first degree if it could be committed by an adult.

(I) Whoever violates division (E) of this section is guilty of improper purchase of a pseudoephedrine product, a misdemeanor of the fourth degree.

**HISTORY: 151 v S 53, § 1, eff. 5-17-06.**

## § 2925.56 Unlawful or improper sales of pseudoephedrine products.

(A)(1) Except as provided in division (A)(2) of this section, no retailer or terminal distributor of dangerous drugs or an employee of a retailer or terminal distributor of dangerous drugs shall knowingly sell, offer to sell, hold for sale, deliver, or otherwise provide to any individual within a period of thirty consecutive days an amount of pseudoephedrine product that is greater than nine grams.

(2) Division (A)(1) of this section does not apply to any quantity of pseudoephedrine product dispensed by a pharmacist pursuant to a valid prescription issued by a licensed health professional authorized to prescribe drugs if the conduct of the pharmacist and the licensed health professional authorized to prescribe drugs is in accordance with Chapter 3719., 4715., 4723., 4729., 4731., or 4741. of the Revised Code.

It is not a violation of division (A)(1) of this section for a retailer, terminal distributor of dangerous drugs, or employee of either to provide to an individual more than nine grams of any pseudoephedrine product within a period of thirty consecutive days if the individual is an employee of the retailer or terminal distributor of dangerous drugs, and the employee receives or accepts from the retailer, terminal distributor of dangerous drugs, or employee the pseudoephedrine product in a sealed container in connection with manufacturing, warehousing, placement, stocking, bagging, loading, or unloading of the product.

(B)(1) Except as provided in division (B)(2) of this section, no retailer or terminal distributor of dangerous drugs or an employee of a retailer or terminal distributor of dangerous drugs shall sell, offer to sell, hold for sale, deliver, or otherwise provide a pseudoephedrine product to an individual who is under eighteen years of age.

(2) Division (B)(1) of this section does not apply to any of the following:

(a) A licensed health professional authorized to prescribe drugs or pharmacist who dispenses, sells, or otherwise provides a pseudoephedrine product to an individual under eighteen years of age and whose conduct is in accordance with Chapter 3719., 4715., 4723., 4729., 4731., or 4741. of the Revised Code;

(b) A parent or guardian of an individual under eighteen years of age who provides a pseudoephedrine product to the individual;

(c) A person who, as authorized by the individual's parent or guardian, dispenses, sells, or otherwise provides a pseudoephedrine product to an individual under eighteen years of age;

(d) The provision by a retailer, terminal distributor of dangerous drugs, or employee of either of a pseudoephedrine product in a sealed container to an employee of the retailer or terminal distributor of dangerous drugs who is under eighteen years of age in connection with manufacturing, warehousing, placement, stocking, bagging, loading, or unloading of the product.

(C) No retailer or terminal distributor of dangerous drugs shall fail to comply with the requirements of division (C)(2) of section 3715.05 of the Revised Code.

(D) Whoever violates division (A)(1) of this section is guilty of unlawfully selling a pseudoephedrine product, a misdemeanor of the first degree.

(E) Whoever violates division (B)(1) of this section is guilty of unlawfully selling a pseudoephedrine product to a minor, a misdemeanor of the fourth degree.

(F) Whoever violates division (C) of this section is guilty of improper sale of a pseudoephedrine product, a misdemeanor of the second degree.

**HISTORY: 151 v S 53, § 1, eff. 5-17-06.**

## § 2925.57 Engaging in illegal pseudoephedrine product transaction scan.

(A) As used in this section and section 2925.58 of the Revised Code:

(1) "Card holder" means any person who presents a driver's or commercial driver's license or an identification card to a seller, or an agent or employee of a seller, to purchase or receive any pseudoephedrine product from the seller, agent, or employee.

(2) "Identification card" and "transaction scan device" have the same meanings as in section 2927.021 [2927.02.1] of the Revised Code.

(3) "Seller" means a retailer or terminal distributor of dangerous drugs.

(4) "Transaction scan" means the process by which a seller or an agent or employee of a seller checks by means of a transaction scan device the validity of a driver's or commercial driver's license or an identification card that is presented as a condition for purchasing or receiving any pseudoephedrine product.

(B)(1) A seller or an agent or employee of a seller may perform a transaction scan by means of a transaction scan device to check the validity of a driver's or commercial driver's license or identification card presented by a card holder as a condition for selling, giving away, or otherwise distributing to the card holder a pseudoephedrine product.

(2) If the information deciphered by the transaction scan performed under division (B)(1) of this section fails to match the information printed on the driver's or commercial driver's license or identification card presented by the card holder, or if the transaction scan indicates that the information so printed is false or fraudulent, neither the seller nor any agent or employee of the seller shall sell, give away, or otherwise distribute any pseudoephedrine product to the card holder.

(3) Division (B)(1) of this section does not preclude a seller or an agent or employee of a seller as a condition for selling, giving away, or otherwise distributing a pseudoephedrine product to the person presenting the document from using a transaction scan device to check the validity of a document other than a driver's or commercial driver's license or an identification card if the document includes a bar code or magnetic strip that may be scanned by the device.

(C) Rules adopted by the registrar of motor vehicles under division (C) of section 4301.61 of the Revised Code apply to the use of transaction scan devices for purposes of this section and section 2925.58 of the Revised Code.

(D)(1) No seller or agent or employee of a seller shall electronically or mechanically record or maintain any information derived from a transaction scan, except the following:

(a) The name and date of birth of the person listed on the driver's or commercial driver's license or identification card presented by a card holder;

(b) The expiration date and identification number of the driver's or commercial driver's license or identification card presented by a card holder.

(2) No seller or agent or employee of a seller shall use the information that is derived from a transaction scan or that is permitted to be recorded and maintained under division (D)(1) of this section except for purposes of section 2925.58 of the Revised Code.

(3) No seller or agent or employee of a seller shall use a transaction scan device for a purpose other than the purpose specified in division (B)(1) of this section.

(4) No seller or agent or employee of a seller shall sell or otherwise disseminate the information derived from a transaction scan to any third party, including, but not limited to, selling or otherwise disseminating that information for any marketing, advertising, or promotional activities, but a seller or agent or employee of a seller may release that information pursuant to a court order or as specifically authorized by section 2925.58 or another section of the Revised Code.

(E) Nothing in this section or section 2925.58 of the Revised Code relieves a seller or an agent or employee of a seller of any responsibility to comply with any other applicable state or federal laws or rules governing the sale, giving away, or other distribution of pseudoephedrine products.

(F) Whoever violates division (B)(2) or (D) of this section is guilty of engaging in an illegal pseudoephedrine product transaction scan, and the court may impose upon the offender a civil penalty of up to one thousand dollars for each violation. The clerk of the court shall pay each collected civil penalty to the county treasurer for deposit into the county treasury.

**HISTORY: 151 v S 53, § 1, eff. 5-17-06.**

## § 2925.58 Affirmative defense where age of purchaser or other recipient of pseudoephedrine product is element of alleged violation.

(A) A seller or an agent or employee of a seller may not be found guilty of a charge of a violation of section 2925.56 of the Revised Code in which the age of the purchaser or other recipient of a pseudoephedrine product is an element of the alleged violation if the seller, agent, or employee raises and proves as an affirmative defense that all of the following occurred:

(1) A card holder attempting to purchase or receive a pseudoephedrine product presented a driver's or commercial driver's license or an identification card.

(2) A transaction scan of the driver's or commercial driver's license or identification card that the card holder presented indicated that the license or card was valid.

(3) The pseudoephedrine product was sold, given away, or otherwise distributed to the card holder in reasonable reliance upon the identification presented and the completed transaction scan.

(B) In determining whether a seller or an agent or employee of a seller has proven the affirmative defense provided by division (A) of this section, the trier of fact in the action for the alleged violation of section 2925.56 of the Revised Code shall consider any written policy that the seller has adopted and implemented and that is intended to prevent violations of section 2925.56 of the Revised Code. For purposes of division (A)(3) of this section, the trier of fact shall consider that reasonable reliance upon the identification presented and the completed transaction scan may require a seller or an agent or employee of a seller to exercise reasonable diligence to determine, and that the use of a transaction scan device does not excuse a seller or an agent or employee of a seller from exercising reasonable diligence to determine, the following:

(1) Whether a person to whom the seller or agent or employee of a seller sells, gives away, or otherwise distributes a pseudoephedrine product is eighteen years of age or older;

(2) Whether the description and picture appearing on the driver's or commercial driver's license or identification card presented by a card holder is that of the card holder.

(C) In any criminal action in which the affirmative defense provided by division (A) of this section is raised, the registrar of motor vehicles or a deputy registrar who issued an identification card under sections 4507.50 to 4507.52 of the Revised Code shall be permitted to submit certified copies of the records of that issuance in lieu of the testimony of the personnel of or contractors with the bureau of motor vehicles in the action.

**HISTORY: 151 v S 53, § 1, eff. 5-17-06.**

# CHAPTER 2927: MISCELLANEOUS OFFENSES



## § 2927.01 Abuse of a corpse.

(A) No person, except as authorized by law, shall treat a human corpse in a way that the person knows would outrage reasonable family sensibilities.

(B) No person, except as authorized by law, shall treat a human corpse in a way that would outrage reasonable community sensibilities.

(C) Whoever violates division (A) of this section is guilty of abuse of a corpse, a misdemeanor of the second degree. Whoever violates division (B) of this section is guilty of gross abuse of a corpse, a felony of the fifth degree.

**HISTORY: 134 v H 511 (Eff 1-1-74); 137 v H 741 (Eff 10-9-78); 146 v S 2. Eff 7-1-96.**

The effective date is set by section 6 of SB 2.

## § 2927.02 Illegal distribution of cigarettes or other tobacco products.

(A) As used in this section and section 2927.021 [2927.02.1] of the Revised Code:

(1) "Child" has the same meaning as in section 2151.011 [2151.01.1] of the Revised Code.

(2) "Cigarette" includes clove cigarettes and hand-rolled cigarettes.

(3) "Distribute" means to furnish, give, or provide cigarettes, other tobacco products, or papers used to roll cigarettes to the ultimate consumer of the cigarettes, other tobacco products, or papers used to roll cigarettes.

(4) "Proof of age" means a driver's license, a commercial driver's license, a military identification card, a passport, or an identification card issued under sections 4507.50 to 4507.52 of the Revised Code that shows that a person is eighteen years of age or older.

(5) "Tobacco product" means any product that is made from tobacco, including, but not limited to, a cigarette, a cigar, pipe tobacco, chewing tobacco, or snuff.

(6) "Vending machine" has the same meaning as "coin machine" in section 2913.01 of the Revised Code.

(B) No manufacturer, producer, distributor, wholesaler, or retailer of cigarettes, other tobacco products, or papers used to roll cigarettes, no agent, employee, or representative of a manufacturer, producer, distributor, wholesaler, or retailer of cigarettes, other tobacco products, or papers used to roll cigarettes, and no other person shall do any of the following:

(1) Give, sell, or otherwise distribute cigarettes, other tobacco products, or papers used to roll cigarettes to any child;

(2) Give away, sell, or distribute cigarettes, other tobacco products, or papers used to roll cigarettes in any place that does not have posted in a conspicuous place a sign stating that giving, selling, or otherwise distributing cigarettes, other tobacco products, or papers used to roll cigarettes to a person under eighteen years of age is prohibited by law;

(3) Knowingly furnish any false information regarding the name, age, or other identification of any child with purpose to obtain cigarettes, other tobacco products, or papers used to roll cigarettes for that child;

(4) Manufacture, sell, or distribute in this state any pack or other container of cigarettes containing fewer than twenty cigarettes or any package of roll-your-own tobacco containing less than six-tenths of one ounce of tobacco;

(5) Sell cigarettes in a smaller quantity than that placed in the pack or other container by the manufacturer.

(C) No person shall sell or offer to sell cigarettes or other tobacco products by or from a vending machine, except in the following locations:

(1) An area within a factory, business, office, or other place not open to the general public;

(2) An area to which children are not generally permitted access;

(3) Any other place not identified in division (C)(1) or (2) of this section, upon all of the following conditions:

(a) The vending machine is located within the immediate vicinity, plain view, and control of the person who owns or operates the place, or an employee of that person, so that all cigarettes and other tobacco product purchases from the vending machine will be readily observed by the person who owns or operates the place or an employee of that person. For the purpose of this section, a vending machine located in any unmonitored area, including an unmonitored coatroom, restroom, hallway, or outer waiting area, shall not be considered located within the immediate vicinity, plain view, and control of the person who owns or operates the place, or an employee of that person.

(b) The vending machine is inaccessible to the public when the place is closed.

(D) The following are affirmative defenses to a charge under division (B)(1) of this section:

(1) The child was accompanied by a parent, spouse who is eighteen years of age or older, or legal guardian of the child.

(2) The person who gave, sold, or distributed cigarettes, other tobacco products, or papers used to roll cigarettes to a child under division (B)(1) of this section is a parent, spouse who is eighteen years of age or older, or legal guardian of the child.

(E) It is not a violation of division (B)(1) or (2) of this section for a person to give or otherwise distribute to a child cigarettes, other tobacco products, or papers used to roll cigarettes while the child is participating in a research protocol if all of the following apply:

(1) The parent, guardian, or legal custodian of the child has consented in writing to the child participating in the research protocol.

(2) An institutional human subjects protection review board, or an equivalent entity, has approved the research protocol.

(3) The child is participating in the research protocol at the facility or location specified in the research protocol.

(F)(1) Whoever violates division (B)(1), (2), (4), or (5) or (C) of this section is guilty of illegal distribution of cigarettes or other tobacco products, a misdemeanor of the fourth degree. If the offender previously has been convicted of a violation of division (B)(1), (2), (4), or (5) or (C) of this section, illegal distribution of cigarettes or other tobacco products is a misdemeanor of the third degree.

(2) Whoever violates division (B)(3) of this section is guilty of permitting children to use cigarettes or other tobacco products, a misdemeanor of the fourth degree. If the offender previously has been convicted of a violation of division (B)(3) of this section, permitting children to use cigarettes or other tobacco products is a misdemeanor of the third degree.

(G) Any cigarettes, other tobacco products, or papers used to roll cigarettes that are given, sold, or otherwise distributed to a child in violation of this section and that are used, possessed, purchased, or received by a child in violation of section 2151.87 of the Revised Code are subject to seizure and forfeiture as contraband under Chapter 2981. of the Revised Code.

**HISTORY: 140 v H 152 (Eff 9-26-84); 144 v S 40 (Eff 10-23-91); 148 v S 218 (Eff 3-15-2001); 149 v H 393 (Eff 7-5-2002); 149 v S 242. Eff 9-19-2002; 151 v H 241, § 1, eff. 7-1-07.**

See provisions of § 4 of 151 v H 241 following RC § 2901.01.
The effective date is set by section 21 of SB 242.
The provisions of § 3 of SB 218 (148 v —) read as follows:
SECTION 3. Except for the provisions set forth in division (C) of section 2927.02 of the Revised Code, nothing in this act shall be construed as limiting or affecting the powers of townships or municipal corporations to regulate the purchase, use, or sale of tobacco.

## § 2927.021 Engaging in illegal tobacco product transaction scan.

(A) As used in this section and section 2927.022 [2927.02.2] of the Revised Code:

(1) "Card holder" means any person who presents a driver's or commercial driver's license or an identification card to a seller, or an agent or employee of a seller, to purchase or receive cigarettes or other tobacco products from the seller, agent, or employee.

(2) "Identification card" means an identification card issued under sections 4507.50 to 4507.52 of the Revised Code.

(3) "Seller" means a seller of cigarettes or other tobacco products and includes any person whose gift of or other distribution of cigarettes or other tobacco products is subject to the prohibitions of section 2927.02 of the Revised Code.

(4) "Transaction scan" means the process by which a seller or an agent or employee of a seller checks, by means of a transaction scan device, the validity of a driver's or commercial driver's license or an identification card that is presented as a condition for purchasing or receiving cigarettes or other tobacco products.

(5) "Transaction scan device" means any commercial device or combination of devices used at a point of sale that is capable of deciphering in an electronically readable format the information encoded on the magnetic strip or bar code of a driver's or commercial driver's license or an identification card.

(B)(1) A seller or an agent or employee of a seller may perform a transaction scan by means of a transaction scan device to check the validity of a driver's or commercial driver's license or identification card presented by a card holder as a condition for selling, giving away, or otherwise distributing to the card holder cigarettes or other tobacco products.

(2) If the information deciphered by the transaction scan performed under division (B)(1) of this section fails to match the information printed on the driver's or commercial driver's license or identification card presented by the card holder, or if the transaction scan indicates that the information so printed is false or fraudulent, neither the seller nor any agent or employee of the seller shall sell, give away, or otherwise distribute any cigarettes or other tobacco products to the card holder.

(3) Division (B)(1) of this section does not preclude a seller or an agent or employee of a seller from using a transaction scan device to check the validity of a document other than a driver's or commercial driver's license or an identification card, if the document includes a bar code or magnetic strip that may be scanned by the device, as a condition for selling, giving away, or otherwise distributing cigarettes or other tobacco products to the person presenting the document.

(C) Rules adopted by the registrar of motor vehicles under division (C) of section 4301.61 of the Revised Code apply to the use of transaction scan devices for purposes of this section and section 2927.022 [2927.02.2] of the Revised Code.

(D)(1) No seller or agent or employee of a seller shall electronically or mechanically record or maintain any information derived from a transaction scan, except the following:

(a) The name and date of birth of the person listed on the driver's or commercial driver's license or identification card presented by a card holder;

(b) The expiration date and identification number of the driver's or commercial driver's license or identification card presented by a card holder.

(2) No seller or agent or employee of a seller shall use the information that is derived from a transaction scan or that is permitted to be recorded and maintained under division (D)(1) of this section, except for purposes of section 2927.022 [2927.02.2] of the Revised Code.

(3) No seller or agent or employee of a seller shall use a transaction scan device for a purpose other than the purpose specified in division (B)(1) of this section.

(4) No seller or agent or employee of a seller shall sell or otherwise disseminate the information derived from a transaction scan to any third party, including, but not limited to, selling or otherwise disseminating that information for any marketing, advertising, or promotional activities, but a seller or agent or employee of a seller may release that information pursuant to a court order or as specifically authorized by section 2927.022 [2927.02.2] or another section of the Revised Code.

(E) Nothing in this section or section 2927.022 [2927.02.2] of the Revised Code relieves a seller or an agent or employee of a seller of any responsibility to comply with any other applicable state or federal laws or rules governing the sale, giving away, or other distribution of cigarettes or other tobacco products.

(F) Whoever violates division (B)(2) or (D) of this section is guilty of engaging in an illegal tobacco product transaction scan, and the court may impose upon the offender a civil penalty of up to one thousand dollars for each violation. The clerk of the court shall pay each collected civil penalty to the county treasurer for deposit into the county treasury.

**HISTORY: 148 v S 200. Eff 9-21-2000.**

## § 2927.022 Transaction scan as affirmative defense to cigarette or tobacco product charge.

(A) A seller or an agent or employee of a seller may not be found guilty of a charge of a violation of section 2927.02 of the Revised Code in which the age of the purchaser or other recipient of cigarettes or other tobacco products is an element of the alleged violation, if the seller, agent, or employee raises and proves as an affirmative defense that all of the following occurred:

(1) A card holder attempting to purchase or receive cigarettes or other tobacco products presented a driver's or commercial driver's license or an identification card.

(2) A transaction scan of the driver's or commercial driver's license or identification card that the card holder presented indicated that the license or card was valid.

(3) The cigarettes or other tobacco products were sold, given away, or otherwise distributed to the card holder in reasonable reliance upon the identification presented and the completed transaction scan.

(B) In determining whether a seller or an agent or employee of a seller has proven the affirmative defense provided by division (A) of this section, the trier of fact in the action for the alleged violation of section 2927.02 of the Revised Code shall consider any written policy that the seller has adopted and implemented and that is intended to prevent violations of section 2927.02 of the Revised Code. For purposes of division (A)(3) of this section, the trier of fact shall consider that reasonable reliance upon the identification presented and the completed transaction scan may require a seller or an agent or employee of a seller to exercise reasonable diligence to determine, and that the use of a transaction scan device does not excuse a seller or an agent or employee of a seller from exercising reasonable diligence to determine, the following:

(1) Whether a person to whom the seller or agent or employee of a seller sells, gives away, or otherwise distributes cigarettes or other tobacco products is eighteen years of age or older;

(2) Whether the description and picture appearing on the driver's or commercial driver's license or identification card presented by a card holder is that of the card holder.

(C) In any criminal action in which the affirmative defense provided by division (A) of this section is raised, the registrar of motor vehicles or a deputy registrar who issued an identification card under sections 4507.50 to 4507.52 of the Revised Code shall be permitted to submit certified copies of the records of that issuance in lieu of the testimony of the personnel of or contractors with the bureau of motor vehicles in the action.

**HISTORY: 148 v S 200. Eff 9-21-2000.**

## § 2927.023 Shipping cigarettes to anyone other than authorized recipient of tobacco products; containers and wrappings.

(A) As used in this section "authorized recipient of tobacco products" means a person who is:

(1) Licensed as a cigarette wholesale dealer under section 5743.15 of the Revised Code;

(2) Licensed as a retail dealer as long as the person purchases cigarettes with the appropriate tax stamp affixed;

(3) An export warehouse proprietor as defined in section 5702 of the Internal Revenue Code;

(4) An operator of a customs bonded warehouse under 19 U.S.C. 1311 or 19 U.S.C. 1555;

(5) An officer, employee, or agent of the federal government or of this state acting in the person's official capacity;

(6) A department, agency, instrumentality, or political subdivision of the federal government or of this state;

(7) A person having a consent for consumer shipment issued by the tax commissioner under section 5743.71 of the Revised Code.

The purpose of this section is to prevent the sale of cigarettes to minors and to ensure compliance with the Master Settlement Agreement, as defined in section 1346.01 of the Revised Code.

(B)(1) No person shall cause to be shipped any cigarettes to any person in this state other than an authorized recipient of tobacco products.

(2) No common carrier, contract carrier, or other person shall knowingly transport cigarettes to any person in this state that the carrier or other person reasonably believes is not an authorized recipient of tobacco products. If cigarettes are transported to a home or residence, it shall be presumed that the common carrier, contract carrier, or other person knew that the person to whom the cigarettes were delivered was not an authorized recipient of tobacco products.

(C) No person engaged in the business of selling cigarettes who ships or causes to be shipped cigarettes to any person in this state in any container or wrapping other than the original container or wrapping of the cigarettes shall fail to plainly and visibly mark the exterior of the container or wrapping in which the cigarettes are shipped with the words "cigarettes."

(D) A court shall impose a fine of up to one thousand dollars for each violation of division (B)(1), (B)(2), or (C) of this section.

**HISTORY: 151 v H 66, § 101.01, eff. 6-30-05; 152 v H 119, § 101.01, eff. 6-30-07.**

The effective date is set by § 815.03 of 152 v H 119.
The effective date is set by § 612.21 of 151 v H 66.

## § 2927.03 Interference with fair housing rights.

(A) No person, whether or not acting under color of law, shall by force or threat of force willfully injure, intimidate, or interfere with, or attempt to injure, intimidate, or interfere with, any of the following:

(1) Any person because of race, color, religion, sex, familial status as defined in section 4112.01 of the Revised Code, national origin, military status as defined in that section, disability as defined in that section, or ancestry and because that person is or has been selling, purchasing, renting, financing, occupying, contracting, or negotiating for the sale, purchase, rental, financing, or occupation of any housing accommodations, or applying for or participating in any service, organization, or facility relating to the business of selling or renting housing accommodations;

(2) Any person because that person is or has been doing, or in order to intimidate that person or any other person or any class of persons from doing, either of the following:

(a) Participating, without discrimination on account of race, color, religion, sex, familial status as defined in section 4112.01 of the Revised Code, national origin, military status as defined in that section, disability as defined in that section, or ancestry, in any of the activities, services, organizations, or facilities described in division (A)(1) of this section;

(b) Affording another person or class of persons opportunity or protection so to participate.

(3) Any person because that person is or has been, or in order to discourage that person or any other person from, lawfully aiding or encouraging other persons to participate, without discrimination on account of race, color, religion, sex, familial status as defined in section 4112.01 of the Revised Code, national origin, military status as defined in that section, disability as defined in that section, or ancestry, in any of the activities, services, organizations, or facilities described in division (A)(1) of this section, or participating lawfully in speech or peaceful assembly opposing any denial of the opportunity to so participate.

(B) Whoever violates division (A) of this section is guilty of a misdemeanor of the first degree.

**HISTORY: 142 v H 5 (Eff 9-28-87); 144 v H 321 (Eff 6-30-92); 146 v S 2 (Eff 7-1-96); 148 v H 264. Eff 3-17-2000; 152 v H 372, § 1, eff. 3-24-08.**

## § 2927.11 Desecration.

(A) No person, without privilege to do so, shall purposely deface, damage, pollute, or otherwise physically mistreat any of the following:

(1) The flag of the United States or of this state;

(2) Any public monument;

(3) Any historical or commemorative marker, or any structure, Indian mound or earthwork, cemetery, thing, or site of great historical or archaeological interest;

(4) A place of worship, its furnishings, or religious artifacts or sacred texts within the place of worship or within the grounds upon which the place of worship is located;

(5) A work of art or museum piece;

(6) Any other object of reverence or sacred devotion.

(B) Whoever violates this section is guilty of desecration. A violation of division (A)(1), (2), (3), (5), or (6) of this section is a misdemeanor of the second degree. Except as otherwise provided in this division, a violation of division (A)(4) of this section is a felony of the fifth degree that is punishable by a fine of up to two thousand five hundred dollars in addition to the penalties specified for a felony of the fifth degree in sections 2929.13 to 2929.18 of the Revised Code. If the value of the property or the amount of physical harm involved in a violation of division (A)(4) of this section is five thousand dollars or more but less than one hundred thousand dollars, a violation of that division is a felony of the fourth degree. If the value of the property or the amount of physical harm involved in a violation of division (A)(4) of this section is one hundred thousand dollars or more, a violation of that division is a felony of the third degree.

(C) As used in this section, "cemetery" means any place of burial and includes burial sites that contain American Indian burial objects placed with or containing American Indian human remains.

**HISTORY: 134 v H 511 (Eff 1-1-74); 136 v H 418 (Eff 8-24-76); 137 v H 741 (Eff 10-9-78); 141 v S 316 (Eff 3-19-87); 147 v H 429 (Eff 9-30-98); 148 v S 51. Eff 9-20-99.**

## § 2927.12 Ethnic intimidation.

(A) No person shall violate section 2903.21, 2903.22, 2909.06, or 2909.07, or division (A)(3), (4), or (5) of section 2917.21 of the Revised Code by reason of the race, color, religion, or national origin of another person or group of persons.

(B) Whoever violates this section is guilty of ethnic intimidation. Ethnic intimidation is an offense of the next higher degree than the offense the commission of which is a necessary element of ethnic intimidation.

**HISTORY: 141 v S 316. Eff 3-19-87.**

## § 2927.13 Selling or donating contaminated blood.

(A) No person, with knowledge that the person is a carrier of a virus that causes acquired immune deficiency syndrome, shall sell or donate the person's blood, plasma, or a product of the person's blood, if the person knows or should know the blood, plasma, or product of the person's blood is being accepted for the purpose of transfusion to another individual.

(B) Whoever violates this section is guilty of selling or donating contaminated blood, a felony of the fourth degree.

**HISTORY: 142 v H 571 (Eff 3-17-89); 146 v S 2. Eff 7-1-96.**

The effective date is set by section 6 of SB 2.

## § 2927.15 Unlawful collection of bodily substance.

(A) No person shall knowingly collect any blood, urine, tissue, or other bodily substance of another person without privilege or consent to do so.

(B)(1) Division (A) of this section does not apply to any of the following:

(a) The collection of any bodily substance of a person by a law enforcement officer, or by another person pursuant to the direction or advice of a law enforcement officer, for purposes of a chemical test or tests of the substance under division (A)(1) of section 1547.111 [1547.11.1] or division (A)(2) of section 4511.191 [4511.19.1] of the Revised Code to determine the alcohol, drug, controlled substance, metabolite of a controlled substance, or combination content of the bodily substance;

(b) The collection of any bodily substance of a person by a peace officer, or by another person pursuant to the direction or advice of a peace officer, for purposes of a test or tests of the substance as provided in division (A) of section 4506.17 of the Revised Code to determine the person's alcohol concentration or the presence of any controlled substance or metabolite of a controlled substance.

(2) Division (B)(1) of this section shall not be construed as implying that the persons identified in divisions (B)(1)(a) and (b) of this section do not have privilege to collect the bodily substance of another person as described in those divisions or as limiting the definition of "privilege" set forth in section 2901.01 of the Revised Code.

(C) Whoever violates division (A) of this section is guilty of unlawful collection of a bodily substance. Except as otherwise provided in this division, unlawful collection of a bodily substance is a misdemeanor of the first degree. If the offender previously has been convicted of or pleaded guilty to a violation of division (A) of this section, unlawful collection of a bodily substance is a felony of the fifth degree.

**HISTORY: 153 v S 58, § 1, eff. 9-17-10.**

## § 2927.21 Duty to report escape of certain animals.

(A) The owner or keeper of any member of a species of the animal kingdom that escapes from the owner's or keeper's custody or control and that is not indigenous to this state or presents a risk of serious physical harm to persons or property, or both, shall, within one hour after the owner or keeper discovers or reasonably should have discovered the escape, report it to:

(1) A law enforcement officer of the municipal corporation or township and the sheriff of the county where the escape occurred; and

(2) The clerk of the municipal legislative authority or the fiscal officer of the township where the escape occurred.

(B) If the office of the clerk of a municipal legislative authority or township fiscal officer is closed to the public at the time a report is required by division (A) of this section, it is sufficient compliance with division (A)(2) of this section if the owner or keeper makes the report within one hour after the office is next open to the public.

(C) Whoever violates this section is guilty of a misdemeanor of the first degree.

**HISTORY: 141 v H 32. Eff 9-11-85; 151 v S 107, § 1, eff. 12-20-05.**

## § 2927.24 Contaminating substance for human consumption or use or contamination with hazardous chemical, biological, or radioactive substance; spreading false report.

(A) As used in this section:

(1) "Poison" has the same meaning as in section 3719.01 of the Revised Code.

(2) "Drug" has the same meaning as in section 4729.01 of the Revised Code.

(3) "Hazardous chemical, biological, or radioactive substance" means any of the following:

(a) Any toxic or poisonous chemical, the precursor of any toxic or poisonous chemical, or any toxin;

(b) Any disease organism or biological agent;

(c) Any substance or item that releases or is designed to release radiation or radioactivity at a level dangerous to human life.

(4) "Biological agent" means any microorganism, virus, infectious substance, or biological product that may be engineered through biotechnology, or any naturally occurring or bioengineered component of any microorganism, virus, infectious substance, or biological product that may be engineered through biotechnology, capable of causing death, disease, or other biological malfunction in a human, an animal, a plant, or another living organism, deterioration of food, water, equipment, supplies, or material of any kind, or deleterious alteration of the environment.

(5) "Toxin" means the toxic material of plants, animals, microorganisms, viruses, fungi, or infectious substances, or a recombinant molecule, whatever its origin or method of reproduction, including, but not limited to, any poisonous substance or biological product that may be engineered through biotechnology or produced by a living organism and any poisonous isomer or biological product, homolog, or derivative of any substance or product of that nature.

(B) Except as provided in division (D) of this section, no person shall do any of the following:

(1) Knowingly mingle a poison, hazardous chemical, biological, or radioactive substance, or other harmful substance with a food, drink, nonprescription drug, prescription drug, or pharmaceutical product, or knowingly place a poison, hazardous chemical, biological, or radioactive substance, or other harmful substance in a spring, well, reservoir, or public water supply, if the person knows or has reason to know that the food, drink, nonprescription drug, prescription drug, pharmaceutical product, or water may be ingested or used by another person. For purposes of this division, a person does not know or have reason to know that water may be ingested or used by another person if it is disposed of as waste into a household drain including the drain of a toilet, sink, tub, or floor.

(2) Knowingly release into the air, knowingly leave in any public place, or knowingly expose one or more persons to any hazardous chemical, biological, or radioactive substance with the intent to cause, or create a risk of, death or serious physical harm to any person.

(C) No person shall do any of the following:

(1) Inform another person that a poison, hazardous chemical, biological, or radioactive substance, or other harmful substance has been or will be placed in a food, drink, nonprescription drug, prescription drug, or other pharmaceutical product, spring, well, reservoir, or public water supply, if the placement of the poison or substance would be a violation of division (B)(1) of this section, and the person knows both that the information is false and that the information likely will be disseminated to the public.

(2) Inform another person that a hazardous chemical, biological, or radioactive substance has been or will be released into the air or left in a public place, or that one or more persons has been or will be exposed to a hazardous chemical, biological, or radioactive substance, if the release, leaving, or exposure of the hazardous chemical, biological, or radioactive substance would be a violation of division (B)(2) of this section, and the person knows both that the information is false and that the information likely will be disseminated to the general public.

(D)(1) A person may mingle a drug with a food or drink for the purpose of causing the drug to be ingested or used in the quantity described by its labeling or prescription.

(2) A person may place a poison or other harmful substance in a spring, well, reservoir, or public water supply in such quantity as is necessary to treat the spring, well, reservoir, or water supply to make it safe for human consumption and use.

(3) The provisions of division (B) of this section shall not be applied in a manner that conflicts with any other state or federal law or rule relating to substances permitted to be applied to or present in any food, raw or processed, any milk or milk product, any meat or meat product, any type of crop, water, or alcoholic or nonalcoholic beverage.

(E)(1) Whoever violates division (B)(1) or (2) of this section is guilty of contaminating a substance for human consumption or use or contamination with a hazardous chemical, biological, or radioactive substance. Except as otherwise provided in this division, contaminating a substance for human consumption or use or contamination with a hazardous chemical, biological, or radioactive substance is a felony of the first degree. If the offense involved an amount of poison, the hazardous chemical, biological, or radioactive substance, or the other harmful substance sufficient to cause death if ingested or used by a person regarding a violation of division (B)(1) of this section or sufficient to cause death to persons who are exposed to it regarding a violation of division (B)(2) of this section or if the offense resulted in serious physical harm to another person, whoever violates division (B)(1) or (2) of this section shall be imprisoned for life with parole eligibility after serving fifteen years of imprisonment.

(2) Whoever violates division (C)(1) or (2) of this section is guilty of spreading a false report of contamination, a felony of the fourth degree.

(F) Divisions (C)(1) and (2) of this section do not limit or affect the application of sections 2917.31 or 2917.32 of the Revised Code. Any act that is a violation of both division (C)(1) or (2) of this section and of section 2917.31 or 2917.32 of the Revised Code may be prosecuted under this section, section 2917.31 or 2917.32 of the Revised Code, or both this section and section 2917.31 or 2917.32 of the Revised Code.

**HISTORY: 145 v H 280 (Eff 6-29-94); 146 v S 2 (Eff 7-1-96); 147 v S 66 (Eff 7-22-98); 148 v S 107 (Eff 3-23-2000); 149 v S 184. Eff 5-15-2002.**

## § 2927.27 Illegal bail bond agent practices.

(A) No person, other than a law enforcement officer, shall apprehend, detain, or arrest a principal on bond, wherever issued, unless that person meets all of the following criteria:

(1) The person is any of the following:

(a) Qualified, licensed, and appointed as a surety bail bond agent under sections 3905.83 to 3905.95 of the Revised Code;

(b) Licensed as a surety bail bond agent by the state where the bond was written;

(c) Licensed as a private investigator under Chapter 4749. of the Revised Code;

(d) Licensed as a private investigator by the state where the bond was written;

(e) An off-duty peace officer, as defined in section 2921.51 of the Revised Code.

(2) The person, prior to apprehending, detaining, or arresting the principal, has entered into a written contract with the surety or with a licensed surety bail bond agent appointed by the surety, which contract sets forth the name of the principal who is to be apprehended, detained, or arrested.

For purposes of division (A)(2) of this section, "surety" has the same meaning as in section 3905.83 of the Revised Code.

(3) The person, prior to apprehending, detaining, or arresting the principal, has notified the local law enforcement agency having jurisdiction over the area in which such activities will be performed and has provided any form of identification or other information requested by the law enforcement agency.

(B) No person shall represent the person's self to be a bail enforcement agent or bounty hunter, or claim any similar title, in this state.

(C)(1) Whoever violates this section is guilty of illegal bail bond agent practices.

(2) A violation of division (A) of this section is a misdemeanor of the first degree or, if the offender previously has been convicted of or pleaded guilty to two or more violations of division (A) of this section, a felony of the third degree.

(3) A violation of division (B) of this section is a misdemeanor of the first degree or, if the offender previously has been convicted of or pleaded guilty to two or more violations of division (B) of this section, a felony of the third degree.

**HISTORY: 148 v H 730. Eff 10-9-2001.**

The effective date is set by section 3 of HB 730.

# CHAPTER 2929: PENALTIES AND SENTENCING



## [IN GENERAL]

### § 2929.01 Definitions.

As used in this chapter:

(A)(1) "Alternative residential facility" means, subject to division (A)(2) of this section, any facility other than an offender's home or residence in which an offender is assigned to live and that satisfies all of the following criteria:

(a) It provides programs through which the offender may seek or maintain employment or may receive education, training, treatment, or habilitation.

(b) It has received the appropriate license or certificate for any specialized education, training, treatment, habilitation, or other service that it provides from the government agency that is responsible for licensing or certifying that type of education, training, treatment, habilitation, or service.

(2) "Alternative residential facility" does not include a community-based correctional facility, jail, halfway house, or prison.

(B) "Basic probation supervision" means a requirement that the offender maintain contact with a person appointed to supervise the offender in accordance with sanctions imposed by the court or imposed by the parole board pursuant to section 2967.28 of the Revised Code. "Basic probation supervision" includes basic parole supervision and basic post-release control supervision.

(C) "Cocaine," "hashish," "L.S.D.," and "unit dose" have the same meanings as in section 2925.01 of the Revised Code.

(D) "Community-based correctional facility" means a community-based correctional facility and program or district community-based correctional facility and program developed pursuant to sections 2301.51 to 2301.58 of the Revised Code.

(E) "Community control sanction" means a sanction that is not a prison term and that is described in section 2929.15, 2929.16, 2929.17, or 2929.18 of the Revised Code or a sanction that is not a jail term and that is described in section 2929.26, 2929.27, or 2929.28 of the Revised Code. "Community control sanction" includes probation if the sentence involved was imposed for a felony that was committed prior to July 1, 1996, or if the sentence involved was imposed for a misdemeanor that was committed prior to January 1, 2004.

(F) "Controlled substance," "marihuana," "schedule I," and "schedule II" have the same meanings as in section 3719.01 of the Revised Code.

(G) "Curfew" means a requirement that an offender during a specified period of time be at a designated place.

(H) "Day reporting" means a sanction pursuant to which an offender is required each day to report to and leave a center or other approved reporting location at specified times in order to participate in work, education or training, treatment, and other approved programs at the center or outside the center.

(I) "Deadly weapon" has the same meaning as in section 2923.11 of the Revised Code.

(J) "Drug and alcohol use monitoring" means a program under which an offender agrees to submit to random chemical analysis of the offender's blood, breath, or urine to determine whether the offender has ingested any alcohol or other drugs.

(K) "Drug treatment program" means any program under which a person undergoes assessment and treatment designed to reduce or completely eliminate the person's physical or emotional reliance upon alcohol, another drug, or alcohol and another drug and under which the person may be required to receive assessment and treatment on an outpatient basis or may be required to reside at a facility other than the person's home or residence while undergoing assessment and treatment.

(L) "Economic loss" means any economic detriment suffered by a victim as a direct and proximate result of the commission of an offense and includes any loss of income due to lost time at work because of any injury caused to the victim, and any property loss, medical cost, or funeral expense incurred as a result of the commission of the offense. "Economic loss" does not include non-economic loss or any punitive or exemplary damages.

(M) "Education or training" includes study at, or in conjunction with a program offered by, a university, college, or technical college or vocational study and also includes the completion of primary school, secondary school, and literacy curricula or their equivalent.

(N) "Firearm" has the same meaning as in section 2923.11 of the Revised Code.

(O) "Halfway house" means a facility licensed by the division of parole and community services of the department of rehabilitation and correction pursuant to section 2967.14 of the Revised Code as a suitable facility for the care and treatment of adult offenders.

(P) "House arrest" means a period of confinement of an offender that is in the offender's home or in other premises specified by the sentencing court or by the parole board pursuant to section 2967.28 of the Revised Code and during which all of the following apply:

(1) The offender is required to remain in the offender's home or other specified premises for the specified period of confinement, except for periods of time during which the offender is at the offender's place of employment or at other premises as authorized by the sentencing court or by the parole board.

(2) The offender is required to report periodically to a person designated by the court or parole board.

(3) The offender is subject to any other restrictions and requirements that may be imposed by the sentencing court or by the parole board.

(Q) "Intensive probation supervision" means a requirement that an offender maintain frequent contact with a person appointed by the court, or by the parole board pursuant to section 2967.28 of the Revised Code, to supervise the offender while the offender is seeking or maintaining necessary employment and participating in training, education, and treatment programs as required in the court's or parole board's order. "Intensive probation supervision" includes intensive parole supervision and intensive post-release control supervision.

(R) "Jail" means a jail, workhouse, minimum security jail, or other residential facility used for the confinement of alleged or convicted offenders that is operated by a political subdivision or a combination of political subdivisions of this state.

(S) "Jail term" means the term in a jail that a sentencing court imposes or is authorized to impose pursuant to section 2929.24 or 2929.25 of the Revised Code or pursuant to any other provision of the Revised Code that authorizes a term in a jail for a misdemeanor conviction.

(T) "Mandatory jail term" means the term in a jail that a sentencing court is required to impose pursuant to division (G) of section 1547.99 of the Revised Code, division (E) of section 2903.06 or division (D) of section 2903.08 of the Revised Code, division (E) or (G) of section 2929.24 of the Revised Code, division (B) of section 4510.14 of the Revised Code, or division (G) of section 4511.19 of the Revised Code or pursuant to any other provision of the Revised Code that requires a term in a jail for a misdemeanor conviction.

(U) "Delinquent child" has the same meaning as in section 2152.02 of the Revised Code.

(V) "License violation report" means a report that is made by a sentencing court, or by the parole board pursuant to section 2967.28 of the Revised Code, to the regulatory or licensing board or agency that issued an offender a professional license or a license or permit to do business in this state and that specifies that the offender has been convicted of or pleaded guilty to an offense that may violate the conditions under which the offender's professional license or license or permit to do business in this state was granted or an offense for which the offender's professional license or license or permit to do business in this state may be revoked or suspended.

(W) "Major drug offender" means an offender who is convicted of or pleads guilty to the possession of, sale of, or offer to sell any drug, compound, mixture, preparation, or substance that consists of or contains at least one thousand grams of hashish; at least one hundred grams of cocaine; at least two thousand five hundred unit doses or two hundred fifty grams of heroin; at least five thousand unit doses of L.S.D. or five hundred grams of L.S.D. in a liquid concentrate, liquid extract, or liquid distillate form;

or at least one hundred times the amount of any other schedule I or II controlled substance other than marihuana that is necessary to commit a felony of the third degree pursuant to section 2925.03, 2925.04, 2925.05, or 2925.11 of the Revised Code that is based on the possession of, sale of, or offer to sell the controlled substance.

(X) "Mandatory prison term" means any of the following:

(1) Subject to division (X)(2) of this section, the term in prison that must be imposed for the offenses or circumstances set forth in divisions (F)(1) to (8) or (F)(12) to (18) of section 2929.13 and division (B) of section 2929.14 of the Revised Code. Except as provided in sections 2925.02, 2925.03, 2925.04, 2925.05, and 2925.11 of the Revised Code, unless the maximum or another specific term is required under section 2929.14 or 2929.142 of the Revised Code, a mandatory prison term described in this division may be any prison term authorized for the level of offense.

(2) The term of sixty or one hundred twenty days in prison that a sentencing court is required to impose for a third or fourth degree felony OVI offense pursuant to division (G)(2) of section 2929.13 and division (G)(1)(d) or (e) of section 4511.19 of the Revised Code or the term of one, two, three, four, or five years in prison that a sentencing court is required to impose pursuant to division (G)(2) of section 2929.13 of the Revised Code.

(3) The term in prison imposed pursuant to division (A) of section 2971.03 of the Revised Code for the offenses and in the circumstances described in division (F)(11) of section 2929.13 of the Revised Code or pursuant to division (B)(1)(a), (b), or (c), (B)(2)(a), (b), or (c), or (B)(3)(a), (b), (c), or (d) of section 2971.03 of the Revised Code and that term as modified or terminated pursuant to section 2971.05 of the Revised Code.

(Y) "Monitored time" means a period of time during which an offender continues to be under the control of the sentencing court or parole board, subject to no conditions other than leading a law-abiding life.

(Z) "Offender" means a person who, in this state, is convicted of or pleads guilty to a felony or a misdemeanor.

(AA) "Prison" means a residential facility used for the confinement of convicted felony offenders that is under the control of the department of rehabilitation and correction but does not include a violation sanction center operated under authority of section 2967.141 of the Revised Code.

(BB) "Prison term" includes either of the following sanctions for an offender:

(1) A stated prison term;

(2) A term in a prison shortened by, or with the approval of, the sentencing court pursuant to section 2929.143, 2929.20, 2967.26, 5120.031, 5120.032, or 5120.073 of the Revised Code.

(CC) "Repeat violent offender" means a person about whom both of the following apply:

(1) The person is being sentenced for committing or for complicity in committing any of the following:

(a) Aggravated murder, murder, any felony of the first or second degree that is an offense of violence, or an attempt to commit any of these offenses if the attempt is a felony of the first or second degree;

(b) An offense under an existing or former law of this state, another state, or the United States that is or was substantially equivalent to an offense described in division (CC)(1)(a) of this section.

(2) The person previously was convicted of or pleaded guilty to an offense described in division (CC)(1)(a) or (b) of this section.

(DD) "Sanction" means any penalty imposed upon an offender who is convicted of or pleads guilty to an offense, as punishment for the offense. "Sanction" includes any sanction imposed pursuant to any provision of sections 2929.14 to 2929.18 or 2929.24 to 2929.28 of the Revised Code.

(EE) "Sentence" means the sanction or combination of sanctions imposed by the sentencing court on an offender who is convicted of or pleads guilty to an offense.

(FF) "Stated prison term" means the prison term, mandatory prison term, or combination of all prison terms and mandatory prison terms imposed by the sentencing court pursuant to section 2929.14, 2929.142, or 2971.03 of the Revised Code or under section 2919.25 of the Revised Code. "Stated prison term" includes any credit received by the offender for time spent in jail awaiting trial, sentencing, or transfer to prison for the offense and any time spent under house arrest or house arrest with electronic monitoring imposed after earning credits pursuant to section 2967.193 of the Revised Code.

(GG) "Victim-offender mediation" means a reconciliation or mediation program that involves an offender and the victim of the offense committed by the offender and that includes a meeting in which the offender and the victim may discuss the offense, discuss restitution, and consider other sanctions for the offense.

(HH) "Fourth degree felony OVI offense" means a violation of division (A) of section 4511.19 of the Revised Code that, under division (G) of that section, is a felony of the fourth degree.

(II) "Mandatory term of local incarceration" means the term of sixty or one hundred twenty days in a jail, a community-based correctional facility, a halfway house, or an alternative residential facility that a sentencing court may impose upon a person who is convicted of or pleads guilty to a fourth degree felony OVI offense pursuant to division (G)(1) of section 2929.13 of the Revised Code and division (G)(1)(d) or (e) of section 4511.19 of the Revised Code.

(JJ) "Designated homicide, assault, or kidnapping offense," "violent sex offense," "sexual motivation specification," "sexually violent offense," "sexually violent predator," and "sexually violent predator specification" have the same meanings as in section 2971.01 of the Revised Code.

(KK) "Sexually oriented offense," "child-victim oriented offense," and "tier III sex offender/child-victim offender," have the same meanings as in section 2950.01 of the Revised Code.

(LL) An offense is "committed in the vicinity of a child" if the offender commits the offense within thirty feet of or within the same residential unit as a child who is under eighteen years of age, regardless of whether the offender knows the age of the child or whether the offender knows the offense is being committed within thirty feet of or within the same residential unit as the child and regardless of whether the child actually views the commission of the offense.

(MM) "Family or household member" has the same meaning as in section 2919.25 of the Revised Code.

(NN) "Motor vehicle" and "manufactured home" have the same meanings as in section 4501.01 of the Revised Code.

(OO) "Detention" and "detention facility" have the same meanings as in section 2921.01 of the Revised Code.

(PP) "Third degree felony OVI offense" means a violation of division (A) of section 4511.19 of the Revised Code that, under division (G) of that section, is a felony of the third degree.

(QQ) "Random drug testing" has the same meaning as in section 5120.63 of the Revised Code.

(RR) "Felony sex offense" has the same meaning as in section 2967.28 of the Revised Code.

(SS) "Body armor" has the same meaning as in section 2941.1411 of the Revised Code.

(TT) "Electronic monitoring" means monitoring through the use of an electronic monitoring device.

(UU) "Electronic monitoring device" means any of the following:

(1) Any device that can be operated by electrical or battery power and that conforms with all of the following:

(a) The device has a transmitter that can be attached to a person, that will transmit a specified signal to a receiver of the type described in division (UU)(1)(b) of this section if the transmitter is removed from the person, turned off, or altered in any manner without prior court approval in relation to electronic monitoring or without prior approval of the department of rehabilitation and correction in relation to the use of an electronic monitoring device for an inmate on transitional control or otherwise is tampered with, that can transmit continuously and periodically a signal to that receiver when the person is within a specified distance from the receiver, and that can transmit an appropriate signal to that receiver if the person to whom it is attached travels a specified distance from that receiver.

(b) The device has a receiver that can receive continuously the signals transmitted by a transmitter of the type described in division (UU)(1)(a) of this section, can transmit continuously those signals by a wireless or landline telephone connection to a central monitoring computer of the type described in division (UU)(1)(c) of this section, and can transmit continuously an appropriate signal to that central monitoring computer if the device has been turned off or altered without prior court approval or otherwise tampered with. The device is designed specifically for use in electronic monitoring, is not a converted wireless phone or another tracking device that is clearly not designed for electronic monitoring, and provides a means of text-based or voice communication with the person.

(c) The device has a central monitoring computer that can receive continuously the signals transmitted by a wireless or landline telephone connection by a receiver of the type described in division (UU)(1)(b) of this section and can monitor continuously the person to whom an electronic monitoring device of the type described in division (UU)(1)(a) of this section is attached.

(2) Any device that is not a device of the type described in division (UU)(1) of this section and that conforms with all of the following:

(a) The device includes a transmitter and receiver that can monitor and determine the location of a subject person at any time, or at a designated point in time, through the use of a central monitoring computer or through other electronic means.

(b) The device includes a transmitter and receiver that can determine at any time, or at a designated point in time, through the use of a central monitoring computer or other electronic means the fact that the transmitter is turned off or altered in any manner without prior approval of the court in relation to the electronic monitoring or without prior approval of the department of rehabilitation and correction in relation to the use of an electronic monitoring device for an inmate on transitional control or otherwise is tampered with.

(3) Any type of technology that can adequately track or determine the location of a subject person at any time and that is approved by the director of rehabilitation and correction, including, but not limited to, any satellite technology, voice tracking system, or retinal scanning system that is so approved.

(VV) "Non-economic loss" means nonpecuniary harm suffered by a victim of an offense as a result of or related to the commission of the offense, including, but not limited to, pain and suffering; loss of society, consortium, companionship, care, assistance, attention, protection, advice, guidance, counsel, instruction, training, or education; mental anguish; and any other intangible loss.

(WW) "Prosecutor" has the same meaning as in section 2935.01 of the Revised Code.

(XX) "Continuous alcohol monitoring" means the ability to automatically test and periodically transmit alcohol consumption levels and tamper attempts at least every hour, regardless of the location of the person who is being monitored.

(YY) A person is "adjudicated a sexually violent predator" if the person is convicted of or pleads guilty to a violent sex offense and also is convicted of or pleads guilty to a sexually violent predator specification that was included in the indictment, count in the indictment, or information charging that violent sex offense or if the person is convicted of or pleads guilty to a designated homicide, assault, or kidnapping offense and also is convicted of or pleads guilty to both a sexual motivation specification and a sexually violent predator specification that were included in the indictment, count in the indictment, or information charging that designated homicide, assault, or kidnapping offense.

(ZZ) An offense is "committed in proximity to a school" if the offender commits the offense in a school safety zone or within five hundred feet of any school building or the boundaries of any school premises, regardless of whether the offender knows the offense is being committed in a school safety zone or within five hundred feet of any school building or the boundaries of any school premises.

(AAA) "Human trafficking" means a scheme or plan to which all of the following apply:

(1) Its object is to subject a victim or victims to involuntary servitude, as defined in section 2905.31 of the Revised Code, to compel a victim or victims to engage in sexual activity for hire, to engage in a performance that is obscene, sexually oriented, or nudity oriented, or to be a model or participant in the production of material that is obscene, sexually oriented, or nudity oriented.

(2) It involves at least two felony offenses, whether or not there has been a prior conviction for any of the felony offenses, to which all of the following apply:

(a) Each of the felony offenses is a violation of section 2905.01, 2905.02, 2905.32, 2907.21, 2907.22, or 2923.32, division (A)(1) or (2) of section 2907.323, or division (B)(1), (2), (3), (4), or (5) of section 2919.22 of the Revised Code or is a violation of a law of any state other than this state that is substantially similar to any of the sections or divisions of the Revised Code identified in this division.

(b) At least one of the felony offenses was committed in this state.

(c) The felony offenses are related to the same scheme or plan and are not isolated instances.

(BBB) "Material," "nudity," "obscene," "performance," and "sexual activity" have the same meanings as in section 2907.01 of the Revised Code.

(CCC) "Material that is obscene, sexually oriented, or nudity oriented" means any material that is obscene, that shows a person participating or engaging in sexual activity, masturbation, or bestiality, or that shows a person in a state of nudity.

(DDD) "Performance that is obscene, sexually oriented, or nudity oriented" means any performance that is obscene, that shows a person participating or engaging in sexual activity, masturbation, or bestiality, or that shows a person in a state of nudity.

**HISTORY: 146 v S 2 (Eff 7-1-96); 146 v S 269 (Eff 7-1-96); 146 v H 445 (Eff 9-3-96); 146 v H 480 (Eff 10-16-96); 146 v S 166 (Eff 10-17-96); 146 v H 180 (Eff 1-1-97); 147 v H 378 (Eff 3-10-98); 147 v S 111 (Eff 3-17-98); 148 v S 9 (Eff 3-8-2000); 148 v S 107 (Eff 3-23-2000); 148 v S 22 (Eff 5-17-2000); 148 v H 349 (Eff 9-22-2000); 148 v S 222 (Eff 3-22-2001); 148 v S 179, § 3 (Eff 1-1-2002); 149 v H 327. Eff 7-8-2002; 149 v H 490, § 1, eff. 1-1-04; 149 v S 123, § 1, eff. 1-1-04; 150 v S 5, § 1, Eff 7-31-03; 150 v S 5, § 3, eff. 1-1-04; 150 v S 57, § 1, eff. 1-1-04; 150 v H 52, § 1, eff. 6-1-04; 150 v H 163, § 1, eff. 9-23-04; 150 v H 473, § 1, eff. 4-29-05; 151 v H 95, § 1, eff. 8-3-06; 151 v H 162, § 1, eff. 10-12-06; 151 v S 260, § 1, eff. 1-2-07; 151 v H 461, § 1, eff. 4-4-07; 152 v S 10, § 1, eff. 1-1-08; 152 v S 220, § 1, eff. 9-30-08; 152 v H 280, § 1, eff. 4-7-09; 152 v H 130, § 1, eff. 4-7-09; 153 v S 162, § 1, eff. 9-13-10; 153 v S 235, § 1, eff. 3-24-11; 2011 HB 86, § 1, eff. Sept. 30, 2011.**

The provisions of § 7 of 153 v S 162 read in part as follows:

SECTION 7. * * * Section 2929.01 of the Revised Code is presented in this act as a composite of the section as amended by both Am. Sub. H.B. 130 and Am. Sub. H.B. 280 of the 127th General Assembly. * * * The General Assembly, applying the principle stated in division (B) of section 1.52 of the Revised Code that amendments are to be harmonized if reasonably capable of simultaneous operation, finds that the composites are the resulting versions of those sections in effect prior to the effective date of those sections as presented in this act.

The effective date is set by § 3 of 152 v S 10.

The provisions of § 6 of 152 v S 10 read as follows:

SECTION 6. * * * Section 2929.01 of the Revised Code is presented in this act as a composite of the section as amended by both Am. Sub. H.B. 461 and Am. Sub. S.B. 260 of the 126th General Assembly. * * * The General Assembly, applying the principle stated in division (B) of section 1.52 of the Revised Code that amendments are to be harmonized if reasonably capable of simultaneous operation, finds that the composites are the resulting versions of the sections in effect prior to the effective date of the sections as presented in this act.

The provisions of § 5(B) of 151 v H 461 read as follows:

SECTION 5. (B) Section 2929.01 of the Revised Code is presented in this act as a composite of the section as amended by both Am. Sub. H.B. 95 and Am. Sub. H.B. 162 of the 126th General Assembly. The General Assembly, applying the principle stated in division (B) of section 1.52 of the Revised Code that amendments are to be harmonized if reasonably capable of simultaneous operation, finds that the composite is the resulting version of the section in effect prior to the effective date of the section as presented in this act.

The provisions of § 3(B) of 151 v S 260 read as follows:

SECTION 3. * * * (B) Section 2929.01 of the Revised Code is presented in this act as a composite of the section as amended by both Am. Sub. H.B. 95 and Am. Sub. H.B. 162 of the 126th General Assembly. The General Assembly, applying the principle stated in division (B) of section 1.52 of the Revised Code that amendments are to be harmonized if reasonably capable of simultaneous operation, finds that the composite is the resulting version of the section in effect prior to the effective date of the section as presented in this act.

The provisions of § 3 of H.B. 473 (150 v —) read as follows:

SECTION 3. * * * Sections 2929.01, 2929.13, and 2929.14 of the Revised Code are presented in this act as composites of the sections as amended by both Sub. H.B. 52 and Am. Sub. H.B. 163 of the 125th General Assembly. * * * The General Assembly, applying the principle stated in division (B) of section 1.52 of the Revised Code that amendments are to be harmonized if reasonably capable of simultaneous operation, finds that the composites are the resulting versions of the sections in effect prior to the effective date of the sections as presented in this act.

The effective date is set by section 4 of H.B. 490.

**Not analogous to former RC § 2929.01 (134 v H 511; 136 v H 300; 137 v H 565; 139 v S 199; 140 v S 210; 142 v H 261; 145 v H 571; 145 v S 186, repealed 146 v S 2, § 2, eff 7-1-96.**

The provisions of § 5 of S.B. 123 (149 v —), as amended by § 3 of H.B. 163 (150 v —), read as follows:

SECTION 5. Notwithstanding division (B) of section 1.58 of the Revised Code, the provisions of the Revised Code amended or enacted in Sections 1 and 2 of this act shall apply only in relation to conduct and offenses committed on or after January 1, 2004. Conduct and offenses committed prior to January 1, 2004, shall be governed by the law in effect on the date the conduct or offense was committed.

See provisions, § 11 of SB 179 (148 v —) following RC § 2923.36.

## [PENALTIES FOR MURDER]

### § 2929.02 Penalties for aggravated murder or murder.

(A) Whoever is convicted of or pleads guilty to aggravated murder in violation of section 2903.01 of the Revised Code shall suffer death or be imprisoned for life, as determined pursuant to sections 2929.022 [2929.02.2], 2929.03, and 2929.04 of the Revised Code, except that no person who raises the matter of age pursuant to section 2929.023 [2929.02.3] of the Revised Code and who is not found to have been eighteen years of age or older at the time of the commission of the offense shall suffer death. In addition, the offender may be fined an amount fixed by the court, but not more than twenty-five thousand dollars.

(B)(1) Except as otherwise provided in division (B)(2) or (3) of this section, whoever is convicted of or pleads guilty to murder in violation of section 2903.02 of the Revised Code shall be imprisoned for an indefinite term of fifteen years to life.

(2) Except as otherwise provided in division (B)(3) of this section, if a person is convicted of or pleads guilty to murder in violation of section 2903.02 of the Revised Code, the victim of the offense was less than thirteen years of age, and the offender also is convicted of or pleads guilty to a sexual motivation specification that was included in the indictment, count in the indictment, or information charging the offense, the court shall impose an indefinite prison term of thirty years to life pursuant to division (B)(3) of section 2971.03 of the Revised Code.

(3) If a person is convicted of or pleads guilty to murder in violation of section 2903.02 of the Revised Code and also is convicted of or pleads guilty to a sexual motivation specification and a sexually violent predator specification that were included in the indictment, count in the indictment, or information that charged the murder, the court shall impose upon the offender a term of life imprisonment without parole that shall be served pursuant to section 2971.03 of the Revised Code.

(4) In addition, the offender may be fined an amount fixed by the court, but not more than fifteen thousand dollars.

(C) The court shall not impose a fine or fines for aggravated murder or murder which, in the aggregate and to the extent not suspended by the court, exceeds the amount which the offender is or will be able to pay by the method and within the time allowed without undue hardship to the offender or to the dependents of the offender, or will prevent the offender from making reparation for the victim's wrongful death.

(D)(1) In addition to any other sanctions imposed for a violation of section 2903.01 or 2903.02 of the Revised Code, if the offender used a motor vehicle as the means to commit the violation, the court shall impose upon the offender a class two suspension of the offender's driver's license, commercial driver's license, temporary instruction permit, probationary license, or nonresident operating privilege as specified in division (A)(2) of section 4510.02 of the Revised Code.

(2) As used in division (D) of this section, "motor vehicle" has the same meaning as in section 4501.01 of the Revised Code.

**HISTORY: 134 v H 511 (Eff 1-1-74); 139 v S 1 (Eff 10-19-81); 146 v H 180 (Eff 1-1-97); 147 v S 107. Eff 7-29-98; 151 v H 461, § 1, eff. 4-4-07; 152 v S 10, § 1, eff. 1-1-08.**

The effective date is set by § 3 of 152 v S 10.

## § 2929.021 Notice to supreme court of indictment charging aggravated murder; plea.

(A) If an indictment or a count in an indictment charges the defendant with aggravated murder and contains one or more specifications of aggravating circumstances listed in division (A) of section 2929.04 of the Revised Code, the clerk of the court in which the indictment is filed, within fifteen days after the day on which it is filed, shall file a notice with the supreme court indicating that the indictment was filed. The notice shall be in the form prescribed by the clerk of the supreme court and shall contain, for each charge of aggravated murder with a specification, at least the following information pertaining to the charge:

(1) The name of the person charged in the indictment or count in the indictment with aggravated murder with a specification;

(2) The docket number or numbers of the case or cases arising out of the charge, if available;

(3) The court in which the case or cases will be heard;

(4) The date on which the indictment was filed.

(B) If the indictment or a count in an indictment charges the defendant with aggravated murder and contains one or more specifications of aggravating circumstances listed in division (A) of section 2929.04 of the Revised Code and if the defendant pleads guilty or no contest to any offense in the case or if the indictment or any count in the indictment is dismissed, the clerk of the court in which the plea is entered or the indictment or count is dismissed shall file a notice with the supreme court indicating what action was taken in the case. The notice shall be filed within fifteen days after the plea is entered or the indictment or count is dismissed, shall be in the form prescribed by the clerk of the supreme court, and shall contain at least the following information:

(1) The name of the person who entered the guilty or no contest plea or who is named in the indictment or count that is dismissed;

(2) The docket numbers of the cases in which the guilty or no contest plea is entered or in which the indictment or count is dismissed;

(3) The sentence imposed on the offender in each case.

**HISTORY: 139 v S 1. Eff 10-19-81.**

## § 2929.022 Determination of aggravating circumstances of prior conviction.

(A) If an indictment or count in an indictment charging a defendant with aggravated murder contains a specification of the aggravating circumstance of a prior conviction listed in division (A)(5) of section 2929.04 of the Revised Code, the defendant may elect to have the panel of three judges, if the defendant waives trial by jury, or the trial judge, if the defendant is tried by jury, determine the existence of that aggravating circumstance at the sentencing hearing held pursuant to divisions (C) and (D) of section 2929.03 of the Revised Code.

(1) If the defendant does not elect to have the existence of the aggravating circumstance determined at the sentencing hearing, the defendant shall be tried on the charge of aggravated murder, on the specification of the aggravating circumstance of a prior conviction listed in division (A)(5) of section 2929.04 of the Revised Code, and on any other specifications of an aggravating circumstance listed in division (A) of section 2929.04 of the Revised Code in a single trial as in any other criminal case in which a person is charged with aggravated murder and specifications.

(2) If the defendant does elect to have the existence of the aggravating circumstance of a prior conviction listed in division (A)(5) of section 2929.04 of the Revised Code determined at the sentencing hearing, then, following a verdict of guilty of the charge of aggravated murder, the panel of three judges or the trial judge shall:

(a) Hold a sentencing hearing pursuant to division (B) of this section, unless required to do otherwise under division (A)(2)(b) of this section;

(b) If the offender raises the matter of age at trial pursuant to section 2929.023 [2929.02.3] of the Revised Code and is not found at trial to have been eighteen years of age or older at the time of the commission of the offense, conduct a hearing to determine if the specification of the aggravating circumstance of a prior conviction listed in division (A)(5) of section 2929.04 of the Revised Code is proven beyond a reasonable doubt. After conducting the hearing, the panel or judge shall proceed as follows:

(i) If that aggravating circumstance is proven beyond a reasonable doubt or if the defendant at trial was convicted of any other specification of an aggravating circumstance, the panel or judge shall impose sentence according to division (E) of section 2929.03 of the Revised Code.

(ii) If that aggravating circumstance is not proven beyond a reasonable doubt and the defendant at trial was not convicted of any other specification of an aggravating circumstance, except as otherwise provided in this division, the panel or judge shall impose sentence of life imprisonment with parole eligibility after serving twenty years of imprisonment on the offender. If that aggravating circumstance is not proven beyond a reasonable doubt, the defendant at trial was not convicted of any other specification of an aggravating circumstance, the victim of the aggravated murder was less than thirteen years of age, and the offender also is convicted of or pleads guilty to a sexual motivation specification that was included in the indictment, count in the indictment, or information charging the offense, the panel or judge shall sentence the offender pursuant to division (B)(3) of section 2971.03 of the Revised Code to an indefinite term consisting of a minimum term of thirty years and a maximum term of life imprisonment.

(B) At the sentencing hearing, the panel of judges, if the defendant was tried by a panel of three judges, or the trial judge, if the defendant was tried by jury, shall, when required pursuant to division (A)(2) of this section, first determine if the specification of the aggravating circumstance of a prior conviction listed in division (A)(5) of section 2929.04 of the Revised Code is proven beyond a reasonable doubt. If the panel of judges or the trial judge determines that the specification of the aggravating circumstance of a prior conviction listed in division (A)(5) of section 2929.04 of the Revised Code is proven beyond a reasonable doubt or if they do not determine that the specification is proven beyond a reasonable doubt but the defendant at trial was convicted of a specification of any other aggravating circumstance listed in division (A) of section 2929.04 of the Revised Code, the panel of judges or the trial judge and trial jury shall impose sentence on the offender pursuant to division (D) of section 2929.03 and section 2929.04 of the Revised Code. If the panel of judges or the trial judge does not determine that the specification of the aggravating circumstance of a prior conviction listed in division (A)(5) of section 2929.04 of the Revised Code is proven beyond a reasonable doubt and the defendant at trial was not convicted of any other specification of an aggravating circumstance listed in division (A) of section 2929.04 of the Revised Code, the panel of judges or the trial judge shall terminate the sentencing hearing and impose sentence on the offender as follows:

(1) Subject to division (B)(2) of this section, the panel or judge shall impose a sentence of life imprisonment with parole eligibility after serving twenty years of imprisonment on the offender.

(2) If the victim of the aggravated murder was less than thirteen years of age and the offender also is convicted of or pleads guilty to a sexual motivation specification that was included in the indictment, count in the indictment, or information charging the offense, the panel or judge shall sentence the offender pursuant to division (B)(3) of section 2971.03 of the Revised Code to an indefinite term consisting of a minimum term of thirty years and a maximum term of life imprisonment.

**HISTORY: 139 v S 1. Eff 10-19-81; 152 v S 10, § 1, eff. 1-1-08.**

The effective date is set by § 3 of 152 v S 10.

## § 2929.023 Defendant may raise matter of age.

A person charged with aggravated murder and one or more specifications of an aggravating circumstance may, at trial, raise the matter of his age at the time of the alleged commission of the offense and may present evidence at trial that he was not eighteen years of age or older at the time of the alleged commission of the offense. The burdens of raising the matter of age, and of going forward with the evidence relating to the matter of age, are upon the defendant. After a defendant has raised the matter of age at trial, the prosecution shall have the burden of proving, by proof beyond a reasonable doubt, that the defendant was eighteen years of age or older at the time of the alleged commission of the offense.

**HISTORY: 139 v S 1. Eff 10-19-81.**

## § 2929.024 Investigation services and experts for indigent.

If the court determines that the defendant is indigent and that investigation services, experts, or other services are reasonably necessary for the proper representation of a defendant charged with aggravated murder at trial or at the sentencing hearing, the court shall authorize the defendant's counsel to obtain the necessary services for the defendant, and shall order that payment of the fees and expenses for the necessary services be made in the same manner that payment for appointed counsel is made pursuant to Chapter 120. of the Revised Code. If the court determines that the necessary services had to be obtained prior to court authorization for payment of the fees and expenses for the necessary services, the court may, after the services have been obtained, authorize the defendant's counsel to obtain the necessary services and order that payment of the fees and expenses for the necessary services be made as provided in this section.

**HISTORY: 139 v S 1. Eff 10-19-81.**

## § 2929.03 Imposing sentence for aggravated murder.

(A) If the indictment or count in the indictment charging aggravated murder does not contain one or more specifications of aggravating circumstances listed in division (A) of section 2929.04 of the Revised Code, then, following a verdict of guilty of the charge of aggravated murder, the trial court shall impose sentence on the offender as follows:

(1) Except as provided in division (A)(2) of this section, the trial court shall impose one of the following sentences on the offender:

(a) Life imprisonment without parole;

(b) Subject to division (A)(1)(e) of this section, life imprisonment with parole eligibility after serving twenty years of imprisonment;

(c) Subject to division (A)(1)(e) of this section, life imprisonment with parole eligibility after serving twenty-five full years of imprisonment;

(d) Subject to division (A)(1)(e) of this section, life imprisonment with parole eligibility after serving thirty full years of imprisonment;

(e) If the victim of the aggravated murder was less than thirteen years of age, the offender also is convicted of or pleads guilty to a sexual motivation specification that was included in the indictment, count in the indictment, or information charging the offense, and the trial court does not impose a sentence of life imprisonment without parole on the offender pursuant to division (A)(1)(a) of this section, the trial court shall sentence the offender pursuant to division (B)(3) of section 2971.03 of the Revised Code to an indefinite term consisting of a minimum term of thirty years and a maximum term of life imprisonment that shall be served pursuant to that section.

(2) If the offender also is convicted of or pleads guilty to a sexual motivation specification and a sexually violent predator specification that are included in the indictment, count in the indictment, or information that charged the aggravated murder, the trial court shall impose upon the offender a sentence of life imprisonment without parole that shall be served pursuant to section 2971.03 of the Revised Code.

(B) If the indictment or count in the indictment charging aggravated murder contains one or more specifications of aggravating circumstances listed in division (A) of section 2929.04 of the Revised Code, the verdict shall separately state whether the accused is found guilty or not guilty of the principal charge and, if guilty of the principal charge, whether the offender was eighteen years of age or older at the time of the commission of the offense, if the matter of age was raised by the offender pursuant to section 2929.023 [2929.02.3] of the Revised Code, and whether the offender is guilty or not guilty of each specification. The jury shall be instructed on its duties in this regard. The instruction to the jury shall include an instruction that a specification shall be proved beyond a reasonable doubt in order to support a guilty verdict on the specification, but the instruction shall not mention the penalty that may be the consequence of a guilty or not guilty verdict on any charge or specification.

(C)(1) If the indictment or count in the indictment charging aggravated murder contains one or more specifications of aggravating circumstances listed in division (A) of section 2929.04 of the Revised Code, then, following a verdict of guilty of the charge but not guilty of each of the specifications, and regardless of whether the offender raised the matter of age pursuant to section 2929.023 [2929.02.3] of the Revised Code, the trial court shall impose sentence on the offender as follows:

(a) Except as provided in division (C)(1)(b) of this section, the trial court shall impose one of the following sentences on the offender:

(i) Life imprisonment without parole;

(ii) Subject to division (C)(1)(a)(v) of this section, life imprisonment with parole eligibility after serving twenty years of imprisonment;

(iii) Subject to division (C)(1)(a)(v) of this section, life imprisonment with parole eligibility after serving twenty-five full years of imprisonment;

(iv) Subject to division (C)(1)(a)(v) of this section, life imprisonment with parole eligibility after serving thirty full years of imprisonment;

(v) If the victim of the aggravated murder was less than thirteen years of age, the offender also is convicted of or pleads guilty to a sexual motivation specification that was included in the indictment, count in the indictment, or information charging the offense, and the trial court does not impose a sentence of life imprisonment without parole on the offender pursuant to division (C)(1)(a)(i) of this section, the trial court shall sentence the offender pursuant to division (B)(3) of section 2971.03 of the Revised Code to an indefinite term consisting of a minimum term of thirty years and a maximum term of life imprisonment.

(b) If the offender also is convicted of or pleads guilty to a sexual motivation specification and a sexually violent predator specification that are included in the indictment, count in the indictment, or information that charged the aggravated murder, the trial court shall impose upon the offender a sentence of life imprisonment without parole that shall be served pursuant to section 2971.03 of the Revised Code.

(2)(a) If the indictment or count in the indictment contains one or more specifications of aggravating circumstances listed in division (A) of section 2929.04 of the Revised Code and if the offender is found guilty of both the charge and one or more of the specifications, the penalty to be imposed on the offender shall be one of the following:

(i) Except as provided in division (C)(2)(a)(ii) or (iii) of this section, the penalty to be imposed on the offender shall be death, life imprisonment without parole, life imprisonment with parole eligibility after serving twenty-five full years of imprisonment, or life imprisonment with parole eligibility after serving thirty full years of imprisonment.

(ii) Except as provided in division (C)(2)(a)(iii) of this section, if the victim of the aggravated murder was less than thirteen years of age, the offender also is convicted of or pleads guilty to a sexual motivation specification that was included in the indictment, count in the indictment, or information charging the offense, and the trial court does not impose a sentence of death or life imprisonment without parole on the offender pursuant to division (C)(2)(a)(i) of this section, the penalty to be imposed on the offender shall be an indefinite term consisting of a minimum term of thirty years and a maximum term of life imprisonment that shall be imposed pursuant to division (B)(3) of section 2971.03 of the Revised Code and served pursuant to that section.

(iii) If the offender also is convicted of or pleads guilty to a sexual motivation specification and a sexually violent predator specification that are included in the indictment, count in the indictment, or information that charged the aggravated murder, the penalty to be imposed on the offender shall be death or life imprisonment without parole that shall be served pursuant to section 2971.03 of the Revised Code.

(b) A penalty imposed pursuant to division (C)(2)(a)(i), (ii), or (iii) of this section shall be determined pursuant to divisions (D) and (E) of this section and shall be determined by one of the following:

(i) By the panel of three judges that tried the offender upon the offender's waiver of the right to trial by jury;

(ii) By the trial jury and the trial judge, if the offender was tried by jury.

(D)(1) Death may not be imposed as a penalty for aggravated murder if the offender raised the matter of age at trial pursuant to section 2929.023 [2929.02.3] of the Revised Code and was not found at trial to have been eighteen years of age or older at the time of the commission of the offense. When death may be imposed as a penalty for aggravated murder, the court shall proceed under this division. When death may be imposed as a penalty, the court, upon the request of the defendant, shall require a pre-sentence investigation to be made and, upon the request of the defendant, shall require a mental examination to be made, and shall require reports of the investigation and of any mental examination submitted to the court, pursuant to section 2947.06 of the Revised Code. No statement made or information provided by a defendant in a mental examination or proceeding conducted pursuant to this division shall be disclosed to any person, except as provided in this division, or be used in evidence against the defendant on the issue of guilt in any retrial. A pre-sentence investigation or mental examination shall not be made except upon request of the defendant. Copies of any reports prepared under this division shall be furnished to the court, to the trial jury if the offender was tried by a jury, to the prosecutor, and to the offender or the offender's counsel for use under this division. The court, and the trial jury if the offender was tried by a jury, shall consider any report prepared pursuant to this division and furnished to it and any evidence raised at trial that is relevant to the aggravating circumstances the offender was found guilty of committing or to any factors in mitigation of the imposition of the sentence of death, shall hear testimony and other evidence that is relevant to the nature and circumstances of the aggravating circumstances the offender was found guilty of committing, the mitigating factors set forth in division (B) of section 2929.04 of the Revised Code, and any other factors in mitigation of the imposition of the sentence of death, and shall hear the statement, if any, of the offender, and the arguments, if any, of counsel for the defense and prosecution, that are relevant to the penalty that should be imposed on the offender. The defendant shall be given great latitude in the presentation of evidence of the mitigating factors set forth in division (B) of section 2929.04 of the Revised Code and of any other factors in mitigation of the imposition of the sentence of death. If the offender chooses to make a statement, the offender is subject to cross-examination only if the offender consents to make the statement under oath or affirmation.

The defendant shall have the burden of going forward with the evidence of any factors in mitigation of the imposition of the sentence of death. The prosecution shall have the burden of proving, by proof beyond a reasonable doubt, that the aggravating circumstances the defendant was found guilty of committing are sufficient to outweigh the factors in mitigation of the imposition of the sentence of death.

(2) Upon consideration of the relevant evidence raised at trial, the testimony, other evidence, statement of the offender, arguments of counsel, and, if applicable, the reports submitted pursuant to division (D)(1) of this section, the trial jury, if the offender was tried by a jury, shall determine whether the aggravating circumstances the offender was found guilty of committing are sufficient to outweigh the mitigating factors present in the case. If the trial jury unanimously finds, by proof beyond a reasonable doubt, that the aggravating circumstances the offender was found guilty of committing outweigh the mitigating factors, the trial jury shall recommend to the court that the sentence of death be imposed on the offender. Absent such a finding, the jury shall recommend that the offender be sentenced to one of the following:

(a) Except as provided in division (D)(2)(b) or (c) of this section, to life imprisonment without parole, life imprisonment with parole eligibility after serving twenty-five full years of imprisonment, or life imprisonment with parole eligibility after serving thirty full years of imprisonment;

(b) Except as provided in division (D)(2)(c) of this section, if the victim of the aggravated murder was less than thirteen years of age, the offender also is convicted of or pleads guilty to a sexual motivation specification that was included in the indictment, count in the indictment, or information charging the offense, and the jury does not recommend a sentence of life imprisonment without parole pursuant to division (D)(2)(a) of this section, to an indefinite term consisting of a minimum term of thirty years and a maximum term of life imprisonment to be imposed pursuant to division (B)(3) of section 2971.03 of the Revised Code and served pursuant to that section.

(c) If the offender also is convicted of or pleads guilty to a sexual motivation specification and a sexually violent predator specification that are included in the indictment, count in the indictment, or information that charged the aggravated murder, to life imprisonment without parole.

If the trial jury recommends that the offender be sentenced to life imprisonment without parole, life imprisonment with parole eligibility after serving twenty-five full years of imprisonment, life imprisonment with parole eligibility after serving thirty full years of imprisonment, or an indefinite term consisting of a minimum term of thirty years and a maximum term of life imprisonment to be imposed pursuant to division (B)(3) of section 2971.03 of the Revised Code, the court shall impose the sentence recommended by the jury upon the offender. If the sentence is an indefinite term consisting of a minimum term of thirty years and a maximum term of life imprisonment imposed as described in division (D)(2)(b) of this section or a sentence of life imprisonment without parole imposed under division (D)(2)(c) of this section, the sentence shall be served pursuant to section 2971.03 of the Revised Code. If the trial jury recommends that the sentence of death be imposed upon the offender, the court shall proceed to impose sentence pursuant to division (D)(3) of this section.

(3) Upon consideration of the relevant evidence raised at trial, the testimony, other evidence, statement of the offender, arguments of counsel, and, if applicable, the reports submitted to the court pursuant to division (D)(1) of this section, if, after receiving pursuant to division (D)(2) of this section the trial jury's recommendation that the sentence of death be imposed, the court finds, by proof beyond a reasonable doubt, or if the panel of three judges unanimously finds, by proof beyond a reasonable doubt, that the aggravating circumstances the offender was found guilty of committing outweigh the mitigating factors, it shall impose sentence of death on the offender. Absent such a finding by the court or panel, the court or the panel shall impose one of the following sentences on the offender:

(a) Except as provided in division (D)(3)(b) of this section, one of the following:

(i) Life imprisonment without parole;

(ii) Subject to division (D)(3)(a)(iv) of this section, life imprisonment with parole eligibility after serving twenty-five full years of imprisonment;

(iii) Subject to division (D)(3)(a)(iv) of this section, life imprisonment with parole eligibility after serving thirty full years of imprisonment;

(iv) If the victim of the aggravated murder was less than thirteen years of age, the offender also is convicted of or pleads guilty to a sexual motivation specification that was included in the indictment, count in the indictment, or information charging the offense, and the trial court does not impose a sentence of life imprisonment without parole on the offender pursuant to division (D)(3)(a)(i) of this section, the court or panel shall sentence the offender pursuant to division (B)(3) of section 2971.03 of the Revised Code to an indefinite term consisting of a minimum term of thirty years and a maximum term of life imprisonment.

(b) If the offender also is convicted of or pleads guilty to a sexual motivation specification and a sexually violent predator specification that are included in the indictment, count in the indictment, or information that charged the aggravated murder, life imprisonment without parole that shall be served pursuant to section 2971.03 of the Revised Code.

(E) If the offender raised the matter of age at trial pursuant to section 2929.023 [2929.02.3] of the Revised Code, was convicted of aggravated murder and one or more specifications of an aggravating circumstance listed in division (A) of section 2929.04 of the Revised Code, and was not found at trial to have been eighteen years of age or older at the time of the commission of the offense, the court or the panel of three judges shall not impose a sentence of death on the offender. Instead, the court or panel shall impose one of the following sentences on the offender:

(1) Except as provided in division (E)(2) of this section, one of the following:

(a) Life imprisonment without parole;

(b) Subject to division (E)(2)(d) of this section, life imprisonment with parole eligibility after serving twenty-five full years of imprisonment;

(c) Subject to division (E)(2)(d) of this section, life imprisonment with parole eligibility after serving thirty full years of imprisonment;

(d) If the victim of the aggravated murder was less than thirteen years of age, the offender also is convicted of or pleads guilty to a sexual motivation specification that was included in the indictment, count in the indictment, or information charging the offense, and the trial court does not impose a sentence of life imprisonment without parole on the offender pursuant to division (E)(2)(a) of this section, the court or panel shall sentence the offender pursuant to division (B)(3) of section 2971.03 of the Revised Code to an indefinite term consisting of a minimum term of thirty years and a maximum term of life imprisonment.

(2) If the offender also is convicted of or pleads guilty to a sexual motivation specification and a sexually violent predator specification that are included in the indictment, count in the indictment, or information that charged the aggravated murder, life imprisonment without parole that shall be served pursuant to section 2971.03 of the Revised Code.

(F) The court or the panel of three judges, when it imposes sentence of death, shall state in a separate opinion its specific findings as to the existence of any of the mitigating factors set forth in division (B) of section 2929.04 of the Revised Code, the existence of any other mitigating factors, the aggravating circumstances the offender was found guilty of committing, and the reasons why the aggravating circumstances the offender was found guilty of committing were sufficient to outweigh the mitigating factors. The court or panel, when it imposes life imprisonment or an indefinite term consisting of a minimum term of thirty years and a maximum term of life imprisonment under division (D) of this section, shall state in a separate opinion its specific findings of which of the mitigating factors set forth in division (B) of section 2929.04 of the Revised Code it found to exist, what other mitigating factors it found to exist, what aggravating circumstances the offender was found guilty of committing, and why it could not find that these aggravating circumstances were sufficient to outweigh the mitigating factors. For cases in which a sentence of death is imposed for an offense committed before January 1, 1995, the court or panel shall file the opinion required to be prepared by this division with the clerk of the appropriate court of appeals and with the clerk of the supreme court within fifteen days after the court or panel imposes sentence. For cases in which a sentence of death is imposed for an offense committed on or after January 1, 1995, the court or panel shall file the opinion required to be prepared by this division with the clerk of the supreme court within fifteen days after the court or panel imposes sentence. The judgment in a case in which a sentencing hearing is held pursuant to this section is not final until the opinion is filed.

(G)(1) Whenever the court or a panel of three judges imposes a sentence of death for an offense committed before January 1, 1995, the clerk of the court in which the judgment is rendered shall deliver the entire record in the case to the appellate court.

(2) Whenever the court or a panel of three judges imposes a sentence of death for an offense committed on or after January 1, 1995, the clerk of the court in which the judgment is rendered shall deliver the entire record in the case to the supreme court.

**HISTORY: 134 v H 511 (Eff 1-1-74); 139 v S 1 (Eff 10-19-81); 146 v S 4 (Eff 9-21-95); 146 v S 2 (Eff 7-1-96); 146 v S 269 (Eff 7-1-96); 146 v H 180. Eff 1-1-97; 150 v H 184, § 1, eff. 3-23-05; 152 v S 10, § 1, eff. 1-1-08.**

The effective date is set by § 3 of 152 v S 10.

The provisions of § 3 of H.B. 184 (150 v —) read as follows:

SECTION 3. Section 2929.03 of the Revised Code is presented in this act as a composite of the section as amended by both Am. Sub. H.B. 180 and Am. Sub. S.B. 269 of the 121st General Assembly. The General Assembly, applying the principle stated in division (B) of section 1.52 of the Revised Code that amendments are to be harmonized if reasonably capable of simultaneous operation, finds that the composite is the resulting version of the section in effect prior to the effective date of the section as presented in this act.

The effective date is set by section 3 of HB 180.

The provisions of §§ 3, 4 of SB 269 read as follows:

SECTION 3. That Section 5 of Am. Sub. S.B. 2 of the 121st General Assembly be amended to read as follows:

"Sec. 5. The provisions of the Revised Code in existence prior to July 1, 1996, shall apply to a person upon whom a court imposed a term of imprisonment prior to that date and, notwithstanding division (B) of section 1.58 of the Revised Code, to a person upon whom a court, on or after that date and in accordance with the law in existence prior to that date, imposes a term of imprisonment for an offense that was committee prior to that date.

The provisions of the Revised Code in existence on and after July 1, 1996, apply to a person who commits an offense on or after that date."

SECTION 4. That existing Section 5 of Am. Sub. S.B. 2 of the 121st General Assembly is hereby repealed.

## § 2929.04 Criteria for imposing death or imprisonment for a capital offense.

(A) Imposition of the death penalty for aggravated murder is precluded unless one or more of the following is specified in the indictment or count in the indictment pursuant to section 2941.14 of the Revised Code and proved beyond a reasonable doubt:

(1) The offense was the assassination of the president of the United States or a person in line of succession to the presidency, the governor or lieutenant governor of this state, the president-elect or vice president-elect of the United States, the governor-elect or lieutenant governor-elect of this state, or a candidate for any of the offices described in this division. For purposes of this division, a person is a candidate if the person has been nominated for election according to law, if the person has filed a petition or petitions according to law to have the person's name placed on the ballot in a primary or general election, or if the person campaigns as a write-in candidate in a primary or general election.

(2) The offense was committed for hire.

(3) The offense was committed for the purpose of escaping detection, apprehension, trial, or punishment for another offense committed by the offender.

(4) The offense was committed while the offender was under detention or while the offender was at large after having broken detention. As used in division (A)(4) of this section, "detention" has the same meaning as in section 2921.01 of the Revised Code, except that detention does not include hospitalization, institutionalization, or confinement in a mental health facility or mental retardation and developmentally disabled facility unless at the time of the commission of the offense either of the following circumstances apply:

(a) The offender was in the facility as a result of being charged with a violation of a section of the Revised Code.

(b) The offender was under detention as a result of being convicted of or pleading guilty to a violation of a section of the Revised Code.

(5) Prior to the offense at bar, the offender was convicted of an offense an essential element of which was the purposeful killing of or attempt to kill another, or the offense at bar was part of a course of conduct involving the purposeful killing of or attempt to kill two or more persons by the offender.

(6) The victim of the offense was a law enforcement officer, as defined in section 2911.01 of the Revised Code, whom the offender had reasonable cause to know or knew to be a law enforcement officer as so defined, and either the victim, at the time of the commission of the offense, was engaged in the victim's duties, or it was the offender's specific purpose to kill a law enforcement officer as so defined.

(7) The offense was committed while the offender was committing, attempting to commit, or fleeing immediately after committing or attempting to commit kidnapping, rape, aggravated arson, aggravated robbery, or aggravated burglary, and either the offender was the principal offender in the commission of the aggravated murder or, if not the principal offender, committed the aggravated murder with prior calculation and design.

(8) The victim of the aggravated murder was a witness to an offense who was purposely killed to prevent the victim's testimony in any criminal proceeding and the aggravated murder was not committed during the commission, attempted commission, or flight immediately after the commission or attempted commission of the offense to which the victim was a witness, or the victim of the aggravated murder was a witness to an offense and was purposely killed in retaliation for the victim's testimony in any criminal proceeding.

(9) The offender, in the commission of the offense, purposefully caused the death of another who was under thirteen years of age at the time of the commission of the offense, and either the offender was the principal offender in the commission of the offense or, if not the principal offender, committed the offense with prior calculation and design.

(10) The offense was committed while the offender was committing, attempting to commit, or fleeing immediately after committing or attempting to commit terrorism.

(B) If one or more of the aggravating circumstances listed in division (A) of this section is specified in the indictment or count in the indictment and proved beyond a reasonable doubt, and if the offender did not raise the matter of age pursuant to section 2929.023 [2929.02.3] of the Revised Code or if the offender, after raising the matter of age, was found at trial to have been eighteen years of age or older at the time of the commission of the offense, the court, trial jury, or panel of three judges shall consider, and weigh against the aggravating circumstances proved beyond a reasonable doubt, the nature and circumstances of the offense, the history, character, and background of the offender, and all of the following factors:

(1) Whether the victim of the offense induced or facilitated it;

(2) Whether it is unlikely that the offense would have been committed, but for the fact that the offender was under duress, coercion, or strong provocation;

(3) Whether, at the time of committing the offense, the offender, because of a mental disease or defect, lacked substantial capacity to appreciate the criminality of the offender's conduct or to conform the offender's conduct to the requirements of the law;

(4) The youth of the offender;

(5) The offender's lack of a significant history of prior criminal convictions and delinquency adjudications;

(6) If the offender was a participant in the offense but not the principal offender, the degree of the offender's participation in the offense and the degree of the offender's participation in the acts that led to the death of the victim;

(7) Any other factors that are relevant to the issue of whether the offender should be sentenced to death.

(C) The defendant shall be given great latitude in the presentation of evidence of the factors listed in division (B) of this section and of any other factors in mitigation of the imposition of the sentence of death.

The existence of any of the mitigating factors listed in division (B) of this section does not preclude the imposition of a sentence of death on the offender but shall be weighed pursuant to divisions (D)(2) and (3) of section 2929.03 of the Revised Code by the trial court, trial jury, or the panel of three judges against the aggravating circumstances the offender was found guilty of committing.

**HISTORY: 134 v H 511 (Eff 1-1-74); 139 v S 1 (Eff 10-19-81); 147 v S 32 (Eff 8-6-97); 147 v H 151 (Eff 9-16-97); 147 v S 193 (Eff 12-29-98); 149 v S 184. Eff 5-15-2002.**

The provisions of § 3 of SB 193 (147 v —) read as follows:

SECTION 3. Section 2929.04 of the Revised Code is presented in this act as a composite of the section as amended by both Sub. H.B. 151 and Am. S.B. 32 of the 122nd General Assembly, with the new language of neither of the acts shown in capital letters. This is in recognition of the principle stated in division (B) of section 1.52 of the Revised Code that such amendments are to be harmonized where not substantively irreconcilable and constitutes a legislative finding that such is the resulting version in effect prior to the effective date of this act.

## § 2929.05 Appellate review of death sentence.

(A) Whenever sentence of death is imposed pursuant to sections 2929.03 and 2929.04 of the Revised Code, the court of appeals, in a case in which a sentence of death was imposed for an offense committed before January 1, 1995, and the supreme court shall review upon appeal the sentence of death at the same time that they review the other issues in the case. The court of appeals and the supreme court shall review the judgment in the case and the sentence of death imposed by the court or panel of three judges in the same manner that they review other criminal cases, except that they shall review and independently weigh all of the facts and other evidence disclosed in the record in the case and consider the offense and the offender to determine whether the aggravating circumstances the offender was found guilty of committing outweigh the mitigating factors in the case, and whether the sentence of death is appropriate. In determining whether the sentence of death is appropriate, the court of appeals, in a case in which a sentence of death was imposed for an offense committed before January 1, 1995, and the supreme court shall consider whether the sentence is excessive or disproportionate to the penalty imposed in similar cases. They also shall review all of the facts and other evidence to determine if the evidence supports the finding of the aggravating circumstances the trial jury or the panel of three judges found the offender guilty of committing, and shall determine whether the sentencing court properly weighed the aggravating circumstances the offender was found guilty of committing and the mitigating factors. The court of appeals, in a case in which a sentence of death was imposed for an offense committed before January 1, 1995, or the supreme court shall affirm a sentence of death only if the particular court is persuaded from the record that the aggravating circumstances the offender was found guilty of committing outweigh the mitigating factors present in the case and that the sentence of death is the appropriate sentence in the case.

A court of appeals that reviews a case in which the sentence of death is imposed for an offense committed before January 1, 1995, shall file a separate opinion as to its findings in the case with the clerk of the supreme court. The opinion shall be filed within fifteen days after the court issues its opinion and shall contain whatever information is required by the clerk of the supreme court.

(B) The court of appeals, in a case in which a sentence of death was imposed for an offense committed before January 1, 1995, and the supreme court shall give priority over all other cases to the review of judgments in which the sentence of death is imposed and, except as otherwise provided in this section, shall conduct the review in accordance with the Rules of Appellate Procedure.

(C) At any time after a sentence of death is imposed pursuant to section 2929.022 [2929.02.2] or 2929.03 of the Revised Code, the court of common pleas that sentenced the offender shall vacate the sentence if the offender did not present evidence at trial that the offender was not eighteen years of age or older at the time of the commission of the aggravated murder for which the offender was sentenced and if the offender shows by a preponderance of the evidence that the offender was less than eighteen years of age at the time of the commission of the aggravated murder for which the offender was sentenced. The court is not required to hold a hearing on a motion filed pursuant to this division unless the court finds, based on the motion and any supporting information submitted by the defendant, any information submitted by the prosecuting attorney, and the record in the case, including any previous hearings and orders, probable cause to believe that the defendant was not eighteen years of age or older at the time of the commission of the aggravated murder for which the defendant was sentenced to death.

**HISTORY: 139 v S 1 (Eff 10-19-81); 146 v S 4 (Eff 9-21-95); 147 v S 107. Eff 7-29-98.**

## § 2929.06 Resentencing after sentence of death or life imprisonment without parole is set aside, nullified, or vacated.

(A) If a sentence of death imposed upon an offender is set aside, nullified, or vacated because the court of appeals, in a case in which a sentence of death was imposed for an offense committed before January 1, 1995, or the supreme court, in cases in which the supreme court reviews the sentence upon appeal, could not affirm the sentence of death under the standards imposed by section 2929.05 of the Revised Code, is set aside, nullified, or vacated for the sole reason that the statutory procedure for imposing the sentence of death that is set forth in sections 2929.03 and 2929.04 of the Revised Code is unconstitutional, is set aside, nullified, or vacated pursuant to division (C) of section 2929.05 of the Revised Code, or is set aside, nullified, or vacated because a court has determined that the offender is mentally retarded under standards set forth in decisions of the supreme court of this state or the United States supreme court, the trial court that sentenced the offender shall conduct a hearing to resentence the offender. At the resentencing hearing, the court shall impose upon the offender a sentence of life imprisonment or an indefinite term consisting of a minimum term of thirty years and a maximum term of life imprisonment that is determined as specified in this division. If division (D) of section 2929.03 of the Revised Code, at the time the offender committed the aggravated murder for which the sentence of death was imposed, required the imposition when a sentence of death was not imposed of a sentence of life imprisonment without parole or a sentence of an indefinite term consisting of a minimum term of thirty years and a maximum term of life imprisonment to be imposed pursuant to division (A) or (B)(3) of section 2971.03 of the Revised Code and served pursuant to that section, the court shall impose the sentence so required. In all other cases, the sentences of life imprisonment that are available at the hearing, and from which the court shall impose sentence, shall be the same sentences of life imprisonment that were available under division (D) of section 2929.03 or under section 2909.24 of the Revised Code at the time the offender committed the offense for which the sentence of death was imposed. Nothing in this division regarding the resentencing of an offender shall affect the operation of section 2971.03 of the Revised Code.

(B) Whenever any court of this state or any federal court sets aside, nullifies, or vacates a sentence of death imposed upon an offender because of error that occurred in the sentencing phase of the trial and if division (A) of this section does not apply, the trial court that sentenced the offender shall conduct a new hearing to resentence the offender. If the offender was tried by a jury, the trial court shall impanel a new jury for the hearing. If the offender was tried by a panel of three judges, that panel or, if necessary, a new panel of three judges shall conduct the hearing. At the hearing, the court or panel shall follow the procedure set forth in division (D) of section 2929.03 of the Revised Code in determining whether to impose upon the offender a sentence of death, a sentence of life imprisonment, or an indefinite term consisting of a minimum term of thirty years and a maximum term of life imprisonment. If, pursuant to that procedure, the court or panel determines that it will impose a sentence other than a sentence of death, the court or panel shall impose upon the offender one of the sentences of life imprisonment that could have been imposed at the time the offender committed the offense for which the sentence of death was imposed, determined as specified in this division, or an indefinite term consisting of a minimum term of thirty years and a maximum term of life imprisonment that is determined as specified in this division. If division (D) of section 2929.03 of the Revised Code, at the time the offender committed the aggravated murder for which the sentence of death was imposed, required the imposition when a sentence of death was not imposed of a sentence of life imprisonment without parole or a sentence of an indefinite term consisting of a minimum term of thirty years and a maximum term of life imprisonment to be imposed pursuant to division (A) or (B)(3) of section 2971.03 of the Revised Code and served pursuant to that section, the court or panel shall impose the sentence so required. In all other cases, the sentences of life imprisonment that are available at the hearing, and from which the court or panel shall impose sentence, shall be the same sentences of life imprisonment that were available under division (D) of section 2929.03 or under section 2909.24 of the Revised Code at the time the offender committed the offense for which the sentence of death was imposed.

(C) If a sentence of life imprisonment without parole imposed upon an offender pursuant to section 2929.021 [2929.02.1] or 2929.03 of the Revised Code is set aside, nullified, or vacated for the sole reason that the statutory procedure for imposing the sentence of life imprisonment without parole that is set forth in sections 2929.03 and 2929.04 of the Revised Code is unconstitutional, the trial court that sentenced the offender shall conduct a hearing to resentence the offender to life imprisonment with parole eligibility after serving twenty-five full years of imprisonment or to life imprisonment with parole eligibility after serving thirty full years of imprisonment.

(D) Nothing in this section limits or restricts the rights of the state to appeal any order setting aside, nullifying, or vacating a conviction or sentence of death, when an appeal of that nature otherwise would be available.

(E) This section, as amended by H.B. 184 of the 125th general assembly, shall apply to all offenders who have been sentenced to death for an aggravated murder that was committed on or after October 19, 1981, or for terrorism that was committed on or after May 15, 2002. This section, as amended by H.B. 184 of the 125th general assembly, shall apply equally to all such offenders sentenced to death prior to, on, or after March 23, 2005, including offenders who, on March 23, 2005, are challenging their sentence of death and offenders whose sentence of death has been set aside, nullified, or vacated by any court of this state or any federal court but who, as of March 23, 2005, have not yet been resentenced.

**HISTORY: 139 v S 1 (Eff 10-19-81); 146 v S 4 (Eff 9-21-95); 146 v S 2 (Eff 7-1-96); 146 v S 269 (Eff 7-1-96); 146 v S 258 (Eff 10-16-96); 146 v H 180 (Eff 1-1-97); 147 v S 107. Eff 7-29-98; 150 v H 184, § 1, eff. 3-23-05; 152 v S 10, § 1, eff. 1-1-08.**

The effective date is set by § 3 of 152 v S 10.

The provisions of § 3 of SB 107 (147 v —) read as follows:

SECTION 3. Section 2929.06 of the Revised Code is presented in this act as a composite of the section as amended by Am. Sub. S.B. 269, Sub. S.B. 258, and Am. Sub. H.B. 180 of the 121st General Assembly, with the new language of none of the acts shown in capital letters. This is in recognition of the principle stated in division (B) of section 1.52 of the Revised Code that such amendments are to be harmonized where not substantively irreconcilable and constitutes a legislative finding that such is the resulting version in effect prior to the effective date of this act.

See provisions, §§ 3, 4 of SB 269 (146 v —) following RC § 2929.03.

## [PENALTIES FOR FELONY]

### § 2929.11 Purposes of felony sentencing; discrimination prohibited.

(A) A court that sentences an offender for a felony shall be guided by the overriding purposes of felony sentencing. The overriding purposes of felony sentencing are to protect the public from future crime by the offender and others and to punish the offender using the minimum sanctions that the court determines accomplish those purposes without imposing an unnecessary burden on state or local government resources. To achieve those purposes, the sentencing court shall consider the need for incapacitating the offender, deterring the offender and others from future crime, rehabilitating the offender, and making restitution to the victim of the offense, the public, or both.

(B) A sentence imposed for a felony shall be reasonably calculated to achieve the two overriding purposes of felony sentencing set forth in division (A) of this section, commensurate with and not demeaning to the seriousness of the offender's conduct and its impact upon the victim, and consistent with sentences imposed for similar crimes committed by similar offenders.

(C) A court that imposes a sentence upon an offender for a felony shall not base the sentence upon the race, ethnic background, gender, or religion of the offender.

**HISTORY: 146 v S 2. Eff 7-1-96; 2011 HB 86, § 1, eff. Sept. 30, 2011.**

**Not analogous to former RC § 2929.11 (134 v H 511; 137 v S 119; 139 v S 199; 140 v S 210; 140 v H 265; 140 v S 4; 141 v H 284; 143 v H 51; 143 v S 258), repealed 146 v S 2, § 2, eff 7-1-96.**

The effective date is set by section 6 of SB 2.

### § 2929.12 Seriousness and recidivism factors.

(A) Unless otherwise required by section 2929.13 or 2929.14 of the Revised Code, a court that imposes a sentence under this chapter upon an offender for a felony has discretion to determine the most effective way to comply with the purposes and principles of sentencing set forth in section 2929.11 of the Revised Code. In exercising that discretion, the court shall consider the factors set forth in divisions (B) and (C) of this section relating to the seriousness of the conduct and the factors provided in divisions (D) and (E) of this section relating to the likelihood of the offender's recidivism and, in addition, may consider any other factors that are relevant to achieving those purposes and principles of sentencing.

(B) The sentencing court shall consider all of the following that apply regarding the offender, the offense, or the victim, and any other relevant factors, as indicating that the offender's conduct is more serious than conduct normally constituting the offense:

(1) The physical or mental injury suffered by the victim of the offense due to the conduct of the offender was exacerbated because of the physical or mental condition or age of the victim.

(2) The victim of the offense suffered serious physical, psychological, or economic harm as a result of the offense.

(3) The offender held a public office or position of trust in the community, and the offense related to that office or position.

(4) The offender's occupation, elected office, or profession obliged the offender to prevent the offense or bring others committing it to justice.

(5) The offender's professional reputation or occupation, elected office, or profession was used to facilitate the offense or is likely to influence the future conduct of others.

(6) The offender's relationship with the victim facilitated the offense.

(7) The offender committed the offense for hire or as a part of an organized criminal activity.

(8) In committing the offense, the offender was motivated by prejudice based on race, ethnic background, gender, sexual orientation, or religion.

(9) If the offense is a violation of section 2919.25 or a violation of section 2903.11, 2903.12, or 2903.13 of the Revised Code involving a person who was a family or household member at the time of the violation, the offender committed the offense in the vicinity of one or more children who are not victims of the offense, and the offender or the victim of the offense is a parent, guardian, custodian, or person in loco parentis of one or more of those children.

(C) The sentencing court shall consider all of the following that apply regarding the offender, the offense, or the victim, and any other relevant factors, as indicating that the offender's conduct is less serious than conduct normally constituting the offense:

(1) The victim induced or facilitated the offense.

(2) In committing the offense, the offender acted under strong provocation.

(3) In committing the offense, the offender did not cause or expect to cause physical harm to any person or property.

(4) There are substantial grounds to mitigate the offender's conduct, although the grounds are not enough to constitute a defense.

(D) The sentencing court shall consider all of the following that apply regarding the offender, and any other relevant factors, as factors indicating that the offender is likely to commit future crimes:

(1) At the time of committing the offense, the offender was under release from confinement before trial or sentencing, under a sanction imposed pursuant to section 2929.16, 2929.17, or 2929.18 of the Revised Code, or under post-release control pursuant to section 2967.28 or any other provision of the Revised Code for an earlier offense or had been unfavorably terminated from post-release control for a prior offense pursuant to division (B) of section 2967.16 or section 2929.141 [2929.14.1] of the Revised Code.

(2) The offender previously was adjudicated a delinquent child pursuant to Chapter 2151. of the Revised Code prior to January 1, 2002, or pursuant to Chapter 2152. of the Revised Code, or the offender has a history of criminal convictions.

(3) The offender has not been rehabilitated to a satisfactory degree after previously being adjudicated a delinquent child pursuant to Chapter 2151. of the Revised Code prior to January 1, 2002, or pursuant to Chapter 2152. of the Revised Code, or the offender has not responded favorably to sanctions previously imposed for criminal convictions.

(4) The offender has demonstrated a pattern of drug or alcohol abuse that is related to the offense, and the offender refuses to acknowledge that the offender has demonstrated that pattern, or the offender refuses treatment for the drug or alcohol abuse.

(5) The offender shows no genuine remorse for the offense.

(E) The sentencing court shall consider all of the following that apply regarding the offender, and any other relevant factors, as factors indicating that the offender is not likely to commit future crimes:

(1) Prior to committing the offense, the offender had not been adjudicated a delinquent child.

(2) Prior to committing the offense, the offender had not been convicted of or pleaded guilty to a criminal offense.

(3) Prior to committing the offense, the offender had led a law-abiding life for a significant number of years.

(4) The offense was committed under circumstances not likely to recur.

(5) The offender shows genuine remorse for the offense.

**HISTORY: 146 v S 2 (Eff 7-1-96); 146 v S 269 (Eff 7-1-96); 148 v S 9 (Eff 3-8-2000); 148 v S 107 (Eff 3-23-2000); 148 v S 179, § 3 (Eff 1-1-2002); 149 v H 327. Eff 7-8-2002.**

**Analogous to former RC § 2929.12 (134 v H 511; 137 v S 119; 138 v S 384; 139 v S 199; 143 v S 258; 145 v S 186), repealed 146 v S 2, § 2, eff 7-1-96.**

See provisions, § 11 of SB 179 (148 v —) following RC § 2923.36.

## § 2929.13 Guidance by degree of felony; monitoring of sexually oriented offenders by global positioning device.

(A) Except as provided in division (E), (F), or (G) of this section and unless a specific sanction is required to be imposed or is precluded from being imposed pursuant to law, a court that imposes a sentence upon an offender for a felony may impose any sanction or combination of sanctions on the offender that are provided in sections 2929.14 to 2929.18 of the Revised Code.

If the offender is eligible to be sentenced to community control sanctions, the court shall consider the appropriateness of imposing a financial sanction pursuant to section 2929.18 of the Revised Code or a sanction of community service pursuant to section 2929.17 of the Revised Code as the sole sanction for the offense. Except as otherwise provided in this division, if the court is required to impose a mandatory prison term for the offense for which sentence is being imposed, the court also shall impose any financial sanction pursuant to section 2929.18 of the Revised Code that is required for the offense and may impose any other financial sanction pursuant to that section but may not impose any additional sanction or combination of sanctions under section 2929.16 or 2929.17 of the Revised Code.

If the offender is being sentenced for a fourth degree felony OVI offense or for a third degree felony OVI offense, in addition to the mandatory term of local incarceration or the mandatory prison term required for the offense by division (G)(1) or (2) of this section, the court shall impose upon the offender a mandatory fine in accordance with division (B)(3) of section 2929.18 of the Revised Code and may impose whichever of the following is applicable:

(1) For a fourth degree felony OVI offense for which sentence is imposed under division (G)(1) of this section, an additional community control sanction or combination of community control sanctions under section 2929.16 or 2929.17 of the Revised Code. If the court imposes upon the offender a community control sanction and the offender violates any condition of the community control sanction, the court may take any action prescribed in division (B) of section 2929.15 of the Revised Code relative to the offender, including imposing a prison term on the offender pursuant to that division.

(2) For a third or fourth degree felony OVI offense for which sentence is imposed under division (G)(2) of this section, an additional prison term as described in division (B)(4) of section 2929.14 of the Revised Code or a community control sanction as described in division (G)(2) of this section.

(B)(1)(a) Except as provided in division (B)(1)(b) of this section, if an offender is convicted of or pleads guilty to a felony of the fourth or fifth degree that is not an offense of violence, the court shall sentence the offender to a community control sanction of at least one year's duration if all of the following apply:

(i) The offender previously has not been convicted of or pleaded guilty to a felony offense or to an offense of violence that is a misdemeanor and that the offender committed within two years prior to the offense for which sentence is being imposed.

(ii) The most serious charge against the offender at the time of sentencing is a felony of the fourth or fifth degree.

(iii) If the court made a request of the department of rehabilitation and correction pursuant to division (B)(1)(c) of this section, the department, within the forty-five-day period specified in that division, provided the court with the names of, contact information for, and program details of one or more community control sanctions of at least one year's duration that are available for persons sentenced by the court.

(b) The court has discretion to impose a prison term upon an offender who is convicted of or pleads guilty to a felony of the fourth or fifth degree that is not an offense of violence if any of the following apply:

(i) The offender committed the offense while having a firearm on or about the offender's person or under the offender's control.

(ii) The offender caused physical harm to another person while committing the offense.

(iii) The offender violated a term of the conditions of bond as set by the court.

(iv) The court made a request of the department of rehabilitation and correction pursuant to division (B)(1)(c) of this section, and the department, within the forty-five-day period specified in that division, did not provide the court with the name of, contact information for, and program details of any community control sanction of at least one year's duration that is available for persons sentenced by the court.

(c) If a court that is sentencing an offender who is convicted of or pleads guilty to a felony of the fourth or fifth degree that is not an offense of violence believes that no community control sanctions are available for its use that, if imposed on the offender, will adequately fulfill the overriding principles and purposes of sentencing, the court shall contact the department of rehabilitation and correction and ask the department to provide the court with the names of, contact information for, and program details of one or more community control sanctions of at least one year's duration that are available for persons sentenced by the court. Not later than forty-five days after receipt of a request from a court under this division, the department shall provide the court with the names of, contact information for, and program details of one or more community control sanctions of at least one year's duration that are available for persons sentenced by the court, if any. Upon making a request under this division that relates to a particular offender, a court shall defer sentencing of that offender until it receives from the department the names of, contact information for, and program details of one or more community control sanctions of at least one year's duration that are available for persons sentenced by the court or for forty-five days, whichever is the earlier.

If the department provides the court with the names of, contact information for, and program details of one or more community control sanctions of at least one year's duration that are available for persons sentenced by the court within the forty-five-day period specified in this division, the court shall impose upon the offender a community control sanction under division (B)(1)(a) of this section, subject to divisions (B)(1)(b)(i) and (ii) of this section. If the department does not provide the court with the names of, contact information for, and program details of one or more community control sanctions of at least one year's duration that are available for persons sentenced by the court within the forty-five-day period specified in this division, the court may impose upon the offender a prison term under division (B)(1)(b)(iii) of this section.

(d) A sentencing court may impose an additional penalty under division (B) of section 2929.15 of the Revised Code upon an offender sentenced to a community control sanction under division (B)(1)(a) of this section if the offender violates the conditions of the community control sanction, violates a law, or leaves the state without the permission of the court or the offender's probation officer.

(2) If division (B)(1) of this section does not apply, except as provided in division (B)(3), (E), (F), or (G) of this section, in sentencing an offender for a felony of the fourth or fifth degree, the sentencing court shall determine whether any of the following apply:

(a) In committing the offense, the offender caused physical harm to a person.

(b) In committing the offense, the offender attempted to cause or made an actual threat of physical harm to a person with a deadly weapon.

(c) In committing the offense, the offender attempted to cause or made an actual threat of physical harm to a person, and the offender previously was convicted of an offense that caused physical harm to a person.

(d) The offender held a public office or position of trust and the offense related to that office or position; the offender's position obliged the offender to prevent the offense or to bring those committing it to justice; or the offender's professional reputation or position facilitated the offense or was likely to influence the future conduct of others.

(e) The offender committed the offense for hire or as part of an organized criminal activity.

(f) The offense is a sex offense that is a fourth or fifth degree felony violation of section 2907.03, 2907.04, 2907.05, 2907.22, 2907.31, 2907.321, 2907.322, 2907.323, or 2907.34 of the Revised Code.

(g) The offender at the time of the offense was serving, or the offender previously had served, a prison term.

(h) The offender committed the offense while under a community control sanction, while on probation, or while released from custody on a bond or personal recognizance.

(i) The offender committed the offense while in possession of a firearm.

(3)(a) If the court makes a finding described in division (B)(2)(a), (b), (c), (d), (e), (f), (g), (h), or (i) of this section and if the court, after considering the factors set forth in section 2929.12 of the Revised Code, finds that a prison term is consistent with the purposes and principles of sentencing set forth in section 2929.11 of the Revised Code and finds that the offender is not amenable to an available community control sanction, the court shall impose a prison term upon the offender.

(b) Except as provided in division (E), (F), or (G) of this section, if the court does not make a finding described in division (B)(2)(a), (b), (c), (d), (e), (f), (g), (h), or (i) of this section and if the court, after considering the factors set forth in section 2929.12 of the Revised Code, finds that a community control sanction or combination of community control sanctions is consistent with the purposes and principles of sentencing set forth in section 2929.11 of the Revised Code, the court shall impose a community control sanction or combination of community control sanctions upon the offender.

(C) Except as provided in division (D), (E), (F), or (G) of this section, in determining whether to impose a prison term as a sanction for a felony of the third degree or a felony drug offense that is a violation of a provision of Chapter 2925. of the Revised Code and that is specified as being subject to this division for purposes of sentencing, the sentencing court shall comply with the purposes and principles of sentencing under section 2929.11 of the Revised Code and with section 2929.12 of the Revised Code.

(D)(1) Except as provided in division (E) or (F) of this section, for a felony of the first or second degree, for a felony drug offense that is a violation of any provision of Chapter 2925., 3719., or 4729. of the Revised Code for which a presumption in favor of a prison term is specified as being applicable, and for a violation of division (A)(4) or (B) of section 2907.05 of the Revised Code for which a presumption in favor of a prison term is specified as being applicable, it is presumed that a prison term is necessary in order to comply with the purposes and principles of sentencing under section 2929.11 of the Revised Code. Division (D)(2) of this section does not apply to a presumption established under this division for a violation of division (A)(4) of section 2907.05 of the Revised Code.

(2) Notwithstanding the presumption established under division (D)(1) of this section for the offenses listed in that division other than a violation of division (A)(4) or (B) of section 2907.05 of the Revised Code, the sentencing court may impose a community control sanction or a combination of community control sanctions instead of a prison term on an offender for a felony of the first or second degree or for a felony drug offense that is a violation of any provision of Chapter 2925., 3719., or 4729. of the Revised Code for which a presumption in favor of a prison term is specified as being applicable if it makes both of the following findings:

(a) A community control sanction or a combination of community control sanctions would adequately punish the offender and protect the public from future crime, because the applicable factors under section 2929.12 of the Revised Code indicating a lesser likelihood of recidivism outweigh the applicable factors under that section indicating a greater likelihood of recidivism.

(b) A community control sanction or a combination of community control sanctions would not demean the seriousness of the offense, because one or more factors under section 2929.12 of the Revised Code that indicate that the offender's conduct was less serious than conduct normally constituting the offense are applicable, and they outweigh the applicable factors under that section that indicate that the offender's conduct was more serious than conduct normally constituting the offense.

(E)(1) Except as provided in division (F) of this section, for any drug offense that is a violation of any provision of Chapter 2925. of the Revised Code and that is a felony of the third, fourth, or fifth degree, the applicability of a presumption under division (D) of this section in favor of a prison term or of division (B) or (C) of this section in determining whether to impose a prison term for the offense shall be determined as specified in section 2925.02, 2925.03, 2925.04, 2925.05, 2925.06, 2925.11, 2925.13, 2925.22, 2925.23, 2925.36, or 2925.37 of the Revised Code, whichever is applicable regarding the violation.

(2) If an offender who was convicted of or pleaded guilty to a felony violates the conditions of a community control sanction imposed for the offense solely by reason of producing positive results on a drug test, the court, as punishment for the violation of the sanction, shall not order that the offender be imprisoned unless the court determines on the record either of the following:

(a) The offender had been ordered as a sanction for the felony to participate in a drug treatment program, in a drug education program, or in narcotics anonymous or a similar program, and the offender continued to use illegal drugs after a reasonable period of participation in the program.

(b) The imprisonment of the offender for the violation is consistent with the purposes and principles of sentencing set forth in section 2929.11 of the Revised Code.

(3) A court that sentences an offender for a drug abuse offense that is a felony of the third, fourth, or fifth degree may require that the offender be assessed by a properly credentialed professional within a specified period of time. The court shall require the professional to file a written assessment of the offender with the court. If the offender is eligible for a community control sanction and after considering the written assessment, the court may impose a community control sanction that includes treatment and recovery support services authorized by section 3793.02 of the Revised Code. If the court imposes treatment and recovery support services as a community control sanction, the court shall direct the level and type of treatment and recovery support services after considering the assessment and recommendation of treatment and recovery support services providers.

(F) Notwithstanding divisions (A) to (E) of this section, the court shall impose a prison term or terms under sections 2929.02 to 2929.06, section 2929.14, section 2929.142, or section 2971.03 of the Revised Code and except as specifically provided in section 2929.20, divisions (C) to (I) of section 2967.19, or section 2967.191 of the Revised Code or when parole is authorized for the offense under section 2967.13 of the Revised Code shall not reduce the term or terms pursuant to section 2929.20, section 2967.19, section 2967.193, or any other provision of Chapter 2967. or Chapter 5120. of the Revised Code for any of the following offenses:

(1) Aggravated murder when death is not imposed or murder;

(2) Any rape, regardless of whether force was involved and regardless of the age of the victim, or an attempt to commit rape if, had the offender completed the rape that was attempted, the offender would have been guilty of a violation of division (A)(1)(b) of section 2907.02 of the Revised Code and would be sentenced under section 2971.03 of the Revised Code;

(3) Gross sexual imposition or sexual battery, if the victim is less than thirteen years of age and if any of the following applies:

(a) Regarding gross sexual imposition, the offender previously was convicted of or pleaded guilty to rape, the former offense of felonious sexual penetration, gross sexual imposition, or sexual battery, and the victim of the previous offense was less than thirteen years of age;

(b) Regarding gross sexual imposition, the offense was committed on or after August 3, 2006, and evidence other than the testimony of the victim was admitted in the case corroborating the violation.

(c) Regarding sexual battery, either of the following applies:

(i) The offense was committed prior to August 3, 2006, the offender previously was convicted of or pleaded guilty to rape, the former offense of felonious sexual penetration, or sexual battery, and the victim of the previous offense was less than thirteen years of age.

(ii) The offense was committed on or after August 3, 2006.

(4) A felony violation of section 2903.04, 2903.06, 2903.08, 2903.11, 2903.12, 2903.13, or 2907.07 of the Revised Code if the section requires the imposition of a prison term;

(5) A first, second, or third degree felony drug offense for which section 2925.02, 2925.03, 2925.04, 2925.05, 2925.06, 2925.11, 2925.13, 2925.22, 2925.23, 2925.36, 2925.37, 3719.99, or 4729.99 of the Revised Code, whichever is applicable regarding the violation, requires the imposition of a mandatory prison term;

(6) Any offense that is a first or second degree felony and that is not set forth in division (F)(1), (2), (3), or (4) of this section, if the offender previously was convicted of or pleaded guilty to aggravated murder, murder, any first or second degree felony, or an offense under an existing or former law of this state, another state, or the United States that is or was substantially equivalent to one of those offenses;

(7) Any offense that is a third degree felony and either is a violation of section 2903.04 of the Revised Code or an attempt to commit a felony of the second degree that is an offense of violence and involved an attempt to cause serious physical harm to a person or that resulted in serious physical harm to a person if the offender previously was convicted of or pleaded guilty to any of the following offenses:

(a) Aggravated murder, murder, involuntary manslaughter, rape, felonious sexual penetration as it existed under section 2907.12 of the Revised Code prior to September 3, 1996, a felony of the first or second degree that resulted in the death of a person or in physical harm to a person, or complicity in or an attempt to commit any of those offenses;

(b) An offense under an existing or former law of this state, another state, or the United States that is or was substantially equivalent to an offense listed in division (F)(7)(a) of this section that resulted in the death of a person or in physical harm to a person.

(8) Any offense, other than a violation of section 2923.12 of the Revised Code, that is a felony, if the offender had a firearm on or about the offender's person or under the offender's control while committing the felony, with respect to a portion of the sentence imposed pursuant to division (B)(1)(a) of section 2929.14 of the Revised Code for having the firearm;

(9) Any offense of violence that is a felony, if the offender wore or carried body armor while committing the felony offense of violence, with respect to the portion of the sentence imposed pursuant to division (B)(1)(d) of section 2929.14 of the Revised Code for wearing or carrying the body armor;

(10) Corrupt activity in violation of section 2923.32 of the Revised Code when the most serious offense in the pattern of corrupt activity that is the basis of the offense is a felony of the first degree;

(11) Any violent sex offense or designated homicide, assault, or kidnapping offense if, in relation to that offense, the offender is adjudicated a sexually violent predator;

(12) A violation of division (A)(1) or (2) of section 2921.36 of the Revised Code, or a violation of division (C) of that section involving an item listed in division (A)(1) or (2) of that section, if the offender is an officer or employee of the department of rehabilitation and correction;

(13) A violation of division (A)(1) or (2) of section 2903.06 of the Revised Code if the victim of the offense is a peace officer, as defined in section 2935.01 of the Revised Code, or an investigator of the bureau of criminal identification and investigation, as defined in section 2903.11 of the Revised Code, with respect to the portion of the sentence imposed pursuant to division (B)(5) of section 2929.14 of the Revised Code;

(14) A violation of division (A)(1) or (2) of section 2903.06 of the Revised Code if the offender has been convicted of or pleaded guilty to three or more violations of division (A) or (B) of section 4511.19 of the Revised Code or an equivalent offense, as defined in section 2941.1415 of the Revised Code, or three or more violations of any combination of those divisions and offenses, with respect to the portion of the sentence imposed pursuant to division (B)(6) of section 2929.14 of the Revised Code;

(15) Kidnapping, in the circumstances specified in section 2971.03 of the Revised Code and when no other provision of division (F) of this section applies;

(16) Kidnapping, abduction, compelling prostitution, promoting prostitution, engaging in a pattern of corrupt activity, illegal use of a minor in a nudity-oriented material or performance in violation of division (A)(1) or (2) of section 2907.323 of the Revised Code, or endangering children in violation of division (B)(1), (2), (3), (4), or (5) of section 2919.22 of the Revised Code, if the offender is convicted of or pleads guilty to a specification as described in section 2941.1422 of the Revised Code that was included in the indictment, count in the indictment, or information charging the offense;

(17) A felony violation of division (A) or (B) of section 2919.25 of the Revised Code if division (D)(3), (4), or (5) of that section, and division (D)(6) of that section, require the imposition of a prison term;

(18) A felony violation of section 2903.11, 2903.12, or 2903.13 of the Revised Code, if the victim of the offense was a woman that the offender knew was pregnant at the time of the violation, with respect to a portion of the sentence imposed pursuant to division (B)(8) of section 2929.14 of the Revised Code.

(G) Notwithstanding divisions (A) to (E) of this section, if an offender is being sentenced for a fourth degree felony OVI offense or for a third degree felony OVI offense, the court shall impose upon the offender a mandatory term of local incarceration or a mandatory prison term in accordance with the following:

(1) If the offender is being sentenced for a fourth degree felony OVI offense and if the offender has not been convicted of and has not pleaded guilty to a specification of the type described in section 2941.1413 of the Revised Code, the court may impose upon the offender a mandatory term of local incarceration of sixty days or one hundred twenty days as specified in division (G)(1)(d) of section 4511.19 of the Revised Code. The court shall not reduce the term pursuant to section 2929.20, 2967.193, or any other provision of the Revised Code. The court that imposes a mandatory term of local incarceration under this division shall specify whether the term is to be served in a jail, a community-based correctional facility, a halfway house, or an alternative residential facility, and the of-

fender shall serve the term in the type of facility specified by the court. A mandatory term of local incarceration imposed under division (G)(1) of this section is not subject to any other Revised Code provision that pertains to a prison term except as provided in division (A)(1) of this section.

(2) If the offender is being sentenced for a third degree felony OVI offense, or if the offender is being sentenced for a fourth degree felony OVI offense and the court does not impose a mandatory term of local incarceration under division (G)(1) of this section, the court shall impose upon the offender a mandatory prison term of one, two, three, four, or five years if the offender also is convicted of or also pleads guilty to a specification of the type described in section 2941.1413 of the Revised Code or shall impose upon the offender a mandatory prison term of sixty days or one hundred twenty days as specified in division (G)(1)(d) or (e) of section 4511.19 of the Revised Code if the offender has not been convicted of and has not pleaded guilty to a specification of that type. Subject to divisions (C) to (I) of section 2967.19 of the Revised Code, the court shall not reduce the term pursuant to section 2929.20, 2967.19, 2967.193, or any other provision of the Revised Code. The offender shall serve the one-, two-, three-, four-, or five-year mandatory prison term consecutively to and prior to the prison term imposed for the underlying offense and consecutively to any other mandatory prison term imposed in relation to the offense. In no case shall an offender who once has been sentenced to a mandatory term of local incarceration pursuant to division (G)(1) of this section for a fourth degree felony OVI offense be sentenced to another mandatory term of local incarceration under that division for any violation of division (A) of section 4511.19 of the Revised Code. In addition to the mandatory prison term described in division (G)(2) of this section, the court may sentence the offender to a community control sanction under section 2929.16 or 2929.17 of the Revised Code, but the offender shall serve the prison term prior to serving the community control sanction. The department of rehabilitation and correction may place an offender sentenced to a mandatory prison term under this division in an intensive program prison established pursuant to section 5120.033 of the Revised Code if the department gave the sentencing judge prior notice of its intent to place the offender in an intensive program prison established under that section and if the judge did not notify the department that the judge disapproved the placement. Upon the establishment of the initial intensive program prison pursuant to section 5120.033 of the Revised Code that is privately operated and managed by a contractor pursuant to a contract entered into under section 9.06 of the Revised Code, both of the following apply:

(a) The department of rehabilitation and correction shall make a reasonable effort to ensure that a sufficient number of offenders sentenced to a mandatory prison term under this division are placed in the privately operated and managed prison so that the privately operated and managed prison has full occupancy.

(b) Unless the privately operated and managed prison has full occupancy, the department of rehabilitation and correction shall not place any offender sentenced to a mandatory prison term under this division in any intensive program prison established pursuant to section 5120.033 of the Revised Code other than the privately operated and managed prison.

(H) If an offender is being sentenced for a sexually oriented offense or child-victim oriented offense that is a felony committed on or after January 1, 1997, the judge shall require the offender to submit to a DNA specimen collection procedure pursuant to section 2901.07 of the Revised Code.

(I) If an offender is being sentenced for a sexually oriented offense or a child-victim oriented offense committed on or after January 1, 1997, the judge shall include in the sentence a summary of the offender's duties imposed under sections 2950.04, 2950.041, 2950.05, and 2950.06 of the Revised Code and the duration of the duties. The judge shall inform the offender, at the time of sentencing, of those duties and of their duration. If required under division (A)(2) of section 2950.03 of the Revised Code, the judge shall perform the duties specified in that section, or, if required under division (A)(6) of section 2950.03 of the Revised Code, the judge shall perform the duties specified in that division.

(J)(1) Except as provided in division (J)(2) of this section, when considering sentencing factors under this section in relation to an offender who is convicted of or pleads guilty to an attempt to commit an offense in violation of section 2923.02 of the Revised Code, the sentencing court shall consider the factors applicable to the felony category of the violation of section 2923.02 of the Revised Code instead of the factors applicable to the felony category of the offense attempted.

(2) When considering sentencing factors under this section in relation to an offender who is convicted of or pleads guilty to an attempt to commit a drug abuse offense for which the penalty is determined by the amount or number of unit doses of the controlled substance involved in the drug abuse offense, the sentencing court shall consider the factors applicable to the felony category that the drug abuse offense attempted would be if that drug abuse offense had been committed and had involved an amount or number of unit doses of the controlled substance that is within the next lower range of controlled substance amounts than was involved in the attempt.

(K) As used in this section, "drug abuse offense" has the same meaning as in section 2925.01 of the Revised Code.

(L) At the time of sentencing an offender for any sexually oriented offense, if the offender is a tier III sex offender/child-victim offender relative to that offense and the offender does not serve a prison term or jail term, the court may require that the offender be monitored by means of a global positioning device. If the court requires such monitoring, the cost of monitoring shall be borne by the offender. If the offender is indigent, the cost of compliance shall be paid by the crime victims reparations fund.

**HISTORY: 146 v S2 (Eff 7-1-96); 146 v S 269 (Eff 7-1-96); 146 v H 445 (Eff 9-3-96); 146 v S 166 (Eff 10-17-96); 146 v H 180 (Eff 1-1-97); 147 v H 32 (Eff 3-10-98); 147 v S 111 (Eff 3-17-98); 147 v H 293 (Eff 3-17-98); 147 v H 122 (Eff 7-29-98); 148 v S 142 (Eff 2-3-2000); 148 v S 107 (Eff 3-23-2000); 148 v S 22 (Eff 5-17-2000); 148 v H 528 (Eff 2-13-2001); 148 v S 222 (Eff 3-22-2001); 149 v H 485 (Eff 6-13-2002); 149 v H 327. Eff 7-8-2002; 149 v S 123, § 1, eff. 1-1-04; 150 v S 5, § 1, Eff 7-31-03; 150 v S 5, § 3, eff. 1-1-04; 150 v H 52, § 1, eff. 6-1-04; 150 v H 163, § 1, eff. 9-23-04; 150 v H 473, § 1, eff. 4-29-05; 151 v H 95, § 1, eff. 8-3-06; 151 v S 260, § 1, eff. 1-2-07; 151 v S 281, § 1, eff. 1-4-07; 151 v H 461, § 1, eff. 4-4-07; 152 v S 10, § 1, eff. 1-1-08; 152 v S 183, § 1, eff. 9-11-08; 152 v H 280, § 1, eff. 4-7-09; 152 v H 130, § 1, eff. 4-7-09; 153 v S 58, § 1, eff. 9-17-10; 2011 HB 86, § 1, eff. Sept. 30, 2011.**

The provisions of § 4 of HB 86 read as follows:

"SECTION 4. The amendments to sections 926.99, 1333.99, 1707.99, 1716.99, 2909.03, 2909.05, 2909.11, 2913.02, 2913.03, 2913.04, 2913.11, 2913.21, 2913.31, 2913.32, 2913.34, 2913.40, 2913.401, 2913.42, 2913.421, 2913.43, 2913.45, 2913.46, 2913.47, 2913.48, 2913.49, 2913.51, 2913.61, 2915.05, 2917.21, 2917.31, 2917.32, 2921.13, 2921.41, 2923.31, and 2981.07, division (B) of section 2929.13, and division (A) of section 2929.14 of the Revised Code that are made in this act apply to a person who commits an offense specified or penalized under those sections on or after the effective date of this section and to a person to whom division (B) of section 1.58 of the Revised Code makes the amendments applicable.

"The provisions of sections 926.99, 1333.99, 1707.99, 1716.99, 2909.03, 2909.05, 2909.11, 2913.02, 2913.03, 2913.04, 2913.11, 2913.21, 2913.31, 2913.32, 2913.34, 2913.40, 2913.401, 2913.42, 2913.421, 2913.43, 2913.45, 2913.46, 2913.47, 2913.48, 2913.49, 2913.51, 2913.61, 2915.05, 2917.21, 2917.31, 2917.32, 2921.13, 2921.41, 2923.31, and 2981.07 of the Revised Code in existence prior to the effective date of this section shall apply to a person upon whom a court imposed sentence prior to the effective date of this section for an offense specified or penalized under those sections. The amendments to sections 926.99, 1333.99, 1707.99, 1716.99, 2909.03, 2909.05, 2909.11, 2913.02, 2913.03, 2913.04, 2913.11, 2913.21, 2913.31, 2913.32, 2913.34, 2913.40, 2913.401, 2913.42, 2913.421, 2913.43, 2913.45, 2913.46, 2913.47, 2913.48, 2913.49, 2913.51, 2913.61, 2915.05, 2917.21, 2917.31, 2917.32, 2921.13, 2921.41, 2923.31, and 2981.07 of the Revised Code that are made in this act do not apply to a person who upon whom a court imposed sentence prior to the effective date of this section for an offense specified or penalized under those sections."

The provisions of § 3 of 153 v S 58 read as follows:

SECTION 3. Section 2929.13 of the Revised Code is presented in this act as a composite of the section as amended by both Am. Sub. H.B. 130 and Am. Sub. H.B. 280 of the 127th General Assembly. The General Assembly, applying the principle stated in division (B) of section 1.52 of the Revised Code that amendments are to be harmonized if reasonably capable of simultaneous operation, finds that the composite is the resulting version of the section in effect prior to the effective date of the section as presented in this act.

The effective date is set by § 3 of 152 v S 10.

The provisions of § 6 of 152 v S 10 read as follows:

SECTION 6. * * * Section 2929.13 of the Revised Code is presented in this act as a composite of the section as amended by Am. Sub. H.B. 461, Am. Sub. S.B. 260, and Sub. S.B. 281 of the 126th General Assembly. * * * The General Assembly, applying the principle stated in division (B) of section 1.52 of the Revised Code that amendments are to be harmonized if reasonably capable of simultaneous operation, finds that the composites are the resulting versions of the sections in effect prior to the effective date of the sections as presented in this act.

The provisions of § 3 of H.B. 473 (150 v —) read as follows:

SECTION 3. * * * Sections 2929.01, 2929.13, and 2929.14 of the Revised Code are presented in this act as composites of the sections as amended by both Sub. H.B. 52 and Am. Sub. H.B. 163 of the 125th General Assembly. * * * The General Assembly, applying the principle stated in division (B) of section 1.52 of the Revised Code that amendments are to be harmonized if reasonably capable of simultaneous operation, finds that the composites are the resulting versions of the sections in effect prior to the effective date of the sections as presented in this act.

The effective date is set by section 4 of S.B. 123.

See provisions of § 5 of S.B. 123 (149 v —) following RC § 2929.01.

**Not analogous to former RC § 2929.13 (139 v S 199), repealed 146 v S 2, § 2, eff 7-1-96.**

The provisions of § 7 of S.B. 5 (150 v —) read as follows:

SECTION 7. (A) * * * Section 2929.13 of the Revised Code is presented in Section 1 of this act as a composite of the section as amended by both Am. Sub. H.B. 327 and Sub. H.B. 485 of the 124th General Assembly. The General Assembly, applying the principle stated in division (B) of section 1.52 of the Revised Code that amendments are to be harmonized if reasonably capable of simultaneous operation, finds that the composites are the resulting versions of the sections in effect prior to the effective date of the sections as presented in Section 1 of this act.

(B) * * * Section 2929.13 of the Revised Code, effective January 1, 2004, is presented in Section 3 of this act as a composite of the section as amended by Am. Sub. H.B. 327, Sub. H.B. 485, and Am. Sub. S.B. 123 of the 124th General Assembly. The General Assembly, applying the principle stated in division (B) of section 1.52 of the Revised Code that amendments are to be harmonized if reasonably capable of simultaneous operation, finds that the composites are the resulting versions of the sections in effect prior to the effective date of the sections as presented in Section 3 of this act.

The provisions of § 3 of HB 485 (149 v —) read as follows:

SECTION 3. Section 2929.13 of the Revised Code is presented in this act as a composite of the section as amended by Am. H.B. 528, Am. Sub. S.B. 22, Am. Sub. S.B. 107, Am. S.B. 142, and Am. Sub. S.B. 222 of the 123rd General Assembly. Sections 2950.01, 2950.04, and 2950.09 of the Revised Code are presented in this act as composites of the sections as amended by both Sub. H.B. 393 and Am. Sub. S.B. 175 of the 124th General Assembly. The General Assembly, applying the principle stated in division (B) of section 1.52 of the Revised Code that amendments are to be harmonized if reasonably capable of simultaneous operation, finds that the composites are the resulting versions of the sections in effect prior to the effective date of the section as presented in this act.

The provisions of § 3 of SB 222 (148 v —) read, in part, as follows:

SECTION 3. * * * Section 2929.13 of the Revised Code is presented in this act as a composite of the section as amended by Am. Sub. S.B. 22, Am. Sub. S.B. 107 and Am. S.B. 142 of the 123rd General Assembly, with the new language of none of the acts shown in capital letters. * * * This is in recognition of the principle stated in division (B) of section 1.52 of the Revised Code that such amendments are to be harmonized where not substantively irreconcilable and constitutes a legislative finding that such is the resulting version in effect prior to the effective date of this act.

## § 2929.14 Basic prison terms.

(A) Except as provided in division (B)(1), (B)(2), (B)(3), (B)(4), (B)(5), (B)(6), (B)(7), (B)(8), (E), (G), (H), or (J) of this section or in division (D)(6) of section 2919.25 of the Revised Code and except in relation to an offense for which a sentence of death or life imprisonment is to be imposed, if the court imposing a sentence upon an offender for a felony elects or is required to impose a prison term on the offender pursuant to this chapter, the court shall impose a definite prison term that shall be one of the following:

(1) For a felony of the first degree, the prison term shall be three, four, five, six, seven, eight, nine, ten, or eleven years.

(2) For a felony of the second degree, the prison term shall be two, three, four, five, six, seven, or eight years.

(3)(a) For a felony of the third degree that is a violation of section 2903.06, 2903.08, 2907.03, 2907.04, or 2907.05 of the Revised Code or that is a violation of section 2911.02 or 2911.12 of the Revised Code if the offender previously has been convicted of or pleaded guilty in two or more separate proceedings to two or more violations of section 2911.01, 2911.02, 2911.11, or 2911.12 of the Revised Code, the prison term shall be twelve, eighteen, twenty-four, thirty, thirty-six, forty-two, forty-eight, fifty-four, or sixty months.

(b) For a felony of the third degree that is not an offense for which division (A)(3)(a) of this section applies, the prison term shall be nine, twelve, eighteen, twenty-four, thirty, or thirty-six months.

(4) For a felony of the fourth degree, the prison term shall be six, seven, eight, nine, ten, eleven, twelve, thir-

teen, fourteen, fifteen, sixteen, seventeen, or eighteen months.

(5) For a felony of the fifth degree, the prison term shall be six, seven, eight, nine, ten, eleven, or twelve months.

(B)(1)(a) Except as provided in division (B)(1)(e) of this section, if an offender who is convicted of or pleads guilty to a felony also is convicted of or pleads guilty to a specification of the type described in section 2941.141, 2941.144, or 2941.145 of the Revised Code, the court shall impose on the offender one of the following prison terms:

(i) A prison term of six years if the specification is of the type described in section 2941.144 of the Revised Code that charges the offender with having a firearm that is an automatic firearm or that was equipped with a firearm muffler or silencer on or about the offender's person or under the offender's control while committing the felony;

(ii) A prison term of three years if the specification is of the type described in section 2941.145 of the Revised Code that charges the offender with having a firearm on or about the offender's person or under the offender's control while committing the offense and displaying the firearm, brandishing the firearm, indicating that the offender possessed the firearm, or using it to facilitate the offense;

(iii) A prison term of one year if the specification is of the type described in section 2941.141 of the Revised Code that charges the offender with having a firearm on or about the offender's person or under the offender's control while committing the felony.

(b) If a court imposes a prison term on an offender under division (B)(1)(a) of this section, the prison term shall not be reduced pursuant to section 2967.19, section 2929.20, section 2967.193, or any other provision of Chapter 2967. or Chapter 5120. of the Revised Code. Except as provided in division (B)(1)(g) of this section, a court shall not impose more than one prison term on an offender under division (B)(1)(a) of this section for felonies committed as part of the same act or transaction.

(c) Except as provided in division (B)(1)(e) of this section, if an offender who is convicted of or pleads guilty to a violation of section 2923.161 of the Revised Code or to a felony that includes, as an essential element, purposely or knowingly causing or attempting to cause the death of or physical harm to another, also is convicted of or pleads guilty to a specification of the type described in section 2941.146 of the Revised Code that charges the offender with committing the offense by discharging a firearm from a motor vehicle other than a manufactured home, the court, after imposing a prison term on the offender for the violation of section 2923.161 of the Revised Code or for the other felony offense under division (A), (B)(2), or (B)(3) of this section, shall impose an additional prison term of five years upon the offender that shall not be reduced pursuant to section 2929.20, section 2967.19, section 2967.193, or any other provision of Chapter 2967. or Chapter 5120. of the Revised Code. A court shall not impose more than one additional prison term on an offender under division (B)(1)(c) of this section for felonies committed as part of the same act or transaction. If a court imposes an additional prison term on an offender under division (B)(1)(c) of this section relative to an offense, the court also shall impose a prison term under division (B)(1)(a) of this section relative to the same offense, provided the criteria specified in that division for imposing an additional prison term are satisfied relative to the offender and the offense.

(d) If an offender who is convicted of or pleads guilty to an offense of violence that is a felony also is convicted of or pleads guilty to a specification of the type described in section 2941.1411 of the Revised Code that charges the offender with wearing or carrying body armor while committing the felony offense of violence, the court shall impose on the offender a prison term of two years. The prison term so imposed, subject to divisions (C) to (I) of section 2967.19 of the Revised Code, shall not be reduced pursuant to section 2929.20, section 2967.19, section 2967.193, or any other provision of Chapter 2967. or Chapter 5120. of the Revised Code. A court shall not impose more than one prison term on an offender under division (B)(1)(d) of this section for felonies committed as part of the same act or transaction. If a court imposes an additional prison term under division (B)(1)(a) or (c) of this section, the court is not precluded from imposing an additional prison term under division (B)(1)(d) of this section.

(e) The court shall not impose any of the prison terms described in division (B)(1)(a) of this section or any of the additional prison terms described in division (B)(1)(c) of this section upon an offender for a violation of section 2923.12 or 2923.123 of the Revised Code. The court shall not impose any of the prison terms described in division (B)(1)(a) or (b) of this section upon an offender for a violation of section 2923.122 that involves a deadly weapon that is a firearm other than a dangerous ordnance, section 2923.16, or section 2923.121 of the Revised Code. The court shall not impose any of the prison terms described in division (B)(1)(a) of this section or any of the additional prison terms described in division (B)(1)(c) of this section upon an offender for a violation of section 2923.13 of the Revised Code unless all of the following apply:

(i) The offender previously has been convicted of aggravated murder, murder, or any felony of the first or second degree.

(ii) Less than five years have passed since the offender was released from prison or post-release control, whichever is later, for the prior offense.

(f) If an offender is convicted of or pleads guilty to a felony that includes, as an essential element, causing or attempting to cause the death of or physical harm to another and also is convicted of or pleads guilty to a specification of the type described in section 2941.1412 of the Revised Code that charges the offender with committing the offense by discharging a firearm at a peace officer as defined in section 2935.01 of the Revised Code or a corrections officer, as defined in section 2941.1412 of the Revised Code, the court, after imposing a prison term on the offender for the felony offense under division (A), (B)(2), or (B)(3) of this section, shall impose an additional prison term of seven years upon the offender that shall not be reduced pursuant to section 2929.20, section 2967.19, section 2967.193, or any other provision of Chapter 2967. or Chapter 5120. of the Revised Code. If an offender is convicted of or pleads guilty to two or more felonies that include, as an essential element, causing or attempting to cause the death or physical harm to another and also is convicted of or pleads guilty to a specification of the type described under division (B)(1)(f) of this section in connection with two or more of the felonies of which the offender is convicted or to which the offender pleads guilty, the sentencing court shall impose on the offender the prison term specified under division (B)(1)(f) of this section for each of two of the specifications of which the offender is convicted or to which the offender pleads guilty and, in its discretion, also may impose on the offender the prison term specified under that division for any or all of the remaining specifications. If a court imposes an additional prison term on an offender under division (B)(1)(f) of this section relative to an offense, the court shall not impose a prison term under division (B)(1)(a) or (c) of this section relative to the same offense.

(g) If an offender is convicted of or pleads guilty to two or more felonies, if one or more of those felonies are aggravated murder, murder, attempted aggravated murder, attempted murder, aggravated robbery, felonious assault, or rape, and if the offender is convicted of or pleads guilty to a specification of the type described under division (B)(1)(a) of this section in connection with two or more of the felonies, the sentencing court shall impose on the offender the prison term specified under division (B)(1)(a) of this section for each of the two most serious specifications of which the offender is convicted or to which the offender pleads guilty and, in its discretion, also may impose on the offender the prison term specified under that division for any or all of the remaining specifications.

(2)(a) If division (B)(2)(b) of this section does not apply, the court may impose on an offender, in addition to the longest prison term authorized or required for the offense, an additional definite prison term of one, two, three, four, five, six, seven, eight, nine, or ten years if all of the following criteria are met:

(i) The offender is convicted of or pleads guilty to a specification of the type described in section 2941.149 of the Revised Code that the offender is a repeat violent offender.

(ii) The offense of which the offender currently is convicted or to which the offender currently pleads guilty is aggravated murder and the court does not impose a sentence of death or life imprisonment without parole, murder, terrorism and the court does not impose a sentence of life imprisonment without parole, any felony of the first degree that is an offense of violence and the court does not impose a sentence of life imprisonment without parole, or any felony of the second degree that is an offense of violence and the trier of fact finds that the offense involved an attempt to cause or a threat to cause serious physical harm to a person or resulted in serious physical harm to a person.

(iii) The court imposes the longest prison term for the offense that is not life imprisonment without parole.

(iv) The court finds that the prison terms imposed pursuant to division (D)(2)(a)(iii) of this section and, if applicable, division (D)(1) or (3) of this section are inadequate to punish the offender and protect the public from future crime, because the applicable factors under section 2929.12 of the Revised Code indicating a greater likelihood of recidivism outweigh the applicable factors under that section indicating a lesser likelihood of recidivism.

(v) The court finds that the prison terms imposed pursuant to division (D)(2)(a)(iii) of this section and, if applicable, division (D)(1) or (3) of this section are demeaning to the seriousness of the offense, because one or more of the factors under section 2929.12 of the Revised Code indicating that the offender's conduct is more serious than conduct normally constituting the offense are present, and they outweigh the applicable factors under that section indicating that the offender's conduct is less serious than conduct normally constituting the offense.

(b) The court shall impose on an offender the longest prison term authorized or required for the offense and shall impose on the offender an additional definite prison term of one, two, three, four, five, six, seven, eight, nine, or ten years if all of the following criteria are met:

(i) The offender is convicted of or pleads guilty to a specification of the type described in section 2941.149 of the Revised Code that the offender is a repeat violent offender.

(ii) The offender within the preceding twenty years has been convicted of or pleaded guilty to three or more offenses described in division (CC)(1) of section 2929.01 of the Revised Code, including all offenses described in that division of which the offender is convicted or to which the offender pleads guilty in the current prosecution and all offenses described in that division of which the offender previously has been convicted or to which the offender previously pleaded guilty, whether prosecuted together or separately.

(iii) The offense or offenses of which the offender currently is convicted or to which the offender currently pleads guilty is aggravated murder and the court does not impose a sentence of death or life imprisonment without parole, murder, terrorism and the court does not impose a sentence of life imprisonment without parole, any felony of the first degree that is an offense of violence and the court does not impose a sentence of life imprisonment without parole, or any felony of the second degree that is an offense of violence and the trier of fact finds that the offense involved an attempt to cause or a threat to cause serious physical harm to a person or resulted in serious physical harm to a person.

(c) For purposes of division (B)(2)(b) of this section, two or more offenses committed at the same time or as part of the same act or event shall be considered one offense, and that one offense shall be the offense with the greatest penalty.

(d) A sentence imposed under division (B)(2)(a) or (b) of this section shall not be reduced pursuant to section 2929.20, section 2967.19, or section 2967.193, or any other provision of Chapter 2967. or Chapter 5120. of the Revised Code. The offender shall serve an additional prison term imposed under this section consecutively to and prior to the prison term imposed for the underlying offense.

(e) When imposing a sentence pursuant to division (B)(2)(a) or (b) of this section, the court shall state its findings explaining the imposed sentence.

(3) Except when an offender commits a violation of section 2903.01 or 2907.02 of the Revised Code and the penalty imposed for the violation is life imprisonment or commits a violation of section 2903.02 of the Revised Code, if the offender commits a violation of section 2925.03 or 2925.11 of the Revised Code and that section classifies the offender as a major drug offender and requires the imposition of a ten-year prison term on the offender, if the offender commits a felony violation of section 2925.02, 2925.04, 2925.05, 2925.36, 3719.07, 3719.08, 3719.16, 3719.161, 4729.37, or 4729.61, division (C) or (D) of section 3719.172, division (C) of section 4729.51, or division (J) of section 4729.54 of the Revised Code that includes the sale, offer to sell, or possession of a schedule I or II controlled substance, with the exception of marihuana, and the court imposing sentence upon the offender finds that the offender is guilty of a specification of the type described in section 2941.1410 of the Revised Code charging that the offender is a major drug offender,

if the court imposing sentence upon an offender for a felony finds that the offender is guilty of corrupt activity with the most serious offense in the pattern of corrupt activity being a felony of the first degree, or if the offender is guilty of an attempted violation of section 2907.02 of the Revised Code and, had the offender completed the violation of section 2907.02 of the Revised Code that was attempted, the offender would have been subject to a sentence of life imprisonment or life imprisonment without parole for the violation of section 2907.02 of the Revised Code, the court shall impose upon the offender for the felony violation a ten-year prison term that, subject to divisions (C) to (I) of section 2967.19 of the Revised Code, cannot be reduced pursuant to section 2929.20, section 2967.19, or any other provision of Chapter 2967. or 5120. of the Revised Code.

(4) If the offender is being sentenced for a third or fourth degree felony OVI offense under division (G)(2) of section 2929.13 of the Revised Code, the sentencing court shall impose upon the offender a mandatory prison term in accordance with that division. In addition to the mandatory prison term, if the offender is being sentenced for a fourth degree felony OVI offense, the court, notwithstanding division (A)(4) of this section, may sentence the offender to a definite prison term of not less than six months and not more than thirty months, and if the offender is being sentenced for a third degree felony OVI offense, the sentencing court may sentence the offender to an additional prison term of any duration specified in division (A)(3) of this section. In either case, the additional prison term imposed shall be reduced by the sixty or one hundred twenty days imposed upon the offender as the mandatory prison term. The total of the additional prison term imposed under division (D)(4) of this section plus the sixty or one hundred twenty days imposed as the mandatory prison term shall equal a definite term in the range of six months to thirty months for a fourth degree felony OVI offense and shall equal one of the authorized prison terms specified in division (A)(3) of this section for a third degree felony OVI offense. If the court imposes an additional prison term under division (B)(4) of this section, the offender shall serve the additional prison term after the offender has served the mandatory prison term required for the offense. In addition to the mandatory prison term or mandatory and additional prison term imposed as described in division (B)(4) of this section, the court also may sentence the offender to a community control sanction under section 2929.16 or 2929.17 of the Revised Code, but the offender shall serve all of the prison terms so imposed prior to serving the community control sanction.

If the offender is being sentenced for a fourth degree felony OVI offense under division (G)(1) of section 2929.13 of the Revised Code and the court imposes a mandatory term of local incarceration, the court may impose a prison term as described in division (A)(1) of that section.

(5) If an offender is convicted of or pleads guilty to a violation of division (A)(1) or (2) of section 2903.06 of the Revised Code and also is convicted of or pleads guilty to a specification of the type described in section 2941.1414 of the Revised Code that charges that the victim of the offense is a peace officer, as defined in section 2935.01 of the Revised Code, or an investigator of the bureau of criminal identification and investigation, as defined in section 2903.11 of the Revised Code, the court shall impose on the offender a prison term of five years. If a court imposes a prison term on an offender under division (B)(5) of this section, the prison term, subject to divisions (C) to (I) of section 2967.19 of the Revised Code, shall not be reduced pursuant to section 2929.20, section 2967.19, section 2967.193, or any other provision of Chapter 2967. or Chapter 5120. of the Revised Code. A court shall not impose more than one prison term on an offender under division (B)(5) of this section for felonies committed as part of the same act.

(6) If an offender is convicted of or pleads guilty to a violation of division (A)(1) or (2) of section 2903.06 of the Revised Code and also is convicted of or pleads guilty to a specification of the type described in section 2941.1415 of the Revised Code that charges that the offender previously has been convicted of or pleaded guilty to three or more violations of division (A) or (B) of section 4511.19 of the Revised Code or an equivalent offense, as defined in section 2941.1415 of the Revised Code, or three or more violations of any combination of those divisions and offenses, the court shall impose on the offender a prison term of three years. If a court imposes a prison term on an offender under division (B)(6) of this section, the prison term, subject to divisions (C) to (I) of section 2967.19 of the Revised Code, shall not be reduced pursuant to section 2929.20, section 2967.19, section 2967.193, or any other provision of Chapter 2967. or Chapter 5120. of the Revised Code. A court shall not impose more than one prison term on an offender under division (B)(6) of this section for felonies committed as part of the same act.

(7)(a) If an offender is convicted of or pleads guilty to a felony violation of section 2905.01, 2905.02, 2907.21, 2907.22, or 2923.32, division (A)(1) or (2) of section 2907.323, or division (B)(1), (2), (3), (4), or (5) of section 2919.22 of the Revised Code and also is convicted of or pleads guilty to a specification of the type described in section 2941.1422 of the Revised Code that charges that the offender knowingly committed the offense in furtherance of human trafficking, the court shall impose on the offender a mandatory prison term that is one of the following:

(i) If the offense is a felony of the first degree, a definite prison term of not less than five years and not greater than ten years;

(ii) If the offense is a felony of the second or third degree, a definite prison term of not less than three years and not greater than the maximum prison term allowed for the offense by division (A) of section 2929.14 of the Revised Code;

(iii) If the offense is a felony of the fourth or fifth degree, a definite prison term that is the maximum prison term allowed for the offense by division (A) of section 2929.14 of the Revised Code.

(b) Subject to divisions (C) to (I) of section 2967.19 of the Revised Code, the prison term imposed under division (B)(7)(a) of this section shall not be reduced pursuant to section 2929.20, section 2967.19, section 2967.193, or any other provision of Chapter 2967. of the Revised Code. A court shall not impose more than one prison term on an offender under division (B)(7)(a) of this section for felonies committed as part of the same act, scheme, or plan.

(8) If an offender is convicted of or pleads guilty to a felony violation of section 2903.11, 2903.12, or 2903.13 of the Revised Code and also is convicted of or pleads guilty to a specification of the type described in section 2941.1423 of the Revised Code that charges that the victim of the violation was a woman whom the offender knew was pregnant at the time of the violation, notwith-

standing the range of prison terms prescribed in division (A) of this section for felonies of the same degree as the violation, the court shall impose on the offender a mandatory prison term that is either a definite prison term of six months or one of the prison terms prescribed in section 2929.14 of the Revised Code for felonies of the same degree as the violation.

(C)(1)(a) Subject to division (C)(1)(b) of this section, if a mandatory prison term is imposed upon an offender pursuant to division (B)(1)(a) of this section for having a firearm on or about the offender's person or under the offender's control while committing a felony, if a mandatory prison term is imposed upon an offender pursuant to division (B)(1)(c) of this section for committing a felony specified in that division by discharging a firearm from a motor vehicle, or if both types of mandatory prison terms are imposed, the offender shall serve any mandatory prison term imposed under either division consecutively to any other mandatory prison term imposed under either division or under division (B)(1)(d) of this section, consecutively to and prior to any prison term imposed for the underlying felony pursuant to division (A), (B)(2), or (B)(3) of this section or any other section of the Revised Code, and consecutively to any other prison term or mandatory prison term previously or subsequently imposed upon the offender.

(b) If a mandatory prison term is imposed upon an offender pursuant to division (B)(1)(d) of this section for wearing or carrying body armor while committing an offense of violence that is a felony, the offender shall serve the mandatory term so imposed consecutively to any other mandatory prison term imposed under that division or under division (B)(1)(a) or (c) of this section, consecutively to and prior to any prison term imposed for the underlying felony under division (A), (B)(2), or (B)(3) of this section or any other section of the Revised Code, and consecutively to any other prison term or mandatory prison term previously or subsequently imposed upon the offender.

(c) If a mandatory prison term is imposed upon an offender pursuant to division (B)(1)(f) of this section, the offender shall serve the mandatory prison term so imposed consecutively to and prior to any prison term imposed for the underlying felony under division (A), (B)(2), or (B)(3) of this section or any other section of the Revised Code, and consecutively to any other prison term or mandatory prison term previously or subsequently imposed upon the offender.

(d) If a mandatory prison term is imposed upon an offender pursuant to division (B)(7) or (8) of this section, the offender shall serve the mandatory prison term so imposed consecutively to any other mandatory prison term imposed under that division or under any other provision of law and consecutively to any other prison term or mandatory prison term previously or subsequently imposed upon the offender.

(2) If an offender who is an inmate in a jail, prison, or other residential detention facility violates section 2917.02, 2917.03, or 2921.35 of the Revised Code or division (A)(1) or (2) of section 2921.34 of the Revised Code, if an offender who is under detention at a detention facility commits a felony violation of section 2923.131 of the Revised Code, or if an offender who is an inmate in a jail, prison, or other residential detention facility or is under detention at a detention facility commits another felony while the offender is an escapee in violation of division (A)(1) or (2) of section 2921.34 of the Revised Code, any prison term imposed upon the offender for one of those violations shall be served by the offender consecutively to the prison term or term of imprisonment the offender was serving when the offender committed that offense and to any other prison term previously or subsequently imposed upon the offender.

(3) If a prison term is imposed for a violation of division (B) of section 2911.01 of the Revised Code, a violation of division (A) of section 2913.02 of the Revised Code in which the stolen property is a firearm or dangerous ordnance, or a felony violation of division (B) of section 2921.331 of the Revised Code, the offender shall serve that prison term consecutively to any other prison term or mandatory prison term previously or subsequently imposed upon the offender.

(4) If multiple prison terms are imposed on an offender for convictions of multiple offenses, the court may require the offender to serve the prison terms consecutively if the court finds that the consecutive service is necessary to protect the public from future crime or to punish the offender and that consecutive sentences are not disproportionate to the seriousness of the offender's conduct and to the danger the offender poses to the public, and if the court also finds any of the following:

(a) The offender committed one or more of the multiple offenses while the offender was awaiting trial or sentencing, was under a sanction imposed pursuant to section 2929.16, 2929.17, or 2929.18 of the Revised Code, or was under post-release control for a prior offense.

(b) At least two of the multiple offenses were committed as part of one or more courses of conduct, and the harm caused by two or more of the multiple offenses so committed was so great or unusual that no single prison term for any of the offenses committed as part of any of the courses of conduct adequately reflects the seriousness of the offender's conduct.

(c) The offender's history of criminal conduct demonstrates that consecutive sentences are necessary to protect the public from future crime by the offender.

(5) If a mandatory prison term is imposed upon an offender pursuant to division (B)(5) or (6) of this section, the offender shall serve the mandatory prison term consecutively to and prior to any prison term imposed for the underlying violation of division (A)(1) or (2) of section 2903.06 of the Revised Code pursuant to division (A) of this section or section 2929.142 of the Revised Code. If a mandatory prison term is imposed upon an offender pursuant to division (B)(5) of this section, and if a mandatory prison term also is imposed upon the offender pursuant to division (B)(6) of this section in relation to the same violation, the offender shall serve the mandatory prison term imposed pursuant to division (B)(5) of this section consecutively to and prior to the mandatory prison term imposed pursuant to division (B)(6) of this section and consecutively to and prior to any prison term imposed for the underlying violation of division (A)(1) or (2) of section 2903.06 of the Revised Code pursuant to division (A) of this section or section 2929.142 of the Revised Code.

(6) When consecutive prison terms are imposed pursuant to division (C)(1), (2), (3), (4), or (5) or division (H)(1) or (2) of this section, the term to be served is the aggregate of all of the terms so imposed.

(D)(1) If a court imposes a prison term for a felony of the first degree, for a felony of the second degree, for a felony sex offense, or for a felony of the third degree that is not a felony sex offense and in the commission of which the offender caused or threatened to cause physical harm to a person, it shall include in the sentence a requirement that the offender be subject to a period of post-release control after the offender's release from imprisonment, in accordance with that division. If a court imposes a sentence including a prison term of a type described in this division on or after July 11, 2006, the failure of a court to include a post-release control requirement in the sentence pursuant to this division does not negate, limit, or otherwise affect the mandatory period of post-release control that is required for the offender under division (B) of section 2967.28 of the Revised Code. Section 2929.191 of the Revised Code applies if, prior to July 11, 2006, a court imposed a sentence including a prison term of a type described in this division and failed to include in the sentence pursuant to this division a statement regarding post-release control.

(2) If a court imposes a prison term for a felony of the third, fourth, or fifth degree that is not subject to division (D)(1) of this section, it shall include in the sentence a requirement that the offender be subject to a period of post-release control after the offender's release from imprisonment, in accordance with that division, if the parole board determines that a period of post-release control is necessary. Section 2929.191 of the Revised Code applies if, prior to July 11, 2006, a court imposed a sentence including a prison term of a type described in this division and failed to include in the sentence pursuant to this division a statement regarding post-release control.

(3) If a court imposes a prison term on or after the effective date of this amendment for a felony, it shall include in the sentence a statement notifying the offender that the offender may be eligible to earn days of credit under the circumstances specified in section 2967.193 of the Revised Code. The statement also shall notify the offender that days of credit are not automatically awarded under that section, but that they must be earned in the manner specified in that section. If a court fails to include the statement in the sentence, the failure does not affect the eligibility of the offender under section 2967.193 of the Revised Code to earn any days of credit as a deduction from the offender's stated prison term or otherwise render any part of that section or any action taken under that section void or voidable. The failure of a court to include in a sentence the statement described in this division does not constitute grounds for setting aside the offender's conviction or sentence or for granting postconviction relief to the offender.

(E) The court shall impose sentence upon the offender in accordance with section 2971.03 of the Revised Code, and Chapter 2971. of the Revised Code applies regarding the prison term or term of life imprisonment without parole imposed upon the offender and the service of that term of imprisonment if any of the following apply:

(1) A person is convicted of or pleads guilty to a violent sex offense or a designated homicide, assault, or kidnapping offense, and, in relation to that offense, the offender is adjudicated a sexually violent predator.

(2) A person is convicted of or pleads guilty to a violation of division (A)(1)(b) of section 2907.02 of the Revised Code committed on or after January 2, 2007, and either the court does not impose a sentence of life without parole when authorized pursuant to division (B) of section 2907.02 of the Revised Code, or division (B) of section 2907.02 of the Revised Code provides that the court shall not sentence the offender pursuant to section 2971.03 of the Revised Code.

(3) A person is convicted of or pleads guilty to attempted rape committed on or after January 2, 2007, and a specification of the type described in section 2941.1418, 2941.1419, or 2941.1420 of the Revised Code.

(4) A person is convicted of or pleads guilty to a violation of section 2905.01 of the Revised Code committed on or after January 1, 2008, and that section requires the court to sentence the offender pursuant to section 2971.03 of the Revised Code.

(5) A person is convicted of or pleads guilty to aggravated murder committed on or after January 1, 2008, and division (A)(2)(b)(ii) of section 2929.022, division (A)(1)(e), (C)(1)(a)(v), (C)(2)(a)(ii), (D)(2)(b), (D)(3)(a)(iv), or (E)(1)(d) of section 2929.03, or division (A) or (B) of section 2929.06 of the Revised Code requires the court to sentence the offender pursuant to division (B)(3) of section 2971.03 of the Revised Code.

(6) A person is convicted of or pleads guilty to murder committed on or after January 1, 2008, and division (B)(2) of section 2929.02 of the Revised Code requires the court to sentence the offender pursuant to section 2971.03 of the Revised Code.

(F) If a person who has been convicted of or pleaded guilty to a felony is sentenced to a prison term or term of imprisonment under this section, sections 2929.02 to 2929.06 of the Revised Code, section 2929.142 of the Revised Code, section 2971.03 of the Revised Code, or any other provision of law, section 5120.163 of the Revised Code applies regarding the person while the person is confined in a state correctional institution.

(G) If an offender who is convicted of or pleads guilty to a felony that is an offense of violence also is convicted of or pleads guilty to a specification of the type described in section 2941.142 of the Revised Code that charges the offender with having committed the felony while participating in a criminal gang, the court shall impose upon the offender an additional prison term of one, two, or three years.

(H)(1) If an offender who is convicted of or pleads guilty to aggravated murder, murder, or a felony of the first, second, or third degree that is an offense of violence also is convicted of or pleads guilty to a specification of the type described in section 2941.143 of the Revised Code that charges the offender with having committed the offense in a school safety zone or towards a person in a school safety zone, the court shall impose upon the offender an additional prison term of two years. The offender shall serve the additional two years consecutively to and prior to the prison term imposed for the underlying offense.

(2)(a) If an offender is convicted of or pleads guilty to a felony violation of section 2907.22, 2907.24, 2907.241, or 2907.25 of the Revised Code and to a specification of the type described in section 2941.1421 of the Revised Code and if the court imposes a prison term on the offender for the felony violation, the court may impose upon the offender an additional prison term as follows:

(i) Subject to division (H)(2)(a)(ii) of this section, an additional prison term of one, two, three, four, five, or six months;

(ii) If the offender previously has been convicted of or pleaded guilty to one or more felony or misdemeanor violations of section 2907.22, 2907.23, 2907.24, 2907.241, or 2907.25 of the Revised Code and also was convicted of or pleaded guilty to a specification of the type described in section 2941.1421 of the Revised Code regarding one or more of those violations, an additional prison term of one, two, three, four, five, six, seven, eight, nine, ten, eleven, or twelve months.

(b) In lieu of imposing an additional prison term under division (H)(2)(a) of this section, the court may directly impose on the offender a sanction that requires the offender to wear a real-time processing, continual tracking electronic monitoring device during the period of time specified by the court. The period of time specified by the court shall equal the duration of an additional prison term that the court could have imposed upon the offender under division (H)(2)(a) of this section. A sanction imposed under this division shall commence on the date specified by the court, provided that the sanction shall not commence until after the offender has served the prison term imposed for the felony violation of section 2907.22, 2907.24, 2907.241, or 2907.25 of the Revised Code and any residential sanction imposed for the violation under section 2929.16 of the Revised Code. A sanction imposed under this division shall be considered to be a community control sanction for purposes of section 2929.15 of the Revised Code, and all provisions of the Revised Code that pertain to community control sanctions shall apply to a sanction imposed under this division, except to the extent that they would by their nature be clearly inapplicable. The offender shall pay all costs associated with a sanction imposed under this division, including the cost of the use of the monitoring device.

(I)(1) At the time of sentencing, the court may recommend the offender for placement in a program of shock incarceration under section 5120.031 of the Revised Code or for placement in an intensive program prison under section 5120.032 of the Revised Code, disapprove placement of the offender in a program of shock incarceration or an intensive program prison of that nature, or make no recommendation on placement of the offender. In no case shall the department of rehabilitation and correction place the offender in a program or prison of that nature unless the department determines as specified in section 5120.031 or 5120.032 of the Revised Code, whichever is applicable, that the offender is eligible for the placement.

If the court disapproves placement of the offender in a program or prison of that nature, the department of rehabilitation and correction shall not place the offender in any program of shock incarceration or intensive program prison.

If the court recommends placement of the offender in a program of shock incarceration or in an intensive program prison, and if the offender is subsequently placed in the recommended program or prison, the department shall notify the court of the placement and shall include with the notice a brief description of the placement.

If the court recommends placement of the offender in a program of shock incarceration or in an intensive program prison and the department does not subsequently place the offender in the recommended program or prison, the department shall send a notice to the court indicating why the offender was not placed in the recommended program or prison.

If the court does not make a recommendation under this division with respect to an offender and if the department determines as specified in section 5120.031 or 5120.032 of the Revised Code, whichever is applicable, that the offender is eligible for placement in a program or prison of that nature, the department shall screen the offender and determine if there is an available program of shock incarceration or an intensive program prison for which the offender is suited. If there is an available program of shock incarceration or an intensive program prison for which the offender is suited, the department shall notify the court of the proposed placement of the offender as specified in section 5120.031 or 5120.032 of the Revised Code and shall include with the notice a brief description of the placement. The court shall have ten days from receipt of the notice to disapprove the placement.

(L) If a person is convicted of or pleads guilty to aggravated vehicular homicide in violation of division (A)(1) of section 2903.06 of the Revised Code and division (B)(2)(c) of that section applies, the person shall be sentenced pursuant to section 2929.142 of the Revised Code.

**HISTORY: 146 v S 2 (Eff 7-1-96); 146 v S 269 (Eff 7-1-96); 146 v H 88 (Eff 9-3-96); 146 v H 445 (Eff 9-3-96); 146 v H 154 (Eff 10-4-96); 146 v S 166 (Eff 10-17-96); 146 v H 180 (Eff 1-1-97); 147 v H 151 (Eff 9-16-97); 147 v H 32 (Eff 3-10-98); 147 v S 111 (Eff 3-17-98); 147 v H 2 (Eff 1-1-99); 148 v S 1 (Eff 8-6-99); 148 v H 29 (Eff 10-29-99); 148 v S 107 (Eff 3-23-2000); 148 v S 22 (Eff 5-17-2000); 148 v S 222 (Eff 3-22-2001); 149 v H 485 (Eff 6-13-2002); 149 v H 327 (Eff 7-8-2002); 149 v H 130. Eff 4-7-2003; 149 v S 123, § 1, eff. 1-1-04; 150 v H 12, §§ 1, 3, eff. 4-8-04†; 150 v H 52, § 1, eff. 6-1-04; 150 v H 163, § 1, eff. 9-23-04; 150 v H 473, § 1, eff. 4-29-05; 151 v H 95, § 1, eff. 8-3-06; 151 v H 137, § 1, eff. 7-11-06; 151 v H 137, § 3, eff. 8-3-06; 151 v S 260, § 1, eff. 1-2-07; 151 v S 281, § 1, eff. 1-4-07; 151 v H 461, § 1, eff. 4-4-07; 152 v S 10, § 1, eff. 1-1-08; 152 v S 184, § 1, eff. 9-9-08; 152 v S 220, § 1, eff. 9-30-08; 152 v H 280, § 1, eff. 4-7-09; 152 v H 130, § 1, eff. 4-7-09; 2011 HB 86, § 1, eff. Sept. 30, 2011.**

† Section 3, H.B. 12, Acts 2004, purported to amend the version of RC § 2929.14 as amended by S.B. 123 (149 v —), which took effect on January 1, 2004. However, H.B. 12, Acts 2004 was approved January 8, 2004, and became effective April 8, 2004.

The provisions of § 4 of HB 86 read as follows:

SECTION 4. The amendments to sections 926.99, 1333.99, 1707.99, 1716.99, 2909.03, 2909.05, 2909.11, 2913.02, 2913.03, 2913.04, 2913.11, 2913.21, 2913.31, 2913.32, 2913.34, 2913.40, 2913.401, 2913.42, 2913.421, 2913.43, 2913.45, 2913.46, 2913.47, 2913.48, 2913.49, 2913.51, 2913.61, 2915.05, 2917.21, 2917.31, 2917.32, 2921.13, 2921.41, 2923.31, and 2981.07, division (B) of section 2929.13, and division (A) of section 2929.14 of the Revised Code that are made in this act apply to a person who commits an offense specified or penalized under those sections on or after the effective date of this section and to a person to whom division (B) of section 1.58 of the Revised Code makes the amendments applicable.

The provisions of sections 926.99, 1333.99, 1707.99, 1716.99, 2909.03, 2909.05, 2909.11, 2913.02, 2913.03, 2913.04, 2913.11, 2913.21, 2913.31, 2913.32, 2913.34, 2913.40, 2913.401, 2913.42, 2913.421, 2913.43, 2913.45, 2913.46, 2913.47, 2913.48, 2913.49, 2913.51, 2913.61, 2915.05, 2917.21, 2917.31, 2917.32, 2921.13, 2921.41, 2923.31, and 2981.07 of the Revised Code in existence prior to the effective date of this section shall apply to a person upon whom a court imposed sentence prior to the effective date of this section for an offense specified or penalized under those sections. The amendments to sections 926.99, 1333.99, 1707.99, 1716.99, 2909.03, 2909.05, 2909.11, 2913.02, 2913.03, 2913.04, 2913.11, 2913.21, 2913.31, 2913.32, 2913.34, 2913.40, 2913.401, 2913.42, 2913.421, 2913.43, 2913.45, 2913.46, 2913.47, 2913.48, 2913.49, 2913.51, 2913.61, 2915.05, 2917.21, 2917.31, 2917.32, 2921.13, 2921.41, 2923.31, and 2981.07 of the Revised Code that are made in this act do not apply to a person who upon whom a court imposed sentence prior to the effective date of this section for an offense specified or penalized under those sections.

The provisions of § 11 of HB 86 read as follows:

"SECTION 11. In amending division (E)(4) of section 2929.14 and division (A) of section 2929.41 of the Revised Code in this act, it is the intent of the General Assembly to simultaneously repeal and revive the amended language in those divisions that was invalidated and severed by the Ohio Supreme Court's decision in

State v. Foster (2006), 109 Ohio St.3d 1. The amended language in those divisions is subject to reenactment under the United States Supreme Court's decision in Oregon v. Ice (2009), 555 U.S. 160, and the Ohio Supreme Court's decision in State v. Hodge (2010), ______ Ohio St.3d ______, Slip Opinion No. 2010-Ohio-6320 and, although constitutional under Hodge, supra, that language is not enforceable until deliberately revived by the General Assembly."

The provisions of § 12 of HB 86 read as follows:

"SECTION 12. Section 2929.14 of the Revised Code is presented in this act as a composite of the section as amended by both Am. Sub. H.B. 130 and Am. Sub. H.B. 280 of the 127th General Assembly. The General Assembly, applying the principle stated in division (B) of section 1.52 of the Revised Code that amendments are to be harmonized if reasonably capable of simultaneous operation, finds that the composites are the resulting versions of the sections in effect prior to the effective date of the sections as presented in this act."

The provisions of § 7 of 152 v H 130 read as follows:

SECTION 7. Section 2929.14 of the Revised Code is presented in this act as a composite of the section as amended by both Sub. S.B. 184 and Sub. S.B. 220 of the 127th General Assembly. The General Assembly, applying the principle stated in division (B) of section 1.52 of the Revised Code that amendments are to be harmonized if reasonably capable of simultaneous operation, finds that the composite is the resulting version of the section in effect prior to the effective date of the section as presented in this act.

The provisions of § 5 of 152 v H 280 read in part as follows:

SECTION 5. * * * Section 2929.14 of the Revised Code is presented in this act as a composite of the section as amended by both Sub. S.B. 184 and Sub. S.B. 220 of the 127th General Assembly. The General Assembly, applying the principle stated in division (B) of section 1.52 of the Revised Code that amendments are to be harmonized if reasonably capable of simultaneous operation, finds that the composite is the resulting version of the section in effect prior to the effective date of the section as presented in this act.

The effective date is set by § 3 of 152 v S 10.

The provisions of § 6 of 152 v S 10 read as follows:

SECTION 6. * * * Section 2929.14 of the Revised Code is presented in this act as a composite of the section as amended by Am. Sub. H.B. 461, Am. Sub. S.B. 260, and Sub. S.B. 281 all of the 126th General Assembly. * * * The General Assembly, applying the principle stated in division (B) of section 1.52 of the Revised Code that amendments are to be harmonized if reasonably capable of simultaneous operation, finds that the composites are the resulting versions of the sections in effect prior to the effective date of the sections as presented in this act.

See provisions of § 5 of 151 v H 137 following RC § 2929.191.

The effective date is set by § 7 of 151 v H 137.

The provisions of § 3 of H.B. 473 (150 v —) read as follows:

SECTION 3. * * * Sections 2929.01, 2929.13, and 2929.14 of the Revised Code are presented in this act as composites of the sections as amended by both Sub. H.B. 52 and Am. Sub. H.B. 163 of the 125th General Assembly. * * * The General Assembly, applying the principle stated in division (B) of section 1.52 of the Revised Code that amendments are to be harmonized if reasonably capable of simultaneous operation, finds that the composites are the resulting versions of the sections in effect prior to the effective date of the sections as presented in this act.

The provisions of § 10, H.B. 12 (150 v —), read as follows:

SECTION 10. If any provision of sections 1547.69, 2911.21, 2913.02, 2921.13, 2923.12, 2923.121, 2923.123, 2923.16, 2929.14, 2953.32, and 4749.10 of the Revised Code, as amended by this act, any provision of sections 109.69, 109.731, 311.41, 311.42, 2923.124, 2923.125, 2923.126, 2923.127, 2923.128, 2923.129, 2923.1210, 2923.1211, 2923.1212, and 2923.1213 of the Revised Code, as enacted by this act, or the application of any provision of those sections to any person or circumstance is held invalid, the invalidity does not affect other provisions or applications of the particular section or related sections that can be given effect without the invalid provision or application, and to this end the provisions of the particular section are severable.

The provisions of § 11, H.B. 12 (150 v —), read as follows:

SECTION 11. (B) Section 2929.14 of the Revised Code, effective on January 1, 2004, is presented in Section 3 of this act as a composite of the section as amended by Sub. H.B. 130, Am. Sub. H.B. 327, Sub. H.B. 485, and Am. Sub. S.B. 123 of the 124th General Assembly. The General Assembly, applying the principle stated in division (B) of section 1.52 of the Revised Code that amendments are to be harmonized if reasonably capable of simultaneous operation, finds that the composite is the resulting version of the section in effect prior to the effective date of the section as presented in Section 3 of this act.

**Not analogous to former RC § 2929.14 (139 v S 199; 145 v S 186), repealed 146 v S 2, § 2, 7-1-96.**

See provisions of § 5 of S.B. 123 (149 v —) following RC § 2929.01.

SECTION 5. Notwithstanding division (B) of section 1.58 of the Revised Code, the provisions of the Revised Code amended or enacted in Sections 1 and 2 of this act shall apply only in relation to conduct and offenses committed on or after January 1, 2004. Conduct and offenses committed prior to January 1, 2004, shall be governed by the law in effect on the date the conduct or offense was committed.

**Comment, Legislative Service Commission**

Section 2929.14 of the Revised Code is amended by Am. Sub. HB 280 and Am. Sub. HB 130 of the 127th General Assembly. Comparison of these amendments in pursuance of section 1.52 of the Revised Code discloses that they are not irreconcilable so that they are required by that section to be harmonized to give effect to each amendment.

## § 2929.141 New felony committed by person on post-release control.

(A) Upon the conviction of or plea of guilty to a felony by a person on post-release control at the time of the commission of the felony, the court may terminate the term of post-release control, and the court may do either of the following regardless of whether the sentencing court or another court of this state imposed the original prison term for which the person is on post-release control:

(1) In addition to any prison term for the new felony, impose a prison term for the post-release control violation. The maximum prison term for the violation shall be the greater of twelve months or the period of post-release control for the earlier felony minus any time the person has spent under post-release control for the earlier felony. In all cases, any prison term imposed for the violation shall be reduced by any prison term that is administratively imposed by the parole board as a post-release control sanction. A prison term imposed for the violation shall be served consecutively to any prison term imposed for the new felony. The imposition of a prison term for the post-release control violation shall terminate the period of post-release control for the earlier felony.

(2) Impose a sanction under sections 2929.15 to 2929.18 of the Revised Code for the violation that shall be served concurrently or consecutively, as specified by the court, with any community control sanctions for the new felony.

**HISTORY: 149 v H 327. Eff 7-8-2002; 152 v H 130, § 1, eff. 4-7-09.**

## § 2929.142 Mandatory prison term for aggravated vehicular homicide where offender has previous OVI-type convictions.

Notwithstanding the definite prison term specified in division (A) of section 2929.14 of the Revised Code for a felony of the first degree, if an offender is convicted of or pleads guilty to aggravated vehicular homicide in violation of division (A)(1) of section 2903.06 of the Revised Code, the court shall impose upon the offender a mandatory prison term of ten, eleven, twelve, thirteen, fourteen, or fifteen years if any of the following apply:

(A) The offender previously has been convicted of or pleaded guilty to three or more prior violations of section 4511.19 of the Revised Code or of a substantially equivalent municipal ordinance within the previous six years.

(B) The offender previously has been convicted of or pleaded guilty to three or more prior violations of division (A) of section 1547.11 of the Revised Code or of a substantially equivalent municipal ordinance within the previous six years.

(C) The offender previously has been convicted of or pleaded guilty to three or more prior violations of division (A)(3) of section 4561.15 of the Revised Code or of a substantially equivalent municipal ordinance within the previous six years.

(D) The offender previously has been convicted of or pleaded guilty to three or more prior violations of division (A)(1) of section 2903.06 of the Revised Code.

(E) The offender previously has been convicted of or pleaded guilty to three or more prior violations of division (A)(1) of section 2903.08 of the Revised Code.

(F) The offender previously has been convicted of or pleaded guilty to three or more prior violations of section 2903.04 of the Revised Code in circumstances in which division (D) of that section applied regarding the violations.

(G) The offender previously has been convicted of or pleaded guilty to three or more violations of any combination of the offenses listed in division (A), (B), (C), (D), (E), or (F) of this section.

(H) The offender previously has been convicted of or pleaded guilty to a second or subsequent felony violation of division (A) of section 4511.19 of the Revised Code.

**HISTORY: 151 v H 461, § 1, eff. 4-4-07.**

## § 2929.143 Eligibility of offender for recommendation to serve risk reduction sentence under section 5120.036 of the Revised Code.

(A) When a court sentences an offender who is convicted of a felony to a term of incarceration in a state correctional institution, the court may recommend that the offender serve a risk reduction sentence under section 5120.036 of the Revised Code if the court determines that a risk reduction sentence is appropriate, and all of the following apply:

(1) The offense for which the offender is being sentenced is not aggravated murder, murder, complicity in committing aggravated murder or murder, an offense of violence that is a felony of the first or second degree, a sexually oriented offense, or an attempt or conspiracy to commit or complicity in committing any offense otherwise identified in this division if the attempt, conspiracy, or complicity is a felony of the first or second degree.

(2) The offender's sentence to the term of incarceration does not consist solely of one or more mandatory prison terms.

(3) The offender agrees to cooperate with an assessment of the offender's needs and risk of reoffending that the department of rehabilitation and correction conducts under section 5120.036 of the Revised Code.

(4) The offender agrees to participate in any programming or treatment that the department of rehabilitation and correction orders to address any issues raised in the assessment described in division (A)(3) of this section.

(B) An offender who is serving a risk reduction sentence is not entitled to any earned credit under section 2967.193 of the Revised Code.

**HISTORY: 2011 HB 86, § 1, eff. Sept. 30, 2011.**

## § 2929.15 Community control sanctions.

(A)(1) If in sentencing an offender for a felony the court is not required to impose a prison term, a mandatory prison term, or a term of life imprisonment upon the offender, the court may directly impose a sentence that consists of one or more community control sanctions authorized pursuant to section 2929.16, 2929.17, or 2929.18 of the Revised Code. If the court is sentencing an offender for a fourth degree felony OVI offense under division (G)(1) of section 2929.13 of the Revised Code, in addition to the mandatory term of local incarceration imposed under that division and the mandatory fine required by division (B)(3) of section 2929.18 of the Revised Code, the court may impose upon the offender a community control sanction or combination of community control sanctions in accordance with sections 2929.16 and 2929.17 of the Revised Code. If the court is sentencing an offender for a third or fourth degree felony OVI offense under division (G)(2) of section 2929.13 of the Revised Code, in addition to the mandatory prison term or mandatory prison term and additional prison term imposed under that division, the court also may impose upon the offender a community control sanction or combination of community control sanctions under section 2929.16 or 2929.17 of the Revised Code, but the offender shall serve all of the prison terms so imposed prior to serving the community control sanction.

The duration of all community control sanctions imposed upon an offender under this division shall not exceed five years. If the offender absconds or otherwise leaves the jurisdiction of the court in which the offender resides without obtaining permission from the court or the offender's probation officer to leave the jurisdiction of the court, or if the offender is confined in any institution for the commission of any offense while under a community control sanction, the period of the community control sanction ceases to run until the offender is brought before the court for its further action. If the court sentences the offender to one or more nonresidential sanctions under section 2929.17 of the Revised Code, the court shall impose as a condition of the nonresidential sanctions that, during the period of the sanctions, the offender must abide by the law and must not leave the state without the permission of the court or the offender's probation officer. The court may impose any other conditions of release under a community control sanction that the court considers appropriate, including, but not limited to, requiring that the offender not ingest or be injected with a drug of abuse and submit to random drug testing as provided in division (D) of this section to determine whether the offender ingested or was injected with a drug of abuse and requiring that the results of the drug test indicate that the offender did not ingest or was not injected with a drug of abuse.

(2)(a) If a court sentences an offender to any community control sanction or combination of community control sanctions authorized pursuant to section 2929.16, 2929.17, or 2929.18 of the Revised Code, the court shall place the offender under the general control and supervision of a department of probation in the county that serves the court for purposes of reporting to the court a violation of any condition of the sanctions, any condition of release under a community control sanction imposed by the court, a violation of law, or the departure of the offender from this state without the permission of the court or the offender's probation officer. Alternatively, if the offender resides in another county and a county department of probation has been established in that county or that county is served by a multicounty probation department established under section 2301.27 of the Revised Code, the court may request the court of common pleas of that county to receive the offender into the general control and supervision of that county or multicounty department of probation for purposes of reporting to the court a violation of any condition of the sanctions, any condition of release under a community control sanction imposed by the court, a violation of law, or the departure of the offender from this state without the permission of the court or the offender's probation officer, subject to the jurisdiction of the trial judge over and with respect to the person of the offender, and to the rules governing that department of probation.

If there is no department of probation in the county that serves the court, the court shall place the offender, regardless of the offender's county of residence, under the general control and supervision of the adult parole authority for purposes of reporting to the court a violation of any of the sanctions, any condition of release under a community control sanction imposed by the court, a violation of law, or the departure of the offender from this state without the permission of the court or the offender's probation officer.

(b) If the court imposing sentence upon an offender sentences the offender to any community control sanction or combination of community control sanctions authorized pursuant to section 2929.16, 2929.17, or 2929.18 of the Revised Code, and if the offender violates any condition of the sanctions, any condition of release under a community control sanction imposed by the court, violates any law, or departs the state without the permission of the court or the offender's probation officer, the public or private person or entity that operates or administers the sanction or the program or activity that comprises the sanction shall report the violation or departure directly to the sentencing court, or shall report the violation or departure to the county or multicounty department of probation with general control and supervision over the offender under division (A)(2)(a) of this section or the officer of that department who supervises the offender, or, if there is no such department with general control and supervision over the offender under that division, to the adult parole authority. If the public or private person or entity that operates or administers the sanction or the program or activity that comprises the sanction reports the violation or departure to the county or multicounty department of probation or the adult parole authority, the department's or authority's officers may treat the offender as if the offender were on probation and in violation of the probation, and shall report the violation of the condition of the sanction, any condition of release under a community control sanction imposed by the court, the violation of law, or the departure from the state without the required permission to the sentencing court.

(3) If an offender who is eligible for community control sanctions under this section admits to being drug addicted or the court has reason to believe that the offender is drug addicted, and if the offense for which the offender is being sentenced was related to the addiction, the court may require that the offender be assessed by a properly credentialed professional within a specified period of time and shall require the professional to file a written assessment of the offender with the court. If a court imposes treatment and recovery support services as a community control sanction, the court shall direct the level and type of treatment and recovery support services after consideration of the written assessment, if available at the time of sentencing, and recommendations of the professional and other treatment and recovery support services providers.

(4) If an assessment completed pursuant to division (A)(3) of this section indicates that the offender is addicted to drugs or alcohol, the court may include in any community control sanction imposed for a violation of section 2925.02, 2925.03, 2925.04, 2925.05, 2925.06, 2925.11, 2925.13, 2925.22, 2925.23, 2925.36, or 2925.37 of the Revised Code a requirement that the offender participate in a treatment and recovery support services program certified under section 3793.06 of the Revised Code or offered by another properly credentialed program provider.

(B)(1) If the conditions of a community control sanction are violated or if the offender violates a law or leaves the state without the permission of the court or the offender's probation officer, the sentencing court may impose upon the violator one or more of the following penalties:

(a) A longer time under the same sanction if the total time under the sanctions does not exceed the five-year limit specified in division (A) of this section;

(b) A more restrictive sanction under section 2929.16, 2929.17, or 2929.18 of the Revised Code;

(c) A prison term on the offender pursuant to section 2929.14 of the Revised Code.

(2) The prison term, if any, imposed upon a violator pursuant to this division shall be within the range of prison terms available for the offense for which the sanction that was violated was imposed and shall not exceed the prison term specified in the notice provided to the offender at the sentencing hearing pursuant to division (B)(2) of section 2929.19 of the Revised Code. The court may reduce the longer period of time that the offender is required to spend under the longer sanction, the more restrictive sanction, or a prison term imposed pursuant to this division by the time the offender successfully spent under the sanction that was initially imposed.

(C) If an offender, for a significant period of time, fulfills the conditions of a sanction imposed pursuant to section 2929.16, 2929.17, or 2929.18 of the Revised Code in an exemplary manner, the court may reduce the period of time under the sanction or impose a less restrictive sanction, but the court shall not permit the offender to violate any law or permit the offender to leave the state without the permission of the court or the offender's probation officer.

(D)(1) If a court under division (A)(1) of this section imposes a condition of release under a community control sanction that requires the offender to submit to random drug testing, the department of probation or the adult parole authority that has general control and supervision of the offender under division (A)(2)(a) of this section may cause the offender to submit to random drug testing performed by a laboratory or entity that has entered into a contract with any of the governmental entities or officers authorized to enter into a contract with that laboratory or entity under section 341.26, 753.33, or 5120.63 of the Revised Code.

(2) If no laboratory or entity described in division (D)(1) of this section has entered into a contract as specified in that division, the department of probation or the adult parole authority that has general control and supervision of the offender under division (A)(2)(a) of this section shall cause the offender to submit to random drug testing performed by a reputable public laboratory to determine whether the individual who is the subject of the drug test ingested or was injected with a drug of abuse.

(3) A laboratory or entity that has entered into a contract pursuant to section 341.26, 753.33, or 5120.63 of the Revised Code shall perform the random drug tests under division (D)(1) of this section in accordance with the applicable standards that are included in the terms of that contract. A public laboratory shall perform the random drug tests under division (D)(2) of this section in accordance with the standards set forth in the policies and procedures established by the department of rehabilitation and correction pursuant to section 5120.63 of the Revised Code. An offender who is required under division (A)(1) of this section to submit to random drug testing as a condition of release under a community control sanction and whose test results indicate that the offender ingested or was injected with a drug of abuse shall pay the fee for the drug test if the department of probation or the adult parole authority that has general control and supervision of the offender requires payment of a fee. A laboratory or entity that performs the random drug testing on an offender under division (D)(1) or (2) of this section shall transmit the results of the drug test to the appropriate department of probation or the adult parole authority that has general control and supervision of the offender under division (A)(2)(a) of this section.

**HISTORY: 146 v S 2 (Eff 7-1-96); 146 v S 269 (Eff 7-1-96); 146 v S 166 (Eff 10-17-96); 148 v S 107 (Eff 3-23-2000); 148 v S 22 (Eff 5-17-2000); 148 v H 349. Eff 9-22-2000; 149 v S 123, § 1, eff. 1-1-04; 150 v H 163, § 1, eff. 9-23-04; 152 v H 130, § 1, eff. 4-7-09; 153 v H 338, § 1, eff. 9-17-10; 2011 HB 86, § 1, eff. Sept. 30, 2011.**

The effective date is set by section 4 of S.B. 123.

See provisions of § 5 of S.B. 123 (149 v —) following RC § 2929.01.

The provisions of § 8 of S.B. 123 read as follows:

SECTION 8. Section 2929.15 of the Revised Code is presented in this act as a composite of the section as amended by Am. Sub. H.B. 349, Am. Sub. S.B. 22, and Am. Sub. S.B. 107 of the 123rd General Assembly. The General Assembly, applying the principle stated in division (B) of section 1.52 of the Revised Code that amendments are to be harmonized if reasonably capable of simultaneous operation, finds that the composites are the resulting versions of the sections in effect prior to the effective date of the sections as presented in this act.

**Not analogous to former RC § 2929.15, amended and renumbered RC § 2929.22.3 in 146 v S 2, eff 7-1-96, repealed 9-6-2002.**

## § 2929.16 Residential sanctions.

(A) Except as provided in this division, the court imposing a sentence for a felony upon an offender who is not required to serve a mandatory prison term may impose any community residential sanction or combination of community residential sanctions under this section. The court imposing a sentence for a fourth degree felony OVI offense under division (G)(1) or (2) of section 2929.13 of the Revised Code or for a third degree felony OVI offense under division (G)(2) of that section may impose upon the offender, in addition to the mandatory term of local incarceration or mandatory prison term imposed under the applicable division, a community residential sanction or combination of community residential sanctions under this section, and the offender shall serve or satisfy the sanction or combination of sanctions after the offender has served the mandatory term of local incarceration or mandatory prison term required for the offense. Community residential sanctions include, but are not limited to, the following:

(1) A term of up to six months at a community-based correctional facility that serves the county;

(2) Except as otherwise provided in division (A)(3) of this section and subject to division (D) of this section, a term of up to six months in a jail;

(3) If the offender is convicted of a fourth degree felony OVI offense and is sentenced under division (G)(1) of section 2929.13 of the Revised Code, subject to division (D) of this section, a term of up to one year in a jail less the mandatory term of local incarceration of sixty or one hundred twenty consecutive days of imprisonment imposed pursuant to that division;

(4) A term in a halfway house;

(5) A term in an alternative residential facility.

(B) The court that assigns any offender convicted of a felony to a residential sanction under this section may authorize the offender to be released so that the offender may seek or maintain employment, receive education or training, or receive treatment. A release pursuant to this division shall be only for the duration of time that is needed to fulfill the purpose of the release and for travel that reasonably is necessary to fulfill the purposes of the release.

(C) If the court assigns an offender to a county jail that is not a minimum security misdemeanant jail in a county that has established a county jail industry program pursuant to section 5147.30 of the Revised Code, the court shall specify, as part of the sentence, whether the sheriff of that county may consider the offender for participation in the county jail industry program. During the offender's term in the county jail, the court shall retain jurisdiction to modify its specification upon a reassessment of the offender's qualifications for participation in the program.

(D) If a court sentences an offender to a term in jail under division (A)(2) or (3) of this section and if the sentence is imposed for a felony of the fourth or fifth degree that is not an offense of violence, the court may specify that it prefers that the offender serve the term in a minimum security jail established under section 341.34 or 753.21 of the Revised Code. If the court includes a specification of that type in the sentence and if the administrator of the appropriate minimum security jail or the designee of that administrator classifies the offender in accordance with section 341.34 or 753.21 of the Revised Code as a minimal security risk, the offender shall serve the term in the minimum security jail established under section 341.34 or 753.21 of the Revised Code. Absent a specification of that type and a finding of that type, the offender shall serve the term in a jail other than a minimum security jail established under section 341.34 or 753.21 of the Revised Code.

(E) If a person who has been convicted of or pleaded guilty to a felony is sentenced to a community residential sanction as described in division (A) of this section, at the time of reception and at other times the person in charge of the operation of the community-based correctional facility, jail, halfway house, alternative residential facility, or other place at which the offender will serve the residential sanction determines to be appropriate, the person in charge of the operation of the community-based correctional facility, jail, halfway house, alternative residential facility, or other place may cause the convicted offender to be examined and tested for tuberculosis, HIV infection, hepatitis, including but not limited to hepatitis A, B, and C, and other contagious diseases. The person in charge of the operation of the community-based correctional facility, jail, halfway house, alternative residential facility, or other place at which the offender will serve the residential sanction may cause a convicted offender in the community-based correctional facility, jail, halfway house, alternative residential facility, or other place who refuses to be tested or treated for tuberculosis, HIV infection, hepatitis, including but not limited to hepatitis A, B, and C, or another contagious disease to be tested and treated involuntarily.

**HISTORY: 146 v S 2 (Eff 7-1-96); 146 v S 269 (Eff 7-1-96); 146 v H 480 (Eff 10-16-96); 146 v S 166 (Eff 10-17-96); 146 v H 72 (Eff 3-18-97); 147 v S 111 (Eff 3-17-98); 148 v S 22. Eff 5-17-2000; 149 v S 123, § 1, eff. 1-1-04; 150 v H 163, § 1, eff. 9-23-04.**

The effective date is set by section 4 of S.B. 123.

See provisions of § 5 of S.B. 123 (149 v —) following RC § 2929.01.

**Analogous in part to former RC § 2929.16 (143 v H 51), repealed 146 v S 2, § 2, eff 7-1-96.**

## § 2929.17 Nonresidential sanctions.

Except as provided in this section, the court imposing a sentence for a felony upon an offender who is not required to serve a mandatory prison term may impose any nonresidential sanction or combination of nonresidential sanctions authorized under this section. If the court imposes one or more nonresidential sanctions authorized under this section, the court shall impose as a condition of the sanction that, during the period of the nonresidential sanction, the offender shall abide by the law and shall not leave the state without the permission of the court or the offender's probation officer.

The court imposing a sentence for a fourth degree felony OVI offense under division (G)(1) or (2) of section 2929.13 of the Revised Code or for a third degree felony OVI offense under division (G)(2) of that section may impose upon the offender, in addition to the mandatory term of local incarceration or mandatory prison term imposed under the applicable division, a nonresidential sanction or combination of nonresidential sanctions under this section, and the offender shall serve or satisfy the sanction or combination of sanctions after the offender has served the mandatory term of local incarceration or mandatory prison term required for the offense. The court shall not impose a term in a drug treatment program as described in division (D) of this section until after considering an assessment by a properly credentialed treatment professional, if available. Nonresidential sanctions include, but are not limited to, the following:

(A) A term of day reporting;

(B) A term of house arrest with electronic monitoring or continuous alcohol monitoring or both electronic monitoring and continuous alcohol monitoring, a term of electronic monitoring or continuous alcohol monitoring without house arrest, or a term of house arrest without electronic monitoring or continuous alcohol monitoring;

(C) A term of community service of up to five hundred hours pursuant to division (B) of section 2951.02 of the Revised Code or, if the court determines that the offender is financially incapable of fulfilling a financial sanction described in section 2929.18 of the Revised Code, a term of community service as an alternative to a financial sanction;

(D) A term in a drug treatment program with a level of security for the offender as determined by the court;

(E) A term of intensive probation supervision;

(F) A term of basic probation supervision;

(G) A term of monitored time;

(H) A term of drug and alcohol use monitoring, including random drug testing;

(I) A curfew term;

(J) A requirement that the offender obtain employment;

(K) A requirement that the offender obtain education or training;

(L) Provided the court obtains the prior approval of the victim, a requirement that the offender participate in victim-offender mediation;

(M) A license violation report;

(N) If the offense is a violation of section 2919.25 or a violation of section 2903.11, 2903.12, or 2903.13 of the Revised Code involving a person who was a family or household member at the time of the violation, if the offender committed the offense in the vicinity of one or more children who are not victims of the offense, and if the offender or the victim of the offense is a parent, guardian, custodian, or person in loco parentis of one or more of those children, a requirement that the offender obtain counseling. This division does not limit the court in requiring the offender to obtain counseling for any offense or in any circumstance not specified in this division.

**HISTORY: 146 v S 2 (Eff 7-1-96); 146 v S 269 (Eff 7-1-96); 146 v S 166 (Eff 10-17-96); 148 v S 9 (Eff 3-8-2000); 148 v S 107 (Eff 3-23-2000); 148 v S 22 (Eff 5-17-2000); 148 v H 349. Eff 9-22-2000; 149 v H 490, § 1, eff. 1-1-04; 149 v S 123, § 1, eff. 1-1-04; 150 v H 163, § 1, eff. 9-23-04; 152 v H 130, § 1, eff. 4-7-09.**

The effective date is set by section 4 of HB 490.

See provisions of § 5 of S.B. 123 (149 v —) following RC § 2929.01.

**Not analogous to former RC § 2929.17, amended and renumbered RC § 2929.24 in 146 v S 2, eff 7-1-96.**

The provisions of § 3 of HB 349 (148 v —) read as follows:

SECTION 3. Sections 2929.01 and 2929.17 of the Revised Code are presented in this act as composites of the sections as amended by both Am. S.B. 9 and Am. Sub. S.B. 107 of the 123rd General Assembly, with the new language of neither of the acts shown in capital letters. Section 2951.02 of the Revised Code is presented in this act as a composite of the section as amended by H.B. 471, Am. S.B. 9, and Am. Sub. S.B. 107 of the 123rd General Assembly, with the new language of none of the acts shown in capital letters. This is in recognition of the principle stated in division (B) of section 1.52 of the Revised Code that such amendments are to be harmonized where not substantively irreconcilable and constitutes a legislative finding that such is the resulting version in effect prior to the effective date of this act.

## § 2929.18 Financial sanctions; restitution; reimbursements.

(A) Except as otherwise provided in this division and in addition to imposing court costs pursuant to section 2947.23 of the Revised Code, the court imposing a sentence upon an offender for a felony may sentence the offender to any financial sanction or combination of financial sanctions authorized under this section or, in the circumstances specified in section 2929.32 of the Revised Code, may impose upon the offender a fine in accordance with that section. Financial sanctions that may be imposed pursuant to this section include, but are not limited to, the following:

(1) Restitution by the offender to the victim of the offender's crime or any survivor of the victim, in an amount based on the victim's economic loss. If the court imposes restitution, the court shall order that the restitution be made to the victim in open court, to the adult probation department that serves the county on behalf of the victim, to the clerk of courts, or to another agency designated by the court. If the court imposes restitution, at sentencing, the court shall determine the amount of restitution to be made by the offender. If the court imposes restitution, the court may base the amount of restitution it orders on an amount recommended by the victim, the offender, a presentence investigation report, estimates or receipts indicating the cost of repairing or replacing property, and other information, provided that the amount the court orders as restitution shall not exceed the amount of the economic loss suffered by the victim as a direct and proximate result of the commission of the offense. If the court decides to impose restitution, the court shall hold a hearing on restitution if the offender, victim, or survivor disputes the amount. All restitution payments shall be credited against any recovery of economic loss in a civil action brought by the victim or any survivor of the victim against the offender.

If the court imposes restitution, the court may order that the offender pay a surcharge of not more than five per cent of the amount of the restitution otherwise ordered to the entity responsible for collecting and processing restitution payments.

The victim or survivor may request that the prosecutor in the case file a motion, or the offender may file a motion, for modification of the payment terms of any restitution ordered. If the court grants the motion, it may modify the payment terms as it determines appropriate.

(2) Except as provided in division (B)(1), (3), or (4) of this section, a fine payable by the offender to the state, to a political subdivision, or as described in division (B)(2) of this section to one or more law enforcement agencies, with the amount of the fine based on a standard percentage of the offender's daily income over a period of time determined by the court and based upon the seriousness of the offense. A fine ordered under this division shall not exceed the maximum conventional fine amount authorized for the level of the offense under division (A)(3) of this section.

(3) Except as provided in division (B)(1), (3), or (4) of this section, a fine payable by the offender to the state, to a political subdivision when appropriate for a felony, or as described in division (B)(2) of this section to one or more law enforcement agencies, in the following amount:

(a) For a felony of the first degree, not more than twenty thousand dollars;

(b) For a felony of the second degree, not more than fifteen thousand dollars;

(c) For a felony of the third degree, not more than ten thousand dollars;

(d) For a felony of the fourth degree, not more than five thousand dollars;

(e) For a felony of the fifth degree, not more than two thousand five hundred dollars.

(4) A state fine or costs as defined in section 2949.111 of the Revised Code.

(5)(a) Reimbursement by the offender of any or all of the costs of sanctions incurred by the government, including the following:

(i) All or part of the costs of implementing any community control sanction, including a supervision fee under section 2951.021 of the Revised Code;

(ii) All or part of the costs of confinement under a sanction imposed pursuant to section 2929.14, 2929.142, or 2929.16 of the Revised Code, provided that the amount of reimbursement ordered under this division shall not exceed the total amount of reimbursement the offender is able to pay as determined at a hearing and shall not exceed the actual cost of the confinement;

(iii) All or part of the cost of purchasing and using an immobilizing or disabling device, including a certified ignition interlock device, or a remote alcohol monitoring device that a court orders an offender to use under section 4510.13 of the Revised Code.

(b) If the offender is sentenced to a sanction of confinement pursuant to section 2929.14 or 2929.16 of the Revised Code that is to be served in a facility operated by a board of county commissioners, a legislative authority of a municipal corporation, or another local governmental entity, if, pursuant to section 307.93, 341.14, 341.19, 341.23, 753.02, 753.04, 753.16, 2301.56, or 2947.19 of the Revised Code and section 2929.37 of the Revised Code, the board, legislative authority, or other local governmental entity requires prisoners to reimburse the county, municipal corporation, or other entity for its expenses incurred by reason of the prisoner's confinement, and if the court does not impose a financial sanction under division (A)(5)(a)(ii) of this section, confinement costs may be assessed pursuant to section 2929.37 of the Revised Code. In addition, the offender may be required to pay the fees specified in section 2929.38 of the Revised Code in accordance with that section.

(c) Reimbursement by the offender for costs pursuant to section 2929.71 of the Revised Code.

(B)(1) For a first, second, or third degree felony violation of any provision of Chapter 2925., 3719., or 4729. of the Revised Code, the sentencing court shall impose upon the offender a mandatory fine of at least one-half of, but not more than, the maximum statutory fine amount authorized for the level of the offense pursuant to division (A)(3) of this section. If an offender alleges in an affidavit filed with the court prior to sentencing that the offender is indigent and unable to pay the mandatory fine and if the court determines the offender is an indigent person and is unable to pay the mandatory fine described in this division, the court shall not impose the mandatory fine upon the offender.

(2) Any mandatory fine imposed upon an offender under division (B)(1) of this section and any fine imposed upon an offender under division (A)(2) or (3) of this section for any fourth or fifth degree felony violation of any provision of Chapter 2925., 3719., or 4729. of the Revised Code shall be paid to law enforcement agencies pursuant to division (F) of section 2925.03 of the Revised Code.

(3) For a fourth degree felony OVI offense and for a third degree felony OVI offense, the sentencing court shall impose upon the offender a mandatory fine in the amount specified in division (G)(1)(d) or (e) of section 4511.19 of the Revised Code, whichever is applicable. The mandatory

fine so imposed shall be disbursed as provided in the division pursuant to which it is imposed.

(4) Notwithstanding any fine otherwise authorized or required to be imposed under division (A)(2) or (3) or (B)(1) of this section or section 2929.31 of the Revised Code for a violation of section 2925.03 of the Revised Code, in addition to any penalty or sanction imposed for that offense under section 2925.03 or sections 2929.11 to 2929.18 of the Revised Code and in addition to the forfeiture of property in connection with the offense as prescribed in Chapter 2981. of the Revised Code, the court that sentences an offender for a violation of section 2925.03 of the Revised Code may impose upon the offender a fine in addition to any fine imposed under division (A)(2) or (3) of this section and in addition to any mandatory fine imposed under division (B)(1) of this section. The fine imposed under division (B)(4) of this section shall be used as provided in division (H) of section 2925.03 of the Revised Code. A fine imposed under division (B)(4) of this section shall not exceed whichever of the following is applicable:

(a) The total value of any personal or real property in which the offender has an interest and that was used in the course of, intended for use in the course of, derived from, or realized through conduct in violation of section 2925.03 of the Revised Code, including any property that constitutes proceeds derived from that offense;

(b) If the offender has no interest in any property of the type described in division (B)(4)(a) of this section or if it is not possible to ascertain whether the offender has an interest in any property of that type in which the offender may have an interest, the amount of the mandatory fine for the offense imposed under division (B)(1) of this section or, if no mandatory fine is imposed under division (B)(1) of this section, the amount of the fine authorized for the level of the offense imposed under division (A)(3) of this section.

(5) Prior to imposing a fine under division (B)(4) of this section, the court shall determine whether the offender has an interest in any property of the type described in division (B)(4)(a) of this section. Except as provided in division (B)(6) or (7) of this section, a fine that is authorized and imposed under division (B)(4) of this section does not limit or affect the imposition of the penalties and sanctions for a violation of section 2925.03 of the Revised Code prescribed under those sections or sections 2929.11 to 2929.18 of the Revised Code and does not limit or affect a forfeiture of property in connection with the offense as prescribed in Chapter 2981. of the Revised Code.

(6) If the sum total of a mandatory fine amount imposed for a first, second, or third degree felony violation of section 2925.03 of the Revised Code under division (B)(1) of this section plus the amount of any fine imposed under division (B)(4) of this section does not exceed the maximum statutory fine amount authorized for the level of the offense under division (A)(3) of this section or section 2929.31 of the Revised Code, the court may impose a fine for the offense in addition to the mandatory fine and the fine imposed under division (B)(4) of this section. The sum total of the amounts of the mandatory fine, the fine imposed under division (B)(4) of this section, and the additional fine imposed under division (B)(6) of this section shall not exceed the maximum statutory fine amount authorized for the level of the offense under division (A)(3) of this section or section 2929.31 of the Revised Code. The clerk of the court shall pay any fine that is imposed under division (B)(6) of this section to the county, township, municipal corporation, park district as created pursuant to section 511.18 or 1545.04 of the Revised Code, or state law enforcement agencies in this state that primarily were responsible for or involved in making the arrest of, and in prosecuting, the offender pursuant to division (F) of section 2925.03 of the Revised Code.

(7) If the sum total of the amount of a mandatory fine imposed for a first, second, or third degree felony violation of section 2925.03 of the Revised Code plus the amount of any fine imposed under division (B)(4) of this section exceeds the maximum statutory fine amount authorized for the level of the offense under division (A)(3) of this section or section 2929.31 of the Revised Code, the court shall not impose a fine under division (B)(6) of this section.

(8)(a) If an offender who is convicted of or pleads guilty to a violation of section 2905.01, 2905.02, 2907.21, 2907.22, or 2923.32, division (A)(1) or (2) of section 2907.323, or division (B)(1), (2), (3), (4), or (5) of section 2919.22 of the Revised Code also is convicted of or pleads guilty to a specification of the type described in section 2941.1422 of the Revised Code that charges that the offender knowingly committed the offense in furtherance of human trafficking, the sentencing court shall sentence the offender to a financial sanction of restitution by the offender to the victim or any survivor of the victim, with the restitution including the costs of housing, counseling, and medical and legal assistance incurred by the victim as a direct result of the offense and the greater of the following:

(i) The gross income or value to the offender of the victim's labor or services;

(ii) The value of the victim's labor as guaranteed under the minimum wage and overtime provisions of the "Federal Fair Labor Standards Act of 1938," 52 Stat. 1060, 20 U.S.C. 207, and state labor laws.

(b) If a court imposing sentence upon an offender for a felony is required to impose upon the offender a financial sanction of restitution under division (B)(8)(a) of this section, in addition to that financial sanction of restitution, the court may sentence the offender to any other financial sanction or combination of financial sanctions authorized under this section, including a restitution sanction under division (A)(1) of this section.

(C)(1) The offender shall pay reimbursements imposed upon the offender pursuant to division (A)(5)(a) of this section to pay the costs incurred by the department of rehabilitation and correction in operating a prison or other facility used to confine offenders pursuant to sanctions imposed under section 2929.14, 2929.142, or 2929.16 of the Revised Code to the treasurer of state. The treasurer of state shall deposit the reimbursements in the confinement cost reimbursement fund that is hereby created in the state treasury. The department of rehabilitation and correction shall use the amounts deposited in the fund to fund the operation of facilities used to confine offenders pursuant to sections 2929.14, 2929.142, and 2929.16 of the Revised Code.

(2) Except as provided in section 2951.021 of the Revised Code, the offender shall pay reimbursements imposed upon the offender pursuant to division (A)(5)(a) of this section to pay the costs incurred by a county pursuant to any sanction imposed under this section or section 2929.16 or 2929.17 of the Revised Code or in operating a facility used to confine offenders pursuant to a sanction imposed under section 2929.16 of the Revised

Code to the county treasurer. The county treasurer shall deposit the reimbursements in the sanction cost reimbursement fund that each board of county commissioners shall create in its county treasury. The county shall use the amounts deposited in the fund to pay the costs incurred by the county pursuant to any sanction imposed under this section or section 2929.16 or 2929.17 of the Revised Code or in operating a facility used to confine offenders pursuant to a sanction imposed under section 2929.16 of the Revised Code.

(3) Except as provided in section 2951.021 of the Revised Code, the offender shall pay reimbursements imposed upon the offender pursuant to division (A)(5)(a) of this section to pay the costs incurred by a municipal corporation pursuant to any sanction imposed under this section or section 2929.16 or 2929.17 of the Revised Code or in operating a facility used to confine offenders pursuant to a sanction imposed under section 2929.16 of the Revised Code to the treasurer of the municipal corporation. The treasurer shall deposit the reimbursements in a special fund that shall be established in the treasury of each municipal corporation. The municipal corporation shall use the amounts deposited in the fund to pay the costs incurred by the municipal corporation pursuant to any sanction imposed under this section or section 2929.16 or 2929.17 of the Revised Code or in operating a facility used to confine offenders pursuant to a sanction imposed under section 2929.16 of the Revised Code.

(4) Except as provided in section 2951.021 of the Revised Code, the offender shall pay reimbursements imposed pursuant to division (A)(5)(a) of this section for the costs incurred by a private provider pursuant to a sanction imposed under this section or section 2929.16 or 2929.17 of the Revised Code to the provider.

(D) Except as otherwise provided in this division, a financial sanction imposed pursuant to division (A) or (B) of this section is a judgment in favor of the state or a political subdivision in which the court that imposed the financial sanction is located, and the offender subject to the financial sanction is the judgment debtor. A financial sanction of reimbursement imposed pursuant to division (A)(5)(a)(ii) of this section upon an offender who is incarcerated in a state facility or a municipal jail is a judgment in favor of the state or the municipal corporation, and the offender subject to the financial sanction is the judgment debtor. A financial sanction of reimbursement imposed upon an offender pursuant to this section for costs incurred by a private provider of sanctions is a judgment in favor of the private provider, and the offender subject to the financial sanction is the judgment debtor. A financial sanction of restitution imposed pursuant to division (A)(1) or (B)(8) of this section is an order in favor of the victim of the offender's criminal act that can be collected through a certificate of judgment as described in division (D)(1) of this section, through execution as described in division (D)(2) of this section, or through an order as described in division (D)(3) of this section, and the offender shall be considered for purposes of the collection as the judgment debtor. Imposition of a financial sanction and execution on the judgment does not preclude any other power of the court to impose or enforce sanctions on the offender. Once the financial sanction is imposed as a judgment or order under this division, the victim, private provider, state, or political subdivision may do any of the following:

(1) Obtain from the clerk of the court in which the judgment was entered a certificate of judgment that shall be in the same manner and form as a certificate of judgment issued in a civil action;

(2) Obtain execution of the judgment or order through any available procedure, including:

(a) An execution against the property of the judgment debtor under Chapter 2329. of the Revised Code;

(b) An execution against the person of the judgment debtor under Chapter 2331. of the Revised Code;

(c) A proceeding in aid of execution under Chapter 2333. of the Revised Code, including:

(i) A proceeding for the examination of the judgment debtor under sections 2333.09 to 2333.12 and sections 2333.15 to 2333.27 of the Revised Code;

(ii) A proceeding for attachment of the person of the judgment debtor under section 2333.28 of the Revised Code;

(iii) A creditor's suit under section 2333.01 of the Revised Code.

(d) The attachment of the property of the judgment debtor under Chapter 2715. of the Revised Code;

(e) The garnishment of the property of the judgment debtor under Chapter 2716. of the Revised Code.

(3) Obtain an order for the assignment of wages of the judgment debtor under section 1321.33 of the Revised Code.

(E) A court that imposes a financial sanction upon an offender may hold a hearing if necessary to determine whether the offender is able to pay the sanction or is likely in the future to be able to pay it.

(F) Each court imposing a financial sanction upon an offender under this section or under section 2929.32 of the Revised Code may designate the clerk of the court or another person to collect the financial sanction. The clerk or other person authorized by law or the court to collect the financial sanction may enter into contracts with one or more public agencies or private vendors for the collection of, amounts due under the financial sanction imposed pursuant to this section or section 2929.32 of the Revised Code. Before entering into a contract for the collection of amounts due from an offender pursuant to any financial sanction imposed pursuant to this section or section 2929.32 of the Revised Code, a court shall comply with sections 307.86 to 307.92 of the Revised Code.

(G) If a court that imposes a financial sanction under division (A) or (B) of this section finds that an offender satisfactorily has completed all other sanctions imposed upon the offender and that all restitution that has been ordered has been paid as ordered, the court may suspend any financial sanctions imposed pursuant to this section or section 2929.32 of the Revised Code that have not been paid.

(H) No financial sanction imposed under this section or section 2929.32 of the Revised Code shall preclude a victim from bringing a civil action against the offender.

**HISTORY: 146 v S 2 (Eff 7-1-96); 146 v S 269 (Eff 7-1-96); 146 v H 480 (Eff 10-16-96); 146 v S 166 (Eff 10-17-96); 147 v H 122 (Eff 7-29-98); 148 v S 107 (Eff 3-23-2000); 148 v S 22 (Eff 5-17-2000); 148 v H 528 (Eff 2-13-2001); 149 v H 170. Eff 9-6-2002; 149 v H 490, § 1, eff. 1-1-04; 149 v S 123, § 1, eff. 1-1-04; 150 v H 52, § 1, eff. 6-1-04; 151 v H 461, § 1, eff. 4-4-07; 151 v H 241, § 1, eff. 7-1-07; 152 v S 17, § 1, eff. 9-30-08; 152 v H 280, § 1, eff. 4-7-09; 2011 HB 5, § 1, eff. Sept. 23, 2011.**

The provisions of § 3 of 152 v S 17 read as follows:

SECTION 3. Section 2929.18 of the Revised Code is presented in this act as a composite of the section as amended by both Sub. H.B. 241 and Am. Sub. H.B. 461 of the 126th General Assembly. * * * The General Assembly, applying the principle stated in division (B) of section 1.52 of the Revised Code that amendments are to be harmonized if reasonably capable of simultaneous operation, finds that the composite is the resulting version of the section in effect prior to the effective date of the section as presented in this act.

See provisions of § 4 of 151 v H 241 following RC § 2901.01.

The effective date is set by section 4 of HB 490.

The provisions of § 5 of HB 490 (149 v —) read as follows:

SECTION 5. Section 2929.18 of the Revised Code is presented in this act as a composite of the section as amended by both Am. Sub. S.B. 123 and Sub. H.B. 170 of the 124th General Assembly. The General Assembly, applying the principle stated in division (B) of section 1.52 of the Revised Code that amendments are to be harmonized if reasonably capable of simultaneous operation, finds that the specified composite is the resulting version of the specified sections in effect prior to the effective date of the section as presented in this act.

See provisions of § 5 of S.B. 123 (149 v —) following RC § 2929.01.

The provisions of § 4 of HB 170 (149 v —) read as follows:

SECTION 4. Section 2929.18 of the Revised Code is presented in this act as a composite of the section as amended by Am. H.B. 528, Am. Sub. S.B. 22, and Am. Sub. S.B. 107 of the 123rd General Assembly. The General Assembly, applying the principle stated in division (B) of section 1.52 of the Revised Code that amendments are to be harmonized if reasonably capable of simultaneous operation, finds that the composite is the resulting version of the section in effect prior to the effective date of the section as presented in this act.

## § 2929.181 Repealed, 146 v S 269, § 2 and by 148 v S 107, § 2 [146 v S 2]. Eff 7-1-96.

This section concerned determination of offender's ability to pay; withholding or deduction orders. See now RC § 2929.18(E).

The provisions of § 3 of SB 107 (148 v —) read as follows:

SECTION 3. The General Assembly hereby declares that the repeal of section 2929.181 of the Revised Code in Section 2 of this act is intended to be a ratification of the repeal of section 2929.181 of the Revised Code by Am. Sub. S.B. 269 of the 121st General Assembly, which was effective on July 1, 1996, and that section 2929.181 of the Revised Code, as enacted by Am. Sub. S.B. 2 of the 121st General Assembly, is not currently in effect.

Section 2929.181 of the Revised Code was enacted by Am. Sub. S.B. 2 of the 121st General Assembly, which was effective on July 1, 1996, was amended by Sub. H.B. 480 of the 121st General Assembly, which was enacted on May 23, 1996, and effective on October 16, 1996, and was repealed by Am. Sub. S.B. 269 of the 121st General Assembly, which was enacted on May 30, 1996, and effective on July 1, 1996. The different enactment dates and effective dates of Sub. H.B. 480 and Am. Sub. S.B. 269 of the 121st General Assembly have caused some confusion as to whether section 2929.181 of the Revised Code continued in effect after the effective date of Sub. H.B. 480 of the 121st General Assembly, despite the repeal of the section by Am. Sub. S.B. 269.

It was the intent of the 121st General Assembly to repeal section 2929.181 of the Revised Code effective on July 1, 1996, by Am. Sub. S.B. 269 of the 121st General Assembly. This repeal is supported by section 1.52 of the Revised Code, which provides that, if statutes enacted by the same session of the General Assembly are irreconcilable, the statute latest in date of enactment prevails. Am. Sub. S.B. 269 of the 121st General Assembly was enacted on May 30, 1996, seven days after the enactment of Sub. H.B. 480 of the 121st General Assembly. Therefore, the repeal of section 2929.181 of the Revised Code contained in Am. Sub. S.B. 269 of the 122nd General Assembly controlled over the amendment of that section by Sub. H.B. 480 of the 121st General Assembly, and the section was repealed effective July 1, 1996.

## § 2929.19 Sentencing hearing.

(A) The court shall hold a sentencing hearing before imposing a sentence under this chapter upon an offender who was convicted of or pleaded guilty to a felony and before resentencing an offender who was convicted of or pleaded guilty to a felony and whose case was remanded pursuant to section 2953.07 or 2953.08 of the Revised Code. At the hearing, the offender, the prosecuting attorney, the victim or the victim's representative in accordance with section 2930.14 of the Revised Code, and, with the approval of the court, any other person may present information relevant to the imposition of sentence in the case. The court shall inform the offender of the verdict of the jury or finding of the court and ask the offender whether the offender has anything to say as to why sentence should not be imposed upon the offender.

(B)(1) At the sentencing hearing, the court, before imposing sentence, shall consider the record, any information presented at the hearing by any person pursuant to division (A) of this section, and, if one was prepared, the presentence investigation report made pursuant to section 2951.03 of the Revised Code or Criminal Rule 32.2, and any victim impact statement made pursuant to section 2947.051 of the Revised Code.

(2) Subject to division (B)(3) of this section, if the sentencing court determines at the sentencing hearing that a prison term is necessary or required, the court shall do all of the following:

(a) Impose a stated prison term and, if the court imposes a mandatory prison term, notify the offender that the prison term is a mandatory prison term;

(b) In addition to any other information, include in the sentencing entry the name and section reference to the offense or offenses, the sentence or sentences imposed and whether the sentence or sentences contain mandatory prison terms, if sentences are imposed for multiple counts whether the sentences are to be served concurrently or consecutively, and the name and section reference of any specification or specifications for which sentence is imposed and the sentence or sentences imposed for the specification or specifications;

(c) Notify the offender that the offender will be supervised under section 2967.28 of the Revised Code after the offender leaves prison if the offender is being sentenced for a felony of the first degree or second degree, for a felony sex offense, or for a felony of the third degree that is not a felony sex offense and in the commission of which the offender caused or threatened to cause physical harm to a person. If a court imposes a sentence including a prison term of a type described in division (B)(2)(c) of this section on or after July 11, 2006, the failure of a court to notify the offender pursuant to division (B)(2)(c) of this section that the offender will be supervised under section 2967.28 of the Revised Code after the offender leaves prison or to include in the judgment of conviction entered on the journal a statement to that effect does not negate, limit, or otherwise affect the mandatory period of supervision that is required for the offender under division (B) of section 2967.28 of the Revised Code. Section 2929.191 of the Revised Code applies if, prior to July 11, 2006, a court imposed a sentence including a prison term of a type described in division (B)(2)(c) of this section and failed to notify the offender pursuant to division (B)(2)(c) of this section regarding post-release control or to include in the judgment of conviction entered on the journal or in the sentence a statement regarding post-release control.

(d) Notify the offender that the offender may be supervised under section 2967.28 of the Revised Code after the offender leaves prison if the offender is being sentenced for a felony of the third, fourth, or fifth degree that is not subject to division (B)(2)(c) of this section.

Section 2929.191 of the Revised Code applies if, prior to July 11, 2006, a court imposed a sentence including a prison term of a type described in division (B)(2)(d) of this section and failed to notify the offender pursuant to division (B)(2)(d) of this section regarding post-release control or to include in the judgment of conviction entered on the journal or in the sentence a statement regarding post-release control.

(e) Notify the offender that, if a period of supervision is imposed following the offender's release from prison, as described in division (B)(2)(c) or (d) of this section, and if the offender violates that supervision or a condition of post-release control imposed under division (B) of section 2967.131 of the Revised Code, the parole board may impose a prison term, as part of the sentence, of up to one-half of the stated prison term originally imposed upon the offender. If a court imposes a sentence including a prison term on or after July 11, 2006, the failure of a court to notify the offender pursuant to division (B)(2)(e) of this section that the parole board may impose a prison term as described in division (B)(2)(e) of this section for a violation of that supervision or a condition of post-release control imposed under division (B) of section 2967.131 of the Revised Code or to include in the judgment of conviction entered on the journal a statement to that effect does not negate, limit, or otherwise affect the authority of the parole board to so impose a prison term for a violation of that nature if, pursuant to division (D)(1) of section 2967.28 of the Revised Code, the parole board notifies the offender prior to the offender's release of the board's authority to so impose a prison term. Section 2929.191 of the Revised Code applies if, prior to July 11, 2006, a court imposed a sentence including a prison term and failed to notify the offender pursuant to division (B)(2)(e) of this section regarding the possibility of the parole board imposing a prison term for a violation of supervision or a condition of post-release control.

(f) Require that the offender not ingest or be injected with a drug of abuse and submit to random drug testing as provided in section 341.26, 753.33, or 5120.63 of the Revised Code, whichever is applicable to the offender who is serving a prison term, and require that the results of the drug test administered under any of those sections indicate that the offender did not ingest or was not injected with a drug of abuse.

(g) Include in the offender's sentence a statement notifying the offender of the information described in division (F)(3) of section 2929.14 of the Revised Code regarding earned credits under section 2967.193 of the Revised Code.

(3)(a) The court shall include in the offender's sentence a statement that the offender is a tier III sex offender/child-victim offender, and the court shall comply with the requirements of section 2950.03 of the Revised Code if any of the following apply:

(i) The offender is being sentenced for a violent sex offense or designated homicide, assault, or kidnapping offense that the offender committed on or after January 1, 1997, and the offender is adjudicated a sexually violent predator in relation to that offense.

(ii) The offender is being sentenced for a sexually oriented offense that the offender committed on or after January 1, 1997, and the offender is a tier III sex offender/child-victim offender relative to that offense.

(iii) The offender is being sentenced on or after July 31, 2003, for a child-victim oriented offense, and the offender is a tier III sex offender/child-victim offender relative to that offense.

(iv) The offender is being sentenced under section 2971.03 of the Revised Code for a violation of division (A)(1)(b) of section 2907.02 of the Revised Code committed on or after January 2, 2007.

(v) The offender is sentenced to a term of life without parole under division (B) of section 2907.02 of the Revised Code.

(vi) The offender is being sentenced for attempted rape committed on or after January 2, 2007, and a specification of the type described in section 2941.1418, 2941.1419, or 2941.1420 of the Revised Code.

(vii) The offender is being sentenced under division (B)(3)(a), (b), (c), or (d) of section 2971.03 of the Revised Code for an offense described in those divisions committed on or after January 1, 2008.

(b) Additionally, if any criterion set forth in divisions (B)(3)(a)(i) to (vii) of this section is satisfied, in the circumstances described in division (E) of section 2929.14 of the Revised Code, the court shall impose sentence on the offender as described in that division.

(4) If the sentencing court determines at the sentencing hearing that a community control sanction should be imposed and the court is not prohibited from imposing a community control sanction, the court shall impose a community control sanction. The court shall notify the offender that, if the conditions of the sanction are violated, if the offender commits a violation of any law, or if the offender leaves this state without the permission of the court or the offender's probation officer, the court may impose a longer time under the same sanction, may impose a more restrictive sanction, or may impose a prison term on the offender and shall indicate the specific prison term that may be imposed as a sanction for the violation, as selected by the court from the range of prison terms for the offense pursuant to section 2929.14 of the Revised Code.

(5) Before imposing a financial sanction under section 2929.18 of the Revised Code or a fine under section 2929.32 of the Revised Code, the court shall consider the offender's present and future ability to pay the amount of the sanction or fine.

(6) If the sentencing court sentences the offender to a sanction of confinement pursuant to section 2929.14 or 2929.16 of the Revised Code that is to be served in a local detention facility, as defined in section 2929.36 of the Revised Code, and if the local detention facility is covered by a policy adopted pursuant to section 307.93, 341.14, 341.19, 341.21, 341.23, 753.02, 753.04, 753.16, 2301.56, or 2947.19 of the Revised Code and section 2929.37 of the Revised Code, both of the following apply:

(a) The court shall specify both of the following as part of the sentence:

(i) If the offender is presented with an itemized bill pursuant to section 2929.37 of the Revised Code for payment of the costs of confinement, the offender is required to pay the bill in accordance with that section.

(ii) If the offender does not dispute the bill described in division (B)(6)(a)(i) of this section and does not pay the bill by the times specified in section 2929.37 of the Revised Code, the clerk of the court may issue a certificate of judgment against the offender as described in that section.

(b) The sentence automatically includes any certificate of judgment issued as described in division (B)(6)(a)(ii) of this section.

(7) The failure of the court to notify the offender that a prison term is a mandatory prison term pursuant to division (B)(2)(a) of this section or to include in the sentencing entry any information required by division (B)(2)(b) of this section does not affect the validity of the imposed sentence or sentences. If the sentencing court notifies the offender at the sentencing hearing that a prison term is mandatory but the sentencing entry does not specify that the prison term is mandatory, the court may complete a corrected journal entry and send copies of the corrected entry to the offender and the department of rehabilitation and correction, or, at the request of the state, the court shall complete a corrected journal entry and send copies of the corrected entry to the offender and department of rehabilitation and correction.

(C)(1) If the offender is being sentenced for a fourth degree felony OVI offense under division (G)(1) of section 2929.13 of the Revised Code, the court shall impose the mandatory term of local incarceration in accordance with that division, shall impose a mandatory fine in accordance with division (B)(3) of section 2929.18 of the Revised Code, and, in addition, may impose additional sanctions as specified in sections 2929.15, 2929.16, 2929.17, and 2929.18 of the Revised Code. The court shall not impose a prison term on the offender except that the court may impose a prison term upon the offender as provided in division (A)(1) of section 2929.13 of the Revised Code.

(2) If the offender is being sentenced for a third or fourth degree felony OVI offense under division (G)(2) of section 2929.13 of the Revised Code, the court shall impose the mandatory prison term in accordance with that division, shall impose a mandatory fine in accordance with division (B)(3) of section 2929.18 of the Revised Code, and, in addition, may impose an additional prison term as specified in section 2929.14 of the Revised Code. In addition to the mandatory prison term or mandatory prison term and additional prison term the court imposes, the court also may impose a community control sanction on the offender, but the offender shall serve all of the prison terms so imposed prior to serving the community control sanction.

(D) The sentencing court, pursuant to division (I)(1) of section 2929.14 of the Revised Code, may recommend placement of the offender in a program of shock incarceration under section 5120.031 of the Revised Code or an intensive program prison under section 5120.032 of the Revised Code, disapprove placement of the offender in a program or prison of that nature, or make no recommendation. If the court recommends or disapproves placement, it shall make a finding that gives its reasons for its recommendation or disapproval.

**HISTORY: 146 v S 2 (Eff 7-1-96); 146 v S 269 (Eff 7-1-96); 146 v S 166 (Eff 10-17-96); 146 v H 180 (Eff 1-1-97); 148 v S 107 (Eff 3-23-2000); 148 v S 22 (Eff 5-17-2000); 148 v H 349 (Eff 9-22-2000); 149 v H 485 (Eff 6-13-2002); 149 v H 327 (Eff 7-8-2002); 149 v H 170. Eff 9-6-2002; 149 v H 490, § 1, eff. 1-1-04; 149 v S 123, § 1, eff. 1-1-04; 150 v S 5, § 1, Eff 7-31-03; 150 v S 5, § 3, eff. 1-1-04; 150 v H 163, § 1, eff. 9-23-04; 150 v H 473, § 1, eff. 4-29-05; 151 v H 137, § 1, eff. 7-11-06; 151 v S 260, § 1, eff. 1-2-07; 151 v H 461, § 1, eff. 4-4-07; 152 v S 10, § 1, eff. 1-1-08; 152 v H 130, § 1, eff. 4-7-09; 2011 HB 86, § 1, eff. Sept. 30, 2011.**

The effective date is set by § 3 of 152 v S 10.

The provisions of § 6 of 152 v S 10 read as follows:

SECTION 6. * * * Section 2929.19 of the Revised Code is presented in this act as a composite of the section as amended by both Am. Sub. H.B. 461 and Am. Sub. S.B. 260 of the 126th General Assembly. The General Assembly, applying the principle stated in division (B) of section 1.52 of the Revised Code that amendments are to be harmonized if reasonably capable of simultaneous operation, finds that the composites are the resulting versions of the sections in effect prior to the effective date of the sections as presented in this act.

See provisions of § 5 of 151 v H 137 following RC § 2929.191.

The effective date is set by § 7 of 151 v H 137.

The effective date is set by section 4 of H.B. 490.

The provisions of § 5 of HB 490 (149 v —) read as follows:

SECTION 5. Section 2929.19 of the Revised Code is presented in this act as a composite of the section as amended by Sub. H.B. 170, Sub. H.B. 485, and Am. Sub. S.B. 123, all of the 124th General Assembly. The General Assembly, applying the principle stated in division (B) of section 1.52 of the Revised Code that amendments are to be harmonized if reasonably capable of simultaneous operation, finds that the specified composite is the resulting version of the specified sections in effect prior to the effective date of the section as presented in this act.

The provisions of § 7 of S.B. 5 (150 v —) read as follows:

SECTION 7. (A) Section 2929.19 of the Revised Code, effective until January 1, 2004, is presented in Section 1 of this act as a composite of the section as amended by both Sub. H.B. 170 and Sub. H.B. 485 of the 124th General Assembly. The General Assembly, applying the principle stated in division (B) of section 1.52 of the Revised Code that amendments are to be harmonized if reasonably capable of simultaneous operation, finds that the composites are the resulting versions of the sections in effect prior to the effective date of the sections as presented in Section 1 of this act.

See provisions of § 5 of S.B. 123 (149 v —) following RC § 2929.01.

The provisions of § 4 of HB 485 (149 v —) read as follows:

SECTION 4. Section 2929.19 of the Revised Code is amended by this act and also by Am. Sub. H.B. 327 of the 124th General Assembly, effective July 8, 2002. The amendments of Am. Sub. H.B. 327 are included in this act to confirm the intention to retain them but are not intended to be effective until July 8, 2002.

**Comment, Legislative Service Commission**

Sections 2929.15 and 2929.19 of the Revised Code are amended by this act [Am. Sub. H.B. 349] and also by Am. Sub. S.B. 22 and Am. Sub. S.B. 107 of the 123rd General Assembly. Comparison of these amendments in pursuance of section 1.52 of the Revised Code discloses that they are not irreconcilable so that they are required by that section to be harmonized to give effect to each amendment.

## § 2929.191 Correction to judgment of conviction concerning post-release control.

(A)(1) If, prior to July 11, 2006, a court imposed a sentence including a prison term of a type described in division (B)(2)(c) of section 2929.19 of the Revised Code and failed to notify the offender pursuant to that division that the offender will be supervised under section 2967.28 of the Revised Code after the offender leaves prison or to include a statement to that effect in the judgment of conviction entered on the journal or in the sentence pursuant to division (D)(1) of section 2929.14 of the Revised Code, at any time before the offender is released from imprisonment under that term and at a hearing conducted in accordance with division (C) of this section, the court may prepare and issue a correction to the judgment of conviction that includes in the judgment of conviction the statement that the offender will be supervised under section 2967.28 of the Revised Code after the offender leaves prison.

If, prior to July 11, 2006, a court imposed a sentence including a prison term of a type described in division (B)(2)(d) of section 2929.19 of the Revised Code and failed to notify the offender pursuant to that division that the offender may be supervised under section 2967.28 of the Revised Code after the offender leaves prison or to include a statement to that effect in the judgment of conviction entered on the journal or in the sentence pursuant to division (D)(2) of section 2929.14 of the Revised Code, at any time before the offender is released from imprisonment under that term and at a hearing conducted in accordance with division (C) of this section, the court may prepare and issue a correction to the judgment of conviction that includes in the judgment of conviction the statement that the offender may be supervised under section 2967.28 of the Revised Code after the offender leaves prison.

(2) If a court prepares and issues a correction to a judgment of conviction as described in division (A)(1) of this section before the offender is released from imprisonment under the prison term the court imposed prior to July 11, 2006, the court shall place upon the journal of the court an entry nunc pro tunc to record the correction to the judgment of conviction and shall provide a copy of the entry to the offender or, if the offender is not physically present at the hearing, shall send a copy of the entry to the department of rehabilitation and correction for delivery to the offender. If the court sends a copy of the entry to the department, the department promptly shall deliver a copy of the entry to the offender. The court's placement upon the journal of the entry nunc pro tunc before the offender is released from imprisonment under the term shall be considered, and shall have the same effect, as if the court at the time of original sentencing had included the statement in the sentence and the judgment of conviction entered on the journal and had notified the offender that the offender will be so supervised regarding a sentence including a prison term of a type described in division (B)(2)(c) of section 2929.19 of the Revised Code or that the offender may be so supervised regarding a sentence including a prison term of a type described in division (B)(2)(d) of that section.

(B)(1) If, prior to July 11, 2006, a court imposed a sentence including a prison term and failed to notify the offender pursuant to division (B)(2)(e) of section 2929.19 of the Revised Code regarding the possibility of the parole board imposing a prison term for a violation of supervision or a condition of post-release control or to include in the judgment of conviction entered on the journal a statement to that effect, at any time before the offender is released from imprisonment under that term and at a hearing conducted in accordance with division (C) of this section, the court may prepare and issue a correction to the judgment of conviction that includes in the judgment of conviction the statement that if a period of supervision is imposed following the offender's release from prison, as described in division (B)(2)(c) or (d) of section 2929.19 of the Revised Code, and if the offender violates that supervision or a condition of post-release control imposed under division (B) of section 2967.131 of the Revised Code the parole board may impose as part of the sentence a prison term of up to one-half of the stated prison term originally imposed upon the offender.

(2) If the court prepares and issues a correction to a judgment of conviction as described in division (B)(1) of this section before the offender is released from imprisonment under the term, the court shall place upon the journal of the court an entry nunc pro tunc to record the correction to the judgment of conviction and shall provide a copy of the entry to the offender or, if the offender is not physically present at the hearing, shall send a copy of the entry to the department of rehabilitation and correction for delivery to the offender. If the court sends a copy of the entry to the department, the department promptly shall deliver a copy of the entry to the offender. The court's placement upon the journal of the entry nunc pro tunc before the offender is released from imprisonment under the term shall be considered, and shall have the same effect, as if the court at the time of original sentencing had included the statement in the judgment of conviction entered on the journal and had notified the offender pursuant to division (B)(2)(e) of section 2929.19 of the Revised Code regarding the possibility of the parole board imposing a prison term for a violation of supervision or a condition of post-release control.

(C) On and after July 11, 2006, a court that wishes to prepare and issue a correction to a judgment of conviction of a type described in division (A)(1) or (B)(1) of this section shall not issue the correction until after the court has conducted a hearing in accordance with this division. Before a court holds a hearing pursuant to this division, the court shall provide notice of the date, time, place, and purpose of the hearing to the offender who is the subject of the hearing, the prosecuting attorney of the county, and the department of rehabilitation and correction. The offender has the right to be physically present at the hearing, except that, upon the court's own motion or the motion of the offender or the prosecuting attorney, the court may permit the offender to appear at the hearing by video conferencing equipment if available and compatible. An appearance by video conferencing equipment pursuant to this division has the same force and effect as if the offender were physically present at the hearing. At the hearing, the offender and the prosecuting attorney may make a statement as to whether the court should issue a correction to the judgment of conviction.

**HISTORY: 151 v H 137, § 1, eff. 7-11-06; 2011 HB 86, § 1, eff. Sept. 30, 2011.**

The provisions of § 5 of 151 v H 137 read as follows:

SECTION 5. (A) The General Assembly hereby declares that its purpose in amending sections 2929.14, 2929.19, and 2967.28 and enacting section 2929.191 of the Revised Code in Sections 1 and 2 of this act and in amending section 2929.14 of the Revised Code in Sections 3 and 4 of this act is to reaffirm that, under the amended sections as they existed prior to the effective date of this act: (1) by operation of law and without need for any prior notification or warning, every convicted offender sentenced to a prison term for a felony of the first or second degree, for a felony sex offense, or for a felony of the third degree that is not a felony sex offense and in the commission of which the offender caused or threatened to cause physical harm to a person always is subject to a period of post-release control after the offender's release from imprisonment pursuant to and for the period of time described in division (B) of section 2967.28 of the Revised Code; (2) by operation of law, every convicted offender sentenced to a prison term for a felony of the third, fourth, or fifth degree that is not subject to the provision described in clause (1) of this sentence is subject to a period of post-release control after the offender's release from imprisonment pursuant to division (C) of section 2967.28 of the Revived Code if the parole board determines in accordance with specified criteria that post-release control is necessary; and (3) by operation of law and without need for any prior notification or warning, every convicted offender sentenced to a prison term and subjected to supervision under a period of post-release control after the offender's release from imprisonment always is subject to having the Parole Board impose in accordance with section 2967.28 of the Revised Code a prison term of up to one-half of the stated prison term originally imposed upon the offender if the offender violates that supervision or a condition of post-release control imposed under division (B) of section 2967.131 of the Revised Code.

(B) The General Assembly hereby declares that it believes that the amendments made to sections 2929.14, 2929.19, and 2967.28 and the enactment of section 2929.191 of the Revised Code in Sections 1 and 2 of this act and the amendment made to section 2929.14 of the Revised Code in Sections 3 and 4 of this act are not substantive in nature and merely clarify that the amended sections operate as described in division (A) of this Section, that the convicted offenders described in clause (1) under division (A) of this Section always are subject by operation of law and without need for any prior notification or warning to a period of post-release control after their release from imprisonment as described in that division, that the convicted offenders described in clause (2) under division (A) of this Section are subject by operation of law to post-release control after their release from imprisonment if the Parole Board makes certain determinations, that the convicted offenders described in clause (3) under division (A) of this Section always are subject by operation of law to having the Parole Board impose a prison term if they violate their supervision or a condition of post-release control as described in that division, and that the amendments made to sections 2929.14, 2929.19, and 2967.28 and the enactment of section 2929.191 of the Revised Code in Sections 1 and 2 of this act and the amendment made to section 2929.14 of the Revised Code in Sections 3 and 4 of this act thus are remedial in nature. The General Assembly declares that it intends that the clarifying, remedial amendments made to sections 2929.14, 2929.19, and 2967.28 and the enactment of section 2929.191 of the Revised Code in Sections 1 and 2 of this act and the amendment made to section 2929.14 of the Revised Code in Sections 3 and 4 of this act apply to all convicted offenders described in division (A) of this Section, regardless of whether they were sentenced prior to, or are sentenced on or after, the effective date of this act.

The effective date is set by § 7 of 151 v H 137.

## § 2929.192 Forfeiture of public retirement system benefits.

(A) If an offender is being sentenced for any felony offense listed in division (D) of this section that was committed on or after May 13, 2008, if the offender committed the offense while serving in a position of honor, trust, or profit, and if the offender, at the time of the commission of the offense, was a member of any public retirement system or a participant in an alternative retirement plan, in addition to any other sanction it imposes under section 2929.14, 2929.15, 2929.16, 2929.17, or 2929.18 of the Revised Code but subject to division (B) of this section, the court shall order the forfeiture to the public retirement system or alternative retirement plan in which the offender was a member or participant of the offender's right to a retirement allowance, pension, disability benefit, or other right or benefit, other than payment of the offender's accumulated contributions, earned by reason of the offender's being a member of the public retirement system or alternative retirement plan. A forfeiture ordered under this division is part of, and shall be included in, the sentence of the offender. The court shall send a copy of the journal entry imposing sentence on the offender to the appropriate public retirement system or alternative retirement plan in which the offender was a member or participant.

(B) In any case in which a sentencing court is required to order forfeiture of an offender's right to a retirement allowance, pension, disability benefit, or other right or benefit under division (A) of this section, the offender may request a hearing regarding the forfeiture by delivering to the court prior to sentencing a written request for a hearing. If a request for a hearing is made by the offender prior to sentencing, the court shall conduct the hearing before sentencing. The court shall notify the offender, the prosecutor who handled the case in which the offender was convicted of or pleaded guilty to the offense for which the forfeiture order was imposed, and the appropriate public retirement system, or alternative retirement plan provider, whichever is applicable, or, if more than one is specified in the motion, the applicable combination of these, of the hearing. A hearing scheduled under this division shall be limited to a consideration of whether there is good cause based on evidence presented by the offender for the forfeiture order not to be issued. If the court determines based on evidence presented by the offender that there is good cause for the forfeiture order not to be issued, the court shall not issue the forfeiture order. If the offender does not request a hearing prior to sentencing or if the court conducts a hearing but does not determine based on evidence presented by the offender that there is good cause for the forfeiture order not to be issued, the court shall order the forfeiture described in division (A) of this section in accordance with that division and shall send a copy of the journal entry imposing sentence on the offender to the appropriate public retirement system or alternative retirement plan in which the offender was a member or participant.

(C) Upon receipt of a copy of the journal entry imposing sentence on an offender under division (A) or (B) of this section that contains an order of forfeiture of a type described in that division, the public retirement system or alternative retirement plan in which the offender was a member or participant shall comply with the forfeiture order on application for a refund of the accumulated contributions of the member or participant.

(D) Division (A) of this section applies regarding an offender who is convicted of or pleads guilty to any of the following offenses committed on or after May 13, 2008, that is a felony and who committed the offense while serving in a position of honor, trust, or profit:

(1) A violation of section 2921.02 or 2923.32 of the Revised Code or a violation of section 2921.41 of the Revised Code that is a felony of the third degree;

(2) A violation of an existing or former municipal ordinance or law of this or any other state or the United States that is substantially equivalent to any violation listed in division (D)(1) of this section;

(3) A conspiracy to commit, attempt to commit, or complicity in committing any violation listed in division (D)(1) or described in division (D)(2) of this section.

(E) For purposes of divisions (A) and (D) of this section, a violation of section 2923.32 of the Revised Code or any other violation or offense that includes as an element a course of conduct or the occurrence of multiple acts is "committed on or after May 13, 2008, " if the course of conduct continues, one or more of the multiple acts occurs, or the subject person's accountability for the course of conduct or for one or more of the multiple acts continues, on or after May 13, 2008.

(F) As used in this section:

(1)(a) For the period beginning May 13, 2008, and ending the day before the effective date of this amendment, "position of honor, trust, or profit" means any of the following:

(i) An elective office of the state or any political subdivision of the state;

(ii) A position on any board or commission of the state that is appointed by the governor or the attorney general;

(iii) A position as a public official or employee, as defined in section 102.01 of the Revised Code, who is required to file a disclosure statement under section 102.02 of the Revised Code;

(iv) A position as a prosecutor, as defined in section 2935.01 of the Revised Code;

(v) A position as a peace officer, as defined in section 2935.01 of the Revised Code, or as the superintendent or a trooper of the state highway patrol.

(b) On and after the effective date of this amendment, "position of honor, trust, or profit" has the same meaning as in division (F)(1)(a) of this section, except that it also includes a position in which, in the course of public employment, an employee has control over the expenditure of public funds of one hundred thousand dollars or more annually.

(2) "Public retirement system" and "alternative retirement plan" have the same meanings as in section 2907.15 of the Revised Code.

(3) "Accumulated contributions" means whichever of the following is applicable:

(a) Regarding an offender who is a member of the public employees retirement system, except as otherwise provided in division (F)(3)(a) of this section, "accumulated contributions" has the same meaning as in section 145.01 of the Revised Code. For a member participating in a PERS defined contribution plan, "accumulated contributions" means the contributions made under section 145.85 of the Revised Code and any earnings on those contributions. For a member participating in a PERS defined contribution plan that includes definitely determinable benefits, "accumulated contributions" means the contributions made under section 145.85 of the Revised Code, any earnings on those contributions, and additionally any amounts paid by the member to purchase service credits.

(b) Regarding an offender who is or was a member of the Ohio police and fire pension fund, "accumulated contributions" means the amount payable to a member under division (G) of section 742.37 of the Revised Code.

(c) Regarding an offender who is a member of the state teachers retirement system, except as otherwise provided in division (F)(3)(c) of this section, "accumulated contributions" has the same meaning as in section 3307.50 of the Revised Code. For a member participating in an STRS defined contribution plan, "accumulated contributions" means the contributions made under section 3307.26 of the Revised Code to participate in a plan established under section 3307.81 of the Revised Code and any earnings on those contributions. For a member participating in a STRS defined contribution plan that includes definitely determinable benefits, "accumulated contributions" means the contributions made under section 3307.26 of the Revised Code to participate in a plan established under section 3307.81 of the Revised Code, any earnings on those contributions, and additionally any amounts paid by the member to purchase service credits.

(d) Regarding an offender who is or was a member of the school employees retirement system, "accumulated contributions" has the same meaning as in section 3309.01 of the Revised Code and also includes employee contributions made under section 3309.85 of the Revised Code and any earnings on those contributions.

(e) Regarding an offender who is or was a member of the state highway patrol retirement system, "accumulated contributions" has the same meaning as in section 5505.01 of the Revised Code.

(f) Regarding an offender who is or was participating in an alternative retirement plan, "accumulated contributions" means the amounts contributed to an alternative retirement plan participant's account by the plan participant pursuant to section 3305.06 of the Revised Code and any earnings on those contributions.

**HISTORY: 152 v S 3, § 1, eff. 5-15-08; 2011 HB 123, § 101, eff. July 29, 2011.**

## § 2929.193 Offender hearing requirements; termination; recovery of benefits paid.

(A) As used in this section:

(1) "Position of honor, trust, or profit" has the same meaning as in division (F)(1)(b) of section 2929.192 of the Revised Code.

(2) "Public retirement system," "alternative retirement plan," and "prosecutor" have the same meanings as in section 2907.15 of the Revised Code.

(B) This section applies to an offender to whom all of the following apply:

(1) The offender is being sentenced for an offense listed in division (D) of section 2929.192 of the Revised Code that is a felony and was committed on or after the effective date of this section.

(2) The offense was committed while the offender was serving in a position of honor, trust, or profit.

(3) At the time of the offense, the offender was one of the following:

(a) A member of a public retirement system;

(b) A contributor to a public retirement system receiving or eligible to receive a benefit under section 145.384, 742.26, 3307.352, or 3309.344 of the Revised Code;

(c) A participant in an alternative retirement plan.

(4) Prior to the final disposition of the case, the offender was granted a disability benefit by a public retirement system or an alternative retirement plan provider.

(C)(1) Prior to sentencing an offender subject to this section, the court shall hold a hearing regarding the condition for which the offender was granted a disability benefit. Not later than ten days prior to the scheduled date of the hearing, the court shall give written notice of the hearing to the offender, the prosecutor who handled the case, and the appropriate public retirement system, alternative retirement plan provider, or, if more than one is providing a disability benefit, the applicable combination of these. The hearing shall be limited to a consideration of whether the offender's disabling condition arose out of the commission of the offense the offender was convicted of or pleaded guilty to.

The system or provider shall submit to the court the offender's medical reports and recommendations, and the offender's disability application. If the court determines based on those documents that the disabling condition arose out of the commission of the offense the offender was convicted of or pleaded guilty to, the court shall order the system or provider to terminate the disability benefit.

(2) Any disability benefit paid the offender prior to its termination may be recovered in accordance with section 145.563, 742.64, 3305.22, 3307.47, 3309.70, or 5505.34 of the Revised Code.

(D) For purposes of this section, a violation of section 2923.32 of the Revised Code or any other violation or offense that includes as an element a course of conduct or the occurrence of multiple acts is "committed on or after the effective date of this section" if the course of conduct continues, one or more of the multiple acts occurs, or the offender's accountability for the course of conduct or for one or more of the multiple acts continues on or after the effective date of this section.

**HISTORY: 2011 HB 123, § 101, eff. July 29, 2011.**

## § 2929.20 Judicial release.

(A) As used in this section:

(1)(a) Except as provided in division (A)(1)(b) of this section, "eligible offender" means any person who, on or after April 7, 2009, is serving a stated prison term that includes one or more nonmandatory prison terms.

(b) "Eligible offender" does not include any person who, on or after April 7, 2009, is serving a stated prison term for any of the following criminal offenses that was a felony and was committed while the person held a public office in this state:

(i) A violation of section 2921.02, 2921.03, 2921.05, 2921.31, 2921.32, 2921.41, 2921.42, or 2923.32 of the Revised Code;

(ii) A violation of section 2913.42, 2921.04, 2921.11, or 2921.12 of the Revised Code, when the conduct constituting the violation was related to the duties of the offender's public office or to the offender's actions as a public official holding that public office;

(iii) A violation of an existing or former municipal ordinance or law of this or any other state or the United States that is substantially equivalent to any violation listed in division (A)(1)(b)(i) of this section;

(iv) A violation of an existing or former municipal ordinance or law of this or any other state or the United States that is substantially equivalent to any violation listed in division (A)(1)(b)(ii) of this section, when the conduct constituting the violation was related to the duties of the offender's public office or to the offender's actions as a public official holding that public office;

(v) A conspiracy to commit, attempt to commit, or complicity in committing any offense listed in division (A)(1)(b)(i) or described in division (A)(1)(b)(iii) of this section;

(vi) A conspiracy to commit, attempt to commit, or complicity in committing any offense listed in division (A)(1)(b)(ii) or described in division (A)(1)(b)(iv) of this section, if the conduct constituting the offense that was the subject of the conspiracy, that would have constituted the offense attempted, or constituting the offense in which the offender was complicit was or would have been related to the duties of the offender's public office or to the offender's actions as a public official holding that public office.

(2) "Nonmandatory prison term" means a prison term that is not a mandatory prison term.

(3) "Public office" means any elected federal, state, or local government office in this state.

(B) On the motion of an eligible offender or upon its own motion, the sentencing court may reduce the eligible offender's aggregated nonmandatory prison term or terms through a judicial release under this section.

(C) An eligible offender may file a motion for judicial release with the sentencing court within the following applicable periods:

(1) If the aggregated nonmandatory prison term or terms is less than two years, the eligible offender may file the motion not earlier than thirty days after the offender is delivered to a state correctional institution or, if the prison term includes a mandatory prison term or terms, not earlier than thirty days after the expiration of all mandatory prison terms.

(2) If the aggregated nonmandatory prison term or terms is at least two years but less than five years, the eligible offender may file the motion not earlier than one hundred eighty days after the offender is delivered to a state correctional institution or, if the prison term includes a mandatory prison term or terms, not earlier than one hundred eighty days after the expiration of all mandatory prison terms.

(3) If the aggregated nonmandatory prison term or terms is five years, the eligible offender may file the motion not earlier than four years after the eligible offender is delivered to a state correctional institution or, if the prison term includes a mandatory prison term or terms, not earlier than four years after the expiration of all mandatory prison terms.

(4) If the aggregated nonmandatory prison term or terms is more than five years but not more than ten years, the eligible offender may file the motion not earlier than five years after the eligible offender is delivered to a state correctional institution or, if the prison term includes a mandatory prison term or terms, not earlier than five years after the expiration of all mandatory prison terms.

(5) If the aggregated nonmandatory prison term or terms is more than ten years, the eligible offender may file the motion not earlier than the later of the date on which the offender has served one-half of the offender's stated prison term or the date specified in division (C)(4) of this section.

(D) Upon receipt of a timely motion for judicial release filed by an eligible offender under division (C) of this section or upon the sentencing court's own motion made within the appropriate time specified in that division, the court may deny the motion without a hearing or schedule a hearing on the motion. The court shall not grant the motion without a hearing. If a court denies a motion without a hearing, the court later may consider judicial release for that eligible offender on a subsequent motion filed by that eligible offender unless the court denies the motion with prejudice. If a court denies a motion with prejudice, the court may later consider judicial release on its own motion. If a court denies a motion after a hearing, the court shall not consider a subsequent motion for that eligible offender. The court shall hold only one hearing for any eligible offender.

A hearing under this section shall be conducted in open court within sixty days after the motion is filed, provided that the court may delay the hearing for one hundred eighty additional days. If the court holds a hearing, the court shall enter a ruling on the motion within ten days after the hearing. If the court denies the motion without a hearing, the court shall enter its ruling on the motion within sixty days after the motion is filed.

(E) If a court schedules a hearing under division (D) of this section, the court shall notify the eligible offender and the head of the state correctional institution in which the eligible offender is confined prior to the hearing. The head of the state correctional institution immediately shall notify the appropriate person at the department of rehabilitation and correction of the hearing, and the department within twenty-four hours after receipt of the notice, shall post on the database it maintains pursuant to section 5120.66 of the Revised Code the offender's name and all of the information specified in division (A)(1)(c)(i) of that section. If the court schedules a hearing for judicial release, the court promptly shall give notice of the hearing to the prosecuting attorney of the county in which the eligible offender was indicted. Upon receipt of the notice from the court, the prosecuting attorney shall notify the victim of the offense or the victim's representative pursuant to section 2930.16 of the Revised Code.

(F) Upon an offender's successful completion of rehabilitative activities, the head of the state correctional institution may notify the sentencing court of the successful completion of the activities.

(G) Prior to the date of the hearing on a motion for judicial release under this section, the head of the state correctional institution in which the eligible offender is confined shall send to the court a report on the eligible offender's conduct in the institution and in any institution from which the eligible offender may have been transferred. The report shall cover the eligible offender's participation in school, vocational training, work, treatment, and other rehabilitative activities and any disciplinary action taken against the eligible offender. The report shall be made part of the record of the hearing.

(H) If the court grants a hearing on a motion for judicial release under this section, the eligible offender shall attend the hearing if ordered to do so by the court. Upon receipt of a copy of the journal entry containing the order, the head of the state correctional institution in which the eligible offender is incarcerated shall deliver the eligible offender to the sheriff of the county in which the hearing is to be held. The sheriff shall convey the eligible offender to and from the hearing.

(I) At the hearing on a motion for judicial release under this section, the court shall afford the eligible offender and the eligible offender's attorney an opportunity to present written and, if present, oral information relevant to the motion. The court shall afford a similar opportunity to the prosecuting attorney, the victim or the victim's representative, as defined in section 2930.01 of the Revised Code, and any other person the court determines is likely to present additional relevant information. The court shall consider any statement of a victim made pursuant to section 2930.14 or 2930.17 of the Revised Code, any victim impact statement prepared pursuant to section 2947.051 of the Revised Code, and any report made under division (G) of this section. The court may consider any written statement of any person submitted to the court pursuant to division (L) of this section. After ruling on the motion, the court shall notify the victim of the ruling in accordance with sections 2930.03 and 2930.16 of the Revised Code.

(J)(1) A court shall not grant a judicial release under this section to an eligible offender who is imprisoned for a felony of the first or second degree, or to an eligible offender who committed an offense under Chapter 2925. or 3719. of the Revised Code and for whom there was a presumption under section 2929.13 of the Revised Code in favor of a prison term, unless the court, with reference to factors under section 2929.12 of the Revised Code, finds both of the following:

(a) That a sanction other than a prison term would adequately punish the offender and protect the public from future criminal violations by the eligible offender because the applicable factors indicating a lesser likelihood of recidivism outweigh the applicable factors indicating a greater likelihood of recidivism;

(b) That a sanction other than a prison term would not demean the seriousness of the offense because factors indicating that the eligible offender's conduct in committing the offense was less serious than conduct normally constituting the offense outweigh factors indicating that the eligible offender's conduct was more serious than conduct normally constituting the offense.

(2) A court that grants a judicial release to an eligible offender under division (J)(1) of this section shall specify on the record both findings required in that division and also shall list all the factors described in that division that were presented at the hearing.

(K) If the court grants a motion for judicial release under this section, the court shall order the release of the eligible offender, shall place the eligible offender under an appropriate community control sanction, under appropriate conditions, and under the supervision of the department of probation serving the court and shall reserve the right to reimpose the sentence that it reduced if the offender violates the sanction. If the court reimposes the reduced sentence, it may do so either concurrently with, or consecutive to, any new sentence imposed upon the eligible offender as a result of the violation that is a new offense. The period of community control shall be no longer than five years. The court, in its discretion, may reduce the period of community control by the amount of time the eligible offender spent in jail or prison for the offense and in prison. If the court made any findings pursuant to division (J)(1) of this section, the court shall serve a copy of the findings upon counsel for the parties within fifteen days after the date on which the court grants the motion for judicial release.

If the court grants a motion for judicial release, the court shall notify the appropriate person at the department of rehabilitation and correction, and the department shall post notice of the release on the database it maintains pursuant to section 5120.66 of the Revised Code.

(L) In addition to and independent of the right of a victim to make a statement pursuant to section 2930.14, 2930.17, or 2946.051 of the Revised Code and any right of a person to present written information or make a statement pursuant to division (I) of this section, any person may submit to the court, at any time prior to the hearing on the offender's motion for judicial release, a written statement concerning the effects of the offender's crime or crimes, the circumstances surrounding the crime or crimes, the manner in which the crime or crimes were perpetrated, and the person's opinion as to whether the offender should be released.

(M) The changes to this section that are made on the effective date of this division apply to any judicial release decision made on or after the effective date of this division for any eligible offender.

**HISTORY: 146 v S 2 (Eff 7-1-96); 146 v S 269 (Eff 7-1-96); 147 v H 151 (Eff 9-16-97); 148 v S 107 (Eff 3-23-2000); 149 v H 327. Eff 7-8-2002; 151 v H 15, § 1, eff. 11-23-05; 152 v S 108, § 1, eff. 4-7-09; 152 v H 130, § 1, eff. 4-7-09; 2011 HB 86, § 1, eff. Sept. 30, 2011.**

The provisions of § 12 of HB 86 read as follows:

"SECTION 12. Section 2929.20 of the Revised Code is presented in this act as a composite of the section as amended by both Am. Sub. H.B. 130 and Sub. S.B. 108 of the 127th General Assembly. The General Assembly, applying the principle stated in division (B) of section 1.52 of the Revised Code that amendments are to be harmonized if reasonably capable of simultaneous operation, finds that the composites are the resulting versions of the sections in effect prior to the effective date of the sections as presented in this act."

**Comment, Legislative Service Commission**

Section 2929.20 of the Revised Code is amended by Sub. SB 108 and Am. Sub. HB 130 of the 127th General Assembly. Comparison of these amendments in pursuance of section 1.52 of the Revised Code discloses that they are not irreconcilable so that they are required by that section to be harmonized to give effect to each amendment.

[PENALTIES FOR MISDEMEANOR]

## § 2929.21 Overriding purposes of misdemeanor sentencing; discrimination prohibited.

(A) A court that sentences an offender for a misdemeanor or minor misdemeanor violation of any provision of the Revised Code, or of any municipal ordinance that is substantially similar to a misdemeanor or minor misdemeanor violation of a provision of the Revised Code, shall be guided by the overriding purposes of misdemeanor sentencing. The overriding purposes of misdemeanor sentencing are to protect the public from future crime by the offender and others and to punish the offender. To achieve those purposes, the sentencing court shall consider the impact of the offense upon the victim and the need for changing the offender's behavior, rehabilitating the offender, and making restitution to the victim of the offense, the public, or the victim and the public.

(B) A sentence imposed for a misdemeanor or minor misdemeanor violation of a Revised Code provision or for a violation of a municipal ordinance that is subject to division (A) of this section shall be reasonably calculated to achieve the two overriding purposes of misdemeanor sentencing set forth in division (A) of this section, commensurate with and not demeaning to the seriousness of the offender's conduct and its impact upon the victim, and consistent with sentences imposed for similar offenses committed by similar offenders.

(C) A court that imposes a sentence upon an offender for a misdemeanor or minor misdemeanor violation of a Revised Code provision or for a violation of a municipal ordinance that is subject to division (A) of this section shall not base the sentence upon the race, ethnic background, gender, or religion of the offender.

(D) Divisions (A) and (B) of this section shall not apply to any offense that is disposed of by a traffic violations bureau of any court pursuant to Traffic Rule 13 and shall not apply to any violation of any provision of the Revised Code that is a minor misdemeanor and that is disposed of without a court appearance. Divisions (A) to (C) of this section do not affect any penalties established by a municipal corporation for a violation of its ordinances.

**HISTORY: 149 v H 490 §§ 1, 2, eff. 1-1-04; 150 v H 52, § 1, eff. 6-1-04.**

The effective date is set by section 4 of H.B. 490.

This section formerly concerned penalties for misdemeanors. See now R.C. § 2929.24.

**Publisher's Note:**

Former R.C. § 2929.21 was repealed and new version enacted by H.B. 490, Acts 2002, effective January 1, 2004.

Former R.C. § 2929.21 was amended by S.B. 5 of Acts 2003, but because of the repeal of the prior version by H.B. 490 of Acts 2002, effective January 1, 2004, the amendment is not set out.

## § 2929.22 Considerations in imposing sentence for misdemeanor.

(A) Unless a mandatory jail term is required to be imposed by division (G) of section 1547.99, division (B) of section 4510.14, division (G) of section 4511.19 of the Revised Code, or any other provision of the Revised Code a court that imposes a sentence under this chapter upon an offender for a misdemeanor or minor misdemeanor has discretion to determine the most effective way to achieve the purposes and principles of sentencing set forth in section 2929.21 of the Revised Code.

Unless a specific sanction is required to be imposed or is precluded from being imposed by the section setting forth an offense or the penalty for an offense or by any provision of sections 2929.23 to 2929.28 of the Revised Code, a court that imposes a sentence upon an offender for a misdemeanor may impose on the offender any sanction or combination of sanctions under sections 2929.24 to 2929.28 of the Revised Code. The court shall not impose a sentence that imposes an unnecessary burden on local government resources.

(B)(1) In determining the appropriate sentence for a misdemeanor, the court shall consider all of the following factors:

(a) The nature and circumstances of the offense or offenses;

(b) Whether the circumstances regarding the offender and the offense or offenses indicate that the offender has a history of persistent criminal activity and that the offender's character and condition reveal a substantial risk that the offender will commit another offense;

(c) Whether the circumstances regarding the offender and the offense or offenses indicate that the offender's history, character, and condition reveal a substantial risk that the offender will be a danger to others and that the offender's conduct has been characterized by a pattern of repetitive, compulsive, or aggressive behavior with heedless indifference to the consequences;

(d) Whether the victim's youth, age, disability, or other factor made the victim particularly vulnerable to the offense or made the impact of the offense more serious;

(e) Whether the offender is likely to commit future crimes in general, in addition to the circumstances described in divisions (B)(1)(b) and (c) of this section.

(2) In determining the appropriate sentence for a misdemeanor, in addition to complying with division (B)(1) of this section, the court may consider any other factors that are relevant to achieving the purposes and principles of sentencing set forth in section 2929.21 of the Revised Code.

(C) Before imposing a jail term as a sentence for a misdemeanor, a court shall consider the appropriateness of imposing a community control sanction or a combination of community control sanctions under sections 2929.25, 2929.26, 2929.27, and 2929.28 of the Revised Code. A court may impose the longest jail term authorized under section 2929.24 of the Revised Code only upon offenders who commit the worst forms of the offense or upon offenders whose conduct and response to prior sanctions for prior offenses demonstrate that the imposition of the longest jail term is necessary to deter the offender from committing a future crime.

(D)(1) A sentencing court shall consider any relevant oral or written statement made by the victim, the defendant, the defense attorney, or the prosecuting authority regarding sentencing for a misdemeanor. This division does not create any rights to notice other than those rights authorized by Chapter 2930. of the Revised Code.

(2) At the time of sentencing for a misdemeanor or as soon as possible after sentencing, the court shall notify the victim of the offense of the victim's right to file an application for an award of reparations pursuant to sections 2743.51 to 2743.72 of the Revised Code.

**HISTORY: 149 v H 490, §§ 1, 2, eff. 1-1-04; 150 v S 57, § 1, eff. 1-1-04.**

The effective date is set by section 4 of H.B. 490.

**Analogous to former RC § 2929.22 (134 v H 511 (Eff 1-1-74); 137 v S 119 (Eff 8-30-78); 143 v S 258 (Eff 11-20-90); 145 v S 186 (Eff 10-12-94); 146 v S 2 (Eff 7-1-96); 148 v S 9. Eff 3-8-2000), repealed, 149 v H 490, § 2, eff 1-1-04.**

**Publisher's Note:**

This section was repealed and reenacted by H.B. 490, Acts 2002, effective January 1, 2004. Section 1 enacted the present version and Section 2 repealed the former version.

## § 2929.221 Amended and renumbered RC § 2929.34 in 149 v H 490. Eff 1-1-04.

## § 2929.223 Repealed, 149 v H 170, § 2 [RC § 2929.15, 140 v H 363; RC § 2929.22.3, 146 v S 2; 146 v S 269; 146 v H 480; 148 v S 107]. Eff 9-6-2002.

This section concerned reimbursement for costs of confinement for an offense other than a minor misdemeanor. See now RC §§ 2929.35-2929.38.

## § 2929.23 Sentencing for sexually oriented offense or child-victim misdemeanor offense committed on or after January 1, 1997.

(A) If an offender is being sentenced for a sexually oriented offense or child-victim oriented offense that is a misdemeanor committed on or after January 1, 1997, and the offender is a tier III sex offender/child-victim offender relative to the offense or the offense is any offense listed in division (D)(1) to (3) of section 2901.07 of the Revised Code, the judge shall include in the offender's sentence a statement that the offender is a tier III sex offender/child-victim offender, shall comply with the requirements of section 2950.03 of the Revised Code, and shall require the offender to submit to a DNA specimen collection procedure pursuant to section 2901.07 of the Revised Code.

(B) If an offender is being sentenced for a sexually oriented offense or a child-victim oriented offense that is a misdemeanor committed on or after January 1, 1997, the judge shall include in the sentence a summary of the offender's duties imposed under sections 2950.04, 2950.041 [2950.04.1], 2950.05, and 2950.06 of the Revised Code and the duration of the duties. The judge shall inform the offender, at the time of sentencing, of those duties and of their duration. If required under division (A)(2) of section 2950.03 of the Revised Code, the judge shall perform the duties specified in that section or, if required under division (A)(6) of section 2950.03 of the Revised Code, the judge shall perform the duties specified in that division.

**HISTORY: 149 v H 490, §§ 1, 2, (eff. 1-1-04); 149 v S 123, § 1, eff. 1-1-04; 150 v S 5, § 3, eff. 1-1-04; 152 v S 10, § 1, eff. 1-1-08.**

The effective date is set by § 3 of 152 v S 10.

This section formerly concerned penalties for misdemeanors.

The effective date is set by section 5 of 150 v S 5.

See provisions of § 5 of S.B. 123 (149 v —) following RC § 2929.01.

## § 2929.24 Definite jail terms for misdemeanor; eligibility for county jail industry program; reimbursement sanction; costs of confinement.

(A) Except as provided in section 2929.22 or 2929.23 of the Revised Code or division (E) or (F) of this section and unless another term is required or authorized pursuant to law, if the sentencing court imposing a sentence upon an offender for a misdemeanor elects or is required to impose a jail term on the offender pursuant to this chapter, the court shall impose a definite jail term that shall be one of the following:

(1) For a misdemeanor of the first degree, not more than one hundred eighty days;

(2) For a misdemeanor of the second degree, not more than ninety days;

(3) For a misdemeanor of the third degree, not more than sixty days;

(4) For a misdemeanor of the fourth degree, not more than thirty days.

(B)(1) A court that sentences an offender to a jail term under this section may permit the offender to serve the sentence in intermittent confinement or may authorize a limited release of the offender as provided in division (B) of section 2929.26 of the Revised Code. The court retains jurisdiction over every offender sentenced to jail to modify the jail sentence imposed at any time, but the court shall not reduce any mandatory jail term.

(2)(a) If a prosecutor, as defined in section 2935.01 of the Revised Code, has filed a notice with the court that the prosecutor wants to be notified about a particular case and if the court is considering modifying the jail sentence of the offender in that case, the court shall notify the prosecutor that the court is considering modifying the jail sentence of the offender in that case. The prosecutor may request a hearing regarding the court's consideration of modifying the jail sentence of the offender in that case, and, if the prosecutor requests a hearing, the court shall notify the eligible offender of the hearing.

(b) If the prosecutor requests a hearing regarding the court's consideration of modifying the jail sentence of the offender in that case, the court shall hold the hearing before considering whether or not to release the offender from the offender's jail sentence.

(C) If a court sentences an offender to a jail term under this section and the court assigns the offender to a county jail that has established a county jail industry program pursuant to section 5147.30 of the Revised Code, the court shall specify, as part of the sentence, whether the offender may be considered for participation in the program. During the offender's term in the county jail, the court retains jurisdiction to modify its specification regarding the offender's participation in the county jail industry program.

(D) If a person is sentenced to a jail term pursuant to this section, the court may impose as part of the sentence pursuant to section 2929.28 of the Revised Code a reimbursement sanction, and, if the local detention facility in which the term is to be served is covered by a policy adopted pursuant to section 307.93, 341.14, 341.19, 341.21, 341.23, 753.02, 753.04, 753.16, 2301.56, or 2947.19 of the Revised Code and section 2929.37 of the Revised Code, both of the following apply:

(1) The court shall specify both of the following as part of the sentence:

(a) If the person is presented with an itemized bill pursuant to section 2929.37 of the Revised Code for payment of the costs of confinement, the person is required to pay the bill in accordance with that section.

(b) If the person does not dispute the bill described in division (D)(1)(a) of this section and does not pay the bill by the times specified in section 2929.37 of the Revised Code, the clerk of the court may issue a certificate of judgment against the person as described in that section.

(2) The sentence automatically includes any certificate of judgment issued as described in division (D)(1)(b) of this section.

(E) If an offender who is convicted of or pleads guilty to a violation of division (B) of section 4511.19 of the Revised Code also is convicted of or also pleads guilty to a specification of the type described in section 2941.1416 of the Revised Code and if the court imposes a jail term on the offender for the underlying offense, the court shall impose upon the offender an additional definite jail term of not more than six months. The additional jail term shall not be reduced pursuant to any provision of the Revised Code. The offender shall serve the additional jail term consecutively to and prior to the jail term imposed for the underlying offense and consecutively to any other mandatory term imposed in relation to the offense.

(F)(1) If an offender is convicted of or pleads guilty to a misdemeanor violation of section 2907.23, 2907.24, 2907.241, or 2907.25 of the Revised Code and to a specification of the type described in section 2941.1421 of the Revised Code and if the court imposes a jail term on the offender for the misdemeanor violation, the court may impose upon the offender an additional definite jail term as follows:

(a) Subject to division (F)(1)(b) of this section, an additional definite jail term of not more than sixty days;

(b) If the offender previously has been convicted of or pleaded guilty to one or more misdemeanor or felony violations of section 2907.22, 2907.23, 2907.24, 2907.241, or 2907.25 of the Revised Code and also was convicted of or pleaded guilty to a specification of the type described in section 2941.1421 of the Revised Code regarding one or more of those violations, an additional definite jail term of not more than one hundred twenty days.

(2) In lieu of imposing an additional definite jail term under division (F)(1) of this section, the court may directly impose on the offender a sanction that requires the offender to wear a real-time processing, continual tracking electronic monitoring device during the period of time specified by the court. The period of time specified by the court shall equal the duration of an additional jail term that the court could have imposed upon the offender under division (F)(1) of this section. A sanction imposed under this division shall commence on the date specified by the court, provided that the sanction shall not commence until after the offender has served the jail term imposed for the misdemeanor violation of section 2907.23, 2907.24, 2907.241, or 2907.25 of the Revised Code and any residential sanction imposed for the violation under section 2929.26 of the Revised Code. A sanction imposed under this division shall be considered to be a community control sanction for purposes of section 2929.25 of the Revised Code, and all provisions of the Revised Code that pertain to community control sanctions shall apply to a sanction imposed under this division, except to the extent that they would by their nature be clearly inapplicable. The offender shall pay all costs associated with a sanction imposed under this division, including the cost of the use of the monitoring device.

(G) If an offender is convicted of or pleads guilty to a misdemeanor violation of section 2903.13 of the Revised Code and also is convicted of or pleads guilty to a specification of the type described in section 2941.1423 of the Revised Code that charges that the victim of the violation was a woman whom the offender knew was pregnant at the time of the violation, the court shall impose on the offender a mandatory jail term that is a definite term of at least thirty days.

(H) If a court sentences an offender to a jail term under this section, the sentencing court retains jurisdiction over the offender and the jail term. Upon motion of either party or upon the court's own motion, the court, in the court's sole discretion and as the circumstances warrant, may substitute one or more community control sanctions under section 2929.26 or 2929.27 of the Revised Code for any jail days that are not mandatory jail days.

**HISTORY: 149 v H 490, § 1, eff. 1-1-04; 150 v H 163, § 1, eff. 9-23-04; 152 v S 220, § 1, eff. 9-30-08; 152 v H 280, § 1, eff. 4-7-09; 153 v H 338, § 1, eff. 9-17-10; 2011 HB 5, § 1, eff. Sept. 23, 2011.**

**Publisher's Note:**

Former RC § 2929.24 was renumbered to RC § 2929.42 and new version enacted by H.B. 490 of Acts 2002, effective January 1, 2004.

## § 2929.25 Community control sanctions.

(A)(1) Except as provided in sections 2929.22 and 2929.23 of the Revised Code or when a jail term is required by law, in sentencing an offender for a misdemeanor, other than a minor misdemeanor, the sentencing court may do either of the following:

(a) Directly impose a sentence that consists of one or more community control sanctions authorized by section 2929.26, 2929.27, or 2929.28 of the Revised Code. The court may impose any other conditions of release under a community control sanction that the court considers appropriate. If the court imposes a jail term upon the offender, the court may impose any community control sanction or combination of community control sanctions in addition to the jail term.

(b) Impose a jail term under section 2929.24 of the Revised Code from the range of jail terms authorized under that section for the offense, suspend all or a portion of the jail term imposed, and place the offender under a community control sanction or combination of community control sanctions authorized under section 2929.26, 2929.27, or 2929.28 of the Revised Code.

(2) The duration of all community control sanctions imposed upon an offender and in effect for an offender at any time shall not exceed five years.

(3) At sentencing, if a court directly imposes a community control sanction or combination of community control sanctions pursuant to division (A)(1)(a) or (B) of this section, the court shall state the duration of the community control sanctions imposed and shall notify the offender that if any of the conditions of the community control sanctions are violated the court may do any of the following:

(a) Impose a longer time under the same community control sanction if the total time under all of the offender's community control sanctions does not exceed the five-year limit specified in division (A)(2) of this section;

(b) Impose a more restrictive community control sanction under section 2929.26, 2929.27, or 2929.28 of the Revised Code, but the court is not required to impose any particular sanction or sanctions;

(c) Impose a definite jail term from the range of jail terms authorized for the offense under section 2929.24 of the Revised Code.

(B) If a court sentences an offender to any community control sanction or combination of community control sanctions pursuant to division (A)(1)(a) of this section, the sentencing court retains jurisdiction over the offender and the period of community control for the duration of the period of community control. Upon the motion of either party or on the court's own motion, the court, in the court's sole discretion and as the circumstances warrant, may modify the community control sanctions or conditions of release previously imposed, substitute a community control sanction or condition of release for another community control sanction or condition of release previously imposed, or impose an additional community control sanction or condition of release.

(C)(1) If a court sentences an offender to any community control sanction or combination of community control sanctions authorized under section 2929.26, 2929.27, or 2929.28 of the Revised Code, the court shall place the offender under the general control and supervision of the court or of a department of probation in the jurisdiction that serves the court for purposes of reporting to the court a violation of any of the conditions of the sanctions imposed. If the offender resides in another jurisdiction and a department of probation has been established to serve the municipal court or county court in that jurisdiction, the sentencing court may request the municipal court or the county court to receive the offender into the general control and supervision of that department of probation for purposes of reporting to the sentencing court a violation of any of the conditions of the sanctions imposed. The sentencing court retains jurisdiction over any offender whom it sentences for the duration of the sanction or sanctions imposed.

(2) The sentencing court shall require as a condition of any community control sanction that the offender abide by the law and not leave the state without the permission of the court or the offender's probation officer. In the interests of doing justice, rehabilitating the offender, and ensuring the offender's good behavior, the court may impose additional requirements on the offender. The offender's compliance with the additional requirements also shall be a condition of the community control sanction imposed upon the offender.

(D)(1) If the court imposing sentence upon an offender sentences the offender to any community control sanction or combination of community control sanctions authorized under section 2929.26, 2929.27, or 2929.28 of the Revised Code, and if the offender violates any of the conditions of the sanctions, the public or private person or entity that supervises or administers the program or activity that comprises the sanction shall report the violation directly to the sentencing court or to the department of probation or probation officer with general control and supervision over the offender. If the public or private person or entity reports the violation to the department of probation or probation officer, the department or officer shall report the violation to the sentencing court.

(2) If an offender violates any condition of a community control sanction, the sentencing court may impose upon the violator one or more of the following penalties:

(a) A longer time under the same community control sanction if the total time under all of the community control sanctions imposed on the violator does not exceed the five-year limit specified in division (A)(2) of this section;

(b) A more restrictive community control sanction;

(c) A combination of community control sanctions, including a jail term.

(3) If the court imposes a jail term upon a violator pursuant to division (D)(2) of this section, the total time spent in jail for the misdemeanor offense and the violation of a condition of the community control sanction shall not exceed the maximum jail term available for the offense for which the sanction that was violated was imposed. The court may reduce the longer period of time that the violator is required to spend under the longer sanction or the more restrictive sanction imposed under division (D)(2) of this section by all or part of the time the violator successfully spent under the sanction that was initially imposed.

(E) Except as otherwise provided in this division, if an offender, for a significant period of time, fulfills the conditions of a community control sanction imposed pursuant to section 2929.26, 2929.27, or 2929.28 of the Revised Code in an exemplary manner, the court may reduce the period of time under the community control sanction or impose a less restrictive community control sanction. Fulfilling the conditions of a community control sanction does not relieve the offender of a duty to make restitution under section 2929.28 of the Revised Code.

**HISTORY: 149 v H 490 § 1, Eff. 1-1-04; 150 v S 57, § 1, eff. 1-1-04; 153 v H 338, § 1, eff. 9-17-10; 2011 HB 5, § 1, eff. Sept. 23, 2011.**

The effective date is set by section 4 of H.B. 490.

**Publisher's Note:**

Former R.C. § 2929.25 was renumbered to R.C. § 2929.32 and new version enacted by H.B. 490, Acts 2002, effective January 1, 2004.

## § 2929.26 Community residential sanctions; testing and treatment for contagious diseases; use of halfway house.

(A) Except when a mandatory jail term is required by law, the court imposing a sentence for a misdemeanor, other than a minor misdemeanor, may impose upon the offender any community residential sanction or combination of community residential sanctions under this section. Community residential sanctions include, but are not limited to, the following:

(1) A term of up to one hundred eighty days in a halfway house or a term in a halfway house not to exceed the longest jail term available for the offense, whichever is shorter, if the political subdivision that would have responsibility for paying the costs of confining the offender in a jail has entered into a contract with the halfway house for use of the facility for misdemeanor offenders;

(2) A term of up to one hundred eighty days in an alternative residential facility or a term in an alternative residential facility not to exceed the longest jail term available for the offense, whichever is shorter. The court may specify the level of security in the alternative residential facility that is needed for the offender.

(3) If the offender is an eligible offender, as defined in section 307.932 of the Revised Code, a term of up to sixty days in a community alternative sentencing center or district community alternative sentencing center established and operated in accordance with that section, in the circumstances specified in that section, with one of the conditions of the sanction being that the offender complete in the center the entire term imposed.

(B) A sentence to a community residential sanction under division (A)(3) of this section shall be in accordance with section 307.932 of the Revised Code. In all other cases, the court that sentences an offender to a community residential sanction under this section may do either or both of the following:

(1) Permit the offender to serve the offender's sentence in intermittent confinement, overnight, on weekends or at any other time or times that will allow the offender to continue at the offender's occupation or care for the offender's family;

(2) Authorize the offender to be released so that the offender may seek or maintain employment, receive education or training, receive treatment, perform community service, or otherwise fulfill an obligation imposed by law or by the court. A release pursuant to this division shall be only for the duration of time that is needed to fulfill the purpose of the release and for travel that reasonably is necessary to fulfill the purposes of the release.

(C) The court may order that a reasonable portion of the income earned by the offender upon a release pursuant to division (B) of this section be applied to any financial sanction imposed under section 2929.28 of the Revised Code.

(D) No court shall sentence any person to a prison term for a misdemeanor or minor misdemeanor or to a jail term for a minor misdemeanor.

(E) If a court sentences a person who has been convicted of or pleaded guilty to a misdemeanor to a community residential sanction as described in division (A) of this section, at the time of reception and at other times the person in charge of the operation of the halfway house, alternative residential facility, community alternative sentencing center, district community alternative sentencing center, or other place at which the offender will serve the residential sanction determines to be appropriate, the person in charge of the operation of the halfway house, alternative residential facility, community alternative sentencing center, district community alternative sentencing center, or other place may cause the convicted offender to be examined and tested for tuberculosis, HIV infection, hepatitis, including, but not limited to, hepatitis A, B, and C, and other contagious diseases. The person in charge of the operation of the halfway house, alternative residential facility, community alternative sentencing center, district community alternative sentencing center, or other place at which the offender will serve the residential sanction may cause a convicted offender in the halfway house, alternative residential facility, community alternative sentencing center, district community alternative sentencing center, or other place who refuses to be tested or treated for tuberculosis, HIV infection, hepatitis, including, but not limited to, hepatitis A, B, and C, or another contagious disease to be tested and treated involuntarily.

(F) A political subdivision may enter into a contract with a halfway house for use of the halfway house to house misdemeanor offenders under a sanction imposed under division (A)(1) of this section.

**HISTORY: 149 v H 490, § 1, eff. 1-1-04; 2011 HB 86, § 1, eff. Sept. 30, 2011.**

The effective date is set by section 4 of H.B. 490.

## § 2929.27 Nonresidential and other sanctions; community service.

(A) Except when a mandatory jail term is required by law, the court imposing a sentence for a misdemeanor, other than a minor misdemeanor, may impose upon the offender any nonresidential sanction or combination of nonresidential sanctions authorized under this division. Nonresidential sanctions include, but are not limited to, the following:

(1) A term of day reporting;

(2) A term of house arrest with electronic monitoring or continuous alcohol monitoring or both electronic monitoring and continuous alcohol monitoring, a term of electronic monitoring or continuous alcohol monitoring without house arrest, or a term of house arrest without electronic monitoring or continuous alcohol monitoring;

(3) A term of community service of up to five hundred hours for a misdemeanor of the first degree or two hundred hours for a misdemeanor of the second, third, or fourth degree;

(4) A term in a drug treatment program with a level of security for the offender as determined necessary by the court;

(5) A term of intensive probation supervision;

(6) A term of basic probation supervision;

(7) A term of monitored time;

(8) A term of drug and alcohol use monitoring, including random drug testing;

(9) A curfew term;

(10) A requirement that the offender obtain employment;

(11) A requirement that the offender obtain education or training;

(12) Provided the court obtains the prior approval of the victim, a requirement that the offender participate in victim-offender mediation;

(13) If authorized by law, suspension of the offender's privilege to operate a motor vehicle, immobilization or forfeiture of the offender's motor vehicle, a requirement that the offender obtain a valid motor vehicle operator's license, or any other related sanction;

(14) A requirement that the offender obtain counseling if the offense is a violation of section 2919.25 or a violation of section 2903.13 of the Revised Code involving a person who was a family or household member at the time of the violation, if the offender committed the offense in the vicinity of one or more children who are not victims of the offense, and if the offender or the victim of the offense is a parent, guardian, custodian, or person in loco parentis of one or more of those children. This division does not limit the court in requiring that the offender obtain counseling for any offense or in any circumstance not specified in this division.

(B) If the court imposes a term of community service pursuant to division (A)(3) of this section, the offender may request that the court modify the sentence to authorize the offender to make a reasonable contribution, as determined by the court, to the general fund of the county, municipality, or other local entity that provides funding to the court. The court may grant the request if the offender demonstrates a change in circumstances from the date the court imposes the sentence or that the modification would otherwise be in the interests of justice. If the court grants the request, the offender shall make a reasonable contribution to the court, and the clerk of the court shall deposit that contribution into the general fund of the county, municipality, or other local entity that provides funding to the court. If more than one entity provides funding to the court, the clerk shall deposit a percentage of the reasonable contribution equal to the percentage of funding the entity provides to the court in that entity's general fund.

(C) In addition to the sanctions authorized under division (A) of this section, the court imposing a sentence for a misdemeanor, other than a minor misdemeanor, upon an offender who is not required to serve a mandatory jail term may impose any other sanction that is intended to discourage the offender or other persons from committing a similar offense if the sanction is reasonably related to the overriding purposes and principles of misdemeanor sentencing.

(D) The court imposing a sentence for a minor misdemeanor may impose a term of community service in lieu of all or part of a fine. The term of community service imposed for a minor misdemeanor shall not exceed thirty hours. After imposing a term of community service, the court may modify the sentence to authorize a reasonable contribution, as determined by the court, to the appropriate general fund as provided in division (B) of this section.

**HISTORY: 149 v H 490, § 1, eff. 1-1-04; 150 v H 163, § 1, eff. 9-23-04; 2011 HB 5, § 1, eff. Sept. 23, 2011.**

The effective date is set by section 4 of H.B. 490.

## § 2929.28 Financial sanctions; court costs.

(A) In addition to imposing court costs pursuant to section 2947.23 of the Revised Code, the court imposing a sentence upon an offender for a misdemeanor, including a minor misdemeanor, may sentence the offender to any financial sanction or combination of financial sanctions authorized under this section. If the court in its discretion imposes one or more financial sanctions, the financial sanctions that may be imposed pursuant to this section include, but are not limited to, the following:

(1) Unless the misdemeanor offense is a minor misdemeanor or could be disposed of by the traffic violations bureau serving the court under Traffic Rule 13, restitution by the offender to the victim of the offender's crime or any survivor of the victim, in an amount based on the victim's economic loss. The court may not impose restitution as a sanction pursuant to this division if the offense is a minor misdemeanor or could be disposed of by the traffic violations bureau serving the court under Traffic Rule 13. If the court requires restitution, the court shall order that the restitution be made to the victim in open court or to the adult probation department that serves the jurisdiction or the clerk of the court on behalf of the victim.

If the court imposes restitution, the court shall determine the amount of restitution to be paid by the offender. If the court imposes restitution, the court may base the amount of restitution it orders on an amount recommended by the victim, the offender, a presentence investigation report, estimates or receipts indicating the cost of repairing or replacing property, and other information, provided that the amount the court orders as restitution shall not exceed the amount of the economic loss suffered by the victim as a direct and proximate result of the commission of the offense. If the court decides to impose restitution, the court shall hold an evidentiary hearing on restitution if the offender, victim, or survivor disputes the amount of restitution. If the court holds an evidentiary hearing, at the hearing the victim or survivor has the burden to prove by a preponderance of the evidence the amount of restitution sought from the offender.

All restitution payments shall be credited against any recovery of economic loss in a civil action brought by the victim or any survivor of the victim against the offender. No person may introduce evidence of an award of restitution under this section in a civil action for purposes of imposing liability against an insurer under section 3937.18 of the Revised Code.

If the court imposes restitution, the court may order that the offender pay a surcharge, of not more than five per cent of the amount of the restitution otherwise ordered, to the entity responsible for collecting and processing restitution payments.

The victim or survivor may request that the prosecutor in the case file a motion, or the offender may file a motion, for modification of the payment terms of any restitution ordered. If the court grants the motion, it may modify the payment terms as it determines appropriate.

(2) A fine of the type described in divisions (A)(2)(a) and (b) of this section payable to the appropriate entity as required by law:

(a) A fine in the following amount:

(i) For a misdemeanor of the first degree, not more than one thousand dollars;

(ii) For a misdemeanor of the second degree, not more than seven hundred fifty dollars;

(iii) For a misdemeanor of the third degree, not more than five hundred dollars;

(iv) For a misdemeanor of the fourth degree, not more than two hundred fifty dollars;

(v) For a minor misdemeanor, not more than one hundred fifty dollars.

(b) A state fine or cost as defined in section 2949.111 of the Revised Code.

(3)(a) Reimbursement by the offender of any or all of the costs of sanctions incurred by the government, including, but not limited to, the following:

(i) All or part of the costs of implementing any community control sanction, including a supervision fee under section 2951.021 of the Revised Code;

(ii) All or part of the costs of confinement in a jail or other residential facility, including, but not limited to, a per diem fee for room and board, the costs of medical and dental treatment, and the costs of repairing property damaged by the offender while confined;

(iii) All or part of the cost of purchasing and using an immobilizing or disabling device, including a certified ignition interlock device, or a remote alcohol monitoring device that a court orders an offender to use under section 4510.13 of the Revised Code.

(b) The amount of reimbursement ordered under division (A)(3)(a) of this section shall not exceed the total amount of reimbursement the offender is able to pay and shall not exceed the actual cost of the sanctions. The court may collect any amount of reimbursement the offender is required to pay under that division. If the court does not order reimbursement under that division, confinement costs may be assessed pursuant to a repayment policy adopted under section 2929.37 of the Revised Code. In addition, the offender may be required to pay the fees specified in section 2929.38 of the Revised Code in accordance with that section.

(B) If the court determines a hearing is necessary, the court may hold a hearing to determine whether the offender is able to pay the financial sanction imposed pursuant to this section or court costs or is likely in the future to be able to pay the sanction or costs.

If the court determines that the offender is indigent and unable to pay the financial sanction or court costs, the court shall consider imposing and may impose a term of community service under division (A) of section 2929.27 of the Revised Code in lieu of imposing a financial sanction or court costs. If the court does not determine that the offender is indigent, the court may impose a term of community service under division (A) of section 2929.27 of the Revised Code in lieu of or in addition to imposing a financial sanction under this section and in addition to imposing court costs. The court may order community service for a minor misdemeanor pursuant to division (D) of section 2929.27 of the Revised Code in lieu of or in addition to imposing a financial sanction under this section and in addition to imposing court costs. If a person fails to pay a financial sanction or court costs, the court may order community service in lieu of the financial sanction or court costs.

(C)(1) The offender shall pay reimbursements imposed upon the offender pursuant to division (A)(3) of this section to pay the costs incurred by a county pursuant to any sanction imposed under this section or section 2929.26 or 2929.27 of the Revised Code or in operating a facility used to confine offenders pursuant to a sanction imposed under section 2929.26 of the Revised Code to the county treasurer. The county treasurer shall deposit the reimbursements in the county's general fund. The county shall use the amounts deposited in the fund to pay the costs incurred by the county pursuant to any sanction imposed under this section or section 2929.26 or 2929.27 of the Revised Code or in operating a facility used to confine offenders pursuant to a sanction imposed under section 2929.26 of the Revised Code.

(2) The offender shall pay reimbursements imposed upon the offender pursuant to division (A)(3) of this section to pay the costs incurred by a municipal corporation pursuant to any sanction imposed under this section or section 2929.26 or 2929.27 of the Revised Code or in operating a facility used to confine offenders pursuant to a sanction imposed under section 2929.26 of the Revised Code to the treasurer of the municipal corporation. The treasurer shall deposit the reimbursements in the municipal corporation's general fund. The municipal corporation shall use the amounts deposited in the fund to pay the costs incurred by the municipal corporation pursuant to any sanction imposed under this section or section 2929.26 or 2929.27 of the Revised Code or in operating a facility used to confine offenders pursuant to a sanction imposed under section 2929.26 of the Revised Code.

(3) The offender shall pay reimbursements imposed pursuant to division (A)(3) of this section for the costs incurred by a private provider pursuant to a sanction imposed under this section or section 2929.26 or 2929.27 of the Revised Code to the provider.

(D) Except as otherwise provided in this division, a financial sanction imposed under division (A) of this section is a judgment in favor of the state or the political subdivision that operates the court that imposed the financial sanction, and the offender subject to the financial sanction is the judgment debtor. A financial sanction of reimbursement imposed pursuant to division (A)(3)(a)(i) of this section upon an offender is a judgment in favor of the entity administering the community control sanction, and the offender subject to the financial sanction is the judgment debtor. A financial sanction of reimbursement imposed pursuant to division (A)(3)(a)(ii) of this section upon an offender confined in a jail or other residential facility is a judgment in favor of the entity operating the jail or other residential facility, and the offender subject to the financial sanction is the judgment debtor. A financial sanction of restitution imposed pursuant to division (A)(1) of this section is an order in favor of the victim of the offender's criminal act that can be collected through a certificate of judgment as described in division (D)(1) of this section, through execution as described in division (D)(2) of this section, or through an order as described in division (D)(3) of this section, and the offender shall be considered for purposes of the collection as the judgment debtor.

Once the financial sanction is imposed as a judgment or order under this division, the victim, private provider, state, or political subdivision may do any of the following:

(1) Obtain from the clerk of the court in which the judgment was entered a certificate of judgment that shall be in the same manner and form as a certificate of judgment issued in a civil action;

(2) Obtain execution of the judgment or order through any available procedure, including any of the procedures identified in divisions (D)(1) and (2) of section 2929.18 of the Revised Code.

(3) Obtain an order for the assignment of wages of the judgment debtor under section 1321.33 of the Revised Code.

(E) The civil remedies authorized under division (D) of this section for the collection of the financial sanction supplement, but do not preclude, enforcement of the criminal sentence.

(F) Each court imposing a financial sanction upon an offender under this section may designate the clerk of the court or another person to collect the financial sanction. The clerk, or another person authorized by law or the court to collect the financial sanction may do the following:

(1) Enter into contracts with one or more public agencies or private vendors for the collection of amounts due under the sanction. Before entering into a contract for the collection of amounts due from an offender pursuant to any financial sanction imposed pursuant to this section, a court shall comply with sections 307.86 to 307.92 of the Revised Code.

(2) Permit payment of all or any portion of the sanction in installments, by financial transaction device if the court is a county court or a municipal court operated by a county, by credit or debit card or by another electronic transfer if the court is a municipal court not operated by a county, or by any other reasonable method, in any time, and on any terms that court considers just, except that the maximum time permitted for payment shall not exceed five years. If the court is a county court or a municipal court operated by a county, the acceptance of payments by any financial transaction device shall be governed by the policy adopted by the board of county commissioners of the county pursuant to section 301.28 of the Revised Code. If the court is a municipal court not operated by a county, the clerk may pay any fee associated with processing an electronic transfer out of public money or may charge the fee to the offender.

(3) To defray administrative costs, charge a reasonable fee to an offender who elects a payment plan rather than a lump sum payment of any financial sanction.

(G) No financial sanction imposed under this section shall preclude a victim from bringing a civil action against the offender.

**HISTORY: 149 v H 490 § 1, Eff. 1-1-04; 150 v S 57, § 1, eff. 1-1-04; 150 v H 52, § 1, eff. 6-1-04; 152 v S 17, § 1, eff. 9-30-08; 2011 HB 5, § 1, eff. Sept. 23, 2011.**

**Publisher's Note:**

Former RC § 2929.28 was amended and renumbered RC § 2929.71 by H.B. 490, effective January 1, 2004.

## § 2929.29 Amended and renumbered RC § 2929.43 in 149 v H 490. Eff 1-1-04.

[ORGANIZATIONAL PENALTIES]

## § 2929.31 Organizational penalties.

(A) Regardless of the penalties provided in sections 2929.02, 2929.14 to 2929.18, and 2929.24 to 2929.28 of the Revised Code, an organization convicted of an offense pursuant to section 2901.23 of the Revised Code shall be fined in accordance with this section. The court shall fix the fine as follows:

(1) For aggravated murder, not more than one hundred thousand dollars;

(2) For murder, not more than fifty thousand dollars;

(3) For a felony of the first degree, not more than twenty-five thousand dollars;

(4) For a felony of the second degree, not more than twenty thousand dollars;

(5) For a felony of the third degree, not more than fifteen thousand dollars;

(6) For a felony of the fourth degree, not more than ten thousand dollars;

(7) For a felony of the fifth degree, not more than seventy-five hundred dollars;

(8) For a misdemeanor of the first degree, not more than five thousand dollars;

(9) For a misdemeanor of the second degree, not more than four thousand dollars;

(10) For a misdemeanor of the third degree, not more than three thousand dollars;

(11) For a misdemeanor of the fourth degree, not more than two thousand dollars;

(12) For a minor misdemeanor, not more than one thousand dollars;

(13) For a felony not specifically classified, not more than ten thousand dollars;

(14) For a misdemeanor not specifically classified, not more than two thousand dollars;

(15) For a minor misdemeanor not specifically classified, not more than one thousand dollars.

(B) When an organization is convicted of an offense that is not specifically classified, and the section defining the offense or penalty plainly indicates a purpose to impose the penalty provided for violation upon organizations, then the penalty so provided shall be imposed in lieu of the penalty provided in this section.

(C) When an organization is convicted of an offense that is not specifically classified, and the penalty provided includes a higher fine than the fine that is provided in this section, then the penalty imposed shall be pursuant to the penalty provided for the violation of the section defining the offense.

(D) This section does not prevent the imposition of available civil sanctions against an organization convicted of an offense pursuant to section 2901.23 of the Revised Code, either in addition to or in lieu of a fine imposed pursuant to this section.

**HISTORY: 134 v H 511 (Eff 1-1-74); 139 v S 199 (Eff 7-1-83); 146 v S 2. Eff 7-1-96; 149 v H 490, § 1, eff. 1-1-04.**

The effective date is set by section 4 of HB 490.

See provisions, § 5 of SB 2 (146 v —) as amended by § 3 of SB 269 (146 v —) following RC § 2929.03.

## § 2929.32 Additional fine for certain offenders; collection of fines; crime victims recovery fund.

(A)(1) Subject to division (A)(2) of this section, notwithstanding the fines prescribed in section 2929.02 of the Revised Code for a person who is convicted of or pleads guilty to aggravated murder or murder, the fines prescribed in section 2929.18 of the Revised Code for a person who is convicted of or pleads guilty to a felony, the fines prescribed in section 2929.28 of the Revised Code for a person who is convicted of or pleads guilty to a misdemeanor, the fines prescribed in section 2929.31 of the Revised Code for an organization that is convicted of or pleads guilty to an offense, and the fines prescribed in any other section of the Revised Code for a person who is convicted of or pleads guilty to an offense, a sentencing court may impose upon the offender a fine of not more than one million dollars if any of the following applies to the offense and the offender:

(a) There are three or more victims, as defined in section 2969.11 of the Revised Code, of the offense for which the offender is being sentenced.

(b) The offender previously has been convicted of or pleaded guilty to one or more offenses, and, for the offense for which the offender is being sentenced and all of the other offenses, there is a total of three or more victims, as defined in section 2969.11 of the Revised Code.

(c) The offense for which the offender is being sentenced is aggravated murder, murder, or a felony of the first degree that, if it had been committed prior to July 1, 1996, would have been an aggravated felony of the first degree.

(2) If the offense in question is a first, second, or third degree felony violation of any provision of Chapter 2925., 3719., or 4729. of the Revised Code, the court shall impose upon the offender the mandatory fine described in division (B) of section 2929.18 of the Revised Code, and, in addition, may impose a fine under division (A) (1) of this section, provided that the total of the mandatory fine and the fine imposed under division (A)(1) of this section shall not exceed one million dollars. The mandatory fine shall be paid as described in division (D) of section 2929.18 of the Revised Code, and the fine imposed under division (A)(1) of this section shall be deposited pursuant to division (B) of this section.

(B) If a sentencing court imposes a fine upon an offender pursuant to division (A)(1) of this section, all moneys paid in satisfaction of the fine or collected pursuant to division (C)(1) of this section in satisfaction of the fine shall be deposited into the crime victims recovery fund created by division (D) of this section and shall be distributed as described in that division.

(C)(1) Subject to division (C)(2) of this section, notwithstanding any contrary provision of any section of the Revised Code, if a sentencing court imposes a fine upon an offender pursuant to division (A)(1) of this section or pursuant to another section of the Revised Code, the fine shall be a judgment against the offender in favor of the state, and both of the following apply to that judgment:

(a) The state may collect the judgment by garnishing, attaching, or otherwise executing against any income, profits, or other real or personal property in which the offender has any right, title, or interest, including property acquired after the imposition of the fine, in the same manner as if the judgment had been rendered against the offender and in favor of the state in a civil action. If the fine is imposed pursuant to division (A)(1) of this section, the moneys collected as a result of the garnishment, attachment, or other execution shall be deposited and distributed as described in divisions (B) and (D) of this section. If the fine is not imposed pursuant to division (A)(1) of this section, the moneys collected as a result of the garnishment, attachment, or other execution shall be distributed as otherwise provided by law for the distribution of money paid in satisfaction of a fine.

(b) The provisions of Chapter 2329. of the Revised Code relative to the establishment of court judgments and decrees as liens and to the enforcement of those liens apply to the judgment.

(2) Division (C) (1) of this section does not apply to any financial sanction imposed pursuant to section 2929.18 of the Revised Code upon a person who is convicted of or pleads guilty to a felony.

(D) There is hereby created in the state treasury the crime victims recovery fund. If a sentencing court imposes a fine upon an offender pursuant to division (A)(1) of this section, all moneys paid in satisfaction of the fine and all moneys collected in satisfaction of the fine pursuant to division (C)(1) of this section shall be deposited into the fund. The fund shall be administered and the moneys in it shall be distributed in accordance with sections 2969.11 to 2969.14 of the Revised Code.

**HISTORY: 146 v S 91, eff. 11-15-95; 146 v S 269, eff. 7-1-96; 149 v H 490, § 1, eff. 1-1-04.**

The effective date is set by section 4 of H.B. 490.

**Publisher's Note:**

This section was formerly RC § 2929.25. It was renumbered by H.B. 490, Acts 2002, effective January 1, 2004.

## § 2929.34 Type of institution where term of imprisonment to be served.

(A) A person who is convicted of or pleads guilty to aggravated murder, murder, or an offense punishable by life imprisonment and who is sentenced to a term of life imprisonment or a prison term pursuant to that conviction shall serve that term in an institution under the control of the department of rehabilitation and correction.

(B)(1) A person who is convicted of or pleads guilty to a felony other than aggravated murder, murder, or an offense punishable by life imprisonment and who is sentenced to a term of imprisonment or a prison term pursuant to that conviction shall serve that term as follows:

(a) Subject to divisions (B)(1)(b) and (B)(2) of this section, in an institution under the control of the department of rehabilitation and correction if the term is a prison term or as otherwise determined by the sentencing court pursuant to section 2929.16 of the Revised Code if the term is not a prison term;

(b) In a facility of a type described in division (G)(1) of section 2929.13 of the Revised Code, if the offender is sentenced pursuant to that division.

(2) If the term is a prison term, the person may be imprisoned in a jail that is not a minimum security jail pursuant to agreement under section 5120.161 of the Revised Code between the department of rehabilitation and correction and the local authority that operates the jail.

(C) A person who is convicted of or pleads guilty to one or more misdemeanors and who is sentenced to a jail term or term of imprisonment pursuant to the conviction or convictions shall serve that term in a county, multicounty, municipal, municipal-county, or multicounty-municipal jail or workhouse; in a community alternative sentencing center or district community alternative sentencing center when authorized by section 307.932 of the Revised Code; or, if the misdemeanor or misdemeanors are not offenses of violence, in a minimum security jail.

(D) Nothing in this section prohibits the commitment, referral, or sentencing of a person who is convicted of or pleads guilty to a felony to a community-based correctional facility.

**HISTORY: 139 v S 199 (Eff 7-1-83); 139 v H 269 (Eff 7-1-83); 140 v S 210 (Eff 7-1-83); 142 v H 455 (Eff 7-20-87); 143 v S 258 (Eff 11-20-90); 145 v H 571 (Eff 10-6-94); 146 v S 2 (Eff 7-1-96); 146 v S 269 (Eff 7-1-96); 146 v S 166. Eff 10-17-96; 149 v H 490, § 1, eff. 1-1-04; 151 v H 162, § 1, eff. 10-12-06; 2011 HB 86, § 1, eff. Sept. 30, 2011.**

The effective date is set by section 4 of HB 490.

See provisions, § 5 of SB 2 (146 v —) as amended by § 3 of SB 269 (146 v —) following RC § 2929.03.

The provisions of § 5 of HB 490 (149 v —) read as follows:

SECTION 5. Section 2929.221 (now 2929.34) of the Revised Code is presented in this act as a composite of the section as amended by both Am. Sub. S.B. 269 and Am. Sub. S.B. 166 of the 121st General Assembly. The General Assembly, applying the principle stated in division (B) of section 1.52 of the Revised Code that amendments are to be harmonized if reasonably capable of simultaneous operation, finds that the specified composite is the resulting version of the specified sections in effect prior to the effective date of the section as presented in this act.

**Publisher's Note:**

This section was formerly RC § 2929.221. It was amended and renumbered by H.B. 490, Acts 2002, effective January 1, 2004.

## [REIMBURSEMENT OF COSTS OF CONFINEMENT IN LOCAL DETENTION FACILITY]

## § 2929.35 Amended and renumbered RC § 2929.36 in 149 v H 490. Eff 1-1-04.

## § 2929.36 Definitions.

As used in sections 2929.36 to 2929.38 of the Revised Code:

(A) "Chief legal officer" includes a prosecuting attorney, village solicitor, city director of law, and attorney for a district of a joint city and county workhouse or county workhouse.

(B) "Clerk of the appropriate court" or "appropriate court clerk" means whichever of the following applies:

(1) If the local detention facility in question is a multicounty correctional center, multicounty-municipal correctional center, district community-based correctional facility, or district workhouse, the clerk of the court of common pleas of the most populous county served by the local detention facility;

(2) If the local detention facility in question is a city workhouse, the clerk of the municipal court for that city;

(3) If neither (B)(1) nor (B)(2) of this section applies, the clerk of the court of common pleas of the county in which the local detention facility in question is located.

(C) "Homestead" has the same meaning as in division (A) of section 323.151 [323.15.1] of the Revised Code.

(D) "Inmate account" has the same meaning as in section 2969.21 of the Revised Code.

(E) "Local detention facility" means a multicounty correctional center, municipal-county correctional center, multicounty-municipal correctional center, community-based correctional facility, district community-based correctional facility, jail, county jail, municipal or county prison, station house, workhouse, city workhouse, county workhouse, joint city and county workhouse, and district workhouse.

**HISTORY: 149 v H 170. Eff 9-6-2002; 149 v H 490, § 1, eff. 1-1-04.**

The effective date is set by section 4 of HB 490.

**Publisher's Note:**

This section was formerly RC § 2929.35. It was renumbered by H.B. 490, Acts 2002, effective January 1, 2004.

## § 2929.37 Policy requiring prisoner to pay costs of confinement.

(A) A board of county commissioners, in an agreement with the sheriff, a legislative authority of a municipal corporation, a corrections commission, a facility governing board, or any other public or private entity that operates a local detention facility at which a prisoner who is convicted of an offense and who is confined in the facility under a sanction or term of imprisonment imposed under section 2929.16, sections 2929.21 to 2929.28, or any other provision of the Revised Code may adopt, pursuant to section 307.93, 341.14, 341.19, 341.21, 341.23, 753.02, 753.04, 753.16, 2301.56, or 2947.19 of the Revised Code, a policy that requires the prisoner to pay all or part of the costs of confinement in that facility. If a board of county commissioners, legislative authority, corrections commission, facility governing board, or other entity adopts a policy for a facility pursuant to one of those sections, the person in charge of that facility shall appoint a reimbursement coordinator to administer the facility's policy.

The costs of confinement may include, but are not limited to, the costs of repairing property damaged by the prisoner while confined, a per diem fee for room and board, medical and dental treatment costs, the fee for a random drug test assessed under division (E) of section 341.26 and division (E) of section 753.33 of the Revised Code, and a one-time reception fee for the costs of processing the prisoner into the facility at the time of the prisoner's initial entry into the facility under the confinement in question, minus any fees deducted under section 2929.38 of the Revised Code. Any policy adopted under this section shall be used when a court does not order reimbursement of confinement costs under section 2929.18 or 2929.28 of the Revised Code. The amount assessed under this section shall not exceed the total amount that the prisoner is able to pay.

(B)(1) Each prisoner covered by a repayment policy adopted as described in division (A) of this section shall receive at the end of the prisoner's confinement an itemized bill of the expenses to be reimbursed. The policy shall allow periodic payments on a schedule to be implemented upon a prisoner's release. The bill also shall state that payment shall be made to the person identified in the bill as the reimbursement coordinator and include a notice that specifies that the prisoner has thirty days in which to dispute the bill by filing a written objection with the reimbursement coordinator and that if the prisoner does not dispute the bill in that manner within that period, the prisoner is required to pay the bill and a certificate of judgment may be obtained against the prisoner for the amount of the unpaid expenses. The prisoner shall sign a copy of the bill, and the reimbursement coordinator shall retain that copy. If the prisoner disputes an item on the bill within thirty days after receiving the bill, the reimbursement coordinator may either concede the disputed item or proceed to a hearing under division (B) (2) of this section.

(2) If the prisoner disputes an item on an itemized bill presented to the prisoner under division (B) (1) of this section and the reimbursement coordinator does not concede the item, the reimbursement coordinator shall submit the bill to the court, and the court shall hold a hearing on the disputed items in the bill. At the end of the hearing, the court shall determine how much of the disputed expenses the prisoner shall reimburse the legislative authority or managing authority and shall issue a judgment in favor of the legislative authority or managing authority for any undisputed expenses and the amount of the disputed expenses for which the prisoner must reimburse the legislative authority or managing authority. The reimbursement coordinator shall not seek to enforce the judgment until at least ninety days after the court issues the judgment.

(C) If a prisoner does not dispute the itemized bill presented to the prisoner under division (B) of this section and does not pay the bill within ninety days, the reimbursement coordinator shall send by mail a notice to the prisoner requesting payment of the expenses as stated in the bill. If the prisoner does not respond to the notice by paying the expenses in full within thirty days of the date the notice was mailed, the reimbursement coordinator shall send by mail a second notice to the prisoner requesting payment of the expenses. If one hundred eighty days elapse from the date that the reimbursement coordinator provides the bill and if the prisoner has not paid the full amount of the expenses pursuant to the bill and the notices, the reimbursement coordinator may notify the clerk of the appropriate court of those facts, and the clerk may issue a certificate of judgment against the prisoner for the balance of the expenses remaining unpaid.

(D) The reimbursement coordinator may collect any amounts remaining unpaid on an itemized bill and any costs associated with the enforcement of the judgment and may enter into a contract with one or more public agencies or private vendors to collect any amounts remaining unpaid. For enforcing a judgment issued under this section, the reimbursement coordinator may assess an additional poundage fee of two per cent of the amount remaining unpaid and may collect costs associated with the enforcement of the judgment.

(E) Neither the reimbursement coordinator nor the legislative authority or the managing authority shall enforce any judgment obtained under this section by means of execution against the prisoner's homestead. Any reimbursement received under this section shall be credited to the general fund of the treasury of the political subdivision that incurred the expense, to be used for general fund purposes.

**HISTORY: 149 v H 170. Eff 9-6-2002; 149 v H 490, § 1, eff. 1-1-04; 151 v H 162, § 1, eff. 10-12-06.**

The effective date is set by section 4 of HB 490.

## § 2929.38 One-time reception fee; fees for medical treatment or service and random drug test.

(A) A board of commissioners of a county, in an agreement with the sheriff, a legislative authority of a municipal corporation, a corrections commission, a facility governing board, or any other public or private entity that operates a local detention facility described in division (A) of section 2929.37 of the Revised Code, may establish a policy that requires any prisoner who is confined in the facility as a result of pleading guilty to or having been convicted of an offense to pay a one-time reception fee for the costs of processing the prisoner into the facility at the time of the prisoner's initial entry into the facility under the confinement in question, to pay a reasonable fee for any medical or dental treatment or service requested by and provided to that prisoner, and to pay the fee for a random drug test assessed under division (E) of section 341.26, and division (E) of section 753.33 of the Revised Code. The fee for the medical treatment or service shall not exceed the actual cost of the treatment or service provided. No prisoner confined in the local detention facility shall be denied any necessary medical care because of inability to pay the fees.

(B) Upon assessment of a one-time reception fee as described in division (A) of this section, the provision of the requested medical treatment or service, or the assessment of a fee for a random drug test, payment of the required fee may be automatically deducted from the prisoner's inmate account in the business office of the local detention facility in which the prisoner is confined. If there is no money in the account, a deduction may be made at a later date during the prisoner's confinement if the money becomes available in the account. If, after release, the prisoner has an unpaid balance of those fees, the sheriff, legislative authority of the municipal corporation, corrections commission, facility governing board, or other entity that operates the local detention facility described in division (A) of section 2929.37 of the Revised Code may bill the prisoner for the payment of the unpaid fees. Fees received for medical or dental treatment or services shall be paid to the commissary fund or resident program fund of a community-based correctional facility, if one exists for the facility, or if no commissary fund or resident program fund exists, to the general fund of the treasury of the political subdivision that incurred the expenses, in the same proportion as those expenses were borne by the political subdivision. Fees received for medical treatment or services that are placed in the commissary fund or resident program fund under this division shall be used for the same purposes as profits from the commissary fund or resident program fund, except that they shall not be used to pay any salary or benefits of any person who works in or is employed for the sole purpose of providing service to the commissary.

(C) Any fee paid by a person under this section shall be deducted from any medical or dental costs that the person is ordered to reimburse under a financial sanction imposed pursuant to section 2929.28 of the Revised Code or to repay under a policy adopted under section 2929.37 of the Revised Code.

(D) As used in this section, "inmate account" has the same meaning as in section 2969.21 of the Revised Code.

**HISTORY: 149 v H 170. Eff 9-6-2002; 150 v H 95, § 1, eff. 9-26-03; 149 v H 490, § 1, eff. 1-1-04; 150 v H 95, § 3.13, eff. 1-1-04; 151 v H 162, § 1, eff. 10-12-06.**

The effective date is set by section 3.13 of HB 95.

## [MULTIPLE SENTENCES]

## § 2929.41 Multiple sentences.

(A) Except as provided in division (B) of this section, division (E) of section 2929.14, or division (D) or (E) of section 2971.03 of the Revised Code, a prison term, jail term, or sentence of imprisonment shall be served concurrently with any other prison term, jail term, or sentence of imprisonment imposed by a court of this state, another state, or the United States. Except as provided in division (B)(3) of this section, a jail term or sentence of imprisonment for misdemeanor shall be served concurrently with a prison term or sentence of imprisonment for felony served in a state or federal correctional institution.

(B)(1) A jail term or sentence of imprisonment for a misdemeanor shall be served consecutively to any other prison term, jail term, or sentence of imprisonment when the trial court specifies that it is to be served consecutively or when it is imposed for a misdemeanor violation of section 2907.322, 2921.34, or 2923.131 of the Revised Code.

When consecutive sentences are imposed for misdemeanor under this division, the term to be served is the aggregate of the consecutive terms imposed, except that the aggregate term to be served shall not exceed eighteen months.

(2) If a court of this state imposes a prison term upon the offender for the commission of a felony and a court of another state or the United States also has imposed a prison term upon the offender for the commission of a felony, the court of this state may order that the offender serve the prison term it imposes consecutively to any prison term imposed upon the offender by the court of another state or the United States.

(3) A jail term or sentence of imprisonment imposed for a misdemeanor violation of section 4510.11, 4510.14, 4510.16, 4510.21, or 4511.19 of the Revised Code shall be served consecutively to a prison term that is imposed for a felony violation of section 2903.06, 2903.07, 2903.08, or 4511.19 of the Revised Code or a felony violation of section 2903.04 of the Revised Code involving the operation of a motor vehicle by the offender and that is served in a state correctional institution when the trial court specifies that it is to be served consecutively.

When consecutive jail terms or sentences of imprisonment and prison terms are imposed for one or more misdemeanors and one or more felonies under this division, the term to be served is the aggregate of the consecutive terms imposed, and the offender shall serve all terms imposed for a felony before serving any term imposed for a misdemeanor.

**HISTORY: 134 v H 511 (Eff 1-1-74); 137 v H 202 (Eff 10-9-78); 139 v S 1 (Eff 10-19-81); 139 v S 199 (Eff 1-5-83); 140 v S 210 (Eff 7-1-83); 142 v H 51 (Eff 3-17-89); 143 v S 258 (Eff 11-20-90); 144 v H 561 (Eff 4-9-93); 145 v H 571 (Eff 10-6-94); 146 v S 2 (Eff 7-1-96); 146 v H 154 (Eff 10-4-96); 146 v H 180 (Eff 1-1-97); 148 v S 107 (Eff 3-23-2000); 148 v S 22. Eff 5-17-2000; 149 v H 490, § 1, eff. 1-1-04; 149 v S 123, § 1, eff. 1-1-04; 2011 HB 86, § 1, eff. Sept. 30, 2011.**

The provisions of § 11 of HB 86 read as follows:

"SECTION 11. In amending division (E)(4) of section 2929.14 and division (A) of section 2929.41 of the Revised Code in this act, it is the intent of the General Assembly to simultaneously repeal and revive the amended language in those divisions that was invalidated and severed by the Ohio Supreme Court's decision in State v. Foster (2006), 109 Ohio St.3d 1. The amended language in those divisions is subject to reenactment under the United States Supreme Court's decision in Oregon v. Ice (2009), 555 U.S. 160, and the Ohio Supreme Court's decision in State v. Hodge (2010), ______ Ohio St.3d ______, Slip Opinion No. 2010-Ohio-6320 and, although constitutional under Hodge, supra, that language is not enforceable until deliberately revived by the General Assembly."

The effective date is set by section 4 of H.B. 490.

See provisions, § 5 of S.B. 123 (149 v —), following RC § 2929.01.

The provisions of § 8 of S.B. 123 read as follows:

SECTION 8. Section 2929.41 of the Revised Code is presented in this act as a composite of the section as amended by both Am. Sub. S.B. 22 and Am. Sub. S.B. 107 of the 123rd General Assembly. The General Assembly, applying the principle stated in division (B) of section 1.52 of the Revised Code that amendments are to be harmonized if reasonably capable of simultaneous operation, finds that the composites are the resulting versions of the sections in effect prior to the effective date of the sections as presented in this act.

See provisions, § 5 of SB 2 (146 v —) as amended by § 3 of SB 269 (146 v —) following RC § 2929.03.

## § 2929.42 Prosecutor to notify appropriate licensing board.

(A) The prosecutor in any case against any person licensed, certified, registered, or otherwise authorized to practice under Chapter 3719., 4715., 4723., 4729., 4730., 4731., 4734., or 4741. of the Revised Code shall notify the appropriate licensing board, on forms provided by the board, of any of the following regarding the person:

(1) A plea of guilty to, or a conviction of, a felony, or a court order dismissing a felony charge on technical or procedural grounds;

(2) A plea of guilty to, or a conviction of, a misdemeanor committed in the course of practice or in the course of business, or a court order dismissing such a misdemeanor charge on technical or procedural grounds;

(3) A plea of guilty to, or a conviction of, a misdemeanor involving moral turpitude, or a court order dismissing such a charge on technical or procedural grounds.

(B) The report required by division (A) of this section shall include the name and address of the person, the nature of the offense, and certified copies of court entries in the action.

**HISTORY: R.C. § 2929.17, 143 v H 615, eff. 3-27-91; 146 v S 143, eff. 3-5-96; R.C. § 2929.24, 146 v S 2, eff. 7-1-96; 146 v S 143, § 5, eff. 7-1-96; 148 v H 506, eff 4-10-01; 149 v H 490, § 1, eff. 1-1-04.**

The effective date is set by section 4 of H.B. 490.

**Publisher's Note:**

This section was formerly RC § 2929.24. It was renumbered by H.B. 490, Acts 2002, effective Jan 1, 2004.

## § 2929.43 Procedure for accepting peace officer's guilty plea to felony or after conviction; negotiated misdemeanor pleas.

(A) As used in this section:

(1) "Peace officer" has the same meaning as in section 109.71 of the Revised Code.

(2) "Felony" has the same meaning as in section 109.511 [109.51.1] of the Revised Code.

(B)(1) Prior to accepting a plea of guilty to an indictment, information, or complaint charging a felony, the court shall determine whether the defendant is a peace officer. If the court determines that the defendant is a peace officer, it shall address the defendant personally and provide the following advisement to the defendant that shall be entered in the record of the court.

"You are hereby advised that conviction of the felony offense to which you are pleading guilty will result in the termination of your employment as a peace officer and in your decertification as a peace officer pursuant to the laws of Ohio."

Upon the request of the defendant, the court shall allow the defendant additional time to consider the appropriateness of the plea of guilty in light of the advisement described in division (B)(1) of this section.

The court shall not accept a plea of guilty of a defendant who is a peace officer unless, in addition to any other procedures required under the Rules of Criminal Procedure, the court determines that the defendant voluntarily and intelligently enters that plea after being given the advisement described in division (B)(1) of this section.

(2) After accepting under division (B)(1) of this section a plea of guilty to an indictment, information, or complaint charging a felony, the court shall provide to the clerk of the court of common pleas a written notice of the plea of guilty of the defendant peace officer, the name and address of the peace officer, the law enforcement agency or other governmental entity that employs the peace officer and its address, the date of the plea, the nature of the felony offense, and certified copies of court entries in the action. Upon receiving the written notice required by division (B)(2) of this section, the clerk of the court of common pleas shall transmit to the employer of the peace officer and to the Ohio peace officer training council a report that includes the information contained in the written notice and the certified copies of the court entries in the action.

(C)(1) Upon the conviction of a defendant, after trial, of a felony, the trial judge shall determine whether the defendant is a peace officer. If the judge determines that the defendant is a peace officer or if the defendant states on the record that the defendant is a peace officer, the judge shall provide to the clerk of the court of common pleas a written notice of the conviction of the defendant peace officer, the name and address of the peace officer, the law enforcement agency or other governmental entity that employs the peace officer and its address, the date of the conviction, the nature of the felony offense, and certified copies of court entries in the action. Upon receiving the written notice required by division (C)(1) of this section, the clerk of the court of common pleas shall transmit to the employer of the peace officer and to the Ohio peace officer training council a report that includes the information contained in the written notice and the certified copies of the court entries in the action.

(2) Upon the conclusion of the final appeal of a defendant who is a peace officer and who has been convicted of a felony, upon expiration of the time period within which that peace officer may appeal the conviction if no appeal is taken, or otherwise upon the final disposition of the criminal action against that peace officer, the trial judge shall provide to the clerk of the court of common pleas a written notice of the final disposition of the action that shall include, as appropriate, notice of the final conviction of the peace officer of the felony, the acquittal of the peace officer of the felony, the conviction of the peace officer of a misdemeanor, or the dismissal of the felony charge against the peace officer. The judge also shall provide to the clerk of the court of common pleas certified copies of the court entries in the action. Upon receiving the written notice required by division (C)(2) of this section, the clerk of the court of common pleas shall transmit to the employer of the peace officer and to the Ohio peace officer training council a report that includes the information contained in the written notice and the certified copies of the court entries in the action.

(D) If pursuant to a negotiated plea agreement between a prosecuting attorney and a defendant who is a peace officer and who is charged with a felony, in which the defendant agrees to enter a plea of guilty to a misdemeanor and to surrender the certificate awarded to the defendant under section 109.77 of the Revised Code, the trial judge issues an order to the defendant to surrender that certificate, the trial judge shall provide to the clerk of the court a written notice of the order, the name and address of the peace officer, the law enforcement agency or other governmental entity that employs the peace officer and its address, the date of the plea, the nature of the misdemeanor to which the peace officer pleaded guilty, and certified copies of court entries in the action. Upon receiving the written notice required by this division, the clerk of the court shall transmit to the employer of the peace officer and to the executive director of the Ohio peace officer training council a report that includes the information contained in the written notice and the certified copies of the court entries in the action.

**HISTORY: 146 v H 566, eff 10-16-96; 149 v H 490, § 1, eff. 1-1-04.**

The effective date is set by section 4 of HB 490.

**Publisher's Note:**

This section was formerly RC § 2929.29. It was renumbered by H.B. 490, Acts 2002, effective January 1, 2004.

## [MODIFICATION OF SENTENCE]

**§ 2929.51** Repealed, 149 v H 490, § 2 [134 v H 511 (Eff 1-1-74); 138 v H 1000 (Eff 4-9-81); 138 v H 682 (Eff 4-9-81); 139 v H 1 (Eff 8-5-81); 139 v S 199 (Eff 7-1-83); 141 v H 475 (Eff 3-7-86); 143 v H 317 (Eff 10-10-89); 143 v S 258 (Eff 11-20-90); 145 v H 152 (Eff 7-1-93); 146 v S 2 (Eff 7-1-96); 146 v S 269 (Eff 7-1-96); 146 v S 223. Eff 3-18-97]. Eff 1-1-04.

This section concerned modification of sentence.

## [OFFENSES PRIOR TO JANUARY 1, 1974, CERTAIN FELONIES PRIOR TO JULY 1, 1983]

### § 2929.61 Offense committed prior to January 1, 1974; third or fourth degree felony committed between that date and July 1, 1983.

(A) Persons charged with a capital offense committed prior to January 1, 1974, shall be prosecuted under the law as it existed at the time the offense was committed, and, if convicted, shall be imprisoned for life, except that whenever the statute under which any such person is prosecuted provides for a lesser penalty under the circumstances of the particular case, such lesser penalty shall be imposed.

(B) Persons charged with an offense, other than a capital offense, committed prior to January 1, 1974, shall be prosecuted under the law as it existed at the time the offense was committed. Persons convicted or sentenced on or after January 1, 1974, for an offense committed prior to January 1, 1974, shall be sentenced according to the penalty for commission of the substantially equivalent offense under Amended Substitute House Bill 511 of the 109th General Assembly. If the offense for which sentence is being imposed does not have a substantial equivalent under that act, or if that act provides a more severe penalty than that originally prescribed for the offense of which the person is convicted, then sentence shall be imposed under the law as it existed prior to January 1, 1974.

(C) Persons charged with an offense that is a felony of the third or fourth degree and that was committed on or after January 1, 1974, and before July 1, 1983, shall be prosecuted under the law as it existed at the time the offense was committed. Persons convicted or sentenced on or after July 1, 1983, for an offense that is a felony of the third or fourth degree and that was committed on or after January 1, 1974, and before July 1, 1983, shall be notified by the court sufficiently in advance of sentencing that they may choose to be sentenced pursuant to either the law in effect at the time of the commission of the offense or the law in effect at the time of sentencing. This notice shall be written and shall include the differences between and possible effects of the alternative sentence forms and the effect of the person's refusal to choose. The person to be sentenced shall then inform the court in writing of his choice, and shall be sentenced accordingly. Any person choosing to be sentenced pursuant to the law in effect at the time of the commission of an offense that is a felony of the third or fourth degree shall then be eligible for parole, and this person cannot at a later date have his sentence converted to a definite sentence. If the person refuses to choose between the two possible sentences, the person shall be sentenced pursuant to the law in effect at the time of the commission of the offense.

(D) Persons charged with an offense that was a felony of the first or second degree at the time it was committed, that was committed on or after January 1, 1974, and that was committed prior to July 1, 1983, shall be prosecuted for that offense and, if convicted, shall be sentenced under the law as it existed at the time the offense was committed.

**HISTORY: 134 v H 511, § 3 (Eff 1-1-74); 136 v H 1 (Eff 6-13-75); 139 v S 199 (Eff 7-1-83); 139 v H 269 (Eff 7-1-83); 140 v S 210. Eff 7-1-83.**

Revised Code § 2929.61 was formerly § 3 of 134 v H 511, eff 1-1-74.

The effective date is set by section 3 of SB 210.

## [REIMBURSEMENT BY ARSONIST]

### § 2929.71 Arsonist to reimburse agencies for costs of investigation and prosecution.

(A) As used in this section:

(1) "Agency" means any law enforcement agency, other public agency, or public official involved in the investigation or prosecution of the offender or in the investigation of the fire or explosion in an aggravated arson, arson, or criminal damaging or endangering case. An "agency" includes, but is not limited to, a sheriff's office, a municipal corporation, township, or township or joint police district police department, the office of a prosecuting attorney, city director of law, village solicitor, or similar chief legal officer of a municipal corporation, the fire marshal's office, a municipal corporation, township, or township fire district fire department, the office of a fire

prevention officer, and any state, county, or municipal corporation crime laboratory.

(2) "Assets" includes all forms of real or personal property.

(3) "Itemized statement" means the statement of costs described in division (B) of this section.

(4) "Offender" means the person who has been convicted of or pleaded guilty to committing, attempting to commit, or complicity in committing a violation of section 2909.02 or 2909.03 of the Revised Code, or, when the means used are fire or explosion, division (A)(2) of section 2909.06 of the Revised Code.

(5) "Costs" means the reasonable value of the time spent by an officer or employee of an agency on the aggravated arson, arson, or criminal damaging or endangering case, any moneys spent by the agency on that case, and the reasonable fair market value of resources used or expended by the agency on that case.

(B) Prior to the sentencing of an offender, the court shall enter an order that directs agencies that wish to be reimbursed by the offender for the costs they incurred in the investigation or prosecution of the offender or in the investigation of the fire or explosion involved in the case, to file with the court within a specified time an itemized statement of those costs. The order also shall require that a copy of the itemized statement be given to the offender or offender's attorney within the specified time. Only itemized statements so filed and given shall be considered at the hearing described in division (C) of this section.

(C) The court shall set a date for a hearing on all the itemized statements filed with it and given to the offender or the offender's attorney in accordance with division (B) of this section. The hearing shall be held prior to the sentencing of the offender, but may be held on the same day as the sentencing. Notice of the hearing date shall be given to the offender or the offender's attorney and to the agencies whose itemized statements are involved. At the hearing, each agency has the burden of establishing by a preponderance of the evidence that the costs set forth in its itemized statement were incurred in the investigation or prosecution of the offender or in the investigation of the fire or explosion involved in the case, and of establishing by a preponderance of the evidence that the offender has assets available for the reimbursement of all or a portion of the costs.

The offender may cross-examine all witnesses and examine all documentation presented by the agencies at the hearing, and the offender may present at the hearing witnesses and documentation the offender has obtained without a subpoena or a subpoena duces tecum or, in the case of documentation, that belongs to the offender. The offender also may issue subpoenas and subpoenas duces tecum for, and present and examine at the hearing, witnesses and documentation, subject to the following applying to the witnesses or documentation subpoenaed:

(1) The testimony of witnesses subpoenaed or documentation subpoenaed is material to the preparation or presentation by the offender of the offender's defense to the claims of the agencies for a reimbursement of costs;

(2) If witnesses to be subpoenaed are personnel of an agency or documentation to be subpoenaed belongs to an agency, the personnel or documentation may be subpoenaed only if the agency involved has indicated, pursuant to this division, that it intends to present the personnel as witnesses or use the documentation at the hearing. The offender shall submit, in writing, a request to an agency as described in this division to ascertain whether the agency intends to present various personnel as witnesses or to use particular documentation. The request shall indicate that the offender is considering issuing subpoenas to personnel of the agency who are specifically named or identified by title or position, or for documentation of the agency that is specifically described or generally identified, and shall request the agency to indicate, in writing, whether it intends to present such personnel as witnesses or to use such documentation at the hearing. The agency shall promptly reply to the request of the offender. An agency is prohibited from presenting personnel as witnesses or from using documentation at the hearing if it indicates to the offender it does not intend to do so in response to a request of the offender under this division, or if it fails to reply or promptly reply to such a request.

(D) Following the hearing, the court shall determine which of the agencies established by a preponderance of the evidence that costs set forth in their itemized statements were incurred as described in division (C) of this section and that the offender has assets available for reimbursement purposes. The court also shall determine whether the offender has assets available to reimburse all such agencies, in whole or in part, for their established costs, and if it determines that the assets are available, it shall order the offender, as part of the offender's sentence, to reimburse the agencies from the offender's assets for all or a specified portion of their established costs.

**HISTORY: 141 v H 284, eff. 3-6-86; 149 v H 490, § 1, eff. 1-1-04; 2011 HB 153, § 101.01, eff. Sept. 29, 2011.**

The effective date is set by section 4 of HB 490.

**Publisher's Note:**

This section was formerly RC § 2929.28. It was renumbered by H.B. 490, Acts 2002, effective January 1, 2004.

## § 2929.72 Repealed, 146 v S 2, § 2 [139 v S 199; 140 v S 210; 142 v H 261; 143 v S 258; 145 v H 571]. Eff 7-1-96.

This section concerned offenses involving firearms.

**For analogous sentencing provisions, see now RC § 2929.14.**

The effective date is set by section 6 of SB 2.

# CHAPTER 2930: VICTIM'S RIGHTS



## § 2930.01 Definitions.

As used in this chapter:

(A) "Crime" means any of the following:

(1) A felony;

(2) A violation of section 2903.05, 2903.06, 2903.13, 2903.21, 2903.211 [2903.21.1], 2903.22, 2907.06, 2919.25, or 2921.04 of the Revised Code, a violation of section 2903.07 of the Revised Code as it existed prior to March 23, 2000, or a violation of a substantially equivalent municipal ordinance;

(3) A violation of division (A) or (B) of section 4511.19, division (A) or (B) of section 1547.11, or division (A)(3) of section 4561.15 of the Revised Code or of a municipal ordinance substantially similar to any of those divisions that is the proximate cause of a vehicle, streetcar, trackless trolley, aquatic device, or aircraft accident in which the victim receives injuries for which the victim receives medical treatment either at the scene of the accident by emergency medical services personnel or at a hospital, ambulatory care facility, physician's office, specialist's office, or other medical care facility.

(4) A motor vehicle accident to which both of the following apply:

(a) The motor vehicle accident is caused by a violation of a provision of the Revised Code that is a misdemeanor of the first degree or higher.

(b) As a result of the motor vehicle accident, the victim receives injuries for which the victim receives medical treatment either at the scene of the accident by emergency medical services personnel or at a hospital, ambulatory care facility, physician's office, specialist's office, or other medical care facility.

(B) "Custodial agency" means one of the following:

(1) The entity that has custody of a defendant or an alleged juvenile offender who is incarcerated for a crime, is under detention for the commission of a specified delinquent act, or who is detained after a finding of incompetence to stand trial or not guilty by reason of insanity relative to a crime, including any of the following:

(a) The department of rehabilitation and correction or the adult parole authority;

(b) A county sheriff;

(c) The entity that administers a jail, as defined in section 2929.01 of the Revised Code;

(d) The entity that administers a community-based correctional facility and program or a district community-based correctional facility and program;

(e) The department of mental health or other entity to which a defendant found incompetent to stand trial or not guilty by reason of insanity is committed.

(2) The entity that has custody of an alleged juvenile offender pursuant to an order of disposition of a juvenile court, including the department of youth services or a school, camp, institution, or other facility operated for the care of delinquent children.

(C) "Defendant" means a person who is alleged to be the perpetrator of a crime in a police report or in a complaint, indictment, or information that charges the commission of a crime and that provides the basis for the criminal prosecution and subsequent proceedings to which this chapter makes reference.

(D) "Member of the victim's family" means a spouse, child, stepchild, sibling, parent, stepparent, grandparent, or other relative of a victim but does not include a person who is charged with, convicted of, or adjudicated to be a delinquent child for the crime or specified delinquent act against the victim or another crime or specified delinquent act arising from the same conduct, criminal episode, or plan.

(E) "Prosecutor" means one of the following:

(1) With respect to a criminal case, it has the same meaning as in section 2935.01 of the Revised Code and also includes the attorney general and, when appropriate, the employees of any person listed in section 2935.01 of the Revised Code or of the attorney general.

(2) With respect to a delinquency proceeding, it includes any person listed in division (C) of section 2935.01 of the Revised Code or an employee of a person listed in that division who prosecutes a delinquency proceeding.

(F) "Public agency" means an office, agency, department, bureau, or other governmental entity of the state or of a political subdivision of the state.

(G) "Public official" has the same meaning as in section 2921.01 of the Revised Code.

(H) "Victim" means either of the following:

(1) A person who is identified as the victim of a crime or specified delinquent act in a police report or in a complaint, indictment, or information that charges the commission of a crime and that provides the basis for the criminal prosecution or delinquency proceeding and subsequent proceedings to which this chapter makes reference.

(2) A person who receives injuries as a result of a vehicle, streetcar, trackless trolley, aquatic device, or aircraft accident that is proximately caused by a violation described in division (A)(3) of this section or a motor vehicle accident that is proximately caused by a violation described in division (A)(4) of this section and who receives medical treatment as described in division (A)(3) or (4) of this section, whichever is applicable.

(I) "Victim's representative" means a member of the victim's family or another person who pursuant to the authority of section 2930.02 of the Revised Code exercises the rights of a victim under this chapter.

(J) "Court" means a court of common pleas, juvenile court, municipal court, or county court.

(K) "Delinquency proceeding" means all proceedings in a juvenile court that are related to a case in which a complaint has been filed alleging that a child is a delinquent child.

(L) "Case" means a delinquency proceeding and all related activity or a criminal prosecution and all related activity.

(M) The "defense" means the defense against criminal charges in a criminal prosecution or the defense against a delinquent child complaint in a delinquency proceeding.

(N) The "prosecution" means the prosecution of criminal charges in a criminal prosecution or the prosecution of a delinquent child complaint in a delinquency proceeding.

(O) "Specified delinquent act" means any of the following:

(1) An act committed by a child that if committed by an adult would be a felony;

(2) An act committed by a child that is a violation of a section listed in division (A)(1) or (2) of this section or is a violation of a substantially equivalent municipal ordinance;

(3) An act committed by a child that is described in division (A)(3) or (4) of this section.

(P)(1) "Alleged juvenile offender" means a child who is alleged to have committed a specified delinquent act in a police report or in a complaint in juvenile court that charges the commission of a specified delinquent act and that provides the basis for the delinquency proceeding and all subsequent proceedings to which this chapter makes reference.

(2) As used in divisions (O) and (P)(1) of this section, "child" has the same meaning as in section 2151.011 [2151.01.1] of the Revised Code.

(Q) "Motor vehicle accident" means any accident involving a motor vehicle.

(R) "Motor vehicle" has the same meaning as in section 4509.01 of the Revised Code.

(S) "Aircraft" has the same meaning as in section 4561.01 of the Revised Code.

(T) "Aquatic device" means any vessel, or any water skis, aquaplane, or similar device.

(U) "Vehicle," "streetcar," and "trackless trolley" have the same meanings as in section 4511.01 of the Revised Code.

(V) "Vehicle, streetcar, trackless trolley, aquatic device, or aircraft accident" means any accident involving a vehicle, streetcar, trackless trolley, aquatic device, or aircraft.

(W) "Vessel" has the same meaning as in section 1547.01 of the Revised Code.

**HISTORY: 145 v S 186 (Eff 10-12-94); 146 v S 2 (Eff 7-1-96); 148 v H 3 (Eff 11-22-99); 148 v S 107. Eff 3-23-2000; 151 v H 108, § 1, eff. 5-17-06.**

## § 2930.02 Exercise of victim's rights by representative.

(A) If a victim is a minor or is incapacitated, incompetent, or deceased, or if the victim chooses to designate another person, a member of a victim's family or another person may exercise the rights of the victim under this chapter as the victim's representative.

If more than one person seeks to act as the victim's representative for a particular victim, the court in which the criminal prosecution or delinquency proceeding is held shall designate one of those persons as the victim's representative. If a victim does not want to have anyone act as the victim's representative, the court shall order that only the victim may exercise the rights of a victim under this chapter.

(B) If pursuant to division (A) of this section a victim's representative is to exercise the rights of a victim, the victim or victim's representative shall notify the prosecutor or, if it is a delinquency proceeding and a prosecutor is not involved in the case, shall notify the court that the victim's representative is to act for the victim. When a victim or victim's representative has so notified the prosecutor or the court, all notice under this chapter shall be sent only to the victim's representative, all rights under this chapter shall be granted only to the victim's representative, and all references in this chapter to a victim shall be interpreted as being references to the victim's representative unless the victim informs the notifying authority that the victim also wishes to receive the notices or exercise the rights. If division (B) of section 2930.03 of the Revised Code requires a victim to make a request in order to receive any notice of a type described in this division and if a victim's representative is to exercise the rights of the victim, the victim's representative shall make the request.

**HISTORY: 145 v S 186 (Eff 10-12-94); 146 v S 2 (Eff 7-1-96); 148 v H 3. Eff 11-22-99.**

## § 2930.03 Means of giving notice to victim; notice of changes.

(A) A person or entity required or authorized under this chapter to give notice to a victim shall give the notice to the victim by any means reasonably calculated to provide prompt actual notice. Except when a provision requires that notice is to be given in a specific manner, a notice may be oral or written.

(B) Except for receipt of the initial information and notice required to be given to a victim under divisions (A) and (B) of section 2930.04, section 2930.05, and divisions (A) and (B) of section 2930.06 of the Revised Code, a victim who wishes to receive any notice authorized by this chapter shall make a request for the notice to the prosecutor or the custodial agency that is to provide the notice, as specified in this chapter. If the victim does not make a request as described in this division, the prosecutor or custodial agency is not required to provide any notice described in this chapter other than the initial information and notice required to be given to a victim under divisions (A) and (B) of section 2930.04, section 2930.05, and divisions (A) and (B) of section 2930.06 of the Revised Code.

(C) A person or agency that is required to furnish notice under this chapter shall give the notice to the victim at the address or telephone number provided to the person or agency by the victim. A victim who requests to receive notice under this chapter as described in division (B) of this section shall inform the person or agency of the name, address, or telephone number of the victim and of any change to that information.

(D) A person or agency that has furnished information to a victim in accordance with any requirement or authorization under this chapter shall notify the victim promptly of any significant changes to that information.

(E) Divisions (A) to (D) of this section do not apply regarding a notice that a prosecutor is required to provide under section 2930.061 [2930.06.1] of the Revised Code. A prosecutor required to provide notice under that section shall provide the notice as specified in that section.

**HISTORY: 145 v S 186 (Eff 10-12-94); 146 v S 2. Eff 7-1-96; 150 v S 178, § 1, eff. 1-30-04.**

The effective date is set by section 6 of SB 2.

## § 2930.04 Information to be given to victim by investigating law enforcement agency.

(A) After its initial contact with a victim of a crime, the law enforcement agency responsible for investigating the crime promptly shall give to the victim, in writing, all of the following information:

(1) An explanation of the victim's rights under this chapter;

(2) Information about medical, counseling, housing, emergency, and any other services that are available to a victim;

(3) Information about compensation for victims under the reparations program in sections 2743.51 to 2743.72 of the Revised Code and the name, street address, and telephone number of the agency to contact to apply for an award of reparations under those sections;

(4) Information about protection that is available to the victim, including protective orders issued by a court.

(B) As soon as practicable after its initial contact with a victim of a crime, the law enforcement agency responsible for investigating the crime shall give to the victim all of the following information:

(1) The business telephone number of the law enforcement officer assigned to investigate the case;

(2) The office address and business telephone number of the prosecutor in the case;

(3) A statement that, if the victim is not notified of the arrest of the offender in the case within a reasonable period of time, the victim may contact the law enforcement agency to learn the status of the case.

(C) To the extent that the information required by this section is provided in the pamphlet prepared pursuant to section 109.42 of the Revised Code or in the information card or other material prepared pursuant to section 2743.71 of the Revised Code, the law enforcement agency may fulfill that portion of its obligations under this section by giving that pamphlet, information card, or other material to the victim.

**HISTORY: 145 v S 186 (Eff 10-12-94); 146 v S 2. Eff 7-1-96.**

The effective date is set by section 6 of SB 2.

## § 2930.05 Notice of arrest of defendant or alleged juvenile offender; affidavit concerning violence or intimidation.

(A) Within a reasonable period of time after the arrest or detention of a defendant or an alleged juvenile offender for a crime or specified delinquent act, the law enforcement agency that investigates the crime or specified delinquent act shall give the victim of the crime or specified delinquent act notice of all of the following:

(1) The arrest or detention;

(2) The name of the defendant or alleged juvenile offender;

(3) Whether the defendant or alleged juvenile offender is eligible for pretrial release or for release from detention;

(4) The telephone number of the law enforcement agency;

(5) The victim's right to telephone the agency to ascertain whether the defendant or alleged juvenile offender has been released from custody or from detention.

(B) If a defendant or alleged juvenile offender has been released from custody on a bond or personal recognizance or has been released from detention and the prosecutor in the case has received the affidavit of a victim stating that the defendant or alleged juvenile offender, or someone acting at the defendant's or alleged juvenile offender's direction, has committed or threatened to commit one or more acts of violence or intimidation against the victim, the victim's family, or the victim's representative, the prosecutor may file a motion asking the court to reconsider the conditions of the bond or personal recognizance granted to the defendant or alleged juvenile offender or to consider returning the defendant or alleged juvenile offender to detention.

**HISTORY: 145 v S 186 (Eff 10-12-94); 146 v S 2 (Eff 7-1-96); 148 v H 3. Eff 11-22-99.**

## § 2930.06 Prosecutor to confer with victim and provide information; notice of court proceedings.

(A) The prosecutor in a case, to the extent practicable, shall confer with the victim in the case before pretrial diversion is granted to the defendant or alleged juvenile offender in the case, before amending or dismissing an indictment, information, or complaint against that defendant or alleged juvenile offender, before agreeing to a negotiated plea for that defendant or alleged juvenile offender, before a trial of that defendant by judge or jury, or before the juvenile court conducts an adjudicatory hearing for that alleged juvenile offender. If the juvenile court disposes of a case prior to the prosecutor's involvement in the case, the court or a court employee shall notify the victim in the case that the alleged juvenile offender will be granted pretrial diversion, the complaint against that alleged juvenile offender will be amended or dismissed, or the court will conduct an adjudicatory hearing for that alleged juvenile offender. If the prosecutor fails to confer with the victim at any of those times, the court, if informed of the failure, shall note on the record the failure and the prosecutor's reasons for the failure. A prosecutor's failure to confer with a victim as required by this division and a court's failure to provide the notice as required by this division do not affect the validity of an agreement between the prosecutor and the defendant or alleged juvenile offender in the case, a pretrial diversion of the defendant or alleged juvenile offender, an amendment or dismissal of an indictment, information, or complaint filed against the defendant or alleged juvenile offender, a plea entered by the defendant or alleged juvenile defender, an admission entered by the defendant or alleged juvenile offender, or any other disposition in the case. A court shall not dismiss a criminal complaint, charge, information, or indictment or a delinquent child complaint solely at the request of the victim and over the objection of the prosecuting attorney, village solicitor, city director of law, or other chief legal officer responsible for the prosecution of the case.

(B) After a prosecution in a case has been commenced, the prosecutor or a designee of the prosecutor other than a court or court employee, to the extent practicable, promptly shall give the victim all of the following information, except that, if the juvenile court disposes of a case prior to the prosecutor's involvement in the case, the court or a court employee, to the extent practicable, promptly shall give the victim all of the following information:

(1) The name of the crime or specified delinquent act with which the defendant or alleged juvenile offender in the case has been charged and the name of the defendant or alleged juvenile offender;

(2) The file number of the case;

(3) A brief statement regarding the procedural steps in a criminal prosecution or delinquency proceeding involving a crime or specified delinquent act similar to the crime or specified delinquent act with which the defendant or alleged juvenile offender has been charged and the right of the victim to be present during all proceedings held throughout the prosecution of the case;

(4) A summary of the rights of a victim under this chapter;

(5) Procedures the victim or the prosecutor may follow if the victim becomes subject to threats or intimidation by the defendant, alleged juvenile offender, or any other person;

(6) The name and business telephone number of a person to contact for further information with respect to the case;

(7) The right of the victim to have a victim's representative exercise the victim's rights under this chapter in accordance with section 2930.02 of the Revised Code and the procedure by which a victim's representative may be designated;

(8) Notice that any notification under division (C) of this section, sections 2930.07 to 2930.19, and section 5139.56 of the Revised Code will be given to the victim only if the victim asks to receive the notification.

(C) Upon the request of the victim, the prosecutor or, if it is a delinquency proceeding and a prosecutor is not involved in the case, the court shall give the victim notice of the date, time, and place of any scheduled criminal or juvenile proceedings in the case and notice of any changes in those proceedings or in the schedule in the case.

(D) A victim who requests notice under division (C) of this section and who elects pursuant to division (B) of section 2930.03 of the Revised Code to receive any further notice from the prosecutor or, if it is a delinquency proceeding and a prosecutor is not involved in the case, the court under this chapter shall keep the prosecutor or the court informed of the victim's current address and telephone number until the case is dismissed or terminated, the defendant is acquitted or sentenced, the delinquent child complaint is dismissed, the defendant is adjudicated a delinquent child, or the appellate process is completed, whichever is the final disposition in the case.

(E) If a defendant is charged with the commission of a misdemeanor offense that is not identified in division (A)(2) of section 2930.01 of the Revised Code and if a police report or a complaint, indictment, or information that charges the commission of that offense and provides the basis for a criminal prosecution of that defendant identifies one or more individuals as individuals against whom that offense was committed, after a prosecution in the case has been commenced, the prosecutor or a designee of the prosecutor other than a court or court employee, to the extent practicable, promptly shall notify each of the individuals so identified in the report, complaint, indictment, or information that, if the defendant is convicted of or pleads guilty to the offense, the individual may make an oral or written statement to the court hearing the case regarding the sentence to be imposed upon the defendant and that the court must consider any statement so made that is relevant. Before imposing sentence in the case, the court shall permit the individuals so identified in the report, complaint, indictment, or information to make an oral or written statement. Division (A) of section 2930.14 of the Revised Code applies regarding any statement so made. The court shall consider a statement so made, in accordance with division (B) of that section and division (D) of section 2929.22 of the Revised Code.

**HISTORY: 145 v S 186 (Eff 10-12-94); 146 v S 2 (Eff 7-1-96); 146 v S 269 (Eff 7-1-96); 147 v S 98 (Eff 3-17-98); 148 v H 3. Eff 11-22-99; 149 v H 490, § 1, eff. 1-1-04.**

The effective date is set by section 4 of HB 490.

## § 2930.061 Written notice of charges sent to department of developmental disabilities.

(A) If a person is charged in a complaint, indictment, or information with any crime or specified delinquent act or with any other violation of law, and if the case involves a victim that the prosecutor in the case knows is a mentally retarded person or a developmentally disabled person, in addition to any other notices required under this chapter or under any other provision of law, the prosecutor in the case shall send written notice of the charges to the department of developmental disabilities. The written notice shall specifically identify the person so charged.

(B) As used in this section, "mentally retarded person" and "developmentally disabled person" have the same meanings as in section 5123.01 of the Revised Code.

**HISTORY: 150 v S 178, § 1, eff. 1-30-04; 153 v S 79, § 1, eff. 10-6-09.**

## § 2930.062 Certain victims of vehicle, streetcar, trackless trolley, aquatic device, or aircraft accident may notify prosecutor or court.

A victim described in division (H)(2) of section 2930.01 of the Revised Code may provide the prosecutor, or if it is a delinquency proceeding and a prosecutor is not involved in the case may provide the court, in the victim's case with written notification of the victim's injuries at any time. Upon receipt of the written notification, the prosecutor or court shall give the victim all of the information specified in division (B) of section 2930.06 if the prosecutor has not already done so.

**HISTORY: 151 v H 108, § 1, eff. 5-17-06.**

## § 2930.07 Concealment of victim's or representative's address, telephone number and similar identifying facts.

(A) If the prosecutor in a case determines that there are reasonable grounds for the victim in a case to be apprehensive regarding acts or threats of violence or intimidation by the defendant or alleged juvenile offender in the case or at the defendant's or alleged juvenile offender's direction against the victim, the victim's family, or the victim's representative, the prosecutor may file a motion with the court requesting that the court issue an order specifying that the victim and other witnesses in the case not be compelled in any phase of the criminal or delinquency proceeding to give testimony that would disclose the victim's or victim's representative's address, place of employment, or similar identifying fact without the victim's or victim's representative's consent. The court shall hold a hearing on the motion in chambers, and a court reporter shall make a record of the proceeding.

(B) If the court, pursuant to division (A) of this section, orders that the victim's or victim's representative's address, telephone number, place of employment, or other identifying fact shall be confidential, the court files or documents shall not contain that information unless it is used to identify the location of the crime or specified delinquent act. The hearing shall be recorded, and the court shall order the transcript sealed.

**HISTORY: 145 v S 186 (Eff 10-12-94); 146 v S 2 (Eff 7-1-96); 146 v S 269 (Eff 7-1-96); 148 v H 3. Eff 11-22-99.**

## § 2930.08 Notice of substantial delay in prosecution; victim's objections.

If a motion, request, or agreement between counsel is made in a case and the motion, request, or agreement might result in a substantial delay in the prosecution of the case, the prosecutor in the case, to the extent practicable and if the victim has requested notice pursuant to division (B) of section 2930.03 of the Revised Code, shall inform the victim that the motion, request, or agreement has been made and that it might result in a delay. If the victim objects to the delay, the prosecutor shall inform the court of the victim's objections, and the court shall consider the victim's objections in ruling on the motion, request, or agreement.

**HISTORY: 145 v S 186 (Eff 10-12-94); 146 v S 2. Eff 7-1-96.**

The effective date is set by section 6 of SB 2.

## § 2930.09 Presence of victim at proceedings; individual providing support.

A victim in a case may be present whenever the defendant or alleged juvenile offender in the case is present during any stage of the case against the defendant or alleged juvenile offender that is conducted on the record, other than a grand jury proceeding, unless the court determines that exclusion of the victim is necessary to protect the defendant's or alleged juvenile offender's right to a fair trial or to a fair delinquency proceeding. At any stage of the case at which the victim is present, the court, at the victim's request, shall permit the victim to be accompanied by an individual to provide support to the victim unless the court determines that exclusion of the individual is necessary to protect the defendant's or alleged juvenile offender's right to a fair trial or to a fair delinquency proceeding.

**HISTORY: 145 v S 186 (Eff 10-12-94); 146 v S 2 (Eff 7-1-96); 146 v S 269 (Eff 7-1-96); 148 v H 3. Eff 11-22-99.**

## § 2930.10 Minimization of unwanted contact between prosecution and defense sides.

(A) The court in which a criminal prosecution or delinquency proceeding is held shall make a reasonable effort to minimize any contact between the victim in the case, members of the victim's family, the victim's representative, or witnesses for the prosecution and the defendant or alleged juvenile offender in the case, members of the defendant's or alleged juvenile offender's family, or witnesses for the defense before, during, and immediately after all court proceedings.

(B) The court shall provide a waiting area for the victim, members of the victim's family, the victim's representative, or witnesses for the prosecution that is separate from the waiting area provided for the defendant or alleged juvenile offender, members of the defendant's or alleged juvenile offender's family, and defense witnesses if a separate waiting area is available and the use of the area is practical.

**HISTORY: 145 v S 186 (Eff 10-12-94); 146 v S 2 (Eff 7-1-96); 148 v H 3. Eff 11-22-99.**

## § 2930.11 Return or retention of victim's property.

(A) Except as otherwise provided in this section or in Chapter 2981. of the Revised Code, the law enforcement agency responsible for investigating a crime or specified delinquent act shall promptly return to the victim of the crime or specified delinquent act any property of the victim that was taken in the course of the investigation. In accordance with Criminal Rule 26 or an applicable juvenile rule, the law enforcement agency may take photographs of the property for use as evidence. If the ownership of the property is in dispute, the agency shall not return the property until the dispute is resolved.

(B) The law enforcement agency responsible for investigating a crime or specified delinquent act shall retain any property of the victim of the crime or specified delinquent act that is needed as evidence in the case, including any weapon used in the commission of the crime or specified delinquent act, if the prosecutor certifies to the court a need to retain the property in lieu of a photograph of the property or of another evidentiary substitute for the property itself.

(C) If the defendant or alleged juvenile offender in a case files a motion requesting the court to order the law enforcement agency to retain property of the victim because the property is needed for the defense in the case, the agency shall retain the property until the court rules on the motion. The court, in making a determination on the motion, shall weigh the victim's need for the property against the defendant's or alleged juvenile offender's assertion that the property has evidentiary value for the defense. The court shall rule on the motion in a timely fashion.

**HISTORY: 145 v S 186 (Eff 10-12-94); 146 v S 2 (Eff 7-1-96); 148 v H 3. Eff 11-22-99; 151 v H 241, § 1, eff. 7-1-07.**

See provisions of § 4 of 151 v H 241 following RC § 2901.01.

## § 2930.12 Notice of acquittal or conviction or of juvenile court dismissal or delinquency adjudication; inclusion of impact statement in presentence investigation report.

At the request of the victim in a criminal prosecution, the prosecutor shall give the victim notice of the defendant's acquittal or conviction. At the request of the victim in a delinquency proceeding, the prosecutor shall give the victim notice of the dismissal of the complaint against the alleged juvenile offender or of the adjudication of the alleged juvenile offender as a delinquent child, except that, if the juvenile court dismisses the complaint against the alleged juvenile offender or adjudicates the alleged juvenile offender a delinquent child prior to the prosecutor's involvement in the case, at the request of the victim, the court or a court employee shall give the victim notice of the dismissal or of the adjudication. If the defendant or alleged juvenile offender is convicted or is adjudicated a delinquent child, the notice shall include all of the following:

(A) The crimes or specified delinquent acts of which the defendant was convicted or for which the alleged juvenile offender was adjudicated a delinquent child;

(B) The address and telephone number of the probation office or other person, if any, that is to prepare a presentence investigation report pursuant to section 2951.03 of the Revised Code or Criminal Rule 32.2, the address and telephone number of the person, if any, who is to prepare a disposition investigation report pursuant to division (C)(1) of section 2152.18 of the Revised Code, and the address and telephone number of the person, if any, who is to prepare a victim impact statement pursuant to division (D)(1) of section 2152.19 or section 2947.051 of the Revised Code;

(C) Notice that the victim may make a statement about the impact of the crime or specified delinquent act to the probation officer or other person, if any, who prepares the presentence investigation report or to the person, if any, who prepares a victim impact statement, that a statement of the victim included in the report will be made available to the defendant or alleged juvenile offender unless the court exempts it from disclosure, and that the court may make the victim impact statement available to the defendant or alleged juvenile offender;

(D) Notice of the victim's right under section 2930.14 of the Revised Code to make a statement about the impact of the crime or specified delinquent act before sentencing or disposition;

(E) The date, time, and place of the sentencing hearing or dispositional hearing;

(F) One of the following:

(1) Any sentence imposed upon the defendant and any subsequent modification of that sentence, including modification under section 2929.20 or 5120.036 of the Revised Code or as a result of the defendant's appeal of the sentence pursuant to section 2953.08 of the Revised Code;

(2) Any disposition ordered for the defendant and any subsequent modification of that disposition, including judicial release or early release in accordance with section 2151.38 of the Revised Code.

**HISTORY: 145 v S 186 (Eff 10-12-94); 146 v S 2 (Eff 7-1-96); 148 v H 3 (Eff 11-22-99); 148 v S 179, § 3. Eff 1-1-2002; 2011 HB 86, § 1, eff. Sept. 30, 2011.**

The effective date is set by section 5 of SB 179.

## § 2930.13 Victim may make written or oral statement to person preparing impact statement.

(A) If the court orders the preparation of a victim impact statement pursuant to division (D)(1) of section 2152.19 or section 2947.051 [2947.05.1] of the Revised Code, the victim in the case may make a written or oral statement regarding the impact of the crime or specified delinquent act to the person whom the court orders to prepare the victim impact statement. A statement made by the victim under this section shall be included in the victim impact statement.

(B) If a probation officer or other person is preparing a presentence investigation report pursuant to section 2947.06 or 2951.03 of the Revised Code or Criminal Rule 32.2, or a disposition investigation report pursuant to section 2152.18 of the Revised Code, concerning the defendant or alleged juvenile offender in the case, the victim may make a written or oral statement regarding the impact of the crime or specified delinquent act to the probation officer or other person. The probation officer or other person shall use the statement in preparing the presentence investigation report or disposition investigation report and, upon the victim's request, shall include a written statement submitted by the victim in the presentence investigation report or disposition investigation report.

(C) A statement made by the victim under division (A) or (B) of this section may include the following:

(1) An explanation of the nature and extent of any physical, psychological, or emotional harm suffered by the victim as a result of the crime or specified delinquent act that is the basis of the case;

(2) An explanation of the extent of any property damage or other economic loss suffered by the victim as a result of that crime or specified delinquent act;

(3) An opinion regarding the extent to which, if any, the victim needs restitution for harm caused by the defendant or alleged juvenile offender as a result of that crime or specified delinquent act and information about whether the victim has applied for or received any compensation for loss or damage caused by that crime or specified delinquent act;

(4) The victim's recommendation for an appropriate sanction or disposition for the defendant or alleged juvenile offender regarding that crime or specified delinquent act.

(D) If a statement made by a victim under division (A) of this section is included in a victim impact statement, the provision, receipt, and retention of copies of, the use of, and the confidentiality, nonpublic record character, and sealing of the victim impact statement is governed by division (B)(2) of section 2152.20 or by division (C) of section 2947.051 [2947.05.1] of the Revised Code, as appropriate. If a statement made by a victim under division (B) of this section is included in a presentence investigation report prepared pursuant to section 2947.06 or 2951.03 of the Revised Code or Criminal Rule 32.2 or in a disposition investigation report pursuant to division (C)(1) of section 2152.18 of the Revised Code, the provision, receipt, and retention of copies of, the use of, and the confidentiality, nonpublic record character, and sealing of the presentence investigation report or disposition investigation report that contains the victim's statement is governed by section 2951.03 of the Revised Code.

**HISTORY: 145 v S 186 (Eff 10-12-94); 146 v S 2 (Eff 7-1-96); 146 v S 269 (Eff 7-1-96); 148 v H 3 (Eff 11-22-99); 148 v S 179, § 3. Eff 1-1-2002; 151 v H 137, § 1, eff. 10-9-06.**

The effective date is set by § 6 of 151 v H 137.
The effective date is set by section 5 of SB 179.

## § 2930.14 Victim may make statement prior to sentencing or disposition of juvenile; defendant's or juvenile's opportunity to respond.

(A) Before imposing sentence upon, or entering an order of disposition for, a defendant or alleged juvenile offender for the commission of a crime or specified delinquent act, the court shall permit the victim of the crime or specified delinquent act to make a statement. The court may give copies of any written statement made by a victim to the defendant or alleged juvenile offender and defendant's or alleged juvenile offender's counsel and may give any written statement made by the defendant or alleged juvenile offender to the victim and the prosecutor. The court may redact any information contained in a written statement that the court determines is not relevant to and will not be relied upon in the sentencing or disposition decision. The written statement of the victim or of the defendant or alleged juvenile offender is confidential and is not a public record as used in section 149.43 of the Revised Code. Any person to whom a copy of a written statement was released by the court shall return it to the court immediately following sentencing or disposition.

(B) The court shall consider a victim's statement made under division (A) of this section along with other factors that the court is required to consider in imposing sentence or in determining the order of disposition. If the statement includes new material facts, the court shall not rely on the new material facts unless it continues the sentencing or dispositional proceeding or takes other appropriate action to allow the defendant or alleged juvenile offender an adequate opportunity to respond to the new material facts.

**HISTORY: 145 v S 186 (Eff 10-12-94); 146 v S 2 (Eff 7-1-96); 148 v H 3. Eff 11-22-99.**

## § 2930.15 Notice of filing of appeal; victim's rights after return to trial court.

(A) If a defendant is convicted of committing a crime against a victim or an alleged juvenile offender is adjudicated a delinquent child for committing a specified delinquent act against a victim, if the victim requests notice of the filing of an appeal, and if the defendant or alleged juvenile offender files an appeal, the prosecutor in the case promptly shall notify the victim of the appeal. The prosecutor also shall give the victim all of the following information:

(1) A brief explanation of the appellate process, including the possible disposition of the case;

(2) Whether the defendant or alleged juvenile offender has been released on bail or other recognizance or under conditions imposed by the juvenile court pending the disposition of the appeal;

(3) The time, place, and location of appellate court proceedings and any subsequent changes in the time, place, or location of those proceedings;

(4) The result of the appeal.

(B) If the appellate court returns the defendant's or alleged juvenile offender's case to the trial court or juvenile court for further proceedings, the victim may exercise all the rights that previously were available to the victim in the trial court or the juvenile court.

**HISTORY: 145 v S 186 (Eff 10-12-94); 146 v S 2 (Eff 7-1-96); 148 v H 3. Eff 11-22-99.**

## § 2930.16 Notice of defendant's incarceration and release date or of juvenile's commitment; prior notice of events affecting release or of defendant's escape or death.

(A) If a defendant is incarcerated, a victim in a case who has requested to receive notice under this section shall be given notice of the incarceration of the defendant. If an alleged juvenile offender is committed to the temporary custody of a school, camp, institution, or other facility operated for the care of delinquent children or to the legal custody of the department of youth services, a victim in a case who has requested to receive notice under this section shall be given notice of the commitment. Promptly after sentence is imposed upon the defendant or the commitment of the alleged juvenile offender is ordered, the prosecutor in the case shall notify the victim of the date on which the defendant will be released from confinement or the prosecutor's reasonable estimate of that date or the date on which the alleged juvenile offender will have served the minimum period of commitment or the prosecutor's reasonable estimate of that date. The prosecutor also shall notify the victim of the name of the custodial agency of the defendant or alleged juvenile offender and tell the victim how to contact that custodial agency. If the custodial agency is the department of rehabilitation and correction, the prosecutor shall notify the victim of the services offered by the office of victims' services pursuant to section 5120.60 of the Revised Code. If the custodial agency is the department of youth services, the prosecutor shall notify the victim of the services provided by the office of victims' services within the release authority of the department pursuant to section 5139.55 of the Revised Code and the victim's right pursuant to section 5139.56 of the Revised Code to submit a written request to the release authority to be notified of actions the release authority takes with respect to the alleged juvenile offender. The victim shall keep the custodial agency informed of the victim's current address and telephone number.

(B)(1) Upon the victim's request, the prosecutor promptly shall notify the victim of any hearing for judicial release of the defendant pursuant to section 2929.20 of the Revised Code, of any hearing for release of the defendant pursuant to section 2967.19 of the Revised Code, or of any hearing for judicial release or early release of the alleged juvenile offender pursuant to section 2151.38 of the Revised Code and of the victim's right to make a statement under those sections. The court shall notify the victim of its ruling in each of those hearings and on each of those applications.

(2) If an offender is sentenced to a prison term pursuant to division (A)(3) or (B) of section 2971.03 of the Revised Code, upon the request of the victim of the crime, the prosecutor promptly shall notify the victim of any hearing to be conducted pursuant to section 2971.05 of the Revised Code to determine whether to modify the requirement that the offender serve the entire prison term in a state correctional facility in accordance with division (C) of that section, whether to continue, revise, or revoke

any existing modification of that requirement, or whether to terminate the prison term in accordance with division (D) of that section. The court shall notify the victim of any order issued at the conclusion of the hearing.

(C) Upon the victim's request made at any time before the particular notice would be due, the custodial agency of a defendant or alleged juvenile offender shall give the victim any of the following notices that is applicable:

(1) At least three weeks before the adult parole authority recommends a pardon or commutation of sentence for the defendant or at least three weeks prior to a hearing before the adult parole authority regarding a grant of parole to the defendant, notice of the victim's right to submit a statement regarding the impact of the defendant's release in accordance with section 2967.12 of the Revised Code and, if applicable, of the victim's right to appear at a full board hearing of the parole board to give testimony as authorized by section 5149.101 of the Revised Code;

(2) At least three weeks before the defendant is transferred to transitional control under section 2967.26 of the Revised Code, notice of the pendency of the transfer and of the victim's right under that section to submit a statement regarding the impact of the transfer;

(3) At least thirty days before the release authority of the department of youth services holds a release review, release hearing, or discharge review for the alleged juvenile offender, notice of the pendency of the review or hearing, of the victim's right to make an oral or written statement regarding the impact of the crime upon the victim or regarding the possible release or discharge, and, if the notice pertains to a hearing, of the victim's right to attend and make statements or comments at the hearing as authorized by section 5139.56 of the Revised Code;

(4) Prompt notice of the defendant's or alleged juvenile offender's escape from a facility of the custodial agency in which the defendant was incarcerated or in which the alleged juvenile offender was placed after commitment, of the defendant's or alleged juvenile offender's absence without leave from a mental health or mental retardation and developmental disabilities facility or from other custody, and of the capture of the defendant or alleged juvenile offender after an escape or absence;

(5) Notice of the defendant's or alleged juvenile offender's death while in confinement or custody;

(6) Notice of the defendant's or alleged juvenile offender's release from confinement or custody and the terms and conditions of the release.

**HISTORY: 145 v S 186 (Eff 10-12-94); 146 v S 2 (Eff 7-1-96); 146 v H 180 (Eff 1-1-97); 147 v S 111 (Eff 3-17-98); 148 v H 3. Eff 11-22-99; 150 v H 375, § 1, eff. 4-29-05; 150 v H 473, § 1, eff. 4-29-05; 151 v S 260, § 1, eff. 1-2-07; 152 v S 10, § 1, eff. 1-1-08; 2011 HB 86, § 1, eff. Sept. 30, 2011.**

The effective date is set by § 3 of 152 v S 10.

The provisions of § 3(A) of 151 v S 260 read as follows:

SECTION 3. (A) Section 2930.16 of the Revised Code is presented in this act as a composite of the section as amended by both Am. Sub. H.B. 375 and Am. Sub. H.B. 473 of the 125th General Assembly. The General Assembly, applying the principle stated in division (B) of section 1.52 of the Revised Code that amendments are to be harmonized if reasonably capable of simultaneous operation, finds that the composite is the resulting version of the section in effect prior to the effective date of the section as presented in this act.

See provisions, § 4 of HB 180 (146 v —) following RC § 2921.34.

## § 2930.17 Victim's statement prior to granting of judicial or early release.

(A) In determining whether to grant a judicial release to a defendant from a prison term pursuant to section 2929.20 of the Revised Code at a time before the defendant's stated prison term expires, in determining whether to grant a release to an offender from a prison term pursuant to section 2967.19 of the Revised Code at a time before the offender's stated prison term expires, or in determining whether to grant a judicial release or early release to an alleged juvenile offender from a commitment to the department of youth services pursuant to section 2151.38 of the Revised Code, the court shall permit a victim of a crime or specified delinquent act for which the defendant or alleged juvenile offender was incarcerated or committed to make a statement, in addition to any other statement made under this chapter, concerning the effects of that crime or specified delinquent act on the victim, the circumstances surrounding the crime or specified delinquent act, the manner in which the crime or specified delinquent act was perpetrated, and the victim's opinion whether the defendant or alleged juvenile offender should be released. The victim may make the statement in writing or orally, at the court's discretion. The court shall give the defendant or alleged juvenile offender and either the adult parole authority or the department of youth services, whichever is applicable, a copy of any written impact statement made by the victim under this division.

(B) In deciding whether to grant a judicial release or early release to the defendant or alleged juvenile offender, the court shall consider a statement made by the victim under division (A) of this section or section 2930.14 or 2947.051 of the Revised Code.

**HISTORY: 145 v S 186 (Eff 10-12-94); 146 v S 2 (Eff 7-1-96); 148 v H 3. Eff 11-22-99; 2011 HB 86, § 1, eff. Sept. 30, 2011.**

## § 2930.18 Prohibited actions by employer of victim.

No employer of a victim shall discharge, discipline, or otherwise retaliate against the victim, a member of the victim's family, or a victim's representative for participating, at the prosecutor's request, in preparation for a criminal or delinquency proceeding or for attendance, pursuant to a subpoena, at a criminal or delinquency proceeding if the attendance is reasonably necessary to protect the interests of the victim. This section generally does not require an employer to pay an employee for time lost as a result of attendance at a criminal or delinquency proceeding. An employer who knowingly violates this section is in contempt of court. This section does not limit or affect the application to any person of section 2151.211 [2151.21.1], 2939.121 [2939.12.1], or 2945.451 [2945.45.1] of the Revised Code.

**HISTORY: 145 v S 186 (Eff 10-12-94); 146 v S 2 (Eff 7-1-96); 148 v H 3. Eff 11-22-99.**

## § 2930.19 Prosecutor's duty to seek compliance; effect of violations; conflicting statutes; incarcerated victims.

(A) In a manner consistent with the duty of a prosecutor to represent the interests of the public as a whole, a prosecutor shall seek compliance with this chapter on behalf of a victim, a member of the victim's family, or the victim's representative.

(B) The failure of a public official or public agency to comply with the requirements of this chapter does not give rise to a claim for damages against that public official or public agency, except that a public agency as an employer may be held responsible for a violation of section 2930.18 of the Revised Code.

(C) The failure of any person or entity to provide a right, privilege, or notice to a victim under this chapter does not constitute grounds for declaring a mistrial or new trial, for setting aside a conviction, sentence, adjudication, or disposition, or for granting postconviction release to a defendant or alleged juvenile offender.

(D) If there is a conflict between a provision in this chapter and a specific statute governing the procedure in a case involving a capital offense, the specific statute supersedes the provision in this chapter.

(E) If the victim of a crime is incarcerated in a state or local correctional facility or is in the legal custody of the department of youth services, the victim's rights under this chapter may be modified by court order to prevent any security risk, hardship, or undue burden upon a public official or public agency with a duty under this chapter.

**HISTORY: 145 v S 186 (Eff 10-12-94); 146 v S 2 (Eff 7-1-96); 148 v H 3. Eff 11-22-99.**

# CHAPTER 2931: JURISDICTION; VENUE

*For text of the Ohio Rules of Criminal Procedure, see page 1629*



## [JURISDICTION]

### § 2931.01 Definition of magistrate.

As used in Chapters 2931. to 2953. of the Revised Code:

(A) "Magistrate" includes county court judges, police justices, mayors of municipal corporation[s], and judges of other courts inferior to the court of common pleas.

(B) "Judge" does not include the probate judge.

(C) "Court" does not include the probate court.

(D) "Clerk" does not include the clerk of the probate court.

**HISTORY: GC § 13422-1; 113 v 123; 114 v 320(479); Bureau of Code Revision, 10-1-53; 127 v 1039(1096) (Eff 1-1-58); 136 v H 205. Eff 1-1-76.**

The effective date is set by section 4 of HB 205.

### § 2931.02 Jurisdiction of county court judges.

A judge of a county court is a conservator of the peace and has jurisdiction in criminal cases throughout his area of jurisdiction. He may hear complaints of [breach of] the peace and issue search warrants. Judges of county courts have jurisdiction on sworn complaint, to issue a warrant for the arrest of a person charged with the commission of a felony where it is made to appear that such person has fled or is outside this state and it is necessary or desirable to extradite such person. Judges of county courts have jurisdiction within their respective areas of jurisdiction in all cases of violation of any law relating to:

(A) Adulteration or deception in the sale of dairy products and other food, drink, drugs, and medicines;

(B) Prevention of cruelty to animals and children;

(C) The abandonment, nonsupport, or ill treatment of a child under eighteen years of age or a physically and mentally handicapped child under the age of eighteen years by its parents;

(D) The abandonment, or ill treatment of a child under eighteen years of age or a physically and mentally handicapped child under the age of eighteen years by its guardian;

(E) The employment of a child under fourteen years of age in public exhibitions or vocations injurious to health, life, or morals, or which will cause or permit him to suffer unnecessary physical or mental pain;

(F) The regulation, restriction, or prohibition of the employment of females and minors;

(G) The torturing, unlawfully punishing, ill treating, or depriving anyone of necessary food, clothing, or shelter;

(H) Any violation of Chapters 4301. and 4303. of the Revised Code, or keeping a place where intoxicating liquor is sold, given away, or furnished in violation of any law prohibiting such acts;

(I) The shipping, selling, using, permitting the use of, branding, or having unlawful quantities of illuminating oil for or in a mine;

(J) The sale, shipment, or adulteration of commercial feeds;

(K) The use of dust-creating machinery in workshops and factories;

(L) The conducting of a pharmacy, or retail drug or chemical store, or the dispensing or selling of drugs, chemicals, poisons, or pharmaceutical preparations therein;

(M) The failure to place and keep in a sanitary condition a bakery, confectionery, creamery, dairy barn, milk depot, laboratory, hotel, restaurant, eating house, packing house, slaughterhouse, ice cream factory, or place where a food product is manufactured, packed, stored, deposited, collected, prepared, produced, or sold for any purpose, or for the violation of any law relating to public health;

(N) Inspection of steam boilers, and of laws licensing steam engineers and boiler operators;

(O) Prevention of short weighing and measuring and all violations of the weights and measures laws;

(P) Laws relating to the practice of medicine or surgery, or any of its branches;

(Q) Laws relating to the filling or refilling of registered containers by other than the owner, or the defacing of the marks of ownership thereon;

(R) Offenses arising from or growing out of the violation of conservation laws.

**HISTORY: GC § 13422-2; 113 v 123; 117 v 586; Bureau of Code Revision, 10-1-53; 127 v 1039(1096) (Eff 1-1-58); 128 v 823(859) (Eff 11-6-59); 132 v S 65 (Eff 11-17-67); 133 v H 1 (Eff 3-18-69); 135 v S 1. Eff 1-1-74.**

### § 2931.03 Jurisdiction of court of common pleas.

The court of common pleas has original jurisdiction of all crimes and offenses, except in cases of minor offenses the exclusive jurisdiction of which is vested in courts inferior to the court of common pleas.

A judge of a court of common pleas does not have the authority to dismiss a criminal complaint, charge, information, or indictment solely at the request of the complaining witness and over the objection of the prosecuting attorney or other chief legal officer who is responsible for the prosecution of the case.

**HISTORY: GC § 13422-5; 113 v 123, § 5; Bureau of Code Revision, 10-1-53; 147 v S 98. Eff 3-17-98.**

## § 2931.04 Jurisdiction of municipal courts not affected.

Sections 2931.01 to 2931.03, inclusive, of the Revised Code, do not affect, modify, or limit the jurisdiction of municipal courts. All municipal court judges have jurisdiction within the territory for which they were elected or appointed in all cases of violation of Chapters 4301. and 4303. of the Revised Code and of prosecutions for keeping a place where intoxicating liquor is sold, given away, or furnished, in violation of any law prohibiting such acts.

**HISTORY: GC § 13422-6; 113 v 123, § 6; 115 v PtII, 118(164), § 62; Bureau of Code Revision, 10-1-53; 128 v 823(861). Eff 11-6-59.**

## § 2931.041 Repealed, 141 v H 158, § 2 [128 v 141; 129 v 582 (748)]. Eff 3-17-87.

This section concerned jurisdiction of municipal courts in criminal cases.

## § 2931.05 Repealed, 128 v 97(116), § 2 [GC § 13423-1; 113 v 123; Bureau of Code Revision, 10-1-53; 127 v 1039]. Eff 1-1-60.

This section concerned bills of exception in summary convictions.

## § 2931.06 Special constables in certain townships.

When the constables in a township situated on and consisting in whole or in part of one or more islands in a lake in this state, or in a township adjoining or abutting on lands belonging to a state or national home for disabled volunteer soldiers or a disabled volunteer soldiers' home, are insufficient to maintain the peace and enforce the laws for the preservation of order therein, a judge of the county court having jurisdiction in [such] township may appoint not more than ten special constables to be conservators of the peace within such township and with powers of constables in criminal causes. The appointing judge shall enter such appointments upon his docket and they shall continue in force for one year unless revoked by him. Such special constables shall receive like fees as are paid for similar services to regular constables.

**HISTORY: GC § 13423-2; 113 v 123, ch 2, § 2; Bureau of Code Revision, 10-1-53; 127 v 1039(1097). Eff 1-1-58.**

## § 2931.07 Recognizance.

Recognizances taken by a judge of a county court or other officer authorized to take them, may be returned to the court of common pleas.

Such recognizances shall be returned to such court forthwith after the commitment of the accused, or after the taking of a recognizance for his appearance before such court. The prosecuting attorney may proceed with the prosecution in such court, and the accused shall appear therein and answer to his recognizance.

**HISTORY: GC §§ 13423-2a, b; 114 v 320(480), § 3; Bureau of Code Revision, 10-1-53; 127 v 1039(1098). Eff 1-1-58.**

## § 2931.08 Repealed, 141 v H 158, § 2 [GC §§ 13423-3½13423-5; 113 v 123, ch 2, §§ 3-5; Bureau of Code Revision, 10-1-53; 125 v S 361; 127 v 1039(1098); 141 v S 54]. Eff 3-17-87.

This section concerned payment of fines to county treasury by judge of county court.

## § 2931.09 Repealed, 141 v H 158, § 2 [GC §§ 13423-3½13423-5; 113 v 123, ch 2, §§ 3-5; Bureau of Code Revision, 10-1-53; 125 v S 361; 127 v 1039(1098); 141 v S 54]. Eff 3-17-87.

This section concerned payment of fines to county treasury by judge of county court.

## § 2931.10 Repealed, 141 v H 158, § 2 [GC §§ 13423-3½13423-5; 113 v 123, ch 2, §§ 3-5; Bureau of Code Revision, 10-1-53; 125 v S 361; 127 v 1039(1098); 141 v S 54]. Eff 3-17-87.

This section concerned payment of fines to county treasury by judge of county court.

## § 2931.11 Repealed, 128 v 97(116), § 2 [GC §§ 13424-1, 13424-2; 113 v 123; Bureau of Code Revision, 10-1-53]. Eff 1-1-60.

This section provided for jury trial before a magistrate and venire of jurors in magistrate's court.

## § 2931.12 Repealed, 128 v 97(116), § 2 [GC §§ 13424-1, 13424-2; 113 v 123; Bureau of Code Revision, 10-1-53]. Eff 1-1-60.

This section provided for jury trial before a magistrate and venire of jurors in magistrate's court.

## § 2931.13 Repealed, 128 v 97(116), § 2 [GC §§ 13424-3, 13424-4; 113 v 123; Bureau of Code Revision, 10-1-53]. Eff 1-1-60.

This section concerned challenges to jurors and the need for the information or affidavit on which charge is based to indicate it is a subsequent offense.

## § 2931.14 Repealed, 128 v 97(116), § 2 [GC §§ 13424-3, 13424-4; 113 v 123; Bureau of Code Revision, 10-1-53]. Eff 1-1-60.

This section concerned challenges to jurors and the need for the information or affidavit on which charge is based to indicate it is a subsequent offense.

## § 2931.15 New trial†.

In prosecutions before a magistrate, a defendant who has been found guilty upon the verdict of a jury or by the decision of the magistrate without the intervention of a jury may[,] upon written application filed within three days after the verdict or decision, be granted a new trial in like manner and for like reasons as provided by sections 2945.79 to 2945.83, inclusive, of the Revised Code.

**HISTORY: GC § 13424-5; 113 v 123, ch 3, § 5; Bureau of Code Revision, 10-1-53; 128 v 141. Eff 1-1-60.**

† This section was repealed by the 103rd General Assembly in S 73 (128 v 97 [116]) passed July 21, 1959, filed August 7, 1959 and effective January 1, 1960. However, amendment in S 133 (128 v 141) was passed July 23, 1959, filed August 12, 1959 and effective January 1, 1960. Apparently, the amendment prevails.

## § 2931.16 Repealed, 128 v 97 (116), § 2 [GC §§ 13424-6, 13424-7; 113 v 123; Bureau of Code Revision, 10-1-53]. Eff 1-1-60.

This section referred to jurors' fees and security for costs of prosecution payable from county treasury.

## § 2931.17 Repealed, 128 v 97 (116), § 2 [GC §§ 13424-6, 13424-7; 113 v 123; Bureau of Code Revision, 10-1-53]. Eff 1-1-60.

This section referred to jurors' fees and security for costs of prosecution payable from county treasury.

## § 2931.18 Humane society may employ attorneys.

A humane society or its agent may employ an attorney, and may also employ one or more assistant attorneys to prosecute violations of law relating to:

(A) Prevention of cruelty to animals or children;

(B) Abandonment, nonsupport, or ill-treatment of a child by its parent;

(C) Employment of a child under fourteen years of age in public exhibitions or vocations injurious to health, life, or morals or which cause or permit such child to suffer unnecessary physical or mental pain;

(D) Neglect or refusal of an adult to support destitute parent. Such attorneys shall be paid out of the county treasury in an amount approved as just and reasonable by the board of county commissioners of that county.

**HISTORY: GC § 13424-8; 113 v 123, ch 3, § 8; Bureau of Code Revision, 10-1-53; 130 v 664 (Eff 10-8-63); 142 v H 246. Eff 12-12-88.**

## § 2931.19 Repealed, 134 v H 511, § 2 [GC §§ 13426-3—13426-5; 113 v 123; Bureau of Code Revision, 10-1-53; 126 v 812]. Eff 1-1-74.

This section concerned venue. See now RC § 2901.12 and Crim R 18.

## § 2931.20 Repealed, 134 v H 511, § 2 [GC §§ 13426-3—13426-5; 113 v 123; Bureau of Code Revision, 10-1-53; 126 v 812]. Eff 1-1-74.

This section concerned venue. See now RC § 2901.12 and Crim R 18.

## § 2931.21 Repealed, 134 v H 511, § 2 [GC §§ 13426-3—13426-5; 113 v 123; Bureau of Code Revision, 10-1-53; 126 v 812]. Eff 1-1-74.

This section concerned venue. See now RC § 2901.12 and Crim R 18.

## § 2931.22 Repealed, 134 v H 511, § 2 [GC §§ 13426-6—13426-8; 113 v 123; Bureau of Code Revision, 10-1-53]. Eff 1-1-74.

This section concerned venue.

## § 2931.23 Repealed, 134 v H 511, § 2 [GC §§ 13426-6—13426-8; 113 v 123; Bureau of Code Revision, 10-1-53]. Eff 1-1-74.

This section concerned venue.

## § 2931.24 Repealed, 134 v H 511, § 2 [GC §§ 13426-6—13426-8; 113 v 123; Bureau of Code Revision, 10-1-53]. Eff 1-1-74.

This section concerned venue.

## § 2931.25 Repealed, 134 v H 511, § 2 [GC §§ 13426-9, 13426-10; 113 v 123; Bureau of Code Revision, 10-1-53]. Eff 1-1-74.

This section concerned venue.

## § 2931.26 Repealed, 134 v H 511, § 2 [GC §§ 13426-9, 13426-10; 113 v 123; Bureau of Code Revision, 10-1-53]. Eff 1-1-74.

This section concerned venue.

## § 2931.27 Repealed, 134 v H 511, § 2 [GC §§ 13426-11, 13426-12; 113 v 123; 115 v 532; Bureau of Code Revision, 10-1-53]. Eff 1-1-74.

This section concerned venue.

## § 2931.28 Repealed, 134 v H 511, § 2 [GC §§ 13426-11, 13426-12; 113 v 123; 115 v 532; Bureau of Code Revision, 10-1-53]. Eff 1-1-74.

This section concerned venue.

### [CHANGE OF VENUE]

## § 2931.29 Procedure on change of venue.

When a change of venue is ordered pursuant to section 2901.12 of the Revised Code, the clerk of the court in which the cause is pending shall make a certified transcript of the proceedings in the case, which, with the original affidavit, complaint, indictment, or information, he shall transmit to the clerk of the court to which said case is sent for trial, and the trial shall be conducted as if the cause had originated in the jurisdiction of the latter court. The prosecuting attorney, city director of law, or other officer who would have prosecuted the case in the court in which the cause originated shall take charge of and try the cause, and the court to which the cause is sent may on application appoint one or more attorneys to assist the prosecutor in the trial, and allow the appointed attorneys reasonable compensation.

**HISTORY: GC § 13427-1; 113 v 123, ch 6; Bureau of Code Revision, 10-1-53; 134 v H 511 (Eff 1-1-74); 137 v H 219. Eff 11-1-77.**

## § 2931.30 Transfer of prisoner on change of venue.

When a change of venue is ordered pursuant to section 2901.12 of the Revised Code, and the accused is in jail, a warrant shall be issued by the clerk of the court in which the cause originated, directed to the proper officer, commanding him to convey the prisoner to the jail of the county or municipal corporation where the prisoner is to be tried, there to be kept until discharged. If the accused is charged with a bailable offense, and at the date of the order changing the venue is under bond for his appearance at the court from which the venue is changed, the court may fix in said order the amount of recognizance which said accused shall give for his appearance at the time the court may designate, in the court to which the venue is changed, and the clerk shall take such recognizance as in other cases, and forward the same with the record. The court shall recognize the witnesses of the prosecution to appear before the court in which the accused is to be tried.

**HISTORY: GC § 13427-2; 113 v 123, ch 6, § 2; Bureau of Code Revision, 10-1-53; 134 v H 511. Eff 1-1-74.**

## § 2931.31 Payment of costs and expenses on change of venue.

The reasonable expenses of the officer acting as prosecutor, incurred in consequence of a change of venue under section 2901.12 of the Revised Code, the fees of the clerk of the court to which the venue is changed, the sheriff or bailiff, and of the jury shall be allowed and paid out of the treasury of the county in which said cause originated.

**HISTORY: GC § 13427-3; 113 v 123, ch 6, § 3; Bureau of Code Revision, 10-1-53; 134 v H 511. Eff 1-1-74.**

## § 2931.32 Repealed, 134 v H 511, § 2 [GC § 13426-2; 113 v 123; Bureau of Code Revision, 10-1-53]. Eff 1-1-74.

This section concerned offenses on or near county boundaries.

# CHAPTER 2933: PEACE WARRANTS; SEARCH WARRANTS



## § 2933.01 Definition of magistrate.

The definition of "magistrate" set forth in section 2931.01 of the Revised Code applies to Chapter 2933 of the Revised Code.

**HISTORY: Bureau of Code Revision. Eff 10-1-53.**

[PEACE WARRANT]

## § 2933.02 Complaint to keep the peace.

When a complaint is made in writing and upon oath, filed with a municipal or county court or a mayor sitting as the judge of a mayor's court, and states that the complainant has just cause to fear and fears that another individual will commit an offense against the person or property of the complainant or his ward or child, a municipal or county court judge or mayor shall issue to the sheriff or to any other appropriate peace officer, as defined in section 2935.01 of the Revised Code, within the territorial jurisdiction of the court, a warrant in the name of the state that commands him forthwith to arrest and take the individual complained of before the court to answer the complaint.

**HISTORY: GC § 13428-1; 113 v 123, ch 7, § 1; Bureau of Code Revision, 10-1-53; 141 v H 412. Eff 3-17-87.**

## § 2933.03 Form of warrant to keep the peace.

Warrants issued under section 2933.02 of the Revised Code shall be substantially in the following form:

The state of Ohio, ....... County, ss:

To the sheriff or other appropriate peace officer, greeting:

Whereas, a complaint has been filed by one C. D., in writing and upon oath, stating that he has just cause to fear and does fear that one E. F. will (here state the threatened injury or violence according to the fact as sworn to).

These are therefore to command you to forthwith arrest E. F. and bring him before this court to show cause why he should not find surety to keep the peace and be of good behavior toward the citizens of the state generally, and C. D. especially, and for his appearance before the proper court.

Given under my hand, this ....... day of...
A. B., Judge,................................County Court;
Judge,.....................................Municipal Court;
Mayor,........................................Mayor's Court

**HISTORY: GC § 13428-2; 113 v 123, ch 7, § 2; Bureau of Code Revision, 10-1-53; 127 v 1039(1099) (Eff 1-1-58); 141 v H 412. Eff 3-17-87.**

## § 2933.04 Arraignment.

When the accused in [is] brought before the municipal, county, or mayor's court pursuant to sections 2933.02 and 2933.03 of the Revised Code, he shall be heard in his defense. If it is necessary for just cause to adjourn the hearing, the municipal or county court judge or mayor involved may order such adjournment. The judge or mayor also may direct the sheriff or other peace officer having custody of the accused to detain him in the county jail or other appropriate detention facility until the cause of delay is removed, unless a bond in a sum fixed by the judge or mayor but not to exceed five hundred dollars, with sufficient surety, is given by the accused. A delay shall not exceed two days.

**HISTORY: GC § 13428-3; 113 v 123(133), ch 7, § 3; Bureau of Code Revision, 10-1-53; 141 v H 412. Eff 3-17-87.**

## § 2933.05 Hearing; discharge, bond, or commitment.

The municipal or county court judge or mayor sitting as the judge of a mayor's court, upon the appearance of the parties pursuant to sections 2933.02 to 2933.04 of the Revised Code, shall hear the witnesses under oath and do one of the following:

(A) Discharge the accused, render judgment against the complainant for costs, and award execution for the costs;

(B) Order the accused to enter into a bond of not less than fifty or more than five hundred dollars, with sufficient surety, to keep the peace and be of good behavior for such time as may be just, render judgment against him for costs, and award execution for the costs.

In default of such bond, the judge or mayor shall commit the accused to the county jail or other appropriate detention facility, until such order is complied with or he is discharged.

**HISTORY: RS §§ 7109, 7110; 66 v 288, §§ 3, 5; 71 v 70, § 2; GC §§ 13428-4, 13428-5; 107 v 402; 113 v 123(133), ch 7, §§ 4, 5; Bureau of Code Revision, 10-1-53; 141 v H 412. Eff 3-17-87.**

## § 2933.06 Appeal; bond; transcript.

The accused under sections 2933.02 to 2933.05 of the Revised Code may appeal from the decision of a municipal or county court judge to the appropriate court of appeals or from the decision of a mayor sitting as the judge of a mayor's court to the appropriate municipal or county court. An appeal from the decision of a municipal or county court judge to the appropriate court of appeals shall be only as to questions of law and, to the extent that sections 2933.06 to 2933.09 of the Revised Code do not contain relevant provisions, shall be made and proceed in accordance with the Rules of Appellate Procedure. An appeal from the decision of a mayor sitting as the judge of a mayor's court to the appropriate municipal or county court shall be as to questions of law and fact, and shall be made and proceed in accordance with sections 2933.06 to 2933.09 of the Revised Code.

In connection with either type of appeal, the accused shall file with the clerk of the municipal, county, or mayor's court, within ten days after the decision is rendered, an appeal bond in a sum to be fixed by the judge or mayor at not less than fifty or more than five hundred dollars, with surety to be approved by the judge or mayor, conditioned that, pending the determination of the appeal, the accused will keep the peace and will be of good behavior generally and especially towards the person named in the complaint. Upon the filing of the appeal bond, the clerk of the municipal, county, or mayor's court forthwith shall make a certified transcript of the proceedings in the action, the appeal bond to be included. Upon the payment by the appellant of the fee for the transcript, the clerk immediately shall file the transcript and all the original papers in the action in the office of the clerk of the appellate court.

**HISTORY: GC § 13428-6; 113 v 123(133), ch 7, § 6; Bureau of Code Revision, 10-1-53; 141 v H 412. Eff 3-17-87.**

## § 2933.07 Discharge on failure to prosecute.

In the case of an appeal from the decision of a mayor sitting as the judge of a mayor's court to the appropriate municipal or county court, no further pleadings shall be required. If the complainant fails to prosecute in such an appeal, the accused shall be discharged unless good cause to the contrary is shown, and the municipal or county court shall render judgment against the complainant for the costs of prosecution and award execution for the costs.

**HISTORY: GC § 13428-7; 113 v 123(134), ch 7, § 7; Bureau of Code Revision, 10-1-53; 141 v H 412. Eff 3-17-87.**

## § 2933.08 Hearing; judgment.

In the case of an appeal from the decision of a mayor sitting as the judge of a mayor's court to the appropriate municipal or county court, the municipal or county court shall set a time for the hearing of that appeal and, at that time, shall hear the witnesses under oath, and either discharge the accused, render judgment against the complainant for costs, and award execution for the costs, or order the accused to enter into a bond, for such time as may be just, to keep the peace and be of good behavior, render judgment against him for costs, and award execution for the costs.

**HISTORY: GC § 13428-8; 113 v 123(134), ch 7, § 8; Bureau of Code Revision, 10-1-53; 141 v H 412. Eff 3-17-87.**

## § 2933.09 Commitment to jail.

In the case of an appeal from the decision of a mayor sitting as the judge of a mayor's court to the appropriate municipal or county court, if the accused fails to enter into a bond ordered pursuant to section 2933.08 of the Revised Code, the municipal or county court shall commit the accused to jail until he enters into a bond or is discharged by law, and shall render judgment against him for costs and award execution for the costs. He shall not be imprisoned longer than one year.

After such a commitment following such an appeal, or after a commitment of not more than one year for not entering into a bond ordered pursuant to section 2933.05 of the Revised Code, if such an appeal was not taken, the court may at any time discharge the accused on his own recognizance.

**HISTORY: GC § 13428-9; 113 v 123(134), ch 7, § 9; Bureau of Code Revision, 10-1-53; 141 v H 412. Eff 3-17-87.**

## § 2933.10 Committing without process.

Whoever, in the presence of a municipal or county court judge, or a mayor sitting as the judge of a mayor's court, makes an affray, threatens to beat or kill another or to commit an offense against the person or property of another, or contends with angry words to the disturbance of the peace, may be ordered without process or other proof to enter into a bond under section 2933.05 of the Revised Code. In default of such a bond, the person may be committed under that section.

**HISTORY: GC § 13428-10; 113 v 123(134), ch 7, § 10; Bureau of Code Revision, 10-1-53; 141 v H 412 (Eff 3-17-87); 142 v H 708. Eff 4-19-88.**

### [PROBATION CONDITIONED UPON TREATMENT]

**§ 2933.16** Repealed, 149 v H 490, § 2 [137 v H 835. Eff 3-27-79]. Eff 1-1-04.

This section concerned treatment as condition of probation after conviction of certain domestic offenses.

### [SEARCH WARRANT]

## § 2933.21 Search warrant.

A judge of a court of record may, within his jurisdiction, issue warrants to search a house or place:

(A) For property stolen, taken by robbers, embezzled, or obtained under false pretense;

(B) For weapons, implements, tools, instruments, articles or property used as a means of the commission of a crime, or when any of the objects or articles are in the possession of another person with the intent to use them as a means of committing crime;

(C) For forged or counterfeit coins, stamps, imprints, labels, trade-marks, bank bills, or other instruments of writing, and dies, plates, stamps, or brands for making them;

(D) For obscene materials and materials harmful to minors involved in a violation of section 2907.31 or 2907.32 of the Revised Code, but only so much of such materials shall be seized as are [is] necessary for evidence in a prosecution of the violation;

(E) For [any] gaming table, establishment, device, or apparatus kept or exhibited for unlawful gaming, or to win or gain money or other property, and for money or property won by unlawful gaming;

(F) For the existence of physical conditions which are or may become hazardous to the public health, safety, or welfare, when governmental inspections of property are authorized or required by law.

The enumeration of certain property and material in this section shall not affect or modify other laws for search and seizure.

**HISTORY: RS § 7120; S&C 455; 56 v 86, § 4; 66 v 289, § 13; 73 v 159, § 3; GC § 13430-1; 113 v 123(136), ch 9; 120 v 230; 124 v 124; Bureau of Code Revision, 10-1-53; 133 v H 84 (Eff 9-15-70); 134 v S 397 (Eff 10-23-72); 135 v H 1 (Eff 3-22-73); 135 v H 989 (Eff 9-16-74); 136 v H 1. Eff 6-13-75.**

## § 2933.22 Probable cause.

(A) A warrant of search or seizure shall issue only upon probable cause, supported by oath or affirmation particularly describing the place to be searched and the property and things to be seized.

(B) A warrant of search to conduct an inspection of property shall issue only upon probable cause to believe that conditions exist upon such property which are or may become hazardous to the public health, safety, or welfare.

**HISTORY: GC § 13430-2; 113 v 123(137), ch 9, § 2; Bureau of Code Revision, 10-1-53; 134 v S 397. Eff 10-23-72.**

## § 2933.23 Affidavit for search warrant.

A search warrant shall not be issued until there is filed with the judge or magistrate an affidavit that particularly describes the place to be searched, names or describes the person to be searched, and names or describes the property to be searched for and seized; that states substantially the offense in relation to the property and that the affiant believes and has good cause to believe that the property is concealed at the place or on the person; and that states the facts upon which the affiant's belief is based. The judge or magistrate may demand other and further evidence before issuing the warrant. If the judge or magistrate is satisfied that grounds for the issuance of the warrant exist or that there is probable cause to believe that they exist, he shall issue the warrant, identifying in it the property and naming or describing the person or place to be searched.

A search warrant issued pursuant to this chapter or Criminal Rule 41 also may contain a provision waiving the statutory precondition for nonconsensual entry, as described in division (C) of section 2933.231 [2933.23.1] of the Revised Code, if the requirements of that section are satisfied.

**HISTORY: GC § 13430-3; 113 v 123(137), ch 9, § 3; Bureau of Code Revision, 10-1-53; 130 v 664 (Eff 10-14-63); 143 v S 258. Eff 11-20-90.**

The effective date is set by section 15 of SB 258.

## § 2933.231 Request for waiver of statutory precondition for nonconsensual entry.

(A) As used in this section:

(1) "Law enforcement officer" has the same meaning as in section 2901.01 of the Revised Code and in Criminal Rule 2.

(2) "Prosecutor" has the same meaning as in section 2935.01 of the Revised Code, and includes any prosecuting attorney as defined in Criminal Rule 2.

(3) "Statutory precondition for nonconsensual entry" means the precondition specified in section 2935.12 of the

Revised Code that requires a law enforcement officer or other authorized individual executing a search warrant to give notice of his intention to execute the warrant and then be refused admittance to a dwelling house or other building before he legally may break down a door or window to gain entry to execute the warrant.

(B) A law enforcement officer, prosecutor, or other authorized individual who files an affidavit for the issuance of a search warrant pursuant to this chapter or Criminal Rule 41 may include in the affidavit a request that the statutory precondition for nonconsensual entry be waived in relation to the search warrant. A request for that waiver shall contain all of the following:

(1) A statement that the affiant has good cause to believe that there is a risk of serious physical harm to the law enforcement officers or other authorized individuals who will execute the warrant if they are required to comply with the statutory precondition for nonconsensual entry;

(2) A statement setting forth the facts upon which the affiant's belief is based, including, but not limited to, the names of all known persons who the affiant believes pose the risk of serious physical harm to the law enforcement officers or other authorized individuals who will execute the warrant at the particular dwelling house or other building;

(3) A statement verifying the address of the dwelling house or other building proposed to be searched as the correct address in relation to the criminal offense or other violation of law underlying the request for the issuance of the search warrant;

(4) A request that, based on those facts, the judge or magistrate waive the statutory precondition for nonconsensual entry.

(C) If an affidavit for the issuance of a search warrant filed pursuant to this chapter or Criminal Rule 41 includes a request for a waiver of the statutory precondition for nonconsensual entry, if the request conforms with division (B) of this section, if division (E) of this section is satisfied, and if the judge or magistrate issues the warrant, the judge or magistrate shall include in it a provision that waives the statutory precondition for nonconsensual entry for purposes of the search and seizure authorized under the warrant only if he determines there is probable cause to believe that, if the law enforcement officers or other authorized individuals who execute the warrant are required to comply with the statutory precondition for nonconsensual entry, they will be subjected to a risk of serious physical harm and to believe that the address of the dwelling house or other building to be searched is the correct address in relation to the criminal offense or other violation of law underlying the issuance of the warrant.

(D)(1) A waiver of the statutory precondition for nonconsensual entry by a judge or magistrate pursuant to division (C) of this section does not authorize, and shall not be construed as authorizing, a law enforcement officer or other authorized individual who executes a search warrant to enter a building other than a building described in the warrant.

(2) The state or any political subdivision associated with a law enforcement officer or other authorized officer who executes a search warrant that contains a provision waiving the statutory precondition for nonconsensual entry is liable in damages in a tort action for any injury, death, or loss to person or property that is proximately caused by the officer's execution of the warrant in accordance with the waiver at an address of a dwelling house or other building that is not described in the warrant.

(E) Any proceeding before a judge or magistrate that involves a request for a waiver of the statutory precondition for nonconsensual entry shall be recorded by shorthand, by stenotype, or by any other mechanical, electronic, or video recording device. The recording of and any transcript of the recording of such a proceeding shall not be a public record for purposes of section 149.43 of the Revised Code until the search warrant is returned by the law enforcement officer or other authorized officer who executes it. This division shall not be construed as requiring, authorizing, or permitting, and does not require, authorize, or permit, the making available for inspection, or the copying, under section 149.43 of the Revised Code of any confidential law enforcement investigatory record or trial preparation record, as defined in that section.

**HISTORY: 143 v S 258. Eff 11-20-90.**

The effective date is set by section 15 of SB 258.

## § 2933.24 Contents of search warrant; report of inspection findings.

(A) A search warrant shall be directed to the proper law enforcement officer or other authorized individual and, by a copy of the affidavit inserted in it or annexed and referred to in it, shall show or recite all the material facts alleged in the affidavit, and particularly name or describe the property to be searched for and seized, the place to be searched, and the person to be searched. If a waiver of the statutory precondition for nonconsensual entry, as defined in division (A) of section 2933.231 [2933.23.1] of the Revised Code, has been granted pursuant to that section, the warrant also shall contain a provision as described in division (C) of that section.

The warrant shall command the officer or individual to search the place or person named or described for the property, and to bring them, together with the person, before the judge or magistrate. The command of the warrant shall be that the search be made in the daytime, unless there is urgent necessity for a search in the night, in which case a search in the night may be ordered.

The warrant shall be returned promptly by the officer or individual holding it. It shall designate the judge or magistrate to whom it shall be returned, if such judge or magistrate is available.

(B) When a search warrant commands a proper law enforcement officer or other authorized individual to inspect physical conditions relating to public health, safety, or welfare, such officer or individual, upon completion of the search, shall complete a report of the conditions and file a copy of such report with the officer's or individual's agency headquarters.

**HISTORY: GC § 13430-4; 113 v 123(137), ch 9, § 4; Bureau of Code Revision, 10-1-53; 130 v 665 (Eff 10-14-63); 134 v S 397 (Eff 10-23-72); 143 v S 258. Eff 11-20-90; 151 v H 34, § 1, eff. 10-21-05.**

The effective date is set by section 15 of SB 258.

## § 2933.241 Inventory of property taken.

The officer taking property under a warrant for search shall give to the person from whom or from whose premises the property was taken a copy of the warrant and a receipt for the property taken or shall leave the copy and receipt at the place from which the property was taken. The return shall be made promptly and shall be accompanied by a written inventory of any property taken. The inventory shall be made in the presence of the applicant for the warrant and the person from whose possession or premises the property was taken, if they are present, or in the presence of at least one credible person other than the applicant for the warrant or the person from whose possession or premises the property was taken and shall be verified by the officer. The judge or magistrate shall upon request deliver a copy of the inventory to the person from whom or from whose premises the property was taken and to the applicant for the warrant.

**HISTORY: 130 v 665. Eff 10-14-63.**

## § 2933.25 Form of search warrant.

Warrants issued under section 2933.21 of the Revised Code shall be substantially in the following form:

State of Ohio, ...................... County, ss:

To the sheriff (or other officer) of said County, greeting:

Whereas there has been filed with me an affidavit, of which the following is a copy (here copy the affidavit).

These are, therefore, to command you in the name of the State of Ohio, with the necessary and proper assistance, to enter, in the daytime (or in the nighttime) into (here describe the house or place as in the affidavit) of the said ......... of the township of .......... in the County aforesaid, and there diligently search for the said goods and chattels, or articles, to wit: (here describe the articles as in the affidavit) and that you bring the same or any part thereof, found on such search, and also the body of E. F., forthwith before me, or some other judge or magistrate of the county having cognizance thereof to be disposed of and dealt with according to law.

Given under my hand, this ............ day of ..........................

A. B., Judge, County Court

**HISTORY: GC § 13430-5; 113 v 123(137), ch 9, § 5; Bureau of Code Revision, 10-1-53; 127 v 1039(1099). Eff 1-1-58.**

## § 2933.26 Property seized to be kept by court.

When a warrant is executed by the seizure of property or things described therein, such property or things shall be kept by the judge, clerk, or magistrate to be used as evidence.

**HISTORY: GC § 13430-6; 113 v 123(138), ch 9, § 6; Bureau of Code Revision. Eff 10-1-53.**

## § 2933.27 Disposition of property before trial.

If, upon examination, the judge or magistrate is satisfied that the offense charged with reference to the things seized under a search warrant has been committed, he shall keep such things or deliver them to the sheriff of the county, to be kept until the accused is tried or the claimant's right is otherwise ascertained.

**HISTORY: GC § 13430-7; 113 v 123(138), ch 9, § 7; Bureau of Code Revision. Eff 10-1-53.**

## § 2933.28 Repealed, 140 v H 632, § 2 [GC § 13430-8; 113 v 123(138), ch 9, § 8; Bureau of Code Revision, 10-1-53]. Eff 3-28-85.

This section concerned disposition of property after trial. See now RC § 2981.01 et seq.

## § 2933.29 Property seized liable for fines.

Upon conviction of a person for keeping a room or place to be used for gambling, or knowingly permitting gambling to be conducted therein, or permitting a game to be played for gain, or a gaming device for gain, money, or other property or for betting, or gambling, or permitting such device to be so used, or for being without a fixed residence and in the habit of gambling, if money or other property won in gaming is found in his possession, such money or other property is subject to seizure and payment of a judgment which may be rendered against him, growing out of such violation.

**HISTORY: GC § 13430-9; 113 v 123(138), ch 9, § 9; Bureau of Code Revision. Eff 10-1-53.**

## § 2933.30 Search for dead bodies.

When an affidavit is filed before a judge or magistrate, alleging that affiant has reason to believe and does believe that a dead human body, procured or obtained contrary to law, is secreted in a building or place in the county, therein particularly specified, such judge or magistrate, taking with him a judge of a county court, or if within a municipal corporation, two officers of such corporation, may enter, inspect, and search said building or place for such body. In making such search, they have the powers of officers executing warrants of search.

**HISTORY: GC § 13430-10; 113 v 123(138), ch 9, § 10; Bureau of Code Revision, 10-1-53; 127 v 1039(1099). Eff 1-1-58.**

## § 2933.31 Search in case of animals.

When complaint is made, on oath or affirmation to a judge or magistrate, that the complainant believes that the law relating to or affecting animals is being, or is about to be violated in a particular building or place, such judge or magistrate shall forthwith issue and deliver a warrant, directed to any sheriff, deputy sheriff, marshal, deputy marshal, watchman, police officer, or agent of a society for the prevention of cruelty to animals, authorizing him to enter and search such building or place and arrest all persons there violating, or attempting to violate, such law, and bring such persons before a judge or magistrate within the county within which such offense has been committed.

An attempt to violate such law relating to animals is a violation thereof.

**HISTORY: GC § 13430-11; 113 v 123(139), ch 9, § 11; Bureau of Code Revision. Eff 10-1-53.**

## § 2933.32 Body cavity and strip searches; conducting unauthorized search; failure to prepare proper report.

(A) As used in this section:

(1) "Body cavity search" means an inspection of the anal or vaginal cavity of a person that is conducted visually, manually, by means of any instrument, apparatus, or object, or in any other manner while the person is detained or arrested for the alleged commission of a misdemeanor or traffic offense.

(2) "Strip search" means an inspection of the genitalia, buttocks, breasts, or undergarments of a person that is preceded by the removal or rearrangement of some or all of the person's clothing that directly covers the person's genitalia, buttocks, breasts, or undergarments and that is conducted visually, manually, by means of any instrument, apparatus, or object, or in any other manner while the person is detained or arrested for the alleged commission of a misdemeanor or traffic offense. "Strip search" does not mean the visual observation of a person who was afforded a reasonable opportunity to secure release on bail or recognizance, who fails to secure such release, and who is to be integrated with the general population of any detention facility, while the person is changing into clothing that is required to be worn by inmates in the facility.

(B)(1) Except as authorized by this division, no law enforcement officer, other employee of a law enforcement agency, physician, or registered nurse or licensed practical nurse shall conduct or cause to be conducted a body cavity search or a strip search.

(2) A body cavity search or strip search may be conducted if a law enforcement officer or employee of a law enforcement agency has probable cause to believe that the person is concealing evidence of the commission of a criminal offense, including fruits or tools of a crime, contraband, or a deadly weapon, as defined in section 2923.11 of the Revised Code, that could not otherwise be discovered. In determining probable cause for purposes of this section, a law enforcement officer or employee of a law enforcement agency shall consider the nature of the offense with which the person to be searched is charged, the circumstances of the person's arrest, and, if known, the prior conviction record of the person.

(3) A body cavity search or strip search may be conducted for any legitimate medical or hygienic reason.

(4) Unless there is a legitimate medical reason or medical emergency justifying a warrantless search, a body cavity search shall be conducted only after a search warrant is issued that authorizes the search. In any case, a body cavity search shall be conducted under sanitary conditions and only by a physician, or a registered nurse or licensed practical nurse, who is registered or licensed to practice in this state.

(5) Unless there is a legitimate medical reason or medical emergency that makes obtaining written authorization impracticable, a body cavity search or strip search shall be conducted only after a law enforcement officer or employee of a law enforcement agency obtains a written authorization for the search from the person in command of the law enforcement agency, or from a person specifically designated by the person in command to give a written authorization for either type of search.

(6) A body cavity search or strip search shall be conducted by a person or persons who are of the same sex as the person who is being searched and the search shall be conducted in a manner and in a location that permits only the person or persons who are physically conducting the search and the person who is being searched to observe the search.

(C)(1) Upon completion of a body cavity search or strip search pursuant to this section, the person or persons who conducted the search shall prepare a written report concerning the search that shall include all of the following:

(a) The written authorization for the search obtained from the person in command of the law enforcement agency or his designee, if required by division (B)(5) of this section;

(b) The name of the person who was searched;

(c) The name of the person or persons who conducted the search, the time and date of the search, and the place at which the search was conducted;

(d) A list of the items, if any, recovered during the search;

(e) The facts upon which the law enforcement officer or employee of the law enforcement agency based his probable cause for the search, including, but not limited to, the officer or employee's review of the nature of the offense with which the searched person is charged, the circumstances of his arrest, and, if known, his prior conviction record;

(f) If the body cavity search was conducted before or without the issuance of a search warrant pursuant to division (B)(4) of this section, or if the body cavity or strip search was conducted before or without the granting of written authorization pursuant to division (B)(5) of this section, the legitimate medical reason or medical emergency that justified the warrantless search or made obtaining written authorization impracticable.

(2) A copy of the written report required by division (C)(1) of this section shall be kept on file in the law enforcement agency, and another copy of it shall be given to the person who was searched.

(D)(1) This section does not preclude the prosecution of a law enforcement officer or employee of a law enforcement agency for the violation of any other section of the Revised Code.

(2) This section does not limit, and shall not be construed to limit, any statutory or common law rights of a person to obtain injunctive relief or to recover damages in a civil action.

(3) If a person is subjected to a body cavity search or strip search in violation of this section, any person may commence a civil action to recover compensatory damages for any injury, death, or loss to person or property or any indignity arising from the violation. In the civil action, the court may award punitive damages to the plaintiffs if they prevail in the action, and it may award reasonable attorney's fees to the parties who prevail in the action.

(4) This section does not apply to body cavity searches or strip searches of persons who have been sentenced to serve a term of imprisonment and who are serving that term in a detention facility, as defined in section 2921.01 of the Revised Code.

(E)(1) Whoever violates division (B) of this section is guilty of conducting an unauthorized search, a misdemeanor of the first degree.

(2) Whoever violates division (C) of this section is guilty of failure to prepare a proper search report, a misdemeanor of the fourth degree.

**HISTORY: 140 v S 268 (Eff 9-26-84); 140 v H 426. Eff 4-4-85.**

## § 2933.33 Exigent circumstances authorizing warrantless search of premises used for illegal manufacture of methamphetamine.

(A) If a law enforcement officer has probable cause to believe that particular premises are used for the illegal manufacture of methamphetamine, for the purpose of conducting a search of the premises without a warrant, the risk of explosion or fire from the illegal manufacture of methamphetamine causing injury to the public constitutes exigent circumstances and reasonable grounds to believe that there is an immediate need to protect the lives, or property, of the officer and other individuals in the vicinity of the illegal manufacture.

(B) As used in this section, "methamphetamine" has the same meaning as in section 2925.01 of the Revised Code.

**HISTORY: 151 v S 53, § 1, eff. 5-17-06.**

**§ 2933.41** Repealed, 151 v H 241, § 2 [134 v H 511 (Eff 1-1-74); 138 v S 50 (Eff 5-29-80); 139 v H 1 (Eff 8-5-81); 140 v H 632 (Eff 3-28-85); 140 v S 65 (Eff 4-4-85); 141 v H 49 (Eff 6-26-86); 141 v S 69 (Eff 9-3-86); 141 v H 428 (Eff 12-23-86); 143 v H 215 (Eff 4-11-90); 143 v S 258 (Eff 11-20-90); 144 v S 98 (Eff 11-12-92); 144 v S 275 (Eff 7-1-93); 145 v H 715 (Eff 7-22-94); 146 v H 1 (Eff 1-1-96); 146 v S 277, § 1 (Eff 3-31-97); 146 v S 162 (Eff 7-1-97); 146 v S 277, § 3 (Eff 7-1-97); 147 v S 164 (Eff 1-15-98); 147 v H 2 (Eff 1-1-99); 147 v H 402 (Eff 3-30-99); 148 v H 55 (Eff 9-29-99); 149 v H 510. Eff 3-31-2003; 150 v H 306, § 1, eff. 7-23-04; 151 v H 374, § 1, eff. 9-28-06]. Eff 7-1-07.

See provisions of § 4 of 151 v H 241 following RC § 2901.01.
This section concerned disposition of property held by law enforcement agency. See now RC § 2981.01 et seq.

**§ 2933.42** Repealed, 151 v H 241, § 2 [141 v S 69 (Eff 9-3-86); 143 v S 258. Eff 8-22-90]. Eff 7-1-07.

See provisions of § 4 of 151 v H 241 following RC § 2901.01.
This section concerned offenses involving contraband; forfeiture of property used in committing violation. See now RC § 2981.01 et seq.

**§ 2933.43** Repealed, 151 v H 241, § 2 [141 v S 69 (Eff 9-3-86); 141 v H 428 (Eff 12-23-86); 143 v H 215 (Eff 4-11-90); 143 v H 261 (Eff 7-18-90); 143 v S 258 (Eff 11-20-90); 144 v S 218 (Eff 10-11-91); 144 v S 174 (Eff 7-31-92); 144 v S 351 (Eff 7-31-92); 146 v H 107 (Eff 6-30-95); 146 v S 162 (Eff 10-29-95); 146 v H 1 (Eff 1-1-96); 146 v S 239 (Eff 9-6-96); 146 v H 670 (Eff 12-2-96); 146 v S 277 (Eff 3-31-97); 147 v H 210 (Eff 6-30-97); 147 v S 164 (Eff 1-15-98); 147 v H 2 (Eff 1-1-99); 148 v H 163 (Eff 6-30-99); 149 v H 7. Eff 8-7-2001; 150 v H 95, § 1, eff. 6-26-03; 151 v H 66, § 101.01, eff. 9-29-05; 151 v H 530, § 101.01, eff. 3-30-06]. Eff 7-1-07.

See provisions of § 4 of 151 v H 241 following RC § 2901.01.
This section concerned procedure for seizure and forfeiture of contraband; law enforcement agency authorized to use, destroy, or sell forfeited contraband; distribution of proceeds of sale. See now RC § 2981.01 et seq.

**§ 2933.44** Repealed, 151 v H 241, § 2 [146 v H 1 (Eff 1-1-96); 147 v H 2. Eff 1-1-99]. Eff 7-1-07.

See provisions of § 4 of 151 v H 241 following RC § 2901.01.
This section concerned annual report by alcohol and drug treatment program receiving juvenile-related forfeiture. See now RC § 2981.01 et seq.

## [WIRETAPPING, ELECTRONIC SURVEILLANCE]

### § 2933.51 Definitions.

As used in sections 2933.51 to 2933.66 of the Revised Code:

(A) "Wire communication" means an aural transfer that is made in whole or in part through the use of facilities for the transmission of communications by the aid of wires or similar methods of connecting the point of origin of the communication and the point of reception of the communication, including the use of a method of connecting the point of origin and the point of reception of the communication in a switching station, if the facilities are furnished or operated by a person engaged in providing or operating the facilities for the transmission of communications. "Wire communication" includes an electronic storage of a wire communication.

(B) "Oral communication" means an oral communication uttered by a person exhibiting an expectation that the communication is not subject to interception under circumstances justifying that expectation. "Oral communication" does not include an electronic communication.

(C) "Intercept" means the aural or other acquisition of the contents of any wire, oral, or electronic communication through the use of an interception device.

(D) "Interception device" means an electronic, mechanical, or other device or apparatus that can be used to intercept a wire, oral, or electronic communication. "Interception device" does not mean any of the following:

(1) A telephone or telegraph instrument, equipment, or facility, or any of its components, if the instrument, equipment, facility, or component is any of the following:

(a) Furnished to the subscriber or user by a provider of wire or electronic communication service in the ordinary course of its business and being used by the subscriber or user in the ordinary course of its business;

(b) Furnished by a subscriber or user for connection to the facilities of a provider of wire or electronic communication service and used in the ordinary course of that subscriber's or user's business;

(c) Being used by a provider of wire or electronic communication service in the ordinary course of its business or by an investigative or law enforcement officer in the ordinary course of the officer's duties that do not involve the interception of wire, oral, or electronic communications.

(2) A hearing aid or similar device being used to correct subnormal hearing to not better than normal.

(E) "Investigative officer" means any of the following:

(1) An officer of this state or a political subdivision of this state, who is empowered by law to conduct investigations or to make arrests for a designated offense;

(2) A person described in divisions (A)(11)(a) and (b) of section 2901.01 of the Revised Code;

(3) An attorney authorized by law to prosecute or participate in the prosecution of a designated offense;

(4) A secret service officer appointed pursuant to section 309.07 of the Revised Code;

(5) An officer of the United States, a state, or a political subdivision of a state who is authorized to conduct investigations pursuant to the "Electronic Communications Privacy Act of 1986," 100 Stat. 1848-1857, 18 U.S.C. 2510-2521 (1986), as amended.

(F) "Interception warrant" means a court order that authorizes the interception of wire, oral, or electronic communications and that is issued pursuant to sections 2933.53 to 2933.56 of the Revised Code.

(G) "Contents," when used with respect to a wire, oral, or electronic communication, includes any information concerning the substance, purport, or meaning of the communication.

(H) "Communications common carrier" means a person who is engaged as a common carrier for hire in intrastate, interstate, or foreign communications by wire, radio, or radio transmission of energy. "Communications common carrier" does not include, to the extent that the person is engaged in radio broadcasting, a person engaged in radio broadcasting.

(I) "Designated offense" means any of the following:

(1) A felony violation of section 1315.53, 1315.55, 2903.01, 2903.02, 2903.11, 2905.01, 2905.02, 2905.11, 2905.22, 2905.32, 2907.02, 2907.21, 2907.22, 2909.02, 2909.03, 2909.04, 2909.22, 2909.23, 2909.24, 2909.26, 2909.27, 2909.28, 2909.29, 2911.01, 2911.02, 2911.11, 2911.12, 2913.02, 2913.04, 2913.42, 2913.51, 2915.02, 2915.03, 2917.01, 2917.02, 2921.02, 2921.03, 2921.04, 2921.32, 2921.34, 2923.20, 2923.32, 2925.03, 2925.04, 2925.05, or 2925.06 or of division (B) of section 2915.05 of the Revised Code;

(2) A violation of section 2919.23 of the Revised Code that, had it occurred prior to July 1, 1996, would have been a violation of section 2905.04 of the Revised Code as it existed prior to that date;

(3) A felony violation of section 2925.11 of the Revised Code that is not a minor drug possession offense, as defined in section 2925.01 of the Revised Code;

(4) Complicity in the commission of a felony violation of a section listed in division (I)(1), (2), or (3) of this section;

(5) An attempt to commit, or conspiracy in the commission of, a felony violation of a section listed in division (I)(1), (2), or (3) of this section, if the attempt or conspiracy is punishable by a term of imprisonment of more than one year.

(J) "Aggrieved person" means a person who was a party to an intercepted wire, oral, or electronic communication or a person against whom the interception of the communication was directed.

(K) "Person" means a person, as defined in section 1.59 of the Revised Code, or a governmental officer, employee, or entity.

(L) "Special need" means a showing that a licensed physician, licensed practicing psychologist, attorney, practicing cleric, journalist, or either spouse is personally engaging in continuing criminal activity, was engaged in continuing criminal activity over a period of time, or is committing, has committed, or is about to commit, a designated offense, or a showing that specified public facilities are being regularly used by someone who is personally engaging in continuing criminal activity, was engaged in continuing criminal activity over a period of time, or is committing, has committed, or is about to commit, a designated offense.

(M) "Journalist" means a person engaged in, connected with, or employed by, any news media, including a newspaper, magazine, press association, news agency, or wire service, a radio or television station, or a similar media, for the purpose of gathering, processing, transmitting, compiling, editing, or disseminating news for the general public.

(N) "Electronic communication" means a transfer of a sign, signal, writing, image, sound, datum, or intelligence of any nature that is transmitted in whole or in part by a wire, radio, electromagnetic, photoelectronic, or photo-optical system. "Electronic communication" does not mean any of the following:

(1) A wire or oral communication;

(2) A communication made through a tone-only paging device;

(3) A communication from an electronic or mechanical tracking device that permits the tracking of the movement of a person or object.

(O) "User" means a person or entity that uses an electronic communication service and is duly authorized by the provider of the service to engage in the use of the electronic communication service.

(P) "Electronic communications system" means a wire, radio, electromagnetic, photoelectronic, or photo-optical facility for the transmission of electronic communications, and a computer facility or related electronic equipment for the electronic storage of electronic communications.

(Q) "Electronic communication service" means a service that provides to users of the service the ability to send or receive wire or electronic communications.

(R) "Readily accessible to the general public" means, with respect to a radio communication, that the communication is none of the following:

(1) Scrambled or encrypted;

(2) Transmitted using a modulation technique, the essential parameters of which have been withheld from the public with the intention of preserving the privacy of the communication;

(3) Carried on a subcarrier or other signal subsidiary to a radio transmission;

(4) Transmitted over a communications system provided by a communications common carrier, unless the communication is a tone-only paging system communication;

(5) Transmitted on a frequency allocated under part 25, subpart D, E, or F of part 74, or part 94 of the Rules of the Federal Communications Commission, as those provisions existed on July 1, 1996, unless, in the case of a communication transmitted on a frequency allocated under part 74 that is not exclusively allocated to broadcast auxiliary services, the communication is a two-way voice communication by radio.

(S) "Electronic storage" means a temporary, intermediate storage of a wire or electronic communication that is incidental to the electronic transmission of the communication, and a storage of a wire or electronic communication by an electronic communication service for the purpose of backup protection of the communication.

(T) "Aural transfer" means a transfer containing the human voice at a point between and including the point of origin and the point of reception.

(U) "Pen register" means a device that records or decodes electronic impulses that identify the numbers dialed, pulsed, or otherwise transmitted on telephone lines to which the device is attached.

(V) "Trap and trace device" means a device that captures the incoming electronic or other impulses that identify the originating number of an instrument or device from which a wire communication or electronic communication was transmitted but that does not intercept the contents of the wire communication or electronic communication.

(W) "Judge of a court of common pleas" means a judge of that court who is elected or appointed as a judge of general jurisdiction or as a judge who exercises both general jurisdiction and probate, domestic relations, or juvenile jurisdiction. "Judge of a court of common pleas" does not mean a judge of that court who is elected or appointed specifically as a probate, domestic relations, or juvenile judge.

**HISTORY: 141 v S 222 (Eff 3-25-87); 146 v H 181, § 1 (Eff 6-13-96); 146 v S 2 (Eff 7-1-96); 146 v H 181, § 3 (Eff 7-1-96); 146 v S 269 (Eff 7-1-96); 146 v S 239 (Eff 9-6-96); 146 v H 333 (Eff 9-19-96); 147 v H 565 (Eff 3-30-99); 149 v S 184. Eff 5-15-2002; 151 v S 9, § 1, eff. 4-14-06; 153 v S 235, § 1, eff. 3-24-11.**

## § 2933.52 Interception of wire, oral or electronic communications.

(A) No person purposely shall do any of the following:

(1) Intercept, attempt to intercept, or procure another person to intercept or attempt to intercept a wire, oral, or electronic communication;

(2) Use, attempt to use, or procure another person to use or attempt to use an interception device to intercept a wire, oral, or electronic communication, if either of the following applies:

(a) The interception device is affixed to, or otherwise transmits a signal through, a wire, cable, satellite, microwave, or other similar method of connection used in wire communications;

(b) The interception device transmits communications by radio, or interferes with the transmission of communications by radio.

(3) Use, or attempt to use, the contents of a wire, oral, or electronic communication, knowing or having reason to know that the contents were obtained through the interception of a wire, oral, or electronic communication in violation of sections 2933.51 to 2933.66 of the Revised Code.

(B) This section does not apply to any of the following:

(1) The interception, disclosure, or use of the contents, or evidence derived from the contents, of an oral, wire, or electronic communication that is obtained through the use of an interception warrant issued pursuant to sections 2933.53 to 2933.56 of the Revised Code, that is obtained pursuant to an oral approval for an interception granted pursuant to section 2933.57 of the Revised Code, or that is obtained pursuant to an order that is issued or an interception that is made in accordance with section 802 of the "Omnibus Crime Control and Safe Streets Act of 1968," 82 Stat. 237, 254, 18 U.S.C. 2510 to 2520 (1968), as amended, the "Electronic Communications Privacy Act of 1986," 100 Stat. 1848-1857, 18 U.S.C. 2510-2521 (1986), as amended, or the "Foreign Intelligence Surveillance Act," 92 Stat. 1783, 50 U.S.C. 1801.11 (1978), as amended;

(2) An operator of a switchboard, or an officer, employee, or agent of a provider of wire or electronic communication service, whose facilities are used in the transmission of a wire or electronic communication to intercept, disclose, or use that communication in the normal course of employment while engaged in an activity that is necessary to the rendition of service or to the protection of the rights or property of the provider of that service, except that a provider of wire or electronic communication service to the public shall not utilize service observing or random monitoring except for mechanical or service quality control checks;

(3) A law enforcement officer who intercepts a wire, oral, or electronic communication, if the officer is a party to the communication or if one of the parties to the communication has given prior consent to the interception by the officer;

(4) A person who is not a law enforcement officer and who intercepts a wire, oral, or electronic communication, if the person is a party to the communication or if one of the parties to the communication has given the person prior consent to the interception, and if the communication is not intercepted for the purpose of committing a criminal offense or tortious act in violation of the laws or Constitution of the United States or this state or for the purpose of committing any other injurious act;

(5) An officer, employee, or agent of a communications common carrier providing information, facilities, or technical assistance to an investigative officer who is authorized to intercept a wire, oral, or electronic communication pursuant to sections 2933.51 to 2933.66 of the Revised Code;

(6) The use of a pen register in accordance with federal or state law;

(7) The use of a trap and trace device in accordance with federal or state law;

(8) A police, fire, or emergency communications system to intercept wire communications coming into and going out of the communications system of a police department, fire department, or emergency center, if both of the following apply:

(a) The telephone, instrument, equipment, or facility is limited to the exclusive use of the communication system for administrative purposes;

(b) At least one telephone, instrument, equipment, or facility that is not subject to interception is made available for public use at each police department, fire department, or emergency center.

(9) The interception or accessing of an electronic communication made through an electronic communication system that is configured so that the electronic communication is readily accessible to the general public.

(10) The interception of a radio communication that is transmitted by any of the following:

(a) A station for the use of the general public;

(b) A governmental, law enforcement, civil defense, private land mobile, or public safety communications system, including a police or fire system, that is readily accessible to the general public;

(c) A station operating on an authorized frequency within the bands allocated to the amateur, citizens band, or general mobile radio services;

(d) A marine or aeronautical communications system.

(11) The interception of a radio communication that relates to a ship, aircraft, vehicle, or person in distress.

(12) The interception of a wire or electronic communication the transmission of which is causing harmful interference to a lawfully operating station or consumer electronic equipment, to the extent necessary to identify the source of that interference.

(13) Other users of the same frequency to intercept a radio communication made through a system that utilizes frequencies monitored by individuals engaged in the provision or the use of that system, if the communication is not scrambled or encrypted.

(C) Whoever violates this section is guilty of interception of wire, oral, or electronic communications, a felony of the fourth degree.

**HISTORY: 141 v S 222 (Eff 3-25-87); 142 v H 231 (Eff 10-5-87); 146 v S 2 (Eff 7-1-96); 146 v H 181, § 3. Eff 7-1-96.**

The effective date is set by section 5 of HB 181.

**Publisher's Note:**

The amendments made by SB 2 (146 v —) and HB 181 (146 v —) have been combined. Please see provisions of RC § 1.52.

## § 2933.521 Divulgence of content of communication by provider of electronic communication service.

(A) Except as provided in division (B) of this section, no person or entity that provides electronic communication service to the public shall purposely divulge the content of a communication, while it is in transmission on that service, to a person or entity other than an addressee or intended recipient of the communication or an agent of an addressee or intended recipient of the communication.

(B)(1) Division (A) of this section does not apply to a communication being transmitted to the person or entity providing the electronic communication service or to an agent of that person or entity.

(2) Notwithstanding division (A) of this section, a person or entity that provides electronic communication service to the public may divulge the content of a communication that is in transmission on that service in any of the following circumstances:

(a) The divulgence is authorized by division (B)(2) of section 2933.52, by section 2933.581 [2933.58.1], by division (C) of section 2933.55, or by division (F) or (G) of section 2933.59 of the Revised Code or by a provision of the "Electronic Communications Privacy Act of 1986," 100 Stat. 1848-1857, 18 U.S.C. 2510-2521 (1986), as amended.

(b) The originator or an addressee or intended recipient of the communication has lawfully consented to the divulgence.

(c) The divulgence is made to a person who is employed or authorized, or whose facilities are used, to forward the communication to its destination.

(d) The content of the communication divulged was inadvertently obtained by the provider of the service, the content appears to pertain to the commission of a crime, and the divulgence is made to a law enforcement agency.

(C) Neither division (A) of this section nor any other provision of sections 2933.51 to 2933.66 of the Revised Code prohibits a provider of electronic communication service from recording the fact that a wire or electronic communication was initiated or completed, in order to protect the provider, another provider furnishing service toward the completion of the wire or electronic communication, or a user of the electronic communication service from fraudulent, unlawful, or abusive use of the electronic communication service.

**HISTORY: 146 v H 181. Eff 6-13-96.**

## § 2933.522 Powers of common pleas court judge.

A judge of a court of common pleas, in accordance with sections 2933.51 to 2933.66 of the Revised Code, may accept applications for interception warrants, may issue interception warrants, may accept applications for extensions of interception warrants, may order extensions of interception warrants, may accept applications for grants of oral orders for interceptions, may grant oral orders for interceptions, and may issue other orders, perform other functions, or engage in other activities authorized or required by sections 2933.51 to 2933.66 of the Revised Code.

**HISTORY: 146 v H 181. Eff 6-13-96.**

## § 2933.53 Application for interception warrant.

(A) The prosecuting attorney of the county in which an interception is to take place or in which an interception device is to be installed, or an assistant to the prosecuting attorney of that county who is specifically designated by the prosecuting attorney to exercise authority under this section, may authorize an application for an interception warrant to a judge of the court of common pleas of the county in which the interception is to take place or in which the interception device is to be installed. If the prosecuting attorney of a county in which an interception is to take place or in which an interception device is to be installed is the subject of an investigation, a special prosecutor appointed by a judge of the court of common pleas of the county served by the prosecuting attorney, without the knowledge of the prosecuting attorney, may apply the procedures of this section. If the subject of an investigation is employed in the office of the prosecuting attorney of the county in which an interception is to take place or in which an interception device is to be installed or the prosecuting attorney of that county believes that the subject has a conflict of interest, the approval of the prosecuting attorney shall be obtained before a special prosecutor is appointed to authorize the application for an interception warrant.

(B) Each application for an interception warrant shall be made in writing upon oath or affirmation to a judge of the court of common pleas of the county in which the interception is to take place or in which the interception device is to be installed, by a person who has received training that satisfies the minimum standards established by the attorney general and the Ohio peace officer training commission under section 2933.64 of the Revised Code. Each application shall contain all of the following:

(1) The name and office of the applicant and the name and office of the prosecuting attorney or assistant prosecuting attorney authorizing the application;

(2) The identity of the investigative officers or law enforcement agency that will intercept the wire, oral, or electronic communications;

(3) A full and complete statement of the objective in seeking the warrant, and a full and complete statement of the facts and circumstances relied on by the applicant to justify the belief that the warrant should be issued, including, but not limited to the following:

(a) The details regarding the designated offense that has been, is being, or is about to be committed;

(b) The identity of the person, if known, who has committed, is committing, or is about to commit the designated offense and whose communications are to be intercepted and the location at which the communications are sought to be intercepted;

(c) Except as provided in division (G)(1) of this section, a particular description of the nature and location of the facilities from which, or the place at which, the communication is to be intercepted;

(d) A particular description of the type of communication sought to be intercepted, and the basis for believing that evidence relating to a designated offense will be obtained through the interception.

(4) A statement as to whether the applicant, or the prosecuting attorney or assistant prosecuting attorney authorizing the application for an interception warrant,

knows or has reason to know that the communications sought to be intercepted are privileged under section 2317.02 of the Revised Code, the nature of any privilege that exists, and the basis of the knowledge of the applicant or authorizing prosecuting attorney or assistant prosecuting attorney of the privileged nature of the communications;

(5) A statement of the use to which the contents of an intercepted wire, oral, or electronic communication, or the evidence derived from the communication, will be put;

(6) A statement of the period of time for which the interception is required to be maintained, and, if the nature of the investigation requires that the authorization for interception not be terminated automatically when the described type of communication first has been intercepted, a particular description of the facts establishing probable cause to believe that additional communications of the same type will occur after the first intercepted communication;

(7) A full and complete statement indicating whether other investigative procedures have been tried and have failed to produce the required evidence or indicating the reason that other investigative procedures reasonably appear to be unlikely to succeed if tried or to be too dangerous to employ in order to obtain evidence;

(8) A full and complete statement of the particular facts concerning all previous applications known to the applicant or the prosecuting attorney or assistant prosecuting attorney authorizing the application for the interception warrant, that have been made to a judge for authorization to intercept wire, oral, or electronic communications involving any of the persons, facilities, or places specified in the application, and the action of the judge with respect to each previous application;

(9) Unless the attorney general is a subject of the investigation, a written statement, signed by the attorney general or an assistant attorney general designated by the attorney general, that the attorney general or assistant attorney general has reviewed the application and either agrees or disagrees with the submission of the application to a judge of the court of common pleas of the county in which the interception is to take place or in which the interception device is to be installed. A disagreement by the attorney general or assistant attorney general does not preclude the making or consideration of an application that otherwise complies with divisions (B)(1) to (8) of this section.

(C) If an application for an interception warrant is for an extension of a warrant, the application shall include, in addition to the information and statements specified in division (B) of this section, a statement setting forth the results thus far obtained from the interceptions of wire, oral, or electronic communications, or a reasonable explanation of the failure to obtain results from the interceptions.

(D) An applicant may submit affidavits of persons other than the applicant in conjunction with the application if the affidavits support a fact or conclusion in the application. The accompanying affidavits shall be based on personal knowledge of the affiant or shall be based on information and belief and specify the source of the information and the reason for the belief. If the applicant or an affiant personally knows of the facts contained in the application or affidavit, the application or affidavit shall state the personal knowledge. If the application or affidavit states the facts based upon information and belief, the application or affidavit shall state that reliance upon information and belief and shall set forth fully the facts supporting the information and belief. If the facts contained in the application or affidavits are derived in whole or in part from the statement of a person other than the applicant or affiant, the application or affidavits shall disclose or describe the sources of the facts and shall contain facts establishing the existence and reliability of the other person or the reliability of the information supplied by the other person. The application also shall state, so far as possible, the basis of the other person's knowledge or belief. If the application or affidavit relies on hearsay to support a fact alleged on information and belief, the application or affidavit shall contain the underlying facts that establish the basis for the conclusions of the source of the hearsay and the factual basis upon which the applicant or the affiant concludes that the source of the hearsay is credible or reliable.

(E) A judge of a court of common pleas to whom an application is made under this section may require the applicant to furnish additional sworn testimony or documentary evidence in support of the application. All sworn testimony furnished shall be recorded and transcribed and shall be made part of the application.

(F) An interception warrant is not required for any of the following:

(1) A pen register used in accordance with federal or state law;

(2) The interception of a wire, oral, or electronic communication by a law enforcement officer if the officer is a party to the communication or if one of the parties to the communication has given prior consent to the interception by the officer;

(3) The interception of a wire, oral, or electronic communication by a person who is not a law enforcement officer if the person is a party to the communication or if one of the parties to the communication has given the person prior consent to the interception, and if the communication is not intercepted for the purpose of committing a criminal offense or tortious act in violation of the laws or constitution of the United States or this state or for the purpose of committing another injurious act.

(4) A trap and trace device used in accordance with federal or state law.

(G)(1) The requirements of division (B)(3)(c) of this section and of division (A)(5) of section 2933.54 of the Revised Code that relate to the specification of facilities from which or the place at which the communication is to be intercepted do not apply if either of the following applies:

(a) In the case of an application with respect to the interception of an oral communication, the application contains a full and complete statement indicating the reason that the specification is not practical and identifies the person committing the designated offense and whose communications are to be intercepted, and the judge of a court of common pleas to whom the application is made finds that the specification is not practical.

(b) In the case of an application with respect to a wire or electronic communication, the application identifies the person believed to be committing the designated offense and whose communications are to be intercepted, the applicant makes a showing of purpose on the part of that person to thwart interception by changing facilities, and the judge of a court of common pleas to whom the application is made finds that that purpose adequately has been shown.

(2) An interception of a communication under an interception warrant with respect to which the requirements of division (B)(3)(c) of this section and division (A)(5) of section 2933.54 of the Revised Code do not apply, due to the application of division (G)(1) of this section, shall not begin until the facilities from which or the place at which the communication is to be intercepted is ascertained by the person implementing the interception warrant.

A provider of wire or electronic communication service that has received an interception warrant that does not specify the facilities from which or the place at which the communication is to be intercepted, due to the application of division (G)(1)(b) of this section, may file a motion with the court requesting the court to modify or quash the interception warrant on the ground that the provider's assistance with respect to the interception cannot be performed in a timely or reasonable manner. The court, upon notice to the applicant for the interception warrant, shall decide the motion expeditiously.

**HISTORY: 141 v S 222 (Eff 3-25-87); 146 v H 181 (Eff 6-13-96); 146 v H 670. Eff 12-2-96.**

## § 2933.54 Conditions for issuance of warrant; denial; termination; finding of objective.

(A) A judge of a court of common pleas to whom an application for an interception warrant is made under section 2933.53 of the Revised Code may issue an interception warrant if the judge determines, on the basis of the facts submitted by the person who made the application and all affiants, that all of the following exist:

(1) The application and affidavits comply with section 2933.53 of the Revised Code.

(2) There is probable cause to believe that a particular person is committing, has committed, or is about to commit a designated offense.

(3) There is probable cause to believe that particular communications concerning the designated offense will be obtained through the interception of wire, oral, or electronic communications.

(4) Normal investigative procedures with respect to the designated offense have been tried and have failed or normal investigative procedures with respect to the designated offense reasonably appear to be unlikely to succeed if tried or to be too dangerous to employ in order to obtain evidence.

(5) Except as provided in division (G)(1) of section 2933.53 of the Revised Code, there is probable cause to believe that the communication facilities from which the communications are to be intercepted, or the place at which oral communications are to be intercepted, are being used or are about to be used in connection with the commission of the designated offense or are leased to, listed in the name of, or commonly used by a person who is the subject of the interception warrant.

(6) The investigative officer has received training that satisfies the minimum standards established by the attorney general and the Ohio peace officer training commission under section 2933.64 of the Revised Code in order to intercept the wire, oral, or electronic communication and is able to execute the interception sought.

(B) If the communication facilities from which a wire or electronic communication is to be intercepted are public facilities, the judge of the court of common pleas to whom the application for an interception warrant is made shall not issue an interception warrant unless the judge, in addition to the findings specified in division (A) of this section, determines that there is a special need to intercept wire or electronic communications made from the facilities.

(C) If the facilities from which, or the place at which, the wire, oral, or electronic communications are to be intercepted are being used by, are about to be used by, are leased to, are listed in the name of, or are commonly used by a licensed physician, a licensed practicing psychologist, an attorney, a practicing clergyman, or a journalist or are used primarily for habitation by a husband and wife, the judge of the court of common pleas to whom the application is made shall not issue an interception warrant unless the judge, in addition to the findings specified in divisions (A) and (B) of this section, determines that there is a special need to intercept wire, oral, or electronic communications over the facilities or in those places. No otherwise privileged wire, oral, or electronic communication shall lose its privileged character because it is intercepted in accordance with or in violation of sections 2933.51 to 2933.66 of the Revised Code.

(D) If an application for an interception warrant does not comply with section 2933.53 of the Revised Code, or if the judge of a court of common pleas with whom an application is filed is not satisfied that grounds exist for issuance of an interception warrant, the judge shall deny the application.

(E) An interception warrant shall terminate when the objective of the warrant has been achieved or upon the expiration of thirty days after the date of commencement of the warrant as specified in this division, whichever occurs first, unless an extension is granted as described in this division. The date of commencement of an interception warrant is the day on which an investigative or law enforcement officer first begins to conduct an interception under the warrant, or the day that is ten days after the warrant is issued, whichever is earlier. A judge of a court of common pleas may grant extensions of a warrant pursuant to section 2933.55 of the Revised Code.

(F) If a judge of a court of common pleas issues an interception warrant, the judge shall make a finding as to the objective of the warrant.

**HISTORY: 141 v S 222 (Eff 3-25-87); 142 v H 708 (Eff 4-19-88); 146 v H 181 (Eff 6-13-96); 146 v H 670. Eff 12-2-96.**

## § 2933.55 Application for extension of warrant; interception concerning other than designated offense.

(A) At any time prior to the expiration of an interception warrant, the person who made the application for the warrant may apply for an extension of the warrant. The person shall file the application for extension with a judge of the court of common pleas of the county in which the interception under the warrant was to take place. An application for extension shall comply with section 2933.53 of the Revised Code.

(B) A judge of a court of common pleas with whom an application for extension of an interception warrant is filed shall determine whether to order an extension of the interception warrant in accordance with section 2933.54 of the Revised Code and shall order an extension for a period no longer than the judge considers necessary to achieve the purposes of the extension. The extension shall terminate upon the attainment of the authorized objective or thirty days after it is granted, whichever occurs first. All provisions of sections 2933.51 to 2933.66 of the Revised

Code that apply to original interception warrants apply to extensions of interception warrants.

(C)(1) When an investigative officer, while intercepting communications pursuant to an interception warrant or pursuant to an oral order for an interception granted under section 2933.57 of the Revised Code, intercepts wire, oral, or electronic communications that pertain to a criminal offense that is other than the designated offense specified in the interception warrant or oral order and that is completely unrelated to the designated offense specified in the interception warrant or oral order, the prosecuting attorney, in order to permit the disclosure or use of the contents, or evidence derived from the contents, of the intercepted communications pursuant to division (G) of section 2933.59 of the Revised Code, may file a motion with the judge who issued the warrant or granted the oral order for an order approving the interception. The judge shall enter an order approving the interception if the judge finds that the communication otherwise was intercepted in accordance with sections 2933.53 to 2933.66 of the Revised Code.

A person may disclose or use the contents, and any evidence derived from the contents, of the intercepted communications dealing with the other, unrelated offense as set forth in division (F) of section 2933.59 of the Revised Code. The person may disclose or use those contents and the evidence derived from those contents as set forth in division (G) of section 2933.59 of the Revised Code only if the issuing judge issues an order approving the interception of the communications concerning the other, unrelated offense.

(2) When an investigative officer, while intercepting communications pursuant to an interception warrant or pursuant to an oral order for an interception granted under section 2933.57 of the Revised Code, intercepts wire, oral, or electronic communications that pertain to a criminal offense that is other than the designated offense specified in the interception warrant or oral order but that is not completely unrelated to the designated offense specified in the interception warrant or oral order, the wire, oral, or electronic communications intercepted shall be treated for all purposes and without the need for further action as if the offense to which they pertain was a designated offense specified in the interception warrant or oral order.

**HISTORY: 141 v S 222 (Eff 3-25-87); 146 v H 181. Eff 6-13-96.**

## § 2933.56 Contents of warrant; sealing of application and warrant; disclosure; retention.

(A) Any interception warrant or extension of an interception warrant that is issued pursuant to sections 2933.53 to 2933.55 of the Revised Code shall contain all of the following:

(1) The name and court of the judge who issued the warrant and the jurisdiction of that court;

(2) If known, the identity of each person whose communications are to be intercepted or, if the identity is unascertainable, a detailed description of each known person whose communications are to be intercepted;

(3) The nature and location of the communications facilities from which or of the place at which the authority to intercept is granted and, in the case of telephone or telegraph communications, a designation of the particular lines involved;

(4) A statement of the objective of the warrant, as found by the issuing judge, and a statement of the designated offenses for which the authority to intercept is granted;

(5) A description of the particular type of communication sought to be intercepted;

(6) The identity of the investigative officer or law enforcement agency that is authorized to intercept communications pursuant to the interception warrant and the identity of the prosecuting attorney or assistant prosecuting attorney authorizing the application for the interception warrant;

(7) The period of time during which the interception is authorized, including a statement as to whether the interception shall terminate automatically when the described communication is first intercepted;

(8) A statement that the interception warrant shall be executed as soon as practicable;

(9) A statement that the interception shall be conducted in a way that minimizes the interception of communications that are not subject to the interception warrant, provided that if the intercepted communication is in a code or a foreign language and an expert in decoding or in that foreign language is not reasonably available during the interception period, minimization may be accomplished as soon as practicable after the interception;

(10) A statement that the interception shall terminate upon attainment of the authorized objective or upon the expiration of the thirty-day period described in division (E) of section 2933.54 of the Revised Code, whichever occurs first, unless an extension of the interception warrant is granted upon application by the judge who issued the original warrant;

(11) A statement that the person who made the application for the warrant or extension and the investigative officer or law enforcement agency authorized to intercept the communications shall provide oral or written progress reports at seven-day intervals to the judge who issued the warrant showing the progress made toward achievement of the authorized objective of the warrant and the need for continued interception;

(12) An authorization to enter private premises, other than the premises of a provider of wire or electronic communication service, for the sole purposes of installing, or of removing and permanently inactivating, interception devices and, if the entry is necessary to execute the interception warrant, a requirement that the time and date of the entry and name of the individual making the entry be reported to the court;

(13) If applicable, a statement directing a provider of wire or electronic communication service, landlord, custodian, or other person forthwith to furnish the applicant all information, facilities, and technical assistance necessary to accomplish the interception unobtrusively and with a minimum of interference with the services that the provider of wire or electronic communication service, landlord, custodian, or other person is providing to the person whose communications are to be intercepted. This assistance by a provider of wire or electronic communication service shall not include assistance in supplying, installing, or removing and permanently inactivating, interception devices. Any provider of wire or electronic communication service and any landlord, custodian, or other person furnishing the facilities or technical assistance shall be compensated for them at the prevailing rates.

(B) The judge of the court of common pleas to whom the application is made or who issued the warrant shall seal all applications for interception warrants that are made and all interception warrants that are issued pursuant to sections 2933.53 to 2933.55 of the Revised Code.

The judge of a court of common pleas who received the application or issued the warrant shall specify who shall have custody of the sealed application and interception warrant. Copies of the interception warrant, together with a copy of the application, shall be delivered to and retained by the person who made the application for the warrant or extension as authority for the interception authorized by the warrant.

Except as otherwise provided in sections 2933.51 to 2933.66 of the Revised Code, the application and interception warrants shall be disclosed only upon a showing of good cause before a judge who is authorized to issue interception warrants. Upon the termination of the authorized interception, the person who made the application for the warrant or extension shall return all applications made and interception warrants issued under sections 2933.53 to 2933.55 of the Revised Code that pertain to the interception to the issuing judge, and the applications and warrants shall be sealed under the issuing judge's direction.

The applications and warrants shall be kept for at least ten years. At the expiration of the ten-year period, the issuing or denying judge may order that the applications and warrants be destroyed.

(C) A violation of division (B) of this section may be punished as contempt of court.

**HISTORY: 141 v S 222 (Eff 3-25-87); 146 v H 181. Eff 6-13-96.**

## § 2933.57 Oral order for interception without warrant.

(A) A judge of the court of common pleas may grant an oral order for an interception without a warrant of a wire, oral, or electronic communication. Upon receipt of an application under this division, the judge of the court of common pleas to whom the application is made may grant an oral order for an interception without a warrant, may include in the order a statement of the type described in division (A)(13) of section 2933.56 of the Revised Code, and shall condition the order upon the filing with the judge, within forty-eight hours, of an application for an interception warrant under section 2933.53 of the Revised Code and division (B) of this section, if the judge determines all of the following:

(1) There appear to be grounds upon which an interception warrant could be issued under section 2933.54 of the Revised Code.

(2) There is probable cause to believe that an emergency situation exists with respect to the investigation of a designated offense.

(3) There is probable cause to believe that the emergency situation involves an immediate danger of death or serious physical harm that justifies the authorization for immediate interception of a private wire, oral, or electronic communication before an application for an interception warrant could, with due diligence, be submitted to the judge and acted upon.

(B) No statement by the attorney general or the attorney general's designee pursuant to division (B)(9) of section 2933.53 is required prior to consideration of an application pursuant to this section.

(C) The judge of a court of common pleas to whom an application is made under division (A) of this section, the applicant, the prosecuting attorney or assistant prosecuting attorney who authorized the application, and any involved provider of wire or electronic communication service may tape record any telephone or other communications between any of them related to the application for, the approval of, and the implementation of an oral order for an interception. All of the provisions of sections 2933.51 to 2933.66 of the Revised Code concerning the sealing, distribution, use, and disclosure of an application for an interception warrant apply to any tape recording between the judge, the applicant, and the prosecuting attorney or the designated assistant concerning the application for and an oral order for an interception.

(D)(1) As soon as possible after granting an oral order for an interception without a warrant, a judge shall place upon the journal of the court an entry nunc pro tunc to record the granting of the oral order. If an interception warrant is issued pursuant to the filing of an application following the granting of an oral order for an interception under this section, the judge shall issue the warrant in accordance with section 2933.54 of the Revised Code, and the warrant shall recite the granting of the oral order and shall be retroactive to the time of the oral order.

(2) Interception pursuant to an oral order under this section shall be made in accordance with section 2933.59 of the Revised Code, except that the interception shall terminate immediately when the communication sought is obtained or when the application for a warrant is denied, whichever is earlier.

(3) If no application for a warrant is made in accordance with this section within forty-eight hours following a grant of an oral order or if an application for a warrant is made in accordance with this section following the grant of an oral order but the application is denied, the content of any private wire, oral, or electronic communication intercepted under the oral order shall be treated as having been obtained in violation of this chapter, and an inventory shall be served in accordance with section 2933.61 of the Revised Code upon the person named in the application. However, a provider of wire or electronic communication service that relies in good faith on the oral order in accordance with division (B) of section 2933.65 of the Revised Code is immune from civil or criminal liability in accordance with that section.

(4) If no application for a warrant is made within forty-eight hours following a grant of an oral order under this section or if an application for a warrant is made but is denied, the judge of a court of common pleas who granted an oral order for the interception shall prepare a journal entry reciting the grant of the oral order that includes as much of the information required to be included in an interception warrant that is practical to include. All of the provisions of sections 2933.51 to 2933.63 of the Revised Code concerning the sealing, distribution, use, and disclosure of an interception warrant apply to the journal entry required by this division. The judge who granted the oral order also shall order the person who received the oral order under this section to prepare an inventory of the recordings and resumes compiled under the oral order and shall require the tape or other recording of the intercepted communication to be delivered to, and sealed by, the judge in accordance with division (B) of section 2933.59 of the Revised Code. The court served by that judge shall retain the evidence, and no person shall use or disclose the evidence in a legal

proceeding, other than a civil action brought by an aggrieved person or as otherwise authorized by the order of a judge of the court of common pleas of the county in which the interception took place. In addition to other remedies or penalties provided by law, a failure to deliver a tape or other recording to the judge in accordance with this division shall be punishable as contempt by the judge directing the delivery.

**HISTORY: 141 v S 222 (Eff 3-25-87); 146 v H 181. Eff 6-13-96.**

## § 2933.58 Instructions to investigative officers; procedure for interception; territorial validity.

(A) Upon the issuance of an interception warrant pursuant to section 2933.54 of the Revised Code and prior to the execution of the warrant or upon a grant of an oral order for an interception under section 2933.57 of the Revised Code, the prosecuting attorney or assistant prosecuting attorney who authorized the application for the warrant or the oral approval shall instruct the investigative officers who are authorized to intercept the communications regarding the application and interpretation of divisions (A), (B), and (C) of section 2317.02 of the Revised Code. The prosecuting attorney or assistant prosecuting attorney who authorized the application or the oral order also shall instruct the officers to minimize the interception of communications that are not subject to the warrant or oral order and shall inform the officers of the procedures to be followed if communications concerning another offense are intercepted. If individuals operating under a contract to provide interception services as described in section 2933.59 of the Revised Code are involved in the interception, the prosecuting attorney or assistant prosecuting attorney who authorized the application for the warrant or the oral order also shall give the instructions and information under this division to those individuals.

(B) Investigative officers who are authorized to intercept communications pursuant to an interception warrant or pursuant to an oral order for an interception granted under section 2933.57 of the Revised Code and individuals who are operating under a contract to provide interception services as described in section 2933.59 of the Revised Code shall monitor the receiver of the interception device at all times during the time period for which the interception is authorized. All communications shall be intercepted only in accordance with the warrant or the oral order.

(C) An interception warrant issued pursuant to sections 2933.53 to 2933.55 of the Revised Code or an oral order for an interception granted under section 2933.57 of the Revised Code authorizes the interception of wire, oral, or electronic communications or the installation of an interception device within the jurisdiction of the court of common pleas served by the judge who issued the warrant or granted the oral order. The warrant or oral order is valid at any place if the interception device is installed within the jurisdiction of the judge who issued the warrant or granted the oral order and is then moved to another place by persons other than the investigative officers.

**HISTORY: 141 v S 222 (Eff 3-25-87); 146 v H 181. Eff 6-13-96.**

**Not analogous to former RC § 2933.58 (133 v H 956), repealed 141 v S 222, § 2, eff 3-25-87.**

## § 2933.581 Persons providing information, facilities or technical assistance to officer; prohibited disclosures; immunity.

(A) Notwithstanding any other provision of law, a provider of wire or electronic communication service, an officer, employee, or agent of a provider of that type, and a landlord, custodian, or other person is authorized to provide information, facilities, or technical assistance to a person who is authorized by the law of this state or the United States to intercept wire, oral, or electronic communications if both of the following apply:

(1) The provider, officer, employee, agent, landlord, custodian, or person has been provided with either of the following:

(a) An interception warrant or extension of an interception warrant that contains a statement of the type described in division (A)(13) of section 2933.56 of the Revised Code;

(b) A written representation of a judge of a court of common pleas or of a prosecuting attorney or specifically designated assistant prosecuting attorney that an oral order for an interception has been granted pursuant to section 2933.57 of the Revised Code, that no interception warrant is required by law, that all applicable statutory requirements have been satisfied, and that the oral order contains a statement of the type described in division (A)(13) of section 2933.56 of the Revised Code that directs the provision of the specified information, facilities, or technical assistance.

(2) The warrant, extension, or representation sets forth the period of time during which the provision of the information, facilities, or technical assistance is authorized and specifies the information, facilities, or technical assistance required.

(B)(1) Except as provided in division (B)(2) of this section, no provider of wire or electronic communication service, no officer, employee, or agent of a provider of that type, and no landlord, custodian, or other person who is authorized to provide information, facilities, or technical assistance under division (A) of this section shall disclose the existence of an interception or the device used to accomplish the interception with respect to which the person has been furnished an interception warrant, an extension of an interception warrant, or a written representation pursuant to that division. A person that makes a disclosure in violation of this division is liable for civil damages of the type described in section 2933.65 of the Revised Code.

(2) Division (B)(1) of this section does not prohibit the disclosure of the existence of an interception or the disclosure of a device used to accomplish an interception when the disclosure is required by legal process, provided the person making the disclosure gives prior notification of the disclosure to the prosecuting attorney of the county in which the interception takes place or in which the interception device is installed.

(C) Except as provided in this section, a provider of wire or electronic communication service, an officer, employee, or agent of a provider of that type, and a landlord, custodian, or other specified person is immune from civil or criminal liability in any action that arises out of its providing information, facilities, or technical assistance in accordance with division (A) of this section and the terms of the interception warrant, extension of an interception warrant, or written representation provided under that division.

**HISTORY: 146 v H 181. Eff 6-13-96.**

## § 2933.59 Execution of warrant or oral order; recording or resume; termination; tampering; destruction of documents; disclosure.

(A) An investigative officer who is, or a member of the law enforcement agency that is, authorized by an interception warrant or a grant of an oral order for an interception pursuant to section 2933.57 of the Revised Code to intercept wire, oral, or electronic communications or an individual who is operating under a contract with that agency and is acting under the supervision of that officer or a member of that agency shall execute the interception warrant or the oral order in accordance with the terms of the warrant or oral order. The officer or member of the law enforcement agency who executes the warrant or oral order or who supervises the execution of the warrant or oral order shall have received training that satisfies the minimum standards established by the attorney general and the Ohio peace officer training commission under section 2933.64 of the Revised Code. The contents of a wire, oral, or electronic communication intercepted pursuant to an interception warrant or pursuant to a grant of an oral order for an interception, if possible, shall be recorded on tape or another similar device. If it is not possible to record the intercepted communication, a detailed resume of that communication immediately shall be reduced to writing. The recording or transcribing of the contents of any wire, oral, or electronic communication pursuant to sections 2933.51 to 2933.66 of the Revised Code shall be done in a way that will protect the recording or transcription from editing or any other alteration.

(B) Immediately upon the expiration of the period of time for which an interception warrant was authorized, or any extensions of that time period, all wire, oral, or electronic communications interceptions shall cease, and any interception device installed pursuant to the interception warrant shall be removed or permanently inactivated as soon as is reasonably practicable. Entry to remove or inactivate an interception device is authorized by the granting of an interception warrant.

Immediately upon the expiration of that period of time or the extension, the recordings or resumes of intercepted communications shall be made available to the issuing judge and shall be sealed under the judge's direction. The issuing judge shall specify who shall have custody of the sealed recordings and resumes. The recordings and resumes shall be kept for at least ten years. At the expiration of the ten-year period, the recordings and resumes may be destroyed upon the order of a judge of the court of common pleas of the county in which the interception took place. Duplicate recordings or resumes may be made for use or disclosure pursuant to divisions (F) and (G) of this section.

(C) No person, with intent to present the altered recording or resume in any judicial proceeding or proceeding under oath or affirmation, shall purposely edit, alter, or tamper with any recording or resume of any intercepted wire, oral, or electronic communications, shall attempt to edit, alter, or tamper with any recording or resume of any intercepted wire, oral, or electronic communications, or shall present or permit the presentation of any altered recording or resume in any judicial proceeding or proceeding under oath or affirmation, without fully indicating the nature of the changes made in the original state of the recording or resume.

(D)(1) Any interception warrant, the existence of lawfully installed interception devices, the application, affidavits, and return prepared in connection with the warrant, and any information concerning the application for, the granting of, or the denial of an interception warrant shall remain secret until they have been disclosed in a criminal trial or in a proceeding that is open to the public or until they have been furnished to the defendant or unless otherwise provided in sections 2933.51 to 2933.66 of the Revised Code.

(2) Any person who violates division (D)(1) of this section may be punished for contempt of court.

(E) When an order for destruction of any documents dealing with an interception warrant is issued, the person directed in the order to destroy the applications, affidavits, interception warrants, any amendments or extensions of the warrants, or recordings or resumes made pursuant to the warrants shall do so in the presence of at least one witness who is not connected with a law enforcement agency. The person who destroys the documents and each witness shall execute affidavits setting forth the facts and circumstances of the destruction. The affidavits shall be filed with and approved by the court having custody of the original materials.

(F) An investigative officer who has obtained knowledge of the contents, or of evidence derived from the contents, of a wire, oral, or electronic communication pursuant to sections 2933.51 to 2933.66 of the Revised Code may disclose the contents or evidence to another investigative officer to the extent that the disclosure is appropriate to the proper performance of the official duties of the officer making or receiving the disclosure and may use the contents or evidence to the extent appropriate to the proper performance of official duties.

(G) A person who has received, pursuant to sections 2933.51 to 2933.66 of the Revised Code, information concerning, or evidence derived from, a wire, oral, or electronic communication intercepted pursuant to an interception warrant may disclose the contents of that communication, or the evidence derived from the contents, while giving testimony under oath or affirmation in a proceeding held under the authority of the United States, this state, another state, or a political subdivision of this state or another state, except that the presence of the seal provided for in division (B) of section 2933.56 of the Revised Code and in division (B) of this section, or a satisfactory explanation of the absence of the seal, shall be a prerequisite for the use or disclosure of the contents of any wire, oral, or electronic communication or evidence derived from the contents. The contents, or evidence derived from the contents, of a wire, oral, or electronic communication intercepted pursuant to an interception warrant and in accordance with sections 2933.51 to 2933.66 of the Revised Code otherwise may be disclosed only upon a showing of good cause before a judge authorized to issue interception warrants.

(H) Whoever violates division (C) of this section is guilty of a felony of the third degree.

**HISTORY: 141 v S 222 (Eff 3-25-87); 146 v H 181 (Eff 6-13-96); 146 v H 670. Eff 12-2-96.**

## § 2933.591 Giving warning of possible surveillance.

(A) No person who knows that an application for an interception warrant has been authorized or made under section 2933.53 of the Revised Code, that an interception warrant has been issued under section 2933.54 of the Revised Code, that an application for an extension of an interception warrant has been filed under section 2933.53 of the Revised Code, that an extension of an interception warrant has been ordered under that section, that an application for a grant of an oral order for an interception has been made under section 2933.57 of the Revised Code, or that oral order for an interception has been granted under section 2933.57 of the Revised Code, with purpose to obstruct, impede, or prevent the interception in question, shall give notice or attempt to give notice of the possible interception to a person.

(B) Whoever violates division (A) of this section is guilty of giving warning of possible surveillance, a felony of the third degree.

**HISTORY: 146 v H 181. Eff 6-13-96.**

## § 2933.60 Reports by judges and prosecuting attorneys.

(A) Within thirty days after the expiration of an interception warrant, the expiration of an extension of an interception warrant, or the denial of an application for an interception warrant, the judge of a court of common pleas who issued the warrant or extension or denied the application shall report all of the following to the administrative office of the United States courts and to the attorney general of this state:

(1) The fact that an application was made for an interception warrant or extension of an interception warrant;

(2) The kind of interception warrant or extension for which application was made, including a statement of whether the warrant or extension was or was not one to which the requirements of division (B)(3)(c) of section 2933.53 and division (A)(5) of section 2933.54 of the Revised Code did not apply due to the application of division (G)(1) of section 2933.53 of the Revised Code;

(3) The fact that the interception warrant or extension was granted as applied for or was denied;

(4) The period of interception authorized by the interception warrant, and the number and duration of any extensions of the warrant;

(5) The designated offenses specified in the interception warrant, application, or extension;

(6) The identity of the person who made the application, any person who executed any accompanying affidavit to an application, and the prosecuting attorney or assistant prosecuting attorney who authorized the application;

(7) The nature of the facilities from which, or the place at which, communications are to be intercepted.

(B) In January of each year, the prosecuting attorney of each county shall report to the administrative office of the United States courts and to the attorney general of this state all information that is required to be reported by subsection (2) of section 2519 of the "Omnibus Crime Control and Safe Streets Act of 1968," 82 Stat. 197, 18 U.S.C. 2519 (1968), as amended.

**HISTORY: 141 v S 222 (Eff 3-25-87); 146 v H 181. Eff 6-13-96.**

## § 2933.61 Service of inventory on interested persons; inspection of materials.

(A) Within a reasonable time not later than ninety days after the filing of an application for an interception warrant that is denied or after the termination of the period of an interception warrant or any extensions of an interception warrant, the judge of a court of common pleas who issued the warrant or extension or denied the application shall cause to be served on the persons named in the application or the interception warrant, and on any other parties to intercepted wire, oral, or electronic communications that the judge determines in the judge's discretion should be notified in the interest of justice, an inventory that shall include notice of all of the following:

(1) The fact that an interception warrant was issued or that application for one was made;

(2) The date the interception warrant was issued and the period of authorized, approved, or disapproved interception or the date of the denial of the application;

(3) The fact that during the stated period wire, oral, or electronic communications were or were not intercepted.

(B) A judge of the court of common pleas of the county, upon the filing of a motion for inspection, in the judge's discretion, may make available for inspection to the person filing the motion or the person's counsel any portions of intercepted wire, oral, or electronic communications, applications for interception warrants, or interception warrants that the judge determines to be in the interest of justice. Upon an ex parte showing of good cause to a judge of a court of common pleas who denied the issuance of or issued an interception warrant, the judge may postpone the serving of the inventory required by this section for a specified period of time.

**HISTORY: 141 v S 222 (Eff 3-25-87); 146 v H 181. Eff 6-13-96.**

## § 2933.62 Conditions for receiving results in evidence or disclosure.

(A) No part of the contents, and no evidence derived from the contents, of any intercepted wire, oral, or electronic communication shall be received in evidence in any trial, hearing, or other proceedings in or before any court, grand jury, department, officer, agency, regulatory body, legislative committee, or other authority of this state or of a political subdivision of this state, if the disclosure of that information is in violation of sections 2933.51 to 2933.66 of the Revised Code.

(B) The contents, or any evidence derived from the contents, of any wire, oral, or electronic communication intercepted pursuant to sections 2933.51 to 2933.66 of the Revised Code shall not be received in evidence or otherwise disclosed in any trial, hearing, or other proceeding held under the authority of this state, other than a proceeding or session of the grand jury, unless each party has been furnished not less than ten days before the trial, hearing, or proceeding, with a copy of the interception warrant and the related application, or a written representation of a judge of a court of common pleas or of a prosecuting attorney or specifically designated assistant prosecuting attorney that an oral order for an interception has been granted pursuant to section 2933.57 of the Revised Code, under which the interception was authorized or approved. The judge or other officer conducting the trial, hearing, or other proceeding may waive the ten-day period if the judge or officer finds that it was not possible to furnish the party with the above information at least ten days before the trial, hearing, or proceeding, and that the party will not be prejudiced by the delay in receiving the information.

**HISTORY: 141 v S 222 (Eff 3-25-87); 146 v H 181. Eff 6-13-96.**

## § 2933.63 Motion to suppress evidence; appeals by state.

(A) Any aggrieved person in any trial, hearing, or proceeding in or before any court, department, officer, agency, regulatory body, or other authority of this state or of a political subdivision of this state, other than a grand jury, may request the involved court, department, officer, agency, body, or authority, by motion, to suppress the contents, or evidence derived from the contents, of a wire, oral, or electronic communication intercepted pursuant to sections 2933.51 to 2933.66 of the Revised Code for any of the following reasons:

(1) The communication was unlawfully intercepted.

(2) The interception warrant under which the communication was intercepted is insufficient on its face.

(3) The interception was not made in conformity with the interception warrant or an oral order for an interception granted under section 2933.57 of the Revised Code.

(4) The communications are of a privileged character and a special need for their interception is not shown or is inadequate as shown.

(B) Any motion filed pursuant to division (A) of this section shall be made before the trial, hearing, or proceeding at which the contents, or evidence derived from the contents, is to be used, unless there was no opportunity to make the motion or the aggrieved person was not aware of the intercepted communications or the grounds of the motion. Upon the filing of the motion by the aggrieved person, the judge or other officer conducting the trial, hearing, or proceeding may make available to the aggrieved person or the person's counsel for inspection any portions of the intercepted communication or evidence derived from the intercepted communication as the judge or other officer determines to be in the interest of justice. If the judge or other officer grants the motion to suppress evidence pursuant to this section, the contents, or the evidence derived from the contents, of the intercepted wire, oral, or electronic communications shall be treated as having been obtained in violation of the law, and the contents and evidence derived from the contents shall not be received in evidence in any trial, hearing, or proceeding.

(C) In addition to any other right to appeal, the state shall have an appeal as of right from an order granting a motion to suppress the contents, or evidence derived from the contents, of a wire, oral, or electronic communication that was intercepted pursuant to an interception warrant or an oral order for an interception granted under section 2933.57 of the Revised Code, or the denial of an application for an interception warrant, if the state's representative certifies to the judge or other official who granted the motion or denied the application that the appeal is not taken for purposes of delay. Any appeal shall be taken within thirty days after the date the order was entered and shall be diligently prosecuted.

**HISTORY: 141 v S 222 (Eff 3-25-87); 146 v H 181. Eff 6-13-96.**

## § 2933.64 Training in wiretapping and electronic surveillance.

The attorney general and the Ohio peace officer training commission, pursuant to Chapter 109. of the Revised Code, shall establish a course of training in the legal and technical aspects of wiretapping and electronic surveillance, shall establish regulations that they find necessary and proper for the training program, and shall establish minimum standards for certification and periodic recertification for investigative officers to be eligible to conduct wiretapping or electronic surveillance under sections 2933.51 to 2933.66 of the Revised Code. The commission shall charge each investigative officer who enrolls in this training a reasonable enrollment fee to offset the cost of the training.

**HISTORY: 141 v S 222 (Eff 3-25-87); 146 v H 181 (Eff 6-13-96); 146 v H 670. Eff 12-2-96.**

## § 2933.65 Civil and criminal actions for violations.

(A) A person whose wire, oral, or electronic communications are intercepted, disclosed, or intentionally used in violation of sections 2933.51 to 2933.66 of the Revised Code may bring a civil action to recover from the person or entity that engaged in the violation any relief that may be appropriate and that includes, but is not limited to, the following:

(1) The preliminary and other equitable or declaratory relief that is appropriate;

(2) Whichever of the following is greater:

(a) Liquidated damages computed at a rate of two hundred dollars per day for each day of violation or liquidated damages of ten thousand dollars, whichever is greater;

(b) The sum of actual damages suffered by the plaintiff and the profits, if any, made as a result of the violation by the person or entity that engaged in the violation.

(3) Punitive damages, if appropriate;

(4) Reasonable attorney's fees and other litigation expenses that are reasonably incurred in bringing the civil action.

(B) Good faith reliance on an interception warrant, extension of an interception warrant, other court order, a grant of an oral order for an interception, a grand jury subpoena, a legislative or statutory authorization, or a good faith determination that divisions (A) and (B) of section 2933.521 [2933.52.1] of the Revised Code permitted the conduct that is the subject of a complaint is a complete defense to a civil action or criminal action that is brought under the laws of this state and that arises out of the execution of the warrant or the oral order.

(C) A claimant who brings a civil action under division (A) of this section shall commence the civil action within two years after the date on which the claimant first has a reasonable opportunity to discover the violation.

(D) The remedies and sanctions described in sections 2933.51 to 2933.66 of the Revised Code with respect to the interception of wire, oral, or electronic communications are the only judicial remedies and sanctions for violations of those sections involving those types of communications that are not violations of the constitution of the United States or of this state.

**HISTORY: 141 v S 222 (Eff 3-25-87); 146 v H 181. Eff 6-13-96.**

## § 2933.66 Judge to conform proceedings to constitutions.

Notwithstanding any provision of sections 2933.51 to 2933.65 of the Revised Code, a judge of a court of common pleas to whom an application for an interception warrant, an extension of an interception warrant, an oral order for an interception, or another purpose is made pursuant to sections 2933.51 to 2933.65 of the Revised Code may take evidence, make a finding, or issue an order to conform the proceedings or the issuance of an order to the constitution of the United States or of this state.

**HISTORY: 141 v S 222 (Eff 3-25-87); 146 v H 181. Eff 6-13-96.**

## [MEDICAID FRAUD FORFEITURES]

**§ 2933.71** Repealed, 151 v H 241, § 2 [145 v H 152. Eff 7-1-93]. Eff 7-1-07.

See provisions of § 4 of 151 v H 241 following RC § 2901.01.
This section concerned definitions. See now RC § 2981.01 et seq.

**§ 2933.72** Repealed, 151 v H 241, § 2 [145 v H 152 (Eff 7-1-93); 145 v H 715. Eff 7-22-94]. Eff 7-1-07.

See provisions of § 4 of 151 v H 241 following RC § 2901.01.
This section concerned order to preserve reachability of property that may be forfeitable; temporary restraining order; post-conviction actions. See now RC § 2981.01 et seq.

**§ 2933.73** Repealed, 151 v H 241, § 2 [145 v H 152 (Eff 7-1-93); 145 v H 715. Eff 7-22-94]. Eff 7-1-07.

See provisions of § 4 of 151 v H 241 following RC § 2901.01.
This section concerned civil hearing; forfeiture order; petition by innocent person claiming interest in property. See now RC § 2981.01 et seq.

**§ 2933.74** Repealed, 151 v H 241, § 2 [145 v H 152 (Eff 7-1-93); 145 v H 715 (Eff 7-22-94); 146 v H 670 (Eff 12-2-96); 147 v S 164. Eff 1-15-98; 151 v H 66, § 101.01, eff. 9-29-05]. Eff 7-1-07.

See provisions of § 4 of 151 v H 241 following RC § 2901.01.
This section concerned settlement of claims; awards to informants; protection of rights of innocent persons; disposal of property; use of proceeds. See now RC § 2981.01 et seq.

**§ 2933.75 Filing of medicaid fraud lien notice; trustees of forfeitable property.**

(A) Upon the institution of any criminal proceeding charging a medicaid fraud offense, the state, at any time during the pendency of the proceeding, may file a medicaid fraud lien notice with the county recorder of any county in which forfeitable property subject to forfeiture may be located. No fee shall be required for filing the notice. The recorder immediately shall record the notice pursuant to section 317.08 of the Revised Code.

(B) A medicaid fraud lien notice shall be signed by the prosecuting attorney or attorney general who will prosecute the case and who files the lien. The notice shall set forth all of the following information:

(1) The name of the person against whom the proceeding has been brought. The prosecuting attorney or attorney general who will prosecute the case may specify in the notice any aliases, names, or fictitious names under which the person may be known.

(2) If known to the prosecuting attorney or attorney general who will prosecute the case, the present residence and business addresses of the person or names set forth in the notice;

(3) A statement that a criminal proceeding for a medicaid fraud offense has been brought against the person named in the notice, the name of the county in which the proceeding has been brought, and the case number of the proceeding;

(4) A statement that the notice is being filed pursuant to this section;

(5) The name and address of the prosecuting attorney or attorney general filing the notice;

(6) A description of the real or personal property subject to the notice and of the interest in that property of the person named in the notice, to the extent the property and the interest of the person in it reasonably is known at the time the proceeding is instituted or at the time the notice is filed.

(C) A medicaid fraud lien notice shall apply only to one person and, to the extent applicable, any aliases, fictitious names, or other names, including names of corporations, partnerships, or other entities, to the extent permitted in this section. A separate medicaid fraud lien notice is required to be filed for any other person.

(D) Within seven days after the filing of each medicaid fraud lien notice, the prosecuting attorney or attorney general who files the notice shall furnish to the person named in the notice by certified mail, return receipt requested, to the last known business or residential address of the person, a copy of the recorded notice with a notation on it of any county in which the notice has been recorded. The failure of the prosecuting attorney or attorney general to furnish a copy of the notice under this section shall not invalidate or otherwise affect the medicaid fraud lien notice when the prosecuting attorney or attorney general did not know and could not reasonably ascertain the address of the person entitled to notice.

After receipt of a copy of the notice under this division, the person named in the notice may petition the court to authorize the person to post a surety bond in lieu of the lien or to otherwise modify the lien as the interests of justice may require. The bond shall be in an amount equal to the value of the property reasonably known to be subject to the notice and conditioned on the payment of any judgment and costs ordered in an action pursuant to Chapter 2981. of the Revised Code up to the value of the bond.

(E) From the date of filing of a medicaid fraud lien notice, the notice creates a lien in favor of the state on any personal or real property or any beneficial interest in the property located in the county in which the notice is filed that then or subsequently is owned by the person named in the notice or under any of the names set forth in the notice.

The lien created in favor of the state is superior and prior to the interest of any other person in the personal or real property or beneficial interest in the property, if the interest is acquired subsequent to the filing of the notice.

(F) If a medicaid fraud lien notice has been filed, and if a forfeiture order is entered subsequent to a conviction or guilty plea in the criminal proceeding pursuant to Chapter 2981. of the Revised Code in favor of the state, the interest of any person in the property that was acquired subsequent to the filing of the notice shall be subject to the notice and order of forfeiture.

(G) Upon the issuance of an order of forfeiture in favor of the state pursuant to Chapter 2981. of the Revised Code, title of the state to the forfeited property shall do either of the following:

(1) In the case of real property, or a beneficial interest in it, relate back to the date of filing of the medicaid fraud lien notice in the county where the property or interest is located. If no medicaid fraud lien notice was filed, title of the state relates back to the date of the recording of the order of forfeiture in the records of the county recorder of the county in which the real property or beneficial interest is located.

(2) In the case of personal property or a beneficial interest in it, relate back to the date on which the property or interest was seized by the state, or the date of filing of a medicaid fraud lien notice in the county in which the property or beneficial interest is located. If the property was not seized and no medicaid fraud lien notice was filed, title of the state relates back to the date of the recording of the order of forfeiture in the county in which the personal property or beneficial interest is located.

(H) If personal or real property, or a beneficial interest in it, that is forfeitable property and is subject to forfeiture pursuant to Chapter 2981. of the Revised Code is conveyed, alienated, disposed of, or otherwise rendered unavailable for forfeiture after the filing of either a medicaid fraud lien notice, or a criminal proceeding for a medicaid fraud offense, whichever is earlier, the state may bring an action in any court of common pleas against the person named in the medicaid fraud lien notice or the defendant in the criminal proceeding to recover the value of the property or interest. The court shall enter final judgment against the person named in the notice or the defendant for an amount equal to the value of the property or interest together with investigative costs and attorney's fees incurred by the state in the action.

(I) If personal or real property, or a beneficial interest in it, that is forfeitable property and is subject to forfeiture pursuant to Chapter 2981. of the Revised Code is alienated or otherwise transferred or disposed of after either the filing of a medicaid fraud lien notice, or the filing of a criminal proceeding for a medicaid fraud offense, whichever is earlier, the transfer or disposal is fraudulent as to the state and the state shall have all the rights granted a creditor under Chapter 1336. of the Revised Code.

(J) No trustee, who acquires actual knowledge that a medicaid fraud lien notice or a criminal proceeding for a medicaid fraud offense has been filed against any person for whom the trustee holds legal or record title to personal or real property, shall recklessly fail to furnish promptly to the prosecuting attorney or attorney general who is prosecuting the case all of the following:

(1) The name and address of the person, as known to the trustee;

(2) The name and address, as known to the trustee, of all other persons for whose benefit the trustee holds title to the property;

(3) If requested by the prosecuting attorney or attorney general who is prosecuting the case, a copy of the trust agreement or other instrument under which the trustee holds title to the property.

Any trustee who fails to comply with division (J) of this section is guilty of failure to provide medicaid fraud lien information, a misdemeanor of the first degree.

(K) If a trustee transfers title to personal or real property after a medicaid fraud lien notice is filed against the property, the lien is filed in the county in which the property is located, and the lien names a person who holds a beneficial interest in the property, the trustee, if the trustee has actual notice of the notice, shall be liable to the state for the greater of the following:

(1) The proceeds received directly by the person named in the notice as a result of the transfer;

(2) The proceeds received by the trustee as a result of the transfer and distributed to the person named in the notice;

(3) The fair market value of the interest of the person named in the notice in the property transferred.

However, if the trustee transfers property for at least its fair market value and holds the proceeds that otherwise would be paid or distributed to the beneficiary, or at the direction of the beneficiary or the beneficiary's designee, the liability of the trustee shall not exceed the amount of the proceeds held by the trustee.

(L) The filing of a medicaid fraud lien notice does not constitute a lien on the record title to personal or real property owned by the trustee, except to the extent the trustee is named in the notice.

The prosecuting attorney for the county or the attorney general may bring a civil action in any court of common pleas to recover from the trustee the amounts set forth in division (H) of this section. The county or state may recover investigative costs and attorney's fees incurred by the prosecuting attorney or the attorney general.

(M)(1) This section does not apply to any transfer by a trustee under a court order, unless the order is entered in an action between the trustee and the beneficiary.

(2) Unless the trustee has actual knowledge that a person owning a beneficial interest in the trust is named in a medicaid fraud lien notice, this section does not apply to either of the following:

(a) Any transfer by a trustee required under the terms of any trust agreement, if the agreement is a matter of public record before the filing of any medicaid fraud lien notice;

(b) Any transfer by a trustee to all of the persons who own a beneficial interest in the trust.

(N) The filing of a medicaid fraud lien notice does not affect the use to which personal or real property, or a beneficial interest in it, that is owned by the person named in the notice may be put or the right of the person to receive any proceeds resulting from the use and ownership, but not the sale, of the property, until a judgment of forfeiture is entered.

(O) The term of a medicaid fraud lien notice is five years from the date the notice is filed, unless a renewal notice has been filed by the prosecuting attorney of the county in which the property or interest is located or by the attorney general. The term of any renewal of a medicaid fraud lien notice granted by the court is five years from the date of its filing. A medicaid fraud lien notice may be renewed any number of times while a criminal proceeding for a medicaid fraud offense, or an appeal from such a proceeding, is pending.

(P) The prosecuting attorney or attorney general who files the medicaid fraud lien notice may terminate, in whole or part, the notice or release any personal or real property or beneficial interest in the property upon any terms that the prosecuting attorney or attorney general determines are appropriate. Any termination or release shall be filed by the prosecuting attorney or attorney general with each county recorder with whom the notice was filed. No fee shall be imposed for the filing.

(Q) The acquittal in a criminal proceeding for a medicaid fraud offense of the person named in the medicaid fraud lien notice or the dismissal of a criminal proceeding for such an offense against the person named in the notice terminates the notice. In such a case, the filing of the notice has no effect.

A person named in a medicaid fraud lien notice may bring an action against the prosecuting attorney or attorney general who filed the notice, in the county where it was filed, seeking a release of the property subject to the notice or termination of the notice. In such a case, the court of common pleas promptly shall set a date for hearing, which shall be not less than five nor more than ten days after the action is filed. The order and a copy of the complaint shall be served on the prosecuting attorney or attorney general within three days after the action is filed. At the hearing, the court shall take evidence as to whether any personal or real property, or beneficial interest in it, that is owned by the person bringing the action is covered by the notice or otherwise is subject to forfeiture. If the person bringing the action shows by a preponderance of the evidence that the notice does not apply to the person or that any personal or real property, or beneficial interest in it, that is owned by the person is not subject to forfeiture, the court shall enter a judgment terminating the notice or releasing the personal or real property or beneficial interest from the notice.

At a hearing, the court may release from the notice any property or beneficial interest upon the posting of security, by the person against whom the notice was filed, in an amount equal to the value of the property or beneficial interest owned by the person.

The court promptly shall enter an order terminating a medicaid fraud lien notice or releasing any personal or real property or beneficial interest in the property, if a sale of the property or beneficial interest is pending and the filing of the notice prevents the sale. However, the proceeds of the sale shall be deposited with the clerk of the court, subject to the further order of the court.

(R) Notwithstanding any provision of this section, any person who has perfected a security interest in personal or real property or a beneficial interest in the property for the payment of an enforceable debt or other similar obligation prior to the filing of a medicaid fraud lien notice in reference to the property or interest may foreclose on the property or interest as otherwise provided by law. The foreclosure, insofar as practical, shall be made so that it otherwise will not interfere with a forfeiture under Chapter 2981. of the Revised Code.

**HISTORY: 145 v H 152 (Eff 7-1-93); 145 v H 715. Eff 7-22-94; 151 v H 241, § 1, eff. 7-1-07.**

See provisions of § 4 of 151 v H 241 following RC § 2901.01.

## [MISCELLANEOUS]

## § 2933.76 Authorization of pen register or trap and trace device.

(A) As used in this section and section 2933.77 of the Revised Code, "electronic communication," "electronic communication service," "investigative officer," "judge of a court of common pleas," "pen register," "trap and trace device," and "wire communication" have the same meanings as in section 2933.51 of the Revised Code.

(B) A judge of a court of common pleas, in accordance with this section, may issue an order authorizing or approving the installation and use, within the jurisdiction of the court, of a pen register or a trap and trace device to obtain information in connection with a criminal investigation.

(C) A law enforcement officer or investigative officer may make an application to a judge of a court of common pleas for an order authorizing the installation and use, within the jurisdiction of the court, of a pen register or a trap and trace device to obtain information in connection with a criminal investigation. The application shall be in writing and shall be under oath or affirmation. Each application shall contain all of the following:

(1) The name of the law enforcement officer or investigative officer making the application and the name of the investigative or law enforcement agency conducting the criminal investigation to which the application relates;

(2) The name, if known, of the person to whom the telephone or other line to which the pen register or trap and trace device is to be attached is leased or in whose name that telephone or other line is listed;

(3) The name, if known, of the person who is the subject of the criminal investigation to which the application relates;

(4) The number and, if known, the physical location of the telephone or other line to which the pen register or the trap and trace device is to be attached;

(5) A statement of the offense to which the information that is likely to be obtained by the installation and use of the pen register or trap and trace device relates;

(6) A certification by the law enforcement officer or investigative officer making the application that the information that is likely to be obtained by the installation and use of the pen register or trap and trace device is relevant to an ongoing criminal investigation being conducted by the investigative or law enforcement agency identified under division (C)(1) of this section.

(D)(1) The judge to whom an application is made under division (C) of this section shall issue and enter an order authorizing the installation and use of a pen register or a trap and trace device if the judge finds that the information relating to an offense that is likely to be obtained by the installation and use of the pen register or trap and trace device is relevant to an ongoing criminal investigation being conducted by the investigative or law enforcement agency identified under division (C)(1) of this section. In the order, the judge shall specify a finding with respect to each of the items required by divisions (C)(1) to (6) of this section to be included in the application.

(2) If the law enforcement officer or investigative officer so requests, the order shall direct the appropriate provider of wire or electronic communication service, landlord, custodian, or other person to furnish the law enforcement officer or investigative officer with all information, facilities, and technical assistance necessary to accomplish the installation and operation of a pen register or trap and trace device unobtrusively and with a minimum of interference of service to the person with respect to whom the installation and operation are to take place. The order further shall direct the person who owns or leases the telephone or other line to which the pen register or trap and trace device is to be attached, or the provider of wire or electronic communication service, landlord, custodian, or other person who is ordered under division (D)(2) of this section to provide information, facilities, or

technical assistance, not to disclose the existence of the criminal investigation or of the installation and use of the pen register or trap and trace device to the listed subscriber of the telephone or other line or to another person unless or until otherwise ordered by the court. If the order pertains to a trap and trace device, the order may require the appropriate provider of wire or electronic communication service to install and operate the device. The order shall be sealed until otherwise ordered by the court.

(E) An order issued pursuant to division (D) of this section shall authorize the installation and use of a pen register or a trap and trace device for a period not to exceed sixty days. The court may grant an extension of the sixty-day period upon application for an order in accordance with division (C) of this section and upon the judicial findings required by division (D)(1) of this section. An extension of an order issued under this division shall be in effect for a period not to exceed sixty days. The court may order further extensions of the sixty-day extended period upon compliance with this division.

(F) A good faith reliance on a court order issued under this section, a legislative authorization, or a statutory authorization is a complete defense against any claim in a civil action or any charge in a criminal action alleging a violation of the requirements of this section or section 2933.77 of the Revised Code.

**HISTORY: 146 v H 181 (Eff 6-13-96); 147 v H 565. Eff 3-30-99.**

## § 2933.77 Duty to provide information, facilities or technical assistance; immunity.

(A) If an order issued under section 2933.76 of the Revised Code authorizing the installation and use of a pen register or a trap and trace device directs a provider of wire or electronic communication service, landlord, custodian, or other person to furnish information, facilities, and technical assistance to accomplish the installation and operation of the pen register or trap and trace device, that provider, landlord, custodian, or other person, in accordance with the order, shall furnish the law enforcement officer or investigative officer with all information, facilities, and technical assistance necessary to accomplish the installation and operation of the pen register or trap and trace device unobtrusively and with a minimum of interference with the service accorded by the provider, landlord, custodian, or other person to the person with respect to whom the installation and operation are to take place. If an order issued under that section requires a provider of wire or electronic communication service to install and operate a trap and trace device, the provider, in accordance with the order, shall install and operate the device.

(B) The investigative or law enforcement agency conducting the criminal investigation to which the order issued under section 2933.76 of the Revised Code for the installation and use of a pen register or a trap and trace device relates shall provide reasonable compensation to a provider of wire or electronic communication service, landlord, custodian, or other person who furnishes facilities or technical assistance in accordance with the order for any reasonable expenses the provider, landlord, custodian, or other person incurs in furnishing the facilities or technical assistance.

(C) A provider of wire or electronic communication service, an officer, employee, or agent of that provider, or a landlord, custodian, or other specified person is immune from civil or criminal liability in any action that arises from the provision of information, facilities, or technical assistance in accordance with the terms of an order of a court issued under section 2933.76 of the Revised Code.

**HISTORY: 146 v H 181 (Eff 6-13-96); 147 v H 565. Eff 3-30-99.**

## § 2933.81 Electronic recording of custodial interrogations; presumption that recorded statements are voluntary.

(A) As used in this section:

(1) "Custodial interrogation" means any interrogation involving a law enforcement officer's questioning that is reasonably likely to elicit incriminating responses and in which a reasonable person in the subject's position would consider self to be in custody, beginning when a person should have been advised of the person's right to counsel and right to remain silent and of the fact that anything the person says could be used against the person, as specified by the United States supreme court in *Miranda v. Arizona*(1966), 384 U.S. 436, and subsequent decisions, and ending when the questioning has completely finished.

(2) "Detention facility" has the same meaning as in section 2921.01 of the Revised Code.

(3) "Electronic recording" or "electronically recorded" means an audio and visual recording that is an authentic, accurate, unaltered record of a custodial interrogation.

(4) "Law enforcement agency" has the same meaning as in section 109.573 [109.57.3] of the Revised Code.

(5) "Law enforcement vehicle" means a vehicle primarily used by a law enforcement agency or by an employee of a law enforcement agency for official law enforcement purposes.

(6) "Local correctional facility" has the same meaning as in section 2903.13 of the Revised Code.

(7) "Place of detention" means a jail, police or sheriff's station, holding cell, state correctional institution, local correctional facility, detention facility, or department of youth services facility. "Place of detention" does not include a law enforcement vehicle.

(8) "State correctional institution" has the same meaning as in section 2967.01 of the Revised Code.

(9) "Statement" means an oral, written, sign language, or nonverbal communication.

(B) All statements made by a person who is the suspect of a violation of or possible violation of section 2903.01, 2903.02, or 2903.03, a violation of section 2903.04 or 2903.06 that is a felony of the first or second degree, a violation of section 2907.02 or 2907.03, or an attempt to commit a violation of section 2907.02 of the Revised Code during a custodial interrogation in a place of detention are presumed to be voluntary if the statements made by the person are electronically recorded. The person making the statements during the electronic recording of the custodial interrogation has the burden of proving that the statements made during the custodial interrogation were not voluntary. There shall be no penalty against the law enforcement agency that employs a law enforcement officer if the law enforcement officer fails to electronically record as required by this division a custodial interrogation. A law enforcement officer's failure to electronically record a custodial interrogation does not create a private cause of action against that law enforcement officer.

(C) A failure to electronically record a statement as required by this section shall not provide the basis to exclude or suppress the statement in any criminal proceeding, delinquent child proceeding, or other legal proceeding.

(D)(1) Law enforcement personnel shall clearly identify and catalog every electronic recording of a custodial interrogation that is recorded pursuant to this section.

(2) If a criminal or delinquent child proceeding is brought against a person who was the subject of a custodial interrogation that was electronically recorded, law enforcement personnel shall preserve the recording until the later of when all appeals, post-conviction relief proceedings, and habeas corpus proceedings are final and concluded or the expiration of the period of time within which such appeals and proceedings must be brought.

(3) Upon motion by the defendant in a criminal proceeding or the alleged delinquent child in a delinquent child proceeding, the court may order that a copy of an electronic recording of a custodial interrogation of the person be preserved for any period beyond the expiration of all appeals, post-conviction relief proceedings, and habeas corpus proceedings.

(4) If no criminal or delinquent child proceeding is brought against a person who was the subject of a custodial interrogation that was electronically recorded pursuant to this section, law enforcement personnel are not required to preserve the related recording.

**HISTORY: 153 v S 77, § 1, eff. 7-6-10.**

## § 2933.82 Preservation of biological evidence; preparation of inventory.

(A) As used in this section:

(1)(a) "Biological evidence" means any of the following:

(i) The contents of a sexual assault examination kit;

(ii) Any item that contains blood, semen, hair, saliva, skin tissue, fingernail scrapings, bone, bodily fluids, or any other identifiable biological material that was collected as part of a criminal investigation or delinquent child investigation and that reasonably may be used to incriminate or exculpate any person for an offense or delinquent act.

(b) The definition of "biological evidence" set forth in division (A)(1)(a) of this section applies whether the material in question is cataloged separately, such as on a slide or swab or in a test tube, or is present on other evidence, including, but not limited to, clothing, ligatures, bedding or other household material, drinking cups or containers, or cigarettes.

(2) "Biological material" has the same meaning as in section 2953.71 of the Revised Code.

(3) "DNA" has the same meaning as in section 109.573 [109.57.3] of the Revised Code.

(4) "Profile" means a unique identifier of an individual, derived from DNA.

(5) "Prosecutor" has the same meaning as in section 2935.01 of the Revised Code.

(6) "Governmental evidence-retention entity" means all of the following:

(a) Any law enforcement agency, prosecutor's office, court, public hospital, crime laboratory, or other governmental or public entity or individual within this state that is charged with the collection, storage, or retrieval of biological evidence;

(b) Any official or employee of any entity or individual described in division (A)(6)(a) of this section.

(B)(1) Each governmental evidence-retention entity that secures any biological evidence in relation to an investigation or prosecution of a criminal offense or delinquent act that is a violation of section 2903.01, 2903.02, or 2903.03, a violation of section 2903.04 or 2903.06 that is a felony of the first or second degree, a violation of section 2907.02 or 2907.03 or division (A)(4) or (B) of section 2907.05 of the Revised Code, or an attempt to commit a violation of section 2907.02 of the Revised Code shall secure the biological evidence for whichever of the following periods of time is applicable:

(a) For a violation of section 2903.01 or 2903.02 of the Revised Code, for the period of time that the offense or act remains unsolved;

(b) For a violation of section 2903.03, a violation of section 2903.04 or 2903.06 that is a felony of the first or second degree, a violation of section 2907.02 or 2907.03 or of division (A)(4) or (B) of section 2907.05 of the Revised Code, or an attempt to commit a violation of section 2907.02 of the Revised Code, for a period of thirty years if the offense or act remains unsolved;

(c) If any person is convicted of or pleads guilty to the offense, or is adjudicated a delinquent child for committing the delinquent act, for the earlier of the following: (i) the expiration of the latest of the following periods of time that apply to the person: the period of time that the person is incarcerated, is in a department of youth services institution or other juvenile facility, is under a community control sanction for that offense, is under any order of disposition for that act, is on probation or parole for that offense, is under judicial release or supervised release for that act, is under post-release control for that offense, is involved in civil litigation in connection with that offense or act, or is subject to registration and other duties imposed for that offense or act under sections 2950.04, 2950.041 [2950.04.1], 2950.05, and 2950.06 of the Revised Code or (ii) thirty years. If after the period of thirty years the person remains incarcerated, then the governmental evidence-retention entity shall secure the biological evidence until the person is released from incarceration or dies.

(2) This section applies to evidence likely to contain biological material that was in the possession of any governmental evidence-retention entity during the investigation and prosecution of a criminal case or delinquent child case involving a violation of section 2903.01, 2903.02, or 2903.03, a violation of section 2903.04 or 2903.06 that is a felony of the first or second degree, a violation of section 2907.02 or 2907.03 or of division (A)(4) or (B) of section 2907.05 of the Revised Code, or an attempt to commit a violation of section 2907.02 of the Revised Code.

(3) A governmental evidence-retention entity that possesses biological evidence shall retain the biological evidence in the amount and manner sufficient to develop a DNA profile from the biological material contained in or included on the evidence.

(4) Upon written request by the defendant in a criminal case or the alleged delinquent child in a delinquent child case involving a violation of section 2903.01, 2903.02, or 2903.03, a violation of section 2903.04 or 2903.06 that is a felony of the first or second degree, a violation of section 2907.02 or 2907.03 or of division (A)(4) or (B) of section 2907.05 of the Revised Code, or an attempt to commit a violation of section 2907.02 of the Revised Code, a governmental evidence-retention entity that possesses biological evidence shall prepare an inventory of the biological evidence that has been preserved in connection with the defendant's criminal case or the alleged delinquent child's delinquent child case.

(5) Except as otherwise provided in division (B)(7) of this section, a governmental evidence-retention entity that possesses biological evidence that includes biological material may destroy the evidence before the expiration of the applicable period of time specified in division (B)(1) of this section if all of the following apply:

(a) No other provision of federal or state law requires the state to preserve the evidence.

(b) The governmental evidence-retention entity, by certified mail, return receipt requested, provides notice of intent to destroy the evidence to all of the following:

(i) All persons who remain in custody, incarcerated, in a department of youth services institution or other juvenile facility, under a community control sanction, under any order of disposition, on probation or parole, under judicial release or supervised release, under post-release control, involved in civil litigation, or subject to registration and other duties imposed for that offense or act under sections 2950.04, 2950.041 [2950.04.1], 2950.05, and 2950.06 of the Revised Code as a result of a criminal conviction, delinquency adjudication, or commitment related to the evidence in question;

(ii) The attorney of record for each person who is in custody in any circumstance described in division (B)(5)(b)(i) of this section if the attorney of record can be located;

(iii) The state public defender;

(iv) The office of the prosecutor of record in the case that resulted in the custody of the person in custody in any circumstance described in division (B)(5)(b)(i) of this section;

(v) The attorney general.

(c) No person who is notified under division (B)(5)(b) of this section does either of the following within one year after the date on which the person receives the notice:

(i) Files a motion for testing of evidence under sections 2953.71 to 2953.81 or section 2953.82 of the Revised Code;

(ii) Submits a written request for retention of evidence to the governmental evidence-retention entity that provided notice of its intent to destroy evidence under division (B)(5)(b) of this section.

(6) Except as otherwise provided in division (B)(7) of this section, if, after providing notice under division (B)(5)(b) of this section of its intent to destroy evidence, a governmental evidence-retention entity receives a written request for retention of the evidence from any person to whom the notice is provided, the governmental evidence-retention entity shall retain the evidence while the person referred to in division (B)(5)(b)(i) of this section remains in custody, incarcerated, in a department of youth services institution or other juvenile facility, under a community control sanction, under any order of disposition, on probation or parole, under judicial release or supervised release, under post-release control, involved in civil litigation, or subject to registration and other duties imposed for that offense or act under sections 2950.04, 2950.041 [2950.04.1], 2950.05, and 2950.06 of the Revised Code as a result of a criminal conviction, delinquency adjudication, or commitment related to the evidence in question.

(7) A governmental evidence-retention entity that possesses biological evidence that includes biological material may destroy the evidence five years after a person pleads guilty or no contest to a violation of section 2903.01, 2903.02, or 2903.03, a violation of 2903.04 or 2903.06 that is a felony of the first or second degree, a violation of section 2907.02, 2907.03, division (A)(4) or (B) of section 2907.05, or an attempt to commit a violation of section 2907.02 of the Revised Code and all appeals have been exhausted unless, upon a motion to the court by the person who pleaded guilty or no contest or the person's attorney and notice to those persons described in division (B)(5)(b) of this section requesting that the evidence not be destroyed, the court finds good cause as to why that evidence must be retained.

(8) A governmental evidence-retention entity shall not be required to preserve physical evidence pursuant to this section that is of such a size, bulk, or physical character as to render retention impracticable. When retention of physical evidence that otherwise would be required to be retained pursuant to this section is impracticable as described in this division, the governmental evidence-retention entity that otherwise would be required to retain the physical evidence shall remove and preserve portions of the material evidence likely to contain biological evidence related to the offense, in a quantity sufficient to permit future DNA testing before returning or disposing of that physical evidence.

(C)(1) The preservation of biological evidence task force established within the bureau of criminal identification and investigation under section 109.561 [109.56.1] of the Revised Code shall establish a system regarding the proper preservation of biological evidence in this state. In establishing the system, the task force shall do all of the following:

(a) Devise standards regarding the proper collection, retention, and cataloguing of biological evidence for ongoing investigations and prosecutions;

(b) Recommend practices, protocols, models, and resources for the cataloging and accessibility of preserved biological evidence already in the possession of governmental evidence-retention entities.

(2) In consultation with the preservation of biological evidence task force described in division (C)(1) of this section, the office of the attorney general shall administer and conduct training programs for law enforcement officers and other relevant employees who are charged with preserving and cataloging biological evidence regarding the methods and procedures referenced in this section.

**HISTORY: 153 v S 77, § 1, eff. 7-6-10; 153 v S 58, § 1, eff. 9-17-10.**

## § 2933.83 Eyewitness identification procedures in lineups; adoption of other scientifically accepted procedures.

(A) As used in this section:

(1) "Administrator" means the person conducting a photo lineup or live lineup.

(2) "Blind administrator" means the administrator does not know the identity of the suspect. "Blind administrator" includes an administrator who conducts a photo lineup through the use of a folder system or a substantially similar system.

(3) "Blinded administrator" means the administrator may know who the suspect is, but does not know which lineup member is being viewed by the eyewitness. "Blinded administrator" includes an administrator who conducts a photo lineup through the use of a folder system or a substantially similar system.

(4) "Eyewitness" means a person who observes another person at or near the scene of an offense.

(5) "Filler" means either a person or a photograph of a person who is not suspected of an offense and is included in an identification procedure.

(6) "Folder system" means a system for conducting a photo lineup that satisfies all of the following:

(a) The investigating officer uses one "suspect photograph" that resembles the description of the suspected perpetrator of the offense provided by the eyewitness, five "filler photographs" of persons not suspected of the offense that match the description of the suspected perpetrator but do not cause the suspect photograph to unduly stand out, four "blank photographs" that contain no images of any person, and ten empty folders.

(b) The investigating officer places one "filler photograph" into one of the empty folders and numbers it as folder 1.

(c) The administrator places the "suspect photograph" and the other four "filler photographs" into five other empty folders, shuffles the five folders so that the administrator is unaware of which folder contains the "suspect photograph," and numbers the five shuffled folders as folders 2 through 6.

(d) The administrator places the four "blank photographs" in the four remaining empty folders and numbers these folders as folders 7 through 10, and these folders serve as "dummy folders."

(e) The administrator provides instructions to the eyewitness as to the lineup procedure and informs the eyewitness that a photograph of the alleged perpetrator of the offense may or may not be included in the photographs the eyewitness is about to see and that the administrator does not know which, if any, of the folders contains the photograph of the alleged perpetrator. The administrator also shall instruct the eyewitness that the administrator does not want to view any of the photographs and will not view any of the photographs and that the eyewitness may not show the administrator any of the photographs. The administrator shall inform the eyewitness that if the eyewitness identifies a photograph as being the person the eyewitness saw the eyewitness shall identify the photograph only by the number of the photograph's corresponding folder.

(f) The administrator hands each of the ten folders to the eyewitness individually without looking at the photograph in the folder. Each time the eyewitness has viewed a folder, the eyewitness indicates whether the photograph is of the person the eyewitness saw, indicates the degree of the eyewitness's confidence in this identification, and returns the folder and the photograph it contains to the administrator.

(g) The administrator follows the procedures specified in this division for a second viewing if the eyewitness requests to view each of the folders a second time, handing them to the eyewitness in the same order as during the first viewing; the eyewitness is not permitted to have more than two viewings of the folders; and the administrator preserves the order of the folders and the photographs they contain in a facedown position in order to document the steps specified in division (A)(6)(h) of this section.

(h) The administrator documents and records the results of the procedure described in divisions (A)(6)(a) to (f) of this section before the eyewitness views each of the folders a second time and before the administrator views any photograph that the eyewitness identifies as being of the person the eyewitness saw. The documentation and record includes the date, time, and location of the lineup procedure; the name of the administrator; the names of all of the individuals present during the lineup; the number of photographs shown to the eyewitness; copies of each photograph shown to the eyewitness; the order in which the folders were presented to the witness; the source of each photograph that was used in the procedure; a statement of the eyewitness's confidence in the eyewitness's own words as to the certainty of the eyewitness's identification of the photographs as being of the person the eyewitness saw that is taken immediately upon the reaction of the eyewitness to viewing the photograph; and any additional information the administrator considers pertinent to the lineup procedure. If the eyewitness views each of the folders a second time, the administrator shall document and record the statement of the eyewitness's confidence in the eyewitness's own words as to the certainty of the eyewitness's identification of a photograph as being of the person the eyewitness saw and document that the identification was made during a second viewing of each of the folders by the eyewitness.

(i) The administrator shall not say anything to the eyewitness or give any oral or nonverbal cues as to whether or not the eyewitness identified the "suspect photograph" until the administrator documents and records the results of the procedure described in divisions (A)(6)(a) to (g) of this section and the photo lineup has concluded.

(7) "Live lineup" means an identification procedure in which a group of persons, including the suspected perpetrator of an offense and other persons not suspected of the offense, is displayed to an eyewitness for the purpose of determining whether the eyewitness identifies the suspect as the perpetrator of the offense.

(8) "Photo lineup" means an identification procedure in which an array of photographs, including a photograph of the suspected perpetrator of an offense and additional photographs of other persons not suspected of the offense, is displayed to an eyewitness for the purpose of determining whether the eyewitness identifies the suspect as the perpetrator of the offense.

(9) "Perpetrator" means the person who committed the offense.

(10) "Suspect" means the person believed by law enforcement to be the possible perpetrator of the offense.

(B) Prior to conducting any live lineup or photo lineup on or after the effective date of this section, any law enforcement agency or criminal justice entity in this state that conducts live lineups or photo lineups shall adopt specific procedures for conducting the lineups. The procedures, at a minimum, shall impose the following requirements:

(1) Unless impracticable, a blind or blinded administrator shall conduct the live lineup or photo lineup.

(2) When it is impracticable for a blind administrator to conduct the live lineup or photo lineup, the administrator shall state in writing the reason for that impracticability.

(3) When it is impracticable for either a blind or blinded administrator to conduct the live lineup or photo lineup, the administrator shall state in writing the reason for that impracticability.

(4) The administrator conducting the lineup shall make a written record that includes all of the following information:

(a) All identification and nonidentification results obtained during the lineup, signed by the eyewitnesses, including the eyewitnesses' confidence statements made immediately at the time of the identification;

(b) The names of all persons present at the lineup;

(c) The date and time of the lineup;

(d) Any eyewitness identification of one or more fillers in the lineup;

(e) The names of the lineup members and other relevant identifying information, and the sources of all photographs or persons used in the lineup.

(5) If a blind administrator is conducting the live lineup or the photo lineup, the administrator shall inform the eyewitness that the suspect may or may not be in the lineup and that the administrator does not know who the suspect is.

(C) For any photo lineup or live lineup that is administered on or after the effective date of this section, all of the following apply:

(1) Evidence of a failure to comply with any of the provisions of this section or with any procedure for conducting lineups that has been adopted by a law enforcement agency or criminal justice agency pursuant to division (B) of this section and that conforms to any provision of divisions (B)(1) to (5) of this section shall be considered by trial courts in adjudicating motions to suppress eyewitness identification resulting from or related to the lineup.

(2) Evidence of a failure to comply with any of the provisions of this section or with any procedure for conducting lineups that has been adopted by a law enforcement agency or criminal justice agency pursuant to division (B) of this section and that conforms to any provision of divisions (B)(1) to (5) of this section shall be admissible in support of any claim of eyewitness misidentification resulting from or related to the lineup as long as that evidence otherwise is admissible.

(3) When evidence of a failure to comply with any of the provisions of this section, or with any procedure for conducting lineups that has been adopted by a law enforcement agency or criminal justice agency pursuant to division (B) of this section and that conforms to any provision of divisions (B)(1) to (5) of this section, is presented at trial, the jury shall be instructed that it may consider credible evidence of noncompliance in determining the reliability of any eyewitness identification resulting from or related to the lineup.

(D) The requirements in this section regarding the procedures for live lineups or photo lineups conducted by a law enforcement agency or criminal justice entity do not prohibit a law enforcement agency or criminal justice entity from adopting other scientifically accepted procedures for conducting live lineups or photo lineups that the scientific community considers more effective.

**HISTORY: 153 v S 77, § 1, eff. 7-6-10.**

## § 2933.831 Rules for live lineups, photo lineups, and showups.

(A) The General Assembly hereby requests the Attorney General to adopt rules pursuant to Chapter 119. of the Revised Code prescribing specific procedures to be followed for the administration by law enforcement agencies and criminal justice entities in this state of photo lineups, live lineups, and showups. The General Assembly also requests that any rules adopted by the Attorney General be consistent with the requirements of divisions (B) and (C) of section 2933.83 of the Revised Code. If the Attorney General adopts rules of the type described in this division, on and after the date on which the rules take effect, law enforcement agencies and criminal justice entities in this state shall comply with the rules in conducting live lineups, photo lineups, and showups.

(B) The General Assembly hereby requests the Ohio Judicial Conference to review existing jury instructions regarding eyewitness identification for compliance with this act.

**HISTORY: 153 v S 77, § 3, eff. 7-6-10.**

**Publisher's Note:**

This section was originally enacted as § 3 of 153 v S 77. It was redesignated as RC § 2933.831 by the Legislative Service Commission.

# CHAPTER 2935: ARREST, CITATION, AND DISPOSITION ALTERNATIVES



## § 2935.01 Definitions.

As used in this chapter:

(A) "Magistrate" has the same meaning as in section 2931.01 of the Revised Code.

(B) "Peace officer" includes, except as provided in section 2935.081 of the Revised Code, a sheriff; deputy sheriff; marshal; deputy marshal; member of the organized police department of any municipal corporation, including a member of the organized police department of a municipal corporation in an adjoining state serving in Ohio under a contract pursuant to section 737.04 of the Revised Code; member of a police force employed by a metropolitan housing authority under division (D) of section 3735.31 of the Revised Code; member of a police force employed by a regional transit authority under division (Y) of section 306.05 of the Revised Code; state university law enforcement officer appointed under section 3345.04 of the Revised Code; enforcement agent of the department of public safety designated under section 5502.14 of the Revised Code; employee of the department of taxation to whom investigation powers have been delegated under section 5743.45 of the Revised Code; employee of the department of natural resources who is a natural resources law enforcement staff officer designated pursuant to section 1501.013 of the Revised Code, a forest officer designated pursuant to section 1503.29 of the Revised Code, a preserve officer designated pursuant to section 1517.10 of the Revised Code, a wildlife officer designated pursuant to section 1531.13 of the Revised Code, a park officer designated pursuant to section 1541.10 of the Revised Code, or a state watercraft officer designated pursuant to section 1547.521 of the Revised Code; individual designated to perform law enforcement duties under section 511.232, 1545.13, or 6101.75 of the Revised Code; veterans' home police officer appointed under section 5907.02 of the Revised Code; special police officer employed by a port authority under section 4582.04 or 4582.28 of the Revised Code; police constable of any township; police officer of a township or joint police district; a special police officer employed by a municipal corporation at a municipal airport, or other municipal air navigation facility, that has scheduled operations, as defined in section 119.3 of Title 14 of the Code of Federal Regulations, 14 C.F.R. 119.3, as amended, and that is required to be under a security program and is governed by aviation security rules of the transportation security administration of the United States department of transportation as provided in Parts 1542. and 1544. of Title 49 of the Code of Federal Regulations, as amended; the house of representatives sergeant at arms if the house of representatives sergeant at arms has arrest authority pursuant to division (E)(1) of section 101.311 of the Revised Code; and an assistant house of representatives sergeant at arms; officer or employee of the bureau of criminal identification and investigation established pursuant to section 109.51 of the Revised Code who has been awarded a certificate by the executive director of the Ohio peace officer training commission attesting to the officer's or employee's satisfactory completion of an approved state, county, municipal, or department of natural resources peace officer basic training program and who is providing assistance upon request to a law enforcement officer or emergency assistance to a peace officer pursuant to section 109.54 or 109.541 of the Revised Code; a state fire marshal law enforcement officer described in division (A)(23) of section 109.71 of the Revised Code; and, for the purpose of arrests within those areas, for the purposes of Chapter 5503. of the Revised Code, and the filing of and service of process relating to those offenses witnessed or investigated by them, the superintendent and troopers of the state highway patrol.

(C) "Prosecutor" includes the county prosecuting attorney and any assistant prosecutor designated to assist the county prosecuting attorney, and, in the case of courts inferior to courts of common pleas, includes the village solicitor, city director of law, or similar chief legal officer of a municipal corporation, any such officer's assistants, or any attorney designated by the prosecuting attorney of the county to appear for the prosecution of a given case.

(D) "Offense," except where the context specifically indicates otherwise, includes felonies, misdemeanors, and violations of ordinances of municipal corporations and other public bodies authorized by law to adopt penal regulations.

**HISTORY: 142 v H 708 (Eff 4-19-88); 144 v H 77 (Eff 9-17-91); 144 v S 144 (Eff 8-8-91); 146 v S 162 (Eff 10-29-95); 146 v S 2 (Eff 7-1-96); 146 v H 72 (Eff 3-18-97); 147 v S 187 (Eff 3-18-99); 148 v H 163 (Eff 6-30-99); 148 v S 137 (Eff 5-17-2000); 148 v S 317 (Eff 3-22-2001); 149 v H 427 (Eff 8-29-2002); 149 v S 200 (Eff 9-6-2002); 149 v H 675 (Eff 3-14-2003); 149 v H 545. Eff 3-19-2003; 152 v H 562, § 101.01, eff. 9-23-08; 2011 HB 153, § 101.01, eff. Sept. 29, 2011.**

The effective date is set by § 812.10 of 152 v H 562.

The provisions of § 815.01 of 152 v H 562 read as follows:

SECTION 815.10. * * * Section 2935.01 of the Revised Code is presented in this act as a composite of the section as amended by both Sub. H.B. 545 and H.B. 675 of the 124th General Assembly. * * * The General Assembly, applying the principle stated in division (B) of section 1.52 of the Revised Code that amendments are to be harmonized if reasonably capable of simultaneous operation, finds that the composites are the resulting versions of the sections in effect prior to the effective date of the sections as presented in this act.

The provisions of § 3 of HB 545 (149 v —) read as follows:

SECTION 3. Section 109.71 of the Revised Code is presented in this act as a composite of the section as amended by both Am. Sub. H.B. 163 and Am. S.B. 137 of the 123rd General Assembly. Section 109.75 of the Revised Code is presented in this act as a composite of the section as amended by both Am. Sub. H.B. 566 and Sub. H.B. 670 of the 121st General Assembly. Section 109.77 of the Revised Code is presented in this act as a composite of the section as amended by Sub. H.B. 148, Am. Sub. H.B. 163, and Am. S.B. 137 of the 123rd General Assembly. Section 2935.01 of the Revised Code is presented in this act as a composite of the section as amended by both Sub. H.B. 427 and Sub. S.B. 200 of the 124th General Assembly. The General Assembly, applying the principle stated in division (B) of section 1.52 of the Revised Code that amendments are to be harmonized if reasonably capable of simultaneous operation, finds that the composites of these sections are the resulting versions of the sections in effect prior to the effective date of the sections as presented in this act.

The provisions of § 36.04 of HB 675 (149 v —) read as follows:

SECTION 36.04. Section 2935.01 of the Revised Code is presented in this act as a composite of the section as amended by both Sub. H.B. 427 and Sub. S.B. 200 of the 124th General Assembly. The General Assembly, applying the principle stated in division (B) of section 1.52 of the Revised Code that amendments are to be harmonized if reasonably capable of simultaneous operation, finds that the composite is the resulting version of the section in effect prior to the effective date of the section as presented in this act.

## § 2935.011 Bureau of criminal identification and investigation personnel as peace officers.

If an officer or employee of the bureau of criminal identification and investigation is included as a "peace officer" under division (B) of section 2935.01 of the Revised Code, both of the following apply:

(A) Division (D)(2) of section 109.541 [109.54.1] applies to the officer or employee while so included.

(B) The officer or employee is not, as a result of the inclusion, a member of a police department for purposes of Chapter 742. of the Revised Code or a law enforcement officer or peace officer for purposes of any state or local retirement system.

**HISTORY: 149 v H 427. Eff 8-29-2002.**

## § 2935.02 Accused may be arrested in any county.

If an accused person flees from justice, or is not found in the county where a warrant for his arrest was issued, the officer holding the same may pursue and arrest him in any county in this state, and convey him before the magistrate or court of the county having cognizance of the case.

If such warrant directs the removal of the accused to the county in which the offense was committed, the officer holding the warrant shall deliver the accused to a court or magistrate of such county.

The necessary expense of such removal and reasonable compensation for his time and trouble, shall be paid to such officer out of the treasury of such county, upon the allowance and order of the county auditor.

**HISTORY: GC § 13432-10; 113 v 123(141), ch 11, § 10; Bureau of Code Revision. Eff 10-1-53.**

## § 2935.03 Officer's authority to arrest without warrant; pursuit outside jurisdiction.

(A)(1) A sheriff, deputy sheriff, marshal, deputy marshal, municipal police officer, township constable, police officer of a township or joint police district, member of a police force employed by a metropolitan housing authority under division (D) of section 3735.31 of the Revised Code, member of a police force employed by a regional transit authority under division (Y) of section 306.35 of the Revised Code, state university law enforcement officer appointed under section 3345.04 of the Revised Code, veterans' home police officer appointed under section 5907.02 of the Revised Code, special police officer employed by a port authority under section 4582.04 or 4582.28 of the Revised Code, or a special police officer employed by a municipal corporation at a municipal airport, or other municipal air navigation facility, that has scheduled operations, as defined in section 119.3 of Title 14 of the Code of Federal Regulations, 14 C.F.R. 119.3, as amended, and that is required to be under a security program and is governed by aviation security rules of the transportation security administration of the United States department of transportation as provided in Parts 1542. and 1544. of Title 49 of the Code of Federal Regulations, as amended, shall arrest and detain, until a warrant can be obtained, a person found violating, within the limits of the political subdivision, metropolitan housing authority housing project, regional transit authority facilities or areas of a municipal corporation that have been agreed to by a regional transit authority and a municipal corporation located within its territorial jurisdiction, college, university, veterans' home operated under Chapter 5907. of the Revised Code, port authority, or municipal airport or other municipal air navigation facility, in which the peace officer is appointed, employed, or elected, a law of this state, an ordinance of a municipal corporation, or a resolution of a township.

(2) A peace officer of the department of natural resources, a state fire marshal law enforcement officer described in division (A)(23) of section 109.71 of the Revised Code, or an individual designated to perform law enforcement duties under section 511.232, 1545.13, or 6101.75 of the Revised Code shall arrest and detain, until a warrant can be obtained, a person found violating, within the limits of the peace officer's, state fire marshal law enforcement officer's, or individual's territorial jurisdiction, a law of this state.

(3) The house sergeant at arms, if the house sergeant at arms has arrest authority pursuant to division (E)(1) of section 101.311 of the Revised Code, and an assistant house sergeant at arms shall arrest and detain, until a warrant can be obtained, a person found violating, within the limits of the sergeant at arms's or assistant sergeant at arms's territorial jurisdiction specified in division (D)(1)(a) of section 101.311 of the Revised Code or while providing security pursuant to division (D)(1)(f) of section 101.311 of the Revised Code, a law of this state, an ordinance of a municipal corporation, or a resolution of a township.

(B)(1) When there is reasonable ground to believe that an offense of violence, the offense of criminal child enticement as defined in section 2905.05 of the Revised Code, the offense of public indecency as defined in section 2907.09 of the Revised Code, the offense of domestic violence as defined in section 2919.25 of the Revised Code, the offense of violating a protection order as defined in section 2919.27 of the Revised Code, the offense of menacing by stalking as defined in section 2903.211 of the Revised Code, the offense of aggravated trespass as defined in section 2911.211 of the Revised Code, a theft offense as defined in section 2913.01 of the Revised Code, or a felony drug abuse offense as defined in section 2925.01 of the Revised Code, has been committed within the limits of the political subdivision, metropolitan housing authority housing project, regional transit authority facilities or those areas of a municipal corporation that have been agreed to by a regional transit authority and a municipal corporation located within its territorial jurisdiction, college, university, veterans' home operated under Chapter 5907. of the Revised Code, port authority, or municipal airport or other municipal air navigation facility, in which the peace officer is appointed, employed, or elected or within the limits of the territorial jurisdiction of the peace officer, a peace officer described in division (A) of this section may arrest and detain until a warrant can be obtained any person who the peace officer has reasonable cause to believe is guilty of the violation.

(2) For purposes of division (B)(1) of this section, the execution of any of the following constitutes reasonable ground to believe that the offense alleged in the statement was committed and reasonable cause to believe that the person alleged in the statement to have committed the offense is guilty of the violation:

(a) A written statement by a person alleging that an alleged offender has committed the offense of menacing by stalking or aggravated trespass;

(b) A written statement by the administrator of the interstate compact on mental health appointed under section 5119.51 of the Revised Code alleging that a person who had been hospitalized, institutionalized, or confined in any facility under an order made pursuant to or under authority of section 2945.37, 2945.371, 2945.38, 2945.39, 2945.40, 2945.401, or 2945.402 of the Revised Code has escaped from the facility, from confinement in a vehicle for transportation to or from the facility, or from supervision by an employee of the facility that is incidental to hospitalization, institutionalization, or confinement in the facility and that occurs outside of the facility, in violation of section 2921.34 of the Revised Code;

(c) A written statement by the administrator of any facility in which a person has been hospitalized, institutionalized, or confined under an order made pursuant to or under authority of section 2945.37, 2945.371, 2945.38, 2945.39, 2945.40, 2945.401, or 2945.402 of the Revised Code alleging that the person has escaped from the facility, from confinement in a vehicle for transportation to or from the facility, or from supervision by an employee of the facility that is incidental to hospitalization, institutionalization, or confinement in the facility and that occurs outside of the facility, in violation of section 2921.34 of the Revised Code.

(3)(a) For purposes of division (B)(1) of this section, a peace officer described in division (A) of this section has reasonable grounds to believe that the offense of domestic violence or the offense of violating a protection order has been committed and reasonable cause to believe that a particular person is guilty of committing the offense if any of the following occurs:

(i) A person executes a written statement alleging that the person in question has committed the offense of domestic violence or the offense of violating a protection order against the person who executes the statement or against a child of the person who executes the statement.

(ii) No written statement of the type described in division (B)(3)(a)(i) of this section is executed, but the peace officer, based upon the peace officer's own knowledge and observation of the facts and circumstances of the alleged incident of the offense of domestic violence or the alleged incident of the offense of violating a protection order or based upon any other information, including, but not limited to, any reasonably trustworthy information given to the peace officer by the alleged victim of the alleged incident of the offense or any witness of the alleged incident of the offense, concludes that there are reasonable grounds to believe that the offense of domestic violence or the offense of violating a protection order has been committed and reasonable cause to believe that the person in question is guilty of committing the offense.

(iii) No written statement of the type described in division (B)(3)(a)(i) of this section is executed, but the peace officer witnessed the person in question commit the offense of domestic violence or the offense of violating a protection order.

(b) If pursuant to division (B)(3)(a) of this section a peace officer has reasonable grounds to believe that the offense of domestic violence or the offense of violating a protection order has been committed and reasonable cause to believe that a particular person is guilty of committing the offense, it is the preferred course of action in this state that the officer arrest and detain that person pursuant to division (B)(1) of this section until a warrant can be obtained.

If pursuant to division (B)(3)(a) of this section a peace officer has reasonable grounds to believe that the offense of domestic violence or the offense of violating a protection order has been committed and reasonable cause to believe that family or household members have committed the offense against each other, it is the preferred course of action in this state that the officer, pursuant to division (B)(1) of this section, arrest and detain until a warrant can be obtained the family or household member who committed the offense and whom the officer has reasonable cause to believe is the primary physical aggressor. There is no preferred course of action in this state regarding any other family or household member who committed the offense and whom the officer does not have reasonable cause to believe is the primary physical aggressor, but, pursuant to division (B)(1) of this section, the peace officer may arrest and detain until a warrant can be obtained any other family or household member who committed the offense and whom the officer does not have reasonable cause to believe is the primary physical aggressor.

(c) If a peace officer described in division (A) of this section does not arrest and detain a person whom the officer has reasonable cause to believe committed the offense of domestic violence or the offense of violating a protection order when it is the preferred course of action in this state pursuant to division (B)(3)(b) of this section that the officer arrest that person, the officer shall articulate in the written report of the incident required by section 2935.032 of the Revised Code a clear statement of the officer's reasons for not arresting and detaining that person until a warrant can be obtained.

(d) In determining for purposes of division (B)(3)(b) of this section which family or household member is the primary physical aggressor in a situation in which family or household members have committed the offense of domestic violence or the offense of violating a protection order against each other, a peace officer described in division (A) of this section, in addition to any other relevant circumstances, should consider all of the following:

(i) Any history of domestic violence or of any other violent acts by either person involved in the alleged offense that the officer reasonably can ascertain;

(ii) If violence is alleged, whether the alleged violence was caused by a person acting in self-defense;

(iii) Each person's fear of physical harm, if any, resulting from the other person's threatened use of force against any person or resulting from the other person's use or history of the use of force against any person, and the reasonableness of that fear;

(iv) The comparative severity of any injuries suffered by the persons involved in the alleged offense.

(e)(i) A peace officer described in division (A) of this section shall not require, as a prerequisite to arresting or charging a person who has committed the offense of domestic violence or the offense of violating a protection order, that the victim of the offense specifically consent to the filing of charges against the person who has committed the offense or sign a complaint against the person who has committed the offense.

(ii) If a person is arrested for or charged with committing the offense of domestic violence or the offense of violating a protection order and if the victim of the offense does not cooperate with the involved law enforcement or prosecuting authorities in the prosecution of the offense or, subsequent to the arrest or the filing of the charges, informs the involved law enforcement or prosecuting authorities that the victim does not wish the prosecution of the offense to continue or wishes to drop charges against the alleged offender relative to the offense, the involved prosecuting authorities, in determining whether to continue with the prosecution of the offense or whether to dismiss charges against the alleged offender relative to the offense and notwithstanding the victim's failure to cooperate or the victim's wishes, shall consider all facts and circumstances that are relevant to the offense, including, but not limited to, the statements and observations of the peace officers who responded to the incident that resulted in the arrest or filing of the charges and of all witnesses to that incident.

(f) In determining pursuant to divisions (B)(3)(a) to (g) of this section whether to arrest a person pursuant to division (B)(1) of this section, a peace officer described in division (A) of this section shall not consider as a factor any possible shortage of cell space at the detention facility to which the person will be taken subsequent to the person's arrest or any possibility that the person's arrest might cause, contribute to, or exacerbate overcrowding at that detention facility or at any other detention facility.

(g) If a peace officer described in division (A) of this section intends pursuant to divisions (B)(3)(a) to (g) of this section to arrest a person pursuant to division (B)(1) of this section and if the officer is unable to do so because the person is not present, the officer promptly shall seek a warrant for the arrest of the person.

(h) If a peace officer described in division (A) of this section responds to a report of an alleged incident of the offense of domestic violence or an alleged incident of the offense of violating a protection order and if the circumstances of the incident involved the use or threatened use of a deadly weapon or any person involved in the incident brandished a deadly weapon during or in relation to the incident, the deadly weapon that was used, threatened to be used, or brandished constitutes contraband, and, to the extent possible, the officer shall seize the deadly weapon as contraband pursuant to Chapter 2981. of the Revised Code. Upon the seizure of a deadly weapon pursuant to division (B)(3)(h) of this section, section 2981.12 of the Revised Code shall apply regarding the treatment and disposition of the deadly weapon. For purposes of that section, the "underlying criminal offense" that was the basis of the seizure of a deadly weapon under division (B)(3)(h) of this section and to which the deadly weapon had a relationship is any of the following that is applicable:

(i) The alleged incident of the offense of domestic violence or the alleged incident of the offense of violating a protection order to which the officer who seized the deadly weapon responded;

(ii) Any offense that arose out of the same facts and circumstances as the report of the alleged incident of the offense of domestic violence or the alleged incident of the offense of violating a protection order to which the officer who seized the deadly weapon responded.

(4) If, in the circumstances described in divisions (B)(3)(a) to (g) of this section, a peace officer described in division (A) of this section arrests and detains a person pursuant to division (B)(1) of this section, or if, pursuant to division (B)(3)(h) of this section, a peace officer described in division (A) of this section seizes a deadly weapon, the officer, to the extent described in and in accordance with section 9.86 or 2744.03 of the Revised Code, is immune in any civil action for damages for injury, death, or loss to person or property that arises from or is related to the arrest and detention or the seizure.

(C) When there is reasonable ground to believe that a violation of division (A)(1), (2), (3), (4), or (5) of section 4506.15 or a violation of section 4511.19 of the Revised Code has been committed by a person operating a motor vehicle subject to regulation by the public utilities commission of Ohio under Title XLIX of the Revised Code, a peace officer with authority to enforce that provision of law may stop or detain the person whom the officer has reasonable cause to believe was operating the motor vehicle in violation of the division or section and, after investigating the circumstances surrounding the operation of the vehicle, may arrest and detain the person.

(D) If a sheriff, deputy sheriff, marshal, deputy marshal, municipal police officer, member of a police force employed by a metropolitan housing authority under division (D) of section 3735.31 of the Revised Code, member of a police force employed by a regional transit authority under division (Y) of section 306.35 of the Revised Code, special police officer employed by a port authority under section 4582.04 or 4582.28 of the Revised Code, special police officer employed by a municipal corporation at a municipal airport or other municipal air navigation facility described in division (A) of this section, township constable, police officer of a township or joint police district, state university law enforcement officer appointed under section 3345.04 of the Revised Code, peace officer of the department of natural resources, individual designated to perform law enforcement duties under section 511.232, 1545.13, or 6101.75 of the Revised Code, the house sergeant at arms if the house sergeant at arms has arrest authority pursuant to division (E)(1) of section 101.311 of the Revised Code, or an assistant house sergeant at arms is authorized by division (A) or (B) of this section to arrest and detain, within the limits of the political subdivision, metropolitan housing authority housing project, regional transit authority facilities or those areas of a municipal corporation that have been agreed to by a regional transit authority and a municipal corporation located within its territorial jurisdiction, port authority, municipal airport or other municipal air navigation facility, college, or university in which the officer is appointed, employed, or elected or within the limits of the territorial jurisdiction of the peace officer, a person until a warrant can be obtained, the peace officer, outside the limits of that territory, may pursue, arrest, and detain that person until a warrant can be obtained if all of the following apply:

(1) The pursuit takes place without unreasonable delay after the offense is committed;

(2) The pursuit is initiated within the limits of the political subdivision, metropolitan housing authority housing project, regional transit authority facilities or those areas of a municipal corporation that have been agreed to by a regional transit authority and a municipal corporation located within its territorial jurisdiction, port authority, municipal airport or other municipal air navigation facility, college, or university in which the peace officer is appointed, employed, or elected or within the limits of the territorial jurisdiction of the peace officer;

(3) The offense involved is a felony, a misdemeanor of the first degree or a substantially equivalent municipal ordinance, a misdemeanor of the second degree or a substantially equivalent municipal ordinance, or any offense for which points are chargeable pursuant to section 4510.036 of the Revised Code.

(E) In addition to the authority granted under division (A) or (B) of this section:

(1) A sheriff or deputy sheriff may arrest and detain, until a warrant can be obtained, any person found violating section 4503.11, 4503.21, or 4549.01, sections 4549.08 to 4549.12, section 4549.62, or Chapter 4511. or 4513. of the Revised Code on the portion of any street or highway that is located immediately adjacent to the boundaries of the county in which the sheriff or deputy sheriff is elected or appointed.

(2) A member of the police force of a township police district created under section 505.48 of the Revised Code, a member of the police force of a joint police district created under section 505.482 of the Revised Code, or a township constable appointed in accordance with section 509.01 of the Revised Code, who has received a certificate from the Ohio peace officer training commission under section 109.75 of the Revised Code, may arrest and detain, until a warrant can be obtained, any person found violating any section or chapter of the Revised Code listed in division (E)(1) of this section, other than sections 4513.33 and 4513.34 of the Revised Code, on the portion of any street or highway that is located immediately adjacent to the boundaries of the township police district or joint police district, in the case of a member of a township police district or joint police district police force, or the unincorporated territory of the township, in the case of a township constable. However, if the population of the township that created the township police district served by the member's police force, or the townships and municipal corporations that created the joint police district served by the member's police force, or the township that is served by the township constable, is sixty thousand or less, the member of the township police district or joint police district police force or the township constable may not make an arrest under division (E)(2) of this section on a state highway that is included as part of the interstate system.

(3) A police officer or village marshal appointed, elected, or employed by a municipal corporation may arrest and detain, until a warrant can be obtained, any person found violating any section or chapter of the Revised Code listed in division (E)(1) of this section on the portion of any street or highway that is located immediately adjacent to the boundaries of the municipal corporation in which the police officer or village marshal is appointed, elected, or employed.

(4) A peace officer of the department of natural resources, a state fire marshal law enforcement officer described in division (A)(23) of section 109.71 of the Revised Code, or an individual designated to perform law enforcement duties under section 511.232, 1545.13, or 6101.75 of the Revised Code may arrest and detain, until a warrant can be obtained, any person found violating any section or chapter of the Revised Code listed in division (E)(1) of this section, other than sections 4513.33 and 4513.34 of the Revised Code, on the portion of any street or highway that is located immediately adjacent to the boundaries of the lands and waters that constitute the territorial jurisdiction of the peace officer or state fire marshal law enforcement officer.

(F)(1) A department of mental health special police officer or a department of developmental disabilities special police officer may arrest without a warrant and detain until a warrant can be obtained any person found committing on the premises of any institution under the jurisdiction of the particular department a misdemeanor under a law of the state.

A department of mental health special police officer or a department of developmental disabilities special police officer may arrest without a warrant and detain until a warrant can be obtained any person who has been hospitalized, institutionalized, or confined in an institution under the jurisdiction of the particular department pursuant to or under authority of section 2945.37, 2945.371, 2945.38, 2945.39, 2945.40, 2945.401, or 2945.402 of the Revised Code and who is found committing on the premises of any institution under the jurisdiction of the particular department a violation of section 2921.34 of the

Revised Code that involves an escape from the premises of the institution.

(2)(a) If a department of mental health special police officer or a department of developmental disabilities special police officer finds any person who has been hospitalized, institutionalized, or confined in an institution under the jurisdiction of the particular department pursuant to or under authority of section 2945.37, 2945.371, 2945.38, 2945.39, 2945.40, 2945.401, or 2945.402 of the Revised Code committing a violation of section 2921.34 of the Revised Code that involves an escape from the premises of the institution, or if there is reasonable ground to believe that a violation of section 2921.34 of the Revised Code has been committed that involves an escape from the premises of an institution under the jurisdiction of the department of mental health or the department of developmental disabilities and if a department of mental health special police officer or a department of developmental disabilities special police officer has reasonable cause to believe that a particular person who has been hospitalized, institutionalized, or confined in the institution pursuant to or under authority of section 2945.37, 2945.371, 2945.38, 2945.39, 2945.40, 2945.401, or 2945.402 of the Revised Code is guilty of the violation, the special police officer, outside of the premises of the institution, may pursue, arrest, and detain that person for that violation of section 2921.34 of the Revised Code, until a warrant can be obtained, if both of the following apply:

(i) The pursuit takes place without unreasonable delay after the offense is committed;

(ii) The pursuit is initiated within the premises of the institution from which the violation of section 2921.34 of the Revised Code occurred.

(b) For purposes of division (F)(2)(a) of this section, the execution of a written statement by the administrator of the institution in which a person had been hospitalized, institutionalized, or confined pursuant to or under authority of section 2945.37, 2945.371, 2945.38, 2945.39, 2945.40, 2945.401, or 2945.402 of the Revised Code alleging that the person has escaped from the premises of the institution in violation of section 2921.34 of the Revised Code constitutes reasonable ground to believe that the violation was committed and reasonable cause to believe that the person alleged in the statement to have committed the offense is guilty of the violation.

(G) As used in this section:

(1) A "department of mental health special police officer" means a special police officer of the department of mental health designated under section 5119.14 of the Revised Code who is certified by the Ohio peace officer training commission under section 109.77 of the Revised Code as having successfully completed an approved peace officer basic training program.

(2) A "department of developmental disabilities special police officer" means a special police officer of the department of developmental disabilities designated under section 5123.13 of the Revised Code who is certified by the Ohio peace officer training council under section 109.77 of the Revised Code as having successfully completed an approved peace officer basic training program.

(3) "Deadly weapon" has the same meaning as in section 2923.11 of the Revised Code.

(4) "Family or household member" has the same meaning as in section 2919.25 of the Revised Code.

(5) "Street" or "highway" has the same meaning as in section 4511.01 of the Revised Code.

(6) "Interstate system" has the same meaning as in section 5516.01 of the Revised Code.

(7) "Peace officer of the department of natural resources" means an employee of the department of natural resources who is a natural resources law enforcement staff officer designated pursuant to section 1501.013 of the Revised Code, a forest officer designated pursuant to section 1503.29 of the Revised Code, a preserve officer designated pursuant to section 1517.10 of the Revised Code, a wildlife officer designated pursuant to section 1531.13 of the Revised Code, a park officer designated pursuant to section 1541.10 of the Revised Code, or a state watercraft officer designated pursuant to section 1547.521 of the Revised Code.

(8) "Portion of any street or highway" means all lanes of the street or highway irrespective of direction of travel, including designated turn lanes, and any berm, median, or shoulder.

**HISTORY: 142 v H 708 (Eff 4-19-88); 143 v H 88 (Eff 3-13-90); 143 v H 669 (Eff 1-10-91); 144 v H 77 (Eff 9-17-91); 144 v H 536 (Eff 11-5-92); 145 v H 42 (Eff 2-9-94); 145 v S 82 (Eff 5-4-94); 145 v H 335 (Eff 12-9-94); 146 v S 2 (Eff 7-1-96); 146 v S 269 (Eff 7-1-96); 146 v H 670 (Eff 12-2-96); 146 v S 285 (Eff 7-1-97); 147 v S 1 (Eff 10-21-97); 147 v S 187 (Eff 3-18-99); 148 v S 137 (Eff 5-17-2000); 148 v S 317 (Eff 3-22-2001); 149 v H 675, § 1.01 (Eff 3-14-2003); 149 v H 545. Eff 3-19-2003; 149 v S 123, § 1, eff. 1-1-04; 151 v H 68, § 101.01, eff. 6-29-05; 151 v H 241, § 1, eff. 7-1-07; 152 v H 119, § 101.01, eff. 9-29-07; 152 v H 562, § 101.01, eff. 9-23-08; 153 v S 79, § 1, eff. 10-6-09; 2011 HB 153, § 101.01, eff. Sept. 29, 2011.**

The effective date is set by § 812.10 of 152 v H 562.
The effective date is set by § 812.03 of 152 v H 119.
See provisions of § 4 of 151 v H 241 following RC § 2901.01.
The effective date is set by § 612.03 of 151 v H 68.
The provisions of § 618.03 of 151 v H 68 read as follows:

SECTION 618.03. The General Assembly, applying the principle stated in division (B) of section 1.52 of the Revised Code that amendments are to be harmonized if reasonably capable of simultaneous operation, finds that the following sections, presented in this act as composites of the sections as amended by the acts indicated, are the resulting versions of the sections in effect prior to the effective date of the sections as presented in this act:

° ° °

Section 2935.03 of the Revised Code as amended by Sub. H.B. 545, H.B. 675, and Am. Sub. S.B. 123 of the 124th General Assembly.

The provisions of § 5 of S.B. 123 (149 v —), as amended by § 3 of H.B. 163 (150 v —), read as follows:

SECTION 5. (A) Notwithstanding division (B) of section 1.58 of the Revised Code, the provisions of the Revised Code amended or enacted in Sections 1 and 2 of Am. Sub. S.B. 123 of the 124th General Assembly shall apply only in relation to conduct and offenses committed on or after January 1, 2004. Conduct and offenses committed prior to January 1, 2004, shall be governed by the law in effect on the date the conduct or offense was committed.

° ° °

**Analogous to former RC § 2935.03 (GC § 13432-1; 113 v 123(140), ch 11; 115 v 530; Bureau of Code Revision, 10-1-53; 132 v S 29; 134 v H 511; 136 v H 300; 137 v H 588; 137 v H 835; 138 v S 355; 140 v S 321; 140 v H 129; 141 v S 33; 141 v H 284; 141 v S 356; 142 v H 231; 142 v H 261), repealed 142 v H 708, § 2, eff 4-19-88.**

## § 2935.031 Policy for pursuit in motor vehicle.

Any agency, instrumentality, or political subdivision of the state that employs a sheriff, deputy sheriff, constable, marshal, deputy marshal, police officer, member of a metropolitan housing authority police force, state university law enforcement officer, or veterans' home police officer with arrest authority under section 2935.03 of the Revised Code or that employs other persons with arrest authority under the Revised Code, shall adopt a policy for the pursuit in a motor vehicle of any person who violates a law of this state or an ordinance of a municipal corporation. The chief law enforcement officer or other chief official of the agency, instrumentality, or political subdivision shall formally advise each peace officer or other person with arrest authority it employs of the pursuit policy adopted by that agency, instrumentality, or political subdivision pursuant to this section.

**HISTORY: 143 v S 49 (Eff 11-3-89); 149 v H 675. Eff 3-14-2003.**

## § 2935.032 Policies and procedures for responding to alleged domestic violence offense or violation of protection order.

(A) Not later than ninety days after the effective date of this amendment, each agency, instrumentality, or political subdivision that is served by any peace officer described in division (B)(1) of section 2935.03 of the Revised Code shall adopt, in accordance with division (E) of this section, written policies, written procedures implementing the policies, and other written procedures for the peace officers who serve it to follow in implementing division (B)(3) of section 2935.03 of the Revised Code and for their appropriate response to each report of an alleged incident of the offense of domestic violence or an alleged incident of the offense of violating a protection order. The policies and procedures shall conform to and be consistent with the provisions of divisions (B)(1) and (B)(3) of section 2935.03 of the Revised Code and divisions (B) to (D) of this section. Each policy adopted under this division shall include, but not be limited to, all of the following:

(1) Provisions specifying that, if a peace officer who serves the agency, instrumentality, or political subdivision responds to an alleged incident of the offense of domestic violence, an alleged incident of the offense of violating a protection order, or an alleged incident of any other offense, both of the following apply:

(a) If the officer determines that there are reasonable grounds to believe that a person knowingly caused serious physical harm to another or to another's unborn or knowingly caused or attempted to cause physical harm to another or to another's unborn by means of a deadly weapon or dangerous ordnance, then, regardless of whether the victim of the offense was a family or household member of the offender, the officer shall treat the incident as felonious assault, shall consider the offender to have committed and the victim to have been the victim of felonious assault, shall consider the offense that was committed to have been felonious assault in determining the manner in which the offender should be treated, and shall comply with whichever of the following is applicable:

(i) Unless the officer has reasonable cause to believe that, during the incident, the offender who committed the felonious assault and one or more other persons committed offenses against each other, the officer shall arrest the offender who committed the felonious assault pursuant to section 2935.03 of the Revised Code and shall detain that offender pursuant to that section until a warrant can be obtained, and the arrest shall be for felonious assault.

(ii) If the officer has reasonable cause to believe that, during the incident, the offender who committed the felonious assault and one or more other persons committed offenses against each other, the officer shall determine in accordance with division (B)(3)(d) of section 2935.03 of the Revised Code which of those persons is the primary physical aggressor. If the offender who committed the felonious assault is the primary physical aggressor, the officer shall arrest that offender for felonious assault pursuant to section 2935.03 of the Revised Code and shall detain that offender pursuant to that section until a warrant can be obtained, and the officer is not required to arrest but may arrest pursuant to section 2935.03 of the Revised Code any other person who committed an offense but who is not the primary physical aggressor. If the offender who committed the felonious assault is not the primary physical aggressor, the officer is not required to arrest that offender or any other person who committed an offense during the incident but may arrest any of them pursuant to section 2935.03 of the Revised Code and detain them pursuant to that section until a warrant can be obtained.

(b) If the officer determines that there are reasonable grounds to believe that a person, while under the influence of sudden passion or in a sudden fit of rage, either of which is brought on by serious provocation occasioned by the victim that is reasonably sufficient to incite the person into using deadly force, knowingly caused serious physical harm to another or to another's unborn or knowingly caused or attempted to cause physical harm to another or to another's unborn by means of a deadly weapon or dangerous ordnance, then, regardless of whether the victim of the offense was a family or household member of the offender, the officer shall treat the incident as aggravated assault, shall consider the offender to have committed and the victim to have been the victim of aggravated assault, shall consider the offense that was committed to have been aggravated assault in determining the manner in which the offender should be treated, and shall comply with whichever of the following is applicable:

(i) Unless the officer has reasonable cause to believe that, during the incident, the offender who committed the aggravated assault and one or more other persons committed offenses against each other, the officer shall arrest the offender who committed the aggravated assault pursuant to section 2935.03 of the Revised Code and shall detain that offender pursuant to that section until a warrant can be obtained, and the arrest shall be for aggravated assault.

(ii) If the officer has reasonable cause to believe that, during the incident, the offender who committed the aggravated assault and one or more other persons committed offenses against each other, the officer shall determine in accordance with division (B)(3)(d) of section 2935.03 of the Revised Code which of those persons is the primary physical aggressor. If the offender who committed the aggravated assault is the primary physical aggressor, the officer shall arrest that offender for aggravated assault pursuant to section 2935.03 of the Revised Code and shall detain that offender pursuant to that section until a warrant can be obtained, and the officer is not required to arrest but may arrest pursuant to section 2935.03 of the Revised Code any other person who committed an offense but who is not the primary physical aggressor. If the offender who committed the aggravated assault is not the primary physical aggressor, the officer is not required to arrest that offender or any other person who committed an offense during the incident but may arrest any of them pursuant to section 2935.03 of the Revised Code and detain them pursuant to that section until a warrant can be obtained.

(2) Provisions requiring the peace officers who serve the agency, instrumentality, or political subdivision to do all of the following:

(a) Respond without undue delay to a report of an alleged incident of the offense of domestic violence or the offense of violating a protection order;

(b) If the alleged offender has been granted pretrial release from custody on a prior charge of the offense of domestic violence or the offense of violating a protection order and has violated one or more conditions of that pretrial release, document the facts and circumstances of the violation in the report to the law enforcement agency that the peace officer makes pursuant to division (D) of this section;

(c) Separate the victim of the offense of domestic violence or the offense of violating a protection order and the alleged offender, conduct separate interviews with the victim and the alleged offender in separate locations, and take a written statement from the victim that indicates the frequency and severity of any prior incidents of physical abuse of the victim by the alleged offender, the number of times the victim has called peace officers for assistance, and the disposition of those calls, if known;

(d) Comply with divisions (B)(1) and (B)(3) of section 2935.03 of the Revised Code and with divisions (B), (C), and (D) of this section.

(3) Sanctions to be imposed upon a peace officer who serves the agency, instrumentality, or political subdivision and who fails to comply with any provision in the policy or with division (B)(1) or (B)(3) of section 2935.03 of the Revised Code or division (B), (C), or (D) of this section.

(4) Examples of reasons that a peace officer may consider for not arresting and detaining until a warrant can be obtained a person who allegedly committed the offense of domestic violence or the offense of violating a protection order when it is the preferred course of action in this state that the officer arrest the alleged offender, as described in division (B)(3)(b) of section 2935.03 of the Revised Code.

(B)(1) Nothing in this section or in division (B)(1) or (B)(3) of section 2935.03 of the Revised Code precludes an agency, instrumentality, or political subdivision that is served by any peace officer described in division (B)(1) of section 2935.03 of the Revised Code from including in the policy it adopts under division (A) of this section either of the following types of provisions:

(a) A provision that requires the peace officers who serve it, if they have reasonable grounds to believe that the offense of domestic violence or the offense of violating a protection order has been committed within the limits of the jurisdiction of the agency, instrumentality, or political subdivision and reasonable cause to believe that a particular person committed the offense, to arrest the alleged offender;

(b) A provision that does not require the peace officers who serve it, if they have reasonable grounds to believe that the offense of domestic violence or the offense of violating a protection order has been committed within the limits of the jurisdiction of the agency, instrumentality, or political subdivision and reasonable cause to believe that a particular person committed the offense, to arrest the alleged offender, but that grants the officers less discretion in those circumstances in deciding whether to arrest the alleged offender than peace officers are granted by divisions (B)(1) and (B)(3) of section 2935.03 of the Revised Code.

(2) If an agency, instrumentality, or political subdivision that is served by any peace officer described in division (B)(1) of section 2935.03 of the Revised Code includes in the policy it adopts under division (A) of this section a provision of the type described in division (B)(1)(a) or (b) of this section, the peace officers who serve the agency, instrumentality, or political subdivision shall comply with the provision in making arrests authorized under division (B)(1) of section 2935.03 of the Revised Code.

(C) When a peace officer described in division (B)(1) of section 2935.03 of the Revised Code investigates a report of an alleged incident of the offense of domestic violence or an alleged incident of the offense of violating a protection order, the officer shall do all of the following:

(1) Complete a domestic violence report in accordance with division (D) of this section;

(2) Advise the victim of the availability of a temporary protection order pursuant to section 2919.26 of the Revised Code or a protection order or consent agreement pursuant to section 3113.31 of the Revised Code;

(3) Give the victim the officer's name, the officer's badge number if the officer has a badge and the badge has a number, the report number for the incident if a report number is available at the time of the officer's investigation, a telephone number that the victim can call for information about the case, the telephone number of a domestic violence shelter in the area, and information on any local victim advocate program.

(D) A peace officer who investigates a report of an alleged incident of the offense of domestic violence or an alleged incident of the offense of violating a protection order shall make a written report of the incident whether or not an arrest is made. The report shall document the officer's observations of the victim and the alleged offender, any visible injuries of the victim or alleged offender, any weapons at the scene, the actions of the alleged offender, any statements made by the victim or witnesses, and any other significant facts or circumstances. If the officer does not arrest and detain until a warrant can be obtained a person who allegedly committed the offense of domestic violence or the offense of violating a protection order when it is the preferred course of action in this state pursuant to division (B)(3)(b) of section 2935.03 of the Revised Code that the alleged offender be arrested, the officer must articulate in the report a clear statement of the officer's reasons for not arresting and detaining that alleged offender until a warrant can be obtained. The officer shall submit the written report to the law enforcement agency to which the officer has been appointed, employed, or elected.

(E) Each agency, instrumentality, or political subdivision that is required to adopt policies and procedures under division (A) of this section shall adopt those policies and procedures in conjunction and consultation with shelters in the community for victims of domestic violence and private organizations, law enforcement agencies, and other public agencies in the community that have expertise in the recognition and handling of domestic violence cases.

(F) To the extent described in and in accordance with section 9.86 or 2744.03 of the Revised Code, a peace officer who arrests an offender for the offense of violating a protection order with respect to a protection order or consent agreement of this state or another state that on its face is valid is immune from liability in a civil action for damages for injury, death, or loss to person or property that allegedly was caused by or related to the arrest.

(G) Each agency, instrumentality, or political subdivision described in division (A) of this section that arrests an offender for an alleged incident of the offense of domestic violence or an alleged incident of the offense of violating a protection order shall consider referring the case to federal authorities for prosecution under 18 U.S.C. 2261 if the incident constitutes a violation of federal law.

(H) As used in this section:

(1) "Another's unborn" has the same meaning as in section 2903.09 of the Revised Code.

(2) "Dangerous ordnance" and "deadly weapon" have the same meanings as in section 2923.11 of the Revised Code.

(3) "The offense of violating a protection order" includes the former offense of violating a protection order or consent agreement or anti-stalking protection order as set forth in section 2919.27 of the Revised Code as it existed prior to the effective date of this amendment.

**HISTORY: 145 v H 335 (Eff 12-9-94); 147 v S 1. Eff 10-21-97.**

## § 2935.033 Peace officer assistance to federal law enforcement officer with arrest authority under Patriot Act.

(A) Any peace officer may render assistance to any federal law enforcement officer who has arrest authority under the "Uniting and Strengthening America by Providing Appropriate Tools Required to Intercept and Obstruct Terrorism (USA Patriot Act) Act of 2001," Pub. L. No. 107-056, 115 Stat. 272, as amended, if both of the following apply:

(1) There is a threat of imminent physical danger to the federal law enforcement officer, a threat of physical harm to another person, or any other serious emergency situation present.

(2) Either the federal law enforcement officer requests emergency assistance or it appears that the federal law enforcement officer is unable to request assistance, and the circumstances reasonably indicate that assistance is appropriate.

(B) "Federal law enforcement officer" has the same meaning as in section 9.88 of the Revised Code.

**HISTORY: 151 v S 9, § 1, eff. 4-14-06.**

## § 2935.04 When any person may arrest.

When a felony has been committed, or there is reasonable ground to believe that a felony has been committed, any person without a warrant may arrest another whom he has reasonable cause to believe is guilty of the offense, and detain him until a warrant can be obtained.

**HISTORY: GC § 13432-2; 113 v 123(140), ch 11, § 2; Bureau of Code Revision. Eff 10-1-53.**

## § 2935.041 Detention, arrest of shoplifters; protection of library, museum and archival institution property; motion picture piracy.

(A) A merchant, or an employee or agent of a merchant, who has probable cause to believe that items offered for sale by a mercantile establishment have been unlawfully taken by a person, may, for the purposes set forth in division (C) of this section, detain the person in a reasonable manner for a reasonable length of time within the mercantile establishment or its immediate vicinity.

(B) Any officer, employee, or agent of a library, museum, or archival institution may, for the purposes set forth in division (C) of this section or for the purpose of conducting a reasonable investigation of a belief that the person has acted in a manner described in divisions (B)(1) and (2) of this section, detain a person in a reasonable manner for a reasonable length of time within, or in the immediate vicinity of, the library, museum, or archival institution, if the officer, employee, or agent has probable cause to believe that the person has either:

(1) Without privilege to do so, knowingly moved, defaced, damaged, destroyed, or otherwise improperly tampered with property owned by or in the custody of the library, museum, or archival institution; or

(2) With purpose to deprive the library, museum, or archival institution of property owned by it or in its custody, knowingly obtained or exerted control over the property without the consent of the owner or person authorized to give consent, beyond the scope of the express or implied consent of the owner or person authorized to give consent, by deception, or by threat.

(C) An officer, agent, or employee of a library, museum, or archival institution pursuant to division (B) of this section or a merchant or employee or agent of a merchant pursuant to division (A) of this section may detain another person for any of the following purposes:

(1) To recover the property that is the subject of the unlawful taking, criminal mischief, or theft;

(2) To cause an arrest to be made by a peace officer;

(3) To obtain a warrant of arrest;

(4) To offer the person, if the person is suspected of the unlawful taking, criminal mischief, or theft and notwithstanding any other provision of the Revised Code, an opportunity to complete a pretrial diversion program and to inform the person of the other legal remedies available to the library, museum, archival institution, or merchant.

(D) The owner or lessee of a facility in which a motion picture is being shown, or the owner's or lessee's employee or agent, who has probable cause to believe that a person is or has been operating an audiovisual recording function of a device in violation of section 2913.07 of the Revised Code may, for the purpose of causing an arrest to be made by a peace officer or of obtaining an arrest warrant, detain the person in a reasonable manner for a reasonable length of time within the facility or its immediate vicinity.

(E) The officer, agent, or employee of the library, museum, or archival institution, the merchant or employee or agent of a merchant, or the owner, lessee, employee, or agent of the facility acting under division (A), (B), or (D) of this section shall not search the person detained, search or seize any property belonging to the person detained without the person's consent, or use undue restraint upon the person detained.

(F) Any peace officer may arrest without a warrant any person that the officer has probable cause to believe has committed any act described in division (B)(1) or (2) of this section, that the officer has probable cause to believe has committed an unlawful taking in a mercantile establishment, or that the officer has reasonable cause to believe has committed an act prohibited by section 2913.07 of the Revised Code. An arrest under this division shall be made within a reasonable time after the commission of the act or unlawful taking.

(G) As used in this section:

(1) "Archival institution" means any public or private building, structure, or shelter in which are stored historical documents, devices, records, manuscripts, or items of public interest, which historical materials are stored to preserve the materials or the information in the materials, to disseminate the information contained in the materials, or to make the materials available for public inspection or for inspection by certain persons who have a particular interest in, use for, or knowledge concerning the materials.

(2) "Museum" means any public or private nonprofit institution that is permanently organized for primarily educational or aesthetic purposes, owns or borrows objects or items of public interest, and cares for and exhibits to the public the objects or items.

(3) "Audiovisual recording function" and "facility" have the same meaning as in section 2913.07 of the Revised Code.

(4) "Pretrial diversion program" means a rehabilitative, educational program designed to reduce recidivism and promote personal responsibility that is at least four hours in length and that has been approved by any court in this state.

**HISTORY: 127 v 765 (Eff 9-13-57); 131 v 676 (Eff 9-15-65); 133 v H 49 (Eff 10-30-69); 137 v H 403. Eff 7-4-78; 150 v H 179, § 1, eff. 3-9-04; 2011 HB 86, § 1, eff. Sept. 30, 2011.**

## § 2935.05 Affidavit filed in case of arrest without warrant.

When a person named in section 2935.03 of the Revised Code has arrested a person without a warrant, he shall, without unnecessary delay, take the person arrested before a court or magistrate having jurisdiction of the offense, and shall file or cause to be filed an affidavit describing the offense for which the person was arrested. Such affidavit shall be filed either with the court or magistrate, or with the prosecuting attorney or other attorney charged by law with prosecution of crimes before such court or magistrate and if filed with such attorney he shall forthwith file with such court or magistrate a complaint, based on such affidavit.

**HISTORY: GC § 13432-3; 113 v 123(140), ch 11, § 3; Bureau of Code Revision, 10-1-53; 128 v 97. Eff 1-1-60.**

## § 2935.06 Duty of private person making arrest.

A private person who has made an arrest pursuant to section 2935.04 of the Revised Code or detention pursuant to section 2935.041 [2935.04.1] of the Revised Code shall forthwith take the person arrested before the most convenient judge or clerk of a court of record or before a magistrate, or deliver such person to an officer authorized to execute criminal warrants who shall, without unnecessary delay, take such person before the court or magistrate having jurisdiction of the offense. The officer may, but if he does not, the private person shall file or cause to be filed in such court or before such magistrate an affidavit stating the offense for which the person was arrested.

**HISTORY: GC § 13432-4; 113 v 123(140), ch 11, § 4; Bureau of Code Revision, 10-1-53; 128 v 97. Eff 1-1-60.**

## § 2935.07 Person arrested without warrant shall be informed of cause of arrest.

When an arrest is made without a warrant by an officer, he shall inform the person arrested of such officer's authority to make the arrest and the cause of the arrest.

When an arrest is made by a private person, he shall, before making the arrest, inform the person to be arrested of the intention to arrest him and the cause of the arrest.

When a person is engaged in the commission of a criminal offense, it is not necessary to inform him of the cause of his arrest.

**HISTORY: GC § 13432-5; 113 v 123(140), ch 11, § 5; Bureau of Code Revision. Eff 10-1-53.**

## § 2935.08 Issuance of warrant.

Upon the filing of an affidavit or complaint as provided in sections 2935.05 or 2935.06 of the Revised Code such judge, clerk, or magistrate shall forthwith issue a warrant to the peace officer making the arrest, or if made by a private person, to the most convenient peace officer who shall receive custody of the person arrested. All further detention and further proceedings shall be pursuant to such affidavit or complaint and warrant.

**HISTORY: GC § 13432-6; 113 v 123(140), ch 11, § 6; Bureau of Code Revision, 10-1-53; 128 v 97 (Eff 1-1-60); 129 v 582(748). Eff 1-10-61.**

## § 2935.081 Administration of oaths, acknowledgment of documents by peace officer.

(A) As used in this section, "peace officer" has the same meaning as in section 2935.01 of the Revised Code, except that "peace officer" does not include, for any purpose, the superintendent or any trooper of the state highway patrol.

(B) A peace officer who has completed a course of in-service training that includes training in the administration of oaths and the acknowledgment of documents and that is approved by the chief legal officer of the political subdivision in which the peace officer is elected or of the political subdivision or other entity in which or by which the peace officer is appointed or employed may administer oaths and acknowledge criminal and juvenile court complaints, summonses, affidavits, and returns of court orders in matters related to the peace officer's official duties.

(C) Except as authorized by division (B) of this section, no peace officer who has completed a course of in-service training of a type described in division (B) of this section shall knowingly perform any act that is specifically required of a notary public unless the peace officer has complied with Chapter 147. of the Revised Code.

**HISTORY: 146 v H 72. Eff 3-18-97.**

## § 2935.09 Accusation by affidavit to cause arrest or prosecution.

(A) As used in this section, "reviewing official" means a judge of a court of record, the prosecuting attorney or attorney charged by law with the prosecution of offenses in a court or before a magistrate, or a magistrate.

(B) In all cases not provided by sections 2935.02 to 2935.08 of the Revised Code, in order to cause the arrest or prosecution of a person charged with committing an offense in this state, a peace officer or a private citizen having knowledge of the facts shall comply with this section.

(C) A peace officer who seeks to cause an arrest or prosecution under this section may file with a reviewing official or the clerk of a court of record an affidavit charging the offense committed.

(D) A private citizen having knowledge of the facts who seeks to cause an arrest or prosecution under this section may file an affidavit charging the offense committed with a reviewing official for the purpose of review to determine if a complaint should be filed by the prosecuting attorney or attorney charged by law with the prosecution of offenses in the court or before the magistrate. A private citizen may file an affidavit charging the offense committed with the clerk of a court of record before or after the normal business hours of the reviewing officials if the clerk's office is open at those times. A clerk who receives an affidavit before or after the normal business hours of the reviewing officials shall forward it to a reviewing official when the reviewing official's normal business hours resume.

**HISTORY: 128 v 97. Eff 1-1-60; 151 v H 214, § 1, eff. 6-30-06.**

**Not analogous to former RC § 2935.09 (GC § 13432-7; 113 v 123(141); Bureau of Code Revision, 10-1-53), repealed 128 v 97(116), § 2, eff 1-1-60.**

The substance of former RC § 2935.09 is now found in RC § 2935.11.

## § 2935.10 Procedure upon filing of affidavit or complaint.

(A) Upon the filing of an affidavit or complaint as provided by section 2935.09 of the Revised Code, if it charges the commission of a felony, such judge, clerk, or magistrate, unless he has reason to believe that it was not filed in good faith, or the claim is not meritorious, shall forthwith issue a warrant for the arrest of the person charged in the affidavit, and directed to a peace officer; otherwise he shall forthwith refer the matter to the prosecuting attorney or other attorney charged by law with prosecution for investigation prior to the issuance of warrant.

(B) If the offense charged is a misdemeanor or violation of a municipal ordinance, such judge, clerk, or magistrate may:

(1) Issue a warrant for the arrest of such person, directed to any officer named in section 2935.03 of the Revised Code but in cases of ordinance violation only to a police officer or marshal or deputy marshal of the municipal corporation;

(2) Issue summons, to be served by a peace officer, bailiff, or court constable, commanding the person against whom the affidavit or complaint was filed to appear forthwith, or at a fixed time in the future, before such court or magistrate. Such summons shall be served in the same manner as in civil cases.

(C) If the affidavit is filed by, or the complaint is filed pursuant to an affidavit executed by, a peace officer who has, at his discretion, at the time of commission of the alleged offense, notified the person to appear before the court or magistrate at a specific time set by such officer, no process need be issued unless the defendant fails to appear at the scheduled time.

(D) Any person charged with a misdemeanor or violation of a municipal ordinance may give bail as provided in sections 2937.22 to 2937.46 of the Revised Code, for his appearance, regardless of whether a warrant, summons, or notice to appear has been issued.

(E) Any warrant, summons, or any notice issued by the peace officer shall state the substance of the charge against the person arrested or directed to appear.

(F) When the offense charged is a misdemeanor, and the warrant or summons issued pursuant to this section is not served within two years of the date of issue, a judge or magistrate may order such warrant or summons withdrawn and the case closed, when it does not appear that the ends of justice require keeping the case open.

**HISTORY: 128 v 97 (Eff 1-1-60); 129 v 582(749) (Eff 1-10-61); 134 v H 511. Eff 3-23-73.**

**Somewhat analogous to former RC §§ 2935.10, 2935.11 (GC §§ 13432-8, 13432-9; 113 v 123(141); Bureau of Code Revision, 10-1-53; analogous to former GC §§ 13494, 13496), repealed 128 v 97(116), § 2, eff 1-1-60.**

## § 2935.11 Failure of person summoned to appear.

If the person summoned to appear as provided in division (B) of section 2935.10 of the Revised Code fails to appear without just cause and personal service of the summons was had upon him, he may be found guilty of contempt of court, and may be fined not to exceed twenty dollars for such contempt. Upon failure to appear the court or magistrate may forthwith issue a warrant for his arrest.

**HISTORY: 128 v 97. Eff 1-1-60.**

**Not analogous to former RC § 2935.11 (GC § 13432-9; 113 v 123(141); Bureau of Code Revision, 10-1-53), repealed 128 v 97(116), § 2, eff 1-1-60; but see former RC § 2935.09 (GC § 13432-7; 113 v 123(141); Bureau of Code Revision, 10-1-53).**

## § 2935.12 Forcible entry in making arrest or executing search warrant.

(A) When making an arrest or executing an arrest warrant or summons in lieu of an arrest warrant, or when executing a search warrant, the peace officer, law enforcement officer, or other authorized individual making the arrest or executing the warrant or summons may break down an outer or inner door or window of a dwelling house or other building, if, after notice of his intention to make the arrest or to execute the warrant or summons, he is refused admittance, but the law enforcement officer or other authorized individual executing a search warrant shall not enter a house or building not described in the warrant.

(B) The precondition for nonconsensual, forcible entry established by division (A) of this section is subject to waiver, as it applies to the execution of a search warrant, in accordance with section 2933.231 [2933.23.1] of the Revised Code.

**HISTORY: 128 v 97 (Eff 1-1-60); 143 v S 258. Eff 11-20-90.**

**Not analogous to former RC § 2935.12 (GC § 13432-11; 113 v 123(141); Bureau of Code Revision, 10-1-53), repealed 128 v 97(116), § 2, eff 1-1-60; but see former RC § 2935.15 (GC § 13432-14; 113 v 123(142); Bureau of Code Revision, 10-1-53).**

The effective date is set by section 15 of SB 258.

The substance of former RC § 2935.12 is now found in RC § 2935.13.

## § 2935.13 Proceedings upon arrest.

Upon the arrest of any person pursuant to warrant, he shall forthwith be taken before the court or magistrate issuing the same, if such court be in session or such magistrate available, and proceedings had as provided in sections 2937.01 to 2937.46, inclusive, of the Revised Code. If such court be not in session and a misdemeanor or ordinance violation is charged, he shall be taken before the clerk or deputy clerk of the court and let to bail, as provided in sections 2937.22 to 2937.46, inclusive, of the Revised Code, if the magistrate be not available, or if the defendant is arrested in a county other than that of the issuing court or magistrate he shall forthwith be taken before the most convenient magistrate, clerk, or deputy clerk of a court of record, and there let to bail for his appearance before the issuing court or magistrate within a reasonable time to be set by such clerk.

**HISTORY: 128 v 97. Eff 1-1-60.**

**Not analogous to former RC § 2935.13 (GC § 13432-12; 113 v 123(142); Bureau of Code Revision, 10-1-53), repealed 128 v 97(116), § 2, eff 1-1-60; but see in part former RC § 2935.12 (GC § 13432-11; 113 v 123(141); Bureau of Code Revision, 10-1-53).**

## § 2935.14 Rights of person arrested.

If the person arrested is unable to offer sufficient bail or, if the offense charged be a felony, he shall, prior to being confined or removed from the county of arrest, as the case may be, be speedily permitted facilities to communicate with an attorney at law of his own choice, or to communicate with at least one relative or other person for the purpose of obtaining counsel (or in cases of misdemeanors or ordinance violation for the purpose of arranging bail). He shall not thereafter be confined or removed from the county or from the situs of initial detention until such attorney has had reasonable opportunity to confer with him privately, or other person to arrange bail, under such security measures as may be necessary under the circumstances.

Whoever, being a police officer in charge of a prisoner, or the custodian of any jail or place of confinement, violates this section shall be fined not less than one hundred nor more than five hundred dollars or imprisoned not more than thirty days, or both.

**HISTORY: 128 v 97. Eff 1-1-60.**

**Not analogous to former RC § 2935.14 (GC § 13432-13; 113 v 123(142); Bureau of Code Revision, 10-1-53), repealed 128 v 97(116), § 2, eff 1-1-60; but see in part former RC § 2935.16 (GC §§ 12856-1, 13432-15; 113 v 123(142); Bureau of Code Revision, 10-1-53) and RC § 2935.17 (GC § 13432-16; 114 v 123(143); Bureau of Code Revision, 10-1-53).**

## § 2935.15 Amount and disposition of bail.

Amount of bail, and nature of security therefor in misdemeanor cases may be set by a schedule fixed by the court or magistrate, or it may be endorsed on the warrant by the magistrate or clerk of the issuing court. If the amount be not endorsed on the warrant, the schedule set by the court or magistrate before whom bail is taken shall prevail. All recognizances taken, or cash received shall be promptly transmitted to the court issuing the warrant, and further proceedings thereon shall be the same as if taken by the issuing court.

**HISTORY: 128 v 97. Eff 1-1-60.**

**Not analogous to former RC § 2935.15 (GC § 13432-14; 113 v 123(142); Bureau of Code Revision, 10-1-53), repealed 128 v 97(116), § 2, eff 1-1-60.**

The substance of former RC § 2935.15 is now found in RC § 2935.12.

## § 2935.16 Prisoners held without process.

When it comes to the attention of any judge or magistrate that a prisoner is being held in any jail or place of custody in his jurisdiction without commitment from a court or magistrate, he shall forthwith, by summary process, require the officer or person in charge of such jail or place of custody to disclose to such court or magistrate, in writing, whether or not he holds the person described or identified in the process and the court under whose process the prisoner is being held. If it appears from the disclosure that the prisoner is held solely under warrant of arrest from any court or magistrate, the judge or magistrate shall order the custodian to produce the prisoner forthwith before the court or magistrate issuing the warrant and if such be impossible for any reason, to produce him before the inquiring judge or magistrate. If it appears from the disclosure that the prisoner is held without process, such judge or magistrate shall require the custodian to produce the prisoner forthwith before him, there to be charged as provided in section 2935.06 of the Revised Code.

Whoever, being the person in temporary or permanent charge of any jail or place of confinement, violates this section shall be fined not less than one hundred nor more than five hundred dollars or imprisoned not more than ninety days, or both.

**HISTORY: 128 v 97. Eff 1-1-60.**

**Not analogous to former RC § 2935.16 (GC § 13432-15; 113 v 123(142); Bureau of Code Revision, 10-1-53), repealed 128 v 97(116), § 2, eff 1-1-60.**

The substance of former RC § 2935.16 is now found in RC § 2935.14.

## § 2935.17 Affidavit forms; authority of supreme court to prescribe.

(A) An affidavit in either of the following forms is sufficient:

(1) "State of Ohio,

........... County, ss:

Before me, A.B., personally came C.D., who being duly sworn according to law deposes and says that on or about the day of .........., ....., at the county of .......... one E.F. (here describe the offense as nearly according to the nature thereof as the case will admit, in ordinary concise language) C.D.

Sworn to and subscribed before me this ..... day of .........., .....

A.B., County Judge
Clerk of ...... Court"

(2) "State of Ohio,

........... County, ss:

Before me, A.B., personally came C.D., who being duly sworn according to law says that on or about the ....... day of ........, ....., one E.F. did: (here listing several common offenses, plainly but tersely described as: fail to stop at stop sign, pass at crest of grade, etc., with a ruled box before each, and then showing an X or distinctive mark in front of the offense claimed to be committed).

C.D.

Sworn to before me and subscribed in my presence this ....... day of ........, .....[.]

A.B., County Judge
Clerk of ....... Court"

(B) A complaint in the following form is sufficient:

"State of Ohio,

........ County, ss:

The undersigned (assistant) prosecuting attorney of ................. County complains that on or about the ...... day of ........, ....., one E.F. did (here describing the offense committed as above) based on affidavit of ............ filed with me.

........................................................

Prosecuting Attorney/City Director of Law"

Provided, that the supreme court of Ohio, may, by rule, provide for the uniform type and language to be used in any affidavit or complaint to be filed in any court inferior to the court of common pleas for violations of the motor vehicle and traffic acts and related ordinances and in any notice to violator to appear in such courts, and may require that such forms and no other, shall be received in such courts, and issued to violators.

**HISTORY: 128 v 97 (Eff 1-1-60); 137 v H 219 (Eff 11-1-77); 148 v H 495. Eff 5-9-2000.**

**Not analogous to former RC § 2935.17 (GC § 13432-16; 113 v 123(143); Bureau of Code Revision, 10-1-53), repealed 128 v 97(116), § 2, eff 1-1-60.**

The substance of former RC § 2935.17 is now found in RC § 2935.14. See also RC § 2937.03.

## § 2935.18 Contents of warrant, summons or notice.

A warrant, summons, or notice of a peace officer shall either contain a copy of the affidavit or recite the substance of the accusation. A warrant shall be directed to a specific officer or to a department designated by its chief, and shall command such officer or member of department to take the accused and bring the accused forthwith before the magistrate or court issuing such warrant to be dealt with according to law. A summons shall be directed to the officer or department, and shall command the officer or department to notify the accused by serving a copy of such summons upon the accused. The following form of warrant is sufficient:

"The State of Ohio,

......... County, ss:

To the Sheriff (other Officer):

Greetings:

Whereas there has been filed with me an affidavit of which the following is a copy (here copy) or the substance, (here set forth the substance, omitting formal parts). These are therefore to command you to take the said E.F., if E.F. is found in your county, or if E.F. is not found in your county, that you pursue after E.F. in any other county in this state and take and safely keep the said E.F. so that you have E.F. forthwith before me or some other magistrate of said county to answer the said complaint and be further dealt with according to law.

Given under my hand this ...... day of ......., ....

A.B., Judge of ...... Court
Clerk of ......... Court"

The following form of summons is sufficient:

"The State of Ohio, ........... County, ss:

To the Bailiff or .............. Constable:

Whereas there has been filed before me an Affidavit (Complaint) of which the following is a copy (here copy) or the substance (here set forth the substance, omitting formal parts). You are commanded to summon one said E.F. to appear before me on the ...... day of ......, ....., at ...... o'clock, .... M., at ...... Building, ....., Ohio, to answer to said charge.

You will make due return of this summons forthwith upon service.

A.B., Judge of ...... Court
Clerk of ......... Court"

**HISTORY: 128 v 97 (Eff 1-1-60); 148 v H 495. Eff 5-9-2000.**

**Not analogous to former RC § 2935.18 (GC § 13432-17; 113 v 123(143); Bureau of Code Revision, 10-1-53), repealed 128 v 97(116), § 2, eff 1-1-60; but see former RC § 2935.20 (GC § 13432-19; 113 v 123(143); Bureau of Code Revision, 10-1-53; analogous to former GC §§ 13500, 13501; RS §§ 7137, 7138; S&C 816, 1402; 35 v 87; 36 v 18; 68 v 3).**

## § 2935.19 Form of affidavit.

An affidavit in the form following is sufficient:

"The State of Ohio,

........... County, ss:

Before me, A. B., personally came C. D., who being duly sworn according to law, deposes and says that on or about the ...... day of ......., .... at the county of ......, one E. F. (here describe the offense committed as nearly according to the nature thereof as the case will admit, in ordinary and concise language.)

Sworn to and subscribed before me, this ..... day of ....., ....

A.B., Judge"

**HISTORY: GC § 13432-18; 113 v 123(143), ch 11, § 18; Bureau of Code Revision, 10-1-53; 127 v 1039(1100) (Eff 1-1-58); 148 v H 495. Eff 5-9-2000.**

## § 2935.20 Right to counsel.

After the arrest, detention, or any other taking into custody of a person, with or without a warrant, such person shall be permitted forthwith facilities to communicate with an attorney at law of his choice who is entitled to practice in the courts of this state, or to communicate with any other person of his choice for the purpose of obtaining counsel. Such communication may be made by a reasonable number of telephone calls or in any other reasonable manner. Such person shall have a right to be visited immediately by any attorney at law so obtained who is entitled to practice in the courts of this state, and to consult with him privately. No officer or any other agent of this state shall prevent, attempt to prevent, or advise such person against the communication, visit, or consultation provided for by this section.

Whoever violates this section shall be fined not less than twenty-five nor more than one hundred dollars or imprisoned not more than thirty days, or both.

**HISTORY: 131 v 677. Eff 11-1-65.**

**Not analogous to former RC § 2935.20 (GC § 13432-19; 113 v 123(143); Bureau of Code Revision, 10-1-53), repealed 128 v 97(116), § 2, eff 1-1-60.**

## § 2935.21 Security for costs.

When the offense charged is a misdemeanor, the magistrate or court, before issuing the warrant, may require the complainant, or if the magistrate considers the complainant irresponsible, may require that said complainant procure a person to be liable for the costs if the complaint is dismissed, and the complainant or other person shall acknowledge himself so liable, and such court or magistrate shall enter such acknowledgment on his docket. Such bond shall not be required of an officer authorized to make arrests when in the discharge of his official duty, or other person or officer authorized to assist the prosecuting attorney in the prosecution of offenders.

**HISTORY: GC § 13432-20; 113 v 123(144), ch 11, § 20; Bureau of Code Revision. Eff 10-1-53.**

## § 2935.22 Repealed, 128 v 97(116), § 2 [GC § 13432-21; 113 v 123(144); Bureau of Code Revision, 10-1-53]. Eff 1-1-60.

This section concerned issuing subpoenas for witnesses.

## § 2935.23 Felony investigation; examination of witnesses.

After a felony has been committed, and before any arrest has been made, the prosecuting attorney of the county, or any judge or magistrate, may cause subpoenas to issue, returnable before any court or magistrate, for any person to give information concerning such felony. The subpoenas shall require the witness to appear forthwith. Before such witness is required to give any information, he must be informed of the purpose of the inquiry, and that he is required to tell the truth concerning the same. He shall then be sworn and be examined under oath by the prosecuting attorney, or the court or magistrate, subject to the constitutional rights of the witness. Such examination shall be taken in writing in any form, and shall be filed with the court or magistrate taking the testimony. Witness fees shall be paid to such persons as in other cases.

**HISTORY: GC § 13432-22; 113 v 123(144), ch 11, § 22; Bureau of Code Revision, 10-1-53; 134 v H 511. Eff 1-1-74.**

## § 2935.24 Arrest by telegraph order.

A judge of a court of record may, by an endorsement under his hand upon a warrant of arrest, authorize the service thereof by telegraph, teletype, wire photo, or other means whereby a written or facsimile copy may be transmitted, and thereafter a copy of such warrant may be sent by any such means to any law enforcement officer. Such copy is effectual in the hands of any law enforcement officer and he shall proceed in the same manner under it as though he held the original warrant issued by the court making the endorsement, except that a state university law enforcement officer shall not arrest for a minor misdemeanor on the basis of a written or facsimile copy of a warrant of arrest. Every officer causing copies of warrants to be sent pursuant to this section, shall certify as correct and file in the office from which such warrant was sent, a copy of such warrant and endorsement thereon, and shall return the original with a statement of his action thereunder.

**HISTORY: GC § 13432-23; 113 v 123(144), ch 11, § 23; Bureau of Code Revision, 10-1-53; 134 v H 511 (Eff 3-23-73); 137 v H 588. Eff 6-19-78.**

## § 2935.25 Power of arrest.

Sections 2935.02 to 2935.24, inclusive, of the Revised Code do not affect or modify the power of arrest vested by law in other persons or officers than those named in section 2935.03 of the Revised Code.

**HISTORY: GC § 13432-24; 113 v 123(145), ch 11, § 24; Bureau of Code Revision. Eff 10-1-53.**

## § 2935.26 Issuance of citation for minor misdemeanor.

(A) Notwithstanding any other provision of the Revised Code, when a law enforcement officer is otherwise authorized to arrest a person for the commission of a minor misdemeanor, the officer shall not arrest the person, but shall issue a citation, unless one of the following applies:

(1) The offender requires medical care or is unable to provide for his own safety.

(2) The offender cannot or will not offer satisfactory evidence of his identity.

(3) The offender refuses to sign the citation.

(4) The offender has previously been issued a citation for the commission of that misdemeanor and has failed to do one of the following:

(a) Appear at the time and place stated in the citation;

(b) Comply with division (C) of this section.

(B) The citation shall contain all of the following:

(1) The name and address of the offender;

(2) A description of the offense and the numerical designation of the applicable statute or ordinance;

(3) The name of the person issuing the citation;

(4) An order for the offender to appear at a stated time and place;

(5) A notice that the offender may comply with division (C) of this section in lieu of appearing at the stated time and place;

(6) A notice that the offender is required to do one of the following and that he may be arrested if he fails to do one of them:

(a) Appear at the time and place stated in the citation;

(b) Comply with division (C) of this section.

(C) In lieu of appearing at the time and place stated in the citation, the offender may, within seven days after the date of issuance of the citation, do either of the following:

(1) Appear in person at the office of the clerk of the court stated in the citation, sign a plea of guilty and a waiver of trial provision that is on the citation, and pay the total amount of the fine and costs;

(2) Sign the guilty plea and waiver of trial provision of the citation, and mail the citation and a check or money order for the total amount of the fine and costs to the office of the clerk of the court stated in the citation.

Remittance by mail of the fine and costs to the office of the clerk of the court stated in the citation constitutes a guilty plea and waiver of trial whether or not the guilty plea and waiver of trial provision of the citation are signed by the defendant.

(D) A law enforcement officer who issues a citation shall complete and sign the citation form, serve a copy of the completed form upon the offender and, without unnecessary delay, file the original citation with the court having jurisdiction over the offense.

(E) Each court shall establish a fine schedule that shall list the fine for each minor misdemeanor, and state the court costs. The fine schedule shall be prominently posted in the place where minor misdemeanor fines are paid.

(F) If an offender fails to appear and does not comply with division (C) of this section, the court may issue a supplemental citation, or a summons or warrant for the arrest of the offender pursuant to the Criminal Rules.

Supplemental citations shall be in the form prescribed by division (B) of this section, but shall be issued and signed by the clerk of the court at which the citation directed the offender to appear and shall be served in the same manner as a summons.

**HISTORY: 137 v S 351. Eff 10-25-78.**

**Not analogous to former RC § 2935.26 (GC § 13434-1; 113 v 123(149); Bureau of Code Revision, 10-1-53), repealed 128 v 97, § 2, eff 1-1-60.**

## § 2935.27 Procedure after issuance of citation; penalties for failure to appear or comply.

(A)(1) If a law enforcement officer issues a citation to a person pursuant to section 2935.26 of the Revised Code and if the minor misdemeanor offense for which the citation is issued is an act prohibited by Chapter 4511., 4513., or 4549. of the Revised Code or an act prohibited by any municipal ordinance that is substantially similar to any section contained in Chapter 4511., 4513., or 4549. of the Revised Code, the officer shall inform the person, if the person has a current valid Ohio driver's or commercial driver's license, of the possible consequences of the person's actions as required under division (E) of this section, and also shall inform the person that the person is required either to appear at the time and place stated in the citation or to comply with division (C) of section 2935.26 of the Revised Code.

(2) If the person is an Ohio resident but does not have a current valid Ohio driver's or commercial driver's license or if the person is a resident of a state that is not a member of the nonresident violator compact, of which this state is a member pursuant to section 4510.71 of the Revised Code, and if the court, by local rule, has prescribed a procedure for the setting of a reasonable security by the court pursuant to division (F) of this section, security shall be set in accordance with that local rule and that division.

A court by local rule may prescribe a procedure for the setting of reasonable security as described in this division. As an alternative to this procedure, a court by local rule may prescribe a procedure for the setting of a reasonable security by the person without the person appearing before the court.

(B) A person who has security set under division (A) (2) of this section shall be given a receipt or other evidence of the deposit of the security by the court.

(C) Upon compliance with division (C) of section 2935.26 of the Revised Code by a person who was issued a citation, the clerk of the court shall notify the court. The court shall immediately return any sum of money, license, or other security deposited in relation to the citation to the person, or to any other person who deposited the security.

(D) If a person who has a current valid Ohio driver's or commercial driver's license and who was issued a citation fails to appear at the time and place specified on the citation, fails to comply with division (C) of section 2935.26 of the Revised Code, or fails to comply with or satisfy any judgment of the court within the time allowed by the court, the court shall declare the forfeiture of the person's license. Thirty days after the declaration of forfeiture, the court shall enter information relative to the forfeiture on a form approved and furnished by the registrar of motor vehicles, and forward the form to the registrar. The registrar shall suspend the person's driver's or commercial driver's license, send written notification of the suspension to the person at the person's last known address, and order the person to surrender the person's driver's or commercial driver's license to the registrar within forty-eight hours. No valid driver's or commercial driver's license shall be granted to the person until the court having jurisdiction of the offense that led to the forfeiture orders that the forfeiture be terminated. The court shall so order if the person, after having failed to appear in court at the required time and place to answer the charge or after having pleaded guilty to or been found guilty of the violation and having failed within the time allowed by the court to pay the fine imposed by the court, thereafter appears to answer the charge and pays any fine imposed by the court or pays the fine originally imposed by the court. The court shall inform the registrar of the termination of the forfeiture by entering information relative to the termination on a form approved and furnished by the registrar and sending the form to the registrar as provided in this division. The person shall pay to the bureau of motor vehicles a fifteen-dollar reinstatement fee to cover the costs of the bureau in administering this section. The registrar shall deposit the fees so paid into the state bureau of motor vehicles fund created by section 4501.25 of the Revised Code.

In addition, upon receipt of the copy of the declaration of forfeiture from the court, neither the registrar nor any deputy registrar shall accept any application for the registration or transfer of registration of any motor vehicle owned or leased by the person named in the declaration of forfeiture until the court having jurisdiction of the offense that led to the forfeiture orders that the forfeiture be terminated. However, for a motor vehicle leased by a person named in a declaration of forfeiture, the registrar shall not implement the preceding sentence until the registrar adopts procedures for that implementation under section 4503.39 of the Revised Code. Upon receipt by the registrar of an order terminating the forfeiture, the registrar shall take such measures as may be necessary to permit the person to register a motor vehicle owned or leased by the person or to transfer the registration of such a motor vehicle, if the person later makes application to take such action and the person otherwise is eligible to register the motor vehicle or to transfer the registration of it.

The registrar is not required to give effect to any declaration of forfeiture or order terminating a forfeiture unless the order is transmitted to the registrar by means of an electronic transfer system. The registrar shall not restore the person's driving or vehicle registration privileges until the person pays the reinstatement fee as provided in this division.

If the person who was issued the citation fails to appear at the time and place specified on the citation and fails to comply with division (C) of section 2935.26 of the Revised Code and the person has deposited a sum of money or other security in relation to the citation under division (A)(2) of this section, the deposit immediately shall be forfeited to the court.

This section does not preclude further action as authorized by division (F) of section 2935.26 of the Revised Code.

(E) A law enforcement officer who issues a person a minor misdemeanor citation for an act prohibited by Chapter 4511., 4513., or 4549. of the Revised Code or an act prohibited by a municipal ordinance that is substantially similar to any section contained in Chapter 4511., 4513., or 4549. of the Revised Code shall inform the person that if the person does not appear at the time and place stated on the citation or does not comply with division (C) of section 2935.26 of the Revised Code, the person's driver's or commercial driver's license will be suspended, the person will not be eligible for the reissuance of the license or the issuance of a new license or the issuance of a certificate of registration for a motor vehicle owned or leased by the person, until the person appears and complies with all orders of the court. The person also is subject to any applicable criminal penalties.

(F) A court setting security under division (A)(2) of this section shall do so in conformity with sections 2937.22 and 2937.23 of the Revised Code and the Rules of Criminal Procedure.

**HISTORY: 137 v S 351 (Eff 10-25-78); 141 v S 356 (Eff 9-24-86); 143 v H 381 (Eff 7-1-89); 143 v S 338 (Eff 11-28-90); 144 v S 275 (Eff 7-1-93)†; 145 v H 687 (Eff 10-12-94); 146 v H 353 (Eff 9-17-96); 146 v S 121 (Eff 11-19-96); 147 v S 85. Eff 5-15-97; 149 v S 123, § 1, eff. 1-1-04; 150 v H 230, § 1, eff. 9-16-04.**

The effective date is set by section 4 of S.B. 123.

See provisions of § 5 of S.B. 123 (149 v —) following RC § 2935.03.

**Analogous to former RC § 2935.27 (GC § 13434-2; 113 v 123(149); Bureau of Code Revision, 10-1-53), repealed 128 v 97, § 2, eff 1-1-60.**

The provisions of § 5 of SB 85 (147 v —) read as follows:

SECTION 5. Sections 2935.27, 2937.221, * * * of the Revised Code are presented in this act as composites of the sections as amended by both Am. Sub. H.B. 353 and Am. Sub. S.B. 121 of the 121st General Assembly, with the new language of neither of the acts shown in capital letters. This is in recognition of the principle stated in division (B) of section 1.52 of the Revised Code that such amendments are to be harmonized where not substantively irreconcilable and constitutes a legislative finding that such is the resulting version in effect prior to the effective date of this act.

† See provisions, §§ 4, 5 of SB 62 (145 v —) changing the effective date of SB 275 from 7-1-93 to 9-1-93, following RC § 2903.04.

## § 2935.28 Names of traffic law violators damaging real property to be provided to owner.

(A) As used in this section, "motor vehicle" has the same meaning as in section 4501.01 of the Revised Code.

(B) If damage is caused to real property by the operation of a motor vehicle in, or during the violation of any section of the Revised Code or of any municipal ordinance, the law enforcement agency that investigates the case, upon request of the real property owner, shall provide the owner with the names of the persons who are charged with the commission of the offense. If a request for the names is made, the agency shall provide the names as soon as possible after the persons are charged with the offense.

(C) The personnel of law enforcement agencies who act pursuant to division (B) of this section in good faith are not liable in damages in a civil action allegedly arising from their actions taken pursuant to that division. Political subdivisions and the state are not liable in damages in a civil action allegedly arising from the actions of personnel of their law enforcement agencies if the personnel have immunity under this division.

**HISTORY: 140 v H 666. Eff 3-14-85.**

**Not analogous to former RC § 2935.28 (GC § 13434-3; 113 v 123(149); Bureau of Code Revision, 10-1-53), repealed 128 v 97(116), § 2, eff 1-1-60.**

[UNIFORM ACT ON FRESH PURSUIT]

## § 2935.29 Definition of fresh pursuit and state.

As used in sections 2935.30 and 2935.31 of the Revised Code:

(A) "Fresh pursuit" includes fresh pursuit as defined by the common law, and also the pursuit of a person who has committed a felony or who is reasonably suspected of having committed a felony. It includes the pursuit of a person suspected of having committed a supposed felony, though no felony has actually been committed, if there is reasonable ground for believing that a felony has been committed. Fresh pursuit does not necessarily imply instant pursuit, but pursuit without unreasonable delay.

(B) "State" includes the District of Columbia.

**HISTORY: GC §§ 13434-7, 13434-8; 117 v 671; Bureau of Code Revision. Eff 10-1-53.**

## § 2935.30 Authority of foreign police.

Any member of an organized state, county, or municipal peace unit of another state of the United States who enters this state in fresh pursuit, and continues within this state in such fresh pursuit, of a person in order to arrest him on the ground that he is believed to have committed a felony in such other state has the same authority to arrest and hold such person in custody as has any member of any organized state, county, or municipal peace unit of this state to arrest and hold in custody a person on the ground that he is believed to have committed a felony in this state.

This section does not make unlawful any arrest in this state which would otherwise be lawful.

**HISTORY: GC §§ 13434-4, 13434-6; 117 v 671; Bureau of Code Revision. Eff 10-1-53.**

## § 2935.31 Hearing before magistrate in county of arrest.

If an arrest is made in this state by an officer of another state under section 2935.30 of the Revised Code, he shall without unnecessary delay take the person arrested before a magistrate of the county in which the arrest was made, who shall conduct a hearing for the purpose of determining the lawfulness of the arrest. If the magistrate determines that the arrest was lawful he shall commit the person arrested to await for a reasonable time the issuance of an extradition warrant by the governor of this state, or admit him to bail for such purposes. If the magistrate determines that the arrest was unlawful he shall discharge the person arrested.

**HISTORY: GC § 13434-5; 117 v 671; Bureau of Code Revision. Eff 10-1-53.**

## § 2935.32 Broadcasting information of crime.

The board of county commissioners or the prosecuting attorney of any county, with the consent of the court of common pleas, may contract with any company engaged in broadcasting by radio, for the purpose of immediate broadcasting of information concerning any violent felony, when the perpetrator thereof has escaped. The sheriff and heads of police departments, immediately upon the commission of any such felony and the escape of such perpetrator, shall furnish all information concerning said crime and the perpetrator thereof, to said company with which such contract may be made, for the purpose of broadcasting. The reasonable cost of such broadcasting shall be paid by the county, out of the county treasury, on the order of the board.

**HISTORY: GC § 13431-1; 113 v 123(139), ch 10, § 1; Bureau of Code Revision. Eff 10-1-53.**

## [ALCOHOLIC TREATMENT]

### § 2935.33 Commitment of alcoholics and intoxicated persons for inpatient care.

(A) If a person charged with a misdemeanor is taken before a judge of a court of record and if it appears to the judge that the person is an alcoholic or is suffering from acute alcohol intoxication and that the person would benefit from services provided by an alcohol and drug addiction program certified under Chapter 3793. of the Revised Code, the judge may place the person temporarily in a program certified under that chapter in the area in which the court has jurisdiction for inpatient care and treatment for an indefinite period not exceeding five days. The commitment does not limit the right to release on bail. The judge may dismiss a charge of a violation of division (B) of section 2917.11 of the Revised Code or of a municipal ordinance substantially equivalent to that division if the defendant complies with all the conditions of treatment ordered by the court.

The court may order that any fines or court costs collected by the court from defendants who have received inpatient care from an alcohol and drug addiction program be paid, for the benefit of the program, to the board of alcohol, drug addiction, and mental health services of the alcohol, drug addiction, and mental health service district in which the program is located or to the director of alcohol and drug addiction services.

(B) If a person is being sentenced for a violation of division (B) of section 2917.11 or section 4511.19 of the Revised Code, a misdemeanor violation of section 2919.25 of the Revised Code, a misdemeanor violation of section 2919.27 of the Revised Code involving a protection order issued or consent agreement approved pursuant to section 2919.26 or 3113.31 of the Revised Code, or a violation of a municipal ordinance substantially equivalent to that division or any of those sections and if it appears to the judge at the time of sentencing that the person is an alcoholic or is suffering from acute alcohol intoxication and that, in lieu of imprisonment, the person would benefit from services provided by an alcohol and drug addiction program certified under Chapter 3793. of the Revised Code, the court may commit the person to close supervision in any facility in the area in which the court has jurisdiction that is, or is operated by, such a program. Such close supervision may include outpatient services and part-time release, except that a person convicted of a violation of division (A) of section 4511.19 of the Revised Code shall be confined to the facility for at least three days and except that a person convicted of a misdemeanor violation of section 2919.25 of the Revised Code, a misdemeanor violation of section 2919.27 of the Revised Code involving a protection order issued or consent agreement approved pursuant to section 2919.26 or 3113.31 of the Revised Code, or a violation of a substantially equivalent municipal ordinance shall be confined to the facility in accordance with the order of commitment. A commitment of a person to a facility for purposes of close supervision shall not exceed the maximum term for which the person could be imprisoned.

(C) A law enforcement officer who finds a person subject to prosecution for violation of division (B) of section 2917.11 of the Revised Code or a municipal ordinance substantially equivalent to that division and who has reasonable cause to believe that the person is an alcoholic or is suffering from acute alcohol intoxication and would benefit from immediate treatment immediately may place the person in an alcohol and drug addiction program certified under Chapter 3793. of the Revised Code in the area in which the person is found, for emergency treatment, in lieu of other arrest procedures, for a maximum period of forty-eight hours. During that time, if the person desires to leave such custody, the person shall be released forthwith.

(D) As used in this section:

(1) "Alcoholic" has the same meaning as in section 3793.01 of the Revised Code;

(2) "Acute alcohol intoxication" means a heavy consumption of alcohol over a relatively short period of time, resulting in dysfunction of the brain centers controlling behavior, speech, and memory and causing characteristic withdrawal symptoms.

**HISTORY: 134 v H 240 (Eff 4-28-72); 136 v H 1 (Eff 6-13-75); 136 v H 907 (Eff 8-25-76); 140 v H 37 (Eff 6-22-84); 141 v H 475 (Eff 3-7-86); 143 v H 317 (Eff 10-10-89); 145 v S 82 (Eff 5-4-94); 146 v S 2. Eff 7-1-96; 149 v H 490, § 1, eff. 1-1-04.**

The effective date is set by section 4 of H.B. 490.

## [PRE-TRIAL DIVERSION PROGRAMS]

### § 2935.36 Pre-trial diversion programs for certain offenders.

(A) The prosecuting attorney may establish pre-trial diversion programs for adults who are accused of committing criminal offenses and whom the prosecuting attorney believes probably will not offend again. The prosecuting attorney may require, as a condition of an accused's participation in the program, the accused to pay a reasonable fee for supervision services that include, but are not limited to, monitoring and drug testing. The programs shall be operated pursuant to written standards approved by journal entry by the presiding judge or, in courts with only one judge, the judge of the court of common pleas and shall not be applicable to any of the following:

(1) Repeat offenders or dangerous offenders;

(2) Persons accused of an offense of violence, of a violation of section 2903.06, 2907.04, 2907.05, 2907.21, 2907.22, 2907.31, 2907.32, 2907.34, 2911.31, 2919.12, 2919.13, 2919.22, 2921.02, 2921.11, 2921.12, 2921.32, or 2923.20 of the Revised Code, or of a violation of section 2905.01, 2905.02, or 2919.23 of the Revised Code that, had it occurred prior to July 1, 1996, would have been a violation of section 2905.04 of the Revised Code as it existed prior to that date, with the exception that the prosecuting attorney may permit persons accused of any such offense to enter a pre-trial diversion program, if the prosecuting attorney finds any of the following:

(a) The accused did not cause, threaten, or intend serious physical harm to any person;

(b) The offense was the result of circumstances not likely to recur;

(c) The accused has no history of prior delinquency or criminal activity;

(d) The accused has led a law-abiding life for a substantial time before commission of the alleged offense;

(e) Substantial grounds tending to excuse or justify the alleged offense.

(3) Persons accused of a violation of Chapter 2925. or 3719. of the Revised Code;

(4) Persons accused of a violation of section 4511.19 of the Revised Code or a violation of any substantially similar municipal ordinance.

(B) An accused who enters a diversion program shall do all of the following:

(1) Waive, in writing and contingent upon the accused's successful completion of the program, the accused's right to a speedy trial, the preliminary hearing, the time period within which the grand jury may consider an indictment against the accused, and arraignment, unless the hearing, indictment, or arraignment has already occurred;

(2) Agree, in writing, to the tolling while in the program of all periods of limitation established by statutes or rules of court, that are applicable to the offense with which the accused is charged and to the conditions of the diversion program established by the prosecuting attorney;

(3) Agree, in writing, to pay any reasonable fee for supervision services established by the prosecuting attorney.

(C) The trial court, upon the application of the prosecuting attorney, shall order the release from confinement of any accused who has agreed to enter a pre-trial diversion program and shall discharge and release any existing bail and release any sureties on recognizances and shall release the accused on a recognizance bond conditioned upon the accused's compliance with the terms of the diversion program. The prosecuting attorney shall notify every victim of the crime and the arresting officers of the prosecuting attorney's intent to permit the accused to enter a pre-trial diversion program. The victim of the crime and the arresting officers shall have the opportunity to file written objections with the prosecuting attorney prior to the commencement of the pre-trial diversion program.

(D) If the accused satisfactorily completes the diversion program, the prosecuting attorney shall recommend to the trial court that the charges against the accused be dismissed, and the court, upon the recommendation of the prosecuting attorney, shall dismiss the charges. If the accused chooses not to enter the prosecuting attorney's diversion program, or if the accused violates the conditions of the agreement pursuant to which the accused has been released, the accused may be brought to trial upon the charges in the manner provided by law, and the waiver executed pursuant to division (B)(1) of this section shall be void on the date the accused is removed from the program for the violation.

(E) As used in this section:

(1) "Repeat offender" means a person who has a history of persistent criminal activity and whose character and condition reveal a substantial risk that the person will commit another offense. It is prima-facie evidence that a person is a repeat offender if any of the following applies:

(a) Having been convicted of one or more offenses of violence and having been imprisoned pursuant to sentence for any such offense, the person commits a subsequent offense of violence;

(b) Having been convicted of one or more sexually oriented offenses or child-victim oriented offenses, both as defined in section 2950.01 of the Revised Code, and having been imprisoned pursuant to sentence for one or more of those offenses, the person commits a subsequent sexually oriented offense or child-victim oriented offense;

(c) Having been convicted of one or more theft offenses as defined in section 2913.01 of the Revised Code and having been imprisoned pursuant to sentence for one or more of those theft offenses, the person commits a subsequent theft offense;

(d) Having been convicted of one or more felony drug abuse offenses as defined in section 2925.01 of the Revised Code and having been imprisoned pursuant to sentence for one or more of those felony drug abuse offenses, the person commits a subsequent felony drug abuse offense;

(e) Having been convicted of two or more felonies and having been imprisoned pursuant to sentence for one or more felonies, the person commits a subsequent offense;

(f) Having been convicted of three or more offenses of any type or degree other than traffic offenses, alcoholic intoxication offenses, or minor misdemeanors and having been imprisoned pursuant to sentence for any such offense, the person commits a subsequent offense.

(2) "Dangerous offender" means a person who has committed an offense, whose history, character, and condition reveal a substantial risk that the person will be a danger to others, and whose conduct has been characterized by a pattern of repetitive, compulsive, or aggressive behavior with heedless indifference to the consequences.

**HISTORY: 137 v H 473 (Eff 6-6-78); 141 v S 262 (Eff 3-20-87); 145 v S 82 (Eff 5-4-94); 146 v S 2 (Eff 7-1-96); 146 v H 180 (Eff 7-1-97); 148 v S 107. Eff 3-23-2000; 150 v S 5, § 1, eff. 7-31-03; 150 v H 95, § 1, eff. 9-26-03; 152 v H 130, § 1, eff. 4-7-09.**

The effective date is set by section 179 of H.B. 95 (150 v —).

Sections 109.57 and 2935.36 of the Revised Code are amended by [Am. Sub. H.B. 95 of the 125th General Assembly] and also by Am. Sub. S.B. 5, both of the 125th General Assembly. Comparison of these amendments in pursuance of section 1.52 of the Revised Code discloses that they are not irreconcilable so that they are required by that section to be harmonized to give effect to each amendment.

# CHAPTER 2937: PRELIMINARY EXAMINATION; BAIL



## § 2937.01 Definitions.

The definition of "magistrate" set forth in section 2931.01 of the Revised Code, and the definitions of "peace officer," "prosecutor," and "offense" set forth in section 2935.01 of the Revised Code apply to Chapter 2937. of the Revised Code.

**HISTORY: Bureau of Code Revision, 10-1-53; 128 v 97. Eff 1-1-60.**

### [PRELIMINARY EXAMINATION]

## § 2937.02 Announcement of charge and rights of accused by court.

When, after arrest, the accused is taken before a court or magistrate, or when the accused appears pursuant to terms of summons or notice, the affidavit or complaint being first filed, the court or magistrate shall, before proceeding further:

(A) Inform the accused of the nature of the charge against him and the identity of the complainant and permit the accused or his counsel to see and read the affidavit or complaint or a copy thereof;

(B) Inform the accused of his right to have counsel and the right to a continuance in the proceedings to secure counsel;

(C) Inform the accused of the effect of pleas of guilty, not guilty, and no contest, of his right to trial by jury, and the necessity of making written demand therefor;

(D) If the charge be a felony, inform the accused of the nature and extent of possible punishment on conviction and of the right to preliminary hearing. Such information may be given to each accused individually or, if at any time there exists any substantial number of defendants to be arraigned at the same session, the judge or magistrate may, by general announcement or by distribution of printed matter, advise all those accused concerning those rights general in their nature, and informing as to individual matters at arraignment.

**HISTORY: 128 v 97. Eff 1-1-60.**

**Analogous to former RC § 2937.02 (GC § 13433-1; 113 v 123(145), ch 12; 115 v 530; Bureau of Code Revision, 10-1-53), repealed 128 v 97(116), § 2, eff 1-1-60.**

## § 2937.03 Arraignment; counsel; bail.

After the announcement, as provided by section 2937.02 of the Revised Code, the accused shall be arraigned by the magistrate, clerk, or prosecutor of the court reading the affidavit or complaint, or reading its substance, omitting purely formal parts, to the accused unless the reading of the affidavit or complaint is waived. The judge or magistrate shall then inquire of the accused whether the accused understands the nature of the charge. If the accused does not indicate understanding, the judge or magistrate shall give explanation in terms of the statute or ordinance claimed violated. If the accused is not represented by counsel and expresses a desire to consult with an attorney at law, the judge or magistrate shall continue the case for a reasonable time to allow the accused to send for or consult with counsel and shall set bail for the later appearance if the offense is bailable. If the accused is not able to make bail, bail is denied, or the offense is not bailable, the court or magistrate shall require the officer having custody of the accused immediately to take a message to any attorney at law within the municipal corporation where the accused is detained, or immediately to make available to the accused use of a telephone for calling to arrange for legal counsel or bail.

**HISTORY: 128 v 97 (Eff 1-1-60); 129 v 582(749) (Eff 1-10-61); 148 v S 8. Eff 7-29-99.**

**Not analogous to former RC** § 2937.03 **(GC § 13433-2; 113 v 123(145); Bureau of Code Revision, 10-1-53), repealed 128 v 97(116), § 2, eff 1-1-60; but see former RC** § 2935.17 **(GC § 13432-16; 113 v 123(143); Bureau of Code Revision, 10-1-53).**

## § 2937.04 Motion for dismissal.

If accused does not desire counsel or, having engaged counsel, appears at the end of granted continuance, he may then raise, by motion to dismiss the affidavit or complaint, any exception thereto which could be asserted against an indictment or information by motion to quash, plea in abatement, or demurrer. Such motion may be made orally and ruled upon by the court or magistrate at the time of presentation, with minute of motion and ruling made in the journal (if a court of record) or on the docket (if a court not of record) or such motion may be presented in writing and set down for argument at later time. Where the motion attacks a defect in the record by facts extrinsic thereto, proof may be offered by testimony or affidavit.

**HISTORY: 128 v 97. Eff 1-1-60.**

**Not analogous to former RC § 2937.04 (GC § 13433-3; 113 v 123(145); Bureau of Code Revision, 10-1-53), repealed 128 v 97(116), § 2, eff 1-1-60.**

## § 2937.05 Discharge on motion to dismiss; amendment of complaint.

If the motion pursuant to section 2937.04 of the Revised Code be sustained, accused shall be discharged unless the court or magistrate finds that the defect can be corrected without changing the nature of the charge, in which case he may order the complaint amended or a proper affidavit filed forthwith and require the accused to plead thereto. The discharge of accused upon the sustaining of a motion to dismiss shall not be considered a bar to further prosecution either of felony or misdemeanor.

**HISTORY: 128 v 97. Eff 1-1-60.**

**Not analogous to former RC § 2937.05 (GC § 13433-4; 113 v 123(145); Bureau of Code Revision, 10-1-53), repealed 128 v 97(116), § 2, eff 1-1-60.**

## § 2937.06 Pleas.

(A) After all motions are disposed of or if no motion is presented, the court or magistrate shall require the accused to plead to the charge.

(1) In cases of felony, only a plea of not guilty or a written plea of guilty shall be received and if the defendant declines to plead, a plea of not guilty shall be entered for the defendant and further proceedings had as set forth in sections 2937.09 to 2937.12 of the Revised Code.

(2) In cases of misdemeanor, the following pleas may be received:

(a) Guilty;

(b) Not guilty;

(c) No contest;

(d) Once in jeopardy, which includes the defenses of former conviction or former acquittal.

(B) Prior to accepting a plea of guilty or a plea of no contest under division (A) of this section, the court shall comply with sections 2943.031 [2943.03.1] and 2943.032 [2943.03.2] of the Revised Code.

(C) Entry of any plea pursuant to this section shall constitute a waiver of any objection that could be taken advantage of by motion pursuant to section 2937.04 of the Revised Code.

**HISTORY: 128 v 97 (Eff 1-1-60); 143 v S 95 (Eff 10-2-89); 146 v S 2. Eff 7-1-96.**

The effective date is set by section 6 of SB 2.

## § 2937.07 Action on pleas of "guilty" and "no contest" in misdemeanor cases.

If the offense is a misdemeanor and the accused pleads guilty to the offense, the court or magistrate shall receive and enter the plea unless the court or magistrate believes that it was made through fraud, collusion, or mistake. If the court or magistrate believes that it was made through fraud, collusion, or mistake, the court or magistrate shall enter a plea of not guilty and set the matter for trial pursuant to Chapter 2938. of the Revised Code. Upon receiving a plea of guilty, the court or magistrate shall call for an explanation of the circumstances of the offense from the affiant or complainant or the affiant's or complainant's representatives unless the offense to which the accused is pleading is a minor misdemeanor in which case the court or magistrate is not required to call for an explanation of the circumstances of the offense. After hearing the explanation of circumstances, together with any statement of the accused or after receiving the plea of guilty if an explanation of the circumstances of the offense is not required, the court or magistrate shall proceed to pronounce the sentence or shall continue the matter for the purpose of imposing the sentence.

A plea to a misdemeanor offense of "no contest" or words of similar import shall constitute an admission of the truth of the facts alleged in the complaint and that the judge or magistrate may make a finding of guilty or not guilty from the explanation of the circumstances of the offense. If the offense to which the accused is entering a plea of "no contest" is a minor misdemeanor, the judge or magistrate is not required to call for an explanation of the circumstances of the offense, and the judge or magistrate may base a finding on the facts alleged in the complaint. If a finding of guilty is made, the judge or magistrate shall impose the sentence or continue the case for sentencing accordingly. A plea of "no contest" or words of similar import shall not be construed as an admission of any fact at issue in the criminal charge in any subsequent civil or criminal action or proceeding.

**HISTORY: 128 v 97. Eff 1-1-60; 149 v H 490, § 1, eff. 1-1-04; 153 v H 338, § 1, eff. 9-17-10.**

The effective date is set by section 4 of HB 490.

**Not analogous to former RC § 2937.07 (GC § 13433-6; 113 v 123(146); Bureau of Code Revision, 10-1-53), repealed 128 v 97(116), § 2, eff 1-1-60; but see former RC § 2937.10 (GC § 13433-9; 113 v 123(146); Bureau of Code Revision, 10-1-53; 127 v 1039(1100)).**

## § 2937.08 Action on pleas of "not guilty" or "once in jeopardy" in misdemeanor cases.

Upon a plea of not guilty or a plea of once in jeopardy, if the charge be a misdemeanor in a court of record, the court shall proceed to set the matter for trial at a future time, pursuant to Chapter 2938. of the Revised Code, and shall let accused to bail pending such trial. Or he may, but only if both prosecutor and accused expressly consent, set the matter for trial forthwith.

Upon the entry of such pleas to a charge of misdemeanor in a court not of record, the magistrate shall forthwith set the matter for future trial or, with the consent of both state and defendant may set trial forthwith, both pursuant to Chapter 2938. of the Revised Code, provided that if the nature of the offense is such that right to jury trial exists, such matter shall not be tried before him unless the accused, by writing subscribed by him, waives a jury and consents to be tried by the magistrate.

If the defendant in such event does not waive right to jury trial, then the magistrate shall require the accused to enter into recognizance to appear before court of record in the county, set by such magistrate, and the magistrate shall thereupon certify all papers filed, together with transcript of proceedings and accrued costs to date, and such recognizance if given, to such designated court of record. Such transfer shall not require the filing of indictment or information and trial shall proceed in the transferee court pursuant to Chapter 2938 of the Revised Code.

**HISTORY: 128 v 97. Eff 1-1-60.**

**Not analogous to former RC § 2937.08 (GC § 13433-7; 113 v 123(146); Bureau of Code Revision, 10-1-53), repealed 128 v 97(116), § 2, eff 1-1-60; but see former RC § 2937.11 (GC § 13433-10; 113 v 123(147); Bureau of Code Revision, 10-1-53; 127 v 1039(1101)).**

## § 2937.081 Repealed, 145 v S 186, § 2 [140 v S 76]. Eff 10-12-94.

This section provided for prosecutor to notify victim or agent of date, time and place of trial or other final disposition. See now RC Chapter 2930.

## § 2937.09 Procedure in felony cases.

If the charge is a felony, the court or magistrate shall, before receiving a plea of guilty, advise the accused that such plea constitutes an admission which may be used against him at a later trial. If the defendant enters a written plea of guilty or, pleading not guilty, affirmatively waives the right to have the court or magistrate take evidence concerning the offense, the court or magistrate forthwith and without taking evidence may find that the crime has been committed and that there is probable and reasonable cause to hold the defendant for trial pursuant to indictment by the grand jury, and, if the offense is bailable, require the accused to enter into recognizance in such amount as it determines to appear before the court of common pleas pursuant to indictment, otherwise to be confined until the grand jury has considered and reported the matter.

**HISTORY: 128 v 97 (Eff 1-1-60); 129 v 582(750); Eff 1-10-61.**

**Not analogous to former RC § 2937.09 (GC § 13433-8; 113 v 123(146); Bureau of Code Revision, 10-1-53), repealed 128 v 97(116), § 2, eff 1-1-60; but see former RC § 2937.11 (GC § 13433-10; 113 v 123(147); Bureau of Code Revision, 10-1-53; 127 v 1039(1101)).**

## § 2937.10 Hearing set in felony cases.

If the charge be a felony and there be no written plea of guilty or waiver of examination, or the court or magistrate refuses to receive such waiver, the court or magistrate, with the consent of the prosecutor and the accused, may set the matter for hearing forthwith, otherwise he shall set the matter for hearing at a fixed time in the future and shall notify both prosecutor and defendant promptly of such time of hearing.

**HISTORY: 128 v 97. Eff 1-1-60.**

**Not analogous to former RC § 2937.10 (GC § 13433-9; 113 v 123(146); Bureau of Code Revision, 10-1-53; 127 v 1039(1100)), repealed 128 v 97(116), § 2, eff 1-1-60.**

## § 2937.11 Presentation of state's case.

(A)(1) As used in this section, "victim" includes any person who was a victim of a felony violation identified in division (B) of this section or a felony offense of violence or against whom was directed any conduct that constitutes, or that is an element of, a felony violation identified in division (B) of this section or a felony offense of violence.

(2) At the preliminary hearing set pursuant to section 2937.10 of the Revised Code and the Criminal Rules, the prosecutor may state, but is not required to state, orally the case for the state and shall then proceed to examine witnesses and introduce exhibits for the state. The accused and the magistrate have full right of cross examination, and the accused has the right of inspection of exhibits prior to their introduction. The hearing shall be conducted under the rules of evidence prevailing in criminal trials generally. On motion of either the state or the accused, witnesses shall be separated and not permitted in the hearing room except when called to testify.

(B) In a case involving an alleged felony violation of section 2905.05, 2907.02, 2907.03, 2907.04, 2907.05, 2907.21, 2907.24, 2907.31, 2907.32, 2907.321 [2907.32.1], 2907.322 [2907.32.2], 2907.323 [2907.32.3], or 2919.22 of the Revised Code or an alleged felony offense of violence and in which an alleged victim of the alleged violation or offense was less than thirteen years of age when the complaint or information was filed, whichever occurred earlier, upon motion of the prosecution, the testimony of the child victim at the preliminary hearing may be taken in a room other than the room in which the preliminary hearing is being conducted and be televised, by closed circuit equipment, into the room in which the preliminary hearing is being conducted, in accordance with division (C) of section 2945.481 [2945.48.1] of the Revised Code.

(C) In a case involving an alleged felony violation listed in division (B) of this section or an alleged felony offense of violence and in which an alleged victim of the alleged violation or offense was less than thirteen years of age when the complaint or information was filed, whichever occurred earlier, the court, on written motion of the prosecutor in the case filed at least three days prior to the hearing, shall order that all testimony of the child victim be recorded and preserved on videotape, in addition to being recorded for purposes of the transcript of the proceeding. If such an order is issued, it shall specifically identify the child victim concerning whose testimony it pertains, apply only during the testimony of the child victim it specifically identifies, and apply to all testimony of the child victim presented at the hearing, regardless of whether the child victim is called as a witness by the prosecution or by the defense.

**HISTORY: 128 v 97 (Eff 1-1-60); 141 v H 108 (Eff 10-14-86); 146 v H 445 (Eff 9-3-96); 147 v S 53. Eff 10-14-97.**

**Not analogous to former RC § 2937.11 (GC § 13433-10; 113 v 123(147); Bureau of Code Revision, 10-1-53; 127 v 1039(1101)), repealed 128 v 97(116), § 2, eff 1-1-60.**

## § 2937.12 Motion for discharge; presentation on behalf of accused; finding of court.

(A) At the conclusion of the presentation of the state's case accused may move for discharge for failure of proof or may offer evidence on his own behalf. Prior to the offering of evidence on behalf of the accused, unless accused is then represented by counsel, the court or magistrate shall advise accused:

(1) That any testimony of witnesses offered by him in the proceeding may, if unfavorable in any particular, be used against him at later trial;

(2) That accused himself may make a statement, not under oath, regarding the charge, for the purpose of explaining the facts in evidence;

(3) That he may refuse to make any statement and such refusal may not be used against him at trials [trial];

(4) That any statement he makes may be used against him at trial.

(B) Upon conclusion of all the evidence and the statement, if any, of the accused, the court or magistrate shall either:

(1) Find that the crime alleged has been committed and that there is probable and reasonable cause to hold or recognize defendant to appear before the court of common pleas of the county or any other county in which venue appears, for trial pursuant to indictment by grand jury;

(2) Find that there is probable cause to hold or recognize defendant to appear before the court of common pleas for trial pursuant to indictment or information on such other charge, felony or misdemeanor, as the evidence indicates was committed by accused;

(3) Find that a misdemeanor was committed and there is probable cause to recognize accused to appear before himself or some other court inferior to the court of common pleas for trial upon such charge;

(4) Order the accused discharged from custody.

**HISTORY: 128 v 97. Eff 1-1-60.**

**Somewhat analogous to former RC §§ 2937.12, 2937.14 (GC §§ 13433-11, 13433-13; 113 v 123(147); Bureau of Code Revision, 10-1-53), repealed 128 v 97(116), § 2, eff 1-1-60.**

## § 2937.13 Basis for finding; no appeal; further prosecution.

In entering a finding, pursuant to section 2937.12 of the Revised Code, the court, while weighing credibility of witness, shall not be required to pass on the weight of the evidence and any finding requiring accused to stand trial on any charge shall be based solely on the presence of substantial credible evidence thereof. No appeal shall lie from such decision nor shall the discharge of defendant be a bar to further prosecution by indictment or otherwise.

**HISTORY: 128 v 97. Eff 1-1-60.**

**Not analogous to former RC § 2937.13 (GC § 13433-12; 113 v 123(147); Bureau of Code Revision, 10-1-53), repealed 128 v 97(116), § 2, eff 1-1-60.**

## § 2937.14 Entry of reason for change in charge.

In any case in which accused is held or recognized to appear for trial on any charge other than the one on which he was arraigned the court or magistrate shall enter the reason for such charge on the journal of the court (if a court of record) or on the docket (if a court not of record) and shall file with the papers in the case the text of the charge found by him to be sustained by the evidence.

**HISTORY: 128 v 97. Eff 1-1-60.**

**Not analogous to former RC § 2937.14 (GC § 13433-13; 113 v 123(147); Bureau of Code Revision, 10-1-53), repealed 128 v 97(116), § 2, eff 1-1-60.**

## § 2937.15 Transcript of proceedings.

Upon the conclusion of the hearing and finding, the magistrate, or if a court of record, the clerk of such court, shall complete all notations of appearance, motions, pleas, and findings on the criminal docket of the court, and shall transmit a transcript of the appearance docket entries, together with a copy of the original complaint and affidavits, if any, filed with the complaint, the journal or docket entry of reason for changes in the charge, if any, together with the order setting bail and the bail deposit, if any, filed, and together with the videotaped testimony, if any, prepared in accordance with division (C) of section 2937.11 of the Revised Code, to the clerk of the court in which the accused is to appear. Such transcript shall contain an itemized account of the costs accrued.

**HISTORY: 128 v 97 (Eff 1-1-60); 141 v H 108. Eff 10-14-86.**

**Not analogous to former RC § 2937.15 (GC § 13433-14; 113 v 123(147); Bureau of Code Revision, 10-1-53), repealed 128 v 97(116), § 2, eff 1-1-60; but see former RC § 2937.19.**

## § 2937.16 When witnesses shall be recognized to appear.

When an accused enters into a recognizance or is committed in default thereof, the judge or magistrate shall require such witnesses against the prisoner as he finds necessary, to enter into a recognizance to appear and testify before the proper court at a proper time, and not depart from such court without leave. If the judge or magistrate finds it necessary he may require such witnesses to give sufficient surety to appear at such court.

**HISTORY: GC § 13433-15; 113 v 123(147), ch 12, § 15; Bureau of Code Revision. Eff 10-1-53.**

## § 2937.17 Recognizance for minor.

A person may be liable in a recognizance for a minor to appear as a witness, or the judge or magistrate may take the minor's recognizance, in a sufficient sum, which is valid notwithstanding the disability of minority.

**HISTORY: GC § 13433-16; 113 v 123(148), ch 12, § 16; Bureau of Code Revision. Eff 10-1-53.**

## § 2937.18 Refusal of witness to enter into a recognizance.

If a witness ordered to give recognizance fails to comply with such order, the judge or magistrate shall commit him to such custody or open or close detention as may be appropriate under the circumstances, until he complies with the order or is discharged. Commitment of the witness may be to the custody of any suitable person or public or private agency, or to an appropriate detention facility other than a jail, or to a jail, but the witness shall not be confined in association with prisoners charged with or convicted of crime. The witness, in lieu of the fee ordinarily allowed witnesses, shall be allowed twenty-five dollars for each day of custody or detention under such order, and shall be allowed mileage as provided for other witnesses, calculated on the distance from his home to the place of giving testimony and return. All proceedings in the case or cases in which the witness is held to appear shall be given priority over other cases and had with all due speed.

**HISTORY: GC § 13433-17; 113 v 123(148), ch 12, § 17; Bureau of Code Revision, 10-1-53; 134 v H 511. Eff 3-23-73.**

## § 2937.19 Subpoena of witnesses or documents.

The magistrate or judge or clerk of the court in which proceedings are being had may issue subpoenas or other process to bring witnesses or documents before the magistrate or court in hearings pending before him either under Chapter 2937. or 2938. of the Revised Code.

In complaints to keep the peace a subpoena must be served within the county, or, in cases of misdemeanors and ordinance offenses, it may be served at any place in this state within one hundred miles of the place where the court or magistrate is scheduled to sit; in felony cases it may be served at any place within this state. In cases where such process is to be served outside the county, it may be issued to be served either by the bailiff or constable of the court or by a sheriff or police officer either by the county in which the court or magistrate sits or in which process is to be served.

**HISTORY: 128 v 97 (Eff 1-1-60); 129 v 582(750). Eff 1-10-61.**

**Not analogous to former RC § 2937.19 (GC § 13433-18; 113 v 123(148); Bureau of Code Revision, 10-1-53), repealed 128 v 97(116), § 2, eff 1-1-60.**

## § 2937.20 Amended and renumbered RC § 2701.03.1 in 146 v S 263. Eff 11-20-96.

## § 2937.21 Continuance.

No continuance at any stage of the proceeding, including that for determination of a motion, shall extend for more than ten days unless both the state and the accused consent thereto. Any continuance or delay in ruling contrary to the provisions of this section shall, unless procured by defendant or his counsel, be grounds for discharge of the defendant forthwith.

**HISTORY: 128 v 97. Eff 1-1-60.**

**Not analogous to former RC § 2937.21 (GC § 13435-1; 113 v 123(149); Bureau of Code Revision, 10-1-53), repealed 128 v 97(116), § 2, eff 1-1-60.**

The substance of former RC § 2937.21 is now found in RC § 2937.22.

### [BAIL AND RECOGNIZANCE]

## § 2937.22 Forms of bail; surcharge; receipt.

(A) Bail is security for the appearance of an accused to appear and answer to a specific criminal or quasi-criminal charge in any court or before any magistrate at a specific time or at any time to which a case may be continued, and not depart without leave. It may take any of the following forms:

(1) The deposit of cash by the accused or by some other person for the accused;

(2) The deposit by the accused or by some other person for the accused in form of bonds of the United States, this state, or any political subdivision thereof in a face amount equal to the sum set by the court or magistrate. In case of bonds not negotiable by delivery such bonds shall be properly endorsed for transfer.

(3) The written undertaking by one or more persons to forfeit the sum of money set by the court or magistrate, if the accused is in default for appearance, which shall be known as a recognizance.

(B) Whenever a person is charged with any offense other than a traffic offense that is not a moving violation and posts bail, the person shall pay a surcharge of twenty-five dollars. The clerk of the court shall retain the twenty-five dollars until the person is convicted, pleads guilty, forfeits bail, is found not guilty, or has the charges dismissed. If the person is convicted, pleads guilty, or forfeits bail, the clerk shall transmit the twenty-five dollars on or before the twentieth day of the month following the month in which the person was convicted, pleaded guilty, or forfeited bail to the treasurer of state, and the treasurer of state shall deposit it into the indigent defense support fund created under section 120.08 of the Revised Code. If the person is found not guilty or the charges are dismissed, the clerk shall return the twenty-five dollars to the person.

(C) All bail shall be received by the clerk of the court, deputy clerk of court, or by the magistrate, or by a special referee appointed by the supreme court pursuant to section 2937.46 of the Revised Code, and, except in cases of recognizances, receipt shall be given therefor.

(D) As used in this section, "moving violation" has the same meaning as in section 2743.70 of the Revised Code.

**HISTORY: 128 v 97. Eff 1-1-60; 153 v H 1, § 101.01, eff. 10-16-09.**

The effective date is set by § 812.10 of 153 v H 1.

**Not analogous to former RC § 2937.22 (GC § 13435-2; 113 v 123(149); Bureau of Code Revision, 10-1-53), repealed 128 v 97(116), § 2, eff 1-1-60; but see former RC § 2937.21 (GC § 13435-1; 113 v 123(149); Bureau of Code Revision, 10-1-53).**

The substance of former RC § 2937.22 is now found in RC § 2937.23.

## § 2937.221 License as bond; notice of penalties.

(A) A person arrested without warrant for any violation listed in division (B) of this section, and having a current valid Ohio driver's or commercial driver's license, if the person has been notified of the possible consequences of the person's actions as required by division (C) of this section, may post bond by depositing the license with the arresting officer if the officer and person so choose, or with the local court having jurisdiction if the court and person so choose. The license may be used as bond only during the period for which it is valid.

When an arresting officer accepts the driver's or commercial driver's license as bond, the officer shall note the date, time, and place of the court appearance on "the violator's notice to appear," and the notice shall serve as a valid Ohio driver's or commercial driver's license until the date and time appearing thereon. The arresting officer immediately shall forward the license to the appropriate court.

When a local court accepts the license as bond or continues the case to another date and time, it shall provide the person with a card in a form approved by the registrar of motor vehicles setting forth the license number, name, address, the date and time of the court appearance, and a statement that the license is being held as bond. The card shall serve as a valid license until the date and time contained in the card.

The court may accept other bond at any time and return the license to the person. The court shall return the license to the person when judgment is satisfied, including, but not limited to, compliance with any court orders, unless a suspension or cancellation is part of the penalty imposed.

Neither "the violator's notice to appear" nor a court — granted card shall continue driving privileges beyond the expiration date of the license.

If the person arrested fails to appear in court at the date and time set by the court or fails to satisfy the judgment of the court, including, but not limited to, compliance with all court orders within the time allowed by the court, the court may declare the forfeiture of the person's license. Thirty days after the declaration of the forfeiture, the court shall forward the person's license to the registrar. The court also shall enter information relative to the forfeiture on a form approved and furnished by the registrar and send the form to the registrar. The registrar shall suspend the person's license and send written notification of the suspension to the person at the person's last known address. No valid driver's or commercial driver's license shall be granted to the person until the court having jurisdiction orders that the forfeiture be terminated. The court shall inform the registrar of the termination of the forfeiture by entering information relative to the termination on a form approved and furnished by the registrar and sending the form to the registrar. Upon the termination, the person shall pay to the bureau of motor vehicles a reinstatement fee of fifteen dollars to cover the costs of the bureau in administering this section. The registrar shall deposit the fees so paid into the state bureau of motor vehicles fund created by section 4501.25 of the Revised Code.

In addition, upon receipt from the court of the copy of the declaration of forfeiture, neither the registrar nor any deputy registrar shall accept any application for the registration or transfer of registration of any motor vehicle owned by or leased in the name of the person named in the declaration of forfeiture until the court having jurisdiction over the offense that led to the suspension issues an order terminating the forfeiture. However, for a motor vehicle leased in the name of a person named in a declaration of forfeiture, the registrar shall not implement the preceding sentence until the registrar adopts procedures for that implementation under section 4503.39 of the Revised Code. Upon receipt by the registrar of such an order, the registrar also shall take the measures necessary to permit the person to register a motor vehicle the person owns or leases or to transfer the registration of a motor vehicle the person owns or leases if the person later makes a proper application and otherwise is eligible to be issued or to transfer a motor vehicle registration.

(B) Division (A) of this section applies to persons arrested for violation of:

(1) Any of the provisions of Chapter 4511. or 4513. of the Revised Code, except sections 4511.19, 4511.20, 4511.251 [4511.25.1], and 4513.36 of the Revised Code;

(2) Any municipal ordinance substantially similar to a section included in division (B)(1) of this section;

(3) Any bylaw, rule, or regulation of the Ohio turnpike commission substantially similar to a section included in division (B)(1) of this section.

Division (A) of this section does not apply to those persons issued a citation for the commission of a minor misdemeanor under section 2935.26 of the Revised Code.

(C) No license shall be accepted as bond by an arresting officer or by a court under this section until the officer or court has notified the person that, if the person deposits the license with the officer or court and either does not appear on the date and at the time set by the officer or the court, if the court sets a time, or does not satisfy any judgment rendered, including, but not limited to, compliance with all court orders, the license will be suspended, and the person will not be eligible for reissuance of the license or issuance of a new license, or the issuance of a certificate of registration for a motor vehicle owned or leased by the person until the person appears and complies with any order issued by the court. The person also is subject to any criminal penalties that may apply to the person.

(D) The registrar shall not restore the person's driving or vehicle registration privileges until the person pays the reinstatement fee as provided in this section.

**HISTORY: 135 v H 234 (Eff 9-24-73); 136 v H 1 (Eff 6-13-75); 137 v S 351 (Eff 10-25-78); 141 v S 356 (Eff 9-24-86); 143 v H 381 (Eff 7-1-89); 143 v S 49 (Eff 11-3-89); 145 v H 687 (Eff 10-12-94); 146 v H 353 (Eff 9-17-96); 146 v S 121 (Eff 11-19-96); 147 v S 85. Eff 5-15-97; 149 v S 123, § 1, eff. 1-1-04; 150 v H 230, § 1, eff. 9-16-04.**

The effective date is set by section 4 of S.B. 123.

See provisions of § 5 of S.B. 123 (149 v —) following RC § 2935.03.

See provisions, § 5 of SB 85 (147 v —) following RC § 2935.27.

## § 2937.222 Hearing on denial of bail to certain alleged offenders; appeal.

(A) On the motion of the prosecuting attorney or on the judge's own motion, the judge shall hold a hearing to determine whether an accused person charged with aggravated murder when it is not a capital offense, murder, a felony of the first or second degree, a violation of section 2903.06 of the Revised Code, a violation of section 2903.211 of the Revised Code that is a felony, or a felony OVI offense shall be denied bail. The judge shall order that the accused be detained until the conclusion of the hearing. Except for good cause, a continuance on the motion of the state shall not exceed three court days. Except for good cause, a continuance on the motion of the accused shall not exceed five court days unless the motion of the accused waives in writing the five-day limit and states in writing a specific period for which the accused requests a continuance. A continuance granted upon a motion of the accused that waives in writing the five-day limit shall not exceed five court days after the period of continuance requested in the motion.

At the hearing, the accused has the right to be represented by counsel and, if the accused is indigent, to have counsel appointed. The judge shall afford the accused an opportunity to testify, to present witnesses and other information, and to cross-examine witnesses who appear at the hearing. The rules concerning admissibility of evidence in criminal trials do not apply to the presentation and consideration of information at the hearing. Regardless of whether the hearing is being held on the motion of the prosecuting attorney or on the court's own motion, the state has the burden of proving that the proof is evident or the presumption great that the accused committed the offense with which the accused is charged, of proving that the accused poses a substantial risk of serious physical harm to any person or to the community, and of proving that no release conditions will reasonably assure the safety of that person and the community.

The judge may reopen the hearing at any time before trial if the judge finds that information exists that was not known to the movant at the time of the hearing and that that information has a material bearing on whether bail should be denied. If a municipal court or county court enters an order denying bail, a judge of the court of common pleas having jurisdiction over the case may continue that order or may hold a hearing pursuant to this section to determine whether to continue that order.

(B) No accused person shall be denied bail pursuant to this section unless the judge finds by clear and convincing evidence that the proof is evident or the presumption great that the accused committed the offense described in division (A) of this section with which the accused is charged, finds by clear and convincing evidence that the accused poses a substantial risk of serious physical harm to any person or to the community, and finds by clear and convincing evidence that no release conditions will reasonably assure the safety of that person and the community.

(C) The judge, in determining whether the accused person described in division (A) of this section poses a substantial risk of serious physical harm to any person or to the community and whether there are conditions of release that will reasonably assure the safety of that person and the community, shall consider all available information regarding all of the following:

(1) The nature and circumstances of the offense charged, including whether the offense is an offense of violence or involves alcohol or a drug of abuse;

(2) The weight of the evidence against the accused;

(3) The history and characteristics of the accused, including, but not limited to, both of the following:

(a) The character, physical and mental condition, family ties, employment, financial resources, length of residence in the community, community ties, past conduct, history relating to drug or alcohol abuse, and criminal history of the accused;

(b) Whether, at the time of the current alleged offense or at the time of the arrest of the accused, the accused was on probation, parole, post-release control, or other release pending trial, sentencing, appeal, or completion of sentence for the commission of an offense under the laws of this state, another state, or the United States or under a municipal ordinance.

(4) The nature and seriousness of the danger to any person or the community that would be posed by the person's release.

(D)(1) An order of the court of common pleas denying bail pursuant to this section is a final appealable order. In an appeal pursuant to division (D) of this section, the court of appeals shall do all of the following:

(a) Give the appeal priority on its calendar;

(b) Liberally modify or dispense with formal requirements in the interest of a speedy and just resolution of the appeal;

(c) Decide the appeal expeditiously;

(d) Promptly enter its judgment affirming or reversing the order denying bail.

(2) The pendency of an appeal under this section does not deprive the court of common pleas of jurisdiction to conduct further proceedings in the case or to further consider the order denying bail in accordance with this section. If, during the pendency of an appeal under division (D) of this section, the court of common pleas sets aside or terminates the order denying bail, the court of appeals shall dismiss the appeal.

(E) As used in this section:

(1) "Court day" has the same meaning as in section 5122.01 of the Revised Code.

(2) "Felony OVI offense" means a third degree felony OVI offense and a fourth degree felony OVI offense.

(3) "Fourth degree felony OVI offense" and "third degree felony OVI offense" have the same meanings as in section 2929.01 of the Revised Code.

**HISTORY: 148 v S 8 (Eff 7-29-99); 148 v H 137 (Eff 3-10-2000); 148 v S 22. Eff 5-17-2000; 149 v S 123, § 1, eff. 1-1-04.**

The effective date is set by section 4 of S.B. 123.

See provisions of § 5 of S.B. 123 (149 v —) following RC § 2935.03.

The provisions of § 8 of S.B. 123 read as follows:

SECTION 8. Section 2937.222 of the Revised Code is presented in this act as a composite of the section as amended by both Am. Sub. H.B. 137 and Am. Sub. S.B. 22 of the 123rd General Assembly. The General Assembly, applying the principle stated in division (B) of section 1.52 of the Revised Code that amendments are to be harmonized if reasonably capable of simultaneous operation, finds that the composites are the resulting versions of the sections in effect prior to the effective date of the sections as presented in this act.

## § 2937.23 Amount of bail.

(A)(1) In a case involving a felony or a violation of section 2903.11, 2903.12, or 2903.13 of the Revised Code when the victim of the offense is a peace officer, the judge or magistrate shall fix the amount of bail.

(2) In a case involving a misdemeanor or a violation of a municipal ordinance and not involving a felony or a violation of section 2903.11, 2903.12, or 2903.13 of the Revised Code when the victim of the offense is a peace officer, the judge, magistrate, or clerk of the court may fix the amount of bail and may do so in accordance with a schedule previously fixed by the judge or magistrate. If the judge, magistrate, or clerk of the court is not readily available, the sheriff, deputy sheriff, marshal, deputy marshal, police officer, or jailer having custody of the person charged may fix the amount of bail in accordance with a schedule previously fixed by the judge or magistrate and shall take the bail only in the county courthouse, the municipal or township building, or the county or municipal jail.

(3) In all cases, the bail shall be fixed with consideration of the seriousness of the offense charged, the previous criminal record of the defendant, and the probability of the defendant appearing at the trial of the case.

(B) In any case involving an alleged violation of section 2903.211 [2903.21.1] of the Revised Code or of a municipal ordinance that is substantially similar to that section, the court shall determine whether it will order an evaluation of the mental condition of the defendant pursuant to section 2919.271 [2919.27.1] of the Revised Code and, if it decides to so order, shall issue the order requiring the evaluation before it sets bail for the person charged with the violation. In any case involving an alleged violation of section 2919.27 of the Revised Code or of a municipal ordinance that is substantially similar to that section and in which the court finds that either of the following criteria applies, the court shall determine whether it will order an evaluation of the mental condition of the defendant pursuant to section 2919.271 [2919.27.1] of the Revised Code and, if it decides to so order, shall issue the order requiring that evaluation before it sets bail for the person charged with the violation:

(1) Regarding an alleged violation of a protection order issued or consent agreement approved pursuant to section 2919.26 or 3113.31 of the Revised Code, that the violation allegedly involves conduct by the defendant that caused physical harm to the person or property of a family or household member covered by the order or agreement or conduct by that defendant that caused a family or household member to believe that the defendant would cause physical harm to that member or that member's property;

(2) Regarding an alleged violation of a protection order issued pursuant to section 2903.213 [2903.21.3] or 2903.214 [2903.21.4] of the Revised Code, or a protection order issued by a court of another state, as defined in section 2919.27 of the Revised Code, that the violation allegedly involves conduct by the defendant that caused physical harm to the person or property of the person covered by the order or conduct by that defendant that caused the person covered by the order to believe that the defendant would cause physical harm to that person or that person's property.

(C) As used in this section, "peace officer" has the same meaning as in section 2935.01 of the Revised Code.

**HISTORY: 128 v 97 (Eff 1-1-60); 129 v 557 (Eff 10-18-61); 141 v H 475 (Eff 3-7-86); 144 v H 536 (Eff 11-5-92); 146 v S 2 (Eff 7-1-96); 147 v S 1 (Eff 10-21-97); 147 v H 302 (Eff 7-29-98); 148 v S 142 (Eff 2-3-2000); 148 v H 202. Eff 2-9-2000.**

**Not analogous to former RC § 2937.23 (GC § 13435-3; 113 v 123(150); Bureau of Code Revision, 10-1-53), repealed 128 v 97(116), § 2, eff 1-1-60; but see former RC § 2937.22 (GC § 13435-2; 113 v 129(149); Bureau of Code Revision, 10-1-53), the substance of which is now found in RC § 2937.281.**

The substance of former RC § 2937.23 is now found in RC § 2937.28.1.

**Comment, Legislative Service Commission**

Section 2937.23 of the Revised Code is amended by this act [Sub. H.B. 202] and also by Am. S.B. 142 of the 123rd General Assembly. Comparison of these amendments in pursuance of section 1.52 of the Revised Code discloses that they are not irreconcilable so that they are required by that section to be harmonized to give effect to each amendment.

## § 2937.24 Oath to surety; form of affidavit.

When a recognizance is offered under section 2937.22 of the Revised Code, the surety on which recognizance qualifies as a real property owner, the judge or magistrate shall require such surety to pledge to this state real property owned by the surety and located in this state. Whenever such pledge of real property has been given by any such proposed surety, he shall execute the usual form of recognizance, and in addition thereto there shall be filed his affidavit of justification of suretyship, to be attached to said recognizance as a part thereof. The surety may be required in such affidavit to depose as to whether he is, at the time of executing the same, surety upon any other recognizance and as to whether there are any unsatisfied judgments or executions against him. He may also be required to state any other fact which the court thinks relevant and material to a correct determination of the surety's sufficiency to act as bail. Such surety shall state in such affidavit where notices under section 2937.38 of the Revised Code may be served on himself, and service of notice of summons at such place is sufficient service for all purposes.

Such affidavit shall be executed by the proposed surety under an oath and may be in the following form:

"State of Ohio, County of .........., ss:

........... residing at ..........., who offers himself as surety for ........... being first duly sworn, says that he owns in his own legal right, real property subject to execution, located in the county of ........... , State of Ohio, consisting of ......... and described as follows to wit: .........; that the title to the same is in his own name; that the value of the same is not less than ......... dollars, and is subject to no encumbrances whatever except ...... ; that he is not surety upon any unpaid or forfeited recognizance, and that he is not a party to any unsatisfied judgment upon any recognizance; that he is worth not less than ......... dollars over and above all debts, liabilities, and lawful claims against him, and all liens, encumbrances, and lawful claims against his property."

**HISTORY: GC § 13435-4; 113 v 123(150), ch 14, § 4; Bureau of Code Revision. Eff 10-1-53.**

## § 2937.25 Lien; form.

Upon the execution of any recognizance in an amount in excess of two hundred dollars in the usual form, and an affidavit of justification under section 2937.24 of the Revised Code, there shall attach to the real property described in said affidavit of justification, a lien in favor of this state in the penal sum of the recognizance, which lien shall remain in full forçe and effect during such time as such recognizance remains effective, or until further order of the court. Upon the acceptance by the judge or magistrate of such recognizance, containing such affidavit of justification, the said recognizance shall be immediately filed with the clerk of said court, if there is a clerk, or with the magistrate. The clerk of the court or the magistrate shall forthwith, upon the filing with him of such recognizance, file with the county recorder of the county in which such real property is located, a notice or lien, in writing, in substance as follows:

"To whom it may concern:

Take notice that the hereinafter described real property, located in the county of ....... , has been pledged for the sum of ....... dollars, to the state of Ohio, by ....... surety upon the recognizance of ....... in a certain cause pending in the ........ court of the county (or city) of ....... , to wit: the state of Ohio, plaintiff, versus ....... defendant, known and identified in such court as cause No .....

Description of real estate: ....... Clerk of the court for the county of ....... or ....... Magistrate.

Dated ..........."

From the time of the filing and recording of such notice it is notice to everyone that the real property therein described has been pledged to this state as security for the performance of the conditions of a criminal recognizance in the penal sum set forth in said recognizance and notice. Such lien does not affect the validity of prior liens on said property.

**HISTORY: GC § 13435-5; 113 v 123(151), ch 14, § 5; Bureau of Code Revision. Eff 10-1-53.**

## § 2937.26 Cancellation of lien; form.

Whenever, by the order of a court, a recognizance under sections 2937.24 and 2937.25 of the Revised Code has been canceled, discharged, or set aside, or the cause in which such recognizance is taken has been dismissed or otherwise terminated the clerk of such court shall forthwith file with the county recorder of the county in which the real property is located, a notice of discharge in writing, in substance as follows:

"To whom it may concern:

Take notice that by the order of the court of ....... (naming court) ........ of the county (or city) of .........., the recognizance of ....... as principal, and ....... as surety, given in the cause of the State of Ohio, plaintiff, versus .........., defendant, known and identified as Cause No......... in said court, is canceled, discharged, and set aside, and the lien of the State of Ohio on the real property therein pledged as security, is hereby waived, discharged, and set aside.

.......... Clerk of the court.

Dated .........."

**HISTORY: GC § 13435-6; 113 v 123(151), ch 14, § 6; Bureau of Code Revision. Eff 10-1-53.**

## § 2937.27 Duties of county recorder.

The county recorder of the county in which the property of a surety on a recognizance is located, shall keep and file all notices of lien and notices of discharge which are filed with him pursuant to section 2937.26 of the Revised Code, and shall keep in addition thereto, a book or record in which he shall index notice of liens and notice of discharges, as they are filed with him. When a lien has been released or discharged for a period of one year, the county recorder may destroy all notices of such lien.

**HISTORY: GC § 13435-7; 113 v 123(152), ch 14, § 7; Bureau of Code Revision, 10-1-53; 129 v 1033. Eff 10-26-61.**

## § 2937.28 Transmission of recognizance.

All recognizances shall be returnable to and all deposits shall be held by or subject to the order of the court or magistrate before whom the accused is to appear initially, and upon the transfer of the case to any other court or magistrate shall be returnable to and transmitted to the transferee court or magistrate.

It is not necessary for the accused to give new recognizance for appearance in common pleas court for arraignment upon indictment or pending appeal after judgment and sentence, unless the magistrate or judge of the trial court or the court to which appeal is taken, shall, for good cause shown, increase or decrease the amount of the recognizance, but such recognizance shall continue and be in full force until trial and appeal therefrom is finally determined. When two or more charges are filed, or indictments returned, against the same person at or about the same time, the recognizance given may be made to include all offenses charged against the accused.

**HISTORY: 128 v 97. Eff 1-1-60.**

**Not analogous to former RC § 2937.28 (GC § 13435-8; 113 v 123(150); Bureau of Code Revision, 10-1-53), repealed 128 v 97(116), § 2, eff 1-1-60.**

## § 2937.281 Requirements of recognizance.

In cases of felony, the recognizance shall be signed by the accused and one or more adult residents of the county in which the case is pending, who shall own, in the aggregate, real property double the amount set as bail, over and above all encumbrances and liable to execution in at least that amount; or it may be signed by the accused and a surety company authorized to do business in this state.

In cases of misdemeanor, the recognizance may be signed by the accused and one or more adult residents, qualified as set forth above or as to personal property ownership, by the accused and surety company, or, if authorized by judge or magistrate, by the accused alone. In cases of misdemeanors arising under Chapters 4501., 4503., 4505., 4507., 4509., 4511., 4513., 4517., and 4549. of the Revised Code, and related ordinance offenses (except those of driving under the influence of intoxicating liquor or controlled substances and leaving the scene of an accident) the court or magistrate shall accept guaranteed arrest bond with respect to which a surety company has become surety as provided in section 3929.141 [3929.14.1] of the Revised Code in lieu of cash bail in an amount not to exceed two hundred dollars.

**HISTORY: 128 v 97 (Eff 1-1-60); 129 v 1401 (Eff 9-5-61); 136 v H 300. Eff 7-1-76.**

**Somewhat analogous to former GC § 13524 and to RC §§ 2937.28.1 (126 v 625; 127 v 847) and 2937.23 (GC § 13435-3; 113 v 123(150); Bureau of Code Revision, 10-1-53), both repealed 128 v 97(116), § 2, eff 1-1-60. See also former RC § 4549.17.**

## § 2937.29 Release on own recognizance.

When from all the circumstances the court is of the opinion that the accused will appear as required, either before or after conviction, the accused may be released on his own recognizance. A failure to appear as required by such recognizance shall constitute an offense subject to the penalty provided in section 2937.99 of the Revised Code.

**HISTORY: 131 v 677. Eff 8-10-65.**

**Not analogous to former RC § 2937.29 (GC § 13435-9; 113 v 123(152); Bureau of Code Revision, 10-1-53), repealed 128 v 97(116), § 2, eff 1-1-60.**

## § 2937.30 Recognizance when accused discharged.

When a defendant is discharged by the trial court otherwise than on a verdict or finding of acquittal, or when the appellate court reverses a conviction and orders the discharge of the defendant and the state or municipality signifies its intention to appeal therefrom, or the record is certified to the supreme court, the defendant shall not be discharged if he is in jail, nor the surety discharged or deposit released if the defendant is on bail, but the trial court, or the court to which appeal is taken may make order for his release on his own recognizance or bail, or recommit him.

**HISTORY: GC § 13435-10; 113 v 123(153), ch 14, § 10; Bureau of Code Revision, 10-1-53; 128 v 97(109). Eff 1-1-60.**

## § 2937.31 Recognizance or deposit for appearance of accused.

If an accused is held to answer and offers sufficient bail, a recognizance or deposit shall be taken for his appearance to answer the charge before such magistrate or before such court to which proceedings may be transferred pursuant to Chapter 2937. of the Revised Code, at a date certain, or from day to day, or in case of the common pleas court on the first day of the next term thereof, and not depart without leave.

**HISTORY: GC § 13435-11; 113 v 123(153), ch 14, § 11; Bureau of Code Revision, 10-1-53; 128 v 97. Eff 1-1-60.**

## § 2937.32 Detention where bail not granted.

If an offense is not bailable, if the court denies bail to the accused, or if the accused does not offer sufficient bail, the court shall order the accused to be detained.

**HISTORY: 148 v S 8. Eff 7-29-99.**

**Analogous to former RC § 2937.32 (GC § 13435-12; 113 v 123(153), ch 14, § 12; Bureau of Code Revision, 10-1-53; 128 v 97), repealed 148 v S 8, § 2, eff 7-29-99.**

## § 2937.33 Receipt of recognizance.

When a transcript or [of] recognizance is received by the clerk of the court of common pleas, or of any court of record to which proceedings are transferred, he shall enter the same upon the appearance docket of the court, with the date of the filing of such transcript or recognizance, the date and amount of the recognizance, the names of the sureties, and the costs. Such recognizance is then of record in such court, and is proceeded on by process issuing therefrom, in a like manner as if it had been entered into before such court. When a court having recognizance of an offense takes a recognizance, it is a sufficient record thereof to enter upon the journal of such court the title of the case, the crime charged, the names of the sureties, the amount of the recognizance, and the time therein required for the appearance of the accused. In making the complete record, when required to be made, recognizances whether returned to or taken in such court shall be recorded in full, if required by the prosecutor or the accused.

**HISTORY: GC § 13435-13; 113 v 123(153), ch 14, § 13; Bureau of Code Revision, 10-1-53; 128 v 97. Eff 1-1-60.**

## § 2937.34 Accused unlawfully detained; examining court to be held.

When a person is committed to jail, charged with an offense for which he has not been indicted, and claims to be unlawfully detained, the sheriff on demand of the accused or his counsel shall forthwith notify the court of common pleas, and the prosecuting attorney, to attend an examining court, the time of which shall be fixed by the judge. The judge shall hear said cause or complaint, examine the witnesses, and make such order as the justice of the case requires, and for such purpose the court may admit to bail, release without bond, or recommit to jail in accordance with the commitment. In the absence of the judge of the court of common pleas, the probate judge shall hold such examining court.

**HISTORY: GC § 13435-14; 113 v 123(154), ch 14, § 14; 114 v 320(479), § 2; Bureau of Code Revision. Eff 10-1-53.**

## § 2937.35 Forfeit of bail.

Upon the failure of the accused or witness to appear in accordance with its terms the bail may in open court be adjudged forfeit, in whole or in part by the court or magistrate before whom he is to appear. But such court or magistrate may, in its discretion, continue the cause to a later date certain, giving notice of such date to him and the bail depositor or sureties, and adjudge the bail forfeit upon failure to appear at such later date.

**HISTORY: 128 v 97. Eff 1-1-60.**

**Not analogous to former RC § 2937.35 (GC § 13435-15; 113 v 123(154); Bureau of Code Revision, 10-1-53), repealed 128 v 97(116), § 2, eff 1-1-60; but see former RC § 2937.38 (GC § 13435-18; 113 v 123(155); Bureau of Code Revision, 10-1-53).**

## § 2937.36 Forfeiture proceedings.

Upon declaration of forfeiture, the magistrate or clerk of the court adjudging forfeiture shall proceed as follows:

(A) As to each bail, the magistrate or clerk shall proceed forthwith to deal with the sum deposited as if the same were imposed as a fine for the offense charged and distribute and account for the same accordingly provided that prior to so doing, the magistrate or clerk may satisfy accrued costs in the case out of the fund.

(B) As to any securities deposited, the magistrate or clerk shall proceed to sell the same, either at public sale advertised in the same manner as sale on chattel execution, or through any state or national bank performing such service upon the over the counter securities market and shall apply proceeds of sale, less costs or brokerage thereof as in cases of forfeited cash bail. Prior to such sale, the clerk shall give notices by ordinary mail to the depositor, at the depositor's address listed of record, if any, of the intention so to do, and such sale shall not proceed if the depositor, within ten days of mailing of such notice appears, and redeems said securities by either producing the body of the defendant in open court or posting the amount set in the recognizance in cash, to be dealt with as forfeited cash bail.

(C) As to recognizances the magistrate or clerk shall notify the accused and each surety within fifteen days after the declaration of the forfeiture by ordinary mail at the address shown by them in their affidavits of qualification or on the record of the case, of the default of the accused and the adjudication of forfeiture and require each of them to show cause on or before a date certain to be stated in the notice, and which shall be not less than forty-five nor more than sixty days from the date of mailing notice, why judgment should not be entered against each of them for the penalty stated in the recognizance. If good cause by production of the body of the accused or otherwise is not shown, the court or magistrate shall thereupon enter judgment against the sureties or either of them, so notified, in such amount, not exceeding the penalty of the bond, as has been set in the adjudication of forfeiture, and shall award execution therefor as in civil cases. The proceeds of sale shall be received by the clerk or magistrate and distributed as on forfeiture of cash bail.

**HISTORY: 128 v 97. Eff 1-1-60; 2011 HB 86, § 1, eff. Sept. 30, 2011.**

**Not analogous to former RC § 2937.36 (GC § 13435-16; 113 v 123(154); Bureau of Code Revision, 10-1-53), repealed 128 v 97(116), § 2, eff 1-1-60; but see former RC § 2937.38**

**(GC § 13435-18; 113 v 123(155); Bureau of Code Revision, 10-1-53).**

The substance of former RC § 2937.36 is now found in RC § 2937.40.

## § 2937.37 Levy on property in judgment against surety.

A magistrate or court of record inferior to the court of common pleas may proceed to judgment against a surety on a recognizance, and levy on his personal property, notwithstanding that the bond may exceed the monetary limitations on the jurisdiction of such court in civil cases, and jurisdiction over the person of surety shall attach from the mailing of the notice specified in section 2937.36 of the Revised Code, notwithstanding that such surety may not be within the territorial jurisdiction of the court; but levy on real property shall be made only through issuance, return, and levy made under certificate of judgment issued to the clerk of the court of common pleas pursuant to section 2329.02 of the Revised Code.

**HISTORY: 128 v 97. Eff 1-1-60.**

**Not analogous to former RC § 2937.37 (GC § 13435-17; 113 v 123(155); Bureau of Code Revision, 10-1-53), repealed 128 v 97(116), § 2, eff 1-1-60; but see former RC § 2937.38 (GC § 13435-18; 113 v 123(155); Bureau of Code Revision, 10-1-53).**

## § 2937.38 Minority no defense in forfeiture proceedings.

In any matter in which a minor is admitted to bail pursuant to Chapter 2937 of the Revised Code, the minority of the accused shall not be available as a defense to judgment against principal or surety, or against the sale of securities or transfer of cash bail, upon forfeiture.

**HISTORY: 128 v 97. Eff 1-1-60.**

**Not analogous to former RC § 2937.38 (GC § 13435-18; 113 v 123(155); Bureau of Code Revision, 10-1-53), repealed 128 v 97(116), § 2, eff 1-1-60.**

The substance of former RC § 2937.38 is now found in RC § 2937.36 (GC § 13435-16; 113 v 123(154); Bureau of Code Revision, 10-1-53) and RC § 2937.37 (GC § 13435-17; 113 v 123(155); Bureau of Code Revision, 10-1-53).

## § 2937.39 Remission of penalty.

After judgment has been rendered against surety or after securities sold or cash bail applied, the court or magistrate, on the appearance, surrender, or rearrest of the accused on the charge, may remit all or such portion of the penalty as it deems just and in the case of previous application and transfer of cash or proceeds, the magistrate or clerk may deduct an amount equal to the amount so transferred from subsequent payments to the agencies receiving such proceeds of forfeiture until the amount is recouped for the benefit of the person or persons entitled thereto under order or remission.

**HISTORY: 128 v 97. Eff 1-1-60.**

**Not analogous to former RC § 2937.39 (GC § 13435-19; 113 v 123(155); Bureau of Code Revision, 10-1-53), repealed 128 v 97(116), § 2, eff 1-1-60; but see former RC § 2937.43 (GC § 13435-23; 113 v 123(156); Bureau of Code Revision, 10-1-53).**

## § 2937.40 Release of bail and sureties.

(A) Bail of any type that is deposited under sections 2937.22 to 2937.45 of the Revised Code or Criminal Rule 46 by a person other than the accused shall be discharged and released, and sureties on recognizances shall be released, in any of the following ways:

(1) When a surety on a recognizance or the depositor of cash or securities as bail for an accused desires to surrender the accused before the appearance date, the surety is discharged from further responsibility or the deposit is redeemed in either of the following ways:

(a) By delivery of the accused into open court;

(b) When, on the written request of the surety or depositor, the clerk of the court to which recognizance is returnable or in which deposit is made issues to the sheriff a warrant for the arrest of the accused and the sheriff indicates on the return that he holds the accused in his jail.

(2) By appearance of the accused in accordance with the terms of the recognizance or deposit and the entry of judgment by the court or magistrate;

(3) By payment into court, after default, of the sum fixed in the recognizance or the sum fixed in the order of forfeiture, if it is less.

(B) When cash or securities have been deposited as bail by a person other than the accused and the bail is discharged and released pursuant to division (A) of this section, or when property has been pledged by a surety on recognizance and the surety on recognizance has been released pursuant to division (A) of this section, the court shall not deduct any amount from the cash or securities or declare forfeited and levy or execute against pledged property. The court shall not apply any of the deposited cash or securities toward, or declare forfeited and levy or execute against property pledged for a recognizance for, the satisfaction of any penalty or fine, and court costs, assessed against the accused upon his conviction or guilty plea, except upon express approval of the person who deposited the cash or securities or the surety.

(C) Bail of any type that is deposited under sections 2937.22 to 2937.45 of the Revised Code or Criminal Rule 46 by an accused shall be discharged and released to the accused, and property pledged by an accused for a recognizance shall be discharged, upon the appearance of the accused in accordance with the terms of the recognizance or deposit and the entry of judgment by the court or magistrate, except that, if the defendant is not indigent, the court may apply deposited bail toward the satisfaction of a penalty or fine, and court costs, assessed against the accused upon his conviction or guilty plea, and may declare forfeited and levy or execute against pledged property for the satisfaction of a penalty or fine, and court costs, assessed against the accused upon his conviction or guilty plea.

(D) Notwithstanding any other provision of this section, an Ohio driver's or commercial driver's license that is deposited as bond may be forfeited and otherwise handled as provided in section 2937.221 [2937.22.1] of the Revised Code.

**HISTORY: 128 v 97 (Eff 1-1-60); 138 v H 402 (Eff 5-13-80); 141 v S 356 (Eff 9-24-86); 143 v H 381 (Eff 7-1-89); 143 v S 338. Eff 11-28-90.**

**Not analogous to former RC § 2937.40 (GC § 13435-20; 113 v 123(155); Bureau of Code Revision, 10-1-53), repealed 128 v 97(116), § 2, eff 1-1-60; but see former RC § 2937.36 (GC § 13435-16; 113 v 123(154); Bureau of Code Revision, 10-1-53).**

## § 2937.41 Return of bail; notice of discharge of recognizance.

On the discharge of bail, the magistrate or clerk of the court shall return, subject to division (B) or (C) of section 2937.40 of the Revised Code, deposited cash or securities to the depositor, but the magistrate or clerk of the court may require presentation of an issued original receipt as a condition to the return. In the case of discharged recognizances, subject to division (B) or (C) of section 2937.40 of the Revised Code, the magistrate or clerk of the court shall endorse the satisfaction on the recognizance and shall forthwith transmit to the county recorder the notice of discharge provided for in section 2937.26 of the Revised Code.

**HISTORY: 128 v 97 (Eff 1-1-60); 138 v H 402. Eff 5-13-80.**

**Not analogous to former RC § 2937.41 (GC § 13435-21; 113 v 123(155); Bureau of Code Revision, 10-1-53), repealed 128 v 97(116), § 2, eff 1-1-60.**

## § 2937.42 Defect in form of recognizance.

Forfeiture of a recognizance shall not be barred or defeated or a judgment thereon reversed by the neglect or omission to note or record the default, or by a defect in the form of such recognizance, if it appears from the tenor thereof at what court the party or witness was bound to appear and that the court or officer before whom it was taken was authorized to require and take such recognizance.

**HISTORY: GC § 13435-22; 113 v 123(156), ch 14, § 22; Bureau of Code Revision, 10-1-53; 128 v 97(112). Eff 1-1-60.**

## § 2937.43 Failure to appear; issuance of warrant.

Should the accused fail to appear as required, after having been released pursuant to section 2937.29 of the Revised Code, the court having jurisdiction at the time of such failure may, in addition to any other action provided by law, issue a warrant for the arrest of such accused.

**HISTORY: 131 v 677. Eff 8-10-65.**

**Not analogous to former RC § 2937.43 (GC § 13435-23; 113 v 123(156); Bureau of Code Revision, 10-1-53), repealed 128 v 97(116), § 2, eff 1-1-60.**

## § 2937.44 Forms of recognizance.

Recognizances substantially in the forms following are sufficient:

RECOGNIZANCE OF THE ACCUSED

The State of Ohio, ....... County, ss:

Be it remembered, that on the .......... day of ...... , in the year .... E. F. and G. H. personally appeared before me, and jointly and severally acknowledged themselves to owe the state of Ohio, the sum of ...... dollars, to be levied on their goods, chattels, lands, and tenements, if default is made in the condition following, to wit:

The condition of this recognizance is such that if the above bound E. F. personally appears before the court of common pleas on the first day of the next term thereof, then and there to answer a charge of (here name the offense with which the accused is charged) and abide the judgment of the court and not depart without leave, then this recognizance shall be void; otherwise it shall be and remain in full force and virtue in law.

Taken and acknowledged before me, on the day and year above written.

A. B., Judge

RECOGNIZANCE OF WITNESS

The State of Ohio, ........ County, ss:

Be it remembered, that on the ......... day of ......., in the year .......... E. F. and G. H. personally appeared before me and jointly and severally acknowledged themselves to owe the state of Ohio, the sum of ...... dollars, to be levied on their goods, chattels, lands, and tenements, if default is made in the condition following, to wit:

The condition of this recognizance is such that if the above bound E. F. personally appears before the court of common pleas on the first day of the next term thereof then and there to give evidence on behalf of the state, touching such matters as shall then and there be required of him, and not depart the court without leave, then this recognizance shall be void, otherwise it shall remain in full force and virtue in law.

Taken and acknowledged before me, on the day and year above written.

A. B., Judge

TO KEEP THE PEACE

The State of Ohio, ........ County, ss:

Be it remembered, that on the ........ day of ........, in the year .... E. F. and G. H. personally appeared before me, and jointly and severally acknowledged themselves to owe the state of Ohio, the sum of ...... dollars, to be levied on their goods, chattels, lands, and tenements, if default is made in the condition following, to wit:

The condition of this recognizance is such that if the above bound E. F. personally appears before the court of common pleas, on the first day of the next term thereof, then and there to answer unto a complaint of C. D. that he has reason to fear, and does fear, that the said E. F. will (here state the charge in the complaint), and abide the order of the court thereon, and in the meantime to keep the peace and be of good behavior toward the citizens of the state generally, and especially toward the said C. D., then this recognizance shall be void; otherwise it shall be and remain in full force and virtue in law.

Taken and acknowledged before me, on the day and year above written.

A. B., Judge

**HISTORY: GC § 13435-24; 113 v 123(156), ch 14, § 24; Bureau of Code Revision, 10-1-53; 127 v 1039(1102). Eff 1-1-58.**

## § 2937.45 Forms of commitments.

Commitments substantially in the forms following are sufficient:

COMMITMENT AFTER EXAMINATION

The State of Ohio, ........ County, ss:

To the Keeper of the Jail of the County aforesaid, greeting:

Whereas, E. F. has been arrested, on the oath of C. D., for (here describe the offense), and has been examined by me on such charge, and required to give bail in the sum of ...... dollars for his appearance before the court of common pleas with which requisition he has failed to comply. Therefore, in the name of the state of Ohio, I command you to receive the said E. F. into your custody, in the jail of the county aforesaid, there to remain until discharged by due course of law.

Given under my hand, this ...... day of .......

COMMITMENT PENDING EXAMINATION

The State of Ohio, ........ County, ss:

To the Keeper of the Jail of the County aforesaid, greeting:

Whereas, E. F. has been arrested on the oath of C. D., for (here describe the offense) and has been brought before me for examination and the same has been necessarily postponed by reason of (here state the cause of delay). Therefore, I command you, in the name of the state of Ohio, to receive the said E. F. into your custody in the jail of the county aforesaid (or in such other place as the justice shall name) there to remain until discharged by due course of law.

Given under my hand, this ...... day of .......

A.B., Judge

**HISTORY: GC § 13435-25; 113 v 123(157), ch 14, § 25; Bureau of Code Revision, 10-1-53; 127 v 1039(1102). Eff 1-1-58.**

## [UNIFORM TRAFFIC PROCEDURE]

## § 2937.46 Supreme court authorized to make uniform rules for practice and procedure in traffic cases.

(A) The supreme court of Ohio, in the interest of uniformity of procedure in the various courts and for the purpose of promoting prompt and efficient disposition of cases arising under the traffic laws of this state and related ordinances, may make uniform rules for practice and procedure in courts inferior to the court of common pleas not inconsistent with the provisions of Chapter 2937. of the Revised Code, including, but not limited to:

(1) Separation of arraignment and trial of traffic and other types of cases;

(2) Consolidation of cases for trial;

(3) Transfer of cases within the same county for the purpose of trial;

(4) Designation of special referees for hearings or for receiving pleas or bail at times when courts are not in session;

(5) Fixing of reasonable bonds, and disposition of cases in which bonds have been forfeited.

(B) Except as otherwise specified in division (N) of section 4511.19 of the Revised Code, all of the rules described in division (A) of this section, when promulgated by the supreme court, shall be fully binding on all courts inferior to the court of common pleas and on the court of common pleas in relation to felony violations of division (A) of section 4511.19 of the Revised Code and shall effect a cancellation of any local court rules inconsistent with the supreme court's rules.

**HISTORY: 128 v 97(112) (Eff 1-1-60); 129 v 582(750). Eff 1-10-61; 149 v S 123, § 1, eff. 1-1-04; 151 v S 8, § 1, eff. 8-17-06.**

The effective date is set by section 4 of S.B. 123.

See provisions of § 5 of S.B. 123 (149 v —) following RC § 2935.03.

## § 2937.99 Failure to appear.

(A) No person shall fail to appear as required, after having been released pursuant to section 2937.29 of the Revised Code. Whoever violates this section is guilty of failure to appear and shall be punished as set forth in division (B) or (C) of this section.

(B) If the release was in connection with a felony charge or pending appeal after conviction of a felony, failure to appear is a felony of the fourth degree.

(C) If the release was in connection with a misdemeanor charge or for appearance as a witness, failure to appear is a misdemeanor of the first degree.

(D) This section does not apply to misdemeanors and related ordinance offenses arising under Chapters 4501., 4503., 4505., 4507., 4509., 4510., 4511., 4513., 4517., 4549., and 5577. of the Revised Code, except that this section does apply to violations of sections 4511.19, 4549.02, and 4549.021 of the Revised Code and ordinance offenses related to sections 4511.19, 4549.02, and 4549.021 of the Revised Code.

**HISTORY: 131 v 677 (Eff 8-10-65); 145 v H 571 (Eff 10-6-94); 148 v S 107. Eff 3-23-2000; 149 v S 123, § 1, eff. 1-1-04.**

The effective date is set by section 4 of S.B. 123.

See provisions of § 5 of S.B. 123 (149 v —) following RC § 2935.03.

# CHAPTER 2938: TRIAL — MAGISTRATE COURTS



## § 2938.01 Definitions.

The definition of "magistrate" set forth in section 2931.01 of the Revised Code, and the definition of "peace officer," "prosecutor," and "offense" set forth in section 2935.01 of the Revised Code applies to Chapter 2938. of the Revised Code.

**HISTORY: 128 v 97(112). Eff 1-1-60.**

## § 2938.02 Applicability of provisions.

The provisions of Chapter 2938. of the Revised Code shall apply to trial on the merits of any misdemeanor, ordinance offense, prosecution for the violation of any rule or regulation of any governmental body authorized to adopt penal regulations, or to complaints to keep the peace, which may be instituted in and retained for trial on the merits in any court or before any magistrate inferior to the court of common pleas; provided that in juvenile courts, where the conduct of any person under the age of eighteen years is made the subject of inquiry and for which special provision is made by Chapter 2151. or 2152. of the Revised Code, such matters shall be tried, adjusted, or disposed of pursuant to Chapter 2151. or 2152. of the Revised Code.

**HISTORY: 128 v 97(113) (Eff 1-1-60); 148 v S 179, § 3. Eff 1-1-2002.**

The effective date is set by section 5 of SB 179.

## § 2938.03 Setting and continuing cases; assignment of additional judges.

The magistrate, or judge or clerk of court of record, shall set all criminal cases for a trial at a date not later than thirty days after plea is received, or in those cases in which the charge has been reduced on preliminary hearing or has been certified by another magistrate, then at a date not later than thirty days from fixing of charge or receipt of transcript as the case may be. Continuances beyond such date shall be granted only upon notice to the opposing party and for good cause shown.

Criminal cases shall be given precedence over civil matters in all assignments for trial and if the volume of contested criminal matters in courts of more than one judge is such as to require it, the chief justice or presiding judge of such court shall assign additional judges from other divisions of the court to assist in the trial of such criminal matters; in the case of county courts, the presiding judge of the court of common pleas shall assign county judges from other areas of jurisdiction within the county to assist those county judges whose volume of criminal cases requires assistance.

**HISTORY: 128 v 97(113). Eff 1-1-60.**

## § 2938.04 Jury trial.

In courts of record right to trial by jury as defined in section 2945.17 of the Revised Code shall be claimed by making demand in writing therefor and filing the same with the clerk of the court not less than three days prior to the date set for trial or on the day following receipt of notice whichever is the later. Failure to claim jury trial as provided in this section is a complete waiver of right thereto. In courts not of record jury trial may not be had, but failure to waive jury in writing where right to jury trial may be asserted shall require the magistrate to certify such case to a court of record as provided in section 2937.08 of the Revised Code.

**HISTORY: 128 v 97(113) (Eff 1-1-60); 129 v 582(751). Eff 1-10-61.**

## § 2938.05 Withdrawal of claim for jury.

Claim of jury, once made, may be withdrawn by written waiver of jury but in such case the court may, if a jury has been summoned, require accused to pay all costs of mileage and fees of members of the venire for one day's service, notwithstanding the outcome of the case. No withdrawal of claim for jury shall effect any re-transfer of a case, once it has been certified to a court of record.

**HISTORY: 128 v 97(113). Eff 1-1-60.**

## § 2938.06 Number of jurors; challenges.

If the number of jurors to be sworn in a case is not stated in the claim, the number to be sworn shall be twelve, but the accused may stipulate for a jury of six, provided in such case the number of peremptory challenges shall be limited to two on each side.

**HISTORY: 128 v 97(114). Eff 1-1-60.**

## § 2938.07 Authority of magistrate or judge.

The magistrate or judge of the trial court shall control all proceedings during a criminal trial and shall limit the introduction of evidence and argument of counsel to relevant and material matters with a view to expeditious and effective ascertainment of truth regarding the matters in issue.

**HISTORY: 128 v 97(114). Eff 1-1-60.**

## § 2938.08 Presumption of innocence.

A defendant in a criminal action is presumed to be innocent until he is proved guilty of the offense charged, and in case of a reasonable doubt whether his guilt is satisfactorily shown, he shall be acquitted. The presumption of innocence places upon the state (or the municipality) the burden of proving him guilty beyond a reasonable doubt.

In charging a jury the trial court shall state the meaning of the presumption of innocence and of reasonable doubt in each case.

**HISTORY: 128 v 97(114). Eff 1-1-60.**

## § 2938.09 Objection to ruling or action.

In the trial of any criminal case, the grounds of an objection to any ruling or action of the judge or magistrate shall be stated if required by him.

**HISTORY: 128 v 97(114) (Eff 1-1-60); 141 v H 412. Eff 3-17-87.**

## § 2938.10 Territorial jurisdiction.

The state or municipality in all cases must prove the offense committed within the territorial jurisdiction of the court, and in ordinance cases within the municipality, except as to those offenses in which the court has county wide jurisdiction created by statute and as to those cases in which certification has been made pursuant to section 2937.08 of the Revised Code.

**HISTORY: 128 v 97(114). Eff 1-1-60.**

## § 2938.11 Order of proceedings of trial.

The trial of an issue shall proceed before the trial court or jury as follows:

(A) Counsel may state the case for the prosecution, including the evidence by which he expects to sustain it.

(B) Counsel for the defendant may state his defense, including the evidence which he expects to offer.

(C) The prosecution then shall produce all its evidence, and the defendant may follow with his evidence, but the court or magistrate, in the furtherance of justice and for good cause shown, may permit evidence to be offered by either side out of its order and may permit rebuttal evidence to be offered by the prosecution.

(D) When the evidence is concluded, unless the case is submitted without argument, counsel for the prosecution shall commence, defendant or his counsel follow, and counsel for the prosecution conclude his argument either to the court or jury. The judge or magistrate may impose a reasonable time limit on argument.

(E) The judge, after argument is concluded in a jury case, forthwith shall charge the jury on the law pertaining to the case and controlling their deliberations, which charge shall not be reduced to writing and taken into the jury room unless the trial judge in his discretion shall so order.

(F) Any verdict arrived at by the jury, or finding determined by the judge or magistrate in trial to the court, shall be announced and received only in open court as soon as it is determined. Any finding by the judge or magistrate shall be announced in open court not more than forty-eight hours after submission of the case to him.

**HISTORY: 128 v 97(114) (Eff 1-1-60); 141 v H 412. Eff 3-17-87.**

## § 2938.12 When accused may be tried in his absence.

A person being tried for a misdemeanor, either to the court, or to a jury, upon request in writing, subscribed by him, may, with the consent of the judge or magistrate, be tried in his absence, but no right shall exist in the defendant to be so tried. If after trial commences a person being tried escapes or departs without leave, the trial shall proceed and verdict or finding be received and sentence passed as if he were personally present.

**HISTORY: 128 v 97(115). Eff 1-1-60.**

## § 2938.13 Responsibility for prosecution.

In any case prosecuted for violation of a municipal ordinance the village solicitor or city director of law, and for a statute, he or the prosecuting attorney, shall present the case for the municipal corporation and the state respectively, but either may delegate the responsibility to some other attorney in a proper case, or, if the defendant be unrepresented by counsel may with leave of court, withdraw from the case. But the magistrate or judge shall not permit prosecution of any criminal case by private attorney employed or retained by a complaining witness.

**HISTORY: 128 v 97(115) (Eff 1-1-60); 137 v H 219. Eff 11-1-77.**

## § 2938.14 Venires for juries.

Venires for juries in courts of record inferior to the court of common pleas shall be drawn and summoned in the manner provided in the various acts creating such courts. But no challenge to the array shall be sustained in any case for the reason that some of the venire are not residents of the territory of the court, if it appears that the venire was regularly drawn and certified by the jury commissioners of county or municipality as the case may be.

**HISTORY: 128 v 97(115) (Eff 1-1-60); 129 v 582(751). Eff 1-10-61.**

## § 2938.15 Rules of evidence and procedure.

The rules of evidence and procedure, including those governing notices, proof of special matters, depositions, and joinder of defendants and offenses set forth in Chapter 2945. of the Revised Code, which are not, by their nature, inapplicable to the trial of misdemeanors, shall prevail in trials under Chapter 2938. of the Revised Code where no special provision is made in such chapter, or where no provision is made by rule of the supreme court adopted pursuant to section 2937.46 of the Revised Code.

**HISTORY: 128 v 97(116) (Eff 1-1-60); 129 v 582(751). Eff 1-10-61.**

# CHAPTER 2939: GRAND JURIES



## § 2939.01 Definition of magistrate.

The definition of "magistrate" set forth in section 2931.01 of the Revised Code applies to Chapter 2939. of the Revised Code.

**HISTORY: Bureau of Code Revision. Eff 10-1-53.**

## § 2939.02 Selection of grand jury.

Grand juries shall consist of fifteen persons who satisfy the qualifications of a juror specified in section 2313.42 of the Revised Code. Persons to serve as grand jurors in the court of common pleas of each county shall be selected from the persons whose names are contained in the annual jury list and from the ballots deposited in the jury wheel, or in the automation data processing storage drawer, or from the names contained in an automated data processing information storage device as prescribed by sections 2313.07, 2313.08, and 2313.35 of the Revised Code.

At the time of the selection of the persons who are to constitute the grand jury, the commissioners of jurors shall draw from the jury wheel, or draw by utilizing the automation data processing equipment and procedures described in section 2313.07 of the Revised Code, ballots containing the names of not less than twenty-five persons. The first fifteen persons whose names are drawn shall constitute the grand jury, if they can be located and served by the sheriff, and if they are not excused by the court or a judge of the court. If any of the first fifteen persons whose names are so drawn are not located or are unable to serve and are for that reason excused by the court or by a judge of the court, whose duty it is to supervise the impaneling of the grand jury, the judge shall then designate the person whose name next appears on the list of persons drawn, to serve in the place of the person not found or excused and shall so continue to substitute the names of the persons drawn in the order in which they were drawn, to fill all vacancies resulting from persons not being found or having been excused by the court or the judge of the court, until the necessary fifteen persons are selected to make up the grand jury. If all of the names appearing on the list of persons drawn are exhausted before the grand jury is complete, the judge shall order the commissioners of jurors to draw such additional names as the judge determines, and shall proceed to fill the vacancies from those names in the order in which they are drawn.

The judge of the court of common pleas may select any person who satisfies the qualifications of a juror and whose name is not included in the annual jury list or on a ballot deposited in the jury wheel or automation data processing storage drawer, or whose name is not contained in an automated data processing information storage device, to preside as foreman of the grand jury, in which event the grand jury shall consist of the foreman so selected and fourteen additional grand jurors selected from the jury wheel or by use of the automation data processing equipment and procedures in the manner provided in this section.

**HISTORY: GC § 11419-34; 114 v 193; Bureau of Code Revision, 10-1-53; 130 v 665 (Eff 8-5-63); 131 v 678 (Eff 11-1-65); 133 v H 424 (Eff 11-25-69); 140 v H 183. Eff 10-1-84.**

## § 2939.03 Grand jurors subject to same provisions and regulations as other jurors.

A grand jury is drawn and notified by the same persons, from the same jury wheel, automation data processing storage drawer, or automated data processing information storage device, and in the same manner as other jurors are drawn and notified under sections 2939.02 to 2939.04 and 2313.01 to 2313.46 of the Revised Code. Grand jurors so drawn and notified are not entitled to an exemption for any reason but may be excused from service or have their service postponed for the same reasons and in the same manner as other jurors under those sections and not otherwise. Grand jurors are subject to the same fines and penalties for nonattendance and otherwise as are other jurors under those sections. The duties and the powers of courts of common pleas, clerks of courts of common pleas, and commissioners of jurors in regard to grand jurors in all respects are the same as in regard to other jurors.

**HISTORY: GC § 11419-35; 114 v 193; Bureau of Code Revision, 10-1-53; 131 v 679 (Eff 11-1-65); 133 v H 424 (Eff 11-25-69); 147 v S 69. Eff 4-16-98.**

## § 2939.031 Selection of additional or alternate juror.

When it appears to the judge impaneling a grand jury that the inquiry is likely to be protracted, or upon direction of the judge, an additional or alternate juror shall be selected in the same manner as the regular jurors in the inquiry are selected. The additional or alternate juror shall be sworn and seated near the jury, with equal opportunity for seeing and hearing the proceedings, shall attend the inquiry at all times and shall obey all orders and admonitions of the court or foreman. When the jurors are ordered kept together, the alternate juror shall be kept with them. The additional or alternate juror shall be liable as a regular juror for failure to attend the inquiry or to obey any order or admonition of the court or foreman. He shall receive the same compensation as other jurors, and except as provided in this section shall be discharged upon the final submission of the bill to the foreman.

If before the final submission of the bill to the jury, a juror dies or is discharged by the judge or foreman due to incapacity, absence, or disqualification of such juror, the additional or alternate juror, upon order of the judge or foreman, shall become one of the jury and serve in all respects as though selected as an original juror during the absence or incapacity of an original juror.

**HISTORY: 125 v H 112. Eff 10-14-53.**

## § 2939.04 Grand jurors; compensation.

The compensation of grand jurors shall be fixed by resolution of the board of county commissioners, not to exceed forty dollars for each day's attendance, payable out of the county treasury. Except in counties of less than one hundred thousand population according to the last federal census, in which counties the judge of the court of common pleas shall make rules in the judge's own county applicable to subsequent grand juror and petit juror service, a person who has served as a grand juror at a term of court is prohibited from serving again, either as a grand juror or petit juror, in that jury year in which the service is rendered or in the next jury year. The person is entitled to a certificate of excuse or postponement in the same manner as a petit juror. The court of common pleas may order the drawing of a special jury to sit at any time public business requires it.

**HISTORY: GC § 11419-36; 114 v 193(204); 116 v 371; Bureau of Code Revision, 10-1-53; 135 v S 465 (Eff 3-4-75); 147 v S 69. Eff 4-16-98.**

## § 2939.05 Repealed, 129 v 1201, § 2 [GC § 13436-1; 113 v 123(158); Bureau of Code Revision, 10-1-53]. Eff 9-11-61.

This section concerned clerk to make list of persons required to appear.

## § 2939.06 Oath to grand jurors.

(A) When a grand jury is impaneled, the court of common pleas shall appoint one of the members of the grand jury as foreperson, and shall administer, or cause to be administered, to the jurors an oath in the following words to which the jurors shall respond "I do solemnly swear" or "I do solemnly affirm":

"Do you solemnly swear or affirm that you will diligently inquire into and carefully deliberate all matters that shall come to your attention concerning this service; and do you solemnly swear or affirm that you will keep secret all proceedings of the grand jury unless you are required in a court of justice to make disclosure; and do you solemnly swear or affirm that you will indict no person through malice, hatred, or ill will; and do you solemnly swear or affirm that you will not leave unindicted any person through fear, favor, or affection, or for any reward or hope thereof; and do you solemnly swear or affirm that in all your deliberations you will present the truth, the whole truth, and nothing but the truth, according to the best of your skill and understanding, as you shall answer unto God or under the penalties of perjury?"

(B) If, on or after the effective date of this amendment, a court impaneling a grand jury uses the grand juror's oath that was in effect prior to the effective date of this amendment instead of the oath set forth in division (A) of this section, the court's use of the former oath does not invalidate or affect the validity of the impanelment of the grand jury, any proceeding, inquiry, or presentation of the grand jury, any indictment or other document found, returned, or issued by the grand jury, or any other action taken by the grand jury.

**HISTORY: GC § 13436-3; 113 v 123(158), ch 15, § 3; Bureau of Code Revision, 10-1-53; 149 v S 218. Eff 3-24-2003.**

**Analogous to former GC §§ 13555 to 13557.**

## § 2939.07 Charge of the court.

The grand jurors, after being sworn, shall be charged as to their duty by the judge of the court of common pleas, who shall call their attention particularly to the obligation of secrecy which their oaths impose, and explain to them the law applicable to such matters as may be brought before them.

**HISTORY: GC § 13436-4; 113 v 123(159), ch 15, § 4; Bureau of Code Revision. Eff 10-1-53.**

## § 2939.08 Duty of grand jury.

After the charge of the court of common pleas, the grand jury shall retire with the officer appointed to attend it, and proceed to inquire of and present all offenses committed within the county.

**HISTORY: GC § 13436-5; 113 v 123(159), ch 15, § 8; Bureau of Code Revision. Eff 10-1-53.**

## § 2939.09 Clerk of grand jury.

The grand jury may appoint one of its members to be its clerk to preserve the minutes of its proceedings and actions in all cases pending before it. Such minutes shall be delivered to the prosecuting attorney before the jury is discharged.

**HISTORY: GC § 13436-6; 113 v 123(159), ch 15, § 6; Bureau of Code Revision. Eff 10-1-53.**

## § 2939.10 Who shall have access to grand jury.

The prosecuting attorney or assistant prosecuting attorney may at all times appear before the grand jury to give information relative to a matter cognizable by it, or advice upon a legal matter when required. The prosecuting attorney may interrogate witnesses before the grand jury when the grand jury or the prosecuting attorney finds it necessary, but no person other than the grand jurors shall be permitted to remain in the room with the jurors while the jurors are expressing their views or giving their votes on a matter before them. In all matters or cases which the attorney general is required to investigate or prosecute by the governor or general assembly, or which a special prosecutor is required by section 177.03 of the Revised Code to investigate and prosecute, the attorney general or the special prosecutor, respectively, shall have and exercise any or all rights, privileges, and powers of prosecuting attorneys, and any assistant or special counsel designated by the attorney general or special prosecutor for that purpose, has the same authority. Proceedings in relation to such matters or cases are under the exclusive supervision and control of the attorney general or the special prosecutor.

**HISTORY: GC § 13436-7; 113 v 123(159), ch 15, § 7; Bureau of Code Revision, 10-1-53; 141 v S 74. Eff 9-3-86.**

## § 2939.11 Official reporters.

The official shorthand reporter of the county, or any shorthand reporter designated by the court of common pleas, at the request of the prosecuting attorney, or any such reporter designated by the attorney general in investigations conducted by him, may take shorthand notes of testimony before the grand jury, and furnish a transcript to the prosecuting attorney or the attorney general, and to no other person. The shorthand reporter shall withdraw from the jury room before the jurors begin to express their views or take their vote on the matter before them. Such reporter shall take an oath to be administered by the judge after the grand jury is sworn, imposing an obligation of secrecy to not disclose any testimony taken or heard except to the grand jury, prosecuting attorney, or attorney general, unless called upon in court to make disclosures.

**HISTORY: GC § 13436-8; 113 v 123(159), ch 15, § 8; Bureau of Code Revision. Eff 10-1-53.**

## § 2939.12 Clerk to issue subpoenas for witnesses.

When required by the grand jury, prosecuting attorney, or judge of the court of common pleas, the clerk of the court of common pleas shall issue subpoenas and other process to any county to bring witnesses to testify before such jury.

**HISTORY: GC § 13436-9; 113 v 123(160), ch 15, § 9; Bureau of Code Revision. Eff 10-1-53.**

## § 2939.121 Employee may not be penalized for being subpoenaed before grand jury.

No employer shall discharge or terminate from employment, threaten to discharge or terminate from employment, or otherwise punish or penalize any employee because of time lost from regular employment as a result of the employee's attendance at any proceeding before a grand jury pursuant to a subpoena. This section generally does not require and shall not be construed to require an employer to pay an employee for time lost resulting from attendance at any grand jury proceeding. However, if an employee is subpoenaed to appear at a grand jury proceeding and the proceeding pertains to an offense against the employer or an offense involving the employee during the course of his employment, the employer shall not decrease or withhold the employee's pay for any time lost as a result of compliance with the subpoena. Any employer who knowingly violates this section is in contempt of court.

**HISTORY: 140 v S 172. Eff 9-26-84.**

## § 2939.13 Oath to witnesses.

Before a witness is examined by the grand jury, an oath shall be administered to him by the foreman of the grand jury or by the judge of the court of common pleas or the clerk of the court of common pleas, truly to testify of such matters and things as may lawfully be inquired of before such jury. A certificate that the oath has been administered shall be indorsed on the subpoena of the witness or otherwise made by the foreman of the grand jury, judge, or clerk certifying the attendance of said witness to the clerk of the court.

**HISTORY: GC § 13436-10; 113 v 123(160), ch 15, § 10; 115 v 417; Bureau of Code Revision. Eff 10-1-53.**

## § 2939.14 Proceedings when witness refuses to testify.

If a witness before a grand jury refuses to answer an interrogatory, the court of common pleas shall be informed in writing, in which such interrogatory shall be stated, with the excuse for the refusal given by the witness. The court shall determine whether the witness is required to answer, and the grand jury shall be forthwith informed of such decision.

**HISTORY: GC § 13436-11; 113 v 123(160), ch 15, § 11; Bureau of Code Revision. Eff 10-1-53.**

## § 2939.15 Court may proceed against witness for contempt.

If the court of common pleas determines that a witness before a grand jury is required to answer an interrogatory and such witness persists in his refusal, he shall be brought before the court, which shall proceed in a like manner as if such witness had been interrogated and refused to answer in open court.

**HISTORY: GC § 13436-12; 113 v 123(160), ch 15, § 12; Bureau of Code Revision. Eff 10-1-53.**

## § 2939.16 Replacement of juror.

In case of sickness, death, discharge, or nonattendance of a grand juror after the grand jury is sworn, the court may cause another to be sworn in his stead. The court shall charge such juror as required by section 2939.07 of the Revised Code.

**HISTORY: GC § 13436-13; 113 v 123(160), ch 15, § 13; Bureau of Code Revision. Eff 10-1-53.**

## § 2939.17 New grand jury may be summoned.

After the grand jury is discharged, the court of common pleas, when necessary, may order the drawing and impaneling of a new grand jury, which shall be summoned and returned as provided by section 2939.03 of the Revised Code and shall be sworn and proceed in the manner provided by sections 2939.06 to 2939.24, inclusive, of the Revised Code. Whenever the governor or general assembly directs the attorney general to conduct any investigation or prosecution, the court of common pleas or any judge thereof, on written request of the attorney general, shall order a special grand jury to be summoned, and such special grand jury may be called and discharge its duties either before, during, or after any session of the regular grand jury, and its proceedings shall be independent of the proceedings of the regular grand jury but of the same force and effect.

Whenever a witness is necessary to a full investigation by the attorney general under this section, or to secure or successfully maintain and conclude a prosecution arising out of any such investigation, the judge of the court of common pleas may grant to such witness immunity from any prosecution based on the testimony or other evidence given by the witness in the course of the investigation or prosecution other than a prosecution for perjury in giving such testimony or evidence.

**HISTORY: GC § 13436-14; 113 v 123(160); Bureau of Code Revision, 10-1-53; 129 v 1201 (Eff 9-11-61); 133 v H 956. Eff 9-16-70.**

## § 2939.18 Fact of indictment shall be kept secret.

No grand juror, officer of the court, or other person shall disclose that an indictment has been found against a person not in custody or under bail, before such indictment is filed and the case docketed, except by the issue of process.

**HISTORY: GC § 13436-15; 113 v 123(161), ch 15, § 15; Bureau of Code Revision. Eff 10-1-53.**

## § 2939.19 Testimony of grand jurors.

No grand juror may state or testify in court in what manner any member of the grand jury voted or what opinion was expressed by any juror on any question before the grand jury.

**HISTORY: GC § 13436-16; 113 v 123(161), ch 15, § 16; Bureau of Code Revision. Eff 10-1-53.**

## § 2939.20 Indictment by twelve jurors.

At least twelve of the grand jurors must concur in the finding of an indictment. When so found, the foreman shall indorse on such indictment the words "A true bill" and subscribe his name as foreman.

**HISTORY: GC § 13436-17; 113 v 123(161), ch 15, § 17; Bureau of Code Revision. Eff 10-1-53.**

## § 2939.21 A grand jury to visit the county jail.

Once every three months, the grand jurors shall visit the county jail, examine its condition, and inquire into the discipline and treatment of the prisoners, their habits, diet, and accommodations. They shall report on these matters to the court of common pleas in writing. The clerk of the court of common pleas shall forward a copy of the report to the department of rehabilitation and correction.

**HISTORY: GC § 13436-20; 113 v 123(161), ch 15, § 20; Bureau of Code Revision, 10-1-53; 136 v H 390 (Eff 8-6-76); 139 v S 23. Eff 7-6-82.**

## § 2939.22 Proceedings when indictments are returned.

Indictments found by a grand jury shall be presented by the foreman to the court of common pleas, and filed with the clerk of the court of common pleas, who shall indorse thereon the date of such filing and enter each case upon the appearance docket and the trial docket of the term when the persons indicted have been arrested. The court shall assign such indictments for trial under section 2945.02 of the Revised Code, and recognizances of defendants and witnesses shall be taken for their appearance in court. When a case is continued to the next term of court, such recognizance shall require the appearance of the defendants and witnesses at a time designated by the court. Secret indictments shall not be docketed by name until after the apprehension of the accused.

**HISTORY: GC § 13436-21; 113 v 123(161), ch 15, § 21; Bureau of Code Revision. Eff 10-1-53.**

## § 2939.23 Report to court when indictment not found.

If an indictment is not found by the grand jury, against an accused who has been held to answer, such fact shall be reported by the foreman to the court of common pleas.

**HISTORY: GC § 13436-22; 113 v 123(162), ch 15, § 22; Bureau of Code Revision. Eff 10-1-53.**

## § 2939.24 Disposition of person in jail and not indicted.

If a person held in jail charged with an indictable offense is not indicted at the term of court at which he is held to answer, he shall be discharged unless:

(A) He was committed on such charge after the discharge of the grand jury.

(B) The transcript has not been filed.

(C) There is not sufficient time at such term of court to investigate said cause.

(D) The grand jury, for good cause, continues the hearing of said charge until the next term of court.

(E) It appears to the court of common pleas that a witness for the state has been enticed or kept away, detained, or prevented from attending court by sickness or unavoidable accident.

**HISTORY: GC § 13436-23; 113 v 123(162), ch 15, § 23; Bureau of Code Revision. Eff 10-1-53.**

### [ATTENDANCE OF WITNESSES FROM WITHOUT STATE]

## § 2939.25 Definition of witness, state, and summons.

As used in sections 2939.25 to 2939.29, inclusive, of the Revised Code:

(A) "Witness" includes a person whose testimony is desired in any proceeding or investigation by a grand jury or in a criminal action, prosecution, or proceeding.

(B) "State" includes any territory of the United States and District of Columbia.

(C) "Summons" includes a subpoena, order, or other notice requiring the appearance of a witness.

**HISTORY: GC § 13436-24; 117 v 668; Bureau of Code Revision. Eff 10-1-53.**

## § 2939.26 Foreign court may compel witnesses.

If a judge of a court of record in any state which by its laws has made provision for commanding persons within that state to attend and testify in this state, certifies under the seal of such court that there is a criminal prosecution pending in such court, or that a grand jury investigation has commenced or is about to commence, that a person being within this state is a material witness in such prosecution or grand jury investigation, and that his presence will be required for a specified number of days, upon presentation of such certificate to any judge of a court of record in the county in this state in which such person is, such judge shall fix a time and place for a hearing and shall make an order directing the witness to appear at a time and place certain for the hearing.

If at a hearing such judge determines that the witness is material and necessary, that it will not cause undue hardship to the witness to be compelled to attend and testify in the prosecution or grand jury investigation in the other state, and that the laws of the state in which the prosecution is pending, or grand jury investigation has commenced or is about to commence, and of any other state through which the witness may be required to pass by ordinary course of travel, will give to him protection from arrest and the service of civil and criminal process, he shall issue a summons, with a copy of the certificate attached, directing the witness to attend and testify in the court where the prosecution is pending, or where a grand jury investigation has commenced or is about to commence, at a time and place specified in the summons. In any such hearing the certificate is prima-facie evidence of all the facts stated therein.

If said certificate recommends that the witness be taken into immediate custody and delivered to an officer of the requesting state to assure his attendance in the requesting state, such judge may, in lieu of notification of the hearing, direct that such witness be forthwith brought before him for said hearing. If the judge at the hearing is satisfied of the desirability of such custody and delivery, for which determination the certificate is prima-facie proof of such desirability, he may, in lieu of issuing subpoena or summons, order that said witness be forthwith taken into custody and delivered to an officer of the requesting state.

If the witness, who is summoned as provided in this section, after being paid or tendered by some properly authorized person the sum of ten cents a mile for each mile by the ordinary traveled route to and from the court where the prosecution is pending and five dollars for each day, that he is required to travel and attend as a witness, fails without good cause to attend and testify as directed in the summons, he shall be punished in the manner provided for the punishment of any witness who disobeys a summons issued from a court of record in this state.

**HISTORY: GC § 13436-25; 117 v 668, § 2; Bureau of Code Revision. Eff 10-1-53.**

## § 2939.27 Certificate to specify time witness will be required; mileage and fees.

If a person in any state, which by its laws has made provision for commanding persons within its borders to attend and testify in criminal prosecutions or grand jury investigations commenced or about to commence, in this state, is a material witness in a prosecution pending in a court of record in this state, or in a grand jury investigation which has commenced or is about to commence, a judge of such court may issue a certificate under the seal of the court stating these facts and specifying the number of days the witness will be required. Said certificate may include a recommendation that the witness be taken into immediate custody and delivered to an officer of this state to assure his attendance in this state. This certificate shall be presented to a judge of a court of record in the county in which the witness is found.

If the witness is summoned to attend and testify in this state he shall be tendered the sum of ten cents a mile for each mile by the ordinary traveled route to and from the court where the prosecution is pending, and five dollars for each day that he is required to travel and attend as a witness. A witness who has appeared in accordance with the summons shall not be required to remain within this state a longer period of time than the period mentioned in the certificate, unless otherwise ordered by the court. If such witness, after coming into this state, fails without good cause to attend and testify as directed in the summons, he shall be punished in the manner provided for the punishment of any witness who disobeys a summons issued from a court of record in this state.

**HISTORY: GC § 13436-26; 117 v 668, § 3; Bureau of Code Revision. Eff 10-1-53.**

## § 2939.28 Exemption from arrest.

If a person comes into this state in obedience to a summons directing him to attend and testify in this state, while in this state pursuant to such summons he is not subject to arrest or the service of process, civil or criminal, in connection with matters which arose before his entrance into this state under the summons.

If a person passes through this state while going to another state in obedience to a summons to attend and testify in that state or while returning therefrom, while so passing through this state he is not subject to arrest or the service of process, civil or criminal, in connection with matters which arose before his entrance into this state under the summons.

**HISTORY: GC § 13436-27; 117 v 668, § 4; Bureau of Code Revision. Eff 10-1-53.**

## § 2939.29 Construction.

Sections 2939.25 to 2939.28, inclusive, of the Revised Code shall be so interpreted and construed as to effectuate their general purpose, to make the law of this state uniform with the law of other states which enact similar uniform legislation.

**HISTORY: GC § 13436-28; 117 v 668, § 5; Bureau of Code Revision. Eff 10-1-53.**

# CHAPTER 2941: INDICTMENT



## [FORM AND SUFFICIENCY]

### § 2941.01 Definition of magistrate.

The definition of "magistrate" set forth in section 2931.01 of the Revised Code applies to Chapter 2941 of the Revised Code.

**HISTORY: Bureau of Code Revision. Eff 10-1-53.**

### § 2941.02 Informations.

All sections of the Revised Code which apply to prosecutions upon indictments, the process thereon, and the issuing and service thereof, to commitments, bails, motions, pleadings, trials, appeals, and punishments, to the execution of any sentence, and all other proceedings in cases of indictments whether in the court of original or appellate jurisdiction, apply to informations, and all prosecutions and proceedings thereon.

**HISTORY: GC § 13437-1; 113 v 123(162), ch 16; Bureau of Code Revision. Eff 10-1-53.**

## § 2941.021 Prosecution by information.

Any criminal offense which is not punishable by death or life imprisonment may be prosecuted by information filed in the common pleas court by the prosecuting attorney if the defendant, after he has been advised by the court of the nature of the charge against him and of his rights under the constitution, is represented by counsel or has affirmatively waived counsel by waiver in writing and in open court, waives in writing and in open court prosecution by indictment.

**HISTORY: 128 v 53. Eff 11-9-59.**

## § 2941.03 Sufficiency of indictments or informations.

An indictment or information is sufficient if it can be understood therefrom:

(A) That it is entitled in a court having authority to receive it, though the name of the court is not stated;

(B) If it is an indictment, that it was found by a grand jury of the county in which the court was held, or if it is an information, that it was subscribed and presented to the court by the prosecuting attorney of the county in which the court was held;

(C) That the defendant is named, or, if his name cannot be discovered, that he is described by a fictitious name, with a statement that his true name is unknown to the jury or prosecuting attorney, but no name shall be stated in addition to one necessary to identify the accused;

(D) That an offense was committed at some place within the jurisdiction of the court, except where the act, though done without the local jurisdiction of the county, is triable therein;

(E) That the offense was committed at some time prior to the time of finding of the indictment or filing of the information.

**HISTORY: GC § 13437-2; 113 v 123(162), ch 16, § 2; Bureau of Code Revision. Eff 10-1-53.**

## § 2941.04 Two or more offenses in one indictment.

An indictment or information may charge two or more different offenses connected together in their commission, or different statements of the same offense, or two or more different offenses of the same class of crimes or offenses, under separate counts, and if two or more indictments or informations are filed in such cases the court may order them to be consolidated.

The prosecution is not required to elect between the different offenses or counts set forth in the indictment or information, but the defendant may be convicted of any number of the offenses charged, and each offense upon which the defendant is convicted must be stated in the verdict. The court in the interest of justice and for good cause shown, may order different offenses or counts set forth in the indictment or information tried separately or divided into two or more groups and each of said groups tried separately. A verdict of acquittal of one or more counts is not an acquittal of any other count.

**HISTORY: GC § 13437-3; 113 v 123(162), ch 16, § 3; Bureau of Code Revision. Eff 10-1-53.**

## § 2941.05 Statement charging an offense.

In an indictment or information charging an offense, each count shall contain, and is sufficient if it contains in substance, a statement that the accused has committed some public offense therein specified. Such statement may be made in ordinary and concise language without any technical averments or any allegations not essential to be proved. It may be in the words of the section of the Revised Code describing the offense or declaring the matter charged to be a public offense, or in any words sufficient to give the accused notice of the offense of which he is charged.

**HISTORY: GC § 13437-4; 113 v 123(163), ch 16, § 4; Bureau of Code Revision, 10-1-53; 126 v 392. Eff 3-17-55.**

## § 2941.06 Form of indictment or information.

An indictment may be substantially in the following form:

"The State of Ohio,)
ss.
........ County)

In the Year ......

The jurors of the Grand Jury of the State of Ohio, within and for the body of the County aforesaid, on their oaths, in the name and by the authority of the State of Ohio, do find and present that A.B., on the ...... day of ..........., at the county of .......... aforesaid, did ....... (here insert the name of the offense if it has one, such as murder, arson, or the like, or if a misdemeanor having no general name, insert a brief description of it as given by law) contrary to the form of the statute in such case made and provided, and against the peace and dignity of the State of Ohio.

....... C.D. .......
Prosecuting Attorney

(Indorsed) A true bill.

E.F., Foreperson of the Grand Jury."

**HISTORY: GC § 13437-5; 113 v 123(163), ch 16, § 5; Bureau of Code Revision, 10-1-53; 136 v H 390 (Eff 8-6-76); 148 v H 495. Eff 5-9-2000.**

## § 2941.07 Bill of particulars.

Upon written request of the defendant made not later than five days prior to the date set for trial, or upon order of the court, the prosecuting attorney shall furnish a bill of particulars setting up specifically the nature of the offense charged and the conduct of the defendant which is alleged to constitute the offense.

**HISTORY: GC § 13437-6; 113 v 123(164), ch 16, § 6; Bureau of Code Revision, 10-1-53; 134 v H 511. Eff 1-1-74.**

## § 2941.08 Certain defects do not render indictment invalid.

An indictment or information is not made invalid, and the trial, judgment, or other proceedings stayed, arrested, or affected:

(A) By the omission of "with force and arms," or words of similar import, or "as appears by the record";

(B) For omitting to state the time at which the offense was committed, in a case in which time is not of the essence of the offense;

(C) For stating the time imperfectly;

(D) For stating imperfectly the means by which the offense was committed except insofar as means is an element of the offense;

(E) For want of a statement of the value or price of a matter or thing, or the amount of damages or injury, where the value or price or the amount of damages or injury is not of the essence of the offense, and in such case it is sufficient to aver that the value or price of the property is less than, equals, or exceeds the certain value or price which determines the offense or grade thereof;

(F) For the want of an allegation of the time or place of a material fact when the time and place have been once stated therein;

(G) Because dates and numbers are represented by figures;

(H) For an omission to allege that the grand jurors were impaneled, sworn, or charged;

(I) For surplusage or repugnant allegations when there is sufficient matter alleged to indicate the crime and person charged;

(J) For want of averment of matter not necessary to be proved;

(K) For other defects or imperfections which do not tend to prejudice the substantial rights of the defendant upon the merits.

**HISTORY: GC § 13437-7; 113 v 123(165), ch 16, § 7; Bureau of Code Revision. Eff 10-1-53.**

## § 2941.09 Identification of corporation.

In any indictment or information it is sufficient for the purpose of identifying any group or association of persons, not incorporated, to state the proper name of such group or association, to state any name or designation by which the group or association has been or is known, to state the names of all persons in such group or association or of one or more of them, or to state the name of one or more persons in such group or association referring to the others as "another" or "others." It is sufficient for the purpose of identifying a corporation to state the corporate name of such corporation, or any name or designation by which such corporation has been or is known.

**HISTORY: GC § 13437-8; 113 v 123(165), ch 16, § 8; Bureau of Code Revision. Eff 10-1-53.**

## § 2941.10 Indictment complete.

No indictment or information for any offense created or defined by statute is objectionable for the reason that it fails to negative any exception, excuse, or proviso contained in the statute creating or defining the offense. The fact that the charge is made is an allegation that no legal excuse for the doing of the act exists in the particular case.

**HISTORY: GC § 13437-9; 113 v 123(165), ch 16, § 9; Bureau of Code Revision. Eff 10-1-53.**

## § 2941.11 Pleading prior conviction.

Whenever it is necessary to allege a prior conviction of the accused in an indictment or information, it is sufficient to allege that the accused was, at a certain stated time, in a certain stated court, convicted of a certain stated offense, giving the name of the offense, or stating the substantial elements thereof.

**HISTORY: GC § 13437-10; 113 v 123(166), ch 16, § 10; Bureau of Code Revision. Eff 10-1-53.**

## § 2941.12 Pleading a statute.

In pleading a statute or right derived therefrom it is sufficient to refer to the statute by its title, or in any other manner which identifies the statute. The court must thereupon take judicial notice of such statute.

**HISTORY: GC § 13437-11; 113 v 123(166), ch 16, § 11; Bureau of Code Revision. Eff 10-1-53.**

## § 2941.13 Pleading a judgment.

In pleading a judgment or other determination of, or a proceeding before, any court or officer, civil or military, it is not necessary to allege the fact conferring jurisdiction on such court or officer. It is sufficient to allege generally that such judgment or determination was given or made or such proceedings had.

**HISTORY: GC § 13437-12; 113 v 123(166), ch 16, § 12; Bureau of Code Revision. Eff 10-1-53.**

## § 2941.14 Allegations in homicide indictment.

(A) In an indictment for aggravated murder, murder, or voluntary or involuntary manslaughter, the manner in which, or the means by which the death was caused need not be set forth.

(B) Imposition of the death penalty for aggravated murder is precluded unless the indictment or count in the indictment charging the offense specifies one or more of the aggravating circumstances listed in division (A) of section 2929.04 of the Revised Code. If more than one aggravating circumstance is specified to an indictment or count, each shall be in a separately numbered specification, and if an aggravating circumstance is specified to a count in an indictment containing more than one count, such specification shall be identified as to the count to which it applies.

(C) A specification to an indictment or count in an indictment charging aggravated murder shall be stated at the end of the body of the indictment or count, and may be in substantially the following form:

"SPECIFICATION (or, SPECIFICATION 1, SPECIFICATION TO THE FIRST COUNT, or SPECIFICATION 1 TO THE FIRST COUNT). The Grand Jurors further find and specify that (set forth the applicable aggravating circumstance listed in divisions (A)(1) to (10) of section 2929.04 of the Revised Code. The aggravating circumstance may be stated in the words of the subdivision in which it appears, or in words sufficient to give the accused notice of the same)."

**HISTORY: GC § 13437-13; 113 v 123(166), ch 16, § 13; Bureau of Code Revision, 10-1-53; 134 v H 511 (Eff 1-1-74); 135 v H 716 (Eff 1-1-74); 139 v S 1 (Eff 10-19-81); 147 v S 32 (Eff 8-6-97); 149 v S 184. Eff 5-15-2002.**

## § 2941.141 Specification that offender had a firearm while committing the offense.

(A) Imposition of a one-year mandatory prison term upon an offender under division (B)(1)(a) of section 2929.14 of the Revised Code is precluded unless the indictment, count in the indictment, or information charging the offense specifies that the offender had a firearm on or about the offender's person or under the offender's control while committing the offense. The specification shall be stated at the end of the body of the indictment, count, or information, and shall be in substantially the following form:

"SPECIFICATION (or, SPECIFICATION TO THE FIRST COUNT). The Grand Jurors (or insert the person's or the prosecuting attorney's name when appropriate) further find and specify that (set forth that the offender had a firearm on or about the offender's person or under the offender's control while committing the offense.)"

(B) Imposition of a one-year mandatory prison term upon an offender under division (B)(1)(a) of section 2929.14 of the Revised Code is precluded if a court imposes a three-year or six-year mandatory prison term on the offender under that division relative to the same felony.

(C) The specification described in division (A) of this section may be used in a delinquent child proceeding in the manner and for the purpose described in section 2152.17 of the Revised Code.

(D) As used in this section, "firearm" has the same meaning as in section 2923.11 of the Revised Code.

**HISTORY: 139 v S 199 (Eff 1-5-83); 143 v S 258 (Eff 11-20-90); 143 v H 669 (Eff 1-10-91); 146 v S 2 (Eff 7-1-96); 148 v S 107 (Eff 3-23-2000); 148 v S 179, § 3. Eff 1-1-2002; 2011 HB 86, § 1, eff. Sept. 30, 2011.**

The effective date is set by section 5 of SB 179.

## § 2941.142 Specification that offender participated in criminal gang.

(A) Imposition of a mandatory prison term of one, two, or three years pursuant to division (G) of section 2929.14 of the Revised Code upon an offender who committed a felony that is an offense of violence while participating in a criminal gang is precluded unless the indictment, count in the indictment, or information charging the felony specifies that the offender committed the felony that is an offense of violence while participating in a criminal gang. The specification shall be stated at the end of the body of the indictment, count, or information, and shall be in substantially the following form:

"SPECIFICATION (or, SPECIFICATION TO THE FIRST COUNT). The grand jurors (or insert the person's or the prosecuting attorney's name when appropriate) further find and specify that (set forth that the offender committed the felony that is an offense of violence while participating in a criminal gang.)"

(B) The specification described in division (A) of this section may be used in a delinquent child proceeding in the manner and for the purpose described in section 2152.17 of the Revised Code.

(C) As used in this section, "criminal gang" has the same meaning as in section 2923.41 of the Revised Code.

**HISTORY: 147 v H 2 (Eff 1-1-99); 148 v S 179, § 3. Eff 1-1-2002; 2011 HB 86, § 1, eff. Sept. 30, 2011.**

**Not analogous to former RC § 2941.14.2 (140 v S 210), repealed 146 v S 2, § 2, eff 7-1-96.**

The effective date is set by section 5 of SB 179.

## § 2941.143 Specification that offense involved school safety zone.

Imposition of a sentence by a court pursuant to division (H) of section 2929.14 of the Revised Code is precluded unless the indictment, count in the indictment, or information charging aggravated murder, murder, or a felony of the first, second, or third degree that is an offense of violence specifies that the offender committed the offense in a school safety zone or towards a person in a school safety zone. The specification shall be stated at the end of the body of the indictment, count, or information and shall be in substantially the following form:

"SPECIFICATION (or, SPECIFICATION TO THE FIRST COUNT). The grand jurors (or insert the person's or the prosecuting attorney's name when appropriate) further find and specify that (set forth that the offender committed aggravated murder, murder, or the felony of the first, second, or third degree that is an offense of violence in a school safety zone or towards a person in a school safety zone)."

**HISTORY: 148 v S 1. Eff 8-6-99; 2011 HB 86, § 1, eff. Sept. 30, 2011.**

**Not analogous to former RC § 2941.14.3 (140 v S 210), repealed 146 v S 2, § 2, eff 7-1-96.**

## § 2941.144 Specification that offender had an automatic firearm or a firearm equipped with a muffler or silencer.

(A) Imposition of a six-year mandatory prison term upon an offender under division (B)(1)(a) of section 2929.14 of the Revised Code is precluded unless the indictment, count in the indictment, or information charging the offense specifies that the offender had a firearm that is an automatic firearm or that was equipped with a firearm muffler or silencer on or about the offender's person or under the offender's control while committing the offense. The specification shall be stated at the end of the body of the indictment, count, or information and shall be stated in substantially the following form:

"SPECIFICATION (or, SPECIFICATION TO THE FIRST COUNT). The Grand Jurors (or insert the person's or the prosecuting attorney's name when appropriate) further find and specify that (set forth that the offender had a firearm that is an automatic firearm or that was equipped with a firearm muffler or silencer on or about the offender's person or under the offender's control while committing the offense)."

(B) Imposition of a six-year mandatory prison term upon an offender under division (B)(1)(a) of section 2929.14 of the Revised Code is precluded if a court imposes a three-year or one-year mandatory prison term on the offender under that division relative to the same felony.

(C) The specification described in division (A) of this section may be used in a delinquent child proceeding in the manner and for the purpose described in section 2152.17 of the Revised Code.

(D) As used in this section, "firearm" and "automatic firearm" have the same meanings as in section 2923.11 of the Revised Code.

**HISTORY: 143 v S 258 (Eff 11-20-90); 146 v S 2 (Eff 7-1-96); 148 v S 107 (Eff 3-23-2000); 148 v S 179, § 3. Eff 1-1-2002; 2011 HB 86, § 1, eff. Sept. 30, 2011.**

The effective date is set by section 5 of SB 179.

## § 2941.145 Specification that offender displayed, brandished, indicated possession of or used firearm.

(A) Imposition of a three-year mandatory prison term upon an offender under division (B)(1)(a) of section

2929.14 of the Revised Code is precluded unless the indictment, count in the indictment, or information charging the offense specifies that the offender had a firearm on or about the offender's person or under the offender's control while committing the offense and displayed the firearm, brandished the firearm, indicated that the offender possessed the firearm, or used it to facilitate the offense. The specification shall be stated at the end of the body of the indictment, count, or information, and shall be stated in substantially the following form:

"SPECIFICATION (or, SPECIFICATION TO THE FIRST COUNT). The Grand Jurors (or insert the person's or the prosecuting attorney's name when appropriate) further find and specify that (set forth that the offender had a firearm on or about the offender's person or under the offender's control while committing the offense and displayed the firearm, brandished the firearm, indicated that the offender possessed the firearm, or used it to facilitate the offense)."

(B) Imposition of a three-year mandatory prison term upon an offender under division (B)(1)(a) of section 2929.14 of the Revised Code is precluded if a court imposes a one-year or six-year mandatory prison term on the offender under that division relative to the same felony.

(C) The specification described in division (A) of this section may be used in a delinquent child proceeding in the manner and for the purpose described in section 2152.17 of the Revised Code.

(D) As used in this section, "firearm" has the same meaning as in section 2923.11 of the Revised Code.

**HISTORY: 146 v S 2 (Eff 7-1-96); 148 v S 107 (Eff 3-23-2000); 148 v S 179, § 3. Eff 1-1-2002; 2011 HB 86, § 1, eff. Sept. 30, 2011.**

The effective date is set by section 5 of SB 179.

## § 2941.146 Specification that offender discharged firearm from motor vehicle.

(A) Imposition of a mandatory five-year prison term upon an offender under division (B)(1)(c) of section 2929.14 of the Revised Code for committing a violation of section 2923.161 of the Revised Code or for committing a felony that includes, as an essential element, purposely or knowingly causing or attempting to cause the death of or physical harm to another and that was committed by discharging a firearm from a motor vehicle other than a manufactured home is precluded unless the indictment, count in the indictment, or information charging the offender specifies that the offender committed the offense by discharging a firearm from a motor vehicle other than a manufactured home. The specification shall be stated at the end of the body of the indictment, count, or information, and shall be stated in substantially the following form:

"SPECIFICATION (or, SPECIFICATION TO THE FIRST COUNT). The Grand Jurors (or insert the person's or prosecuting attorney's name when appropriate) further find and specify that (set forth that the offender committed the violation of section 2923.161 of the Revised Code or the felony that includes, as an essential element, purposely or knowingly causing or attempting to cause the death of or physical harm to another and that was committed by discharging a firearm from a motor vehicle other than a manufactured home)."

(B) The specification described in division (A) of this section may be used in a delinquent child proceeding in the manner and for the purpose described in section 2152.17 of the Revised Code.

(C) As used in this section:

(1) "Firearm" has the same meaning as in section 2923.11 of the Revised Code;

(2) "Motor vehicle" and "manufactured home" have the same meanings as in section 4501.01 of the Revised Code.

**HISTORY: 146 v S 2 (Eff 7-1-96); 148 v S 107 (Eff 3-23-2000); 148 v S 179, § 3. Eff 1-1-2002; 2011 HB 86, § 1, eff. Sept. 30, 2011.**

The effective date is set by section 5 of SB 179.

## § 2941.147 Specification of sexual motivation.

(A) Whenever a person is charged with an offense that is a violation of section 2903.01, 2903.02, 2903.11, or 2905.01 of the Revised Code, a violation of division (A) of section 2903.04 of the Revised Code, an attempt to violate or complicity in violating section 2903.01, 2903.02, 2903.11, or 2905.01 of the Revised Code when the attempt or complicity is a felony, or an attempt to violate or complicity in violating division (A) of section 2903.04 of the Revised Code when the attempt or complicity is a felony, the indictment, count in the indictment, information, or complaint charging the offense may include a specification that the person committed the offense with a sexual motivation. The specification shall be stated at the end of the body of the indictment, count, information, or complaint and shall be in substantially the following form:

"SPECIFICATION (OR, SPECIFICATION TO THE FIRST COUNT). The Grand Jurors (or insert the person's or the prosecuting attorney's name when appropriate) further find and specify that the offender committed the offense with a sexual motivation."

(B) As used in this section, "sexual motivation" has the same meaning as in section 2971.01 of the Revised Code.

**HISTORY: 146 v H 180. Eff 1-1-97.**

The effective date is set by section 3 of HB 180.
See provisions, § 4 of HB 180 (146 v —), following RC § 2921.34.

## § 2941.148 Specification that offender is a sexually violent predator.

(A)(1) The application of Chapter 2971. of the Revised Code to an offender is precluded unless one of the following applies:

(a) The offender is charged with a violent sex offense, and the indictment, count in the indictment, or information charging the violent sex offense also includes a specification that the offender is a sexually violent predator, or the offender is charged with a designated homicide, assault, or kidnapping offense, and the indictment, count in the indictment, or information charging the designated homicide, assault, or kidnapping offense also includes both a specification of the type described in section 2941.147 [2941.14.7] of the Revised Code and a specification that the offender is a sexually violent predator.

(b) The offender is convicted of or pleads guilty to a violation of division (A)(1)(b) of section 2907.02 of the Revised Code committed on or after January 2, 2007, and division (B) of section 2907.02 of the Revised Code does not prohibit the court from sentencing the offender pursuant to section 2971.03 of the Revised Code.

(c) The offender is convicted of or pleads guilty to attempted rape committed on or after January 2, 2007, and to a specification of the type described in section 2941.1418 [2941.14.18], 2941.1419 [2941.14.19], or 2941.1420 [2941.14.20] of the Revised Code.

(d) The offender is convicted of or pleads guilty to a violation of section 2905.01 of the Revised Code and to a specification of the type described in section 2941.147 [2941.14.7] of the Revised Code, and section 2905.01 of the Revised Code requires a court to sentence the offender pursuant to section 2971.03 of the Revised Code.

(e) The offender is convicted of or pleads guilty to aggravated murder and to a specification of the type described in section 2941.147 [2941.14.7] of the Revised Code, and division (A)(2)(b)(ii) of section 2929.022 [2929.02.2], division (A)(1)(e), (C)(1)(a)(v), (C)(2)(a)(ii), (D)(2)(b), (D)(3)(a)(iv), or (E)(1)(d) of section 2929.03, or division (A) or (B) of section 2929.06 of the Revised Code requires a court to sentence the offender pursuant to division (B)(3) of section 2971.03 of the Revised Code.

(f) The offender is convicted of or pleads guilty to murder and to a specification of the type described in section 2941.147 [2941.14.7] of the Revised Code, and division (B)(2) of section 2929.02 of the Revised Code requires a court to sentence the offender pursuant to section 2971.03 of the Revised Code.

(2) A specification required under division (A)(1)(a) of this section that an offender is a sexually violent predator shall be stated at the end of the body of the indictment, count, or information and shall be stated in substantially the following form:

"SPECIFICATION (OR, SPECIFICATION TO THE FIRST COUNT). The grand jury (or insert the person's or prosecuting attorney's name when appropriate) further find and specify that the offender is a sexually violent predator."

(B) In determining for purposes of this section whether a person is a sexually violent predator, all of the factors set forth in divisions (H)(1) to (6) of section 2971.01 of the Revised Code that apply regarding the person may be considered as evidence tending to indicate that it is likely that the person will engage in the future in one or more sexually violent offenses.

(C) As used in this section, "designated homicide, assault, or kidnapping offense," "violent sex offense," and "sexually violent predator" have the same meanings as in section 2971.01 of the Revised Code.

**HISTORY: 146 v H 180. Eff 1-1-97; 150 v H 473, § 1, eff. 4-29-05; 151 v S 260, § 1, eff. 1-2-07; 152 v S 10, § 1, eff. 1-1-08.**

The effective date is set by § 3 of 152 v S 10.
The effective date is set by section 3 of HB 180.

## § 2941.149 Specification that offender is repeat violent offender.

(A) The determination by a court that an offender is a repeat violent offender is precluded unless the indictment, count in the indictment, or information charging the offender specifies that the offender is a repeat violent offender. The specification shall be stated at the end of the body of the indictment, count, or information, and shall be stated in substantially the following form:

"SPECIFICATION (or, SPECIFICATION TO THE FIRST COUNT). The Grand Jurors (or insert the person's or prosecuting attorney's name when appropriate) further find and specify that (set forth that the offender is a repeat violent offender)."

(B) The court shall determine the issue of whether an offender is a repeat violent offender.

(C) At the arraignment of the defendant or as soon thereafter as is practicable, the prosecuting attorney may give notice to the defendant of the prosecuting attorney's intention to use a certified copy of the entry of judgment of a prior conviction as proof of that prior conviction. The defendant must then give notice to the prosecuting attorney of the defendant's intention to object to the use of the entry of judgment. If the defendant pursuant to Criminal Rule 12 does not give notice of that intention to the prosecuting attorney before trial, the defendant waives the objection to the use of an entry of judgment as proof of the defendant's prior conviction, as shown on the entry of judgment.

(D) As used in this section, "repeat violent offender" has the same meaning as in section 2929.01 of the Revised Code.

**HISTORY: 146 v S 269. Eff 7-1-96; 151 v H 95, § 1, eff. 8-3-06.**

The effective date is set by section 5 of SB 269.

## § 2941.1410 Specification that offender is a major drug offender.

(A) Except as provided in sections 2925.03 and 2925.11 of the Revised Code, the determination by a court that an offender is a major drug offender is precluded unless the indictment, count in the indictment, or information charging the offender specifies that the offender is a major drug offender. The specification shall be stated at the end of the body of the indictment, count, or information, and shall be stated in substantially the following form:

"SPECIFICATION (or, SPECIFICATION TO THE FIRST COUNT). The Grand Jurors (or insert the person's or prosecuting attorney's name when appropriate) further find and specify that (set forth that the offender is a major drug offender)."

(B) The court shall determine the issue of whether an offender is a major drug offender.

(C) As used in this section, "major drug offender" has the same meaning as in section 2929.01 of the Revised Code.

**HISTORY: 146 v S 269 (Eff 7-1-96); 148 v S 107. Eff 3-23-2000.**

## § 2941.1411 Specification that offender wore or carried body armor.

(A) Imposition of a two-year mandatory prison term upon an offender under division (B)(1)(d) of section 2929.14 of the Revised Code is precluded unless the indictment, count in the indictment, or information charging the offense specifies that the offender wore or carried body armor while committing the offense and that the offense is an offense of violence that is a felony. The specification shall be stated at the end of the body of the indictment, count, or information and shall be stated in substantially the following form:

"SPECIFICATION (or, SPECIFICATION TO THE FIRST COUNT). The Grand Jurors (or insert the person's or the prosecuting attorney's name when appropriate) further find and specify that (set forth that the offender wore or carried body armor while committing the specified offense and that the specified offense is an offense of violence that is a felony)."

(B) As used in this section, "body armor" means any vest, helmet, shield, or similar item that is designed or specifically carried to diminish the impact of a bullet or projectile upon the offender's body.

**HISTORY: 148 v S 222. Eff 3-22-2001; 2011 HB 86, § 1, eff. Sept. 30, 2011.**

## § 2941.1412 Specification that offender discharged firearm at peace officer or corrections officer.

(A) Imposition of a seven-year mandatory prison term upon an offender under division (B)(1)(f) of section 2929.14 of the Revised Code is precluded unless the indictment, count in the indictment, or information charging the offense specifies that the offender discharged a firearm at a peace officer or a corrections officer while committing the offense. The specification shall be stated at the end of the body of the indictment, count, or information and shall be in substantially the following form:

"SPECIFICATION (or, SPECIFICATION TO THE FIRST COUNT).

The Grand Jurors (or insert the person's or the prosecuting attorney's name when appropriate) further find and specify that (set forth that the offender discharged a firearm at a peace officer or a corrections officer while committing the offense)."

(B) As used in this section:

(1) "Firearm" has the same meaning as in section 2923.11 of the Revised Code.

(2) "Peace officer" has the same meaning as in section 2935.01 of the Revised Code.

(3) "Corrections officer" means a person employed by a detention facility as a corrections officer.

(4) "Detention facility" has the same meaning as in section 2921.01 of the Revised Code.

**HISTORY: 149 v H 130. Eff 4-7-2003; 2011 HB 86, § 1, eff. Sept. 30, 2011.**

## § 2941.1413 Specification concerning additional prison term for certain repeat OVI offenders.

(A) Imposition of a mandatory additional prison term of one, two, three, four, or five years upon an offender under division (G)(2) of section 2929.13 of the Revised Code is precluded unless the indictment, count in the indictment, or information charging a felony violation of division (A) of section 4511.19 of the Revised Code specifies that the offender, within twenty years of the offense, previously has been convicted of or pleaded guilty to five or more equivalent offenses. The specification shall be stated at the end of the body of the indictment, count, or information and shall be stated in substantially the following form:

"SPECIFICATION (or, SPECIFICATION TO THE FIRST COUNT). The Grand Jurors (or insert the person's or the prosecuting attorney's name when appropriate) further find and specify that (set forth that the offender, within twenty years of committing the offense, previously had been convicted of or pleaded guilty to five or more equivalent offenses)."

(B) As used in division (A) of this section, "equivalent offense" has the same meaning as in section 4511.181 [4511.18.1] of the Revised Code.

**HISTORY: 150 v H 163, § 1, eff. 9-23-04.**

## § 2941.1414 Specification that victim of aggravated vehicular homicide was a peace officer or investigator of bureau of criminal identification and investigation.

(A) Imposition of a five-year mandatory prison term upon an offender under division (B)(5) of section 2929.14 of the Revised Code is precluded unless the offender is convicted of or pleads guilty to violating division (A)(1) or (2) of section 2903.06 of the Revised Code and unless the indictment, count in the indictment, or information charging the offense specifies that the victim of the offense is a peace officer or an investigator of the bureau of criminal identification and investigation. The specification shall be stated at the end of the body of the indictment, count, or information and shall be stated in substantially the following form:

"SPECIFICATION (or, SPECIFICATION TO THE FIRST COUNT). The Grand Jurors (or insert the person's or the prosecuting attorney's name when appropriate) further find and specify that (set forth that the victim of the offense is a peace officer or an investigator of the bureau of criminal identification and investigation)."

(B) The specification described in division (A) of this section may be used in a delinquent child proceeding in the manner and for the purpose described in section 2152.17 of the Revised Code.

(C) As used in this section:

(1) "Peace officer" has the same meaning as in section 2935.01 of the Revised Code.

(2) "Investigator of the bureau of criminal identification and investigation" has the same meaning as in section 2903.11 of the Revised Code.

**HISTORY: 150 v H 52, § 1, eff. 6-1-04; 151 v S 281, § 1, eff. 1-4-07; 2011 HB 86, § 1, eff. Sept. 30, 2011.**

## § 2941.1415 Specification in prosecution for aggravated vehicular homicide that offender had three or more previous convictions of driving under the influence.

(A) Imposition of a three-year mandatory prison term upon an offender under division (B)(6) of section 2929.14 of the Revised Code is precluded unless the offender is convicted of or pleads guilty to violating division (A)(1) or (2) of section 2903.06 of the Revised Code and unless the indictment, count in the indictment, or information charging the offense specifies that the offender previously has been convicted of or pleaded guilty to three or more violations of division (A) or (B) of section 4511.19 of the Revised Code or an equivalent offense, or three or more violations of any combination of those divisions and offenses. The specification shall be stated at the end of the body of the indictment, count, or information and shall be stated in substantially the following form:

"SPECIFICATION (or, SPECIFICATION TO THE FIRST COUNT). The Grand Jurors (or insert the person's or the prosecuting attorney's name when appropriate) further find and specify that (set forth that the offender previously has been convicted of or pleaded guilty to three or more violations of division (A) or (B) of section 4511.19 of the Revised Code or an equivalent offense, or three or more violations of any combination of those divisions and offenses)."

(B) The specification described in division (A) of this section may be used in a delinquent child proceeding in the manner and for the purpose described in section 2152.17 of the Revised Code.

(C) As used in this section, "equivalent offense" has the same meaning as in section 4511.181 of the Revised Code.

**HISTORY: 150 v H 52, § 1, eff. 6-1-04; 2011 HB 86, § 1, eff. Sept. 30, 2011.**

## § 2941.1416 Specification concerning additional jail term where offender has prior misdemeanor OVI offenses.

(A) Imposition of a mandatory, additional, definite jail term of up to six months upon an offender under division (E) of section 2929.24 of the Revised Code is precluded unless the information charging a violation of division (B) of section 4511.19 of the Revised Code specifies that the offender, within twenty years of the offense, previously has been convicted of or pleaded guilty to five or more equivalent offenses. The specification shall be stated at the end of the body of the information and shall be stated in substantially the following form:

"SPECIFICATION. (Insert the person's or the prosecuting attorney's name as appropriate) further finds and specifies that (set forth that the offender, within twenty years of committing the offense, previously had been convicted of or pleaded guilty to five or more equivalent offenses)."

(B) As used in division (A) of this section, "equivalent offense" has the same meaning as in section 4511.181 [4511.18.1] of the Revised Code.

**HISTORY: 150 v H 163, § 1, eff. 9-23-04.**

## § 2941.1417 Specification that property is subject to forfeiture.

(A) Property is not subject to forfeiture in a criminal case unless the indictment, count in the indictment, or information charging the offense specifies, to the extent it is reasonably known at the time of filing, the nature and extent of the alleged offender's interest in the property, a description of the property, and, if the property is alleged to be an instrumentality, the alleged use or intended use of the property in the commission or facilitation of the offense. The specification shall be stated at the end of the body of the indictment, count, or information and shall be in substantially the following form:

"SPECIFICATION (or SPECIFICATION TO THE FIRST COUNT). The grand jurors (or insert the person's or prosecuting attorney's name when appropriate) further find and specify that (set forth the alleged offender's interest in the property, a description of the property subject to forfeiture, and any alleged use or intended use of the property in the commission or facilitation of the offense)."

(B) The trier of fact shall determine whether the property is subject to forfeiture.

(C) The specification described in division (A) of this section may be used in a delinquent child proceeding.

**HISTORY: 151 v H 241, § 1, eff. 7-1-07.**

See provisions of § 4 of 151 v H 241 following RC § 2901.01.

## § 2941.1418 Specification that had attempted rape been completed, offender would have been guilty of child rape.

(A) Imposition of a mandatory indefinite prison term consisting of a minimum term of five years and a maximum term of twenty-five years upon an offender pursuant to division (A)(3)(e)(ii) or (B)(2)(a) of section 2971.03 of the Revised Code is precluded unless the offender is convicted of or pleads guilty to attempted rape and unless the indictment, count in the indictment, or information charging the offense specifies that the offender was sixteen years of age or older at the time of the commission of the offense and that, had the offender completed the rape that was attempted, the offender would have been guilty of rape in violation of division (A)(1)(b) of section 2907.02 of the Revised Code.

(B) The specification shall be stated at the end of the body of the indictment, count, or information and shall be stated in substantially the following form:

"SPECIFICATION (or, SPECIFICATION TO THE FIRST COUNT). The Grand Jurors (or insert the person's or the prosecuting attorney's name when appropriate) further find and specify that (set forth that the offender was sixteen years of age or older at the time of the commission of the offense and that, had the offender completed the rape that was attempted, the offender would have been guilty of a violation of division (A)(1)(b) of section 2907.02 of the Revised Code)."

**HISTORY: 151 v S 260, § 1, eff. 1-2-07.**

## § 2941.1419 Specification that had attempted rape been completed, offender would have been guilty of child rape and victim was under ten or that offender purposely compelled victim to submit by force or threat of force.

Imposition of a mandatory indefinite prison term consisting of a minimum term of ten years and a maximum term of life imprisonment upon an offender pursuant to division (A)(3)(e)(iii) or (B)(2)(b) of section 2971.03 of the Revised Code is precluded unless the offender is convicted of or pleads guilty to attempted rape and unless the indictment, count in the indictment, or information charging the offense specifies that, had the offender completed the rape that was attempted, the offender would have been guilty of rape in violation of division (A)(1)(b) of section 2907.02 of the Revised Code and specifies that one of the following applies:

(A) The victim was under ten years of age.

(B) The offender attempted to commit rape by purposely compelling the victim to submit by force or threat of force, and the offender was sixteen years of age or older at the time of the commission of the offense.

The specification shall be stated at the end of the body of the indictment, count, or information and shall be stated in substantially the following form:

"SPECIFICATION (or, SPECIFICATION TO THE FIRST COUNT). The Grand Jurors (or insert the person's or the prosecuting attorney's name when appropriate) further find and specify that (set forth that, had the offender completed the rape that was attempted, the offender would have been guilty of a violation of division (A)(1)(b) of section 2907.02 of the Revised Code, and the victim was under ten years of age or the offender attempted to commit rape by purposely compelling the victim to submit by force or threat of force, and the offender was sixteen years of age or older at the time of the commission of the offense)."

**HISTORY: 151 v S 260, § 1, eff. 1-2-07.**

## § 2941.1420 Specification that had attempted rape been completed, offender would have been guilty of child rape and that certain other circumstances applied.

(A) Imposition of a mandatory indefinite prison term consisting of a minimum term of fifteen years and a maximum term of life imprisonment upon an offender pursuant to division (A)(3)(e)(iv) or (B)(2)(c) of section 2971.03 of the Revised Code is precluded unless the offender is convicted of or pleads guilty to attempted rape and unless the indictment, count in the indictment, or information charging the offense specifies that, had the offender completed the rape that was attempted, the offender would have been guilty of rape in violation of division (A)(1)(b) of section 2907.02 of the Revised Code, and any of the following apply:

(1) The offender previously has been convicted of or pleaded guilty to one of the following:

(a) Attempted rape and previously has been convicted of or pleaded guilty to a specification of the type described in this section or section 2941.1418 [2941.14.18] or 2941.1419 [2941.14.19] of the Revised Code;

(b) Attempted rape under circumstances that are substantially similar to the circumstances described in this section or section 2941.1419 [2941.14.19] or 2941.1420 [2941.14.20] of the Revised Code;

(c) A violation of an existing or former law of this state, another state, or the United States that is substantially similar to any of the offenses described in divisions (A)(1)(a) and (b) of this section.

(2) The offender previously has been convicted of or pleaded guilty to violating division (A)(1)(b) of section 2907.02 of the Revised Code or to violating a substantially similar existing or former law of this state, another state, or the United States.

(3) The offender during or immediately after the commission of the offense caused serious physical harm to the victim.

(B) The specification shall be stated at the end of the body of the indictment, count, or information and shall be stated in substantially the following form:

"SPECIFICATION (or, SPECIFICATION TO THE FIRST COUNT). The Grand Jurors (or insert the person's or the prosecuting attorney's name when appropriate) further find and specify that (set forth that, had the offender completed the rape that was attempted, the offender would have been guilty of a violation of division (A)(1)(b) of section 2907.02 of the Revised Code, and the offender previously has been convicted of or pleaded guilty to attempted rape and previously has been convicted of or pleaded guilty to a specification of the type described in this section or section 2941.1418 [2941.14.18] or 2941.1419 [2941.14.19] of the Revised Code, previously has been convicted of or pleaded guilty to attempted rape under circumstances that are substantially similar to the circumstances described in this section or section 2941.1419 [2941.14.19] or 2941.1420 [2941.14.20] of the Revised Code, or previously has been convicted of or pleaded guilty to violating a substantially similar existing or former law of this state, another state, or the United States; previously has been convicted of or pleaded guilty to violating division (A)(1)(b) of section 2907.02 of the Revised Code or to violating a substantially similar existing or former law of this state, another state, or the United States; or the offender during or immediately after the commission of the offense caused serious physical harm to the victim)."

**HISTORY: 151 v S 260, § 1, eff. 1-2-07.**

## § 2941.1421 Specification that prostitution-related offense was committed in proximity to school.

(A) Imposition of an additional prison term of one, two, three, four, five, or six months under division (H)(2)(a)(i) of section 2929.14 of the Revised Code, an additional prison term of one, two, three, four, five, six, seven, eight, nine, ten, eleven, or twelve months under division (H)(2)(a)(ii) of section 2929.14 of the Revised Code, an additional definite jail term of not more than sixty days under division (F)(1)(a) of section 2929.24 of the Revised Code, or an additional definite jail term of not more than one hundred twenty days under division (F)(1)(b) of section 2929.24 of the Revised Code is precluded unless the indictment, count in the indictment, or information charging a felony violation of section 2907.22, 2907.24, 2907.241, or 2907.25 of the Revised Code or a misdemeanor violation of section 2907.23, 2907.24, 2907.241, or 2907.25 of the Revised Code, whichever is applicable, specifies that the violation was committed in proximity to a school. The specification shall be stated at the end of the body of the indictment, count, or information and shall be in substantially the following form:

"SPECIFICATION (or, SPECIFICATION TO THE FIRST COUNT). The Grand Jurors (or insert the person's or the prosecuting attorney's name when appropriate) further find and specify that (set forth that the specified offense was committed in proximity to a school).

(B) As used in this section, "committed in proximity to a school" has the same meaning as in section 2929.01 of the Revised Code.

**HISTORY: 152 v S 220, § 1, eff. 9-30-08; 2011 HB 86, § 1, eff. Sept. 30, 2011.**

## § 2941.1422 Human trafficking specification.

(A) Imposition of a mandatory prison term under division (B)(7) of section 2929.14 of the Revised Code is precluded unless the offender is convicted of or pleads guilty to a felony violation of section 2905.01, 2905.02, 2907.21, 2907.22, or 2923.32, division (A)(1) or (2) of section 2907.323, or division (B)(1), (2), (3), (4), or (5) of section 2919.22 of the Revised Code and unless the indictment, count in the indictment, or information charging the offense specifies that the offender knowingly committed the offense in furtherance of human trafficking. The specification shall be stated at the end of the body of the indictment, count, or information and shall be stated in substantially the following form:

"SPECIFICATION (or, SPECIFICATION TO THE FIRST COUNT). The Grand Jurors (or insert the person's or the prosecuting attorney's name when appropriate) further find and specify that (set forth that the defendant knowingly committed the offense in furtherance of human trafficking)."

(B) As used in this section, "human trafficking" has the same meaning as in section 2929.01 of the Revised Code.

**HISTORY: 152 v H 280, § 1, eff. 4-7-09; 2011 HB 86, § 1, eff. Sept. 30, 2011.**

The provisions of § 3 of 152 v H 280 read as follows:

SECTION 3. (A) The General Assembly strongly encourages the Attorney General to establish a Trafficking in Persons Study Commission. If the Attorney General establishes the Commission, it shall be composed of the number of members determined by the Attorney General. The Attorney General shall appoint the members, and each member shall be qualified by education or experience in subject matters that are relevant to the functions and duties of the Commission specified in division (B) of this section. If the Attorney General establishes the Commission, the Attorney General shall notify the Governor, the President and Minority Leader of the Senate, and the Speaker and Minority Leader of the House of Representatives. When all members of the Commission have been appointed, the Commission promptly shall meet, select a chairperson and a vice-chairperson, and organize its activities.

(B) If the Attorney General establishes a Trafficking in Persons Study Commission under division (A) of this section, the Commission shall: (1) study and review the problem of trafficking in persons, particularly as it affects this state or occurs in this state; (2) study and review the criminal law of this state to determine the manner and extent to which it currently applies to conduct that involves or is related to trafficking in persons, including the criminal offenses of this state that currently apply to such conduct and the penalties for those offenses; and (3) develop recommendations to address the problem of trafficking in persons and to improve and expand as necessary the criminal law of this state to better address conduct that involves or is related to trafficking in persons.

(C) If the Attorney General establishes a Trafficking in Persons Study Commission under division (A) of this section, upon completing its functions and duties under division (B) of this section, the Commission shall prepare a report that summarizes its findings and its recommendations for changes in the law of this state. The Commission shall deliver a copy of the report to the Governor, the Attorney General, the President and Minority Leader of the Senate, and the Speaker and Minority Leader of the House of Representatives.

## § 2941.1423 Pregnant victim specification.

Imposition of a mandatory prison term under division (B)(8) of section 2929.14 of the Revised Code or a mandatory jail term under division (F) of section 2929.24 of the Revised Code is precluded unless the offender is convicted of or pleads guilty to a violation of section 2903.11, 2903.12, or 2903.13 of the Revised Code and unless the indictment, count in the indictment, or information charging the offense specifies the victim of the offense was a woman whom the offender knew was pregnant at the time of the offense. The specification shall be stated at the end of the body of the indictment, count, or information and shall be stated in substantially the following form:

"SPECIFICATION (or, SPECIFICATION TO THE FIRST COUNT). The Grand Jurors (or insert the person's or prosecuting attorney's name when appropriate) further find and specify that (set forth that the victim of the offense was a woman whom the defendant knew was pregnant at the time of the offense)."

**HISTORY: 152 v H 280, § 1, eff. 4-7-09; 2011 HB 86, § 1, eff. Sept. 30, 2011.**

## § 2941.15 Sufficiency of indictment for forgery.

In an indictment or information for falsely making, altering, forging, printing, photographing, uttering, disposing of, or putting off an instrument, it is sufficient to set forth the purport and value thereof. Where the instrument is a promise to pay money conditionally, it is not necessary to allege that the condition has been performed.

**HISTORY: GC § 13437-14; 113 v 123(166), ch 16, § 14; Bureau of Code Revision. Eff 10-1-53.**

## § 2941.16 Sufficient description for forgery.

In an indictment or information for engraving or making the whole or part of an instrument, matter, or thing, or for using or having the unlawful custody or possession of a plate or other material upon which the whole or part of an instrument, matter, or thing was engraved or made, or for having the unlawful custody or possession of a paper upon which the whole or part of an instrument, matter, or thing was made or printed, it is sufficient to describe such instrument, matter, or thing by any name or designation by which it is usually known.

**HISTORY: GC § 13437-15; 113 v 123(166), ch 16, § 15; Bureau of Code Revision. Eff 10-1-53.**

## § 2941.17 Description by usual name or purport.

In all cases when it is necessary to make an averment in an indictment or information as to a writing, instrument, tool, or thing, it is sufficient to describe it by any name or designation by which it is usually known, or by the purport thereof.

**HISTORY: GC § 13437-16; 113 v 123(167), ch 16, § 16; Bureau of Code Revision, 10-1-53; 134 v H 511. Eff 1-1-74.**

## § 2941.18 Allegations in perjury indictment.

In an indictment or information for perjury or falsification, it is not necessary to set forth any part of a record or proceeding, or the commission or authority of the court or other authority before which perjury or falsification was committed.

**HISTORY: GC § 13437-17; 113 v 123(167), ch 16, § 17; Bureau of Code Revision, 10-1-53; 134 v H 511. Eff 1-1-74.**

## § 2941.19 Alleging intent to defraud.

It is sufficient in an indictment or information where it is necessary to allege an intent to defraud, to allege that the accused did the act with intent to defraud, without alleging an intent to defraud a particular person or corporation. On the trial of such an indictment or information, an intent to defraud a particular person need not be proved. It is sufficient to prove that the accused did the act charged with intent to defraud.

**HISTORY: GC § 13437-18; 113 v 123(167), ch 16, § 18; Bureau of Code Revision. Eff 10-1-53.**

## § 2941.20 Allegations sufficient for unlawfully selling liquor.

An indictment, information, or affidavit charging a violation of law relative to the sale, possession, transportation, buying, or giving intoxicating liquor to any person, need not allege the kind of liquor sold, nor the person by whom bought except that such charge must be sufficient to inform the accused of the particular offense with which he is charged.

**HISTORY: GC § 13437-19; 113 v 123(167), ch 16, § 19; Bureau of Code Revision. Eff 10-1-53.**

## § 2941.21 Averments as to joint ownership.

In an indictment or information for an offense committed upon, or in relation to, property belonging to partners or joint owners, it is sufficient to allege the ownership of such property to be in such partnership by its firm name, or in one or more of such partners or owners without naming all of them.

**HISTORY: GC § 13437-20; 113 v 123(167), ch 16, § 20; Bureau of Code Revision. Eff 10-1-53.**

## § 2941.22 Averments as to will or codicil.

In an indictment or information for stealing a will, codicil, or other testamentary instrument, or for forgery thereof, or, for a fraudulent purpose, keeping, destroying, or secreting it, whether in relation to real or personal property, or during the life of a testator or after his death, it is not necessary to allege the ownership or value thereof.

**HISTORY: GC § 13437-21; 113 v 123(167), ch 16, § 21; Bureau of Code Revision. Eff 10-1-53.**

## § 2941.23 Averments as to election.

In an indictment or information for an offense committed in relation to an election, it is sufficient to allege that such election was authorized by law, without stating the names of the officers holding it or the person voted for or the offices to be filled at the election.

**HISTORY: GC § 13437-22; 113 v 123(167), ch 16, § 22; Bureau of Code Revision. Eff 10-1-53.**

## § 2941.24 Repealed, 135 v H 716, § 2 [GC § 13437-23; 113 v 123(168); Bureau of Code Revision, 10-1-53]. Eff 1-1-74.

This section concerned counts for embezzlement and larceny.

## § 2941.25 Multiple counts.

(A) Where the same conduct by defendant can be construed to constitute two or more allied offenses of similar import, the indictment or information may contain counts for all such offenses, but the defendant may be convicted of only one.

(B) Where the defendant's conduct constitutes two or more offenses of dissimilar import, or where his conduct results in two or more offenses of the same or similar kind committed separately or with a separate animus as to each, the indictment or information may contain counts for all such offenses, and the defendant may be convicted of all of them.

**HISTORY: 134 v H 511. Eff 1-1-74.**

**Not analogous to former RC § 2941.25 (GC § 13437-24; 113 v 123(168); Bureau of Code Revision, 10-1-53), repealed 134 v H 511, § 2, eff 1-1-74.**

## § 2941.26 Variance.

When, on the trial of an indictment or information, there appears to be a variance between the statement in such indictment or information and the evidence offered in proof thereof, in the Christian name or surname, or other description of a person therein named or described, or in the name or description of a matter or thing therein named or described, such variance is not ground for an acquittal of the defendant unless the court before which the trial is had finds that such variance is material to the merits of the case or may be prejudicial to the defendant.

**HISTORY: GC § 13437-25; 113 v 123(168), ch 16, § 25; Bureau of Code Revision. Eff 10-1-53.**

## § 2941.27 Proof of dilatory plea.

No plea in abatement, or other dilatory plea to the indictment or information, shall be received by any court unless the party offering such plan proves the truth thereof by affidavit, or by some other sworn evidence.

**HISTORY: GC § 13437-26; 113 v 123(168), ch 16, § 26; Bureau of Code Revision. Eff 10-1-53.**

## § 2941.28 Misjoinder of parties or offenses.

No indictment or information shall be quashed, set aside, or dismissed for any of the following defects:

(A) That there is a misjoinder of the parties accused;

(B) That there is a misjoinder of the offenses charged in the indictment or information, or duplicity therein;

(C) That any uncertainty exists therein.

If the court is of the opinion that either defect referred to in division (A) or (B) of this section exists in any indictment or information, it may sever such indictment or information into separate indictments or informations or into separate counts.

If the court is of the opinion that the defect referred to in division (C) of this section exists in the indictment or information, it may order the indictment or information amended to cure such defect, provided no change is made in the name or identity of the crime charged.

**HISTORY: GC § 13437-27; 113 v 123(168), ch 16, § 27; Bureau of Code Revision. Eff 10-1-53.**

## § 2941.29 Time for objecting to defect in indictment.

No indictment or information shall be quashed, set aside, or dismissed, or motion to quash be sustained, or any motion for delay of sentence for the purpose of review be granted, nor shall any conviction be set aside or reversed on account of any defect in form or substance of the indictment or information, unless the objection to such indictment or information, specifically stating the defect claimed, is made prior to the commencement of the trial, or at such time thereafter as the court permits.

**HISTORY: GC § 13437-28; 113 v 123(169), ch 16, § 28; Bureau of Code Revision. Eff 10-1-53.**

## § 2941.30 Amending an indictment.

The court may at any time before, during, or after a trial amend the indictment, information, or bill of particulars, in respect to any defect, imperfection, or omission in form or substance, or of any variance with the evidence, provided no change is made in the name or identity of the crime charged. If any amendment is made to the substance of the indictment or information or to cure a variance between the indictment or information and the proof, the accused is entitled to a discharge of the jury on his motion, if a jury has been impaneled, and to a reasonable continuance of the cause, unless it clearly appears from the whole proceedings that he has not been misled or prejudiced by the defect or variance in respect to which the amendment is made, or that his rights will be fully protected by proceeding with the trial, or by a postponement thereof to a later day with the same or another jury. In case a jury is discharged from further consideration of a case under this section, the accused was not in jeopardy. No action of the court in refusing a continuance or postponement under this section is reviewable except after motion to and refusal by the trial court to grant a new trial therefor, and no appeal based upon such action of the court shall be sustained, nor reversal had, unless from consideration of the whole proceedings, the reviewing court finds that the accused was prejudiced in his defense or that a failure of justice resulted.

**HISTORY: GC § 13437-29; 113 v 123(169), ch 16, § 29; Bureau of Code Revision. Eff 10-1-53.**

## § 2941.31 Record of quashed indictment.

In criminal prosecutions, when the indictment or information has been quashed or the prosecuting attorney has entered a nolle prosequi thereon, or the cause or indictment is disposed of otherwise than upon trial, a complete record shall not be made by the clerk of the court of common pleas unless ordered to do so by the court of common pleas.

**HISTORY: GC § 13437-30; 113 v 123(169), ch 16, § 30; 115 v 530; Bureau of Code Revision. Eff 10-1-53.**

## § 2941.32 Proceedings when two indictments pending.

If two or more indictments or informations are pending against the same defendant for the same criminal act, the prosecuting attorney must elect upon which he will proceed, and upon trial being had upon one of them, the remaining indictments or information shall be quashed.

**HISTORY: GC § 13437-31; 113 v 123(170), ch 16, § 31; Bureau of Code Revision. Eff 10-1-53.**

## § 2941.33 Nolle prosequi.

The prosecuting attorney shall not enter a nolle prosequi in any cause without leave of the court, on good cause shown, in open court. A nolle prosequi entered contrary to this section is invalid.

**HISTORY: GC § 13437-32; 113 v 123(170), ch 16, § 32; Bureau of Code Revision. Eff 10-1-53.**

## § 2941.34 Lost or destroyed indictment.

If an indictment or information is mutilated, obliterated, lost, mislaid, destroyed, or stolen, or for any other reason cannot be produced at the arraignment or trial of the defendant, the court may substitute a copy.

**HISTORY: GC § 13437-33; 113 v 123(170), ch 16, § 33; Bureau of Code Revision, 10-1-53; 127 v 847. Eff 9-16-57.**

## § 2941.35 Prosecutions for misdemeanor.

Prosecutions for misdemeanors may be instituted by a prosecuting attorney by affidavit or such other method as is provided by law in such courts as have original jurisdiction in misdemeanors. Laws as to form, sufficiency, amendments, objections, and exceptions to indictments and as to the service thereof apply to such affidavits and warrants issued thereon.

**HISTORY: GC § 13437-34; 113 v 123(170), ch 16, § 34; 121 v 121; Bureau of Code Revision. Eff 10-1-53.**

### [PROCESS ON INDICTMENTS]

## § 2941.36 Warrant for arrest of accused.

A warrant may be issued at any time by an order of a court, or on motion of a prosecuting attorney after the indictment, information, or affidavit is filed. When directed to the sheriff of the county where such indictment was found or information or affidavit filed, he may pursue and arrest the accused in any county and commit him to jail or present him in open court, if court is in session.

**HISTORY: GC § 13438-1; 113 v 123(170), ch 17; Bureau of Code Revision. Eff 10-1-53.**

## § 2941.37 Warrant when accused is nonresident.

When an accused resides out of the county in which the indictment was found or information filed, a warrant may issue thereon, directed to the sheriff of the county where such accused resides or is found. Such sheriff shall arrest the accused and convey him to the county from which such warrant was issued, and there commit him to jail or present him in open court, if court is in session.

**HISTORY: GC § 13438-2; 113 v 123(170), ch 17, § 2; Bureau of Code Revision. Eff 10-1-53.**

## § 2941.38 Warrant when accused escapes.

When an accused escapes and forfeits his recognizance after the jury is sworn, a warrant reciting the facts may issue at the request of the prosecuting attorney, to the sheriff of any county, who shall pursue, arrest, and commit the accused to the jail of the county from which such warrant issued, until he is discharged.

**HISTORY: GC § 13438-3; 113 v 123(171), ch 17, § 3; Bureau of Code Revision. Eff 10-1-53.**

## § 2941.39 Indictment of convicts.

When a convict in a state correctional institution is indicted for a felony committed while confined in the correctional institution, the convict shall remain in the custody of the department of rehabilitation and correction, subject to sections 2941.40 to 2941.46 of the Revised Code.

**HISTORY: GC § 13438-4; 113 v 123(171), ch 17, § 4; Bureau of Code Revision, 10-1-53; 145 v H 571 (Eff 10-6-94); 147 v S 111. Eff 3-17-98.**

## § 2941.40 Convicts removed for sentence or trial.

A convict in a state correctional institution, who escaped, forfeited his recognizance before receiving sentence for a felony, or against whom an indictment or information for felony is pending, may be removed to the county in which the conviction was had or the indictment or information was pending for sentence or trial, upon the warrant of the court of common pleas of the county.

**HISTORY: GC § 13438-5; 113 v 123(171), ch 17, § 5; Bureau of Code Revision, 10-1-53; 133 v H 508 (Eff 10-24-69); 145 v H 571. Eff 10-6-94.**

## § 2941.401 Prisoner may request trial on pending charges.

When a person has entered upon a term of imprisonment in a correctional institution of this state, and when during the continuance of the term of imprisonment there is pending in this state any untried indictment, information, or complaint against the prisoner, he shall be brought to trial within one hundred eighty days after he causes to be delivered to the prosecuting attorney and the appropriate court in which the matter is pending, written notice of the place of his imprisonment and a request for a final disposition to be made of the matter, except that for good cause shown in open court, with the prisoner or his counsel present, the court may grant any necessary or reasonable continuance. The request of the prisoner shall be accompanied by a certificate of the warden or superintendent having custody of the prisoner, stating the term of commitment under which the prisoner is being held, the time served and remaining to be served on the sentence, the amount of good time earned, the time of parole eligibility of the prisoner, and any decisions of the adult parole authority relating to the prisoner.

The written notice and request for final disposition shall be given or sent by the prisoner to the warden or superintendent having custody of him, who shall promptly forward it with the certificate to the appropriate prosecuting attorney and court by registered or certified mail, return receipt requested.

The warden or superintendent having custody of the prisoner shall promptly inform him in writing of the source and contents of any untried indictment, information, or complaint against him, concerning which the warden or superintendent has knowledge, and of his right to make a request for final disposition thereof.

Escape from custody by the prisoner, subsequent to his execution of the request for final disposition, voids the request.

If the action is not brought to trial within the time provided, subject to continuance allowed pursuant to this section, no court any longer has jurisdiction thereof, the indictment, information, or complaint is void, and the court shall enter an order dismissing the action with prejudice.

This section does not apply to any person adjudged to be mentally ill or who is under sentence of life imprisonment or death, or to any prisoner under sentence of death.

**HISTORY: 133 v S 355 (Eff 11-18-69); 145 v H 571. Eff 10-6-94.**

## § 2941.41 Warrant for removal.

A warrant for removal specified in section 2941.40 of the Revised Code shall be in the usual form, except that it shall set forth that the accused is in a state correctional institution. The warrant shall be directed to the sheriff of the county in which the conviction was had or the indictment or information is pending. When a copy of the warrant is presented to the warden or the superintendent of a state correctional institution, he shall deliver the convict to the sheriff who shall convey him to the county and commit him to the county jail. For removing and returning the convict, the sheriff shall receive the fees allowed for conveying convicts to a state correctional institution.

**HISTORY: GC § 13438-6; 113 v 123(171), ch 17, § 6; Bureau of Code Revision, 10-1-53; 139 v H 145 (Eff 5-28-81); 145 v H 571. Eff 10-6-94.**

## § 2941.42 Convict to be confined.

A convict removed as provided by section 2941.41 of the Revised Code shall be kept in jail subject to be taken into court for sentence or trial. If the case is continued or the execution of the sentence is suspended, the court may order him to be returned to the state correctional institution by the sheriff, who shall deliver him, with a certified copy of the order, to the warden, who shall again deliver the convict to the sheriff upon another certified order of the court.

**HISTORY: GC § 13438-7; 113 v 123(171), ch 17, § 7; Bureau of Code Revision, 10-1-53; 145 v H 571. Eff 10-6-94.**

## § 2941.43 Disposition of prisoner following trial for another offense.

If the convict referred to in section 2941.40 of the Revised Code is acquitted, he shall [be]† forthwith returned by the sheriff to the state correctional institution to serve out the remainder of his sentence. If he is sentenced to imprisonment in a state correctional institution, he shall be returned to the state correctional institution by the sheriff to serve his new term. If he is sentenced to death, the death sentence shall be executed as if he were not under sentence of imprisonment in a state correctional institution.

**HISTORY: GC § 13438-8; 113 v 123(172), ch 17, § 8; Bureau of Code Revision, 10-1-53; 131 v 679 (Eff 10-30-65); 134 v H 511 (Eff 1-1-74); 145 v H 571. Eff 10-6-94.**

† So in enrolled bill. But see version in 134 v H 511.

## § 2941.44 Arrest and return of escaped convicts; expenses.

Sheriffs, deputy sheriffs, marshals, deputy marshals, watchmen, police officers, and coroners may arrest a convict escaping from a state correctional institution and forthwith convey him to the institution and deliver him to the warden of the institution. They shall be allowed ten cents per mile going to and returning from the institution and additional compensation that the warden finds reasonable for the necessary expense incurred.

**HISTORY: GC § 13438-9; 113 v 123(172), ch 17, § 9; Bureau of Code Revision, 10-1-53; 128 v 542 (Eff 7-17-59); 145 v H 571. Eff 10-6-94.**

## § 2941.45 Trial of persons serving sentence.

Any person serving a sentence in jail or the workhouse, who is indicted or informed against for another offense, may be brought before the court of common pleas upon warrant for that purpose, for arraignment and trial. Such person shall remain in the custody of the jailer or keeper of the workhouse, but may be temporarily confined in the jail, if a prisoner in the workhouse.

If such prisoner is convicted and sentenced upon trial, he shall be returned to the jail or workhouse to serve out the former sentence before the subsequent sentence is executed.

**HISTORY: GC § 13438-10; 113 v 123(172), ch 17, § 10; Bureau of Code Revision. Eff 10-1-53.**

## § 2941.46 Arrest of convict or prisoner violating pardon or parole.

(A) If a convict has been conditionally pardoned or a prisoner has been paroled from any state correctional institution, any peace officer may arrest the convict or prisoner without a warrant if the peace officer has reasonable ground to believe that the convict or prisoner has violated or is violating any rule governing the conduct of paroled prisoners prescribed by the adult parole authority or any of the following that is a condition of his pardon or parole:

(1) A condition that prohibits his ownership, possession, or use of a firearm, deadly weapon, ammunition, or dangerous ordnance;

(2) A condition that prohibits him from being within a specified structure or geographic area;

(3) A condition that confines him to a residence, facility, or other structure;

(4) A condition that prohibits him from contacting or communicating with any specified individual;

(5) A condition that prohibits him from associating with a specified individual.

(B) Upon making an arrest under this section, the arresting peace officer or his department or agency promptly shall notify the authority that the convict or prisoner has been arrested.

(C) Nothing in this section limits, or shall be construed to limit, the powers of arrest granted to certain law enforcement officers and citizens under sections 2935.03 and 2935.04 of the Revised Code.

(D) As used in this section:

(1) "State correctional institution," "pardon," "parole," "convict," and "prisoner" have the same meanings as in section 2967.01 of the Revised Code.

(2) "Peace officer" has the same meaning as in section 2935.01 of the Revised Code.

(3) "Firearm," "deadly weapon," and "dangerous ordnance" have the same meanings as in section 2923.11 of the Revised Code.

**HISTORY: GC § 13438-11; 113 v 123(172), ch 17, § 11; 118 v 288(302), § 25; Bureau of Code Revision, 10-1-53; 130 v PtII, 146 (Eff 3-18-65); 144 v S 49 (Eff 7-21-92); 145 v H 571. Eff 10-6-94.**

## § 2941.47 Summons on indictments against corporations.

When an indictment is returned or information filed against a corporation, a summons commanding the sheriff to notify the accused thereof, returnable on the seventh day after its date, shall issue on praecipe of the prosecuting attorney. Such summons with a copy of the indictment shall be served and returned in the manner provided for service of summons upon corporations in civil actions. If the service cannot be made in the county where the prosecution began, the sheriff may make service in any other county of the state, upon the president, secretary, superintendent, clerk, treasurer, cashier, managing agent, or other chief officer thereof, or by leaving a copy at a general or branch office or usual place of doing business of such corporation, with the person having charge thereof. Such corporation shall appear by one of its officers or by counsel on or before the return day of the summons served and answer to the indictment or information by motion, demurrer, or plea, and upon failure to make such appearance and answer, the clerk of the court of common pleas shall enter a plea of "not guilty." Upon such appearance being made or plea entered, the corporation is before the court until the case is finally disposed of. On said indictment or information no warrant of arrest may issue except for individuals who may be included in such indictment or information.

**HISTORY: GC § 13438-12; 113 v 123(172), ch 17, § 12; Bureau of Code Revision. Eff 10-1-53.**

## § 2941.48 Recognizance of witnesses.

In any case pending in the court of common pleas, the court, either before or after indictment, may require any witness designated by the prosecuting attorney to enter into a recognizance, with or without surety, in such sum as the court thinks proper for his appearance to testify in such cause. A witness failing or refusing to comply with such order shall be committed to the county jail until he gives his testimony in such case or is ordered discharged by the court. If a witness is committed to jail upon order of court for want of such recognizance, he shall be paid while so confined like fees as are allowed witnesses by section 2335.08 of the Revised Code. The trial of such case has precedence over other cases and the court shall designate any early day for such trial.

**HISTORY: GC § 13438-13; 113 v 123(173), ch 17, § 13; Bureau of Code Revision. Eff 10-1-53.**

### [SERVICE OF INDICTMENT AND EXCEPTIONS]

## § 2941.49 Indictment to be served on accused.

Within three days after the filing of an indictment for felony and in every other case when requested, the clerk of the court of common pleas shall make and deliver to the sheriff, defendant, or the defendant's counsel, a copy of such indictment. The sheriff, on receiving such copy, shall serve it on the defendant. A defendant, without his assent, shall not be arraigned or called on to answer to an indictment until one day has elapsed after receiving or having an opportunity to receive in person or by counsel, a copy of such indictment.

**HISTORY: GC § 13439-1; 113 v 123(173), ch 18; Bureau of Code Revision. Eff 10-1-53.**

## § 2941.50 Repealed, 136 v H 164, § 2 [GC § 13439-2; 113 v 123(173); Bureau of Code Revision, 10-1-53; 130 v 666; 131 v 679; 132 v S 486]. Eff 1-13-76.

This section concerned assigning counsel to defend.

## § 2941.51 Payment of appointed or selected counsel.

(A) Counsel appointed to a case or selected by an indigent person under division (E) of section 120.16 or division (E) of section 120.26 of the Revised Code, or otherwise appointed by the court, except for counsel appointed by the court to provide legal representation for a person charged with a violation of an ordinance of a municipal corporation, shall be paid for their services by the county the compensation and expenses that the trial court approves. Each request for payment shall be accompanied by a financial disclosure form and an affidavit of indigency that are completed by the indigent person on forms prescribed by the state public defender. Compensation and expenses shall not exceed the amounts fixed by the board of county commissioners pursuant to division (B) of this section.

(B) The board of county commissioners shall establish a schedule of fees by case or on an hourly basis to be paid by the county for legal services provided by appointed counsel. Prior to establishing such schedule, the board shall request the bar association or associations of the county to submit a proposed schedule. The schedule submitted shall be subject to the review, amendment, and approval of the board of county commissioners.

(C) In a case where counsel have been appointed to conduct an appeal under Chapter 120. of the Revised Code, such compensation shall be fixed by the court of appeals or the supreme court, as provided in divisions (A) and (B) of this section.

(D) The fees and expenses approved by the court under this section shall not be taxed as part of the costs and shall be paid by the county. However, if the person represented has, or reasonably may be expected to have, the means to meet some part of the cost of the services rendered to the person, the person shall pay the county an amount that the person reasonably can be expected to pay. Pursuant to section 120.04 of the Revised Code, the county shall pay to the state public defender a percentage of the payment received from the person in an amount proportionate to the percentage of the costs of the person's case that were paid to the county by the state public defender pursuant to this section. The money paid to the state public defender shall be credited to the client payment fund created pursuant to division (B)(5) of section 120.04 of the Revised Code.

(E) The county auditor shall draw a warrant on the county treasurer for the payment of such counsel in the amount fixed by the court, plus the expenses that the court fixes and certifies to the auditor. The county auditor shall report periodically, but not less than annually, to the board of county commissioners and to the Ohio public defender commission the amounts paid out pursuant to the approval of the court under this section, separately stating costs and expenses that are reimbursable under section 120.35 of the Revised Code. The board, after review and approval of the auditor's report, may then certify it to the state public defender for reimbursement. The request for reimbursement shall be accompanied by a financial disclosure form completed by each indigent person for whom counsel was provided on a form prescribed by the state public defender. The state public defender shall review the report and, in accordance with the standards, guidelines, and maximums established pursuant to divisions (B)(7) and (8) of section 120.04 of the Revised Code, pay fifty per cent of the total cost, other than costs and expenses that are reimbursable under section 120.35 of the Revised Code, if any, of paying appointed counsel in each county and pay fifty per cent of costs and expenses that are reimbursable under section 120.35 of the Revised Code, if any, to the board.

(F) If any county system for paying appointed counsel fails to maintain the standards for the conduct of the system established by the rules of the Ohio public defender commission pursuant to divisions (B) and (C) of section 120.03 of the Revised Code or the standards established by the state public defender pursuant to division (B)(7) of section 120.04 of the Revised Code, the commission shall notify the board of county commissioners of the county that the county system for paying appointed counsel has failed to comply with its rules. Unless the board corrects the conduct of its appointed counsel system to comply with the rules within ninety days after the date of the notice, the state public defender may deny all or part of the county's reimbursement from the state provided for in this section.

**HISTORY: GC § 13439-3; 113 v 123(173), ch 18, § 3; 117 v 279; 122 v 301; Bureau of Code Revision, 10-1-53; 128 v 54 (Eff 11-9-59); 131 v 680 (Eff 11-11-65); 132 v H 1 (Eff 2-21-67); 136 v H 164; (Eff 1-13-76); 140 v H 291 (Eff 7-1-83); 140 v S 271 (Eff 9-26-84); 141 v H 201 (Eff 7-1-85); 146 v H 117 (Eff 6-30-95); 147 v H 215 (Eff 9-29-97); 148 v H 283. Eff 9-29-99.**

The effective date is set by section 162 of HB 283.

## § 2941.52 Repealed, 136 v H 164, § 2 [GC § 13439-4; 113 v 123(174); Bureau of Code Revision, 10-1-53]. Eff 1-13-76.

This section concerned reasonable time to except.

## § 2941.53 Exceptions to an indictment.

An accused may except to an indictment by:

(A) A motion to quash;

(B) A plea in abatement;

(C) A demurrer.

**HISTORY: GC § 13439-5; 113 v 123(174), ch 18, § 5; Bureau of Code Revision. Eff 10-1-53.**

## § 2941.54 Motion to quash.

A motion to quash may be made when there is a defect apparent upon the face of the record, within the meaning of sections 2941.02 to 2941.35, inclusive, of the Revised

Code, including defects in the form of indictment and in the manner in which an offense is charged.

**HISTORY: GC § 13439-6; 113 v 123(174), ch 18, § 6; Bureau of Code Revision. Eff 10-1-53.**

## § 2941.55 Plea in abatement.

Plea in abatement may be made when there is a defect in the record shown by facts extrinsic thereto.

**HISTORY: GC § 13439-7; 113 v 123(174), ch 18, § 7; Bureau of Code Revision. Eff 10-1-53.**

## § 2941.56 Misnomer.

If the accused pleads in abatement that he is not indicted by his true name, he must plead his true name which shall be entered on the minutes of the court. After such entry, the trial and proceedings on the indictment shall be had against him by that name, referring also to the name by which he is indicted, as if he had been indicted by his true name.

**HISTORY: GC § 13439-8; 113 v 123(174), ch 18, § 8; Bureau of Code Revision. Eff 10-1-53.**

## § 2941.57 Demurrer.

The accused may demur:

(A) When the facts stated in the indictment do not constitute an offense punishable by the laws of this state;

(B) When the intent is not alleged and proof thereof is necessary to make out the offense charged;

(C) When it appears on the face of the indictment that the offense charged is not within the jurisdiction of the court.

**HISTORY: GC § 13439-9; 113 v 123(174), ch 18, § 9; Bureau of Code Revision. Eff 10-1-53.**

## § 2941.58 Accused not discharged when indictment quashed.

When a motion to quash or a plea in abatement is adjudged in favor of the accused, the trial court may order the case to be resubmitted to the grand jury, if then pending, or to the next succeeding grand jury. The accused then may be committed to jail or held to bail in such sum as the trial court requires for his appearance to answer at a time to be fixed by the court.

**HISTORY: GC § 13439-10; 113 v 123(174), ch 18, § 10; Bureau of Code Revision. Eff 10-1-53.**

## § 2941.59 Waiver of defects.

The accused waives all defects which may be excepted to by a motion to quash or a plea in abatement, by demurring to an indictment, or by pleading in bar or the general issue.

**HISTORY: GC § 13439-11; 113 v 123(175), ch 18, § 11; Bureau of Code Revision. Eff 10-1-53.**

## § 2941.60 Answer to plea in abatement.

The prosecuting attorney may demur to a plea in abatement if it is not sufficient in substance, or he may reply, setting forth any facts which may show there is no defect in the record as charged in the plea.

**HISTORY: GC § 13439-12; 113 v 123(175), ch 18, § 12; Bureau of Code Revision. Eff 10-1-53.**

## § 2941.61 After demurrer accused may plead.

After a demurrer to an indictment is overruled, the accused may plead under section 2943.03 of the Revised Code.

**HISTORY: GC § 13439-13; 113 v 123(175), ch 18, § 13; Bureau of Code Revision. Eff 10-1-53.**

## § 2941.62 Hearing on motions and demurrers.

Motions to quash, pleas in abatement, and demurrers shall be heard immediately upon their filing, unless the trial court, for good cause shown, sets another time for such hearing.

**HISTORY: GC § 13439-14; 113 v 123(175), ch 18, § 14; Bureau of Code Revision. Eff 10-1-53.**

## § 2941.63 Counsel to assist prosecutor.

The court of common pleas, or the court of appeals, whenever it is of the opinion that the public interest requires it, may appoint an attorney to assist the prosecuting attorney in the trial of a case pending in such court. The board of county commissioners shall pay said assistant to the prosecuting attorney such compensation for his services as the court approves.

**HISTORY: GC § 13439-15; 113 v 123(175), ch 18, § 15; Bureau of Code Revision. Eff 10-1-53.**

# CHAPTER 2943: ARRAIGNMENT; PLEAS



## § 2943.01 Definition of magistrate.

The definition of "magistrate" set forth in section 2931.01 of the Revised Code applies to Chapter 2943. of the Revised Code.

**HISTORY: Bureau of Code Revision. Eff 10-1-53.**

## § 2943.02 Arraignment.

An accused person shall be arraigned by the clerk of the court of common pleas, or his deputy, reading the indictment or information to the accused, unless the accused or his attorney waives the reading thereof. He shall then be asked to plead thereto. Arraignment shall be made immediately after the disposition of exceptions to the indictment, if any are filed, or, if no exceptions are filed, after reasonable opportunity has been given the accused to file such exceptions.

**HISTORY: GC § 13440-1; 113 v 123(175), ch 19; Bureau of Code Revision. Eff 10-1-53.**

## § 2943.03 Pleas to indictment.

Pleas to an indictment or information are:

(A) Guilty;

(B) Not guilty;

(C) A former judgment of conviction or acquittal of the offense;

(D) Once in jeopardy;

(E) Not guilty by reason of insanity.

A defendant who does not plead guilty may enter one or more of the other pleas. A defendant who does not plead not guilty by reason of insanity is conclusively presumed to have been sane at the time of the commission of the offense charged. The court may, for good cause shown, allow a change of plea at any time before the commencement of the trial.

**HISTORY: GC § 13440-2; 113 v 123(175), ch 19, § 2; Bureau of Code Revision. Eff 10-1-53.**

## § 2943.031 Advice as to possible deportation, exclusion or denial of naturalization upon guilty or no contest plea.

(A) Except as provided in division (B) of this section, prior to accepting a plea of guilty or a plea of no contest to an indictment, information, or complaint charging a felony or a misdemeanor other than a minor misdemeanor if the defendant previously has not been convicted of or pleaded guilty to a minor misdemeanor, the court shall address the defendant personally, provide the following advisement to the defendant that shall be entered in the record of the court, and determine that the defendant understands the advisement:

"If you are not a citizen of the United States you are hereby advised that conviction of the offense to which you are pleading guilty (or no contest, when applicable) may have the consequences of deportation, exclusion from admission to the United States, or denial of naturalization pursuant to the laws of the United States."

Upon request of the defendant, the court shall allow him additional time to consider the appropriateness of the plea in light of the advisement described in this division.

(B) The court is not required to give the advisement described in division (A) of this section if either of the following applies:

(1) The defendant enters a plea of guilty on a written form, the form includes a question asking whether the defendant is a citizen of the United States, and the defendant answers that question in the affirmative;

(2) The defendant states orally on the record that he is a citizen of the United States.

(C) Except as provided in division (B) of this section, the defendant shall not be required at the time of entering a plea to disclose to the court his legal status in the United States.

(D) Upon motion of the defendant, the court shall set aside the judgment and permit the defendant to withdraw a plea of guilty or no contest and enter a plea of not guilty or not guilty by reason of insanity, if, after the effective date of this section, the court fails to provide the defendant the advisement described in division (A) of this section, the advisement is required by that division, and the defendant shows that he is not a citizen of the United States and that the conviction of the offense to which he pleaded guilty or no contest may result in his being subject to deportation, exclusion from admission to the United States, or denial of naturalization pursuant to the laws of the United States.

(E) In the absence of a record that the court provided the advisement described in division (A) of this section and if the advisement is required by that division, the defendant shall be presumed not to have received the advisement.

(F) Nothing in this section shall be construed as preventing a court, in the sound exercise of its discretion pursuant to Criminal Rule 32.1, from setting aside the judgment of conviction and permitting a defendant to withdraw his plea.

**HISTORY: 143 v S 95. Eff 10-2-89.**

## § 2943.032 Advice as to possible residential sanction for violation of condition.

Prior to accepting a guilty plea or a plea of no contest to an indictment, information, or complaint that charges a felony, the court shall inform the defendant personally that, if the defendant pleads guilty or no contest to the felony so charged or any other felony, if the court imposes a prison term upon the defendant for the felony, and if the offender violates the conditions of a post-release control sanction imposed by the parole board upon the completion of the stated prison term, the parole board may impose upon the offender a residential sanction that includes a new prison term of up to nine months.

**HISTORY: 146 v S 2. Eff 7-1-96; 152 v H 130, § 1, eff. 4-7-09.**

The effective date is set by section 6 of SB 2.

## § 2943.033 Notice of federal firearms provisions prior to guilty or no contest plea to certain misdemeanor offenses of violence.

(A) As used in this section, "person living as a spouse" means a person who is living or has lived with the defendant in a common law marital relationship, who otherwise is cohabiting with the defendant, or who otherwise has cohabited with the defendant within five years prior to the date of the alleged commission of the act in question.

(B) The notice required under division (C) of this section shall be provided to a defendant when the alleged victim is any of the following:

(1) A spouse, person living as a spouse, or former spouse of the defendant;

(2) A parent or child of the defendant;

(3) A parent or child of a spouse, person living as a spouse, or former spouse of the defendant;

(4) The natural parent of any child of whom the defendant is the other natural or putative natural parent.

(C) Prior to accepting a guilty plea or plea of no contest to an indictment, information, or complaint that charges a person with a misdemeanor offense of violence, the court shall inform the defendant either personally or in writing that under 18 U.S.C. 922(g)(9) it may be unlawful for the person to ship, transport, purchase, or possess a firearm or ammunition as a result of any conviction for a misdemeanor offense of violence. The plea may not be vacated based on a failure to inform the person so charged regarding the restrictions under 18 U.S.C. 922(g)(9).

**HISTORY: 152 v H 562, § 101.01, eff. 6-24-08.**

The effective date is set by § 812.20 of 152 v H 562.

## § 2943.04 Form of plea.

Pleas of guilty or not guilty may be oral. Pleas in all other cases shall be in writing, subscribed by the defendant or his counsel, and shall immediately be entered upon the minutes of the court.

**HISTORY: GC § 13440-3; 113 v 123(176), ch 19, § 3; Bureau of Code Revision. Eff 10-1-53.**

## § 2943.041 Repealed, 145 v S 186, § 2 [140 v S 172; 142 v S 6; 145 v H 571]. Eff 10-12-94.

This section concerned rights of victim or representative family member present at hearing or proceeding. See now RC Chapter 2930.

[DOUBLE JEOPARDY]

## § 2943.05 Form of plea of former conviction.

If a defendant pleads that he has had former judgment of conviction or acquittal, or has been once in jeopardy, he must set forth in his plea the court, time, and place of such conviction, acquittal, or jeopardy. No claim of former judgment of conviction or acquittal, or jeopardy may be given in evidence under the plea of not guilty.

**HISTORY: GC § 13440-4; 113 v 123(176), ch 19, § 4; Bureau of Code Revision. Eff 10-1-53.**

## § 2943.06 Trial of issue on plea of former conviction.

If a defendant pleads a judgment of conviction, acquittal, or former jeopardy, the prosecuting attorney may reply that there is no such conviction, acquittal, or jeopardy. The issue thus made shall be tried to a jury, and on such trial the defendant must produce the record of such conviction, acquittal, or jeopardy, and prove that he is the person charged in such record, and he may also introduce other evidence to establish the identity of such offense. If the prosecuting attorney demurs to said plea and said demurrer is overruled, the prosecuting attorney may then reply to said plea.

**HISTORY: GC § 13440-5; 113 v 123(176), ch 19, § 5; Bureau of Code Revision. Eff 10-1-53.**

## § 2943.07 What is not former acquittal.

If a defendant was formerly acquitted on the ground of variance between the indictment or information and the proof, or if the indictment or information was dismissed, without a judgment of acquittal, upon an objection to its form or substance, or in order to hold the defendant for a higher offense, it is not an acquittal of the same offense.

**HISTORY: GC § 13440-6; 113 v 123(176), ch 19, § 6; Bureau of Code Revision. Eff 10-1-53.**

## § 2943.08 What is former acquittal.

Whenever a defendant is acquitted on the merits, he is acquitted of the same offense, notwithstanding any defect in form or substance in the indictment or information on which the trial was had.

**HISTORY: GC § 13440-7; 113 v 123(176), ch 19, § 7; Bureau of Code Revision. Eff 10-1-53.**

## § 2943.09 Conviction or acquittal of a higher offense.

When a defendant has been convicted or acquitted, or has been once in jeopardy upon an indictment or information, the conviction, acquittal, or jeopardy is a bar to another indictment or information for the offense charged in the former indictment or information, or for an attempt to commit the same offense, or for an offense necessarily included therein, of which he might have been convicted under the former indictment or information.

**HISTORY: GC § 13440-8; 113 v 123(176), ch 19, § 8; Bureau of Code Revision. Eff 10-1-53.**

## § 2943.10 Proceedings after verdict on plea in bar.

If the issue on the plea in bar under section 2943.06 of the Revised Code is found for the defendant he shall be discharged. If the issue is found against the defendant the case shall proceed and be disposed of upon his other pleas.

**HISTORY: GC § 13440-9; 113 v 123(177), ch 19, § 9; Bureau of Code Revision. Eff 10-1-53.**

# CHAPTER 2945: TRIAL



## § 2945.01 Definition of magistrate.

The definition of "magistrate" set forth in section 2931.01 of the Revised Code applies to Chapter 2945. of the Revised Code.

**HISTORY: Bureau of Code Revision. Eff 10-1-53.**

## § 2945.02 Setting and continuing cases.

The court of common pleas shall set all criminal cases for trial for a day not later than thirty days after the date of entry of the plea of the defendant. No continuance of the trial shall be granted except upon affirmative proof in open court, upon reasonable notice, that the ends of justice require a continuance.

No continuance shall be granted for any other time than it is affirmatively proved the ends of justice require.

Whenever any continuance is granted, the court shall enter on the journal the reason for the same.

Criminal cases shall be given precedence over civil matters and proceedings. The failure of the court to set such criminal cases for trial, as required by this section, does not operate as an acquittal, but upon notice of such failure or upon motion of the prosecuting attorney or a defendant, such case shall forthwith be set for trial within a reasonable time, not exceeding thirty days thereafter.

**HISTORY: GC § 13442-1; 113 v 123(178), ch 21; Bureau of Code Revision. Eff 10-1-53.**

## § 2945.03 Control of trial.

The judge of the trial court shall control all proceedings during a criminal trial, and shall limit the introduction of evidence and the argument of counsel to relevant and material matters with a view to expeditious and effective ascertainment of the truth regarding the matters in issue.

**HISTORY: GC § 13442-2; 113 v 123(178), ch 21, § 2; Bureau of Code Revision. Eff 10-1-53.**

## § 2945.04 Orders to prevent intimidation of victim or witness; orders to prevent offenses against complainant or his ward, child or property.

(A) If a motion is filed with a court before which a criminal case is pending alleging that a person has committed or is reasonably likely to commit any act prohibited by section 2921.04 of the Revised Code in relation to the case, if the court holds a hearing on the motion, and if the court determines that the allegations made in the motion are true, the court may issue an order doing any or any combination of the following, subject to division (C) of this section:

(1) Directing the defendant in the case not to violate or to cease a violation of section 2921.04 of the Revised Code;

(2) Directing a person other than a defendant who is before the court, including, but not limited to, a subpoenaed witness or other person entering the courtroom of the court, not to violate or to cease a violation of section 2921.04 of the Revised Code;

(3) Directing the defendant or a person described in division (A)(2) of this section to maintain a prescribed geographic distance from any specified person who is before the court, including, but not limited to, the victim of the offense that is the basis of the case or a subpoenaed witness in the case;

(4) Directing the defendant or a person described in division (A)(2) of this section not to communicate with any specified person who is before the court, including, but not limited to, the victim of the offense or a subpoenaed witness in the case;

(5) Directing a specified law enforcement agency that serves a political subdivision within the territorial jurisdiction of the court to provide protection for any specified person who is before the court, including, but not limited to, the victim of the offense or a subpoenaed witness in the case;

(6) Any other reasonable order that would assist in preventing or causing the cessation of a violation of section 2921.04 of the Revised Code.

(B) If a motion is filed with a court in which a criminal complaint has been filed alleging that the offender or another person acting in concert with the offender has committed or is reasonably likely to commit any act that would constitute an offense against the person or property of the complainant, his ward, or his child, if the court holds a hearing on the motion, and if the court determines that the allegations made in the motion are true, the court may issue an order doing one or more of the following, subject to division (C) of this section:

(1) Directing the defendant in the case not to commit an act or to cease committing an act that constitutes an offense against the person or property of the complainant, his ward, or child;

(2) Directing a person other than the defendant who is before the court, including, but not limited to, a subpoenaed witness or other person entering the courtroom, not to commit an act or to cease committing an act that constitutes an offense against the person or property of the complainant, his ward, or child;

(3) Directing the defendant or a person described in division (B)(2) of this section to maintain a prescribed geographic distance from any specified person who is before the court, including, but not limited to, the complainant or the victim of the offense, or a subpoenaed witness in the case;

(4) Directing the defendant or a person described in division (B)(2) of this section not to communicate with any specified person who is before the court, including, but not limited to, the complainant, the victim of the offense, or a subpoenaed witness in the case;

(5) Directing a specified law enforcement agency that serves a political subdivision within the territorial jurisdiction of the court to provide protection for any specified person who is before the court, including, but not limited to, the complainant, the victim of the offense, or a subpoenaed witness in the case;

(6) When the complainant and the defendant cohabit with one another but the complainant is not a family or household member, as defined in section 2919.25 of the Revised Code, granting possession of the residence or household to the complainant to the exclusion of the defendant by evicting the defendant when the residence or household is owned or leased solely by the complainant or by ordering the defendant to vacate the premises when the residence or household is jointly owned or leased by the complainant and the defendant;

(7) Any other reasonable order that would assist in preventing or causing the cessation of an act that constitutes an offense against the person or property of the complainant, his ward, or child.

(C) No order issued under authority of division (A) or (B) of this section shall prohibit or be construed as prohibiting any attorney for the defendant in the case or for a person described in division (A)(2) or (B)(2) of this section from conducting any investigation of the pending criminal case, from preparing or conducting any defense of the pending criminal case, or from attempting to zealously represent his client in the pending criminal case within the bounds of the law. However, this division does not exempt any person from the prohibitions contained in section 2921.04 or any section of the Revised Code that constitutes an offense against the person or property of the complainant, his ward, or his child, or provide a defense to a charge of any violation of that section or of an offense of that nature.

(D)(1) A person who violates an order issued pursuant to division (A) of this section is subject to the following sanctions:

(a) Criminal prosecution for a violation of section 2921.04 of the Revised Code, if the violation of the court order constitutes a violation of that section;

(b) Punishment for contempt of court.

(2) A person who violates an order issued pursuant to division (B) of this section is subject to the following sanctions:

(a) Criminal prosecution for a violation of a section of the Revised Code that constitutes an offense against the person or property of the complainant, his ward, or child;

(b) Punishment for contempt of court.

(E)(1) The punishment of a person for contempt of court for violation of an order issued pursuant to division (A) of this section does not bar criminal prosecution of the person for a violation of section 2921.04 of the Revised Code.

(2) The punishment of a person for contempt of court for a violation of an order issued pursuant to division (B) of this section does not bar criminal prosecution of the person for an offense against the person or property of the complainant, his ward, or child.

(3) A person punished for contempt of court under this section is entitled to credit for the punishment imposed upon conviction of a violation of the offense arising out of the same activity, and a person convicted of such a violation shall not subsequently be punished for contempt of court arising out of the same activity.

**HISTORY: 140 v S 172 (Eff 9-26-84); 145 v H 335. Eff 12-9-94.**

**Not analogous to former RC § 2945.04 (GC § 13442-3; 113 v 123(179); Bureau of Code Revision, 10-1-53), repealed 135 v H 716, § 2, eff 1-1-74.**

## [TRIAL BY COURT]

### § 2945.05 Defendant may waive jury trial.

In all criminal cases pending in courts of record in this state, the defendant may waive a trial by jury and be tried by the court without a jury. Such waiver by a defendant, shall be in writing, signed by the defendant, and filed in said cause and made a part of the record thereof. It shall be entitled in the court and cause, and in substance as follows: "I ........, defendant in the above cause, hereby voluntarily waive and relinquish my right to a trial by jury, and elect to be tried by a Judge of the Court in which the said cause may be pending. I fully understand that under the laws of this state, I have a constitutional right to a trial by jury."

Such waiver of trial by jury must be made in open court after the defendant has been arraigned and has had opportunity to consult with counsel. Such waiver may be withdrawn by the defendant at any time before the commencement of the trial.

**HISTORY: GC § 13442-4; 113 v 123(179), ch 21, § 4; Bureau of Code Revision. Eff 10-1-53.**

### § 2945.06 Jurisdiction of judge when jury trial is waived; three-judge court.

In any case in which a defendant waives his right to trial by jury and elects to be tried by the court under section 2945.05 of the Revised Code, any judge of the court in which the cause is pending shall proceed to hear, try, and determine the cause in accordance with the rules and in like manner as if the cause were being tried before a jury. If the accused is charged with an offense punishable with death, he shall be tried by a court to be composed of three judges, consisting of the judge presiding at the time in the trial of criminal cases and two other judges to be designated by the presiding judge or chief justice of that court, and in case there is neither a presiding judge nor a chief justice, by the chief justice of the supreme court. The judges or a majority of them may decide all questions of fact and law arising upon the trial; however the accused shall not be found guilty or not guilty of any offense unless the judges unanimously find the accused guilty or not guilty. If the accused pleads guilty of aggravated murder, a court composed of three judges shall examine the witnesses, determine whether the accused is guilty of aggravated murder or any other offense, and pronounce sentence accordingly. The court shall follow the procedures contained in sections 2929.03 and 2929.04 of the Revised Code in all cases in which the accused is charged with an offense punishable by death. If in the composition of the court it is necessary that a judge from another county be assigned by the chief justice, the judge from another county shall be compensated for his services as provided by section 141.07 of the Revised Code.

**HISTORY: GC § 13442-5; 113 v 123(179), ch 21, § 5; 115 v 531; Bureau of Code Revision, 10-1-53; 139 v S 1. Eff 10-19-81.**

### § 2945.07 Repealed, 145 v S 186, § 2 [140 v S 172; 142 v S 6; 145 v H 571]. Eff 10-12-94.

This section concerned rights of victim or representative family member present at trial. See now RC Chapter 2930.

## [TRIAL PROCEEDINGS]

### § 2945.08 Prosecution in wrong county; proceeding.

If it appears, on the trial of a criminal cause, that the offense was committed within the exclusive jurisdiction of another county of this state, the court must direct the defendant to be committed to await a warrant from the proper county for his arrest, but if the offense is a bailable offense the court may admit the defendant to bail with sufficient sureties conditioned, that he will, within such time as the court appoints, render himself amenable to a warrant for his arrest from the proper county, and if not sooner arrested thereon, will appear in court at the time fixed to surrender himself upon the warrant.

The clerk of the court of common pleas shall forthwith notify the prosecuting attorney of the county in which such offense was committed, in order that proper proceedings may be had in the case. A defendant in such case shall not be committed nor held under bond for a period of more than ten days.

**HISTORY: GC § 13442-6; 113 v 123(180), ch 21, § 6; Bureau of Code Revision. Eff 10-1-53.**

### § 2945.09 Grounds of objection to be stated.

In the trial of any criminal case, the grounds of an objection to any ruling or action of the court shall be stated if required by the court.

**HISTORY: GC § 13442-7; 113 v 123(180), ch 21, § 7; Bureau of Code Revision, Eff 10-1-53; 141 v H 412. Eff 3-17-87.**

## § 2945.10 Order of proceedings of trial.

The trial of an issue upon an indictment or information shall proceed before the trial court or jury as follows:

(A) Counsel for the state must first state the case for the prosecution, and may briefly state the evidence by which he expects to sustain it.

(B) The defendant or his counsel must then state his defense, and may briefly state the evidence which he expects to offer in support of it.

(C) The state must first produce its evidence and the defendant shall then produce his evidence.

(D) The state will then be confined to rebutting evidence, but the court, for good reason, in furtherance of justice, may permit evidence to be offered by either side out of its order.

(E) When the evidence is concluded, either party may request instructions to the jury on the points of law, which instructions shall be reduced to writing if either party requests it.

(F) When the evidence is concluded, unless the case is submitted without argument, the counsel for the state shall commence, the defendant or his counsel follow, and the counsel for the state conclude the argument to the jury.

(G) The court, after the argument is concluded and before proceeding with other business, shall forthwith charge the jury. Such charge shall be reduced to writing by the court if either party requests it before the argument to the jury is commenced. Such charge, or other charge or instruction provided for in this section, when so written and given, shall not be orally qualified, modified, or explained to the jury by the court. Written charges and instructions shall be taken by the jury in their retirement and returned with their verdict into court and remain on file with the papers of the case.

The court may deviate from the order of proceedings listed in this section.

**HISTORY: GC § 13442-8; 113 v 123(180), ch 21, § 8; Bureau of Code Revision. Eff 10-1-53.**

## § 2945.11 Charge to the jury as to law and fact.

In charging the jury, the court must state to it all matters of law necessary for the information of the jury in giving its verdict. The court must also inform the jury that the jury is the exclusive judge of all questions of fact. The court must state to the jury that in determining the question of guilt, it must not consider the punishment but that punishment rests with the judge except in cases of murder in the first degree or burglary of an inhabited dwelling.

**HISTORY: GC § 13442-9; 113 v 123(181), ch 21, § 9; Bureau of Code Revision. Eff 10-1-53.**

## § 2945.12 When accused may be tried in his absence.

A person indicted for a misdemeanor, upon request in writing subscribed by him and entered in the journal, may be tried in his absence by a jury or by the court. No other person shall be tried unless personally present, but if a person indicted escapes or forfeits his recognizance after the jury is sworn, the trial shall proceed and the verdict be received and recorded. If the offense charged is a misdemeanor, judgment and sentence shall be pronounced as if he were personally present. If the offense charged is a felony, the case shall be continued until the accused appears in court, or is retaken.

**HISTORY: GC § 13442-10; 113 v 123(181), ch 21, § 10; Bureau of Code Revision. Eff 10-1-53.**

## § 2945.13 Joint trials in felony cases.

When two or more persons are jointly indicted for a felony, except a capital offense, they shall be tried jointly unless the court, for good cause shown on application therefor by the prosecuting attorney or one or more of said defendants, orders one or more of said defendants to be tried separately.

**HISTORY: GC § 13442-11; 113 v 123(181), ch 21, § 11; Bureau of Code Revision. Eff 10-1-53.**

## § 2945.14 Mistake in charging offense.

If it appears during the trial and before submission to the jury or court, that a mistake has been made in charging the proper offense in the indictment or information, the court may order a discontinuance of trial without prejudice to the prosecution. The accused, if there is good cause to detain him, may be recognized to appear at the same or next succeeding term of court, or in default thereof committed to jail. In such case the court shall recognize the witnesses for the state to appear at the same time and testify.

**HISTORY: GC § 13442-12; 113 v 123(181), ch 21, § 12; Bureau of Code Revision. Eff 10-1-53.**

## § 2945.15 Discharge of defendant.

When two or more persons are tried jointly, before any of the accused has gone into his defense the trial court may direct one or more of such accused to be discharged that he may be a witness for the state.

An accused person, when there is not sufficient evidence to put him upon his defense, may be discharged by the court, but if not so discharged, shall be entitled to the immediate verdict of the jury in his favor. Such order of discharge, in either case, is a bar to another prosecution for the same offense.

**HISTORY: GC § 13442-13; 113 v 123(181), ch 21, § 13; Bureau of Code Revision. Eff 10-1-53.**

## § 2945.16 View of the premises.

When it is proper for the jurors to have a view of the place at which a material fact occurred, the trial court may order them to be conducted in a body, under the charge of the sheriff or other officer, to such place, which shall be shown to them by a person designated by the court. While the jurors are absent on such view no person other than such officer and such person so appointed, shall speak to them on any subject connected with the trial. The accused has the right to attend such view by the jury, but may waive this right.

The expense of such view as approved by the court shall be taxed as other costs in the case.

HISTORY: GC § 13442-14; 113 v 123(182), ch 21, § 14; Bureau of Code Revision, 10-1-53; 129 v 1201. Eff 9-11-61.

[JURY TRIAL]

## § 2945.17 Right to trial by jury.

(A) At any trial, in any court, for the violation of any statute of this state, or of any ordinance of any municipal corporation, except as provided in divisions (B) and (C) of this section, the accused has the right to be tried by a jury.

(B) The right to be tried by a jury that is granted under division (A) of this section does not apply to a violation of a statute or ordinance that is any of the following:

(1) A violation that is a minor misdemeanor;

(2) A violation for which the potential penalty does not include the possibility of a prison term or jail term and for which the possible fine does not exceed one thousand dollars.

(C) Division (A) of this section does not apply to, and there is no right to a jury trial for, a person who is the subject of a complaint filed under section 2151.27 of the Revised Code against both a child and the parent, guardian, or other person having care of the child.

HISTORY: GC § 13443; 115 v 78; Bureau of Code Revision, 10-1-53; 134 v H 511 (Eff 1-1-74); 148 v S 179, § 1. Eff 4-9-2001; 149 v H 490, § 1, eff. 1-1-04.

The effective date is set by section 4 of HB 490.

**Publisher's Note:**

RC § 2945.17 appears in the amending section of SB 179 (148 v —) but does not appear in the body of the act for sections effective 1-1-2002.

## § 2945.171 Verdict in writing.

In all criminal cases the verdict of the jury shall be in writing and signed by each of the jurors concurring therein.

HISTORY: 129 v 336. Eff 9-28-61.

## § 2945.18 Repealed, 145 v H 41, § 2 [139 v S 1]. Eff 9-27-93.

This section concerned venire for jury in capital cases.

The provisions of § 3 of HB 41 (145 v —) read as follows:

SECTION 3. The provisions of this act apply to any case that is filed on or after the effective date of this act and in which the defendant is charged with the commission of a capital offense, regardless of when the alleged capital offense occurred.

## § 2945.19 Repealed, 145 v H 41, § 2 [139 v S 1]. Eff 9-27-93.

This section concerned special venire in capital cases.

## § 2945.20 Separate trial for capital offense.

When two or more persons are jointly indicted for a capital offense, each of such persons shall be tried separately. The court, for good cause shown on application therefor by the prosecuting attorney or one or more of the defendants, may order said defendants to be tried jointly.

HISTORY: GC § 13443-3; 113 v 123(183), ch 22, § 3; 116 v 301; Bureau of Code Revision. Eff 10-1-53.

## § 2945.21 Peremptory challenges.

(A)(1) In criminal cases in which there is only one defendant, each party, in addition to the challenges for cause authorized by law, may peremptorily challenge three of the jurors in misdemeanor cases and four of the jurors in felony cases other than capital cases. If there is more than one defendant, each defendant may peremptorily challenge the same number of jurors as if he were the sole defendant.

(2) Notwithstanding Criminal Rule 24, in capital cases in which there is only one defendant, each party, in addition to the challenges for cause authorized by law, may peremptorily challenge twelve of the jurors. If there is more than one defendant, each defendant may peremptorily challenge the same number of jurors as if he were the sole defendant.

(3) In any case in which there are multiple defendants, the prosecuting attorney may peremptorily challenge a number of jurors equal to the total number of peremptory challenges allowed to all of the defendants.

(B) If any indictments, informations, or complaints are consolidated for trial, the consolidated cases shall be considered, for purposes of exercising peremptory challenges, as though the defendants or offenses had been joined in the same indictment, information, or complaint.

(C) The exercise of peremptory challenges authorized by this section shall be in accordance with the procedures of Criminal Rule 24.

HISTORY: GC § 13443-4; 113 v 123(183), ch 22, § 4; 119 v 594; Bureau of Code Revision, 10-1-53; 139 v S 1. Eff 10-19-81.

## § 2945.22 Repealed, 139 v S 1, § 2 [GC § 13443-6; 113 v 123(183); Bureau of Code Revision, 10-1-53]. Eff 10-19-81.

This section concerned peremptory challenges.

## § 2945.23 When peremptory challenges required.

Except by agreement, neither the state nor the defendant shall be required to exercise any peremptory challenge until twelve jurors have been passed for cause and are in the panel.

HISTORY: GC § 13443-7; 113 v 123(183), ch 22, § 7; Bureau of Code Revision. Eff 10-1-53.

## § 2945.24 Juries.

In all criminal cases, a jury summoned and impaneled under sections 2313.01 to 2313.47 of the Revised Code shall try the accused.

HISTORY: GC § 13443-5; 113 v 123(183), ch 22, § 5; Bureau of Code Revision, 10-1-53; 136 v H 133 (Eff 6-3-76); 139 v S 1 (Eff 10-19-81); 145 v H 41. Eff 9-27-93.

See provisions, § 3 of HB 41 (145 v —) following RC § 2945.18.

## § 2945.25 Causes of challenging of jurors.

A person called as a juror in a criminal case may be challenged for the following causes:

(A) That he was a member of the grand jury that found the indictment in the case;

(B) That he is possessed of a state of mind evincing enmity or bias toward the defendant or the state; but no person summoned as a juror shall be disqualified by reason of a previously formed or expressed opinion with reference to the guilt or innocence of the accused, if the court is satisfied, from examination of the juror or from other evidence, that he will render an impartial verdict according to the law and the evidence submitted to the jury at the trial;

(C) In the trial of a capital offense, that he unequivocally states that under no circumstances will he follow the instructions of a trial judge and consider fairly the imposition of a sentence of death in a particular case. A prospective juror's conscientious or religious opposition to the death penalty in and of itself is not grounds for a challenge for cause. All parties shall be given wide latitude in voir dire questioning in this regard.

(D) That he is related by consanguinity or affinity within the fifth degree to the person alleged to be injured or attempted to be injured by the offense charged, or to the person on whose complaint the prosecution was instituted, or to the defendant;

(E) That he served on a petit jury drawn in the same cause against the same defendant, and that [petit]† jury was discharged after hearing the evidence or rendering a verdict on the evidence that was set aside;

(F) That he served as a juror in a civil case brought against the defendant for the same act;

(G) That he has been subpoenaed in good faith as a witness in the case;

(H) That he is a chronic alcoholic, or drug dependent person;

(I) That he has been convicted of a crime that by law disqualifies him from serving on a jury;

(J) That he has an action pending between him and the state or the defendant;

(K) That he or his spouse is a party to another action then pending in any court in which an attorney in the cause then on trial is an attorney, either for or against him;

(L) That he is the person alleged to be injured or attempted to be injured by the offense charged, or is the person on whose complaint the prosecution was instituted, or the defendant;

(M) That he is the employer or employee, or the spouse, parent, son, or daughter of the employer or employee, or the counselor, agent, or attorney of any person included in division (L) of this section;

(N) That English is not his native language, and his knowledge of English is insufficient to permit him to understand the facts and law in the case;

(O) That he otherwise is unsuitable for any other cause to serve as a juror.

The validity of each challenge listed in this section shall be determined by the court.

**HISTORY: GC § 13443-8; 113 v 123(183), ch 22, § 8; 118 v 429; Bureau of Code Revision, 10-1-53; 138 v H 965 (Eff 4-9-81); 139 v S 1. Eff 10-19-81.**

† Division (E), S 1 failed to contain the word "petit" here. It was added in H 965.

## § 2945.26 Challenge for cause.

Challenges for cause shall be tried by the court on the oath of the person challenged, or other evidence, and shall be made before the jury is sworn.

**HISTORY: GC § 13443-9; 113 v 123(184), ch 22, § 9; Bureau of Code Revision. Eff 10-1-53.**

## § 2945.27 Examination of jurors by the court.

The judge of the trial court shall examine the prospective jurors under oath or upon affirmation as to their qualifications to serve as fair and impartial jurors, but he shall permit reasonable examination of such jurors by the prosecuting attorney and by the defendant or his counsel.

**HISTORY: GC § 13443-10; 113 v 123(184), ch 22, § 10; Bureau of Code Revision, 10-1-53; 127 v 419. Eff 9-9-57.**

## § 2945.28 Form of oath or affirmation by juror.

(A) In criminal cases jurors and the jury shall take the following oath to be administered by the trial court or the clerk of the court of common pleas, and the jurors shall respond to the oath "I do swear" or "I do affirm": "Do you swear or affirm that you will diligently inquire into and carefully deliberate all matters between the State of Ohio and the defendant (giving the defendant's name)? Do you swear or affirm you will do this to the best of your skill and understanding, without bias or prejudice? So help you God."

A juror shall be allowed to make affirmation and the words "this you do as you shall answer under the pains and penalties of perjury" shall be substituted for the words, "So help you God."

(B) If, on or after the effective date of this amendment, a court that impanels a jury in a criminal case uses the oath that was in effect prior to the effective date of this amendment instead of the oath set forth in division (A) of this section, the court's use of the former oath does not invalidate or affect the validity of the impanelment of the jury or any action taken by the jury.

**HISTORY: RS §§ 7281, 7282; 66 v 308, §§ 137, 138; GC §§ 13443-11, 13443-12; 113 v 123(184), ch 22, §§ 11, 12; Bureau of Code Revision. Eff 10-1-53; 150 v S 71, § 1, eff. 5-18-05.**

## § 2945.29 Jurors becoming unable to perform duties.

If, before the conclusion of the trial, a juror becomes sick, or for other reason is unable to perform his duty, the court may order him to be discharged. In that case, if alternate jurors have been selected, one of them shall be designated to take the place of the juror so discharged. If, after all alternate jurors have been made regular jurors, a juror becomes too incapacitated to perform his duty, and has been discharged by the court, a new juror may be sworn and the trial begin anew, or the jury may be discharged and a new jury then or thereafter impaneled.

**HISTORY: GC § 13443-13; 113 v 123(184), ch 22, § 13; Bureau of Code Revision. Eff 10-1-53.**

## § 2945.30 Medical attendance of juror.

In case of sickness of any juror before the conclusion of the trial, the court may order that such juror receive medical attendance and shall order the payment of a reasonable charge for such medical attendance out of the judiciary fund.

**HISTORY: GC § 13443-14; 113 v 123(184), ch 22, § 14; Bureau of Code Revision. Eff 10-1-53.**

## § 2945.31 Separation of jurors.

After the trial has commenced, before or after the jury is sworn, the court may order the jurors to be kept in charge of proper officers, or they may be permitted to separate during the trial. If the jurors are kept in charge of officers of the court, proper arrangements shall be made for their care, maintenance, and comfort, under the orders and direction of the court. In case of necessity the court may permit temporary separation of the jurors.

**HISTORY: GC § 13443-15; 113 v 123(185), ch 22, § 15; Bureau of Code Revision. Eff 10-1-53.**

## § 2945.32 Oath to officers if jury sequestered.

When an order has been entered by the court of common pleas in any criminal cause, directing the jurors to be kept in charge of the officers of the court, the following oath shall be administered by the clerk of the court of common pleas to said officers: "You do solemnly swear that you will, to the best of your ability, keep the persons sworn as jurors on this trial, from separating from each other; that you will not suffer any communications to be made to them, or any of them, orally or otherwise; that you will not communicate with them, or any of them, orally or otherwise, except by the order of this court, or to ask them if they have agreed on their verdict, until they shall be discharged, and that you will not, before they render their verdict communicate to any person the state of their deliberations or the verdict they have agreed upon, so help you God." Any officer having taken such oath who willfully violates the same, or permits the same to be violated, is guilty of perjury and shall be imprisoned not less than one nor more than ten years.

**HISTORY: GC § 13443-16; 113 v 123(185), ch 22, § 16; Bureau of Code Revision. Eff 10-1-53.**

## § 2945.33 Keeping and conduct of jury after case submitted.

When a cause is finally submitted the jurors must be kept together in a convenient place under the charge of an officer until they agree upon a verdict, or are discharged by the court. The court, except in cases where the offense charged may be punishable by death, may permit the jurors to separate during the adjournment of court overnight, under proper cautions, or under supervision of an officer. Such officer shall not permit a communication to be made to them, nor make any himself except to ask if they have agreed upon a verdict, unless he does so by order of the court. Such officer shall not communicate to any person, before the verdict is delivered, any matter in relation to their deliberation. Upon the trial of any prosecution for misdemeanor, the court may permit the jury to separate during their deliberation, or upon adjournment of the court overnight.

In cases where the offense charged may be punished by death, after the case is finally submitted to the jury, the jurors shall be kept in charge of the proper officer and proper arrangements for their care and maintenance shall be made as under section 2945.31 of the Revised Code.

**HISTORY: GC § 13448-1; 113 v 123(194), ch 27; 115 v 531; Bureau of Code Revision, 10-1-53; 131 v 681. Eff 11-9-65.**

## § 2945.34 Admonition if jurors separate during trial.

If the jurors are permitted to separate during a trial, they shall be admonished by the court not to converse with, nor permit themselves to be addressed by any person, nor to listen to any conversation on the subject of the trial, nor form or express any opinion thereon, until the case is finally submitted to them.

**HISTORY: GC § 13443-17; 113 v 123(185), ch 22, § 17; Bureau of Code Revision. Eff 10-1-53.**

## § 2945.35 Papers the jury may take.

Upon retiring for deliberation, the jury, at the discretion of the court, may take with it all papers except depositions, and all articles, photographs, and maps which have been offered in evidence. No article or paper identified but not admitted in evidence shall be taken by the jury upon its retirement.

**HISTORY: GC § 13444-26; 113 v 123(191), ch 23, § 26; Bureau of Code Revision. Eff 10-1-53.**

## § 2945.36 For what cause jury may be discharged.

The trial court may discharge a jury without prejudice to the prosecution:

(A) For the sickness or corruption of a juror or other accident or calamity;

(B) Because there is no probability of such jurors agreeing;

(C) If it appears after the jury has been sworn that one of the jurors is a witness in the case;

(D) By the consent of the prosecuting attorney and the defendant.

The reason for such discharge shall be entered on the journal.

**HISTORY: GC § 13443-18; 113 v 123(185), ch 22, § 18; Bureau of Code Revision. Eff 10-1-53.**

### [COMPETENCY TO STAND TRIAL]

## § 2945.37 Definitions; hearing on competence to stand trial.

(A) As used in sections 2945.37 to 2945.402 [2945.40.2] of the Revised Code:

(1) "Prosecutor" means a prosecuting attorney or a city director of law, village solicitor, or similar chief legal officer of a municipal corporation who has authority to prosecute a criminal case that is before the court or the criminal case in which a defendant in a criminal case has been found incompetent to stand trial or not guilty by reason of insanity.

(2) "Examiner" means either of the following:

(a) A psychiatrist or a licensed clinical psychologist who satisfies the criteria of division (I)(1) of section 5122.01 of the Revised Code or is employed by a certified forensic center designated by the department of mental health to conduct examinations or evaluations.

(b) For purposes of a separate mental retardation evaluation that is ordered by a court pursuant to division (H) of section 2945.371 [2945.37.1] of the Revised Code, a psychologist designated by the director of developmental disabilities pursuant to that section to conduct that separate mental retardation evaluation.

(3) "Nonsecured status" means any unsupervised, off-grounds movement or trial visit from a hospital or institution, or any conditional release, that is granted to a person who is found incompetent to stand trial and is committed pursuant to section 2945.39 of the Revised Code or to a person who is found not guilty by reason of insanity and is committed pursuant to section 2945.40 of the Revised Code.

(4) "Unsupervised, off-grounds movement" includes only off-grounds privileges that are unsupervised and that have an expectation of return to the hospital or institution on a daily basis.

(5) "Trial visit" means a patient privilege of a longer stated duration of unsupervised community contact with an expectation of return to the hospital or institution at designated times.

(6) "Conditional release" means a commitment status under which the trial court at any time may revoke a person's conditional release and order the rehospitalization or reinstitutionalization of the person as described in division (A) of section 2945.402 [2945.40.2] of the Revised Code and pursuant to which a person who is found incompetent to stand trial or a person who is found not guilty by reason of insanity lives and receives treatment in the community for a period of time that does not exceed the maximum prison term or term of imprisonment that the person could have received for the offense in question had the person been convicted of the offense instead of being found incompetent to stand trial on the charge of the offense or being found not guilty by reason of insanity relative to the offense.

(7) "Licensed clinical psychologist," "mentally ill person subject to hospitalization by court order," and "psychiatrist" have the same meanings as in section 5122.01 of the Revised Code.

(8) "Mentally retarded person subject to institutionalization by court order" has the same meaning as in section 5123.01 of the Revised Code.

(B) In a criminal action in a court of common pleas, a county court, or a municipal court, the court, prosecutor, or defense may raise the issue of the defendant's competence to stand trial. If the issue is raised before the trial has commenced, the court shall hold a hearing on the issue as provided in this section. If the issue is raised after the trial has commenced, the court shall hold a hearing on the issue only for good cause shown or on the court's own motion.

(C) The court shall conduct the hearing required or authorized under division (B) of this section within thirty days after the issue is raised, unless the defendant has been referred for evaluation in which case the court shall conduct the hearing within ten days after the filing of the report of the evaluation or, in the case of a defendant who is ordered by the court pursuant to division (H) of section 2945.371 [2945.37.1] of the Revised Code to undergo a separate mental retardation evaluation conducted by a psychologist designated by the director of developmental disabilities, within ten days after the filing of the report of the separate mental retardation evaluation under that division. A hearing may be continued for good cause.

(D) The defendant shall be represented by counsel at the hearing conducted under division (C) of this section. If the defendant is unable to obtain counsel, the court shall appoint counsel under Chapter 120. of the Revised Code or under the authority recognized in division (C) of section 120.06, division (E) of section 120.16, division (E) of section 120.26, or section 2941.51 of the Revised Code before proceeding with the hearing.

(E) The prosecutor and defense counsel may submit evidence on the issue of the defendant's competence to stand trial. A written report of the evaluation of the defendant may be admitted into evidence at the hearing by stipulation, but, if either the prosecution or defense objects to its admission, the report may be admitted under sections 2317.36 to 2317.38 of the Revised Code or any other applicable statute or rule.

(F) The court shall not find a defendant incompetent to stand trial solely because the defendant is receiving or has received treatment as a voluntary or involuntary mentally ill patient under Chapter 5122. or a voluntary or involuntary mentally retarded resident under Chapter 5123. of the Revised Code or because the defendant is receiving or has received psychotropic drugs or other medication, even if the defendant might become incompetent to stand trial without the drugs or medication.

(G) A defendant is presumed to be competent to stand trial. If, after a hearing, the court finds by a preponderance of the evidence that, because of the defendant's present mental condition, the defendant is incapable of understanding the nature and objective of the proceedings against the defendant or of assisting in the defendant's defense, the court shall find the defendant incompetent to stand trial and shall enter an order authorized by section 2945.38 of the Revised Code.

(H) Municipal courts shall follow the procedures set forth in sections 2945.37 to 2945.402 [2945.40.2] of the Revised Code. Except as provided in section 2945.371 [2945.37.1] of the Revised Code, a municipal court shall not order an evaluation of the defendant's competence to stand trial or the defendant's mental condition at the time of the commission of the offense to be conducted at any hospital operated by the department of mental health. Those evaluations shall be performed through community resources including, but not limited to, certified forensic centers, court probation departments, and community mental health agencies. All expenses of the evaluations shall be borne by the legislative authority of the municipal court, as defined in section 1901.03 of the Revised Code, and shall be taxed as costs in the case. If a defendant is found incompetent to stand trial or not guilty by reason of insanity, a municipal court may commit the defendant as provided in sections 2945.38 to 2945.402 [2945.40.2] of the Revised Code.

**HISTORY: 137 v H 565 (Eff 11-1-78); 138 v S 297 (Eff 4-30-80); 139 v H 694 (Eff 11-15-81); 142 v S 156 (Eff 7-1-89); 146 v S 285. Eff 7-1-97; 153 v S 79, § 1, eff. 10-6-09.**

**Analogous to former RC § 2945.37 (GC § 13441-1; 113 v 123; Bureau of Code Revision, 10-1-53; 136 v S 368), repealed 137 v H 565, § 2, eff 11-1-78.**

The effective date is set by section 4 of SB 285.

## § 2945.371 Evaluations of defendant's mental condition at relevant time; separate mental retardation evaluation.

(A) If the issue of a defendant's competence to stand trial is raised or if a defendant enters a plea of not guilty by reason of insanity, the court may order one or more evaluations of the defendant's present mental condition or, in the case of a plea of not guilty by reason of insanity, of the defendant's mental condition at the time of the offense charged. An examiner shall conduct the evaluation.

(B) If the court orders more than one evaluation under division (A) of this section, the prosecutor and the defendant may recommend to the court an examiner whom each prefers to perform one of the evaluations. If a defendant enters a plea of not guilty by reason of insanity and if the court does not designate an examiner recommended by the defendant, the court shall inform the defendant that the defendant may have independent expert evaluation and that, if the defendant is unable to obtain independent expert evaluation, it will be obtained for the defendant at public expense if the defendant is indigent.

(C) If the court orders an evaluation under division (A) of this section, the defendant shall be available at the times and places established by the examiners who are to conduct the evaluation. The court may order a defendant who has been released on bail or recognizance to submit to an evaluation under this section. If a defendant who has been released on bail or recognizance refuses to submit to a complete evaluation, the court may amend the conditions of bail or recognizance and order the sheriff to take the defendant into custody and deliver the defendant to a center, program, or facility operated or certified by the department of mental health or the department of developmental disabilities where the defendant may be held for evaluation for a reasonable period of time not to exceed twenty days.

(D) A defendant who has not been released on bail or recognizance may be evaluated at the defendant's place of detention. Upon the request of the examiner, the court may order the sheriff to transport the defendant to a program or facility operated or certified by the department of mental health or the department of developmental disabilities, where the defendant may be held for evaluation for a reasonable period of time not to exceed twenty days, and to return the defendant to the place of detention after the evaluation. A municipal court may make an order under this division only upon the request of a certified forensic center examiner.

(E) If a court orders the evaluation to determine a defendant's mental condition at the time of the offense charged, the court shall inform the examiner of the offense with which the defendant is charged.

(F) In conducting an evaluation of a defendant's mental condition at the time of the offense charged, the examiner shall consider all relevant evidence. If the offense charged involves the use of force against another person, the relevant evidence to be considered includes, but is not limited to, any evidence that the defendant suffered, at the time of the commission of the offense, from the "battered woman syndrome."

(G) The examiner shall file a written report with the court within thirty days after entry of a court order for evaluation, and the court shall provide copies of the report to the prosecutor and defense counsel. The report shall include all of the following:

(1) The examiner's findings;

(2) The facts in reasonable detail on which the findings are based;

(3) If the evaluation was ordered to determine the defendant's competence to stand trial, all of the following findings or recommendations that are applicable:

(a) Whether the defendant is capable of understanding the nature and objective of the proceedings against the defendant or of assisting in the defendant's defense;

(b) If the examiner's opinion is that the defendant is incapable of understanding the nature and objective of the proceedings against the defendant or of assisting in the defendant's defense, whether the defendant presently is mentally ill or mentally retarded and, if the examiner's opinion is that the defendant presently is mentally retarded, whether the defendant appears to be a mentally retarded person subject to institutionalization by court order;

(c) If the examiner's opinion is that the defendant is incapable of understanding the nature and objective of the proceedings against the defendant or of assisting in the defendant's defense, the examiner's opinion as to the likelihood of the defendant becoming capable of understanding the nature and objective of the proceedings against the defendant and of assisting in the defendant's defense within one year if the defendant is provided with a course of treatment;

(d) If the examiner's opinion is that the defendant is incapable of understanding the nature and objective of the proceedings against the defendant or of assisting in the defendant's defense and that the defendant presently is mentally ill or mentally retarded, the examiner's recommendation as to the least restrictive placement or commitment alternative, consistent with the defendant's treatment needs for restoration to competency and with the safety of the community;

(e) If the defendant is charged with a misdemeanor offense that is not an offense of violence and the examiner's opinion is that the defendant is incapable of understanding the nature and objective of the proceedings against the defendant or of assisting in the defendant's defense and that the defendant is presently mentally ill or mentally retarded, the examiner's recommendation as to whether the defendant is amenable to engagement in mental health treatment or developmental disability services.

(4) If the evaluation was ordered to determine the defendant's mental condition at the time of the offense charged, the examiner's findings as to whether the defendant, at the time of the offense charged, did not know, as a result of a severe mental disease or defect, the wrongfulness of the defendant's acts charged.

(H) If the examiner's report filed under division (G) of this section indicates that in the examiner's opinion the defendant is incapable of understanding the nature and objective of the proceedings against the defendant or of assisting in the defendant's defense and that in the examiner's opinion the defendant appears to be a mentally retarded person subject to institutionalization by court order, the court shall order the defendant to undergo a separate mental retardation evaluation conducted by a psychologist designated by the director of developmental disabilities. Divisions (C) to (F) of this section apply in relation to a separate mental retardation evaluation conducted under this division. The psychologist appointed under this division to conduct the separate mental retardation evaluation shall file a written report with the court within thirty days after the entry of the court order requiring the separate mental retardation evaluation, and the court shall provide copies of the report to the prosecutor and defense counsel. The report shall include all of the information described in divisions (G)(1) to (4) of this section. If the court orders a separate mental retardation evaluation of a defendant under this division, the court shall not conduct a hearing under divisions (B) to (H) of section 2945.37 of the Revised Code regarding that defendant until a report of the separate mental retardation evaluation conducted under this division has been filed. Upon the filing of that report, the court shall conduct the hearing within the period of time specified in division (C) of section 2945.37 of the Revised Code.

(I) An examiner appointed under divisions (A) and (B) of this section or under division (H) of this section to evaluate a defendant to determine the defendant's competence to stand trial also may be appointed to evaluate a defendant who has entered a plea of not guilty by reason of insanity, but an examiner of that nature shall prepare separate reports on the issue of competence to stand trial and the defense of not guilty by reason of insanity.

(J) No statement that a defendant makes in an evaluation or hearing under divisions (A) to (H) of this section relating to the defendant's competence to stand trial or to the defendant's mental condition at the time of the offense charged shall be used against the defendant on the issue of guilt in any criminal action or proceeding, but, in a criminal action or proceeding, the prosecutor or defense counsel may call as a witness any person who evaluated the defendant or prepared a report pursuant to a referral under this section. Neither the appointment nor the testimony of an examiner appointed under this section precludes the prosecutor or defense counsel from calling other witnesses or presenting other evidence on competency or insanity issues.

(K) Persons appointed as examiners under divisions (A) and (B) of this section or under division (H) of this section shall be paid a reasonable amount for their services and expenses, as certified by the court. The certified amount shall be paid by the county in the case of county courts and courts of common pleas and by the legislative authority, as defined in section 1901.03 of the Revised Code, in the case of municipal courts.

**HISTORY: 137 v H 565 (Eff 11-1-78); 138 v S 297 (Eff 4-30-80); 138 v H 900 (Eff 7-1-80); 138 v H 965 (Eff 4-9-81); 146 v S 285 (Eff 7-1-97); 149 v S 122. Eff 2-20-2002; 153 v S 79, § 1, eff. 10-6-09; 2011 HB 153, § 101.01, eff. Sept. 29, 2011.**

See provisions, § 2 of SB 122 (149 v —) following RC § 2945.38.

## § 2945.38 Disposition of defendant after competency hearing; treatment and evaluation orders.

(A) If the issue of a defendant's competence to stand trial is raised and if the court, upon conducting the hearing provided for in section 2945.37 of the Revised Code, finds that the defendant is competent to stand trial, the defendant shall be proceeded against as provided by law. If the court finds the defendant competent to stand trial and the defendant is receiving psychotropic drugs or other medication, the court may authorize the continued administration of the drugs or medication or other appropriate treatment in order to maintain the defendant's competence to stand trial, unless the defendant's attending physician advises the court against continuation of the drugs, other medication, or treatment.

(B)(1)(a) If, after taking into consideration all relevant reports, information, and other evidence, the court finds that the defendant is incompetent to stand trial and that there is a substantial probability that the defendant will become competent to stand trial within one year if the defendant is provided with a course of treatment, the court shall order the defendant to undergo treatment. If the defendant has been charged with a felony offense and if, after taking into consideration all relevant reports, information, and other evidence, the court finds that the defendant is incompetent to stand trial, but the court is unable at that time to determine whether there is a substantial probability that the defendant will become competent to stand trial within one year if the defendant is provided with a course of treatment, the court shall order continuing evaluation and treatment of the defendant for a period not to exceed four months to determine whether there is a substantial probability that the defendant will become competent to stand trial within one year if the defendant is provided with a course of treatment.

(b) The court order for the defendant to undergo treatment or continuing evaluation and treatment under division (B)(1)(a) of this section shall specify that the defendant, if determined to require mental health treatment or continuing evaluation and treatment, shall be committed to the department of mental health for treatment or continuing evaluation and treatment at a hospital, facility, or agency, as determined to be clinically appropriate by the department of mental health and, if determined to require treatment or continuing evaluation and treatment for a developmental disability, shall receive treatment or continuing evaluation and treatment at an institution or facility operated by the department of developmental disabilities, at a facility certified by the department of developmental disabilities as being qualified to treat mental retardation, at a public or private community mental retardation facility, or by a mental retardation professional. The order may restrict the defendant's freedom of movement as the court considers necessary. The prosecutor in the defendant's case shall send to the chief clinical officer of the hospital , facility, or agency where the defendant is placed by the department of mental health, or to the managing officer of the institution, the director of the facility, or the person to which the defendant is committed, copies of relevant police reports and other background information that pertains to the defendant and is available to the prosecutor unless the prosecutor determines that the release of any of the information in the police reports or any of the other background information to unauthorized persons would interfere with the effective prosecution of any person or would create a substantial risk of harm to any person.

In committing the defendant to the department of mental health, the court shall consider the extent to which the person is a danger to the person and to others, the need for security, and the type of crime involved and, if the court finds that restrictions on the defendant's freedom of movement are necessary, shall specify the least restrictive limitations on the person's freedom of movement determined to be necessary to protect public safety. In determining commitment alternatives for defendants determined to require treatment or continuing evaluation and treatment for developmental disabilities, the court shall consider the extent to which the person is a danger to the person and to others, the need for security, and the type of crime involved and shall order the least restrictive alternative available that is consistent with public safety and treatment goals. In weighing these factors, the court shall give preference to protecting public safety.

(c) If the defendant is found incompetent to stand trial, if the chief clinical officer of the hospital , facility, or agency where the defendant is placed, or the managing officer of the institution, the director of the facility, or the person to which the defendant is committed for treatment or continuing evaluation and treatment under division (B)(1)(b) of this section determines that medication is necessary to restore the defendant's competency to stand trial, and if the defendant lacks the capacity to give informed consent or refuses medication, the chief clinical officer of the hospital, facility, or agency where the defendant is placed, or the managing officer of the institution, the director of the facility, or the person to which the defendant is committed for treatment or continuing evaluation and treatment may petition the court for authorization for the involuntary administration of medication. The court shall hold a hearing on the petition within five days of the filing of the petition if the petition was filed in a municipal court or a county court regarding an incompetent defendant charged with a misdemeanor or within ten days of the filing of the petition if the petition was filed in a court of common pleas regarding an incompetent defendant charged with a felony offense. Following the hearing, the court may authorize the involuntary administration of medication or may dismiss the petition.

(d) If the defendant is charged with a misdemeanor offense that is not an offense of violence, the prosecutor may hold the charges in abeyance while the defendant engages in mental health treatment or developmental disability services.

(2) If the court finds that the defendant is incompetent to stand trial and that, even if the defendant is provided with a course of treatment, there is not a substantial probability that the defendant will become competent to stand trial within one year, the court shall order the discharge of the defendant, unless upon motion of the prosecutor or on its own motion, the court either seeks to retain jurisdiction over the defendant pursuant to section 2945.39 of the Revised Code or files an affidavit in the probate court for the civil commitment of the defendant pursuant to Chapter 5122. or 5123. of the Revised Code alleging that the defendant is a mentally ill person subject to hospitalization by court order or a mentally retarded person subject to institutionalization by court order. If an affidavit is filed in the probate court, the trial court shall send to the probate court copies of all written reports of the defendant's mental condition that were prepared pursuant to section 2945.371 of the Revised Code.

The trial court may issue the temporary order of detention that a probate court may issue under section 5122.11 or 5123.71 of the Revised Code, to remain in effect until the probable cause or initial hearing in the probate court. Further proceedings in the probate court are civil proceedings governed by Chapter 5122. or 5123. of the Revised Code.

(C) No defendant shall be required to undergo treatment, including any continuing evaluation and treatment, under division (B)(1) of this section for longer than whichever of the following periods is applicable:

(1) One year, if the most serious offense with which the defendant is charged is one of the following offenses:

(a) Aggravated murder, murder, or an offense of violence for which a sentence of death or life imprisonment may be imposed;

(b) An offense of violence that is a felony of the first or second degree;

(c) A conspiracy to commit, an attempt to commit, or complicity in the commission of an offense described in division (C)(1)(a) or (b) of this section if the conspiracy, attempt, or complicity is a felony of the first or second degree.

(2) Six months, if the most serious offense with which the defendant is charged is a felony other than a felony described in division (C)(1) of this section;

(3) Sixty days, if the most serious offense with which the defendant is charged is a misdemeanor of the first or second degree;

(4) Thirty days, if the most serious offense with which the defendant is charged is a misdemeanor of the third or fourth degree, a minor misdemeanor, or an unclassified misdemeanor.

(D) Any defendant who is committed pursuant to this section shall not voluntarily admit the defendant or be voluntarily admitted to a hospital or institution pursuant to section 5122.02, 5122.15, 5123.69, or 5123.76 of the Revised Code.

(E) Except as otherwise provided in this division, a defendant who is charged with an offense and is committed by the court under this section to the department of mental health with restrictions on the defendant's freedom of movement or is committed to an institution or facility for the treatment of developmental disabilities shall not be granted unsupervised on-grounds movement, supervised off-grounds movement, or nonsecured status except in accordance with the court order. The court may grant a defendant supervised off-grounds movement to obtain medical treatment or specialized habilitation treatment services if the person who supervises the treatment or the continuing evaluation and treatment of the defendant ordered under division (B)(1)(a) of this section informs the court that the treatment or continuing evaluation and treatment cannot be provided at the hospital or facility where the defendant is placed by the department of mental health or the institution or facility to which the defendant is committed. The chief clinical officer of the hospital or facility where the defendant is placed by the department of mental health or the managing officer of the institution or director of the facility to which the defendant is committed, or a designee of any of those persons, may grant a defendant movement to a medical facility for an emergency medical situation with appropriate supervision to ensure the safety of the defendant, staff, and community during that emergency medical situation. The chief clinical officer of the hospital or facility where the defendant is placed by the department of mental health or the managing officer of the institution or director of the facility to which the defendant is committed shall notify the court within twenty-four hours of the defendant's movement to the medical facility for an emergency medical situation under this division.

(F) The person who supervises the treatment or continuing evaluation and treatment of a defendant ordered to undergo treatment or continuing evaluation and treatment under division (B)(1)(a) of this section shall file a written report with the court at the following times:

(1) Whenever the person believes the defendant is capable of understanding the nature and objective of the proceedings against the defendant and of assisting in the defendant's defense;

(2) For a felony offense, fourteen days before expiration of the maximum time for treatment as specified in division (C) of this section and fourteen days before the expiration of the maximum time for continuing evaluation

and treatment as specified in division (B)(1)(a) of this section, and, for a misdemeanor offense, ten days before the expiration of the maximum time for treatment, as specified in division (C) of this section;

(3) At a minimum, after each six months of treatment;

(4) Whenever the person who supervises the treatment or continuing evaluation and treatment of a defendant ordered under division (B)(1)(a) of this section believes that there is not a substantial probability that the defendant will become capable of understanding the nature and objective of the proceedings against the defendant or of assisting in the defendant's defense even if the defendant is provided with a course of treatment.

(G) A report under division (F) of this section shall contain the examiner's findings, the facts in reasonable detail on which the findings are based, and the examiner's opinion as to the defendant's capability of understanding the nature and objective of the proceedings against the defendant and of assisting in the defendant's defense. If, in the examiner's opinion, the defendant remains incapable of understanding the nature and objective of the proceedings against the defendant and of assisting in the defendant's defense and there is a substantial probability that the defendant will become capable of understanding the nature and objective of the proceedings against the defendant and of assisting in the defendant's defense if the defendant is provided with a course of treatment, if in the examiner's opinion the defendant remains mentally ill or mentally retarded, and if the maximum time for treatment as specified in division (C) of this section has not expired, the report also shall contain the examiner's recommendation as to the least restrictive placement or commitment alternative that is consistent with the defendant's treatment needs for restoration to competency and with the safety of the community. The court shall provide copies of the report to the prosecutor and defense counsel.

(H) If a defendant is committed pursuant to division (B)(1) of this section, within ten days after the treating physician of the defendant or the examiner of the defendant who is employed or retained by the treating facility advises that there is not a substantial probability that the defendant will become capable of understanding the nature and objective of the proceedings against the defendant or of assisting in the defendant's defense even if the defendant is provided with a course of treatment, within ten days after the expiration of the maximum time for treatment as specified in division (C) of this section, within ten days after the expiration of the maximum time for continuing evaluation and treatment as specified in division (B)(1)(a) of this section, within thirty days after a defendant's request for a hearing that is made after six months of treatment, or within thirty days after being advised by the treating physician or examiner that the defendant is competent to stand trial, whichever is the earliest, the court shall conduct another hearing to determine if the defendant is competent to stand trial and shall do whichever of the following is applicable:

(1) If the court finds that the defendant is competent to stand trial, the defendant shall be proceeded against as provided by law.

(2) If the court finds that the defendant is incompetent to stand trial, but that there is a substantial probability that the defendant will become competent to stand trial if the defendant is provided with a course of treatment, and the maximum time for treatment as specified in division (C) of this section has not expired, the court, after consideration of the examiner's recommendation, shall order that treatment be continued, may change the least restrictive limitations on the defendant's freedom of movement, and, if applicable, shall specify whether the treatment for developmental disabilities is to be continued at the same or a different facility or institution.

(3) If the court finds that the defendant is incompetent to stand trial, if the defendant is charged with an offense listed in division (C)(1) of this section, and if the court finds that there is not a substantial probability that the defendant will become competent to stand trial even if the defendant is provided with a course of treatment, or if the maximum time for treatment relative to that offense as specified in division (C) of this section has expired, further proceedings shall be as provided in sections 2945.39, 2945.401, and 2945.402 of the Revised Code.

(4) If the court finds that the defendant is incompetent to stand trial, if the most serious offense with which the defendant is charged is a misdemeanor or a felony other than a felony listed in division (C)(1) of this section, and if the court finds that there is not a substantial probability that the defendant will become competent to stand trial even if the defendant is provided with a course of treatment, or if the maximum time for treatment relative to that offense as specified in division (C) of this section has expired, the court shall dismiss the indictment, information, or complaint against the defendant. A dismissal under this division is not a bar to further prosecution based on the same conduct. The court shall discharge the defendant unless the court or prosecutor files an affidavit in probate court for civil commitment pursuant to Chapter 5122. or 5123. of the Revised Code. If an affidavit for civil commitment is filed, the court may detain the defendant for ten days pending civil commitment. All of the following provisions apply to persons charged with a misdemeanor or a felony other than a felony listed in division (C)(1) of this section who are committed by the probate court subsequent to the court's or prosecutor's filing of an affidavit for civil commitment under authority of this division:

(a) The chief clinical officer of the entity, hospital, or facility, the managing officer of the institution, or the person to which the defendant is committed or admitted shall do all of the following:

(i) Notify the prosecutor, in writing, of the discharge of the defendant, send the notice at least ten days prior to the discharge unless the discharge is by the probate court, and state in the notice the date on which the defendant will be discharged;

(ii) Notify the prosecutor, in writing, when the defendant is absent without leave or is granted unsupervised, off-grounds movement, and send this notice promptly after the discovery of the absence without leave or prior to the granting of the unsupervised, off-grounds movement, whichever is applicable;

(iii) Notify the prosecutor, in writing, of the change of the defendant's commitment or admission to voluntary status, send the notice promptly upon learning of the change to voluntary status, and state in the notice the date on which the defendant was committed or admitted on a voluntary status.

(b) Upon receiving notice that the defendant will be granted unsupervised, off-grounds movement, the prosecutor either shall re-indict the defendant or promptly notify the court that the prosecutor does not intend to prosecute the charges against the defendant.

(I) If a defendant is convicted of a crime and sentenced to a jail or workhouse, the defendant's sentence shall be reduced by the total number of days the defendant is confined for evaluation to determine the defendant's competence to stand trial or treatment under this section and sections 2945.37 and 2945.371 of the Revised Code or by the total number of days the defendant is confined for evaluation to determine the defendant's mental condition at the time of the offense charged.

**HISTORY: GC § 13441-2; 113 v 123(177), ch 20, § 2; Bureau of Code Revision, 10-1-53; 136 v S 185 (Eff 8-29-75); 137 v H 565 (Eff 11-1-78); 138 v S 297 (Eff 4-30-80); 138 v H 900 (Eff 7-1-80); 138 v H 965 (Eff 4-9-81); 142 v S 156 (Eff 7-1-89); 146 v S 269 (Eff 7-1-96); 146 v S 285 (Eff 7-1-97); 149 v S 122. Eff 2-20-2002; 153 v S 79, § 1, eff. 10-6-09; 2011 HB 153, § 101.01, eff. Sept. 29, 2011.**

The provisions of §§ 2, 3 of SB 122 (149 v —) read as follows:

SECTION 2. That existing sections 2945.371 and 2945.39 and section 2945.38 of the Revised Code as it results from Am. Sub. S.B. 285 of the 121st General Assembly are hereby repealed.

SECTION 3. This act presents section 2945.38 of the Revised Code as it existed prior to its amendment by Am. Sub. S.B. 285 of the 121st General Assembly. The revived version of that section supersedes the version of that section repealed by Section 2 of this act and omits and repeals all changes made to that section by Am. Sub. S.B. 285 of the 121st General Assembly. The omission and repeal of those changes is not intended to have any substantive effect and is intended to present in this act the version of section 2945.38 of the Revised Code that is currently effective. The repeal of section 2945.38 of the Revised Code by Section 2 of this act is to give effect to the holding of the Ohio Supreme Court in *State v. Sullivan* (2001), 90 Ohio St.3d 502, that section 2945.38 of the Revised Code, as amended by Am. Sub. S.B. 285 of the 121st General Assembly, is unconstitutional.

**Publisher's Note:**

Section 2 of SB 122 repeals the SB 285 (146 v —) version and section 3 revives and amends the former version.

## § 2945.381 Repealed, 137 v H 565, § 2 [136 v S 185]. Eff 11-1-78.

This section concerned the disposition of a mentally ill person accused of committing a crime.

## § 2945.39 Proceedings after expiration of maximum time for treatment after finding of incompetency.

(A) If a defendant who is charged with an offense described in division (C)(1) of section 2945.38 of the Revised Code is found incompetent to stand trial, after the expiration of the maximum time for treatment as specified in division (C) of that section or after the court finds that there is not a substantial probability that the defendant will become competent to stand trial even if the defendant is provided with a course of treatment, one of the following applies:

(1) The court or the prosecutor may file an affidavit in probate court for civil commitment of the defendant in the manner provided in Chapter 5122. or 5123. of the Revised Code. If the court or prosecutor files an affidavit for civil commitment, the court may detain the defendant for ten days pending civil commitment. If the probate court commits the defendant subsequent to the court's or prosecutor's filing of an affidavit for civil commitment, the chief clinical officer of the entity, hospital, or facility, the managing officer of the institution, or the person to which the defendant is committed or admitted shall send to the prosecutor the notices described in divisions (H)(4)(a)(i) to (iii) of section 2945.38 of the Revised Code within the periods of time and under the circumstances specified in those divisions.

(2) On the motion of the prosecutor or on its own motion, the court may retain jurisdiction over the defendant if, at a hearing, the court finds both of the following by clear and convincing evidence:

(a) The defendant committed the offense with which the defendant is charged.

(b) The defendant is a mentally ill person subject to hospitalization by court order or a mentally retarded person subject to institutionalization by court order.

(B) In making its determination under division (A)(2) of this section as to whether to retain jurisdiction over the defendant, the court may consider all relevant evidence, including, but not limited to, any relevant psychiatric, psychological, or medical testimony or reports, the acts constituting the offense charged, and any history of the defendant that is relevant to the defendant's ability to conform to the law.

(C) If the court conducts a hearing as described in division (A)(2) of this section and if the court does not make both findings described in divisions (A)(2)(a) and (b) of this section by clear and convincing evidence, the court shall dismiss the indictment, information, or complaint against the defendant. Upon the dismissal, the court shall discharge the defendant unless the court or prosecutor files an affidavit in probate court for civil commitment of the defendant pursuant to Chapter 5122. or 5123. of the Revised Code. If the court or prosecutor files an affidavit for civil commitment, the court may order that the defendant be detained for up to ten days pending the civil commitment. If the probate court commits the defendant subsequent to the court's or prosecutor's filing of an affidavit for civil commitment, the chief clinical officer of the entity, hospital, or facility, the managing officer of the institution, or the person to which the defendant is committed or admitted shall send to the prosecutor the notices described in divisions (H)(4)(a)(i) to (iii) of section 2945.38 of the Revised Code within the periods of time and under the circumstances specified in those divisions. A dismissal of charges under this division is not a bar to further criminal proceedings based on the same conduct.

(D)(1) If the court conducts a hearing as described in division (A)(2) of this section and if the court makes the findings described in divisions (A)(2)(a) and (b) of this section by clear and convincing evidence, the court shall commit the defendant, if determined to require mental health treatment, to the department of mental health for treatment at a hospital, facility, or agency as determined clinically appropriate by the department of mental health or, if determined to require treatment for developmental disabilities, to a facility operated by the department of developmental disabilities, or another facility, as appropriate. In committing the defendant to the department of mental health, the court shall specify the least restrictive limitations on the defendant's freedom of movement determined to be necessary to protect public safety. In determining the place and nature of the commitment to a facility operated by the department of developmental disabilities or another facility for treatment of developmental disabilities, the court shall order the least restrictive commitment alternative available that is consistent with public safety and the welfare of the defendant. In weighing these factors, the court shall give preference to protecting public safety.

(2) If a court makes a commitment of a defendant under division (D)(1) of this section, the prosecutor shall send to the hospital, facility, or agency where the defendant is placed by the department of mental health or to the defendant's place of commitment all reports of the defendant's current mental condition and, except as otherwise provided in this division, any other relevant information, including, but not limited to, a transcript of the hearing held pursuant to division (A)(2) of this section, copies of relevant police reports, and copies of any prior arrest and conviction records that pertain to the defendant and that the prosecutor possesses. The prosecutor shall send the reports of the defendant's current mental condition in every case of commitment, and, unless the prosecutor determines that the release of any of the other relevant information to unauthorized persons would interfere with the effective prosecution of any person or would create a substantial risk of harm to any person, the prosecutor also shall send the other relevant information.

(3) If a court makes a commitment under division (D)(1) of this section, all further proceedings shall be in accordance with sections 2945.401 and 2945.402 of the Revised Code.

**HISTORY: 146 v S 285 (Eff 7-1-97); 149 v S 122. Eff 2-20-2002; 153 v S 79, § 1, eff. 10-6-09; 2011 HB 153, § 101.01, eff. Sept. 29, 2011.**

**Not analogous to former RC § 2945.39 (137 v H 565; 138 v S 297; 138 v H 900; 138 v H 736; 138 v H 965; 139 v H 1; 143 v H 484), repealed 146 v S 285, § 1, eff 7-1-97.**

See provisions, § 2 of SB 122 (149 v —) following RC § 2945.38.

## § 2945.391 Finding of not guilty by reason of insanity.

For purposes of sections 2945.371 [2945.37.1], 2945.40, 2945.401 [2945.40.1], and 2945.402 [2945.40.2] and Chapters 5122. and 5123. of the Revised Code, a person is "not guilty by reason of insanity" relative to a charge of an offense only as described in division (A)(14) of section 2901.01 of the Revised Code. Proof that a person's reason, at the time of the commission of an offense, was so impaired that the person did not have the ability to refrain from doing the person's act or acts, does not constitute a defense.

**HISTORY: 143 v S 24 (Eff 7-24-90); 146 v S 239 (Eff 9-6-96); 146 v S 285. Eff 7-1-97.**

The effective date is set by section 4 of SB 285.

## § 2945.392 Battered woman syndrome testimony.

(A) The declarations set forth in division (A) of section 2901.06 of the Revised Code apply in relation to this section.

(B) If a defendant is charged with an offense involving the use of force against another and the defendant enters a plea to the charge of not guilty by reason of insanity, the defendant may introduce expert testimony of the "battered woman syndrome" and expert testimony that the defendant suffered from that syndrome as evidence to establish the requisite impairment of the defendant's reason, at the time of the commission of the offense, that is necessary for a finding that the defendant is not guilty by reason of insanity. The introduction of any expert testimony under this division shall be in accordance with the Ohio Rules of Evidence.

**HISTORY: 143 v H 484 (Eff 11-5-90); 146 v S 285. Eff 7-1-97.**

The effective date is set by section 4 of SB 285.

## § 2945.40 Procedure upon acquittal by reason of insanity.

(A) If a person is found not guilty by reason of insanity, the verdict shall state that finding, and the trial court shall conduct a full hearing to determine whether the person is a mentally ill person subject to hospitalization by court order or a mentally retarded person subject to institutionalization by court order. Prior to the hearing, if the trial judge believes that there is probable cause that the person found not guilty by reason of insanity is a mentally ill person subject to hospitalization by court order or mentally retarded person subject to institutionalization by court order, the trial judge may issue a temporary order of detention for that person to remain in effect for ten court days or until the hearing, whichever occurs first.

Any person detained pursuant to a temporary order of detention issued under this division shall be held in a suitable facility, taking into consideration the place and type of confinement prior to and during trial.

(B) The court shall hold the hearing under division (A) of this section to determine whether the person found not guilty by reason of insanity is a mentally ill person subject to hospitalization by court order or a mentally retarded person subject to institutionalization by court order within ten court days after the finding of not guilty by reason of insanity. Failure to conduct the hearing within the ten-day period shall cause the immediate discharge of the respondent, unless the judge grants a continuance for not longer than ten court days for good cause shown or for any period of time upon motion of the respondent.

(C) If a person is found not guilty by reason of insanity, the person has the right to attend all hearings conducted pursuant to sections 2945.37 to 2945.402 of the Revised Code. At any hearing conducted pursuant to one of those sections, the court shall inform the person that the person has all of the following rights:

(1) The right to be represented by counsel and to have that counsel provided at public expense if the person is indigent, with the counsel to be appointed by the court under Chapter 120. of the Revised Code or under the authority recognized in division (C) of section 120.06, division (E) of section 120.16, division (E) of section 120.26, or section 2941.51 of the Revised Code;

(2) The right to have independent expert evaluation and to have that independent expert evaluation provided at public expense if the person is indigent;

(3) The right to subpoena witnesses and documents, to present evidence on the person's behalf, and to cross-examine witnesses against the person;

(4) The right to testify in the person's own behalf and to not be compelled to testify;

(5) The right to have copies of any relevant medical or mental health document in the custody of the state or of any place of commitment other than a document for which the court finds that the release to the person of information contained in the document would create a substantial risk of harm to any person.

(D) The hearing under division (A) of this section shall be open to the public, and the court shall conduct the hearing in accordance with the Rules of Civil Procedure. The court shall make and maintain a full transcript and record of the hearing proceedings. The court may consider all relevant evidence, including, but not limited to, any relevant psychiatric, psychological, or medical testimony or reports, the acts constituting the offense in relation to which the person was found not guilty by reason of insanity, and any history of the person that is relevant to the person's ability to conform to the law.

(E) Upon completion of the hearing under division (A) of this section, if the court finds there is not clear and convincing evidence that the person is a mentally ill person subject to hospitalization by court order or a mentally retarded person subject to institutionalization by court order, the court shall discharge the person, unless a detainer has been placed upon the person by the department of rehabilitation and correction, in which case the person shall be returned to that department.

(F) If, at the hearing under division (A) of this section, the court finds by clear and convincing evidence that the person is a mentally ill person subject to hospitalization by court order, the court shall commit the person to the department of mental health for placement in a hospital, facility, or agency as determined clinically appropriate by the department of mental health. If, at the hearing under division (A) of this section, the court finds by clear and convincing evidence that the person is a mentally retarded person subject to institutionalization by court order, it shall commit the person to a facility operated by the department of developmental disabilities or another facility, as appropriate. Further proceedings shall be in accordance with sections 2945.401 and 2945.402 of the Revised Code. In committing the person to the department of mental health, the court shall specify the least restrictive limitations to the defendant's freedom of movement determined to be necessary to protect public safety. In determining the place and nature of the commitment of a mentally retarded person subject to institutionalization by court order, the court shall order the least restrictive commitment alternative available that is consistent with public safety and the welfare of the person. In weighing these factors, the court shall give preference to protecting public safety.

(G) If a court makes a commitment of a person under division (F) of this section, the prosecutor shall send to the hospital, facility, or agency where the person is placed by the department of mental health or to the defendant's place of commitment all reports of the person's current mental condition, and, except as otherwise provided in this division, any other relevant information, including, but not limited to, a transcript of the hearing held pursuant to division (A) of this section, copies of relevant police reports, and copies of any prior arrest and conviction records that pertain to the person and that the prosecutor possesses. The prosecutor shall send the reports of the person's current mental condition in every case of commitment, and, unless the prosecutor determines that the release of any of the other relevant information to unauthorized persons would interfere with the effective prosecution of any person or would create a substantial risk of harm to any person, the prosecutor also shall send the other relevant information.

(H) A person who is committed pursuant to this section shall not voluntarily admit the person or be voluntarily admitted to a hospital or institution pursuant to section 5122.02, 5122.15, 5123.69, or 5123.76 of the Revised Code.

**HISTORY: 137 v H 565 (Eff 11-1-78); 138 v S 297 (Eff 4-30-80); 138 v H 965 (Eff 4-9-81); 139 v H 1 (Eff 8-5-81); 142 v S 156 (Eff 7-1-89); 143 v S 24 (Eff 7-24-90); 145 v H 571 (Eff 10-6-94); 146 v H 567 (Eff 10-29-96); 146 v S 285. Eff 7-1-97; 153 v S 79, § 1, eff. 10-6-09; 2011 HB 153, § 101.01, eff. Sept. 29, 2011.**

**Analogous to former RC § 2945.40 (GC § 13441-4; 113 v 123; Bureau of Code Revision, 10-1-53), repealed 137 v H 565, § 2, eff 11-1-78.**

The effective date is set by section 4 of SB 285.

## § 2945.401 Continuing jurisdiction of court after incompetency finding or insanity acquittal; application of other laws; termination of commitment or change in conditions.

(A) A defendant found incompetent to stand trial and committed pursuant to section 2945.39 of the Revised Code or a person found not guilty by reason of insanity and committed pursuant to section 2945.40 of the Revised Code shall remain subject to the jurisdiction of the trial court pursuant to that commitment, and to the provisions of this section, until the final termination of the commitment as described in division (J)(1) of this section. If the jurisdiction is terminated under this division because of the final termination of the commitment resulting from the expiration of the maximum prison term or term of imprisonment described in division (J)(1)(b) of this section, the court or prosecutor may file an affidavit for the civil commitment of the defendant or person pursuant to Chapter 5122. or 5123. of the Revised Code.

(B) A hearing conducted under any provision of sections 2945.37 to 2945.402 of the Revised Code shall not be conducted in accordance with Chapters 5122. and 5123. of the Revised Code. Any person who is committed pursuant to section 2945.39 or 2945.40 of the Revised Code shall not voluntarily admit the person or be voluntarily admitted to a hospital or institution pursuant to section 5122.02, 5122.15, 5123.69, or 5123.76 of the Revised Code. All other provisions of Chapters 5122. and 5123. of the Revised Code regarding hospitalization or institutionalization shall apply to the extent they are not in conflict with this chapter. A commitment under section 2945.39 or 2945.40 of the Revised Code shall not be terminated and the conditions of the commitment shall not be changed except as otherwise provided in division (D)(2) of this section with respect to a mentally retarded person subject to institutionalization by court order or except by order of the trial court.

(C) The department of mental health or the institution or facility to which a defendant or person has been committed under section 2945.39 or 2945.40 of the Revised Code shall report in writing to the trial court, at the times specified in this division, as to whether the defendant or person remains a mentally ill person subject to hospitalization by court order or a mentally retarded person subject to institutionalization by court order and, in the case of a defendant committed under section 2945.39 of the Revised Code, as to whether the defendant remains incompetent to stand trial. The department, institution, or facility shall make the reports after the initial six months of treatment and every two years after the initial report is made. The trial court shall provide copies of the reports to the prosecutor and to the counsel for the defendant or person. Within thirty days after its receipt pursuant to this division of a report from the department, institution, or facility, the trial court shall hold a hearing on the continued commitment of the defendant or person or on any changes in the conditions of the commitment of the defendant or person. The defendant or person may request a change in the conditions of confinement, and the trial court shall conduct a hearing on that request if six months or more have elapsed since the most recent hearing was conducted under this section.

(D)(1) Except as otherwise provided in division (D)(2) of this section, when a defendant or person has been committed under section 2945.39 or 2945.40 of the Revised Code, at any time after evaluating the risks to public safety and the welfare of the defendant or person, the designee of the department of mental health or the managing officer of the institution or director of the facility to which the defendant or person is committed may recommend a termination of the defendant's or person's commitment or a change in the conditions of the defendant's or person's commitment.

Except as otherwise provided in division (D)(2) of this section, if the designee of the department of mental health recommends on-grounds unsupervised movement, off-grounds supervised movement, or nonsecured status for the defendant or person or termination of the defendant's or person's commitment, the following provisions apply:

(a) If the department's designee recommends on-grounds unsupervised movement or off-grounds supervised movement, the department's designee shall file with the trial court an application for approval of the movement and shall send a copy of the application to the prosecutor. Within fifteen days after receiving the application, the prosecutor may request a hearing on the application and, if a hearing is requested, shall so inform the department's designee. If the prosecutor does not request a hearing within the fifteen-day period, the trial court shall approve the application by entering its order approving the requested movement or, within five days after the expiration of the fifteen-day period, shall set a date for a hearing on the application. If the prosecutor requests a hearing on the application within the fifteen-day period, the trial court shall hold a hearing on the application within thirty days after the hearing is requested. If the trial court, within five days after the expiration of the fifteen-day period, sets a date for a hearing on the application, the trial court shall hold the hearing within thirty days after setting the hearing date. At least fifteen days before any hearing is held under this division, the trial court shall give the prosecutor written notice of the date, time, and place of the hearing. At the conclusion of each hearing conducted under this division, the trial court either shall approve or disapprove the application and shall enter its order accordingly.

(b) If the department's designee recommends termination of the defendant's or person's commitment at any time or if the department's designee recommends the first of any nonsecured status for the defendant or person, the department's designee shall send written notice of this recommendation to the trial court and to the local forensic center. The local forensic center shall evaluate the committed defendant or person and, within thirty days after its receipt of the written notice, shall submit to the trial court and the department's designee a written report of the evaluation. The trial court shall provide a copy of the department's designee's written notice and of the local forensic center's written report to the prosecutor and to the counsel for the defendant or person. Upon the local forensic center's submission of the report to the trial court and the department's designee, all of the following apply:

(i) If the forensic center disagrees with the recommendation of the department's designee, it shall inform the department's designee and the trial court of its decision and the reasons for the decision. The department's designee, after consideration of the forensic center's decision, shall either withdraw, proceed with, or modify and proceed with the recommendation. If the department's designee proceeds with, or modifies and proceeds with, the recommendation, the department's designee shall proceed in accordance with division (D)(1)(b)(iii) of this section.

(ii) If the forensic center agrees with the recommendation of the department's designee, it shall inform the department's designee and the trial court of its decision and the reasons for the decision, and the department's designee shall proceed in accordance with division (D)(1)(b)(iii) of this section.

(iii) If the forensic center disagrees with the recommendation of the department's designee and the department's designee proceeds with, or modifies and proceeds with, the recommendation or if the forensic center agrees with the recommendation of the department's designee, the department's designee shall work with community mental health agencies, programs, facilities, or boards of alcohol, drug addiction, and mental health services to develop a plan to implement the recommendation. If the defendant or person is on medication, the plan shall include, but shall not be limited to, a system to monitor the defendant's or person's compliance with the prescribed medication treatment plan. The system shall include a schedule that clearly states when the defendant or person shall report for a medication compliance check. The medication compliance checks shall be based upon the effective duration of the prescribed medication, taking into account the route by which it is taken, and shall be scheduled at intervals sufficiently close together to detect a potential increase in mental illness symptoms that the medication is intended to prevent.

The department's designee shall send the recommendation and plan developed under division (D)(1)(b)(iii) of this section, in writing, to the trial court, the prosecutor and the counsel for the committed defendant or person. The trial court shall conduct a hearing on the recommendation and plan developed under division (D)(1)(b)(iii) of this section. Divisions (D)(1)(c) and (d) and (E) to (J) of this section apply regarding the hearing.

(c) If the department's designee's recommendation is for nonsecured status or termination of commitment, the prosecutor may obtain an independent expert evaluation of the defendant's or person's mental condition, and the trial court may continue the hearing on the recommendation for a period of not more than thirty days to permit time for the evaluation.

The prosecutor may introduce the evaluation report or present other evidence at the hearing in accordance with the Rules of Evidence.

(d) The trial court shall schedule the hearing on a department's designee's recommendation for nonsecured status or termination of commitment and shall give reasonable notice to the prosecutor and the counsel for the defendant or person. Unless continued for independent evaluation at the prosecutor's request or for other good cause, the hearing shall be held within thirty days after the trial court's receipt of the recommendation and plan.

(2)(a) Division (D)(1) of this section does not apply to on-grounds unsupervised movement of a defendant or person who has been committed under section 2945.39 or 2945.40 of the Revised Code, who is a mentally retarded person subject to institutionalization by court order, and who is being provided residential habilitation, care, and treatment in a facility operated by the department of developmental disabilities.

(b) If, pursuant to section 2945.39 of the Revised Code, the trial court commits a defendant who is found incompetent to stand trial and who is a mentally retarded person subject to institutionalization by court order, if the defendant is being provided residential habilitation, care, and treatment in a facility operated by the department of developmental disabilities, if an individual who is conducting a survey for the department of health to determine the facility's compliance with the certification requirements of the medicaid program under Chapter 5111. of the Revised Code and Title XIX of the "Social Security Act," 49 Stat. 620 (1935), 42 U.S.C.A. 301, as amended, cites the defendant's receipt of the residential habilitation, care, and treatment in the facility as being inappropriate under the certification requirements, if the defendant's receipt of the residential habilitation, care, and treatment in the facility potentially jeopardizes the facility's continued receipt of federal medicaid moneys, and if as a result of the citation the chief clinical officer of the facility determines that the conditions of the defendant's commitment should be changed, the department of developmental disabilities may cause the defendant to be removed from the particular facility and, after evaluating the risks to public safety and the welfare of the defendant and after determining whether another type of placement is consistent with the certification requirements, may place the defendant in another facility that the department selects as an appropriate facility for the defendant's continued receipt of residential habilitation, care, and treatment and that is a no less secure setting than the facility in which the defendant had been placed at the time of the citation. Within three days after the defendant's removal and alternative placement under the circumstances described in division (D)(2)(b) of this section, the department of developmental disabilities shall notify the trial court and the prosecutor in writing of the removal and alternative placement.

The trial court shall set a date for a hearing on the removal and alternative placement, and the hearing shall be held within twenty-one days after the trial court's receipt of the notice from the department of developmental disabilities. At least ten days before the hearing is held, the trial court shall give the prosecutor, the department of developmental disabilities, and the counsel for the defendant written notice of the date, time, and place of the hearing. At the hearing, the trial court shall consider the citation issued by the individual who conducted the survey for the department of health to be prima-facie evidence of the fact that the defendant's commitment to the particular facility was inappropriate under the certification requirements of the medicaid program under Chapter 5111. of the Revised Code and Title XIX of the "Social Security Act," 49 Stat. 620 (1935), 42 U.S.C.A. 301, as amended, and potentially jeopardizes the particular facility's continued receipt of federal medicaid moneys. At the conclusion of the hearing, the trial court may approve or disapprove the defendant's removal and alternative placement. If the trial court approves the defendant's removal and alternative placement, the department of developmental disabilities may continue the defendant's alternative placement. If the trial court disapproves the defendant's removal and alternative placement, it shall enter an order modifying the defendant's removal and alternative placement, but that order shall not require the department of developmental disabilities to replace the defendant for purposes of continued residential habilitation, care, and treatment in the facility associated with the citation issued by the individual who conducted the survey for the department of health.

(E) In making a determination under this section regarding nonsecured status or termination of commitment, the trial court shall consider all relevant factors, including, but not limited to, all of the following:

(1) Whether, in the trial court's view, the defendant or person currently represents a substantial risk of physical harm to the defendant or person or others;

(2) Psychiatric and medical testimony as to the current mental and physical condition of the defendant or person;

(3) Whether the defendant or person has insight into the dependant's or person's condition so that the defendant or person will continue treatment as prescribed or seek professional assistance as needed;

(4) The grounds upon which the state relies for the proposed commitment;

(5) Any past history that is relevant to establish the defendant's or person's degree of conformity to the laws, rules, regulations, and values of society;

(6) If there is evidence that the defendant's or person's mental illness is in a state of remission, the medically suggested cause and degree of the remission and the probability that the defendant or person will continue treatment to maintain the remissive state of the defendant's or person's illness should the defendant's or person's commitment conditions be altered.

(F) At any hearing held pursuant to division (C) or (D)(1) or (2) of this section, the defendant or the person shall have all the rights of a defendant or person at a commitment hearing as described in section 2945.40 of the Revised Code.

(G) In a hearing held pursuant to division (C) or (D)(1) of this section, the prosecutor has the burden of proof as follows:

(1) For a recommendation of termination of commitment, to show by clear and convincing evidence that the defendant or person remains a mentally ill person subject to hospitalization by court order or a mentally retarded person subject to institutionalization by court order;

(2) For a recommendation for a change in the conditions of the commitment to a less restrictive status, to show by clear and convincing evidence that the proposed change represents a threat to public safety or a threat to the safety of any person.

(H) In a hearing held pursuant to division (C) or (D)(1) or (2) of this section, the prosecutor shall represent the state or the public interest.

(I) At the conclusion of a hearing conducted under division (D)(1) of this section regarding a recommendation from the designee of the department of mental health, managing officer of the institution, or director of a facility, the trial court may approve, disapprove, or modify the recommendation and shall enter an order accordingly.

(J)(1) A defendant or person who has been committed pursuant to section 2945.39 or 2945.40 of the Revised Code continues to be under the jurisdiction of the trial court until the final termination of the commitment. For purposes of division (J) of this section, the final termination of a commitment occurs upon the earlier of one of the following:

(a) The defendant or person no longer is a mentally ill person subject to hospitalization by court order or a mentally retarded person subject to institutionalization by court order, as determined by the trial court;

(b) The expiration of the maximum prison term or term of imprisonment that the defendant or person could have received if the defendant or person had been convicted of the most serious offense with which the defendant or person is charged or in relation to which the defendant or person was found not guilty by reason of insanity;

(c) The trial court enters an order terminating the commitment under the circumstances described in division (J)(2)(a)(ii) of this section.

(2)(a) If a defendant is found incompetent to stand trial and committed pursuant to section 2945.39 of the Revised Code, if neither of the circumstances described in divisions (J)(1)(a) and (b) of this section applies to that defendant, and if a report filed with the trial court pursuant to division (C) of this section indicates that the defendant presently is competent to stand trial or if, at any other time during the period of the defendant's commitment, the prosecutor, the counsel for the defendant, or the designee of the department of mental health or the managing officer of the institution or director of the facility to which the defendant is committed files an application with the trial court alleging that the defendant presently is competent to stand trial and requesting a hearing on the competency issue or the trial court otherwise has reasonable cause to believe that the defendant presently is competent to stand trial and determines on its own motion to hold a hearing on the competency issue, the trial court shall schedule a hearing on the competency of the defendant to stand trial, shall give the prosecutor, the counsel for the defendant, and the department's designee or the managing officer of the institution or the director of the facility to which the defendant is committed notice of the date, time, and place of the hearing at least fifteen days before the hearing, and shall conduct the hearing within thirty days of the filing of the application or of its own motion. If, at the conclusion of the hearing, the trial court determines that the defendant presently is capable of understanding the nature and objective of the proceedings against the defendant and of assisting in the defendant's defense, the trial court shall order that the defendant is competent to stand trial and shall be proceeded against as provided by law with respect to the applicable offenses described in division (C)(1) of section 2945.38 of the Revised Code and shall enter whichever of the following additional orders is appropriate:

(i) If the trial court determines that the defendant remains a mentally ill person subject to hospitalization by court order or a mentally retarded person subject to institutionalization by court order, the trial court shall order that the defendant's commitment to the department of mental health or to an institution or facility for the treatment of developmental disabilities be continued during the pendency of the trial on the applicable offenses described in division (C)(1) of section 2945.38 of the Revised Code.

(ii) If the trial court determines that the defendant no longer is a mentally ill person subject to hospitalization by court order or a mentally retarded person subject to institutionalization by court order, the trial court shall order that the defendant's commitment to the department of mental health or to an institution or facility for the treatment of developmental disabilities shall not be continued during the pendency of the trial on the applicable offenses described in division (C)(1) of section 2945.38 of the Revised Code. This order shall be a final termination of the commitment for purposes of division (J)(1)(c) of this section.

(b) If, at the conclusion of the hearing described in division (J)(2)(a) of this section, the trial court determines that the defendant remains incapable of understanding the nature and objective of the proceedings against the defendant or of assisting in the defendant's defense, the trial court shall order that the defendant continues to be incompetent to stand trial, that the defendant's commitment to the department of mental health or to an institution or facility for the treatment of developmental disabilities shall be continued, and that the defendant remains subject to the jurisdiction of the trial court pursuant to that commitment, and to the provisions of this section, until the final termination of the commitment as described in division (J)(1) of this section.

**HISTORY: 146 v S 285. Eff 7-1-97; 153 v S 79, § 1, eff. 10-6-09; 2011 HB 153, § 101.01, eff. Sept. 29, 2011.**

The effective date is set by section 4 of SB 285.

## § 2945.402 Conditional release.

(A) In approving a conditional release, the trial court may set any conditions on the release with respect to the treatment, evaluation, counseling, or control of the defendant or person that the court considers necessary to protect the public safety and the welfare of the defendant or person. The trial court may revoke a defendant's or person's conditional release and order reinstatement of the previous placement or reinstitutionalization at any time the conditions of the release have not been satisfied, provided that the revocation shall be in accordance with this section.

(B) A conditional release is a commitment. The hearings on continued commitment as described in section 2945.401 of the Revised Code apply to a defendant or person on conditional release.

(C) A person, agency, or facility that is assigned to monitor a defendant or person on conditional release immediately shall notify the trial court on learning that the defendant or person being monitored has violated the terms of the conditional release. Upon learning of any violation of the terms of the conditional release, the trial court may issue a temporary order of detention or, if necessary, an arrest warrant for the defendant or person. Within ten court days after the defendant's or person's detention or arrest, the trial court shall conduct a hearing to determine whether the conditional release should be modified or terminated. At the hearing, the defendant or person shall have the same rights as are described in division (C) of section 2945.40 of the Revised Code. The trial court may order a continuance of the ten-court-day period for no longer than ten days for good cause shown or for any period on motion of the defendant or person. If the trial court fails to conduct the hearing within the ten-court-day period and does not order a continuance in accordance with this division, the defendant or person shall be restored to the prior conditional release status.

(D) The trial court shall give all parties reasonable notice of a hearing conducted under this section. At the hearing, the prosecutor shall present the case demonstrating that the defendant or person violated the terms of the conditional release. If the court finds by a preponderance of the evidence that the defendant or person violated the terms of the conditional release, the court may continue, modify, or terminate the conditional release and shall enter its order accordingly.

**HISTORY: 146 v S 285. Eff 7-1-97; 2011 HB 153, § 101.01, eff. Sept. 29, 2011.**

The effective date is set by section 4 of SB 285.

[WITNESSES]

## § 2945.41 Rules applicable in criminal cases.

The rules of evidence in civil causes, where applicable, govern in all criminal causes.

**HISTORY: GC § 13444-1; 113 v 123(185), ch 23; Bureau of Code Revision. Eff 10-1-53.**

## § 2945.42 Competency of witnesses.

No person is disqualified as a witness in a criminal prosecution by reason of the person's interest in the prosecution as a party or otherwise or by reason of the person's conviction of crime. Husband and wife are competent witnesses to testify in behalf of each other in all criminal prosecutions and to testify against each other in all actions, prosecutions, and proceedings for personal injury of either by the other, bigamy, or failure to provide for, neglect of, or cruelty to their children under eighteen years of age or their physically or mentally handicapped child under twenty-one years of age. A spouse may testify against his or her spouse in a prosecution under a provision of sections 2903.11 to 2903.13, 2919.21, 2919.22, or 2919.25 of the Revised Code for cruelty to, neglect of, or abandonment of such spouse, in a prosecution against his or her spouse under section 2903.211 [2903.21.1] or 2911.211 [2911.21.1], of the Revised Code for the commission of the offense against the spouse who is testifying, in a prosecution under section 2919.27 of the Revised Code involving a protection order issued or consent agreement approved pursuant to section 2919.26 or 3113.31 of the Revised Code for the commission of the offense against the spouse who is testifying, or in a prosecution under section 2907.02 of the Revised Code for the commission of rape or under former section 2907.12 of the Revised Code for felonious sexual penetration against such spouse in a case in which the offense can be committed against a spouse. Such interest, conviction, or relationship may be shown for the purpose of affecting the credibility of the witness. Husband or wife shall not testify concerning a communication made by one to the other, or act done by either in the presence of the other, during coverture, unless the communication was made or act done in the known presence or hearing of a third person competent to be a witness, or in case of personal injury by either the husband or wife to the other, or rape or the former offense of felonious sexual penetration in a case in which the offense can be committed against a spouse, or bigamy, or failure to provide for, or neglect or cruelty of either to their children under eighteen years of age or their physically or mentally handicapped child under twenty-one years of age, violation of a protection order or consent agreement, or neglect or abandonment of a spouse under a provision of those sections. The presence or whereabouts of the husband or wife is not an act under this section. The rule is the same if the marital relation has ceased to exist.

**HISTORY: GC § 13444-2; 113 v 123(186), ch 23, § 2; Bureau of Code Revision, 10-1-53; 134 v S 312 (Eff 1-26-72); 136 v H 1 (Eff 6-13-75); 138 v H 920 (Eff 4-9-81); 141 v H 475 (Eff 3-7-86); 144 v H 536 (Eff 11-5-92); 146 v S 2 (Eff 7-1-96); 146 v H 445. Eff 9-3-96.**

## § 2945.43 Defendant may testify.

On the trial of a criminal cause, a person charged with an offense may, at his own request, be a witness, but not otherwise. The failure of such person to testify may be considered by the court and jury and may be made the subject of comment by counsel.

**HISTORY: GC § 13444-3; 113 v 123(186), ch 23, § 3; Bureau of Code Revision. Eff 10-1-53.**

## § 2945.44 Immunity of witnesses turning state's evidence.

(A) In any criminal proceeding in this state or in any criminal or civil proceeding brought pursuant to Chapter 2981. of the Revised Code, if a witness refuses to answer or produce information on the basis of the witness's privilege against self-incrimination, the court of common pleas of the county in which the proceeding is being held, unless it finds that to do so would not further the administration of justice, shall compel the witness to answer or produce the information, if both of the following apply:

(1) The prosecuting attorney of the county in which the proceedings are being held makes a written request to the court of common pleas to order the witness to answer or produce the information, notwithstanding the witness's claim of privilege;

(2) The court of common pleas informs the witness that by answering, or producing the information the witness will receive immunity under division (B) of this section.

(B) If, but for this section, the witness would have been privileged to withhold an answer or any information given in any criminal proceeding, and the witness complies with an order under division (A) of this section compelling the witness to give an answer or produce any information, the witness shall not be prosecuted or subjected to any criminal penalty in the courts of this state for or on account of any transaction or matter concerning which, in compliance with the order, the witness gave an answer or produced any information.

(C) A witness granted immunity under this section may be subjected to a criminal penalty for any violation of section 2921.11, 2921.12, or 2921.13 of the Revised Code, or for contempt committed in answering, failing to answer, or failing to produce information in compliance with the order.

**HISTORY: 137 v H 491 (Eff 5-30-78); 141 v H 5. Eff 1-1-86; 151 v H 241, § 1, eff. 7-1-07.**

See provisions of § 4 of 151 v H 241 following RC § 2901.01.

**Analogous to former RC § 2945.44 (134 v H 511; 136 v S 234), repealed 137 v H 491, § 2, eff 5-30-78; and RC § 2945.44 (GC § 13444-4; 113 v 123(186); Bureau of Code Revision, 10-1-53; 126 v 168), repealed 134 v H 511, § 2, eff 1-1-74.**

The effective date is set by section 3 of HB 5.

## § 2945.45 Subpoenas to issue to any county.

In all criminal cases, the clerk of the court of common pleas, upon a praecipe being filed, shall issue writs of subpoena for the witnesses named therein, directed to the sheriff of such county, or the county where such witnesses reside or are found, which shall be served and returned as in other cases. Such sheriff, by writing indorsed on the writs, may depute a disinterested person to serve and return them. The person so deputed to serve such subpoenas shall make a return of the service made, and make oath thereto before a person competent to administer oaths, which shall be indorsed on the writ. The return may be forwarded through the post office, or otherwise.

**HISTORY: GC § 13444-5; 113 v 123(187), ch 23, § 5; Bureau of Code Revision. Eff 10-1-53.**

## § 2945.451 Employee may not be penalized for being subpoenaed to criminal proceeding.

No employer shall discharge or terminate from employment, threaten to discharge or terminate from employment, or otherwise punish or penalize any employee because of time lost from regular employment as a result of the employee's attendance at any proceeding in a criminal case pursuant to a subpoena. This section generally does not require and shall not be construed to require an employer to pay an employee for time lost as a result of attendance at any criminal proceeding. However, if an employee is subpoenaed to appear at a criminal proceeding and the proceeding pertains to an offense against the employer or an offense involving the employee during the course of his employment, the employer shall not decrease or withhold the employee's pay for any time lost as a result of compliance with the subpoena. Any employer who knowingly violates this section is in contempt of court.

**HISTORY: 140 v S 172. Eff 9-26-84.**

## § 2945.46 Attendance of witness enforced.

Civil procedure relative to compelling the attendance and testimony of witnesses, their examination, the administering of oaths and affirmations, and proceedings for contempt to enforce the remedies and protect the rights of parties, extend to criminal cases as far as applicable.

**HISTORY: GC § 13444-6; 113 v 123(187), ch 23, § 6; Bureau of Code Revision. Eff 10-1-53.**

## § 2945.47 Deposition or subpoena of prisoner.

(A)(1) As used in this section, "detention facility" has the same meaning as in section 2921.01 of the Revised Code.

(2) If it is necessary in a criminal proceeding before the court to procure the testimony of a person who is imprisoned in a detention facility or state correctional institution within this state, or who is in the custody of the department of youth services, the court may require that the person's testimony be taken by deposition pursuant to Criminal Rule 15 at the place of the person's confinement, if the person is not a defendant in the case and if the court determines that the interests of justice do not demand that the person be brought before the court for the presentation of the person's testimony. All witnesses for the prosecution shall be brought before the court. The defendant may waive any right to compel the appearance of a person brought before the court pursuant to this division.

(B) Subject to division (C) of this section, if it is necessary in a criminal proceeding before the court to procure the testimony of a person who is imprisoned in a detention facility within this state, the court may order a subpoena to be issued, directed to the keeper of the institution, commanding the keeper to bring the prisoner named in the subpoena before the court.

The keeper, upon receiving the subpoena, shall take the witness before the court at the time and place named in the subpoena, and hold the witness until the witness is discharged by the court. When discharged, the witness shall be returned in the custody of such officer to the place of imprisonment from which the witness was taken, and the officer may command any assistance that the officer considers proper for the transportation of the witness.

(C) If it is necessary in a criminal proceeding before the court to procure the testimony of a person who is imprisoned in a state correctional institution within this state, or who is in the custody of the department of youth services, the court may order a subpoena to be issued directed to the sheriff of the county in which the indictment or grand jury proceeding is pending. When a copy of the subpoena is presented by the sheriff to the warden or superintendent of a state correctional institution, or to the person in charge of the facility in which a juvenile is confined, the witness shall be delivered at the institution or facility to the sheriff who shall take the witness before the court at the time and place named in the subpoena and hold the witness until the witness is discharged by the court. When discharged, the witness shall be returned in the custody of the sheriff to the place of imprisonment from which the witness was taken.

(D) The court, in the manner provided in Chapter 120. of the Revised Code, shall either assign counsel or designate a public defender to represent a juvenile subpoenaed as a witness under this section. Compensation for assigned counsel shall be made pursuant to section 2941.51 of the Revised Code.

(E) When a person's testimony is taken by deposition pursuant to division (A) of this section, the deposition shall be upon oral examination if either the prosecuting authority or the defendant who is taking the deposition requests that the deposition be upon oral examination, and may be videotaped if either the prosecuting authority or the defendant who is taking the deposition requests that it be recorded by means of videotape.

The person requesting the testimony of the person whose deposition is taken pursuant to division (A) of this section shall pay the expense of taking the deposition, except that the court may tax the expense as court costs in appropriate cases.

**HISTORY: RS §§ 7290, 7291; 70 v 78; GC §§ 13444-7, 13444-8; 113 v 123(187), ch 23, §§ 7, 8; Bureau of Code Revision, 10-1-53; 129 v 322 (Eff 7-14-61); 136 v S 393 (Eff 9-27-76); 139 v H 145 (Eff 5-28-81); 139 v H 440 (Eff 11-23-81); 145 v H 571 (Eff 10-6-94); 147 v H 293. Eff 3-17-98.**

## § 2945.48 Witness may be placed in jail.

When a witness mentioned in section 2945.47 of the Revised Code is in attendance upon a court he may be placed in the jail of the county. The expenses of the officer in transporting him to and from such court, including compensation for the guard or attendant of such prisoner not exceeding the per diem salary of such guard for the time he is away from said institution, shall be allowed by the court and taxed and paid as other costs against the state.

**HISTORY: GC § 13444-9; 113 v 123(188), ch 23, § 9; Bureau of Code Revision. Eff 10-1-53.**

### § 2945.481 Deposition of child victim; videotaping; testimony taken outside courtroom and televised into it or replayed in courtroom.

(A)(1) As used in this section, "victim" includes any person who was a victim of a violation identified in division (A)(2) of this section or an offense of violence or against whom was directed any conduct that constitutes, or that is an element of, a violation identified in division (A)(2) of this section or an offense of violence.

(2) In any proceeding in the prosecution of a charge of a violation of section 2905.03, 2905.05, 2907.02, 2907.03, 2907.04, 2907.05, 2907.06, 2907.07, 2907.09, 2907.21, 2907.23, 2907.24, 2907.31, 2907.32, 2907.321 [2907.32.1], 2907.322 [2907.32.2], 2907.323 [2907.32.3], or 2919.22 of the Revised Code or an offense of violence and in which an alleged victim of the violation or offense was a child who was less than thirteen years of age when the complaint, indictment, or information was filed, whichever occurred earlier, the judge of the court in which the prosecution is being conducted, upon motion of an attorney for the prosecution, shall order that the testimony of the child victim be taken by deposition. The prosecution also may request that the deposition be videotaped in accordance with division (A)(3) of this section. The judge shall notify the child victim whose deposition is to be taken, the prosecution, and the defense of the date, time, and place for taking the deposition. The notice shall identify the child victim who is to be examined and shall indicate whether a request that the deposition be videotaped has been made. The defendant shall have the right to attend the deposition and the right to be represented by counsel. Depositions shall be taken in the manner provided in civil cases, except that the judge shall preside at the taking of the deposition and shall rule at that time on any objections of the prosecution or the attorney for the defense. The prosecution and the attorney for the defense shall have the right, as at trial, to full examination and cross-examination of the child victim whose deposition is to be taken. If a deposition taken under this division is intended to be offered as evidence in the proceeding, it shall be filed in the court in which the action is pending and is admissible in the manner described in division (B) of this section. If a deposition of a child victim taken under this division is admitted as evidence at the proceeding under division (B) of this section, the child victim shall not be required to testify in person at the proceeding. However, at any time before the conclusion of the proceeding, the attorney for the defense may file a motion with the judge requesting that another deposition of the child victim be taken because new evidence material to the defense has been discovered that the attorney for the defense could not with reasonable diligence have discovered prior to the taking of the admitted deposition. A motion for another deposition shall be accompanied by supporting affidavits. Upon the filing of a motion for another deposition and affidavits, the court may order that additional testimony of the child victim relative to the new evidence be taken by another deposition. If the court orders the taking of another deposition under this provision, the deposition shall be taken in accordance with this division; if the admitted deposition was a videotaped deposition taken in accordance with division (A)(3) of this section, the new deposition also shall be videotaped in accordance with that division and in other cases, the new deposition may be videotaped in accordance with that division.

(3) If the prosecution requests that a deposition to be taken under division (A)(2) of this section be videotaped, the judge shall order that the deposition be videotaped in accordance with this division. If a judge issues an order that the deposition be videotaped, the judge shall exclude from the room in which the deposition is to be taken every person except the child victim giving the testimony, the judge, one or more interpreters if needed, the attorneys for the prosecution and the defense, any person needed to operate the equipment to be used, one person chosen by the child victim giving the deposition, and any person whose presence the judge determines would contribute to the welfare and well-being of the child victim giving the deposition. The person chosen by the child victim shall not be a witness in the proceeding and, both before and during the deposition, shall not discuss the testimony of the child victim with any other witness in the proceeding. To the extent feasible, any person operating the recording equipment shall be restricted to a room adjacent to the room in which the deposition is being taken, or to a location in the room in which the deposition is being taken that is behind a screen or mirror, so that the person operating the recording equipment can see and hear, but cannot be seen or heard by, the child victim giving the deposition during the deposition. The defendant shall be permitted to observe and hear the testimony of the child victim giving the deposition on a monitor, shall be provided with an electronic means of immediate communication with the defendant's attorney during the testimony, and shall be restricted to a location from which the defendant cannot be seen or heard by the child victim giving the deposition, except on a monitor provided for that purpose. The child victim giving the deposition shall be provided with a monitor on which the child victim can observe, during the testimony, the defendant. The judge, at the judge's discretion, may preside at the deposition by electronic means from outside the room in which the deposition is to be taken; if the judge presides by electronic means, the judge shall be provided with monitors on which the judge can see each person in the room in which the deposition is to be taken and with an electronic means of communication with each person, and each person in the room shall be provided with a monitor on which that person can see the judge and with an electronic means of communication with the judge. A deposition that is videotaped under this division shall be taken and filed in the manner described in division (A)(2) of this section and is admissible in the manner described in this division and division (B) of this section, and, if a deposition that is videotaped under this division is admitted as evidence at the proceeding, the child victim shall not be required to testify in person at the proceeding. No deposition videotaped under this division shall be admitted as evidence at any proceeding unless division (B) of this section is satisfied relative to the deposition and all of the following apply relative to the recording:

(a) The recording is both aural and visual and is recorded on film or videotape, or by other electronic means.

(b) The recording is authenticated under the Rules of Evidence and the Rules of Criminal Procedure as a fair and accurate representation of what occurred, and the recording is not altered other than at the direction and under the supervision of the judge in the proceeding.

(c) Each voice on the recording that is material to the testimony on the recording or the making of the recording, as determined by the judge, is identified.

(d) Both the prosecution and the defendant are afforded an opportunity to view the recording before it is shown in the proceeding.

(B)(1) At any proceeding in a prosecution in relation to which a deposition was taken under division (A) of this section, the deposition or a part of it is admissible in evidence upon motion of the prosecution if the testimony in the deposition or the part to be admitted is not excluded by the hearsay rule and if the deposition or the part to be admitted otherwise is admissible under the Rules of Evidence. For purposes of this division, testimony is not excluded by the hearsay rule if the testimony is not hearsay under Evidence Rule 801; if the testimony is within an exception to the hearsay rule set forth in Evidence Rule 803; if the child victim who gave the testimony is unavailable as a witness, as defined in Evidence Rule 804, and the testimony is admissible under that rule; or if both of the following apply:

(a) The defendant had an opportunity and similar motive at the time of the taking of the deposition to develop the testimony by direct, cross, or redirect examination.

(b) The judge determines that there is reasonable cause to believe that, if the child victim who gave the testimony in the deposition were to testify in person at the proceeding, the child victim would experience serious emotional trauma as a result of the child victim's participation at the proceeding.

(2) Objections to receiving in evidence a deposition or a part of it under division (B) of this section shall be made as provided in civil actions.

(3) The provisions of divisions (A) and (B) of this section are in addition to any other provisions of the Revised Code, the Rules of Criminal Procedure, or the Rules of Evidence that pertain to the taking or admission of depositions in a criminal proceeding and do not limit the admissibility under any of those other provisions of any deposition taken under division (A) of this section or otherwise taken.

(C) In any proceeding in the prosecution of any charge of a violation listed in division (A)(2) of this section or an offense of violence and in which an alleged victim of the violation or offense was a child who was less than thirteen years of age when the complaint, indictment, or information was filed, whichever occurred earlier, the prosecution may file a motion with the judge requesting the judge to order the testimony of the child victim to be taken in a room other than the room in which the proceeding is being conducted and be televised, by closed circuit equipment, into the room in which the proceeding is being conducted to be viewed by the jury, if applicable, the defendant, and any other persons who are not permitted in the room in which the testimony is to be taken but who would have been present during the testimony of the child victim had it been given in the room in which the proceeding is being conducted. Except for good cause shown, the prosecution shall file a motion under this division at least seven days before the date of the proceeding. The judge may issue the order upon the motion of the prosecution filed under this section, if the judge determines that the child victim is unavailable to testify in the room in which the proceeding is being conducted in the physical presence of the defendant, for one or more of the reasons set forth in division (E) of this section. If a judge issues an order of that nature, the judge shall exclude from the room in which the testimony is to be taken every person except a person described in division (A)(3) of this section. The judge, at the judge's discretion, may preside during the giving of the testimony by electronic means from outside the room in which it is being given, subject to the limitations set forth in division (A)(3) of this section. To the extent feasible, any person operating the televising equipment shall be hidden from the sight and hearing of the child victim giving the testimony, in a manner similar to that described in division (A)(3) of this section. The defendant shall be permitted to observe and hear the testimony of the child victim giving the testimony on a monitor, shall be provided with an electronic means of immediate communication with the defendant's attorney during the testimony, and shall be restricted to a location from which the defendant cannot be seen or heard by the child victim giving the testimony, except on a monitor provided for that purpose. The child victim giving the testimony shall be provided with a monitor on which the child victim can observe, during the testimony, the defendant.

(D) In any proceeding in the prosecution of any charge of a violation listed in division (A)(2) of this section or an offense of violence and in which an alleged victim of the violation or offense was a child who was less than thirteen years of age when the complaint, indictment, or information was filed, whichever occurred earlier, the prosecution may file a motion with the judge requesting the judge to order the testimony of the child victim to be taken outside of the room in which the proceeding is being conducted and be recorded for showing in the room in which the proceeding is being conducted before the judge, the jury, if applicable, the defendant, and any other persons who would have been present during the testimony of the child victim had it been given in the room in which the proceeding is being conducted. Except for good cause shown, the prosecution shall file a motion under this division at least seven days before the date of the proceeding. The judge may issue the order upon the motion of the prosecution filed under this division, if the judge determines that the child victim is unavailable to testify in the room in which the proceeding is being conducted in the physical presence of the defendant, for one or more of the reasons set forth in division (E) of this section. If a judge issues an order of that nature, the judge shall exclude from the room in which the testimony is to be taken every person except a person described in division (A)(3) of this section. To the extent feasible, any person operating the recording equipment shall be hidden from the sight and hearing of the child victim giving the testimony, in a manner similar to that described in division (A)(3) of this section. The defendant shall be permitted to observe and hear the testimony of the child victim who is giving the testimony on a monitor, shall be provided with an electronic means of immediate communication with the defendant's attorney during the testimony, and shall be restricted to a location from which the defendant cannot be seen or heard by the child victim giving the testimony, except on a monitor provided for that purpose. The child victim giving the testimony shall be provided with a monitor on which the child victim can observe, during the testimony, the defendant. No order for the taking of testimony by recording shall be issued under this division unless the provisions set forth in divisions (A)(3)(a), (b), (c), and (d) of this section apply to the recording of the testimony.

(E) For purposes of divisions (C) and (D) of this section, a judge may order the testimony of a child victim to be taken outside the room in which the proceeding is being conducted if the judge determines that the child victim is unavailable to testify in the room in the physical presence of the defendant due to one or more of the following:

(1) The persistent refusal of the child victim to testify despite judicial requests to do so;

(2) The inability of the child victim to communicate about the alleged violation or offense because of extreme fear, failure of memory, or another similar reason;

(3) The substantial likelihood that the child victim will suffer serious emotional trauma from so testifying.

(F)(1) If a judge issues an order pursuant to division (C) or (D) of this section that requires the testimony of a child victim in a criminal proceeding to be taken outside of the room in which the proceeding is being conducted, the order shall specifically identify the child victim to whose testimony it applies, the order applies only during the testimony of the specified child victim, and the child victim giving the testimony shall not be required to testify at the proceeding other than in accordance with the order.

(2) A judge who makes any determination regarding the admissibility of a deposition under divisions (A) and (B) of this section, the videotaping of a deposition under division (A)(3) of this section, or the taking of testimony outside of the room in which a proceeding is being conducted under division (C) or (D) of this section, shall enter the determination and findings on the record in the proceeding.

**HISTORY: RC § 2907.41, 141 v H 108 (Eff 10-14-86); 146 v H 445 (Eff 9-3-96); RC § 2945.48.1, 147 v S 53. Eff 10-14-97.**

## § 2945.482 Deposition of mentally retarded or developmentally disabled victim; taking of testimony outside room where proceeding is being conducted.

(A) As used in this section:

(1) "Mentally retarded person" and "developmentally disabled person" have the same meanings as in section 5123.01 of the Revised Code.

(2) "Mentally retarded or developmentally disabled victim" includes a mentally retarded or developmentally disabled person who was a victim of a violation identified in division (B)(1) of this section or an offense of violence or against whom was directed any conduct that constitutes, or that is an element of, a violation identified in division (B)(1) of this section or an offense of violence.

(B)(1) In any proceeding in the prosecution of a charge of a violation of section 2903.16, 2903.34, 2903.341 [2903.34.1], 2905.03, 2907.02, 2907.03, 2907.05, 2907.06, 2907.09, 2907.21, 2907.23, 2907.24, 2907.32, 2907.321 [2907.32.1], 2907.322 [2907.32.2], or 2907.323 [2907.32.3] of the Revised Code or an offense of violence and in which an alleged victim of the violation or offense was a mentally retarded or developmentally disabled person, the judge of the court in which the prosecution is being conducted, upon motion of an attorney for the prosecution, shall order that the testimony of the mentally retarded or developmentally disabled victim be taken by deposition. The prosecution also may request that the deposition be videotaped in accordance with division (B)(2) of this section. The judge shall notify the mentally retarded or developmentally disabled victim whose deposition is to be taken, the prosecution, and the defense of the date, time, and place for taking the deposition. The notice shall identify the mentally retarded or developmentally disabled victim who is to be examined and shall indicate whether a request that the deposition be videotaped has been made. The defendant shall have the right to attend the deposition and the right to be represented by counsel. Depositions shall be taken in the manner provided in civil cases, except that the judge shall preside at the taking of the deposition and shall rule at the time on any objections of the prosecution or the attorney for the defense. The prosecution and the attorney for the defense shall have the right, as at trial, to full examination and cross-examination of the mentally retarded or developmentally disabled victim whose deposition is to be taken. If a deposition taken under this division is intended to be offered as evidence in the proceeding, it shall be filed in the court in which the action is pending and is admissible in the manner described in division (C) of this section.

If a deposition of a mentally retarded or developmentally disabled victim taken under this division is admitted as evidence at the proceeding under division (C) of this section, the mentally retarded or developmentally disabled victim shall not be required to testify in person at the proceeding.

At any time before the conclusion of the proceeding, the attorney for the defense may file a motion with the judge requesting that another deposition of the mentally retarded or developmentally disabled victim be taken because new evidence material to the defense has been discovered that the attorney for the defense could not with reasonable diligence have discovered prior to the taking of the admitted deposition. If the court orders the taking of another deposition under this provision, the deposition shall be taken in accordance with this division. If the admitted deposition was a videotaped deposition taken in accordance with division (B)(2) of this section, the new deposition shall be videotaped in accordance with that division. In other cases, the new deposition may be videotaped in accordance with that division.

(2) If the prosecution requests that a deposition to be taken under division (B)(2) of this section be videotaped, the judge shall order that the deposition be videotaped in accordance with this division. If a judge issues an order that the deposition be videotaped, the judge shall exclude from the room in which the deposition is to be taken every person except the mentally retarded or developmentally disabled victim giving the testimony, the judge, one or more interpreters if needed, the attorneys for the prosecution and the defense, any person needed to operate the equipment to be used, one person chosen by the mentally retarded or developmentally disabled victim giving the deposition, and any person whose presence the judge determines would contribute to the welfare and well-being of the mentally retarded or developmentally disabled victim giving the deposition. The person chosen by the mentally retarded or developmentally disabled victim shall not be a witness in the proceeding and, both before and during the deposition, shall not discuss the testimony of the mentally retarded or developmentally disabled victim with any other witness in the proceeding. To the extent feasible, any person operating the recording equipment shall be restricted to a room adjacent to the room in which the deposition is being taken, or to a location in the room in which the deposition is being taken that is behind a screen or mirror, so that the person operating the

recording equipment can see and hear, but cannot be seen or heard by, the mentally retarded or developmentally disabled victim giving the deposition during the deposition.

The defendant shall be permitted to observe and hear the testimony of the mentally retarded or developmentally disabled victim giving the deposition on a monitor, shall be provided with an electronic means of immediate communication with the defendant's attorney during the testimony, and shall be restricted to a location from which the defendant cannot be seen or heard by the mentally retarded or developmentally disabled victim giving the deposition, except on a monitor provided for that purpose. The mentally retarded or developmentally disabled victim giving the deposition shall be provided with a monitor on which the victim can observe, during the testimony, the defendant. The judge, at the judge's discretion, may preside at the deposition by electronic means from outside the room in which the deposition is to be taken. If the judge presides by electronic means, the judge shall be provided with monitors on which the judge can see each person in the room in which the deposition is to be taken and with an electronic means of communication with each person, and each person in the room shall be provided with a monitor on which that person can see the judge and with an electronic means of communication with the judge. A deposition that is videotaped under this division shall be taken and filed in the manner described in division (B)(1) of this section and is admissible in the manner described in this division and division (C) of this section, and, if a deposition that is videotaped under this division is admitted as evidence at the proceeding, the mentally retarded or developmentally disabled victim shall not be required to testify in person at the proceeding. No deposition videotaped under this division shall be admitted as evidence at any proceeding unless division (C) of this section is satisfied relative to the deposition and all of the following apply relative to the recording:

(a) The recording is both aural and visual and is recorded on film or videotape, or by other electronic means.

(b) The recording is authenticated under the Rules of Evidence and the Rules of Criminal Procedure as a fair and accurate representation of what occurred, and the recording is not altered other than at the direction and under the supervision of the judge in the proceeding.

(c) Each voice on the recording that is material to the testimony on the recording or the making of the recording, as determined by the judge, is identified.

(d) Both the prosecution and the defendant are afforded an opportunity to view the recording before it is shown in the proceeding.

(C)(1) At any proceeding in a prosecution in relation to which a deposition was taken under division (B) of this section, the deposition or a part of it is admissible in evidence upon motion of the prosecution if the testimony in the deposition or the part to be admitted is not excluded by the hearsay rule and if the deposition or the part to be admitted otherwise is admissible under the Rules of Evidence. For purposes of this division, testimony is not excluded by the hearsay rule if the testimony is not hearsay under Evidence Rule 801; the testimony is within an exception to the hearsay rule set forth in Evidence Rule 803; the mentally retarded or developmentally disabled victim who gave the testimony is unavailable as a witness, as defined in Evidence Rule 804, and the testimony is admissible under that rule; or both of the following apply:

(a) The defendant had an opportunity and similar motive at the time of the taking of the deposition to develop the testimony by direct, cross, or redirect examination.

(b) The judge determines that there is reasonable cause to believe that, if the mentally retarded or developmentally disabled victim who gave the testimony in the deposition were to testify in person at the proceeding, the mentally retarded or developmentally disabled victim would experience serious emotional trauma as a result of the mentally retarded or developmentally disabled victim's participation at the proceeding.

(2) Objections to receiving in evidence a deposition or a part of it under division (C) of this section shall be made as provided in civil actions.

(3) The provisions of divisions (B) and (C) of this section are in addition to any other provisions of the Revised Code, the Rules of Criminal Procedure, or the Rules of Evidence that pertain to the taking or admission of depositions in a criminal proceeding and do not limit the admissibility under any of those other provisions of any deposition taken under division (B) of this section or otherwise taken.

(D) In any proceeding in the prosecution of any charge of a violation listed in division (B)(1) of this section or an offense of violence and in which an alleged victim of the violation or offense was a mentally retarded or developmentally disabled person, the prosecution may file a motion with the judge requesting the judge to order the testimony of the mentally retarded or developmentally disabled victim to be taken in a room other than the room in which the proceeding is being conducted and be televised, by closed circuit equipment, into the room in which the proceeding is being conducted to be viewed by the jury, if applicable, the defendant, and any other persons who are not permitted in the room in which the testimony is to be taken but who would have been present during the testimony of the mentally retarded or developmentally disabled victim had it been given in the room in which the proceeding is being conducted. Except for good cause shown, the prosecution shall file a motion under this division at least seven days before the date of the proceeding. The judge may issue the order upon the motion of the prosecution filed under this section, if the judge determines that the mentally retarded or developmentally disabled victim is unavailable to testify in the room in which the proceeding is being conducted in the physical presence of the defendant for one or more of the reasons set forth in division (F) of this section. If a judge issues an order of that nature, the judge shall exclude from the room in which the testimony is to be taken every person except a person described in division (B)(2) of this section. The judge, at the judge's discretion, may preside during the giving of the testimony by electronic means from outside the room in which it is being given, subject to the limitations set forth in division (B)(2) of this section. To the extent feasible, any person operating the televising equipment shall be hidden from the sight and hearing of the mentally retarded or developmentally disabled victim giving the testimony, in a manner similar to that described in division (B)(2) of this section. The defendant shall be permitted to observe and hear the testimony of the mentally retarded or developmentally disabled victim giving the testimony on a monitor, shall be provided with an electronic means of immediate communication with the defendant's attorney during the testimony, and shall be restricted to a location from which the defendant cannot be seen or heard by the mentally retarded or developmentally disabled victim giving the testimony, except on a monitor provided for that purpose. The mentally retarded or developmentally disabled victim giving the testimony shall be provided with a monitor on which the mentally retarded or developmentally disabled victim can observe, during the testimony, the defendant.

(E) In any proceeding in the prosecution of any charge of a violation listed in division (B)(1) of this section or an offense of violence and in which an alleged victim of the violation or offense was a mentally retarded or developmentally disabled victim, the prosecution may file a motion with the judge requesting the judge to order the testimony of the mentally retarded or developmentally disabled victim to be taken outside of the room in which the proceeding is being conducted and be recorded for showing in the room in which the proceeding is being conducted before the judge, the jury, if applicable, the defendant, and any other persons who would have been present during the testimony of the mentally retarded or developmentally disabled victim had it been given in the room in which the proceeding is being conducted. Except for good cause shown, the prosecution shall file a motion under this division at least seven days before the date of the proceeding. The judge may issue the order upon the motion of the prosecution filed under this division, if the judge determines that the mentally retarded or developmentally disabled victim is unavailable to testify in the room in which the proceeding is being conducted in the physical presence of the defendant, for one or more of the reasons set forth in division (F) of this section. If a judge issues an order of that nature, the judge shall exclude from the room in which the testimony is to be taken every person except a person described in division (B)(2) of this section. To the extent feasible, any person operating the recording equipment shall be hidden from the sight and hearing of the mentally retarded or developmentally disabled victim giving the testimony, in a manner similar to that described in division (B)(2) of this section. The defendant shall be permitted to observe and hear the testimony of the mentally retarded or developmentally disabled victim who is giving the testimony on a monitor, shall be provided with an electronic means of immediate communication with the defendant's attorney during the testimony, and shall be restricted to a location from which the defendant cannot be seen or heard by the mentally retarded or developmentally disabled victim giving the testimony, except on a monitor provided for that purpose. The mentally retarded or developmentally disabled victim giving the testimony shall be provided with a monitor on which the victim can observe, during the testimony, the defendant. No order for the taking of testimony by recording shall be issued under this division unless the provisions set forth in divisions (B)(2)(a), (b), (c), and (d) of this section apply to the recording of the testimony.

(F) For purposes of divisions (D) and (E) of this section, a judge may order the testimony of a mentally retarded or developmentally disabled victim to be taken outside the room in which the proceeding is being conducted if the judge determines that the mentally retarded or developmentally disabled victim is unavailable to testify in the room in the physical presence of the defendant due to one or more of the following:

(1) The persistent refusal of the mentally retarded or developmentally disabled victim to testify despite judicial requests to do so;

(2) The inability of the mentally retarded or developmentally disabled victim to communicate about the alleged violation or offense because of extreme fear, failure of memory, or another similar reason;

(3) The substantial likelihood that the mentally retarded or developmentally disabled victim will suffer serious emotional trauma from so testifying.

(G)(1) If a judge issues an order pursuant to division (D) or (E) of this section that requires the testimony of a mentally retarded or developmentally disabled victim in a criminal proceeding to be taken outside of the room in which the proceeding is being conducted, the order shall specifically identify the mentally retarded or developmentally disabled victim to whose testimony it applies, the order applies only during the testimony of the specified mentally retarded or developmentally disabled victim, and the mentally retarded or developmentally disabled victim giving the testimony shall not be required to testify at the proceeding other than in accordance with the order.

(2) A judge who makes any determination regarding the admissibility of a deposition under divisions (B) and (C) of this section, the videotaping of a deposition under division (B)(2) of this section, or the taking of testimony outside of the room in which a proceeding is being conducted under division (D) or (E) of this section shall enter the determination and findings on the record in the proceeding.

**HISTORY: 150 v S 178, § 1, eff. 1-30-04.**

## § 2945.49 Testimony of deceased or absent witness; videotaped preliminary hearing testimony of child victim.

(A)(1) As used in this section, "victim" includes any person who was a victim of a felony violation identified in division (B)(1) of this section or a felony offense of violence or against whom was directed any conduct that constitutes, or that is an element of, a felony violation identified in division (B)(1) of this section or a felony offense of violence.

(2) Testimony taken at an examination or a preliminary hearing at which the defendant is present, or at a former trial of the cause, or taken by deposition at the instance of the defendant or the state, may be used whenever the witness giving the testimony dies or cannot for any reason be produced at the trial or whenever the witness has, since giving that testimony, become incapacitated to testify. If the former testimony is contained within an authenticated transcript of the testimony, it shall be proven by the transcript, otherwise by other testimony.

(B)(1) At a trial on a charge of a felony violation of section 2905.05, 2907.02, 2907.03, 2907.04, 2907.05, 2907.21, 2907.24, 2907.31, 2907.32, 2907.321 [2907.32.1], 2907.322 [2907.32.2], 2907.323 [2907.32.3], or 2919.22 of the Revised Code or a felony offense of violence and in which an alleged victim of the alleged violation or offense was less than thirteen years of age when the complaint or information was filed, whichever occurred earlier, the court, upon motion of the prosecutor in the case, may admit videotaped preliminary hearing testimony of the child victim as evidence at the trial, in lieu of the child victim appearing as a witness and testifying at the trial, if all of the following apply:

(a) The videotape of the testimony was made at the preliminary hearing at which probable cause of the violation charged was found;

(b) The videotape of the testimony was made in accordance with division (C) of section 2937.11 of the Revised Code;

(c) The testimony in the videotape is not excluded by the hearsay rule and otherwise is admissible under the Rules of Evidence. For purposes of this division, testimony is not excluded by the hearsay rule if the testimony is not hearsay under Evidence Rule 801, if the testimony is within an exception to the hearsay rule set forth in Evidence Rule 803, if the child victim who gave the testimony is unavailable as a witness, as defined in Evidence Rule 804, and the testimony is admissible under that rule, or if both of the following apply:

(i) The accused had an opportunity and similar motive at the preliminary hearing to develop the testimony of the child victim by direct, cross, or redirect examination;

(ii) The court determines that there is reasonable cause to believe that if the child victim who gave the testimony at the preliminary hearing were to testify in person at the trial, the child victim would experience serious emotional trauma as a result of the child victim's participation at the trial.

(2) If a child victim of an alleged felony violation of section 2905.05, 2907.02, 2907.03, 2907.04, 2907.05, 2907.21, 2907.24, 2907.31, 2907.32, 2907.321 [2907.32.1], 2907.322 [2907.32.2], 2907.323 [2907.32.3], or 2919.22 of the Revised Code or an alleged felony offense of violence testifies at the preliminary hearing in the case, if the testimony of the child victim at the preliminary hearing was videotaped pursuant to division (C) of section 2937.11 of the Revised Code, and if the defendant in the case files a written objection to the use, pursuant to division (B)(1) of this section, of the videotaped testimony at the trial, the court, immediately after the filing of the objection, shall hold a hearing to determine whether the videotaped testimony of the child victim should be admissible at trial under division (B)(1) of this section and, if it is admissible, whether the child victim should be required to provide limited additional testimony of the type described in this division. At the hearing held pursuant to this division, the defendant and the prosecutor in the case may present any evidence that is relevant to the issues to be determined at the hearing, but the child victim shall not be required to testify at the hearing.

After the hearing, the court shall not require the child victim to testify at the trial, unless it determines that both of the following apply:

(a) That the testimony of the child victim at trial is necessary for one or more of the following reasons:

(i) Evidence that was not available at the time of the testimony of the child victim at the preliminary hearing has been discovered;

(ii) The circumstances surrounding the case have changed sufficiently to necessitate that the child victim testify at the trial.

(b) That the testimony of the child victim at the trial is necessary to protect the right of the defendant to a fair trial.

The court shall enter its finding and the reasons for it in the journal. If the court requires the child victim to testify at the trial, the testimony of the victim shall be limited to the new evidence and changed circumstances, and the child victim shall not otherwise be required to testify at the trial. The required testimony of the child victim may be given in person or, upon motion of the prosecution, may be taken by deposition in accordance with division (A) of section 2945.481 [2945.48.1] of the Revised Code provided the deposition is admitted as evidence under division (B) of that section, may be taken outside of the courtroom and televised into the courtroom in accordance with division (C) of that section, or may be taken outside of the courtroom and recorded for showing in the courtroom in accordance with division (D) of that section.

(3) If videotaped testimony of a child victim is admitted at trial in accordance with division (B)(1) of this section, the child victim shall not be compelled in any way to appear as a witness at the trial, except as provided in division (B)(2) of this section.

(C) An order issued pursuant to division (B) of this section shall specifically identify the child victim concerning whose testimony it pertains. The order shall apply only during the testimony of the child victim it specifically identifies.

(D) As used in this section, "prosecutor" has the same meaning as in section 2935.01 of the Revised Code.

**HISTORY: GC § 13444-10; 113 v 123(188), ch 23, § 10; Bureau of Code Revision, 10-1-53; 141 v H 108 (Eff 10-14-86); 146 v H 445 (Eff 9-3-96); 147 v S 53. Eff 10-14-97.**

## § 2945.491 Admission at trial of videotaped preliminary hearing testimony of mentally retarded or developmentally disabled victim.

(A) As used in this section:

(1) "Mentally retarded person" and "developmentally disabled person" have the same meanings as in section 5123.01 of the Revised Code.

(2) "Mentally retarded or developmentally disabled victim" includes a mentally retarded or developmentally disabled person who was a victim of a felony violation identified in division (B)(1) of this section or a felony offense of violence or against whom was directed any conduct that constitutes, or that is an element of, a felony violation identified in division (B)(1) of this section or a felony offense of violence.

(B)(1) At a trial on a charge of a felony violation of section 2903.16, 2903.34, 2903.341 [2903.34.1], 2907.02, 2907.03, 2907.05, 2907.21, 2907.23, 2907.24, 2907.32, 2907.321 [2907.32.1], 2907.322 [2907.32.2], or 2907.323 [2907.32.3] of the Revised Code or an offense of violence and in which an alleged victim of the violation or offense was a mentally retarded or developmentally disabled person, the court, upon motion of the prosecutor in the case, may admit videotaped preliminary hearing testimony of the mentally retarded or developmentally disabled victim as evidence at the trial, in lieu of the mentally retarded or developmentally disabled victim appearing as a witness and testifying at trial, if all of the following apply:

(a) The videotape of the testimony was made at the preliminary hearing at which probable cause of the violation charged was found.

(b) The videotape of the testimony was made in accordance with division (C) of section 2937.11 of the Revised Code.

(c) The testimony in the videotape is not excluded by the hearsay rule and otherwise is admissible under the Rules of Evidence. For purposes of this division, testimony is not excluded by the hearsay rule if the testimony is not hearsay under Evidence Rule 801, the testimony is within an exception to the hearsay rule set forth in Evidence Rule 803, the mentally retarded or developmentally disabled victim who gave the testimony is unavailable as a witness, as defined in Evidence Rule 804, and the testimony is admissible under that rule, or both of the following apply:

(i) The accused had an opportunity and similar motive at the preliminary hearing to develop the testimony of the mentally retarded or developmentally disabled victim by direct, cross, or redirect examination.

(ii) The court determines that there is reasonable cause to believe that if the mentally retarded or developmentally disabled victim who gave the testimony at the preliminary hearing were to testify in person at the trial, the mentally retarded or developmentally disabled victim would experience serious emotional trauma as a result of the victim's participation at the trial.

(2) If a mentally retarded or developmentally disabled victim of an alleged felony violation of section 2903.16, 2903.34, 2903.341 [2903.34.1], 2907.02, 2907.03, 2907.05, 2907.21, 2907.23, 2907.24, 2907.32, 2907.321 [2907.32.1], 2907.322 [2907.32.2], or 2907.323 [2907.32.3] of the Revised Code or an alleged felony offense of violence testifies at the preliminary hearing in the case, if the testimony of the mentally retarded or developmentally disabled victim at the preliminary hearing was videotaped pursuant to division (C) of section 2937.11 of the Revised Code, and if the defendant in the case files a written objection to the use, pursuant to division (B)(1) of this section, of the videotaped testimony at the trial, the court, immediately after the filing of the objection, shall hold a hearing to determine whether the videotaped testimony of the mentally retarded or developmentally disabled victim should be admissible at trial under division (B)(1) of this section and, if it is admissible, whether the mentally retarded or developmentally disabled victim should be required to provide limited additional testimony of the type described in this division. At the hearing held pursuant to this division, the defendant and the prosecutor in the case may present any evidence that is relevant to the issues to be determined at the hearing, but the mentally retarded or developmentally disabled victim shall not be required to testify at the hearing.

After the hearing, the court shall not require the mentally retarded or developmentally disabled victim to testify at the trial, unless it determines that both of the following apply:

(a) That the testimony of the mentally retarded or developmentally disabled victim at trial is necessary for one or more of the following reasons:

(i) Evidence that was not available at the time of the testimony of the mentally retarded or developmentally disabled victim at the preliminary hearing has been discovered.

(ii) The circumstances surrounding the case have changed sufficiently to necessitate that the mentally retarded or developmentally disabled victim testify at the trial.

(b) That the testimony of the mentally retarded or developmentally disabled victim at the trial is necessary to protect the right of the defendant to a fair trial.

The court shall enter its finding and the reasons for it in the journal. If the court requires the mentally retarded or developmentally disabled victim to testify at the trial, the testimony of the victim shall be limited to the new evidence and changed circumstances, and the mentally retarded or developmentally disabled victim shall not otherwise be required to testify at the trial. The required testimony of the mentally retarded or developmentally disabled victim may be given in person or, upon motion of the prosecution, may be taken by deposition in accordance with division (B) of section 2945.482 [2945.48.2] of the Revised Code provided the deposition is admitted as evidence under division (C) of that section, may be taken outside of the courtroom and televised into the courtroom in accordance with division (D) of that section, or may be taken outside of the courtroom and recorded for showing in the courtroom in accordance with division (E) of that section.

(3) If videotaped testimony of a mentally retarded or developmentally disabled victim is admitted at trial in accordance with division (B)(1) of this section, the mentally retarded or developmentally disabled victim shall not be compelled in any way to appear as a witness at the trial, except as provided in division (B)(2) of this section.

(C) An order issued pursuant to division (B) of this section shall specifically identify the mentally retarded or developmentally disabled victim concerning whose testimony it pertains. The order shall apply only during the testimony of the mentally retarded or developmentally disabled victim it specifically identifies.

**HISTORY: 150 v S 178, § 1, eff. 1-30-04.**

## § 2945.50 Deposition in criminal cases.

At any time after an issue of fact is joined upon an indictment, information, or an affidavit, the prosecution or the defendant may apply in writing to the court in which such indictment, information, or affidavit is pending for a commission to take the depositions of any witness. The court or a judge thereof may grant such commission and make an order stating in what manner and for what length of time notice shall be given to the prosecution or to the defendant, before such witness shall be examined.

**HISTORY: RS § 7293; 70 v 145, § 144; GC § 13444-11; 103 v 443; 113 v 123(188), ch 23, § 11; Bureau of Code Revision, 10-1-53; 131 v 681. Eff 10-13-65.**

## § 2945.51 When defendant may be taken; expenses.

When a deposition is to be taken in this state, and a commission is granted under section 2945.50 of the Revised Code while the defendant is confined in jail, the sheriff or deputy or other person having custody of the defendant shall be ordered by the court to take the defendant to the place of the taking of the deposition, and have him before the officer at the time of taking such deposition. Such sheriff or deputy or other person having custody of the defendant shall be reimbursed for actual reasonable traveling expenses for himself and the defendant, the bills for the same, upon the approval of the board of county commissioners, to be paid from the county treasury on the warrant of the county auditor. Such sheriff shall receive as fees therefor, one dollar for each day in attendance thereat. Such fees and traveling expenses shall be taxed and collected as other fees and costs in the case.

**HISTORY: GC § 13444-12; 103 v 443; 107 v 451; 113 v 123(188), ch 23, § 12; Bureau of Code Revision, 10-1-53; 131 v 681. Eff 10-13-65.**

## § 2945.52 Counsel appointed shall represent the defendant.

Counsel assigned by the court to represent the defendant may attend upon and represent the defendant at the taking of a deposition under section 2945.50 of the

Revised Code, and said counsel shall be paid a reasonable fee for his services in taking such deposition, in addition to the compensation allowed for defending such defendant, to be fixed by the court. He shall also be allowed his actual expenses incurred in going to and from the place of taking the deposition.

**HISTORY: GC § 13444-13; 113 v 123(189), ch 23, § 13; Bureau of Code Revision. Eff 10-1-53.**

## § 2945.53 Right of accused to examine witness.

In all cases in which depositions are taken by the state or the accused, to be used by or against the accused, as provided in sections 2945.50 to 2945.52, inclusive, of the Revised Code, the court shall by proper order provide and secure to the accused the means and opportunity to be present in person and with counsel at the taking of such deposition, and to examine the witness face to face, as fully and in the same manner as if in court. All expenses necessarily incurred in the securing of such means and opportunity, and the expenses of the prosecuting attorney in attending the taking of such deposition, shall be paid out of the county treasury upon the certificate of the court making such order.

**HISTORY: GC § 13444-14; 113 v 123(189), ch 23, § 14; Bureau of Code Revision. Eff 10-1-53.**

## § 2945.54 Conduct of examination.

The examination of witnesses by deposition in criminal cases shall be taken and certified, and the return thereof to the court made as for taking depositions under sections 2319.05 to 2319.31, inclusive, of the Revised Code. The commissioners appointed under section 2945.50 of the Revised Code to take depositions shall receive such compensation as the court directs, to be paid out of the county treasury and taxed as part of the costs in the case.

**HISTORY: GC § 13444-15; 113 v 123(189), ch 23, § 15; Bureau of Code Revision. Eff 10-1-53.**

This section is referred to in section 3 of HB No. 1201, effective July 1, 1970, although it was not repealed by section 1 of such act. Section 3 reads as follows:

"That the taking effect of the Rules of Civil Procedure on July 1, 1970, is prima-facie evidence that the sections of the Revised Code to be repealed by Section 1 are in conflict with such rules and shall have no further force or effect except that for the purposes of depositions in criminal cases under section 2945.54 of the Revised Code, procedures adopted by reference to sections 2319.05 to 2319.31, inclusive, of the Revised Code, and, for the purposes of an offer to confess judgment in an appropriation case under section 163.16 of the Revised Code, procedures adopted by reference to sections 2311.14 to 2311.20, inclusive, of the Revised Code, shall continue effective without change, unless a court shall determine that one of such sections, or some part thereof, has clearly not been superseded by such rules and that in the absence of such section or part thereof being effective, there would be no applicable standard of procedure prescribed by either statutory law or rule of court. The failure to repeal or amend any other section establishes no evidence concerning its conflict with such rules."

## § 2945.55 Testimony of previous identification.

When identification of the defendant is an issue, a witness who has on previous occasion identified such person may testify to such previous identification. Such identification may be proved by other witnesses.

**HISTORY: GC § 13444-16; 113 v 123(189), ch 23, § 16; Bureau of Code Revision. Eff 10-1-53.**

## § 2945.56 Rebuttal of defendant's character evidence.

When the defendant offers evidence of his character or reputation, the prosecution may offer, in rebuttal thereof, proof of his previous conviction of a crime involving moral turpitude, in addition to other competent evidence.

**HISTORY: GC § 13444-17; 113 v 123(189), ch 23, § 17; Bureau of Code Revision. Eff 10-1-53.**

## § 2945.57 Number of witnesses to character.

The number of witnesses who are expected to testify upon the subject of character or reputation, for whom subpoenas are issued, shall be designated upon the praecipe and, except in cases of murder in the first and second degree, manslaughter, rape, assault with intent to commit rape, or selling intoxicating liquor to a person in the habit of becoming intoxicated, shall not exceed ten upon each side, unless a deposit of at least one per diem and mileage fee for each of such additional witnesses is first made with the clerk of the court of common pleas. Not more than ten witnesses upon each side shall be permitted to testify upon the question of character or reputation in a criminal cause unless their full per diem and mileage fees have been deposited or paid by the party in whose behalf they are sworn, and the clerk shall not issue a certificate for compensation to be paid out of the county treasury to a witness who has testified upon the subject of character or reputation, except as provided in this section.

**HISTORY: GC § 13444-18; 113 v 123(189), ch 23, § 18; Bureau of Code Revision. Eff 10-1-53.**

## § 2945.58 Alibi.

Whenever a defendant in a criminal cause proposes to offer in his defense, testimony to establish an alibi on his behalf, such defendant shall, not less than three days before the trial of such cause, file and serve upon the prosecuting attorney a notice in writing of his intention to claim such alibi. Notice shall include specific information as to the place at which the defendant claims to have been at the time of the alleged offense. If the defendant fails to file such written notice, the court may exclude evidence offered by the defendant for the purpose of proving such alibi.

**HISTORY: GC § 13444-20; 113 v 123(190), ch 23, § 20; Bureau of Code Revision. Eff 10-1-53.**

## § 2945.59 Proof of defendant's motive.

In any criminal case in which the defendant's motive or intent, the absence of mistake or accident on his part, or the defendant's scheme, plan, or system in doing an act is material, any acts of the defendant which tend to show his motive or intent, the absence of mistake or accident on his part, or the defendant's scheme, plan, or system in doing the act in question may be proved, whether they are contemporaneous with or prior or subsequent thereto, notwithstanding that such proof may show or tend to show the commission of another crime by the defendant.

**HISTORY: GC § 13444-19; 113 v 123(190), ch 23, § 19; Bureau of Code Revision. Eff 10-1-53.**

## § 2945.60 Repealed, 134 v H 511, § 2 [RS § 7298; S&S 262; 58 v 110; 66 v 309; GC § 13444-21; 113 v 123; Bureau of Code Revision, 10-1-53]. Eff 1-1-74.

This section established procedure for proof of treason.

## § 2945.61 Repealed, 134 v H 511, § 2 [RS § 7298; S&S 262; 58 v 110; 66 v 309; GC § 13444-21; 113 v 123; Bureau of Code Revision, 10-1-53]. Eff 1-1-74.

This section established proof in case of setting on foot or providing means for an unauthorized military expedition.

## § 2945.62 Repealed, 134 v H 511, § 2 [GC §§ 13444-22, 13444-23; 113 v 123; Bureau of Code Revision, 10-1-53]. Eff 1-1-74.

This section established procedure for proof in case of perjury.

## § 2945.63 Repealed, 134 v H 511, § 2 [GC §§ 13444-22, 13444-23; 113 v 123; Bureau of Code Revision, 10-1-53]. Eff 1-1-74.

This section established proof in a trial for seduction of a female.

## § 2945.64 Prima-facie evidence of embezzlement.

Failure or refusal to pay over or produce public money by a person charged with the collection, receipt, transfer, disbursement, or safekeeping of such money, whether belonging to this state, a county, township, municipal corporation, or board of education, or other public money, or to account to or make settlement with a legal authority of the official accounts of such person, is prima-facie evidence of the embezzlement thereof. Upon the trial of such person for the embezzlement of public money, it is sufficient evidence for the purpose of showing a balance against him, to produce a transcript from the records of the auditor of state, director of budget and management, county auditor, or board of county commissioners. The refusal of such person, whether in or out of office, to pay a draft, order, or warrant drawn upon him by an authorized officer, for public money in his hands, or a refusal by a person promptly to pay over to his successor public money or securities on the legal requirement of an authorized officer of the state or county, on the trial of an indictment against him for embezzlement, is prima-facie evidence thereof.

**HISTORY: GC § 13444-25; 113 v 123(191), ch 23, § 25; Bureau of Code Revision, 10-1-53; 141 v H 201. Eff 7-1-85.**

## [BILL OF EXCEPTIONS]

## § 2945.65 Repealed, 141 v H 412, § 2 [GC §§ 13445-1-13445-2; 113 v 123(191), ch. 24; Bureau of Code Revision, 10-1-53; 125 v S 112; 128 v 141; 129 v 1398; 131 v 682; 137 v H 219]. Eff 3-17-87.

This section described a bill of exceptions.

## § 2945.66 Repealed, 141 v H 412, § 2 [GC §§ 13445-1-13445-2; 113 v 123(191), ch. 24; Bureau of Code Revision, 10-1-53; 125 v S 112; 128 v 141; 129 v 1398; 131 v 682; 137 v H 219]. Eff 3-17-87.

This section outlined procedures for filing a bill of exceptions.

## § 2945.67 Appeal by state.

(A) A prosecuting attorney, village solicitor, city director of law, or the attorney general may appeal as a matter of right any decision of a trial court in a criminal case, or any decision of a juvenile court in a delinquency case, which decision grants a motion to dismiss all or any part of an indictment, complaint, or information, a motion to suppress evidence, or a motion for the return of seized property or grants post conviction relief pursuant to sections 2953.21 to 2953.24† of the Revised Code, and may appeal by leave of the court to which the appeal is taken any other decision, except the final verdict, of the trial court in a criminal case or of the juvenile court in a delinquency case. In addition to any other right to appeal under this section or any other provision of law, a prosecuting attorney, city director of law, village solicitor, or similar chief legal officer of a municipal corporation, or the attorney general may appeal, in accordance with section 2953.08 of the Revised Code, a sentence imposed upon a person who is convicted of or pleads guilty to a felony.

(B) In any proceeding brought pursuant to division (A) of this section, the court, in accordance with Chapter 120. of the Revised Code, shall appoint the county public defender, joint county public defender, or other counsel to represent any person who is indigent, is not represented by counsel, and does not waive the person's right to counsel.

**HISTORY: 137 v H 1168 (Eff 11-1-78); 146 v S 2. Eff 7-1-96.**

† Division (A), RC § 2953.24 was repealed by HB 164 (136 v —), § 2, effective 1-13-76.

**Analogous to former RC § 2945.67 (GC § 13446-1; 113 v 123; Bureau of Code Revision, 10-1-53; 131 v 682; 137 v H 219), repealed 137 v H 1168, § 2, eff 11-1-78.**

The effective date is set by section 6 of SB 2.

## § 2945.68 Repealed, 137 v H 1168, § 2 [GC §§ 13446-2—13446-4; 113 v 123; Bureau of Code Revision, 10-1-53; 131 v 682; 134 v H 511; 137 v H 219]. Eff 11-1-78.

This section concerned application to file bill of exceptions.

*Note: RC § 2945.68 was also repealed by 146 v S 2, § 2. Eff 7-1-96.*

## § 2945.69 Repealed, 137 v H 1168, § 2 [GC §§ 13446-2—13446-4; 113 v 123; Bureau of Code Revision, 10-1-53; 131 v 682; 134 v H 511; 137 v H 219]. Eff 11-1-78.

This section concerned appointment of attorney.

## § 2945.70 Repealed, 137 v H 1168, § 2 [GC §§ 13446-2—13446-4; 113 v 123; Bureau of Code Revi-

sion, 10-1-53; 131 v 682; 134 v H 511; 137 v H 219]. Eff 11-1-78.

This section concerned decision of the court.

[TIME FOR TRIAL]

## § 2945.71 Time within which hearing or trial must be held.

(A) Subject to division (D) of this section, a person against whom a charge is pending in a court not of record, or against whom a charge of minor misdemeanor is pending in a court of record, shall be brought to trial within thirty days after the person's arrest or the service of summons.

(B) Subject to division (D) of this section, a person against whom a charge of misdemeanor, other than a minor misdemeanor, is pending in a court of record, shall be brought to trial as follows:

(1) Within forty-five days after the person's arrest or the service of summons, if the offense charged is a misdemeanor of the third or fourth degree, or other misdemeanor for which the maximum penalty is imprisonment for not more than sixty days;

(2) Within ninety days after the person's arrest or the service of summons, if the offense charged is a misdemeanor of the first or second degree, or other misdemeanor for which the maximum penalty is imprisonment for more than sixty days.

(C) A person against whom a charge of felony is pending:

(1) Notwithstanding any provisions to the contrary in Criminal Rule 5(B), shall be accorded a preliminary hearing within fifteen consecutive days after the person's arrest if the accused is not held in jail in lieu of bail on the pending charge or within ten consecutive days after the person's arrest if the accused is held in jail in lieu of bail on the pending charge;

(2) Shall be brought to trial within two hundred seventy days after the person's arrest.

(D) A person against whom one or more charges of different degrees, whether felonies, misdemeanors, or combinations of felonies and misdemeanors, all of which arose out of the same act or transaction, are pending shall be brought to trial on all of the charges within the time period required for the highest degree of offense charged, as determined under divisions (A), (B), and (C) of this section.

(E) For purposes of computing time under divisions (A), (B), (C)(2), and (D) of this section, each day during which the accused is held in jail in lieu of bail on the pending charge shall be counted as three days. This division does not apply for purposes of computing time under division (C)(1) of this section.

(F) This section shall not be construed to modify in any way section 2941.401 or sections 2963.30 to 2963.35 of the Revised Code.

**HISTORY: 134 v H 511 (Eff 1-1-74); 135 v H 716 (Eff 1-1-74); 136 v S 83 (Eff 10-17-75); 138 v S 288 (Eff 10-22-80); 139 v S 119 (Eff 3-17-82); 148 v S 49. Eff 10-29-99.**

**Analogous to RC § 2945.71 (GC § 13447-1; 113 v 123(193); Bureau of Code Revision, 10-1-53), repealed 134 v H 511, § 2, eff 1-1-74.**

## § 2945.72 Extension of time for hearing or trial.

The time within which an accused must be brought to trial, or, in the case of felony, to preliminary hearing and trial, may be extended only by the following:

(A) Any period during which the accused is unavailable for hearing or trial, by reason of other criminal proceedings against him, within or outside the state, by reason of his confinement in another state, or by reason of the pendency of extradition proceedings, provided that the prosecution exercises reasonable diligence to secure his availability;

(B) Any period during which the accused is mentally incompetent to stand trial or during which his mental competence to stand trial is being determined, or any period during which the accused is physically incapable of standing trial;

(C) Any period of delay necessitated by the accused's lack of counsel, provided that such delay is not occasioned by any lack of diligence in providing counsel to an indigent accused upon his request as required by law;

(D) Any period of delay occasioned by the neglect or improper act of the accused;

(E) Any period of delay necessitated by reason of a plea in bar or abatement, motion, proceeding, or action made or instituted by the accused;

(F) Any period of delay necessitated by a removal or change of venue pursuant to law;

(G) Any period during which trial is stayed pursuant to an express statutory requirement, or pursuant to an order of another court competent to issue such order;

(H) The period of any continuance granted on the accused's own motion, and the period of any reasonable continuance granted other than upon the accused's own motion;

(I) Any period during which an appeal filed pursuant to section 2945.67 of the Revised Code is pending.

**HISTORY: 134 v H 511 (Eff 1-1-74); 136 v H 164 (Eff 1-13-76); 136 v S 368 (Eff 9-27-76); 137 v H 1168. Eff 11-1-78.**

**Analogous to former RC § 2945.72 (GC § 13447-2; 113 v 123(193); Bureau of Code Revision, 10-1-53), repealed 134 v H 511, § 2, eff 1-1-74.**

## § 2945.73 Discharge for delay in trial.

(A) A charge of felony shall be dismissed if the accused is not accorded a preliminary hearing within the time required by sections 2945.71 and 2945.72 of the Revised Code.

(B) Upon motion made at or prior to the commencement of trial, a person charged with an offense shall be discharged if he is not brought to trial within the time required by sections 2945.71 and 2945.72 of the Revised Code.

(C) Regardless of whether a longer time limit may be provided by sections 2945.71 and 2945.72 of the Revised Code, a person charged with misdemeanor shall be discharged if he is held in jail in lieu of bond awaiting trial on the pending charge:

(1) For a total period equal to the maximum term of imprisonment which may be imposed for the most serious misdemeanor charged;

(2) For a total period equal to the term of imprisonment allowed in lieu of payment of the maximum fine which may be imposed for the most serious misdemeanor

charged, when the offense or offenses charged constitute minor misdemeanors.

(D) When a charge of felony is dismissed pursuant to division (A) of this section, such dismissal has the same effect as a nolle prosequi. When an accused is discharged pursuant to division (B) or (C) of this section, such discharge is a bar to any further criminal proceedings against him based on the same conduct.

**HISTORY: 134 v H 511. Eff 1-1-74.**

**Analogous to former RC § 2945.73 (GC § 13447-3; 113 v 123(193); Bureau of Code Revision, 10-1-53), repealed 134 v H 511, § 2, eff 1-1-74.**

## [VERDICT]

### § 2945.74 Defendant may be convicted of lesser offense.

The jury may find the defendant not guilty of the offense charged, but guilty of an attempt to commit it if such attempt is an offense at law. When the indictment or information charges an offense, including different degrees, or if other offenses are included within the offense charged, the jury may find the defendant not guilty of the degree charged but guilty of an inferior degree thereof or lesser included offense.

If the offense charged is murder and the accused is convicted by confession in open court, the court shall examine the witnesses, determine the degree of the crime, and pronounce sentence accordingly.

**HISTORY: GC § 13448-2; 113 v 123(194), ch 27, § 2; Bureau of Code Revision. Eff 10-1-53.**

### § 2945.75 Degree of offense; charge and verdict; proof of prior conviction.

(A) When the presence of one or more additional elements makes an offense one of more serious degree:

(1) The affidavit, complaint, indictment, or information either shall state the degree of the offense which the accused is alleged to have committed, or shall allege such additional element or elements. Otherwise such affidavit, complaint, indictment, or information is effective to charge only the least degree of the offense.

(2) A guilty verdict shall state either the degree of the offense of which the offender is found guilty, or that such additional element or elements are present. Otherwise, a guilty verdict constitutes a finding of guilty of the least degree of the offense charged.

(B)(1) Whenever in any case it is necessary to prove a prior conviction, a certified copy of the entry of judgment in such prior conviction together with evidence sufficient to identify the defendant named in the entry as the offender in the case at bar, is sufficient to prove such prior conviction.

(2) Whenever in any case it is necessary to prove a prior conviction of an offense for which the registrar of motor vehicles maintains a record, a certified copy of the record that shows the name, date of birth, and social security number of the accused is prima-facie evidence of the identity of the accused and prima-facie evidence of all prior convictions shown on the record. The accused may offer evidence to rebut the prima-facie evidence of the accused's identity and the evidence of prior convictions. Proof of a prior conviction of an offense for which the registrar maintains a record may also be proved as provided in division (B)(1) of this section.

(3) If the defendant claims a constitutional defect in any prior conviction, the defendant has the burden of proving the defect by a preponderance of the evidence.

**HISTORY: 134 v H 511. Eff 1-1-74; 151 v H 461, § 1, eff. 4-4-07; 152 v S 17, § 1, eff. 9-30-08.**

**Analogous to former RC § 2945.75 (GC § 13448-3; 113 v 123(194), ch 27, § 3; Bureau of Code Revision, 10-1-53), repealed 134 v H 511, § 2, eff 1-1-74.**

### § 2945.76 Repealed, 134 v H 511, § 2 [GC § 13448-4; 113 v 123(194); Bureau of Code Revision, 10-1-53; 133 v H 288]. Eff 1-1-74.

This section concerned circumstances for acquittal for carrying concealed weapon.

### § 2945.77 Polling jury.

When the jurors agree upon their verdict, they must be conducted into court by the officer having them in charge.

Before the verdict is accepted, the jury may be polled at the request of either the prosecuting attorney or the defendant. If one of the jurors upon being polled declare that said verdict is not his verdict, the jury must further deliberate upon the case.

**HISTORY: GC § 13448-5; 113 v 123(195), ch 27, § 5; Bureau of Code Revision. Eff 10-1-53.**

### § 2945.78 Recording the verdict.

When the verdict given is such as the court may receive, it must be immediately entered in full upon the minutes.

**HISTORY: GC § 13448-6; 113 v 123(195), ch 27, § 6; Bureau of Code Revision. Eff 10-1-53.**

## [NEW TRIAL]

### § 2945.79 Causes for new trial.

A new trial, after a verdict of conviction, may be granted on the application of the defendant for any of the following causes affecting materially his substantial rights:

(A) Irregularity in the proceedings of the court, jury, prosecuting attorney, or the witnesses for the state, or for any order of the court, or abuse of discretion by which the defendant was prevented from having a fair trial;

(B) Misconduct of the jury, prosecuting attorney, or the witnesses for the state;

(C) Accident or surprise which ordinary prudence could not have guarded against;

(D) That the verdict is not sustained by sufficient evidence or is contrary to law; but if the evidence shows the defendant is not guilty of the degree of crime for which he was convicted, but guilty of a lesser degree thereof, or of a lesser crime included therein, the court may modify the verdict or finding accordingly, without granting or ordering a new trial, and pass sentence on such verdict or finding as modified, provided that this power extends to any court to which the cause may be taken on appeal;

(E) Error of law occurring at the trial;

(F) When new evidence is discovered material to the defendant, which he could not with reasonable diligence have discovered and produced at the trial. When a motion for a new trial is made upon the ground of newly discovered evidence, the defendant must produce at the hearing of said motion, in support thereof, the affidavits of the witnesses by whom such evidence is expected to be given, and if time is required by the defendant to procure such affidavits, the court may postpone the hearing of the motion for such length of time as under all the circumstances of the case is reasonable. The prosecuting attorney may produce affidavits or other evidence to impeach the affidavits of such witnesses.

**HISTORY: GC § 13449-1; 113 v 123(195), ch 28; Bureau of Code Revision. Eff 10-1-53.**

## § 2945.80 Application for new trial.

Application for a new trial shall be made by motion upon written grounds, and except for the cause of newly discovered evidence material for the person applying, which he could not with reasonable diligence have discovered and produced at the trial, shall be filed within three days after the verdict was rendered, or the decision of the court where a trial by jury has been waived, unless it is made to appear by clear and convincing proof that the defendant was unavoidably prevented from filing his motion for a new trial in which case it shall be filed within three days from the order of the court finding that he was unavoidably prevented from filing such motion within the time provided herein.

Motions for new trial on account of newly discovered evidence shall be filed within one hundred twenty days following the day upon which the verdict was rendered, or the decision of the court where trial by jury has been waived. If it is made to appear by clear and convincing proof that the defendant was unavoidably prevented from the discovery of the evidence upon which he must rely, such motion shall be filed within three days from an order of the court finding that he was unavoidably prevented from discovering the evidence within the one hundred twenty day period.

**HISTORY: GC § 13449-2; 113 v 123(196), ch 28, § 2; Bureau of Code Revision, 10-1-53; 128 v 141 (Eff 1-1-60); 131 v 683. Eff 11-1-65.**

## § 2945.81 Causes to be sustained by affidavits.

The causes enumerated in divisions (B) and (C) of section 2945.79 of the Revised Code must be sustained by affidavit showing their truth, and may be controverted by affidavits.

**HISTORY: GC § 13449-3; 113 v 123(196), ch 28, § 3; Bureau of Code Revision. Eff 10-1-53.**

## § 2945.82 New trial.

When a new trial is granted by the trial court, or when a new trial is awarded on appeal, the accused shall stand for trial upon the indictment or information as though there had been no previous trial thereof.

**HISTORY: GC § 13449-4; 113 v 123(196), ch 28, § 4; Bureau of Code Revision. Eff 10-1-53.**

## § 2945.83 When new trial shall not be granted.

No motion for a new trial shall be granted or verdict set aside, nor shall any judgment of conviction be reversed in any court because of:

(A) An inaccuracy or imperfection in the indictment, information, or warrant, provided that the charge is sufficient to fairly and reasonably inform the accused of the nature and cause of the accusation against him;

(B) A variance between the allegations and the proof thereof unless the accused is misled or prejudiced thereby;

(C) The admission or rejection of any evidence offered against or for the accused unless it affirmatively appears on the record that the accused was or may have been prejudiced thereby;

(D) A misdirection of the jury unless the accused was or may have been prejudiced thereby;

(E) Any other cause unless it appears affirmatively from the record that the accused was prejudiced thereby or was prevented from having a fair trial.

**HISTORY: GC § 13449-5; 113 v 123(196), ch 28, § 5; Bureau of Code Revision. Eff 10-1-53.**

## § 2945.831 Motion not necessary for appellate review.

A motion for a new trial is not a necessary prerequisite to obtain appellate review of the sufficiency or weight of the evidence in the trial of a criminal case.

**HISTORY: 128 v 141. Eff 1-1-60.**

## § 2945.832 Repealed, 141 v H 412, § 2 [128 v 141]. Eff 3-17-87.

This section dealt with other sections governing exceptions.

# CHAPTER 2947: JUDGMENT; SENTENCE



## § 2947.01 Definition of magistrate.

The definition of "magistrate" set forth in section 2931.01 of the Revised Code applies to Chapter 2947. of the Revised Code.

**HISTORY: Bureau of Code Revision. Eff 10-1-53.**

## [ARREST OF JUDGMENT]

## § 2947.02 Motion in arrest.

A judgment may be arrested by the court upon motion of the defendant, or upon the court's own motion, for either of the following causes:

(A) The offense charged is not within the jurisdiction of the court;

(B) The facts stated in the indictment or information do not constitute an offense.

**HISTORY: GC § 13450-1; 113 v 123(196), ch 29; Bureau of Code Revision. Eff 10-1-53.**

## § 2947.03 When judgment not arrested.

A judgment shall not be arrested for a defect in form. Motions in arrest of judgment shall be made within three days after the verdict is rendered.

**HISTORY: GC § 13450-2; 113 v 123(197), ch 29, § 2; Bureau of Code Revision. Eff 10-1-53.**

## § 2947.04 Effect of arrest of judgment.

When a judgment is arrested, it places the defendant in a like position with respect to the prosecution as before the indictment or information was found. If, from the evidence at the trial, there is reason to believe that the defendant is guilty of an offense, the trial court shall order him to enter into a recognizance with sufficient surety for his appearance at the first day of the next term of such court, or the court having jurisdiction of the offense if within this state, otherwise the defendant shall be discharged.

**HISTORY: GC § 13450-3; 113 v 123(197), ch 29, § 3; Bureau of Code Revision. Eff 10-1-53.**

## [SENTENCE AND PROCEEDINGS]

**§ 2947.05** Repealed, 146 v S 2, § 2 [GC § 13451-1; 113 v 123 (197), ch. 30; Bureau of Code Revision, 10-1-53; 145 v S 186]. Eff 7-1-96.

This section gave defendant, prosecutor and victim right to make statement prior to sentencing.
The effective date is set by section 6 of SB 2.

## § 2947.051 Victim impact statement to be considered in imposing sentence.

(A) In all criminal cases in which a person is convicted of or pleads guilty to a felony, if the offender, in committing the offense, caused, attempted to cause, threatened to cause, or created a risk of physical harm to the victim of the offense, the court, prior to sentencing the offender, shall order the preparation of a victim impact statement by the department of probation of the county in which the victim of the offense resides, by the court's own regular probation officer, or by a victim assistance program that is operated by the state, any county or municipal corporation, or any other governmental entity. The court, in accordance with sections 2929.13 and 2929.19 of the Revised Code, shall consider the victim impact statement in determining the sentence to be imposed upon the offender.

(B) Each victim impact statement prepared under this section shall identify the victim of the offense, itemize any economic loss suffered by the victim as a result of the offense, identify any physical injury suffered by the victim as a result of the offense and the seriousness and permanence of the injury, identify any change in the victim's personal welfare or familial relationships as a result of the offense and any psychological impact experienced by the victim or the victim's family as a result of the offense, and contain any other information related to the impact of the offense upon the victim that the court requires. Each victim impact statement prepared under this section shall include any statement made by the victim pursuant to section 2930.13 of the Revised Code.

(C) A victim impact statement prepared under this section shall be kept confidential and is not a public record as defined in section 149.43 of the Revised Code. However, the court may furnish copies of the statement to both the defendant or the defendant's counsel and the prosecuting attorney. Immediately following the imposition of sentence upon the defendant, the defendant, the defendant's counsel, and the prosecuting attorney shall return to the court the copies of the victim impact statement that were made available to the defendant, the counsel, or the prosecuting attorney.

**HISTORY: 138 v S 384 (Eff 10-22-80); 139 v S 199 (Eff 1-5-83); 145 v S 186 (Eff 10-12-94); 146 v S 2. Eff 7-1-96.**

The effective date is set by section 6 of SB 2.

## § 2947.052 Repealed, 145 v S 186, § 2 [144 v H 725]. Eff 10-12-94.

This section provided that victim or representative present at sentencing may request notice of intended electronically monitored early release. See now RC § 2930.16.

## § 2947.06 Testimony in mitigation of sentence; presentence investigation report; psychological reports.

(A)(1) The trial court may hear testimony in mitigation of a sentence at the term of conviction or plea or at the next term. The prosecuting attorney may offer testimony on behalf of the state to give the court a true understanding of the case. The court shall determine whether sentence should immediately be imposed. The court on its own motion may direct the department of probation of the county in which the defendant resides, or its own regular probation officer, to make any inquiries and presentence investigation reports that the court requires concerning the defendant.

(2) The provisions of section 2951.03 of the Revised Code shall govern the preparation of, the provision, receipt, and retention of copies of, the use of, and the confidentiality, nonpublic record character, and sealing of a presentence investigation report prepared pursuant to division (A) (1) of this section.

(B) The court may appoint not more than two psychologists or psychiatrists to make any reports concerning the defendant that the court requires for the purpose of determining the disposition of the case. Each psychologist or psychiatrist shall receive a fee to be fixed by the court and taxed in the costs of the case. The psychologist's or psychiatrist's reports shall be made in writing, in open court, and in the presence of the defendant, except in misdemeanor cases in which sentence may be pronounced in the absence of the defendant. A copy of each report of a psychologist or psychiatrist may be furnished to the defendant, if present, who may examine the persons making the report, under oath, as to any matter or thing contained in the report.

**HISTORY: GC § 13451-2; 113 v 123(197), ch 30, § 2; Bureau of Code Revision, 10-1-53; 130 v 667 (Eff 9-24-63); 142 v H 73, § 1 (Eff 10-1-87); 142 v H 73, § 5 (Eff 10-1-89); 146 v S 2 (Eff 7-1-96); 146 v S 269. Eff 7-1-96; 149 v H 490, § 1, eff. 1-1-04.**

The effective date is set by section 4 of H.B. 490.

**RC § 2947.06 was repealed in 139 v S 199, § 2, file 256, eff 1-1-83. Repeal rescinded in 1982 by 139 v H 269, § 4.**

## § 2947.061 Repealed, 146 v S 2, § 6 [131 v 684; 133 v H 686; 133 v H 1136; 136 v H 837; 139 v s 199; 139 v H 269; 140 v H 291; 145 v H 571; 145 v S 186; 146 v H 4]. Eff 7-1-96.

This section set regulations for probation after serving thirty days or six months of sentence, —shock probation—, and attendance at hearing for probation.

The repeal of RC § 2947.06.1 by SB 2 (146 v —) is confirmed in § 2 of SB 269 (146 v —), effective 7-1-96. The provisions of § 12 of SB 269 (146 v —) read as follows:

SECTION 12. The repeal by this act of section 2947.061 of the Revised Code is intended to confirm the result intended by the General Assembly in enacting Am. Sub. S.B. 2 and Sub. H.B. 4 of the 121st General Assembly. Both acts passed on June 29, 1995. Am. Sub. S.B. 2 repealed the section while Sub. H.B. 4 amended it. The existence of the section is therefore uncertain. The intention of the General Assembly was for the section to be neither continued nor revived as the result of its amendment by Sub. H.B. 4, but rather for the section to be repealed as provided in Am. Sub. S.B. 2.

## § 2947.062 Repealed, 146 v S 2, § 6 [131 v 684; 133 v H 686; 133 v H 1136; 136 v H 837; 139 v s 199; 139 v H 269; 140 v H 291; 145 v H 571; 145 v S 186; 146 v H 4]. Eff 7-1-96.

This section set regulations for transportation of prisoner.

The repeal of RC § 2947.06.1 by SB 2 (146 v —) is confirmed in § 2 of SB 269 (146 v —), effective 7-1-96. The provisions of § 12 of SB 269 (146 v —) read as follows:

SECTION 12. The repeal by this act of section 2947.061 of the Revised Code is intended to confirm the result intended by the General Assembly in enacting Am. Sub. S.B. 2 and Sub. H.B. 4 of the 121st General Assembly. Both acts passed on June 29, 1995. Am. Sub. S.B. 2 repealed the section while Sub. H.B. 4 amended it. The existence of the section is therefore uncertain. The intention of the General Assembly was for the section to be neither continued nor revived as the result of its amendment by Sub. H.B. 4, but rather for the section to be repealed as provided in Am. Sub. S.B. 2.

## § 2947.07 When court to pronounce judgment.

If a convicted defendant does not show sufficient cause as to why judgment should not be pronounced, the court shall pronounce the judgment.

**HISTORY: GC § 13451-4; 113 v 123(198), ch 30, § 4; Bureau of Code Revision. Eff 10-1-53.**

## § 2947.08 Time of execution in capital cases.

In cases where the death sentence is imposed, at least one hundred twenty days shall intervene between the day of sentence and the day appointed for the execution thereof.

**HISTORY: GC § 13451-5; 113 v 123(198), ch 30, § 5; Bureau of Code Revision, 10-1-53; 131 v 684. Eff 8-10-65.**

## § 2947.09 Repealed, 134 v H 511, § 2 [GC §§ 13451-6—13451-8; 113 v 123; 115 v 542; Bureau of Code Revision, 10-1-53; 133 v S 460]. Eff 1-1-74.

This section concerned sentence to hard labor.

## § 2947.10 Repealed, 134 v H 511, § 2 [GC §§ 13451-6—13451-8; 113 v 123; 115 v 542; Bureau of Code Revision, 10-1-53; 133 v S 460]. Eff 1-1-74.

This section concerned punishment by fine and imprisonment.

**§ 2947.11** Repealed, 134 v H 511, § 2 [GC §§ 13451-6—13451-8; 113 v 123; 115 v 542; Bureau of Code Revision, 10-1-53; 133 v S 460]. Eff 1-1-74.

This section concerned conditional sentence for a misdemeanor.

**§ 2947.12** Repealed, 134 v H 511, § 2 [GC §§ 13451-8a—13451-8b; 113 v 123; 115 v 543; Bureau of Code Revision, 10-1-53; 134 v H 139]. Eff 1-1-74.

This section established time and manner of payment of fine.

**§ 2947.13** Repealed, 134 v H 511, § 2 [GC §§ 13451-8a—13451-8b; 113 v 123; 115 v 543; Bureau of Code Revision, 10-1-53; 134 v H 139]. Eff 1-1-74.

This section established procedure for remission or suspension of sentence.

## § 2947.14 Satisfaction of fine.

(A) If a fine is imposed as a sentence or a part of a sentence, the court or magistrate that imposed the fine may order that the offender be committed to the jail or workhouse until the fine is paid or secured to be paid, or the offender is otherwise legally discharged, if the court or magistrate determines at a hearing that the offender is able, at that time, to pay the fine but refuses to do so. The hearing required by this section shall be conducted at the time of sentencing.

(B) At the hearing, the offender has the right to be represented by counsel and to testify and present evidence as to the offender's ability to pay the fine. If a court or magistrate determines after considering the evidence presented by an offender, that the offender is able to pay a fine, the determination shall be supported by findings of fact set forth in a judgment entry that indicate the offender's income, assets, and debts, as presented by the offender, and the offender's ability to pay.

(C) If the court or magistrate has found the offender able to pay a fine at a hearing conducted in compliance with divisions (A) and (B) of this section, and the offender fails to pay the fine, a warrant may be issued for the arrest of the offender. Any offender held in custody pursuant to such an arrest shall be entitled to a hearing on the first regularly scheduled court day following the date of arrest in order to inform the court or magistrate of any change of circumstances that has occurred since the time of sentencing and that affects the offender's ability to pay the fine. The right to the hearing on any change of circumstances may be waived by the offender.

At the hearing to determine any change of circumstances, the offender has the right to testify and present evidence as to any portion of the offender's income, assets, or debts that has changed in such a manner as to affect the offender's ability to pay the fine. If a court or magistrate determines, after considering any evidence presented by the offender, that the offender remains able to pay the fine, that determination shall be supported by a judgment entry that includes findings of fact upon which such a determination is based.

(D) No person shall be ordered to be committed to a jail or workhouse or otherwise be held in custody in satisfaction of a fine imposed as the whole or a part of a sentence except as provided in this section. Any person imprisoned pursuant to this section shall receive credit upon the fine at the rate of fifty dollars per day or fraction of a day. If the unpaid fine is less than fifty dollars, the person shall be imprisoned one day.

(E) No commitment pursuant to this section shall exceed six months.

**HISTORY: GC § 13451-9; 113 v 123(199), ch 30, § 9; 120 v 320; Bureau of Code Revision, 10-1-53; 133 v S 460 (Eff 9-3-70); 140 v H 277 (Eff 9-20-84); 140 v H 113 (Eff 1-8-85); 149 v H 170. Eff 9-6-2002.**

## § 2947.15 Labor by jail inmates; vocational training, rehabilitation.

Persons committed to jail by a judge or magistrate for nonpayment of fine, or convicts sentenced to hard labor in the county jail, shall perform labor under the direction of the board of county commissioners within or outside the jail, within the county, and the board shall adopt orders and rules in relation to the performance of labor and the sheriff or other officer having the custody of the persons or convicts shall be governed by the orders and rules. The sheriff of the county shall collect the proceeds of the labor of the persons or convicts, pay it into the county treasury, take the county treasurer's duplicate receipts for the amount paid, and forthwith deposit one of them with the county auditor. The sheriff, with the approval of the board, may provide for the vocational training and rehabilitation of prisoners confined in the county jail.

This section does not apply to prisoners participating in a county jail industry program established under section 5147.30 of the Revised Code.

**HISTORY: GC § 13451-10; 113 v 123(199), ch 30, § 10; Bureau of Code Revision, 10-1-53; 125 v S 275 (Eff 10-15-53); 133 v S 460 (Eff 9-3-70); 143 v H 588 (Eff 10-31-90); 143 v H 51. Eff 11-8-90.**

## § 2947.151 Reduction of jail sentence.

The sheriff in charge of a county jail may, upon a consideration of the quality and amount of work done in the kitchen, in the jail offices, on the jail premises, or elsewhere, allow reductions of inmates' sentences as follows:

(A) On sentences of ninety days or less, up to three days for each thirty days of sentence;

(B) On sentences longer than ninety days but not longer than six months, up to four days for each thirty days of sentence;

(C) On sentences longer than six months, up to five days for each thirty days of sentence.

The reduction of the inmate's sentence shall become effective only upon the written concurrence of the presiding or sentencing judge or magistrate of the court where the sentence was imposed.

This section shall in no way restrict any other powers vested in the presiding or sentencing judge or magistrate of the court where the sentence was imposed.

**HISTORY: 128 v 595. Eff 10-1-59.**

## § 2947.16 Recognizance.

A person convicted of a misdemeanor may be required by the judge or magistrate to enter into a recognizance, with sufficient surety, in such sum as the judge or magistrate finds proper, to keep the peace and be of good behavior for such time, not exceeding two years, as the court directs. The court may order such person to stand committed until such order is complied with or he is discharged by law, but the court may discharge such person at any time on his own recognizance, or cancel such recognizance.

**HISTORY: GC § 13451-11; 113 v 123(199), ch 30, § 11; Bureau of Code Revision. Eff 10-1-53.**

## § 2947.17 Breach of condition of a recognizance.

In case of a breach of the condition of any recognizance given under section 2947.16 of the Revised Code, the same proceedings shall be had as are prescribed in relation to forfeiture of other recognizances.

**HISTORY: GC § 13451-12; 113 v 123(199), ch 30, § 12; Bureau of Code Revision, 10-1-53; 133 v H 228 (Eff 1-1-70); 138 v H 736. Eff 10-16-80.**

## § 2947.18 Sentence to workhouse for jail offense.

Where the board of county commissioners of a county, or legislative authority of a municipal corporation having no workhouse, has made provisions for receiving prisoners into the workhouse of a city in any other county or district in the state, a court or magistrate, where imprisonment in jail may lawfully be imposed in such case, may sentence persons convicted of a misdemeanor, including a violation of a municipal ordinance, to such workhouse.

**HISTORY: GC § 13451-13; 113 v 123(199), ch 30, § 13; Bureau of Code Revision, 10-1-53; 133 v S 460. Eff 9-3-70.**

## § 2947.19 Confinement of county prisoners in city workhouse; reimbursement by prisoner; testing and treatment for certain diseases.

(A) In a county that has no workhouse but in which is located a city that has a workhouse maintained by the city, the board of county commissioners may agree with the proper authorities of that city upon terms under which persons convicted of misdemeanors shall be maintained in the city workhouse at the expense of the county. In the case of persons committed to the city workhouse for the violation of a law of this state, whether the commitment is from the court of common pleas, magistrate's court, or other court, the cost of maintaining those persons committed shall be paid out of the general fund of the county, on the allowance of the board of county commissioners, provided that all persons committed to the city workhouse for the violation of ordinances of the city shall be maintained in that workhouse at the sole cost of the city.

(B) Pursuant to section 2929.37 of the Revised Code, the board of county commissioners or the legislative authority of the city may require a person who was convicted of an offense and who is confined in the city workhouse as provided in division (A) of this section to reimburse the county or the city, as the case may be, for its expenses incurred by reason of the person's confinement. If a person is convicted of or pleads guilty to a felony and the court imposes a sanction that requires the offender to serve a term in a city workhouse, sections 341.23, 753.02, 753.04, and 753.16 of the Revised Code govern the determination of whether the court may impose a sanction under section 2929.18 of the Revised Code that requires the offender to reimburse the expenses of confinement.

(C) Notwithstanding any contrary provision in this section or section 2929.18, 2929.28, or 2929.37 of the Revised Code, the board of county commissioners or the legislative authority of the city may establish a policy that complies with section 2929.38 of the Revised Code and that requires any person who is not indigent and who is confined in the city workhouse to pay a reception fee or a fee for any medical treatment or service requested by and provided to that person.

(D) If a person who has been convicted of or pleaded guilty to an offense is confined in the workhouse as provided in division (A) of this section, at the time of reception and at other times the person in charge of the operation of the workhouse determines to be appropriate, the person in charge of the operation of the workhouse may cause the convicted offender to be examined and tested for tuberculosis, HIV infection, hepatitis, including but not limited to hepatitis A, B, and C, and other contagious diseases. The person in charge of the operation of the workhouse may cause a convicted offender in the workhouse who refuses to be tested or treated for tuberculosis, HIV infection, hepatitis, including but not limited to hepatitis A, B, and C, or another contagious disease to be tested and treated involuntarily.

**HISTORY: GC § 13451-14; 113 v 123(200), ch 30, § 14; Bureau of Code Revision, 10-1-53; 136 v H 205 (Eff 1-1-76); 140 v H 363 (Eff 9-26-84); 146 v S 2 (Eff 7-1-96); 146 v S 269 (Eff 7-1-96); 146 v H 480 (Eff 10-16-96); 147 v S 111 (Eff 3-17-98); 149 v H 170. Eff 9-6-2002; 149 v H 490, § 1, eff. 1-1-04.**

The effective date is set by section 4 of HB 490.

## § 2947.20 Submission of health insurance claims of inmates.

(A) For each person who is confined in a city workhouse as provided in section 2947.19 of the Revised Code, the county or the city, as the case may be, may make a determination as to whether the person is covered under a health insurance or health care policy, contract, or plan and, if the person has such coverage, what terms and conditions are imposed by it for the filing and payment of claims.

(B) If, pursuant to division (A) of this section, it is determined that the person is covered under a policy, contract, or plan and, while that coverage is in force, the workhouse renders or arranges for the rendering of health care services to the person in accordance with the terms and conditions of the policy, contract, or plan, then the person, county, city, or provider of the health care services, as appropriate under the terms and conditions of the policy, contract, or plan, shall promptly submit a claim for payment for the health care services to the appropriate third-party payer and shall designate, or make any other arrangement necessary to ensure, that payment of any amount due on the claim be made to the county, city, or provider, as the case may be.

(C) Any payment made to the county or the city pursuant to division (B) of this section shall be paid into the treasury of the governmental entity that incurred the expenses.

(D) This section also applies to any person who is under the custody of a law enforcement officer, as defined in section 2901.01 of the Revised Code, prior to the person's confinement in the workhouse.

**HISTORY: 146 v S 163. Eff 10-16-96.**

**Not analogous to former RC § 2947.20 (GC § 13451-15; 113 v 123(200), ch 30, § 15; 120 v 320; Bureau of Code Revision, 10-1-53; 133 v S 460; 134 v H 511; 140 v H 277), repealed 140 v H 113, § 2, eff 1-8-85.**

## § 2947.21 Officer's warrant for detention in workhouse or jail.

When a person is sentenced to a workhouse by the court of common pleas, the clerk of the court of common pleas shall make and deliver to the sheriff a certified copy of the judgment. The copy shall describe the crime charged and the sentence of the court. The sheriff shall deliver the copy to the officer in charge of the workhouse, and the copy shall be that officer's warrant for detaining the person in custody. In case of such a conviction by any other court or magistrate, the court or magistrate shall make a certified transcript of the docket in the case, which, in like manner, shall be delivered to the marshal, constable, or sheriff to be delivered by the marshal, constable, or sheriff to the proper officer in charge of the workhouse and be that officer's warrant for detaining the person in custody.

When a person is sentenced to a jail or workhouse under section 2929.24 of the Revised Code, the court shall certify a transcript of the docket in the case, and the court shall deliver the certified transcript to the proper officer in charge of the workhouse or jail, and the certified transcript is the officer's warrant for detaining the person in custody during the prescribed period or periods.

**HISTORY: GC § 13451-16; 113 v 123(200), ch 30, § 16; Bureau of Code Revision, 10-1-53; 133 v H 228 (Eff 1-1-70); 138 v H 736 (Eff 10-16-80); 146 v S 2. Eff 7-1-96; 149 v H 490, § 1, eff. 1-1-04.**

The effective date is set by section 4 of H.B. 490.

## § 2947.22 Person may be confined in jail temporarily.

A person sentenced to a workhouse may be confined in the jail of the county in which he was convicted, for such period as is necessary to procure the papers and make arrangements to transport him to the workhouse.

**HISTORY: GC § 13451-17; 113 v 123(200), ch 30, § 17; Bureau of Code Revision. Eff 10-1-53.**

## § 2947.23 Judgment for costs and jury fees.

(A)(1) In all criminal cases, including violations of ordinances, the judge or magistrate shall include in the sentence the costs of prosecution, including any costs under section 2947.231 [2947.23.1] of the Revised Code, and render a judgment against the defendant for such costs. At the time the judge or magistrate imposes sentence, the judge or magistrate shall notify the defendant of both of the following:

(a) If the defendant fails to pay that judgment or fails to timely make payments towards that judgment under a payment schedule approved by the court, the court may order the defendant to perform community service in an amount of not more than forty hours per month until the judgment is paid or until the court is satisfied that the defendant is in compliance with the approved payment schedule.

(b) If the court orders the defendant to perform the community service, the defendant will receive credit upon the judgment at the specified hourly credit rate per hour of community service performed, and each hour of community service performed will reduce the judgment by that amount.

(2) The following shall apply in all criminal cases:

(a) If a jury has been sworn at the trial of a case, the fees of the jurors shall be included in the costs, which shall be paid to the public treasury from which the jurors were paid.

(b) If a jury has not been sworn at the trial of a case because of a defendant's failure to appear without good cause, the costs incurred in summoning jurors for that particular trial may be included in the costs of prosecution. If the costs incurred in summoning jurors are assessed against the defendant, those costs shall be paid to the public treasury from which the jurors were paid.

(B) If a judge or magistrate has reason to believe that a defendant has failed to pay the judgment described in division (A) of this section or has failed to timely make payments towards that judgment under a payment schedule approved by the judge or magistrate, the judge or magistrate shall hold a hearing to determine whether to order the offender to perform community service for that failure. The judge or magistrate shall notify both the defendant and the prosecuting attorney of the place, time, and date of the hearing and shall give each an opportunity to present evidence. If, after the hearing, the judge or magistrate determines that the defendant has failed to pay the judgment or to timely make payments under the payment schedule and that imposition of community service for the failure is appropriate, the judge or magistrate may order the offender to perform community service in an amount of not more than forty hours per month until the judgment is paid or until the judge or magistrate is satisfied that the offender is in compliance with the approved payment schedule. If the judge or magistrate orders the defendant to perform community service under this division, the defendant shall receive credit upon the judgment at the specified hourly credit rate per hour of community service performed, and each hour of community service performed shall reduce the judgment by that amount. Except for the credit and reduction provided in this division, ordering an offender to perform community service under this division does not lessen the amount of the judgment and does not preclude the state from taking any other action to execute the judgment.

(C) As used in this section, "specified hourly credit rate" means the wage rate that is specified in 26 U.S.C.A. 206(a)(1) under the federal Fair Labor Standards Act of 1938, that then is in effect, and that an employer subject to that provision must pay per hour to each of the employer's employees who is subject to that provision.

**HISTORY: GC § 13451-18; 113 v 123(201), ch 30, § 18; 120 v 320; Bureau of Code Revision, 10-1-53; 149 v H 271. Eff 3-24-2003; 150 v S 71, § 1, eff. 5-18-05; 152 v H 283, § 1, eff. 9-12-08.**

## § 2947.231 State board of pharmacy investigation costs.

If a business entity described in division (B)(1)(j) or (k) of section 4729.51 of the Revised Code pleads guilty or no contest to or is found guilty of any criminal offense, the judge or magistrate shall include in the sentence any costs incurred by the state board of pharmacy in an investigation leading to the plea or conviction. Investigative costs include staff salaries, administrative costs, travel expenses, attorney's fees, and any other reasonable expense incurred by the board. The board shall set forth the costs the entity is required to pay in an itemized statement provided to the judge or magistrate.

**HISTORY: 152 v H 283, § 1, eff. 9-12-08.**

**§ 2947.24** Repealed, 137 v H 565, § 2 [GC §§ 13451-19, 13451-20; 118 v 686; 121 v 443; 124 v 382; Bureau of Code Revision, 10-1-53; 125 v S 155; 126 v 392; 129 v 1448; 130 v 667; 133 v H 688; 134 v H 494; 134 v H 511; 136 v H 244; 137 v H 1]. Eff 11-1-78.

This section defined mentally deficient offenders. See related provisions in RC Chapters 5120., 5122., and 5123.

**§ 2947.25** Repealed, 137 v H 565, § 2 [GC §§ 13451-19, 13451-20; 118 v 686; 121 v 443; 124 v 382; Bureau of Code Revision, 10-1-53; 125 v S 155; 126 v 392; 129 v 1448; 130 v 667; 133 v H 688; 134 v H 494; 134 v H 511; 136 v H 244; 137 v H 1]. Eff 11-1-78.

This section required psychiatric examination before sentence. See related provisions in RC Chapters 5120., 5122., and 5123.

**§ 2947.26** Repealed, 137 v H 565, § 2 [GC §§ 13451-21, 13451-22; 118 v 686; 121 v 443; 124 v 382; Bureau of Code Revision, 10-1-53; 125 v S 155; 132 v H 1; 132 v S 316; 133 v H 688; 133 v S 272; 134 v H 494; 136 v H 1; 137 v H 1]. Eff 11-1-78.

This section provided for postponement of commitment, conditions for release, and procedures upon recovery or improvement of inmate. See related provisions in RC Chapters 5120., 5122., and 5123.

**§ 2947.27** Repealed, 137 v H 565, § 2 [GC §§ 13451-21, 13451-22; 118 v 686; 121 v 443; 124 v 382; Bureau of Code Revision, 10-1-53; 125 v S 155; 132 v H 1; 132 v S 316; 133 v H 688; 133 v S 272; 134 v H 494; 136 v H 1; 137 v H 1]. Eff 11-1-78.

This section provided for postponement of commitment, conditions for release, and procedures upon recovery or improvement of inmate. See related provisions in RC Chapters 5120., 5122., and 5123.

**§ 2947.271** Repealed, 137 v H 565, § 2 [134 v H 511; 136 v H 1]. Eff 11-1-78.

This section concerned annual case review of mentally deficient offender.

**§ 2947.28** Repealed, 137 v H 565, § 2 [GC §§ 13451-22a, 13451-23; 118 v 686; 121 v 443; Bureau of Code Revision, 10-1-53; 125 v S 155; 133 v H 688; 134 v H 494]. Eff 11-1-78.

This section concerned application for release.

**§ 2947.29** Repealed, 137 v H 565, § 2 [GC §§ 13451-22a, 13451-23; 118 v 686; 121 v 443; Bureau of Code Revision, 10-1-53; 125 v S 155; 133 v H 688; 134 v H 494]. Eff 11-1-78.

This section concerned application for release.

**§ 2947.30** Repealed, 134 v H 511, § 2 [132 v H 996; 133 v H 228; 134 v H 143]. Eff 1-1-74.

This section concerned additional penalty for possessing firearms while rioting.

**§ 2947.31** Repealed, 134 v H 511, § 2 [132 v H 996; 133 v H 228; 134 v H 143]. Eff 1-1-74.

This section concerned periodic sentences.

# CHAPTER 2949: EXECUTION OF SENTENCE



## § 2949.01 Definition of magistrate.

The definition of "magistrate" set forth in section 2931.01 of the Revised Code applies to Chapter 2949. of the Revised Code.

**HISTORY: Bureau of Code Revision. Eff 10-1-53.**

## [SUSPENSION OF SENTENCE]

## § 2949.02 Execution suspended pending appeal.

(A) If a person is convicted of any bailable offense, including, but not limited to, a violation of an ordinance of a municipal corporation, in a municipal or county court or in a court of common pleas and if the person gives to the trial judge or magistrate a written notice of the person's intention to file or apply for leave to file an appeal to the court of appeals, the trial judge or magistrate may suspend, subject to division (A)(2)(b) of section 2953.09 of the Revised Code, execution of the sentence or judgment imposed for any fixed time that will give the person time either to prepare and file, or to apply for leave to file, the appeal. In all bailable cases, except as provided in division (B) of this section, the trial judge or magistrate may release the person on bail in accordance with Criminal Rule 46, and the bail shall at least be conditioned that the person will appeal without delay and abide by the judgment and sentence of the court.

(B) Notwithstanding any provision of Criminal Rule 46 to the contrary, a trial judge of a court of common pleas shall not release on bail pursuant to division (A) of this section a person who is convicted of a bailable offense if the person is sentenced to imprisonment for life or if that offense is a violation of section 2903.01, 2903.02, 2903.03, 2903.04, 2903.11, 2905.01, 2905.02, 2905.11, 2907.02, 2909.02, 2911.01, 2911.02, or 2911.11 of the Revised Code or is felonious sexual penetration in violation of former section 2907.12 of the Revised Code.

(C) If a trial judge of a court of common pleas is prohibited by division (B) of this section from releasing on bail pursuant to division (A) of this section a person who is convicted of a bailable offense and not sentenced to imprisonment for life, the appropriate court of appeals or two judges of it, upon motion of such a person and for good cause shown, may release the person on bail in accordance with Appellate Rule 8 and Criminal Rule 46, and the bail shall at least be conditioned as described in division (A) of this section.

**HISTORY: GC § 13453-1; 113 v 123(203), ch 32; Bureau of Code Revision, 10-1-53; 139 v S 199 (Eff 7-1-83); 141 v H 412 (Eff 3-17-87); 146 v H 445. Eff 9-3-96.**

## § 2949.03 Further suspending execution.

If a judgment of conviction by a court of common pleas, municipal court, or county court is affirmed by a court of appeals and remanded to the trial court for execution of the sentence or judgment imposed, and the person so convicted gives notice of his intention to file a notice of appeal to the supreme court, the trial court, on the filing of a motion by such person within three days after the rendition by the court of appeals of the judgment of affirmation, may further suspend, subject to division (A)(2)(b) of section 2953.09 of the Revised Code, the execution of the sentence or judgment imposed for a time sufficient to give such person an opportunity to file a notice of appeal to the supreme court, but the sentence or judgment imposed shall not be suspended more than thirty days for that purpose.

**HISTORY: GC § 13453-2; 113 v 123(204), ch 32, § 2; Bureau of Code Revision, 10-1-53; 141 v H 412. Eff 3-17-87.**

## § 2949.04 Increase or decrease in bail.

When bail is fixed pursuant to division (B) of section 2953.03 or section 2949.02 or 2953.09 of the Revised Code in connection with an appeal, a reduction or increase in the amount of that bail or other change in that bail shall not be required of the accused during the pendency of the appeal unless the trial judge or magistrate, or the court in which the appeal is being prosecuted, finds that there is good cause to reduce or increase the amount of that bail or good cause for any other change in that bail. If the court in which the appeal is being prosecuted finds there is good cause to reduce or increase the amount of that bail or good cause for any other change in that bail, it shall order the reduction, increase, or other change in accordance with Criminal Rule 46, and the new bail shall be in the amount and form so ordered and otherwise be to the approval of and filed with the clerk of the court in which the appeal is being prosecuted.

**HISTORY: GC § 13453-3; 113 v 123(204), ch 32, § 3; Bureau of Code Revision, 10-1-53; 129 v 423 (Eff 10-19-61); 141 v H 412. Eff 3-17-87.**

## § 2949.05 Execution of sentence.

If no appeal is filed, if leave to file an appeal or certification of a case is denied, if the judgment of the trial court is affirmed on appeal, or if post-conviction relief under section 2953.21 of the Revised Code is denied, the trial court or magistrate shall carry into execution the sentence or judgment which had been pronounced against the defendant.

**HISTORY: GC § 13453-4; 113 v 123(204), ch 32, § 4; Bureau of Code Revision, 10-1-53; 129 v 423 (Eff 10-19-61); 133 v S 354 (Eff 11-18-69); 141 v H 412. Eff 3-17-87.**

## § 2949.06 Escape after sentencing; resentencing.

If a person escapes after sentence and before confinement in a state correctional institution or jail, the clerk of the trial court, upon application of the prosecuting attorney or by order of the court, shall issue a warrant stating the conviction and sentence and commanding the sheriff to pursue the person into any county of this state. The sheriff shall take into custody the person so escaping and shall make return of the warrant to the court if it is in session, and if it is not in session he shall commit the accused to the jail of the county and bring him before the court at the next session of the court. The court shall set aside the former sentence and again pronounce judgment upon the verdict.

**HISTORY: GC § 13453-5; 113 v 123(204), ch 32, § 5; Bureau of Code Revision, 10-1-53; 145 v H 571. Eff 10-6-94.**

## § 2949.07 No credit for time absent.

If a convict escapes from a state correctional institution, the time the convict is absent from the institution because of his escape shall not be credited as a part of the time for which he was sentenced.

**HISTORY: GC § 13453-6; 113 v 123(204), ch 32, § 6; Bureau of Code Revision, 10-1-53; 145 v H 571. Eff 10-6-94.**

## § 2949.08 Confinement upon conviction; reduction of sentence for prior confinement.

(A) When a person who is convicted of or pleads guilty to a felony is sentenced to a community residential sanction in a community-based correctional facility pursuant to section 2929.16 of the Revised Code or when a person who is convicted of or pleads guilty to a felony or a misdemeanor is sentenced to a term of imprisonment in a jail, the judge or magistrate shall order the person into the custody of the sheriff or constable, and the sheriff or constable shall deliver the person with the record of the person's conviction to the jailer, administrator, or keeper, in whose custody the person shall remain until the term of imprisonment expires or the person is otherwise legally discharged.

(B) The record of the person's conviction shall specify the total number of days, if any, that the person was confined for any reason arising out of the offense for which the person was convicted and sentenced prior to delivery to the jailer, administrator, or keeper under this section. The record shall be used to determine any reduction of sentence under division (C) of this section.

(C)(1) If the person is sentenced to a jail for a felony or a misdemeanor, the jailer in charge of a jail shall reduce the sentence of a person delivered into the jailer's custody pursuant to division (A) of this section by the total number of days the person was confined for any reason arising out of the offense for which the person was convicted and sentenced, including confinement in lieu of bail while awaiting trial, confinement for examination to determine the person's competence to stand trial or to determine sanity, and confinement while awaiting transportation to the place where the person is to serve the sentence.

(2) If the person is sentenced to a community-based correctional facility for a felony, the total amount of time that a person shall be confined in a community-based correctional facility, in a jail, and for any reason arising out of the offense for which the person was convicted and sentenced prior to delivery to the jailer, administrator, or keeper shall not exceed the maximum prison term available for that offense. Any term in a jail shall be reduced first pursuant to division (C)(1) of this section by the total number of days the person was confined prior to delivery to the jailer, administrator, or keeper. Only after the term in a jail has been entirely reduced may the term in a community-based correctional facility be reduced pursuant to this division. This division does not affect the limitations placed on the duration of a term in a jail or a community-based correctional facility under divisions (A)(1), (2), and (3) of section 2929.16 of the Revised Code.

(D) For purposes of divisions (B) and (C) of this section, a person shall be considered to have been confined for a day if the person was confined for any period or periods of time totaling more than eight hours during that day.

(E) As used in this section, "community-based correctional facility" and "jail" have the same meanings as in section 2929.01 of the Revised Code.

**HISTORY: GC § 13454-1; 113 v 123(205), ch 33; Bureau of Code Revision, 10-1-53; 138 v S 23 (Eff 3-27-80); 148 v S 107. Eff 3-23-2000.**

[FINES AND COSTS]

## § 2949.09 Execution for fine and costs.

When a judge or magistrate renders judgment for a fine, an execution may issue for such judgment and costs of prosecution, to be levied on the property, or in default thereof, upon the body of the defendant for nonpayment of the fine. The officer holding such writ may arrest such defendant in any county and commit him to the jail of the county in which such writ issued, until such time fine is paid or secured to be paid or he is otherwise legally discharged.

**HISTORY: GC § 13454-2; 113 v 123(205), ch 33, § 2; Bureau of Code Revision, 10-1-53; 133 v S 460. Eff 9-3-70.**

## § 2949.091 Additional court costs or bail.

(A)(1)(a) The court in which any person is convicted of or pleads guilty to any offense shall impose one of the following sums as costs in the case in addition to any other court costs that the court is required by law to impose upon the offender:

(i) Thirty dollars if the offense is a felony;

(ii) Twenty dollars if the offense is a misdemeanor other than a traffic offense that is not a moving violation;

(iii) Ten dollars if the offense is a traffic offense that is not a moving violation, excluding parking violations.

(b) All moneys collected pursuant to division (A)(1)(a) of this section during a month shall be transmitted on or before the twentieth day of the following month by the clerk of the court to the treasurer of state and deposited by the treasurer of state to the credit of the indigent defense support fund established under section 120.08 of the Revised Code. The court shall not waive the payment of the additional thirty-, twenty-, or ten-dollar court costs, unless the court determines that the offender is indigent and waives the payment of all court costs imposed upon the indigent offender.

(2)(a) The juvenile court in which a child is found to be a delinquent child or a juvenile traffic offender for an act that, if committed by an adult, would be an offense, shall impose one of the following sums as costs in the case in addition to any other court costs that the court is required or permitted by law to impose upon the delinquent child or juvenile traffic offender:

(i) Thirty dollars if the offense is a felony;

(ii) Twenty dollars if the offense is a misdemeanor other than a traffic offense that is not a moving violation;

(iii) Ten dollars if the offense is a traffic offense that is not a moving violation, excluding parking violations.

(b) All moneys collected pursuant to division (A)(2)(a) of this section during a month shall be transmitted on or before the twentieth day of the following month by the clerk of the court to the treasurer of state and deposited by the treasurer of state to the credit of the indigent defense support fund established under section 120.08 of the Revised Code. The thirty-, twenty-, or ten-dollar court costs shall be collected in all cases unless the court determines the juvenile is indigent and waives the payment of all court costs, or enters an order on its journal stating that it has determined that the juvenile is indigent, that no other court costs are to be taxed in the case, and that the payment of the thirty-, twenty-, or ten-dollar court costs is waived.

(B) Whenever a person is charged with any offense described in division (A)(1) of this section, the court shall add to the amount of the bail the thirty, twenty, or ten dollars required to be paid by division (A)(1) of this section. The thirty, twenty, or ten dollars shall be retained by the clerk of the court until the person is convicted, pleads guilty, forfeits bail, is found not guilty, or has the charges dismissed. If the person is convicted, pleads guilty, or forfeits bail, the clerk shall transmit the thirty, twenty, or ten dollars on or before the twentieth day of the month following the month in which the person was convicted, pleaded guilty, or forfeited bail to the treasurer of state, who shall deposit it to the credit of the indigent defense support fund established under section 120.08 of the Revised Code. If the person is found not guilty or the charges are dismissed, the clerk shall return the thirty, twenty, or ten dollars to the person.

(C) No person shall be placed or held in a detention facility for failing to pay the additional thirty-, twenty-, or ten-dollar court costs or bail that are required to be paid by this section.

(D) As used in this section:

(1) "Moving violation" and "bail" have the same meanings as in section 2743.70 of the Revised Code.

(2) "Detention facility" has the same meaning as in section 2921.01 of the Revised Code.

**HISTORY: 140 v H 291 (Eff 7-1-83); 142 v H 171 (Eff 7-1-87); 143 v H 111 (Eff 7-1-89); 143 v S 131 (Eff 7-25-90); 144 v H 298 (Eff 7-26-91); 147 v H 426. Eff 7-22-98; 150 v H 95, § 1, eff. 9-26-03; 153 v H 1, § 101.01, eff. 10-16-09.**

The effective date is set by § 812.10 of 153 v H 1.
The effective date is set by section 179 of H.B. 95 (150 v —).

## § 2949.092 Condition for waiver of specified additional court costs.

If a person is convicted of or pleads guilty to an offense and the court specifically is required, pursuant to section 2743.70 or 2949.091 [2949.09.1], 2949.093 [2949.09.3], or 2949.094 [2949.09.4] of the Revised Code or pursuant to any other section of the Revised Code to impose a specified sum of money as costs in the case in addition to any other costs that the court is required or permitted by law to impose in the case, the court shall not waive the payment of the specified additional court costs that the section of the Revised Code specifically requires the court to impose unless the court determines that the offender is indigent and the court waives the payment of all court costs imposed upon the offender.

**HISTORY: 143 v S 131. Eff 7-25-90; 151 v H 66, § 101.01, eff. 9-29-05; 152 v H 562, § 101.01, eff. 9-23-08.**

The effective date is set by § 812.10 of 152 v H 562.
The effective date is set by § 612.03 of 151 v H 66.

## § 2949.093 County participation in criminal justice regional information system.

(A) A board of county commissioners of any county containing fifty-five or more law enforcement agencies by resolution may elect to participate in a criminal justice regional information system, either by creating and maintaining a new criminal justice regional information system or by participating in an existing criminal justice regional information system.

(B) A county is not eligible to participate in any criminal justice regional information system unless it creates in its county treasury, pursuant to section 305.28 of the Revised Code, a criminal justice regional information fund.

(C) A county that elects to participate in a criminal justice regional information system shall obtain revenues to fund its participation by establishing an additional court cost not exceeding five dollars to be imposed for moving violations that occur in that county. The board of county commissioners of that county shall establish the amount of the additional court cost by resolution. The board shall give written notice to all courts located in that county that adjudicate or otherwise process moving violations that occur in that county of the county's election to participate in the system and of the amount of the additional court cost. Upon receipt of such notice, each recipient court shall impose that amount as an additional court cost for all moving violations the court adjudicates or otherwise processes, in accordance with divisions (D) and (E) of this section.

(D)(1) The court in which any person is convicted of or pleads guilty to any moving violation that occurs in a county that has elected to participate in a criminal justice regional information system shall impose the sum established by the board pursuant to division (C) of this section as costs in the case in addition to any other court costs that the court is required by law to impose upon the offender. The court shall not waive the payment of the additional court cost established by the board pursuant to division (C) of this section unless the court determines that the offender is indigent and waives the payment of all court costs imposed upon the indigent offender.

All such money collected during a month shall be transmitted on the first business day of the following month by the clerk of the court to the county treasurer of the county in which the court is located and thereafter the county treasurer shall deposit the money in that county's criminal justice regional information fund.

(2) The juvenile court in which a child is found to be a juvenile traffic offender for an act that is a moving violation occurring in a county participating in a criminal justice regional information system shall impose the sum established by the board pursuant to division (C) of this section as costs in the case in addition to any other court costs that the court is required by law to impose upon the juvenile traffic offender. The juvenile court shall not waive the payment of the additional court cost established by the board pursuant to division (C) of this section unless the court determines that the juvenile is indigent and waives the payment of all court costs imposed upon the indigent offender.

All such money collected during a month shall be transmitted on the first business day of the following month by the clerk of the court to the county treasurer of the county in which the juvenile court is located and thereafter the county treasurer shall deposit the money in that county's criminal justice regional information fund.

(E) Whenever a person is charged with any offense that is a moving violation and posts bail, the court shall add to the amount of the bail the set sum required to be paid by division (D)(1) of this section. The clerk of the court shall retain that set sum until the person is convicted, pleads guilty, forfeits bail, is found not guilty, or has the charges dismissed. If the person is convicted, pleads guilty, or forfeits bail, the clerk shall transmit the set sum to the county treasurer, who shall deposit it in the county criminal justice regional information fund. If the person is found not guilty or the charges are dismissed, the clerk shall return the set sum to the person.

(F) No person shall be placed or held in a detention facility as defined in section 2921.01 of the Revised Code for failing to pay the court cost or bail that is required to be paid by this section.

(G)(1) Except as provided in division (G)(2) of this section, all funds collected by a county under this section shall be used by that county only to pay the costs it incurs in creating and maintaining a new criminal justice regional information system or to pay the costs it incurs in participating in an existing criminal justice regional information system.

(2) If the board of county commissioners of a county determines that the funds in that county's criminal justice regional information fund are more than sufficient to satisfy the purpose for which the additional court cost described in division (C) of this section was imposed, the board may declare a surplus in the fund. The county may expend the surplus only to pay the costs it incurs in improving the law enforcement computer technology of local law enforcement agencies located in that county.

(H) As used in this section:

(1) "Moving violation" means any violation of any statute or ordinance, other than section 4513.263 [4513.26.3] of the Revised Code or an ordinance that is substantially equivalent to that section, that regulates the operation of vehicles, streetcars, or trackless trolleys on highways or streets or that regulates size or load limitations or fitness requirements of vehicles. "Moving violation" does not include the violation of any statute or ordinance that regulates pedestrians or the parking of vehicles.

(2) "Bail" means cash, a check, a money order, a credit card, or any other form of money that is posted by or for an offender pursuant to sections 2937.22 to 2937.46 of the Revised Code, Criminal Rule 46, or Traffic Rule 4 to prevent the offender from being placed or held in a detention facility, as defined in section 2921.01 of the Revised Code.

(3) "Criminal justice regional information system" means a governmental computer system that serves as a cooperative between political subdivisions in a particular region for the purpose of providing a consolidated computerized information system for criminal justice agencies in that region.

**HISTORY: 151 v H 66, § 101.01, eff. 9-29-05.**

The effective date is set by § 612.03 of 151 v H 66.

## § 2949.094 Additional court costs for drug law enforcement, justice program services, and indigent drivers alcohol treatment funds.

(A) The court in which any person is convicted of or pleads guilty to any moving violation shall impose an additional court cost of ten dollars upon the offender. The court shall not waive the payment of the ten dollars unless the court determines that the offender is indigent and waives the payment of all court costs imposed upon the indigent offender.

The clerk of the court shall transmit thirty-five per cent of all additional court costs collected pursuant to this division during a month on or before the twenty-third day of the following month to the state treasury of which ninety-seven per cent shall be credited to the drug law enforcement fund created under section 5502.68 of the

Revised Code and the remaining three per cent shall be credited to the justice program services fund created under section 5502.67 of the Revised Code. The clerk shall transmit fifteen per cent of all additional court costs so collected during a month on or before the twenty-third day of the following month to the county or municipal indigent drivers alcohol treatment fund under the control of that court, as created by the county or municipal corporation under division (H) of section 4511.191 [4511.19.1] of the Revised Code. The clerk shall transmit fifty per cent of all additional court costs so collected during a month on or before the twenty-third day of the following month to the state treasury to be credited to the indigent defense support fund created pursuant to section 120.08 of the Revised Code.

(B) The juvenile court in which a child is found to be a juvenile traffic offender for an act that is a moving violation shall impose an additional court cost of ten dollars upon the juvenile traffic offender. The juvenile court shall not waive the payment of the ten dollars unless the court determines that the juvenile is indigent and waives the payment of all court costs imposed upon the indigent offender.

The clerk of the court shall transmit thirty-five per cent of all additional court costs collected pursuant to this division during a month on or before the twenty-third day of the following month to the state treasury of which ninety-seven per cent shall be credited to the drug law enforcement fund created under section 5502.68 of the Revised Code and the remaining three per cent shall be credited to the justice program services fund created under section 5502.67 of the Revised Code. The clerk shall transmit fifteen per cent of all additional court costs so collected during a month on or before the twenty-third day of the following month to the county juvenile indigent drivers alcohol treatment fund under the control of that court, as created by the county under division (H) of section 4511.191 [4511.19.1] of the Revised Code. The clerk shall transmit fifty per cent of all additional court costs so collected during a month on or before the twenty-third day of the following month to the state treasury to be credited to the indigent defense support fund created pursuant to section 120.08 of the Revised Code.

(C) Whenever a person is charged with any offense that is a moving violation and posts bail, the court shall add to the amount of the bail the ten dollars required to be paid by division (A) of this section. The clerk of the court shall retain the ten dollars until the person is convicted, pleads guilty, forfeits bail, is found not guilty, or has the charges dismissed. If the person is convicted, pleads guilty, or forfeits bail, the clerk shall transmit three dollars and fifty cents out of the ten dollars to the state treasury of which ninety-seven per cent shall be credited to the drug law enforcement fund created under section 5502.68 of the Revised Code and the remaining three per cent shall be credited to the justice program services fund created under section 5502.67 of the Revised Code, the clerk shall transmit one dollar and fifty cents out of the ten dollars to the county, municipal, or county juvenile indigent drivers alcohol treatment fund under the control of that court, as created by the county or municipal corporation under division (H) of section 4511.191 [4511.19.1] of the Revised Code, and the clerk shall transmit five dollars out of the ten dollars to the state treasury to be credited to the indigent defense support fund created under section 120.08 of the Revised Code. If the person is found not guilty or the charges are dismissed, the clerk shall return the ten dollars to the person.

(D) No person shall be placed or held in a detention facility for failing to pay the court cost or bail that is required to be paid by this section.

(E) As used in this section:

(1) "Bail" and "moving violation" have the same meanings as in section 2949.093 [2949.09.3] of the Revised Code.

(2) "Detention facility" has the same meaning as in section 2921.01 of the Revised Code.

(3) "Division of criminal justice services" means the division of criminal justice services of the department of public safety, created by section 5502.62 of the Revised Code.

**HISTORY: 152 v H 562, § 101.01, eff. 9-23-08; 152 v H 215, § 1, eff. 4-7-09; 153 v H 2, § 101.01, eff. 7-1-09.**

The effective date is set by § 812.10 of 153 v H 2.
The effective date is set by § 812.10 of 152 v H 562.

## § 2949.10 Execution for fine to issue to other county.

An execution under section 2949.09 of the Revised Code may issue to the sheriff of any county in which the defendant resides, is found, or has property, and the sheriff shall execute the writ. If the defendant is taken, the sheriff shall commit him to the jail of the county in which the writ issued and deliver a certified copy of the writ to the sheriff of such county, who shall detain the offender until he is discharged as provided in such section.

**HISTORY: GC § 13454-3; 113 v 123(205), ch 33, § 3; Bureau of Code Revision. Eff 10-1-53.**

## § 2949.11 Fines paid into county treasury.

Unless otherwise required in the Revised Code, an officer who collects a fine shall pay it into the treasury of the county in which such fine was assessed, within twenty days after the receipt of the fine, to the credit of the county general fund. The county treasurer shall issue duplicate receipts for the fine, and the officer making the collection shall deposit one of these receipts with the county auditor.

**HISTORY: GC § 13454-4; 113 v 123(205), ch 33, § 4; Bureau of Code Revision, 10-1-53; 125 v S 361 (Eff 10-1-53); 141 v S 54. Eff 5-6-86.**

## § 2949.111 Assignment of offender's payments toward satisfaction of costs, restitution, fine or supervision fees.

(A) As used in this section:

(1) "Court costs" means any assessment that the court requires an offender to pay to defray the costs of operating the court.

(2) "State fines or costs" means any costs imposed or forfeited bail collected by the court under section 2743.70 of the Revised Code for deposit into the reparations fund or under section 2949.091 [2949.09.1] of the Revised Code for deposit into the indigent defense support fund established under section 120.08 of the Revised Code and all fines, penalties, and forfeited bail collected by the court and paid to a law library association under section 307.515 [307.51.5] of the Revised Code.

(3) "Reimbursement" means any reimbursement for the costs of confinement that the court orders an offender to pay pursuant to section 2929.28 of the Revised Code, any supervision fee, any fee for the costs of house arrest with electronic monitoring that an offender agrees to pay, any reimbursement for the costs of an investigation or prosecution that the court orders an offender to pay pursuant to section 2929.71 of the Revised Code, or any other costs that the court orders an offender to pay.

(4) "Supervision fees" means any fees that a court, pursuant to sections 2929.18, 2929.28, and 2951.021 [2951.02.1] of the Revised Code, requires an offender who is under a community control sanction to pay for supervision services.

(5) "Community control sanction" has the same meaning as in section 2929.01 of the Revised Code.

(B) Unless the court, in accordance with division (C) of this section, enters in the record of the case a different method of assigning payments, if a person who is charged with a misdemeanor is convicted of or pleads guilty to the offense, if the court orders the offender to pay any combination of court costs, state fines or costs, restitution, a conventional fine, or any reimbursement, and if the offender makes any payment of any of them to a clerk of court, the clerk shall assign the offender's payment in the following manner:

(1) If the court ordered the offender to pay any court costs, the offender's payment shall be assigned toward the satisfaction of those court costs until they have been entirely paid.

(2) If the court ordered the offender to pay any state fines or costs and if all of the court costs that the court ordered the offender to pay have been paid, the remainder of the offender's payment shall be assigned on a pro rata basis toward the satisfaction of the state fines or costs until they have been entirely paid.

(3) If the court ordered the offender to pay any restitution and if all of the court costs and state fines or costs that the court ordered the offender to pay have been paid, the remainder of the offender's payment shall be assigned toward the satisfaction of the restitution until it has been entirely paid.

(4) If the court ordered the offender to pay any fine and if all of the court costs, state fines or costs, and restitution that the court ordered the offender to pay have been paid, the remainder of the offender's payment shall be assigned toward the satisfaction of the fine until it has been entirely paid.

(5) If the court ordered the offender to pay any reimbursement and if all of the court costs, state fines or costs, restitution, and fines that the court ordered the offender to pay have been paid, the remainder of the offender's payment shall be assigned toward the satisfaction of the reimbursements until they have been entirely paid.

(C) If a person who is charged with a misdemeanor is convicted of or pleads guilty to the offense and if the court orders the offender to pay any combination of court costs, state fines or costs, restitution, fines, or reimbursements, the court, at the time it orders the offender to make those payments, may prescribe an order of payments that differs from the order set forth in division (B) of this section by entering in the record of the case the order so prescribed. If a different order is entered in the record, on receipt of any payment, the clerk of the court shall assign the payment in the manner prescribed by the court.

**HISTORY: 145 v H 406 (Eff 11-11-94); 146 v S 2 (Eff 7-1-96); 149 v H 170. Eff 9-6-2002; 149 v H 490, § 1, eff. 1-1-04; 152 v H 420, § 101.01, eff. 1-1-10; 153 v H 1, § 110.10, eff. 1-1-10.**

The effective date is set by § 812.10 of 153 v H 1.

The provisions of § 503 of 152 v H 420 read in part as follows:

SECTION 503. The amendment, enactment, or repeal by this act of the following sections takes effect on the dates specified below:

° ° °

The amendment of sections 733.40, 1901.024, 1901.31, 1907.20, 2949.111, 3375.50 (307.515), and 4513.35 of the Revised Code, on January 1, 2010;

° ° °

The effective date is set by section 4 of HB 490.

## [TRANSPORTATION OF FELONS; COSTS]

### § 2949.12 Delivery of convict to reception facility; assignment to institution, jail or workhouse.

Unless the execution of sentence is suspended or the convicted felon has less than thirty days to serve in prison and the department of rehabilitation and correction, the county sheriff, and the court agree otherwise, a convicted felon who is sentenced to serve a term of imprisonment in a state correctional institution shall be conveyed, within five days after sentencing, excluding Saturdays, Sundays, and legal holidays, by the sheriff of the county in which the conviction was had to the facility that is designated by the department of rehabilitation and correction for the reception of convicted felons. The sheriff shall deliver the convicted felon into the custody of the managing officer of the reception facility and, at that time, unless the department and the sheriff have agreed to electronically processed prisoner commitment, shall present the managing officer with a copy of the convicted felon's sentence that clearly describes each offense for which the felon was sentenced to a correctional institution, designates each section of the Revised Code that the felon violated and that resulted in the felon's conviction and sentence to a correctional institution, designates the sentence imposed for each offense for which the felon was sentenced to a correctional institution, and, pursuant to section 2967.191 [2967.19.1] of the Revised Code, specifies the total number of days, if any, that the felon was confined for any reason prior to conviction and sentence. The sheriff, at that time, also shall present the managing officer with a copy of the indictment. The clerk of the court of common pleas shall furnish the copies of the sentence and indictment. In the case of a person under the age of eighteen years who is certified to the court of common pleas by the juvenile court, the clerk of the court of common pleas also shall attach a copy of the certification to the copy of the indictment.

The convicted felon shall be assigned to an institution or designated to be housed in a county, multicounty, municipal, municipal-county, or multicounty-municipal jail or workhouse, if authorized pursuant to section 5120.161 [5120.16.1] of the Revised Code, shall be conveyed to the institution, jail, or workhouse, and shall be kept within the institution, jail, or workhouse until the term of the felon's imprisonment expires, the felon is pardoned, paroled, or placed under a post-release control sanction, or the felon is transferred under laws permitting the transfer of prisoners. If the execution of the felon's sentence is suspended, and the judgment thereafter affirmed, the felon shall be conveyed, in the same manner as if the execution of the felon's sentence had not been suspended, to the reception facility as soon as practicable after the judge directs the execution of sentence. The trial judge or other judge of the court, in the judge's discretion and for good cause shown, may extend the time of the conveyance.

**HISTORY: GC § 13455-1; 113 v 123(205), ch 34; 120 v 628; Bureau of Code Revision, 10-1-53; 135 v S 254 (Eff 8-21-73); 136 v H 685 (Eff 5-21-76); 139 v S 199 (Eff 7-1-83); 140 v S 210 (Eff 7-1-83); 140 v S 172 (Eff 9-26-84); 142 v H 455 (Eff 7-20-87); 142 v H 261 (Eff 11-1-87); 142 v H 708 (Eff 4-19-88); 145 v H 571 (Eff 10-6-94); 146 v S 2. Eff 7-1-96; 152 v H 130, § 1, eff. 4-7-09.**

The effective date is set by section 6 of SB 2.

## § 2949.13 Sheriff may require assistance.

During the time the sheriff is conveying a convicted felon to an institution for imprisonment therein, he may secure him in a jail and demand the assistance of a sheriff, jailer, or other person in keeping such prisoner, as if he were in his own county. Such sheriff, jailer, or other person is liable, on refusal, to like penalties as if the sheriff making the demand were in his own county.

**HISTORY: GC § 13455-2; 113 v 123(206), ch 34, § 2; Bureau of Code Revision. Eff 10-1-53.**

## § 2949.14 Cost bill in case of felony.

Upon conviction of a nonindigent person for a felony, the clerk of the court of common pleas shall make and certify under the clerk's hand and seal of the court, a complete itemized bill of the costs made in such prosecution, including the sum paid by the board of county commissioners, certified by the county auditor, for the arrest and return of the person on the requisition of the governor, or on the request of the governor to the president of the United States, or on the return of the fugitive by a designated agent pursuant to a waiver of extradition except in cases of parole violation. The clerk shall attempt to collect the costs from the person convicted.

**HISTORY: GC § 13455-3; 113 v 123(206), ch 34, § 3; Bureau of Code Revision, 10-1-53; 132 v S 447 (Eff 2-5-68); 140 v H 291. Eff 7-1-83; 2011 HB 153, § 101.01, eff. Sept. 29, 2011.**

## § 2949.15 Writs of execution to issue.

If a nonindigent person convicted of a felony fails to pay the costs of prosecution pursuant to section 2949.14 of the Revised Code, the clerk of the court of common pleas shall forthwith issue to the sheriff of the county in which the indictment was found, and to the sheriff of any other county in which the person has property, executions against his property for fines and the costs of prosecution, which shall be served and returned within ten days, with the proceedings of such sheriff or the certification that there is no property upon which to levy, indorsed thereon.

When a levy is made upon property under such execution, a writ shall forthwith be issued by the clerk for the sale thereof, and such sheriff shall sell the property and make return thereof, and after paying the costs of conviction, execution, and sale, pay the balance to the person authorized to receive it.

**HISTORY: GC § 13455-4; 113 v 123(206), ch 34, § 4; Bureau of Code Revision, 10-1-53; 140 v H 291. Eff 7-1-83.**

## § 2949.16 Repealed, 140 v H 291, § 2 [GC § 13455-5; 113 v 123 (206), ch 34, § 5; Bureau of Code Revision, 10-1-53]. Eff 7-1-83.

This section concerned costs on execution for felony.

## § 2949.17 Transportation of prisoners; expenses.

(A) The sheriff may take one guard for every two convicted felons to be transported to a correctional institution. The trial judge may authorize a larger number of guards upon written application of the sheriff, in which case a transcript of the order of the judge shall be certified by the clerk of the court of common pleas under the seal of the court, and the sheriff shall deliver the order with the convict to the person in charge of the correctional institution.

(B) In order to obtain reimbursement for the county for the expenses of transportation for indigent convicted felons, the clerk of the court of common pleas shall prepare a transportation cost bill for each indigent convicted felon transported pursuant to this section for an amount equal to not less than one dollar a mile from the county seat to the state correctional institution and return for each prisoner. The number of miles shall be computed by the usual route of travel. The clerk's duties under this division are subject to division (B) of section 2949.19 of the Revised Code.

**HISTORY: GC § 13455-6; 113 v 123(207), ch 34, § 6; Bureau of Code Revision, 10-1-53; 128 v 542 (Eff 7-17-59); 138 v H 204 (Eff 7-30-79); 139 v H 694 (Eff 11-15-81); 140 v H 291 (Eff 7-1-83); 145 v H 571 (Eff 10-6-94); 148 v H 283. Eff 9-29-99; 153 v H 1, § 101.01, eff. 10-16-09.**

The effective date is set by § 812.10 of 153 v H 1.
The effective date is set by section 162 of HB 283.

## § 2949.18 Repealed, 140 v H 291, § 2 [GC § 13455-7; 113 v 123 (207), ch 34, § 7; Bureau of Code Revision, 10-1-53; 138 v H 204; 139 v H 694]. Eff 7-1-83.

This section concerned certification and payment of cost bill.

## § 2949.19 State payment of criminal costs.

(A) Subject to division (B) of this section, the clerk of the court of common pleas shall report to the state public defender all cases in which an indigent person was convicted of a felony, all cases in which reimbursement is required by section 2949.20 of the Revised Code, and all cost bills for transportation that are prepared pursuant to section 2949.17 of the Revised Code. The reports shall be filed for each fiscal quarter within thirty days after the end of the quarter on a form prescribed by the state public defender and shall be accompanied by a certification of a judge of the court that in all cases listed in the report the defendant was determined to be indigent and convicted of a felony or that the case is reported pursuant to section 2949.20 of the Revised Code and that for each transportation cost bill submitted pursuant to section 2949.17 of the Revised Code that the convicted felon was determined to be indigent. The state public defender shall review the reports received under this division and prepare a transportation cost voucher and a quarterly subsidy voucher for each county for the amounts the state public defender finds to be correct. To compute the quarterly subsidy, the state public defender first shall subtract the total of all transportation cost vouchers that the state public defender approves for payment for the quarter from one-fourth of the state public defender's total appropriation for criminal costs subsidy for the fiscal year of which the quarter is part. The state public defender then shall compute a base subsidy amount per case by dividing the remainder by the total number of cases from all counties the state public defender approves for subsidy for the quarter. The quarterly subsidy voucher for each county shall then be the product of the base subsidy amount times the number of cases submitted by the county and approved for subsidy for the quarter. Payment shall be made to the clerk.

The clerk shall keep a record of all cases submitted for the subsidy in which the defendant was bound over to the court of common pleas from the municipal court. Upon receipt of the quarterly subsidy, the clerk shall pay to the clerk of the municipal court, for municipal court costs in such cases, an amount that does not exceed fifteen dollars per case, shall pay foreign sheriffs for their services, and shall deposit the remainder of the subsidy to the credit of the general fund of the county. The clerk of the court of common pleas then shall stamp the clerk's records "subsidy costs satisfied."

(B) If notified by the state public defender under section 2949.201 [2949.20.1] of the Revised Code that, for a specified state fiscal year, the general assembly has not appropriated funding for reimbursement payments pursuant to division (A) of this section, the clerk of the court of common pleas is exempt for that state fiscal year from the duties imposed upon the clerk by division (A) of this section and by sections 2949.17 and 2949.20 of the Revised Code. Upon providing the notice described in this division, the state public defender is exempt for that state fiscal year from the duties imposed upon the state public defender by division (A) of this section.

**HISTORY: GC § 13455-8; 113 v 123(207), ch 34, § 8; Bureau of Code Revision, 10-1-53; 130 v 668 (Eff 10-14-63); 138 v H 204 (Eff 7-30-79); 139 v H 694 (Eff 11-15-81); 140 v H 291 (Eff 7-1-83); 140 v H 462 (Eff 3-28-85); 141 v H 201 (Eff 7-1-85); 142 v H 171 (Eff 7-1-87); 148 v H 283. Eff 9-29-99.**

The effective date is set by section 162 of HB 283.

## § 2949.20 Costs in case of reversal.

In any case of final judgment of reversal as provided in section 2953.07 of the Revised Code, whenever the state of Ohio is the appellee, the clerk of the court of common pleas of the county in which sentence was imposed shall certify the case to the state public defender for reimbursement in the report required by section 2949.19 of the Revised Code, subject to division (B) of section 2949.19 of the Revised Code.

**HISTORY: GC § 13455-9; 115 v 532, § 2; Bureau of Code Revision, 10-1-53; 138 v H 204 (Eff 7-30-79); 139 v H 694 (Eff 11-15-81); 140 v H 291 (Eff 7-1-83); 148 v H 283. Eff 9-29-99.**

The effective date is set by section 162 of HB 283.

## § 2949.201 Notification to clerks of courts of common pleas as to status of state appropriations.

(A) On or before the date specified in division (B) of this section, in each state fiscal year, the state public defender shall notify the clerk of the court of common pleas of each county whether the general assembly has, or has not, appropriated funding for that state fiscal year for reimbursement payments pursuant to division (A) of section 2949.19 of the Revised Code.

(B) The state public defender shall provide the notification required by division (A) of this section on or before whichever of the following dates is applicable:

(1) If, on the first day of July of the fiscal year in question, the main operating appropriations act that covers that fiscal year is in effect, on or before the thirty-first day of July;

(2) If, on the first day of July of the fiscal year in question, the main operating appropriations act that covers that fiscal year is not in effect, on or before the day that is thirty days after the effective date of the main operating appropriations act that covers that fiscal year.

**HISTORY: 139 v H 694 (Eff 11-15-81); 140 v H 291 (Eff 7-1-83); 148 v H 283. Eff 9-29-99.**

The effective date is set by section 162 of HB 283.

[DEATH SENTENCE]

## § 2949.21 Conveyance to reception facility; assignment to institution.

A writ for the execution of the death penalty shall be directed to the sheriff by the court issuing it, and the sheriff, within thirty days and in a private manner, shall convey the prisoner to the facility designated by the director of rehabilitation and correction for the reception of the prisoner. For conducting the prisoner to the facility, the sheriff shall receive like fees and mileage as in other cases, when approved by the warden of the facility. After the procedures performed at the reception facility are completed, the prisoner shall be assigned to an appropriate correctional institution, conveyed to the institution, and kept within the institution until the execution of his sentence.

**HISTORY: GC § 13456-1; 113 v 123(207), ch 35; Bureau of Code Revision, 10-1-53; 144 v S 359 (Eff 12-22-92); 145 v H 571. Eff 10-6-94.**

## § 2949.22 Execution of death sentence.

(A) Except as provided in division (C) of this section, a death sentence shall be executed by causing the application to the person, upon whom the sentence was imposed, of a lethal injection of a drug or combination of drugs of sufficient dosage to quickly and painlessly cause death. The application of the drug or combination of drugs shall be continued until the person is dead. The warden of the correctional institution in which the sentence is to be executed or another person selected by the director of rehabilitation and correction shall ensure that the death sentence is executed.

(B) A death sentence shall be executed within the walls of the state correctional institution designated by the director of rehabilitation and correction as the location for executions, within an enclosure to be prepared for that purpose, under the direction of the warden of the institution or, in the warden's absence, a deputy warden, and on the day designated by the judge passing sentence or otherwise designated by a court in the course of any appellate or postconviction proceedings. The enclosure shall exclude public view.

(C) If a person is sentenced to death, and if the execution of a death sentence by lethal injection has been determined to be unconstitutional, the death sentence shall be executed by using any different manner of execution prescribed by law subsequent to the effective date of this amendment instead of by causing the application to the person of a lethal injection of a drug or combination of drugs of sufficient dosage to quickly and painlessly cause death, provided that the subsequently prescribed different manner of execution has not been determined to be unconstitutional. The use of the subsequently prescribed different manner of execution shall be continued until the person is dead. The warden of the state correctional institution in which the sentence is to be executed or another person selected by the director of rehabilitation and correction shall ensure that the sentence of death is executed.

(D) No change in the law made by the amendment to this section that took effect on October 1, 1993, or by this amendment constitutes a declaration by or belief of the general assembly that execution of a death sentence by electrocution is a cruel and unusual punishment proscribed by the Ohio Constitution or the United States Constitution.

**HISTORY: GC § 13456-2; 113 v 123(208), ch 35, § 2; Bureau of Code Revision, 10-1-53; 144 v S 359 (Eff 12-22-92); 145 v H 11 (Eff 10-1-93); 145 v H 571 (Eff 10-6-94); 149 v H 362. Eff 11-21-2001.**

## § 2949.23 Repealed, 144 v S 359, § 2 [GC § 13456-3; 113 v 123(208), ch 35, § 3; Bureau of Code Revision, 10-1-53]. Eff 12-22-92.

This section concerned time of execution. See now RC § 2949.22.

## § 2949.24 Execution and return of warrant.

Unless a suspension of execution is ordered by the court of appeals in which the cause is pending on appeal or the supreme court for a case in which a sentence of death is imposed for an offense committed before January 1, 1995, or by the supreme court for a case in which a sentence of death is imposed for an offense committed on or after January 1, 1995, or is ordered by two judges or four justices of that court, the warden or another person selected by the director of rehabilitation and correction shall proceed at the time and place named in the warrant to ensure that the death sentence of the prisoner under death sentence is executed in accordance with section 2949.22 of the Revised Code. The warden shall make the return to the clerk of the court of common pleas of the county immediately from which the prisoner was sentenced of the manner of the execution of the warrant. The clerk shall record the warrant and the return in the records of the case.

**HISTORY: GC § 13456-4; 113 v 123(208), ch 35, § 4; Bureau of Code Revision, 10-1-53; 144 v S 359 (Eff 12-22-92); 146 v S 4. Eff 9-21-95.**

## § 2949.25 Attendance at execution.

(A) At the execution of a death sentence, only the following persons may be present:

(1) The warden of the state correctional institution in which the sentence is executed or a deputy warden, any other person selected by the director of rehabilitation and correction to ensure that the death sentence is executed, any persons necessary to execute the death sentence by lethal injection, and the number of correction officers that the warden thinks necessary;

(2) The sheriff of the county in which the prisoner was tried and convicted;

(3) The director of rehabilitation and correction, or the director's agent;

(4) Physicians of the state correctional institution in which the sentence is executed;

(5) The clergyperson in attendance upon the prisoner, and not more than three other persons, to be designated by the prisoner, who are not confined in any state institution;

(6) Not more than three persons to be designated by the immediate family of the victim;

(7) Representatives of the news media as authorized by the director of rehabilitation and correction.

(B) The director shall authorize at least one representative of a newspaper, at least one representative of a television station, and at least one representative of a radio station to be present at the execution of the sentence under division (A)(7) of this section.

**HISTORY: GC § 13456-5; 113 v 123(208), ch 35, § 5; Bureau of Code Revision, 10-1-53; 125 v S 155 (Eff 7-1-54); 134 v H 494 (Eff 7-12-72); 144 v S 359 (Eff 12-22-92); 145 v H 11 (Eff 10-1-93); 145 v H 571 (Eff 10-6-94); 149 v H 362. Eff 11-21-2001.**

## § 2949.26 Disposition of body of executed convict.

The body of an executed convict shall be returned for burial in any county of the state, to friends who made written request therefor, if made to the warden the day before or on the morning of the execution. The warden may pay the transportation and other funeral expenses, not to exceed fifty dollars.

If no request is made by such friends therefor, such body shall be disposed of as provided by section 1713.34 of the Revised Code and the rules of the director of job and family services.

**HISTORY: GC § 13456-6; 113 v 123(208), ch 35, § 6; Bureau of Code Revision, 10-1-53; 141 v H 201 (Eff 7-1-85); 148 v H 471. Eff 7-1-2000.**

The effective date is set by section 12(A) of HB 471.

## § 2949.27 Escape, rearrest, and execution.

If a convicted felon escapes after sentence of death, and is not retaken before the time fixed for his execution, any sheriff may rearrest and commit him to the county jail, and make return thereof to the court in which the sentence was passed. Such court shall again fix the time for execution, which shall be carried into effect as provided in sections 2949.21 to 2949.26, inclusive, of the Revised Code.

**HISTORY: GC § 13456-7; 113 v 123(209), ch 35, § 7; Bureau of Code Revision. Eff 10-1-53.**

## § 2949.28 Suspension of execution of death sentence of insane convict.

(A) As used in this section and section 2949.29 of the Revised Code, "insane" means that the convict in question does not have the mental capacity to understand the nature of the death penalty and why it was imposed upon the convict.

(B)(1) If a convict sentenced to death appears to be insane, the warden or the sheriff having custody of the convict, the convict's counsel, or a psychiatrist or psychologist who has examined the convict shall give notice of the apparent insanity to whichever of the following is applicable:

(a) If the convict was tried by a jury, to the judge who imposed the sentence upon the convict or, if that judge is unavailable, to another judge of the same court of common pleas;

(b) If the convict was tried by a three-judge panel, to any of the three judges who imposed the sentence upon the convict or, if each of those judges is unavailable, to another judge of the same court of common pleas.

(2) Upon receiving a notice pursuant to division (B)(1) of this section, a judge shall determine, based on the notice and any supporting information, any information submitted by the prosecuting attorney, and the record in the case, including previous hearings and orders, whether probable cause exists to believe that the convict is insane. If the judge finds that probable cause exists to believe that the convict is insane, the judge shall hold a hearing to determine whether the convict is insane. If the judge does not find that probable cause of that nature exists, the judge may dismiss the matter without a hearing.

(3) If the judge who is given notice under division (B)(1) of this section finds probable cause to believe that the convict is insane, the judge shall inquire into the convict's insanity at a time and place to be fixed by the judge and shall give immediate notice of the inquiry to the prosecuting attorney who prosecuted the case, or that prosecuting attorney's successor, and to the convict and the convict's counsel. The judge may hold the inquiry at the place at which the convict is confined. If the convict does not have counsel, the court shall appoint an attorney to represent the convict in the inquiry. The court may appoint one or more psychiatrists or psychologists to examine the convict. The court shall not appoint a psychiatrist or psychologist who is an employee of the department of rehabilitation and correction to examine the convict. The court shall conduct any hearing under this section and section 2949.29 of the Revised Code and issue any ruling in the matter no later than sixty days from the date of the notice given under division (B)(1) of this section.

(4) Execution of the sentence shall be suspended pending completion of the inquiry only upon an order of the supreme court. If the supreme court issues an order granting a stay of execution, the supreme court in that order also may authorize the court of common pleas to continue the stay of execution or to set a new date for execution as provided in this section or section 2949.29 of the Revised Code.

(C) If the court appoints a psychiatrist or psychologist to examine the convict, the court shall inform the psychiatrist or psychologist of the location of the convict and of the purpose of the examination. The examiner shall have access to any available psychiatric or psychological report previously submitted to the court with respect to the mental condition of the convict, including, if applicable, a report regarding the convict's competency to stand trial or the convict's plea of not guilty by reason of insanity. The examiner also shall have access to any available current mental health and medical records of the convict.

The examiner shall conduct a thorough examination of the convict and shall submit a report to the court within thirty days of the examiner's appointment. The report shall contain the examiner's findings as to whether the convict has the mental capacity to understand the nature of the death penalty and why it was imposed upon the convict and the facts, in reasonable detail, upon which the findings are based.

**HISTORY: GC § 13456-8; 113 v 123(209), ch 35, § 8; Bureau of Code Revision, 10-1-53; 133 v S 354 (Eff 11-18-69); 147 v S 107. Eff 7-29-98.**

## § 2949.29 Proceedings on insanity inquiry.

(A) The prosecuting attorney, the convict, and the convict's counsel shall attend an inquiry commenced as provided in section 2949.28 of the Revised Code. The prosecuting attorney and the convict or the convict's counsel may produce, examine, and cross-examine witnesses, and all findings shall be in writing signed by the judge. If it is found that the convict is not insane, the sentence shall be executed at the time previously appointed, unless that time has passed pending completion of the inquiry, in which case the judge conducting the inquiry, if authorized by the supreme court, shall appoint a time for execution of the sentence to be effective fifteen days from the date of the entry of the judge's findings in the inquiry.

(B) If it is found that the convict is insane and if authorized by the supreme court, the judge shall continue any stay of execution of the sentence previously issued, order the convict to be confined in the area at which other convicts sentenced to death are confined or in a maximum security medical or psychiatric facility operated by the department of rehabilitation and correction, and order treatment of the convict. Thereafter, the court at any time may conduct and, on motion of the prosecuting attorney, shall conduct a hearing pursuant to division (A) of this section to continue the inquiry into the convict's insanity and, as provided in section 2949.28 of the Revised Code, may appoint one or more psychiatrists or psychologists to make a further examination of the convict and to submit a report to the court. If the court finds at the hearing that the convict is not insane and if the time previously appointed for execution of the sentence has not passed, the sentence shall be executed at the previously appointed time. If the court finds at the hearing that the convict is not insane and if the time previously appointed for execution of the sentence has passed, the judge who conducts the hearing, if authorized by the supreme court, shall appoint a new time for execution of the sentence to be effective fifteen days from the date of the entry of the judge's findings in the hearing.

(C) In all proceedings under this section, the convict is presumed not to be insane, and the court shall find that the convict is not insane unless the court finds by a preponderance of the evidence that the convict is insane.

(D) Proceedings for inquiry into the insanity of any convict sentenced to death shall be exclusively pursuant to this section, section 2949.28 of the Revised Code, and the Rules of Evidence. Neither Chapter 5122. or 5123. of the Revised Code nor any other provision of the Revised Code nor any other rule concerning mentally ill persons, mentally retarded persons, or insane persons applies to any proceeding for inquiry into the insanity of any convict sentenced to death.

**HISTORY: GC § 13456-9; 113 v 123(209), ch 35, § 9; Bureau of Code Revision, 10-1-53; 133 v S 354 (Eff 11-18-69); 147 v S 107. Eff 7-29-98.**

## § 2949.30 Repealed, 147 v S 107, § 2 [GC § 13456-10; 113 v 123 (209), ch 35, § 10; Bureau of Code Revision, 10-1-53; 130 v 669]. Eff 7-29-98.

This section concerned the restoration of insane convicts to sanity and the governor's order of their execution. See now RC § 2949.29.

## § 2949.31 Pregnant prisoners sentenced to death.

If a female convict sentenced to death appears to be pregnant, the warden or sheriff having custody of the convict, her counsel, or a physician who has examined the convict shall give notice of the apparent pregnancy to the appropriate judge of the appropriate court of common pleas as determined in the same manner as is provided in divisions (B)(1)(a) and (b) of section 2949.28 of the Revised Code, and like proceedings shall be had as are provided under sections 2949.28 and 2949.29 of the Revised Code in case of an insane convict sentenced to death, except to the extent that they by their nature clearly would be inapplicable.

If it is found at the inquiry held in accordance with sections 2949.28 and 2949.29 of the Revised Code that the convict is not pregnant, the sentence shall be executed at the time previously appointed, unless that time has passed pending completion of the inquiry, in which case the judge conducting the inquiry, if authorized by the supreme court, shall appoint a new time for execution of the sentence to be effective fifteen days from the date of the entry of the judge's ruling in the inquiry.

If it is found at the inquiry that the convict is pregnant, the judge shall suspend execution of the sentence and order the convict to be confined in the area at which other convicts sentenced to death are confined or in an appropriate medical facility. When the court finds that the convict no longer is pregnant, if the time previously appointed for execution of the sentence has not passed, the sentence shall be executed at the previously appointed time. When the court finds that the convict no longer is pregnant, if the time previously appointed for execution of the sentence has passed, the judge who conducts the inquiry, if authorized by the supreme court, shall appoint a new time for execution of the sentence to be effective fifteen days from the date of the entry of the judge's ruling in the inquiry.

**HISTORY: GC § 13456-11; 113 v 123(209), ch 35, § 11; Bureau of Code Revision, 10-1-53; 147 v S 107. Eff 7-29-98.**

## § 2949.32 Repealed, 147 v S 107, § 2 [GC § 13456-12; 113 v 123 (209), ch 35, § 12; Bureau of Code Revision, 10-1-53; 133 v S 354]. Eff 7-29-98.

This section concerned execution of a convict after she was no longer pregnant. See now RC § 2949.31.

## § 2949.33 Repealed, 135 v H 716, § 2 [GC §§ 13457-1, 13457-2; 113 v 123; Bureau of Code Revision, 10-1-53; 133 v S 460]. Eff 1-1-74.

This section determined when cumulative sentence may be imposed.

## § 2949.34 Repealed, 135 v H 716, § 2 [GC §§ 13457-1, 13457-2; 113 v 123; Bureau of Code Revision, 10-1-53; 133 v S 460]. Eff 1-1-74.

This section established sentencing of habitual offenders.

## § 2949.35 Repealed, 135 v H 716, § 2 [GC §§ 13457-3, 13457-4; 113 v 123; Bureau of Code Revision, 10-1-53]. Eff 1-1-74.

This section outlined exemptions for convictions under RC §§ 2949.33 and 2949.34.

## § 2949.36 Repealed, 135 v H 716, § 2 [GC §§ 13457-3, 13457-4; 113 v 123; Bureau of Code Revision, 10-1-53]. Eff 1-1-74.

This section provided for parole from workhouse.

# CHAPTER 2950: SEX OFFENDER REGISTRATION AND NOTIFICATION



## § 2950.01 Definitions.

As used in this chapter, unless the context clearly requires otherwise:

(A) "Sexually oriented offense" means any of the following violations or offenses committed by a person, regardless of the person's age:

(1) A violation of section 2907.02, 2907.03, 2907.05, 2907.06, 2907.07, 2907.08, 2907.21, 2907.32, 2907.321 [2907.32.1], 2907.322 [2907.32.2], or 2907.323 [2907.32.3] of the Revised Code;

(2) A violation of section 2907.04 of the Revised Code when the offender is less than four years older than the other person with whom the offender engaged in sexual conduct, the other person did not consent to the sexual conduct, and the offender previously has not been convicted of or pleaded guilty to a violation of section 2907.02, 2907.03, or 2907.04 of the Revised Code or a violation of former section 2907.12 of the Revised Code;

(3) A violation of section 2907.04 of the Revised Code when the offender is at least four years older than the other person with whom the offender engaged in sexual conduct or when the offender is less than four years older than the other person with whom the offender engaged in sexual conduct and the offender previously has been convicted of or pleaded guilty to a violation of section 2907.02, 2907.03, or 2907.04 of the Revised Code or a violation of former section 2907.12 of the Revised Code;

(4) A violation of section 2903.01, 2903.02, or 2903.11 of the Revised Code when the violation was committed with a sexual motivation;

(5) A violation of division (A) of section 2903.04 of the Revised Code when the offender committed or attempted to commit the felony that is the basis of the violation with a sexual motivation;

(6) A violation of division (A)(3) of section 2903.211 [2903.21.1] of the Revised Code;

(7) A violation of division (A)(1), (2), (3), or (5) of section 2905.01 of the Revised Code when the offense is committed with a sexual motivation;

(8) A violation of division (A)(4) of section 2905.01 of the Revised Code;

(9) A violation of division (B) of section 2905.01 of the Revised Code when the victim of the offense is under eighteen years of age and the offender is not a parent of the victim of the offense;

(10) A violation of division (B) of section 2905.02, of division (B) of section 2905.03, of division (B) of section 2905.05, or of division (B)(5) of section 2919.22 of the Revised Code;

(11) A violation of any former law of this state, any existing or former municipal ordinance or law of another state or the United States, any existing or former law applicable in a military court or in an Indian tribal court, or any existing or former law of any nation other than the United States that is or was substantially equivalent to any offense listed in division (A)(1), (2), (3), (4), (5), (6), (7), (8), (9), or (10) of this section;

(12) Any attempt to commit, conspiracy to commit, or complicity in committing any offense listed in division (A)(1), (2), (3), (4), (5), (6), (7), (8), (9), (10), or (11) of this section.

(B)(1) "Sex offender" means, subject to division (B)(2) of this section, a person who is convicted of, pleads guilty to, has been convicted of, has pleaded guilty to, is adjudicated a delinquent child for committing, or has been adjudicated a delinquent child for committing any sexually oriented offense.

(2) "Sex offender" does not include a person who is convicted of, pleads guilty to, has been convicted of, has pleaded guilty to, is adjudicated a delinquent child for committing, or has been adjudicated a delinquent child for committing a sexually oriented offense if the offense involves consensual sexual conduct or consensual sexual contact and either of the following applies:

(a) The victim of the sexually oriented offense was eighteen years of age or older and at the time of the sexually oriented offense was not under the custodial authority of the person who is convicted of, pleads guilty to, has been convicted of, has pleaded guilty to, is adjudicated a delinquent child for committing, or has been adjudicated a delinquent child for committing the sexually oriented offense.

(b) The victim of the offense was thirteen years of age or older, and the person who is convicted of, pleads guilty to, has been convicted of, has pleaded guilty to, is adjudicated a delinquent child for committing, or has been adjudicated a delinquent child for committing the sexually oriented offense is not more than four years older than the victim.

(C) "Child-victim oriented offense" means any of the following violations or offenses committed by a person, regardless of the person's age, when the victim is under eighteen years of age and is not a child of the person who commits the violation:

(1) A violation of division (A)(1), (2), (3), or (5) of section 2905.01 of the Revised Code when the violation is not included in division (A)(7) of this section;

(2) A violation of division (A) of section 2905.02, division (A) of section 2905.03, or division (A) of section 2905.05 of the Revised Code;

(3) A violation of any former law of this state, any existing or former municipal ordinance or law of another state or the United States, any existing or former law applicable in a military court or in an Indian tribal court, or any existing or former law of any nation other than the United States that is or was substantially equivalent to any offense listed in division (C)(1) or (2) of this section;

(4) Any attempt to commit, conspiracy to commit, or complicity in committing any offense listed in division (C)(1), (2), or (3) of this section.

(D) "Child-victim offender" means a person who is convicted of, pleads guilty to, has been convicted of, has pleaded guilty to, is adjudicated a delinquent child for committing, or has been adjudicated a delinquent child for committing any child-victim oriented offense.

(E) "Tier I sex offender/child-victim offender" means any of the following:

(1) A sex offender who is convicted of, pleads guilty to, has been convicted of, or has pleaded guilty to any of the following sexually oriented offenses:

(a) A violation of section 2907.06, 2907.07, 2907.08, or 2907.32 of the Revised Code;

(b) A violation of section 2907.04 of the Revised Code when the offender is less than four years older than the other person with whom the offender engaged in sexual conduct, the other person did not consent to the sexual conduct, and the offender previously has not been convicted of or pleaded guilty to a violation of section 2907.02, 2907.03, or 2907.04 of the Revised Code or a violation of former section 2907.12 of the Revised Code;

(c) A violation of division (A)(1), (2), (3), or (5) of section 2907.05 of the Revised Code;

(d) A violation of division (A)(3) of section 2907.323 [2907.32.3] of the Revised Code;

(e) A violation of division (A)(3) of section 2903.211 [2903.21.1], of division (B) of section 2905.03, or of division (B) of section 2905.05 of the Revised Code;

(f) A violation of any former law of this state, any existing or former municipal ordinance or law of another state or the United States, any existing or former law applicable in a military court or in an Indian tribal court, or any existing or former law of any nation other than the United States, that is or was substantially equivalent to any offense listed in division (E)(1)(a), (b), (c), (d), or (e) of this section;

(g) Any attempt to commit, conspiracy to commit, or complicity in committing any offense listed in division (E)(1)(a), (b), (c), (d), (e), or (f) of this section.

(2) A child-victim offender who is convicted of, pleads guilty to, has been convicted of, or has pleaded guilty to a child-victim oriented offense and who is not within either category of child-victim offender described in division (F)(2) or (G)(2) of this section.

(3) A sex offender who is adjudicated a delinquent child for committing or has been adjudicated a delinquent child for committing any sexually oriented offense and who a juvenile court, pursuant to section 2152.82, 2152.83, 2152.84, or 2152.85 of the Revised Code, classifies a tier I sex offender/child-victim offender relative to the offense.

(4) A child-victim offender who is adjudicated a delinquent child for committing or has been adjudicated a delinquent child for committing any child-victim oriented offense and who a juvenile court, pursuant to section 2152.82, 2152.83, 2152.84, or 2152.85 of the Revised Code, classifies a tier I sex offender/child-victim offender relative to the offense.

(F) "Tier II sex offender/child-victim offender" means any of the following:

(1) A sex offender who is convicted of, pleads guilty to, has been convicted of, or has pleaded guilty to any of the following sexually oriented offenses:

(a) A violation of section 2907.21, 2907.321 [2907.32.1], or 2907.322 [2907.32.2] of the Revised Code;

(b) A violation of section 2907.04 of the Revised Code when the offender is at least four years older than the other person with whom the offender engaged in sexual conduct, or when the offender is less than four years older than the other person with whom the offender engaged in sexual conduct and the offender previously has been convicted of or pleaded guilty to a violation of section 2907.02, 2907.03, or 2907.04 of the Revised Code or former section 2907.12 of the Revised Code;

(c) A violation of division (A)(4) of section 2907.05 or of division (A)(1) or (2) of section 2907.323 [2907.32.3] of the Revised Code;

(d) A violation of division (A)(1), (2), (3), or (5) of section 2905.01 of the Revised Code when the offense is committed with a sexual motivation;

(e) A violation of division (A)(4) of section 2905.01 of the Revised Code when the victim of the offense is eighteen years of age or older;

(f) A violation of division (B) of section 2905.02 or of division (B)(5) of section 2919.22 of the Revised Code;

(g) A violation of any former law of this state, any existing or former municipal ordinance or law of another state or the United States, any existing or former law applicable in a military court or in an Indian tribal court, or any existing or former law of any nation other than the United States that is or was substantially equivalent to any offense listed in division (F)(1)(a), (b), (c), (d), (e), or (f) of this section;

(h) Any attempt to commit, conspiracy to commit, or complicity in committing any offense listed in division (F)(1)(a), (b), (c), (d), (e), (f), or (g) of this section;

(i) Any sexually oriented offense that is committed after the sex offender previously has been convicted of, pleaded guilty to, or has been adjudicated a delinquent child for committing any sexually oriented offense or child-victim oriented offense for which the offender was classified a tier I sex offender/child-victim offender.

(2) A child-victim offender who is convicted of, pleads guilty to, has been convicted of, or has pleaded guilty to any child-victim oriented offense when the child-victim oriented offense is committed after the child-victim offender previously has been convicted of, pleaded guilty to, or been adjudicated a delinquent child for committing any sexually oriented offense or child-victim oriented offense for which the offender was classified a tier I sex offender/child-victim offender.

(3) A sex offender who is adjudicated a delinquent child for committing or has been adjudicated a delinquent child for committing any sexually oriented offense and who a juvenile court, pursuant to section 2152.82, 2152.83, 2152.84, or 2152.85 of the Revised Code, classifies a tier II sex offender/child-victim offender relative to the offense.

(4) A child-victim offender who is adjudicated a delinquent child for committing or has been adjudicated a delinquent child for committing any child-victim oriented offense and whom a juvenile court, pursuant to section 2152.82, 2152.83, 2152.84, or 2152.85 of the Revised Code, classifies a tier II sex offender/child-victim offender relative to the current offense.

(5) A sex offender or child-victim offender who is not in any category of tier II sex offender/child-victim offender set forth in division (F)(1), (2), (3), or (4) of this section, who prior to January 1, 2008, was adjudicated a delinquent child for committing a sexually oriented offense or child-victim oriented offense, and who prior to that date was determined to be a habitual sex offender or determined to be a habitual child-victim offender, unless either of the following applies:

(a) The sex offender or child-victim offender is reclassified pursuant to section 2950.031 [2950.03.1] or 2950.032 [2950.03.2] of the Revised Code as a tier I sex offender/child-victim offender or a tier III sex offender/child-victim offender relative to the offense.

(b) A juvenile court, pursuant to section 2152.82, 2152.83, 2152.84, or 2152.85 of the Revised Code, classifies the child a tier I sex offender/child-victim offender or a tier III sex offender/child-victim offender relative to the offense.

(G) "Tier III sex offender/child-victim offender" means any of the following:

(1) A sex offender who is convicted of, pleads guilty to, has been convicted of, or has pleaded guilty to any of the following sexually oriented offenses:

(a) A violation of section 2907.02 or 2907.03 of the Revised Code;

(b) A violation of division (B) of section 2907.05 of the Revised Code;

(c) A violation of section 2903.01, 2903.02, or 2903.11 of the Revised Code when the violation was committed with a sexual motivation;

(d) A violation of division (A) of section 2903.04 of the Revised Code when the offender committed or attempted to commit the felony that is the basis of the violation with a sexual motivation;

(e) A violation of division (A)(4) of section 2905.01 of the Revised Code when the victim of the offense is under eighteen years of age;

(f) A violation of division (B) of section 2905.01 of the Revised Code when the victim of the offense is under eighteen years of age and the offender is not a parent of the victim of the offense;

(g) A violation of any former law of this state, any existing or former municipal ordinance or law of another state or the United States, any existing or former law applicable in a military court or in an Indian tribal court, or any existing or former law of any nation other than the United States that is or was substantially equivalent to any offense listed in division (G)(1)(a), (b), (c), (d), (e), or (f) of this section;

(h) Any attempt to commit, conspiracy to commit, or complicity in committing any offense listed in division (G)(1)(a), (b), (c), (d), (e), (f), or (g) of this section;

(i) Any sexually oriented offense that is committed after the sex offender previously has been convicted of, pleaded guilty to, or been adjudicated a delinquent child for committing any sexually oriented offense or child-victim oriented offense for which the offender was classified a tier II sex offender/child-victim offender or a tier III sex offender/child-victim offender.

(2) A child-victim offender who is convicted of, pleads guilty to, has been convicted of, or has pleaded guilty to any child-victim oriented offense when the child-victim oriented offense is committed after the child-victim offender previously has been convicted of, pleaded guilty to, or been adjudicated a delinquent child for committing any sexually oriented offense or child-victim oriented offense for which the offender was classified a tier II sex offender/child-victim offender or a tier III sex offender/child-victim offender.

(3) A sex offender who is adjudicated a delinquent child for committing or has been adjudicated a delinquent child for committing any sexually oriented offense and who a juvenile court, pursuant to section 2152.82, 2152.83, 2152.84, or 2152.85 of the Revised Code, classifies a tier III sex offender/child-victim offender relative to the offense.

(4) A child-victim offender who is adjudicated a delinquent child for committing or has been adjudicated a delinquent child for committing any child-victim oriented offense and whom a juvenile court, pursuant to section 2152.82, 2152.83, 2152.84, or 2152.85 of the Revised Code, classifies a tier III sex offender/child-victim offender relative to the current offense.

(5) A sex offender or child-victim offender who is not in any category of tier III sex offender/child-victim offender set forth in division (G)(1), (2), (3), or (4) of this section, who prior to January 1, 2008, was convicted of or pleaded guilty to a sexually oriented offense or child-victim oriented offense or was adjudicated a delinquent child for committing a sexually oriented offense or child-victim oriented offense and classified a juvenile offender registrant, and who prior to that date was adjudicated a sexual predator or adjudicated a child-victim predator, unless either of the following applies:

(a) The sex offender or child-victim offender is reclassified pursuant to section 2950.031 [2950.03.1] or 2950.032 [2950.03.2] of the Revised Code as a tier I sex offender/child-victim offender or a tier II sex offender/child-victim offender relative to the offense.

(b) The sex offender or child-victim offender is a delinquent child, and a juvenile court, pursuant to section

2152.82, 2152.83, 2152.84, or 2152.85 of the Revised Code, classifies the child a tier I sex offender/child-victim offender or a tier II sex offender/child-victim offender relative to the offense.

(6) A sex offender who is convicted of, pleads guilty to, was convicted of, or pleaded guilty to a sexually oriented offense, if the sexually oriented offense and the circumstances in which it was committed are such that division (F) of section 2971.03 of the Revised Code automatically classifies the offender as a tier III sex offender/child-victim offender;

(7) A sex offender or child-victim offender who is convicted of, pleads guilty to, was convicted of, pleaded guilty to, is adjudicated a delinquent child for committing, or was adjudicated a delinquent child for committing a sexually oriented offense or child-victim offense in another state, in a federal court, military court, or Indian tribal court, or in a court in any nation other than the United States if both of the following apply:

(a) Under the law of the jurisdiction in which the offender was convicted or pleaded guilty or the delinquent child was adjudicated, the offender or delinquent child is in a category substantially equivalent to a category of tier III sex offender/child-victim offender described in division (G)(1), (2), (3), (4), (5), or (6) of this section.

(b) Subsequent to the conviction, plea of guilty, or adjudication in the other jurisdiction, the offender or delinquent child resides, has temporary domicile, attends school or an institution of higher education, is employed, or intends to reside in this state in any manner and for any period of time that subjects the offender or delinquent child to a duty to register or provide notice of intent to reside under section 2950.04 or 2950.041 [2950.04.1] of the Revised Code.

(H) "Confinement" includes, but is not limited to, a community residential sanction imposed pursuant to section 2929.16 or 2929.26 of the Revised Code.

(I) "Prosecutor" has the same meaning as in section 2935.01 of the Revised Code.

(J) "Supervised release" means a release of an offender from a prison term, a term of imprisonment, or another type of confinement that satisfies either of the following conditions:

(1) The release is on parole, a conditional pardon, under a community control sanction, under transitional control, or under a post-release control sanction, and it requires the person to report to or be supervised by a parole officer, probation officer, field officer, or another type of supervising officer.

(2) The release is any type of release that is not described in division (J)(1) of this section and that requires the person to report to or be supervised by a probation officer, a parole officer, a field officer, or another type of supervising officer.

(K) "Sexually violent predator specification," "sexually violent predator," "sexually violent offense," "sexual motivation specification," "designated homicide, assault, or kidnapping offense," and "violent sex offense" have the same meanings as in section 2971.01 of the Revised Code.

(L) "Post-release control sanction" and "transitional control" have the same meanings as in section 2967.01 of the Revised Code.

(M) "Juvenile offender registrant" means a person who is adjudicated a delinquent child for committing on or after January 1, 2002, a sexually oriented offense or a child-victim oriented offense, who is fourteen years of age or older at the time of committing the offense, and who a juvenile court judge, pursuant to an order issued under section 2152.82, 2152.83, 2152.84, 2152.85, or 2152.86 of the Revised Code, classifies a juvenile offender registrant and specifies has a duty to comply with sections 2950.04, 2950.041 [2950.04.1], 2950.05, and 2950.06 of the Revised Code. "Juvenile offender registrant" includes a person who prior to January 1, 2008, was a "juvenile offender registrant" under the definition of the term in existence prior to January 1, 2008, and a person who prior to July 31, 2003, was a "juvenile sex offender registrant" under the former definition of that former term.

(N) "Public registry-qualified juvenile offender registrant" means a person who is adjudicated a delinquent child and on whom a juvenile court has imposed a serious youthful offender dispositional sentence under section 2152.13 of the Revised Code before, on, or after January 1, 2008, and to whom all of the following apply:

(1) The person is adjudicated a delinquent child for committing, attempting to commit, conspiring to commit, or complicity in committing one of the following acts:

(a) A violation of section 2907.02 of the Revised Code, division (B) of section 2907.05 of the Revised Code, or section 2907.03 of the Revised Code if the victim of the violation was less than twelve years of age;

(b) A violation of section 2903.01, 2903.02, or 2905.01 of the Revised Code that was committed with a purpose to gratify the sexual needs or desires of the child.

(2) The person was fourteen, fifteen, sixteen, or seventeen years of age at the time of committing the act.

(3) A juvenile court judge, pursuant to an order issued under section 2152.86 of the Revised Code, classifies the person a juvenile offender registrant, specifies the person has a duty to comply with sections 2950.04, 2950.05, and 2950.06 of the Revised Code, and classifies the person a public registry-qualified juvenile offender registrant, and the classification of the person as a public registry-qualified juvenile offender registrant has not been terminated pursuant to division (D) of section 2152.86 of the Revised Code.

(O) "Secure facility" means any facility that is designed and operated to ensure that all of its entrances and exits are locked and under the exclusive control of its staff and to ensure that, because of that exclusive control, no person who is institutionalized or confined in the facility may leave the facility without permission or supervision.

(P) "Out-of-state juvenile offender registrant" means a person who is adjudicated a delinquent child in a court in another state, in a federal court, military court, or Indian tribal court, or in a court in any nation other than the United States for committing a sexually oriented offense or a child-victim oriented offense, who on or after January 1, 2002, moves to and resides in this state or temporarily is domiciled in this state for more than five days, and who has a duty under section 2950.04 or 2950.041 [2950.04.1] of the Revised Code to register in this state and the duty to otherwise comply with that applicable section and sections 2950.05 and 2950.06 of the Revised Code. "Out-of-state juvenile offender registrant" includes a person who prior to January 1, 2008, was an "out-of-state juvenile offender registrant" under the definition of the term in existence prior to January 1, 2008, and a person who prior to July 31, 2003, was an "out-of-state juvenile sex offender registrant" under the former definition of that former term.

(Q) "Juvenile court judge" includes a magistrate to whom the juvenile court judge confers duties pursuant to division (A)(15) of section 2151.23 of the Revised Code.

(R) "Adjudicated a delinquent child for committing a sexually oriented offense" includes a child who receives a serious youthful offender dispositional sentence under section 2152.13 of the Revised Code for committing a sexually oriented offense.

(S) "School" and "school premises" have the same meanings as in section 2925.01 of the Revised Code.

(T) "Residential premises" means the building in which a residential unit is located and the grounds upon which that building stands, extending to the perimeter of the property. "Residential premises" includes any type of structure in which a residential unit is located, including, but not limited to, multi-unit buildings and mobile and manufactured homes.

(U) "Residential unit" means a dwelling unit for residential use and occupancy, and includes the structure or part of a structure that is used as a home, residence, or sleeping place by one person who maintains a household or two or more persons who maintain a common household. "Residential unit" does not include a halfway house or a community-based correctional facility.

(V) "Multi-unit building" means a building in which is located more than twelve residential units that have entry doors that open directly into the unit from a hallway that is shared with one or more other units. A residential unit is not considered located in a multi-unit building if the unit does not have an entry door that opens directly into the unit from a hallway that is shared with one or more other units or if the unit is in a building that is not a multi-unit building as described in this division.

(W) "Community control sanction" has the same meaning as in section 2929.01 of the Revised Code.

(X) "Halfway house" and "community-based correctional facility" have the same meanings as in section 2929.01 of the Revised Code.

**HISTORY: 146 v H 180 (Eff 1-1-97); 147 v S 111 (Eff 3-17-98); 147 v H 565 (Eff 3-30-99); 148 v H 502 (Eff 3-15-2001); 149 v S 3 (Eff 1-1-2002); 149 v S 175 (Eff 5-7-2002); 149 v H 485 (Eff 6-13-2002); 149 v H 393. Eff 7-5-2002; 149 v H 490, § 1, eff. 1-1-04; 150 v S 5, § 1, eff. 7-31-03; 150 v S 5, § 3, eff. 1-1-04; 150 v S 57, § 1, eff. 1-1-04; 150 v H 473, § 1, eff. 4-29-05; 151 v S 260, § 1, eff. 1-2-07; 152 v S 10, § 1, eff. 1-1-08.**

The effective date is set by § 3 of 152 v S 10.

The effective date is set by section 3 of S.B. 5.

**Analogous to former RC § 2950.01 (130 v 669; 134 v H 511), repealed 146 v H 180, § 2, eff 1-1-97.**

## § 2950.011 Statutory references to sexually oriented or child-victim oriented offense.

Except as specifically provided to the contrary in sections 2950.02 to 2950.99 of the Revised Code, all references in any of those sections to "sexually oriented offense" include, in addition to the violations specified in division (A) of section 2950.01 of the Revised Code on and after January 1, 2008, any sexually oriented offense, as that term was defined in section 2950.01 of the Revised Code prior to January 1, 2008, that was committed prior to that date and that was not a registration exempt sexually oriented offense, as that term was defined in that section prior to January 1, 2008.

Except as specifically provided to the contrary in sections 2950.02 to 2950.99 of the Revised Code, all references in any of those sections to "child-victim oriented offense" include, in addition to the violations specified in division (C) of section 2950.01 of the Revised Code on and after January 1, 2008, any child-victim oriented offense, as that term was defined in section 2950.01 of the Revised Code prior to January 1, 2008, that was committed prior to that date.

**HISTORY: 152 v S 10, § 1, eff. 1-1-08.**

The effective date is set by § 3 of 152 v S 10.

## § 2950.02 Legislative determinations and intent to provide information to protect public safety.

(A) The general assembly hereby determines and declares that it recognizes and finds all of the following:

(1) If the public is provided adequate notice and information about offenders and delinquent children who commit sexually oriented offenses or who commit child-victim oriented offenses, members of the public and communities can develop constructive plans to prepare themselves and their children for the offender's or delinquent child's release from imprisonment, a prison term, or other confinement or detention. This allows members of the public and communities to meet with members of law enforcement agencies to prepare and obtain information about the rights and responsibilities of the public and the communities and to provide education and counseling to their children.

(2) Sex offenders and child-victim offenders pose a risk of engaging in further sexually abusive behavior even after being released from imprisonment, a prison term, or other confinement or detention, and protection of members of the public from sex offenders and child-victim offenders is a paramount governmental interest.

(3) The penal, juvenile, and mental health components of the justice system of this state are largely hidden from public view, and a lack of information from any component may result in the failure of the system to satisfy this paramount governmental interest of public safety described in division (A)(2) of this section.

(4) Overly restrictive confidentiality and liability laws governing the release of information about sex offenders and child-victim offenders have reduced the willingness to release information that could be appropriately released under the public disclosure laws and have increased risks of public safety.

(5) A person who is found to be a sex offender or a child-victim offender has a reduced expectation of privacy because of the public's interest in public safety and in the effective operation of government.

(6) The release of information about sex offenders and child-victim offenders to public agencies and the general public will further the governmental interests of public safety and public scrutiny of the criminal, juvenile, and mental health systems as long as the information released is rationally related to the furtherance of those goals.

(B) The general assembly hereby declares that, in providing in this chapter for registration regarding offenders and certain delinquent children who have committed sexually oriented offenses or who have committed child-victim oriented offenses and for community notification regarding tier III sex offenders/child-victim offenders who are criminal offenders, public registry-qualified juvenile offender registrants, and certain other juvenile offender registrants who are about to be or have been released from imprisonment, a prison term, or other confinement or detention and who will live in or near a particular neighborhood or who otherwise will live in or near a particular neighborhood, it is the general assembly's intent to protect the safety and general welfare of the people of this state. The general assembly further declares that it is the policy of this state to require the exchange in accordance with this chapter of relevant information about sex offenders and child-victim offenders among public agencies and officials and to authorize the release in accordance with this chapter of necessary and relevant information about sex offenders and child-victim offenders to members of the general public as a means of assuring public protection and that the exchange or release of that information is not punitive.

**HISTORY: 146 v H 180 (Eff 7-1-97); 149 v S 3. Eff 1-1-2002; 150 v S 5, § 1, eff. 7-31-03; 152 v S 10, § 1, eff. 1-1-08.**

The effective date is set by § 3 of 152 v S 10.

**Analogous to former RC § 2950.02 (130 v 669), repealed 146 v H 180, § 2, eff 7-1-97.**

## § 2950.021 Repealed, 152 v S 10, § 2 [150 v S 5, § 1, eff. 7-31-03]. Eff 1-1-08.

This section concerned determination removing presumptive exemption from registration.

## § 2950.03 Notice to offender or delinquent child of duty to register and update address.

(A) Each person who has been convicted of, is convicted of, has pleaded guilty to, or pleads guilty to a sexually oriented offense or a child-victim oriented offense and who has a duty to register pursuant to section 2950.04 or 2950.041 [2950.04.1] of the Revised Code and each person who is adjudicated a delinquent child for committing a sexually oriented offense or a child-victim oriented offense and who is classified a juvenile offender registrant based on that adjudication shall be provided notice in accordance with this section of the offender's or delinquent child's duties imposed under sections 2950.04, 2950.041 [2950.04.1], 2950.05, and 2950.06 of the Revised Code and of the offender's duties to similarly register, provide notice of a change, and verify addresses in another state if the offender resides, is temporarily domiciled, attends a school or institution of higher education, or is employed in a state other than this state. The following official shall provide the notice required under this division to the specified person at the following time:

(1) Regardless of when the person committed the sexually oriented offense or child-victim oriented offense, if the person is an offender who is sentenced to a prison term, a term of imprisonment, or any other type of confinement for any offense, and if on or after January 1, 2008, the offender is serving that term or is under that confinement, subject to division (A)(5) of this section, the official in charge of the jail, workhouse, state correctional institution, or other institution in which the offender serves the prison term, term of imprisonment, or confinement, or a designee of that official, shall provide the notice to the offender before the offender is released pursuant to any type of supervised release or before the offender otherwise is released from the prison term, term of imprisonment, or confinement.

(2) Regardless of when the person committed the sexually oriented offense or child-victim oriented offense, if the person is an offender who is sentenced on or after January 1, 2008 for any offense, and if division (A)(1) of this section does not apply, the judge shall provide the notice to the offender at the time of sentencing.

(3) If the person is a delinquent child who is classified a juvenile offender registrant on or after January 1, 2008, the judge shall provide the notice to the delinquent child at the time specified in division (B) of section 2152.82, division (C) of section 2152.83, division (C) of section 2152.84, or division (E) of section 2152.85 of the Revised Code, whichever is applicable.

(4) If the person is a delinquent child who is classified as both a juvenile offender registrant and a public registry-qualified juvenile offender registrant on or after January 1, 2008, the judge shall provide the notice to the delinquent child at the time specified in division (B) of section 2152.86 of the Revised Code.

(5) If the person is an offender or delinquent child in any of the following categories, the attorney general, department of rehabilitation and correction, or department of youth services shall provide the notice to the offender or delinquent child at the time and in the manner specified in section 2950.031 [2950.03.1] or division (A) or (B) of section 2950.032 [2950.03.2] of the Revised Code, whichever is applicable:

(a) An offender or delinquent child who prior to December 1, 2007, has registered a residence, school, institution of higher education, or place of employment address pursuant to section 2950.04, 2950.041 [2950.04.1], or 2950.05 of the Revised Code;

(b) An offender or delinquent child who registers with a sheriff pursuant to section 2950.04 or 2950.041 [2950.04.1] of the Revised Code on or after December 1, 2007, previously had not registered under either section with that sheriff or any other sheriff, and was convicted of, pleaded guilty to, or was classified a juvenile offender registrant relative to the sexually oriented offense or child-victim oriented offense upon which the registration was based prior to December 1, 2007;

(c) An offender who on December 1, 2007, is serving a prison term in a state correctional institution for a sexually oriented offense or child-victim oriented offense or each delinquent child who has been classified a juvenile offender registrant relative to a sexually oriented offense or child-victim oriented offense and who on that date is confined in an institution of the department of youth services for the sexually oriented offense or child-victim oriented offense;

(d) An offender or delinquent child who on or after December 2, 2007, commences a prison term in a state correctional institution or confinement in an institution of the department of youth services for a sexually oriented offense or child-victim oriented offense and who was convicted of, pleaded guilty to, or was classified a juvenile offender registrant relative to the sexually oriented offense or child-victim oriented offense prior to that date.

(6) If the person is an offender or delinquent child who on or after July 1, 2007, and prior to January 1, 2008, is convicted of or pleads guilty to a sexually oriented offense or a child-victim oriented offense and is not sentenced to a prison term for that offense or is classified a juvenile offender registrant relative to a sexually oriented offense or child-victim oriented offense and is not committed to the custody of the department of youth services for that offense, the sentencing court or juvenile court shall provide the notice to the offender or delinquent child at the time and in the manner specified in division (C) of section 2950.032 [2950.03.2] of the Revised Code.

(7) If the person is an offender or delinquent child who has a duty to register in this state pursuant to division (A)(4) of section 2950.04 or 2950.041 [2950.04.1] of the Revised Code, the offender or delinquent child is presumed to have knowledge of the law and of the offender's or delinquent child's duties imposed under sections 2950.04, 2950.041 [2950.04.1], 2950.05, and 2950.06 of the Revised Code.

(B)(1) The notice provided under division (A) of this section shall inform the offender or delinquent child of the offender's or delinquent child's duty to register, to provide notice of a change in the offender's or delinquent child's residence address or in the offender's school, institution of higher education, or place of employment address, as applicable, and register the new address, to periodically verify the offender's or delinquent child's residence address or the offender's school, institution of higher education, or place of employment address, as applicable, and, if applicable, to provide notice of the offender's or delinquent child's intent to reside, pursuant to sections 2950.04, 2950.041 [2950.04.1], 2950.05, and 2950.06 of the Revised Code. The notice shall specify that, for an offender, it applies regarding residence addresses or school, institution of higher education, and place of employment addresses and that, for a delinquent child, it applies regarding residence addresses. Additionally, it shall inform the offender of the offender's duties to similarly register, provide notice of a change in, and verify those addresses in states other than this state as described in division (A) of this section. A notice provided under division (A)(1), (2), (3), or (4) of this section shall comport with the following:

(a) If the notice is provided to an offender under division (A)(1) or (2) of this section, the official, official's designee, or judge shall require the offender to read and sign a form stating that the offender's duties to register, to file a notice of intent to reside, if applicable, to register a new residence address or new school, institution of higher education, or place of employment address, and to periodically verify those addresses, and the offender's duties in other states as described in division (A) of this section have been explained to the offender. If the offender is unable to read, the official, official's designee, or judge shall certify on the form that the official, designee, or judge specifically informed the offender of those duties and that the offender indicated an understanding of those duties.

(b) If the notice is provided to a delinquent child under division (A)(3) or (4) of this section, the judge shall require the delinquent child and the delinquent child's parent, guardian, or custodian to read and sign a form stating that the delinquent child's duties to register, to file a notice of intent to reside, if applicable, to register a new residence address, and to periodically verify that address have been explained to the delinquent child and to the delinquent child's parent, guardian, or custodian. If the delinquent child or the delinquent child's parent, guardian, or custodian is unable to read, the judge shall certify on the form that the judge specifically informed the delinquent child or the delinquent child's parent, guardian, or custodian of those duties and that the delinquent child or the delinquent child's parent, guardian, or custodian indicated an understanding of those duties.

(2) The notice provided under divisions (A)(1) to (4) of this section shall be on a form prescribed by the bureau of criminal identification and investigation and shall contain all of the information specified in division (A) of this section and all of the information required by the bureau. The notice provided under divisions (A)(1) to (4) of this section shall include, but is not limited to, all of the following:

(a) For any notice provided under divisions (A)(1) to (4) of this section, an explanation of the offender's periodic residence address or periodic school, institution of higher education, or place of employment address verification process or of the delinquent child's periodic residence address verification process, an explanation of the frequency with which the offender or delinquent child will be required to verify those addresses under that process, a statement that the offender or delinquent child must verify those addresses at the times specified under that process or face criminal prosecution or a delinquent child proceeding, and an explanation of the offender's duty to similarly register, verify, and reregister those addresses in another state if the offender resides in another state, attends a school or institution of higher education in another state, or is employed in another state.

(b) If the notice is provided under division (A)(3) or (4) of this section, a statement that the delinquent child has been classified by the adjudicating juvenile court judge or the judge's successor in office a juvenile offender registrant and, if applicable, a public-registry qualified juvenile offender registrant and has a duty to comply with sections 2950.04, 2950.041 [2950.04.1], 2950.05, and 2950.06 of the Revised Code;

(c) If the notice is provided under division (A)(3) or (4) of this section, a statement that, if the delinquent child fails to comply with the requirements of sections 2950.04, 2950.041 [2950.04.1], 2950.05, and 2950.06 of the Revised Code, both of the following apply:

(i) If the delinquent child's failure occurs while the child is under eighteen years of age, the child is subject to proceedings under Chapter 2152. of the Revised Code based on the failure, but if the failure occurs while the child is eighteen years of age or older, the child is subject to criminal prosecution based on the failure.

(ii) If the delinquent child's failure occurs while the child is under eighteen years of age, unless the child is emancipated, as defined in section 2919.121 [2919.12.1] of the Revised Code, the failure of the parent, guardian, or custodian to ensure that the child complies with those requirements is a violation of section 2919.24 of the Revised Code and may result in the prosecution of the parent, guardian, or custodian for that violation.

(3)(a) After an offender described in division (A)(1) or (2) of this section has signed the form described in divisions (B)(1) and (2) of this section or the official, official's designee, or judge has certified on the form that the form has been explained to the offender and that the offender indicated an understanding of the duties indicated on it, the official, official's designee, or judge shall give one copy of the form to the offender, within three days shall send one copy of the form to the bureau of criminal identification and investigation in accordance with the procedures adopted pursuant to section 2950.13 of the Revised Code, shall send one copy of the form to the sheriff of the county in which the offender expects to reside, and shall send one copy of the form to the sheriff of the county in which the offender was convicted or pleaded guilty if the offender has a duty to register pursuant to division (A)(1) of section 2950.04 or 2950.041 [2950.04.1] of the Revised Code.

(b) After a delinquent child described in division (A)(3) or (4) of this section and the delinquent child's parent, guardian, or custodian have signed the form described in divisions (B)(1) and (2) of this section or the judge has certified on the form that the form has been explained to the delinquent child or the delinquent child's parent, guardian, or custodian and that the delinquent child or the delinquent child's parent, guardian, or custodian indicated an understanding of the duties and information indicated on the form, the judge shall give a copy of the form to both the delinquent child and to the delinquent child's parent, guardian, or custodian, within three days shall send one copy of the form to the bureau of criminal identification and investigation in accordance with the procedures adopted pursuant to section 2950.13 of the Revised Code, shall send one copy of the form to the sheriff of the county in which the delinquent child expects to reside, and shall send one copy of the form to the sheriff of the county in which the child was adjudicated a delinquent child if the delinquent child has a duty to register pursuant to division (A)(1) of section 2950.04 or 2950.041 [2950.04.1] of the Revised Code.

(C) The official, official's designee, judge, chief of police, or sheriff who is required to provide notice to an offender or delinquent child under divisions (A)(1) to (4) of this section shall determine the offender's or delinquent child's name, identifying factors, and expected future residence address in this state or any other state, shall obtain the offender's or delinquent child's criminal and delinquency history, and shall obtain a photograph and the fingerprints of the offender or delinquent child. Regarding an offender, the official, designee, or judge also shall obtain from the offender the offender's current or expected future school, institution of higher education, or place of employment address in this state, if any. If the notice is provided by a judge under division (A)(2), (3), or (4) of this section, the sheriff shall provide the offender's or delinquent child's criminal and delinquency history to the judge. The official, official's designee, or judge shall obtain this information and these items prior to giving the notice, except that a judge may give the notice prior to obtaining the offender's or delinquent child's criminal and delinquency history. Within three days after receiving this information and these items, the official, official's designee, or judge shall forward the information and items to the bureau of criminal identification and investigation in accordance with the forwarding procedures adopted pursuant to section 2950.13 of the Revised Code, to the sheriff of the county in which the offender or delinquent child expects to reside and to the sheriff of the county in which the offender or delinquent child was convicted, pleaded guilty, or adjudicated a delinquent child if the offender or delinquent child has a duty to register pursuant to division (A)(1) of section 2950.04 or 2950.041 [2950.04.1] of the Revised Code, and, regarding an offender, to the sheriff of the county, if any, in which the offender attends or will attend a school or institution of higher education or is or will be employed. If the notice is provided under division (A)(3) or (4) of this section and if the delinquent child has been committed to the department of youth services or to a secure facility, the judge, in addition to the other information and items described in this division, also shall forward to the bureau and to the sheriff notification that the child has been so committed. If it has not already done so, the bureau of criminal identification and investigation shall forward a copy of the fingerprints and conviction data received under this division to the federal bureau of investigation.

**HISTORY: 146 v H 180 (Eff 1-1-97); 147 v H 93 (Eff 12-31-97); 148 v H 502 (Eff 3-15-2001); 149 v S 3 (Eff 1-1-2002); 149 v H 485. Eff 6-13-2002; 150 v S 5, § 1, eff. 7-31-03; 150 v H 473, § 1, eff. 4-29-05; 152 v S 10, § 1, eff. 1-1-08.**

The effective date is set by § 3 of 152 v S 10.

**Not analogous to former RC § 2950.03 (130 v 670; 145 v H 571), repealed 146 v H 180, § 2, eff 1-1-97.**

## § 2950.031 Attorney general to determine application of new SORN Law to each offender or delinquent child; registered letter to be sent; right to court hearing to contest application.

(A)(1) At any time on or after July 1, 2007, and not later than December 1, 2007, the attorney general shall determine for each offender or delinquent child who prior to December 1, 2007, has registered a residence, school, institution of higher education, or place of employment address pursuant to section 2950.04, 2950.041 [2950.04.1], or 2950.05 of the Revised Code the offender's or delinquent child's new classification as a tier I sex offender/child-victim offender, a tier II sex offender/child-victim offender, or a tier III sex offender/child-victim offender under Chapter 2950. of the Revised Code as it will exist under the changes that will be implemented on January 1, 2008, the offender's or delinquent child's duties under Chapter 2950. of the Revised Code as so changed, and, regarding a delinquent child, whether the child is a public registry-qualified juvenile offender registrant.

(2) At any time on or after July 1, 2007, and not later than December 1, 2007, the attorney general shall send to each offender or delinquent child who prior to December 1, 2007, has registered a residence, school, institution of higher education, or place of employment address pursuant to section 2950.04, 2950.041 [2950.04.1], or 2950.05 of the Revised Code a registered letter that contains the information described in this division. The registered letter shall be sent return receipt requested to the last reported address of the person and, if the person is a delinquent child, the last reported address of the parents of the delinquent child. The letter sent to an offender or to a delinquent child and the delinquent child's parents pursuant to this division shall notify the offender or the delinquent child and the delinquent child's parents of all of the following:

(a) The changes in Chapter 2950. of the Revised Code that will be implemented on January 1, 2008;

(b) Subject to division (A)(2)(c) of this section, the offender's or delinquent child's new classification as a tier I sex offender/child-victim offender, a tier II sex offender/child-victim offender, or a tier III sex offender/child-victim offender under Chapter 2950. of the Revised Code as it will exist under the changes that will be implemented on January 1, 2008, the offender's or delinquent child's duties under Chapter 2950. of the Revised Code as so changed and the duration of those duties, whether the delinquent child is classified a public registry-qualified juvenile offender registrant, and the information specified in division (B) of section 2950.03 of the Revised Code to the extent it is relevant to the offender or delinquent child;

(c) The fact that the offender or delinquent child has a right to a hearing as described in division (E) of this section, the procedures for requesting the hearing, and the period of time within which the request for the hearing must be made.

(d) If the offender's or delinquent child's duty to comply with sections 2950.04, 2950.041 [2950.04.1], 2950.05, and 2950.06 of the Revised Code is scheduled to terminate on or after July 1, 2007, and prior to January 1, 2008, under the version of section 2950.07 of the Revised Code that is in effect prior to January 1, 2008, a summary of the provisions of section 2950.033 [2950.03.3] of the Revised Code and the application of those provisions to the offender or delinquent child, provided that this division applies to a delinquent child only if the child is in a category specified in division (C) of section 2950.033 [2950.03.3] of the Revised Code.

(3) The attorney general shall make the determinations described in division (A)(1) of this section for each offender or delinquent child who has registered an address as described in that division, even if the offender's duty to comply with sections 2950.04, 2950.041 [2950.04.1], 2950.05, and 2950.06 of the Revised Code is scheduled to terminate prior to January 1, 2008, under the version of section 2950.07 of the Revised Code that is in effect prior to that date or the delinquent child is in a category specified in division (C) of section 2950.033 [2950.03.3] of the Revised Code and the child's duty to comply with those sections is scheduled to terminate prior to January 1, 2008, under the version of section 2950.07 of the Revised Code that is in effect prior to that date. The attorney general shall send the registered letter described in division (A)(2) of this section to each offender or delinquent child who has registered an address as described in that division even if the offender's duty to comply with sections 2950.04, 2950.041 [2950.04.1], 2950.05, and 2950.06 of the Revised Code is scheduled to terminate prior to January 1, 2008, under the version of section 2950.07 of the Revised Code that is in effect prior to that date, or the delinquent child is in a category specified in division (C) of section 2950.033 [2950.03.3] of the Revised Code, and the child's duty to comply with those sections is scheduled to terminate prior to January 1, 2008, under the version of section 2950.07 of the Revised Code that is in effect prior to that date. Section 2950.033 [2950.03.3] of the Revised Code applies to any offender who has registered an address as described in division (A)(1) or (2) of this section and whose duty to comply with sections 2950.04, 2950.041 [2950.04.1], 2950.05, and 2950.06 of the Revised Code is scheduled to terminate prior to January 1, 2008, under the version of section 2950.07 of the Revised Code that is in effect prior to that date, or the delinquent child is in a category specified in division (C) of section 2950.033 [2950.03.3] of the Revised Code, and the child's duty to comply with those sections is scheduled to terminate prior to January 1, 2008, under the version of section 2950.07 of the Revised Code that is in effect prior to that date.

(B) If a sheriff informs the attorney general pursuant to section 2950.043 [2950.04.3] of the Revised Code that an offender or delinquent child registered with the sheriff pursuant to section 2950.04 or 2950.041 [2950.04.1] of the Revised Code on or after December 1, 2007, that the offender or delinquent child previously had not registered under either section with that sheriff or any other sheriff, and that the offender or delinquent child was convicted of, pleaded guilty to, or was classified a juvenile offender registrant relative to the sexually oriented offense or child-victim oriented offense upon which the registration was based prior to December 1, 2007, within fourteen days after being so informed of the registration and receiving the information and material specified in division (D) of that section, the attorney general shall determine for the offender or delinquent child all of the matters specified in division (A)(1) of this section. Upon making the determinations, the attorney general immediately shall send to the offender or to the delinquent child and the delinquent child's parents a registered letter pursuant to division (A)(2) of this section that contains the information specified in that division.

(C) The attorney general shall maintain the return receipts for all offenders, delinquent children, and parents of delinquent children who are sent a registered letter under division (A) or (B) of this section. For each offender, delinquent child, and parents of a delinquent child, the attorney general shall send a copy of the return receipt for the offender, delinquent child, or parents to the sheriff with whom the offender or delinquent child most recently registered a residence address and, if applicable, a school, institution of higher education, or place of employment address and to the prosecutor who handled the case in which the offender or delinquent child was convicted of, pleaded guilty to, or was adjudicated a delinquent child for committing the sexually oriented offense or child-victim oriented offense that resulted in the offender's or child's registration duty under section 2950.04 or 2950.041 [2950.04.1] of the Revised Code. If a return receipt indicates that the offender, delinquent child, or parents of a delinquent child to whom the registered letter was sent does not reside or have temporary domicile at the listed address, the attorney general immediately shall provide notice of that fact to the sheriff with whom the offender or delinquent child registered that residence address.

(D) The attorney general shall mail to each sheriff a list of all offenders and delinquent children who have registered a residence address or a school, institution of higher education, or place of employment address with that sheriff and to whom a registered letter is sent under division (A) or (B) of this section. The list shall specify the offender's or delinquent child's new classification as a tier I sex offender/child-victim offender, a tier II sex offender/child-victim offender, or a tier III sex offender/child-victim offender under Chapter 2950. of the Revised Code as it will exist under the changes that will be implemented on January 1, 2008, the offender's or delinquent child's duties under Chapter 2950. of the Revised Code as so changed, and, regarding a delinquent child, whether the child is a public registry-qualified juvenile offender registrant.

(E) An offender or delinquent child who is in a category described in division (A)(2) or (B) of this section may request as a matter of right a court hearing to contest the application to the offender or delinquent child of the new registration requirements under Chapter 2950. of the Revised Code as it will exist under the changes that will be implemented on January 1, 2008. The offender or delinquent child may contest the manner in which the letter sent to the offender or delinquent child pursuant to division (A) or (B) of this section specifies that the new registration requirements apply to the offender or delinquent child or may contest whether those new registration requirements apply at all to the offender or delinquent child. To request the hearing, the offender or delinquent child not later than the date that is sixty days after the offender or delinquent child received the registered letter sent by the attorney general pursuant to division (A)(2) of this section shall file a petition with the court specified in this division. If the offender or delinquent child resides in or is temporarily domiciled in this state and requests a hearing, the offender or delinquent child shall file the petition with, and the hearing shall be held in, the court of common pleas or, for a delinquent child, the juvenile court of the county in which the offender or delinquent child resides or temporarily is domiciled. If the offender does not reside in and is not temporarily domiciled in this state, the offender or delinquent child shall file the petition with, and the hearing shall be held in, the court of common pleas of the county in which the offender registered a school, institution of higher education, or place of employment address, but if the offender has registered addresses of that nature in more than one county, the offender may file such a petition in the court of only one of those counties.

If the offender or delinquent child requests a hearing by timely filing a petition with the appropriate court, the offender or delinquent child shall serve a copy of the petition on the prosecutor of the county in which the petition is filed. The prosecutor shall represent the interests of the state in the hearing. In any hearing under this division, the Rules of Civil Procedure or, if the hearing is in a juvenile court, the Rules of Juvenile Procedure apply, except to the extent that those Rules would by their nature be clearly inapplicable. The court shall schedule a hearing, and shall provide notice to the offender or delinquent child and prosecutor of the date, time, and place of the hearing.

If an offender or delinquent child requests a hearing in accordance with this division, until the court issues its decision at or subsequent to the hearing, the offender or delinquent child shall comply prior to January 1, 2008, with Chapter 2950. of the Revised Code as it exists prior to that date and shall comply on and after January 1, 2008, with Chapter 2950. of the Revised Code as it will exist under the changes that will be implemented on that date. If an offender or delinquent child requests a hearing in accordance with this division, at the hearing, all parties are entitled to be heard, and the court shall consider all relevant information and testimony presented relative to the application to the offender or delinquent child of the new registration requirements under Chapter 2950. of the Revised Code as it will exist under the changes that will be implemented on January 1, 2008. If, at the conclusion of the hearing, the court finds that the offender or delinquent child has proven by clear and convincing evidence that the new registration requirements do not apply to the offender or delinquent child in the manner specified in the letter sent to the offender or delinquent child pursuant to division (A) or (B) of this section, the court shall issue an order that specifies the manner in which the court has determined that the new registration requirements do apply to the offender or delinquent child. If at the conclusion of the hearing the court finds that the offender or delinquent child has proven by clear and convincing evidence that the new registration requirements do not apply to the offender or delinquent child, the court shall issue an order that specifies that the new registration requirements do not apply to the offender or delinquent child. The court promptly shall serve a copy of an order issued under this division upon the sheriff with whom the offender or delinquent child most recently registered under section 2950.04, 2950.041 [2950.04.1], or 2950.05 of the Revised Code and upon the bureau of criminal identification and investigation. The offender or delinquent child and the prosecutor have the right to appeal the decision of the court issued under this division.

If an offender or delinquent child fails to request a hearing in accordance with this division within the applicable sixty-day period specified in this division, the failure constitutes a waiver by the offender or delinquent child of the offender's or delinquent child's right to a hearing under this division, and the offender or delinquent child is bound by the determinations of the attorney general contained in the registered letter sent to the offender or child.

If a juvenile court issues an order under division (A)(2) or (3) of section 2152.86 of the Revised Code that classifies a delinquent child a public-registry qualified juvenile offender registrant and if the child's delinquent act was committed prior to January 1, 2008, a challenge to the classification contained in the order shall be made pursuant to division (D) of section 2152.86 of the Revised Code.

**HISTORY: 152 v S 10, § 1, eff. 7-1-07.**

The effective date is set by § 3 of 152 v S 10.

**Not analogous to former RC § 2950.031, amended and renumbered to RC § 2950.034 by 152 v S 10, eff 7-1-07.**

## § 2950.032 Attorney general to determine tier classification for each offender or delinquent child; notice of provisions implemented on January 1, 2008.

(A)(1) At any time on or after July 1, 2007, and not later than December 1, 2007, the attorney general shall do all of the following:

(a) For each offender who on December 1, 2007, will be serving a prison term in a state correctional institution for a sexually oriented offense or child-victim oriented offense, determine the offender's classification relative to that offense as a tier I sex offender/child-victim offender, a tier II sex offender/child-victim offender, or a tier III sex offender/child-victim offender under Chapter 2950. of the Revised Code as it will exist under the changes in that chapter that will be implemented on January 1, 2008, and the offender's duties under Chapter 2950. of the Revised Code as so changed and provide to the department of rehabilitation and correction a document that describes that classification and those duties;

(b) For each delinquent child who has been classified a juvenile offender registrant relative to a sexually oriented offense or child-victim oriented offense and who on December 1, 2007, will be confined in an institution of the department of youth services for the sexually oriented offense or child-victim oriented offense, determine the delinquent child's classification relative to that offense as a tier I sex offender/child-victim offender, a tier II sex offender/child-victim offender, or a tier III sex offender/child-victim offender under Chapter 2950. of the Revised Code as it will exist under the changes in that chapter that will be implemented on January 1, 2008, the delinquent child's duties under Chapter 2950. of the Revised Code as so changed, and whether the delinquent child is a public registry-qualified juvenile offender registrant and provide to the department a document that describes that classification, those duties, and whether the delinquent child is a public registry-qualified juvenile offender registrant.

(c) For each offender and delinquent child described in division (A)(1)(a) or (b) of this section, determine whether the attorney general is required to send a registered letter to that offender or that delinquent child and delinquent child's parents pursuant to section 2950.031 [2950.03.1] of the Revised Code relative to the sexually oriented offense or child-victim oriented offense for which the offender or delinquent child is serving the prison term or is confined and, if the attorney general is required to send such a letter to that offender or that delinquent child and delinquent child's parents relative to that offense, include in the document provided to the department of rehabilitation and correction or the department of youth services under division (A)(1)(a) or (b) of this section a conspicuous notice that the attorney general will be sending the offender or delinquent child and delinquent child's parent the registered letter and that the department is not required to provide to the offender or delinquent child the written notice described in division (A)(2) of this section.

(2) At any time on or after July 1, 2007, and not later than December 1, 2007, except as otherwise described in this division, the department of rehabilitation and correction shall provide to each offender described in division (A)(1)(a) of this section and the department of youth services shall provide to each delinquent child described in division (A)(1)(b) of this section and to the delinquent child's parents a written notice that contains the information described in this division. The department of rehabilitation and correction and the department of youth services are not required to provide the written notice to an offender or a delinquent child and the delinquent child's parents if the attorney general included in the document provided to the particular department under division (A)(1)(a) or (b) of this section notice that the attorney general will be sending that offender or that delinquent child and the delinquent child's parents a registered letter and that the department is not required to provide to that offender or that delinquent child and parents the written notice. The written notice provided to an offender or a delinquent child and the delinquent child's parents pursuant to this division shall notify the offender or delinquent child of all of the following:

(a) The changes in Chapter 2950. of the Revised Code that will be implemented on January 1, 2008;

(b) Subject to division (A)(2)(c) of this section, the offender's or delinquent child's classification as a tier I sex offender/child-victim offender, a tier II sex offender/child-victim offender, or a tier III sex offender/child-victim offender under Chapter 2950. of the Revised Code as it will exist under the changes that will be implemented on January 1, 2008, the offender's or delinquent child's duties under Chapter 2950. of the Revised Code as so changed and the duration of those duties, whether the delinquent child is classified a public registry-qualified juvenile offender registrant, and the information specified in division (B) of section 2950.03 of the Revised Code to the extent it is relevant to the offender or delinquent child;

(c) The fact that the offender or delinquent child has a right to a hearing as described in division (E) of this section, the procedures for requesting the hearing, and the period of time within which the request for the hearing must be made;

(d) If the offender's or delinquent child's duty to comply with sections 2950.04, 2950.041 [2950.04.1], 2950.05, and 2950.06 of the Revised Code is scheduled to terminate on or after July 1, 2007, and prior to January 1, 2008, under the version of section 2950.07 of the Revised Code that is in effect prior to January 1, 2008, a summary of the provisions of section 2950.033 [2950.03.3] of the Revised Code and the application of those provisions to the offender or delinquent child, provided that this division applies regarding a delinquent child only if the child is in a category specified in division (A) of section 2950.033 [2950.03.3] of the Revised Code.

(3) The attorney general shall make the determinations described in divisions (A)(1)(a) and (b) of this section for each offender or delinquent child who is described in either of those divisions even if the offender's duty to comply with sections 2950.04, 2950.041 [2950.04.1], 2950.05, and 2950.06 of the Revised Code is scheduled to terminate prior to January 1, 2008, under the version of section 2950.07 of the Revised Code that is in effect prior to that date, or the delinquent child is in a category specified in division (C) of section 2950.033 [2950.03.3] of the Revised Code, and the child's duty to comply with those sections is scheduled to terminate prior to January 1, 2008, under the version of section 2950.07 of the Revised Code that is in effect prior to that date. The department of rehabilitation and correction shall provide to each offender described in division (A)(1)(a) of this section and the department of youth services shall provide to each delinquent child described in division (A)(1)(b) of this section the notice described in division (A)(2) of this section, even if the offender's duty to comply with sections 2950.04, 2950.041 [2950.04.1], 2950.05, and 2950.06 of the Revised Code is scheduled to terminate prior to January 1, 2008, under the version of section 2950.07 of the Revised Code that is in effect prior to that date, or the delinquent child is in a category specified in division (C) of section 2950.033 [2950.03.3] of the Revised Code, and the child's duty to comply with those sections is scheduled to terminate prior to January 1, 2008, under the version of section 2950.07 of the Revised Code that is in effect prior to that date. Section 2950.033 [2950.03.3] of the Revised Code applies regarding any offender described in division (A)(1)(a) or (b) of this section whose duty to comply with sections 2950.04, 2950.041 [2950.04.1], 2950.05, and 2950.06 of the Revised Code is scheduled to terminate prior to January 1, 2008, under the version of section 2950.07 of the Revised Code that is in effect prior to that date and any delinquent child who is in a category specified in division (A) of section 2950.033 [2950.03.3] of the Revised Code and whose duty to comply with those sections is scheduled to terminate prior to January 1, 2008, under the version of section 2950.07 of the Revised Code that is in effect prior to that date.

(B) If on or after December 2, 2007, an offender commences a prison term in a state correctional institution or a delinquent child commences confinement in an institution of the department of youth services for a sexually oriented offense or a child-victim oriented offense and if the offender or delinquent child was convicted of, pleaded guilty to, or was classified a juvenile offender registrant relative to the sexually oriented offense or child-victim oriented offense on or before that date, as soon as practicable, the department of rehabilitation and correction or the department of youth services, as applicable, shall contact the attorney general, inform the attorney general of the commencement of the prison term or institutionalization, and forward to the attorney general information and material that identifies the offender or delinquent child and that describes the sexually oriented offense resulting in the prison term or institutionalization, the facts and circumstances of it, and the offender's or delinquent child's criminal or delinquency history. Within fourteen days after being so informed of the commencement of the prison term or institutionalization and receiving the information and material specified in this division, the attorney general shall determine for the offender or delinquent child all of the matters specified in division (A)(1)(a), (b), or (c) of this section and immediately provide to the appropriate department a document that describes the offender's or delinquent child's classification and duties as so determined.

Upon receipt from the attorney general of a document described in this division that pertains to an offender or delinquent child, the department of rehabilitation and correction shall provide to the offender or the department of youth services shall provide to the delinquent child, as applicable, a written notice that contains the information specified in division (A)(2) of this section.

(C) If, on or after July 1, 2007, and prior to January 1, 2008, an offender is convicted of or pleads guilty to a sexually oriented offense or a child-victim oriented offense and the court does not sentence the offender to a prison term for that offense or if, on or after July 1, 2007, and prior to January 1, 2008, a delinquent child is classified a juvenile offender registrant relative to a sexually oriented offense or a child-victim oriented offense and the juvenile court does not commit the child to the custody of the department of youth services for that offense, the court at the time of sentencing or the juvenile court at the time specified in division (B) of section 2152.82, division (C) of section 2152.83, division (C) of section 2152.84, division (E) of section 2152.85, or division (A) of section 2152.86 of the Revised Code, whichever is applicable, shall do all of the following:

(1) Provide the offender or the delinquent child and the delinquent child's parents with the notices required under section 2950.03 of the Revised Code, as it exists prior to January 1, 2008, regarding the offender's or delinquent child's duties under this chapter as it exists prior to that date;

(2) Provide the offender or the delinquent child and the delinquent child's parents with a written notice that contains the information specified in divisions (A)(2)(a) and (b) of this section;

(3) Provide the offender or the delinquent child and the delinquent child's parents a written notice that clearly indicates that the offender or delinquent child is required to comply with the duties described in the notice provided under division (C)(1) of this section until January 1, 2008, and will be required to comply with the duties described in the notice provided under division (C)(2) of this section on and after that date.

(D)(1) Except as otherwise provided in this division, the officer or employee of the department of rehabilitation and correction or the department of youth services who provides an offender or a delinquent child and the delinquent child's parents with the notices described in division (A)(2) or (B) of this section shall require the offender or delinquent child to read and sign a form stating that the changes in Chapter 2950. of the Revised Code that will be implemented on January 1, 2008, the offender's or delinquent child's classification as a tier I sex offender, a tier II sex offender, or a tier III sex offender, the offender's or delinquent child's duties under Chapter 2950. of the Revised Code as so changed and the duration of those duties, the delinquent child's classification as a public registry-qualified juvenile offender registrant if applicable, the information specified in division (B) of section 2950.03 of the Revised Code to the extent it is relevant to the offender or delinquent child, and the right to a hearing, procedures for requesting the hearing, and period of time within which the request for the hearing must be made have been explained to the offender or delinquent child.

Except as otherwise provided in this division, the judge who provides an offender or delinquent child with the notices described in division (C) of this section shall require the offender or delinquent child to read and sign a form stating that all of the information described in divisions (C)(1) to (3) of this section has been explained to the offender or delinquent child.

If the offender or delinquent child is unable to read, the official, employee, or judge shall certify on the form that the official, employee, or judge specifically informed the offender or delinquent child of all of that information and that the offender or delinquent child indicated an understanding of it.

(2) After an offender or delinquent child has signed the form described in division (D)(1) of this section or the official, employee, or judge has certified on the form that the form has been explained to the offender or delinquent child and that the offender or delinquent child indicated an understanding of the specified information, the official, employee, or judge shall give one copy of the form to the offender or delinquent child, within three days shall send one copy of the form to the bureau of criminal identification and investigation in accordance with the procedures adopted pursuant to section 2950.13 of the Revised Code, and shall send one copy of the form to the sheriff of the county in which the offender or delinquent child expects to reside and one copy to the prosecutor who handled the case in which the offender or delinquent child was convicted of, pleaded guilty to, or was adjudicated a delinquent child for committing the sexually oriented offense or child-victim oriented offense that resulted in the offender's or child's registration duty under section 2950.04 or 2950.041 [2950.04.1] of the Revised Code.

(E) An offender or delinquent child who is provided a notice under division (A)(2) or (B) of this section may request as a matter of right a court hearing to contest the application to the offender or delinquent child of the new registration requirements under Chapter 2950. of the Revised Code as it will exist under the changes that will be implemented on January 1, 2008. The offender or delinquent child may contest the matters that are identified in division (E) of section 2950.031 [2950.03.1] of the Revised Code. To request the hearing, an offender or delinquent child who is provided a notice under division (A)(2) of this section shall file a petition with the appropriate court not later than the date that is sixty days after the offender or delinquent child is provided the notice under that division, and an offender or delinquent child who is provided a notice under division (B) of this section shall file a petition with the appropriate court not later than the date that is sixty days after the offender or delinquent child is provided the notice under that division. The request for the hearing shall be made in the manner and with the court specified in division (E) of section 2950.031 [2950.03.1] of the Revised Code, and, except as otherwise provided in this division, the provisions of that division regarding the service of process and notice regarding the hearing, the conduct of the hearing, the determinations to be made at the hearing, and appeals of those determinations also apply to a hearing requested under this division. If a hearing is requested as described in this division, the offender or delinquent child shall appear at the hearing by video conferencing equipment if available and compatible, except that, upon the court's own motion or the motion of the offender or delinquent child or the prosecutor representing the interests of the state and a determination by the court that the interests of justice require that the offender or delinquent child be present, the court may permit the offender or delinquent child to be physically present at the hearing. An appearance by video conferencing equipment pursuant to this division has the same force and effect as if the offender or delinquent child were physically present at the hearing. The provisions of division (E) of section 2950.031 [2950.03.1] of the Revised Code regarding the effect of a failure to timely request a hearing also apply to a failure to timely request a hearing under this division.

If a juvenile court issues an order under division (A)(2) or (3) of section 2152.86 of the Revised Code that classifies a delinquent child a public-registry qualified juvenile offender registrant and if the child's delinquent act was committed prior to January 1, 2008, a challenge to the classification contained in the order shall be made pursuant to division (D) of section 2152.86 of the Revised Code.

**HISTORY: 152 v S 10, § 1, eff. 7-1-07.**

The effective date is set by § 3 of 152 v S 10.

## § 2950.033 Offenders and delinquent children whose SORN Law duties are scheduled to terminate on or after 7-1-07 and prior to 1-1-08.

(A) If, on or before July 1, 2007, an offender who has been convicted of or pleaded guilty to a sexually oriented offense or a child-victim oriented offense or a delinquent child in a category specified in division (C) of this section has a duty to comply with sections 2950.04, 2950.041 [2950.04.1], 2950.05, and 2950.06 of the Revised Code based on that offense and if the offender's or delinquent child's duty to comply with those sections based on that offense is scheduled to terminate on or after July 1, 2007, and prior to January 1, 2008, under the version of section 2950.07 of the Revised Code that is in effect prior to January 1, 2008, notwithstanding that scheduled termination of those duties, the offender's or delinquent child's duties under those sections shall not terminate as scheduled and shall remain in effect for the following period of time:

(1) If the offender or delinquent child is in a category described in division (A)(1) of section 2950.031 [2950.03.1] of the Revised Code, receives a registered letter from the attorney general pursuant to division (A)(2) of that section, and timely requests a hearing in accordance with division (E) of that section to contest the application to the offender or delinquent child of the new registration requirements under Chapter 2950. of the Revised Code as it will exist under the changes that will be implemented on January 1, 2008, or the tier classification of the offender or delinquent child specified by the attorney general, the offender's or delinquent child's duty to comply with sections 2950.04, 2950.041 [2950.04.1], 2950.05, and 2950.06 of the Revised Code shall continue at least until the court issues its decision at or subsequent to the hearing. The offender's or delinquent child's duty to comply with those sections shall continue in accordance with, and for the duration specified in, the determinations of the attorney general that are specified in the registered letter the offender or delinquent child received from the attorney general, unless the court's decision terminates the offender's or delinquent child's duty to comply with those sections or provides a different duration for which the offender or delinquent child has a duty to comply with them.

(2) If the offender or delinquent child is in a category described in division (A)(1) of section 2950.031 [2950.03.1] of the Revised Code, receives a registered letter from the attorney general pursuant to division (A)(2) of that section, and does not timely request a hearing in accordance with division (E) of that section to contest the application to the offender or delinquent child of the new registration requirements under Chapter 2950. of the Revised Code as it will exist under the changes that will be implemented on January 1, 2008, or the tier classification of the offender or delinquent child specified by the attorney general, the offender's or delinquent child's duty to comply with sections 2950.04, 2950.041 [2950.04.1], 2950.05, and 2950.06 of the Revised Code shall continue in accordance with, and for the duration specified in, the determinations of the attorney general that are specified in the registered letter the offender or delinquent child received from the attorney general.

(3) If the offender or delinquent child is in a category described in division (A)(1)(a) or (b) of section 2950.032 [2950.03.2] of the Revised Code, receives a notice from the department of rehabilitation and correction or department of youth services pursuant to division (A)(2) of that section, and timely requests a hearing in accordance with division (E) of that section to contest the application to the offender or delinquent child of the new registration requirements under Chapter 2950. of the Revised Code as it will exist under the changes that will be implemented on January 1, 2008, or the tier classification of the delinquent child specified by the attorney general the offender's or delinquent child's duty to comply with sections 2950.04, 2950.041 [2950.04.1], 2950.05, and 2950.06 of the Revised Code shall continue in the same manner and for the same duration as is described in division (A)(1) of this section regarding offenders and delinquent children in a category described in division (A)(1) of section 2950.031 [2950.03.1] of the Revised Code, who receive a registered letter from the attorney general pursuant to division (A)(2) of that section, and who timely request a hearing in accordance with division (E) of that section.

(4) If the offender or delinquent child is in a category described in division (A)(1)(a) or (b) of section 2950.032 [2950.03.2] of the Revised Code, receives a notice from the department of rehabilitation and correction or department of youth services pursuant to division (A)(2) of that section, and does not timely request a hearing in accordance with division (E) of that section to contest the application to the offender or delinquent child of the new registration requirements under Chapter 2950. of the Revised Code as it will exist under the changes that will be implemented on January 1, 2008, or the tier classification of the delinquent child specified by the attorney general the offender's or delinquent child's duty to comply with sections 2950.04, 2950.041 [2950.04.1], 2950.05, and 2950.06 of the Revised Code shall continue in the same manner and for the same duration as is described in division (A)(2) of this section regarding offenders and delinquent children in a category described in division (A)(1) of section 2950.031 [2950.03.1] of the Revised Code, who receive a registered letter from the attorney general pursuant to division (A)(2) of that section, and who do not timely request a hearing in accordance with division (E) of that section.

(5) If the offender or delinquent child is in a category described in division (A)(1) of section 2950.031 [2950.03.1] of the Revised Code but does not receive a registered letter from the attorney general pursuant to division (A)(2) of that section, or if the offender or delinquent child is in a category described in division

(A)(1)(a) or (b) of section 2950.032 [2950.03.2] of the Revised Code but does not receive a notice from the department of rehabilitation and correction or department of youth services pursuant to division (A)(2) of that section, notwithstanding the failure of the offender or delinquent child to receive the registered letter or the notice, the offender's or delinquent child's duty to comply with sections 2950.04, 2950.041 [2950.04.1], 2950.05, and 2950.06 of the Revised Code shall continue in accordance with, and for the duration specified in, the provisions of Chapter 2950. of the Revised Code as they will exist under the changes to the provisions that will be implemented on January 1, 2008.

(B) An offender or a delinquent child in a category specified in division (C) of this section who, on or before July 1, 2007, has a duty to comply with sections 2950.04, 2950.041 [2950.04.1], 2950.05, and 2950.06 of the Revised Code based on a conviction of, plea of guilty to, or adjudication as a delinquent child for committing a sexually oriented offense or a child-victim oriented offense and whose duty to comply with those sections is scheduled to terminate on or after July 1, 2007, and prior to January 1, 2008, under the version of section 2950.07 of the Revised Code that is in effect prior to January 1, 2008, is presumed to have knowledge of the law, the content of division (A) of this section and its application to the offender or delinquent child, and the offender's or delinquent child's duties under Chapter 2950. of the Revised Code as it will exist under the changes that will be implemented on January 1, 2008. Any failure of any such offender or delinquent child to receive a registered letter from the attorney general pursuant to division (A)(2) of section 2950.031 [2950.03.1] of the Revised Code or to receive a written notice from the department of rehabilitation and correction or department of youth services pursuant to division (A)(2) of section 2950.032 [2950.03.2] of the Revised Code does not negate, limit, or modify the presumption specified in this division.

(C) Divisions (A) and (B) of this section apply to a person who is adjudicated a delinquent child for committing a sexually oriented offense or child-victim oriented offense only if the person is so adjudicated prior to January 1, 2008, and, under the version of section 2950.01 of the Revised Code that is to take effect on January 1, 2008, will be a public registry-qualified juvenile offender registrant relative to that offense.

**HISTORY: 152 v S 10, § 1, eff. 7-1-07.**

The effective date is set by § 3 of 152 v S 10.

## § 2950.034 Residing within 1,000 feet of school, preschool, or child day-care center premises prohibited.

(A) No person who has been convicted of, is convicted of, has pleaded guilty to, or pleads guilty to a sexually oriented offense or a child-victim oriented offense shall establish a residence or occupy residential premises within one thousand feet of any school premises or preschool or child day-care center premises.

(B) If a person to whom division (A) of this section applies violates division (A) of this section by establishing a residence or occupying residential premises within one thousand feet of any school premises or preschool or child day-care center premises, an owner or lessee of real property that is located within one thousand feet of those school premises or preschool or child day-care center premises, or the prosecuting attorney, village solicitor, city or township director of law, similar chief legal officer of a municipal corporation or township, or official designated as a prosecutor in a municipal corporation that has jurisdiction over the place at which the person establishes the residence or occupies the residential premises in question, has a cause of action for injunctive relief against the person. The plaintiff shall not be required to prove irreparable harm in order to obtain the relief.

(C) As used in this section:

(1) "Child day-care center" has the same meaning as in section 5104.01 of the Revised Code.

(2) "Preschool" means any public or private institution or center that provides early childhood instructional or educational services to children who are at least three years of age but less than six years of age and who are not enrolled in or are not eligible to be enrolled in kindergarten, whether or not those services are provided in a child day-care setting. "Preschool" does not include any place that is the permanent residence of the person who is providing the early childhood instructional or educational services to the children described in this division.

(3) "Preschool or child day-care center premises" means all of the following:

(a) Any building in which any preschool or child day-care center activities are conducted if the building has signage that indicates that the building houses a preschool or child day-care center, is clearly visible and discernable without obstruction, and meets any local zoning ordinances which may apply;

(b) The parcel of real property on which a preschool or child day-care center is situated if the parcel of real property has signage that indicates that a preschool or child day-care center is situated on the parcel, is clearly visible and discernable without obstruction, and meets any local zoning ordinances which may apply;

(c) Any grounds, play areas, and other facilities of a preschool or child day-care center that are regularly used by the children served by the preschool or child day-care center if the grounds, play areas, or other facilities have signage that indicates that they are regularly used by children served by the preschool or child day-care center, is clearly visible and discernable without obstruction, and meets any local zoning ordinances which may apply.

**HISTORY: 150 v S 5, § 1, eff. 7-31-03; 150 v H 473, § 1, eff. 4-29-05; 152 v S 10, § 1, eff. 7-1-07.**

The effective date is set by § 3 of 152 v S 10.

This section was renumbered from RC § 2950.031 by 152 v S 10, effective July 1, 2007.

The provisions of § 8 of S.B. 5 (150 v —) read as follows:

SECTION 8. Sections 1923.01, 1923.02, 1923.051, 5321.01, and 5321.03 of the Revised Code, as amended by this act, and sections 2950.031 and 5321.051 of the Revised Code, as enacted by this act, apply to rental agreements entered into on or after the effective date of this act.

## § 2950.04 Duty to register and comply with registration requirements.

(A)(1)(a) Immediately after a sentencing hearing is held on or after January 1, 2008, for an offender who is convicted of or pleads guilty to a sexually oriented offense and is sentenced to a prison term, a term of imprisonment, or any other type of confinement and before the offender is transferred to the custody of the department of rehabilitation and correction or to the official in charge of the jail, workhouse, state correctional institution, or other institution where the offender will be confined, the offender shall register personally with the sheriff, or the sheriff's designee, of the county in which the offender was convicted of or pleaded guilty to the sexually oriented offense.

(b) Immediately after a dispositional hearing is held on or after January 1, 2008, for a child who is adjudicated a delinquent child for committing a sexually oriented offense, is classified a juvenile offender registrant based on that adjudication, and is committed to the custody of the department of youth services or to a secure facility that is not operated by the department and before the child is transferred to the custody of the department of youth services or the secure facility to which the delinquent child is committed, the delinquent child shall register personally with the sheriff, or the sheriff's designee, of the county in which the delinquent child was classified a juvenile offender registrant based on that sexually oriented offense.

(c) A law enforcement officer shall be present at the sentencing hearing or dispositional hearing described in division (A)(1)(a) or (b) of this section to immediately transport the offender or delinquent child who is the subject of the hearing to the sheriff, or the sheriff's designee, of the county in which the offender or delinquent child is convicted, pleads guilty, or is adjudicated a delinquent child.

(d) After an offender who has registered pursuant to division (A)(1)(a) of this section is released from a prison term, a term of imprisonment, or any other type of confinement, the offender shall register as provided in division (A)(2) of this section. After a delinquent child who has registered pursuant to division (A)(1)(b) of this section is released from the custody of the department of youth services or from a secure facility that is not operated by the department, the delinquent child shall register as provided in division (A)(3) of this section.

(2) Regardless of when the sexually oriented offense was committed, each offender who is convicted of, pleads guilty to, has been convicted of, or has pleaded guilty to a sexually oriented offense shall comply with the following registration requirements described in divisions (A)(2)(a), (b), (c), (d), and (e) of this section:

(a) The offender shall register personally with the sheriff, or the sheriff's designee, of the county within three days of the offender's coming into a county in which the offender resides or temporarily is domiciled for more than three days.

(b) The offender shall register personally with the sheriff, or the sheriff's designee, of the county immediately upon coming into a county in which the offender attends a school or institution of higher education on a full-time or part-time basis regardless of whether the offender resides or has a temporary domicile in this state or another state.

(c) The offender shall register personally with the sheriff, or the sheriff's designee, of the county in which the offender is employed if the offender resides or has a temporary domicile in this state and has been employed in that county for more than three days or for an aggregate period of fourteen or more days in that calendar year.

(d) The offender shall register personally with the sheriff, or the sheriff's designee, of the county in which the offender then is employed if the offender does not reside or have a temporary domicile in this state and has been employed at any location or locations in this state more than three days or for an aggregate period of fourteen or more days in that calendar year.

(e) The offender shall register with the sheriff, or the sheriff's designee, or other appropriate person of the other state immediately upon entering into any state other than this state in which the offender attends a school or institution of higher education on a full-time or part-time basis or upon being employed in any state other than this state for more than three days or for an aggregate period of fourteen or more days in that calendar year regardless of whether the offender resides or has a temporary domicile in this state, the other state, or a different state

(3)(a) Each child who is adjudicated a delinquent child for committing a sexually oriented offense and who is classified a juvenile offender registrant based on that adjudication shall register personally with the sheriff, or the sheriff's designee, of the county within three days of the delinquent child's coming into a county in which the delinquent child resides or temporarily is domiciled for more than three days.

(b) In addition to the registration duty imposed under division (A)(3)(a) of this section, each public registry-qualified juvenile offender registrant shall comply with the following additional registration requirements:

(i) The public registry-qualified juvenile offender registrant shall register personally with the sheriff, or the sheriff's designee, of the county immediately upon coming into a county in which the registrant attends a school or institution of higher education on a full-time or part-time basis regardless of whether the registrant resides or has a temporary domicile in this state or another state.

(ii) The public registry-qualified juvenile offender registrant shall register personally with the sheriff, or the sheriff's designee, of the county in which the registrant is employed if the registrant resides or has a temporary domicile in this state and has been employed in that county for more than three days or for an aggregate period of fourteen or more days in that calendar year.

(iii) The public registry-qualified juvenile offender registrant shall register personally with the sheriff, or the sheriff's designee, of the county in which the registrant then is employed if the registrant does not reside or have a temporary domicile in this state and has been employed at any location or locations in this state more than three days or for an aggregate period of fourteen or more days in that calendar year.

(iv) The public registry-qualified juvenile offender registrant shall register with the sheriff, or the sheriff's designee, or other appropriate person of the other state immediately upon entering into any state other than this state in which the registrant attends a school or institution of higher education on a full-time or part-time basis or upon being employed in any state other than this state for more than three days or for an aggregate period of fourteen or more days in that calendar year regardless of whether the registrant resides or has a temporary domicile in this state, the other state, or a different state.

(c) If the delinquent child is committed for the sexually oriented offense to the department of youth services or to a secure facility that is not operated by the department, this duty begins when the delinquent child is discharged or released in any manner from custody in a department of youth services secure facility or from the secure facility that is not operated by the department if pursuant to the discharge or release the delinquent child is not committed to any other secure facility of the department or any other secure facility.

(4) Regardless of when the sexually oriented offense was committed, each person who is convicted, pleads

guilty, or is adjudicated a delinquent child in a court in another state, in a federal court, military court, or Indian tribal court, or in a court in any nation other than the United States for committing a sexually oriented offense shall comply with the following registration requirements if, at the time the offender or delinquent child moves to and resides in this state or temporarily is domiciled in this state for more than three days, the offender or public registry-qualified juvenile offender registrant enters this state to attend a school or institution of higher education, or the offender or public registry-qualified juvenile offender registrant is employed in this state for more than the specified period of time, the offender or delinquent child has a duty to register as a sex offender or child-victim offender under the law of that other jurisdiction as a result of the conviction, guilty plea, or adjudication:

(a) Each offender and delinquent child shall register personally with the sheriff, or the sheriff's designee, of the county within three days of the offender's or delinquent child's coming into the county in which the offender or delinquent child resides or temporarily is domiciled for more than three days.

(b) Each offender or public registry-qualified juvenile offender registrant shall register personally with the sheriff, or the sheriff's designee, of the county immediately upon coming into a county in which the offender or public registry-qualified juvenile offender registrant attends a school or institution of higher education on a full-time or part-time basis regardless of whether the offender or public registry-qualified juvenile offender registrant resides or has a temporary domicile in this state or another state.

(c) Each offender or public registry-qualified juvenile offender registrant shall register personally with the sheriff, or the sheriff's designee, of the county in which the offender or public registry-qualified juvenile offender registrant is employed if the offender resides or has a temporary domicile in this state and has been employed in that county for more than three days or for an aggregate period of fourteen days or more in that calendar year.

(d) Each offender or public registry-qualified juvenile offender registrant shall register personally with the sheriff, or the sheriff's designee, of the county in which the offender or public registry-qualified juvenile offender registrant then is employed if the offender or public registry-qualified juvenile offender registrant does not reside or have a temporary domicile in this state and has been employed at any location or locations in this state for more than three days or for an aggregate period of fourteen or more days in that calendar year.

(5) An offender or a delinquent child who is a public registry-qualified juvenile offender registrant is not required to register under division (A)(2), (3), or (4) of this section if a court issues an order terminating the offender's or delinquent child's duty to comply with sections 2950.04, 2950.041 [2950.04.1], 2950.05, and 2950.06 of the Revised Code pursuant to section 2950.15 of the Revised Code. A delinquent child who is a juvenile offender registrant but is not a public registry-qualified juvenile offender registrant is not required to register under any of those divisions if a juvenile court issues an order declassifying the delinquent child as a juvenile offender registrant pursuant to section 2152.84 or 2152.85 of the Revised Code.

(B) An offender or delinquent child who is required by division (A) of this section to register in this state personally shall obtain from the sheriff or from a designee of the sheriff a registration form that conforms to division (C) of this section, shall complete and sign the form, and shall return the completed form together with the offender's or delinquent child's photograph, copies of travel and immigration documents, and any other required material to the sheriff or the designee. The sheriff or designee shall sign the form and indicate on the form the date on which it is so returned. The registration required under this division is complete when the offender or delinquent child returns the form, containing the requisite information, photograph, other required material, signatures, and date, to the sheriff or designee.

(C) The registration form to be used under divisions (A) and (B) of this section shall include or contain all of the following for the offender or delinquent child who is registering:

(1) The offender's or delinquent child's name and any aliases used by the offender or delinquent child;

(2) The offender's or delinquent child's social security number and date of birth, including any alternate social security numbers or dates of birth that the offender or delinquent child has used or uses;

(3) Regarding an offender or delinquent child who is registering under a duty imposed under division (A)(1) of this section, a statement that the offender is serving a prison term, term of imprisonment, or any other type of confinement or a statement that the delinquent child is in the custody of the department of youth services or is confined in a secure facility that is not operated by the department;

(4) Regarding an offender or delinquent child who is registering under a duty imposed under division (A)(2), (3), or (4) of this section as a result of the offender or delinquent child residing in this state or temporarily being domiciled in this state for more than three days, the current residence address of the offender or delinquent child who is registering, the name and address of the offender's or delinquent child's employer if the offender or delinquent child is employed at the time of registration or if the offender or delinquent child knows at the time of registration that the offender or delinquent child will be commencing employment with that employer subsequent to registration, any other employment information, such as the general area where the offender or delinquent child is employed, if the offender or delinquent child is employed in many locations, and the name and address of the offender's or public registry-qualified juvenile offender registrant's school or institution of higher education if the offender or public registry-qualified juvenile offender registrant attends one at the time of registration or if the offender or public registry-qualified juvenile offender registrant knows at the time of registration that the offender or public registry-qualified juvenile offender registrant will be commencing attendance at that school or institution subsequent to registration;

(5) Regarding an offender or public registry-qualified juvenile offender registrant who is registering under a duty imposed under division (A)(2), (3), or (4) of this section as a result of the offender or public registry-qualified juvenile offender registrant attending a school or institution of higher education in this state on a full-time or part-time basis or being employed in this state or in a particular county in this state, whichever is applicable, for more than three days or for an aggregate of fourteen or more days in any calendar year, the name and current address of the school, institution of higher education, or place of employment of the offender or public registry-qualified juvenile

offender registrant who is registering, including any other employment information, such as the general area where the offender or public registry-qualified juvenile offender registrant is employed, if the offender or public registry-qualified juvenile offender registrant is employed in many locations;

(6) The identification license plate number of each vehicle the offender or delinquent child owns, of each vehicle registered in the offender's or delinquent child's name, of each vehicle the offender or delinquent child operates as a part of employment, and of each other vehicle that is regularly available to be operated by the offender or delinquent child; a description of where each vehicle is habitually parked, stored, docked, or otherwise kept; and, if required by the bureau of criminal identification and investigation, a photograph of each of those vehicles;

(7) If the offender or delinquent child has a driver's or commercial driver's license or permit issued by this state or any other state or a state identification card issued under section 4507.50 or 4507.51 of the Revised Code or a comparable identification card issued by another state, the driver's license number, commercial driver's license number, or state identification card number;

(8) If the offender or delinquent child was convicted of, pleaded guilty to, or was adjudicated a delinquent child for committing the sexually oriented offense resulting in the registration duty in a court in another state, in a federal court, military court, or Indian tribal court, or in a court in any nation other than the United States, a DNA specimen, as defined in section 109.573 [109.57.3] of the Revised Code, from the offender or delinquent child, a citation for, and the name of, the sexually oriented offense resulting in the registration duty, and a certified copy of a document that describes the text of that sexually oriented offense;

(9) A description of each professional and occupational license, permit, or registration, including those licenses, permits, and registrations issued under Title XLVII of the Revised Code, held by the offender or delinquent child;

(10) Any email addresses, internet identifiers, or telephone numbers registered to or used by the offender or delinquent child;

(11) Any other information required by the bureau of criminal identification and investigation.

(D) After an offender or delinquent child registers with a sheriff, or the sheriff's designee, pursuant to this section, the sheriff, or the sheriff's designee, shall forward the signed, written registration form, photograph, and other material to the bureau of criminal identification and investigation in accordance with the forwarding procedures adopted pursuant to section 2950.13 of the Revised Code. If an offender registers a school, institution of higher education, or place of employment address, or provides a school or institution of higher education address under division (C)(4) of this section, the sheriff also shall provide notice to the law enforcement agency with jurisdiction over the premises of the school, institution of higher education, or place of employment of the offender's name and that the offender has registered that address as a place at which the offender attends school or an institution of higher education or at which the offender is employed. The bureau shall include the information and materials forwarded to it under this division in the state registry of sex offenders and child victim offenders established and maintained under section 2950.13 of the Revised Code.

(E) No person who is required to register pursuant to divisions (A) and (B) of this section, and no person who is required to send a notice of intent to reside pursuant to division (G) of this section, shall fail to register or send the notice of intent as required in accordance with those divisions or that division.

(F) An offender or delinquent child who is required to register pursuant to divisions (A) and (B) of this section shall register pursuant to this section for the period of time specified in section 2950.07 of the Revised Code, with the duty commencing on the date specified in division (A) of that section.

(G) If an offender or delinquent child who is required by division (A) of this section to register is a tier III sex offender/child-victim offender, the offender or delinquent child also shall send the sheriff, or the sheriff's designee, of the county in which the offender or delinquent child intends to reside written notice of the offender's or delinquent child's intent to reside in the county. The offender or delinquent child shall send the notice of intent to reside at least twenty days prior to the date the offender or delinquent child begins to reside in the county. The notice of intent to reside shall contain the following information:

(1) The offender's or delinquent child's name;

(2) The address or addresses at which the offender or delinquent child intends to reside;

(3) The sexually oriented offense of which the offender was convicted, to which the offender pleaded guilty, or for which the child was adjudicated a delinquent child

(H) If, immediately prior to January 1, 2008, an offender or delinquent child who was convicted of, pleaded guilty to, or was adjudicated a delinquent child for committing a sexually oriented offense or a child-victim oriented offense as those terms were defined in section 2950.01 of the Revised Code prior to January 1, 2008, was required by division (A) of this section or section 2950.041 [2950.04.1] of the Revised Code to register and if, on or after January 1, 2008, that offense is a sexually oriented offense as that term is defined in section 2950.01 of the Revised Code on and after January 1, 2008, the duty to register that is imposed pursuant to this section on and after January 1, 2008, shall be considered, for purposes of section 2950.07 of the Revised Code and for all other purposes, to be a continuation of the duty imposed upon the offender or delinquent child prior to January 1, 2008, under this section or section 2950.041 [2950.04.1] of the Revised Code.

**HISTORY: 146 v H 180 (Eff 7-1-97); 147 v H 565 (Eff 3-30-99); 148 v H 502 (Eff 3-15-2001); 149 v S 3 (Eff 1-1-2002); 149 v S 175 (Eff 5-7-2002); 149 v H 485 (Eff 6-13-2002); 149 v H 393. Eff 7-5-2002; 150 v S 5, § 1, eff. 7-31-03; 150 v H 473, § 1, eff. 4-29-05; 152 v S 10, § 1, eff. 1-1-08.**

The effective date is set by § 3 of 152 v S 10.

**Not analogous to former RC § 2950.04 (130 v 670), repealed 146 v H 180, § 2, eff 7-1-97.**

See provisions, § 3 of HB 485 (149 v —) following RC § 2929.13.

## § 2950.041 Duty to register resulting from child-victim oriented offense; notice of intent to reside.

(A)(1)(a) Immediately after a sentencing hearing is held on or after January 1, 2008, for an offender who is convicted of or pleads guilty to a child-victim oriented offense and is sentenced to a prison term, a term of imprisonment, or any other type of confinement and before the offender is transferred to the custody of the department of rehabilitation and correction or to the official in charge of the jail, workhouse, state correctional institution, or other institution where the offender will be confined, the offender shall register personally with the sheriff, or the sheriff's designee, of the county in which the offender was convicted of or pleaded guilty to the child-victim offense.

(b) Immediately after a dispositional hearing is held on or after January 1, 2008, for a child who is adjudicated a delinquent child for committing a child-victim oriented offense, is classified a juvenile offender registrant based on that adjudication, and is committed to the custody of the department of youth services or to a secure facility that is not operated by the department and before the child is transferred to the custody of the department of youth services or the secure facility to which the delinquent child is committed, the delinquent child shall register personally with the sheriff, or the sheriff's designee, of the county in which the delinquent child was classified a juvenile offender registrant based on that child-victim oriented offense.

(c) A law enforcement officer shall be present at the sentencing hearing or dispositional hearing described in division (A)(1)(a) or (b) of this section to immediately transport the offender or delinquent child who is the subject of the hearing to the sheriff, or the sheriff's designee, of the county in which the offender or delinquent child is convicted, pleads guilty, or is adjudicated a delinquent child.

(d) After an offender who has registered pursuant to division (A)(1)(a) of this section is released from a prison term, a term of imprisonment, or any other type of confinement, the offender shall register as provided in division (A)(2) of this section. After a delinquent child who has registered pursuant to division (A)(1)(b) of this section is released from the custody of the department of youth services or from a secure facility that is not operated by the department, the delinquent child shall register as provided in division (A)(3) of this section.

(2) Regardless of when the child-victim oriented offense was committed, each offender who is convicted of, pleads guilty to, has been convicted of, or has pleaded guilty to a child-victim oriented offense shall comply with all of the following registration requirements:

(a) The offender shall register personally with the sheriff, or the sheriff's designee, of the county within three days of the offender's coming into a county in which the offender resides or temporarily is domiciled for more than three days.

(b) The offender shall register personally with the sheriff, or the sheriff's designee, of the county immediately upon coming into a county in which the offender attends a school or institution of higher education on a full-time or part-time basis regardless of whether the offender resides or has a temporary domicile in this state or another state.

(c) The offender shall register personally with the sheriff, or the sheriff's designee, of the county in which the offender is employed if the offender resides or has a temporary domicile in this state and has been employed in that county for more than three days or for an aggregate period of fourteen or more days in that calendar year.

(d) The offender shall register personally with the sheriff, or the sheriff's designee, of the county in which the offender then is employed if the offender does not reside or have a temporary domicile in this state and has been employed at any location or locations in this state for more than three days or for an aggregate period of fourteen or more days in that calendar year.

(e) The offender shall register personally with the sheriff, or the sheriff's designee, or other appropriate person of the other state immediately upon entering into any state other than this state in which the offender attends a school or institution of higher education on a full-time or part-time basis or upon being employed in any state other than this state for more than three days or for an aggregate period of fourteen or more days in that calendar year regardless of whether the offender resides or has a temporary domicile in this state, the other state, or a different state.

(3) Regardless of when the child-victim oriented offense was committed, each child who on or after July 31, 2003, is adjudicated a delinquent child for committing a child-victim oriented offense and who is classified a juvenile offender registrant based on that adjudication shall register personally with the sheriff, or the sheriff's designee, of the county within three days of the delinquent child's coming into a county in which the delinquent child resides or temporarily is domiciled for more than three days. If the delinquent child is committed for the child-victim oriented offense to the department of youth services or to a secure facility that is not operated by the department, this duty begins when the delinquent child is discharged or released in any manner from custody in a department of youth services secure facility or from the secure facility that is not operated by the department if pursuant to the discharge or release the delinquent child is not committed to any other secure facility of the department or any other secure facility.

(4) Regardless of when the child-victim oriented offense was committed, each person who is convicted, pleads guilty, or is adjudicated a delinquent child in a court in another state, in a federal court, military court, or Indian tribal court, or in a court in any nation other than the United States for committing a child-victim oriented offense shall comply with all of the following registration requirements if, at the time the offender or delinquent child moves to and resides in this state or temporarily is domiciled in this state for more than three days, the offender enters this state to attend the school or institution of higher education, or the offender is employed in this state for more than the specified period of time, the offender or delinquent child has a duty to register as a child-victim offender or sex offender under the law of that other jurisdiction as a result of the conviction, guilty plea, or adjudication:

(a) Each offender and delinquent child shall register personally with the sheriff, or the sheriff's designee, of the county within three days of the offender's or delinquent child's coming into the county in which the offender or delinquent child resides or temporarily is domiciled for more than three days.

(b) Each offender shall register personally with the sheriff, or the sheriff's designee, of the county immediately upon coming into a county in which the offender attends a school or institution of higher education on a full-time or part-time basis regardless of whether the offender resides or has a temporary domicile in this state or another state.

(c) Each offender shall register personally with the sheriff, or the sheriff's designee, of the county in which the offender is employed if the offender resides or has a temporary domicile in this state and has been employed in that county for more than three days or for an aggregate period of fourteen days or more in that calendar year.

(d) Each offender shall register personally with the sheriff, or the sheriff's designee, of the county in which the offender then is employed if the offender does not reside or have a temporary domicile in this state and has not been employed at any location or locations in this state for more than three days or for an aggregate period of fourteen or more days in that calendar year.

(5) An offender is not required to register under division (A)(2), (3), or (4) of this section if a court issues an order terminating the offender's duty to comply with sections 2950.04, 2950.041 [2950.04.1], 2950.05, and 2950.06 of the Revised Code pursuant to section 2950.15 of the Revised Code. A delinquent child who is a juvenile offender registrant but is not a public registry-qualified juvenile offender registrant is not required to register under any of those divisions if a juvenile court issues an order declassifying the delinquent child as a juvenile offender registrant pursuant to section 2152.84 or 2152.85 of the Revised Code.

(B) An offender or delinquent child who is required by division (A) of this section to register in this state personally shall do so in the manner described in division (B) of section 2950.04 of the Revised Code, and the registration is complete as described in that division.

(C) The registration form to be used under divisions (A) and (B) of this section shall include or contain all of the following for the offender or delinquent child who is registering:

(1) The offender's or delinquent child's name, any aliases used by the offender or delinquent child, and a photograph of the offender or delinquent child;

(2) The offender's or delinquent child's social security number and date of birth, including any alternate social security numbers or dates of birth that the offender or delinquent child has used or uses;

(3) Regarding an offender or delinquent child who is registering under a duty imposed under division (A)(1) of this section, a statement that the offender is serving a prison term, term of imprisonment, or any other type of confinement or a statement that the delinquent child is in the custody of the department of youth services or is confined in a secure facility that is not operated by the department;

(4) Regarding an offender or delinquent child who is registering under a duty imposed under division (A)(2), (3), or (4) of this section as a result of the offender or delinquent child residing in this state or temporarily being domiciled in this state for more than three days, all of the information described in division (C)(4) of section 2950.04 of the Revised Code;

(5) Regarding an offender who is registering under a duty imposed under division (A)(2) or (4) of this section as a result of the offender attending a school or institution of higher education on a full-time or part-time basis or being employed in this state or in a particular county in this state, whichever is applicable, for more than three days or for an aggregate of fourteen or more days in any calendar year, all of the information described in division (C)(5) of section 2950.04 of the Revised Code;

(6) The identification license plate number issued by this state or any other state of each vehicle the offender or delinquent child owns, of each vehicle registered in the offender's or delinquent child's name, of each vehicle the offender or delinquent child operates as a part of employment, and of each other vehicle that is regularly available to be operated by the offender or delinquent child; a description of where each vehicle is habitually parked, stored, docked, or otherwise kept; and, if required by the bureau of criminal identification and investigation, a photograph of each of those vehicles;

(7) If the offender or delinquent child has a driver's or commercial driver's license or permit issued by this state or any other state or a state identification card issued under section 4507.50 or 4507.51 of the Revised Code or a comparable identification card issued by another state, the driver's license number, commercial driver's license number, or state identification card number;

(8) If the offender or delinquent child was convicted of, pleaded guilty to, or was adjudicated a delinquent child for committing the child-victim oriented offense resulting in the registration duty in a court in another state, in a federal court, military court, or Indian tribal court, or in a court in any nation other than the United States, a DNA specimen, as defined in section 109.573 [109.57.3] of the Revised Code, from the offender or delinquent child, a citation for, and the name of, the child-victim oriented offense resulting in the registration duty, and a certified copy of a document that describes the text of that child-victim oriented offense;

(9) Copies of travel and immigration documents;

(10) A description of each professional and occupational license, permit, or registration, including those licenses, permits, and registrations issued under Title XLVII of the Revised Code, held by the offender or delinquent child;

(11) Any email addresses, internet identifiers, or telephone numbers registered to or used by the offender or delinquent child;

(12) Any other information required by the bureau of criminal identification and investigation.

(D) Division (D) of section 2950.04 of the Revised Code applies when an offender or delinquent child registers with a sheriff pursuant to this section.

(E) No person who is required to register pursuant to divisions (A) and (B) of this section, and no person who is required to send a notice of intent to reside pursuant to division (G) of this section, shall fail to register or send the notice as required in accordance with those divisions or that division.

(F) An offender or delinquent child who is required to register pursuant to divisions (A) and (B) of this section shall register pursuant to this section for the period of time specified in section 2950.07 of the Revised Code, with the duty commencing on the date specified in division (A) of that section.

(G) If an offender or delinquent child who is required by division (A) of this section to register is a tier III sex offender/child-victim offender, the offender or delinquent child also shall send the sheriff, or the sheriff's designee, of the county in which the offender or delinquent child intends to reside written notice of the offender's or delinquent child's intent to reside in the county. The offender or delinquent child shall send the notice of intent to reside at least twenty days prior to the date the offender or delinquent child begins to reside in the county. The notice of intent to reside shall contain all of the following information:

(1) The information specified in divisions (G)(1) and (2) of section 2950.04 of the Revised Code;

(2) The child-victim oriented offense of which the offender was convicted, to which the offender pleaded guilty, or for which the child was adjudicated a delinquent child

(H) If, immediately prior to January 1, 2008, an offender or delinquent child who was convicted of, pleaded guilty to, or was adjudicated a delinquent child for committing a child-victim oriented offense or a sexually oriented offense as those terms were defined in section 2950.01 of the Revised Code prior to January 1, 2008, was required by division (A) of this section or section 2950.04 of the Revised Code to register and if, on or after January 1, 2008, that offense is a child-victim oriented offense as that term is defined in section 2950.01 of the Revised Code on and after January 1, 2008, the duty to register that is imposed pursuant to this section on and after January 1, 2008, shall be considered, for purposes of section 2950.07 of the Revised Code and for all other purposes, to be a continuation of the duty imposed upon the offender or delinquent child prior to January 1, 2008, under this section or section 2950.04 of the Revised Code.

**HISTORY: 150 v S 5, § 1, eff. 7-31-03; 150 v H 473, § 1, eff. 4-29-05; 152 v S 10, § 1, eff. 1-1-08.**

The effective date is set by § 3 of 152 v S 10.

## § 2950.042 Parole officers to verify compliance with registration requirements.

By January 1, 2008, the department of rehabilitation and correction, the adult parole authority, and the department of youth services shall adopt rules to require parole officers to verify within three days of an offender's or delinquent child's release that the offender or delinquent child has registered as provided in divisions (A)(2) and (3) of section 2950.04 of the Revised Code or in divisions (A)(2) and (3) of section 2950.041 [2950.04.1] of the Revised Code, whichever is applicable.

**HISTORY: 152 v S 10, § 1, eff. 7-1-07.**

The effective date is set by § 3 of 152 v S 10.

## § 2950.043 Sheriff to notify attorney general of registration on or after 12-1-07.

If an offender or delinquent child registers with a sheriff pursuant to section 2950.04 or 2950.041 [2950.04.1] of the Revised Code on or after December 1, 2007, if the offender or delinquent child previously has not registered under either section with that sheriff or any other sheriff, and if the offender or delinquent child was convicted of, pleaded guilty to, or was classified a juvenile offender registrant relative to the sexually oriented offense or child-victim oriented offense upon which the registration was based prior to December 1, 2007, as soon as practicable after the registration, the sheriff shall contact the attorney general, inform the attorney general of the registration, and forward to the attorney general in the manner specified in division (D) of section 2950.04 of the Revised Code all of the information and material specified in that division. Upon being informed of the registration and receiving the information and material, the attorney general shall comply with division (B) of section 2950.031 [2950.03.1] of the Revised Code.

**HISTORY: 152 v S 10, § 1, eff. 7-1-07.**

The effective date is set by § 3 of 152 v S 10.

## § 2950.05 Notice of change of address; registration of new address; notice of change in vehicle information, email addresses, internet identifiers, or telephone numbers.

(A) If an offender or delinquent child is required to register pursuant to division (A)(2), (3), or (4) of section 2950.04 or 2950.041 [2950.04.1] of the Revised Code, the delinquent child if not a public registry-qualified juvenile offender registrant shall provide written notice of any change of residence address, and the offender and public registry-qualified juvenile offender registrant shall provide notice of any change of residence, school, institution of higher education, or place of employment address, to the sheriff with whom the offender or delinquent child most recently registered the address under division (A)(2), (3), or (4) of section 2950.04 or 2950.041 [2950.04.1] of the Revised Code or under division (B) of this section. A written notice of a change of school, institution of higher education, or place of employment address also shall include the name of the new school, institution of higher education, or place of employment. The delinquent child if not a public registry-qualified juvenile offender registrant shall provide the written notice at least twenty days prior to changing the residence address, and the offender and public registry-qualified juvenile offender registrant shall provide the written notice at least twenty days prior to changing the address of the residence, school, or institution of higher education and not later than three days after changing the address of the place of employment. They shall provide the written notices during the period they are required to register. If a residence address change is not to a fixed address, the offender or delinquent child shall include in that notice a detailed description of the place or places at which the offender or delinquent child intends to stay and, not later than the end of the first business day immediately following the day on which the person obtains a fixed residence address, shall provide that sheriff written notice of that fixed residence address. If a person whose residence address change is not to a fixed address describes in a notice under this division the place or places at which the person intends to stay, for purposes of divisions (C) to (I) of this section, sections 2950.06 to 2950.13 of the Revised Code, and sections 311.171 [311.17.1] and 2919.24 of the Revised Code, the place or places so described in the notice shall be considered the person's residence address and registered residence address until the person provides the written notice of a fixed residence address as described in this division.

(B) If an offender or public registry-qualified juvenile offender registrant is required to provide notice of a residence, school, institution of higher education, or place of employment address change under division (A) of this section, or a delinquent child who is not a public registry-qualified juvenile offender registrant is required to provide notice of a residence address change under that division, the offender or delinquent child, at least twenty days prior to changing the residence, school, or institution of higher education address and not later than three days after changing the place of employment address, as applicable, also shall register the new address in the manner, and using the form, described in divisions (B) and (C) of section 2950.04 or 2950.041 [2950.04.1] of the Revised Code, whichever is applicable, with the sheriff of the county in which the offender's or delinquent child's new address is located, subject to division (C) of this section. If a residence address change is not to a fixed address, the offender or delinquent child shall include in the registration a detailed description of the place or places at which the offender or delinquent child intends to stay and, not later than the end of the first business day immediately following the day on which the person obtains a fixed residence address, shall register with that sheriff that fixed residence address. If a person whose residence address change is not to a fixed address describes in a registration under this division the place or places at which the person intends to stay, for purposes of divisions (C) to (I) of this section, sections 2950.06 to 2950.13 of the Revised Code, and sections 311.171 [311.17.1] and 2919.24 of the Revised Code, the place or places so described in the registration shall be considered the person's residence address and registered residence address, until the person registers a fixed residence address as described in this division.

(C) Divisions (A) and (B) of this section apply to a person who is required to register pursuant to division (A)(2), (3), or (4) of section 2950.04 or 2950.041 [2950.04.1] of the Revised Code regardless of whether the new residence, school, institution of higher education, or place of employment address is in this state or in another state. If the new address is in another state, the person shall register with the appropriate law enforcement officials in that state in the manner required under the law of that state and within the earlier of the period of time required under the law of that state or at least seven days prior to changing the address.

(D) If an offender or delinquent child who is a public registry-qualified juvenile offender registrant is required to register pursuant to division (A)(2), (3), or (4) of section 2950.04 or 2950.041 [2950.04.1] of the Revised Code, the offender or public registry-qualified juvenile offender registrant shall provide written notice, within three days of the change, of any change in vehicle information, email addresses, internet identifiers, or telephone numbers registered to or used by the offender or registrant to the sheriff with whom the offender or registrant has most recently registered under division (A)(2), (3), or (4) of section 2950.04 or 2950.041 [2950.04.1] of the Revised Code.

(E)(1) Upon receiving from an offender or delinquent child pursuant to division (A) of this section notice of a change of the offender's or public registry-qualified juvenile offender registrant's residence, school, institution of higher education, or place of employment address or the residence address of a delinquent child who is not a public registry-qualified juvenile offender registrant, a sheriff promptly shall forward the new address to the bureau of criminal identification and investigation in accordance with the forwarding procedures adopted pursuant to section 2950.13 of the Revised Code if the new address is in another state or, if the new address is located in another county in this state, to the sheriff of that county. Upon receiving from an offender or public registry-qualified juvenile offender registrant notice of vehicle and identifier changes pursuant to division (D) of this section, a sheriff promptly shall forward the new information to the bureau of criminal identification and investigation in accordance with the forwarding procedures adopted pursuant to section 2950.13 of the Revised Code. The bureau shall include all information forwarded to it under this division in the state registry of sex offenders and child-victim offenders established and maintained under section 2950.13 of the Revised Code and shall forward notice of the offender's or delinquent child's new residence, school, institution of higher education, or place of employment address, as applicable, to the appropriate officials in the other state.

(2) When an offender or public registry-qualified juvenile offender registrant registers a new residence, school, institution of higher education, or place of employment address or a delinquent child who is not a public registry-qualified juvenile offender registrant registers a new residence address pursuant to division (B) of this section, the sheriff with whom the offender or delinquent child registers and the bureau of criminal identification and investigation shall comply with division (D) of section 2950.04 or 2950.041 [2950.04.1] of the Revised Code, whichever is applicable.

(F)(1) No person who is required to notify a sheriff of a change of address pursuant to division (A) of this section or a change in vehicle information or identifiers pursuant to division (D) of this section shall fail to notify the appropriate sheriff in accordance with that division.

(2) No person who is required to register a new residence, school, institution of higher education, or place of employment address with a sheriff or with an official of another state pursuant to divisions (B) and (C) of this section shall fail to register with the appropriate sheriff or official of the other state in accordance with those divisions.

(G)(1) It is an affirmative defense to a charge of a violation of division (F)(1) of this section that it was impossible for the person to provide the written notice to the sheriff as required under division (A) of this section because of a lack of knowledge, on the date specified for the provision of the written notice, of a residence, school, institution of higher education, or place of employment address change, and that the person provided notice of the residence, school, institution of higher education, or place of employment address change to the sheriff specified in division (A) of this section as soon as possible, but not later than the end of the first business day, after learning of the address change by doing either of the following:

(a) The person provided notice of the address change to the sheriff specified in division (A) of this section by telephone immediately upon learning of the address change or, if the person did not have reasonable access to a telephone at that time, as soon as possible, but not later than the end of the first business day, after learning of the address change and having reasonable access to a telephone, and the person, as soon as possible, but not later than the end of the first business day, after providing notice of the address change to the sheriff by telephone, provided written notice of the address change to that sheriff.

(b) The person, as soon as possible, but not later than the end of the first business day, after learning of the address change, provided written notice of the address change to the sheriff specified in division (A) of this section.

(2) It is an affirmative defense to a charge of a violation of division (F)(2) of this section that it was impossible for the person to register the new address with the sheriff or the official of the other state as required under division (B) or (C) of this section because of a lack of knowledge, on the date specified for the registration of the new address, of a residence, school, institution of higher education, or place of employment address change, and that the person registered the new residence, school, institution of higher education, or place of employment address with the sheriff or the official of the other state specified in division (B) or

(C) of this section as soon as possible, but not later than the end of the first business day, after learning of the address change by doing either of the following:

(a) The person provided notice of the new address to the sheriff or official specified in division (B) or (C) of this section by telephone immediately upon learning of the new address or, if the person did not have reasonable access to a telephone at that time, as soon as possible, but not later than the end of the first business day, after learning of the new address and having reasonable access to a telephone, and the person, as soon as possible, but not later than the end of the first business day, after providing notice of the new address to the sheriff or official by telephone, registered the new address with that sheriff or official in accordance with division (B) or (C) of this section.

(b) The person, as soon as possible, but not later than the end of the first business day, after learning of the new address, registered the new address with the sheriff or official specified in division (B) or (C) of this section, in accordance with that division.

(H) An offender or delinquent child who is required to comply with divisions (A), (B), and (C) of this section shall do so for the period of time specified in section 2950.07 of the Revised Code.

(I) As used in this section, and in all other sections of the Revised Code that refer to the duties imposed on an offender or delinquent child under this section relative to a change in the offender's or delinquent child's residence, school, institution of higher education, or place of employment address, "change in address" includes any circumstance in which the old address for the person in question no longer is accurate, regardless of whether the person in question has a new address.

**HISTORY: 146 v H 180 (Eff 7-1-97); 149 v S 3 (Eff 1-1-2002); 149 v S 175. Eff 5-7-2002; 150 v S 5, § 1, eff. 7-31-03; 150 v H 473, § 1, eff. 4-29-05; 152 v S 10, § 1, eff. 1-1-08.**

The effective date is set by § 3 of 152 v S 10.

**Analogous to former RC § 2950.05 (130 v 671), repealed 146 v H 180, § 2, eff 7-1-97.**

## § 2950.06 Periodic verification of current address.

(A) An offender or delinquent child who is required to register a residence address pursuant to division (A)(2), (3), or (4) of section 2950.04 or 2950.041 [2950.04.1] of the Revised Code shall periodically verify the offender's or delinquent child's current residence address, and an offender or public registry-qualified juvenile offender registrant who is required to register a school, institution of higher education, or place of employment address pursuant to any of those divisions shall periodically verify the address of the offender's or public registry-qualified juvenile offender registrant's current school, institution of higher education, or place of employment, in accordance with this section. The frequency of verification shall be determined in accordance with division (B) of this section, and the manner of verification shall be determined in accordance with division (C) of this section.

(B) The frequency with which an offender or delinquent child must verify the offender's or delinquent child's current residence, school, institution of higher education, or place of employment address pursuant to division (A) of this section shall be determined as follows:

(1) Regardless of when the sexually oriented offense or child-victim oriented offense for which the offender or delinquent child is required to register was committed, if the offender or delinquent child is a tier I sex offender/child-victim offender, the offender shall verify the offender's current residence address or current school, institution of higher education, or place of employment address, and the delinquent child shall verify the delinquent child's current residence address, in accordance with division (C) of this section on each anniversary of the offender's or delinquent child's initial registration date during the period the offender or delinquent child is required to register

(2) Regardless of when the sexually oriented offense or child-victim oriented offense for which the offender or delinquent child is required to register was committed, if the offender or delinquent child is a tier II sex offender/child-victim offender, the offender shall verify the offender's current residence address or current school, institution of higher education, or place of employment address, and the delinquent child shall verify the delinquent child's current residence address, in accordance with division (C) of this section every one hundred eighty days after the offender's or delinquent child's initial registration date during the period the offender or delinquent child is required to register.

(3) Regardless of when the sexually oriented offense or child-victim oriented offense for which the offender or delinquent child is required to register was committed, if the offender or delinquent child is a tier III sex offender/child-victim offender, the offender shall verify the offender's current residence address or current school, institution of higher education, or place of employment address, and the delinquent child shall verify the delinquent child's current residence address and, if the delinquent child is a public registry-qualified juvenile offender registrant, the current school, institution of higher education, or place of employment address, in accordance with division (C) of this section every ninety days after the offender's or delinquent child's initial registration date during the period the offender or delinquent child is required to register.

(4) If, prior to January 1, 2008, an offender or delinquent child registered with a sheriff under a duty imposed under section 2950.04 or 2950.041 [2950.04.1] of the Revised Code as a result of a conviction of, plea of guilty to, or adjudication as a delinquent child for committing a sexually oriented offense or a child-victim oriented offense as those terms were defined in section 2950.01 of the Revised Code prior to January 1, 2008, the duty to register that is imposed on the offender or delinquent child pursuant to section 2950.04 or 2950.041 [2950.04.1] of the Revised Code on and after January 1, 2008, is a continuation of the duty imposed upon the offender prior to January 1, 2008, under section 2950.04 or 2950.041 [2950.04.1] of the Revised Code and, for purposes of divisions (B)(1), (2), and (3) of this section, the offender's initial registration date related to that offense is the date on which the offender initially registered under section 2950.04 or 2950.041 [2950.04.1] of the Revised Code.

(C)(1) An offender or delinquent child who is required to verify the offender's or delinquent child's current residence, school, institution of higher education, or place of employment address pursuant to division (A) of this section shall verify the address with the sheriff with whom the offender or delinquent child most recently registered the address by personally appearing before the sheriff or a designee of the sheriff, no earlier than ten days before the date on which the verification is required pursuant to division (B) of this section and no later than the date so required for verification, and completing and signing a copy of the verification form prescribed by the bureau of criminal identification and investigation. The sheriff or designee shall sign the completed form and indicate on the form the date on which it is so completed. The verification required under this division is complete when the offender or delinquent child personally appears before the sheriff or designee and completes and signs the form as described in this division.

(2) To facilitate the verification of an offender's or delinquent child's current residence, school, institution of higher education, or place of employment address, as applicable, under division (C)(1) of this section, the sheriff with whom the offender or delinquent child most recently registered the address may mail a nonforwardable verification form prescribed by the bureau of criminal identification and investigation to the offender's or delinquent child's last reported address and to the last reported address of the parents of the delinquent child, with a notice that conspicuously states that the offender or delinquent child must personally appear before the sheriff or a designee of the sheriff to complete the form and the date by which the form must be so completed. Regardless of whether a sheriff mails a form to an offender or delinquent child and that child's parents, each offender or delinquent child who is required to verify the offender's or delinquent child's current residence, school, institution of higher education, or place of employment address, as applicable, pursuant to division (A) of this section shall personally appear before the sheriff or a designee of the sheriff to verify the address in accordance with division (C)(1) of this section.

(D) The verification form to be used under division (C) of this section shall contain all of the following:

(1) Except as provided in division (D)(2) of this section, the current residence address of the offender or delinquent child, the name and address of the offender's or delinquent child's employer if the offender or delinquent child is employed at the time of verification or if the offender or delinquent child knows at the time of verification that the offender or delinquent child will be commencing employment with that employer subsequent to verification, the name and address of the offender's or public registry-qualified juvenile offender registrant's school or institution of higher education if the offender or public registry-qualified juvenile offender registrant attends one at the time of verification or if the offender or public registry-qualified juvenile offender registrant knows at the time of verification that the offender will be commencing attendance at that school or institution subsequent to verification, and any other information required by the bureau of criminal identification and investigation.

(2) Regarding an offender or public registry-qualified juvenile offender registrant who is verifying a current school, institution of higher education, or place of employment address, the name and current address of the school, institution of higher education, or place of employment of the offender or public registry-qualified juvenile offender registrant and any other information required by the bureau of criminal identification and investigation.

(E) Upon an offender's or delinquent child's personal appearance and completion of a verification form under division (C) of this section, a sheriff promptly shall forward a copy of the verification form to the bureau of criminal identification and investigation in accordance with the forwarding procedures adopted by the attorney general pursuant to section 2950.13 of the Revised Code. If an offender or public registry-qualified juvenile offender registrant verifies a school, institution of higher education, or place of employment address, or provides a school or institution of higher education address under division (D)(1) of this section, the sheriff also shall provide notice to the law enforcement agency with jurisdiction over the premises of the school, institution of higher education, or place of employment of the offender's or public registry-qualified juvenile offender registrant's name and that the offender or public registry-qualified juvenile offender registrant has verified or provided that address as a place at which the offender or public registry-qualified juvenile offender registrant attends school or an institution of higher education or at which the offender or public registry-qualified juvenile offender registrant is employed. The bureau shall include all information forwarded to it under this division in the state registry of sex offenders and child-victim offenders established and maintained under section 2950.13 of the Revised Code.

(F) No person who is required to verify a current residence, school, institution of higher education, or place of employment address, as applicable, pursuant to divisions (A) to (C) of this section shall fail to verify a current residence, school, institution of higher education, or place of employment address, as applicable, in accordance with those divisions by the date required for the verification as set forth in division (B) of this section, provided that no person shall be prosecuted or subjected to a delinquent child proceeding for a violation of this division, and that no parent, guardian, or custodian of a delinquent child shall be prosecuted for a violation of section 2919.24 of the Revised Code based on the delinquent child's violation of this division, prior to the expiration of the period of time specified in division (G) of this section.

(G)(1) If an offender or delinquent child fails to verify a current residence, school, institution of higher education, or place of employment address, as applicable, as required by divisions (A) to (C) of this section by the date required for the verification as set forth in division (B) of this section, the sheriff with whom the offender or delinquent child is required to verify the current address, on the day following that date required for the verification, shall send a written warning to the offender or to the delinquent child and that child's parents, at the offender's or delinquent child's and that child's parents' last known residence, school, institution of higher education, or place of employment address, as applicable, regarding the offender's or delinquent child's duty to verify the offender's or delinquent child's current residence, school, institution of higher education, or place of employment address, as applicable.

The written warning shall do all of the following:

(a) Identify the sheriff who sends it and the date on which it is sent;

(b) State conspicuously that the offender or delinquent child has failed to verify the offender's or public registry-qualified juvenile offender registrant's current residence, school, institution of higher education, or place of employment address or the current residence address of a delinquent child who is not a public registry-qualified juvenile offender registrant by the date required for the verification;

(c) Conspicuously state that the offender or delinquent child has seven days from the date on which the warning is sent to verify the current residence, school, institution of higher education, or place of employment address, as applicable, with the sheriff who sent the warning;

(d) Conspicuously state that a failure to timely verify the specified current address or addresses is a felony offense;

(e) Conspicuously state that, if the offender or public registry-qualified juvenile offender registrant verifies the current residence, school, institution of higher education, or place of employment address or the delinquent child who is not a public registry-qualified juvenile offender registrant verifies the current residence address with that sheriff within that seven-day period, the offender or delinquent child will not be prosecuted or subjected to a delinquent child proceeding for a failure to timely verify a current address and the delinquent child's parent, guardian, or custodian will not be prosecuted based on a failure of the delinquent child to timely verify an address;

(f) Conspicuously state that, if the offender or public registry-qualified juvenile offender registrant does not verify the current residence, school, institution of higher education, or place of employment address or the delinquent child who is not a public registry-qualified juvenile offender registrant does not verify the current residence address with that sheriff within that seven-day period, the offender or delinquent child will be arrested or taken into custody, as appropriate, and prosecuted or subjected to a delinquent child proceeding for a failure to timely verify a current address and the delinquent child's parent, guardian, or custodian may be prosecuted for a violation of section 2919.24 of the Revised Code based on the delinquent child's failure to timely verify a current residence address.

(2) If an offender or delinquent child fails to verify a current residence, school, institution of higher education, or place of employment address, as applicable, as required by divisions (A) to (C) of this section by the date required for the verification as set forth in division (B) of this section, the offender or delinquent child shall not be prosecuted or subjected to a delinquent child proceeding for a violation of division (F) of this section, and the delinquent child's parent, guardian, or custodian shall not be prosecuted for a violation of section 2919.24 of the Revised Code based on the delinquent child's failure to timely verify a current residence address and, if the delinquent child is a public registry-qualified juvenile offender registrant, the current school, institution of higher education, or place of employment address, as applicable, unless the seven-day period subsequent to that date that the offender or delinquent child is provided under division (G)(1) of this section to verify the current address has expired and the offender or delinquent child, prior to the expiration of that seven-day period, has not verified the current address. Upon the expiration of the seven-day period that the offender or delinquent child is provided under division (G)(1) of this section to verify the current address, if the offender or delinquent child has not verified the current address, all of the following apply:

(a) The sheriff with whom the offender or delinquent child is required to verify the current residence, school, institution of higher education, or place of employment address, as applicable, promptly shall notify the bureau of criminal identification and investigation of the failure.

(b) The sheriff with whom the offender or delinquent child is required to verify the current residence, school, institution of higher education, or place of employment address, as applicable, the sheriff of the county in which the offender or delinquent child resides, the sheriff of the county in which is located the offender's or public registry-qualified juvenile offender registrant's school, institution of higher education, or place of employment address that was to be verified, or a deputy of the appropriate sheriff, shall locate the offender or delinquent child, promptly shall seek a warrant for the arrest or taking into custody, as appropriate, of the offender or delinquent child for the violation of division (F) of this section and shall arrest the offender or take the child into custody, as appropriate.

(c) The offender or delinquent child is subject to prosecution or a delinquent child proceeding for the violation of division (F) of this section, and the delinquent child's parent, guardian, or custodian may be subject to prosecution for a violation of section 2919.24 of the Revised Code based on the delinquent child's violation of that division.

(H) An offender or public registry-qualified juvenile offender registrant who is required to verify the offender's or public registry-qualified juvenile offender registrant's current residence, school, institution of higher education, or place of employment address pursuant to divisions (A) to (C) of this section and a delinquent child who is not a public registry-qualified juvenile offender registrant who is required to verify the delinquent child's current residence address pursuant to those divisions shall do so for the period of time specified in section 2950.07 of the Revised Code.

**HISTORY: 146 v H 180 (Eff 7-1-97); 147 v H 565 (Eff 3-30-99); 149 v S 3 (Eff 1-1-2002); 149 v H 485. Eff 6-13-2002; 150 v S 5, § 1, eff. 7-31-03; 152 v S 10, § 1, eff. 1-1-08.**

The effective date is set by § 3 of 152 v S 10.

**Not analogous to former RC § 2950.06 (130 v 671), repealed 146 v H 180, § 2, eff 7-1-97.**

## § 2950.07 Commencement of duty to register; duration.

(A) The duty of an offender who is convicted of, pleads guilty to, has been convicted of, or has pleaded guilty to a sexually oriented offense or a child-victim oriented offense and the duty of a delinquent child who is or has been adjudicated a delinquent child for committing a sexually oriented offense or a child-victim oriented offense and is classified a juvenile offender registrant or who is an out-of-state juvenile offender registrant to comply with sections 2950.04, 2950.041 [2950.04.1], 2950.05, and 2950.06 of the Revised Code commences on whichever of the following dates is applicable:

(1) If the offender's duty to register is imposed pursuant to division (A)(1)(a) of section 2950.04 or division (A)(1)(a) of section 2950.041 [2950.04.1] of the Revised Code, the offender's duty to comply with those sections commences immediately after the entry of the judgment of conviction.

(2) If the delinquent child's duty to register is imposed pursuant to division (A)(1)(b) of section 2950.04 or division (A)(1)(b) of section 2950.041 [2950.04.1] of the Revised Code, the delinquent child's duty to comply with those sections commences immediately after the order of disposition.

(3) If the offender's duty to register is imposed pursuant to division (A)(2) of section 2950.04 or division (A)(2) of section 2950.041 [2950.04.1] of the Revised Code,

subject to division (A)(7) of this section, the offender's duty to comply with those sections commences on the date of the offender's release from a prison term, a term of imprisonment, or any other type of confinement, or if the offender is not sentenced to a prison term, a term of imprisonment, or any other type of confinement, on the date of the entry of the judgment of conviction of the sexually oriented offense or child-victim oriented offense.

(4) If the offender's or delinquent child's duty to register is imposed pursuant to division (A)(4) of section 2950.04 or division (A)(4) of section 2950.041 [2950.04.1] of the Revised Code, the offender's duty to comply with those sections commences regarding residence addresses on the date that the offender begins to reside or becomes temporarily domiciled in this state, the offender's duty regarding addresses of schools, institutions of higher education, and places of employment commences on the date the offender begins attending any school or institution of higher education in this state on a full-time or part-time basis or becomes employed in this state, and the delinquent child's duty commences on the date the delinquent child begins to reside or becomes temporarily domiciled in this state.

(5) If the delinquent child's duty to register is imposed pursuant to division (A)(3) of section 2950.04 or division (A)(3) of section 2950.041 [2950.04.1] of the Revised Code, if the delinquent child's classification as a juvenile offender registrant is made at the time of the child's disposition for that sexually oriented offense or child-victim oriented offense, whichever is applicable, and if the delinquent child is committed for the sexually oriented offense or child-victim oriented offense to the department of youth services or to a secure facility that is not operated by the department, the delinquent child's duty to comply with those sections commences on the date of the delinquent child's discharge or release from custody in the department of youth services secure facility or from the secure facility not operated by the department as described in that division.

(6) If the delinquent child's duty to register is imposed pursuant to division (A)(3) of section 2950.04 or division (A)(3) of section 2950.041 [2950.04.1] of the Revised Code and if either the delinquent child's classification as a juvenile offender registrant is made at the time of the child's disposition for that sexually oriented offense or child-victim oriented offense, whichever is applicable, and the delinquent child is not committed for the sexually oriented offense or child-victim oriented offense to the department of youth services or to a secure facility that is not operated by the department or the child's classification as a juvenile offender registrant is made pursuant to section 2152.83 or division (A)(2) of section 2152.86 of the Revised Code, subject to divisions (A)(7) of this section, the delinquent child's duty to comply with those sections commences on the date of entry of the court's order that classifies the delinquent child a juvenile offender registrant.

(7) If the offender's or delinquent child's duty to register is imposed pursuant to division (A)(2), (3), or (4) of section 2950.04 or section 2950.041 [2950.04.1] of the Revised Code and if the offender or delinquent child prior to January 1, 2008, has registered a residence, school, institution of higher education, or place of employment address pursuant to section 2950.04, 2950.041 [2950.04.1], or 2950.05 of the Revised Code as they existed prior to that date, the offender or delinquent child initially shall register in accordance with section 2950.04 or 2950.041 of the Revised Code, whichever is applicable, as it exists on and after January 1, 2008, not later than the earlier of the dates specified in divisions (A)(7)(a) and (b) of this section. The offender's or delinquent child's duty to comply thereafter with sections 2950.04, 2950.041 [2950.04.1], 2950.05, and 2950.06 of the Revised Code as they exist on and after January 1, 2008, commences on the date of that initial registration. The offender or delinquent child initially shall register under section 2950.04 or 2950.041 [2950.04.1] of the Revised Code as it exists on and after January 1, 2008, not later than the earlier of the following:

(a) The date that is six months after the date on which the offender or delinquent child received a registered letter from the attorney general under division (A)(2) or (B) of section 2950.031 [2950.03.1] of the Revised Code;

(b) The earlier of the date on which the offender or delinquent child would be required to verify a previously registered address under section 2950.06 of the Revised Code as it exists on and after January 1, 2008, or, if the offender or delinquent child has changed a previously registered address, the date on which the offender or delinquent child would be required to register a new residence, school, institution of higher education, or place of employment address under section 2950.05 of the Revised Code as it exists on and after January 1, 2008.

(8) If the offender's or delinquent child's duty to register was imposed pursuant to section 2950.04 or 2950.041 [2950.04.1] of the Revised Code as they existed prior to January 1, 2008, the offender's or delinquent child's duty to comply with sections 2950.04, 2950.041 [2950.04.1], 2950.05, and 2950.06 of the Revised Code as they exist on and after January 1, 2008, is a continuation of the offender's or delinquent child's former duty to register imposed prior to January 1, 2008, under section 2950.04 or 2950.041 [2950.04.1] of the Revised Code and shall be considered for all purposes as having commenced on the date that the offender's duty under that section commenced.

(B) The duty of an offender who is convicted of, pleads guilty to, has been convicted of, or has pleaded guilty to a sexually oriented offense or a child-victim oriented offense and the duty of a delinquent child who is or has been adjudicated a delinquent child for committing a sexually oriented offense or a child-victim oriented offense and is classified a juvenile offender registrant or who is an out-of-state juvenile offender registrant to comply with sections 2950.04, 2950.041 [2950.04.1], 2950.05, and 2950.06 of the Revised Code continues, after the date of commencement, for whichever of the following periods is applicable:

(1) Except as otherwise provided in this division, if the person is an offender who is a tier III sex offender/child-victim offender relative to the sexually oriented offense or child-victim oriented offense, if the person is a delinquent child who is a tier III sex offender/child-victim offender relative to the sexually oriented offense or child-victim oriented offense, or if the person is a delinquent child who is a public registry-qualified juvenile offender registrant relative to the sexually oriented offense, the offender's or delinquent child's duty to comply with those sections continues until the offender's or delinquent child's death. Regarding a delinquent child who is a tier III sex offender/child-victim offender relative to the offense but is not a public registry-qualified juvenile offender registrant relative to the offense, if the judge who made the disposition for the delinquent child or that judge's successor in office subsequently enters a determination pursuant to section

2152.84 or 2152.85 of the Revised Code that the delinquent child no longer is a tier III sex offender/child-victim offender, the delinquent child's duty to comply with those sections continues for the period of time that is applicable to the delinquent child under division (B)(2) or (3) of this section, based on the reclassification of the child pursuant to section 2152.84 or 21562.85 of the Revised Code as a tier I sex offender/child-victim offender or a tier II sex offender/child-victim offender. In no case shall the lifetime duty to comply that is imposed under this division on an offender who is a tier III sex offender/child-victim offender be removed or terminated. A delinquent child who is a public registry-qualified juvenile offender registrant may have the lifetime duty to register terminated only pursuant to section 2950.15 of the Revised Code.

(2) If the person is an offender who is a tier II sex offender/child-victim offender relative to the sexually oriented offense or child-victim oriented offense, the offender's duty to comply with those sections continues for twenty-five years. Except as otherwise provided in this division, if the person is a delinquent child who is a tier II sex offender/child-victim offender relative to the sexually oriented offense or child-victim oriented offense, the delinquent child's duty to comply with those sections continues for twenty years. Regarding a delinquent child who is a tier II sex offender/child-victim offender relative to the offense but is not a public registry-qualified juvenile offender registrant relative to the offense, if the judge who made the disposition for the delinquent child or that judge's successor in office subsequently enters a determination pursuant to section 2152.84 or 2152.85 of the Revised Code that the delinquent child no longer is a tier II sex offender/child-victim offender but remains a juvenile offender registrant, the delinquent child's duty to comply with those sections continues for the period of time that is applicable to the delinquent child under division (B)(3) of this section, based on the reclassification of the child pursuant to section 2152.84 or 2152.85 of the Revised Code as a tier I sex offender/child-victim offender.

(3) Except as otherwise provided in this division, if the person is an offender who is a tier I sex offender/child-victim offender relative to the sexually oriented offense or child-victim oriented offense, the offender's duty to comply with those sections continues for fifteen years. Except as otherwise provided in this division, if the person is a delinquent child who is a tier I sex offender/child-victim offender relative to the sexually oriented offense or child-victim oriented offense, the delinquent child's duty to comply with those sections continues for ten years. Regarding a delinquent child who is a juvenile offender registrant and a tier I sex offender/child-victim offender but is not a public registry-qualified juvenile offender registrant, if the judge who made the disposition for the delinquent child or that judge's successor in office subsequently enters a determination pursuant to section 2152.84 or 2152.85 of the Revised Code that the delinquent child no longer is to be classified a juvenile offender registrant, the delinquent child's duty to comply with those sections terminates upon the court's entry of the determination. A person who is an offender who is a tier I sex offender/child-victim offender may have the fifteen-year duty to register terminated only pursuant to section 2950.15 of the Revised Code.

(C)(1) If an offender has been convicted of or pleaded guilty to a sexually oriented offense and the offender subsequently is convicted of or pleads guilty to another sexually oriented offense or a child-victim oriented offense, if an offender has been convicted of or pleaded guilty to a child-victim oriented offense and the offender subsequently is convicted of or pleads guilty to another child-victim oriented offense or a sexually oriented offense, if a delinquent child has been adjudicated a delinquent child for committing a sexually oriented offense and is classified a juvenile offender registrant or is an out-of-state juvenile offender registrant and the child subsequently is adjudicated a delinquent child for committing another sexually oriented offense or a child-victim oriented offense and is classified a juvenile offender registrant relative to that offense or subsequently is convicted of or pleads guilty to another sexually oriented offense or a child-victim oriented offense, or if a delinquent child has been adjudicated a delinquent child for committing a child-victim oriented offense and is classified a juvenile offender registrant or is an out-of-state juvenile offender registrant and the child subsequently is adjudicated a delinquent child for committing another child-victim oriented offense or a sexually oriented offense and is classified a juvenile offender registrant relative to that offense or subsequently is convicted of or pleads guilty to another child-victim oriented offense or a sexually oriented offense, the period of time for which the offender or delinquent child must comply with the sections specified in division (A) of this section shall be separately calculated pursuant to divisions (A)(1) to (8) and (B)(1) to (3) of this section for each of the sexually oriented offenses and child-victim oriented offenses, and the offender or delinquent child shall comply with each separately calculated period of time independently.

If a delinquent child has been adjudicated a delinquent child for committing a sexually oriented offense or a child-victim oriented offense, is classified a juvenile offender registrant or is an out-of-state juvenile offender registrant relative to that offense, and, after attaining eighteen years of age, subsequently is convicted of or pleads guilty to another sexually oriented offense or child-victim oriented offense, the subsequent conviction or guilty plea does not limit, affect, or supersede the duties imposed upon the delinquent child under this chapter relative to the delinquent child's classification as a juvenile offender registrant or as an out-of-state juvenile offender registrant, and the delinquent child shall comply with both those duties and the duties imposed under this chapter relative to the subsequent conviction or guilty plea.

(2) If a delinquent child has been adjudicated a delinquent child for committing a sexually oriented offense or a child-victim oriented offense and is classified a juvenile offender registrant relative to the offense and if the juvenile judge or the judge's successor in office subsequently reclassifies the offense tier in which the child is classified pursuant to section 2152.84 or 2152.85 of the Revised Code, the judge's subsequent determination to reclassify the child does not affect the date of commencement of the delinquent child's duty to comply with sections 2950.04, 2950.041 [2950.04.1], 2950.05, and 2950.06 of the Revised Code as determined under division (A) of this section. The child's duty to comply with those sections after the reclassification is a continuation of the child's duty to comply with the sections that was in effect prior to the reclassification, and the duty shall continue for the period of time specified in division (B)(1), (2), or (3) of this section, whichever is applicable.

If, prior to January 1, 2008, an offender had a duty to comply with the sections specified in division (A) of this section as a result of a conviction of or plea of guilty to a sexually oriented offense or child-victim oriented offense as those terms were defined in section 2950.01 of the Revised Code prior to January 1, 2008, or a delinquent child had a duty to comply with those sections as a result of an adjudication as a delinquent child for committing one of those offenses as they were defined prior to January 1, 2008, the period of time specified in division (B)(1), (2), or (3) of this section on and after January 1, 2008, for which a person must comply with sections 2950.04, 2950.041 [2950.04.1], 2950.05, and 2950.06 of the Revised Code applies to the person, automatically replaces the period of time for which the person had to comply with those sections prior to January 1, 2008, and is a continuation of the person's duty to comply with the sections that was in effect prior to the reclassification. If, prior to January 1, 2008, an offender or a delinquent child had a duty to comply with the sections specified in division (A) of this section, the offender's or delinquent child's classification as a tier I sex offender/child-victim offender, a tier II sex offender/child-victim offender, or a tier III sex offender/child-victim offender for purposes of that period of time shall be determined as specified in section 2950.031 [2950.03.1] or 2950.032 [2950.03.2] of the Revised Code, as applicable.

(D) The duty of an offender or delinquent child to register under this chapter is tolled for any period during which the offender or delinquent child is returned to confinement in a secure facility for any reason or imprisoned for an offense when the confinement in a secure facility or imprisonment occurs subsequent to the date determined pursuant to division (A) of this section. The offender's or delinquent child's duty to register under this chapter resumes upon the offender's or delinquent child's release from confinement in a secure facility or imprisonment.

(E) An offender or delinquent child who has been or is convicted, has pleaded or pleads guilty, or has been or is adjudicated a delinquent child, in a court in another state, in a federal court, military court, or Indian tribal court, or in a court of any nation other than the United States for committing a sexually oriented offense or a child-victim oriented offense may apply to the sheriff of the county in which the offender or delinquent child resides or temporarily is domiciled, or in which the offender attends a school or institution of higher education or is employed, for credit against the duty to register for the time that the offender or delinquent child has complied with the sex offender or child-victim offender registration requirements of another jurisdiction. The sheriff shall grant the offender or delinquent child credit against the duty to register for time for which the offender or delinquent child provides adequate proof that the offender or delinquent child has complied with the sex offender or child-victim offender registration requirements of another jurisdiction. If the offender or delinquent child disagrees with the determination of the sheriff, the offender or delinquent child may appeal the determination to the court of common pleas of the county in which the offender or delinquent child resides or is temporarily domiciled, or in which the offender attends a school or institution of higher education or is employed.

**HISTORY: 146 v H 180 (Eff 7-1-97); 147 v H 565 (Eff 3-30-99); 149 v S 3 (Eff 1-1-2002); 149 v H 485. Eff 6-13-2002; 150 v S 5, § 1, eff. 7-31-03; 152 v S 10, § 1, eff. 1-1-08.**

The effective date is set by § 3 of 152 v S 10.

**Not analogous to former RC § 2950.07 (130 v 671), repealed 146 v H 180, § 2, eff 7-1-97.**

## § 2950.08 Persons authorized to inspect information and records.

(A) Subject to division (B) of this section, the statements, information, photographs, fingerprints, and material required by sections 2950.04, 2950.041 [2950.04.1], 2950.05, and 2950.06 of the Revised Code and provided by a person who registers, who provides notice of a change of residence, school, institution of higher education, or place of employment address and registers the new residence, school, institution of higher education, or place of employment address, or who provides verification of a current residence, school, institution of higher education, or place of employment address pursuant to those sections and that are in the possession of the bureau of criminal identification and investigation and the information in the possession of the bureau that was received by the bureau pursuant to section 2950.14 of the Revised Code shall not be open to inspection by the public or by any person other than the following persons:

(1) A regularly employed peace officer or other law enforcement officer;

(2) An authorized employee of the bureau of criminal identification and investigation for the purpose of providing information to a board, administrator, or person pursuant to division (F) or (G) of section 109.57 of the Revised Code;

(3) The registrar of motor vehicles, or an employee of the registrar of motor vehicles, for the purpose of verifying and updating any of the information so provided, upon the request of the bureau of criminal identification and investigation.

(B) Division (A) of this section does not apply to any information that is contained in the internet sex offender and child-victim offender database established by the attorney general under division (A)(11) of section 2950.13 of the Revised Code regarding offenders and that is disseminated as described in that division.

**HISTORY: 130 v 671 (Eff 10-4-63); 143 v S 140 (Eff 10-2-89); 146 v S 160 (Eff 1-27-97); 146 v H 180. Eff 7-1-97; 150 v S 5, § 1, Eff 7-31-03; 152 v S 10, § 1, eff. 1-1-08.**

The effective date is set by § 3 of 152 v S 10.

The provisions of § 7 of S.B. 5 (150 v —) read as follows:

SECTION 7. (A) Section 2950.08 of the Revised Code is presented in Section 1 of this act as a composite of the section as amended by both Am. Sub. H.B. 180 and Am. Sub. S.B. 160 of the 121st General Assembly. The General Assembly, applying the principle stated in division (B) of section 1.52 of the Revised Code that amendments are to be harmonized if reasonably capable of simultaneous operation, finds that the composites are the resulting versions of the sections in effect prior to the effective date of the sections as presented in Section 1 of this act.

The effective date is set by section 5 of HB 180.

## § 2950.081 Disclosure of sex offender registration information in possession of sheriff; internet database provisions.

(A) Any statements, information, photographs, fingerprints, or materials that are required to be provided, and that are provided, by an offender or delinquent child pursuant to section 2950.04, 2950.041 [2950.04.1], 2950.05, or 2950.06 of the Revised Code and that are in the possession of a county sheriff are public records open to public inspection under section 149.43 of the Revised Code and shall be included in the internet sex offender and child-victim offender database established and maintained under section 2950.13 of the Revised Code to the extent provided in that section.

(B) Except when the child is classified a public registry-qualified juvenile offender registrant, the sheriff shall not cause to be publicly disseminated by means of the internet any statements, information, photographs, fingerprints, or materials that are provided by a delinquent child who sends a notice of intent to reside, registers, provides notice of a change of residence address and registers the new residence address, or provides verification of a current residence address pursuant to this chapter and that are in the possession of a county sheriff.

(C) If a sheriff establishes on the internet a sex offender and child-victim offender database for the public dissemination of some or all of the materials that are described in division (A) of this section, that are not prohibited from inclusion by division (B) of this section, and that pertain to offenders or delinquent children who register in the sheriff's county, in addition to all of the other information and materials included, the sheriff shall include in the database a chart describing which sexually oriented offenses and child-victim oriented offenses are included in the definitions of tier I sex offender/child-victim offender, tier II sex offender/child-victim offender, and tier III sex offender/child-victim offender and for each offender or delinquent child in relation to whom information and materials are provided a statement as to whether the offender or delinquent child is a tier I sex offender/child-victim offenders, a tier II sex offender/child-victim offenders, or a tier III sex offender/child-victim offenders.

**HISTORY: 149 v S 3. Eff 1-1-2002; 150 v S 5, § 1, Eff 7-31-03; 152 v S 10, § 1, eff. 1-1-08.**

The effective date is set by § 3 of 152 v S 10.

## § 2950.09 Repealed, 152 v S 10, § 2 [146 v H 180 (Eff 1-1-97); 147 v H 565 (Eff 3-30-99); 148 v H 502 (Eff 3-15-2001); 149 v S 3 (Eff 1-1-2002); 149 v S 175 (Eff 5-7-2002); 149 v H 485 (Eff 6-13-2002); 149 v H 393. Eff 7-5-2002; 150 v S 5, § 1, eff. 7-31-03; 150 v H 473, § 1, eff. 4-29-05; 151 v S 260, § 1, eff. 1-2-07]. Eff 1-1-08.

The effective date is set by § 3 of 152 v S 10.
This section concerned classification as a sexual predator, determination hearings, and petitions for removal from classification.

## § 2950.091 Repealed, 152 v S 10, § 2 [150 v S 5, § 1, eff. 7-31-03]. Eff 1-1-08.

The effective date is set by § 3 of 152 v S 10.
This section concerned classification as a child-victim predator or habitual child-victim offender.

## § 2950.10 Notice to victim of offender's or delinquent child's registration or change of information.

(A)(1) Regardless of when the sexually oriented offense or child-victim oriented offense was committed, if a person is convicted of, pleads guilty to, has been convicted of, or has pleaded guilty to a sexually oriented offense or a child-victim oriented offense or a person is or has been adjudicated a delinquent child for committing a sexually oriented offense or a child-victim oriented offense and is classified a juvenile offender registrant or is an out-of-state juvenile offender registrant based on that adjudication, if the offender or delinquent child is in any category specified in division (B)(1)(a), (b), or (c) of this section, if the offender or delinquent child registers with a sheriff pursuant to section 2950.04, 2950.041 [2950.04.1], or 2950.05 of the Revised Code, and if the victim of the sexually oriented offense or child-victim oriented offense has made a request in accordance with rules adopted by the attorney general that specifies that the victim would like to be provided the notices described in this section, the sheriff shall notify the victim of the sexually oriented offense or child-victim oriented offense, in writing, that the offender or delinquent child has registered and shall include in the notice the offender's name and photograph, and the address or addresses of the offender's residence, school, institution of higher education, or place of employment, as applicable, or the delinquent child's name, photograph, and residence address or addresses. The sheriff shall provide the notice required by this division to the victim at the most recent residence address available for that victim and not later than five days after the offender or delinquent child registers with the sheriff.

(2) Regardless of when the sexually oriented offense or child-victim oriented offense was committed, if a person is convicted of, pleads guilty to, has been convicted of, or has pleaded guilty to a sexually oriented offense or a child-victim oriented offense or a person is or has been adjudicated a delinquent child for committing a sexually oriented offense or a child-victim oriented offense and is classified a juvenile offender registrant or is an out-of-state juvenile offender registrant based on that adjudication, if the offender or delinquent child is in any category specified in division (B)(1)(a), (b), or (c) of this section, if the offender or delinquent child registers with a sheriff pursuant to section 2950.04, 2950.041 [2950.04.1], or 2950.05 of the Revised Code, if the victim of the sexually oriented offense or child-victim oriented offense has made a request in accordance with rules adopted by the attorney general that specifies that the victim would like to be provided the notices described in this section, and if the offender notifies the sheriff of a change of residence, school, institution of higher education, or place of employment address or the delinquent child notifies the sheriff of a change of residence address pursuant to section 2950.05 of the Revised Code, the sheriff shall notify the victim of the sexually oriented offense or child-victim oriented offense, in writing, that the offender's or delinquent child's address has changed and shall include in the notice the offender's name and photograph, and the new address or addresses of the offender's residence, school, institution of higher education, or place of employment, as applicable, or the delinquent child's name, photograph, and new residence address or addresses. The sheriff shall provide the notice required by this division to the victim at the most recent residence address available for that victim and no later than five days after the offender or delinquent child notifies the sheriff of the change in the offender's or delinquent child's residence, school, institution of higher education, or place of employment address.

(3) Regardless of when the sexually oriented offense or child-victim oriented offense was committed, if a person is convicted of, pleads guilty to, has been convicted of, or has pleaded guilty to a sexually oriented offense or a child-victim oriented offense or a person is or has been adjudicated a delinquent child for committing a sexually oriented offense or a child-victim oriented offense and is classified a juvenile offender registrant or is an out-of-state juvenile

offender registrant based on that adjudication, and if the offender or delinquent child is in any category specified in division (B)(1)(a), (b), or (c) of this section, the victim of the offense may make a request in accordance with rules adopted by the attorney general pursuant to section 2950.13 of the Revised Code that specifies that the victim would like to be provided the notices described in divisions (A)(1) and (2) of this section. If the victim makes a request in accordance with those rules, the sheriff described in divisions (A)(1) and (2) of this section shall provide the victim with the notices described in those divisions.

(4) If a victim makes a request as described in division (A)(3) of this section that specifies that the victim would like to be provided the notices described in divisions (A)(1) and (2) of this section, all information a sheriff obtains regarding the victim from or as a result of the request is confidential, and the information is not a public record open for inspection under section 149.43 of the Revised Code.

(5) The notices described in divisions (A)(1) and (2) of this section are in addition to any notices regarding the offender or delinquent child that the victim is entitled to receive under Chapter 2930. of the Revised Code.

(B)(1) The duties to provide the notices described in divisions (A)(1) and (2) of this section apply regarding any offender or delinquent child who is in any of the following categories:

(a) The offender is a tier III sex offender/child-victim offender relative to the offense described in division (A) of this section for which a victim requested to be provided notice under that division, or the delinquent child is a public registry-qualified juvenile offender registrant, and a juvenile court has not removed pursuant to section 2950.15 of the Revised Code the delinquent child's duty to comply with sections 2950.04, 2950.041 [2950.04.1], 2950.05, and 2950.06 of the Revised Code.

(b) The delinquent child is a tier III sex offender/child-victim offender who is not a public-registry qualified juvenile offender registrant, the delinquent child was subjected to this section prior to the effective date of this amendment as a sexual predator, habitual sex offender, child-victim predator, or habitual child-victim offender, as those terms were defined in section 2950.01 of the Revised Code as it existed prior to the effective date of this amendment, and a juvenile court has not removed pursuant to section 2152.84 or 2152.85 of the Revised Code the delinquent child's duty to comply with sections 2950.04, 2950.041 [2950.04.1], 2950.05, and 2950.06 of the Revised Code.

(c) The delinquent child is a tier III sex offender/child-victim offender who is not a public registry-qualified juvenile offender registrant, the delinquent child was classified a juvenile offender registrant on or after the effective date of this amendment, the court has imposed a requirement under section 2152.82, 2152.83, or 2152.84 of the Revised Code subjecting the delinquent child to this section, and a juvenile court has not removed pursuant to section 2152.84 or 2152.85 of the Revised Code the delinquent child's duty to comply with sections 2950.04, 2950.041 [2950.04.1], 2950.05, and 2950.06 of the Revised Code.

(2) A victim of a sexually oriented offense or of a child-victim oriented offense is not entitled to be provided any notice described in division (A)(1) or (2) of this section unless the offender or delinquent child is in a category specified in division (B)(1)(a), (b), or (c) of this section. A victim of a sexually oriented offense or of a child-victim oriented offense is not entitled to any notice described in division (A)(1) or (2) of this section unless the victim makes a request in accordance with rules adopted by the attorney general pursuant to section 2950.13 of the Revised Code that specifies that the victim would like to be provided the notices described in divisions (A)(1) and (2) of this section. This division does not affect any rights of a victim of a sexually oriented offense or child-victim oriented offense to be provided notice regarding an offender or delinquent child that are described in Chapter 2930. of the Revised Code.

**HISTORY: 146 v H 180 (Eff 7-1-97); 147 v H 565 (Eff 3-30-99); 149 v S 3 (Eff 1-1-2002); 149 v H 485. Eff 6-13-2002; 150 v S 5, § 1, Eff 7-31-03; 151 v H 15, § 1, eff. 11-23-05; 152 v S 10, § 1, eff. 1-1-08.**

The effective date is set by § 3 of 152 v S 10.

## § 2950.11 Community notification provisions.

(A) Regardless of when the sexually oriented offense or child-victim oriented offense was committed, if a person is convicted of, pleads guilty to, has been convicted of, or has pleaded guilty to a sexually oriented offense or a child-victim oriented offense or a person is or has been adjudicated a delinquent child for committing a sexually oriented offense or a child-victim oriented offense and is classified a juvenile offender registrant or is an out-of-state juvenile offender registrant based on that adjudication, and if the offender or delinquent child is in any category specified in division (F)(1)(a), (b), or (c) of this section, the sheriff with whom the offender or delinquent child has most recently registered under section 2950.04, 2950.041 [2950.04.1], or 2950.05 of the Revised Code and the sheriff to whom the offender or delinquent child most recently sent a notice of intent to reside under section 2950.04 or 2950.041 [2950.04.1] of the Revised Code, within the period of time specified in division (C) of this section, shall provide a written notice containing the information set forth in division (B) of this section to all of the persons described in divisions (A)(1) to (10) of this section. If the sheriff has sent a notice to the persons described in those divisions as a result of receiving a notice of intent to reside and if the offender or delinquent child registers a residence address that is the same residence address described in the notice of intent to reside, the sheriff is not required to send an additional notice when the offender or delinquent child registers. The sheriff shall provide the notice to all of the following persons:

(1)(a) Any occupant of each residential unit that is located within one thousand feet of the offender's or delinquent child's residential premises, that is located within the county served by the sheriff, and that is not located in a multi-unit building. Division (D)(3) of this section applies regarding notices required under this division.

(b) If the offender or delinquent child resides in a multi-unit building, any occupant of each residential unit that is located in that multi-unit building and that shares a common hallway with the offender or delinquent child. For purposes of this division, an occupant's unit shares a common hallway with the offender or delinquent child if the entrance door into the occupant's unit is located on the same floor and opens into the same hallway as the entrance door to the unit the offender or delinquent child occupies. Division (D)(3) of this section applies regarding notices required under this division.

(c) The building manager, or the person the building owner or condominium unit owners association authorizes to exercise management and control, of each multi-unit building that is located within one thousand feet of the offender's or delinquent child's residential premises, including a multi-unit building in which the offender or delinquent child resides, and that is located within the county served by the sheriff. In addition to notifying the building manager or the person authorized to exercise management and control in the multi-unit building under this division, the sheriff shall post a copy of the notice prominently in each common entryway in the building and any other location in the building the sheriff determines appropriate. The manager or person exercising management and control of the building shall permit the sheriff to post copies of the notice under this division as the sheriff determines appropriate. In lieu of posting copies of the notice as described in this division, a sheriff may provide notice to all occupants of the multi-unit building by mail or personal contact; if the sheriff so notifies all the occupants, the sheriff is not required to post copies of the notice in the common entryways to the building. Division (D)(3) of this section applies regarding notices required under this division.

(d) All additional persons who are within any category of neighbors of the offender or delinquent child that the attorney general by rule adopted under section 2950.13 of the Revised Code requires to be provided the notice and who reside within the county served by the sheriff;

(2) The executive director of the public children services agency that has jurisdiction within the specified geographical notification area and that is located within the county served by the sheriff;

(3)(a) The superintendent of each board of education of a school district that has schools within the specified geographical notification area and that is located within the county served by the sheriff;

(b) The principal of the school within the specified geographical notification area and within the county served by the sheriff that the delinquent child attends;

(c) If the delinquent child attends a school outside of the specified geographical notification area or outside of the school district where the delinquent child resides, the superintendent of the board of education of a school district that governs the school that the delinquent child attends and the principal of the school that the delinquent child attends.

(4)(a) The appointing or hiring officer of each chartered nonpublic school located within the specified geographical notification area and within the county served by the sheriff or of each other school located within the specified geographical notification area and within the county served by the sheriff and that is not operated by a board of education described in division (A)(3) of this section;

(b) Regardless of the location of the school, the appointing or hiring officer of a chartered nonpublic school that the delinquent child attends.

(5) The director, head teacher, elementary principal, or site administrator of each preschool program governed by Chapter 3301. of the Revised Code that is located within the specified geographical notification area and within the county served by the sheriff;

(6) The administrator of each child day-care center or type A family day-care home that is located within the specified geographical notification area and within the county served by the sheriff, and the provider of each certified type B family day-care home that is located within the specified geographical notification area and within the county served by the sheriff. As used in this division, "child day-care center," "type A family day-care home," and "certified type B family day-care home" have the same meanings as in section 5104.01 of the Revised Code.

(7) The president or other chief administrative officer of each institution of higher education, as defined in section 2907.03 of the Revised Code, that is located within the specified geographical notification area and within the county served by the sheriff, and the chief law enforcement officer of the state university law enforcement agency or campus police department established under section 3345.04 or 1713.50 of the Revised Code, if any, that serves that institution;

(8) The sheriff of each county that includes any portion of the specified geographical notification area;

(9) If the offender or delinquent child resides within the county served by the sheriff, the chief of police, marshal, or other chief law enforcement officer of the municipal corporation in which the offender or delinquent child resides or, if the offender or delinquent child resides in an unincorporated area, the constable or chief of the police department or police district police force of the township in which the offender or delinquent child resides;

(10) Volunteer organizations in which contact with minors or other vulnerable individuals might occur or any organization, company, or individual who requests notification as provided in division (J) of this section.

(B) The notice required under division (A) of this section shall include all of the following information regarding the subject offender or delinquent child:

(1) The offender's or delinquent child's name;

(2) The address or addresses of the offender's or public registry-qualified juvenile offender registrant's residence, school, institution of higher education, or place of employment, as applicable, or the residence address or addresses of a delinquent child who is not a public registry-qualified juvenile offender registrant;

(3) The sexually oriented offense or child-victim oriented offense of which the offender was convicted, to which the offender pleaded guilty, or for which the child was adjudicated a delinquent child;

(4) A statement that identifies the category specified in division (F)(1)(a), (b), or (c) of this section that includes the offender or delinquent child and that subjects the offender or delinquent child to this section;

(5) The offender's or delinquent child's photograph.

(C) If a sheriff with whom an offender or delinquent child registers under section 2950.04, 2950.041 [2950.04.1], or 2950.05 of the Revised Code or to whom the offender or delinquent child most recently sent a notice of intent to reside under section 2950.04 or 2950.041 [2950.04.1] of the Revised Code is required by division (A) of this section to provide notices regarding an offender or delinquent child and if, pursuant to that requirement, the sheriff provides a notice to a sheriff of one or more other counties in accordance with division (A)(8) of this section, the sheriff of each of the other counties who is provided notice under division (A)(8) of this section shall provide the notices described in divisions (A)(1) to (7) and (A)(9) and (10) of this section to each person or entity identified within those divisions that is located within the specified geographical notification area and within the county served by the sheriff in question.

(D)(1) A sheriff required by division (A) or (C) of this section to provide notices regarding an offender or delinquent child shall provide the notice to the neighbors that are described in division (A)(1) of this section and the notices to law enforcement personnel that are described in divisions (A)(8) and (9) of this section as soon as practicable, but no later than five days after the offender sends the notice of intent to reside to the sheriff and again no later than five days after the offender or delinquent child registers with the sheriff or, if the sheriff is required by division (C) of this section to provide the notices, no later than five days after the sheriff is provided the notice described in division (A)(8) of this section.

A sheriff required by division (A) or (C) of this section to provide notices regarding an offender or delinquent child shall provide the notices to all other specified persons that are described in divisions (A)(2) to (7) and (A)(10) of this section as soon as practicable, but not later than seven days after the offender or delinquent child registers with the sheriff or, if the sheriff is required by division (C) of this section to provide the notices, no later than five days after the sheriff is provided the notice described in division (A)(8) of this section.

(2) If an offender or delinquent child in relation to whom division (A) of this section applies verifies the offender's or delinquent child's current residence, school, institution of higher education, or place of employment address, as applicable, with a sheriff pursuant to section 2950.06 of the Revised Code, the sheriff may provide a written notice containing the information set forth in division (B) of this section to the persons identified in divisions (A)(1) to (10) of this section. If a sheriff provides a notice pursuant to this division to the sheriff of one or more other counties in accordance with division (A)(8) of this section, the sheriff of each of the other counties who is provided the notice under division (A)(8) of this section may provide, but is not required to provide, a written notice containing the information set forth in division (B) of this section to the persons identified in divisions (A)(1) to (7) and (A)(9) and (10) of this section.

(3) A sheriff may provide notice under division (A)(1)(a) or (b) of this section, and may provide notice under division (A)(1)(c) of this section to a building manager or person authorized to exercise management and control of a building, by mail, by personal contact, or by leaving the notice at or under the entry door to a residential unit. For purposes of divisions (A)(1)(a) and (b) of this section, and the portion of division (A)(1)(c) of this section relating to the provision of notice to occupants of a multi-unit building by mail or personal contact, the provision of one written notice per unit is deemed as providing notice to all occupants of that unit.

(E) All information that a sheriff possesses regarding an offender or delinquent child who is in a category specified in division (F)(1)(a), (b), or (c) of this section that is described in division (B) of this section and that must be provided in a notice required under division (A) or (C) of this section or that may be provided in a notice authorized under division (D)(2) of this section is a public record that is open to inspection under section 149.43 of the Revised Code.

The sheriff shall not cause to be publicly disseminated by means of the internet any of the information described in this division that is provided by a delinquent child unless that child is in a category specified in division (F)(1)(a), (b), or (c) of this section.

(F)(1) Except as provided in division (F)(2) of this section, the duties to provide the notices described in divisions (A) and (C) of this section apply regarding any offender or delinquent child who is in any of the following categories:

(a) The offender is a tier III sex offender/child-victim offender, or the delinquent child is a public registry-qualified juvenile offender registrant, and a juvenile court has not removed pursuant to section 2950.15 of the Revised Code the delinquent child's duty to comply with sections 2950.04, 2950.041 [2950.04.1], 2950.05, and 2950.06 of the Revised Code.

(b) The delinquent child is a tier III sex offender/child-victim offender who is not a public-registry qualified juvenile offender registrant, the delinquent child was subjected to this section prior to the effective date of this amendment as a sexual predator, habitual sex offender, child-victim predator, or habitual child-victim offender, as those terms were defined in section 2950.01 of the Revised Code as it existed prior to the effective date of this amendment, and a juvenile court has not removed pursuant to section 2152.84 or 2152.85 of the Revised Code the delinquent child's duty to comply with sections 2950.04, 2950.041 [2950.04.1], 2950.05, and 2950.06 of the Revised Code.

(c) The delinquent child is a tier III sex offender/child-victim offender who is not a public registry-qualified juvenile offender registrant, the delinquent child was classified a juvenile offender registrant on or after the effective date of this amendment, the court has imposed a requirement under section 2152.82, 2152.83, or 2152.84 of the Revised Code subjecting the delinquent child to this section, and a juvenile court has not removed pursuant to section 2152.84 or 2152.85 of the Revised Code the delinquent child's duty to comply with sections 2950.04, 2950.041 [2950.04.1], 2950.05, and 2950.06 of the Revised Code.

(2) The notification provisions of this section do not apply to a person described in division (F)(1)(a), (b), or (c) of this section if a court finds at a hearing after considering the factors described in this division that the person would not be subject to the notification provisions of this section that were in the version of this section that existed immediately prior to the effective date of this amendment. In making the determination of whether a person would have been subject to the notification provisions under prior law as described in this division, the court shall consider the following factors:

(a) The offender's or delinquent child's age;

(b) The offender's or delinquent child's prior criminal or delinquency record regarding all offenses, including, but not limited to, all sexual offenses;

(c) The age of the victim of the sexually oriented offense for which sentence is to be imposed or the order of disposition is to be made;

(d) Whether the sexually oriented offense for which sentence is to be imposed or the order of disposition is to be made involved multiple victims;

(e) Whether the offender or delinquent child used drugs or alcohol to impair the victim of the sexually oriented offense or to prevent the victim from resisting;

(f) If the offender or delinquent child previously has been convicted of or pleaded guilty to, or been adjudicated a delinquent child for committing an act that if committed by an adult would be, a criminal offense, whether the offender or delinquent child completed any sentence or dispositional order imposed for the prior offense or act and, if the prior offense or act was a sex offense or a sexually oriented offense, whether the offender or delinquent child participated in available programs for sexual offenders;

(g) Any mental illness or mental disability of the offender or delinquent child;

(h) The nature of the offender's or delinquent child's sexual conduct, sexual contact, or interaction in a sexual context with the victim of the sexually oriented offense and whether the sexual conduct, sexual contact, or interaction in a sexual context was part of a demonstrated pattern of abuse;

(i) Whether the offender or delinquent child, during the commission of the sexually oriented offense for which sentence is to be imposed or the order of disposition is to be made, displayed cruelty or made one or more threats of cruelty;

(j) Whether the offender or delinquent child would have been a habitual sex offender or a habitual child victim offender under the definitions of those terms set forth in section 2950.01 of the Revised Code as that section existed prior to the effective date of this amendment;

(k) Any additional behavioral characteristics that contribute to the offender's or delinquent child's conduct.

(G)(1) The department of job and family services shall compile, maintain, and update in January and July of each year, a list of all agencies, centers, or homes of a type described in division (A)(2) or (6) of this section that contains the name of each agency, center, or home of that type, the county in which it is located, its address and telephone number, and the name of an administrative officer or employee of the agency, center, or home.

(2) The department of education shall compile, maintain, and update in January and July of each year, a list of all boards of education, schools, or programs of a type described in division (A)(3), (4), or (5) of this section that contains the name of each board of education, school, or program of that type, the county in which it is located, its address and telephone number, the name of the superintendent of the board or of an administrative officer or employee of the school or program, and, in relation to a board of education, the county or counties in which each of its schools is located and the address of each such school.

(3) The Ohio board of regents shall compile, maintain, and update in January and July of each year, a list of all institutions of a type described in division (A)(7) of this section that contains the name of each such institution, the county in which it is located, its address and telephone number, and the name of its president or other chief administrative officer.

(4) A sheriff required by division (A) or (C) of this section, or authorized by division (D)(2) of this section, to provide notices regarding an offender or delinquent child, or a designee of a sheriff of that type, may request the department of job and family services, department of education, or Ohio board of regents, by telephone, in person, or by mail, to provide the sheriff or designee with the names, addresses, and telephone numbers of the appropriate persons and entities to whom the notices described in divisions (A)(2) to (7) of this section are to be provided. Upon receipt of a request, the department or board shall provide the requesting sheriff or designee with the names, addresses, and telephone numbers of the appropriate persons and entities to whom those notices are to be provided.

(H)(1) Upon the motion of the offender or the prosecuting attorney of the county in which the offender was convicted of or pleaded guilty to the sexually oriented offense or child-victim oriented offense for which the offender is subject to community notification under this section, or upon the motion of the sentencing judge or that judge's successor in office, the judge may schedule a hearing to determine whether the interests of justice would be served by suspending the community notification requirement under this section in relation to the offender. The judge may dismiss the motion without a hearing but may not issue an order suspending the community notification requirement without a hearing. At the hearing, all parties are entitled to be heard, and the judge shall consider all of the factors set forth in division (K) of this section. If, at the conclusion of the hearing, the judge finds that the offender has proven by clear and convincing evidence that the offender is unlikely to commit in the future a sexually oriented offense or a child-victim oriented offense and if the judge finds that suspending the community notification requirement is in the interests of justice, the judge may suspend the application of this section in relation to the offender. The order shall contain both of these findings.

The judge promptly shall serve a copy of the order upon the sheriff with whom the offender most recently registered under section 2950.04, 2950.041 [2950.04.1], or 2950.05 of the Revised Code and upon the bureau of criminal identification and investigation.

An order suspending the community notification requirement does not suspend or otherwise alter an offender's duties to comply with sections 2950.04, 2950.041 [2950.04.1], 2950.05, and 2950.06 of the Revised Code and does not suspend the victim notification requirement under section 2950.10 of the Revised Code.

(2) A prosecuting attorney, a sentencing judge or that judge's successor in office, and an offender who is subject to the community notification requirement under this section may initially make a motion under division (H)(1) of this section upon the expiration of twenty years after the offender's duty to comply with division (A)(2), (3), or (4) of section 2950.04, division (A)(2), (3), or (4) of section 2950.041 [2950.04.1] and sections 2950.05 and 2950.06 of the Revised Code begins in relation to the offense for which the offender is subject to community notification. After the initial making of a motion under division (H)(1) of this section, thereafter, the prosecutor, judge, and offender may make a subsequent motion under that division upon the expiration of five years after the judge has entered an order denying the initial motion or the most recent motion made under that division.

(3) The offender and the prosecuting attorney have the right to appeal an order approving or denying a motion made under division (H)(1) of this section.

(4) Divisions (H)(1) to (3) of this section do not apply to any of the following types of offender:

(a) A person who is convicted of or pleads guilty to a violent sex offense or designated homicide, assault, or kidnapping offense and who, in relation to that offense, is adjudicated a sexually violent predator;

(b) A person who is convicted of or pleads guilty to a sexually oriented offense that is a violation of division (A)(1)(b) of section 2907.02 of the Revised Code committed on or after January 2, 2007, and either who is sentenced under section 2971.03 of the Revised Code or upon whom a sentence of life without parole is imposed under division (B) of section 2907.02 of the Revised Code;

(c) A person who is convicted of or pleads guilty to a sexually oriented offense that is attempted rape committed on or after January 2, 2007, and who also is convicted of or pleads guilty to a specification of the type described in section 2941.1418 [2941.14.18], 2941.1419 [2941.14.19], or 2941.1420 [2941.14.20] of the Revised Code;

(d) A person who is convicted of or pleads guilty to an offense described in division (B)(3)(a), (b), (c), or (d) of section 2971.03 of the Revised Code and who is sentenced for that offense pursuant to that division;

(e) An offender who is in a category specified in division (F)(1)(a), (b), or (c) of this section and who, subsequent to being subjected to community notification, has pleaded guilty to or been convicted of a sexually oriented offense or child-victim oriented offense.

(I) If a person is convicted of, pleads guilty to, has been convicted of, or has pleaded guilty to a sexually oriented offense or a child-victim oriented offense or a person is or has been adjudicated a delinquent child for committing a sexually oriented offense or a child-victim oriented offense and is classified a juvenile offender registrant or is an out-of-state juvenile offender registrant based on that adjudication, and if the offender or delinquent child is not in any category specified in division (F)(1)(a), (b), or (c) of this section, the sheriff with whom the offender or delinquent child has most recently registered under section 2950.04, 2950.041 [2950.04.1], or 2950.05 of the Revised Code and the sheriff to whom the offender or delinquent child most recently sent a notice of intent to reside under section 2950.04 or 2950.041 [2950.04.1] of the Revised Code, within the period of time specified in division (D) of this section, shall provide a written notice containing the information set forth in division (B) of this section to the executive director of the public children services agency that has jurisdiction within the specified geographical notification area and that is located within the county served by the sheriff.

(J) Each sheriff shall allow a volunteer organization or other organization, company, or individual who wishes to receive the notice described in division (A)(10) of this section regarding a specific offender or delinquent child or notice regarding all offenders and delinquent children who are located in the specified geographical notification area to notify the sheriff by electronic mail or through the sheriff's web site of this election. The sheriff shall promptly inform the bureau of criminal identification and investigation of these requests in accordance with the forwarding procedures adopted by the attorney general pursuant to section 2950.13 of the Revised Code.

(K) In making a determination under division (H)(1) of this section as to whether to suspend the community notification requirement under this section for an offender, the judge shall consider all relevant factors, including, but not limited to, all of the following:

(1) The offender's age;

(2) The offender's prior criminal or delinquency record regarding all offenses, including, but not limited to, all sexually oriented offenses or child-victim oriented offenses;

(3) The age of the victim of the sexually oriented offense or child-victim oriented offense the offender committed;

(4) Whether the sexually oriented offense or child-victim oriented offense the offender committed involved multiple victims;

(5) Whether the offender used drugs or alcohol to impair the victim of the sexually oriented offense or child-victim oriented the offender committed or to prevent the victim from resisting;

(6) If the offender previously has been convicted of, pleaded guilty to, or been adjudicated a delinquent child for committing an act that if committed by an adult would be a criminal offense, whether the offender completed any sentence or dispositional order imposed for the prior offense or act and, if the prior offense or act was a sexually oriented offense or a child-victim oriented offense, whether the offender or delinquent child participated in available programs for sex offenders or child-victim offenders;

(7) Any mental illness or mental disability of the offender;

(8) The nature of the offender's sexual conduct, sexual contact, or interaction in a sexual context with the victim of the sexually oriented offense the offender committed or the nature of the offender's interaction in a sexual context with the victim of the child-victim oriented offense the offender committed, whichever is applicable, and whether the sexual conduct, sexual contact, or interaction in a sexual context was part of a demonstrated pattern of abuse;

(9) Whether the offender, during the commission of the sexually oriented offense or child-victim oriented offense the offender committed, displayed cruelty or made one or more threats of cruelty;

(10) Any additional behavioral characteristics that contribute to the offender's conduct.

(L) As used in this section, "specified geographical notification area" means the geographic area or areas within which the attorney general, by rule adopted under section 2950.13 of the Revised Code, requires the notice described in division (B) of this section to be given to the persons identified in divisions (A)(2) to (8) of this section.

**HISTORY: 146 v H 180 (Eff 7-1-97); 147 v H 396 (Eff 1-30-98); 147 v H 565 (Eff 3-30-99); 148 v H 471 (Eff 7-1-2000); 149 v S 3 (Eff 1-1-2002); 149 v S 175 (Eff 5-7-2002); 149 v H 485. Eff 6-13-2002; 150 v S 5, § 1, Eff 7-31-03; 150 v H 473, § 1, eff. 4-29-05; 151 v H 15, § 1, eff. 11-23-05; 151 v S 17, § 1, eff. 8-3-06; 151 v S 260, § 1, eff. 1-2-07; 152 v S 10, § 1, eff. 1-1-08.**

The effective date is set by § 3 of 152 v S 10.

## § 2950.111 Sheriff or designee may request confirmation of offender or delinquent child's address.

(A) If an offender or delinquent child registers a residence address, provides notice of a change of any residence address, or verifies a current residence address pursuant to section 2950.04, 2950.041 [2950.04.1], 2950.05, or 2950.06 of the Revised Code, all of the following apply:

(1) At any time after the registration, provision of the notice, or verification, the sheriff with whom the offender or delinquent child so registered or to whom the offender or delinquent child so provided the notice or verified the current address, or a designee of that sheriff, may contact a person who owns, leases, or otherwise has custody, control, or supervision of the premises at the address provided by the offender or delinquent child in the registration, the notice, or the verification and request that the person confirm or deny that the offender or delinquent child currently resides at that address.

(2) Upon receipt of a request under division (A)(1) of this section, notwithstanding any other provision of law, the person who owns, leases, or otherwise has custody, control, or supervision of the premises, or an agent of that person, shall comply with the request and inform the sheriff or designee who made the request whether or not the offender or delinquent child currently resides at that address.

(3) Section 2950.12 of the Revised Code applies to a person who, in accordance with division (A)(2) of this section, provides information of the type described in that division.

(B) Division (A) of this section applies regarding any public or private residential premises, including, but not limited to, a private residence, a multi-unit residential facility, a halfway house, a homeless shelter, or any other type of residential premises. Division (A) of this section does not apply regarding an offender's registration, provision of notice of a change in, or verification of a school, institution of higher education, or place of employment address pursuant to section 2950.04, 2950.041 [2950.04.1], 2950.05, or 2950.06 of the Revised Code.

(C) A sheriff or designee of a sheriff may attempt to confirm that an offender or delinquent child who registers a residence address, provides notice of a change of any residence address, or verifies a current residence address as described in division (A) of this section currently resides at the address in question in manners other than the manner provided in this section. A sheriff or designee of a sheriff is not limited in the number of requests that may be made under this section regarding any registration, provision of notice, or verification, or in the number of times that the sheriff or designee may attempt to confirm, in manners other than the manner provided in this section, that an offender or delinquent child currently resides at the address in question.

**HISTORY: 150 v S 5, § 1, Eff 7-31-03.**

## § 2950.12 Immunity.

(A) Except as provided in division (B) of this section, any of the following persons shall be immune from liability in a civil action to recover damages for injury, death, or loss to person or property allegedly caused by an act or omission in connection with a power, duty, responsibility, or authorization under this chapter or under rules adopted under authority of this chapter:

(1) An officer or employee of the bureau of criminal identification and investigation;

(2) The attorney general, a chief of police, marshal, or other chief law enforcement officer of a municipal corporation, a sheriff, a constable or chief of police of a township police department or police district police force, and a deputy, officer, or employee of the office of the attorney general, the law enforcement agency served by the marshal or the municipal or township chief, the office of the sheriff, or the constable;

(3) A prosecutor and an officer or employee of the office of a prosecutor;

(4) A supervising officer and an officer or employee of the adult parole authority of the department of rehabilitation and correction;

(5) A supervising officer and an officer or employee of the department of youth services;

(6) A supervisor and a caseworker or employee of a public children services agency acting pursuant to section 5153.16 of the Revised Code;

(7) A managing officer of a state correctional institution and an officer or employee of the department of rehabilitation and correction;

(8) A person identified in division (A)(2), (3), (4), (5), (6), or (7) of section 2950.11 of the Revised Code, an organization or person identified in division (A)(10) of that section, or the agent of that person or organization;

(9) A person identified in division (A)(2) of section 2950.111 [2950.11.1] of the Revised Code, regarding the person's provision of information pursuant to that division to a sheriff or a designee of a sheriff.

(B) The immunity described in division (A) of this section does not apply to a person described in divisions (A)(1) to (8) of this section if, in relation to the act or omission in question, any of the following applies:

(1) The act or omission was manifestly outside the scope of the person's employment or official responsibilities.

(2) The act or omission was with malicious purpose, in bad faith, or in a wanton or reckless manner.

(3) Liability for the act or omission is expressly imposed by a section of the Revised Code.

**HISTORY: 146 v H 180 (Eff 7-1-97); 149 v S 3 (Eff 1-1-2002); 149 v S 175. Eff 5-7-2002; 150 v S 5, § 1, eff. 7-31-03; 152 v S 10, § 1, eff. 1-1-08.**

The effective date is set by § 3 of 152 v S 10.

## § 2950.13 General duties of attorney general concerning SORN Law.

(A) The attorney general shall do all of the following:

(1) No later than July 1, 1997, establish and maintain a state registry of sex offenders and child-victim offenders that is housed at the bureau of criminal identification and investigation and that contains all of the registration, change of residence, school, institution of higher education, or place of employment address, and verification information the bureau receives pursuant to sections 2950.04, 2950.041 [2950.04.1], 2950.05, and 2950.06 of the Revised Code regarding each person who is convicted of, pleads guilty to, has been convicted of, or has pleaded guilty to a sexually oriented offense or a child-victim oriented offense and each person who is or has been adjudicated a delinquent child for committing a sexually oriented offense or a child-victim oriented offense and is classified a juvenile offender registrant or is an out-of-state juvenile offender registrant based on that adjudication, all of the information the bureau receives pursuant to section 2950.14 of the Revised Code, and any notice of an order terminating or modifying an offender's or delinquent child's duty to comply with sections 2950.04, 2950.041 [2950.04.1], 2950.05, and 2950.06 of the Revised Code the bureau receives pursuant to section 2152.84, 2152.85, or 2950.15 of the Revised Code. For a person who was convicted of or pleaded guilty to the sexually oriented offense or child-victim related offense, the registry also shall indicate whether the person was convicted of or pleaded guilty to the offense in a criminal prosecution or in a serious youthful offender case. The registry shall not be open to inspection by the public or by any person other than a person identified in division (A) of section 2950.08 of the Revised Code. In addition to the information and material previously identified in this division, the registry shall include all of the following regarding each person who is listed in the registry:

(a) A citation for, and the name of, all sexually oriented offenses or child-victim oriented offenses of which the person was convicted, to which the person pleaded guilty, or for which the person was adjudicated a delinquent child and that resulted in a registration duty, and the date on which those offenses were committed;

(b) The text of the sexually oriented offenses or child-victim oriented offenses identified in division (A)(1)(a) of this section as those offenses existed at the time the person was convicted of, pleaded guilty to, or was adjudicated a delinquent child for committing those offenses, or a link to a database that sets forth the text of those offenses;

(c) A statement as to whether the person is a tier I sex offender/child-victim offender, a tier II sex offender/child-victim offender, or a tier III sex offender/child-victim offender for the sexually oriented offenses or child-victim oriented offenses identified in division (A)(1)(a) of this section;

(d) The community supervision status of the person, including, but not limited to, whether the person is serving a community control sanction and the nature of any such sanction, whether the person is under supervised release and the nature of the release, or regarding a juvenile, whether the juvenile is under any type of release authorized under Chapter 2152. or 5139. of the Revised Code and the nature of any such release;

(e) The offense and delinquency history of the person, as determined from information gathered or provided under sections 109.57 and 2950.14 of the Revised Code;

(f) The bureau of criminal identification and investigation tracking number assigned to the person if one has been so assigned, the federal bureau of investigation number assigned to the person if one has been assigned and the bureau of criminal identification and investigation is aware of the number, and any other state identification number assigned to the person of which the bureau is aware;

(g) Fingerprints and palmprints of the person;

(h) A DNA specimen, as defined in section 109.573 [109.57.3] of the Revised Code, from the person;

(i) Whether the person has any outstanding arrest warrants;

(j) Whether the person is in compliance with the person's duties under this chapter.

(2) In consultation with local law enforcement representatives and no later than July 1, 1997, adopt rules that contain guidelines necessary for the implementation of this chapter;

(3) In consultation with local law enforcement representatives, adopt rules for the implementation and administration of the provisions contained in section 2950.11 of the Revised Code that pertain to the notification of neighbors of an offender or a delinquent child who has committed a sexually oriented offense or a child-victim oriented offense and and† is in a category specified in division (F)(1) of that section and rules that prescribe a manner in which victims of a sexually oriented offense or a child-victim oriented offense committed by an offender or a delinquent child who is in a category specified in division (B)(1) of section 2950.10 of the Revised Code may make a request that specifies that the victim would like to be provided the notices described in divisions (A)(1) and (2) of section 2950.10 of the Revised Code;

(4) In consultation with local law enforcement representatives and through the bureau of criminal identification and investigation, prescribe the forms to be used by judges and officials pursuant to section 2950.03 or 2950.032 [2950.03.2] of the Revised Code to advise offenders and delinquent children of their duties of filing a notice of intent to reside, registration, notification of a change of residence, school, institution of higher education, or place of employment address and registration of the new, school, institution of higher education, or place of employment address, as applicable, and address verification under sections 2950.04, 2950.041 [2950.04.1], 2950.05, and 2950.06 of the Revised Code, and prescribe the forms to be used by sheriffs relative to those duties of filing a notice of intent to reside, registration, change of residence, school, institution of higher education, or place of employment address notification, and address verification;

(5) Make copies of the forms prescribed under division (A)(4) of this section available to judges, officials, and sheriffs;

(6) Through the bureau of criminal identification and investigation, provide the notifications, the information and materials, and the documents that the bureau is required to provide to appropriate law enforcement officials and to the federal bureau of investigation pursuant to sections 2950.04, 2950.041 [2950.04.1], 2950.05, and 2950.06 of the Revised Code;

(7) Through the bureau of criminal identification and investigation, maintain the verification forms returned under the address verification mechanism set forth in section 2950.06 of the Revised Code;

(8) In consultation with representatives of the officials, judges, and sheriffs, adopt procedures for officials, judges, and sheriffs to use to forward information, photographs, and fingerprints to the bureau of criminal identification and investigation pursuant to the requirements of sections 2950.03, 2950.04, 2950.041 [2950.04.1], 2950.05, 2950.06, and 2950.11 of the Revised Code;

(9) In consultation with the director of education, the director of job and family services, and the director of rehabilitation and correction, adopt rules that contain guidelines to be followed by boards of education of a school district, chartered nonpublic schools or other schools not operated by a board of education, preschool programs, child day-care centers, type A family day-care homes, certified type B family day-care homes, and institutions of higher education regarding the proper use and administration of information received pursuant to section 2950.11 of the Revised Code relative to an offender or delinquent child who has committed a sexually oriented offense or a child-victim oriented offense and is in a category specified in division (F)(1) of that section;

(10) In consultation with local law enforcement representatives and no later than July 1, 1997, adopt rules that designate a geographic area or areas within which the notice described in division (B) of section 2950.11 of the Revised Code must be given to the persons identified in divisions (A)(2) to (8) and (A)(10) of that section;

(11) Through the bureau of criminal identification and investigation, not later than January 1, 2004, establish and operate on the internet a sex offender and child-victim offender database that contains information for every offender who has committed a sexually oriented offense or a child-victim oriented offense and registers in any county in this state pursuant to section 2950.04 or 2950.041 [2950.04.1] of the Revised Code and for every delinquent child who has committed a sexually oriented offense, is a public registry-qualified juvenile offender registrant, and registers in any county in this state pursuant to either such section. The bureau shall not include on the database the

identity of any offender's or public registry-qualified juvenile offender registrant's victim, any offender's or public registry-qualified juvenile offender registrant's social security number, the name of any school or institution of higher education attended by any offender or public registry-qualified juvenile offender registrant, the name of the place of employment of any offender or public registry-qualified juvenile offender registrant, any tracking or identification number described in division (A)(1)(f) of this section, or any information described in division (C)(7) of section 2950.04 or 2950.041 [2950.04.1] of the Revised Code. The bureau shall provide on the database, for each offender and each public registry-qualified juvenile offender registrant, at least the information specified in divisions (A)(11)(a) to (h) of this section. Otherwise, the bureau shall determine the information to be provided on the database for each offender and public registry-qualified juvenile offender registrant and shall obtain that information from the information contained in the state registry of sex offenders and child-victim offenders described in division (A)(1) of this section, which information, while in the possession of the sheriff who provided it, is a public record open for inspection as described in section 2950.081 [2950.08.1] of the Revised Code. The database is a public record open for inspection under section 149.43 of the Revised Code, and it shall be searchable by offender or public registry-qualified juvenile offender registrant name, by county, by zip code, and by school district. The database shall provide a link to the web site of each sheriff who has established and operates on the internet a sex offender and child-victim offender database that contains information for offenders and public registry-qualified juvenile offender registrants who register in that county pursuant to section 2950.04 or 2950.041 [2950.04.1] of the Revised Code, with the link being a direct link to the sex offender and child-victim offender database for the sheriff. The bureau shall provide on the database, for each offender and public registry-qualified juvenile offender registrant, at least the following information:

(a) The information described in divisions (A)(1)(a), (b), (c), and (d) of this section relative to the offender or public registry-qualified juvenile offender registrant;

(b) The address of the offender's or public registry-qualified juvenile offender registrant's school, institution of higher education, or place of employment provided in a registration form;

(c) The information described in division (C)(6) of section 2950.04 or 2950.041 [2950.04.1] of the Revised Code;

(d) A chart describing which sexually oriented offenses and child-victim oriented offenses are included in the definitions of tier I sex offender/child-victim offender, tier II sex offender/child-victim offender, and tier III sex offender/child-victim offender;

(e) Fingerprints and palm prints of the offender or public registry-qualified juvenile offender registrant and a DNA specimen from the offender or public registry-qualified juvenile offender registrant;

(f) The information set forth in division (B) of section 2950.11 of the Revised Code;

(g) Any outstanding arrest warrants for the offender or public registry-qualified juvenile offender registrant;

(h) The offender's or public registry-qualified juvenile offender registrant's compliance status with duties under this chapter.

(12) Develop software to be used by sheriffs in establishing on the internet a sex offender and child-victim offender database for the public dissemination of some or all of the information and materials described in division (A) of section 2950.081 [2950.08.1] of the Revised Code that are public records under that division, that are not prohibited from inclusion by division (B) of that section, and that pertain to offenders and public registry-qualified juvenile offender registrants who register in the sheriff's county pursuant to section 2950.04 or 2950.041 [2950.04.1] of the Revised Code and for the public dissemination of information the sheriff receives pursuant to section 2950.14 of the Revised Code and, upon the request of any sheriff, provide technical guidance to the requesting sheriff in establishing on the internet such a database;

(13) Through the bureau of criminal identification and investigation, not later than January 1, 2004, establish and operate on the internet a database that enables local law enforcement representatives to remotely search by electronic means the state registry of sex offenders and child-victim offenders described in division (A)(1) of this section and any information and materials the bureau receives pursuant to sections 2950.04, 2950.041 [2950.04.1], 2950.05, 2950.06, and 2950.14 of the Revised Code. The database shall enable local law enforcement representatives to obtain detailed information regarding each offender and delinquent child who is included in the registry, including, but not limited to the offender's or delinquent child's name, aliases, residence address, name and address of any place of employment, school, institution of higher education, if applicable, license plate number of each vehicle identified in division (C)(5) of section 2950.04 or 2950.041 [2950.04.1] of the Revised Code to the extent applicable, victim preference if available, date of most recent release from confinement if applicable, fingerprints, and palmprints, all of the information and material described in division (A)(1)(a) to (h) of this section regarding the offender or delinquent child, and other identification parameters the bureau considers appropriate. The database is not a public record open for inspection under section 149.43 of the Revised Code and shall be available only to law enforcement representatives as described in this division. Information obtained by local law enforcement representatives through use of this database is not open to inspection by the public or by any person other than a person identified in division (A) of section 2950.08 of the Revised Code.

(14) Through the bureau of criminal identification and investigation, maintain a list of requests for notice about a specified offender or delinquent child or specified geographical notification area made pursuant to division (J) of section 2950.11 of the Revised Code and, when an offender or delinquent child changes residence to another county, forward any requests for information about that specific offender or delinquent child to the appropriate sheriff;

(15) Through the bureau of criminal identification and investigation, establish and operate a system for the immediate notification by electronic means of the appropriate officials in other states specified in this division each time an offender or delinquent child registers a residence, school, institution of higher education, or place of employment address under section 2950.04 or 2950.041 [2950.04.1] of the revised Code or provides a notice of a change of address or registers a new address under division (A) or (B) of section 2950.05 of the Revised Code.

The immediate notification by electronic means shall be provided to the appropriate officials in each state in which the offender or delinquent child is required to register a residence, school, institution of higher education, or place of employment address. The notification shall contain the offender's or delinquent child's name and all of the information the bureau receives from the sheriff with whom the offender or delinquent child registered the address or provided the notice of change of address or registered the new address.

(B) The attorney general in consultation with local law enforcement representatives, may adopt rules that establish one or more categories of neighbors of an offender or delinquent child who, in addition to the occupants of residential premises and other persons specified in division (A)(1) of section 2950.11 of the Revised Code, must be given the notice described in division (B) of that section.

(C) No person, other than a local law enforcement representative, shall knowingly do any of the following:

(1) Gain or attempt to gain access to the database established and operated by the attorney general, through the bureau of criminal identification and investigation, pursuant to division (A)(13) of this section.

(2) Permit any person to inspect any information obtained through use of the database described in division (C)(1) of this section, other than as permitted under that division.

(D) As used in this section, "local law enforcement representatives" means representatives of the sheriffs of this state, representatives of the municipal chiefs of police and marshals of this state, and representatives of the township constables and chiefs of police of the township police departments or police district police forces of this state.

**HISTORY: 146 v H 180 (Eff 7-1-97); 146 v H 72 (Eff 7-1-97); 148 v H 471 (Eff 7-1-2000); 149 v S 3 (Eff 1-1-2002); 149 v H 485. Eff 6-13-2002; 150 v S 5, § 1, Eff 7-31-03; 151 v S 260, § 1, eff. 1-2-07; 152 v S 10, § 1, eff. 1-1-08.**

† As enrolled in (A)(3) by 152 v S 10.
The effective date is set by § 3 of 152 v S 10.

## § 2950.131 Link to educational information on current research about sex offenders and child-victim offenders; notice to offenders regarding correcting information.

(A) By January 1, 2008, the bureau of criminal identification and investigation, with the assistance of the office of criminal justice services, shall include on the internet sex offender and child-victim offender database established and operated pursuant to division (A)(11) of section 2950.13 of the Revised Code a link to educational information for the public on current research about sex offenders and child-victim offenders. Each sheriff who has established on the internet a sex offender and child-victim offender database may include a link to this information on the sheriff's internet database.

(B) By January 1, 2008, the internet sex offender and child-victim offender database established and operated pursuant to division (A)(11) of section 2950.13 of the Revised Code and each sheriff's internet sex offender and child-victim offender database is required to inform offenders and public registry-qualified juvenile offender registrants that they may contact the sheriff of the county in which the offender or delinquent child registered an address if the offender or delinquent child believes that information contained on the internet sex offender and child-victim offender database or sheriff's internet sex offender and child-victim offender database pertaining to the offender or delinquent child is incorrect.

**HISTORY: 152 v S 97, § 1, eff. 1-1-08.**

The effective date is set by § 3 of 152 v S 97.

## § 2950.132 Conformance to federal regulations, guidelines, or standards.

If, on or after the effective date of this section, the United States attorney general or an office established under the authority of the United States attorney general adopts any regulation, guideline, or standard that interprets or applies the federal Sex Offender Registration and Notification Act, Pub. L. No. 109-249, to require additional sex offender registration and notification than otherwise required by Chapter 2950. of the Revised Code, as amended by this act, or notifies the attorney general of this state that the amendments made by this act are not in substantial compliance with the federal Sex Offender Registration and Notification Act or regulations, guidelines or standards interpreting or applying the federal Sex Offender Registration and Notification Act, the attorney general of this state within one hundred eighty days after notification or the adoption of any regulation, guideline or standard that interprets or applies the federal Sex Offender Registration and Notification Act, shall adopt rules in accordance with Chapter 119. of the Revised Code to require additional sex offender registration or notification so that Ohio's sex offender registration and notification requirements are consistent with, and not less stringent than, the federal Sex Offender Registration and Notification Act and any regulation, guideline or standard that interprets or applies the federal Sex Offender Registration and Notification Act.

**HISTORY: 152 v S 10, § 1, eff. 7-1-07.**

The effective date is set by § 3 of 152 v S 10.

**Publisher's Note:**

Renumbered from 2950.131 by the Ohio Legislative Service Commission.

## § 2950.14 Information to be provided to bureau of criminal identification and investigation prior to release; information to be entered on internet database.

(A) Prior to releasing an offender who is under the custody and control of the department of rehabilitation and correction and who has been convicted of or pleaded guilty to committing, either prior to, on, or after January 1, 1997, any sexually oriented offense or any child-victim oriented offense, the department of rehabilitation and correction shall provide all of the information described in division (B) of this section to the bureau of criminal identification and investigation regarding the offender and to the sheriff of the county in which the offender's anticipated future residence is located. Prior to releasing a delinquent child who is in the custody of the department of youth services who has been adjudicated a delinquent child for committing any sexually oriented offense or any child-victim oriented offense, regardless of when the offense was committed, and who has been classified a juvenile offender registrant based on that adjudication, the department of youth services shall provide all of the information described in division (B) of this section to the bureau of criminal identification and investigation regarding the delinquent child.

(B) The department of rehabilitation and correction and the department of youth services shall provide all of the following information to the bureau of criminal identification and investigation regarding an offender or delinquent child described in division (A) of this section:

(1) The offender's or delinquent child's name and any aliases used by the offender or delinquent child;

(2) All identifying factors concerning, and a physical description of, the offender or delinquent child;

(3) The offender's or delinquent child's anticipated future residence;

(4) The offense and delinquency history and the terms and conditions of release of the offender or delinquent child;

(5) Whether the offender or delinquent child was treated for a mental abnormality or personality disorder while under the custody and control of the department;

(6) Any other information that the bureau indicates is relevant and that the department possesses.

(C) Upon receipt of the information described in division (B) of this section regarding an offender or delinquent child, the bureau immediately shall enter the information into the state registry of sex offenders and child-victim offenders that the bureau maintains pursuant to section 2950.13 of the Revised Code and into the records that the bureau maintains pursuant to division (A) of section 109.57 of the Revised Code. Upon receipt of that information regarding an offender, the bureau immediately shall enter the information on the sex offender and child-victim offender database it establishes and operates on the internet pursuant to division (A)(11) of section 2950.13 of the Revised Code.

(D) Upon receipt of the information described in division (B) of this section regarding an offender, a sheriff who has established on the internet a sex offender and child-victim offender database for the public dissemination of information regarding such offenders shall enter that information on the database.

**HISTORY: 146 v H 180 (Eff 1-1-97); 147 v H 565 (Eff 3-30-99); 149 v S 3 (Eff 1-1-2002); 149 v H 393. Eff 7-5-2002; 150 v S 5, § 1, Eff 7-31-03; 151 v S 260, § 1, eff. 1-2-07; 152 v S 10, § 1, eff. 1-1-08.**

The effective date is set by § 3 of 152 v S 10.

## § 2950.15 Motion requesting court to terminate duty to comply with registration requirements.

(A) As used in this section and section 2950.16 of the Revised Code, "eligible offender" means a person who is convicted of, pleads guilty to, was convicted of, or pleaded guilty to a sexually oriented offense or child-victim oriented offense, regardless of when the offense was committed, and is a tier I sex offender/child-victim offender or a child who is or was adjudicated a delinquent child for committing a sexually oriented offense or child-victim oriented offense, regardless of when the offense was committed, and is a public registry-qualified juvenile offender registrant.

(B) Pursuant to this section, an eligible offender may make a motion to the court of common pleas or, for a delinquent child, the juvenile court of the county in which the eligible offender resides requesting that the court terminate the eligible offender's duty to comply with sections 2950.04, 2950.041 [2950.04.1], 2950.05, and 2950.06 of the Revised Code. If the eligible offender is not a resident of this state, the eligible offender may make a motion to the court of common pleas of the county in which the eligible offender has registered pursuant to section 2950.04 or 2950.041 [2950.04.1] of the Revised Code, but if the eligible offender has registered addresses of that nature in more than one county, the eligible offender may make such a motion in the court of only one of those counties. Notwithstanding any state or local rule assigning costs and fees for filing and processing civil and criminal cases, the fee for filing the motion shall be one hundred fifty dollars. This fee shall be applied to any further processing of the motion, including, but not limited to, the costs associated with investigating the motion, notifying relevant parties, scheduling hearings, and recording and reporting the court's determination.

(C)(1) Except as provided in division (C)(2) of this section, an eligible offender who is classified a tier I sex offender/child-victim offender may make a motion under division (B) of this section upon the expiration of ten years after the eligible offender's duty to comply with division (A)(2) or (4) of section 2950.04 or division (A)(2) or (4) of section 2950.041 and sections 2950.05 and 2950.06 of the Revised Code begins in relation to the offense for which the eligible offender is subject to those provisions.

(2) An eligible offender who is a delinquent child and is classified a public registry-qualified juvenile offender registrant may make a motion under division (B) of this section upon the expiration of twenty-five years after the eligible offender's duty to comply with division (A)(3) or (4) of section 2950.04 and sections 2950.05 and 2950.06 of the Revised Code begins in relation to the offense for which the eligible offender is subject to those provisions.

(D) An eligible offender who makes a motion under division (B) of this section shall include all of the following with the motion:

(1) A certified copy of the judgment entry and any other documentation of the sentence or disposition given for the offense or offenses for which the eligible offender was convicted, pleaded guilty, or was adjudicated a delinquent child;

(2) Documentation of the date of discharge from supervision or release, whichever is applicable;

(3) Evidence that the eligible offender has completed a sex offender or child-victim offender treatment program certified by the department of rehabilitation and correction or the department of youth services pursuant to section 2950.16 of the Revised Code;

(4) Evidence that the eligible offender has not been convicted of, pleaded guilty to, or been adjudicated a delinquent child for committing any subsequent sexually oriented offense, child-victim oriented offense, or other criminal offense, except for a minor misdemeanor traffic offense;

(5) Evidence that the eligible offender has paid any financial sanctions imposed upon the offender pursuant to section 2929.18 or 2929.28 of the Revised Code.

(E) Upon the filing of a motion pursuant to division (B) of this section, the offender or delinquent child shall serve a copy of the motion on the prosecutor who handled the case in which the eligible offender was convicted of, pleaded guilty to, or was adjudicated a delinquent child for committing the sexually oriented offense or child-victim oriented offense. Upon the filing of the motion, the court shall set a tentative date for a hearing on the motion that is not later than one hundred eighty days from the date the motion is filed unless good cause exists to hold the hearing at a later date and shall notify the eligible offender and the prosecutor of the date, time, and place of the hearing. The court shall then forward a copy of the motion and its supporting documentation to the court's probation department or another appropriate agency to investigate the merits of the motion. The probation department or agency shall submit a written report detailing its investigation to the court within sixty days of receiving the motion and supporting documentation.

Upon receipt of the written report from the probation department or other appropriate agency, the court shall forward a copy of the motion, supporting documentation, and the written report to the prosecutor.

(F)(1) After the prosecutor is served with a copy of the motion as described in division (E) of this section, the prosecutor shall notify the victim of any offense for which the eligible offender is requesting a termination of duties under sections 2950.04, 2950.041 [2950.04.1], 2950.05, and 2950.06 of the Revised Code. The victim may submit a written statement to the prosecutor regarding any knowledge the victim has of the eligible offender's conduct while subject to the duties imposed by sections 2950.04, 2950.041 [2950.04.1], 2950.05, and 2950.06 of the Revised Code.

(2) At least seven days before the hearing date, the prosecutor may file an objection to the motion with the court and serve a copy of the objection to the motion to the eligible offender or the eligible offender's attorney.

(G) In addition to the evidence that accompanies the motion described in division (D) of this section and the written report submitted pursuant to division (E) of this section, in determining whether to grant a motion made under division (B) of this section, the court may consider any other evidence the court considers relevant, including, but not limited to, evidence of the following while the eligible offender has been subject to the duties imposed under sections 2950.04, 2950.041 [2950.04.1], 2950.05, and 2950.06 of the Revised Code:

(1) Whether the eligible offender's driver's license, commercial driver's license, temporary instruction permit, probationary license, or nonresident operating privilege has ever been suspended;

(2) Whether the eligible offender has maintained financial responsibility for a motor vehicle as required by section 4509.101 [4509.10.1] of the Revised Code;

(3) Whether the eligible offender has satisfied any child or spousal support obligations, if applicable;

(4) Whether the eligible offender has paid all local, state, and federal income taxes, and has timely filed all associated income tax returns, as required by local, state, or federal law;

(5) Whether there is evidence that the eligible offender has adequately addressed sex offending or child-victim offending behaviors;

(6) Whether the eligible offender has maintained a residence for a substantial period of time;

(7) Whether the eligible offender has maintained employment or, if the eligible offender has not been employed while under a duty to comply with sections 2950.04, 2950.041 [2950.04.1], 2950.05, and 2950.06 of the Revised Code, whether the eligible offender has satisfied the offender's financial obligations through other manners of support such as disability payments, a pension, spousal or child support, or scholarships or grants;

(8) Whether the eligible offender has adequately addressed any drug or alcohol abuse or addiction;

(9) Letters of reference;

(10) Documentation of the eligible offender's service to the community or to specific individuals in need.

(H)(1) The court, without a hearing, may issue an order denying the eligible offender's motion to terminate the eligible offender's duty to comply with sections 2950.04, 2950.041 [2950.04.1], 2950.05, and 2950.06 of the Revised Code if the court, based on the evidence submitted with the motion pursuant to division (D) of this section and the written report submitted pursuant to division (E) of this section and after considering the factors described in division (G) of this section, finds that those duties should not be terminated.

(2) If the prosecutor does not file an objection to the eligible offender's application as provided in division (F)(2) of this section, the court, without a hearing, may issue an order that terminates the eligible offender's duty to comply with sections 2950.04, 2950.041 [2950.04.1], 2950.05, and 2950.06 of the Revised Code if the court, based on the evidence submitted with the motion pursuant to division (D) of this section and the written report submitted pursuant to division (E) of this section and after considering the factors described in division (G) of this section, finds that those duties should be terminated.

(3) If the court does not issue an order under division (H)(1) or (2) of this section, the court shall hold a hearing to determine whether to grant or deny the motion. At the hearing, the Rules of Civil Procedure or, if the hearing is in a juvenile court, the Rules of Juvenile Procedure apply, except to the extent that those Rules would by their nature be clearly inapplicable. At the hearing, the eligible offender has the burden of going forward with the evidence and the burden of proof by a preponderance of the evidence. If, after considering the evidence submitted with the motion pursuant to division (D) of this section, the written report submitted pursuant to division (E) of this section, and the factors described in division (G) of this section, the court finds that the eligible offender has satisfied the burden of proof, the court shall issue an order that terminates the eligible offender's duty to comply with sections 2950.04, 2950.041 [2950.04.1], 2950.05, and 2950.06 of the Revised Code. If the court finds that the eligible offender has not satisfied the burden of proof, the court shall issue an order denying the motion.

(4)(a) The court shall provide prompt notice of its order issued pursuant to division (H)(1), (2), or (3) of this section to the eligible offender or the eligible offender's attorney.

(b) If the court issues an order terminating the eligible offender's duty to comply with sections 2950.04, 2950.041 [2950.04.1], 2950.05, and 2950.06 of the Revised Code, the court shall promptly forward a copy of the order to the bureau of criminal identification and investigation. Upon receipt of the order, the bureau shall update all records pertaining to the eligible offender to reflect the termination order. The bureau also shall notify every sheriff with whom the eligible offender has most recently registered under section 2950.04, 2950.041 [2950.04.1], or 2950.05 of the Revised Code of the termination order.

(c) If the court issues an order terminating the eligible offender's duty to comply with sections 2950.04, 2950.041 [2950.04.1], 2950.05, and 2950.06 of the Revised Code, the court shall promptly forward a copy of the order to any court that sentenced the offender or adjudicated the child a delinquent child for a sexually oriented offense or child-victim oriented offense that is the basis of the termination order. The court that receives this notice shall retain a copy of the order in the eligible offender's original case file.

**HISTORY: 152 v S 10, § 1, eff. 1-1-08.**

The effective date is set by § 3 of 152 v S 10.

## § 2950.16 Certification of sex offender and child-victim offender treatment programs.

By July 1, 2008, the department of rehabilitation and correction and the department of youth services shall adopt rules pertaining to the certification of sex offender and child-victim offender treatment programs. The rules shall include a requirement that the departments periodically inspect and certify sex offender and child-victim offender treatment programs. The rules shall also include a requirement that the departments maintain a list of certified sex offender and child-victim offender treatment programs that is open to public inspection.

**HISTORY: 152 v S 10, § 1, eff. 1-1-08.**

The effective date is set by § 3 of 152 v S 10.

## § 2950.17 Possession of photograph of victim of sexually oriented offense or child-victim oriented offense prohibited while person serving term of confinement imposed for offense; possession of photograph of any minor child prohibited; penalty.

(A) Regardless of when the sexually oriented offense or child-victim oriented offense was committed, a person who is convicted of, pleads guilty to, has been convicted of, or has pleaded guilty to a sexually oriented offense or a child-victim oriented offense or a person who is or has been adjudicated a delinquent child for committing a sexually oriented offense or a child-victim oriented offense shall not possess a photograph of the victim of the sexually oriented offense or child-victim oriented offense while the person is serving any prison term, jail term, community residential sanction, or other term of confinement imposed on the offender for the offense.

(B) Regardless of when the child-victim oriented offense was committed, a person who is convicted of, pleads guilty to, has been convicted of, or has pleaded guilty to a child-victim oriented offense or a person who is or has been adjudicated a delinquent child for committing a child-victim oriented offense shall not possess a photograph of any minor child while the person is serving any prison term, jail term, community residential sanction, or other term of confinement imposed on the offender for the offense.

(C) Whoever violates this section is guilty of illegal possession of a prohibited photograph, a misdemeanor of the first degree.

**HISTORY: 2011 HB 86, § 1, eff. Sept. 30, 2011.**

## § 2950.99 Penalties.

(A)(1)(a) Except as otherwise provided in division (A)(1)(b) of this section, whoever violates a prohibition in section 2950.04, 2950.041, 2950.05, or 2950.06 of the Revised Code shall be punished as follows:

(i) If the most serious sexually oriented offense that was the basis of the registration, notice of intent to reside, change of address notification, or address verification requirement that was violated under the prohibition is aggravated murder or murder if committed by an adult or a comparable category of offense committed in another jurisdiction, the offender is guilty of a felony of the first degree.

(ii) If the most serious sexually oriented offense or child-victim oriented offense that was the basis of the registration, notice of intent to reside, change of address notification, or address verification requirement that was violated under the prohibition is a felony of the first, second, third, or fourth degree if committed by an adult or a comparable category of offense committed in another jurisdiction, the offender is guilty of a felony of the same degree as the most serious sexually oriented offense or child-victim oriented offense that was the basis of the registration, notice of intent to reside, change of address, or address verification requirement that was violated under the prohibition, or, if the most serious sexually oriented offense or child-victim oriented offense that was the basis of the registration, notice of intent to reside, change of address, or address verification requirement that was violated under the prohibition is a comparable category of offense committed in another jurisdiction, the offender is guilty of a felony of the same degree as that offense committed in the other jurisdiction would constitute if committed in this state.

(iii) If the most serious sexually oriented offense or child-victim oriented offense that was the basis of the registration, notice of intent to reside, change of address notification, or address verification requirement that was violated under the prohibition is a felony of the fifth degree or a misdemeanor if committed by an adult or a comparable category of offense committed in another jurisdiction, the offender is guilty of a felony of the fourth degree.

(b) If the offender previously has been convicted of or pleaded guilty to, or previously has been adjudicated a delinquent child for committing, a violation of a prohibition in section 2950.04, 2950.041, 2950.05, or 2950.06 of the Revised Code, whoever violates a prohibition in section 2950.04, 2950.041, 2950.05, or 2950.06 of the Revised Code shall be punished as follows:

(i) If the most serious sexually oriented offense that was the basis of the registration, notice of intent to reside, change of address notification, or address verification requirement that was violated under the prohibition is aggravated murder or murder if committed by an adult or a comparable category of offense committed in another jurisdiction, the offender is guilty of a felony of the first degree.

(ii) If the most serious sexually oriented offense or child-victim oriented offense that was the basis of the registration, notice of intent to reside, change of address notification, or address verification requirement that was violated under the prohibition is a felony of the first, second, or third degree if committed by an adult or a comparable category of offense committed in another jurisdiction, the offender is guilty of a felony of the same degree as the most serious sexually oriented offense or child-victim oriented offense that was the basis of the registration, notice of intent to reside, change of address, or address verification requirement that was violated under the prohibition, or, if the most serious sexually oriented offense or child-victim oriented offense that was the basis of the registration, notice of intent to reside, change of address, or address verification requirement that was violated under the prohibition is a comparable category of offense committed in another jurisdiction, the offender is guilty of a felony of the same degree as that offense committed in the other jurisdiction would constitute if committed in this state.

(iii) If the most serious sexually oriented offense or child-victim oriented offense that was the basis of the registration, notice of intent to reside, change of address notification, or address verification requirement that was violated under the prohibition is a felony of the fourth or fifth degree if committed by an adult or a comparable category of offense committed in another jurisdiction, the offender is guilty of a felony of the third degree.

(iv) If the most serious sexually oriented offense or child-victim oriented offense that was the basis of the registration, notice of intent to reside, change of address notification, or address verification requirement that was violated under the prohibition is a misdemeanor if committed by an adult or a comparable category of offense committed in another jurisdiction, the offender is guilty of a felony of the fourth degree.

(2)(a) In addition to any penalty or sanction imposed under division (A)(1) of this section or any other provision of law for a violation of a prohibition in section 2950.04, 2950.041, 2950.05, or 2950.06 of the Revised Code, if the offender or delinquent child is subject to a community control sanction, is on parole, is subject to one or more post-release control sanctions, or is subject to any other type of supervised release at the time of the violation, the violation shall constitute a violation of the terms and conditions of the community control sanction, parole, post-release control sanction, or other type of supervised release.

(b) In addition to any penalty or sanction imposed under division (A)(1)(b)(i), (ii), or (iii) of this section or any other provision of law for a violation of a prohibition in section 2950.04, 2950.041, 2950.05, or 2950.06 of the Revised Code, if the offender previously has been convicted of or pleaded guilty to, or previously has been adjudicated a delinquent child for committing, a violation of a prohibition in section 2950.04, 2950.041, 2950.05, or 2950.06 of the Revised Code when the most serious sexually oriented offense or child-victim oriented offense that was the basis of the requirement that was violated under the prohibition is a felony if committed by an adult or a comparable category of offense committed in another jurisdiction, the court imposing a sentence upon the offender shall impose a definite prison term of no less than three years. The definite prison term imposed under this section, subject to divisions (C) to (I) of section 2967.19 of the Revised Code, shall not be reduced to less than three years pursuant to any provision of Chapter 2967. or any other provision of the Revised Code.

(3) As used in division (A)(1) of this section, "comparable category of offense committed in another jurisdiction" means a sexually oriented offense or child-victim oriented offense that was the basis of the registration, notice of intent to reside, change of address notification, or address verification requirement that was violated, that is a violation of an existing or former law of another state or the United States, an existing or former law applicable in a military court or in an Indian tribal court, or an existing or former law of any nation other than the United States, and that, if it had been committed in this state, would constitute or would have constituted aggravated murder or murder for purposes of division (A)(1)(a)(i) of this section, a felony of the first, second, third, or fourth degree for purposes of division (A)(1)(a)(ii) of this section, a felony of the fifth degree or a misdemeanor for purposes of division (A)(1)(a)(iii) of this section, aggravated murder or murder for purposes of division (A)(1)(b)(i) of this section, a felony of the first, second, or third degree for purposes of division (A)(1)(b)(ii) of this section, a felony of the fourth or fifth degree for purposes of division (A)(1)(b)(iii) of this section, or a misdemeanor for purposes of division (A)(1)(b)(iv) of this section.

(B) If a person violates a prohibition in section 2950.04, 2950.041, 2950.05, or 2950.06 of the Revised Code that applies to the person as a result of the person being adjudicated a delinquent child and being classified a juvenile offender registrant or an out-of-state juvenile offender registrant, both of the following apply:

(1) If the violation occurs while the person is under eighteen years of age, the person is subject to proceedings under Chapter 2152. of the Revised Code based on the violation.

(2) If the violation occurs while the person is eighteen years of age or older, the person is subject to criminal prosecution based on the violation.

(C) Whoever violates division (C) of section 2950.13 of the Revised Code is guilty of a misdemeanor of the first degree.

**HISTORY: 130 v 671 (Eff 10-4-63); 134 v H 511 (Eff 1-1-74); 146 v S 2 (Eff 7-1-96); 146 v H 180 (Eff 7-1-97); 149 v S 3. Eff 1-1-2002; 149 v H 490, § 1, eff. 1-1-04; 150 v S 5, § 1, Eff 7-31-03; 150 v S 5, § 3, eff. 1-1-04; 150 v H 473, § 1, eff. 4-29-05; 152 v S 97, § 1, eff. 1-1-08; 2011 HB 86, § 1, eff. Sept. 30, 2011.**

The effective date is set by § 3 of 152 v S 97.
The effective date is set by section 4 of H.B. 490.

# CHAPTER 2951: PROBATION



## § 2951.01 Definitions.

As used in this chapter:

(A) "Magistrate" has the same meaning as in section 2931.01 of the Revised Code.

(B) "Community control sanction" has the same meaning as in section 2929.01 of the Revised Code.

(C) "Ignition interlock device" has the same meaning as in section 4511.83 of the Revised Code.

(D) "Multicounty department of probation" means a probation department established under section 2301.27 of the Revised Code to serve more than one county.

(E) "Probation agency" means a county department of probation, a multicounty department of probation, a municipal court department of probation established under section 1901.33 of the Revised Code, or the adult parole authority.

(F) "County-operated municipal court" and "legislative authority" have the same meanings as in section 1901.03 of the Revised Code.

(G) "Detention facility" has the same meaning as in section 2921.01 of the Revised Code.

(H) "Repeat offender" and "dangerous offender" have the same meanings as in section 2935.36 of the Revised Code.

(I) "Minor drug possession offense" has the same meaning as in section 2925.01 of the Revised Code.

(J) "Peace officer" has the same meaning as in section 2935.01 of the Revised Code.

(K) "Firearm," "deadly weapon," and "dangerous ordnance" have the same meanings as in section 2923.11 of the Revised Code.

**HISTORY: Bureau of Code Revision. Eff 10-1-53; 149 v H 490, § 1, eff. 1-1-04.**

The effective date is set by section 4 of HB 490.

## § 2951.011 Application of 7-1-96 amendments.

(A)(1) Chapter 2951. of the Revised Code, as it existed prior to July 1, 1996, applies to a person upon whom a court imposed a term of imprisonment prior to July 1, 1996, and a person upon whom a court, on or after July 1, 1996, and in accordance with law existing prior to July 1, 1996, imposed a term of imprisonment for an offense that was committed prior to July 1, 1996.

(2) Chapter 2951. of the Revised Code as it exists on and after July 1, 1996, applies to a person upon whom a court imposed a stated prison term for an offense committed on or after July 1, 1996.

(B)(1) Except as provided in division (A)(1) of this section, Chapter 2951. of the Revised Code, as it existed prior to January 1, 2004, applies to a person upon whom a court imposed a sentence for a misdemeanor offense prior to January 1, 2004, and a person upon whom a court, on or after January 1, 2004, and in accordance with law existing prior to January 1, 2004, imposed a sentence for a misdemeanor offense that was committed prior to January 1, 2004.

(2) Except as provided in division (A)(2) of this section, Chapter 2951. of the Revised Code as it exists on and after January 1, 2004, applies to a person upon whom a court imposes a sentence for a misdemeanor offense committed on or after January 1, 2004.

**HISTORY: 146 v S 2. Eff 7-1-96; 149 v H 490, § 1, eff. 1-1-04; 150 v S 57, § 1, eff. 1-1-04.**

The effective date is set by section 4 of H.B. 490.

See provisions, § 5 of SB 2 (146 v —), as amended by § 3 of SB 269 (146 v —), following RC § 2929.03.

## § 2951.02 Authorized searches during offender's misdemeanor community control sanction or felony nonresidential sanction; community service; ignition interlock devices.

(A) During the period of a misdemeanor offender's community control sanction or during the period of a felony offender's nonresidential sanction, authorized probation officers who are engaged within the scope of their supervisory duties or responsibilities may search, with or without a warrant, the person of the offender, the place of residence of the offender, and a motor vehicle, another item of tangible or intangible personal property, or other real property in which the offender has a right, title, or interest or for which the offender has the express or implied permission of a person with a right, title, or interest to use, occupy, or possess if the probation officers have reasonable grounds to believe that the offender is not abiding by the law or otherwise is not complying with the conditions of the misdemeanor offender's community control sanction or the conditions of the felony offender's nonresidential sanction. If a felony offender who is sentenced to a nonresidential sanction is under the general control and supervision of the adult parole authority, as described in division (A)(2)(a) of section 2929.15 of the Revised Code, adult parole authority field officers with supervisory responsibilities over the felony offender shall have the same search authority relative to the felony offender during the period of the sanction that is described under this division for probation officers. The court that places the misdemeanor offender under a community control sanction pursuant to section 2929.25 of the Revised Code or that sentences the felony offender to a nonresidential sanction pursuant to section 2929.17 of the Revised Code shall provide the offender with a written notice that informs the offender that authorized probation officers or adult parole authority field officers with supervisory responsibilities over the offender who are engaged within the scope of their supervisory duties or responsibilities may conduct those types of searches during the period of community control sanction or the nonresidential sanction if they have reasonable grounds to believe that the offender is not abiding by the law or otherwise is not complying with the conditions of the offender's community control sanction or nonresidential sanction.

(B) If an offender is convicted of or pleads guilty to a misdemeanor, the court may require the offender, as a condition of the offender's sentence of a community control sanction, to perform supervised community service work in accordance with this division. If an offender is convicted of or pleads guilty to a felony, the court, pursuant to sections 2929.15 and 2929.17 of the Revised Code, may impose a sanction that requires the offender to perform supervised community service work in accordance with this division. The supervised community service work shall be under the authority of health districts, park districts, counties, municipal corporations, townships, other political subdivisions of the state, or agencies of the state or any of its political subdivisions, or under the authority of charitable organizations that render services to the community or its citizens, in accordance with this division. The court may require an offender who is ordered to perform the work to pay to it a reasonable fee to cover the costs of the offender's participation in the work, including, but not limited to, the costs of procuring a policy or policies of liability insurance to cover the period during which the offender will perform the work.

A court may permit any offender convicted of a felony or a misdemeanor to satisfy the payment of a fine imposed for the offense pursuant to section 2929.18 or 2929.28 of the Revised Code by performing supervised community service work as described in this division if the offender requests an opportunity to satisfy the payment by this means and if the court determines that the offender is financially unable to pay the fine.

After imposing a term of community service, the court may modify the sentence to authorize a reasonable contribution to the appropriate general fund as provided in division (B) of section 2929.27 of the Revised Code.

The supervised community service work that may be imposed under this division shall be subject to the following limitations:

(1) The court shall fix the period of the work and, if necessary, shall distribute it over weekends or over other appropriate times that will allow the offender to continue at the offender's occupation or to care for the offender's family. The period of the work as fixed by the court shall not exceed in the aggregate the number of hours of community service imposed by the court pursuant to section 2929.17 or 2929.27 of the Revised Code.

(2) An agency, political subdivision, or charitable organization must agree to accept the offender for the work before the court requires the offender to perform the work for the entity. A court shall not require an offender to perform supervised community service work for an agency, political subdivision, or charitable organization at a location that is an unreasonable distance from the offender's residence or domicile, unless the offender is provided with transportation to the location where the work is to be performed.

(3) A court may enter into an agreement with a county department of job and family services for the management, placement, and supervision of offenders eligible for community service work in work activities, developmental activities, and alternative work activities under sections 5107.40 to 5107.69 of the Revised Code. If a court and a county department of job and family services have entered into an agreement of that nature, the clerk of that court is authorized to pay directly to the county department all or a portion of the fees collected by the court pursuant to this division in accordance with the terms of its agreement.

(4) Community service work that a court requires under this division shall be supervised by an official of the agency, political subdivision, or charitable organization for which the work is performed or by a person designated by the agency, political subdivision, or charitable organization. The official or designated person shall be qualified for the supervision by education, training, or experience, and periodically shall report, in writing, to the court and to the offender's probation officer concerning the conduct of the offender in performing the work.

(5) The total of any period of supervised community service work imposed on an offender under division (B) of this section plus the period of all other sanctions imposed pursuant to sections 2929.15, 2929.16, 2929.17, and 2929.18 of the Revised Code for a felony, or pursuant to sections 2929.25, 2929.26, 2929.27, and 2929.28 of the Revised Code for a misdemeanor, shall not exceed five years.

(C)(1) If an offender is convicted of a violation of section 4511.19 of the Revised Code, a municipal ordinance relating to operating a vehicle while under the influence of alcohol, a drug of abuse, or a combination of them, or a municipal ordinance relating to operating a vehicle with a prohibited concentration of alcohol, a controlled substance, or a metabolite of a controlled substance in the whole blood, blood serum or plasma, breath, or urine, the court may require, as a condition of a community control sanction, any suspension of a driver's or commercial driver's license or permit or nonresident operating privilege, and all other penalties provided by law or by ordinance, that the offender operate only a motor vehicle equipped with an ignition interlock device that is certified pursuant to section 4510.43 of the Revised Code.

(2) If a court requires an offender, as a condition of a community control sanction pursuant to division (C)(1) of this section, to operate only a motor vehicle equipped with an ignition interlock device that is certified pursuant to section 4510.43 of the Revised Code, the offender immediately shall surrender the offender's driver's or commercial driver's license or permit to the court. Upon the receipt of the offender's license or permit, the court shall issue an order authorizing the offender to operate a motor vehicle equipped with a certified ignition interlock device, deliver the offender's license or permit to the bureau of motor vehicles, and include in the abstract of the case forwarded to the bureau pursuant to section 4510.036 of the Revised Code the conditions of the community control sanction imposed pursuant to division (C)(1) of this section. The court shall give the offender a copy of its order, and that copy shall be used by the offender in lieu of a driver's or commercial driver's license or permit until the bureau issues a restricted license to the offender.

(3) Upon receipt of an offender's driver's or commercial driver's license or permit pursuant to division (C)(2) of this section, the bureau of motor vehicles shall issue a restricted license to the offender. The restricted license shall

be identical to the surrendered license, except that it shall have printed on its face a statement that the offender is prohibited from operating a motor vehicle that is not equipped with an ignition interlock device that is certified pursuant to section 4510.43 of the Revised Code. The bureau shall deliver the offender's surrendered license or permit to the court upon receipt of a court order requiring it to do so, or reissue the offender's license or permit under section 4510.52 of the Revised Code if the registrar destroyed the offender's license or permit under that section. The offender shall surrender the restricted license to the court upon receipt of the offender's surrendered license or permit.

(4) If an offender violates a requirement of the court imposed under division (C)(1) of this section, the court may impose a class seven suspension of the offender's driver's or commercial driver's license or permit or nonresident operating privilege from the range specified in division (A)(7) of section 4510.02 of the Revised Code. On a second or subsequent violation, the court may impose a class four suspension of the offender's driver's or commercial driver's license or permit or nonresident operating privilege from the range specified in division (A)(4) of section 4510.02 of the Revised Code.

**HISTORY: 134 v H 511 (Eff 1-1-74); 136 v S 144 (Eff 8-27-75); 137 v S 119 (Eff 8-30-78); 138 v H 892 (Eff 10-10-80); 138 v H 682 (Eff 4-9-81); 139 v H 1 (Eff 8-5-81); 139 v S 432 (Eff 3-16-83); 140 v S 210 (Eff 7-1-83); 142 v H 429 (Eff 6-20-88); 142 v H 322 (Eff 9-9-88); 143 v H 381 (Eff 7-1-89); 143 v S 258 (Eff 11-20-90); 145 v H 152 (Eff 7-1-93); 145 v H 571 (Eff 10-6-94); 145 v H 687 (Eff 10-12-94); 145 v H 687 (Eff 10-17-94); 146 v H 4 (Eff 11-9-95); 146 v H 167 (Eff 11-15-95); 146 v S 2 (Eff 7-1-96); 146 v S 269 (Eff 7-1-96); 147 v H 408 (Eff 10-1-97); 148 v S 9 (Eff 3-8-2000); 148 v S 107 (Eff 3-23-2000); 148 v H 471 (Eff 7-1-2000); 148 v H 349. Eff 9-22-2000; 149 v S 123, § 1, eff. 1-1-04; 149 v H 490, § 1, eff. 1-1-04; 151 v S 8, § 1, eff. 8-17-06; 2011 HB 5, § 1, eff. Sept. 23, 2011.**

The effective date is set by section 4 of H.B. 490.

The provisions of § 5 of S.B. 123 (149 v —), as amended by § 3 of H.B. 163 (150 v —), read as follows:

SECTION 5. (A) Notwithstanding division (B) of section 1.58 of the Revised Code, the provisions of the Revised Code amended or enacted in Sections 1 and 2 of Am. Sub. S.B. 123 of the 124th General Assembly shall apply only in relation to conduct and offenses committed on or after January 1, 2004. Conduct and offenses committed prior to January 1, 2004, shall be governed by the law in effect on the date the conduct or offense was committed.

° ° °

The provisions of § 3 of HB 349 (148 v —) read as follows:

SECTION 3. Sections 2929.01 and 2929.17 of the Revised Code are presented in this act as composites of the sections as amended by both Am. S.B. 9 and Am. Sub. S.B. 107 of the 123rd General Assembly, with the new language of neither of the acts shown in capital letters. Section 2951.02 of the Revised Code is presented in this act as a composite of the section as amended by H.B. 471, Am. S.B. 9, and Am. Sub. S.B. 107 of the 123rd General Assembly, with the new language of none of the acts shown in capital letters. This is in recognition of the principle stated in division (B) of section 1.52 of the Revised Code that such amendments are to be harmonized where not substantively irreconcilable and constitutes a legislative finding that such is the resulting version in effect prior to the effective date of this act.

## § 2951.021 Offender may be required to pay monthly supervision fee.

(A)(1) If a court places a misdemeanor offender under a community control sanction under section 2929.26, 2929.27, or 2929.28 of the Revised Code or places a felony offender under a community control sanction under section 2929.16, 2929.17, or 2929.18 of the Revised Code and if the court places the offender under the control and supervision of a probation agency, the court may require the offender, as a condition of community control, to pay a monthly supervision fee of not more than fifty dollars for supervision services. If the court requires an offender to pay a monthly supervision fee and the offender will be under the control of a county department of probation, a multicounty department of probation, or a municipal court department of probation established under section 1901.33 of the Revised Code, the court shall specify whether the offender is to pay the fee to the probation agency that will have control over the offender or to the clerk of the court for which the supervision agency is established. If the court requires an offender to pay a monthly probation fee and the offender will be under the control of the adult parole authority, the court shall specify that the offender is to pay the fee to the clerk of the court of common pleas.

(2) No person shall be assessed, in any month, more than fifty dollars in supervision fees.

(3) The prosecuting attorney of the county or the chief legal officer of a municipal corporation in which is located the court that imposed sentence upon an offender may bring a civil action to recover unpaid monthly supervision fees that the offender was required to pay. Any amount recovered in the civil action shall be paid into the appropriate county or municipal probation services fund in accordance with division (B) of this section.

(4) The failure of an offender to comply with a condition of community control that requires the offender to pay a monthly supervision fee and that is imposed under division (A) (1) of this section shall not constitute the basis for the modification of the offender's community control sanctions pursuant to section 2929.15 or 2929.25 of the Revised Code but may be considered with any other factors that form the basis of a modification of a sanction for violating a community control sanction under those sections. If the court determines that a misdemeanor offender on community control failed to pay a monthly supervision fee imposed under division (A) (1) of this section and that no other factors warranting the modification of the offender's community control sanction are present, the court shall remand the offender to the custody of the probation agency and may impose any additional conditions of community control upon the offender, including a requirement that the offender perform community service, as the ends of justice require. Any requirement imposed pursuant to division (A) (4) of this section that the offender perform community service shall be in addition to and shall not limit or otherwise affect any order that the offender perform community service pursuant to division (B) of section 2951.02 of the Revised Code.

(B) Prior to the last day of the month in each month during the period of community control, an offender who is ordered to pay a monthly supervision fee under this section shall pay the fee to the probation agency that has control and supervision over the offender or to the clerk of the court for which the probation agency is established, as specified by the court, except that, if the probation agency is the adult parole authority, the offender shall pay the fee to the clerk of the court of common pleas. Each probation agency or clerk of a court that receives any monthly supervision fees shall keep a record of the monthly supervision fees that are paid to the agency or the clerk and shall give a written receipt to each person who pays a supervision fee to the agency or clerk.

(C) Subject to division (E) of this section, all monthly supervision fees collected under this section by a probation agency or the clerk of a court shall be disposed of in the following manner:

(1) For offenders who are under the control and supervision of a county department of probation or a municipal court department of probation in a county-operated municipal court, on or before the fifth business day of each month, the chief probation officer, the chief probation officer's designee, or the clerk of the court shall pay all monthly supervision fees collected in the previous month to the county treasurer of the county in which the county department of probation or municipal court department of probation is established for deposit into the county probation services fund established in the county treasury of that county pursuant to division (A) (1) section 321.44 of the Revised Code.

(2) For offenders who are under the control and supervision of a multicounty department of probation, on or before the fifth business day of each month, the chief probation officer, the chief probation officer's designee, or the clerk of the court shall pay all monthly supervision fees collected in the previous month to the county treasurer of the county in which is located the court of common pleas that placed the offender under a community control sanction under the control of the department for deposit into the county probation services fund established in the county treasury of that county pursuant to division (A) (1) of section 321.44 of the Revised Code and for subsequent appropriation and transfer in accordance with division (A) (2) of that section to the appropriate multicounty probation services fund established pursuant to division (B) of that section.

(3) For offenders who are under the control and supervision of a municipal court department of probation in a municipal court that is not a county-operated municipal court, on or before the fifth business day of each month, the chief probation officer, the chief probation officer's designee, or the clerk of the court shall pay all monthly supervision fees collected in the previous month to the treasurer of the municipal corporation for deposit into the municipal probation services fund established pursuant to section 737.41 of the Revised Code.

(4) For offenders who are under the control and supervision of the adult parole authority, the clerk of the court of common pleas, on or before the fifth business day of January, April, July, and October, shall pay all monthly supervision fees collected by the clerk in the previous three months to the treasurer of the county in which is located the court of common pleas that placed the offender under a community control sanction under the control of the authority for deposit into the county probation services fund established in the county treasury of that county pursuant to division (A) (1) of section 321.44 of the Revised Code.

(D) Not later than the first day of December of each year, each probation agency or the court of common pleas of a county in which the court has entered into an agreement with the adult parole authority pursuant to section 2301.32 of the Revised Code shall prepare a report regarding its use of money from a county probation services account, a multicounty probation services account, or a municipal probation services account, whichever is applicable. The report shall specify the amount appropriated from the fund to the probation agency or court during the current calendar year, an estimate of the amount that the probation agency or court will expend by the end of the year, a summary of how the amount appropriated has been expended for probation services, and an estimate of the amount of supervision fees that the probation agency or court will collect and pay to the appropriate treasurer for deposit in the appropriate fund in the next calendar year. The report shall be filed with one of the following:

(1) If the probation agency is a county department of probation or a municipal court department of probation in a county-operated municipal court, with the board of county commissioners of that county;

(2) If the probation agency is a multicounty department of probation, with the board of county commissioners of the county whose treasurer, in accordance with section 2301.27 of the Revised Code, is designated as the treasurer to whom supervision fees collected under this section are to be appropriated and transferred under division (A) (2) of section 321.44 of the Revised Code;

(3) If the probation agency is a department of probation of a municipal court that is not a county-operated municipal court, with the legislative authority of the municipal corporation that operates the court;

(4) If the court of common pleas has entered into an agreement with the adult parole authority, with the director of rehabilitation and correction, the chief of the adult parole authority, and the board of county commissioners in each county for which the adult parole authority provides probation services.

(E) If the clerk of a court of common pleas or the clerk of a municipal court collects any monthly supervision fees under this section, the clerk may retain up to two per cent of the fees so collected to cover any administrative costs experienced in complying with the clerk's duties under this section.

**HISTORY: 145 v H 406 (Eff 11-11-94); 146 v S 2 (Eff 7-1-96); 146 v S 269. Eff 7-1-96; 149 v H 490, § 1, eff. 1-1-04; 152 v H 130, § 1, eff. 4-7-09.**

The effective date is set by section 4 of H.B. 490.

## § 2951.022 Determination of court responsibility for supervision of concurrent supervision offender; enforcement of financial obligations; terms of supervision; agreement with adult parole authority.

(A) As used in this section:

(1) "Concurrent supervision offender" means any offender who has been sentenced to community control for one or more misdemeanor violations or has been placed under a community control sanction pursuant to section 2929.16, 2929.17, 2929.18, or 2929.20 of the Revised Code and who is simultaneously subject to supervision by any of the following:

(a) Two or more municipal courts or county courts in this state;

(b) Two or more courts of common pleas in this state;

(c) One or more courts of common pleas in this state and one or more municipal courts or county courts in this state.

"Concurrent supervision offender" does not include a parolee or releasee.

(2) "Parolee" and "releasee" have the same meanings as in section 2967.01 of the Revised Code.

(B)(1) Except as otherwise provided in divisions (B)(2), (3), and (4) of this section, a concurrent supervision offender shall be supervised by the court that imposed the longest possible sentence and shall not be supervised by any other court.

(2) In the case of a concurrent supervision offender subject to supervision by two or more municipal or county courts in the same county, the municipal or county court in the territorial jurisdiction in which the offender resides shall supervise the offender. In the case of a concurrent supervision offender subject to supervision by a municipal court or county court and a court of common pleas for two or more equal possible sentences, the municipal or county court shall supervise the offender. In the case of a concurrent supervision offender subject to supervision by two or more courts of common pleas in separate counties in this state, the court that lies within the same territorial jurisdiction in which the offender resides shall supervise the offender.

(3) Separate courts within the same county may enter into an agreement or adopt local rules of procedure specifying, generally, that concurrent supervision offenders will be supervised in a manner other than that provided for in divisions (B)(1) and (2) of this section.

(4)(a) The judges of the various courts of this state having jurisdiction over a concurrent supervision offender may agree by journal entry to transfer jurisdiction over a concurrent supervision offender from one court to another court in any manner the courts consider appropriate, if the offender is supervised by only a single supervising authority at all times. An agreement to transfer supervision of an offender under division (B)(4)(a) of this section shall not take effect until approved by every court having authority to supervise the offender and may provide for the transfer of supervision to the offender's jurisdiction of residence whether or not the offender was subject to supervision in that jurisdiction prior to transfer. In the case of a subsequent conviction in a court other than the supervising court, the supervising court may agree to accept a transfer of jurisdiction from the court of conviction prior to sentencing and proceed to sentence the offender according to law.

(b) If the judges of the various courts of this state having authority to supervise a concurrent supervision offender cannot reach agreement with respect to the supervision of the offender, the offender may be subject to concurrent supervision in the interest of justice upon the courts' consideration of the provisions set forth in division (C) of this section.

(C) In determining whether a court maintains authority to supervise an offender or transfers authority to supervise the offender pursuant to division (B)(3) or (4) of this section, the court shall consider all of the following:

(1) The safety of the community;

(2) The risk that the offender might reoffend;

(3) The nature of the offenses committed by the offender;

(4) The likelihood that the offender will remain in the jurisdiction;

(5) The ability of the offender to travel to and from the offender's residence and place of employment or school to the offices of the supervising authority;

(6) The resources for residential and nonresidential sanctions or rehabilitative treatment available to the various courts having supervising authority;

(7) Any other factors consistent with the purposes of sentencing.

(D) The court having sole authority over a concurrent supervision offender pursuant to this section shall have complete authority for enforcement of any financial obligations imposed by any other court, shall set a payment schedule consistent with the offender's ability to pay, and shall cause payments of the offender's financial obligations to be directed to the sentencing court in proportion to the total amounts ordered by all sentencing courts, or as otherwise agreed by the sentencing courts. Financial obligations include financial sanctions imposed pursuant to sections 2929.18 and 2929.28 of the Revised Code, court costs, and any other financial order or fee imposed by a sentencing court. A supervision fee may be charged only by the agency providing supervision of the case.

(E) Unless the local residential sanction is suspended, the offender shall complete any local residential sanction before jurisdiction is transferred in accordance with this section. The supervising court shall respect all conditions of supervision established by a sentencing court, but any conflicting or inconsistent order of the supervising court shall supersede any other order of a sentencing court. In the case of a concurrent supervision offender, the supervising court shall determine when supervision will be terminated but shall not terminate supervision until all financial obligations are paid pursuant to sections 2929.18 and 2929.28 of the Revised Code.

(F) The adult parole authority and one or more courts may enter into an agreement whereby a releasee or parolee who is simultaneously under the supervision of the adult parole authority and the court or courts is supervised exclusively by either the authority or a court.

**HISTORY: 2011 HB 86, § 1, eff. Sept. 30, 2011.**

## § 2951.03 Presentence investigation report in felony case.

(A)(1) No person who has been convicted of or pleaded guilty to a felony shall be placed under a community control sanction until a written presentence investigation report has been considered by the court. If a court orders the preparation of a presentence investigation report pursuant to this section, section 2947.06 of the Revised Code, or Criminal Rule 32.2, the officer making the report shall inquire into the circumstances of the offense and the criminal record, social history, and present condition of the defendant, all information available regarding any prior adjudications of the defendant as a delinquent child and regarding the dispositions made relative to those adjudications, and any other matters specified in Criminal Rule 32.2. Whenever the officer considers it advisable, the officer's investigation may include a physical and mental examination of the defendant. A physical examination of the defendant may include a drug test consisting of a chemical analysis of a blood or urine specimen of the defendant to determine whether the defendant ingested or was injected with a drug of abuse. If, pursuant to section 2930.13 of the Revised Code, the victim of the offense of which the defendant has been convicted wishes to make a statement regarding the impact of the offense for the officer's use in preparing the presentence investigation report, the officer shall comply with the requirements of that section.

(2) If a defendant is committed to any institution, the presentence investigation report shall be sent to the institution with the entry of commitment. If a defendant is committed to any institution and a presentence investiga-

tion report is not prepared regarding that defendant pursuant to this section, section 2947.06 of the Revised Code, or Criminal Rule 32.2, the director of the department of rehabilitation and correction or the director's designee may order that an offender background investigation and report be conducted and prepared regarding the defendant pursuant to section 5120.16 of the Revised Code. An offender background investigation report prepared pursuant to this section shall be considered confidential information and is not a public record under section 149.43 of the Revised Code.

(3) The department of rehabilitation and correction may use any presentence investigation report and any offender background investigation report prepared pursuant to this section for penological and rehabilitative purposes. The department may disclose any presentence investigation report and any offender background investigation report to courts, law enforcement agencies, community-based correctional facilities, halfway houses, and medical, mental health, and substance abuse treatment providers. The department shall make the disclosure in a manner calculated to maintain the report's confidentiality. Any presentence investigation report or offender background investigation report that the department discloses to a community-based correctional facility, a halfway house, or a medical, mental health, or substance abuse treatment provider shall not include a victim impact section or information identifying a witness.

(B)(1) If a presentence investigation report is prepared pursuant to this section, section 2947.06 of the Revised Code, or Criminal Rule 32.2, the court, at a reasonable time before imposing sentence, shall permit the defendant or the defendant's counsel to read the report, except that the court shall not permit the defendant or the defendant's counsel to read any of the following:

(a) Any recommendation as to sentence;

(b) Any diagnostic opinions that, if disclosed, the court believes might seriously disrupt a program of rehabilitation for the defendant;

(c) Any sources of information obtained upon a promise of confidentiality;

(d) Any other information that, if disclosed, the court believes might result in physical harm or some other type of harm to the defendant or to any other person.

(2) Prior to sentencing, the court shall permit the defendant and the defendant's counsel to comment on the presentence investigation report and, in its discretion, may permit the defendant and the defendant's counsel to introduce testimony or other information that relates to any alleged factual inaccuracy contained in the report.

(3) If the court believes that any information in the presentence investigation report should not be disclosed pursuant to division (B)(1) of this section, the court, in lieu of making the report or any part of the report available, shall state orally or in writing a summary of the factual information contained in the report that will be relied upon in determining the defendant's sentence. The court shall permit the defendant and the defendant's counsel to comment upon the oral or written summary of the report.

(4) Any material that is disclosed to the defendant or the defendant's counsel pursuant to this section shall be disclosed to the prosecutor who is handling the prosecution of the case against the defendant.

(5) If the comments of the defendant or the defendant's counsel, the testimony they introduce, or any of the other information they introduce alleges any factual inaccuracy in the presentence investigation report or the summary of the report, the court shall do either of the following with respect to each alleged factual inaccuracy:

(a) Make a finding as to the allegation;

(b) Make a determination that no finding is necessary with respect to the allegation, because the factual matter will not be taken into account in the sentencing of the defendant.

(C) A court's decision as to the content of a summary under division (B)(3) of this section or as to the withholding of information under division (B)(1)(a), (b), (c), or (d) of this section shall be considered to be within the discretion of the court. No appeal can be taken from either of those decisions, and neither of those decisions shall be the basis for a reversal of the sentence imposed.

(D)(1) The contents of a presentence investigation report prepared pursuant to this section, section 2947.06 of the Revised Code, or Criminal Rule 32.2 and the contents of any written or oral summary of a presentence investigation report or of a part of a presentence investigation report described in division (B)(3) of this section are confidential information and are not a public record. The court, an appellate court, authorized probation officers, investigators, and court personnel, the defendant, the defendant's counsel, the prosecutor who is handling the prosecution of the case against the defendant, and authorized personnel of an institution to which the defendant is committed may inspect, receive copies of, retain copies of, and use a presentence investigation report or a written or oral summary of a presentence investigation only for the purposes of or only as authorized by Criminal Rule 32.2 or this section, division (F)(1) of section 2953.08, section 2947.06, or another section of the Revised Code.

(2) Immediately following the imposition of sentence upon the defendant, the defendant or the defendant's counsel and the prosecutor shall return to the court all copies of a presentence investigation report and of any written summary of a presentence investigation report or part of a presentence investigation report that the court made available to the defendant or the defendant's counsel and to the prosecutor pursuant to this section. The defendant or the defendant's counsel and the prosecutor shall not make any copies of the presentence investigation report or of any written summary of a presentence investigation report or part of a presentence investigation report that the court made available to them pursuant to this section.

(3) Except when a presentence investigation report or a written or oral summary of a presentence investigation report is being used for the purposes of or as authorized by Criminal Rule 32.2 or this section, division (F)(1) of section 2953.08, section 2947.06, or another section of the Revised Code, the court or other authorized holder of the report or summary shall retain the report or summary under seal.

(E) In inquiring into the information available regarding any prior adjudications of the defendant as a delinquent child and regarding the dispositions made relative to those adjudications, the officer making the report shall consider all information that is relevant, including, but not limited to, the materials described in division (B) of section 2151.14, division (C)(3) of section 2152.18, division (D)(3) of section 2152.19, and division (E) of section 2152.71 of the Revised Code.

(F) As used in this section:

(1) "Prosecutor" has the same meaning as in section 2935.01 of the Revised Code.

(2) "Community control sanction" has the same meaning as in section 2929.01 of the Revised Code.

(3) "Public record" has the same meaning as in section 149.43 of the Revised Code.

**HISTORY: GC § 13452-1a; 121 v 381; Bureau of Code Revision, 10-1-53; 130 v 672 (Eff 9-24-63); 142 v H 73, § 1 (Eff 10-1-87); 142 v H 73, § 3 (Eff 10-1-89); 143 v S 258 (Eff 11-20-90); 145 v H 571 (Eff 10-6-94); 145 v S 186 (Eff 10-12-94); 146 v S 2 (Eff 7-1-96); 146 v S 269 (Eff 7-1-96); 148 v H 349 (Eff 9-22-2000); 149 v H 247 (Eff 5-30-2002); 149 v H 510. Eff 3-31-2003.**

## § 2951.04 Repealed, 146 v S 269, § 2 [136 v H 300; 138 v H 900; 141 v H 475; 143 v H 317; 143 v S 258; 145 v H 385; 146 v S 2]. Eff 7-1-96.

This section regulated conditional probation for treatment and rehabilitation of drug dependent persons.

The effective date is set by section 5 of SB 269.

## § 2951.041 Intervention in lieu of conviction.

(A)(1) If an offender is charged with a criminal offense, including but not limited to a violation of section 2913.02, 2913.03, 2913.11, 2913.21, 2913.31, or 2919.21 of the Revised Code, and the court has reason to believe that drug or alcohol usage by the offender was a factor leading to the criminal offense with which the offender is charged or that, at the time of committing that offense, the offender had a mental illness or was a person with intellectual disability and that the mental illness or status as a person with intellectual disability was a factor leading to the offender's criminal behavior, the court may accept, prior to the entry of a guilty plea, the offender's request for intervention in lieu of conviction. The request shall include a statement from the offender as to whether the offender is alleging that drug or alcohol usage by the offender was a factor leading to the criminal offense with which the offender is charged or is alleging that, at the time of committing that offense, the offender had a mental illness or was a person with intellectual disability and that the mental illness or status as a person with intellectual disability was a factor leading to the criminal offense with which the offender is charged. The request also shall include a waiver of the defendant's right to a speedy trial, the preliminary hearing, the time period within which the grand jury may consider an indictment against the offender, and arraignment, unless the hearing, indictment, or arraignment has already occurred. The court may reject an offender's request without a hearing. If the court elects to consider an offender's request, the court shall conduct a hearing to determine whether the offender is eligible under this section for intervention in lieu of conviction and shall stay all criminal proceedings pending the outcome of the hearing. If the court schedules a hearing, the court shall order an assessment of the offender for the purpose of determining the offender's eligibility for intervention in lieu of conviction and recommending an appropriate intervention plan.

If the offender alleges that drug or alcohol usage by the offender was a factor leading to the criminal offense with which the offender is charged, the court may order that the offender be assessed by a program certified pursuant to section 3793.06 of the Revised Code or a properly credentialed professional for the purpose of determining the offender's eligibility for intervention in lieu of conviction and recommending an appropriate intervention plan. The program or the properly credentialed professional shall provide a written assessment of the offender to the court.

(2) The victim notification provisions of division (C) of section 2930.08 of the Revised Code apply in relation to any hearing held under division (A)(1) of this section.

(B) An offender is eligible for intervention in lieu of conviction if the court finds all of the following:

(1) The offender previously has not been convicted of or pleaded guilty to a felony offense of violence or previously has been convicted of or pleaded guilty to any felony that is not an offense of violence and the prosecuting attorney recommends that the offender be found eligible for participation in intervention in lieu of treatment under this section, previously has not been through intervention in lieu of conviction under this section or any similar regimen, and is charged with a felony for which the court, upon conviction, would impose sentence under division (B)(2)(b) of section 2929.13 of the Revised Code or with a misdemeanor.

(2) The offense is not a felony of the first, second, or third degree, is not an offense of violence, is not a violation of division (A)(1) or (2) of section 2903.06 of the Revised Code, is not a violation of division (A)(1) of section 2903.08 of the Revised Code, is not a violation of division (A) of section 4511.19 of the Revised Code or a municipal ordinance that is substantially similar to that division, and is not an offense for which a sentencing court is required to impose a mandatory prison term, a mandatory term of local incarceration, or a mandatory term of imprisonment in a jail.

(3) The offender is not charged with a violation of section 2925.02, 2925.04, or 2925.06 of the Revised Code, is not charged with a violation of section 2925.03 of the Revised Code that is a felony of the first, second, third, or fourth degree, and is not charged with a violation of section 2925.11 of the Revised Code that is a felony of the first, second, or third degree.

(4) If an offender alleges that drug or alcohol usage by the offender was a factor leading to the criminal offense with which the offender is charged, the court has ordered that the offender be assessed by a program certified pursuant to section 3793.06 of the Revised Code or a properly credentialed professional for the purpose of determining the offender's eligibility for intervention in lieu of conviction and recommending an appropriate intervention plan, the offender has been assessed by a program of that nature or a properly credentialed professional in accordance with the court's order, and the program or properly credentialed professional has filed the written assessment of the offender with the court.

(5) If an offender alleges that, at the time of committing the criminal offense with which the offender is charged, the offender had a mental illness or was a person with intellectual disability and that the mental illness or status as a person with intellectual disability was a factor leading to that offense, the offender has been assessed by a psychiatrist, psychologist, independent social worker, or professional clinical counselor for the purpose of determining the offender's eligibility for intervention in lieu of conviction and recommending an appropriate intervention plan.

(6) The offender's drug usage, alcohol usage, mental illness, or intellectual disability, whichever is applicable, was a factor leading to the criminal offense with which the

offender is charged, intervention in lieu of conviction would not demean the seriousness of the offense, and intervention would substantially reduce the likelihood of any future criminal activity.

(7) The alleged victim of the offense was not sixty-five years of age or older, permanently and totally disabled, under thirteen years of age, or a peace officer engaged in the officer's official duties at the time of the alleged offense.

(8) If the offender is charged with a violation of section 2925.24 of the Revised Code, the alleged violation did not result in physical harm to any person, and the offender previously has not been treated for drug abuse.

(9) The offender is willing to comply with all terms and conditions imposed by the court pursuant to division (D) of this section.

(C) At the conclusion of a hearing held pursuant to division (A) of this section, the court shall enter its determination as to whether the offender is eligible for intervention in lieu of conviction and as to whether to grant the offender's request. If the court finds under division (B) of this section that the offender is eligible for intervention in lieu of conviction and grants the offender's request, the court shall accept the offender's plea of guilty and waiver of the defendant's right to a speedy trial, the preliminary hearing, the time period within which the grand jury may consider an indictment against the offender, and arraignment, unless the hearing, indictment, or arraignment has already occurred. In addition, the court then may stay all criminal proceedings and order the offender to comply with all terms and conditions imposed by the court pursuant to division (D) of this section. If the court finds that the offender is not eligible or does not grant the offender's request, the criminal proceedings against the offender shall proceed as if the offender's request for intervention in lieu of conviction had not been made.

(D) If the court grants an offender's request for intervention in lieu of conviction, the court shall place the offender under the general control and supervision of the county probation department, the adult parole authority, or another appropriate local probation or court services agency, if one exists, as if the offender was subject to a community control sanction imposed under section 2929.15, 2929.18, or 2929.25 of the Revised Code. The court shall establish an intervention plan for the offender. The terms and conditions of the intervention plan shall require the offender, for at least one year from the date on which the court grants the order of intervention in lieu of conviction, to abstain from the use of illegal drugs and alcohol, to participate in treatment and recovery support services, and to submit to regular random testing for drug and alcohol use and may include any other treatment terms and conditions, or terms and conditions similar to community control sanctions, which may include community service or restitution, that are ordered by the court.

(E) If the court grants an offender's request for intervention in lieu of conviction and the court finds that the offender has successfully completed the intervention plan for the offender, including the requirement that the offender abstain from using illegal drugs and alcohol for a period of at least one year from the date on which the court granted the order of intervention in lieu of conviction, the requirement that the offender participate in treatment and recovery support services, and all other terms and conditions ordered by the court, the court shall dismiss the proceedings against the offender. Successful completion of the intervention plan and period of abstinence under this section shall be without adjudication of guilt and is not a criminal conviction for purposes of any disqualification or disability imposed by law and upon conviction of a crime, and the court may order the sealing of records related to the offense in question in the manner provided in sections 2953.31 to 2953.36 of the Revised Code.

(F) If the court grants an offender's request for intervention in lieu of conviction and the offender fails to comply with any term or condition imposed as part of the intervention plan for the offender, the supervising authority for the offender promptly shall advise the court of this failure, and the court shall hold a hearing to determine whether the offender failed to comply with any term or condition imposed as part of the plan. If the court determines that the offender has failed to comply with any of those terms and conditions, it shall enter a finding of guilty and shall impose an appropriate sanction under Chapter 2929. of the Revised Code. If the court sentences the offender to a prison term, the court, after consulting with the department of rehabilitation and correction regarding the availability of services, may order continued court-supervised activity and treatment of the offender during the prison term and, upon consideration of reports received from the department concerning the offender's progress in the program of activity and treatment, may consider judicial release under section 2929.20 of the Revised Code.

(G) As used in this section:

(1) "Community control sanction" has the same meaning as in section 2929.01 of the Revised Code.

(2) "Intervention in lieu of conviction" means any court-supervised activity that complies with this section.

(3) "Peace officer" has the same meaning as in section 2935.01 of the Revised Code.

(4) "Mental illness" and "psychiatrist" have the same meanings as in section 5122.01 of the Revised Code.

(5) "Person with intellectual disability" means a person having significantly subaverage general intellectual functioning existing concurrently with deficiencies in adaptive behavior, manifested during the developmental period.

(6) "Psychologist" has the same meaning as in section 4732.01 of the Revised Code.

(H) Whenever the term "mentally retarded person" is used in any statute, rule, contract, grant, or other document, the reference shall be deemed to include a "person with intellectual disability," as defined in this section.

**HISTORY: 148 v H 202 (Eff 2-9-2000); 148 v S 107 (Eff 3-23-2000); 149 v H 327. Eff 7-8-2002; 149 v H 490, § 1, eff. 1-1-04; 152 v H 130, § 1, eff. 4-7-09; 2011 HB 86, § 1, eff. Sept. 30, 2011.**

The effective date is set by section 4 of H.B. 490.

**Analogous to former RC § 2951.04.1 (136 v H 300; 138 v H 900; 143 v H 317; 143 v S 258; 145 v H 385; 146 v S 2; 146 v S 269), repealed 148 v S 107, § 2, eff 3-23-2000.**

## § 2951.05 Random drug testing.

(A)(1) A county department of probation, a multicounty department of probation, or the adult parole authority that has general control and supervision of offenders who are required to submit to random drug testing under division (A)(1)(a) of section 2929.25 of the Revised Code or who are subject to a nonresidential sanction that includes random drug testing under section 2929.17 or 2929.27 of the Revised Code, may cause each offender to submit to random drug testing performed by a laboratory or entity that has entered into a contract with any of the governmental entities or officers authorized to enter into a contract with that laboratory or entity under section 341.26, 753.33, or 5120.63 of the Revised Code.

(2) If no laboratory or entity described in division (A)(1) of this section has entered into a contract as specified in that division, the county department of probation, the multicounty department of probation, or the adult parole authority, as appropriate, that has general control and supervision of offenders shall cause the offender to submit to random drug testing performed by a reputable public laboratory to determine whether the individual who is the subject of the drug test ingested or was injected with a drug of abuse.

(3) A laboratory or entity that has entered into a contract as specified in division (A)(1) of this section shall perform the random drug testing in accordance with the applicable standards that are included in the terms of that contract. A public laboratory shall perform the random drug tests in accordance with the standards set forth in the policies and procedures established by the department of rehabilitation and correction pursuant to section 5120.63 of the Revised Code. An offender who is subject to a nonresidential sanction that includes random drug testing under section 2929.17 or 2929.27 of the Revised Code shall pay the fee for the drug test if the test results indicate that the offender ingested or was injected with a drug of abuse and if the county department of probation, the multicounty department of probation, or the adult parole authority that has general control and supervision of the offender requires payment of a fee. A laboratory or entity that performs the random drug testing on an offender shall transmit the results of the drug test to the appropriate county probation department, multicounty probation department, or adult parole authority that has general control and supervision of the offender.

(B) As used in this section:

(1) "Multicounty department of probation" means a probation department established under section 2301.27 of the Revised Code to serve more than one county.

(2) "Random drug testing" has the same meaning as in section 5120.63 of the Revised Code.

**HISTORY: GC § 13452-3; 113 v 123(201), ch 31, § 3; 121 v 381; Bureau of Code Revision, 10-1-53; 125 v S 155 (Eff 7-1-54); 128 v 959 (Eff 10-1-59); 129 v 481 (Eff 10-18-61); 130 v PtII, 146 (Eff 3-18-65); 145 v H 406 (Eff 11-11-94); 148 v H 349. Eff 9-22-2000; 149 v H 490, § 1, eff. 1-1-04.**

The effective date is set by section 4 of H.B. 490.

## § 2951.06 Release from custody.

Upon entry in the records of the judge or magistrate of the sentence of a community control sanction provided for in section 2929.15 or 2929.25 of the Revised Code, the defendant shall be released from custody as soon as the requirements and conditions required by the judge supervising the community control sanction have been met. The defendant shall continue under the control and supervision of the appropriate probation agency, to the extent required by law, the conditions of the community control sanction, and the rules and regulations governing the probation agency.

**HISTORY: GC § 13452-4; 113 v 123(202), ch 31, § 4; 121 v 381; Bureau of Code Revision, 10-1-53; 125 v S 155 (Eff 7-1-54); 129 v 481 (Eff 10-18-61); 130 v PtII, 147. Eff 3-18-65; 149 v H 490, § 1, eff. 1-1-04.**

The effective date is set by section 4 of HB 490.

## § 2951.07 Period of community control.

A community control sanction continues for the period that the judge or magistrate determines and, subject to the five-year limit specified in section 2929.15 or 2929.25 of the Revised Code, may be extended. If the offender under community control absconds or otherwise leaves the jurisdiction of the court without permission from the probation officer, the probation agency, or the court to do so, or if the offender is confined in any institution for the commission of any offense, the period of community control ceases to run until the time that the offender is brought before the court for its further action.

**HISTORY: GC § 13452-5; 113 v 123(202), ch 31, § 5; 115 v 531; Bureau of Code Revision, 10-1-53; 143 v S 258 (Eff 11-20-90); 146 v S 2 (Eff 7-1-96); 146 v S 269. Eff 7-1-96; 149 v H 490, § 1, eff. 1-1-04.**

The effective date is set by section 4 of H.B. 490.

## § 2951.08 Arrest of person under community control sanction.

(A) During a period of community control, any field officer or probation officer may arrest the person under a community control sanction without a warrant and bring the person before the judge or magistrate before whom the cause was pending. During a period of community control, any peace officer may arrest the person under a community control sanction without a warrant upon the written order of the chief probation officer of the probation agency if the person under a community control sanction is under the supervision of that probation agency or on the order of an officer of the adult parole authority created pursuant to section 5149.02 of the Revised Code if the person under a community control sanction is under the supervision of the authority. During a period of community control, any peace officer may arrest the person under a community control sanction on the warrant of the judge or magistrate before whom the cause was pending.

During a period of community control, any peace officer may arrest the person under a community control sanction without a warrant if the peace officer has reasonable ground to believe that the person has violated or is violating any of the following that is a condition of the person's community control sanction:

(1) A condition that prohibits ownership, possession, or use of a firearm, deadly weapon, ammunition, or dangerous ordnance;

(2) A condition that prohibits the person from being within a specified structure or geographic area;

(3) A condition that confines the person to a residence, facility, or other structure;

(4) A condition that prohibits the person from contacting or communicating with any specified individual;

(5) A condition that prohibits the person from associating with a specified individual;

(6) A condition as provided in division (A)(1)(a) of section 2929.25 of the Revised Code or in division (A)(1) of section 2929.15 or (A)(8) of section 2929.27 of the Revised Code that requires that the person not ingest or be injected with a drug of abuse and submit to random drug testing and requires that the results of the drug test

indicate that the person did not ingest or was not injected with a drug of abuse.

(B) Within three business days after making an arrest under this section, the arresting field officer, probation officer, or peace officer or the department or agency of the arresting officer shall notify the chief probation officer or the chief probation officer's designee that the person has been arrested. Within thirty days of being notified that a field officer, probation officer, or peace officer has made an arrest under this section, the chief probation officer or designee, or another probation officer designated by the chief probation officer, promptly shall bring the person who was arrested before the judge or magistrate before whom the cause was pending.

(C) Nothing in this section limits the powers of arrest granted to certain law enforcement officers and citizens under sections 2935.03 and 2935.04 of the Revised Code.

(D) A probation officer shall receive the actual and necessary expenses incurred in the performance of the officer's duties.

(E) As used in this section, "random drug testing" has the same meaning as in section 5120.63 of the Revised Code.

**HISTORY: GC § 13452-6; 113 v 123(202), ch 31, § 6; 121 v 381; Bureau of Code Revision, 10-1-53; 125 v S 155 (Eff 7-1-54); 129 v 481 (Eff 10-18-61); 130 v PtII, 147 (Eff 3-18-65); 144 v S 49 (Eff 7-21-92); 145 v H 406 (Eff 11-11-94); 146 v S 269 (Eff 7-1-96); 148 v H 349. Eff 9-22-2000; 149 v H 490, § 1, eff. 1-1-04; 2011 HB 86, § 1, eff. Sept. 30, 2011.**

The effective date is set by section 4 of HB 490.

## § 2951.09 Repealed, 149 v H 490, § 2 [GC § 13452-7; 113 v 123(202), ch 31, § 7; 115 v 532; Bureau of Code Revision, 10-1-53; 143 v S 258 (Eff 11-20-90); 146 v S 2. Eff 7-1-96]. Eff 1-1-04.

This section concerned proceedings after arrest of probationer.

## § 2951.10 Final order.

An order suspending the imposition of a sentence for a misdemeanor under section 2929.25 of the Revised Code and placing the defendant under a community control sanction is a final order from which appeal may be prosecuted.

**HISTORY: GC § 13452-9; 113 v 123(202), ch 31, § 9; Bureau of Code Revision. Eff 10-1-53; 149 v H 490, § 1, eff. 1-1-04.**

The effective date is set by section 4 of H.B. 490.

## § 2951.11 Repealed, 134 v H 511, § 2 [GC § 13452-10; 113 v 123(203); Bureau of Code Revision, 10-1-53; 133 v S 460]. Eff 1-1-74.

This section concerned parole by board of county commissioners.

## § 2951.12 Repealed, 136 v H 1, § 2 [GC § 13452-11; 113 v 123(203); Bureau of Code Revision, 10-1-53; 133 v S 460]. Eff 6-13-75.

This section concerned recommitment for failure to comply with conditions of parole.

## § 2951.13 Attendance at revocation hearing.

A convict confined in a state correctional institution for a felony committed while the convict was under a community control sanction imposed for a former conviction may be removed from the institution for the purpose of attending a hearing on revocation of the community control sanction. When a copy of the journal entry ordering the revocation hearing is presented to the warden or superintendent of the institution where the convict is confined, the warden or superintendent shall deliver the convict to the sheriff of the county where the hearing is to be held, and the sheriff shall convey the convict to and from the hearing. The approval of the governor on the journal entry is not required.

**HISTORY: 133 v H 1136 (Eff 5-26-70); 140 v H 291 (Eff 7-1-83); 145 v H 571 (Eff 10-6-94); 146 v S 2. Eff 7-1-96.**

The effective date is set by section 6 of SB 2.

# CHAPTER 2953: APPEALS; OTHER POSTCONVICTION REMEDIES



## § 2953.01 Definition of magistrate.

The definition of "magistrate" set forth in section 2931.01 of the Revised Code applies to Chapter 2953. of the Revised Code.

**HISTORY: Bureau of Code Revision. Eff 10-1-53.**

## § 2953.02 Review of judgments.

In a capital case in which a sentence of death is imposed for an offense committed before January 1, 1995, and in any other criminal case, including a conviction for the violation of an ordinance of a municipal corporation, the judgment or final order of a court of record inferior to the court of appeals may be reviewed in the court of appeals. A final order of an administrative officer or agency may be reviewed in the court of common pleas. A judgment or final order of the court of appeals involving a question arising under the Constitution of the United States or of this state may be appealed to the supreme court as a matter of right. This right of appeal from judgments and final orders of the court of appeals shall extend to cases in which a sentence of death is imposed for an offense committed before January 1, 1995, and in which the death penalty has been affirmed, felony cases in which the supreme court has directed the court of appeals to certify its record, and in all other criminal cases of public or general interest wherein the supreme court has granted a motion to certify the record of the court of appeals. In a capital case in which a sentence of death is imposed for an offense committed on or after January 1, 1995, the judgment or final order may be appealed from the trial court directly to the supreme court as a matter of right. The supreme court in criminal cases shall not be required to determine as to the weight of the evidence, except that, in cases in which a sentence of death is imposed for an offense committed on or after January 1, 1995, and in which the question of the weight of the evidence to support the judgment has been raised on appeal, the supreme court shall determine as to the weight of the evidence to support the judgment and shall determine as to the weight of the evidence to support the sentence of death as provided in section 2929.05 of the Revised Code.

**HISTORY: GC § 13459-1; 113 v 123(211), ch 38; Bureau of Code Revision, 10-1-53; 128 v 141 (Eff 1-1-60); 133 v S 530 (Eff 6-12-70); 139 v S 1 (Eff 10-19-81); 146 v S 4. Eff 9-21-95.**

## § 2953.03 Motion for new trial or filing of appeal if defendant on bail.

(A) If a motion for a new trial is filed pursuant to Criminal Rule 33 by a defendant who is convicted of a misdemeanor under the Revised Code or an ordinance of a municipal corporation, and if that defendant was on bail at the time of the conviction of that offense, the trial judge or magistrate shall suspend execution of the sentence or judgment imposed pending the determination on the motion for a new trial and shall determine the amount and nature of any bail that is required of the defendant in accordance with Criminal Rule 46.

(B) If a notice of appeal is filed pursuant to the Rules of Appellate Procedure or Chapter 1905. of the Revised Code by a defendant who is convicted in a municipal, county, or mayor's court or a court of common pleas of a misdemeanor under the Revised Code or an ordinance of a municipal corporation, if that defendant was on bail at the time of the conviction of that offense, and if execution of the sentence or judgment imposed is suspended, the trial court or magistrate or the court in which the appeal is being prosecuted shall determine the amount and nature of any bail that is required of the defendant as follows:

(1) In the case of an appeal to a court of appeals by a defendant who is convicted in a municipal or county court or a court of common pleas, in accordance with Appellate Rule 8 and Criminal Rule 46;

(2) In the case of an appeal to a municipal or county court by a defendant who is convicted in a mayor's court, in accordance with Criminal Rule 46.

**HISTORY: 141 v H 412. Eff 3-17-87.**

**Not analogous to former RC § 2953.03 (GC § 13459-2; 113 v 123(212), ch 38, § 2; Bureau of Code Revision, 10-1-53; 128 v 144; 129 v 305; 130 v 672; 136 v H 164), repealed 141 v H 412, § 2, eff 3-17-87.**

## § 2953.04 Repealed, 141 v H 412, § 2 [GC §§ 13459-3, 13459-4; 113 v 123(212), ch 38, §§ 3, 4; 116 v 104 (116, 117), § 2; Bureau of Code Revision, 10-1-53; 128 v 141]. Eff 3-17-87.

This section concerned proceedings to review and appeal.

## § 2953.05 Repealed, 141 v H 412, § 2 [GC §§ 13459-3, 13459-4; 113 v 123(212), ch 38, §§ 3, 4; 116 v 104 (116, 117), § 2; Bureau of Code Revision, 10-1-53; 128 v 141]. Eff 3-17-87.

This section concerned proceedings to review and appeal.

## § 2953.051 Repealed, 141 v H 412, § 2 [128 v 141]. Eff 3-17-87.

This section concerned suspension of sentence and continuance of bail.

## § 2953.06 Repealed, 141 v H 412, § 2 [GC § 13459-5; 113 v 123(212), ch 38, § 5; 116 v 104(117), § 2; Bureau of Code Revision, 10-1-53]. Eff 3-17-87.

This section concerned notice of appeal served upon prosecuting attorney.

## § 2953.07 Disposition of appeal; setting of execution date.

Upon the hearing of an appeal other than an appeal from a mayor's court, the appellate court may affirm the judgment or reverse it, in whole or in part, or modify it, and order the accused to be discharged or grant a new trial. The appellate court may remand the accused for the sole purpose of correcting a sentence imposed contrary to law, provided that, on an appeal of a sentence imposed upon a person who is convicted of or pleads guilty to a felony that is brought under section 2953.08 of the Revised Code, division (G) of that section applies to the court. If the judgment is reversed, the appellant shall recover from the appellee all court costs incurred to secure the reversal, including the cost of transcripts. In capital cases, when the judgment is affirmed and the day fixed for the execution is passed, the appellate court shall appoint a day for it, and the clerk of the appellate court shall issue a warrant under the seal of the appellate court, to the sheriff of the proper county, or the warden of the appropriate state correctional institution, commanding the sheriff or warden to carry the sentence into execution on the day so appointed. The sheriff or warden shall execute and return the warrant as in other cases, and the clerk shall record the warrant and return.

(B) As used in this section, "appellate court" means, for a case in which a sentence of death is imposed for an offense committed before January 1, 1995, both the court of appeals and the supreme court, and for a case in which a sentence of death is imposed for an offense committed on or after January 1, 1995, the supreme court.

**HISTORY: GC § 13459-6; 113 v 123(213), ch 38, § 6; 116 v 104(117), § 2; Bureau of Code Revision, 10-1-53; 141 v H 412 (Eff 3-17-87); 145 v H 571 (Eff 10-6-94); 146 v S 4 (Eff 9-21-95); 146 v S 2. Eff 7-1-96.**

The effective date is set by section 6 of SB 2.

See provisions, § 5 of SB 2 (146 v —) as amended by § 3 of SB 269 (146 v —), following RC § 2929.03.

## § 2953.08 Grounds for appeal by defendant or prosecutor of sentence for felony; appeal cost oversight committee.

(A) In addition to any other right to appeal and except as provided in division (D) of this section, a defendant who is convicted of or pleads guilty to a felony may appeal as a matter of right the sentence imposed upon the defendant on one of the following grounds:

(1) The sentence consisted of or included the maximum prison term allowed for the offense by division (A) of section 2929.14 or section 2929.142 of the Revised Code, the maximum prison term was not required for the offense pursuant to Chapter 2925. or any other provision of the Revised Code, and the court imposed the sentence under one of the following circumstances:

(a) The sentence was imposed for only one offense.

(b) The sentence was imposed for two or more offenses arising out of a single incident, and the court imposed the maximum prison term for the offense of the highest degree.

(2) The sentence consisted of or included a prison term, the offense for which it was imposed is a felony of the fourth or fifth degree or is a felony drug offense that is a violation of a provision of Chapter 2925. of the Revised Code and that is specified as being subject to division (B) of section 2929.13 of the Revised Code for purposes of sentencing, and the court did not specify at sentencing that it found one or more factors specified in divisions (B)(1)(a) to (i) of section 2929.13 of the Revised Code to apply relative to the defendant. If the court specifies that it found one or more of those factors to apply relative to the defendant, the defendant is not entitled under this division to appeal as a matter of right the sentence imposed upon the offender.

(3) The person was convicted of or pleaded guilty to a violent sex offense or a designated homicide, assault, or kidnapping offense, was adjudicated a sexually violent predator in relation to that offense, and was sentenced pursuant to division (A)(3) of section 2971.03 of the Revised Code, if the minimum term of the indefinite term imposed pursuant to division (A)(3) of section 2971.03 of the Revised Code is the longest term available for the offense from among the range of terms listed in section 2929.14 of the Revised Code. As used in this division, "designated homicide, assault, or kidnapping offense" and "violent sex offense" have the same meanings as in section 2971.01 of the Revised Code. As used in this division, "adjudicated a sexually violent predator" has the same meaning as in section 2929.01 of the Revised Code, and a person is "adjudicated a sexually violent predator" in the same manner and the same circumstances as are described in that section.

(4) The sentence is contrary to law.

(5) The sentence consisted of an additional prison term of ten years imposed pursuant to division (B)(2)(a) of section 2929.14 of the Revised Code.

(B) In addition to any other right to appeal and except as provided in division (D) of this section, a prosecuting attorney, a city director of law, village solicitor, or similar chief legal officer of a municipal corporation, or the attorney general, if one of those persons prosecuted the case, may appeal as a matter of right a sentence imposed upon a defendant who is convicted of or pleads guilty to a felony or, in the circumstances described in division (B)(3) of this section the modification of a sentence imposed upon such a defendant, on any of the following grounds:

(1) The sentence did not include a prison term despite a presumption favoring a prison term for the offense for which it was imposed, as set forth in section 2929.13 or Chapter 2925. of the Revised Code.

(2) The sentence is contrary to law.

(3) The sentence is a modification under section 2929.20 of the Revised Code of a sentence that was imposed for a felony of the first or second degree.

(C)(1) In addition to the right to appeal a sentence granted under division (A) or (B) of this section, a defendant who is convicted of or pleads guilty to a felony may seek leave to appeal a sentence imposed upon the defendant on the basis that the sentencing judge has imposed consecutive sentences under division (C)(3) of section 2929.14 of the Revised Code and that the consecutive sentences exceed the maximum prison term allowed by division (A) of that section for the most serious offense of which the defendant was convicted. Upon the filing of a motion under this division, the court of appeals may grant leave to appeal the sentence if the court determines that the allegation included as the basis of the motion is true.

(2) A defendant may seek leave to appeal an additional sentence imposed upon the defendant pursuant to division (B)(2)(a) or (b) of section 2929.14 of the Revised Code if the additional sentence is for a definite prison term that is longer than five years.

(D)(1) A sentence imposed upon a defendant is not subject to review under this section if the sentence is authorized by law, has been recommended jointly by the defendant and the prosecution in the case, and is imposed by a sentencing judge.

(2) Except as provided in division (C)(2) of this section, a sentence imposed upon a defendant is not subject to review under this section if the sentence is imposed pursuant to division (B)(2)(b) of section 2929.14 of the Revised Code. Except as otherwise provided in this division, a defendant retains all rights to appeal as provided under this chapter or any other provision of the Revised Code. A defendant has the right to appeal under this chapter or any other provision of the Revised Code the court's application of division (B)(2)(c) of section 2929.14 of the Revised Code.

(3) A sentence imposed for aggravated murder or murder pursuant to sections 2929.02 to 2929.06 of the Revised Code is not subject to review under this section.

(E) A defendant, prosecuting attorney, city director of law, village solicitor, or chief municipal legal officer shall file an appeal of a sentence under this section to a court of appeals within the time limits specified in Rule 4(B) of the Rules of Appellate Procedure, provided that if the appeal is pursuant to division (B)(3) of this section, the time limits specified in that rule shall not commence running until the court grants the motion that makes the sentence modification in question. A sentence appeal under this section shall be consolidated with any other appeal in the case. If no other appeal is filed, the court of appeals may review only the portions of the trial record that pertain to sentencing.

(F) On the appeal of a sentence under this section, the record to be reviewed shall include all of the following, as applicable:

(1) Any presentence, psychiatric, or other investigative report that was submitted to the court in writing before the sentence was imposed. An appellate court that reviews a presentence investigation report prepared pursuant to section 2947.06 or 2951.03 of the Revised Code or Criminal Rule 32.2 in connection with the appeal of a sentence under this section shall comply with division (D)(3) of section 2951.03 of the Revised Code when the appellate court is not using the presentence investigation report, and the appellate court's use of a presentence investigation report of that nature in connection with the appeal of a sentence under this section does not affect the otherwise confidential character of the contents of that

report as described in division (D)(1) of section 2951.03 of the Revised Code and does not cause that report to become a public record, as defined in section 149.43 of the Revised Code, following the appellate court's use of the report.

(2) The trial record in the case in which the sentence was imposed;

(3) Any oral or written statements made to or by the court at the sentencing hearing at which the sentence was imposed;

(4) Any written findings that the court was required to make in connection with the modification of the sentence pursuant to a judicial release under division (I) of section 2929.20 of the Revised Code.

(G)(1) If the sentencing court was required to make the findings required by division (B) or (D) of section 2929.13 or division (I) of section 2929.20 of the Revised Code, or to state the findings of the trier of fact required by division (B)(2)(e) of section 2929.14 of the Revised Code, relative to the imposition or modification of the sentence, and if the sentencing court failed to state the required findings on the record, the court hearing an appeal under division (A), (B), or (C) of this section shall remand the case to the sentencing court and instruct the sentencing court to state, on the record, the required findings.

(2) The court hearing an appeal under division (A), (B), or (C) of this section shall review the record, including the findings underlying the sentence or modification given by the sentencing court.

The appellate court may increase, reduce, or otherwise modify a sentence that is appealed under this section or may vacate the sentence and remand the matter to the sentencing court for resentencing. The appellate court's standard for review is not whether the sentencing court abused its discretion. The appellate court may take any action authorized by this division if it clearly and convincingly finds either of the following:

(a) That the record does not support the sentencing court's findings under division (B) or (D) of section 2929.13, division (B)(2)(e) or (C)(4) of section 2929.14, or division (I) of section 2929.20 of the Revised Code, whichever, if any, is relevant;

(b) That the sentence is otherwise contrary to law.

(H) A judgment or final order of a court of appeals under this section may be appealed, by leave of court, to the supreme court.

(I)(1) There is hereby established the felony sentence appeal cost oversight committee, consisting of eight members. One member shall be the chief justice of the supreme court or a representative of the court designated by the chief justice, one member shall be a member of the senate appointed by the president of the senate, one member shall be a member of the house of representatives appointed by the speaker of the house of representatives, one member shall be the director of budget and management or a representative of the office of budget and management designated by the director, one member shall be a judge of a court of appeals, court of common pleas, municipal court, or county court appointed by the chief justice of the supreme court, one member shall be the state public defender or a representative of the office of the state public defender designated by the state public defender, one member shall be a prosecuting attorney appointed by the Ohio prosecuting attorneys association, and one member shall be a county commissioner appointed by the county commissioners association of Ohio. No more than three of the appointed members of the committee may be members of the same political party.

The president of the senate, the speaker of the house of representatives, the chief justice of the supreme court, the Ohio prosecuting attorneys association, and the county commissioners association of Ohio shall make the initial appointments to the committee of the appointed members no later than ninety days after July 1, 1996. Of those initial appointments to the committee, the members appointed by the speaker of the house of representatives and the Ohio prosecuting attorneys association shall serve a term ending two years after July 1, 1996, the member appointed by the chief justice of the supreme court shall serve a term ending three years after July 1, 1996, and the members appointed by the president of the senate and the county commissioners association of Ohio shall serve terms ending four years after July 1, 1996. Thereafter, terms of office of the appointed members shall be for four years, with each term ending on the same day of the same month as did the term that it succeeds. Members may be reappointed. Vacancies shall be filled in the same manner provided for original appointments. A member appointed to fill a vacancy occurring prior to the expiration of the term for which that member's predecessor was appointed shall hold office as a member for the remainder of the predecessor's term. An appointed member shall continue in office subsequent to the expiration date of that member's term until that member's successor takes office or until a period of sixty days has elapsed, whichever occurs first.

If the chief justice of the supreme court, the director of the office of budget and management, or the state public defender serves as a member of the committee, that person's term of office as a member shall continue for as long as that person holds office as chief justice, director of the office of budget and management, or state public defender. If the chief justice of the supreme court designates a representative of the court to serve as a member, the director of budget and management designates a representative of the office of budget and management to serve as a member, or the state public defender designates a representative of the office of the state public defender to serve as a member, the person so designated shall serve as a member of the commission for as long as the official who made the designation holds office as chief justice, director of the office of budget and management, or state public defender or until that official revokes the designation.

The chief justice of the supreme court or the representative of the supreme court appointed by the chief justice shall serve as chairperson of the committee. The committee shall meet within two weeks after all appointed members have been appointed and shall organize as necessary. Thereafter, the committee shall meet at least once every six months or more often upon the call of the chairperson or the written request of three or more members, provided that the committee shall not meet unless moneys have been appropriated to the judiciary budget administered by the supreme court specifically for the purpose of providing financial assistance to counties under division (I)(2) of this section and the moneys so appropriated then are available for that purpose.

The members of the committee shall serve without compensation, but, if moneys have been appropriated to the judiciary budget administered by the supreme court specifically for the purpose of providing financial assistance to counties under division (I)(2) of this section, each member shall be reimbursed out of the moneys so appropriated that then are available for actual and necessary expenses incurred in the performance of official duties as a committee member.

(2) The state criminal sentencing commission periodically shall provide to the felony sentence appeal cost oversight committee all data the commission collects pursuant to division (A)(5) of section 181.25 of the Revised Code. Upon receipt of the data from the state criminal sentencing commission, the felony sentence appeal cost oversight committee periodically shall review the data; determine whether any money has been appropriated to the judiciary budget administered by the supreme court specifically for the purpose of providing state financial assistance to counties in accordance with this division for the increase in expenses the counties experience as a result of the felony sentence appeal provisions set forth in this section or as a result of a postconviction relief proceeding brought under division (A)(2) of section 2953.21 of the Revised Code or an appeal of a judgment in that proceeding; if it determines that any money has been so appropriated, determine the total amount of moneys that have been so appropriated specifically for that purpose and that then are available for that purpose; and develop a recommended method of distributing those moneys to the counties. The committee shall send a copy of its recommendation to the supreme court. Upon receipt of the committee's recommendation, the supreme court shall distribute to the counties, based upon that recommendation, the moneys that have been so appropriated specifically for the purpose of providing state financial assistance to counties under this division and that then are available for that purpose.

**HISTORY: 146 v S 2 (Eff 7-1-96); 146 v S 269 (Eff 7-1-96); 146 v H 180 (Eff 1-1-97); 147 v H 151 (Eff 9-16-97); 148 v S 107 (Eff 3-23-2000); 148 v H 331. Eff 10-10-2000; 150 v H 473, § 1, eff. 4-29-05; 151 v H 95, § 1, eff. 8-3-06; 151 v H 461, § 1, eff. 4-4-07; 152 v H 130, § 1, eff. 4-7-09; 2011 HB 86, § 1, eff. Sept. 30, 2011.**

The provisions of § 3 of H.B. 473 (150 v —) read as follows:

SECTION 3. * * * Section 2953.08 of the Revised Code is presented in this act as a composite of the section as amended by both Sub. H.B. 331 and Am. Sub. S.B. 107 of the 123rd General Assembly. The General Assembly, applying the principle stated in division (B) of section 1.52 of the Revised Code that amendments are to be harmonized if reasonably capable of simultaneous operation, finds that the composites are the resulting versions of the sections in effect prior to the effective date of the sections as presented in this act.

## § 2953.09 Suspension of sentence in criminal cases; bail.

(A)(1) Upon filing an appeal in the supreme court, the execution of the sentence or judgment imposed in cases of felony is suspended.

(2)(a) If a notice of appeal is filed pursuant to the Rules of Appellate Procedure by a defendant who is convicted in a municipal or county court or a court of common pleas of a felony or misdemeanor under the Revised Code or an ordinance of a municipal corporation, the filing of the notice of appeal does not suspend execution of the sentence or judgment imposed. However, consistent with divisions (A)(2)(b), (B), and (C) of this section, Appellate Rule 8, and Criminal Rule 46, the municipal or county court, court of common pleas, or court of appeals may suspend execution of the sentence or judgment imposed during the pendency of the appeal and shall determine whether that defendant is entitled to bail and the amount and nature of any bail that is required. The bail shall at least be conditioned that the defendant will prosecute the appeal without delay and abide by the judgment and sentence of the court.

(b)(i) A court of common pleas or court of appeals may suspend the execution of a sentence of death imposed for an offense committed before January 1, 1995, only if no date for execution has been set by the supreme court, good cause is shown for the suspension, the defendant files a motion requesting the suspension, and notice has been given to the prosecuting attorney of the appropriate county.

(ii) A court of common pleas may suspend the execution of a sentence of death imposed for an offense committed on or after January 1, 1995, only if no date for execution has been set by the supreme court, good cause is shown, the defendant files a motion requesting the suspension, and notice has been given to the prosecuting attorney of the appropriate county.

(iii) A court of common pleas or court of appeals may suspend the execution of the sentence or judgment imposed for a felony in a capital case in which a sentence of death is not imposed only if no date for execution of the sentence has been set by the supreme court, good cause is shown for the suspension, the defendant files a motion requesting the suspension, and only after notice has been given to the prosecuting attorney of the appropriate county.

(B) Notwithstanding any provision of Criminal Rule 46 to the contrary, a trial judge of a court of common pleas shall not release on bail pursuant to division (A)(2)(a) of this section a defendant who is convicted of a bailable offense if the defendant is sentenced to imprisonment for life or if that offense is a violation of section 2903.01, 2903.02, 2903.03, 2903.04, 2903.11, 2905.01, 2905.02, 2905.11, 2907.02, 2909.02, 2911.01, 2911.02, or 2911.11 of the Revised Code or is felonious sexual penetration in violation of former section 2907.12 of the Revised Code.

(C) If a trial judge of a court of common pleas is prohibited by division (B) of this section from releasing on bail pursuant to division (A)(2)(a) of this section a defendant who is convicted of a bailable offense and not sentenced to imprisonment for life, the appropriate court of appeals or two judges of it, upon motion of the defendant and for good cause shown, may release the defendant on bail in accordance with division (A)(2) of this section.

**HISTORY: GC § 13459-8; 113 v 123(213), ch 38, § 8; 116 v 104(118), § 2; Bureau of Code Revision, 10-1-53; 129 v 423 (Eff 10-19-61); 139 v S 199 (Eff 7-1-83); 141 v H 412 (Eff 3-17-87); 146 v S 4 (Eff 9-21-95); 146 v H 445. Eff 9-3-96.**

## § 2953.10 Power to suspend sentence.

When an appeal is taken from a court of appeals to the supreme court, the supreme court has the same power and authority to suspend the execution of sentence during the pendency of the appeal and admit the defendant to bail as does the court of appeals unless another section of the Revised Code or the Rules of Practice of the Supreme Court specify a distinct bail or suspension of sentence authority.

When an appeal in a case in which a sentence of death is imposed for an offense committed on or after January 1, 1995, is taken directly from the trial court to the supreme court, the supreme court has the same power and authority to suspend the execution of the sentence during the pendency of the appeal and admit the defendant to bail as does the court of appeals for cases in which a sentence of death is imposed for an offense committed before January 1, 1995, unless another section of the Revised Code or the Rules of Practice of the Supreme Court specify a distinct bail or suspension of sentence authority.

**HISTORY: GC § 13459-8a; 123 v 748; Bureau of Code Revision, 10-1-53; 141 v H 412 (Eff 3-17-87); 146 v S 4. Eff 9-21-95.**

## § 2953.11 Custody of defendant under suspended sentence.

In cases of conviction of felony, except for aggravated murder or murder, if the defendant has been committed to a state correctional institution and sentence is suspended, the clerk of the court in which the entry is made suspending the sentence under the seal of the court shall forthwith certify the suspension to the warden of the state correctional institution, who shall deliver the defendant to the sheriff of the county in which the defendant was convicted. The sheriff thereupon shall convey the defendant to the jail of the county in which the defendant was convicted and keep the defendant in custody unless admitted to bail pending the decision on the appeal or the termination of the suspension of sentence. If the judgment is affirmed or if the suspension of sentence is terminated, the sheriff shall convey the defendant to the state correctional institution to serve the balance of the defendant's term of sentence. The supreme court in the order allowing the filing of an appeal may provide that the defendant shall remain in the custody of the warden of the state correctional institution pending the decision of the court in such case.

**HISTORY: GC § 13459-9; 113 v 123(213), ch 38, § 9; 116 v 104(118), § 2; Bureau of Code Revision, 10-1-53; 129 v 322 (Eff 7-14-61); 145 v H 571 (Eff 10-6-94); 146 v S 2. Eff 7-1-96.**

The effective date is set by section 6 of SB 2.

See provisions, § 5 of SB 2 (146 v —), as amended by § 3 of SB 269 (146 v —), effective 7-1-96, following RC § 2929.03.

## § 2953.12 Repealed, 141 v H 412, § 2 [GC § 13459-10; 113 v 123(214), ch 38, § 10; 116 v 104(118), § 2; Bureau of Code Revision, 10-1-53]. Eff 3-17-87.

This section ruled suspending execution of sentence in misdemeanor cases did not take effect until recognizance given.

## § 2953.13 Procedure when conviction is reversed or when case is remanded to trial court.

When a defendant has been committed to a state correctional institution and the judgment by virtue of which the commitment was made is reversed on appeal, and the defendant is entitled to discharge or a new trial, or when the case is remanded to the trial court for any reason, the clerk of the court reversing the judgment or remanding the case, under the seal of the court, shall forthwith certify the reversal or remand to the warden of the state correctional institution.

The warden, on receipt of the certificate, if a discharge of the defendant is ordered, shall forthwith discharge the defendant from the state correctional institution.

If a new trial is ordered or the case is remanded, the warden shall forthwith cause the defendant to be conveyed to the jail of the county in which the defendant was convicted, and committed to the custody of the sheriff of that county.

**HISTORY: GC §§ 13459-11—13459-13; 113 v 123(214), ch 38, §§ 11-13; 116 v 104(118), § 2; Bureau of Code Revision, 10-1-53; 145 v H 571. Eff 10-6-94; 152 v H 130, § 1, eff. 4-7-09.**

## § 2953.14 State may seek review.

Whenever a court superior to the trial court renders judgment adverse to the state in a criminal action or proceeding, the state, through either the prosecuting attorney or the attorney general, may institute an appeal to reverse such judgment in the next higher court. If the conviction was for a violation of a municipal ordinance, such appeal may be brought by the village solicitor, city director of law, or other chief legal officer of the municipal corporation. Like proceedings shall be had in the higher court at the hearing of the appeal as in the review of other criminal actions or proceedings. The clerk of the court rendering the judgment sought to be reversed, on application of the prosecuting attorney, attorney general, solicitor, director of law, or other chief legal officer shall make a transcript of the docket and journal entries in the action or proceeding, and transmit it with all papers and files in the action or proceeding to the higher court.

**HISTORY: GC § 13459-14; 113 v 123(214), ch 38, § 14; 116 v 104(119), § 2; Bureau of Code Revision, 10-1-53; 137 v H 219 (Eff 11-1-77); 141 v H 412. Eff 3-17-87.**

### [POSTCONVICTION REMEDIES]

## § 2953.21 Petition for postconviction relief.

(A)(1)(a) Any person who has been convicted of a criminal offense or adjudicated a delinquent child and who claims that there was such a denial or infringement of the person's rights as to render the judgment void or voidable under the Ohio Constitution or the Constitution of the United States, and any person who has been convicted of a criminal offense that is a felony and who is an offender, for whom DNA testing that was performed under sections 2953.71 to 2953.81 of the Revised Code or under former section 2953.82 of the Revised Code and analyzed in the context of and upon consideration of all available admissible evidence related to the person's case as described in division (D) of section 2953.74 of the Revised Code provided results that establish, by clear and convincing evidence, actual innocence of that felony offense or, if the person was sentenced to death, establish, by clear and convincing evidence, actual innocence of the aggravating circumstance or circumstances the person was found guilty of committing and that is or are the basis of that sentence of death, may file a petition in the court that imposed sentence, stating the grounds for relief relied upon, and asking the court to vacate or set aside the judgment or sentence or to grant other appropriate relief. The petitioner may file a supporting affidavit and other documentary evidence in support of the claim for relief.

(b) As used in division (A)(1)(a) of this section, "actual innocence" means that, had the results of the DNA testing conducted under sections 2953.71 to 2953.81 of the

Revised Code or under former section 2953.82 of the Revised Code been presented at trial, and had those results been analyzed in the context of and upon consideration of all available admissible evidence related to the person's case as described in division (D) of section 2953.74 of the Revised Code no reasonable factfinder would have found the petitioner guilty of the offense of which the petitioner was convicted, or, if the person was sentenced to death, no reasonable factfinder would have found the petitioner guilty of the aggravating circumstance or circumstances the petitioner was found guilty of committing and that is or are the basis of that sentence of death.

(c) As used in divisions (A)(1)(a) and (b) of this section, "former section 2953.82 of the Revised Code" means section 2953.82 of the Revised Code as it existed prior to the effective date of this amendment.

(2) Except as otherwise provided in section 2953.23 of the Revised Code, a petition under division (A)(1) of this section shall be filed no later than one hundred eighty days after the date on which the trial transcript is filed in the court of appeals in the direct appeal of the judgment of conviction or adjudication or, if the direct appeal involves a sentence of death, the date on which the trial transcript is filed in the supreme court. If no appeal is taken, except as otherwise provided in section 2953.23 of the Revised Code, the petition shall be filed no later than one hundred eighty days after the expiration of the time for filing the appeal.

(3) In a petition filed under division (A) of this section, a person who has been sentenced to death may ask the court to render void or voidable the judgment with respect to the conviction of aggravated murder or the specification of an aggravating circumstance or the sentence of death.

(4) A petitioner shall state in the original or amended petition filed under division (A) of this section all grounds for relief claimed by the petitioner. Except as provided in section 2953.23 of the Revised Code, any ground for relief that is not so stated in the petition is waived.

(5) If the petitioner in a petition filed under division (A) of this section was convicted of or pleaded guilty to a felony, the petition may include a claim that the petitioner was denied the equal protection of the laws in violation of the Ohio Constitution or the United States Constitution because the sentence imposed upon the petitioner for the felony was part of a consistent pattern of disparity in sentencing by the judge who imposed the sentence, with regard to the petitioner's race, gender, ethnic background, or religion. If the supreme court adopts a rule requiring a court of common pleas to maintain information with regard to an offender's race, gender, ethnic background, or religion, the supporting evidence for the petition shall include, but shall not be limited to, a copy of that type of information relative to the petitioner's sentence and copies of that type of information relative to sentences that the same judge imposed upon other persons.

(B) The clerk of the court in which the petition is filed shall docket the petition and bring it promptly to the attention of the court. The clerk of the court in which the petition is filed immediately shall forward a copy of the petition to the prosecuting attorney of that county.

(C) The court shall consider a petition that is timely filed under division (A)(2) of this section even if a direct appeal of the judgment is pending. Before granting a hearing on a petition filed under division (A) of this section, the court shall determine whether there are substantive grounds for relief. In making such a determination, the court shall consider, in addition to the petition, the supporting affidavits, and the documentary evidence, all the files and records pertaining to the proceedings against the petitioner, including, but not limited to, the indictment, the court's journal entries, the journalized records of the clerk of the court, and the court reporter's transcript. The court reporter's transcript, if ordered and certified by the court, shall be taxed as court costs. If the court dismisses the petition, it shall make and file findings of fact and conclusions of law with respect to such dismissal.

(D) Within ten days after the docketing of the petition, or within any further time that the court may fix for good cause shown, the prosecuting attorney shall respond by answer or motion. Within twenty days from the date the issues are raised, either party may move for summary judgment. The right to summary judgment shall appear on the face of the record.

(E) Unless the petition and the files and records of the case show the petitioner is not entitled to relief, the court shall proceed to a prompt hearing on the issues even if a direct appeal of the case is pending. If the court notifies the parties that it has found grounds for granting relief, either party may request an appellate court in which a direct appeal of the judgment is pending to remand the pending case to the court.

(F) At any time before the answer or motion is filed, the petitioner may amend the petition with or without leave or prejudice to the proceedings. The petitioner may amend the petition with leave of court at any time thereafter.

(G) If the court does not find grounds for granting relief, it shall make and file findings of fact and conclusions of law and shall enter judgment denying relief on the petition. If no direct appeal of the case is pending and the court finds grounds for relief or if a pending direct appeal of the case has been remanded to the court pursuant to a request made pursuant to division (E) of this section and the court finds grounds for granting relief, it shall make and file findings of fact and conclusions of law and shall enter a judgment that vacates and sets aside the judgment in question, and, in the case of a petitioner who is a prisoner in custody, shall discharge or resentence the petitioner or grant a new trial as the court determines appropriate. The court also may make supplementary orders to the relief granted, concerning such matters as rearraignment, retrial, custody, and bail. If the trial court's order granting the petition is reversed on appeal and if the direct appeal of the case has been remanded from an appellate court pursuant to a request under division (E) of this section, the appellate court reversing the order granting the petition shall notify the appellate court in which the direct appeal of the case was pending at the time of the remand of the reversal and remand of the trial court's order. Upon the reversal and remand of the trial court's order granting the petition, regardless of whether notice is sent or received, the direct appeal of the case that was remanded is reinstated.

(H) Upon the filing of a petition pursuant to division (A) of this section by a person sentenced to death, only the supreme court may stay execution of the sentence of death.

(I)(1) If a person sentenced to death intends to file a petition under this section, the court shall appoint counsel to represent the person upon a finding that the person is indigent and that the person either accepts the appointment of counsel or is unable to make a competent decision whether to accept or reject the appointment of counsel. The court may decline to appoint counsel for the person only upon a finding, after a hearing if necessary, that the person rejects the appointment of counsel and understands the legal consequences of that decision or upon a finding that the person is not indigent.

(2) The court shall not appoint as counsel under division (I)(1) of this section an attorney who represented the petitioner at trial in the case to which the petition relates unless the person and the attorney expressly request the appointment. The court shall appoint as counsel under division (I)(1) of this section only an attorney who is certified under Rule 20 of the Rules of Superintendence for the Courts of Ohio to represent indigent defendants charged with or convicted of an offense for which the death penalty can be or has been imposed. The ineffectiveness or incompetence of counsel during proceedings under this section does not constitute grounds for relief in a proceeding under this section, in an appeal of any action under this section, or in an application to reopen a direct appeal.

(3) Division (I) of this section does not preclude attorneys who represent the state of Ohio from invoking the provisions of 28 U.S.C. 154 with respect to capital cases that were pending in federal habeas corpus proceedings prior to July 1, 1996, insofar as the petitioners in those cases were represented in proceedings under this section by one or more counsel appointed by the court under this section or section 120.06, 120.16, 120.26, or 120.33 of the Revised Code and those appointed counsel meet the requirements of division (I)(2) of this section.

(J) Subject to the appeal of a sentence for a felony that is authorized by section 2953.08 of the Revised Code, the remedy set forth in this section is the exclusive remedy by which a person may bring a collateral challenge to the validity of a conviction or sentence in a criminal case or to the validity of an adjudication of a child as a delinquent child for the commission of an act that would be a criminal offense if committed by an adult or the validity of a related order of disposition.

**HISTORY: 131 v 684 (Eff 7-21-65); 132 v H 742 (Eff 12-9-67); 141 v H 412 (Eff 3-17-87); 145 v H 571 (Eff 10-6-94); 146 v S 4 (Eff 9-21-95); 146 v S 2 (Eff 7-1-96); 146 v S 269 (Eff 7-1-96); 146 v S 258 (Eff 10-16-96); 149 v H 94. Eff 9-5-2001; 150 v S 11, § 1, eff. 10-29-03; 151 v S 262, § 1, eff. 7-11-06; 153 v S 77, § 1, eff. 7-6-10.**

See provisions of § 4 of 151 v S 262 following RC § 2901.07.
The effective date is set by section 204 of HB 94.
The provisions of § 237 of HB 94 (149 v —) read as follows:
SECTION 237. Section 2953.21 of the Revised Code is presented in this act as a composite of the section as amended by both Sub. S.B. 258 and Am. Sub. S.B. 269 of the 121st General Assembly. The General Assembly, applying the principle stated in division (B) of section 1.52 of the Revised Code that amendments are to be harmonized if reasonably capable of simultaneous operation, finds that the composite is the resulting version of the section in effect prior to the effective date of the section as presented in this act.

## § 2953.22 Hearing.

If a hearing is granted pursuant to section 2953.21 of the Revised Code, the petitioner shall be permitted to attend the hearing. Testimony of the prisoner or other witnesses may be offered by deposition.

If the petitioner is in a state correctional institution, he may be returned for the hearing upon the warrant of the court of common pleas of the county where the hearing is to be held. The approval of the governor on the warrant shall not be required. The warrant shall be directed to the sheriff of the county in which the hearing is to be held. When a copy of the warrant is presented to the warden or other head of a state correctional institution, he shall deliver the convict to the sheriff, who shall convey him to the county. For removing and returning the convict, the sheriff shall receive the fees allowed for conveying convicts to the correctional institution.

**HISTORY: 132 v H 742 (Eff 12-9-67); 145 v H 571. Eff 10-6-94.**

**Analogous to former RC § 2953.22 (131 v 685), repealed 132 v H 742, § 2, eff 12-9-67.**

## § 2953.23 Time for filing petition; appeals.

(A) Whether a hearing is or is not held on a petition filed pursuant to section 2953.21 of the Revised Code, a court may not entertain a petition filed after the expiration of the period prescribed in division (A) of that section or a second petition or successive petitions for similar relief on behalf of a petitioner unless division (A)(1) or (2) of this section applies:

(1) Both of the following apply:

(a) Either the petitioner shows that the petitioner was unavoidably prevented from discovery of the facts upon which the petitioner must rely to present the claim for relief, or, subsequent to the period prescribed in division (A)(2) of section 2953.21 of the Revised Code or to the filing of an earlier petition, the United States Supreme Court recognized a new federal or state right that applies retroactively to persons in the petitioner's situation, and the petition asserts a claim based on that right.

(b) The petitioner shows by clear and convincing evidence that, but for constitutional error at trial, no reasonable factfinder would have found the petitioner guilty of the offense of which the petitioner was convicted or, if the claim challenges a sentence of death that, but for constitutional error at the sentencing hearing, no reasonable factfinder would have found the petitioner eligible for the death sentence.

(2) The petitioner was convicted of a felony, the petitioner is an offender for whom DNA testing was performed under sections 2953.71 to 2953.81 of the Revised Code or under former section 2953.82 of the Revised Code and analyzed in the context of and upon consideration of all available admissible evidence related to the inmate's case as described in division (D) of section 2953.74 of the Revised Code, and the results of the DNA testing establish, by clear and convincing evidence, actual innocence of that felony offense or, if the person was sentenced to death, establish, by clear and convincing evidence, actual innocence of the aggravating circumstance or circumstances the person was found guilty of committing and that is or are the basis of that sentence of death.

As used in this division, "actual innocence" has the same meaning as in division (A)(1)(b) of section 2953.21 of the Revised Code, and "former section 2953.82 of the Revised Code" has the same meaning as in division (A)(1)(c) of section 2953.21 of the Revised Code.

(B) An order awarding or denying relief sought in a petition filed pursuant to section 2953.21 of the Revised Code is a final judgment and may be appealed pursuant to Chapter 2953. of the Revised Code.

**HISTORY: 132 v H 742 (Eff 12-9-67); 146 v S 4. Eff 9-21-95; 150 v S 11, § 1, eff. 10-29-03; 151 v S 262, § 1, eff. 7-11-06; 153 v S 77, § 1, eff. 7-6-10.**

See provisions of § 4 of 151 v S 262 following RC § 2901.07.

**Analogous to former RC § 2953.23 (131 v 685), repealed 132 v H 742, § 2, eff 12-9-67.**

## § 2953.24 Repealed, 136 v H 164, § 2 [132 v H 742]. Eff 1-13-76.

This section concerned compensation of counsel.

## [SEALING OF RECORD OF CONVICTION]

## § 2953.31 Definitions.

As used in sections 2953.31 to 2953.36 of the Revised Code:

(A) "First offender" means anyone who has been convicted of an offense in this state or any other jurisdiction and who previously or subsequently has not been convicted of the same or a different offense in this state or any other jurisdiction. When two or more convictions result from or are connected with the same act or result from offenses committed at the same time, they shall be counted as one conviction. When two or three convictions result from the same indictment, information, or complaint, from the same plea of guilty, or from the same official proceeding, and result from related criminal acts that were committed within a three-month period but do not result from the same act or from offenses committed at the same time, they shall be counted as one conviction, provided that a court may decide as provided in division (C) (1) (a) of section 2953.32 of the Revised Code that it is not in the public interest for the two or three convictions to be counted as one conviction.

For purposes of, and except as otherwise provided in, this division, a conviction for a minor misdemeanor, for a violation of any section in Chapter 4507., 4510., 4511., 4513., or 4549. of the Revised Code, or for a violation of a municipal ordinance that is substantially similar to any section in those chapters is not a previous or subsequent conviction. However, a conviction for a violation of section 4511.19, 4511.251, 4549.02, 4549.021, 4549.03, 4549.042, or 4549.62 or sections 4549.41 to 4549.46 of the Revised Code, for a violation of section 4510.11 or 4510.14 of the Revised Code that is based upon the offender's operation of a vehicle during a suspension imposed under section 4511.191 or 4511.196 of the Revised Code, for a violation of a substantially equivalent municipal ordinance, for a felony violation of Title XLV of the Revised Code, or for a violation of a substantially equivalent former law of this state or former municipal ordinance shall be considered a previous or subsequent conviction.

(B) "Prosecutor" means the county prosecuting attorney, city director of law, village solicitor, or similar chief legal officer, who has the authority to prosecute a criminal case in the court in which the case is filed.

(C) "Bail forfeiture" means the forfeiture of bail by a defendant who is arrested for the commission of a misdemeanor, other than a defendant in a traffic case as defined in Traffic Rule 2, if the forfeiture is pursuant to an agreement with the court and prosecutor in the case.

(D) "Official records" has the same meaning as in division (D) of section 2953.51 of the Revised Code.

(E) "Official proceeding" has the same meaning as in section 2921.01 of the Revised Code.

(F) "Community control sanction" has the same meaning as in section 2929.01 of the Revised Code.

(G) "Post-release control" and "post-release control sanction" have the same meanings as in section 2967.01 of the Revised Code.

(H) "DNA database," "DNA record," and "law enforcement agency" have the same meanings as in section 109.573 [109.57.3] of the Revised Code.

(I) "Fingerprints filed for record" means any fingerprints obtained by the superintendent of the bureau of criminal identification and investigation pursuant to sections 109.57 and 109.571 [109.57.1] of the Revised Code.

**HISTORY: 135 v S 5 (Eff 1-1-74); 140 v H 227 (Eff 9-26-84); 142 v H 175 (Eff 6-29-88); 143 v S 49 (Eff 11-3-89); 143 v S 382 (Eff 12-31-90); 146 v H 274 (Eff 8-8-96); 148 v S 13. Eff 3-23-2000; 149 v H 490, § 1, eff. 1-1-04; 153 v S 77, § 1, eff. 7-6-10.**

The effective date is set by section 4 of H.B. 490.

The provisions of § 5 of S.B. 123 (149 v —), as amended by § 3 of H.B. 163 (150 v —), read as follows:

SECTION 5. (A) Notwithstanding division (B) of section 1.58 of the Revised Code, the provisions of the Revised Code amended or enacted in Sections 1 and 2 of Am. Sub. S.B. 123 of the 124th General Assembly shall apply only in relation to conduct and offenses committed on or after January 1, 2004. Conduct and offenses committed prior to January 1, 2004, shall be governed by the law in effect on the date the conduct or offense was committed. ° ° °

The provisions of § 7 of S.B. 123 (149 v —) read as follows:

SECTION 7. (A) If, on or after March 31, 1999, a person filed an application in a court that requested the sealing of a conviction record under sections 2953.31 to 2953.36 of the Revised Code, if at the time the application was filed section 2953.36 did not make sections 2953.31 to 2953.35 of the Revised Code inapplicable to the conviction that was the subject of the application, if the person withdrew the application prior to March 31, 2001, and if the person refiles an application in the appropriate court within ninety days after the effective date of this section that requests the sealing of the same conviction record under sections 2953.31 to 2953.36 of the Revised Code, all of the following apply:

(1) Divisions (C), (D), and (E) of section 2953.36 of the Revised Code, as they have existed since March 23, 2000, do not apply regarding the application or the determination of whether it should be accepted or granted, and the court may accept and grant the application regardless of whether the conviction that is the subject of the application is a conviction to which any of those divisions, but for the operation of this division, makes sections 2953.31 to 2953.35 of the Revised Code inapplicable.

(2) Except as provided in division (A)(1) of this section, the provisions of sections 2953.31 to 2953.36 of the Revised Code that are in effect at the time of the refiling of the application apply regarding the application and the determination of whether it should be granted.

(B) This section shall expire one year after this act becomes law.

## § 2953.32 Sealing of record of conviction or bail forfeiture.

(A)(1) Except as provided in section 2953.61 of the Revised Code, a first offender may apply to the sentencing court if convicted in this state, or to a court of common pleas if convicted in another state or in a federal court, for the sealing of the conviction record. Application may be made at the expiration of three years after the offender's final discharge if convicted of a felony, or at the expiration of one year after the offender's final discharge if convicted of a misdemeanor.

(2) Any person who has been arrested for any misdemeanor offense and who has effected a bail forfeiture may apply to the court in which the misdemeanor criminal case was pending when bail was forfeited for the sealing of the record of the case. Except as provided in section 2953.61 of the Revised Code, the application may be filed at any time after the expiration of one year from the date on which the bail forfeiture was entered upon the minutes of the court or the journal, whichever entry occurs first.

(B) Upon the filing of an application under this section, the court shall set a date for a hearing and shall notify the prosecutor for the case of the hearing on the application. The prosecutor may object to the granting of the application by filing an objection with the court prior to the date set for the hearing. The prosecutor shall specify in the objection the reasons for believing a denial of the application is justified. The court shall direct its regular probation officer, a state probation officer, or the department of probation of the county in which the applicant resides to make inquiries and written reports as the court requires concerning the applicant.

(C)(1) The court shall do each of the following:

(a) Determine whether the applicant is a first offender or whether the forfeiture of bail was agreed to by the applicant and the prosecutor in the case. If the applicant applies as a first offender pursuant to division (A)(1) of this section and has two or three convictions that result from the same indictment, information, or complaint, from the same plea of guilty, or from the same official proceeding, and result from related criminal acts that were committed within a three-month period but do not result from the same act or from offenses committed at the same time, in making its determination under this division, the court initially shall determine whether it is not in the public interest for the two or three convictions to be counted as one conviction. If the court determines that it is not in the public interest for the two or three convictions to be counted as one conviction, the court shall determine that the applicant is not a first offender; if the court does not make that determination, the court shall determine that the offender is a first offender.

(b) Determine whether criminal proceedings are pending against the applicant;

(c) If the applicant is a first offender who applies pursuant to division (A)(1) of this section, determine whether the applicant has been rehabilitated to the satisfaction of the court;

(d) If the prosecutor has filed an objection in accordance with division (B) of this section, consider the reasons against granting the application specified by the prosecutor in the objection;

(e) Weigh the interests of the applicant in having the records pertaining to the applicant's conviction sealed against the legitimate needs, if any, of the government to maintain those records.

(2) If the court determines, after complying with division (C)(1) of this section, that the applicant is a first offender or the subject of a bail forfeiture, that no criminal proceeding is pending against the applicant, and that the interests of the applicant in having the records pertaining to the applicant's conviction or bail forfeiture sealed are not outweighed by any legitimate governmental needs to maintain those records, and that the rehabilitation of an applicant who is a first offender applying pursuant to division (A)(1) of this section has been attained to the satisfaction of the court, the court, except as provided in divisions (G) and (H) of this section, shall order all official records pertaining to the case sealed and, except as provided in division (F) of this section, all index references to the case deleted and, in the case of bail forfeitures, shall dismiss the charges in the case. The proceedings in the case shall be considered not to have occurred and the conviction or bail forfeiture of the person who is the subject of the proceedings shall be sealed, except that upon conviction of a subsequent offense, the sealed record of prior conviction or bail forfeiture may be considered by the court in determining the sentence or other appropriate disposition, including the relief provided for in sections 2953.31 to 2953.33 of the Revised Code.

(3) Upon the filing of an application under this section, the applicant, unless indigent, shall pay a fee of fifty dollars. The court shall pay thirty dollars of the fee into the state treasury. It shall pay twenty dollars of the fee into the county general revenue fund if the sealed conviction or bail forfeiture was pursuant to a state statute, or into the general revenue fund of the municipal corporation involved if the sealed conviction or bail forfeiture was pursuant to a municipal ordinance.

(D) Inspection of the sealed records included in the order may be made only by the following persons or for the following purposes:

(1) By a law enforcement officer or prosecutor, or the assistants of either, to determine whether the nature and character of the offense with which a person is to be charged would be affected by virtue of the person's previously having been convicted of a crime;

(2) By the parole or probation officer of the person who is the subject of the records, for the exclusive use of the officer in supervising the person while on parole or under a community control sanction or a post-release control sanction, and in making inquiries and written reports as requested by the court or adult parole authority;

(3) Upon application by the person who is the subject of the records, by the persons named in the application;

(4) By a law enforcement officer who was involved in the case, for use in the officer's defense of a civil action arising out of the officer's involvement in that case;

(5) By a prosecuting attorney or the prosecuting attorney's assistants, to determine a defendant's eligibility to enter a pre-trial diversion program established pursuant to section 2935.36 of the Revised Code;

(6) By any law enforcement agency or any authorized employee of a law enforcement agency or by the department of rehabilitation and correction as part of a background investigation of a person who applies for employment with the agency as a law enforcement officer or with the department as a corrections officer;

(7) By any law enforcement agency or any authorized employee of a law enforcement agency, for the purposes set forth in, and in the manner provided in, section 2953.321 [2953.32.1] of the Revised Code;

(8) By the bureau of criminal identification and investigation or any authorized employee of the bureau for the purpose of providing information to a board or person pursuant to division (F) or (G) of section 109.57 of the Revised Code;

(9) By the bureau of criminal identification and investigation or any authorized employee of the bureau for the purpose of performing a criminal history records check on a person to whom a certificate as prescribed in section 109.77 of the Revised Code is to be awarded;

(10) By the bureau of criminal identification and investigation or any authorized employee of the bureau for the purpose of conducting a criminal records check of an

individual pursuant to division (B) of section 109.572 [109.57.2] of the Revised Code that was requested pursuant to any of the sections identified in division (B)(1) of that section;

(11) By the bureau of criminal identification and investigation, an authorized employee of the bureau, a sheriff, or an authorized employee of the sheriff in connection with a criminal records check described in section 311.41 of the Revised Code;

(12) By the attorney general or an authorized employee of the attorney general or a court for purposes of determining a person's classification pursuant to Chapter 2950. of the Revised Code.

When the nature and character of the offense with which a person is to be charged would be affected by the information, it may be used for the purpose of charging the person with an offense.

(E) In any criminal proceeding, proof of any otherwise admissible prior conviction may be introduced and proved, notwithstanding the fact that for any such prior conviction an order of sealing previously was issued pursuant to sections 2953.31 to 2953.36 of the Revised Code.

(F) The person or governmental agency, office, or department that maintains sealed records pertaining to convictions or bail forfeitures that have been sealed pursuant to this section may maintain a manual or computerized index to the sealed records. The index shall contain only the name of, and alphanumeric identifiers that relate to, the persons who are the subject of the sealed records, the word "sealed," and the name of the person, agency, office, or department that has custody of the sealed records, and shall not contain the name of the crime committed. The index shall be made available by the person who has custody of the sealed records only for the purposes set forth in divisions (C), (D), and (E) of this section.

(G) Notwithstanding any provision of this section or section 2953.33 of the Revised Code that requires otherwise, a board of education of a city, local, exempted village, or joint vocational school district that maintains records of an individual who has been permanently excluded under sections 3301.121 [3301.12.1] and 3313.662 [3313.66.2] of the Revised Code is permitted to maintain records regarding a conviction that was used as the basis for the individual's permanent exclusion, regardless of a court order to seal the record. An order issued under this section to seal the record of a conviction does not revoke the adjudication order of the superintendent of public instruction to permanently exclude the individual who is the subject of the sealing order. An order issued under this section to seal the record of a conviction of an individual may be presented to a district superintendent as evidence to support the contention that the superintendent should recommend that the permanent exclusion of the individual who is the subject of the sealing order be revoked. Except as otherwise authorized by this division and sections 3301.121 [3301.12.1] and 3313.662 [3313.66.2] of the Revised Code, any school employee in possession of or having access to the sealed conviction records of an individual that were the basis of a permanent exclusion of the individual is subject to section 2953.35 of the Revised Code.

(H) For purposes of sections 2953.31 to 2953.36 of the Revised Code, DNA records collected in the DNA database and fingerprints filed for record by the superintendent of the bureau of criminal identification and investigation shall not be sealed unless the superintendent receives a certified copy of a final court order establishing that the offender's conviction has been overturned. For purposes of this section, a court order is not "final" if time remains for an appeal or application for discretionary review with respect to the order.

**HISTORY: 135 v S 5 (Eff 1-1-74); 137 v H 219 (Eff 11-1-77); 138 v H 105 (Eff 10-25-79); 140 v H 227 (Eff 9-26-84); 142 v H 8 (Eff 7-31-87); 142 v H 175 (Eff 6-29-88); 143 v S 140 (Eff 10-2-89); 144 v H 154 (Eff 7-31-92); 145 v H 571 (Eff 10-6-94); 146 v H 566 (Eff 10-16-96); 146 v S 160 (Eff 1-27-97); 148 v S 13. Eff 3-23-2000; 149 v H 490, § 1, eff. 1-1-04; 150 v H 12, §§ 1, 3, eff. 4-8-04†; 152 v S 10, § 1, eff. 7-1-07; 152 v H 104, § 1, eff. 3-24-08; 152 v H 195, § 1, eff. 9-30-08; 153 v S 77, § 1, eff. 7-6-10.**

† Section 3, H.B. 12, Acts 2004, purported to amend the version of RC § 2953.32 as amended by S.B. 123 (149 v —), which took effect on January 1, 2004. However, H.B. 12, Acts 2004 was approved January 8, 2004, and became effective April 8, 2004.

The effective date is set by § 3 of 152 v S 10.

See the provisions of §§ 7, 9, and 10 of H.B. 12 (150 v —) following RC § 2923.12.

## § 2953.321 Disposition and use of investigatory work product.

(A) As used in this section, "investigatory work product" means any records or reports of a law enforcement officer or agency that are excepted from the definition of "official records" contained in section 2953.51 of the Revised Code and that pertain to a case the records of which have been ordered sealed pursuant to division (C)(2) of section 2953.32 of the Revised Code or have been ordered expunged pursuant to division (D)(2) of section 2953.37 of the Revised Code.

(B) Upon the issuance of an order by a court pursuant to division (C)(2) of section 2953.32 of the Revised Code directing that all official records pertaining to a case be sealed or an order by a court pursuant to division (D)(2) of section 2953.37 of the Revised Code directing that all official records pertaining to a case be expunged:

(1) Every law enforcement officer who possesses investigatory work product immediately shall deliver that work product to the law enforcement officer's employing law enforcement agency.

(2) Except as provided in division (B)(3) of this section, every law enforcement agency that possesses investigatory work product shall close that work product to all persons who are not directly employed by the law enforcement agency and shall treat that work product, in relation to all persons other than those who are directly employed by the law enforcement agency, as if it did not exist and never had existed.

(3) A law enforcement agency that possesses investigatory work product may permit another law enforcement agency to use that work product in the investigation of another offense if the facts incident to the offense being investigated by the other law enforcement agency and the facts incident to an offense that is the subject of the case are reasonably similar. The agency that permits the use of investigatory work product may provide the other agency with the name of the person who is the subject of the case if it believes that the name of the person is necessary to the conduct of the investigation by the other agency.

(C)(1) Except as provided in division (B)(3) of this section, no law enforcement officer or other person employed by a law enforcement agency shall knowingly release, disseminate, or otherwise make the investigatory work product or any information contained in that work product available to, or discuss any information contained in it with, any person not employed by the employing law enforcement agency.

(2) No law enforcement agency, or person employed by a law enforcement agency, that receives investigatory work product pursuant to division (B)(3) of this section shall use that work product for any purpose other than the investigation of the offense for which it was obtained from the other law enforcement agency, or disclose the name of the person who is the subject of the work product except when necessary for the conduct of the investigation of the offense, or the prosecution of the person for committing the offense, for which it was obtained from the other law enforcement agency.

(3) It is not a violation of division (C)(1) or (2) of this section for the bureau of criminal identification and investigation or any authorized employee of the bureau participating in the investigation of criminal activity to release, disseminate, or otherwise make available to, or discuss with, a person directly employed by a law enforcement agency DNA records collected in the DNA database or fingerprints filed for record by the superintendent of the bureau of criminal identification and investigation.

(D) Whoever violates division (C)(1) or (2) of this section is guilty of divulging confidential investigatory work product, a misdemeanor of the fourth degree.

**HISTORY: 142 v H 175. Eff 6-29-88; 153 v S 77, § 1, eff. 7-6-10; 2011 SB 17, § 1, eff. Sept. 30, 2011.**

## § 2953.33 Rights and privileges restored; answering questions.

(A) An order issued under section 2953.37 of the Revised Code to expunge the record of a person's conviction or, except as provided in division (G) of section 2953.32 of the Revised Code, an order issued under that section to seal the record of a person's conviction restores the person who is the subject of the order to all rights and privileges not otherwise restored by termination of the sentence or community control sanction or by final release on parole or post-release control.

(B)(1) In any application for employment, license, or other right or privilege, any appearance as a witness, or any other inquiry, except as provided in division (E) of section 2953.32 and in section 3319.292 of the Revised Code and subject to division (B)(2) of this section, a person may be questioned only with respect to convictions not sealed, bail forfeitures not expunged under section 2953.42 of the Revised Code as it existed prior to June 29, 1988, and bail forfeitures not sealed, unless the question bears a direct and substantial relationship to the position for which the person is being considered.

(2) A person may not be questioned in any application, appearance, or inquiry of a type described in division (B)(1) of this section with respect to any conviction expunged under section 2953.37 of the Revised Code.

**HISTORY: 135 v S 5 (Eff 1-1-74); 138 v H 105 (Eff 10-25-79); 142 v H 175 (Eff 6-29-88); 144 v H 154. Eff 7-31-92; 149 v H 490, § 1, eff. 1-1-04; 152 v H 428, § 1, eff. 9-12-08; 2011 SB 17, § 1, eff. Sept. 30, 2011.**

The effective date is set by section 4 of H.B. 490.

The provisions of § 7 of S.B. 123 (149 v —) read as follows:

SECTION 7. (A) If, on or after March 31, 1999, a person filed an application in a court that requested the sealing of a conviction record under sections 2953.31 to 2953.36 of the Revised Code, if at the time the application was filed section 2953.36 did not make sections 2953.31 to 2953.35 of the Revised Code inapplicable to the conviction that was the subject of the application, if the person withdrew the application prior to March 31, 2001, and if the person refiles an application in the appropriate court within ninety days after the effective date of this section that requests the sealing of the same conviction record under sections 2953.31 to 2953.36 of the Revised Code, all of the following apply:

(1) Divisions (C), (D), and (E) of section 2953.36 of the Revised Code, as they have existed since March 23, 2000, do not apply regarding the application or the determination of whether it should be accepted or granted, and the court may accept and grant the application regardless of whether the conviction that is the subject of the application is a conviction to which any of those divisions, but for the operation of this division, makes sections 2953.31 to 2953.35 of the Revised Code inapplicable.

(2) Except as provided in division (A)(1) of this section, the provisions of sections 2953.31 to 2953.36 of the Revised Code that are in effect at the time of the refiling of the application apply regarding the application and the determination of whether it should be granted.

(B) This section shall expire one year after this act becomes law.

## § 2953.34 First offender may still take appeal or seek relief.

Nothing in sections 2953.31 to 2953.33 of the Revised Code precludes a first offender from taking an appeal or seeking any relief from his conviction or from relying on it in lieu of any subsequent prosecution for the same offense.

**HISTORY: 135 v S 5, § 2. Eff 1-1-74.**

The provisions of § 7 of S.B. 123 (149 v —) read as follows:

SECTION 7. (A) If, on or after March 31, 1999, a person filed an application in a court that requested the sealing of a conviction record under sections 2953.31 to 2953.36 of the Revised Code, if at the time the application was filed section 2953.36 did not make sections 2953.31 to 2953.35 of the Revised Code inapplicable to the conviction that was the subject of the application, if the person withdrew the application prior to March 31, 2001, and if the person refiles an application in the appropriate court within ninety days after the effective date of this section that requests the sealing of the same conviction record under sections 2953.31 to 2953.36 of the Revised Code, all of the following apply:

(1) Divisions (C), (D), and (E) of section 2953.36 of the Revised Code, as they have existed since March 23, 2000, do not apply regarding the application or the determination of whether it should be accepted or granted, and the court may accept and grant the application regardless of whether the conviction that is the subject of the application is a conviction to which any of those divisions, but for the operation of this division, makes sections 2953.31 to 2953.35 of the Revised Code inapplicable.

(2) Except as provided in division (A)(1) of this section, the provisions of sections 2953.31 to 2953.36 of the Revised Code that are in effect at the time of the refiling of the application apply regarding the application and the determination of whether it should be granted.

(B) This section shall expire one year after this act becomes law.

## § 2953.35 Divulging confidential information.

(A) Except as authorized by divisions (D), (E), and (F) of section 2953.32 of the Revised Code or by Chapter 2950. of the Revised Code, any officer or employee of the state, or a political subdivision of the state, who releases or otherwise disseminates or makes available for any purpose involving employment, bonding, or licensing in connection with any business, trade, or profession to any person, or to any department, agency, or other instrumentality of the state, or any political subdivision of the state, any information or other data concerning any arrest, complaint, indictment, trial, hearing, adjudication, conviction, or correctional supervision the records with respect to which the officer or employee had knowledge of were sealed by an existing order issued pursuant to sections 2953.31 to 2953.36 of the Revised Code, were expunged by an order issued pursuant to section 2953.37 of the Revised Code, or were expunged by an order issued pursuant to section 2953.42 of the Revised Code as it existed prior to June 29, 1988, is guilty of divulging confidential information, a misdemeanor of the fourth degree.

(B) Any person who, in violation of section 2953.32 of the Revised Code, uses, disseminates, or otherwise makes available any index prepared pursuant to division (F) of section 2953.32 of the Revised Code is guilty of a misdemeanor of the fourth degree.

(C) It is not a violation of this section for the bureau of criminal identification and investigation or any authorized employee of the bureau participating in the investigation of criminal activity to release, disseminate, or otherwise make available to, or discuss with, a person directly employed by a law enforcement agency DNA records collected in the DNA database or fingerprints filed for record by the superintendent of the bureau of criminal identification and investigation.

**HISTORY: 135 v S 5 (Eff 1-1-74); 136 v H 1 (Eff 6-13-75); 138 v H 105 (Eff 10-25-79); 142 v H 175 (Eff 6-29-88); 146 v H 180. Eff 7-1-97; 153 v S 77, § 1, eff. 7-6-10; 2011 SB 17, § 1, eff. Sept. 30, 2011.**

## § 2953.36 Exceptions to preceding sections.

Sections 2953.31 to 2953.35 of the Revised Code do not apply to any of the following:

(A) Convictions when the offender is subject to a mandatory prison term;

(B) Convictions under section 2907.02, 2907.03, 2907.04, 2907.05, 2907.06, 2907.321, 2907.322, or 2907.323, former section 2907.12, or Chapter 4507., 4510., 4511., or 4549. of the Revised Code, or a conviction for a violation of a municipal ordinance that is substantially similar to any section contained in any of those chapters;

(C) Convictions of an offense of violence when the offense is a misdemeanor of the first degree or a felony and when the offense is not a violation of section 2917.03 of the Revised Code and is not a violation of section 2903.13, 2917.01 or 2917.31 of the Revised Code that is a misdemeanor of the first degree;

(D) Convictions on or after the effective date of this amendment under section 2907.07 of the Revised Code or a conviction on or after the effective date of this amendment for a violation of a municipal ordinance that is substantially similar to that section;

(E) Convictions on or after the effective date of this amendment under section 2907.08, 2907.09, 2907.21, 2907.22, 2907.23, 2907.31, 2907.311 [2907.31.1], 2907.32, or 2907.33 of the Revised Code when the victim of the offense was under eighteen years of age;

(F) Convictions of an offense in circumstances in which the victim of the offense was under eighteen years of age when the offense is a misdemeanor of the first degree or a felony;

(G) Convictions of a felony of the first or second degree;

(H) Bail forfeitures in a traffic case as defined in Traffic Rule 2.

**HISTORY: 135 v S 5 (Eff 1-1-74); 142 v H 175 (Eff 6-29-88); 145 v H 335 (Eff 12-9-94); 146 v S 269 (Eff 7-1-96); 146 v H 445 (Eff 9-3-96); 146 v H 353 (Eff 9-17-96); 148 v S 13. Eff 3-23-2000; 149 v S 123, § 1, eff. 1-1-04; 152 v S 18, § 1, eff. 10-10-07.**

The effective date is set by section 4 of S.B. 123.

See provisions, § 5 of S.B. 123 (149 v —), following RC § 2953.31.

## § 2953.37 Expungement of a prior conviction of improperly handling firearms in a motor vehicle that is no longer a crime.

(A) As used in this section:

(1) "Expunge" means to destroy, delete, and erase a record as appropriate for the record's physical or electronic form or characteristic so that the record is permanently irretrievable.

(2) "Official records" has the same meaning as in section 2953.51 of the Revised Code.

(3) "Prosecutor" has the same meaning as in section 2953.31 of the Revised Code.

(4) "Record of conviction" means the record related to a conviction of or plea of guilty to an offense.

(B) Any person who is convicted of, was convicted of, pleads guilty to, or has pleaded guilty to a violation of division (B), (C), or (E) of section 2923.16 of the Revised Code as the division existed prior to the effective date of this section and who is authorized by division (H)(2)(a) of that section to file an application under this section for the expungement of the conviction record may apply to the sentencing court for the expungement of the record of conviction. The person may file the application at any time on or after the effective date of this section. The application shall do all of the following:

(1) Identify the applicant, the offense for which the expungement is sought, the date of the conviction of or plea of guilty to that offense, and the court in which the conviction occurred or the plea of guilty was entered;

(2) Include evidence that the offense was a violation of division (B), (C), or (E) of section 2923.16 of the Revised Code as the division existed prior to the effective date of this section and that the applicant is authorized by division (H)(2)(a) of that section to file an application under this section;

(3) Include a request for expungement of the record of conviction of that offense under this section.

(C) Upon the filing of an application under division (B) of this section and the payment of the fee described in division (D)(3) of this section if applicable, the court shall set a date for a hearing and shall notify the prosecutor for the case of the hearing on the application. The prosecutor may object to the granting of the application by filing an objection with the court prior to the date set for the hearing. The prosecutor shall specify in the objection the reasons for believing a denial of the application is justified. The court shall direct its regular probation officer, a state probation officer, or the department of probation of the county in which the applicant resides to make inquiries and written reports as the court requires concerning the applicant. The court shall hold the hearing scheduled under this division.

(D)(1) At the hearing held under division (C) of this section, the court shall do each of the following:

(a) Determine whether the applicant has been convicted of or pleaded guilty to a violation of division (E) of section 2923.16 of the Revised Code as the division existed prior to the effective date of this section and whether the conduct that was the basis of the violation no longer would be a violation of that division on or after the effective date of this section;

(b) Determine whether the applicant has been convicted of or pleaded guilty to a violation of division (B) or (C) of section 2923.16 of the Revised Code as the division existed prior to the effective date of this section and whether the conduct that was the basis of the violation no longer would be a violation of that division on or after the effective date of this section due to the application of division (F)(5) of that section as it exists on and after the effective date of this section;

(c) If the prosecutor has filed an objection in accordance with division (C) of this section, consider the reasons against granting the application specified by the prosecutor in the objection;

(d) Weigh the interests of the applicant in having the records pertaining to the applicant's conviction or guilty plea expunged against the legitimate needs, if any, of the government to maintain those records.

(2)(a) The court may order the expungement of all official records pertaining to the case and the deletion of all index references to the case and, if it does order the expungement, shall send notice of the order to each public office or agency that the court has reason to believe may have an official record pertaining to the case if the court, after complying with division (D)(1) of this section, determines both of the following:

(i) That the applicant has been convicted of or pleaded guilty to a violation of division (E) of section 2923.16 of the Revised Code as it existed prior to the effective date of this section and the conduct that was the basis of the violation no longer would be a violation of that division on or after the effective date of this section, or that the applicant has been convicted of or pleaded guilty to a violation of division (B) or (C) of section 2923.16 of the Revised Code as the division existed prior to the effective date of this section and the conduct that was the basis of the violation no longer would be a violation of that division on or after the effective date of this section due to the application of division (F)(5) of that section as it exists on and after the effective date of this section;

(ii) That the interests of the applicant in having the records pertaining to the applicant's conviction or guilty plea expunged are not outweighed by any legitimate needs of the government to maintain those records.

(b) The proceedings in the case that is the subject of an order issued under division (D)(2)(a) of this section shall be considered not to have occurred and the conviction or guilty plea of the person who is the subject of the proceedings shall be expunged. The record of the conviction shall not be used for any purpose, including, but not limited to, a criminal records check under section 109.572 of the Revised Code or a determination under section 2923.125 or 2923.1212 of the Revised Code of eligibility for a license or temporary emergency license to carry a concealed handgun. The applicant may, and the court shall, reply that no record exists with respect to the applicant upon any inquiry into the matter.

(3) Upon the filing of an application under this section, the applicant, unless indigent, shall pay a fee of fifty dollars. The court shall pay thirty dollars of the fee into the state treasury and shall pay twenty dollars of the fee into the county general revenue fund.

**HISTORY: 2011 SB 17, § 1, eff. Sept. 30, 2011.**

## § 2953.41 Repealed, 142 v H 175, § 2 [137 v S 192]. Eff 6-29-88.

This section concerned expungement after agreed bail forfeiture. See now RC § 2953.31 et seq.

## § 2953.42 Repealed, 142 v H 175, § 2 [137 v S 192]. Eff 6-29-88.

This section concerned expungement after agreed bail forfeiture. See now RC § 2953.31 et seq.

## § 2953.43 Repealed, 142 v H 175, § 2 [137 v S 192]. Eff 6-29-88.

This section concerned expungement after agreed bail forfeiture. See now RC § 2953.31 et seq.

## [SEALING OF RECORDS AFTER NOT GUILTY FINDING OR DISMISSAL]

## § 2953.51 Definitions.

As used in sections 2953.51 to 2953.56 of the Revised Code:

(A) "No bill" means a report by the foreperson or deputy foreperson of a grand jury that an indictment is not found by the grand jury against a person who has been held to answer before the grand jury for the commission of an offense.

(B) "Prosecutor" has the same meaning as in section 2953.31 of the Revised Code.

(C) "Court" means the court in which a case is pending at the time a finding of not guilty in the case or a dismissal of the complaint, indictment, or information in the case is entered on the minutes or journal of the court, or the court to which the foreperson or deputy foreperson of a grand jury reports, pursuant to section 2939.23 of the Revised Code, that the grand jury has returned a no bill.

(D) "Official records" means all records that are possessed by any public office or agency that relate to a criminal case, including, but not limited to: the notation to the case in the criminal docket; all subpoenas issued in the case; all papers and documents filed by the defendant or the prosecutor in the case; all records of all testimony and evidence presented in all proceedings in the case; all court files, papers, documents, folders, entries, affidavits, or writs that pertain to the case; all computer, microfilm, microfiche, or microdot records, indices, or references to the case; all index references to the case; all fingerprints and photographs; all records and investigative reports pertaining to the case that are possessed by any law enforcement officer or agency, except that any records or reports that are the specific investigatory work product of a law enforcement officer or agency are not and shall not be considered to be official records when they are in the possession of that officer or agency; and all investigative records and reports other than those possessed by a law enforcement officer or agency pertaining to the case. "Official records" does not include records or reports maintained pursuant to section 2151.421 [2151.42.1] of the Revised Code by a public children services agency or the department of job and family services.

(E) "DNA database," "DNA record," and "law enforcement agency" have the same meanings as in section 109.573 [109.57.3] of the Revised Code.

(F) "Fingerprints filed for record" has the same meaning as in section 2953.31 of the Revised Code.

**HISTORY: 140 v H 227 (Eff 9-26-84); 146 v H 274 (Eff 8-8-96); 148 v H 471. Eff 7-1-2000; 153 v S 77, § 1, eff. 7-6-10.**

The effective date is set by section 12(A) of HB 471.

## § 2953.52 Sealing of official records after not guilty finding, dismissal of proceedings or no bill.

(A)(1) Any person, who is found not guilty of an offense by a jury or a court or who is the defendant named in a dismissed complaint, indictment, or information, may apply to the court for an order to seal his official records in the case. Except as provided in section 2953.61 of the Revised Code, the application may be filed at any time after the finding of not guilty or the dismissal of the complaint, indictment, or information is entered upon the minutes of the court or the journal, whichever entry occurs first.

(2) Any person, against whom a no bill is entered by a grand jury, may apply to the court for an order to seal his official records in the case. Except as provided in section 2953.61 of the Revised Code, the application may be filed at any time after the expiration of two years after the date on which the foreman or deputy foreman of the grand jury reports to the court that the grand jury has reported a no bill.

(B)(1) Upon the filing of an application pursuant to division (A) of this section, the court shall set a date for a hearing and shall notify the prosecutor in the case of the hearing on the application. The prosecutor may object to the granting of the application by filing an objection with the court prior to the date set for the hearing. The prosecutor shall specify in the objection the reasons he believes justify a denial of the application.

(2) The court shall do each of the following:

(a) Determine whether the person was found not guilty in the case, or the complaint, indictment, or information in the case was dismissed, or a no bill was returned in the case and a period of two years or a longer period as required by section 2953.61 of the Revised Code has expired from the date of the report to the court of that no bill by the foreman or deputy foreman of the grand jury;

(b) Determine whether criminal proceedings are pending against the person;

(c) If the prosecutor has filed an objection in accordance with division (B)(1) of this section, consider the reasons against granting the application specified by the prosecutor in the objection;

(d) Weigh the interests of the person in having the official records pertaining to the case sealed against the legitimate needs, if any, of the government to maintain those records.

(3) If the court determines, after complying with division (B)(2) of this section, that the person was found not guilty in the case, that the complaint, indictment, or information in the case was dismissed, or that a no bill was returned in the case and that the appropriate period of time has expired from the date of the report to the court of the no bill by the foreman or deputy foreman of the grand jury; that no criminal proceedings are pending against the person; and the interests of the person in having the records pertaining to the case sealed are not outweighed by any legitimate governmental needs to maintain such records, or if division (E)(2)(b) of section 4301.69 of the Revised Code applies, the court shall issue an order directing that all official records pertaining to the case be sealed and that, except as provided in section 2953.53 of the Revised Code, the proceedings in the case be deemed not to have occurred.

**HISTORY: 140 v H 227 (Eff 9-26-84); 142 v H 175 (Eff 6-29-88); 149 v H 17. Eff 10-11-2002.**

## § 2953.53 Order to seal records; index of sealed records.

(A) The court shall send notice of any order to seal official records issued pursuant to section 2953.52 of the Revised Code to any public office or agency that the court knows or has reason to believe may have any record of the case, whether or not it is an official record, that is the subject of the order. The notice shall be sent by certified mail, return receipt requested.

(B) A person whose official records have been sealed pursuant to an order issued pursuant to section 2953.52 of the Revised Code may present a copy of that order and a written request to comply with it, to a public office or agency that has a record of the case that is the subject of the order.

(C) An order to seal official records issued pursuant to section 2953.52 of the Revised Code applies to every public office or agency that has a record of the case that is the subject of the order, regardless of whether it receives notice of the hearing on the application for the order to seal the official records or receives a copy of the order to seal the official records pursuant to division (A) or (B) of this section.

(D) Upon receiving a copy of an order to seal official records pursuant to division (A) or (B) of this section or upon otherwise becoming aware of an applicable order to seal official records issued pursuant to section 2953.52 of the Revised Code, a public office or agency shall comply with the order and, if applicable, with the provisions of section 2953.54 of the Revised Code, except that it may maintain a record of the case that is the subject of the order if the record is maintained for the purpose of compiling statistical data only and does not contain any reference to the person who is the subject of the case and the order.

A public office or agency also may maintain an index of sealed official records, in a form similar to that for sealed records of conviction as set forth in division (F) of section 2953.32 of the Revised Code, access to which may not be afforded to any person other than the person who has custody of the sealed official records. The sealed official records to which such an index pertains shall not be available to any person, except that the official records of a case that have been sealed may be made available to the following persons for the following purposes:

(1) To the person who is the subject of the records upon written application, and to any other person named in the application, for any purpose;

(2) To a law enforcement officer who was involved in the case, for use in the officer's defense of a civil action arising out of the officer's involvement in that case;

(3) To a prosecuting attorney or the prosecuting attorney's assistants to determine a defendant's eligibility to enter a pre-trial diversion program established pursuant to section 2935.36 of the Revised Code;

(4) To a prosecuting attorney or the prosecuting attorney's assistants to determine a defendant's eligibility to enter a pre-trial diversion program under division (E)(2)(b) of section 4301.69 of the Revised Code.

**HISTORY: 140 v H 227 (Eff 9-26-84); 142 v H 8 (Eff 7-31-87); 142 v H 175 (Eff 6-29-88); 149 v H 17. Eff 10-11-2002.**

## § 2953.54 Disposition and use of specific investigatory work product; divulging confidential information.

(A) Except as otherwise provided in Chapter 2950. of the Revised Code, upon the issuance of an order by a court under division (B) of section 2953.52 of the Revised Code directing that all official records pertaining to a case be sealed and that the proceedings in the case be deemed not to have occurred:

(1) Every law enforcement officer possessing records or reports pertaining to the case that are the officer's specific investigatory work product and that are excepted from the definition of "official records" contained in section 2953.51 of the Revised Code shall immediately deliver the records and reports to the officer's employing law enforcement agency. Except as provided in division (A)(3) of this section, no such officer shall knowingly release, disseminate, or otherwise make the records and reports or any information contained in them available to, or discuss any information contained in them with, any person not employed by the officer's employing law enforcement agency.

(2) Every law enforcement agency that possesses records or reports pertaining to the case that are its specific investigatory work product and that are excepted from the definition of "official records" contained in section 2953.51 of the Revised Code, or that are the specific investigatory work product of a law enforcement officer it employs and that were delivered to it under division (A)(1) of this section shall, except as provided in division (A)(3) of this section, close the records and reports to all persons who are not directly employed by the law enforcement agency and shall, except as provided in division (A)(3) of this section, treat the records and reports, in relation to all persons other than those who are directly employed by the law enforcement agency, as if they did not exist and had never existed. Except as provided in division (A)(3) of this section, no person who is employed by the law enforcement agency shall knowingly release, disseminate, or otherwise make the records and reports in the possession of the employing law enforcement agency or any information contained in them available to, or discuss any information contained in them with, any person not employed by the employing law enforcement agency.

(3) A law enforcement agency that possesses records or reports pertaining to the case that are its specific investigatory work product and that are excepted from the definition of "official records" contained in division (D) of section 2953.51 of the Revised Code, or that are the specific investigatory work product of a law enforcement officer it employs and that were delivered to it under division (A)(1) of this section may permit another law enforcement agency to use the records or reports in the investigation of another offense, if the facts incident to the offense being investigated by the other law enforcement agency and the facts incident to an offense that is the subject of the case are reasonably similar. The agency that provides the records and reports may provide the other agency with the name of the person who is the subject of the case, if it believes that the name of the person is necessary to the conduct of the investigation by the other agency.

No law enforcement agency, or person employed by a law enforcement agency, that receives from another law enforcement agency records or reports pertaining to a case the records of which have been ordered sealed pursuant to division (B) of section 2953.52 of the Revised Code shall use the records and reports for any purpose other than the investigation of the offense for which they were obtained from the other law enforcement agency, or disclose the name of the person who is the subject of the records or reports except when necessary for the conduct of the investigation of the offense, or the prosecution of the person for committing the offense, for which they were obtained from the other law enforcement agency.

(B) Whoever violates division (A)(1), (2), or (3) of this section is guilty of divulging confidential information, a misdemeanor of the fourth degree.

(C) It is not a violation of this section for the bureau of criminal identification and investigation or any authorized employee of the bureau participating in the investigation of criminal activity to release, disseminate, or otherwise make available to, or discuss with, a person directly employed by a law enforcement agency DNA records collected in the DNA database or fingerprints filed for record by the superintendent of the bureau of criminal identification and investigation.

**HISTORY: 140 v H 227 (Eff 9-26-84); 146 v H 180. Eff 7-1-97; 153 v S 77, § 1, eff. 7-6-10.**

The effective date is set by section 5 of HB 180.

## § 2953.55 Inquiry as to sealed records prohibited; divulging confidential information.

(A) In any application for employment, license, or any other right or privilege, any appearance as a witness, or any other inquiry, a person may not be questioned with respect to any record that has been sealed pursuant to section 2953.52 of the Revised Code. If an inquiry is made in violation of this section, the person whose official record was sealed may respond as if the arrest underlying the case to which the sealed official records pertain and all other proceedings in that case did not occur, and the person whose official record was sealed shall not be subject to any adverse action because of the arrest, the proceedings, or the person's response.

(B) An officer or employee of the state or any of its political subdivisions who knowingly releases, disseminates, or makes available for any purpose involving employment, bonding, licensing, or education to any person or to any department, agency, or other instrumentality of the state, or of any of its political subdivisions, any information or other data concerning any arrest, complaint, indictment, information, trial, adjudication, or correctional supervision, the records of which have been sealed pursuant to section 2953.52 of the Revised Code, is guilty of divulging confidential information, a misdemeanor of the fourth degree.

(C) It is not a violation of this section for the bureau of criminal identification and investigation or any authorized employee of the bureau participating in the investigation of criminal activity to release, disseminate, or otherwise make available to, or discuss with, a person directly employed by a law enforcement agency DNA records collected in the DNA database or fingerprints filed for record by the superintendent of the bureau of criminal identification and investigation.

**HISTORY: 140 v H 227. Eff 9-26-84; 153 v S 77, § 1, eff. 7-6-10.**

### § 2953.56 Violation of provisions does not provide basis to exclude or suppress certain evidence.

Violations of sections 2953.31 to 2953.61 of the Revised Code shall not provide the basis to exclude or suppress any of the following evidence that is otherwise admissible in a criminal proceeding, delinquent child proceeding, or other legal proceeding:

(A) DNA records collected in the DNA database;

(B) Fingerprints filed for record by the superintendent of the bureau of criminal identification and investigation;

(C) Other evidence that was obtained or discovered as the direct or indirect result of divulging or otherwise using the records described in divisions (A) and (B) of this section.

**HISTORY: 153 v S 77, § 1, eff. 7-6-10.**

## [SEALING OF RECORDS WHEN COURT ENTERS JUDGMENT VACATING AND SETTING ASIDE CONVICTION BECAUSE OF DNA TESTING]

### § 2953.57 Sealing of records when court enters judgment vacating and setting aside conviction because of DNA testing.

(A) A court that enters a judgment that vacates and sets aside the conviction of a person because of DNA testing that was performed under sections 2953.71 to 2953.81 of the Revised Code or under section 2953.82 of the Revised Code shall issue ninety days after the court vacates and sets aside the conviction an order directing that all official records pertaining to the case involving the vacated conviction be sealed and that the proceedings in the case shall be deemed not to have occurred.

(B) As used in sections 2953.57 to 2953.60 of the Revised Code, "official records" has the same meaning as in section 2953.51 of the Revised Code.

**HISTORY: 153 v S 77, § 1, eff. 7-6-10.**

### § 2953.58 Transmission of order to public office or agency; office or agency may maintain index of sealed records.

(A) The court shall send notice of an order to seal official records issued pursuant to section 2953.57 of the Revised Code to any public office or agency that the court knows or has reason to believe may have any record of the case, whether or not it is an official record, that is the subject of the order. The notice shall be sent by certified mail, return receipt requested.

(B) A person whose official records have been sealed pursuant to an order issued pursuant to section 2953.57 of the Revised Code may present a copy of that order and a written request to comply with it, to a public office or agency that has a record of the case that is the subject of the order.

(C) An order to seal official records issued pursuant to section 2953.57 of the Revised Code applies to every public office or agency that has a record of the case that is the subject of the order, regardless of whether it receives a copy of the order to seal the official records pursuant to division (A) or (B) of this section.

(D) Upon receiving a copy of an order to seal official records pursuant to division (A) or (B) of this section or upon otherwise becoming aware of an applicable order to seal official records issued pursuant to section 2953.57 of the Revised Code, a public office or agency shall comply with the order and, if applicable, with the provisions of section 2953.59 of the Revised Code, except that it may maintain a record of the case that is the subject of the order if the record is maintained for the purpose of compiling statistical data only and does not contain any reference to the person who is the subject of the case and the order.

A public office or agency also may maintain an index of sealed official records, in a form similar to that for sealed records of conviction as set forth in division (F) of section 2953.32 of the Revised Code, access to which may not be afforded to any person other than the person who has custody of the sealed official records. The sealed official records to which such an index pertains shall not be available to any person, except that the official records of a case that have been sealed may be made available to the following persons for the following purposes:

(1) To the person who is the subject of the records upon written application, and to any other person named in the application, for any purpose;

(2) To a law enforcement officer who was involved in the case, for use in the officer's defense of a civil action arising out of the officer's involvement in that case.

**HISTORY: 153 v S 77, § 1, eff. 7-6-10.**

### § 2953.59 Duties of law enforcement officer or agency upon issuance of order; divulging confidential information.

(A) Except as otherwise provided in Chapter 2950. of the Revised Code, upon the issuance of an order by a court under section 2953.57 of the Revised Code directing that all official records pertaining to a case be sealed and that the proceedings in the case be deemed not to have occurred:

(1) Every law enforcement officer possessing records or reports pertaining to the case that are the officer's specific investigatory work product and that are excepted from the definition of "official records" contained in section 2953.51 of the Revised Code shall immediately deliver the records and reports to the officer's employing law enforcement agency. Except as provided in division (A)(3) of this section, no such officer shall knowingly release, disseminate, or otherwise make the records and reports or any information contained in them available to, or discuss any information contained in them with, any person not employed by the officer's employing law enforcement agency.

(2) Every law enforcement agency that possesses records or reports pertaining to the case that are its specific investigatory work product and that are excepted from the definition of "official records" contained in section 2953.51 of the Revised Code, or that are the specific

investigatory work product of a law enforcement officer it employs and that were delivered to it under division (A)(1) of this section shall, except as provided in division (A)(3) of this section, close the records and reports to all persons who are not directly employed by the law enforcement agency and shall, except as provided in division (A)(3) of this section, treat the records and reports, in relation to all persons other than those who are directly employed by the law enforcement agency, as if they did not exist and had never existed. Except as provided in division (A)(3) of this section, no person who is employed by the law enforcement agency shall knowingly release, disseminate, or otherwise make the records and reports in the possession of the employing law enforcement agency or any information contained in them available to, or discuss any information contained in them with, any person not employed by the employing law enforcement agency.

(3) A law enforcement agency that possesses records or reports pertaining to the case that are its specific investigatory work product and that are excepted from the definition of "official records" contained in division (D) of section 2953.51 of the Revised Code, or that are the specific investigatory work product of a law enforcement officer it employs and that were delivered to it under division (A)(1) of this section may permit another law enforcement agency to use the records or reports in the investigation of another offense, if the facts incident to the offense being investigated by the other law enforcement agency and the facts incident to an offense that is the subject of the case are reasonably similar and if all references to the name or identifying information of the person whose records were sealed are redacted from the records or reports. The agency that provides the records and reports may not provide the other agency with the name of the person who is the subject of the case the records of which were sealed.

(B) Whoever violates division (A)(1), (2), or (3) of this section is guilty of divulging confidential information, a misdemeanor of the fourth degree.

**HISTORY: 153 v S 77, § 1, eff. 7-6-10.**

## § 2953.60 Inquiry as to sealed records prohibited; divulging confidential information.

(A) In any application for employment, license, or any other right or privilege, any appearance as a witness, or any other inquiry, a person may not be questioned with respect to any record that has been sealed pursuant to section 2953.57 of the Revised Code. If an inquiry is made in violation of this section, the person whose official record was sealed may respond as if the arrest underlying the case to which the sealed official records pertain and all other proceedings in that case did not occur, and the person whose official record was sealed shall not be subject to any adverse action because of the arrest, the proceedings, or the person's response.

(B) An officer or employee of the state or any of its political subdivisions who knowingly releases, disseminates, or makes available for any purpose involving employment, bonding, licensing, or education to any person or to any department, agency, or other instrumentality of the state, or of any of its political subdivisions, any information or other data concerning any arrest, complaint, indictment, information, trial, adjudication, or correctional supervision, the records of which have been sealed pursuant to section 2953.57 of the Revised Code, is guilty of divulging confidential information, a misdemeanor of the fourth degree.

**HISTORY: 153 v S 77, § 1, eff. 7-6-10.**

## § 2953.61 Sealing of records in cases of multiple charges.

When a person is charged with two or more offenses as a result of or in connection with the same act and at least one of the charges has a final disposition that is different than the final disposition of the other charges, the person may not apply to the court for the sealing of his record in any of the cases until such time as he would be able to apply to the court and have all of the records in all of the cases pertaining to those charges sealed pursuant to divisions (A)(1) and (2) of section 2953.32 and divisions (A)(1) and (2) of section 2953.52 of the Revised Code.

**HISTORY: 142 v H 175. Eff 6-29-88.**

# [POSTCONVICTION DNA TESTING FOR ELIGIBLE OFFENDERS]

## § 2953.71 Definitions.

As used in sections 2953.71 to 2953.83 of the Revised Code:

(A) "Application" or "application for DNA testing" means a request through postconviction relief for the state to do DNA testing on biological material from the case in which the offender was convicted of the offense for which the offender is an eligible offender and is requesting the DNA testing under sections 2953.71 to 2953.81 of the Revised Code.

(B) "Biological material" means any product of a human body containing DNA.

(C) "Chain of custody" means a record or other evidence that tracks a subject sample of biological material from the time the biological material was first obtained until the time it currently exists in its place of storage and, in relation to a DNA sample, a record or other evidence that tracks the DNA sample from the time it was first obtained until it currently exists in its place of storage. For purposes of this division, examples of when biological material or a DNA sample is first obtained include, but are not limited to, obtaining the material or sample at the scene of a crime, from a victim, from an offender, or in any other manner or time as is appropriate in the facts and circumstances present.

(D) "Custodial agency" means the group or entity that has the responsibility to maintain biological material in question.

(E) "Custodian" means the person who is the primary representative of a custodial agency.

(F) "Eligible offender" means an offender who is eligible under division (C) of section 2953.72 of the Revised Code to request DNA testing to be conducted under sections 2953.71 to 2953.81 of the Revised Code.

(G) "Exclusion" or "exclusion result" means a result of DNA testing that scientifically precludes or forecloses the subject offender as a contributor of biological material recovered from the crime scene or victim in question, in relation to the offense for which the offender is an eligible offender and for which the sentence of death or prison term was imposed upon the offender.

(H) "Extracting personnel" means medically approved personnel who are employed to physically obtain an offender's DNA specimen for purposes of DNA testing under sections 2953.71 to 2953.81 of the Revised Code.

(I) "Inclusion" or "inclusion result" means a result of DNA testing that scientifically cannot exclude, or that holds accountable, the subject offender as a contributor of biological material recovered from the crime scene or victim in question, in relation to the offense for which the offender is an eligible offender and for which the sentence of death or prison term was imposed upon the offender.

(J) "Inconclusive" or "inconclusive result" means a result of DNA testing that is rendered when a scientifically appropriate and definitive DNA analysis or result, or both, cannot be determined.

(K) "Offender" means a criminal offender who was sentenced by a court, or by a jury and a court, of this state.

(L) "Outcome determinative" means that had the results of DNA testing of the subject offender been presented at the trial of the subject offender requesting DNA testing and been found relevant and admissible with respect to the felony offense for which the offender is an eligible offender and is requesting the DNA testing, and had those results been analyzed in the context of and upon consideration of all available admissible evidence related to the offender's case as described in division (D) of section 2953.74 of the Revised Code, there is a strong probability that no reasonable factfinder would have found the offender guilty of that offense or, if the offender was sentenced to death relative to that offense, would have found the offender guilty of the aggravating circumstance or circumstances the offender was found guilty of committing and that is or are the basis of that sentence of death.

(M) "Parent sample" means the biological material first obtained from a crime scene or a victim of an offense for which an offender is an eligible offender, and from which a sample will be presently taken to do a DNA comparison to the DNA of the subject offender under sections 2953.71 to 2953.81 of the Revised Code.

(N) "Prison" and "community control sanction" have the same meanings as in section 2929.01 of the Revised Code.

(O) "Prosecuting attorney" means the prosecuting attorney who, or whose office, prosecuted the case in which the subject offender was convicted of the offense for which the offender is an eligible offender and is requesting the DNA testing.

(P) "Prosecuting authority" means the prosecuting attorney or the attorney general.

(Q) "Reasonable diligence" means a degree of diligence that is comparable to the diligence a reasonable person would employ in searching for information regarding an important matter in the person's own life.

(R) "Testing authority" means a laboratory at which DNA testing will be conducted under sections 2953.71 to 2953.81 of the Revised Code.

(S) "Parole" and "post-release control" have the same meanings as in section 2967.01 of the Revised Code.

(T) "Sexually oriented offense" and "child-victim oriented offense" have the same meanings as in section 2950.01 of the Revised Code.

(U) "Definitive DNA test" means a DNA test that clearly establishes that biological material from the perpetrator of the crime was recovered from the crime scene and also clearly establishes whether or not the biological material is that of the eligible offender. A prior DNA test is not definitive if the eligible offender proves by a preponderance of the evidence that because of advances in DNA technology there is a possibility of discovering new biological material from the perpetrator that the prior DNA test may have failed to discover. Prior testing may have been a prior "definitive DNA test" as to some biological evidence but may not have been a prior "definitive DNA test" as to other biological evidence.

**HISTORY: 150 v S 11, § 1, Eff 10-29-03; 151 v S 262, § 1, eff. 7-11-06; 153 v S 77, § 1, eff. 7-6-10.**

See provisions of § 4 of 151 v S 262 following RC § 2901.07.

## § 2953.72 Eligible offender may submit application and acknowledgment for DNA testing.

(A) Any eligible offender who wishes to request DNA testing under sections 2953.71 to 2953.81 of the Revised Code shall submit an application for the testing to the court of common pleas specified in section 2953.73 of the Revised Code, on a form prescribed by the attorney general for this purpose. The eligible offender shall submit the application in accordance with the procedures set forth in section 2953.73 of the Revised Code. The eligible offender shall specify on the application the offense or offenses for which the offender is an eligible offender and is requesting the DNA testing. Along with the application, the eligible offender shall submit an acknowledgment that is on a form prescribed by the attorney general for this purpose and that is signed by the offender. The acknowledgment shall set forth all of the following:

(1) That sections 2953.71 to 2953.81 of the Revised Code contemplate applications for DNA testing of an eligible offender at a stage of a prosecution or case after the offender has been sentenced, that any exclusion or inclusion result of DNA testing rendered pursuant to those sections may be used by a party in any proceeding as described in section 2953.81 of the Revised Code, and that all requests for any DNA testing made at trial will continue to be handled by the prosecuting attorney in the case;

(2) That the process of conducting postconviction DNA testing for an eligible offender under sections 2953.71 to 2953.81 of the Revised Code begins when the offender submits an application under section 2953.73 of the Revised Code and the acknowledgment described in this section;

(3) That the eligible offender must submit the application and acknowledgment to the court of common pleas that heard the case in which the offender was convicted of the offense for which the offender is an eligible offender and is requesting the DNA testing;

(4) That the state has established a set of criteria set forth in section 2953.74 of the Revised Code by which eligible offender applications for DNA testing will be screened and that a judge of a court of common pleas upon receipt of a properly filed application and accompanying acknowledgment will apply those criteria to determine whether to accept or reject the application;

(5) That the results of DNA testing conducted under sections 2953.71 to 2953.81 of the Revised Code will be provided as described in section 2953.81 of the Revised Code to all parties in the postconviction proceedings and will be reported to various courts;

(6) That, if DNA testing is conducted with respect to an offender under sections 2953.71 to 2953.81 of the Revised Code, the state will not offer the offender a retest if an inclusion result is achieved relative to the testing and that,

if the state were to offer a retest after an inclusion result, the policy would create an atmosphere in which endless testing could occur and in which postconviction proceedings could be stalled for many years;

(7) That, if the court rejects an eligible offender's application for DNA testing because the offender does not satisfy the acceptance criteria described in division (A)(4) of this section, the court will not accept or consider subsequent applications;

(8) That the acknowledgment memorializes the provisions of sections 2953.71 to 2953.81 of the Revised Code with respect to the application of postconviction DNA testing to offenders, that those provisions do not give any offender any additional constitutional right that the offender did not already have, that the court has no duty or obligation to provide postconviction DNA testing to offenders, that the court of common pleas has the sole discretion subject to an appeal as described in this division to determine whether an offender is an eligible offender and whether an eligible offender's application for DNA testing satisfies the acceptance criteria described in division (A)(4) of this section and whether the application should be accepted or rejected, that if the court of common pleas rejects an eligible offender's application, the offender may seek leave of the supreme court to appeal the rejection to that court if the offender was sentenced to death for the offense for which the offender is requesting the DNA testing and, if the offender was not sentenced to death for that offense, may appeal the rejection to the court of appeals, and that no determination otherwise made by the court of common pleas in the exercise of its discretion regarding the eligibility of an offender or regarding postconviction DNA testing under those provisions is reviewable by or appealable to any court;

(9) That the manner in which sections 2953.71 to 2953.81 of the Revised Code with respect to the offering of postconviction DNA testing to offenders are carried out does not confer any constitutional right upon any offender, that the state has established guidelines and procedures relative to those provisions to ensure that they are carried out with both justice and efficiency in mind, and that an offender who participates in any phase of the mechanism contained in those provisions, including, but not limited to, applying for DNA testing and being rejected, having an application for DNA testing accepted and not receiving the test, or having DNA testing conducted and receiving unfavorable results, does not gain as a result of the participation any constitutional right to challenge, or, except as provided in division (A)(8) of this section, any right to any review or appeal of, the manner in which those provisions are carried out;

(10) That the most basic aspect of sections 2953.71 to 2953.81 of the Revised Code is that, in order for DNA testing to occur, there must be an offender sample against which other evidence may be compared, that, if an eligible offender's application is accepted but the offender subsequently refuses to submit to the collection of the sample of biological material from the offender or hinders the state from obtaining a sample of biological material from the offender, the goal of those provisions will be frustrated, and that an offender's refusal or hindrance shall cause the court to rescind its prior acceptance of the application for DNA testing for the offender and deny the application.

(B) The attorney general shall prescribe a form to be used to make an application for DNA testing under division (A) of this section and section 2953.73 of the Revised Code and a form to be used to provide the acknowledgment described in division (A) of this section. The forms shall include all information described in division (A) of this section, spaces for an offender to insert all information necessary to complete the forms, including, but not limited to, specifying the offense or offenses for which the offender is an eligible offender and is requesting the DNA testing, and any other information or material the attorney general determines is necessary or relevant. The attorney general shall distribute copies of the prescribed forms to the department of rehabilitation and correction, the department shall ensure that each prison in which offenders are housed has a supply of copies of the forms, and the department shall ensure that copies of the forms are provided free of charge to any offender who requests them.

(C)(1) An offender is eligible to request DNA testing to be conducted under sections 2953.71 to 2953.81 of the Revised Code only if all of the following apply:

(a) The offense for which the offender claims to be an eligible offender is a felony, and the offender was convicted by a judge or jury of that offense.

(b) One of the following applies:

(i) The offender was sentenced to a prison term or sentence of death for the felony described in division (C)(1)(a) of this section, and the offender is in prison serving that prison term or under that sentence of death, has been paroled or is on probation regarding that felony, is under post-release control regarding that felony, or has been released from that prison term and is under a community control sanction regarding that felony.

(ii) The offender was not sentenced to a prison term or sentence of death for the felony described in division (C)(1)(a) of this section, but was sentenced to a community control sanction for that felony and is under that community control sanction.

(iii) The felony described in division (C)(1)(a) of this section was a sexually oriented offense or child-victim oriented offense, and the offender has a duty to comply with sections 2950.04, 2950.041 [2950.04.1], 2950.05, and 2950.06 of the Revised Code relative to that felony.

(2) An offender is not an eligible offender under division (C)(1) of this section regarding any offense to which the offender pleaded guilty or no contest.

(3) An offender is not an eligible offender under division (C)(1) of this section regarding any offense if the offender dies prior to submitting an application for DNA testing related to that offense under section 2953.73 of the Revised Code.

**HISTORY: 150 v S 11, § 1, eff. 10-29-03; 151 v S 262, § 1, eff. 7-11-06; 153 v S 77, § 1, eff. 7-6-10.**

See provisions of § 4 of 151 v S 262 following RC § 2901.07.

## § 2953.73 Submission of application; response; court determination as to whether to accept or reject application; appeals.

(A) An eligible offender who wishes to request DNA testing to be conducted under sections 2953.71 to 2953.81 of the Revised Code shall submit an application for DNA testing on a form prescribed by the attorney general for this purpose and shall submit the form to the court of common pleas that sentenced the offender for the offense for which the offender is an eligible offender and is requesting DNA testing.

(B) If an eligible offender submits an application for DNA testing under division (A) of this section, upon the submission of the application, all of the following apply:

(1) The eligible offender shall serve a copy of the application on the prosecuting attorney and the attorney general.

(2) The application shall be assigned to the judge of that court of common pleas who was the trial judge in the case in which the eligible offender was convicted of the offense for which the offender is requesting DNA testing, or, if that judge no longer is a judge of that court, it shall be assigned according to court rules. The judge to whom the application is assigned shall decide the application. The application shall become part of the file in the case.

(C) If an eligible offender submits an application for DNA testing under division (A) of this section, regardless of whether the offender has commenced any federal habeas corpus proceeding relative to the case in which the offender was convicted of the offense for which the offender is an eligible offender and is requesting DNA testing, any response to the application by the prosecuting attorney or the attorney general shall be filed not later than forty-five days after the date on which the eligible offender submits the application. The prosecuting attorney or the attorney general, or both, may, but are not required to, file a response to the application. If the prosecuting attorney or the attorney general files a response under this division, the prosecuting attorney or attorney general, whoever filed the response, shall serve a copy of the response on the eligible offender.

(D) If an eligible offender submits an application for DNA testing under division (A) of this section, the court shall make the determination as to whether the application should be accepted or rejected. The court shall expedite its review of the application. The court shall make the determination in accordance with the criteria and procedures set forth in sections 2953.74 to 2953.81 of the Revised Code and, in making the determination, shall consider the application, the supporting affidavits, and the documentary evidence and, in addition to those materials, shall consider all the files and records pertaining to the proceedings against the applicant, including, but not limited to, the indictment, the court's journal entries, the journalized records of the clerk of the court, and the court reporter's transcript and all responses to the application filed under division (C) of this section by a prosecuting attorney or the attorney general, unless the application and the files and records show the applicant is not entitled to DNA testing, in which case the application may be denied. The court is not required to conduct an evidentiary hearing in conducting its review of, and in making its determination as to whether to accept or reject, the application. Upon making its determination, the court shall enter a judgment and order that either accepts or rejects the application and that includes within the judgment and order the reasons for the acceptance or rejection as applied to the criteria and procedures set forth in sections 2953.71 to 2953.81 of the Revised Code. The court shall send a copy of the judgment and order to the eligible offender who filed it, the prosecuting attorney, and the attorney general.

(E) A judgment and order of a court entered under division (D) of this section is appealable only as provided in this division. If an eligible offender submits an application for DNA testing under section 2953.73 of the Revised Code and the court of common pleas rejects the application under division (D) of this section, one of the following applies:

(1) If the offender was sentenced to death for the offense for which the offender claims to be an eligible offender and is requesting DNA testing, the offender may seek leave of the supreme court to appeal the rejection to the supreme court. Courts of appeals do not have jurisdiction to review any rejection if the offender was sentenced to death for the offense for which the offender claims to be an eligible offender and is requesting DNA testing.

(2) If the offender was not sentenced to death for the offense for which the offender claims to be an eligible offender and is requesting DNA testing, the rejection is a final appealable order, and the offender may appeal it to the court of appeals of the district in which is located that court of common pleas.

(F) Notwithstanding any provision of law regarding fees and costs, no filing fee shall be required of, and no court costs shall be assessed against, an eligible offender who is indigent and who submits an application under this section.

(G) If a court rejects an eligible offender's application for DNA testing under division (D) of this section, unless the rejection is overturned on appeal, no court shall require the state to administer a DNA test under sections 2953.71 to 2953.81 of the Revised Code on the eligible offender.

**HISTORY: 150 v S 11, § 1, Eff 10-29-03; 150 v H 525, § 1, eff. 5-18-05; 151 v S 262, § 1, eff. 7-11-06; 153 v S 77, § 1, eff. 7-6-10.**

See provisions of § 4 of 151 v S 262 following RC § 2901.07.

### § 2953.74 Grounds for accepting or rejecting application; comparing test results to federal combined DNA index system.

(A) If an eligible offender submits an application for DNA testing under section 2953.73 of the Revised Code and a prior definitive DNA test has been conducted regarding the same biological evidence that the offender seeks to have tested, the court shall reject the offender's application. If an eligible offender files an application for DNA testing and a prior inconclusive DNA test has been conducted regarding the same biological evidence that the offender seeks to have tested, the court shall review the application and has the discretion, on a case-by-case basis, to either accept or reject the application. The court may direct a testing authority to provide the court with information that the court may use in determining whether prior DNA test results were definitive or inconclusive and whether to accept or reject an application in relation to which there were prior inconclusive DNA test results.

(B) If an eligible offender submits an application for DNA testing under section 2953.73 of the Revised Code, the court may accept the application only if one of the following applies:

(1) The offender did not have a DNA test taken at the trial stage in the case in which the offender was convicted of the offense for which the offender is an eligible offender and is requesting the DNA testing regarding the same biological evidence that the offender seeks to have tested, the offender shows that DNA exclusion when analyzed in the context of and upon consideration of all available admissible evidence related to the subject offender's case as described in division (D) of this section

would have been outcome determinative at that trial stage in that case, and, at the time of the trial stage in that case, DNA testing was not generally accepted, the results of DNA testing were not generally admissible in evidence, or DNA testing was not yet available.

(2) The offender had a DNA test taken at the trial stage in the case in which the offender was convicted of the offense for which the offender is an eligible offender and is requesting the DNA testing regarding the same biological evidence that the offender seeks to have tested, the test was not a prior definitive DNA test that is subject to division (A) of this section, and the offender shows that DNA exclusion when analyzed in the context of and upon consideration of all available admissible evidence related to the subject offender's case as described in division (D) of this section would have been outcome determinative at the trial stage in that case.

(C) If an eligible offender submits an application for DNA testing under section 2953.73 of the Revised Code, the court may accept the application only if all of the following apply:

(1) The court determines pursuant to section 2953.75 of the Revised Code that biological material was collected from the crime scene or the victim of the offense for which the offender is an eligible offender and is requesting the DNA testing and that the parent sample of that biological material against which a sample from the offender can be compared still exists at that point in time.

(2) The testing authority determines all of the following pursuant to section 2953.76 of the Revised Code regarding the parent sample of the biological material described in division (C)(1) of this section:

(a) The parent sample of the biological material so collected contains scientifically sufficient material to extract a test sample.

(b) The parent sample of the biological material so collected is not so minute or fragile as to risk destruction of the parent sample by the extraction described in division (C)(2)(a) of this section; provided that the court may determine in its discretion, on a case-by-case basis, that, even if the parent sample of the biological material so collected is so minute or fragile as to risk destruction of the parent sample by the extraction, the application should not be rejected solely on the basis of that risk.

(c) The parent sample of the biological material so collected has not degraded or been contaminated to the extent that it has become scientifically unsuitable for testing, and the parent sample otherwise has been preserved, and remains, in a condition that is scientifically suitable for testing.

(3) The court determines that, at the trial stage in the case in which the offender was convicted of the offense for which the offender is an eligible offender and is requesting the DNA testing, the identity of the person who committed the offense was an issue.

(4) The court determines that one or more of the defense theories asserted by the offender at the trial stage in the case described in division (C)(3) of this section or in a retrial of that case in a court of this state was of such a nature that, if DNA testing is conducted and an exclusion result is obtained, the exclusion result will be outcome determinative.

(5) The court determines that, if DNA testing is conducted and an exclusion result is obtained, the results of the testing will be outcome determinative regarding that offender.

(6) The court determines pursuant to section 2953.76 of the Revised Code from the chain of custody of the parent sample of the biological material to be tested and of any test sample extracted from the parent sample, and from the totality of circumstances involved, that the parent sample and the extracted test sample are the same sample as collected and that there is no reason to believe that they have been out of state custody or have been tampered with or contaminated since they were collected.

(D) If an eligible offender submits an application for DNA testing under section 2953.73 of the Revised Code, the court, in determining whether the "outcome determinative" criterion described in divisions (B)(1) and (2) of this section has been satisfied, shall consider all available admissible evidence related to the subject offender's case.

(E) If an eligible offender submits an application for DNA testing under section 2953.73 of the Revised Code and the court accepts the application, the eligible offender may request the court to order, or the court on its own initiative may order, the bureau of criminal identification and investigation to compare the results of DNA testing of biological material from an unidentified person other than the offender that was obtained from the crime scene or from a victim of the offense for which the offender has been approved for DNA testing to the combined DNA index system maintained by the federal bureau of investigation.

If the bureau, upon comparing the test results to the combined DNA index system, determines the identity of the person who is the contributor of the biological material, the bureau shall provide that information to the court that accepted the application, the offender, and the prosecuting attorney. The offender or the state may use the information for any lawful purpose.

If the bureau, upon comparing the test results to the combined DNA index system, is unable to determine the identity of the person who is the contributor of the biological material, the bureau may compare the test results to other previously obtained and acceptable DNA test results of any person whose identity is known other than the eligible offender. If the bureau, upon comparing the test results to the DNA test results of any person whose identity is known, determines that the person whose identity is known is the contributor of the biological material, the bureau shall provide that information to the court that accepted the application, the offender, and the prosecuting attorney. The offender or the state may use the information for any lawful purpose.

**HISTORY: 150 v S 11, § 1, Eff 10-29-03; 151 v S 262, § 1, eff. 7-11-06; 153 v S 77, § 1, eff. 7-6-10.**

See provisions of § 4 of 151 v S 262 following RC § 2901.07.

## § 2953.75 Determinations by prosecuting attorney as to whether biological material was collected and whether parent sample still exists.

(A) If an eligible offender submits an application for DNA testing under section 2953.73 of the Revised Code, the court shall require the prosecuting attorney to use reasonable diligence to determine whether biological material was collected from the crime scene or victim of the offense for which the offender is an eligible offender and is requesting the DNA testing against which a sample from the offender can be compared and whether the parent sample of that biological material still exists at that point in time. In using reasonable diligence to make those determinations, the prosecuting attorney shall rely upon all relevant sources, including, but not limited to, all of the following:

(1) All prosecuting authorities in the case in which the offender was convicted of the offense for which the offender is an eligible offender and is requesting the DNA testing and in the appeals of, and postconviction proceedings related to, that case;

(2) All law enforcement authorities involved in the investigation of the offense for which the offender is an eligible offender and is requesting the DNA testing;

(3) All custodial agencies involved at any time with the biological material in question;

(4) The custodian of all custodial agencies described in division (A)(3) of this section;

(5) All crime laboratories involved at any time with the biological material in question;

(6) All other reasonable sources.

(B) The prosecuting attorney shall prepare a report that contains the prosecuting attorney's determinations made under division (A) of this section and shall file a copy of the report with the court and provide a copy to the eligible offender and the attorney general.

**HISTORY: 150 v S 11, § 1, Eff 10-29-03; 153 v S 77, § 1, eff. 7-6-10.**

## § 2953.76 Findings and determinations concerning quantity, quality, chain of custody, and reliability of parent sample.

If an eligible offender submits an application for DNA testing under section 2953.73 of the Revised Code, the court shall require the prosecuting attorney to consult with the testing authority and to prepare findings regarding the quantity and quality of the parent sample of the biological material collected from the crime scene or victim of the offense for which the offender is an eligible offender and is requesting the DNA testing and that is to be tested, and of the chain of custody and reliability regarding that parent sample, as follows:

(A) The testing authority shall determine whether there is a scientifically sufficient quantity of the parent sample to test and whether the parent sample is so minute or fragile that there is a substantial risk that the parent sample could be destroyed in testing. The testing authority may determine that there is not a sufficient quantity to test in order to preserve the state's ability to present in the future the original evidence presented at trial, if another trial is required. Upon making its determination under this division, the testing authority shall prepare a written document that contains its determination and the reasoning and rationale for that determination and shall provide a copy to the court, the eligible offender, the prosecuting attorney, and the attorney general. The court may determine in its discretion, on a case-by-case basis, that, even if the parent sample of the biological material so collected is so minute or fragile as to risk destruction of the parent sample by the extraction, the application should not be rejected solely on the basis of that risk.

(B) The testing authority shall determine whether the parent sample has degraded or been contaminated to the extent that it has become scientifically unsuitable for testing and whether the parent sample otherwise has been preserved, and remains, in a condition that is suitable for testing. Upon making its determination under this division, the testing authority shall prepare a written document that contains its determination and the reasoning and rationale for that determination and shall provide a copy to the court, the eligible offender, the prosecuting attorney, and the attorney general.

(C) The court shall determine, from the chain of custody of the parent sample of the biological material to be tested and of any test sample extracted from the parent sample and from the totality of circumstances involved, whether the parent sample and the extracted test sample are the same sample as collected and whether there is any reason to believe that they have been out of state custody or have been tampered with or contaminated since they were collected. Upon making its determination under this division, the court shall prepare and retain a written document that contains its determination and the reasoning and rationale for that determination.

**HISTORY: 150 v S 11, § 1, Eff 10-29-03; 153 v S 77, § 1, eff. 7-6-10.**

## § 2953.77 Precautions concerning chain of custody and against contamination during transport or testing; documentation.

(A) If an eligible offender submits an application for DNA testing under section 2953.73 of the Revised Code and if the application is accepted and DNA testing is to be performed, the court shall require that the chain of custody remain intact and that all of the applicable following precautions are satisfied to ensure that the parent sample of the biological material collected from the crime scene or the victim of the offense for which the offender is an eligible offender and requested the DNA testing, and the test sample of the parent sample that is extracted and actually is to be tested, are not contaminated during transport or the testing process:

(1) The court shall require that the chain of custody be maintained and documented relative to the parent sample and the test sample actually to be tested between the time they are removed from their place of storage or the time of their extraction to the time at which the DNA testing will be performed.

(2) The court, the testing authority, and the law enforcement and prosecutorial personnel involved in the process, or any combination of those entities and persons, shall coordinate the transport of the parent sample and the test sample actually to be tested between their place of storage and the place where the DNA testing will be performed, and the court and testing authority shall document the transport procedures so used.

(3) The testing authority shall determine and document the custodian of the parent sample and the test sample actually to be tested after they are in the possession of the testing authority.

(4) The testing authority shall maintain and preserve the parent sample and the test sample actually to be tested after they are in the possession of the testing authority and shall document the maintenance and preservation procedures used.

(5) After the DNA testing, the court, the testing authority, and the original custodial agency of the parent sample, or any combination of those entities, shall coordinate the return of the remaining parent sample back to its place of storage with the original custodial agency or to any other place determined in accordance with this division and section 2953.81 of the Revised Code. The court shall determine, in consultation with the testing authority, the

custodial agency to maintain any newly created, extracted, or collected DNA material resulting from the testing. The court and testing authority shall document the return procedures for original materials and for any newly created, extracted, or collected DNA material resulting from the testing, and also the custodial agency to which those materials should be taken.

(B) A court or testing authority shall provide the documentation required under division (A) of this section in writing and shall maintain that documentation.

**HISTORY: 150 v S 11, § 1, Eff 10-29-03; 153 v S 77, § 1, eff. 7-6-10.**

## § 2953.78 Selection of testing authority; effect of offender's objection; approval or designation of testing authorities.

(A) If an eligible offender submits an application for DNA testing under section 2953.73 of the Revised Code and if the application is accepted and DNA testing is to be performed, the court shall select the testing authority to be used for the testing. A court shall not select or use a testing authority for DNA testing unless the attorney general approves or designates the testing authority pursuant to division (C) of this section and unless the testing authority satisfies the criteria set forth in section 2953.80 of the Revised Code.

(B) If a court selects a testing authority pursuant to division (A) of this section and the eligible offender for whom the test is to be performed objects to the use of the selected testing authority, the court shall rescind its prior acceptance of the application for DNA testing for the offender and deny the application. An objection as described in this division, and the resulting rescission and denial, do not preclude a court from accepting in the court's discretion, a subsequent application by the same eligible offender requesting DNA testing.

(C) The attorney general shall approve or designate testing authorities that may be selected and used to conduct DNA testing, shall prepare a list of the approved or designated testing authorities, and shall provide copies of the list to all courts of common pleas. The attorney general shall update the list as appropriate to reflect changes in the approved or designated testing authorities and shall provide copies of the updated list to all courts of common pleas. The attorney general shall not approve or designate a testing authority under this division unless the testing authority satisfies the criteria set forth in section 2953.80 of the Revised Code. A testing authority that is equipped to handle advanced DNA testing may be approved or designated under this division, provided it satisfies the criteria set forth in that section.

(D) The attorney general's approval or designation of testing authorities under division (C) of this section, and the selection and use of any approved or designated testing authority, do not afford an offender any right to subsequently challenge the approval, designation, selection, or use, and an offender may not appeal to any court the approval, designation, selection, or use of a testing authority.

**HISTORY: 150 v S 11, § 1, Eff 10-29-03; 151 v S 262, § 1, eff. 7-11-06; 153 v S 77, § 1, eff. 7-6-10.**

See provisions of § 4 of 151 v S 262 following RC § 2901.07.

## § 2953.79 Obtaining biological material from offender; offender's refusal or hindrance.

(A) If an eligible offender submits an application for DNA testing under section 2953.73 of the Revised Code and if the application is accepted and DNA testing is to be performed, a sample of biological material shall be obtained from the offender in accordance with this section, to be compared with the parent sample of biological material collected from the crime scene or the victim of the offense for which the offender is an eligible offender and requested the DNA testing. The offender's filing of the application constitutes the offender's consent to the obtaining of the sample of biological material from the offender. The testing authority shall obtain the sample of biological material from the offender in accordance with medically accepted procedures.

(B) If DNA testing is to be performed for an offender as described in division (A) of this section, the court shall require the state to coordinate with the department of rehabilitation and correction or the other state agency or entity of local government with custody of the offender, whichever is applicable, as to the time and place at which the sample of biological material will be obtained from the offender. If the offender is in prison or is in custody in another facility at the time the DNA testing is to be performed, the sample of biological material shall be obtained from the offender at the facility in which the offender is housed, and the department of rehabilitation and correction or the other state agency or entity of local government with custody of the offender, whichever is applicable, shall make the offender available at the specified time. The court shall require the state to provide notice to the offender and to the offender's counsel of the date on which, and the time and place at which, the sample will be so obtained.

The court also shall require the state to coordinate with the testing authority regarding the obtaining of the sample from the offender.

(C)(1) If DNA testing is to be performed for an offender as described in division (A) of this section, and the offender refuses to submit to the collection of the sample of biological material from the offender or hinders the state from obtaining a sample of biological material from the offender, the court shall rescind its prior acceptance of the application for DNA testing for the offender and deny the application.

(2) For purposes of division (C)(1) of this section:

(a) An offender's "refusal to submit to the collection of a sample of biological material from the offender" includes, but is not limited to, the offender's rejection of the physical manner in which a sample of the offender's biological material is to be taken.

(b) An offender's "hindrance of the state in obtaining a sample of biological material from the offender" includes, but is not limited to, the offender being physically or verbally uncooperative or antagonistic in the taking of a sample of the offender's biological material.

(D) The extracting personnel shall make the determination as to whether an eligible offender for whom DNA testing is to be performed is refusing to submit to the collection of a sample of biological material from the offender or is hindering the state from obtaining a sample of biological material from the offender at the time and date of the scheduled collection of the sample. If the extracting personnel determine that an offender is refusing to submit to the collection of a sample or is hindering the state from obtaining a sample, the extracting personnel shall document in writing the conditions that constitute the refusal or hindrance, maintain the documentation, and notify the court of the offender's refusal or hindrance.

**HISTORY: 150 v S 11, § 1, Eff 10-29-03; 153 v S 77, § 1, eff. 7-6-10.**

## § 2953.80 Criteria for approval, designation, selection, or use of testing authority.

(A) The attorney general shall not approve or designate a testing authority for conducting DNA testing under section 2953.78 of the Revised Code, and a court shall not select or use a testing authority for DNA testing under that section, unless the testing authority satisfies all of the following criteria:

(1) It is in compliance with nationally accepted quality assurance standards for forensic DNA testing or advanced DNA testing, as published in the quality assurance standards for forensic DNA testing laboratories issued by the director of the federal bureau of investigation.

(2) It undergoes an annual internal or external audit for quality assurance in conformity with the standards identified in division (A)(1) of this section.

(3) At least once in the preceding two-year period, and at least once each two-year period thereafter, it undergoes an external audit for quality assurance in conformity with the standards identified in division (A)(1) of this section.

(B) As used in division (A) of this section:

(1) "External audit" means a quality assurance review of a testing authority that is conducted by a forensic DNA testing agency outside of, and not affiliated with, the testing authority.

(2) "Internal audit" means an internal review of a testing authority that is conducted by the testing authority itself.

**HISTORY: 150 v S 11, § 1, Eff 10-29-03; 151 v S 262, § 1, eff. 7-11-06.**

See provisions of § 4 of 151 v S 262 following RC § 2901.07.

## § 2953.81 Maintaining of results and samples; access to results and distribution of copies; use as evidence.

If an eligible inmate submits an application for DNA testing under section 2953.73 of the Revised Code and if DNA testing is performed based on that application, upon completion of the testing, all of the following apply:

(A) The court or a designee of the court shall require the state to maintain the results of the testing and to maintain and preserve both the parent sample of the biological material used and the offender sample of the biological material used. The testing authority may be designated as the person to maintain the results of the testing or to maintain and preserve some or all of the samples, or both. The results of the testing remain state's evidence. The samples shall be preserved during the entire period of time for which the offender is imprisoned or confined relative to the sentence in question, is on parole or probation relative to that sentence, is under post-release control or a community control sanction relative to that sentence, or has a duty to comply with sections 2950.04, 2950.041 [2950.04.1], 2950.05, and 2950.06 of the Revised Code relative to that sentence. Additionally, if the prison term or confinement under the sentence in question expires, if the sentence in question is a sentence of death and the offender is executed, or if the parole or probation period, the period of post-release control, the community control sanction, or the duty to comply with sections 2950.04, 2950.041 [2950.04.1], 2950.05, and 2950.06 of the Revised Code under the sentence in question ends, the samples shall be preserved for a reasonable period of time of not less than twenty-four months after the term or confinement expires, the offender is executed, or the parole or probation period, the period of post-release control, the community control sanction, or the duty to comply with sections 2950.04, 2950.041 [2950.04.1], 2950.05, and 2950.06 of the Revised Code ends, whichever is applicable. The court shall determine the period of time that is reasonable for purposes of this division, provided that the period shall not be less than twenty-four months after the term or confinement expires, the offender is executed, or the parole or probation period, the period of post-release control, the community control sanction, or the duty to comply with sections 2950.04, 2950.041 [2950.04.1], 2950.05, and 2950.06 of the Revised Code ends, whichever is applicable.

(B) The results of the testing are a public record.

(C) The court or the testing authority shall provide a copy of the results of the testing to the prosecuting attorney, the attorney general, and the subject offender.

(D) If the postconviction proceeding in question is pending at that time in a court of this state, the court of common pleas that decided the DNA application or the testing authority shall provide a copy of the results of the testing to any court of this state, and, if it is pending in a federal court, the court of common pleas that decided the DNA application or the testing authority shall provide a copy of the results of the testing to that federal court.

(E) The testing authority shall provide a copy of the results of the testing to the court of common pleas that decided the DNA application.

(F) The offender or the state may enter the results of the testing into any proceeding.

**HISTORY: 150 v S 11, § 1, Eff 10-29-03; 153 v S 77, § 1, eff. 7-6-10.**

## § 2953.82 Repealed, 153 v S 77, § 2 [150 v S 11, § 1, Eff 10-29-03; 150 v H 525, § 1, eff. 5-18-05; 151 v S 262, § 1, eff. 7-11-06]. Eff 7-6-10.

This section concerned request by an inmate who pleaded guilty or no contest to felony.

## § 2953.83 Application of Rules of Criminal Procedure.

In any court proceeding under sections 2953.71 to 2953.81 of the Revised Code, the Rules of Criminal Procedure apply, except to the extent that sections 2953.71 to 2953.81 of the Revised Code provide a different procedure or to the extent that the Rules would by their nature be clearly inapplicable.

**HISTORY: 150 v S 11, § 1, Eff 10-29-03; 153 v S 77, § 1, eff. 7-6-10.**

## § 2953.84 Effect on other means of obtaining postconviction DNA testing.

The provisions of sections 2953.71 to 2953.81 of the Revised Code by which an offender may obtain postconviction DNA testing are not the exclusive means by which an offender may obtain postconviction DNA testing, and the provisions of those sections do not limit or affect any other means by which an offender may obtain postconviction DNA testing.

**HISTORY: 151 v S 262, § 1, eff. 7-11-06; 153 v S 77, § 1, eff. 7-6-10.**

See provisions of § 4 of 151 v S 262 following RC § 2901.07.

# CHAPTER 2961: DISFRANCHISED CONVICTS; HABITUAL CRIMINALS



## § 2961.01 Civil rights of convicted felons.

(A)(1) A person who pleads guilty to a felony under the laws of this or any other state or the United States and whose plea is accepted by the court or a person against whom a verdict or finding of guilt for committing a felony under any law of that type is returned, unless the plea, verdict, or finding is reversed or annulled, is incompetent to be an elector or juror or to hold an office of honor, trust, or profit.

(2) When any person who under division (A)(1) of this section is incompetent to be an elector or juror or to hold an office of honor, trust, or profit is granted parole, judicial release, or a conditional pardon or is released under a non-jail community control sanction or a post-release control sanction, the person is competent to be an elector during the period of community control, parole, post-release control, or release or until the conditions of the pardon have been performed or have transpired and is competent to be an elector thereafter following final discharge. The full pardon of a person who under division (A)(1) of this section is incompetent to be an elector or juror or to hold an office of honor, trust, or profit restores the rights and privileges so forfeited under division (A)(1) of this section, but a pardon shall not release the person from the costs of a conviction in this state, unless so specified.

(B) A person who pleads guilty to a felony under laws of this state or any other state or the United States and whose plea is accepted by the court or a person against whom a verdict or finding of guilt for committing a felony under any law of that type is returned is incompetent to circulate or serve as a witness for the signing of any declaration of candidacy and petition, voter registration application, or nominating, initiative, referendum, or recall petition.

(C) As used in this section:

(1) "Community control sanction" has the same meaning as in section 2929.01 of the Revised Code.

(2) "Non-jail community control sanction" means a community control sanction that is neither a term in a community-based correctional facility nor a term in a jail.

(3) "Post-release control" and "post-release control sanction" have the same meanings as in section 2967.01 of the Revised Code.

**HISTORY: GC § 13458-1; 113 v 123(211), ch 37; Bureau of Code Revision, 10-1-53; 134 v H 511 (Eff 1-1-74); 147 v S 111. Eff 3-17-98; 149 v H 490, § 1, eff. 1-1-04; 151 v H 3, § 1, eff. 5-2-06; 152 v H 195, § 1, eff. 9-30-08.**

The effective date is set by section 4 of H.B. 490.

## § 2961.02 Conviction of disqualifying offense as bar to holding public office or position of public employment or serving as volunteer.

(A) As used in this section:

(1) "Disqualifying offense" means an offense that has both of the following characteristics:

(a) It is one of the following:

(i) A theft offense that is a felony;

(ii) A felony under the laws of this state, another state, or the United States, that is not covered by division (A)(1)(a)(i) of this section and that involves fraud, deceit, or theft.

(b) It is an offense for which the laws of this state, another state, or the United States do not otherwise contain a provision specifying permanent disqualification, or disqualification for a specified period, from holding a public office or position of public employment, or from serving as an unpaid volunteer, as a result of conviction of the offense, including, but not limited to, a provision such as that in division (C)(1) of section 2921.41 of the Revised Code.

(2) "Political subdivision" has the same meaning as in section 2744.01 of the Revised Code.

(3) "Private entity" includes an individual, corporation, limited liability company, business trust, estate, trust, partnership, or association that receives any funds from a state agency or political subdivision to perform an activity on behalf of the state agency or political subdivision.

(4) "State agency" has the same meaning as in section 1.60 of the Revised Code.

(5) "Theft offense" has the same meaning as in section 2913.01 of the Revised Code.

(6) "Volunteer" means a person who serves as a volunteer without compensation with a state agency or political subdivision or who serves as a volunteer without compensation with a private entity, including, but not limited to, an uncompensated auxiliary police officer, auxiliary deputy sheriff, or volunteer firefighter.

(B) Any person who pleads guilty to a disqualifying offense and whose plea is accepted by the court or any person against whom a verdict or finding of guilt for committing a disqualifying offense is returned is incompetent to hold a public office or position of public employment or to serve as a volunteer, if holding the public office or position of public employment or serving as the volunteer involves substantial management or control over the property of a state agency, political subdivision, or private entity.

(C) Division (B) of this section does not apply if a plea, verdict, or finding of the type described in that division regarding a disqualifying offense is reversed, expunged, or annulled. The full pardon of a person who has pleaded guilty to a disqualifying offense and whose plea was accepted by the court or a person against whom a verdict or finding of guilt for committing a disqualifying offense was returned restores the privileges forfeited under division (B) of this section, but the pardon does not release the person from the costs of the person's conviction in this state, unless so specified.

**HISTORY: 150 v H 181, § 1, eff. 5-18-05; 152 v H 195, § 1, eff. 9-30-08.**

## § 2961.03 Revocation of license in certain cases.

Whenever a person engaged in business as a second-hand dealer, junk dealer, transient dealer, peddler, itinerant vendor, or pawnbroker, under a license issued under any law of this state or under any ordinance of a municipal corporation, is convicted and sentenced for knowingly and fraudulently buying, receiving, or concealing goods or property which has been stolen, taken by robbers, embezzled, or obtained by false pretenses, such judgment of conviction, in addition to the other penalties provided by law for such offense, acts as a cancellation and revocation of such license to conduct such business, and the court in which such conviction was had shall forthwith certify to the authority which issued such license, the fact of such conviction. A person who has been so convicted and whose license has been canceled or revoked, shall not again be licensed to engage in such business, or any of the businesses enumerated in this section, unless such person is pardoned by the governor.

**HISTORY: GC § 13458-3; 113 v 123(211), ch 37, § 3; Bureau of Code Revision. Eff 10-1-53.**

## § 2961.11 Repealed, 134 v H 511, § 2 [GC §§ 13744-1—13744-3; 113 v 40; Bureau of Code Revision, 10-1-53; 132 v S 36]. Eff 1-1-74.

This section concerned habitual criminals, see RC § 2929.11 et seq for similar provisions.

## § 2961.12 Repealed, 134 v H 511, § 2 [GC §§ 13744-1—13744-3; 113 v 40; Bureau of Code Revision, 10-1-53; 132 v S 36]. Eff 1-1-74.

This section concerned habitual criminals, see RC § 2929.11 et seq for similar provisions.

## § 2961.13 Repealed, 134 v H 511, § 2 [GC §§ 13744-1—13744-3; 113 v 40; Bureau of Code Revision, 10-1-53; 132 v S 36]. Eff 1-1-74.

This section concerned habitual criminals, see RC § 2929.11 et seq for similar provisions.

## § 2961.21 Definitions.

As used in sections 2961.21 to 2961.24 of the Revised Code:

(A)(1) "Discretionary civil impact" means any section of the Revised Code or the Administrative Code that creates a penalty, disability, or disadvantage, however denominated, to which all of the following apply:

(a) It is triggered in whole or in part by a person's conviction of an offense, whether or not the penalty, disability, or disadvantage is included in the judgment or sentence.

(b) It is imposed on a person, licensing agency, or employer.

(c) It permits, but does not require, that the person with the conviction record have a license denied or revoked, permits an agency to deny or revoke a license or certification to the person with the conviction record or business, or permits a business to refuse to employ the person with the conviction record.

(2) "Discretionary civil impact" does not include imprisonment, probation, parole, supervised release, forfeiture, restitution, fine, assessment, or costs of prosecution.

(B) "Eligible prisoner" means any of the following:

(1) A prisoner who is serving a prison term in a state correctional institution and who satisfies all of the criteria specified in division (A)(1) of section 2961.22 of the Revised Code to be eligible to apply to the department of rehabilitation and correction or the sentencing court for a certificate of achievement and employability;

(2) A prisoner who has been released from a state correctional institution, who is under supervision on parole or under a post-release control sanction, and who satisfies all of the criteria specified in division (A)(1) of section 2961.22 of the Revised Code to be eligible to apply to the adult parole authority for a certificate of achievement and employability.

(C) "Licensing agency" means any of the following:

(1) Any agency identified as a "licensing agency" under section 4776.01 of the Revised Code.

(2) Any regulatory or licensing board or agency not included in division (C)(1) of this section that has the administrative authority to issue, suspend, or revoke any professional license or certification or any license or certification that enables a person or entity to engage in any profession or occupation to attain a specified status or position.

(D)(1) "Mandatory civil impact" means any section of the Revised Code or the Administrative Code that creates a penalty, disability, or disadvantage, however denominated, to which all of the following apply:

(a) It is triggered automatically solely by a person's conviction of an offense, whether or not the penalty, disability, or disadvantage is included in the judgment or sentence.

(b) It is imposed on a person, licensing agency, or employer.

(c) It precludes the person with the criminal record from maintaining or obtaining licensure or employment, precludes the agency from issuing a license or certification to the person with the criminal record or business, or precludes a business from being certified or from employing the person with the criminal record.

(2) "Mandatory civil impact" does not include imprisonment, probation, parole, supervised release, forfeiture, restitution, fine, assessment, or costs of prosecution.

**HISTORY: 2011 HB 86, § 1, eff. Sept. 30, 2011.**

## § 2961.22 Eligibility of prisoner to apply for certificate of achievement and employability; application; relief from mandatory civil impacts.

(A)(1) Any prisoner serving a prison term in a state correctional institution who satisfies all of the following is eligible to apply to the department of rehabilitation and correction at a time specified in division (A)(2) of this section and in accordance with division (D) of this section for a certificate of achievement and employability:

(a) The prisoner has satisfactorily completed one or more in-prison vocational programs approved by rule by the department of rehabilitation and correction.

(b) The prisoner has demonstrated exemplary performance as determined by completion of one or more cognitive or behavioral improvement programs approved by rule by the department while incarcerated in a state correctional institution, while under supervision, or during both periods of time.

(c) The prisoner has completed community service hours.

(d) The prisoner shows other evidence of achievement and rehabilitation while under the jurisdiction of the department.

(2) An eligible prisoner may apply to the department of rehabilitation and correction under division (A)(1) of this section for a certificate of achievement and employability no earlier than one year prior to the date scheduled for the release of the prisoner from department custody and no later than the date of release of the prisoner.

(B)(1) Any prisoner who has been released from a state correctional institution, who is under supervision on parole or under a post-release control sanction, and who satisfies all of the criteria set forth in division (A)(1) of this section is eligible to apply to the adult parole authority at a time specified in division (B)(2) of this section and in accordance with division (D) of this section for a certificate of achievement and employability.

(2) An eligible prisoner may apply to the adult parole authority under division (B)(1) of this section for a certificate of achievement and employability at any time while the prisoner is under supervision on parole or under a post-release control sanction.

(C)(1) An eligible prisoner may apply to the department of rehabilitation and correction or to the adult parole authority at a time specified in division (A) or (B) of this section, whichever is applicable, for a certificate of achievement and employability that grants the prisoner relief from one or more mandatory civil impacts that would affect a potential job within a field in which the prisoner trained as part of the prisoner's in-prison vocational program. The prisoner shall specify the mandatory civil impacts from which the prisoner is requesting relief under the certificate. Upon application by a prisoner in accordance with this division, if the mandatory civil impact of any licensing agency would be affected by the issuance of the certificate to the prisoner, the department or authority shall notify the licensing agency of the filing of the application, provide the licensing agency with a copy of the application and all evidence that the department, authority, or court has regarding the prisoner, and afford the licensing agency with an opportunity to object in writing to the issuance of the certificate to the prisoner.

(2) Upon application by a prisoner in accordance with division (C)(1) of this section, the department of rehabilitation and correction or the adult parole authority, whichever is applicable, shall consider the application and all objections to the issuance of a certificate of achievement and employability to the prisoner, if any, that were made by a licensing agency under division (C)(1) of this section. If the department or authority determines that the prisoner is an eligible prisoner, that the application was filed at a time specified in division (B) of this section, and that any licensing agency objections to the issuance of the certificate to the prisoner are not sufficient to deny the issuance of the certificate to the prisoner, subject to division (C)(3) of this section, the department or authority shall issue the prisoner a certificate of achievement and employability that grants the prisoner relief from the mandatory civil impacts that are specified in the prisoner's application and that would affect a potential job within a field in which the prisoner trained as part of the prisoner's in-prison vocational program.

(3) The mandatory civil impacts identified in division (A)(1) of section 2961.01 and in division (B) of section 2961.02 of the Revised Code shall not be affected by any certificate of achievement and employability issued under this section. No certificate of achievement and employability issued to a prisoner under this section grants the prisoner relief from the mandatory civil impacts identified in division (A)(1) of section 2961.01 and in division (B) of section 2961.02 of the Revised Code.

(E) The department of rehabilitation and correction shall adopt rules that define in-prison vocational programs and cognitive or behavioral improvement programs that a prisoner may complete to satisfy the criteria described in divisions (A)(1)(a) and (b) of this section.

**HISTORY: 2011 HB 86, § 1, eff. Sept. 30, 2011.**

## § 2961.23 Effect of issuance of certificate of achievement and employability where licensure or certification otherwise barred by mandatory civil impacts; effect of presentation of certificate to employer; liability of employer.

(A)(1) If a person who has been issued a certificate of achievement and employability under section 2961.22 of the Revised Code applies to a licensing agency for a license or certificate and the person has a conviction or guilty plea that otherwise would bar licensure or certification for the person because of a mandatory civil impact, the agency shall give the person individualized consideration for the license or certification, notwithstanding the mandatory civil impact, the mandatory civil impact shall be considered for all purposes to be a discretionary civil impact, and the certificate constitutes a rebuttable presumption that the person's criminal convictions are insufficient evidence that the person is unfit for the license or certification in question. Notwithstanding the presumption established under this division, the agency may deny the license or certification for the person if it determines that the person is unfit for issuance of the license.

(2) If an employer that has hired a person who has been issued a certificate of achievement and employability under section 2961.22 of the Revised Code applies to a licensing agency for a license or certification and the person has a conviction or guilty plea that otherwise would bar the person's employment with the employer or licensure for the employer because of a mandatory civil impact, the agency shall give the person individualized consideration, notwithstanding the mandatory civil impact, the mandatory civil impact shall be considered for all purposes to be a discretionary civil impact, and the certificate constitutes a rebuttable presumption that the person's criminal convictions are insufficient evidence that the person is unfit for the employment, or that the employer is unfit for the license or certification, in question. Notwithstanding the presumption established under this division, the agency may deny the license or certification for the employer if it determines that the person is unfit for the employment or that the employer is unfit for the license or certification.

(B) If an employer hires a person who has been issued a certificate of achievement and employability under section 2961.22 of the Revised Code and if the person presents the employer with a copy of the certificate, all of the following apply:

(1) If a subsequent civil action against the employer alleges that the employer was negligent in hiring the person and if the civil action includes as an element of the alleged negligence that the employer had actual or constructive knowledge of the incompetence or dangerousness of the person, the person's presentation of the certificate to the employer is an absolute defense for the employer to the element of the employer's actual or constructive knowledge of the incompetence or dangerousness of the person.

(2) If the person, after being hired, subsequently demonstrates dangerousness and if the employer retains the person as an employee after the demonstration of dangerousness, the employer may be held liable in a civil action that is based on or relates to the retention of the person as an employee only if it is proved by a preponderance of the evidence that the person having hiring and firing responsibility for the employer had actual knowledge that the employee was dangerous and was willful in retaining the person as an employee after the demonstration of dangerousness of which the person had actual knowledge.

**HISTORY: 2011 HB 86, § 1, eff. Sept. 30, 2011.**

## § 2961.24 Adoption of rules specifying standards and criteria for revocation of certificate of achievement and employability.

The department of rehabilitation and correction shall adopt rules that specify standards and criteria for the revocation of a certificate of achievement and employability issued under section 2961.22 of the Revised Code. The rules shall require revocation of a certificate that has been issued to a person if the person is convicted of or pleads guilty to any offense other than a minor misdemeanor or a traffic offense. The rules shall not provide for revocation of a certificate that has been issued to a person based on a violation of a condition of conditional pardon, parole, other form of authorized release, transitional control, or post-release control under section 2967.15 of the Revised Code that is not also a criminal offense under any other section of the Revised Code.

**HISTORY: 2011 HB 86, § 1, eff. Sept. 30, 2011.**

# CHAPTER 2963: EXTRADITION



## § 2963.01 Definitions.

As used in sections 2963.01 to 2963.27 of the Revised Code:

(A) "Governor" includes any person performing the functions of governor by authority of the law of this state.

(B) "Executive authority" includes the governor, and any person performing the functions of governor in a state other than this state.

(C) "State," referring to a state other than this state, includes any state or territory, organized or unorganized, of the United States.

(D) "Community control sanction" has the same meaning as in section 2929.01 of the Revised Code.

(E) "Post-release control" and "post-release control sanction" have the same meanings as in section 2967.01 of the Revised Code.

**HISTORY: GC § 109-1; 117 v 588; Bureau of Code Revision. Eff 10-1-53; 149 v H 490, § 1, eff. 1-1-04.**

The effective date is set by section 4 of H.B. 490.

[FUGITIVE FROM ANOTHER STATE]

## § 2963.02 Governor to deliver fugitives from justice.

Subject to sections 2963.01 to 2963.27, inclusive, of the Revised Code, the constitution of the United States and all acts of congress enacted in pursuance thereof, the governor shall have arrested and delivered to the executive authority of any other state of the United States, any person charged in that state with treason, felony, or other crime, who has fled from justice and is found in this state.

**HISTORY: GC § 109-2; 117 v 108, § 2; Bureau of Code Revision. Eff 10-1-53.**

## § 2963.03 Demand for extradition.

No demand for the extradition of a person charged with crime in another state shall be recognized by the governor unless the demand is in writing alleging, except in cases arising under section 2963.06 of the Revised Code, that the accused was present in the demanding state at the time of the commission of the alleged crime, and that thereafter he fled from the state, and unless the demand is accompanied by:

(A) A copy of an indictment found or by information supported by affidavit in the state having jurisdiction of the crime, or by a copy of an affidavit made before a magistrate there, together with a copy of any warrant which was issued thereupon;

(B) A copy of a judgment of conviction or of a sentence imposed in execution thereof, together with a statement by the executive authority of the demanding state that the person claimed has escaped from confinement or has broken the terms of his bail, probation, or parole. The indictment, information, or affidavit made before the magistrate must substantially charge the person demanded with having committed a crime under the law of that state. The copy of indictment, information, affidavit, judgment of conviction, or sentence must be authenticated by the executive authority making the demand.

**HISTORY: GC § 109-3; 117 v 588, § 3; Bureau of Code Revision. Eff 10-1-53.**

## § 2963.04 Demand investigated by order of governor.

When a demand is made upon the governor of this state by the executive authority of another state for the surrender of a person charged with crime, the governor may call upon the attorney general or any prosecuting officer in this state to investigate or assist in investigating the demand, and to report to him the situation and circumstances of the person so demanded, and whether such person ought to be surrendered.

**HISTORY: GC § 109-4; 117 v 588, § 4; Bureau of Code Revision. Eff 10-1-53.**

## § 2963.05 Extradition upon agreement to return prisoner.

When it is desired to have returned to this state a person charged in this state with a crime, and such person is imprisoned or is held under criminal proceedings then pending against him in another state, the governor may agree with the executive authority of such other state for the extradition of such person before the conclusion of such proceedings or his term of sentence in such other state, upon condition that such person be returned to such other state at the expense of this state as soon as the prosecution in this state is terminated.

The governor may also surrender, on demand of the executive authority of any other state, any person in this state who is charged under section 2963.21 of the Revised Code with having violated the laws of the state whose executive authority is making the demand, even though such person left the demanding state involuntarily. This section shall be carried out by conforming to the procedure outlined in sections 2963.01 to 2963.27, inclusive, of the Revised Code.

**HISTORY: GC § 109-5; 117 v 588, § 5; Bureau of Code Revision. Eff 10-1-53.**

## § 2963.06 Governor may surrender anyone charged with crime against another state.

The governor may surrender, on demand of the executive authority of any other state, any person in this state charged in such other state in the manner provided in section 2963.03 of the Revised Code with committing an act in this state, or in a third state, intentionally resulting in a crime in the state whose executive authority is making the demand, and sections 2963.01 to 2963.27, inclusive, of the Revised Code, apply to such cases, even though the accused was not in that state at the time of the commission of the crime, and has not fled therefrom.

**HISTORY: GC § 109-6; 117 v 588, § 6; Bureau of Code Revision. Eff 10-1-53.**

## § 2963.07 Warrant for arrest.

If the governor decides that a demand for extradition should be complied with, he shall sign a warrant of arrest, which shall be sealed with the state seal and be directed to any peace officer or other person whom the governor finds fit to entrust with the execution thereof. The warrant must substantially recite the facts necessary to the validity of its issuance.

Such warrant shall authorize the peace officer or other person to whom directed to arrest the accused at any time and any place where he may be found within the state and to command the aid of all peace officers or other persons in the execution of the warrant, and to deliver the accused, subject to sections 2963.01 to 2963.27, inclusive, of the Revised Code, to the authorized agent of the demanding state.

**HISTORY: GC §§ 109-7, 109-8; 117 v 588, §§ 7, 8; Bureau of Code Revision. Eff 10-1-53.**

## § 2963.08 Authority to arrest accused.

Every peace officer or other person empowered to make an arrest under section 2963.07 of the Revised Code has the same authority, in arresting the accused, to command assistance therein as peace officers have in the execution of any criminal process directed to them, with like penalties against those who refuse their assistance.

**HISTORY: GC § 109-9; 117 v 588, § 9; Bureau of Code Revision. Eff 10-1-53.**

## § 2963.09 Mandatory hearing.

No person arrested upon a warrant under section 2963.07 of the Revised Code shall be delivered to the agent whom the executive authority demanding him appointed to receive him unless such person is first taken forthwith before a judge of a court of record in this state, who shall inform him of the demand made for his surrender and of the crime with which he is charged, and that he has the right to demand and procure legal counsel. If the prisoner or his counsel desires to test the legality of his arrest, the judge shall fix a reasonable time to be allowed him within which to apply for a writ of habeas corpus. When such writ is applied for, notice thereof and of the time and place of hearing thereon, shall be given to the prosecuting officer of the county in which the arrest is made and in which the accused is in custody, and to the said agent of the demanding state.

Whoever violates this section by willfully delivering a person arrested upon the governor's warrant to an agent for extradition of the demanding state before a hearing, shall be fined not more than one thousand dollars or imprisoned not more than six months, or both.

**HISTORY: GC § 109-10; 117 v 588, § 10; Bureau of Code Revision. Eff 10-1-53.**

## § 2963.10 Prisoner may be confined while en route.

A peace officer or other person executing a warrant of arrest issued by the governor, or an agent of the demanding state to whom the prisoner has been delivered, may, when necessary, confine the prisoner in the jail of any county or city through which he may pass.

The officer or agent of a demanding state to whom a prisoner has been delivered following extradition proceedings in another state, or to whom a prisoner has been delivered after waiving extradition in such other state, and who is passing through this state with such a prisoner for the purpose of immediately returning such prisoner to the demanding state may, when necessary, confine the prisoner in the jail of any county or city through which he may pass. Such officer or agent shall produce and show to the keeper of such jail his warrant and other written evidence of the fact that he is actually transporting such prisoner to the demanding state after a requisition by the executive authority of such demanding state. Such prisoner may not demand a new requisition while in this state.

The keeper of such jail must receive and safely keep a prisoner delivered to him under this section, until the officer or agent having charge of him is ready to proceed on his route. Such officer or agent is chargeable with the expense of such keeping.

**HISTORY: GC § 109-12; 117 v 588, § 12; Bureau of Code Revision. Eff 10-1-53.**

## § 2963.11 Fugitive from justice.

When, on the oath of a credible person before any judge or magistrate of this state, any person within this state is charged with the commission of any crime in any other state and with having fled from justice, or with having been convicted of a crime in that state and having escaped from confinement, or having broken the terms of the person's bail or parole or violated the conditions of a community control sanction or post-release control sanction, or whenever complaint has been made before any judge or magistrate in this state setting forth on the affidavit of any credible person in another state that a crime has been committed in the other state and that the accused has been charged in that state with the commission of the crime, and has fled from justice, or with having been convicted of a crime in that state and having escaped from confinement, or having broken the terms of bail, probation, or parole, and is believed to be in this state, the judge or magistrate shall issue a warrant directed to any peace officer, commanding the peace officer to apprehend the person named in the warrant, wherever the person may be found in this state, and to bring the person before the same or any other judge, magistrate, or court that may be available in or convenient of access to the place where the arrest may be made, to answer the charge or complaint and affidavit, and a certified copy of the sworn charge or complaint and upon which the warrant is issued shall be attached to the warrant.

This section does not apply to cases arising under section 2963.06 of the Revised Code.

**HISTORY: GC § 109-13; 117 v 588, § 13; Bureau of Code Revision, Eff 10-1-53; 146 v S 2. Eff 7-1-96; 149 v H 490, § 1, eff. 1-1-04.**

The effective date is set by section 4 of H.B. 490.

## § 2963.12 Arrest without warrant.

An arrest may be made by any peace officer or a private person without a warrant upon reasonable information that the accused stands charged in the courts of any state with a crime punishable by death or imprisonment for a term exceeding one year. When so arrested the accused must be taken before a judge or magistrate with all practicable speed and complaint must be made against him under oath setting forth the ground for the arrest, as provided in section 2963.11 of the Revised Code. Thereafter his answer shall be heard as if he had been arrested on a warrant.

**HISTORY: GC § 109-14; 117 v 588, § 14; Bureau of Code Revision. Eff 10-1-53.**

## § 2963.13 Fugitive to be confined pending requisition.

If from the examination before the judge or magistrate it appears that the person held under section 2963.11 or 2963.12 of the Revised Code is the person charged with having committed the crime alleged and that he has fled from justice, the judge or magistrate must, by a warrant reciting the accusation, commit him to the county jail for such a time, not to exceed thirty days and specified in the warrant, as will enable the arrest of the accused to be made under a warrant of the governor on a requisition of the executive authority of the state having jurisdiction of the offense, unless the accused furnishes bail or until he is legally discharged.

**HISTORY: GC § 109-15; 117 v 588, § 15; Bureau of Code Revision. Eff 10-1-53.**

## § 2963.14 Bail.

Unless the offense with which the prisoner is charged under sections 2963.11 and 2963.12 of the Revised Code is shown to be an offense punishable by death or life imprisonment under the laws of the state in which it was committed, a judge or magistrate in this state may admit the person arrested to bail by bond, with sufficient sureties and in such sum as he deems proper, conditioned for his appearance before said judge or magistrate at a time specified in such bond, and for his surrender, to be arrested upon the warrant of the governor of this state.

**HISTORY: GC § 109-16; 117 v 588, § 16; Bureau of Code Revision. Eff 10-1-53.**

## § 2963.15 Release of accused.

If the accused mentioned in section 2963.14 of the Revised Code is not arrested under warrant of the governor by the expiration of the time specified in the warrant or bond, a judge or magistrate may discharge him or may recommit him for a further period not to exceed sixty days, or a judge or magistrate may again take bail for his appearance and surrender, under said section, but within a period not to exceed sixty days after the date of such new bond.

**HISTORY: GC § 109-17; 117 v 588, § 17; Bureau of Code Revision. Eff 10-1-53.**

## § 2963.16 Forfeited recognizance.

If a prisoner admitted to bail under section 2963.14 of the Revised Code fails to appear and surrender himself according to the conditions of his bond, the judge or magistrate, by proper order, shall declare the bond forfeited and order his immediate arrest without warrant if he is within this state. Recovery may be had on such bond in the name of the state as in the case of other bonds given by the accused in criminal proceedings.

**HISTORY: GC § 109-18; 117 v 588, § 18; Bureau of Code Revision. Eff 10-1-53.**

## § 2963.17 Governor may hold fugitive indicted in this state or surrender him.

If a criminal prosecution has been instituted under the laws of this state against a person sought by another state under sections 2963.01 to 2963.27, inclusive, of the Revised Code, and is still pending, the governor may surrender him on demand of the executive authority of another state or hold him until he has been tried and discharged or convicted and punished in this state.

**HISTORY: GC § 109-19; 117 v 588, § 19; Bureau of Code Revision. Eff 10-1-53.**

## § 2963.18 Guilt not to be inquired into by governor or in extradition proceedings.

The guilt or innocence of an accused as to the crime of which he is charged may not be inquired into by the governor or in any proceeding after a demand for extradition accompanied by a charge of crime under section 2963.03 of the Revised Code has been presented to the governor, except as it may be involved in identifying the person held as the person charged with the crime.

**HISTORY: GC § 109-20; 117 v 588, § 20; Bureau of Code Revision. Eff 10-1-53.**

## § 2963.19 Governor may recall warrant for arrest.

The governor may recall his warrant of arrest issued under section 2963.07 of the Revised Code or may issue another warrant whenever he thinks is proper.

**HISTORY: GC § 109-21; 117 v 588, § 21; Bureau of Code Revision. Eff 10-1-53.**

[FUGITIVE FROM THIS STATE]

## § 2963.20 Governor to demand fugitive from this state.

Whenever the governor demands a person charged with crime, with escaping from confinement, or with breaking the terms of the person's bail or parole in this state or violating the conditions of a community control sanction or post-release control sanction imposed in this state, from the executive authority of any other state, or from the chief justice or an associate justice of the supreme court of the District of Columbia authorized to receive that demand under the laws of the United States, the governor shall issue a warrant under the seal of this state, to an agent, commanding the agent to receive the person so charged and convey that person to the proper officer of the county in which the offense was committed.

**HISTORY: GC § 109-22; 117 v 588, § 22; Bureau of Code Revision. Eff 10-1-53; 149 v H 490, § 1, eff. 1-1-04.**

The effective date is set by section 4 of H.B. 490.

## § 2963.21 Application for requisition for return of fugitive.

When the return to this state of a person charged with crime in this state is required, the prosecuting attorney shall present to the governor a written application for a requisition for the return of the person charged. The application shall state the name of the person charged, the crime charged against the person, the approximate time, place, and circumstances of its commission, the state in which the person charged is believed to be located, and the location of the person in that state at the time the application is made. The prosecuting attorney shall certify that in the prosecuting attorney's opinion the ends of justice require the arrest and return of the person charged to this state for trial and that the proceeding is not instituted to enforce a private claim.

When the return to this state is required of a person who has been convicted of a crime in this state and has escaped from confinement or broken the terms of the person's bail, parole, community control sanction, or post-release control sanction, the prosecuting attorney of the county in which the offense was committed, the adult parole authority, or the warden of the institution or sheriff of the county from which escape was made shall present to the governor a written application for a requisition for the return of the person. The application shall state the person's name, the crime of which the person was convicted, the circumstances of the person's escape from confinement or of the breach of the terms of the person's bail, parole, community control sanction, or post-release control sanction, the state in which the person is believed to be located, and the location of the person in that state at the time the application is made.

An application presented under this section shall be verified by affidavit, executed in duplicate, and accompanied by two certified copies of the indictment returned, of the information and affidavit filed, of the complaint made to the judge or magistrate, stating the offense with which the accused is charged, of the judgment of conviction, or of the sentence. The prosecuting attorney, adult parole authority, warden, or sheriff also may attach any other affidavits or documents in duplicate that the prosecuting attorney, adult parole authority, warden, or sheriff finds proper to be submitted with the application. One copy of the application, with the action of the governor indicated by indorsement on the application, and one of the certified copies of the indictment, complaint, information, and affidavits, of the judgment of conviction, or of the sentence shall be filed in the office of the secretary of state to remain of record in that office. The other copies of all papers shall be forwarded with the governor's requisition.

**HISTORY: GC § 109-23; 117 v 588, § 23; Bureau of Code Revision, 10-1-53; 146 v S 269. Eff 7-1-96; 149 v H 490, § 1, eff. 1-1-04.**

The effective date is set by section 4 of H.B. 490.

## § 2963.22 Reimbursement of fees.

The director of budget and management shall provide for reimbursement of the fees to the officers of the state on whose governor the requisition is made under section 2963.21 of the Revised Code, and all necessary travel in returning the prisoner at the rates governing travel that have been adopted pursuant to section 126.31 of the Revised Code, on the certificate of the governor of such state.

**HISTORY: GC § 109-24; 117 v 588, § 24; Bureau of Code Revision, 10-1-53; 141 v H 201 (Eff 7-1-85); 143 v S 336. Eff 4-10-90.**

## § 2963.23 Accused immune from civil suits until conviction or return home.

A person brought into this state by, or after waiver of, extradition based on a criminal charge is not subject to service of personal process in any civil action in this state until he has been convicted in the criminal proceeding, or, if acquitted, until he has had reasonable opportunity to return to the state from which he was extradited.

**HISTORY: GC § 109-25; 117 v 588, § 25; Bureau of Code Revision. Eff 10-1-53.**

## § 2963.24 Extradition hearing waived.

Any person arrested in this state charged with having committed any crime in another state or alleged to have escaped from confinement, or broken the terms of his bail, probation, or parole may waive the issuance and service of the warrant provided for in section 2963.07 of the Revised Code and all other procedure incidental to extradition proceedings, by executing or subscribing in the presence of a judge of any court of record within this state, a writing which states that he consents to return to the demanding state. Before such waiver is executed or subscribed by such person the judge in open court shall inform such person of his rights to the issuance and service of a warrant of extradition and to obtain a writ of habeas corpus as provided for in section 2963.09 of the Revised Code.

When such consent has been executed it shall forthwith be forwarded to the office of the governor and filed therein. The judge shall direct the officer having such person in custody to deliver forthwith such person to the accredited agent of the demanding state, and shall deliver to such agent a copy of such consent. This section does not limit the rights of the accused person to return voluntarily and without formality to the demanding state before any such demand has been made, nor is this waiver procedure an exclusive procedure or a limitation on the powers, rights, or duties of the officers of the demanding state or of this state.

**HISTORY: GC § 109-26; 117 v 588, § 26; Bureau of Code Revision. Eff 10-1-53.**

## § 2963.25 Right to punish or regain custody by this state not waived.

Sections 2963.01 to 2963.27, inclusive, of the Revised Code do not constitute a waiver by this state of its right, power, or privilege to try such demanded person for crime committed within this state, or of its right, power, or privilege to regain custody of such person by extradition proceedings or otherwise for the purpose of trial, sentence, or punishment for any crime committed within this state, nor are any proceedings had under such sections, which result in, or fail to result in, extradition, a waiver by this state of any of its rights, privileges, or jurisdiction.

**HISTORY: GC § 109-27; 117 v 588, § 27; Bureau of Code Revision. Eff 10-1-53.**

## § 2963.26 Extradited fugitive may be tried for other crimes committed in this state.

A person returned to this state by, or after waiver of, extradition proceedings, may be tried in this state for other crimes which he may be charged with having committed here, as well as that specified in the requisition for his extradition.

**HISTORY: GC § 109-28; 117 v 588, § 28; Bureau of Code Revision. Eff 10-1-53.**

## § 2963.27 Uniform interpretation.

Sections 2963.01 to 2963.26, inclusive, of the Revised Code shall be so interpreted and construed as to make the law of this state uniform with the law of those states which enact similar legislation.

**HISTORY: GC § 109-29; 117 v 588, § 29; Bureau of Code Revision. Eff 10-1-53.**

## § 2963.28 Request by governor for extradition of criminal.

If it appears to the governor by sworn evidence in writing that a person has committed a crime within this state for which such person may be delivered to the United States or its authorities by a foreign government or its authorities, because of laws of the United States, or of a treaty between the United States and a foreign government, and that such person is a fugitive from justice of this state, and may be found within the territory of such foreign government, the governor, under the great seal of Ohio, shall request the president of the United States, or the secretary of state of the United States, to take any steps necessary for the extradition of such person and his delivery to any agent of this state appointed by the governor, or to the proper officer of the county within which he is charged with the commission of such crime.

**HISTORY: RS § 97-1; 81 v 208; GC § 116; Bureau of Code Revision. Eff 10-1-53.**

## § 2963.29 Governor must be satisfied by evidence of good faith.

The governor shall not request the extradition of a person under section 2963.28 of the Revised Code unless he is satisfied by sworn evidence that extradition is sought in good faith for the punishment of the crime named and not for the purpose of collecting a debt or pecuniary mulct or of bringing the alleged fugitive within this state to serve him with civil process, or with criminal process other than for the crime for which his extradition is sought.

**HISTORY: RS § 97-1; 81 v 208; GC § 117; Bureau of Code Revision. Eff 10-1-53.**

### [INTERSTATE AGREEMENT ON DETAINERS]

## § 2963.30 Interstate agreement on detainers.

The Interstate Agreement on Detainers is hereby enacted into law and entered into by this state with all other jurisdictions legally joining therein, in the form substantially as follows:

### THE INTERSTATE AGREEMENT ON DETAINERS

The contracting states solemnly agree that:

#### Article I

The party states find that charges outstanding against a prisoner, detainers based on untried indictments, informations or complaints, and difficulties in securing speedy trials of persons already incarcerated in other jurisdictions, produce uncertainties which obstruct programs of prisoner treatment and rehabilitation. Accordingly, it is the policy of the party states and the purpose of this agreement to encourage the expeditious and orderly disposition of such charges and determination of the proper status of any and all detainers based on untried indictments, informations or complaints. The party states also find that proceedings with reference to such charges and detainers, when emanating from another jurisdiction, cannot properly be had in the absence of cooperative procedures. It is the further purpose of this agreement to provide such cooperative procedures.

#### Article II

As used in this agreement:

(a) "State" shall mean a state of the United States:[;] the United States of America:[;] a territory or possession of the United States:[;] the District of Columbia:[;] the Commonwealth of Puerto Rico.

(b) "Sending state" shall mean a state in which a prisoner is incarcerated at the time that he initiates a request for final disposition pursuant to Article III hereof or at the time that a request for custody or availability is initiated pursuant to Article IV hereof.

(c) "Receiving state" shall mean the state in which trial is to be had on an indictment, information or complaint pursuant to Article III or Article IV hereof.

## Article III

(a) Whenever a person has entered upon a term of imprisonment in a penal or correctional institution of a party state, and whenever during the continuance of the term of imprisonment there is pending in any other party state any untried indictment, information or complaint on the basis of which a detainer has been lodged against the prisoner, he shall be brought to trial within one hundred eighty days after he shall have caused to be delivered to the prosecuting officer and the appropriate court of the prosecuting officer's jurisdiction written notice of the place of his imprisonment and his request for a final disposition to be made of the indictment, information or complaint: provided that for good cause shown in open court, the prisoner or his counsel being present, the court having jurisdiction of the matter may grant any necessary or reasonable continuance. The request of the prisoner shall be accompanied by a certificate of the appropriate official having custody of the prisoner, stating the term of commitment under which the prisoner is being held, the time already served, the time remaining to be served on the sentence, the amount of good time earned, the time of parole eligibility of the prisoner, and any decisions of the state parole agency relating to the prisoner.

(b) The written notice and request for final disposition referred to in paragraph (a) hereof shall be given or sent by the prisoner to the warden, commissioner of corrections or other official having custody of him, who shall promptly forward it together with the certificate to the appropriate prosecuting official and court by registered or certified mail, return receipt requested.

(c) The warden, commissioner of corrections or other official having custody of the prisoner shall promptly inform him of the source and contents of any detainer lodged against him and shall also inform him of his rights to make a request for final disposition of the indictment, information or complaint on which the detainer is based.

(d) Any request or [for] final disposition made by a prisoner pursuant to paragraph (a) hereof shall operate as a request for final disposition of all untried indictments, informations or complaints on the basis of which detainers have been lodged against the prisoner from the state to whose prosecuting official the request for final disposition is specifically directed. The warden, commissioner of corrections or other officials having custody of the prisoner shall forthwith notify all appropriate prosecuting officers and courts in the several jurisdictions within the state to which the prisoner's request for final disposition is being sent of the proceeding being initiated by the prisoner. Any notification sent pursuant to this paragraph shall be accompanied by copies of the prisoner's written notice, request, and the certificate. If trial is not had on any indictment, information or complaint contemplated hereby prior to the return of the prisoner to the original place of imprisonment, such indictment, information or complaint shall not be of any further force or effect, and the court shall enter an order dismissing the same with prejudice.

(e) Any request for final disposition made by a prisoner pursuant to paragraph (a) hereof shall also be deemed to be a waiver of extradition with respect to any charge or proceeding contemplated thereby or included therein by reason of paragraph (d) hereof, and a waiver of extradition to the receiving state to serve any sentence there imposed upon him, after completion of his term of imprisonment in the sending state. The request for final disposition shall also constitute a consent by the prisoner to the production of his body in any court where his presence may be required in order to effectuate the purposes of this agreement and a further consent voluntarily to be returned to the original place of imprisonment in accordance with the provisions of this agreement. Nothing in this paragraph shall prevent the imposition of a concurrent sentence if otherwise permitted by law.

(f) Escape from custody by the prisoner subsequent to his execution of the request for final disposition referred to in paragraph (a) hereof shall void the request.

## Article IV

(a) The appropriate officer of the jurisdiction in which an untried indictment, information or complaint is pending shall be entitled to have a prisoner against whom he has lodged a detainer and who is serving a term of imprisonment in any party state made available in accordance with Article V (a) hereof upon presentation of a written request for temporary custody or availability to the appropriate authorities of the state in which the prisoner is incarcerated:[,] provided that the court having jurisdiction of such indictment, information or complaint shall have duly approved, recorded and transmitted the request:[,] and provided further that there shall be a period of thirty days after receipt by the appropriate authorities before the request be honored, within which period the governor of the sending state may disapprove the request for temporary custody or availability, either upon his own motion or upon motion of the prisoner.

(b) Upon receipt of the officer's written request as provided in paragraph (a) hereof, the appropriate authorities having the prisoner in custody shall furnish the officer with a certificate stating the term of commitment under which the prisoner is being held, the time already served, the time remaining to be served on the sentence, the amount of good time earned, the time of parole eligibility of the prisoner, and any decisions of the state parole agency relating to the prisoner. Said authorities simultaneously shall furnish all other officers and appropriate courts in the receiving state who have lodged detainers against the prisoner with similar certificates and with notices informing them of the request for custody or availability and of the reasons therefor.

(c) In respect of any proceeding made possible by this Article, trial shall be commenced within one hundred twenty days of the arrival of the prisoner in the receiving state, but for good cause shown in open court, the prisoner or his counsel being present, the court having jurisdiction of the matter may grant any necessary or reasonable continuance.

(d) Nothing contained in this Article shall be construed to deprive any prisoner of any right which he may have to contest the legality of his delivery as provided in paragraph (a) hereof, but such delivery may not be opposed or denied on the ground that the executive authority of the sending state has not affirmatively consented to or ordered such delivery.

(e) If trial is not had on any indictment, information or complaint contemplated hereby prior to the prisoner's being returned to the original place of imprisonment pursuant to Article V (e) hereof, such indictment, information or complaint shall not be of any further force or effect, and the court shall enter an order dismissing the same with prejudice.

### Article V

(a) In response to a request made under Article III or Article IV hereof, the appropriate authority in a sending state shall offer to deliver temporary custody of such prisoner to the appropriate authority in the state where such indictment, information or complaint is pending against such person in order that speedy and efficient prosecution may be had. If the request for final disposition is made by the prisoner, the offer of temporary custody shall accompany the written notice provided for in Article III of this agreement. In the case of a federal prisoner, the appropriate authority in the receiving state shall be entitled to temporary custody as provided by this agreement or to the prisoner's presence in federal custody at the place of trial, whichever custodian arrangement may be approved by the custodian.

(b) The officer or other representative of a state accepting an offer of temporary custody shall present the following upon demand:

(1) Proper identification and evidence of his authority to act for the state into whose temporary custody the prisoner is to be given.

(2) A duly certified copy of the indictment, information or complaint on the basis of which the detainer has been lodged and on the basis of which the request for temporary custody of the prisoner has been made.

(c) If the appropriate authority shall refuse or fail to accept temporary custody of said person, or in the event that an action on the indictment, information or complaint on the basis of which the detainer has been lodged is not brought to trial within the period provided in Article III or Article IV hereof, the appropriate court of the jurisdiction where the indictment, information or complaint has been pending shall enter an order dismissing the same with prejudice, and any detainer based thereon shall cease to be of any force or effect.

(d) The temporary custody referred to in this agreement shall be only for the purpose of permitting prosecution on the charge or charges contained in one or more untried indictments, informations or complaints which form the basis of the detainer or detainers or for prosecution on any other charge or charges arising out of the same transaction,[;] except for his attendance at court and while being transported to or from any place at which his presence may be required, the prisoner shall be held in a suitable jail or other facility regularly used for persons awaiting prosecution.

(e) At the earliest practicable time consonant with the purposes of this agreement, the prisoner shall be returned to the sending state.

(f) During the continuance of temporary custody or while the prisoner is otherwise being made available for trial as required by this agreement, time being served on the sentence shall continue to run but good time shall be earned by the prisoner only if, and to the extent that, the law and practice of the jurisdiction which imposed the sentence may allow.

(g) For all purposes other than that for which temporary custody as provided in this agreement is exercised, the prisoner shall be deemed to remain in the custody of and subject to the jurisdiction of the sending state and any escape from temporary custody may be dealt with in the same manner as an escape from the original place of imprisonment or in any other manner permitted by law.

(h) From the time that a party state receives custody of a prisoner pursuant to this agreement until such prisoner is returned to the territory and custody of the sending state, the state in which the one or more untried indictments, informations or complaints are pending or in which trial is being had shall be responsible for the prisoner and shall also pay all costs of transporting, caring for, keeping and returning the prisoner,[;] the provisions of this paragraph shall govern unless the states concerned shall have entered into a supplementary agreement providing for a different allocation of costs and responsibilities as between or among themselves. Nothing herein contained shall be construed to alter or affect any internal relationship among the departments, agencies and officers of and in the government of a party state, or between a party state and its subdivisions, as to the payment of costs, or responsibilities therefor.

### Article VI

(a) In determining the duration and expiration dates of the time periods provided in Articles III and IV of this agreement, the running of said time periods shall be tolled whenever and for as long as the prisoner is unable to stand trial, as determined by the court having jurisdiction of the matter.

(b) No provision of this agreement, and no remedy made available by this agreement, shall apply to any person who is adjudged to be mentally ill, or who is under sentence of death.

### Article VII

Each state party to this agreement shall designate an officer who, acting jointly with like officers of other party states, shall promulgate rules and regulations to carry out more effectively the terms and provisions of this agreement, and who shall provide, within and without the state, information necessary to the effective operation of this agreement.

### Article VIII

This agreement shall enter into full force and effect as to a party state when such state has enacted the same into law. A state party to this agreement may withdraw herefrom by enacting a statute repealing the same. However, the withdrawal of any state shall not affect the status of any proceedings already initiated by inmates or by state officers at the time such withdrawal takes effect, nor shall it affect their rights in respect thereof.

### Article IX

This agreement shall be liberally construed so as to effectuate its purposes. The provisions of this agreement shall be severable and if any phrase, clause, sentence or provision of this agreement is declared to be contrary to the constitution of any party state or of the United States or the applicability thereof to any government, agency, person or circumstance is held invalid, the validity of the remainder of this agreement and the applicability thereof to any agreement, agency, person or circumstance shall not be affected thereby. If this agreement shall be held contrary to the constitution of any state party hereto, the agreement shall remain in full force and effect as to the remaining states and in full force and effect as to the state affected as to all severable matters.

**HISTORY: 133 v S 356. Eff 11-18-69.**

## § 2963.31 Definitions.

As used in section 2963.30 of the Revised Code, with reference to the courts of this state, "appropriate court" means the court of record having jurisdiction of the indictment, information, or complaint.

**HISTORY: 133 v S 356. Eff 11-18-69.**

## § 2963.32 Duty to effectuate agreement.

The courts, departments, agencies, and officers of this state and its political subdivisions shall do all things that are necessary to effectuate the agreement adopted pursuant to section 2963.30 of the Revised Code and that are appropriate within their respective jurisdictions and consistent with their duties and authority. The warden or other official in charge of a correctional institution in this state shall give over the person of any inmate of the institution when so required by the operation of the agreement.

**HISTORY: 133 v S 356 (Eff 11-18-69); 145 v H 571. Eff 10-6-94.**

## § 2963.33 Repealed, 134 v H 511, § 2 [133 v S 356]. Eff 1-1-74.

This section concerned habitual offenders.

## § 2963.34 Escape and aiding escape.

A person, while in another state pursuant to the agreement, adopted pursuant to section 2963.30 of the Revised Code, is subject to the prohibitions and penalties provided by sections 2921.34 and 2921.35 of the Revised Code.

**HISTORY: 133 v S 356 (Eff 11-18-69); 134 v H 511. Eff 1-1-74.**

## § 2963.35 Administrator of agreement; rules and regulations.

The chief of the bureau of sentence computation or another individual specified by the director of rehabilitation and correction is designated as the administrator as required by Article VII of the agreement adopted pursuant to section 2963.30 of the Revised Code. The administrator, acting jointly with like officers of other party states, shall, in accordance with Chapter 119. of the Revised Code, promulgate rules and regulations to carry out the terms of the agreement. The administrator is authorized and empowered to cooperate with all departments, agencies, and officers of this state and its political subdivisions, in facilitating the proper administration of the agreement or of any supplementary agreement or agreements entered into by this state thereunder.

**HISTORY: 133 v S 356 (Eff 11-18-69); 147 v S 111. Eff 3-17-98.**

# CHAPTER 2965: PARDON; PAROLE [REPEALED]



**§ 2965.01** Repealed, 130 v PtII, 147, § 2 [GC §§ 2209, 2209-1, 2209-2; 118 v 288; Bureau of Code Revision, 10-1-53; 126 v 307; 128 v 960; 129 v 1667]. Eff 3-18-65.

**§ 2965.02** Repealed, 130 v PtII, 147, § 2 [GC §§ 2209, 2209-1, 2209-2; 118 v 288; Bureau of Code Revision, 10-1-53; 126 v 307; 128 v 960; 129 v 1667]. Eff 3-18-65.

**§ 2965.03** Repealed, 130 v PtII, 147, § 2 [GC §§ 2209, 2209-1, 2209-2; 118 v 288; Bureau of Code Revision, 10-1-53; 126 v 307; 128 v 960; 129 v 1667]. Eff 3-18-65.

**§ 2965.04** Repealed, 130 v PtII, 147, § 2 [GC §§ 2209-3, 2209-4, 2209-5; 118 v 288; Bureau of Code Revision, 10-1-53; 128 v 960; 129 v 1668]. Eff 3-18-65.

**§ 2965.05** Repealed, 130 v PtII, 147, § 2 [GC §§ 2209-3, 2209-4, 2209-5; 118 v 288; Bureau of Code Revision, 10-1-53; 128 v 960; 129 v 1668]. Eff 3-18-65.

**§ 2965.06** Repealed, 130 v PtII, 147, § 2 [GC §§ 2209-3, 2209-4, 2209-5; 118 v 288; Bureau of Code Revision, 10-1-53; 128 v 960; 129 v 1668]. Eff 3-18-65.

**§ 2965.07** Repealed, 130 v PtII, 147, § 2 [GC §§ 2209-6, 2209-7, 2209-8; 118 v 288; 123 v 862; 124 v 825; Bureau of Code Revision, 10-1-53; 125 v 289, 823; 126 v 640; 127 v 8, 383; 128 v 960; 129 v 484]. Eff 3-18-65.

**§ 2965.08** Repealed, 130 v PtII, 147, § 2 [GC §§ 2209-6, 2209-7, 2209-8; 118 v 288; 123 v 862; 124 v 825; Bureau of Code Revision, 10-1-53; 125 v 289, 823; 126 v 640; 127 v 8, 383; 128 v 960; 129 v 484]. Eff 3-18-65.

**§ 2965.09** Repealed, 130 v PtII, 147, § 2 [GC §§ 2209-6, 2209-7, 2209-8; 118 v 288; 123 v 862; 124 v 825; Bureau of Code Revision, 10-1-53; 125 v 289, 823; 126 v 640; 127 v 8, 383; 128 v 960; 129 v 484]. Eff 3-18-65.

**§ 2965.10** Repealed, 130 v PtII, 147, § 2 [GC §§ 2209-9, 2209-10, 2209-11; 118 v 288; Bureau of Code Revision, 10-1-53]. Eff 3-18-65.

**§ 2965.11** Repealed, 130 v PtII, 147, § 2 [GC §§ 2209-9, 2209-10, 2209-11; 118 v 288; Bureau of Code Revision, 10-1-53]. Eff 3-18-65.

**§ 2965.12** Repealed, 130 v PtII, 147, § 2 [GC §§ 2209-9, 2209-10, 2209-11; 118 v 288; Bureau of Code Revision, 10-1-53]. Eff 3-18-65.

**§ 2965.13** Repealed, 130 v PtII, 147, § 2 [GC §§ 2209-12, 2209-13, 2209-14; 118 v 288; Bureau of Code Revision, 10-1-53]. Eff 3-18-65.

**§ 2965.14** Repealed, 130 v PtII, 147, § 2 [GC §§ 2209-12, 2209-13, 2209-14; 118 v 288; Bureau of Code Revision, 10-1-53]. Eff 3-18-65.

**§ 2965.15** Repealed, 130 v PtII, 147, § 2 [GC §§ 2209-12, 2209-13, 2209-14; 118 v 288; Bureau of Code Revision, 10-1-53]. Eff 3-18-65.

**§ 2965.16** Repealed, 130 v PtII, 147, § 2 [GC §§ 2209-15, 2209-16, 2209-17; 118 v 288; Bureau of Code Revision, 10-1-53; 128 v 960]. Eff 3-18-65.

**§ 2965.17** Repealed, 130 v PtII, 147, § 2 [GC §§ 2209-15, 2209-16, 2209-17; 118 v 288; Bureau of Code Revision, 10-1-53; 128 v 960]. Eff 3-18-65.

**§ 2965.18** Repealed, 130 v PtII, 147, § 2 [GC §§ 2209-15, 2209-16, 2209-17; 118 v 288; Bureau of Code Revision, 10-1-53; 128 v 960]. Eff 3-18-65.

**§ 2965.19** Repealed, 130 v PtII, 147, § 2 [GC §§ 2209-18, 2209-19; 118 v 288; Bureau of Code Revision, 10-1-53; 127 v 118; 128 v 960; 129 v 484; 130 v 673]. Eff 3-18-65.

**§ 2965.20** Repealed, 130 v PtII, 147, § 2 [GC §§ 2209-18, 2209-19; 118 v 288; Bureau of Code Revision, 10-1-53; 127 v 118; 128 v 960; 129 v 484; 130 v 673]. Eff 3-18-65.

**§ 2965.201** Repealed, 130 v PtII, 147, § 2 [129 v S 468]. Eff 3-18-65.

**§ 2965.21** Repealed, 130 v PtII, 147, § 2 [GC § 2209-20; 118 v 288, § 21; Bureau of Code Revision, 10-1-53; 128 v 960]. Eff 3-18-65.

**§ 2965.211** Repealed, 130 v PtII, 147, § 2 [129 v H 1093]. Eff 3-18-65.

**§ 2965.22** Repealed, 130 v PtII, 147, § 2 [GC §§ 2209-21, 2210-1; 114 v 530, § 2; 118 v 288 (297, 300), §§ 22, 25; 121 v 402; Bureau of Code Revision, 10-1-53]. Eff 3-18-65.

**§ 2965.23** Repealed, 130 v PtII, 147, § 2 [GC §§ 2209-21, 2210-1; 114 v 530, § 2; 118 v 288 (297, 300), §§ 22, 25; 121 v 402; Bureau of Code Revision, 10-1-53]. Eff 3-18-65.

**§ 2965.31** Repealed, 130 v PtII, 147, § 2 [GC §§ 2210, 2210-2; 114 v 530; Bureau of Code Revision, 10-1-53; 125 v 836]. Eff 3-18-65.

**§ 2965.32** Repealed, 130 v PtII, 147, § 2 [GC §§ 2210, 2210-2; 114 v 530; Bureau of Code Revision, 10-1-53; 125 v 836]. Eff 3-18-65.

**§ 2965.33** Repealed, 130 v PtII, 147, § 2 [GC §§ 2210-3, 108-1; 114 v 530; 117 v 596; Bureau of Code Revision, 10-1-53; 127 v 115]. Eff 3-18-65.

**§ 2965.34** Repealed, 130 v PtII, 147, § 2 [GC §§ 2210-3, 108-1; 114 v 530; 117 v 596; Bureau of Code Revision, 10-1-53; 127 v 115]. Eff 3-18-65.

**§ 2965.341** Repealed, 130 v PtII, 147, § 2 [127 v S 165]. Eff 3-18-65.

**§ 2965.35** Repealed, 130 v PtII, 147, § 2 [127 v 213; 129 v 1669; 130 v H 1 (673, 674)]. Eff 3-18-65.

See RC Chapter 2967: PARDON; PAROLE; PROBATION.

**§ 2965.36** Repealed, 130 v PtII, 147, § 2 [127 v 213; 129 v 1669; 130 v H 1 (673, 674)]. Eff 3-18-65.

See RC Chapter 2967: PARDON; PAROLE; PROBATION.

**§ 2965.37** Repealed, 130 v PtII, 147, § 2 [127 v 213; 129 v 1669; 130 v H 1 (673, 674)]. Eff 3-18-65.

See RC Chapter 2967: PARDON; PAROLE; PROBATION.

# CHAPTER 2967: PARDON; PAROLE; PROBATION



## § 2967.01 Definitions.

As used in this chapter:

(A) "State correctional institution" includes any institution or facility that is operated by the department of rehabilitation and correction and that is used for the custody, care, or treatment of criminal, delinquent, or psychologically or psychiatrically disturbed offenders.

(B) "Pardon" means the remission of penalty by the governor in accordance with the power vested in the governor by the constitution.

(C) "Commutation" or "commutation of sentence" means the substitution by the governor of a lesser for a greater punishment. A stated prison term may be commuted without the consent of the convict, except when granted upon the acceptance and performance by the convict of conditions precedent. After commutation, the commuted prison term shall be the only one in existence. The commutation may be stated in terms of commuting from a named offense to a lesser included offense with a shorter prison term, in terms of commuting from a stated prison term in months and years to a shorter prison term in months and years, or in terms of commuting from any other stated prison term to a shorter prison term.

(D) "Reprieve" means the temporary suspension by the governor of the execution of a sentence or prison term. The governor may grant a reprieve without the consent of and against the will of the convict.

(E) "Parole" means, regarding a prisoner who is serving a prison term for aggravated murder or murder, who is serving a prison term of life imprisonment for rape or for felonious sexual penetration as it existed under section 2907.12 of the Revised Code prior to September 3, 1996, or who was sentenced prior to July 1, 1996, a release of the prisoner from confinement in any state correctional institution by the adult parole authority that is subject to the eligibility criteria specified in this chapter and that is under the terms and conditions, and for the period of time, prescribed by the authority in its published rules and official minutes or required by division (A) of section 2967.131 [2967.13.1] of the Revised Code or another provision of this chapter.

(F) "Head of a state correctional institution" or "head of the institution" means the resident head of the institution and the person immediately in charge of the institution, whether designated warden, superintendent, or any other name by which the head is known.

(G) "Convict" means a person who has been convicted of a felony under the laws of this state, whether or not actually confined in a state correctional institution, unless the person has been pardoned or has served the person's sentence or prison term.

(H) "Prisoner" means a person who is in actual confinement in a state correctional institution.

(I) "Parolee" means any inmate who has been released from confinement on parole by order of the adult parole authority or conditionally pardoned, who is under supervision of the adult parole authority and has not been granted a final release, and who has not been declared in violation of the inmate's parole by the authority or is performing the prescribed conditions of a conditional pardon.

(J) "Releasee" means an inmate who has been released from confinement pursuant to section 2967.28 of the Revised Code under a period of post-release control that includes one or more post-release control sanctions.

(K) "Final release" means a remission by the adult parole authority of the balance of the sentence or prison term of a parolee or prisoner or the termination by the authority of a term of post-release control of a releasee.

(L) "Parole violator" or "release violator" means any parolee or releasee who has been declared to be in violation of the condition of parole or post-release control specified in division (A) or (B) of section 2967.131 [2967.13.1] of the Revised Code or in violation of any other term, condition, or rule of the parolee's or releasee's parole or of the parolee's or releasee's post-release control sanctions, the determination of which has been made by the adult parole authority and recorded in its official minutes.

(M) "Administrative release" means a termination of jurisdiction over a particular sentence or prison term by the adult parole authority for administrative convenience.

(N) "Post-release control" means a period of supervision by the adult parole authority after a prisoner's release from imprisonment that includes one or more post-release control sanctions imposed under section 2967.28 of the Revised Code.

(O) "Post-release control sanction" means a sanction that is authorized under sections 2929.16 to 2929.18 of the Revised Code and that is imposed upon a prisoner upon the prisoner's release from a prison term.

(P) "Community control sanction," "prison term," "mandatory prison term," and "stated prison term" have the same meanings as in section 2929.01 of the Revised Code.

(Q) "Transitional control" means control of a prisoner under the transitional control program established by the department of rehabilitation and correction under section 2967.26 of the Revised Code, if the department establishes a program of that nature under that section.

(R) "Random drug testing" has the same meaning as in section 5120.63 of the Revised Code.

**HISTORY: 130 v PtII, 149 (Eff 3-18-65); 131 v 685 (Eff 10-20-65); 134 v H 494 (Eff 7-12-72); 138 v S 52 (Eff 1-9-81); 139 v S 199 (Eff 7-1-83); 145 v H 571 (Eff 10-6-94); 146 v H 4 (Eff 11-9-95); 146 v S 2 (Eff 7-1-96); 146 v S 269 (Eff 7-1-96); 147 v S 111 (Eff 3-17-98); 148 v H 349. Eff 9-22-2000.**

See provisions, § 5 of SB 2 (146 v —) as amended by § 3 of SB 269 (146 v —) following RC § 2929.03.

## § 2967.02 Administration of provisions; pardons.

(A) The adult parole authority created by section 5149.02 of the Revised Code shall administer sections 2967.01 to 2967.28 of the Revised Code, and other sections of the Revised Code governing pardon, community control sanctions, post-release control, and parole.

(B) The governor may grant a pardon after conviction, may grant an absolute and entire pardon or a partial pardon, and may grant a pardon upon conditions precedent or subsequent.

(C) The adult parole authority shall supervise all parolees. The department of rehabilitation and correction has legal custody of a parolee until the authority grants the parolee a final release pursuant to section 2967.16 of the Revised Code.

(D) The department of rehabilitation and correction has legal custody of a releasee until the adult parole authority grants the releasee a final release pursuant to section 2967.16 of the Revised Code.

**HISTORY: 130 v PtII, 150 (Eff 3-18-65); 146 v S 2. Eff 7-1-96; 149 v H 490, § 1, eff. 1-1-04.**

The effective date is set by section 4 of H.B. 490.

See provisions, § 5 of SB 2 (146 v —), as amended by § 3 of SB 269 (146 v —), following RC § 2929.03.

## § 2967.021 Application of provisions effective 7-1-96.

(A) Chapter 2967. of the Revised Code, as it existed prior to July 1, 1996, applies to a person upon whom a court imposed a term of imprisonment prior to July 1, 1996, and a person upon whom a court, on or after July 1, 1996, and in accordance with law existing prior to July 1, 1996, imposed a term of imprisonment for an offense that was committed prior to July 1, 1996.

(B) Chapter 2967. of the Revised Code, as it exists on and after July 1, 1996, applies to a person upon whom a court imposed a stated prison term for an offense committed on or after July 1, 1996.

**HISTORY: 146 v S 2. Eff 7-1-96.**

The effective date is set by section 6 of SB 2.

## § 2967.03 Pardon, commutation, medical release, or reprieve.

The adult parole authority may exercise its functions and duties in relation to the pardon, commutation of sentence, or reprieve of a convict upon direction of the governor or upon its own initiative. It may exercise its functions and duties in relation to the parole of a prisoner who is eligible for parole upon the initiative of the head of the institution in which the prisoner is confined or upon its own initiative. When a prisoner becomes eligible for parole, the head of the institution in which the prisoner is confined shall notify the authority in the manner prescribed by the authority. The authority may investigate and examine, or cause the investigation and examination of, prisoners confined in state correctional institutions concerning their conduct in the institutions, their mental and moral qualities and characteristics, their knowledge of a trade or profession, their former means of livelihood, their family relationships, and any other matters affecting their fitness to be at liberty without being a threat to society.

The authority may recommend to the governor the pardon, commutation of sentence, medical release, or reprieve of any convict or prisoner or grant a parole to any prisoner for whom parole is authorized, if in its judgment there is reasonable ground to believe that granting a pardon, commutation, medical release, or reprieve to the convict or paroling the prisoner would further the interests of justice and be consistent with the welfare and security of society. However, the authority shall not recommend a pardon, commutation of sentence, or medical release of, or grant a parole to, any convict or prisoner until the authority has complied with the applicable notice requirements of sections 2930.16 and 2967.12 of the Revised Code and until it has considered any statement made by a victim or a victim's representative that is relevant to the convict's or prisoner's case and that was sent to the authority pursuant to section 2930.17 of the Revised Code, any other statement made by a victim or a victim's representative that is relevant to the convict's or prisoner's case and that was received by the authority after it provided notice of the pendency of the action under sections 2930.16 and 2967.12 of the Revised Code, and any written statement of any person submitted to the court pursuant to division (G) of section 2967.12 of the Revised Code. If a victim, victim's representative, or the victim's spouse, parent, sibling, or child appears at a full board hearing of the parole board and gives testimony as authorized by section 5149.101 [5149.10.1] of the Revised Code, the authority shall consider the testimony in determining whether to grant a parole. The trial judge and prosecuting attorney of the trial court in which a person was convicted shall furnish to the authority, at the request of the authority, a summarized statement of the facts proved at the trial and of all other facts having reference to the propriety of recommending a pardon, commutation, or medical release, or granting a parole, together with a recommendation for or against a pardon, commutation, medical release, or parole, and the reasons for the recommendation. The trial judge, the prosecuting attorney, specified law enforcement agency members, and a representative of the prisoner may appear at a full board hearing of the parole board and give testimony in regard to the grant of a parole to the prisoner as authorized by section 5149.101 [5149.10.1] of the Revised Code. All state and local officials shall furnish information to the authority, when so requested by it in the performance of its duties.

The adult parole authority shall exercise its functions and duties in relation to the release of prisoners who are serving a stated prison term in accordance with section 2967.28 of the Revised Code.

**HISTORY: 130 v PtII, 151 (Eff 3-18-65); 140 v S 172 (Eff 9-26-84); 142 v S 6 (Eff 6-10-87); 145 v H 571 (Eff 10-6-94); 145 v S 186 (Eff 10-12-94); 146 v S 2. Eff 7-1-96; 150 v H 375, § 1, eff. 4-29-05; 151 v H 15, § 1, eff. 11-23-05; 152 v H 130, § 1, eff. 4-7-09.**

The provisions of § 10 of HB 86 read as follows:

(A) Within ninety days after the effective date of this section, the Department of Rehabilitation and Correction shall thoroughly review the cases of all parole-eligible inmates who are sixty-five years of age or older and who have had a statutory first parole consideration hearing.

(B) Upon completion of the review described in division (A) of this section, the Department shall send a report to the President and Minority Leader of the Senate and to the Speaker and Minority Leader of the House of Representatives that summarizes the findings of its review and that explains why each of those inmates has not been paroled or otherwise released from custody of the Department.

(C) Upon completion of the review described in division (A) of this section, the Chair of the Parole Board shall present to the Board the cases of the inmates described in that division. Upon presentation of the case of an inmate, the Board, by majority vote, may choose to rehear the inmate's case for possible release on parole.

The effective date is set by section 6 of SB 2.

See provisions, § 5 of SB 2 (146 v —), as amended by § 3 of SB 269 (146 v —), following RC § 2929.03.

## § 2967.04 Pardons and commutations; conditions; effect.

(A) A pardon or commutation may be granted upon such conditions precedent or subsequent as the governor may impose, which conditions shall be stated in the warrant. Such pardon or commutation shall not take effect until the conditions so imposed are accepted by the convict or prisoner so pardoned or having his sentence commuted, and his acceptance is indorsed upon the warrant, signed by him, and attested by one witness. Such witness shall go before the clerk of the court of common pleas in whose office the sentence is recorded and prove the signature of the convict. The clerk shall thereupon record the warrant, indorsement, and proof in the journal of the court, which record, or a duly certified transcript thereof, shall be evidence of such pardon or commutation, the conditions thereof, and the acceptance of the conditions.

(B) An unconditional pardon relieves the person to whom it is granted of all disabilities arising out of the conviction or convictions from which it is granted. For purposes of this section, "unconditional pardon" includes a conditional pardon with respect to which all conditions have been performed or have transpired.

**HISTORY: 130 v PtII, 151 (Eff 3-18-65); 134 v H 511. Eff 1-1-74.**

## § 2967.05 Release when inmate is terminally ill, medically incapacitated, or in imminent danger of death.

(A) As used in this section:

(1) "Imminent danger of death" means that the inmate has a medically diagnosable condition that will cause death to occur within a short period of time.

As used in division (A)(1) of this section, "within a short period of time" means generally within six months.

(2)(a) "Medically incapacitated" means any diagnosable medical condition, including mental dementia and severe, permanent medical or cognitive disability, that prevents the inmate from completing activities of daily living without significant assistance, that incapacitates the inmate to the extent that institutional confinement does not offer additional restrictions, that is likely to continue throughout the entire period of parole, and that is unlikely to improve noticeably.

(b) "Medically incapacitated" does not include conditions related solely to mental illness unless the mental illness is accompanied by injury, disease, or organic defect.

(3)(a) "Terminal illness" means a condition that satisfies all of the following criteria:

(i) The condition is irreversible and incurable and is caused by disease, illness, or injury from which the inmate is unlikely to recover.

(ii) In accordance with reasonable medical standards and a reasonable degree of medical certainty, the condition is likely to cause death to the inmate within twelve months.

(iii) Institutional confinement of the inmate does not offer additional protections for public safety or against the inmate's risk to reoffend.

(b) The department of rehabilitation and correction shall adopt rules pursuant to Chapter 119. of the Revised Code to implement the definition of "terminal illness" in division (A)(3)(a) of this section.

(B) Upon the recommendation of the director of rehabilitation and correction, accompanied by a certificate of the attending physician that an inmate is terminally ill, medically incapacitated, or in imminent danger of death, the governor may order the inmate's release as if on parole, reserving the right to return the inmate to the institution pursuant to this section. If, subsequent to the inmate's release, the inmate's health improves so that the inmate is no longer terminally ill, medically incapacitated, or in imminent danger of death, the inmate shall be returned, by order of the governor, to the institution from which the inmate was released. If the inmate violates any rules or conditions applicable to the inmate, the inmate may be returned to an institution under the control of the department of rehabilitation and correction. The governor may direct the adult parole authority to investigate or cause to be investigated the inmate and make a recommendation in the manner set forth in section 2967.03 of the Revised Code. An inmate released under this section shall be subject to supervision by the adult parole authority in accordance with any recommendation of the adult parole authority that is approved by the governor. The adult parole authority shall adopt rules pursuant to section 119.03 of the Revised Code to establish the procedure for medical release of an inmate when an inmate is terminally ill, medically incapacitated, or in imminent danger of death.

(C) No inmate is eligible for release under this section if the inmate is serving a death sentence, a sentence of life without parole, a sentence under Chapter 2971. of the Revised Code for a felony of the first or second degree, a sentence for aggravated murder or murder, or a mandatory prison term for an offense of violence or any specification described in Chapter 2941. of the Revised Code.

**HISTORY: 132 v S 395 (Eff 12-13-67); 139 v S 199 (Eff 7-1-83); 145 v H 571. Eff 10-6-94; 152 v H 130, § 1, eff. 4-7-09.**

**Analogous to former RC § 2967.05 (130 v PtII, 152), repealed 132 v S 395, § 2, eff 12-13-67.**

## § 2967.06 Warrants of pardon and commutation.

Warrants of pardon and commutation shall be issued in triplicate, one to be given to the convict, one to be filed with the clerk of the court of common pleas in whose office the sentence is recorded, and one to be filed with the head of the institution in which the convict was confined, in case he was confined.

All warrants of pardon, whether conditional or otherwise, shall be recorded by said clerk and the officer of the institution with whom such warrants and copies are filed, in a book provided for that purpose, which record shall include the indorsements on such warrants. A copy of such a warrant with all indorsements, certified by said clerk under seal, shall be received in evidence as proof of the facts set forth in such copy with indorsements.

**HISTORY: 130 v PtII, 152. Eff 3-18-65.**

## § 2967.07 Applications for executive pardon, commutation, or reprieve.

All applications for pardon, commutation of sentence, or reprieve shall be made in writing to the adult parole authority. Upon the filing of such application, or when directed by the governor in any case, a thorough investigation into the propriety of granting a pardon, commutation, or reprieve shall be made by the authority, which shall report in writing to the governor a brief statement of the facts in the case, together with the recommendation of the authority for or against the granting of a pardon, commutation, or reprieve, the grounds therefor and the records or minutes relating to the case.

**HISTORY: 130 v PtII, 152. Eff 3-18-65.**

## § 2967.08 Reprieve to a person under sentence of death.

The governor may grant a reprieve for a definite time to a person under sentence of death, with or without notices or application.

**HISTORY: 130 v PtII, 153. Eff 3-18-65.**

## § 2967.09 Warrant of reprieve.

On receiving a warrant of reprieve, the head of the institution, sheriff, or other officer having custody of the person reprieved, shall file it forthwith with the clerk of the court of common pleas in which the sentence is recorded, who shall thereupon record the warrant in the journal of the court.

**HISTORY: 130 v PtII, 153. Eff 3-18-65.**

## § 2967.10 Confinement of prisoner during reprieve.

When the governor directs in a warrant of reprieve that the prisoner be confined in a state correctional institution for the time of the reprieve or any part thereof, the sheriff or other officer having the prisoner in custody shall convey him to the state correctional institution in the manner provided for the conveyance of convicts, and the warden shall receive the prisoner and warrant and proceed as the warrant directs. At the expiration of the time specified in the warrant for the confinement of the prisoner in the state correctional institution, the warden shall deal with him according to the sentence as originally imposed, or as modified by executive clemency as shown by a new warrant of pardon, commutation, or reprieve executed by the governor.

**HISTORY: 130 v PtII, 153 (Eff 3-18-65); 145 v H 571. Eff 10-6-94.**

## § 2967.11 Repealed, 152 v H 130, § 2 [146 v S 2 (Eff 7-1-96); 146 v S 269. Eff 7-1-96]. Eff 4-7-09.

This section concerned bad time added to prison term for violations and the rules infraction board at each institution.

## § 2967.12 Notice of pendency of pardon, commutation, or parole; right to give testimony, present information, or make statement.

(A) Except as provided in division (G) of this section, at least three weeks before the adult parole authority recommends any pardon or commutation of sentence, or grants any parole, the authority shall provide a notice of the pendency of the pardon, commutation, or parole, setting forth the name of the person on whose behalf it is made, the offense of which the person was convicted or to which the person pleaded guilty, the time of conviction or the guilty plea, and the term of the person's sentence, to the prosecuting attorney and the judge of the court of common pleas of the county in which the indictment against the person was found. If there is more than one judge of that court of common pleas, the authority shall provide the notice to the presiding judge. The department of rehabilitation and correction may utilize electronic means to provide this notice. The department of rehabilitation and correction, at the same time that it provides the notice to the prosecuting attorney and judge under this division, also shall post on the database it maintains pursuant to section 5120.66 of the Revised Code the offender's name and all of the information specified in division (A)(1)(c)(iii) of that section.

(B) If a request for notification has been made pursuant to section 2930.16 of the Revised Code, the office of victim services or the adult parole authority also shall provide notice to the victim or the victim's representative at least three weeks prior to recommending any pardon or commutation of sentence for, or granting any parole to, the person. The notice shall include the information required by division (A) of this section and may be provided by telephone or through electronic means. The notice also shall inform the victim or the victim's representative that the victim or representative may send a written statement relative to the victimization and the pending action to the adult parole authority and that, if the authority receives any written statement prior to recommending a pardon or commutation or granting a parole for a person, the authority will consider the statement before it recommends a pardon or commutation or grants a parole. If the person is being considered for parole, the notice shall inform the victim or the victim's representative that a full board hearing of the parole board may be held and that the victim or victim's representative may contact the office of victims' services for further information. If the person being considered for parole was convicted of or pleaded guilty to violating section 2903.01 or 2903.02 of the Revised Code, the notice shall inform the victim of that offense, the victim's representative, or a member of the victim's immediate family that the victim, the victim's representative, and the victim's immediate family have the right to give testimony at a full board hearing of the parole board and that the victim or victim's representative may contact the office of victims' services for further information. As used in this division, "the victim's immediate family" means the mother, father, spouse, sibling, or child of the victim.

(C) When notice of the pendency of any pardon, commutation of sentence, or parole has been provided to a judge or prosecutor or posted on the database as required in division (A) of this section and a hearing on the pardon, commutation, or parole is continued to a date certain, the authority shall provide notice of the further consideration of the pardon, commutation, or parole at least three weeks before the further consideration. The notice of the further consideration shall be provided to the proper judge and prosecuting attorney at least three weeks before the further consideration, and may be provided using electronic means, and, if the initial notice was posted on the database as provided in division (A) of this section, the notice of the further consideration shall be posted on the database at least three weeks before the further consideration. When notice of the pendency of any pardon, commutation, or parole has been given as provided in division (B) of this section and the hearing on it is continued to a date certain, the authority shall give notice of the further consideration to the victim or the victim's representative in accordance with section 2930.03 of the Revised Code.

(D) In case of an application for the pardon or commutation of sentence of a person sentenced to capital punishment, the governor may modify the requirements of notification and publication if there is not sufficient time for compliance with the requirements before the date fixed for the execution of sentence.

(E) If an offender is serving a prison term imposed under division (A)(3), (B)(1)(a), (b), or (c), (B)(2)(a), (b), or (c), or (B)(3)(a), (b), (c), or (d) of section 2971.03 of the Revised Code and if the parole board terminates its control over the offender's service of that term pursuant to section 2971.04 of the Revised Code, the parole board immediately shall provide written notice of its termination of control or the transfer of control to the entities and persons specified in section 2971.04 of the Revised Code.

(F) The failure of the adult parole authority to comply with the notice or posting provisions of division (A), (B), or (C) of this section or the failure of the parole board to comply with the notice provisions of division (E) of this section do not give any rights or any grounds for appeal or post-conviction relief to the person serving the sentence.

(G) Divisions (A), (B), and (C) of this section do not apply to any release of a person that is of the type described in division (B)(2)(b) of section 5120.031 [5120.03.1] of the Revised Code.

(H) In addition to and independent of the right of a victim to make a statement as described in division (A) of this section or pursuant to section 2930.17 of the Revised Code or to otherwise make a statement, the authority for a judge or prosecuting attorney to furnish statements and information, make recommendations, and give testimony as described in division (A) of this section, the right of a prosecuting attorney, judge, or victim to give testimony or submit a statement at a full parole board hearing pursuant to section 5149.101 [5149.10.1] of the Revised Code, and any other right or duty of a person to present information or make a statement, any person may send to the adult parole authority at any time prior to the authority's recommending a pardon or commutation or granting a parole for the offender a written statement relative to the offense and the pending action.

**HISTORY: 130 v PtII, 153 (Eff 3-18-65); 140 v S 172 (Eff 9-26-84); 143 v S 258 (Eff 11-20-90); 145 v S 186 (Eff 10-12-94); 146 v S 2 (Eff 7-1-96); 146 v H 180. Eff 1-1-97; 150 v H 375, § 1, eff. 4-29-05; 151 v H 15, § 1, eff. 11-23-05; 151 v S 260, § 1, eff. 1-2-07; 152 v S 10, § 1, eff. 1-1-08; 152 v H 130, § 1, eff. 4-7-09.**

The effective date is set by § 3 of 152 v S 10.
The effective date is set by section 3 of HB 180.
See provisions, § 5 of SB 2 (146 v —) as amended by § 3 of SB 269 (146 v —) following RC § 2929.03.

## § 2967.121 Notice of scheduled release of certain felons.

(A) Subject to division (C) of this section, at least two weeks before any convict who is serving a sentence for committing a felony of the first, second, or third degree is released from confinement in any state correctional institution pursuant to a pardon, commutation of sentence, parole, or completed prison term, the adult parole authority shall provide notice of the release to the prosecuting attorney of the county in which the indictment of the convict was found.

(B) The notice required by division (A) of this section may be contained in a weekly list of all felons of the first, second, or third degree who are scheduled for release. The notice shall contain all of the following:

(1) The name of the convict being released;

(2) The date of the convict's release;

(3) The offense for the violation of which the convict was convicted and incarcerated;

(4) The date of the convict's conviction pursuant to which the convict was incarcerated;

(5) The sentence imposed for that conviction;

(6) The length of any supervision that the convict will be under;

(7) The name, business address, and business phone number of the convict's supervising officer;

(8) The address at which the convict will reside.

(C)(1) Divisions (A) and (B) of this section do not apply to the release from confinement of an offender if the offender is serving a prison term imposed under division (A)(3), (B)(1)(a), (b), or (c), (B)(2)(a), (b), or (c), or (B)(3)(a), (b), (c), or (d) of section 2971.03 of the Revised Code, if the court pursuant to section 2971.05 of the

Revised Code modifies the requirement that the offender serve that entire term in a state correctional institution, and if the release from confinement is pursuant to that modification. In a case of that type, the court that modifies the requirement promptly shall provide written notice of the modification and the order that modifies the requirement or revises the modification to the offender, the department of rehabilitation and correction, the prosecuting attorney, and any state agency or political subdivision that is affected by the order.

(2) Divisions (A) and (B) of this section do not apply to the release from confinement of an offender if, upon admission to the state correctional institution, the offender has less than fourteen days to serve on the sentence.

**HISTORY: 140 v H 399 (Eff 9-26-84); 145 v H 571 (Eff 10-6-94); 146 v S 2 (Eff 7-1-96); 146 H 180 (Eff 1-1-97); 148 v S 107. Eff 3-23-2000; 151 v S 260, § 1, eff. 1-2-07; 152 v S 10, § 1, eff. 1-1-08; 152 v H 130, § 1, eff. 4-7-09.**

The effective date is set by § 3 of 152 v S 10.

See provisions, § 5 of SB 2 (146 v —) as amended by § 3 of SB 269 (146 v —) following RC § 2929.03.

## § 2967.13 Parole eligibility.

(A) Except as provided in division (G) of this section, a prisoner serving a sentence of imprisonment for life for an offense committed on or after July 1, 1996, is not entitled to any earned credit under section 2967.193 [2967.19.3] of the Revised Code and becomes eligible for parole as follows:

(1) If a sentence of imprisonment for life was imposed for the offense of murder, at the expiration of the prisoner's minimum term;

(2) If a sentence of imprisonment for life with parole eligibility after serving twenty years of imprisonment was imposed pursuant to section 2929.022 [2929.02.2] or 2929.03 of the Revised Code, after serving a term of twenty years;

(3) If a sentence of imprisonment for life with parole eligibility after serving twenty-five full years of imprisonment was imposed pursuant to section 2929.022 [2929.02.2] or 2929.03 of the Revised Code, after serving a term of twenty-five full years;

(4) If a sentence of imprisonment for life with parole eligibility after serving thirty full years of imprisonment was imposed pursuant to section 2929.022 [2929.02.2] or 2929.03 of the Revised Code, after serving a term of thirty full years;

(5) If a sentence of imprisonment for life was imposed for rape, after serving a term of ten full years' imprisonment;

(6) If a sentence of imprisonment for life with parole eligibility after serving fifteen years of imprisonment was imposed for a violation of section 2927.24 of the Revised Code, after serving a term of fifteen years.

(B) Except as provided in division (G) of this section, a prisoner serving a sentence of imprisonment for life with parole eligibility after serving twenty years of imprisonment or a sentence of imprisonment for life with parole eligibility after serving twenty-five full years or thirty full years of imprisonment imposed pursuant to section 2929.022 [2929.02.2] or 2929.03 of the Revised Code for an offense committed on or after July 1, 1996, consecutively to any other term of imprisonment, becomes eligible for parole after serving twenty years, twenty full years, or thirty full years, as applicable, as to each such sentence of life imprisonment, which shall not be reduced for earned credits under section 2967.193 [2967.19.3] of the Revised Code, plus the term or terms of the other sentences consecutively imposed or, if one of the other sentences is another type of life sentence with parole eligibility, the number of years before parole eligibility for that sentence.

(C) Except as provided in division (G) of this section, a prisoner serving consecutively two or more sentences in which an indefinite term of imprisonment is imposed becomes eligible for parole upon the expiration of the aggregate of the minimum terms of the sentences.

(D) Except as provided in division (G) of this section, a prisoner serving a term of imprisonment who is described in division (A) of section 2967.021 [2967.02.1] of the Revised Code becomes eligible for parole as described in that division or, if the prisoner is serving a definite term of imprisonment, shall be released as described in that division.

(E) A prisoner serving a sentence of life imprisonment without parole imposed pursuant to section 2907.02 or section 2929.03 or 2929.06 of the Revised Code is not eligible for parole and shall be imprisoned until death.

(F) A prisoner serving a stated prison term shall be released in accordance with section 2967.28 of the Revised Code.

(G) A prisoner serving a prison term or term of life imprisonment without parole imposed pursuant to section 2971.03 of the Revised Code never becomes eligible for parole during that term of imprisonment.

**HISTORY: 134 v H 511 (Eff 1-1-74); 139 v S 1 (Eff 10-19-81); 139 v S 199 (Eff 7-1-83); 139 v H 269 (Eff 7-1-83); 140 v S 210 (Eff 7-1-83); 142 v H 5 (Eff 9-28-87); 142 v H 261 (Eff 11-1-87); 142 v H 708 (Eff 4-19-88); 144 v S 331 (Eff 11-13-92); 145 v H 571 (Eff 10-6-94); 146 v S 2 (Eff 7-1-96); 146 v S 269 (Eff 7-1-96); 146 v H 445 (Eff 9-3-96); 146 v H 180 (Eff 1-1-97); 148 v S 107 (Eff 3-23-2000); 149 v H 485. Eff 6-13-2002.**

The provisions of § 4 of SB 107 (148 v —) read in part as follows:

SECTION 4. * * * Section 2967.13 of the Revised Code is presented in this act as a composite of the section as amended by Am. Sub. H.B. 180, Am. Sub. H.B. 445, and Am. Sub. S.B. 269 of the 121st General Assembly, with the new language of none of the acts shown in capital letters. * * * This is in recognition of the principle stated in division (B) of section 1.52 of the Revised Code that such amendments are to be harmonized where not substantively irreconcilable and constitutes a legislative finding that such is the resulting version in effect prior to the effective date of this act.

See provisions, § 5 of SB 2 (146 v —), as amended by § 3 of SB 269 (146 v —), following RC § 2929.03.

## § 2967.131 Additional conditions of release; searches.

(A) In addition to any other terms and conditions of a conditional pardon or parole, of transitional control, or of another form of authorized release from confinement in a state correctional institution that is granted to an individual and that involves the placement of the individual under the supervision of the adult parole authority, and in addition to any other sanctions of post-release control of a felon imposed under section 2967.28 of the Revised Code, the authority or, in the case of a conditional pardon, the governor shall include in the terms and conditions of the conditional pardon, parole, transitional control, or other form of authorized release or shall include as conditions of the post-release control the conditions that the individual or felon not leave the state without permission of the court or the individual's or felon's parole or probation officer and that the individual or felon abide by the law during the period of the individual's or felon's conditional pardon, parole, transitional control, other form of authorized release, or post-release control.

(B)(1) The department of rehabilitation and correction, as a condition of parole or post-release control, may require that the individual or felon shall not ingest or be injected with a drug of abuse and shall submit to random drug testing as provided in divisions (B)(2), (3), and (4) of this section and that the results of the drug test indicate that the individual or felon did not ingest or was not injected with a drug of abuse.

(2) If the adult parole authority has general control and supervision of an individual or felon who is required to submit to random drug testing as a condition of parole or post-release control under division (B)(1) of this section, the authority may cause the individual or felon to submit to random drug testing performed by a laboratory or entity that has entered into a contract with any of the governmental entities or officers authorized to enter into a contract with that laboratory or entity under section 341.26, 753.33, or 5120.63 of the Revised Code.

(3) If no laboratory or entity described in division (B)(2) of this section has entered into a contract as specified in that division, the adult parole authority shall cause the individual or felon to submit to random drug testing performed by a reputable public laboratory to determine whether the individual or felon who is the subject of the drug test ingested or was injected with a drug of abuse.

(4) If a laboratory or entity has entered into a contract with a governmental entity or officer as specified in division (B)(2) of this section, the laboratory or entity shall perform the random drug testing under division (B)(2) of this section in accordance with the applicable standards that are included in the terms of that contract. A public laboratory shall perform the random drug tests under division (B)(3) of this section in accordance with the standards set forth in the policies and procedures established by the department of rehabilitation and correction pursuant to section 5120.63 of the Revised Code. An individual or felon who is required under division (B)(1) of this section to submit to random drug testing as a condition of parole or post-release control and whose test results indicate that the individual or felon ingested or was injected with a drug of abuse shall pay the fee for the drug test if the adult parole authority requires payment of a fee. A laboratory or entity that performs the random drug testing on a parolee or releasee under division (B)(2) or (3) of this section shall transmit the results of the drug test to the adult parole authority.

(C) During the period of a conditional pardon or parole, of transitional control, or of another form of authorized release from confinement in a state correctional institution that is granted to an individual and that involves the placement of the individual under the supervision of the adult parole authority, and during a period of post-release control of a felon imposed under section 2967.28 of the Revised Code, authorized field officers of the authority who are engaged within the scope of their supervisory duties or responsibilities may search, with or without a warrant, the person of the individual or felon, the place of residence of the individual or felon, and a motor vehicle, another item of tangible or intangible personal property, or other real property in which the individual or felon has a right, title, or interest or for which the individual or felon has the express or implied permission of a person with a right, title, or interest to use, occupy, or possess, if the field officers have reasonable grounds to believe that the individual or felon has left the state, is not abiding by the law, or otherwise is not complying with the terms and conditions of the individual's or felon's conditional pardon, parole, transitional control, other form of authorized release, or post-release control. The authority shall provide each individual who is granted a conditional pardon or parole, transitional control, or another form of authorized release from confinement in a state correctional institution and each felon who is under post-release control with a written notice that informs the individual or felon that authorized field officers of the authority who are engaged within the scope of their supervisory duties or responsibilities may conduct those types of searches during the period of the conditional pardon, parole, transitional control, other form of authorized release, or post-release control if they have reasonable grounds to believe that the individual or felon has left the state, is not abiding by the law, or otherwise is not complying with the terms and conditions of the individual's or felon's conditional pardon, parole, transitional control, other form of authorized release, or post-release control.

**HISTORY: 146 v H 4 (Eff 11-9-95); 146 v S 269 (Eff 7-1-96); 147 v S 111 (Eff 3-17-98); 148 v S 107 (Eff 3-23-2000); 148 v H 349. Eff 9-22-2000.**

## § 2967.14 Time to be served at halfway house or community residential center; licensing and reimbursement of facilities.

(A) The department of rehabilitation and correction or the adult parole authority may require or allow a parolee, a releasee, or a prisoner otherwise released from a state correctional institution to reside in a halfway house or other suitable community residential center that has been licensed by the division of parole and community services pursuant to division (C) of this section during a part or for the entire period of the offender's or parolee's conditional release or of the releasee's term of post-release control. The court of common pleas that placed an offender under a sanction consisting of a term in a halfway house or in an alternative residential sanction may require the offender to reside in a halfway house or other suitable community residential center that is designated by the court and that has been licensed by the division pursuant to division (C) of this section during a part or for the entire period of the offender's residential sanction.

(B) The division of parole and community services may negotiate and enter into agreements with any public or private agency or a department or political subdivision of the state that operates a halfway house, reentry center, or community residential center that has been licensed by the division pursuant to division (C) of this section. An agreement under this division shall provide for the purchase of beds, shall set limits of supervision and levels of occupancy, and shall determine the scope of services for all eligible offenders, including those subject to a residential sanction, as defined in rules adopted by the director of rehabilitation and correction in accordance with Chapter 119. of the Revised Code, or those released from prison without supervision. The payments for beds and services shall not exceed the total operating costs of the halfway house, reentry center, or community residential center during the term of an agreement. The director of rehabilitation and correction shall adopt rules in accordance with

Chapter 119. of the Revised Code for determining includable and excludable costs and income to be used in computing the agency's average daily per capita costs with its facility at full occupancy.

The department of rehabilitation and correction may use no more than ten per cent of the amount appropriated to the department each fiscal year for the halfway house, reentry center, and community residential center program to pay for contracts for nonresidential services for offenders under the supervision of the adult parole authority. The nonresidential services may include, but are not limited to, treatment for substance abuse, mental health counseling, counseling for sex offenders, and electronic monitoring services.

(C) The division of parole and community services may license a halfway house, reentry center, or community residential center as a suitable facility for the care and treatment of adult offenders, including offenders sentenced under section 2929.16 or 2929.26 of the Revised Code, only if the halfway house, reentry center, or community residential center complies with the standards that the division adopts in accordance with Chapter 119. of the Revised Code for the licensure of halfway houses, reentry centers, and community residential centers. The division shall annually inspect each licensed halfway house, licensed reentry center, and licensed community residential center to determine if it is in compliance with the licensure standards.

**HISTORY: 136 v H 637 (Eff 8-27-76); 139 v H 694 (Eff 11-15-81); 144 v S 331 (Eff 11-13-92); 145 v H 571 (Eff 10-6-94); 146 v S 2 (Eff 7-1-96); 147 v S 111 (Eff 3-17-98); 149 v H 510. Eff 3-31-2003; 150 v S 57, § 1, eff. 1-1-04; 2011 HB 86, § 1, eff. Sept. 30, 2011.**

## § 2967.141 Violation sanction centers.

(A) As used in this section, "alternative residential facility" has the same meaning as in section 2929.01 of the Revised Code.

(B) The department of rehabilitation and correction, through its division of parole and community services, may operate or contract for the operation of one or more violation sanction centers as an alternative residential facility. A violation sanction center operated under authority of this division is not a prison as defined in section 2929.01 of the Revised Code. A violation sanction center operated under authority of this division may be used for either of the following purposes:

(1) Service of the term of a more restrictive post-release control sanction that the parole board, subsequent to a hearing, imposes pursuant to division (F)(2) of section 2967.28 of the Revised Code upon a releasee who has violated a post-release control sanction imposed upon the releasee under that section;

(2) Service of a sanction that the adult parole authority or parole board imposes upon a parolee whom the authority determines to be a parole violator because of a violation of the terms and conditions of the parolee's parole or conditional pardon.

(C) If a violation sanction center is established under the authority of this section, notwithstanding the fact that the center is an alternative residential facility for the purposes described in division (B) of this section, the center shall be used only for the purposes described in that division. A violation sanction center established under the authority of this section is not an alternative residential facility for the purpose of imposing sentence on an offender who is convicted of or pleads guilty to a felony, and a court that is sentencing an offender for a felony pursuant to sections 2929.11 to 2929.19 of the Revised Code shall not sentence the offender to a community residential sanction that requires the offender to serve a term in the center.

(D) If a releasee is ordered to serve a sanction in a violation sanction center, as described in division (B)(1) of this section, all of the following apply:

(1) The releasee shall not be considered to be under a new prison term for a violation of post-release control.

(2) The time the releasee serves in the center shall not count toward, and shall not be considered in determining, the maximum cumulative prison term for all violations that is described in division (F)(3) of section 2967.28 of the Revised Code.

(3) The time the releasee serves in the center shall count as part of, and shall be credited toward, the remaining period of post-release control that is applicable to the releasee.

**HISTORY: 147 v S 111 (Eff 3-17-98); 148 v S 107. Eff 3-23-2000; 152 v H 130, § 1, eff. 4-7-09.**

## § 2967.15 Arrest of parolee or other releasee for violation; hearing; disposition.

(A) If an adult parole authority field officer has reasonable cause to believe that a person who is a parolee or releasee, who is under transitional control, or who is under another form of authorized release and who is under the supervision of the adult parole authority has violated or is violating the condition of a conditional pardon, parole, other form of authorized release, transitional control, or post-release control specified in division (A) of section 2967.131 [2967.13.1] of the Revised Code or any other term or condition of the person's conditional pardon, parole, other form of authorized release, transitional control, or post-release control, the field officer may arrest the person without a warrant or order a peace officer to arrest the person without a warrant. A person so arrested shall be confined in the jail of the county in which the person is arrested or in another facility designated by the chief of the adult parole authority until a determination is made regarding the person's release status. Upon making an arrest under this section, the arresting or supervising adult parole authority field officer promptly shall notify the superintendent of parole supervision or the superintendent's designee, in writing, that the person has been arrested and is in custody and submit an appropriate report of the reason for the arrest.

(B) Except as otherwise provided in this division, prior to the revocation by the adult parole authority of a person's pardon, parole, or other release and prior to the imposition by the parole board or adult parole authority of a new prison term as a post-release control sanction for a person, the adult parole authority shall grant the person a hearing in accordance with rules adopted by the department of rehabilitation and correction under Chapter 119. of the Revised Code. The adult parole authority is not required to grant the person a hearing if the person is convicted of or pleads guilty to an offense that the person committed while released on a pardon, on parole, or another form of release, or on post-release control and upon which the revocation of the person's pardon, parole, other release, or post-release control is based.

If a person who has been pardoned is found to be a violator of the conditions of the parolee's conditional pardon or commutation of sentence, the authority forthwith shall transmit to the governor its recommendation concerning that violation, and the violator shall be retained in custody until the governor issues an order concerning that violation.

If the authority fails to make a determination of the case of a parolee or releasee alleged to be a violator of the terms and conditions of the parolee's or releasee's conditional pardon, parole, other release, or post-release control sanctions within a reasonable time, the parolee or releasee shall be released from custody under the same terms and conditions of the parolee's or releasee's original conditional pardon, parole, other release, or post-release control sanctions.

(C)(1) If a person who is a parolee or releasee, who is under transitional control, or who is under another form of authorized release under the supervision of the adult parole authority absconds from supervision, the supervising adult parole authority field officer shall report that fact to the superintendent of parole supervision, in writing, and the authority shall declare that person to be a violator at large. Upon being advised of the apprehension and availability for return of a violator at large, the superintendent of parole supervision shall determine whether the violator at large should be restored to parole, transitional control, another form of authorized release, or post-release control.

The time between the date on which a person who is a parolee or other releasee is declared to be a violator or violator at large and the date on which that person is returned to custody in this state under the immediate control of the adult parole authority shall not be counted as time served under the sentence imposed on that person or as a part of the term of post-release control.

(2) A person who is under transitional control or who is under any form of authorized release under the supervision of the adult parole authority is considered to be in custody while under the transitional control or on release, and, if the person absconds from supervision, the person may be prosecuted for the offense of escape.

(D) A person who is a parolee or releasee, who is under transitional control, or who is under another form of authorized release under the supervision of the adult parole authority and who has violated a term or condition of the person's conditional pardon, parole, transitional control, other form of authorized release, or post-release control shall be declared to be a violator if the person is committed to a correctional institution outside the state to serve a sentence imposed upon the person by a federal court or a court of another state or if the person otherwise leaves the state.

(E) As used in this section, "peace officer" has the same meaning as in section 2935.01 of the Revised Code.

**HISTORY: 130 v PtII, 154 (Eff 3-18-65); 144 v S 49 (Eff 7-21-92); 145 v H 571 (Eff 10-6-94); 146 v H 117 (Eff 6-30-95); 146 v H 4 (Eff 11-9-95); 146 v S 2 (Eff 7-1-96); 146 v S 269 (Eff 7-1-96); 147 v S 111. Eff 3-17-98; 152 v H 130, § 1, eff. 4-7-09.**

The provisions of § 7(C) of SB 269 (146 v —) read as follows: (C) Section 2967.15 of the Revised Code was amended by Am. Sub. H.B. 117, Sub. H.B. 4, and Am. Sub. S.B. 2 of the 121st General Assembly. Comparison of these amendments in pursuance of section 1.52 of the Revised Code discloses that while certain of the amendments of these acts are reconcilable, certain other of the amendments are substantively irreconcilable. Am. Sub. H.B. 117 was passed on June 28, 1995; Sub. H.B. 4 and Am. Sub. S.B. 2 both were passed on June 29, 1995. Section 2967.15 of the Revised Code is presented in this act as it results from Sub. H.B. 4 and such of the amendments of Am. Sub. H.B. 117 and Am. Sub. S.B. 2 as are not in conflict with the amendments of Sub. H.B. 4. This is in recognition of the principles stated in division (B) of section 1.52 of the Revised Code that amendments are to be harmonized where not substantively irreconcilable, and that where amendments are substantively irreconcilable, the latest amendment is to prevail. This division constitutes a legislative finding that such harmonized and reconciled section was the resulting version in effect prior to the effective date of this act.

## § 2967.16 Final release; restoration of rights and privileges.

(A) Except as provided in division (D) of this section, when a paroled prisoner has faithfully performed the conditions and obligations of the paroled prisoner's parole and has obeyed the rules and regulations adopted by the adult parole authority that apply to the paroled prisoner, the authority upon the recommendation of the superintendent of parole supervision may enter upon its minutes a final release and thereupon shall issue to the paroled prisoner a certificate of final release, but the authority shall not grant a final release earlier than one year after the paroled prisoner is released from the institution on parole, and, in the case of a paroled prisoner whose minimum sentence is life imprisonment, the authority shall not grant a final release earlier than five years after the paroled prisoner is released from the institution on parole.

(B)(1) When a prisoner who has been released under a period of post-release control pursuant to section 2967.28 of the Revised Code has faithfully performed the conditions and obligations of the released prisoner's post-release control sanctions and has obeyed the rules and regulations adopted by the adult parole authority that apply to the released prisoner or has the period of post-release control terminated by a court pursuant to section 2929.141 [2929.14.1] of the Revised Code, the authority, upon the recommendation of the superintendent of parole supervision, may enter upon its minutes a final release and, upon the entry of the final release, shall issue to the released prisoner a certificate of final release. In the case of a prisoner who has been released under a period of post-release control pursuant to division (B) of section 2967.28 of the Revised Code, the authority shall not grant a final release earlier than one year after the released prisoner is released from the institution under a period of post-release control. The authority shall classify the termination of post-release control as favorable or unfavorable depending on the offender's conduct and compliance with the conditions of supervision. In the case of a released prisoner whose sentence is life imprisonment, the authority shall not grant a final release earlier than five years after the released prisoner is released from the institution under a period of post-release control.

(2) The department of rehabilitation and correction, no later than six months after July 8, 2002, shall adopt a rule in accordance with Chapter 119. of the Revised Code that establishes the criteria for the classification of a post-release control termination as "favorable" or "unfavorable."

(C)(1) Except as provided in division (C)(2) of this section, the following prisoners or person shall be restored to the rights and privileges forfeited by a conviction:

(a) A prisoner who has served the entire prison term that comprises or is part of the prisoner's sentence and has not been placed under any post-release control sanctions;

(b) A prisoner who has been granted a final release by the adult parole authority pursuant to division (A) or (B) of this section;

(c) A person who has completed the period of a community control sanction or combination of community control sanctions, as defined in section 2929.01 of the Revised Code, that was imposed by the sentencing court.

(2)(a) As used in division (C)(2)(c) of this section:

(i) "Position of honor, trust, or profit" has the same meaning as in section 2929.192 [2929.19.2] of the Revised Code.

(ii) "Public office" means any elected federal, state, or local government office in this state.

(b) For purposes of division (C)(2)(c) of this section, a violation of section 2923.32 of the Revised Code or any other violation or offense that includes as an element a course of conduct or the occurrence of multiple acts is "committed on or after the effective date of this amendment" if the course of conduct continues, one or more of the multiple acts occurs, or the subject person's accountability for the course of conduct or for one or more of the multiple acts continues, on or after the effective date of this amendment.

(c) Division (C)(1) of this section does not restore a prisoner or person to the privilege of holding a position of honor, trust, or profit if the prisoner or person was convicted of or pleaded guilty to committing on or after the effective date of this amendment any of the following offenses that is a felony:

(i) A violation of section 2921.02, 2921.03, 2921.05, 2921.41, 2921.42, or 2923.32 of the Revised Code;

(ii) A violation of section 2913.42, 2921.04, 2921.11, 2921.12, 2921.31, or 2921.32 of the Revised Code, when the person committed the violation while the person was serving in a public office and the conduct constituting the violation was related to the duties of the person's public office or to the person's actions as a public official holding that public office;

(iii) A violation of an existing or former municipal ordinance or law of this or any other state or the United States that is substantially equivalent to any violation listed in division (C)(2)(c)(i) of this section;

(iv) A violation of an existing or former municipal ordinance or law of this or any other state or the United States that is substantially equivalent to any violation listed in division (C)(2)(c)(ii) of this section, when the person committed the violation while the person was serving in a public office and the conduct constituting the violation was related to the duties of the person's public office or to the person's actions as a public official holding that public office;

(v) A conspiracy to commit, attempt to commit, or complicity in committing any offense listed in division (C)(2)(c)(i) or described in division (C)(2)(c)(iii) of this section;

(vi) A conspiracy to commit, attempt to commit, or complicity in committing any offense listed in division (C)(2)(c)(ii) or described in division (C)(2)(c)(iv) of this section, if the person committed the violation while the person was serving in a public office and the conduct constituting the offense that was the subject of the conspiracy, that would have constituted the offense attempted, or constituting the offense in which the person was complicit was or would have been related to the duties of the person's public office or to the person's actions as a public official holding that public office.

(D) Division (A) of this section does not apply to a prisoner in the shock incarceration program established pursuant to section 5120.031 [5120.03.1] of the Revised Code.

(E) The adult parole authority shall record the final release of a parolee or prisoner in the official minutes of the authority.

**HISTORY: 130 v PtII, 156 (Eff 3-18-65); 131 v 687 (Eff 11-1-65); 145 v H 314 (Eff 9-29-94); 146 v S 2 (Eff 7-1-96); 146 v S 269 (Eff 7-1-96); 148 v S 107 (Eff 3-23-2000); 149 v H 327. Eff 7-8-2002; 152 v S 3, § 1, eff. 5-15-08.**

See provisions, § 5 of SB 2 (146 v —), as amended by section 3 of SB 269 (146 v —), following RC § 2929.03.

## § 2967.17 Parole authority may grant administrative release.

(A) The adult parole authority, in its discretion, may grant an administrative release to any of the following:

(1) A parole violator or release violator serving another felony sentence in a correctional institution within or without this state for the purpose of consolidation of the records or if justice would best be served;

(2) A parole violator at large or release violator at large whose case has been inactive for at least ten years following the date of declaration of the parole violation or the violation of a post-release control sanction;

(3) A parolee taken into custody by the immigration and naturalization service of the United States department of justice and deported from the United States.

(B)(1)(a) As used in divisions (B)(2) and (3) of this section, "position of honor, trust, or profit" has the same meaning as in section 2929.192 [2929.19.2] of the Revised Code.

(b) For purposes of divisions (B)(2) and (3) of this section, a violation of section 2923.32 of the Revised Code or any other violation or offense that includes as an element a course of conduct or the occurrence of multiple acts is "committed on or after the effective date of this amendment" if the course of conduct continues, one or more of the multiple acts occurs, or the subject person's accountability for the course of conduct or for one or more of the multiple acts continues, on or after the effective date of this amendment.

(2) The adult parole authority shall not grant an administrative release except upon the concurrence of a majority of the parole board and approval of the chief of the adult parole authority. An administrative release does not restore for the person to whom it is granted the rights and privileges forfeited by conviction as provided in section 2961.01 of the Revised Code. Any person granted an administrative release under this section may subsequently apply for a commutation of sentence for the purpose of regaining the rights and privileges forfeited by conviction, except that the privilege of circulating or serving as a witness for the signing of any declaration of candidacy and petition, voter registration application, or nominating, initiative, referendum, or recall petition forfeited under section 2961.01 of the Revised Code may not be restored under this section and except that the privilege of holding a position of honor, trust, or profit may not be restored under this section to a person in the circumstances described in division (B)(3) of this section.

(3) The privilege of holding a position of honor, trust, or profit may not be restored under this section to a person who was convicted of or pleaded guilty to committing on or after the effective date of this amendment any violation or offense listed in divisions (C)(2)(c)(i) to (vi) of section 2967.16 of the Revised Code that is a felony.

**HISTORY: 131 v 687 (Eff 10-20-65); 145 v H 571 (Eff 10-6-94); 145 v S 242 (Eff 10-6-94); 146 v S 2. Eff 7-1-96; 151 v H 3, § 1, eff. 5-2-06; 152 v S 3, § 1, eff. 5-15-08.**

The effective date is set by section 6 of SB 2.

See provisions, § 5 of SB 2 (146 v —), as amended by § 3 of SB 269 (146 v —), following RC § 2929.03.

## § 2967.18 Sentence reduction or early release due to overcrowding emergency.

(A) Whenever the director of rehabilitation and correction determines that the total population of the state correctional institutions for males and females, the total population of the state correctional institutions for males, or the total population of the state correctional institutions for females exceeds the capacity of those institutions and that an overcrowding emergency exists, the director shall notify the correctional institution inspection committee of the emergency and provide the committee with information in support of the director's determination. The director shall not notify the committee that an overcrowding emergency exists unless the director determines that no other reasonable method is available to resolve the overcrowding emergency.

(B) On receipt of the notice given pursuant to division (A) of this section, the correctional institution inspection committee promptly shall review the determination of the director of rehabilitation and correction. Notwithstanding any other provision of the Revised Code or the Administrative Code that governs the lengths of criminal sentences, sets forth the time within which a prisoner is eligible for parole or within which a prisoner may apply for release, or regulates the procedure for granting parole or release to prisoners confined in state correctional institutions, the committee may recommend to the governor that the prison terms of eligible male, female, or all prisoners, as determined under division (E) of this section, be reduced by thirty, sixty, or ninety days, in the manner prescribed in that division.

(C) If the correctional institution inspection committee disagrees with the determination of the director of rehabilitation and correction that an overcrowding emergency exists, if the committee finds that an overcrowding emergency exists but does not make a recommendation pursuant to division (B) of this section, or if the committee does not make a finding or a recommendation pursuant to that division within thirty days of receipt of the notice given pursuant to division (A) of this section, the director may recommend to the governor that the action set forth in division (B) of this section be taken.

(D) Upon receipt of a recommendation from the correctional institution inspection committee or the director of rehabilitation and correction made pursuant to this section, the governor may declare in writing that an overcrowding emergency exists in all of the institutions within the control of the department in which men are confined, in which women are confined, or both. The declaration shall state that the adult parole authority shall take the action set forth in division (B) of this section. After the governor makes the declaration, the director shall file a copy of it with the secretary of state, and the copy is a public record.

The department may begin to implement the declaration of the governor made pursuant to this section on the date that it is filed with the secretary of state. The department shall begin to implement the declaration within thirty days after the date of filing. The declaration shall be implemented in accordance with division (E) of this section.

(E)(1) No reduction of sentence pursuant to division (B) of this section shall be granted to any of the following:

(a) A person who is serving a term of imprisonment for aggravated murder, murder, voluntary manslaughter, involuntary manslaughter, felonious assault, kidnapping, rape, aggravated arson, aggravated robbery, or any other offense punishable by life imprisonment or by an indefinite term of a specified number of years to life, or for conspiracy in, complicity in, or attempt to commit any of those offenses;

(b) A person who is serving a term of imprisonment for any felony other than carrying a concealed weapon that was committed while the person had a firearm, as defined in section 2923.11 of the Revised Code, on or about the offender's person or under the offender's control;

(c) A person who is serving a term of imprisonment for a violation of section 2925.03 of the Revised Code;

(d) A person who is serving a term of imprisonment for engaging in a pattern of corrupt activity;

(e) A person who is serving a prison term or term of life imprisonment without parole imposed pursuant to section 2971.03 of the Revised Code;

(f) A person who was denied parole or release pursuant to section 2929.20 of the Revised Code during the term of imprisonment the person currently is serving.

(2) A declaration of the governor that requires the adult parole authority to take the action set forth in division (B) of this section shall be implemented only by reducing the prison terms of prisoners who are not in any of the categories set forth in division (E)(1) of this section, and only by granting reductions of prison terms in the following order:

(a) Under any such declaration, prison terms initially shall be reduced only for persons who are not in any of the categories set forth in division (E)(1) of this section and who are not serving a term of imprisonment for any of the following offenses:

(i) An offense of violence that is a felony of the first, second, or third degree or that, under the law in existence prior to the effective date of this amendment, was an aggravated felony of the first, second, or third degree or a felony of the first or second degree;

(ii) An offense set forth in Chapter 2925. of the Revised Code that is a felony of the first or second degree.

(b) If every person serving a term of imprisonment at the time of the implementation of any such declaration who is in the class of persons eligible for the initial reduction of prison terms, as described in division (E)(2)(a) of this section, has received a total of ninety days of term reduction for each three years of imprisonment actually served, then prison terms may be reduced for all other persons serving a term of imprisonment at that time who are not in any of the categories set forth in division (E)(1) of this section.

(F) An offender who is released from a state correctional institution pursuant to this section is subject to post-release control sanctions imposed by the adult parole authority as if the offender was a prisoner described in division (B) of section 2967.28 of the Revised Code who was being released from imprisonment.

(G) If more than one overcrowding emergency is declared while a prisoner is serving a prison term, the total term reduction for that prisoner as the result of multiple declarations shall not exceed ninety days for each three years of imprisonment actually served.

**HISTORY: 139 v S 199 (Eff 1-5-83); 139 v H 269 (Eff 3-1-83); 142 v H 262 (Eff 10-20-87); 144 v H 298 (Eff 7-26-91); 145 v H 152 (Eff 7-1-93); 145 v H 571 (Eff 10-6-94); 146 v S 2 (Eff 7-1-96); 146 v H 445 (Eff 9-3-96); 146 v H 180. Eff 1-1-97.**

The effective date is set by section 3 of HB 180.

See provisions, § 5 of SB 2 (146 v —) as amended by § 3 of SB 269 (146 v —) following RC § 2929.03.

**Comment, Legislative Service Commission**

Section 2967.18 of the Revised Code is amended by this act [Am. Sub. H.B. 180] and also by Am. Sub. H.B. 445 of the 121st General Assembly. Comparison of these amendments in pursuance of section 1.52 of the Revised Code discloses that they are not irreconcilable so that they are required by that section to be harmonized to give effect to each amendment.

## § 2967.19 Petition by director of rehabilitation and correction to sentencing court to release offender confined in state correctional institution under stated prison term of one year or more.

(A) As used in this section:

(1) "Deadly weapon" and "dangerous ordnance" have the same meanings as in section 2923.11 of the Revised.

(2) "Disqualifying prison term" means any of the following:

(a) A prison term imposed for aggravated murder, murder, voluntary manslaughter, involuntary manslaughter, felonious assault, kidnapping, rape, aggravated arson, aggravated burglary, or aggravated robbery;

(b) A prison term imposed for complicity in, an attempt to commit, or conspiracy to commit any offense listed in division (A)(2)(a) of this section;

(c) A prison term of life imprisonment, including any term of life imprisonment that has parole eligibility;

(d) A prison term imposed for any felony other than carrying a concealed weapon an essential element of which is any conduct or failure to act expressly involving any deadly weapon or dangerous ordnance;

(e) A prison term imposed for any violation of section 2925.03 of the Revised Code that is a felony of the first or second degree;

(f) A prison term imposed for engaging in a pattern of corrupt activity in violation of section 2923.32 of the Revised Code;

(g) A prison term imposed pursuant to section 2971.03 of the Revised Code;

(h) A prison term imposed for any sexually oriented offense.

(3) "Eligible prison term" means any prison term that is not a disqualifying prison term and is not a restricting prison term.

(4) "Restricting prison term" means any of the following:

(a) A mandatory prison term imposed under division (D)(1)(a), (D)(1)(c), (D)(1)(f), (D)(1)(g), (D)(2), or (D)(7) of section 2929.14 of the Revised Code for a specification of the type described in that division;

(b) In the case of an offender who has been sentenced to a mandatory prison term for a specification of the type described in division (A)(4)(a) of this section, the prison term imposed for the felony offense for which the specification was stated at the end of the body of the indictment, count in the indictment, or information charging the offense;

(c) A prison term imposed for trafficking in persons;

(d) A prison term imposed for any offense that is described in division (A)(4)(d)(i) of this section if division (A)(4)(d)(ii) of this section applies to the offender:

(i) The offense is a felony of the first or second degree that is an offense of violence and that is not described in division (A)(2)(a) or (b) of this section, an attempt to commit a felony of the first or second degree that is an offense of violence and that is not described in division (A)(2)(a) or (b) of this section if the attempt is a felony of the first or second degree, or an offense under an existing or former law of this state, another state, or the United States that is or was substantially equivalent to any other offense described in this division.

(ii) The offender previously was convicted of or pleaded guilty to any offense listed in division (A)(2) or (A)(4)(d)(i) of this section.

(5) "Sexually oriented offense" has the same meaning as in section 2950.01 of the Revised Code.

(B) The director of rehabilitation and correction may petition the sentencing court for the release from prison of any offender confined in a state correctional institution under a stated prison term of one year or more who is eligible under division (C) of this section for a release under this section and who has served at least eighty per cent of that stated prison term that remains to be served after the offender becomes eligible as described in that division. If the director wishes to submit a petition for release under this section, the director shall submit the petition not earlier than ninety days prior to the date on which the offender has served eighty per cent of the offender's stated prison term that remains to be served after the offender becomes eligible as described in division (C) of this section. The director's submission of a petition for release under this section constitutes a recommendation by the director that the court strongly consider release of the offender consistent with the purposes and principles of sentencing set forth in sections 2929.11 and 2929.13 of the Revised Code.

(C)(1) An offender serving a stated prison term of one year or more and who has commenced service of that stated prison term becomes eligible for release from prison under this section only as described in this division. An offender serving a stated prison term that includes a disqualifying prison term is not eligible for release from prison under this section. An offender serving a stated prison term that consists solely of one or more restricting prison terms is not eligible for release under this section. An offender serving a stated prison term of one year or more that includes one or more restricting prison terms and one or more eligible prison terms becomes eligible for release under this section after having fully served each restricting prison term. An offender serving a stated prison term that consists solely of one or more eligible prison terms becomes eligible for release under this section upon the offender's commencement of service of that stated prison term. After an offender becomes eligible for release under this section, the director of rehabilitation and correction may petition for the release of the offender under division (C)(2) of this section no earlier than ninety days before the offender has served the portion of the offender's stated prison term specified in that division. For purposes of determining an offender's eligibility for release under this section, if the offender's stated prison term includes consecutive prison terms, any restricting prison terms shall be deemed served prior to any eligible prison terms that run consecutively to the restricting prison terms, and the eligible prison terms are deemed to commence after all of the restricting prison terms have been fully served.

An offender serving a stated prison term one one year or more that includes a mandatory prison term that is not a disqualifying prison term and is not a restricting prison term is not automatically ineligible as a result of the offender's service of that mandatory term for release from prison under this section, and the offender's eligibility for release from prison under this section is determined in accordance with this division.

(2) If an offender confined in a state correctional institution under a stated prison term is eligible for release under this section as described in division (C)(1) of this section, the director of rehabilitation and correction may petition the sentencing court pursuant to division (B) of this section for the release from prison of the offender.

(D) The director shall include with any petition submitted to the sentencing court under this section an institutional summary report that covers the offender's participation while confined in a state correctional institution in school, training, work, treatment, and other rehabilitative activities and any disciplinary action taken against the offender while so confined. The director shall include with the petition a post-release control assessment and placement plan, when relevant, and any other documentation requested by the court, if available.

(E) When the director submits a petition under this section for release of an offender, the department promptly shall provide to the prosecuting attorney of the county in which the offender was indicted a copy of the petition, a copy of the institutional summary report, and any other information provided to the court. The department also promptly shall give notice of the filing of the petition to any victim of the offender or victim's representative of any victim of the offender who is registered with the office of victim's services.

The department also shall post notice of the petition on the database it maintains under section 5120.66 of the Revised Code and include information on where a person may send comments regarding the petition.

(F) Upon receipt of a petition for release of an offender submitted by the director under this section, the court may deny the petition without a hearing. The court shall not grant a petition for release of an offender without a hearing. If a court denies a petition for release of an offender without a hearing, the court may later consider release of that offender on a subsequent petition. The court shall enter its ruling within thirty days after the petition is filed.

(G) If the court grants a hearing on a petition for release of an offender submitted under this section, the court shall notify the head of the state correctional institution in which the offender is confined of the hearing prior to the hearing. If the court makes a journal entry ordering the offender to be conveyed to the hearing, except as otherwise provided in this division, the head of the correctional institution shall deliver the offender to the sheriff of the county in which the hearing is to be held, and the sheriff shall convey the offender to and from the hearing. Upon the court's own motion or the motion of the offender or the prosecuting attorney of the county in which the offender was indicted, the court may permit the offender to appear at the hearing by video conferencing equipment if equipment of that nature is available and compatible.

Upon receipt of notice from a court of a hearing on the release of an offender under this division, the head of the state correctional institution in which the offender is confined immediately shall notify the appropriate person at the department of rehabilitation and correction of the hearing, and the department within twenty-four hours after receipt of the notice shall post on the database it maintains pursuant to section 5120.66 of the Revised Code the offender's name and all of the information specified in division (A)(1)(c)(i) of that section. If the court grants a hearing on a petition for release of an offender under this section, the court promptly shall give notice of the hearing to the prosecuting attorney of the county in which the offender was indicted. Upon receipt of the notice from the court, the prosecuting attorney shall notify pursuant to section 2930.16 of the Revised Code any victim of the offender or the victim's representative of the hearing.

(H) If the court grants a hearing on a petition for release of an offender under this section, at the hearing, the court shall afford the offender and the offender's attorney an opportunity to present written information and, if present, oral information relevant to the motion. The court shall afford a similar opportunity to the prosecuting attorney, victim or victim's representative, as defined in section 2930.01 of the Revised Code, and any other person the court determines is likely to present additional relevant information. If the court pursuant to division (G) of this section permits the offender to appear at the hearing by video conferencing equipment, the offender's opportunity to present oral information shall be as a part of the video conferencing. The court shall consider any statement of a victim made under section 2930.14 or 2930.17 of the Revised Code, any victim impact statement prepared under 2947.051 of the Revised Code, and any report, plan, and other documentation submitted by the director under division (D) of this section. After ruling on the motion, the court shall notify the victim in accordance with sections 2930.03 and 2930.16 of the Revised Code.

(I) If the court grants a petition for release of an offender under this section, it shall order the release of the offender, shall place the offender under one or more appropriate community control sanctions, under appropriate conditions, and under the supervision of the department of probation that serves the court, and shall reserve the right to reimpose the sentence that it reduced and from which the offender was released if the offender violates the sanction. The court shall not make a release under this section effective prior to the date on which the offender has served at least eighty per cent of the offender's stated prison term that remains to be served after the offender becomes eligible as described in division (C) of this section. If the sentence under which the offender is confined in a state correctional institution and from which the offender is being released was imposed for a felony of the first or second degree, the court shall consider ordering that the offender be monitored by means of a global positioning device. If the court reimposes the sentence that it reduced and from which the offender was released and if the violation of the sanction is a new offense, the court may order that the reimposed sentence be served either concurrently with, or consecutive to, any new sentence imposed upon the offender as a result of the violation that is a new offense. The period of all community control sanctions imposed under this division shall not exceed five years. The court, in its discretion, may reduce the period of community control sanctions by the amount of time the offender spent in jail or prison for the offense.

If the court grants a petition for release of an offender under this section, it shall notify the appropriate person at the department of rehabilitation and correction of the release, and the department shall post notice of the release on the database it maintains pursuant to section 5120.66 of the Revised Code.

(J) The department shall adopt under Chapter 119. of the Revised Code any rules necessary to implement this section.

**HISTORY: 2011 HB 86, § 1, eff. Sept. 30, 2011.**

This section established procedure for calculating time off for good behavior.

The effective date is set by section 6 of SB 2.

## § 2967.191 Reduction of prison term for related days of confinement.

The department of rehabilitation and correction shall reduce the stated prison term of a prisoner or, if the prisoner is serving a term for which there is parole eligibility, the minimum and maximum term or the parole eligibility date of the prisoner by the total number of days that the prisoner was confined for any reason arising out of the offense for which the prisoner was convicted and sentenced, including confinement in lieu of bail while awaiting trial, confinement for examination to determine the prisoner's competence to stand trial or sanity, and confinement while awaiting transportation to the place where the prisoner is to serve the prisoner's prison term.

**HISTORY: 131 v 688 (Eff 10-20-65); 134 v H 511 (Eff 3-23-73); 137 v H 565 (Eff 11-1-78); 138 v H 1000 (Eff 4-9-81); 139 v S 199 (Eff 7-1-83); 146 v S 2 (Eff 7-1-96); 146 v S 269 (Eff 7-1-96); 147 v S 111. Eff 3-17-98.**

See provisions, § 5 of SB 2 (146 v —) as amended by § 3 of SB 269 (146 v —) following RC § 2929.03.

## § 2967.192 Repealed, 146 v S 2, § 2 [139 v S 199; 139 v H 269, § 4; 142 v H 261; 145 v H 571]. Eff 7-1-96.

This section described the effect of time of offense on calculation of credit for good behavior.

The effective date is set by section 6 of SB 2.

## § 2967.193 Days of credit may be earned.

(A)(1) Except as provided in division (C) of this section and subject to the maximum aggregate total specified in division (A)(2) of this section, a person confined in a state correctional institution may provisionally earn one day or five days of credit, based on the category set forth in division (D)(1), (2), (3), (4), or (5) of this section in which the person is included, toward satisfaction of the person's stated prison term for each completed month during which the person productively participates in an education program, vocational training, employment in prison industries, treatment for substance abuse, or any other constructive program developed by the department with specific standards for performance by prisoners. Except as provided in division (C) of this section and subject to the maximum aggregate total specified in division (A)(2) of this section, a person so confined who successfully completes two programs or activities of that type may, in addition, provisionally earn up to five days of credit toward satisfaction of the person's stated prison term for the successful completion of the second program or activity. The person shall not be awarded any provisional days of credit for the successful completion of the first program or activity or for the successful completion of any program or activity that is completed after the second program or activity. At the end of each calendar month in which a prisoner productively participates in a program or activity listed in this division or successfully completes a program or activity listed in this division, the department of rehabilitation and correction shall determine and record the total number of days credit that the prisoner provisionally earned in that calendar month. If the prisoner violates prison rules, the department may deny the prisoner a credit that otherwise could have been provisionally awarded to the prisoner or may withdraw one or more credits previously provisionally earned by the prisoner. Days of credit provisionally earned by a prisoner shall be finalized and awarded by the department subject to administrative review by the department of the prisoner's conduct.

(2) The aggregate days of credit provisionally earned by a person for program or activity participation and program and activity completion under this section and the aggregate days of credit finally credited to a person under this section shall not exceed eight per cent of the total number of days in the person's stated prison term.

(B) The department of rehabilitation and correction shall adopt rules that specify the programs or activities for which credit may be earned under this section, the criteria for determining productive participation in, or completion of, the programs or activities and the criteria for awarding credit, including criteria for awarding additional credit for successful program or activity completion, and the criteria for denying or withdrawing previously provisionally earned credit as a result of a violation of prison rules.

(C) No person confined in a state correctional institution to whom any of the following applies shall be awarded any days of credit under division (A) of this section:

(1) The person is serving a prison term that section 2929.13 or section 2929.14 of the Revised Code specifies cannot be reduced pursuant to this section or this Chapter or is serving a sentence for which section 2967.13 or division (B) of section 2929.143 of the Revised Code specifies that the person is not entitled to any earned credit under this section.

(2) The person is sentenced to death or is serving a prison term or a term of life imprisonment for aggravated murder, murder, or a conspiracy or attempt to commit, or complicity in committing, aggravated murder or murder.

(3) The person is serving a sentence of life imprisonment without parole imposed pursuant to section 2929.03 or 2929.06 of the Revised Code, a prison term or a term of life imprisonment without parole imposed pursuant to section 2971.03 of the Revised Code, or a sentence for a sexually oriented offense that was committed on or after the effective date of this amendment.

(D) This division does not apply to a determination of whether a person confined in a state correctional institution may earn any days of credit under division (A) of this section for successful completion of a second program or activity. The determination of whether a person confined in a state correctional institution may earn one day of credit or five days of credit under division (A) of this section for each completed month during which the person productively participates in a program or activity specified under that division shall be made in accordance with the following:

(1) The offender may earn one day of credit under division (A) of this section, except as provided in division (C) of this section, if the most serious offense for which the offender is confined is any of the following that is a felony of the first or second degree:

(a) A violation of division (A) of section 2903.04 or of section 2903.03, 2903.11, 2903.15, 2905.01, 2907.24, 2907.25, 2909.02, 2909.09, 2909.10, 2909.101, 2909.26, 2909.27, 2909.29, 2911.01, 2911.02, 2911.11, 2911.12, 2919.13, 2919.151, 2919.22, 2921.34, 2923.01, 2923.131, 2923.162, 2923.32, 2925.24, or 2927.24 of the Revised Code;

(b) A conspiracy or attempt to commit, or complicity in committing, any other offense for which the maximum penalty is imprisonment for life or any offense listed in division (D)(1)(a) of this section.

(2) The offender may earn one day of credit under division (A) of this section, except as provided in division (C) of this section, if the offender is serving a stated prison term that includes a prison term imposed for a sexually oriented offense that the offender committed prior to the effective date of this amendment.

(3) The offender may earn one day of credit under division (A) of this section, except as provided in division (C) of this section, if the offender is serving a stated prison term that includes a prison term imposed for a felony other than carrying a concealed weapon an essential element of which is any conduct or failure to act expressly involving any deadly weapon or dangerous ordnance.

(4) Except as provided in division (C) of this section, if the most serious offense for which the offender is confined is a felony of the first or second degree and divisions (D)(1), (2), and (3) of this section do not apply to the offender, the offender may earn one day of credit under division (A) of this section if the offender committed that offense prior to the effective date of this amendment, and the offender may earn five days of credit under division (A) of this section if the offender committed that offense on or after the effective date of this amendment.

(5) Except as provided in division (C) of this section, if the most serious offense for which the offender is confined is a felony of the third, fourth, or fifth degree or an unclassified felony and neither division (D)(2) nor (3) of this section applies to the offender, the offender may earn one day of credit under division (A) of this section if the offender committed that offense prior to the effective date of this amendment, and the offender may earn five days of credit under division (A) of this section if the offender committed that offense on or after the effective date of this amendment.

(E) If a court imposes a sentence including a prison term on or after the effective date of this amendment for a felony, and if the court is required to include notice of the type described in division (F)(3) of section 2929.14 of the Revised Code in the offender's sentence, the failure of the court to include the notice does not affect the eligibility of the offender under this section to earn any days of credit as a deduction from the offender's stated prison term or otherwise render any part of this section or any action taken under this section void or voidable and does not constitute grounds for setting aside the offender's conviction or sentence or for granting postconviction relief to the offender.

(F) The department annually shall seek and consider the written feedback of the Ohio prosecuting attorneys association, the Ohio judicial conference, the Ohio public defender, the Ohio association of criminal defense lawyers, and other organizations and associations that have an interest in the operation of the corrections system and the earned credits program under this section as part of its evaluation of the program and in determining whether to modify the program.

(G) As used in this section, "sexually oriented offense" has the same meaning as in section 2950.01 of the Revised Code.

**HISTORY: 142 v H 261 (Eff 11-1-87); 143 v S 258 (Eff 11-20-90); 144 v H 725 (Eff 4-16-93); 145 v H 571 (Eff 10-6-94); 146 v S 2 (Eff 7-1-96); 146 v S 269 (Eff 7-1-96); 146 v H 180. Eff 1-1-97; 2011 HB 86, § 1, eff. Sept. 30, 2011.**

The provisions of § 12 of HB 86 read as follows:

SECTION 12. Section 2967.193 of the Revised Code is presented in this act as a composite of the section as amended by both Am. Sub. S.B. 269 and Am. Sub. H.B. 180 of the 121st General Assembly. The General Assembly, applying the principle stated in division (B) of section 1.52 of the Revised Code that amendments are to be harmonized if reasonably capable of simultaneous operation, finds that the composites are the resulting versions of the sections in effect prior to the effective date of the sections as presented in this act.

The effective date is set by section 3 of HB 180.

See provisions, § 5 of SB 2 (146 v —) as amended by § 3 of SB 269 (146 v —) following RC § 2929.03.

**Comment, Legislative Service Commission**

Section 2967.193 of the Revised Code is amended by this act [Am. Sub. S.B. 269] and also by Am. Sub. H.B. 180 of the 121st General Assembly. Comparison of these amendments in pursuance of section 1.52 of the Revised Code discloses that they are not irreconcilable so that they are required by that section to be harmonized to give effect to each amendment.

## § 2967.20 Repealed, 145 v H 571, § 2 [130 v PtII, 157; 134 v H 494]. Eff 10-6-94.

This section concerned transfer of prisoners.

## § 2967.21 Term of sentence unaffected by transfer.

Any prisoner sentenced or committed to a state correctional institution may be transferred from that institution to another state correctional institution, but the prisoner shall continue to be subject to the same conditions as to the stated prison term, parole, and release as if the prisoner were confined in the institution to which the prisoner originally was sentenced or committed.

**HISTORY: 130 v PtII, 157 (Eff 3-18-65); 145 v H 571 (Eff 10-6-94); 146 v S 2. Eff 7-1-96.**

The effective date is set by section 6 of SB 2.

See provisions, § 5 of SB 2 (146 v —), as amended by § 3 of SB 269 (146 v —), following RC § 2929.03.

## § 2967.22 Involuntary commitment of mentally ill or retarded releasee.

Whenever it is brought to the attention of the adult parole authority or a department of probation that a parolee, person under a community control sanction, person under transitional control, or releasee appears to be a mentally ill person subject to hospitalization by court order, as defined in section 5122.01 of the Revised Code, or a mentally retarded person subject to institutionalization by court order, as defined in section 5123.01 of the

Revised Code, the parole or probation officer, subject to the approval of the chief of the adult parole authority, the designee of the chief of the adult parole authority, or the chief probation officer, may file an affidavit under section 5122.11 or 5123.71 of the Revised Code. A parolee, person under a community control sanction, or releasee who is involuntarily detained under Chapter 5122. or 5123. of the Revised Code shall receive credit against the period of parole or community control or the term of post-release control for the period of involuntary detention.

If a parolee, person under a community control sanction, person under transitional control, or releasee escapes from an institution or facility within the department of mental health or the department of developmental disabilities, the superintendent of the institution immediately shall notify the chief of the adult parole authority or the chief probation officer. Notwithstanding the provisions of section 5122.26 of the Revised Code, the procedure for the apprehension, detention, and return of the parolee, person under a community control sanction, person under transitional control, or releasee is the same as that provided for the apprehension, detention, and return of persons who escape from institutions operated by the department of rehabilitation and correction. If the escaped parolee, person under transitional control, or releasee is not apprehended and returned to the custody of the department of mental health or the department of developmental disabilities within ninety days after the escape, the parolee, person under transitional control, or releasee shall be discharged from the custody of the department of mental health or the department of developmental disabilities and returned to the custody of the department of rehabilitation and correction. If the escaped person under a community control sanction is not apprehended and returned to the custody of the department of mental health or the department of developmental disabilities within ninety days after the escape, the person under a community control sanction shall be discharged from the custody of the department of mental health or the department of developmental disabilities and returned to the custody of the court that sentenced that person.

**HISTORY: 130 v PtII, 157 (Eff 3-18-65); 134 v H 494 (Eff 7-12-72); 137 v H 565 (Eff 11-1-78); 138 v S 52 (Eff 1-9-81); 138 v H 965 (Eff 4-9-81); 143 v H 569 (Eff 7-1-91); 146 v S 2 (Eff 7-1-96); 147 v S 111. Eff 3-17-98; 149 v H 490, § 1, eff. 1-1-04; 153 v S 79, § 1, eff. 10-6-09.**

The effective date is set by section 4 of H.B. 490.

See provisions, § 5 of SB 2 (146 v —), as amended by § 3 of SB 269 (146 v —), following RC § 2929.03.

## § 2967.23 Repealed, 147 v S 111, § 2 [144 v S 331; 145 v H 571; 146 v S 2; 146 v S 269]. Eff 3-17-98.

This section allowed for release of prisoner to halfway house or community-based correctional facility by the department of rehabilitation and correction.

## § 2967.25 Repealed, 146 v S 2, § 2 [130 v PtII, 158; 132 v H 65; 133 v H 1; 134 v H 511]. Eff 7-1-96.

This section determined parole eligibility when serving consecutive sentences.

The effective date is set by section 6 of SB 2.

## § 2967.26 Transitional control program; passes.

(A)(1) The department of rehabilitation and correction, by rule, may establish a transitional control program for the purpose of closely monitoring a prisoner's adjustment to community supervision during the final one hundred eighty days of the prisoner's confinement. If the department establishes a transitional control program under this division, the adult parole authority may transfer eligible prisoners to transitional control status under the program during the final one hundred eighty days of their confinement and under the terms and conditions established by the department, shall provide for the confinement as provided in this division of each eligible prisoner so transferred, and shall supervise each eligible prisoner so transferred in one or more community control sanctions. Each eligible prisoner who is transferred to transitional control status under the program shall be confined in a suitable facility that is licensed pursuant to division (C) of section 2967.14 of the Revised Code, or shall be confined in a residence the department has approved for this purpose and be monitored pursuant to an electronic monitoring device, as defined in section 2929.01 of the Revised Code. If the department establishes a transitional control program under this division, the rules establishing the program shall include criteria that define which prisoners are eligible for the program, criteria that must be satisfied to be approved as a residence that may be used for confinement under the program of a prisoner that is transferred to it and procedures for the department to approve residences that satisfy those criteria, and provisions of the type described in division (C) of this section. At a minimum, the criteria that define which prisoners are eligible for the program shall provide all of the following:

(a) That a prisoner is eligible for the program if the prisoner is serving a prison term or term of imprisonment for an offense committed prior to March 17, 1998, and if, at the time at which eligibility is being determined, the prisoner would have been eligible for a furlough under this section as it existed immediately prior to March 17, 1998, or would have been eligible for conditional release under former section 2967.23 of the Revised Code as that section existed immediately prior to March 17, 1998;

(b) That no prisoner who is serving a mandatory prison term is eligible for the program until after expiration of the mandatory term;

(c) That no prisoner who is serving a prison term or term of life imprisonment without parole imposed pursuant to section 2971.03 of the Revised Code is eligible for the program.

(2) At least three weeks prior to transferring to transitional control under this section a prisoner who is serving a term of imprisonment or prison term for an offense committed on or after July 1, 1996, the adult parole authority shall give notice of the pendency of the transfer to transitional control to the court of common pleas of the county in which the indictment against the prisoner was found and of the fact that the court may disapprove the transfer of the prisoner to transitional control and shall include a report prepared by the head of the state correctional institution in which the prisoner is confined. The head of the state correctional institution in which the prisoner is confined, upon the request of the adult parole authority, shall provide to the authority for inclusion in the notice sent to the court under this division a report on the prisoner's conduct in the institution and in any institution from which the prisoner may have been transferred. The

report shall cover the prisoner's participation in school, vocational training, work, treatment, and other rehabilitative activities and any disciplinary action taken against the prisoner. If the court disapproves of the transfer of the prisoner to transitional control, the court shall notify the authority of the disapproval within thirty days after receipt of the notice. If the court timely disapproves the transfer of the prisoner to transitional control, the authority shall not proceed with the transfer. If the court does not timely disapprove the transfer of the prisoner to transitional control, the authority may transfer the prisoner to transitional control.

(3) If the victim of an offense for which a prisoner was sentenced to a prison term or term of imprisonment has requested notification under section 2930.16 of the Revised Code and has provided the department of rehabilitation and correction with the victim's name and address, the adult parole authority, at least three weeks prior to transferring the prisoner to transitional control pursuant to this section, shall notify the victim of the pendency of the transfer and of the victim's right to submit a statement to the authority regarding the impact of the transfer of the prisoner to transitional control. If the victim subsequently submits a statement of that nature to the authority, the authority shall consider the statement in deciding whether to transfer the prisoner to transitional control.

(4) The department of rehabilitation and correction, at least three weeks prior to transferring a prisoner to transitional control pursuant to this section, shall post on the database it maintains pursuant to section 5120.66 of the Revised Code the prisoner's name and all of the information specified in division (A)(1)(c)(iv) of that section. In addition to and independent of the right of a victim to submit a statement as described in division (A)(3) of this section or to otherwise make a statement and in addition to and independent of any other right or duty of a person to present information or make a statement, any person may send to the adult parole authority at any time prior to the authority's transfer of the prisoner to transitional control a written statement regarding the transfer of the prisoner to transitional control. In addition to the information, reports, and statements it considers under divisions (A)(2) and (3) of this section or that it otherwise considers, the authority shall consider each statement submitted in accordance with this division in deciding whether to transfer the prisoner to transitional control.

(B) Each prisoner transferred to transitional control under this section shall be confined in the manner described in division (A) of this section during any period of time that the prisoner is not actually working at the prisoner's approved employment, engaged in a vocational training or another educational program, engaged in another program designated by the director, or engaged in other activities approved by the department.

(C) The department of rehabilitation and correction shall adopt rules for transferring eligible prisoners to transitional control, supervising and confining prisoners so transferred, administering the transitional control program in accordance with this section, and using the moneys deposited into the transitional control fund established under division (E) of this section.

(D) The department of rehabilitation and correction may adopt rules for the issuance of passes for the limited purposes described in this division to prisoners who are transferred to transitional control under this section. If the department adopts rules of that nature, the rules shall govern the granting of the passes and shall provide for the supervision of prisoners who are temporarily released pursuant to one of those passes. Upon the adoption of rules under this division, the department may issue passes to prisoners who are transferred to transitional control status under this section in accordance with the rules and the provisions of this division. All passes issued under this division shall be for a maximum of forty-eight hours and may be issued only for the following purposes:

(1) To visit a relative in imminent danger of death;

(2) To have a private viewing of the body of a deceased relative;

(3) To visit with family;

(4) To otherwise aid in the rehabilitation of the prisoner.

(E) The adult parole authority may require a prisoner who is transferred to transitional control to pay to the division of parole and community services the reasonable expenses incurred by the division in supervising or confining the prisoner while under transitional control. Inability to pay those reasonable expenses shall not be grounds for refusing to transfer an otherwise eligible prisoner to transitional control. Amounts received by the division of parole and community services under this division shall be deposited into the transitional control fund, which is hereby created in the state treasury and which hereby replaces and succeeds the furlough services fund that formerly existed in the state treasury. All moneys that remain in the furlough services fund on March 17, 1998, shall be transferred on that date to the transitional control fund. The transitional control fund shall be used solely to pay costs related to the operation of the transitional control program established under this section. The director of rehabilitation and correction shall adopt rules in accordance with section 111.15 of the Revised Code for the use of the fund.

(F) A prisoner who violates any rule established by the department of rehabilitation and correction under division (A), (C), or (D) of this section may be transferred to a state correctional institution pursuant to rules adopted under division (A), (C), or (D) of this section, but the prisoner shall receive credit towards completing the prisoner's sentence for the time spent under transitional control.

If a prisoner is transferred to transitional control under this section, upon successful completion of the period of transitional control, the prisoner may be released on parole or under post-release control pursuant to section 2967.13 or 2967.28 of the Revised Code and rules adopted by the department of rehabilitation and correction. If the prisoner is released under post-release control, the duration of the post-release control, the type of post-release control sanctions that may be imposed, the enforcement of the sanctions, and the treatment of prisoners who violate any sanction applicable to the prisoner are governed by section 2967.28 of the Revised Code.

**HISTORY: 134 v H 567 (Eff 3-7-72); 136 v H 637 (Eff 8-27-76); 139 v S 1 (Eff 10-19-81); 139 v H 694 (Eff 11-15-81); 139 v S 199 (Eff 7-1-83); 140 v S 210 (Eff 7-1-83); 142 v S 94 (Eff 7-20-88); 145 v H 152 (Eff 7-1-93); 145 v H 571 (Eff 10-6-94); 145 v S 186 (Eff 10-12-94); 146 v S 2 (Eff 7-1-96); 146 v H 180 (Eff 1-1-97); 147 v S 111 (Eff 3-17-98); 148 v S 107 (Eff 3-23-2000); 149 v H 510. Eff 3-31-2003; 149 v H 490, § 1, eff. 1-1-04; 151 v H 15, § 1, eff. 11-23-05; 152 v H 130, § 1, eff. 4-7-09.**

The provisions of § 3 of 151 v H 15 read as follows:

SECTION 3. Section 2967.26 of the Revised Code is presented in this act as a composite of the section as amended by both Am. Sub. H.B. 490 and Sub. H.B. 510 of the 124th General Assembly. The General Assembly, applying the principle stated in division (B)

of section 1.52 of the Revised Code that amendments are to be harmonized if reasonably capable of simultaneous operation, finds that the composite is the resulting version of the section in effect prior to the effective date of the section as presented in this act.
The effective date is set by section 4 of H.B. 490.

## § 2967.27 Escorted visits.

(A)(1) The department of rehabilitation and correction may grant escorted visits to prisoners confined in any state correctional facility for the limited purpose of visiting a relative in imminent danger of death or having a private viewing of the body of a deceased relative.

(2) Prior to granting any prisoner an escorted visit for the limited purpose of visiting a relative in imminent danger of death or having a private viewing of the body of a deceased relative under this section, the department shall notify its office of victims' services so that the office may provide assistance to any victim or victims of the offense committed by the prisoner and to members of the family of the victim.

(B) The department of rehabilitation and correction shall adopt rules for the granting of escorted visits under this section and for supervising prisoners on an escorted visit.

(C) No prisoner shall be granted an escorted visit under this section if the prisoner is likely to pose a threat to the public safety or has a record of more than two felony commitments (including the present charge), not more than one of which may be for a crime of an assaultive nature.

(D) The procedure for granting an escorted visit under this section is separate from, and independent of, the transitional control program described in section 2967.26 of the Revised Code.

**HISTORY: 135 v H 217 (Eff 9-26-74); 139 v S 1 (Eff 10-19-81); 145 v H 571 (Eff 10-6-94); 145 v S 186 (Eff 10-12-94); 146 v S 2 (Eff 7-1-96); 146 v S 269 (Eff 7-1-96); 146 v H 180 (Eff 1-1-97); 147 v S 111 (Eff 3-17-98); 149 v H 510. Eff 3-31-2003.**

## § 2967.28 Period of post-release control for certain offenders; sanctions; proceedings upon violation.

(A) As used in this section:

(1) "Monitored time" means the monitored time sanction specified in section 2929.17 of the Revised Code.

(2) "Deadly weapon" and "dangerous ordnance" have the same meanings as in section 2923.11 of the Revised Code.

(3) "Felony sex offense" means a violation of a section contained in Chapter 2907. of the Revised Code that is a felony.

(B) Each sentence to a prison term for a felony of the first degree, for a felony of the second degree, for a felony sex offense, or for a felony of the third degree that is not a felony sex offense and in the commission of which the offender caused or threatened to cause physical harm to a person shall include a requirement that the offender be subject to a period of post-release control imposed by the parole board after the offender's release from imprisonment. If a court imposes a sentence including a prison term of a type described in this division on or after July 11, 2006, the failure of a sentencing court to notify the offender pursuant to division (B)(2)(c) of section 2929.19 of the Revised Code of this requirement or to include in the judgment of conviction entered on the journal a statement that the offender's sentence includes this requirement does not negate, limit, or otherwise affect the mandatory period of supervision that is required for the offender under this division. Section 2929.191 of the Revised Code applies if, prior to July 11, 2006, a court imposed a sentence including a prison term of a type described in this division and failed to notify the offender pursuant to division (B)(2)(c) of section 2929.19 of the Revised Code regarding post-release control or to include in the judgment of conviction entered on the journal or in the sentence pursuant to division (D)(1) of section 2929.14 of the Revised Code a statement regarding post-release control. Unless reduced by the parole board pursuant to division (D) of this section when authorized under that division, a period of post-release control required by this division for an offender shall be of one of the following periods:

(1) For a felony of the first degree or for a felony sex offense, five years;

(2) For a felony of the second degree that is not a felony sex offense, three years;

(3) For a felony of the third degree that is not a felony sex offense and in the commission of which the offender caused or threatened physical harm to a person, three years.

(C) Any sentence to a prison term for a felony of the third, fourth, or fifth degree that is not subject to division (B)(1) or (3) of this section shall include a requirement that the offender be subject to a period of post-release control of up to three years after the offender's release from imprisonment, if the parole board, in accordance with division (D) of this section, determines that a period of post-release control is necessary for that offender. Section 2929.191 of the Revised Code applies if, prior to July 11, 2006, a court imposed a sentence including a prison term of a type described in this division and failed to notify the offender pursuant to division (B)(2)(d) of section 2929.19 of the Revised Code regarding post-release control or to include in the judgment of conviction entered on the journal or in the sentence pursuant to division (D)(2) of section 2929.14 of the Revised Code a statement regarding post-release control. Pursuant to an agreement entered into under section 2967.29 of the Revised Code, a court of common pleas or parole board may impose sanctions or conditions on an offender who is placed on post-release control under this division.

(D)(1) Before the prisoner is released from imprisonment, the parole board or, pursuant to an agreement under section 2967.29 of the Revised Code, the court shall impose upon a prisoner described in division (B) of this section, may impose upon a prisoner described in division (C) of this section, and shall impose upon a prisoner described in division (B)(2)(b) of section 5120.031 or in division (B)(1) of section 5120.032 of the Revised Code, one or more post-release control sanctions to apply during the prisoner's period of post-release control. Whenever the board or court imposes one or more post-release control sanctions upon a prisoner, the board or court, in addition to imposing the sanctions, also shall include as a condition of the post-release control that the offender not leave the state without permission of the court or the offender's parole or probation officer and that the offender abide by the law. The board or court may impose any other conditions of release under a post-release control sanction that the board or court considers appropriate, and the conditions of release may include any community residential sanction, community nonresidential sanction, or financial sanction that the sentencing court was authorized to impose pursuant to sections 2929.16, 2929.17, and 2929.18 of the Revised Code. Prior to the release of a prisoner for whom it will impose one or more post-release control sanctions under this division, the parole board or court shall review the prisoner's criminal history, results from the single validated risk assessment tool selected by the department of rehabilitation and correction under section 5120.114 of the Revised Code, all juvenile court adjudications finding the prisoner, while a juvenile, to be a delinquent child, and the record of the prisoner's conduct while imprisoned. The parole board or court shall consider any recommendation regarding post-release control sanctions for the prisoner made by the office of victims' services. After considering those materials, the board or court shall determine, for a prisoner described in division (B) of this section, division (B)(2)(b) of section 5120.031, or division (B)(1) of section 5120.032 of the Revised Code, which post-release control sanction or combination of post-release control sanctions is reasonable under the circumstances or, for a prisoner described in division (C) of this section, whether a post-release control sanction is necessary and, if so, which post-release control sanction or combination of post-release control sanctions is reasonable under the circumstances. In the case of a prisoner convicted of a felony of the fourth or fifth degree other than a felony sex offense, the board or court shall presume that monitored time is the appropriate post-release control sanction unless the board or court determines that a more restrictive sanction is warranted. A post-release control sanction imposed under this division takes effect upon the prisoner's release from imprisonment.

Regardless of whether the prisoner was sentenced to the prison term prior to, on, or after July 11, 2006, prior to the release of a prisoner for whom it will impose one or more post-release control sanctions under this division, the parole board shall notify the prisoner that, if the prisoner violates any sanction so imposed or any condition of post-release control described in division (B) of section 2967.131 of the Revised Code that is imposed on the prisoner, the parole board may impose a prison term of up to one-half of the stated prison term originally imposed upon the prisoner.

(2) If a prisoner who is placed on post-release control under this section is released before the expiration of the prisoner's stated prison term by reason of credit earned under section 2967.193 of the Revised Code and if the prisoner earned sixty or more days of credit, the adult parole authority shall supervise the offender with an active global positioning system device for the first fourteen days after the offender's release from imprisonment. This division does not prohibit or limit the imposition of any post-release control sanction otherwise authorized by this section.

(3) At any time after a prisoner is released from imprisonment and during the period of post-release control applicable to the releasee, the adult parole authority or, pursuant to an agreement under section 2967.29 of the Revised Code, the court may review the releasee's behavior under the post-release control sanctions imposed upon the releasee under this section. The authority or court may determine, based upon the review and in accordance with the standards established under division (E) of this section, that a more restrictive or a less restrictive sanction is appropriate and may impose a different sanction. The authority also may recommend that the parole board or court increase or reduce the duration of the period of post-release control imposed by the court. If the authority recommends that the board or court increase the duration of post-release control, the board or court shall review the releasee's behavior and may increase the duration of the period of post-release control imposed by the court up to eight years. If the authority recommends that the board or court reduce the duration of control for an offense described in division (B) or (C) of this section, the board or court shall review the releasee's behavior and may reduce the duration of the period of control imposed by the court. In no case shall the board or court reduce the duration of the period of control imposed for an offense described in division (B)(1) of this section to a period less than the length of the stated prison term originally imposed, and in no case shall the board or court permit the releasee to leave the state without permission of the court or the releasee's parole or probation officer.

(E) The department of rehabilitation and correction, in accordance with Chapter 119. of the Revised Code, shall adopt rules that do all of the following:

(1) Establish standards for the imposition by the parole board of post-release control sanctions under this section that are consistent with the overriding purposes and sentencing principles set forth in section 2929.11 of the Revised Code and that are appropriate to the needs of releasees;

(2) Establish standards by which the parole board can determine which prisoners described in division (C) of this section should be placed under a period of post-release control;

(3) Establish standards to be used by the parole board in reducing the duration of the period of post-release control imposed by the court when authorized under division (D) of this section, in imposing a more restrictive post-release control sanction than monitored time upon a prisoner convicted of a felony of the fourth or fifth degree other than a felony sex offense, or in imposing a less restrictive control sanction upon a releasee based on the releasee's activities including, but not limited to, remaining free from criminal activity and from the abuse of alcohol or other drugs, successfully participating in approved rehabilitation programs, maintaining employment, and paying restitution to the victim or meeting the terms of other financial sanctions;

(4) Establish standards to be used by the adult parole authority in modifying a releasee's post-release control sanctions pursuant to division (D)(2) of this section;

(5) Establish standards to be used by the adult parole authority or parole board in imposing further sanctions under division (F) of this section on releasees who violate post-release control sanctions, including standards that do the following:

(a) Classify violations according to the degree of seriousness;

(b) Define the circumstances under which formal action by the parole board is warranted;

(c) Govern the use of evidence at violation hearings;

(d) Ensure procedural due process to an alleged violator;

(e) Prescribe nonresidential community control sanctions for most misdemeanor and technical violations;

(f) Provide procedures for the return of a releasee to imprisonment for violations of post-release control.

(F)(1) Whenever the parole board imposes one or more post-release control sanctions upon an offender under this section, the offender upon release from imprisonment shall be under the general jurisdiction of the adult parole authority and generally shall be supervised by the field services section through its staff of parole and field officers as described in section 5149.04 of the Revised Code, as if the offender had been placed on parole. If the offender upon release from imprisonment violates the post-release control sanction or any conditions described in division (A) of section 2967.131 of the Revised Code that are imposed on the offender, the public or private person or entity that operates or administers the sanction or the program or activity that comprises the sanction shall report the violation directly to the adult parole authority or to the officer of the authority who supervises the offender. The authority's officers may treat the offender as if the offender were on parole and in violation of the parole, and otherwise shall comply with this section.

(2) If the adult parole authority or, pursuant to an agreement under section 2967.29 of the Revised Code, the court determines that a releasee has violated a post-release control sanction or any conditions described in division (A) of section 2967.131 of the Revised Code imposed upon the releasee and that a more restrictive sanction is appropriate, the authority or court may impose a more restrictive sanction upon the releasee, in accordance with the standards established under division (E) of this section or in accordance with the agreement made under section 2967.29 of the Revised Code, or may report the violation to the parole board for a hearing pursuant to division (F)(3) of this section. The authority or court may not, pursuant to this division, increase the duration of the releasee's post-release control or impose as a post-release control sanction a residential sanction that includes a prison term, but the authority or court may impose on the releasee any other residential sanction, nonresidential sanction, or financial sanction that the sentencing court was authorized to impose pursuant to sections 2929.16, 2929.17, and 2929.18 of the Revised Code.

(3) The parole board or, pursuant to an agreement under section 2967.29 of the Revised Code, the court may hold a hearing on any alleged violation by a releasee of a post-release control sanction or any conditions described in division (A) of section 2967.131 of the Revised Code that are imposed upon the releasee. If after the hearing the board or court finds that the releasee violated the sanction or condition, the board or court may increase the duration of the releasee's post-release control up to the maximum duration authorized by division (B) or (C) of this section or impose a more restrictive post-release control sanction. When appropriate, the board or court may impose as a post-release control sanction a residential sanction that includes a prison term. The board or court shall consider a prison term as a post-release control sanction imposed for a violation of post-release control when the violation involves a deadly weapon or dangerous ordnance, physical harm or attempted serious physical harm to a person, or sexual misconduct, or when the releasee committed repeated violations of post-release control sanctions. Unless a releasee's stated prison term was reduced pursuant to section 5120.032 of the Revised Code, the period of a prison term that is imposed as a post-release control sanction under this division shall not exceed nine months, and the maximum cumulative prison term for all violations under this division shall not exceed one-half of the stated prison term originally imposed upon the offender as part of this sentence. If a releasee's stated prison term was reduced pursuant to section 5120.032 of the Revised Code, the period of a prison term that is imposed as a post-release control sanction under this division and the maximum cumulative prison term for all violations under this division shall not exceed the period of time not served in prison under the sentence imposed by the court. The period of a prison term that is imposed as a post-release control sanction under this division shall not count as, or be credited toward, the remaining period of post-release control.

If an offender is imprisoned for a felony committed while under post-release control supervision and is again released on post-release control for a period of time determined by division (F)(4)(d) of this section, the maximum cumulative prison term for all violations under this division shall not exceed one-half of the total stated prison terms of the earlier felony, reduced by any prison term administratively imposed by the parole board or court, plus one-half of the total stated prison term of the new felony.

(4) Any period of post-release control shall commence upon an offender's actual release from prison. If an offender is serving an indefinite prison term or a life sentence in addition to a stated prison term, the offender shall serve the period of post-release control in the following manner:

(a) If a period of post-release control is imposed upon the offender and if the offender also is subject to a period of parole under a life sentence or an indefinite sentence, and if the period of post-release control ends prior to the period of parole, the offender shall be supervised on parole. The offender shall receive credit for post-release control supervision during the period of parole. The offender is not eligible for final release under section 2967.16 of the Revised Code until the post-release control period otherwise would have ended.

(b) If a period of post-release control is imposed upon the offender and if the offender also is subject to a period of parole under an indefinite sentence, and if the period of parole ends prior to the period of post-release control, the offender shall be supervised on post-release control. The requirements of parole supervision shall be satisfied during the post-release control period.

(c) If an offender is subject to more than one period of post-release control, the period of post-release control for all of the sentences shall be the period of post-release control that expires last, as determined by the parole board or court. Periods of post-release control shall be served concurrently and shall not be imposed consecutively to each other.

(d) The period of post-release control for a releasee who commits a felony while under post-release control for an earlier felony shall be the longer of the period of post-release control specified for the new felony under division (B) or (C) of this section or the time remaining under the period of post-release control imposed for the earlier felony as determined by the parole board or court.

**HISTORY: 146 v S 2 (Eff 7-1-96); 146 v S 269 (Eff 7-1-96); 147 v S 111 (Eff 3-17-98); 148 v S 107 (Eff 3-23-2000); 149 v H 327 (Eff 7-8-2002); 149 v H 510; Eff 3-31-2003; 151 v H 137, § 1, eff. 7-11-06; 152 v H 130, § 1, eff. 4-7-09; 2011 HB 86, § 1, eff. Sept. 30, 2011.**

See provisions of § 5 of 151 v H 137 following RC § 2929.191. The effective date is set by § 7 of 151 v H 137.

**§ 2967.29 Court, after consultation with county commissioners, may agree to making joint decisions with parole board relating to parole and post-release control.**

(A) A court of common pleas may cooperate with the department of rehabilitation and correction in the supervision of offenders who return to the court's territorial jurisdiction after serving a prison term. The court, after consultation with the board of county commissioners, may enter into an agreement with the department allowing the court and the parole board to make joint decisions relating to parole and post-release control to the extent permitted by section 2967.28 of the Revised Code.

(B) An agreement made under this section shall include at least all of the following:

(1) The categories of offenders with regard to which the court may participate in making decisions;

(2) The process by which the offenders in each category will be identified;

(3) The process by which the court and the parole board will monitor offenders and make recommendations regarding programming while the offenders are in prison;

(4) The process by which the court will participate in setting appropriate sanctions and conditions on offenders who leave prison on post-release control or parole;

(5) The process by which the court may participate in reducing the duration of the period of post-release control;

(6) Guidelines for the supervision of offenders under post-release control or parole supervision;

(7) Guidelines for sanctions for violations of parole or post-release control;

(8) Provisions that take into account the perspective of affected victims.

(C) A court that enters into an agreement under this section shall provide the department of rehabilitation and correction with a presentence investigation upon the offender's admission to prison. The department shall provide the court with a summary of an offender's progress while in prison prior to the release of the offender.

**HISTORY: 152 v H 130, § 1, eff. 4-7-09.**

**§ 2967.31** Repealed, 146 v S 2, § 2 [134 v H 511; 136 v H 1; 139 v S 199; 139 v 432; 145 v H 571]. Eff 7-1-96.

This section set guidelines for shock parole.

The effective date is set by section 6 of SB 2.

# CHAPTER 2969: RECOVERY OF OFFENDER'S PROFITS FUND; CRIME VICTIMS RECOVERY FUND



## § 2969.01 Definitions.

As used in sections 2969.01 to 2969.06 of the Revised Code:

(A) "Offender" means a person who pleads guilty to, is convicted of, or is found not guilty by reason of insanity of an offense in this state or a person against whom a complaint or information has been filed or an indictment has been returned in this state.

(B) "Victim" means a person who suffers personal injury, death, or property loss as a result of any of the following, or the beneficiaries of an action for the wrongful death of any person killed as a result of any of the following:

(1) An offense;

(2) The good faith effort of a person to prevent an offense;

(3) The good faith effort of any person to apprehend a person suspected of engaging in an offense.

(C) "Member of the family of an offender" means an individual who is related by consanguinity or affinity to an offender.

**HISTORY: 140 v S 172 (Eff 9-26-84); 146 v S 91. Eff 11-15-95.**

## § 2969.02 Payment of proceeds of contract with offender or allied person into recovery of offender's profits fund.

(A) Except as provided in section 2969.05 of the Revised Code, a person that enters into a contract with an offender, an agent, assignee, conspirator, or accomplice of an offender, a member of the family of an offender, or an agent or assignee of a member of the family of an offender shall pay the money, and the monetary value of the property other than money, due under the contract to the clerk of the court of claims for deposit in the recovery of offender's profits fund, if the terms of the contract provide for any of the following:

(1) The reenactment or description by the offender or by a member of the family of the offender in any of the following of an offense that the offender committed:

(a) A movie, book, magazine, newspaper, article, or other form of literary expression;

(b) A program on television, radio, or another broadcasting medium;

(c) A play, speech, or another form of live entertainment, instruction, or presentation.

(2) The expression or description of the thoughts, feelings, opinions, or emotions of the offender or of a member of the family of the offender regarding or experienced during the offense in a material, performance, or program described in division (A)(1)(a), (b), or (c) of this section;

(3) The life story or a part of the life story of the offender or of a member of the family of the offender or an interview or a part of an interview with the offender, an agent, assignee, conspirator, or accomplice of the offender, a member of the family of the offender, or an agent or assignee of a member of the family of an offender that is to be used in a material, performance, or program described in division (A)(1)(a), (b), or (c) of this section, if the publication value of the story or interview results in part from the notoriety brought by the commission of an offense.

(B) An offender, an agent, assignee, conspirator, or accomplice of an offender, a member of the family of an offender, or an agent or assignee of a member of the family of an offender who enters into a contract described in division (A) of this section or a person who receives money or property other than money pursuant to a contract of that nature shall pay the money or the monetary value of the property received pursuant to the contract to the clerk of the court of claims for deposit in the recovery of offender's profits fund. If a person receives money or property pursuant to a contract described in division (A) of this section and fails to pay it or its monetary value to the clerk of the court of claims for deposit in the fund as required by this division, the state has a lien upon the money or property and upon property that is purchased or otherwise obtained with the money or property. The attorney general shall enforce the lien in the same manner as a judgment lien may be enforced by a private individual.

(C)(1) A person who fails to pay money or the monetary value of property other than money to the clerk of the court of claims for deposit as required by this section is liable to the state for the money or the monetary value of the property.

(2) If a person who is required by this section to pay money or the monetary value of property other than money to the clerk of the court of claims for deposit in the recovery of offender's profits fund fails to do so, the attorney general shall bring an action to recover the money or the monetary value of the property against the person

who has possession, custody, or control of the money or property or against the person who failed to pay the money or the monetary value of the property to the clerk for deposit in the fund as required by this section. The action shall be brought in the appropriate court. If the court determines in an action brought pursuant to this division that money or the monetary value of property is to be paid to the clerk for deposit in the fund, it shall order that the money be paid to the clerk for deposit in the fund and that the property be sold and the money received from the sale be paid to the clerk for deposit in the fund.

**HISTORY: 140 v S 172 (Eff 9-26-84); 141 v H 201 (Eff 7-1-85); 146 v S 91. Eff 11-15-95.**

## § 2969.03 Declaratory judgment to determine application.

Any person may bring an action for a declaratory judgment to determine if section 2969.02 of the Revised Code applies to a particular contract. The action for a declaratory judgment shall be brought in the Franklin county court of common pleas.

**HISTORY: 140 v S 172. Eff 9-26-84.**

## § 2969.04 Administration and distribution of funds; action by victim.

(A) The clerk of the court of claims shall administer the recovery of offender's profits fund created by section 2969.06 of the Revised Code and shall maintain in the fund in the name of each offender a separate account for money received, or money received from the sale or other disposition of property, pursuant to section 2969.02 or 2969.03 of the Revised Code. The clerk shall distribute the money in each account in accordance with division (C) of this section.

If money is deposited in the fund and maintained in a separate account in the name of an offender and if the offender is found not guilty of all of the charges against the offender in this state, all of the charges against the offender in this state are dismissed, or the offender is found not guilty of some of the charges against the offender in this state and the remaining charges against the offender in this state are dismissed, the clerk shall return all of the money in the separate account plus the interest earned on the money to the persons from whom it was obtained.

(B) Notwithstanding a contrary provision of any section of the Revised Code that deals with the limitation of actions, a victim of an offense committed by an offender in whose name a separate account is maintained in the recovery of offender's profits fund may bring a civil action against the offender or the representatives of the offender, and, if money in the separate account was obtained from a member of the family of the offender or an agent or assignee of a member of the family of the offender, against the family member, agent, or assignee at any time within three years after the establishment of the separate account.

In order to recover from a separate account maintained in the fund in the name of an offender, a victim of that offender shall do all of the following:

(1) Within the three-year period or, if the action was initiated before the separate account was established, within ninety days after the separate account is established, notify the clerk of the court of claims that a civil action has been brought against the offender or the representatives of the offender and, if money in the separate account was obtained from a member of the family of the offender or an agent or assignee of a member of the family of the offender, against the family member, agent, or assignee;

(2) Notify the clerk of the court of claims of the entry of any judgment in the civil action;

(3) Within ninety days after the judgment in the civil action is final or, if the judgment was obtained before the separate account was established, within ninety days after the separate account is established, request the clerk of the court of claims to pay from the separate account the judgment that the victim is awarded in the civil action.

If a civil action is brought against an offender or the representatives of the offender and, if money in the separate account was obtained from a member of the family of the offender or an agent or assignee of a member of the family of the offender, against the family member, agent, or assignee and if the civil action is brought after the expiration of the statute of limitations that would apply to the civil action but for this division, the court shall state in a judgment in favor of the victim that the judgment may be enforced only against the separate account maintained in the name of that offender in the recovery of offender's profits fund.

(C)(1) The clerk of the court of claims shall not make a payment from the separate account maintained in the name of an offender in the recovery of offender's profits fund to a victim of the offender until the expiration of the later of the following periods:

(a) The expiration of three years after the establishment of the separate account, provided that no action of which the clerk was notified under division (B)(1) of this section is pending;

(b) If three years has elapsed since the establishment of the separate account and if one or more actions of which the clerk was notified under division (B)(1) of this section is pending at the expiration of that three-year period, the date of the final disposition of the last of those pending actions.

(2) Upon the expiration of the applicable period of time set forth in division (C)(1) of this section, the clerk of the court of claims shall make payments from the separate account maintained in the name of an offender in the recovery of offender's profits fund to any victim of the offender who has obtained a judgment against the offender or the representatives of the offender and, if money in the separate account was obtained from a member of the family of the offender or an agent or assignee of a member of the family of the offender, against the family member, agent, or assignee for damages resulting from an offense committed by the offender. The payments shall be made as provided in this division.

After an offender in whose name a separate account is maintained in the recovery of offender's profits fund is convicted of or found not guilty by reason of insanity of any offense in this state, the clerk of the court of claims shall determine on the second day of January and the first day of April, July, and October of each year the amount of money in that separate account. After the expiration of the applicable period of time set forth in division (C)(1) of this section, the clerk shall pay from that separate account any judgment for which a victim of that offender has requested payment pursuant to division (B)(3) of this section and has requested payment prior to the date of the most recent quarterly determination described in this division. If, at a time that payments would be made from that separate account, there are insufficient funds in that separate account to pay all of the applicable judgments against the offender or the representatives of the offender and, if money in the separate account was obtained from a member of the family of the offender or an agent or asignee† of a member of the family of the offender, against the family member, agent, or assignee, the clerk of the court of claims shall pay the judgments on a pro rata basis.

**HISTORY: 140 v S 172 (Eff 9-26-84); 141 v H 201 (Eff 7-1-85); 146 v S 91. Eff 11-15-95.**

† As enrolled, subsection (C)(2), 146 v S 91.

## § 2969.05 Payment of unexpended funds to person from whom obtained.

If a separate account has been maintained in the recovery of offender's profits fund and if there is no further requirement to pay money or the monetary value of property into the fund pursuant to section 2969.02 of the Revised Code, unless otherwise ordered by a court of record in which a judgment has been rendered against the offender or the representatives of the offender and, if money in the separate account was obtained from a member of the family of the offender or an agent or assignee of a member of the family of the offender, against the family member, agent, or assignee, the clerk of the court of claims shall pay the money remaining in the separate account to the persons from whom the money was obtained, if all of the following apply:

(A) The applicable period of time that governs the making of payments from the separate account, as set forth in division (C)(1) of section 2969.04 of the Revised Code, has elapsed.

(B) None of the civil actions against the offender or the representatives of the offender and, if money in the separate account was obtained from a member of the family of the offender or an agent or assignee of a member of the family of the offender, against the family member, agent, or assignee of which the clerk of the court of claims has been notified pursuant to division (B)(1) of section 2969.04 of the Revised Code is pending.

(C) All judgments for which payment was requested pursuant to division (B)(3) of section 2969.04 of the Revised Code have been paid.

**HISTORY: 140 v S 172 (Eff 9-26-84); 141 v H 201 (Eff 7-1-85); 146 v S 91. Eff 11-15-95.**

## § 2969.06 Recovery of offender's profits fund.

All moneys collected pursuant to sections 2969.02 and 2969.03 of the Revised Code shall be credited by the treasurer of state to the recovery of offender's profits fund, which is hereby created in the state treasury. Except as provided in division (A) of section 2969.04 of the Revised Code, any interest earned on the money in the fund shall be credited to the fund.

**HISTORY: 140 v S 172 (Eff 9-26-84); 141 v H 201. Eff 7-1-85.**

[CRIME VICTIMS RECOVERY FUND]

## § 2969.11 Definitions.

As used in sections 2969.11 to 2969.14 of the Revised Code:

(A) "Crime victims recovery fund" means the fund created by division (D) of section 2929.32 of the Revised Code.

(B) "Victim" means a person who suffers personal injury, death, or property loss as a result of any of the following, or the beneficiaries of an action for the wrongful death of any person killed as a result of any of the following:

(1) An offense committed by an offender in whose name a separate account is maintained in the crime victims recovery fund pursuant to section 2969.12 of the Revised Code;

(2) The good faith effort of a person to prevent an offense committed by an offender in whose name a separate account is maintained in the crime victims recovery fund pursuant to section 2969.12 of the Revised Code;

(3) The good faith effort of a person to apprehend a person suspected of engaging in an offense committed by an offender in whose name a separate account is maintained in the crime victims recovery fund pursuant to section 2969.12 of the Revised Code.

**HISTORY: 146 v S 91. Eff 11-15-95; 149 v H 490, § 1, eff. 1-1-04.**

The effective date is set by section 4 of H.B. 490.

## § 2969.12 Administration and distribution of crime victims recovery fund.

(A) The clerk of the court of claims shall administer the crime victims recovery fund and shall maintain in the fund in the name of each offender a separate account for money received, or money received from the sale or other disposition of property, pursuant to section 2929.32 of the Revised Code in connection with that offender. The clerk shall distribute the money in that separate account in accordance with division (C) of this section.

(B) Notwithstanding a contrary provision of any section of the Revised Code that deals with the limitation of actions, a victim of an offense committed by an offender in whose name a separate account is maintained in the crime victims recovery fund may bring a civil action against the offender or the representatives of the offender at any time within three years after the establishment of the separate account.

In order to recover from a separate account maintained in the fund in the name of an offender, a victim of that offender shall do all of the following:

(1) Within the three-year period or, if the action was initiated before the separate account was established, within ninety days after the separate account is established, notify the clerk of the court of claims that a civil action has been brought against the offender or the representatives of the offender;

(2) Notify the clerk of the court of claims of the entry of any judgment in the civil action;

(3) Within ninety days after the judgment in the civil action is final or, if the judgment was obtained before the separate account was established, within ninety days after the separate account is established, request the clerk of the court of claims to pay from the separate account the judgment that the victim is awarded in the civil action.

If a civil action is brought against an offender or the representatives of the offender after the expiration of the statute of limitations that would apply to the civil action but for this division, the court shall state in a judgment in favor of the victim that the judgment may be enforced only against the separate account maintained in the name of that offender in the crime victims recovery fund.

(C)(1) The clerk of the court of claims shall not make a payment from the separate account maintained in the name of an offender in the crime victims recovery fund to a victim of the offender until the expiration of the later of the following periods:

(a) The expiration of three years after the establishment of the separate account, provided that no action of which the clerk was notified under division (B) (1) of this section is pending;

(b) If three years has elapsed since the establishment of the separate account and if one or more actions of which the clerk was notified under division (B) (1) of this section is pending at the expiration of that three-year period, the date of the final disposition of the last of those pending actions.

(2) Upon the expiration of the applicable period of time set forth in division (C) (1) of this section, the clerk of the court of claims shall make payments from the separate account maintained in the name of the offender in the crime victims recovery fund to the victims of the offender who obtained a judgment against the offender or the representatives of the offender for damages resulting from the offense committed by the offender. The payments shall be made as provided in this division.

When a separate account is maintained in the name of an offender in the crime victims recovery fund, the clerk of the court of claims shall determine on the second day of January and the first day of April, July, and October of each year the amount of money in that separate account. After the expiration of the applicable period of time set forth in division (C) (1) of this section, the clerk shall pay from that separate account any judgment for which a victim of that offender has requested payment pursuant to division (B) (3) of this section and has requested payment prior to the date of the most recent quarterly determination described in this division. If at a time that payments would be made from that separate account there are insufficient funds in that separate account to pay all of the applicable judgments against the offender or the representatives of the offender, the clerk of the court of claims shall pay the judgments on a pro rata basis.

**HISTORY: 146 v S 91. Eff 11-15-95; 149 v H 490, § 1, eff. 1-1-04.**

The effective date is set by section 4 of H.B. 490.

## § 2969.13 Crediting of moneys collected and interest to fund.

All moneys that are collected pursuant to section 2929.32 of the Revised Code and required to be deposited in the crime victims recovery fund shall be credited by the treasurer of state to the fund. Any interest earned on the money in the fund shall be credited to the fund.

**HISTORY: 146 v S 91. Eff 11-15-95; 149 v H 490, § 1, eff. 1-1-04.**

The effective date is set by section 4 of H.B. 490.

## § 2969.14 Payment of cost of confinement from unexpended funds; disposition of residue.

(A) If a separate account has been maintained in the name of an offender in the crime victims recovery fund and if there is no further requirement to pay into the fund money, or the monetary value of property, pursuant to section 2929.32 of the Revised Code, unless otherwise ordered by a court of record in which a judgment has been rendered against the offender or the representatives of the offender, the clerk of the court of claims shall pay the money remaining in the separate account in accordance with division (B) of this section, if all of the following apply:

(1) The applicable period of time that governs the making of payments from the separate account, as set forth in division (C) (1) of section 2969.12 of the Revised Code, has elapsed.

(2) None of the civil actions against the offender or the representatives of the offender of which the clerk of the court of claims has been notified pursuant to division (B) (1) of section 2969.12 of the Revised Code is pending.

(3) All judgments for which payment was requested pursuant to division (B) (3) of section 2969.12 of the Revised Code have been paid.

(B) If the clerk of the court of claims is required by division (A) of this section to pay the money remaining in the separate account established in the name of an offender in accordance with this division, the clerk shall pay the money as follows:

(1) If the offender was confined for a felony in a prison or other facility operated by the department of rehabilitation and correction under a sanction imposed pursuant to section 2929.14 or 2929.16 of the Revised Code, the clerk shall pay the money to the treasurer of state, in accordance with division (C) (1) of section 2929.18 of the Revised Code, to cover the costs of the confinement. If any money remains in the separate account after the payment of the costs of the confinement pursuant to this division, the clerk shall pay the remaining money in accordance with divisions (B) (2), (3), and (5) of this section.

(2) If the offender was confined for a felony in a facility operated by a county or a municipal corporation, after payment of any costs required to be paid under division (B) (1) of this section, the clerk shall pay the money to the treasurer of the county or of the municipal corporation that operated the facility, in accordance with division (C) (2) or (3) of section 2929.18 of the Revised Code, to cover the costs of the confinement. If more than one county or municipal corporation operated a facility in which the offender was confined, the clerk shall equitably apportion the money among each of those counties and municipal corporations. If any money remains in the separate account after the payment of the costs of the confinement pursuant to this division, the clerk shall pay the remaining money in accordance with divisions (B) (3) and (5) of this section.

(3) If the offender was sentenced for a felony to any community control sanction other than a sanction described in division (B) (2) of this section, after payment of any costs required to be paid under division (B) (1) or (2) of this section, the clerk shall pay the money to the treasurer of the county or of the municipal corporation that incurred costs pursuant to the sanction, in accordance with division (C) (2) or (3) of section 2929.18 of the Revised Code, to cover the costs so incurred. If more than one county or municipal corporation incurred costs pursuant to the sanction, the clerk shall equitably apportion the money among each of those counties and municipal corporations. If any money remains in the separate account after the payment of the costs of the sanction pursuant to this division, the clerk shall pay the remaining money in accordance with division (B) (5) of this section.

(4) If the offender was imprisoned or incarcerated for a misdemeanor, to the treasurer of the political subdivision that operates the facility in which the offender was imprisoned or incarcerated, to cover the costs of the imprisonment or incarceration. If more than one political subdivision operated a facility in which the offender was confined, the clerk shall equitably apportion the money among each of those political subdivisions. If any money remains in the separate account after the payment of the costs of the imprisonment or incarceration under this division, the clerk shall pay the remaining money in accordance with division (B) (5) of this section.

(5) If any money remains in the separate account after payment of any costs required to be paid under division (B) (1), (2), (3), or (4) of this section, or if no provision of division (B) (1), (2), (3), or (4) of this section applies, the clerk shall distribute the amount of the money remaining in the separate account as otherwise provided by law for the distribution of money paid in satisfaction of a fine, as if that amount was a fine paid by the offender.

**HISTORY: 146 v S 91. Eff 11-15-95; 149 v H 490, § 1, eff. 1-1-04.**

The effective date is set by section 4 of H.B. 490.

## [CIVIL ACTIONS BY INMATE AGAINST GOVERNMENTAL ENTITY OR EMPLOYEE]

### § 2969.21 Definitions.

As used in sections 2969.21 to 2969.27 of the Revised Code:

(A) "Clerk" means the elected or appointed clerk of any court in this state, except the court of claims or the supreme court, in which an inmate has commenced a civil action against a government entity or employee or has filed an appeal of the judgment or order in a civil action of that nature.

(B)(1) "Civil action or appeal against a government entity or employee" means any of the following:

(a) A civil action that an inmate commences against the state, a political subdivision, or an employee of the state or a political subdivision in a court of common pleas, court of appeals, county court, or municipal court;

(b) An appeal of the judgment or order in a civil action of the type described in division (B)(1)(a) of this section that an inmate files in a court of appeals.

(2) "Civil action or appeal against a governmental entity or employee" does not include any civil action that an inmate commences against the state, a political subdivision, or an employee of the state or a political subdivision in the court of claims or the supreme court or an appeal of the judgment or order entered by the court of claims in a civil action of that nature, that an inmate files in a court of appeals or the supreme court.

(C) "Employee" means an officer or employee of the state or of a political subdivision who is acting under color of state law.

(D) "Inmate" means a person who is in actual confinement in a state correctional institution or in a county, multicounty, municipal, municipal-county, or multicounty-municipal jail or workhouse or a releasee who is serving a sanction in a violation sanction center.

(E) "Inmate account" means an account maintained by the department of rehabilitation and correction under rules adopted by the director of rehabilitation and correction pursuant to section 5120.01 of the Revised Code or a similar account maintained by a sheriff or any other administrator of a jail or workhouse or by the administrator of a violation sanction center.

(F) "Political subdivision" means a county, township, city, or village; the office of an elected officer of a county, township, city, or village; or a department, board, office, commission, agency, institution, or other instrumentality of a county, township, city, or village.

(G) "State" has the same meaning as in section 2743.01 of the Revised Code.

(H) "State correctional institution" has the same meaning as in section 2967.01 of the Revised Code.

(I) "Violation sanction center" means an alternative residential facility that houses releasees who have violated a post-release control sanction or the terms and conditions of parole or of a conditional pardon and that is operated pursuant to section 2967.141 [2967.14.1] of the Revised Code.

**HISTORY: 146 v H 455 (Eff 10-17-96); 147 v S 111 (Eff 3-17-98); 149 v S 168. Eff 6-28-2002.**

### § 2969.22 Deductions from inmate account and procedure when inmate sues governmental entity or employee.

(A)(1) Whenever an inmate commences a civil action or appeal against a government entity or employee on or after October 17, 1996, all of the following apply:

(a) The clerk of the court in which the civil action or appeal is filed shall notify the inmate and either the department of rehabilitation and correction, the sheriff or other administrator of the jail or workhouse, or the administrator of the violation sanction center, whichever has physical custody of the inmate, of the deductions and procedures required by divisions (A) to (D) of this section, and shall identify in the notice the civil action or appeal by case name, case number, name of each party, and the court in which the civil action or appeal was brought.

(b) The clerk of the court in which the civil action or appeal is filed shall charge to the inmate either the total payment of the requisite fees that are described in section 2303.20 of the Revised Code or that otherwise are applicable to actions or appeals filed in that court or, if the inmate has submitted an affidavit of indigency, all funds in the inmate account of that inmate in excess of ten dollars, and shall notify the inmate of the charge.

(c) Unless the amount charged under division (A)(1)(b) of this section constitutes the total amount of the requisite fees, all income in the inmate account of the inmate shall be forwarded to the clerk of the court during each calendar month following the month in which the inmate filed the civil action or appeal until the total payment of the requisite fees occurs. The first ten dollars in the inmate account of the inmate each month shall be excluded from that forwarding requirement. If multiple charges are assessed to an inmate account under this division, charges shall be calculated on the basis of the inmate's total income and shall be paid as described in this division until the charges exceed one hundred per cent of nonexcluded funds in the inmate account; thereafter, all unpaid fees shall be paid simultaneously from the inmate account of the inmate to the appropriate court or courts pro rata.

(d) Upon receipt of the notice of the requisite fees payable pursuant to divisions (A)(1)(a) to (c) of this section, the department, sheriff or other administrator of the jail or workhouse, or the administrator of the violation sanction center shall deduct from the inmate account of the inmate and transmit to the clerk of the appropriate court the appropriate amounts of the requisite fees as described in divisions (A)(1)(b) and (c) of this section.

(2) The procedures described in this section apply notwithstanding any contrary court rule or the filing of a poverty affidavit.

(3) This section does not limit the clerk of a court of common pleas, court of appeals, county court, or municipal court from considering any other inmate resources separate and apart from an inmate account of an inmate in evaluating the inmate's ability to pay court costs, fees, awards, or other amounts.

(B) An inmate who commences a civil action or appeal against a governmental entity or employee on or after October 17, 1996, shall be considered to have authorized payment as the plaintiff in the civil action or the appellant in the appeal of the requisite fees that are described in section 2303.20 of the Revised Code or that otherwise are applicable to actions or appeals filed in the court in which the action or appeal is filed, using the procedures set forth in this section, until total payment of the requisite fees.

(C)(1) If an inmate files a civil action or appeal against a government entity or employee on or after October 17, 1996, upon the termination of the civil action or appeal, the clerk of the court in which the action or appeal was filed shall notify the department of rehabilitation and correction, the sheriff or other administrator of the jail or workhouse, or the administrator of the violation sanction center of the outcome of the civil action or appeal and shall identify the civil action or appeal by case name, case number, name of each party, and the court in which the civil action or appeal was brought.

(2) The department of rehabilitation and correction, the sheriff or other administrator of a jail or workhouse, or the administrator of the violation sanction center shall keep in the inmate's file a record of the information supplied by the clerk of the appropriate court under division (C)(1) of this section.

(D) If an inmate is to be released from confinement prior to the total payment of the requisite fees as provided in divisions (A) and (B) of this section, the department of rehabilitation and correction, the sheriff or other administrator of the jail or workhouse, or the administrator of the violation sanction center, whichever has physical custody of the inmate, shall inform the clerk of the court of common pleas, court of appeals, county court, or municipal court of the release. The department, sheriff or other administrator of the jail or workhouse, or administrator of the violation sanction center shall deduct from the inmate account of the inmate in the month of the inmate's release from custody an amount sufficient to pay the remainder of the requisite fees owed and transmit that amount to the clerk. If there are insufficient funds in the inmate account of the inmate to totally pay the requisite fees, the department, sheriff or other administrator of the jail or workhouse, or administrator of the violation sanction center shall deduct the balance of the account and transmit that amount to the clerk. The clerk shall inform the court of the amount of the requisite fees still owed.

**HISTORY: 146 v H 455 (Eff 10-17-96); 147 v S 111 (Eff 3-17-98); 149 v S 168. Eff 6-28-2002.**

## § 2969.23 Clerk to collect fees and expenses from inmate.

If an inmate files a civil action or appeal against a government entity or employee on or after the effective date of this section and if the inmate is ordered to pay court costs, an award of reasonable attorney's fees, or any other fees or expenses the clerk of the court in which the action or appeal is filed shall collect the court costs, reasonable attorney's fees, and other fees or expenses from the inmate using the procedures set forth in section 2969.22 of the Revised Code regarding the collection of fees.

**HISTORY: 146 v H 455. Eff 10-17-96.**

## § 2969.24 Grounds for dismissal of inmate's action or appeal; hearing.

(A) If an inmate files a civil action or appeal against a government entity or employee, the court in which the action or appeal is filed, on its own motion or on the motion of a party, may dismiss the civil action or appeal at any stage in the proceedings if the court finds any of the following:

(1) The allegation of indigency in a poverty affidavit filed by the inmate is false.

(2) The claim that is the basis of the civil action or the issues of law that are the basis of the appeal are frivolous or malicious.

(3) The inmate filed an affidavit required by section 2969.25 or 2969.26 of the Revised Code that was materially false.

(B) For the purposes of this section, in determining whether a claim that is the basis of the civil action or the issues of law that are the basis of the appeal are frivolous or malicious, the court may consider whether any of the following applies:

(1) The claim fails to state a claim or the issues of law fail to state any issues of law.

(2) The claim has no arguable basis in law or fact or the issues of law have no arguable basis in law.

(3) It is clear that the inmate cannot prove material facts in support of the claim or in support of the issues of law.

(4) The claim that is the basis of the civil action is substantially similar to a claim in a previous civil action filed by the inmate or the issues of law that are the basis of the appeal are substantially similar to issues of law raised in a previous appeal filed by the inmate, in that the claim that is the basis of the current civil action or the issues of law that are the basis of the current appeal involve the same parties or arise from the same operative facts as the claim or issues of law in the previous civil action or appeal.

(C) If a party files a motion requesting the dismissal of a civil action or appeal under division (A) of this section, the court shall hold a hearing on the motion. If the court raises the issue of the dismissal of a civil action or appeal under division (A) of this section by its own motion, the court may hold a hearing on the motion. If practicable, the court may hold the hearing described in this division by telephone or, in the alternative, at the state correctional institution, jail, workhouse, or violation sanction center in which the inmate is confined.

(D) On the filing of a motion for dismissal of a civil action under division (A) of this section, the court may suspend discovery relating to the civil action pending the determination of the motion.

(E) Divisions (A) to (D) of this section do not limit the authority of the court in which the civil action or appeal is filed to otherwise dismiss the civil action or appeal.

**HISTORY: 146 v H 455 (Eff 10-17-96); 147 v S 111. Eff 3-17-98.**

### § 2969.25 Inmate's affidavit as to prior actions; review of multiple actions; waiver of prepayment.

(A) At the time that an inmate commences a civil action or appeal against a government entity or employee, the inmate shall file with the court an affidavit that contains a description of each civil action or appeal of a civil action that the inmate has filed in the previous five years in any state or federal court. The affidavit shall include all of the following for each of those civil actions or appeals:

(1) A brief description of the nature of the civil action or appeal;

(2) The case name, case number, and the court in which the civil action or appeal was brought;

(3) The name of each party to the civil action or appeal;

(4) The outcome of the civil action or appeal, including whether the court dismissed the civil action or appeal as frivolous or malicious under state or federal law or rule of court, whether the court made an award against the inmate or the inmate's counsel of record for frivolous conduct under section 2323.51 of the Revised Code, another statute, or a rule of court, and, if the court so dismissed the action or appeal or made an award of that nature, the date of the final order affirming the dismissal or award.

(B) If an inmate who files a civil action in a court of common pleas, court of appeals, county court, or municipal court or an inmate who files an appeal from a judgment or order in a civil action in any of those courts has filed three or more civil actions or appeals of civil actions in a court of record in this state in the preceding twelve months or previously has been subject to the review procedure described in this division, the court may appoint a member of the bar to review the claim that is the basis of the civil action or the issues of law that are the basis of the appeal and to make a recommendation regarding whether the claim asserted in the action or the issues of law raised in the appeal are frivolous or malicious under section 2969.24 of the Revised Code, any other provision of law, or rule of court.

(C) If an inmate who files a civil action or appeal against a government entity or employee seeks a waiver of the prepayment of the full filing fees assessed by the court in which the action or appeal is filed, the inmate shall file with the complaint or notice of appeal an affidavit that the inmate is seeking a waiver of the prepayment of the court's full filing fees and an affidavit of indigency. The affidavit of waiver and the affidavit of indigency shall contain all of the following:

(1) A statement that sets forth the balance in the inmate account of the inmate for each of the preceding six months, as certified by the institutional cashier;

(2) A statement that sets forth all other cash and things of value owned by the inmate at that time.

**HISTORY: 146 v H 455 (Eff 10-17-96); 149 v S 168. Eff 6-28-2002.**

### § 2969.26 Claims subject to grievance system.

(A) If an inmate commences a civil action or appeal against a government entity or employee and if the inmate's claim in the civil action or the inmate's claim in the civil action that is being appealed is subject to the grievance system for the state correctional institution, jail, workhouse, or violation sanction center in which the inmate is confined, the inmate shall file both of the following with the court:

(1) An affidavit stating that the grievance was filed and the date on which the inmate received the decision regarding the grievance.

(2) A copy of any written decision regarding the grievance from the grievance system.

(B) If the civil action or appeal is commenced before the grievance system process is complete, the court shall stay the civil action or appeal for a period not to exceed one hundred eighty days to permit the completion of the grievance system process.

**HISTORY: 146 v H 455 (Eff 10-17-96); 147 v S 111. Eff 3-17-98.**

### § 2969.27 Deductions from judgment awarded to inmate.

If an inmate commences a civil action or appeal against a government entity or employee and is granted a judgment for damages in the civil action or appeal, the court shall order that the following be deducted and paid from the award on a pro rata basis before any payment is made to the inmate or the inmate's counsel:

(A) Any fine, court costs, or court-ordered restitution imposed upon the inmate for an offense for which the inmate is confined or for any previous offense committed by the inmate;

(B) The amount of an award of reparations made under sections 2743.51 to 2743.71 of the Revised Code to a victim of the inmate relative to the offense for which the inmate is confined or any previous offense committed by the inmate;

(C) Any other award ordered by a court against the inmate in any other criminal or civil action or proceeding in any court in this state.

**HISTORY: 146 v H 455. Eff 10-17-96.**

# CHAPTER 2971: SENTENCING OF SEXUALLY VIOLENT PREDATORS



## § 2971.01 Definitions.

As used in this chapter:

(A) "Mandatory prison term" has the same meaning as in section 2929.01 of the Revised Code.

(B) "Designated homicide, assault, or kidnapping offense" means any of the following:

(1) A violation of section 2903.01, 2903.02, 2903.11, or 2905.01 of the Revised Code or a violation of division (A) of section 2903.04 of the Revised Code;

(2) An attempt to commit or complicity in committing a violation listed in division (B)(1) of this section, if the attempt or complicity is a felony.

(C) "Examiner" has the same meaning as in section 2945.371 [2945.37.1] of the Revised Code.

(D) "Peace officer" has the same meaning as in section 2935.01 of the Revised Code.

(E) "Prosecuting attorney" means the prosecuting attorney who prosecuted the case of the offender in question or the successor in office to that prosecuting attorney.

(F) "Sexually oriented offense" and "child-victim oriented offense" have the same meanings as in section 2950.01 of the Revised Code.

(G) "Sexually violent offense" means any of the following:

(1) A violent sex offense;

(2) A designated homicide, assault, or kidnapping offense that the offender commits with a sexual motivation.

(H)(1) "Sexually violent predator" means a person who, on or after January 1, 1997, commits a sexually violent offense and is likely to engage in the future in one or more sexually violent offenses.

(2) For purposes of division (H)(1) of this section, any of the following factors may be considered as evidence tending to indicate that there is a likelihood that the person will engage in the future in one or more sexually violent offenses:

(a) The person has been convicted two or more times, in separate criminal actions, of a sexually oriented offense or a child-victim oriented offense. For purposes of this division, convictions that result from or are connected with the same act or result from offenses committed at the same time are one conviction, and a conviction set aside pursuant to law is not a conviction.

(b) The person has a documented history from childhood, into the juvenile developmental years, that exhibits sexually deviant behavior.

(c) Available information or evidence suggests that the person chronically commits offenses with a sexual motivation.

(d) The person has committed one or more offenses in which the person has tortured or engaged in ritualistic acts with one or more victims.

(e) The person has committed one or more offenses in which one or more victims were physically harmed to the degree that the particular victim's life was in jeopardy.

(f) Any other relevant evidence.

(I) "Sexually violent predator specification" means a specification, as described in section 2941.148 [2941.14.8] of the Revised Code, that charges that a person charged with a violent sex offense, or a person charged with a designated homicide, assault, or kidnapping offense and a sexual motivation specification, is a sexually violent predator.

(J) "Sexual motivation" means a purpose to gratify the sexual needs or desires of the offender.

(K) "Sexual motivation specification" means a specification, as described in section 2941.147 [2941.14.7] of the Revised Code, that charges that a person charged with a designated homicide, assault, or kidnapping offense committed the offense with a sexual motivation.

(L) "Violent sex offense" means any of the following:

(1) A violation of section 2907.02, 2907.03, or 2907.12† or of division (A)(4) or (B) of section 2907.05 of the Revised Code;

(2) A felony violation of a former law of this state that is substantially equivalent to a violation listed in division (L)(1) of this section or of an existing or former law of the United States or of another state that is substantially equivalent to a violation listed in division (L)(1) of this section;

(3) An attempt to commit or complicity in committing a violation listed in division (L)(1) or (2) of this section if the attempt or complicity is a felony.

**HISTORY: 146 v H 180. Eff 1-1-97; 150 v S 5, § 1, eff. 7-31-03; 150 v H 473, § 1, eff. 4-29-05; 152 v S 10, § 1, eff. 1-1-08.**

The effective date is set by § 3 of 152 v S 10.

The effective date is set by section 3 of HB 180.

† Division (L)(1), RC § 2907.12 repealed 9-3-96, but see RC § 2907.01(A).

## § 2971.02 Determination of sexually violent predator specification by court or by jury.

In any case in which a sexually violent predator specification is included in the indictment, count in the indictment, or information charging a violent sex offense or a designated homicide, assault, or kidnapping offense and in which the defendant is tried by a jury, the defendant may elect to have the court instead of the jury determine the sexually violent predator specification.

If the defendant does not elect to have the court determine the sexually violent predator specification, the defendant shall be tried before the jury on the charge of the offense and, if the offense is a designated homicide, assault, or kidnapping offense, on the sexual motivation specification that is included in the indictment, count in the indictment, or information charging the offense. Following a verdict of guilty on the charge of the offense and, if the offense is a designated homicide, assault, or kidnapping offense, on the related sexual motivation specification, the defendant shall be tried before the jury on the sexually violent predator specification.

If the defendant elects to have the court determine the sexually violent predator specification, the defendant shall be tried before the jury on the charge of the offense and, if the offense is a designated homicide, assault, or kidnapping offense, on the sexual motivation specification that is included in the indictment, count in the indictment, or information charging the offense. Following a verdict of guilty on the charge of the offense and, if the offense if a designated homicide, assault, or kidnapping offense, on the related sexual motivation specification, the court shall conduct a proceeding at which it shall determine the sexually violent predator specification.

**HISTORY: 146 v H 180. Eff 1-1-97; 150 v H 473, § 1, eff. 4-29-05.**

The effective date is set by section 3 of HB 180.

See provisions, § 4 of HB 180 (146 v —) following RC § 2921.34.

## § 2971.03 Sentencing of sexually violent offender with predator specification.

(A) Notwithstanding divisions (A) and (D) of section 2929.14, section 2929.02, 2929.03, 2929.06, 2929.13, or another section of the Revised Code, other than divisions (B) and (C) of section 2929.14 of the Revised Code, that authorizes or requires a specified prison term or a mandatory prison term for a person who is convicted of or pleads guilty to a felony or that specifies the manner and place of service of a prison term or term of imprisonment, the court shall impose a sentence upon a person who is convicted of or pleads guilty to a violent sex offense and who also is convicted of or pleads guilty to a sexually violent predator specification that was included in the indictment, count in the indictment, or information charging that offense, and upon a person who is convicted of or pleads guilty to a designated homicide, assault, or kidnapping offense and also is convicted of or pleads guilty to both a sexual motivation specification and a sexually violent predator specification that were included in the indictment, count in the indictment, or information charging that offense, as follows:

(1) If the offense for which the sentence is being imposed is aggravated murder and if the court does not impose upon the offender a sentence of death, it shall impose upon the offender a term of life imprisonment without parole. If the court sentences the offender to death and the sentence of death is vacated, overturned, or otherwise set aside, the court shall impose upon the offender a term of life imprisonment without parole.

(2) If the offense for which the sentence is being imposed is murder; or if the offense is rape committed in violation of division (A)(1)(b) of section 2907.02 of the Revised Code when the offender purposely compelled the victim to submit by force or threat of force, when the victim was less than ten years of age, when the offender previously has been convicted of or pleaded guilty to either rape committed in violation of that division or a violation of an existing or former law of this state, another state, or the United States that is substantially similar to division (A)(1)(b) of section 2907.02 of the Revised Code, or when the offender during or immediately after the commission of the rape caused serious physical harm to the victim; or if the offense is an offense other than aggravated murder or murder for which a term of life imprisonment may be imposed, it shall impose upon the offender a term of life imprisonment without parole.

(3)(a) Except as otherwise provided in division (A)(3)(b), (c), (d), or (e) or (A)(4) of this section, if the offense for which the sentence is being imposed is an offense other than aggravated murder, murder, or rape and other than an offense for which a term of life imprisonment may be imposed, it shall impose an indefinite prison term consisting of a minimum term fixed by the court from among the range of terms available as a definite term for the offense, but not less than two years, and a maximum term of life imprisonment.

(b) Except as otherwise provided in division (A)(4) of this section, if the offense for which the sentence is being imposed is kidnapping that is a felony of the first degree, it shall impose an indefinite prison term as follows:

(i) If the kidnapping is committed on or after January 1, 2008, and the victim of the offense is less than thirteen years of age, except as otherwise provided in this division, it shall impose an indefinite prison term consisting of a minimum term of fifteen years and a maximum term of life imprisonment. If the kidnapping is committed on or after January 1, 2008, the victim of the offense is less than thirteen years of age, and the offender released the victim in a safe place unharmed, it shall impose an indefinite prison term consisting of a minimum term of ten years and a maximum term of life imprisonment.

(ii) If the kidnapping is committed prior to January 1, 2008, or division (A)(3)(b)(i) of this section does not apply, it shall impose an indefinite term consisting of a minimum term fixed by the court that is not less than ten years and a maximum term of life imprisonment.

(c) Except as otherwise provided in division (A)(4) of this section, if the offense for which the sentence is being imposed is kidnapping that is a felony of the second degree, it shall impose an indefinite prison term consisting of a minimum term fixed by the court that is not less than eight years, and a maximum term of life imprisonment.

(d) Except as otherwise provided in division (A)(4) of this section, if the offense for which the sentence is being imposed is rape for which a term of life imprisonment is not imposed under division (A)(2) of this section or division (B) of section 2907.02 of the Revised Code, it shall impose an indefinite prison term as follows:

(i) If the rape is committed on or after January 2, 2007, in violation of division (A)(1)(b) of section 2907.02 of the Revised Code, it shall impose an indefinite prison term consisting of a minimum term of twenty-five years and a maximum term of life imprisonment.

(ii) If the rape is committed prior to January 2, 2007, or the rape is committed on or after January 2, 2007, other than in violation of division (A)(1)(b) of section 2907.02 of the Revised Code, it shall impose an indefinite prison term consisting of a minimum term fixed by the court that is not less than ten years, and a maximum term of life imprisonment.

(e) Except as otherwise provided in division (A)(4) of this section, if the offense for which sentence is being imposed is attempted rape, it shall impose an indefinite prison term as follows:

(i) Except as otherwise provided in division (A)(3)(e)(ii), (iii), or (iv) of this section, it shall impose an indefinite prison term pursuant to division (A)(3)(a) of this section.

(ii) If the attempted rape for which sentence is being imposed was committed on or after January 2, 2007, and if the offender also is convicted of or pleads guilty to a specification of the type described in section 2941.1418 of the Revised Code, it shall impose an indefinite prison term consisting of a minimum term of five years and a maximum term of twenty-five years.

(iii) If the attempted rape for which sentence is being imposed was committed on or after January 2, 2007, and if the offender also is convicted of or pleads guilty to a specification of the type described in section 2941.1419 of the Revised Code, it shall impose an indefinite prison term consisting of a minimum term of ten years and a maximum of life imprisonment.

(iv) If the attempted rape for which sentence is being imposed was committed on or after January 2, 2007, and if the offender also is convicted of or pleads guilty to a specification of the type described in section 2941.1420 of the Revised Code, it shall impose an indefinite prison term consisting of a minimum term of fifteen years and a maximum of life imprisonment.

(4) For any offense for which the sentence is being imposed, if the offender previously has been convicted of or pleaded guilty to a violent sex offense and also to a sexually violent predator specification that was included in the indictment, count in the indictment, or information charging that offense, or previously has been convicted of or pleaded guilty to a designated homicide, assault, or kidnapping offense and also to both a sexual motivation specification and a sexually violent predator specification that were included in the indictment, count in the indictment, or information charging that offense, it shall impose upon the offender a term of life imprisonment without parole.

(B)(1) Notwithstanding section 2929.13, division (A) or (D) of section 2929.14, or another section of the Revised Code other than division (B) of section 2907.02 or divisions (B) and (C) of section 2929.14 of the Revised Code that authorizes or requires a specified prison term or a mandatory prison term for a person who is convicted of or pleads guilty to a felony or that specifies the manner and place of service of a prison term or term of imprisonment, if a person is convicted of or pleads guilty to a violation of division (A)(1)(b) of section 2907.02 of the Revised Code committed on or after January 2, 2007, if division (A) of this section does not apply regarding the person, and if the court does not impose a sentence of life without parole when authorized pursuant to division (B) of section 2907.02 of the Revised Code, the court shall impose upon the person an indefinite prison term consisting of one of the following:

(a) Except as otherwise required in division (B)(1)(b) or (c) of this section, a minimum term of ten years and a maximum term of life imprisonment.

(b) If the victim was less than ten years of age, a minimum term of fifteen years and a maximum of life imprisonment.

(c) If the offender purposely compels the victim to submit by force or threat of force, or if the offender previously has been convicted of or pleaded guilty to violating division (A)(1)(b) of section 2907.02 of the Revised Code or to violating an existing or former law of this state, another state, or the United States that is substantially similar to division (A)(1)(b) of that section, or if the offender during or immediately after the commission of the offense caused serious physical harm to the victim, a minimum term of twenty-five years and a maximum of life imprisonment.

(2) Notwithstanding section 2929.13, division (A) or (D) of section 2929.14, or another section of the Revised Code other than divisions (B) and (C) of section 2929.14 of the Revised Code that authorizes or requires a specified prison term or a mandatory prison term for a person who is convicted of or pleads guilty to a felony or that specifies the manner and place of service of a prison term or term of imprisonment and except as otherwise provided in division (B) of section 2907.02 of the Revised Code, if a person is convicted of or pleads guilty to attempted rape committed on or after January 2, 2007, and if division (A) of this section does not apply regarding the person, the court shall impose upon the person an indefinite prison term consisting of one of the following:

(a) If the person also is convicted of or pleads guilty to a specification of the type described in section 2941.1418 of the Revised Code, the court shall impose upon the person an indefinite prison term consisting of a minimum term of five years and a maximum term of twenty-five years.

(b) If the person also is convicted of or pleads guilty to a specification of the type described in section 2941.1419 of the Revised Code, the court shall impose upon the person an indefinite prison term consisting of a minimum term of ten years and a maximum term of life imprisonment.

(c) If the person also is convicted of or pleads guilty to a specification of the type described in section 2941.1420 of the Revised Code, the court shall impose upon the person an indefinite prison term consisting of a minimum term of fifteen years and a maximum term of life imprisonment.

(3) Notwithstanding section 2929.13, division (A) or (D) of section 2929.14, or another section of the Revised Code other than divisions (B) and (C) of section 2929.14 of the Revised Code that authorizes or requires a specified prison term or a mandatory prison term for a person who is convicted of or pleads guilty to a felony or that specifies the manner and place of service of a prison term or term of imprisonment, if a person is convicted of or pleads guilty to an offense described in division (B)(3)(a), (b), (c), or (d) of this section committed on or after January 1, 2008, if the person also is convicted of or pleads guilty to a sexual motivation specification that was included in the indictment, count in the indictment, or information charging that offense, and if division (A) of this section does not apply regarding the person, the court shall impose upon the person an indefinite prison term consisting of one of the following:

(a) An indefinite prison term consisting of a minimum of ten years and a maximum term of life imprisonment if the offense for which the sentence is being imposed is kidnapping, the victim of the offense is less than thirteen years of age, and the offender released the victim in a safe place unharmed;

(b) An indefinite prison term consisting of a minimum of fifteen years and a maximum term of life imprisonment if the offense for which the sentence is being imposed is kidnapping when the victim of the offense is less than thirteen years of age and division (B)(3)(a) of this section does not apply;

(c) An indefinite term consisting of a minimum of thirty years and a maximum term of life imprisonment if the offense for which the sentence is being imposed is aggravated murder, when the victim of the offense is less than thirteen years of age, a sentence of death or life imprisonment without parole is not imposed for the offense, and division (A)(2)(b)(ii) of section 2929.022, division (A)(1)(e), (C)(1)(a)(v), (C)(2)(a)(ii), (D)(2)(b), (D)(3)(a)(iv), or (E)(1)(d) of section 2929.03, or division (A) or (B) of section 2929.06 of the Revised Code requires that the sentence for the offense be imposed pursuant to this division;

(d) An indefinite prison term consisting of a minimum of thirty years and a maximum term of life imprisonment if the offense for which the sentence is being imposed is murder when the victim of the offense is less than thirteen years of age.

(C)(1) If the offender is sentenced to a prison term pursuant to division (A)(3), (B)(1)(a), (b), or (c), (B)(2)(a), (b), or (c), or (B)(3)(a), (b), (c), or (d) of this section, the parole board shall have control over the offender's service of the term during the entire term unless the parole board terminates its control in accordance with section 2971.04 of the Revised Code.

(2) Except as provided in division (C)(3) of this section, an offender sentenced to a prison term or term of life imprisonment without parole pursuant to division (A) of this section shall serve the entire prison term or term of life imprisonment in a state correctional institution. The offender is not eligible for judicial release under section 2929.20 of the Revised Code.

(3) For a prison term imposed pursuant to division (A)(3), (B)(1)(a), (b), or (c), (B)(2)(a), (b), or (c), or (B)(3)(a), (b), (c), or (d) of this section, the court, in accordance with section 2971.05 of the Revised Code, may terminate the prison term or modify the requirement that the offender serve the entire term in a state correctional institution if all of the following apply:

(a) The offender has served at least the minimum term imposed as part of that prison term.

(b) The parole board, pursuant to section 2971.04 of the Revised Code, has terminated its control over the offender's service of that prison term.

(c) The court has held a hearing and found, by clear and convincing evidence, one of the following:

(i) In the case of termination of the prison term, that the offender is unlikely to commit a sexually violent offense in the future;

(ii) In the case of modification of the requirement, that the offender does not represent a substantial risk of physical harm to others.

(4) An offender who has been sentenced to a term of life imprisonment without parole pursuant to division (A)(1), (2), or (4) of this section shall not be released from the term of life imprisonment or be permitted to serve a portion of it in a place other than a state correctional institution.

(D) If a court sentences an offender to a prison term or term of life imprisonment without parole pursuant to division (A) of this section and the court also imposes on the offender one or more additional prison terms pursuant to division (B) of section 2929.14 of the Revised Code, all of the additional prison terms shall be served consecutively with, and prior to, the prison term or term of life imprisonment without parole imposed upon the offender pursuant to division (A) of this section.

(E) If the offender is convicted of or pleads guilty to two or more offenses for which a prison term or term of life imprisonment without parole is required to be imposed pursuant to division (A) of this section, divisions (A) to (D) of this section shall be applied for each offense. All minimum terms imposed upon the offender pursuant to division (A)(3) or (B) of this section for those offenses shall be aggregated and served consecutively, as if they were a single minimum term imposed under that division.

(F)(1) If an offender is convicted of or pleads guilty to a violent sex offense and also is convicted of or pleads guilty to a sexually violent predator specification that was included in the indictment, count in the indictment, or information charging that offense, or is convicted of or pleads guilty to a designated homicide, assault, or kidnapping offense and also is convicted of or pleads guilty to both a sexual motivation specification and a sexually violent predator specification that were included in the indictment, count in the indictment, or information charging that offense, the conviction of or plea of guilty to the offense and the sexually violent predator specification automatically classifies the offender as a tier III sex offender/child-victim offender for purposes of Chapter 2950. of the Revised Code.

(2) If an offender is convicted of or pleads guilty to committing on or after January 2, 2007, a violation of division (A)(1)(b) of section 2907.02 of the Revised Code and either the offender is sentenced under section 2971.03 of the Revised Code or a sentence of life without parole is imposed under division (B) of section 2907.02 of the Revised Code, the conviction of or plea of guilty to the offense automatically classifies the offender as a tier III sex offender/child-victim offender for purposes of Chapter 2950. of the Revised Code.

(3) If a person is convicted of or pleads guilty to committing on or after January 2, 2007, attempted rape and also is convicted of or pleads guilty to a specification of the type described in section 2941.1418, 2941.1419, or 2941.1420 of the Revised Code, the conviction of or plea of guilty to the offense and the specification automatically classify the offender as a tier III sex offender/child-victim offender for purposes of Chapter 2950. of the Revised Code.

(4) If a person is convicted of or pleads guilty to one of the offenses described in division (B)(3)(a), (b), (c), or (d) of this section and a sexual motivation specification related to the offense and the victim of the offense is less than thirteen years of age, the conviction of or plea of guilty to the offense automatically classifies the offender as a tier III sex offender/child-victim offender for purposes of Chapter 2950. of the Revised Code.

**HISTORY: 146 v H 180. Eff 1-1-97; 150 v H 473, § 1, eff. 4-29-05; 151 v S 260, § 1, eff. 1-2-07; 152 v S 10, § 1, eff. 1-1-08; 2011 HB 86, § 1, eff. Sept. 30, 2011.**

The effective date is set by § 3 of 152 v S 10.
The effective date is set by section 3 of HB 180.

## § 2971.04 Termination of parole board's control after offender has served minimum prison term; transfer to court.

(A) If an offender is serving a prison term imposed under division (A)(3), (B)(1)(a), (b), or (c), (B)(2)(a), (b), or (c), or (B)(3)(a), (b), (c), or (d) of section 2971.03 of the Revised Code, at any time after the offender has served the minimum term imposed under that sentence, the parole board may terminate its control over the offender's service of the prison term. The parole board initially shall determine whether to terminate its control over the offender's service of the prison term upon the completion of the offender's service of the minimum term under the sentence and shall make subsequent determinations at least once every two years after that first determination. The parole board shall not terminate its control over the offender's service of the prison term unless it finds at a hearing that the offender does not represent a substantial risk of physical harm to others. Prior to determining whether to terminate its control over the offender's service of the prison term, the parole board shall request the department of rehabilitation and correction to prepare pursuant to section 5120.61 of the Revised Code an update of the most recent risk assessment and report relative to the offender. The offender has the right to be present at any hearing held under this section. At the hearing, the offender and the prosecuting attorney may make a statement and present evidence as to whether the parole board should terminate its control over the offender's service of the prison term. In making its determination as to whether to terminate its control over the offender's service of the prison term, the parole board may follow the standards and guidelines adopted by the department of rehabilitation and correction under section 5120.49 of the Revised Code and shall consider the updated risk assessment and report relating to the offender prepared by the department pursuant to section 5120.61 of the Revised Code in response to the request made under this division and any statements or evidence submitted by the offender or the prosecuting attorney. If the parole board terminates its control over an offender's service of a prison term imposed under division (A)(3), (B)(1)(a), (b), or (c), (B)(2)(a), (b), or (c), or (B)(3)(a), (b), (c), or (d) of section 2971.03 of the Revised Code, it shall recommend to the court modifications to the requirement that the offender serve the entire term in a state correctional institution. The court is not bound by the recommendations submitted by the parole board.

(B) If the parole board terminates its control over an offender's service of a prison term imposed pursuant to division (A)(3), (B)(1)(a), (b), or (c), (B)(2)(a), (b), or (c), or (B)(3)(a), (b), (c), or (d) of section 2971.03 of the Revised Code, the parole board immediately shall provide written notice of its termination of control to the department of rehabilitation and correction, the court, and the prosecuting attorney, and, after the board's termination of its control, the court shall have control over the offender's service of that prison term.

After the transfer, the court shall have control over the offender's service of that prison term for the offender's entire life, subject to the court's termination of the term pursuant to section 2971.05 of the Revised Code.

(C) If control over the offender's service of the prison term is transferred to the court, all of the following apply:

(1) The offender shall not be released solely as a result of the transfer of control over the service of that prison term.

(2) The offender shall not be permitted solely as a result of the transfer to serve a portion of that term in a place other than a state correctional institution.

(3) The offender shall continue serving that term in a state correctional institution, subject to the following:

(a) A release pursuant to a pardon, commutation, or reprieve;

(b) A modification or termination of the term by the court pursuant to this chapter.

**HISTORY: 146 v H 180. Eff 1-1-97; 150 v H 473, § 1, eff. 4-29-05; 151 v S 260, § 1, eff. 1-2-07; 152 v S 10, § 1, eff. 1-1-08.**

The effective date is set by § 3 of 152 v S 10.

The effective date is set by section 3 of HB 180.

### § 2971.05 Hearing on modification or termination of prison term after transfer of control to court; conditional release; final release; supervision of sexually violent offenders with active global positioning system.

(A)(1) After control over an offender's service of a prison term imposed pursuant to division (A)(3), (B)(1)(a), (b), or (c), (B)(2)(a), (b), or (c), or (B)(3)(a), (b), (c), or (d) of section 2971.03 of the Revised Code has been transferred pursuant to section 2971.04 of the Revised Code to the court, the court shall schedule, within thirty days of any of the following, a hearing on whether to modify in accordance with division (C) of this section the requirement that the offender serve the entire prison term in a state correctional institution or to terminate the prison term in accordance with division (D) of this section:

(a) Control over the offender's service of a prison term is transferred pursuant to section 2971.04 of the Revised Code to the court, and no hearing to modify the requirement has been held;

(b) Two years elapse after the most recent prior hearing held pursuant to division (A)(1) or (2) of this section;

(c) The prosecuting attorney, the department of rehabilitation and correction, or the adult parole authority requests the hearing, and recommends that the requirement be modified or that the offender's prison term be terminated.

(2) After control over the offender's service of a prison term has been transferred pursuant to section 2971.04 of the Revised Code to the court, the court, within thirty days of either of the following, shall conduct a hearing on whether to modify in accordance with division (C) of this section the requirement that the offender serve the entire prison term in a state correctional institution, whether to continue, revise, or revoke an existing modification of that requirement, or whether to terminate the term in accordance with division (D) of this section:

(a) The requirement that the offender serve the entire prison term in a state correctional institution has been modified, and the offender is taken into custody for any reason.

(b) The department of rehabilitation and correction or the prosecuting attorney notifies the court pursuant to section 2971.06 of the Revised Code regarding a known or suspected violation of a term or condition of the modification or a belief that there is a substantial likelihood that the offender has committed or is about to commit a sexually violent offense.

(3) After control over the offender's service of a prison term has been transferred pursuant to section 2971.04 of the Revised Code to the court, the court, in any of the following circumstances, may conduct a hearing within thirty days to determine whether to modify in accordance with division (C) of this section the requirement that the offender serve the entire prison term in a state correctional institution, whether to continue, revise, or revoke an existing modification of that requirement, or whether to terminate the sentence in accordance with division (D) of this section:

(a) The offender requests the hearing;

(b) Upon the court's own motion;

(c) One or more examiners who have conducted a psychological examination and assessment of the offender file a statement that states that there no longer is a likelihood that the offender will engage in the future in a sexually violent offense.

(B)(1) Before a court holds a hearing pursuant to division (A) of this section, the court shall provide notice of the date, time, place, and purpose of the hearing to the offender, the prosecuting attorney, the department of rehabilitation and correction, and the adult parole authority and shall request the department to prepare pursuant to section 5120.61 of the Revised Code an update of the most recent risk assessment and report relative to the offender. The offender has the right to be present at any hearing held under this section. At the hearing, the offender and the prosecuting attorney may make a statement and present evidence as to whether the requirement that the offender serve the entire prison term in a state correctional institution should or should not be modified, whether the existing modification of the requirement should be continued, revised, or revoked, and whether the prison term should or should not be terminated.

(2) At a hearing held pursuant to division (A) of this section, the court may and, if the hearing is held pursuant to division (A)(1)(a), (1)(b), or (3)(c) of this section, shall determine by clear and convincing evidence whether the offender is unlikely to commit a sexually violent offense in the future.

(3) At the conclusion of the hearing held pursuant to division (A) of this section, the court may order that the requirement that the offender serve the entire prison term in a state correctional institution be continued, that the requirement be modified pursuant to division (C) of this section, that an existing modification be continued, revised, or revoked pursuant to division (C) of this section, or that the prison term be terminated pursuant to division (D) of this section.

(C)(1) If, at the conclusion of a hearing held pursuant to division (A) of this section, the court determines by clear and convincing evidence that the offender will not represent a substantial risk of physical harm to others, the court may modify the requirement that the offender serve the entire prison term imposed under division (A)(3), (B)(1)(a), (b), or (c), (B)(2)(a), (b), or (c), or (B)(3)(a), (b), (c), or (d) of section 2971.03 of the Revised Code in a state correctional institution in a manner that the court considers appropriate. If the court modifies the requirement for an offender whose prison term was imposed pursuant to division (A)(3) of section 2971.03 of the Revised Code, the court shall order the adult parole authority to supervise the offender and shall require that the authority's supervision of the offender be pursuant to division (E) of this section. If the court modifies the requirement for an offender whose prison term was imposed pursuant to division (B)(1)(a), (b), or (c), (2)(a), (b), or (c), or (3)(a), (b), (c), or (d) of section 2971.03 of the Revised Code, the court shall order the adult parole authority to supervise the offender and may require that the authority's supervision of the offender be pursuant to division (E) of this section.

(2) The modification of the requirement does not terminate the prison term but serves only to suspend the requirement that the offender serve the entire term in a state correctional institution. The prison term shall remain in effect for the offender's entire life unless the court terminates the prison term pursuant to division (D) of this section. The offender shall remain under the jurisdiction of the court for the offender's entire life unless the court so terminates the prison term. The modification of the requirement does not terminate the classification of the offender, as described in division (F) of section 2971.03 of the Revised Code, as a sexual predator for purposes of Chapter 2950. of the Revised Code, and the offender is subject to supervision, including supervision under division (E) of this section if the court required the supervision of the offender to be pursuant to that division.

(3) If the court revokes the modification under consideration, the court shall order that the offender be returned to the custody of the department of rehabilitation and correction to continue serving the prison term to which the modification applied, and section 2971.06 of the Revised Code applies regarding the offender.

(D)(1) If, at the conclusion of a hearing held pursuant to division (A) of this section, the court determines by clear and convincing evidence that the offender is unlikely to commit a sexually violent offense in the future, the court may terminate the offender's prison term imposed under division (A)(3), (B)(1)(a), (b), or (c), (B)(2)(a), (b), or (c), or (B)(3)(a), (b), (c), or (d) of section 2971.03 of the Revised Code, subject to the offender satisfactorily completing the period of conditional release required by this division and, if applicable, compliance with division (E) of this section. If the court terminates the prison term, the court shall place the offender on conditional release for five years, notify the adult parole authority of its determination and of the termination of the prison term, and order the adult parole authority to supervise the offender during the five-year period of conditional release or, if division (E) applies to the offender, to supervise the offender pursuant to and for the period of time specified in that division. If the court terminates the prison term for an offender whose prison term was imposed pursuant to division (A)(3) of section 2971.03 of the Revised Code, the court shall require that the authority's supervision of the offender be pursuant to division (E) of this section. If the court terminates the prison term for an offender whose prison term was imposed pursuant to division (B)(1)(a), (b), or (c), (2)(a), (b), or (c), or (3)(a), (b), (c), or (d) of section 2971.03 of the Revised Code, the court may require that the authority's supervision of the offender be pursuant to division (E) of this section. Upon receipt of a notice from a court pursuant to this division, the adult parole authority shall supervise the offender who is the subject of the notice during the five-year period of conditional release, periodically notify the court of the offender's activities during that five-year period of conditional release, and file with the court no later than thirty days prior to the expiration of the five-year period of conditional release a written recommendation as to whether the termination of the offender's prison term should be finalized, whether the period of conditional release should be extended, or whether another type of action authorized pursuant to this chapter should be taken.

(2) Upon receipt of a recommendation of the adult parole authority filed pursuant to division (D)(1) of this section, the court shall hold a hearing to determine whether to finalize the termination of the offender's prison term, to extend the period of conditional release, or to take another type of action authorized pursuant to this chapter. The court shall hold the hearing no later than the date on which the five-year period of conditional release terminates and shall provide notice of the date, time, place, and purpose of the hearing to the offender and to the prosecuting attorney. At the hearing, the offender, the prosecuting attorney, and the adult parole authority employee who supervised the offender during the period of conditional release may make a statement and present evidence.

If the court determines at the hearing to extend an offender's period of conditional release, it may do so for additional periods of one year in the same manner as the original period of conditional release, and except as otherwise described in this division, all procedures and requirements that applied to the original period of conditional release apply to the additional period of extended conditional release unless the court modifies a procedure or requirement. If an offender's period of conditional release is extended as described in this division, all references to a five-year period of conditional release that are contained in division (D)(1) of this section shall be construed, in applying the provisions of that division to the extension, as being references to the one-year period of the extension of the conditional release.

If the court determines at the hearing to take another type of action authorized pursuant to this chapter, it may do so in the same manner as if the action had been taken at any other stage of the proceedings under this chapter. As used in this division, "another type of action" includes the revocation of the conditional release and the return of the offender to a state correctional institution to continue to serve the prison term.

If the court determines at the hearing to finalize the termination of the offender's prison term, it shall notify the department of rehabilitation and correction, the department shall enter into its records a final release and issue to the offender a certificate of final release, and the prison term thereafter shall be considered completed and terminated in every way.

(3) The termination of an offender's prison term pursuant to division (D)(1) or (2) of this section does not affect the classification of the offender, as described in division (F) of section 2971.03 of the Revised Code, as a tier III sex offender/child-victim offender for purposes of Chapter 2950. of the Revised Code, does not terminate the adult parole authority's supervision of the offender, and, if the court had required the supervision of the offender to be pursuant to division (E) of this section, does not terminate the supervision of the offender with an active global positioning system device, pursuant to that division.

(E) If a prison term imposed upon an offender pursuant to division (A)(3) of section 2971.03 of the Revised Code is modified as provided in division (C) of this section or terminated as provided in division (D) of this section, the adult parole authority shall supervise the offender with an active global positioning system device during any time period in which the offender is not incarcerated in a state correctional institution. If a prison term imposed upon an offender pursuant to division (B)(1)(a), (b), or (c), (2)(a), (b), or (c), or (3)(a), (b), (c), or (d) of section 2971.03 of the Revised Code is modified as provided in division (C) of this section or terminated as provided in division (D) of this section, and if the court requires that the adult parole authority's supervision of the offender be pursuant to this division, the authority shall supervise the offender with an active global positioning system device during any time period in which the offender is not incarcerated in a state correctional institution. If the adult parole authority is required to supervise the offender with an active global positioning system device as described in this division, unless the court removes the offender's classification as a sexually violent predator regarding an offender whose prison term was imposed under division (A)(3) of section 2971.03 of the Revised Code or terminates the requirement that supervision of the offender be pursuant to this division regarding an offender whose prison term was imposed under division (B)(1)(a), (b), or (c), (2)(a), (b), or (c), or (3)(a), (b), (c), or (d) of section 2971.03 of the Revised Code, the offender is subject to supervision with an active global positioning system pursuant to this division for the offender's entire life. The costs of administering the supervision of offenders with an active global positioning system device pursuant to this division shall be paid out of funds from the reparations fund, created pursuant to section 2743.191 [2743.19.1] of the Revised Code. This division shall only apply to a sexually violent predator sentenced pursuant to division (A)(3) of section 2971.03 of the Revised Code who is released from the custody of the department of rehabilitation and correction on or after September 29, 2005 or an offender sentenced pursuant to division (B)(1) or (2) of section 2971.03 of the Revised Code on or after January 2, 2007.

**HISTORY: 146 v H 180. Eff 1-1-97; 150 v H 473, § 1, eff. 4-29-05; 151 v H 66, § 101.01, eff. 9-29-05; 151 v S 260, § 1, eff. 1-2-07; 152 v S 10, § 1, eff. 1-1-08.**

The effective date is set by § 3 of 152 v S 10.
The effective date is set by § 612.03 of 151 v H 66.
The effective date is set by section 3 of HB 180.

## § 2971.06 Detention of offender for violation of condition of modification or conditional release or upon likelihood of additional offense.

If an offender is serving a prison term imposed under division (A)(3), (B)(1)(a), (b), or (c), (B)(2)(a), (b), or (c), or (B)(3)(a), (b), (c), or (d) of section 2971.03 of the Revised Code, if, pursuant to section 2971.05 of the Revised Code, the court modifies the requirement that the offender serve the entire prison term in a state correctional institution or places the offender on conditional release and if, at any time after the offender has been released from serving the term in an institution, the department of rehabilitation and correction or the prosecuting attorney learns or obtains information indicating that the offender has violated a term or condition of the modification or conditional release or believes there is a substantial likelihood that the offender has committed or is about to commit a sexually violent offense, all of the following apply:

(A) The department or the prosecuting attorney may contact a peace officer, parole officer, or probation officer and request the officer to take the offender into custody. If the department contacts a peace officer, parole officer, or probation officer and requests that the offender be taken into custody, the department shall notify the prosecuting attorney that it made the request and shall provide the reasons for which it made the request. Upon receipt of a request that an offender be taken into custody, a peace officer, parole officer, or probation officer shall take the offender in question into custody and promptly shall notify the department and the prosecuting attorney, in writing, that the offender was taken into custody. After the offender has been taken into custody, the department or the prosecuting attorney shall notify the court of the violation or the belief that there is a substantial likelihood that the offender has committed or is about to commit a sexually violent offense, and the prosecuting attorney may request that the court, pursuant to section 2971.05 of the Revised Code, revise the modification. An offender may be held in custody under this provision for no longer than thirty days, pending a determination pursuant to section 2971.05 of the Revised Code of whether the modification of the requirement that the offender serve the entire prison term in a state correctional institution should be revised. If the court fails to make a determination under that section regarding the prosecuting attorney's request within thirty days after the offender was taken into custody, the offender shall be released from custody and shall be subject to the same terms and conditions as existed under the then-existing modification of the requirement that the offender serve the entire prison term in a state correctional institution, provided that if the act that resulted in the offender being taken into custody under this division is a criminal offense and if the offender is arrested for that act, the offender may be retained in custody in accordance with the applicable law.

(B) If the offender is not taken into custody pursuant to division (A) of this section, the department or the prosecuting attorney shall notify the court of the known or suspected violation or of the belief that there is a substantial likelihood that the offender has committed or is about to commit a sexually violent offense. If the department provides the notification to the court, it also shall notify the prosecuting attorney that it provided the notification and shall provide the reasons for which it provided the notification. The prosecuting attorney may request that the court, pursuant to section 2971.05 of the Revised Code, revise the modification.

**HISTORY: 146 v H 180. Eff 1-1-97; 151 v S 260, § 1, eff. 1-2-07; 152 v S 10, § 1, eff. 1-1-08.**

The effective date is set by § 3 of 152 v S 10.
The effective date is set by section 3 of HB 180.

## § 2971.07 Application of chapter; warrantless searches after modification or conditional release.

(A) This chapter does not apply to any offender unless the offender is one of the following:

(1) The offender is convicted of or pleads guilty to a violent sex offense and also is convicted of or pleads guilty to a sexually violent predator specification that was included in the indictment, count in the indictment, or information charging that offense.

(2) The offender is convicted of or pleads guilty to a designated homicide, assault, or kidnapping offense and also is convicted of or pleads guilty to both a sexual motivation specification and a sexually violent predator specification that were included in the indictment, count in the indictment, or information charging that offense.

(3) The offender is convicted of or pleads guilty to a violation of division (A)(1)(b) of section 2907.02 of the Revised Code committed on or after January 2, 2007, and the court does not sentence the offender to a term of life without parole pursuant to division (B) of section 2907.02 of the Revised Code or division (B) of that section prohibits the court from sentencing the offender pursuant to section 2971.03 of the Revised Code.

(4) The offender is convicted of or pleads guilty to attempted rape committed on or after January 2, 2007, and also is convicted of or pleads guilty to a specification of the type described in section 2941.1418 [2941.14.18], 2941.1419 [2941.14.19], or 2941.1420 [2941.14.20] of the Revised Code.

(5) The offender is convicted of or pleads guilty to a violation of section 2905.01 of the Revised Code and also is convicted of or pleads guilty to a sexual motivation specification that was included in the indictment, count in the indictment, or information charging that offense, and that section requires a court to sentence the offender pursuant to section 2971.03 of the Revised Code.

(6) The offender is convicted of or pleads guilty to aggravated murder and also is convicted of or pleads guilty to a sexual motivation specification that was included in the indictment, count in the indictment, or information charging that offense, and division (A)(2)(b)(ii) of section 2929.022 [2929.02.2], division (A)(1)(e), (C)(1)(a)(v), (C)(2)(a)(ii), (D)(2)(b), (D)(3)(a)(iv), or (E)(1)(d) of section 2929.03, or division (A) or (B) of section 2929.06 of the Revised Code requires a court to sentence the offender pursuant to division (B)(3) of section 2971.03 of the Revised Code.

(7) The offender is convicted of or pleads guilty to murder and also is convicted of or pleads guilty to a sexual motivation specification that was included in the indictment, count in the indictment, or information charging that offense, and division (B)(2) of section 2929.02 of the Revised Code requires a court to sentence the offender pursuant to section 2971.03 of the Revised Code.

(B) This chapter does not limit or affect a court in imposing upon an offender described in divisions (A)(1) to (9) of this section any financial sanction under section 2929.18 or any other section of the Revised Code, or, except as specifically provided in this chapter, any other sanction that is authorized or required for the offense or violation by any other provision of law.

(C) If an offender is sentenced to a prison term under division (A)(3), (B)(1)(a), (b), or (c), (B)(2)(a), (b), or (c), or (B)(3)(a), (b), (c), or (d) of section 2971.03 of the Revised Code and if, pursuant to section 2971.05 of the Revised Code, the court modifies the requirement that the offender serve the entire prison term in a state correctional institution or places the offender on conditional release that involves the placement of the offender under the supervision of the adult parole authority, authorized field officers of the authority who are engaged within the scope of their supervisory duties or responsibilities may search, with or without a warrant, the person of the offender, the place of residence of the offender, and a motor vehicle, another item of tangible or intangible personal property, or any other real property in which the offender has the express or implied permission of a person with a right, title, or interest to use, occupy, or possess if the field officer has reasonable grounds to believe that the offender is not abiding by the law or otherwise is not complying with the terms and conditions of the offender's modification or release. The authority shall provide each offender with a written notice that informs the offender that authorized field officers of the authority who are engaged within the scope of their supervisory duties or responsibilities may conduct those types of searches during the period of the modification or release if they have reasonable grounds to believe that the offender is not abiding by the law or otherwise is not complying with the terms and conditions of the offender's modification or release.

**HISTORY: 146 v H 180. Eff 1-1-97; 151 v S 260, § 1, eff. 1-2-07; 152 v S 10, § 1, eff. 1-1-08.**

The effective date is set by § 3 of 152 v S 10.
The effective date is set by section 3 of HB 180.
See provisions, § 4 of HB 180 (146 v —) following RC § 2921.34.

# CHAPTER 2981: FORFEITURE LAW

Section



## § 2981.01 Purposes of forfeitures; definitions.

(A) Forfeitures under this chapter shall be governed by all of the following purposes:

(1) To provide economic disincentives and remedies to deter and offset the economic effect of offenses by seizing and forfeiting contraband, proceeds, and certain instrumentalities;

(2) To ensure that seizures and forfeitures of instrumentalities are proportionate to the offense committed;

(3) To protect third parties from wrongful forfeiture of their property;

(4) To prioritize restitution for victims of offenses.

(B) As used in this chapter:

(1) "Aircraft" has the same meaning as in section 4561.01 of the Revised Code.

(2) "Computers," "computer networks," "computer systems," "computer software," and "telecommunications device" have the same meanings as in section 2913.01 of the Revised Code.

(3) "Financial institution" means a bank, credit union, savings and loan association, or a licensee or registrant under Chapter 1321. of the Revised Code.

(4) "Firearm" and "dangerous ordnance" have the same meanings as in section 2923.11 of the Revised Code.

(5) "Innocent person" includes any bona fide purchaser of property that is subject to forfeiture, including any person who establishes a valid claim to or interest in the property in accordance with section 2923.04 of the Revised Code, and any victim of an alleged offense.

(6) "Instrumentality" means property otherwise lawful to possess that is used in or intended to be used in an offense. An "instrumentality" may include, but is not limited to, a firearm, a mobile instrumentality, a computer, a computer network, a computer system, computer software, a telecommunications device, money, and any other means of exchange.

(7) "Law enforcement agency" includes, but is not limited to, the state board of pharmacy, the enforcement division of the department of taxation, and the office of the prosecutor.

(8) "Mobile instrumentality" means an instrumentality that is inherently mobile and used in the routine transport of persons. "Mobile instrumentality" includes, but is not limited to, any vehicle, any watercraft, and any aircraft.

(9) "Money" has the same meaning as in section 1301.201 of the Revised Code.

(10) "Offense" means any act or omission that could be charged as a criminal offense or a delinquent act, whether or not a formal criminal prosecution or delinquent child proceeding began at the time the forfeiture is initiated. Except as otherwise specified, an offense for which property may be forfeited includes any felony and any misdemeanor. The commission of an "offense" includes the commission of a delinquent act.

(11) "Proceeds" means both of the following:

(a) In cases involving unlawful goods, services, or activities, "proceeds" means any property derived directly or indirectly from an offense. "Proceeds" may include, but is not limited to, money or any other means of exchange. "Proceeds" is not limited to the net gain or profit realized from the offense.

(b) In cases involving lawful goods or services that are sold or provided in an unlawful manner, "proceeds" means the amount of money or other means of exchange acquired through the illegal transactions resulting in the forfeiture, less the direct costs lawfully incurred in providing the goods or services. The lawful costs deduction does not include any part of the overhead expenses of, or income taxes paid by, the entity providing the goods or services. The alleged offender or delinquent child has the burden to prove that any costs are lawfully incurred.

(12) "Property" means "property" as defined in section 2901.01 of the Revised Code and any benefit, privilege, claim, position, interest in an enterprise, or right derived, directly or indirectly, from the offense.

(13) "Property subject to forfeiture" includes contraband and proceeds and may include instrumentalities as provided in this chapter.

(14) "Prosecutor" has the same meaning as in section 2935.01 of the Revised Code. When relevant, "prosecutor" also includes the attorney general.

(15) "Vehicle" has the same meaning as in section 4501.01 of the Revised Code.

(16) "Watercraft" has the same meaning as in section 1547.01 of the Revised Code.

(C) The penalties and procedures under Chapters 2923., 2925., and 2933. of the Revised Code remain in effect to the extent that they do not conflict with this chapter.

**HISTORY: 151 v H 241, § 1, eff. 7-1-07; 152 v H 120, § 1, eff. 7-1-07; 2011 HB 9, § 1, eff. June 29, 2011.**

Acts 2011, HB 9, § 3 provides: "This act applies to transactions entered into on or after the effective date of this act."

The effective date is set by § 3 of 152 v H 120.

See provisions of § 4 of 151 v H 241 following RC § 2901.01.

## § 2981.02 Property subject to forfeiture; determination of use or intended use of instrumentality; motor vehicle law exclusion.

(A) The following property is subject to forfeiture to the state or a political subdivision under either the criminal or delinquency process in section 2981.04 of the Revised Code or the civil process in section 2981.05 of the Revised Code:

(1) Contraband involved in an offense;

(2) Proceeds derived from or acquired through the commission of an offense;

(3) An instrumentality that is used in or intended to be used in the commission or facilitation of any of the following offenses when the use or intended use, consistent with division (B) of this section, is sufficient to warrant forfeiture under this chapter:

(a) A felony;

(b) A misdemeanor, when forfeiture is specifically authorized by a section of the Revised Code or by a municipal ordinance that creates the offense or sets forth its penalties;

(c) An attempt to commit, complicity in committing, or a conspiracy to commit an offense of the type described in divisions (A)(3)(a) and (b) of this section.

(B) In determining whether an alleged instrumentality was used in or was intended to be used in the commission or facilitation of an offense or an attempt, complicity, or conspiracy to commit an offense in a manner sufficient to warrant its forfeiture, the trier of fact shall consider the following factors the trier of fact determines are relevant:

(1) Whether the offense could not have been committed or attempted but for the presence of the instrumentality;

(2) Whether the primary purpose in using the instrumentality was to commit or attempt to commit the offense;

(3) The extent to which the instrumentality furthered the commission of, or attempt to commit, the offense.

(C) This chapter does not apply to or limit forfeitures under Title XLV of the Revised Code, including forfeitures relating to section 2903.06 or 2903.08 of the Revised Code.

**HISTORY: 151 v H 241, § 1, eff. 7-1-07.**

See provisions of § 4 of 151 v H 241 following RC § 2901.01.

## § 2981.03 Provisional title of state or subdivision; vesting; seizure; preservation of reachability; stay of other actions; conditional release; filing of action by prosecutor; records.

(A)(1) The state or political subdivision acquires provisional title to property subject to forfeiture under this chapter upon a person's commission of an offense giving rise to forfeiture, subject to third party claims and a final adjudication under section 2981.04 or 2981.05 of the Revised Code. Provisional title authorizes the state or political subdivision to seize and hold the property, and to act to protect the property, under this section before any proceeding under this chapter. Title to the property vests with the state or political subdivision when the trier of fact renders a final forfeiture verdict or order under section 2981.04 or 2981.05 of the Revised Code, but that title is subject to third party claims adjudicated under those sections.

(2) A law enforcement officer may seize property that the officer has probable cause to believe is property subject to forfeiture. If a law enforcement officer seizes property that is titled or registered under law, the officer or the law enforcement agency that employs the officer shall notify the property owner of the seizure. The agency shall give notice to the property owner at the owner's last known address as soon as practical after the seizure and may give the notice by certified mail or orally by any means, including telephone. If the officer or agency is unable to provide the notice required by this division despite reasonable, good faith efforts, those efforts constitute fulfillment of the notice requirement.

(3) In a civil forfeiture case under this chapter in which the state or political subdivision seeks to seize real property, the property owner may request a hearing before the seizure, and in the hearing the state or political subdivision shall show probable cause that the real property is subject to forfeiture.

(4) A person aggrieved by an alleged unlawful seizure of property may seek relief from the seizure by filing a motion in the appropriate court that shows the person's interest in the property, states why the seizure was unlawful, and requests the property's return. If the motion is filed before an indictment, information, or a complaint seeking forfeiture of the property is filed, the court shall promptly schedule a hearing on the motion, and at the hearing the person shall demonstrate by a preponderance of the evidence that the seizure was unlawful and that the person is entitled to the property. If the motion is filed by a defendant after an indictment, information, or a complaint seeking forfeiture of the property has been filed, the court shall treat the motion as a motion to suppress evidence. If the motion is filed by a third party after an indictment, information, or complaint seeking forfeiture of the property has been filed, the court shall treat the motion as a petition of a person with an alleged interest in the subject property, pursuant to divisions (E) and (F) of section 2981.04 of the Revised Code.

(5)(a) In any action under section 2981.04 or 2981.05 of the Revised Code, if a property owner or third party claims lawful interest in the subject property alleged to be proceeds, the state or political subdivision has provisional title and a right to hold property if it proves both of the following by a preponderance of the evidence:

(i) The interest in the property was acquired by the alleged offender or delinquent child during the commission of the offense or within a reasonable time after that period.

(ii) There is no likely source for the interest in the property other than as proceeds derived from or acquired through the commission of the offense.

(b) The alleged offender or delinquent child shall have the burden to prove the amount of any direct costs lawfully incurred.

(B)(1) Upon application by the prosecutor who prosecutes or brings an action that allows forfeiture under this chapter, the court in which the action is prosecuted or filed may issue an order taking any reasonable action necessary to preserve the reachability of the property including, but not limited to, a restraining order or injunction, an order requiring execution of a satisfactory bond or insurance policy, an order to inspect, photograph, or inventory the property, an order placing a lien or lis pendens against the property, or an order appointing a receiver or trustee. The court may issue an order of this nature at any of the following times:

(a) Upon the filing of a complaint, indictment, or information alleging the property to be subject to forfeiture under section 2981.02 of the Revised Code;

(b) Prior to the filing of a complaint, an indictment, or information alleging the property to be subject to forfeiture under section 2981.02 of the Revised Code, if, after giving notice to all persons known to have a interest in the property and giving those persons an opportunity to be heard, the court determines that all of the following apply:

(i) There is a substantial probability the state or political subdivision will prevail on the forfeiture issue.

(ii) There is a substantial probability that failure to enter the order will result in the property being destroyed, being removed from the court's jurisdiction, or otherwise being made unavailable for forfeiture.

(iii) The need to preserve the availability of the property outweighs the hardship on the person against whom the order is to be entered.

(c) As a condition of releasing the property based on a determination of substantial hardship under division (D) of this section.

(2) Except as otherwise provided in division (B)(3) of this section, the court shall make an order under division (B)(1)(b) of this section effective for not more than ninety days, but the court may extend the order if the prosecutor demonstrates that the need to preserve the reachability of the property still exists or for other good cause shown and shall extend the order if an indictment, information, or a complaint is filed alleging that the property is subject to forfeiture.

(3) A court may issue an order under division (B)(1) of this section without giving notice or a hearing to a person known to have a interest in the property if the prosecutor demonstrates that the property is subject to forfeiture and that giving notice and a hearing will jeopardize the availability of the property for forfeiture. Notwithstanding the ninety-day limit described in division (B)(2) of this section, the court shall make an order under division (B)(3) of this section effective for not more than ten days, but the court may extend the order if the prosecutor again demonstrates that the property is subject to forfeiture and that a hearing will jeopardize the availability of the property or for other good cause shown or if the person subject to the order consents to a longer period. If a party requests a hearing on the order, the court shall hold the hearing at the earliest possible time before the order expires.

(4) At any hearing under division (B) of this section, the court may receive and consider evidence and information that is inadmissible under the Rules of Evidence. The court shall cause the hearing to be recorded and shall cause a transcript to be made. If property is to be seized as a result of the hearing, the recording and transcript shall not be a public record for purposes of section 149.43 of the Revised Code until the property is seized. This section does not authorize making available for inspection any confidential law enforcement investigatory record or trial preparation record, as defined in section 149.43 of the Revised Code.

(C) Except as otherwise provided in division (E) of this section, any replevin, conversion, or other civil action brought concerning property subject to a criminal or civil forfeiture action under this chapter shall be stayed until the forfeiture action is resolved.

(D)(1) A person with an interest in property that is subject to forfeiture and that is seized under this chapter may seek conditional release of the property by requesting possession from the person with custody of the property. The request shall demonstrate how the person meets the requirements specified in divisions (D)(3)(a), (b), and (c) of this section.

(2) If the person with custody of the property does not release the property within fifteen days after a person makes a request under division (D)(1) of this section, or within seven days after a person makes the request if the property was seized as a mobile instrumentality or if the request is to copy records, the person who made the request may file a petition for conditional release with the court in which the complaint, indictment, or information is filed or, if no complaint, indictment, or information is filed, the court that issued the seizure warrant for the property. The petition shall demonstrate how the person meets the requirements specified in divisions (D)(3)(a), (b), and (c) of this section and the steps the person has taken to secure release of the property from the official. Unless extended for good cause shown, the petition shall be filed either within thirty days of the filing of a complaint, an indictment, or information in the forfeiture action or, if no complaint, indictment, or information is filed, within thirty days of the issuance of the seizure warrant of the property.

If the court finds that the person meets the criteria specified in divisions (D)(3)(a), (b), and (c) of this section, the court shall order the property's conditional return to the person pending completion of the forfeiture action. In issuing this order, the court shall notify the person of the prohibitions against interfering with or diminishing property in section 2981.07 of the Revised Code and may make any order necessary to ensure that the value of the property is maintained.

If personal, business, or governmental records are seized, including those contained in computer files, a person may petition the court for a prompt opportunity to copy, at the person's expense, any records that are not contraband. The court may grant the petition if the person demonstrates how the person meets the requirements specified in divisions (D)(3)(a) and (c) of this section. The court shall order a competent person to supervise the copying.

(3) Except when there is probable cause that the property is contraband, property that must be held for a reasonable time as evidence related to an offense, or property that is likely to be used in additional offenses or except when the state or political subdivision meets the burden imposed under division (A)(5) of this section regarding alleged proceeds, a court may conditionally release property subject to forfeiture to a person who demonstrates all of the following:

(a) A possessory interest in the property;

(b) Sufficient ties to the community to provide assurance that the property will be available at the time of trial;

(c) That failure to conditionally release the property will cause a substantial hardship to the claimant.

(4) In determining whether a substantial hardship exists, the court shall weigh the claimant's likely hardship from the state's or political subdivision's continued possession of the property against the risk that the property will be destroyed, damaged, lost, concealed, or transferred if returned to the claimant. The court shall consider in favor of release the possibility that withholding the property would prevent a legitimate business from functioning, prevent the claimant's or an innocent person from maintaining employment, or leave the claimant or an innocent person homeless.

(5) If the state or political subdivision shows that the claimant's petition is frivolous, the court shall deny the

petition. Otherwise, the state or political subdivision may respond to the petition by submitting evidence ex parte to avoid disclosing any matter that may adversely affect an ongoing criminal investigation or pending trial.

(6) The court shall decide on the petition not more than thirty days after it is filed. If the property seized is alleged to be a mobile instrumentality, the court shall decide on the petition as soon as practicable within the thirty-day period. If personal, business, or governmental records were seized and a person files a petition to copy the records, the court shall decide on the petition as soon as practicable. In any case, the court may extend the time for deciding on the petition by consent of the parties or for good cause shown.

(E) Nothing in this section precludes a financial institution that has or purports to have a security interest in or lien on property described in section 2981.02 of the Revised Code from filing an action in connection with the property, prior to its disposition under this chapter, to obtain possession of the property in order to foreclose or otherwise enforce the security interest or lien.

If a financial institution commences a civil action or takes any other appropriate legal action to sell the property prior to its seizure or prior to its disposition under this chapter, if the person who is responsible for conducting the sale has actual knowledge of the commencement of a forfeiture action under either section 2981.04 or 2981.05 of the Revised Code, and if the property is sold, then the person shall dispose of the proceeds of the sale in the following order:

(1) First, to the payment of the costs of the sale, excluding any associated attorney's fees, and to the payment of the costs incurred by law enforcement agencies and financial institutions in connection with the seizure, storage, and maintenance of, and provision of security for, the property;

(2) Second, in the order of priority of the security interests and liens, to the payment of valid security interests and liens pertaining to the property that, at the time at which the state or political subdivision gains provisional title, are held by known secured parties and lienholders;

(3) Third, to the court that has or would have jurisdiction in a case or proceeding under section 2981.04 or section 2981.05 of the Revised Code for disposition under this chapter.

(F) A prosecutor may file a forfeiture action under section 2981.04 or 2981.05 of the Revised Code, or both. If property is seized pursuant to this section and a criminal forfeiture has not begun under section 2981.04 of the Revised Code, the prosecutor of the county in which the seizure occurred shall commence a civil action to forfeit that property under section 2981.05 of the Revised Code.

If the property seized includes property alleged to be a mobile instrumentality or includes personal, business, or governmental records, the civil forfeiture action shall be brought within thirty days of seizure. Otherwise, the action shall be brought within sixty days of seizure. In either case, the period within which the action shall be brought may be extended by agreement of the parties or by the court for good cause shown.

A prosecutor may file an appropriate charging instrument under section 2981.04 of the Revised Code to seek a criminal forfeiture after a civil forfeiture action begins. Filing a charging instrument for an offense that is also the basis of a civil forfeiture action shall stay the civil action.

A civil action to obtain civil forfeiture may be commenced as described in section 2981.05 of the Revised Code regardless of whether the offender or delinquent child has pleaded guilty to, been convicted of, or been adjudicated a delinquent child for the act that is the basis of the order.

(G) The prosecutor shall maintain an accurate record of each item disposed of under section 2981.04 or 2981.05 of the Revised Code. The record shall not identify or enable the identification of the officer who seized the property. The record is a public record open for inspection under section 149.43 of the Revised Code.

**HISTORY: 151 v H 241, § 1, eff. 7-1-07.**

See provisions of § 4 of 151 v H 241 following RC § 2901.01.

## § 2981.04 Criminal forfeiture proceedings.

(A)(1) Property described in division (A) of section 2981.02 of the Revised Code may be forfeited under this section only if the complaint, indictment, or information charging the offense or municipal violation, or the complaint charging the delinquent act, contains a specification of the type described in section 2941.1417 [2941.14.17] of the Revised Code that sets forth all of the following to the extent it is reasonably known at the time of the filing:

(a) The nature and extent of the alleged offender's or delinquent child's interest in the property;

(b) A description of the property;

(c) If the property is alleged to be an instrumentality, the alleged use or intended use of the property in the commission or facilitation of the offense.

(2) If any property is not reasonably foreseen to be subject to forfeiture at the time of filing the indictment, information, or complaint, the trier of fact still may return a verdict of forfeiture concerning that property in the hearing described in division (B) of this section if the prosecutor, upon discovering the property to be subject to forfeiture, gave prompt notice of this fact to the alleged offender or delinquent child under Criminal Rule 7(E) or Juvenile Rule 10(B).

(3) For good cause shown, the court may consider issues of the guilt of the alleged offender or the delinquency of the alleged delinquent child separate from whether property specified as subject to forfeiture should be forfeited.

(B) If a person pleads guilty to or is convicted of an offense or is adjudicated a delinquent child for committing a delinquent act and the complaint, indictment, or information charging the offense or act contains a specification covering property subject to forfeiture under section 2981.02 of the Revised Code, the trier of fact shall determine whether the person's property shall be forfeited. If the state or political subdivision proves by a preponderance of the evidence that the property is in whole or part subject to forfeiture under section 2981.02 of the Revised Code, after a proportionality review under section 2981.09 of the Revised Code when relevant, the trier of fact shall return a verdict of forfeiture that specifically describes the extent of the property subject to forfeiture. If the trier of fact is a jury, on the offender's or delinquent child's motion, the court shall make the determination of whether the property shall be forfeited.

(C) If the court enters a verdict of forfeiture under this section, the court imposing sentence or disposition, in addition to any other sentence authorized by Chapter 2929. of the Revised Code or any disposition authorized by

Chapter 2152. of the Revised Code, shall order that the offender or delinquent child forfeit to the state or political subdivision the offender's or delinquent child's interest in the property. The property vests with the state or political subdivision subject to the claims of third parties. The court may issue any additional order to affect the forfeiture, including, but not limited to, an order under section 2981.06 of the Revised Code.

(D) After the entry of a forfeiture order under this section, the prosecutor shall attempt to identify any person with an interest in the property subject to forfeiture by searching appropriate public records and making reasonably diligent inquiries. The prosecutor shall give notice of the forfeiture that remains subject to the claims of third parties and proposed disposal of the forfeited property to any person known to have an interest in the property. The prosecutor also shall publish notice of the forfeiture that remains subject to the claims of third parties and proposed disposal of the forfeited property once each week for two consecutive weeks in a newspaper of general circulation in the county in which the property was seized.

(E)(1) Any person, other than the offender or delinquent child whose conviction or plea of guilty or delinquency adjudication is the basis of the forfeiture order, who asserts a legal interest in the property that is the subject of the order may petition the court that issued the order for a hearing under division (E)(3) of this section to adjudicate the validity of the person's alleged interest in the property. All of the following apply to the petition:

(a) It shall be filed within thirty days after the final publication of notice or the person's receipt of notice under division (D) of this section.

(b) It shall be signed by the petitioner under the penalties for falsification specified in section 2921.13 of the Revised Code.

(c) It shall describe the nature and extent of the petitioner's interest in the property, the time and circumstances of the petitioner's acquisition of that interest, any additional facts supporting the petitioner's claim, and the relief sought.

(2)(a) In lieu of filing a petition as described in division (E)(1) of this section, a person, other than the offender or delinquent child whose conviction or plea of guilty or delinquency adjudication is the basis of the forfeiture order, may file an affidavit as described in this division to establish the validity of the alleged right, title, or interest in the property that is the subject of the forfeiture order if the person is a secured party or other lienholder of record that asserts a legal interest in the property, including, but not limited to, a mortgage, security interest, or other type of lien. The affidavit shall contain averments that the secured party or other lienholder acquired its alleged right, title, or interest in the property in the regular course of its business, for a specified valuable consideration, without actual knowledge of any facts pertaining to the offense that was the basis of the forfeiture order, in good faith, and without the intent to prevent or otherwise impede the state or political subdivision from seizing or obtaining a forfeiture of the property. The person shall file the affidavit within thirty days after the earlier of the final publication of notice or the receipt of notice under division (D) of this section.

(b) Except as otherwise provided in this section, the affidavit shall constitute prima-facie evidence of the validity of the affiant's alleged interest in the property.

(c) Unless the prosecutor files a motion challenging the affidavit within ten days after its filing and unless the prosecutor establishes by a preponderance of the evidence at the hearing held under division (E)(3) of this section that the affiant does not possess the alleged interest in the property or that the affiant had actual knowledge of facts pertaining to the offense or delinquent act that was the basis of the forfeiture order, the affidavit shall constitute conclusive evidence of the validity of the affiant's interest in the property.

(d) Any subsequent purchaser or other transferee of property pursuant to forfeiture under this section shall take the property subject to the continued validity of the interest of the affiant.

(3) Upon receipt of a petition or affidavit filed under division (E)(1) or (2) of this section, the court shall hold a hearing to determine the validity of the petitioner's interest in the property that is the subject of the forfeiture order or, if the affidavit was challenged, to determine the validity of the affiant's interest in the property. To the extent practicable and consistent with the interests of justice, the court shall hold the hearing within thirty days after the filing of the petition or within thirty days after the prosecutor files the motion challenging the affidavit. The court may consolidate the hearing with a hearing on any other petition or affidavit that is filed by a person other than the offender or delinquent child whose conviction or plea of guilty or delinquency adjudication is the basis of the forfeiture order and that relates to the property that is the subject of the forfeiture order.

At the hearing, the petitioner or affiant may testify, present evidence and witnesses on the petitioner's or affiant's behalf, and cross-examine witnesses for the state or political subdivision. In regards to a petition, the state or political subdivision may present evidence and witnesses in rebuttal and in defense of its claim to the property and may cross-examine witnesses for the petitioner. In regards to an affidavit, the prosecutor may present evidence and witnesses and cross-examine witnesses for the affiant.

In addition to the evidence and testimony presented at the hearing, the court also shall consider the relevant portions of the record in the criminal or delinquent child case that resulted in the forfeiture order.

(F)(1) If the hearing involves a petition, the court shall amend its forfeiture order if it determines at the hearing held pursuant to division (E)(3) of this section that the petitioner has established either of the following by a preponderance of the evidence:

(a) The petitioner has a legal interest in the property that is subject to the forfeiture order that renders the order completely or partially invalid because the legal interest in the property was vested in the petitioner, rather than the offender or delinquent child whose conviction or plea of guilty or delinquency adjudication is the basis of the order, or was superior to any interest of that offender or delinquent child, at the time of the commission of the offense or delinquent act that is the basis of the order.

(b) The petitioner is a bona fide purchaser for value of the interest in the property that is subject to the forfeiture order and was, at the time of the purchase, reasonably without cause to believe that it was subject to forfeiture.

(2) The court also shall amend its forfeiture order to reflect any interest of a secured party or other lienholder of record in the property subject to forfeiture who prevails at a hearing on the petition or affidavit filed pursuant to division (E)(1) or (2) of this section.

(G) If the court disposes of all petitions or affidavits timely filed under this section in favor of the state or political subdivision, the state or political subdivision shall have clear title to the property that is the subject of a forfeiture order issued under this section, but only to the extent that other parties' lawful interests in the property are not infringed. To the extent that the state or political subdivision has clear title to the property, the state or political subdivision may warrant good title to any subsequent purchaser or other transferee.

**HISTORY: 151 v H 241, § 1, eff. 7-1-07.**

See provisions of § 4 of 151 v H 241 following RC § 2901.01.

## § 2981.05 Civil forfeiture proceedings.

(A) The prosecutor of the political subdivision in which property described in division (A) of section 2981.02 of the Revised Code is located may commence a civil forfeiture action under this section by filing in the court of common pleas of the county in which the property is located a complaint requesting an order that forfeits the property to the state or a political subdivision. The filing shall be consistent with division (F) of section 2981.03 of the Revised Code.

(B) Prior to or upon the commencement of a civil forfeiture action, the prosecutor shall attempt to identify any person with an interest in the property subject to forfeiture by searching appropriate public records and making reasonably diligent inquiries. The prosecutor shall give notice of the commencement of the civil action, together with a copy of the complaint, to each person who is reasonably known to have any interest in the property, by certified mail, return receipt requested, or by personal service. The prosecutor shall cause a similar notice to be published once each week for two consecutive weeks in a newspaper of general circulation in the county in which the property is located.

(C) A person with an interest in the property subject to forfeiture may petition the court to release the property pursuant to division (D) of section 2981.03 of the Revised Code. The court shall consider the petition as provided in that section. If a timely petition for pretrial hardship release is not filed, or if a petition is filed but not granted, the person may file a claim for the release of the property under the Rules of Civil Procedure. The court shall dispose of any petitions timely filed under this division.

(D) The court shall issue a civil forfeiture order if it determines that the prosecutor has proved by a preponderance of the evidence that the property is subject to forfeiture under section 2981.02 of the Revised Code, and, after a proportionality review under section 2981.09 of the Revised Code when relevant, the trier of fact specifically describes the extent of the property to be forfeited. A civil forfeiture order shall state that all interest in the property in question of the adult or juvenile who committed the act that is the basis of the order is forfeited to the state or political subdivision and shall make due provision for the interest in that property of any other person, when appropriate under this section. The court may issue any additional order to affect the forfeiture, including, but not limited to, one or more orders under section 2981.06 of the Revised Code.

(E) If the court disposes of all petitions timely filed under this section in favor of the state or political subdivision, the state or political subdivision shall have clear title to the property that is the subject of a forfeiture order under this section, but only to the extent that other parties' lawful interests in the property are not infringed. To the extent that the state or political subdivision has clear title to the property, the state or political subdivision may warrant good title to any subsequent purchaser or other transferee.

**HISTORY: 151 v H 241, § 1, eff. 7-1-07.**

See provisions of § 4 of 151 v H 241 following RC § 2901.01.

## § 2981.06 Proceedings upon entry of forfeiture order.

(A) Upon the entry of a forfeiture order under section 2981.04 or 2981.05 of the Revised Code, if necessary, the court shall order an appropriate law enforcement officer to seize the forfeited property on conditions that the court considers proper. If necessary, the court shall order the person in possession of the property to deliver the property by a specific date to the law enforcement agency involved in the initial seizure of the property. The court shall deliver the order by personal service or certified mail.

(B) With respect to property that is the subject of a forfeiture order issued under section 2981.04 or 2981.05 of the Revised Code, the court that issued the order, upon petition of the prosecutor who prosecuted the underlying offense or act or brought the civil forfeiture action, may do any of the following:

(1) Enter any appropriate restraining orders or injunctions; require execution of satisfactory performance bonds; appoint receivers, conservators, appraisers, accountants, or trustees; or take any other action necessary to safeguard and maintain the forfeited property;

(2) Authorize the payment of rewards to persons who provide information resulting in forfeiture of the property under this chapter from funds provided under division (F) of section 2981.12 of the Revised Code;

(3) Authorize the prosecutor to settle claims;

(4) Restore forfeited property to victims and grant petitions for mitigation or remission of forfeiture;

(5) Authorize a stay of the forfeiture order pending appeal or resolution of any claim to the property if requested by a person other than the defendant or a person acting in concert with, or on behalf of, the defendant.

(C) To facilitate the identification and location of property that is the subject of a forfeiture order and to facilitate the disposition of petitions for remission or mitigation issued under this section, after the issuance of a forfeiture order and upon application by the prosecutor, the court, consistent with the Civil Rules, may order that the testimony of any witness relating to the forfeited property be taken by deposition and that any designated material that is not privileged be produced at the same time and place as the testimony.

(D) The court shall order forfeiture of any other property of the offender or delinquent child up to the value of the unreachable property if any of the following describe any property subject to a forfeiture order under section 2981.04 or 2981.05 of the Revised Code:

(1) It cannot be located through due diligence.

(2) It has been transferred, sold, or deposited with a third party.

(3) It has been placed beyond the jurisdiction of the court.

(4) It has been substantially diminished in value or has been commingled with other property and cannot be divided without difficulty or undue injury to innocent persons.

(E) After the state or political subdivision is granted clear title under section 2981.04 or 2981.05 of the Revised Code, the prosecutor shall direct disposition of the property pursuant to this chapter, making due provisions for the rights of innocent persons.

(F) Any interest in property not exercisable by, or transferable for value to, the state or political subdivision shall expire and shall not revert to the offender or delinquent child who forfeited the property. The offender or delinquent child is not eligible to purchase the property at a sale under this chapter.

(G) Any income accruing to or derived from forfeited property may be used to offset ordinary and necessary expenses related to the property that are required by law or necessary to protect the interest of the state, political subdivision, or third parties.

**HISTORY: 151 v H 241, § 1, eff. 7-1-07.**

See provisions of § 4 of 151 v H 241 following RC § 2901.01.

## § 2981.07 Interference with or diminishing forfeitable property.

(A) No person shall destroy, damage, remove, or transfer property that is subject to forfeiture or otherwise take any action in regard to property that is subject to forfeiture with purpose to do any of the following:

(1) Prevent or impair the state's or political subdivision's lawful authority to take the property into its custody or control under this chapter or to continue holding the property under its lawful custody or control;

(2) Impair or defeat the court's continuing jurisdiction over the person and property;

(3) Devalue property that the person knows, or has reasonable cause to believe, is subject to forfeiture proceedings under this chapter.

(B)(1) Whoever violates this section is guilty of interference with or diminishing forfeitable property.

(2) Except as otherwise provided in divisions (B)(3), (4), and (5) of this section, interference with or diminishing forfeitable property is a misdemeanor of the first degree.

(3) If the value of the property is one thousand dollars or more but less than seven thousand five hundred dollars, interference with or diminishing forfeitable property is a felony of the fifth degree.

(4) If the value of the property is seven thousand five hundred dollars or more but less than one hundred fifty thousand dollars, interference with or diminishing forfeitable property is a felony of the fourth degree.

(5) If the value of the property is one hundred fifty thousand dollars or more, interference with or diminishing forfeitable property is a felony of the third degree.

**HISTORY: 151 v H 241, § 1, eff. 7-1-07; 2011 HB 86, § 1, eff. Sept. 30, 2011.**

The provisions of § 4 of HB 86 read as follows:

"SECTION 4. The amendments to sections 926.99, 1333.99, 1707.99, 1716.99, 2909.03, 2909.05, 2909.11, 2913.02, 2913.03, 2913.04, 2913.11, 2913.21, 2913.31, 2913.32, 2913.34, 2913.40, 2913.401, 2913.42, 2913.421, 2913.43, 2913.45, 2913.46, 2913.47, 2913.48, 2913.49, 2913.51, 2913.61, 2915.05, 2917.21, 2917.31, 2917.32, 2921.13, 2921.41, 2923.31, and 2981.07, division (B) of section 2929.13, and division (A) of section 2929.14 of the Revised Code that are made in this act apply to a person who commits an offense specified or penalized under those sections on or after the effective date of this section and to a person to whom division (B) of section 1.58 of the Revised Code makes the amendments applicable.

"The provisions of sections 926.99, 1333.99, 1707.99, 1716.99, 2909.03, 2909.05, 2909.11, 2913.02, 2913.03, 2913.04, 2913.11, 2913.21, 2913.31, 2913.32, 2913.34, 2913.40, 2913.401, 2913.42, 2913.421, 2913.43, 2913.45, 2913.46, 2913.47, 2913.48, 2913.49, 2913.51, 2913.61, 2915.05, 2917.21, 2917.31, 2917.32, 2921.13, 2921.41, 2923.31, and 2981.07 of the Revised Code in existence prior to the effective date of this section shall apply to a person upon whom a court imposed sentence prior to the effective date of this section for an offense specified or penalized under those sections. The amendments to sections 926.99, 1333.99, 1707.99, 1716.99, 2909.03, 2909.05, 2909.11, 2913.02, 2913.03, 2913.04, 2913.11, 2913.21, 2913.31, 2913.32, 2913.34, 2913.40, 2913.401, 2913.42, 2913.421, 2913.43, 2913.45, 2913.46, 2913.47, 2913.48, 2913.49, 2913.51, 2913.61, 2915.05, 2917.21, 2917.31, 2917.32, 2921.13, 2921.41, 2923.31, and 2981.07 of the Revised Code that are made in this act do not apply to a person who upon whom a court imposed sentence prior to the effective date of this section for an offense specified or penalized under those sections."

See provisions of § 4 of 151 v H 241 following RC § 2901.01.

## § 2981.08 Right to trial by jury.

Parties to a forfeiture action under this chapter have a right to trial by jury as follows:

(A) In a criminal forfeiture action, the defendant has the right to trial by jury.

(B) In a civil forfeiture action, the defendant, the state or political subdivision, and third party claimants have the right to trial by jury.

**HISTORY: 151 v H 241, § 1, eff. 7-1-07.**

See provisions of § 4 of 151 v H 241 following RC § 2901.01.

## § 2981.09 Proportionality review regarding possible forfeiture of instrumentality.

(A) Property may not be forfeited as an instrumentality under this chapter to the extent that the amount or value of the property is disproportionate to the severity of the offense. The owner of the property shall have the burden of going forward with the evidence and the burden to prove by a preponderance of the evidence that the amount or value of the property subject to forfeiture is disproportionate to the severity of the offense.

(B) Contraband and any proceeds obtained from the offense are not subject to proportionality review under this section.

(C) In determining the severity of the offense for purposes of forfeiture of an instrumentality, the court shall consider all relevant factors including, but not limited to, the following:

(1) The seriousness of the offense and its impact on the community, including the duration of the activity and the harm caused or intended by the person whose property is subject to forfeiture;

(2) The extent to which the person whose property is subject to forfeiture participated in the offense;

(3) Whether the offense was completed or attempted.

(D) In determining the value of the property that is an instrumentality and that is subject to forfeiture, the court shall consider relevant factors including, but not limited to, the following:

(1) The fair market value of the property;

(2) The value of the property to the person whose property is subject to forfeiture, including hardship to the person or to innocent persons if the property were forfeited.

**HISTORY: 151 v H 241, § 1, eff. 7-1-07.**

See provisions of § 4 of 151 v H 241 following RC § 2901.01.

## § 2981.11 Custody and disposition of property; internal control policy; reports to attorney general; locating persons entitled to possession; definitions.

(A)(1) Any property that has been lost, abandoned, stolen, seized pursuant to a search warrant, or otherwise lawfully seized or forfeited and that is in the custody of a law enforcement agency shall be kept safely by the agency, pending the time it no longer is needed as evidence or for another lawful purpose, and shall be disposed of pursuant to sections 2981.12 and 2981.13 of the Revised Code.

(2) This chapter does not apply to the custody and disposal of any of the following:

(a) Vehicles subject to forfeiture under Title XLV of the Revised Code, except as provided in division (A)(6) of section 2981.12 of the Revised Code;

(b) Abandoned junk motor vehicles or other property of negligible value;

(c) Property held by a department of rehabilitation and correction institution that is unclaimed, that does not have an identified owner, that the owner agrees to dispose of, or that is identified by the department as having little value;

(d) Animals taken, and devices used in unlawfully taking animals, under section 1531.20 of the Revised Code;

(e) Controlled substances sold by a peace officer in the performance of the officer's official duties under section 3719.141 of the Revised Code;

(f) Property recovered by a township law enforcement agency under sections 505.105 to 505.109 of the Revised Code;

(g) Property held and disposed of under an ordinance of the municipal corporation or under sections 737.29 to 737.33 of the Revised Code, except that a municipal corporation that has received notice of a citizens' reward program as provided in division (F) of section 2981.12 of the Revised Code and disposes of property under an ordinance shall pay twenty-five per cent of any moneys acquired from any sale or auction to the citizens' reward program.

(B)(1) Each law enforcement agency that has custody of any property that is subject to this section shall adopt and comply with a written internal control policy that does all of the following:

(a) Provides for keeping detailed records as to the amount of property acquired by the agency and the date property was acquired;

(b) Provides for keeping detailed records of the disposition of the property, which shall include, but not be limited to, both of the following:

(i) The manner in which it was disposed, the date of disposition, detailed financial records concerning any property sold, and the name of any person who received the property. The record shall not identify or enable identification of the individual officer who seized any item of property.

(ii) The general types of expenditures made with amounts that are gained from the sale of the property and that are retained by the agency, including the specific amount expended on each general type of expenditure, except that the policy shall not provide for or permit the identification of any specific expenditure that is made in an ongoing investigation.

(c) Complies with section 2981.13 of the Revised Code if the agency has a law enforcement trust fund or similar fund created under that section.

(2) Each law enforcement agency that during any calendar year has any seized or forfeited property covered by this section in its custody, including amounts distributed under section 2981.13 of the Revised Code to its law enforcement trust fund or a similar fund created for the state highway patrol, department of public safety, department of taxation, or state board of pharmacy, shall prepare a report covering the calendar year that cumulates all of the information contained in all of the public records kept by the agency pursuant to this section for that calendar year. The agency shall send a copy of the cumulative report to the attorney general not later than the first day of March in the calendar year following the calendar year covered by the report.

(3) The records kept under the internal control policy shall be open to public inspection during the agency's regular business hours. The policy adopted under this section and each report received by the attorney general is a public record open for inspection under section 149.43 of the Revised Code.

(4) Not later than the fifteenth day of April in each calendar year in which reports are sent to the attorney general under division (B)(2) of this section, the attorney general shall send to the president of the senate and the speaker of the house of representatives a written notice that indicates that the attorney general received reports that cover the previous calendar year, that the reports are open for inspection under section 149.43 of the Revised Code, and that the attorney general will provide a copy of any or all of the reports to the president of the senate or the speaker of the house of representatives upon request.

(C) A law enforcement agency with custody of property to be disposed of under section 2981.12 or 2981.13 of the Revised Code shall make a reasonable effort to locate persons entitled to possession of the property, to notify them of when and where it may be claimed, and to return the property to them at the earliest possible time. In the absence of evidence identifying persons entitled to possession, it is sufficient notice to advertise in a newspaper of general circulation in the county and to briefly describe the nature of the property in custody and inviting persons to view and establish their right to it.

(D) As used in sections 2981.11 to 2981.13 of the Revised Code:

(1) "Citizens' reward program" has the same meaning as in section 9.92 of the Revised Code.

(2) "Law enforcement agency" includes correctional institutions.

(3) "Township law enforcement agency" means an organized police department of a township, a township police district, a joint police district, or the office of a township constable.

**HISTORY: 151 v H 241, § 1, eff. 7-1-07; 152 v H 120, § 1, eff. 7-1-07; 2011 HB 153, § 101.01, eff. Sept. 29, 2011.**

The effective date is set by § 3 of 152 v H 120.
See provisions of § 4 of 151 v H 241 following RC § 2901.01.

## § 2981.12 Disposal of unclaimed or forfeited property other than contraband, proceeds, and instrumentalities; citizen's reward program.

(A) Unclaimed or forfeited property in the custody of a law enforcement agency, other than property described in division (A)(2) of section 2981.11 of the Revised Code, shall be disposed of by order of any court of record that has territorial jurisdiction over the political subdivision that employs the law enforcement agency, as follows:

(1) Drugs shall be disposed of pursuant to section 3719.11 of the Revised Code or placed in the custody of the secretary of the treasury of the United States for disposal or use for medical or scientific purposes under applicable federal law.

(2) Firearms and dangerous ordnance suitable for police work may be given to a law enforcement agency for that purpose. Firearms suitable for sporting use or as museum pieces or collectors' items may be sold at public auction pursuant to division (B) of this section. The agency may sell other firearms and dangerous ordnance to a federally licensed firearms dealer in a manner that the court considers proper. The agency shall destroy any firearms or dangerous ordnance not given to a law enforcement agency or sold or shall send them to the bureau of criminal identification and investigation for destruction by the bureau.

(3) Obscene materials shall be destroyed.

(4) Beer, intoxicating liquor, or alcohol seized from a person who does not hold a permit issued under Chapters 4301. and 4303. of the Revised Code or otherwise forfeited to the state for an offense under section 4301.45 or 4301.53 of the Revised Code shall be sold by the division of liquor control if the division determines that it is fit for sale or shall be placed in the custody of the investigations unit in the department of public safety and be used for training relating to law enforcement activities. The department, with the assistance of the division of liquor control, shall adopt rules in accordance with Chapter 119. of the Revised Code to provide for the distribution to state or local law enforcement agencies upon their request. If any tax imposed under Title XLIII of the Revised Code has not been paid in relation to the beer, intoxicating liquor, or alcohol, any moneys acquired from the sale shall first be used to pay the tax. All other money collected under this division shall be paid into the state treasury. Any beer, intoxicating liquor, or alcohol that the division determines to be unfit for sale shall be destroyed.

(5) Money received by an inmate of a correctional institution from an unauthorized source or in an unauthorized manner shall be returned to the sender, if known, or deposited in the inmates' industrial and entertainment fund of the institution if the sender is not known.

(6)(a) Any mobile instrumentality forfeited under this chapter may be given to the law enforcement agency that initially seized the mobile instrumentality for use in performing its duties, if the agency wants the mobile instrumentality. The agency shall take the mobile instrumentality subject to any security interest or lien on the mobile instrumentality.

(b) Vehicles and vehicle parts forfeited under sections 4549.61 to 4549.63 of the Revised Code may be given to a law enforcement agency for use in performing its duties. Those parts may be incorporated into any other official vehicle. Parts that do not bear vehicle identification numbers or derivatives of them may be sold or disposed of as provided by rules of the director of public safety. Parts from which a vehicle identification number or derivative of it has been removed, defaced, covered, altered, or destroyed and that are not suitable for police work or incorporation into an official vehicle shall be destroyed and sold as junk or scrap.

(7) Computers, computer networks, computer systems, and computer software suitable for police work may be given to a law enforcement agency for that purpose or disposed of under division (B) of this section.

(B) Unclaimed or forfeited property that is not described in division (A) of this section or division (A)(2) of section 2981.11 of the Revised Code, with court approval, may be used by the law enforcement agency in possession of it. If it is not used by the agency, it may be sold without appraisal at a public auction to the highest bidder for cash or disposed of in another manner that the court considers proper.

(C) Except as provided in divisions (A) and (F) of this section and after compliance with division (D) of this section when applicable, any moneys acquired from the sale of property disposed of pursuant to this section shall be placed in the general revenue fund of the state, or the general fund of the county, the township, or the municipal corporation of which the law enforcement agency involved is an agency.

(D) If the property was in the possession of the law enforcement agency in relation to a delinquent child proceeding in a juvenile court, ten per cent of any moneys acquired from the sale of property disposed of under this section shall be applied to one or more alcohol and drug addiction treatment programs that are certified by the department of alcohol and drug addiction services under section 3793.06 of the Revised Code. A juvenile court shall not specify a program, except as provided in this division, unless the program is in the same county as the court or in a contiguous county. If no certified program is located in any of those counties, the juvenile court may specify a certified program anywhere in Ohio. The remaining ninety per cent of the proceeds or cash shall be applied as provided in division (C) of this section.

Each treatment program that receives in any calendar year forfeited money under this division shall file an annual report for that year with the attorney general and with the court of common pleas and board of county commissioners of the county in which the program is located and of any other county from which the program received forfeited money. The program shall file the report on or before the first day of March in the calendar year following the calendar year in which the program received the money. The report shall include statistics on the number of persons the program served, identify the types of treatment services it provided to them, and include a specific accounting of the purposes for which it used the money so received. No information contained in the report shall identify, or enable a person to determine the identity of, any person served by the program.

(E) Each certified alcohol and drug addiction treatment program that receives in any calendar year money under this section or under section 2981.13 of the Revised Code as the result of a juvenile forfeiture order shall file an annual report for that calendar year with the attorney general and with the court of common pleas and board of county commissioners of the county in which the program is located and of any other county from which the program received the money. The program shall file the report on or before the first day of March in the calendar year following the year in which the program received the money. The report shall include statistics on the number of persons served with the money, identify the types of treatment services provided, and specifically account for how the money was used. No information in the report shall identify or enable a person to determine the identity of anyone served by the program.

As used in this division, "juvenile-related forfeiture order" means any forfeiture order issued by a juvenile court under section 2981.04 or 2981.05 of the Revised Code and any disposal of property ordered by a court under section 2981.11 of the Revised Code regarding property that was in the possession of a law enforcement agency in relation to a delinquent child proceeding in a juvenile court.

(F) Each board of county commissioners that recognizes a citizens' reward program under section 9.92 of the Revised Code shall notify each law enforcement agency of that county and of a township or municipal corporation wholly located in that county of the recognition by filing a copy of its resolution conferring that recognition with each of those agencies. When the board recognizes a citizens' reward program and the county includes a part, but not all, of the territory of a municipal corporation, the board shall so notify the law enforcement agency of that municipal corporation of the recognition of the citizens' reward program only if the county contains the highest percentage of the municipal corporation's population.

Upon being so notified, each law enforcement agency shall pay twenty-five per cent of any forfeited proceeds or cash derived from each sale of property disposed of pursuant to this section to the citizens' reward program for use exclusively to pay rewards. No part of the funds may be used to pay expenses associated with the program. If a citizens' reward program that operates in more than one county or in another state in addition to this state receives funds under this section, the funds shall be used to pay rewards only for tips and information to law enforcement agencies concerning offenses committed in the county from which the funds were received.

Receiving funds under this section or section 2981.11 of the Revised Code does not make the citizens' reward program a governmental unit or public office for purposes of section 149.43 of the Revised Code.

(G) Any property forfeited under this chapter shall not be used to pay any fine imposed upon a person who is convicted of or pleads guilty to an underlying criminal offense or a different offense arising out of the same facts and circumstances.

**HISTORY: 151 v H 241, § 1, eff. 7-1-07; 2011 HB 153, § 101.01, eff. Sept. 29, 2011.**

See provisions of § 4 of 151 v H 241 following RC § 2901.01.

## § 2981.13 Disposal of contraband, proceeds, and instrumentalities; local and state funds; community preventive education programs.

(A) Except as otherwise provided in this section, property ordered forfeited as contraband, proceeds, or an instrumentality pursuant to this chapter shall be disposed of, used, or sold pursuant to section 2981.12 of the Revised Code. If the property is to be sold under that section, the prosecutor shall cause notice of the proposed sale to be given in accordance with law.

(B) If the contraband or instrumentality forfeited under this chapter is sold, any moneys acquired from a sale and any proceeds forfeited under this chapter shall be applied in the following order:

(1) First, to pay costs incurred in the seizure, storage, maintenance, security, and sale of the property and in the forfeiture proceeding;

(2) Second, in a criminal forfeiture case, to satisfy any restitution ordered to the victim of the offense or, in a civil forfeiture case, to satisfy any recovery ordered for the person harmed, unless paid from other assets;

(3) Third, to pay the balance due on any security interest preserved under this chapter;

(4) Fourth, apply the remaining amounts as follows:

(a) If the forfeiture was ordered by a juvenile court, ten per cent to one or more certified alcohol and drug addiction treatment programs as provided in division (D) of section 2981.12 of the Revised Code;

(b) If the forfeiture was ordered in a juvenile court, ninety per cent, and if the forfeiture was ordered in a court other than a juvenile court, one hundred per cent to the law enforcement trust fund of the prosecutor and to the following fund supporting the law enforcement agency that substantially conducted the investigation: the law enforcement trust fund of the county sheriff, municipal corporation, township, or park district created under section 511.18 or 1545.01 of the Revised Code; the state highway patrol contraband, forfeiture, and other fund; the department of public safety investigative unit contraband, forfeiture, and other fund; the department of taxation enforcement fund; the board of pharmacy drug law enforcement fund created by division (B)(1) of section 4729.65 of the Revised Code; the medicaid fraud investigation and prosecution fund; or the treasurer of state for deposit into the peace officer training commission fund if any other state law enforcement agency substantially conducted the investigation. In the case of property forfeited for medicaid fraud, any remaining amount shall be used by the attorney general to investigate and prosecute medicaid fraud offenses.

If the prosecutor declines to accept any of the remaining amounts, the amounts shall be applied to the fund of the agency that substantially conducted the investigation.

(c) If more than one law enforcement agency is substantially involved in the seizure of property forfeited under this chapter, the court ordering the forfeiture shall equitably divide the amounts, after calculating any distribution to the law enforcement trust fund of the prosecutor pursuant to division (B)(4) of this section, among the entities that the court determines were substantially involved in the seizure.

(C)(1) A law enforcement trust fund shall be established by the prosecutor of each county who intends to receive any remaining amounts pursuant to this section, by the sheriff of each county, by the legislative authority of each municipal corporation, by the board of township trustees of each township that has a township police department, township or joint police district police force, or office of the constable, and by the board of park commissioners of each park district created pursuant to section 511.18 or 1545.01 of the Revised Code that has a park district police force or law enforcement department, for the purposes of this section.

There is hereby created in the state treasury the state highway patrol contraband, forfeiture, and other fund, the department of public safety investigative unit contraband, forfeiture, and other fund, the medicaid fraud investigation and prosecution fund, the department of taxation enforcement fund, and the peace officer training commission fund, for the purposes of this section.

Amounts distributed to any municipal corporation, township, or park district law enforcement trust fund shall be allocated from the fund by the legislative authority only to the police department of the municipal corporation, by the board of township trustees only to the township police department, township police district police force, or office of the constable, by the joint police district board only to the joint police district, and by the board of park commissioners only to the park district police force or law enforcement department.

(2)(a) No amounts shall be allocated to a fund created under this section or used by an agency unless the agency has adopted a written internal control policy that addresses the use of moneys received from the appropriate fund. The appropriate fund shall be expended only in accordance with that policy and, subject to the requirements specified in this section, only for the following purposes:

(i) To pay the costs of protracted or complex investigations or prosecutions;

(ii) To provide reasonable technical training or expertise;

(iii) To provide matching funds to obtain federal grants to aid law enforcement, in the support of DARE programs or other programs designed to educate adults or children with respect to the dangers associated with the use of drugs of abuse;

(iv) To pay the costs of emergency action taken under section 3745.13 of the Revised Code relative to the operation of an illegal methamphetamine laboratory if the forfeited property or money involved was that of a person responsible for the operation of the laboratory;

(v) For other law enforcement purposes that the superintendent of the state highway patrol, department of public safety, prosecutor, county sheriff, legislative authority, department of taxation, board of township trustees, or board of park commissioners determines to be appropriate.

(b) The board of pharmacy drug law enforcement fund shall be expended only in accordance with the written internal control policy so adopted by the board and only in accordance with section 4729.65 of the Revised Code, except that it also may be expended to pay the costs of emergency action taken under section 3745.13 of the Revised Code relative to the operation of an illegal methamphetamine laboratory if the forfeited property or money involved was that of a person responsible for the operation of the laboratory.

(c) The state highway patrol contraband, forfeiture, and other fund, the department of public safety investigative unit contraband, forfeiture, and other fund, the department of taxation enforcement fund, the board of pharmacy drug law enforcement fund, and a law enforcement trust fund shall not be used to meet the operating costs of the state highway patrol, of the investigative unit of the department of public safety, of the state board of pharmacy, of any political subdivision, or of any office of a prosecutor or county sheriff that are unrelated to law enforcement.

(d) Forfeited moneys that are paid into the state treasury to be deposited into the peace officer training commission fund shall be used by the commission only to pay the costs of peace officer training.

(3) Any of the following offices or agencies that receive amounts under this section during any calendar year shall file a report with the specified entity, not later than the thirty-first day of January of the next calendar year, verifying that the moneys were expended only for the purposes authorized by this section or other relevant statute and specifying the amounts expended for each authorized purpose:

(a) Any sheriff or prosecutor shall file the report with the county auditor.

(b) Any municipal corporation police department shall file the report with the legislative authority of the municipal corporation.

(c) Any township police department, township or joint police district police force, or office of the constable shall file the report with the board of township trustees of the township.

(d) Any park district police force or law enforcement department shall file the report with the board of park commissioners of the park district.

(e) The superintendent of the state highway patrol and the tax commissioner shall file the report with the attorney general.

(f) The executive director of the state board of pharmacy shall file the report with the attorney general, verifying that cash and forfeited proceeds paid into the board of pharmacy drug law enforcement fund were used only in accordance with section 4729.65 of the Revised Code.

(g) The peace officer training commission shall file a report with the attorney general, verifying that cash and forfeited proceeds paid into the peace officer training commission fund pursuant to this section during the prior calendar year were used by the commission during the prior calendar year only to pay the costs of peace officer training.

(D) The written internal control policy of a county sheriff, prosecutor, municipal corporation police department, township police department, township or joint police district police force, office of the constable, or park district police force or law enforcement department shall provide that at least ten per cent of the first one hundred thousand dollars of amounts deposited during each calendar year in the agency's law enforcement trust fund under this section, and at least twenty per cent of the amounts exceeding one hundred thousand dollars that are so deposited, shall be used in connection with community preventive education programs. The manner of use shall be determined by the sheriff, prosecutor, department, police force, or office of the constable after receiving and considering advice on appropriate community preventive education programs from the county's board of alcohol, drug addiction, and mental health services, from the county's alcohol and drug addiction services board, or through appropriate community dialogue.

The financial records kept under the internal control policy shall specify the amount deposited during each calendar year in the portion of that amount that was used pursuant to this division, and the programs in connection with which the portion of that amount was so used.

As used in this division, "community preventive education programs" include, but are not limited to, DARE programs and other programs designed to educate adults or children with respect to the dangers associated with using drugs of abuse.

(E) Upon the sale, under this section or section 2981.12 of the Revised Code, of any property that is required by law to be titled or registered, the state shall issue an appropriate certificate of title or registration to the purchaser. If the state is vested with title and elects to retain property that is required to be titled or registered under law, the state shall issue an appropriate certificate of title or registration.

(F) Any failure of a law enforcement officer or agency, prosecutor, court, or the attorney general to comply with this section in relation to any property seized does not affect the validity of the seizure and shall not be considered to be the basis for suppressing any evidence resulting from the seizure, provided the seizure itself was lawful.

**HISTORY: 151 v H 241, § 1, eff. 7-1-07; 152 v H 120, § 1, eff. 7-1-07; 153 v H 1, § 101.01, eff. 10-16-09; 2011 HB 153, § 101.01, eff. Sept. 29, 2011.**

The effective date is set by § 812.10 of 153 v H 1.
The effective date is set by § 3 of 152 v H 120.
See provisions of § 4 of 151 v H 241 following RC § 2901.01.

## § 2981.14 Forfeiture under federal law.

(A) Nothing in this chapter precludes the head of a law enforcement agency that seizes property from seeking forfeiture under federal law. If the property is forfeitable under this chapter and federal forfeiture is not sought, the property is subject only to this chapter.

(B) Any law enforcement agency that receives moneys from a sale of forfeited property under federal law shall deposit, use, and account for the amounts, including any interest derived, in accordance with applicable federal law. If the state highway patrol or the investigative unit of the department of public safety receives such federal forfeiture moneys, the appropriate official shall deposit all interest or other earnings derived from the investment of the moneys into the contraband, forfeiture, and other fund of the highway patrol or the department, whichever is appropriate.

**HISTORY: 151 v H 241, § 1, eff. 7-1-07.**

See provisions of § 4 of 151 v H 241 following RC § 2901.01.

# MISCELLANEOUS STATUTORY PROVISIONS

## CHAPTER 1: DEFINITIONS; RULES OF CONSTRUCTION



### § 1.01 "Revised Code".

All statutes of a permanent and general nature of the state as revised and consolidated into general provisions, titles, chapters, and sections shall be known and designated as the "Revised Code," for which designation "R.C." may be substituted. Except as otherwise provided in section 1301.107 of the Revised Code, Title, Chapter, and section headings and marginal General Code section numbers do not constitute any part of the law as contained in the "Revised Code."

The enactment of the Revised Code shall not be construed to affect a right or liability accrued or incurred under any section of the General Code prior to the effective date of such enactment, or an action or proceeding for the enforcement of such right or liability. Such enactment shall not be construed to relieve any person from punishment for an act committed in violation of any section of the General Code, nor to affect an indictment or prosecution therefor. For such purposes, any such section of the General Code shall continue in full force notwithstanding its repeal for the purpose of revision.

**HISTORY: Bureau of Code Revision. Eff 10-1-53; 2011 HB 9, § 1, eff. June 29, 2011.**

Acts 2011, HB 9, § 3 provides: "This act applies to transactions entered into on or after the effective date of this act."

[DEFINITIONS]

### § 1.02 General definitions.

As used in the Revised Code, unless the context otherwise requires:

(A) "Whoever" includes all persons, natural and artificial; partners; principals, agents, and employees; and all officials, public or private.

(B) "Another," when used to designate the owner of property which is the subject of an offense, includes not only natural persons but also every other owner of property.

(C) "Of unsound mind" includes all forms of mental retardation or derangement.

(D) "Bond" includes an undertaking.

(E) "Undertaking" includes a bond.

(F) "And" may be read "or," and "or" may be read "and" if the sense requires it.

(G) "Registered mail" includes certified mail and "certified mail" includes registered mail.

**HISTORY: Bureau of Code Revision, 10-1-53; 126 v 1164 (Eff 6-27-55); 129 v 582 (Eff 1-10-61); 133 v H 688 (Eff 11-21-69); 134 v H 607. Eff 1-3-72.**

### § 1.03 Definition of "anything of value."

As used in any section of the Revised Code for the violation of which there is provided a penalty or forfeiture, unless the context otherwise requires, "anything of value" includes:

(A) Money, bank bills or notes, United States treasury notes, and other bills, bonds, or notes issued by lawful authority and intended to pass and circulate as money;

(B) Goods and chattels;

(C) Promissory notes, bills of exchange, orders, drafts, warrants, checks, or bonds given for the payment of money;

(D) Receipts given for the payment of money or other property;

(E) Rights in action;

(F) Things which savor of the realty and are, at the time they are taken, a part of the freehold, whether they are of the substance or produce thereof or affixed thereto, although there may be no interval between the severing and taking away;

(G) Any interest in realty, including fee simple and partial interests, present and future, contingent or vested interest, beneficial interests, leasehold interests, and any other interest in realty;

(H) Any promise of future employment;

(I) Every other thing of value.

**HISTORY: RS § 6794; 60 v 20; 66 v 29, 341; 68 v 87; 69 v 67; GC § 12369; Bureau of Code Revision, 10-1-53; 136 v H 1040. Eff 8-27-76.**

## § 1.04 Definition of standard time for Ohio.

The standard time throughout this state shall be the mean astronomical time of the seventy-fifth degree of longitude west from Greenwich. Courts, public offices, and official legal proceedings subject to the laws of this state shall be regulated thereby. Whenever the time of performance of any act, or the time of accrual or determination of any rights, is fixed or governed by the statutes of this state or by any resolutions, rules, regulations, or orders in effect under authority of such statutes, such time shall be the standard time provided in this section.

All clocks maintained in or upon public buildings, existing as such under the laws of this state, shall be set and run according to this section.

**HISTORY: RS § 4446-3; 90 v 115; GC § 5979; 112 v 3; 120 v 3; Bureau of Code Revision. Eff 10-1-53.**

**Comment, Legislative Service Commission**

The standard time fixed by this act shall be placed in operation at 2:00 o'clock antemeridian, by mean astronomical time of the seventy-fifth degree of longitude west from Greenwich, of the first Sunday after the enactment date of this act. (120 v 3 [4], § 2)

## § 1.05 "Imprisoned" defined.

(A) As used in the Revised Code, unless the context otherwise requires, "imprisoned" or "imprisonment" means being imprisoned under a sentence imposed for an offense or serving a term of imprisonment, prison term, jail term, term of local incarceration, or other term under a sentence imposed for an offense in an institution under the control of the department of rehabilitation and correction, a county, multicounty, municipal, municipal-county, or multicounty-municipal jail or workhouse, a minimum security jail, a community-based correctional facility, a halfway house, an alternative residential facility, or another facility described or referred to in section 2929.34 of the Revised Code for the type of criminal offense and under the circumstances specified or referred to in that section.

(B) As used in division (A) of this section, "community-based correctional facility," "halfway house," and "alternative residential facility" have the same meanings as in section 2929.01 of the Revised Code.

**HISTORY: RS § 6794; Revised Statutes of 1880 and Codifying Commission; GC § 12370; Bureau of Code Revision, 10-1-53; 134 v H 511 (Eff 1-1-74); 139 v S 199 (Eff 1-5-83); 140 v S 210 (Eff 7-1-83); 142 v H 455 (Eff 7-20-87); 143 v S 258 (Eff 11-20-90); 145 v H 571 (Eff 10-6-94); 146 v S 2 (Eff 7-1-96); 146 v S 269 (Eff 7-1-96); 146 v S 166. Eff 10-17-96; 149 v H 490, § 1, eff. 1-1-04.**

The effective date is set by section 4 of HB 490.

The provisions of § 5 of HB 490 (149 v —) read as follows:

SECTION 5. Section 1.05 of the Revised Code is presented in this act as a composite of the section as amended by both Am. Sub. S.B. 166 and Am. Sub. S.B. 269 of the 121st General Assembly. The General Assembly, applying the principle stated in division (B) of section 1.52 of the Revised Code that amendments are to be harmonized if reasonably capable of simultaneous operation, finds that the specified composite is the resulting version of the specified sections in effect prior to the effective date of the section as presented in this act.

## § 1.06 Repealed, 134 v H 511, § 2 [RS § 6795; 66 v 324, § 230; GC § 12372; 121 v 125; Bureau of Code Revision, 10-1-53]. Eff 1-1-74.

This section defined felonies, misdemeanors, and minor offenses. See now RC § 2901.02.

## § 1.07 Value of written instrument or evidence of debt.

Except as provided in sections 2909.11 and 2913.61 of the Revised Code, when an evidence of debt or a written instrument is the subject of a criminal act, the amount of money due on the evidence of debt or the written instrument or secured thereby, or the amount of money or the value of property affected thereby, shall be deemed the value of the evidence of debt or the written instrument.

**HISTORY: RS § 6796; 74 v 241, § 3; GC § 12373; Bureau of Code Revision, 10-1-53; 134 v H 511. Eff 1-1-74.**

## § 1.08 "Blighted area," "slum," and "blighted parcel" defined; restrictions on determination.

As used in the Revised Code:

(A) "Blighted area" and "slum" mean an area in which at least seventy per cent of the parcels are blighted parcels and those blighted parcels substantially impair or arrest the sound growth of the state or a political subdivision of the state, retard the provision of housing accommodations, constitute an economic or social liability, or are a menace to the public health, safety, morals, or welfare in their present condition and use.

(B) "Blighted parcel" means either of the following:

(1) A parcel that has one or more of the following conditions:

(a) A structure that is dilapidated, unsanitary, unsafe, or vermin infested and that because of its condition has been designated by an agency that is responsible for the enforcement of housing, building, or fire codes as unfit for human habitation or use;

(b) The property poses a direct threat to public health or safety in its present condition by reason of environmentally hazardous conditions, solid waste pollution, or contamination;

(c) Tax or special assessment delinquencies exceeding the fair value of the land that remain unpaid thirty-five days after notice to pay has been mailed.

(2) A parcel that has two or more of the following conditions that, collectively considered, adversely affect surrounding or community property values or entail land use relationships that cannot reasonably be corrected through existing zoning codes or other land use regulations:

(a) Dilapidation and deterioration;

(b) Age and obsolescence;

(c) Inadequate provision for ventilation, light, air, sanitation, or open spaces;

(d) Unsafe and unsanitary conditions;

(e) Hazards that endanger lives or properties by fire or other causes;

(f) Noncompliance with building, housing, or other codes;

(g) Nonworking or disconnected utilities;

(h) Is vacant or contains an abandoned structure;

(i) Excessive dwelling unit density;

(j) Is located in an area of defective or inadequate street layout;

(k) Overcrowding of buildings on the land;

(l) Faulty lot layout in relation to size, adequacy, accessibility, or usefulness;

(m) Vermin infestation;

(n) Extensive damage or destruction caused by a major disaster when the damage has not been remediated within a reasonable time;

(o) Identified hazards to health and safety that are conducive to ill health, transmission of disease, juvenile delinquency, or crime;

(p) Ownership or multiple ownership of a single parcel when the owner, or a majority of the owners of a parcel in the case of multiple ownership, cannot be located.

(C) When determining whether a property is a blighted parcel or whether an area is a blighted area or slum for the purposes of this section, no person shall consider whether there is a comparatively better use for any premises, property, structure, area, or portion of an area, or whether the property could generate more tax revenues if put to another use.

(D)(1) Notwithstanding any other provision of this section, absent any environmental or public health hazard that cannot be corrected under its current use or ownership, a property is not a blighted parcel because of any condition listed in division (B) of this section if the condition is consistent with conditions that are normally incident to generally accepted agricultural practices and the land is used for agricultural purposes as defined in section 303.01 or 519.01 of the Revised Code, or the county auditor of the county in which the land is located has determined under section 5713.31 of the Revised Code that the land is "land devoted exclusively to agricultural use" as defined in section 5713.30 of the Revised Code.

(2) A property that under division (D)(1) of this section is not a blighted parcel shall not be included in a blighted area or slum.

**HISTORY: 152 v S 7, § 1, eff. 10-10-07.**

The provisions of § 4 of 152 v S 7 read as follows:

SECTION 4. In accordance with *City of Norwood v. Horney* (2006), 110 Ohio St.3d 353, in which the Supreme Court held the right of property to be a fundamental right protected by the United States and Ohio Constitutions, the General Assembly finds that the exercise of the power of eminent domain at any level of government is a matter of statewide importance and hereby declares its intention that this act be construed to apply generally throughout the state.

The provisions of § 5 of 152 v S 7 read as follows:

SECTION 5. Sections 1 and 2 of this act do not apply to appropriation proceedings pending on the effective date of this act. This section is not intended to indicate that such appropriation proceedings do not have to comply with the constitutional requirements set forth in *City of Norwood v. Horney* (2006), 110 Ohio St.3d 353.

## [CONSTRUCTION]

### § 1.11 Liberal construction of remedial laws.

Remedial laws and all proceedings under them shall be liberally construed in order to promote their object and assist the parties in obtaining justice. The rule of the common law that statutes in derogation of the common law must be strictly construed has no application to remedial laws; but this section does not require a liberal construction of laws affecting personal liberty, relating to amercement, or of a penal nature.

**HISTORY: RS § 4948; S&C 940; 51 v 57, § 2; GC 10214; Bureau of Code Revision. Eff 10-1-53.**

### § 1.12 Special provision governs unless cumulative.

When a special provision is made in a remedial law as to service, pleadings, competency of witnesses, or in any other respect inconsistent with the general provisions of sections of the Revised Code relating to procedure in the court of common pleas and procedure on appeal, the special provision shall govern, unless it appears that the provisions are cumulative.

**HISTORY: RS § 4956; GC § 10222; Bureau of Code Revision. Eff 10-1-53.**

### § 1.14 First day excluded and last day included in computing time; exceptions; legal holiday defined.

The time within which an act is required by law to be done shall be computed by excluding the first and including the last day; except that, when the last day falls on Sunday or a legal holiday, the act may be done on the next succeeding day that is not Sunday or a legal holiday.

When a public office in which an act, required by law, is to be performed is closed to the public for the entire day that constitutes the last day for doing the act or before its usual closing time on that day, the act may be performed on the next succeeding day that is not a Sunday or a legal holiday as defined in this section.

"Legal holiday" as used in this section means the following days:

(A) The first day of January, known as New Year's day;

(B) The third Monday in January, known as Martin Luther King day;

(C) The third Monday in February, known as Washington-Lincoln day;

(D) The day designated in the "Act of June 28, 1968," 82 Stat. 250, 5 U.S.C. 6103, as amended, for the commemoration of Memorial day;

(E) The fourth day of July, known as Independence day;

(F) The first Monday in September, known as Labor day;

(G) The second Monday in October, known as Columbus day;

(H) The eleventh day of November, known as Veterans' day;

(I) The fourth Thursday in November, known as Thanksgiving day;

(J) The twenty-fifth day of December, known as Christmas day;

(K) Any day appointed and recommended by the governor of this state or the president of the United States as a holiday.

If any day designated in this section as a legal holiday falls on Sunday, the next succeeding day is a legal holiday.

**HISTORY: RS § 4951; S&C 1130; 51 v 57, § 597; GC § 10216; Bureau of Code Revision, 10-1-53; 129 v 1073 (Eff 10-11-61); 133 v H 5 (Eff 1-1-71); 135 v H 460 (Eff 7-1-74); 136 v S 18 (Eff 8-1-75); 138 v S 93 (Eff 4-14-81); 139 v S 68 (Eff 5-17-81); 140 v H 364 (Eff 3-14-85); 148 v H 738. Eff 4-10-2001.**

The provisions of § 3 of HB 364 (140 v —) read as follows:

SECTION 3. In the case of collective bargaining agreements between private employers and bona fide labor organizations that are in effect on the effective date of sections 1.14 and 124.19 of the Revised Code as amended by this act, the day designated in the "Act of September 18, 1975," 89 Stat. 479, 5 U.S.C. 6103, as now or hereafter amended, for the commemoration of Memorial Day shall be observed as Decoration or Memorial Day unless the agreement specifically identifies another day as the one on which Decoration or Memorial Day will be observed.

## § 1.15 Effective date; priority of legal rights.

When an act is to take effect or become operative from and after a day named, no part of that day shall be included. If priority of legal rights depends upon the order of events on the same day, such priority shall be determined by the times in the day at which they respectively occurred.

**HISTORY: Codifying Commission; GC § 10217; Bureau of Code Revision. Eff 10-1-53.**

## § 1.22 Change in judicial construction does not affect prior valid obligations.

When an officer or board of a county, township, or municipal corporation by ordinance, resolution, order, or other proceeding, in pursuance of a statute of the state, has authorized or caused the issue and delivery of any bonds, obligations, or instruments of such county, township, or municipal corporation, or has caused any county, township, or municipal contracts, grants, franchises, rights, or privileges to be made or given, which were valid according to judicial construction and adjudication at the date of such action or proceeding, and loans or other things of value have been effected or acquired or expenditures have been made by other persons in reliance upon such construction or adjudication, such bonds, obligations, contracts, grants, franchises, rights, and privileges shall be valid and binding, notwithstanding subsequent change of such rule of judicial construction and adjudication with respect to other similar legislation.

**HISTORY: RS § 22b-1; 95 v 444; GC § 22; Bureau of Code Revision. Eff 10-1-53.**

## § 1.23 Construction of section references.

(A) Wherever in a penalty section reference is made to a violation of a series of sections, or of divisions or subdivisions of a section, such reference shall be construed to mean a violation of any section, division, or subdivision included in such reference.

(B) References in the Revised Code to action taken or authorized under designated sections of the Revised Code include, in every case, action taken or authorized under the applicable section of the General Code which is superseded by the Revised Code.

**HISTORY: Senate Judiciary Committee; 134 v H 607 (Eff 1-3-72); 136 v H 837 (Eff 5-25-76); 137 v H 1. Eff 8-26-77.**

## § 1.30 Intent of Code revision acts is nonsubstantive.

(A) In enacting any legislation with the stated purpose of correcting nonsubstantive errors in the Revised Code, it is the intent of the general assembly not to make substantive changes in the law in effect on the date of such enactment. A section of the Revised Code affected by any such act shall be construed as a restatement and correction of, and substituted in a continuing way for, the corresponding statutory provision existing on its date of enactment.

(B) Acts of the general assembly with the purpose described in division (A) of this section include:

(1) House Bill No. 1 of the 100th general assembly;
(2) House Bill No. 1 of the 104th general assembly;
(3) House Bill No. 1 of the 105th general assembly;
(4) House Bill No. 5 of the 105th general assembly special session;
(5) House Bill No. 1 of the 107th general assembly;
(6) House Bill No. 1 of the 108th general assembly;
(7) House Bill No. 1 of the 109th general assembly;
(8) House Bill No. 1 of the 110th general assembly;
(9) House Bill No. 1 of the 111th general assembly;
(10) House Bill No. 1 of the 112th general assembly;
(11) House Bill No. 1 of the 113th general assembly;
(12) House Bill No. 1 of the 114th general assembly;
(13) House Bill No. 37 of the 115th general assembly;
(14) House Bill No. 428 of the 116th general assembly;
(15) House Bill No. 708 of the 117th general assembly.

**HISTORY: 134 v H 1 (Eff 3-26-71); 135 v H 1 (Eff 3-22-73); 136 v H 1 (Eff 6-13-75); 137 v H 1 (Eff 8-26-77); 138 v H 1 (Eff 5-16-79); 139 v H 1 (Eff 8-5-81); 140 v H 37 (Eff 6-22-84); 141 v H 428 (Eff 12-23-86); 142 v H 708. Eff 4-19-88.**

## § 1.41 Applicability of sections 1.41 to 1.59.

Sections 1.41 to 1.59, inclusive, of the Revised Code apply to all statutes, subject to the conditions stated in section 1.51 of the Revised Code, and to rules adopted under them.

**HISTORY: 134 v H 607. Eff 1-3-72.**

## § 1.42 Common and technical use.

Words and phrases shall be read in context and construed according to the rules of grammar and common usage. Words and phrases that have acquired a technical or particular meaning, whether by legislative definition or otherwise, shall be construed accordingly.

**HISTORY: 134 v H 607. Eff 1-3-72.**

**Analogous to former RC § 1.10 (Bureau of Code Revision, 10-1-53), repealed, 134 v H 607, § 2, eff 1-3-72.**

## § 1.43 Singular and plural; gender; tense.

(A) The singular includes the plural, and the plural includes the singular.

(B) Words of one gender include the other genders.

(C) Words in the present tense include the future.

**HISTORY: 134 v H 607. Eff 1-3-72.**

**Analogous to former RC § 1.10 (Bureau of Code Revision, 10-1-53), repealed, 134 v H 607, § 2, eff 1-3-72.**

## § 1.44 Week; year.

(A) "Week" means seven consecutive days.

(B) "Year" means twelve consecutive months.

**HISTORY: 134 v H 607. Eff 1-3-72.**

## § 1.45 Computation of time.

If a number of months is to be computed by counting the months from a particular day, the period ends on the same numerical day in the concluding month as the day of the month from which the computation is begun, unless there are not that many days in the concluding month, in which case the period ends on the last day of that month.

**HISTORY: 134 v H 607. Eff 1-3-72.**

## § 1.46 Words govern expression of numbers.

If there is a conflict between figures and words in expressing a number, the words govern.

**HISTORY: 134 v H 607. Eff 1-3-72.**

## § 1.47 Intentions in the enactment of statutes.

In enacting a statute, it is presumed that:

(A) Compliance with the constitutions of the state and of the United States is intended;

(B) The entire statute is intended to be effective;

(C) A just and reasonable result is intended;

(D) A result feasible of execution is intended.

**HISTORY: 134 v H 607. Eff 1-3-72.**

## § 1.48 Statute presumed prospective.

A statute is presumed to be prospective in its operation unless expressly made retrospective.

**HISTORY: 134 v H 607. Eff 1-3-72.**

## § 1.49 Ambiguous statutes.

If a statute is ambiguous, the court, in determining the intention of the legislature, may consider among other matters:

(A) The object sought to be attained;

(B) The circumstances under which the statute was enacted;

(C) The legislative history;

(D) The common law or former statutory provisions, including laws upon the same or similar subjects;

(E) The consequences of a particular construction;

(F) The administrative construction of the statute.

**HISTORY: 134 v H 607. Eff 1-3-72.**

## § 1.50 Severability of Code section provisions.

If any provisions of a section of the Revised Code or the application thereof to any person or circumstance is held invalid, the invalidity does not affect other provisions or applications of the section or related sections which can be given effect without the invalid provision or application, and to this end the provisions are severable.

**HISTORY: 134 v H 607. Eff 1-3-72.**

**Analogous to former RC § 1.13 (GC § 26-2; 122 v 239; Bureau of Code Revision, 10-1-53), repealed, 134 v H 607, eff 1-3-72.**

## § 1.51 Special or local provision prevails over general; exception.

If a general provision conflicts with a special or local provision, they shall be construed, if possible, so that effect is given to both. If the conflict between the provisions is irreconcilable, the special or local provision prevails as an exception to the general provision, unless the general provision is the later adoption and the manifest intent is that the general provision prevail.

**HISTORY: 134 v H 607. Eff 1-3-72.**

## § 1.52 Irreconcilable statutes or amendments.

(A) If statutes enacted at the same or different sessions of the legislature are irreconcilable, the statute latest in date of enactment prevails.

(B) If amendments to the same statute are enacted at the same or different sessions of the legislature, one amendment without reference to another, the amendments are to be harmonized, if possible, so that effect may be given to each. If the amendments are substantively irreconcilable, the latest in date of enactment prevails. The fact that a later amendment restates language deleted by an earlier amendment, or fails to include language inserted by an earlier amendment, does not of itself make the amendments irreconcilable. Amendments are irreconcilable only when changes made by each cannot reasonably be put into simultaneous operation.

**HISTORY: 134 v H 607. Eff 1-3-72.**

## § 1.53 Language of enrolled act prevails in conflicts.

If the language of the enrolled act deposited with the secretary of state, including any code section number designated pursuant to section 103.131 [103.13.1] of the Revised Code, conflicts with the language of any subsequent printing or reprinting of the statute, the language and any such designated section number of the enrolled act prevails.

**HISTORY: 134 v H 607. Eff 1-3-72.**

## § 1.54 Continuation of prior statute.

A statute which is reenacted or amended is intended to be a continuation of the prior statute and not a new enactment, so far as it is the same as the prior statute.

**HISTORY: 134 v H 607. Eff 1-3-72.**

## § 1.55 Intent of reference.

A reference to any portion of a statute of this state applies to all reenactments or amendments thereof.

**HISTORY: 134 v H 607. Eff 1-3-72.**

## § 1.56 Reference to series.

If a statute refers to a series of numbers or letters, the first and the last numbers or letters are included.

**HISTORY: 134 v H 607. Eff 1-3-72.**

## § 1.57 Repeal of repealing statute.

The repeal of a repealing statute does not revive the statute originally repealed nor impair the effect of any saving clause therein.

**HISTORY: 134 v H 607. Eff 1-3-72.**

**Analogous to former RC** § 1.19 **(RS § 78; S&C 59; 29 v 513; GC § 25; Bureau of Code Revision, 10-1-53), repealed, 134 v H 607, § 2, eff 1-3-72.**

## § 1.58 Effect of reenactment, amendment, or repeal.

(A) The reenactment, amendment, or repeal of a statute does not, except as provided in division (B) of this section:

(1) Affect the prior operation of the statute or any prior action taken thereunder;

(2) Affect any validation, cure, right, privilege, obligation, or liability previously acquired, accrued, accorded, or incurred thereunder;

(3) Affect any violation thereof or penalty, forfeiture, or punishment incurred in respect thereto, prior to the amendment or repeal;

(4) Affect any investigation, proceeding, or remedy in respect of any such privilege, obligation, liability, penalty, forfeiture, or punishment; and the investigation, proceeding, or remedy may be instituted, continued, or enforced, and the penalty, forfeiture, or punishment imposed, as if the statute had not been repealed or amended.

(B) If the penalty, forfeiture, or punishment for any offense is reduced by a reenactment or amendment of a statute, the penalty, forfeiture, or punishment, if not already imposed, shall be imposed according to the statute as amended.

**HISTORY: 134 v H 607. Eff 1-3-72.**

**Analogous to former RC** §§ 1.20, 1.21 **(RS § 79; S&S 1; 63 v 22; GC §§ 26, 26-1; 122 v 28; Bureau of Code Revision, 10-1-53), repealed, 134 v H 607, § 2, eff 1-3-72.**

## § 1.59 Definitions.

As used in any statute, unless another definition is provided in that statute or a related statute:

(A) "Child" includes child by adoption.

(B) "Oath" includes affirmation and "swear" includes affirm.

(C) "Person" includes an individual, corporation, business trust, estate, trust, partnership, and association.

(D) "Population" means that shown by the most recent regular federal census.

(E) "Property" means real and personal property.

(F) "Rule" includes regulation.

(G) "State," when applied to a part of the United States, includes any state, district, commonwealth, territory, insular possession thereof, and any area subject to the legislative authority of the United States of America. "This state" or "the state" means the state of Ohio.

(H) "United States" includes all the states.

(I) "Will" includes codicil.

(J) "Written" or "in writing" includes any representation of words, letters, symbols, or figures; this provision does not affect any law relating to signatures.

(K) "Internet" means the international computer network of both federal and nonfederal interoperable packet switched data networks, including the graphical subnetwork known as the world wide web.

**HISTORY: 134 v H 607. Eff 1-3-72; 150 v H 204, § 1, eff. 11-5-04.**

## § 1.60 "State agency" defined.

As used in Title I of the Revised Code, "state agency," except as otherwise provided in the title, means every organized body, office, or agency established by the laws of the state for the exercise of any function of state government. "State agency" does not include the nonprofit corporation formed under section 187.01 of the Revised Code.

**HISTORY: 141 v H 201. Eff 7-1-85; 2011 HB 1, § 1, eff. Feb. 18, 2011.**

The provisions of § 3 of 2011 HB 1 read as follows:

SECTION 3. The Supreme Court of Ohio shall have exclusive, original jurisdiction over any claim asserting that any one or more sections of the Revised Code amended or enacted by this act, or any portion of one or more of those sections, or any rule adopted under one or more of those sections, violates any provision of the Ohio Constitution; and over any claim asserting that any action taken pursuant to those sections by the Governor or the nonprofit corporation formed under section 187.01 of the Revised Code violates any provision of the Ohio Constitution or any provision of the Revised Code. Any such claim shall be filed as otherwise required by the Court's rules of practice not later than the sixtieth day after the effective date of this act. If any claim over which the Supreme Court is granted exclusive, original jurisdiction by this section is filed in any lower court, the claim shall be dismissed by the court on the ground that the court lacks jurisdiction to review it.

# CHAPTER 9: MISCELLANEOUS

Section



[CONSTRUCTION MANAGEMENT SERVICES]



## § 9.06 Contracts for private operation and management of correctional facilities.

(A)(1) The department of rehabilitation and correction may contract for the private operation and management pursuant to this section of the initial intensive program prison established pursuant to section 5120.033 of the Revised Code, if one or more intensive program prisons are established under that section, and may contract for the private operation and management of any other facility under this section. Counties and municipal corporations to the extent authorized in sections 307.93, 341.35, 753.03, and 753.15 of the Revised Code may contract for the private operation and management of a facility under this section. A contract entered into under this section shall be for an initial term specified in the contract with an option to renew for additional periods of two years.

(2) The department of rehabilitation and correction, by rule, shall adopt minimum criteria and specifications that a person or entity, other than a person or entity that satisfies the criteria set forth in division (A)(3)(a) of this section and subject to division (I) of this section, must satisfy in order to apply to operate and manage as a

contractor pursuant to this section the initial intensive program prison established pursuant to section 5120.033 of the Revised Code, if one or more intensive program prisons are established under that section.

(3) Subject to division (I) of this section, any person or entity that applies to operate and manage a facility as a contractor pursuant to this section shall satisfy one or more of the following criteria:

(a) The person or entity, at the time of the application, operates and manages one or more facilities accredited by the American correctional association.

(b) The person or entity satisfies all of the minimum criteria and specifications adopted by the department of rehabilitation and correction pursuant to division (A)(2) of this section, provided that this alternative shall be available only in relation to the initial intensive program prison established pursuant to section 5120.033 of the Revised Code, if one or more intensive program prisons are established under that section.

(4) Subject to division (I) of this section, before a public entity may enter into a contract under this section, the contractor shall convincingly demonstrate to the public entity that it can operate the facility with the inmate capacity required by the public entity and provide the services required in this section and realize at least a five per cent savings over the projected cost to the public entity of providing these same services to operate the facility that is the subject of the contract. No out-of-state prisoners may be housed in any facility that is the subject of a contract entered into under this section.

(B) Subject to division (I) of this section, any contract entered into under this section shall include all of the following:

(1) A requirement that, if the contractor applied pursuant to division (A)(3)(b) of this section, the contractor continue complying with the applicable criteria and specifications adopted by the department of rehabilitation and correction pursuant to division (A)(2) of this section;

(2) A requirement that all of the following conditions be met:

(a) The contractor begins the process of accrediting the facility with the American correctional association no later than sixty days after the facility receives its first inmate.

(b) The contractor receives accreditation of the facility within twelve months after the date the contractor applies to the American correctional association for accreditation.

(c) Once the accreditation is received, the contractor maintains it for the duration of the contract term.

(d) If the contractor does not comply with divisions (B)(2)(a) to (c) of this section, the contractor is in violation of the contract, and the public entity may revoke the contract at its discretion.

(3) A requirement that the contractor comply with all rules promulgated by the department of rehabilitation and correction that apply to the operation and management of correctional facilities, including the minimum standards for jails in Ohio and policies regarding the use of force and the use of deadly force, although the public entity may require more stringent standards, and comply with any applicable laws, rules, or regulations of the federal, state, and local governments, including, but not limited to, sanitation, food service, safety, and health regulations. The contractor shall be required to send copies of reports of inspections completed by the appropriate authorities regarding compliance with rules and regulations to the director of rehabilitation and correction or the director's designee and, if contracting with a local public entity, to the governing authority of that entity.

(4) A requirement that the contractor report for investigation all crimes in connection with the facility to the public entity, to all local law enforcement agencies with jurisdiction over the place at which the facility is located, and, for a crime committed at a state correctional institution, to the state highway patrol;

(5) A requirement that the contractor immediately report all escapes from the facility, and the apprehension of all escapees, by telephone and in writing to all local law enforcement agencies with jurisdiction over the place at which the facility is located, to the prosecuting attorney of the county in which the facility is located, to the state highway patrol, to a daily newspaper having general circulation in the county in which the facility is located, and, if the facility is a state correctional institution, to the department of rehabilitation and correction. The written notice may be by either facsimile transmission or mail. A failure to comply with this requirement regarding an escape is a violation of section 2921.22 of the Revised Code.

(6) A requirement that, if the facility is a state correctional institution, the contractor provide a written report within specified time limits to the director of rehabilitation and correction or the director's designee of all unusual incidents at the facility as defined in rules promulgated by the department of rehabilitation and correction or, if the facility is a local correctional institution, that the contractor provide a written report of all unusual incidents at the facility to the governing authority of the local public entity;

(7) A requirement that the contractor maintain proper control of inmates' personal funds pursuant to rules promulgated by the department of rehabilitation and correction for state correctional institutions or pursuant to the minimum standards for jails along with any additional standards established by the local public entity for local correctional institutions and that records pertaining to these funds be made available to representatives of the public entity for review or audit;

(8) A requirement that the contractor prepare and distribute to the director of rehabilitation and correction or, if contracting with a local public entity, to the governing authority of the local entity annual budget income and expenditure statements and funding source financial reports;

(9) A requirement that the public entity appoint and supervise a full-time contract monitor, that the contractor provide suitable office space for the contract monitor at the facility, and that the contractor allow the contract monitor unrestricted access to all parts of the facility and all records of the facility except the contractor's financial records;

(10) A requirement that if the facility is a state correctional institution designated department of rehabilitation and correction staff members be allowed access to the facility in accordance with rules promulgated by the department;

(11) A requirement that the contractor provide internal and perimeter security as agreed upon in the contract;

(12) If the facility is a state correctional institution, a requirement that the contractor impose discipline on inmates housed in the facility only in accordance with rules promulgated by the department of rehabilitation and correction;

(13) A requirement that the facility be staffed at all times with a staffing pattern approved by the public entity

and adequate both to ensure supervision of inmates and maintenance of security within the facility and to provide for programs, transportation, security, and other operational needs. In determining security needs, the contractor shall be required to consider, among other things, the proximity of the facility to neighborhoods and schools.

(14) If the contract is with a local public entity, a requirement that the contractor provide services and programs, consistent with the minimum standards for jails promulgated by the department of rehabilitation and correction under section 5120.10 of the Revised Code;

(15) A clear statement that no immunity from liability granted to the state, and no immunity from liability granted to political subdivisions under Chapter 2744. of the Revised Code, shall extend to the contractor or any of the contractor's employees;

(16) A statement that all documents and records relevant to the facility shall be maintained in the same manner required for, and subject to the same laws, rules, and regulations as apply to, the records of the public entity;

(17) Authorization for the public entity to impose a fine on the contractor from a schedule of fines included in the contract for the contractor's failure to perform its contractual duties or to cancel the contract, as the public entity considers appropriate. If a fine is imposed, the public entity may reduce the payment owed to the contractor pursuant to any invoice in the amount of the imposed fine.

(18) A statement that all services provided or goods produced at the facility shall be subject to the same regulations, and the same distribution limitations, as apply to goods and services produced at other correctional institutions;

(19) If the facility is a state correctional institution, authorization for the department to establish one or more prison industries at the facility;

(20) A requirement that, if the facility is an intensive program prison established pursuant to section 5120.033 of the Revised Code, the facility shall comply with all criteria for intensive program prisons of that type that are set forth in that section;

(21) If the facility is a state correctional institution, a requirement that the contractor provide clothing for all inmates housed in the facility that is conspicuous in its color, style, or color and style, that conspicuously identifies its wearer as an inmate, and that is readily distinguishable from clothing of a nature that normally is worn outside the facility by non-inmates, that the contractor require all inmates housed in the facility to wear the clothing so provided, and that the contractor not permit any inmate, while inside or on the premises of the facility or while being transported to or from the facility, to wear any clothing of a nature that does not conspicuously identify its wearer as an inmate and that normally is worn outside the facility by non-inmates.

(C) No contract entered into under this section may require, authorize, or imply a delegation of the authority or responsibility of the public entity to a contractor for any of the following:

(1) Developing or implementing procedures for calculating inmate release and parole eligibility dates and recommending the granting or denying of parole, although the contractor may submit written reports that have been prepared in the ordinary course of business;

(2) Developing or implementing procedures for calculating and awarding earned credits, approving the type of work inmates may perform and the wage or earned credits, if any, that may be awarded to inmates engaging in that work, and granting, denying, or revoking earned credits;

(3) For inmates serving a term imposed for a felony offense committed prior to July 1, 1996, or for a misdemeanor offense, developing or implementing procedures for calculating and awarding good time, approving the good time, if any, that may be awarded to inmates engaging in work, and granting, denying, or revoking good time;

(4) Classifying an inmate or placing an inmate in a more or a less restrictive custody than the custody ordered by the public entity;

(5) Approving inmates for work release;

(6) Contracting for local or long distance telephone services for inmates or receiving commissions from those services at a facility that is owned by or operated under a contract with the department.

(D) A contractor that has been approved to operate a facility under this section, and a person or entity that enters into a contract for specialized services, as described in division (I) of this section, relative to an intensive program prison established pursuant to section 5120.033 of the Revised Code to be operated by a contractor that has been approved to operate the prison under this section, shall provide an adequate policy of insurance specifically including, but not limited to, insurance for civil rights claims as determined by a risk management or actuarial firm with demonstrated experience in public liability for state governments. The insurance policy shall provide that the state, including all state agencies, and all political subdivisions of the state with jurisdiction over the facility or in which a facility is located are named as insured, and that the state and its political subdivisions shall be sent any notice of cancellation. The contractor may not self-insure.

A contractor that has been approved to operate a facility under this section, and a person or entity that enters into a contract for specialized services, as described in division (I) of this section, relative to an intensive program prison established pursuant to section 5120.033 of the Revised Code to be operated by a contractor that has been approved to operate the prison under this section, shall indemnify and hold harmless the state, its officers, agents, and employees, and any local government entity in the state having jurisdiction over the facility or ownership of the facility, shall reimburse the state for its costs in defending the state or any of its officers, agents, or employees, and shall reimburse any local government entity of that nature for its costs in defending the local government entity, from all of the following:

(1) Any claims or losses for services rendered by the contractor, person, or entity performing or supplying services in connection with the performance of the contract;

(2) Any failure of the contractor, person, or entity or its officers or employees to adhere to the laws, rules, regulations, or terms agreed to in the contract;

(3) Any constitutional, federal, state, or civil rights claim brought against the state related to the facility operated and managed by the contractor;

(4) Any claims, losses, demands, or causes of action arising out of the contractor's, person's, or entity's activities in this state;

(5) Any attorney's fees or court costs arising from any habeas corpus actions or other inmate suits that may arise from any event that occurred at the facility or was a result of such an event, or arise over the conditions, manage-

ment, or operation of the facility, which fees and costs shall include, but not be limited to, attorney's fees for the state's representation and for any court-appointed representation of any inmate, and the costs of any special judge who may be appointed to hear those actions or suits.

(E) Private correctional officers of a contractor operating and managing a facility pursuant to a contract entered into under this section may carry and use firearms in the course of their employment only after being certified as satisfactorily completing an approved training program as described in division (A) of section 109.78 of the Revised Code.

(F) Upon notification by the contractor of an escape from, or of a disturbance at, the facility that is the subject of a contract entered into under this section, the department of rehabilitation and correction and state and local law enforcement agencies shall use all reasonable means to recapture escapees or quell any disturbance. Any cost incurred by the state or its political subdivisions relating to the apprehension of an escapee or the quelling of a disturbance at the facility shall be chargeable to and borne by the contractor. The contractor shall also reimburse the state or its political subdivisions for all reasonable costs incurred relating to the temporary detention of the escapee following recapture.

(G) Any offense that would be a crime if committed at a state correctional institution or jail, workhouse, prison, or other correctional facility shall be a crime if committed by or with regard to inmates at facilities operated pursuant to a contract entered into under this section.

(H) A contractor operating and managing a facility pursuant to a contract entered into under this section shall pay any inmate workers at the facility at the rate approved by the public entity. Inmates working at the facility shall not be considered employees of the contractor.

(I) In contracting for the private operation and management pursuant to division (A) of this section of any intensive program prison established pursuant to section 5120.033 of the Revised Code, the department of rehabilitation and correction may enter into a contract with a contractor for the general operation and management of the prison and may enter into one or more separate contracts with other persons or entities for the provision of specialized services for persons confined in the prison, including, but not limited to, security or training services or medical, counseling, educational, or similar treatment programs. If, pursuant to this division, the department enters into a contract with a contractor for the general operation and management of the prison and also enters into one or more specialized service contracts with other persons or entities, all of the following apply:

(1) The contract for the general operation and management shall comply with all requirements and criteria set forth in this section, and all provisions of this section apply in relation to the prison operated and managed pursuant to the contract.

(2) Divisions (A)(2), (B), and (C) of this section do not apply in relation to any specialized services contract, except to the extent that the provisions of those divisions clearly are relevant to the specialized services to be provided under the specialized services contract. Division (D) of this section applies in relation to each specialized services contract.

(J) If, on or after the effective date of this amendment, a contractor enters into a contract with the department of rehabilitation and correction under this section for the operation and management of any facility described in Section 753.10 of the act in which this amendment was adopted, if the contract provides for the sale of the facility to the contractor, if the facility is sold to the contractor subsequent to the execution of the contract, and if the contractor is privately operating and managing the facility, notwithstanding the contractor's private operation and management of the facility, all of the following apply:

(1) Except as expressly provided to the contrary in this section, the facility being privately operated and managed by the contractor shall be considered for purposes of the Revised Code as being under the control of, or under the jurisdiction of, the department of rehabilitation and correction.

(2) Any reference in this section to "state correctional institution," any reference in Chapter 2967. of the Revised Code to "state correctional institution," other than the definition of that term set forth in section 2967.01 of the Revised Code, or to "prison," and any reference in Chapter 2929., 5120., 5145., 5147., or 5149. or any other provision of the Revised Code to "state correctional institution" or "prison" shall be considered to include a reference to the facility being privately operated and managed by the contractor, unless the context makes the inclusion of that facility clearly inapplicable.

(3) Upon the sale and conveyance of the facility, the facility shall be returned to the tax list and duplicate maintained by the county auditor, and the facility shall be subject to all real property taxes and assessments. No exemption from real property taxation pursuant to Chapter 5709. of the Revised Code shall apply to the facility conveyed. The gross receipts and income of the contractor to whom the facility is conveyed that are derived from operating and managing the facility under this section shall be subject to gross receipts and income taxes levied by the state and its subdivisions, including the taxes levied pursuant to Chapters 718., 5747., 5748., and 5751. of the Revised Code. Unless exempted under another section of the Revised Code, transactions involving a contractor as a consumer or purchaser are subject to any tax levied under Chapters 5739. and 5741. of the Revised Code.

(4) After the sale and conveyance of the facility, all of the following apply:

(a) Before the contractor may resell or otherwise transfer the facility and the real property on which it is situated, any surrounding land that also was transferred under the contract, or both the facility and real property on which it is situated plus the surrounding land that was transferred under the contract, the contractor first must offer the state the opportunity to repurchase the facility, real property, and surrounding land that is to be resold or transferred and must sell the facility, real property, and surrounding land to the state if the state so desires, pursuant to and in accordance with the repurchase clause included in the contract.

(b) Upon the default by the contractor of any financial agreement for the purchase of the facility and the real property on which it is situated, any surrounding land that also was transferred under the contract, or both the facility and real property on which it is situated plus the surrounding land that was transferred under the contract, upon the default by the contractor of any other term in the contract, or upon the financial insolvency of the contractor or inability of the contractor to meet its contractual obligations, the state may repurchase the facility, real property, and surrounding land, if the state so desires, pursuant to and in accordance with the repurchase clause included in the contract.

(c) If the contract entered into under this section for the operation and management of a state correctional institution is terminated, both of the following apply:

(i) The operation and management responsibilities of the state correctional institution shall be transferred to another contractor under the same terms and conditions as applied to the original contractor or to the department of rehabilitation and correction.

(ii) The department of rehabilitation and correction or the new contractor, whichever is applicable, may enter into an agreement with the terminated contractor to purchase the terminated contractor's equipment, supplies, furnishings, and consumables.

(K) Any action asserting that section 9.06 of the Revised Code or section 753.10 of the act in which this amendment was adopted violates any provision of the Ohio constitution and any claim asserting that any action taken by the governor or the department of administrative services or the department of rehabilitation and correction pursuant to section 9.06 of the Revised Code or section 753.10 of the act in which this amendment was adopted violates any provision of the Ohio constitution or any provision of the Revised Code shall be brought in the court of common pleas of Franklin county. The court shall give any action filed pursuant to this division priority over all other civil cases pending on its docket and expeditiously make a determination on the claim. If an appeal is taken from any final order issued in a case brought pursuant to this division, the court of appeals shall give the case priority over all other civil cases pending on its docket and expeditiously make a determination on the appeal.

(L) As used in this section:

(1) "Public entity" means the department of rehabilitation and correction, or a county or municipal corporation or a combination of counties and municipal corporations, that has jurisdiction over a facility that is the subject of a contract entered into under this section.

(2) "Local public entity" means a county or municipal corporation, or a combination of counties and municipal corporations, that has jurisdiction over a jail, workhouse, or other correctional facility used only for misdemeanants that is the subject of a contract entered into under this section.

(3) "Governing authority of a local public entity" means, for a county, the board of county commissioners; for a municipal corporation, the legislative authority; for a combination of counties and municipal corporations, all the boards of county commissioners and municipal legislative authorities that joined to create the facility.

(4) "Contractor" means a person or entity that enters into a contract under this section to operate and manage a jail, workhouse, or other correctional facility.

(5) "Facility" means any of the following:

(a) The specific county, multicounty, municipal, municipal-county, or multicounty-municipal jail, workhouse, prison, or other type of correctional institution or facility used only for misdemeanants that is the subject of a contract entered into under this section;

(b) Any state correctional institution that is the subject of a contract entered into under this section, including any facility described in Section 753.10 of the act in which this amendment was adopted at any time prior to or after any sale to a contractor of the state's right, title, and interest in the facility, the land situated thereon, and specified surrounding land.

(6) "Person or entity" in the case of a contract for the private operation and management of a state correctional institution, includes an employee organization, as defined in section 4117.01 of the Revised Code, that represents employees at state correctional institutions.

**HISTORY: 146 v H 117 (Eff 9-29-95); 147 v H 215 (Eff 9-29-97); 147 v H 293 (Eff 3-17-98); 148 v H 283 (Eff 6-30-99); 149 v H 94. Eff 9-5-2001; 152 v H 130, § 1, eff. 4-7-09; 153 v H 1, § 101.01, eff. 10-16-09; 153 v H 1, § 101.01, eff. 10-16-09; 2011 HB 153, § 101.01, eff. June 30, 2011.**

Acts 2011, HB 153, § 815.20 provides: "The General Assembly, applying the principle stated in division (B) of section 1.52 of the Revised Code that amendments are to be harmonized if reasonably capable of simultaneous operation, finds that the following sections, presented in this act as composites of the sections as amended by the acts indicated, are the resulting versions of the sections in effect prior to the effective date of the sections as presented in this act:

"Section 9.06 of the Revised Code as amended by Am. Sub. H.B. 130 of the 127th General Assembly and Am. Sub. H.B. 1 of the 128th General Assembly."

The effective date is set by § 812.10 of 153 v H 1.

The effective date is set by section 204 of HB 94.

**Comment, Legislative Service Commission**

Section 9.06 of the Revised Code is amended by Am. Sub. H.B. 1 of the 128th General Assembly and Am. Sub. H.B. 130 of the 127th General Assembly. Comparison of these amendments in pursuance of section 1.52 of the Revised Code discloses that they are not irreconcilable so that they are required by that section to be harmonized to give effect to each amendment.

## § 9.07 Entities authorized to operate correctional facility housing out-of-state prisoners; requirements for operation.

(A) As used in this section:

(1) "Deadly weapon" has the same meaning as in section 2923.11 of the Revised Code.

(2) "Governing authority of a local public entity" means whichever of the following is applicable:

(a) For a county, the board of county commissioners of the county;

(b) For a municipal corporation, the legislative authority of the municipal corporation;

(c) For a combination of counties, a combination of municipal corporations, or a combination of one or more counties and one or more municipal corporations, all boards of county commissioners and legislative authorities of all of the counties and municipal corporations that combined to form a local public entity for purposes of this section.

(3) "Local public entity" means a county, a municipal corporation, a combination of counties, a combination of municipal corporations, or a combination of one or more counties and one or more municipal corporations.

(4) "Non-contracting political subdivision" means any political subdivision to which all of the following apply:

(a) A correctional facility for the housing of out-of-state prisoners in this state is or will be located in the political subdivision.

(b) The correctional facility described in division (A)(4)(a) of this section is being operated and managed, or will be operated and managed, by a local public entity or a private contractor pursuant to a contract entered into prior to March 17, 1998, or a contract entered into on or after March 17, 1998, under this section.

(c) The political subdivision is not a party to the contract described in division (A)(4)(b) of this section for the management and operation of the correctional facility.

(5) "Out-of-state jurisdiction" means the United States, any state other than this state, and any political subdivision or other jurisdiction located in a state other than this state.

(6) "Out-of-state prisoner" means a person who is convicted of a crime in another state or under the laws of the United States or who is found under the laws of another state or of the United States to be a delinquent child or the substantially equivalent designation.

(7) "Private contractor" means either of the following:

(a) A person who, on or after March 17, 1998, enters into a contract under this section with a local public entity to operate and manage a correctional facility in this state for out-of-state prisoners.

(b) A person who, pursuant to a contract with a local public entity entered into prior to March 17, 1998, operates and manages on March 17, 1998, a correctional facility in this state for housing out-of-state prisoners.

(B) Subject to division (I) of this section, the only entities other than this state that are authorized to operate a correctional facility to house out-of-state prisoners in this state are a local public entity that operates a correctional facility pursuant to this section or a private contractor that operates a correctional facility pursuant to this section under a contract with a local public entity.

Subject to division (I) of this section, a private entity may operate a correctional facility in this state for the housing of out-of-state prisoners only if the private entity is a private contractor that enters into a contract that comports with division (D) of this section with a local public entity for the management and operation of the correctional facility.

(C)(1) Except as provided in this division, on and after March 17, 1998, a local public entity shall not enter into a contract with an out-of-state jurisdiction to house out-of-state prisoners in a correctional facility in this state. On and after March 17, 1998, a local public entity may enter into a contract with an out-of-state jurisdiction to house out-of-state prisoners in a correctional facility in this state only if the local public entity and the out-of-state jurisdiction with which the local public entity intends to contract jointly submit to the department of rehabilitation and correction a statement that certifies the correctional facility's intended use, intended prisoner population, and custody level, and the department reviews and comments upon the plans for the design or renovation of the correctional facility regarding their suitability for the intended prisoner population specified in the submitted statement.

(2) If a local public entity and an out-of-state jurisdiction enter into a contract to house out-of-state prisoners in a correctional facility in this state as authorized under division (C)(1) of this section, in addition to any other provisions it contains, the contract shall include whichever of the following provisions is applicable:

(a) If a private contractor will operate the facility in question pursuant to a contract entered into in accordance with division (D) of this section, a requirement that, if the facility is closed or ceases to operate for any reason and if the conversion plan described in division (D)(16) of this section is not complied with, the out-of-state jurisdiction will be responsible for housing and transporting the prisoners who are in the facility at the time it is closed or ceases to operate and for the cost of so housing and transporting those prisoners;

(b) If a private contractor will not operate the facility in question pursuant to a contract entered into in accordance with division (D) of this section, a conversion plan that will be followed if, for any reason, the facility is closed or ceases to operate. The conversion plan shall include, but is not limited to, provisions that specify whether the local public entity or the out-of-state jurisdiction will be responsible for housing and transporting the prisoners who are in the facility at the time it is closed or ceases to operate and for the cost of so housing and transporting those prisoners.

(3) If a local public entity and an out-of-state jurisdiction intend to enter into a contract to house out-of-state prisoners in a correctional facility in this state as authorized under division (C)(1) of this section, or if a local public entity and a private contractor intend to enter into a contract pursuant to division (D) of this section for the private contractor's management and operation of a correctional facility in this state to house out-of-state prisoners, prior to entering into the contract the local public entity and the out-of-state jurisdiction, or the local public entity and the private contractor, whichever is applicable, shall conduct a public hearing in accordance with this division, and, prior to entering into the contract, the governing authority of the local public entity in which the facility is or will be located shall authorize the location and operation of the facility. The hearing shall be conducted at a location within the municipal corporation or township in which the facility is or will be located. At least one week prior to conducting the hearing, the local public entity and the out-of-state jurisdiction or private contractor with the duty to conduct the hearing shall cause notice of the date, time, and place of the hearing to be made by publication in the newspaper with the largest general circulation in the county in which the municipal corporation or township is located. The notice shall be of a sufficient size that it covers at least one-quarter of a page of the newspaper in which it is published. This division applies to a private contractor that, pursuant to the requirement set forth in division (I) of this section, is required to enter into a contract under division (D) of this section.

(D) Subject to division (I) of this section, on and after March 17, 1998, if a local public entity enters into a contract with a private contractor for the management and operation of a correctional facility in this state to house out-of-state prisoners, the contract, at a minimum, shall include all of the following provisions:

(1) A requirement that the private contractor seek and obtain accreditation from the American correctional association for the correctional facility within two years after accepting the first out-of-state prisoner at the correctional facility under the contract and that it maintain that accreditation for the term of the contract;

(2) A requirement that the private contractor comply with all applicable laws, rules, or regulations of the government of this state, political subdivisions of this state, and the United States, including, but not limited to, all sanitation, food service, safety, and health regulations;

(3) A requirement that the private contractor send copies of reports of inspections completed by appropriate authorities regarding compliance with laws, rules, and regulations of the type described in division (D)(2) of this section to the director of rehabilitation and correction or the director's designee and to the governing authority of the local public entity in which the correctional facility is located;

(4) A requirement that the private contractor report to the local law enforcement agencies with jurisdiction over the place at which the correctional facility is located, for investigation, all criminal offenses or delinquent acts that are committed in or on the grounds of, or otherwise in

connection with, the correctional facility and report to the department of rehabilitation and correction all disturbances at the facility;

(5) A requirement that the private contractor immediately report all escapes from the facility, and the apprehension of all escapees, by telephone and in writing to the department of rehabilitation and correction, to all local law enforcement agencies with jurisdiction over the place at which the facility is located, to the state highway patrol, to the prosecuting attorney of the county in which the facility is located, and to a daily newspaper having general circulation in the county in which the facility is located. The written notice may be by either facsimile transmission or mail. A failure to comply with this requirement is a violation of section 2921.22 of the Revised Code.

(6) A requirement that the private contractor provide a written report to the director of rehabilitation and correction or the director's designee and to the governing authority of the local public entity in which the correctional facility is located of all unusual incidents occurring at the correctional facility. The private contractor shall report the incidents in accordance with the incident reporting rules that, at the time of the incident, are applicable to state correctional facilities for similar incidents occurring at state correctional facilities.

(7) A requirement that the private contractor provide internal and perimeter security to protect the public, staff members of the correctional facility, and prisoners in the correctional facility;

(8) A requirement that the correctional facility be staffed at all times with a staffing pattern that is adequate to ensure supervision of inmates and maintenance of security within the correctional facility and to provide for appropriate programs, transportation, security, and other operational needs. In determining security needs for the correctional facility, the private contractor and the contract requirements shall fully take into account all relevant factors, including, but not limited to, the proximity of the facility to neighborhoods and schools.

(9) A requirement that the private contractor provide an adequate policy of insurance that satisfies the requirements set forth in division (D) of section 9.06 of the Revised Code regarding contractors who operate and manage a facility under that section, and that the private contractor indemnify and hold harmless the state, its officers, agents, and employees, and any local public entity in the state with jurisdiction over the place at which the correctional facility is located or that owns the correctional facility, reimburse the state for its costs in defending the state or any of its officers, agents, or employees, and reimburse any local government entity of that nature for its costs in defending the local government entity, in the manner described in division (D) of that section regarding contractors who operate and manage a facility under that section;

(10) A requirement that the private contractor adopt for prisoners housed in the correctional facility the security classification system and schedule adopted by the department of rehabilitation and correction under section 5145.03 of the Revised Code, classify in accordance with the system and schedule each prisoner housed in the facility, and house all prisoners in the facility in accordance with their classification under this division;

(11) A requirement that the private contractor will not accept for housing, and will not house, in the correctional facility any out-of-state prisoner in relation to whom any of the following applies:

(a) The private entity has not obtained from the out-of-state jurisdiction that imposed the sentence or sanction under which the prisoner will be confined in this state a copy of the institutional record of the prisoner while previously confined in that out-of-state jurisdiction or a statement that the prisoner previously has not been confined in that out-of-state jurisdiction and a copy of all medical records pertaining to that prisoner that are in the possession of the out-of-state jurisdiction.

(b) The prisoner, while confined in any out-of-state jurisdiction, has a record of institutional violence involving the use of a deadly weapon or a pattern of committing acts of an assaultive nature against employees of, or visitors to, the place of confinement or has a record of escape or attempted escape from secure custody.

(c) Under the security classification system and schedule adopted by the department of rehabilitation and correction under section 5145.03 of the Revised Code and adopted by the private contractor under division (B)(10) of this section, the out-of-state prisoner would be classified as being at a security level higher than medium security.

(12) A requirement that the private contractor, prior to housing any out-of-state prisoner in the correctional facility under the contract, enter into a written agreement with the department of rehabilitation and correction that sets forth a plan and procedure that will be used to coordinate law enforcement activities of state law enforcement agencies and of local law enforcement agencies with jurisdiction over the place at which the facility is located in response to any riot, rebellion, escape, insurrection, or other emergency occurring inside or outside the facility;

(13) A requirement that the private contractor cooperate with the correctional institution inspection committee in the committee's performance of its duties under section 103.73 of the Revised Code and provide the committee, its subcommittees, and its staff members, in performing those duties, with access to the correctional facility as described in that section;

(14) A requirement that the private contractor permit any peace officer who serves a law enforcement agency with jurisdiction over the place at which the correctional facility is located to enter into the facility to investigate any criminal offense or delinquent act that allegedly has been committed in or on the grounds of, or otherwise in connection with, the facility;

(15) A requirement that the private contractor will not employ any person at the correctional facility until after the private contractor has submitted to the bureau of criminal identification and investigation, on a form prescribed by the superintendent of the bureau, a request that the bureau conduct a criminal records check of the person and a requirement that the private contractor will not employ any person at the facility if the records check or other information possessed by the contractor indicates that the person previously has engaged in malfeasance;

(16) A requirement that the private contractor will not accept for housing, and will not house, in the correctional facility any out-of-state prisoner unless the private contractor and the out-of-state jurisdiction that imposed the sentence for which the prisoner is to be confined agree that, if the out-of-state prisoner is confined in the facility in this state, commits a criminal offense while confined in the facility, is convicted of or pleads guilty to that offense, and is sentenced to a term of confinement for that offense but is not sentenced to death for that offense, the private contractor and the out-of-state jurisdiction will do all of the following:

(a) Unless section 5120.50 of the Revised Code does not apply in relation to the offense the prisoner committed while confined in this state and the term of confinement imposed for that offense, the out-of-state jurisdiction will accept the prisoner pursuant to that section for service of that term of confinement and for any period of time remaining under the sentence for which the prisoner was confined in the facility in this state, the out-of-state jurisdiction will confine the prisoner pursuant to that section for that term and that remaining period of time, and the private contractor will transport the prisoner to the out-of-state jurisdiction for service of that term and that remaining period of time.

(b) If section 5120.50 of the Revised Code does not apply in relation to the offense the prisoner committed while confined in this state and the term of confinement imposed for that offense, the prisoner shall be returned to the out-of-state jurisdiction or its private contractor for completion of the period of time remaining under the out-of-state sentence for which the prisoner was confined in the facility in this state before starting service of the term of confinement imposed for the offense committed while confined in this state, the out-of-state jurisdiction or its private contractor will confine the prisoner for that remaining period of time and will transport the prisoner outside of this state for service of that remaining period of time, and, if the prisoner is confined in this state in a facility operated by the department of rehabilitation and correction, the private contractor will be financially responsible for reimbursing the department at the per diem cost of confinement for the duration of that incarceration, with the amount of the reimbursement so paid to be deposited in the department's prisoner programs fund.

(17) A requirement that the private contractor, prior to housing any out-of-state prisoner in the correctional facility under the contract, enter into an agreement with the local public entity that sets forth a conversion plan that will be followed if, for any reason, the facility is closed or ceases to operate. The conversion plan shall include, but is not limited to, provisions that specify whether the private contractor, the local public entity, or the out-of-state jurisdictions that imposed the sentences for which the out-of-state prisoners are confined in the facility will be responsible for housing and transporting the prisoners who are in the facility at the time it is closed or ceases to operate and for the cost of so housing and transporting those prisoners.

(18) A schedule of fines that the local public entity shall impose upon the private contractor if the private contractor fails to perform its contractual duties, and a requirement that, if the private contractor fails to perform its contractual duties, the local public entity shall impose a fine on the private contractor from the schedule of fines and, in addition to the fine, may exercise any other rights it has under the contract. Division (F)(2) of this section applies regarding a fine described in this division.

(19) A requirement that the private contractor adopt and use in the correctional facility the drug testing and treatment program that the department of rehabilitation and correction uses for inmates in state correctional institutions;

(20) A requirement that the private contractor provide clothing for all out-of-state prisoners housed in the correctional facility that is conspicuous in its color, style, or color and style, that conspicuously identifies its wearer as a prisoner, and that is readily distinguishable from clothing of a nature that normally is worn outside the facility by non-prisoners, that the private contractor require all out-of-state prisoners housed in the facility to wear the clothing so provided, and that the private contractor not permit any out-of-state prisoner, while inside or on the premises of the facility or while being transported to or from the facility, to wear any clothing of a nature that does not conspicuously identify its wearer as a prisoner and that normally is worn outside the facility by non-prisoners;

(21) A requirement that, at the time the contract is made, the private contractor provide to all parties to the contract adequate proof that it has complied with the requirement described in division (D)(9) of this section, and a requirement that, at any time during the term of the contract, the private contractor upon request provide to any party to the contract adequate proof that it continues to be in compliance with the requirement described in division (D)(9) of this section.

(E) A private correctional officer or other designated employee of a private contractor that operates a correctional facility that houses out-of-state prisoners in this state under a contract entered into prior to, on, or after March 17, 1998, may carry and use firearms in the course of the officer's or employee's employment only if the officer or employee is certified as having satisfactorily completed an approved training program designed to qualify persons for positions as special police officers, security guards, or persons otherwise privately employed in a police capacity, as described in division (A) of section 109.78 of the Revised Code.

(F)(1) Upon notification by the private contractor of an escape from, or of a disturbance at, a correctional facility that is operated by a private contractor under a contract entered into prior to, on, or after March 17, 1998, and that houses out-of-state prisoners in this state, the department of rehabilitation and correction and state and local law enforcement agencies shall use all reasonable means to recapture persons who escaped from the facility or quell any disturbance at the facility, in accordance with the plan and procedure included in the written agreement entered into under division (D)(12) of this section in relation to contracts entered into on or after March 17, 1998, and in accordance with their normal procedures in relation to contracts entered into prior to March 17, 1998. Any cost incurred by this state or a political subdivision of this state relating to the apprehension of a person who escaped from the facility, to the quelling of a disturbance at the facility, or to the investigation or prosecution as described in division (G)(2) of this section of any offense relating to the escape or disturbance shall be chargeable to and borne by the private contractor. The contractor also shall reimburse the state or its political subdivisions for all reasonable costs incurred relating to the temporary detention of a person who escaped from the facility, following the person's recapture.

(2) If a private contractor that, on or after March 17, 1998, enters into a contract under this section with a local public entity for the operation of a correctional facility that houses out-of-state prisoners fails to perform its contractual duties, the local public entity shall impose upon the private contractor a fine from the schedule of fines included in the contract and may exercise any other rights it has under the contract. A fine imposed under this division shall be paid to the local public entity that enters into the contract, and the local public entity shall deposit the money so paid into its treasury to the credit of the fund used to pay for community policing. If a fine is imposed under this division, the local public entity may reduce the

payment owed to the private contractor pursuant to any invoice in the amount of the fine.

(3) If a private contractor, on or after March 17, 1998, enters into a contract under this section with a local public entity for the operation of a correctional facility that houses out-of-state prisoners in this state, the private contractor shall comply with the insurance, indemnification, hold harmless, and cost reimbursement provisions described in division (D)(9) of this section.

(G)(1) Any act or omission that would be a criminal offense or a delinquent act if committed at a state correctional institution or at a jail, workhouse, prison, or other correctional facility operated by this state or by any political subdivision or group of political subdivisions of this state shall be a criminal offense or delinquent act if committed by or with regard to any out-of-state prisoner who is housed at any correctional facility operated by a private contractor in this state pursuant to a contract entered into prior to, on, or after March 17, 1998.

(2) If any political subdivision of this state experiences any cost in the investigation or prosecution of an offense committed by an out-of-state prisoner housed in a correctional facility operated by a private contractor in this state pursuant to a contract entered into prior to, on, or after March 17, 1998, the private contractor shall reimburse the political subdivision for the costs so experienced.

(3)(a) Except as otherwise provided in this division, the state, and any officer or employee, as defined in section 109.36 of the Revised Code, of the state is not liable in damages in a civil action for any injury, death, or loss to person or property that allegedly arises from, or is related to, the establishment, management, or operation of a correctional facility to house out-of-state prisoners in this state pursuant to a contract between a local public entity and an out-of-state jurisdiction, a local public entity and a private contractor, or a private contractor and an out-of-state jurisdiction that was entered into prior to March 17, 1998, or that is entered into on or after March 17, 1998, in accordance with its provisions. The immunity provided in this division does not apply regarding an act or omission of an officer or employee, as defined in section 109.36 of the Revised Code, of the state that is manifestly outside the scope of the officer's or employee's official responsibilities or regarding an act or omission of the state, or of an officer or employee, as so defined, of the state that is undertaken with malicious purpose, in bad faith, or in a wanton or reckless manner.

(b) Except as otherwise provided in this division, a non-contracting political subdivision, and any employee, as defined in section 2744.01 of the Revised Code, of a non-contracting political subdivision is not liable in damages in a civil action for any injury, death, or loss to person or property that allegedly arises from, or is related to, the establishment, management, or operation of a correctional facility to house out-of-state prisoners in this state pursuant to a contract between a local public entity other than the non-contracting political subdivision and an out-of-state jurisdiction, a local public entity other than the non-contracting political subdivision and a private contractor, or a private contractor and an out-of-state jurisdiction that was entered into prior to March 17, 1998, or that is entered into on or after March 17, 1998, in accordance with its provisions. The immunity provided in this division does not apply regarding an act or omission of an employee, as defined in section 2744.01 of the Revised Code, of a non-contracting political subdivision that is manifestly outside the scope of the employee's employment or official responsibilities or regarding an act or omission of a non-contracting political subdivision or an employee, as so defined, of a non-contracting political subdivision that is undertaken with malicious purpose, in bad faith, or in a wanton or reckless manner.

(c) Divisions (G)(3)(a) and (b) of this section do not affect any immunity or defense that the state and its officers and employees or a non-contracting political subdivision and its employees may be entitled to under another section of the Revised Code or the common law of this state, including, but not limited to, section 9.86 or Chapter 2744. of the Revised Code.

(H)(1) Upon the completion of an out-of-state prisoner's term of detention at a correctional facility operated by a private contractor in this state pursuant to a contract entered into prior to, on, or after March 17, 1998, the operator of the correctional facility shall transport the prisoner to the out-of-state jurisdiction that imposed the sentence for which the prisoner was confined before it releases the prisoner from its custody.

(2) No private contractor that operates and manages a correctional facility housing out-of-state prisoners in this state pursuant to a contract entered into prior to, on, or after March 17, 1998, shall fail to comply with division (H)(1) of this section.

(3) Whoever violates division (H)(2) of this section is guilty of a misdemeanor of the first degree.

(I) Except as otherwise provided in this division, the provisions of divisions (A) to (H) of this section apply in relation to any correctional facility operated by a private contractor in this state to house out-of-state prisoners, regardless of whether the facility is operated pursuant to a contract entered into prior to, on, or after March 17, 1998. Division (C)(1) of this section shall not apply in relation to any correctional facility for housing out-of-state prisoners in this state that is operated by a private contractor under a contract entered into with a local public entity prior to March 17, 1998. If a private contractor operates a correctional facility in this state for the housing of out-of-state prisoners under a contract entered into with a local public entity prior to March 17, 1998, no later than thirty days after the effective date of this amendment, the private contractor shall enter into a contract with the local public entity that comports to the requirements and criteria of division (D) of this section.

**HISTORY: 147 v H 293 (Eff 3-17-98); 148 v H 283. Eff 6-30-99.**

The effective date is set by section 164 of HB 283.

## § 9.08 Restrictions on prisoner access to internet.

(A) As used in this section:

(1) "Computer," "computer network," "computer system," "computer services," "telecommunications service," and "information service" have the same meanings as in section 2913.01 of the Revised Code.

(2) "Contractor" means either of the following:

(a) A person who enters into a contract under section 9.06 of the Revised Code.

(b) A person who enters into a contract under section 9.07 of the Revised Code to operate and manage a correctional facility in this state for out-of-state prisoners.

(3) "Private correctional facility" means a correctional facility that is operated by a contractor under a contract pursuant to section 9.06 or 9.07 of the Revised Code.

(B) No officer or employee of a contractor who is operating and managing a private correctional facility shall provide a prisoner in the private correctional facility access to or permit a prisoner in the private correctional facility to have access to the internet through the use of a computer, computer network, computer system, computer services, telecommunications service, or information service unless both of the following apply:

(1) The prisoner is participating in an approved educational program with direct supervision that requires the use of the internet for training or research purposes.

(2) The provision of and access to the internet is in accordance with rules promulgated by the department of rehabilitation and correction pursuant to section 5120.62 of the Revised Code.

(C)(1) No prisoner in a private correctional facility shall access the internet through the use of a computer, computer network, computer system, computer services, telecommunications service, or information service unless both of the following apply:

(a) The prisoner is participating in an approved educational program with direct supervision that requires the use of the internet for training or research purposes.

(b) The provision of and access to the internet is in accordance with rules promulgated by the department of rehabilitation and correction pursuant to section 5120.62 of the Revised Code.

(2) Whoever violates division (C)(1) of this section is guilty of improper internet access, a misdemeanor of the first degree.

**HISTORY: 148 v S 12. Eff 6-8-2000; 150 v H 204, § 1, eff. 11-5-04.**

## [CONSTRUCTION MANAGEMENT SERVICES]

### § 9.62 Purchase of police dog or horse by assigned officer.

(A) As used in this section:

(1) "Police dog or horse" means a dog or horse that has been trained, and may be used, to assist law enforcement officers in the performance of their official duties.

(2) "Law enforcement agency" means an organization or unit made up of law enforcement officers as defined in section 2901.01 of the Revised Code.

(B) Upon the disbanding of the canine or equine unit of a law enforcement agency, the agency shall give the law enforcement officer to whom a police dog or horse is assigned the first chance to purchase the animal, for one dollar. An officer who purchases an animal under this section shall assume all responsibility for the animal thereafter.

(C) If a police dog or horse is injured in the line of duty, becomes disabled and is unfit for duty, or grows too old to be fit for duty, the law enforcement officer to whom the animal is assigned may purchase the animal, for one dollar. If an officer chooses not to purchase an animal as authorized by this division or division (B) of this section, the disposition of the animal shall be as otherwise provided by law.

(D) A law enforcement officer who leaves an equine or canine unit of a law enforcement agency while the police dog or horse assigned to the officer is still fit for duty forfeits the right to purchase the animal under this section.

**HISTORY: 147 v H 219. Eff 6-1-98.**

# TITLE 1: STATE GOVERNMENT

## CHAPTER 101: GENERAL ASSEMBLY



### [POWERS OF COMMITTEES]

### § 101.44 Testimony before committee not to be used in criminal prosecution of witness; exception.

Except a person who, in writing, requests permission to appear before a committee or subcommittee of the general assembly, or of either house thereof, or who, in writing, waives the rights, privileges, and immunities granted by this section, the testimony of a witness examined before a committee or subcommittee shall not be used as evidence in a criminal proceeding against such witness. This section does not exempt a witness from the penalties for perjury.

**HISTORY: RS § 53; 69 v 61, § 5; 98 v 268; GC § 60; 122 v 321; Bureau of Code Revision, 10-1-53; 136 v S 545. Eff 1-17-77.**

### [LEGISLATIVE LOBBYING]

### § 101.81 Power to secure information.

(A) In order to secure information with respect to any pending or contemplated legislative action, or any alleged breach of its privileges or misconduct by its members, the general assembly may order any person in Ohio to appear and testify before it, before either of its houses, or before any of its standing or select committees, and may order such person to produce books, papers, and other tangible evidence.

(B) An order under division (A) of this section, to appear or to produce books, papers, and other tangible evidence, may be issued by the general assembly, by either of its houses, or, within the limits of its charge by the general assembly or either of its houses, by a standing or a select committee. Such order shall be in writing, and may be directed to an appropriate officer anywhere in Ohio, for service and return in the same manner as a subpoena.

(C) No person shall fail to obey an order issued under this section, or, having appeared pursuant to such order, refuse to answer a question pertinent to the matter under inquiry.

(D) Whoever violates division (C) of this section is guilty of contempt of the general assembly, a misdemeanor of the fourth degree.

**HISTORY: 134 v H 511. Eff 1-1-74.**

**Analogous to former RC § 2917.42 (RS § 6981-1; 98 v 99; GC § 12845; Bureau of Code Revision, 10-1-53), repealed 134 v H 511, § 2, eff 1-1-74.**

## CHAPTER 108: LIEUTENANT GOVERNOR



### § 108.05 Cabinet member; appointment for special assignment.

(A) The lieutenant governor shall be a member of the governor's cabinet and shall preside at its meetings in the absence of the governor.

(B) The governor may appoint the lieutenant governor as an administrative department head listed in section 121.03 of the Revised Code, as the governor's representative on any board, agency, committee, or commission of which the governor is a member and has the authority to appoint a representative, or in an advisory capacity to any nonelective board, agency, committee, or commission in the executive department or may give the lieutenant governor any special assignment as the governor considers in the interest of the state.

(C) When carrying out any of the functions described in division (B) of this section, the lieutenant governor shall be reimbursed from funds of the particular authority for necessary expenses incurred in the conduct of authority [authorized] business.

**HISTORY: 133 v S 353 (Eff 11-6-69); 137 v S 115 (Eff 1-8-79); 139 v S 550 (Eff 11-26-82); 147 v S 193. Eff 12-29-98; 151 v H 66, § 101.01, eff. 6-30-05.**

The effective date is set by § 612.12 of 151 v H 66.

# CHAPTER 109: ATTORNEY GENERAL

[ORGANIZATION]

## § 109.01 Election; term.

The attorney general shall be elected quadrennially, and shall hold his office for a term of four years. The term of office of the attorney general shall commence on the second Monday of January next after his election.

**HISTORY: RS § 214; S&C 91; Const. Art. III, § 2; 50 v 267, § 24; GC § 331; Bureau of Code Revision, 10-1-53; 129 v 582. Eff 1-10-61.**

## § 109.02 Duties as chief law officer.

The attorney general is the chief law officer for the state and all its departments and shall be provided with adequate office space in Columbus. Except as provided in division (E) of section 120.06 and in sections 3517.152 [3517.15.2] to 3517.157 [3517.15.7] of the Revised Code, no state officer or board, or head of a department or institution of the state shall employ, or be represented by, other counsel or attorneys at law. The attorney general shall appear for the state in the trial and argument of all civil and criminal causes in the supreme court in which the state is directly or indirectly interested. When required by the governor or the general assembly, the attorney general shall appear for the state in any court or tribunal in a cause in which the state is a party, or in which the state is directly interested. Upon the written request of the governor, the attorney general shall prosecute any person indicted for a crime.

**HISTORY: RS § 202; S&C 88; 50 v 267, §§ 3-5; 73 v 189, 191; 93 v 127; 97 v 59; GC § 333; Bureau of Code Revision, 10-1-53; 133 v S 438 (Eff 11-17-69); 144 v H 210 (Eff 5-1-92); 146 v S 9. Eff 8-24-95.**

## § 109.03 Appointment of assistant attorney general and chief counsel; duties.

The attorney general may appoint a first assistant attorney general, a chief counsel, and assistant attorneys general, each of whom shall be an attorney at law, to serve for the term for which the attorney general is elected, unless sooner discharged by him, and each shall perform such duties, not otherwise provided by law, as are assigned him by the attorney general.

**HISTORY: RS § 202a; 92 v 172; 97 v 59; GC § 334; 100 v 93; 110 v 10; 114 v 53; Bureau of Code Revision. Eff 10-1-53.**

## § 109.04 Powers and duties of first assistant attorney general.

During the absence or disability of the attorney general, or when so directed by the attorney general, including all the rights, privileges, and powers conferred upon the attorney general by sections 2939.10, 2939.11, and 2939.17 of the Revised Code, the first assistant attorney general shall perform the duties of the attorney general.

**HISTORY: RS § 202a; 92 v 172; 97 v 59; GC § 335; 100 v 93; 101 v 97; 114 v 53; Bureau of Code Revision. Eff 10-1-53.**

## § 109.05 Employees.

The attorney general may appoint such employees as are necessary.

**HISTORY: RS § 202a; 92 v 172; 97 v 59; GC § 337; 100 v 93; 107 v 503; Bureau of Code Revision. Eff 10-1-53.**

## § 109.06 Bond.

Before entering upon the discharge of the duties of his office, the attorney general shall give a bond to the state in the sum of five thousand dollars, with two or more sureties approved by the governor, conditioned for the faithful discharge of the duties of his office. Such bond, with the approval of the governor and the oath of office indorsed thereon, shall be deposited with the secretary of state and kept in his office.

The first assistant attorney general shall give a bond to the state in the sum of five thousand dollars, and such other employees as are designated by the attorney general shall give a bond to the state in such amounts as the attorney general determines. Such bonds shall be approved by the attorney general, conditioned for the faithful discharge of the duties of their offices, and shall be deposited with the secretary of state and kept in his office.

**HISTORY: RS § 201; S&C 88; 50 v 267; GC § 332; Bureau of Code Revision. Eff 10-1-53.**

## § 109.07 Special counsel.

Except under the circumstances described in division (E) of section 120.06 of the Revised Code, the attorney general may appoint special counsel to represent the state in civil actions, criminal prosecutions, or other proceedings in which the state is a party or directly interested. The special counsel shall be paid for their services from funds appropriated by the general assembly for that purpose.

**HISTORY: RS § 202a; 92 v 172; 97 v 59; GC § 336; 100 v 93; Bureau of Code Revision, 10-1-53; 144 v H 210. Eff 5-1-92.**

## § 109.08 Special counsel to collect claims.

The attorney general may appoint special counsel to represent the state in connection with all claims of whatsoever nature which are certified to the attorney general for collection under any law or which the attorney general is authorized to collect.

Such special counsel shall be paid for their services from funds collected by them in an amount approved by the attorney general.

The attorney general shall provide to the special counsel appointed to represent the state in connection with claims arising out of Chapters 5733., 5739., 5741., and 5747. of the Revised Code the official letterhead stationery of the attorney general. The special counsel shall use the letterhead stationery, but only in connection with the collection of such claims arising out of those taxes.

**HISTORY: GC § 336-1; 117 v 304; Bureau of Code Revision, 10-1-53; 143 v S 147. Eff 1-1-90.**

The effective date is set by section 3 of SB 147.

## § 109.081 Attorney general claims fund.

Up to eleven per cent of all amounts collected by the attorney general, whether by employees or agents of the attorney general or by special counsel pursuant to section 109.08 of the Revised Code, on claims due the state shall be paid into the state treasury to the credit of the attorney general claims fund, which is hereby created. The attorney general, after consultation with the director of budget and management, shall determine the exact percentage of those collected amounts that shall be paid into the state treasury to the credit of the fund. The fund shall be used for the payment of expenses incurred by the office of the attorney general.

**HISTORY: 140 v H 291 (Eff 7-1-83); 141 v H 201 (Eff 7-1-85); 144 v H 298 (Eff 7-26-91); 148 v H 283. Eff 6-30-99.**

The effective date is set by section 164 of HB 283.

## § 109.082 Problem resolution officers for certain taxes.

The attorney general shall appoint one or more problem resolution officers from among the employees of the office of the attorney general. These officers shall receive and review inquiries and complaints concerning collections made pursuant to Chapters 5733., 5739., 5741., 5747., and 5751. of the Revised Code regarding which the taxpayer has been unable to obtain satisfactory information after several attempts to communicate with the employee of the office assigned to the taxpayer's collection case or the employee's immediate supervisor, or the special counsel assigned to the case.

**HISTORY: 143 v S 147. Eff 1-1-90; 151 v H 390, § 1, eff. 9-28-06.**

The provisions of § 3 of 151 v H 390 read as follows:

SECTION 3. The amendment or enactment by this act of sections 109.082, 131.02, 5703.06, and 5703.58 of the Revised Code apply to assessments made, or if no assessment was made, to liabilities arising, before, on, or after the effective date of this act. However, the statute of limitations to collection in section 131.02 of the Revised Code, as amended by this act, and to assessment in section 5703.58 of the Revised Code, as enacted by this act, expire not earlier than three years after the effective date of this act, notwithstanding any provisions in such sections to the contrary.

The effective date is set by section 3 of SB 147.

## § 109.09 Action on official bonds.

When so directed, the attorney general shall bring an action on the official bond of a delinquent officer, and shall also prosecute any officer for an offense against the revenue laws of the state that come to his knowledge. Such action may be brought by him in the court of common pleas of Franklin county, or of any county in which one or more of the defendants reside, or can be summoned.

**HISTORY: RS § 203; S&C 89; 50 v 267, §§ 6-8; GC § 338; Bureau of Code Revision. Eff 10-1-53.**

## § 109.10 Proceedings in quo warranto.

The attorney general may prosecute a proceeding in quo warranto in the supreme court of the state, the court of appeals of Franklin county, or the court of appeals of any county wherein a defendant company has a place of business, or the officers or persons made defendants reside or may be found.

**HISTORY: RS § 204; S&C 89; 50 v 267; 82 v 16, 18; GC § 339; 103 v 405; Bureau of Code Revision. Eff 10-1-53.**

## § 109.11 Attorney general reimbursement fund.

There is hereby created in the state treasury the attorney general reimbursement fund that shall be used for the expenses of the office of the attorney general in providing legal services and other services on behalf of the state. All amounts received by the attorney general as reimbursement for legal services and other services that have been rendered to other state agencies shall be paid into the state treasury to the credit of the attorney general reimbursement fund. All amounts awarded by a court to the attorney general for attorney's fees, investigation costs, expert witness fees, fines, and all other costs and fees associated with representation provided by the attorney general and all amounts awarded to the attorney general by a court shall be paid into the state treasury to the credit of the attorney general reimbursement fund.

**HISTORY: 144 v S 351. Eff 7-1-92.**

**Not analogous to former RC § 109.11 (128 v 317; 135 v S 174), repealed 143 v H 111, § 2, eff 7-1-89.**

## § 109.111 Court order fund.

There is hereby created the attorney general court order fund, which shall be in the custody of the treasurer of state but shall not be part of the state treasury. The fund shall consist of all money collected or received as a result of an order of any court to be received or secured by, or delivered to, the attorney general for transfer, distribution, disbursement, or allocation pursuant to court order. All money in the fund, including investment earnings thereon, shall be used solely to make payment as directed pursuant to court order.

**HISTORY: 146 v S 310. Eff 9-19-96.**

## § 109.12 Legal advice to state officers and boards.

The attorney general, when so requested, shall give legal advice to a state officer, board, commission, the warden of a state correctional institution, the superintendent, trustees, or directors of a benevolent institution of the state, and the trustees of the Ohio state university, in all matters relating to their official duties.

**HISTORY: RS § 206; S&C 90; 67 v 20, § 15; 70 v 19, § 15; GC § 341; Bureau of Code Revision, 10-1-53; 145 v H 571. Eff 10-6-94.**

## § 109.121 Land title review and opinion.

Prior to the acquisition by the state of any right, title, or interest in real property, except highway rights-of-way, evidence of such right, title, or interest shall be submitted to the attorney general for his review and opinion. Such evidence shall be that customarily and generally used in the community in which the real property is situated and may consist of, but not be limited to, attorneys' opinions of title, abstracts of title, title guarantees, or title insurance.

**HISTORY: 133 v S 205. Eff 11-12-69.**

## § 109.122 Expositions commission duties.

(A) The attorney general may review for form, content, and legality and provide legal advice concerning any proposed entertainment or sponsorship contracts of the Ohio expositions commission that the commission provides as required by section 991.03 of the Revised Code.

(B) The commission shall reimburse the attorney general for all legal expenses associated with reviewing proposed entertainment or sponsorship contracts under division (A) of this section.

**HISTORY: 145 v H 152. Eff 7-1-93.**

**Not analogous to former RC § 109.122 (134 v H 1170; 135 v H 1), repealed 138 v S 76, § 2, eff 3-13-80.**

## § 109.13 General assembly may require written opinions.

When so required by resolution, the attorney general shall give his written opinion on questions of law to either house of the general assembly.

**HISTORY: RS § 207; S&C 90; 50 v 267, § 16; GC § 342; Bureau of Code Revision. Eff 10-1-53.**

## § 109.14 Advising of prosecuting attorneys, township law directors.

When requested by them, the attorney general shall advise the prosecuting attorneys of the several counties respecting their duties in all complaints, suits, and controversies in which the state is, or may be a party, and shall advise the township law director of a township that has adopted a limited home rule government under Chapter 504. of the Revised Code.

**HISTORY: RS § 208; S&C 90; 50 v 267, § 17; 88 v 11; GC § 343; Bureau of Code Revision, 10-1-53; 146 v H 501 (Eff 11-6-96); 148 v H 187. Eff 9-15-99.**

## § 109.15 Forms of contracts.

The attorney general shall prepare suitable forms of contracts, obligations, and other like instruments of writing for the use of state officers, when requested by the governor, secretary of state, auditor of state, or treasurer of state.

**HISTORY: RS § 209; S&C 90; 50 v 267, § 18; GC § 344; Bureau of Code Revision. Eff 10-1-53.**

## § 109.16 Suits may be brought in Franklin county.

The attorney general may prosecute an action, information, or other proceeding in behalf of the state, or in which the state is interested, except prosecutions by indictment, in the proper court of Franklin county, or of any other county in which one or more of the defendants reside or may be found. No civil action, unless elsewhere specially provided, shall be commenced in Franklin county, if one or more of the defendants do not reside or cannot be found therein, unless the attorney general certifies on the writ that he believes the amount in controversy exceeds five hundred dollars.

**HISTORY: RS § 210; S&C 90; 50 v 267, § 19; GC § 345; Bureau of Code Revision. Eff 10-1-53.**

## § 109.17 Writs in other counties.

In all cases instituted by the attorney general under sections 109.01 to 109.22, inclusive, of the Revised Code, the writ may be sent by mail to the sheriff of any county, and returned by him in like manner. For such service, the sheriff shall be allowed the same mileage and fees as if the writ had been issued from the court of common pleas or the court of appeals of his county, and made returnable thereto.

**HISTORY: RS § 211; S&C 90; 50 v 267, § 20; 82 v 16, 18; GC § 346; 103 v 405; Bureau of Code Revision. Eff 10-1-53.**

## § 109.18 Service by publication.

If a writ of mesne process in proceedings in quo warranto is returned "not found" by the sheriff of the county in which the company is authorized by law to have its place of business, the clerk of the court in which the information or other proceeding is filed shall issue a notice of the filing and substance thereof, and cause it to be published once a week for six consecutive weeks in a newspaper published in and of general circulation in the county wherein such company is authorized to have its place of business. An affidavit of the publication together with a copy of the notice shall be filed in the office of the clerk. If the defendant company fails to answer or plead to such information of proceeding within thirty days from the filing of the affidavit and copy, judgment shall be given upon the default as if the writ or mesne process had been served and returned.

**HISTORY: RS § 212; S&C 91; 50 v 267, § 21; GC § 347; Bureau of Code Revision, 10-1-53; 137 v H 42. Eff 10-7-77.**

## § 109.19 Security for costs and verification of pleadings.

No undertaking or security is required on behalf of the state or an officer thereof, in the prosecution or defense of any action, writ, or proceeding. In an action, writ, or proceeding it is not necessary to verify the pleadings on the part of the state or any officer thereof.

**HISTORY: RS § 213; S&C 91; 56 v 240, § 22; GC § 348; Bureau of Code Revision. Eff 10-1-53.**

## § 109.20 Actions to be taken out of their order.

Upon motion of the attorney general, embodying a statement that the public interests require it, a civil action, brought or prosecuted by him on behalf of the state, or an officer, board, or commission thereof, or an action in which the state is a party, shall be taken out of its order upon the docket and assigned for trial at as early a day as practicable.

**HISTORY: RS § 217; 75 v 125; GC § 349; Bureau of Code Revision. Eff 10-1-53.**

## § 109.21 Disposition of receipts.

The attorney general shall pay all moneys collected or received by the attorney general on behalf of the state into the state treasury to the credit of the general revenue fund.

**HISTORY: RS §§ 216, 218; S&C 91, 1233; 50 v 267, § 26; 57 v 83, § 4; GC § 350; Bureau of Code Revision. Eff 10-1-53; 147 v S 164, Eff 1-15-98.**

## § 109.22 Registers shall be kept.

The attorney general shall keep a register of all actions, demands, complaints, writs, informations, and other proceedings, prosecuted or defended by him, noting therein the proceedings under each, and a register of all official opinions in writing given by him. He shall deliver to his successor the registers, papers, documents, books, and other property belonging to his office.

**HISTORY: RS § 215; S&C 91; 50 v 267, § 25; GC § 351; Bureau of Code Revision. Eff 10-1-53.**

# [DUTIES CONCERNING CHARITABLE TRUSTS]

## § 109.23 Charitable trust defined.

As used in sections 109.23 to 109.33 of the Revised Code:

(A) "Charitable trust" means any fiduciary relationship with respect to property arising under the law of this state or of another jurisdiction as a result of a manifestation of intention to create it, and subjecting the person by whom the property is held to fiduciary duties to deal with the property within this state for any charitable, religious or educational purpose.

(B) "Charitable trust" includes the fiduciary relationship, the entity serving as trustee, the status as trustee, the corpus of such trust, or a combination of any or all of such meanings, regardless of the primary meaning of any use of the term, that is necessary in any circumstances to effect the purposes of such sections.

(C) An executor, administrator, guardian, or other conservator of the estate of a decedent, incompetent, or other similarly protected person is, when holding assets in which a charitable trust has a vested or contingent interest and to the extent that such sections are not clearly inapplicable, to be considered a fiduciary of a charitable trust.

(D) The fact that any person sought to be charged with fiduciary duties is a corporation, association, foundation, or any other type of organization that has, under judicial decisions or other statutes, been distinguished from a charitable trust does not provide a presumption against its being a charitable trust as defined in this section.

**HISTORY: 125 v 351 (Eff 10-14-53); 136 v H 347. Eff 11-19-75.**

## § 109.231 Acts prohibited in administration.

(A) In the administration of any trust which is a "private foundation" as defined in section 509 of the internal revenue code of 1954, a trust for charitable purposes described in section 4947(a)(1) of the internal revenue code of 1954 to the extent that it is treated for federal tax purposes as such a private foundation, or a "split-interest trust" as described in section 4947(a)(2) of the internal revenue code of 1954, the following acts are prohibited:

(1) Engaging in any act of "self-dealing," as defined in section 4941(d) of the internal revenue code of 1954, which would give rise to any liability for any tax imposed by section 4941 of the internal revenue code of 1954;

(2) Retaining any "excess business holdings," as defined in section 4943(c) of the internal revenue code of 1954, which would give rise to any liability for any tax imposed by section 4943 of the internal revenue code of 1954;

(3) Making any investments which would jeopardize the carrying out of any of the exempt purposes of the trust, within the meaning of section 4944 of the internal revenue code of 1954, so as to give rise to any liability for any tax

imposed by section 4944 of the internal revenue code of 1954; or

(4) Making any "taxable expenditures," as defined in section 4945(d) of the internal revenue code of 1954, which would give rise to any liability for any tax imposed by section 4945 of the internal revenue code of 1954. The prohibitions of this division do not apply to split-interest trusts, or to amounts thereof, to the extent that such prohibitions are inapplicable thereto by reason of section 4947 of the internal revenue code of 1954.

(B) In the administration of any trust which is a "private foundation" as defined in section 509 of the internal revenue code of 1954, or a trust for charitable purposes described in section 4947(a)(1) of the internal revenue code of 1954 to the extent that it is treated for federal tax purposes as such a private foundation, there shall, for the purposes specified in the governing instrument, be distributed at such time and in such manner, for each taxable year, amounts of income and principal at least sufficient to avoid liability for any tax imposed by section 4942 of the internal revenue code of 1954.

(C) Divisions (A) and (B) of this section express the continuing policy of this state with respect to charitable trust interests and are enacted to assist such trusts in maintaining various tax benefits extended to them, and apply to all trusts described therein, whether or not contrary to the provisions of the governing instrument of such a trust, provided that divisions (A) and (B) of this section do not apply to a trust in existence on the effective date of this section to the extent that the attorney general, the trustor, or any beneficiary of such trust, on or before November 30, 1971, files with the trustee of such trust a written objection to application to such trust of one or more provisions of said divisions, and if the trustee receiving such written objection commences an action on or before December 31, 1971, in the court having jurisdiction over such trust to reform, or to excuse such trust from compliance with, its governing instrument or any other instrument in order to meet the requirements of said divisions. A trustee receiving such written objection shall commence such an action, and the one or more provisions of said divisions specified in such written objection will not apply to such trust unless and until said court determines that their application to such trust is in the best interests of all parties in interest.

(D) No trustee of a trust to which division (A) or (B) of this section is applicable shall be surcharged for a violation of a prohibition or requirement of said divisions, unless he participated in such violation knowing that it was a violation, nor shall such trustee be surcharged if such violation was not willful and was due to reasonable cause, provided that this division does not exonerate a trustee from any responsibility or liability to which he is subject under any other rule of law whether or not duplicated in division (A) or (B) of this section.

(E) As used in this section, "trust" includes a trust or any other organization, other than a corporation, which is a "private foundation" as defined in section 509 of the internal revenue code of 1954, and "trustee" includes any member of the governing body of such organization.

(F) Except as provided in division (D) of this section, nothing in this section impairs the rights and powers of the courts or the attorney general of this state with respect to any trust.

**HISTORY: 134 v S 198. Eff 9-17-71.**

## § 109.232 Amendment of trust.

(A) The governing instrument of a trust described in division (A) of section 109.231 [109.23.1] of the Revised Code may be amended to permit the trust to acquire the characteristics of a trust described in section 664(D)(1) or (2) of the internal revenue code of 1954, or to conform to the requirements of, or to obtain benefits available under, section 507, 508, or 509 of the internal revenue code of 1954. Such amendment may be made by the trustee with the approval of the attorney general, of the trustor, and, if one or more beneficiaries are named in the governing instrument of such trust, of each named beneficiary. If the trustor is not then living or is not then competent to give such approval, such amendment may be made by the trustee with the approval of the attorney general and, if one or more beneficiaries are named in the governing instrument of such trust, of each named beneficiary. If one or more of said required approvals is not obtained, the trustee may apply to the court having jurisdiction over such trust for approval of such amendment. Said governing instrument may also be amended in any respect and by any method set forth therein or as otherwise provided by law.

(B) Nothing in this section impairs the rights and powers of the courts or the attorney general of this state with respect to any trust.

(C) For the purposes of sections 109.231 [109.23.1] and 109.232 [109.23.2] of the Revised Code, all references to sections of the internal revenue code of 1954 include all amendments or reenactments thereof.

**HISTORY: 134 v S 198 (Eff 9-17-71); 134 v S 533. Eff 7-15-72.**

## § 109.24 Administration and enforcement of charitable trusts.

The powers of the attorney general under sections 109.23 to 109.33 of the Revised Code shall be in addition to and not in limitation of his powers held at common law. The attorney general may investigate transactions and relationships of trustees of a charitable trust for the purpose of determining whether the property held for charitable, religious, or educational purposes has been and is being properly administered in accordance with fiduciary principles as established by the courts and statutes of this state. The attorney general is empowered to require the production of any books or papers which are relevant to the inquiry. Each such request shall be in writing, and shall do all of the following:

(A) Identify the person to whom the request is directed;

(B) State the specific purpose of the investigation;

(C) Describe any books and the papers to be produced with such definiteness and certainty as to permit such material to be fairly identified;

(D) Prescribe a return date which will provide at least ten days' notice within which the books or papers to be produced may be assembled;

(E) State the place where and the time within which any books or papers are to be produced, provided, however, that copies of such books and papers may be produced in lieu of the originals.

No request shall contain any requirement which would be held to be unreasonable or oppressive or which would be privileged from disclosure if contained in a subpoena duces tecum issued by a court of this state pursuant to the Rules of Civil Procedure. If the production of documents required by the request would be unduly burdensome, the person upon whom the request is served, in lieu of producing such books or papers at the place designated in the request, shall make such books or papers available for inspection, copying, or reproduction at the place where such books or papers are kept.

Whenever a request fails to meet the requirements enumerated in this section, any person upon whom the request is served may file a complaint to quash such request in the court of common pleas of the county in which the trust, institution, association, or corporation has its principal place of business in this state. The complaint shall contain a brief statement of facts entitling such person to have such requests quashed. No answer to such complaint is required. Upon the filing of the complaint, the court, on motion of the complainant, shall enter an order fixing a date for a hearing on the complaint and requiring that a copy of the complaint and a notice of the filing and of the date for hearing be given to the attorney general or his assistant in the manner in which summons is required to be served or substituted services required to be made in other cases. On the day fixed for the hearing on the complaint, the court shall determine from the complaint and from such evidence as is submitted by either party whether the person upon whom the request was served is entitled to have the request quashed. The proceeding is a special proceeding, and final orders in the proceeding may be vacated, modified, or reversed on appeal pursuant to the Rules of Appellate Procedure and, to the extent not in conflict with those rules, Chapter 2505. of the Revised Code.

The attorney general shall institute and prosecute a proper action to enforce the performance of any charitable trust, and to restrain the abuse of it whenever he considers such action advisable or if directed to do so by the governor, the supreme court, the general assembly, or either house of the general assembly. Such action may be brought in his own name, on behalf of the state, or in the name of a beneficiary of the trust, in the court of common pleas of any county in which the trust property or any part of it is situated or invested, or in which the trustee resides; provided that in the case of a charitable trust created by, arising as a result of, or funded by a will, such action may be brought in either the court of common pleas of any such county, or the probate division of it, at the election of the attorney general. No such action shall abate or discontinue by virtue of the discontinuance in office of the attorney general in whose name such actions may be brought. This section is intended to allow the attorney general full discretion concerning the manner in which the action is to be prosecuted, including the authority to settle an action when he considers that advisable.

**HISTORY: 125 v 352 (Eff 10-14-53); 136 v H 347 (Eff 11-19-75); 141 v H 412. Eff 3-17-87.**

## § 109.25 Necessary party to charitable trust proceedings.

The attorney general is a necessary party to and shall be served with process or with summons by registered mail in all judicial proceedings, the object of which is to:

(A) Terminate a charitable trust or distribute assets;

(B) Depart from the objects or purposes of a charitable trust as the same are set forth in the instrument creating the trust, including any proceeding for the application of the doctrine of cy pres or deviation;

(C) Construe the provisions of an instrument with respect to a charitable trust;

(D) Determine the validity of a will having provisions for a charitable trust.

A judgment rendered in such proceedings without service of process or summons upon the attorney general is void, unenforceable, and shall be set aside upon the attorney general's motion seeking such relief. The attorney general shall intervene in any judicial proceeding affecting a charitable trust when requested to do so by the court having jurisdiction of the proceeding, and may intervene in any judicial proceeding affecting a charitable trust when he determines that the public interest should be protected in such proceeding.

**HISTORY: 125 v 352 (Eff 10-14-53); 129 v 582 (Eff 1-10-61); 136 v H 347. Eff 11-19-75.**

## § 109.26 Register of charitable trusts.

Except as provided in this section, every charitable trust established or active in this state shall register with the attorney general. The attorney general shall prepare and maintain a register of such charitable trusts. The following are not required to register under this section:

(A) Charitable remainder trusts created after July 31, 1969, gifts to which are deductible for federal income, gift, or estate tax purposes;

(B) Charitable trusts in which all charitable interests are contingent and will vest only upon conditions which have not occurred;

(C) Decedent's estates;

(D) Such other classes of charitable trusts as the attorney general may exempt from registration by regulation pursuant to section 109.27 of the Revised Code.

County or independent agricultural societies organized under Chapter 1711. of the Revised Code are not charitable trusts.

Every charitable trust shall be registered with the attorney general in accordance with this section within six months after the effective date of this section, November 19, 1975, within six months after the creation of such trust, or within six months after occurrence of an event by reason of which such trust is required to register by this section, whichever is later, provided that all registrations of charitable trusts made prior to November 19, 1975, shall be deemed in full compliance with this section and no further registration shall be required.

No trustee of a charitable trust shall willfully fail to register such charitable trust as required by this section.

**HISTORY: 125 v 353 (Eff 10-14-53); 129 v 582 (Eff 1-10-61); 136 v H 347 (Eff 11-19-75); 137 v H 1 (Eff 8-26-77); 137 v H 659. Eff 1-10-78.**

## § 109.27 Rules concerning charitable trusts.

The attorney general shall make such rules subject to the provisions of sections 119.01 to 119.13 of the Revised Code, as are necessary to administer sections 109.23 to 109.33 of the Revised Code.

**HISTORY: 125 v 353 (Eff 10-14-53); 136 v H 347. Eff 11-19-75.**

## § 109.28 Inspection of register of charitable trusts.

The register established by section 109.26 shall be open to the inspection of any person at such reasonable times and for such legitimate purposes as the attorney general may determine; provided, however, that any investigation of a charitable trust shall not be open to public inspection.

**HISTORY: 125 v 353. Eff 10-14-53.**

## § 109.29 Furnish information relating to charitable trusts.

The clerk of each court of common pleas or the judge of the probate division thereof, and of each court of appeals shall furnish copies of papers and such information as to the records and files of his office relating to charitable trusts as the attorney general may require.

**HISTORY: 125 v 353 (Eff 10-14-53); 136 v H 347. Eff 11-19-75.**

## § 109.30 Notice to attorney general and specified persons after probate of will.

After admission to probate of a will creating or purporting to create a charitable trust that must be registered under section 109.26 of the Revised Code, or containing a gift valued in excess of one thousand dollars to any charitable trust, notice shall be given to the attorney general, as well as to the persons specified in division (A)(1) of section 2107.19 of the Revised Code, in accordance with that section. If probate of a will creating or purporting to create any charitable trust is refused by interlocutory order under section 2107.181 [2107.18.1] of the Revised Code, notice of the further hearing under that section shall be given to the attorney general as well as to the other necessary parties.

**HISTORY: 136 v H 347 (Eff 11-19-75); 143 v H 346. Eff 5-31-90.**

**Analogous to former RC § 109.30 (125 v 353), repealed 136 v H 347, § 2, eff 11-19-75.**

The provisions of § 3 of HB 346 (143 v —) read as follows:

SECTION 3. (A) Sections 1 and 2 of this act shall apply only to the estates of decedents who die on or after the effective date of this act.

(B) It is the intent of the General Assembly in the outright repeal of sections 2107.13 and 2107.14 of the Revised Code and the amendments to sections 109.30, 2107.18, 2107.19, 2107.22, 2107.27, 2107.76, 2115.16, and 2703.14 of the Revised Code by this act, to respond to the dicta of the Supreme Court in Palazzi v. Estate of Gardner (1987), 32 Ohio St.3d 169 and to enact statutory provisions relating to notice of probate proceedings that are not unconstitutional as potentially violative of the due process of law rights of nonresidents of this state.

(C) Chapter 2106. of the Revised Code, as enacted by this act, shall be known as "Rights of Surviving Spouses."

## § 109.31 Trustee's report to attorney general; fees.

Except as otherwise provided by this section, the trustees of a charitable trust required to register under section 109.26 of the Revised Code shall file annual reports on forms prescribed by the attorney general, on or before the fifteenth day of the fifth month following the close of the trust's taxable year as established for federal tax purposes; or, in lieu of filing those reports, the trustees may file complete copies of all annual federal returns required to be filed by the trust with the internal revenue service for the taxable year, together with all schedules, attachments, and reports due with the return or returns. The federal returns shall be filed with the attorney general at the same time as required by the internal revenue service, taking into account any applicable extension of the federal filing date.

The annual report shall be signed by the trustee who is authorized to sign it. The annual report shall be considered certified by the trustee and the trustee's signature on the report shall have the same effect as though made under oath.

A charitable trust required to register under section 109.26 of the Revised Code is not required to file the reports required by this section if any of the following apply:

(A) It is organized and operated exclusively for religious purposes.

(B) It is an educational institution that normally maintains a regular faculty and curriculum and normally has a regularly organized body of pupils or students in attendance at the place where its educational activities are regularly carried on.

(C) For any taxable year it has gross receipts of less than twenty-five thousand dollars and at the end of which it has gross assets of less than twenty-five thousand dollars.

The attorney general, by rule pursuant to section 109.27 of the Revised Code, may exempt other classes of charitable trusts from the requirements of this section, and may by rule increase monetary limits set forth in division (C) of this section, that require filing with the attorney general's office.

The attorney general may institute judicial proceedings to secure compliance with this section and to secure the proper administration of any trust or other relationship to which this section applies. The willful failure of any trustee to file reports as required by this section may be grounds for judicial removal of the trustee responsible for such failure.

The attorney general shall charge the following fees for filing the annual report:

| Assets | Fee |
|---|---|
| Less than $25,000 | $ 0 |
| $25,000 but less than $100,000 | 50 |
| $100,000 but less than $500,000 | 100 |
| $500,000 or more | 200 |

For the purposes of this section, "assets" refers to the total fair market value of the charitable trust's assets at the end of that trust's taxable year as established for federal tax purposes.

Any charitable trust that fails to pay the fee required by this section at the time required shall pay an additional fee of two hundred dollars, except that the attorney general may waive the two-hundred dollar fee upon a showing that the trustees of the charitable trust failed to pay the fee for filing the annual report at the time required by this section for reasons that were beyond the control of the trustees of the charitable trust or of a designee of the trustees.

This section shall not be subject to section 119.12 of the Revised Code.

**HISTORY: 136 v H 347 (Eff 11-19-75); 143 v H 486 (Eff 11-7-90); 145 v S 71. Eff 10-29-93; 153 v H 519, § 1, eff. 9-10-10.**

**Analogous to former RC § 109.31 (125 v 353), repealed 136 v 347, § 2, eff 11-19-75.**

## § 109.32 Charitable law fund; expenses of charitable law section.

All annual filing fees obtained by the attorney general pursuant to section 109.31 of the Revised Code, all receipts obtained from the sale of the charitable foundations directory, all registration fees received by the attorney general, bond forfeitures, awards of costs and attorney's fees, and civil penalties assessed under Chapter 1716. of the Revised Code, and all license fees received by the attorney general under section 2915.08, 2915.081 [2915.08.1], or 2915.082 [2915.08.2] of the Revised Code shall be paid into the state treasury to the credit of the charitable law fund. The charitable law fund shall be used insofar as its moneys are available for the expenses of the charitable law section of the office of the attorney general, except that all annual license fees that are received by the attorney general under section 2915.08, 2915.081 [2915.08.1], or 2915.082 [2915.08.2] of the Revised Code and that are credited to the fund shall be used by the attorney general, or any law enforcement agency in cooperation with the attorney general, for the purposes specified in division (H) of section 2915.10 of the Revised Code and to administer and enforce Chapter 2915. of the Revised Code. The expenses of the charitable law section in excess of moneys available in the charitable law fund shall be paid out of regular appropriations to the office of the attorney general.

**HISTORY: 136 v H 347 (Eff 11-19-75); 143 v H 486 (Eff 11-7-90); 148 v H 59 (Eff 10-29-99); 149 v H 512. Eff 4-3-2003; 150 v H 95, § 1, eff. 7-1-03.**

**Analogous to former RC § 109.32 (125 v 354), repealed 136 v H 347, § 2, eff 11-19-75.**

The effective date is set by section 182 of H.B. 95.

## § 109.33 Assistants; appointments, compensation.

The attorney general may appoint, with salaries fixed pursuant to section 124.15 or 124.152 [124.15.2] of the Revised Code, such assistants and may employ such stenographers and clerks as may be necessary to carry out sections 109.23 to 109.33 of the Revised Code. The attorney general may also employ experts for assistance in any specific matter at a reasonable rate of compensation.

**HISTORY: 125 v 354 (Eff 10-14-53); 132 v H 93 (Eff 5-17-67); 137 v H 1 (Eff 8-26-77); 141 v H 831. Eff 4-9-86.**

This section was amended by Senate Bill 5 of the 2011 legislative session. However, referendum petitions were filed to prevent SB 5 from taking effect as scheduled on July 1, 2011. The provisions of SB 5 were rejected by the voters at the referendum election on November 8, 2011.

## [NONPROFIT HEALTH CARE ENTITY TRANSACTIONS]

## § 109.34 Nonprofit health care entity proposing certain transactions to notify attorney general and obtain approval.

(A) As used in this section and in section 109.35 of the Revised Code:

(1) "Fair market value" means the price that the assets being transferred would bring in a competitive and open market under a fair sale with the buyer and seller acting prudently, knowledgeably, and in their own best interest and a reasonable time being allowed for exposure in the market.

(2) "Nonprofit health care entity" means any of the following that was created for any charitable or social welfare purpose related to health care:

(a) A hospital, as defined in section 3727.01 of the Revised Code, that is owned or operated by a corporation organized under Chapter 1702. of the Revised Code or the nonprofit corporation law of another state;

(b) Either of the following that is or has been exempt from taxation under section 501(a) of the Internal Revenue Code:

(i) An entity that is or has been granted a certificate of authority under Chapter 1742. of the Revised Code;

(ii) An entity that is authorized or has been authorized to transact business in this state under Title XXXIX [39] of the Revised Code, that is in the business of providing sickness and accident insurance, and that was previously a hospital service association under former Chapter 1739. of the Revised Code or Chapter 669. of the General Code, has merged or otherwise consolidated with a former hospital service association, or any of whose predecessors in interest has merged or otherwise consolidated with a former hospital service association.

(3) "Party" includes a nonprofit health care entity that is the subject of a transaction or proposed transaction, an acquiring person, and the resulting entity, if any.

(4) "Transaction" means a transfer of ownership or control of assets of a nonprofit health care entity, whether by purchase, merger, consolidation, lease, gift, joint venture, or other transfer, including any binding obligation in furtherance of the transaction, that is equal to at least twenty per cent of the assets of the entity and occurs in the twenty-four-month period prior to the date notice is submitted to the attorney general in accordance with division (B) of this section. "Transaction" also means a transfer of ownership or control of any assets of a nonprofit health care entity, whether by purchase, merger, consolidation, lease, gift, joint venture, or other transfer, including any binding obligation in furtherance of the transaction, if the entity is unable to fulfill its stated or actual purpose without the assets. "Transaction" does not include either of the following:

(a) A transfer of ownership or control of assets of a nonprofit health care entity between nonprofit health care entities and persons exempt from taxation under section 501(a) of the "Internal Revenue Code of 1986," 100 Stat. 2085, 26 U.S.C. 501, as amended;

(b) A transfer of ownership or control of assets of a nonprofit health care entity in relation to which the nonprofit health care entity, prior to the effective date of this section, has entered into a consent decree with the attorney general that requires distribution of the charitable assets of the entity to an appropriate health-related charity. The exemption in division (A)(4)(b) of this section does not limit the authority of the attorney general to seek remedies for breaches of fiduciary duty or other violations of law.

(B) A nonprofit health care entity proposing to enter into a transaction shall provide notice of the proposed transaction to the attorney general and obtain written approval of the transaction in accordance with this section. The nonprofit health care entity shall submit the notice on forms provided by the attorney general, and the notice shall include all of the following:

(1) The names and addresses of the parties, including a list of all individuals who are or have been chosen as directors, officers, or board members of the parties;

(2) The terms of the proposed transaction, including a summary of all contracts or other agreements of the parties;

(3) The amount, source, and nature of consideration to be paid to the nonprofit health care entity, its directors, officers, board members, executives, or experts retained by the nonprofit health care entity.

(4) A statement acknowledging that the nonprofit health care entity is under a continuing duty to notify the attorney general of any changes in the information contained in the notice or other documents required by this section and that a violation of this duty may delay approval of the proposed transaction. The statement shall be signed by a representative of the nonprofit health care entity at the time the notice is submitted to the attorney general.

(C) In addition to the notice described in division (B) of this section, the nonprofit health care entity shall submit all of the following:

(1) Audited financial statements for the nonprofit health care entity for the three fiscal years prior to the date the nonprofit health care entity submitted the notice to the attorney general;

(2) A valuation statement prepared by an independent, qualified expert, including an investment banker, actuary, appraiser, certified public accountant, or other expert, that assesses the full and fair market value of the nonprofit health care entity;

(3) Copies of all contracts and other agreements between the parties or their officers, directors, board members, or other fiduciaries, including any contracts or other final agreements relating to the close of the proposed transaction;

(4) Any additional information the attorney general considers necessary to value the nonprofit health care entity's assets as required in rules adopted by the attorney general in accordance with Chapter 119. of the Revised Code.

(D) The notice and all other documents or materials submitted pursuant to this section are public records provided they meet the definition set forth in section 149.43 of the Revised Code.

(E) Not later than two business days after the discovery of any changes in information contained in the notice or other documents required by this section, the nonprofit health care entity shall provide copies to the attorney general of any documents and other material relevant to the changes. In addition to the ninety-day extension authorized by division (A) of section 109.35 of the Revised Code, the attorney general for good cause may delay approval of the proposed transaction up to thirty days following receipt of the documents and other material relevant to the changes.

(F) Not later than seven days after submitting the notice and other documents required by this section, the nonprofit health care entity shall publish notice of the proposed transaction in at least one daily newspaper of general circulation in the county where the nonprofit health care entity has its principal place of business. The notice shall state the names of the parties and a description of the proposed transaction.

(G) Notwithstanding division (A)(4)(a) of this section, as used in this division, "nonprofit combination" means a transaction between a nonprofit health care entity and another unrelated nonprofit health care entity.

Not less than sixty days before the closing of a nonprofit combination, a nonprofit health care entity that is a party to the combination and is the party to be acquired shall provide notice of the nonprofit combination to the attorney general by submitting the information described in divisions (B)(1) and (3) of this section.

Not later than seven days after the information required by this section is submitted to the attorney general, each of the nonprofit health care entities that is a party to a nonprofit combination shall publish the notice described in division (F) of this section.

**HISTORY: 147 v H 242. Eff 5-7-97.**

The provisions of § 4 of HB 597 (148 v —) read as follows:

SECTION 4. The General Assembly hereby declares that the General Assembly, by enacting any provision of this act, does not intend to repeal any provision of sections 109.34, 109.35, and 109.99 of the Revised Code.

## § 109.35 Approval or disapproval of transactions; prohibitions.

(A) Not later than sixty days after receipt of a notice and other documents required by section 109.34 of the Revised Code, the attorney general shall approve or disapprove the proposed transaction, except that the attorney general for good cause may extend this period an additional ninety days.

(B) In determining whether to approve or disapprove a proposed transaction, the attorney general shall consider:

(1) Whether the proposed transaction will result in a breach of fiduciary duty, as determined by the attorney general, including conflicts of interest related to payments or benefits to officers, directors, board members, executives, and experts employed or retained by the parties;

(2) Whether the nonprofit health care entity will receive full and fair market value for its charitable or social welfare assets;

(3) Whether the proceeds of the proposed transaction will be used consistent with the nonprofit health care entity's original charitable purpose;

(4) Any other criteria the attorney general considers necessary to determine whether the nonprofit health care entity will receive full and fair market value for its charitable or social welfare assets as required in rules adopted by the attorney general in accordance with Chapter 119. of the Revised Code.

(C) The attorney general may retain, at the nonprofit health care entity's expense, one or more independently qualified experts, including an investment banker, actuary, appraiser, certified public accountant, or other expert, as the attorney general considers reasonably necessary to provide assistance in making a decision under this section. The nonprofit health care entity shall promptly reimburse the attorney general for the cost of retaining experts. The cost of retaining an expert shall not exceed an amount that is reasonable and necessary to make a determination under this section. The contract to retain an expert is exempt from Chapter 125. of the Revised Code.

At any time while considering a proposed transaction under this section, the attorney general may request any additional information from the nonprofit health care entity that the attorney general considers appropriate to the valuation of the entity's charitable or social welfare assets. The nonprofit health care entity shall provide the information not later than ten days after the date of the request. The attorney general for good cause may delay approval of the proposed transaction up to thirty days, in addition to the ninety-day extension authorized by division (A) of this section, following receipt of documents and other material containing the information requested.

(D) The attorney general shall approve or disapprove a proposed transaction on the basis of the criteria set forth in division (B) of this section. Once a proposed transaction is approved, any substantial alteration is a new transaction subject to approval by the attorney general.

The nonprofit health care entity may resubmit a notice and other documents seeking approval of a proposed transaction disapproved by the attorney general but may not submit a notice and other documents that are identical or substantially similar to the original submission.

If the attorney general disapproves the proposed transaction, the nonprofit health care entity may appeal the disapproval pursuant to division (H) of this section.

(E) If the attorney general approves the proposed transaction, the nonprofit health care entity shall hold a public hearing to receive comment on the proposed use of the proceeds of the transaction. The hearing shall be held in the county where the nonprofit health care entity has its principal place of business not later than forty-five days after receipt of written notice of the attorney general's approval.

At least thirty days prior to the date set for the hearing, the nonprofit health care entity shall publish notice of the hearing in at least one daily newspaper of general circulation in the county where the nonprofit health care entity has its principal place of business. The notice shall include a statement that a transaction has been approved by the attorney general, the names of the parties, a description of the proposed transaction, and the date, time, and place of the hearing.

(F)(1) The proceeds of an approved transaction shall be dedicated and transferred to one or more existing or new charitable organizations exempt from taxation under section 501(a) and described in section 501(c)(3) of the "Internal Revenue Code of 1986," 100 Stat. 2085, 26 U.S.C.A. 501, as amended.

(2) The attorney general may authorize a dedication and transfer to a person exempt from taxation under section 501(a) and described in section 501(c)(4) of the "Internal Revenue Code of 1986," 100 Stat. 2085, 26 U.S.C.A. 501, as amended, if all of the following conditions are met:

(a) The attorney general determines that the dedication and transfer is necessary to ensure effective management and monetization of the equity ownership, if any, in the nonprofit health care entity;

(b) The person described in division (F)(2) of this section agrees to all of the following conditions:

(i) The person described in division (F)(2) of this section will receive from the nonprofit health care entity only the amount of proceeds of the transaction as are necessary to fund the level of activity necessary to preserve the person's tax-exempt status;

(ii) No proceeds of the transaction, or any other funds or resources controlled by the person described in division (F)(2) of this section, will be disbursed for campaign contributions, lobbying expenditures, or other political activity;

(iii) The person described in division (F)(2) of this section agrees to abide by any requirements imposed on persons exempt from taxation under section 501(a) and described in section 501(c)(3) of the "Internal Revenue Code of 1986," 100 Stat. 2085, 26 U.S.C.A. 501, as amended, that the attorney general determines appropriate.

(G)(1) No nonprofit health care entity shall enter into a transaction subject to this section without the approval of the attorney general granted in accordance with this section.

(2) No person who is an officer, director, board member, or other fiduciary of a nonprofit health care entity shall receive anything of substantial value that relates to a transaction described in this section and section 109.34 of the Revised Code and is of such a character as to manifest a substantial and improper influence on the person with respect to the person's duties.

(3) The attorney general may institute and prosecute a civil or criminal action to enforce this section and section 109.34 of the Revised Code in the court of common pleas of the county in which the nonprofit health care entity has its principal place of business or the Franklin county court of common pleas. In addition to any civil remedies that exist under common law or the Revised Code, a court may rescind the transaction, grant injunctive relief, assess a civil penalty in an amount not exceeding ten million dollars, or impose any combination of these remedies.

(H) A nonprofit health care entity that is a party to a proposed transaction that has been disapproved by the attorney general may appeal the disapproval only by following the procedure set forth in this division. The disapproval may be appealed to the court of common pleas of the county in which the nonprofit health entity has its principal place of business. The court of common pleas may reverse, vacate, or modify the attorney general's decision to disapprove a transaction if the court finds that the decision was unlawful or unreasonable. This appeal shall proceed as an appeal de novo. To bring an appeal under this division, a nonprofit health care entity shall file a notice of appeal with the court and the attorney general not later than fifteen days after the entity's receipt of notice of the attorney general's disapproval of the transaction. Not later than thirty days after receipt of the notice of appeal, the attorney general shall prepare and certify to the court of common pleas a complete record of all of the documents submitted by the nonprofit health care entity to the attorney general and any documents generated by consultants at the request of the attorney general or other materials produced by the attorney general as part of the attorney general's determination of whether to approve or disapprove the transaction.

The judgment of the court of common pleas is final unless reversed, vacated, or modified on appeal. An appeal may be taken by either the nonprofit health care entity or the attorney general, shall proceed as in the case of appeals in civil actions, and shall be pursuant to the rules of appellate procedure and, to the extent not in conflict with those rules, Chapter 2505. of the Revised Code.

(I)(1) The powers of the attorney general under this section and section 109.34 of the Revised Code are in addition to the attorney general's powers held at common law and under sections 109.23 to 109.33 of the Revised Code.

This section and section 109.34 of the Revised Code do not limit or otherwise affect any of the following:

(a) Any other civil or criminal right, claim, or defense that the attorney general or parties may assert under common law or the Revised Code;

(b) The authority of the attorney general to institute and prosecute an action to enforce sections 109.23 to 109.33 of the Revised Code;

(c) The authority of the attorney general to investigate and prosecute violations of any state or federal antitrust law.

(2) Nothing in this section shall be construed to grant to the attorney general any authority of the superintendent of insurance under Title XVII [17] or Title XXXIX [39] of the Revised Code relating to the superintendent's review of an entity described in division (A)(2)(b) of section 109.34 of the Revised Code.

(3) Nothing in this section or section 109.34 of the Revised Code shall be construed to limit the independent authority of the attorney general to protect charitable trusts and charitable assets in this state.

**HISTORY: 147 v H 242. Eff 5-7-97.**

See provisions, § 4 of HB 597 (148 v —), following RC § 109.34.

## [DEFENSE OF OFFICERS AND EMPLOYEES]

### § 109.36 Definitions.

As used in this section and sections 109.361 to 109.366 of the Revised Code:

(A)(1) "Officer or employee" means any of the following:

(a) A person who, at the time a cause of action against the person arises, is serving in an elected or appointed office or position with the state or is employed by the state.

(b) A person that, at the time a cause of action against the person, partnership, or corporation arises, is rendering medical, nursing, dental, podiatric, optometric, physical therapeutic, psychiatric, or psychological services pursuant to a personal services contract or purchased service contract with a department, agency, or institution of the state.

(c) A person that, at the time a cause of action against the person, partnership, or corporation arises, is rendering peer review, utilization review, or drug utilization review services in relation to medical, nursing, dental, podiatric, optometric, physical therapeutic, psychiatric, or psychological services pursuant to a personal services contract or purchased service contract with a department, agency, or institution of the state.

(d) A person who, at the time a cause of action against the person arises, is rendering medical, nursing, dental, podiatric, optometric, physical therapeutic, psychiatric, or psychological services to patients in a state institution operated by the department of mental health pursuant to an agreement with the department.

(2) "Officer or employee" does not include any person elected, appointed, or employed by any political subdivision of the state.

(B) "State" means the state of Ohio, including but not limited to, the general assembly, the supreme court, courts of appeals, the offices of all elected state officers, and all departments, boards, offices, commissions, agencies, institutions, and other instrumentalities of the state of Ohio. "State" does not include political subdivisions.

(C) "Political subdivisions" of the state means municipal corporations, townships, counties, school districts, and all other bodies corporate and politic responsible for governmental activities only in geographical areas smaller than that of the state.

(D) "Employer" means the general assembly, the supreme court, courts of appeals, any office of an elected state officer, or any department, board, office, commission, agency, institution, or other instrumentality of the state of Ohio that employs or contracts with an officer or employee or to which an officer or employee is elected or appointed.

**HISTORY: 138 v S 76 (Eff 3-13-80); 139 v S 204 (Eff 7-26-82); 145 v H 715 (Eff 7-22-94); 145 v H 571 (Eff 10-6-94); 146 v H 350 (Eff 1-27-97); 149 v S 108, § 2.01 (Eff 7-6-2001); 149 v S 179. Eff 4-9-2003; 153 v H 10, § 1, eff. 6-17-10; 2011 HB 153, § 101.01, eff. Sept. 29, 2011.**

### § 109.361 Duty to defend state officer or employee in civil action upon request.

Upon the receipt of a written request by any officer or employee, the attorney general, except as provided in section 109.362 [109.36.2] of the Revised Code, except under the circumstances described in division (E) of section 120.06 of the Revised Code, and except for civil actions in which the state is the plaintiff, shall represent and defend the officer or employee in any civil action instituted against the officer or employee. All expenses and court costs, including the reasonable compensation of special counsel, incurred by the attorney general in the defense of an officer or employee shall be paid by the employer that employed the officer or employee at the time the alleged act or omission occurred.

The defense of the officer or employee may be rendered by the attorney general, an assistant attorney general, or any special counsel appointed by the attorney general, who, in addition to providing the defense of the officer or employee, may file counterclaims and cross-claims and engage in third-party practice on behalf of the officer or employee. If the officer or employee recovers any money pursuant to any counterclaim or cross-claim so filed, the officer or employee, to the extent of the recovery on the counterclaim or cross-claim, shall reimburse the attorney general for all expenses and court costs, including the reasonable compensation of assistant attorneys general and special counsel, incurred in bringing the counterclaim or cross-claim. The officer or employee shall cooperate fully with the attorney general's defense. Sections 109.36 to 109.366 [109.36.6] of the Revised Code do not deprive any officer or employee of the right to select counsel of his own choice or settle his case at his own expense at any time, and, except under the circumstances described in division (E) of section 120.06 of the Revised Code, do not prohibit the attorney general from entering his appearance in a case to protect the interest of the state even though no request for the appearance has been made by the officer or employee.

**HISTORY: 138 v S 76 (Eff 3-13-80); 144 v H 210. Eff 5-1-92.**

### § 109.362 Investigation as to whether action was outside scope of duties or in bad faith; effect of insurance; notice of denial.

(A) Prior to undertaking any defense under section 109.361 [109.36.1] of the Revised Code, the attorney general shall conduct an investigation of the facts to determine whether the requirements of this section have been met. If the attorney general determines that any officer who holds an elective state office was acting manifestly outside the scope of his official responsibilities or that any other officer or employee was acting manifestly outside the scope of his employment or official responsibilities, with malicious purpose, in bad faith, or in a wanton or reckless manner, the attorney general shall not represent and defend the officer or employee. An initial determination to represent and defend the officer or employee does not prohibit a later determination that the requirements of this section have not been met.

(B) The attorney general shall also deny a request for representation upon a determination that the requesting officer or employee is covered by a policy of insurance purchased by the state requiring the insurer to provide counsel in the action and that the amount of the claim against the officer or employee is not in excess of the amount of coverage under the policy of insurance. If the amount of the claim against the officer or employee is in excess of the amount of coverage under the policy of insurance, the state is not the plaintiff, and the officer or employee is not otherwise prohibited by this section from being represented and defended by the attorney general, the attorney general shall represent and defend the officer or employee for the amount of the claim in excess of the amount of coverage.

(C) If the attorney general denies representation to an employee or officer who makes a request in accordance with the provisions of section 109.361 [109.36.1] of the Revised Code, the attorney general shall notify the requesting officer or employee in writing of the denial setting forth the reasons for the denial within a reasonable time after the attorney general's receipt of the written request from the officer or employee.

**HISTORY: 138 v S 76. Eff 3-13-80.**

## § 109.363 Employer to provide report and information.

The employer of the defendant officer or employee shall provide the attorney general with a written report indicating the present or former position, job title, or classification of the officer or employee with the state and, citing pertinent facts, whether in its opinion the officer or employee meets the requirements of section 109.362 [109.36.2] of the Revised Code. In addition, the employer shall provide any additional information that is requested by the attorney general.

**HISTORY: 138 v S 76. Eff 3-13-80.**

## § 109.364 Action to recover expenses from employer upon denial.

If the attorney general denies representation to an officer or employee who made a request for representation under section 109.361 [109.36.1] of the Revised Code, the officer or employee may, upon the termination of the action for which he requested the representation, commence an action in the court of claims against the employer pursuant to sections 2743.01 to 2743.20 of the Revised Code for the reasonable expenses incurred in providing his own defense.

An action brought pursuant to this section shall be commenced no later than two years after the cause of action arising under this section accrues. A cause of action arising under this section accrues upon the conclusion of the civil action instituted against the officer or employee for which the attorney general denied the officer's or employee's request for representation if the time for filing an appeal in the action lapses without the filing of an appeal or upon the conclusion of the final appeal in the civil action instituted against the officer or employee for which the attorney general denied the officer's or employee's request for representation if an appeal is filed in the action.

If the court of claims finds that the officer or employee was entitled to have the attorney general represent and defend him under section 109.361 [109.36.1] of the Revised Code, the court shall enter judgment against the employer in favor of the officer or employee in the amount of the reasonable expenses incurred by the officer or employee in providing his own defense and in bringing the action authorized by this section. The reasonable expenses may include, but are not limited to, payment of court costs, attorney's fees, investigative costs, and expert witness fees.

**HISTORY: 138 v S 76. Eff 3-13-80.**

## § 109.365 Privileged information; no reference to decision whether to defend.

Information obtained by the attorney general pursuant to his investigation to determine whether to defend an officer or employee is privileged and is not admissible as evidence against the officer or employee in any legal action or proceeding and no reference to the information may be made in any trial or hearing. The decision of the attorney general to defend or not defend an officer or employee is not admissible as evidence in any trial or hearing. This section does not apply to any trial or hearing to determine the right of an officer or employee to reimbursement pursuant to section 109.364 [109.36.4] of the Revised Code or to any trial or hearing held as a result of an action filed pursuant to division (F) of section 9.87 of the Revised Code.

**HISTORY: 138 v S 76. Eff 3-13-80.**

## § 109.366 Rules for implementation.

The attorney general may promulgate any rules that are necessary for the implementation of sections 109.36 to 109.366 [109.36.6] of the Revised Code.

**HISTORY: 138 v S 76. Eff 3-13-80.**

## § 109.37 Legal representation of department of rehabilitation and correction employee in criminal proceeding.

(A) An employee of the department of rehabilitation and correction may be represented in a criminal proceeding by an attorney selected pursuant to division (B) of this section when all of the following apply:

(1) The employee used deadly force that resulted in the death of another.

(2) The use of deadly force occurred within the scope and in the course of the employee's assigned duties.

(3) The employee's use of deadly force is being investigated by a prosecuting attorney or other criminal investigating authority for possible criminal charges.

(B) When all of the conditions set forth in division (A) of this section apply, the employee may submit a request for legal representation to the director of rehabilitation and correction. If the director determines that all of the conditions in that division apply, and if the director considers the requested legal representation to be appropriate, the director may approve the request and submit it to the attorney general. Upon receipt of the request, the attorney general shall furnish the employee the names of three attorneys who are admitted to the practice of law in this state and are experienced in the defense of criminal charges. The employee may select one of the attorneys to represent the employee until the grand jury concludes its proceedings or the case is disposed of before the grand jury concludes its proceedings.

(C) An attorney who represents an employee pursuant to division (B) of this section shall be paid at the usual rate for like services in the community in which the criminal proceedings occur or at the usual rate paid to special counsel under section 109.07 of the Revised Code, as the attorney general decides. The department of rehabilitation and correction shall pay the attorney's compensation and all reasonable expenses and court costs incurred in the defense of the employee. The attorney general may adopt rules concerning the compensation of attorneys pursuant to this division.

(D) If a criminal investigation described in division (A)(3) of this section of an employee results in an indictment based on the employee's use of deadly force, an attorney who represents the employee pursuant to division (B) of this section may continue to represent the employee in the criminal proceeding on any terms to which the attorney and employee mutually agree. Subject to section 9.871 [9.87.1] of the Revised Code, neither the attorney general nor the department of rehabilitation and correction is obligated to provide the employee with legal representation or to pay attorney's fees, expenses, or court costs incurred by the employee following the indictment of the employee.

(E) If an employee is represented by an attorney as described in division (B) of this section and if the employee is subsequently convicted of or pleads guilty to a criminal offense based on the employee's use of deadly force, the attorney general or the department of rehabilitation and correction may seek to recover, including by means of a civil action, from the employee the costs of legal representation paid by the department pursuant to division (B) of this section.

**HISTORY: 152 v H 130, § 1, eff. 4-7-09.**

## § 109.40 Compilation and distribution of obscenity laws.

The attorney general shall compile all statutes relative to obscenity in a convenient pamphlet or paper and may distribute this compilation, without charge, to such sheriffs, police chiefs, county prosecutors, city prosecutors, mayors, constables, judges of the courts of common pleas, county court judges, municipal judges, and other interested parties, as may request such distribution, and make available a reasonable number of such compilations to fill such requests.

The attorney general shall, from time to time, supplement and keep the compilation current and he may, upon request, distribute such supplemental material in the manner provided in this section.

**HISTORY: 128 v 554. Eff 11-5-59.**

## § 109.41 Agent in certain escheat matters.

Whenever any state begins procedure to escheat property of any person who is an Ohio citizen, corporation, firm, or resident, or whose last known address was in Ohio, on the ground that the property has been abandoned, or on any other grounds, the attorney general may, after making diligent effort to notify the owner of the property and failing in the same, act as attorney in fact for the Ohio owner to claim the property. Upon taking custody of the property, the attorney general shall deposit same in the general fund of Ohio, or if the property be in kind, the attorney general shall cause the same to be sold pursuant to section 2113.40 of the Revised Code, and deposit the proceeds of the sale in the general fund. Claims to the property shall thereafter be made in the manner provided for in Chapter 2743. of the Revised Code.

**HISTORY: 129 v 497 (Eff 10-12-61); 135 v H 800. Eff 1-1-75.**

## § 109.42 Victim's bill of rights pamphlet.

(A) The attorney general shall prepare and have printed a pamphlet that contains a compilation of all statutes relative to victim's rights in which the attorney general lists and explains the statutes in the form of a victim's bill of rights. The attorney general shall distribute the pamphlet to all sheriffs, marshals, municipal corporation and township police departments, constables, and other law enforcement agencies, to all prosecuting attorneys, city directors of law, village solicitors, and other similar chief legal officers of municipal corporations, and to organizations that represent or provide services for victims of crime. The victim's bill of rights set forth in the pamphlet shall contain a description of all of the rights of victims that are provided for in Chapter 2930. or in any other section of the Revised Code and shall include, but not be limited to, all of the following:

(1) The right of a victim or a victim's representative to attend a proceeding before a grand jury, in a juvenile case, or in a criminal case pursuant to a subpoena without being discharged from the victim's or representative's employment, having the victim's or representative's employment terminated, having the victim's or representative's pay decreased or withheld, or otherwise being punished, penalized, or threatened as a result of time lost from regular employment because of the victim's or representative's attendance at the proceeding pursuant to the subpoena, as set forth in section 2151.211, 2930.18, 2939.121, or 2945.451 of the Revised Code;

(2) The potential availability pursuant to section 2151.359 or 2152.61 of the Revised Code of a forfeited recognizance to pay damages caused by a child when the delinquency of the child or child's violation of probation or community control is found to be proximately caused by the failure of the child's parent or guardian to subject the child to reasonable parental authority or to faithfully discharge the conditions of probation or community control;

(3) The availability of awards of reparations pursuant to sections 2743.51 to 2743.72 of the Revised Code for injuries caused by criminal offenses;

(4) The right of the victim in certain criminal or juvenile cases or a victim's representative to receive, pursuant to section 2930.06 of the Revised Code, notice of the date, time, and place of the trial or delinquency proceeding in the case or, if there will not be a trial or delinquency proceeding, information from the prosecutor, as defined in section 2930.01 of the Revised Code, regarding the disposition of the case;

(5) The right of the victim in certain criminal or juvenile cases or a victim's representative to receive,

pursuant to section 2930.04, 2930.05, or 2930.06 of the Revised Code, notice of the name of the person charged with the violation, the case or docket number assigned to the charge, and a telephone number or numbers that can be called to obtain information about the disposition of the case;

(6) The right of the victim in certain criminal or juvenile cases or of the victim's representative pursuant to section 2930.13 or 2930.14 of the Revised Code, subject to any reasonable terms set by the court as authorized under section 2930.14 of the Revised Code, to make a statement about the victimization and, if applicable, a statement relative to the sentencing or disposition of the offender;

(7) The opportunity to obtain a court order, pursuant to section 2945.04 of the Revised Code, to prevent or stop the commission of the offense of intimidation of a crime victim or witness or an offense against the person or property of the complainant, or of the complainant's ward or child;

(8) The right of the victim in certain criminal or juvenile cases or a victim's representative pursuant to sections 2151.38, 2929.20, 2930.10, 2930.16, and 2930.17 of the Revised Code to receive notice of a pending motion for judicial release, release pursuant to section 2967.19 of the Revised Code, or other early release of the person who committed the offense against the victim, to make an oral or written statement at the court hearing on the motion, and to be notified of the court's decision on the motion;

(9) The right of the victim in certain criminal or juvenile cases or a victim's representative pursuant to section 2930.16, 2967.12, 2967.26, or 5139.56 of the Revised Code to receive notice of any pending commutation, pardon, parole, transitional control, discharge, other form of authorized release, post-release control, or supervised release for the person who committed the offense against the victim or any application for release of that person and to send a written statement relative to the victimization and the pending action to the adult parole authority or the release authority of the department of youth services;

(10) The right of the victim to bring a civil action pursuant to sections 2969.01 to 2969.06 of the Revised Code to obtain money from the offender's profit fund;

(11) The right, pursuant to section 3109.09 of the Revised Code, to maintain a civil action to recover compensatory damages not exceeding ten thousand dollars and costs from the parent of a minor who willfully damages property through the commission of an act that would be a theft offense, as defined in section 2913.01 of the Revised Code, if committed by an adult;

(12) The right, pursuant to section 3109.10 of the Revised Code, to maintain a civil action to recover compensatory damages not exceeding ten thousand dollars and costs from the parent of a minor who willfully and maliciously assaults a person;

(13) The possibility of receiving restitution from an offender or a delinquent child pursuant to section 2152.20, 2929.18, or 2929.28 of the Revised Code;

(14) The right of the victim in certain criminal or juvenile cases or a victim's representative, pursuant to section 2930.16 of the Revised Code, to receive notice of the escape from confinement or custody of the person who committed the offense, to receive that notice from the custodial agency of the person at the victim's last address or telephone number provided to the custodial agency, and to receive notice that, if either the victim's address or telephone number changes, it is in the victim's interest to provide the new address or telephone number to the custodial agency;

(15) The right of a victim of domestic violence to seek the issuance of a civil protection order pursuant to section 3113.31 of the Revised Code, the right of a victim of a violation of section 2903.14, 2909.06, 2909.07, 2911.12, 2911.211, or 2919.22 of the Revised Code, a violation of a substantially similar municipal ordinance, or an offense of violence who is a family or household member of the offender at the time of the offense to seek the issuance of a temporary protection order pursuant to section 2919.26 of the Revised Code, and the right of both types of victims to be accompanied by a victim advocate during court proceedings;

(16) The right of a victim of a sexually oriented offense or of a child-victim oriented offense that is committed by a person who is convicted of, pleads guilty to, or is adjudicated a delinquent child for committing the offense and who is in a category specified in division (B) of section 2950.10 of the Revised Code to receive, pursuant to that section, notice that the person has registered with a sheriff under section 2950.04, 2950.041, or 2950.05 of the Revised Code and notice of the person's name, the person's residence that is registered, and the offender's school, institution of higher education, or place of employment address or addresses that are registered, the person's photograph, and a summary of the manner in which the victim must make a request to receive the notice. As used in this division, "sexually oriented offense" and "child-victim oriented offense" have the same meanings as in section 2950.01 of the Revised Code.

(17) The right of a victim of certain sexually violent offenses committed by an offender who also is convicted of or pleads guilty to a sexually violent predator specification and who is sentenced to a prison term pursuant to division (A)(3) of section 2971.03 of the Revised Code, of a victim of a violation of division (A)(1)(b) of section 2907.02 of the Revised Code committed on or after January 2, 2007, by an offender who is sentenced for the violation pursuant to division (B)(1)(a), (b), or (c) of section 2971.03 of the Revised Code, of a victim of an attempted rape committed on or after January 2, 2007, by an offender who also is convicted of or pleads guilty to a specification of the type described in section 2941.1418, 2941.1419, or 2941.1420 of the Revised Code and is sentenced for the violation pursuant to division (B)(2)(a), (b), or (c) of section 2971.03 of the Revised Code, and of a victim of an offense that is described in division (B)(3)(a), (b), (c), or (d) of section 2971.03 of the Revised Code and is committed by an offender who is sentenced pursuant to one of those divisions to receive, pursuant to section 2930.16 of the Revised Code, notice of a hearing to determine whether to modify the requirement that the offender serve the entire prison term in a state correctional facility, whether to continue, revise, or revoke any existing modification of that requirement, or whether to terminate the prison term. As used in this division, "sexually violent offense" and "sexually violent predator specification" have the same meanings as in section 2971.01 of the Revised Code.

(B)(1)(a) Subject to division (B)(1)(c) of this section, a prosecuting attorney, assistant prosecuting attorney, city director of law, assistant city director of law, village solicitor, assistant village solicitor, or similar chief legal officer of a municipal corporation or an assistant of any of those officers who prosecutes an offense committed in this state, upon first contact with the victim of the offense, the victim's family, or the victim's dependents, shall give the victim, the victim's family, or the victim's dependents a copy of the pamphlet prepared pursuant to division (A) of this section and explain, upon request, the information in the pamphlet to the victim, the victim's family, or the victim's dependents.

(b) Subject to division (B)(1)(c) of this section, a law enforcement agency that investigates an offense or delinquent act committed in this state shall give the victim of the offense or delinquent act, the victim's family, or the victim's dependents a copy of the pamphlet prepared pursuant to division (A) of this section at one of the following times:

(i) Upon first contact with the victim, the victim's family, or the victim's dependents;

(ii) If the offense or delinquent act is an offense of violence, if the circumstances of the offense or delinquent act and the condition of the victim, the victim's family, or the victim's dependents indicate that the victim, the victim's family, or the victim's dependents will not be able to understand the significance of the pamphlet upon first contact with the agency, and if the agency anticipates that it will have an additional contact with the victim, the victim's family, or the victim's dependents, upon the agency's second contact with the victim, the victim's family, or the victim's dependents.

If the agency does not give the victim, the victim's family, or the victim's dependents a copy of the pamphlet upon first contact with them and does not have a second contact with the victim, the victim's family, or the victim's dependents, the agency shall mail a copy of the pamphlet to the victim, the victim's family, or the victim's dependents at their last known address.

(c) In complying on and after December 9, 1994, with the duties imposed by division (B)(1)(a) or (b) of this section, an official or a law enforcement agency shall use copies of the pamphlet that are in the official's or agency's possession on December 9, 1994, until the official or agency has distributed all of those copies. After the official or agency has distributed all of those copies, the official or agency shall use only copies of the pamphlet that contain at least the information described in divisions (A)(1) to (17) of this section.

(2) The failure of a law enforcement agency or of a prosecuting attorney, assistant prosecuting attorney, city director of law, assistant city director of law, village solicitor, assistant village solicitor, or similar chief legal officer of a municipal corporation or an assistant to any of those officers to give, as required by division (B)(1) of this section, the victim of an offense or delinquent act, the victim's family, or the victim's dependents a copy of the pamphlet prepared pursuant to division (A) of this section does not give the victim, the victim's family, the victim's dependents, or a victim's representative any rights under section 2743.51 to 2743.72, 2945.04, 2967.12, 2969.01 to 2969.06, 3109.09, or 3109.10 of the Revised Code or under any other provision of the Revised Code and does not affect any right under those sections.

(3) A law enforcement agency, a prosecuting attorney or assistant prosecuting attorney, or a city director of law, assistant city director of law, village solicitor, assistant village solicitor, or similar chief legal officer of a municipal corporation that distributes a copy of the pamphlet prepared pursuant to division (A) of this section shall not be required to distribute a copy of an information card or other printed material provided by the clerk of the court of claims pursuant to section 2743.71 of the Revised Code.

(C) The cost of printing and distributing the pamphlet prepared pursuant to division (A) of this section shall be paid out of the reparations fund, created pursuant to section 2743.191 of the Revised Code, in accordance with division (D) of that section.

(D) As used in this section:

(1) "Victim's representative" has the same meaning as in section 2930.01 of the Revised Code;

(2) "Victim advocate" has the same meaning as in section 2919.26 of the Revised Code.

**HISTORY: 141 v H 657 (Eff 9-12-86); 142 v H 207 (Eff 9-24-87); 142 v H 708 (Eff 4-19-88); 143 v S 3 (Eff 4-11-91); 145 v H 152 (Eff 7-1-93); 145 v S 186 (Eff 10-12-94); 145 v H 335 (Eff 12-9-94); 146 v H 18 (Eff 11-24-95); 146 v S 2 (Eff 7-1-96); 146 v H 601 (Eff 10-29-96); 146 v H 180 (Eff 1-1-97); 147 v S 111 (Eff 3-17-98); 148 v H 3 (Eff 11-22-99); 148 v S 179, § 3. Eff 1-1-2002; 149 v H 490, § 1, eff. 1-1-04; 150 v S 5, § 1, eff. 7-31-03; 150 v S 5, § 3, eff. 1-1-04; 150 v S 50, § 1, eff. 1-8-04; 150 v H 427, § 1, eff. 6-9-04; 150 v H 473, § 1, eff. 4-29-05; 151 v H 15, § 1, eff. 11-23-05; 151 v S 260, § 1, eff. 1-2-07; 152 v S 10, § 1, eff. 1-1-08; 2011 HB 86, § 1, eff. Sept. 30, 2011.**

The effective date is set by § 3 of 152 v S 10.

The provisions of § 14 of H.B. 427 (150 v —) read as follows:

SECTION 14. Section 109.42 of the Revised Code is presented in this act as a composite of the section as amended by Am. Sub. H.B. 490 of the 124th General Assembly and Section 3 of Am. Sub. S.B. 5 and Section 1 of Sub. S.B. 50, both of the 125th General Assembly. * * * The General Assembly, applying the principle stated in division (B) of section 1.52 of the Revised Code that amendments are to be harmonized if reasonably capable of simultaneous operation, finds that the composites are the resulting versions of the sections in effect prior to the effective date of the sections as presented in this act.

## § 109.43 Training for elected officials or appropriate designees regarding public records law and sunshine laws.

(A) As used in this section:

(1) "Designee" means a designee of the elected official in the public office if that elected official is the only elected official in the public office involved or a designee of all of the elected officials in the public office if the public office involved includes more than one elected official.

(2) "Elected official" means an official elected to a local or statewide office. "Elected official" does not include the chief justice or a justice of the supreme court, a judge of a court of appeals, court of common pleas, municipal court, or county court, or a clerk of any of those courts.

(3) "Public office" has the same meaning as in section 149.011 of the Revised Code.

(4) "Public record" has the same meaning as in section 149.43 of the Revised Code.

(B) The attorney general shall develop, provide, and certify training programs and seminars for all elected officials or their appropriate designees in order to enhance the officials' knowledge of the duty to provide access to public records as required by section 149.43 of the Revised Code. The training shall be three hours for every term of office for which the elected official was appointed or elected to the public office involved. The training shall provide elected officials or their appropriate designees with guidance in developing and updating their offices' policies as required under section 149.43 of the Revised Code. The successful completion by an elected official or by an elected official's appropriate designee of the training requirements established by the attorney general under this section shall satisfy the education requirements imposed on elected officials or their appropriate designees under division (E) of section 149.43 of the Revised Code. Prior to providing the training programs and seminars under this section to satisfy the education requirements imposed on elected officials or their appropriate designees under division (E) of section 149.43 of the Revised Code, the attorney general shall ensure that the training programs and seminars are accredited by the commission on continuing legal education established by the supreme court.

(C) The attorney general shall not charge any elected official or the appropriate designee of any elected official any fee for attending the training programs and seminars that the attorney general conducts under this section. The attorney general may allow the attendance of any other interested persons at any of the training programs or seminars that the attorney general conducts under this section and shall not charge the person any fee for attending the training program or seminar.

(D) In addition to developing, providing, and certifying training programs and seminars as required under division (B) of this section, the attorney general may contract with one or more other state agencies, political subdivisions, or other public or private entities to conduct the training programs and seminars for elected officials or their appropriate designees under this section. The contract may provide for the attendance of any other interested persons at any of the training programs or seminars conducted by the contracting state agency, political subdivision, or other public or private entity. The contracting state agency, political subdivision, or other public or private entity may charge an elected official, an elected official's appropriate designee, or an interested person a registration fee for attending the training program or seminar conducted by that contracting agency, political subdivision, or entity pursuant to a contract entered into under this division. The attorney general shall determine a reasonable amount for the registration fee based on the actual and necessary expenses associated with the training programs and seminars. If the contracting state agency, political subdivision, or other public or private entity charges an elected official or an elected official's appropriate designee a registration fee for attending the training program or seminar conducted pursuant to a contract entered into under this division by that contracting agency, political subdivision, or entity, the public office for which the elected official was appointed or elected to represent may use the public office's own funds to pay for the cost of the registration fee.

(E) The attorney general shall develop and provide to all public offices a model public records policy for responding to public records requests in compliance with section 149.43 of the Revised Code in order to provide guidance to public offices in developing their own public record policies for responding to public records requests in compliance with that section.

(F) The attorney general may provide any other appropriate training or educational programs about Ohio's "Sunshine Laws," sections 121.22, 149.38, 149.381, and 149.43 of the Revised Code, as may be developed and offered by the attorney general or by the attorney general in collaboration with one or more other state agencies, political subdivisions, or other public or private entities.

(G) The auditor of state, in the course of an annual or biennial audit of a public office pursuant to Chapter 117. of the Revised Code, shall audit the public office for compliance with this section and division (E) of section 149.43 of the Revised Code.

**HISTORY: 151 v H 9, § 1, eff. 9-29-07; 2011 HB 153, § 101.01, eff. Sept. 29, 2011.**

The effective date is set by § 5 of 151 v H 9.

## [BUREAU OF CRIMINAL IDENTIFICATION AND INVESTIGATION]

### § 109.51 Creation of bureau of criminal identification and investigation.

There is hereby created in the office of the attorney general, a bureau of criminal identification and investigation to be located at the site of the London correctional institution. The attorney general shall appoint a superintendent of said bureau. The superintendent shall appoint, with the approval of the attorney general, such assistants as are necessary to carry out the functions and duties of the bureau as contained in sections 109.51 to 109.63, inclusive, of the Revised Code.

**HISTORY: 130 v 9. Eff 9-24-63.**

**For provisions analogous to RC § 109.51 et seq, see former RC § 5149.01 et seq, repealed 130 v H 263, pp. 1669-70, § 3, eff 9-24-63.**

### § 109.511 Felony precludes or terminates employment as investigator or special agent.

(A) As used in this section, "felony" means any of the following:

(1) An offense committed in this state that is a felony under the law of this state;

(2) An offense committed in a state other than this state, or under the law of the United States, that, if committed in this state, would be a felony under the law of this state.

(B) The superintendent of the bureau of criminal identification and investigation shall not appoint or employ any person as an investigator or a special agent on a permanent basis, on a temporary basis, for a probationary term, or on other than a permanent basis if the person previously has been convicted of or has pleaded guilty to a felony.

(C)(1) The superintendent shall terminate the employment of an investigator or a special agent who does either of the following:

(a) Pleads guilty to a felony;

(b) Pleads guilty to a misdemeanor pursuant to a negotiated plea agreement as provided in division (D) of section 2929.43 of the Revised Code in which the investigator or special agent agrees to surrender the certificate awarded to the investigator or special agent under section 109.77 of the Revised Code.

(2) The superintendent shall suspend from employment an investigator or a special agent who is convicted, after trial, of a felony. If the investigator or special agent files an appeal from that conviction and the conviction is upheld by the highest court to which the appeal is taken or if the investigator or special agent does not file a timely appeal, the superintendent shall terminate the employment of that investigator or special agent. If the investigator or special agent files an appeal that results in that

investigator's or special agent's acquittal of the felony or conviction of a misdemeanor, or in the dismissal of the felony charge against the investigator or special agent, the superintendent shall reinstate that investigator or special agent. An investigator or a special agent who is reinstated under this division shall not receive any back pay unless that investigator's or special agent's conviction of the felony was reversed on appeal, or the felony charge was dismissed, because the court found insufficient evidence to convict the investigator or special agent of the felony.

(D) This section does not apply regarding an offense that was committed prior to January 1, 1997.

(E) The suspension from employment or the termination of the employment of an investigator or a special agent under division (C) of this section shall be in accordance with Chapter 119. of the Revised Code.

**HISTORY: 146 v H 566. Eff 10-16-96; 149 v H 490, § 1, eff. 1-1-04.**

The effective date is set by section 4 of HB 490.

## § 109.52 Operations of bureau.

The bureau of criminal identification and investigation may operate and maintain a criminal analysis laboratory and mobile units thereof, create a staff of investigators and technicians skilled in the solution and control of crimes and criminal activity, keep statistics and other necessary data, assist in the prevention of crime, and engage in such other activities as will aid law enforcement officers in solving crimes and controlling criminal activity.

**HISTORY: 130 v 9. Eff 9-24-63.**

## § 109.521 Asset forfeiture and cost reimbursement fund.

There is hereby created in the state treasury the bureau of criminal identification and investigation asset forfeiture and cost reimbursement fund. All amounts awarded to the bureau of criminal identification and investigation as a result of shared federal asset forfeiture and state and local moneys designated as restitution for reimbursement of the costs of investigations shall be deposited into this fund. The moneys in this fund shall be used in accordance with federal asset forfeiture rules, regulations, and laws. Interest earned on the money in this fund shall be credited to the fund.

**HISTORY: 152 v H 119, § 101.01, eff. 9-29-07.**

The effective date is set by § 812.03 of 152 v H 119.

## § 109.53 Equipment and furnishings of bureau.

The bureau of criminal identification and investigation shall be supplied with furniture, fixtures, apparatus, vehicles, and materials necessary to carry out the functions and duties of the bureau as contained in sections 109.51 to 109.63, inclusive, of the Revised Code.

**HISTORY: 130 v 9. Eff 9-24-63.**

## § 109.54 Intergovernmental cooperation; list of persons experienced in questioning children.

(A) The bureau of criminal identification and investigation may investigate any criminal activity in this state that is of statewide or intercounty concern when requested by local authorities and may aid federal authorities, when requested, in their investigation of any criminal activity in this state. The bureau may investigate any criminal activity in this state related to the conduct of elections when requested by the secretary of state. The bureau may investigate any criminal activity in this state involving drug abuse or illegal drug distribution prohibited under Chapter 3719. or 4729. of the Revised Code. The superintendent and any agent of the bureau may participate, as the director of an organized crime task force established under section 177.02 of the Revised Code or as a member of the investigatory staff of a task force established under that section, in an investigation of organized criminal activity anywhere within this state under sections 177.01 to 177.03 of the Revised Code.

(B) The bureau may provide any trained investigative personnel and specialized equipment that are requested by any sheriff or chief of police, by the authorized designee of any sheriff or chief of police, or by any other authorized law enforcement officer to aid and assist the officer in the investigation and solution of any crime or the control of any criminal activity occurring within the officer's jurisdiction. This assistance shall be furnished by the bureau without disturbing or impairing any of the existing law enforcement authority or the prerogatives of local law enforcement authorities or officers. Investigators provided pursuant to this section, or engaged in an investigation pursuant to section 109.83 of the Revised Code, may go armed in the same manner as sheriffs and regularly appointed police officers under section 2923.12 of the Revised Code.

(C)(1) The bureau shall obtain recording equipment that can be used to record depositions of the type described in division (A) of section 2152.81 and division (A) of section 2945.481 [2945.48.1] of the Revised Code, or testimony of the type described in division (D) of section 2152.81 and division (D) of section 2945.481 [2945.48.1] or in division (C) of section 2937.11 of the Revised Code, shall obtain closed circuit equipment that can be used to televise testimony of the type described in division (C) of section 2152.81 and division (C) of section 2945.481 [2945.48.1] or in division (B) of section 2937.11 of the Revised Code, and shall provide the equipment, upon request, to any court for use in recording any deposition or testimony of one of those types or in televising the testimony in accordance with the applicable division.

(2) The bureau shall obtain the names, addresses, and telephone numbers of persons who are experienced in questioning children in relation to an investigation of a violation of section 2905.03, 2905.05, 2907.02, 2907.03, 2907.04, 2907.05, 2907.06, 2907.07, 2907.09, 2907.21, 2907.23, 2907.24, 2907.31, 2907.32, 2907.321 [2907.32.1], 2907.322 [2907.32.2], 2907.323 [2907.32.3], or 2919.22 of the Revised Code or an offense of violence and shall maintain a list of those names, addresses, and telephone numbers. The list shall include a classification of the names, addresses, and telephone numbers by appellate district. Upon request, the bureau shall provide any county sheriff, chief of police, prosecuting attorney, village solicitor, city director of law, or similar chief legal officer with the name, address, and telephone number of any person contained in the list.

**HISTORY: 130 v 9 (Eff 9-24-63); 141 v S 74 (Eff 9-3-86); 141 v H 108 (Eff 10-14-86); 146 v H 445 (Eff 9-3-96); 146 v H 480 (Eff 10-16-96); 147 v S 53 (Eff 10-14-97); 148 v S 179, § 3. Eff 1-1-2002; 151 v H 66, § 101.01, eff. 9-29-05.**

The effective date is set by § 612.03 of 151 v H 66.
The effective date is set by section 5 of SB 179.

## § 109.541 Arrest authority of investigator while assisting law enforcement officer; emergency assistance.

(A) As used in this section:

(1) "Investigator" means an officer or employee of the bureau of criminal identification and investigation described in section 109.54 of the Revised Code.

(2) "Peace officer" has the same meaning as in section 2935.01 of the Revised Code.

(B) An investigator, while providing assistance to a law enforcement officer pursuant to division (B) of section 109.54 of the Revised Code, has the same arrest authority as a peace officer of the law enforcement agency served by the law enforcement officer requesting the assistance. The investigator may exercise this arrest authority only in connection with the investigation or activities for which the investigator's assistance was requested.

(C)(1) No state official shall command, order, or direct an investigator to perform any duty or service that is not authorized by law. The power and duties conferred by this section on the bureau of criminal identification and investigation are supplementary to, and in no way a limitation on, the power and duties of sheriffs or other peace officers of the state or a political subdivision of the state.

(2) An investigator, pursuant to the policy established by the superintendent of the bureau of criminal identification and investigation under division (D)(1) of this section, may render emergency assistance to any peace officer who has arrest authority under section 2935.03 of the Revised Code if both of the following apply:

(a) There is a threat of imminent physical harm to the peace officer, a threat of physical harm to another person, or any serious emergency situation.

(b) The peace officer requests emergency assistance, or it appears to the investigator that the peace officer is unable to request emergency assistance and that the circumstances reasonably indicate that emergency assistance is appropriate.

(D)(1) The superintendent of the bureau of criminal identification and investigation, not later than sixty days after the effective date of this section, shall establish a policy specifying the manner and procedures by which an investigator may render emergency assistance to a peace officer pursuant to division (C)(2) of this section.

(2) An investigator who renders assistance to a law enforcement officer pursuant to division (B) of section 109.54 of the Revised Code or renders emergency assistance to any peace officer pursuant to division (C)(2) of this section and under the policy established under division (D)(1) of this section shall be considered to be engaged in the investigator's regular employment for the purpose of compensation, retirement benefits, indemnification rights, workers' compensation, and any other rights or benefits to which the investigator may be entitled incident to the investigator's regular employment.

(3) An investigator who renders emergency assistance to a peace officer pursuant to division (C)(2) of this section and under the policy established under division (D)(1) of this section has the same authority as the peace officer to whom the assistance is rendered.

(4) An investigator who renders emergency assistance to a peace officer pursuant to division (C)(2) of this section and under the policy established under division (D)(1) of this section retains personal immunity from liability as described in sections 9.85 to 9.87 of the Revised Code, the right to defense under sections 109.36 to 109.366 [109.36.6] of the Revised Code, and the right to indemnification under section 9.87 of the Revised Code. This section does not affect the provisions of section 2743.02 of the Revised Code that pertain to the commencement of a civil action against a state officer or employee.

**HISTORY: 146 v H 480. Eff 10-16-96.**

## § 109.542 Investigative personnel to be considered peace officers.

If an officer or employee of the bureau of criminal identification and investigation is investigative personnel of the bureau and has been awarded a certificate by the executive director of the Ohio peace officer training commission attesting to the officer's or employee's satisfactory completion of an approved state, county, municipal, or department of natural resources peace officer basic training program, both of the following apply:

(A) The officer or employee shall be considered a peace officer during the term of the officer's or employee's appointment or employment with the bureau in that capacity for the purposes of maintaining a current and valid basic training certificate pursuant to rules adopted under section 109.74 of the Revised Code.

(B) Sections 109.71 to 109.77 of the Revised Code apply to the officer or employee as if the officer or employee was included in the definition of "peace officer" set forth in section 109.71 of the Revised Code.

**HISTORY: 149 v H 427. Eff 8-29-2002.**

## § 109.55 Coordination of law enforcement activities.

The superintendent of the bureau of criminal identification and investigation shall recommend cooperative policies for the coordination of the law enforcement work and crime prevention activities of all state and local agencies and officials having law enforcement duties to promote cooperation between such agencies and officials, to secure effective and efficient law enforcement, to eliminate duplication of work, and to promote economy of operation in such agencies.

In formulating and recommending cooperative policies, the superintendent shall emphasize the provisions of section 2901.30 of the Revised Code.

The superintendent shall develop procedures and forms to implement section 2901.30 of the Revised Code.

**HISTORY: 130 v 9 (Eff 9-24-63); 140 v S 321. Eff 4-9-85.**

## § 109.56 Training local law enforcement authorities.

The bureau of criminal identification and investigation shall, where practicable, assist in training local law enforcement officers in crime prevention, detection, and solution when requested by local authorities, and, where practicable, furnish instruction to sheriffs, chiefs of police, and other law officers in the establishment of efficient local bureaus of identification in their districts.

**HISTORY: 130 v 9. Eff 9-24-63.**

## § 109.561 Preservation of biological evidence task force.

There is hereby established within the bureau of criminal identification and investigation a preservation of biological evidence task force. The task force shall consist of officers and employees of the bureau; a representative from the Ohio prosecutors association; a representative from the Ohio state coroners association; a representative from the Ohio association of chiefs of police; a representative from the Ohio public defenders office, in consultation with the Ohio innocence project; a representative from the division of criminal justice services of the department of public safety; and a representative from the buckeye state sheriffs association. The task force shall perform the duties and functions specified in division (C) of section 2933.82 of the Revised Code.

**HISTORY: 153 v S 77, § 1, eff. 7-6-10; 153 v S 58, § 1, eff. 9-17-10.**

## § 109.57 Duties of superintendent of bureau.

(A)(1) The superintendent of the bureau of criminal identification and investigation shall procure from wherever procurable and file for record photographs, pictures, descriptions, fingerprints, measurements, and other information that may be pertinent of all persons who have been convicted of committing within this state a felony, any crime constituting a misdemeanor on the first offense and a felony on subsequent offenses, or any misdemeanor described in division (A)(1)(a), (A)(8)(a), or (A)(10)(a) of section 109.572 of the Revised Code, of all children under eighteen years of age who have been adjudicated delinquent children for committing within this state an act that would be a felony or an offense of violence if committed by an adult or who have been convicted of or pleaded guilty to committing within this state a felony or an offense of violence, and of all well-known and habitual criminals. The person in charge of any county, multicounty, municipal, municipal-county, or multicounty-municipal jail or workhouse, community-based correctional facility, halfway house, alternative residential facility, or state correctional institution and the person in charge of any state institution having custody of a person suspected of having committed a felony, any crime constituting a misdemeanor on the first offense and a felony on subsequent offenses, or any misdemeanor described in division (A)(1)(a), (A)(8)(a), or (A)(10)(a) of section 109.572 of the Revised Code or having custody of a child under eighteen years of age with respect to whom there is probable cause to believe that the child may have committed an act that would be a felony or an offense of violence if committed by an adult shall furnish such material to the superintendent of the bureau. Fingerprints, photographs, or other descriptive information of a child who is under eighteen years of age, has not been arrested or otherwise taken into custody for committing an act that would be a felony or an offense of violence who is not in any other category of child specified in this division, if committed by an adult, has not been adjudicated a delinquent child for committing an act that would be a felony or an offense of violence if committed by an adult, has not been convicted of or pleaded guilty to committing a felony or an offense of violence, and is not a child with respect to whom there is probable cause to believe that the child may have committed an act that would be a felony or an offense of violence if committed by an adult shall not be procured by the superintendent or furnished by any person in charge of any county, multicounty, municipal, municipal-county, or multicounty-municipal jail or workhouse, community-based correctional facility, halfway house, alternative residential facility, or state correctional institution, except as authorized in section 2151.313 of the Revised Code.

(2) Every clerk of a court of record in this state, other than the supreme court or a court of appeals, shall send to the superintendent of the bureau a weekly report containing a summary of each case involving a felony, involving any crime constituting a misdemeanor on the first offense and a felony on subsequent offenses, involving a misdemeanor described in division (A)(1)(a), (A)(8)(a), or (A)(10)(a) of section 109.572 of the Revised Code, or involving an adjudication in a case in which a child under eighteen years of age was alleged to be a delinquent child for committing an act that would be a felony or an offense of violence if committed by an adult. The clerk of the court of common pleas shall include in the report and summary the clerk sends under this division all information described in divisions (A)(2)(a) to (f) of this section regarding a case before the court of appeals that is served by that clerk. The summary shall be written on the standard forms furnished by the superintendent pursuant to division (B) of this section and shall include the following information:

(a) The incident tracking number contained on the standard forms furnished by the superintendent pursuant to division (B) of this section;

(b) The style and number of the case;

(c) The date of arrest, offense, summons, or arraignment;

(d) The date that the person was convicted of or pleaded guilty to the offense, adjudicated a delinquent child for committing the act that would be a felony or an offense of violence if committed by an adult, found not guilty of the offense, or found not to be a delinquent child for committing an act that would be a felony or an offense of violence if committed by an adult, the date of an entry dismissing the charge, an entry declaring a mistrial of the offense in which the person is discharged, an entry finding that the person or child is not competent to stand trial, or an entry of a nolle prosequi, or the date of any other determination that constitutes final resolution of the case;

(e) A statement of the original charge with the section of the Revised Code that was alleged to be violated;

(f) If the person or child was convicted, pleaded guilty, or was adjudicated a delinquent child, the sentence or terms of probation imposed or any other disposition of the offender or the delinquent child.

If the offense involved the disarming of a law enforcement officer or an attempt to disarm a law enforcement officer, the clerk shall clearly state that fact in the summary, and the superintendent shall ensure that a clear statement of that fact is placed in the bureau's records.

(3) The superintendent shall cooperate with and assist sheriffs, chiefs of police, and other law enforcement officers in the establishment of a complete system of criminal identification and in obtaining fingerprints and other means of identification of all persons arrested on a charge of a felony, any crime constituting a misdemeanor on the first offense and a felony on subsequent offenses, or a misdemeanor described in division (A)(1)(a), (A)(8)(a), or (A)(10)(a) of section 109.572 of the Revised Code and of all children under eighteen years of age arrested or otherwise taken into custody for committing an act that would be a felony or an offense of violence if committed by an adult. The superintendent also shall file for record

the fingerprint impressions of all persons confined in a county, multicounty, municipal, municipal-county, or multicounty-municipal jail or workhouse, community-based correctional facility, halfway house, alternative residential facility, or state correctional institution for the violation of state laws and of all children under eighteen years of age who are confined in a county, multicounty, municipal, municipal-county, or multicounty-municipal jail or workhouse, community-based correctional facility, halfway house, alternative residential facility, or state correctional institution or in any facility for delinquent children for committing an act that would be a felony or an offense of violence if committed by an adult, and any other information that the superintendent may receive from law enforcement officials of the state and its political subdivisions.

(4) The superintendent shall carry out Chapter 2950. of the Revised Code with respect to the registration of persons who are convicted of or plead guilty to a sexually oriented offense or a child-victim oriented offense and with respect to all other duties imposed on the bureau under that chapter.

(5) The bureau shall perform centralized recordkeeping functions for criminal history records and services in this state for purposes of the national crime prevention and privacy compact set forth in section 109.571 of the Revised Code and is the criminal history record repository as defined in that section for purposes of that compact. The superintendent or the superintendent's designee is the compact officer for purposes of that compact and shall carry out the responsibilities of the compact officer specified in that compact.

(B) The superintendent shall prepare and furnish to every county, multicounty, municipal, municipal-county, or multicounty-municipal jail or workhouse, community-based correctional facility, halfway house, alternative residential facility, or state correctional institution and to every clerk of a court in this state specified in division (A)(2) of this section standard forms for reporting the information required under division (A) of this section. The standard forms that the superintendent prepares pursuant to this division may be in a tangible format, in an electronic format, or in both tangible formats and electronic formats.

(C)(1) The superintendent may operate a center for electronic, automated, or other data processing for the storage and retrieval of information, data, and statistics pertaining to criminals and to children under eighteen years of age who are adjudicated delinquent children for committing an act that would be a felony or an offense of violence if committed by an adult, criminal activity, crime prevention, law enforcement, and criminal justice, and may establish and operate a statewide communications network to be known as the Ohio law enforcement gateway to gather and disseminate information, data, and statistics for the use of law enforcement agencies and for other uses specified in this division. The superintendent may gather, store, retrieve, and disseminate information, data, and statistics that pertain to children who are under eighteen years of age and that are gathered pursuant to sections 109.57 to 109.61 of the Revised Code together with information, data, and statistics that pertain to adults and that are gathered pursuant to those sections.

(2) The superintendent or the superintendent's designee shall gather information of the nature described in division (C)(1) of this section that pertains to the offense and delinquency history of a person who has been convicted of, pleaded guilty to, or been adjudicated a delinquent child for committing a sexually oriented offense or a child-victim oriented offense for inclusion in the state registry of sex offenders and child-victim offenders maintained pursuant to division (A)(1) of section 2950.13 of the Revised Code and in the internet database operated pursuant to division (A)(13) of that section and for possible inclusion in the internet database operated pursuant to division (A)(11) of that section.

(3) In addition to any other authorized use of information, data, and statistics of the nature described in division (C)(1) of this section, the superintendent or the superintendent's designee may provide and exchange the information, data, and statistics pursuant to the national crime prevention and privacy compact as described in division (A)(5) of this section.

(4) The attorney general may adopt rules under Chapter 119. of the Revised Code establishing guidelines for the operation of and participation in the Ohio law enforcement gateway. The rules may include criteria for granting and restricting access to information gathered and disseminated through the Ohio law enforcement gateway. The attorney general shall permit the state medical board and board of nursing to access and view, but not alter, information gathered and disseminated through the Ohio law enforcement gateway.

The attorney general may appoint a steering committee to advise the attorney general in the operation of the Ohio law enforcement gateway that is comprised of persons who are representatives of the criminal justice agencies in this state that use the Ohio law enforcement gateway and is chaired by the superintendent or the superintendent's designee.

(D)(1) The following are not public records under section 149.43 of the Revised Code:

(a) Information and materials furnished to the superintendent pursuant to division (A) of this section;

(b) Information, data, and statistics gathered or disseminated through the Ohio law enforcement gateway pursuant to division (C)(1) of this section;

(c) Information and materials furnished to any board or person under division (F) or (G) of this section.

(2) The superintendent or the superintendent's designee shall gather and retain information so furnished under division (A) of this section that pertains to the offense and delinquency history of a person who has been convicted of, pleaded guilty to, or been adjudicated a delinquent child for committing a sexually oriented offense or a child-victim oriented offense for the purposes described in division (C)(2) of this section.

(E) The attorney general shall adopt rules, in accordance with Chapter 119. of the Revised Code, setting forth the procedure by which a person may receive or release information gathered by the superintendent pursuant to division (A) of this section. A reasonable fee may be charged for this service. If a temporary employment service submits a request for a determination of whether a person the service plans to refer to an employment position has been convicted of or pleaded guilty to an offense listed in division (A)(1), (3), (4), (5), or (6) of section 109.572 of the Revised Code, the request shall be treated as a single request and only one fee shall be charged.

(F)(1) As used in division (F)(2) of this section, "head start agency" means an entity in this state that has been approved to be an agency for purposes of subchapter II of the "Community Economic Development Act," 95 Stat. 489 (1981), 42 U.S.C.A. 9831, as amended.

(2)(a) In addition to or in conjunction with any request that is required to be made under section 109.572, 2151.86, 3301.32, 3301.541, division (C) of section 3310.58, or section 3319.39, 3319.391, 3327.10, 3701.881, 5104.012, 5104.013, 5123.081, 5126.28, 5126.281, or 5153.111 of the Revised Code or that is made under section 3314.41, 3319.392, 3326.25, or 3328.20 of the Revised Code, the board of education of any school district; the director of developmental disabilities; any county board of developmental disabilities; any entity under contract with a county board of developmental disabilities; the chief administrator of any chartered nonpublic school; the chief administrator of a registered private provider that is not also a chartered nonpublic school; the chief administrator of any home health agency; the chief administrator of or person operating any child day-care center, type A family day-care home, or type B family day-care home licensed or certified under Chapter 5104. of the Revised Code; the administrator of any type C family day-care home certified pursuant to Section 1 of Sub. H.B. 62 of the 121st general assembly or Section 5 of Am. Sub. S.B. 160 of the 121st general assembly; the chief administrator of any head start agency; the executive director of a public children services agency; a private company described in section 3314.41, 3319.392, 3326.25, or 3328.20 of the Revised Code; or an employer described in division (J)(2) of section 3327.10 of the Revised Code may request that the superintendent of the bureau investigate and determine, with respect to any individual who has applied for employment in any position after October 2, 1989, or any individual wishing to apply for employment with a board of education may request, with regard to the individual, whether the bureau has any information gathered under division (A) of this section that pertains to that individual. On receipt of the request, the superintendent shall determine whether that information exists and, upon request of the person, board, or entity requesting information, also shall request from the federal bureau of investigation any criminal records it has pertaining to that individual. The superintendent or the superintendent's designee also may request criminal history records from other states or the federal government pursuant to the national crime prevention and privacy compact set forth in section 109.571 of the Revised Code. Within thirty days of the date that the superintendent receives a request, the superintendent shall send to the board, entity, or person a report of any information that the superintendent determines exists, including information contained in records that have been sealed under section 2953.32 of the Revised Code, and, within thirty days of its receipt, shall send the board, entity, or person a report of any information received from the federal bureau of investigation, other than information the dissemination of which is prohibited by federal law.

(b) When a board of education or a registered private provider is required to receive information under this section as a prerequisite to employment of an individual pursuant to division (C) of section 3310.58 or section 3319.39 of the Revised Code, it may accept a certified copy of records that were issued by the bureau of criminal identification and investigation and that are presented by an individual applying for employment with the district in lieu of requesting that information itself. In such a case, the board shall accept the certified copy issued by the bureau in order to make a photocopy of it for that individual's employment application documents and shall return the certified copy to the individual. In a case of that nature, a district or provider only shall accept a certified copy of records of that nature within one year after the date of their issuance by the bureau.

(c) Notwithstanding division (F)(2)(a) of this section, in the case of a request under section 3319.39, 3319.391, or 3327.10 of the Revised Code only for criminal records maintained by the federal bureau of investigation, the superintendent shall not determine whether any information gathered under division (A) of this section exists on the person for whom the request is made.

(3) The state board of education may request, with respect to any individual who has applied for employment after October 2, 1989, in any position with the state board or the department of education, any information that a school district board of education is authorized to request under division (F)(2) of this section, and the superintendent of the bureau shall proceed as if the request has been received from a school district board of education under division (F)(2) of this section.

(4) When the superintendent of the bureau receives a request for information under section 3319.291 of the Revised Code, the superintendent shall proceed as if the request has been received from a school district board of education and shall comply with divisions (F)(2)(a) and (c) of this section.

(5) When a recipient of a classroom reading improvement grant paid under section 3301.86 of the Revised Code requests, with respect to any individual who applies to participate in providing any program or service funded in whole or in part by the grant, the information that a school district board of education is authorized to request under division (F)(2)(a) of this section, the superintendent of the bureau shall proceed as if the request has been received from a school district board of education under division (F)(2)(a) of this section.

(G) In addition to or in conjunction with any request that is required to be made under section 3701.881, 3712.09, 3721.121, 5119.693, or 5119.85 of the Revised Code with respect to an individual who has applied for employment in a position that involves providing direct care to an older adult or adult resident, the chief administrator of a home health agency, hospice care program, home licensed under Chapter 3721. of the Revised Code, adult day-care program operated pursuant to rules adopted under section 3721.04 of the Revised Code, adult foster home, or adult care facility may request that the superintendent of the bureau investigate and determine, with respect to any individual who has applied after January 27, 1997, for employment in a position that does not involve providing direct care to an older adult or adult resident, whether the bureau has any information gathered under division (A) of this section that pertains to that individual.

In addition to or in conjunction with any request that is required to be made under section 173.27 of the Revised Code with respect to an individual who has applied for employment in a position that involves providing ombudsperson services to residents of long-term care facilities or recipients of community-based long-term care services, the state long-term care ombudsperson, ombudsperson's designee, or director of health may request that the superintendent investigate and determine, with respect to any individual who has applied for employment in a position that does not involve providing such ombudsperson services, whether the bureau has any information gathered under division (A) of this section that pertains to that applicant.

In addition to or in conjunction with any request that is required to be made under section 173.394 of the Revised Code with respect to an individual who has applied for employment in a position that involves providing direct care to an individual, the chief administrator of a community-based long-term care agency may request that the superintendent investigate and determine, with respect to any individual who has applied for employment in a position that does not involve providing direct care, whether the bureau has any information gathered under division (A) of this section that pertains to that applicant.

On receipt of a request under this division, the superintendent shall determine whether that information exists and, on request of the individual requesting information, shall also request from the federal bureau of investigation any criminal records it has pertaining to the applicant. The superintendent or the superintendent's designee also may request criminal history records from other states or the federal government pursuant to the national crime prevention and privacy compact set forth in section 109.571 of the Revised Code. Within thirty days of the date a request is received, the superintendent shall send to the requester a report of any information determined to exist, including information contained in records that have been sealed under section 2953.32 of the Revised Code, and, within thirty days of its receipt, shall send the requester a report of any information received from the federal bureau of investigation, other than information the dissemination of which is prohibited by federal law.

(H) Information obtained by a government entity or person under this section is confidential and shall not be released or disseminated.

(I) The superintendent may charge a reasonable fee for providing information or criminal records under division (F)(2) or (G) of this section.

(J) As used in this section:

(1) "Sexually oriented offense" and "child-victim oriented offense" have the same meanings as in section 2950.01 of the Revised Code.

(2) "Registered private provider" means a nonpublic school or entity registered with the superintendent of public instruction under section 3310.41 of the Revised Code to participate in the autism scholarship program or section 3310.58 of the Revised Code to participate in the Jon Peterson special needs scholarship program.

**HISTORY: 130 v 11 (Eff 9-24-63); 130 v 10 (Eff 10-4-63); 133 v H 956 (Eff 9-16-70); 137 v H 1 (Eff 8-26-77); 138 v H 736 (Eff 10-16-80); 140 v H 235 (Eff 6-7-84); 143 v S 140 (Eff 10-2-89); 145 v H 152 (Eff 7-1-93); 145 v H 162 (Eff 10-1-93); 145 v S 38 (Eff 10-29-93); 145 v H 571 (Eff 10-6-94); 145 v H 694 (Eff 11-11-94); 146 v H 1 (Eff 1-1-96); 146 v H 223 (Eff 11-15-95); 146 v S 160 (Eff 1-27-97); 146 v H 124, § 1 (Eff 3-31-97); 146 v H 180 (Eff 7-1-97); 146 v H 124, § 4 (Eff 7-1-97); 147 v H 151 (Eff 9-16-97); 147 v H 342 (Eff 12-31-97); 147 v H 2 (Eff 1-1-99); 148 v H 1 (Eff 3-30-99); 148 v H 282 (Eff 9-28-99); 148 v H 3 (Eff 11-22-99); 148 v H 538. Eff 9-22-2000; 150 v S 5, § 1, eff. 7-31-03; 150 v H 95, § 1, eff. 9-26-03; 150 v S 53, § 1, eff. 4-7-04; 150 v H 106, § 1, eff. 9-16-04; 151 v H 66, § 101.01, eff. 6-30-05; 151 v H 530, § 101.01, eff. 6-30-06; 151 v S 238, § 1, eff. 9-21-06; 152 v H 190, § 1, eff. 11-14-07; 152 v S 10, § 1, eff. 1-1-08; 152 v S 163, § 1, eff. 8-14-08; 152 v H 428, § 1, eff. 9-12-08; 153 v S 79, § 1, eff. 10-6-09; 153 v H 1, § 101.01, eff. 10-16-09, 1-1-10; 153 v H 10, § 1, eff. 6-17-10; 2011 HB 93, § 1, eff. May 20, 2011; 2011 HB 153, § 101.01, eff. Sept. 29, 2011.**

Pursuant to 2011 HB 153, §812.30, the amendment to subdivision (G) is effective July 1, 2011.

The provisions of § 4 of 153 v H 10 read in part as follows:

SECTION 4. Section 109.57 of the Revised Code is presented in this act as a composite of the section as amended by both Am. Sub. H.B. 1 and Sub. S.B. 79 of the 128th General Assembly. * * * The General Assembly, applying the principle stated in division (B) of section 1.52 of the Revised Code that amendments are to be harmonized if reasonably capable of simultaneous operation, finds that the composites are the resulting versions of the sections in effect prior to the effective date of the sections as presented in this act.

The effective date is set by § 812.50 of 153 v H 1.

The provisions of 815.10 of 153 v H 1 read as follows:

SECTION 815.10. The General Assembly, applying the principle stated in division (B) of section 1.52 of the Revised Code that amendments are to be harmonized if reasonably capable of simultaneous operation, finds that the following sections, presented in this act as composites of the sections as amended by the acts indicated, are the resulting versions of the sections in effect prior to the effective date of the sections as presented in this act: * * *

Section 109.57 of the Revised Code as amended by both Sub. H.B. 428 and Sub. S.B. 163 of the 127th General Assembly.

* * *

The provisions of § 15 of 153 v S 79 read as follows:

SECTION 15. The General Assembly, applying the principle stated in division (B) of section 1.52 of the Revised Code that amendments are to be harmonized if reasonably capable of simultaneous operation, finds that the following sections, presented in this act as composites of the sections as amended by the acts indicated, are the resulting versions of the sections in effect prior to the effective date of the sections as presented in this act:

Section 109.57 of the Revised Code as amended by both Sub. H.B. 428 and Sub. S.B. 163 of the 127th General Assembly.

* * *

The effective date is set by § 3 of 152 v S 10.

The effective date is set by § 812.03 of 151 v H 530.

The effective date is set by § 612.12 of 151 v H 66.

The effective date is set by section 179 of H.B. 95 (150 v —).

The provisions of § 3, S.B. 53 (150 v —), read as follows:

SECTION 3. Section 109.57 of the Revised Code is presented in this act as a composite of the section as amended by both Am. Sub. H.B. 95 and Am. Sub. S.B. 5 of the 125th General Assembly. The General Assembly, applying the principle stated in division (B) of section 1.52 of the Revised Code that amendments are to be harmonized if reasonably capable of simultaneous operation, finds that the composite is the resulting version of the section in effect prior to the effective date of the section as presented in this act.

The provisions of § 7 of HB 538 (148 v —) read as follows:

SECTION 7. Section 109.57 of the Revised Code is presented in this act as a composite of the section as amended by both Am. Sub. H.B. 3 and Am. Sub. H.B. 282 of the 123rd General Assembly with the new language of neither of the acts shown in capital letters. This is in recognition of the principle stated in division (B) of section 1.52 of the Revised Code that such amendments are to be harmonized where not substantively irreconcilable and constitutes a legislative finding that such are the resulting versions of those sections in effect prior to the effective date of this act.

The provisions of § 3 of SB 160 (146 v —) read as follows:

SECTION 3. Sections 109.57, 109.572, 2950.08, 2953.32, and 3701.881 of the Revised Code, as amended by this act regarding employment of persons who provide direct care to older adults, and sections 173.41, 3712.09, 3721.121, and 3722.151 of the Revised Code, as enacted by this act, apply only to persons who apply for employment on or after the effective date of this act.

**Publisher's Note:**

The amendment of RC § 109.57 by 152 v H 119 was disapproved by the Governor.

**Comment, Legislative Service Commission**

Section 109.57 of the Revised Code is amended by Am. Sub. H.B. 1 and Sub. S.B. 79 of the 128th General Assembly. Comparison of these amendments in pursuance of section 1.52 of the Revised Code discloses that they are not irreconcilable so that they are required by that section to be harmonized to give effect to each amendment.

## § 109.571 National crime prevention and privacy compact.

The "national crime prevention and privacy compact" is hereby ratified, enacted into law, and entered into by the state of Ohio as a party to the compact with any other state that has legally joined in the compact as follows:

NATIONAL CRIME PREVENTION AND PRIVACY COMPACT

The contracting states agree to the following:

Overview

(a) This compact organizes an electronic information sharing system among the federal government and the states to exchange criminal history records for noncriminal justice purposes authorized by federal or state law, such as background checks for governmental licensing and employment.

(b) Under this compact, the FBI and the party states agree to maintain detailed databases of their respective criminal history records, including arrests and dispositions, and to make them available to the federal government and to party states for authorized purposes. The FBI shall also manage the federal data facilities that provide a significant part of the infrastructure for the system.

Article I

As used in this compact:

(1) "Attorney general" means the attorney general of the United States.

(2) "Compact officer" means:

(A) With respect to the federal government, an official so designated by the director of the FBI; and

(B) With respect to a party state, the chief administrator of the state's criminal history record repository or a designee of the chief administrator who is a regular full-time employee of the repository.

(3) "Council" means the compact council established under Article VI of the compact.

(4)(A) "Criminal history records" means information collected by criminal justice agencies on individuals consisting of identifiable descriptions and notations of arrests, detentions, indictments, or other formal criminal charges, and any disposition arising therefrom, including acquittal, sentencing, correctional supervision, or release.

(B) "Criminal history records" does not include identification information such as fingerprint records if the information does not indicate involvement of the individual with the criminal justice system.

(5) "Criminal history record repository" means the state agency designated by the governor or other appropriate executive official or the legislature of a state to perform centralized recordkeeping functions for criminal history records and services in the state.

(6) "Criminal justice" includes activities relating to the detection, apprehension, detention, pretrial release, post-trial release, prosecution, adjudication, correctional supervision, or rehabilitation of accused persons or criminal offenders. The administration of criminal justice includes criminal identification activities and the collection, storage, and dissemination of criminal history records.

(7) "Criminal justice agency" means courts and a governmental agency or any subunit of a governmental agency that performs the administration of criminal justice pursuant to a statute or executive order and allocates a substantial part of its annual budget to the administration of criminal justice. "Criminal justice agency" also includes federal and state inspectors general offices.

(8) "Criminal justice services" means services provided by the FBI to criminal justice agencies in response to a request for information about a particular individual or as an update to information previously provided for criminal justice purposes.

(9) "Criterion offense" means any felony or misdemeanor offense not included on the list of nonserious offenses published periodically by the FBI.

(10) "Direct access" means access to the national identification index by computer terminal or other automated means not requiring the assistance of or intervention by any other party or agency.

(11) "Executive order" means an order of the president of the United States or the chief executive officer of a state that has the force of law and that is promulgated in accordance with applicable law.

(12) "FBI" means the federal bureau of investigation.

(13) "Interstate identification system" or "III system" means the cooperative federal-state system for the exchange of criminal history records and includes the national identification index, the national fingerprint file, and, to the extent of their participation in that system, the criminal history record repositories of the states and the FBI.

(14) "National fingerprint file" means a database of fingerprints, or other uniquely personal identifying information, relating to an arrested or charged individual maintained by the FBI to provide positive identification of record subjects indexed in the III system.

(15) "National identification index" means an index maintained by the FBI consisting of names, identifying numbers, and other descriptive information relating to record subjects about whom there are criminal history records in the III system.

(16) "National indices" means the national identification index and the national fingerprint file.

(17) "Nonparty state" means a state that has not ratified this compact.

(18) "Noncriminal justice purposes" means uses of criminal history records for purposes authorized by federal or state law other than purposes relating to criminal justice activities, including employment suitability, licensing determinations, immigration and naturalization matters, and national security clearances.

(19) "Party state" means a state that has ratified this compact.

(20) "Positive identification" means a determination, based upon a comparison of fingerprints or other equally reliable biometric identification techniques, that the subject of a record search is the same person as the subject of a criminal history record or records indexed in the III system. Identifications based solely upon a comparison of subject's names or other nonunique identification characteristics or numbers, or combinations thereof, shall not constitute positive identification.

(21) "Sealed record information" means both of the following:

(A) With respect to adults, that portion of a record that is not available for criminal justice uses, not supported by fingerprints or other accepted means of positive identification, or subject to restrictions on dissemination for noncriminal justice purposes pursuant to a court order related to a particular subject or pursuant to a federal or state statute that requires action on a sealing petition filed by a particular record subject;

(B) With respect to juveniles, whatever each state determines is a sealed record under its own law and procedure.

(22) "State" means any state, territory, or possession of the United States, the District of Columbia, and the Commonwealth of Puerto Rico.

Article II

The purposes of this compact are to do all of the following:

(1) Provide a legal framework for the establishment of a cooperative federal-state system for the interstate and federal-state exchange of criminal history records for noncriminal justice uses;

(2) Require the FBI to permit use of the national identification index and the national fingerprint file by each party state, and to provide, in a timely fashion, federal and state criminal history records to requesting states, in accordance with the terms of this compact and with rules, procedures, and standards established by the council under Article VI;

(3) Require party states to provide information and records for the national identification index and the national fingerprint file and to provide criminal history records, in a timely fashion, to criminal history record repositories of other states and the federal government for noncriminal justice purposes, in accordance with the terms of this compact and with rules, procedures, and standards established by the council under Article VI;

(4) Provide for the establishment of a council to monitor III system operations and to prescribe system rules and procedures for the effective and proper operation of the III system for noncriminal justice purposes;

(5) Require the FBI and each party state to adhere to III system standards concerning record dissemination and use, response times, system security, data quality, and other duly established standards, including those that enhance the accuracy and privacy of such records.

Article III

(a) The director of the FBI shall do all of the following:

(1) Appoint an FBI compact officer who shall do all of the following:

(A) Administer this compact within the department of justice and among federal agencies and other agencies and organizations that submit search requests to the FBI pursuant to Article V(c);

(B) Ensure that compact provisions and rules, procedures, and standards prescribed by the council under Article VI are complied with by the department of justice and the federal agencies and other agencies and organizations referred to in Article III(1)(A);

(C) Regulate the use of records received by means of the III system from party states when those records are supplied by the FBI directly to other federal agencies;

(2) Provide to federal agencies and to state criminal history record repositories criminal history records maintained in its database for the noncriminal justice purposes described in Article IV, including both of the following:

(A) Information from nonparty states;

(B) Information from party states that is available from the FBI through the III system, but is not available from the party state through the III system;

(3) Provide a telecommunications network and maintain centralized facilities for the exchange of criminal history records for both criminal justice purposes and the noncriminal justice purposes described in Article IV, and ensure that the exchange of criminal history records for criminal justice purposes has priority over exchange for noncriminal justice purposes;

(4) Modify or enter into user agreements with nonparty state criminal history record repositories to require them to establish record request procedures conforming to those prescribed in Article V.

(b) Each party state shall do all of the following:

(1) Appoint a compact officer who shall do all of the following:

(A) Administer this compact within that state;

(B) Ensure that the compact provisions and rules, procedures, and standards established by the council under Article VI are complied with in the state;

(C) Regulate the in-state use of records received by means of the III system from the FBI or from other party states;

(2) Establish and maintain a criminal history record repository, which shall provide both of the following:

(A) Information and records for the national identification index and the national fingerprint file;

(B) The state's III system-indexed criminal history records for noncriminal justice purposes described in Article IV;

(3) Participate in the national fingerprint file;

(4) Provide and maintain telecommunications links and related equipment necessary to support the services set forth in this compact.

(c) In carrying out their responsibilities under this compact, the FBI and each party state shall comply with the III system rules, procedures, and standards duly established by the council concerning record dissemination and use, response times, data quality, system security, accuracy, privacy protection, and other aspects of III system operation.

(d)(1) Use of the III system for noncriminal justice purposes authorized in this compact shall be managed so as not to diminish the level of services provided in support of criminal justice purposes.

(2) Administration of compact provisions shall not reduce the level of service available to authorized noncriminal justice users on the effective date of this compact.

Article IV

(a) To the extent authorized by section 552a of title 5, United States Code (commonly known as the 'Privacy Act of 1974'), the FBI shall provide on request criminal history records (excluding sealed records) to state criminal history record repositories for noncriminal justice purposes allowed by federal statute, federal executive order, or a state statute that has been approved by the attorney general and that authorizes national indices checks.

(b) The FBI, to the extent authorized by section 552a of title 5, United States Code (commonly known as the 'Privacy Act of 1974') and state criminal history record repositories, shall provide criminal history records (excluding sealed records) to criminal justice agencies and other governmental or nongovernmental agencies for noncriminal justice purposes allowed by federal statute, federal executive order, or a state statute that has been approved by the attorney general, that authorizes national indices checks.

(c) Any record obtained under this compact may be used only for the official purposes for which the record was requested. Each compact officer shall establish procedures, consistent with this compact, and with rules, procedures, and standards established by the council under Article VI, which procedures shall protect the accuracy and privacy of the records, and shall do all of the following:

(1) Ensure that records obtained under this compact are used only by authorized officials for authorized purposes;

(2) Require that subsequent record checks are requested to obtain current information whenever a new need arises;

(3) Ensure that record entries that may not legally be used for a particular noncriminal justice purpose are deleted from the response and, if no information authorized for release remains, an appropriate 'no record' response is communicated to the requesting official.

Article V

(a) Subject fingerprints or other approved forms of positive identification shall be submitted with all requests for criminal history record checks for noncriminal justice purposes.

(b) Each request for a criminal history record check utilizing the national indices made under any approved state statute shall be submitted through that state's criminal history record repository. A state criminal history record repository shall process an interstate request for noncriminal justice purposes through the national indices only if the request is transmitted through another state criminal history record repository or the FBI.

(c) Each request for criminal history record checks utilizing the national indices made under federal authority shall be submitted through the FBI or, if the state criminal history record repository consents to process fingerprint submissions, through the criminal history record repository in the state in which the request originated. Direct access to the national identification index by entities other than the FBI or state criminal history record repositories shall not be permitted for noncriminal justice purposes.

(d) A state criminal history record repository for the FBI may charge a fee, in accordance with applicable law, for handling a request involving fingerprint processing for noncriminal justice purposes and may not charge a fee for providing criminal history records in response to an electric request for a record that does not involve a request to process fingerprints.

(e)(1) If a state criminal history record repository cannot positively identify the subject of a record request made for noncriminal justice purposes, the request, together with fingerprints or other approved identifying information, shall be forwarded to the FBI for a search of the national indices.

(2) If, with respect to a request forwarded by a state criminal history record repository under paragraph (1), the FBI positively identifies the subject as having a III system-indexed record or records, the FBI shall so advise the state criminal history repository; and the state criminal history record repository shall be entitled to obtain the additional criminal history record information from the FBI or other state criminal history record repositories.

Article VI

(a)(1) There is established a council to be known as the 'compact council,' which shall have the authority to promulgate rules and procedures governing the use of the III system for noncriminal justice purposes, not to conflict with the FBI administration of the III system for criminal justice purposes.

(2) The council shall do all of the following:

(A) Continue in existence as long as this compact remains in effect;

(B) Be located, for administrative purposes, within the FBI;

(C) Be organized and hold its first meeting as soon as practicable after the effective date of this compact.

(b) The council shall be composed of fifteen members, each of whom shall be appointed by the attorney general as follows:

(1) Nine members, each of whom shall serve a two-year term, who shall be selected from among the compact officers of party states based on the recommendation of the compact officers of all party states, except that, in the absence of the requisite number of compact officers available to serve, the chief administrators of the criminal history record repositories of nonparty states shall be eligible to serve on an interim basis;

(2) Two at-large members, nominated by the director of the FBI, each of whom shall serve a three-year term, of whom one shall be a representative of the criminal justice agencies of the federal government and may not be employed by the FBI; and one shall be a representative of the noncriminal justice agencies of the federal government;

(3) Two at-large members, nominated by the chairman of the council, once the chairman is elected pursuant to Article VI(c), each of whom shall serve a three-year term, of whom one shall be a representative of state or local criminal justice agencies; and one shall be a representative of state or local noncriminal justice agencies;

(4) One member, who shall serve a three-year term, and who shall simultaneously be a member of the FBI's advisory policy board on criminal justice information services, nominated by the membership of that policy board;

(5) One member, nominated by the director of the FBI, who shall serve a three-year term, and who shall be an employee of the FBI.

(c)(1) From its membership, the council shall elect a chairman and a vice chairman of the council, respectively. Both the chairman and the vice chairman shall be a compact officer, unless there is no compact officer on the council who is willing to serve, in which case the chairman may be an at-large member; and shall serve a two-year term and may be reelected to only one additional two-year term.

(2) The vice chairman of the council shall serve as the chairman of the council in the absence of the chairman.

(d)(1) The council shall meet at least once each year at the call of the chairman. Each meeting of the council shall be open to the public. The council shall provide prior public notice in the federal register of each meeting of the council, including the matters to be addressed at the meeting.

(2) A majority of the council or any committee of the council shall constitute a quorum of the council or of such committee, respectively, for the conduct of business. A lesser number may meet to hold hearings, take testimony, or conduct any business not requiring a vote.

(e) The council shall make available for public inspection and copying at the council office with the FBI, and shall publish in the federal register, any rules, procedures, or standards established by the council.

(f) The council may request from the FBI any reports, studies, statistics, or other information or materials that the council determines to be necessary to enable the council to perform its duties under this compact. The FBI, to the extent authorized by law, may provide such assistance or information upon such a request.

(g) The chairman may establish committees as necessary to carry out this compact and may prescribe their membership, responsibilities, and duration.

Article VII

This compact shall take effect upon being entered into by two or more states as between those states and the federal government. Upon subsequent entering into this compact by additional states, it shall become effective among those states and the federal government and each party state that has previously ratified it. When ratified, this compact shall have the full force and effect of law within the ratifying jurisdictions. The form of ratification shall be in accordance with the laws of the executing state.

Article VIII

(a) Administration of this compact shall not interfere with the management and control of the director of the FBI over the FBI's collection and dissemination of criminal history records and the advisory function of the FBI's advisory policy board chartered under the Federal Advisory Committee Act (5 U.S.C. App.) for all purposes other than noncriminal justice.

(b) Nothing in this compact shall require the FBI to obligate or expend funds beyond those appropriated to the FBI.

(c) Nothing in this compact shall diminish or lessen the obligations, responsibilities, and authorities of any state, whether a party state or a nonparty state, or of any criminal history record repository or other subdivision or component thereof, under the Departments of State, Justice, and Commerce, the Judiciary, and Related Agencies Appropriation Act, 1973 (Public Law 92-544), or regulations and guidelines promulgated thereunder, including the rules and procedures promulgated by the council under Article VI(a), regarding the use and dissemination of criminal history records and information.

Article IX

(a) This compact shall bind each party state until renounced by the party state.

(b) Any renunciation of this compact by a party state shall be effected in the same manner by which the party state ratified this compact and shall become effective one hundred and eighty days after written notice of renunciation is provided by the party state to each other party state and to the federal government.

Article X

The provisions of this compact shall be severable, and if any phrase, clause, sentence, or provision of this compact is declared to be contrary to the constitution of any participating state, or to the Constitution of the United States, or the applicability of any phrase, clause, sentence, or provision of this compact to any government, agency, person, or circumstance is held invalid, the validity of the remainder of this compact and the applicability of the remainder of this compact to any government, agency, person, or circumstance shall not be affected thereby. If a portion of this compact is held contrary to the constitution of any party state, all other portions of this compact shall remain in full force and effect as to the remaining party states and in full force and effect as to the party states affected, as to all other provisions.

Article XI

(a) The council shall do both of the following:

(1) Have initial authority to make determinations with respect to any dispute regarding all of the following:

(A) Interpretation of this compact;

(B) Any rule or standard established by the council pursuant to Article V;

(C) Any dispute or controversy between any parties to this compact;

(2) Hold a hearing concerning any dispute described in paragraph (1) at a regularly scheduled meeting of the council and only render a decision based upon a majority vote of the members of the council. The decision shall be published pursuant to the requirements of Article VI(e).

(b) The FBI shall exercise immediate and necessary action to preserve the integrity of the III system, maintain system policy and standards, protect the accuracy and privacy of records, and to prevent abuses, until the council holds a hearing on such matters.

(c) The FBI or a party state may appeal any decision of the council to the attorney general, and thereafter may file suit in the appropriate district court of the United States, which shall have original jurisdiction of all cases or controversies arising under this compact. Any suit arising under this compact and initiated in a state court shall be removed to the appropriate district court of the United States in the manner provided by section 1446 of title 28, United States Code, or other statutory authority.

**HISTORY: 150 v S 53, § 1, eff. 4-7-04.**

**Not analogous to former RC § 109.571 (133 v H 956; 135 v S 174; 143 v H 552), repealed 146 v H 670, § 2, eff. 12-2-96.**

## § 109.572 Criminal records check and fingerprinting generally.

(A)(1) Upon receipt of a request pursuant to section 121.08, 3301.32, 3301.541, or 3319.39 of the Revised Code, a completed form prescribed pursuant to division (C)(1) of this section, and a set of fingerprint impressions obtained in the manner described in division (C)(2) of this section, the superintendent of the bureau of criminal identification and investigation shall conduct a criminal records check in the manner described in division (B) of this section to determine whether any information exists that indicates that the person who is the subject of the request previously has been convicted of or pleaded guilty to any of the following:

(a) A violation of section 2903.01, 2903.02, 2903.03, 2903.04, 2903.11, 2903.12, 2903.13, 2903.16, 2903.21, 2903.34, 2905.01, 2905.02, 2905.05, 2907.02, 2907.03, 2907.04, 2907.05, 2907.06, 2907.07, 2907.08, 2907.09, 2907.21, 2907.22, 2907.23, 2907.25, 2907.31, 2907.32, 2907.321, 2907.322, 2907.323, 2911.01, 2911.02, 2911.11, 2911.12, 2919.12, 2919.22, 2919.24, 2919.25, 2923.12, 2923.13, 2923.161, 2925.02, 2925.03, 2925.04, 2925.05, 2925.06, or 3716.11 of the Revised Code, felonious sexual penetration in violation of former section 2907.12 of the Revised Code, a violation of section 2905.04 of the Revised Code as it existed prior to July 1, 1996, a violation of section 2919.23 of the Revised Code that would have been a violation of section 2905.04 of the Revised Code as it existed prior to July 1, 1996, had the violation been committed prior to that date, or a violation of section 2925.11 of the Revised Code that is not a minor drug possession offense;

(b) A violation of an existing or former law of this state, any other state, or the United States that is substantially equivalent to any of the offenses listed in division (A)(1)(a) of this section.

(2) On receipt of a request pursuant to section 5123.081 of the Revised Code with respect to an applicant for employment in any position with the department of developmental disabilities, pursuant to section 5126.28 of

the Revised Code with respect to an applicant for employment in any position with a county board of developmental disabilities, or pursuant to section 5126.281 of the Revised Code with respect to an applicant for employment in a direct services position with an entity contracting with a county board for employment, a completed form prescribed pursuant to division (C)(1) of this section, and a set of fingerprint impressions obtained in the manner described in division (C)(2) of this section, the superintendent of the bureau of criminal identification and investigation shall conduct a criminal records check. The superintendent shall conduct the criminal records check in the manner described in division (B) of this section to determine whether any information exists that indicates that the person who is the subject of the request has been convicted of or pleaded guilty to any of the following:

(a) A violation of section 2903.01, 2903.02, 2903.03, 2903.04, 2903.11, 2903.12, 2903.13, 2903.16, 2903.21, 2903.34, 2903.341, 2905.01, 2905.02, 2905.04, 2905.05, 2907.02, 2907.03, 2907.04, 2907.05, 2907.06, 2907.07, 2907.08, 2907.09, 2907.12, 2907.21, 2907.22, 2907.23, 2907.25, 2907.31, 2907.32, 2907.321, 2907.322, 2907.323, 2911.01, 2911.02, 2911.11, 2911.12, 2919.12, 2919.22, 2919.24, 2919.25, 2923.12, 2923.13, 2923.161, 2925.02, 2925.03, or 3716.11 of the Revised Code;

(b) An existing or former municipal ordinance or law of this state, any other state, or the United States that is substantially equivalent to any of the offenses listed in division (A)(2)(a) of this section.

(3) On receipt of a request pursuant to section 173.27, 173.394, 3712.09, 3721.121, 5119.693, or 5119.85 of the Revised Code, a completed form prescribed pursuant to division (C)(1) of this section, and a set of fingerprint impressions obtained in the manner described in division (C)(2) of this section, the superintendent of the bureau of criminal identification and investigation shall conduct a criminal records check with respect to any person who has applied for employment in a position for which a criminal records check is required by those sections. The superintendent shall conduct the criminal records check in the manner described in division (B) of this section to determine whether any information exists that indicates that the person who is the subject of the request previously has been convicted of or pleaded guilty to any of the following:

(a) A violation of section 2903.01, 2903.02, 2903.03, 2903.04, 2903.11, 2903.12, 2903.13, 2903.16, 2903.21, 2903.34, 2905.01, 2905.02, 2905.11, 2905.12, 2907.02, 2907.03, 2907.05, 2907.06, 2907.07, 2907.08, 2907.09, 2907.12, 2907.25, 2907.31, 2907.32, 2907.321, 2907.322, 2907.323, 2911.01, 2911.02, 2911.11, 2911.12, 2911.13, 2913.02, 2913.03, 2913.04, 2913.11, 2913.21, 2913.31, 2913.40, 2913.43, 2913.47, 2913.51, 2919.25, 2921.36, 2923.12, 2923.13, 2923.161, 2925.02, 2925.03, 2925.11, 2925.13, 2925.22, 2925.23, or 3716.11 of the Revised Code;

(b) An existing or former law of this state, any other state, or the United States that is substantially equivalent to any of the offenses listed in division (A)(3)(a) of this section.

(4) On receipt of a request pursuant to section 3701.881 of the Revised Code with respect to an applicant for employment with a home health agency as a person responsible for the care, custody, or control of a child, a completed form prescribed pursuant to division (C)(1) of this section, and a set of fingerprint impressions obtained in the manner described in division (C)(2) of this section, the superintendent of the bureau of criminal identification and investigation shall conduct a criminal records check. The superintendent shall conduct the criminal records check in the manner described in division (B) of this section to determine whether any information exists that indicates that the person who is the subject of the request previously has been convicted of or pleaded guilty to any of the following:

(a) A violation of section 2903.01, 2903.02, 2903.03, 2903.04, 2903.11, 2903.12, 2903.13, 2903.16, 2903.21, 2903.34, 2905.01, 2905.02, 2905.04, 2905.05, 2907.02, 2907.03, 2907.04, 2907.05, 2907.06, 2907.07, 2907.08, 2907.09, 2907.12, 2907.21, 2907.22, 2907.23, 2907.25, 2907.31, 2907.32, 2907.321, 2907.322, 2907.323, 2911.01, 2911.02, 2911.11, 2911.12, 2919.12, 2919.22, 2919.24, 2919.25, 2923.12, 2923.13, 2923.161, 2925.02, 2925.03, 2925.04, 2925.05, 2925.06, or 3716.11 of the Revised Code or a violation of section 2925.11 of the Revised Code that is not a minor drug possession offense;

(b) An existing or former law of this state, any other state, or the United States that is substantially equivalent to any of the offenses listed in division (A)(4)(a) of this section.

(5) On receipt of a request pursuant to section 5111.032, 5111.033, or 5111.034 of the Revised Code, a completed form prescribed pursuant to division (C)(1) of this section, and a set of fingerprint impressions obtained in the manner described in division (C)(2) of this section, the superintendent of the bureau of criminal identification and investigation shall conduct a criminal records check. The superintendent shall conduct the criminal records check in the manner described in division (B) of this section to determine whether any information exists that indicates that the person who is the subject of the request previously has been convicted of, has pleaded guilty to, or has been found eligible for intervention in lieu of conviction for any of the following, regardless of the date of the conviction, the date of entry of the guilty plea, or the date the person was found eligible for intervention in lieu of conviction:

(a) A violation of section 959.13, 2903.01, 2903.02, 2903.03, 2903.04, 2903.041, 2903.11, 2903.12, 2903.13, 2903.15, 2903.16, 2903.21, 2903.211, 2903.22, 2903.34, 2905.01, 2905.02, 2905.05, 2905.11, 2905.12, 2907.02, 2907.03, 2907.04, 2907.05, 2907.06, 2907.07, 2907.08, 2907.09, 2907.21, 2907.22, 2907.23, 2907.24, 2907.25, 2907.31, 2907.32, 2907.321, 2907.322, 2907.323, 2909.02, 2909.03, 2909.04, 2909.05, 2909.22, 2909.23, 2909.24, 2911.01, 2911.02, 2911.11, 2911.12, 2911.13, 2913.02, 2913.03, 2913.04, 2913.05, 2913.11, 2913.21, 2913.31, 2913.32, 2913.40, 2913.41, 2913.42, 2913.43, 2913.44, 2913.441, 2913.45, 2913.46, 2913.47, 2913.48, 2913.49, 2913.51, 2917.01, 2917.02, 2917.03, 2917.11, 2917.31, 2919.12, 2919.22, 2919.23, 2919.24, 2919.25, 2921.03, 2921.11, 2921.13, 2921.34, 2921.35, 2921.36, 2923.01, 2923.02, 2923.03, 2923.12, 2923.13, 2923.161, 2923.32, 2925.02, 2925.03, 2925.04, 2925.05, 2925.06, 2925.11, 2925.13, 2925.14, 2925.22, 2925.23, 2927.12, or 3716.11 of the Revised Code, felonious sexual penetration in violation of former section 2907.12 of the Revised Code, a violation of section 2905.04 of the Revised Code as it existed prior to July 1, 1996, a violation of section 2919.23 of the Revised Code that would have been a violation of section 2905.04 of the Revised Code as it existed prior to July 1, 1996, had the violation been committed prior to that date;

(b) A violation of an existing or former municipal ordinance or law of this state, any other state, or the

United States that is substantially equivalent to any of the offenses listed in division (A)(5)(a) of this section.

(6) On receipt of a request pursuant to section 3701.881 of the Revised Code with respect to an applicant for employment with a home health agency in a position that involves providing direct care to an older adult, a completed form prescribed pursuant to division (C)(1) of this section, and a set of fingerprint impressions obtained in the manner described in division (C)(2) of this section, the superintendent of the bureau of criminal identification and investigation shall conduct a criminal records check. The superintendent shall conduct the criminal records check in the manner described in division (B) of this section to determine whether any information exists that indicates that the person who is the subject of the request previously has been convicted of or pleaded guilty to any of the following:

(a) A violation of section 2903.01, 2903.02, 2903.03, 2903.04, 2903.11, 2903.12, 2903.13, 2903.16, 2903.21, 2903.34, 2905.01, 2905.02, 2905.11, 2905.12, 2907.02, 2907.03, 2907.05, 2907.06, 2907.07, 2907.08, 2907.09, 2907.12, 2907.25, 2907.31, 2907.32, 2907.321, 2907.322, 2907.323, 2911.01, 2911.02, 2911.11, 2911.12, 2911.13, 2913.02, 2913.03, 2913.04, 2913.11, 2913.21, 2913.31, 2913.40, 2913.43, 2913.47, 2913.51, 2919.25, 2921.36, 2923.12, 2923.13, 2923.161, 2925.02, 2925.03, 2925.11, 2925.13, 2925.22, 2925.23, or 3716.11 of the Revised Code;

(b) An existing or former law of this state, any other state, or the United States that is substantially equivalent to any of the offenses listed in division (A)(6)(a) of this section.

(7) When conducting a criminal records check upon a request pursuant to section 3319.39 of the Revised Code for an applicant who is a teacher, in addition to the determination made under division (A)(1) of this section, the superintendent shall determine whether any information exists that indicates that the person who is the subject of the request previously has been convicted of or pleaded guilty to any offense specified in section 3319.31 of the Revised Code.

(8) On receipt of a request pursuant to section 2151.86 of the Revised Code, a completed form prescribed pursuant to division (C)(1) of this section, and a set of fingerprint impressions obtained in the manner described in division (C)(2) of this section, the superintendent of the bureau of criminal identification and investigation shall conduct a criminal records check in the manner described in division (B) of this section to determine whether any information exists that indicates that the person who is the subject of the request previously has been convicted of or pleaded guilty to any of the following:

(a) A violation of section 959.13, 2903.01, 2903.02, 2903.03, 2903.04, 2903.11, 2903.12, 2903.13, 2903.15, 2903.16, 2903.21, 2903.211, 2903.22, 2903.34, 2905.01, 2905.02, 2905.05, 2907.02, 2907.03, 2907.04, 2907.05, 2907.06, 2907.07, 2907.08, 2907.09, 2907.21, 2907.22, 2907.23, 2907.25, 2907.31, 2907.32, 2907.321, 2907.322, 2907.323, 2909.02, 2909.03, 2909.22, 2909.23, 2909.24, 2911.01, 2911.02, 2911.11, 2911.12, 2913.49, 2917.01, 2917.02, 2919.12, 2919.22, 2919.24, 2919.25, 2923.12, 2923.13, 2923.161, 2925.02, 2925.03, 2925.04, 2925.05, 2925.06, 2927.12, or 3716.11 of the Revised Code, a violation of section 2905.04 of the Revised Code as it existed prior to July 1, 1996, a violation of section 2919.23 of the Revised Code that would have been a violation of section 2905.04 of the Revised Code as it existed prior to July 1, 1996, had the violation been committed prior to that date, a violation of section 2925.11 of the Revised Code that is not a minor drug possession offense, two or more OVI or OVUAC violations committed within the three years immediately preceding the submission of the application or petition that is the basis of the request, or felonious sexual penetration in violation of former section 2907.12 of the Revised Code;

(b) A violation of an existing or former law of this state, any other state, or the United States that is substantially equivalent to any of the offenses listed in division (A)(8)(a) of this section.

(9) Upon receipt of a request pursuant to section 5104.012 or 5104.013 of the Revised Code, a completed form prescribed pursuant to division (C)(1) of this section, and a set of fingerprint impressions obtained in the manner described in division (C)(2) of this section, the superintendent of the bureau of criminal identification and investigation shall conduct a criminal records check in the manner described in division (B) of this section to determine whether any information exists that indicates that the person who is the subject of the request has been convicted of or pleaded guilty to any of the following:

(a) A violation of section 2903.01, 2903.02, 2903.03, 2903.04, 2903.11, 2903.12, 2903.13, 2903.16, 2903.21, 2903.22, 2903.34, 2905.01, 2905.02, 2905.05, 2907.02, 2907.03, 2907.04, 2907.05, 2907.06, 2907.07, 2907.08, 2907.09, 2907.21, 2907.22, 2907.23, 2907.25, 2907.31, 2907.32, 2907.321, 2907.322, 2907.323, 2911.01, 2911.02, 2911.11, 2911.12, 2913.02, 2913.03, 2913.04, 2913.041, 2913.05, 2913.06, 2913.11, 2913.21, 2913.31, 2913.32, 2913.33, 2913.34, 2913.40, 2913.41, 2913.42, 2913.43, 2913.44, 2913.441, 2913.45, 2913.46, 2913.47, 2913.48, 2913.49, 2919.12, 2919.22, 2919.24, 2919.25, 2921.11, 2921.13, 2923.01, 2923.12, 2923.13, 2923.161, 2925.02, 2925.03, 2925.04, 2925.05, 2925.06, or 3716.11 of the Revised Code, felonious sexual penetration in violation of former section 2907.12 of the Revised Code, a violation of section 2905.04 of the Revised Code as it existed prior to July 1, 1996, a violation of section 2919.23 of the Revised Code that would have been a violation of section 2905.04 of the Revised Code as it existed prior to July 1, 1996, had the violation been committed prior to that date, a violation of section 2925.11 of the Revised Code that is not a minor drug possession offense, a violation of section 2923.02 or 2923.03 of the Revised Code that relates to a crime specified in this division, or a second violation of section 4511.19 of the Revised Code within five years of the date of application for licensure or certification.

(b) A violation of an existing or former law of this state, any other state, or the United States that is substantially equivalent to any of the offenses or violations described in division (A)(9)(a) of this section.

(10) Upon receipt of a request pursuant to section 5153.111 of the Revised Code, a completed form prescribed pursuant to division (C)(1) of this section, and a set of fingerprint impressions obtained in the manner described in division (C)(2) of this section, the superintendent of the bureau of criminal identification and investigation shall conduct a criminal records check in the manner described in division (B) of this section to determine whether any information exists that indicates that the person who is the subject of the request previously has been convicted of or pleaded guilty to any of the following:

(a) A violation of section 2903.01, 2903.02, 2903.03, 2903.04, 2903.11, 2903.12, 2903.13, 2903.16, 2903.21, 2903.34, 2905.01, 2905.02, 2905.05, 2907.02, 2907.03,

2907.04, 2907.05, 2907.06, 2907.07, 2907.08, 2907.09, 2907.21, 2907.22, 2907.23, 2907.25, 2907.31, 2907.32, 2907.321, 2907.322, 2907.323, 2909.02, 2909.03, 2911.01, 2911.02, 2911.11, 2911.12, 2919.12, 2919.22, 2919.24, 2919.25, 2923.12, 2923.13, 2923.161, 2925.02, 2925.03, 2925.04, 2925.05, 2925.06, or 3716.11 of the Revised Code, felonious sexual penetration in violation of former section 2907.12 of the Revised Code, a violation of section 2905.04 of the Revised Code as it existed prior to July 1, 1996, a violation of section 2919.23 of the Revised Code that would have been a violation of section 2905.04 of the Revised Code as it existed prior to July 1, 1996, had the violation been committed prior to that date, or a violation of section 2925.11 of the Revised Code that is not a minor drug possession offense;

(b) A violation of an existing or former law of this state, any other state, or the United States that is substantially equivalent to any of the offenses listed in division (A)(10)(a) of this section.

(11) On receipt of a request for a criminal records check from an individual pursuant to section 4749.03 or 4749.06 of the Revised Code, accompanied by a completed copy of the form prescribed in division (C)(1) of this section and a set of fingerprint impressions obtained in a manner described in division (C)(2) of this section, the superintendent of the bureau of criminal identification and investigation shall conduct a criminal records check in the manner described in division (B) of this section to determine whether any information exists indicating that the person who is the subject of the request has been convicted of or pleaded guilty to a felony in this state or in any other state. If the individual indicates that a firearm will be carried in the course of business, the superintendent shall require information from the federal bureau of investigation as described in division (B)(2) of this section. The superintendent shall report the findings of the criminal records check and any information the federal bureau of investigation provides to the director of public safety.

(12) On receipt of a request pursuant to section 1321.37, 1321.53, 1321.531, 1322.03, 1322.031, or 4763.05 of the Revised Code, a completed form prescribed pursuant to division (C)(1) of this section, and a set of fingerprint impressions obtained in the manner described in division (C)(2) of this section, the superintendent of the bureau of criminal identification and investigation shall conduct a criminal records check with respect to any person who has applied for a license, permit, or certification from the department of commerce or a division in the department. The superintendent shall conduct the criminal records check in the manner described in division (B) of this section to determine whether any information exists that indicates that the person who is the subject of the request previously has been convicted of or pleaded guilty to any of the following: a violation of section 2913.02, 2913.11, 2913.31, 2913.51, or 2925.03 of the Revised Code; any other criminal offense involving theft, receiving stolen property, embezzlement, forgery, fraud, passing bad checks, money laundering, or drug trafficking, or any criminal offense involving money or securities, as set forth in Chapters 2909., 2911., 2913., 2915., 2921., 2923., and 2925. of the Revised Code; or any existing or former law of this state, any other state, or the United States that is substantially equivalent to those offenses.

(13) On receipt of a request for a criminal records check from the treasurer of state under section 113.041 of the Revised Code or from an individual under section 4701.08, 4715.101, 4717.061, 4725.121, 4725.501, 4729.071, 4730.101, 4730.14, 4730.28, 4731.081, 4731.15, 4731.171, 4731.222, 4731.281, 4731.296, 4731.531, 4732.091, 4734.202, 4740.061, 4741.10, 4755.70, 4757.101, 4759.061, 4760.032, 4760.06, 4761.051, 4762.031, 4762.06, or 4779.091 of the Revised Code, accompanied by a completed form prescribed under division (C)(1) of this section and a set of fingerprint impressions obtained in the manner described in division (C)(2) of this section, the superintendent of the bureau of criminal identification and investigation shall conduct a criminal records check in the manner described in division (B) of this section to determine whether any information exists that indicates that the person who is the subject of the request has been convicted of or pleaded guilty to any criminal offense in this state or any other state. The superintendent shall send the results of a check requested under section 113.041 of the Revised Code to the treasurer of state and shall send the results of a check requested under any of the other listed sections to the licensing board specified by the individual in the request.

(14) On receipt of a request pursuant to section 1121.23, 1155.03, 1163.05, 1315.141, 1733.47, or 1761.26 of the Revised Code, a completed form prescribed pursuant to division (C)(1) of this section, and a set of fingerprint impressions obtained in the manner described in division (C)(2) of this section, the superintendent of the bureau of criminal identification and investigation shall conduct a criminal records check in the manner described in division (B) of this section to determine whether any information exists that indicates that the person who is the subject of the request previously has been convicted of or pleaded guilty to any criminal offense under any existing or former law of this state, any other state, or the United States.

(15) On receipt of a request for a criminal records check from an appointing or licensing authority under section 3772.07 of the Revised Code, a completed form prescribed under division (C)(1) of this section, and a set of fingerprint impressions obtained in the manner prescribed in division (C)(2) of this section, the superintendent of the bureau of criminal identification and investigation shall conduct a criminal records check in the manner described in division (B) of this section to determine whether any information exists that indicates that the person who is the subject of the request previously has been convicted of or pleaded guilty or no contest to any offense under any existing or former law of this state, any other state, or the United States that is a disqualifying offense as defined in section 3772.07 of the Revised Code or substantially equivalent to such an offense.

(16) Not later than thirty days after the date the superintendent receives a request of a type described in division (A)(1), (2), (3), (4), (5), (6), (7), (8), (9), (10), (11), (12), (14), or (15) of this section, the completed form, and the fingerprint impressions, the superintendent shall send the person, board, or entity that made the request any information, other than information the dissemination of which is prohibited by federal law, the superintendent determines exists with respect to the person who is the subject of the request that indicates that the person previously has been convicted of or pleaded guilty to any offense listed or described in division (A)(1), (2), (3), (4), (5), (6), (7), (8), (9), (10), (11), (12), (14), or (15) of this section, as appropriate. The superintendent shall send the person, board, or entity that made the request a copy of the list of offenses specified in division (A)(1), (2), (3), (4), (5), (6), (7), (8), (9), (10), (11), (12), (14), or (15) of this

section, as appropriate. If the request was made under section 3701.881 of the Revised Code with regard to an applicant who may be both responsible for the care, custody, or control of a child and involved in providing direct care to an older adult, the superintendent shall provide a list of the offenses specified in divisions (A)(4) and (6) of this section.

Not later than thirty days after the superintendent receives a request for a criminal records check pursuant to section 113.041 of the Revised Code, the completed form, and the fingerprint impressions, the superintendent shall send the treasurer of state any information, other than information the dissemination of which is prohibited by federal law, the superintendent determines exist with respect to the person who is the subject of the request that indicates that the person previously has been convicted of or pleaded guilty to any criminal offense in this state or any other state.

(B) The superintendent shall conduct any criminal records check requested under section 113.041, 121.08, 173.27, 173.394, 1121.23, 1155.03, 1163.05, 1315.141, 1321.53, 1321.531, 1322.03, 1322.031, 1733.47, 1761.26, 2151.86, 3301.32, 3301.541, 3319.39, 3701.881, 3712.09, 3721.121, 3772.07, 4701.08, 4715.101, 4717.061, 4725.121, 4725.501, 4729.071, 4730.101, 4730.14, 4730.28, 4731.081, 4731.15, 4731.171, 4731.222, 4731.281, 4731.296, 4731.531, 4732.091, 4734.202, 4740.061, 4741.10, 4749.03, 4749.06, 4755.70, 4757.101, 4759.061, 4760.032, 4760.06, 4761.051, 4762.031, 4762.06, 4763.05, 4779.091, 5104.012, 5104.013, 5111.032, 5111.033, 5111.034, 5119.693, 5119.85, 5123.081, 5126.28, 5126.281, or 5153.111 of the Revised Code as follows:

(1) The superintendent shall review or cause to be reviewed any relevant information gathered and compiled by the bureau under division (A) of section 109.57 of the Revised Code that relates to the person who is the subject of the request, including, if the criminal records check was requested under section 113.041, 121.08, 173.27, 173.394, 1121.23, 1155.03, 1163.05, 1315.141, 1321.37, 1321.53, 1321.531, 1322.03, 1322.031, 1733.47, 1761.26, 2151.86, 3301.32, 3301.541, 3319.39, 3701.881, 3712.09, 3721.121, 3772.07, 4749.03, 4749.06, 4763.05, 5104.012, 5104.013, 5111.032, 5111.033, 5111.034, 5119.693, 5119.85, 5123.081, 5126.28, 5126.281, or 5153.111 of the Revised Code, any relevant information contained in records that have been sealed under section 2953.32 of the Revised Code;

(2) If the request received by the superintendent asks for information from the federal bureau of investigation, the superintendent shall request from the federal bureau of investigation any information it has with respect to the person who is the subject of the request, including fingerprint-based checks of national crime information databases as described in 42 U.S.C. 671 if the request is made pursuant to section 2151.86, 5104.012, or 5104.013 of the Revised Code or if any other Revised Code section requires fingerprint-based checks of that nature, and shall review or cause to be reviewed any information the superintendent receives from that bureau. If a request under section 3319.39 of the Revised Code asks only for information from the federal bureau of investigation, the superintendent shall not conduct the review prescribed by division (B)(1) of this section.

(3) The superintendent or the superintendent's designee may request criminal history records from other states or the federal government pursuant to the national crime prevention and privacy compact set forth in section 109.571 of the Revised Code.

(C)(1) The superintendent shall prescribe a form to obtain the information necessary to conduct a criminal records check from any person for whom a criminal records check is requested under section 113.041 of the Revised Code or required by section 121.08, 173.27, 173.394, 1121.23, 1155.03, 1163.05, 1315.141, 1321.53, 1321.531, 1322.03, 1322.031, 1733.47, 1761.26, 2151.86, 3301.32, 3301.541, 3319.39, 3701.881, 3712.09, 3721.121, 3772.07, 4701.08, 4715.101, 4717.061, 4725.121, 4725.501, 4729.071, 4730.101, 4730.14, 4730.28, 4731.081, 4731.15, 4731.171, 4731.222, 4731.281, 4731.296, 4731.531, 4732.091, 4734.202, 4740.061, 4741.10, 4749.03, 4749.06, 4755.70, 4757.101, 4759.061, 4760.032, 4760.06, 4761.051, 4762.031, 4762.06, 4763.05, 4779.091, 5104.012, 5104.013, 5111.032, 5111.033, 5111.034, 5119.693, 5119.85, 5123.081, 5126.28, 5126.281, or 5153.111 of the Revised Code. The form that the superintendent prescribes pursuant to this division may be in a tangible format, in an electronic format, or in both tangible and electronic formats.

(2) The superintendent shall prescribe standard impression sheets to obtain the fingerprint impressions of any person for whom a criminal records check is requested under section 113.041 of the Revised Code or required by section 121.08, 173.27, 173.394, 1121.23, 1155.03, 1163.05, 1315.141, 1321.53, 1321.531, 1322.03, 1322.031, 1733.47, 1761.26, 2151.86, 3301.32, 3301.541, 3319.39, 3701.881, 3712.09, 3721.121, 3772.07, 4701.08, 4715.101, 4717.061, 4725.121, 4725.501, 4729.071, 4730.101, 4730.14, 4730.28, 4731.081, 4731.15, 4731.171, 4731.222, 4731.281, 4731.296, 4731.531, 4732.091, 4734.202, 4740.061, 4741.10, 4749.03, 4749.06, 4755.70, 4757.101, 4759.061, 4760.032, 4760.06, 4761.051, 4762.031, 4762.06, 4763.05, 4779.091, 5104.012, 5104.013, 5111.032, 5111.033, 5111.034, 5119.693, 5119.85, 5123.081, 5126.28, 5126.281, or 5153.111 of the Revised Code. Any person for whom a records check is requested under or required by any of those sections shall obtain the fingerprint impressions at a county sheriff's office, municipal police department, or any other entity with the ability to make fingerprint impressions on the standard impression sheets prescribed by the superintendent. The office, department, or entity may charge the person a reasonable fee for making the impressions. The standard impression sheets the superintendent prescribes pursuant to this division may be in a tangible format, in an electronic format, or in both tangible and electronic formats.

(3) Subject to division (D) of this section, the superintendent shall prescribe and charge a reasonable fee for providing a criminal records check requested under section 113.041, 121.08, 173.27, 173.394, 1121.23, 1155.03, 1163.05, 1315.141, 1321.53, 1321.531, 1322.03, 1322.031, 1733.47, 1761.26, 2151.86, 3301.32, 3301.541, 3319.39, 3701.881, 3712.09, 3721.121, 3772.07, 4701.08, 4715.101, 4717.061, 4725.121, 4725.501, 4729.071, 4730.101, 4730.14, 4730.28, 4731.081, 4731.15, 4731.171, 4731.222, 4731.281, 4731.296, 4731.531, 4732.091, 4734.202, 4740.061, 4741.10, 4749.03, 4749.06, 4755.70, 4757.101, 4759.061, 4760.032, 4760.06, 4761.051, 4762.031, 4762.06, 4763.05, 4779.091, 5104.012, 5104.013, 5111.032, 5111.033, 5111.034, 5119.693, 5119.85, 5123.081, 5126.28, 5126.281, or 5153.111 of the Revised Code. The person making a criminal records request under any of those sections shall pay the fee prescribed pursuant to this division. A person making a request under

section 3701.881 of the Revised Code for a criminal records check for an applicant who may be both responsible for the care, custody, or control of a child and involved in providing direct care to an older adult shall pay one fee for the request. In the case of a request under section 1121.23, 1155.03, 1163.05, 1315.141, 1733.47, 1761.26, or 5111.032 of the Revised Code, the fee shall be paid in the manner specified in that section.

(4) The superintendent of the bureau of criminal identification and investigation may prescribe methods of forwarding fingerprint impressions and information necessary to conduct a criminal records check, which methods shall include, but not be limited to, an electronic method.

(D) A determination whether any information exists that indicates that a person previously has been convicted of or pleaded guilty to any offense listed or described in division (A)(1)(a) or (b), (A)(2)(a) or (b), (A)(3)(a) or (b), (A)(4)(a) or (b), (A)(5)(a) or (b), (A)(6)(a) or (b), (A)(7), (A)(8)(a) or (b), (A)(9)(a) or (b), (A)(10)(a) or (b), (A)(12), (A)(14), or (A)(15) of this section, or that indicates that a person previously has been convicted of or pleaded guilty to any criminal offense in this state or any other state regarding a criminal records check of a type described in division (A)(13) of this section, and that is made by the superintendent with respect to information considered in a criminal records check in accordance with this section is valid for the person who is the subject of the criminal records check for a period of one year from the date upon which the superintendent makes the determination. During the period in which the determination in regard to a person is valid, if another request under this section is made for a criminal records check for that person, the superintendent shall provide the information that is the basis for the superintendent's initial determination at a lower fee than the fee prescribed for the initial criminal records check.

(E) When the superintendent receives a request for information from a registered private provider, the superintendent shall proceed as if the request was received from a school district board of education under section 3319.39 of the Revised Code. The superintendent shall apply division (A)(7) of this section to any such request for an applicant who is a teacher.

(F) As used in this section:

(1) "Criminal records check" means any criminal records check conducted by the superintendent of the bureau of criminal identification and investigation in accordance with division (B) of this section.

(2) "Minor drug possession offense" has the same meaning as in section 2925.01 of the Revised Code.

(3) "Older adult" means a person age sixty or older.

(4) "OVI or OVUAC violation" means a violation of section 4511.19 of the Revised Code or a violation of an existing or former law of this state, any other state, or the United States that is substantially equivalent to section 4511.19 of the Revised Code.

(5) "Registered private provider" means a nonpublic school or entity registered with the superintendent of public instruction under section 3310.41 of the Revised Code to participate in the autism scholarship program or section 3310.58 of the Revised Code to participate in the Jon Peterson special needs scholarship program.

**HISTORY: 145 v S 38 (Eff 10-29-93); 145 v H 694 (Eff 11-11-94); 146 v S 2 (Eff 7-1-96); 146 v S 269 (Eff 7-1-96); 146 v H 445 (Eff 9-3-96); 146 v S 160 (Eff 1-27-97); 147 v S 96 (Eff 6-11-97); 148 v H 538 (Eff 9-22-2000); 148 v H 448. Eff 10-5-2000; 150 v H 95, § 1, eff. 9-26-03; 150 v S 178, § 1, eff. 1-30-04; 150 v S 53, § 1, eff. 4-7-04; 150 v H 306, § 1, eff. 7-23-04; 150 v H 117, § 1, eff. 9-3-04; 150 v H 11, § 1, eff. 5-18-05; 151 v H 68, § 101.01, eff. 7-1-05; 151 v H 530, § 101.01, eff. 3-30-06; 151 v S 238, § 1, eff. 9-21-06; 151 v S 185, § 1, eff. 1-1-07; 152 v H 119, § 101.01, eff. 9-29-07; 152 v H 104, § 1, eff. 3-24-08; 152 v S 163, § 1, eff. 8-14-08; 152 v H 545, § 1, eff. 9-1-08; 152 v S 247, § 1, eff. 9-11-08; 152 v H 195, § 1, eff. 9-30-08; 153 v S 79, § 1, eff. 10-6-09; 153 v H 1, § 101.01, eff. 10-16-09, 1-1-10; 153 v H 519, § 1, eff. 9-10-10; 2011 HB 153, § 101.01, eff. July 1, 2011.**

The provisions of § 6 of 153 v H 519 read in part as follows:

SECTION 6. The General Assembly, applying the principle stated in division (B) of section 1.52 of the Revised Code that amendments are to be harmonized if reasonably capable of simultaneous operation, finds that the following sections, presented in this act as composites of the sections as amended by the acts indicated, are the resulting versions of the sections in effect before the effective date of the sections as presented in this act:

Section 109.572 of the Revised Code as amended by both Am. Sub. H.B. 1 and Sub. S.B. 79 of the 128th General Assembly.

° ° °

The effective date is set by § 812.50 of 153 v H 1.

The provisions of 815.10 of 153 v H 1 read as follows:

SECTION 815.10. The General Assembly, applying the principle stated in division (B) of section 1.52 of the Revised Code that amendments are to be harmonized if reasonably capable of simultaneous operation, finds that the following sections, presented in this act as composites of the sections as amended by the acts indicated, are the resulting versions of the sections in effect prior to the effective date of the sections as presented in this act:

° ° °

Section 109.572 of the Revised Code as amended by Sub. H.B. 195, Sub. H.B. 545, and Sub. S.B. 247, all of the 127th General Assembly.

° ° °

The provisions of § 15 of 153 v S 79 read as follows:

SECTION 15. The General Assembly, applying the principle stated in division (B) of section 1.52 of the Revised Code that amendments are to be harmonized if reasonably capable of simultaneous operation, finds that the following sections, presented in this act as composites of the sections as amended by the acts indicated, are the resulting versions of the sections in effect prior to the effective date of the sections as presented in this act:

° ° °

Section 109.572 of the Revised Code as amended by Sub. H.B. 195, Sub. H.B. 545, and Sub. S.B. 247, all of the 127th General Assembly.

° ° °

The provisions of § 7 of 152 v S 163 read as follows:

SECTION 7. Section 109.572 of the Revised Code is presented in this act as a composite of the section as amended by both Am. Sub. S.B. 185 and Am. Sub. S.B. 238 of the 126th General Assembly. Section 2151.86 of the Revised Code is presented in this act as a composite of the section as amended by both Am. Sub. H.B. 106 and Am. Sub. H.B. 117 of the 125th General Assembly. The General Assembly, applying the principle stated in division (B) of section 1.52 of the Revised Code that amendments are to be harmonized if reasonably capable of simultaneous operation, finds that the composites are the resulting versions of the sections in effect prior to the effective date of the sections as presented in this act.

The provisions of § 3 of 152 v H 104 read as follows:

SECTION 3. Section 109.572 of the Revised Code is presented in this act as a composite of the section as amended by both Am. Sub. S.B. 185 and Am. Sub. S.B. 238 of the 126th General Assembly. The General Assembly, applying the principle stated in division (B) of section 1.52 of the Revised Code that amendments are to be harmonized if reasonably capable of simultaneous operation, finds that the composite is the resulting version of the section in effect prior to the effective date of the section as presented in this act.

The effective date is set by § 812.03 of 152 v H 119.

The provisions of § 824.03 of 152 v H 119 read in part as follows:

SECTION 824.03. The General Assembly, applying the principle stated in division (B) of section 1.52 of the Revised Code that amendments are to be harmonized if reasonably capable of simultaneous operation, finds that the following sections, presented in this act as composites of the sections as amended by the acts indicated, are the resulting versions of the sections in effect prior to the effective date of the sections as presented in this act:

Section 109.572 of the Revised Code as amended by both Am. Sub. S.B. 185 and Am. Sub. S.B. 238 of the 126th General Assembly.

* * *

The finding in this section takes effect at the same time as the section referenced in the finding takes effect.

The effective date is set by § 812.03 of 151 v H 530.

The provisions of § 831.03 of 151 v H 530 read in part as follows:

SECTION 831.03. The General Assembly, applying the principle stated in division (B) of section 1.52 of the Revised Code that amendments are to be harmonized if reasonably capable of simultaneous operation, finds that the following sections, presented in this act as composites of the sections as amended by the acts indicated, are the resulting versions of the sections in effect prior to the effective date of the sections as presented in this act:

Section 109.572 of the Revised Code as amended by both Am. Sub. H.B. 11 and Am. Sub. H.B. 117 of the 125th General Assembly and Am. Sub. H.B. 68 of the 126th General Assembly.

* * *

The finding in this section takes effect at the same time as the section referenced in the finding takes effect.

The effective date is set by § 612.09 of 151 v H 68.

The provisions of § 618.03 of 151 v H 68 read as follows:

SECTION 618.03. The General Assembly, applying the principle stated in division (B) of section 1.52 of the Revised Code that amendments are to be harmonized if reasonably capable of simultaneous operation, finds that the following sections, presented in this act as composites of the sections as amended by the acts indicated, are the resulting versions of the sections in effect prior to the effective date of the sections as presented in this act:

Section 109.572 of the Revised Code as amended by Am. Sub. H.B. 117, Am. Sub. H.B. 306, Am. Sub. S.B. 53, and Am. S.B. 178, all of the 125th General Assembly.

The provisions of § 4 of H.B. 11 (150 v —) read as follows:

SECTION 4. Section 109.572 of the Revised Code is presented in this act as a composite of the section as amended by Am. Sub. H.B. 117, Am. Sub. H.B. 306, Am. Sub. S.B. 53 and Am. S.B. 178 of the 125th General Assembly. * * * The General Assembly, applying the principle stated in division (B) of section 1.52 of the Revised Code that amendments are to be harmonized if reasonably capable of simultaneous operation, finds that the composites are the resulting versions of the sections in effect prior to the effective date of the sections as presented in this act.

The provisions of § 214 of H.B. 95 (150 v —) read as follows:

SECTION 214. * * * Section 109.572 of the Revised Code is presented in this act as a composite of the section as amended by both Sub. H.B. 448 and Sub. H.B. 538 of the 123rd General Assembly. The General Assembly, applying the principle stated in division (B) of section 1.52 of the Revised Code that amendments are to be harmonized if reasonably capable of simultaneous operation, finds that the composite is the resulting version of the section in effect prior to the effective date of the section as presented in this act.

**Publisher's Note:**

The insertion of subsections (E) and (F)(4) of RC § 109.572 by 152 v H 119 was disapproved by the Governor.

## § 109.5721 Retained applicant fingerprint database.

(A) As used in this section:

(1) "Employment" includes volunteer service.

(2) "Licensure" means the authorization, evidenced by a license, certificate, registration, permit, or other authority that is issued or conferred by a public office, to engage in a profession, occupation, or occupational activity, to be a foster caregiver, or to have control of and operate certain specific equipment, machinery, or premises over which a public office has jurisdiction.

(3) "Participating public office" means a public office that requires a fingerprint background check as a condition of employment with, licensure by, or approval for adoption by the public office and that elects to receive notice under division (C) of this section in accordance with rules adopted by the attorney general.

(4) "Public office" has the same meaning as in section 117.01 of the Revised Code.

(B) Within six months after August 15, 2007, the superintendent of the bureau of criminal identification and investigation shall establish and maintain a database of fingerprints of individuals on whom the bureau has conducted criminal records checks for the purpose of determining eligibility for employment with, licensure by, or approval for adoption by a public office. The superintendent shall maintain the database separate and apart from other records maintained by the bureau. The database shall be known as the retained applicant fingerprint database.

(C) When the superintendent receives information that an individual whose name is in the retained applicant fingerprint database has been arrested for, convicted of, or pleaded guilty to any offense, the superintendent shall promptly notify any participating public office that employs, licensed, or approved the individual of the arrest, conviction, or guilty plea. The public office that receives the notification and its employees and officers shall use the information contained in the notification solely to determine the individual's eligibility for continued employment with the public office, to retain licensure issued by the public office, or to be approved for adoption by the public office. The public office and its employees and officers shall not disclose that information to any person for any other purpose.

(D) If an individual has submitted fingerprint impressions for employment with, licensure by, or approval for adoption by a participating public office and seeks employment with, licensure by, or approval for adoption by another participating public office, the other public office shall reprint the individual. If an individual has been reprinted, the superintendent shall update that individual's information accordingly.

(E) The bureau of criminal identification and investigation and the participating public office shall use information contained in the retained applicant fingerprint database and in the notice described in division (C) of this section for the purpose of employment with, licensure by, or approval for adoption by the participating public office. This information is otherwise confidential and not a public record under section 149.43 of the Revised Code.

(F) The attorney general shall adopt rules in accordance with Chapter 119. of the Revised Code governing the operation and maintenance of the database. The rules shall provide for, but not be limited to, both of the following:

(1) The expungement or sealing of records of individuals who are deceased or who are no longer employed, granted licensure, or approved for adoption by the public office that required submission of the individual's fingerprints;

(2) The terms under which a public office may elect to receive notification under division (C) of this section, including payment of any reasonable fee that may be charged for the purpose.

(G) No public office or employee of a public office shall be considered negligent in a civil action solely because the public office did not elect to be a participating public office.

(H)(1) No person shall knowingly use information contained in or received from the retained applicant fingerprint database for purposes not authorized by this section.

(2) No person shall knowingly use information contained in or received from the retained applicant fingerprint database with the intent to harass or intimidate another person.

(3) Whoever violates division (H)(1) or (H)(2) of this section is guilty of unlawful use of retained applicant fingerprint database records. A violation of division (H)(1) of this section is a misdemeanor of the fourth degree. A violation of division (H)(2) of this section is a misdemeanor of the first degree.

**HISTORY: 152 v S 97, § 1, eff. 8-15-07; 152 v S 163, § 1, eff. 8-14-08.**

The effective date is set by § 3 of 152 v S 97.

## § 109.573 DNA laboratory and database; unidentified person database; relatives of missing persons database.

(A) As used in this section:

(1) "DNA" means human deoxyribonucleic acid.

(2) "DNA analysis" means a laboratory analysis of a DNA specimen to identify DNA characteristics and to create a DNA record.

(3) "DNA database" means a collection of DNA records from forensic casework or from crime scenes, specimens from anonymous and unidentified sources, and records collected pursuant to sections 2152.74 and 2901.07 of the Revised Code and a population statistics database for determining the frequency of occurrence of characteristics in DNA records.

(4) "DNA record" means the objective result of a DNA analysis of a DNA specimen, including representations of DNA fragment lengths, digital images of autoradiographs, discrete allele assignment numbers, and other DNA specimen characteristics that aid in establishing the identity of an individual.

(5) "DNA specimen" includes human blood cells or physiological tissues or body fluids.

(6) "Unidentified person database" means a collection of DNA records, and, on and after May 21, 1998, of fingerprint and photograph records, of unidentified human corpses, human remains, or living individuals.

(7) "Relatives of missing persons database" means a collection of DNA records of persons related by consanguinity to a missing person.

(8) "Law enforcement agency" means a police department, the office of a sheriff, the state highway patrol, a county prosecuting attorney, or a federal, state, or local governmental body that enforces criminal laws and that has employees who have a statutory power of arrest.

(9) "Administration of criminal justice" means the performance of detection, apprehension, detention, pretrial release, post-trial release, prosecution, adjudication, correctional supervision, or rehabilitation of accused persons or criminal offenders. "Administration of criminal justice" also includes criminal identification activities and the collection, storage, and dissemination of criminal history record information.

(B)(1) The superintendent of the bureau of criminal identification and investigation may do all of the following:

(a) Establish and maintain a state DNA laboratory to perform DNA analyses of DNA specimens;

(b) Establish and maintain a DNA database;

(c) Establish and maintain an unidentified person database to aid in the establishment of the identity of unknown human corpses, human remains, or living individuals;

(d) Establish and maintain a relatives of missing persons database for comparison with the unidentified person database to aid in the establishment of the identity of unknown human corpses, human remains, and living individuals.

(2) If the bureau of criminal identification and investigation establishes and maintains a DNA laboratory and a DNA database, the bureau may use or disclose information regarding DNA records for the following purposes:

(a) The bureau may disclose information to a law enforcement agency for the administration of criminal justice.

(b) The bureau shall disclose pursuant to a court order issued under section 3111.09 of the Revised Code any information necessary to determine the existence of a parent and child relationship in an action brought under sections 3111.01 to 3111.18 of the Revised Code.

(c) The bureau may use or disclose information from the population statistics database, for identification research and protocol development, or for quality control purposes.

(3) If the bureau of criminal identification and investigation establishes and maintains a relatives of missing persons database, all of the following apply:

(a) If a person has disappeared and has been continuously absent from the person's place of last domicile for a thirty-day or longer period of time without being heard from during the period, persons related by consanguinity to the missing person may submit to the bureau a DNA specimen, the bureau may include the DNA record of the specimen in the relatives of missing persons database, and, if the bureau does not include the DNA record of the specimen in the relatives of missing persons database, the bureau shall retain the DNA record for future reference and inclusion as appropriate in that database.

(b) The bureau shall not charge a fee for the submission of a DNA specimen pursuant to division (B)(3)(a) of this section.

(c) If the DNA specimen submitted pursuant to division (B)(3)(a) of this section is collected by withdrawing blood from the person or a similarly invasive procedure, a physician, registered nurse, licensed practical nurse, duly licensed clinical laboratory technician, or other qualified medical practitioner shall conduct the collection procedure for the DNA specimen submitted pursuant to division (B)(3)(a) of this section and shall collect the DNA specimen in a medically approved manner. If the DNA specimen is collected by swabbing for buccal cells or a similarly noninvasive procedure, division (B)(3)(c) of this section does not require that the DNA specimen be collected by a qualified medical practitioner of that nature. No later than fifteen days after the date of the collection of the DNA specimen, the person conducting the DNA specimen collection procedure shall cause the DNA specimen to be forwarded to the bureau of criminal identification and investigation in accordance with procedures established by the superintendent of the bureau under division (H) of this section. The bureau may provide the specimen vials, mailing tubes, labels, postage, and instruction needed for the collection and forwarding of the DNA specimen to the bureau.

(d) The superintendent, in the superintendent's discretion, may compare DNA records in the relatives of missing persons database with the DNA records in the unidentified person database.

(4) If the bureau of criminal identification and investigation establishes and maintains an unidentified person database and if the superintendent of the bureau identifies a matching DNA record for the DNA record of a person or deceased person whose DNA record is contained in the unidentified person database, the superintendent shall inform the coroner who submitted or the law enforcement agency that submitted the DNA specimen to the bureau of the match and, if possible, of the identity of the unidentified person.

(5) The bureau of criminal identification and investigation may enter into a contract with a qualified public or private laboratory to perform DNA analyses, DNA specimen maintenance, preservation, and storage, DNA record keeping, and other duties required of the bureau under this section. A public or private laboratory under contract with the bureau shall follow quality assurance and privacy requirements established by the superintendent of the bureau.

(C) The superintendent of the bureau of criminal identification and investigation shall establish procedures for entering into the DNA database the DNA records submitted pursuant to sections 2152.74 and 2901.07 of the Revised Code and for determining an order of priority for entry of the DNA records based on the types of offenses committed by the persons whose records are submitted and the available resources of the bureau.

(D) When a DNA record is derived from a DNA specimen provided pursuant to section 2152.74 or 2901.07 of the Revised Code, the bureau of criminal identification and investigation shall attach to the DNA record personal identification information that identifies the person from whom the DNA specimen was taken. The personal identification information may include the subject person's fingerprints and any other information the bureau determines necessary. The DNA record and personal identification information attached to it shall be used only for the purpose of personal identification or for a purpose specified in this section.

(E) DNA records, DNA specimens, fingerprints, and photographs that the bureau of criminal identification and investigation receives pursuant to this section and sections 313.08, 2152.74, and 2901.07 of the Revised Code and personal identification information attached to a DNA record are not public records under section 149.43 of the Revised Code.

(F) The bureau of criminal identification and investigation may charge a reasonable fee for providing information pursuant to this section to any law enforcement agency located in another state.

(G)(1) No person who because of the person's employment or official position has access to a DNA specimen, a DNA record, or other information contained in the DNA database that identifies an individual shall knowingly disclose that specimen, record, or information to any person or agency not entitled to receive it or otherwise shall misuse that specimen, record, or information.

(2) No person without authorization or privilege to obtain information contained in the DNA database that identifies an individual person shall purposely obtain that information.

(H) The superintendent of the bureau of criminal identification and investigation shall establish procedures for all of the following:

(1) The forwarding to the bureau of DNA specimens collected pursuant to division (H) of this section and sections 313.08, 2152.74, and 2901.07 of the Revised Code and of fingerprints and photographs collected pursuant to section 313.08 of the Revised Code;

(2) The collection, maintenance, preservation, and analysis of DNA specimens;

(3) The creation, maintenance, and operation of the DNA database;

(4) The use and dissemination of information from the DNA database;

(5) The creation, maintenance, and operation of the unidentified person database;

(6) The use and dissemination of information from the unidentified person database;

(7) The creation, maintenance, and operation of the relatives of missing persons database;

(8) The use and dissemination of information from the relatives of missing persons database;

(9) The verification of entities requesting DNA records and other DNA information from the bureau and the authority of the entity to receive the information;

(10) The operation of the bureau and responsibilities of employees of the bureau with respect to the activities described in this section.

(I) In conducting DNA analyses of DNA specimens, the state DNA laboratory and any laboratory with which the bureau has entered into a contract pursuant to division (B)(5) of this section shall give DNA analyses of DNA specimens that relate to ongoing criminal investigations or prosecutions priority over DNA analyses of DNA specimens that relate to applications made pursuant to section 2953.73 of the Revised Code.

(J) The attorney general may develop procedures for entering into the national DNA index system the DNA records submitted pursuant to division (B)(1) of section 2901.07 of the Revised Code.

**HISTORY: 146 v H 5 (Eff 8-30-95); 146 v H 124 (Eff 3-31-97); 147 v S 140 (Eff 5-21-98); 148 v S 180 (Eff 3-22-2001); 148 v S 179, § 3 (Eff 1-1-2002); 149 v H 427. Eff 8-29-2002; 150 v S 11, § 1, eff. 10-29-03; 150 v H 525, § 1, eff. 5-18-05; 153 v S 77, § 1, eff. 7-6-10.**

## [VOLUNTEERS HAVING UNSUPERVISED ACCESS TO CHILDREN]

## § 109.574 Definitions.

As used in sections 109.574 [109.57.4] to 109.577 [109.57.7] of the Revised Code:

(A) "Organization or entity" means a religious, charitable, scientific, educational, athletic, or service institution or organization or local government entity that provides care, treatment, education, training, instruction, supervision, or recreation to children.

(B) "Unsupervised access to a child" means that the person in question has access to a child and that either of the following applies:

(1) No other person eighteen years of age or older is present in the same room with the child.

(2) If outdoors, no other person eighteen years of age or older is within a thirty-yard radius of the child or has visual contact with the child.

HISTORY: 148 v S 187. Eff 3-22-2001.

## § 109.575 Information to be provided to volunteers having unsupervised access to child on regular basis.

At the time of a person's initial application to an organization or entity to be a volunteer in a position in which the person on a regular basis will have unsupervised access to a child, the organization or entity shall inform the person that, at any time, the person might be required to provide a set of impressions of the person's fingerprints and a criminal records check might be conducted with respect to the person. Not later than thirty days after the effective date of this section, each organization or entity shall notify each current volunteer who is in a position in which the person on a regular basis has unsupervised access to a child that, at any time, the volunteer might be required to provide a set of impressions of the volunteer's fingerprints and a criminal records check might be conducted with respect to the volunteer.

HISTORY: 148 v S 187. Eff 3-22-2001.

## § 109.576 Notice to parent or guardian of volunteer's conviction.

(A) If a person has applied to an organization or entity to be a volunteer in a position in which the person on a regular basis has unsupervised access to a child, if the organization or entity subjects the person to a criminal records check, if the report of the results of the criminal records check indicates that the person has been convicted of or pleaded guilty to any of the offenses described in division (A)(1) of section 109.572 [109.57.2] of the Revised Code, and if the organization or entity accepts the person as a volunteer in a position in which the person on a regular basis has unsupervised access to a child, the organization or entity shall notify the parent or guardian of each child for whom it provides services that the volunteer has been convicted of one or more of those offenses but that, nonetheless, the person will be serving the organization or entity in that position. The notification required by this division shall be in writing, and the organization or entity shall send the notice to the parent or guardian on the date the organization or entity commences providing services to the child or on the date the organization or entity decides to accept the person as a volunteer after receiving the report of the results of the criminal records check, whichever is later.

(B) If a person is serving an organization or entity as a volunteer in a position in which the person on a regular basis has unsupervised access to a child, if the organization or entity subjects the person to a criminal records check, if the report of the results of the criminal records check indicates that the person has been convicted of or pleaded guilty to any of the offenses described in division (A)(1) of section 109.572 [109.57.2] of the Revised Code, and if the organization or entity retains the person as a volunteer in the same position or in any other position in which the person on a regular basis has unsupervised access to a child, the organization or entity shall notify the parent or guardian of each child for whom it provides services that the volunteer has been convicted of one or more of those offenses but that, nonetheless, the person will be retained by the organization or entity in that position. The notification required by this division shall be in writing, and the organization or entity shall send the notice to the parent or guardian on the date the organization or entity commences providing services to the child or on the date the organization or entity decides to retain the person after receiving the report of the results of the criminal records check, whichever is later.

(C) A notification to a parent or guardian of a child that is required by division (A) or (B) of this section shall identify by name the person who is accepted or retained as a volunteer in a position in which the person on a regular basis has unsupervised access to a child, shall state the fact that the person has been convicted of or pleaded guilty to one or more of the offenses described in division (A)(1) of section 109.572 [109.57.2] of the Revised Code, but shall not identify the offense or offenses in question.

(D) Divisions (A) to (C) of this section apply regarding any criminal records check performed by the bureau of criminal identification and investigation pursuant to section 109.57, section 109.572 [109.57.2], or rules adopted under division (E) of section 109.57 of the Revised Code, any criminal records check performed in any manner by the organization or entity or any of its officers or employees, or any criminal records check performed in any manner by any person upon the request of the organization or entity or any of its officers or employees.

HISTORY: 148 v S 187. Eff 3-22-2001.

## § 109.577 Immunity where volunteer has been subjected to criminal records check.

(A) If an organization or entity uses a volunteer in a position in which the person on a regular basis has unsupervised access to a child and if the volunteer has been subjected to a criminal records check performed by the bureau of criminal identification and investigation pursuant to section 109.57, section 109.572 [109.57.2], or rules adopted under division (E) of section 109.57 of the Revised Code, the organization or entity, and its officials and employees, are immune from civil liability that might otherwise be incurred or imposed for any death or any injury or loss to person or property that is caused by any act or omission of the volunteer and that results from or is related to the volunteer having unsupervised access to a child on a regular basis. This immunity does not apply to a person, organization, or entity that has immunity from civil liability in accordance with section 9.86, 2744.02, or 2744.03 of the Revised Code for the good faith compliance, attempted compliance, or failure to comply.

(B) This section does not create a new cause of action or substantive legal right against a person, organization, or entity and does not affect any immunities from civil liability or defenses established by another section of the Revised Code or available at common law, to which a person, organization, or entity may be entitled under circumstances not covered by this section.

HISTORY: 148 v S 187. Eff 3-22-2001.

## § 109.578 Criminal records check concerning prospective firefighter or EMT.

(A) On receipt of a request pursuant to section 505.381 [505.38.1], 737.081 [737.08.1], 737.221 [737.22.1], or 4765.301 [4765.30.1] of the Revised Code, a completed form prescribed pursuant to division (C)(1) of this section, and a set of fingerprint impressions obtained in the manner described in division (C)(2) of this section, the superintendent of the bureau of criminal identification and investigation shall conduct a criminal records check in the manner described in division (B) of this section to determine whether any information exists that indicates that the person who is the subject of the request previously has been convicted of or pleaded guilty to any of the following:

(1) A felony;

(2) A violation of section 2909.03 of the Revised Code;

(3) A violation of an existing or former law of this state, any other state, or the United States that is substantially equivalent to any of the offenses listed in division (A)(1) or (2) of this section.

(B) The superintendent shall conduct any criminal records check pursuant to division (A) of this section as follows:

(1) The superintendent shall review or cause to be reviewed any relevant information gathered and compiled by the bureau under division (A) of section 109.57 of the Revised Code that relates to the person who is the subject of the request, including any relevant information contained in records that have been sealed under section 2953.32 of the Revised Code.

(2) If the request received by the superintendent asks for information from the federal bureau of investigation, the superintendent shall request from the federal bureau of investigation any information it has with respect to the person who is the subject of the request and shall review or cause to be reviewed any information the superintendent receives from that bureau.

(C)(1) The superintendent shall prescribe a form to obtain the information necessary to conduct a criminal records check from any person for whom a criminal records check is requested pursuant to section 505.381 [505.38.1], 737.081 [737.08.1], 737.221 [737.22.1], or 4765.301 [4765.30.1] of the Revised Code. The form that the superintendent prescribes pursuant to this division may be in a tangible format, in an electronic format, or in both tangible and electronic formats.

(2) The superintendent shall prescribe standard impression sheets to obtain the fingerprint impressions of any person for whom a criminal records check is requested pursuant to section 505.381 [505.38.1], 737.081 [737.08.1], 737.221 [737.22.1], or 4765.301 [4765.30.1] of the Revised Code. Any person for whom a records check is requested pursuant to any of those sections shall obtain the fingerprint impressions at a county sheriff's office, a municipal police department, or any other entity with the ability to make fingerprint impressions on the standard impression sheets prescribed by the superintendent. The office, department, or entity may charge the person a reasonable fee for making the impressions. The standard impression sheets the superintendent prescribes pursuant to this division may be in a tangible format, in an electronic format, or in both tangible and electronic formats.

(3) Subject to division (D) of this section, the superintendent shall prescribe and charge a reasonable fee for providing a criminal records check requested under section 505.381 [505.38.1], 737.081 [737.08.1], 737.221 [737.22.1], or 4765.301 [4765.30.1] of the Revised Code. The person making the criminal records request shall pay the fee prescribed pursuant to this division.

(4) The superintendent may prescribe methods of forwarding fingerprint impressions and information necessary to conduct a criminal records check. The methods shall include, but are not limited to, an electronic method.

(D) A determination whether any information exists that indicates that a person previously has been convicted of or pleaded guilty to any offense listed or described in division (A) of this section and that the superintendent made with respect to information considered in a criminal records check in accordance with this section is valid for the person who is the subject of the criminal records check for a period of one year from the date upon which the superintendent makes the determination. During the period in which the determination in regard to a person is valid, if another request under this section is made for a criminal records check for that person, the superintendent shall provide the information that is the basis for the superintendent's initial determination at a lower fee than the fee prescribed for the initial criminal records check.

(E) As used in this section, "criminal records check" means any criminal records check conducted by the superintendent of the bureau of criminal identification and investigation in accordance with division (B) of this section.

**HISTORY: 149 v S 258. Eff 4-9-2003.**

## § 109.579 Criminal records checks relating to investment of bureau of workers' compensation funds.

(A) On receipt of a request pursuant to division (B) of section 4123.444 [4123.44.4] of the Revised Code, a completed form prescribed pursuant to division (C)(1) of this section, and a set of fingerprint impressions obtained in the manner described in division (C)(2) of this section, the superintendent of the bureau of criminal identification and investigation shall conduct a criminal records check in the manner described in division (B) of this section to determine whether any information exists that indicates that the person who is the subject of the request previously has been convicted of or pleaded guilty to any criminal offense involving theft, receiving stolen property, embezzlement, forgery, fraud, passing bad checks, money laundering, drug trafficking, or any criminal offense involving money or securities, as set forth in Chapters 2909., 2911., 2913., 2915., 2921., 2923., and 2925. of the Revised Code or other law of this state, or the laws of any other state or of the United States that are substantially equivalent to those offenses.

(B) The superintendent shall conduct a criminal records check pursuant to division (A) of this section as follows:

(1) The superintendent shall review or cause to be reviewed any relevant information gathered and compiled by the bureau under division (A) of section 109.57 of the Revised Code that relates to the person who is the subject of the request, including any relevant information contained in records that have been sealed under section 2953.32 of the Revised Code.

(2) If the request received by the superintendent asks for information from the federal bureau of investigation, the superintendent shall request from the federal bureau of investigation any information it has with respect to the person who is the subject of the request. The superintendent shall review or cause to be reviewed any information that the superintendent receives from the federal bureau of investigation.

(3) The superintendent shall forward the results of a criminal records check conducted pursuant to this division to the administrator of workers' compensation.

(C)(1) The superintendent shall prescribe a form to obtain the information necessary to conduct a criminal records check from any person for whom a criminal records check is requested pursuant to division (B) of section 4123.444 [4123.44.4] of the Revised Code. The form that the superintendent prescribes pursuant to this division may be in a tangible format, in an electronic format, or in both tangible and electronic formats.

(2) The superintendent shall prescribe standard impression sheets to obtain the fingerprint impressions of any person for whom a criminal records check is requested pursuant to section 4123.444 [4123.44.4] of the Revised Code. Any person for whom the administrator requests the superintendent to conduct a criminal records check pursuant to that section shall have the person's fingerprint impressions made at a county sheriff's office, a municipal police department, or any other entity with the ability to make fingerprint impressions on the standard impression sheets prescribed by the superintendent. The office, department, or entity may charge the person a reasonable fee for making the impressions. The standard impression sheets the superintendent prescribes pursuant to this division may be in a tangible format, in an electronic format, or in both tangible and electronic formats.

(3) The superintendent may prescribe methods of forwarding fingerprint impressions and information necessary to conduct a criminal records check. The methods shall include, but are not limited to, electronic methods.

(D) A determination whether any information exists that indicates that a person previously has been convicted of or pleaded guilty to any offense listed or described in division (A) of this section that the superintendent makes pursuant to information considered in a criminal records check under this section is valid for the person who is the subject of that criminal records check for a period of one year after the date the superintendent makes that determination.

(E) The superintendent shall prescribe and charge a reasonable fee for providing a criminal records check requested under section 4123.444 [4123.44.4] of the Revised Code. If another request for a criminal records check is made under this section for a person for whom a valid determination under division (D) of this section is available, the superintendent shall provide the determination for a reduced fee.

**HISTORY: 151 v H 66, § 101.01, eff. 9-29-05.**

The effective date is set by § 612.03 of 151 v H 66.

## § 109.58 Superintendent shall prepare a standard fingerprint impression sheet.

The superintendent of the bureau of criminal identification and investigation shall prepare standard impression sheets on which fingerprints may be made in accordance with the fingerprint system of identification. The impression sheets may provide for other descriptive matter that the superintendent may prescribe. The superintendent shall furnish the impression sheets to each sheriff, chief of police, and person in charge of every county, multicounty, municipal, municipal-county, or multicounty-municipal jail or workhouse, community-based correctional facility, halfway house, alternative residential facility, or state correctional institution within the state. Upon the request of the board of education of a school district or of the principal or chief administrative officer of a nonpublic school, the superintendent shall provide standard impression sheets to the district or school for use in their fingerprinting programs under section 3313.96 of the Revised Code.

**HISTORY: 130 v 11 (Eff 9-24-63); 140 v S 321 (Eff 4-9-85); 145 v H 571 (Eff 10-6-94); 147 v H 342. Eff 12-31-97.**

## § 109.59 Fingerprint impression and descriptive measurement records.

The sheriff, chief of police, or other person in charge of each prison, workhouse, or state correctional institution shall send to the bureau of criminal identification and investigation, on forms furnished by the superintendent of the bureau, any fingerprint impressions and other descriptive measurements that the superintendent may require. The information shall be filed, classified, and preserved by the bureau.

**HISTORY: 130 v 11 (Eff 9-24-63); 145 v H 571. Eff 10-6-94.**

## § 109.60 Duty of sheriffs and police chiefs to take and forward fingerprints and descriptions; annual reports of arrests relating to methamphetamine production and manufacturing laboratories.

(A)(1) The sheriffs of the several counties and the chiefs of police of cities, immediately upon the arrest of any person for any felony, on suspicion of any felony, for a crime constituting a misdemeanor on the first offense and a felony on subsequent offenses, or for any misdemeanor described in division (A)(1)(a), (A)(8)(a), or (A)(10)(a) of section 109.572 [109.57.2] of the Revised Code, and immediately upon the arrest or taking into custody of any child under eighteen years of age for committing an act that would be a felony or an offense of violence if committed by an adult or upon probable cause to believe that a child of that age may have committed an act that would be a felony or an offense of violence if committed by an adult, shall take the person's or child's fingerprints, or cause the same to be taken, according to the fingerprint system of identification on the forms furnished by the superintendent of the bureau of criminal identification and investigation, and immediately shall forward copies of the completed forms, any other description that may be required, and the history of the offense committed to the bureau to be classified and filed and to the clerk of the court having jurisdiction over the prosecution of the offense or over the adjudication relative to the act.

(2) Except as provided in division (B) of this section, if a person or child has not been arrested and first appears before a court or magistrate in response to a summons, or if a sheriff or chief of police has not taken, or caused to be taken, a person's or child's fingerprints in accordance with division (A)(1) of this section by the time of the arraignment or first appearance of the person or child, the court shall order the person or child to appear before the sheriff or chief of police within twenty-four hours to have the person's or child's fingerprints taken. The sheriff or chief of police shall take the person's or child's fingerprints, or cause the fingerprints to be taken, according to the fingerprint system of identification on the forms furnished by the superintendent of the bureau of criminal identification and investigation and, immediately after the person's or child's arraignment or first appearance, forward copies of the completed forms, any other description that may be required, and the history of the offense committed

to the bureau to be classified and filed and to the clerk of the court.

(3) Every court with jurisdiction over a case involving a person or child with respect to whom division (A)(1) or (2) of this section requires a sheriff or chief of police to take the person's or child's fingerprints shall inquire at the time of the person's or child's sentencing or adjudication whether or not the person or child has been fingerprinted pursuant to division (A)(1) or (2) of this section for the original arrest or court appearance upon which the sentence or adjudication is based. If the person or child was not fingerprinted for the original arrest or court appearance upon which the sentence or adjudication is based, the court shall order the person or child to appear before the sheriff or chief of police within twenty-four hours to have the person's or child's fingerprints taken. The sheriff or chief of police shall take the person's or child's fingerprints, or cause the fingerprints to be taken, according to the fingerprint system of identification on the forms furnished by the superintendent of the bureau of criminal identification and investigation and immediately forward copies of the completed forms, any other description that may be required, and the history of the offense committed to the bureau to be classified and filed and to the clerk of the court.

(4) If a person or child is in the custody of a law enforcement agency or a detention facility, as defined in section 2921.01 of the Revised Code, and the chief law enforcement officer or chief administrative officer of the detention facility discovers that a warrant has been issued or a bill of information has been filed alleging the person or child to have committed an offense or act other than the offense or act for which the person or child is in custody, and the other alleged offense or act is one for which fingerprints are to be taken pursuant to division (A)(1) of this section, the law enforcement agency or detention facility shall take the fingerprints of the person or child, or cause the fingerprints to be taken, according to the fingerprint system of identification on the forms furnished by the superintendent of the bureau of criminal identification and investigation and immediately forward copies of the completed forms, any other description that may be required, and the history of the offense committed to the bureau to be classified and filed and to the clerk of the court that issued the warrant or with which the bill of information was filed.

(5) If an accused is found not guilty of the offense charged or a nolle prosequi is entered in any case, or if any accused child under eighteen years of age is found not to be a delinquent child for committing an act that would be a felony or an offense of violence if committed by an adult or not guilty of the felony or offense of violence charged or a nolle prosequi is entered in that case, the fingerprints and description shall be given to the accused upon the accused's request.

(6) The superintendent shall compare the description received with those already on file in the bureau, and, if the superintendent finds that the person arrested or taken into custody has a criminal record or a record as a delinquent child for having committed an act that would be a felony or an offense of violence if committed by an adult or is a fugitive from justice or wanted by any jurisdiction in this or another state, the United States, or a foreign country for any offense, the superintendent at once shall inform the arresting officer, the officer taking the person into custody, or the chief administrative officer of the county, multicounty, municipal, municipal-county, or multicounty-municipal jail or workhouse, community-based correctional facility, halfway house, alternative residential facility, or state correctional institution in which the person or child is in custody of that fact and give appropriate notice to the proper authorities in the jurisdiction in which the person is wanted, or, if that jurisdiction is a foreign country, give appropriate notice to federal authorities for transmission to the foreign country. The names, under which each person whose identification is filed is known, shall be alphabetically indexed by the superintendent.

(B) Division (A) of this section does not apply to a violator of a city ordinance unless the officers have reason to believe that the violator is a past offender or the crime is one constituting a misdemeanor on the first offense and a felony on subsequent offenses, or unless it is advisable for the purpose of subsequent identification. This section does not apply to any child under eighteen years of age who was not arrested or otherwise taken into custody for committing an act that would be a felony or an offense of violence if committed by an adult or upon probable cause to believe that a child of that age may have committed an act that would be a felony or an offense of violence if committed by an adult, except as provided in section 2151.313 [2151.31.3] of the Revised Code.

(C)(1) For purposes of division (C) of this section, a law enforcement agency shall be considered to have arrested a person if any law enforcement officer who is employed by, appointed by, or serves that agency arrests the person. As used in division (C) of this section:

(a) "Illegal methamphetamine manufacturing laboratory" has the same meaning as in section 3745.13 of the Revised Code.

(b) "Methamphetamine or a methamphetamine product" means methamphetamine, any salt, isomer, or salt of an isomer of methamphetamine, or any compound, mixture, preparation, or substance containing methamphetamine or any salt, isomer, or salt of an isomer of methamphetamine.

(2) Each law enforcement agency that, in any calendar year, arrests any person for a violation of section 2925.04 of the Revised Code that is based on the manufacture of methamphetamine or a methamphetamine product, a violation of section 2925.041 [2925.04.1] of the Revised Code that is based on the possession of chemicals sufficient to produce methamphetamine or a methamphetamine product, or a violation of any other provision of Chapter 2925. or 3719. of the Revised Code that is based on the possession of chemicals sufficient to produce methamphetamine or a methamphetamine product shall prepare an annual report covering the calendar year that contains the information specified in division (C)(3) of this section relative to all arrests for violations of those sections committed under those circumstances during that calendar year and relative to illegal methamphetamine manufacturing laboratories, dump sites, and chemical caches as specified in that division and shall send the annual report, not later than the first day of March in the calendar year following the calendar year covered by the report, to the bureau of criminal identification and investigation.

The law enforcement agency shall write any annual report prepared and filed under this division on the standard forms furnished by the superintendent of the bureau of criminal identification and investigation pursuant to division (C)(4) of this section. The annual report shall be a statistical report, and nothing in the report or in the information it contains shall identify, or enable the identification of, any person who was arrested and whose arrest is included in the information contained in the report. The annual report in the possession of the bureau and the information it contains are public records for the purpose of section 149.43 of the Revised Code.

(3) The annual report prepared and filed by a law enforcement agency under division (C)(2) of this section shall contain all of the following information for the calendar year covered by the report:

(a) The total number of arrests made by the agency in that calendar year for a violation of section 2925.04 of the Revised Code that is based on the manufacture of methamphetamine or a methamphetamine product, a violation of section 2925.041 [2925.04.1] of the Revised Code that is based on the possession of chemicals sufficient to produce methamphetamine or a methamphetamine product, or a violation of any other provision of Chapter 2925. or 3719. of the Revised Code that is based on the possession of chemicals sufficient to produce methamphetamine or a methamphetamine product;

(b) The total number of illegal methamphetamine manufacturing laboratories at which one or more of the arrests reported under division (C)(3)(a) of this section occurred, or that were discovered in that calendar year within the territory served by the agency but at which none of the arrests reported under division (C)(3)(a) of this section occurred;

(c) The total number of dump sites and chemical caches that are, or that are reasonably believed to be, related to illegal methamphetamine manufacturing and that were discovered in that calendar year within the territory served by the agency.

(4) The superintendent of the bureau of criminal identification and investigation shall prepare and furnish to each law enforcement agency in this state standard forms for making the annual reports required by division (C)(2) of this section. The standard forms that the superintendent prepares pursuant to this division may be in a tangible format, in an electronic format, or in both a tangible format and an electronic format.

(5) The annual report required by division (C)(2) of this section is separate from, and in addition to, any report, materials, or information required under division (A) of this section or under any other provision of sections 109.57 to 109.62 of the Revised Code.

**HISTORY: 130 v 12 (Eff 9-24-63); 133 v H 956 (Eff 9-16-70); 137 v S 170 (Eff 11-16-77); 146 v H 1 (Eff 1-1-96); 146 v H 124 (Eff 3-31-97); 147 v H 342 (Eff 12-31-97); 147 v H 2. Eff 1-1-99; 151 v S 53, § 1, eff. 5-17-06; 151 v S 238, § 1, eff. 9-21-06; 152 v S 163, § 1, eff. 8-14-08.**

The effective date is set by section 4 of HB 2.

## § 109.61 Duty of sheriffs and police chiefs to send descriptions, fingerprints, photographs and measurements to bureau.

Each sheriff or chief of police shall furnish the bureau of criminal identification and investigation with descriptions, fingerprints, photographs, and measurements of the following:

(A)(1) Persons arrested who in that sheriff's or chief of police's judgment are wanted for serious offenses, are fugitives from justice, or in whose possession at the time of arrest are found goods or property reasonably believed to have been stolen;

(2) Children arrested or otherwise taken into custody who in that sheriff's or chief of police's judgment are under eighteen years of age and have committed an act that would be a felony or an offense of violence if committed by an adult.

(B) All persons in whose possession are found burglar outfits, burglar tools, or burglar keys, or who have in their possession high power explosives reasonably believed to be intended to be used for unlawful purposes;

(C) Persons who are in possession of infernal machines or other contrivances in whole or in part and reasonably believed by the sheriff or chief of police to be intended to be used for unlawful purposes;

(D) All persons carrying concealed firearms or other deadly weapons reasonably believed to be carried for unlawful purposes;

(E) All persons who have in their possession inks, dies, paper, or other articles necessary in the making of counterfeit bank notes or in the alteration of bank notes, or dies, molds, or other articles necessary in the making of counterfeit money and reasonably believed to be intended to be used by them for those types of unlawful purposes.

**HISTORY: 130 v 12 (Eff 9-24-63); 146 v H 1 (Eff 1-1-96); 146 v H 124 (Eff 3-31-97); 147 v H 2. Eff 1-1-99.**

The effective date is set by section 4 of HB 2.

## § 109.62 Interstate, national, and international cooperation.

The superintendent of the bureau of criminal identification and investigation shall co-operate with bureaus in other states and with the federal bureau of investigation to develop and carry on a complete interstate, national, and international system of criminal identification and investigation.

**HISTORY: 130 v 12. Eff 9-24-63.**

## § 109.63 Superintendent of bureau and assistants may testify in court.

The superintendent of the bureau of criminal identification and investigation and his assistants employed in accordance with section 109.51 of the Revised Code may testify in any court in this state to the same extent as any law enforcement officer in this state.

**HISTORY: 130 v 12. Eff 9-24-63.**

## § 109.64 Periodic information bulletins concerning missing children.

The bureau of criminal identification and investigation shall prepare a periodic information bulletin concerning missing children whom it determines may be present in this state. The bureau shall compile the bulletin from information contained in the national crime information center computer. The bulletin shall indicate the names and addresses of these minors who are the subject of missing children cases and other information that the superintendent of the bureau considers appropriate. The bulletin shall contain a reminder to law enforcement agencies of their responsibilities under section 2901.30 of the Revised Code.

The bureau shall send a copy of each periodic information bulletin to the missing children clearinghouse established under section 109.65 of the Revised Code for use in connection with its responsibilities under division (E) of that section. Upon receipt of each periodic information bulletin from the bureau, the missing children clearinghouse shall send a copy of the bulletin to each sheriff, marshal, police department of a municipal corporation, police force of a township police district or joint police district, and township constable in this state, to the board of education of each school district in this state, and to each nonpublic school in this state. The bureau shall provide a copy of the bulletin, upon request, to other persons or entities. The superintendent of the bureau, with the approval of the attorney general, may establish a reasonable fee for a copy of a bulletin provided to persons or entities other than law enforcement agencies in this or other states or of the federal government, the department of education, governmental entities of this state, and libraries in this state. The superintendent shall deposit all such fees collected into the missing children fund created by section 109.65 of the Revised Code.

As used in this section, "missing children," "information," and "minor" have the same meanings as in section 2901.30 of the Revised Code.

**HISTORY: 140 v S 321 (Eff 4-9-85); 145 v S 63. Eff 10-1-93; 2011 HB 153, § 101.01, eff. Sept. 29, 2011.**

## § 109.65 Missing children clearinghouse; educational program; fund.

(A) As used in this section, "minor," "missing child," and "missing children" have the same meanings as in section 2901.30 of the Revised Code.

(B) There is hereby created within the office of the attorney general the missing children clearinghouse. The attorney general shall administer the clearinghouse. The clearinghouse is established as a central repository of information to coordinate and improve the availability of information regarding missing children, which information shall be collected and disseminated by the clearinghouse to assist in the location of missing children. The clearinghouse shall act as an information repository separate from and in addition to law enforcement agencies within this state.

(C) The missing children clearinghouse may perform any of the following functions:

(1) The establishment of services to aid in the location of missing children that include, but are not limited to, any of the following services:

(a) Assistance in the preparation and dissemination of flyers identifying and describing missing children and their abductors;

(b) The development of informational forms for the reporting of missing children that may be used by parents, guardians, and law enforcement officials to facilitate the location of a missing child;

(c) The provision of assistance to public and private organizations, boards of education, nonpublic schools, preschools, child care facilities, and law enforcement agencies in planning and implementing voluntary programs to fingerprint children.

(2) The establishment and operation of a toll-free telephone line for supplemental reports of missing children and reports of sightings of missing children;

(3) Upon the request of any person or entity and upon payment of any applicable fee established by the attorney general under division (H) of this section, the provision to the person or entity who makes the request of a copy of any information possessed by the clearinghouse that was acquired or prepared pursuant to division (E)(3) of this section;

(4) The performance of liaison services between individuals and public and private agencies regarding procedures for handling and responding to missing children reports;

(5) The participation as a member in any networks of other missing children centers or clearinghouses;

(6) The creation and operation of an intrastate network of communication designed for the speedy collection and processing of information concerning missing children.

(D) If a board of education is notified by school personnel that a missing child is attending any school under the board's jurisdiction, or if the principal or chief administrative officer of a nonpublic school is notified by school personnel that a missing child is attending that school, the board or the principal or chief administrative officer immediately shall give notice of that fact to the missing children clearinghouse and to the law enforcement agency with jurisdiction over the area where the missing child resides.

(E)(1) The attorney general, in cooperation with the department of job and family services, shall establish a "missing child educational program" within the missing children clearinghouse that shall perform the functions specified in divisions (E)(1) to (3) of this section. The program shall operate under the supervision and control of the attorney general in accordance with procedures that the attorney general shall develop to implement divisions (E)(1) to (3) of this section. The attorney general shall cooperate with the department of education in developing and disseminating information acquired or prepared pursuant to division (E)(3) of this section.

(2) Upon the request of any board of education in this state or any nonpublic school in this state, the missing child educational program shall provide to the board or school a reasonable number of copies of the information acquired or prepared pursuant to division (E)(3) of this section.

Upon the request of any board of education in this state or any nonpublic school in this state that, pursuant to section 3313.96 of the Revised Code, is developing an information program concerning missing children issues and matters, the missing child educational program shall provide to the board or nonpublic school assistance in developing the information program. The assistance may include, but is not limited to, the provision of any or all of the following:

(a) If the requesting entity is a board of education of a school district, sample policies on missing and exploited children issues to assist the board in complying with section 3313.205 [3313.20.5] of the Revised Code;

(b) Suggested safety curricula regarding missing children issues, including child safety and abduction prevention issues;

(c) Assistance in developing, with local law enforcement agencies, prosecuting attorneys, boards of education, school districts, and nonpublic schools, cooperative programs for fingerprinting children;

(d) Other assistance to further the goals of the program.

(3) The missing child educational program shall acquire or prepare informational materials relating to missing children issues and matters. These issues and matters include, but are not limited to, the following:

(a) The types of missing children;

(b) The reasons why and how minors become missing children, the potential adverse consequences of a minor becoming a missing child, and, in the case of minors who are considering running away from home or from the care, custody, and control of their parents, parent who is the residential parent and legal custodian, guardian, legal custodian, or another person responsible for them, alternatives that may be available to address their concerns and problems;

(c) Offenses under federal law that could relate to missing children and other provisions of federal law that focus on missing children;

(d) Offenses under the Revised Code that could relate to missing children, including, but not limited to, kidnapping, abduction, unlawful restraint, child stealing, interference with custody, endangering children, domestic violence, abuse of a child and contributing to the dependency, neglect, unruliness, or delinquency of a child, sexual offenses, drug offenses, prostitution offenses, and obscenity offenses, and other provisions of the Revised Code that could relate to missing children;

(e) Legislation being considered by the general assembly, legislatures of other states, the congress of the United States, and political subdivisions in this or any other state to address missing children issues;

(f) Sources of information on missing children issues;

(g) State, local, federal, and private systems for locating and identifying missing children;

(h) Law enforcement agency programs, responsibilities, and investigative techniques in missing children matters;

(i) Efforts on the community level in this and other states, concerning missing children issues and matters, by governmental entities and private organizations;

(j) The identification of private organizations that, among their primary objectives, address missing children issues and matters;

(k) How to avoid becoming a missing child and what to do if one becomes a missing child;

(l) Efforts that schools, parents, and members of a community can undertake to reduce the risk that a minor will become a missing child and to quickly locate or identify a minor if he becomes a missing child, including, but not limited to, fingerprinting programs.

(F) Each year the missing children clearinghouse shall issue a report describing its performance of the functions specified in division (E) of this section and shall provide a copy of the report to the speaker of the house of representatives, the president of the senate, the governor, the superintendent of the bureau of criminal identification and investigation, and the director of job and family services.

(G) Any state agency or political subdivision of this state that operates a missing children program or a clearinghouse for information about missing children shall coordinate its activities with the missing children clearinghouse.

(H) The attorney general shall determine a reasonable fee to be charged for providing to any person or entity other than a state or local law enforcement agency of this or any other state, a law enforcement agency of the United States, a board of education of a school district in this state, a nonpublic school in this state, a governmental entity in this state, or a public library in this state, pursuant to division (A)(3) of this section, copies of any information acquired or prepared pursuant to division (E)(3) of this section. The attorney general shall collect the fee prior to sending or giving copies of any information to any person or entity for whom or which this division requires the fee to be charged and shall deposit the fee into the missing children fund created by division (I) of this section.

(I) There is hereby created in the state treasury the missing children fund that shall consist of all moneys awarded to the state by donation, gift, or bequest, all other moneys received for purposes of this section, and all fees collected pursuant to this section or section 109.64 of the Revised Code. The attorney general shall use the moneys in the missing children fund only for purposes of the office of the attorney general acquiring or preparing information pursuant to division (E)(3) of this section.

(J) The failure of the missing children clearinghouse to undertake any function or activity authorized in this section does not create a cause of action against the state.

**HISTORY: RC § 3301.25, 140 v S 321 (Eff 4-9-85); 142 v H 231 (Eff 10-5-87); 143 v S 3 (Eff 4-11-91); RC § 109.65, 145 v S 63 (Eff 10-1-93); 148 v H 471. Eff 7-1-2000.**

The effective date is set by section 12(A) of HB 471.

## § 109.69 Reciprocity agreements with states issuing licenses to carry concealed handguns.

(A)(1) The attorney general shall negotiate and enter into a reciprocity agreement with any other license-issuing state under which a license to carry a concealed handgun that is issued by the other state is recognized in this state if the attorney general determines that both of the following apply:

(a) The eligibility requirements imposed by that license-issuing state for that license are substantially comparable to the eligibility requirements for a license to carry a concealed handgun issued under section 2923.125 [2923.12.5] of the Revised Code.

(b) That license-issuing state recognizes a license to carry a concealed handgun issued under section 2923.125 [2923.12.5] of the Revised Code.

(2) A reciprocity agreement entered into under division (A)(1) of this section also may provide for the recognition in this state of a license to carry a concealed handgun issued on a temporary or emergency basis by the other license-issuing state, if the eligibility requirements imposed by that license-issuing state for the temporary or emergency license are substantially comparable to the eligibility requirements for a license or temporary emergency license to carry a concealed handgun issued under section 2923.125 [2923.12.5] or 2923.1213 [2923.12.13] of the Revised Code and if that license-issuing state recognizes a temporary emergency license to carry a concealed handgun issued under section 2923.1213 [2923.12.13] of the Revised Code.

(3) The attorney general shall not negotiate any agreement with any other license-issuing state under which a license to carry a concealed handgun that is issued by the other state is recognized in this state other than as provided in divisions (A)(1) and (2) of this section.

(B) As used in this section:

(1) "Handgun" has the same meaning as in section 2923.11 of the Revised Code.

(2) "License-issuing state" means a state other than this state that, pursuant to law, provides for the issuance of a license to carry a concealed handgun.

**HISTORY: 150 v H 12, § 1, eff. 4-8-04.**

The provisions of § 6, H.B. 12 (150 v —), read as follows:
SECTION 6. In amending sections 1547.69, 2911.21, 2921.13,

2923.12, 2923.121, 2923.123, 2923.13, 2923.16, 2953.32, and 4749.10 of the Revised Code and in enacting sections 109.69, 109.731, 311.41, 311.42, and 2923.124 to 2923.1213 of the Revised Code in this act, the General Assembly hereby declares its intent to recognize both of the following:

(A) The inalienable and fundamental right of an individual to defend the individual's person and the members of the individual's family;

(B) The fact that the right described in division (A) of this section predates the adoption of the United States Constitution, the adoption of the Ohio Constitution, and the enactment of all statutory laws by the General Assembly and may not be infringed by any enactment of the General Assembly.

The provisions of § 7, H.B. 12 (150 v —), read as follows:

SECTION 7. In enacting sections 109.69, 109.731, 311.41, 311.42, and 2923.124 to 2923.1213 of the Revised Code in this act and in amending sections 1547.69, 2911.21, 2921.13, 2923.12, 2923.121, 2923.123, 2923.13, 2923.16, 2953.32, and 4749.10 of the Revised Code in this act relative to licenses to carry a concealed handgun, the General Assembly hereby declares that it is not its intent to declare or otherwise give the impression that, prior to the effective date of this act, an individual did not have an inalienable and fundamental right, or a right under the Ohio Constitution or the United States Constitution, to carry a concealed handgun or other firearm for the defense of the individual's person or a member of the individual's family while engaged in lawful activity. Further, the General Assembly declares that it is not its intent to invalidate any prior convictions for violating any section of the Revised Code or a municipal ordinance prior to the effective date of this act or to prevent the prosecution of any violation committed prior to the effective date of this act.

The provisions of § 9, H.B. 12 (150 v —), read as follows:

SECTION 9. The General Assembly finds that licenses to carry concealed handguns are a matter of statewide concern and wishes to ensure uniformity throughout the state regarding the qualifications for a person to hold a license to carry a concealed handgun and the authority granted to a person holding a license of that nature. It is the intent of the General Assembly in amending sections 1547.69, 2911.21, 2921.13, 2923.12, 2923.121, 2923.123, 2923.16, 2953.32, and 4749.10 and enacting sections 109.69, 109.731, 311.41, 311.42, and 2923.124 to 2923.1213 of the Revised Code to enact laws of a general nature, and, by enacting those laws of a general nature, the state occupies and preempts the field of issuing licenses to carry a concealed handgun and the validity of licenses of that nature. No municipal corporation may adopt or continue in existence any ordinance, and no township may adopt or continue in existence any resolution, that is in conflict with those sections, including, but not limited to, any ordinance or resolution that attempts to restrict the places where a person possessing a valid license to carry a concealed handgun may carry a handgun concealed.

The provisions of § 10, H.B. 12 (150 v —), read as follows:

SECTION 10. If any provision of sections 1547.69, 2911.21, 2913.02, 2921.13, 2923.12, 2923.121, 2923.123, 2923.16, 2929.14, 2953.32, and 4749.10 of the Revised Code, as amended by this act, any provision of sections 109.69, 109.731, 311.41, 311.42, 2923.124, 2923.125, 2923.126, 2923.127, 2923.128, 2923.129, 2923.1210, 2923.1211, 2923.1212, and 2923.1213 of the Revised Code, as enacted by this act, or the application of any provision of those sections to any person or circumstance is held invalid, the invalidity does not affect other provisions or applications of the particular section or related sections that can be given effect without the invalid provision or application, and to this end the provisions of the particular section are severable.

## [OHIO PEACE OFFICER TRAINING COMMISSION]

### § 109.71 Creation of peace officer training commission; definitions.

There is hereby created in the office of the attorney general the Ohio peace officer training commission. The commission shall consist of nine members appointed by the governor with the advice and consent of the senate and selected as follows: one member representing the public; two members who are incumbent sheriffs; two members who are incumbent chiefs of police; one member from the bureau of criminal identification and investigation; one member from the state highway patrol; one member who is the special agent in charge of a field office of the federal bureau of investigation in this state; and one member from the department of education, trade and industrial education services, law enforcement training.

This section does not confer any arrest authority or any ability or authority to detain a person, write or issue any citation, or provide any disposition alternative, as granted under Chapter 2935. of the Revised Code.

As used in sections 109.71 to 109.801 of the Revised Code:

(A) "Peace officer" means:

(1) A deputy sheriff, marshal, deputy marshal, member of the organized police department of a township or municipal corporation, member of a township police district or joint police district police force, member of a police force employed by a metropolitan housing authority under division (D) of section 3735.31 of the Revised Code, or township constable, who is commissioned and employed as a peace officer by a political subdivision of this state or by a metropolitan housing authority, and whose primary duties are to preserve the peace, to protect life and property, and to enforce the laws of this state, ordinances of a municipal corporation, resolutions of a township, or regulations of a board of county commissioners or board of township trustees, or any of those laws, ordinances, resolutions, or regulations;

(2) A police officer who is employed by a railroad company and appointed and commissioned by the secretary of state pursuant to sections 4973.17 to 4973.22 of the Revised Code;

(3) Employees of the department of taxation engaged in the enforcement of Chapter 5743. of the Revised Code and designated by the tax commissioner for peace officer training for purposes of the delegation of investigation powers under section 5743.45 of the Revised Code;

(4) An undercover drug agent;

(5) Enforcement agents of the department of public safety whom the director of public safety designates under section 5502.14 of the Revised Code;

(6) An employee of the department of natural resources who is a natural resources law enforcement staff officer designated pursuant to section 1501.013, a park officer designated pursuant to section 1541.10, a forest officer designated pursuant to section 1503.29, a preserve officer designated pursuant to section 1517.10, a wildlife officer designated pursuant to section 1531.13, or a state watercraft officer designated pursuant to section 1547.521 of the Revised Code;

(7) An employee of a park district who is designated pursuant to section 511.232 or 1545.13 of the Revised Code;

(8) An employee of a conservancy district who is designated pursuant to section 6101.75 of the Revised Code;

(9) A police officer who is employed by a hospital that employs and maintains its own proprietary police department or security department, and who is appointed and commissioned by the secretary of state pursuant to sections 4973.17 to 4973.22 of the Revised Code;

(10) Veterans' homes police officers designated under section 5907.02 of the Revised Code;

(11) A police officer who is employed by a qualified nonprofit corporation police department pursuant to section 1702.80 of the Revised Code;

(12) A state university law enforcement officer appointed under section 3345.04 of the Revised Code or a person serving as a state university law enforcement officer on a permanent basis on June 19, 1978, who has been awarded a certificate by the executive director of the Ohio peace officer training commission attesting to the person's satisfactory completion of an approved state, county, municipal, or department of natural resources peace officer basic training program;

(13) A special police officer employed by the department of mental health pursuant to section 5119.14 of the Revised Code or the department of developmental disabilities pursuant to section 5123.13 of the Revised Code;

(14) A member of a campus police department appointed under section 1713.50 of the Revised Code;

(15) A member of a police force employed by a regional transit authority under division (Y) of section 306.35 of the Revised Code;

(16) Investigators appointed by the auditor of state pursuant to section 117.091 of the Revised Code and engaged in the enforcement of Chapter 117. of the Revised Code;

(17) A special police officer designated by the superintendent of the state highway patrol pursuant to section 5503.09 of the Revised Code or a person who was serving as a special police officer pursuant to that section on a permanent basis on October 21, 1997, and who has been awarded a certificate by the executive director of the Ohio peace officer training commission attesting to the person's satisfactory completion of an approved state, county, municipal, or department of natural resources peace officer basic training program;

(18) A special police officer employed by a port authority under section 4582.04 or 4582.28 of the Revised Code or a person serving as a special police officer employed by a port authority on a permanent basis on May 17, 2000, who has been awarded a certificate by the executive director of the Ohio peace officer training commission attesting to the person's satisfactory completion of an approved state, county, municipal, or department of natural resources peace officer basic training program;

(19) A special police officer employed by a municipal corporation who has been awarded a certificate by the executive director of the Ohio peace officer training commission for satisfactory completion of an approved peace officer basic training program and who is employed on a permanent basis on or after March 19, 2003, at a municipal airport, or other municipal air navigation facility, that has scheduled operations, as defined in section 119.3 of Title 14 of the Code of Federal Regulations, 14 C.F.R. 119.3, as amended, and that is required to be under a security program and is governed by aviation security rules of the transportation security administration of the United States department of transportation as provided in Parts 1542. and 1544. of Title 49 of the Code of Federal Regulations, as amended;

(20) A police officer who is employed by an owner or operator of an amusement park that has an average yearly attendance in excess of six hundred thousand guests and that employs and maintains its own proprietary police department or security department, and who is appointed and commissioned by a judge of the appropriate municipal court or county court pursuant to section 4973.17 of the Revised Code;

(21) A police officer who is employed by a bank, savings and loan association, savings bank, credit union, or association of banks, savings and loan associations, savings banks, or credit unions, who has been appointed and commissioned by the secretary of state pursuant to sections 4973.17 to 4973.22 of the Revised Code, and who has been awarded a certificate by the executive director of the Ohio peace officer training commission attesting to the person's satisfactory completion of a state, county, municipal, or department of natural resources peace officer basic training program;

(22) An investigator, as defined in section 109.541 of the Revised Code, of the bureau of criminal identification and investigation who is commissioned by the superintendent of the bureau as a special agent for the purpose of assisting law enforcement officers or providing emergency assistance to peace officers pursuant to authority granted under that section;

(23) A state fire marshal law enforcement officer appointed under section 3737.22 of the Revised Code or a person serving as a state fire marshal law enforcement officer on a permanent basis on or after July 1, 1982, who has been awarded a certificate by the executive director of the Ohio peace officer training commission attesting to the person's satisfactory completion of an approved state, county, municipal, or department of natural resources peace officer basic training program;

(24) A gaming agent employed under section 3772.03 of the Revised Code.

(B) "Undercover drug agent" has the same meaning as in division (B)(2) of section 109.79 of the Revised Code.

(C) "Crisis intervention training" means training in the use of interpersonal and communication skills to most effectively and sensitively interview victims of rape.

(D) "Missing children" has the same meaning as in section 2901.30 of the Revised Code.

**HISTORY: 142 v H 708 (Eff 4-19-88); 143 v H 110 (Eff 5-31-90); 143 v H 271 (Eff 4-10-91); 143 v H 669 (Eff 1-10-91); 144 v H 77 (Eff 9-17-91); 144 v S 49 (Eff 7-21-92); 144 v H 758 (Eff 1-15-93); 145 v S 182 (Eff 10-20-94); 146 v S 162 (Eff 10-29-95); 146 v S 2 (Eff 7-1-96); 146 v H 445 (Eff 9-3-96); 146 v H 670 (Eff 12-2-96); 146 v H 351 (Eff 1-14-97); 146 v S 285 (Eff 3-13-97); 147 v S 60 (Eff 10-21-97); 147 v S 213 (Eff 7-29-98); 147 v S 187 (Eff 3-18-99); 148 v H 163 (Eff 6-30-99); 148 v S 137 (Eff 5-17-2000); 149 v H 675 (Eff 3-14-2003); 149 v H 545. Eff 3-19-2003; 151 v H 58, § 1, eff. 5-3-05; 151 v H 81, § 1, eff. 4-14-06; 151 v H 347, § 1, eff. 3-14-07; 151 v H 454, § 1, eff. 4-6-07; 152 v H 562, § 101.01, eff. 9-23-08; 153 v S 79, § 1, eff. 10-6-09; 153 v H 519, § 1, eff. 9-10-10; 2011 HB 153, § 101.01, eff. Sept. 29, 2011.**

The effective date is set by § 812.10 of 152 v H 562.

The provisions of § 815.01 of 152 v H 562 read as follows:

SECTION 815.10. Section 109.71 of the Revised Code is presented in this act as a composite of the section as amended by both Sub. H.B. 347 and Sub. H.B. 454 of the 126th General Assembly. ° ° ° The General Assembly, applying the principle stated in division (B) of section 1.52 of the Revised Code that amendments are to be harmonized if reasonably capable of simultaneous operation, finds that the composites are the resulting versions of the sections in effect prior to the effective date of the sections as presented in this act.

Governor Taft's veto of HB 347 was overridden by the Ohio General Assembly.

The provisions of § 3 of 151 v H 58 read as follows:

SECTION 3. Section 109.71 of the Revised Code is presented in this act as a composite of the section as amended by both Sub. H.B. 545 and H.B. 675 of the 124th General Assembly. The General Assembly, applying the principle stated in division (B) of section 1.52 of the Revised Code that amendments are to be harmonized if reasonably capable of simultaneous operation, finds that the composite is the resulting version of the section in effect prior to the effective date of the section as presented in this act.

The effective date is set by § 4 of 151 v H 58.

**Analogous to former RC § 109.71 (131 v 8; 133 v H 111; 133 v H 575; 136 v S 272; 137 v S 141; 139 v H 44; 140 v S 85; 140 v H 759; 140 v H 435; 140 v S 321; 140 v H 129; 141 v S 278; 141 v S 364; 142 v H 231; 142 v H 261), repealed 142 v H 708, § 2, eff 4-19-88.**

The provisions of § 4 of H.B. 516 (150 v —) read in part as follows:

SECTION 4. The following agencies shall be retained pursuant to division (D) of section 101.83 of the Revised Code and shall expire on December 31, 2010:

| AGENCY NAME | REVISED CODE OR UNCODIFIED SECTION |
|---|---|
| ○○○ | ○○○ |
| Ohio Peace Officer Training Commission | 109.71 |
| ○○○ | ○○○ |

The provisions of § 36.01 of HB 675 (149 v —) read as follows:

SECTION 36.01. Section 109.71 of the Revised Code is presented in this act as a composite of the section as amended by both Am. Sub. H.B. 163 and Am. S.B. 137 of the 123rd General Assembly. The General Assembly, applying the principle stated in division (B) of section 1.52 of the Revised Code that amendments are to be harmonized if reasonably capable of simultaneous operation, finds that the composite is the resulting version of the section in effect prior to the effective date of the section as presented in this act.

The provisions of § 3 of HB 545 (149 v —) read as follows:

SECTION 3. Section 109.71 of the Revised Code is presented in this act as a composite of the section as amended by both Am. Sub. H.B. 163 and Am. S.B. 137 of the 123rd General Assembly. Section 109.75 of the Revised Code is presented in this act as a composite of the section as amended by both Am. Sub. H.B. 566 and Sub. H.B. 670 of the 121st General Assembly. Section 109.77 of the Revised Code is presented in this act as a composite of the section as amended by Sub. H.B. 148, Am. Sub. H.B. 163, and Am. S.B. 137 of the 123rd General Assembly. Section 2935.01 of the Revised Code is presented in this act as a composite of the section as amended by both Sub. H.B. 427 and Sub. S.B. 200 of the 124th General Assembly. The General Assembly, applying the principle stated in division (B) of section 1.52 of the Revised Code that amendments are to be harmonized if reasonably capable of simultaneous operation, finds that the composites of these sections are the resulting versions of the sections in effect prior to the effective date of the sections as presented in this act.

## § 109.72 Terms of members; meetings; expenses.

Ohio peace officer training commission member terms shall be for three years, commencing on the twentieth day of September and ending on the nineteenth day of September. Each member shall hold office from the date of appointment until the end of the term to which the member was appointed. Any member appointed to fill a vacancy occurring prior to the expiration of the term for which the member's predecessor was appointed shall hold office for the remainder of such term. Any member shall continue in office subsequent to the expiration date of the member's term until the member's successor takes office, or until a period of sixty days has elapsed, whichever occurs first. An interim chairperson shall be appointed by the governor until such time as the commission elects a permanent chairperson.

Any member of the commission appointed pursuant to section 109.71 of the Revised Code as an incumbent sheriff, incumbent chief of police, representative of the state highway patrol, state department of education, federal bureau of investigation, and bureau of criminal identification and investigation, shall immediately, upon termination of holding such office, cease to be a member of the commission, and a successor shall be appointed.

The commission shall meet at least four times each year. Special meetings may be called by the chairperson and shall be called by the chairperson at the request of the attorney general or upon the written request of five members of the commission. The commission may establish its own requirements as to quorum and its own procedures with respect to the conduct of its meetings and other affairs; provided, that all recommendations by the commission to the attorney general pursuant to section 109.74 of the Revised Code shall require the affirmative vote of five members of the commission.

Membership on the commission does not constitute the holding of an office, and members of the commission shall not be required to take and file oaths of office before serving on the commission. The commission shall not exercise any portion of the sovereign power of the state.

The members of the commission shall receive no compensation for their services but shall be allowed their actual and necessary expenses incurred in the performance of their duties.

No member of the commission shall be disqualified from holding any public office or employment, nor shall the member forfeit any such office or employment, by reason of appointment to the commission, notwithstanding any general, special, or local law, ordinance, or city charter to the contrary.

**HISTORY: 131 v 8 (Eff 9-6-65); 135 v S 131 (Eff 8-21-73); 146 v H 670. Eff 12-2-96.**

## § 109.73 Commission to recommend rules; executive director; powers.

(A) The Ohio peace officer training commission shall recommend rules to the attorney general with respect to all of the following:

(1) The approval, or revocation of approval, of peace officer training schools administered by the state, counties, municipal corporations, public school districts, technical college districts, and the department of natural resources;

(2) Minimum courses of study, attendance requirements, and equipment and facilities to be required at approved state, county, municipal, and department of natural resources peace officer training schools;

(3) Minimum qualifications for instructors at approved state, county, municipal, and department of natural resources peace officer training schools;

(4) The requirements of minimum basic training that peace officers appointed to probationary terms shall complete before being eligible for permanent appointment, which requirements shall include training in the handling of the offense of domestic violence, other types of domestic violence-related offenses and incidents, and protection orders and consent agreements issued or approved under section 2919.26 or 3113.31 of the Revised Code; crisis intervention training; and training in the handling of missing children and child abuse and neglect cases; and the time within which such basic training shall be completed following appointment to a probationary term;

(5) The requirements of minimum basic training that peace officers not appointed for probationary terms but appointed on other than a permanent basis shall complete

in order to be eligible for continued employment or permanent appointment, which requirements shall include training in the handling of the offense of domestic violence, other types of domestic violence-related offenses and incidents, and protection orders and consent agreements issued or approved under section 2919.26 or 3113.31 of the Revised Code, crisis intervention training, and training in the handling of missing children and child abuse and neglect cases, and the time within which such basic training shall be completed following appointment on other than a permanent basis;

(6) Categories or classifications of advanced in-service training programs for peace officers, including programs in the handling of the offense of domestic violence, other types of domestic violence-related offenses and incidents, and protection orders and consent agreements issued or approved under section 2919.26 or 3113.31 of the Revised Code, in crisis intervention, and in the handling of missing children and child abuse and neglect cases, and minimum courses of study and attendance requirements with respect to such categories or classifications;

(7) Permitting persons, who are employed as members of a campus police department appointed under section 1713.50 of the Revised Code; who are employed as police officers by a qualified nonprofit corporation police department pursuant to section 1702.80 of the Revised Code; who are appointed and commissioned as bank, savings and loan association, savings bank, credit union, or association of banks, savings and loan associations, savings banks, or credit unions police officers, as railroad police officers, or as hospital police officers pursuant to sections 4973.17 to 4973.22 of the Revised Code; or who are appointed and commissioned as amusement park police officers pursuant to section 4973.17 of the Revised Code, to attend approved peace officer training schools, including the Ohio peace officer training academy, and to receive certificates of satisfactory completion of basic training programs, if the private college or university that established the campus police department; qualified nonprofit corporation police department; bank, savings and loan association, savings bank, credit union, or association of banks, savings and loan associations, savings banks, or credit unions; railroad company; hospital; or amusement park sponsoring the police officers pays the entire cost of the training and certification and if trainee vacancies are available;

(8) Permitting undercover drug agents to attend approved peace officer training schools, other than the Ohio peace officer training academy, and to receive certificates of satisfactory completion of basic training programs, if, for each undercover drug agent, the county, township, or municipal corporation that employs that undercover drug agent pays the entire cost of the training and certification;

(9)(a) The requirements for basic training programs for bailiffs and deputy bailiffs of courts of record of this state and for criminal investigators employed by the state public defender that those persons shall complete before they may carry a firearm while on duty;

(b) The requirements for any training received by a bailiff or deputy bailiff of a court of record of this state or by a criminal investigator employed by the state public defender prior to June 6, 1986, that is to be considered equivalent to the training described in division (A)(9)(a) of this section.

(10) Establishing minimum qualifications and requirements for certification for dogs utilized by law enforcement agencies;

(11) Establishing minimum requirements for certification of persons who are employed as correction officers in a full-service jail, five-day facility, or eight-hour holding facility or who provide correction services in such a jail or facility;

(12) Establishing requirements for the training of agents of a county humane society under section 1717.06 of the Revised Code, including, without limitation, a requirement that the agents receive instruction on traditional animal husbandry methods and training techniques, including customary owner-performed practices.

(B) The commission shall appoint an executive director, with the approval of the attorney general, who shall hold office during the pleasure of the commission. The executive director shall perform such duties assigned by the commission. The executive director shall receive a salary fixed pursuant to Chapter 124. of the Revised Code and reimbursement for expenses within the amounts available by appropriation. The executive director may appoint officers, employees, agents, and consultants as the executive director considers necessary, prescribe their duties, and provide for reimbursement of their expenses within the amounts available for reimbursement by appropriation and with the approval of the commission.

(C) The commission may do all of the following:

(1) Recommend studies, surveys, and reports to be made by the executive director regarding the carrying out of the objectives and purposes of sections 109.71 to 109.77 of the Revised Code;

(2) Visit and inspect any peace officer training school that has been approved by the executive director or for which application for approval has been made;

(3) Make recommendations, from time to time, to the executive director, the attorney general, and the general assembly regarding the carrying out of the purposes of sections 109.71 to 109.77 of the Revised Code;

(4) Report to the attorney general from time to time, and to the governor and the general assembly at least annually, concerning the activities of the commission;

(5) Establish fees for the services the commission offers under sections 109.71 to 109.79 of the Revised Code, including, but not limited to, fees for training, certification, and testing;

(6) Perform such other acts as are necessary or appropriate to carry out the powers and duties of the commission as set forth in sections 109.71 to 109.77 of the Revised Code.

(D) In establishing the requirements, under division (A)(12) of this section, the commission may consider any portions of the curriculum for instruction on the topic of animal husbandry practices, if any, of the Ohio state university college of veterinary medicine. No person or entity that fails to provide instruction on traditional animal husbandry methods and training techniques, including customary owner-performed practices, shall qualify to train a humane agent for appointment under section 1717.06 of the Revised Code.

**HISTORY: 131 v 11 (Eff 9-6-65); 132 v H 93 (Eff 5-17-67); 134 v S 396 (Eff 2-17-72); 136 v S 272 (Eff 8-19-76); 137 v H 835 (Eff 3-27-79); 139 v H 44 (Eff 5-8-81); 140 v H 759 (Eff 3-28-85); 140 v H 435 (Eff 4-4-85); 140 v S 321 (Eff 4-9-85); 141 v S 149 (Eff 6-6-86); 141 v S 364 (Eff 3-17-87); 143 v H 110 (Eff 5-31-90); 143 v S 3 (Eff 4-11-91); 143 v H 669 (Eff 1-10-91); 144 v S 359 (Eff 12-22-92); 144 v H 758 (Eff 1-15-93); 146 v H 670 (Eff 12-2-96); 149 v S 221. Eff 4-9-2003; 151 v H 58, § 1, eff. 5-3-05; 151 v H 81, § 1, eff. 4-14-06; 153 v H 1, § 101.01, eff. 10-16-09.**

The effective date is set by § 812.10 of 153 v H 1.

The effective date is set by § 4 of 151 v H 58.

## § 109.731 Duties of commission concerning licenses to carry concealed handgun.

(A) The Ohio peace officer training commission shall prescribe, and shall make available to sheriffs, all of the following:

(1) An application form that is to be used under section 2923.125 [2923.12.5] of the Revised Code by a person who applies for a license to carry a concealed handgun and an application form that is to be used under section 2923.125 [2923.12.5] of the Revised Code by a person who applies for the renewal of a license of that nature, both of which shall conform substantially to the forms prescribed in section 2923.1210 [2923.12.10] of the Revised Code;

(2) A form for the license to carry a concealed handgun that is to be issued by sheriffs to persons who qualify for a license to carry a concealed handgun under section 2923.125 [2923.12.5] of the Revised Code and that conforms to the following requirements:

(a) It has space for the licensee's full name, residence address, and date of birth and for a color photograph of the licensee.

(b) It has space for the date of issuance of the license, its expiration date, its county of issuance, the name of the sheriff who issues the license, and the unique combination of letters and numbers that identify the county of issuance and the license given to the licensee by the sheriff in accordance with division (A)(4) of this section.

(c) It has space for the signature of the licensee and the signature or a facsimile signature of the sheriff who issues the license.

(d) It does not require the licensee to include serial numbers of handguns, other identification related to handguns, or similar data that is not pertinent or relevant to obtaining the license and that could be used as a de facto means of registration of handguns owned by the licensee.

(3) A series of three-letter county codes that identify each county in this state;

(4) A procedure by which a sheriff shall give each license, replacement license, or renewal license to carry a concealed handgun and each temporary emergency license or replacement temporary emergency license to carry a concealed handgun the sheriff issues under section 2923.125 [2923.12.5] or 2923.1213 [2923.12.13] of the Revised Code a unique combination of letters and numbers that identifies the county in which the license or temporary emergency license was issued and that uses the county code and a unique number for each license and each temporary emergency license the sheriff of that county issues;

(5) A form for the temporary emergency license to carry a concealed handgun that is to be issued by sheriffs to persons who qualify for a temporary emergency license under section 2923.1213 [2923.12.13] of the Revised Code, which form shall conform to all the requirements set forth in divisions (A)(2)(a) to (d) of this section and shall additionally conspicuously specify that the license is a temporary emergency license and the date of its issuance.

(B)(1) The Ohio peace officer training commission, in consultation with the attorney general, shall prepare a pamphlet that does all of the following, in everyday language:

(a) Explains the firearms laws of this state;

(b) Instructs the reader in dispute resolution and explains the laws of this state related to that matter;

(c) Provides information to the reader regarding all aspects of the use of deadly force with a firearm, including, but not limited to, the steps that should be taken before contemplating the use of, or using, deadly force with a firearm, possible alternatives to using deadly force with a firearm, and the law governing the use of deadly force with a firearm.

(2) The attorney general shall consult with and assist the commission in the preparation of the pamphlet described in division (B)(1) of this section and, as necessary, shall recommend to the commission changes in the pamphlet to reflect changes in the law that are relevant to it. The attorney general shall publish the pamphlet on the web site of the attorney general and shall provide the address of the web site to any person who requests the pamphlet.

(C) The Ohio peace officer training commission shall maintain statistics with respect to the issuance, renewal, suspension, revocation, and denial of licenses to carry a concealed handgun and the suspension of processing of applications for those licenses, and with respect to the issuance, suspension, revocation, and denial of temporary emergency licenses to carry a concealed handgun, as reported by the sheriffs pursuant to division (C) of section 2923.129 [2923.12.9] of the Revised Code. Not later than the first day of March in each year, the commission shall submit a statistical report to the governor, the president of the senate, and the speaker of the house of representatives indicating the number of licenses to carry a concealed handgun that were issued, renewed, suspended, revoked, and denied in the previous calendar year, the number of applications for those licenses for which processing was suspended in accordance with division (D)(3) of section 2923.125 [2923.12.5] of the Revised Code in the previous calendar year, and the number of temporary emergency licenses to carry a concealed handgun that were issued, suspended, revoked, or denied in the previous calendar year. Nothing in the statistics or the statistical report shall identify, or enable the identification of, any individual who was issued or denied a license, for whom a license was renewed, whose license was suspended or revoked, or for whom application processing was suspended. The statistics and the statistical report are public records for the purpose of section 149.43 of the Revised Code.

(D) As used in this section, "handgun" has the same meaning as in section 2923.11 of the Revised Code.

**HISTORY: 150 v H 12, § 1, eff. 4-8-04; 151 v H 347, § 1, eff. 3-14-07; 153 v H 1, § 101.01, eff. 10-16-09.**

The effective date is set by § 812.10 of 153 v H 1.

Governor Taft's veto of HB 347 was overridden by the Ohio General Assembly.

See provisions of H.B. 12 following § 109.69.

## § 109.74 Attorney general may adopt and promulgate rules and regulations.

The attorney general, in accordance with Chapter 119. of the Revised Code, has discretion to adopt and promulgate any or all of the rules and regulations recommended by the Ohio peace officer training commission to the attorney general pursuant to section 109.73 of the Revised Code. When the attorney general promulgates any rule or regulation recommended by the commission, the attorney general shall transmit a certified copy thereof to the secretary of state.

**HISTORY: 131 v 11 (Eff 9-6-65); 146 v H 670. Eff 12-2-96.**

## § 109.741 Training in missing children, missing persons, child abuse and neglect cases.

The attorney general shall adopt, in accordance with Chapter 119. or pursuant to section 109.74 of the Revised Code, rules governing the training of peace officers in the handling of missing children, missing persons, and child abuse and neglect cases. The rules shall specify the amount of that training necessary for the satisfactory completion of basic training programs at approved peace officer training schools, other than the Ohio peace officer training academy and the time within which a peace officer is required to receive that training, if the peace officer is appointed as a peace officer before receiving that training.

**HISTORY: 140 v S 321 (Eff 4-9-85); 141 v S 84. Eff 4-9-85; 151 v H 571, § 1, eff. 4-5-07.**

The effective date is set by section 3 of SB 84.

## § 109.742 Crisis intervention training.

The attorney general shall adopt, in accordance with Chapter 119. or pursuant to section 109.74 of the Revised Code, rules governing the training of peace officers in crisis intervention. The rules shall specify the amount of training necessary for the satisfactory completion of basic training programs at approved peace officer training schools, other than the Ohio peace officer training academy.

**HISTORY: 140 v H 435. Eff 4-4-85; 153 v H 1, § 101.01, eff. 10-16-09.**

The effective date is set by § 812.10 of 153 v H 1.

## § 109.743 Rules for firearms requalification programs.

The attorney general shall adopt, in accordance with Chapter 119. of the Revised Code or pursuant to section 109.74 of the Revised Code, rules governing firearms requalification programs that are required by section 109.801 [109.80.1] of the Revised Code. At a minimum, the rules shall prohibit a firearms requalification program from being used to fulfill the requirements of section 109.801 [109.80.1] of the Revised Code until after the program is approved by the executive director of the Ohio peace officer training commission pursuant to section 109.75 of the Revised Code.

**HISTORY: 143 v H 271 (Eff 4-10-91); 146 v H 670. Eff 12-2-96.**

## § 109.744 Training relating to domestic violence.

The attorney general shall adopt, in accordance with Chapter 119. of the Revised Code or pursuant to section 109.74 of the Revised Code, rules governing the training of peace officers in the handling of the offense of domestic violence, other types of domestic violence-related offenses and incidents, and protection orders and consent agreements issued or approved under section 2919.26 or 3113.31 of the Revised Code. The provisions of the rules shall include, but shall not be limited to, all of the following:

(A) A specified amount of training that is necessary for the satisfactory completion of basic training programs at approved peace officer training schools, other than the Ohio peace officer training academy;

(B) A requirement that the training include, but not be limited to, training in all of the following:

(1) All recent amendments to domestic violence-related laws;

(2) Notifying a victim of domestic violence of the victim's rights;

(3) Processing protection orders and consent agreements issued or approved under section 2919.26 or 3113.31 of the Revised Code.

**HISTORY: 143 v S 3. Eff 4-11-91; 153 v H 1, § 101.01, eff. 10-16-09.**

The effective date is set by § 812.10 of 153 v H 1.

## § 109.75 Powers and duties of executive director.

The executive director of the Ohio peace officer training commission, on behalf of the commission, shall have the following powers and duties, which shall be exercised with the general advice of the commission and only in accordance with section 109.751 [109.75.1] of the Revised Code and the rules adopted pursuant to that section, and with the rules adopted by the attorney general pursuant to sections 109.74, 109.741 [109.74.1], 109.742 [109.74.2], and 109.743 [109.74.3] of the Revised Code:

(A) To approve peace officer training schools and firearms requalification programs administered by the state, counties, municipal corporations, and the department of natural resources, to issue certificates of approval to approved schools, and to revoke an approval or certificate;

(B) To certify, as qualified, instructors at approved peace officer training schools, to issue appropriate certificates to these instructors, and to revoke for good cause shown certificates of these instructors;

(C) To certify, as qualified, commanders at approved peace officer training schools, to issue appropriate certificates to these commanders, and to revoke for good cause shown certificates of these commanders. As used in this division, "commander" means the director or other head of an approved peace officer training school.

(D) To certify peace officers and sheriffs who have satisfactorily completed basic training programs and to issue appropriate certificates to these peace officers and sheriffs;

(E) To cause studies and surveys to be made relating to the establishment, operation, and approval of state, county, and municipal peace officer training schools;

(F) To consult and cooperate with state, county, and municipal peace officer training schools for the development of advanced in-service training programs for peace officers;

(G) To consult and cooperate with universities, colleges, and institutes for the development of specialized courses of study in the state for peace officers in police science and police administration;

(H) To consult and cooperate with other departments and agencies of the state and federal government concerned with peace officer training;

(I) To perform any other acts that may be necessary or appropriate to carry out the executive director's powers and duties as set forth in sections 109.71 to 109.77 of the Revised Code;

(J) To report to the commission at each regular meeting of the commission and at any other times that the commission may require;

(K) To certify persons who have satisfactorily completed approved training programs for correction officers in full-service jails, five-day facilities, or eight-hour holding facilities or approved training programs for others who provide correction services in those jails or facilities and to issue appropriate certificates to those persons;

(L) To maintain any records associated with the powers and duties set forth in this section. Certification examinations, either before or after completion, are not public records for purposes of section 149.43 of the Revised Code, but the results of such examinations are public records under that section.

**HISTORY: 131 v 11 (Eff 9-6-65); 139 v H 44 (Eff 5-8-81); 140 v H 759 (Eff 3-28-85); 140 v H 435 (Eff 4-4-85); 140 v S 321 (Eff 4-9-85); 141 v H 428 (Eff 12-23-86); 143 v H 271 (Eff 4-10-91); 143 v H 669 (Eff 1-10-91); 146 v H 566 (Eff 10-16-96); 146 v H 670 (Eff 12-2-96); 149 v H 545. Eff 3-19-2003.**

See provisions, § 3 of HB 545 (149 v —) following RC § 109.71.

## § 109.751 Attendance of undercover drug agents, bailiffs, deputy bailiffs or public defender investigators.

(A) The executive director of the Ohio peace officer training commission shall neither approve nor issue a certificate of approval to a peace officer training school pursuant to section 109.75 of the Revised Code unless the school agrees to permit, in accordance with rules adopted by the attorney general pursuant to division (C) of this section, undercover drug agents to attend its basic training programs. The executive director shall revoke approval, and the certificate of approval of, a peace officer training school that does not permit, in accordance with rules adopted by the attorney general pursuant to division (C) of this section, undercover drug agents to attend its basic training programs.

This division does not apply to peace officer training schools for employees of conservancy districts who are designated pursuant to section 6101.75 of the Revised Code or for a natural resources law enforcement staff officer, park officers, forest officers, preserve officers, wildlife officers, or state watercraft officers of the department of natural resources.

(B)(1) A peace officer training school is not required to permit an undercover drug agent, a bailiff or deputy bailiff of a court of record of this state, or a criminal investigator employed by the state public defender to attend its basic training programs if either of the following applies:

(a) In the case of the Ohio peace officer training academy, the employer county, township, municipal corporation, court, or state public defender or the particular undercover drug agent, bailiff, deputy bailiff, or criminal investigator has not paid the tuition costs of training in accordance with section 109.79 of the Revised Code;

(b) In the case of other peace officer training schools, the employing county, township, municipal corporation, court, or state public defender fails to pay the entire cost of the training and certification.

(2) A training school shall not permit a bailiff or deputy bailiff of a court of record of this state or a criminal investigator employed by the state public defender to attend its basic training programs unless the employing court of the bailiff or deputy bailiff or the state public defender, whichever is applicable, has authorized the bailiff, deputy bailiff, or investigator to attend the school.

(C) The attorney general shall adopt, in accordance with Chapter 119. or pursuant to section 109.74 of the Revised Code, rules governing the attendance of undercover drug agents at approved peace officer training schools, other than the Ohio peace officer training academy, and the certification of the agents upon their satisfactory completion of basic training programs.

**HISTORY: 139 v H 44 (Eff 5-8-81); 140 v H 759 (Eff 3-28-85); 141 v S 149 (Eff 6-6-86); 141 v S 278 (Eff 3-6-86); 141 v H 428 (Eff 12-23-86); 145 v S 182 (Eff 10-20-94); 146 v H 670 (Eff 12-2-96); 147 v S 187. Eff 3-18-99; 153 v H 1, § 101.01, eff. 10-16-09.**

The effective date is set by § 812.10 of 153 v H 1.

## § 109.752 Sheriff may attend peace officer basic training programs.

Any sheriff may attend and be awarded a certificate by the executive director of the Ohio peace officer training commission attesting to the satisfactory completion of any state, county, municipal, or department of natural resources peace officer basic training program that has been approved by the executive director under section 109.75 of the Revised Code or is offered at the Ohio peace officer training academy.

**HISTORY: 143 v H 271 (Eff 4-10-91); 143 v H 669 (Eff 1-10-91); 146 v H 670. Eff 12-2-96.**

## § 109.76 Provisions not to exempt officers from civil service provisions.

Nothing in sections 109.71 to 109.77 of the Revised Code shall be construed to except any peace officer, or other officer or employee from the provisions of Chapter 124. of the Revised Code.

**HISTORY: 131 v 12 (Eff 9-6-65); 137 v H 1. Eff 8-26-77.**

## § 109.761 Agency or entity appointing or employing peace officers to provide reports and roster to commission.

(A)(1) Each agency or entity that appoints or employs one or more peace officers shall report to the Ohio peace officer training commission all of the following that occur on or after February 20, 2002:

(a) The appointment or employment of any person to serve the agency or entity as a peace officer in any full-time, part-time, reserve, auxiliary, or other capacity;

(b) The termination, resignation, felony conviction, death, or guilty plea as specified in division (F) of section 109.77 of the Revised Code of any person who has been appointed to or employed by the agency or entity as a peace officer in any full-time, part-time, reserve, auxiliary, or other capacity and is serving the agency or entity in any of those peace officer capacities.

(2) An agency or entity shall make each report required by this division not later than ten days after the occurrence of the event being reported. The agency or entity shall

make the report in the manner and format prescribed by the executive director of the Ohio peace officer training commission.

(B) Each agency or entity that appoints or employs one or more peace officers or state highway patrol troopers shall annually provide to the Ohio peace officer training commission a roster of all persons who have been appointed to or employed by the agency or entity as peace officers or troopers in any full-time, part-time, reserve, auxiliary, or other capacity and are serving, or during the year covered by the report have served, the agency or entity in any of those peace officer or trooper capacities. The agency or entity shall provide the roster in the manner and format, and by the date, prescribed by the executive director of the Ohio peace officer training commission.

(C) The Ohio peace officer training commission shall prescribe the manner and format of making reports under division (A) of this section and providing annual rosters under division (B) of this section and shall prescribe the date by which the annual rosters must be provided.

**HISTORY: 149 v S 119. Eff 2-20-2002; 151 v S 281, § 1, eff. 1-4-07; 153 v H 1, § 101.01, eff. 10-16-09.**

The effective date is set by § 812.10 of 153 v H 1.

## § 109.77 Certificate necessary for appointment; prohibitions.

(A) As used in this section, "felony" has the same meaning as in section 109.511 [109.51.1] of the Revised Code.

(B)(1) Notwithstanding any general, special, or local law or charter to the contrary, and except as otherwise provided in this section, no person shall receive an original appointment on a permanent basis as any of the following unless the person previously has been awarded a certificate by the executive director of the Ohio peace officer training commission attesting to the person's satisfactory completion of an approved state, county, municipal, or department of natural resources peace officer basic training program:

(a) A peace officer of any county, township, municipal corporation, regional transit authority, or metropolitan housing authority;

(b) A natural resources law enforcement staff officer, park officer, forest officer, preserve officer, wildlife officer, or state watercraft officer of the department of natural resources;

(c) An employee of a park district under section 511.232 [511.23.2] or 1545.13 of the Revised Code;

(d) An employee of a conservancy district who is designated pursuant to section 6101.75 of the Revised Code;

(e) A state university law enforcement officer;

(f) A special police officer employed by the department of mental health pursuant to section 5119.14 of the Revised Code or the department of developmental disabilities pursuant to section 5123.13 of the Revised Code;

(g) An enforcement agent of the department of public safety whom the director of public safety designates under section 5502.14 of the Revised Code;

(h) A special police officer employed by a port authority under section 4582.04 or 4582.28 of the Revised Code;

(i) A special police officer employed by a municipal corporation at a municipal airport, or other municipal air navigation facility, that has scheduled operations, as defined in section 119.3 of Title 14 of the Code of Federal Regulations, 14 C.F.R. 119.3, as amended, and that is required to be under a security program and is governed by aviation security rules of the transportation security administration of the United States department of transportation as provided in Parts 1542. and 1544. of Title 49 of the Code of Federal Regulations, as amended;

(j) A gaming agent employed under section 3772.03 of the Revised Code.

(2) Every person who is appointed on a temporary basis or for a probationary term or on other than a permanent basis as any of the following shall forfeit the appointed position unless the person previously has completed satisfactorily or, within the time prescribed by rules adopted by the attorney general pursuant to section 109.74 of the Revised Code, satisfactorily completes a state, county, municipal, or department of natural resources peace officer basic training program for temporary or probationary officers and is awarded a certificate by the director attesting to the satisfactory completion of the program:

(a) A peace officer of any county, township, municipal corporation, regional transit authority, or metropolitan housing authority;

(b) A natural resources law enforcement staff officer, park officer, forest officer, preserve officer, wildlife officer, or state watercraft officer of the department of natural resources;

(c) An employee of a park district under section 511.232 [511.23.2] or 1545.13 of the Revised Code;

(d) An employee of a conservancy district who is designated pursuant to section 6101.75 of the Revised Code;

(e) A special police officer employed by the department of mental health pursuant to section 5119.14 of the Revised Code or the department of developmental disabilities pursuant to section 5123.13 of the Revised Code;

(f) An enforcement agent of the department of public safety whom the director of public safety designates under section 5502.14 of the Revised Code;

(g) A special police officer employed by a port authority under section 4582.04 or 4582.28 of the Revised Code;

(h) A special police officer employed by a municipal corporation at a municipal airport, or other municipal air navigation facility, that has scheduled operations, as defined in section 119.3 of Title 14 of the Code of Federal Regulations, 14 C.F.R. 119.3, as amended, and that is required to be under a security program and is governed by aviation security rules of the transportation security administration of the United States department of transportation as provided in Parts 1542. and 1544. of Title 49 of the Code of Federal Regulations, as amended.

(3) For purposes of division (B) of this section, a state, county, municipal, or department of natural resources peace officer basic training program, regardless of whether the program is to be completed by peace officers appointed on a permanent or temporary, probationary, or other nonpermanent basis, shall include training in the handling of the offense of domestic violence, other types of domestic violence-related offenses and incidents, and protection orders and consent agreements issued or approved under section 2919.26 or 3113.31 of the Revised Code and crisis intervention training. The requirement to complete training in the handling of the offense of domestic violence, other types of domestic violence-related offenses and incidents, and protection orders and consent agreements issued or approved under section 2919.26 or 3113.31 of the Revised Code does not apply to any person serving as a peace officer on March 27, 1979,

and the requirement to complete training in crisis intervention does not apply to any person serving as a peace officer on April 4, 1985. Any person who is serving as a peace officer on April 4, 1985, who terminates that employment after that date, and who subsequently is hired as a peace officer by the same or another law enforcement agency shall complete training in crisis intervention as prescribed by rules adopted by the attorney general pursuant to section 109.742 [109.74.2] of the Revised Code. No peace officer shall have employment as a peace officer terminated and then be reinstated with intent to circumvent this section.

(4) Division (B) of this section does not apply to any person serving on a permanent basis on March 28, 1985, as a park officer, forest officer, preserve officer, wildlife officer, or state watercraft officer of the department of natural resources or as an employee of a park district under section 511.232 [511.23.2] or 1545.13 of the Revised Code, to any person serving on a permanent basis on March 6, 1986, as an employee of a conservancy district designated pursuant to section 6101.75 of the Revised Code, to any person serving on a permanent basis on January 10, 1991, as a preserve officer of the department of natural resources, to any person employed on a permanent basis on July 2, 1992, as a special police officer by the department of mental health pursuant to section 5119.14 of the Revised Code or by the department of developmental disabilities pursuant to section 5123.13 of the Revised Code, to any person serving on a permanent basis on May 17, 2000, as a special police officer employed by a port authority under section 4582.04 or 4582.28 of the Revised Code, to any person serving on a permanent basis on March 19, 2003, as a special police officer employed by a municipal corporation at a municipal airport or other municipal air navigation facility described in division (A)(19) of section 109.71 of the Revised Code, to any person serving on a permanent basis on June 19, 1978, as a state university law enforcement officer pursuant to section 3345.04 of the Revised Code and who, immediately prior to June 19, 1978, was serving as a special police officer designated under authority of that section, or to any person serving on a permanent basis on September 20, 1984, as a liquor control investigator, known after June 30, 1999, as an enforcement agent of the department of public safety, engaged in the enforcement of Chapters 4301. and 4303. of the Revised Code.

(5) Division (B) of this section does not apply to any person who is appointed as a regional transit authority police officer pursuant to division (Y) of section 306.35 of the Revised Code if, on or before July 1, 1996, the person has completed satisfactorily an approved state, county, municipal, or department of natural resources peace officer basic training program and has been awarded a certificate by the executive director of the Ohio peace officer training commission attesting to the person's satisfactory completion of such an approved program and if, on July 1, 1996, the person is performing peace officer functions for a regional transit authority.

(C) No person, after September 20, 1984, shall receive an original appointment on a permanent basis as a veterans' home police officer designated under section 5907.02 of the Revised Code unless the person previously has been awarded a certificate by the executive director of the Ohio peace officer training commission attesting to the person's satisfactory completion of an approved police officer basic training program. Every person who is appointed on a temporary basis or for a probationary term or on other than a permanent basis as a veterans' home police officer designated under section 5907.02 of the Revised Code shall forfeit that position unless the person previously has completed satisfactorily or, within one year from the time of appointment, satisfactorily completes an approved police officer basic training program.

(D) No bailiff or deputy bailiff of a court of record of this state and no criminal investigator who is employed by the state public defender shall carry a firearm, as defined in section 2923.11 of the Revised Code, while on duty unless the bailiff, deputy bailiff, or criminal investigator has done or received one of the following:

(1) Has been awarded a certificate by the executive director of the Ohio peace officer training commission, which certificate attests to satisfactory completion of an approved state, county, or municipal basic training program for bailiffs and deputy bailiffs of courts of record and for criminal investigators employed by the state public defender that has been recommended by the Ohio peace officer training commission;

(2) Has successfully completed a firearms training program approved by the Ohio peace officer training commission prior to employment as a bailiff, deputy bailiff, or criminal investigator;

(3) Prior to June 6, 1986, was authorized to carry a firearm by the court that employed the bailiff or deputy bailiff or, in the case of a criminal investigator, by the state public defender and has received training in the use of firearms that the Ohio peace officer training commission determines is equivalent to the training that otherwise is required by division (D) of this section.

(E)(1) Before a person seeking a certificate completes an approved peace officer basic training program, the executive director of the Ohio peace officer training commission shall request the person to disclose, and the person shall disclose, any previous criminal conviction of or plea of guilty of that person to a felony.

(2) Before a person seeking a certificate completes an approved peace officer basic training program, the executive director shall request a criminal history records check on the person. The executive director shall submit the person's fingerprints to the bureau of criminal identification and investigation, which shall submit the fingerprints to the federal bureau of investigation for a national criminal history records check.

Upon receipt of the executive director's request, the bureau of criminal identification and investigation and the federal bureau of investigation shall conduct a criminal history records check on the person and, upon completion of the check, shall provide a copy of the criminal history records check to the executive director. The executive director shall not award any certificate prescribed in this section unless the executive director has received a copy of the criminal history records check on the person to whom the certificate is to be awarded.

(3) The executive director of the commission shall not award a certificate prescribed in this section to a person who has been convicted of or has pleaded guilty to a felony or who fails to disclose any previous criminal conviction of or plea of guilty to a felony as required under division (E)(1) of this section.

(4) The executive director of the commission shall revoke the certificate awarded to a person as prescribed in this section, and that person shall forfeit all of the benefits derived from being certified as a peace officer under this section, if the person, before completion of an approved peace officer basic training program, failed to disclose any

previous criminal conviction of or plea of guilty to a felony as required under division (E)(1) of this section.

(F)(1) Regardless of whether the person has been awarded the certificate or has been classified as a peace officer prior to, on, or after October 16, 1996, the executive director of the Ohio peace officer training commission shall revoke any certificate that has been awarded to a person as prescribed in this section if the person does either of the following:

(a) Pleads guilty to a felony committed on or after January 1, 1997;

(b) Pleads guilty to a misdemeanor committed on or after January 1, 1997, pursuant to a negotiated plea agreement as provided in division (D) of section 2929.43 of the Revised Code in which the person agrees to surrender the certificate awarded to the person under this section.

(2) The executive director of the commission shall suspend any certificate that has been awarded to a person as prescribed in this section if the person is convicted, after trial, of a felony committed on or after January 1, 1997. The executive director shall suspend the certificate pursuant to division (F)(2) of this section pending the outcome of an appeal by the person from that conviction to the highest court to which the appeal is taken or until the expiration of the period in which an appeal is required to be filed. If the person files an appeal that results in that person's acquittal of the felony or conviction of a misdemeanor, or in the dismissal of the felony charge against that person, the executive director shall reinstate the certificate awarded to the person under this section. If the person files an appeal from that person's conviction of the felony and the conviction is upheld by the highest court to which the appeal is taken or if the person does not file a timely appeal, the executive director shall revoke the certificate awarded to the person under this section.

(G)(1) If a person is awarded a certificate under this section and the certificate is revoked pursuant to division (E)(4) or (F) of this section, the person shall not be eligible to receive, at any time, a certificate attesting to the person's satisfactory completion of a peace officer basic training program.

(2) The revocation or suspension of a certificate under division (E)(4) or (F) of this section shall be in accordance with Chapter 119. of the Revised Code.

(H)(1) A person who was employed as a peace officer of a county, township, or municipal corporation of the state on January 1, 1966, and who has completed at least sixteen years of full-time active service as such a peace officer, or equivalent service as determined by the executive director of the Ohio peace officer training commission, may receive an original appointment on a permanent basis and serve as a peace officer of a county, township, or municipal corporation, or as a state university law enforcement officer, without complying with the requirements of division (B) of this section.

(2) Any person who held an appointment as a state highway trooper on January 1, 1966, may receive an original appointment on a permanent basis and serve as a peace officer of a county, township, or municipal corporation, or as a state university law enforcement officer, without complying with the requirements of division (B) of this section.

(I) No person who is appointed as a peace officer of a county, township, or municipal corporation on or after April 9, 1985, shall serve as a peace officer of that county, township, or municipal corporation unless the person has received training in the handling of missing children and child abuse and neglect cases from an approved state, county, township, or municipal police officer basic training program or receives the training within the time prescribed by rules adopted by the attorney general pursuant to section 109.741 [109.74.1] of the Revised Code.

(J) No part of any approved state, county, or municipal basic training program for bailiffs and deputy bailiffs of courts of record and no part of any approved state, county, or municipal basic training program for criminal investigators employed by the state public defender shall be used as credit toward the completion by a peace officer of any part of the approved state, county, or municipal peace officer basic training program that the peace officer is required by this section to complete satisfactorily.

(K) This section does not apply to any member of the police department of a municipal corporation in an adjoining state serving in this state under a contract pursuant to section 737.04 of the Revised Code.

**HISTORY: 142 v H 708 (Eff 4-19-88); 143 v H 271 (Eff 4-10-91); 143 v S 3 (Eff 4-11-91); 143 v H 669 (Eff 1-10-91); 144 v S 49 (Eff 7-21-92); 145 v S 182 (Eff 10-20-94); 146 v S 162 (Eff 10-29-95); 146 v S 2 (Eff 7-1-96); 146 v S 269 (Eff 7-1-96); 146 v H 566 (Eff 10-16-96); 146 v H 670 (Eff 12-2-96); 146 v S 285 (Eff 3-13-97); 147 v S 187 (Eff 3-18-99); 148 v H 163 (Eff 6-30-99); 148 v H 148 (Eff 7-15-99); 148 v S 137 (Eff 5-17-2000); 149 v H 675 (Eff 3-14-2003); 149 v H 545. Eff 3-19-2003; 149 v H 490, § 1, eff. 1-1-04; 153 v S 79, § 1, eff. 10-6-09; 153 v H 1, § 101.01, eff. 10-16-09; 153 v H 519, § 1, eff. 9-10-10.**

The provisions of § 6 of 153 v H 519 read in part as follows:

SECTION 6. The General Assembly, applying the principle stated in division (B) of section 1.52 of the Revised Code that amendments are to be harmonized if reasonably capable of simultaneous operation, finds that the following sections, presented in this act as composites of the sections as amended by the acts indicated, are the resulting versions of the sections in effect before the effective date of the sections as presented in this act:

° ° °

Section 109.77 of the Revised Code as amended by both Am. Sub. H.B. 1 and Sub. S.B. 79 of the 128th General Assembly.

° ° °

The effective date is set by § 812.10 of 153 v H 1.

The provisions of 815.10 of 153 v H 1 read as follows:

SECTION 815.10. The General Assembly, applying the principle stated in division (B) of section 1.52 of the Revised Code that amendments are to be harmonized if reasonably capable of simultaneous operation, finds that the following sections, presented in this act as composites of the sections as amended by the acts indicated, are the resulting versions of the sections in effect prior to the effective date of the sections as presented in this act:

° ° °

Section 109.77 of the Revised Code as amended by Am. Sub. H.B. 490, Sub. H.B. 545, and H.B. 675, all of the 124th General Assembly.

° ° °

The provisions of § 15 of 153 v S 79 read as follows:

SECTION 15. The General Assembly, applying the principle stated in division (B) of section 1.52 of the Revised Code that amendments are to be harmonized if reasonably capable of simultaneous operation, finds that the following sections, presented in this act as composites of the sections as amended by the acts indicated, are the resulting versions of the sections in effect prior to the effective date of the sections as presented in this act:

° ° °

Section 109.77 of the Revised Code as amended by Am. Sub. H.B. 490, Sub. H.B. 545, and H.B. 675, all of the 124th General Assembly.

° ° °

The effective date is set by section 4 of HB 490.

The provisions of § 5 of HB 490 (149 v —) read as follows:

SECTION 5. Section 109.77 of the Revised Code is presented

in this act as a composite of the section as amended by Sub. H.B. 148, Am. Sub. H.B. 163, and Am. S.B. 137 of the 123rd General Assembly. The General Assembly, applying the principle stated in division (B) of section 1.52 of the Revised Code that amendments are to be harmonized if reasonably capable of simultaneous operation, finds that the specified composite is the resulting version of the specified sections in effect prior to the effective date of the section as presented in this act.

**Analogous to former RC § 109.77 (131 v 12; 133 v H 575; 137 v H 588; 137 v H 835; 139 v H 738; 140 v S 85; 140 v H 759; 140 v H 435; 140 v S 321; 140 v H 129; 141 v S 84; 141 v S 149; 141 v S 278; 141 v H 428; 142 v H 231; 142 v H 261), repealed 142 v H 708, § 2, eff 4-19-88.**

## § 109.78 Certification of special police, security guards, private police; firearms training; private security fund.

(A) The executive director of the Ohio peace officer training commission, on behalf of the commission and in accordance with rules promulgated by the attorney general, shall certify persons who have satisfactorily completed approved training programs designed to qualify persons for positions as special police, security guards, or persons otherwise privately employed in a police capacity and issue appropriate certificates to such persons. Application for approval of a training program designed to qualify persons for such positions shall be made to the commission. An application for approval shall be submitted to the commission with a fee of one hundred twenty-five dollars, which fee shall be refunded if the application is denied. Such programs shall cover only duties and jurisdiction of such security guards and special police privately employed in a police capacity when such officers do not qualify for training under section 109.71 of the Revised Code. A person attending an approved basic training program administered by the state shall pay to the agency administering the program the cost of the person's participation in the program as determined by the agency. A person attending an approved basic training program administered by a county or municipal corporation shall pay the cost of the person's participation in the program, as determined by the administering subdivision, to the county or the municipal corporation. A person who is issued a certificate for satisfactory completion of an approved basic training program shall pay to the commission a fee of fifteen dollars. A duplicate of a lost, spoliated, or destroyed certificate may be issued upon application and payment of a fee of fifteen dollars. Such certificate or the completion of twenty years of active duty as a peace officer shall satisfy the educational requirements for appointment or commission as a special police officer or special deputy of a political subdivision of this state.

(B)(1) The executive director of the Ohio peace officer training commission, on behalf of the commission and in accordance with rules promulgated by the attorney general, shall certify basic firearms training programs, and shall issue certificates to class A, B, or C licensees or prospective class A, B, or C licensees under Chapter 4749. of the Revised Code and to registered or prospective employees of such class A, B, or C licensees who have satisfactorily completed a basic firearms training program of the type described in division (A)(1) of section 4749.10 of the Revised Code.

Application for approval of a basic firearms training program shall be made to the commission. An application shall be submitted to the commission with a fee of one hundred dollars, which fee shall be refunded if the application is denied.

A person who is issued a certificate for satisfactory completion of an approved basic firearms training program shall pay a fee of ten dollars to the commission. A duplicate of a lost, spoliated, or destroyed certificate may be issued upon application and payment of a fee of five dollars.

(2) The executive director, on behalf of the commission and in accordance with rules promulgated by the attorney general, also shall certify firearms requalification training programs and instructors for the annual requalification of class A, B, or C licensees under Chapter 4749. of the Revised Code and registered or prospective employees of such class A, B, or C licensees who are authorized to carry a firearm under section 4749.10 of the Revised Code. Application for approval of a training program or instructor for such purpose shall be made to the commission. Such an application shall be submitted to the commission with a fee of fifty dollars, which fee shall be refunded if the application is denied.

(3) The executive director, upon request, also shall review firearms training received within three years prior to November 23, 1985, by any class A, B, or C licensee or prospective class A, B, or C licensee, or by any registered or prospective employee of any class A, B, or C licensee under Chapter 4749. of the Revised Code to determine if the training received is equivalent to a basic firearms training program that includes twenty hours of handgun training and five hours of training in the use of other firearms, if any other firearm is to be used. If the executive director determines the training was received within the three-year period and that it is equivalent to such a program, the executive director shall issue written evidence of approval of the equivalency training to the licensee or employee.

(C) There is hereby established in the state treasury the peace officer private security fund, which shall be used by the Ohio peace officer training commission to administer the training program to qualify persons for positions as special police, security guards, or other private employment in a police capacity, as described in division (A) of this section, and the training program in basic firearms and the training program for firearms requalification, both as described in division (B) of this section. All fees paid to the commission by applicants for approval of a training program designed to qualify persons for such private police positions, basic firearms training program, or a firearms requalification training program or instructor, as required by division (A) or (B) of this section, by persons who satisfactorily complete a private police training program or a basic firearms training program, as required by division (A) or (B) of this section, or by persons who satisfactorily requalify in firearms use, as required by division (B)(2) of section 4749.10 of the Revised Code, shall be transmitted to the treasurer of state for deposit in the fund. The fund shall be used only for the purpose set forth in this division.

(D) No public or private educational institution, or superintendent of the state highway patrol shall employ a person as a special police officer, security guard, or other position in which such person goes armed while on duty, who has not received a certificate of having satisfactorily completed an approved basic peace officer training program, unless the person has completed twenty years of active duty as a peace officer.

**HISTORY: 133 v H 575 (Eff 11-21-69); 134 v H 1 (Eff 3-26-71); 134 v H 633 (Eff 4-3-72); 135 v S 192 (Eff 9-23-74);**

**137 v S 194 (Eff 7-8-77); 141 v H 402 (Eff 11-27-85); 141 v H 428 (Eff 12-23-86); 142 v H 419 (Eff 7-1-87); 146 v S 2 (Eff 7-1-96); 146 v H 670 (Eff 12-2-96); 148 v S 137. Eff 5-17-2000.**

## § 109.79 Training academy.

(A) The Ohio peace officer training commission shall establish and conduct a training school for law enforcement officers of any political subdivision of the state or of the state public defender's office. The school shall be known as the Ohio peace officer training academy. No bailiff or deputy bailiff of a court of record of this state and no criminal investigator employed by the state public defender shall be permitted to attend the academy for training unless the employing court of the bailiff or deputy bailiff or the state public defender, whichever is applicable, has authorized the bailiff, deputy bailiff, or investigator to attend the academy.

The Ohio peace officer training commission shall develop the training program, which shall include courses in both the civil and criminal functions of law enforcement officers, a course in crisis intervention with six or more hours of training, and training in the handling of missing children and child abuse and neglect cases, and shall establish rules governing qualifications for admission to the academy. The commission may require competitive examinations to determine fitness of prospective trainees, so long as the examinations or other criteria for admission to the academy are consistent with the provisions of Chapter 124. of the Revised Code.

The Ohio peace officer training commission shall determine tuition costs sufficient in the aggregate to pay the costs of operating the academy. The costs of acquiring and equipping the academy shall be paid from appropriations made by the general assembly to the Ohio peace officer training commission for that purpose, from gifts or grants received for that purpose, or from fees for goods related to the academy.

The Ohio peace officer training commission shall create a gaming-related curriculum for gaming agents. The Ohio peace officer training commission shall use money distributed to the Ohio peace officer training academy from the Ohio law enforcement training fund to first support the academy's training programs for gaming agents and gaming-related curriculum. The Ohio peace officer training commission may utilize existing training programs in other states that specialize in training gaming agents.

The law enforcement officers, during the period of their training, shall receive compensation as determined by the political subdivision that sponsors them or, if the officer is a criminal investigator employed by the state public defender, as determined by the state public defender. The political subdivision may pay the tuition costs of the law enforcement officers they sponsor and the state public defender may pay the tuition costs of criminal investigators of that office who attend the academy.

If trainee vacancies exist, the academy may train and issue certificates of satisfactory completion to peace officers who are employed by a campus police department pursuant to section 1713.50 of the Revised Code, by a qualified nonprofit corporation police department pursuant to section 1702.80 of the Revised Code, or by a railroad company, who are amusement park police officers appointed and commissioned by a judge of the appropriate municipal court or county court pursuant to section 4973.17 of the Revised Code, or who are bank, savings and loan association, savings bank, credit union, or association of banks, savings and loan associations, savings banks, or credit unions, or hospital police officers appointed and commissioned by the secretary of state pursuant to sections 4973.17 to 4973.22 of the Revised Code, provided that no such officer shall be trained at the academy unless the officer meets the qualifications established for admission to the academy and the qualified nonprofit corporation police department; bank, savings and loan association, savings bank, credit union, or association of banks, savings and loan associations, savings banks, or credit unions; railroad company; hospital; or amusement park or the private college or university that established the campus police department prepays the entire cost of the training. A qualified nonprofit corporation police department; bank, savings and loan association, savings bank, credit union, or association of banks, savings and loan associations, savings banks, or credit unions; railroad company; hospital; or amusement park or a private college or university that has established a campus police department is not entitled to reimbursement from the state for any amount paid for the cost of training the bank, savings and loan association, savings bank, credit union, or association of banks, savings and loan associations, savings banks, or credit unions peace officers; the railroad company's peace officers; or the peace officers of the qualified nonprofit corporation police department, campus police department, hospital, or amusement park.

The academy shall permit investigators employed by the state medical board to take selected courses that the board determines are consistent with its responsibilities for initial and continuing training of investigators as required under sections 4730.26 and 4731.05 of the Revised Code. The board shall pay the entire cost of training that investigators receive at the academy.

(B) As used in this section:

(1) "Law enforcement officers" include any undercover drug agent, any bailiff or deputy bailiff of a court of record, and any criminal investigator who is employed by the state public defender.

(2) "Undercover drug agent" means any person who:

(a) Is employed by a county, township, or municipal corporation for the purposes set forth in division (B)(2)(b) of this section but who is not an employee of a county sheriff's department, of a township constable, or of the police department of a municipal corporation or township;

(b) In the course of the person's employment by a county, township, or municipal corporation, investigates and gathers information pertaining to persons who are suspected of violating Chapter 2925. or 3719. of the Revised Code, and generally does not wear a uniform in the performance of the person's duties.

(3) "Crisis intervention training" has the same meaning as in section 109.71 of the Revised Code.

(4) "Missing children" has the same meaning as in section 2901.30 of the Revised Code.

**HISTORY: 133 v H 1160 (Eff 8-31-70); 136 v S 272 (Eff 8-19-76); 138 v H 83 (Eff 9-26-79); 139 v H 44 (Eff 5-8-81); 140 v H 435 (Eff 4-4-85); 140 v S 321 (Eff 4-9-85); 141 v S 149 (Eff 6-6-86); 141 v H 769 (Eff 3-17-87); 141 v S 364 (Eff 3-17-87); 142 v H 708 (Eff 4-19-88); 143 v H 110 (Eff 5-31-90); 144 v H 758 (Eff 1-15-93); 146 v H 670 (Eff 12-2-96); 147 v H 606. Eff 3-9-99; 151 v H 58, § 1, eff. 5-3-05; 151 v H 66, § 101.01, eff. 9-29-05; 151 v H 81, § 1, eff. 4-14-06; 153 v H 519, § 1, eff. 9-10-10.**

The effective date is set by § 612.03 of 151 v H 66.
The effective date is set by § 4 of 151 v H 58.

## § 109.80 Basic training course for sheriffs; continuing education required.

(A) The Ohio peace officer training commission shall develop and conduct a basic training course lasting at least three weeks for sheriffs appointed or elected on or after January 1, 1988 and shall establish criteria for what constitutes successful completion of the course. The basic training course shall include instruction in contemporary law enforcement, criminal investigations, the judicial process, civil rules, corrections, and other topics relevant to the duties and operations of the office of sheriff. The commission shall offer the course every four years within six months after the general election of sheriffs in each county and at other times when it is needed to permit sheriffs to attend within six months after appointment or election. The course shall be conducted by the Ohio peace officer training academy. The council shall provide that not less than two weeks of the course conducted within six months after the general election of sheriffs in each county shall be conducted prior to the first Monday in January next after that general election.

(B) The attorney general shall appoint a continuing education committee, consisting of not fewer than five nor more than seven members, including but not limited to, members of the Ohio peace officer training commission and sheriffs. The commission and the committee jointly shall determine the type of continuing education required for sheriffs to complete the requirements of division (E) of section 311.01 of the Revised Code and shall establish criteria for what constitutes successful completion of the requirement. The committee shall approve the courses that sheriffs may attend to complete the continuing education requirement and shall publish an approved list of those courses. The commission shall maintain a list of approved training schools that sheriffs may attend to complete the continuing education requirement. Upon request, the committee may approve courses other than those courses conducted as part of a certified law enforcement manager program.

(C) Upon presentation of evidence by a sheriff that because of medical disability or for other good cause that † the sheriff is unable to complete the basic or continuing education requirement, the commission may waive the requirement until the disability or cause terminates.

(D) As used in this section, "newly elected sheriff" means a person who did not hold the office of sheriff of a county on the date the person was elected sheriff of that county.

**HISTORY: 141 v H 683 (Eff 3-11-87); 142 v H 708 (Eff 4-19-88); 146 v H 670 (Eff 12-2-96); 146 v H 351. Eff 1-14-97.**

† The language, in division (C), is the result of combining HB 670 (146 v —) and HB 351 (146 v —).

The provisions of § 4 of H.B. 516 (150 v —) read in part as follows:

SECTION 4. The following agencies shall be retained pursuant to division (D) of section 101.83 of the Revised Code and shall expire on December 31, 2010:

| AGENCY NAME | REVISED CODE OR UNCODIFIED SECTION |
|---|---|
| ○○○ | ○○○ |
| Continuing Education Committee (for Sheriffs) | 109.80 |
| ○○○ | ○○○ |

**Comment, Legislative Service Commission**

Sections * * * 109.80 of the Revised Code is amended by this act [Sub. H.B. 670] and also by Sub. H.B. 351 of the 121st General Assembly. Comparison of these amendments in pursuance of section 1.52 of the Revised Code discloses that they are not irreconcilable so that they are required by that section to be harmonized to give effect to each amendment.

## § 109.801 Annual firearms requalification.

(A)(1) Each year, any of the following persons who are authorized to carry firearms in the course of their official duties shall complete successfully a firearms requalification program approved by the executive director of the Ohio peace officer training commission in accordance with rules adopted by the attorney general pursuant to section 109.743 of the Revised Code: any peace officer, sheriff, chief of police of an organized police department of a municipal corporation or township, chief of police of a township police district or joint police district police force, superintendent of the state highway patrol, state highway patrol trooper, or chief of police of a university or college police department; any parole or probation officer who carries a firearm in the course of official duties; the house of representatives sergeant at arms if the house of representatives sergeant at arms has arrest authority pursuant to division (E)(1) of section 101.311 of the Revised Code; any assistant house of representatives sergeant at arms; or any employee of the department of youth services who is designated pursuant to division (A)(2) of section 5139.53 of the Revised Code as being authorized to carry a firearm while on duty as described in that division.

(2) No person listed in division (A)(1) of this section shall carry a firearm during the course of official duties if the person does not comply with division (A)(1) of this section.

(B) The hours that a sheriff spends attending a firearms requalification program required by division (A) of this section are in addition to the sixteen hours of continuing education that are required by division (E) of section 311.01 of the Revised Code.

(C) As used in this section, "firearm" has the same meaning as in section 2923.11 of the Revised Code.

**HISTORY: 143 v H 271 (Eff 4-10-91); 145 v S 182 (Eff 10-20-94); 145 v H 406 (Eff 11-11-94); 146 v H 670 (Eff 12-2-96); 147 v H 1 (Eff 7-1-98); 147 v S 187 (Eff 3-18-99); 148 v S 317 (Eff 3-22-2001); 149 v H 545. Eff 3-19-2003; 150 v H 230, § 1, eff. 9-16-04; 151 v H 347, § 1, eff. 3-14-07; 2011 HB 153, § 101.01, eff. Sept. 29, 2011.**

Governor Taft's veto of HB 347 was overridden by the Ohio General Assembly.

## § 109.802 Law enforcement assistance fund to pay reimbursement for continuing professional training programs.

(A) There is hereby created in the state treasury the law enforcement assistance fund. The attorney general shall use the fund to pay reimbursements for continuing professional training programs for peace officers and troopers as provided in this section and section 109.803 [109.80.3] of the Revised Code, compensation of any employees of the attorney general required to administer those sections, and any other administrative costs incurred by the attorney general to administer those sections.

(B) The attorney general shall adopt rules in accordance with Chapter 119. of the Revised Code establishing application procedures, standards, and guidelines, and prescribing an application form, for the reimbursement of public appointing authorities for the cost of continuing professional training programs for their peace officers and troopers. The rules shall include, but are not limited to, all of the following:

(1) A requirement that applications for reimbursement be submitted on a calendar-year basis;

(2) The documentation required to substantiate any costs for which the applicant seeks reimbursement;

(3) Procedures for submitting applications for reimbursement for the cost of continuing professional training programs completed by a peace officer or trooper for whom the executive director of the Ohio peace officer training commission granted pursuant to division (A)(2) of section 109.803 [109.80.3] of the Revised Code an extension of the time for compliance with the continuing professional training requirement specified in division (A) of that section and who complied with the requirement prior to the date on which the extension ends;

(4) Any other requirements necessary for the proper administration of the reimbursement program.

(C) The Ohio peace officer training commission shall administer a program for reimbursing public appointing authorities for the costs of continuing professional training programs that are successfully completed by the appointing authority's peace officers or troopers. The commission shall administer the reimbursement program in accordance with rules adopted by the attorney general pursuant to division (B) of this section.

(D) Each public appointing authority may apply each calendar year to the peace officer training commission for reimbursement for the costs of continuing professional training programs that are successfully completed by the appointing authority's peace officers or troopers. Each application shall be made in accordance with, on an application form prescribed in, and be supported by the documentation required by, the rules adopted by the attorney general pursuant to division (B) of this section.

(E)(1) The Ohio peace officer training commission, in accordance with rules of the attorney general adopted under division (B) of this section, shall review each application for reimbursement made under division (D) of this section to determine if the applicant is entitled to reimbursement for the training programs for which the applicant seeks reimbursement. Except as provided in division (E)(2) of this section, a public appointing authority that complies with division (B) of section 109.761 [109.76.1] of the Revised Code and applies under division (D) of this section for reimbursement is entitled to reimbursement for each of the appointing authority's peace officers or troopers who timely complies with the continuing professional training requirement specified in division (A)(1) of section 109.803 [109.80.3] of the Revised Code by completing the minimum number of hours of training directed by the Ohio peace officer training commission under that division and with the other requirements described in that division.

(2) If a peace officer or trooper of the public appointing authority for whom the executive director of the commission granted an extension pursuant to division (A)(2) of section 109.803 [109.80.3] of the Revised Code complies prior to the date on which the extension ends with the continuing professional training requirement, and if the peace officer or trooper also has complied with the other requirements described in division (A)(1) of section 109.803 [109.80.3] of the Revised Code, the public appointing authority is entitled to reimbursement for the training programs completed by that peace officer or trooper. An application for reimbursement of the type described in this division shall be made in accordance with rules adopted by the attorney general pursuant to division (B) of section 109.802 [109.80.2] of the Revised Code.

(3) If a public appointing authority that applies under division (D) of this section for reimbursement is entitled to reimbursement under division (E)(1) or (2) of this section for each peace officer and trooper who successfully completes a training program, the commission shall approve reimbursing the appointing authority for the cost of that program. The actual amount of reimbursement for each authorized training program shall be determined by rules adopted by the attorney general under division (B) of this section.

If the public appointing authority is entitled to reimbursement under division (E)(2) of this section, payment of the reimbursement shall not be withheld during the period of the extension granted to the other peace officers or troopers of the authority pursuant to division (A)(2) of section 109.803 [109.80.3] of the Revised Code, pending their compliance with the requirement. If the public appointing authority is entitled to reimbursement under division (E)(2) of this section and if one or more of its peace officers or troopers who were granted an extension pursuant to division (A)(2) of section 109.803 [109.80.3] of the Revised Code fails to complete prior to the date on which the extension ends the required minimum number of hours of continuing professional training set by the commission under division (A)(1) of section 109.803 [109.80.3] of the Revised Code, the failure does not affect the reimbursement made to the public appointing authority, and the public appointing authority is not required to return the reimbursement or any portion of it.

(F) Each public appointing authority that receives funds under this section shall keep those funds separate from any other funds of the appointing authority and shall use those funds only for paying the cost of continuing professional training programs.

(G) As used in this section and section 109.803 [109.80.3] of the Revised Code:

(1) "Peace officer" has the same meaning as in section 109.71 of the Revised Code.

(2) "Trooper" means an individual appointed as a state highway patrol trooper under section 5503.01 of the Revised Code.

(3) "Appointing authority" means any agency or entity that appoints a peace officer or trooper.

**HISTORY: 143 v H 271 (Eff 4-10-91); 145 v S 182 (Eff 10-20-94); 145 v H 406 (Eff 11-11-94); 146 v H 566 (Eff 10-16-96); 146 v H 670 (Eff 12-2-96); 147 v S 187. Eff 3-18-99; 151 v S 281, § 1, eff. 1-4-07; 153 v H 1, § 101.01, eff. 10-16-09.**

The effective date is set by § 812.10 of 153 v H 1.

The provisions of § 9 of SB 187 (147 v —) read in part as follows:

SECTION 9. * * * Section 109.802 of the Revised Code is presented in this act as a composite of the section as amended by both Am. Sub. H.B. 566 and Sub. H.B. 670 of the 121st General Assembly, with the new language of neither of the acts shown in capital letters. * * * This is in recognition of the principle stated in division (B) of section 1.52 of the Revised Code that such amendments are to be harmonized where not substantively irreconcilable and constitutes a legislative finding that such is the resulting version in effect prior to the effective date of this act.

## § 109.803 Minimum annual required hours of continuing professional training; standards for training and programs.

(A)(1) Subject to division (A)(2) of this section, every appointing authority shall require each of its appointed peace officers and troopers to complete up to twenty-four hours of continuing professional training each calendar year, as directed by the Ohio peace officer training commission. The number of hours directed by the commission, up to twenty-four hours, is intended to be a minimum requirement, and appointing authorities are encouraged to exceed the number of hours the commission directs as the minimum. The commission shall set the required minimum number of hours based upon available funding for reimbursement as described in this division. If no funding for the reimbursement is available, no continuing professional training will be required.

(2) An appointing authority may submit a written request to the peace officer training commission that requests for a calendar year because of emergency circumstances an extension of the time within which one or more of its appointed peace officers or troopers must complete the required minimum number of hours of continuing professional training set by the commission, as described in division (A)(1) of this section. A request made under this division shall set forth the name of each of the appointing authority's peace officers or troopers for whom an extension is requested, identify the emergency circumstances related to that peace officer or trooper, include documentation of those emergency circumstances, and set forth the date on which the request is submitted to the commission. A request shall be made under this division not later than the fifteenth day of December in the calendar year for which the extension is requested.

Upon receipt of a written request made under this division, the executive director of the commission shall review the request and the submitted documentation. If the executive director of the commission is satisfied that emergency circumstances exist for any peace officer or trooper for whom a request was made under this division, the executive director may approve the request for that peace officer or trooper and grant an extension of the time within which that peace officer or trooper must complete the required minimum number of hours of continuing professional training set by the commission. An extension granted under this division may be for any period of time the executive director believes to be appropriate, and the executive director shall specify in the notice granting the extension the date on which the extension ends. Not later than thirty days after the date on which a request is submitted to the commission, for each peace officer and trooper for whom an extension is requested, the executive director either shall approve the request and grant an extension or deny the request and deny an extension and shall send to the appointing authority that submitted the request written notice of the executive director's decision.

If the executive director grants an extension of the time within which a particular appointed peace officer or trooper of an appointing authority must complete the required minimum number of hours of continuing professional training set by the commission, the appointing authority shall require that peace officer or trooper to complete the required minimum number of hours of training not later than the date on which the extension ends.

(B) With the advice of the Ohio peace officer training commission, the attorney general shall adopt in accordance with Chapter 119. of the Revised Code rules setting forth minimum standards for continuing professional training for peace officers and troopers and governing the administration of continuing professional training programs for peace officers and troopers. The attorney general shall transmit a certified copy of any rule adopted under this section to the secretary of state.

**HISTORY: 151 v S 281, § 1, eff. 1-4-07; 153 v H 1, § 101.01, eff. 10-16-09.**

The effective date is set by § 812.10 of 153 v H 1.

**Not analogous to former RC § 109.803 (143 v H 271 (Eff 4-10-91); 145 v H 406 (Eff 11-11-94); 146 v H 670. Eff 12-2-96), repealed 151 v S 281, § 2, eff 1-4-07.**

# [ANTITRUST SECTION IN OFFICE OF ATTORNEY GENERAL]

## § 109.81 Antitrust cases; special counsel.

(A) The attorney general shall act as the attorney at law in any antitrust case for the state. He may act as the attorney at law in any antitrust case for any political subdivision of the state, for the governing body of any political subdivision of the state, or, as parens patriae, for any natural person residing in the state. The attorney general shall do all things necessary under the laws of any state or the federal government to properly conduct any antitrust case in which he acts as attorney at law, including the bringing of an action for equitable relief or for the recovery of damages.

(B) The attorney general may appoint special counsel to act as attorney at law in any antitrust case described in division (A) of this section. A special counsel appointed under this section shall be paid in either or both of the following ways:

(1) At an hourly rate determined by the attorney general;

(2) At a percentage determined by the attorney general of the monetary relief or economic benefit recovered from conducting the antitrust case.

**HISTORY: 132 v H 556 (Eff 12-14-67); 145 v H 152. Eff 7-1-93.**

## § 109.82 Antitrust section.

There is hereby created in the office of the attorney general a section of antitrust. Ten per cent of all recoveries obtained by the attorney general pursuant to section 109.81 of the Revised Code by settlement or by judgment in any court and the full amount of all related civil penalties, attorney's fees, and reimbursements of investigative, litigation, or expert witness costs shall be paid into the state treasury to the credit of the attorney general antitrust fund, which is hereby created. The fund shall be used for expenses of the antitrust section. The expenses of the antitrust section in excess of the money available in the fund shall be paid out of the regular appropriation to the office of the attorney general.

**HISTORY: 132 v H 556 (Eff 12-14-67); 137 v S 221 (Eff 11-23-77); 141 v H 201 (Eff 7-1-85); 144 v H 298 (Eff 7-26-91); 144 v S 351. Eff 7-1-92.**

[ORGANIZED CRIMINAL ACTIVITY]

## § 109.83 Investigation of organized criminal activity.

(A) When directed by the governor or general assembly, the attorney general may investigate any organized criminal activity in this state. When it appears to the attorney general, as a result of an investigation conducted pursuant to this division, that there is cause to prosecute for the commission of a crime, the attorney general shall refer the evidence to the prosecuting attorney having jurisdiction of the matter, to a regular grand jury drawn and impaneled pursuant to sections 2939.01 to 2939.24 of the Revised Code, or to a special grand jury drawn and impaneled pursuant to section 2939.17 of the Revised Code. When the crime or the elements of the crime were committed in two or more counties, the referral shall be to the prosecuting attorney, the regular grand jury, or a special grand jury of the county in which the most significant portion of the crime or the elements of the crime occurred or, if it is not possible to determine that county, the county with the largest population. When evidence is referred directly to a grand jury pursuant to this section, the attorney general and any assistant or special counsel designated by the attorney general has the exclusive right to appear at any time before the grand jury to give information relative to a legal matter cognizable by it, or to advise upon a legal matter when required, and may exercise all rights, privileges, and powers of prosecuting attorneys in such cases.

(B)(1) When information is referred to the attorney general by an organized crime task force or the organized crime investigations commission pursuant to section 177.03 of the Revised Code, the attorney general shall review the information so referred and upon a determination that there is cause to prosecute for the commission of a crime, the attorney general either shall refer the information as evidence to a regular or special grand jury in the manner described in, and in the county determined in accordance with the provisions of, division (A) of this section or shall initiate a criminal action or proceeding in a court of proper jurisdiction. If an indictment is returned by a grand jury pursuant to a referral made under this division, the attorney general has sole responsibility to prosecute the accused offender.

(2) The attorney general, and any assistant or special counsel designated by the attorney general who appears under this division in any county for the prosecution of any crime has the same powers and authority as a prosecuting attorney, including, but not limited to, powers relating to attendance before the courts and grand juries of the county, preparation and trial of indictments for crimes, and representation of the state in any criminal proceeding, in any civil proceeding related to the crime, or in any appeal from a criminal case or from a civil case related to the crime in any court of this state.

(C) When proceeding under the authority of this section, the attorney general may appear for the state in any court or tribunal of proper jurisdiction for the purpose of conducting investigations under division (A) of this section, or for the purpose of conducting criminal proceedings, civil proceedings, or any other proceeding that is necessary to promote and safeguard the public interests of the citizens of this state.

(D) This section shall not be construed to prevent the attorney general and prosecuting attorneys or special prosecutors from cooperating in the investigation and prosecution of offenses under this section. However, in cases in which information was referred to the attorney general by an organized crime task force because the office of a prosecuting attorney was implicated by an investigation conducted by the task force, the attorney general shall not inform the implicated prosecutor of the investigation or referral and shall not cooperate with the prosecutor on the matter.

(E) As used in this section, "organized criminal activity" has the same meaning as in section 177.01 of the Revised Code.

**HISTORY: 133 v H 956 (Eff 9-16-70); 141 v S 74 (Eff 9-3-86); 147 v H 2. Eff 1-1-99.**

The effective date is set by section 4 of HB 2.

[WORKER'S COMPENSATION]

## § 109.84 Investigation and prosecution of violation of law.

(A) Upon the written request of the governor, the industrial commission, the administrator of workers' compensation, or upon the attorney general's becoming aware of criminal or improper activity related to Chapter 4121. or 4123. of the Revised Code, the attorney general shall investigate any criminal or civil violation of law related to Chapter 4121. or 4123. of the Revised Code.

(B) When it appears to the attorney general, as a result of an investigation under division (A) of this section, that there is cause to prosecute for the commission of a crime or to pursue a civil remedy, he may refer the evidence to the prosecuting attorney having jurisdiction of the matter, or to a regular grand jury drawn and impaneled pursuant to sections 2939.01 to 2939.24 of the Revised Code, or to a special grand jury drawn and impaneled pursuant to section 2939.17 of the Revised Code, or he may initiate and prosecute any necessary criminal or civil actions in any court or tribunal of competent jurisdiction in this state. When proceeding under this section, the attorney general has all rights, privileges, and powers of prosecuting attorneys, and any assistant or special counsel designated by him for that purpose has the same authority.

(C) The attorney general shall be reimbursed by the bureau of workers' compensation for all actual and necessary costs incurred in conducting investigations requested by the governor, the commission, or the administrator and all actual and necessary costs in conducting the prosecution arising out of such investigation.

**HISTORY: 136 v S 545 (Eff 1-17-77); 143 v H 222. Eff 11-3-89.**

[MEDICAID INVESTIGATIONS]

## § 109.85 Medicaid investigations.

(A) Upon the written request of the governor, the general assembly, the auditor of state, the director of job and family services, the director of health, or the director of budget and management, or upon the attorney general's becoming aware of criminal or improper activity related to Chapter 3721. and the medical assistance program established under section 5111.01 of the Revised Code, the attorney general shall investigate any criminal or civil violation of law related to Chapter 3721. of the Revised Code or the medical assistance program.

(B) When it appears to the attorney general, as a result of an investigation under division (A) of this section, that there is cause to prosecute for the commission of a crime or to pursue a civil remedy, the attorney general may refer the evidence to the prosecuting attorney having jurisdiction of the matter, or to a regular grand jury drawn and impaneled pursuant to sections 2939.01 to 2939.24 of the Revised Code, or to a special grand jury drawn and impaneled pursuant to section 2939.17 of the Revised Code, or the attorney general may initiate and prosecute any necessary criminal or civil actions in any court or tribunal of competent jurisdiction in this state. When proceeding under this section, the attorney general, and any assistant or special counsel designated by the attorney general for that purpose, have all rights, privileges, and powers of prosecuting attorneys. The attorney general shall have exclusive supervision and control of all investigations and prosecutions initiated by the attorney general under this section. The forfeiture provisions of Chapter 2981. of the Revised Code apply in relation to any such criminal action initiated and prosecuted by the attorney general.

(C) Nothing in this section shall prevent a county prosecuting attorney from investigating and prosecuting criminal activity related to Chapter 3721. of the Revised Code and the medical assistance program established under section 5111.01 of the Revised Code. The forfeiture provisions of Chapter 2981. of the Revised Code apply in relation to any prosecution of criminal activity related to the medical assistance program undertaken by the prosecuting attorney.

**HISTORY: 137 v S 159 (Eff 4-24-78); 138 v H 176 (Eff 7-1-80); 141 v H 201 (Eff 7-1-85); 143 v H 672 (Eff 11-14-89); 145 v H 152 (Eff 7-1-93); 148 v H 471. Eff 7-1-2000; 151 v H 241, § 1, eff. 7-1-07.**

The provisions of § 4 of 151 v H 241 read as follows:

SECTION 4. Sections 1, 2, and 3 of this act shall take effect on July 1, 2007. If a criminal or civil forfeiture action relating to misconduct under Title XXIX of the Revised Code was or is commenced before July 1, 2007, and is still pending on that date, the court in which the case is pending shall, to the extent practical, apply the provisions of Chapter 2981. of the Revised Code in the case.

The effective date is set by section 12(A) of HB 471.

## [PATIENT ABUSE OR NEGLECT]

### § 109.86 Investigation of abuse or neglect of care facility patient; prosecution.

(A) The attorney general shall investigate any activity the attorney general has reasonable cause to believe is in violation of section 2903.34 of the Revised Code. Upon written request of the governor, the general assembly, the auditor of state, or the director of health, job and family services, aging, mental health, or developmental disabilities, the attorney general shall investigate any activity these persons believe is in violation of section 2903.34 of the Revised Code. If after an investigation the attorney general has probable cause to prosecute for the commission of a crime, the attorney general shall refer the evidence to the prosecuting attorney, director of law, or other similar chief legal officer having jurisdiction over the matter. If the prosecuting attorney decides to present the evidence to a grand jury, the prosecuting attorney shall notify the attorney general in writing of the decision within thirty days after referral of the matter and shall present the evidence prior to the discharge of the next regular grand jury. If the director of law or other chief legal officer decides to prosecute the case, the director or officer shall notify the attorney general in writing of the decision within thirty days and shall initiate prosecution within sixty days after the matter was referred to the director or officer.

(B) If the prosecuting attorney, director of law, or other chief legal officer fails to notify the attorney general or to present evidence or initiate prosecution in accordance with division (A) of this section, the attorney general may present the evidence to a regular grand jury drawn and impaneled pursuant to sections 2939.01 to 2939.24 of the Revised Code, or to a special grand jury drawn and impaneled pursuant to section 2939.17 of the Revised Code, or the attorney general may initiate and prosecute any action in any court or tribunal of competent jurisdiction in this state. The attorney general, and any assistant or special counsel designated by the attorney general, have all the powers of a prosecuting attorney, director of law, or other chief legal officer when proceeding under this section. Nothing in this section shall limit or prevent a prosecuting attorney, director of law, or other chief legal officer from investigating and prosecuting criminal activity committed against a resident or patient of a care facility.

**HISTORY: 141 v H 566 (Eff 9-17-86); 148 v H 471. Eff 7-1-2000; 153 v S 79, § 1, eff. 10-6-09.**

The effective date is set by section 12(A) of HB 471.

## [TELEMARKETING]

### § 109.87 Violation of federal laws concerning telemarketing prohibited; investigations and enforcement by attorney general.

(A)(1) As used in this section, "federal act or rule" means the "Telemarketing and Consumer Fraud and Abuse Prevention Act," 108 Stat. 1545 to 1551, 15 U.S.C. 6101 to 6108, the "Telephone Consumer Protection Act of 1991," 105 Stat. 2395, 47 U.S.C. 227, any amendment or reenactment of either of those acts, any rule adopted or issued pursuant to either of those acts, or any amendment of that rule.

(2) The terms that are used in this section have the same meanings as in the applicable federal act or rule.

(B)(1) No seller or telemarketer shall engage in any act or practice in violation of any provision of a federal act or rule.

(2) The attorney general, in any proceedings under this section, shall recognize any exemptions recognized by the federal communications commission under the "Telephone Consumer Protection Act of 1991," 105 Stat. 2395, 47 U.S.C. 227, any amendment or reenactment of that act, any rule adopted or issued pursuant to that act, or any amendment of that rule.

(C)(1) If the attorney general, as a result of complaints or the attorney general's own inquiries, has reason to believe that a person has engaged, is engaging, or is preparing to engage in a violation of any provision of a federal act or rule, the attorney general may investigate the alleged violation. For purposes of an investigation under division (C)(1) of this section, the attorney general may administer oaths, subpoena witnesses, adduce evidence, and require the production of any relevant matter.

(2) If the matter to be produced under division (C)(1) of this section is located outside this state, the attorney general may designate any representative, including any official of the state in which the matter is located, to inspect the matter on the behalf of the attorney general. The person subpoenaed may make the matter available to the attorney general at a convenient location within the state or pay the reasonable and necessary expenses for the attorney general or the attorney general's representative to examine the matter at the place where it is located, provided that those expenses shall not be charged to a party that subsequently is not found to have engaged in a violation of any provision of a federal act or rule.

(3) A person subpoenaed under division (C)(1) of this section may file a motion to extend the day on which the subpoena is to be returned or to modify or quash the subpoena, for good cause shown, in the court of common pleas of Franklin county or of the county in this state in which the person resides or in which the person's principal place of business is located. The person may file the motion not later than twenty days after the service of the subpoena.

(4) A person subpoenaed under division (C)(1) of this section shall comply with the terms of the subpoena unless the parties agree to modify the terms of the subpoena or unless the court has modified or quashed the subpoena, extended the day on which the subpoena is to be returned, or issued any other order with respect to the subpoena prior to the day on which the subpoena is to be returned. If a person fails without lawful excuse to testify or to produce relevant matter pursuant to a subpoena, the attorney general may apply to the court of common pleas of the county in which the person subpoenaed resides or in which the person's principal place of business is located for an order that compels compliance with the subpoena.

(5) If an individual subpoenaed under division (C)(1) of this section refuses to testify or to produce relevant matter pursuant to the subpoena on the ground that the testimony or matter may incriminate the individual, the attorney general may request the court to order the individual to provide the testimony or matter. With the exception of a prosecution for perjury or a civil action for damages under division (D)(1) of this section, an individual who complies with a court order to provide testimony or matter, after asserting a privilege against self-incrimination to which the individual is entitled by law, shall not be subjected to a criminal proceeding or a civil penalty or forfeiture on the basis of the testimony or matter required to be disclosed or testimony or matter discovered through that testimony or matter required to be disclosed.

(6) The attorney general may do either of the following:

(a) During an investigation under division (C) of this section, afford the person who is the subject of the investigation, in a manner considered appropriate to that person, an opportunity to cease and desist from any suspected violation of any provision of a federal act or rule. The attorney general may suspend the investigation during the period that the attorney general permits the person to cease and desist from that suspected violation. The suspension of the investigation or the affording of an opportunity to cease and desist shall not prejudice or prohibit any further investigation by the attorney general under division (C) of this section.

(b) Terminate an investigation under division (C) of this section upon acceptance of a written assurance of voluntary compliance from a person who is suspected of a violation of any provision of a federal act or rule. The acceptance of an assurance under division (C)(6)(b) of this section may be conditioned upon an undertaking to reimburse or to take other appropriate corrective action with respect to identifiable telephone service subscribers who are damaged by an alleged violation of any provision of a federal act or rule. An assurance of compliance given by a person under division (C)(6)(b) of this section is not evidence of a violation of any provision of a federal act or rule. The attorney general, at any time, may reopen an investigation terminated by the acceptance of an assurance of voluntary compliance, if the attorney general believes that further proceedings are in the public interest. Evidence of a violation of an assurance of voluntary compliance is prima-facie evidence of an act or practice in violation of the applicable provision of a federal act or rule if the evidence is presented after the violation in a civil action brought under division (D)(1) of this section. An assurance of voluntary compliance may be filed with the court and if approved by the court, entered as a consent judgment in the action.

(7) The procedures that are available to the attorney general under division (C) of this section are cumulative and concurrent, and the exercise of one procedure by the attorney general does not preclude or require the exercise of any other procedure.

(D)(1) If, by the attorney general's own inquiries or as a result of complaints or an investigation conducted under division (C) of this section, the attorney general has reasonable cause to believe that a person has engaged or is engaging in a violation of any provision of this section or of a federal act or rule, the attorney general, subject to division (D)(2) or (3) of this section, may bring in the appropriate court of common pleas of this state or in the appropriate district court of the United States, but not in both courts, a civil action against the alleged violator for injunctive relief or a civil action against the alleged violator for damages, or both, pursuant to the federal act or rule, on behalf of the residents of this state who have been subjected to telemarketing acts or practices in violation of this section. The attorney general may bring the action under this section or under the applicable federal act or rule, but the attorney general shall not plead a violation of both this section and the applicable federal act or rule in the action. On the motion of the attorney general or on its own motion, a court may impose a civil penalty for a violation of the provision of this section or of the federal act or rule that is the subject of the action. The amount of any award of damages made or civil penalty imposed under division (D)(1) of this section shall not exceed any maximum allowable amount of damages or civil penalty that is specified in the applicable federal act or rule. An award of damages or civil penalties may be recovered under this section or under the applicable federal act or rule, but an award of damages or civil penalties shall not be recovered under both this section and the applicable federal act or rule.

(2) If a civil action has been instituted by or on behalf of the federal trade commission or the federal communications commission for a violation of any provision of an applicable federal act or rule, the attorney general, during the pendency of that action, shall not institute any civil action under division (D)(1) of this section against any defendant that is named in the complaint in the civil action that has been instituted by or on behalf of the federal trade commission or the federal communications commission,

whichever is applicable, for any violation that is alleged in that complaint.

(3) If a civil action that has been instituted by or on behalf of the federal trade commission or the federal communications commission for a violation of any provision of an applicable federal act or rule affecting the residents of this state is litigated to its conclusion and the federal trade commission or the federal communications commission recovers an award of damages or civil penalties or obtains any relief under the applicable federal act or rule, the attorney general shall not institute any civil action under division (D)(1) of this section for any violation within the same time period that is alleged in the civil action that was instituted as described in division (D)(3) of this section and in which the federal trade commission or federal communications commission has recovered the damages or civil penalties or obtained the relief.

(E) Any civil action that the attorney general brings in a federal court under division (D)(1) of this section shall comply with the applicable provisions of the federal act or rule the violation of which is the subject of the action.

(F) The attorney general shall deposit any civil penalties that are imposed under division (D)(1) of this section to the credit of the telephone solicitation protection fund, which is hereby created in the state treasury, to be used to pay the costs of the office of the attorney general in investigating any violation of, and in enforcing, any federal act or rule or this section.

**HISTORY: 150 v S 28, § 1, eff. 4-13-04.**

## [CRIME VICTIMS ASSISTANCE]

## § 109.90 Drug take-back Program; attorney general duties.

(A) The attorney general shall collaborate with the state board of pharmacy and director of alcohol and drug addiction services in the establishment and administration of a drug take-back program, as provided under section 4729.69 of the Revised Code. The office of the attorney general is solely responsible for the costs incurred in the establishment and administration of the program.

(B) The attorney general may accept grants, gifts, or donations for purposes of the program. Money received under this division or section 3793.22 or 4729.69 of the Revised Code shall be deposited into the state treasury to the credit of the drug take-back program fund, which is hereby created. Money credited to the fund shall be used solely for purposes of the program.

**HISTORY: 2011 HB 93, § 1, eff. May 20, 2011.**

Acts 2011, HB 93, § 8 provides: "(A) Not later than one year after the effective date of this section, and annually each year for four years thereafter, the State Board of Pharmacy shall prepare a report on all of the following:

(A)(1) The total number of applications received by the Board for a terminal distributor of dangerous drugs license with a pain management clinic classification;

(2) The total number of licenses with a pain management clinic classification granted or denied by the Board;

(3) Any disciplinary actions taken by the Board against holders of licenses with a pain management clinic classification;

(4) Total revenues generated from fees for licenses with a pain management clinic classification, fines and penalties paid by license holders, or other disciplinary actions taken against license holders;

(5) Any other relevant information regarding the implementation of this act.

(B) On completion of each report, the Board shall submit a copy of the report to the Governor and, in accordance with section 101.68 of the Revised Code, the General Assembly. In accordance with that section, the Board shall display the report on the Board's internet web site."

## § 109.91 Crime victims assistance office; state victims assistance advisory committee.

(A) There is hereby established within the office of the attorney general the crime victims assistance office.

(B) There is hereby established the state victims assistance advisory council. The council shall consist of a chairperson, to be appointed by the attorney general, three ex officio members, and fifteen members to be appointed by the attorney general as follows: one member who represents the Ohio victim-witness association; three members who represent local victim assistance programs, including one from a municipally operated program and one from a county-operated program; one member who represents the interests of elderly victims; one member who is a board member of any statewide or local organization that exists primarily to aid victims of domestic violence, or who is an employee of, or counselor for, such an organization; one member who is an employee or officer of a county probation department or a probation department operated by the department of rehabilitation and correction; one member who is a county prosecuting attorney; one member who is a city law director; one member who is a county sheriff; one member who is a member or officer of a township or municipal police department; one member who is a court of common pleas judge; one member who is a municipal court judge or county court judge; and two members who are private citizens and are not government employees.

The council shall include the following ex officio, nonvoting members: the attorney general, one member of the senate to be designated by the president of the senate, and one member of the house of representatives to be designated by the speaker of the house.

Members of the council shall serve without compensation, but shall be reimbursed for travel and other necessary expenses that are incurred in the conduct of their official duties as members of the council. The chairperson and members of the council appointed by the attorney general shall serve at the pleasure of the attorney general. The attorney general shall serve on the council until the end of the term of office that qualified the attorney general for membership on the council. The member of the senate and the member of the house of representatives shall serve at the pleasure of the president of the senate and the speaker of the house of representatives, respectively.

(C) The victims assistance advisory council shall perform both of the following duties:

(1) Advise the crime victims assistance office in determining crime and delinquency victim service needs, determining crime and delinquency victim policies for the state, and improving and exercising leadership in the quality of crime and delinquency victim programs in the state;

(2) Review and recommend to the crime victims assistance office the victim assistance programs that should be considered for the receipt of state financial assistance pursuant to section 109.92 of the Revised Code. The

financial assistance allocation recommendations of the council shall be based on the following priorities:

(a) Programs in existence on July 1, 1985, shall be given first priority;

(b) Programs offering or proposing to offer the broadest range of services and referrals to the community served, including medical, psychological, financial, educational, vocational, and legal services that were not in existence on July 1, 1985, shall be given second priority;

(c) Other qualified programs shall be given last priority.

(D) As used in this section and section 109.92 of the Revised Code, "victim assistance program" includes, but is not limited to a program that provides at least one of the following:

(1) Services to victims of any offense of violence or delinquent act that would be an offense of violence if committed by an adult;

(2) Financial assistance or property repair services to victims of crime or delinquent acts;

(3) Assistance to victims of crime or delinquent acts in judicial proceedings;

(4) Assistance to victims of crime or delinquent acts under the operation of any political subdivision of the state or a branch of the criminal justice system set forth in division (B)(1)(a), (b), or (c) of section 5502.61 of the Revised Code;

(5) Technical assistance to persons or organizations that provide services to victims of crime or delinquent acts under the operation of a branch of the criminal justice system set forth in division (B)(1)(a), (b), or (c) of section 5502.61 of the Revised Code.

A victim assistance program does not include the program for the reparation of crime victims established pursuant to Chapter 2743. of the Revised Code.

**HISTORY: 140 v S 195 (Eff 7-1-85); 142 v H 171 (Eff 7-1-87); 142 v H 231 (Eff 10-5-87); 145 v H 152 (Eff 7-1-93); 146 v H 670. Eff 12-2-96; 151 v H 66, § 101.01, eff. 6-30-05; 2011 SB 171, § 1, eff. June 30, 2011.**

The effective date is set by § 612.12 of 151 v H 66.

The provisions of § 4 of H.B. 516 (150 v —) read in part as follows:

SECTION 4. The following agencies shall be retained pursuant to division (D) of section 101.83 of the Revised Code and shall expire on December 31, 2010:

| AGENCY NAME | REVISED CODE OR UNCODIFIED SECTION |
| --- | --- |
| ○○○ | ○○○ |
| State Victims Assistance Advisory Committee | 109.91 |
| ○○○ | ○○○ |

## § 109.92 Financial assistance to victim assistance programs.

(A) Appropriations may be made by the general assembly to the office of the attorney general for the purpose of providing state financial assistance to victim assistance programs that operate in the state. All amounts so appropriated shall be used to provide financial assistance to victim assistance programs in accordance with section 109.91 of the Revised Code and this section. The program for the provision of such financial assistance shall be administered by the crime victims assistance office established pursuant to section 109.91 of the Revised Code.

(B) A victim assistance program may apply to the crime victims assistance office for state financial assistance out of funds appropriated to the office of the attorney general for that purpose by the general assembly. Each application for such financial assistance shall include all of the following information:

(1) Evidence that the program is incorporated in this state as a nonprofit corporation or is a program established by a unit of state or local government;

(2) The proposed budget of the program for the period during which the financial assistance is sought;

(3) A summary of services offered by the program;

(4) An estimate of the number of persons served by the program.

(C) Within thirty days of receipt of an application for financial assistance from a victim assistance program in accordance with division (B) of this section, the crime victims assistance office, based in part on the recommendations of the victim assistance advisory board made pursuant to section 109.91 of the Revised Code, shall notify the program in writing whether it is eligible for financial assistance and, if eligible, estimate the amount that will be made available to the program and the time when the financial assistance will be made available.

(D) Each victim assistance program that receives any financial assistance pursuant to this section shall use the financial assistance only to provide the services identified in its application for such assistance as being services it offered and to cover a reasonable cost of administration of the program. Each victim assistance program that receives any such financial assistance shall make a good faith effort to minimize its costs of administration.

**HISTORY: 140 v S 195 (Eff 7-1-85); 143 v H 111 (Eff 7-1-89); 148 v S 153. Eff 7-1-2000.**

The effective date is set by section 4 of SB 153.

### [MISCELLANEOUS]

## § 109.93 Attorney general education fund.

The attorney general education fund is hereby created in the state treasury. The fund shall consist of gifts and grants received by the attorney general for the purposes of the fund. The fund shall be administered by the attorney general and shall be used to support various educational programs. These educational programs may include programs for consumer protection, victims of crime, environmental protection, drug abuse, child abuse, peace officer training, crime prevention, and law. The fund may also be used to pay costs associated with the solicitation of gifts and grants for the purposes of the fund, and the costs of administering the fund. The fund shall not be used to replace money spent by local programs for similar purposes.

**HISTORY: 144 v S 351. Eff 7-1-92; 152 v H 119, § 101.01, eff. 9-29-07.**

The provisions of § 512.41 of 152 v H 119 read as follows:

SECTION 512.41. For purposes of sections 109.93, 111.18, and 173.85 of the Revised Code, as amended by this act, the Director of Budget and Management, in collaboration with the Treasurer of State, may take any action necessary to establish funds in the state treasury that were previously held in the custody of the Treasurer of State, including, but not limited to, the transfer of cash from the custodial funds to the state treasury and the establishment of appropriations and encumbrances to support outstanding obligations. The amounts necessary to support outstanding obligations are hereby appropriated. Agencies may request additional appropriation authority, but it shall be subject to approval by the Controlling Board.

The effective date is set by § 812.03 of 152 v H 119.

**Not analogous to former RC § 109.93 renumbered from RC § 122.21 in 142 v H 171 and renumbered to RC § 122.21 in 142 v H 231, eff 10-5-87.**

## § 109.94 Identity fraud passport.

(A) The attorney general, in cooperation with any law enforcement agency, may issue an identity fraud passport to a person who is a victim in this state of identity fraud or identity fraud against an elderly person or disabled adult and has filed a police report with any law enforcement agency citing that the person is a victim of a violation of section 2913.49 of the Revised Code. Once a police report of that nature has been filed with any law enforcement agency, the victim may apply for an identity fraud passport through any law enforcement agency. The law enforcement agency shall send a copy of the police report and the application for an identity fraud passport to the attorney general. The attorney general shall process the application and supporting police report and may issue the victim of identity fraud or identity fraud against an elderly person or disabled adult an identity fraud passport in the form of a card or certificate.

(B)(1) A victim of identity fraud or identity fraud against an elderly person or disabled adult may present the victim's identity fraud passport issued by the attorney general in accordance with division (A) of this section to both of the following:

(a) A law enforcement agency to help prevent the victim's arrest or detention for offenses committed by someone other than the victim who is using the victim's identity;

(b) Any of the victim's creditors to aid in the creditors' investigation and establishment of whether fraudulent charges were made against accounts in the victim's name or whether accounts were opened using the victim's identity.

(2) Acceptance of the identity fraud passport presented by the victim to a law enforcement agency or creditors pursuant to division (B)(1) of this section is at the discretion of the law enforcement agency or creditor. A law enforcement agency or creditor may consider the surrounding circumstances and available information regarding the offense of identity fraud pertaining to the victim.

(C)(1) Subject to its use for statistical purposes pursuant to division (C)(2) of this section, an application made with the attorney general pursuant to division (A) of this section, including any supporting documentation, is not a public record pursuant to section 149.43 of the Revised Code. The attorney general may provide access to the applications and supporting documentation filed with the attorney general's office to other criminal justice agencies in this or another state.

(2) The attorney general shall maintain statistics with respect to the number of applications for identity fraud passports submitted, and the number of identity fraud passports issued, pursuant to division (A) of this section. Not later than the first day of November in each year, the attorney general shall submit a statistical report to the governor, the president and minority leader of the senate, and the speaker and minority leader of the house of representatives indicating the number of applications for identity fraud passports submitted, and the number of identity fraud passports issued, pursuant to division (A) of this section in the previous fiscal year. Nothing in the statistics maintained or the statistical report submitted by the attorney general pursuant to this division shall identify, or enable the identification of, any individual who applied for, was issued, or was denied an identity fraud passport. The statistics and the statistical report are public records for the purpose of section 149.43 of the Revised Code.

**HISTORY: 151 v H 48, § 1, eff. 9-16-05.**

## § 109.941 Enforcement of identity fraud crimes.

The attorney general shall cooperate with and provide technical assistance to any local law enforcement agency in the state, upon that agency's request, with respect to enforcement of identity fraud crimes.

**HISTORY: 152 v H 46, § 1, eff. 9-1-08.**

**Not analogous to former RC § 109.941, amended and renumbered to RC § 122.23 by 142 v H 231, eff 10-5-87.**

The effective date is set by § 3 of 152 v H 46.

## § 109.95 Authority of attorney general to commence actions for election fraud.

Notwithstanding any provision of the Revised Code to the contrary pertaining to prosecutorial authority, the attorney general may initiate criminal proceedings for election fraud under section 3599.42 of the Revised Code which results from a violation of any provision of Title XXXV of the Revised Code, other than Chapter 3517. of the Revised Code, involving voting, an initiative or referendum petition process, or the conducting of an election, by presenting evidence of criminal violations in question to the prosecuting attorney of any county in which the violations may be prosecuted. If the prosecuting attorney does not prosecute the violations within a reasonable time or requests the attorney general to do so, the attorney general may proceed with the prosecution of the violations with all of the rights, privileges, and powers conferred by law on a prosecuting attorney, including, but not limited to, the power to appear before a grand jury and to interrogate witnesses before a grand jury.

**HISTORY: 151 v H 3, § 1, eff. 5-2-06.**

**Not analogous to former RC § 109.95, amended and renumbered to RC § 122.25 by 142 v H 231, eff 10-5-87.**

## § 109.96 [Invalid].

**Publisher's Note:**

The enactment of § 109.96 in 151 v H 694 was held to be invalid in United Auto Workers, Local Union 1112 v. Brunner, 182 Ohio App. 3d 1, 2009 Ohio 1750. That enactment was not analogous to former RC § 109.96, amended and renumbered to RC § 122.26 by 142 v H 231, eff. 10-5-87.

## § 109.97 Annual capital case status report.

(A) As used in this section:

(1) "Commutation," "pardon," "prisoner," and "state correctional institution" have the same meanings as in section 2967.01 of the Revised Code.

(2) "Individual's present legal status" means whichever of the following circumstances apply on the thirty-first day of December of the calendar year covered by a capital case status report described in divisions (B) and (C) of this section to an individual who was sentenced to death pursuant to sections 2929.02 to 2929.04 or section 2929.06 of the Revised Code for an aggravated murder committed on or after October 19, 1981:

(a) The individual was executed in accordance with section 2949.22 of the Revised Code for the aggravated murder, or the individual otherwise is deceased.

(b) The individual continues to be confined in a state correctional institution waiting for the execution of the sentence of death.

(c) The individual has been released from confinement in a state correctional institution pursuant to a pardon granted in connection with the aggravated murder, or the individual has been granted a commutation in connection with the aggravated murder and has been released from confinement or is serving a prison term or sentence of imprisonment pursuant to the commutation.

(d) The individual has had the sentence of death vacated or reversed on appeal or pursuant to division (C) of section 2929.05 of the Revised Code or otherwise has been relieved of the sentence of death by a court of this state or the United States.

(e) The individual has had the sentence of death vacated as described in section 2929.06 of the Revised Code or otherwise, the individual has been resentenced pursuant to that section or otherwise to a sentence other than a sentence of death, and the individual is a prisoner serving a prison term or sentence of imprisonment in a state correctional institution.

(f) The individual is confined in a correctional institution of another state or the United States for the commission of another offense or has been executed in accordance with a sentence of death imposed by a court of another state or the United States for the commission of another offense.

(g) The individual has escaped from confinement in a state correctional institution or a correctional institution of another state or the United States and currently is at-large.

(B) The attorney general annually shall prepare or cause to be prepared a capital case status report that pertains to all individuals who were sentenced to death pursuant to sections 2929.02 to 2929.04 or section 2929.06 of the Revised Code for an aggravated murder committed on or after October 19, 1981, and that contains for each of those individuals the information described in division (C)(1) of this section. The attorney general shall file a copy of each annual capital case status report with the governor, the chief justice of the supreme court, the president of the senate, and the speaker of the house of representatives no later than the first day of April of the calendar year following the calendar year covered by the report. Each annual capital case status report shall be a public record subject to inspection and copying in accordance with section 149.43 of the Revised Code.

(C)(1) An annual capital case status report prepared pursuant to division (B) of this section shall contain all of the following information that pertains as of the thirty-first day of December of the calendar year covered by the report to each individual who was sentenced to death pursuant to sections 2929.02 to 2929.04 or 2929.06 of the Revised Code for an aggravated murder committed on or after October 19, 1981:

(a) A citation to and brief summary of the facts of each case in which the individual was sentenced to death pursuant to sections 2929.02 to 2929.04 or section 2929.06 of the Revised Code for an aggravated murder committed on or after October 19, 1981;

(b) A statement as to the individual's present legal status;

(c) A summary history of the individual's legal actions to vacate, reverse, or otherwise be relieved from the sentence of death described in division (C)(1)(a) of this section, including, but not limited to, motions to vacate the sentence of death, appeals, petitions for postconviction relief, and petitions for habeas corpus relief filed with a court of this state or a court of the United States under section 2929.05, 2953.21, or another section of the Revised Code, the Ohio Constitution, federal statutes, or the United States Constitution;

(d) Any other information that the attorney general determines is relevant, including, but not limited to, a tentatively scheduled date for the execution of the individual's sentence of death in accordance with section 2949.22 of the Revised Code.

(2) In each annual capital case status report prepared pursuant to division (B) of this section, the attorney general shall set forth or cause to be set forth the information described in division (C)(1) of this section in the form that the attorney general considers most appropriate to present that information, including, but not limited to, charts, tables, graphs, and narrative summaries.

(D) All officers and employees of the government of this state and its political subdivisions shall cooperate, upon request of the attorney general, in providing information that facilitates the attorney general in the performance of the attorney general's responsibilities under this section.

**HISTORY: 147 v H 18. Eff 1-30-98.**

**Not analogous to former RC § 109.97, amended and renumbered RC § 122.27 in 142 v H 231, eff 10-5-87. RC § 122.27 was renumbered to RC § 181.56 in 145 v H 152, eff 7-1-93.**

## § 109.98 Civil action against state retirement board member.

As used in this section, "state retirement board" means the public employees retirement board, board of trustees of the Ohio police and fire pension fund, school employees retirement board, state teachers retirement board, and state highway patrol retirement board.

If a member of a state retirement board breaches the member's fiduciary duty to the retirement system, the attorney general may maintain a civil action against the board member for harm resulting from that breach. Notwithstanding sections 145.10, 742.09, 3307.13, 3309.13, and 5505.23 of the Revised Code, after being informed of an allegation that the entire board has breached its fiduciary duty, the state retirement board may retain independent legal counsel, including legal counsel provided by the board's fiduciary insurance carrier, to advise the board and to represent the board.

The attorney general may recover damages or be granted injunctive relief, which shall include the enjoinment of specified activities and the removal of the member from the board. Any damages awarded shall be paid to the retirement system. The authority to maintain a civil action created by this section is in addition to any authority the attorney general possesses under any other provision of the Revised Code.

**HISTORY: 150 v S 133, § 1, eff. 9-15-04; 151 v H 66, § 101.01, eff. 9-29-05.**

The effective date is set by § 612.03 of 151 v H 66.

**Not analogous to former RC § 109.98 (142 v H 171), repealed 142 v H 231, § 2, eff 10-5-87.**

## § 109.981 Civil action against member of bureau of workers' compensation board of directors.

If a member of the bureau of workers' compensation board of directors breaches the member's fiduciary duty to the bureau of workers' compensation, the attorney general may maintain a civil action against the board member for harm resulting from that breach. Notwithstanding section 4121.128 [4121.12.8] of the Revised Code, after being informed of an allegation that the entire board has breached its fiduciary duty, the board may retain independent legal counsel, including legal counsel provided by the board's fiduciary insurance carrier, to advise the board and to represent the board. The attorney general may recover damages or be granted injunctive relief, which shall include the enjoinment of specified activities and the removal of the member from the board. Any damages awarded shall be paid to the bureau. The authority to maintain a civil action created by this section is in addition to any authority the attorney general possesses under any other provision of the Revised Code.

**HISTORY: 151 v H 66, § 101.01, eff. 9-29-05; 152 v H 100, § 101.01, eff. 9-10-07.**

The effective date is set by § 609.03 of 152 v H 100.
The effective date is set by § 612.03 of 151 v H 66.

## § 109.99 Penalties.

(A) Whoever violates section 109.26 of the Revised Code shall be fined not less than five hundred nor more than ten thousand dollars or be imprisoned not less than one month nor more than one year, or both.

(B) Whoever violates division (G)(1) of section 109.573 [109.57.3] of the Revised Code is guilty of unlawful disclosure of DNA database information, a misdemeanor of the first degree.

(C) Whoever violates division (G)(2) of section 109.573 [109.57.3] of the Revised Code is guilty of unlawful possession of DNA database information, a misdemeanor of the first degree.

(D)(1) Whoever violates division (G)(1) of section 109.35 of the Revised Code is guilty of entering into a transaction involving a nonprofit health care entity without the approval of the attorney general, a felony of the third degree.

(2) Whoever violates division (G)(2) of section 109.35 of the Revised Code is guilty of receiving improper compensation relating to a transaction involving a nonprofit health care entity, a felony of the third degree.

**HISTORY: 125 v 354 (Eff 10-14-53); 146 v H 5 (Eff 8-30-95); 147 v H 242. Eff 5-7-97.**

See provisions, § 4 of HB 597 (148 v —), following RC § 109.34.

# CHAPTER 120: PUBLIC DEFENDERS

## [OHIO PUBLIC DEFENDER COMMISSION]

### § 120.01 Ohio public defender commission.

There is hereby created the Ohio public defender commission to provide, supervise, and coordinate legal representation at state expense for indigent and other persons. The commission shall consist of nine members, one of whom shall be chairman. The chairman shall be appointed by the governor with the advice and consent of the senate. Four members shall be appointed by the governor, two of whom shall be from each of the two major political parties. Four members shall be appointed by the supreme court, two of whom shall be from each of the two major political parties. The chairman, and not less than two of the members appointed by the governor, and not less than two of the members appointed by the supreme court shall be attorneys admitted to the practice of law in this state.

Within thirty days after the effective date of this section, the governor and the supreme court shall make initial appointments to the commission. Of the initial appointments made to the commission by the governor, the appointment of the chairman shall be for a term of two years. Of the other four appointments, one shall be for a term ending one year after the effective date of this section, one shall be for a term ending two years after that date, one shall be for a term ending three years after that date, and one shall be for a term ending four years after that date. Of the initial appointments made to the commission by the supreme court, one shall be for a term ending one year after the effective date of this section, one shall be for a term ending two years after that date, one shall be for a term ending three years after that date, and one shall be for a term ending four years after that date. Thereafter, terms of office shall be for four years, each term ending on the same day of the same month of the year as did the term which it succeeds. Any member appointed to fill a vacancy occurring prior to the expiration of the term for which his predecessor was appointed shall hold office for the remainder of such term. Any member shall continue in office subsequent to the expiration date of his term until his successor takes office or until a period of sixty days has elapsed, whichever occurs first.

**HISTORY: 136 v H 164. Eff 1-13-76.**

The provisions of § 4 of H.B. 516 (150 v —) read in part as follows:

SECTION 4. The following agencies shall be retained pursuant to division (D) of section 101.83 of the Revised Code and shall expire on December 31, 2010:

| AGENCY NAME | REVISED CODE OR UNCODIFIED SECTION |
|---|---|
| ○○○ | ○○○ |
| Ohio Public Defender Commission | 120.01 |
| ○○○ | ○○○ |

### § 120.02 Meetings; compensation.

The members of the Ohio public defender commission shall meet at least quarterly, and shall meet at other times pursuant to the call of the chairman of the commission or at the request of the state public defender. The members of the commission shall receive an amount fixed pursuant to section 124.14 of the Revised Code per diem for every meeting of the commission that they attend, together with the actual and necessary expenses that they incur, and mileage for each mile necessarily traveled, in connection with every meeting of the commission that they attend.

**HISTORY: 136 v H 164 (Eff 1-13-76); 144 v H 210. Eff 5-1-92.**

### § 120.03 Powers and duties.

(A) The Ohio public defender commission shall appoint the state public defender, who shall serve at the pleasure of the commission.

(B) The Ohio public defender commission shall establish rules for the conduct of the offices of the county and joint county public defenders and for the conduct of county appointed counsel systems in the state. These rules shall include, but are not limited to, the following:

(1) Standards of indigency and minimum qualifications for legal representation by a public defender or appointed counsel. In establishing standards of indigency and determining who is eligible for legal representation by a public defender or appointed counsel, the commission shall consider an indigent person to be an individual who at the time his need is determined is unable to provide for the payment of an attorney and all other necessary expenses of representation. Release on bail shall not prevent a person from being determined to be indigent.

(2) Standards for the hiring of outside counsel;

(3) Standards for contracts by a public defender with law schools, legal aid societies, and nonprofit organizations for providing counsel;

(4) Standards for the qualifications, training, and size of the legal and supporting staff for a public defender, facilities, and other requirements needed to maintain and operate an office of a public defender;

(5) Minimum caseload standards;

(6) Procedures for the assessment and collection of the costs of legal representation that is provided by public defenders or appointed counsel;

(7) Standards and guidelines for determining whether a client is able to make an up-front contribution toward the cost of his legal representation;

(8) Procedures for the collection of up-front contributions from clients who are able to contribute toward the cost of their legal representation, as determined pursuant to the standards and guidelines developed under division (B)(7) of this section. All of such up-front contributions shall be paid into the appropriate county fund.

(9) Standards for contracts between a board of county commissioners, a county public defender commission, or a joint county public defender commission and a municipal corporation for the legal representation of indigent persons charged with violations of the ordinances of the municipal corporation.

(C) The Ohio public defender commission shall adopt rules prescribing minimum qualifications of counsel appointed pursuant to this chapter or appointed by the courts. Without limiting its general authority to prescribe different qualifications for different categories of appointed counsel, the commission shall prescribe, by rule, special qualifications for counsel and co-counsel appointed in capital cases.

(D) In administering the office of the Ohio public defender commission:

(1) The commission shall do the following:

(a) Approve an annual operating budget;

(b) Make an annual report to the governor, the general assembly, and the supreme court of Ohio on the operation of the state public defender's office, the county appointed counsel systems, and the county and joint county public defenders' offices.

(2) The commission may do the following:

(a) Accept the services of volunteer workers and consultants at no compensation other than reimbursement of actual and necessary expenses;

(b) Prepare and publish statistical and case studies and other data pertinent to the legal representation of indigent persons;

(c) Conduct programs having a general objective of training and educating attorneys and others in the legal representation of indigent persons.

(E) There is hereby established in the state treasury the public defender training fund for the deposit of fees received by the Ohio public defender commission from educational seminars, and the sale of publications, on topics concerning criminal law and procedure. Expenditures from this fund shall be made only for the operation of activities authorized by division (D)(2)(c) of this section.

(F)(1) In accordance with sections 109.02, 109.07, and 109.361 [109.36.1] to 109.366 [109.36.6] of the Revised Code, but subject to division (E) of section 120.06 of the Revised Code, the attorney general shall represent or provide for the representation of the Ohio public defender commission, the state public defender, assistant state public defenders, and other employees of the commission or the state public defender.

(2) Subject to division (E) of section 120.06 of the Revised Code, the attorney general shall represent or provide for the representation of attorneys described in division (C) of section 120.41 of the Revised Code in malpractice or other civil actions or proceedings that arise from alleged actions or omissions related to responsibilities derived pursuant to this chapter, or in civil actions that are based upon alleged violations of the constitution or statutes of the United States, including section 1983 of Title 42 of the United States Code, 93 Stat. 1284 (1979), 42 U.S.C.A. 1983, as amended, and that arise from alleged actions or omissions related to responsibilities derived pursuant to this chapter. For purposes of the representation, sections 109.361 [109.36.1] to 109.366 [109.36.6] of the Revised Code shall apply to an attorney described in division (C) of section 120.41 of the Revised Code as if he were an officer or employee, as defined in section 109.36 of the Revised Code, and the Ohio public defender commission or the state public defender, whichever contracted with the attorney, shall be considered his employer.

**HISTORY: 136 v H 164 (Eff 1-13-76); 138 v H 204 (Eff 7-30-79); 139 v H 694 (Eff 11-15-81); 140 v H 291 (Eff 7-1-83); 140 v S 271 (Eff 9-26-84); 141 v H 201 (Eff 7-1-85); 144 v H 210 (Eff 5-1-92); 145 v H 152. Eff 7-1-93.**

## § 120.04 State public defender; powers and duties.

(A) The state public defender shall serve at the pleasure of the Ohio public defender commission and shall be an attorney with a minimum of four years of experience in the practice of law and be admitted to the practice of law in this state at least one year prior to appointment.

(B) The state public defender shall do all of the following:

(1) Maintain a central office in Columbus. The central office shall be provided with a library of adequate size, considering the needs of the office and the accessibility of other libraries, and other necessary facilities and equipment.

(2) Appoint assistant state public defenders, all of whom shall be attorneys admitted to the practice of law in this state, and other personnel necessary for the operation of the state public defender office. Assistant state public defenders shall be appointed on a full-time basis. The state public defender, assistant state public defenders, and employees appointed by the state public defender shall not engage in the private practice of law.

(3) Supervise the compliance of county public defender offices, joint county public defender offices, and county appointed counsel systems with standards established by rules of the Ohio public defender commission pursuant to division (B) of section 120.03 of the Revised Code;

(4) Keep and maintain financial records of all cases handled and develop records for use in the calculation of direct and indirect costs, in the operation of the office, and report periodically, but not less than annually, to the commission on all relevant data on the operations of the office, costs, projected needs, and recommendations for legislation or amendments to court rules, as may be appropriate to improve the criminal justice system;

(5) Collect all moneys due the state for reimbursement for legal services under this chapter and under section 2941.51 of the Revised Code and institute any actions in court on behalf of the state for the collection of such sums that the state public defender considers advisable. Except as provided otherwise in division (D) of section 120.06 of the Revised Code, all moneys collected by the state public defender under this chapter and section 2941.51 of the Revised Code shall be deposited in the state treasury to the credit of the client payment fund, which is hereby created. All moneys credited to the fund shall be used by the state public defender to appoint assistant state public defenders and to provide other personnel, equipment, and facilities necessary for the operation of the state public defender office, to reimburse counties for the operation of county public defender offices, joint county public defender offices, and county appointed counsel systems pursuant to sections 120.18, 120.28, and 120.33 of the Revised Code, or to provide assistance to counties in the operation of county indigent defense systems.

(6) With respect to funds appropriated to the commission to pay criminal costs, perform the duties imposed by sections 2949.19 and 2949.201 [2949.20.1] of the Revised Code;

(7) Establish standards and guidelines for the reimbursement, pursuant to sections 120.18, 120.28, 120.33, 2941.51, and 2949.19 of the Revised Code, of counties for the operation of county public defender offices, joint county public defender offices, and county appointed counsel systems and for other costs related to felony prosecutions;

(8) Establish maximum amounts that the state will reimburse the counties pursuant to sections 120.18, 120.28, 120.33, and 2941.51 of the Revised Code;

(9) Establish maximum amounts that the state will reimburse the counties pursuant to section 120.33 of the Revised Code for each specific type of legal service performed by a county appointed counsel system;

(10) Administer sections 120.18, 120.28, 120.33, 2941.51, and 2949.19 of the Revised Code and make reimbursements pursuant to those sections;

(11) Administer the program established pursuant to sections 120.51 to 120.55 of the Revised Code for the charitable public purpose of providing financial assistance to legal aid societies. Neither the state public defender nor any of the state public defender's employees who is responsible in any way for the administration of that program and who performs those administrative responsibilities in good faith is in any manner liable if a legal aid society that is provided financial assistance under the program uses the financial assistance other than in accordance with sections 120.51 to 120.55 of the Revised Code or fails to comply with the requirements of those sections.

(12) Establish an office for the handling of appeal and postconviction matters;

(13) Provide technical aid and assistance to county public defender offices, joint county public defender offices, and other local counsel providing legal representation to indigent persons, including representation and assistance on appeals.

(C) The state public defender may do any of the following:

(1) In providing legal representation, conduct investigations, obtain expert testimony, take depositions, use other discovery methods, order transcripts, and make all other preparations which are appropriate and necessary to an adequate defense or the prosecution of appeals and other legal proceedings;

(2) Seek, solicit, and apply for grants for the operation of programs for the defense of indigent persons from any public or private source, and may receive donations, grants, awards, and similar funds from any lawful source. Such funds shall be deposited in the state treasury to the credit of the public defender gifts and grants fund, which is hereby created.

(3) Make all the necessary arrangements to coordinate the services of the office with any federal, county, or private programs established to provide legal representation to indigent persons and others, and to obtain and provide all funds allowable under any such programs;

(4) Consult and cooperate with professional groups concerned with the causes of criminal conduct, the reduction of crime, the rehabilitation and correction of persons convicted of crime, the administration of criminal justice, and the administration and operation of the state public defender's office;

(5) Accept the services of volunteer workers and consultants at no compensation other than reimbursement for actual and necessary expenses;

(6) Prescribe any forms that are necessary for the uniform operation of this chapter;

(7) Contract with a county public defender commission or a joint county public defender commission to provide all or any part of the services that a county public defender or joint county public defender is required or permitted to provide by this chapter, or contract with a board of county commissioners of a county that is not served by a county public defender commission or a joint county public defender commission for the provision of services in accordance with section 120.33 of the Revised Code. All money received by the state public defender pursuant to such a contract shall be credited to either the multicounty: county share fund or, if received as a result of a contract with Trumbull county, the Trumbull county: county share fund.

(8) Authorize persons employed as criminal investigators to attend the Ohio peace officer training academy or any other peace officer training school for training;

(9) Procure a policy or policies of malpractice insurance that provide coverage for the state public defender and assistant state public defenders in connection with malpractice claims that may arise from their actions or omissions related to responsibilities derived pursuant to this chapter.

(D) No person employed by the state public defender as a criminal investigator shall attend the Ohio peace officer training academy or any other peace officer training school unless authorized to do so by the state public defender.

**HISTORY: 136 v H 164 (Eff 1-13-76); 138 v H 204 (Eff 7-30-79); 139 v H 694 (Eff 11-15-81); 140 v H 291 (Eff 7-1-83); 140 v S 271 (Eff 9-26-84); 140 v S 219 (Eff 1-8-85); 141 v H 201 (Eff 7-1-85); 141 v S 149 (Eff 6-6-86); 141 v H 428 (Eff 12-23-86); 142 v H 171 (Eff 7-1-87); 144 v H 210 (Eff 5-1-92); 147 v H 215 (Eff 9-29-97); 148 v H 283. Eff 9-29-99.**

The effective date is set by section 162 of HB 283.

## § 120.05 Determination of indigency.

(A) The determination of indigency shall be made by the state public defender, subject to review by the court. This section does not apply in relation to sections 120.51 to 120.55 of the Revised Code.

(B) The state public defender shall investigate the financial status of each person to be represented, at the earliest time the circumstances permit, and may require the person represented to disclose the records of public or private income sources and property, otherwise confidential, which may be of aid in determining indigency. The state public defender may obtain information from any public record contained in any office of the state, or any political subdivision or agency thereof, on request without payment of any fees ordinarily required by law. He shall make the results of the investigation available to the court upon request. The court, before whom a person seeking representation is taken, may determine the person's eligibility for legal representation by the state public defender.

(C) If a determination of eligibility cannot be made before the time when the first services are to be rendered by the state public defender, he shall render such services on a provisional basis. If the state public defender, or the court on review, subsequently determines that the person receiving the services is ineligible, the public defender shall notify the person of the termination of his services.

(D) Where the person represented has, or may reasonably be expected to have, the means to meet some part of the cost of the services rendered to him, he shall reimburse the state public defender in an amount which he can reasonably be expected to pay.

(E) If it is determined by the state public defender, or by the court, that the legal representation was provided to a person not entitled thereto, the person may be required to reimburse the public defender for the costs of the representation provided. Any action filed by the state public defender to collect legal fees hereunder, must be brought within two years from the last date legal representation was provided.

**HISTORY: 136 v H 164 (Eff 1-13-76); 140 v S 219. Eff 1-8-85.**

**§ 120.06 State public defender to provide representation to indigents; defense of malpractice and similar actions.**

(A)(1) The state public defender, when designated by the court or requested by a county public defender or joint county public defender, may provide legal representation in all courts throughout the state to indigent adults and juveniles who are charged with the commission of an offense or act for which the penalty or any possible adjudication includes the potential loss of liberty.

(2) The state public defender may provide legal representation to any indigent person who, while incarcerated in any state correctional institution, is charged with a felony offense, for which the penalty or any possible adjudication that may be imposed by a court upon conviction includes the potential loss of liberty.

(3) The state public defender may provide legal representation to any person incarcerated in any correctional institution of the state, in any matter in which the person asserts the person is unlawfully imprisoned or detained.

(4) The state public defender, in any case in which the state public defender has provided legal representation or is requested to do so by a county public defender or joint county public defender, may provide legal representation on appeal.

(5) The state public defender, when designated by the court or requested by a county public defender, joint county public defender, or the director of rehabilitation and correction, shall provide legal representation in parole and probation revocation matters or matters relating to the revocation of community control or post-release control under a community control sanction or post-release control sanction, unless the state public defender finds that the alleged parole or probation violator or alleged violator of a community control sanction or post-release control sanction has the financial capacity to retain the alleged violator's own counsel.

(6) If the state public defender contracts with a county public defender commission, a joint county public defender commission, or a board of county commissioners for the provision of services, under authority of division (C)(7) of section 120.04 of the Revised Code, the state public defender shall provide legal representation in accordance with the contract.

(B) The state public defender shall not be required to prosecute any appeal, postconviction remedy, or other proceeding pursuant to division (A)(3), (4), or (5) of this section, unless the state public defender first is satisfied that there is arguable merit to the proceeding.

(C) A court may appoint counsel or allow an indigent person to select the indigent's own personal counsel to assist the state public defender as co-counsel when the interests of justice so require. When co-counsel is appointed to assist the state public defender, the co-counsel shall receive any compensation that the court may approve, not to exceed the amounts provided for in section 2941.51 of the Revised Code.

(D)(1) When the state public defender is designated by the court or requested by a county public defender or joint county public defender to provide legal representation for an indigent person in any case, other than pursuant to a contract entered into under authority of division (C)(7) of section 120.04 of the Revised Code, the state public defender shall send to the county in which the case is filed a bill detailing the actual cost of the representation that separately itemizes legal fees and expenses. The county, upon receipt of an itemized bill from the state public defender pursuant to this division, shall pay the state public defender each of the following amounts:

(a) For the amount identified as legal fees in the itemized bill, one hundred per cent of the amount identified as legal fees less the state reimbursement rate as calculated by the state public defender pursuant to section 120.34 of the Revised Code for the month the case terminated, as set forth in the itemized bill;

(b) For the amount identified as expenses in the itemized bill, one hundred per cent.

(2) Upon payment of the itemized bill under division (D)(1) of this section, the county may submit the cost of the expenses, excluding legal fees, to the state public defender for reimbursement pursuant to section 120.33 of the Revised Code.

(3) When the state public defender provides investigation or mitigation services to private appointed counsel or to a county or joint county public defender as approved by the appointing court, other than pursuant to a contract entered into under authority of division (C)(7) of section 120.04 of the Revised Code, the state public defender shall send to the county in which the case is filed a bill itemizing the actual cost of the services provided. The county, upon receipt of an itemized bill from the state public defender pursuant to this division, shall pay one hundred per cent of the amount as set forth in the itemized bill. Upon payment of the itemized bill received pursuant to this division, the county may submit the cost of the investigation and mitigation services to the state public defender for reimbursement pursuant to section 120.33 of the Revised Code.

(4) There is hereby created in the state treasury the county representation fund for the deposit of moneys received from counties under this division. All moneys credited to the fund shall be used by the state public defender to provide legal representation for indigent persons when designated by the court or requested by a county or joint county public defender or to provide investigation or mitigation services, including investigation or mitigation services to private appointed counsel or a county or joint county public defender, as approved by the court.

(E)(1) Notwithstanding any contrary provision of sections 109.02, 109.07, 109.361 [109.36.1] to 109.366 [109.36.6], and 120.03 of the Revised Code that pertains to representation by the attorney general, an assistant attorney general, or special counsel of an officer or employee, as defined in section 109.36 of the Revised Code, or of an entity of state government, the state public defender may elect to contract with, and to have the state pay pursuant to division (E)(2) of this section for the services of, private legal counsel to represent the Ohio public defender commission, the state public defender, assistant state public defenders, other employees of the commission or the state public defender, and attorneys described in division (C) of section 120.41 of the Revised Code in a malpractice or other civil action or proceeding that arises from alleged actions or omissions related to responsibilities derived pursuant to this chapter, or in a civil action that is based upon alleged violations of the constitution or statutes of the United States, including section 1983 of Title 42 of the United States Code, 93 Stat. 1284 (1979), 42 U.S.C.A. 1983, as amended, and that arises from alleged actions or omissions related to responsibilities derived pursuant to this chapter, if the state public defender determines, in good faith, that the defendant in the civil action or proceeding did not act manifestly outside the scope of the defendant's employment or official responsibilities, with malicious purpose, in bad faith, or in a wanton or reckless manner. If the state public defender elects not to contract pursuant to this division for private legal counsel in a civil action or proceeding, then, in accordance with sections 109.02, 109.07, 109.361 [109.36.1] to 109.366 [109.36.6], and 120.03 of the Revised Code, the attorney general shall represent or provide for the representation of the Ohio public defender commission, the state public defender, assistant state public defenders, other employees of the commission or the state public defender, or attorneys described in division (C) of section 120.41 of the Revised Code in the civil action or proceeding.

(2)(a) Subject to division (E)(2)(b) of this section, payment from the state treasury for the services of private legal counsel with whom the state public defender has contracted pursuant to division (E)(1) of this section shall be accomplished only through the following procedure:

(i) The private legal counsel shall file with the attorney general a copy of the contract; a request for an award of legal fees, court costs, and expenses earned or incurred in connection with the defense of the Ohio public defender commission, the state public defender, an assistant state public defender, an employee, or an attorney in a specified civil action or proceeding; a written itemization of those fees, costs, and expenses, including the signature of the state public defender and the state public defender's attestation that the fees, costs, and expenses were earned or incurred pursuant to division (E)(1) of this section to the best of the state public defender's knowledge and information; a written statement whether the fees, costs, and expenses are for all legal services to be rendered in connection with that defense, are only for legal services rendered to the date of the request and additional legal services likely will have to be provided in connection with that defense, or are for the final legal services rendered in connection with that defense; a written statement indicating whether the private legal counsel previously submitted a request for an award under division (E)(2) of this section in connection with that defense and, if so, the date and the amount of each award granted; and, if the fees, costs, and expenses are for all legal services to be rendered in connection with that defense or are for the final legal services rendered in connection with that defense, a certified copy of any judgment entry in the civil action or proceeding or a signed copy of any settlement agreement entered into between the parties to the civil action or proceeding.

(ii) Upon receipt of a request for an award of legal fees, court costs, and expenses and the requisite supportive documentation described in division (E)(2)(a)(i) of this section, the attorney general shall review the request and documentation; determine whether any of the limitations specified in division (E)(2)(b) of this section apply to the request; and, if an award of legal fees, court costs, or expenses is permissible after applying the limitations, prepare a document awarding legal fees, court costs, or expenses to the private legal counsel. The document shall name the private legal counsel as the recipient of the award; specify the total amount of the award as determined by the attorney general; itemize the portions of the award that represent legal fees, court costs, and expenses; specify any limitation applied pursuant to division (E)(2)(b) of this section to reduce the amount of the award sought by the private legal counsel; state that the award is payable from the state treasury pursuant to division (E)(2)(a)(iii) of this section; and be approved by the inclusion of the signatures of the attorney general, the state public defender, and the private legal counsel.

(iii) The attorney general shall forward a copy of the document prepared pursuant to division (E)(2)(a)(ii) of this section to the director of budget and management. The award of legal fees, court costs, or expenses shall be paid out of the state public defender's appropriations, to the extent there is a sufficient available balance in those appropriations. If the state public defender does not have a sufficient available balance in the state public defender's appropriations to pay the entire award of legal fees, court costs, or expenses, the director shall make application for a transfer of appropriations out of the emergency purposes account or any other appropriation for emergencies or contingencies in an amount equal to the portion of the award that exceeds the sufficient available balance in the state public defender's appropriations. A transfer of appropriations out of the emergency purposes account or any other appropriation for emergencies or contingencies shall be authorized if there are sufficient moneys greater than the sum total of then pending emergency purposes account requests, or requests for releases from the other appropriation. If a transfer of appropriations out of the emergency purposes account or other appropriation for emergencies or contingencies is made to pay an amount equal to the portion of the award that exceeds the sufficient available balance in the state public defender's appropriations, the director shall cause the payment to be made to the private legal counsel. If sufficient moneys do not exist in the emergency purposes account or other appropriation for emergencies or contingencies to pay an amount equal to the portion of the award that exceeds the sufficient available balance in the state public defender's appropriations, the private legal counsel shall request the general assembly to make an appropriation sufficient to pay an amount equal to the portion of the award that exceeds the sufficient available balance in the state public defender's appropriations, and no payment in that amount shall be made until the appropriation has been made. The private legal counsel shall make the request during the current biennium and during each succeeding biennium until a sufficient appropriation is made.

(b) An award of legal fees, court costs, and expenses pursuant to division (E) of this section is subject to the following limitations:

(i) The maximum award or maximum aggregate of a series of awards of legal fees, court costs, and expenses to the private legal counsel in connection with the defense of the Ohio public defender commission, the state public defender, an assistant state public defender, an employee, or an attorney in a specified civil action or proceeding shall not exceed fifty thousand dollars.

(ii) The private legal counsel shall not be awarded legal fees, court costs, or expenses to the extent the fees, costs, or expenses are covered by a policy of malpractice or other insurance.

(iii) The private legal counsel shall be awarded legal fees and expenses only to the extent that the fees and expenses are reasonable in light of the legal services rendered by the private legal counsel in connection with the defense of the Ohio public defender commission, the state public defender, an assistant state public defender, an employee, or an attorney in a specified civil action or proceeding.

(c) If, pursuant to division (E)(2)(a) of this section, the attorney general denies a request for an award of legal fees, court costs, or expenses to private legal counsel because of the application of a limitation specified in division (E)(2)(b) of this section, the attorney general shall notify the private legal counsel in writing of the denial and of the limitation applied.

(d) If, pursuant to division (E)(2)(c) of this section, a private legal counsel receives a denial of an award notification or if a private legal counsel refuses to approve a document under division (E)(2)(a)(ii) of this section because of the proposed application of a limitation specified in division (E)(2)(b) of this section, the private legal counsel may commence a civil action against the attorney general in the court of claims to prove the private legal counsel's entitlement to the award sought, to prove that division (E)(2)(b) of this section does not prohibit or otherwise limit the award sought, and to recover a judgment for the amount of the award sought. A civil action under division (E)(2)(d) of this section shall be commenced no later than two years after receipt of a denial of award notification or, if the private legal counsel refused to approve a document under division (E)(2)(a)(ii) of this section because of the proposed application of a limitation specified in division (E)(2)(b) of this section, no later than two years after the refusal. Any judgment of the court of claims in favor of the private legal counsel shall be paid from the state treasury in accordance with division (E)(2)(a) of this section.

(F) If a court appoints the office of the state public defender to represent a petitioner in a postconviction relief proceeding under section 2953.21 of the Revised Code, the petitioner has received a sentence of death, and the proceeding relates to that sentence, all of the attorneys who represent the petitioner in the proceeding pursuant to the appointment, whether an assistant state public defender, the state public defender, or another attorney, shall be certified under Rule 20 of the Rules of Superintendence for the Courts of Ohio to represent indigent defendants charged with or convicted of an offense for which the death penalty can be or has been imposed.

(G) As used in this section:

(1) "Community control sanction" has the same meaning as in section 2929.01 of the Revised Code.

(2) "Post-release control sanction" has the same meaning as in section 2967.01 of the Revised Code.

**HISTORY: 136 v H 164 (Eff 1-13-76); 138 v H 204 (Eff 7-30-79); 139 v H 694 (Eff 11-15-81); 140 v H 291 (Eff 7-1-83); 140 v S 271 (Eff 9-26-84); 141 v H 201 (Eff 7-1-85); 144 v H 210 (Eff 5-1-92); 145 v H 571 (Eff 10-6-94); 146 v S 258 (Eff 10-16-96); 148 v H 283 (Eff 9-29-99); 149 v H 94. Eff 9-5-2001; 149 v H 490, § 1, eff. 1-1-04; 151 v H 66, § 101.01, eff. 9-29-05.**

The effective date is set by § 612.03 of 151 v H 66.
The effective date is set by section 4 of H.B. 490.

## § 120.07 Civil case filing fee fund.

There is hereby created in the state treasury the civil case filing fee fund to receive all funds deposited in the fund pursuant to sections 1901.26, 1907.24, and 2303.201 [2303.20.1] of the Revised Code. All money credited to the fund shall be used by the state public defender for the purpose of appointing assistant state public defenders and for providing other personnel, equipment, and facilities necessary for the operation of the state public defender office.

**HISTORY: 151 v H 66, § 101.01, eff. 9-29-05.**

The effective date is set by § 612.03 of 151 v H 66.

## § 120.08 Indigent defense support fund created.

There is hereby created in the state treasury the indigent defense support fund, consisting of money paid into the fund pursuant to sections 4507.45, 4509.101 [4509.10.1], 4510.22, and 4511.19 of the Revised Code and pursuant to sections 2937.22, 2949.091 [2949.09.1], and 2949.094 [2949.09.4] of the Revised Code out of the additional court costs imposed under those sections. The state public defender shall use at least ninety per cent of the money in the fund for the purpose of reimbursing county governments for expenses incurred pursuant to sections 120.18, 120.28, and 120.33 of the Revised Code. Disbursements from the fund to county governments shall be made at least once per year and shall be allocated proportionately so that each county receives an equal percentage of its total cost for operating its county public defender system, its joint county public defender system, its county appointed counsel system, or its system operated under division (C)(7) of section 120.04 of the Revised Code and division (B) of section 120.33 of the Revised Code. The state public defender may use not more than ten per cent of the money in the fund for the purposes of appointing assistant state public defenders or for providing other personnel, equipment, and facilities necessary for the operation of the state public defender office.

**HISTORY: 152 v S 209, § 1, eff. 3-26-08; 152 v H 562, § 101.01, eff. 9-23-08; 153 v H 1, § 101.01, eff. 10-16-09.**

The effective date is set by § 812.10 of 153 v H 1.
The effective date is set by § 812.10 of 152 v H 562.
The effective date is set by § 6 of 152 v S 209.

### [COUNTY PUBLIC DEFENDER COMMISSION]

## § 120.13 County public defender commission.

(A) The county commissioners in any county may establish a county public defender commission. The commission shall have five members, three of whom shall be appointed by the board of county commissioners, and two by the judge, or the presiding judge if there is one, of the court of common pleas of the county. At least one member appointed by each of these appointing bodies shall be an attorney admitted to the practice of law in this state.

(B) The board of county commissioners shall select a specific day for the county public defender commission to be established and on which all members' appointments shall take effect, and shall notify the Ohio public defender commission of the date.

(C) Of the initial appointments made to the county public defender commission, two appointments by the county commissioners and one appointment by the court shall be for a term of two years ending two years after the date the commission is established, and one appointment by each of the appointing bodies shall be for a term ending four years after the date the commission is established. Thereafter, terms of office shall be for four years, each term ending on the same day of the same month of the year as did the term which it succeeds. Each member shall hold office from the date of appointment until the end of the term for which the member was appointed. Any member appointed to fill a vacancy occurring prior to the expiration of the term for which the member's predecessor was appointed shall hold office for the remainder of such term. Any member shall continue in office subsequent to the expiration date of the member's term until a successor takes office, or until a period of sixty days has elapsed, whichever occurs first.

(D) The members of the commission shall choose as chairperson one of the commission members, who shall serve as chairperson for two years. Meetings shall be held at least quarterly and at such other times as called by the chairperson or by request of the county public defender. Members of the commission may receive an amount fixed by the county commissioners, but not in excess of the amounts set for the members of the Ohio public defender commission pursuant to section 124.14 of the Revised Code per diem for every meeting of the board they attend, and necessary expenses including mileage for each mile necessarily traveled.

(E) The county commissioners may terminate the county public defender commission at any time if at least ninety days prior to termination, the commissioners notify the Ohio public defender commission in writing of the termination date. Upon the termination date all pending county public defender matters shall be transferred to the state public defender, a joint county public defender, or appointed counsel.

(F) The cost of representation in all matters assumed by the state public defender shall be charged to the counties in accordance with division (D) of section 120.06 of the Revised Code.

**HISTORY: 136 v H 164 (Eff 1-13-76); 139 v H 694. Eff 11-15-81; 151 v H 66, § 101.01, eff. 9-29-05.**

The effective date is set by § 612.03 of 151 v H 66.

## § 120.14 Powers and duties.

(A)(1) Except as provided in division (A)(2) of this section, the county public defender commission shall appoint the county public defender and may remove him from office only for good cause.

(2) If a county public defender commission contracts with the state public defender or with one or more nonprofit organizations for the state public defender or the organizations to provide all of the services that the county public defender is required or permitted to provide by this chapter, the commission shall not appoint a county public defender.

(B) The commission shall determine the qualifications and size of the supporting staff and facilities and other requirements needed to maintain and operate the office of the county public defender.

(C) In administering the office of county public defender, the commission shall:

(1) Recommend to the county commissioners an annual operating budget which is subject to the review, amendment, and approval of the board of county commissioners;

(2)(a) Make an annual report to the county commissioners and the Ohio public defender commission on the operation of the county public defender's office, including complete and detailed information on finances and costs that separately states costs and expenses that are reimbursable under section 120.35 of the Revised Code, and any other data and information requested by the state public defender;

(b) Make monthly reports relating to reimbursement and associated case data pursuant to the rules of the Ohio public defender commission to the board of county commissioners and the Ohio public defender commission on the total costs of the public defender's office.

(3) Cooperate with the Ohio public defender commission in maintaining the standards established by rules of the Ohio public defender commission pursuant to divisions (B) and (C) of section 120.03 of the Revised Code, and cooperate with the state public defender in his programs providing technical aid and assistance to county systems.

(D) The commission may accept the services of volunteer workers and consultants at no compensation except reimbursement for actual and necessary expenses.

(E) The commission may contract with any municipal corporation, within the county served by the county public defender, for the county public defender to provide legal representation for indigent persons who are charged with a violation of the ordinances of the municipal corporation.

(F) A county public defender commission, with the approval of the board of county commissioners regarding all provisions that pertain to the financing of defense counsel for indigent persons, may contract with the state public defender or with any nonprofit organization, the primary purpose of which is to provide legal representation to indigent persons, for the state public defender or the organization to provide all or any part of the services that a county public defender is required or permitted to provide by this chapter. A contract entered into pursuant to this division may provide for payment for the services provided on a per case, hourly, or fixed contract basis. The state public defender and any nonprofit organization that contracts with a county public defender commission pursuant to this division shall do all of the following:

(1) Comply with all standards established by the rules of the Ohio public defender commission;

(2) Comply with all standards established by the state public defender;

(3) Comply with all statutory duties and other laws applicable to county public defenders.

**HISTORY: 136 v H 164 (Eff 1-13-76); 140 v H 291 (Eff 7-1-83); 140 v S 271. Eff 9-26-84.**

## § 120.15 County public defender; powers and duties; determination of indigency.

(A) The county public defender shall be appointed by the county public defender commission for a term not to exceed four years. He shall be an attorney with a minimum of two years experience in the practice of law and be admitted to the practice of law in Ohio at least one year prior to his appointment.

(B) In carrying out the responsibilities and performing the duties of his office, the county public defender shall:

(1) Maintain an office, approved by the commission, provided with a library of adequate size, considering the needs of the office and the accessibility of other libraries, and other necessary facilities and equipment;

(2) Keep and maintain financial records of all cases handled and develop records for use in the calculation of direct and indirect costs in the operation of the office and report monthly pursuant to the rules of the Ohio public defender commission to the county public defender com-

mission and to the Ohio public defender commission on all relevant data on the operations of the office, costs, projected needs, and recommendations for legislation or amendments to court rules, as may be appropriate to improve the criminal justice system;

(3) Collect all moneys due from contracts with municipal corporations or for reimbursement for legal services under this chapter and institute such actions in court for the collection of such sums as he considers advisable. All moneys collected or received by the public defender shall be paid into the county treasury to the credit of the general revenue fund.

(4) Appoint assistant county public defenders and all other personnel necessary to the functioning of the county public defender's office, subject to the authority of the county public defender commission to determine the size and qualifications of the staff pursuant to division (B) of section 120.14 of the Revised Code. All assistant county public defenders shall be admitted to the practice of law in Ohio, and may be appointed on a full or part-time basis.

(C) The county public defender may exercise the rights authorized in division (C) of section 120.04 of the Revised Code.

(D) The county public defender shall determine indigency of persons, subject to review by the court, in the same manner as provided in section 120.05 of the Revised Code. Each monthly report submitted to the board of county commissioners and the state public defender shall include a certification by the county public defender that all persons provided representation by the county public defender's office during the month covered by the report were indigent under the standards of the Ohio public defender commission.

**HISTORY: 136 v H 164 (Eff 1-13-76); 140 v S 271. Eff 9-26-84.**

## § 120.16 When representation to be provided; notice to accused.

(A)(1) The county public defender shall provide legal representation to indigent adults and juveniles who are charged with the commission of an offense or act that is a violation of a state statute and for which the penalty or any possible adjudication includes the potential loss of liberty and in postconviction proceedings as defined in this section.

(2) The county public defender may provide legal representation to indigent adults and juveniles charged with the violation of an ordinance of a municipal corporation for which the penalty or any possible adjudication includes the potential loss of liberty, if the county public defender commission has contracted with the municipal corporation to provide legal representation for indigent persons charged with a violation of an ordinance of the municipal corporation.

(B) The county public defender shall provide the legal representation authorized by division (A) of this section at every stage of the proceedings following arrest, detention, service of summons, or indictment.

(C) The county public defender may request the state public defender to prosecute any appeal or other remedy before or after conviction that the county public defender decides is in the interests of justice, and may provide legal representation in parole and probation revocation matters and matters relating to the revocation of community control or post-release control under a community control sanction or post-release control sanction.

(D) The county public defender shall not be required to prosecute any appeal, postconviction remedy, or other proceeding, unless the county public defender is first satisfied there is arguable merit to the proceeding.

(E) Nothing in this section shall prevent a court from appointing counsel other than the county public defender or from allowing an indigent person to select the indigent person's own personal counsel to represent the indigent person. A court may also appoint counsel or allow an indigent person to select the indigent person's own personal counsel to assist the county public defender as co-counsel when the interests of justice so require.

(F) Information as to the right to legal representation by the county public defender or assigned counsel shall be afforded to an accused person immediately upon arrest, when brought before a magistrate, or when formally charged, whichever occurs first.

(G) If a court appoints the office of the county public defender to represent a petitioner in a postconviction relief proceeding under section 2953.21 of the Revised Code, the petitioner has received a sentence of death, and the proceeding relates to that sentence, all of the attorneys who represent the petitioner in the proceeding pursuant to the appointment, whether an assistant county public defender or the county public defender, shall be certified under Rule 20 of the Rules of Superintendence for the Courts of Ohio to represent indigent defendants charged with or convicted of an offense for which the death penalty can be or has been imposed.

(H) As used in this section:

(1) "Community control sanction" has the same meaning as in section 2929.01 of the Revised Code.

(2) "Post-release control sanction" has the same meaning as in section 2967.01 of the Revised Code.

**HISTORY: 136 v H 164 (Eff 1-13-76); 138 v H 204 (Eff 7-30-79); 140 v S 271 (Eff 9-26-84); 146 v S 258 (Eff 10-16-96); 149 v H 94. Eff 9-5-2001; 149 v H 490, § 1, eff. 1-1-04.**

The effective date is set by section 4 of HB 490.

## § 120.17 County public defender precludes representation by state public defender; exceptions.

In any county in which the county commissioners choose to establish a county public defender's office, the Ohio public defender shall not be required to defend indigent persons in that county, except as set forth in division (A) of section 120.06 of the Revised Code, or if the court finds that it is required in the interests of justice.

**HISTORY: 136 v H 164. Eff 1-13-76.**

## § 120.18 Cost of county public defender's office; reimbursement.

(A) The county public defender commission's report to the board of county commissioners shall be audited by the county auditor. The board of county commissioners, after review and approval of the audited report, may then certify it to the state public defender for reimbursement. If a request for the reimbursement of any operating expenditure incurred by a county public defender office is not received by the state public defender within sixty days after the end of the calendar month in which the expenditure is incurred, the state public defender shall not pay the requested reimbursement, unless the county has requested, and the state public defender has granted, an extension of the sixty-day time limit. Each request for reimbursement shall include a certification by the county public defender that the persons provided representation by the county public defender's office during the period covered by the report were indigent and, for each person provided representation during that period, a financial disclosure form completed by the person on a form prescribed by the state public defender. The state public defender shall also review the report and, in accordance with the standards, guidelines, and maximums established pursuant to divisions (B)(7) and (8) of section 120.04 of the Revised Code, prepare a voucher for fifty per cent of the total cost of each county public defender's office for the period of time covered by the certified report and a voucher for fifty per cent of the costs and expenses that are reimbursable under section 120.35 of the Revised Code, if any, or, if the amount of money appropriated by the general assembly to reimburse counties for the operation of county public defender offices, joint county public defender offices, and county appointed counsel systems is not sufficient to pay fifty per cent of the total cost of all of the offices and systems, for the lesser amount required by section 120.34 of the Revised Code. For the purposes of this section, "total cost" means total expenses minus costs and expenses reimbursable under section 120.35 of the Revised Code and any funds received by the county public defender commission pursuant to a contract, except a contract entered into with a municipal corporation pursuant to division (E) of section 120.14 of the Revised Code, gift, or grant.

(B) If the county public defender fails to maintain the standards for the conduct of the office established by rules of the Ohio public defender commission pursuant to divisions (B) and (C) of section 120.03 or the standards established by the state public defender pursuant to division (B)(7) of section 120.04 of the Revised Code, the Ohio public defender commission shall notify the county public defender commission and the board of county commissioners of the county that the county public defender has failed to comply with its rules or the standards of the state public defender. Unless the county public defender commission or the county public defender corrects the conduct of the county public defender's office to comply with the rules and standards within ninety days after the date of the notice, the state public defender may deny payment of all or part of the county's reimbursement from the state provided for in division (A) of this section.

**HISTORY: 136 v H 164 (Eff 1-13-76); 138 v H 204 (Eff 7-30-79); 139 v H 694 (Eff 11-15-81); 140 v H 291 (Eff 7-1-83); 140 v S 271 (Eff 9-26-84); 141 v H 201 (Eff 7-1-85); 146 v H 117 (Eff 6-30-95); 148 v H 283. Eff 9-29-99.**

The effective date is set by section 162 of HB 283.

## [JOINT COUNTY PUBLIC DEFENDER COMMISSION]

### § 120.23 Joint county public defender commission.

(A) The boards of county commissioners in two or more adjoining or neighboring counties may form themselves into a joint board and proceed to organize a district for the establishment of a joint county public defender commission. The commission shall have three members from each county, who shall be appointed by the board of county commissioners of the county.

(B) The boards shall agree on a specific date for the joint county public defender commission to be established, on which date the appointments of all members shall take effect. The joint board shall notify the Ohio public defender commission of the date.

(C) Of the initial appointments made by each county to the joint county public defender commission, one appointment shall be for a term of one year ending one year after the date the commission is established, one appointment shall be for a term of two years ending two years after the date the commission is established, and one appointment shall be for a period of three years, ending three years after the date the commission is established. Thereafter, terms of office shall be for three years, each term ending on the same day of the same month of the year as did the term which it succeeds. Each member shall hold office from the date of appointment until the end of the term for which the member was appointed. Any member appointed to fill a vacancy occurring prior to the expiration of the term for which the member's predecessor was appointed shall hold office for the remainder of the term. Any member shall continue in office subsequent to the expiration date of the member's term until a successor takes office, or until a period of sixty days has elapsed, whichever occurs first.

(D) The members of the commission shall choose as chairperson one of the commission members, who shall serve as chairperson for two years. Meetings shall be held at least quarterly and at such other times as called by the chairperson or by request of the joint county public defender. Members of the commission may receive an amount fixed by the agreement of the boards of commissioners of the counties in the district, but not in excess of the amount set for the members of the Ohio public defender commission pursuant to section 124.14 of the Revised Code per diem for every meeting of the commission they attend, and necessary expenses including mileage for each mile necessarily traveled.

(E) The agreement of the boards of county commissioners establishing the joint county public defender commission shall provide for the allocation of the proportion of expenses to be paid by each county, which may be based upon population, number of cases, or such other factors as the commissioners determine to be appropriate. The county commissioners may amend their agreement from time to time to provide for a different allocation of the proportion of expenses to be paid by each county.

(F) The county auditor of the county, with the greatest population is hereby designated as the fiscal officer of a joint county public defender district organized under this section. The county auditors of the several counties composing the joint county public defender commission district shall meet at the commission office not less than once in each six months, to adjust accounts and to transact such other duties in connection with the commission as pertain to the business of their office.

(G) Each member of the board of county commissioners who meets by appointment to consider the organization of a joint county public defender commission shall, upon presentation of properly certified accounts, be paid the member's necessary expenses upon a warrant drawn by the county auditor of the member's county.

(H) The board of county commissioners of any county within a joint county public defender commission district may withdraw from the district. Such withdrawal shall not be effective until at least ninety days after the board has notified the Ohio public defender commission, the joint county public defender commission of the district, and each board of county commissioners in the district, in writing of the termination date. The failure of a board of county commissioners to approve an annual operating budget for the office of the joint county public defender as provided in division (C)(1) of section 120.24 of the Revised Code constitutes a notice of withdrawal by the county from the district, effective on the ninetieth day after commencement of the next fiscal year. Upon the termination date, all joint county public defender matters relating to the withdrawing county shall be transferred to the state public defender, a county public defender, or appointed counsel.

(I) The cost of representation in all matters assumed by the state public defender shall be charged to the counties in accordance with division (D) of section 120.06 of the Revised Code.

Members of the joint county public defender commission who are residents of a county withdrawing from such district are deemed to have resigned their positions upon the completion of the withdrawal procedure provided by this section. Vacancies thus created shall not be filled.

If two or more counties remain within the district after the withdrawal, the boards of county commissioners of the remaining adjoining or neighboring counties may agree to continue the operation of the joint county public defender commission and to reallocate the proportionate share of expenses to be paid by each participating county.

**HISTORY: 136 v H 164 (Eff 1-13-76); 139 v H 694. Eff 11-15-81; 151 v H 66, § 101.01, eff. 9-29-05.**

The effective date is set by § 612.03 of 151 v H 66.

## § 120.24 Powers and duties.

(A)(1) Except as provided in division (A)(2) of this section, the joint county public defender commission shall appoint the joint county public defender and may remove him from office only for good cause.

(2) If a joint county public defender commission contracts with the state public defender or with one or more nonprofit organizations for the state public defender or the organizations to provide all of the services that the joint county public defender is required or permitted to provide by this chapter, the commission shall not appoint a joint county public defender.

(B) The commission shall determine the qualifications and size of the supporting staff and facilities and other requirements needed to maintain and operate the office.

(C) In administering the office of joint county public defender, the commission shall:

(1) Recommend to the boards of county commissioners in the district an annual operating budget which is subject to the review, amendment, and approval of the boards of county commissioners in the district;

(2)(a) Make an annual report to the boards of county commissioners in the district and the Ohio public defender commission on the operation of the public defender's office, including complete and detailed information on finances and costs that separately states costs and expenses that are reimbursable under section 120.35 of the Revised Code, and such other data and information requested by the state public defender;

(b) Make monthly reports relating to reimbursement and associated case data pursuant to the rules of the Ohio public defender commission to the boards of county commissioners in the district and the Ohio public defender commission on the total costs of the public defender's office.

(3) Cooperate with the Ohio public defender commission in maintaining the standards established by rules of the Ohio public defender commission pursuant to divisions (B) and (C) of section 120.03 of the Revised Code, and cooperate with the state public defender in his programs providing technical aid and assistance to county systems.

(D) The commission may accept the services of volunteer workers and consultants at no compensation except reimbursement for actual and necessary expenses.

(E) The commission may contract with any municipal corporation, within the counties served by the joint county public defender, for the joint county public defender to provide legal representation for indigent persons who are charged with a violation of the ordinances of the municipal corporation.

(F) A joint county public defender commission, with the approval of each participating board of county commissioners regarding all provisions that pertain to the financing of defense counsel for indigent persons, may contract with the state public defender or with any nonprofit organization, the primary purpose of which is to provide legal representation to indigent persons, for the state public defender or the organization to provide all or any part of the services that a joint county public defender is required or permitted to provide by this chapter. A contract entered into pursuant to this division may provide for payment for the services provided on a per case, hourly, or fixed contract basis. The state public defender and any nonprofit organization that contracts with a joint county public defender commission pursuant to this division shall do all of the following:

(1) Comply with all standards established by the rules of the Ohio public defender commission;

(2) Comply with all standards established by the Ohio public defender;

(3) Comply with all statutory duties and other laws applicable to joint county public defenders.

**HISTORY: 136 v H 164 (Eff 1-13-76); 140 v H 291 (Eff 7-1-83); 140 v S 271. Eff 9-26-84.**

## § 120.25 Joint county public defender; powers and duties; determination of indigency.

(A) The joint county public defender shall be appointed by the joint county public defender commission for a term not to exceed four years. He shall be an attorney with a minimum of two years experience in the practice of law and be admitted to the practice of law in Ohio at least one year prior to his appointment.

(B) In carrying out the responsibilities and performing the duties of his office, the joint county public defender shall:

(1) Maintain an office, approved by the commission, provided with a library of adequate size, considering the needs of the office and the accessibility of other libraries, and other necessary facilities and equipment;

(2) Keep and maintain financial records of all cases handled and develop records for use in the calculation of direct and indirect costs in the operation of the office, and report monthly pursuant to the rules of the Ohio public defender commission to the joint county defender commission and to the Ohio public defender commission on all

relevant data on the operations of the office, costs, projected needs, and recommendations for legislation or amendments to court rules, as may be appropriate to improve the criminal justice system;

(3) Collect all moneys due from contracts with municipal corporations or for reimbursement for legal services under this chapter and institute such actions in court for the collection of such sums as he considers advisable. The public defender shall pay into the treasury of each county in the district, to the credit of the general revenue fund, the county's proportionate share of all moneys collected or received by him.

(4) Appoint assistant joint county public defenders and all other personnel necessary to the functioning of the joint county public defender office, subject to the authority of the joint county public defender commission to determine the size and qualifications of the staff pursuant to division (B) of section 120.24 of the Revised Code. All assistant joint county public defenders shall be admitted to the practice of law in Ohio, and may be appointed on a full or part-time basis.

(C) The joint county public defender may exercise the rights authorized in division (C) of section 120.04 of the Revised Code.

(D) The joint county public defender shall determine indigency of persons, subject to review by the court, in the same manner as provided in section 120.05 of the Revised Code. Each monthly report submitted to the board of county commissioners and the state public defender shall include a certification by the joint county public defender that all persons provided representation by the joint county public defender's office during the month covered by the report were indigent under the standards of the Ohio public defender commission.

**HISTORY: 136 v H 164 (Eff 1-13-76); 140 v S 271. Eff 9-26-84.**

## § 120.26 When representation to be provided; notice to accused.

(A)(1) The joint county public defender shall provide legal representation to indigent adults and juveniles who are charged with the commission of an offense or act that is a violation of a state statute and for which the penalty or any possible adjudication includes the potential loss of liberty and in postconviction proceedings as defined in this section.

(2) The joint county public defender may provide legal representation to indigent adults and juveniles charged with the violation of an ordinance of a municipal corporation for which the penalty or any possible adjudication includes the potential loss of liberty, if the joint county public defender commission has contracted with the municipal corporation to provide legal representation for indigent persons charged with a violation of an ordinance of the municipal corporation.

(B) The joint county public defender shall provide the legal representation authorized by division (A) of this section at every stage of the proceedings following arrest, detention, service of summons, or indictment.

(C) The joint county public defender may request the Ohio public defender to prosecute any appeal or other remedy before or after conviction that the joint county public defender decides is in the interests of justice and may provide legal representation in parole and probation revocation matters and matters relating to the revocation of community control or post-release control under a community control sanction or post-release control sanction.

(D) The joint county public defender shall not be required to prosecute any appeal, postconviction remedy, or other proceeding, unless the joint county public defender is first satisfied that there is arguable merit to the proceeding.

(E) Nothing in this section shall prevent a court from appointing counsel other than the joint county public defender or from allowing an indigent person to select the indigent person's own personal counsel to represent the indigent person. A court may also appoint counsel or allow an indigent person to select the indigent person's own personal counsel to assist the joint county public defender as co-counsel when the interests of justice so require.

(F) Information as to the right to legal representation by the joint county public defender or assigned counsel shall be afforded to an accused person immediately upon arrest, when brought before a magistrate, or when formally charged, whichever occurs first.

(G) If a court appoints the office of the joint county public defender to represent a petitioner in a postconviction relief proceeding under section 2953.21 of the Revised Code, the petitioner has received a sentence of death, and the proceeding relates to that sentence, all of the attorneys who represent the petitioner in the proceeding pursuant to the appointment, whether an assistant joint county defender or the joint county public defender, shall be certified under Rule 20 of the Rules of Superintendence for the Courts of Ohio to represent indigent defendants charged with or convicted of an offense for which the death penalty can be or has been imposed.

(H) As used in this section:

(1) "Community control sanction" has the same meaning as in section 2929.01 of the Revised Code.

(2) "Post-release control sanction" has the same meaning as in section 2967.01 of the Revised Code.

**HISTORY: 136 v H 164 (Eff 1-13-76); 138 v H 204 (Eff 7-30-79); 140 v S 271 (Eff 9-26-84); 146 v S 258 (Eff 10-16-96); 149 v H 94. Eff 9-5-2001; 149 v H 490, § 1, eff. 1-1-04.**

The effective date is set by section 4 of HB 490.

## § 120.27 Joint county public defender precludes representation by state public defender.

In any counties in which the boards of county commissioners choose to establish a joint county public defender's office, the Ohio public defender shall not be required to defend indigent persons in those counties, except as set forth in division (A) of section 120.06 of the Revised Code, or if the court finds that it is required in the interests of justice.

**HISTORY: 136 v H 164. Eff 1-13-76.**

## § 120.28 Cost of joint county public defender's office; reimbursement.

(A) The joint county public defender commission's report to the joint board of county commissioners shall be audited by the fiscal officer of the district. The joint board of county commissioners, after review and approval of the audited report, may then certify it to the state public defender for reimbursement. If a request for the reimbursement of any operating expenditure incurred by a joint county public defender office is not received by the state public defender within sixty days after the end of the calendar month in which the expenditure is incurred, the state public defender shall not pay the requested reimbursement, unless the joint board of county commissioners has requested, and the state public defender has granted, an extension of the sixty-day time limit. Each request for reimbursement shall include a certification by the joint county public defender that all persons provided representation by the joint county public defender's office during the period covered by the request were indigent and, for each person provided representation during that period, a financial disclosure form completed by the person on a form prescribed by the state public defender. The state public defender shall also review the report and, in accordance with the standards, guidelines, and maximums established pursuant to divisions (B)(7) and (8) of section 120.04 of the Revised Code, prepare a voucher for fifty per cent of the total cost of each joint county public defender's office for the period of time covered by the certified report and a voucher for fifty per cent of the costs and expenses that are reimbursable under section 120.35 of the Revised Code, if any, or, if the amount of money appropriated by the general assembly to reimburse counties for the operation of county public defender offices, joint county public defender offices, and county appointed counsel systems is not sufficient to pay fifty per cent of the total cost of all of the offices and systems, for the lesser amount required by section 120.34 of the Revised Code. For purposes of this section, "total cost" means total expenses minus costs and expenses reimbursable under section 120.35 of the Revised Code and any funds received by the joint county public defender commission pursuant to a contract, except a contract entered into with a municipal corporation pursuant to division (E) of section 120.24 of the Revised Code, gift, or grant. Each county in the district shall be entitled to a share of such state reimbursement in proportion to the percentage of the total cost it has agreed to pay.

(B) If the joint county public defender fails to maintain the standards for the conduct of the office established by the rules of the Ohio public defender commission pursuant to divisions (B) and (C) of section 120.03 or the standards established by the state public defender pursuant to division (B)(7) of section 120.04 of the Revised Code, the Ohio public defender commission shall notify the joint county public defender commission and the board of county commissioners of each county in the district that the joint county public defender has failed to comply with its rules or the standards of the state public defender. Unless the joint public defender commission or the joint county public defender corrects the conduct of the joint county public defender's office to comply with the rules and standards within ninety days after the date of the notice, the state public defender may deny all or part of the counties' reimbursement from the state provided for in division (A) of this section.

**HISTORY: 136 v H 164 (Eff 1-13-76); 138 v H 204 (Eff 7-30-79); 139 v H 694 (Eff 11-15-81); 140 v H 291 (Eff 7-1-83); 140 v S 271 (Eff 9-26-84); 141 v H 201 (Eff 7-1-85); 146 v H 117 (Eff 6-30-95); 148 v H 283. Eff 9-29-99.**

The effective date is set by section 162 of HB 283.

## [COUNTY SELECTED OR APPOINTED COUNSEL SYSTEM]

### § 120.33 County selected or appointed counsel system; contract with state public defender.

(A) In lieu of using a county public defender or joint county public defender to represent indigent persons in the proceedings set forth in division (A) of section 120.16 of the Revised Code, the board of county commissioners of any county may adopt a resolution to pay counsel who are either personally selected by the indigent person or appointed by the court. The resolution shall include those provisions the board of county commissioners considers necessary to provide effective representation of indigent persons in any proceeding for which counsel is provided under this section. The resolution shall include provisions for contracts with any municipal corporation under which the municipal corporation shall reimburse the county for counsel appointed to represent indigent persons charged with violations of the ordinances of the municipal corporation.

(1) In a county that adopts a resolution to pay counsel, an indigent person shall have the right to do either of the following:

(a) To select the person's own personal counsel to represent the person in any proceeding included within the provisions of the resolution;

(b) To request the court to appoint counsel to represent the person in such a proceeding.

(2) The court having jurisdiction over the proceeding in a county that adopts a resolution to pay counsel shall, after determining that the person is indigent and entitled to legal representation under this section, do either of the following:

(a) By signed journal entry recorded on its docket, enter the name of the lawyer selected by the indigent person as counsel of record;

(b) Appoint counsel for the indigent person if the person has requested the court to appoint counsel and, by signed journal entry recorded on its dockets, enter the name of the lawyer appointed for the indigent person as counsel of record.

(3) The board of county commissioners shall establish a schedule of fees by case or on an hourly basis to be paid to counsel for legal services provided pursuant to a resolution adopted under this section. Prior to establishing the schedule, the board of county commissioners shall request the bar association or associations of the county to submit a proposed schedule. The schedule submitted shall be subject to the review, amendment, and approval of the board of county commissioners.

(4) Counsel selected by the indigent person or appointed by the court at the request of an indigent person in a county that adopts a resolution to pay counsel, except for counsel appointed to represent a person charged with any violation of an ordinance of a municipal corporation that has not contracted with the county commissioners for the payment of appointed counsel, shall be paid by the county and shall receive the compensation and expenses the court approves. Each request for payment shall be accompanied by a financial disclosure form and an affida-

vit of indigency that are completed by the indigent person on forms prescribed by the state public defender. Compensation and expenses shall not exceed the amounts fixed by the board of county commissioners in the schedule adopted pursuant to division (A)(3) of this section. No court shall approve compensation and expenses that exceed the amount fixed pursuant to division (A)(3) of this section.

The fees and expenses approved by the court shall not be taxed as part of the costs and shall be paid by the county. However, if the person represented has, or may reasonably be expected to have, the means to meet some part of the cost of the services rendered to the person, the person shall pay the county an amount that the person reasonably can be expected to pay. Pursuant to section 120.04 of the Revised Code, the county shall pay to the state public defender a percentage of the payment received from the person in an amount proportionate to the percentage of the costs of the person's case that were paid to the county by the state public defender pursuant to this section. The money paid to the state public defender shall be credited to the client payment fund created pursuant to division (B)(5) of section 120.04 of the Revised Code.

The county auditor shall draw a warrant on the county treasurer for the payment of counsel in the amount fixed by the court, plus the expenses the court fixes and certifies to the auditor. The county auditor shall report periodically, but not less than annually, to the board of county commissioners and to the state public defender the amounts paid out pursuant to the approval of the court. The board of county commissioners, after review and approval of the auditor's report, or the county auditor, with permission from and notice to the board of county commissioners, may then certify it to the state public defender for reimbursement. The state public defender may pay a requested reimbursement only if the request for reimbursement is accompanied by a financial disclosure form and an affidavit of indigency completed by the indigent person on forms prescribed by the state public defender or if the court certifies by electronic signature as prescribed by the state public defender that a financial disclosure form and affidavit of indigency have been completed by the indigent person and are available for inspection. If a request for the reimbursement of the cost of counsel in any case is not received by the state public defender within ninety days after the end of the calendar month in which the case is finally disposed of by the court, unless the county has requested and the state public defender has granted an extension of the ninety-day limit, the state public defender shall not pay the requested reimbursement. The state public defender shall also review the report and, in accordance with the standards, guidelines, and maximums established pursuant to divisions (B)(7) and (8) of section 120.04 of the Revised Code, prepare a voucher for fifty per cent of the total cost of each county appointed counsel system in the period of time covered by the certified report and a voucher for fifty per cent of the costs and expenses that are reimbursable under section 120.35 of the Revised Code, if any, or, if the amount of money appropriated by the general assembly to reimburse counties for the operation of county public defender offices, joint county public defender offices, and county appointed counsel systems is not sufficient to pay fifty per cent of the total cost of all of the offices and systems other than costs and expenses that are reimbursable under section 120.35 of the Revised Code, for the lesser amount required by section 120.34 of the Revised Code.

(5) If any county appointed counsel system fails to maintain the standards for the conduct of the system established by the rules of the Ohio public defender commission pursuant to divisions (B) and (C) of section 120.03 or the standards established by the state public defender pursuant to division (B)(7) of section 120.04 of the Revised Code, the Ohio public defender commission shall notify the board of county commissioners of the county that the county appointed counsel system has failed to comply with its rules or the standards of the state public defender. Unless the board of county commissioners corrects the conduct of its appointed counsel system to comply with the rules and standards within ninety days after the date of the notice, the state public defender may deny all or part of the county's reimbursement from the state provided for in division (A)(4) of this section.

(B) In lieu of using a county public defender or joint county public defender to represent indigent persons in the proceedings set forth in division (A) of section 120.16 of the Revised Code, and in lieu of adopting the resolution and following the procedure described in division (A) of this section, the board of county commissioners of any county may contract with the state public defender for the state public defender's legal representation of indigent persons. A contract entered into pursuant to this division may provide for payment for the services provided on a per case, hourly, or fixed contract basis.

(C) If a court appoints an attorney pursuant to this section to represent a petitioner in a postconviction relief proceeding under section 2953.21 of the Revised Code, the petitioner has received a sentence of death, and the proceeding relates to that sentence, the attorney who represents the petitioner in the proceeding pursuant to the appointment shall be certified under Rule 20 of the Rules of Superintendence for the Courts of Ohio to represent indigent defendants charged with or convicted of an offense for which the death penalty can be or has been imposed.

**HISTORY: 136 v H 164 (Eff 1-13-76); 138 v H 204 (Eff 7-30-79); 139 v H 694 (Eff 11-15-81); 140 v H 291 (Eff 7-1-83); 140 v S 271 (Eff 9-26-84); 141 v H 201 (Eff 7-1-85); 146 v H 117 (Eff 6-30-95); 146 v S 258 (Eff 10-16-96); 147 v H 215 (Eff 9-29-97); 148 v H 283 (Eff 9-29-99); 149 v H 94. Eff 9-5-2001; 152 v H 119, § 101.01, eff. 9-29-07.**

The effective date is set by § 812.03 of 152 v H 119.
The effective date is set by section 204 of HB 94.

## § 120.34 Total reimbursement not to exceed appropriation; pro rata reduction when funds insufficient; annual estimate.

The total amount of money paid to all counties in any fiscal year pursuant to sections 120.18, 120.28, and 120.33 of the Revised Code for the reimbursement of a percentage of the counties' cost of operating county public defender offices, joint county public defender offices, and county appointed counsel systems shall not exceed the total amount appropriated for that fiscal year by the general assembly for the reimbursement of the counties for the operation of the offices and systems. If the amount appropriated by the general assembly in any fiscal year is insufficient to pay fifty per cent of the total cost in the fiscal year of all county public defender offices, all joint county public defender offices, and all county appointed counsel systems, the amount of money paid in that fiscal year pursuant to sections 120.18, 120.28, and 120.33 of the

Revised Code to each county for the fiscal year shall be reduced proportionately so that each county is paid an equal percentage of its total cost in the fiscal year for operating its county public defender system, its joint county public defender system, and its county appointed counsel system.

The total amount of money paid to all counties in any fiscal year pursuant to section 120.35 of the Revised Code for the reimbursement of a percentage of the counties' costs and expenses of conducting the defense in capital cases shall not exceed the total amount appropriated for that fiscal year by the general assembly for the reimbursement of the counties for conducting the defense in capital cases. If the amount appropriated by the general assembly in any fiscal year is insufficient to pay fifty per cent of the counties' total costs and expenses of conducting the defense in capital cases in the fiscal year, the amount of money paid in that fiscal year pursuant to section 120.35 of the Revised Code to each county for the fiscal year shall be reduced proportionately so that each county is paid an equal percentage of its costs and expenses of conducting the defense in capital cases in the fiscal year.

If any county receives an amount of money pursuant to section 120.18, 120.28, 120.33, or 120.35 of the Revised Code that is in excess of the amount of reimbursement it is entitled to receive pursuant to this section, the state public defender shall request the board of county commissioners to return the excess payment and the board of county commissioners, upon receipt of the request, shall direct the appropriate county officer to return the excess payment to the state.

Within thirty days of the end of each fiscal quarter, the state public defender shall provide to the office of budget and management and the legislative budget office of the legislative service commission an estimate of the amount of money that will be required for the balance of the fiscal year to make the payments required by sections 120.18, 120.28, 120.33, and 120.35 of the Revised Code.

**HISTORY: 138 v H 204 (Eff 7-30-79); 140 v H 291. Eff 7-1-83.**

## § 120.35 Reimbursement in capital cases.

The state public defender shall, pursuant to section 120.18, 120.28, 120.33, or 2941.51 of the Revised Code, reimburse fifty per cent of all costs and expenses of conducting the defense in capital cases. If appropriations are insufficient to pay fifty per cent of such costs and expenses, the state public defender shall reimburse such costs and expenses as provided in section 120.34 of the Revised Code.

**HISTORY: 140 v H 291. Eff 7-1-83.**

## § 120.36 Application fee for indigent defendants and parties in juvenile court.

(A)(1) Subject to division (A)(2), (3), (4), (5), or (6) of this section, if a person who is a defendant in a criminal case or a party in a case in juvenile court requests or is provided a state public defender, a county or joint county public defender, or any other counsel appointed by the court, the court in which the criminal case is initially filed or the juvenile court, whichever is applicable, shall assess, unless the application fee is waived or reduced, a non-refundable application fee of twenty-five dollars.

The court shall direct the person to pay the application fee to the clerk of court. The person shall pay the application fee to the clerk of court at the time the person files an affidavit of indigency or a financial disclosure form with the court, a state public defender, a county or joint county public defender, or any other counsel appointed by the court or within seven days of that date. If the person does not pay the application fee within that seven-day period, the court shall assess the application fee at sentencing or at the final disposition of the case.

(2) For purposes of this section, a criminal case includes any case involving a violation of any provision of the Revised Code or of an ordinance of a municipal corporation for which the potential penalty includes loss of liberty and includes any contempt proceeding in which a court may impose a term of imprisonment.

(3) In a juvenile court proceeding, the court shall not assess the application fee against a child if the court appoints a guardian ad litem for the child or the court appoints an attorney to represent the child at the request of a guardian ad litem.

(4) The court shall not assess an application fee for a postconviction proceeding or when the defendant files an appeal.

(5)(a) Except when the court assesses an application fee pursuant to division (A)(5)(b) of this section, the court shall assess an application fee when a person is charged with a violation of a community control sanction or a violation of a post-release control sanction.

(b) If a charge of violating a community control sanction or post-release control sanction described in division (A)(5)(a) of this section results in a person also being charged with violating any provision of the Revised Code or an ordinance of a municipal corporation, the court shall only assess an application fee for the case that results from the additional charge.

(6) If a case is transferred from one court to another court and the person failed to pay the application fee to the court that initially assessed the application fee, the court that initially assessed the fee shall remove the assessment, and the court to which the case was transferred shall assess the application fee.

(7) The court shall assess an application fee pursuant to this section one time per case. For purposes of assessing the application fee, a case means one complete proceeding or trial held in one court for a person on an indictment, information, complaint, petition, citation, writ, motion, or other document initiating a case that arises out of a single incident or a series of related incidents, or when one individual is charged with two or more offenses that the court handles simultaneously. The court may waive or reduce the fee for a specific person in a specific case upon a finding that the person lacks financial resources that are sufficient to pay the fee or that payment of the fee would result in an undue hardship.

(B) No court, state public defender, county or joint county public defender, or other counsel appointed by the court shall deny a person the assistance of counsel solely due to the person's failure to pay the application fee assessed pursuant to division (A) of this section. A person's present inability, failure, or refusal to pay the application fee shall not disqualify that person from legal representation.

(C) The application fee assessed pursuant to division (A) of this section is separate from and in addition to any other amount assessed against a person who is found to be able to contribute toward the cost of the person's legal representation pursuant to division (D) of section 2941.51 of the Revised Code.

(D) The clerk of the court that assessed the fees shall forward all application fees collected pursuant to this section to the county treasurer for deposit in the county treasury. The county shall retain eighty per cent of the application fees so collected to offset the costs of providing legal representation to indigent persons. Not later than the last day of each month, the county auditor shall remit twenty per cent of the application fees so collected in the previous month to the state public defender. The state public defender shall deposit the remitted fees into the state treasury to the credit of the client payment fund created pursuant to division (B)(5) of section 120.04 of the Revised Code. The state public defender may use that money in accordance with that section.

(E) On or before the twentieth day of each month beginning in February of the year 2007, each clerk of court shall provide to the state public defender a report including all of the following:

(1) The number of persons in the previous month who requested or were provided a state public defender, county or joint county public defender, or other counsel appointed by the court;

(2) The number of persons in the previous month for whom the court waived the application fee pursuant to division (A) of this section;

(3) The dollar value of the application fees assessed pursuant to division (A) of this section in the previous month;

(4) The amount of assessed application fees collected in the previous month;

(5) The balance of unpaid assessed application fees at the open and close of the previous month.

(F) As used in this section:

(1) "Clerk of court" means the clerk of the court of common pleas of the county, the clerk of the juvenile court of the county, the clerk of the domestic relations division of the court of common pleas of the county, the clerk of the probate court of the county, the clerk of a municipal court in the county, the clerk of a county-operated municipal court, or the clerk of a county court in the county, whichever is applicable.

(2) "County-operated municipal court" has the same meaning as in section 1901.03 of the Revised Code.

**HISTORY: 151 v H 66, § 101.01, eff. 9-29-05; 151 v H 530, § 101.01, eff. 6-30-06.**

The effective date is set by § 812.03 of 151 v H 530.

The provisions of § 701.03 of 151 v H 530 read as follows:

SECTION 701.03. On or before February 20, 2007, each clerk of court, as defined in section 120.36 of the Revised Code, shall provide to the State Public Defender a report including all of the following for the calendar year 2006:

(A) The number of persons who requested or were provided a state public defender, county or joint county public defender, or other counsel appointed by the court;

(B) The number of persons for whom the court waived the application fee pursuant to division (A) of section 120.36 of the Revised Code;

(C) The dollar value of the application fees assessed pursuant to division (A) of section 120.36 of the Revised Code;

(D) The amount of assessed application fees collected;

(E) The balance of unpaid assessed application fees at the open and close of the calendar year.

The effective date is set by § 612.03 of 151 v H 66.

## § 120.38 Attorney-client privilege applicable.

(A) All information obtained by a public defender when determining if a person is indigent, shall be held confidential within the ethical standards of attorney-client communications, unless previously on public record, or made available to the court as provided in section 120.05 of the Revised Code.

(B) All communications between the individual defendant and a public defender shall be fully protected by the attorney-client privilege to the same extent and degree as though counsel had been privately engaged.

**HISTORY: 136 v H 164. Eff 1-13-76.**

## § 120.39 Restrictions.

(A) Except as provided in division (B) of this section, counsel appointed by the court, co-counsel appointed to assist the state public defender or a county or joint county public defender, and any public defender, county public defender, or joint county defender, or member of their offices, shall not be a partner or employee of any prosecuting attorney, city director of law, village solicitor, or similar chief legal officer.

(B) A partner or employee of a village solicitor or of a law firm, legal professional association, or legal clinic with which the village solicitor is affiliated may be appointed by the court, assist a public defender, or serve as public defender in any criminal proceedings in which the village solicitor is not acting as prosecuting attorney.

(C) No prosecuting attorney, city director of law or similar officer or their assistants and employees, and no judge or court employee shall serve on the state public defender commission, or any county or joint county public defender commission.

**HISTORY: 136 v H 164 (Eff 1-13-76); 137 v H 219 (Eff 11-1-77); 139 v S 38. Eff 3-15-82.**

## § 120.40 Pay ranges; limitation.

(A) The pay ranges established by the board of county commissioners for the county public defender and those established by the joint board of county commissioners for the joint county public defender shall not exceed the pay ranges assigned under section 325.11 of the Revised Code for county prosecutors.

(B) The pay ranges established by the board of county commissioners for the staff of the county public defender and those established by the joint board of county commissioners for the staff of the joint county public defender shall not exceed the pay ranges assigned under section 124.14 of the Revised Code for comparable positions of the staff of the Ohio public defender.

**HISTORY: 136 v H 164. Eff 1-13-76; 2011 HB 153, § 101.01, eff. Sept. 29, 2011.**

## § 120.41 Indemnification of public defenders in malpractice action.

(A) In connection with any malpractice action filed against a state, county, or joint county public defender or assistant public defender, the state, or the county or district in which the defender office is located when the action is brought against a county or joint county public defender or assistant public defender, shall indemnify the attorney, if he acted in good faith and in the scope of his employment, for any judgment awarded in the malpractice action or amount negotiated in settlement of the malpractice claim asserted in the action, and for any court costs or legal fees incurred in the defense of the malpractice claim asserted in the action.

(B)(1) In connection with any malpractice action filed against an attorney who was either personally selected by an indigent person or appointed by a court pursuant to section 120.33 of the Revised Code, the attorney shall be indemnified in accordance with division (B) of this section for any judgment awarded in the malpractice action or amount negotiated in settlement of the malpractice claim asserted in the action, and for any court costs or legal fees incurred in defense of the malpractice claim asserted in the action.

(2) Subject to division (B)(3) of this section, an indemnification as described in division (B)(1) of this section shall be accomplished only through the following procedure:

(a) The attorney who was either personally selected by an indigent person or appointed by a court pursuant to section 120.33 of the Revised Code, or his counsel in the malpractice action, shall file with the attorney general a request for indemnification pursuant to division (B)(1) of this section, which shall be accompanied by the following types of supportive documentation to the extent that they relate to the request for indemnification:

(i) A certified copy of the judgment entry in the malpractice action;

(ii) A signed copy of any settlement agreement entered into between the parties to the malpractice action;

(iii) A written itemization of all court costs and legal fees incurred in the defense of the malpractice claim asserted in the action.

(b) Upon receipt of a request for indemnification and the requisite supportive documentation required by division (B)(2)(a) of this section, the attorney general shall review the request and documentation; determine whether any of the limitations specified in division (B)(3) of this section apply to the requested indemnification; and, if an indemnification in any amount is permitted under division (B)(1) of this section after applying those limitations, prepare an indemnity agreement. The indemnity agreement shall specify whether the indemnification will be for a judgment awarded in a malpractice action, an amount negotiated in settlement of the malpractice claim asserted in a malpractice action, court costs or legal fees incurred in the defense of the malpractice claim asserted in a malpractice action, or a combination of those items. The indemnity agreement additionally shall specify the total amount of permissible indemnification as determined by the attorney general; itemize the portions of the permissible indemnification that represent the judgment, settlement, court costs, or legal fees covered by the indemnity agreement; specify any limitations applied pursuant to division (B)(3) of this section to reduce the amount of indemnification sought by the attorney involved; name the persons to whom the entire permissible indemnification or portions of it will be paid; state that the permissible indemnification is payable from the state treasury pursuant to division (B)(2)(c) of this section; and be approved by the inclusion of the signatures of the attorney general and the attorney involved.

(c) The attorney general shall forward a copy of the indemnity agreement prepared pursuant to division (B)(2)(b) of this section to the director of budget and management. The director shall make application for the payment of the amount of the permissible indemnification out of the emergency purposes account or any other appropriation for emergencies or contingencies, and payment out of that account or any other appropriation for emergencies or contingencies shall be authorized if there are sufficient moneys greater than the sum total of then pending emergency purposes account requests, or requests for releases from the other appropriation. If sufficient moneys exist in the emergency purposes account or any other appropriation for emergencies or contingencies to pay the permissible indemnification, the director shall cause payment of the appropriate amounts specified in the indemnity agreement to be made to the persons named in it. If sufficient moneys do not exist in the emergency purposes account or any other appropriation for emergencies or contingencies to pay the permissible indemnification, the attorney involved or his counsel in the malpractice action shall request the general assembly to make an appropriation sufficient to pay the indemnification, and no payment shall be made until the appropriation has been made. The attorney involved or his counsel in the malpractice action shall make the request during the current biennium and during each succeeding biennium until a sufficient appropriation is made.

(3) An indemnification pursuant to divisions (B)(1) and (2) of this section is subject to the following limitations:

(a) The maximum aggregate amount of the indemnification, whether paid to or on behalf of the attorney who was either personally selected by an indigent person or appointed by a court pursuant to section 120.33 of the Revised Code, shall be one million dollars per occurrence, regardless of the number of persons who suffer injury, death, or loss to person or property as a result of the malpractice involved.

(b) The attorney described in division (B)(3)(a) of this section shall not be indemnified to the extent of any amounts covered by a policy of malpractice insurance, for any portion of a judgment that represents punitive or exemplary damages, for any portion of an amount negotiated in settlement of a malpractice claim that is unreasonable, or for any amount described in division (B)(1) of this section unless he acted in good faith and in the scope of his employment.

(c) The attorney described in division (B)(3)(a) of this section shall be indemnified only for the portion of legal fees that is reasonable.

(4) If, pursuant to division (B)(2) of this section, the attorney general denies any indemnification to an attorney who was either personally selected by an indigent person or appointed by a court pursuant to section 120.33 of the Revised Code because of the application of a limitation specified in division (B)(3) of this section, he shall notify that attorney or his counsel in the malpractice action in writing of the denial and of the limitation applied.

(5) If, pursuant to division (B)(4) of this section, an attorney who was either personally selected by an indigent person or appointed by a court pursuant to section 120.33 of the Revised Code or his counsel in the malpractice action receives a denial of indemnification notification, or if that attorney refuses to approve an indemnity agreement under division (B)(2) of this section because of the proposed application of a limitation specified in division (B)(3) of this section, the attorney may commence a civil action against the attorney general in the court of claims to prove his entitlement to the indemnification sought, to prove that division (B)(3) of this section does not prohibit or otherwise limit the indemnification sought, and to recover a judgment for the amount of indemnification sought. A civil action under this division shall be commenced no later than two years after the receipt of a denial

of indemnification notification or, if the attorney refused to approve an indemnity agreement under division (B)(2) of this section because of the proposed application of a limitation specified in division (B)(3) of this section, no later than two years after the refusal. Any judgment of the court of claims in favor of the attorney shall be paid from the state treasury in accordance with division (B)(2) of this section.

(C) In connection with any malpractice action filed against an attorney who has contracted with the Ohio public defender commission or the state public defender, pursuant to authority granted by this chapter, to provide legal services to indigent or other persons, the state shall indemnify the attorney, if he acted in good faith and in the scope of his employment, for any judgment awarded in the malpractice action or amount negotiated in settlement of the malpractice claim asserted in the action, and for any court costs or legal fees incurred in the defense of the malpractice claim asserted in the action.

**HISTORY: 139 v H 694 (Eff 11-15-81); 144 v H 210. Eff 5-1-92.**

## [LEGAL AID SOCIETY FUNDING]

### § 120.51 Definitions.

As used in sections 120.51 to 120.55 of the Revised Code:

(A) "Legal aid society" means a nonprofit corporation that satisfies all of the following:

(1) It is chartered to provide general legal services to the poor, it is incorporated and operated exclusively in this state, its primary purpose or function is to provide civil legal services, without charge, to indigents, and, in addition to providing civil legal services to indigents, it may provide legal training or legal technical assistance to other legal aid societies in this state.

(2) It has a board of trustees, a majority of its board of trustees are attorneys, and at least one-third of its board of trustees, when selected, are eligible to receive legal services from the legal aid society.

(3) It receives funding from the legal services corporation or otherwise provides civil legal services to indigents.

(B) "Indigent" means a person or persons whose income is not greater than one hundred twenty-five per cent of the current poverty threshold established by the United States office of management and budget.

(C) "Fee generating case" means any case or matter which, if undertaken on behalf of an indigent by an attorney in private practice, reasonably would be expected to result in payment of a fee for legal services from an award to a client, from public funds, or from the opposing party. A case shall not be considered a fee generating case if adequate representation is unavailable or if any of the following circumstances exist concerning the case:

(1) The legal aid society that represents the indigent in the case has determined that free referral is not possible for any of the following reasons:

(a) The case has been rejected by the local lawyer referral service, or if there is no such service, by two attorneys in private practice who have experience in the subject matter of the case.

(b) Neither the local lawyer referral service, if one exists, nor any attorney will consider the case without payment of a consultation fee.

(c) The case is of a type that attorneys in private practice in the area ordinarily do not accept, or do not accept without prepayment of a fee.

(d) Emergency circumstances compel immediate action before referral can be made, but the client is advised that, if appropriate and consistent with professional responsibility, referral will be attempted at a later time.

(2) Recovery of damages is not the principal object of the case and a request for damages is merely ancillary to an action for equitable or other nonpecuniary relief, or inclusion of a counterclaim requesting damages is necessary for effective defense or because of applicable rules governing joinder of counterclaims.

(3) A court has appointed a legal aid society or its employee to represent the indigent in the case pursuant to a statute, or a court rule or practice of equal applicability to all attorneys in the jurisdiction.

(4) The case involves the rights of a claimant under a publicly supported benefit program for which entitlement is based on need.

**HISTORY: 140 v S 219 (Eff 1-8-85); 145 v H 152 (Eff 7-1-93); 146 v H 151. Eff 12-4-95.**

### § 120.52 Legal aid fund.

There is hereby established in the state treasury the legal aid fund, which shall be for the charitable public purpose of providing financial assistance to legal aid societies that provide civil legal services to indigents. The fund shall contain all funds credited to it by the treasurer of state pursuant to sections 1901.26, 1907.24, 2303.201 [2303.20.1], 3953.231 [3953.23.1], 4705.09 and 4705.10 of the Revised Code.

The treasurer of state may invest moneys contained in the legal aid fund in any manner authorized by the Revised Code for the investment of state moneys. However, no such investment shall interfere with any apportionment, allocation, or payment of moneys as required by section 120.53 of the Revised Code.

The state public defender, through the Ohio legal assistance foundation, shall administer the payment of moneys out of the fund. Four and one-half per cent of the moneys in the fund shall be reserved for the actual, reasonable costs of administering sections 120.51 to 120.55 and sections 1901.26, 1907.24, 2303.201 [2303.20.1], 3953.231 [3953.23.1], 4705.09, and 4705.10 of the Revised Code. Moneys that are reserved for administrative costs but that are not used for actual, reasonable administrative costs shall be set aside for use in the manner described in division (A) of section 120.521 [120.52.1] of the Revised Code. The remainder of the moneys in the legal aid fund shall be distributed in accordance with section 120.53 of the Revised Code. The Ohio legal assistance foundation shall establish, in accordance with Chapter 119. of the Revised Code, rules governing the administration of the legal aid fund, including the programs established under sections 1901.26, 1907.24, 2303.201 [2303.20.1], 4705.09, and 4705.10 of the Revised Code regarding interest on interest-bearing trust accounts of an attorney, law firm, or legal professional association.

**HISTORY: 140 v S 219 (Eff 1-8-85); 141 v H 201 (Eff 7-1-85); 141 v H 201, § 12 (Eff 1-1-87); 142 v H 708 (Eff 4-19-88); 145 v H 152 (Eff 7-1-93); 146 v H 117 (Eff 6-30-95); 146 v H 151. Eff 12-4-95; 151 v H 66, § 101.01, eff. 10-1-05; 151 v H 530, § 101.01, eff. 6-30-06.**

The effective date is set by § 812.03 of 151 v H 530.
The effective date is set by § 612.09 of 151 v H 66.

## § 120.521 Legal assistance foundation; fund.

(A) The state public defender shall establish a charitable, tax exempt foundation, named the Ohio legal assistance foundation, to actively solicit and accept gifts, bequests, donations, and contributions for use in providing financial assistance to legal aid societies, enhancing or improving the delivery of civil legal services to indigents, and operating the foundation. The Ohio legal assistance foundation shall deposit all gifts, bequests, donations, and contributions accepted by it into the legal assistance foundation fund established under this section. If the state public defender, pursuant to section 120.52 of the Revised Code as it existed prior to the effective date of this section, established a charitable, tax exempt foundation named the Ohio legal assistance foundation and if that foundation is in existence on the day before the effective date of this section, that foundation shall continue in existence and shall serve as the Ohio legal assistance foundation described in this section.

There is hereby established the legal assistance foundation fund, which shall be under the custody and control of the Ohio legal assistance foundation. The fund shall contain all moneys distributed to the Ohio legal assistance foundation pursuant to section 120.53 of the Revised Code and all gifts, bequests, donations, and contributions accepted by the Ohio legal assistance foundation under this section.

The Ohio legal assistance foundation shall distribute or use all moneys in the legal assistance foundation fund for the charitable public purpose of providing financial assistance to legal aid societies that provide civil legal services to indigents, enhancing or improving the delivery of civil legal services to indigents, and operating the foundation. The Ohio legal assistance foundation shall establish rules governing the administration of the legal assistance foundation fund.

The Ohio legal assistance foundation shall include, in the annual report it is required to make to the governor, the general assembly, and the supreme court pursuant to division (G)(2) of section 120.53 of the Revised Code, an audited financial statement on the distribution and use of the legal assistance foundation fund. No information contained in the statement shall identify or enable the identification of any person served by a legal aid society or in any way breach confidentiality.

(B) A foundation is tax exempt for purposes of this section if the foundation is exempt from federal income taxation under subsection 501(a) of the "Internal Revenue Code of 1986," 100 Stat. 2085, 26 U.S.C. 501(a), as amended, and if the foundation has received from the internal revenue service a determination letter that is in effect stating that the foundation is exempt from federal income taxation under that subsection.

**HISTORY: 146 v H 117. Eff 6-30-95; 151 v H 530, § 101.01, eff. 6-30-06.**

The effective date is set by § 812.03 of 151 v H 530.

## § 120.53 Legal aid society may apply for financial assistance; allocation and distribution of funds; annual reports.

(A) A legal aid society that operates within the state may apply to the Ohio legal assistance foundation for financial assistance from the legal aid fund established by section 120.52 of the Revised Code to be used for the funding of the society during the calendar year following the calendar year in which application is made.

(B) An application for financial assistance made under division (A) of this section shall be submitted by the first day of November of the calendar year preceding the calendar year for which financial assistance is desired and shall include all of the following:

(1) Evidence that the applicant is incorporated in this state as a nonprofit corporation;

(2) A list of the trustees of the applicant;

(3) The proposed budget of the applicant for these funds for the following calendar year;

(4) A summary of the services to be offered by the applicant in the following calendar year;

(5) A specific description of the territory or constituency served by the applicant;

(6) An estimate of the number of persons to be served by the applicant during the following calendar year;

(7) A general description of the additional sources of the applicant's funding;

(8) The amount of the applicant's total budget for the calendar year in which the application is filed that it will expend in that calendar year for legal services in each of the counties it serves;

(9) A specific description of any services, programs, training, and legal technical assistance to be delivered by the applicant or by another person pursuant to a contract with the applicant, including, but not limited to, by private attorneys or through reduced fee plans, judicare panels, organized pro bono programs, and mediation programs.

(C) The Ohio legal assistance foundation shall determine whether each applicant that filed an application for financial assistance under division (A) of this section in a calendar year is eligible for financial assistance under this section. To be eligible for such financial assistance, an applicant shall satisfy the criteria for being a legal aid society and shall be in compliance with the provisions of sections 120.51 to 120.55 of the Revised Code and with the rules and requirements the foundation establishes pursuant to section 120.52 of the Revised Code. The Ohio legal assistance foundation then, on or before the fifteenth day of December of the calendar year in which the application is filed, shall notify each such applicant, in writing, whether it is eligible for financial assistance under this section, and if it is eligible, estimate the amount that will be available for that applicant for each six-month distribution period, as determined under division (D) of this section.

(D) The Ohio legal assistance foundation shall allocate moneys contained in the legal aid fund monthly for distribution to applicants that filed their applications in the previous calendar year and are determined to be eligible applicants.

All moneys contained in the fund on the first day of each month shall be allocated, after deduction of the costs of administering sections 120.51 to 120.55 and sections 1901.26, 1907.24, 2303.201 [2303.20.1], 3953.231 [3953.23.1], 4705.09, and 4705.10 of the Revised Code that are authorized by section 120.52 of the Revised Code, according to this section and shall be distributed accordingly not later than the last day of the month following the month the moneys were received. In making the allocations under this section, the moneys in the fund that were generated pursuant to sections 1901.26, 1907.24, 2303.201 [2303.20.1], 3953.231 [3953.23.1], 4705.09, and 4705.10 of the Revised Code shall be apportioned as follows:

(1) After deduction of the amount authorized and used for actual, reasonable administrative costs under section 120.52 of the Revised Code:

(a) Five per cent of the moneys remaining in the fund shall be reserved for use in the manner described in division (A) of section 120.521 [120.52.1] of the Revised Code or for distribution to legal aid societies that provide assistance to special population groups of their eligible clients, engage in special projects that have a substantial impact on their local service area or on significant segments of the state's poverty population, or provide legal training or support to other legal aid societies in the state;

(b) After deduction of the amount described in division (D)(1)(a) of this section, one and three-quarters per cent of the moneys remaining in the fund shall be apportioned among entities that received financial assistance from the legal aid fund prior to the effective date of this amendment but that, on and after the effective date of this amendment, no longer qualify as a legal aid society that is eligible for financial assistance under this section.

(c) After deduction of the amounts described in divisions (D)(1)(a) and (b) of this section, fifteen per cent of the moneys remaining in the fund shall be placed in the legal assistance foundation fund for use in the manner described in division (A) of section 120.521 [120.52.1] of the Revised Code.

(2) After deduction of the actual, reasonable administrative costs under section 120.52 of the Revised Code and after deduction of the amounts identified in divisions (D)(1)(a), (b), and (c) of this section, the remaining moneys shall be apportioned among the counties that are served by eligible legal aid societies that have applied for financial assistance under this section so that each such county is apportioned a portion of those moneys, based upon the ratio of the number of indigents who reside in that county to the total number of indigents who reside in all counties of this state that are served by eligible legal aid societies that have applied for financial assistance under this section. Subject to division (E) of this section, the moneys apportioned to a county under this division then shall be allocated to the eligible legal aid society that serves the county and that has applied for financial assistance under this section. For purposes of this division, the source of data identifying the number of indigent persons who reside in a county shall be the most recent decennial census figures from the United States department of commerce, division of census.

(E) If the Ohio legal assistance foundation, in attempting to make an allocation of moneys under division (D)(2) of this section, determines that a county that has been apportioned money under that division is served by more than one eligible legal aid society that has applied for financial assistance under this section, the Ohio legal assistance foundation shall allocate the moneys that have been apportioned to that county under division (D)(2) of this section among all eligible legal aid societies that serve that county and that have applied for financial assistance under this section on a pro rata basis, so that each such eligible society is allocated a portion based upon the amount of its total budget expended in the prior calendar year for legal services in that county as compared to the total amount expended in the prior calendar year for legal services in that county by all eligible legal aid societies that serve that county and that have applied for financial assistance under this section.

(F) Moneys allocated to eligible applicants under this section shall be paid monthly beginning the calendar year following the calendar year in which the application is filed.

(G)(1) A legal aid society that receives financial assistance in any calendar year under this section shall file an annual report with the Ohio legal assistance foundation detailing the number and types of cases handled, and the amount and types of legal training, legal technical assistance, and other service provided, by means of that financial assistance. No information contained in the report shall identify or enable the identification of any person served by the legal aid society or in any way breach client confidentiality.

(2) The Ohio legal assistance foundation shall make an annual report to the governor, the general assembly, and the supreme court on the distribution and use of the legal aid fund. The foundation also shall include in the annual report an audited financial statement of all gifts, bequests, donations, contributions, and other moneys the foundation receives. No information contained in the report shall identify or enable the identification of any person served by a legal aid society, or in any way breach confidentiality.

(H) A legal aid society may enter into agreements for the provision of services, programs, training, or legal technical assistance for the legal aid society or to indigent persons.

**HISTORY: 140 v S 219 (Eff 1-8-85); 141 v H 201 (Eff 7-1-85); 141 v H 201, § 17 (Eff 3-1-87); 142 v H 708 (Eff 4-19-88); 145 v H 152 (Eff 7-1-93); 146 v H 117. Eff 6-30-95; 151 v H 66, § 101.01, eff. 10-1-05; 151 v H 530, § 101.01, eff. 6-30-06.**

The effective date is set by § 812.03 of 151 v H 530.
The effective date is set by § 612.09 of 151 v H 66.

## § 120.54 Permitted uses of financial assistance.

(A) A legal aid society that receives financial assistance from the legal aid fund under section 120.53 of the Revised Code shall use the financial assistance for only the following purposes:

(1) To defray the costs of providing legal services to indigents;

(2) To provide legal training and legal technical assistance to other eligible legal aid societies; and

(3) If the legal aid society has entered into an agreement pursuant to division (H) of section 120.53 of the Revised Code and in accordance with the description and list of conditions set forth in its application pursuant to division (B)(9) of that section, to provide funds for the services, programs, training, and legal technical assistance provided to the legal aid society under the contract.

(B) No financial assistance received by a legal aid society from the legal aid fund pursuant to section 120.53 of the Revised Code shall be used for the provision of legal services in relation to any criminal case or proceeding or in relation to the provision of legal assistance in any fee generating case.

**HISTORY: 140 v S 219 (Eff 1-8-85); 145 v H 152 (Eff 7-1-93); 146 v H 117. Eff 6-30-95.**

## § 120.55 Conditions to be ensured by society.

In providing legal assistance, each legal aid society that receives financial assistance from the legal aid fund under section 120.53 of the Revised Code shall ensure all of the following:

(A) The maintenance of quality service and professional standards;

(B) That no person shall interfere with any attorney funded in whole or in part by sections 120.51 to 120.55 of the Revised Code in carrying out his professional responsibility to his client as established by the rules of professional responsibility;

(C) The expenditure of the financial assistance only in accordance with sections 120.51 to 120.55 of the Revised Code;

(D) The preservation of client confidentiality.

**HISTORY: 140 v S 219 (Eff 1-8-85); 146 v H 117. Eff 6-30-95.**

# CHAPTER 124: DEPARTMENT OF ADMINISTRATIVE SERVICES — PERSONNEL

Section



## [LAYOFF PROCEDURE]

### § 124.34 Tenure of office; reduction, suspension, removal and demotion.

(A) The tenure of every officer or employee in the classified service of the state and the counties, civil service townships, cities, city health districts, general health districts, and city school districts of the state, holding a position under this chapter, shall be during good behavior and efficient service. No officer or employee shall be reduced in pay or position, fined, suspended, or removed, or have the officer's or employee's longevity reduced or eliminated, except as provided in section 124.32 of the Revised Code, and for incompetency, inefficiency, dishonesty, drunkenness, immoral conduct, insubordination, discourteous treatment of the public, neglect of duty, violation of any policy or work rule of the officer's or employee's appointing authority, violation of this chapter or the rules of the director of administrative services or the commission, any other failure of good behavior, any other acts of misfeasance, malfeasance, or nonfeasance in office, or conviction of a felony. The denial of a one-time pay supplement or a bonus to an officer or employee is not a reduction in pay for purposes of this section.

This section does not apply to any modifications or reductions in pay or work week authorized by division (Q) of section 124.181 or section 124.392, 124.393, or 124.394 of the Revised Code.

An appointing authority may require an employee who is suspended to report to work to serve the suspension. An employee serving a suspension in this manner shall continue to be compensated at the employee's regular rate of pay for hours worked. The disciplinary action shall be recorded in the employee's personnel file in the same manner as other disciplinary actions and has the same effect as a suspension without pay for the purpose of recording disciplinary actions.

A finding by the appropriate ethics commission, based upon a preponderance of the evidence, that the facts alleged in a complaint under section 102.06 of the Revised Code constitute a violation of Chapter 102., section 2921.42, or section 2921.43 of the Revised Code may constitute grounds for dismissal. Failure to file a statement or falsely filing a statement required by section 102.02 of the Revised Code may also constitute grounds for dismissal. The tenure of an employee in the career professional service of the department of transportation is subject to section 5501.20 of the Revised Code.

Conviction of a felony is a separate basis for reducing in pay or position, suspending, or removing an officer or employee, even if the officer or employee has already been reduced in pay or position, suspended, or removed for the same conduct that is the basis of the felony. An officer or employee may not appeal to the state personnel board of review or the commission any disciplinary action taken by an appointing authority as a result of the officer's or employee's conviction of a felony. If an officer or employee removed under this section is reinstated as a result of an appeal of the removal, any conviction of a felony that occurs during the pendency of the appeal is a basis for further disciplinary action under this section upon the officer's or employee's reinstatement.

A person convicted of a felony immediately forfeits the person's status as a classified employee in any public employment on and after the date of the conviction for the felony. If an officer or employee is removed under this section as a result of being convicted of a felony or is subsequently convicted of a felony that involves the same conduct that was the basis for the removal, the officer or employee is barred from receiving any compensation after the removal notwithstanding any modification or disaffirmance of the removal, unless the conviction for the felony is subsequently reversed or annulled.

Any person removed for conviction of a felony is entitled to a cash payment for any accrued but unused sick, personal, and vacation leave as authorized by law. If subsequently reemployed in the public sector, the person shall qualify for and accrue these forms of leave in the manner specified by law for a newly appointed employee and shall not be credited with prior public service for the purpose of receiving these forms of leave.

As used in this division, "felony" means any of the following:

(1) A felony that is an offense of violence as defined in section 2901.01 of the Revised Code;

(2) A felony that is a felony drug abuse offense as defined in section 2925.01 of the Revised Code;

(3) A felony under the laws of this or any other state or the United States that is a crime of moral turpitude;

(4) A felony involving dishonesty, fraud, or theft;

(5) A felony that is a violation of section 2921.05, 2921.32, or 2921.42 of the Revised Code.

(B) In case of a reduction, a suspension of more than forty work hours in the case of an employee exempt from the payment of overtime compensation, a suspension of more than twenty-four work hours in the case of an employee required to be paid overtime compensation, a fine of more than forty hours' pay in the case of an employee exempt from the payment of overtime compensation, a fine of more than twenty-four hours' pay in the case of an employee required to be paid overtime compensation, or removal, except for the reduction or removal of a probationary employee, the appointing authority shall serve the employee with a copy of the order of reduction, fine, suspension, or removal, which order shall state the reasons for the action.

Within ten days following the date on which the order is served or, in the case of an employee in the career professional service of the department of transportation, within ten days following the filing of a removal order, the employee, except as otherwise provided in this section, may file an appeal of the order in writing with the state personnel board of review or the commission. For purposes of this section, the date on which an order is served is the date of hand delivery of the order or the date of delivery of the order by certified United States mail, whichever occurs first. If an appeal is filed, the board or commission shall forthwith notify the appointing authority and shall hear, or appoint a trial board to hear, the appeal within thirty days from and after its filing with the board or commission. The board, commission, or trial board may affirm, disaffirm, or modify the judgment of the appointing authority. However, in an appeal of a removal order based upon a violation of a last chance agreement, the board, commission, or trial board may only determine if the employee violated the agreement and thus affirm or disaffirm the judgment of the appointing authority.

In cases of removal or reduction in pay for disciplinary reasons, either the appointing authority or the officer or employee may appeal from the decision of the state personnel board of review or the commission, and any such appeal shall be to the court of common pleas of the county in which the appointing authority is located, or to the court of common pleas of Franklin county, as provided by section 119.12 of the Revised Code.

(C) In the case of the suspension for any period of time, or a fine, demotion, or removal, of a chief of police, a chief of a fire department, or any member of the police or fire department of a city or civil service township, who is in the classified civil service, the appointing authority shall furnish the chief or member with a copy of the order of suspension, fine, demotion, or removal, which order shall state the reasons for the action. The order shall be filed with the municipal or civil service township civil service commission. Within ten days following the filing of the order, the chief or member may file an appeal, in writing, with the commission. If an appeal is filed, the commission shall forthwith notify the appointing authority and shall hear, or appoint a trial board to hear, the appeal within thirty days from and after its filing with the commission, and it may affirm, disaffirm, or modify the judgment of the appointing authority. An appeal on questions of law and fact may be had from the decision of the commission to the court of common pleas in the county in which the city or civil service township is situated. The appeal shall be taken within thirty days from the finding of the commission.

(D) A violation of division (A)(7) of section 2907.03 of the Revised Code is grounds for termination of employment of a nonteaching employee under this section.

(E) As used in this section, "last chance agreement" means an agreement signed by both an appointing authority and an officer or employee of the appointing authority that describes the type of behavior or circumstances that, if it occurs, will automatically lead to removal of the officer or employee without the right of appeal to the state personnel board of review or the appropriate commission.

**HISTORY: GC § 486-17a; 106 v 400(412); 114 v 224; Bureau of Code Revision, RC § 143.27, 10-1-53; 126 v 90; 128 v 1049(1064) (Eff 11-2-59); 129 v 1330 (Eff 10-27-61); 131 v 128 (Eff 9-13-65); 132 v S 271 (Eff 12-13-67); RC § 124.34, 135 v S 174 (Eff 12-4-73); 135 v H 55 (Eff 1-1-74); 135 v S 243 (Eff 7-23-74); 135 v H 513 (Eff 8-9-74); 136 v H 1 (Eff 6-13-75); 137 v H 47 (Eff 3-13-78); 138 v H 155 (Eff 5-16-79); 141 v H 300 (Eff 9-17-86); 145 v H 454 (Eff 7-19-94); 147 v H 215 (Eff 9-29-97); 147 v S 229 (Eff 9-16-98); 147 v H 348 (Eff 3-22-99); 147 v S 144 (Eff 3-30-99); 148 v H 640. Eff 6-15-2000; 151 v H 187, § 1, eff. 7-1-07; 153 v H 16, § 101, eff. 6-30-09; 153 v H 1, § 101.01, eff. 7-17-09; 2011 HB 153 § 101.01, eff. Sept. 29, 2011.**

This section was amended by Senate Bill 5 of the 2011 legislative session. However, referendum petitions were filed to prevent SB 5 from taking effect as scheduled on July 1, 2011. The provisions of SB 5 were rejected by the voters at the referendum election on November 8, 2011.

Acts 2011, HB 153, § 815.20 provides: "The General Assembly, applying the principle stated in division (B) of section 1.52 of the Revised Code that amendments are to be harmonized if reasonably capable of simultaneous operation, finds that the following sections, presented in this act as composites of the sections as amended by the acts indicated, are the resulting versions of the sections in effect prior to the effective date of the sections as presented in this act:

"Section 124.34 of the Revised Code as amended by Am. Sub. H.B. 1 and Am. Sub. H.B. 16 of the 128th General Assembly."

The effective date is set by § 812.20 of 153 v H 1.

The effective date is set by § 809.10 of 153 v H 16.

The effective date is set by § 7 of 151 v H 187.

**Analogous in part to former RC § 143.26, repealed 129 v 1334, § 2.**

The effective date is set by section 81 of HB 640.

The provisions of § 87 of HB 640 (148 v —) read as follows:

SECTION 87. Section 124.34 of the Revised Code is presented in this act as a composite of the section as amended by both Am. Sub. H.B. 348 and Am. Sub. S.B. 144 of the 122nd General Assembly, with the new language of neither of the acts shown in capital letters. This is in recognition of the principle stated in division (B) of section 1.52 of the Revised Code that such amendments are to be harmonized where not substantively irreconcilable and constitutes a legislative finding that such is the resulting version in effect prior to the effective date of this act.

**Comment, Legislative Service Commission**

Section 124.34 of the Revised Code is amended by Am. Sub. H.B. 1 and Am. Sub. H.B. 16 of the 128th General Assembly. Comparison of these amendments in pursuance of section 1.52 of the Revised Code discloses that they are not irreconcilable so that they are required by that section to be harmonized to give effect to each amendment.

# CHAPTER 141: SALARIES OF STATE OFFICERS

Section

[EXECUTIVE OFFICERS]



## [EXECUTIVE OFFICERS]

### § 141.011 Salaries beginning in 2001; payment upon death of elected executive officer.

Beginning in calendar year 2001, the annual salaries of the elective officers of the state shall be as follows rather than as prescribed by divisions (A) to (F) of section 141.01 of the Revised Code:

(A)(1) In calendar year 2001 the annual salary of the governor shall be one hundred twenty-six thousand four hundred ninety-seven dollars.

(2) In calendar years 2002 through 2006 the annual salary of the governor shall be one hundred thirty thousand two hundred ninety-two dollars.

(3) In calendar year 2007 the annual salary of the governor shall be the annual salary in 2006 increased by each of the following percentages in succession:

(a) The lesser of three per cent or the percentage increase, if any, in the consumer price index from October 1, 2001, to September 30, 2002, rounded to the nearest one-tenth of one per cent;

(b) The lesser of three per cent or the percentage increase, if any, in the consumer price index from October 1, 2002, to September 30, 2003, rounded to the nearest one-tenth of one per cent;

(c) The lesser of three per cent or the percentage increase, if any, in the consumer price index from October 1, 2003, to September 30, 2004, rounded to the nearest one-tenth of one per cent;

(d) The lesser of three per cent or the percentage increase, if any, in the consumer price index from October 1, 2004, to September 30, 2005, rounded to the nearest one-tenth of one per cent;

(e) The lesser of three per cent or the percentage increase, if any, in the consumer price index from October 1, 2005, to September 30, 2006, rounded to the nearest one-tenth of one per cent.

(4) In calendar year 2008 and thereafter, the annual salary of the governor shall be the annual salary in 2007 increased by the lesser of the following:

(a) Three per cent;

(b) The percentage increase, if any, in the consumer price index from October 1, 2006, to September 30, 2007, rounded to the nearest one-tenth of one per cent.

(B)(1) In calendar year 2001 the annual salary of the lieutenant governor shall be sixty-six thousand three hundred six dollars.

(2) In calendar years 2002 through 2006 the annual salary of the lieutenant governor shall be sixty-eight thousand two hundred ninety-five dollars.

(3) In calendar year 2007 the annual salary of the lieutenant governor shall be the annual salary in 2006 increased by each of the following percentages in succession:

(a) The lesser of three per cent or the percentage increase, if any, in the consumer price index from October 1, 2001, to September 30, 2002, rounded to the nearest one-tenth of one per cent;

(b) The lesser of three per cent or the percentage increase, if any, in the consumer price index from October 1, 2002, to September 30, 2003, rounded to the nearest one-tenth of one per cent;

(c) The lesser of three per cent or the percentage increase, if any, in the consumer price index from October 1, 2003, to September 30, 2004, rounded to the nearest one-tenth of one per cent;

(d) The lesser of three per cent or the percentage increase, if any, in the consumer price index from October 1, 2004, to September 30, 2005, rounded to the nearest one-tenth of one per cent;

(e) The lesser of three per cent or the percentage increase, if any, in the consumer price index from October 1, 2005, to September 30, 2006, rounded to the nearest one-tenth of one per cent.

(4) In calendar year 2008 and thereafter, the annual salary of the lieutenant governor shall be the annual salary in 2007 increased by the lesser of the following:

(a) Three per cent;

(b) The percentage increase, if any, in the consumer price index from October 1, 2006, to September 30, 2007, rounded to the nearest one-tenth of one per cent.

If the governor appoints the lieutenant governor as an administrative department head, the lieutenant governor may accept the salary for that office while serving as its head in lieu of the salary for the office of lieutenant governor.

(C)(1) In calendar year 2001 the annual salary of the secretary of state, auditor of state, treasurer of state, and attorney general shall be ninety-three thousand four hundred forty-seven dollars.

(2) In calendar year 2002 the annual salary of the secretary of state, auditor of state, treasurer of state, and attorney general shall be ninety-six thousand two hundred fifty dollars.

(3) In each calendar year from 2003 through 2008, the annual salary of the secretary of state, auditor of state, treasurer of state, and attorney general shall be increased by the lesser of the following:

(a) Three per cent;

(b) The percentage increase, if any, in the consumer price index over the twelve-month period that ends on the thirtieth day of September of the immediately preceding year, rounded to the nearest one-tenth of one per cent.

(D) Upon the death of an elected executive officer of the state listed in divisions (A) to (F) of section 141.01 of the Revised Code during that person's term of office, an amount shall be paid in accordance with section 2113.04 of the Revised Code, or to that person's estate. The amount shall equal the amount of the salary that the officer would have received during the remainder of the officer's unexpired term or an amount equal to the salary of that person's office for two years, whichever is less.

(E) As used in this section, "consumer price index" has the same meaning as in section 101.27 of the Revised Code.

**HISTORY: 140 v H 897 (Eff 12-26-84); 141 v H 850 (Eff 9-17-86); 142 v S 452 (Eff 12-15-88); 146 v H 408 (Eff 5-8-96); 147 v S 193 (Eff 12-29-98); 148 v H 712. Eff 12-8-2000; 151 v H 66, § 101.01, eff. 6-30-05.**

The effective date is set by § 612.12 of 151 v H 66.

# CHAPTER 149: DOCUMENTS, REPORTS, AND RECORDS



## [RECORDS COMMISSIONS]

### § 149.43 Availability of public records.

(A) As used in this section:

(1) "Public record" means records kept by any public office, including, but not limited to, state, county, city, village, township, and school district units, and records pertaining to the delivery of educational services by an alternative school in this state kept by the nonprofit or for-profit entity operating the alternative school pursuant to section 3313.533 of the Revised Code. "Public record" does not mean any of the following:

(a) Medical records;

(b) Records pertaining to probation and parole proceedings or to proceedings related to the imposition of community control sanctions and post-release control sanctions;

(c) Records pertaining to actions under section 2151.85 and division (C) of section 2919.121 of the Revised Code and to appeals of actions arising under those sections;

(d) Records pertaining to adoption proceedings, including the contents of an adoption file maintained by the department of health under section 3705.12 of the Revised Code;

(e) Information in a record contained in the putative father registry established by section 3107.062 of the Revised Code, regardless of whether the information is held by the department of job and family services or, pursuant to section 3111.69 of the Revised Code, the office of child support in the department or a child support enforcement agency;

(f) Records listed in division (A) of section 3107.42 of the Revised Code or specified in division (A) of section 3107.52 of the Revised Code;

(g) Trial preparation records;

(h) Confidential law enforcement investigatory records;

(i) Records containing information that is confidential under section 2710.03 or 4112.05 of the Revised Code;

(j) DNA records stored in the DNA database pursuant to section 109.573 of the Revised Code;

(k) Inmate records released by the department of rehabilitation and correction to the department of youth services or a court of record pursuant to division (E) of section 5120.21 of the Revised Code;

(l) Records maintained by the department of youth services pertaining to children in its custody released by the department of youth services to the department of rehabilitation and correction pursuant to section 5139.05 of the Revised Code;

(m) Intellectual property records;

(n) Donor profile records;

(o) Records maintained by the department of job and family services pursuant to section 3121.894 of the Revised Code;

(p) Peace officer, parole officer, probation officer, bailiff, prosecuting attorney, assistant prosecuting attorney, correctional employee, youth services employee, firefighter, EMT, or investigator of the bureau of criminal identification and investigation residential and familial information;

(q) In the case of a county hospital operated pursuant to Chapter 339. of the Revised Code or a municipal hospital operated pursuant to Chapter 749. of the Revised Code, information that constitutes a trade secret, as defined in section 1333.61 of the Revised Code;

(r) Information pertaining to the recreational activities of a person under the age of eighteen;

(s) Records provided to, statements made by review board members during meetings of, and all work products of a child fatality review board acting under sections 307.621 to 307.629 of the Revised Code, and child fatality review data submitted by the child fatality review board to the department of health or a national child death review database, other than the report prepared pursuant to division (A) of section 307.626 of the Revised Code;

(t) Records provided to and statements made by the executive director of a public children services agency or a prosecuting attorney acting pursuant to section 5153.171 of the Revised Code other than the information released under that section;

(u) Test materials, examinations, or evaluation tools used in an examination for licensure as a nursing home administrator that the board of examiners of nursing home administrators administers under section 4751.04 of the Revised Code or contracts under that section with a private or government entity to administer;

(v) Records the release of which is prohibited by state or federal law;

(w) Proprietary information of or relating to any person that is submitted to or compiled by the Ohio venture capital authority created under section 150.01 of the Revised Code;

(x) Information reported and evaluations conducted pursuant to section 3701.072 of the Revised Code;

(y) Financial statements and data any person submits for any purpose to the Ohio housing finance agency or the controlling board in connection with applying for, receiving, or accounting for financial assistance from the agency, and information that identifies any individual who benefits directly or indirectly from financial assistance from the agency;

(z) Records listed in section 5101.29 of the Revised Code;

(aa) Discharges recorded with a county recorder under section 317.24 of the Revised Code, as specified in division (B)(2) of that section;

(bb) Usage information including names and addresses of specific residential and commercial customers of a municipally owned or operated public utility.

(2) "Confidential law enforcement investigatory record" means any record that pertains to a law enforcement matter of a criminal, quasi-criminal, civil, or administrative nature, but only to the extent that the release of the record would create a high probability of disclosure of any of the following:

(a) The identity of a suspect who has not been charged with the offense to which the record pertains, or of an information source or witness to whom confidentiality has been reasonably promised;

(b) Information provided by an information source or witness to whom confidentiality has been reasonably promised, which information would reasonably tend to disclose the source's or witness's identity;

(c) Specific confidential investigatory techniques or procedures or specific investigatory work product;

(d) Information that would endanger the life or physical safety of law enforcement personnel, a crime victim, a witness, or a confidential information source.

(3) "Medical record" means any document or combination of documents, except births, deaths, and the fact of admission to or discharge from a hospital, that pertains to the medical history, diagnosis, prognosis, or medical condition of a patient and that is generated and maintained in the process of medical treatment.

(4) "Trial preparation record" means any record that contains information that is specifically compiled in reasonable anticipation of, or in defense of, a civil or criminal action or proceeding, including the independent thought processes and personal trial preparation of an attorney.

(5) "Intellectual property record" means a record, other than a financial or administrative record, that is produced or collected by or for faculty or staff of a state institution of higher learning in the conduct of or as a result of study or research on an educational, commercial, scientific, artistic, technical, or scholarly issue, regardless of whether the study or research was sponsored by the institution alone or in conjunction with a governmental body or private concern, and that has not been publicly released, published, or patented.

(6) "Donor profile record" means all records about donors or potential donors to a public institution of higher education except the names and reported addresses of the actual donors and the date, amount, and conditions of the actual donation.

(7) "Peace officer, parole officer, probation officer, bailiff, prosecuting attorney, assistant prosecuting attorney, correctional employee, youth services employee, firefighter, EMT, or investigator of the bureau of criminal identification and investigation residential and familial information" means any information that discloses any of the following about a peace officer, parole officer, probation officer, bailiff, prosecuting attorney, assistant prosecuting attorney, correctional employee, youth services employee, firefighter, EMT, or investigator of the bureau of criminal identification and investigation:

(a) The address of the actual personal residence of a peace officer, parole officer, probation officer, bailiff, assistant prosecuting attorney, correctional employee, youth services employee, firefighter, EMT, or an investigator of the bureau of criminal identification and investigation, except for the state or political subdivision in which the peace officer, parole officer, probation officer, bailiff, assistant prosecuting attorney, correctional employee, youth services employee, firefighter, EMT, or investigator of the bureau of criminal identification and investigation resides;

(b) Information compiled from referral to or participation in an employee assistance program;

(c) The social security number, the residential telephone number, any bank account, debit card, charge card, or credit card number, or the emergency telephone number of, or any medical information pertaining to, a peace officer, parole officer, probation officer, bailiff, prosecuting attorney, assistant prosecuting attorney, correctional employee, youth services employee, firefighter, EMT, or investigator of the bureau of criminal identification and investigation;

(d) The name of any beneficiary of employment benefits, including, but not limited to, life insurance benefits, provided to a peace officer, parole officer, probation officer, bailiff, prosecuting attorney, assistant prosecuting attorney, correctional employee, youth services employee, firefighter, EMT, or investigator of the bureau of criminal identification and investigation by the peace officer's, parole officer's, probation officer's, bailiff's, prosecuting attorney's, assistant prosecuting attorney's, correctional employee's, youth services employee's, firefighter's, EMT's, or investigator of the bureau of criminal identification and investigation's employer;

(e) The identity and amount of any charitable or employment benefit deduction made by the peace officer's, parole officer's, probation officer's, bailiff's, prosecuting attorney's, assistant prosecuting attorney's, correctional employee's, youth services employee's, firefighter's, EMT's, or investigator of the bureau of criminal identification and investigation's employer from the peace officer's, parole officer's, probation officer's, bailiff's, prosecuting attorney's, assistant prosecuting attorney's, correctional employee's, youth services employee's, firefighter's, EMT's, or investigator of the bureau of criminal identification and investigation's compensation unless the amount of the deduction is required by state or federal law;

(f) The name, the residential address, the name of the employer, the address of the employer, the social security number, the residential telephone number, any bank account, debit card, charge card, or credit card number, or the emergency telephone number of the spouse, a former spouse, or any child of a peace officer, parole officer, probation officer, bailiff, prosecuting attorney, assistant prosecuting attorney, correctional employee, youth services employee, firefighter, EMT, or investigator of the bureau of criminal identification and investigation;

(g) A photograph of a peace officer who holds a position or has an assignment that may include undercover or plain clothes positions or assignments as determined by the peace officer's appointing authority.

As used in divisions (A)(7) and (B)(9) of this section, "peace officer" has the same meaning as in section 109.71 of the Revised Code and also includes the superintendent and troopers of the state highway patrol; it does not include the sheriff of a county or a supervisory employee who, in the absence of the sheriff, is authorized to stand in for, exercise the authority of, and perform the duties of the sheriff.

As used in divisions (A)(7) and (B)(5) of this section, "correctional employee" means any employee of the department of rehabilitation and correction who in the course of performing the employee's job duties has or has had contact with inmates and persons under supervision.

As used in divisions (A)(7) and (B)(5) of this section, "youth services employee" means any employee of the department of youth services who in the course of performing the employee's job duties has or has had contact with children committed to the custody of the department of youth services.

As used in divisions (A)(7) and (B)(9) of this section, "firefighter" means any regular, paid or volunteer, member of a lawfully constituted fire department of a municipal corporation, township, fire district, or village.

As used in divisions (A)(7) and (B)(9) of this section, "EMT" means EMTs-basic, EMTs-I, and paramedics that provide emergency medical services for a public emergency medical service organization. "Emergency medical service organization," "EMT-basic," "EMT-I," and "paramedic" have the same meanings as in section 4765.01 of the Revised Code.

As used in divisions (A)(7) and (B)(9) of this section, "investigator of the bureau of criminal identification and investigation" has the meaning defined in section 2903.11 of the Revised Code.

(8) "Information pertaining to the recreational activities of a person under the age of eighteen" means information that is kept in the ordinary course of business by a public office, that pertains to the recreational activities of a person under the age of eighteen years, and that discloses any of the following:

(a) The address or telephone number of a person under the age of eighteen or the address or telephone number of that person's parent, guardian, custodian, or emergency contact person;

(b) The social security number, birth date, or photographic image of a person under the age of eighteen;

(c) Any medical record, history, or information pertaining to a person under the age of eighteen;

(d) Any additional information sought or required about a person under the age of eighteen for the purpose of allowing that person to participate in any recreational activity conducted or sponsored by a public office or to use or obtain admission privileges to any recreational facility owned or operated by a public office.

(9) "Community control sanction" has the same meaning as in section 2929.01 of the Revised Code.

(10) "Post-release control sanction" has the same meaning as in section 2967.01 of the Revised Code.

(11) "Redaction" means obscuring or deleting any information that is exempt from the duty to permit public inspection or copying from an item that otherwise meets the definition of a "record" in section 149.011 of the Revised Code.

(12) "Designee" and "elected official" have the same meanings as in section 109.43 of the Revised Code.

(B)(1) Upon request and subject to division (B)(8) of this section, all public records responsive to the request shall be promptly prepared and made available for inspection to any person at all reasonable times during regular business hours. Subject to division (B)(8) of this section, upon request, a public office or person responsible for public records shall make copies of the requested public record available at cost and within a reasonable period of time. If a public record contains information that is exempt from the duty to permit public inspection or to copy the public record, the public office or the person responsible for the public record shall make available all of the information within the public record that is not exempt. When making that public record available for public inspection or copying that public record, the public office or the person responsible for the public record shall notify the requester of any redaction or make the redaction plainly visible. A redaction shall be deemed a denial of a request to inspect or copy the redacted information, except if federal or state law authorizes or requires a public office to make the redaction.

(2) To facilitate broader access to public records, a public office or the person responsible for public records shall organize and maintain public records in a manner that they can be made available for inspection or copying in accordance with division (B) of this section. A public office also shall have available a copy of its current records retention schedule at a location readily available to the public. If a requester makes an ambiguous or overly broad request or has difficulty in making a request for copies or inspection of public records under this section such that the public office or the person responsible for the requested public record cannot reasonably identify what public records are being requested, the public office or the person responsible for the requested public record may deny the request but shall provide the requester with an opportunity to revise the request by informing the requester of the manner in which records are maintained by the public office and accessed in the ordinary course of the public office's or person's duties.

(3) If a request is ultimately denied, in part or in whole, the public office or the person responsible for the requested public record shall provide the requester with an explanation, including legal authority, setting forth why the request was denied. If the initial request was provided in writing, the explanation also shall be provided to the requester in writing. The explanation shall not preclude the public office or the person responsible for the requested public record from relying upon additional reasons or legal authority in defending an action commenced under division (C) of this section.

(4) Unless specifically required or authorized by state or federal law or in accordance with division (B) of this section, no public office or person responsible for public records may limit or condition the availability of public records by requiring disclosure of the requester's identity or the intended use of the requested public record. Any requirement that the requester disclose the requestor's identity or the intended use of the requested public record constitutes a denial of the request.

(5) A public office or person responsible for public records may ask a requester to make the request in writing, may ask for the requester's identity, and may inquire about the intended use of the information requested, but may do so only after disclosing to the requester that a written request is not mandatory and that the requester may decline to reveal the requester's identity or the intended use and when a written request or disclosure of the identity or intended use would benefit the requester by enhancing the ability of the public office or person responsible for public records to identify, locate, or deliver the public records sought by the requester.

(6) If any person chooses to obtain a copy of a public record in accordance with division (B) of this section, the public office or person responsible for the public record may require that person to pay in advance the cost involved in providing the copy of the public record in accordance with the choice made by the person seeking the copy under this division. The public office or the person responsible for the public record shall permit that person to choose to have the public record duplicated upon paper, upon the same medium upon which the public office or person responsible for the public record keeps it, or upon any other medium upon which the public office or person responsible for the public record determines that it reasonably can be duplicated as an integral part of the normal operations of the public office or person responsible for the public record. When the person seeking the copy makes a choice under this division, the public office or person responsible for the public record shall provide a copy of it in accordance with the choice made by the person seeking the copy. Nothing in this section requires a public office or person responsible for the public record to allow the person seeking a copy of the public record to make the copies of the public record.

(7) Upon a request made in accordance with division (B) of this section and subject to division (B)(6) of this section, a public office or person responsible for public records shall transmit a copy of a public record to any person by United States mail or by any other means of delivery or transmission within a reasonable period of time after receiving the request for the copy. The public office or person responsible for the public record may require the person making the request to pay in advance the cost of postage if the copy is transmitted by United States mail or the cost of delivery if the copy is transmitted other than by United States mail, and to pay in advance the costs incurred for other supplies used in the mailing, delivery, or transmission.

Any public office may adopt a policy and procedures that it will follow in transmitting, within a reasonable period of time after receiving a request, copies of public records by United States mail or by any other means of delivery or transmission pursuant to this division. A public office that adopts a policy and procedures under this division shall comply with them in performing its duties under this division.

In any policy and procedures adopted under this division, a public office may limit the number of records requested by a person that the office will transmit by United States mail to ten per month, unless the person certifies to the office in writing that the person does not intend to use or forward the requested records, or the information contained in them, for commercial purposes. For purposes of this division, "commercial" shall be narrowly construed and does not include reporting or gathering news, reporting or gathering information to assist citizen oversight or understanding of the operation or activities of government, or nonprofit educational research.

(8) A public office or person responsible for public records is not required to permit a person who is incarcerated pursuant to a criminal conviction or a juvenile adjudication to inspect or to obtain a copy of any public record concerning a criminal investigation or prosecution or concerning what would be a criminal investigation or prosecution if the subject of the investigation or prosecution were an adult, unless the request to inspect or to obtain a copy of the record is for the purpose of acquiring information that is subject to release as a public record under this section and the judge who imposed the sentence or made the adjudication with respect to the person, or the judge's successor in office, finds that the information sought in the public record is necessary to support what appears to be a justiciable claim of the person.

(9)(a) Upon written request made and signed by a journalist on or after December 16, 1999, a public office, or person responsible for public records, having custody of the records of the agency employing a specified peace officer, parole officer, probation officer, bailiff, prosecuting attorney, assistant prosecuting attorney, correctional employee, youth services employee, firefighter, EMT, or investigator of the bureau of criminal identification and investigation shall disclose to the journalist the address of the actual personal residence of the peace officer, parole officer, probation officer, bailiff, prosecuting attorney, assistant prosecuting attorney, correctional employee, youth services employee, firefighter, EMT, or investigator of the bureau of criminal identification and investigation and, if the peace officer's, parole officer's, probation officer's, bailiff's, prosecuting attorney's, assistant prosecuting attorney's, correctional employee's, youth services employee's, firefighter's, EMT's, or investigator of the bureau of criminal identification and investigation's spouse, former spouse, or child is employed by a public office, the name and address of the employer of the peace officer's, parole officer's, probation officer's, bailiff's, prosecuting attorney's, assistant prosecuting attorney's, correctional employee's, youth services employee's, firefighter's, EMT's, or investigator of the bureau of criminal identification and investigation's spouse, former spouse, or child. The request shall include the journalist's name and title and the name and address of the journalist's employer and shall state that disclosure of the information sought would be in the public interest.

(b) Division (B)(9)(a) of this section also applies to journalist requests for customer information maintained by a municipally owned or operated public utility, other than social security numbers and any private financial information such as credit reports, payment methods, credit card numbers, and bank account information.

(c) As used in division (B)(9) of this section, "journalist" means a person engaged in, connected with, or employed by any news medium, including a newspaper, magazine, press association, news agency, or wire service, a radio or television station, or a similar medium, for the purpose of gathering, processing, transmitting, compiling, editing, or disseminating information for the general public.

(C)(1) If a person allegedly is aggrieved by the failure of a public office or the person responsible for public records to promptly prepare a public record and to make it available to the person for inspection in accordance with division (B) of this section or by any other failure of a public office or the person responsible for public records to comply with an obligation in accordance with division (B) of this section, the person allegedly aggrieved may commence a mandamus action to obtain a judgment that orders the public office or the person responsible for the public record to comply with division (B) of this section, that awards court costs and reasonable attorney's fees to the person that instituted the mandamus action, and, if applicable, that includes an order fixing statutory damages under division (C)(1) of this section. The mandamus action may be commenced in the court of common pleas of the county in which division (B) of this section allegedly was not complied with, in the supreme court pursuant to its original jurisdiction under Section 2 of Article IV, Ohio Constitution, or in the court of appeals for the appellate district in which division (B) of this section allegedly was not complied with pursuant to its original jurisdiction under Section 3 of Article IV, Ohio Constitution.

If a requestor transmits a written request by hand delivery or certified mail to inspect or receive copies of any public record in a manner that fairly describes the public record or class of public records to the public office or person responsible for the requested public records, except as otherwise provided in this section, the requestor shall be entitled to recover the amount of statutory damages set forth in this division if a court determines that the public office or the person responsible for public records failed to comply with an obligation in accordance with division (B) of this section.

The amount of statutory damages shall be fixed at one hundred dollars for each business day during which the public office or person responsible for the requested public records failed to comply with an obligation in accordance with division (B) of this section, beginning with the day on which the requester files a mandamus action to recover statutory damages, up to a maximum of one thousand dollars. The award of statutory damages shall not be construed as a penalty, but as compensation for injury arising from lost use of the requested information. The existence of this injury shall be conclusively presumed. The award of statutory damages shall be in addition to all other remedies authorized by this section.

The court may reduce an award of statutory damages or not award statutory damages if the court determines both of the following:

(a) That, based on the ordinary application of statutory law and case law as it existed at the time of the conduct or threatened conduct of the public office or person responsible for the requested public records that allegedly constitutes a failure to comply with an obligation in accordance with division (B) of this section and that was the basis of the mandamus action, a well-informed public office or person responsible for the requested public records reasonably would believe that the conduct or threatened conduct of the public office or person responsible for the requested public records did not constitute a failure to comply with an obligation in accordance with division (B) of this section;

(b) That a well-informed public office or person responsible for the requested public records reasonably would believe that the conduct or threatened conduct of the public office or person responsible for the requested public records would serve the public policy that underlies the authority that is asserted as permitting that conduct or threatened conduct.

(2)(a) If the court issues a writ of mandamus that orders the public office or the person responsible for the public record to comply with division (B) of this section and determines that the circumstances described in division (C)(1) of this section exist, the court shall determine and award to the relator all court costs.

(b) If the court renders a judgment that orders the public office or the person responsible for the public record to comply with division (B) of this section, the court may award reasonable attorney's fees subject to reduction as described in division (C)(2)(c) of this section. The court shall award reasonable attorney's fees, subject to reduction as described in division (C)(2)(c) of this section when either of the following applies:

(i) The public office or the person responsible for the public records failed to respond affirmatively or negatively to the public records request in accordance with the time allowed under division (B) of this section.

(ii) The public office or the person responsible for the public records promised to permit the relator to inspect or receive copies of the public records requested within a specified period of time but failed to fulfill that promise within that specified period of time.

(c) Court costs and reasonable attorney's fees awarded under this section shall be construed as remedial and not punitive. Reasonable attorney's fees shall include reasonable fees incurred to produce proof of the reasonableness and amount of the fees and to otherwise litigate entitlement to the fees. The court may reduce an award of attorney's fees to the relator or not award attorney's fees to the relator if the court determines both of the following:

(i) That, based on the ordinary application of statutory law and case law as it existed at the time of the conduct or threatened conduct of the public office or person responsible for the requested public records that allegedly constitutes a failure to comply with an obligation in accordance with division (B) of this section and that was the basis of the mandamus action, a well-informed public office or person responsible for the requested public records reasonably would believe that the conduct or threatened conduct of the public office or person responsible for the requested public records did not constitute a failure to comply with an obligation in accordance with division (B) of this section;

(ii) That a well-informed public office or person responsible for the requested public records reasonably would believe that the conduct or threatened conduct of the public office or person responsible for the requested public records as described in division (C)(2)(c)(i) of this section would serve the public policy that underlies the authority that is asserted as permitting that conduct or threatened conduct.

(D) Chapter 1347. of the Revised Code does not limit the provisions of this section.

(E)(1) To ensure that all employees of public offices are appropriately educated about a public office's obligations under division (B) of this section, all elected officials or their appropriate designees shall attend training approved by the attorney general as provided in section 109.43 of the Revised Code. In addition, all public offices shall adopt a public records policy in compliance with this section for responding to public records requests. In adopting a public records policy under this division, a public office may obtain guidance from the model public records policy developed and provided to the public office by the attorney general under section 109.43 of the Revised Code. Except as otherwise provided in this section, the policy may not limit the number of public records that the public office will make available to a single person, may not limit the number of public records that it will make available during a fixed period of time, and may not establish a fixed period of time before it will respond to a request for inspection or copying of public records, unless that period is less than eight hours.

(2) The public office shall distribute the public records policy adopted by the public office under division (E)(1) of this section to the employee of the public office who is the records custodian or records manager or otherwise has custody of the records of that office. The public office shall require that employee to acknowledge receipt of the copy of the public records policy. The public office shall create a poster that describes its public records policy and shall post the poster in a conspicuous place in the public office and in all locations where the public office has branch offices. The public office may post its public records policy on the internet web site of the public office if the public office maintains an internet web site. A public office that has established a manual or handbook of its general policies and procedures for all employees of the public office shall include the public records policy of the public office in the manual or handbook.

(F)(1) The bureau of motor vehicles may adopt rules pursuant to Chapter 119. of the Revised Code to reasonably limit the number of bulk commercial special extraction requests made by a person for the same records or for updated records during a calendar year. The rules may include provisions for charges to be made for bulk commercial special extraction requests for the actual cost of the bureau, plus special extraction costs, plus ten per cent. The bureau may charge for expenses for redacting information, the release of which is prohibited by law.

(2) As used in division (F)(1) of this section:

(a) "Actual cost" means the cost of depleted supplies, records storage media costs, actual mailing and alternative delivery costs, or other transmitting costs, and any direct equipment operating and maintenance costs, including actual costs paid to private contractors for copying services.

(b) "Bulk commercial special extraction request" means a request for copies of a record for information in a format other than the format already available, or information that cannot be extracted without examination of all items in a records series, class of records, or data base by a person who intends to use or forward the copies for surveys, marketing, solicitation, or resale for commercial purposes. "Bulk commercial special extraction request" does not include a request by a person who gives assurance to the bureau that the person making the request does not intend to use or forward the requested copies for surveys, marketing, solicitation, or resale for commercial purposes.

(c) "Commercial" means profit-seeking production, buying, or selling of any good, service, or other product.

(d) "Special extraction costs" means the cost of the time spent by the lowest paid employee competent to perform the task, the actual amount paid to outside private contractors employed by the bureau, or the actual cost incurred to create computer programs to make the special extraction. "Special extraction costs" include any charges paid to a public agency for computer or records services.

(3) For purposes of divisions (F)(1) and (2) of this section, "surveys, marketing, solicitation, or resale for commercial purposes" shall be narrowly construed and does not include reporting or gathering news, reporting or gathering information to assist citizen oversight or understanding of the operation or activities of government, or nonprofit educational research.

**HISTORY: 130 v 155 (Eff 9-27-63); 138 v S 62 (Eff 1-18-80); 140 v H 84 (Eff 3-19-85); 141 v H 238 (Eff 7-1-85); 141 v H 319 (Eff 3-24-86); 142 v S 275 (Eff 10-15-87); 145 v H 152 (Eff 7-1-93); 146 v H 5 (Eff 8-30-95); 146 v S 269 (Eff 7-1-96); 146 v H 353 (Eff 9-17-96); 146 v H 419 (Eff 9-18-96); 146 v S 277, § 1 (Eff 3-31-97); 146 v H 438, § 3 (Eff 7-1-97); 146 v S 277, § 6 (Eff 7-1-97); 147 v H 352 (Eff 1-1-98); 147 v H 421 (Eff 5-6-98); 148 v S 55 (Eff 10-26-99); 148 v S 78 (Eff 12-16-99); 148 v H 471 (Eff 7-1-2000); 148 v H 539 (Eff 6-21-2000); 148 v H 640 (Eff 9-14-2000); 148 v H 448 (Eff 10-5-2000); 148 v S 180 (Eff 3-22-2001); 149 v H 196 (Eff 11-20-2001); 149 v S 180 (Eff 4-9-2003); 149 v S 258. Eff 4-9-2003; 149 v H 490, § 1, eff. 1-1-04; 150 v H 6, § 1, eff. 2-12-04; 150 v H 431, § 1, eff. 7-1-05; 150 v H 303, § 1, eff. 10-29-05; 151 v H 141, § eff. 3-30-07; 151 v H 9, § 1, eff. 9-29-07; 152 v H 214, § 1, eff. 5-14-08; 152 v S 248, § 1, eff. 4-7-09; 153 v H 1, § 101.01, eff. 10-16-09; 2011 HB 153, § 101.01, eff. Sept. 29, 2011; 2011 HB 64, § 1, eff. Oct. 17, 2011.**

The effective date is set by § 812.10 of 153 v H 1.

The provisions of 815.10 of 153 v H 1 read as follows:

SECTION 815.10. The General Assembly, applying the principle stated in division (B) of section 1.52 of the Revised Code that amendments are to be harmonized if reasonably capable of simultaneous operation, finds that the following sections, presented in this act as composites of the sections as amended by the acts indicated, are the resulting versions of the sections in effect prior to the effective date of the sections as presented in this act:

* * *

Section 149.43 of the Revised Code as amended by Am. Sub. H.B. 214 and Am. Sub. S.B. 248, both of the 127th General Assembly.

* * *

The provisions of § 4 of 152 v S 248 read as follows:

SECTION 4. Section 149.43 of the Revised Code is presented in this act as a composite of the section as amended by both Sub. H.B. 9 and Sub. H.B. 141 of the 126th General Assembly. The General Assembly, applying the principle stated in division (B) of section 1.52 of the Revised Code that amendments are to be harmonized if reasonably capable of simultaneous operation, finds that the composite is the resulting version of the section in effect prior to the effective date of the section as presented in this act.

The provisions of § 9 of 152 v H 214 read as follows:

SECTION 9. Section 149.43 of the Revised Code is presented in this act as a composite of the section as amended by both Sub. H.B. 9 and Sub. H.B. 141 of the 126th General Assembly. * * * The General Assembly, applying the principle stated in division (B) of section 1.52 of the Revised Code that amendments are to be harmonized if reasonably capable of simultaneous operation, finds that the composites are the resulting versions of the sections in effect prior to the effective date of the sections as presented in this act.

The effective date is set by § 5 of 151 v H 9.

The provisions of § 6 of 151 v H 9 read as follows:

SECTION 6. Section 149.43 of the Revised Code is presented in this act as a composite of the section as amended by Am. Sub. H.B. 303, Am. Sub. H.B. 431, and Sub. S.B. 222, all of the 125th General Assembly. The General Assembly, applying the principle stated in division (B) of section 1.52 of the Revised Code that amendments are to be harmonized if reasonably capable of simultaneous operation, finds that the composite is the resulting version of the section in effect prior to the effective date of this act.

The provisions of § 3 of 151 v H 141 read as follows:

SECTION 3. Section 149.43 of the Revised Code is presented in this act as a composite of the section as amended by Am. Sub. H.B. 303, Am. Sub. H.B. 431, and Sub. S.B. 222, all of the 125th General Assembly. The General Assembly, applying the principle stated in division (B) of section 1.52 of the Revised Code that amendments are to be harmonized if reasonably capable of simultaneous operation, finds that the composite is the resulting version of the section in effect prior to the effective date of the section as presented in this act.

The effective date is set by section 5 of H.B. 303 (150 v —).

The provisions of § 3 of H.B. 6 (150 v —) read as follows:

SECTION 3. Section 149.43 of the Revised Code is presented in this act as a composite of the section as amended by Am. Sub. H.B. 490, Am. Sub. S.B. 180, and Sub. S.B. 258 of the 124th General Assembly. The General Assembly, applying the principle stated in division (B) of section 1.52 of the Revised Code that amendments are to be harmonized if reasonably capable of simultaneous operation, finds that the composite is the resulting version of the section in effect prior to the effective date of the section as presented in this act.

# CHAPTER 173: DEPARTMENT OF AGING

Section



## § 173.121 Center may conduct bingo games.

(A) As used in this section, "bingo," "bingo game operator," and "participant" have the same meanings as in section 2915.01 of the Revised Code.

(B) Notwithstanding sections 2915.07 to 2915.13 of the Revised Code, a multipurpose senior center may conduct bingo games described in division (S)(1) of section 2915.01 of the Revised Code, but only if it complies with all of the following requirements:

(1) All bingo games are conducted only on the premises of the facility.

(2) All participants are sixty years of age or older.

(3) All bingo game operators are sixty years of age or older and receive no compensation for serving as operators.

(4) No participant is charged an admission fee, and no participant is charged more than twenty-five cents to purchase a bingo card or sheet.

(5) All proceeds from games are used only for any of the following:

(a) To pay winners monetary or nonmonetary prizes;

(b) To provide refreshments;

(c) To defray any costs directly related to conducting the games;

(d) To defray costs of services the facility provides in accordance with section 173.12 of the Revised Code.

**HISTORY: 143 v H 573 (Eff 4-10-91); 149 v H 512. Eff 7-1-03; 150 v H 87, § 24, eff. 3-31-03.**

The provisions of § 24 of H.B. 87 (150 v —) read as follows:

SECTION 24. Sections 1 to 9 of Am.Sub. H.B. 512 of the 124th General Assembly take effect July 1, 2003.

This section is not subject to the referendum. Therefore, under Ohio Constitution, Article II, Section 1d and section 1.471 of the Revised Code, this section goes into immediate effect when this act becomes law.

# CHAPTER 177: INVESTIGATION AND PROSECUTION OF ORGANIZED CRIMINAL ACTIVITY

Section



## § 177.01 Organized crime investigations commission created.

(A) The organized crime investigations commission, consisting of seven members, is hereby established in the office of the attorney general. One of the members shall be the attorney general. Of the remaining members, each of whom shall be appointed by the governor with the advice and consent of the senate, two shall be prosecuting attorneys, two shall be county sheriffs, and two shall be chief municipal law enforcement officers. No more than four members of the commission shall be members of the same political party.

Of the initial appointments to the commission, one member who is a prosecuting attorney and one who is a county sheriff each shall be appointed for terms ending September 3, 1987, one member who is a prosecuting attorney and one who is a chief municipal law enforcement officer each shall be appointed for terms ending September 3, 1988, and one member who is a county sheriff and one who is a chief municipal law enforcement officer each shall be appointed for terms ending September 3, 1989. Thereafter, terms of office of persons appointed to the commission shall be for three years, with each term ending on the same day of the same month of the year as did the term that it succeeds. Members may be reappointed. Each appointed member shall hold office from the date of the member's appointment until the end of the term for which the member was appointed, except that an appointed member who ceases to hold the office or position of prosecuting attorney, county sheriff, or chief municipal law enforcement officer prior to the expiration of the member's term of office on the commission shall cease to be a member of the commission on the date that the member ceases to hold the office or position. Vacancies shall be filled in the manner provided for original appointments. Any member appointed to fill a vacancy occurring prior to the expiration of the term for which the member's predecessor was appointed shall take office on the commission when the member is confirmed by the senate and shall hold office for the remainder of such term. Any member shall continue in office subsequent to the expiration date of the member's term until the member's successor takes office, or until a period of sixty days has elapsed, whichever occurs first.

The attorney general shall become a member of the commission on September 3, 1986. Successors in office to that attorney general shall become members of the commission on the day they assume the office of attorney general. An attorney general's term of office as a member of the commission shall continue for as long as the person in question holds the office of attorney general.

Each member of the commission may designate, in writing, another person to represent the member on the commission. If a member makes such a designation, either the member or the designee may perform the member's duties and exercise the member's authority on the commission. If a member makes such a designation, the member may revoke the designation by sending written notice of the revocation to the commission. Upon such a revocation, the member may designate a different person to represent the member on the commission by sending written notice of the designation to the commission at least two weeks prior to the date on which the new designation is to take effect.

The attorney general or a person the attorney general designates pursuant to this division to represent the attorney general on the commission shall serve as chairperson of the commission. The commission shall meet within two weeks after all appointed members have been appointed, at a time and place determined by the governor. The commission shall organize by selecting a vice-chairperson and other officers who are necessary and shall adopt rules to govern its procedures. Thereafter, the commission shall meet at least once every six months, or more often upon the call of the chairperson or the written request of two or more members. Each member of the commission shall have one vote. Four members constitute a quorum, and four votes are required to validate an action of the commission.

The members of the commission shall serve without compensation, but each member shall be reimbursed for actual and necessary expenses incurred in the performance of official duties. In the absence of the chairperson, the vice-chairperson shall perform the duties of the chairperson.

(B) The commission shall coordinate investigations of organized criminal activity and perform all of the functions and duties relative to the investigations that are set forth in section 177.02 of the Revised Code, and it shall cooperate with departments and officers of the government of the United States in the suppression of organized criminal activity.

(C) The commission shall appoint and fix the compensation of a director and such technical and clerical employees who are necessary to exercise the powers and carry out the duties of the commission, may enter into contracts with one or more consultants to assist in exercising those powers and carrying out those duties, and may enter into contracts and purchase any equipment necessary to the performance of its duties. The director and employees of the commission shall be members of the unclassified service as defined in section 124.11 of the Revised Code. The commission shall require the director and each employee, prior to commencing employment with the commission, to undergo an investigation for the purpose of obtaining a security clearance and, after the initial investigation, may require the director and each employee to undergo an investigation for that purpose at any time during the director's or employee's employment with the commission. The commission may require any consultant with whom it contracts to undergo an investigation for the purpose of obtaining a security clearance. An investigation under this division may include, but is not limited to, a polygraph examination and shall be conducted by an organization designated by the commission.

(D) An appointed commission member may be removed from office as a member of the commission by the vote of four members of the commission or by the governor for any of the following reasons:

(1) Neglect of duty, misconduct, incompetence, or malfeasance in office;

(2) Conviction of or a plea of guilty to a felony or an offense of moral turpitude;

(3) Being mentally ill or mentally incompetent;

(4) Being the subject of an investigation by a task force established by the commission or another law enforcement agency, where the proof of criminal activity is evident or the presumption great;

(5) Engaging in any activity or associating with any persons or organization inappropriate to the member's position as a member of the commission.

(E) As used in sections 177.01 to 177.03 of the Revised Code:

(1) "Organized criminal activity" means any combination or conspiracy to engage in activity that constitutes "engaging in a pattern of corrupt activity;" any violation, combination of violations, or conspiracy to commit one or more violations of section 2925.03, 2925.04, 2925.05, 2925.06, or 2925.11 of the Revised Code other than a violation of section 2925.11 of the Revised Code that is a minor drug possession offense; or any criminal activity that relates to the corruption of a public official, as defined in section 2921.01 of the Revised Code, or of a public servant of the type described in division (B)(3) of that section.

(2) A person is engaging in an activity that constitutes "engaging in a pattern of corrupt activity" if any of the following apply:

(a) The person is or was employed by, or associated with, an enterprise and the person conducts or participates in, directly or indirectly, the affairs of the enterprise through a pattern of corrupt activity or the collection of an unlawful debt.

(b) The person, through a pattern of corrupt activity or the collection of an unlawful debt, acquires or maintains, directly or indirectly, an interest in, or control of, an enterprise or real property.

(c) The person knowingly has received proceeds derived, directly or indirectly, from a pattern of corrupt activity or the collection of an unlawful debt and the person uses or invests, directly or indirectly, a part of those proceeds, or proceeds derived from the use or investment of any of those proceeds, in the acquisition of title to, or a right, interest, or equity in, real property or the establishment or operation of an enterprise. A purchase of securities on the open market with intent to make an investment, without intent to control or participate in the control of the issuer, and without intent to assist another to do so is not an activity that constitutes "engaging in a pattern of corrupt activity" if the securities of the issuer held after the purchase by the purchaser, the members of the purchaser's immediate family, and the purchaser's or members' accomplices in any pattern of corrupt activity or the collection of an unlawful debt, do not aggregate one per cent of the outstanding securities of any one class of the issuer and do not confer, in law or in fact, the power to elect one or more directors of the issuer.

(3) "Pattern of corrupt activity" means two or more incidents of corrupt activity, whether or not there has been a prior conviction, that are related to the affairs of the same enterprise, are not isolated, and are not so closely related to each other and connected in time and place that they constitute a single event. At least one of the incidents forming the pattern shall occur on or after September 3, 1986. Unless any incident was an aggravated murder or murder, the most recent of the incidents forming the pattern shall occur within six years after the commission of any prior incident forming the pattern, excluding any period of imprisonment served by any person engaging in the corrupt activity.

(4) "Corrupt activity," "unlawful debt," "enterprise," "person," "real property," and "beneficial interest" have the same meanings as in section 2923.31 of the Revised Code.

(5) "Minor drug possession offense" has the same meaning as in section 2925.01 of the Revised Code.

**HISTORY: 141 v S 74 (Eff 9-3-86); 142 v H 708 (Eff 4-19-88); 143 v H 215 (Eff 4-11-90); 144 v H 298 (Eff 7-26-91); 146 v S 2 (Eff 7-1-96); 147 v H 2. Eff 1-1-99.**

The effective date is set by section 4 of HB 2.

The provisions of § 4 of H.B. 516 (150 v —) read in part as follows:

SECTION 4. The following agencies shall be retained pursuant to division (D) of section 101.83 of the Revised Code and shall expire on December 31, 2010:

| *AGENCY NAME* | *REVISED CODE OR UNCODIFIED SECTION* |
|---|---|
| ○○ | ○○○ |
| Organized Crime Investigations Commission | 177.01 |
| ○○ | ○○○ |

## § 177.011 Organized crime commission fund.

There is hereby created in the state treasury the organized crime commission fund. The fund shall consist of moneys paid to the treasurer of state pursuant to the judgment of a court in a criminal case as reimbursement of expenses that the organized crime investigations commission or an organized crime task force established by the commission incurred in the investigation of the criminal activity upon which the prosecution of the criminal case was based. All investment earnings on moneys in the fund shall be credited to the fund. The organized crime investigations commission shall use the moneys in the fund to reimburse political subdivisions for the expenses the political subdivisions incur when their law enforcement officers participate in an organized crime task force.

**HISTORY: 147 v H 215. Eff 6-30-97.**

## § 177.02 Complaint alleging organized criminal activity; task force; investigatory staff; confidentiality.

(A) Any person may file with the organized crime investigations commission a complaint that alleges that organized criminal activity has occurred in a county. A person who files a complaint under this division also may file with the commission information relative to the complaint.

(B) Upon the filing of a complaint under division (A) of this section or upon its own initiative, the commission may establish an organized crime task force to investigate organized criminal activity in a single county or in two or more counties if it determines, based upon the complaint filed and the information relative to it or based upon any information that it may have received, that there is reason to believe that organized criminal activity has occurred and continues to occur in that county or in each of those counties. The commission shall not establish an organized crime task force to investigate organized criminal activity in any single county unless it makes the determination required under this division relative to that county and shall not establish an organized crime task force to investigate organized criminal activity in two or more counties unless it makes the determination required under this division relative to each of those counties. The commission, at any time, may terminate an organized crime task force it has established under this section.

(C)(1) If the commission establishes an organized crime task force to investigate organized criminal activity in a single county or in two or more counties pursuant to division (B) of this section, the commission initially shall appoint a task force director to directly supervise the investigation. The task force director shall be either the sheriff or a deputy sheriff of any county in the state, the chief law enforcement officer or a member of a law enforcement agency of any municipal corporation or township in the state, or an agent of the bureau of criminal identification and investigation. No person shall be appointed as task force director without the person's consent and, if applicable, the consent of the person's employing sheriff or law enforcement agency or of the superintendent of the bureau of criminal identification and investigation if the person is an employee of the bureau. Upon appointment of a task force director, the commission shall meet with the director and establish the scope and limits of the investigation to be conducted by the task force and the size of the task force investigatory staff to be appointed by the task force director. The commission, at any time, may remove a task force director appointed under this division and may replace any director so removed according to the guidelines for the initial appointment of a director.

(2) A task force director appointed under this section shall assemble a task force investigatory staff, of a size determined by the commission and the director, to conduct the investigation. Unless it appears to the commission and the director, based upon the complaint filed and any information relative to it or based upon any information that the commission may have received, that there is reason to believe that the office of the prosecuting attorney of the county or one of the counties served by the task force is implicated in the organized criminal activity to be investigated, one member of the investigatory staff shall be the prosecuting attorney or an assistant prosecuting attorney of the county or one of the counties served by the task force. If a prosecuting attorney or assistant prosecuting attorney is not a participating member of the task force, the office of the attorney general shall provide legal assistance to the task force upon request. Each of the other members of the investigatory staff shall be either the sheriff or a deputy sheriff of any county in the state, the chief law enforcement officer or a member of a law enforcement agency of any municipal corporation or township in the state, or an agent of the bureau of criminal identification and investigation. No person shall be appointed to the investigatory staff without the person's consent and, if applicable, the consent of the person's employing sheriff or law enforcement agency or the superintendent of the bureau of criminal identification and investigation if the person is an employee of the bureau. To the extent possible, the investigatory staff shall be composed of persons familiar with investigatory techniques that generally would be utilized in an investigation of organized criminal activity. To the extent practicable, the investigatory staff shall be assembled in such a manner that numerous law enforcement agencies within the county or the counties served by the task force are represented on the investigatory staff. The investigatory staff shall be assembled in such a manner that at least one sheriff, deputy sheriff, municipal corporation law enforcement officer, or township law enforcement officer from each of the counties served by the task force is represented on the investigatory staff. A task force director, at any time, may remove any member of the investigatory staff the task force director has assembled under this division and may replace any member so removed according to the guidelines for the initial assembly of the investigatory staff.

(3) The commission may provide an organized crime task force established under this section with technical and clerical employees and with equipment necessary to efficiently conduct its investigation into organized criminal activity.

(4) Upon the establishment of a task force, the commission shall issue to the task force director and each member of the task force investigatory staff appropriate credentials stating the person's identity, position, and authority.

(D) A task force investigatory staff, during the period of the investigation for which it is assembled, is responsible only to the task force director and shall operate under the direction and control of the task force director. Any necessary and actual expenses incurred by a task force director or investigatory staff, including any such expenses incurred for food, lodging, or travel, and any other necessary and actual expenses of an investigation into organized criminal activity conducted by a task force, shall be paid by the commission. For purposes of workers' compensation and the allocation of liability for any death, injury, or damage they may cause in the performance of their duties, a task force director and investigatory staff, during the period of the investigation for which the task force is assembled, shall be considered to be employees of the commission and of the state. However, for purposes of compensation, pension or indemnity fund rights, and other rights and benefits to which they may be entitled, a task force director and investigatory staff, during the period of the performance of their duties as director and investigatory staff, shall be considered to be performing their duties in their normal capacity as prosecuting attorney, assistant prosecuting attorney, sheriff, deputy sheriff, chief law enforcement officer or member of a law enforcement agency of a municipal corporation or township, or agent of the bureau of criminal identification and investigation.

(E) Except as provided in this division, upon the establishment of a task force, the commission shall provide the prosecuting attorney of each of the counties served by the task force with written notice that the task force has been established to investigate organized criminal activity in that county. Such notice shall not be provided to a prosecuting attorney if it appears to the commission, based upon the complaint filed and any information relative to it or based upon any information that the commission may have received, that there is reason to believe that the office of that prosecuting attorney is implicated in the organized criminal activity to be investigated.

(F) The filing of a complaint alleging organized criminal activity, the establishment of an organized crime task force, the appointment of a task force director and the identity of the task force director, the assembly of an investigatory staff and the identity of its members, the conduct of an investigation into organized criminal activity, and the identity of any person who is being or is expected to be investigated by the task force shall be kept confidential by the commission and its director and employees, and by the task force and its director, investigatory staff, and employees until an indictment is returned or a criminal action or proceeding is initiated in a court of proper jurisdiction.

(G) For purposes of divisions (C) and (E) of this section, the office of a prosecuting attorney shall be considered as being implicated in organized criminal activity only if the prosecuting attorney, one or more of the prosecuting attorney's assistants, or one or more of the prosecuting attorney's employees has committed or attempted or conspired to commit, is committing or attempting or conspiring to commit, or has engaged in or is engaging in complicity in the commission of, organized criminal activity.

**HISTORY: 141 v S 74 (Eff 9-3-86); 147 v H 2. Eff 1-1-99.**

The effective date is set by section 4 of HB 2.

## § 177.03 Authority and powers of task force; notice to local law enforcement agency; action on results of investigation; special prosecutor.

(A) An organized crime task force established under section 177.02 of the Revised Code to investigate organized criminal activity in a single county or in two or more counties shall investigate organized criminal activity within the county or counties in accordance with the scope and limits established by the organized crime investigations commission and the task force director. For purposes of the investigation, the task force director and investigatory staff shall have the powers of a peace officer throughout the county or counties in which the investigation is to be undertaken. However, the authority and powers granted to the director and investigatory staff under this section do not supplant or diminish the authority and power provided by the Revised Code to other law enforcement agencies or their officers or investigators.

An organized crime task force, in the conduct of its investigation, may issue subpoenas and subpoenas duces tecum. The task force may compel the attendance of witnesses and the production of records and papers of all kinds and description that are relevant to the investigation, including, but not limited to, any books, accounts, documents, and memoranda pertaining to the subject of the investigation. Upon the failure of any person to comply with any lawful order of the task force, the task force may apply to the court of common pleas of the proper county for a contempt order, as in the case of disobedience of the requirements of a subpoena issued from the court of common pleas, or a refusal to testify thereon.

(B) This section and section 177.02 of the Revised Code do not prevent an organized crime task force from cooperating with other law enforcement agencies of this state, a political subdivision of this state, another state, a political subdivision of another state, or the United States, or their officers or investigators in the investigation and prosecution of any offenses comprising organized criminal activity.

(C)(1) If an organized crime task force, either prior to the commencement of or during the course of its investigation of organized criminal activity in a single county or in two or more counties, has reason to believe that the investigation will require it to engage in substantial investigative activities in a particular municipal corporation or township in the county or any of the counties, the task force director shall notify the commission chairperson of that belief and the reasons for that belief. The chairperson shall present that belief and those reasons to the commission, and, if the commission determines that there is a compelling reason to notify a local law enforcement agency that has jurisdiction within that municipal corporation or township that the task force will be engaging in investigative activities in the municipal corporation or township, the commission, subject to division (C)(2) of this section, shall provide written notice of that fact as follows:

(a) If the investigative activities will be engaged in in a township or in a municipal corporation that does not have a police department or similar law enforcement agency, the commission shall provide the notice to the sheriff of the county in which the township or municipal corporation is located.

(b) If the investigative activities will be engaged in in a municipal corporation that has a police department or similar law enforcement agency, the commission shall provide the notice to the chief law enforcement officer of the department or agency.

(2) The notice described in division (C)(1) of this section shall not be provided to a sheriff or chief law enforcement officer if it appears to the commission, based upon the complaint filed and any information relative to it or based upon any information that the commission may have received, that there is reason to believe that the office of that sheriff or chief law enforcement officer is implicated in the organized criminal activity being investigated.

(D)(1) If an organized crime task force determines, pursuant to its investigation of organized criminal activity in a single county or in two or more counties, that there is not reasonable cause to believe that organized criminal activity has occurred or is occurring in the county or in any of the counties, it shall report its determination to the commission, terminate its task force activities, and disband.

(2)(a) If a task force determines, pursuant to its investigation of organized criminal activity in a single county or in two or more counties, that there is reasonable cause to believe that organized criminal activity has occurred or is occurring in the county or in any of the counties, it shall report its determination to the commission and, except as provided in division (D)(3) of this section, shall refer a copy of all of the information gathered during the course of the investigation to the prosecuting attorney who has jurisdiction over the matter and inform the prosecuting attorney that the prosecuting attorney has thirty days to decide whether the prosecuting attorney should present the information to a grand jury and that, if the prosecuting attorney intends to make a presentation of the information to the grand jury, the prosecuting attorney has to give the commission written notice of that intention. If the organized criminal activity occurred or is occurring in two or more counties, the referral of the information shall be to the prosecuting attorney of the county in which the most significant portion of the activity occurred or is occurring or, if it is not possible to determine that county, the county with the largest population.

If a prosecuting attorney who has been referred information under this division fails to notify the commission in writing, within thirty days after the referral, that the prosecuting attorney will present the information to the grand jury of the prosecuting attorney's county, the task force, except as provided in division (D)(2)(b) of this section, shall refer a copy of all of the information to the attorney general, who shall proceed according to division (B) of section 109.83 of the Revised Code. If the prosecuting attorney fails to notify the commission in writing within that time that the prosecuting attorney will present the information to the grand jury, the prosecuting attorney promptly shall return all of the information that the task force referred to the prosecuting attorney under this division.

If a prosecuting attorney who has been referred information under this division notifies the commission in writing, within thirty days after the referral, of the prosecuting attorney's intention to present the information referred to the prosecuting attorney to the grand jury of the prosecuting attorney's county, the prosecuting attorney shall proceed promptly to present the information as evidence to the grand jury and shall notify the commission of the grand jury's final actions, findings of indictments, or reports. The prosecuting attorney may disclose to the attorney general any matters occurring before the grand jury that are disclosed to the prosecuting attorney for use in the performance of the prosecuting attorney's duties. The prosecuting attorney shall present the information as evidence to the grand jury prior to the discharge of the next regular grand jury. If the prosecuting attorney fails to present the information as evidence within that time, the commission, except as provided in division (D)(2)(b) of this section, shall notify the attorney general, the task force shall refer a copy of all of the information to the attorney general, and the attorney general may proceed as if the prosecuting attorney had declined under this division to accept the matter. If the prosecuting attorney fails to present the information as evidence within that time, the prosecuting attorney promptly shall return to the task force all of the information that the task force had referred to the prosecuting attorney under this division.

(b) If a prosecuting attorney who has been referred information under division (D)(2)(a) of this section fails to notify the commission in accordance with that division that the prosecuting attorney will present the information to the grand jury, and the task force that conducted the investigation determines, pursuant to its investigation, that the office of the attorney general is implicated in organized criminal activity, the task force shall not contact or refer any information to the attorney general but shall report its determinations and refer all of the information to the commission. If a prosecuting attorney who has been referred information under division (D)(2)(a) of this section notifies the commission in accordance with that division that the prosecuting attorney intends to present the information to the grand jury but fails to do so prior to the discharge of the next regular grand jury, and the task force that conducted the investigation determines, pursuant to the investigation, that the office of the attorney general is implicated in organized criminal activity, neither the commission nor the task force shall contact or refer any information to the attorney general. Instead, the task force shall report its determinations and refer all of the information gathered during the course of the investigation to the commission.

In either such case, the commission shall review the information, and, if a majority of the members of the commission determine that the office of the attorney general is implicated, the chairperson of the commission shall appear before the presiding judge of the court of common pleas or of the court of appeals for the county in which the prosecuting attorney who was referred the information serves and request the appointment of a special prosecutor to handle the matter. If the presiding judge finds that there is reasonable cause to believe that organized criminal activity has occurred or is occurring in the county or in any of the counties served by the task force and that the office of the attorney general is implicated, the judge shall appoint a special prosecutor to perform the functions of prosecuting attorney of the county in relation to the matter. The commission shall refer a copy of all of the information gathered during the course of the investigation to the special prosecutor. The special prosecutor shall review the information so referred and, upon a determination that there is cause to prosecute for the commission of a crime, the special prosecutor shall proceed promptly to present the information so referred to the grand jury and shall notify the commission of the grand jury's final actions, findings of indictments, or reports. A special prosecutor appointed under this division shall not inform the attorney general of the investigation or referral of information and shall not cooperate with the attorney general on the matter.

(3) If a task force determines, pursuant to its investigation of organized criminal activity in a single county or in two or more counties, that there is reasonable cause to believe that organized criminal activity has occurred or is occurring in the county or in any of the counties, and that the office of a prosecuting attorney who normally would be referred the information gathered during the course of the investigation pursuant to division (D)(2) of this section is implicated by the information in organized criminal activity, the task force shall not contact or refer any information to the prosecuting attorney. Instead it shall report its determinations and refer all of the information gathered during the course of the investigation to the commission. The commission shall review the information, and if a majority of the members of the commission determine

that the office of the prosecuting attorney is implicated in organized criminal activity, the chairperson of the commission shall appear before the presiding judge of the court of common pleas or of the court of appeals for the county in which that prosecuting attorney serves and request the appointment of a special prosecutor to handle the matter. If the presiding judge finds that there is reasonable cause to believe that organized criminal activity has occurred or is occurring in the county or in any of the counties served by the task force and that the office of the prosecuting attorney in question is implicated in organized criminal activity, the judge shall appoint a special prosecutor to perform the functions of prosecuting attorney of the county in relation to the matter, and the commission shall refer a copy of all of the information gathered during the course of the investigation to the special prosecutor. It shall inform the special prosecutor that the special prosecutor has thirty days to decide whether the special prosecutor should present the information to a grand jury and that if the special prosecutor intends to make a presentation of the information to the grand jury, the special prosecutor has to give the commission written notice of that intention. A special prosecutor appointed under this division shall not inform the implicated prosecuting attorney of the investigation or referral of information and shall not cooperate with the prosecutor on the matter.

If a special prosecutor who has been referred information under this division fails to notify the commission in writing, within thirty days after the referral, that the special prosecutor will present the information to the grand jury of the county, or if the presiding judge is requested pursuant to this division to appoint a special prosecutor but the judge does not do so, the commission shall refer a copy of all of the information to the attorney general, who shall proceed according to division (B) of section 109.83 of the Revised Code. Upon such a failure of a special prosecutor to notify the commission, the special prosecutor promptly shall return to the commission all of the information that the commission had referred to the special prosecutor under this division.

If a special prosecutor who has been referred information under this division notifies the commission in writing, within thirty days after the referral, of the special prosecutor's intention to present the information referred to the special prosecutor to the grand jury of the county, the special prosecutor shall proceed promptly to present the information as evidence to the grand jury and shall notify the commission of the grand jury's final actions, findings of indictments, or reports. The special prosecutor may disclose to the attorney general any matters occurring before the grand jury that are disclosed to the special prosecutor for use in the performance of the special prosecutor's duties. The information shall be presented as evidence to the grand jury prior to the discharge of the next regular grand jury. If the special prosecutor fails to present the information as evidence within that time, the commission shall notify the attorney general and refer a copy of all of the information to the attorney general, the attorney general may proceed as if the special prosecutor had declined under this division to accept the matter, and the special prosecutor promptly shall return to the commission all of the information that the commission had referred to the special prosecutor under this division.

(4) The referral of information by a task force to a prosecuting attorney, to the attorney general, to the commission, or to a special prosecutor under this division, the content, scope, and subject of any information so referred, and the identity of any person who was investigated by the task force shall be kept confidential by the task force and its director, investigatory staff, and employees, by the commission and its director, employees, and consultants, by the prosecuting attorney and the prosecuting attorney's assistants and employees, by the special prosecutor and the special prosecutor's assistants and employees, and by the attorney general and the attorney general's assistants and employees until an indictment is returned or a criminal action or proceeding is initiated in a court of proper jurisdiction.

(5) Any information gathered by a task force during the course of its investigation that is in the possession of the task force, a prosecuting attorney, the attorney general, the commission, or a special prosecutor, and any record that pertains to any such information and that is maintained by the task force, a prosecuting attorney, the attorney general, the commission, or a special prosecutor is a confidential law enforcement investigatory record for purposes of section 149.43 of the Revised Code. However, no provision contained in this division or that section affects or limits or shall be construed as affecting or limiting any right of discovery granted to any person under the Revised Code, the Rules of Criminal Procedure, or the Rules of Juvenile Procedure.

(6) In no case shall the commission, a task force, a prosecuting attorney, a special prosecutor, or the attorney general publicly issue a report or summary that identifies or enables the identification of any person who has been or is being investigated under sections 177.01 to 177.03 of the Revised Code unless an indictment is returned against the person or a criminal action or proceeding is initiated against the person in a court of proper jurisdiction.

(7) For purposes of divisions (C) and (D) of this section, the office of a prosecuting attorney, the attorney general, a sheriff, or a chief law enforcement officer shall be considered as being implicated in organized criminal activity only if the prosecuting attorney, attorney general, sheriff, or chief law enforcement officer, one or more of the assistants, deputies, or officers thereof, or one or more of the employees thereof has committed or attempted or conspired to commit, is committing or attempting or conspiring to commit, or has engaged in or is engaging in complicity in the commission of, organized criminal activity.

(8) For purposes of this section, notification by a prosecuting attorney or special prosecutor may be accomplished by certified mail or any other documentation that is agreed upon by the prosecuting attorney or special prosecutor and the commission or their representatives. Notice by certified mail is complete upon mailing.

(E) If an organized crime task force has probable cause to believe, pursuant to its investigation of organized criminal activity in a single county or in two or more counties, that a law of another state or the United States has been or is being violated, the task force director shall notify the commission chairperson of that belief and the reasons for that belief. The chairperson shall present that belief and those reasons to the commission and, if the commission determines that there is probable cause to believe that such a law has been or is being violated, the commission may refer the matter to the attorney general of the other state or to the appropriate United States attorney, whichever is applicable, and provide that attorney general or United States attorney with a copy of relevant information.

**HISTORY: 141 v S 74 (Eff 9-3-86); 147 v H 2. Eff 1-1-99.**

The effective date is set by section 4 of HB 2.

# CHAPTER 181: CRIMINAL SENTENCING COMMISSION; CRIMINAL JUSTICE SERVICES

Section



## [CRIMINAL SENTENCING]

### § 181.21 State criminal sentencing commission; juvenile committee.

(A) There is hereby created within the supreme court the state criminal sentencing commission, consisting of thirty-one members. One member shall be the chief justice of the supreme court, who shall be the chairperson of the commission. The following ten members of the commission, no more than six of whom shall be members of the same political party, shall be appointed by the chief justice: one judge of a court of appeals, three judges of courts of common pleas who are not juvenile court judges, three judges of juvenile courts, and three judges of municipal courts or county courts. Four members shall be the superintendent of the state highway patrol, the state public defender, the director of youth services, and the director of rehabilitation and correction, or their individual designees. The following twelve members, no more than seven of whom shall be members of the same political party, shall be appointed by the governor after consulting with the appropriate state associations, if any, that are represented by these members: one sheriff; two county prosecuting attorneys, at least one of whom shall be experienced in the prosecution of cases in juvenile court involving alleged delinquent children, unruly children, and juvenile traffic offenders; two peace officers of a municipal corporation or township, at least one of whom shall be experienced in the investigation of cases involving juveniles; one former victim of a violation of Title XXIX [29] of the Revised Code; one attorney whose practice of law primarily involves the representation of criminal defendants; one member of the Ohio state bar association; one attorney whose practice of law primarily involves the representation in juvenile court of alleged delinquent children, unruly children, and juvenile traffic offenders; one full-time city prosecuting attorney; one county commissioner; and one mayor, city manager, or member of a legislative authority of a municipal corporation. Two members shall be members of the senate, one appointed by the president of the senate and one appointed by the minority leader of the senate. Two members shall be members of the house of representatives, one appointed by the speaker of the house of representatives and one appointed by the minority leader of the house of representatives.

The chief justice shall become a member of the commission on August 22, 1990, and the chief justice's successors in office shall become members of the commission on the day that they assume the office of chief justice. The term of office of the chief justice as a member of the commission shall continue for as long as that person holds the office of chief justice. The term of office of the member who is an attorney whose practice of law primarily involves the representation of criminal defendants, the term of office of the member who is an attorney whose practice of law primarily involves the representation in juvenile court of alleged delinquent children, unruly children, and juvenile traffic offenders, and the term of office of the former victim of a violation of Title XXIX [29] of the Revised Code shall be four years. The term of office of the superintendent of the state highway patrol, the state public defender, the director of youth services, and the director of rehabilitation and correction, or their individual designees, as members of the commission shall continue for as long as they hold the office of superintendent of the state highway patrol, state public defender, director of youth services, or director of rehabilitation and correction. The term of office of a municipal corporation or township peace officer as a member of the commission shall be the lesser of four years or until that person ceases to be a peace officer of a municipal corporation or township. Unless the full-time city prosecuting attorney is an elected official, the term of office of the full-time city prosecuting attorney shall be the lesser of four years or until the full-time city prosecuting attorney ceases to be a full-time city prosecuting attorney. All of the members of the commission who are elected officials shall serve the lesser of four years or until the expiration of their term of office. Any vacancy on the commission shall be filled in the same manner as the original appointment.

When the chief justice and governor make their appointments to the commission, they shall consider adequate representation by race and gender.

(B) The commission shall select a vice-chairperson and any other necessary officers and adopt rules to govern its proceedings. The commission shall meet as necessary at the call of the chairperson or on the written request of eight or more of its members. Sixteen members of the commission constitute a quorum, and the votes of a majority of the quorum present shall be required to validate any action of the commission. All business of the commission shall be conducted in public meetings.

The members of the commission shall serve without compensation, but each member shall be reimbursed for the member's actual and necessary expenses incurred in the performance of the member's official duties on the commission. In the absence of the chairperson, the vice-chairperson shall perform the duties of the chairperson.

(C) The commission shall establish an office and shall appoint and fix the compensation of a project director and any other employees necessary to assist the commission in the execution of its authority under sections 181.21 to 181.26 of the Revised Code. The project director shall have a thorough understanding of the criminal laws of this state and experience in committee-oriented research. The other employees may include a research coordinator with experience and training in policy-oriented research; professional staff employees with backgrounds in criminal law, criminal justice, political science, or related fields of expertise; administrative assistants; and secretaries. The commission also may appoint and fix the compensation of part-time data collectors, clerical employees, and other temporary employees as needed to enable the commission to execute its authority under sections 181.21 to 181.26 of the Revised Code.

(D) The sentencing commission shall establish a standing juvenile committee. The committee shall consist of the following commission members: the chief justice of the supreme court or the chief justice's designee, the director of youth services, the three juvenile court judges, one court of common pleas judge who is not a juvenile court judge, one county prosecuting attorney who is experienced in the prosecution of cases in juvenile court involving alleged delinquent children, unruly children, and juvenile traffic offenders, the attorney whose practice of law primarily involves the representation in juvenile court of alleged delinquent children, unruly children, and juvenile traffic offenders, the former victim of a violation of Title XXIX [29] of the Revised Code, the county commissioner, one legislator from each political party, the sheriff, and one municipal corporation or township peace officer who is experienced in the investigation of cases involving juveniles. The members of the commission may serve on the committee by designation of the chief justice. The chief justice shall designate a member to serve as chairperson of the committee. The committee shall meet as necessary at the call of the chairperson or on the written request of four or more of the committee's members. A majority of the members of the committee shall constitute a quorum, and the votes of a majority of the quorum present shall be required to validate any action of the committee, including recommendations to the commission. The committee and the commission shall comply with section 181.26 of the Revised Code.

**HISTORY: 143 v S 258 (Eff 8-22-90); 145 v H 152 (Eff 7-1-93); 145 v H 21 (Eff 2-4-94); 146 v H 670 (Eff 12-2-96); 146 v H 591 (Eff 3-13-97); 148 v S 107. Eff 3-23-2000.**

The provisions of § 4 of H.B. 516 (150 v —) read in part as follows:

SECTION 4. The following agencies shall be retained pursuant to division (D) of section 101.83 of the Revised Code and shall expire on December 31, 2010:

| *AGENCY NAME* | *REVISED CODE OR UNCODIFIED SECTION* |
|---|---|
| ooo | ooo |
| State Criminal Sentencing Commission | 181.21 |
| ooo | ooo |

The provisions of § 4 of SB 107 (148 v —) read in part as follows:

SECTION 4. Sections 181.21 and 181.22 of the Revised Code are presented in this act as composites of the sections as amended by both Sub. H.B. 591 and Sub. H.B. 670 of the 121st General Assembly, with the new language of neither of the acts shown in capital letters. * * * This is in recognition of the principle stated in division (B) of section 1.52 of the Revised Code that such amendments are to be harmonized where not substantively irreconcilable and constitutes a legislative finding that such is the resulting version in effect prior to the effective date of this act.

## § 181.22 Criminal sentencing advisory committee.

There is hereby created the criminal sentencing advisory committee. The committee shall be comprised of the chairperson of the parole board, the director of the office of the correctional institution inspection committee, a juvenile detention facility operator, a provider of juvenile probation or community control services, a provider of juvenile parole or aftercare services, a superintendent of a state institution operated by the department of youth services, a community-based juvenile services provider, a person who is a member of a youth advocacy organization, a victim of a violation of Title XXIX [29] of the Revised Code that was committed by a juvenile offender, a representative of community corrections programming appointed by the governor, and any other members appointed by the chairperson of the state criminal sentencing commission upon the advice of the commission. The committee shall serve as an advisory body to the state criminal sentencing commission and to the commission's standing juvenile committee.

The members of the committee shall serve without compensation, but each member shall be reimbursed for the member's actual and necessary expenses incurred in the performance of the member's official duties.

**HISTORY: 143 v S 258 (Eff 8-22-90); 144 v H 298 (Eff 7-26-91); 145 v H 152 (Eff 7-1-93); 145 v H 21 (Eff 2-4-94); 146 v H 670 (Eff 12-2-96); 146 v H 591 (Eff 3-13-97); 148 v S 107 (Eff 3-23-2000); 148 v S 179, § 3. Eff 1-1-2002.**

The effective date is set by section 5 of SB 179.

The provisions of § 4 of H.B. 516 (150 v —) read in part as follows:

SECTION 4. The following agencies shall be retained pursuant to division (D) of section 101.83 of the Revised Code and shall expire on December 31, 2010:

| *AGENCY NAME* | *REVISED CODE OR UNCODIFIED SECTION* |
|---|---|
| ooo | ooo |
| Criminal Sentencing Advisory Committee | 181.22 |
| ooo | ooo |

## § 181.23 Study by commission; recommendation; sentencing policy.

(A) The state criminal sentencing commission shall study the existing criminal statutes and law of this state, sentencing patterns throughout the state, and available correctional resources. The commission shall use the results of its study to develop and recommend to the general assembly a comprehensive criminal sentencing structure. As part of its study, the commission shall do all of the following:

(1) Evaluate the effectiveness of the sentencing structure of the state;

(2) Systematically review each criminal statute to determine if the penalty provided is proportional to the seriousness of the offense committed and to penalties provided for other offenses;

(3) Review any existing sentencing guidelines;

(4) Determine the number, capacity, and quality of all available state, regional, and local correctional facilities and resources, including, but not limited to, detention facilities, probation services, pretrial diversion programs, and other nonfacility correctional programs;

(5) Collect a profile of the populations of state, regional, and local correctional facilities, services, and programs;

(6) Coordinate available correctional facilities, services, and programs with the criminal sentencing goals of the state, including, but not limited to, punishment, deterrence, fairness, rehabilitation, and treatment;

(7) Identify any additional correctional resources that are necessary to balance the needs of criminal sentencing and the available correctional resources.

(B) The commission shall develop a sentencing policy for the state that is based upon the findings and conclusions of its study under division (A) of this section. The policy shall be designed to enhance public safety by achieving certainty in sentencing, deterrence, and a reasonable use of correctional facilities, programs, and services and shall be designed to achieve fairness in sentencing.

**HISTORY: 143 v S 258 (Eff 8-22-90); 146 v H 670 (Eff 12-2-96); 148 v S 107. Eff 3-23-2000.**

## § 181.24 Recommendation of comprehensive criminal sentencing structure; projections; draft version.

(A) No later than July 1, 1993, the state criminal sentencing commission shall recommend to the general assembly a comprehensive criminal sentencing structure for the state that is consistent with the sentencing policy developed pursuant to division (B) of section 181.23 of the Revised Code and the conclusions of the study conducted pursuant to division (A) of that section. The sentencing structure shall be designed to enhance public safety, to assist in the management of prison overcrowding and correctional resources, to simplify the sentencing structure of the state that is in existence on August 22, 1990, and to result in a new sentencing structure that is readily understandable by the citizens of the state, to simplify the criminal code of the state, to assure proportionality, uniformity, and other fairness in criminal sentencing, and to provide increased certainty in criminal sentencing.

(B) The comprehensive criminal sentencing structure recommended by the commission shall provide for all of the following:

(1) Proportionate sentences, with increased penalties for offenses based upon the seriousness of the offense and the criminal history of the offender;

(2) Procedures for ensuring that the penalty imposed for a criminal offense upon similar offenders is uniform in all jurisdictions in the state;

(3) Retention of reasonable judicial discretion within established limits that are consistent with the goals of the overall criminal sentencing structure;

(4) Procedures for matching criminal penalties with the available correctional facilities, programs, and services;

(5) A structure and procedures that control the use and duration of a full range of sentencing options that is consistent with public safety, including, but not limited to, long terms of imprisonment, probation, fines, and other sanctions that do not involve incarceration;

(6) Appropriate reasons for judicial discretion in departing from the general sentencing structure.

(C) The commission shall project the impact of all aspects of the comprehensive criminal sentencing structure upon the capacities of existing correctional facilities. It also shall project the effect of parole release patterns and patterns of release from regional and local jails, workhouses, and other correctional facilities upon the sentencing structure. Additionally, the commission shall determine whether any additional correctional facilities are necessary to implement the sentencing structure.

(D) The commission shall determine whether any special appellate procedures are necessary for reviewing departures from, or the misapplication of, the general sentencing structure recommended pursuant to this section.

(E) The commission shall submit a draft version of the comprehensive criminal sentencing structure to selected judges, prosecuting attorneys, defense attorneys, law enforcement officials, correctional officials, bar associations, and other persons with experience or expertise in criminal sentencing and solicit their comments on the draft.

**HISTORY: 143 v S 258 (Eff 8-22-90); 144 v S 273 (Eff 3-6-92); 146 v H 670 (Eff 12-2-96); 148 v S 107. Eff 3-23-2000.**

## § 181.25 Duties of commission if sentencing structure is enacted.

(A) If the comprehensive criminal sentencing structure that it recommends to the general assembly pursuant to section 181.24 of the Revised Code or any aspects of that sentencing structure are enacted into law, the state criminal sentencing commission shall do all of the following:

(1) Assist the general assembly in the implementation of those aspects of the sentencing structure that are enacted into law;

(2) Monitor the operation of the aspects of the sentencing structure that are enacted into law and report to the general assembly no later than January 1, 1997, and biennially thereafter, on all of the following matters:

(a) The impact of the sentencing structure in effect on and after July 1, 1996, on political subdivisions and other relevant aspects of local government in this state, including all of the following information:

(i) The number and type of offenders who were being imprisoned in a state correctional institution under the law in effect prior to July 1, 1996, but who are being punished under a community control sanction, as defined in section 2929.01 of the Revised Code, under the law in effect on and after July 1, 1996;

(ii) The fiscal and other impact of the law in effect on and after July 1, 1996, on political subdivisions and other relevant aspects of local government in this state, including law enforcement agencies, the court system, prosecutors, as defined in section 2935.01 of the Revised Code, the public defender and assigned counsel system, jails and workhouses, probation departments, the drug and alcohol abuse intervention and treatment system, and the mental health intervention and treatment system.

(b) The impact of the sentencing structure in effect on and after July 1, 1996, on the population of state correctional institutions, including information regarding the number and types of offenders who are being imprisoned under the law in effect on and after July 1, 1996, and the amount of space in state correctional institutions that is necessary to house those offenders;

(c) The impact of the sentencing structure and the sentence appeal provisions in effect on and after July 1, 1996, on the appellate courts of this state, including information regarding the number of sentence-based appeals, the cost of reviewing appeals of that nature, whether a special court should be created to review sentences, and whether changes should be made to ensure that sentence-based appeals are conducted expeditiously.

(3) Review all bills that are introduced in the general assembly that provide for new criminal offenses or that change the penalty for any criminal offense, determine if those bills are consistent with the sentencing policy adopted under division (B) of section 181.23 of the Revised Code, determine the impact of those bills upon the correctional resources of the state, and recommend to the general assembly any necessary amendments to those bills. When the commission recommends any amendment for a bill before the general assembly, it shall do so in a manner that is consistent with the requirements of section 181.24 of the Revised Code.

(4) Study criminal sentencing structures in this state, other states, and the federal government, recommend necessary changes to the sentencing structure of the state, and determine the costs and effects of any proposed changes in the sentencing structure of the state;

(5) Collect and maintain data that pertains to the cost to counties of the felony sentence appeal provisions set forth in section 2953.08 of the Revised Code, of the postconviction relief proceeding provisions set forth in division (A)(2) of section 2953.21 of the Revised Code, and of appeals from judgments entered in such postconviction relief proceedings. The data so collected and maintained shall include, but shall not be limited to, the increase in expenses that counties experience as a result of those provisions and those appeals and the number of felony sentence appeals made, postconviction relief proceedings filed, and appeals of postconviction relief proceeding judgments made in each county under those provisions. The commission periodically shall provide to the felony sentence appeal cost oversight committee, in accordance with division (I) of section 2953.08 of the Revised Code, all data the commission collects pursuant to this division.

(B) In addition to its duties set forth in section 181.24 of the Revised Code and division (A) of this section, the state criminal sentencing commission shall review all forfeiture statutes in Titles XXIX [29] and XLV [45] of the Revised Code and, not later than July 1, 2002, recommend to the general assembly any necessary changes to those statutes.

**HISTORY: 143 v S 258 (Eff 8-22-90); 146 v S 2 (Eff 7-1-96); 146 v H 670 (Eff 12-2-96); 148 v S 107 (Eff 3-23-2000); 149 v H 327. Eff 7-8-2002.**

**§ 181.251** Amended and renumbered RC § 5502.63 by 151 v H 66. Eff 6-30-05

**HISTORY: 150 v H 12, § 1, eff. 4-8-04; 151 v H 66, § 101.01, eff. 6-30-05.**

The effective date is set by § 612.12 of 151 v H 66.

### § 181.26 Additional duties of commission concerning juveniles.

(A) In addition to its duties set forth in sections 181.23 to 181.25 of the Revised Code, the state criminal sentencing commission shall do all of the following:

(1) Review all statutes governing delinquent child, unruly child, and juvenile traffic offender dispositions in this state;

(2) Review state and local resources, including facilities and programs, used for delinquent child, unruly child, and juvenile traffic offender dispositions and profile the populations of youthful offenders in the facilities and programs;

(3) Report to the general assembly no later than October 1, 1999, a comprehensive plan containing recommendations based on the reviews required under divisions (A)(1) and (2) of this section. The recommendations shall do all of the following:

(a) Assist in the managing of the number of persons in, and costs of, the facilities, the programs, and other resources used in delinquent child, unruly child, and juvenile traffic offender dispositions;

(b) Foster rehabilitation, public safety, sanctions, accountability, and other reasonable goals;

(c) Provide greater certainty, proportionality, uniformity, fairness, and simplicity in delinquent child, unruly child, and juvenile traffic offender dispositions while retaining reasonable judicial discretion;

(d) Provide for the restoration of victims of juvenile offenses.

(B) The commission shall project the impact of the comprehensive plan recommended by the commission under this section on state and local resources used in delinquent child, unruly child, and juvenile traffic offender dispositions. The commission shall determine whether any additional facilities, programs, or other resources are needed to implement the comprehensive plan.

(C) If the general assembly enacts all or a substantial part of the comprehensive plan recommended by the commission under this section, the commission shall do all of the following:

(1) Assist in the implementation of the enacted plan;

(2) Monitor the operation of the plan, periodically report to the general assembly on the plan's operation and the plan's impact on resources used in delinquent child, unruly child, and juvenile traffic offender dispositions, and periodically recommend changes in the plan to the general assembly based on this monitoring;

(3) Review all bills that are introduced in the general assembly that relate to delinquent child, unruly child, and juvenile traffic offender dispositions and assist the general assembly in making legislation consistent with the plan.

**HISTORY: 146 v H 591 (Eff 3-13-97); 147 v H 1 (Eff 11-25-97); 147 v H 484. Eff 3-18-99.**

## [CRIMINAL JUSTICE SERVICES]

**§ 181.51** Amended and renumbered RC § 5502.61 by 151 v H 66. Eff 6-30-05

**HISTORY: RC § 122.21, 137 v H 1277 (Eff 12-14-78); 139 v H 440 (Eff 11-23-81); RC § 109.93, 142 v H 171 (Eff 7-1-87); RC § 122.21, 142 v H 231 (Eff 10-5-87); 142 v H 708 (Eff 4-19-88); 144 v H 298 (Eff 7-26-91); RC § 181.51, 145 v H 152 (Eff 7-1-93); 149 v H 94. Eff 9-5-2001; 151 v H 66, § 101.01, eff. 6-30-05.**

The effective date is set by § 612.12 of 151 v H 66.
The effective date is set by section 204 of HB 94.

**§ 181.52** Amended and renumbered RC § 5502.62 by 151 v H 66. Eff 6-30-05

The effective date is set by § 612.12 of 151 v H 66.

**§ 181.53** Repealed, 151 v H 66, § 105.01 [RC § 122.24, 137 v H 1277 (Eff 12-14-78); RC § 109.94.2, 142 v H 171 (Eff 7-1-87); RC § 122.24, 142 v H 231 (Eff 10-5-87); 142 v H 708 (Eff 4-19-88); 144 v H 298 (Eff 7-26-91); RC § 181.53, 145 v H 152. Eff 7-1-93]. Eff 6-30-05.

This section concerned advisory committees.
The effective date is set by § 612.15 of 151 v H 66.

**§ 181.54** Amended and renumbered RC § 5502.64 by 151 v H 66. Eff 6-30-05

**HISTORY: RC § 122.25, 137 v H 1277 (Eff 12-14-78); RC § 109.95, 142 v H 171 (Eff 7-1-87); RC § 122.25, 142 v H 231 (Eff 10-5-87); 144 v H 298 (Eff 7-26-91); RC § 181.54, 145 v H 152 (Eff 7-1-93); 149 v H 94. Eff 9-5-2001; 151 v H 66, § 101.01, eff. 6-30-05.**

The effective date is set by § 612.12 of 151 v H 66.
The effective date is set by section 204 of HB 94.

**§ 181.55** Amended and renumbered RC § 5502.65 by 151 v H 66. Eff 6-30-05

**HISTORY: RC § 122.26, 137 v H 1277 (Eff 12-14-78); 139 v H 536 (Eff 8-12-82); RC § 109.96, 142 v H 171 (Eff 7-1-87); RC § 122.26, 142 v H 231 (Eff 10-5-87); 144 v H 298 (Eff 7-26-91); RC § 181.55, 145 v H 152 (Eff 7-1-93); 149 v H 94. Eff 9-5-2001; 151 v H 66, § 101.01, eff. 6-30-05.**

The effective date is set by § 612.12 of 151 v H 66.
The effective date is set by section 204 of HB 94.

**§ 181.56** Amended and renumbered RC § 5502.66 by 151 v H 66. Eff 6-30-05

**HISTORY: RC § 122.27, 137 v H 1277 (Eff 12-14-78); RC § 109.97, 142 v H 171 (Eff 7-1-87); RC § 122.27, 142 v H 231 (Eff 10-5-87); 142 v H 708 (Eff 4-19-88); RC § 181.56, 145 v H 152 (Eff 7-1-93); 149 v H 94. Eff 9-5-2001; 151 v H 66, § 101.01, eff. 6-30-05.**

The effective date is set by § 612.12 of 151 v H 66.
The effective date is set by section 204 of HB 94.

# TITLE 3: COUNTIES

## CHAPTER 306: COUNTY TRANSIT SYSTEM; REGIONAL TRANSIT AUTHORITY; REGIONAL TRANSIT COMMISSION



### [REGIONAL TRANSIT AUTHORITIES]

### § 306.35 Powers and duties of authority.

Upon the creation of a regional transit authority as provided by section 306.32 of the Revised Code, and upon the qualifying of its board of trustees and the election of a president and a vice-president, the authority shall exercise in its own name all the rights, powers, and duties vested in and conferred upon it by sections 306.30 to 306.53 of the Revised Code. Subject to any reservations, limitations, and qualifications that are set forth in those sections, the regional transit authority:

(A) May sue or be sued in its corporate name;

(B) May make contracts in the exercise of the rights, powers, and duties conferred upon it;

(C) May adopt and at will alter a seal and use such seal by causing it to be impressed, affixed, reproduced, or otherwise used, but failure to affix the seal shall not affect the validity of any instrument;

(D)(1) May adopt, amend, and repeal bylaws for the administration of its affairs and rules for the control of the administration and operation of transit facilities under its jurisdiction, and for the exercise of all of its rights of ownership in those transit facilities;

(2) The regional transit authority also may adopt bylaws and rules for the following purposes:

(a) To prohibit selling, giving away, or using any beer or intoxicating liquor on transit vehicles or transit property;

(b) For the preservation of good order within or on transit vehicles or transit property;

(c) To provide for the protection and preservation of all property and life within or on transit vehicles or transit property;

(d) To regulate and enforce the collection of fares.

(3) Before a bylaw or rule adopted under division (D)(2) of this section takes effect, the regional transit authority shall provide for a notice of its adoption to be published once a week for two consecutive weeks in a newspaper of general circulation within the territorial boundaries of the regional transit authority, or as provided in section 7.16 of the Revised Code.

(4) No person shall violate any bylaw or rule of a regional transit authority adopted under division (D)(2) of this section.

(E) May fix, alter, and collect fares, rates, and rentals and other charges for the use of transit facilities under its jurisdiction to be determined exclusively by it for the purpose of providing for the payment of the expenses of the regional transit authority, the acquisition, construction, improvement, extension, repair, maintenance, and operation of transit facilities under its jurisdiction, the payment of principal and interest on its obligations, and to fulfill the terms of any agreements made with purchasers or holders of any such obligations, or with any person or political subdivision;

(F) Shall have jurisdiction, control, possession, and supervision of all property, rights, easements, licenses, moneys, contracts, accounts, liens, books, records, maps, or other property rights and interests conveyed, delivered, transferred, or assigned to it;

(G)(1) Except as provided in division (G)(2) of this section, may acquire, construct, improve, extend, repair, lease, operate, maintain, or manage transit facilities within or without its territorial boundaries, considered necessary to accomplish the purposes of its organization and make charges for the use of transit facilities.

(2) Beginning on July 1, 2011, a regional transit authority shall not extend its service or facilities into a political subdivision outside the territorial boundaries of the authority without giving prior notice to the legislative authority of the political subdivision. The legislative authority shall have thirty days after receiving the notice to comment on the proposal.

(H) May levy and collect taxes as provided in sections 306.40 and 306.49 of the Revised Code;

(I) May issue bonds secured by its general credit as provided in section 306.40 of the Revised Code;

(J) May hold, encumber, control, acquire by donation, by purchase for cash or by installment payments, by lease-purchase agreement, by lease with option to purchase, or by condemnation, and may construct, own, lease as lessee or lessor, use, and sell, real and personal property, or any interest or right in real and personal property, within or without its territorial boundaries, for the location or protection of transit facilities and improvements and access to transit facilities and improvements, the relocation of buildings, structures, and improvements situated on lands acquired by the regional transit authority, or for any other necessary purpose, or for obtaining or storing materials to be used in constructing, maintaining, and improving transit facilities under its jurisdiction;

(K) May exercise the power of eminent domain to acquire property or any interest in property, within or without its territorial boundaries, that is necessary or proper for the construction or efficient operation of any transit facility or access to any transit facility under its jurisdiction in accordance with section 306.36 of the Revised Code;

(L) May provide by agreement with any county, including the counties within its territorial boundaries, or any municipal corporation or any combination of counties or municipal corporations for the making of necessary surveys, appraisals, and examinations preliminary to the acquisition or construction of any transit facility and the amount of the expense for the surveys, appraisals, and examinations to be paid by each such county or municipal corporation;

(M) May provide by agreement with any county, including the counties within its territorial boundaries, or any municipal corporation or any combination of those counties or municipal corporations for the acquisition, construction, improvement, extension, maintenance, or operation of any transit facility owned or to be owned and operated by it or owned or to be owned and operated by any such county or municipal corporation and the terms on which it shall be acquired, leased, constructed, maintained, or operated, and the amount of the cost and expense of the acquisition, lease, construction, maintenance, or operation to be paid by each such county or municipal corporation;

(N) May issue revenue bonds for the purpose of acquiring, replacing, improving, extending, enlarging, or constructing any facility or permanent improvement that it is authorized to acquire, replace, improve, extend, enlarge, or construct, including all costs in connection with and incidental to the acquisition, replacement, improvement, extension, enlargement, or construction, and their financing, as provided by section 306.37 of the Revised Code;

(O) May enter into and supervise franchise agreements for the operation of a transit system;

(P) May accept the assignment of and supervise an existing franchise agreement for the operation of a transit system;

(Q) May exercise a right to purchase a transit system in accordance with the acquisition terms of an existing franchise agreement; and in connection with the purchase the regional transit authority may issue revenue bonds as provided by section 306.37 of the Revised Code or issue bonds secured by its general credit as provided in section 306.40 of the Revised Code;

(R) May apply for and accept grants or loans from the United States, the state, or any other public body for the purpose of providing for the development or improvement of transit facilities, mass transportation facilities, equipment, techniques, methods, or services, and grants or loans needed to exercise a right to purchase a transit system pursuant to agreement with the owner of those transit facilities, or for providing lawful financial assistance to existing transit systems; and may provide any consideration that may be required in order to obtain those grants or loans from the United States, the state, or other public body, either of which grants or loans may be evidenced by the issuance of revenue bonds as provided by section 306.37 of the Revised Code or general obligation bonds as provided by section 306.40 of the Revised Code;

(S) May employ and fix the compensation of consulting engineers, superintendents, managers, and such other engineering, construction, accounting and financial experts, attorneys, and other employees and agents necessary for the accomplishment of its purposes;

(T) May procure insurance against loss to it by reason of damages to its properties resulting from fire, theft, accident, or other casualties or by reason of its liability for any damages to persons or property occurring in the construction or operation of transit facilities under its jurisdiction or the conduct of its activities;

(U) May maintain funds that it considers necessary for the efficient performance of its duties;

(V) May direct its agents or employees, when properly identified in writing, after at least five days' written notice, to enter upon lands within or without its territorial boundaries in order to make surveys and examinations preliminary to the location and construction of transit facilities, without liability to it or its agents or employees except for actual damage done;

(W) On its own motion, may request the appropriate zoning board, as defined in section 4563.03 of the Revised Code, to establish and enforce zoning regulations pertaining to any transit facility under its jurisdiction in the manner prescribed by sections 4563.01 to 4563.21 of the Revised Code;

(X) If it acquires any existing transit system, shall assume all the employer's obligations under any existing labor contract between the employees and management of the system. If the board acquires, constructs, controls, or operates any such facilities, it shall negotiate arrangements to protect the interests of employees affected by the acquisition, construction, control, or operation. The arrangements shall include, but are not limited to:

(1) The preservation of rights, privileges, and benefits under existing collective bargaining agreements or otherwise, the preservation of rights and benefits under any existing pension plans covering prior service, and continued participation in social security in addition to participation in the public employees retirement system as required in Chapter 145. of the Revised Code;

(2) The continuation of collective bargaining rights;

(3) The protection of individual employees against a worsening of their positions with respect to their employment;

(4) Assurances of employment to employees of those transit systems and priority reemployment of employees terminated or laid off;

(5) Paid training or retraining programs;

(6) Signed written labor agreements.

The arrangements may include provisions for the submission of labor disputes to final and binding arbitration.

(Y) May provide for and maintain security operations, including a transit police department, subject to section 306.352 of the Revised Code. Regional transit authority police officers shall have the power and duty to act as peace officers within transit facilities owned, operated, or leased by the transit authority to protect the transit authority's property and the person and property of passengers, to preserve the peace, and to enforce all laws of the state and ordinances and regulations of political subdivisions in which the transit authority operates. Regional transit authority police officers also shall have the power and duty to act as peace officers when they render emergency assistance outside their jurisdiction to any other peace officer who is not a regional transit authority police officer and who has arrest authority under section 2935.03 of the Revised Code. Regional transit authority police officers may render emergency assistance if there is a threat of imminent physical danger to the peace officer, a threat of physical harm to another person, or any other serious emergency situation and if either the peace officer who is assisted requests emergency assistance or it appears that the peace officer who is assisted is unable to request emergency assistance and the circumstances observed by the regional transit authority police officer reasonably indicate that emergency assistance is appropriate.

Before exercising powers of arrest and the other powers and duties of a peace officer, each regional transit authority police officer shall take an oath and give bond to the state in a sum that the board of trustees prescribes for the proper performance of the officer's duties.

Persons employed as regional transit authority police officers shall complete training for the position to which they have been appointed as required by the Ohio peace officer training commission as authorized in section 109.77 of the Revised Code, or be otherwise qualified. The cost of the training shall be provided by the regional transit authority.

(Z) May procure a policy or policies insuring members of its board of trustees against liability on account of damages or injury to persons and property resulting from any act or omission of a member in the member's official capacity as a member of the board or resulting solely out of the member's membership on the board;

(AA) May enter into any agreement for the sale and leaseback or lease and leaseback of transit facilities, which agreement may contain all necessary covenants for the security and protection of any lessor or the regional transit authority including, but not limited to, indemnification of the lessor against the loss of anticipated tax benefits arising from acts, omissions, or misrepresentations of the regional transit authority. In connection with that transaction, the regional transit authority may contract for insurance and letters of credit and pay any premiums or other charges for the insurance and letters of credit. The fiscal officer shall not be required to furnish any certificate under section 5705.41 of the Revised Code in connection with the execution of any such agreement.

(BB) In regard to any contract entered into on or after March 19, 1993, for the rendering of services or the supplying of materials or for the construction, demolition, alteration, repair, or reconstruction of transit facilities in which a bond is required for the faithful performance of the contract, may permit the person awarded the contract to utilize a letter of credit issued by a bank or other financial institution in lieu of the bond;

(CC) May enter into agreements with municipal corporations located within the territorial jurisdiction of the regional transit authority permitting regional transit authority police officers employed under division (Y) of this section to exercise full arrest powers, as provided in section 2935.03 of the Revised Code, for the purpose of preserving the peace and enforcing all laws of the state and ordinances and regulations of the municipal corporation within the areas that may be agreed to by the regional transit authority and the municipal corporation.

**HISTORY: 131 v 192 (Eff 11-1-65); 133 v S 125 (Eff 8-25-70); 136 v S 427 (Eff 8-9-76); 137 v S 194 (Eff 7-8-77); 139 v S 543 (Eff 5-24-82); 144 v S 164 (Eff 3-19-93); 146 v S 2 (Eff 7-1-96); 146 v S 269 (Eff 7-1-96); 146 v H 566 (Eff 10-16-96); 146 v H 670 (Eff 12-2-96); 147 v H 228. Eff 5-7-97; 150 v H 95, § 1, eff. 9-26-03; 2011 HB 153, § 101.01, eff. June 30, 2011.**

The effective date is set by section 179 of H.B. 95 (150 v —).

### § 306.352 Felony precludes or terminates employment as police officer.

(A) As used in this section, "felony" has the same meaning as in section 109.511 of the Revised Code.

(B)(1) In the exercise of its authority under division (Y) of section 306.35 of the Revised Code, a regional transit authority shall not employ a person as a regional transit authority police officer on a permanent basis, on a temporary basis, for a probationary term, or on other than a permanent basis if the person previously has been convicted of or has pleaded guilty to a felony.

(2)(a) The transit authority shall terminate the employment of a person as a regional transit authority police officer if the person does either of the following:

(i) Pleads guilty to a felony;

(ii) Pleads guilty to a misdemeanor pursuant to a negotiated plea agreement as provided in division (D) of section 2929.43 of the Revised Code in which the police officer agrees to surrender the certificate awarded to that police officer under section 109.77 of the Revised Code.

(b) The transit authority shall suspend from employment a person designated as a regional transit authority police officer if that person is convicted, after trial, of a felony. If the police officer files an appeal from that conviction and the conviction is upheld by the highest court to which the appeal is taken or if the police officer does not file a timely appeal, the transit authority shall terminate the employment of that police officer. If the police officer files an appeal that results in the police officer's acquittal of the felony or conviction of a misdemeanor, or in the dismissal of the felony charge against the police officer, the transit authority shall reinstate that police officer. A police officer who is reinstated under division (B)(2)(b) of this section shall not receive any back pay unless that officer's conviction of the felony was reversed on appeal, or the felony charge was dismissed, because the court found insufficient evidence to convict the police officer of the felony.

(3) Division (B) of this section does not apply regarding an offense that was committed prior to January 1, 1997.

(4) The suspension from employment, or the termination of the employment, of a regional transit authority police officer under division (B)(2) of this section shall be in accordance with Chapter 119. of the Revised Code.

**HISTORY: 146 v H 566. Eff 10-16-96; 149 v H 490, § 1, eff. 1-1-04.**

The effective date is set by section 4 of H.B. 490.

## CHAPTER 307: BOARD OF COUNTY COMMISSIONERS — POWERS

Section



### § 307.62 Appropriations and grants for crime victim assistance programs.

(A) As used in this section:

(1) "County agency" includes any department, authority, commission, office, or board of the county.

(2) "Crisis intervention services" means short-term emotional or psychological aid provided in the form of counseling or referral for crime victims.

(3) "Emergency services" means the provision of aid including temporary shelter for victims who cannot safely remain in their current lodgings, repair of locks or boarding up of windows to prevent the immediate reburglarization of a home or an apartment, or provision of petty cash for meeting immediate needs related to transportation, food, shelter, and other necessities.

(4) "Support services" includes follow-up counseling, guidance for resolution of problems caused by the crime, and assistance in obtaining aid and services from social service agencies, criminal justice agencies, and the police.

(5) "Court-related services" means services calculated to assist crime victims in participating in criminal justice proceedings involving crimes committed against such victims, including transportation to court, child care while in

court or at a court-related proceeding, escort services, and the filing of requests for restraining orders. "Court-related services" does not include the provision of an attorney to represent the crime victim in any criminal prosecution based upon the crime committed against such victim.

(6) "Crime prevention services" means educational programs and materials to help avoid and prevent the commission of criminal acts in the future.

(7) "Victim and offender mediation services" means services designed to provide victims the opportunity for a meeting to ask questions, express feelings, or discuss restitution agreements with the convicted offenders or delinquent juveniles involved in the crimes against such victims.

(B) In addition to any money from another source appropriated for the same purpose, the board of county commissioners of any county may appropriate to a county agency, or grant to a private, nonprofit corporation or association, the money derived from a tax levied pursuant to division (II) of section 5705.19 of the Revised Code, for the public purpose of providing and maintaining in the county a crime victim assistance program offering crisis intervention services, emergency services, support services, court-related services, crime prevention services, or victim and offender mediation services. Money appropriated or granted under this section may be used to pay the salaries of employees of the county agency or of the private, nonprofit corporation or association who provide those services to clients of the agency, corporation, or association, but shall not be used to pay the fees of attorneys, doctors, mental health counselors, or other professionals who are not employees of the agency, corporation, or association.

All or some of the money may be given by the board in the form of a grant to a private, nonprofit corporation or association, if such corporation or association applies, on an application form prescribed by the board, for a grant to provide and maintain a crime victim assistance program. The board shall evaluate the application, and if such application is approved, the board shall enter into an agreement with the corporation or association granting all or some of the money. The agreement shall specify the following conditions for use of the money granted:

(1) That the recipient of the grant money shall keep current and accurate accounts of its use of the grant money;

(2) That, in accordance with rules adopted by the auditor of state pursuant to section 117.20 of the Revised Code, at least annually the recipient shall audit its crime victim assistance program. The recipient may contract with private auditors for performance of these audits. The cost of the audits shall be paid out of the grant money, except that no more than ten thousand dollars of the grant money may be expended per year on audits. A copy of the fiscal audit report shall be provided to the director of the recipient providing the crime victim assistance program, the board, the auditor of state, and the county auditor.

(3) That the recipient is liable to repay to the board any grant money that is improperly used;

(4) That the recipient shall repay to the board all grant money remaining unused at the end of the fiscal year or other accounting period for which the board granted the money. However, when the recipient is to receive grant money in the next succeeding fiscal year or other accounting period following the fiscal year or other accounting period for which the board granted the money, the recipient need not repay the grant money remaining unused.

(5) That a summary of program activities offered under the recipient crime victim assistance program annually be provided to the board.

The board shall not expend any money granted under this section until it has received a written agreement, signed by an officer or agent of the recipient authorized to legally bind the recipient, embodying all conditions stated in division (B) of this section and any other conditions specified in the agreement, regarding the use of the money granted by the board.

Upon discovering that money granted under this section is being or has been improperly used, the board, by resolution, shall demand that the recipient repay the improperly used money and shall transmit a certified copy of the resolution to the recipient. If the recipient does not repay the improperly used money within a reasonable period of time, the board shall direct the prosecuting attorney to bring a civil action to recover the improperly used money.

**HISTORY: 144 v S 32. Eff 7-1-92.**

**Not analogous to former RC § 307.62 (RS §§ 633-12,633-13; 92 v 212; GC §§ 2498, 2499; Bureau of Code Revision, 10-1-53), repealed 139 v S 114, § 2, eff 10-27-81.**

# CHAPTER 309: PROSECUTING ATTORNEY

Section



Section



## § 309.01 Election of prosecuting attorney.

There shall be elected quadrennially in each county, a prosecuting attorney, who shall hold his office for four years, beginning on the first Monday of January next after his election.

**HISTORY: RS § 1267; S&C 1225; 50 v 215; 78 v 260; 93 v 125; 98 v 273; GC § 2909; 116 v PtII, 184; Bureau of Code Revision. Eff 10-1-53.**

## § 309.02 Qualifications of candidate for prosecuting attorney.

No person shall be eligible as a candidate for the office of prosecuting attorney, or shall be elected to such office, who is not an attorney at law licensed to practice law in this state. No prosecuting attorney shall be a member of the general assembly of this state or mayor of a municipal corporation.

**HISTORY: RS § 1268; S&C 1227; 77 v 42; GC § 2910; Bureau of Code Revision, 10-1-53; 144 v S 243. Eff 8-19-92.**

## § 309.03 Bond of prosecuting attorney; oath.

Before entering upon the discharge of his duties, the prosecuting attorney shall give a bond, signed by a bonding or surety company approved by the court of common pleas or the probate court and authorized to do business in this state, or, at his option, signed by two or more freeholders having real estate in the value of double the amount of the bond over and above all encumbrances to the state. Such bond shall be in a sum not less than one thousand dollars, to be fixed by the court of common pleas or the probate court and conditioned that such prosecuting attorney will faithfully discharge all the duties enjoined upon him by law, and pay over all moneys received by him in his official capacity. The expense or premium for such bond shall be paid by the board of county commissioners, and shall be charged to the general fund of the county. Such bond, with the approval of such court and the oath of office required by sections 3.22 and 3.23 of the Revised Code indorsed thereon, shall be deposited with the county treasurer.

**HISTORY: RS § 1269; S&C 1225; 50 v 215, § 3; GC § 2911; 112 v 111; Bureau of Code Revision. Eff 10-1-53.**

## § 309.05 Removal of prosecuting attorney for neglect or misconduct.

On complaint, in writing, signed by one or more taxpayers, containing distinct charges and specifications of wanton and willful neglect of duty or gross misconduct in office by the prosecuting attorney, supported by affidavit and filed in the court of common pleas, the court shall assign the complaint for hearing and shall cause reasonable notice of the hearing to be given to the prosecuting attorney of the time fixed by the court for the hearing. At the time so fixed, or to which the court adjourns the hearing, the court shall hear the evidence adduced by the complainants and the prosecuting attorney. The court may consider motions for judgment on the pleadings made pursuant to Civil Rule 12, motions to dismiss made pursuant to Civil Rule 41, and motions for summary judgment made pursuant to Civil Rule 56 that are filed before the hearing. If it appears that the prosecuting attorney has willfully and wantonly neglected to perform the prosecuting attorney's duties, or has been guilty of gross misconduct in office, the court shall remove the prosecuting attorney from office and declare the office vacant. Otherwise the complaint shall be dismissed, and the court shall render judgment against the losing party for costs.

If a complaint to remove a prosecuting attorney is dismissed because the complainant or complainants failed to file an affidavit in support of the complaint, the dismissal shall be without prejudice.

**HISTORY: RS § 1272; S&C 1227; 50 v 215, § 8; GC § 2913; Bureau of Code Revision. Eff 10-1-53; 150 v H 252, § 1, eff. 9-16-04.**

## § 309.06 Assistant prosecuting attorneys; clerks; stenographers.

(A) On or before the first Monday in January of each year, the judge of the court of common pleas or, if there is more than one judge, the judges of the court of common pleas in joint session may fix an aggregate sum to be expended for the incoming year for the compensation of assistants, clerks, and stenographers of the prosecuting attorney's office.

The prosecuting attorney may appoint any assistants, clerks, and stenographers who are necessary for the proper performance of the duties of his office and fix their compensation, not to exceed, in the aggregate, the amount fixed by the judges of the court of common pleas. The compensation, after being so fixed, shall be paid to the assistants, clerks, and stenographers biweekly from the general fund of the county treasury, upon the warrant of the county auditor.

(B) Subject to section 2921.421 [2921.42.1] of the Revised Code, a prosecuting attorney may appoint, as an assistant prosecuting attorney, clerk, stenographer, or other employee, a person who is an associate or partner of, or who is employed by, the prosecuting attorney or an assistant prosecuting attorney in the private practice of law in a partnership, professional association, or other law business arrangement.

**HISTORY: RS § 1271; 75 v 520; 77 v 319; 79 v 79; 86 v 4; 86 v 66; 90 v 73; 92 v 37; 94 v 30; 95 v 240; 97 v 315; GC §§ 2914, 2915; Bureau of Code Revision, 10-1-53; 139 v S 114 (Eff 10-27-81); 144 v S 359 (Eff 12-22-92); 145 v H 285. Eff 3-2-94.**

## § 309.07 Appointment of secret service officer.

The prosecuting attorney may appoint secret service officers whose duty it shall be to aid him in the collection and discovery of evidence to be used in the trial of criminal cases and matters of a criminal nature. Such appointment shall be made for such term as the prosecuting attorney deems advisable, and subject to termination at any time by such prosecuting attorney. The compensation of said officers shall be fixed by the judge of the court of common pleas, or, if there is more than one judge, such compensation shall be fixed by the judges of such court in joint session, and shall not be less than one hundred twenty-five dollars per month for the time actually occupied in such service nor more than seventy-five per cent of the salary of the prosecuting attorney for a year. Such salary shall be payable monthly, out of the county fund, upon the warrant of the county auditor.

**HISTORY: GC § 2915-1; 102 v 77, 78; 103 v 501; Bureau of Code Revision, 10-1-53; 133 v S 94. Eff 10-24-69.**

## § 309.08 Powers and duties of prosecuting attorney; rewards for information as to drug-related offenses.

(A) The prosecuting attorney may inquire into the commission of crimes within the county. The prosecuting attorney shall prosecute, on behalf of the state, all complaints, suits, and controversies in which the state is a party, except for those required to be prosecuted by a special prosecutor pursuant to section 177.03 of the Revised Code or by the attorney general pursuant to section 109.83 of the Revised Code, and other suits, matters, and controversies that the prosecuting attorney is required to prosecute within or outside the county, in the probate court, court of common pleas, and court of appeals. In conjunction with the attorney general, the prosecuting attorney shall prosecute in the supreme court cases arising in the prosecuting attorney's county, except for those cases required to be prosecuted by a special prosecutor pursuant to section 177.03 of the Revised Code or by the attorney general pursuant to section 109.83 of the Revised Code.

In every case of conviction, the prosecuting attorney forthwith shall cause execution to be issued for the fine and costs, or costs only, as the case may be, and faithfully shall urge the collection until it is effected or found to be impracticable to collect. The prosecuting attorney forthwith shall pay to the county treasurer all moneys belonging to the state or county which come into the prosecuting attorney's possession.

The prosecuting attorney or an assistant prosecuting attorney of a county may participate, as a member of the investigatory staff of an organized crime task force established under section 177.02 of the Revised Code that has jurisdiction in that county, in an investigation of organized criminal activity under sections 177.01 to 177.03 of the Revised Code.

(B) The prosecuting attorney may pay a reward to a person who has volunteered any tip or information to a law enforcement agency in the county concerning a drug-related offense that is planned to occur, is occurring, or has occurred, in whole or in part, in the county. The prosecuting attorney may provide for the payment, out of the following sources, of rewards to a person who has volunteered tips and information to a law enforcement agency in the county concerning a drug-related offense that is planned to occur, is occurring, or has occurred, in whole or in part, in the county:

(1) The law enforcement trust fund established by the prosecuting attorney pursuant to division (C)(1) of section 2981.13 of the Revised Code;

(2) The portion of any mandatory fines imposed pursuant to divisions (B)(1) and (2) of section 2929.18 or Chapter 2925. of the Revised Code that is paid to the prosecuting attorney pursuant to that division or chapter, the portion of any additional fines imposed under division (A) of section 2929.18 of the Revised Code that is paid to the prosecuting attorney pursuant to that division, or the portion of any fines imposed pursuant to division (A) of section 2925.42 of the Revised Code that is paid to the prosecuting attorney pursuant to division (B) of that section;

(3) The furtherance of justice fund allowed to the prosecuting attorney under section 325.12 of the Revised Code or any additional funds allowed to the prosecuting attorney under section 325.13 of the Revised Code;

(4) Any other moneys lawfully in the possession or control of the prosecuting attorney.

(C) As used in division (B) of this section, "drug-related offense" means any violation of Chapter 2925. or 3719. of the Revised Code or any violation of a municipal ordinance that is substantially equivalent to any section in either of those chapters.

**HISTORY: RS § 1273; S&C 1125, 1185; 33 v 44, §§ 1, 2, 3; 50 v 215, § 2; 82 v 27; 98 v 160; GC § 2916; 102 v 77; 103 v 405(419); Bureau of Code Revision, 10-1-53; 141 v S 74 (Eff 9-3-86); 143 v S 258 (Eff 11-20-90); 145 v H 152 (Eff 7-1-93); 146 v S 2 (Eff 7-1-96); 146 v S 166. Eff 10-17-96; 151 v H 241, § 1, eff. 7-1-07.**

The provisions of § 4 of 151 v H 241 read as follows:

SECTION 4. Sections 1, 2, and 3 of this act shall take effect on July 1, 2007. If a criminal or civil forfeiture action relating to misconduct under Title XXIX of the Revised Code was or is commenced before July 1, 2007, and is still pending on that date, the court in which the case is pending shall, to the extent practical, apply the provisions of Chapter 2981. of the Revised Code in the case.

The provisions of § 4 of SB 166 read as follows:

SECTION 4. The amendments made by this act to sections 309.08, 2925.03, 2929.18, 3719.21, 3793.06, and 3793.11 of the Revised Code apply to offenses that are committed on or after the effective date of this act.

## § 309.09 Legal adviser; additional counsel.

(A) The prosecuting attorney shall be the legal adviser of the board of county commissioners, board of elections, all other county officers and boards, and all tax-supported public libraries, and any of them may require written opinions or instructions from the prosecuting attorney in matters connected with their official duties. The prosecuting attorney shall prosecute and defend all suits and actions that any such officer, board, or tax-supported public library directs or to which it is a party, and no county officer may employ any other counsel or attorney at the expense of the county, except as provided in section 305.14 of the Revised Code.

(B)(1) The prosecuting attorney shall be the legal adviser for all township officers, boards, and commissions, unless, subject to division (B)(2) of this section, the township has adopted a limited home rule government pursuant to Chapter 504. of the Revised Code and has not entered into a contract to have the prosecuting attorney serve as the township law director, in which case, subject to division (B)(2) of this section, the township law director, whether serving full-time or part-time, shall be the legal adviser for all township officers, boards, and commissions. When the board of township trustees finds it advisable or necessary to have additional legal counsel, it may employ an attorney other than the township law director or the prosecuting attorney of the county, either for a particular matter or on an annual basis, to represent the township and its officers, boards, and commissions in their official capacities and to advise them on legal matters. No such legal counsel may be employed, except on the order of the board of township trustees, duly entered upon its journal, in which the compensation to be paid for the legal services shall be fixed. The compensation shall be paid from the township fund.

Nothing in this division confers any of the powers or duties of a prosecuting attorney under section 309.08 of the Revised Code upon a township law director.

(2)(a) If any township in the county served by the prosecuting attorney has adopted any resolution regarding the operation of adult entertainment establishments pursuant to the authority that is granted under section 503.52 of the Revised Code or if a resolution of that nature has been adopted under section 503.53 of the Revised Code in a township in the county served by the prosecuting attorney, all of the following apply:

(i) Upon the request of a township in the county that has adopted, or in which has been adopted, a resolution of that nature that is made pursuant to division (E)(1)(c) of section 503.52 of the Revised Code, the prosecuting attorney shall prosecute and defend on behalf of the township in the trial and argument in any court or tribunal of any challenge to the validity of the resolution. If the challenge to the validity of the resolution is before a federal court, the prosecuting attorney may request the attorney general to assist the prosecuting attorney in prosecuting and defending the challenge and, upon the prosecuting attorney's making of such a request, the attorney general shall assist the prosecuting attorney in performing that service if the resolution was drafted in accordance with legal guidance provided by the attorney general as described in division (B)(2) of section 503.52 of the Revised Code. The attorney general shall provide this assistance without charge to the township for which the service is performed. If a township adopts a resolution without the legal guidance of the attorney general, the attorney general is not required to provide assistance as described in this division to a prosecuting attorney.

(ii) Upon the request of a township in the county that has adopted, or in which has been adopted, a resolution of that nature that is made pursuant to division (E)(1)(a) of section 503.52 of the Revised Code, the prosecuting attorney shall prosecute and defend on behalf of the township a civil action to enjoin the violation of the resolution in question.

(iii) Upon the request of a township in the county that has adopted, or in which has been adopted, a resolution of that nature that is made pursuant to division (E)(1)(b) of section 503.52 of the Revised Code, the prosecuting attorney shall prosecute and defend on behalf of the township a civil action under Chapter 3767. of the Revised Code to abate as a nuisance the place in the unincorporated area of the township at which the resolution is being or has been violated. Proceeds from the sale of personal property or contents seized pursuant to the action shall be applied and deposited in accordance with division (E)(1)(b) of section 503.52 of the Revised Code.

(b) The provisions of division (B)(2)(a) of this section apply regarding all townships, including townships that have adopted a limited home rule government pursuant to Chapter 504. of the Revised Code, and regardless of whether a township that has so adopted a limited home rule government has entered into a contract with the prosecuting attorney as described in division (B) of section 504.15 of the Revised Code or has appointed a law director as described in division (A) of that section.

The prosecuting attorney shall prosecute and defend in the actions and proceedings described in division (B)(2)(a) of this section without charge to the township for which the services are performed.

(C) Whenever the board of county commissioners employs an attorney other than the prosecuting attorney of the county, without the authorization of the court of common pleas as provided in section 305.14 of the Revised Code, either for a particular matter or on an annual basis, to represent the board in its official capacity and to advise it on legal matters, the board shall enter upon its journal an order of the board in which the compensation to be paid for the legal services shall be fixed. The compensation shall be paid from the county general fund. The total compensation paid, in any year, by the board for legal services under this division shall not exceed the total annual compensation of the prosecuting attorney for that county.

(D) The prosecuting attorney and the board of county commissioners jointly may contract with a board of park commissioners under section 1545.07 of the Revised Code for the prosecuting attorney to provide legal services to the park district the board of park commissioners operates.

(E) The prosecuting attorney may be, in the prosecuting attorney's discretion and with the approval of the board of county commissioners, the legal adviser of a joint fire district created under section 505.371 of the Revised Code at no cost to the district or may be the legal adviser to the district under a contract that the prosecuting attorney and the district enter into, and that the board of county commissioner approves, to authorize the prosecuting attorney to provide legal services to the district.

(F) The prosecuting attorney may be, in the prosecuting attorney's discretion and with the approval of the board of county commissioners, the legal adviser of a joint ambulance district created under section 505.71 of the Revised Code at no cost to the district or may be the legal adviser to the district under a contract that the prosecuting attorney and the district enter into, and that the board of county commissioners approves, to authorize the prosecuting attorney to provide legal services to the district.

(G) The prosecuting attorney may be, in the prosecuting attorney's discretion and with the approval of the board of county commissioners, the legal adviser of a joint emergency medical services district created under section 307.052 of the Revised Code at no cost to the district or may be the legal adviser to the district under a contract that the prosecuting attorney and the district enter into, and that the board of county commissioners approves, to authorize the prosecuting attorney to provide legal services to the district.

(H) The prosecuting attorney may be, in the prosecuting attorney's discretion and with the approval of the board of county commissioners, the legal adviser of a fire and ambulance district created under section 505.375 of the Revised Code at no cost to the district or may be the legal adviser to the district under a contract that the prosecuting attorney and the district enter into, and that the board of county commissioners approves, to authorize the prosecuting attorney to provide legal services to the district.

(I) All money received pursuant to a contract entered into under division (D), (E), (F), (G), or (H) of this section shall be deposited into the prosecuting attorney's legal services fund, which shall be established in the county treasury of each county in which such a contract exists. Moneys in that fund may be appropriated only to the prosecuting attorney for the purpose of providing legal services to a park district, joint fire district, joint ambulance district, joint emergency medical services district, or a fire and ambulance district, as applicable, under a contract entered into under the applicable division.

**HISTORY: RS § 1274; 98 v 160; GC § 2917; Bureau of Code Revision, 10-1-53; 125 v H 251 (Eff 10-2-53); 128 v 597 (Eff 11-9-59); 129 v 1557 (Eff 10-27-61); 137 v H 316 (Eff 10-25-78); 141 v H 428 (Eff 12-23-86); 144 v H 77 (Eff 9-17-91); 146 v H 268 (Eff 5-8-96); 146 v H 501 (Eff 11-6-96); 147 v S 201 (Eff 12-21-98); 148 v H 187. Eff 9-20-99; 150 v H 299, § 1, eff. 6-10-04; 151 v H 33, § 1, eff. 12-20-05; 151 v H 23, § 1, eff. 8-17-06; 2011 SB 120, § 1, eff. Sept. 30, 2011.**

## § 309.10 Provisions for other counsel.

Sections 309.08 and 309.09 of the Revised Code do not prevent a school board from employing counsel to represent it, but when counsel is employed, the counsel shall be paid by the school board from the school fund. Sections 309.08 and 309.09 of the Revised Code do not prevent a county board of developmental disabilities from employing counsel to represent it, but that counsel shall be employed in accordance with division (C) of section 305.14 and paid in accordance with division (A)(7) of section 5126.05 of the Revised Code.

Sections 309.08 and 309.09 of the Revised Code do not prevent a board of county hospital trustees from employing counsel with the approval of the county commissioners to bring legal action for the collection of delinquent accounts of the hospital, but when counsel is employed, the counsel shall be paid from the hospital's funds. Sections 309.08 and 309.09 of the Revised Code do not prevent a board of library trustees from employing counsel to represent it, but when counsel is employed, the counsel shall be paid from the library's funds. Sections 309.08 and 309.09 of the Revised Code do not prevent the appointment and employment of assistants, clerks, and stenographers to assist the prosecuting attorney as provided in sections 309.01 to 309.16 of the Revised Code, or the appointment by the court of common pleas or the court of appeals of an attorney to assist the prosecuting attorney in the trial of a criminal cause pending in that court, or the board of county commissioners from paying for those services.

**HISTORY: RS § 1274; 98 v 160; GC § 2918; Bureau of Code Revision, 10-1-53; 127 v 440; 128 v 597 (Eff 11-9-59); 142 v S 155 (Eff 6-24-88); 143 v H 569 (Eff 11-11-90); 145 v H 694 (Eff 11-11-94); 146 v H 629 (Eff 3-13-97); 148 v H 400. Eff 8-29-2000; 153 v S 79, § 1, eff. 10-6-09.**

## § 309.11 Official bonds.

The prosecuting attorney shall prepare, in legal form, the official bonds for all county officers, and shall see that the acceptance of such bonds by the proper authorities, the signing thereof, and all the indorsements thereon, are in conformity to law, and that they are deposited with the proper officer. No bond shall be accepted or approved for any county officer by the person or tribunal authorized to approve it, until the prosecuting attorney has inspected it, and certified thereon that such bond is sufficient. In case of a vacancy in the office of prosecuting attorney or of the absence or disability of the prosecuting attorney, such duties shall be discharged by the probate judge.

**HISTORY: RS § 1276; S&S 634; S&C 1226; 62 v 173, § 5; 81 v 198; GC § 2920; Bureau of Code Revision. Eff 10-1-53.**

## § 309.12 Protection of public funds.

Upon being satisfied that funds of the county, or public moneys in the hands of the county treasurer or belonging to the county, are about to be or have been misapplied, or that any such public moneys have been illegally drawn or withheld from the county treasury, or that a contract, in contravention of law, has been executed or is about to be entered into, or that such a contract was procured by fraud or corruption, or that any property, real or personal, belonging to the county is being illegally used or occupied, or that such property is being used or occupied in violation of contract, or that the terms of a contract made by or on behalf of the county are being or have been violated, or that money is due the county, the prosecuting attorney may, by civil action in the name of the state, apply to a court of competent jurisdiction, to restrain such contemplated misapplication of funds, or the completion of such illegal contract, or to recover, for the use of the county, all public moneys so misapplied or illegally drawn or withheld from the county treasury, or to recover damages, for the benefit of the county, resulting from the execution of such illegal contract, or to recover, for the benefit of the county, such real or personal property so used or occupied, or to recover for the benefit of the county, damages resulting from the nonperformance of the terms of such contract, or to otherwise enforce it, or to recover such money as is due the county.

**HISTORY: RS § 1277; 70 v 38, § 1; 93 v 408; 95 v 558; GC § 2921; Bureau of Code Revision. Eff 10-1-53.**

## § 309.13 Taxpayer's suit.

If the prosecuting attorney fails, upon the written request of a taxpayer of the county, to make the application or institute the civil action contemplated in section 309.12 of the Revised Code, the taxpayer may make such application or institute such civil action in the name of the state, or, in any case wherein the prosecuting attorney is authorized to make such application, such taxpayer may bring any suit or institute any such proceedings against any county officer or person who holds or has held a county office, for misconduct in office or neglect of his duty, to recover money illegally drawn or illegally withheld from the county treasury, and to recover damages resulting from the execution of such illegal contract.

If such prosecuting attorney fails upon the written request of a taxpayer of the county, to bring such suit or institute such proceedings, or if for any reason the prosecuting attorney cannot bring such action, or if he has received and unlawfully withheld moneys belonging to the county, or has received or drawn public moneys out of the county treasury which he is not lawfully entitled to demand and receive, a taxpayer, upon securing the costs, may bring such suit or institute such proceedings, in the name of the state. Such action shall be for the benefit of the county, as if brought by the prosecuting attorney.

If the court hearing such case is satisfied that such taxpayer is entitled to the relief prayed for in his petition, and judgment is ordered in his favor, he shall be allowed his costs, including a reasonable compensation to his attorney.

**HISTORY: RS §§ 1278a, 1278; 70 v 38, § 2; 92 v 337; 93 v 408; GC §§ 2922, 2923; 106 v 105; Bureau of Code Revision. Eff 10-1-53.**

## § 309.14 Injuries to timber.

When trees standing or growing on any land belonging to the state, or to any school district, are, without lawful authority, cut down, or in any way injured, the prosecuting attorney shall prosecute the wrongdoer, and shall seize all timber so cut down, if it can be found, and sell it at public vendue, on five days' notice. The prosecuting attorney shall pay the proceeds of such sale into the state treasury to the credit of the general revenue fund, or into the county treasury to the credit of the school district, as the case may be.

**HISTORY: RS § 1279; S&C 442, 445; 40 v 57, §§ 1, 3; GC § 2924; Bureau of Code Revision, 10-1-53; 141 v H 201. Eff 7-1-85.**

## § 309.15 Annual report to attorney general.

On or before the first day of September in each year, if so required by the attorney general by a written notice given on or before the first day of August, the prosecuting attorney shall transmit to the attorney general a report of all crimes prosecuted by indictment or information in his county for the year ending the first day of July, specifying:

(A) Under the head of felonies:

(1) The number convicted;

(2) The number acquitted;

(3) The amount of costs incurred;

(4) The amount of costs collected.

(B) Under the head of misdemeanors:

(1) The number convicted;

(2) The number acquitted;

(3) The amount of fines imposed;

(4) The amount of fines collected;

(5) The amount of costs incurred;

(6) The amount of costs collected.

(C) Such other information as the attorney general requires.

The attorney general may prepare and forward to the prosecuting attorney the necessary blanks and instructions for such annual reports. Prosecuting attorneys shall furnish to the attorney general any information he requires in the execution of his office, whenever such information is requested by him.

**HISTORY: RS § 1282; 90 v 225; GC § 2925; Bureau of Code Revision. Eff 10-1-53.**

## § 309.16 Annual report to county commissioners; certain information to be transmitted to state fire marshal.

(A) On the first Monday of September in each year, each prosecuting attorney shall make a certified statement to the board of county commissioners specifying:

(1) The number of criminal prosecutions pursued to final conviction and sentence under his official care, during the year next preceding the time of making such statement. In such statement the prosecuting attorney shall name the parties to each prosecution, the amount of fine assessed in each case, the number of recognizances forfeited, and the amount of money collected in each case.

(2) With respect to the offenses set forth in sections 2909.02 and 2909.03 of the Revised Code, such statement shall also include the following information:

(a) The number of fires occurring in the county for which the state fire marshal or an assistant state fire marshal has determined there was evidence sufficient to charge a person with aggravated arson or arson;

(b) The number of cases under sections 2909.02 and 2909.03 of the Revised Code presented by the prosecuting attorney to the grand jury for indictment;

(c) The number of indictments under such sections returned by the grand jury;

(d) The number of cases under such sections prosecuted either by indictment or by information by the prosecuting attorney;

(e) The number of cases under such sections resulting in final conviction and sentence and the number of cases resulting in acquittals;

(f) The number of cases under such sections dismissed or terminated without a final adjudication as to guilt or innocence.

(B) The prosecuting attorney shall also transmit to the state fire marshal on or before the first Monday of September in each year all information relative to the crimes under such sections required to be reported to the board of county commissioners pursuant to division (A)(2) of this section.

(C) For purposes of divisions (A)(2) and (B) of this section, sections 2909.02 and 2909.03 of the Revised Code include a conspiracy or attempt to commit, or complicity in the commission of, arson or aggravated arson under sections 2923.01 to 2923.03 of the Revised Code.

(D) If the prosecuting attorney fails to make reports at the time and in the manner required by this section, he shall forfeit and pay not less than one hundred nor more than five hundred dollars, to be recovered in a civil action in the name of the board.

**HISTORY: RS § 881; S&S 90; S&C 248; 58 v 69; GC § 2926; Bureau of Code Revision, 10-1-53; 138 v S 198. Eff 7-31-80.**

## § 309.17 Action to reclaim property.

When the prosecuting attorney of a county is informed that a person has in his possession money or other property belonging to a person found dead within such county, upon whose estate no letters of administration have been issued, the prosecuting attorney, by notice in writing, shall require the person having such money or other property to deposit it with the probate court. If within fifteen days such person does not comply with such requirement, the prosecuting attorney shall bring suit in the court of common pleas, in the name of the state, for the recovery thereof, and, when recovered, it shall be at the disposition of the probate court.

**HISTORY: RS § 1229; S&C 1405; 53 v 48, § 6; GC § 2865; Bureau of Code Revision. Eff 10-1-53.**

## § 309.18 Victim to be notified of escape of violent offender.

(A) If a prosecuting attorney of a county receives notice from the sheriff of the county pursuant to section 341.011 of the Revised Code that a person indicted for or otherwise charged with an offense of violence that is a felony and that was committed in the county has escaped from the county jail or workhouse or otherwise has escaped from the custody of the sheriff or receives notice from a chief of police or other chief law enforcement officer of a municipal corporation pursuant to section 753.19 of the Revised Code that a person indicted for or otherwise charged with an offense of violence that is a felony and that was committed in the county has escaped from a jail or workhouse of that municipal corporation or otherwise has escaped from the custody of that municipal corporation, the prosecuting attorney shall notify each victim of an offense of violence that is a felony committed by that person of the person's escape and, if applicable, of the person's subsequent apprehension. The notice of escape shall be given as soon as possible after receipt of the notice from the department, sheriff, or chief law enforcement officer of the municipal corporation and shall be given by telephone or in person, except that, if a prosecuting attorney tries and fails to give the notice of escape by telephone at the victim's last known telephone number or tries and fails to give the notice of escape in person at the victim's last known address, the notice of escape shall be given to the victim at the victim's last known address by certified mail, return receipt requested. The notice of apprehension shall be given as soon as possible after the person is apprehended and shall be given in the same manner as is the notice of escape.

Any prosecuting attorney who fails to give any notice required by this division is immune from civil liability for any injury, death, or loss to person or property that might be incurred as a result of that failure to give notice.

(B) If a prosecuting attorney of a county receives notice from the department of rehabilitation and correction pursuant to section 5120.14 of the Revised Code or otherwise receives notice from the department that a person who was convicted of or pleaded guilty in that county to an offense of violence that is a felony has escaped from a correctional institution under the control of the department or otherwise has escaped from the custody of the department, and if the office of victim services of the department requests assistance from the prosecuting attorney in identifying and locating the victim of the offense, the prosecuting attorney promptly shall provide the information requested, if available, to the office of victim services.

**HISTORY: 142 v H 207 (Eff 9-24-87); 145 v H 571. Eff 10-6-94; 2011 HB 86, § 1, eff. Sept. 30, 2011.**

# CHAPTER 311: SHERIFF

Section



## § 311.01 Qualifications for sheriff; basic training course; continuing education.

(A) A sheriff shall be elected quadrennially in each county. A sheriff shall hold office for a term of four years, beginning on the first Monday of January next after the sheriff's election.

(B) Except as otherwise provided in this section, no person is eligible to be a candidate for sheriff, and no person shall be elected or appointed to the office of sheriff, unless that person meets all of the following requirements:

(1) The person is a citizen of the United States.

(2) The person has been a resident of the county in which the person is a candidate for or is appointed to the office of sheriff for at least one year immediately prior to the qualification date.

(3) The person has the qualifications of an elector as specified in section 3503.01 of the Revised Code and has complied with all applicable election laws.

(4) The person has been awarded a high school diploma or a certificate of high school equivalence issued for achievement of specified minimum scores on the general educational development test of the American council on education.

(5) The person has not been convicted of or pleaded guilty to a felony or any offense involving moral turpitude under the laws of this or any other state or the United States, and has not been convicted of or pleaded guilty to an offense that is a misdemeanor of the first degree under the laws of this state or an offense under the laws of any other state or the United States that carries a penalty that is substantially equivalent to the penalty for a misdemeanor of the first degree under the laws of this state.

(6) The person has been fingerprinted and has been the subject of a search of local, state, and national fingerprint files to disclose any criminal record. Such fingerprints shall be taken under the direction of the administrative judge of the court of common pleas who, prior to the applicable qualification date, shall notify the board of elections, board of county commissioners, or county central committee of the proper political party, as applicable, of the judge's findings.

(7) The person has prepared a complete history of the person's places of residence for a period of six years immediately preceding the qualification date and a complete history of the person's places of employment for a period of six years immediately preceding the qualification date, indicating the name and address of each employer and the period of time employed by that employer. The residence and employment histories shall be filed with the administrative judge of the court of common pleas of the county, who shall forward them with the findings under division (B)(6) of this section to the appropriate board of elections, board of county commissioners, or county cen-

tral committee of the proper political party prior to the applicable qualification date.

(8) The person meets at least one of the following conditions:

(a) Has obtained or held, within the four-year period ending immediately prior to the qualification date, a valid basic peace officer certificate of training issued by the Ohio peace officer training commission or has been issued a certificate of training pursuant to section 5503.05 of the Revised Code, and, within the four-year period ending immediately prior to the qualification date, has been employed as an appointee pursuant to section 5503.01 of the Revised Code or as a full-time peace officer as defined in section 109.71 of the Revised Code performing duties related to the enforcement of statutes, ordinances, or codes;

(b) Has obtained or held, within the three-year period ending immediately prior to the qualification date, a valid basic peace officer certificate of training issued by the Ohio peace officer training commission and has been employed for at least the last three years prior to the qualification date as a full-time law enforcement officer, as defined in division (A)(11) of section 2901.01 of the Revised Code, performing duties related to the enforcement of statutes, ordinances, or codes.

(9) The person meets at least one of the following conditions:

(a) Has at least two years of supervisory experience as a peace officer at the rank of corporal or above, or has been appointed pursuant to section 5503.01 of the Revised Code and served at the rank of sergeant or above, in the five-year period ending immediately prior to the qualification date;

(b) Has completed satisfactorily at least two years of post-secondary education or the equivalent in semester or quarter hours in a college or university authorized to confer degrees by the Ohio board of regents or the comparable agency of another state in which the college or university is located or in a school that holds a certificate of registration issued by the state board of career colleges and schools under Chapter 3332. of the Revised Code.

(C) Persons who meet the requirements of division (B) of this section, except the requirement of division (B)(2) of this section, may take all actions otherwise necessary to comply with division (B) of this section. If, on the applicable qualification date, no person has met all the requirements of division (B) of this section, then persons who have complied with and meet the requirements of division (B) of this section, except the requirement of division (B)(2) of this section, shall be considered qualified candidates under division (B) of this section.

(D) Newly elected sheriffs shall attend a basic training course conducted by the Ohio peace officer training commission pursuant to division (A) of section 109.80 of the Revised Code. A newly elected sheriff shall complete not less than two weeks of this course before the first Monday in January next after the sheriff's election. While attending the basic training course, a newly elected sheriff may, with the approval of the board of county commissioners, receive compensation, paid for from funds established by the sheriff's county for this purpose, in the same manner and amounts as if carrying out the powers and duties of the office of sheriff.

Appointed sheriffs shall attend the first basic training course conducted by the Ohio peace officer training commission pursuant to division (A) of section 109.80 of the Revised Code within six months following the date of appointment or election to the office of sheriff. While attending the basic training course, appointed sheriffs shall receive regular compensation in the same manner and amounts as if carrying out their regular powers and duties.

Five days of instruction at the basic training course shall be considered equal to one week of work. The costs of conducting the basic training course and the costs of meals, lodging, and travel of appointed and newly elected sheriffs attending the course shall be paid from state funds appropriated to the commission for this purpose.

(E) In each calendar year, each sheriff shall attend and successfully complete at least sixteen hours of continuing education approved under division (B) of section 109.80 of the Revised Code. A sheriff who receives a waiver of the continuing education requirement from the commission under division (C) of section 109.80 of the Revised Code because of medical disability or for other good cause shall complete the requirement at the earliest time after the disability or cause terminates.

(F)(1) Each person who is a candidate for election to or who is under consideration for appointment to the office of sheriff shall swear before the administrative judge of the court of common pleas as to the truth of any information the person provides to verify the person's qualifications for the office. A person who violates this requirement is guilty of falsification under section 2921.13 of the Revised Code.

(2) Each board of elections shall certify whether or not a candidate for the office of sheriff who has filed a declaration of candidacy, a statement of candidacy, or a declaration of intent to be a write-in candidate meets the qualifications specified in divisions (B) and (C) of this section.

(G) The office of a sheriff who is required to comply with division (D) or (E) of this section and who fails to successfully complete the courses pursuant to those divisions is hereby deemed to be vacant.

(H) As used in this section:

(1) "Qualification date" means the last day on which a candidate for the office of sheriff can file a declaration of candidacy, a statement of candidacy, or a declaration of intent to be a write-in candidate, as applicable, in the case of a primary election for the office of sheriff; the last day on which a person may be appointed to fill a vacancy in a party nomination for the office of sheriff under Chapter 3513. of the Revised Code, in the case of a vacancy in the office of sheriff; or a date thirty days after the day on which a vacancy in the office of sheriff occurs, in the case of an appointment to such a vacancy under section 305.02 of the Revised Code.

(2) "Newly elected sheriff" means a person who did not hold the office of sheriff of a county on the date the person was elected sheriff of that county.

**HISTORY: RS § 1202; S&C 1403; 55 v 150; 93 v 351; GC § 2823; 116 v PtII, 184; Bureau of Code Revision, 10-1-53; 141 v H 683 (Eff 3-11-87); 146 v S 2 (Eff 7-1-96); 146 v H 670 (Eff 12-2-96); 146 v H 351 (Eff 1-14-97); 148 v H 283. Eff 9-29-99; 150 v H 75, § 1, eff. 12-9-03.**

The effective date is set by section 3 of H.B. 75.

## § 311.02 Bond.

The sheriff shall, within ten days after receiving his commission and before the first Monday of January next after his election, give a bond, signed by a bonding or surety company authorized to do business in this state and to be approved by the board of county commissioners, or, at the option of such sheriff, signed by two or more freeholders having real estate in the value of double the amount of the bond, over and above all encumbrances to the state, in a sum not less than five thousand nor more than fifty thousand dollars, which sum shall be fixed by the board, and such bond shall be conditioned for the faithful performance of the duties of his office. The expense or premium for such bond shall be paid by the board and charged to the general fund of the county. Such bonds, with the approval of the board and the oath of office required by sections 3.22 and 3.23 of the Revised Code, and Section 7 of Article XV, Ohio Constitution, indorsed thereon, shall be filed with the county auditor and kept in his office.

The board may require the sheriff, at any time during his term of office, to give additional sureties on his bond, or to give a new bond.

No judge or clerk of any court or attorney at law shall be received as surety on such bond.

If the sheriff fails to give a bond within the time required, or fails to give additional sureties on such bond or a new bond within ten days after he has received written notice that the board so requires, the board shall declare the office of such sheriff vacant.

**HISTORY: RS §§ 1203 to 1206; S&C 190, 191, 1404; 51 v 301, §§ 1-7; 55 v 150, § 3; GC §§ 2824 to 2827; 112 v 111; Bureau of Code Revision, 10-1-53; 129 v 1365. Eff 10-12-61.**

## § 311.03 Disability or absence.

When the sheriff, by reason of absence, sickness, or other disability, is incapable of serving any process required to be served, or by reason of interest is incompetent to serve it, the court of common pleas, if in session, or, if not in session, a judge of such court may appoint a suitable person to serve such process or to perform the duties of sheriff during the continuance of such disability. Such appointee shall give such bond as the court or judge requires, conditioned for the faithful performance of his duties, and take the oath of office.

**HISTORY: RS § 1208; S&C 539, 1402; 29 v 410, §§ 1, 2; 50 v 311, § 35; 84 v 208; GC § 2828; 121 v 343; Bureau of Code Revision, 10-1-53; 126 v 205 (Eff 1-1-56); 129 v 582 (625) (Eff 1-10-61); 129 v 1365. Eff 10-12-61.**

## § 311.04 Deputy sheriffs.

(A) As used in this section, "felony" has the same meaning as in section 109.511 [109.51.1] of the Revised Code.

(B)(1) Subject to division (C) of this section, the sheriff may appoint, in writing, one or more deputies. At the time of the appointment, the sheriff shall file the writing upon which the appointment is made with the clerk of the court of common pleas, and the clerk of the court shall enter it upon the journal of the court. The sheriff shall pay the clerk's fees for the filing and journal entry of the writing. In cases of emergency, the sheriff may request of the sheriff of another county the aid of qualified deputies serving in those other counties of the state, and, if the consent of the sheriff of that other county is received, the deputies while so assigned shall be considered to be the deputies of the sheriff of the county requesting aid. No judge of a county court or mayor shall be appointed a deputy.

(2) Notwithstanding section 2335.33 of the Revised Code, the sheriff shall retain the fee charged pursuant to division (B) of section 311.37 of the Revised Code for the purpose of training deputies appointed pursuant to this section.

(C)(1) The sheriff shall not appoint a person as a deputy sheriff pursuant to division (B)(1) of this section on a permanent basis, on a temporary basis, for a probationary term, or on other than a permanent basis if the person previously has been convicted of or has pleaded guilty to a felony.

(2)(a) The sheriff shall terminate the employment of a deputy sheriff appointed under division (B)(1) of this section if the deputy sheriff does either of the following:

(i) Pleads guilty to a felony;

(ii) Pleads guilty to a misdemeanor pursuant to a negotiated plea agreement as provided in division (D) of section 2929.43 of the Revised Code in which the deputy sheriff agrees to surrender the certificate awarded to the deputy sheriff under section 109.77 of the Revised Code.

(b) The sheriff shall suspend from employment any deputy sheriff appointed under division (B)(1) of this section if the deputy sheriff is convicted, after trial, of a felony. If the deputy sheriff files an appeal from that conviction and the conviction is upheld by the highest court to which the appeal is taken or if the deputy sheriff does not file a timely appeal, the sheriff shall terminate the employment of that deputy sheriff. If the deputy sheriff files an appeal that results in that deputy sheriff's acquittal of the felony or conviction of a misdemeanor, or in the dismissal of the felony charge against the deputy sheriff, the sheriff shall reinstate that deputy sheriff. A deputy sheriff who is reinstated under division (C)(2)(b) of this section shall not receive any back pay unless that deputy sheriff's conviction of the felony was reversed on appeal, or the felony charge was dismissed, because the court found insufficient evidence to convict the deputy sheriff of the felony.

(3) Division (C) of this section does not apply regarding an offense that was committed prior to January 1, 1997.

(4) The suspension from employment, or the termination of the employment, of a deputy sheriff under division (C)(2) of this section shall be in accordance with Chapter 119. of the Revised Code.

**HISTORY: RS § 1209; S&C 500; 29 v 410, § 4; 66 v 35, § 3; 83 v 29; GC § 2830; Bureau of Code Revision, 10-1-53; 127 v 1039 (Eff 1-1-58); 128 v 688 (Eff 10-1-59); 133 v H 1106 (Eff 9-7-70); 141 v S 247 (Eff 7-9-86); 146 v H 566. Eff 10-16-96; 149 v H 490, § 1, eff. 1-1-04.**

The effective date is set by section 4 of HB 490.

## § 311.05 Conduct of deputies.

The sheriff shall only be responsible for the neglect of duty or misconduct in office of any of his deputies if he orders, has prior knowledge of, participates in, acts in reckless disregard of, or ratifies the neglect of duty or misconduct in office of the deputy.

**HISTORY: RS § 1210; S&C 500; 29 v 410, §§ 4, 5; GC § 2831; Bureau of Code Revision, 10-1-53; 140 v H 273. Eff 10-5-83.**

## § 311.06 Location of sheriff's office.

(A) The sheriff's office shall be maintained at the county seat of justice, or at another location as provided in division (B) of this section, in such rooms as the board of county commissioners provides for that purpose. Such office shall be furnished with all necessary furniture, blankbooks, stationery, and blanks at the expense of the county.

(B) With the consent of the sheriff, the board of county commissioners may provide by resolution for establishment of the primary office of the sheriff at a location outside the county seat of justice. The adoption of the resolution and the location of the sheriff's primary office shall be entered on the journal of the board. The board shall give reasonable public notice of its action taken pursuant to this division in accordance with division (F) of section 121.22 of the Revised Code.

**HISTORY: RS § 1217; 70 v 292; GC § 2832; Bureau of Code Revision. Eff 10-1-53; 153 v H 393, § 1, eff. 6-18-10.**

The effective date is set by § 8 of 153 v H 393.

## § 311.07 General powers and duties of sheriff.

(A) Each sheriff shall preserve the public peace and cause all persons guilty of any breach of the peace, within the sheriff's knowledge or view, to enter into recognizance with sureties to keep the peace and to appear at the succeeding term of the court of common pleas, and the sheriff shall commit such persons to jail in case they refuse to do so. The sheriff shall return a transcript of all the sheriff's proceedings with the recognizance so taken to such court. The sheriff shall, except as provided in division (C) of this section, execute all warrants, writs, and other process directed to the sheriff by any proper and lawful authority of this state, and those issued by a proper and lawful authority of any other state. The sheriff shall attend upon the court of common pleas and the court of appeals during their sessions, and, when required, shall attend upon the probate court. In the execution of official duties of the sheriff, the sheriff may call to the sheriff's aid such persons or power of the county as is necessary. Under the direction and control of the board of county commissioners, such sheriff shall have charge of the court house. A sheriff or deputy sheriff of a county may participate, as the director of an organized crime task force established under section 177.02 of the Revised Code or as a member of the investigatory staff of such a task force, in an investigation of organized criminal activity in any county or counties in this state under sections 177.01 to 177.03 of the Revised Code.

(B) The sheriff of a county may call upon the sheriff of any other county, the mayor or other chief executive of any municipal corporation, and the chairperson of the board of township trustees of any township within this state, to furnish such law enforcement or fire protection personnel, or both, together with appropriate equipment and apparatus, as may be necessary to preserve the public peace and protect persons and property in the requesting sheriff's county. Such aid shall be furnished to the sheriff requesting it, insofar as possible without withdrawing from the political subdivision furnishing such aid the minimum police and fire protection appearing necessary under the circumstances. Law enforcement and fire protection personnel acting outside the territory of their regular employment shall be considered as performing services within the territory of their regular employment for the purposes of compensation, pension or indemnity fund rights, workers' compensation, and other rights or benefits to which they may be entitled as incidents of their regular employment. The county receiving aid shall reimburse, as provided in this section, the political subdivision furnishing it the cost of furnishing such aid, including compensation of personnel, expenses incurred by reason of the injury or death of any such personnel while rendering such aid, expenses of furnishing equipment and apparatus, compensation for damage to or loss of equipment or apparatus while in service outside the territory of its regular use, and such other reasonable expenses as may be incurred by any such political subdivision in furnishing aid. The cost of furnishing such aid may be paid from the sheriff's furtherance of justice fund created pursuant to section 325.071 [325.07.1] of the Revised Code or from the law enforcement trust fund created pursuant to section 2981.13 of the Revised Code, or from the county general fund to the extent moneys have been appropriated for such purposes pursuant to section 5705.38 of the Revised Code unless the board of county commissioners adopts a resolution restricting or prohibiting the use of general fund moneys without the prior approval of the board of county commissioners. Nothing in this section shall be construed as superseding or modifying in any way any provision of a contract entered into pursuant to section 311.29 of the Revised Code. Law enforcement officers acting pursuant to this section outside the territory of their regular employment have the same authority to enforce the law as when acting within the territory of their regular employment.

(C) The sheriff shall not execute process that is issued in a state other than this state, unless the process contains either of the following:

(1) A certification by the judge of the court that issued the process stating that the issuing court has jurisdiction to issue the process and that the documents being forwarded conform to the laws of the state in which the court is located;

(2) If the process is an initial summons to appear and defend issued after the filing of a complaint commencing an action, a certification by the clerk of the court that issued the process stating that the process was issued in conformance with the laws of the state in which the court is located.

(D) As used in this section and section 311.08 of the Revised Code, "proper and lawful authority" means any authority authorized by law to issue any process and "process" means those documents issued in this state in accordance with section 7.01 of the Revised Code and those documents, other than executions of judgments or decrees, issued in a state other than this state that conform to the laws of the state of issuance governing the issuance of process in that state.

**HISTORY: RS § 1211; S&C 1229, 1397; 29 v 112, § 2; 29 v 315, § 6; 82 v 16, 26; GC § 2833; 103 v 405(419); Bureau of Code Revision, 10-1-53; 132 v H 996 (Eff 6-13-68); 136 v S 545 (Eff 1-17-77); 138 v H 278 (Eff 6-12-80); 140 v S 23 (Eff 7-29-83); 141 v S 74 (Eff 9-3-86); 147 v H 342. Eff 12-31-97; 151 v H 241, § 1, eff. 7-1-07.**

See provisions of § 4 of 151 v H 241 following RC § 309.08.

## § 311.08 Execution and return of process.

(A) The sheriff shall, except as provided in division (B) of this section, execute every summons, order, or other process directed to him by a proper and lawful authority of this state or issued by a proper and lawful authority of any other state, make return thereof, and exercise the powers conferred and perform the duties enjoined upon him by statute and by the common law.

In an action in which the sheriff is a party, or is interested, process shall be directed to and executed by a person appointed by the court of common pleas or a judge of the court of common pleas.

(B) The sheriff shall not execute process that is issued in a state other than this state, unless the process contains either of the following:

(1) A certification by the judge of the court that issued the process stating that the issuing court has jurisdiction to issue the process and that the documents being forwarded conform to the laws of the state in which the court is located;

(2) If the process is an initial summons to appear and defend issued after the filing of a complaint commencing an action, a certification by the clerk of the court that issued the process stating that the process was issued in conformance with the laws of the state in which the court is located.

**HISTORY: RS §§ 4967, 4970; S&C 1128, 1130; S&S 572; 51 v 57, §§ 582, 593, 594; 65 v 96, § 592; GC §§ 2834, 2835; Bureau of Code Revision, 10-1-53; 138 v H 278 (Eff 6-12-80); 139 v S 114. Eff 10-27-81.**

## § 311.09 Indorsement on writs.

The sheriff shall indorse upon every writ or order the day and hour such writ or order was received by him.

**HISTORY: RS § 4966; S&C 1130; 51 v 57, § 591; GC § 2836; Bureau of Code Revision. Eff 10-1-53.**

## § 311.10 Foreign execution docket.

(A) There shall be kept in the office of the sheriff a foreign execution docket, furnished by the county, in which, on the receipt by the sheriff of any execution, order of sale, or other process issuing from any court of any county, other than the county in which he resides, the sheriff shall make an entry of the date of such writ, when it was received by him, from what court and county it was issued, and the date and amount of the judgment or decree. The sheriff shall copy in such book, the same as indorsed upon or contained in such writ, the full description of the property and real estate that he levies upon or offers for sale. He shall also copy into such book his return on such writ when he makes a return, and shall include the bill of costs. The sheriff shall make a direct and reverse index of each case entered in such book. The entries shall be notice to subsequent purchasers and creditors of the matters contained in them, but if the lien of any judgment is kept alive in the county of rendition beyond the period of five years, purchasers and creditors in such foreign county shall not be deemed to have notice of such lien unless written notice of it is filed by the judgment creditor with the sheriff of the foreign county, who shall certify such fact upon the foreign execution docket and index such notice at the place of the original entry.

(B) The sheriff shall also enter in the foreign execution docket the receipt of any process issued by a proper and lawful authority of a state other than this state, the date of issuance and the date of his receipt of the process, the court and state in which the process was issued, and the nature of the process. The sheriff shall also enter in the docket all action taken in relation to such process by his office.

(C) For making such entries the sheriff shall receive twenty-five cents in each case, to be taxed in the fee bill.

(D) For the use of the persons entitled to such fees, the sheriff shall retain all fees due in such cases to residents of his county, and, on demand, he shall pay them to such persons.

**HISTORY: RS §§ 1212, 1213; S&C 1402; 36 v 18, § 3; 57 v 6, § 2; 84 v 208, 209; GC §§ 2837, 2838; 111 v 31; Bureau of Code Revision, 10-1-53; 128 v 542 (Eff 7-17-59); 138 v H 278. Eff 6-12-80.**

## § 311.11 Cashbook.

There shall be kept in the office of the sheriff a cashbook, to be furnished by the county, in which, on receipt by him of any money in his official capacity, the sheriff shall make an entry of the date, the amount thereof, the title of the cause, and the name and number of the writ or process on which such money was received. If such money is received on the sale of real estate, in partition or otherwise, where the sale has been for part cash and other evidences of indebtedness are taken for part of the purchase money, such sheriff shall make an entry on such book of the date, number, and amount of such evidences of indebtedness.

**HISTORY: RS § 1214; S&S 734; 65 v 115; 84 v 208, 209; GC § 2839; Bureau of Code Revision. Eff 10-1-53.**

## § 311.12 Inspection of books; certified copies of entries.

The books required to be kept by sections 311.01 to 311.23 of the Revised Code, shall be open to the search and inspection of all persons. The sheriff shall furnish a certified copy of any entry in such books upon request and shall charge and collect a fee of twenty-five cents for each such certification or copy thereof.

**HISTORY: RS § 1216; S&C 1402; 36 v 18, § 4; 84 v 208, 209; GC § 2841; Bureau of Code Revision, 10-1-53; 128 v 542 (Eff 7-17-59); 139 v S 114. Eff 10-27-81.**

## § 311.13 Books to be delivered to successor.

The books required to be kept by sections 311.01 to 311.23 of the Revised Code, shall not be removed from the sheriff's office. Such books shall be delivered over, without mutilation, as public property to each succeeding sheriff. No sheriff shall willfully fail to comply with this section or section 311.11 of the Revised Code.

**HISTORY: RS § 1215; S&S 734; 65 v 115, §§ 2, 4, 5; 84 v 208; 86 v 239; GC § 2840; Bureau of Code Revision, 10-1-53; 139 v S 114. Eff 10-27-81.**

## § 311.14 Moneys, books, and papers to be delivered to successor.

Upon retiring from office, the sheriff shall pay over to his successor in office all moneys received by such sheriff and remaining in his hands. He shall deliver to his successor all evidences of indebtedness and all books, blanks, and stationery belonging to his office. Each sheriff shall demand and receive such books and papers from his predecessor.

**HISTORY: RS § 1218; S&C 1402; 36 v 18, § 5; 69 v 168, § 5; 84 v 208, 210; GC § 2842; Bureau of Code Revision. Eff 10-1-53.**

## § 311.15 Process, goods, and prisoners to be delivered to successor.

When the term of office for which a sheriff has been elected expires, or he resigns or moves outside the county, such sheriff shall deliver all writs of execution and all other processes, of whatever description, whether executed or not, and all goods and chattels taken by him, in execution or on attachment, which remain in his hands, together with all bonds, to the person elected or appointed and qualified to discharge the duties of sheriff, and he shall make the necessary and proper return upon each such writ or other process so far as executed. Such sheriff shall also deliver to his successor all prisoners in the county jail or otherwise in his custody, with all bail bonds taken by him and remaining in his possession. The new sheriff shall receive all such prisoners, writs, or other processes, and he shall execute such writs and processes as remain unexecuted in whole or in part as if they had been directed to him originally. No process shall be directed to or executed by a sheriff whose term of office has expired.

**HISTORY: RS § 1219; S&C 1390; 29 v 112, § 8; 84 v 208, 210; GC § 2843; Bureau of Code Revision. Eff 10-1-53.**

## § 311.16 Annual report of sheriff.

On the first Monday in September of each year, the sheriff shall make a certified statement to the board of county commissioners of all fines and costs in criminal prosecutions collected by him, on execution or otherwise, during the year next preceding such date, and he shall also report in such statement the amount of fines and costs so collected and paid over to the clerk of the court of common pleas or to the county treasurer.

If the sheriff fails to make reports at the time and in the manner required by this section, he shall forfeit and pay not less than fifty nor more than one hundred dollars, to be recovered in a civil action in the name of the board.

**HISTORY: RS § 884; S&S 91; 58 v 70, § 3; GC § 2844; Bureau of Code Revision. Eff 10-1-53.**

## § 311.17 Fees.

Except as provided in a contract entered into under division (A) of section 3125.141 [3125.14.1] of the Revised Code, for the services specified in this section, the sheriff shall charge the following fees, which the court or its clerk shall tax in the bill of costs against the judgment debtor or those legally liable therefor for the judgment:

(A) For the service and return of the following writs and orders:

(1) Execution:

(a) When money is paid without levy or when no property is found, thirty dollars;

(b) When levy is made on real property, for the first tract, twenty-five dollars, and for each additional tract, ten dollars;

(c) When levy is made on goods and chattels, including inventory, fifty dollars.

(2) Writ of attachment of property, except for purpose of garnishment, forty dollars;

(3) Writ of attachment for the purpose of garnishment, ten dollars;

(4) Writ of replevin, forty dollars;

(5) Warrant to arrest, for each person named in the writ, twenty dollars;

(6) Attachment for contempt, for each person named in the writ, six dollars;

(7) Writ of possession or restitution, sixty dollars;

(8) Subpoena, for each person named in the writ, in either a civil or criminal case, ten dollars;

(9) Venire, for each person named in the writ, in either a civil or criminal case, six dollars;

(10) Summoning each juror, other than on venire, in either a civil or criminal case, six dollars;

(11) Writ of partition, twenty-five dollars;

(12) Order of sale on partition, for the first tract, fifty dollars, and for each additional tract, twenty-five dollars;

(13) Other order of sale of real property, for the first tract, fifty dollars, and for each additional tract, twenty-five dollars;

(14) Administering oath to appraisers, three dollars each;

(15) Furnishing copies for advertisements, one dollar for each hundred words;

(16) Copy of indictment, for each defendant, five dollars;

(17) All summons, writs, orders, or notices, for the first name, six dollars, and for each additional name, one dollar.

(B) In addition to the fee for service and return:

(1) On each summons, writ, order, or notice, a fee of two dollars per mile for the first mile, and one dollar per mile for each additional mile, going and returning, actual mileage to be charged on each additional name;

(2) Taking bail bond, three dollars;

(3) Jail fees, as follows:

(a) For receiving a prisoner, five dollars each time a prisoner is received, and for discharging or surrendering a prisoner, five dollars each time a prisoner is discharged or surrendered. The departure or return of a prisoner from or to a jail in connection with a program established under section 5147.28 of the Revised Code is not a receipt, discharge, or surrender of the prisoner for purposes of this division.

(b) Taking a prisoner before a judge or court, per day, five dollars;

(c) Calling action, one dollar;

(d) Calling jury, three dollars;

(e) Calling each witness, three dollars;

(f) Bringing prisoner before court on habeas corpus, six dollars.

(4) Poundage on all moneys actually made and paid to the sheriff on execution, decree, or sale of real estate, one and one-half per cent;

(5) Making and executing a deed of land sold on execution, decree, or order of the court, to be paid by the purchaser, fifty dollars.

When any of the services described in division (A) or (B) of this section are rendered by an officer or employee, whose salary or per diem compensation is paid by the county, the applicable legal fees and any other extraordinary expenses, including overtime, provided for the service shall be taxed in the costs in the case and, when collected, shall be paid into the general fund of the county.

The sheriff shall charge the same fees for the execution of process issued in any other state as the sheriff charges for the execution of process of a substantively similar nature that is issued in this state.

**HISTORY: RS § 1230; S&S 364; S&C 639; 73 v 127, § 11; 76 v 117, § 20; 77 v 116; GC § 2845; 102 v 277; 108 v PtII, 1203(1214); Bureau of Code Revision, 10-1-53; 128 v 542 (Eff 7-17-59); 135 v S 208 (Eff 12-17-73); 138 v H 278 (Eff 6-12-80); 140 v H 897. Eff 12-26-84; 150 v H 95, § 1, eff.**

**9-26-03; 150 v H 200, § 1, eff. 12-21-04; 153 v H 1, § 101.01, eff. 10-16-09.**

The effective date is set by § 812.10 of 153 v H 1.
The effective date is set by section 4 of H.B. 200 (150 v —).
The effective date is set by section 179 of H.B. 95 (150 v —).

## § 311.171 Fees to pay costs of registering sex offenders and child-victim offenders and providing community notification.

(A) As used in this section:

(1) "Federal poverty level" means the income level represented by the poverty guidelines as revised annually by the United States department of health and human services in accordance with section 673(2) of the "Omnibus Reconciliation Act of 1981," 95 Stat. 511, 42 U.S.C.A. 9902, as amended, for a family size equal to the size of the family of the person whose income is being determined.

(2) "Registration year" of an offender means one of the following:

(a) The twelve-month period beginning on the anniversary, occurring on or after January 1, 2004, of the date on which an offender's registration period began in accordance with section 2950.07 of the Revised Code;

(b) The twelve-month period beginning on the date on which an offender's registration period begins, on or after January 1, 2004, in accordance with section 2950.07 of the Revised Code.

(3) "Sexually oriented offense," "child-victim oriented offense," and "tier III sex offender/child-victim offender" have the same meanings as in section 2950.01 of the Revised Code.

(B) The sheriff may charge a fee each time a person does any of the following:

(1) Registers under section 2950.04 or 2950.041 of the Revised Code;

(2) Registers a new residence address under section 2950.05 of the Revised Code;

(3) Verifies a current residence address under section 2950.06 of the Revised Code.

(C) If the sheriff charges one or more fees provided for in division (B) of this section, all of the following apply:

(1) The sheriff shall not require the payment of any fee from a delinquent child until the delinquent child reaches eighteen years of age. When a delinquent child reaches eighteen years of age and the sheriff charges a fee to the delinquent child, the provisions of this section applicable to "offenders" shall be construed to apply to the delinquent child.

(2) For an offender who is a tier III sex offender/child-victim offender, the fees may not exceed a total of one hundred dollars for each registration year.

(3) For an offender who has been convicted of or pleaded guilty to a sexually oriented offense or a child-victim offense and who is not described in division (C)(2) of this section, the fees may not exceed a total of twenty-five dollars for each registration year.

(4) An offender who is required to pay a fee shall retain the receipts received under section 325.28 of the Revised Code for payments made during the offender's registration year to establish that the payment of any fee will exceed the maximum annual amount permissible under this division.

(5) The sheriff shall not refuse to register a person, register a new residence address of a person, or verify the current residence address of a person, who does not pay a fee the sheriff requires under this section.

(6) The sheriff shall report unpaid fees in accordance with division (C) of section 325.31 of the Revised Code, and the county may recover those fees in a civil action in the same manner as other money due the county.

(D) Each time a person appears before the sheriff to provide any registration or verification specified in division (B) of this section for which the sheriff charges a fee, the sheriff shall determine whether the person is able to pay the fee. In making that determination, the sheriff shall determine whether the person's income is less than one hundred twenty-five per cent of the federal poverty level. A person whose income is equal to or greater than one hundred twenty-five per cent of the federal poverty level shall be considered able to pay the fee.

(E) If a sheriff determines a person's income is less than one hundred twenty-five per cent of the federal poverty level, the sheriff shall waive payment of the fee. If the sheriff determines a person's income is equal to or greater than one hundred twenty-five per cent of the federal poverty level, the sheriff may allow the person to pay the fee in accordance with a payment schedule the sheriff establishes based on the person's ability to pay. The sheriff shall document any waiver or alternative fee arrangement in the official registration records of the sheriff's office and shall provide the offender with a written copy of any waiver or alternative fee arrangement.

(F) All fees paid to a sheriff under this section shall be paid into the county treasury to the credit of the county general fund and shall be allocated to the sheriff to be used to defray the costs of registering sex offenders and child-victim offenders and providing community notification under Chapter 2950. of the Revised Code.

(G) If an offender has registered with a sheriff and subsequently relocates to a different county during a registration year, the annual maximum amounts set forth in division (C) of this section shall apply to the sheriff in the new county, and that sheriff shall consider any payments already made by the offender for purposes of determining when the applicable maximum has been met for the offender's registration year.

**HISTORY: 150 v S 5, § 1, eff. 7-31-03; 152 v S 10, § 1, eff. 1-1-08.**

The effective date is set by § 3 of 152 v S 10.

## § 311.18 Mileage fees on foreign process.

When a sheriff returns, in any manner other than by himself or his deputy personally, any process issued from the court of common pleas or other court of a county other than that in which he resides, such sheriff shall receive only mileage on such return of process, to be computed from his office to the place of service and back to his office.

**HISTORY: RS § 1232; 73 v 127, § 14; 76 v 117, § 22; GC § 2847; Bureau of Code Revision. Eff 10-1-53.**

## § 311.19 Fees of appraisers.

In all cases in which an attachment is issued, the freeholders required to be called by the sheriff to appraise property shall be allowed such fees for their services as the court directs.

**HISTORY: RS § 1233; S&C 634; 73 v 127, § 15; 76 v 117, § 23; GC § 2848; 102 v 277; Bureau of Code Revision. Eff 10-1-53.**

## § 311.20 Allowance for prisoners.

On or before the twenty-first day of June of each year, the sheriff shall prepare and submit to the board of county commissioners a budget estimating the cost of operating the jail and feeding its inmates for the ensuing fiscal year.

On the fifth day of each month the sheriff shall render to the board an itemized and accurate account, with all bills attached, showing the actual cost of keeping and feeding prisoners and other persons placed in his charge and the number of meals served to each such prisoner or other person during the preceding month. The number of days for which allowance shall be made shall be computed on the basis of one day for each three meals actually served.

**HISTORY: RS § 1235; S&S 366, 441; S&C 635; 62 v 60; 73 v 127, § 17; 76 v 117, § 25; 92 v 288; 98 v 255; GC § 2850; 112 v 62; 121 v 335; Bureau of Code Revision, 10-1-53; 125 v H 198 (Eff 10-2-53); 131 v 207 (Eff 9-6-65); 139 v S 23. Eff 7-6-82.**

## § 311.21 Fees in cases relating to dower.

The sheriff shall be allowed fees as follows for service relating to dower: For summoning and swearing the board of county commissioners, traveling fees, to be computed from the place of return of his proceedings to the place where the land lies in which dower is to be assigned, at the rate of ten cents per mile.

**HISTORY: RS § 1237; S&C 642; 73 v 127, § 37; 76 v 117, § 27; GC § 2852; Bureau of Code Revision. Eff 10-1-53.**

## § 311.22 Service of process.

The court or judge may, for good cause, appoint a person to serve a particular process or order, and such person shall have the same power to execute such process or order which the sheriff has. Such person may be appointed on the motion of the party who obtains the process or order, and the return must be verified by affidavit. He shall be entitled to the fees allowed to the sheriff for similar services.

**HISTORY: RS § 4968; S&C 1128; 51 v 57, § 583; GC § 2854; Bureau of Code Revision. Eff 10-1-53.**

## § 311.23 Adjournment of court.

If the judge of the court of common pleas, or a quorum of the judges of the court of appeals, fails to attend at the time and place appointed for holding such court, or if, after the calling of the court, the judge of the court of common pleas or a quorum of the judges of the court of appeals is unable, on account of sickness or from any other cause, to attend the daily sessions of such court, the sheriff shall adjourn the court from day to day, until such judge attends or such quorum is convened.

**HISTORY: RS § 4969; S&C 1130; 51 v 57, § 593; 79 v 15; 82 v 16, 31; GC § 2855; 103 v 405 (419); Bureau of Code Revision, 10-1-53; 136 v H 390. Eff 8-6-76.**

# [SHERIFFS' STANDARD CAR-MARKING AND UNIFORM COMMISSION]

## § 311.25 Sheriffs' standard car-marking and uniform commission.

A commission is hereby established to be known as the county sheriffs' standard car-marking and uniform commission. It shall consist of three members, not more than two of whom shall be members of the same political party. To be eligible for appointment a person shall be an elected and acting county sheriff. Each member shall be appointed by the governor, with the advice and consent of the senate, and shall serve at the pleasure of the governor.

**HISTORY: 128 v 310. Eff 10-23-59.**

The provisions of § 4 of H.B. 516 (150 v —) read in part as follows:

SECTION 4. The following agencies shall be retained pursuant to division (D) of section 101.83 of the Revised Code and shall expire on December 31, 2010:

| *AGENCY NAME* | *REVISED CODE OR UNCODIFIED SECTION* |
|---|---|
| ○○○ | ○○○ |
| County Sheriffs' Standard Car-Marking and Uniform Commission | 311.25 |
| ○○○ | ○○○ |

## § 311.26 Organization.

The county sheriffs' standard car-marking and uniform commission shall elect one of its members as president, who shall preside at its meetings and who may call meetings. The commission may make its own bylaws.

**HISTORY: 128 v 310 (Eff 10-23-59); 129 v 582 (626) (Eff 1-10-61); 130 v 199. Eff 9-27-63.**

## § 311.27 No compensation.

The members of the county sheriffs' standard car-marking and uniform commission shall receive no compensation for their services.

**HISTORY: 128 v 310 (Eff 10-23-59); 129 v 582 (626) (Eff 1-10-61); 130 v 199. Eff 9-27-63.**

## § 311.28 Duties.

The county sheriffs' standard car-marking and uniform commission shall prescribe a uniform of standard design and color for the use of all county sheriffs and shall prescribe a standard color and design of car-marking for all motor vehicles used by county sheriffs.

On and after January 1, 1961, the standard uniform shall be worn by the county sheriffs and their deputies and the standard car-markings shall be used on all cars operated by the county sheriffs and their deputies while in the performance of their duties.

**HISTORY: 128 v 310 (Eff 10-23-59); 129 v 582 (626). Eff 1-10-61.**

## § 311.281 Use of sheriff's uniform and vehicle markings prohibited.

(A) No person, except a county sheriff or the deputies of a county sheriff, shall wear the badge, the standard uniform, or any distinctive part of the standard uniform prescribed for county sheriffs and their deputies by the county sheriffs' standard car-marking and uniform commission.

(B) No person, except a county sheriff or the deputies of a county sheriff, shall mark a motor vehicle in a manner similar to that prescribed for county sheriffs and their deputies by the county sheriffs' standard car-marking and uniform commission.

(C) Whoever violates division (A) of this section is guilty of a violation of section 2921.51 of the Revised Code. Whoever violates division (B) of this section is guilty of a violation of section 2913.441 [2913.44.1] of the Revised Code.

**HISTORY: 133 v H 625 (Eff 11-21-69); 146 v S 2. Eff 7-1-96.**

The effective date is set by section 6 of SB 2.

## § 311.29 Contracts to perform police functions; payments; deputy sheriffs.

(A) As used in this section, "Chautauqua assembly" has the same meaning as in section 4511.90 of the Revised Code.

(B) The sheriff may, from time to time, enter into contracts with any municipal corporation, township, township police district, joint police district, metropolitan housing authority, port authority, water or sewer district, school district, library district, health district, park district created pursuant to section 511.18 or 1545.01 of the Revised Code, soil and water conservation district, water conservancy district, or other taxing district or with the board of county commissioners of any contiguous county with the concurrence of the sheriff of the other county, and such subdivisions, authorities, and counties may enter into agreements with the sheriff pursuant to which the sheriff undertakes and is authorized by the contracting subdivision, authority, or county to perform any police function, exercise any police power, or render any police service in behalf of the contracting subdivision, authority, or county, or its legislative authority, that the subdivision, authority, or county, or its legislative authority, may perform, exercise, or render.

Upon the execution of an agreement under this division and within the limitations prescribed by it, the sheriff may exercise the same powers as the contracting subdivision, authority, or county possesses with respect to such policing that by the agreement the sheriff undertakes to perform or render, and all powers necessary or incidental thereto, as amply as such powers are possessed and exercised by the contracting subdivision, authority, or county directly.

Any agreement authorized by division (A), (B), or (C) of this section shall not suspend the possession by a contracting subdivision, authority, or county of any police power performed or exercised or police service rendered in pursuance to the agreement nor limit the authority of the sheriff.

(C) The sheriff may enter into contracts with any Chautauqua assembly that has grounds located within the county, and the Chautauqua assembly may enter into agreements with the sheriff pursuant to which the sheriff undertakes to perform any police function, exercise any police power, or render any police service upon the grounds of the Chautauqua assembly that the sheriff is authorized by law to perform, exercise, or render in any other part of the county within the sheriff's territorial jurisdiction. Upon the execution of an agreement under this division, the sheriff may, within the limitations prescribed by the agreement, exercise such powers with respect to such policing upon the grounds of the Chautauqua assembly, provided that any limitation contained in the agreement shall not be construed to limit the authority of the sheriff.

(D) Contracts entered into under division (A), (B), or (C) of this section shall provide for the reimbursement of the county for the costs incurred by the sheriff for such policing including, but not limited to, the salaries of deputy sheriffs assigned to such policing, the current costs of funding retirement pensions and of providing workers' compensation, the cost of training, and the cost of equipment and supplies used in such policing, to the extent that such equipment and supplies are not directly furnished by the contracting subdivision, authority, county, or Chautauqua assembly. Each such contract shall provide for the ascertainment of such costs and shall be of any duration, not in excess of four years, and may contain any other terms that may be agreed upon. All payments pursuant to any such contract in reimbursement of the costs of such policing shall be made to the treasurer of the county to be credited to a special fund to be known as the "sheriff's policing revolving fund," hereby created. Any moneys coming into the fund shall be used for the purposes provided in divisions (A) to (D) of this section and paid out on vouchers by the county commissioners as other funds coming into their possession. Any moneys credited to the fund and not obligated at the termination of the contract shall be credited to the county general fund.

The sheriff shall assign the number of deputies as may be provided for in any contract made pursuant to division (A), (B), or (C) of this section. The number of deputies regularly assigned to such policing shall be in addition to and an enlargement of the sheriff's regular number of deputies. Nothing in divisions (A) to (D) of this section shall preclude the sheriff from temporarily increasing or decreasing the deputies so assigned as emergencies indicate a need for shifting assignments to the extent provided by the contracts.

All such deputies shall have the same powers and duties, the same qualifications, and be appointed and paid and receive the same benefits and provisions and be governed by the same laws as all other deputy sheriffs.

Contracts under division (A), (B), or (C) of this section may be entered into jointly with the board of county commissioners, and sections 307.14 to 307.19 of the Revised Code apply to this section insofar as they may be applicable.

(E)(1) As used in division (E) of this section:

(a) "Ohio prisoner" has the same meaning as in section 5120.64 of the Revised Code.

(b) "Out-of-state prisoner" and "private contractor" have the same meanings as in section 9.07 of the Revised Code.

(2) The sheriff may enter into a contract with a private person or entity for the return of Ohio prisoners who are the responsibility of the sheriff from outside of this state to a location in this state specified by the sheriff, if there are adequate funds appropriated by the board of county commissioners and there is a certification pursuant to

division (D) of section 5705.41 of the Revised Code that the funds are available for this purpose. A contract entered into under this division is within the coverage of section 325.07 of the Revised Code. If a sheriff enters into a contract as described in this division, subject to division (E)(3) of this section, the private person or entity in accordance with the contract may return Ohio prisoners from outside of this state to locations in this state specified by the sheriff. A contract entered into under this division shall include all of the following:

(a) Specific provisions that assign the responsibility for costs related to medical care of prisoners while they are being returned that is not covered by insurance of the private person or entity;

(b) Specific provisions that set forth the number of days, not exceeding ten, within which the private person or entity, after it receives the prisoner in the other state, must deliver the prisoner to the location in this state specified by the sheriff, subject to the exceptions adopted as described in division (E)(2)(c) of this section;

(c) Any exceptions to the specified number of days for delivery specified as described in division (E)(2)(b) of this section;

(d) A requirement that the private person or entity immediately report all escapes of prisoners who are being returned to this state, and the apprehension of all prisoners who are being returned and who have escaped, to the sheriff and to the local law enforcement agency of this state or another state that has jurisdiction over the place at which the escape occurs;

(e) A schedule of fines that the sheriff shall impose upon the private person or entity if the private person or entity fails to perform its contractual duties, and a requirement that, if the private person or entity fails to perform its contractual duties, the sheriff shall impose a fine on the private person or entity from the schedule of fines and, in addition, may exercise any other rights the sheriff has under the contract.

(f) If the contract is entered into on or after the effective date of the rules adopted by the department of rehabilitation and correction under section 5120.64 of the Revised Code, specific provisions that comport with all applicable standards that are contained in those rules.

(3) If the private person or entity that enters into the contract fails to perform its contractual duties, the sheriff shall impose upon the private person or entity a fine from the schedule, the money paid in satisfaction of the fine shall be paid into the county treasury, and the sheriff may exercise any other rights the sheriff has under the contract. If a fine is imposed under this division, the sheriff may reduce the payment owed to the private person or entity pursuant to any invoice in the amount of the fine.

(4) Upon the effective date of the rules adopted by the department of rehabilitation and correction under section 5120.64 of the Revised Code, notwithstanding the existence of a contract entered into under division (E)(2) of this section, in no case shall the private person or entity that is a party to the contract return Ohio prisoners from outside of this state into this state for a sheriff unless the private person or entity complies with all applicable standards that are contained in the rules.

(5) Divisions (E)(1) to (4) of this section do not apply regarding any out-of-state prisoner who is brought into this state to be housed pursuant to section 9.07 of the Revised Code in a correctional facility in this state that is managed and operated by a private contractor.

**HISTORY: 129 v 1362 (Eff 8-18-61); 130 v 199 (Eff 1-23-63); 133 v H 1 (Eff 3-18-69); 136 v S 545 (Eff 1-17-77); 137 v S 221 (Eff 11-23-77); 138 v H 948 (Eff 5-22-80); 144 v S 174 (Eff 7-31-92); 145 v S 200 (Eff 12-7-93); 148 v H 661. Eff 3-15-2001; 2011 HB 153, § 101.01, eff. Sept. 29, 2011.**

## § 311.30 Parking enforcement unit.

(A) The board of county commissioners may establish, by resolution, a parking enforcement unit within the office of the sheriff to operate in the unincorporated areas of the county, and may provide for the regulation of parking enforcement officers. The sheriff shall be the executive head of the parking enforcement unit, shall make all appointments and removals of parking enforcement officers, subject to any general rules prescribed by the board of county commissions by resolution, and shall prescribe rules for the organization, training, administration, control, and conduct of the parking enforcement unit. The sheriff may appoint parking enforcement officers who agree to serve for nominal compensation, and persons with physical disabilities may receive appointments as parking enforcement officers.

(B) The authority of the parking enforcement officers shall be limited to the enforcement of section 4511.69 of the Revised Code and any other parking laws specified in the resolution creating the parking enforcement unit. Parking enforcement officers shall have no other powers.

(C) The training the parking enforcement officers shall receive shall include instruction in general administrative rules and procedures governing the parking enforcement unit, the role of the judicial system as it relates to parking regulation and enforcement, proper techniques and methods relating to the enforcement of parking laws, human interaction skills, and first aid.

**HISTORY: 143 v S 174. Eff 7-13-90.**

**Not analogous to former RC § 311.30 (131 v 208; 133 v S 218), repealed 134 v H 24, § 2, eff 10-6-71.**

## § 311.31 Voluntary motor vehicle decal registration program.

(A) The board of county commissioners of a county may establish, by resolution, a voluntary motor vehicle decal registration program to be controlled and conducted by the sheriff within the unincorporated areas of the county. The board may establish a fee for participation in the program in an amount sufficient to cover the cost of administering the program and the cost of the decals. The board shall coordinate its program with any pre-existing program established by a township located within the county under section 505.67 of the Revised Code.

(B) Any resident of the county may enroll a motor vehicle that the resident owns in the program by signing a consent form, displaying the decal issued under this section, and paying the prescribed fee. The motor vehicle owner shall remove the decal to withdraw from the program and also prior to the sale or transfer of ownership of the vehicle. Any law enforcement officer may conduct, at any place within this state at which the officer would be permitted to arrest the person operating the vehicle, an investigatory stop of any motor vehicle displaying a decal issued under this section when the vehicle is being driven between the hours of one a.m. and five a.m. A law enforcement officer may conduct an investigatory stop under this division regardless of whether the officer observes a violation of law involving the vehicle or whether the officer has probable cause to believe that any violation of law involving the vehicle has occurred.

(C) The consent form required under division (B) of this section shall:

(1) Describe the conditions for participation in the program, including a description of an investigatory stop and a statement that any law enforcement officer may conduct, at any place within this state at which the officer would be permitted to arrest the person operating the vehicle, an investigatory stop of the motor vehicle when it is being driven between the hours of one a.m. and five a.m.

(2) Contain other information identifying the vehicle and owner as the sheriff considers necessary.

(D) The state director of public safety, in accordance with Chapter 119. of the Revised Code, shall adopt rules governing the color, size, and design of decals issued under this section and the location where the decals shall be displayed on vehicles that are enrolled in the program.

(E) Divisions (A) to (D) of this section do not require a law enforcement officer to conduct an investigatory stop of a vehicle displaying a decal issued under this section.

(F) As used in this section:

(1) "Investigatory stop" means a temporary stop of a motor vehicle and its operator and occupants for purposes of determining the identity of the person who is operating the vehicle and, if the person who is operating it is not its owner, whether any violation of law has occurred or is occurring. An "investigatory stop" is not an arrest, but, if an officer who conducts an investigatory stop determines that illegal conduct has occurred or is occurring, an "investigatory stop" may be the basis for an arrest.

(2) "Law enforcement officer" means a sheriff, deputy sheriff, constable, police officer of a township or joint police district, marshal, deputy marshal, municipal police officer, or state highway patrol trooper.

**HISTORY: 145 v S 75. Eff 10-20-94; 2011 HB 153, § 101.01, eff. Sept. 29, 2011.**

**Not analogous to former RC** § 311.31 **(131 v 208; 133 v S 218), repealed 134 v H 24, § 2, eff 10-6-71.**

## § 311.37 Transient vendors to file information and bond; municipal regulation.

(A) No transient vendor, as defined in section 5739.17 of the Revised Code, who obtains a transient vendor's license pursuant to section 5739.17 of the Revised Code, intending to provide goods and services of a retail value of more than five hundred dollars, shall negligently fail to file with the county sheriff all of the following before doing business as a transient vendor anywhere in that county:

(1) Proof of the transient vendor's identity and proof that a transient vendor's license has been obtained in this state;

(2) A statement describing the goods or services to be provided by the transient vendor and an estimate of the amount of the goods or services that the vendor expects to sell in that county, as documented by invoices indicating the wholesale value of goods to be sold;

(3) The transient vendor's permanent business address;

(4) The times and days during which, and the temporary places of business, as defined in section 5739.17 of the Revised Code, at which the transient vendor plans to do business in that county.

(B) The sheriff shall maintain a record of the information required under division (A) of this section for a period of two years, which shall be open to the inspection of any person. The sheriff shall be allowed a fee of up to one hundred dollars for collection of the bond required by this section. The bond shall be fifty per cent of the wholesale value of the goods and services provided, but in no case shall the bond exceed ten thousand dollars. The bond shall be in a form approved by the attorney general. The bond shall remain in effect for two years after the transient vendor last does business in that county.

(C) No transient vendor, as defined in section 5739.17 of the Revised Code, intending to provide goods and services of a retail value of more than five hundred dollars, shall negligently fail to file a bond within ten days before doing business as a transient vendor anywhere in that county.

(D) The bond filed by any transient vendor pursuant to this section shall be given to the attorney general by the county sheriff within ten working days after a transient vendor ceases to do business in that county, and shall be in favor of the state for the benefit of any person who suffers loss or damage as a result of the purchase of goods from the transient vendor or as the result of the negligent or intentionally tortious acts of the transient vendor in the conduct of business in the county. The bond may be used to compensate any state or local agency for damages caused by the transient vendor, for costs incurred by the agency for the illegal acts of the transient vendor, or for failure to pay any amount owed by the transient vendor to the state or local agency. The bond also may be used to compensate the state for any sales tax not paid by the transient vendor. Except for the amount of unpaid sales taxes to be deducted from the bond, if any, the attorney general shall pay any portion of the bond to any person or agency in accordance with the order of a court without making an independent finding as to the amount of the bond that is payable to that person or agency.

(E) This section does not apply to any of the following:

(1) A transient vendor making retail sales at a temporary exhibition, show, fair, world trade center, flea market, or similar event, as permitted by section 5739.17 of the Revised Code;

(2) Any nonprofit corporation, community chest, fund, or foundation organized and operated exclusively for religious, charitable, scientific, literary, or educational purposes when no part of the entity's earnings benefit any private shareholder or individual;

(3) Any person who operates a permanent business in this state, occupies temporary premises, and prominently displays the permanent business' name and permanent address while business is conducted from the temporary premises.

(4) Any person who sells goods by sample, brochure, or catalog for future delivery or any person who makes sales as the result of the invitation of an owner or occupant of a residence to the person.

(5) Any person who sells handmade or handcrafted items, or who sells fresh farm produce.

Nothing in this section shall prohibit the legislative authority of a municipal corporation from adopting an ordinance regulating transient vendors, as defined in section 5739.17 of the Revised Code, except that a municipal corporation may not require a transient vendor who obtains a bond in compliance with this section to obtain or pay for any additional bond or require that persons exempt pursuant to division (E) of this section obtain a bond. A municipal corporation may require that a transient vendor exhibit the transient vendor's license and any proof of bond required to such officer or employee of the municipal corporation as the municipal corporation designates by ordinance.

**HISTORY: 141 v S 247 (Eff 7-9-86); 142 v H 153 (Eff 10-20-87); 149 v S 143. Eff 6-21-2002.**

## § 311.41 Criminal records and incompetency checks of applicants for license to carry concealed handgun.

(A)(1) Upon receipt of an application for a license to carry a concealed handgun under division (C) of section 2923.125 [2923.12.5] of the Revised Code, an application to renew a license to carry a concealed handgun under division (F) of that section, or an application for a temporary emergency license to carry a concealed handgun under section 2923.1213 [2923.12.13] of the Revised Code, the sheriff shall conduct a criminal records check and an incompetency check of the applicant to determine whether the applicant fails to meet the criteria described in division (D)(1) of section 2923.125 [2923.12.5] of the Revised Code. The sheriff shall conduct the criminal records check and the incompetency records check required by this division through use of an electronic fingerprint reading device or, if the sheriff does not possess and does not have ready access to the use of an electronic fingerprint reading device, by requesting the bureau of criminal identification and investigation to conduct the checks as described in this division.

In order to conduct the criminal records check and the incompetency records check, the sheriff shall obtain the fingerprints of at least four fingers of the applicant by using an electronic fingerprint reading device for the purpose of conducting the criminal records check and the incompetency records check or, if the sheriff does not possess and does not have ready access to the use of an electronic fingerprint reading device, shall obtain from the applicant a completed standard fingerprint impression sheet prescribed pursuant to division (C)(2) of section 109.572 [109.57.2] of the Revised Code. The fingerprints so obtained, along with the applicant's social security number, shall be used to conduct the criminal records check and the incompetency records check. If the sheriff does not use an electronic fingerprint reading device to obtain the fingerprints and conduct the records checks, the sheriff shall submit the completed standard fingerprint impression sheet of the applicant, along with the applicant's social security number, to the superintendent of the bureau of criminal identification and investigation and shall request the bureau to conduct the criminal records check and the incompetency records check of the applicant and, if necessary, shall request the superintendent of the bureau to obtain information from the federal bureau of investigation as part of the criminal records check for the applicant. If it is not possible to use an electronic fingerprint reading device to conduct an incompetency records check, the sheriff shall submit the completed standard fingerprint impression sheet of the applicant, along with the applicant's social security number, to the superintendent of the bureau of criminal identification and investigation and shall request the bureau to conduct the incompetency records check. The sheriff shall not retain the applicant's fingerprints as part of the application.

(2) Except as otherwise provided in this division, if at any time the applicant decides not to continue with the application process, the sheriff immediately shall cease any investigation that is being conducted under division (A)(1) of this section. The sheriff shall not cease that investigation if, at the time of the applicant's decision not to continue with the application process, the sheriff had determined from any of the sheriff's investigations that the applicant then was engaged in activity of a criminal nature.

(B) If a criminal records check and an incompetency records check conducted under division (A) of this section do not indicate that the applicant fails to meet the criteria described in division (D)(1) of section 2923.125 [2923.12.5] of the Revised Code, except as otherwise provided in this division, the sheriff shall destroy or cause a designated employee to destroy all records other than the application for a license to carry a concealed handgun, the application to renew a license to carry a concealed handgun, or the affidavit submitted regarding an application for a temporary emergency license to carry a concealed handgun that were made in connection with the criminal records check and incompetency records check within twenty days after conducting the criminal records check and incompetency records check. If an applicant appeals a denial of an application as described in division (D)(2) of section 2923.125 [2923.12.5] of the Revised Code or challenges the results of a criminal records check pursuant to section 2923.127 [2923.12.7] of the Revised Code, records of fingerprints of the applicant shall not be destroyed during the pendency of the appeal or the challenge and review. When an applicant appeals a denial as described in that division, the twenty-day period described in this division commences regarding the fingerprints upon the determination of the appeal. When required as a result of a challenge and review performed pursuant to section 2923.127 [2923.12.7] of the Revised Code, the source the sheriff used in conducting the criminal records check shall destroy or the chief operating officer of the source shall cause an employee of the source designated by the chief to destroy all records other than the application for a license to carry a concealed handgun, the application to renew a license to carry a concealed handgun, or the affidavit submitted regarding an application for a temporary emergency license to carry a concealed handgun that were made in connection with the criminal records check within twenty days after completion of that challenge and review.

(C) If division (B) of this section applies to a particular criminal records check or incompetency records check, no sheriff, employee of a sheriff designated by the sheriff to destroy records under that division, source the sheriff used in conducting the criminal records check or incompetency records check, or employee of the source designated by the chief operating officer of the source to destroy records under that division shall fail to destroy or cause to be destroyed within the applicable twenty-day period specified in that division all records other than the application for a license to carry a concealed handgun, the application to renew a license to carry a concealed handgun, or the affidavit submitted regarding an application for a temporary emergency license to carry a concealed handgun made in connection with the particular criminal records check or incompetency records check.

(D) Whoever violates division (C) of this section is guilty of failure to destroy records, a misdemeanor of the second degree.

(E) As used in this section, "handgun" has the same meaning as in section 2923.11 of the Revised Code.

**HISTORY: 150 v H 12, § 1, eff. 4-8-04; 151 v H 347, § 1, eff. 3-14-07.**

Governor Taft's veto of HB 347 was overridden by the Ohio General Assembly.

The provisions of § 6, H.B. 12 (150 v —), read as follows:

SECTION 6. In amending sections 1547.69, 2911.21, 2921.13, 2923.12, 2923.121, 2923.123, 2923.13, 2923.16, 2953.32, and 4749.10 of the Revised Code and in enacting sections 109.69, 109.731, 311.41, 311.42, and 2923.124 to 2923.1213 of the Revised Code in this act, the General Assembly hereby declares its intent to recognize both of the following:

(A) The inalienable and fundamental right of an individual to defend the individual's person and the members of the individual's family;

(B) The fact that the right described in division (A) of this section predates the adoption of the United States Constitution, the adoption of the Ohio Constitution, and the enactment of all statutory laws by the General Assembly and may not be infringed by any enactment of the General Assembly.

The provisions of § 7, H.B. 12 (150 v —), read as follows:

SECTION 7. In enacting sections 109.69, 109.731, 311.41, 311.42, and 2923.124 to 2923.1213 of the Revised Code in this act and in amending sections 1547.69, 2911.21, 2921.13, 2923.12, 2923.121, 2923.123, 2923.13, 2923.16, 2953.32, and 4749.10 of the Revised Code in this act relative to licenses to carry a concealed handgun, the General Assembly hereby declares that it is not its intent to declare or otherwise give the impression that, prior to the effective date of this act, an individual did not have an inalienable and fundamental right, or a right under the Ohio Constitution or the United States Constitution, to carry a concealed handgun or other firearm for the defense of the individual's person or a member of the individual's family while engaged in lawful activity. Further, the General Assembly declares that it is not its intent to invalidate any prior convictions for violating any section of the Revised Code or a municipal ordinance prior to the effective date of this act or to prevent the prosecution of any violation committed prior to the effective date of this act.

The provisions of § 9, H.B. 12 (150 v —), read as follows:

SECTION 9. The General Assembly finds that licenses to carry concealed handguns are a matter of statewide concern and wishes to ensure uniformity throughout the state regarding the qualifications for a person to hold a license to carry a concealed handgun and the authority granted to a person holding a license of that nature. It is the intent of the General Assembly in amending sections 1547.69, 2911.21, 2921.13, 2923.12, 2923.121, 2923.123, 2923.16, 2953.32, and 4749.10 and enacting sections 109.69, 109.731, 311.41, 311.42, and 2923.124 to 2923.1213 of the Revised Code to enact laws of a general nature, and, by enacting those laws of a general nature, the state occupies and preempts the field of issuing licenses to carry a concealed handgun and the validity of licenses of that nature. No municipal corporation may adopt or continue in existence any ordinance, and no township may adopt or continue in existence any resolution, that is in conflict with those sections, including, but not limited to, any ordinance or resolution that attempts to restrict the places where a person possessing a valid license to carry a concealed handgun may carry a handgun concealed.

The provisions of § 10, H.B. 12 (150 v —), read as follows:

SECTION 10. If any provision of sections 1547.69, 2911.21, 2913.02, 2921.13, 2923.12, 2923.121, 2923.123, 2923.16, 2929.14, 2953.32, and 4749.10 of the Revised Code, as amended by this act, any provision of sections 109.69, 109.731, 311.41, 311.42, 2923.124, 2923.125, 2923.126, 2923.127, 2923.128, 2923.129, 2923.1210, 2923.1211, and 2923.1213 of the Revised Code, as enacted by this act, or the application of any provision of those sections to any person or circumstance is held invalid, the invalidity does not affect other provisions or applications of the particular section or related sections that can be given effect without the invalid provision or application, and to this end the provisions of the particular section are severable.

## § 311.42 Sheriff's concealed handgun license issuance expense fund.

(A) Each county shall establish in the county treasury a sheriff's concealed handgun license issuance expense fund. The sheriff of that county shall deposit into that fund all fees paid by applicants for the issuance or renewal of a license or duplicate license to carry a concealed handgun under section 2923.125 [2923.12.5] of the Revised Code and all fees paid by the person seeking a temporary emergency license to carry a concealed handgun under section 2923.1213 [2923.12.13] of the Revised Code. The county shall distribute all fees deposited into the fund except forty dollars of each fee paid by an applicant under division (B) of section 2923.125 [2923.12.5] of the Revised Code, fifteen dollars of each fee paid under section 2923.1213 [2923.12.13] of the Revised Code, and thirty-five dollars of each fee paid under division (F) of section 2923.125 [2923.12.5] of the Revised Code to the attorney general to be used to pay the cost of background checks performed by the bureau of criminal identification and investigation and the federal bureau of investigation and to cover administrative costs associated with issuing the license.

(B) The sheriff, with the approval of the board of county commissioners, may expend any county portion of the fees deposited into the sheriff's concealed handgun license issuance expense fund for any costs incurred by the sheriff in connection with performing any administrative functions related to the issuance of licenses or temporary emergency licenses to carry a concealed handgun under section 2923.125 [2923.12.5] or 2923.1213 [2923.12.13] of the Revised Code, including, but not limited to, personnel expenses and the costs of any handgun safety education program that the sheriff chooses to fund.

**HISTORY: 150 v H 12, § 1, eff. 4-8-04; 153 v H 1, § 101.01, eff. 10-16-09.**

The effective date is set by § 812.10 of 153 v H 1.

See the provisions of H.B. 12 following § 311.41.

## § 311.99 Penalties.

(A) Whoever violates section 311.13 of the Revised Code shall be fined not more than one thousand dollars and imprisoned in the county jail not less than thirty days or more than two years.

(B) Whoever violates division (A) or (C) of section 311.37 of the Revised Code is guilty of failure to file a transient vendor's information or bond, a minor misdemeanor. If the offender previously has been convicted of a violation of division (A) of section 311.37 of the Revised Code, failure to file a transient vendor's information or bond is a misdemeanor of the second degree. If the offender previously has been convicted of two or more violations of division (A) of section 311.37 of the Revised Code, failure to file a transient vendor's information or bond is a misdemeanor of the first degree. A sheriff or police officer in a municipal corporation may enforce this division. The prosecuting attorney of a county shall inform the tax commissioner of any instance when a complaint is brought against a transient vendor pursuant to this division.

**HISTORY: Bureau of Code Revision, 10-1-53; 133 v H 625 (Eff 11-21-69); 133 v H 926 (Eff 7-14-70); 134 v H 24 (Eff 10-6-71); 141 v S 247 (Eff 7-9-86); 141 v H 683 (Eff 3-11-87); 146 v S 2 (Eff 7-1-96); 149 v S 143. Eff 6-21-2002.**

# CHAPTER 313: CORONER

Section



## § 313.09 Records.

The coroner shall keep a complete record of and shall fill in the cause of death on the death certificate, in all cases coming under his jurisdiction. All records shall be kept in the office of the coroner, but, if no such office is maintained, then such records shall be kept in the office of the clerk of the court of common pleas. Such records shall be properly indexed, and shall state the name, if known, of every deceased person as described in section 313.12 of the Revised Code, the place where the body was found, date of death, cause of death, and all other available information. The report of the coroner and the detailed findings of the autopsy shall be attached to the report of each case. The coroner shall promptly deliver, to the prosecuting attorney of the county in which such death occurred, copies of all necessary records relating to every death in which, in the judgment of the coroner or prosecuting attorney, further investigation is advisable. The sheriff of the county, the police of the city, the constable of the township, or marshal of the village in which the death occurred may be requested to furnish more information or make further investigation when requested by the coroner or his deputy. The prosecuting attorney may obtain copies of records and such other information as is necessary from the office of the coroner. All records of the coroner are the property of the county.

**HISTORY: GC § 2855-10; 121 v 591; Bureau of Code Revision, 10-1-53; 136 v H 750. Eff 8-26-75.**

## § 313.091 Request for decedent's medical and psychiatric records.

In connection with the performance of duties under this chapter, a coroner, deputy coroner, or representative of a coroner or deputy coroner may request, in writing, to inspect and receive a copy of the deceased person's medical and psychiatric records. The person to whom the request is delivered shall make such records in the person's custody available during normal business hours to the coroner, deputy coroner, or representative for purposes of inspection and copying. A person who provides copies of medical or psychiatric records pursuant to a request made under this section may request, in writing, reimbursement in a specified amount for the necessary and reasonable costs of copying the records, in which case the coroner, deputy coroner, or representative shall remit that amount to the person upon receipt of the copies.

Any medical or psychiatric record provided to a coroner, deputy coroner, or representative of a coroner or deputy coroner under this section is not a public record subject to section 149.43 of the Revised Code. The release of a deceased person's medical or psychiatric records to a coroner, deputy coroner, or representative of a coroner or deputy coroner in accordance with this section does not violate division (B)(4) of section 4731.22 or section 5122.31 of the Revised Code.

As used in this section and section 313.10 of the Revised Code, "medical record" has the same meaning as in division (A)(3) of section 149.43 of the Revised Code.

**HISTORY: 148 v H 499 (Eff 2-13-2001); 149 v H 94. Eff 9-5-2001.**

The effective date is set by section 204 of HB 94.

## § 313.10 Records to be public; certified copies as evidence; exceptions; request by next of kin of decedent, journalist, or insurer.

(A)(1) Except as otherwise provided in this section, the records of the coroner who has jurisdiction over the case, including, but not limited to, the detailed descriptions of the observations written during the progress of an autopsy and the conclusions drawn from those observations filed in the office of the coroner under division (A) of section 313.13 of the Revised Code, made personally by the coroner or by anyone acting under the coroner's direction or supervision, are public records. Those records, or transcripts or photostatic copies of them, certified by the coroner shall be received as evidence in any criminal or civil action or proceeding in a court in this state, as to the facts contained in those records. The coroner of the county where the death was pronounced shall be responsible for the release of all public records relating to that death.

(2) Except as otherwise provided in division (D) or (E) of this section, the following records in a coroner's office are not public records:

(a) Preliminary autopsy and investigative notes and findings made by the coroner or by anyone acting under the coroner's direction or supervision;

(b) Photographs of a decedent made by the coroner or by anyone acting under the coroner's direction or supervision;

(c) Suicide notes;

(d) Medical and psychiatric records provided to the coroner, a deputy coroner, or a representative of the coroner or a deputy coroner under section 313.091 [313.09.1] of the Revised Code;

(e) Records of a deceased individual that are confidential law enforcement investigatory records as defined in section 149.43 of the Revised Code;

(f) Laboratory reports generated from the analysis of physical evidence by the coroner's laboratory that is discoverable under Criminal Rule 16.

(3) In the coroner's discretion, photographs of a decedent may be used for medical, legal, or educational purposes.

(B) All records in the coroner's office that are public records are open to inspection by the public, and any person may receive a copy of any such record or part of it upon demand in writing, accompanied by payment of a record retrieval and copying fee, at the rate of twenty-five cents per page or a minimum fee of one dollar.

(C)(1) The coroner shall provide a copy of the full and complete records of the coroner with respect to a decedent to a person who makes a written request as the next of kin of the decedent. The following persons may make a request pursuant to this division as the next of kin of a decedent:

(a) The surviving spouse of the decedent;

(b) If there is no surviving spouse, or if the surviving spouse has died without having made a request pursuant to this division, any child of the decedent over eighteen years of age, with each child over eighteen years of age having an independent right to make a request pursuant to this division;

(c) If there is no surviving spouse or child over eighteen years of age, or if the surviving spouse and all children over eighteen years of age have died without having made a request pursuant to this division, the parents of the decedent, with each parent having an independent right to make a request pursuant to this division;

(d) If there is no surviving spouse, child over eighteen years of age, or parents of the decedent, or if all have died without having made a request pursuant to this division, the brothers and sisters of the decedent, whether of the whole or the half blood, with each having an independent right to make a request pursuant to this division.

(2) If there is no surviving person who may make a written request as next of kin for a copy of the full and complete records of the coroner pursuant to division (C)(1) of this section, or if all next of kin of the decedent have died without having made a request pursuant to that division, the coroner shall provide a copy of the full and complete records of the coroner with respect to a decedent to the representative of the estate of the decedent who is the subject of the records upon written request made by the representative.

(D) A journalist may submit to the coroner a written request to view preliminary autopsy and investigative notes and findings, suicide notes, or photographs of the decedent made by the coroner or by anyone acting under the coroner's discretion or supervision. The request shall include the journalist's name and title and the name and address of the journalist's employer and state that the granting of the request would be in the best interest of the public. If a journalist submits a written request to the coroner to view the records described in this division, the coroner shall grant the journalist's request. The journalist shall not copy the preliminary autopsy and investigative notes and findings, suicide notes, or photographs of the decedent.

(E)(1) An insurer may submit to the coroner a written request to obtain a copy of the full and complete records of the coroner with respect to a deceased person. The request shall include the name of the deceased person, the type of policy to which the written request relates, and the name and address of the insurer.

(2) If an insurer submits a written request to the coroner to obtain a copy of records pursuant to division (E)(1) of this section, the coroner shall grant that request.

(3) Upon the granting of a written request to obtain a copy of records by the coroner, the insurer may utilize the records for the following purposes:

(a) To investigate any first party claim or third party claim asserted under a policy of insurance issued by the insurer that arises from the death of the deceased person;

(b) To determine coverage for any first party claim or third party claim asserted under a policy of insurance issued by the insurer that arises from the death of the deceased person;

(c) To determine the insurer's liability for any first party claim or third party claim asserted under a policy of insurance issued by the insurer that arises from the death of the deceased person.

(4) Prior to the delivery of records that are the subject of a request made pursuant to division (E)(1) of this section, the coroner may require the insurer who submitted the written request for the records to provide a payment to the coroner of a record retrieval and copying fee at the rate of twenty-five cents per page or a minimum fee of one dollar.

(5) Any records produced by the coroner in response to a written request under division (E)(1) of this section shall remain in the care, custody, and control of the insurer and its employees or representatives at all times. The insurer may not release or disclose the records to any other person unless any of the following apply:

(a) The release of the records is reasonably necessary to further a purpose described in division (E)(3) of this section.

(b) A court of competent jurisdiction orders the insurer to produce the records.

(c) The insurer is required to produce the records in response to a civil or criminal subpoena.

(d) The insurer is responding to a request for the records from a law enforcement agency, the department of insurance or a department of insurance from another state, or another governmental authority.

(F) The coroner may contact the decedent's next of kin to inform the next of kin that a journalist or an insurer has submitted a written request pursuant to division (D) or (E) of this section and whether the coroner has granted the journalist's or the insurer's request.

(G) As used in this section:

(1) "Full and complete records of the coroner" includes, but is not limited to, the following:

(a) The detailed descriptions of the observations written by the coroner or by anyone acting under the coroner's direction or supervision during the progress of an autopsy and the conclusions drawn from those observations that are filed in the office of the coroner under division (A) of section 313.13 of the Revised Code;

(b) Preliminary autopsy and investigative notes and findings made by the coroner or by anyone acting under the coroner's direction or supervision;

(c) Photographs of a decedent made by the coroner or by anyone acting under the coroner's direction or supervision;

(d) Suicide notes;

(e) Medical and psychiatric records provided to the coroner, a deputy coroner, or a representative of the coroner or a deputy coroner under section 313.091 [313.09.1] of the Revised Code;

(f) Records of a deceased individual that are confidential law enforcement investigatory records as defined in section 149.43 of the Revised Code;

(g) Laboratory reports generated from the analysis of physical evidence by the coroner's laboratory that is discoverable under Criminal Rule 16.

(2) "Insurer" has the same meaning as in section 3901.07 of the Revised Code.

(3) "Journalist" has the same meaning as in section 149.43 of the Revised Code.

**HISTORY: GC § 2855-11; 121 v 591; Bureau of Code Revision, 10-1-53; 148 v H 499. Eff 2-13-2001; 151 v H 235, § 1, eff. 8-17-06; 152 v H 471, § 1, eff. 4-7-09.**

## § 313.11 Removal or disturbing of body or effects prohibited.

(A) No person, without an order from the coroner, any deputy coroner, or an investigator or other person designated by the coroner as having authority to issue an order under this section, shall purposely remove or disturb the body of any person who has died in the manner described in section 313.12 of the Revised Code, or purposely and without such an order disturb the clothing or any article upon or near such a body or any of the possessions that the coroner has a duty to store under section 313.14 of the Revised Code.

(B) It is an affirmative defense to a charge under this section that the offender attempted in good faith to rescue or administer life-preserving assistance to the deceased person, even though it is established he was dead at the time of the attempted rescue or assistance.

(C) Whoever violates this section is guilty of unlawfully disturbing a body, a misdemeanor of the fourth degree.

**HISTORY: 136 v H 750 (Eff 8-26-75); 139 v H 55 (Eff 8-19-82); 143 v H 639. Eff 9-26-90.**

**Analogous to former RC § 313.11 (121 v 591; Bureau of Code Revision, 10-1-53), repealed 134 v H 511, eff 1-1-74.**

## § 313.12 Notice to coroner of violent, suspicious, unusual or sudden death or any death of a mentally retarded or developmentally disabled person.

(A) When any person dies as a result of criminal or other violent means, by casualty, by suicide, or in any suspicious or unusual manner, when any person, including a child under two years of age, dies suddenly when in apparent good health, or when any mentally retarded person or developmentally disabled person dies regardless of the circumstances, the physician called in attendance, or any member of an ambulance service, emergency squad, or law enforcement agency who obtains knowledge thereof arising from the person's duties, shall immediately notify the office of the coroner of the known facts concerning the time, place, manner, and circumstances of the death, and any other information that is required pursuant to sections 313.01 to 313.22 of the Revised Code. In such cases, if a request is made for cremation, the funeral director called in attendance shall immediately notify the coroner.

(B) As used in this section, "mentally retarded person" and "developmentally disabled person" have the same meanings as in section 5123.01 of the Revised Code.

**HISTORY: GC § 2855-5; 121 v 591; Bureau of Code Revision, 10-1-53; 136 v H 750 (Eff 8-26-75); 144 v H 244. Eff 11-1-92; 150 v S 178, § 1, eff. 1-30-04.**

The effective date is set by section 4 of HB 244.

## § 313.121 Death of apparently healthy child under age of two to be reported; autopsy; supportive services for parents; information on sudden infant death syndrome.

(A) As used in this section, "parent" means either parent, except that if one parent has been designated the residential parent and legal custodian of the child, "parent" means the designated residential parent and legal custodian, and if a person other than a parent is the child's legal guardian, "parent" means the legal guardian.

(B) If a child under two years of age dies suddenly when in apparent good health, the death shall be reported immediately to the coroner of the county in which the death occurred, as required by section 313.12 of the Revised Code. Except as provided in division (C) of this section, the coroner or deputy coroner shall perform an autopsy on the child. The autopsy shall be performed in accordance with public health council rules adopted under section 313.122 [313.12.2] of the Revised Code. The coroner or deputy coroner may perform research procedures and tests when performing the autopsy.

(C) A coroner or deputy coroner is not required to perform an autopsy if the coroner of the county in which the death occurred or a court with jurisdiction over the deceased body determines under section 313.131 [313.13.1] of the Revised Code that an autopsy is contrary to the religious beliefs of the child. If the coroner or the court makes such a determination, the coroner shall notify the health district or department of health with jurisdiction in the area in which the child's parent resides. For purposes of this division, the religious beliefs of the parents of a child shall be considered to be the religious beliefs of the child.

(D) If the child's parent makes a written or verbal request for the preliminary results of the autopsy after the results are available, the coroner, or a person designated by him, shall give the parent an oral statement of the preliminary results.

The coroner, within a reasonable time after the final results of the autopsy are reported, shall send written notice of the results to the state department of health, the health district or department with jurisdiction in the area in which the child's parent resides, and, upon the request of a parent of the child, to the child's attending physician. Upon the written request of a parent of the child and the payment of the transcript fee required by section 313.10 of the Revised Code, the coroner shall send written notice of the final results to that parent. The notice sent to the state department of health shall include all of the information specified by rule of the public health council adopted under section 313.122 [313.12.2] of the Revised Code.

(E) On the occurrence of any of the following, the health district or department with jurisdiction in the area in which the child's parent resides shall offer the parent any counseling or other supportive services it has available:

(1) When it learns through any source that an autopsy is being performed on a child under two years of age who died suddenly when in apparent good health;

(2) When it receives notice that the final result of an autopsy performed pursuant to this section concluded that the child died of sudden infant death syndrome;

(3) When it is notified by the coroner that, pursuant to division (C) of this section, an autopsy was not performed.

(F) When a health district or department receives notice that the final result of an autopsy performed pursuant to this section concluded that the child died of sudden infant death syndrome or that, pursuant to division (C) of this section, an autopsy was not performed but sudden infant death syndrome may have been the cause of death, it shall offer the child's parent information about sudden infant death syndrome. The state department of health shall ensure that current information on sudden infant death syndrome is available for distribution by health districts and departments.

**HISTORY: 144 v H 244. Eff 11-1-92.**

The effective date is set by section 4 of HB 244.

## § 313.122 Protocol for autopsies after sudden infant death.

The public health council, after reviewing and considering any recommendations made by the Ohio state coroners association, shall adopt rules in accordance with Chapter 119. of the Revised Code establishing a protocol governing the performance of autopsies under section 313.121 [313.12.1] of the Revised Code. The rules shall specify the information derived from an autopsy that a coroner is required to report to the state department of health. The public health council shall not amend the rules adopted under this section unless it notifies the Ohio state coroners association of the proposed changes and consults with the association.

**HISTORY: 144 v H 244. Eff 11-1-92.**

The effective date is set by section 4 of HB 244.

## § 313.123 Autopsy defined; disposal of medical waste; autopsy contrary to decedent's religious beliefs; retention of DNA specimens; immunity of employee.

(A)(1) As used in this chapter, "autopsy" means the external and internal examination of the body of a deceased person, including, but not limited to, gross visual inspection and dissection of the body and its internal organs, photographic or narrative documentation of findings, microscopic, radiological, toxicological, chemical, or other laboratory analyses performed in the discretion of the examining individual upon tissues, organs, blood, other bodily fluids, gases, or any other specimens and the retention for diagnostic and documentary purposes of tissues, organs, blood, other bodily fluids, gases, or any other specimens as the examining individual considers necessary to establish and defend against challenges to the cause and manner of death of the deceased person.

(2) As used in this section, "DNA specimen" has the same meaning as in section 109.573 [109.57.3] of the Revised Code.

(B)(1) Except as otherwise provided in division (B)(2) of this section, retained tissues, organs, blood, other bodily fluids, gases, or any other specimens from an autopsy are medical waste and shall be disposed of in accordance with applicable federal and state laws, including any protocol rules adopted under section 313.122 [313.12.2] of the Revised Code.

(2) If an autopsy is performed on a deceased person and pursuant to section 313.131 [313.13.1] of the Revised Code the coroner has reason to believe that the autopsy is contrary to the deceased person's religious beliefs, the coroner shall not remove any specimens, including, but not limited to, tissues, organs, blood, or other bodily fluids, from the body of the deceased person unless removing those specimens from the body of the deceased person is a compelling public necessity. Except as otherwise provided in division (B)(3) of this section, if the coroner removes any specimens from the body of the deceased person, the coroner shall return the specimens, as soon as is practicable, to the person who has the right to the disposition of the body.

(3) The coroner may retain a DNA specimen for diagnostic, evidentiary, or confirmatory purposes.

(C) A cause of action shall not lie against any employee of a coroner's office for requesting, ordering, or performing an autopsy in good faith under the authority of this chapter.

**HISTORY: 151 v H 235, § 1, eff. 8-17-06.**

## § 313.13 Autopsy; blood test of decedent killed in motor vehicle accident.

(A) The coroner, any deputy coroner, an investigator appointed pursuant to section 313.05 of the Revised Code, or any other person the coroner designates as having the authority to act under this section may go to the dead body and take charge of it. Whether and when an autopsy is performed shall be determined under sections 313.121 [313.12.1] and 313.131 [313.13.1] of the Revised Code. If an autopsy is performed by the coroner, deputy coroner, or pathologists, a detailed description of the observations written during the progress of such autopsy, or as soon after such autopsy as reasonably possible, and the conclusions drawn from the observations shall be filed in the office of the coroner.

(B) If the office of the coroner is notified that a person who was the operator of a motor vehicle that was involved in an accident or crash was killed in the accident or crash or died as a result of injuries suffered in it, the coroner, deputy coroner, or pathologist shall go to the dead body and take charge of it and administer a chemical test to the blood of the deceased person to determine the alcohol, drug, or alcohol and drug content of the blood. This division does not authorize the coroner, deputy coroner, or pathologist to perform an autopsy, and does not affect and shall not be construed as affecting the provisions of section 313.131 [313.13.1] of the Revised Code that govern the determination of whether and when an autopsy is to be performed.

**HISTORY: GC § 2855-6; 121 v 591; Bureau of Code Revision, 10-1-53; 136 v H 1182 (Eff 5-4-76); 141 v S 283 (Eff 3-25-87); 143 v S 131 (Eff 7-25-90); 143 v H 639 (Eff 9-26-90); 144 v H 244. Eff 11-1-92; 152 v H 529, § 1, eff. 4-7-09.**

The effective date is set by section 4 of HB 244.

## § 313.131 Procedure when autopsy is contrary to decedent's religious belief.

(A) As used in this section:

(1) "Friend" means any person who maintained regular contact with the deceased person, and who was familiar with the deceased person's activities, health, and religious beliefs at the time of the deceased person's death, any person who assumes custody of the body for burial, and any person authorized by written instrument, executed by the deceased person to make burial arrangements.

(2) "Relative" means any of the following persons: the deceased person's surviving spouse, children, parents, or siblings.

(B) The coroner, deputy coroner, or pathologist shall perform an autopsy if, in the opinion of the coroner, or, in his absence, in the opinion of the deputy coroner, an autopsy is necessary, except for certain circumstances provided for in this section where a relative or friend of the deceased person informs the coroner that an autopsy is contrary to the deceased person's religious beliefs, or the coroner otherwise has reason to believe that an autopsy is contrary to the deceased person's religious beliefs. The coroner has such reason to believe an autopsy is contrary to the deceased person's religious beliefs if a document signed by the deceased and stating an objection to an autopsy is found on the deceased's person or in his effects. For the purposes of this division, a person is a relative or friend of the deceased person if the person presents an affidavit stating that he is a relative or friend as defined in division (A) of this section.

(C)(1) Except as provided in division (F) of this section, if a relative or friend of the deceased person informs the coroner that an autopsy is contrary to the deceased person's religious beliefs, or the coroner otherwise has reason to believe that an autopsy is contrary to the deceased person's religious beliefs, and the coroner concludes the autopsy is a compelling public necessity, no autopsy shall be performed for forty-eight hours after the coroner takes charge of the deceased person. An autopsy is a compelling public necessity if it is necessary to the conduct of an investigation by law enforcement officials of a homicide or suspected homicide, or any other criminal investigation, or is necessary to establish the cause of the deceased person's death for the purpose of protecting against an immediate and substantial threat to the public health. During the forty-eight hour period, the objecting relative or friend may file suit to enjoin the autopsy, and shall give notice of any such filing to the coroner. The coroner may seek an order waiving the forty-eight hour waiting period. If the coroner seeks such an order, the court shall give notice of the coroner's motion, by telephone if necessary, to the objecting relative or friend, or, if none objected, to all of the deceased person's relatives whose addresses or telephone numbers can be obtained through the exercise of reasonable diligence. The court may grant the coroner's motion if the court determines that no friend or relative of the deceased person objects to the autopsy or if the court is satisfied that any objections of a friend or relative have been heard, and if it also determines that the delay may prejudice the accuracy of the autopsy, or if law enforcement officials are investigating the deceased person's death as a homicide and suspect the objecting party committed the homicide or aided or abetted in the homicide. If no friend or relative files suit within the forty-eight hour period, the coroner may proceed with the autopsy.

(2) The court shall hear a petition to enjoin an autopsy within forty-eight hours after the filing of the petition. The Rules of Civil Procedure shall govern all aspects of the proceedings, except as otherwise provided in division (C)(2) of this section. The court is not bound by the Rules of Evidence in the conduct of the hearing. The court shall order the autopsy if the court finds that under the circumstances the coroner has demonstrated a need for the autopsy. If the court enjoins the autopsy, the coroner shall immediately proceed under section 313.14 of the Revised Code.

(D)(1) If a relative or friend of the decedent informs the coroner that an autopsy is contrary to the deceased person's religious beliefs, or the coroner otherwise has reason to believe that an autopsy is contrary to the deceased person's religious beliefs, and the coroner concludes the autopsy is necessary, but not a compelling public necessity, the coroner may file a petition in a court of common pleas seeking a declaratory judgment authorizing the autopsy. Upon the filing of the petition, the court shall schedule a hearing on the petition, and shall issue a summons to the objecting relative or friend, or, if none objected, to all of the deceased person's relatives whose addresses can be obtained through the exercise of reasonable diligence. The court shall hold the hearing no later than forty-eight hours after the filing of the petition. The court shall conduct the hearing in the manner provided in division (C)(2) of this section.

(2) Each person claiming to be a relative or friend of the deceased person shall immediately upon receipt of the summons file an affidavit with the court stating the facts upon which the claim is based. If the court finds that any person is falsely representing himself as a relative or friend of the deceased person, the court shall dismiss the person from the action. If after dismissal no objecting party remains, and the coroner does not have reason to believe that an autopsy is contrary to the deceased person's religious beliefs, the court shall dismiss the action and the coroner may proceed with the autopsy. The court shall order the autopsy after hearing the petition if the court finds that under the circumstances the coroner has demonstrated a need for the autopsy. The court shall waive the payment of all court costs in the action. If the petition is denied, the coroner shall immediately proceed under section 313.14 of the Revised Code.

Any autopsy performed pursuant to a court order granting an autopsy shall be performed using the least intrusive procedure.

(E) For purposes of divisions (B), (C)(1), and (D)(1) of this section, any time the friends or relatives of a deceased person disagree about whether an autopsy is contrary to the deceased person's religious beliefs, the coroner shall consider only the information provided to him by the person of highest priority, as determined by which is listed first among the following:

(1) The deceased person's surviving spouse;

(2) An adult son or daughter of the deceased person;

(3) Either parent of the deceased person;

(4) An adult brother or sister of the deceased person;

(5) The guardian of the person of the deceased person at the time of death;

(6) A person other than those listed in divisions (E)(1) to (5) of this section who is a friend as defined in division (A)[(1)] of this section.

If two or more persons of equal priority disagree about whether an autopsy is contrary to the deceased person's religious beliefs, and those persons are also of the highest priority among those who provide the coroner with information the coroner has reason to believe that an autopsy is contrary to the deceased person's religious beliefs.

(F)(1) Divisions (C)(1) and (2) of this section do not apply in any case involving aggravated murder, suspected aggravated murder, murder, suspected murder, manslaughter offenses, or suspected manslaughter offenses.

(2) This section does not prohibit the coroner, deputy coroner, or pathologist from administering a chemical test to the blood of a deceased person to determine the alcohol, drug, or alcohol and drug content of the blood, when required by division (B) of section 313.13 of the Revised Code, and does not limit the coroner, deputy coroner, or pathologist in the performance of his duties in administering a chemical test under that division.

**HISTORY: 141 v S 283 (Eff 3-25-87); 143 v S 131. Eff 7-25-90.**

## § 313.14 Notice to relatives; disposition of property.

The coroner shall notify any known relatives of a deceased person who meets death in the manner described by section 313.12 of the Revised Code by letter or otherwise. The next of kin, other relatives, or friends of the deceased person, in the order named, shall have prior right as to disposition of the body of such deceased person. If relatives of the deceased are unknown, the coroner shall make a diligent effort to ascertain the next of kin, other relatives, or friends of the deceased person. The coroner shall take charge and possession of all moneys, clothing, and other valuable personal effects of such deceased person, found in connection with or pertaining to such body, and shall store such possessions in the county coroner's office or such other suitable place as is provided for such storage by the board of county commissioners. If the coroner considers it advisable, he may[,] after taking adequate precautions for the security of such possessions, store the possessions where he finds them until other storage space becomes available. After using such of the clothing as is necessary in the burial of the body, in case the cost of the burial is paid by the county, the coroner shall sell at public auction the valuable personal effects of such deceased persons, found in connection with or pertaining to the unclaimed dead body, except firearms, which shall be disposed of as provided by section 313.141 [313.14.1] of the Revised Code, and he shall make a verified inventory of such effects. Such effects shall be sold within eighteen months after burial, or after delivery of such body in accordance with section 1713.34 of the Revised Code. All moneys derived from such sale shall be deposited in the county treasury. A notice of such sale shall be given in one newspaper of general circulation in the county, for five days in succession, and the sale shall be held immediately thereafter. The cost of such advertisement and notices shall be paid by the board upon the submission of a verified statement therefor, certified to the coroner.

This section does not invalidate section 1713.34 of the Revised Code.

**HISTORY: GC § 2855-13; 121 v 591; 123 v 766; Bureau of Code Revision, 10-1-53; 136 v H 750 (Eff 8-26-75); 136 v H 1182 (Eff 8-1-76); 139 v H 55. Eff 8-19-82.**

## § 313.141 Firearms in personal effects of deceased person.

If firearms are included in the valuable personal effects of a deceased person who met death in the manner described by section 313.12 of the Revised Code, the coroner shall deliver the firearms to the chief of police of the municipal corporation within which the body is found, or to the sheriff of the county if the body is not found within a municipal corporation. The firearms shall be used for law enforcement purposes only or they shall be destroyed. Upon delivery of the firearms to the chief of police or the sheriff, the law enforcement officer to whom the delivery is made shall give the coroner a receipt for the firearms that states the date of delivery and an accurate description of the firearms.

**HISTORY: 136 v H 1182. Eff 8-1-76.**

## § 313.15 Determination of responsibility for death.

All dead bodies in the custody of the coroner shall be held until such time as the coroner, after consultation with the prosecuting attorney, or with the police department of a municipal corporation, if the death occurred in a municipal corporation, or with the sheriff, has decided that it is no longer necessary to hold such body to enable him to decide on a diagnosis giving a reasonable and true cause of death, or to decide that such body is no longer necessary to assist any of such officials in his duties.

**HISTORY: GC § 2855-14; 121 v 591; Bureau of Code Revision. Eff 10-1-53.**

## § 313.17 Subpoenas; oath and testimony of witnesses.

The coroner or deputy coroner may issue subpoenas for such witnesses as are necessary, administer to such witnesses the usual oath, and proceed to inquire how the deceased came to his death, whether by violence to self or from any other persons, by whom, whether as principals or accessories before or after the fact, and all circumstances relating thereto. The testimony of such witnesses shall be reduced to writing and subscribed to by them, and with the findings and recognizances mentioned in this section, shall be kept on file in the coroner's office, unless the county fails to provide such an office, in which event all such records, findings and recognizances shall be kept on file in the office of the clerk of the court of common pleas. The coroner may cause such witnesses to enter into recognizance, in such sum as is proper, for their appearance to give testimony concerning the matter. He may require any such witnesses to give security for their attendance, and, if any of them fails to comply with his requirements he shall commit such person to the county jail until discharged by due course of law. In case of the failure of any person to comply with such subpoena, or on the refusal of a witness to testify to any matter regarding which he may lawfully be interrogated, the probate judge, or a judge of the court of common pleas, on application of the coroner, shall compel obedience to such subpoena by attachment proceedings as for contempt. A report shall be made from the personal observation by the coroner or his deputy of the corpse, from the statements of relatives or other persons having any knowledge of the facts, and from such other sources of information as are available, or from the autopsy.

**HISTORY: GC § 2855-7; 121 v 591; 123 v 769; Bureau of Code Revision, 10-1-53; 136 v H 390. Eff 8-6-76.**

## § 313.18 Disinterment of body.

The prosecuting attorney or coroner may order the disinterment of any dead body, under the direction and supervision of the coroner, and may authorize the removal of such body by the coroner to the quarters established for the use of such coroner, for the purpose of examination and autopsy.

**HISTORY: GC § 2855-8; 121 v 591; Bureau of Code Revision. Eff 10-1-53.**

## § 313.19 Coroner's verdict the legally accepted cause of death.

The cause of death and the manner and mode in which the death occurred, as delivered by the coroner and incorporated in the coroner's verdict and in the death certificate filed with the division of vital statistics, shall be the legally accepted manner and mode in which such death occurred, and the legally accepted cause of death, unless the court of common pleas of the county in which the death occurred, after a hearing, directs the coroner to change his decision as to such cause and manner and mode of death.

**HISTORY: GC § 2855-16; 121 v 591; Bureau of Code Revision. Eff 10-1-53.**

## § 313.20 Coroner's writs.

The coroner may issue any writ required by sections 313.01 to 313.22, of the Revised Code, to any constable of the county in which a body is found as described in section 313.12 of the Revised Code, or if the emergency so requires, to any discreet person of the county, and such person is entitled to receive for the services rendered the same fees as elected constables. Every constable, or other person so appointed, who fails to execute any warrant directed to him, shall forfeit and pay twenty-five dollars, which amount shall be recovered upon the complaint of the coroner, before any court having jurisdiction thereof. All such forfeitures shall be for the use of the county.

**HISTORY: RS § 1223; 75 v 570, § 11; GC § 2858; 106 v 448; Bureau of Code Revision, 10-1-53; 136 v H 750. Eff 8-26-75.**

## § 313.21 Testing for suspected toxic substances or for law enforcement purposes; records.

(A) The coroner may use or may allow the use of the coroner's laboratory and facilities for tests in an emergency involving suspected toxic substances or for law enforcement-related testing, and may direct his assistants and other personnel to perform such testing in addition to testing performed in execution of their duties as set forth in sections 313.01 to 313.22 of the Revised Code. Nothing in this division shall permit such testing except in compliance with state and federal quality assurance requirements for medical laboratories.

(B) The coroner shall keep a complete record of all chemical tests and other tests performed each fiscal year pursuant to division (A) of this section, the public agency, hospital, or person for whom the test was performed, and the cost incurred for each test. This record shall be kept in the office of the coroner.

**HISTORY: 137 v H 1118 (Eff 3-8-79); 142 v H 499, §§ 1, 3 (Eff 6-30-87); 143 v H 332 (Eff 8-5-89); 144 v S 233. Eff 11-15-91.**

**Somewhat analogous to former RC § 313.21 (Bureau of Code Revision, 10-1-53; 132 v H 1), repealed 134 v H 511, § 2, eff 1-1-74.**

## § 313.211 Disposition of dangerous drugs.

The coroner may secure, catalog, record, and, with the approval of the prosecuting attorney, destroy any dangerous drugs found at the scene of an investigation the coroner conducts, if the dangerous drugs are no longer needed for investigative or scientific purposes.

**HISTORY: 152 v H 471, § 1, eff. 4-7-09.**

## § 313.212 Drug overdose determination of death; coroner.

If the coroner determines that a drug overdose is the cause of death of a person, the coroner may provide a notice of the death to the state medical board. The coroner may include in the notice any information relating to the drug that resulted in the overdose, including the individual authorized under Chapter 4731. of the Revised Code to practice medicine or surgery, osteopathic medicine or surgery, or podiatric medicine or surgery who prescribed the drug to the decedent.

**HISTORY: 2011 HB 93, § 1, eff. May 20, 2011.**

Acts 2011, HB 93, § 8 provides: "(A) Not later than one year after the effective date of this section, and annually each year for four years thereafter, the State Board of Pharmacy shall prepare a report on all of the following:

(A)(1) The total number of applications received by the Board for a terminal distributor of dangerous drugs license with a pain management clinic classification;

(2) The total number of licenses with a pain management clinic classification granted or denied by the Board;

(3) Any disciplinary actions taken by the Board against holders of licenses with a pain management clinic classification;

(4) Total revenues generated from fees for licenses with a pain management clinic classification, fines and penalties paid by license holders, or other disciplinary actions taken against license holders;

(5) Any other relevant information regarding the implementation of this act.

(B) On completion of each report, the Board shall submit a copy of the report to the Governor and, in accordance with section 101.68 of the Revised Code, the General Assembly. In accordance with that section, the Board shall display the report on the Board's internet web site."

## § 313.23 Interested person may view autopsy without permission of next of kin; minors.

(A) As used in this section:

(1) "Interested person" means an employee of the coroner's office, a physician, dentist, nurse, professor at a medical school, medical student, medical resident, nursing student, an employee of a procurement organization, a member of a law enforcement agency, or any other person the coroner, in the coroner's discretion, determines is appropriate.

(2) "Procurement organization" has the same meaning as in section 2108.01 of the Revised Code.

(B) The coroner may allow an interested person to view an autopsy of a decedent without the interested person receiving permission to view the decedent's autopsy from the decedent's next of kin.

(C) No person who is under eighteen years of age and who is not an interested person may view an autopsy.

**HISTORY: 151 v H 235, § 1, eff. 8-17-06; 152 v H 529, § 1, eff. 4-7-09.**

# CHAPTER 341: JAILS

Section



## [DUTIES OF SHERIFFS]

### § 341.01 Sheriff to have charge of jail.

The sheriff shall have charge of the county jail and all persons confined therein. He shall keep such persons safely, attend to the jail, and govern and regulate the jail according to the minimum standards for jails in Ohio promulgated by the department of rehabilitation and correction.

The sheriff's responsibilities under this section do not extend to a jail or workhouse that is the subject of a contract entered into under section 9.06 of the Revised Code.

**HISTORY: RS § 7368; S&S 746; S&C 1398; 29 v 112, § 4; 41 v 74, § 5; GC § 3157; Bureau of Code Revision, 10-1-53; 139 v S 23 (Eff 7-6-82); 146 v H 117. Eff 9-29-95.**

The effective date is set by section 197 of HB 117.

### § 341.011 Duty to give notice of escape and apprehension of escapee.

(A) If a person who was convicted of or pleaded guilty to an offense or was indicted or otherwise charged with the commission of an offense escapes from a county jail or workhouse or otherwise escapes from the custody of a sheriff, the sheriff immediately after the escape shall report the escape, by telephone and in writing, to all local law enforcement agencies with jurisdiction over the place where the person escaped from custody, to the state highway patrol, to the department of rehabilitation and correction if the escaped person is a prisoner under the custody of the department who is in the jail or workhouse, to the prosecuting attorney of the county, and to a newspaper of general circulation in the county. The written notice may be by either facsimile transmission or mail. A failure to comply with this requirement is a violation of section 2921.22 of the Revised Code.

(B) Upon the apprehension of the escaped person, the sheriff shall give notice of the apprehension of the escaped person by telephone and in writing to the persons notified under division (A) of this section.

**HISTORY: 142 v H 207 (Eff 9-24-87); 148 v H 283. Eff 6-30-99.**

The effective date is set by section 164 of HB 283.

### § 341.02 Jail register; operational policies and procedures; prisoner rules of conduct.

The sheriff shall make the following entries in a suitable book, which shall be known as the "jail register," kept in the office of the jailer, and delivered to the successor in office of such jailer:

(A) The name of each prisoner, and the date and cause of his commitment;

(B) The date and manner of his discharge.

The sheriff or jail administrator shall prepare written operational policies and procedures and prisoner rules of conduct, and maintain the records prescribed by these policies and procedures in accordance with the minimum standards for jails in Ohio promulgated by the department of rehabilitation and correction.

The court of common pleas shall review the jail's operational policies and procedures and prisoner rules of conduct. If the court approves the policies, procedures, and rules of conduct, they shall be adopted.

**HISTORY: RS § 7369; S&C 746; 41 v 74, § 6; GC § 3158; Bureau of Code Revision, 10-1-53; 131 v 229 (Eff 9-6-65); 139 v S 23. Eff 7-6-82.**

## § 341.04 Sheriff shall visit jail.

The sheriff shall visit the county jail and examine the condition of each prisoner, at least once during each month.

**HISTORY: RS § 7371; S&C 748; 41 v 74, § 12; GC § 3160; Bureau of Code Revision, 10-1-53; 139 v S 114 (Eff 10-27-81); 139 v S 23. Eff 7-6-82.**

## § 341.05 Assignment, compensation of staff; administrator; civilian officers; female staff.

(A) The sheriff shall assign sufficient staff to ensure the safe and secure operation of the county jail, but staff shall be assigned only to the extent such staff can be provided with funds appropriated to the sheriff at the discretion of the board of county commissioners. The staff may include any of the following:

(1) An administrator for the jail;

(2) Jail officers, including civilian jail officers who are not sheriff's deputies, to conduct security duties;

(3) Other necessary employees to assist in the operation of the county jail.

(B) The sheriff shall employ a sufficient number of female staff to be available to perform all reception and release procedures for female prisoners. These female employees shall be on duty for the duration of the confinement of the female prisoners.

(C) The jail administrator and civilian jail officers appointed by the sheriff shall have all the powers of police officers on the jail grounds as are necessary for the proper performance of the duties relating to their positions at the jail and as are consistent with their level of training.

(D) The sheriff may authorize civilian jail officers to wear a standard uniform consistent with their prescribed authority, in accordance with section 311.281 [311.28.1] of the Revised Code. Civilian jail officer uniforms shall be differentiated clearly from the uniforms worn by sheriff's deputies.

(E) Except as provided in division (B) of section 341.25 of the Revised Code, the compensation of jail staff shall be payable from the general fund of the county, upon the warrant of the auditor, in accordance with standard county payroll procedures.

**HISTORY: RS § 7372; S&C 748; 41 v 74, § 13; GC § 3161; Bureau of Code Revision, 10-1-53; 139 v S 23 (Eff 7-6-82); 146 v H 480. Eff 10-16-96; 150 v H 95, § 1, eff. 9-26-03.**

The effective date is set by section 179 of H.B. 95 (150 v —).

[RULES AND REGULATIONS]

## § 341.06 Repealed, 149 v S 170, § 2 [146 v H 480; 148 v H 349]. Eff 9-6-2002.

This section concerned prisoner reimbursement policy; coordinator; and medical treatment or service. See now RC §§ 2929.35-2929.38.

## § 341.07 Copies of minimum standards for jails; notice of prisoner rules of conduct.

The department of rehabilitation and correction shall provide a copy of the minimum standards for jails in Ohio to the board of county commissioners, the common pleas court, and the sheriff.

The sheriff shall ensure that the prisoner rules of conduct are placed in a conspicuous location within each jail confinement area or are given to each prisoner in written form.

**HISTORY: RS §§ 7375, 7376; S&C 746; 41 v 74, §§ 2, 3; GC §§ 3163, 3164; Bureau of Code Revision, 10-1-53; 139 v S 23. Eff 7-6-82.**

## § 341.08 Minimum standards may be revised, altered or amended.

The department of rehabilitation and correction may, by rule, revise, alter, or amend the minimum standards for jails in Ohio to reflect changes in case law or public policy. Such revised, altered, or amended standards shall be printed and distributed to the board of county commissioners, the court of common pleas, and the sheriff in the manner directed by section 341.07 of the Revised Code.

**HISTORY: RS § 7377; S&C 746; 41 v 74, § 4; GC § 3165; Bureau of Code Revision, 10-1-53; 139 v S 23. Eff 7-6-82.**

## § 341.09 Separation of prisoners in county jails.

When the design of a county jail will permit, the separation of prisoners shall be as required in the minimum standards for jails in Ohio.

The department of rehabilitation and correction shall, when necessary, initiate appropriate judicial proceedings for the enforcement of this section.

**HISTORY: RS §§ 7377-1, 7377-2; 88 v 150, §§ 1, 2; GC §§ 3166, 3167; Bureau of Code Revision, 10-1-53; 139 v S 23. Eff 7-6-82.**

## § 341.10 Separate confinement in new county jails.

County officers having charge of the construction of a new jail shall provide for the separate confinement of prisoners, as required by section 341.09 of the Revised Code.

**HISTORY: RS § 7377-3; 88 v 150, § 3; GC § 3168; Bureau of Code Revision, 10-1-53.**

## § 341.11 Confinement of minors.

Except as provided in division (C) of section 2151.311 [2151.31.1] of the Revised Code, no child taken into custody shall be held in a county, multicounty, or municipal jail or workhouse or other place for the confinement of adults convicted of crime, under arrest, or charged with crime.

Except as provided in division (C) of section 2151.311 [2151.31.1] of the Revised Code, a child confined pursuant to section 2151.311 [2151.31.1] of the Revised Code shall be held in a room or cell totally separate and removed by sight and sound from all adult prisoners.

**HISTORY: RS § 7377-4; 80 v 102; GC § 3169; Bureau of Code Revision, 10-1-53; 139 v S 23 (Eff 7-6-82); 143 v H 166 (Eff 2-14-90); 146 v H 480. Eff 10-16-96.**

## [USE OF OTHER JAILS]

### § 341.12 Confinement of persons in custody in jail of another county.

In a county not having a sufficient jail or staff, the sheriff shall convey any person charged with the commission of an offense, sentenced to imprisonment in the county jail, or in custody upon civil process to a jail in any county the sheriff considers most convenient and secure. As used in this paragraph, any county includes a contiguous county in an adjoining state.

The sheriff may call such aid as is necessary in guarding, transporting, or returning such person. Whoever neglects or refuses to render such aid, when so called upon, shall forfeit and pay the sum of ten dollars, to be recovered by an action in the name and for the use of the county.

Such sheriff and his assistants shall receive such compensation for their services as the county auditor of the county from which such person was removed considers reasonable. The compensation shall be paid from the county treasury on the warrant of the auditor.

The receiving sheriff shall not, pursuant to this section, convey the person received to any county other than the one from which the person was removed.

**HISTORY: RS § 7382; S&C 1399; 29 v 112, § 5; 93 v 131; GC § 3170; Bureau of Code Revision, 10-1-53; 139 v S 23. Eff 7-6-82; 152 v H 215, § 1, eff. 4-7-09; 2011 HB 86, § 1, eff. Sept. 30, 2011.**

### § 341.13 Reception of person conveyed.

The sheriff of a county in this state to which a prisoner has been removed as provided by section 341.12 of the Revised Code shall, on being furnished a copy of the process or commitment, receive the prisoner into custody. The sheriff of a contiguous county of an adjoining state to which a prisoner has been removed as provided in section 341.12 of the Revised Code may, on being furnished a copy of the commitment, receive the prisoner into the sheriff's custody. Each receiving sheriff shall be liable for escapes or other neglect of duty in relation to the prisoner, as in other cases, and neither the conveying sheriff nor any county commissioner of the county that employs the conveying sheriff is liable in damages in a civil action for any injury, death, or loss to person or property suffered or caused by the prisoner while the prisoner is in the custody of the receiving sheriff. Each receiving sheriff shall receive from the treasury of the county from which the prisoner was removed, such fees as are allowed in other cases.

**HISTORY: RS § 7383; S&C 1399; 29 v 112, § 6; GC § 3171; Bureau of Code Revision, 10-1-53; 152 v H 215, § 1, eff. 4-7-09.**

### § 341.14 Advance deposit of prisoner costs; reimbursement by prisoner; testing and treatment for certain diseases.

(A) The sheriff of an adjoining county in this state shall not receive prisoners as provided by section 341.12 of the Revised Code unless there is deposited weekly with the sheriff an amount equal to the actual cost of keeping and feeding each prisoner so committed for the use of the jail of that county, and the same amount for a period of time less than one week. If a prisoner is discharged before the expiration of the term for which the prisoner was committed, the excess of the amount advanced shall be refunded.

(B) Pursuant to section 2929.37 of the Revised Code, the board of county commissioners of the county of this state that receives pursuant to section 341.12 of the Revised Code for confinement in its jail, a prisoner who was convicted of an offense, may require the prisoner to reimburse the county for its expenses incurred by reason of the prisoner's confinement.

(C) Notwithstanding any contrary provision in this section or section 2929.18, 2929.28, or 2929.37 of the Revised Code, the board of county commissioners in this state may establish a policy that complies with section 2929.38 of the Revised Code and that requires any prisoner who is not indigent and who is confined in the county's jail under this section to pay a reception fee, a fee for medical treatment or service requested by and provided to that prisoner, or the fee for a random drug test assessed under division (E) of section 341.26 of the Revised Code.

(D) If a county in this state receives pursuant to section 341.12 of the Revised Code for confinement in its jail a person who has been convicted of or pleaded guilty to an offense and has been sentenced to a term in a jail or a person who has been arrested for an offense, who has been denied bail or has had bail set and has not been released on bail, and who is confined in jail pending trial, at the time of reception and at other times the sheriff or other person in charge of the operation of the jail determines to be appropriate, the sheriff or other person in charge of the operation of the jail may cause the convicted or accused offender to be examined and tested for tuberculosis, HIV infection, hepatitis, including but not limited to hepatitis A, B, and C, and other contagious diseases. The sheriff or other person in charge of the operation of the jail may cause a convicted or accused offender in the jail who refuses to be tested or treated for tuberculosis, HIV infection, hepatitis, including but not limited to hepatitis A, B, and C, or another contagious disease to be tested and treated involuntarily.

**HISTORY: RS § 7384; S&C 748; 50 v 212; GC § 3172; Bureau of Code Revision, 10-1-53; 140 v H 363 (Eff 9-26-84); 146 v S 2 (Eff 7-1-96); 146 v S 269 (Eff 7-1-96); 146 v H 480 (Eff 10-16-96); 147 v S 111 (Eff 3-17-98); 149 v H 170. Eff 9-6-2002; 149 v H 490, § 1, eff. 1-1-04; 152 v H 215, § 1, eff. 4-7-09.**

The effective date is set by section 4 of HB 490.

### § 341.141 Provisions concerning transfer to contiguous county in another state.

(A) The sheriff of a county in this state shall not transfer a prisoner to a contiguous county in an adjoining state as provided in section 341.12 of the Revised Code unless there is deposited weekly with the sheriff of the contiguous county an amount equal to the actual cost of keeping and feeding each prisoner committed to the custody of that sheriff for the use of the jail of that county, and the same amount for a period of time less than one week. If a prisoner is discharged before the expiration of a week for which the cost of keeping and feeding the prisoner has been deposited, the excess of the amount shall be refunded.

(B) The minimum standards for jails that are applicable for jails in the adjoining state shall apply to a jail in that adjoining state that receives prisoners as provided in section 341.13 of the Revised Code.

(C) All other terms of the transfer of a prisoner from a county in this state to a contiguous county in an adjoining state shall be as agreed upon by the board of county commissioners, any applicable governmental entity in the receiving county, and the sheriffs involved in the transfer.

(D) If a prisoner is transferred to a contiguous county of an adjoining state as provided in section 341.12 of the Revised Code, jurisdiction over the transferred prisoner shall remain with the Ohio governmental agencies and entities that would have jurisdiction over the prisoner if the prisoner had not been so transferred, including the Ohio court to which the prisoner's case is assigned.

**HISTORY: 152 v H 215, § 1, eff. 4-7-09.**

## § 341.15 Quarterly account of fees of sheriff.

At the end of each quarter, of each calendar year, a sheriff in this state shall account for and pay to the county treasurer all money received by the sheriff as provided by sections 341.13 and 341.14 of the Revised Code.

**HISTORY: RS § 7385; S&C 740; 50 v 212, § 2; GC § 3173; Bureau of Code Revision. Eff 10-1-53; 152 v H 215, § 1, eff. 4-7-09.**

## § 341.16 Process for the return of prisoner.

The prosecuting attorney of the county from which a person charged with the commission of an offense has been removed for safekeeping, may file a praecipe with the clerk of the court of common pleas thereof, directing that a warrant be issued to the sheriff having the custody of such person, and commanding him to deliver the prisoner to the sheriff of the county from which the prisoner was removed, or to the sheriff of the county in which the trial is to take place upon change of venue.

**HISTORY: RS § 7386; S&C 1399; 29 v 112, § 7; 93 v 132; GC § 3174; Bureau of Code Revision. Eff 10-1-53.**

## § 341.17 Payment of costs of habeas corpus.

When a writ of habeas corpus is issued for a person removed and confined in a county jail as provided by section 341.12 of the Revised Code, the county from which such person was sent shall pay all the costs of such proceeding. Upon the presentation of the certificate of the clerk of the court of common pleas, showing the amount of such costs, to the county auditor of the county from which such person was sent, the auditor shall draw his order for such costs on the county treasurer in favor of such clerk, or in favor of such person as the clerk orders, and the clerk shall pay such costs to the persons entitled to them.

**HISTORY: RS § 7387; S&C 749; 50 v 212, § 3; GC § 3175; Bureau of Code Revision. Eff 10-1-53.**

## § 341.18 County using jail of another county liable for damages.

The county in which a prisoner was confined as provided by sections 341.12 and 341.13 of the Revised Code, shall have a right of action against the county from which such prisoner was sent, for damages done by him to the jail or other property of the county.

**HISTORY: RS § 7388; S&C 749; 50 v 212, § 4; GC § 3176; Bureau of Code Revision. Eff 10-1-53.**

### [MISCELLANEOUS]

## § 341.19 Reimbursement of county by prisoner; testing and treatment for certain diseases.

(A) Pursuant to section 2929.37 of the Revised Code, the board of county commissioners may require a person who was convicted of an offense and who is confined in the county jail to reimburse the county for its expenses incurred by reason of the person's confinement.

(B) Notwithstanding any contrary provision in this section or section 2929.18, 2929.28, or 2929.37 of the Revised Code, the board of county commissioners may establish a policy that complies with section 2929.38 of the Revised Code and that requires any prisoner who is not indigent and who is confined in the county's jail under this section to pay a reception fee, a fee for any medical treatment or service requested by and provided to that prisoner, or the fee for a random drug test assessed under division (E) of section 341.26 of the Revised Code.

(C) If a person who is convicted of or pleads guilty to an offense is sentenced to a term in a jail, or if a person who has been arrested for an offense, and who has been denied bail or has had bail set and has not been released on bail is confined in jail pending trial, at the time of reception and at other times the sheriff or other person in charge of the operation of the jail determines to be appropriate, the sheriff or other person in charge of the operation of the jail may cause the convicted or accused offender to be examined and tested for tuberculosis, HIV infection, hepatitis, including but not limited to hepatitis A, B, and C, and other contagious diseases. The sheriff or other person in charge of the operation of the jail may cause a convicted or accused offender in the jail who refuses to be tested or treated for tuberculosis, HIV infection, hepatitis, including but not limited to hepatitis A, B, and C, or another contagious disease to be tested and treated involuntarily.

**HISTORY: RS § 7378; S&C 747; 41 v 74, § 10; 87 v 186; GC § 3177; Bureau of Code Revision, 10-1-53; 131 v 230 (Eff 9-6-65); 140 v H 363 (Eff 9-26-84); 146 v S 2 (Eff 7-1-96); 146 v S 269 (Eff 7-1-96); 146 v H 480 (Eff 10-16-96); 147 v S 111 (Eff 3-17-98); 149 v H 170. Eff 9-6-2002; 149 v H 490, § 1, eff. 1-1-04.**

The effective date is set by section 4 of HB 490.

## § 341.191 Submission of health insurance claims for jail inmates.

(A) For each person who is confined in a county jail, the county may make a determination as to whether the person is covered under a health insurance or health care policy, contract, or plan and, if the person has such coverage, what terms and conditions are imposed by it for the filing and payment of claims.

(B) If, pursuant to division (A) of this section, it is determined that the person is covered under a policy, contract, or plan and, while that coverage is in force, the county jail renders or arranges for the rendering of health care services to the person in accordance with the terms and conditions of the policy, contract, or plan, then the person, county, or provider of the health care services, as appropriate under the terms and conditions of the policy, contract, or plan, shall promptly submit a claim for payment for the health care services to the appropriate third-party payer and shall designate, or make any other arrangement necessary to ensure, that payment of any amount due on the claim be made to the county or the provider, as the case may be.

(C) Any payment made to the county pursuant to division (B) of this section shall be paid into the county treasury.

(D) This section also applies to any person who is under the custody of a law enforcement officer, as defined in section 2901.01 of the Revised Code, prior to the person's confinement in the county jail.

**HISTORY: 146 v S 163. Eff 10-16-96.**

## § 341.192 Payment for necessary medical care of county or state prisoners at medicaid reimbursement rate.

(A) As used in this section:

(1) "Jail" means a county jail, or a multicounty, municipal-county, or multicounty-municipal correctional center.

(2) "Medical assistance program" has the same meaning as in section 2913.40 of the Revised Code.

(3) "Medical provider" means a physician, hospital, laboratory, pharmacy, or other health care provider that is not employed by or under contract to a county, municipal corporation, township, the department of youth services, or the department of rehabilitation and correction to provide medical services to persons confined in a jail or state correctional institution, or is in the custody of a law enforcement officer.

(4) "Necessary care" means medical care of a nonelective nature that cannot be postponed until after the period of confinement of a person who is confined in a jail or state correctional institution, or is in the custody of a law enforcement officer without endangering the life or health of the person.

(B) If a physician employed by or under contract to a county, municipal corporation, township, the department of youth services, or the department of rehabilitation and correction to provide medical services to persons confined in a jail or state correctional institution determines that a person who is confined in the jail or state correctional institution or who is in the custody of a law enforcement officer prior to the person's confinement in a jail or state correctional institution requires necessary care that the physician cannot provide, the necessary care shall be provided by a medical provider. The county, municipal corporation, township, the department of youth services, or the department of rehabilitation and correction shall pay a medical provider for necessary care an amount not exceeding the authorized reimbursement rate for the same service established by the department of job and family services under the medical assistance program.

**HISTORY: 151 v H 66, § 101.01, eff. 9-29-05; 152 v H 130, § 1, eff. 4-7-09; 2011 HB 153, § 101.01, eff. Sept. 29, 2011.**

The effective date is set by § 612.03 of 151 v H 66.

## § 341.20 Contracts for food, medical, other services; cook.

The board of county commissioners, with the consent of the sheriff, may contract with commercial providers for the provision to prisoners and other persons of food services, medical services, and other programs and services necessary for the care and welfare of prisoners and other persons placed in the sheriff's charge.

In the absence of a commercial food service contract, the sheriff shall appoint a cook who shall have charge over the preparation of food for the feeding of prisoners and other persons placed in the sheriff's charge. The cook need not, but may be, required to perform other staff duties provided for in this section. The compensation of the cook shall be payable semimonthly from the general fund of the county, upon the warrant of the county auditor.

**HISTORY: RS § 7388a; 93 v 577; 95 v 467, § 7388a; 97 v 86; GC § 3178; 108 v PtII, 1125; 120 v 706; 123 v 370; Bureau of Code Revision, 10-1-53; 125 v H 273 (Eff 10-2-53); 131 v 231 (Eff 9-6-65); 132 v S 117 (Eff 10-13-67); 138 v H 965 (Eff 4-9-81); 139 v S 23 (Eff 7-6-82); 146 v H 480. Eff 10-16-96.**

## § 341.21 Confinement of federal or state prisoners; medical care; drug tests; testing and treatment for certain diseases.

(A) The board of county commissioners may direct the sheriff to receive into custody prisoners charged with or convicted of crime by the United States, and to keep those prisoners until discharged.

The board of the county in which prisoners charged with or convicted of crime by the United States may be so committed may negotiate and conclude any contracts with the United States for the use of the jail as provided by this section and as the board sees fit.

A prisoner so committed shall be supported at the expense of the United States during the prisoner's confinement in the county jail. No greater compensation shall be charged by a sheriff for the subsistence of that type of prisoner than is provided by section 311.20 of the Revised Code to be charged for the subsistence of state prisoners.

A sheriff or jailer who neglects or refuses to perform the services and duties directed by the board by reason of this division, shall be liable to the same penalties, forfeitures, and actions as if the prisoner had been committed under the authority of this state.

(B) Prior to the acceptance for housing into the county jail of persons who are designated by the department of rehabilitation and correction, who plead guilty to or are convicted of a felony of the fourth or fifth degree, and who satisfy the other requirements listed in section 5120.161 [5120.16.1] of the Revised Code, the board of county commissioners shall enter into an agreement with the department of rehabilitation and correction under section 5120.161 [5120.16.1] of the Revised Code for the housing in the county jail of persons designated by the department who plead guilty to or are convicted of a felony of the fourth or fifth degree and who satisfy the other requirements listed in that section in exchange for a per diem fee per person. Persons incarcerated in the county jail pursuant to an agreement entered into under this division shall be subject to supervision and control in the manner described in section 5120.161 [5120.16.1] of the Revised Code. This division does not affect the authority of a court to directly sentence a person who is convicted of or pleads guilty to a felony to the county jail in accordance with section 2929.16 of the Revised Code.

(C) Notwithstanding any contrary provision in section 2929.18, 2929.28, or 2929.37 or in any other section of the Revised Code, the board of county commissioners may establish a policy that complies with section 2929.38 of the Revised Code and that requires any person who is not indigent and who is confined in the jail under division (B) of this section to pay a reception fee, a fee for any medical treatment or service requested by and provided to that person, or the fee for a random drug test assessed under division (E) of section 341.26 of the Revised Code.

(D) If a sheriff receives into custody a prisoner convicted of crime by the United States as described in division (A) of this section, if a person who has been convicted of or pleaded guilty to an offense is incarcerated in the jail in the manner described in division (B) of this section, if a sheriff receives into custody a prisoner charged with a crime by the United States and the prisoner has had bail denied or has had bail set, has not been released on bail, and is confined in jail pending trial, or if a person who has been arrested for an offense, and who has been denied bail or has had bail set and has not been released on bail is confined in jail pending trial, at the time of reception and at other times the sheriff or other person in charge of the operation of the jail determines to be appropriate, the sheriff or other person in charge of the operation of the jail may cause the convicted or accused offender to be examined and tested for tuberculosis, HIV infection, hepatitis, including, but not limited to, hepatitis A, B, and C, and other contagious diseases. The sheriff or other person in charge of the operation of the jail may cause a convicted or accused offender in the jail who refuses to be tested or treated for tuberculosis, HIV infection, hepatitis, including, but not limited to, hepatitis A, B, and C, or another contagious disease to be tested and treated involuntarily.

**HISTORY: RS § 7381; S&C 749; 57 v 108; GC § 3179; 113 v 35; Bureau of Code Revision, 10-1-53; 139 v S 199 (Eff 1-1-83); 146 v S 2 (Eff 7-1-96); 146 v H 480 (Eff 10-16-96); 147 v S 111 (Eff 3-17-98); 148 v H 349 (Eff 9-22-2000); 149 v H 170. Eff 9-6-2002; 149 v H 490, § 1, eff. 1-1-04.**

The effective date is set by section 4 of HB 490.

## § 341.22 Religious services and welfare work in county jail.

Each administrative board or other authority in the state, having control of a county jail, shall provide for the holding of religious services and the conducting of other welfare work in such jail, by such persons or organizations, and at such times, as the probate judge directs.

**HISTORY: 99 v 225, § 3; GC § 3180; 109 v 526; Bureau of Code Revision. Eff 10-1-53.**

## § 341.23 Confinement of prisoners from county or municipal corporation having no workhouse; reimbursement policy; testing and treatment for certain diseases.

(A) The board of county commissioners of any county or the legislative authority of any municipal corporation in which there is no workhouse may agree with the legislative authority of any municipal corporation or other authority having control of the workhouse of any other city, or with the directors of any district of a joint city and county workhouse or county workhouse, upon terms on which persons convicted of a misdemeanor by any court or magistrate of a county or municipal corporation having no workhouse, may be received into that workhouse, under sentence of the court or magistrate. The board or legislative authority may pay the expenses incurred under the agreement out of the general fund of that county or municipal corporation, upon the certificate of the proper officer of the workhouse.

(B) The sheriff or other officer transporting any person to the workhouse described in division (A) of this section shall receive six cents per mile for the sheriff or officer, going and returning, five cents per mile for transporting the convict, and five cents per mile, going and coming, for the service of each deputy, to be allowed as in cases in which a person is transported to a state correctional institution. The number of miles shall be computed by the usual routes of travel and, in state cases, shall be paid out of the general fund of the county, on the allowance of the board, and for the violation of the ordinances of any municipal corporation, shall be paid by that municipal corporation on the order of its legislative authority.

(C) Pursuant to section 2929.37 of the Revised Code, the board of county commissioners, the directors of the district of a joint city and county workhouse or county workhouse, or the legislative authority of the municipal corporation may require a person who was convicted of an offense and who is confined in a workhouse as provided in division (A) of this section, to reimburse the county, district, or municipal corporation, as the case may be, for its expenses incurred by reason of the person's confinement.

(D) Notwithstanding any contrary provision in this section or section 2929.18, 2929.28, or 2929.37 of the Revised Code, the appropriate board of county commissioners and legislative authorities may include in their agreement entered into under division (A) of this section a policy that complies with section 2929.38 of the Revised Code and that requires any person who is not indigent and who is confined in the county, city, district, or joint city and county workhouse under this section to pay a reception fee, a fee for any medical treatment or service requested by and provided to that person, or the fee for a random drug test assessed under division (E) of section 341.26 of the Revised Code.

(E) If a person who has been convicted of or pleaded guilty to an offense is incarcerated in the workhouse as provided in division (A) of this section, at the time of reception and at other times the person in charge of the operation of the workhouse determines to be appropriate, the person in charge of the operation of the workhouse may cause the convicted offender to be examined and tested for tuberculosis, HIV infection, hepatitis, including but not limited to hepatitis A, B, and C, and other contagious diseases. The person in charge of the operation of the workhouse may cause a convicted offender in the workhouse who refuses to be tested or treated for tuberculosis, HIV infection, hepatitis, including but not limited to hepatitis A, B, and C, or another contagious disease to be tested and treated involuntarily.

**HISTORY: 84 v 136, 139; 91 v 180; GC § 14564; Bureau of Code Revision, 10-1-53; 140 v H 363 (Eff 9-26-84); 145 v H 571 (Eff 10-6-94); 146 v S 2 (Eff 7-1-96); 146 v S 269 (Eff 7-1-96); 146 v H 480 (Eff 10-16-96); 147 v S 111 (Eff 3-17-98); 148 v H 349 (Eff 9-22-2000); 149 v H 170. Eff 9-6-2002; 149 v H 490, § 1, eff. 1-1-04.**

The effective date is set by section 4 of HB 490.

## § 341.24 Submission of health insurance claims for workhouse inmates.

(A) For each person who is confined in a workhouse as provided in section 341.23 of the Revised Code, the county, district, or municipal corporation, as the case may be, may make a determination as to whether the person is covered under a health insurance or health care policy, contract, or plan and, if the person has such coverage, what terms and conditions are imposed by it for the filing and payment of claims.

(B) If, pursuant to division (A) of this section, it is determined that the person is covered under a policy, contract, or plan and, while that coverage is in force, the workhouse renders or arranges for the rendering of health care services to the person in accordance with the terms and conditions of the policy, contract, or plan, then the person, county, district, municipal corporation, or provider of the health care services, as appropriate under the terms and conditions of the policy, contract, or plan, shall promptly submit a claim for payment for the health care services to the appropriate third-party payer and shall designate, or make any other arrangement necessary to ensure, that payment of any amount due on the claim be made to the county, district, municipal corporation, or provider, as the case may be.

(C) Any payment made to the county, district, or municipal corporation pursuant to division (B) of this section shall be paid into the treasury of the governmental entity that incurred the expenses.

(D) This section also applies to any person who is under the custody of a law enforcement officer, as defined in section 2901.01 of the Revised Code, prior to the person's confinement in the workhouse.

**HISTORY: 146 v S 163. Eff 10-16-96.**

## § 341.25 Commissary; fund.

(A) The sheriff may establish a commissary for the jail. The commissary may be established either in-house or by another arrangement. If a commissary is established, all persons incarcerated in the jail shall receive commissary privileges. A person's purchases from the commissary shall be deducted from the person's account record in the jail's business office. The commissary shall provide for the distribution to indigent persons incarcerated in the jail necessary hygiene articles and writing materials.

(B) If a commissary is established, the sheriff shall establish a commissary fund for the jail. The management of funds in the commissary fund shall be strictly controlled in accordance with procedures adopted by the auditor of state. Commissary fund revenue over and above operating costs and reserve shall be considered profits. All profits from the commissary fund shall be used to purchase supplies and equipment, and to provide life skills training and education or treatment services, or both, for the benefit of persons incarcerated in the jail, and to pay salary and benefits for employees of the sheriff who work in or are employed for the purpose of providing service to the commissary. The sheriff shall adopt rules for the operation of any commissary fund the sheriff establishes.

**HISTORY: 146 v H 480 (Eff 10-16-96); 147 v H 215. Eff 6-30-97; 150 v H 95, § 1, eff. 9-26-03.**

The effective date is set by section 179 of H.B. 95 (150 v —).

## § 341.26 Random drug testing of prisoners.

(A) As used in this section:

(1) "Random drug testing" has the same meaning as in section 5120.63 of the Revised Code.

(2) "Prisoner" means a person confined in a jail or multicounty correctional center following a conviction of or plea of guilty to a criminal offense.

(B) The board of county commissioners of the county, with the consent of the sheriff of the county, or the boards of county commissioners of two or more adjacent counties that have jointly established a multicounty correctional center pursuant to section 307.93 of the Revised Code, with the consent of the sheriffs of those adjacent counties, may enter into a contract with a laboratory or entity to perform blood or urine specimen collection, documentation, maintenance, transportation, preservation, storage, and analyses and other duties required in the performance of random drug testing of prisoners. The terms of any contract entered into under this division shall include a requirement that the laboratory or entity and its employees, the sheriff, deputy sheriffs, the corrections commission or the administrator of the multicounty correctional center specified in division (D) of this section, the employees of the jail and multicounty correctional center, and all other persons comply with the standards for the performance of random drug testing as specified in rules adopted under division (C) of this section.

(C) Prior to entering into a contract with a laboratory or entity under division (B) of this section, a board of county commissioners or, in the case of a multicounty correctional center, the boards of county commissioners of the counties that have established the center shall adopt rules for the random drug testing of prisoners. The rules shall include, but are not limited to, provisions that do the following:

(1) Require the laboratory or entity to seek, obtain, and maintain accreditation from the national institute on drug abuse;

(2) Establish standards for the performance of random drug testing that include, but are not limited to, standards governing the following:

(a) The collection by the laboratory or entity of blood or urine specimens of individuals in a scientifically or medically approved manner and under reasonable and sanitary conditions;

(b) The collection and testing by the laboratory or entity of blood or urine specimens with due regard for the privacy of the individual being tested and in a manner reasonably calculated to prevent substitutions or interference with the collection and testing of the specimens;

(c) The documentation of blood or urine specimens collected by the laboratory or entity and documentation procedures that reasonably preclude the possibility of erroneous identification of test results and that provide the individual being tested an opportunity to furnish information identifying any prescription or nonprescription drugs used by the individual in connection with a medical condition;

(d) The collection, maintenance, storage, and transportation by the laboratory or entity of blood or urine specimens in a manner that reasonably precludes the possibility of contamination or adulteration of the specimens;

(e) The testing by the laboratory or entity of a blood or urine specimen of an individual to determine whether the individual ingested or was injected with a drug of abuse, in a manner that conforms to scientifically accepted analytical methods and procedures and that may include verification or confirmation of any positive test result by a reliable analytical method;

(f) The analysis of an individual's blood or urine specimen by an employee of the laboratory or entity who is qualified by education, training, and experience to perform that analysis and whose regular duties include the analysis of blood or urine specimens to determine the presence of a drug of abuse and whether the individual who is the subject of the test ingested or was injected with a drug of abuse.

(3) Specify the frequency of performing random drug testing on prisoners in the jail or multicounty correctional center;

(4) Prescribe procedures for the automatic, random selection of prisoners in the jail or multicounty correctional center to submit to random drug testing under this section;

(5) Provide for reasonable safeguards for transmitting the results of the random drug testing of prisoners in the jail or multicounty correctional center from the contracting laboratory or entity to the sheriff, the corrections commission, or the administrator of the multicounty correctional center pursuant to division (E) of this section;

(6) Establish a reasonable fee to cover the costs associated with random drug testing and analysis performed by a contracting laboratory or entity under this section and establish procedures pursuant to division (E) of this section for the collection of those fees from the prisoners subjected to the drug tests.

(D) If a board of county commissioners enters into a contract pursuant to division (B) of this section, the sheriff of that county, pursuant to the terms of the contract and the rules adopted under division (C) of this section, shall facilitate the collection, documentation, maintenance, and transportation by the contracting laboratory or entity of the blood or urine specimens of the prisoners who are confined in the jail and who are subject to random drug testing. If the boards of county commissioners that have jointly established a multicounty correctional center enter into a contract pursuant to division (B) of this section, the corrections commission or the administrator of the multicounty correctional center, pursuant to the terms of the contract and the rules adopted under division (C) of this section, shall facilitate the collection, documentation, maintenance, and transportation by the contracting laboratory or entity of the blood or urine specimens of the prisoners who are confined in the multicounty correctional center and who are subject to random drug testing.

(E) If a county or two or more adjacent counties enter into a contract pursuant to division (B) of this section and the contracting laboratory or entity performs the random drug testing as provided in the contract, the laboratory or entity shall transmit the results of the drug tests to the sheriff, corrections commission, or administrator who facilitated the collection, documentation, maintenance, and transportation of blood or urine specimens under division (D) of this section. The sheriff, corrections commission, or administrator shall file for record the results of the random drug tests that indicate whether or not each prisoner who is confined in the jail or multicounty correctional center and who was subjected to the drug test ingested or was injected with a drug of abuse. The sheriff, corrections commission, or administrator shall give appropriate notice of the drug test results to each prisoner who was subjected to the drug test and whose drug test results indicate that the prisoner ingested or was injected with a drug of abuse. The sheriff, corrections commission, or administrator shall afford that prisoner an opportunity to be heard regarding the results of the drug test and to present contrary evidence at a hearing held before the sheriff, corrections commission, or administrator within thirty days after notification of the prisoner under this division. After the hearing, if a hearing is held, the sheriff, corrections commission, or administrator shall make a determination regarding any evidence presented by the prisoner. If the sheriff, corrections commission, or administrator rejects the evidence presented by the prisoner at the hearing or if no hearing is held under this division, the sheriff, corrections commission, or administrator may assess a reasonable fee, determined pursuant to division (C) of this section, for the costs associated with the random drug test to be paid by the prisoner whose drug test results indicate that the prisoner ingested or was injected with a drug of abuse. The sheriff, corrections commission, or administrator may collect the fee pursuant to section 307.93, 341.14, 341.19, 341.21, or 341.23 of the Revised Code.

**HISTORY: 148 v H 349 (Eff 9-22-2000); 149 v H 170. Eff 9-6-2002.**

## § 341.27 Immunity concerning prisoners or adult offenders on work detail.

(A) As used in this section:

(1) "County correctional facility" has the same meaning as in section 341.42 of the Revised Code.

(2) "County correctional officer" has the same meaning as in section 341.41 of the Revised Code.

(B) If all the prisoners or adult offenders working on a work detail administered by a county correctional facility and outside the facility have volunteered for the work detail and are imprisoned or reside in that facility for an offense other than a felony of the first or second degree and if the applicable county correctional officer complies with division (C) of this section, both of the following apply:

(1) No sheriff, deputy sheriff, or county correctional officer is liable for civil damages for injury, death, or loss to person or property caused or suffered by a prisoner or adult offender working on the work detail unless the injury, death, or loss results from malice or wanton or reckless misconduct of the sheriff, deputy sheriff, or county correctional officer.

(2) The county in which the prisoners or adult offenders work on the work detail and that employs the sheriff, deputy sheriff, or county correctional officer is not liable for civil damages for injury, death, or loss to person or property caused or suffered by a prisoner or adult offender working on the work detail unless the injury, death, or loss results from malice or wanton or reckless misconduct of the sheriff or any deputy sheriff or county correctional officer.

(C) To qualify for the immunity described in division (B)(1) of this section regarding a work detail, a county correctional officer, prior to having the prisoners or adult offenders of the county correctional facility, work outside the facility on the work detail, shall inform each prisoner or adult offender on the work detail of the provisions of this section, including notifying the prisoner or adult offender that, by volunteering for the work detail, the prisoner or adult offender cannot hold the sheriff, deputy sheriff, or county correctional officer or the county liable for civil damages for injury, death, or loss to person or property unless the injury, death, or loss results from malice or wanton or reckless misconduct of the sheriff, deputy sheriff, or county correctional officer.

**HISTORY: 150 v H 316, § 1, eff. 3-31-05.**

[REHABILITATION WORK CAMPS]

## § 341.31 County rehabilitation work camps.

In addition to its other powers, the board of county commissioners of any county may construct, maintain, equip, furnish, appoint the necessary personnel of, and supervise the operation of county rehabilitation work camps for the purpose of the rehabilitation of persons who have been sentenced to imprisonment for a misdemeanor.

**HISTORY: 128 v 1043 (Eff 11-5-59); 143 v S 258. Eff 8-22-90.**

## § 341.32 Agreement with other counties and municipal corporations.

The board of county commissioners of any county not having a county rehabilitation work camp or the legislative authority of any municipal corporation may agree upon the terms on which persons convicted of a misdemeanor by any court or magistrate of such county or municipal corporation may be received into a county rehabilitation work camp under sentence of such court or magistrate. Such board or legislative authority may pay the expenses, including the cost of transportation of prisoners, incurred under such agreement out of the general fund of such county or municipal corporation, upon the certificate of the proper officer of such county work rehabilitation camp.

**HISTORY: 128 v 1043. Eff 11-5-59.**

## § 341.33 Use of county rehabilitation work camps by municipal corporations.

Imprisonment under the ordinances of a municipal corporation, in addition to the manner provided for in section 1905.35 of the Revised Code, may be in a county rehabilitation work camp, provided an agreement for the use of such camp has been entered into between the board of county commissioners of the county wherein such camp is located and the legislative authority of such municipal corporation.

**HISTORY: 128 v 1043. Eff 11-5-59.**

## § 341.34 Minimum security jails.

(A) As used in this section, "building or structure" includes, but is not limited to, a modular unit, building, or structure and a movable unit, building, or structure.

(B)(1) The board of county commissioners of any county, by resolution, may dedicate and permit the use, as a minimum security jail, of any vacant or abandoned public building or structure owned by the county that has not been dedicated to or is not then in use for any county or other public purpose, or any building or structure rented or leased by the county. The board of county commissioners of any county, by resolution, also may dedicate and permit the use, as a minimum security jail, of any building or structure purchased by or constructed by or for the county. Subject to divisions (B)(3) and (C) of this section, upon the effective date of such a resolution, the specified building or structure shall be used, in accordance with this section, for the confinement of persons who meet one of the following conditions:

(a) The person is sentenced to a term of imprisonment for a traffic violation or a misdemeanor or is sentenced to a residential sanction in the jail for a felony of the fourth or fifth degree pursuant to sections 2929.11 to 2929.19 of the Revised Code, and the jail administrator or the jail administrator's designee has classified the person as a minimal security risk. In determining the person's classification under this division, the administrator or designee shall consider all relevant factors, including, but not limited to, the person's escape risk and propensity for assaultive or violent behavior, based upon the person's prior and current behavior.

(b) The person is an inmate transferred by order of a judge of the sentencing court upon the request of the sheriff, administrator, jailer, or other person responsible for operating the jail other than a contractor as defined in section 9.06 of the Revised Code, who is named in the request as being suitable for confinement in a minimum security facility.

(2) The board of county commissioners of any county, by resolution, may affiliate with one or more adjacent counties, or with one or more municipal corporations located within the county or within an adjacent county, and dedicate and permit the use, as a minimum security jail, of any vacant or abandoned public building or structure owned by any of the affiliating counties or municipal corporations that has not been dedicated to or is not then in use for any public purpose, or any building or structure rented or leased by any of the affiliating counties or municipal corporations. The board of county commissioners of any county, by resolution, also may affiliate with one or more adjacent counties or with one or more municipal corporations located within the county or within an adjacent county and dedicate and permit the use, as a minimum security jail, of any building or structure purchased by or constructed by or for any of the affiliating counties or municipal corporations. Any counties and municipal corporations that affiliate for purposes of this division shall enter into an agreement that establishes the responsibilities for the operation and for the cost of operation of the minimum security jail. Subject to divisions (B)(3) and (C) of this section, upon the effective date of a resolution adopted under this division, the specified building or structure shall be used, in accordance with this section, for the confinement of persons who meet one of the following conditions:

(a) The person is sentenced to a term of imprisonment for a traffic violation, a misdemeanor, or a violation of an ordinance of any municipal corporation, or is sentenced to a residential sanction in the jail for a felony of the fourth or fifth degree pursuant to sections 2929.11 to 2929.19 of the Revised Code, and the jail administrator or the jail administrator's designee has classified the person as a minimal security risk. In determining the person's classification under this division, the administrator or designee shall consider all relevant factors, including, but not limited to, the person's escape risk and propensity for assaultive or violent behavior, based upon the person's prior and current behavior.

(b) The person is an inmate transferred by order of a judge of the sentencing court upon the request of the sheriff, administrator, jailer, or other person responsible for operating the jail other than a contractor as defined in section 9.06 of the Revised Code, who is named in the request as being suitable for confinement in a minimum security facility.

(3) No person shall be confined in a building or structure dedicated as a minimum security jail under division (B)(1) or (2) of this section unless the judge who sentenced the person to the term of imprisonment for the traffic violation or the misdemeanor specifies that the term of imprisonment is to be served in that jail, and division (B)(1) or (2) of this section permits the confinement of the person in that jail or unless the judge who sentenced the person to the residential sanction for the felony specifies that the residential sanction is to be served in a jail, and division (B)(1) or (2) of this section permits the confinement of the person in that jail. If a rented or leased building or structure is so dedicated, the building or structure may be used as a minimum security jail only during the period that it is rented or leased by the county or by an affiliated county or municipal corporation. If a person convicted of a misdemeanor is confined to a building or structure dedicated as a minimum security jail under division (B)(1) or (2) of this section and the sheriff, administrator, jailer, or other person responsible for operating the jail other than a contractor as defined in section 9.06 of the Revised Code determines that it would be more appropriate for the person so confined to be confined in another jail or workhouse facility, the sheriff, administrator, jailer, or other person may transfer the person so confined to a more appropriate jail or workhouse facility.

(C) All of the following apply to a building or structure that is dedicated pursuant to division (B)(1) or (2) of this section for use as a minimum security jail:

(1) To the extent that the use of the building or structure as a minimum security jail requires a variance from any county, municipal corporation, or township zoning regulations or ordinances, the variance shall be granted.

(2) Except as provided in this section, the building or structure shall not be used to confine any person unless it is in substantial compliance with any applicable housing, fire prevention, sanitation, health, and safety codes, regulations, or standards.

(3) Unless such satisfaction or compliance is required under the standards described in division (C)(4) of this section, and notwithstanding any other provision of state or local law to the contrary, the building or structure need not satisfy or comply with any state or local building standard or code in order to be used to confine a person for the purposes specified in division (B) of this section.

(4) The building or structure shall not be used to confine any person unless it is in compliance with all minimum standards and minimum renovation, modification, and construction criteria for minimum security jails that have been proposed by the department of rehabilitation and correction, through its bureau of adult detention, under section 5120.10 of the Revised Code.

(5) The building or structure need not be renovated or modified into a secure detention facility in order to be used solely to confine a person for the purposes specified in divisions (B)(1)(a) and (B)(2)(a) of this section.

(6) The building or structure shall be used, equipped, furnished, and staffed in the manner necessary to provide adequate and suitable living, sleeping, food service or preparation, drinking, bathing and toilet, sanitation, and other necessary facilities, furnishings, and equipment.

(D) Except as provided in this section, a minimum security jail dedicated and used under this section shall be considered to be part of the jail, workhouse, or other correctional facilities of the county or the affiliated counties and municipal corporations for all purposes under the law. All persons confined in such a minimum security jail shall be and shall remain, in all respects, under the control of the county authority that has responsibility for the management and operation of the jail, workhouse, or other correctional facilities of the county or, if it is operated by any affiliation of counties or municipal corporations, under the control of the specified county or municipal corporation with that authority, provided that, if the person was convicted of a felony and is serving a residential sanction in the facility, all provisions of law that pertain to persons convicted of a felony that would not by their nature clearly be inapplicable apply regarding the person. A minimum security jail dedicated and used under this section shall be managed and maintained in accordance with policies and procedures adopted by the board of county commissioners or the affiliated counties and municipal corporations governing the safe and healthful operation of the jail, the confinement and supervision of the persons sentenced to it, and their participation in work release or similar rehabilitation programs. In addition to other rules of conduct and discipline, the rights of ingress and egress of persons confined in a minimum security jail dedicated and used under this section shall be subject to reasonable restrictions. Every person confined in a minimum security jail dedicated and used under this section shall be given verbal and written notification, at the time of the person's admission to the jail, that purposely leaving, or purposely failing to return to, the jail without proper authority or permission constitutes the felony offense of escape.

(E) If a person who has been convicted of or pleaded guilty to an offense is sentenced to a term of imprisonment or a residential sanction in a minimum security jail as described in division (B)(1)(a) or (B)(2)(a) of this section, or if a person is an inmate transferred to a minimum security jail by order of a judge of the sentencing court as described in division (B)(1)(b) or (2)(b) of this section, at the time of reception and at other times the person in charge of the operation of the jail determines to be appropriate, the sheriff or other person in charge of the operation of the jail may cause the convicted offender to be examined and tested for tuberculosis, HIV infection, hepatitis, including but not limited to hepatitis A, B, and C, and other contagious diseases. The person in charge of the operation of the jail may cause a convicted offender in the jail who refuses to be tested or treated for tuberculosis, HIV infection, hepatitis, including but not limited to hepatitis A, B, and C, or another contagious disease to be tested and treated involuntarily.

**HISTORY: 143 v S 131 (Eff 7-25-90); 143 v H 837 (Eff 7-25-90); 143 v S 258 (Eff 8-22-90); 144 v S 351 (Eff 7-1-92); 146 v H 117 (Eff 9-29-95); 146 v S 269 (Eff 7-1-96); 146 v H 480 (Eff 10-16-96); 147 v S 111 (Eff 3-17-98); 147 v H 293. Eff 3-17-98.**

## § 341.35 Contract for private operation of facility.

The board of county commissioners of a county with a county jail, workhouse, minimum security misdemeanant jail, or other correctional facility may enter into a contract under section 9.06 of the Revised Code for the private operation and management of that facility, but only if the facility is used to house only misdemeanant inmates.

**HISTORY: 146 v H 117. Eff 9-29-95.**

The effective date is set by section 197 of HB 117.

## § 341.41 Prisoner access to exercise equipment or participation in fighting skills programs.

(A) As used in this section:

(1) "Free weight exercise equipment" means any equipment or device that is designed to increase the muscle mass and physical strength of the person using it. "Free weight exercise equipment" includes, but is not limited to, barbells, dumbbells, weight plates, and similar free weight-type equipment and other devices that the department of rehabilitation and correction, in rules adopted under section 5120.423 [5120.42.3] of the Revised Code, designates as enabling a person to increase muscle mass and physical strength.

(2) "Fixed weight exercise equipment" means any equipment, machine, or device that is not designed primarily to increase muscle mass and physical strength but rather to keep a person in relatively good physical condition. "Fixed weight exercise equipment" includes, but is not limited to, weight machines that utilize weight plates, tension bands, or similar devices that provide weight training resistance like universal and nautilus equipment. "Fixed weight exercise equipment" includes machines that are usually assembled as a unit, are not readily dismantled, and have been specifically modified for prison use so as to make them secure and immobile.

(3) "County correctional officer" means a person who is employed by a county as an employee or officer of a county jail, county workhouse, minimum security jail, joint city and county workhouse, municipal-county correctional center, multicounty-municipal correctional center, municipal-county jail or workhouse, or multicounty-municipal jail or workhouse.

(4) A person is "employed by a county" if the person is employed by, or receives any compensation or benefits from, any official, officer, office, agency, board, commission, department, or other entity that is a branch of county government, that is established by a county, or that serves a county, including, but not limited to, a sheriff.

(5) "Multicounty-municipal" has the same meaning as in section 307.93 of the Revised Code.

(B) No county correctional officer shall do any of the following:

(1) Provide a prisoner access to free weight or fixed weight exercise equipment;

(2) Allow a prisoner to provide or receive instruction in boxing, wrestling, karate, judo, or another form of martial arts, or any other program that the department of rehabilitation and correction, in rules adopted under section 5120.423 [5120.42.3] of the Revised Code, designates as enabling a person to improve fighting skills.

(C) Nothing in this section prohibits a county correctional officer from allowing a prisoner to participate in jogging, basketball, stationary exercise bicycling, supervised calisthenics, or other physical activities that are not designed to increase muscle mass and physical strength or improve fighting skills.

**HISTORY: 146 v H 152 (Eff 10-4-96); 147 v H 293. Eff 3-17-98.**

## § 341.42 Restrictions on prisoner access to Internet.

(A) As used in this section:

(1) "County correctional officer" has the same meaning as in section 341.41 of the Revised Code.

(2) "Computer," "computer network," "computer system," "computer services," "telecommunications service," and "information service" have the same meanings as in section 2913.01 of the Revised Code.

(3) "County correctional facility" means a county jail, county workhouse, minimum security jail, joint city and county workhouse, municipal-county correctional center, multicounty-municipal correctional center, municipal-county jail or workhouse, or multicounty-municipal jail or workhouse.

(B) No county correctional officer shall provide a prisoner access to or permit a prisoner to have access to the internet through the use of a computer, computer network, computer system, computer services, telecommunications service, or information service unless both of the following apply:

(1) The prisoner is participating in an approved educational program with direct supervision that requires the use of the internet for training or research purposes.

(2) The provision of and access to the internet is in accordance with rules promulgated by the department of rehabilitation and correction pursuant to section 5120.62 of the Revised Code.

(C)(1) No prisoner in a county correctional facility under the control of a county shall access the internet through the use of a computer, computer network, computer system, computer services, telecommunications service, or information service unless both of the following apply:

(a) The prisoner is participating in an approved educational program with direct supervision that requires the use of the internet for training or research purposes.

(b) The provision of and access to the internet is in accordance with rules promulgated by the department of rehabilitation and correction pursuant to section 5120.62 of the Revised Code.

(2) Whoever violates division (C)(1) of this section is guilty of improper internet access, a misdemeanor of the first degree.

**HISTORY: 148 v S 12. Eff 6-8-2000; 150 v H 204, § 1, eff. 11-5-04.**

# TITLE 5: TOWNSHIPS

## CHAPTER 503: GENERAL PROVISIONS



[MASSAGE ESTABLISHMENTS]

### § 503.40 Definitions.

As used in sections 503.40 to 503.49 of the Revised Code:

(A) "Massage" means any method of exerting pressure on, stroking, kneading, rubbing, tapping, pounding, vibrating, or stimulating the external soft tissue of the body with the hands, or with the aid of any mechanical or electrical apparatus or appliance.

(B) "Massage establishment" means any fixed place of business where a person offers massages:

(1) In exchange for anything of value; or

(2) In connection with the provision of another legitimate service.

(C) "Masseur" or "masseuse" means any individual who performs massages at a massage establishment.

(D) "Sexual or genital area" includes the genitalia, pubic area, anus, perineum of any person, and the breasts of a female.

**HISTORY: 144 v H 247. Eff 6-3-92.**

### § 503.41 Resolution regulating massage establishments and their employees; licensed health professionals excepted.

(A) A board of township trustees, by resolution, may regulate and require the registration of massage establishments and their employees within the unincorporated territory of the township. In accordance with sections 503.40 to 503.49 of the Revised Code, for that purpose, the board, by a majority vote of all members, may adopt, amend, administer, and enforce regulations within the unincorporated territory of the township.

(B) A board may adopt regulations and amendments under this section only after public hearing at not fewer than two regular sessions of the board. The board shall cause to be published in a newspaper of general circulation in the township, or as provided in section 7.16 of the Revised Code, notice of the public hearings, including the time, date, and place, once a week for two weeks immediately preceding the hearings. The board shall make available proposed regulations or amendments to the public at the office of the board.

(C) Regulations or amendments adopted by the board are effective thirty days after the date of adoption unless, within thirty days after the adoption of the regulations or amendments, the township fiscal officer receives a petition, signed by a number of qualified electors residing in the unincorporated area of the township equal to not less than ten per cent of the total vote cast for all candidates for governor in the area at the most recent general election at which a governor was elected, requesting the board to submit the regulations or amendments to the electors of the area for approval or rejection at the next primary or general election occurring at least ninety days after the board receives the petition.

No regulation or amendment for which the referendum vote has been requested is effective unless a majority of the votes cast on the issue is in favor of the regulation or amendment. Upon certification by the board of elections that a majority of the votes cast on the issue was in favor of the regulation or amendment, the regulation or amendment takes immediate effect.

(D) The board shall make available regulations it adopts or amends to the public at the office of the board and shall cause to be published once a notice of the availability of the regulations in a newspaper of general circulation in the township within ten days after their adoption or amendment.

(E) Nothing in sections 503.40 to 503.49 of the Revised Code shall be construed to allow a board of township trustees to regulate the practice of any limited branch of medicine specified in section 4731.15 of the Revised Code or the practice of providing therapeutic massage by a licensed physician, a licensed chiropractor, a licensed podiatrist, a licensed nurse, or any other licensed health professional. As used in this division, "licensed" means licensed, certified, or registered to practice in this state.

**HISTORY: 144 v H 247 (Eff 6-3-92); 146 v H 99 (Eff 8-22-95); 147 v H 606. Eff 3-9-99; 151 v S 107, § 1, eff. 12-20-05; 153 v H 48, § 1, eff. 7-2-10; 2011 HB 153, § 101.01, eff. Sept. 29, 2011.**

### § 503.42 Permit to operate establishment; masseur or masseuse's license; prohibited activities.

If a board of township trustees has adopted a resolution under section 503.41 of the Revised Code:

(A) No person shall engage in, conduct or carry on, or permit to be engaged in, conducted or carried on in the unincorporated areas of the township, the operation of a massage establishment without first having obtained a permit from the board of township trustees as provided in section 503.43 of the Revised Code.

(B) No individual shall act as a masseur or masseuse for a massage establishment located in the unincorporated areas of the township without first having obtained a license from the board of township trustees as provided in section 503.45 of the Revised Code.

(C) No owner or operator of a massage establishment located in the unincorporated areas of the township shall knowingly do any of the following:

(1) Employ an unlicensed masseur or masseuse;

(2) Refuse to allow appropriate state or local authorities, including police officers, access to the massage establishment for any health or safety inspection conducted pursuant to a regulation adopted by the township under section 503.41 of the Revised Code;

(3) Operate during the hours designated as prohibited hours of operation by the board of township trustees;

(4) Employ any person under the age of eighteen.

(D) No person employed in a massage establishment located in the unincorporated area of the township shall knowingly do any of the following in the performance of duties at the massage establishment:

(1) Place his or her hand upon, touch with any part of his or her body, fondle in any manner, or massage the sexual or genital area of any other person;

(2) Perform, offer, or agree to perform any act which would require the touching of the sexual or genital area of any other person;

(3) Touch, offer, or agree to touch the sexual or genital area of any other person with any mechanical or electrical apparatus or appliance;

(4) Wear unclean clothing, no clothing, transparent clothing, or clothing that otherwise reveals the sexual or genital areas of the masseur or masseuse;

(5) Uncover or allow the sexual or genital area of any other person to be uncovered while providing massages.

(E) No licensed masseur or masseuse shall accept or continue employment at a massage establishment that does not have a current, valid permit issued by the board of township trustees.

**HISTORY: 144 v H 247. Eff 6-3-92.**

## § 503.43 Application for permit; contents and expiration of permit.

If a board of township trustees has adopted a resolution under section 503.41 of the Revised Code, the application for a permit to operate a massage establishment shall be made to the board and shall include the following:

(A) An initial, nonrefundable filing fee of two hundred fifty dollars and an annual nonrefundable renewal fee of one hundred twenty-five dollars;

(B) A health and safety report of an inspection of the premises performed within thirty days of the application to determine compliance with applicable health and safety codes, which inspection appropriate state or local authorities acting pursuant to an agreement with the board shall perform;

(C) The full name and address of any person applying for a permit, including any partner or limited partner of a partnership applicant, any officer or director of a corporate applicant, and any stockholder holding more than two per cent of the stock of a corporate applicant, the date of birth and social security number of each individual, and the federal identification number of any partnership or corporation;

(D) Authorization for an investigation into the criminal record of any person applying for a permit;

(E) Any other information determined by the board to be necessary.

A permit issued under this section to a massage establishment shall expire one year after the date of issuance, except that no massage establishment shall be required to discontinue business because of the failure of the board to act on a renewal application filed in a timely manner and pending before the board on the expiration date of the establishment's permit. Each permit shall contain the name of the applicant, the address of the massage establishment, and the expiration date of the permit.

**HISTORY: 144 v H 247. Eff 6-3-92.**

## § 503.44 Reasons for denial or revocation of permit.

If a board of township trustees has adopted a resolution under section 503.41 of the Revised Code, it shall deny any application for a permit to operate a massage establishment or revoke a previously issued permit, for any of the following reasons:

(A) Falsification of any of the information required for the application or failure to fully complete the application;

(B) Failure to cooperate with any required health or safety inspection;

(C) Any one of the persons named on the application is under the age of eighteen;

(D) Any one of the persons named on the application has been convicted of or pleaded guilty to any violation of Chapter 2907. of the Revised Code, or violation of any municipal ordinance that is substantially equivalent to any offense contained in Chapter 2907. of the Revised Code, within five years preceding the application;

(E) Any masseur or masseuse employed at the licensed massage establishment has been convicted of or pleaded guilty to a violation of division (D) of section 503.42 of the Revised Code.

**HISTORY: 144 v H 247. Eff 6-3-92.**

## § 503.45 Application for license as a massager; contents and expiration of license.

If a board of township trustees has adopted a resolution under section 503.41 of the Revised Code, the application for a license as a massager shall be made to the board and shall include the following:

(A) An initial, nonrefundable filing fee of one hundred dollars and an annual nonrefundable renewal fee of fifty dollars;

(B) The results of a physical examination performed by a licensed physician, a physician assistant, a clinical nurse specialist, a certified nurse practitioner, or a certified nurse-midwife within thirty days of the application certifying that the applicant is free from communicable diseases;

(C) The full name, date of birth, address, and social security number of the applicant;

(D) The results of an investigation by appropriate police agencies into the criminal record of the applicant, including a photograph taken no later than thirty days prior to the application, fingerprints, and background investigation;

(E) Any other information determined by the board to be necessary.

A license issued under this section to a massager shall expire one year after the date of issuance, except that no massager shall be required to discontinue performing massages because of the failure of the board to act on a renewal application filed in a timely manner and pending before the board on the expiration date of the person's license. Each license shall contain the full name of the applicant, a color photograph and a brief description of the person, and the expiration date of the license.

**HISTORY: 144 v H 247 (Eff 6-3-92); 149 v S 245. Eff 3-31-2003.**

## § 503.46 Reasons for denial or revocation of license.

If a board of township trustees has adopted a resolution under section 503.41 of the Revised Code, it shall deny the application for a masseur or masseuse license or revoke a previously issued license for any of the following reasons:

(A) Falsification of any of the information required for the application or failure to fully complete the application;

(B) The applicant is under the age of twenty-one.

(C) The applicant has been convicted of or pleaded guilty to any violation of Chapter 2907. of the Revised Code, or violation of any municipal ordinance that is substantially equivalent to any offense contained in Chapter 2907. of the Revised Code, within five years preceding the application.

(D) The applicant has been convicted of or pleaded guilty to a violation of division (D) of section 503.42 of the Revised Code.

**HISTORY: 144 v H 247. Eff 6-3-92.**

## § 503.47 Requirements that may be adopted.

If a board of township trustees has adopted a resolution under section 503.41 of the Revised Code, the regulations adopted for that purpose may require any of the following:

(A) A massage establishment to display its current permit in an area open to the public;

(B) Each massager to display the massager's license at all times in the areas where the licensee is providing massages;

(C) Massage establishments to undergo periodic health and safety inspections to determine continual compliance with applicable health and safety codes;

(D) Massagers to undergo periodic physical examinations performed by a licensed physician, a physician assistant, a clinical nurse specialist, a certified nurse practitioner, or a certified nurse-midwife certifying that the massager continues to be free from communicable diseases;

(E) Any other requirement reasonably thought necessary by the board.

**HISTORY: 144 v H 247 (Eff 6-3-92); 149 v S 245. Eff 3-31-2003.**

## § 503.48 Hearing not required; record of proceedings; appeals.

A board of township trustees acting under sections 503.40 to 503.49 of the Revised Code need not hold any hearing in connection with an order denying or revoking a permit to operate a massage establishment or masseur or masseuse license. The board shall maintain a complete record of each proceeding and shall notify the applicant in writing of its order. Any person adversely affected by an order of the board denying or revoking a permit to operate a massage establishment or masseur or masseuse license may appeal from the order of the board to the court of common pleas of the county in which the township is located, the place of business of the permit holder is located, or the person is a resident. The appeal shall be in accordance with Chapter 2506. of the Revised Code.

**HISTORY: 144 v H 247. Eff 6-3-92.**

## § 503.49 Deposit and use of fees.

If a board of township trustees has adopted a resolution under section 503.41 of the Revised Code, the board shall deposit the fees collected by the township for massage establishment permits and masseur and masseuse licenses in the township general fund and first use the fees for the cost of administering and enforcing regulations adopted under section 503.41 of the Revised Code.

**HISTORY: 144 v H 247. Eff 6-3-92.**

## § 503.50 Penalties.

(A) Whoever violates division (A) or (B) of section 503.42 of the Revised Code is guilty of a misdemeanor of the first degree.

(B) Whoever violates division (C), (D), or (E) of section 503.42 of the Revised Code is guilty of a misdemeanor of the third degree.

**HISTORY: 144 v H 247 (Eff 6-3-92); 146 v S 2. Eff 7-1-96.**

The effective date is set by section 6 of SB 2.

### [ADULT ENTERTAINMENT ESTABLISHMENTS]

## § 503.51 Definitions.

As used in sections 503.51 to 503.53 of the Revised Code, "adult arcade," "adult bookstore," "adult novelty store," "adult video store," "adult cabaret," "adult entertainment establishment," "adult motion picture theater," "adult theater," "distinguished or characterized by their emphasis upon," "nude or seminude model studio," "nudity," "nude," "state of nudity," "regularly features," "regularly shown," "seminude," "state of seminudity," "sexual encounter establishment," "specified anatomical areas," and "specified sexual activity" have the same meanings as in section 2907.39 of the Revised Code.

**HISTORY: 151 v H 23, § 1, eff. 8-17-06.**

**Analogous to former RC § 503.51 (145 v H 3. Eff 10-1-93), repealed 151 v H 23, § 2, eff 8-17-06.**

See provisions of § 3 of 151 v H 23 following RC § 503.52.

## § 503.52 Authority to regulate adult entertainment establishments; request to prosecuting attorney; indemnification by state.

(A) Townships have authority to exercise all powers of local self-government regarding the operation of adult entertainment establishments within their limits and to adopt and enforce within their limits any local police, sanitary, and similar regulations regarding the operation of adult entertainment establishments that are not in conflict with general laws. The regulations may include, but are not limited to, antinudity restrictions, limitations on hours of operation, interior configuration requirements, and requirements that adult entertainment establishments and their employees obtain licenses or permits to operate as or to be employed by an adult entertainment establishment. The authority granted under this division shall be exercised by the adoption of resolutions and may include the adoption of resolutions that create one or more criminal offenses and impose criminal penalties related to the operation of adult entertainment establishments or may provide for civil sanction for violations of regulations established under the resolutions. Townships have the same rights, powers, and duties pursuant to the authority granted under this division as municipal corporations have under Section 3, Article XVIII, Ohio Constitution relative to their authority to exercise powers of local self-government and to adopt and enforce within their limits local police, sanitary, and similar regulations, except to the extent that the rights, powers, and duties that the municipal corporations have by their nature clearly are inapplicable to townships and to the exercise by townships of their authority granted under this division. No regulation adopted under authority of this division shall be in conflict with any provision in Chapter 4303. of the Revised Code, or with any rule adopted by the division of liquor control pursuant to that chapter, that regulates establishments that hold a liquor permit.

(B)(1) The authority of a township granted under division (A) of this section applies to all townships. If a township has adopted a limited home rule government pursuant to Chapter 504. of the Revised Code, the authority granted under division (A) of this section is in addition to the powers and authority granted to the township under Chapter 504. of the Revised Code.

(2) Upon the request of any township, the attorney general shall provide legal guidance and assistance to the township in developing, formulating, and drafting a resolution regarding the operation of adult entertainment establishments of a type described in division (A) of this section. The attorney general shall provide this service without charge to the township for which the service is performed.

(C) In case of conflict between any resolution enacted by a board of township trustees under the authority granted under division (A) of this section and a municipal ordinance or resolution, the ordinance or resolution enacted by the municipal corporation prevails. In case of conflict between any resolution enacted by a board of township trustees under the authority granted under division (A) of this section and a county resolution, the resolution enacted by the board of township trustees prevails.

(D) All proceeds from criminal and civil sanctions for violation of a regulation established by a township under a resolution adopted under division (A) of this section that are paid to the township shall be applied initially to the payment of costs incurred in the prosecution and enforcement of the resolution, including, but not limited to, court costs, reasonable attorney's fees, and other litigation expenses incurred by the county or township.

(E)(1)(a) When it appears that a resolution adopted under division (A) of this section or section 503.53 of the Revised Code is being or is about to be violated, the township in which the violation is taking place may request the prosecuting attorney of the county in which the township is located to prosecute and defend on behalf of the township a civil action to enjoin the violation. If the township does not request the prosecuting attorney to prosecute and defend an action to enjoin the violation, the legal counsel of that township, if other than the prosecuting attorney, may prosecute and defend a civil action to enjoin the violation.

(b) A township may request the prosecuting attorney of the county in which the township is located to prosecute and defend on behalf of the township a civil action under Chapter 3767. of the Revised Code to abate as a nuisance any place in the unincorporated area of the township at which a resolution adopted under division (A) of this section or section 503.53 of the Revised Code is being or has been violated. If the township does not request the prosecuting attorney to prosecute and defend an action under that chapter, the legal counsel of the township, if other than the prosecuting attorney, may prosecute and defend an action under that chapter for that purpose. All proceeds from the sale of personal property or contents seized pursuant to the action shall be applied initially to the payment of costs incurred in the prosecution of the action and the costs associated with the abatement and sale ordered under division (A) of section 3767.06 of the Revised Code, including, but not limited to, court costs, reasonable attorney's fees, and other litigation expenses incurred by the county or township. Any proceeds remaining after that initial application shall be deposited into the township treasury and credited to the general fund.

(c) If a township has adopted one or more resolutions regarding the operation of adult entertainment establishments pursuant to the authority that is granted under division (A) of this section or if a township resolution of that nature has been adopted under section 503.53 of the Revised Code and the validity of the resolution is challenged, the township may request the prosecuting attorney of the county in which the township is located to prosecute and defend on behalf of the township in the trial and argument in any court or tribunal of the challenge to the validity of the resolution.

(2) Division (E)(1) of this section applies regarding all townships, including townships that have adopted a limited home rule government pursuant to Chapter 504. of the Revised Code and regardless of whether a township that has so adopted a limited home rule government has entered into a contract with the prosecuting attorney as described in division (B) of section 504.15 of the Revised Code or has appointed a law director as described in division (A) of that section.

Upon the request of any township in the county served by the prosecuting attorney made pursuant to division (E)(1)(a), (b), or (c) of this section, the prosecuting attorney shall prosecute and defend in the action or proceeding as requested, as specified in division (B)(2) of section 309.09 of the Revised Code, without charge to the township for which the service is performed.

If a prosecuting attorney is prosecuting and defending a challenge to the validity of a resolution of a township pursuant to a request made pursuant to division (E)(1)(c) of this section and if the challenge is before a federal court, the prosecuting attorney may request the attorney general to assist the prosecuting attorney in prosecuting and defending the challenge, and, upon the prosecuting attorney's making of such a request, the attorney general shall assist the prosecuting attorney in performing that service if the resolution was drafted in accordance with legal guidance provided by the attorney general as described in division (B)(2) of this section. The attorney general shall provide this assistance without charge to the township for which the service is performed. If a township adopts a resolution without the legal guidance of the attorney general, the attorney general is not being required to provide assistance as described in this division to a prosecuting attorney.

(F) Except as otherwise provided in this division, the state shall indemnify a township and its trustees from liability incurred in the enforcement of a resolution that is authorized by this section, that was drafted in accordance with legal guidance provided by the attorney general as described in division (B)(2) of this section, and that a court finds to be unconstitutional or otherwise legally defective by paying any judgment in, or amount negotiated in settlement of, any civil action arising from the enforcement of the resolution. The state shall not indemnify a township or its trustees until all appeals have been exhausted or the action has otherwise been finally resolved.

The state shall not indemnify a township or its trustees for any of the following or to the extent that any of the following apply:

(1) Any part of the judgment or settlement that represents damages that are covered by a policy of insurance for civil liability;

(2) Any part of the judgment or settlement that is based upon an officer or employee of the township acting manifestly outside the scope of the officer's or employee's employment or official responsibilities, with malicious purpose, in bad faith, or in a wanton or reckless manner;

(3) Any part of the judgment that is for punitive damages;

(4) Any part of a consent judgment or settlement that the attorney general determines is unreasonable.

**HISTORY: 151 v H 23, § 1, eff. 8-17-06; 152 v S 16, § 1, eff. 9-4-07.**

**Analogous in part to former RC § 503.52 (145 v H 3. Eff 10-1-93; 151 v S 107, § 1, eff. 12-20-05), repealed 151 v H 23, § 2, eff 8-17-06.**

The provisions of § 3 of 151 v H 23 read as follows:

SECTION 3. In enacting new sections 503.51 and 503.52 and sections 2907.38 and 2907.39 of the Revised Code, the General Assembly makes the following statement of intent and findings:

(A)(1) Adult entertainment establishments require special supervision from the public safety agencies of this state in order to protect and preserve the health, safety, morals, and welfare of the patrons and employees of the businesses as well as the citizens of this state.

(2) The General Assembly finds that adult entertainment establishments are frequently used for unlawful sexual activities, including prostitution and sexual liaisons of a casual nature.

(3) The concern over sexually transmitted diseases is a legitimate health concern of this state that demands reasonable regulation of adult entertainment establishments by the state in the specified manner, and expanded authority for reasonable regulation of adult entertainment establishments by local governments, in order to protect the health and well-being of the citizens.

(4) Minimal regulations enacted by local governments or the state are a legitimate and reasonable means of accountability to ensure that operators of adult entertainment establishments comply with reasonable regulations and to ensure that operators do not knowingly allow their establishments to be used as places of illegal sexual activity or solicitation.

(5) There is convincing documented evidence that adult entertainment establishments, because of their very nature, have a deleterious effect on both the existing businesses around them and the surrounding residential areas adjacent to them and cause increased crime, particularly in the overnight hours, and the downgrading of property values.

(6) The General Assembly desires to minimize and control these adverse effects by regulating adult entertainment establishments in the specified manner and by expanding the authority of local governments to regulate adult entertainment establishments and, by minimizing and controlling these adverse effects, to protect the health, safety, and welfare of the citizenry; protect the citizens from increased crime; preserve the quality of life; preserve the property values and character of surrounding neighborhoods; and deter the spread of urban blight.

(7) The General Assembly has determined that current local zoning and other locational criteria do not adequately protect the health, safety, and general welfare of the people of this state and that expanded local government authority to regulate adult entertainment establishments is necessary.

(8) It is not the intent of the General Assembly in enacting this act to suppress, or authorize the suppression of, any speech activities protected by the First Amendment but to enact content-neutral statutes that expand local government authority to address the secondary effects of adult entertainment establishments.

(9) It is not the intent of the General Assembly to condone or legitimize the distribution of obscene material, and the General Assembly recognizes that state and federal law prohibits the distribution of obscene materials and expects and encourages state law enforcement officials to enforce state obscenity statutes against any such illegal activities in this state.

(B) It is the intent of the General Assembly in enacting new sections 503.51 and 503.52 and sections 2907.38 and 2907.39 of the Revised Code to regulate in the specified manner, and to expand the authority of local governments to regulate, adult entertainment establishments in order to promote the health, safety, morals, and general welfare of the citizens of this state and establish reasonable regulations to prevent the deleterious secondary effects of adult entertainment establishments within this state. The provisions of new sections 503.51 and 503.52 and sections 2907.38 and 2907.39 of the Revised Code have neither the purpose nor effect of imposing a limitation or restriction on the content of any communicative materials, including sexually oriented materials. Similarly, it is not the intent nor effect of the General Assembly in enacting new sections 503.51 and 503.52 and sections 2907.38 and 2907.39 of the Revised Code to restrict or deny, or authorize the restriction or denial of, access by adults to sexually oriented materials protected by the First Amendment, or to deny, or authorize the denial of, access by the distributors and exhibitors of adult entertainment and adult materials to their intended market. Neither is it the intent nor effect of the General Assembly in enacting new sections 503.51 and 503.52 and sections 2907.38 and 2907.39 of the Revised Code to condone or legitimize the distribution or exhibition of obscene material.

(C) Based on evidence concerning the adverse secondary effects of adult uses on communities presented in hearings and in reports made available to the legislature and on findings incorporated in the cases of *City of Littleton, Colorado v. Z.J. Gifts D-4, L.L.C. (2004), 541 U.S. 774, City of Erie v. Pap's A.M.* (2000), 529 U.S. 277; *Barnes v. Glen Theatre, Inc.* (1991), 501 U.S. 560; *City of Renton v. Playtime Theatres, Inc.* (1986), 475 U.S. 41; *Young v. American Mini Theatres* (1976), 426 U.S. 50; *California v. LaRue* (1972), 409 U.S. 109; *DLS, Inc. v. City of Chattanooga* (6th Cir. 1997) 107 F.3d 403; *East Brooks Books, Inc. v. City of Memphis,* (6th Cir. 1995), 48 F.3d 220; *Harris v. Fitchville Township Trustees* (N.D. Ohio 2000), 99 F. Supp.2d 837; *Bamon Corp. v. City of Dayton* (S.D. Ohio 1990), 730 F. Supp. 90, *aff'd* (6th Cir. 1991), 923 F.2d 470; *Broadway Books v. Roberts* (E.D. Tenn. 1986), 642 F. Supp. 486; *Bright Lights, Inc. v. City of Newport* (E.D. Ky. 1993), 830 F. Supp. 378; *Richland Bookmart v. Nichols* (6th Cir. 1998), 137 F.3d 435; *Deja Vu v. Metro Government* (6th Cir. 1999), 1999 U.S. App. LEXIS 535; *Threesome Entertainment v. Strittmather* (N.D. Ohio 1998), 4 F.Supp.2d 710; *J.L. Spoons, Inc. v. City of Brunswick* (N.D. Ohio 1999), 49 F. Supp.2d 1032; *Triplett Grille, Inc. v. City of Akron* (6th Cir. 1994) 40 F.3d 129; *Nightclubs, Inc. v. City of Paducah* (6th Cir. 2000), 202 F.3d 884; *O'Connor v. City and County of Denver* (10th Cir. 1990), 894 F.2d 1210; *Deja Vu of Nashville, Inc., et al. v. Metropolitan Government of Nashville and Davidson County* (6th Cir. 2001), 2001 U.S. App. LEXIS 26007; *State of Ohio ex rel. Rothal v. Smith* (Ohio C.P.

2002), Summit C.P. No. CV 01094594; *Z.J. Gifts D-2, L.L.C. v. City of Aurora* (10th Cir. 1998), 136 F.3d 683; *Connection Distrib. Co. v. Reno* (6th Cir. 1998), 154 F.3d 281; *Sundance Assocs. v. Reno* (10th Cir. 1998), 139 F.3d 804; *American Library Association v. Reno* (D.C. Cir. 1994), 33 F.3d 78; *American Target Advertising, Inc. v. Giani* (10th Cir. 2000), 199 F.3d 1241; and other cases and on reports of secondary effects occurring in and around adult entertainment establishments in Phoenix, Arizona (1984); Minneapolis, Minnesota (1980); Houston, Texas (1983); Indianapolis, Indiana (1984); Amarillo, Texas (1977); Garden Grove, California (1991); Los Angeles, California (1977); Whittier, California (1978); Austin, Texas (1986); Seattle, Washington (1989); Oklahoma City, Oklahoma (1986); Cleveland, Ohio (1977); Dallas, Texas (1997); St. Croix County, Wisconsin (1993); Bellevue, Washington (1998); Newport News, Virginia (1996); Tucson, Arizona (1990); St. Paul, Minnesota (1988); Oklahoma City, Oklahoma (1986 and 1992); Beaumont, Texas (1982); New York, New York (1994); Ellicottville, New York (1998); Des Moines, Iowa (1984); Islip, New York (1980); Adams County, Colorado (1987); Manatee County, Florida (1987); New Hanover County, North Carolina (1989); Las Vegas, Nevada (1978); Cattaraugas County, New York (1998); Cleburne, Texas (1997); Dallas, Texas (1997); El Paso, Texas (1986); New York Times Square study (1994); Report to ACLJ on the Secondary Impacts of Sex Oriented Businesses (1996); the findings from the Report of the Attorney General's Working Group On The Regulation Of Sexually Oriented Businesses (June 6, 1989, State of Minnesota); and on testimony to Congress in 136 Cong. Rec. S. 8987; 135 Cong. Rec. S. 14519; 135 Cong. Rec. S. 5636, 134 Cong. Rec. E. 3750; and also on findings from the paper entitled "Stripclubs According to Strippers: Exposing Workplace Sexual Violence," by Kelly Holsopple, Program Director, Freedom and Justice Center for Prostitution Resources, Minneapolis, Minnesota; and from "Sexually Oriented Businesses: An Insider's View," by David Sherman, presented to the Michigan House Committee on Ethics and Constitutional Law, Jan. 12, 2000; and from various other police reports, testimony, newspaper reports, and other documentary evidence, the General Assembly finds:

(1) Adult entertainment establishments lend themselves to ancillary unlawful and unhealthy activities that are presently uncontrolled by the operators of the establishments. Further, there is presently no statewide mechanism, and no general or comprehensive grant of authority enabling local governments, to make the owners of these establishments responsible for the activities that occur on their premises.

(2) Certain employees of adult entertainment establishments, as defined in section 2907.39 of the Revised Code as adult theaters and cabarets, engage in a higher incidence of certain types of illicit sexual behavior than employees of other establishments.

(3) Sexual acts, including masturbation and oral and anal sex, occur at adult entertainment establishments, especially those that provide private or semiprivate booths or cubicles for viewing films, videos, or live sex shows. The "couch dances" or "lap dances" that frequently occur in adult entertainment establishments featuring live nude or seminude dancers constitute or may constitute the offense of "engaging in prostitution" under section 2907.25 of the Revised Code.

(4) Offering and providing such space encourages such activities, which creates unhealthy conditions.

(5) Persons frequent certain adult theaters, adult arcades, and other adult entertainment establishments for the purpose of engaging in sexual activity within the premises of those adult entertainment establishments.

(6) Numerous communicable diseases may be spread by activities occurring in sexually oriented businesses, including, but not limited to, syphilis, gonorrhea, human immunodeficiency virus infection (HIV-AIDS), genital herpes, hepatitis salmonella, campylobacter and shigella infections, chlamydial, myoplasmal and ureoplasmal infections, trichomoniasis, and chancroid.

(7) Since 1981 and to the present, there has been an increasing cumulative number of reported cases of AIDS caused by the human immunodeficiency virus (HIV) in the United States: 600 in 1982, 2,200 in 1983, 4,600 in 1984, 8,555 in 1985, and 253,448 through December 31, 1992.

(8) A total of 10,255 AIDS cases had been reported in Ohio as of January 1999. Ohio has required HIV case reporting since 1990, and the reported information shows 7,969 people living with (HIV) (4,213) and (AIDS) (3,756) in the state.

(9) Since 1981 and to the present, there have been an increasing cumulative number of persons testing positive for the HIV antibody test in Ohio.

(10) The number of cases of early (less than one year) syphilis in the United States reported annually has risen. 33,613 cases were reported in 1982, and 45,200 cases were reported through November 1990.

(11) The number of cases of gonorrhea in the United States reported annually remains at a high level, with over one-half million cases being reported in 1990.

(12) The Surgeon General of the United States in his report of October 22, 1986, has advised the American public that AIDS and HIV infection may be transmitted through sexual contact, intravenous drug abuse, and exposure to infected blood and blood components, and from an infected mother to her newborn.

(13) According to the best scientific evidence, AIDS and HIV infection, as well as syphilis and gonorrhea, are principally transmitted by sexual acts.

(14) Sanitary conditions in some adult entertainment establishments are unhealthy, in part, because the activities conducted there are unhealthy, and, in part, because of the unregulated nature of the activities and the failure of the owners and the operators of the facilities to self-regulate those activities and maintain those facilities.

(15) The findings noted in divisions (C)(1) to (14) of this section raise substantial governmental concerns.

(16) Adult entertainment establishments have operational characteristics that should subject them to reasonable government regulation in order to protect those substantial governmental concerns.

(17) The enactment of new sections 503.51 and 503.52 and sections 2907.38 and 2907.39 of the Revised Code will promote the general welfare, health, morals, and safety of the citizens of this state.

## § 503.53 Election on resolution regulating adult entertainment establishments.

(A) Resolutions of the type described in division (A) of section 503.52 of the Revised Code may be proposed by initiative petition by the electors of a township and adopted by election by these electors, under the same circumstances, in the same manner, and subject to the same penalties as provided in sections 731.28 to 731.40 and 731.99 of the Revised Code for ordinances and other measures of municipal corporations, insofar as those sections are applicable to townships, except as follows:

(1) The board of township trustees shall perform the duties imposed on the legislative authority of the municipal corporation under those sections.

(2) Initiative petitions shall be filed with the township fiscal officer, who shall perform the duties imposed under those sections upon the city auditor or village clerk.

(3) Initiative petitions shall contain the signatures of electors of the township equal in number to at least ten per cent of the total vote cast in the township for the office of governor at the most recent general election for that office.

(4) Each signer of an initiative petition shall be an elector of the township in which the election on the proposed resolution is to be held.

(B) A resolution proposed under division (A) of this section may provide for the following:

(1) Modification of the administrative procedures, including administrative zoning procedures, of the township as those procedures apply to adult entertainment establishments to ensure that constitutional requirements are met;

(2) Criminal and civil sanctions for adult entertainment establishments that violate regulations established by the resolution.

**HISTORY: 146 v H 50. Eff 10-25-95; 151 v S 107, § 1, eff. 12-20-05; 151 v H 23, § 1, eff. 8-17-06.**

**Not analogous to former RC § 503.29 (RS § 1449; S & C 1569; 51 v 489; GC § 3267; Bureau of Code Revision, 10-1-53; 129 v 582), repealed 139 v S 114, § 2, eff 10-27-81.**

**Publisher's Note:**

This section was amended and renumbered from RC § 503.29 by 151 v H 23, effective August 17, 2006.

## § 503.54 Repealed, 151 v H 23, § 2 [145 v H 3. Eff 10-1-93]. Eff 8-17-06.

This section concerned application for permit and expiration.
See now RC §§ 503.51 to 503.53.

## § 503.55 Repealed, 151 v H 23, § 2 [145 v H 3. Eff 10-1-93]. Eff 8-17-06.

This section concerned reasons for denial or revocation of permit.
See now RC §§ 503.51 to 503.53.

## § 503.56 Repealed, 151 v H 23, § 2 [145 v H 3. Eff 10-1-93]. Eff 8-17-06.

This section concerned requirements that may be imposed on cabaret.
See now RC §§ 503.51 to 503.53.

## § 503.57 Repealed, 151 v H 23, § 2 [145 v H 3. Eff 10-1-93]. Eff 8-17-06.

This section concerned hearing on denial or revocation not required, record, notice of proceedings, and appeals.
See now RC §§ 503.51 to 503.53.

## § 503.58 Repealed, 151 v H 23, § 2 [145 v H 3. Eff 10-1-93]. Eff 8-17-06.

This section concerned deposit and use of fees.
See now RC §§ 503.51 to 503.53.

## § 503.59 Repealed, 151 v H 23, § 2 [145 v H 3. Eff 10-1-93]. Eff 8-17-06.

This section concerned penalties.
See now RC §§ 503.51 to 503.53.

## § 503.60 Township authority to regulate residency of sex offenders and child-victim offenders.

(A) Townships have authority to exercise all powers of local self-government within their limits regarding the residency of a person who has been convicted of or pleaded guilty to either a sexually oriented offense or a child-victim oriented offense and to adopt and enforce within their limits any local police, sanitary, and similar regulations regarding the residency of such persons that are not in conflict with general laws. The authority granted under this division shall be exercised by the adoption of resolutions. Townships have the same rights, powers, and duties pursuant to the authority granted under this division as municipal corporations have under Section 3 of Article XVIII, Ohio Constitution relative to their authority to exercise powers of local self-government and to adopt and enforce within their limits local police, sanitary, and similar regulations, except to the extent that the rights, powers, and duties that the municipal corporations have by their nature clearly are inapplicable to townships and to the exercise by townships of their authority granted under this division.

(B) The authority of a township granted under division (A) of this section applies to all townships. If a township has adopted a limited home rule government pursuant to Chapter 504. of the Revised Code, the authority granted under division (A) of this section is in addition to the powers and authority granted to the township under Chapter 504. of the Revised Code.

(C) As used in this section, "child-victim oriented offense" and "sexually oriented offense" have the same meanings as in section 2950.01 of the Revised Code.

**HISTORY: 152 v S 97, § 1, eff. 1-1-08.**

The effective date is set by § 3 of 152 v S 97.

**Not analogous to former RC § 503.60 (145 v H 3. Eff 10-1-93), repealed 151 v H 23, § 2, eff 8-17-06.**

# CHAPTER 504: LIMITED HOME RULE GOVERNMENT

Section



## § 504.04 Exercise of home rule powers; limitations; officers; conflicts with municipal or county laws.

(A) A township that adopts a limited home rule government may do all of the following by resolution, provided that any of these resolutions, other than a resolution to supply water or sewer services in accordance with sections 504.18 to 504.20 of the Revised Code, may be enforced only by the imposition of civil fines as authorized in this chapter:

(1) Exercise all powers of local self-government within the unincorporated area of the township, other than powers that are in conflict with general laws, except that the township shall comply with the requirements and prohibitions of this chapter, and shall enact no taxes other than those authorized by general law, and except that no resolution adopted pursuant to this chapter shall encroach upon the powers, duties, and privileges of elected township officers or change, alter, combine, eliminate, or otherwise modify the form or structure of the township government unless the change is required or permitted by this chapter;

(2) Adopt and enforce within the unincorporated area of the township local police, sanitary, and other similar regulations that are not in conflict with general laws or otherwise prohibited by division (B) of this section;

(3) Supply water and sewer services to users within the unincorporated area of the township in accordance with sections 504.18 to 504.20 of the Revised Code;

(4) Adopt and enforce within the unincorporated area of the township any resolution of a type described in section 503.52 or 503.60 of the Revised Code.

(B) No resolution adopted pursuant to this chapter shall do any of the following:

(1) Create a criminal offense or impose criminal penalties, except as authorized by division (A) of this section or by section 503.52 of the Revised Code;

(2) Impose civil fines other than as authorized by this chapter;

(3) Establish or revise subdivision regulations, road construction standards, urban sediment rules, or storm water and drainage regulations, except as provided in section 504.21 of the Revised Code;

(4) Establish or revise building standards, building codes, and other standard codes except as provided in section 504.13 of the Revised Code;

(5) Increase, decrease, or otherwise alter the powers or duties of a township under any other chapter of the Revised Code pertaining to agriculture or the conservation or development of natural resources;

(6) Establish regulations affecting hunting, trapping, fishing, or the possession, use, or sale of firearms;

(7) Establish or revise water or sewer regulations, except in accordance with section 504.18, 504.19, or 504.21 of the Revised Code.

Nothing in this chapter shall be construed as affecting the powers of counties with regard to the subjects listed in divisions (B)(3) to (5) of this section.

(C) Under a limited home rule government, all officers shall have the qualifications, and be nominated, elected, or appointed, as provided in Chapter 505. of the Revised Code, except that the board of township trustees shall appoint a full-time or part-time law director pursuant to section 504.15 of the Revised Code, and except that a five-member board of township trustees approved for the township before September 26, 2003, shall continue to serve as the legislative authority with successive members serving for four-year terms of office until a termination of a limited home rule government under section 504.03 of the Revised Code.

(D) In case of conflict between resolutions enacted by a board of township trustees and municipal ordinances or resolutions, the ordinance or resolution enacted by the municipal corporation prevails. In case of conflict between resolutions enacted by a board of township trustees and any county resolution, the resolution enacted by the board of township trustees prevails.

**HISTORY: 144 v H 77 (Eff 9-17-91); 145 v H 579 (Eff 7-13-94); 148 v H 187 (Eff 9-20-99); 149 v H 94. Eff 9-5-2001; 150 v H 95, § 1, eff. 9-26-03; 150 v H 411, § 1, eff. 5-6-05; 151 v H 23, § 1, eff. 8-17-06; 152 v S 97, § 1, eff. 1-1-08.**

The effective date is set by § 3 of 152 v S 97.
The effective date is set by section 179 of H.B. 95 (150 v —).

## § 504.05 Civil fine for violation.

The board of township trustees may impose a civil fine for a violation of a resolution adopted pursuant to this chapter, and may graduate the amount of the fine based on the number of previous violations of the resolution. No fine shall exceed one thousand dollars. Any resolution that imposes a fine shall clearly state the amount of the fine for the first and for subsequent violations.

**HISTORY: 144 v H 77. Eff 9-17-91.**

## § 504.06 Citation issued to violator.

(A) Peace officers serving the township pursuant to section 504.16 of the Revised Code may issue citations to persons who violate township resolutions adopted pursuant to this chapter. Each citation shall contain provisions that:

(1) Advise the person upon whom it is served that the person must answer in relation to the violation charged in the citation within fourteen days after the citation is served upon the person;

(2) Indicate the allowable answers that may be made and that the person will be afforded a court hearing if the person denies in the person's answer having committed the violation;

(3) Specify that the answer must be made in person or by mail to the township fiscal officer;

(4) Indicate the amount of the fine that arises from the violation.

(B) A peace officer who issues a citation for a violation of a township resolution shall complete the citation by identifying the violation charged and by indicating the date, time, and place of the violation charged. The officer shall sign the citation, affirm the facts that it contains, and without unnecessary delay file the original citation with the court having jurisdiction over the violation. A copy of a citation issued pursuant to this section shall be served pursuant to the Rules of Civil Procedure upon the person who violated the resolution. No peace officer is entitled to receive witness fees in a cause prosecuted under a township resolution adopted pursuant to this chapter.

**HISTORY: 144 v H 77. Eff 9-17-91; 151 v S 107, § 1, eff. 12-20-05.**

## § 504.07 Answer; scheduling of hearing; judgment or default judgment; appeal.

(A)(1) A person who is served with a citation pursuant to division (B) of section 504.06 of the Revised Code shall answer the charge by personal appearance before, or by mail addressed to, the township fiscal officer, who shall immediately notify the township law director. An answer shall be made within fourteen days after the citation is served upon the person and shall be in one of the following forms:

(a) An admission that the person committed the violation, by payment of any fine arising from the violation. Payment of a fine pursuant to division (A)(1)(a) of this section shall be payable to the fiscal officer of the township and deposited by the fiscal officer into the township general fund.

(b) A denial that the person committed the violation.

(2) Whenever a person pays a fine pursuant to division (A)(1)(a) of this section or whenever a person answers by denying the violation or does not submit payment of the fine within the time required by division (A)(1) of this section, the township fiscal officer shall notify the court having jurisdiction over the violation.

(B) If a person answers by denying the violation or does not submit payment of the fine within the time required by division (A)(1) of this section, the court having jurisdiction over the violation shall, upon receiving the notification required by division (A)(2) of this section, schedule a hearing on the violation and send notice of the date and time of the hearing to the person charged with the violation and to the township law director. If the person charged with the violation fails to appear for the scheduled hearing, the court may hold the person in contempt, or issue a summons or a warrant for the person's arrest pursuant to Criminal Rule 4. If the court issues a summons and the person charged with the violation fails to appear, the court may enter a default judgment against the person and require the person to pay the fine arising from the violation.

(C) The court shall hold the scheduled hearing in accordance with the Rules of Civil Procedure and the rules of the court, and shall determine whether the township has established, by a preponderance of the evidence, that the person committed the violation. If the court determines that the person committed the violation, it shall enter a judgment against the person requiring the person to pay the fine arising from the violation.

If the court determines that the township has not established, by a preponderance of the evidence, that the person committed the violation, the court shall enter judgment against the township whose resolution allegedly was violated, shall dismiss the charge of the violation against the person, and shall assess costs against the township.

(D) Payment of any judgment or default judgment entered against a person pursuant to this section shall be made to the clerk of the court that entered the judgment, within ten days after the date of entry. All money paid in satisfaction of a judgment or default judgment shall be disbursed by the clerk as required by law and the clerk shall enter the fact of payment of the money and its disbursement in the records of the court. If payment of a judgment or default judgment is not made within this time period, execution may be levied, and such other measures may be taken for its collection as are authorized for the collection of an unpaid money judgment in a civil action rendered in that court. The municipal or county court shall assess costs against the judgment debtor, to be paid upon satisfaction of the judgment.

(E) Any person against whom a judgment or default judgment is entered pursuant to this section and any township against which a judgment is entered pursuant to this section may appeal the judgment or default judgment to the court of appeals within whose territorial jurisdiction the resolution allegedly was violated. An appeal shall be made by filing a notice of appeal with the trial court and with the court of appeals within thirty days after the entry of judgment by the trial court and by the payment of reasonable costs as the court requires. Upon the filing of an appeal, the court shall schedule a hearing date and notify the parties of the date, time, and place of the hearing. The hearing shall be held by the court in accordance with the rules of the court. Service of a notice of appeal under this division does not stay enforcement and collection of the judgment or default judgment from which appeal is taken by the person unless the person who files the appeal posts bond with the trial court, in the amount of the judgment, plus court costs, at or before service of the notice of appeal.

Notwithstanding any other provision of law, the judgment on appeal of the court of appeals is final.

**HISTORY: 144 v H 77. Eff 9-17-91; 151 v S 107, § 1, eff. 12-20-05.**

# CHAPTER 505: TRUSTEES

[PROPERTY RECOVERED BY POLICE DEPARTMENT]

### § 505.105 Disposition of stolen or other property recovered by police department.

Stolen or other property recovered by members of an organized police department of a township, a township police district, a joint police district, or the office of a township constable shall be deposited and kept in a place designated by the head of the department, district, or office. Each article of property shall be entered in a book kept for that purpose, with the name of its owner, if ascertained, the person from whom it was taken, the place where it was found with general circumstances, the date of its receipt, and the name of the officer receiving it.

An inventory of all money or other property shall be given to the party from whom it was taken, and, if it is not claimed by some person within thirty days after arrest and seizure, it shall be delivered to the person from whom it was taken, and to no other person, either attorney, agent, factor, or clerk, except by special order of the head of the department, district, or office.

**HISTORY: 148 v H 55. Eff 9-29-99; 2011 HB 153, § 101.01, eff. Sept. 29, 2011.**

### § 505.106 Neglect or refusal to deposit property.

No officer, or other member of an organized police department of a township, a township police district, a joint police district, or the office of a township constable shall neglect or refuse to deposit property taken or found by the officer or other member in possession of a person arrested. Any conviction for a violation of this section shall vacate the office of the person so convicted.

**HISTORY: 148 v H 55. Eff 9-29-99; 2011 HB 153, § 101.01, eff. Sept. 29, 2011.**

### § 505.107 Return of property to claimant or accused person.

If, within thirty days, the money or property recovered under section 505.105 of the Revised Code is claimed by any other person, it shall be retained by its custodian until after the discharge or conviction of the person from whom it was taken and as long as it is required as evidence in any case in court. If that claimant establishes to the satisfaction of the court that the claimant is the rightful owner, the money or property shall be restored to the claimant; otherwise, it shall be returned to the accused person, personally, and not to any attorney, agent, factor, or clerk of the accused person, except upon special order of the head of the organized police department of the township, township police district, joint police district, or office of a township constable, as the case may be, after all liens and claims in favor of the township have first been discharged and satisfied.

**HISTORY: 148 v H 55. Eff 9-29-99; 2011 HB 153, § 101.01, eff. Sept. 29, 2011.**

### § 505.108 Sale or donation of unclaimed property.

Except as otherwise provided in this section and unless the property involved is required to be disposed of pursuant to another section of the Revised Code, property that is unclaimed for ninety days or more shall be sold by the chief of police or other head of the organized police department of the township, township police district, joint police district, or office of a township constable at public auction, after notice of the sale has been provided by publication once a week for three successive weeks in a newspaper of general circulation, or as provided in section 7.16 of the Revised Code, in the county, or counties, if appropriate, in the case of a joint police district. The proceeds of the sale shall be paid to the fiscal officer of the township and credited to the township general fund, except that, in the case of a joint police district, the proceeds of a sale shall be paid to the treasurer of the joint police district board and credited to the appropriate fund according to agreement of the participating townships and municipal corporations.

If authorized to do so by a resolution adopted by the board of township trustees or, in the case of a joint police district, the joint police district board, and if the property involved is not required to be disposed of pursuant to another section of the Revised Code, the head of the department, district, or office may contribute property that is unclaimed for ninety days or more to one or more public agencies, to one or more nonprofit organizations no part of the net income of which inures to the benefit of any private shareholder or individual and no substantial part of the activities of which consists of carrying on propaganda or otherwise attempting to influence legislation, or to one or more organizations satisfying section 501(c)(3) or (c)(19) of the Internal Revenue Code of 1986.

**HISTORY: 148 v H 55. Eff 9-29-99; 151 v S 107, § 1, eff. 12-20-05; 2011 HB 153, § 101.01, eff. Sept. 29, 2011.**

### § 505.109 Payment of removal, storage and selling expenses.

Upon the sale of any unclaimed property as provided in section 505.108 of the Revised Code, if any of the unclaimed property was ordered removed to a place of storage or stored, or both, by or under the direction of the head of the organized police department of the township, township police district, joint police district, or office of a township constable, any expenses or charges for the removal or storage, or both, and costs of sale, provided they are approved by the head of the department, district, or office, shall first be paid from the proceeds of the sale. Notice shall be given by certified mail, thirty days before the date of the sale, to the owner and mortgagee, or other lienholder, at their last known addresses.

**HISTORY: 148 v H 55. Eff 9-29-99; 2011 HB 153, § 101.01, eff. Sept. 29, 2011.**

### § 505.17 Regulations for engine noise and vehicle parking.

(A) Except in a township or portion of a township that is within the limits of a municipal corporation, the board of township trustees may make regulations and orders as are necessary to control passenger car, motorcycle, and internal combustion engine noise, as permitted under section

4513.221 of the Revised Code, and all vehicle parking in the township. This authorization includes, among other powers, the power to regulate parking on established roadways proximate to buildings on private property as necessary to provide access to the property by public safety vehicles and equipment, if the property is used for commercial purposes, the public is permitted to use the parking area, and accommodation for more than ten motor vehicles is provided, and the power to authorize the issuance of orders limiting or prohibiting parking on any township street or highway during a snow emergency declared pursuant to a snow-emergency authorization adopted under this division. All such regulations and orders shall be subject to the limitations, restrictions, and exceptions in sections 4511.01 to 4511.76 and 4513.02 to 4513.37 of the Revised Code.

A board of township trustees may adopt a general snow-emergency authorization, which becomes effective under division (B)(1) of this section, allowing the president of the board or some other person specified in the authorization to issue an order declaring a snow emergency and limiting or prohibiting parking on any township street or highway during the snow emergency. Any such order becomes effective under division (B)(2) of this section. Each general snow-emergency authorization adopted under this division shall specify the weather conditions under which a snow emergency may be declared in that township.

(B)(1) All regulations and orders, including any snow-emergency authorization established by the board under this section, except for an order declaring a snow emergency as provided in division (B)(2) of this section, shall be posted by the township fiscal officer in five conspicuous public places in the township for thirty days before becoming effective, and shall be published in a newspaper of general circulation in the township for three consecutive weeks or as provided in section 7.16 of the Revised Code. In addition to these requirements, no general snow-emergency authorization shall become effective until permanent signs giving notice that parking is limited or prohibited during a snow emergency are properly posted, in accordance with any applicable standards adopted by the department of transportation, along streets or highways specified in the authorization.

(2) Pursuant to the adoption of a snow-emergency authorization under this section, an order declaring a snow emergency becomes effective two hours after the president of the board or the other person specified in the general snow-emergency authorization makes an announcement of a snow emergency to the local news media. The president or other specified person shall request the local news media to announce that a snow emergency has been declared, the time the declaration will go into effect, and whether the snow emergency will remain in effect for a specified period of time or indefinitely until canceled by a subsequent announcement to the local news media by the president or other specified person.

(C) Such regulations and orders may be enforced where traffic control devices conforming to section 4511.09 of the Revised Code are prominently displayed. Parking regulations authorized by this section do not apply to any state highway unless the parking regulations are approved by the director of transportation.

(D) A board of township trustees or its designated agent may order into storage any vehicle parked in violation of a township parking regulation or order, if the violation is not one that is required to be handled pursuant to Chapter 4521. of the Revised Code. The owner or any lienholder of a vehicle ordered into storage may claim the vehicle upon presentation of proof of ownership, which may be evidenced by a certificate of title to the vehicle, and payment of all expenses, charges, and fines incurred as a result of the parking violation and removal and storage of the vehicle.

(E) Whoever violates any regulation or order adopted pursuant to this section is guilty of a minor misdemeanor, unless the township has enacted a regulation pursuant to division (A) of section 4521.02 of the Revised Code, that specifies that the violation shall not be considered a criminal offense and shall be handled pursuant to Chapter 4521. of the Revised Code. Fines levied and collected under this section shall be paid into the township general revenue fund.

**HISTORY: GC § 3287; 123 v 265; Bureau of Code Revision, 10-1-53; 135 v H 200 (Eff 9-23-73); 135 v H 300 (Eff 1-1-74); 138 v S 257 (Eff 6-25-80); 139 v H 707 (Eff 1-1-83); 141 v H 131 (Eff 6-26-86); 142 v H 113. Eff 6-20-88; 151 v S 107, § 1, eff. 12-20-05; 2011 HB 153, § 101.01, eff. Sept. 29, 2011.**

## [FIRE AND POLICE PROTECTION]

### § 505.373 Adoption of standard code.

The board of township trustees may, by resolution, adopt by incorporation by reference a standard code pertaining to fire, fire hazards, and fire prevention prepared and promulgated by the state or any department, board, or other agency of the state, or any such code prepared and promulgated by a public or private organization that publishes a model or standard code.

After the adoption of the code by the board, a notice clearly identifying the code, stating the purpose of the code, and stating that a complete copy of the code is on file with the township fiscal officer for inspection by the public and also on file in the law library of the county in which the township is located and that the fiscal officer has copies available for distribution to the public at cost, shall be posted by the fiscal officer in five conspicuous places in the township for thirty days before becoming effective. The notice required by this section shall also be published in a newspaper of general circulation in the township once a week for three consecutive weeks or as provided in section 7.16 of the Revised Code. If the adopting township amends or deletes any provision of the code, the notice shall contain a brief summary of the deletion or amendment.

If the agency that originally promulgated or published the code thereafter amends the code, any township that has adopted the code pursuant to this section may adopt the amendment or change by incorporation by reference in the same manner as provided for adoption of the original code.

**HISTORY: 135 v H 739 (Eff 7-26-74); 148 v H 187. Eff 9-20-99; 151 v S 107, § 1, eff. 12-20-05; 2011 HB 153, § 101.01, eff. June 30, 2011.**

### § 505.374 Violation prohibited.

No person shall violate a provision of a standard code or regulation adopted under section 505.373 [505.37.3] or division (C) of section 505.375 [505.37.5] of the Revised

Code. Each day of continued violation of this section shall constitute a separate offense.

**HISTORY: 135 v H 739 (Eff 7-26-74); 146 v H 192. Eff 11-21-95.**

## [TOWNSHIP POLICE DISTRICTS]

### § 505.48 Township police districts.

(A) The board of township trustees of any township may, by resolution adopted by two-thirds of the members of the board, create a township police district comprised of all or a portion of the unincorporated territory of the township as the resolution may specify. If the township police district does not include all of the unincorporated territory of the township, the resolution creating the district shall contain a complete and accurate description of the territory of the district and a separate and distinct name for the district.

At any time not less than one hundred twenty days after a township police district is created and operative, the territorial limits of the district may be altered in the manner provided in division (B) of this section or, if applicable, as provided in section 505.482 of the Revised Code.

(B) Except as otherwise provided in section 505.481 of the Revised Code, the territorial limits of a township police district may be altered by a resolution adopted by a two-thirds vote of the board of township trustees. If the township police district imposes a tax, any territory proposed for addition to the district shall become part of the district only after all of the following have occurred:

(1) Adoption by two-thirds vote of the board of township trustees of a resolution approving the expansion of the territorial limits of the district;

(2) Adoption by a two-thirds vote of the board of township trustees of a resolution recommending the extension of the tax to the additional territory;

(3) Approval of the tax by the electors of the territory proposed for addition to the district.

Each resolution of the board adopted under division (B)(2) of this section shall state the name of the township police district, a description of the territory to be added, and the rate and termination date of the tax, which shall be the rate and termination date of the tax currently in effect in the district.

The board of trustees shall certify each resolution adopted under division (B)(2) of this section to the board of elections in accordance with section 5705.19 of the Revised Code. The election required under division (B)(3) of this section shall be held, canvassed, and certified in the manner provided for the submission of tax levies under section 5705.25 of the Revised Code, except that the question appearing on the ballot shall read:

"Shall the territory within..............................
..............................................................
(description of the proposed territory to be added)
be added to..................................................
(name)
township police district, and a property tax at a rate of taxation not exceeding ................ (here insert tax rate) be in effect for ................. (here insert the number of years the tax is to be in effect or "a continuing period of time," as applicable)?"

If the question is approved by at least a majority of the electors voting on it, the joinder shall be effective as of the first day of January of the year following approval, and, on that date, the township police district tax shall be extended to the taxable property within the territory that has been added.

**HISTORY: 130 v 211 (Eff 9-24-63); 141 v H 743. Eff 3-10-87; 150 v H 148, § 1, eff. 11-5-04; 2011 HB 153, § 101.01, eff. Sept. 29, 2011.**

### § 505.482 Joint township police district board.

(A) The boards of township trustees of any two or more contiguous townships, or the boards of township trustees of one or more contiguous townships and the legislative authorities of one or more contiguous municipal corporations, whether or not within the same county, by adoption of a joint resolution by a majority favorable vote of each such board and of the members of the legislative authority of each such municipal corporation, may form themselves into a joint police district comprising all or any part of the townships or municipal corporations as are mutually agreed upon. The governing body of the joint police district shall be a joint police district board, which shall include either all of the township trustees of each township and all of the members of the legislative authority of each municipal corporation in the district, as agreed to and established in the joint resolution creating the joint police district; or an odd number of members as agreed to and established in the joint resolution, as long as the members are representatives from each board of township trustees of each township and from the legislative authority of each municipal corporation in the joint police district.

(B) The joint police district board shall organize within thirty days after the favorable vote by the last board of township trustees or the members of the legislative authority of the last municipal corporation joining itself into the joint police district board. The president of the board of township trustees of the most populous participating township or the legislative authority of the most populous participating municipal corporation shall give notice of the time and place of organization to each pending member of the joint police district board, as established in the joint resolution. Such notice shall be signed and shall be sent by certified mail to each such pending member of the board at least five days prior to the organization meeting, which meeting shall be held in one of the participating townships or municipal corporations. Two-thirds of the joint police district board members constitutes a quorum. The members of the joint police district board shall, at the organization meeting, proceed with the election of a president, a secretary, and a treasurer, and such other officers as they consider necessary and proper, and shall transact such other business as properly comes before the board.

(C) In the formation of a joint police district, such action may be taken by or on behalf of part of a township, by excluding that portion of the township lying within a municipal corporation. The joint police district board may exercise the same powers as are granted to a board of township trustees in the operation of a township police district under sections 505.49 to 505.55 of the Revised Code, including, but not limited to, the power to employ, train, and discipline personnel, to acquire equipment and buildings, to levy a tax, to issue bonds and notes, and to dissolve the district.

**HISTORY: 144 v H 77. Eff 9-17-91; 2011 HB 153, § 101.01, eff. Sept. 29, 2011.**

This section was formerly codified as RC § 505.481.

This section was renumbered as RC § 505.481 by 2011 HB 153, § 101.01, effective June 30, 2011.

## § 505.483 Joint police district; adoption resolution.

A township or municipal corporation, or parts thereof, may join an existing joint police district by the adoption of a resolution by the township or of an ordinance by the municipal corporation requesting participation in the district and upon approval of the existing joint police district board.

**HISTORY: 2011 HB 153, § 101.01, eff. Sept. 29, 2011.**

## § 505.484 Joint police district board bond.

The treasurer of the joint police district board, before entering upon the duties of that office, shall execute a bond payable to the state, in the amount and with surety to be approved by the joint police district board, conditioned for the faithful performance of all the official duties required by the treasurer. The bond shall be deposited with the president of the joint police district board, and a copy thereof, certified by the president, shall be filed with the county auditor.

**HISTORY: 2011 HB 153, § 101.01, eff. Sept. 29, 2011.**

## § 505.49 Contract for police protection; status of police department members.

(A) As used in this section, "felony" has the same meaning as in section 109.511 of the Revised Code.

(B)(1) The township trustees of a township police district, by a two-thirds vote of the board, or a joint police district board, by majority vote of its members, may adopt rules necessary for the operation of the township or joint police district, including a determination of the qualifications of the chief of police, patrol officers, and others to serve as members of the district police force.

(2) Except as otherwise provided in division (E) of this section and subject to division (D) of this section, the township trustees of a township police district, by a two-thirds vote of the board or the joint police district board, by majority vote of its members, shall appoint a chief of police for the district, determine the number of patrol officers and other personnel required by the district, and establish salary schedules and other conditions of employment for the employees of the township or joint police district. The chief of police of the district shall serve at the pleasure of the township trustees or the joint police district board and shall appoint patrol officers and other personnel that the district may require, subject to division (D) of this section and to the rules and limits as to qualifications, salary ranges, and numbers of personnel established by the board of township trustees or the joint police district board. The township trustees may include in the township police district and under the direction and control of the chief of police any constable appointed pursuant to section 509.01 of the Revised Code, or may designate the chief of police or any patrol officer appointed by the chief of police as a constable, as provided for in section 509.01 of the Revised Code, for the township police district.

(3) Except as provided in division (D) of this section, a patrol officer, other police district employee, or police constable, who has been awarded a certificate attesting to the satisfactory completion of an approved state, county, or municipal police basic training program, as required by section 109.77 of the Revised Code, may be removed or suspended only under the conditions and by the procedures in sections 505.491 to 505.495 of the Revised Code. Any other patrol officer, police district employee, or police constable shall serve at the pleasure of the township trustees or joint police district board. In case of removal or suspension of an appointee by the board of township trustees of a township police district or the joint police district board, that appointee may appeal the decision of either board to the court of common pleas of the county in which the district is situated to determine the sufficiency of the cause of removal or suspension. The appointee shall take the appeal within ten days of written notice to the appointee of the decision of the board.

(C)(1) Division (B) of this section does not apply to a township that has a population of ten thousand or more persons residing within the township and outside of any municipal corporation, that has its own police department employing ten or more full-time paid employees, and that has a civil service commission established under division (B) of section 124.40 of the Revised Code. The township shall comply with the procedures for the employment, promotion, and discharge of police personnel provided by Chapter 124. of the Revised Code, except as otherwise provided in divisions (C)(2) and (3) of this section.

(2) The board of township trustees of the township may appoint the chief of police, and a person so appointed shall be in the unclassified service under section 124.11 of the Revised Code and shall serve at the pleasure of the board. A person appointed chief of police under these conditions who is removed by the board or who resigns from the position shall be entitled to return to the classified service in the township police department, in the position that person held previous to the person's appointment as chief of police.

(3) The appointing authority of an urban township, as defined in section 504.01 of the Revised Code, may appoint to a vacant position any one of the three highest scorers on the eligible list for a promotional examination.

(4) The board of township trustees of a township described in this division shall determine the number of personnel required and establish salary schedules and conditions of employment not in conflict with Chapter 124. of the Revised Code.

(5) Persons employed as police personnel in a township described in this division on the date a civil service commission is appointed pursuant to division (B) of section 124.40 of the Revised Code, without being required to pass a competitive examination or a police training program, shall retain their employment and any rank previously granted them by action of the township trustees or otherwise, but those persons are eligible for promotion only by compliance with Chapter 124. of the Revised Code.

(6) This division does not apply to constables appointed pursuant to section 509.01 of the Revised Code. This division is subject to division (D) of this section.

(D)(1) The board of township trustees or a joint police district board shall not appoint or employ a person as a chief of police, and the chief of police shall not appoint or employ a person as a patrol officer or other peace officer of a township police district, township police department, or joint police district on a permanent basis, on a temporary basis, for a probationary term, or on other than a permanent basis if the person previously has been convicted of or has pleaded guilty to a felony.

(2)(a) The board of township trustees or joint police district board shall terminate the appointment or employment of a chief of police, patrol officer, or other peace officer of a township police district, township police department, or joint police district who does either of the following:

(i) Pleads guilty to a felony;

(ii) Pleads guilty to a misdemeanor pursuant to a negotiated plea agreement as provided in division (D) of section 2929.43 of the Revised Code in which the chief of police, patrol officer, or other peace officer of a township police district, township police department, or joint police district agrees to surrender the certificate awarded to that chief of police, patrol officer, or other peace officer under section 109.77 of the Revised Code.

(b) The board shall suspend the appointment or employment of a chief of police, patrol officer, or other peace officer of a township police district, township police department, or joint police district who is convicted, after trial, of a felony. If such chief of police, patrol officer, or other peace officer files an appeal from that conviction and the conviction is upheld by the highest court to which the appeal is taken, or, if no timely appeal is filed, the board shall terminate the appointment or employment of that chief of police, patrol officer, or other peace officer. If the chief of police, patrol officer, or other peace officer of a township police district, township police department, or joint police district files an appeal that results in that chief of police's, patrol officer's, or other peace officer's acquittal of the felony or conviction of a misdemeanor, or in the dismissal of the felony charge against the chief of police, patrol officer, or other peace officer, the board shall reinstate that chief of police, patrol officer, or other peace officer. A chief of police, patrol officer, or other peace officer who is reinstated under division (D)(2)(b) of this section shall not receive any back pay unless the conviction of that chief of police, patrol officer, or other peace officer of the felony was reversed on appeal, or the felony charge was dismissed, because the court found insufficient evidence to convict the chief of police, patrol officer, or other peace officer of the felony.

(3) Division (D) of this section does not apply regarding an offense that was committed prior to January 1, 1997.

(4) The suspension or termination of the appointment or employment of a chief of police, patrol officer, or other peace officer under division (D)(2) of this section shall be in accordance with Chapter 119. of the Revised Code.

(E) The board of township trustees or the joint police district board may enter into a contract under section 505.43 or 505.50 of the Revised Code to obtain all police protection for the township police district or joint police district from one or more municipal corporations, county sheriffs, or other townships. If the board enters into such a contract, subject to division (D) of this section, it may, but is not required to, appoint a police chief for the district.

(F) The members of the police force of a township police district of a township, or of a joint police district board comprised of a township, that adopts the limited self-government form of township government shall serve as peace officers for the township territory included in the district.

(G) A chief of police or patrol officer of a township police district, township police department, or joint police district may participate, as the director of an organized crime task force established under section 177.02 of the Revised Code or as a member of the investigatory staff of that task force, in an investigation of organized criminal activity in any county or counties in this state under sections 177.01 to 177.03 of the Revised Code.

**HISTORY: 130 v 211 (Eff 9-24-63); 132 v H 191 (Eff 11-24-67); 135 v H 513 (Eff 8-9-74); 137 v H 671 (Eff 1-13-78); 137 v H 1074 (Eff 4-20-78); 141 v S 74 (Eff 9-3-86); 144 v H 77 (Eff 9-17-91); 144 v S 125 (Eff 4-16-93); 146 v H 566 (Eff 10-16-96); 149 v H 515. Eff 3-31-2003; 149 v H 490, § 1, eff. 1-1-04; 2011 HB 153, § 101.01, eff. Sept. 29, 2011.**

This section was amended by Senate Bill 5 of the 2011 legislative session. However, referendum petitions were filed to prevent SB 5 from taking effect as scheduled on July 1, 2011. The provisions of SB 5 were rejected by the voters at the referendum election on November 8, 2011.

Acts 2011, HB 153, § 815.20 provides: "The General Assembly, applying the principle stated in division (B) of section 1.52 of the Revised Code that amendments are to be harmonized if reasonably capable of simultaneous operation, finds that the following sections, presented in this act as composites of the sections as amended by the acts indicated, are the resulting versions of the sections in effect prior to the effective date of the sections as presented in this act:

"Section 505.49 of the Revised Code as amended by both Am. Sub. H.B. 490 and Am. H.B. 515 of the 124th General Assembly."

The effective date is set by section 4 of HB 490.

**Comment, Legislative Service Commission**

Section 505.49 of the Revised Code is amended by this act [Am. Sub. H.B. 490] (effective January 1, 2004) and also by Am. H.B. 515, both of the 124th General Assembly. * * * Comparison of these amendments in pursuance of section 1.52 of the Revised Code discloses that they are not irreconcilable so that they are required by that section to be harmonized to give effect to each amendment.

## § 505.491 Trustees to prefer charges against delinquent police personnel.

Except as provided in division (D) of section 505.49 or in division (C) of section 509.01 of the Revised Code for a board of township trustees, and except as provided in division (D) of section 505.49 of the Revised Code for a joint police district board, if the board has reason to believe that a chief of police, patrol officer, or other township or joint police district employee appointed under division (B) of section 505.49 of the Revised Code or a police constable appointed under division (B) of section 509.01 of the Revised Code has been guilty, in the performance of the official duty of that chief of police, patrol officer, other township or joint police district employee, or police constable, of bribery, misfeasance, malfeasance, nonfeasance, misconduct in office, neglect of duty, gross immorality, habitual drunkenness, incompetence, or failure to obey orders given that person by the proper authority, the board immediately shall file written charges against that person. The written charges shall set forth in detail a statement of the alleged guilt and, at the same time, or as soon thereafter as possible, serve a true copy of those charges upon the person against whom they are made. The service may be made on the person or by leaving a copy of the charges at the office or residence of that person. Return of the service shall be made to the board in the same manner that is provided for the return of the service of summons in a civil action.

**HISTORY: 132 v H 191 (Eff 11-24-67); 133 v H 1 (Eff 3-18-69); 135 v H 513 (Eff 8-9-74); 146 v H 566. Eff 10-16-96; 2011 HB 153, § 101.01, eff. Sept. 29, 2011.**

## § 505.492 Hearing of charges; action of township trustees.

Charges filed by the board of township trustees or joint police district board under section 505.491 of the Revised Code shall be heard at the next regular meeting thereof, unless the board extends the time for the hearing, which shall be done only on the application of the accused. The accused may appear in person and by counsel, examine all witnesses, and answer all charges against the accused.

**HISTORY: 132 v H 191. Eff 11-24-67; 2011 HB 153, § 101.01, eff. Sept. 29, 2011.**

## § 505.493 Suspension of accused pending hearing.

Pending any proceedings under sections 505.491 and 505.492 of the Revised Code, an accused person may be suspended by the board of township trustees or joint police district board, but such suspension shall be for a period not longer than fifteen days, unless the hearing of such charges is extended upon the application of the accused, in which event the suspension shall not exceed thirty days.

**HISTORY: 132 v H 191. Eff 11-24-67; 2011 HB 153, § 101.01, eff. Sept. 29, 2011.**

## § 505.494 Power of township trustees as to process.

For the purpose of investigating charges filed pursuant to section 505.491 of the Revised Code, the board of township trustees or joint police district board may issue subpoenas or compulsory process to compel the attendance of persons and the production of books and papers before it and provide by resolution for exercising and enforcing this section.

**HISTORY: 132 v H 191. Eff 11-24-67; 2011 HB 153, § 101.01, eff. Sept. 29, 2011.**

## § 505.495 Oaths; compulsory testimony; witness fees and mileage; costs.

In all cases in which the attendance of witnesses may be compelled for an investigation, under section 505.494 of the Revised Code, any member of the board of township trustees or of the joint police district board may administer the requisite oaths. The board has the same power to compel the giving of testimony by attending witnesses as is conferred upon courts. In all such cases, witnesses shall be entitled to the same privileges and immunities as are allowed witnesses in civil cases. Witnesses shall be paid the fees and mileage provided for under section 1901.26 of the Revised Code, and the costs of all such proceedings shall be payable from the general fund of the township or joint police district.

**HISTORY: 132 v H 191. Eff 11-24-67; 152 v H 525, § 1, eff. 7-1-09; 2011 HB 153, § 101.01, eff. Sept. 29, 2011.**

The effective date is set by § 3 of 152 v H 525.

## § 505.50 Acquisition of equipment and buildings; emergency police protection.

The board of township trustees of a township or of a township police district, or a joint police district board, may purchase, lease, lease with an option to purchase, or otherwise acquire any police apparatus, equipment, including a public communications system, or materials that the township, township police district, or joint police district requires and may build, purchase, lease, or lease with an option to purchase any building or buildings and site of the building or buildings that are necessary for the police operations of the township or either district.

The boards of trustees of any two or more contiguous townships, or the boards of township trustees of one or more contiguous townships and the legislative authorities of one or more contiguous municipal corporations, by joint agreement, may unite in the joint purchase, lease, lease with an option to purchase, maintenance, use, and operation of police equipment for any other police purpose designated in sections 505.48 to 505.55 of the Revised Code, and to prorate the expense of that joint action on terms mutually agreed upon by the trustees in each affected township and the legislative authorities of each affected municipal corporation.

The board of trustees of a township or of a township police district, or a joint police district board, may enter into a contract with one or more townships, a municipal corporation, a park district created pursuant to section 511.18 or 1545.01 of the Revised Code, or the county sheriff upon any terms that are mutually agreed upon for the provision of police protection services or additional police protection services either on a regular basis or for additional protection in times of emergency. The contract shall be agreed to in each instance by the respective board or boards of township trustees, the board of county commissioners, the board of park commissioners, the joint police district board, or the legislative authority of the municipal corporation involved. The contract may provide for a fixed annual charge to be paid at the time agreed upon in the contract.

Chapter 2744. of the Revised Code, insofar as it is applicable to the operation of police departments, applies to the contracting political subdivisions and police department members when the members are serving outside their own political subdivision pursuant to such a contract. Police department members acting outside the political subdivision in which they are employed may participate in any pension or indemnity fund established by their employer and are entitled to all the rights and benefits of Chapter 4123. of the Revised Code, to the same extent as while performing services within the political subdivision.

**HISTORY: 130 v 212 (Eff 9-24-63); 141 v H 176 (Eff 11-20-85); 141 v H 743 (Eff 12-10-86); 144 v S 174. Eff 7-31-92; 150 v H 97, § 1, eff. 10-21-03; 150 v H 148, § 1, eff. 11-5-04; 2011 HB 153, § 101.01, eff. Sept. 29, 2011.**

## § 505.51 Police district tax levy authorized.

(A) In the case of a township police district, the board of trustees of the township police district may levy a tax upon all of the taxable property in the township police district pursuant to sections 5705.19 and 5705.25 of the Revised Code to defray all or a portion of expenses of the township police district in providing police protection.

(B) In the case of a joint police district, the joint police district board may levy a tax upon all of the taxable property in the joint police district pursuant to sections 5705.19 and 5705.25 of the Revised Code to defray all or a portion of expenses of the joint police district in providing police protection.

**HISTORY: 130 v 213. Eff 9-24-63; 2011 HB 153, § 101.01, eff. Sept. 29, 2011.**

## § 505.511 Charges for responding to security alarm system false alarms.

(A) A board of township trustees that operates a township police department , the board of township trustees of a township police district, or a joint police district board may, after police constables, the township police, a law enforcement agency with which the township contracts for police services, the joint police district police, and the county sheriff or the sheriff's deputy have answered a combined total of three false alarms from the same commercial or residential security alarm system within the township in the same calendar year, cause the township fiscal officer to mail the manager of the commercial establishment or the occupant, lessee, agent, or tenant of the residence a bill for each subsequent false alarm from the same alarm system during that year, to defray the costs incurred. The bill's amount shall be as follows:

(1) For the fourth false alarm of that year ...... $50.00;

(2) For the fifth false alarm of that year ...... $100.00;

(3) For all false alarms in that year occurring after the fifth false alarm ...... $150.00.

If payment of the bill is not received within thirty days, the township fiscal officer or joint police district treasurer shall send a notice by certified mail to the manager and to the owner, if different, of the real estate of which the commercial establishment is a part, or to the occupant, lessee, agent, or tenant and to the owner, if different, of the real estate of which the residence is a part, indicating that failure to pay the bill within thirty days, or to show just cause why the bill should not be paid, will result in the assessment of a lien upon the real estate in the amount of the bill. If payment is not received within those thirty days or if just cause is not shown, the amount of the bill shall be entered upon the tax duplicate, shall be a lien upon the real estate from the date of the entry, and shall be collected as other taxes and returned to the township treasury to be earmarked for use for police services.

The board of township trustees shall not cause the township fiscal officer, or the joint police district board shall not cause the joint police district treasurer, to send a bill pursuant to this division if a bill has already been sent pursuant to division (B) of this section for the same false alarm.

(B) The county sheriff may, after the county sheriff or the sheriff's deputy, police constables, the township police, the joint police district police, and a law enforcement agency with which the township contracts for police services have answered a combined total of three false alarms from the same commercial or residential security alarm system within the unincorporated area of the county in the same calendar year, mail the manager of the commercial establishment or the occupant, lessee, agent, or tenant of the residence a bill for each subsequent false alarm from the same alarm system during that year, to defray the costs incurred. The bill's amount shall be as follows:

(1) For the fourth false alarm of that year ...... $50.00;

(2) For the fifth false alarm of that year ...... $100.00;

(3) For all false alarms in that year occurring after the fifth false alarm ...... $150.00.

If payment of the bill is not received within thirty days, the sheriff shall send a notice by certified mail to the manager and to the owner, if different, of the real estate of which the commercial establishment is a part, or to the occupant, lessee, agent, or tenant and to the owner, if different, of the real estate of which the residence is a part, indicating that failure to pay the bill within thirty days, or to show just cause why the bill should not be paid, will result in the assessment of a lien upon the real estate in the amount of the bill. If payment is not received within those thirty days or if just cause is not shown, the amount of the bill shall be entered upon the tax duplicate, shall be a lien upon the real estate from the date of the entry, and shall be collected as other taxes and returned to the county treasury.

The sheriff shall not send a bill pursuant to this division if a bill has already been sent pursuant to division (A) of this section for the same false alarm.

(C) As used in this section, "commercial establishment" has the same meaning as in section 505.391 of the Revised Code.

**HISTORY: 141 v H 150 (Eff 9-17-86); 142 v H 420 (Eff 6-14-88); 147 v H 259. Eff 12-18-97; 150 v H 255, § 1, eff. 3-31-05; 151 v S 107, § 1, eff. 12-20-05; 2011 HB 153, § 101.01, eff. Sept. 29, 2011.**

## § 505.52 Bond issues by police district.

The board of trustees of a township police district or a joint police district board may issue bonds for the purpose of buying police equipment in the manner provided for in section 133.18 and pursuant to Chapter 133. of the Revised Code. The proceeds of the bonds issued under this section, other than any premium and accrued interest which is credited to the sinking fund, shall be placed in the township treasury or joint police district board treasury to the credit of a fund to be known as the "police equipment fund." Money from the police equipment fund shall be paid out only upon order of the township board of trustees of the township police district or of the joint police district board.

**HISTORY: 130 v 213 (Eff 9-24-63); 143 v H 230. Eff 10-30-89; 2011 HB 153, § 101.01, eff. Sept. 29, 2011.**

## § 505.53 Issuance of notes by police district.

The board of trustees of a township police district or a joint police district board may issue notes for a period not to exceed three years for the purpose of buying police equipment or a building or site to house police equipment. One-third of the purchase price of the equipment, building, or site shall be paid at the time of purchase, and the remainder of the purchase price shall be covered by notes maturing in two and three years respectively. Notes may bear interest not to exceed the rate determined as provided in section 9.95 of the Revised Code, and shall not be subject to Chapter 133. of the Revised Code. Such notes shall be offered for sale on the open market or given to a vendor if no sale is made.

**HISTORY: 130 v 213 (Eff 9-24-63); 138 v H 275 (Eff 11-1-79); 139 v H 95 (Eff 5-13-81); 143 v H 230. Eff 10-30-89; 2011 HB 153, § 101.01, eff. Sept. 29, 2011.**

## § 505.54 Additional training for police district personnel.

The board of trustees of the township or the joint police district board may, upon nomination by the chief of police, send one or more of the officers, patrol officers, or other employees of the township police district or the joint police district to a school of instruction designed to provide additional training or skills related to the employees work assignment in the district. The trustees may make advance tuition payments for any employee so nominated and may defray all or a portion of the employee's expenses while receiving this instruction.

**HISTORY: 130 v 213. Eff 9-24-63; 2011 HB 153, § 101.01, eff. Sept. 29, 2011.**

## § 505.541 Parking enforcement unit.

(A) The board of township trustees or a joint police district board, respectively, may establish, by resolution, a parking enforcement unit within a township police district or within a joint police district, and provide for the regulation of parking enforcement officers. The chief of police of the district shall be the executive head of the parking enforcement unit, shall make all appointments and removals of parking enforcement officers, subject to any general rules prescribed by the board of township trustees by resolution or joint police district board, as appropriate, and shall prescribe rules for the organization, training, administration, control, and conduct of the parking enforcement unit. The chief of police may appoint parking enforcement officers who agree to serve for nominal compensation, and persons with physical disabilities may receive appointments as parking enforcement officers.

(B) The authority of the parking enforcement officers shall be limited to the enforcement of section 4511.69 of the Revised Code and any other parking laws specified in the resolution creating the parking enforcement unit. Parking enforcement officers shall have no other powers.

(C) The training the parking enforcement officers shall receive shall include instruction in general administrative rules and procedures governing the parking enforcement unit, the role of the judicial system as it relates to parking regulation and enforcement, proper techniques and methods relating to the enforcement of parking laws, human interaction skills, and first aid.

**HISTORY: 143 v S 174. Eff 7-13-90; 2011 HB 153, § 101.01, eff. Sept. 29, 2011.**

## § 505.55 Dissolution of police district.

In the event that need for a township police district ceases to exist, the township trustees by a two-thirds vote of the board shall adopt a resolution specifying the date that the township police district shall cease to exist and provide for the disposal of all property belonging to the district by public sale. Such sale must be by public auction and upon notice thereof being published once a week for three weeks in a newspaper of general circulation in such township or as provided in section 7.16 of the Revised Code. The last of such publications shall be made at least five days before the date of the sale. Any moneys remaining after the dissolution of the district or received from the public sale of property shall be paid into the treasury of the township and may be expended for any public purpose when duly authorized by the township board of trustees.

**HISTORY: 130 v 213. Eff 9-24-63; 2011 HB 153, § 101.01, eff. Sept. 29, 2011.**

## § 505.551 Withdrawal from joint police district.

(A) Any township or municipal corporation may withdraw from a joint police district created under section 505.482 of the Revised Code by adopting a resolution or an ordinance, respectively, ordering withdrawal. On or after the first day of January of the year following the adoption of the resolution or ordinance of withdrawal, the township or municipal corporation withdrawing ceases to be a part of the district, and the power of the district to levy a tax upon the taxable property in the withdrawing township or municipal corporation terminates, except that the district shall continue to levy and collect taxes for the payment of indebtedness within the territory of the district as it was comprised at the time the indebtedness was incurred.

(B) Upon the withdrawal of any township or municipal corporation from a joint police district, the county auditor shall ascertain, apportion, and order a division of the funds on hand and moneys and taxes in the process of collection, except for taxes levied for the payment of indebtedness, credits, and real and personal property, either in money or in kind, on the basis of the valuation of the respective tax duplicates of the withdrawing township or municipal corporation and the remaining territory of the joint police district.

(C) When the number of townships or municipal corporations comprising a joint police district is reduced to one, the joint police district ceases to exist by operation of law, and the funds, credits, and property remaining after apportionments to withdrawing townships or municipal corporations shall be assumed by the one remaining township or municipal corporation. When a joint police district ceases to exist and an indebtedness remains unpaid, the board of county commissioners shall continue to levy and collect taxes for the payment of that indebtedness within the territory of the joint police district as it was comprised at the time the indebtedness was incurred.

**HISTORY: 2011 HB 153, § 101.01, eff. Sept. 29, 2011.**

### [TOWNSHIP BUILDING CODE]

## § 505.73 Existing structures code.

(A) The board of township trustees may, by resolution, adopt by incorporation by reference, administer, and enforce within the unincorporated area of the township an existing structures code pertaining to the repair and continued maintenance of structures and the premises of those structures. For that purpose, the board shall adopt any model or standard code prepared and promulgated by this state, any department, board, or agency of this state, or any public or private organization that publishes a recognized model or standard code on the subject. The board shall ensure that the code adopted governs subject matter not addressed by the state residential building code and that it is fully compatible with the state residential and nonresidential building codes the board of building standards adopts pursuant to section 3781.10 of the Revised Code.

(B) The board shall assign the duties of administering and enforcing the existing structures code to a township officer or employee who is trained and qualified for those duties and shall establish by resolution the minimum qualifications necessary to perform those duties.

(C)(1) After the board adopts an existing structures code, the township fiscal officer shall post a notice that clearly identifies the code, states the code's purpose, and states that a complete copy of the code is on file for inspection by the public with the fiscal officer and in the county law library and that the fiscal officer has copies available for distribution to the public at cost.

(2) The township fiscal officer shall post the notice in five conspicuous places in the township for thirty days before the code becomes effective and shall publish the notice in a newspaper of general circulation in the township for three consecutive weeks or as provided in section 7.16 of the Revised Code. If the adopting township amends or deletes any provision of the code, the notice shall contain a brief summary of the deletion or amendment.

(D) If the agency that originally promulgated or published the existing structures code amends the code, the board may adopt the amendment or change by incorporation by reference in the manner provided for the adoption of the original code.

**HISTORY: 142 v H 285. Eff 10-20-87; 150 v H 175, § 1, eff. 5-27-05; 151 v S 107, § 1, eff. 12-20-05; 2011 HB 153, § 101.01, eff. Sept. 29, 2011.**

## § 505.74 Violations prohibited.

No person shall violate a standard existing structures code as adopted pursuant to section 505.73 of the Revised Code. Each day of continued violation of this section constitutes a separate offense.

**HISTORY: 142 v H 285. Eff 10-20-87.**

## § 505.75 Local residential building regulations; building department; inspector; contracts with municipal corporations or counties.

(A)(1) A board of township trustees may adopt local residential building regulations governing residential buildings as defined in section 3781.06 of the Revised Code. No regulation shall differ from the state residential building code unless the regulation addresses subject matter not addressed by the state residential building code or is adopted pursuant to section 3781.01 of the Revised Code.

(2) The board may adopt regulations that are necessary for participation in the national flood insurance program and that do not conflict with the residential and nonresidential building codes, governing the prohibition, location, erection, construction, or floodproofing of new buildings or structures, or substantial improvements to existing buildings or structures, in unincorporated territory within flood hazard areas identified under the "Flood Disaster Protection Act of 1973," 87 Stat. 975, 42 U.S.C.A. 4002, as amended, including, but not limited to, residential, commercial, or industrial buildings or structures.

(B)(1) Regulations or amendments to regulations may be adopted under this section only after a public hearing† at not fewer than two regular or special sessions of the board of township trustees and upon an affirmative vote of all members of the board. The board shall cause notice of a public hearing to be published in a newspaper of general circulation in the township once a week for two weeks immediately preceding a hearing, except that if the board posts the hearing notice on the board's internet site, the board need publish only one notice of the hearing in a newspaper of general circulation if that newspaper notice includes that internet site and a statement that the notice is also posted on the internet site. Any notice the board publishes or posts shall include the time, date, and place of the public hearing.

(2) The proposed regulations shall be made available to the public at the board office.

(C)(1) The board of township trustees may create a building department and employ personnel it determines necessary to administer and enforce any local residential building regulations or existing structures code the board adopts pursuant to this section. The building department may enforce state residential and nonresidential building codes the board of building standards establishes pursuant to Chapter 3781. of the Revised Code if the department is certified pursuant to section 3781.10 of the Revised Code to enforce those codes. Upon certification of the building department under section 3781.10 of the Revised Code, the board of township trustees†† may direct the building department to exercise enforcement authority and to accept and approve plans pursuant to sections 3781.03 and 3791.04 of the Revised Code for the classes of buildings for which the building department and personnel are certified.

(2) To administer and enforce any local residential building regulations, or existing structures code and the state residential and nonresidential building codes, the board may create, establish, fill, and fix the compensation of the position of township building inspector to serve as the chief administrative officer of the building department. In lieu of creating the position of township building inspector, the board may assign the duties of the inspector to an existing township officer who is certified pursuant to division (E) of section 3781.10 of the Revised Code.

(D)(1) The board of township trustees may enter into a contract with any other township, any municipal corporation, or board of county commissioners for the municipal corporation or board of county commissioners to administer and enforce local residential building regulations or existing structures code in the township or to enforce the state residential and nonresidential building codes in the township if the building department of the municipal corporation or county is certified to enforce those codes.

(2) Any other township, any municipal corporation, or a board of county commissioners may contract with a board of township trustees to administer and enforce local building regulations or an existing structures code in the municipal corporation or county and, if certified, to enforce the state residential and nonresidential building codes in the municipal corporation or unincorporated areas of the county.

**HISTORY: 137 v S 155 (Eff 11-16-77); 146 v H 99. Eff 8-22-95; 150 v S 115, § 1, eff. 4-15-05; 150 v H 175, § 1, eff. 5-27-05.**

† Amended in (B)(1) as "after public hearings" by 150 v S 115, effective April 15, 2005.

†† Amended in (C)(1) as "the board may direct" by 150 v S 115, effective April 15, 2005.

**Comment, Legislative Service Commission**

Section 505.75 of the Revised Code is amended by Sub. S.B. 115 and Am. Sub. H.B. 175 of the 125th General Assembly. There are no substantive conflicts, but the Legislative Service Commission is carrying two versions.

### § 505.76 Availability of regulations and code; publication of information.

Local residential building regulations a board of township trustees adopts under section 505.75 of the Revised Code and an existing structures code the board adopts pursuant to section 505.73 of the Revised Code shall be made available to the public at the office of the board, and the section headings and numbers and a notice of the availability of the regulations shall be published in at least one newspaper of general townshipwide circulation within ten days after their adoption or amendment.

**HISTORY: 137 v S 155. Eff 11-16-77; 150 v H 175, § 1, eff. 5-27-05.**

### § 505.77 Prohibitions; action for injunction, abatement, or other appropriate relief; exemption for public utility or railroad property.

(A)(1) No person shall erect, construct, alter, repair, or maintain any residential building, as defined in section 3781.06 of the Revised Code, within the unincorporated portion of any township in which a building department has authority to administer and enforce local residential building regulations or an existing structures code unless that person complies with the regulations and code.

(2) No person shall erect, construct, alter, repair, or maintain any residential building, as defined in section 3781.06 of the Revised Code, within the unincorporated portion of any township in which a certified building department has jurisdiction to enforce the state residential building code unless that person fully complies with the state residential building code.

(3) No person shall erect, construct, alter, repair, or maintain any residential, commercial, or industrial buildings or structures within the unincorporated area of any township, if a board of township trustees has enacted building regulations under section 505.75 of the Revised Code that are necessary for participation in the national flood insurance program, without complying with those regulations.

(4) In addition to any remedies provided by law, if any building is being erected, constructed, altered, repaired, or maintained in violation of the building regulations, existing structures code, or state residential building code in townships in which a certified building department has jurisdiction, the board, the township building inspector, or any owner of an adjacent, contiguous, or neighboring property who would be especially damaged by the violation may institute a suit for injunction, abatement, or other appropriate action to prevent the violation of the building regulations or the state residential building code relating to the erection, construction, alteration, repair, or maintenance of that building.

(B) Sections 505.75 to 505.77 of the Revised Code do not confer any power on any board with respect to the location, erection, construction, reconstruction, change, alteration, maintenance, removal, use, or enlargement of any buildings or structures of any public utility or railroad, whether publicly or privately owned, or the use of land by any public utility or railroad for the operation of its business. Local building regulations the board adopts and the building code that the building department administers and enforces do not affect buildings or structures that exist or on which construction has begun on or before the date on which the building department begins enforcement of the building code or the date the board adopts the building regulations.

(C) No person shall violate any building regulation the board adopts under division (A) of section 505.75 of the Revised Code. Each day during which an illegal location, erection, construction, floodproofing, repair, alteration, or maintenance continues may be considered a separate offense.

**HISTORY: 137 v S 155. Eff 11-16-77; 150 v H 175, § 1, eff. 5-27-05.**

### § 505.99 Penalty.

Whoever violates section 505.374 [505.37.4], 505.74, 505.75, 505.76, 505.77, or 505.94 of the Revised Code is guilty of a minor misdemeanor.

**HISTORY: 135 v H 739 (Eff 7-26-74); 137 v S 155 (Eff 11-16-77); 139 v S 80 (Eff 3-15-82); 141 v H 85 (Eff 3-6-86); 142 v H 285 (Eff 10-20-87); 146 v S 2. Eff 7-1-96.**

The effective date is set by section 6 of SB 2.

### § 505.991 Penalties.

Whoever violates section 505.106 [505.10.6] of the Revised Code shall be fined not less than twice the value of any property not deposited as provided by that section, but not more than three thousand dollars, or imprisoned not more than thirty days, or both.

**HISTORY: 148 v H 55. Eff 9-29-99.**

## CHAPTER 509: CONSTABLES

Section



Section



### § 509.01 Constables; compensation.

(A) As used in this section, "felony" has the same meaning as in section 109.511 of the Revised Code.

(B) Subject to division (C) of this section, the board of township trustees may designate any qualified persons as police constables and may provide them with the automobiles, communication systems, uniforms, and police equipment that the board considers necessary. Except as provided in division (C) of this section, police constables designated under this division, who have been awarded a certificate attesting to the satisfactory completion of an approved state, county, or municipal police basic training program, as required by section 109.77 of the Revised Code, may be removed or suspended only under the conditions and by the procedures in sections 505.491 to 505.495 of the Revised Code. Any other police constable shall serve at the pleasure of the township trustees. In case of removal or suspension of a police constable by the board of township trustees, that police constable may appeal the decision of the board to the court of common pleas of the county to determine the sufficiency of the cause of removal or suspension. The police constable shall take the appeal within ten days of written notice to the police constable of the decision of the board. The board may pay each police constable, from the general funds of the township, the compensation that the board by resolution prescribes for the time actually spent in keeping the peace, protecting property, and performing duties as a police constable, including duties as an ex officio deputy bailiff of a municipal court pursuant to section 1901.32 of the Revised Code and duties as a ministerial officer of a county court. The police constable shall not be paid fees in addition to the compensation allowed by the board for services rendered as a police constable, including services as an ex officio deputy bailiff of a municipal court pursuant to section 1901.32 of the Revised Code and as a ministerial officer of a county court. All constable fees provided for by section 509.15 of the Revised Code, if due for services rendered while the police constable performing those services is being compensated as a police constable for that performance, shall be paid into the general fund of the township.

(C)(1) The board of township trustees shall not designate a person as a police constable pursuant to division (B) of this section on a permanent basis, on a temporary basis, for a probationary term, or on other than a permanent basis if the person previously has been convicted of or has pleaded guilty to a felony.

(2)(a) The board of township trustees shall terminate the employment of a police constable designated under division (B) of this section if the police constable does either of the following:

(i) Pleads guilty to a felony;

(ii) Pleads guilty to a misdemeanor pursuant to a negotiated plea agreement as provided in division (D) of section 2929.43 of the Revised Code in which the police constable agrees to surrender the certificate awarded to the police constable under section 109.77 of the Revised Code.

(b) The board shall suspend from employment a police constable designated under division (B) of this section if the police constable is convicted, after trial, of a felony. If the police constable files an appeal from that conviction and the conviction is upheld by the highest court to which the appeal is taken or if the police constable does not file a timely appeal, the board shall terminate the employment of that police constable. If the police constable files an appeal that results in that police constable's acquittal of the felony or conviction of a misdemeanor, or in the dismissal of the felony charge against the police constable, the board shall reinstate that police constable. A police constable who is reinstated under division (C)(2)(b) of this section shall not receive any back pay unless that police constable's conviction of the felony was reversed on appeal, or the felony charge was dismissed, because the court found insufficient evidence to convict the police constable of the felony.

(3) Division (C) of this section does not apply regarding an offense that was committed prior to January 1, 1997.

(4) The suspension from employment, or the termination of the employment, of a police constable under division (C)(2) of this section shall be in accordance with Chapter 119. of the Revised Code.

**HISTORY: 128 v 823 (Eff 11-6-59); 132 v H 191 (Eff 11-24-67); 141 v H 159 (Eff 3-19-87); 146 v H 566. Eff 10-16-96; 149 v H 490, § 1, eff. 1-1-04.**

The effective date is set by section 4 of HB 490.

**Not analogous to former RC § 509.01 (RS §§ 1442, 1448; S&S 914; S&C 85, 802, 1566, 1567; 51 v 179, § 182; 51 v 489, §§ 5, 8; 56 v 156; 65 v 87, § 7; 83 v 28; 85 v 131; 86 v 94; 87 v 118; 89 v 65; 89 v 195; 90 v 144; 97 v 39; 97 v 62; 97 v 187; 98 v 171; 98 v 172; GC § 3327; Bureau of Code Revision, 10-1-53), repealed 128 v 823(862), § 2, eff 11-6-59.**

## § 509.02 Bond.

Each constable, before entering upon the discharge of official duties, shall give bond to the state in a sum of not less than five hundred nor more than two thousand dollars, conditioned for the faithful and diligent discharge of official duties, and with sureties resident of the township. The amount of the bond and its sureties shall be approved by the board of township trustees. The bond shall be deposited with the township fiscal officer.

**HISTORY: RS § 1516; S&C 802, 1567; 51 v 179, §§ 183 to 185; 51 v 489, § 9; GC § 3328; Bureau of Code Revision. Eff 10-1-53; 151 v S 107, § 1, eff. 12-20-05.**

## § 509.04 Parking enforcement unit.

(A) The board of township trustees may establish, by resolution, a parking enforcement unit within the office of a township constable, and provide for the regulation of parking enforcement officers. The board of township trustees shall appoint a police constable as executive head of the parking enforcement unit, who shall make all appointments and removals of parking enforcement officers, subject to any general rules prescribed by the board of township trustees by resolution, and shall prescribe rules for the organization, training, administration, control, and conduct of the parking enforcement unit. The executive head of the parking enforcement unit may appoint parking enforcement officers who agree to serve for nominal compensation, and persons with physical disabilities may receive appointments as parking enforcement officers.

(B) The authority of the parking enforcement officers shall be limited to the enforcement of section 4511.69 of the Revised Code and any other parking laws specified in the resolution creating the parking enforcement unit. Parking enforcement officers shall have no other powers.

(C) The training the parking enforcement officers shall receive shall include instruction in general administrative rules and procedures governing the parking enforcement unit, the role of the judicial system as it relates to parking regulation and enforcement, proper techniques and methods relating to the enforcement of parking laws, human interaction skills, and first aid.

**HISTORY: 143 v S 174. Eff 7-13-90.**

**Not analogous to former RC § 509.04 (RS §§ 6685—6687; S&C 803; 51 v 179, §§ 188—190; GC §§ 3331—3333; 124 v 353; Bureau of Code Revision, 10-1-53), repealed 128 v 823, § 2, eff 11-6-59.**

## § 509.05 Sheriffs and constables ministerial officers of county court; powers and duties of constables.

In addition to the county sheriff, constables shall be ministerial officers of the county court in all cases in their respective townships, and in criminal cases, they shall be such officers within the county. They shall apprehend and bring to justice felons and disturbers of the peace, suppress riots, and keep and preserve the peace within the county. They may execute all writs and process, in criminal cases, throughout the county in which they reside, and in which they were elected or appointed. If a person charged with the commission of a crime or offense flees from justice, any constable of the county wherein such crime or offense was committed shall pursue and arrest such fugitive in any other county of the state and convey him before the county court of the county where such crime or offense was committed.

Such constables shall serve and execute all warrants, writs, precepts, executions, and other process directed and delivered to them, and shall do all things pertaining to the office of constable.

The authority of a constable in serving any process, either civil or criminal, and in doing his duties generally shall extend throughout the county in which he is appointed, and in executing and serving process issued by a judge of the county court, he may exercise the same authority and powers over goods and chattels, and the persons of parties, as is granted to a sheriff or coroner, under like process issued from courts of record.

A constable may participate, as the director of an organized crime task force established under section 177.02 of the Revised Code or as a member of the investigatory staff of such a task force, in an investigation of organized criminal activity in any county or counties in this state under sections 177.01 to 177.03 of the Revised Code.

**HISTORY: 127 v 1039 (Eff 1-1-58); 141 v S 74. Eff 9-3-86.**

**Analogous to former RC § 509.05 (RS §§ 6689, 6699, 6995; S&C 803, 804, 814; 35 v 87, § 25; 51 v 179, §§ 192, 198; GC §§ 3335, 3341, 3345; Bureau of Code Revision, 10-1-53), repealed in 127 v 978, § 2, eff 1-1-58.**

## § 509.06 Aid of sheriff.

Constables, marshals, chiefs of police, and other police officers, in discharging their duties, may call the sheriff or a deputy sheriff to their aid in state cases.

**HISTORY: RS § 6690; S&C 803; 51 v 179, § 193; GC § 3336; 108 v PtII, 1203; Bureau of Code Revision. Eff 10-1-53.**

## § 509.07 Return of process.

Each constable shall, at the proper office and on the proper return day, make due return of all process directed and delivered to him. If the judgment upon which such constable has an execution is docketed in the court of common pleas, appealed, or stayed, on notice to return the execution, he shall state such fact on the execution.

**HISTORY: RS § 6691; S&C 803; 51 v 179, § 194; GC § 3337; Bureau of Code Revision. Eff 10-1-53.**

## § 509.08 Time of receiving writ.

Each constable, on the receipt of any writ or other process, except subpoenas, shall note thereon the time of receiving it. He shall also state in his return on such writ or process the time and manner of executing it.

**HISTORY: RS § 6692; S&C 804; 51 v 179, § 195; GC § 3338; Bureau of Code Revision. Eff 10-1-53.**

## § 509.09 Return of "not found."

No constable shall make a return on any process of "not found," as to any defendant, unless he has been to the usual place of residence of the defendant at least once, if such defendant has a residence in the county.

**HISTORY: RS § 6693; S&C 804; 51 v 179, § 196; GC § 3339; Bureau of Code Revision. Eff 10-1-53.**

## § 509.10 Arrest on view or warrant; keep the peace.

Each constable shall apprehend, on view or warrant, and bring to justice, all felons, disturbers, and violators of the criminal laws of this state, and shall suppress all riots, affrays, and unlawful assemblies which come to his knowledge, and shall generally keep the peace in his township.

**HISTORY: RS § 6694; S&C 804; 51 v 179, § 197; GC § 3340; Bureau of Code Revision, 10-1-53; 128 v 823. Eff 11-6-59.**

## § 509.11 Copy of process to be left with jailer.

When it becomes the duty of the constable to take a person to the county jail, such constable shall deliver to the sheriff or jailer a certified copy of the execution, commitment, or other process, whereby he holds such person in custody, and shall return the original to the judge who issued it. Such copy is sufficient authority to the sheriff or jailer to keep the prisoner in jail until discharged.

**HISTORY: RS § 6696; S&C 804; 51 v 179, § 199; GC § 3342; Bureau of Code Revision, 10-1-53; 132 v H 2. Eff 2-14-67.**

## § 509.12 Payment of moneys.

A constable shall pay over to the party entitled thereto, all moneys received by such constable in his official capacity, if demand is made by such party, his agent, or attorney, at any time before the constable returns the writ upon which he has received such moneys. If the money is not paid over by that time, the constable shall pay it to the judge of the county court when he returns the writ.

**HISTORY: RS § 6697; S&C 804; 51 v 179, § 200; GC § 3343; Bureau of Code Revision, 10-1-53; 128 v 823. Eff 11-6-59.**

## § 509.13 Forfeiture.

Constables shall be liable to a ten per cent forfeiture upon the amount of damages for which judgment may be entered against them, for failing to make return, making a false return, or failing to pay over money collected or received by them in their official capacity. Such judgment must include, in addition to the damages and costs, the forfeiture provided by this section.

**HISTORY: RS § 6698; S&C 804; 51 v 179, § 201; GC § 3344; Bureau of Code Revision. Eff 10-1-53.**

## § 509.15 Fees of constables.

The following fees and expenses shall be taxed as costs, collected from the judgment debtor, and paid to the general fund of the appropriate township or district as compensation due for services rendered by township constables or members of the police force of a township police district or joint police district:

(A) Serving and making return of each of the following:

(1) Order to commit to jail, order on jailer for prisoner, or order of ejectment, including copies to complete service, one dollar for each defendant named therein;

(2) Search warrant or warrant of arrest, for each person named in the writ, five dollars;

(3) Writ of attachment of property, except for purpose of garnishment, twenty dollars;

(4) Writ of attachment for the purpose of garnishment, five dollars;

(5) Writ of possession or restitution, twenty dollars;

(6) Attachment for contempt, for each person named in the writ, three dollars;

(7) Writ of replevin, twenty dollars;

(8) Summons and writs, subpoena, venire, and notice to garnishee, including copies to complete service, three dollars for each person named therein;

(9) Execution against property or person, eighty cents, and six per cent of all money thus collected;

(10) Any other writ, order, or notice required by law, for each person named therein, including copies to complete service, three dollars for the first name and fifty cents for each additional name.

(B) Mileage for the distance actually and necessarily traveled in serving and returning any of the preceding writs, orders, and notices, fifty cents for the first mile and for each additional mile, twenty cents;

(C) For attending a criminal case during the trial or hearing and having charge of prisoners, each case, two dollars and fifty cents, but, when so acting, such constable shall not be entitled to a witness fee if called upon to testify;

(D) For attending civil court during a jury trial, each case, two dollars;

(E) For attending civil court during a trial without jury, each case, one dollar and fifty cents;

(F) The actual amount paid solely for the transportation, meals, and lodging of prisoners, and for the moving and storage of goods and the care of animals taken on any legal process, such expense shall be specifically itemized on the back of the writs and sworn to;

(G) For summoning and swearing appraisers, each case, two dollars;

(H) For advertising property for sale, by posting, taken on any legal process, one dollar;

(I) For taking and making return of any bond required by law, eighty cents.

Notwithstanding anything to the contrary in this section, if any comparable fee or expense specified under section 311.17 of the Revised Code is increased to an amount greater than that set forth in this section, the board of township trustees, board of trustees of the township police district, or joint police district board, as appropriate, may require that the amount taxed as costs under this section equal the amount specified under section 311.17 of the Revised Code.

**HISTORY: RS § 622; S&S 368; S&C 638; 62 v 89, § 2; GC § 3347; 108 v PtII, 1203; 109 v 303; Bureau of Code Revision, 10-1-53; 130 v 214 (Eff 8-19-63); 146 v H 56. Eff 8-23-95; 2011 HB 153, § 101.01, eff. Sept. 29, 2011.**

# TITLE 7: MUNICIPAL CORPORATIONS

## CHAPTER 715: GENERAL POWERS



### [PEACE AND MORALS]

### § 715.48 Regulation by license of shows and games; trafficking in tickets; exceptions.

Any municipal corporation may:

(A) Regulate, by license or otherwise, restrain, or prohibit theatrical exhibitions, public shows, and athletic games, of whatever name or nature, for which money or other reward is demanded or received;

(B) Regulate, by license or otherwise, the business of trafficking in theatrical tickets, or other tickets of licensed amusements, by parties not acting as agents of those issuing them.

Public school entertainments, lecture courses, and lectures on historic, literary, or scientific subjects do not come within this section.

**HISTORY: Bates § 1536-100; 96 v 22, § 7-7; 97 v 505, § 7-7; 99 v 5, § 7g; GC § 3657; 102 v 88; Bureau of Code Revision. Eff 10-1-53.**

### § 715.49 Preservation of peace and protection of property.

(A) Any municipal corporation may prevent riot, gambling, noise and disturbance, and indecent and disorderly conduct or assemblages, preserve the peace and good order, and protect the property of the municipal corporation and its inhabitants.

(B) Anytime a noise ordinance of a municipal corporation is violated, but the source of the noise is located outside the borders of that municipal corporation in an adjoining municipal corporation, the municipal corporation with the ordinance may enforce the ordinance against that source as long as there is a written agreement between the two municipal corporations permitting such enforcement.

**HISTORY: Bates § 1536-100; 96 v 22, § 7-1; 97 v 504, § 7-1; 99 v 5, § 7a; GC § 3658; Bureau of Code Revision, 10-1-53; 145 v S 264. Eff 9-29-94.**

### § 715.50 Police jurisdiction outside municipal corporation.

A municipal corporation owning and using lands beyond its limits for a municipal purpose may provide, by ordinance or resolution, all needful police or sanitary regulations for the protection of such property and may prosecute violations thereof in the municipal court of such municipal corporation.

**HISTORY: GC § 3658-1; 120 v 150; Bureau of Code Revision, 10-1-53; 136 v H 205. Eff 1-1-76.**

### § 715.51 Billiards, pool, and gambling.

Any municipal corporation may:

(A) Regulate billiard and pool tables, nine or ten pin alleys or tables, and shooting and ball alleys;

(B) Authorize the destruction of instruments or devices used for the purpose of gambling.

**HISTORY: Bates § 1536-100; 96 v 22, § 7-2; 97 v 505, § 7-2; 99 v 5, § 7b; GC § 3659; Bureau of Code Revision. Eff 10-1-53.**

### § 715.52 Houses of ill fame.

Any municipal corporation may:

(A) Suppress and restrain disorderly houses and houses of ill fame;

(B) Provide for the punishment of all lewd and lascivious behavior in the streets and other public places.

**HISTORY: Bates § 1536-100; 96 v 22, § 7-5; 97 v 505, § 7-5; 99 v 5, § 7d; GC § 3660; Bureau of Code Revision. Eff 10-1-53.**

### § 715.53 Taverns.

Any municipal corporation may regulate taverns and other houses for public entertainment.

**HISTORY: Bates § 1536-100; 96 v 22, § 7-6; 97 v 505, § 7-6; 99 v 5, § 7f; GC § 3662; Bureau of Code Revision. Eff 10-1-53.**

### § 715.54 Vicious literature.

Any municipal corporation may restrain and prohibit the distribution, sale, and exposure for sale of books, papers, pictures, and periodicals or advertising matters of an obscene or immoral nature.

HISTORY: Bates § 1536-100; 96 v 25, § 7-24; 97 v 509, § 7-24; 99 v 9, § 7x; GC § 3663; Bureau of Code Revision. Eff 10-1-53.

## § 715.55 Assistance by attorney general concerning ordinance regulating adult entertainment establishments; indemnification by state.

(A) As used in this section, "adult entertainment establishment" has the same meaning as in section 2907.39 of the Revised Code.

(B) The legislative authority of a municipal corporation may request the attorney general to provide legal guidance and assistance in developing, formulating, and drafting an ordinance regarding the operation of adult entertainment establishments that does not conflict with general laws, with any provision in Chapter 4303. of the Revised Code, or with any provision in a rule adopted by the division of liquor control pursuant to that chapter that regulates establishments that hold a liquor permit. Upon the request of a legislative authority pursuant to this division, the attorney general shall provide legal guidance and assistance to the municipal corporation in developing, formulating, and drafting an ordinance regarding adult entertainment establishments. The ordinance may include, but need not be limited to, antinudity restrictions, limitations on hours of operation, interior configuration requirements, and requirements that an adult entertainment establishment and its employees obtain licenses or permits to operate as an adult entertainment establishment or to be employed by an adult entertainment establishment. The ordinance may create one or more criminal offenses and impose criminal penalties related to the operation of adult entertainment establishments or may provide for civil sanctions for violations of the ordinance.

(C) Except as otherwise provided in this division, the state shall indemnify a municipal corporation and the members of the municipal corporation's legislative authority from liability incurred in the enforcement of an ordinance that is authorized by this section, that was drafted in accordance with legal guidance provided by the attorney general as described in division (B) of this section, and that a court finds to be unconstitutional or otherwise legally defective by paying any judgment in, or amount negotiated in settlement of, any civil action arising from the enforcement of the ordinance. The state shall not indemnify a municipal corporation or the members of the municipal corporation's legislative authority until all appeals have been exhausted or the action has otherwise been finally resolved.

The state shall not indemnify a municipal corporation or the members of the municipal corporation's legislative authority for any of the following or to the extent that any of the following apply:

(1) Any part of the judgment or settlement that represents damages that are covered by a policy of insurance for civil liability;

(2) Any part of the judgment or settlement that is based upon an officer or employee of the municipal corporation acting manifestly outside the scope of the officer's or employee's employment or official responsibilities, with malicious purpose, in bad faith, or in a wanton or reckless manner;

(3) Any part of the judgment that is for punitive damages;

(4) Any part of a consent judgment or settlement that the attorney general determines is unreasonable.

HISTORY: 152 v S 16, § 1, eff. 9-4-07.

Not analogous to former RC § 715.55 (RS §§ 2108, 2109; S&C 1554, 1555; Bates §§ 1536-318, 1536-319; 66 v 183, § 200, 201; GC §§ 3664, 3665; 103 v 168; Bureau of Code Revision, 10-1-53), repealed 146 v S 2, § 2, eff 7-1-96.

## § 715.59 Hospitals for diseased prisoners.

The legislative authority of a municipal corporation may provide suitable hospitals for the reception and care of such prisoners as are diseased or disabled, under such regulations and the charge of such persons as the legislative authority directs.

HISTORY: RS § 2112; S&C 1555; Bates § 1536-322; 66 v 183, § 204; GC § 3668; Bureau of Code Revision. Eff 10-1-53.

[LICENSES]

## § 715.60 Regulation of explosives.

Any municipal corporation may regulate the transportation, keeping, and sale of gunpowder and other explosives or dangerous combustibles and materials, and provide or license magazines therefor.

HISTORY: Bates § 1536-100; 96 v 23, § 7-11; 97 v 506, § 7-11; 99 v 6, § 7k; GC § 3669; Bureau of Code Revision. Eff 10-1-53.

## § 715.61 Regulation and licensing of certain occupations and premises.

Any municipal corporation may regulate and license manufacturers and dealers in explosives, chattel mortgage and salary loan brokers, peddlers, public ballrooms, scavengers, intelligence officers, billiard rooms, bowling alleys, livery, sale, and boarding stables, dancing or riding academies or schools, race courses, ball grounds, street musicians, secondhand dealers, junk shops, and all persons engaged in the trade, business, or profession of manicuring, massaging, or chiropody. In the granting of any license a municipal corporation may charge such fees as the legislative authority deems proper and expedient.

HISTORY: Bates § 1536-100; 97 v 509, § 7-30; 99 v 9, § 7dd; GC § 3670; 101 v 232; Bureau of Code Revision, 10-1-53; 145 v H 376. Eff 7-22-94.

## § 715.62 Evidence.

In the trial of any action brought under section 715.61 of the Revised Code, the fact that any party to such action represented himself as engaged in any business or occupation, for the transaction of which a license is required, or as the keeper, proprietor, or manager of the thing for which a license is required, or that such party exhibits a sign indicating such business or calling, or such proprietorship or management, shall be conclusive evidence of the liability of the party to pay such license fee.

HISTORY: Bates § 1536-100; 97 v 509, § 7-30; 99 v 9, § 7dd; GC § 3671; Bureau of Code Revision. Eff 10-1-53.

## § 715.63 License power; exception.

Any municipal corporation may license exhibitors of shows or performances of any kind, hawkers, peddlers, auctioneers of horses and other animals on the highways or public grounds of the municipal corporation, vendors of gunpowder and other explosives, taverns, houses of public entertainment, and hucksters in the public streets or markets. The municipal corporation may, in granting such license, charge such fee as is reasonable. No municipal corporation may require of the owner of any product of his own raising, or the manufacturer of any article manufactured by him, a license to vend or sell, by himself or his agent, any such article or product. The legislative authority of such municipal corporation may delegate to the mayor of the municipal corporation the authority to grant, issue, and revoke licenses.

**HISTORY: RS § 2669; Bates § 1536-327; 66 v 223, § 447; 76 v 167, § 1; 77 v 74; 82 v 148; 86 v 164; GC § 3672; 101 v 37; Bureau of Code Revision. Eff 10-1-53.**

### § 715.64 Licensing transient dealers and solicitors.

Any municipal corporation may license transient dealers, persons who temporarily open stores or places for the sale of goods, wares, or merchandise, and each person who, on the streets or traveling from place to place about such municipal corporation, sells, bargains to sell, or solicits orders for goods, wares, or merchandise by retail. Such license shall be granted as provided by section 715.63 of the Revised Code.

This section does not apply to persons selling by sample only, nor to any agricultural articles or products offered or exposed for sale by the producer.

**HISTORY: RS §§ 2669b, 2670-1 (Bates' Edition, 1902); Bates §§ 1536-328, 1536-331; 86 v 244; 87 v 100, § 1; 90 v 311; GC §§ 3673, 3676; Bureau of Code Revision. Eff 10-1-53.**

### § 715.65 Licensing of advertising mediums and matters.

Any municipal corporation may license billposters, advertising sign painters, bill distributors, card tackers, and advertising matter of any article or compound which has not been manufactured or compounded within such municipal corporation. In granting such license the legislative authority of such municipal corporation may fix such license fees as are expedient, and may delegate to the mayor thereof the authority to grant, issue, and revoke such license.

This section does not authorize such legislative authority to charge merchants doing business therein a license fee for advertising their own business.

**HISTORY: RS § 2669c; Bates § 1536-329; 91 v 362; GC § 3674; Bureau of Code Revision. Eff 10-1-53.**

### § 715.66 Vehicle license for undertakers; money to be used for street repairs.

Any municipal corporation may license the owners of vehicles used for the transportation of persons or property, for hire, and all undertakers and owners of hearses.

The owners of such vehicles may be made liable for the breach of any ordinance regulating the conduct of the drivers thereof.

All moneys and receipts, in any municipal corporation, which are derived from the enforcement of any ordinance or law requiring the payment of a vehicle license fee, shall be credited and paid into a separate fund, which fund shall be known as "the public service street repair fund." All moneys and receipts credited to such fund shall be used for the sole purpose of repairing streets, avenues, alleys, and lanes within such municipal corporation.

**HISTORY: RS § 2670; Bates § 1536-330; 66 v 224, § 448; GC § 3675; 101 v 147; Bureau of Code Revision. Eff 10-1-53.**

[MISDEMEANOR]

### § 715.67 Violation of ordinances may be made a misdemeanor.

Any municipal corporation may make the violation of any of its ordinances a misdemeanor, and provide for the punishment thereof by fine or imprisonment, or both. The fine, imposed under authority of this section, shall not exceed five hundred dollars and imprisonment shall not exceed six months.

**HISTORY: Bates § 1536-100; 96 v 25, § 7-29; 97 v 509, § 7-29; 99 v 9, § 7cc; GC § 3628; Bureau of Code Revision. Eff 10-1-53.**

## CHAPTER 731: ORGANIZATION

Section



[INITIATIVE AND REFERENDUM]

### § 731.36 Prohibited practices relative to petitions.

No person shall, directly or indirectly:

(A) Willfully misrepresent the contents of any initiative or referendum petition;

(B) Pay or offer to pay any elector anything of value for signing an initiative or referendum petition;

(C) Promise to help another person to obtain appointment to any office provided for by the constitution or laws of this state or by the ordinances of any municipal corporation, or to any position or employment in the service of the state or any political subdivision thereof as a consideration for obtaining signatures to an initiative or referendum petition;

(D) Obtain signatures to any initiative or referendum petition as a consideration for the assistance or promise of assistance of another person in securing an appointment to any office or position provided for by the constitution or laws of this state or by the ordinance of any municipal corporation therein, or employment in the service of the state or any subdivision thereof;

(E) Alter, add to, or erase any signatures or names on the parts of a petition after such parts have been filed with the city auditor or village clerk;

(F) Fail to file the sworn itemized statement required in section 731.35 of the Revised Code.

**HISTORY: GC § 4227-10; 104 v 238; 106 v 443; Bureau of Code Revision. Eff 10-1-53.**

## § 731.38 Prohibition against accepting premium for signing.

No person shall accept anything of value for signing an initiative or referendum petition.

**HISTORY: GC § 4227-11; 104 v 238; Bureau of Code Revision. Eff 10-1-53.**

## § 731.40 Prohibition against threats in securing signatures.

No person shall, directly or indirectly, by intimidation or threats, influence or seek to influence any person to sign or abstain from signing, or to solicit signatures to or abstain from soliciting signatures to an initiative or referendum petition.

**HISTORY: GC § 4227-11; 104 v 238; Bureau of Code Revision. Eff 10-1-53.**

### [PENALTIES]

## § 731.99 Penalties.

(A) Whoever violates section 731.36 of the Revised Code shall be fined not less than one hundred nor more than five hundred dollars.

(B) Whoever violates section 731.40 of the Revised Code is guilty of a minor misdemeanor.

(C) Whoever violates section 731.38 of the Revised Code shall be fined not more than twenty-five dollars.

**HISTORY: Bureau of Code Revision, 10-1-53; 126 v 575 (Eff 10-6-55); 138 v H 1062 (Eff 3-23-81); 139 v S 199 (Eff 1-1-83); 146 v S 2. Eff 7-1-96.**

The effective date is set by section 6 of SB 2.

# CHAPTER 733: OFFICERS

Section



### [CITY DIRECTOR OF LAW]

## § 733.51 Powers and duties of city director of law.

The city director of law shall prepare all contracts, bonds, and other instruments in writing in which the city is concerned, and shall serve the several directors and officers provided in Title VII [7] of the Revised Code as legal counsel and attorney.

The director of law shall be prosecuting attorney of the mayor's court. When the legislative authority of the city allows assistants to the director of law, he may designate the assistants to act as prosecuting attorneys of the mayor's court. The person designated shall be subject to the approval of the legislative authority.

**HISTORY: RS Bates § 1536-663; 96 v 65, § 137; 99 v 458, § 137; GC §§ 4305, 4306; 102 v 131; Bureau of Code Revision, 10-1-53; 136 v H 205 (Eff 1-1-76); 137 v H 219. Eff 11-1-77.**

## § 733.52 Prosecuting attorney of mayor's court.

The city director of law as prosecuting attorney of the mayor's court shall prosecute all cases brought before the court, and perform the same duties, as far as they are applicable thereto, as required of the prosecuting attorney of the county.

The director of law or the assistants whom he designates to act as prosecuting attorneys of the mayor's court shall receive such compensation for the service provided by this section as the legislative authority of the city prescribes, and such additional compensation as the board of county commissioners allows.

**HISTORY: RS § 1813; Bates § 1536-844; S&C 1536; 66 v 179, § 191; 84 v 26, 28; 95 v 86; GC § 4307; 102 v 131; Bureau of Code Revision, 10-1-53; 136 v H 205 (Eff 1-1-76); 137 v H 219. Eff 11-1-77.**

## § 733.53 Duties as to suits.

The city director of law, when required to do so by resolution of the legislative authority of the city, shall prosecute or defend on behalf of the city, all complaints, suits, and controversies in which the city is a party, and such other suits, matters, and controversies as he is, by resolution or ordinance, directed to prosecute. He shall not be required to prosecute any action before the mayor of the city for the violation of an ordinance without first advising such action.

**HISTORY: RS § 1774; Bates § 1536-664; 66 v 175, § 157; 85 v 249; 90 v 132; GC § 4308; Bureau of Code Revision, 10-1-53; 137 v H 219. Eff 11-1-77.**

## § 733.54 City director of law shall give opinions.

When an officer of a city entertains doubts concerning the law in any matter before him in his official capacity, and desires the opinion of the city director of law, he shall clearly state to the director of law, in writing, the question upon which the opinion is desired, and thereupon the director of law shall, within a reasonable time, reply orally or in writing to such inquiry. The right conferred upon such officers by this section extends to the legislative authority of the city, and to each board provided for in Title VII [7] of the Revised Code.

**HISTORY: RS § 1775; Bates § 1536-665; 85 v 225; GC § 4309; Bureau of Code Revision, 10-1-53; 137 v H 219. Eff 11-1-77.**

[MISCONDUCT IN OFFICE]

## § 733.72 Charges against municipal officers filed with probate judge; proceedings.

When a complaint under oath is filed with the probate judge of the county in which a municipal corporation or the larger part thereof is situated, by any elector of the municipal corporation, signed and approved by four other electors thereof, the judge shall forthwith issue a citation to any person charged in the complaint for his appearance before the judge within ten days from the filing thereof, and shall also furnish the accused and the village solicitor or city director of law with a copy thereof. The complaint shall charge any of the following:

(A) That a member of the legislative authority of the municipal corporation has received, directly or indirectly, compensation for his services as a member thereof, as a committeeman, or otherwise, contrary to law;

(B) That a member of the legislative authority or an officer of the municipal corporation is or has been interested, directly or indirectly, in the profits of a contract, job, work, or service, or is or has been acting as a commissioner, architect, superintendent, or engineer in work undertaken or prosecuted by the municipal corporation, contrary to law;

(C) That a member of the legislative authority or an officer of the municipal corporation has been guilty of misfeasance or malfeasance in office.

Before acting upon such complaint, the judge shall require the party complaining to furnish sufficient security for costs.

**HISTORY: RS § 1732; Bates § 1536-989; 68 v 113, § 1; GC § 4670; Bureau of Code Revision, 10-1-53; 137 v H 219. Eff 11-1-77.**

## § 733.73 Appearance of counsel; jury.

On the day fixed by the probate judge for the return of the citation issued pursuant to section 733.72 of the Revised Code, the village solicitor or city director of law shall appear on behalf of the complainant to conduct the prosecution, and the accused may also appear by counsel. A time shall be set for hearing the case, which shall be not more than ten days after such return. If a jury is demanded by either party, the probate judge shall direct the summoning of twelve men [jurors] in the manner provided by sections 2313.19 to 2313.26 of the Revised Code. In a municipal corporation having no village solicitor or city director of law, or in case the village solicitor or city director of law is accused of any misfeasance or malfeasance in his office, the prosecuting attorney shall appear on behalf of the complainant to conduct the prosecution.

**HISTORY: RS § 1733; Bates § 1536-990; 68 v 113, § 2; GC § 4671; Bureau of Code Revision, 10-1-53; 129 v 582(641) (Eff 1-10-61); 131 v 269 (Eff 1-1-66); 137 v H 219. Eff 11-1-77.**

# CHAPTER 737: PUBLIC SAFETY

Section
737.99 Repealed.

## [DEPARTMENT OF PUBLIC SAFETY IN CITY]

### § 737.01 Director of public safety.

In each city there shall be a department of public safety, which shall be administered by a director of public safety. The director shall be appointed by the mayor and need not be a resident of the city at the time of his appointment but shall become a resident thereof within six months after his appointment unless such residence requirement is waived by ordinance.

**HISTORY: RS Bates § 1536-682; 96 v 68, § 146; 99 v 564, § 146; GC § 4367; Bureau of Code Revision, 10-1-53; 133 v H 279. Eff 10-2-69.**

### § 737.02 General duties; records; contracts.

Under the direction of the mayor, the director of public safety shall be the executive head of the police and fire departments and the chief administrative authority of the charity, correction, and building departments. He shall have all powers and duties connected with and incident to the appointment, regulation, and government of such departments except as otherwise provided by law. He shall keep a record of his proceedings, a copy of which, certified by him, shall be competent evidence in all courts.

Such director shall make all contracts in the name of the city with reference to the management of such departments, for the erection or repair of all buildings or improvements in connection therewith, and for the purchase of all supplies necessary for such departments.

**HISTORY: RS Bates §§ 1536-683, 1536-684, 1536-686; 96 v 69, §§ 147, 148; 96 v 70, § 150; 99 v 564, § 147; GC §§ 4368, 4369; Bureau of Code Revision. Eff 10-1-53.**

### § 737.021 Division of traffic engineering and safety in department of public safety.

The legislative authority of a city may create and abolish, by ordinance, a division of traffic engineering and safety within the department of public safety. The director of public safety of such city shall be the executive head of such division. He shall have all powers and duties connected with and incident to the appointment, regulation, and government of such division, and shall make such rules and regulations as he may deem necessary for the government and operation of the division. He shall keep a record of all his proceedings in connection with the administration of such division. A copy of such proceedings, when certified by him, shall be competent evidence in all courts. Such division may be staffed by traffic and safety engineers and such other employees as determined by the legislative authority.

**HISTORY: 131 v 274. Eff 11-1-65.**

### § 737.022 Authority of director to promulgate certain traffic regulations.

(A) As used in this section:

(1) "Occupy or use," with respect to a public way, means to create parking spaces and install, repair, maintain, replace, and operate parking meters or other similar devices for the purpose of providing on-street parking.

(2) "Public agency" includes any county, municipal corporation, port authority, regional transit authority, airport authority, or transportation improvement district created pursuant to the laws of this state.

(3) "Public parking franchise" means a property right and privilege to occupy and use one or more public ways for the operation of an on-street parking system in all or in one or more portions of the area within the corporate limits of a municipal corporation or to construct, install, repair, maintain, and operate parking meters or other devices or facilities on public property owned or controlled by the municipal corporation.

(4) "Public way" means the surface of, and the space within, through, on, across, above, or below, any public street, road, highway, lane, path, alley, court, sidewalk, boulevard, parkway, or drive owned or controlled by a municipal corporation.

(B) In order to expedite the flow and direction of traffic, to eliminate congestion on public ways, and to provide for the safety of passengers in motor vehicles and pedestrians, the legislative authority of a municipal corporation may by ordinance make and issue, or, in the case of the legislative authority of a city, authorize the director of public safety to make and issue rules and regulations concerning:

(1) The number, type, and location of traffic control devices and signs;

(2) The regulation or prohibition of parking on public ways or public property;

(3) The regulation of the right-of-way at intersections of streets, alleys, and highways;

(4) The regulation or prohibition of turns at intersections;

(5) The creation, abolition, and regulation of through routes and truck routes;

(6) The creation, abolition, and regulation of pedestrian crosswalk and safety zones;

(7) The creation, abolition, and regulation of bus loading and unloading zones and business loading zones;

(8) The creation, abolition, and regulation of traffic lanes, and passing zones;

(9) The regulation of the direction of traffic on public ways and the creation and abolition of one way public streets, roads, alleys, courts, or drives;

(10) Such other subjects as may be provided by ordinance, which shall not be limited by the specific enumeration of subjects by this section.

(C) The legislative authority of a municipal corporation having rules and regulations with respect to parking on public ways or public property for the purposes specified in division (B) of this section may establish and maintain reasonable fees and charges for the privilege of parking in locations permitted by those rules and regulations and may construct, install, maintain, repair, replace, and operate parking meters or other devices or facilities on public ways and public property for the collection of those fees and charges. The operation of meters, devices, and facilities may be managed and operated by municipal officials and employees or by any other person or public agency retained by the municipal corporation for those purposes, as determined by the legislative authority.

(D) As an alternative to the operation of parking meters, devices, and facilities in the manner specified in division (C) of this section, the legislative authority of a municipal corporation having rules and regulations with respect to parking on public ways or public property for the purposes specified in division (B) of this section may grant to a person or public agency a public parking franchise permitting that person or agency to occupy and use certain public ways or to construct, install, maintain, repair, replace, and operate parking meters or other devices or facilities on public property on and subject to terms and conditions specified in a franchise agreement approved by the legislative authority; provided, that no such public parking franchise shall be granted for a term of more than thirty years. The legislative authority may require the person or public agency receiving such a public parking franchise to pay to the municipal corporation a lump sum fee, a periodic fee, or both for the property rights and privileges granted. Public parking franchises shall be subject to regulation by the legislative authority of the municipal corporation and shall not be deemed to be a public utility or an entity otherwise subject to regulation by any state agency or commission.

(E) Rules and regulations made and issued in accordance with division (B) of this section shall be issued in the manner and subject to the conditions and limitations as prescribed by ordinance of the legislative authority of such city. Copies of rules and regulations issued pursuant to this section, when certified by the director of public safety, shall be competent evidence in all courts. Violation of any such rules and regulations shall be as specified by the legislative authority, either a criminal misdemeanor punishable as provided by the ordinances of such municipal corporation or a civil infraction for which a charge is prescribed. The enforcement of rules and regulations violations of which constitute criminal misdemeanors shall be by authorized law enforcement officers.

**HISTORY: 131 v 275. Eff 11-1-65; 2011 HB 153, § 101.01, eff. Sept. 29, 2011.**

Acts 2011, HB 153, § 737.30 provides: "The authority provided in section 737.022 of the Revised Code as amended by this act is in addition and supplemental to provisions for the subject matter that may also be the subject of other laws, and is supplemental to and not in derogation of any similar authority provided by, derived from, or implied by, the Constitution of the state of Ohio or any other laws, including the law amended by this act, or any charter, order, resolution, or ordinance, and no inference shall be drawn to negate the authority thereunder by reason of express provisions contained in section 737.022 of the Revised Code."

## § 737.03 Management of certain institutions; contracts and expenditures.

The director of public safety shall manage and make all contracts with reference to police stations, fire houses, reform schools, infirmaries, hospitals other than municipal hospitals operated pursuant to Chapter 749. of the Revised Code, workhouses, farms, pesthouses, and all other charitable and reformatory institutions. In the control and supervision of those institutions, the director shall be governed by the provisions of Title VII of the Revised Code relating to those institutions.

The director may make all contracts and expenditures of money for acquiring lands for the erection or repairing of station houses, police stations, fire department buildings, fire cisterns, and plugs, that are required, for the purchase of engines, apparatus, and all other supplies necessary for the police and fire departments, and for other undertakings and departments under the director's supervision, but no obligation involving an expenditure of more than twenty-five thousand dollars shall be created unless first authorized and directed by ordinance. In making, altering, or modifying those contracts, the director shall be governed by sections 735.05 to 735.09 of the Revised Code, except that all bids shall be filed with and opened by the director. The director shall make no sale or disposition of any property belonging to the city without first being authorized by resolution or ordinance of the city legislative authority.

**HISTORY: Bates §§ 1536-683, 1536-690; 96 v 69, § 147; 96 v 71, § 154; 97 v 388, § 154; 99 v 564, §§ 147, 154; GC §§ 4370, 4371; 123 v 495; Bureau of Code Revision, 10-1-53; 132 v S 378 (Eff 4-29-68); 136 v H 8 (Eff 8-11-75); 138 v H 371 (Eff 3-14-80); 142 v H 527 (Eff 3-17-89); 149 v H 94. Eff 9-5-2001; 150 v H 95, § 1, eff. 9-26-03; 150 v S 222, § 1, eff. 4-27-05.**

The effective date is set by section 179 of H.B. 95 (150 v —).

[CONTRACT FOR POLICE PROTECTION]

## § 737.04 Mutual aid contracts with other political subdivisions for law enforcement purposes.

The legislative authority of any municipal corporation, in order to obtain police protection or to obtain additional police protection, or to allow its police officers to work in multijurisdictional drug, gang, or career criminal task forces, may enter into contracts with one or more municipal corporations, townships, township police districts, joint police districts, or county sheriffs in this state, with one or more park districts created pursuant to section 511.18 or 1545.01 of the Revised Code, with one or more port authorities, or with a contiguous municipal corporation in an adjoining state, upon any terms that are agreed upon, for services of police departments or the use of police equipment or for the interchange of services of police departments or police equipment within the several territories of the contracting subdivisions.

Chapter 2744. of the Revised Code, insofar as it applies to the operation of police departments, shall apply to the contracting political subdivisions and to the police department members when they are rendering service outside their own subdivisions pursuant to the contracts.

Police department members acting outside the subdivision in which they are employed, pursuant to a contract entered into under this section, shall be entitled to participate in any indemnity fund established by their employer to the same extent as while acting within the employing subdivision. Those members shall be entitled to all the rights and benefits of Chapter 4123. of the Revised Code, to the same extent as while performing service within the subdivision.

The contracts may provide for:

(A) A fixed annual charge to be paid at the times agreed upon and stipulated in the contract;

(B) Compensation based upon:

(1) A stipulated price for each call or emergency;

(2) The number of members or pieces of equipment employed;

(3) The elapsed time of service required in each call or emergency.

(C) Compensation for loss or damage to equipment while engaged in rendering police services outside the limits of the subdivision owning and furnishing the equipment;

(D) Reimbursement of the subdivision in which the police department members are employed for any indemnity award or premium contribution assessed against the employing subdivision for workers' compensation benefits for injuries or death of its police department members occurring while engaged in rendering police services pursuant to the contract.

**HISTORY: GC § 4371-1; 122 v 288; Bureau of Code Revision, 10-1-53; 136 v S 545 (Eff 1-17-77); 138 v H 279 (Eff 10-26-79); 139 v H 738 (Eff 6-25-82); 141 v H 201 (Eff 7-1-85); 141 v H 176 (Eff 11-20-85); 144 v S 174 (Eff 7-31-92); 147 v H 342. Eff 12-31-97; 152 v H 67, § 101.01, eff. 6-30-07; 2011 HB 153, § 101.01, eff. Sept. 29, 2011.**

The effective date is set by § 609.10 of 152 v H 67.

## § 737.041 Resolution to provide police services without a contract.

The police department of any municipal corporation may provide police protection to any county, municipal corporation, township, township police district, or joint police district of this state, to a park district created pursuant to section 511.18 or 1545.01 of the Revised Code, to a port authority, to any multijurisdictional drug, gang, or career criminal task force, or to a governmental entity of an adjoining state without a contract to provide police protection, upon the approval, by resolution, of the legislative authority of the municipal corporation in which the department is located and upon authorization by an officer or employee of the police department providing the police protection who is designated by title of office or position, pursuant to the resolution of the legislative authority of the municipal corporation, to give the authorization.

Chapter 2744. of the Revised Code, insofar as it applies to the operation of police departments, shall apply to any municipal corporation and to members of its police department when the members are rendering police services pursuant to this section outside the municipal corporation by which they are employed.

Police department members acting, as provided in this section, outside the municipal corporation by which they are employed shall be entitled to participate in any pension or indemnity fund established by their employer to the same extent as while acting within the municipal corporation by which they are employed. Those members shall be entitled to all the rights and benefits of Chapter 4123. of the Revised Code to the same extent as while performing services within the municipal corporation by which they are employed.

**HISTORY: 138 v S 98 (Eff 10-6-80); 139 v H 103 (Eff 5-19-82); 141 v H 176 (Eff 11-20-85); 144 v S 174 (Eff 7-31-92); 147 v H 342. Eff 12-31-97; 152 v H 67, § 101.01, eff. 6-30-07; 2011 HB 153, § 101.01, eff. Sept. 29, 2011.**

The effective date is set by § 609.10 of 152 v H 67.

# [POLICE AND FIRE DEPARTMENTS IN CITY]

## § 737.05 Composition and control of police department.

The police department of each city shall be composed of a chief of police and such other officers, patrolmen, and employees as the legislative authority thereof provides by ordinance.

The director of public safety of such city shall have the exclusive management and control of all other officers, surgeons, secretaries, clerks, and employees in the police department as provided by ordinances or resolution of such legislative authority. He may commission private policemen, who may not be in the classified list of the department, under such rules and regulations as the legislative authority prescribes.

**HISTORY: RS Bates § 1536-685; 96 v 70, § 149; GC § 4374, 4375; 118 v 319; Bureau of Code Revision. Eff 10-1-53.**

## § 737.051 City auxiliary police unit; parking enforcement unit.

(A) The legislative authority of a city may establish, by ordinance, an auxiliary police unit within the police department of the city, and provide for the regulation of auxiliary police officers. The director of public safety shall be the executive head of the auxiliary police unit, shall make all appointments and removals of auxiliary police officers, subject to any general rules prescribed by the legislative authority by ordinance, and shall prescribe rules for the organization, training, administration, control, and conduct of the auxiliary police unit. Members of the auxiliary police unit shall not be in the classified service of the city.

(B)(1) The legislative authority of a city may establish, by ordinance, a parking enforcement unit within the police department of the city, and provide for the regulation of parking enforcement officers. The director of public safety shall be the executive head of the parking enforcement unit, shall make all appointments and removals of parking enforcement officers, subject to any general rules prescribed by the legislative authority by ordinance, and shall prescribe rules for the organization, training, administration, control and conduct of the parking enforcement unit. The director may appoint parking enforcement officers who agree to serve for nominal compensation, and persons with physical disabilities may receive appointments as parking enforcement officers.

(2) The authority of the parking enforcement officers shall be limited to the enforcement of ordinances governing parking in handicapped parking locations and fire lanes and any other parking ordinances specified in the ordinance creating the parking enforcement unit. Parking enforcement officers shall have no other powers.

(3) The training the parking enforcement officers shall receive shall include instruction in general administrative rules and procedures governing the parking enforcement unit. The role of the judicial system as it relates to parking regulation and enforcement, proper techniques and methods relating to the enforcement of parking ordinances, human interaction skills, and first aid.

**HISTORY: 130 v 241 (Eff 5-6-63); 141 v H 201 (Eff 7-1-85); 143 v S 174. Eff 7-13-90.**

## § 737.052 Felony precludes or terminates employment as chief, police officer or auxiliary officer.

(A) As used in this section, "felony" has the same meaning as in section 109.511 [109.51.1] of the Revised Code.

(B)(1) The director of public safety shall not appoint a person as a chief of police, a member of the police department of the municipal corporation, or an auxiliary police officer on a permanent basis, on a temporary basis, for a probationary term, or on other than a permanent basis if the person previously has been convicted of or has pleaded guilty to a felony.

(2)(a) The director of public safety shall terminate the employment of a chief of police, member of the police department, or auxiliary police officer who does either of the following:

(i) Pleads guilty to a felony;

(ii) Pleads guilty to a misdemeanor pursuant to a negotiated plea agreement as provided in division (D) of section 2929.43 of the Revised Code in which the chief of police, member of the police department, or auxiliary police officer agrees to surrender the certificate awarded to the chief of police, member of the police department, or auxiliary police officer under section 109.77 of the Revised Code.

(b) The director shall suspend from employment a chief of police, member of the police department, or auxiliary police officer who is convicted, after trial, of a felony. If the chief of police, member of the police department, or auxiliary police officer files an appeal from that conviction and the conviction is upheld by the highest court to which the appeal is taken or if the chief of police, member of the police department, or auxiliary police officer does not file a timely appeal, the director shall terminate that person's employment. If the chief of police, member of the police department, or auxiliary police officer files an appeal that results in that person's acquittal of the felony or conviction of a misdemeanor, or in the dismissal of the felony charge against that person, the director shall reinstate that person. A chief of police, member of the police department, or auxiliary police officer who is reinstated under division (B)(2)(b) of this section shall not receive any back pay unless that person's conviction of the felony was reversed on appeal, or the felony charge was dismissed, because the court found insufficient evidence to convict that person of the felony.

(3) Division (B) of this section does not apply regarding an offense that was committed prior to January 1, 1997.

(4) The suspension from employment, or the termination of the employment, of the chief of police, member of the police department, or auxiliary police officer under division (B)(2) of this section shall be in accordance with Chapter 119. of the Revised Code.

**HISTORY: 146 v H 566. Eff 10-16-96; 149 v H 490, § 1, eff. 1-1-04.**

The effective date is set by section 4 of HB 490.

## § 737.06 Chief of police.

The chief of police shall have exclusive control of the stationing and transfer of all patrolmen, auxiliary police officers, and other officers and employees in the police department, and police auxiliary unit, under such general rules and regulations as the director of public safety prescribes.

**HISTORY: RS Bates § 1536-684; 96 v 69, § 148; GC § 4372; Bureau of Code Revision, 10-1-53; 130 v 242. Eff 5-6-63.**

## § 737.07 Hours of work for policemen in cities; leave of absence.

In each city, except in case of necessary appearances in court and emergency special duty assignments, not to exceed eight hours constitute a day's work and not to exceed forty-four hours constitute a week's work for policemen. Annually, in each city, each policeman shall be given not less than two weeks' leave of absence with full pay.

**HISTORY: GC § 4374-1; 119 v 132; Bureau of Code Revision, 10-1-53; 133 v S 28. Eff 11-19-69.**

## § 737.08 Composition and control of city fire department.

(A) The fire department of each city shall be composed of a chief of the fire department and other officers, firefighters, and employees provided for by ordinance. Neither this section nor any other section of the Revised Code requires, or shall be construed to require, that the fire chief be a resident of the city.

(B) No person shall be appointed as a permanent full-time paid member, whose duties include fire fighting, of the fire department of any city, unless either of the following applies:

(1) The person has received a certificate issued under former section 3303.07 of the Revised Code or section 4765.55 of the Revised Code evidencing satisfactory completion of a firefighter training program.

(2) The person began serving as a permanent full-time paid firefighter with the fire department of a village or other city prior to July 2, 1970, and receives a fire training certificate issued under section 4765.55 of the Revised Code.

(C) No person who is appointed as a volunteer firefighter of a city fire department shall remain in that position, unless either of the following applies:

(1) Within one year of the appointment, the person has received a certificate issued under former section 3303.07 of the Revised Code or section 4765.55 of the Revised Code evidencing satisfactory completion of a firefighter training program.

(2) The person began serving as a permanent full-time paid firefighter with the fire department of a village or other city prior to July 2, 1970, or as a volunteer firefighter with the fire department of a township, fire district, village, or other city prior to July 2, 1979, and receives a fire training certificate issued under section 4765.55 of the Revised Code.

(D) The director of public safety shall have the exclusive management and control of other surgeons, secretaries, clerks, and employees provided for by ordinance or resolution of the legislative authority of the city.

**HISTORY: RS Bates § 1536-686; 96 v 70, § 150; GC § 4377; 118 v 320; Bureau of Code Revision, 10-1-53; 133 v S 226 (Eff 11-19-69); 137 v H 590 (Eff 7-1-79); 144 v S 98 (Eff 11-12-92); 146 v H 405 (Eff 10-1-96); 149 v H 143. Eff 1-25-2002; 151 v H 401, § 1, eff. 4-5-07.**

## § 737.081 Criminal records check for prospective firefighter.

(A) The fire chief of a city fire department may request the superintendent of BCII to conduct a criminal records check with respect to any person who is under consideration for appointment or employment as a permanent, full-time paid firefighter or any person who is under consideration for appointment as a volunteer firefighter.

(B)(1) The fire chief of the city fire department may request that the superintendent of BCII obtain information from the federal bureau of investigation as a part of the criminal records check requested pursuant to division (A) of this section.

(2) A fire chief authorized by division (A) of this section to request a criminal records check shall provide to each person for whom the fire chief intends to request a criminal records check a copy of the form prescribed pursuant to division (C)(1) of section 109.578 [109.57.8] of the Revised Code and a standard impression sheet to obtain fingerprint impressions prescribed pursuant to division (C)(2) of section 109.578 [109.57.8] of the Revised Code, obtain the completed form and impression sheet from the person, and forward the completed form and impression sheet to the superintendent of BCII at the time the criminal records check is requested.

(3) Any person subject to a criminal records check who receives a copy of the form and a copy of the impression sheet pursuant to division (B)(2) of this section and who is requested to complete the form and provide a set of fingerprint impressions shall complete the form or provide all the information necessary to complete the form and shall provide the impression sheet with the impressions of the person's fingerprints. If a person fails to provide the information necessary to complete the form or fails to provide impressions of the person's fingerprints, the appointing authority shall not appoint or employ the person as a permanent full-time paid firefighter or a volunteer firefighter.

(C)(1) Except as otherwise provided in division (C)(2) of this section, an appointing authority shall not appoint or employ a person as a permanent, full-time paid firefighter or a volunteer firefighter if the fire chief has requested a criminal records check pursuant to division (A) of this section and the criminal records check indicates that the person previously has been convicted of or pleaded guilty to any of the following:

(a) A felony;

(b) A violation of section 2909.03 of the Revised Code;

(c) A violation of an existing or former law of this state, any other state, or the United States that is substantially equivalent to any of the offenses described in division (C)(1)(a) or (b) of this section.

(2) Notwithstanding division (C)(1) of this section, an appointing authority may appoint or employ a person as a permanent, full-time paid firefighter or a volunteer firefighter if all of the following apply:

(a) The fire chief has requested a criminal records check pursuant to division (A) of this section.

(b) The criminal records check indicates that the person previously has been convicted of or pleaded guilty to any of the offenses described in division (C)(1) of this section.

(c) The person meets rehabilitation standards established in rules adopted under division (E) of this section.

(3) If a fire chief requests a criminal records check pursuant to division (A) of this section, an appointing authority may appoint or employ a person as a permanent, full-time paid firefighter or volunteer firefighter conditionally until the criminal records check is completed and the fire chief receives the results. If the results of the criminal records check indicate that, pursuant to division (C)(1) of this section, the person subject to the criminal records check is disqualified from appointment or employment, the fire chief shall release the person from appointment or employment.

(D) The fire chief shall pay to the bureau of criminal identification and investigation the fee prescribed pursuant to division (C)(3) of section 109.578 [109.57.8] of the Revised Code for each criminal records check conducted in accordance with that section. The fire chief may charge the applicant who is subject to the criminal records check a fee for the costs the fire chief incurs in obtaining the criminal records check. A fee charged under this division shall not exceed the amount of fees the fire chief pays for the criminal records check. If a fee is charged under this division, the fire chief shall notify the applicant at the time of the applicant's initial application for appointment or employment of the amount of the fee and that, unless the fee is paid, the applicant will not be considered for appointment or employment.

(E) The appointing authority shall adopt rules in accordance with Chapter 119. of the Revised Code to implement this section. The rules shall include rehabilitation standards a person who has been convicted of or pleaded guilty to an offense listed in division (C)(1) of this section must meet for the appointing authority to appoint or employ the person as a permanent, full-time paid firefighter or a volunteer firefighter.

(F) A fire chief who intends to request a criminal records check for an applicant shall inform each applicant, at the time of the person's initial application for appointment or employment, that the applicant is required to provide a set of impressions of the person's fingerprints and that the fire chief requires a criminal records check to be conducted and satisfactorily completed in accordance with section 109.578 [109.57.8] of the Revised Code.

(G) As used in this section:

(1) "Appointing authority" means any person or body that has the authority to hire, appoint, or employ permanent, full-time paid firefighters and volunteer firefighters under section 737.08 of the Revised Code.

(2) "Criminal records check" has the same meaning as in section 109.578 [109.57.8] of the Revised Code.

(3) "Superintendent of BCII" has the same meaning as in section 2151.86 of the Revised Code.

**HISTORY: 149 v S 258. Eff 4-9-2003.**

## § 737.09 Chief of fire department.

The chief of the fire department shall have exclusive control of the stationing and transferring of all firemen and other officers and employees in the department, under such general rules and regulations as the director of public safety prescribes.

**HISTORY: RS Bates § 1536-686; 96 v 70, § 150; GC § 4376; Bureau of Code Revision. Eff 10-1-53.**

## § 737.10 Additional patrolmen and firemen in emergency situation.

In case of riot or other like emergency, the mayor may appoint additional patrolmen and officers for temporary service in the police department, or additional firemen and officers for temporary service in the fire department, who need not be in the classified list of such department. Such additional persons shall be employed only for the time during which the emergency exists.

The mayor may call upon the sheriff of the county in which all or part of the municipal corporation lies or the sheriff of any adjoining county, the mayor or other chief executive of any municipal corporation in the same or any adjoining county, and the chairman of the board of township trustees of any township in the same or any adjoining county, to furnish such law enforcement or fire protection personnel, or both, together with appropriate equipment and apparatus, as may be necessary to preserve the public peace and protect persons and property in the requesting municipal corporation in the event of riot. Such aid shall be furnished to the mayor requesting it, insofar as possible without withdrawing from the political subdivision furnishing such aid the minimum police and fire protection appearing necessary under the circumstances. In such case, law enforcement and fire protection personnel acting outside the territory of their regular employment shall be considered as performing services within the territory of their regular employment for purposes of compensation, pension or indemnity fund rights, workers' compensation, and other rights or benefits to which they may be entitled as incidents of their regular employment. The municipal corporation receiving such aid shall reimburse the political subdivision furnishing it the cost of furnishing such aid, including compensation of personnel, expenses incurred by reason of the injury or death of any such personnel while rendering such aid, expenses of furnishing equipment and apparatus, compensation for damage to or loss of equipment or apparatus while in service outside the territory of its regular use, and such other reasonable expenses as may be incurred by any such political subdivision in furnishing such aid. Nothing in this section shall be construed as superseding or modifying in any way any provision of a contract entered into pursuant to section 737.04 of the Revised Code. Law enforcement officers acting pursuant to this section outside the territory of their regular employment have the same authority to enforce the law as when acting within the territory of their regular employment.

**HISTORY: RS Bates § 1536-684; 96 v 69, § 148; GC § 4373; Bureau of Code Revision, 10-1-53; 132 v H 996 (Eff 6-13-68); 136 v S 545. Eff 1-17-77.**

## § 737.11 General duties of police and fire departments.

The police force of a municipal corporation shall preserve the peace, protect persons and property, and obey and enforce all ordinances of the legislative authority of the municipal corporation, all criminal laws of the state and the United States, all court orders issued and consent agreements approved pursuant to sections 2919.26 and 3113.31 of the Revised Code, all protection orders issued pursuant to section 2903.213 [2903.21.3] or 2903.214 [2903.21.4] of the Revised Code, and protection orders issued by courts of another state, as defined in section 2919.27 of the Revised Code. The fire department shall protect the lives and property of the people in case of fire. Both the police and fire departments shall perform any other duties that are provided by ordinance. The police and fire departments in every city shall be maintained under the civil service system.

A chief or officer of a police force of a municipal corporation may participate, as the director of an organized crime task force established under section 177.02 of the Revised Code or as a member of the investigatory staff of such a task force, in an investigation of organized criminal activity in any county or counties in this state under sections 177.01 to 177.03 of the Revised Code.

**HISTORY: RS Bates § 1536-687; 96 v 71, § 151 GC § 4378; Bureau of Code Revision, 10-1-53; 137 v H 835 (Eff 3-27-79); 141 v S 74 (Eff 9-3-86); 144 v H 536 (Eff 11-5-92); 147 v S 1 (Eff 10-21-97); 147 v H 302. Eff 7-29-98.**

## § 737.111 Disposition of funds received by police department.

All fines imposed as discipline or punishment upon members of the police department of a municipal corporation by the authority having charge or control thereof, all rewards, fees, or proceeds of gifts and emoluments allowed by such authority paid and given for or on account of any extraordinary service of any member of the department, and moneys arising from the sale of unclaimed property or money, after deducting all expenses incident thereto, shall be credited to the general fund of the municipal corporation.

**HISTORY: RS Bates § 1536-597(c); 95 v 227, § 22(c); 97 v 247, § 2(c); GC § 4623; 120 v 248; Bureau of Code Revision, RC § 741.41, 10-1-53; 131 v 285 (Eff 11-5-65); RC § 737.11.1, 141 v H 201. Eff 7-1-85.**

## § 737.112 Disposition of funds received by fire department.

All fines imposed as discipline or punishment upon members of the fire department of a municipal corporation by the authority having charge or control thereof, the proceeds of all suits for penalties for the violation of state statutes and municipal ordinances with the execution of which such department is charged, license fees or other fees payable thereunder, and fees received by such municipal corporation for any services performed or inspections made by the fire department, except fees charged and received by the municipal corporation from other subdivisions for fire protection or fire fighting therein shall be credited to the general fund of the municipal corporation.

**HISTORY: RS Bates § 1536-596(c); 95 v 224, § 1(c); 97 v 243, § 1(c); GC § 4607; 118 v 283; Bureau of Code Revision, RC § 741.10, 10-1-53; 131 v 278 (Eff 11-5-65); RC § 737.11.2, 141 v H 201. Eff 7-1-85.**

## § 737.12 Suspension of police and fire personnel.

Except as provided in section 737.052 [737.05.2] of the Revised Code, the chief of police and the chief of the fire department have the exclusive right to suspend any of the deputies, officers, or employees in their respective departments and under their management and control, for incompetence, gross neglect of duty, gross immorality, habitual drunkenness, failure to obey orders given them by the proper authority, or for any other reasonable and just cause.

If an employee is suspended under this section, the chief of police or the chief of the fire department, as the case may be, shall forthwith certify that fact in writing, together with the cause for the suspension, to the director of public safety, who, within five days from the receipt of that certification, shall proceed to inquire into the cause of the suspension and render judgment on it. If the charge is sustained, the judgment may be for the person's suspension, reduction in rank, or dismissal from the department. The judgment shall be final except as otherwise provided by law.

The director, in any investigation of charges against a member of the police or fire department, shall have the same powers to administer oaths and to secure the attendance of witnesses and the production of books and papers that are conferred upon the mayor.

**HISTORY: RS Bates § 1536-688; 96 v 71, § 152; GC §§ 4379, 4380; 101 v 297; Bureau of Code Revision, 10-1-53; 146 v H 566. Eff 10-16-96.**

## § 737.13 Classification of service; rules and regulations.

The director of public safety of a city shall classify the service in the police and fire departments in conformity with the ordinance of the legislative authority thereof determining the number of persons to be employed in the departments, and shall make all rules for the regulation and discipline of such departments, except as otherwise provided by law.

**HISTORY: RS Bates § 1536-689; 96 v 71, § 153; 99 v 564, § 153; GC § 4382; Bureau of Code Revision. Eff 10-1-53.**

## § 737.14 Relief for members of police or fire department.

The legislative authority of a municipal corporation may provide by general ordinance for the relief, out of the police or fire funds, of members of either department temporarily or permanently disabled in the discharge of their duty. This section does not impair, restrict, or repeal any law authorizing the levy of taxes in municipal corporations to provide for firemen, police, and sanitary police pension funds, and to create and perpetuate boards of trustees for the administration of such funds.

**HISTORY: RS Bates § 1536-691; 96 v 72, § 155; GC § 4383; Bureau of Code Revision. Eff 10-1-53.**

### [VILLAGE MARSHAL]

## § 737.15 Appointment of village marshal.

Each village shall have a marshal, designated chief of police, appointed by the mayor with the advice and consent of the legislative authority of the village, who need not be a resident of the village at the time of appointment but shall become a resident thereof within six months after appointment by the mayor and confirmation by the legislative authority unless such residence requirement is waived by ordinance, and who shall continue in office until removed therefrom as provided by section 737.171 [737.17.1] of the Revised Code.

No person shall receive an appointment under this section after January 1, 1970, unless, not more than sixty days prior to receiving such appointment, the person has passed a physical examination, given by a licensed physician, a physician assistant, a clinical nurse specialist, a certified nurse practitioner, or a certified nurse-midwife, showing that the person meets the physical requirements necessary to perform the duties of village marshal as established by the legislative authority of the village. The appointing authority shall, prior to making any such appointment, file with the Ohio police and fire pension fund a copy of the report or findings of said licensed physician, physician assistant, clinical nurse specialist, certified nurse practitioner, or certified nurse-midwife. The professional fee for such physical examination shall be paid for by such legislative authority.

**HISTORY: RS Bates §§ 1536-860, 1536-978; 96 v 86, § 206; 98 v 172, § 222; GC § 4384; 119 v 699; Bureau of Code Revision, 10-1-53; 130 v 242 (Eff 9-16-63); 131 v 276 (Eff 9-6-65); 133 v S 86 (Eff 10-24-69); 148 v H 222 (Eff 11-2-99); 149 v S 245. Eff 3-31-2003.**

## § 737.16 Deputy marshals, police officers, night guards and special police officers.

The mayor shall, when provided for by the legislative authority of a village, and subject to its confirmation, appoint all deputy marshals, police officers, night guards, and special police officers. All such officers shall continue in office until removed therefrom for the cause and in the manner provided by section 737.19 of the Revised Code.

No person shall receive an appointment under this section after January 1, 1970, unless the person has, not more than sixty days prior to receiving such appointment, passed a physical examination, given by a licensed physician, a physician assistant, a clinical nurse specialist, a certified nurse practitioner, or a certified nurse-midwife, showing that the person meets the physical requirements necessary to perform the duties of the position to which the person is to be appointed as established by the legislative authority of the village. The appointing authority shall, prior to making any such appointment, file with the Ohio police and fire pension fund a copy of the report or findings of said licensed physician, physician assistant, clinical nurse specialist, certified nurse practitioner, or certified nurse-midwife. The professional fee for such physical examination shall be paid for by the legislative authority.

**HISTORY: GC § 4384-1; 119 v 699; Bureau of Code Revision, 10-1-53; 130 v 242 (Eff 9-6-63); 133 v S 86 (Eff 10-24-69); 137 v H 812 (Eff 8-1-78); 148 v H 222 (Eff 11-2-99); 149 v S 245. Eff 3-31-2003.**

## § 737.161 Village auxiliary police unit; parking enforcement unit.

(A) The legislative authority of a village may establish, by ordinance, an auxiliary police unit within the police department of the village, and provide for the regulation of auxiliary police officers. The mayor shall be the executive head of the auxiliary police unit, shall make all appointments and removals of auxiliary police officers, subject to any general rules prescribed by the legislative authority by ordinance, and shall prescribe rules for the organization, training, administration, control, and conduct of the auxiliary police unit. The village marshal shall have exclusive control of the stationing and transferring of all auxiliary police officers, under such general rules as the mayor prescribes.

(B)(1) The legislative authority of a village may establish, by ordinance, a parking enforcement unit within the police department of the village, and provide for the regulation of parking enforcement officers. The mayor shall be the executive head of the parking enforcement unit, shall make all appointments and removals of parking enforcement officers, subject to any general rules prescribed by the legislative authority by ordinance, and shall prescribe rules for the organization, training, administration, control, and conduct of the parking enforcement unit. The mayor may appoint parking enforcement officers who agree to serve for nominal compensation, and persons with physical disabilities may receive appointments as parking enforcement officers.

(2) The authority of the parking enforcement officers shall be limited to the enforcement of ordinances govern-

ing parking in handicapped parking locations and fire lanes and any other parking ordinances specified in the ordinance creating the parking enforcement unit. Parking enforcement officers shall have no other powers.

(3) The training the parking enforcement officers shall receive shall include instruction in general administrative rules and procedures governing the parking enforcement unit, the role of the judicial system as it relates to parking regulation and enforcement, proper techniques and methods relating to the enforcement of parking ordinances, human interaction skills, and first aid.

**HISTORY: 130 v 242 (Eff 5-6-63); 141 v H 201 (Eff 7-1-85); 143 v S 174. Eff 7-13-90.**

## § 737.162 Felony precludes or terminates employment in law enforcement capacity.

(A) As used in this section, "felony" has the same meaning as in section 109.511 of the Revised Code.

(B)(1) The mayor shall not appoint a person as a marshal, a deputy marshal, a police officer, a night watchperson, a special police officer, or an auxiliary police officer on a permanent basis, on a temporary basis, for a probationary term, or on other than a permanent basis if the person previously has been convicted of or has pleaded guilty to a felony.

(2)(a) The mayor shall terminate the employment of a marshal, deputy marshal, police officer, night watchperson, special police officer, or auxiliary police officer who does either of the following:

(i) Pleads guilty to a felony;

(ii) Pleads guilty to a misdemeanor pursuant to a negotiated plea agreement as provided in division (D) of section 2929.43 of the Revised Code in which the marshal, deputy marshal, police officer, night watchperson, special police officer, or auxiliary police officer agrees to surrender the certificate awarded to that person under section 109.77 of the Revised Code.

(b) The mayor shall suspend from employment a marshal, deputy marshal, police officer, night watchperson, special police officer, or auxiliary police officer who is convicted, after trial, of a felony. If the marshal, deputy marshal, police officer, night watchperson, special police officer, or auxiliary police officer files an appeal from that conviction and the conviction is upheld by the highest court to which the appeal is taken or if that person does not file a timely appeal, the mayor shall terminate that person's employment. If the marshal, deputy marshal, police officer, night watchperson, special police officer, or auxiliary police officer files an appeal that results in that person's acquittal of the felony or conviction of a misdemeanor, or in the dismissal of the felony charge against that person, the mayor shall reinstate that person. A marshal, deputy marshal, police officer, night watchperson, special police officer, or auxiliary police officer who is reinstated under division (B)(2)(b) of this section shall not receive any back pay unless that person's conviction of the felony was reversed on appeal, or the felony charge was dismissed, because the court found insufficient evidence to convict that person of the felony.

(3) Division (B) of this section does not apply regarding an offense that was committed prior to January 1, 1997.

(4) The suspension from employment, or the termination of the employment, of a marshal, deputy marshal, police officer, night watchperson, special police officer, or auxiliary police officer under division (B)(2) of this section shall be in accordance with Chapter 119. of the Revised Code.

**HISTORY: 146 v H 566. Eff 10-16-96; 149 v H 490, § 1, eff. 1-1-04.**

The effective date is set by section 4 of HB 490.

## § 737.17 Probationary period; final appointment.

All appointments made under sections 737.15 and 737.16 of the Revised Code shall be for a probationary period of six months' continuous service, and none shall be finally made until the appointee has satisfactorily served his probationary period. At the end of the probationary period the mayor shall transmit to the legislative authority of the village a record of such employee's service with his recommendations thereon and he may, with the concurrence of the legislative authority, remove or finally appoint the employee.

**HISTORY: GC § 4384-2; 119 v 699; Bureau of Code Revision. Eff 10-1-53.**

## § 737.171 Removal proceedings; suspension; appeals.

Except as provided in section 737.162 [737.16.2] of the Revised Code, if the mayor of a village has reason to believe that a duly appointed marshal of the village has been guilty of incompetency, inefficiency, dishonesty, drunkenness, immoral conduct, insubordination, discourteous treatment of the public, neglect of duty, or any other acts of misfeasance, malfeasance, or nonfeasance in the performance of the marshal's official duty, the mayor shall file with the legislative authority of the village written charges against that person setting forth in detail the reason for the charges, and immediately shall serve a true copy of the charges upon the person against whom they are made.

Charges filed under this section shall be heard at the next regular meeting of the legislative authority occurring not less than five days after the date those charges have been served on the person against whom they are made. The person against whom those charges are filed may appear in person and by counsel at the hearing, examine all witnesses, and answer all charges against that person.

At the conclusion of the hearing, the legislative authority may dismiss the charges, suspend the accused from office for not more than sixty days, or remove the accused from office.

Action of the legislative authority removing or suspending the accused from office requires the affirmative vote of two-thirds of all members elected to it.

In the case of removal from office, the person so removed may appeal on questions of law and fact the decision of the legislative authority to the court of common pleas of the county in which the village is situated. The person shall take the appeal within ten days from the date of the finding of the legislative authority.

**HISTORY: 130 v 243 (Eff 9-16-63); 130 v Pt.II, 57 (Eff 12-16-64); 137 v H 812 (Eff 8-1-78); 146 v H 566. Eff 10-16-96.**

## § 737.18 General powers of village police officers.

The marshal shall be the peace officer of a village and the executive head, under the mayor, of the police force.

The marshal, and the deputy marshals, policemen, or night watchmen under him shall have the powers conferred by law upon police officers in all villages of the state, and such other powers, not inconsistent with the nature of their offices, as are conferred by ordinance.

A marshal, deputy marshal, or police officer of a village may participate, as the director of an organized crime task force established under section 177.02 of the Revised Code or as a member of the investigatory staff of such a task force, in an investigation of organized criminal activity in any county or counties in this state under sections 177.01 to 177.03 of the Revised Code.

**HISTORY: RS Bates § 1536-860; 96 v 86, § 206; GC § 4385; Bureau of Code Revision, 10-1-53; 141 v S 74. Eff 9-3-86.**

## § 737.19 Powers and duties of marshal.

(A) The marshal of a village has exclusive authority over the stationing and transfer of all deputies, officers, and employees within the police department of the village, under the general rules that the mayor prescribes.

(B) Except as provided in section 737.162 [737.16.2] of the Revised Code, the marshal of a village has the exclusive right to suspend any of the deputies, officers, or employees in the village police department who are under the management and control of the marshal for incompetence, gross neglect of duty, gross immorality, habitual drunkenness, failure to obey orders given them by the proper authority, or for any other reasonable or just cause.

If an employee is suspended under this section, the marshal immediately shall certify this fact in writing, together with the cause for the suspension, to the mayor of the village and immediately shall serve a true copy of the charges upon the person against whom they are made. Within five days after receiving this certification, the mayor shall inquire into the cause of the suspension and shall render a judgment on it. If the mayor sustains the charges, the judgment of the mayor may be for the person's suspension, reduction in rank, or removal from the department.

Suspensions of more than three days, reduction in rank, or removal from the department under this section may be appealed to the legislative authority of the village within five days from the date of the mayor's judgment. The legislative authority shall hear the appeal at its next regularly scheduled meeting. The person against whom the judgment has been rendered may appear in person and by counsel at the hearing, examine all witnesses, and answer all charges against that person.

At the conclusion of the hearing, the legislative authority may dismiss the charges, uphold the mayor's judgment, or modify the judgment to one of suspension for not more than sixty days, reduction in rank, or removal from the department.

Action of the legislative authority removing or suspending the accused from the department requires the affirmative vote of two-thirds of all members elected to it.

In the case of removal from the department, the person so removed may appeal on questions of law and fact the decision of the legislative authority to the court of common pleas of the county in which the village is situated. The person shall take the appeal within ten days from the date of the finding of the legislative authority.

(C) The marshal of a village shall suppress all riots, disturbances, and breaches of the peace, and to that end may call upon the citizens to aid the marshal. The marshal shall arrest all disorderly persons in the village and pursue and arrest any person fleeing from justice in any part of the state. The marshal shall arrest any person in the act of committing an offense against the laws of the state or the ordinances of the village and forthwith bring that person before the mayor or other competent authority for examination or trial. The marshal shall receive and execute proper authority for the arrest and detention of criminals fleeing or escaping from other places or states.

In the discharge of the marshal's duties, the marshal shall have the powers and be subject to the responsibilities of constables, and, for services performed by the marshal or the marshal's deputies, the same fees and expenses shall be taxed as are allowed constables.

**HISTORY: RS §§ 1849, 1850; Bates §§ 1536-862, 1536-863; 66 v 173, §§ 142, 143; GC §§ 4386, 4387; 108 v Pt.II, 1203; Bureau of Code Revision, 10-1-53; 137 v H 812 (Eff 8-1-78); 146 v H 566. Eff 10-16-96.**

## § 737.20 Disposition of fines and penalties.

All fees, costs, fines, and penalties collected by the marshal shall immediately be paid to the mayor, who shall report to the legislative authority of the village monthly the amount thereof, from whom, and for what purpose collected, and when paid to the mayor.

**HISTORY: RS § 1851; Bates § 1536-864; 66 v 173, § 144; GC § 4388; Bureau of Code Revision. Eff 10-1-53.**

### [FIRE DEPARTMENT IN CITY OR VILLAGE]

## § 737.27 Investigation of fires.

The legislative authority of a municipal corporation may invest any officer of the fire or police department with the power, and impose on him the duty, to be present at all fires, investigate the cause thereof, examine witnesses, compel the attendance of witnesses and the production of books and papers, and to do and perform all other acts necessary to the effective discharge of such duties.

Such officer may administer oaths, make arrests, and enter, for the purpose of examination, any building which, in his opinion, is in danger from fire. The officer shall report his proceedings to the legislative authority at such times as are required.

**HISTORY: RS §§ 2474, 2475; Bates §§ 1536-873, 1536-874; 66 v 205, §§ 330, 331; GC §§ 4396, 4397; Bureau of Code Revision. Eff 10-1-53.**

### [PROPERTY RECOVERED BY POLICE; DISPOSITION]

## § 737.29 Property recovered by police.

Stolen or other property recovered by members of the police force of a municipal corporation shall be deposited and kept in a place designated by the mayor. Each such article shall be entered in a book kept for that purpose, with the name of the owner, if ascertained, the person from whom taken, the place where found with general circumstances, the date of its receipt, and the name of the officer receiving it.

An inventory of all money or other property shall be given to the party from whom taken, and in case it is not claimed by some person within thirty days after arrest and seizure it shall be delivered to the person from whom taken, and to no other person, either attorney, agent, factor, or clerk, except by special order of the mayor.

**HISTORY: RS § 6858-1; 98 v 60; GC §§ 4398, 4399; Bureau of Code Revision. Eff 10-1-53.**

## § 737.30 Repealed, 149 v H 490, § 2. [RS § 6858-2; 98 v 61; GC § 12937; Bureau of Code Revision. Eff 10-1-53.] Eff 1-1-04.

This section concerned deposit of stolen property.

## § 737.31 Disposition to claimant.

If, within thirty days, the money or property recovered under section 737.29 of the Revised Code is claimed by any other person, it shall be retained by the custodian thereof until after the discharge or conviction of the person from whom it was taken and so long as it is required as evidence in any case in court. If such claimant establishes to the satisfaction of the court that he is the rightful owner, the money or property shall be restored to him, otherwise it shall be returned to the accused person, personally, and not to any attorney, agent, factor, or clerk of such accused person, except upon special order of the mayor after all liens and claims in favor of the municipal corporation have first been discharged and satisfied.

**HISTORY: RS § 6858-1; 98 v 60; GC § 4400; Bureau of Code Revision. Eff 10-1-53.**

## § 737.32 Sale or donation of unclaimed property.

Except as otherwise provided in this section and unless the property involved is required to be disposed of pursuant to another section of the Revised Code, property that is unclaimed for ninety days or more shall be sold by the chief of police of the municipal corporation, marshal of the village, or licensed auctioneer at public auction, after notice of the sale has been provided by publication once a week for three successive weeks in a newspaper of general circulation in the county or as provided in section 7.16 of the Revised Code. The proceeds of the sale shall be paid to the treasurer of the municipal corporation and shall be credited to the general fund of the municipal corporation.

If authorized to do so by an ordinance adopted by the legislative authority of the municipal corporation and if the property involved is not required to be disposed of pursuant to another section of the Revised Code, the chief of police or marshal may contribute property that is unclaimed for ninety days or more to one or more public agencies, to one or more nonprofit organizations no part of the net income of which inures to the benefit of any private shareholder or individual and no substantial part of the activities of which consists of carrying on propaganda or otherwise attempting to influence legislation, or to one or more organizations satisfying section 501(c)(3) or (c)(19) of the Internal Revenue Code of 1986.

**HISTORY: RS § 6858-3; 98 v 61; GC § 4401; 112 v 254; Bureau of Code Revision, 10-1-53; 125 v 346 (Eff 10-1-53); 131 v 276 (Eff 9-29-65); 133 v H 13 (Eff 7-14-69); 134 v H 24 (Eff 10-6-71); 148 v H 55. Eff 9-29-99; 2011 HB 153, § 101.01, eff. Sept. 29, 2011.**

## § 737.33 Expenses of storage and sale; notice.

Upon the sale of any unclaimed or impounded property as provided in section 737.32 of the Revised Code, if any such unclaimed or impounded property was ordered removed to a place of storage or stored, or both, by or under the direction of a chief of police of the municipal corporation or marshal of the village, any expenses or charges for such removal or storage, or both, and costs of sale, provided the same are approved by such chief of police or marshal, shall first be paid from the proceeds of such sale. Notice shall be given by registered mail, thirty days before the date of such sale, to the owner and mortgagee, or other lien holder, at their last known address.

**HISTORY: GC § 4401-1; 124 v 377; Bureau of Code Revision. Eff 10-1-53.**

# [PUBLIC BUILDINGS, INSPECTION FOR FIRE SAFETY]

## § 737.37 Power of legislative authority to regulate.

The legislative authority of a municipal corporation may make such regulations pertaining to public buildings as it considers necessary for the public safety.

**HISTORY: RS Bates § 1536-317f; 97 v 266, § 6; GC § 4664; Bureau of Code Revision. Eff 10-1-53.**

## § 737.41 Municipal probation services fund.

(A) The legislative authority of a municipal corporation in which is established a municipal court, other than a county-operated municipal court, that has a department of probation shall establish in the municipal treasury a municipal probation services fund. The fund shall contain all moneys paid to the treasurer of the municipal corporation under section 2951.021 of the Revised Code for deposit into the fund. The treasurer of the municipal corporation shall disburse the money contained in the fund at the request of the municipal court department of probation, for use only by that department for specialized staff, purchase of equipment, purchase of services, reconciliation programs for offenders and victims, other treatment programs, including alcohol and drug addiction programs certified under section 3793.06 of the Revised Code, determined to be appropriate by the chief probation officer, and other similar expenses related to placing offenders under a community control sanction.

(B) Any money in a municipal probation services fund at the end of a fiscal year shall not revert to the treasury of the municipal corporation but shall be retained in the fund.

(C) As used in this section:

(1) "County-operated municipal court" has the same meaning as in section 1901.03 of the Revised Code.

(2) "Community control sanction" has the same meaning as in section 2929.01 of the Revised Code.

**HISTORY: 145 v H 406. Eff 11-11-94; 149 v H 490, § 1, eff. 1-1-04.**

The effective date is set by section 4 of HB 490.

**§ 737.99** Repealed, 149 v H 490, § 2 [Bureau of Code Revision, 10-1-53; 127 v 285, § 2 (Eff 9-7-57); 133 v H 290 (Eff 7-14-70); 134 v H 24. Eff 10-6-71.] Eff 1-1-04.

This section concerned the penalty for any property not deposited as provided by section 737.30.

# CHAPTER 753: REFORMATORY INSTITUTIONS

Section



## [PRISONS AND STATION HOUSES]

### § 753.02 Municipal liability for sustaining inmates in prison or station house; reimbursement by inmate; drug tests; testing and treatment for certain diseases.

(A) The legislative authority of a municipal corporation shall provide by ordinance for sustaining all persons sentenced to or confined in a prison or station house at the expense of the municipal corporation, and in counties where prisons or station houses are in quarters leased from the board of county commissioners, may contract with the board for the care and maintenance of those persons by the sheriff or other person charged with the care and maintenance of county prisoners. On the presentation of bills for food, sustenance, and necessary supplies, to the proper officer, certified by the person whom the legislative authority designates, the officer shall audit the bills under the rules prescribed by the legislative authority, and draw the officer's order on the treasurer of the municipal corporation in favor of the person presenting the bill.

(B) Pursuant to section 2929.37 of the Revised Code, the legislative authority of the municipal corporation may require a person who was convicted of an offense and who is confined in a prison or station house as provided in division (A) of this section, or a person who was convicted of an offense and who is confined in the county jail as provided in section 1905.35 of the Revised Code, to reimburse the municipal corporation for its expenses incurred by reason of the person's confinement.

(C) Notwithstanding any contrary provision in this section or section 2929.18, 2929.28, or 2929.37 of the Revised Code, the legislative authority of the municipal corporation may establish a policy that complies with section 2929.38 of the Revised Code and that requires any person who is not indigent and who is confined in a prison or station house to pay a reception fee, a fee for any medical treatment or service requested by and provided to that person, or the fee for a random drug test assessed under division (E) of section 753.33 of the Revised Code.

(D) If a person who has been convicted of or pleaded guilty to an offense is sentenced to a term of imprisonment in a prison or station house as described in division (A) of this section, or if a person who has been arrested for an offense, and who has been denied bail or has had bail set and has not been released on bail is confined in a prison or station house as described in division (A) of this section pending trial, at the time of reception and at other times the person in charge of the operation of the prison or station house determines to be appropriate, the person in charge of the operation of the prison or station house may cause the convicted or accused offender to be examined and tested for tuberculosis, HIV infection, hepatitis, including, but not limited to, hepatitis A, B, and C, and other contagious diseases. The person in charge of the operation of the prison or station house may cause a convicted or accused offender in the prison or station house who refuses to be tested or treated for tuberculosis, HIV infection, hepatitis, including, but not limited to, hepatitis A, B, and C, or another contagious disease to be tested and treated involuntarily.

**HISTORY: RS § 2093; Bates § 1536-367; 66 v 186, § 217; GC § 4126; 107 v 502; 124 v 127; Bureau of Code Revision, 10-1-53; 134 v H 172 (Eff 11-25-71); 140 v H 363 (Eff 9-26-84); 146 v S 2 (Eff 7-1-96); 146 v S 269 (Eff 7-1-96); 146 v H 480 (Eff 10-16-96); 147 v S 111 (Eff 3-17-98); 148 v H 349 (Eff 9-22-2000); 149 v H 170. Eff 9-6-2002; 149 v H 490, § 1, eff. 1-1-04.**

The effective date is set by section 4 of HB 490.

### § 753.021 Submission of health insurance claims for inmates.

(A) For each person who is confined in a prison or station house as provided in section 753.02 of the Revised Code or in a county jail as provided in section 1905.35 of the Revised Code, the municipal corporation may make a determination as to whether the person is covered under a health insurance or health care policy, contract, or plan and, if the person has such coverage, what terms and conditions are imposed by it for the filing and payment of claims.

(B) If, pursuant to division (A) of this section, it is determined that the person is covered under a policy, contract, or plan and, while that coverage is in force, the prison, station house, or county jail renders or arranges for the rendering of health care services to the person, in accordance with the terms and conditions of the policy, contract, or plan, then the person, municipal corporation, or provider of the health care services, as appropriate under the terms and conditions of the policy, contract, or plan, shall promptly submit a claim for payment for the health care services to the appropriate third-party payer and shall designate, or make any other arrangement necessary to ensure, that payment of any amount due on the claim be made to the municipal corporation or the provider, as the case may be.

(C) Any payment made to the municipal corporation pursuant to division (B) of this section shall be paid into the treasury of the municipal corporation.

(D) This section also applies to any person who is under the custody of a law enforcement officer, as defined in section 2901.01 of the Revised Code, prior to the person's confinement in the prison, station house, or county jail.

**HISTORY: 146 v S 163. Eff 10-16-96.**

## § 753.03 Disposition of prisoners sentenced for misdemeanors.

A municipal legislative authority may, by ordinance, provide for the keeping of persons convicted and sentenced for misdemeanors, during the term of their imprisonment, at such place as the legislative authority determines, provided that the place selected is in substantial compliance with the minimum standards for jails in Ohio promulgated by the department of rehabilitation and correction. The legislative authority may enter into a contract under section 9.06 of the Revised Code for the private operation and management of any municipal correctional facility, but only if the facility is used to house only misdemeanant inmates.

**HISTORY: RS § 2094; Bates § 1536-368; 66 v 186, § 218; GC § 4127; Bureau of Code Revision, 10-1-53; 139 v S 23 (Eff 7-6-82); 146 v H 117. Eff 9-29-95.**

The effective date is set by section 197 of HB 117.

[WORKHOUSES]

## § 753.04 Commitment to workhouse; drug tests; testing and treatment for certain diseases.

(A) When a person over sixteen years of age is convicted of an offense under the law of this state or an ordinance of a municipal corporation, and the tribunal before which the conviction is had is authorized by law to commit the offender to the county jail or municipal corporation prison, the court, mayor, or judge of the county court, as the case may be, may sentence the offender to a workhouse.

When a commitment is made from a municipal corporation or township in the county, other than in a municipal corporation having a workhouse, the legislative authority of the municipal corporation or the board of township trustees shall transmit with the mittimus a sum of money equal to not less than seventy cents per day for the time of the commitment, to be placed in the hands of the superintendent of a workhouse for the care and maintenance of the prisoner.

(B) Pursuant to section 2929.37 of the Revised Code, the legislative authority of the municipal corporation or the board of township trustees may require a person who is convicted of an offense and who is confined in a workhouse as provided in division (A) of this section, to reimburse the municipal corporation or the township, as the case may be, for its expenses incurred by reason of the person's confinement.

(C) Notwithstanding any contrary provision in this section or section 2929.18, 2929.28, or 2929.37 of the Revised Code, the legislative authority of the municipal corporation or board of township trustees may establish a policy that complies with section 2929.38 of the Revised Code and that requires any person who is not indigent and who is confined in the workhouse under division (A) of this section to pay a reception fee, a fee for any medical treatment or service requested by and provided to that person, or the fee for a random drug test assessed under division (E) of section 753.33 of the Revised Code.

(D) If a person who has been convicted of or pleaded guilty to an offense is incarcerated in a workhouse or if a person who has been arrested for an offense, and who has not been denied bail or has had bail set and has not been released on bail is confined in a workhouse pending trial, at the time of reception and at other times the person in charge of the operation of the workhouse determines to be appropriate, the person in charge of the operation of the workhouse may cause the convicted or accused offender to be examined and tested for tuberculosis, HIV infection, hepatitis, including, but not limited to, hepatitis A, B, and C, and other contagious diseases. The person in charge of the operation of the workhouse may cause a convicted or accused offender in the workhouse who refuses to be tested or treated for tuberculosis, HIV infection, hepatitis, including, but not limited to, hepatitis A, B, and C, or another contagious disease to be tested and treated involuntarily.

**HISTORY: RS § 2099; Bates § 1536-369; 99 v 125; 73 v 211, § 275; GC § 4128; 110 v 12; Bureau of Code Revision, 10-1-53; 126 v 320; 127 v 1039 (Eff 1-1-58); 140 v H 363 (Eff 9-26-84); 146 v S 2 (Eff 7-1-96); 146 v S 269 (Eff 7-1-96); 146 v H 480 (Eff 10-16-96); 147 v S 111 (Eff 3-17-98); 148 v H 349 (Eff 9-22-2000); 149 v H 170. Eff 9-6-2002; 149 v H 490, § 1, eff. 1-1-04.**

The effective date is set by section 4 of HB 490.

## § 753.041 Submission of health insurance claims for workhouse inmates.

(A) For each person who is confined in a workhouse as provided in section 753.04 of the Revised Code, the municipal corporation or the township, as the case may be, may make a determination as to whether the person is covered under a health insurance or health care policy, contract, or plan and, if the person has such coverage, what terms and conditions are imposed by it for the filing and payment of claims.

(B) If, pursuant to division (A) of this section, it is determined that the person is covered under a policy, contract, or plan and, while that coverage is in force, the workhouse renders or arranges for the rendering of health care services to the person in accordance with the terms and conditions of the policy, contract, or plan, then the person, municipal corporation, township, or provider of the health care services, as appropriate under the terms and conditions of the policy, contract, or plan, shall promptly submit a claim for payment for the health care services to the appropriate third-party payer and shall designate, or make any other arrangement necessary to ensure, that payment of any amount due on the claim be made to the municipal corporation, township, or provider, as the case may be.

(C) Any payment made to the municipal corporation or township pursuant to division (B) of this section shall be paid into the treasury of the governmental entity that incurred the expenses.

(D) This section also applies to any person who is under the custody of a law enforcement officer, as defined in section 2901.01 of the Revised Code, prior to the person's confinement in the workhouse.

**HISTORY: 146 v S 163. Eff 10-16-96.**

## § 753.05 Employment of prisoners.

A person sentenced under section 753.04 of the Revised Code shall be received into the workhouse, and shall be kept and confined at labor therein, or if such labor cannot be furnished he may be employed at labor elsewhere when such employment is authorized by ordinance, and shall be subject to the rules, regulations, and discipline thereof until the expiration of his sentence, when he shall be discharged.

**HISTORY: RS § 2100; Bates § 1536-370; 66 v 195, § 276; 82 v 117; GC § 4129; 110 v 12; Bureau of Code Revision. Eff 10-1-53.**

## § 753.06 Immunity concerning prisoners or adult offenders on work detail.

(A) As used in this section:

(1) "Municipal correctional facility" has the same meaning as in section 753.32 of the Revised Code.

(2) "Municipal correctional officer" has the same meaning as in section 753.31 of the Revised Code.

(B) If all the prisoners working on a work detail administered by a municipal correctional facility and outside the facility have volunteered for the work detail and are imprisoned in that facility for an offense other than a felony of the first or second degree and if the applicable municipal correctional officer complies with division (C) of this section, both of the following apply:

(1) No member of the organized police department of the municipal corporation and no municipal correctional officer is liable for civil damages for injury, death, or loss to person or property caused or suffered by a prisoner working on the work detail unless the injury, death, or loss results from malice or wanton or reckless misconduct of the member of the organized police department of the municipal corporation or the municipal correctional officer.

(2) A municipal corporation in which the prisoners work on the work detail and that employs the member of the organized police department or the municipal correctional officer or a township in which the prisoners work on the work detail is not liable for civil damages for injury, death, or loss to person or property caused or suffered by a prisoner working on the work detail unless the injury, death, or loss results from malice or wanton or reckless misconduct of the member of the organized police department of the municipal corporation or a municipal correctional officer.

(C) To qualify for the immunity described in division (B)(1) of this section regarding a work detail, a municipal correctional officer, prior to having the prisoners of the municipal correctional facility work outside the facility on the work detail, shall inform each prisoner on the work detail of the provisions of this section, including notifying the prisoner that, by volunteering for the work detail, the prisoner cannot hold any member of the organized police department of the municipal corporation or any municipal correctional officer or the municipal corporation or township liable for civil damages for injury, death, or loss to person or property unless the injury, death, or loss results from malice or wanton or reckless misconduct of the member of the organized police department of the municipal corporation or the municipal correctional officer.

**HISTORY: 150 v H 316, § 1, eff. 3-31-05.**

This section referred to cumulative sentences and habitual offenders.

## § 753.08 Prompt commitment; fees.

The officer having the execution of the final sentence of a court, magistrate, or mayor shall cause the convicted person to be conveyed to the workhouse as soon as practicable after the sentence is pronounced, and all officers shall be paid the fees therefor allowed by law for similar services in other cases. Such fees shall be paid, when the sentence is by the court, from the county treasury, and when by the magistrate, from the township treasury.

**HISTORY: RS § 2101; Bates § 1536-372; 66 v 196, § 277; GC § 4132; Bureau of Code Revision. Eff 10-1-53.**

## § 753.09 Discharge.

The director of public safety may discharge, for good and sufficient cause, a person committed to the workhouse. A record of all such discharges shall be kept and reported to the legislative authority of the municipal corporation in the annual report of such director, with a brief statement of the reasons therefor.

**HISTORY: RS § 2102; Bates § 1536-373; 66 v 196, § 278; 97 v 488; GC § 4133; Bureau of Code Revision. Eff 10-1-53.**

## § 753.10 Parole of inmates.

The director of public safety may establish rules and regulations under which, and specify the conditions on which, a prisoner may be allowed to go upon parole outside of the buildings and enclosures of the workhouse. While on parole such person shall remain in the legal custody and under the control of such director, and subject at any time to be taken back within the enclosure of the institution. Full power to enforce the rules, regulations, and conditions, and to retake and reimprison any convict so paroled, is hereby conferred upon such director, whose written order shall be sufficient warrant for all officers named therein to authorize them to return to actual custody any conditionally released or paroled prisoner. All such officers shall execute such order the same as ordinary criminal process.

No parole shall be granted by such director without previous notice thereof to the trial judge.

**HISTORY: RS § 2102; Bates § 1536-373; 66 v 196, § 278; 97 v 488; GC § 4134; Bureau of Code Revision. Eff 10-1-53.**

## § 753.11 Violation of parole.

The director of public safety may employ or authorize any person to see that the conditions of a parole are not violated, and in case of violation to return to the workhouse any prisoner so violating his parole. The time between the violation of the conditions of such parole, or conditional release by whatever name, as entered by order of such director on the records of the workhouse, and the reimprisonment or return of the prisoner, shall not be counted as any part or portion of time served under his sentence.

**HISTORY: RS § 2102; Bates § 1536-373; 66 v 196, § 278; 97 v 488; GC § 4135; Bureau of Code Revision. Eff 10-1-53.**

## § 753.13 Joint municipal and county workhouse.

The board of county commissioners may unite with any municipal corporation located in the county in the acquisition or erection, management, and maintenance of a workhouse for the joint use of such county and municipal corporation, upon such terms as they may agree, and the board may levy and collect the necessary funds therefor from the taxable property of the county.

**HISTORY: RS § 2107; Bates § 1536-377; 68 v 114, § 1; 81 v 129; 97 v 448; GC § 4139; Bureau of Code Revision. Eff 10-1-53.**

## § 753.14 Withdrawal from support and maintenance of joint workhouse.

In any county in which, prior to May 20, 1920, there has been constructed and maintained a joint municipal and county workhouse, either the municipal corporation or the county may withdraw therefrom, may decline to further participate in the expense of maintaining such institution, and may sell its interest in such institution.

In the event of a sale thereof by such municipal corporation or county, the proceeds thereof shall be used in the payment of such indebtedness as was incurred in behalf of such municipal corporation or county in the management, control, and operation of such workhouse, and any balance remaining shall be placed in the general fund of such municipal corporation or county.

**HISTORY: GC § 4139-1; 108 v Pt.II, 1232; Bureau of Code Revision. Eff 10-1-53.**

## § 753.15 Workhouses; management by joint board; privatization.

(A) Except as provided in division (B) of this section, in a city, a workhouse erected for the joint use of the city and the county in which such city is located shall be managed and controlled by a joint board composed of the board of county commissioners and the board of control of the city, and in a village by the board of county commissioners and the board of trustees of public affairs. Such joint board shall have all the powers and duties in the management, control, and maintenance of such workhouse as are conferred upon the director of public safety in cities, and in addition thereto it may construct sewers for such workhouse and pay therefor from funds raised by taxation for the maintenance of such institution.

The joint board may lease or purchase suitable property and buildings for a workhouse, or real estate for the purpose of erecting and maintaining a workhouse thereon, but it shall not expend more than ten thousand dollars for any such purpose unless such amount is approved by a majority of the voters of the county, exclusive of the municipal corporation, voting at a general election.

(B) In lieu of forming a joint board to manage and control a workhouse erected for the joint use of the city and the county in which the city is located, the board of county commissioners and the legislative authority of the city may enter into a contract for the private operation and management of the workhouse as provided in section 9.06 of the Revised Code, but only if the workhouse is used solely for misdemeanant inmates. In order to enter into a contract under section 9.06 of the Revised Code, both the board and the legislative authority shall approve and be parties to the contract.

**HISTORY: RS § 2107; Bates § 1536-377; 68 v 114, § 1; 81 v 129; 97 v 448; GC § 4140; 101 v 240; Bureau of Code Revision, 10-1-53; 146 v H 117. Eff 9-29-95.**

The effective date is set by section 197 of HB 117.

## § 753.16 Agreement to receive prisoners from another county or state prisoners; reimbursement policy; testing and treatment for certain diseases.

(A) Any city or district having a workhouse may receive as inmates of the workhouse persons sentenced or committed to it from counties other than the one in which the workhouse is situated, upon the terms and during the length of time agreed upon by the boards of county commissioners of those counties, or by the legislative authority of a municipal corporation in those counties and the legislative authority of the city, or the board of the district workhouse, or other authority having the management and control of the workhouse. Prisoners so received shall in all respects be and remain under the control of that authority, and shall be subject to the rules and discipline of the workhouse to which the other prisoners detained in the workhouse are subject.

(B) Prior to the acceptance for housing into a jail or workhouse of persons who are designated by the department of rehabilitation and correction, who plead guilty to or are convicted of a felony of the fourth or fifth degree, and who satisfy the other requirements listed in section 5120.161 [5120.16.1] of the Revised Code, the legislative authority of a municipal corporation having a jail or workhouse, or the joint board managing and controlling a workhouse for the joint use of a municipal corporation and a county shall enter into an agreement with the department of rehabilitation and correction under section 5120.161 [5120.16.1] of the Revised Code for the housing in the jail or workhouse of persons who are designated by the department, who plead guilty to or are convicted of a felony of the fourth or fifth degree, and who satisfy the other requirements listed in that section, in exchange for a per diem fee per person. Persons incarcerated in the jail or workhouse pursuant to an agreement of that nature shall be subject to supervision and control in the manner described in section 5120.161 [5120.16.1] of the Revised Code. This division does not affect the authority of a court to directly sentence a person who is convicted of or pleads guilty to a felony to the jail or workhouse in accordance with section 2929.16 of the Revised Code.

(C) Pursuant to section 2929.37 of the Revised Code, the board of county commissioners, the legislative authority of the municipal corporation, or the board or other managing authority of the district workhouse may require a person who was convicted of an offense and who is confined in the workhouse as provided in division (A) of this section, to reimburse the county, municipal corporation, or district, as the case may be, for its expenses incurred by reason of the person's confinement.

(D) Notwithstanding any contrary provision in this section or section 2929.18, 2929.28, or 2929.37 of the Revised Code, the board of county commissioners, the legislative authority of a municipal corporation, or the board or other managing authority of the district workhouse may establish a policy that complies with section 2929.38 of the Revised Code and that requires any person who is not indigent and who is confined in the jail or workhouse under division (A) or (B) of this section to pay a reception fee, a fee for any medical treatment or service requested by and provided to that person, or the fee for a random drug test assessed under division (E) of section 753.33 of the Revised Code.

(E) If a person who has been convicted of or pleaded guilty to an offense is confined in the workhouse as provided in division (A) of this section or is incarcerated in the workhouse in the manner described in division (B) of this section, or if a person who has been arrested for an offense, and who has been denied bail or has had bail set and has not been released on bail is confined in the workhouse pending trial, at the time of reception and at other times the person in charge of the operation of the workhouse determines to be appropriate, the person in charge of the operation of the workhouse may cause the convicted or accused offender to be examined and tested for tuberculosis, HIV infection, hepatitis, including but not limited to hepatitis A, B, and C, and other contagious diseases. The person in charge of the operation of the workhouse may cause a convicted or accused offender in the workhouse who refuses to be tested or treated for tuberculosis, HIV infection, hepatitis, including but not limited to hepatitis A, B, and C, or another contagious disease to be tested and treated involuntarily.

**HISTORY: RS § 2107a; Bates § 1536-378; 80 v 220; GC § 4141; 110 v 12; Bureau of Code Revision, 10-1-53; 139 v S 23 (Eff 7-6-82); 139 v S 199 (Eff 1-1-83); 140 v H 363 (Eff 9-26-84); 146 v S 2 (Eff 7-1-96); 146 v S 269 (Eff 7-1-96); 146 v H 480 (Eff 10-16-96); 147 v S 111 (Eff 3-17-98); 148 v H 349 (Eff 9-22-2000); 149 v H 170. Eff 9-6-2002; 149 v H 490, § 1, eff. 1-1-04.**

The effective date is set by section 4 of HB 490.

## § 753.161 Submission of health insurance claims of out-of-county inmates.

(A) For each person who is confined in a workhouse as provided in section 753.16 of the Revised Code, the county, municipal corporation, or district, as the case may be, may make a determination as to whether the person is covered under a health insurance or health care policy, contract, or plan and, if the person has such coverage, what terms and conditions are imposed by it for the filing and payment of claims.

(B) If, pursuant to division (A) of this section, it is determined that the person is covered under a policy, contract, or plan and, while that coverage is in force, the workhouse renders or arranges for the rendering of health care services to the person in accordance with the terms and conditions of the policy, contract, or plan, then the person, county, municipal corporation, district, or provider of the health care services, as appropriate under the terms and conditions of the policy, contract, or plan, shall promptly submit a claim for payment for the health care services to the appropriate third-party payer and shall designate, or make any other arrangement necessary to ensure, that payment of any amount due on the claim be made to the county, municipal corporation, district, or provider, as the case may be.

(C) Any payment made to the county, municipal corporation, or district pursuant to division (B) of this section shall be paid into the treasury of the governmental entity that incurred the expenses.

(D) This section also applies to any person who is under the custody of a law enforcement officer, as defined in section 2901.01 of the Revised Code, prior to the person's confinement in the workhouse.

**HISTORY: 146 v S 163. Eff 10-16-96.**

## § 753.17 Officers to have police powers.

The superintendent, assistant superintendent, and each guard of a workhouse shall have such powers of policemen as are necessary for the proper performance of the duties of their positions.

**HISTORY: RS § 2105; Bates § 1536-375; 66 v 196, § 281; GC § 4137; Bureau of Code Revision. Eff 10-1-53.**

## § 753.18 Religious services in jail or workhouse.

Each administrative board or other authority in the state having charge or control of a city jail or workhouse shall provide for holding religious services therein each week, and may employ a clergyman or religious organization to conduct such services. Any expense so incurred by such board or authority shall be paid from the general fund of the city.

**HISTORY: GC § 4153; 99 v 225, § 3; Bureau of Code Revision, 10-1-53; 139 v S 23. Eff 7-6-82.**

## § 753.19 Deputy to give notice of escape and of apprehension of escapee.

(A) If a person who was convicted of or pleaded guilty to an offense or was indicted or otherwise charged with the commission of an offense escapes from a jail or workhouse of a municipal corporation or otherwise escapes from the custody of a municipal corporation, the chief of police or other chief law enforcement officer of that municipal corporation immediately after the escape shall report the escape, by telephone and in writing, to all local law enforcement agencies with jurisdiction over the place where the person escaped from custody, to the state highway patrol, to the department of rehabilitation and correction if the escaped person is a prisoner under the custody of the department who is in the jail or workhouse, to the prosecuting attorney of the county, and to a newspaper of general circulation in the municipal corporation in a newspaper of general circulation in each county in which part of the municipal corporation is located. The written notice may be by either facsimile transmission or mail. A failure to comply with this requirement is a violation of section 2921.22 of the Revised Code.

(B) Upon the apprehension of the escaped person, the chief law enforcement officer shall give notice of the apprehension of the escaped person by telephone and in writing to the persons notified under division (A) of this section.

**HISTORY: 142 v H 207 (Eff 9-24-87); 148 v H 283. Eff 6-30-99.**

The effective date is set by section 164 of HB 283.

## § 753.21 Minimum security jails.

(A) As used in this section, "building or structure" includes, but is not limited to, a modular unit, building, or structure and a movable unit, building, or structure.

(B)(1) The legislative authority of a municipal corporation, by ordinance, may dedicate and permit the use, as a minimum security jail, of any vacant or abandoned public building or structure owned by the municipal corporation that has not been dedicated to or is not then in use for any municipal or other public purpose, or any building or structure rented or leased by the municipal corporation. The legislative authority of a municipal corporation, by ordinance, also may dedicate and permit the use, as a minimum security jail, of any building or structure purchased by or constructed by or for the municipal corporation. Subject to divisions (B)(3) and (C) of this section, upon the effective date of such an ordinance, the specified building or structure shall be used, in accordance with this section, for the confinement of persons who meet one of the following conditions:

(a) The person is sentenced to a term of imprisonment for a traffic violation, a misdemeanor, or a violation of a municipal ordinance and is under the jurisdiction of the municipal corporation or is sentenced to a residential sanction in the jail for a felony of the fourth or fifth degree pursuant to sections 2929.11 to 2929.19 of the Revised Code, and the jail administrator or the jail administrator's designee has classified the person as a minimal security risk. In determining the person's classification under this division, the administrator or designee shall consider all relevant factors, including, but not limited to, the person's escape risk and propensity for assaultive or violent behavior, based upon the person's prior and current behavior.

(b) The person is an inmate transferred by order of a judge of the sentencing court upon the request of the sheriff, administrator, jailer, or other person responsible for operating the jail other than a contractor as defined in section 9.06 of the Revised Code, who is named in the request as being suitable for confinement in a minimum security facility.

(2) The legislative authority of a municipal corporation, by ordinance, may affiliate with the county in which it is located, with one or more counties adjacent to the county in which it is located, or with one or more municipal corporations located within the county in which it is located or within an adjacent county, and dedicate and permit the use, as a minimum security jail, of any vacant or abandoned public building or structure owned by any of the affiliating counties or municipal corporations that has not been dedicated to or is not then in use for any public purpose, or any building or structure rented or leased by any of the affiliating counties or municipal corporations. The legislative authority of a municipal corporation, by ordinance, also may affiliate with one or more counties adjacent to the county in which it is located or with one or more municipal corporations located within the county in which it is located or within an adjacent county and dedicate and permit the use, as a minimum security jail, of any building or structure purchased by or constructed by or for any of the affiliating counties or municipal corporations. Any counties and municipal corporations that affiliate for purposes of this division shall enter into an agreement that establishes the responsibilities for the operation and for the cost of operation of the minimum security jail. Subject to divisions (B)(3) and (C) of this section, upon the effective date of an ordinance adopted under this division, the specified building or structure shall be used, in accordance with this section, for the confinement of persons who meet one of the following conditions:

(a) The person is sentenced to a term of imprisonment for a traffic violation, a misdemeanor, or a violation of an ordinance of a municipal corporation and is under the jurisdiction of any of the affiliating counties or municipal corporations or is sentenced to a residential sanction in the jail for a felony of the fourth or fifth degree pursuant to sections 2929.11 to 2929.19 of the Revised Code, and the jail administrator or the jail administrator's designee has classified the person as a minimal security risk. In determining the person's classification under this division, the administrator or designee shall consider all relevant factors, including, but not limited to, the person's escape risk and propensity for assaultive or violent behavior, based upon the person's prior and current behavior.

(b) The person is an inmate transferred by order of a judge of the sentencing court upon the request of the sheriff, administrator, jailer, or other person responsible for operating the jail other than a contractor as defined in section 9.06 of the Revised Code, who is named in the request as being suitable for confinement in a minimum security facility.

(3) No person shall be confined in a building or structure dedicated as a minimum security jail under division (B)(1) or (2) of this section unless the judge who sentenced the person to the term of imprisonment for the traffic violation or the misdemeanor specifies that the term of imprisonment is to be served in that jail, and division (B)(1) or (2) of this section permits the confinement of the person in that jail or unless the judge who sentenced the person to the residential sanction for the felony specifies that the residential sanction is to be served in a jail, and division (B)(1) or (2) of this section permits the confinement of the person in that jail. If a rented or leased building or structure is so dedicated, the building or structure may be used as a minimum security jail only during the period that it is rented or leased by the municipal corporation or by an affiliated county or municipal corporation. If a person convicted of a misdemeanor is confined to a building or structure dedicated as a minimum security jail under division (B)(1) or (2) of this section and the sheriff, administrator, jailer, or other person responsible for operating the jail other than a contractor as defined in division (H) of † section 9.06 of the Revised Code determines that it would be more appropriate for the person so confined to be confined in

another jail or workhouse facility, the sheriff, administrator, jailer, or other person may transfer the person so confined to a more appropriate jail or workhouse facility.

(C) All of the following apply in relation to a building or structure that is dedicated pursuant to division (B)(1) or (2) of this section for use as a minimum security jail:

(1) To the extent that the use of the building or structure as a minimum security jail requires a variance from any municipal corporation, county, or township zoning ordinances or regulations, the variance shall be granted.

(2) Except as provided in this section, the building or structure shall not be used to confine any person unless it is in substantial compliance with any applicable housing, fire prevention, sanitation, health, and safety codes, regulations, or standards.

(3) Unless such satisfaction or compliance is required under the standards described in division (C)(4) of this section, and notwithstanding any other provision of state or local law to the contrary, the building or structure need not satisfy or comply with any state or local building standard or code in order to be used to confine a person for the purposes specified in division (B) of this section.

(4) The building or structure shall not be used to confine any person unless it is in compliance with all minimum standards and minimum renovation, modification, and construction criteria for minimum security jails that have been proposed by the department of rehabilitation and correction, through its bureau of adult detention, under section 5120.10 of the Revised Code.

(5) The building or structure need not be renovated or modified into a secure detention facility in order to be used solely to confine a person for the purposes specified in divisions (B)(1)(a) and (B)(2)(a) of this section.

(6) The building or structure shall be used, equipped, furnished, and staffed to provide adequate and suitable living, sleeping, food service or preparation, drinking, bathing and toilet, sanitation, and other necessary facilities, furnishings, and equipment.

(D) Except as provided in this section, a minimum security jail dedicated and used under this section shall be considered to be part of the jail, workhouse, or other correctional facilities of the municipal corporation or the affiliated counties and municipal corporations for all purposes under the law. All persons confined in such a minimum security jail shall be and shall remain, in all respects, under the control of the authority of the municipal corporation that has responsibility for the management and operation of the jail, workhouse, or other correctional facilities of the municipal corporation or, if it is operated by any affiliation of counties or municipal corporations, under the control of the specified county or municipal corporation with that authority, provided that, if the person was convicted of a felony and is serving a residential sanction in the facility, all provisions of law that pertain to persons convicted of a felony that would not by their nature clearly be inapplicable apply regarding the person. A minimum security jail dedicated and used under this section shall be managed and maintained in accordance with policies and procedures adopted by the legislative authority of the municipal corporation or the affiliated counties and municipal corporations governing the safe and healthful operation of the jail, the confinement and supervision of the persons sentenced to it, and their participation in work release or similar rehabilitation programs. In addition to other rules of conduct and discipline, the rights of ingress and egress of persons confined in a minimum security jail dedicated and used under this section shall be subject to reasonable restrictions. Every person confined in a minimum security jail dedicated and used under this section shall be given verbal and written notification, at the time of the person's admission to the jail, that purposely leaving, or purposely failing to return to, the jail without proper authority or permission constitutes the felony offense of escape.

(E) If a person who has been convicted of or pleaded guilty to an offense is sentenced to a term of imprisonment or a residential sanction in a minimum security jail as described in division (B)(1)(a) or (B)(2)(a) of this section, or if a person is an inmate transferred to a minimum security jail by order of a judge of the sentencing court as described in division (B)(1)(b) or (2)(b) of this section, at the time of reception and at other times the person in charge of the operation of the jail determines to be appropriate, the person in charge of the operation of the jail may cause the convicted offender to be examined and tested for tuberculosis, HIV infection, hepatitis, including but not limited to hepatitis A, B, and C, and other contagious diseases. The person in charge of the operation of the jail may cause a convicted offender in the jail who refuses to be tested or treated for tuberculosis, HIV infection, hepatitis, including but not limited to hepatitis A, B, and C, or another contagious disease to be tested and treated involuntarily.

**HISTORY: 143 v S 131 (Eff 7-25-90); 143 v H 837 (Eff 7-25-90); 143 v S 258 (Eff 8-22-90); 144 v S 351 (Eff 7-1-92); 146 v H 117 (Eff 9-29-95); 146 v S 269 (Eff 7-1-96); 146 v H 480 (Eff 10-16-96); 147 v S 111 (Eff 3-17-98); 147 v H 293. Eff 3-17-98.**

† So in enrolled bill, division (B)(3). The words "division (H) of" were deleted in (B)(1)(b) and (B)(2)(b). The definitions now appear in division (J).

## § 753.22 Commissary; fund.

(A) The director of public safety or the joint board established pursuant to section 753.15 of the Revised Code may establish a commissary for the workhouse. The commissary may be established either in-house or by another arrangement. If a commissary is established, all persons incarcerated in the workhouse shall receive commissary privileges. A person's purchases from the commissary shall be deducted from the person's account record in the workhouse's business office. The commissary shall provide for the distribution to indigent persons incarcerated in the workhouse necessary hygiene articles and writing materials.

(B) If a commissary is established, the director of public safety or the joint board established pursuant to section 753.15 of the Revised Code shall establish a commissary fund for the workhouse. The management of funds in the commissary fund shall be strictly controlled in accordance with procedures adopted by the auditor of state. Commissary fund revenue over and above operating costs and reserve shall be considered profits. All profits from the commissary fund shall be used to purchase supplies and equipment for the benefit of persons incarcerated in the workhouse and to pay salary and benefits for employees of the workhouse, or for any other persons, who work in or are employed for the sole purpose of providing service to the commissary. The director of public safety or the joint board established pursuant to section 753.15 of the Revised Code shall adopt rules and regulations for the operation of any commissary fund the director or the joint board establishes.

**HISTORY: 146 v H 480. Eff 10-16-96; 150 v H 95, § 1, eff. 9-26-03.**

The effective date is set by section 179 of H.B. 95 (150 v —).

## § 753.31 Prisoner access to exercise equipment or participation in fighting skills programs.

(A) As used in this section:

(1) "Free weight exercise equipment" means any equipment or device that is designed to increase the muscle mass and physical strength of the person using it. "Free weight exercise equipment" includes, but is not limited to, barbells, dumbbells, weight plates, and similar free weight-type equipment and other devices that the department of rehabilitation and correction, in rules adopted under section 5120.423 [5120.42.3] of the Revised Code, designates as enabling a person to increase muscle mass and physical strength.

(2) "Fixed weight exercise equipment" means any equipment, machine, or device that is not designed primarily to increase muscle mass and physical strength but rather to keep a person in relatively good physical condition. "Fixed weight exercise equipment" includes, but is not limited to, weight machines that utilize weight plates, tension bands, or similar devices that provide weight training resistance like universal and nautilus equipment. "Fixed weight exercise equipment" includes machines that are usually assembled as a unit, are not readily dismantled, and have been specifically modified for prison use so as to make them secure and immobile.

(3) "Municipal correctional officer" means a person who is employed by a municipal corporation as an employee or officer of a municipal jail, municipal workhouse, minimum security jail, joint city and county workhouse, municipal-county correctional center, multicounty-municipal correctional center, municipal-county jail or workhouse, or multicounty-municipal jail or workhouse.

(4) A person is "employed by a municipal corporation" if the person is employed by, or receives any compensation or benefits from, any official, officer, office, agency, board, commission, department, or other entity that is a branch of municipal government, that is established by a municipal corporation, or that serves a municipal corporation, including, but not limited to, a chief law enforcement officer of a municipal corporation.

(5) "Multicounty-municipal" has the same meaning as in section 307.93 of the Revised Code.

(B) No municipal correctional officer shall do any of the following:

(1) Provide a prisoner access to free weight or fixed weight exercise equipment;

(2) Allow a prisoner to provide or receive instruction in boxing, wrestling, karate, judo, or another form of martial arts, or any other program that the department of rehabilitation and correction, in rules adopted under section 5120.423 [5120.42.3] of the Revised Code, designates as enabling a person to improve fighting skills.

(C) Nothing in this section prohibits a municipal correctional officer from allowing a prisoner to participate in jogging, basketball, stationary exercise bicycling, supervised calisthenics, or other physical activities that are not designed to increase muscle mass and physical strength or improve fighting skills.

**HISTORY: 146 v H 152 (Eff 10-4-96); 147 v H 293. Eff 3-17-98.**

The provisions of § 6 of HB 152 (146 v —) read as follows:

SECTION 6. On and after the effective date of this act, no moneys in the treasury of the state, or moneys coming lawfully into the possession or custody of the Treasurer of State, except moneys donated by gift, devise, or bequest specifically for this purpose, shall be used to purchase any fixed weight exercise equipment authorized by the act, and no moneys in the treasury of any subdivision of the state, or moneys coming lawfully into the possession or custody of the treasurer of any subdivision, shall be used to purchase any fixed weight exercise equipment for use at any facility described in Section 5 of this act.

## § 753.32 Restrictions on prisoner access to internet.

(A) As used in this section:

(1) "Municipal correctional officer" has the same meaning as in section 753.31 of the Revised Code.

(2) "Computer," "computer network," "computer system," "computer services," "telecommunications service," and "information service" have the same meanings as in section 2913.01 of the Revised Code.

(3) "Municipal correctional facility" means a municipal jail, municipal workhouse, minimum security jail, joint city and county workhouse, municipal-county correctional center, multicounty-municipal correctional center, municipal-county jail or workhouse, or multicounty-municipal jail or workhouse.

(B) No municipal correctional officer shall provide a prisoner access to or permit a prisoner to have access to the internet through the use of a computer, computer network, computer system, computer services, telecommunications service, or information service unless both of the following apply:

(1) The prisoner is participating in an approved educational program with direct supervision that requires the use of the internet for training or research purposes.

(2) The provision of and access to the internet is in accordance with rules promulgated by the department of rehabilitation and correction pursuant to section 5120.62 of the Revised Code.

(C)(1) No prisoner in a municipal correctional facility under the control of a municipal corporation shall access the internet through the use of a computer, computer network, computer system, computer services, telecommunications service, or information service unless both of the following apply:

(a) The prisoner is participating in an approved educational program with direct supervision that requires the use of the internet for training or research purposes.

(b) The provision of and access to the internet is in accordance with rules promulgated by the department of rehabilitation and correction pursuant to section 5120.62 of the Revised Code.

(2) Whoever violates division (C)(1) of this section is guilty of improper internet access, a misdemeanor of the first degree.

**HISTORY: 148 v S 12. Eff 6-8-2000; 150 v H 204, § 1, eff. 11-5-04.**

## § 753.33 Random drug testing of municipal prisoners.

(A) As used in this section:

(1) "Joint board" means the joint board established pursuant to section 753.15 of the Revised Code.

(2) "Municipal prisoner" means a prisoner who is confined in a municipal jail, municipal workhouse, minimum security jail, joint city and county workhouse, municipal-county correctional center, multicounty-municipal correctional center, municipal-county jail or workhouse, or multicounty-municipal jail or workhouse for being convicted of or pleading guilty to a criminal offense.

(3) "Multicounty-municipal" has the same meaning as in section 307.93 of the Revised Code.

(4) "Random drug testing" has the same meaning as in section 5120.63 of the Revised Code.

(B) The director of public safety or a joint board may enter into a contract with a laboratory or entity to perform blood or urine specimen collection, documentation, maintenance, transportation, preservation, storage, and analyses and other duties required in the performance of random drug testing of municipal prisoners. The terms of any contract entered into under this division shall include a requirement that the laboratory or entity and its employees, the director of public safety or the joint board, the superintendent or chief administrative officer specified in division (D) of this section, the employees of the correctional facilities listed in division (A)(1) of this section, and all other persons comply with the standards for the performance of random drug testing as specified in rules adopted under division (C) of this section.

(C) Prior to entering into a contract with a laboratory or entity under division (B) of this section, a director of public safety or a joint board shall adopt rules for the random drug testing of municipal prisoners. The rules shall include, but are not limited to, provisions that do the following:

(1) Require the laboratory or entity to seek, obtain, and maintain accreditation from the national institute on drug abuse;

(2) Establish standards for the performance of random drug testing of municipal prisoners that include, but are not limited to, standards governing the following:

(a) The collection by the laboratory or entity of blood or urine specimens of individuals in a scientifically or medically approved manner and under reasonable and sanitary conditions;

(b) The collection and testing by the laboratory or entity of blood or urine specimens with due regard for the privacy of the individual being tested and in a manner reasonably calculated to prevent substitutions or interference with the collection and testing of the specimens;

(c) The documentation of blood or urine specimens collected by the laboratory or entity and documentation procedures that reasonably preclude the possibility of erroneous identification of test results and that provide the individual being tested an opportunity to furnish information identifying any prescription or nonprescription drugs used by the individual in connection with a medical condition;

(d) The collection, maintenance, storage, and transportation by the laboratory or entity of blood or urine specimens in a manner that reasonably precludes the possibility of contamination or adulteration of the specimens;

(e) The testing by the laboratory or entity of a blood or urine specimen of an individual to determine whether the individual ingested or was injected with a drug of abuse, in a manner that conforms to scientifically accepted analytical methods and procedures and that may include verification or confirmation of any positive test result by a reliable analytical method;

(f) The analysis of an individual's blood or urine specimen by an employee of the laboratory or entity who is qualified by education, training, and experience to perform that analysis and whose regular duties include the analysis of blood or urine specimens to determine the presence of a drug of abuse and whether the individual who is the subject of the test ingested or was injected with a drug of abuse.

(3) Specify the frequency of performing random drug testing on municipal prisoners;

(4) Prescribe procedures for the automatic, random selection of municipal prisoners to submit to random drug testing under this section;

(5) Provide for reasonable safeguards for the transmittal of the results of the random drug testing of municipal prisoners from the contracting laboratory or entity to the director of public safety or the joint board pursuant to division (E) of this section;

(6) Establish a reasonable fee to cover the costs associated with random drug testing and analysis performed by a contracting laboratory or entity under this section and establish procedures pursuant to division (E) of this section for the collection of those fees from the municipal prisoners subjected to the drug tests.

(D) If a director of public safety or a joint board enters into a contract pursuant to division (B) of this section, the superintendent or chief administrative officer of a correctional facility listed in division (A)(2) of this section in which municipal prisoners are confined, pursuant to the terms of the contract and the rules adopted under division (C) of this section, shall facilitate the collection, documentation, maintenance, and transportation by the contracting laboratory or entity of the blood or urine specimens of the municipal prisoners who are confined in that correctional facility and who are subject to random drug testing.

(E) If a director of public safety or a joint board enters into a contract pursuant to division (B) of this section and the contracting laboratory or entity performs the random drug testing as provided in the contract, the laboratory or entity shall transmit the results of the drug test to the director of public safety or the joint board, as appropriate, that entered into the contract. The director or the joint board shall file for record the results of the random drug tests that indicate whether or not each municipal prisoner who was subjected to the drug test ingested or was injected with a drug of abuse. The director or the joint board shall give appropriate notice of the drug test results to each municipal prisoner who was subjected to a drug test and whose drug test results indicate that the municipal prisoner ingested or was injected with a drug of abuse. The director or the joint board shall afford that municipal prisoner an opportunity to be heard regarding the results of the drug test and to present contrary evidence at a hearing held before the director or the joint board within thirty days after notification of the municipal prisoner under this division. After the hearing, if a hearing is held, the director or the joint board shall make a determination regarding any evidence presented by the municipal prisoner. If the director or the joint board rejects the evidence presented by the municipal prisoner at the hearing or if no hearing is held under this division, the director or the joint board may assess a reasonable fee, determined pursuant to division (C) of this section, for the costs associated with the random drug test to be paid by the municipal prisoner whose drug test results indicate that the prisoner ingested or was injected with a drug of abuse. The director or the joint board may collect the fee pursuant to section 753.02, 753.04, or 753.16 of the Revised Code.

**HISTORY: 148 v H 349. Eff 9-22-2000.**

# TITLE 9: AGRICULTURE — ANIMALS — FENCES

## CHAPTER 901: DEPARTMENT OF AGRICULTURE



[RURAL REHABILITATION]

### § 901.51 Injuring vines, bushes, trees, or crops.

No person, without privilege to do so, shall recklessly cut down, destroy, girdle, or otherwise injure a vine, bush, shrub, sapling, tree, or crop standing or growing on the land of another or upon public land.

In addition to the penalty provided in section 901.99 of the Revised Code, whoever violates this section is liable in treble damages for the injury caused.

**HISTORY: 134 v H 511. Eff 1-1-74.**

The effective date of HB 511 is set by section 4 of the act.

### § 901.511 Terrorism involving agricultural products or equipment.

(A) As used in this section:

(1) "Agricultural product" means any of the following items that is produced for testing or research in the context of a product development program in conjunction or coordination with a private research facility, a university, or any federal, state, or local governmental agency or that is produced for personal, commercial, pharmaceutical, or educational purposes: field crop or field crop product; timber or timber product; forestry product; livestock or livestock product; meat or meat product; milk or dairy product; poultry or poultry product; equine animal; wool; fruit or vegetable crop; aquacultural product; horticultural crop, including plant materials grown in a greenhouse, nursery stock grown inside or outside of a container, ornamental grass, turf grass, ornamental trees, ornamental shrubs, or flowers; sod; mushrooms; viticultural product; apicultural product; tobacco; pasture; wild animal or domestic deer, as "wild animal" and "domestic deer" are defined in section 1531.01 of the Revised Code; or any combination of those items.

(2) "Equipment" means any implement, machinery, real or personal property, building, or structure that is used in the production, growing, harvesting, or housing of any agricultural product. "Equipment" also includes any laboratory, research, product, samples, supplies, or fixed equipment that is used to test, develop, or analyze the process of producing, growing, or maintaining any agricultural product.

(3) "Material support or resources" means currency, payment instruments, other financial securities, financial services, lodging, training, safehouses, false documentation or identification, communications equipment, facilities, weapons, lethal substances, explosives, personnel, transportation, and other physical assets, except medicine or religious materials.

(4) "Payment instrument" means a check, draft, money order, traveler's check, cashier's check, teller's check, or other instrument or order for the transmission or payment of money regardless of whether the item in question is negotiable.

(5) "Specified offense" means either of the following:

(a) A violation of section 2909.02, 2909.03, 2909.05, 2909.06, 2909.07, 2911.13, 2911.21, 2913.02, 2913.04, or 2913.42 of the Revised Code;

(b) An attempt to commit, complicity in committing, or a conspiracy to commit an offense listed in division (A)(5)(a) of this section.

(B) No person shall commit a specified offense involving any agricultural product or equipment with the intent to do any of the following:

(1) Intimidate or coerce a civilian population;

(2) Influence the policy of any government by intimidation or coercion;

(3) Affect the conduct of any government;

(4) Interrupt or interfere with agricultural production, agricultural research, or equipment for purposes of disrupting or influencing, through intimidation or other means, consumer confidence or agricultural production methods.

Division (B) of this section does not apply to the practice of veterinary medicine by a person who has been issued a valid license, temporary permit, or registration certificate to practice veterinary medicine under Chapter 4741. of the Revised Code. As used in this division, "practice of veterinary medicine" has the same meaning as in section 4741.01 of the Revised Code.

(C) No person shall raise, solicit, collect, donate, or provide any material support or resources with the purpose that the material support or resources will be used in whole or in part to plan, prepare, carry out, or aid in either a violation of division (B) of this section or in the concealment of, or an escape from, a violation of that division.

(D)(1) In addition to the penalties established in section 901.99 of the Revised Code for a violation of this section, the court may require any person who violates this section to pay the victim of the offense an amount up to triple the value of the agricultural product or equipment that was the subject of the violation.

(2) In ordering restitution under division (D)(1) of this section, the court shall consider as part of the value of the agricultural product or equipment the market value of the agricultural product or equipment prior to the violation and the production, research, testing, replacement, and development costs directly related to the agricultural product or equipment that was the subject of the violation.

(E) The enactment of this section is not intended to require the prosecution exclusively under this section of an act, series of acts, or course of behavior that could be prosecuted either under this section or under another section of the Revised Code. One or more acts, series of acts, or courses of behavior that may be prosecuted either under this section or under another section of the Revised Code may be prosecuted under this section, the other section, or both sections.

**HISTORY: 150 v S 67, § 1, eff. 10-13-04.**

## [LIVESTOCK EXHIBITIONS]

### § 901.73 Inspection and investigation where exhibition apparently intended; period of ownership required to exhibit.

(A)(1) The director of agriculture may inspect and investigate any matter involving livestock that is not present at an exhibition, but is registered or entered in an exhibition, or raised with the apparent intent of being so registered or entered, when the director reasonably suspects any of the following:

(a) There has been a violation of section 901.76 or 2925.09 of the Revised Code or a rule adopted under section 901.72 of the Revised Code;

(b) The livestock's health, safety, or welfare may be threatened;

(c) The livestock constitutes a threat to or may adversely affect food safety.

(2) The director may conduct random inspections and investigations regarding any matter involving livestock present at an exhibition.

(3) With the consent of the property owner and the livestock owner, the director or the director's designee may enter at all reasonable times any premises, facility, pen, yard, vehicle, or means of conveyance for the purpose of sampling and testing livestock registered or entered in an exhibition or raised with the apparent intent of being so registered or entered. If the director or the director's designee is denied access to any premises, facility, pen, yard, vehicle, or means of conveyance by the property owner or to livestock by the livestock owner, and if the director reasonably suspects that food safety or the health, safety, or welfare of livestock is threatened, the director may apply to a court of competent jurisdiction in the county in which the premises, facility, pen, yard, vehicle, means of conveyance, or livestock are located for a search warrant authorizing access to the premises, facility, pen, yard, vehicle, means of conveyance, or livestock for the purposes of this section. The court shall issue the search warrant for the purposes requested if there is probable cause to believe that livestock is involved that is registered or entered in an exhibition or raised with the apparent intent of being so registered or entered, and that food safety or the health, safety, or welfare of livestock is threatened. The finding of probable cause may be based on hearsay, provided there is a substantial basis for believing that the source of the hearsay is credible and that there is a factual basis for the information furnished.

The director may designate employees of the department of agriculture, employees of the United States department of agriculture, licensed veterinarians, or employees or students of an approved or accredited veterinary school or college to perform the inspecting, sampling, and testing. The director may contract with laboratories, universities, or other persons or institutions, both public and private, to perform the livestock testing.

(B) While the director or the director's designee is sampling or testing the livestock, the owner or custodian of the livestock shall render assistance in accordance with sections 941.05 and 941.08 of the Revised Code. Any person who refuses to cooperate with the director or the director's designee in the inspection, sampling, and testing of livestock may be prohibited by the director acting under section 901.74 of the Revised Code from participating in any exhibition.

(C) A person may register, enter, or exhibit at an exhibition only livestock owned by that person for the length of time specified by rule of the director, unless one of the following applies:

(1) The livestock owner suffers from a recognized physical handicap that prevents the owner from showing the livestock;

(2) The sponsor provides written permission to someone other than the livestock owner to register, enter, or exhibit the livestock;

(3) A rule of the director provides that this division shall not apply to an exhibition.

**HISTORY: 146 v H 202 (Eff 6-14-95); 146 v S 269. Eff 7-1-96.**

### § 901.75 Exhibition after disqualification prohibited.

No person shall exhibit livestock owned or raised by another person if the person owning or raising the livestock has been disqualified by the director of agriculture under section 901.74 of the Revised Code or has been disqualified from exhibiting livestock by any court having jurisdiction.

**HISTORY: 146 v H 202. Eff 6-14-95.**

### § 901.76 Tampering with or sabotaging livestock prohibited.

(A) No person shall tamper with any livestock.

(B) No person shall sabotage any livestock exhibited at an exhibition.

(C) In addition to the penalties established in section 901.99 of the Revised Code, whoever violates division (A) or (B) of this section is subject to disciplinary action by the director of agriculture under section 901.74 of the Revised Code.

(D) This section does not apply to either of the following:

(1) Any action taken or activity performed or administered by a licensed veterinarian or in accordance with instructions of a licensed veterinarian if the action or activity was undertaken for accepted medical purposes during the course of a valid veterinarian-client-patient relationship;

(2) Accepted grooming, commercial, or medical practices as defined by rules of the director adopted under section 901.72 of the Revised Code.

(E) As used in this section:

(1) "Tamper" means any of the following:

(a) Treatment of livestock in such a manner that food derived from the livestock would be considered adulterated as defined in division (A), (B), (C), (D), (E), (H), (I), or (J) of section 3715.59 of the Revised Code;

(b) The injection, use, or administration of any drug that is prohibited under any federal law or law of this state, or any drug that is used in any manner that is not authorized under any federal law or law of this state. Whenever the commissioner of the United States food and drug administration or the secretary of the United States department of agriculture, pursuant to the "Federal Food, Drug, and Cosmetic Act," 52 Stat. 1040 (1938), 21 U.S.C.A. 301, as amended, or the federal "Virus-Serum-Toxin Act," 37 Stat. 832 (1913), 21 U.S.C.A. 151, as amended, approves, disapproves, or modifies the conditions of the approved use of a drug, the approval, disapproval, or modification automatically is effective for the purposes of division (E)(1)(b) of this section, unless the director, in accordance with Chapter 119. of the Revised Code, adopts a rule to alter for the purposes of that division the action taken by the commissioner or secretary. The director may adopt such a rule if the director considers it to be necessary or appropriate for the protection of food safety or the health, safety, or welfare of livestock or to prevent the use of a drug for the purpose of concealing, enhancing, transforming, or changing the true conformation, configuration, or condition of livestock. No such rule shall authorize the use of any drug the use of which is prohibited by, or authorize the use of any drug in a manner not authorized by, the commissioner or secretary under either of those acts.

(c) The injection, or other internal or external administration of any product or material, whether gas, solid, or liquid, to livestock for the purpose of concealing, enhancing, transforming, or changing the true conformation, configuration, condition, or age of the livestock or making the livestock appear more sound than it actually is;

(d) The use or administration, for cosmetic purposes, of steroids, growth stimulants, or internal artificial filling, including paraffin, silicone injection, or any other substance;

(e) The use or administration of any drug or feed additive affecting the central nervous system of the livestock;

(f) The use or administration of diuretics for cosmetic purposes;

(g) The surgical manipulation or removal of tissue so as to change, transform, or enhance the true conformation or configuration of, or to conceal the age of, the livestock.

(2) "Sabotage" means intentionally tampering with any livestock belonging to or owned by another person that has been registered, entered in, or exhibited in any exhibition, or raised with the apparent intent of being entered in an exhibition.

**HISTORY: 146 v H 202. Eff 6-14-95.**

## § 901.99 Penalties.

(A) Whoever violates section 901.51 of the Revised Code is guilty of a misdemeanor of the fourth degree.

(B) Whoever violates section 901.75 or division (C) of section 901.73 of the Revised Code is guilty of a misdemeanor of the first degree.

(C) Whoever violates division (A) of section 901.76 of the Revised Code is guilty of a felony of the fifth degree on a first offense and of a felony of the fourth degree on each subsequent offense.

(D) Whoever violates division (B) of section 901.76 of the Revised Code is guilty of a felony of the fourth degree.

(E) Whoever violates division (B) of section 901.511 [901.51.1] of the Revised Code is guilty on a first offense of a misdemeanor or a felony that is one degree higher than the penalty for the most serious underlying specified offense that is involved in the violation. However, if on such an initial violation the penalty for the most serious underlying specified offense is a felony of the first degree, the violator is guilty of a felony of the first degree.

On each subsequent violation of division (B) of that section, the violator is guilty of a misdemeanor or a felony that is two degrees higher than the penalty for the most serious underlying specified offense that is involved in the subsequent violation. However, if on such a subsequent violation the penalty for the most serious underlying specified offense is a felony of the first or second degree, the violator is guilty of a felony of the first degree.

As used in this division, "specified offense" has the same meaning as in section 901.511 [901.51.1] of the Revised Code, and "most serious underlying specified offense" refers to the underlying specified offense that carries the highest maximum penalty.

(F) Whoever violates division (C) of section 901.511 [901.51.1] of the Revised Code is guilty of a felony of the third degree.

**HISTORY: Bureau of Code Revision, 10-1-53; 128 v 604 (Eff 8-1-59); 131 v 335 (Eff 11-3-65); 134 v H 511 (Eff 1-1-74); 136 v H 1 (Eff 6-13-75); 145 v S 134 (Eff 6-20-94); 146 v H 202 (Eff 6-14-95); 146 v S 269. Eff 7-1-96; 150 v S 67, § 1, eff. 10-13-04.**

This section was derived from GC § 1103. See also RC § 901.27.

# CHAPTER 951: ANIMALS RUNNING AT LARGE; STRAYS

Section



### [ANIMALS RUNNING AT LARGE]

## § 951.01 Prohibition against animals running at large [Repealed].

Repealed by 2011 HB 22, § 2, effective September 23, 2011.

**HISTORY: RS § 4201; S&S 11; S&C 70; 29 v 467, §§ 1, 2, 3; 70 v 286; GC § 5808; Bureau of Code Revision, 10-1-53; 129 v 582(661) (Eff 1-10-61); 137 v H 531. Eff 11-3-78.**

## § 951.02 Animals running at large on public roads; grazing on another's land.

No person, who is the owner or keeper of horses, mules, cattle, bison, sheep, goats, swine, llamas, alpacas, or geese, shall permit them to run at large in the public road, highway, street, lane, or alley, or upon unenclosed land, or cause the animals to be herded, kept, or detained for the purpose of grazing on premises other than those owned or lawfully occupied by the owner or keeper of the animals.

**HISTORY: RS §§ 4202, 4207; S&S 7, 8; S&C 76; 56 v 77, §§ 1, 2, 3; 62 v 185; 72 v 170; 78 v 18; 81 v 105; 93 v 129; 98 v 334; GC §§ 5809, 5818; 110 v 119; Bureau of Code Revision, 10-1-53; 137 v H 531. Eff 11-3-78; 2011 HB 22, § 1, eff. Sept. 23, 2011.**

## § 951.99 Penalty.

Whoever recklessly violates section 951.02 of the Revised Code is guilty of a misdemeanor of the fourth degree.

**HISTORY: Bureau of Code Revision, 10-1-53; 137 v H 531. Eff 11-3-78; 2011 HB 22, § 1, eff. Sept. 23, 2011.**

**Publisher's Note:**

This section was derived from GC § 12938. See also RC § 951.03.

# CHAPTER 955: DOGS

Section



## [DOG AND KENNEL LICENSES]

## § 955.01 Registration of dogs.

(A)(1) Except as otherwise provided in this section or in sections 955.011 [955.01.1], 955.012 [955.01.2], and 955.16 of the Revised Code, every person who owns, keeps, or harbors a dog more than three months of age, shall file, on or after the first day of the preceding December but before the thirty-first day of January of each year, in the office of the county auditor of the county in which the dog is kept or harbored, an application for registration for the following year, beginning the thirty-first day of January of that year. The board of county commissioners, by resolution, may extend the period for filing the application. The application shall state the age, sex, color, character of hair, whether short or long, and breed, if known, of the dog and the name and address of the owner of the dog. A registration fee of two dollars for each dog shall accompany the application, unless a greater fee has been established under division (A)(2) of this section or under section 955.14 of the Revised Code.

(2) A board of county commissioners may establish a registration fee higher than the one provided for in division (A)(1) of this section for dogs more than nine months of age that have not been spayed or neutered, except that the higher registration fee permitted by this division shall not apply if a person registering a dog furnishes with the application either a certificate from a licensed veterinarian verifying that the dog should not be spayed or neutered because of its age or medical condition or because the dog is used or intended for use for show or breeding purposes or a certificate from the owner of the dog declaring that the owner holds a valid hunting license issued by the division of wildlife of the department of natural resources and that the dog is used or intended for use for hunting purposes. If the board establishes such a fee, the application for registration shall state whether the dog is spayed or neutered, and whether a licensed veterinarian has certified that the dog should not be spayed or neutered or the owner has stated that the dog is used or intended to be used for hunting purposes. The board may require a person who is registering a spayed or neutered dog to furnish with the application a certificate from a licensed veterinarian verifying that the dog is spayed or neutered. No person shall furnish a certificate under this division which the person knows to be false.

(B) If the application for registration is not filed and the registration fee paid, on or before the thirty-first day of January of each year or, if the board of county commissioners by resolution has extended the date to a date later than the thirty-first day of January, the date established by the board, the auditor shall assess a penalty in an amount equal to the registration fee upon the owner, keeper, or harborer, which must be paid with the registration fee.

(C) An animal shelter that keeps or harbors a dog more than three months of age is exempt from paying any fees imposed under division (A) or (B) of this section if it is a nonprofit organization that is exempt from federal income taxation under subsection 501(a) and described in subsection 501(c)(3) of the "Internal Revenue Code of 1986," 100 Stat. 285, 261.

**HISTORY: RS § 2833; 74 v 177, §§ 1, 3; 76 v 85, § 14; 87 v 160; 97 v 275; 98 v 87; 99 v 484; GC § 5652; 107 v 534; 108 v Pt.I 534; 112 v 347; 124 v 428; Bureau of Code Revision, 10-1-53; 127 v 444 (Eff 7-18-57); 127 v 681 (Eff 9-13-57); 130 v 275 (Eff 10-10-63); 135 v H 152 (Eff 11-21-73); 137 v H 775 (Eff 1-1-79); 141 v H 454 (Eff 11-1-85); 142 v H 246 (Eff 12-12-88); 147 v H 219. Eff 6-1-98.**

## § 955.012 Registration of law enforcement canines.

(A) As used in this section:

(1) "Controlled substance" has the same meaning as in section 3719.01 of the Revised Code.

(2) "Law enforcement agency" means the state highway patrol, the office of a county sheriff, the police department of a municipal corporation or township, or a township or joint police district.

(3) "Law enforcement canine" means a dog regularly utilized by a law enforcement agency for general law enforcement purposes, tracking, or detecting the presence of a controlled substance or explosive.

(B) Instead of obtaining an annual registration under section 955.01 of the Revised Code, a law enforcement agency owning, keeping, or harboring a law enforcement canine may obtain an annual registration for the dog as a law enforcement canine under this section. The application for a law enforcement canine registration shall be submitted to the county auditor of the county in which the central office of the law enforcement agency that owns, keeps, or harbors the dog is located, except that for a dog owned, kept, or harbored by the state highway patrol, the application shall be submitted to the county auditor of the county in which is located the state highway patrol post to which the dog and its handler primarily are assigned. The application shall be submitted on or after the first day of December immediately preceding the beginning of the registration year and before the thirty-first day of January of that year. If the period for filing registration applications under division (A)(1) of section 955.01 of the Revised Code is extended in the county in which a law enforcement canine is to be registered, an application for registration under this section shall be submitted to the county auditor not later than the registration deadline for that year, as so extended.

The application for registration of a law enforcement canine shall state the age, sex, hair color, character of hair, whether short or long, and breed, if known, of the dog, the name and address of the owner of the dog, and, if the law enforcement agency keeping or harboring the dog is different from the owner, the name of that law enforcement agency. For a dog owned, kept, or harbored by the police department of a municipal corporation or township or by a township or joint police district, the application shall be signed by the chief of the police department or district. For a dog owned, kept, or harbored by the office of a county sheriff, the application shall be signed by the sheriff. For a dog owned, kept, or harbored by the state highway patrol, the application shall be signed by the officer in charge of the post of the state highway patrol to which the dog and its handler primarily are assigned. The application shall include a certification by the chief of the police department or district, sheriff, or officer of the state highway patrol post, as applicable, that the dog described in the application has been properly trained to carry out one or more of the purposes described in division (A)(3) of this section and actually is used for one or more of those purposes by the law enforcement agency making the application.

No fee is required for issuance of a law enforcement canine registration. Upon proper proof of loss, a duplicate certificate and tag shall be issued for a dog registered under this section, and no fee shall be required.

If an application for registration of a law enforcement canine is not filed under this section on or before the thirty-first day of January of the registration year, or the extended registration deadline established under division (A)(1) of section 955.01 of the Revised Code, as applicable, the law enforcement canine shall be registered under that section, and the registration fee and late registration penalty applicable under divisions (A) and (B) of that section shall accompany the application.

(C) If a law enforcement agency becomes the owner, keeper, or harborer of a law enforcement canine or brings a law enforcement canine into the state after the thirty-first day of January of a registration year or the extended registration deadline established under division (A)(1) of section 955.01 of the Revised Code, as applicable, the law enforcement agency, within thirty days after becoming the owner, keeper, or harborer or bringing the dog into the state, may submit an application for registration of the dog under this section. Upon submission of the application, the law enforcement agency shall be issued such a registration in the manner provided in division (B) of this section. If such an application is not filed within the thirty-day period, the dog shall be registered under section 955.05 of the Revised Code, and the registration fee and late registration penalty applicable under that section or section 955.06 of the Revised Code shall accompany the application.

**HISTORY: 147 v H 219. Eff 6-1-98; 2011 HB 153, § 101.01, eff. Sept. 29, 2011.**

## § 955.10 Tags to be worn.

No owner of a dog, except a dog constantly confined to a registered kennel, shall fail to require the dog to wear, at all times, a valid tag issued in connection with a certificate of registration. A dog's failure at any time to wear a valid tag shall be prima-facie evidence of lack of registration and shall subject any dog found not wearing such tag to impounding, sale, or destruction.

**HISTORY: GC § 5652-6; 107 v 534; Bureau of Code Revision. Eff 10-1-53; 142 v H 246. Eff 12-12-88.**

## § 955.11 Transfer of ownership or possession of dog.

(A) As used in this section:

(1)(a) "Dangerous dog" means a dog that, without provocation, and subject to division (A)(1)(b) of this section, has chased or approached in either a menacing fashion or an apparent attitude of attack, or has attempted to bite or otherwise endanger any person, while that dog is off the premises of its owner, keeper, or harborer and not under the reasonable control of its owner, keeper, harborer, or some other responsible person, or not physically restrained or confined in a locked pen which has a top, locked fenced yard, or other locked enclosure which has a top.

(b) "Dangerous dog" does not include a police dog that has chased or approached in either a menacing fashion or an apparent attitude of attack, or has attempted to bite or otherwise endanger any person while the police dog is being used to assist one or more law enforcement officers in the performance of their official duties.

(2) "Menacing fashion" means that a dog would cause any person being chased or approached to reasonably believe that the dog will cause physical injury to that person.

(3) "Police dog" means a dog that has been trained, and may be used, to assist one or more law enforcement officers in the performance of their official duties.

(4)(a) "Vicious dog" means a dog that, without provocation and subject to division (A)(4)(b) of this section, meets any of the following:

(i) Has killed or caused serious injury to any person;

(ii) Has caused injury, other than killing or serious injury, to any person, or has killed another dog.

(iii) Belongs to a breed that is commonly known as a pit bull dog. The ownership, keeping, or harboring of such a breed of dog shall be prima-facie evidence of the ownership, keeping, or harboring of a vicious dog.

(b) "Vicious dog" does not include either of the following:

(i) A police dog that has killed or caused serious injury to any person or that has caused injury, other than killing or serious injury, to any person while the police dog is being used to assist one or more law enforcement officers in the performance of their official duties;

(ii) A dog that has killed or caused serious injury to any person while a person was committing or attempting to commit a trespass or other criminal offense on the property of the owner, keeper, or harborer of the dog.

(5) "Without provocation" means that a dog was not teased, tormented, or abused by a person, or that the dog was not coming to the aid or the defense of a person who was not engaged in illegal or criminal activity and who was not using the dog as a means of carrying out such activity.

(B) Upon the transfer of ownership of any dog, the seller of the dog shall give the buyer a transfer of ownership certificate that shall be signed by the seller. The certificate shall contain the registration number of the dog, the name of the seller, and a brief description of the dog. Blank forms of the certificate may be obtained from the county auditor. A transfer of ownership shall be recorded by the auditor upon presentation of a transfer of ownership certificate that is signed by the former owner of a dog and that is accompanied by a fee of twenty-five cents.

(C) Prior to the transfer of ownership or possession of any dog, upon the buyer's or other transferee's request, the seller or other transferor of the dog shall give to the person a written notice relative to the behavior and propensities of the dog.

(D) Within ten days after the transfer of ownership or possession of any dog, if the seller or other transferor of the dog has knowledge that the dog is a dangerous or vicious dog, he shall give to the buyer or other transferee, the board of health for the district in which the buyer or other transferee resides, and the dog warden of the county in which the buyer or other transferee resides, a completed copy of a written form on which the seller shall furnish the following information:

(1) The name and address of the buyer or other transferee of the dog;

(2) The age, sex, color, breed, and current registration number of the dog.

In addition, the seller shall answer the following questions which shall be specifically stated on the form as follows:

"Has the dog ever chased or attempted to attack or bite a person? if yes, describe the incident(s) in which the behavior occurred."

"Has the dog ever bitten a person? if yes, describe the incident(s) in which the behavior occurred."

"Has the dog ever seriously injured or killed a person? if yes, describe the incident(s) in which the behavior occurred."

The dog warden of the county in which the seller resides shall furnish the form to the seller at no cost.

(E) No seller or other transferor of a dog shall fail to comply with the applicable requirements of divisions (B) to (D) of this section.

**HISTORY: GC § 5652-7c; 112 v 347; Bureau of Code Revision, 10-1-53; 135 v H 152 (Eff 11-21-73); 142 v H 352. Eff 7-10-87.**

[IMPOUNDING]

## § 955.21 Prohibition against failure to register dog kennel.

No owner, keeper, or harborer of a dog more than three months of age, nor owner of a dog kennel, shall fail to file the application for registration required by section 955.01 of the Revised Code, nor shall he fail to pay the legal fee therefor.

**HISTORY: GC § 5652-14; 107 v 534; 108 v PtI 534; 112 v 347; Bureau of Code Revision. Eff 10-1-53.**

## § 955.22 Confinement or restraint of dog; liability insurance; debarking or surgically silencing dog.

(A) As used in this section, "dangerous dog" and "vicious dog" have the same meanings as in section 955.11 of the Revised Code.

(B) No owner, keeper, or harborer of any female dog shall permit it to go beyond the premises of the owner, keeper, or harborer at any time the dog is in heat unless the dog is properly in leash.

(C) Except when a dog is lawfully engaged in hunting and accompanied by the owner, keeper, harborer, or handler of the dog, no owner, keeper, or harborer of any dog shall fail at any time to do either of the following:

(1) Keep the dog physically confined or restrained upon the premises of the owner, keeper, or harborer by a leash, tether, adequate fence, supervision, or secure enclosure to prevent escape;

(2) Keep the dog under the reasonable control of some person.

(D) Except when a dangerous or vicious dog is lawfully engaged in hunting or training for the purpose of hunting and is accompanied by the owner, keeper, harborer, or handler of the dog, no owner, keeper, or harborer of a dangerous or vicious dog shall fail to do either of the following:

(1) While that dog is on the premises of the owner, keeper, or harborer, securely confine it at all times in a locked pen that has a top, locked fenced yard, or other locked enclosure that has a top, except that a dangerous dog may, in the alternative, be tied with a leash or tether so that the dog is adequately restrained;

(2) While that dog is off the premises of the owner, keeper, or harborer, keep that dog on a chain-link leash or tether that is not more than six feet in length and additionally do at least one of the following:

(a) Keep that dog in a locked pen that has a top, locked fenced yard, or other locked enclosure that has a top;

(b) Have the leash or tether controlled by a person who is of suitable age and discretion or securely attach, tie, or affix the leash or tether to the ground or a stationary object or fixture so that the dog is adequately restrained and station such a person in close enough proximity to that dog so as to prevent it from causing injury to any person;

(c) Muzzle that dog.

(E) No owner, keeper, or harborer of a vicious dog shall fail to obtain liability insurance with an insurer authorized to write liability insurance in this state providing coverage in each occurrence, subject to a limit, exclusive of interest and costs, of not less than one hundred thousand dollars because of damage or bodily injury to or death of a person caused by the vicious dog.

(F) No person shall do any of the following:

(1) Debark or surgically silence a dog that the person knows or has reason to believe is a vicious dog;

(2) Possess a vicious dog if the person knows or has reason to believe that the dog has been debarked or surgically silenced;

(3) Falsely attest on a waiver form provided by the veterinarian under division (G) of this section that the person's dog is not a vicious dog or otherwise provide false information on that written waiver form.

(G) Before a veterinarian debarks or surgically silences a dog, the veterinarian may give the owner of the dog a written waiver form that attests that the dog is not a vicious dog. The written waiver form shall include all of the following:

(1) The veterinarian's license number and current business address;

(2) The number of the license of the dog if the dog is licensed;

(3) A reasonable description of the age, coloring, and gender of the dog as well as any notable markings on the dog;

(4) The signature of the owner of the dog attesting that the owner's dog is not a vicious dog;

(5) A statement that division (F) of section 955.22 of the Revised Code prohibits any person from doing any of the following:

(a) Debarking or surgically silencing a dog that the person knows or has reason to believe is a vicious dog;

(b) Possessing a vicious dog if the person knows or has reason to believe that the dog has been debarked or surgically silenced;

(c) Falsely attesting on a waiver form provided by the veterinarian under division (G) of section 955.22 of the Revised Code that the person's dog is not a vicious dog or otherwise provide false information on that written waiver form.

(H) It is an affirmative defense to a charge of a violation of division (F) of this section that the veterinarian who is charged with the violation obtained, prior to debarking or surgically silencing the dog, a written waiver form that complies with division (G) of this section and that attests that the dog is not a vicious dog.

**HISTORY: GC § 5652-14a; 112 v 347; Bureau of Code Revision, 10-1-53; 131 v 387 (Eff 9-1-65); 142 v H 352 (Eff 7-10-87); 148 v H 350. Eff 10-10-2000.**

The provisions of § 3 of HB 350 (148 v —) read as follows:

SECTION 3. A person who possesses a debarked or surgically silenced vicious dog, as defined in section 955.11 of the Revised Code, shall, within ninety days of the effective date of this act, have that vicious dog humanely destroyed by a licensed veterinarian, the county dog warden, or the county humane society.

## § 955.221 Local ordinances or resolutions to control dogs.

(A) For the purposes of this section, ordinances or resolutions to control dogs include, but are not limited to, ordinances or resolutions concerned with the ownership, keeping, or harboring of dogs, the restraint of dogs, dogs as public nuisances, and dogs as a threat to public health, safety, and welfare, except that such ordinances or resolutions as permitted in division (B) of this section shall not prohibit the use of any dog which is lawfully engaged in hunting or training for the purpose of hunting while accompanied by a licensed hunter. However, such dogs at all other times and in all other respects shall be subject to the ordinance or resolution permitted by this section, unless actually in the field and engaged in hunting or in legitimate training for such purpose.

(B)(1) A board of county commissioners may adopt and enforce resolutions to control dogs within the unincorporated areas of the county that are not otherwise in conflict with any other provision of the Revised Code.

(2) A board of township trustees may adopt and enforce resolutions to control dogs within the township that are not otherwise in conflict with any other provision of the Revised Code, if the township is located in a county where the board of county commissioners has not adopted resolutions to control dogs within the unincorporated areas of the county under this section. In the event that the board of county commissioners adopts resolutions to control dogs in the county after a board of township trustees has adopted resolutions to control dogs within the township, the resolutions adopted by the county board of commissioners prevail over the resolutions adopted by the board of township trustees.

(3) A municipal corporation may adopt and enforce ordinances to control dogs within the municipal corporation that are not otherwise in conflict with any other provision of the Revised Code.

(C) No person shall violate any resolution or ordinance adopted under this section.

**HISTORY: 142 v H 352 (Eff 7-10-87); 143 v H 291. Eff 6-21-90.**

## § 955.25 Unlawful tag.

No person shall own, keep, or harbor a dog wearing a fictitious, altered, or invalid registration tag or a registration tag not issued by the county auditor in connection with the registration of such animal.

**HISTORY: GC § 5652-15; 107 v 534; 108 v PtI 534; 112 v 347; Bureau of Code Revision. Eff 10-1-53.**

## § 955.26 Confinement of dogs.

Whenever, in the judgment of the director of health, any city or general health district board of health, or persons performing the duties of a board of health, rabies is prevalent, the director of health, the board, or those persons shall declare a quarantine of all dogs in the health district or in a part of it. During the quarantine, the owner, keeper, or harborer of any dog shall keep it confined on the premises of the owner, keeper, or harborer, or in a suitable pound or kennel, at the expense of the owner, keeper, or harborer, except that a dog may be permitted to leave the premises of its owner, keeper, or harborer if it is under leash or under the control of a responsible person. The quarantine order shall be considered an emergency and need not be published.

When the quarantine has been declared, the director of health, the board, or those persons may require vaccination for rabies of all dogs within the health district or part of it. Proof of rabies vaccination within a satisfactory period shall be demonstrated to the county auditor before any registration is issued under section 955.01 of the Revised Code for any dog that is required to be vaccinated.

The public health council shall determine appropriate methods of rabies vaccination and satisfactory periods for purposes of quarantines under this section.

When a quarantine of dogs has been declared in any health district or part of a health district, the county dog warden and all other persons having the authority of police officers shall assist the health authorities in enforcing the quarantine order. When rabies vaccination has been declared compulsory in any health district or part of a health district, the dog warden shall assist the health authorities in enforcing the vaccination order.

Notwithstanding the provisions of this section, a city or general health district board of health may make orders pursuant to sections 3709.20 and 3709.21 of the Revised Code requiring the vaccination of dogs.

**HISTORY: GC § 5652-16; 112 v 347; 124 v 413; Bureau of Code Revision, 10-1-53; 128 v 295 (Eff 9-18-59); 129 v 582(662) (Eff 1-10-61); 129 v 1190 (Eff 9-26-61); 142 v H 352. Eff 7-10-87.**

## § 955.261 Duties after dog bites person; quarantine.

(A)(1) No person shall remove a dog that has bitten any person from the county in which the bite occurred until a quarantine period as specified in division (B) of this section has been completed. No person shall transfer a dog that has bitten any person until a quarantine period as specified in division (B) of this section has been completed, except that a person may transfer the dog to the county dog warden or to any other animal control authority.

(2)(a) Subject to division (A)(2)(b) of this section, no person shall kill a dog that has bitten any person until a quarantine period as specified in division (B) of this section has been completed.

(b) Division (A)(2)(a) of this section does not apply to the killing of a dog in order to prevent further injury or death or if the dog is diseased or seriously injured.

(3) No person who has killed a dog that has bitten any person in order to prevent further injury or death or if the dog is diseased or seriously injured shall fail to do both of the following:

(a) Immediately after the killing of the dog, notify the board of health for the district in which the bite occurred of the facts relative to the bite and the killing;

(b) Hold the body of the dog until that board of health claims it to perform tests for rabies.

(B) The quarantine period for a dog that has bitten any person shall be ten days or another period that the board of health for the district in which the bite occurred determines is necessary to observe the dog for rabies.

(C)(1) To enable persons to comply with the quarantine requirements specified in divisions (A) and (B) of this section, boards of health shall make provision for the quarantine of individual dogs under the circumstances described in those divisions.

(2) Upon the receipt of a notification pursuant to division (A)(3) of this section that a dog that has bitten any person has been killed, the board of health for the district in which the bite occurred shall claim the body of the dog from its killer and then perform tests on the body for rabies.

(D) This section does not apply to a police dog that has bitten a person while the police dog is under the care of a licensed veterinarian or has bitten a person while the police dog is being used for law enforcement, corrections, prison or jail security, or investigative purposes. If, after biting a person, a police dog exhibits any abnormal behavior, the law enforcement agency and the law enforcement officer the police dog assists, within a reasonable time after the person is bitten, shall make the police dog available for the board of health for the district in which the bite occurred to perform tests for rabies.

(E) As used in this section, "police dog" has the same meaning as in section 2921.321 [2921.32.1] of the Revised Code.

**HISTORY: 142 v H 352 (Eff 7-10-87); 148 v H 701. Eff 4-9-2001.**

## [PROHIBITIONS]

## § 955.39 Prohibition against violating a rabies quarantine.

No person shall violate a rabies quarantine order issued under section 955.26 of the Revised Code.

**HISTORY: Bureau of Code Revision. Eff 10-1-53.**

**Publisher's Note:**

This section was derived from GC § 5652-16. See also RC § 955.26.

## [FINES AND PENALTIES]

## § 955.99 Penalties.

(A)(1) Whoever violates division (E) of section 955.11 of the Revised Code because of a failure to comply with division (B) of that section is guilty of a minor misdemeanor.

(2) Whoever violates division (E) of section 955.11 of the Revised Code because of a failure to comply with division (C) or (D) of that section is guilty of a minor misdemeanor on a first offense and of a misdemeanor of the fourth degree on each subsequent offense.

(B) Whoever violates section 955.10, 955.23, 955.24, or 955.25 of the Revised Code is guilty of a minor misdemeanor.

(C) Whoever violates section 955.261 [955.26.1], 955.39, or 955.50 of the Revised Code is guilty of a minor misdemeanor on a first offense and of a misdemeanor of the fourth degree on each subsequent offense.

(D) Whoever violates division (F) of section 955.16 or division (B) of section 955.43 of the Revised Code is guilty of a misdemeanor of the fourth degree.

(E)(1) Whoever violates section 955.21 or division (B) or (C) of section 955.22 of the Revised Code shall be fined not less than twenty-five dollars or more than one hundred dollars on a first offense, and on each subsequent offense shall be fined not less than seventy-five dollars or more than two hundred fifty dollars and may be imprisoned for not more than thirty days.

(2) In addition to the penalties prescribed in division (E)(1) of this section, if the offender is guilty of a violation of division (B) or (C) of section 955.22 of the Revised Code, the court may order the offender to personally supervise the dog that the offender owns, keeps, or harbors, to cause that dog to complete dog obedience training, or to do both.

(F) If a violation of division (D) of section 955.22 of the Revised Code involves a dangerous dog, whoever violates that division is guilty of a misdemeanor of the fourth degree on a first offense and of a misdemeanor of the third degree on each subsequent offense. Additionally, the court may order the offender to personally supervise the dangerous dog that the offender owns, keeps, or harbors, to cause that dog to complete dog obedience training, or to do both, and the court may order the offender to obtain liability insurance pursuant to division (E) of section 955.22 of the Revised Code. The court, in the alternative, may order the dangerous dog to be humanely destroyed by a licensed veterinarian, the county dog warden, or the county humane society.

(G) If a violation of division (D) of section 955.22 of the Revised Code involves a vicious dog, whoever violates that division is guilty of one of the following:

(1) A felony of the fourth degree on a first or subsequent offense if the dog kills or seriously injures a person. Additionally, the court shall order that the vicious dog be humanely destroyed by a licensed veterinarian, the county dog warden, or the county humane society.

(2) A misdemeanor of the first degree on a first offense and a felony of the fourth degree on each subsequent offense. Additionally, the court may order the vicious dog to be humanely destroyed by a licensed veterinarian, the county dog warden, or the county humane society.

(3) A misdemeanor of the first degree if the dog causes injury, other than killing or serious injury, to any person.

(H) Whoever violates division (A)(2) of section 955.01 or division (E) of section 955.22 of the Revised Code is guilty of a misdemeanor of the first degree.

(I) Whoever violates division (C) of section 955.221 [955.22.1] of the Revised Code is guilty of a minor misdemeanor. Each day of continued violation constitutes a separate offense. Fines levied and collected for violations of that division shall be distributed by the mayor or clerk of the municipal or county court in accordance with section 733.40, division (F) of section 1901.31, or division (C) of section 1907.20 of the Revised Code to the treasury of the county, township, or municipal corporation whose resolution or ordinance was violated.

(J) Whoever violates division (F)(1), (2), or (3) of section 955.22 of the Revised Code is guilty of a felony of the fourth degree. Additionally, the court shall order that the vicious dog be humanely destroyed by a licensed veterinarian, the county dog warden, or the county humane society.

**HISTORY: Bureau of Code Revision, 10-1-53; 133 v S 514 (Eff 7-16-70); 134 v H 511 (Eff 1-1-74); 136 v S 256 (Eff 6-4-76); 138 v H 854 (Eff 1-1-81); 141 v H 454 (Eff 11-1-85); 141 v H 428 (Eff 12-23-86); 142 v H 352 (Eff 7-10-87); 142 v H 246 (Eff 12-12-88); 143 v H 291 (Eff 6-21-90); 148 v H 350. Eff 10-10-2000.**

# CHAPTER 959: OFFENSES RELATING TO DOMESTIC ANIMALS

Section



## § 959.01 Abandoning animals.

No owner or keeper of a dog, cat, or other domestic animal, shall abandon such animal.

**HISTORY: GC § 13368; 124 v 428, § 2; Bureau of Code Revision. Eff 10-1-53.**

**Not analogous to former GC § 13368 [97 v 128, § 4], repealed in 101 v 332.**

## § 959.02 Injuring animals.

No person shall maliciously, or willfully, and without the consent of the owner, kill or injure a horse, mare, foal, filly, jack, mule, sheep, goat, cow, steer, bull, heifer, ass, ox, swine, dog, cat, or other domestic animal that is the property of another. This section does not apply to a licensed veterinarian acting in an official capacity.

**HISTORY: RS § 6851; S&C 74, 75; 53 v 192, §§ 1, 2; 54 v 126, §§ 1, 2; GC § 13361; 124 v 428; Bureau of Code Revision. Eff 10-1-53.**

## § 959.03 Poisoning animals.

No person shall maliciously, or willfully and without the consent of the owner, administer poison, except a licensed veterinarian acting in such capacity, to a horse, mare, foal, filly, jack, mule, sheep, goat, cow, steer, bull, heifer, ass, ox, swine, dog, cat, poultry, or any other domestic animal that is the property of another; and no person shall, willfully and without the consent of the owner, place any poisoned food where it may be easily found and eaten by any of such animals, either upon his own lands or the lands of another.

**HISTORY: RS § 6852; S&C 75; 53 v 192, § 3; GC § 13362; 108 v PtII 1231; 124 v 428; Bureau of Code Revision. Eff 10-1-53.**

## § 959.04 Trespassing animals.

Sections 959.02 and 959.03 of the Revised Code do not extend to a person killing or injuring an animal or attempting to do so while endeavoring to prevent it from trespassing upon his enclosure, or while it is so trespassing, or while driving it away from his premises; provided within fifteen days thereafter, payment is made for damages done to such animal by such killing or injuring, less the actual amount of damage done by such animal while so trespassing, or a sufficient sum of money is deposited with the nearest judge of a county court or judge of a municipal court having jurisdiction within such time to cover such damages. Such deposit shall remain in the custody of such judge until there is a determination of the damages resulting from such killing or injury and from such trespass. Such judge and his bondsmen shall be responsible for the safekeeping of such money and for the payment thereof as for money collected upon a judgment.

**HISTORY: RS § 6853; S&C 74, 75; 53 v 192, § 4; 54 v 126, § 3; 90 v 140; GC § 13363; Bureau of Code Revision, 10-1-53; 129 v 582(662). Eff 1-10-61.**

## § 959.05 Drugging animal prior to competition restricted.

No person shall administer to any animal within forty-eight hours prior to the time that the animal competes at a fair or exhibition conducted by a county or independent agricultural society authorized under Chapter 1711. of the Revised Code or by the Ohio expositions commission any drug or medicament not specifically permitted under rules of the state racing commission promulgated pursuant to Chapter 3769. of the Revised Code or under rules of the society, in respect to a county or independent agricultural society, or of the Ohio expositions commission, in respect to the Ohio state fair. This section does not apply to any horse racing meeting conducted under a permit issued pursuant to Chapter 3769. of the Revised Code.

**HISTORY: 136 v H 894. Eff 2-26-76.**

**Not analogous to former RC § 959.05 [RS § 6855; S&S 11; S&C 71; 54 v 14; 64 v 207; GC § 13364; Bureau of Code Revision, 10-1-53], repealed 132 v H 842, eff 12-14-67.**

## § 959.06 Prohibited methods of destroying domestic animals.

(A) No person shall destroy any domestic animal by the use of a high altitude decompression chamber or by any method other than a method that immediately and painlessly renders the domestic animal initially unconscious and subsequently dead.

(B) This section does not apply to or prohibit the slaughtering of livestock under Chapter 945. of the Revised Code, or the taking of any wild animal, as defined in section 1531.01 of the Revised Code, when taken in accordance with Chapter 1533. of the Revised Code.

**HISTORY: 138 v H 854. Eff 1-1-81.**

**Not analogous to former RC § 959.06 [RS § 4211-26; 85 v 336; GC § 13365; Bureau of Code Revision, 10-1-53], repealed, 132 v H 842, § 2, eff 12-14-67.**
The effective date of HB 854 is set by section 3 of the act.

## § 959.12 Alteration of brands.

No person shall maliciously alter or deface an artificial earmark or brand upon a horse, mare, foal, filly, jack, mule, sheep, goat, cow, steer, bull, heifer, ass, ox, swine, that is the property of another.

**HISTORY: RS § 6850; S&C 430; 29 v 144, § 20; GC § 13375; Bureau of Code Revision. Eff 10-1-53.**

## § 959.13 Cruelty to animals.

(A) No person shall:

(1) Torture an animal, deprive one of necessary sustenance, unnecessarily or cruelly beat, needlessly mutilate or kill, or impound or confine an animal without supplying it during such confinement with a sufficient quantity of good wholesome food and water;

(2) Impound or confine an animal without affording it, during such confinement, access to shelter from wind, rain, snow, or excessive direct sunlight if it can reasonably be expected that the animals would otherwise become sick or in some other way suffer. Division (A)(2) of this section does not apply to animals impounded or confined prior to slaughter. For the purpose of this section, shelter means a man-made enclosure, windbreak, sunshade, or natural windbreak or sunshade that is developed from the earth's contour, tree development, or vegetation.[;]

(3) Carry or convey an animal in a cruel or inhuman[e] manner;

(4) Keep animals other than cattle, poultry or fowl, swine, sheep, or goats in an enclosure without wholesome exercise and change of air, † nor or feed cows on food that produces impure or unwholesome milk;

(5) Detain livestock in railroad cars or compartments longer than twenty-eight hours after they are so placed without supplying them with necessary food, water, and attention, nor permit such stock to be so crowded as to overlie, crush, wound, or kill each other.

(B) Upon the written request of the owner or person in custody of any particular shipment of livestock, which written request shall be separate and apart from any printed bill of lading or other railroad form, the length of time in which such livestock may be detained in any cars or compartment without food, water, and attention, may be extended to thirty-six hours without penalty therefor. This section does not prevent the dehorning of cattle.

(C) All fines collected for violations of this section shall be paid to the society or association for the prevention of cruelty to animals, if there be such in the county, township, or municipal corporation where such violation occurred.

**HISTORY: RS § 6951; 72 v 129, §§ 1, 2, 4, 5, 6, 8, 22; 78 v 134; 89 v 140; 93 v 15; GC § 13376; 101 v 118; 109 v 152; Bureau of Code Revision, 10-1-53; 136 v H 858. Eff 1-17-77.**

† So in 136 v H 858.

## § 959.131 Prohibitions concerning companion animals.

(A) As used in this section:

(1) "Companion animal" means any animal that is kept inside a residential dwelling and any dog or cat regardless of where it is kept. "Companion animal" does not include livestock or any wild animal.

(2) "Cruelty," "torment," and "torture" have the same meanings as in section 1717.01 of the Revised Code.

(3) "Residential dwelling" means a structure or shelter or the portion of a structure or shelter that is used by one or more humans for the purpose of a habitation.

(4) "Practice of veterinary medicine" has the same meaning as in section 4741.01 of the Revised Code.

(5) "Wild animal" has the same meaning as in section 1531.01 of the Revised Code.

(6) "Federal animal welfare act" means the "Laboratory Animal Act of 1966," Pub. L. No. 89-544, 80 Stat. 350 (1966), 7 U.S.C.A. 2131 et seq., as amended by the "Animal Welfare Act of 1970," Pub. L. No. 91-579, 84 Stat. 1560 (1970), the "Animal Welfare Act Amendments of 1976," Pub. L. No. 94-279, 90 Stat. 417 (1976), and the "Food Security Act of 1985," Pub. L. No. 99-198, 99 Stat. 1354 (1985), and as it may be subsequently amended.

(B) No person shall knowingly torture, torment, needlessly mutilate or maim, cruelly beat, poison, needlessly kill, or commit an act of cruelty against a companion animal.

(C) No person who confines or who is the custodian or caretaker of a companion animal shall negligently do any of the following:

(1) Torture, torment, needlessly mutilate or maim, cruelly beat, poison, needlessly kill, or commit an act of cruelty against the companion animal;

(2) Deprive the companion animal of necessary sustenance, confine the companion animal without supplying it during the confinement with sufficient quantities of good, wholesome food and water, or impound or confine the companion animal without affording it, during the impoundment or confinement, with access to shelter from heat, cold, wind, rain, snow, or excessive direct sunlight, if it can reasonably be expected that the companion animal would become sick or suffer in any other way as a result of or due to the deprivation, confinement, or impoundment or confinement in any of those specified manners.

(D) Divisions (B) and (C) of this section do not apply to any of the following:

(1) A companion animal used in scientific research conducted by an institution in accordance with the federal animal welfare act and related regulations;

(2) The lawful practice of veterinary medicine by a person who has been issued a license, temporary permit, or registration certificate to do so under Chapter 4741. of the Revised Code;

(3) Dogs being used or intended for use for hunting or field trial purposes, provided that the dogs are being treated in accordance with usual and commonly accepted practices for the care of hunting dogs;

(4) The use of common training devices, if the companion animal is being treated in accordance with usual and commonly accepted practices for the training of animals;

(5) The administering of medicine to a companion animal that was properly prescribed by a person who has been issued a license, temporary permit, or registration certificate under Chapter 4741. of the Revised Code.

(E) Notwithstanding any section of the Revised Code that otherwise provides for the distribution of fine moneys, the clerk of court shall forward all fines the clerk collects that are so imposed for any violation of this section to the treasurer of the political subdivision or the state, whose county humane society or law enforcement agency is to be paid the fine money as determined under this division. The treasurer to whom the fines are forwarded shall pay the fine moneys to the county humane society or the county, township, municipal corporation, or state law enforcement agency in this state that primarily was responsible for or involved in the investigation and prosecution of the violation. If a county humane society receives any fine moneys under this division, the county humane society shall use the fine moneys to provide the training that is required for humane agents under section 1717.06 of the Revised Code.

**HISTORY: 149 v S 221. Eff 4-9-2003.**

## § 959.132 Procedures for seizure and impoundment of companion animals.

(A) As used in this section:

(1) "Companion animal" has the same meaning as in section 959.131 [959.13.1] of the Revised Code.

(2) "Impounding agency" means a county humane society organized under section 1717.05 of the Revised Code, an animal shelter, or a law enforcement agency that has impounded a companion animal in accordance with this section.

(3) "Offense" means a violation of section 959.131 [959.13.1] of the Revised Code or an attempt, in violation of section 2923.02 of the Revised Code, to violate section 959.131 [959.13.1] of the Revised Code.

(4) "Officer" means any law enforcement officer, agent of a county humane society, or other person appointed to act as an animal control officer for a municipal corporation or township in accordance with state law, an ordinance, or a resolution.

(B) An officer may seize and cause to be impounded at an impounding agency a companion animal that the officer has probable cause to believe is the subject of an offense. No officer or impounding agency shall impound a companion animal that is the subject of an offense in a shelter owned, operated, or controlled by a board of county commissioners pursuant to Chapter 955. of the Revised Code unless the board, by resolution, authorizes the impoundment of such a companion animal in a shelter owned, operated, or controlled by that board and has executed, in the case when the officer is other than a dog warden or assistant dog warden, a contract specifying the terms and conditions of the impoundment.

(C) The officer shall give written notice of the seizure and impoundment to the owner, keeper, or harborer of the companion animal that was seized and impounded. If the officer is unable to give the notice to the owner, keeper, or harborer of the companion animal, the officer shall post the notice on the door of the residence or in another conspicuous place on the premises at which the companion animal was seized. The notice shall include a statement that a hearing will be held not later than ten days after the notice is provided or at the next available court date to determine whether the officer had probable cause to seize the companion animal and, if applicable, to determine the amount of a bond or cash deposit that is needed to provide for the companion animal's care and keeping for not less than thirty days beginning on the date on which the companion animal was impounded.

(D) A companion animal that is seized under this section may be humanely destroyed immediately or at any time during impoundment if a licensed veterinarian determines it to be necessary because the companion animal is suffering.

(E)(1) Not later than ten days after notice is provided or at the next available court date, the court shall hold a hearing to determine whether the officer impounding a companion animal had probable cause to seize the companion animal. If the court determines that probable cause exists, the court shall determine the amount of a bond or cash deposit that is needed to provide for the companion animal's care and keeping for not less than thirty days beginning on the date on which the companion animal was impounded.

(2) If the court determines that probable cause does not exist, the court immediately shall order the impounding agency to return the companion animal to its owner if possible. If the companion animal cannot be returned because it has died as a result of neglect or other misconduct by the impounding agency or if the companion animal is injured as a result of neglect or other misconduct by the impounding agency, the court shall order the impounding agency to pay the owner an amount

determined by the court to be equal to the reasonable market value of the companion animal at the time that it was impounded plus statutory interest as defined in section 1343.03 of the Revised Code from the date of the impoundment or an amount determined by the court to be equal to the reasonable cost of treatment of the injury to the companion animal, as applicable. The requirement established in division (E)(2) of this section regarding the payment of the reasonable market value of the companion animal shall not apply in the case of a dog that, in violation of section 955.01 of the Revised Code, was not registered at the time it was seized and impounded.

(3) If the court determines that probable cause exists and determines the amount of a bond or cash deposit, the case shall continue and the owner shall post a bond or cash deposit to provide for the companion animal's care and keeping for not less than thirty days beginning on the date on which the companion animal was impounded. The owner may renew a bond or cash deposit by posting, not later than ten days following the expiration of the period for which a previous bond or cash deposit was posted, a new bond or cash deposit in an amount that the court, in consultation with the impounding agency, determines is sufficient to provide for the companion animal's care and keeping for not less than thirty days beginning on the date on which the previous period expired. If no bond or cash deposit is posted or if a bond or cash deposit expires and is not renewed, the impounding agency may determine the disposition of the companion animal unless the court issues an order that specifies otherwise.

(F) If a person is convicted of committing an offense, the court may impose the following additional penalties against the person:

(1) A requirement that the person pay for the costs incurred by the impounding agency in caring for a companion animal involved in the applicable offense, provided that the costs were incurred during the companion animal's impoundment. A bond or cash deposit posted under this section may be applied to the costs.

(2) An order permanently terminating the person's right to possession, title, custody, or care of the companion animal that was involved in the offense. If the court issues such an order, the court shall order the disposition of the companion animal.

(G) If a person is found not guilty of committing an offense, the court immediately shall order the impounding agency to return the companion animal to its owner if possible and to return the entire amount of any bond or cash deposit posted under division (E) of this section. If the companion animal cannot be returned because it has died as a result of neglect or other misconduct by the impounding agency or if the companion animal is injured as a result of neglect or other misconduct by the impounding agency, the court shall order the impounding agency to pay the owner an amount determined by the court to be equal to the reasonable market value of the companion animal at the time that it was impounded plus statutory interest as defined in section 1343.03 of the Revised Code from the date of the impoundment or an amount determined by the court to be equal to the reasonable cost of treatment of the injury to the companion animal, as applicable. The requirements established in this division regarding the return of a bond or cash deposit and the payment of the reasonable market value of the companion animal shall not apply in the case of a dog that, in violation of section 955.01 of the Revised Code, was not registered at the time it was seized and impounded.

(H) If charges are filed under section 959.131 [959.13.1] of the Revised Code against the custodian or caretaker of a companion animal, but the companion animal that is the subject of the charges is not impounded, the court in which the charges are pending may order the owner or person having custody of the companion animal to provide to the companion animal the necessities described in division (C)(2) of section 959.131 [959.13.1] of the Revised Code until the final disposition of the charges. If the court issues an order of that nature, the court also may authorize an officer or another person to visit the place where the companion animal is being kept, at the times and under the conditions that the court may set, to determine whether the companion animal is receiving those necessities and to remove and impound the companion animal if the companion animal is not receiving those necessities.

**HISTORY: 152 v H 71, § 1, eff. 9-30-08.**

**Analogous to former RC § 959.132 (149 v S 221. Eff 4-9-2003), repealed 152 v H 71, § 2, eff 9-30-08.**

## § 959.14 Horse tails.

No owner or person having the custody, control, or possession of a horse, nor an agent or employee of such owner or custodian, shall cut off or cause to be cut off or amputated the skin, flesh, muscles, bone, or integuments of the dock or tail of the horse in order to shorten its natural length or proportions .

No person shall pull out the hairs of the foretop, mane, or withers of a horse except minimum quantities required for medical testing.

This section does not prohibit the cutting or amputation of the dock or tail of a horse when necessary because of accident, malformation, or disease or as a proactive measure to prevent injury if performed by a veterinarian that is licensed under Chapter 4741. of the Revised Code or in another state.

**HISTORY: RS § 6951-1; 90 v 138; GC § 13377; Bureau of Code Revision. Eff 10-1-53; 2011 HB 229, § 1, eff. Oct. 17, 2011.**

## § 959.15 Animal fights.

No person shall knowingly engage in or be employed at cockfighting, bearbaiting, or pitting an animal against another; no person shall receive money for the admission of another to a place kept for such purpose; no person shall use, train, or possess any animal for seizing, detaining, or maltreating a domestic animal. Any person who knowingly purchases a ticket of admission to such place, or is present thereat, or witnesses such spectacle, is an aider and abettor.

**HISTORY: RS § 6952; S&C 449; 29 v 161, §§ 11, 12; 72 v 129, §§ 7, 10, 22; GC § 13378; Bureau of Code Revision, 10-1-53; 138 v S 233. Eff 6-10-80.**

## § 959.16 Dogfighting offenses; investigations; seizure and impoundment of dogs, confiscation of equipment.

(A) No person shall knowingly do any of the following:

(1) Promote, engage in, or be employed at dogfighting;

(2) Receive money or anything else of value for the admission of another person to a dogfighting event or a place kept for dogfighting;

(3) Sell, purchase, possess, or train a dog for dogfighting;

(4) Use, train, or possess a dog for seizing, detaining, or maltreating a domestic animal;

(5) Pay money or give anything else of value in exchange for admission to or be present at a dogfight;

(6) Witness a dogfight if it is presented as a public spectacle.

(B) The department of agriculture may investigate complaints and follow up rumors of dogfighting activities and may report any information so gathered to an appropriate prosecutor or law enforcement agency.

(C) Any peace officer, as defined in section 2935.01 of the Revised Code, may seize and cause to be impounded in accordance with section 959.161 [959.16.1] of the Revised Code any dogs that have been, are, or are intended to be used in dogfighting. In addition, any peace officer shall confiscate any equipment or devices used in training such dogs or as part of dogfights.

**HISTORY: 138 v S 233. Eff 6-10-80; 152 v H 71, § 1, eff. 9-30-08.**

**Not analogous to former RC § 959.16 [RS § 6854; S&S 279; 65 v 200; GC § 13379; Bureau of Code Revision, 10-1-53], repealed, 134 v H 511, § 2, eff 1-1-74.**

## § 959.161 Procedures for seizure and impoundment of fighting dogs.

(A) As used in this section:

(1) "Fighting dog" means a dog that a peace officer has probable cause to believe has been, is, or is intended to be used in dogfighting in violation of section 959.16 of the Revised Code.

(2) "Impounding entity" means the entity that has possession of an impounded fighting dog during its impoundment.

(3) "Peace officer" has the same meaning as in section 2935.01 of the Revised Code.

(4) "Violation" means a violation of section 959.16 of the Revised Code or an attempt, in violation of section 2923.02 of the Revised Code, to violate section 959.16 of the Revised Code.

(B) A peace officer may seize and cause to be impounded with an impounding entity a fighting dog that the peace officer has probable cause to believe is involved in a violation.

(C) A fighting dog that is seized under this section may be humanely destroyed under either of the following circumstances:

(1) During its seizure if it is necessary because the fighting dog is suffering;

(2) At any time during its impoundment if a licensed veterinarian determines it to be necessary because the fighting dog is suffering.

(D) Procedures, requirements, and other provisions that are established in divisions (C), (E), (F), and (G) of section 959.132 [959.13.2] of the Revised Code shall apply to the seizure, impoundment, and disposition of a fighting dog. For purposes of that application, references in those divisions of section 959.132 [959.13.2] of the Revised Code to "companion animal," "impounding agency," "officer," and "offense" shall be deemed to be replaced, respectively, with references to "fighting dog," "impounding entity," "peace officer," and "violation" as defined in this section. Likewise, references in those divisions of section 959.132 [959.13.2] of the Revised Code to "section 959.131 [959.13.1] of the Revised Code" shall be deemed to be replaced with references to section 959.16 of the Revised Code, as applicable.

**HISTORY: 152 v H 71, § 1, eff. 9-30-08.**

## § 959.17 Trapshooting.

Live birds or fowl shall not be used as targets in trapshooting.

**HISTORY: RC §§ 6952-1, 6952-2; 95 v 254, §§ 1, 2; GC § 13380; Bureau of Code Revision. Eff 10-1-53.**

## § 959.18 Prohibition against killing a carrier pigeon.

No person who is not the owner thereof, shall shoot, kill, or maim an Antwerp or homing pigeon, commonly known as "carrier" pigeon, nor shall such person entrap, catch, or detain a carrier pigeon, provided it has the name of the owner stamped upon its wing or tail, or has a band with the owner's name, initial, or number on its leg.

**HISTORY: RS § 7017-2; 93 v 218; GC § 13381; Bureau of Code Revision. Eff 10-1-53.**

## § 959.19 Prohibition against servicing mare in public street.

No owner of a stallion or jack or the agent of such owner, shall permit it to serve a mare within thirty feet of a public street or alley in a municipal corporation.

**HISTORY: RS § 7038-1; 88 v 394; GC § 13414; Bureau of Code Revision. Eff 10-1-53.**

## § 959.20 Use of certain devices on animals prohibited.

As used in this section:

(A) "Work animal" includes a horse, pony, mule, donkey, mare, ox, bull, gelding, or other animal used or intended to be used for a work purpose.

(B) "Work purpose" means the performance by a work animal of some work or labor, including showing, performing, or being used in any exhibition, show, circus, rodeo, or similar use.

(C) "Owner" includes any person, firm, association, or corporation owning or having a proprietary interest in or possession, custody, or charge of a work animal.

No person shall directly or indirectly or by aiding, abetting, or permitting the doing thereof put, place, fasten, use, or fix upon or to any work animal used or readied for use for a work purpose, twisted wire snaffles, unpadded bucking straps, unpadded flank straps, electric or other prods, or similar devices.

The commission or performance of any act prohibited by this section is the act of the owner of the work animal upon or to which such act was done.

**HISTORY: 131 v 387 (Eff 10-8-65); 141 v H 797. Eff 7-24-86.**

## § 959.99 Penalties.

(A) Whoever violates section 959.18 or 959.19 of the Revised Code is guilty of a minor misdemeanor.

(B) Except as otherwise provided in this division, whoever violates section 959.02 of the Revised Code is guilty of a misdemeanor of the second degree. If the value of the animal killed or the injury done amounts to three hundred dollars or more, whoever violates section 959.02 of the Revised Code is guilty of a misdemeanor of the first degree.

(C) Whoever violates section 959.03, 959.06, 959.12, 959.15, or 959.17 of the Revised Code is guilty of a misdemeanor of the fourth degree.

(D) Whoever violates division (A) of section 959.13 of the Revised Code is guilty of a misdemeanor of the second degree. In addition, the court may order the offender to forfeit the animal or livestock and may provide for its disposition, including, but not limited to, the sale of the animal or livestock. If an animal or livestock is forfeited and sold pursuant to this division, the proceeds from the sale first shall be applied to pay the expenses incurred with regard to the care of the animal from the time it was taken from the custody of the former owner. The balance of the proceeds from the sale, if any, shall be paid to the former owner of the animal.

(E)(1) Whoever violates division (B) of section 959.131 [959.13.1] of the Revised Code is guilty of a misdemeanor of the first degree on a first offense and a felony of the fifth degree on each subsequent offense.

(2) Whoever violates section 959.01 of the Revised Code or division (C) of section 959.131 [959.13.1] of the Revised Code is guilty of a misdemeanor of the second degree on a first offense and a misdemeanor of the first degree on each subsequent offense.

(3)(a) A court may order a person who is convicted of or pleads guilty to a violation of section 959.131 [959.13.1] of the Revised Code to forfeit to an impounding agency, as defined in section 959.132 [959.13.2] of the Revised Code, any or all of the companion animals in that person's ownership or care. The court also may prohibit or place limitations on the person's ability to own or care for any companion animals for a specified or indefinite period of time.

(b) A court may order a person who is convicted of or pleads guilty to a violation of section 959.131 [959.13.1] of the Revised Code to reimburse an impounding agency for the reasonably necessary costs incurred by the agency for the care of a companion animal that the agency impounded as a result of the investigation or prosecution of the violation, provided that the costs were not otherwise paid under section 959.132 [959.13.2] of the Revised Code.

(4) If a court has reason to believe that a person who is convicted of or pleads guilty to a violation of section 959.131 [959.13.1] of the Revised Code suffers from a mental or emotional disorder that contributed to the violation, the court may impose as a community control sanction or as a condition of probation a requirement that the offender undergo psychological evaluation or counseling. The court shall order the offender to pay the costs of the evaluation or counseling.

(F) Whoever violates section 959.14 of the Revised Code is guilty of a misdemeanor of the second degree on a first offense and a misdemeanor of the first degree on each subsequent offense.

(G) Whoever violates section 959.05 or 959.20 of the Revised Code is guilty of a misdemeanor of the first degree.

(H) Whoever violates section 959.16 of the Revised Code is guilty of a felony of the fourth degree for a first offense and a felony of the third degree on each subsequent offense.

**HISTORY: Bureau of Code Revision, 10-1-53; 125 v 215 (Eff 10-2-53); 131 v 387 (Eff 10-8-65); 132 v H 1 (Eff 2-21-67); 132 v H 842 (Eff 12-14-67); 134 v H 511 (Eff 1-1-74); 136 v H 894 (Eff 2-26-76); 138 v S 233 (Eff 6-10-80); 138 v H 854 (Eff 1-1-81); 139 v S 199 (Eff 7-1-83); 143 v H 12 (Eff 9-15-89); 146 v S 2 (Eff 7-1-96); 147 v H 219 (Eff 6-1-98); 148 v H 350 (Eff 10-10-2000); 149 v S 221. Eff 4-9-2003.**

# TITLE 11: FINANCIAL INSTITUTIONS

## CHAPTER 1127: BANKS — CRIMES AND PROHIBITED ACTIVITIES



### § 1127.02 Receipt of deposits when bank is insolvent.

No regulated person shall receive, or permit to be received, money, checks, drafts, or other property as a deposit in a bank, when the regulated person knows the bank is insolvent.

**HISTORY: RC § 1129.04, 132 v S 97 (Eff 1-1-68); RC § 1127.02, 146 v H 538. Eff 1-1-97.**

**Not analogous to former RC § 1127.02, amended and renumbered RC** § 1123.01 **in 146 v H 538, eff 1-1-97.**
The effective date is set by section 10 of HB 538.

### § 1127.03 Compensation for procuring certain bank or trust company services prohibited.

(A) No regulated person shall, except as provided by law, stipulate for or receive any fee, commission, gift, or thing of value from any person for procuring or endeavoring to procure for that person, or for any other person, any loan, extension or renewal of a loan, or substitution of security from any bank or trust company, or the purchase, discount, or acceptance of any paper, note, draft, check, or bill of exchange by any bank or trust company.

(B) Division (A) of this section does not prohibit any bona fide salary, wages, fees, or other compensation paid, or expenses reimbursed, in the usual course of business by a bank or trust company to a regulated person, or normal business amenities that facilitate the discussion of business, foster good business relations, or serve some other demonstrable business purpose.

**HISTORY: RC § 1129.12, 142 v S 149 (Eff 7-14-87); RC § 1127.03, 146 v H 538. Eff 1-1-97.**

**Not analogous to former RC § 1127.03, amended and renumbered, RC** § 1123.02 **in 146 v H 538, eff 1-1-97.**
The effective date is set by section 10 of HB 538.

### § 1127.06 Violation of participation order.

No person subject to an order issued by the superintendent of financial institutions under section 1121.33 or 1121.34 of the Revised Code shall knowingly participate, directly or indirectly, in any manner, including by engaging in an activity specifically prohibited in the order, in the conduct of the affairs of any bank or trust company.

**HISTORY: 146 v H 538. Eff 1-1-97.**

**Not analogous to former RC § 1127.06 (132 v S 97), repealed 146 v H 538, § 2, eff 1-1-97.**
The effective date is set by section 10 of HB 538.

### § 1127.08 Falsification, forgery or counterfeiting.

No person, for the purpose of influencing in any manner the actions or decisions of the superintendent of financial institutions in the superintendent's capacity as chief executive officer of the division of financial institutions, shall knowingly make or provide to the superintendent or any employee or agent of the division, or knowingly invite reliance by any of them upon, a statement, document, or other thing the person knows to be false, misleading, forged, or counterfeit.

**HISTORY: 146 v H 538. Eff 1-1-97.**

The effective date is set by section 10 of HB 538.

### § 1127.09 False communications.

No person shall knowingly make, publish, or otherwise communicate any statement, report, information, or data relating to the financial or other condition of any bank or trust company that the person knows to be false or misleading.

**HISTORY: 146 v H 538. Eff 1-1-97.**

The effective date is set by section 10 of HB 538.

### § 1127.11 Concealment of assets or placing beyond official's reach; impeding official.

No person shall knowingly do any of the following:

(A) Conceal or attempt to conceal an asset or property from a conservator, receiver, or liquidating agent appointed by the superintendent of financial institutions with respect to any asset acquired or liability assumed by the conservator, receiver, or liquidating agent;

(B) Impede or attempt to impede the functions of the conservator, receiver, or liquidating agent;

(C) Place or attempt to place any asset or property beyond the reach of the conservator, receiver, or liquidating agent.

**HISTORY: 146 v H 538. Eff 1-1-97.**

The effective date is set by section 10 of HB 538.

### § 1127.99 Penalties.

(A) Whoever violates section 1127.06, 1127.08, or 1127.11 of the Revised Code is guilty of a felony of the third degree.

(B) Whoever violates section 1127.02 or 1127.03 of the Revised Code is guilty of a felony of the fourth degree.

(C) Whoever violates section 1127.09 of the Revised Code is guilty of a felony of the fifth degree.

**HISTORY: 146 v H 538. Eff 1-1-97.**

The effective date is set by section 10 of HB 538.

# CHAPTER 1153: SAVINGS AND LOAN ASSOCIATIONS — MISCELLANEOUS PROVISIONS

Section



## § 1153.03 Declaration of excessive dividend.

No director of a building and loan association shall vote to declare, and no financial or first secretary of such an association shall declare or advise its board of directors to declare, for the purpose of deceiving the people or defrauding the members of the association, a greater dividend than has been actually earned by such association.

**HISTORY: GC § 13189; 99 v 536, § 46; Bureau of Code Revision. Eff 10-1-53.**

## § 1153.06 Failure to make reports; unlawful solicitation of business.

No officer of a building and loan association shall fail to make the reports required of him by the laws provided for the organization, regulation, and inspection of building and loan associations, and no person shall solicit business for such association, or aid it to do business, contrary to such laws, or without having complied therewith.

**HISTORY: GC § 13192; 99 v 536, § 46; Bureau of Code Revision. Eff 10-1-53.**

## § 1153.07 Civil liability for violations.

Suit under section 1.16 of the Revised Code, based on a violation of sections 1153.03 and 1153.06 of the Revised Code, may be brought against the violator and the sureties on the bond given by the violator to the savings and loan association for the faithful performance of his duty.

**HISTORY: GC § 13193; 99 v 536, § 46; Bureau of Code Revision, 10-1-53; 134 v H 511 (Eff 1-1-74); 136 v H 1 (Eff 6-13-75); 146 v S 2. Eff 7-1-96.**

The effective date is set by section 6 of SB 2.

## § 1153.99 Penalties.

(A) Whoever violates section 1153.03 of the Revised Code is guilty of a felony of the fifth degree.

(B) Whoever violates section 1153.06 of the Revised Code is guilty of a misdemeanor of the first degree.

**HISTORY: Bureau of Code Revision, 10-1-53; 134 v H 511 (Eff 1-1-74); 136 v H 1 (Eff 6-13-75); 146 v S 2. Eff 7-1-96.**

The effective date is set by section 6 of SB 2.

# TITLE 13: COMMERCIAL TRANSACTIONS — OTHER COMMERCIAL TRANSACTIONS

## CHAPTER 1315: MONEY TRANSMITTERS LAW; CHECK-CASHING BUSINESSES

Section



### [TRANSACTION REPORTING, MONEY LAUNDERING]

### § 1315.53 Duty to report transactions, keep records; money laundering prohibitions.

(A) A money transmitter that is required to file a report regarding business conducted in this state pursuant to the "Currency and Foreign Transactions Reporting Act," 84 Stat. 1118 (1970), 31 U.S.C.A. 5311 to 5326 and 31 C.F.R. part 103 or 12 C.F.R. 21.11, shall file a duplicate of that report with the attorney general.

(B) All persons engaged in a trade or business, who receive more than ten thousand dollars in money in one transaction or who receive more than ten thousand dollars in money through two or more related transactions, and who are required to file returns under 26 U.S.C.A. 6050I and 26 C.F.R. 1.6050I, shall complete and file with the attorney general the information required by 26 U.S.C.A. 6050I and C.F.R. 1.6050I.

(C) A money transmitter that is regulated under the "Currency and Foreign Transactions Reporting Act," 84 Stat. 1118 (1970), 31 U.S.C.A. 5325 and 31 C.F.R. part 103 and that is required to make available prescribed records to the secretary of the United States department of treasury upon request at any time shall follow the same prescribed procedures and create and maintain the same prescribed records relating to a transaction and shall make those records available to the attorney general on request at any time.

(D)(1) The good faith filing of a report required by this section with the appropriate federal agency shall be considered compliance with the reporting requirements of this section.

(2) This section does not preclude a money transmitter or a person engaged in a trade or business, in their discretion, from instituting contact with, and thereafter communicating with and disclosing customer financial records to, appropriate state or local law enforcement agencies if the money transmitter or person has information that may be relevant to a possible violation of a section of the Revised Code or a municipal ordinance or to the evasion or attempted evasion of a reporting requirement of this section.

(3) A money transmitter, a person engaged in a trade or business, or an officer, employee, agent, or authorized delegate of an entity or person of that nature, or a public official or governmental employee who keeps or files a record pursuant to this section or who communicates or discloses information or records under division (D)(2) of this section is not liable to its customer, a state or local agency, or a person for loss or damage caused in whole or in part by the making, filing, or governmental use of the report or of information contained in that report.

(E)(1) The attorney general may report possible violations indicated by analysis of the reports required by this section to an appropriate law enforcement agency for use in the proper discharge of its official duties. The attorney general shall provide copies of the reports required by this section to an appropriate prosecutorial or law enforcement agency upon being provided with a written request for records relating to a specific individual or entity and stating that the agency has an articulable suspicion that the specific individual or entity has committed an offense to which the reports appear to be relevant.

(2) No person shall release information received pursuant to division (E) of this section, except in the proper discharge of the person's official duties.

(F)(1) No person shall do any of the following:

(a) Purposely violate or fail to comply with this section;

(b) With the intent to conceal or disguise the fact that money or a payment instrument is the proceeds of unlawful activity, or to promote, manage, establish, carry on, or facilitate the promotion, management, establishment, or carrying on of an unlawful activity, knowingly furnish or provide to a money transmitter, a person engaged in a trade or business, an officer, employee, agent, or authorized delegate of a money transmitter or person engaged in a trade or business, or the attorney general, false, inaccurate, or incomplete information or knowingly conceal a material fact in connection with a transaction for which a report is required to be filed pursuant to this section;

(c) With the intent to conceal or disguise the fact that money or a payment instrument is the proceeds of unlawful activity, or to promote, manage, establish, carry on, or facilitate the promotion, management, establishment, or carrying on of unlawful activity, or to avoid the making or filing of a report required under this section, or to cause the making or filing of a report required under this section that contains a material omission or misstatement, conduct or structure or attempt to conduct or structure a transaction by or through one or more money transmitters or persons engaged in a trade or business.

(2) In addition to the criminal sanctions imposed under section 1315.99 of the Revised Code, the sentencing court may impose upon a person who violates division (F)(1) of this section an additional fine of three times the value of the property involved in the transaction or, if no transaction is involved, five thousand dollars. The fine shall be paid to the state treasury to the credit of the general revenue fund.

(G) Notwithstanding any other section of the Revised Code, each transaction conducted or attempted to be conducted and each exemption from reporting claimed in violation of this section constitutes a separate, punishable offense.

(H) A report, record, information, analysis, or request obtained by the attorney general or an agency pursuant to this section is not a public record subject to section 149.43 of the Revised Code and is not subject to disclosure.

**HISTORY: 146 v H 333. Eff 9-19-96.**

**Not analogous to former RC § 1315.53 (GC § 8432; 99 v 427, § 52; Bureau of Code Revision, 10-1-53), repealed 129 v S 5, § 2, eff 7-1-62.**

## § 1315.54 Investigations.

(A) The attorney general may conduct investigations within or outside this state to determine if a money transmitter or person engaged in a trade or business has failed to file a report required by section 1315.53 of the Revised Code or has engaged or is engaging in an act, practice, or transaction that constitutes a violation of a provision of sections 1315.51 to 1315.55 of the Revised Code.

(B) On request of the attorney general, a money transmitter shall make the money transmitter's books and records available to the attorney general during normal business hours for inspection and examination in connection with an investigation conducted under this section. No person shall purposely fail to comply with this division.

(C) Any record or other document or information obtained by the attorney general pursuant to an investigation conducted under this section is not a public record subject to section 149.43 of the Revised Code and is not subject to disclosure.

(D) This section does not apply to any bank, bank holding company, or affiliate of a bank or bank holding company, that is subject to examination by the comptroller of the currency, the federal reserve, or the federal deposit insurance corporation, or to any savings and loan association, savings and loan holding company, or affiliate of a savings and loan association or savings and loan holding company, that is subject to examination by the office of thrift supervision.

**HISTORY: 146 v H 333. Eff 9-19-96.**

**Not analogous to former RC § 1315.54 (GC § 8433; 99 v 427, § 53; Bureau of Code Revision, 10-1-53), repealed 129 v S 5, § 2, eff 7-1-62.**

## § 1315.55 Additional money laundering prohibitions.

(A)(1) No person shall conduct or attempt to conduct a transaction knowing that the property involved in the transaction is the proceeds of some form of unlawful activity with the purpose of committing or furthering the commission of corrupt activity.

(2) No person shall conduct or attempt to conduct a transaction knowing that the property involved in the transaction is the proceeds of some form of unlawful activity with the intent to conceal or disguise the nature, location, source, ownership, or control of the property or the intent to avoid a transaction reporting requirement under section 1315.53 of the Revised Code or federal law.

(3) No person shall conduct or attempt to conduct a transaction with the purpose to promote, manage, establish, carry on, or facilitate the promotion, management, establishment, or carrying on of corrupt activity.

(4) No person shall conduct or structure or attempt to conduct or structure a transaction that involves the proceeds of corrupt activity that is of a value greater than ten thousand dollars if the person knows or has reasonable cause to know that the transaction involves the proceeds of corrupt activity.

(5) No person shall conduct or attempt to conduct a transaction that involves what has been represented to the person by a law enforcement officer or another person at the direction of or with the approval of a law enforcement officer to be the proceeds of corrupt activity or property used to conduct or facilitate corrupt activity with the intent to promote, manage, establish, carry on, or facilitate promotion, management, establishment, or carrying on of corrupt activity, to conceal or disguise the nature, location, source, ownership, or control of the property believed to be the proceeds of corrupt activity, or to avoid a transaction reporting requirement under section 1315.53 of the Revised Code or federal law.

(B) In addition to the criminal sanctions imposed under section 1315.99 of the Revised Code, the sentencing court may impose upon a person who violates division (A) of this section an additional fine of three times the value of the property involved in the transaction. The fine shall be paid to the state treasury to the credit of the general revenue fund.

(C) For the purposes of division (A) of this section, a person shall be considered to know or have reasonable cause to know that proceeds are from corrupt activity if either of the following apply:

(1) The person knows or has reasonable cause to know that the proceeds are from some form of activity that constitutes corrupt activity, though not necessarily which form of corrupt activity;

(2) As a part of a covert investigation, a law enforcement officer in his undercover capacity represents to the person that the proceeds are from some form of activity that constitutes corrupt activity.

**HISTORY: 146 v H 333. Eff 9-19-96.**

**Not analogous to former RC § 1315.55 (GC § 8434; 99 v 427, § 54; Bureau of Code Revision, 10-1-53), repealed 129 v S 5, § 2, eff 7-1-62.**

[PENALTIES]

## § 1315.99 Penalties.

(A) Whoever violates division (A) or (B) of section 1315.28 or division (E)(2) of section 1315.53 of the Revised Code is guilty of a misdemeanor of the first degree.

(B) Whoever violates division (F)(1) of section 1315.53 or division (B) of section 1315.54 of the Revised Code is guilty of a felony of the fourth degree.

(C) Whoever violates division (A) of section 1315.55 of the Revised Code is guilty of money laundering. A violation of division (A)(1), (2), (3), (4), or (5) of that section is a felony of the third degree, and, in addition, the court may impose a fine of seven thousand five hundred dollars or twice the value of the property involved, whichever is greater.

(D) Whoever knowingly violates division (A) of section 1315.02, or intentionally violates division (B)(1) of section 1315.081 [1315.08.1], of the Revised Code is guilty of a felony of the fourth degree.

**HISTORY: RC § 1310.99, 126 v 756 (Eff 10-13-55); 137 v H 1134 (Eff 7-1-79); 144 v H 332 (Eff 10-6-92); RC § 1315.99, 144 v H 693 (Eff 11-6-92); 145 v H 266 (Eff 7-30-93); 146 v H 313 (Eff 12-5-95); 146 v H 333 (Eff 9-19-96); 146 v H 538. Eff 1-1-97; 151 v H 454, § 1, eff. 4-6-07; 152 v H 545, § 1, eff. 9-1-08.**

The provisions of § 5 of 151 v H 454 read in part as follows:

SECTION 5. * * * Section 1315.99 of the Revised Code is presented in this act as a composite of the section as amended by both Am. Sub. H.B. 333 and Am. Sub. H.B. 538 of the 121st General Assembly. The General Assembly, applying the principle stated in division (B) of section 1.52 of the Revised Code that amendments are to be harmonized if reasonably capable of simultaneous operation, finds that the composites are the resulting versions of the sections in effect prior to the effective date of the sections as presented in this act.

See Comment, Legislative Service Commission, following RC § 1315.21.

# CHAPTER 1333: TRADE PRACTICES

Section



## [PYRAMID SALES PLAN OR PROGRAM]

### § 1333.91 Definitions.

As used in sections 1333.91 to 1333.94 of the Revised Code:

(A) "Pyramid sales plan or program" means any scheme, whether or not for the disposal or distribution of property, whereby a person pays a consideration for the chance or opportunity to receive compensation, regardless of whether he also receives other rights or property, under either of the following circumstances:

(1) For introducing one or more persons into participation in the plan or program;

(2) When another participant has introduced a person into participation in the plan or program.

(B) "Compensation" means money, financial benefit, or anything of value. Compensation does not include payment based upon sales made to persons who are not participants in a pyramid sales plan or program, and who are not purchasing in order to participate in the plan or program.

(C) "Consideration" does not include:

(1) Payment for sales demonstration equipment and materials furnished at cost, whereby no profit, commission, fee, rebate or other benefit is realized by any person in the sales plan, for use in making sales and not for resale;

(2) Payment for promotional and administrative fees not to exceed twenty-five dollars when computed on an annual basis.

(D) "Participant" means a person who purchases, proposes, plans, prepares, or offers the opportunity to take part in, or advance into, a pyramid sales plan or program.

**HISTORY: 135 v H 609. Eff 9-27-74.**

### § 1333.92 Pyramid sales prohibited.

No person shall propose, plan, prepare, or operate a pyramid sales plan or program.

**HISTORY: 135 v H 609. Eff 9-27-74.**

### § 1333.93 Contract void; civil action recovery.

Any contract made in violation of section 1333.92 of the Revised Code is void. Any person who has paid consideration for the chance or opportunity to participate in a pyramid sales plan or program may recover, in a civil action, the amount of the consideration paid, together with reasonable attorney fees, from any participant who has received compensation under either of the following circumstances:

(A) For introducing the person into participation in a pyramid sales plan or program;

(B) When another participant has introduced the person into participation in a pyramid sales plan or program.

**HISTORY: 135 v H 609. Eff 9-27-74.**

### § 1333.94 Temporary restraining order.

Whenever it appears that a person is violating or about to violate section 1333.92 of the Revised Code, the attorney general may bring an action in the court of common pleas to enjoin the violation. Upon a proper showing, a temporary restraining order, or a preliminary or permanent injunction shall be granted without bond. The court may impose a penalty of not more than five thousand dollars for each day of violation of a temporary restraining order or preliminary or permanent injunction issued under this section.

**HISTORY: 135 v H 609. Eff 9-27-74.**

### § 1333.95 Additional remedies.

The remedies in sections 1333.91 to 1333.95 of the Revised Code are in addition to remedies otherwise available.

**HISTORY: 135 v H 609. Eff 9-27-74.**

## [PENALTIES]

### § 1333.99 Penalties.

(A) Whoever violates sections 1333.01 to 1333.04 of the Revised Code is guilty of a minor misdemeanor.

(B) Whoever violates section 1333.12 or 1333.71 of the Revised Code is guilty of a misdemeanor of the fourth degree.

(C) Whoever violates section 1333.36 of the Revised Code is guilty of a misdemeanor of the third degree.

(D) A prosecuting attorney may file an action to restrain any person found in violation of section 1333.36 of the Revised Code. Upon the filing of such an action, the common pleas court may receive evidence of such violation and forthwith grant a temporary restraining order as may be prayed for, pending a hearing on the merits of said cause.

(E) Whoever violates division (A)(1) of section 1333.52 or section 1333.81 of the Revised Code is guilty of a misdemeanor of the first degree.

(F) Whoever violates division (A)(2) or (B) of section 1333.52 of the Revised Code is guilty of a misdemeanor of the second degree.

(G) Except as otherwise provided in this division, whoever violates section 1333.92 of the Revised Code is guilty of a misdemeanor of the first degree. If the value of the compensation is one thousand dollars or more and less than seven thousand five hundred dollars, whoever violates section 1333.92 of the Revised Code is guilty of a felony of the fifth degree. If the value of the compensation is seven thousand five hundred dollars or more and less than one hundred fifty thousand dollars, whoever violates section 1333.92 of the Revised Code is guilty of a felony of the fourth degree. If the value of the compensation is one hundred fifty thousand dollars or more, whoever violates section 1333.92 of the Revised Code is guilty of a felony of the third degree.

**HISTORY: Bureau of Code Revision, 10-1-53; 129 v H 342 (Eff 10-24-61); 132 v H 730 (Eff 11-14-67); 134 v H 511 (Eff 1-1-74); 135 v H 609 (Eff 9-27-74); 136 v H 159 (Eff 5-10-76); 137 v H 478 (Eff 11-8-77); 137 v H 1147 (Eff 1-5-79); 139 v S 199 (Eff 7-1-83); 139 v H 269 (Eff 1-5-83); 146 v S 2. Eff 7-1-96; 150 v H 95, § 1, eff. 9-26-03; 152 v S 171, § 1, eff. 9-11-08; 2011 HB 86, § 1, eff. Sept. 30, 2011.**

The provisions of § 4 of HB 86 read as follows:

"SECTION 4. The amendments to sections 926.99, 1333.99, 1707.99, 1716.99, 2909.03, 2909.05, 2909.11, 2913.02, 2913.03, 2913.04, 2913.11, 2913.21, 2913.31, 2913.32, 2913.34, 2913.40, 2913.401, 2913.42, 2913.421, 2913.43, 2913.45, 2913.46, 2913.47, 2913.48, 2913.49, 2913.51, 2913.61, 2915.05, 2917.21, 2917.31, 2917.32, 2921.13, 2921.41, 2923.31, and 2981.07, division (B) of section 2929.13, and division (A) of section 2929.14 of the Revised Code that are made in this act apply to a person who commits an offense specified or penalized under those sections on or after the effective date of this section and to a person to whom division (B) of section 1.58 of the Revised Code makes the amendments applicable.

"The provisions of sections 926.99, 1333.99, 1707.99, 1716.99, 2909.03, 2909.05, 2909.11, 2913.02, 2913.03, 2913.04, 2913.11, 2913.21, 2913.31, 2913.32, 2913.34, 2913.40, 2913.401, 2913.42, 2913.421, 2913.43, 2913.45, 2913.46, 2913.47, 2913.48, 2913.49, 2913.51, 2913.61, 2915.05, 2917.21, 2917.31, 2917.32, 2921.13, 2921.41, 2923.31, and 2981.07 of the Revised Code in existence prior to the effective date of this section shall apply to a person upon whom a court imposed sentence prior to the effective date of this section for an offense specified or penalized under those sections. The amendments to sections 926.99, 1333.99, 1707.99, 1716.99, 2909.03, 2909.05, 2909.11, 2913.02, 2913.03, 2913.04, 2913.11, 2913.21, 2913.31, 2913.32, 2913.34, 2913.40, 2913.401, 2913.42, 2913.421, 2913.43, 2913.45, 2913.46, 2913.47, 2913.48, 2913.49, 2913.51, 2913.61, 2915.05, 2917.21, 2917.31, 2917.32, 2921.13, 2921.41, 2923.31, and 2981.07 of the Revised Code that are made in this act do not apply to a person who upon whom a court imposed sentence prior to the effective date of this section for an offense specified or penalized under those sections."

The effective date is set by section 179 of H.B. 95 (150 v —).

# CHAPTER 1345: CONSUMER SALES PRACTICES

Section



## § 1345.02 Unfair or deceptive consumer sales practices prohibited.

(A) No supplier shall commit an unfair or deceptive act or practice in connection with a consumer transaction. Such an unfair or deceptive act or practice by a supplier violates this section whether it occurs before, during, or after the transaction.

(B) Without limiting the scope of division (A) of this section, the act or practice of a supplier in representing any of the following is deceptive:

(1) That the subject of a consumer transaction has sponsorship, approval, performance characteristics, accessories, uses, or benefits that it does not have;

(2) That the subject of a consumer transaction is of a particular standard, quality, grade, style, prescription, or model, if it is not;

(3) That the subject of a consumer transaction is new, or unused, if it is not;

(4) That the subject of a consumer transaction is available to the consumer for a reason that does not exist;

(5) That the subject of a consumer transaction has been supplied in accordance with a previous representation, if it has not, except that the act of a supplier in furnishing similar merchandise of equal or greater value as a good faith substitute does not violate this section;

(6) That the subject of a consumer transaction will be supplied in greater quantity than the supplier intends;

(7) That replacement or repair is needed, if it is not;

(8) That a specific price advantage exists, if it does not;

(9) That the supplier has a sponsorship, approval, or affiliation that the supplier does not have;

(10) That a consumer transaction involves or does not involve a warranty, a disclaimer of warranties or other rights, remedies, or obligations if the representation is false.

(C) In construing division (A) of this section, the court shall give due consideration and great weight to federal trade commission orders, trade regulation rules and guides, and the federal courts' interpretations of subsection 45(a)(1) of the "Federal Trade Commission Act," 38 Stat. 717 (1914), 15 U.S.C.A. 41, as amended.

(D) No supplier shall offer to a consumer or represent that a consumer will receive a rebate, discount, or other benefit as an inducement for entering into a consumer transaction in return for giving the supplier the names of prospective consumers, or otherwise helping the supplier to enter into other consumer transactions, if earning the benefit is contingent upon an event occurring after the consumer enters into the transaction.

(E)(1) No supplier, in connection with a consumer transaction involving natural gas service or public telecommunications service to a consumer in this state, shall request or submit, or cause to be requested or submitted, a change in the consumer's provider of natural gas service or public telecommunications service, without first obtaining, or causing to be obtained, the verified consent of the consumer. For the purpose of this division and with respect to public telecommunications service only, the procedures necessary for verifying the consent of a consumer shall be those prescribed by rule by the public utilities commission for public telecommunications service under division (D) of section 4905.72 of the Revised Code. Also, for the purpose of this division, the act, omission, or failure of any officer, agent, or other individual, acting for or employed by another person, while acting within the scope of that authority or employment, is the act or failure of that other person.

(2) Consistent with the exclusion, under 47 C.F.R. 64.1100(a)(3), of commercial mobile radio service providers from the verification requirements adopted in 47 C.F.R. 64.1100, 64.1150, 64.1160, 64.1170, 64.1180, and 64.1190 by the federal communications commission, division (E)(1) of this section does not apply to a provider of commercial mobile radio service insofar as such provider is engaged in the provision of commercial mobile radio service. However, when that exclusion no longer is in effect, division (E)(1) of this section shall apply to such a provider.

(3) The attorney general may initiate criminal proceedings for a prosecution under division (C) of section 1345.99 of the Revised Code by presenting evidence of criminal violations to the prosecuting attorney of any county in which the offense may be prosecuted. If the prosecuting attorney does not prosecute the violations, or at the request of the prosecuting attorney, the attorney general may proceed in the prosecution with all the rights, privileges, and powers conferred by law on prosecuting attorneys, including the power to appear before grand juries and to interrogate witnesses before grand juries.

(F) Concerning a consumer transaction in connection with a residential mortgage, and without limiting the scope of division (A) or (B) of this section, the act of a supplier in doing either of the following is deceptive:

(1) Knowingly failing to provide disclosures required under state and federal law;

(2) Knowingly providing a disclosure that includes a material misrepresentation.

**HISTORY: 134 v H 103 (Eff 7-14-72); 137 v H 681 (Eff 8-11-78); 148 v H 177. Eff 5-17-2000; 151 v S 185, § 1, eff. 1-1-07.**

## [NATURAL GAS AND PUBLIC TELECOMMUNICATIONS SERVICE PROVIDER CHANGES]

### § 1345.18 Consumer's prior, verified consent required to switch natural gas or public telecommunications service provider.

(A) As used in this section:

(1) "Consumer," "person," and "supplier" have the same meanings as in section 1345.01 of the Revised Code.

(2) "Consumer transaction" has the same meaning as in section 1345.01 of the Revised Code except that the sale, lease, assignment, award by chance, or other transfer of an item of goods, a service, a franchise, or an intangible, or solicitation to supply any of those things, to an individual is for purposes that are primarily other than personal, family, or household.

(3) "Natural gas service" means the sale of natural gas, exclusive of any distribution or ancillary service.

(4) "Public telecommunications service" means the transmission by electromagnetic or other means, other than by a telephone company as defined in section 4927.01 of the Revised Code, of signs, signals, writings, images, sounds, messages, or data originating in this state regardless of actual call routing. "Public telecommunications service" excludes a system, including its construction, maintenance, or operation, for the provision of telecommunications service, or any portion of such service, by any entity for the sole and exclusive use of that entity, its parent, a subsidiary, or an affiliated entity, and not for resale, directly or indirectly; the provision of terminal equipment used to originate telecommunications service; broadcast transmission by radio, television, or satellite broadcast stations regulated by the federal government; or cable television service.

(B)(1) No supplier, in connection with a consumer transaction involving natural gas service or public telecommunications service to a consumer in this state, shall request or submit, or cause to be requested or submitted, a change in the consumer's provider of natural gas service or public telecommunications service, without first obtaining, or causing to be obtained, the verified consent of the consumer. For the purpose of this division and with respect to public telecommunications service only, the procedures necessary for verifying the consent of a consumer shall be those prescribed by rule by the public utilities commission for public telecommunications service under division (D) of section 4905.72 of the Revised Code. Also, for the purpose of this division, the act, omission, or failure of any officer, agent, or other individual, acting for or employed by another person, while acting within the scope of that authority or employment, is the act or failure of that other person.

(2) Consistent with the exclusion, under 47 C.F.R. 64.1100(a)(3), of commercial mobile radio service providers from the verification requirements adopted in 47 C.F.R. 64.1100, 64.1150, 64.1160, 64.1170, 64.1180, and 64.1190 by the federal communications commission, division (B)(1) of this section does not apply to a provider of commercial mobile radio service insofar as such provider is engaged in the provision of commercial mobile radio service. However, when that exclusion no longer is in effect, division (B)(1) of this section shall apply to such a provider.

**HISTORY: 148 v H 177. Eff 5-17-2000.**

## [HOME SOLICITATION SALE]

### § 1345.23 Writing required; contents, warning.

(A) Every home solicitation shall be evidenced by a written agreement or offer to purchase in the same language as that principally used in the oral sales presentation and shall contain the name and address of the seller. The seller shall present the writing to the buyer and obtain the buyer's signature to it. The writing shall state the date on which the buyer actually signs. The seller shall leave with the buyer a copy of the writing which has been signed by the seller and complies with division (B) of this section.

(B) In connection with every home solicitation sale:

(1) The following statement shall appear clearly and conspicuously on the copy of the contract left with the buyer in bold-face type of the minimum size of ten points, in substantially the following form and in immediate proximity to the space reserved in the contract for the signature of the buyer: "You, the buyer, may cancel this transaction at any time prior to midnight of the third business day after the date of this transaction. See the attached notice of cancellation for an explanation of this right."

(2) A completed form, in duplicate, captioned "notice of cancellation", shall be attached to the contract signed by the buyer and be easily detachable, and shall contain in ten-point, boldface type, the following information and statements in the same language as that used in the contract:

NOTICE OF CANCELLATION

(enter date of transaction)

.......................................

(Date)

You may cancel this transaction, without any penalty or obligation, within three business days from the above date.

If you cancel, any property traded in, any payments made by you under the contract or sale, and any negotiable instrument executed by you will be returned within ten business days following receipt by the seller of your cancellation notice, and any security interest arising out of the transaction will be cancelled. If you cancel, you must make available to the seller at your residence, in substantially as good condition as when received, any goods delivered to you under this contract or sale; or you may if you wish, comply with the instructions of the seller regarding the return shipment of the goods at the seller's expense and risk.

If you do make the goods available to the seller and the seller does not pick them up within twenty days of the date of your notice of cancellation, you may retain or dispose of the goods without any further obligation. If you fail to make the goods available to the seller, or if you agree to return the goods to the seller and fail to do so, then you remain liable for performance of all obligations under the contract.

To cancel this transaction, mail or deliver a signed and dated copy of this cancellation notice or any other written notice, or send a telegram, to (Name of seller), at (address of seller's place of business)

.................. ..................

not later than midnight of...............................

(Date)

I hereby cancel this transaction.

..................................

(Date)

(Buyer's signature)

...........................................

(3) Before furnishing copies of the notice of cancellation to the buyer, the seller shall complete both copies by entering the name of the seller, the address of the seller's place of business, the date of the transaction which is the date the buyer signed the contract and the date, not earlier than the third business day following the date of the transaction, by which the buyer may give notice of cancellation.

(4) A home solicitation sales contract which contains the notice of buyer's right to cancel and notice of cancellation in the form and language provided in the federal trade commission's trade regulation rule providing a cooling-off period for door-to-door sales shall be deemed to comply with the requirements of divisions (B)(1), (2), and (3) of this section with respect to the form and language of such notices so long as the federal trade commission language provides at least equal information to the consumer concerning his right to cancel as is required by divisions (B)(1), (2), and (3) of this section.

(C) Until the seller has complied with divisions (A) and (B) of this section the buyer may cancel the home solicitation sale by notifying the seller by mailing, delivering, or telegraphing written notice to the seller of his intention to cancel. The three day period prescribed by section 1345.22 of the Revised Code begins to run from the time the seller complies with divisions (A) and (B) of this section.

(D) In connection with any home solicitation sale, no seller shall:

(1) Include in any home solicitation sales contract, any confession of judgment or any waiver of any rights to which the buyer is entitled under this section, including specifically his right to cancel the sale in accordance with this section.

(2) Fail to inform each buyer orally, at the time he signs the contract for the goods or services, of his right to cancel.

(3) Misrepresent in any manner the buyer's right to cancel.

(4) Fail or refuse to honor any valid notice of cancellation by a buyer and within ten business days after receipt of such notice to:

(a) Refund all payments made under the contract or sale;

(b) Return any goods or property traded in, in substantially as good condition as when received by the seller;

(c) Cancel and return any note, negotiable instrument, or other evidence of indebtedness executed by the buyer in connection with the contract or sale and take any action necessary or appropriate to reflect the termination of any security interest or lien created under the sale or offer to purchase.

(5) Negotiate, transfer, sell, or assign any note or other evidence of indebtedness to a finance company or other third party prior to midnight of the fifth business day following the day the contract for the goods or services was signed.

(6) Fail to notify the buyer, within ten business days of receipt of the buyer's notice of cancellation, whether the seller intends to repossess or abandon any shipped or delivered goods.

**HISTORY: 134 v 24 (Eff 1-1-73); 135 v H 241. Eff 9-30-74.**

## § 1345.24 Seller to retain notice of cancellation.

In a home solicitation sale, the seller shall retain, for the period in which an action to enforce the sale could be commenced, any notice of cancellation made pursuant to section 1345.22 of the Revised Code. The seller shall also retain the envelope in which any notice of cancellation is sent or delivered. If the date of delivery is not indicated or recorded on the notice of cancellation or on the envelope, the seller shall record the date of delivery on the notice of cancellation.

**HISTORY: 134 v S 24 (Eff 1-1-73); 135 v H 241. Eff 9-30-74.**

[PENALTIES]

## § 1345.99 Penalties.

(A) Whoever violates section 1345.23 or 1345.24 of the Revised Code is guilty of a minor misdemeanor.

(B) Whoever violates division (D) of section 1345.76 of the Revised Code shall be fined not more than one thousand dollars.

(C) Whoever knowingly violates division (E) of section 1345.02 or knowingly violates section 1345.18 of the Revised Code is guilty of a misdemeanor of the third degree for a first offense and a misdemeanor of the second degree for any subsequent offense.

**HISTORY: 134 v S 24 (Eff 1-1-73); 135 v H 241 (Eff 9-30-74); 148 v H 21 (Eff 9-15-99); 148 v H 177. Eff 5-17-2000.**

# CHAPTER 1349: CONSUMER PROTECTION

Section



## § 1349.06 Records of person offering new and unused personal property for sale at flea market or other location.

(A) As used in this section, "flea market" has the same meaning as in section 3715.52 of the Revised Code.

(B)(1) Each person that offers new and unused personal property for sale to the general public at a flea market or other location shall maintain, in accordance with division (B) of this section, a record of the person's purchases of that property.

For each purchase transaction, the record shall include at least all of the following:

(a) The date of the transaction;

(b) The name and address of the individual from whom, or the entity from which, the property was purchased;

(c) A full and accurate description of the property purchased, including any identifying letters or marks on the property;

(d) The price paid for the property.

(2) With respect to a single purchase of property for five hundred dollars or more, a bill of sale associated with the purchase that contains the information listed in division (B)(1) of this section is sufficient to satisfy the requirements of that division.

(3) The record of each purchase transaction shall be maintained for at least two years.

(C) No person shall do any of the following:

(1) Knowingly falsify, obliterate, or destroy the record required to be maintained by this section;

(2) Knowingly refuse or otherwise fail, upon the request of a law enforcement officer, to make the record required to be maintained by this section available for inspection within a period of time that is reasonable under the circumstances surrounding the request. Nothing in division (C)(2) of this section requires that a law enforcement officer be given immediate access to the record without reasonable notice.

(3) Fail to comply with this section.

(D)(1) If the record required to be maintained by this section is lost, stolen, or destroyed, and the circumstances surrounding the loss, theft, or destruction do not constitute a violation of division (C)(1), (2), or (3) of this section, the person shall do both of the following:

(a) Within thirty days after the loss, theft, or destruction, give notice of the loss, theft, or destruction to the sheriff of the county in which the person's principal residence in this state or principal place of business in this state is located;

(b) Immediately begin maintaining a new record as required by this section.

(2) A person that notifies the sheriff in accordance with division (D)(1) of this section is in compliance with division (B) of this section as to the record that was lost, stolen, or destroyed and is a subject of the notice.

(E) This section does not apply to any of the following:

(1) The sale of a motor vehicle, trailer, or semitrailer that is required to be registered under Chapter 4503. of the Revised Code or for which a certificate of title is required under Chapter 4505. of the Revised Code;

(2) The sale of food products, agricultural products, or forestry products;

(3) Any business conducted at an industry or association trade show;

(4) The sale of handmade or handcrafted items by the individual who produced the items.

**HISTORY: 148 v S 64. Eff 10-29-99.**

The provisions of § 3 of SB 64 (148 v —) read as follows:
SECTION 3. Section 1349.06 of the Revised Code, as enacted

by this act, shall apply to all new and unused personal property that a person on or after the effective date of this act purchases for sale to the general public.

### § 1349.17 Restrictions on recording credit card, telephone or social security numbers.

(A) No person shall record or cause to be recorded either of the following:

(1) A credit card account number of the other party to a transaction, when a check, bill of exchange, or other draft is presented for payment;

(2) The telephone number or social security account number of the other party to a transaction, when payment is made by credit card charge agreement, check, bill of exchange, or other draft.

(B) Division (A) of this section does not apply to a transaction, if all of the following conditions are met:

(1) The credit card account number, social security account number, or telephone number is recorded for a legitimate business purpose, including collection purposes.

(2) The other party to the transaction consents to the recording of the credit card account number, social security account number, or telephone number.

(3) The credit card account number, social security account number, or telephone number that is recorded during the course of the transaction is not disclosed to any third party for any purposes other than collection purposes and is not used to market goods or services unrelated to the goods or services purchased in the transaction.

(C) Nothing in this section prohibits the recording of the number of a credit card account when given in lieu of a deposit to secure payment in the event of default, loss, damage, or other occurrence, or requires a person to accept a check presented for payment, if the other party to the transaction refuses to consent to the recording of the number of the party's social security account or license to operate a motor vehicle.

**HISTORY: 144 v H 20 (Eff 8-20-91); 145 v H 266. Eff 7-30-93.**

## [DISCLOSURE OR NOTIFICATION OF BREACH OF SECURITY OF PERSONAL INFORMATION SYSTEM]

### § 1349.19 Disclosure or notification of breach of security of computerized personal information system.

(A) As used in this section:

(1)(a) "Breach of the security of the system" means unauthorized access to and acquisition of computerized data that compromises the security or confidentiality of personal information owned or licensed by a person and that causes, reasonably is believed to have caused, or reasonably is believed will cause a material risk of identity theft or other fraud to the person or property of a resident of this state.

(b) For purposes of division (A)(1)(a) of this section:

(i) Good faith acquisition of personal information by an employee or agent of the person for the purposes of the person is not a breach of the security of the system, provided that the personal information is not used for an unlawful purpose or subject to further unauthorized disclosure.

(ii) Acquisition of personal information pursuant to a search warrant, subpoena, or other court order, or pursuant to a subpoena, order, or duty of a regulatory state agency, is not a breach of the security of the system.

(2) "Business entity" means a sole proprietorship, partnership, corporation, association, or other group, however organized and whether operating for profit or not for profit, including a financial institution organized, chartered, or holding a license authorizing operation under the laws of this state, any other state, the United States, or any other country, or the parent or subsidiary of a financial institution.

(3) "Consumer reporting agency that compiles and maintains files on consumers on a nationwide basis" means a consumer reporting agency that regularly engages in the practice of assembling or evaluating, and maintaining, for the purpose of furnishing consumer reports to third parties bearing on a consumer's creditworthiness, credit standing, or credit capacity, each of the following regarding consumers residing nationwide:

(a) Public record information;

(b) Credit account information from persons who furnish that information regularly and in the ordinary course of business.

(4) "Encryption" means the use of an algorithmic process to transform data into a form in which there is a low probability of assigning meaning without use of a confidential process or key.

(5) "Individual" means a natural person.

(6) "Person" has the same meaning as in section 1.59 of the Revised Code, except that "person" includes a business entity only if the business entity conducts business in this state.

(7)(a) "Personal information" means an individual's name, consisting of the individual's first name or first initial and last name, in combination with and linked to any one or more of the following data elements, when the data elements are not encrypted, redacted, or altered by any method or technology in such a manner that the data elements are unreadable:

(i) Social security number;

(ii) Driver's license number or state identification card number;

(iii) Account number or credit or debit card number, in combination with and linked to any required security code, access code, or password that would permit access to an individual's financial account.

(b) "Personal information" does not include publicly available information that is lawfully made available to the general public from federal, state, or local government records or any of the following media that are widely distributed:

(i) Any news, editorial, or advertising statement published in any bona fide newspaper, journal, or magazine, or broadcast over radio or television;

(ii) Any gathering or furnishing of information or news by any bona fide reporter, correspondent, or news bureau to news media described in division (A)(7)(b)(i) of this section;

(iii) Any publication designed for and distributed to members of any bona fide association or charitable or fraternal nonprofit corporation;

(iv) Any type of media similar in nature to any item, entity, or activity identified in division (A)(7)(b)(i), (ii), or (iii) of this section.

(8) "Record" means any information that is stored in an electronic medium and is retrievable in perceivable form. "Record" does not include any publicly available directory containing information an individual voluntarily has consented to have publicly disseminated or listed, such as name, address, or telephone number.

(9) "Redacted" means altered or truncated so that no more than the last four digits of a social security number, driver's license number, state identification card number, account number, or credit or debit card number is accessible as part of the data.

(10) "System" means any collection or group of related records that are kept in an organized manner, that are maintained by a person, and from which personal information is retrieved by the name of the individual or by some identifying number, symbol, or other identifier assigned to the individual. "System" does not include any published directory, any reference material or newsletter, or any routine information that is maintained for the purpose of internal office administration of the person, if the use of the directory, material, newsletter, or information would not adversely affect an individual, and there has been no unauthorized external breach of the directory, material, newsletter, or information.

(B)(1) Any person that owns or licenses computerized data that includes personal information shall disclose any breach of the security of the system, following its discovery or notification of the breach of the security of the system, to any resident of this state whose personal information was, or reasonably is believed to have been, accessed and acquired by an unauthorized person if the access and acquisition by the unauthorized person causes or reasonably is believed will cause a material risk of identity theft or other fraud to the resident. The disclosure described in this division may be made pursuant to any provision of a contract entered into by the person with another person prior to the date the breach of the security of the system occurred if that contract does not conflict with any provision of this section and does not waive any provision of this section. For purposes of this section, a resident of this state is an individual whose principal mailing address as reflected in the records of the person is in this state.

(2) The person shall make the disclosure described in division (B)(1) of this section in the most expedient time possible but not later than forty-five days following its discovery or notification of the breach in the security of the system, subject to the legitimate needs of law enforcement activities described in division (D) of this section and consistent with any measures necessary to determine the scope of the breach, including which residents' personal information was accessed and acquired, and to restore the reasonable integrity of the data system.

(C) Any person that, on behalf of or at the direction of another person or on behalf of or at the direction of any governmental entity, is the custodian of or stores computerized data that includes personal information shall notify that other person or governmental entity of any breach of the security of the system in an expeditious manner, if the personal information was, or reasonably is believed to have been, accessed and acquired by an unauthorized person and if the access and acquisition by the unauthorized person causes or reasonably is believed will cause a material risk of identity theft or other fraud to a resident of this state.

(D) The person may delay the disclosure or notification required by division (B), (C), or (G) of this section if a law enforcement agency determines that the disclosure or notification will impede a criminal investigation or jeopardize homeland or national security, in which case, the person shall make the disclosure or notification after the law enforcement agency determines that disclosure or notification will not compromise the investigation or jeopardize homeland or national security.

(E) For purposes of this section, a person may disclose or make a notification by any of the following methods:

(1) Written notice;

(2) Electronic notice, if the person's primary method of communication with the resident to whom the disclosure must be made is by electronic means;

(3) Telephone notice;

(4) Substitute notice in accordance with this division, if the person required to disclose demonstrates that the person does not have sufficient contact information to provide notice in a manner described in division (E)(1), (2), or (3) of this section, or that the cost of providing disclosure or notice to residents to whom disclosure or notification is required would exceed two hundred fifty thousand dollars, or that the affected class of subject residents to whom disclosure or notification is required exceeds five hundred thousand persons. Substitute notice under this division shall consist of all of the following:

(a) Electronic mail notice if the person has an electronic mail address for the resident to whom the disclosure must be made;

(b) Conspicuous posting of the disclosure or notice on the person's web site, if the person maintains one;

(c) Notification to major media outlets, to the extent that the cumulative total of the readership, viewing audience, or listening audience of all of the outlets so notified equals or exceeds seventy-five per cent of the population of this state.

(5) Substitute notice in accordance with this division, if the person required to disclose demonstrates that the person is a business entity with ten employees or fewer and that the cost of providing the disclosures or notices to residents to whom disclosure or notification is required will exceed ten thousand dollars. Substitute notice under this division shall consist of all of the following:

(a) Notification by a paid advertisement in a local newspaper that is distributed in the geographic area in which the business entity is located, which advertisement shall be of sufficient size that it covers at least one-quarter of a page in the newspaper and shall be published in the newspaper at least once a week for three consecutive weeks;

(b) Conspicuous posting of the disclosure or notice on the business entity's web site, if the entity maintains one;

(c) Notification to major media outlets in the geographic area in which the business entity is located.

(F)(1) A financial institution, trust company, or credit union or any affiliate of a financial institution, trust company, or credit union that is required by federal law, including, but not limited to, any federal statute, regulation, regulatory guidance, or other regulatory action, to notify its customers of an information security breach with respect to information about those customers and that is subject to examination by its functional government regulatory agency for compliance with the applicable federal law, is exempt from the requirements of this section.

(2) This section does not apply to any person or entity that is a covered entity as defined in 45 C.F.R. 160.103, as amended.

(G) If a person discovers circumstances that require disclosure under this section to more than one thousand residents of this state involved in a single occurrence of a breach of the security of the system, the person shall notify, without unreasonable delay, all consumer reporting agencies that compile and maintain files on consumers on a nationwide basis of the timing, distribution, and content of the disclosure given by the person to the residents of this state. In no case shall a person that is required to make a notification required by this division delay any disclosure or notification required by division (B) or (C) of this section in order to make the notification required by this division.

(H) Any waiver of this section is contrary to public policy and is void and unenforceable.

(I) The attorney general may conduct pursuant to sections 1349.191 [1349.19.1] and 1349.192 [1349.19.2] of the Revised Code an investigation and bring a civil action upon an alleged failure by a person to comply with the requirements of this section.

**HISTORY: 151 v H 104, § 1, eff. 2-17-06; 151 v S 126, § 1, eff. 3-30-07.**

See provisions of § 3 of 151 v H 104 following RC § 1347.12.

## § 1349.191 Investigation by attorney general.

(A) As used in this section and section 1349.192 [1349.19.2] of the Revised Code:

(1) "Agency of a political subdivision" has the same meaning as in section 1347.12 of the Revised Code.

(2) "Business" has the same meaning as in section 1349.19 of the Revised Code.

(3) "State agency" has the same meaning as in section 1.60 of the Revised Code.

(B) The attorney general may conduct an investigation if the attorney general, based on complaints or the attorney general's own inquiries, has reason to believe that a state agency or an agency of a political subdivision has failed or is failing to comply with section 1347.12 of the Revised Code or that a person has failed or is failing to comply with section 1349.19 of the Revised Code.

(C) In any investigation conducted pursuant to this section, the attorney general may administer oaths, subpoena witnesses, adduce evidence, and subpoena the production of any book, document, record, or other relevant matter.

(D)(1) If the attorney general under division (C) of this section subpoenas the production of any relevant matter that is located outside this state, the attorney general may designate a representative, including an official of the state in which that relevant matter is located, to inspect the relevant matter on the attorney general's behalf. The attorney general may carry out similar requests received from officials of other states.

(2) Any person who is subpoenaed to produce relevant matter pursuant to division (C) of this section shall make that relevant matter available at a convenient location within this state or the state of the representative designated under division (D)(1) of this section.

(E) Any person who is subpoenaed as a witness or to produce relevant matter pursuant to division (C) of this section may file in the court of common pleas of Franklin county, the county in this state in which the person resides, or the county in this state in which the person's principal place of business is located a petition to extend for good cause shown the date on which the subpoena is to be returned or to modify or quash for good cause shown that subpoena. The person may file the petition at any time prior to the date specified for the return of the subpoena or within twenty days after the service of the subpoena, whichever is earlier.

(F) Any person who is subpoenaed as a witness or to produce relevant matter pursuant to division (C) of this section shall comply with the terms of the subpoena unless the court orders otherwise prior to the date specified for the return of the subpoena or, if applicable, that date as extended. If a person fails without lawful excuse to obey a subpoena, the attorney general may apply to the court of common pleas for an order that does one or more of the following:

(1) Compels the requested discovery;

(2) Adjudges the person in contempt of court;

(3) Grants injunctive relief to restrain the person from failing to comply with section 1347.12 or 1349.19 of the Revised Code, whichever is applicable;

(4) Grants injunctive relief to preserve or restore the status quo;

(5) Grants other relief that may be required until the person obeys the subpoena.

(G) The court shall impose a civil penalty on any person who violates an order of a court issued under division (F) of this section in the same manner as the imposition of a civil penalty under section 1349.192 [1349.19.2] of the Revised Code for a failure to comply with section 1347.12 or 1349.19 of the Revised Code, whichever is applicable.

**HISTORY: 151 v H 104, § 1, eff. 2-17-06.**

See provisions of § 3 of 151 v H 104 following RC § 1347.12.

## § 1349.192 Civil action by attorney general; penalties; liability for costs of investigation and action.

(A)(1) The attorney general shall have the exclusive authority to bring a civil action in a court of common pleas for appropriate relief under this section, including a temporary restraining order, preliminary or permanent injunction, and civil penalties, if it appears that a state agency or an agency of a political subdivision has failed or is failing to comply with section 1347.12 of the Revised Code or that a person has failed or is failing to comply with section 1349.19 of the Revised Code. Upon its finding that a state agency or an agency of a political subdivision has failed to comply with section 1347.12 of the Revised Code or that a person has failed to comply with section 1349.19 of the Revised Code, the court shall impose a civil penalty upon the state agency, agency of a political subdivision, or person as follows:

(a) For each day that the state agency, agency of a political subdivision, or person has intentionally or recklessly failed to comply with the applicable section, subject to divisions (A)(1)(b) and (c) of this section, a civil penalty of up to one thousand dollars for each day the agency or person fails to comply with the section;

(b) If the state agency, agency of a political subdivision, or person has intentionally or recklessly failed to comply with the applicable section for more than sixty days, subject to division (A)(1)(c) of this section, a civil penalty in the amount specified in division (A)(1)(a) of this section for each day of the first sixty days that the agency or person fails to comply with the section and, for each day commencing with the sixty-first day that the state agency, agency of a political subdivision, or person has failed to comply with the section, a civil penalty of up to five thousand dollars for each such day the agency or person fails to comply with the section;

(c) If the state agency, agency of a political subdivision, or person has intentionally or recklessly failed to comply with the applicable section for more than ninety days, a civil penalty in the amount specified in division (A)(1)(a) of this section for each day of the first sixty days that the agency or person fails to comply with the section, a civil penalty of up to five thousand dollars for each day commencing with the sixty-first day and continuing through the ninetieth day that the agency or person fails to comply with the section, and, for each day commencing with the ninety-first day that the state agency, agency of a political subdivision, or person has failed to comply with the section, a civil penalty of up to ten thousand dollars for each such day the agency or person fails to comply with the section.

(2) Any civil penalty that is assessed under division (A)(1) of this section shall be deposited into the consumer protection enforcement fund created by section 1345.51 of the Revised Code.

(3) In determining the appropriate civil penalty to assess under division (A)(1) of this section, the court shall consider all relevant factors, including the following:

(a) If the defendant in the civil action is a state agency, an agency of a political subdivision, or a person that is a business entity, whether or not the high managerial officer, agent, or employee of the agency or business entity having supervisory responsibility for compliance with section 1347.12 or 1349.19 of the Revised Code, whichever is applicable, acted in bad faith in failing to comply with the section.

(b) If the defendant in the civil action is a person other than a business entity, whether or not the person acted in bad faith in failing to comply with section 1349.19 of the Revised Code.

(B) Any state agency or agency of a political subdivision that is found by the court to have failed to comply with section 1347.12 of the Revised Code or any person that is found by the court to have failed to comply with section 1349.19 of the Revised Code shall be liable to the attorney general for the attorney general's costs in conducting an investigation under section 1349.191 [1349.19.1] of the Revised Code and bringing an action under this section.

(C) The rights and remedies that are provided under this section are in addition to any other rights or remedies that are provided by law.

**HISTORY: 151 v H 104, § 1, eff. 2-17-06.**

See provisions of § 3 of 151 v H 104 following RC § 1347.12.

## [CONSUMER REPORTING AGENCY INSURANCE DISCLOSURES]

### § 1349.51 Consumer reporting agency not to disclose certain information obtained from insurance inquiry; indemnification of agents.

(A) As used in this section:

(1) "Consumer report" and "consumer reporting agency" have the same meanings as in the "Fair Credit Reporting Act," 84 Stat. 1128 (1970), 15 U.S.C.A. 1681a, as amended.

(2) "Licensed resident insurance agent" means any natural person or business entity licensed as a resident insurance agent under section 3905.06 of the Revised Code.

(B) No consumer reporting agency shall sell or otherwise furnish any information relative to an individual's insurance coverage that was submitted, in whole or in part, in conjunction with an insurance company's inquiry into an individual's credit history or request for a consumer report. This information includes, but is not limited to, the expiration date of an insurance policy, information that may be used to find a policy's expiration date or approximate expiration date, and the terms and conditions of an insurance policy.

(C) Division (B) of this section does not prohibit a consumer reporting agency from furnishing information relative to an individual's insurance coverage to the agent or producer that supplied the information.

(D) Division (B) of this section does not prohibit a consumer reporting agency from furnishing information relative to an individual's insurance coverage to an insurance company, the insurer's affiliates, or members of a holding company in which the insurer is a member, if the information was supplied by an agent or producer acting on behalf of the insurer.

(E) Nothing in this section shall be construed to prohibit an insurance company from obtaining a claims history or motor vehicle report.

(F) An insurance company shall indemnify, defend, and hold harmless its licensed resident insurance agent from and against all liability, damages, fees, and costs arising out of or relating to the actions, errors, or omissions of its licensed resident insurance agent resulting from the use of credit information or insurance scores for the insurance company, provided that its licensed resident insurance agent follows the procedures and instructions established by the insurance company for its licensed resident insurance agent, works within the authority granted by the insurance company to its licensed resident insurance agent, and complies with all applicable laws and regulations. Nothing in this section shall be construed to provide a consumer or insured with a cause of action that does not exist in the absence of this section.

**HISTORY: 150 v S 151, § 1, eff. 9-23-04.**

## [SECURITY FREEZES ON CONSUMER CREDIT REPORTS]

### § 1349.52 Consumer may elect to place security freeze on credit report.

(A) As used in this section:

(1) "Consumer credit reporting agency" means any person that, for monetary fees, dues, or on a cooperative nonprofit basis, regularly engages in whole or in part in the practice of maintaining consumers' credit information for the purpose of furnishing credit reports to third parties.

(2) "Credit report" means any written, oral, or other communication of any credit information by a consumer credit reporting agency that operates or maintains a database of consumer credit information bearing on a consumer's credit worthiness, credit standing, or credit capacity.

(3) "Security freeze" means a restriction placed in a consumer's credit report at the request of the consumer that prohibits a consumer credit reporting agency from releasing all or any part of the consumer's credit report or

any information derived from the consumer's credit report relating to the extension of credit without the express authorization of the consumer.

(4) "Other comparable service" means a service for which a receipt of delivery is provided.

(B) A consumer may elect to place a security freeze on the consumer's credit report by making a request to a consumer credit reporting agency in writing by certified mail or other comparable service or by any secured electronic method authorized by the consumer credit reporting agency.

(C) A consumer credit reporting agency shall place a security freeze on a credit report not later than three business days after receiving a request pursuant to division (B) of this section. The consumer credit reporting agency shall send a written confirmation of the security freeze to the consumer within five business days of placing the security freeze and, at the same time, shall provide the consumer with a unique personal identification number or password. The number or password shall not be the consumer's social security number.

(D) A consumer may allow the consumer's credit report to be accessed for a specific party or period of time while a security freeze is in place by contacting the consumer credit reporting agency by certified mail or other comparable service, secure electronic method selected by the consumer credit reporting agency, or telephone and requesting that the security freeze be temporarily lifted, and providing all of the following:

(1) Information generally considered sufficient to identify the consumer;

(2) The unique personal identification number or password provided by the consumer credit reporting agency pursuant to division (C) of this section;

(3) The proper information regarding the third party who is to receive the consumer credit report or the time period for which the consumer credit report shall be available to users of the credit report.

(E)(1) A consumer credit reporting agency that receives a request in writing by certified mail or other comparable service from a consumer to temporarily lift a security freeze on a credit report pursuant to division (D) of this section shall comply with the request not later than three business days after receiving the request.

(2) Except as otherwise provided in this section, a consumer credit reporting agency that receives a request by secure electronic method selected by the consumer credit reporting agency, telephone, or another means authorized by the consumer credit reporting agency from a consumer to temporarily lift a security freeze on a credit report pursuant to division (D) of this section shall comply with the request not later than fifteen minutes after receiving the request unless any of the following applies:

(a) The consumer fails to meet the requirements of division (D) of this section.

(b) The consumer credit reporting agency's ability to temporarily lift the security freeze within fifteen minutes is prevented by an act of God, including fire, earthquakes, hurricanes, storms, or similar natural disaster or phenomena; unauthorized or illegal acts by a third party, including terrorism, sabotage, riot, vandalism, labor strikes or disputes disrupting operations, or similar occurrence; operational interruption, including electrical failure, unanticipated delay in equipment or replacement part delivery, computer hardware or software failures inhibiting response time, or similar disruption; governmental action, including emergency orders or regulations, judicial or law enforcement action, or similar directives; regularly scheduled maintenance, during other than normal business hours of, or updates to, the consumer credit reporting agency's systems; or commercially reasonable maintenance of, or repair to, the consumer credit reporting agency's systems that is unexpected or unscheduled.

(3) A consumer credit reporting agency shall remove or temporarily lift a security freeze placed on a credit report only in the following cases:

(a) Upon consumer request pursuant to division (D) of this section;

(b) If the credit report was frozen due to a material misrepresentation of fact by the consumer. If a consumer credit reporting agency intends to remove a security freeze upon a credit report pursuant to division (E)(3)(b) of this section, the consumer credit reporting agency shall notify the consumer in writing at least five business days prior to removing the security freeze on the credit report.

(F) A consumer credit reporting agency, when required by the "Fair Credit Reporting Act," 84 Stat. 1128 (1970), 15 U.S.C. 1681g(c), to provide a summary of rights, or when receiving a request from a consumer for information about a security freeze, shall provide the following written notice:

"Ohio Consumers Have the Right to Obtain a Security Freeze:

You may obtain a security freeze on your credit report to protect your privacy and ensure that credit is not granted in your name without your knowledge. You have a right to place a "security freeze" on your credit report pursuant to Ohio law. The security freeze will prohibit a consumer credit reporting agency from releasing any information in your credit report without your express authorization or approval. The security freeze is designed to prevent credit, loans, and services from being approved in your name without your consent. When you place a security freeze on your credit report, within five business days you will be provided a personal identification number or password to use if you choose to remove the security freeze on your credit report or to temporarily authorize the release of your credit report for a specific party or parties or for a specific period of time after the security freeze is in place. To provide that authorization, you must contact the consumer credit reporting agency and provide all of the following:

(a) Information generally considered sufficient to identify the consumer;

(b) The unique personal identification number or password provided by the consumer credit reporting agency;

(c) The proper information regarding the third party who is to receive the consumer credit report or the time period for which the credit report shall be available to users of the credit report.

A consumer credit reporting agency that receives a request from a consumer to temporarily lift a security freeze on a credit report shall comply with the request not later than fifteen minutes after receiving the request.

A security freeze does not apply to circumstances in which you have an existing account relationship and a copy of your report is requested by your existing creditor or its agents or affiliates for certain types of account review, collection, fraud control, or similar activities.

If you are actively seeking credit, you should understand that the procedures involved in lifting a security freeze may slow your own applications for credit. You should plan ahead and lift a freeze, either completely if you are shopping around, or specifically for a certain creditor, a few days before actually applying for new credit."

(G) Except as otherwise provided in division (E) of this section, a consumer credit reporting agency shall keep a security freeze in place until the consumer requests that the security freeze be removed. A consumer credit reporting agency shall remove a security freeze within three business days of receiving a request by telephone or by any other means authorized by the consumer credit reporting agency for removal from the consumer when the consumer provides the following:

(1) Information generally considered sufficient to identify the consumer;

(2) The unique personal identification number or password provided by the consumer credit reporting agency pursuant to division (C) of this section.

(H) A consumer credit reporting agency may release a credit report on which a security freeze has been placed to the following:

(1) A person, or subsidiary, affiliate, or agent of that person, or an assignee of a financial obligation owing by the consumer to that person, or a prospective assignee of a financial obligation owing by the consumer to that person in conjunction with the proposed purchase of the financial obligation, with which the consumer has or had prior to assignment an account or contract, including a demand deposit account, or to whom the consumer issued a negotiable instrument, for the purposes of reviewing the account or collecting the financial obligation owing for the account, contract, or negotiable instrument. For purposes of this paragraph, "reviewing the account" includes activities related to account maintenance, monitoring, credit line increases, and account upgrades and enhancements.

(2) A subsidiary, affiliate, agent, assignee, or prospective assignee of a person to whom access has been granted under division (D) of this section, for purposes of facilitating the extension of credit or other permissible use;

(3) Any state or local law enforcement agency, trial court, or private collection agency acting pursuant to a court order, warrant, or subpoena;

(4) Any federal, state, or local governmental entity, agency, or instrumentality that is acting within the entity's, agency's, or instrumentality's authority;

(5) A state or local child support enforcement agency;

(6) A person seeking to use the information contained in the consumer's credit report for the purpose of prescreening pursuant to the "Fair Credit Reporting Act," 84 Stat. 1128 (1970), 15 U.S.C. 1681 et seq.;

(7) Any person or entity administering a credit file monitoring subscription service to which the consumer has subscribed;

(8) Any person or entity providing a consumer with a copy of the consumer's credit report upon the consumer's request;

(9) Any person or entity for use in setting or adjusting a rate, adjusting a claim, or underwriting for insurance purposes;

(10) Any person or entity acting to investigate fraud or acting to investigate or collect delinquent taxes or unpaid court orders provided those responsibilities are consistent with section 1681b of the "Fair Credit Reporting Act," 15 U.S.C. 1681 et seq.

(I)(1) A consumer credit reporting agency may charge a consumer a reasonable fee not to exceed five dollars for placing a security freeze on that consumer's credit report. If the consumer is a victim of a violation of section 2913.49 of the Revised Code, the consumer credit reporting agency shall not charge a fee to place a security freeze on that consumer's credit report, but that consumer shall send a copy of the police report related to the violation of section 2913.49 of the Revised Code to the consumer credit reporting agency.

(2) A consumer credit reporting agency may charge a consumer a reasonable fee not to exceed five dollars for removing or temporarily lifting a security freeze on that consumer's credit report if the consumer elects to remove or temporarily lift the security freeze on the consumer's credit report for a specific creditor and may charge a consumer a reasonable fee not to exceed five dollars if the consumer elects to temporarily lift the security freeze for a specified period of time.

(3) A consumer credit reporting agency may charge a reasonable fee not to exceed five dollars to a consumer who fails to retain the original personal identification number provided by the consumer credit reporting agency and must be reissued the same or a new personal identification number.

(J) If a security freeze is in place, a consumer credit reporting agency shall not change any of the following official information in a credit report without sending a written confirmation of the change to the consumer within thirty days of the change being posted to the consumer's file: name; date of birth; social security number; or address. Written confirmation is not required for technical modifications of a consumer's official information, including name and street abbreviations, complete spellings, or transposition of numbers or letters. In the case of an address change, the written confirmation shall be sent to both the new address and to the former address.

(K) The provisions of this section do not apply to a consumer credit reporting agency that acts only as a reseller of credit information by assembling and merging information contained in the database of another consumer credit reporting agency or multiple consumer credit reporting agencies and does not maintain a permanent database of credit information from which new credit reports are produced, except that the reseller of credit information shall honor any security freeze placed on a credit report by another consumer credit reporting agency.

(L) The following entities are not required to place a security freeze in a credit report:

(1) A check services company or fraud prevention services company that issues reports on incidents of fraud or authorizations for the purpose of approving or processing negotiable instruments, electronic funds transfers, or similar methods of payments;

(2) A demand deposit account information service company that issues reports, regarding account closures due to fraud, substantial overdrafts, automated teller machine abuse, or similar negative information regarding a consumer, to inquiring banks or other financial institutions for use only in reviewing a consumer request for a demand deposit account at the inquiring bank or financial institution.

(M)(1) The attorney general may conduct an investigation if the attorney general, based on complaints or the attorney general's own inquiries, has reason to believe that a consumer credit reporting agency has failed or is failing to comply with this section.

(2) In any investigation conducted pursuant to this section, the attorney general may administer oaths, subpoena witnesses, adduce evidence, and subpoena the production of any book, document, record, or other relevant matter.

(3) If the attorney general under division (M)(2) of this section subpoenas the production of any relevant matter that is located outside this state, the attorney general may designate a representative, including an official of the state in which that relevant matter is located, to inspect the relevant matter on the attorney general's behalf. The attorney general may carry out similar requests received from officials of other states.

(4) Any person who is subpoenaed to produce relevant matter pursuant to division (M)(2) of this section shall make that relevant matter available at a convenient location within this state or the state of the representative designated under division (M)(3) of this section.

(5) Any person who is subpoenaed as a witness or to produce relevant matter pursuant to division (M)(2) of this section may file in the court of common pleas of Franklin county, the county in this state in which the person resides, or the county in this state in which the person's principal place of business is located a petition to extend for good cause shown the date on which the subpoena is to be returned or to modify or quash for good cause shown that subpoena. The person may file the petition at any time prior to the date specified for the return of the subpoena or within twenty days after the service of the subpoena, whichever is earlier.

(6) Any person who is subpoenaed as a witness or to produce relevant matter pursuant to division (M)(2) of this section shall comply with the terms of the subpoena unless the court orders otherwise prior to the date specified for the return of the subpoena or, if applicable, that date as extended. If a person fails without lawful excuse to obey a subpoena, the attorney general may apply to the court of common pleas for an order that does one or more of the following:

(a) Compels the requested discovery;

(b) Adjudges the person in contempt of court;

(c) Grants injunctive relief to restrain the person from failing to comply with section 1347.12 or 1349.19 of the Revised Code, whichever is applicable;

(d) Grants injunctive relief to preserve or restore the status quo;

(e) Grants other relief that may be required until the person obeys the subpoena.

(N)(1) The attorney general has the authority to bring a civil action in a court of common pleas for appropriate relief under this section, including a temporary restraining order, preliminary or permanent injunction, and civil penalties, if it appears that a consumer credit reporting agency has failed or is failing to comply with this section. Upon its finding that a consumer credit reporting agency has intentionally or recklessly failed to comply with this section, the court shall impose a civil penalty upon the consumer credit reporting agency of up to two thousand five hundred dollars for each instance that the consumer credit reporting agency fails to comply.

(2) Any civil penalty that is assessed under division (N)(1) of this section shall be deposited into the consumer protection enforcement fund created by section 1345.51 of the Revised Code.

(3) In determining the appropriate civil penalty to assess under division (N)(1) of this section, the court shall consider all relevant factors, including the degree of the defendant's culpability, any history of prior violations of this section by the defendant, the defendant's ability to pay, the effect of the court's decision on the defendant's ability to continue to conduct the defendant's business, and whether or not the defendant acted in bad faith in failing to comply with this section.

(O) Any consumer credit reporting agency that is found by the court to have failed to comply with this section is liable to the attorney general for the attorney general's costs in conducting an investigation and bringing an action under this section.

(P) The rights and remedies that are provided under this section are in addition to any other rights or remedies that are provided by law.

**HISTORY: 152 v H 46, § 1, eff. 9-1-08.**

The effective date is set by § 3 of 152 v H 46.

## [PENALTIES]

## § 1349.99 Penalties.

(A) Whoever violates section 1349.06 or 1349.17 of the Revised Code is guilty of a minor misdemeanor.

(B)(1) Whoever violates section 1349.45 of the Revised Code is guilty of a misdemeanor of the first degree.

(2) Notwithstanding division (B)(1) of this section, the only remedies that are available for a violation of section 1349.45 of the Revised Code by a registrant or licensee under sections 1322.01 to 1322.12 of the Revised Code are those set forth in section 1322.10 of the Revised Code or otherwise provided by statute or common law.

(3) The provisions of division (B) of this section are not intended to be exclusive remedies and do not preclude the use of any other remedy provided by law.

**HISTORY: 144 v H 20 (Eff 8-20-91); 148 v S 64. Eff 10-29-99; 150 v H 420, § 1, eff. 11-5-04.**

# TITLE 15: CONSERVATION OF NATURAL RESOURCES

## CHAPTER 1531: DIVISION OF WILDLIFE



### § 1531.02 State ownership of wild animals; prohibitions.

The ownership of and the title to all wild animals in this state, not legally confined or held by private ownership legally acquired, is in the state, which holds such title in trust for the benefit of all the people. Individual possession shall be obtained only in accordance with the Revised Code or division rules. No person at any time of the year shall take in any manner or possess any number or quantity of wild animals, except wild animals that the Revised Code or division rules permit to be taken, hunted, killed, or had in possession, and only at the time and place and in the manner that the Revised Code or division rules prescribe. No person shall buy, sell, or offer any part of wild animals for sale, or transport any part of wild animals, except as permitted by the Revised Code or division rules. No person shall possess or transport a wild animal that has been taken or possessed unlawfully outside the state.

A person doing anything prohibited or neglecting to do anything required by this chapter or Chapter 1533. of the Revised Code or contrary to any division rule violates this section. A person who counsels, aids, shields, or harbors an offender under those chapters or any division rule, or who knowingly shares in the proceeds of such a violation, or receives or possesses any wild animal in violation of the Revised Code or division rule, violates this section.

**HISTORY: GC § 1391; 108 v PtI, 577, § 2; 116 v 310; 119 v 369; 123 v 84 (129), § 2; Bureau of Code Revision, 10-1-53; 130 v H 573 (Eff 9-30-63); 130 v PtII, 102 (Eff 12-16-64); 131 v 514 (Eff 11-9-65); 132 v H 1 (Eff 2-21-67); 141 v H 848 (Eff 2-27-87); 142 v S 256 (Eff 7-20-88); 145 v S 182 (Eff 10-20-94); 147 v S 103. Eff 6-1-98; 151 v H 443, § 1, eff. 4-6-07.**

[DIVISION OF WILDLIFE]

### § 1531.07 Jurisdiction of division.

All lakes, reservoirs, and state lands dedicated to the use of the public for park and pleasure resort purposes shall be under the supervision and control of the chief of the division of wildlife with respect to the enforcement of all laws relating to the protection of birds, fish, and game. All laws for the protection of fish in inland rivers and streams of the state, and all laws for the protection of the birds, fish, and game and fur-bearing animals, shall apply to all such state reservoirs and lakes. No person shall disturb, injure, or destroy a tree, plant, lawn, embankment, decoration, or other property or kill, injure, or disturb a waterfowl, water animal, bird, or game or fur-bearing animal, kept as a semidomestic pet upon an island or within the boundary lines of Buckeye Lake, Indian Lake, The Portage Lakes, Lake St. Marys, Guilford Lake, and Lake Loramie, or any other territory over which the state has jurisdiction or an embankment or state land adjacent thereto. No person shall take or disturb fish in any lagoon or any other portion of any of the waters over which the state has jurisdiction and which have been set aside by the chief for the propagation of fish.

**HISTORY: GC § 1446; 108 v PtI, 577 (601), § 56; 113 v 551 (588); 118 v 83 (96); 123 v 84 (158), § 2; Bureau of Code Revision, 10-1-53; 130 v H 573. Eff 9-30-63.**

[PROSECUTIONS AND PENALTIES]

### § 1531.201 Action to recover possession or restitution value of wild animal; revocation of license, permit, or stamp.

(A) As used in this section:

(1) "Gross score" means the number derived by calculating the measurements of the antlers of a white-tailed deer in accordance with division (C)(2) of this section.

(2) "Point" means a projection on the antler of a white-tailed deer that is at least one-inch long as measured from its tip to the nearest edge of antler beam and the length of which exceeds the length of its base. "Point" does not include an antler beam tip.

(3) "Abnormal point" means a point that is nontypical in shape or location.

(4) "Normal point" means a point that projects from the main antler beam in a typical shape or location.

(5) "Inside spread of main antler beams" means the measurement at right angles to the center line of the skull of a white-tailed deer at the widest point between main antler beams.

(6) "Length of main antler beam" means the measurement from the lowest outside edge of the antler burr of a white-tailed deer over the outer curve to the most distant point of what is or appears to be the main antler beam beginning at the place on the antler burr where the center line along the outer curve of the beam intersects the antler burr.

(7) "Antler burr" means the elevated bony rim around the antler base of a white-tailed deer that is just above the skin of the pedicle.

(B) The chief of the division of wildlife or the chief's authorized representative may bring a civil action to recover possession of or the restitution value of any wild animal held, taken, bought, sold, or possessed in violation of this chapter or Chapter 1533. of the Revised Code or any division rule against any person who held, took, bought, sold, or possessed the wild animal.

The minimum restitution value to the state for wild animals that are unlawfully held, taken, bought, sold, or possessed shall be established in division rule.

(C)(1) In addition to any restitution value established in division rule, a person who is convicted of a violation of this chapter or Chapter 1533. of the Revised Code or a division rule governing the holding, taking, buying, sale, or possession of an antlered white-tailed deer with a gross score of more than one hundred twenty-five inches also shall pay an additional restitution value that is calculated using the following formula:

Additional restitution value = ((gross score — 100)$^2$ x $1.65).

(2) The gross score of an antlered white-tailed deer shall be determined by taking and adding together all of the following measurements, which shall be made to the nearest one-eighth of an inch using a one-quarter-inch wide flexible steel tape:

(a) Inside spread of the main antler beams, not to exceed the length of the longest main antler beam;

(b) Length of the right main antler beam;

(c) Length of the left main antler beam;

(d) Total length of all abnormal points;

(e) Total length of all normal points as measured from the nearest edge of the main antler beam over the outer curve to the tip. To determine the baseline for normal point measurement, the tape shall be laid along the outer curve of the antler beam so that the top edge of the tape coincides with the top edge of the antler beam on both sides of the point.

(f) Circumference taken at the narrowest place between the antler burr and the first normal point on the right main antler beam. If the first normal point is missing, the circumference shall be taken at the narrowest place between the antler burr and the second normal point.

(g) Circumference taken at the narrowest place between the first normal point and the second normal point on the right main antler beam. If the first normal point is missing, the circumference shall be taken at the narrowest place between the antler burr and the second normal point.

(h) Circumference taken at the narrowest place between the second normal point and the third normal point on the right main antler beam;

(i) Circumference taken at the narrowest place between the third normal point and the fourth normal point on the right main antler beam. If the fourth normal point is missing, the circumference shall be taken halfway between the third normal point and the tip of the main antler beam.

(j) Circumference taken at the narrowest place between the antler burr and the first normal point on the left main antler beam. If the first normal point is missing, the circumference shall be taken at the narrowest place between the antler burr and the second normal point.

(k) Circumference taken at the narrowest place between the first normal point and the second normal point on the left main antler beam. If the first normal point is missing, the circumference shall be taken at the narrowest place between the antler burr and the second normal point.

(l) Circumference taken at the narrowest place between the second normal point and the third normal point on the left main antler beam;

(m) Circumference taken at the narrowest place between the third normal point and the fourth normal point on the left main antler beam. If the fourth normal point is missing, the circumference shall be taken halfway between the third normal point and the tip of the main antler beam.

Antlers may be measured at any time; no drying time is required.

(D) Upon conviction of holding, taking, buying, selling, or possessing a wild animal in violation of this chapter, Chapter 1533. of the Revised Code, or a division rule, the chief shall revoke until payment of the restitution value is made each hunting license, fur taker permit, deer permit, wild turkey permit, wetlands habitat stamp, and fishing license issued to that person under this chapter or Chapter 1533. of the Revised Code. No fee paid for such a license, permit, or stamp shall be returned to the person.

Upon revoking a person's license, permit, or stamp or a combination thereof under this division, the chief immediately shall send a notice of that action by certified mail to the last known address of the person. The notice shall state the action taken, order the person to surrender the revoked license, permit, or stamp or combination thereof, and state that the department of natural resources will not afford a hearing as required under section 119.06 of the Revised Code.

(E) Nothing in this section affects the right of seizure under any other section of the Revised Code.

**HISTORY: 141 v H 848 (Eff 2-27-87); 145 v S 182. Eff 10-20-94; 152 v H 238, § 1, eff. 3-4-08.**

## § 1531.23 Judgment for costs and fine or forfeiture; failure to pay.

If the defendant in a prosecution or condemnation proceeding under a division rule or this chapter or Chapter 1533. of the Revised Code is convicted, judgment shall be rendered against him for costs in addition to the fine imposed or forfeiture declared. The judgment shall be the first lien upon the property of the person convicted, and no exemption shall be claimed or allowed against that lien. If he fails to pay the fine and costs imposed or if execution issued is returned unsatisfied, the person convicted shall be committed to the county jail or to a workhouse and there confined one day for the amount of the fine adjudged against him, determined as provided in section 2747.14 of the Revised Code. The person convicted shall not be discharged or paroled therefrom by any board or officer except upon payment of the fine remaining unpaid or upon written permission of the chief of the division of wildlife.

**HISTORY: GC § 1453; 108 v PtI, 577 (604), § 63; 113 v 551 (590); 123 v 84 (160), § 2; Bureau of Code Revision, 10-1-53; 130 v PtII, 108 (Eff 12-16-64); 132 v H 195 (Eff 8-31-67); 133 v 460 (Eff 9-3-70); 135 v H 453 (Eff 11-20-73); 140 v H 113 (Eff 1-8-85); 145 v S 182. Eff 10-20-94.**

### [PROPAGATION AND PRESERVATION]

## § 1531.25 Protection of species threatened with statewide extinction.

The chief of the division of wildlife, with the approval of the wildlife council, shall adopt and may modify and repeal rules, in accordance with Chapter 119. of the Revised Code, restricting the taking or possession of native wildlife, or any eggs or offspring thereof, that he finds to be threatened with statewide extinction. The rules shall identify the common and scientific names of each endangered species and shall be modified from time to time to include all species on the list of endangered fish and wildlife pursuant to Section 4 of the "Endangered Species Act of 1973," 87 Stat. 884, 16 U.S.C. 1531, as amended, and that are native to this state, or that migrate or are otherwise reasonably likely to occur within the state.

The rules shall provide for the taking of species threatened with statewide extinction, for zoological, educational, and scientific purposes, and for propagation in captivity to preserve the species, under written permits from the chief. The rules shall in no way restrict the taking or possession of species listed on such United States list for zoological, educational, or scientific purposes, or for propagation in captivity to preserve the species, under a permit or license from the United States or any instrumentality thereof.

No person shall violate any rule adopted pursuant to this section.

**HISTORY: 135 v S 35 (Eff 1-1-74); 140 v H 5 (Eff 10-14-83); 142 v S 256. Eff 7-20-88.**

**Not analogous to former RC § 1531.25 (GC § 1435-2; 109 v 326; 113 v 551; 118 v 83; 123 v 84; Bureau Code Revision, 10-1-53) repealed 130 v H 573, § 2, eff 9-30-63.**

## § 1531.29 Polluting state land or water.

No person shall place or dispose of in any manner, any garbage, waste, peelings of vegetables or fruits, rubbish, ashes, cans, bottles, wire, paper, cartons, boxes, parts of automobiles, wagons, furniture, glass, oil, or anything else of an unsightly or unsanitary nature on any state owned, controlled, or administered land, or in any ditch, stream, river, lake, pond, or other watercourse, except those waters which do not combine or effect a junction with natural surface or underground waters, or upon the bank thereof where the same is liable to be washed into the water either by ordinary flow or floods. This section does not apply to any substance placed under authority of a permit issued under section 6111.04 of the Revised Code or exempted by such section from its terms.

**HISTORY: 133 v H 503 (Eff 10-30-69); 135 v H 453. Eff 11-20-73.**

[PENALTIES]

## § 1531.99 Penalties.

(A) Whoever violates section 1531.02 of the Revised Code, or any division rule, other than a rule adopted under section 1531.25 of the Revised Code, is guilty of a misdemeanor of the fourth degree.

(B) Whoever violates section 1531.02 of the Revised Code concerning the taking or possession of deer or violates division (K) of section 1531.06 or section 1531.07 or 1531.29 of the Revised Code is guilty of a misdemeanor of the third degree on a first offense; on each subsequent offense, that person is guilty of a misdemeanor of the first degree.

(C) Whoever violates section 1531.25 of the Revised Code is guilty of a misdemeanor of the first degree.

(D) Whoever violates section 1531.02 of the Revised Code concerning the buying, selling, or offering for sale of any wild animals or parts of wild animals, the minimum value of which animals or parts, in the aggregate, is one thousand dollars or more as established under section 1531.201 [1531.20.1] of the Revised Code, is guilty of a felony of the fifth degree.

(E) A court that imposes sentence for a violation of any section of this chapter governing the holding, taking, buying, selling, or possession of wild animals, including, without limitation, section 1531.11 of the Revised Code, may require the person who is convicted of or pleads guilty to the offense, in addition to any fine, term of imprisonment, seizure, and forfeiture imposed, to make restitution for the minimum value of the wild animal illegally held, taken, bought, sold, or possessed as established under section 1531.201 [1531.20.1] of the Revised Code. An officer who collects moneys paid as restitution under this section shall pay those moneys to the treasurer of state who shall deposit them in the state treasury to the credit of the wildlife fund established under section 1531.17 of the Revised Code.

**HISTORY: Bureau of Code Revision, 10-1-53; 129 v 1310 (Eff 10-12-61); 131 v 519 (Eff 9-1-65); 131 v 520 (Eff 11-4-65); 133 v H 503 (Eff 10-30-69); 135 v S 35 (Eff 1-1-74); 135 v H 453 (Eff 1-1-74); 136 v H 1316 (Eff 8-31-76); 141 v H 848 (Eff 2-27-87); 145 v S 182 (Eff 10-20-94); 146 v S 2 (Eff 7-1-96); 147 v S 187. Eff 3-18-99; 151 v H 443, § 1, eff. 4-6-07; 152 v H 238, § 1, eff. 3-4-08.**

# CHAPTER 1547: WATERCRAFT AND WATERWAYS

Section



[DIVISION OF WATERCRAFT]

## § 1547.01 Definitions.

(A) As used in sections 1541.03, 1547.26, 1547.39, 1547.40, 1547.53, 1547.54, 1547.541, 1547.542, 1547.543, 1547.56, 1547.57, 1547.66, and 5311.01 of the Revised Code, "watercraft" means any of the following when used or capable of being used for transportation on the water:

(1) A vessel operated by machinery either permanently or temporarily affixed;

(2) A sailboat other than a sailboard;

(3) An inflatable, manually propelled boat that is required by federal law to have a hull identification number meeting the requirements of the United States coast guard;

(4) A canoe or rowboat.

"Watercraft" does not include ferries as referred to in Chapter 4583. of the Revised Code.

Watercraft subject to section 1547.54 of the Revised Code shall be divided into five classes as follows:

Class A: Less than sixteen feet in length;

Class 1: At least sixteen feet, but less than twenty-six feet in length;

Class 2: At least twenty-six feet, but less than forty feet in length;

Class 3: At least forty feet, but less than sixty-five feet in length;

Class 4: At least sixty-five feet in length.

(B) As used in this chapter:

(1) "Vessel" includes every description of craft, including nondisplacement craft and seaplanes, designed to be used as a means of transportation on water.

(2) "Rowboat" means any vessel, except a canoe, that is designed to be rowed and that is propelled by human muscular effort by oars or paddles and upon which no mechanical propulsion device, electric motor, internal combustion engine, or sail has been affixed or is used for the operation of the vessel.

(3) "Sailboat" means any vessel, equipped with mast and sails, dependent upon the wind to propel it in the normal course of operation.

(a) Any sailboat equipped with an inboard engine is deemed a powercraft with auxiliary sail.

(b) Any sailboat equipped with a detachable motor is deemed a sailboat with auxiliary power.

(c) Any sailboat being propelled by mechanical power, whether under sail or not, is deemed a powercraft and subject to all laws and rules governing powercraft operation.

(4) "Powercraft" means any vessel propelled by machinery, fuel, rockets, or similar device.

(5) "Person" includes any legal entity defined as a person in section 1.59 of the Revised Code and any body politic, except the United States and this state, and includes any agent, trustee, executor, receiver, assignee, or other representative thereof.

(6) "Owner" includes any person who claims lawful possession of a vessel by virtue of legal title or equitable interest therein that entitled the person to that possession.

(7) "Operator" includes any person who navigates or has under the person's control a vessel, or vessel and detachable motor, on the waters in this state.

(8) "Visible" means visible on a dark night with clear atmosphere.

(9) "Waters in this state" means all streams, rivers, lakes, ponds, marshes, watercourses, waterways, and other bodies of water, natural or humanmade, that are situated wholly or partially within this state or within its jurisdiction and are used for recreational boating.

(10) "Navigable waters" means waters that come under the jurisdiction of the department of the army of the United States and any waterways within or adjacent to this state, except inland lakes having neither a navigable inlet nor outlet.

(11) "In operation" in reference to a vessel means that the vessel is being navigated or otherwise used on the waters in this state.

(12) "Sewage" means human body wastes and the wastes from toilets and other receptacles intended to receive or retain body waste.

(13) "Canoe" means a narrow vessel of shallow draft, pointed at both ends and propelled by human muscular effort, and includes kayaks, racing shells, and rowing sculls.

(14) "Coast guard approved" means bearing an approval number assigned by the United States coast guard.

(15) "Type one personal flotation device" means a device that is designed to turn an unconscious person floating in water from a face downward position to a vertical or slightly face upward position and that has at least nine kilograms, approximately twenty pounds, of buoyancy.

(16) "Type two personal flotation device" means a device that is designed to turn an unconscious person in the water from a face downward position to a vertical or slightly face upward position and that has at least seven kilograms, approximately fifteen and four-tenths pounds, of buoyancy.

(17) "Type three personal flotation device" means a device that is designed to keep a conscious person in a vertical or slightly face upward position and that has at least seven kilograms, approximately fifteen and four-tenths pounds, of buoyancy.

(18) "Type four personal flotation device" means a device that is designed to be thrown to a person in the water and not worn and that has at least seven and five-tenths kilograms, approximately sixteen and five-tenths pounds, of buoyancy.

(19) "Type five personal flotation device" means a device that, unlike other personal flotation devices, has limitations on its approval by the United States coast guard, including, without limitation, all of the following:

(a) The approval label on the type five personal flotation device indicates that the device is approved for the activity in which the vessel is being used or as a substitute for a personal flotation device of the type required on the vessel in use.

(b) The personal flotation device is used in accordance with any requirements on the approval label.

(c) The personal flotation device is used in accordance with requirements in its owner's manual if the approval label refers to such a manual.

(20) "Inflatable watercraft" means any vessel constructed of rubber, canvas, or other material that is designed to be inflated with any gaseous substance, constructed with two or more air cells, and operated as a vessel. Inflatable watercraft propelled by a motor shall be classified as powercraft and shall be registered by length. Inflatable watercraft propelled by a sail shall be classified as a sailboat and shall be registered by length.

(21) "Idle speed" means the slowest possible speed needed to maintain steerage or maneuverability.

(22) "Diver's flag" means a red flag not less than one foot square having a diagonal white stripe extending from the masthead to the opposite lower corner that when displayed indicates that divers are in the water.

(23) "Muffler" means an acoustical suppression device or system that is designed and installed to abate the sound of exhaust gases emitted from an internal combustion engine and that prevents excessive or unusual noise.

(24) "Law enforcement vessel" means any vessel used in law enforcement and under the command of a law enforcement officer.

(25) "Personal watercraft" means a vessel, less than sixteen feet in length, that is propelled by machinery and designed to be operated by an individual sitting, standing, or kneeling on the vessel rather than by an individual sitting or standing inside the vessel.

(26) "No wake" has the same meaning as "idle speed."

(27) "Watercraft dealer" means any person who is regularly engaged in the business of manufacturing, selling, displaying, offering for sale, or dealing in vessels at an established place of business. "Watercraft dealer" does not include a person who is a marine salvage dealer or any other person who dismantles, salvages, or rebuilds vessels using used parts.

(28) "Electronic" includes electrical, digital, magnetic, optical, electromagnetic, or any other form of technology that entails capabilities similar to these technologies.

(29) "Electronic record" means a record generated, communicated, received, or stored by electronic means for use in an information system or for transmission from one information system to another.

(30) "Electronic signature" means a signature in electronic form attached to or logically associated with an electronic record.

(31) "Drug of abuse" has the same meaning as in section 4506.01 of the Revised Code.

(32) "Watercourse" means a substantially natural channel with recognized banks and bottom in which a flow of water occurs, with an average of at least ten feet mean surface water width and at least five miles of length.

(33) "Impoundment" means the reservoir created by a dam or other artificial barrier across a watercourse that causes water to be stored deeper than and generally beyond the banks of the natural channel of the watercourse during periods of normal flow, but does not include water stored behind rock piles, rock riffle dams, and low channel dams where the depth of water is less than ten feet above the channel bottom and is essentially confined within the banks of the natural channel during periods of normal stream flow.

(34) "Wild river area" means an area declared a wild river area by the director of natural resources under this chapter and includes those rivers or sections of rivers that are free of impoundments and generally inaccessible except by trail, with watersheds or shorelines essentially primitive and waters unpolluted, representing vestiges of primitive America.

(35) "Scenic river area" means an area declared a scenic river area by the director under this chapter and includes those rivers or sections of rivers that are free of impoundments, with shorelines or watersheds still largely primitive and shorelines largely undeveloped, but accessible in places by roads.

(36) "Recreational river area" means an area declared a recreational river area by the director under this chapter and includes those rivers or sections of rivers that are readily accessible by road or railroad, that may have some development along their shorelines, and that may have undergone some impoundment or diversion in the past.

**HISTORY: 128 v 1004 (Eff 3-5-59); 129 v 582(694) (Eff 1-10-61); 129 v 1350 (Eff 11-2-61); 133 v H 1002 (Eff 9-4-70); 136 v H 957 (Eff 9-3-76); 137 v S 387 (Eff 3-15-79); 138 v S 65 (Eff 1-1-80); 139 v H 782 (Eff 3-4-83); 140 v H 682 (Eff 3-28-85); 141 v H 400 (Eff 6-12-85); 143 v H 522 (Eff 6-13-90); 146 v H 117 (Eff 6-30-95); 146 v S 295 (Eff 3-18-97); 147 v S 187 (Eff 3-18-99); 148 v H 306 (Eff 11-22-99); 148 v S 242 (Eff 9-14-2000); 149 v S 150. Eff 7-5-2002; 151 v S 8, § 1, eff. 8-17-06; 153 v H 1, § 101.01, eff. 7-17-09; 2011 HB 153, § 101.01, eff. Sept. 29, 2011.**

The effective date is set by § 812.20 of 153 v H 1.

## § 1547.02 Applicability of chapter; relationship to federal law; right to regulate equipment.

Unless otherwise provided, this chapter applies to all vessels operating on the waters in this state. Nothing in this chapter shall be construed in contravention of any valid federal act or regulation, but is in addition to the act or regulation where not inconsistent.

The state reserves to itself the exclusive right to regulate the minimum equipment requirements of watercraft and vessels operated on the waters in this state.

**HISTORY: 153 v H 1, § 101.01, eff. 7-17-09.**

**Not analogous to former RC § 1547.02 (128 v 1004; 132 v H 617; 136 v H 1; 136 v H 957; 137 v H 1), repealed 143 v H 522, § 2, eff 6-13-90.**

The effective date is set by § 812.20 of 153 v H 1.

## § 1547.05 Requirements for operation of certain powercraft by persons born in 1982 or later.

No person born on or after January 1, 1982, shall operate on the waters in this state a powercraft powered by more than ten horsepower, unless the operator successfully has completed either a safe boater course approved by the national association of state boating law administrators or a proctored or nonproctored proficiency examination that tests knowledge of information included in the curriculum of such a course, and has received a certificate as evidence of successful completion of the course or examination.

No person shall permit a powercraft to be operated on the waters in this state in violation of this section.

**HISTORY: 147 v H 502. Eff 1-1-2000; 151 v H 443, § 1, eff. 4-6-07.**

**Not analogous to former RC § 1547.05 (128 v 1004; 139 v H 782; 140 v H 682), repealed 143 v H 522, § 2, eff 6-13-90.**

The effective date is set by section 3 of HB 502.

## § 1547.051 Duty to present certificate or proof of holding it.

A person born on or after January 1, 1982, who is operating on the waters in this state a powercraft powered by more than ten horsepower and who is stopped by a law enforcement officer in the enforcement of Chapter 1547. of the Revised Code or rules adopted under it shall present to the law enforcement officer, not later than seventy-two hours after being stopped, a certificate obtained by the person pursuant to section 1547.05 of the Revised Code prior to being stopped or proof of holding such a certificate. Failure of the person to present the certificate or proof of holding it within seventy-two hours constitutes prima-facie evidence of a violation of section 1547.05 of the Revised Code.

**HISTORY: 147 v H 502. Eff 1-1-2000.**

The effective date is set by section 3 of HB 502.

## § 1547.052 Powercraft rentals to persons born in 1982 or later.

(A) No rental business shall lease, hire, or rent a powercraft powered by more than ten horsepower for operation on the waters in this state to a person born on or after January 1, 1982, unless the person meets one of the following requirements:

(1) The person signs a statement on the rental agreement or attached to the rental agreement that the person has successfully completed a safe boater course approved by the national association of state boating law administrators or has successfully completed a proficiency examination as provided in section 1547.05 of the Revised Code.

(2) The person receives educational materials from the rental business and successfully passes, with a score of ninety per cent or better, an abbreviated examination given by the rental business. The achievement of a passing score on the examination shall be indicated on or attached to the powercraft rental agreement.

(B) Any person born on or after January 1, 1982, operating or supervising the operation of a leased, hired, or rented powercraft shall:

(1) Meet the requirements for boater education of division (A) of this section.

(2) Be named as an operator on the agreement that leases, hires, or rents the powercraft.

(C) The division of watercraft shall make available to all watercraft rental businesses in Ohio boater safety educational materials and an abbreviated examination that shall be used by the watercraft rental business for the purposes of division (A)(2) of this section.

**HISTORY: 147 v H 502 (Eff 1-1-2000); 148 v H 306. Eff 1-1-2000.**

The effective date is set by section 3 of HB 306.

## § 1547.06 Restrictions on child operators; duty of supervisory adult.

(A) Except as otherwise provided in this division, no person under sixteen years of age shall operate a personal watercraft on the waters in this state. A person who is not less than twelve, nor more than fifteen years of age may operate a personal watercraft if a supervising person eighteen years of age or older is aboard the personal watercraft and, in the case of a supervising person born on or after January 1, 1982, if the supervising person holds a certificate obtained under section 1547.05 of the Revised Code or, in the case of a rented powercraft, meets the requirements of section 1547.052 [1547.05.2] of the Revised Code.

(B) No person under twelve years of age shall operate any vessel on the waters in this state unless the person is under the direct visual and audible supervision, during the operation, of a person who is eighteen years of age or older. This division does not apply to a personal watercraft, which shall be governed by division (A) of this section, or to a powercraft, other than a personal watercraft, powered by more than ten horsepower, which shall be governed by division (C) of this section.

(C) No person under twelve years of age shall operate on the waters in this state a powercraft, other than a personal watercraft, powered by more than ten horsepower unless the person is under the direct visual and audible supervision, during the operation, of a person eighteen years of age or older who is aboard the powercraft and, in the case of such a supervising person born on or after January 1, 1982, who holds a certificate obtained under section 1547.05 of the Revised Code or, in the case of a rented powercraft, meets the requirements of section 1547.052 [1547.05.2] of the Revised Code.

(D) No supervising person eighteen years of age or older shall permit any person who is under the supervising person's supervision and who is operating a vessel on the waters in this state to violate any section of this chapter or a rule adopted under it.

**HISTORY: 128 v 1004 (Eff 8-5-59); 136 v H 957 (Eff 9-3-76); 139 v H 782 (Eff 3-4-83); 143 v H 522 (Eff 6-13-90); 146 v S 295 (Eff 3-18-97); 147 v H 502. Eff 1-1-2000.**

The effective date is set by section 3 of HB 502.

## § 1547.07 Reckless or unsafe operation.

(A) Any person who operates any vessel or manipulates any water skis, aquaplane, or similar device on the waters in this state carelessly or heedlessly, or in disregard of the rights or safety of any person, vessel, or property, or without due caution, at a rate of speed or in a manner so as to endanger any person, vessel, or property is guilty of reckless operation of the vessel or other device.

(B) No person shall operate or permit the operation of a vessel in an unsafe manner. A vessel shall be operated in a reasonable and prudent manner at all times.

Unsafe vessel operation includes, without limitation, any of the following:

(1) A vessel becoming airborne or completely leaving the water while crossing the wake of another vessel at a distance of less than one hundred feet, or at an unsafe distance, from the vessel creating the wake;

(2) Operating at such a speed and proximity to another vessel or to a person attempting to ride on one or more water skis, surfboard, inflatable device, or similar device being towed by a vessel so as to require the operator of either vessel to swerve or turn abruptly to avoid collision;

(3) Operating less than two hundred feet directly behind a person water skiing or attempting to water ski;

(4) Weaving through congested traffic.

**HISTORY: 128 v 1004 (Eff 8-5-59); 133 v H 1002 (Eff 9-4-70); 139 v H 782 (Eff 3-4-83); 143 v H 522 (Eff 6-13-90); 146 v S 295. Eff 3-18-97.**

## § 1547.071 Authority of officer when especially hazardous condition exists.

(A) If a law enforcement officer observes a vessel being used and determines that at least one of the unsafe conditions identified in division (C) of this section is present and that an especially hazardous condition exists, the officer may direct the operator of the vessel to take whatever immediate and reasonable actions are necessary for the safety of the persons aboard the vessel, including directing the operator to return the vessel to mooring and remain there until the situation creating the hazardous condition is corrected or has ended.

For the purposes of this section, an especially hazardous condition is one in which a reasonably prudent person would believe that the continued operation of a vessel would create a special hazard to the safety of the persons aboard the vessel.

(B) The refusal by an operator of a vessel to terminate use of the vessel after being ordered to do so by a law enforcement officer under division (A) of this section is prima-facie evidence of a violation of section 1547.07 of the Revised Code.

(C) For the purposes of this section, any of the following is an unsafe condition:

(1) Insufficient personal flotation devices;

(2) Insufficient fire extinguishers;

(3) Overloaded, insufficient freeboard for the water conditions in which the vessel is operating;

(4) Improper display of navigation lights;

(5) Fuel leaks, including fuel leaking from either the engine or the fuel system;

(6) Accumulation of or an abnormal amount of fuel in the bilges;

(7) Inadequate backfire flame control;

(8) Improper ventilation.

(D) This section does not apply to any of the following:

(1) Foreign vessels temporarily using waters that are subject to the jurisdiction of the United States;

(2) Military vessels, vessels owned by the state or a political subdivision, or other public vessels, except those that are used for recreation;

(3) A ship's lifeboats, as defined in section 1548.01 of the Revised Code;

(4) Vessels that are solely commercial and that are carrying more than six passengers for hire.

**HISTORY: 146 v S 295. Eff 3-18-97.**

## § 1547.072 Failure to maintain sufficient control prohibited.

No person shall operate or permit the operation of a vessel on the waters in this state without maintaining sufficient control to avoid an incident that results in property damage, physical injury, loss of life, or any combination of them.

**HISTORY: 152 v S 271, § 1, eff. 6-13-08.**

## § 1547.10 Operator to stop and furnish information upon accident or collision.

In case of accident to or collision with persons or property on the waters of this state, due to the operation of any vessel, the operator having knowledge of the accident or collision shall immediately stop the vessel at the scene of the accident or collision, to the extent that it is safe and practical, and shall remain at the scene of the accident or collision until he has given his name and address and, if he is not the owner, the name and address of the owner of the vessel, together with the registration number of the vessel, if any, to any person injured in the accident or collision or to the operator, occupant, owner, or attendant of any vessel damaged in the accident or collision, or to any law enforcement officer at the scene of the accident or collision.

If the injured person is unable to comprehend and record the information required to be given by this section, the other operator involved in the accident or collision shall forthwith notify the nearest law enforcement agency having authority concerning the location of the accident or collision, and his name, address, and the registration number, if any, of the vessel he was operating, and then remain at the scene of the accident or collision or at the nearest location from which notification is possible until a law enforcement officer arrives, unless removed from the scene by an emergency vehicle operated by the state or a political subdivision or by an ambulance.

If the accident or collision is with an unoccupied or unattended vessel, the operator so colliding with the vessel shall securely attach the information required to be given in this section, in writing, to a conspicuous place in or on the unoccupied or unattended vessel.

**HISTORY: 140 v H 682 (Eff 3-28-85); 143 v H 522. Eff 6-13-90.**

**Not analogous to former RC § 1547.10 (128 v 1004; 133 v H 1002), repealed 136 v H 957, § 2, eff 9-3-76.**

## § 1547.11 Operation, physical control, or manipulation under influence of alcohol or drug.

(A) No person shall operate or be in physical control of any vessel underway or shall manipulate any water skis, aquaplane, or similar device on the waters in this state if, at the time of the operation, control, or manipulation, any of the following applies:

(1) The person is under the influence of alcohol, a drug of abuse, or a combination of them.

(2) The person has a concentration of eight-hundredths of one per cent or more by weight of alcohol per unit volume in the person's whole blood.

(3) The person has a concentration of ninety-six-thousandths of one per cent or more by weight per unit volume of alcohol in the person's blood serum or plasma.

(4) The person has a concentration of eleven-hundredths of one gram or more by weight of alcohol per one hundred milliliters of the person's urine.

(5) The person has a concentration of eight-hundredths of one gram or more by weight of alcohol per two hundred ten liters of the person's breath.

(6) Except as provided in division (H) of this section, the person has a concentration of any of the following controlled substances or metabolites of a controlled substance in the person's whole blood, blood serum or plasma, or urine that equals or exceeds any of the following:

(a) The person has a concentration of amphetamine in the person's urine of at least five hundred nanograms of amphetamine per milliliter of the person's urine or has a concentration of amphetamine in the person's whole blood or blood serum or plasma of at least one hundred nanograms of amphetamine per milliliter of the person's whole blood or blood serum or plasma.

(b) The person has a concentration of cocaine in the person's urine of at least one hundred fifty nanograms of cocaine per milliliter of the person's urine or has a concentration of cocaine in the person's whole blood or blood serum or plasma of at least fifty nanograms of cocaine per milliliter of the person's whole blood or blood serum or plasma.

(c) The person has a concentration of cocaine metabolite in the person's urine of at least one hundred fifty nanograms of cocaine metabolite per milliliter of the person's urine or has a concentration of cocaine metabolite in the person's whole blood or blood serum or plasma of at least fifty nanograms of cocaine metabolite per milliliter of the person's whole blood or blood serum or plasma.

(d) The person has a concentration of heroin in the person's urine of at least two thousand nanograms of heroin per milliliter of the person's urine or has a concentration of heroin in the person's whole blood or blood serum or plasma of at least fifty nanograms of heroin per milliliter of the person's whole blood or blood serum or plasma.

(e) The person has a concentration of heroin metabolite (6-monoacetyl morphine) in the person's urine of at least ten nanograms of heroin metabolite (6-monoacetyl morphine) per milliliter of the person's urine or has a concentration of heroin metabolite (6-monoacetyl morphine) in the person's whole blood or blood serum or plasma of at least ten nanograms of heroin metabolite (6-monoacetyl morphine) per milliliter of the person's whole blood or blood serum or plasma.

(f) The person has a concentration of L.S.D. in the person's urine of at least twenty-five nanograms of L.S.D. per milliliter of the person's urine or has a concentration of L.S.D. in the person's whole blood or blood serum or plasma of at least ten nanograms of L.S.D. per milliliter of the person's whole blood or blood serum or plasma.

(g) The person has a concentration of marihuana in the person's urine of at least ten nanograms of marihuana per milliliter of the person's urine or has a concentration of marihuana in the person's whole blood or blood serum or plasma of at least two nanograms of marihuana per milliliter of the person's whole blood or blood serum or plasma.

(h) The state board of pharmacy has adopted a rule pursuant to section 4729.041 [4729.04.1] of the Revised Code that specifies the amount of salvia divinorum and the amount of salvinorin A that constitute concentrations of salvia divinorum and salvinorin A in a person's urine, in a person's whole blood, or in a person's blood serum or plasma at or above which the person is impaired for purposes of operating or being in physical control of any vessel underway or manipulating any water skis, aquaplane, or similar device on the waters of this state, the rule is in effect, and the person has a concentration of salvia divinorum or salvinorin A of at least that amount so specified by rule in the person's urine, in the person's whole blood, or in the person's blood serum or plasma.

(i) Either of the following applies:

(i) The person is under the influence of alcohol, a drug of abuse, or a combination of them, and, as measured by gas chromatography mass spectrometry, the person has a concentration of marihuana metabolite in the person's urine of at least fifteen nanograms of marihuana metabolite per milliliter of the person's urine or has a concentration of marihuana metabolite in the person's whole blood or blood serum or plasma of at least five nanograms of marihuana metabolite per milliliter of the person's whole blood or blood serum or plasma.

(ii) As measured by gas chromatography mass spectrometry, the person has a concentration of marihuana metabolite in the person's urine of at least thirty-five nanograms of marihuana metabolite per milliliter of the person's urine or has a concentration of marihuana metabolite in the person's whole blood or blood serum or plasma of at least fifty nanograms of marihuana metabolite per milliliter of the person's whole blood or blood serum or plasma.

(j) The person has a concentration of methamphetamine in the person's urine of at least five hundred nanograms of methamphetamine per milliliter of the person's urine or has a concentration of methamphetamine in the person's whole blood or blood serum or plasma of at least one hundred nanograms of methamphetamine per milliliter of the person's whole blood or blood serum or plasma.

(k) The person has a concentration of phencyclidine in the person's urine of at least twenty-five nanograms of phencyclidine per milliliter of the person's urine or has a concentration of phencyclidine in the person's whole blood or blood serum or plasma of at least ten nanograms of phencyclidine per milliliter of the person's whole blood or blood serum or plasma.

(B) No person under twenty-one years of age shall operate or be in physical control of any vessel underway or shall manipulate any water skis, aquaplane, or similar device on the waters in this state if, at the time of the operation, control, or manipulation, any of the following applies:

(1) The person has a concentration of at least two-hundredths of one per cent, but less than eight-hundredths of one per cent by weight per unit volume of alcohol in the person's whole blood.

(2) The person has a concentration of at least three-hundredths of one per cent but less than ninety-six-thousandths of one per cent by weight per unit volume of alcohol in the person's blood serum or plasma.

(3) The person has a concentration of at least twenty-eight one-thousandths of one gram, but less than eleven-hundredths of one gram by weight of alcohol per one hundred milliliters of the person's urine.

(4) The person has a concentration of at least two-hundredths of one gram, but less than eight-hundredths of one gram by weight of alcohol per two hundred ten liters of the person's breath.

(C) In any proceeding arising out of one incident, a person may be charged with a violation of division (A)(1) and a violation of division (B)(1), (2), (3), or (4) of this section, but the person shall not be convicted of more than one violation of those divisions.

(D)(1)(a) In any criminal prosecution or juvenile court proceeding for a violation of division (A) or (B) of this section or for an equivalent offense that is watercraft-related, the result of any test of any blood or urine withdrawn and analyzed at any health care provider, as defined in section 2317.02 of the Revised Code, may be admitted with expert testimony to be considered with any other relevant and competent evidence in determining the guilt or innocence of the defendant.

(b) In any criminal prosecution or juvenile court proceeding for a violation of division (A) or (B) of this section or for an equivalent offense that is watercraft-related, the court may admit evidence on the concentration of alcohol, drugs of abuse, controlled substances, metabolites of a controlled substance, or a combination of them in the defendant's or child's whole blood, blood serum or plasma, urine, or breath at the time of the alleged violation as shown by chemical analysis of the substance withdrawn, or specimen taken within three hours of the time of the alleged violation. The three-hour time limit specified in this division regarding the admission of evidence does not extend or affect the two-hour time limit specified in division (C) of section 1547.111 [1547.11.1] of the Revised Code as the maximum period of time during which a person may consent to a chemical test or tests as described in that section. The court may admit evidence on the concentration of alcohol, drugs of abuse, or a combination of them as described in this division when a person submits to a blood, breath, urine, or other bodily substance test at the request of a law enforcement officer under section 1547.111 [1547.11.1] of the Revised Code or a blood or urine sample is obtained pursuant to a search warrant. Only a physician, a registered nurse, an emergency medical technician-intermediate, an emergency medical technician-paramedic, or a qualified technician, chemist, or phlebotomist shall withdraw blood for the purpose of determining the alcohol, drug, controlled substance, metabolite of a controlled substance, or combination content of the whole blood, blood serum, or blood plasma. This limitation does not apply to the taking of breath or urine specimens. A person authorized to withdraw blood under this division may refuse to withdraw blood under this division if, in that person's opinion, the physical welfare of the defendant or child would be endangered by withdrawing blood.

The whole blood, blood serum or plasma, urine, or breath withdrawn under division (D)(1)(b) of this section shall be analyzed in accordance with methods approved by the director of health by an individual possessing a valid permit issued by the director pursuant to section 3701.143 [3701.14.3] of the Revised Code.

(2) In a criminal prosecution or juvenile court proceeding for a violation of division (A) of this section or for an equivalent offense that is watercraft-related, if there was at the time the bodily substance was taken a concentration of less than the applicable concentration of alcohol specified for a violation of division (A)(2), (3), (4), or (5) of this section or less than the applicable concentration of a listed controlled substance or a listed metabolite of a controlled substance specified for a violation of division (A)(6) of this section, that fact may be considered with other competent evidence in determining the guilt or innocence of the defendant or in making an adjudication for the child. This division does not limit or affect a criminal prosecution or juvenile court proceeding for a violation of division (B) of this section or for a violation of a prohibition that is substantially equivalent to that division.

(3) Upon the request of the person who was tested, the results of the chemical test shall be made available to the person or the person's attorney immediately upon completion of the test analysis.

If the chemical test was administered pursuant to division (D)(1)(b) of this section, the person tested may have a physician, a registered nurse, or a qualified technician, chemist, or phlebotomist of the person's own choosing administer a chemical test or tests in addition to any administered at the direction of a law enforcement officer, and shall be so advised. The failure or inability to obtain an additional test by a person shall not preclude the admission of evidence relating to the test or tests taken at the direction of a law enforcement officer.

(E)(1) In any criminal prosecution or juvenile court proceeding for a violation of division (A) or (B) of this section, of a municipal ordinance relating to operating or being in physical control of any vessel underway or to manipulating any water skis, aquaplane, or similar device on the waters of this state while under the influence of alcohol, a drug of abuse, or a combination of them, or of a municipal ordinance relating to operating or being in physical control of any vessel underway or to manipulating any water skis, aquaplane, or similar device on the waters of this state with a prohibited concentration of alcohol, a controlled substance, or a metabolite of a controlled substance in the whole blood, blood serum or plasma, breath, or urine, if a law enforcement officer has administered a field sobriety test to the operator or person found to be in physical control of the vessel underway involved in the violation or the person manipulating the water skis, aquaplane, or similar device involved in the violation and if it is shown by clear and convincing evidence that the officer administered the test in substantial compliance with the testing standards for reliable, credible, and generally accepted field sobriety tests for vehicles that were in effect at the time the tests were administered, including, but not limited to, any testing standards then in effect that have been set by the national highway traffic safety administration, that by their nature are not clearly inapplicable regarding the operation or physical control of vessels underway or the manipulation of water skis, aquaplanes, or similar devices, all of the following apply:

(a) The officer may testify concerning the results of the field sobriety test so administered.

(b) The prosecution may introduce the results of the field sobriety test so administered as evidence in any proceedings in the criminal prosecution or juvenile court proceeding.

(c) If testimony is presented or evidence is introduced under division (E)(1)(a) or (b) of this section and if the testimony or evidence is admissible under the Rules of Evidence, the court shall admit the testimony or evidence, and the trier of fact shall give it whatever weight the trier of fact considers to be appropriate.

(2) Division (E)(1) of this section does not limit or preclude a court, in its determination of whether the arrest of a person was supported by probable cause or its determination of any other matter in a criminal prosecution or juvenile court proceeding of a type described in that division, from considering evidence or testimony that is not otherwise disallowed by division (E)(1) of this section.

(F)(1) Subject to division (F)(3) of this section, in any criminal prosecution or juvenile court proceeding for a violation of division (A) or (B) of this section or for an equivalent offense that is substantially equivalent to either of those divisions, the court shall admit as prima-facie evidence a laboratory report from any laboratory personnel issued a permit by the department of health authorizing an analysis as described in this division that contains an analysis of the whole blood, blood serum or plasma, breath, urine, or other bodily substance tested and that contains all of the information specified in this division. The laboratory report shall contain all of the following:

(a) The signature, under oath, of any person who performed the analysis;

(b) Any findings as to the identity and quantity of alcohol, a drug of abuse, a controlled substance, a metabolite of a controlled substance, or a combination of them that was found;

(c) A copy of a notarized statement by the laboratory director or a designee of the director that contains the name of each certified analyst or test performer involved with the report, the analyst's or test performer's employment relationship with the laboratory that issued the report, and a notation that performing an analysis of the type involved is part of the analyst's or test performer's regular duties;

(d) An outline of the analyst's or test performer's education, training, and experience in performing the type of analysis involved and a certification that the laboratory satisfies appropriate quality control standards in general and, in this particular analysis, under rules of the department of health.

(2) Notwithstanding any other provision of law regarding the admission of evidence, a report of the type described in division (F)(1) of this section is not admissible against the defendant or child to whom it pertains in any proceeding, other than a preliminary hearing or a grand jury proceeding, unless the prosecutor has served a copy of the report on the defendant's or child's attorney or, if the defendant or child has no attorney, on the defendant or child.

(3) A report of the type described in division (F)(1) of this section shall not be prima-facie evidence of the contents, identity, or amount of any substance if, within seven days after the defendant or child to whom the report pertains or the defendant's or child's attorney receives a copy of the report, the defendant or child or the defendant's or child's attorney demands the testimony of the person who signed the report. The judge in the case may extend the seven-day time limit in the interest of justice.

(G) Except as otherwise provided in this division, any physician, registered nurse, emergency medical technician-intermediate, emergency medical technician-paramedic, or qualified technician, chemist, or phlebotomist who withdraws blood from a person pursuant to this section or section 1547.111 [1547.11.1] of the Revised Code, and a hospital, first-aid station, or clinic at which blood is withdrawn from a person pursuant to this section or section 1547.111 [1547.11.1] of the Revised Code, is immune from criminal and civil liability based upon a claim of assault and battery or any other claim that is not a claim of malpractice, for any act performed in withdrawing blood from the person. The immunity provided in this division also extends to an emergency medical service organization that employs an emergency medical technician-intermediate, an emergency medical technician-paramedic who withdraws blood under this section. The immunity provided in this division is not available to a person who withdraws blood if the person engages in willful or wanton misconduct.

(H) Division (A)(6) of this section does not apply to a person who operates or is in physical control of a vessel underway or manipulates any water skis, aquaplane, or similar device while the person has a concentration of a listed controlled substance or a listed metabolite of a controlled substance in the person's whole blood, blood serum or plasma, or urine that equals or exceeds the amount specified in that division, if both of the following apply:

(1) The person obtained the controlled substance pursuant to a prescription issued by a licensed health professional authorized to prescribe drugs.

(2) The person injected, ingested, or inhaled the controlled substance in accordance with the health professional's directions.

(I) As used in this section and section 1547.111 [1547.11.1] of the Revised Code:

(1) "Equivalent offense" has the same meaning as in section 4511.181 [4511.18.1] of the Revised Code.

(2) "National highway traffic safety administration" has the same meaning as in section 4511.19 of the Revised Code.

(3) "Operate" means that a vessel is being used on the waters in this state when the vessel is not securely affixed to a dock or to shore or to any permanent structure to which the vessel has the right to affix or that a vessel is not anchored in a designated anchorage area or boat camping area that is established by the United States coast guard, this state, or a political subdivision and in which the vessel has the right to anchor.

(4) "Controlled substance" and "marihuana" have the same meanings as in section 3719.01 of the Revised Code.

(5) "Cocaine" and "L.S.D." have the same meanings as in section 2925.01 of the Revised Code.

(6) "Equivalent offense that is watercraft-related" means an equivalent offense that is one of the following:

(a) A violation of division (A) or (B) of this section;

(b) A violation of a municipal ordinance prohibiting a person from operating or being in physical control of any vessel underway or from manipulating any water skis, aquaplane, or similar device on the waters of this state while under the influence of alcohol, a drug of abuse, or a combination of them or prohibiting a person from operating or being in physical control of any vessel underway or from manipulating any water skis, aquaplane, or similar device on the waters of this state with a prohibited concentration of alcohol, a controlled substance, or a metabolite of a controlled substance in the whole blood, blood serum or plasma, breath, or urine;

(c) A violation of an existing or former municipal ordinance, law of another state, or law of the United States that is substantially equivalent to division (A) or (B) of this section;

(d) A violation of a former law of this state that was substantially equivalent to division (A) or (B) of this section.

(7) "Emergency medical technician-intermediate" and "emergency medical technician-paramedic" have the same meanings as in section 4765.01 of the Revised Code.

**HISTORY: 128 v 1004 (Eff 8-5-59); 133 v H 1002 (Eff 9-4-70); 136 v H 957 (Eff 9-3-76); 139 v H 782 (Eff 3-4-83); 141 v H 265 (Eff 7-24-86); 143 v H 522 (Eff 6-13-90); 146 v S 295 (Eff 3-18-97); 149 v S 163, § 1. Eff 4-9-2003; 149 v S 123, § 1, eff. 1-1-04; 149 v S 163, § 3, eff. 1-1-04; 150 v H 87, § 1, eff. 6-30-03; 150 v H 87, § 4, eff. 1-1-04; 150 v H 163, § 1, eff. 9-23-04; 151 v S 8, § 1, eff. 8-17-06; 152 v S 17, § 1, eff. 9-30-08; 152 v H 215, § 1, eff. 4-7-09; 153 v S 58, § 1, eff. 9-17-10.**

The effective date is set by section 26 of H.B. 87.

The provisions of § 5 of S.B. 123 (149 v —), as amended by § 3 of H.B. 163 (150 v —), read as follows:

SECTION 5. (A) Notwithstanding division (B) of section 1.58 of the Revised Code, the provisions of the Revised Code amended or enacted in Sections 1 and 2 of Am. Sub. S.B. 123 of the 124th General Assembly shall apply only in relation to conduct and offenses committed on or after January 1, 2004. Conduct and offenses committed prior to January 1, 2004, shall be governed by the law in effect on the date the conduct or offense was committed. * * *

## § 1547.111 Implied consent.

(A)(1)(a) Any person who operates or is in physical control of a vessel or manipulates any water skis, aquaplane, or similar device upon any waters in this state shall be deemed to have given consent to a chemical test or tests to determine the alcohol, drug of abuse, controlled substance, metabolite of a controlled substance, or combination content of the person's whole blood, blood serum or plasma, breath, or urine if arrested for operating or being in physical control of a vessel or manipulating any water skis, aquaplane, or similar device in violation of section 1547.11 of the Revised Code or a substantially equivalent municipal ordinance.

(b) The test or tests under division (A)(1) of this section shall be administered at the request of a law enforcement officer having reasonable grounds to believe the person was operating or in physical control of a vessel or manipulating any water skis, aquaplane, or similar device in violation of section 1547.11 of the Revised Code or a substantially equivalent municipal ordinance. The law enforcement agency by which the officer is employed shall designate which test or tests shall be administered.

(2) Any person who is dead or unconscious or who otherwise is in a condition rendering the person incapable of refusal shall be deemed to have consented as provided in division (A)(1) of this section, and the test or tests may be administered, subject to sections 313.12 to 313.16 of the Revised Code.

(B)(1) If a law enforcement officer arrests a person for operating or being in physical control of a vessel or manipulating any water skis, aquaplane, or similar device in violation of section 1547.11 of the Revised Code or a substantially equivalent municipal ordinance and if the person previously has been convicted of or pleaded guilty to two or more violations of section 1547.11 of the Revised Code or other equivalent offenses, the law enforcement officer shall request the person to submit, and the person shall submit, to a chemical test or tests of the person's whole blood, blood serum or plasma, breath, or urine for the purpose of determining the alcohol, drug of abuse, controlled substance, metabolite of a controlled substance, or combination content of the person's whole blood, blood serum or plasma, breath, or urine. A law enforcement officer who makes a request pursuant to this division that a person submit to a chemical test or tests is not required to advise the person of the consequences of refusing to submit to the test or tests and is not required to give the person the form described in division (C) of this section, but the officer shall advise the person at the time of the arrest that if the person refuses to take a chemical test the officer may employ whatever reasonable means are necessary to ensure that the person submits to a chemical test of the person's whole blood or blood serum or plasma. The officer shall also advise the person at the time of the arrest that the person may have an independent chemical test taken at the person's own expense. The advice shall be in written form prescribed by the chief of the division of watercraft and shall be read to the person. The form shall contain a statement that the form was shown to the person under arrest and read to the person by the arresting officer. The reading of the form shall be witnessed by one or more persons, and the witnesses shall certify to this fact by signing the form. Divisions (A)(1)(b) and (A)(2) of this section apply to the administration of a chemical test or tests pursuant to this division.

(2) If a person refuses to submit to a chemical test upon a request made pursuant to division (B)(1) of this section, the law enforcement officer who made the request may employ whatever reasonable means are necessary to ensure that the person submits to a chemical test of the person's whole blood or blood serum or plasma. A law enforcement officer who acts pursuant to this division to ensure that a person submits to a chemical test of the person's whole blood or blood serum or plasma is immune from criminal and civil liability based upon a claim for assault and battery or any other claim for the acts, unless the officer so acted with malicious purpose, in bad faith, or in a wanton or reckless manner.

(C) Except as provided in division (B) of this section, any person under arrest for violating section 1547.11 of the Revised Code or a substantially equivalent municipal ordinance shall be advised of the consequences of refusing to submit to a chemical test or tests designated as provided in division (A) of this section. The advice shall be in a written form prescribed by the chief of the division of watercraft and shall be read to the person. The form shall contain a statement that the form was shown to the person under arrest and read to the person by the arresting officer. The reading of the form shall be witnessed by one or more persons, and the witnesses shall certify to this fact by signing the form. The person must submit to the chemical test or tests, subsequent to the request of the arresting officer, within two hours of the time of the alleged violation, and if the person does not submit to the test or tests within that two-hour time limit, the failure to submit automatically constitutes a refusal to submit to the test or tests.

(D) Except as provided in division (B) of this section, if a law enforcement officer asks a person under arrest for violating section 1547.11 of the Revised Code or a substantially equivalent municipal ordinance to submit to a chemical test or tests as provided in division (A) of this section, if the arresting officer advises the person of the consequences of the person's refusal as provided in division (C) of this section, and if the person refuses to submit, no chemical test shall be given. Upon receipt of a sworn statement of the officer that the arresting law enforcement officer had reasonable grounds to believe the arrested person, violated section 1547.11 of the Revised Code or a substantially equivalent municipal ordinance and that the person refused to submit to the chemical test upon the request of the officer, and upon receipt of the form as provided in division (C) of this section certifying that the arrested person was advised of the consequences of the refusal, the chief of the division of watercraft shall inform the person by written notice that the person is prohibited from operating or being in physical control of a vessel, from manipulating any water skis, aquaplane, or similar device, and from registering any watercraft in accordance with section 1547.54 of the Revised Code, for one year following the date of the alleged violation. The suspension of these operation, physical control, manipulation, and registration privileges shall continue for the entire one-year period, subject to review as provided in this section.

If the person under arrest is the owner of the vessel involved in the alleged violation, the law enforcement officer who arrested the person shall seize the watercraft registration certificate and tags from the vessel involved in the violation and forward them to the chief. The chief shall retain the impounded registration certificate and tags and shall impound all other registration certificates and tags issued to the person in accordance with sections 1547.54 and 1547.57 of the Revised Code, for a period of one year following the date of the alleged violation, subject to review as provided in this section.

If the arrested person fails to surrender the registration certificate because it is not on the person of the arrested person or in the watercraft, the law enforcement officer who made the arrest shall order the person to surrender it within twenty-four hours to the law enforcement officer or the law enforcement agency that employs the law enforcement officer. If the person fails to do so, the law enforcement officer shall notify the chief of that fact in the statement the officer submits to the chief under this division.

(E) Upon suspending a person's operation, physical control, manipulation, and registration privileges in accordance with division (D) of this section, the chief shall notify the person in writing, at the person's last known address, and inform the person that the person may petition for a hearing in accordance with division (F) of this section. If a person whose operation, physical control, manipulation, and registration privileges have been suspended petitions for a hearing or appeals any adverse decision, the suspension shall begin at the termination of any hearing or appeal unless the hearing or appeal results in a decision favorable to the person.

(F) Any person who has been notified by the chief that the person is prohibited from operating or being in physical control of a vessel or manipulating any water skis, aquaplane, or similar device and from registering any watercraft in accordance with section 1547.54 of the Revised Code, or who has had the registration certificate and tags of the person's watercraft impounded pursuant to division (D) of this section, within twenty days of the notification or impoundment, may file a petition in the municipal court or the county court, or if the person is a minor in juvenile court, with jurisdiction over the place at which the arrest occurred, agreeing to pay the cost of the proceedings and alleging error in the action taken by the chief under division (D) of this section or alleging one or more of the matters within the scope of the hearing as provided in this section, or both. The petitioner shall notify the chief of the filing of the petition and send the chief a copy of the petition.

The scope of the hearing is limited to the issues of whether the law enforcement officer had reasonable grounds to believe the petitioner was operating or in physical control of a vessel or manipulating any water skis, aquaplane, or similar device in violation of section 1547.11 of the Revised Code or a substantially equivalent municipal ordinance, whether the petitioner was placed under arrest, whether the petitioner refused to submit to the chemical test upon request of the officer, and whether the petitioner was advised of the consequences of the petitioner's refusal.

(G)(1) The chief shall furnish the court a copy of the affidavit as provided in division (C) of this section and any other relevant information requested by the court.

(2) In hearing the matter and in determining whether the person has shown error in the decision taken by the chief as provided in division (D) of this section, the court shall decide the issue upon the relevant, competent, and material evidence submitted by the chief or the person whose operation, physical control, manipulation, and registration privileges have been suspended.

In the proceedings, the chief shall be represented by the prosecuting attorney of the county in which the petition is filed if the petition is filed in a county court or juvenile court, except that if the arrest occurred within a city or village within the jurisdiction of the county court in which the petition is filed, the city director of law or village solicitor of that city or village shall represent the chief. If the petition is filed in the municipal court, the chief shall be represented as provided in section 1901.34 of the Revised Code.

(3) If the court finds from the evidence submitted that the person has failed to show error in the action taken by the chief under division (D) of this section or in one or more of the matters within the scope of the hearing as provided in division (F) of this section, or both, the court shall assess the cost of the proceeding against the person and shall uphold the suspension of the operation, physical control, use, and registration privileges provided in division (D) of this section. If the court finds that the person has shown error in the action taken by the chief under division (D) of this section or in one or more of the matters within the scope of the hearing as provided in division (F) of this section, or both, the cost of the proceedings shall be paid out of the county treasury of the county in which the proceedings were held, the chief shall reinstate the operation, physical control, manipulation, and registration privileges of the person without charge, and the chief shall return the registration certificate and tags, if impounded, without charge.

(4) The court shall give information in writing of any action taken under this section to the chief.

(H) At the end of any period of suspension or impoundment imposed under this section, and upon request of the person whose operation, physical control, use, and registration privileges were suspended or whose registration certificate and tags were impounded, the chief shall reinstate the person's operation, physical control, manipulation, and registration privileges by written notice and return the certificate and tags.

(I) No person who has received written notice from the chief that the person is prohibited from operating of being in physical control of a vessel, from manipulating any water skis, aquaplane, or similar device, and from registering a watercraft, or who has had the registration certificate and tags of the person's watercraft impounded, in accordance with division (D) of this section, shall operate or be in physical control of a vessel or manipulate any water skis, aquaplane, or similar device for a period of one year following the date of the person's alleged violation of section 1547.11 of the Revised Code or the substantially equivalent municipal ordinance.

**HISTORY: 141 v H 265 (Eff 7-24-86); 143 v H 522 (Eff 6-13-90); 147 v S 187 (Eff 3-18-99); 149 v S 163, § 1. Eff 4-9-2003; 149 v S 123, § 1, eff. 1-1-04; 149 v S 163, § 3, eff. 1-1-04; 151 v S 8, § 1, eff. 8-17-06; 152 v S 17, § 1, eff. 9-30-08; 152 v H 215, § 1, eff. 4-7-09.**

The effective date is set by section 5 of S.B. 163 (149 v —).

See provisions, § 5 of S.B. 123 (149 v —), following RC § 1547.11.

## § 1547.12 Incapacitated operators prohibited.

No person shall operate any vessel if the person is so mentally or physically incapacitated as to be unable to operate the vessel in a safe and competent manner.

No person shall permit any vessel to be operated on the waters in this state in violation of this section.

**HISTORY: 128 v 1004 (Eff 8-5-59); 143 v H 522 (Eff 6-13-90); 147 v S 187. Eff 3-18-99.**

## § 1547.13 Failure to comply with law enforcement order; fleeing.

(A) No person shall fail to comply with any lawful order or direction of any law enforcement officer having authority to direct, control, or regulate the operation or use of vessels.

(B) No person shall operate any vessel so as to purposely elude or flee from a law enforcement officer after receiving a visible or audible signal from a law enforcement officer to bring the vessel to a stop.

(C) No person shall operate or permit to be operated any vessel on the waters in this state in violation of this section.

**HISTORY: 143 v H 522 (Eff 6-13-90); 147 v S 187. Eff 3-18-99.**

**Not analogous to former RC § 1547.13 (128 v 1004; 129 v 582; 133 v H 1002), repealed 134 v H 511, § 2, eff 1-1-74.**

## § 1547.131 Duty upon approach of law enforcement vessel.

Upon the approach of a law enforcement vessel with at least one flashing, rotating, or oscillating light of a color conforming with the requirements of federal law, the operator of any vessel shall stop if followed or give way in any crossing, head-on, or overtaking situation and shall remain in that position until the law enforcement vessel has passed, except when otherwise directed by a law enforcement officer. If traffic conditions warrant, a siren or other sound producing device also may be operated as an additional signaling device. This section does not relieve the operator of any law enforcement vessel from the duty to operate with due regard for the safety of all persons and property on the waters in this state.

No person shall operate or permit to be operated any vessel on the waters in this state in violation of this section.

**HISTORY: 143 v H 522 (Eff 6-13-90); 147 v S 187. Eff 3-18-99.**

## § 1547.132 Creating wake within 100 feet of certain vessels.

(A) As used in this section, "public service" means activities that include, but are not limited to, escorting or patrolling special water events, traffic control, salvage, firefighting, medical assistance, assisting disabled vessels, and search and rescue.

(B) No person shall operate a vessel at a speed that creates a wake within one hundred feet of a stationary law enforcement vessel displaying at least one flashing, oscillating, or rotating light conforming with 33 C.F.R. 88.11.

(C) No person shall operate a vessel at a speed that creates a wake within one hundred feet of a vessel that is being used to provide public service and that displays at least one flashing, oscillating, or rotating light conforming with 33 C.F.R. 88.12.

(D) No person shall permit any vessel to be operated on the waters in this state in violation of this section.

**HISTORY: 152 v S 271, § 1, eff. 6-13-08.**

## § 1547.14 Water skiing confined to ski zones or where not specifically restricted.

(A) Except on the waters of the Ohio River or Lake Erie and immediately connected harbors and bays, any person who rides or attempts to ride upon one or more water skis, surfboard, or similar device, or who engages or attempts to engage in barefoot skiing, and any person who operates a vessel towing a person riding or attempting to ride on one or more water skis, surfboard, or similar device, or engaging or attempting to engage in barefoot skiing, shall confine that activity to the water area within a designated ski zone on all bodies of water on which a ski zone has been established.

(B) On all bodies of water where no specific activity zones have been established, the activities described in division (A) of this section shall be confined to areas where the activities are not specifically restricted by this chapter and rules adopted under it.

(C) Divisions (A) and (B) of this section do not apply to an activity described in division (A) of this section if the vessel involved in the activity is traveling at idle speed in a designated no wake zone and the activity is not being conducted in any of the following areas:

(1) Within three hundred feet of a gas dock, marina, launch ramp, or harbor entrance;

(2) Within a designated anchorage area, swim zone, boat swim zone, or boat camping area;

(3) Under a bridge or within three hundred feet of a bridge underpass;

(4) Any area designated as a no ski zone.

(D) No person shall operate or permit to be operated any vessel on the waters in this state in violation of this section.

**HISTORY: 128 v 1004 (Eff 8-5-59); 139 v H 782 (Eff 3-4-83); 140 v H 682 (Eff 3-28-85); 143 v H 522 (Eff 6-13-90); 147 v S 187. Eff 3-18-99; 152 v S 271, § 1, eff. 6-13-08.**

## § 1547.15 Observer required when towing skier.

Any person who operates a vessel towing any person riding or attempting to ride upon one or more water skis or upon a surfboard or similar device, or engaging or attempting to engage in barefoot skiing, on the waters in this state shall have present in the vessel a person or persons other than the operator, ten years of age or older, who shall at all times observe the progress of the person being towed. The operator of the towing vessel shall at all times observe the traffic pattern toward which the vessel is approaching.

No person shall operate or permit to be operated any vessel on the waters in this state in violation of this section.

**HISTORY: 128 v 1004 (Eff 8-5-59); 133 v H 1002 (Eff 9-4-70); 139 v H 782 (Eff 3-4-83); 140 v H 682 (Eff 3-28-85); 143 v H 522 (Eff 6-13-90); 147 v S 187. Eff 3-18-99.**

## § 1547.16 Water skiing after dark prohibited.

No person shall ride or attempt to ride upon water skis, surfboard, or similar device, or engage or attempt to engage in barefoot skiing, or use or operate any vessel to tow any person thereon on the waters in this state during that period of the day between sunset and sunrise, except upon special permit issued by the state department, conservancy district, or political subdivision having jurisdiction and control of such water.

**HISTORY: 128 v 1004 (Eff 8-5-59); 139 v H 782 (Eff 3-4-83); 140 v H 682 (Eff 3-28-85); 143 v H 522. Eff 6-13-90.**

## § 1547.18 Personal flotation device required for towed person.

(A) No person shall ride or attempt to ride on one or more water skis, surfboard, inflatable device, or similar device being towed by a vessel without wearing an adequate and effective coast guard approved type one, two, or three personal flotation device or type five personal flotation device specifically designed for water skiing, in good and serviceable condition and of appropriate size, except upon special permit issued by the state department, conservancy district, or political subdivision having jurisdiction and control of the water.

(B) No person shall engage or attempt to engage in barefoot skiing without wearing an adequate and effective coast guard approved type one, two, or three personal flotation device or type five personal flotation device specifically designed for water skiing, in good and serviceable condition and of appropriate size, or a wet suit specifically designed for barefoot skiing.

(C) No operator of a vessel shall tow any person who fails to comply with division (A) or (B) of this section.

**HISTORY: 128 v 1004 (Eff 8-5-59); 129 v 582(695) (Eff 1-10-61); 133 v H 1002 (Eff 9-4-70); 136 v H 957 (Eff 9-3-76); 140 v H 682 (Eff 3-28-85); 143 v H 522 (Eff 6-13-90); 146 v S 295. Eff 3-18-97.**

## § 1547.24 Children under 10 must wear appropriate size personal flotation device.

No person shall operate or permit to be operated any vessel under eighteen feet in length while there is present in the vessel any person under ten years of age, not wearing a coast guard approved type one, two, three, or five personal flotation device in good and serviceable condition of appropriate size securely attached to the person under ten years of age.

**HISTORY: 128 v 1004 (Eff 8-5-59); 136 v H 957 (Eff 9-3-76); 143 v H 522. Eff 6-13-90; 152 v S 271, § 1, eff. 6-13-08.**

## § 1547.25 Operation without personal flotation devices prohibited.

(A) No person shall operate or permit to be operated any vessel, other than a commercial vessel or other vessel exempted by rules adopted under section 1547.52 of the Revised Code, on the waters in this state:

(1) That is sixteen feet or greater in length without carrying aboard one type one, two, or three personal flotation device for each person aboard and one type four personal flotation device;

(2) That is less than sixteen feet in length, including canoes and kayaks of any length, without carrying aboard one type one, two, or three personal flotation device for each person aboard.

(B) A type five personal flotation device may be carried in lieu of a type one, two, or three personal flotation device required under division (A) of this section.

(C) No person shall operate or permit to be operated any commercial vessel on the waters in this state:

(1) That is less than forty feet in length and is not carrying persons for hire without carrying aboard at least one type one, two, or three personal flotation device for each person aboard;

(2) That is carrying persons for hire or is forty feet in length or longer and is not carrying persons for hire without carrying aboard at least one type one personal flotation device for each person aboard;

(3) That is twenty-six feet in length or longer without carrying aboard at least one type four ring life buoy in addition to the applicable requirements of divisions (C)(1) and (2) of this section.

(D) Each personal flotation device carried aboard a vessel, including a commercial vessel, pursuant to this section shall be coast guard approved and in good and serviceable condition, of appropriate size for the wearer, and readily accessible to each person aboard the vessel at all times.

(E) As used in this section, "commercial vessel" means any vessel used in the carriage of any person or property for a valuable consideration whether flowing directly or indirectly from the owner, partner, or agent or any other person interested in the vessel. "Commercial vessel" does not include any vessel that is manufactured or used primarily for noncommercial use or that is leased, rented, or chartered to another for noncommercial use.

**HISTORY: 128 v 1004 (Eff 8-5-59); 129 v 1712 (Eff 3-31-62); 133 v H 1002 (Eff 9-4-70); 136 v H 957 (Eff 9-3-76); 137 v S 173 (Eff 5-20-77); 139 v H 782 (Eff 3-4-83); 143 v H 522 (Eff 6-13-90); 146 v S 295 (Eff 3-18-97); 147 v S 187 (Eff 3-18-99); 149 v S 150. Eff 7-5-2002.**

# [DIVISION OF WATERCRAFT]

## § 1547.523 Felony precludes or terminates employment as state watercraft officer.

(A) As used in this section, "felony" has the same meaning as in section 109.511 [109.51.1] of the Revised Code.

(B)(1) The chief of the division of watercraft shall not appoint a person as a state watercraft officer on a permanent basis, on a temporary basis, for a probationary term, or on other than a permanent basis if the person previously has been convicted of or has pleaded guilty to a felony.

(2)(a) The chief of the division of watercraft shall terminate the employment of a state watercraft officer who does either of the following:

(i) Pleads guilty to a felony;

(ii) Pleads guilty to a misdemeanor pursuant to a negotiated plea agreement as provided in division (D) of section 2929.43 of the Revised Code in which the state watercraft officer agrees to surrender the certificate awarded to that officer under section 109.77 of the Revised Code.

(b) The chief shall suspend from employment a state watercraft officer who is convicted, after trial, of a felony. If the state watercraft officer files an appeal from that conviction and the conviction is upheld by the highest court to which the appeal is taken or if the state watercraft officer does not file a timely appeal, the chief shall terminate the employment of that state watercraft officer. If the state watercraft officer files an appeal that results in the state watercraft officer's acquittal of the felony or conviction of a misdemeanor, or in the dismissal of the felony charge against the state watercraft officer, the chief shall reinstate that state watercraft officer. A state watercraft officer who is reinstated under division (B)(2)(b) of this section shall not receive any back pay unless that state watercraft officer's conviction of the felony was reversed on appeal, or the felony charge was dismissed, because the court found insufficient evidence to convict the state watercraft officer of the felony.

(3) Division (B) of this section does not apply regarding an offense that was committed prior to January 1, 1997.

(4) The suspension from employment, or the termination of the employment, of a state watercraft officer under division (B)(2) of this section shall be in accordance with Chapter 119. of the Revised Code.

**HISTORY: 146 v H 566. Eff 10-16-96; 149 v H 490, § 1, eff. 1-1-04.**

The effective date is set by section 4 of H.B. 490.

## § 1547.63 Enforcement.

Every sheriff, deputy sheriff, marshal, deputy marshal, member of the organized police department of any municipal corporation, police constable of any township, wildlife officer, park officer, preserve officer, conservancy district police officer, and other law enforcement officer, within the area of his authority, may enforce this chapter and rules adopted by the chief of the division of watercraft and, in the exercise thereof, may stop and board any vessel subject to this chapter and rules adopted under it.

**HISTORY: 129 v 582(702) (Eff 1-10-61); 131 v 546 (Eff 11-1-65); 143 v H 522 (Eff 6-13-90); 145 v S 182. Eff 10-20-94.**

**Analogous to former RC § 1501.25 (128 v H 928), repealed 129 v H 1, § 2, eff 1-10-61.**

## § 1547.69 Firearms offenses; signaling devices.

(A) As used in this section:

(1) "Firearm" and "handgun" have the same meanings as in section 2923.11 of the Revised Code.

(2) "Unloaded" has the same meaning as in section 2923.16 of the Revised Code.

(B) No person shall knowingly discharge a firearm while in or on a vessel.

(C) No person shall knowingly transport or have a loaded firearm in a vessel in a manner that the firearm is accessible to the operator or any passenger.

(D) No person shall knowingly transport or have a firearm in a vessel unless it is unloaded and is carried in one of the following ways:

(1) In a closed package, box, or case;

(2) In plain sight with the action opened or the weapon stripped, or, if the firearm is of a type on which the action will not stay open or that cannot easily be stripped, in plain sight.

(E)(1) The affirmative defenses authorized in divisions (D)(1) and (2) of section 2923.12 of the Revised Code are affirmative defenses to a charge under division (C) or (D) of this section that involves a firearm other than a handgun. It is an affirmative defense to a charge under division (C) or (D) of this section of transporting or having a firearm of any type, including a handgun, in a vessel that the actor transported or had the firearm in the vessel for any lawful purpose and while the vessel was on the actor's own property, provided that this affirmative defense is not available unless the actor, prior to arriving at the vessel on the actor's own property, did not transport or possess the firearm in the vessel or in a motor vehicle in a manner prohibited by this section or division (B) or (C) of section 2923.16 of the Revised Code while the vessel was being operated on a waterway that was not on the actor's own property or while the motor vehicle was being operated on a street, highway, or other public or private property used by the public for vehicular traffic.

(2) No person who is charged with a violation of division (C) or (D) of this section shall be required to obtain a license or temporary emergency license to carry a concealed handgun under section 2923.125 [2923.12.5] or 2923.1213 [2923.12.13] of the Revised Code as a condition for the dismissal of the charge.

(F) Divisions (B), (C), and (D) of this section do not apply to the possession or discharge of a United States coast guard approved signaling device required to be carried aboard a vessel under section 1547.251 [1547.25.1] of the Revised Code when the signaling device is possessed or used for the purpose of giving a visual distress signal. No person shall knowingly transport or possess any signaling device of that nature in or on a vessel in a loaded condition at any time other than immediately prior to the discharge of the signaling device for the purpose of giving a visual distress signal.

(G) No person shall operate or permit to be operated any vessel on the waters in this state in violation of this section.

(H)(1) This section does not apply to any of the following:

(a) An officer, agent, or employee of this or any other state or of the United States, or to a law enforcement officer, when authorized to carry or have loaded or accessible firearms in a vessel and acting within the scope of the officer's, agent's, or employee's duties;

(b) Any person who is employed in this state, who is authorized to carry or have loaded or accessible firearms in a vessel, and who is subject to and in compliance with the requirements of section 109.801 [109.80.1] of the Revised Code, unless the appointing authority of the person has expressly specified that the exemption provided in division (H)(1)(b) of this section does not apply to the person;

(c) Any person legally engaged in hunting.

(2) Divisions (C) and (D) of this section do not apply to a person who transports or possesses a handgun in a vessel and who, at the time of that transportation or possession, is carrying a valid license or temporary emergency license to carry a concealed handgun issued to the person under section 2923.125 [2923.12.5] or 2923.1213 [2923.12.13] of the Revised Code or a license to carry a concealed handgun that was issued by another state with which the attorney general has entered into a reciprocity agreement under section 109.69 of the Revised Code, unless the person knowingly is in a place on the vessel described in division (B) of section 2923.126 [2923.12.6] of the Revised Code.

(I) If a law enforcement officer stops a vessel for a violation of this section or any other law enforcement purpose, if any person on the vessel surrenders a firearm to the officer, either voluntarily or pursuant to a request or demand of the officer, and if the officer does not charge the person with a violation of this section or arrest the person for any offense, the person is not otherwise prohibited by law from possessing the firearm, and the firearm is not contraband, the officer shall return the firearm to the person at the termination of the stop.

**HISTORY: 143 v H 522 (Eff 6-13-90); 147 v S 187. Eff 3-18-99; 150 v H 12, § 1, eff. 4-8-04; 151 v H 347, § 1, eff. 3-14-07.**

Governor Taft's veto of HB 347 was overridden by the Ohio General Assembly.

The provisions of § 6, H.B. 12 (150 v —), read as follows:

SECTION 6. In amending sections 1547.69, 2911.21, 2921.13, 2923.12, 2923.121, 2923.123, 2923.13, 2923.16, 2953.32, and 4749.10 of the Revised Code and in enacting sections 109.69,

109.731, 311.41, 311.42, and 2923.124 to 2923.1213 of the Revised Code in this act, the General Assembly hereby declares its intent to recognize both of the following:

(A) The inalienable and fundamental right of an individual to defend the individual's person and the members of the individual's family;

(B) The fact that the right described in division (A) of this section predates the adoption of the United States Constitution, the adoption of the Ohio Constitution, and the enactment of all statutory laws by the General Assembly and may not be infringed by any enactment of the General Assembly.

The provisions of § 7, H.B. 12 (150 v —), read as follows:

SECTION 7. In enacting sections 109.69, 109.731, 311.41, 311.42, and 2923.124 to 2923.1213 of the Revised Code in this act and in amending sections 1547.69, 2911.21, 2921.13, 2923.12, 2923.121, 2923.123, 2923.13, 2923.16, 2953.32, and 4749.10 of the Revised Code in this act relative to licenses to carry a concealed handgun, the General Assembly hereby declares that it is not its intent to declare or otherwise give the impression that, prior to the effective date of this act, an individual did not have an inalienable and fundamental right, or a right under the Ohio Constitution or the United States Constitution, to carry a concealed handgun or other firearm for the defense of the individual's person or a member of the individual's family while engaged in lawful activity. Further, the General Assembly declares that it is not its intent to invalidate any prior convictions for violating any section of the Revised Code or a municipal ordinance prior to the effective date of this act or to prevent the prosecution of any violation committed prior to the effective date of this act.

The provisions of § 9, H.B. 12 (150 v —), read as follows:

SECTION 9. The General Assembly finds that licenses to carry concealed handguns are a matter of statewide concern and wishes to ensure uniformity throughout the state regarding the qualifications for a person to hold a license to carry a concealed handgun and the authority granted to a person holding a license of that nature. It is the intent of the General Assembly in amending sections 1547.69, 2911.21, 2921.13, 2923.12, 2923.121, 2923.123, 2923.16, 2953.32, and 4749.10 and enacting sections 109.69, 109.731, 311.41, 311.42, and 2923.124 to 2923.1213 of the Revised Code to enact laws of a general nature, and, by enacting those laws of a general nature, the state occupies and preempts the field of issuing licenses to carry a concealed handgun and the validity of licenses of that nature. No municipal corporation may adopt or continue in existence any ordinance, and no township may adopt or continue in existence any resolution, that is in conflict with those sections, including, but not limited to, any ordinance or resolution that attempts to restrict the places where a person possessing a valid license to carry a concealed handgun may carry a handgun concealed.

The provisions of § 10, H.B. 12 (150 v —), read as follows:

SECTION 10. If any provision of sections 1547.69, 2911.21, 2913.02, 2921.13, 2923.12, 2923.121, 2923.123, 2923.16, 2929.14, 2953.32, and 4749.10 of the Revised Code, as amended by this act, any provision of sections 109.69, 109.731, 311.41, 311.42, 2923.124, 2923.125, 2923.126, 2923.127, 2923.128, 2923.129, 2923.1210, 2923.1211, 2923.1212, and 2923.1213 of the Revised Code, as enacted by this act, or the application of any provision of those sections to any person or circumstance is held invalid, the invalidity does not affect other provisions or applications of the particular section or related sections that can be given effect without the invalid provision or application, and to this end the provisions of the particular section are severable.

## § 1547.80 Rules regarding security of ports and associated facilities.

(A) Notwithstanding any provision of the Revised Code to the contrary, the department of natural resources, division of watercraft, in consultation with the department of public safety, shall adopt rules regarding the security of ports on waterways in this state and the facilities associated with those ports. The rules shall include but not be limited to provisions that do the following:

(1) Designate the ports, located in whole or in part within this state, to which the requirements of this section apply, considering the size and activity of the port, its proximity to a metropolitan location, its proximity to a sensitive site as defined in section 4563.30 of the Revised Code, and any other criteria related to security that the department considers reasonable;

(2) Require the designated ports to register biennially with the department of natural resources;

(3) Require the designated ports to do all of the following:

(a) Prepare a written security plan that is consistent with the most recent security guidelines established pursuant to the national maritime transportation security plan by the secretary in the department in which the United States coast guard is located;

(b) Develop a written list of emergency contacts and telephone numbers;

(c) Restrict access to vessels by unauthorized persons;

(d) Require those piloting or renting vessels to provide identification;

(e) Create an emergency locater map that identifies areas of the port facilities;

(f) Familiarize local law enforcement agencies with the facilities and consult with them in the development of the port's security procedures.

(4) Require all owners of vessels or pilots to secure their vessels;

(5) Require all persons who rent a vessel to present government-issued identification, in addition to any required license, to the person who rents them the vessel;

(6) Address the security of port facilities located in whole or in part in this state in any other manner the department determines to be necessary.

(B) The security plan and the emergency locator map this section describes shall display prominently the following statement: "This document may contain information that, if disclosed, could endanger the life or safety of the public; therefore, this document is to be maintained and used in a manner that preserves the confidentiality of the information it contains in a manner consistent with law."

(C) Each port facility designated pursuant to division (A) of this section shall provide a copy of the registration this section requires and the port's security plan and emergency locator map to the department of public safety, to the department of natural resources, to the sheriff of the county in which the port is located in whole or in part, and if the facility is located in whole or in part in a municipal corporation, to the chief of police of each municipal corporation in which the port is located. Copies of registration, emergency locator maps, and security plans provided under this division are not public records under section 149.43 of the Revised Code and are not subject to mandatory disclosure under that section.

(D) This section shall not be construed to replace or supersede any standards for facilities the United States department of homeland security and the transportation security administration require, safety standards of the United States department of transportation, or any standard or law related to maritime security enforced by the secretary of the department in which the United States coast guard is located.

**HISTORY: 151 v S 9, § 1, eff. 4-14-06.**

[MISCELLANEOUS]

## § 1547.91 Wrecking.

No person, with purpose to unlawfully damage, ground, or sink a vessel afloat, shall do any of the following:

(A) Employ any false signal, buoy, or other aid to navigation;

(B) Tamper with any signal, buoy, or other aid to navigation;

(C) Do any act which creates an imminent and substantial risk that any vessel afloat will be damaged, grounded, sunk, or scuttled.

**HISTORY: 134 v H 511 (Eff 1-1-74); 143 v H 522. Eff 6-13-90.**

## § 1547.92 Tampering with navigation aid or vessel prohibited.

No person shall knowingly:

(A) Damage, remove, or tamper with any signal, buoy, or other aid to navigation;

(B) Sever the mooring lines of, set adrift, or tamper with any vessel that is moored or tied up on the waters in this state.

**HISTORY: 139 v H 782 (Eff 3-4-83); 143 v H 522. Eff 6-13-90.**

**Analogous to former RC § 1547.92 (134 v H 511), repealed in 136 v H 957, § 2, eff 9-3-76.**

[PENALTIES]

## § 1547.99 Penalties.

(A) Whoever violates section 1547.91 of the Revised Code is guilty of a felony of the fourth degree.

(B) Whoever violates division (F) of section 1547.08, section 1547.10, division (I) of section 1547.111 [1547.11.1], section 1547.13, or section 1547.66 of the Revised Code is guilty of a misdemeanor of the first degree.

(C) Whoever violates a provision of this chapter or a rule adopted thereunder, for which no penalty is otherwise provided, is guilty of a minor misdemeanor.

(D) Whoever violates section 1547.07, 1547.132 [1547.13.2], or 1547.12 of the Revised Code without causing injury to persons or damage to property is guilty of a misdemeanor of the fourth degree.

(E) Whoever violates section 1547.07, 1547.132 [1547.13.2], or 1547.12 of the Revised Code causing injury to persons or damage to property is guilty of a misdemeanor of the third degree.

(F) Whoever violates division (N) of section 1547.54, division (G) of section 1547.30, or section 1547.131 [1547.13.1], 1547.25, 1547.33, 1547.38, 1547.39, 1547.40, 1547.65, 1547.69, or 1547.92 of the Revised Code or a rule adopted under division (A)(2) of section 1547.52 of the Revised Code is guilty of a misdemeanor of the fourth degree.

(G) Whoever violates section 1547.11 of the Revised Code is guilty of a misdemeanor of the first degree and shall be punished as provided in division (G)(1), (2), or (3) of this section.

(1) Except as otherwise provided in division (G)(2) or (3) of this section, the court shall sentence the offender to a jail term of three consecutive days and may sentence the offender pursuant to section 2929.24 of the Revised Code to a longer jail term. In addition, the court shall impose upon the offender a fine of not less than one hundred fifty nor more than one thousand dollars.

The court may suspend the execution of the mandatory jail term of three consecutive days that it is required to impose by division (G)(1) of this section if the court, in lieu of the suspended jail term, places the offender under a community control sanction pursuant to section 2929.25 of the Revised Code and requires the offender to attend, for three consecutive days, a drivers' intervention program that is certified pursuant to section 3793.10 of the Revised Code. The court also may suspend the execution of any part of the mandatory jail term of three consecutive days that it is required to impose by division (G)(1) of this section if the court places the offender under a community control sanction pursuant to section 2929.25 of the Revised Code for part of the three consecutive days; requires the offender to attend, for that part of the three consecutive days, a drivers' intervention program that is certified pursuant to section 3793.10 of the Revised Code; and sentences the offender to a jail term equal to the remainder of the three consecutive days that the offender does not spend attending the drivers' intervention program. The court may require the offender, as a condition of community control, to attend and satisfactorily complete any treatment or education programs, in addition to the required attendance at a drivers' intervention program, that the operators of the drivers' intervention program determine that the offender should attend and to report periodically to the court on the offender's progress in the programs. The court also may impose any other conditions of community control on the offender that it considers necessary.

(2) If, within six years of the offense, the offender has been convicted of or pleaded guilty to one violation of section 1547.11 of the Revised Code or one other equivalent offense, the court shall sentence the offender to a jail term of ten consecutive days and may sentence the offender pursuant to section 2929.24 of the Revised Code to a longer jail term. In addition, the court shall impose upon the offender a fine of not less than one hundred fifty nor more than one thousand dollars.

In addition to any other sentence that it imposes upon the offender, the court may require the offender to attend a drivers' intervention program that is certified pursuant to section 3793.10 of the Revised Code.

(3) If, within six years of the offense, the offender has been convicted of or pleaded guilty to more than one violation or offense identified in division (G)(2) of this section, the court shall sentence the offender to a jail term of thirty consecutive days and may sentence the offender to a longer jail term of not more than one year. In addition, the court shall impose upon the offender a fine of not less than one hundred fifty nor more than one thousand dollars.

In addition to any other sentence that it imposes upon the offender, the court may require the offender to attend a drivers' intervention program that is certified pursuant to section 3793.10 of the Revised Code.

(4) Upon a showing that serving a jail term would seriously affect the ability of an offender sentenced pursuant to division (G)(1), (2), or (3) of this section to continue the offender's employment, the court may autho-

rize that the offender be granted work release after the offender has served the mandatory jail term of three, ten, or thirty consecutive days that the court is required by division (G)(1), (2), or (3) of this section to impose. No court shall authorize work release during the mandatory jail term of three, ten, or thirty consecutive days that the court is required by division (G)(1), (2), or (3) of this section to impose. The duration of the work release shall not exceed the time necessary each day for the offender to commute to and from the place of employment and the place in which the jail term is served and the time actually spent under employment.

(5) Notwithstanding any section of the Revised Code that authorizes the suspension of the imposition or execution of a sentence or the placement of an offender in any treatment program in lieu of being imprisoned or serving a jail term, no court shall suspend the mandatory jail term of ten or thirty consecutive days required to be imposed by division (G)(2) or (3) of this section or place an offender who is sentenced pursuant to division (G)(2) or (3) of this section in any treatment program in lieu of being imprisoned or serving a jail term until after the offender has served the mandatory jail term of ten or thirty consecutive days required to be imposed pursuant to division (G)(2) or (3) of this section. Notwithstanding any section of the Revised Code that authorizes the suspension of the imposition or execution of a sentence or the placement of an offender in any treatment program in lieu of being imprisoned or serving a jail term, no court, except as specifically authorized by division (G)(1) of this section, shall suspend the mandatory jail term of three consecutive days required to be imposed by division (G)(1) of this section or place an offender who is sentenced pursuant to division (G)(1) of this section in any treatment program in lieu of imprisonment until after the offender has served the mandatory jail term of three consecutive days required to be imposed pursuant to division (G)(1) of this section.

(6) As used in division (G) of this section:

(a) "Equivalent offense" has the same meaning as in section 4511.181 [4511.18.1] of the Revised Code.

(b) "Jail term" and "mandatory jail term" have the same meanings as in section 2929.01 of the Revised Code.

(H) Whoever violates section 1547.304 [1547.30.4] of the Revised Code is guilty of a misdemeanor of the fourth degree and also shall be assessed any costs incurred by the state or a county, township, municipal corporation, or other political subdivision in disposing of an abandoned junk vessel or outboard motor, less any money accruing to the state, county, township, municipal corporation, or other political subdivision from that disposal.

(I) Whoever violates division (B) or (C) of section 1547.49 of the Revised Code is guilty of a minor misdemeanor.

(J) Whoever violates section 1547.31 of the Revised Code is guilty of a misdemeanor of the fourth degree on a first offense. On each subsequent offense, the person is guilty of a misdemeanor of the third degree.

(K) Whoever violates section 1547.05 or 1547.051 [1547.05.1] of the Revised Code is guilty of a misdemeanor of the fourth degree if the violation is not related to a collision, injury to a person, or damage to property and a misdemeanor of the third degree if the violation is related to a collision, injury to a person, or damage to property.

(L) The sentencing court, in addition to the penalty provided under this section for a violation of this chapter or a rule adopted under it that involves a powercraft powered by more than ten horsepower and that, in the opinion of the court, involves a threat to the safety of persons or property, shall order the offender to complete successfully a boating course approved by the national association of state boating law administrators before the offender is allowed to operate a powercraft powered by more than ten horsepower on the waters in this state. Violation of a court order entered under this division is punishable as contempt under Chapter 2705. of the Revised Code.

**HISTORY: 128 v 1004 (Eff 8-5-59); 129 v 582(703) (Eff 1-10-61); 129 v 1388 (Eff 1-1-62); 131 v 547 (Eff 11-1-65); 134 v S 397 (Eff 10-23-72); 134 v H 511 (Eff 1-1-74); 137 v H 1 (Eff 8-26-77); 139 v H 782 (Eff 3-4-83); 140 v H 682 (Eff 3-28-85); 141 v H 265 (Eff 7-24-86); 141 v H 428 (Eff 12-23-86); 143 v H 317 (Eff 10-10-89); 143 v H 522 (Eff 6-13-90); 146 v S 2 (Eff 7-1-96); 146 v S 295 (Eff 3-18-97); 148 v S 107 (Eff 3-23-2000); 149 v S 150. Eff 7-5-2002; 149 v S 123, § 1, eff. 1-1-04; 149 v H 490, § 1, eff. 1-1-04; 151 v S 8, § 1, eff. 8-17-06; 151 v H 443, § 1, eff. 4-6-07; 152 v S 271, § 1, eff. 6-13-08; 152 v S 17, § 1, eff. 9-30-08; 153 v H 1, § 101.01, eff. 7-17-09.**

The effective date is set by § 812.20 of 153 v H 1.

The provisions of 815.10 of 153 v H 1 read as follows:

SECTION 815.10. The General Assembly, applying the principle stated in division (B) of section 1.52 of the Revised Code that amendments are to be harmonized if reasonably capable of simultaneous operation, finds that the following sections, presented in this act as composites of the sections as amended by the acts indicated, are the resulting versions of the sections in effect prior to the effective date of the sections as presented in this act:

° ° °

Section 1547.99 of the Revised Code as amended by Am. Sub. S.B. 17 and Am. Sub. S.B. 271, both of the 127th General Assembly.

° ° °

The effective date is set by section 4 of H.B. 490.

See provisions, § 5 of S.B. 123 (149 v —), following RC § 1547.11.

# CHAPTER 1548: WATERCRAFT CERTIFICATES OF TITLE

Section



## § 1548.01 Definitions; exceptions to chapter; forms.

(A) As used in this chapter, "electronic" and "watercraft" have the same meanings as in section 1547.01 of the Revised Code.

(B) This chapter does not apply to any of the following:

(1) A watercraft covered by a marine document in effect that has been assigned to it by the United States government pursuant to federal law;

(2) A watercraft from a country other than the United States temporarily using the waters in this state;

(3) A watercraft whose owner is the United States, a state, or a political subdivision of a state;

(4) A ship's lifeboat. As used in division (B)(4) of this section, "lifeboat" means a watercraft that is held aboard another vessel and used exclusively for emergency purposes.

(5) A canoe;

(6) A watercraft less than fourteen feet in length without a permanently affixed mechanical means of propulsion;

(7) A watercraft less than fourteen feet in length with a permanently fixed mechanical means of propulsion of less than ten horsepower as determined by the manufacturer's rating;

(8) Outboard motors of less than ten horsepower as determined by the manufacturer's rating.

(C) The various certificates, applications, and assignments necessary to provide certificates of title for watercraft and outboard motors shall be made on appropriate forms approved by the chief of the division of watercraft.

**HISTORY: 130 v H 289 (Eff 10-10-63); 131 v 548 (Eff 9-9-65); 134 v S 350 (Eff 12-21-71); 139 v H 782 (Eff 3-4-83); 143 v H 522 (Eff 6-13-90); 145 v S 182 (Eff 10-20-94); 146 v S 295 (Eff 3-18-97); 147 v S 187 (Eff 3-18-99); 149 v S 59. Eff 10-31-2001.**

## § 1548.18 Prohibitions.

No person shall do any of the following:

(A) Operate in this state a watercraft for which a certificate of title is required or a watercraft powered by an outboard motor for which a certificate of title is required without having the certificate, or a valid temporary permit and number, in accordance with this chapter or, if a physical certificate of title has not been issued for it, operate the watercraft or outboard motor in this state knowing that the ownership information relating to the watercraft or outboard motor has not been entered into the automated title processing system by a clerk of a court of common pleas;

(B) Operate in this state a watercraft for which a certificate of title is required or a watercraft powered by an outboard motor for which a certificate of title is required upon which the certificate of title has been canceled;

(C) Fail to surrender any certificate of title upon cancellation of it by the chief of the division of watercraft and notice of the cancellation as prescribed in this chapter;

(D) Fail to surrender the certificate of title to a clerk of a court of common pleas as provided in this chapter, in case of the destruction or dismantling or change of a watercraft or outboard motor in such respect that it is not the watercraft or outboard motor described in the certificate of title;

(E) Violate any provision of this chapter for which no penalty is otherwise provided, or any lawful rules adopted pursuant to this chapter;

(F) Operate in this state a watercraft or outboard motor knowing that the certificate of title to or ownership of the watercraft or outboard motor as otherwise reflected in the automated title processing system has been canceled.

**HISTORY: 130 v H 289 (Eff 10-10-63); 131 v 556 (Eff 9-9-65); 134 v S 350 (Eff 12-21-71); 135 v S 251 (Eff 1-1-74); 149 v S 59. Eff 10-31-2001.**

See provisions of § 6 of H.B. 230 (150 v —) following RC § 1548.02.

## § 1548.19 Offenses concerning stolen property, serial numbers, and certificates of title.

No person shall do any of the following:

(A) Procure or attempt to procure a certificate of title to a watercraft or outboard motor, or pass or attempt to pass a certificate of title or any assignment of a certificate of title to a watercraft or outboard motor, or in any other manner gain or attempt to gain ownership of a watercraft or outboard motor, knowing or having reason to believe that the watercraft or outboard motor has been stolen;

(B) Sell or offer for sale in this state a watercraft or outboard motor on which the manufacturer's or assigned serial number has been destroyed, removed, covered, altered, or defaced with knowledge of the destruction, removal, covering, alteration, or defacement of the manufacturer's or assigned serial number;

(C) Sell or transfer a watercraft or outboard motor without delivering to the purchaser or transferee of it a certificate of title, or a manufacturer's or importer's certificate to it, assigned to the purchaser as provided for in this chapter, except as otherwise provided in this chapter.

**HISTORY: 130 v H 289 (Eff 10-10-63); 134 v H 511 (Eff 1-1-74); 135 v S 251 (Eff 1-1-74); 137 v S 387 (Eff 3-15-79); 138 v S 65 (Eff 1-1-80); 149 v S 59. Eff 10-31-2001.**

See provisions of § 6 of H.B. 230 (150 v —) following RC § 1548.02.

## § 1548.99 Penalties.

(A) Whoever violates section 1548.18 of the Revised Code is guilty of a misdemeanor of the fourth degree.

(B) Whoever violates section 1548.19 of the Revised Code is guilty of a felony of the fifth degree.

**HISTORY: 130 v H 289 (Eff 10-10-63); 143 v H 522 (Eff 6-13-90); 146 v S 2. Eff 7-1-96.**

The effective date is set by section 6 of SB 2.

# TITLE 19: COURTS — MUNICIPAL — MAYOR'S — COUNTY

## CHAPTER 1901: MUNICIPAL COURT



[JURISDICTION]

### § 1901.20 Criminal and traffic jurisdiction.

(A)(1) The municipal court has jurisdiction of the violation of any ordinance of any municipal corporation within its territory, unless the violation is required to be handled by a parking violations bureau or joint parking violations bureau pursuant to Chapter 4521. of the Revised Code, and of the violation of any misdemeanor committed within the limits of its territory. The municipal court has jurisdiction of the violation of a vehicle parking or standing resolution or regulation if a local authority, as defined in division (D) of section 4521.01 of the Revised Code, has specified that it is not to be considered a criminal offense, if the violation is committed within the limits of the court's territory, and if the violation is not required to be handled by a parking violations bureau or joint parking violations bureau pursuant to Chapter 4521. of the Revised Code. The municipal court, if it has a housing or environmental division, has jurisdiction of any criminal action over which the housing or environmental division is given jurisdiction by section 1901.181 [1901.18.1] of the Revised Code, provided that, except as specified in division (B) of that section, no judge of the court other than the judge of the division shall hear or determine any action over which the division has jurisdiction. In all such prosecutions and cases, the court shall proceed to a final determination of the prosecution or case.

(2) A judge of a municipal court does not have the authority to dismiss a criminal complaint, charge, information, or indictment solely at the request of the complaining witness and over the objection of the prosecuting attorney, village solicitor, city director of law, or other chief legal officer who is responsible for the prosecution of the case.

(B) The municipal court has jurisdiction to hear felony cases committed within its territory. In all felony cases, the court may conduct preliminary hearings and other necessary hearings prior to the indictment of the defendant or prior to the court's finding that there is probable and reasonable cause to hold or recognize the defendant to appear before a court of common pleas and may discharge, recognize, or commit the defendant.

(C) A municipal court has jurisdiction of an appeal from a judgment or default judgment entered pursuant to Chapter 4521. of the Revised Code, as authorized by division (D) of section 4521.08 of the Revised Code. The appeal shall be placed on the regular docket of the court and shall be determined by a judge of the court.

**HISTORY: GC § 1598; 124 v 589; Bureau of Code Revision, 10-1-53; 128 v 823 (Eff 11-6-59); 139 v H 707 (Eff 1-1-83); 141 v H 159 (Eff 3-19-87); 144 v S 105 (Eff 3-24-92); 146 v H 350, § 1 (Eff 1-27-97); 146 v H 350, § 13 (Eff 7-1-97); 146 v H 438 (Eff 7-1-97); 147 v S 98. Eff 3-17-98.**

See provisions, § 2.02(B) and § 3(B)(1) of SB 108 (149 v —), following RC § 1901.04.1.

[PROCEDURE]

### § 1901.21 Criminal and civil procedure; bond.

(A) In a criminal case or proceeding, the practice, procedure, and mode of bringing and conducting prosecutions for offenses shall be as provided in the criminal rules, and the power of the court in relation to the prosecution is the same as the power that is conferred upon county courts.

In any civil case or proceeding for which no special provision is made in this chapter, the practice and procedure in the case or proceeding shall be the same as in courts of common pleas. If no practice or procedure for the case or proceeding is provided for in the courts of common pleas, then the practice or procedure of county courts shall apply.

(B) In the Cleveland municipal court, all bonds for the appearance of a defendant charged with an offense, when the offense is bailable, shall be entered into before the clerk of the municipal court and approved by him; and the surety in them shall be qualified by the clerk. One surety in every such bond shall be a resident within the jurisdiction of the court; the sureties shall own property worth double the sum to be secured and shall have real estate within Cuyahoga county liable to execution of a value equal to the sum to be secured; and when two or more sureties are offered to the same bond, they shall have in the aggregate the qualification prescribed. The bond shall require the defendant to appear before the court to answer the charge against him, or before the court of common pleas when the defendant is held to the grand jury.

The bond shall clearly disclose the full name of each surety, together with the residence address, and there shall be indorsed on it a brief, but pertinent, description of the real estate owned by each surety.

When the bond is entered into, approved, and accepted, it becomes a subsisting lien on the real estate of the surety in it, upon which he has qualified, until the bond has been exonerated or discharged.

A copy of every such bond, certified under the seal of the court by the clerk as a true copy, shall be filed by him with the county recorder of Cuyahoga county forthwith unless in the meantime the defendant has been acquitted or discharged by the court. The recorder shall provide a suitable record book, properly indexed, in which he shall record all bonds certified to him. The recorder shall be entitled to receive from the clerk, such fees and record charges as are now authorized by law for recording deeds and mortgages; and such fees and charges shall be taxed by the clerk in the costs of the respective cases, and shall be paid to the recorder by the clerk from funds in his hands upon certified vouchers or bills rendered by the recorder.

The clerk shall transmit to the recorder each day a certified list, under the seal of the court, of all bonds which have been exonerated or discharged, and the recorder shall note on the margin of the record of each bond the discharge or satisfaction of it, and the lien on the real estate of the surety in such bond shall thereby be canceled and discharged.

The clerk shall not approve or accept as surety, on any such bond, any person who is then liable on any bond previously executed in the municipal court, unless it appears to the satisfaction of the clerk that the person offering himself as surety has sufficient equity in his real estate over and above his liability on the prior bonds, to justify the subsequent bond, or unless the prior bonds have been exonerated and discharged.

The clerk may tax in the costs of the case, such fees for making the copies and certificates required in this section as the court by rule provides.

In all misdemeanor cases, the clerk, in lieu of the sureties required by this section, may accept a deposit of money, in United States legal tender, in an amount equal to the penal sum stipulated in the bond, and in any felony case a judge of the municipal court may direct the clerk to accept such a deposit in an amount fixed by the judge, which amount shall be the sum stipulated in the bond, and such deposit shall be retained by the clerk as security on it until the bond has been exonerated and discharged. If any such bond is forfeited, the clerk shall apply the money so deposited in satisfaction of any judgment that may be rendered on the bond, and the depositor of such fund shall surrender and forfeit all right in and to the deposit to the extent of such judgment.

**HISTORY: GC § 1599; 124 v 589; Bureau of Code Revision, 10-1-53; 125 v 903 (952); 128 v 823 (Eff 11-6-59); 129 v 423 (Eff 10-19-61); 135 v H 1 (Eff 3-22-73); 136 v H 205 (Eff 1-1-76); 141 v H 412 (Eff 3-17-87); 141 v H 159 (Eff 3-19-87); 142 v H 708. Eff 4-19-88.**

## § 1901.23 Issuance of writs and process.

Writs and process in a municipal court shall be served, returned, and publication made in the manner provided for service, return, and publication of summons, writs, and process in the court of common pleas.

In any civil action or proceeding in which the subject matter of the action or proceeding is located within the territory or a defendant resides or is served with summons within the territory, the court may issue summons, orders of interpleader, all other writs, and mesne and final process, including executions necessary or proper for the complete adjudication of the issues and determination of the action, to the bailiff for service in the county or counties in which the court is situated and to the sheriff of any other county against one or more of the remaining defendants.

All warrants, executions, subpoenas, writs, and processes in all criminal and quasi-criminal cases may be issued to the bailiff of the court, a police officer of the appropriate municipal corporation, or to the sheriff of the appropriate county.

In any civil action in which the bailiff is a party or is interested, writs and process shall be directed to the sheriff. If both of these officers are interested, the writs and process shall be directed to and executed by a person appointed by the court or a judge of the court, and that person has the same power to execute the writs and process that the bailiff has. The return of the appointee shall be verified by affidavit, and he is entitled to the fees allowed to the bailiff for similar service.

**HISTORY: GC § 1603; 124 v 589; Bureau of Code Revision, 10-1-53; 128 v 823 (Eff 11-6-59); 141 v H 159. Eff 3-19-87.**

## § 1901.24 Jury demand; number of jurors; verdict.

(A) A jury trial in a municipal court shall be demanded in the manner prescribed in the Rules of Civil Procedure or the Rules of Criminal Procedure. The number of persons composing a jury and the verdicts of jurors shall be governed by those rules.

(B) The right of a person to a jury trial in a municipal court is waived under the circumstances prescribed in the Rules of Civil Procedure or the Rules of Criminal Procedure.

**HISTORY: 141 v H 159. Eff 3-19-87.**

**Analogous in part to former RC § 1901.24 (GC § 1604; 124 v 589; Bureau of Code Revision, 10-1-53; 125 v 903(954); 129 v 423; 130 v 605; 130 v PtII, 138; 140 v H 183), repealed 141 v H 159, § 2, eff 3-19-87.**

## § 1901.25 Selection and impaneling of jury.

A municipal court may provide by rule the manner in which jurors shall be chosen, and may provide that jurors to be used in the court may be chosen and summoned by the jury commissioners of the county as provided in sections 2313.01 to 2313.26 of the Revised Code. Selection shall be made from residents within the territory and those appearing to reside outside the territory shall be returned to the jury wheel, to the automation data processing storage drawer, or to any other automated data processing information storage device used pursuant to division (C) of section 2313.21 of the Revised Code. Jurors shall be impaneled in the same manner, shall have the same qualifications, shall be challenged for the same causes, and shall receive the same fees as jurors in the court of common pleas. The fees of jurors in any criminal case involving the violation of state law shall be paid out of the county treasury. The fees of jurors in any criminal case involving a violation of a municipal ordinance shall be paid out of the treasury of the municipal corporation in which the violation occurred.

**HISTORY: GC § 1604; 124 v 589; Bureau of Code Revision, 10-1-53; 131 v 605 (Eff 11-1-65); 133 v H 424 (Eff 11-25-69); 141 v H 159. Eff 3-19-87.**

## § 1901.26 Costs.

(A) Subject to division (E) of this section, costs in a municipal court shall be fixed and taxed as follows:

(1)(a) The municipal court shall require an advance deposit for the filing of any new civil action or proceeding when required by division (C) of this section, and in all other cases, by rule, shall establish a schedule of fees and costs to be taxed in any civil or criminal action or proceeding.

(b)(i) The legislative authority of a municipal corporation may by ordinance establish a schedule of fees to be taxed as costs in any civil, criminal, or traffic action or proceeding in a municipal court for the performance by officers or other employees of the municipal corporation's police department or marshal's office of any of the services specified in sections 311.17 and 509.15 of the Revised Code. No fee in the schedule shall be higher than the fee specified in section 311.17 of the Revised Code for the performance of the same service by the sheriff. If a fee established in the schedule conflicts with a fee for the same service established in another section of the Revised Code or a rule of court, the fee established in the other section of the Revised Code or the rule of court shall apply.

(ii) When an officer or employee of a municipal police department or marshal's office performs in a civil, criminal, or traffic action or proceeding in a municipal court a service specified in section 311.17 or 509.15 of the Revised Code for which a taxable fee has been established under this or any other section of the Revised Code, the applicable legal fees and any other extraordinary expenses, including overtime, provided for the service shall be taxed as costs in the case. The clerk of the court shall pay those legal fees and other expenses, when collected, into the general fund of the municipal corporation that employs the officer or employee.

(iii) If a bailiff of a municipal court performs in a civil, criminal, or traffic action or proceeding in that court a service specified in section 311.17 or 509.15 of the Revised Code for which a taxable fee has been established under this section or any other section of the Revised Code, the fee for the service is the same and is taxable to the same extent as if the service had been performed by an officer or employee of the police department or marshal's office of the municipal corporation in which the court is located. The clerk of that court shall pay the fee, when collected, into the general fund of the entity or entities that fund the bailiff's salary, in the same prorated amount as the salary is funded.

(iv) Division (A)(1)(b) of this section does not authorize or require any officer or employee of a police department or marshal's office of a municipal corporation or any bailiff of a municipal court to perform any service not otherwise authorized by law.

(2) The municipal court, by rule, may require an advance deposit for the filing of any civil action or proceeding and publication fees as provided in section 2701.09 of the Revised Code. The court may waive the requirement for advance deposit upon affidavit or other evidence that a party is unable to make the required deposit.

(3) When a jury trial is demanded in any civil action or proceeding, the party making the demand may be required to make an advance deposit as fixed by rule of court, unless, upon affidavit or other evidence, the court concludes that the party is unable to make the required deposit. If a jury is called, the fees of a jury shall be taxed as costs.

(4) In any civil or criminal action or proceeding, each witness shall receive twelve dollars for each full day's attendance and six dollars for each half day's attendance. Each witness in a municipal court that is not a county-operated municipal court also shall receive fifty and one-half cents for each mile necessarily traveled to and from the witness's place of residence to the action or proceeding.

(5) A reasonable charge for driving, towing, carting, storing, keeping, and preserving motor vehicles and other personal property recovered or seized in any proceeding may be taxed as part of the costs in a trial of the cause, in an amount that shall be fixed by rule of court.

(6) Chattel property seized under any writ or process issued by the court shall be preserved pending final disposition for the benefit of all persons interested and may be placed in storage when necessary or proper for that preservation. The custodian of any chattel property so stored shall not be required to part with the possession of the property until a reasonable charge, to be fixed by the court, is paid.

(7) The municipal court, as it determines, may refund all deposits and advance payments of fees and costs, including those for jurors and summoning jurors, when they have been paid by the losing party.

(8) Charges for the publication of legal notices required by statute or order of court may be taxed as part of the costs, as provided by section 7.13 of the Revised Code.

(B)(1) The municipal court may determine that, for the efficient operation of the court, additional funds are necessary to acquire and pay for special projects of the court including, but not limited to, the acquisition of additional facilities or the rehabilitation of existing facilities, the acquisition of equipment, the hiring and training of staff, community service programs, mediation or dispute resolution services, the employment of magistrates, the training and education of judges, acting judges, and magistrates, and other related services. Upon that determination, the court by rule may charge a fee, in addition to all other court costs, on the filing of each criminal cause, civil action or proceeding, or judgment by confession.

If the municipal court offers a special program or service in cases of a specific type, the municipal court by rule may assess an additional charge in a case of that type, over and above court costs, to cover the special program or service. The municipal court shall adjust the special assessment periodically, but not retroactively, so that the amount assessed in those cases does not exceed the actual cost of providing the service or program.

All moneys collected under division (B) of this section shall be paid to the county treasurer if the court is a county-operated municipal court or to the city treasurer if the court is not a county-operated municipal court for deposit into either a general special projects fund or a fund established for a specific special project. Moneys from a fund of that nature shall be disbursed upon an order of the court in an amount no greater than the actual cost to the court of a project. If a specific fund is terminated because of the discontinuance of a program or service established under division (B) of this section, the municipal court may order that moneys remaining in the fund be transferred to an account established under this division for a similar purpose.

(2) As used in division (B) of this section:

(a) "Criminal cause" means a charge alleging the violation of a statute or ordinance, or subsection of a statute or ordinance, that requires a separate finding of fact or a separate plea before disposition and of which the defendant may be found guilty, whether filed as part of a multiple charge on a single summons, citation, or complaint or as a separate charge on a single summons, citation, or complaint. "Criminal cause" does not include separate violations of the same statute or ordinance, or subsection of the same statute or ordinance, unless each charge is filed on a separate summons, citation, or complaint.

(b) "Civil action or proceeding" means any civil litigation that must be determined by judgment entry.

(C) The municipal court shall collect in all its divisions except the small claims division the sum of twenty-six dollars as additional filing fees in each new civil action or proceeding for the charitable public purpose of providing financial assistance to legal aid societies that operate within the state and to support the office of the state public defender. The municipal court shall collect in its small claims division the sum of eleven dollars as additional filing fees in each new civil action or proceeding for the charitable public purpose of providing financial assistance to legal aid societies that operate within the state and to support the office of the state public defender. This division does not apply to any execution on a judgment, proceeding in aid of execution, or other post-judgment proceeding arising out of a civil action. The filing fees required to be collected under this division shall be in addition to any other court costs imposed in the action or proceeding and shall be collected at the time of the filing of the action or proceeding. The court shall not waive the payment of the additional filing fees in a new civil action or proceeding unless the court waives the advanced payment of all filing fees in the action or proceeding. All such moneys collected during a month except for an amount equal to up to one per cent of those moneys retained to cover administrative costs shall be transmitted on or before the twentieth day of the following month by the clerk of the court to the treasurer of state in a manner prescribed by the treasurer of state or by the Ohio legal assistance foundation. The treasurer of state shall deposit four per cent of the funds collected under this division to the credit of the civil case filing fee fund established under section 120.07 of the Revised Code and ninety-six per cent of the funds collected under this division to the credit of the legal aid fund established under section 120.52 of the Revised Code.

The court may retain up to one per cent of the moneys it collects under this division to cover administrative costs, including the hiring of any additional personnel necessary to implement this division. If the court fails to transmit to the treasurer of state the moneys the court collects under this division in a manner prescribed by the treasurer of state or by the Ohio legal assistance foundation, the court shall forfeit the moneys the court retains under this division to cover administrative costs, including the hiring of any additional personnel necessary to implement this division, and shall transmit to the treasurer of state all moneys collected under this division, including the forfeited amount retained for administrative costs, for deposit in the legal aid fund.

(D) In the Cleveland municipal court, reasonable charges for investigating titles of real estate to be sold or disposed of under any writ or process of the court may be taxed as part of the costs.

(E) Under the circumstances described in sections 2969.21 to 2969.27 of the Revised Code, the clerk of the municipal court shall charge the fees and perform the other duties specified in those sections.

(F) As used in this section:

(1) "Full day's attendance" means a day on which a witness is required or requested to be present at an action or proceeding before and after twelve noon, regardless of whether the witness actually testifies.

(2) "Half day's attendance" means a day on which a witness is required or requested to be present at an action or proceeding either before or after twelve noon, but not both, regardless of whether the witness actually testifies.

**HISTORY: GC § 1605; 124 v 589; Bureau of Code Revision, 10-1-53; 140 v S 219 (Eff 2-22-85); 141 v H 201 (Eff 7-1-85); 141 v H 201, § 14 (Eff 1-1-87); 141 v H 159, § 3 (Eff 1-1-87); 141 v H 159 (Eff 3-19-87); 142 v H 171 (Eff 7-1-87); 143 v H 111 (Eff 7-1-89); 144 v H 298 (Eff 7-26-91); 144 v H 405 (Eff 1-1-93); 146 v H 455 (Eff 10-17-96); 146 v H 423 (Eff 10-31-96); 146 v H 438 (Eff 7-1-97); 147 v H 507 (Eff 3-22-99); 149 v H 94. Eff 9-5-2001; 151 v H 66, § 101.01, eff. 10-1-05; 151 v H 226, § 1, eff. 2-27-06; 152 v H 525, § 1, eff. 7-1-09; 153 v H 1, § 101.01, eff. 10-16-09.**

The effective date is set by § 812.10 of 153 v H 1.

The effective date is set by § 3 of 152 v H 525.

The provisions of § 4 of 152 v H 525 reads as follows:

SECTION 4. Section 1901.26 of the Revised Code is presented in this act as a composite of the section as amended by both Am. Sub. H.B. 66 and Am. H.B. 226 of the 126th General Assembly. The General Assembly, applying the principle stated in division (B) of section 1.52 of the Revised Code that amendments are to be harmonized if reasonably capable of simultaneous operation, finds that the composite is the resulting version of the section in effect prior to the effective date of the section as presented in this act.

The effective date is set by § 612.09 of 151 v H 66.

The effective date is set by section 204 of HB 94.

## § 1901.30 Appeals.

Appeals from the municipal court may be taken as follows:

(A) To the court of appeals in accordance with the Rules of Appellate Procedure and any relevant sections of the Revised Code, including, but not limited to, Chapter 2505. of the Revised Code to the extent it is not in conflict with those rules.

(B) When an appeal is taken from the municipal court, the clerk of the municipal court shall transmit, pursuant to the rules of appellate procedure, the record on appeal to the clerk of the appellate court to be filed.

(C) In all appeal proceedings relating to judgments or orders of a municipal court, the reviewing courts shall take judicial notice of all rules relating to pleadings, practice, or procedure of the municipal court.

**HISTORY: GC § 1609; 124 v 589; Bureau of Code Revision, 10-1-53; 128 v 823 (Eff 11-6-59); 131 v 606 (Eff 11-1-65); 133 v S 530 (Eff 6-12-70); 137 v H 1168 (Eff 11-1-78); 141 v H 412 (Eff 3-17-87); 141 v H 159 (Eff 3-19-87); 142 v H 708. Eff 4-19-88.**

## § 1901.33 Court employees; department of probation.

(A) The judge or judges of a municipal court may appoint one or more interpreters, one or more mental health professionals, one or more probation officers, an assignment commissioner, deputy assignment commissioners, and other court aides on a full-time, part-time, hourly, or other basis. Each appointee shall receive the compensation out of the city treasury that the legislative authority prescribes in either biweekly installments or semimonthly installments, as determined by the payroll administrator, except that in a county-operated municipal court they shall receive the compensation out of the treasury of the county in which the court is located that the board of county commissioners prescribes. Probation officers have all the powers of regular police officers and shall perform any duties that are designated by the judge or judges of the court. Assignment commissioners shall assign cases for trial and perform any other duties that the court directs.

The judge or judges may appoint one or more typists, stenographers, statistical clerks, and official court reporters, each of whom shall be paid the compensation out of the city treasury that the legislative authority prescribes, except that in a county-operated municipal court they shall be paid the compensation out of the treasury of the county in which the court is located that the board of county commissioners prescribes.

(B) If a municipal court appoints one or more probation officers, those officers shall constitute the municipal court department of probation unless the court designates other employees as the department of probation for the court.

(C) The chief probation officer may grant permission to a probation officer to carry firearms when required in the discharge of the probation officer's official duties if the probation officer has successfully completed a basic firearm training program that is approved by the executive director of the Ohio peace officer training commission. A probation officer who has been granted permission to carry a firearm in the discharge of the probation officer's official duties annually shall successfully complete a firearms requalification program in accordance with section 109.801 [109.80.1] of the Revised Code.

(D) The judge or judges of a municipal court in which the clerk of the court is elected as provided in division (A)(1)(a) or (d) or (A)(2)(b) of section 1901.31 of the Revised Code may appoint an administrative assistant. The administrative assistant shall have charge of personnel related matters of the court and shall perform any other administrative duties assigned by the court. The administrative assistant shall receive the compensation out of the city treasury that the court prescribes, except that, in a county-operated municipal court, the administrative assistant shall receive the compensation out of the treasury of the county in which the court is located that the court prescribes.

**HISTORY: GC § 1612; 124 v 589; Bureau of Code Revision, 10-1-53; 125 v 903 (Eff 10-1-53); 137 v H 517 (Eff 1-16-78); 141 v H 159 (Eff 3-19-87); 145 v H 406 (Eff 11-11-94); 146 v H 670 (Eff 12-2-96); 146 v H 438 (Eff 7-1-97); 148 v S 325 (Eff 4-9-2001); 149 v H 510. Eff 3-31-2003; 151 v H 530, § 101.01, eff. 6-30-06.**

The effective date is set by § 812.03 of 151 v H 530.

## § 1901.34 Criminal prosecutions; compensation of prosecuting officers.

(A) Except as provided in divisions (B) and (D) of this section, the village solicitor, city director of law, or similar chief legal officer for each municipal corporation within the territory of a municipal court shall prosecute all cases brought before the municipal court for criminal offenses occurring within the municipal corporation for which that person is the solicitor, director of law, or similar chief legal officer. Except as provided in division (B) of this section, the village solicitor, city director of law, or similar chief legal officer of the municipal corporation in which a municipal court is located shall prosecute all criminal cases brought before the court arising in the unincorporated areas within the territory of the municipal court.

(B) The Auglaize county, Brown county, Clermont county, Hocking county, Holmes county, Jackson county, Morrow county, Ottawa county, Portage county, and Putnam county prosecuting attorneys and, effective January 1, 2011, the Putnam county prosecuting attorney shall prosecute in municipal court all violations of state law arising in their respective counties. The Carroll county, Crawford county, Hamilton county, Madison county, and Wayne county prosecuting attorneys and beginning January 1, 2008, the Erie county prosecuting attorney shall prosecute all violations of state law arising within the unincorporated areas of their respective counties. The Columbiana county prosecuting attorney shall prosecute in the Columbiana county municipal court all violations of state law arising in the county, except for violations arising in the municipal corporation of East Liverpool, Liverpool township, or St. Clair township. The Darke county prosecuting attorney shall prosecute in the Darke county municipal court all violations of state law arising in the county, except for violations of state law arising in the municipal corporation of Greenville and violations of state law arising in the village of Versailles. The Greene county board of county commissioners may provide for the prosecution of all violations of state law arising within the territorial jurisdiction of any municipal court located in Greene county. The Montgomery county prosecuting attorney shall prosecute in the Montgomery county municipal court all felony, misdemeanor, and traffic violations arising in the unincorporated townships of Jefferson, Jackson, Perry, and Clay and all felony violations of state law and all violations involving a state or county agency arising within the jurisdiction of the court. All other violations arising in the territory of the Montgomery county municipal court shall be prosecuted by the village solicitor, city director of law, or similar chief legal officer for each municipal corporation within the territory of the Montgomery county municipal court.

The prosecuting attorney of any county given the duty of prosecuting in municipal court violations of state law shall receive no additional compensation for assuming these additional duties, except that the prosecuting attorney of Hamilton, Portage, and Wayne counties shall receive compensation at the rate of four thousand eight hundred dollars per year, and the prosecuting attorney of Auglaize county shall receive compensation at the rate of one thousand eight hundred dollars per year, each payable from the county treasury of the respective counties in semimonthly installments.

(C) The village solicitor, city director of law, or similar chief legal officer shall perform the same duties, insofar as they are applicable to the village solicitor, city director of law, or similar chief legal officer, as are required of the prosecuting attorney of the county. The village solicitor, city director of law, similar chief legal officer or any assistants who may be appointed shall receive for such services additional compensation to be paid from the treasury of the county as the board of county commissioners prescribes.

(D) The prosecuting attorney of any county, other than Auglaize, Brown, Clermont, Hocking, Holmes, Jackson, Morrow, Ottawa, Portage, or Putnam county, may enter into an agreement with any municipal corporation in the county in which the prosecuting attorney serves pursuant to which the prosecuting attorney prosecutes all criminal cases brought before the municipal court that has territorial jurisdiction over that municipal corporation for criminal offenses occurring within the municipal corporation. The prosecuting attorney of Auglaize, Brown, Clermont, Hocking, Holmes, Jackson, Morrow, Ottawa, Portage, or Putnam county or, effective January 1, 2011, the prosecuting attorney of Putnam county may enter into an agreement with any municipal corporation in the county in which the prosecuting attorney serves pursuant to which the respective prosecuting attorney prosecutes all cases brought before the Auglaize county, Brown county, Clermont county, Hocking county, Holmes county, Jackson county, Morrow county, Ottawa county, Portage county, or Putnam county municipal court for violations of the ordinances of the municipal corporation or for criminal offenses other than violations of state law occurring within the municipal corporation. For prosecuting these cases, the prosecuting attorney and the municipal corporation may agree upon a fee to be paid by the municipal corporation, which fee shall be paid into the county treasury, to be used to cover expenses of the office of the prosecuting attorney.

**HISTORY: GC § 1613; 124 v 589; Bureau of Code Revision, 10-1-53; 125 v 496; 132 v H 361 (Eff 7-25-67); 132 v S 493 (Eff 6-11-68); 133 v H 749 (Eff 11-19-69); 136 v H 205 (Eff 1-1-76); 136 v H 1558 (Eff 1-17-77); 137 v H 219 (Eff 11-1-77); 137 v H 312 (Eff 1-1-78); 137 v H 517 (Eff 1-16-78); 138 v H 961 (Eff 9-29-80); 138 v S 357 (Eff 1-9-81); 139 v H 1 (Eff 8-5-81); 141 v H 159 (Eff 3-19-87); 144 v H 200 (Eff 7-8-91); 145 v H 21 (Eff 2-4-94); 148 v H 599 (Eff 1-1-2002); 149 v H 530. Eff 12-18-2002; 150 v H 38, § 1, eff. 6-17-04; 151 v S 147, § 1, eff. 11-15-05; 151 v S 171, § 1, eff. 1-2-07; 151 v H 336, § 1, eff. 1-18-07; 151 v S 171, § 3, 1-18-07; 152 v H 119, § 101.01, eff. 9-29-07; 153 v H 238, § 1, eff. 7-1-10; 153 v H 338, § 1, eff. 1-1-11.**

See provisions of § 3 of 153 v H 338 following RC § 1901.01.
The effective date is set by § 4 of 153 v H 338.
The effective date is set by § 5 of 153 v H 238.
See provisions of §§ 2, 3, 4, and 6 following RC § 1901.01.
The effective date is set by § 812.03 of 152 v H 119.
See provisions of §§ 4 and 5 following RC § 1901.01.
See provisions of § 3 of 151 v H 336 following RC § 1901.02.
The effective date set by § 9 of 151 v S 171, which is the effective date for § 1, was not applicable because the act was not filed with the Secretary of State until January 2, 2007.
The effective date is set by § 8 of 151 v S 147.

# CHAPTER 1905: MAYOR'S COURT

Section



## § 1905.01 Mayor's Court.

(A) In Georgetown in Brown county, in Mount Gilead in Morrow county, and in all other municipal corporations having a population of more than one hundred, other than Batavia in Clermont county, not being the site of a municipal court nor a place where a judge of the Auglaize county, Crawford county, Jackson county, Miami county, Montgomery county, Portage county, or Wayne county municipal court sits as required pursuant to section 1901.021 [1901.02.1] of the Revised Code or by designation of the judges pursuant to section 1901.021 [1901.02.1] of the Revised Code, the mayor of the municipal corporation has jurisdiction, except as provided in divisions (B), (C), and (E) of this section and subject to the limitation contained in section 1905.03 and the limitation contained in section 1905.031 [1905.03.1] of the Revised Code, to hear and determine any prosecution for the violation of an ordinance of the municipal corporation, to hear and determine any case involving a violation of a vehicle parking or standing ordinance of the municipal corporation unless the violation is required to be handled by a parking violations bureau or joint parking violations bureau pursuant to Chapter 4521. of the Revised Code, and to hear and determine all criminal causes involving any moving traffic violation occurring on a state highway located within the boundaries of the municipal corporation, subject to the limitations of sections 2937.08 and 2938.04 of the Revised Code.

(B)(1) In Georgetown in Brown county, in Mount Gilead in Morrow county, and in all other municipal corporations having a population of more than one hundred, other than Batavia in Clermont county, not being the site of a municipal court nor a place where a judge of a court listed in division (A) of this section sits as required pursuant to section 1901.021 [1901.02.1] of the Revised Code or by designation of the judges pursuant to section 1901.021 [1901.02.1] of the Revised Code, the mayor of the municipal corporation has jurisdiction, subject to the limitation contained in section 1905.03 of the Revised Code, to hear and determine prosecutions involving a violation of an ordinance of the municipal corporation relating to operating a vehicle while under the influence of alcohol, a drug of abuse, or a combination of them, or relating to operating a vehicle with a prohibited concentration of alcohol, a controlled substance, or a metabolite of a controlled substance in the whole blood, blood serum or plasma, breath, or urine, and to hear and determine criminal causes involving a violation of section 4511.19 of the Revised Code that occur on a state highway located within the boundaries of the municipal corporation, subject to the limitations of sections 2937.08 and 2938.04 of the Revised Code, only if the person charged with the violation, within six years of the date of the violation charged, has not been convicted of or pleaded guilty to any of the following:

(a) A violation of an ordinance of any municipal corporation relating to operating a vehicle while under the influence of alcohol, a drug of abuse, or a combination of them or relating to operating a vehicle with a prohibited concentration of alcohol, a controlled substance, or a metabolite of a controlled substance in the whole blood, blood serum or plasma, breath, or urine;

(b) A violation of section 4511.19 of the Revised Code;

(c) A violation of any ordinance of any municipal corporation or of any section of the Revised Code that regulates the operation of vehicles, streetcars, and trackless trolleys upon the highways or streets, to which all of the following apply:

(i) The person, in the case in which the conviction was obtained or the plea of guilty was entered, had been charged with a violation of an ordinance of a type described in division (B)(1)(a) of this section, or with a violation of section 4511.19 of the Revised Code;

(ii) The charge of the violation described in division (B)(1)(c)(i) of this section was dismissed or reduced;

(iii) The violation of which the person was convicted or to which the person pleaded guilty arose out of the same facts and circumstances and the same act as did the charge that was dismissed or reduced.

(d) A violation of a statute of the United States or of any other state or a municipal ordinance of a municipal corporation located in any other state that is substantially similar to section 4511.19 of the Revised Code.

(2) The mayor of a municipal corporation does not have jurisdiction to hear and determine any prosecution or criminal cause involving a violation described in division (B)(1)(a) or (b) of this section, regardless of where the violation occurred, if the person charged with the violation, within six years of the violation charged, has been convicted of or pleaded guilty to any violation listed in division (B)(1)(a), (b), (c), or (d) of this section.

If the mayor of a municipal corporation having a population of more than one hundred, in hearing a prosecution involving a violation of an ordinance of the municipal corporation the mayor serves relating to operating a vehicle while under the influence of alcohol, a drug of abuse, or a combination of them or relating to operating a vehicle with a prohibited concentration of alcohol, a controlled substance, or a metabolite of a controlled substance in the whole blood, blood serum or plasma, breath, or urine, or in hearing a criminal cause involving a violation of section 4511.19 of the Revised Code, determines that the person charged, within six years of the violation charged, has been convicted of or pleaded guilty to any violation listed in division (B)(1)(a), (b), (c), or (d) of this section, the mayor immediately shall transfer the case to the county court or municipal court with jurisdiction over the violation charged, in accordance with section 1905.032 [1905.03.2] of the Revised Code.

(C)(1) In Georgetown in Brown county, in Mount Gilead in Morrow county, and in all other municipal corporations having a population of more than one hundred, other than Batavia in Clermont county, not being the site of a municipal court and not being a place where a judge of a court listed in division (A) of this section sits as required pursuant to section 1901.021 [1901.02.1] of the Revised Code or by designation of the judges pursuant to section 1901.021 [1901.02.1] of the Revised Code, the mayor of the municipal corporation, subject to sections 1901.031 [1901.03.1], 2937.08, and 2938.04 of the Revised Code, has jurisdiction to hear and determine prosecutions involving a violation of a municipal ordinance that is substantially equivalent to division (A) of section 4510.14 or section 4510.16 of the Revised Code and to hear and determine criminal causes that involve a moving traffic violation, that involve a violation of division (A) of section 4510.14 or section 4510.16 of the Revised Code, and that occur on a state highway located within the boundaries of the municipal corporation only if all of the following apply regarding the violation and the person charged:

(a) Regarding a violation of section 4510.16 of the Revised Code or a violation of a municipal ordinance that is substantially equivalent to that division, the person charged with the violation, within six years of the date of the violation charged, has not been convicted of or pleaded guilty to any of the following:

(i) A violation of section 4510.16 of the Revised Code;

(ii) A violation of a municipal ordinance that is substantially equivalent to section 4510.16 of the Revised Code;

(iii) A violation of any municipal ordinance or section of the Revised Code that regulates the operation of vehicles, streetcars, and trackless trolleys upon the highways or streets, in a case in which, after a charge against the person of a violation of a type described in division (C)(1)(a)(i) or (ii) of this section was dismissed or reduced, the person is convicted of or pleads guilty to a violation that arose out of the same facts and circumstances and the same act as did the charge that was dismissed or reduced.

(b) Regarding a violation of division (A) of section 4510.14 of the Revised Code or a violation of a municipal ordinance that is substantially equivalent to that division, the person charged with the violation, within six years of the date of the violation charged, has not been convicted of or pleaded guilty to any of the following:

(i) A violation of division (A) of section 4510.14 of the Revised Code;

(ii) A violation of a municipal ordinance that is substantially equivalent to division (A) of section 4510.14 of the Revised Code;

(iii) A violation of any municipal ordinance or section of the Revised Code that regulates the operation of vehicles, streetcars, and trackless trolleys upon the highways or streets in a case in which, after a charge against the person of a violation of a type described in division (C)(1)(b)(i) or (ii) of this section was dismissed or reduced, the person is convicted of or pleads guilty to a violation that arose out of the same facts and circumstances and the same act as did the charge that was dismissed or reduced.

(2) The mayor of a municipal corporation does not have jurisdiction to hear and determine any prosecution or criminal cause involving a violation described in division (C)(1)(a)(i) or (ii) of this section if the person charged with the violation, within six years of the violation charged, has been convicted of or pleaded guilty to any violation listed in division (C)(1)(a)(i), (ii), or (iii) of this section and does not have jurisdiction to hear and determine any prosecu-

tion or criminal cause involving a violation described in division (C)(1)(b)(i) or (ii) of this section if the person charged with the violation, within six years of the violation charged, has been convicted of or pleaded guilty to any violation listed in division (C)(1)(b)(i), (ii), or (iii) of this section.

(3) If the mayor of a municipal corporation, in hearing a prosecution involving a violation of an ordinance of the municipal corporation the mayor serves that is substantially equivalent to division (A) of section 4510.14 or section 4510.16 of the Revised Code or a violation of division (A) of section 4510.14 or section 4510.16 of the Revised Code, determines that, under division (C)(2) of this section, mayors do not have jurisdiction of the prosecution, the mayor immediately shall transfer the case to the county court or municipal court with jurisdiction over the violation in accordance with section 1905.032 [1905.03.2] of the Revised Code.

(D) If the mayor of a municipal corporation has jurisdiction pursuant to division (B)(1) of this section to hear and determine a prosecution or criminal cause involving a violation described in division (B)(1)(a) or (b) of this section, the authority of the mayor to hear or determine the prosecution or cause is subject to the limitation contained in division (C) of section 1905.03 of the Revised Code. If the mayor of a municipal corporation has jurisdiction pursuant to division (A) or (C) of this section to hear and determine a prosecution or criminal cause involving a violation other than a violation described in division (B)(1)(a) or (b) of this section, the authority of the mayor to hear or determine the prosecution or cause is subject to the limitation contained in division (C) of section 1905.031 [1905.03.1] of the Revised Code.

(E)(1) The mayor of a municipal corporation does not have jurisdiction to hear and determine any prosecution or criminal cause involving any of the following:

(a) A violation of section 2919.25 or 2919.27 of the Revised Code;

(b) A violation of section 2903.11, 2903.12, 2903.13, 2903.211, or 2911.211 [2903.21.1, or 2911.21.1] of the Revised Code that involves a person who was a family or household member of the defendant at the time of the violation;

(c) A violation of a municipal ordinance that is substantially equivalent to an offense described in division (E)(1)(a) or (b) of this section and that involves a person who was a family or household member of the defendant at the time of the violation.

(2) The mayor of a municipal corporation does not have jurisdiction to hear and determine a motion filed pursuant to section 2919.26 of the Revised Code or filed pursuant to a municipal ordinance that is substantially equivalent to that section or to issue a protection order pursuant to that section or a substantially equivalent municipal ordinance.

(3) As used in this section, "family or household member" has the same meaning as in section 2919.25 of the Revised Code.

(F) In keeping a docket and files, the mayor, and a mayor's court magistrate appointed under section 1905.05 of the Revised Code, shall be governed by the laws pertaining to county courts.

**HISTORY: RS § 1816; Bates § 1536-776; 66 v 169, § 114; 69 v 192, § 117; GC § 4527; 109 v PtII, 1203; Bureau of Code Revision, 10-1-53; 128 v 823 (Eff 11-6-59); 130 v 608 (Eff 10-14-63); 132 v H 361 (Eff 7-25-67); 136 v H 205 (Eff 1-1-76); 137 v H 312 (Eff 1-1-78); 139 v H 707 (Eff 1-1-83); 143 v S 131 (Eff 7-25-90); 143 v H 837 (Eff 7-25-90); 145 v S 62 (Eff 9-1-93); 146 v H 353 (Eff 9-17-96); 146 v H 670 (Eff 12-2-96); 147 v S 1 (Eff 10-21-97); 147 v S 60 (Eff 10-21-97); 148 v H 105 (Eff 7-29-99); 149 v H 530, § 1. Eff 12-18-2002; 149 v S 123, § 1, eff. 1-1-04; 150 v H 24, § 1, eff. 8-29-03; 150 v H 24, § 3, eff. 1-1-04; 151 v S 8, § 1, eff. 8-17-06; 153 v H 238, § 1, eff. 7-1-10.**

The effective date is set by § 5 of 153 v H 238.

The effective date is set by section 5 of H.B. 24.

The provisions of § 5 of S.B. 123 (149 v —), as amended by § 3 of H.B. 163 (150 v —), read as follows:

SECTION 5. (A) Notwithstanding division (B) of section 1.58 of the Revised Code, the provisions of the Revised Code amended or enacted in Sections 1 and 2 of Am. Sub. S.B. 123 of the 124th General Assembly shall apply only in relation to conduct and offenses committed on or after January 1, 2004. Conduct and offenses committed prior to January 1, 2004, shall be governed by the law in effect on the date the conduct or offense was committed. ° ° °

## § 1905.02 County court provisions.

The provisions of Chapter 1907. of the Revised Code, insofar as they are relevant, apply in proceedings in a mayor's court, if the municipal corporation in which the mayor's court is located is within the jurisdiction of a county court.

**HISTORY: 141 v H 158. Eff 3-17-87.**

**Not analogous to former RC § 1905.02 (RS § 1817; Bates § 1536-777; 66 v 169; 69 v 192; GC § 4528; 108 v PtII, 1203; 109 v 173; Bureau of Code Revision, 10-1-53), repealed 128 v 823(862), § 2, eff 11-6-59.**

The effective date is set by section 4 of HB 158.

## § 1905.03 Supreme Court rules prescribing educational standards for mayor wishing to exercise OVI jurisdiction; continuing education.

(A) The supreme court may adopt rules prescribing educational standards for mayors of municipal corporations who conduct a mayor's court and who wish to exercise the jurisdiction granted by section 1905.01 of the Revised Code over a prosecution or criminal cause involving a violation of section 4511.19 of the Revised Code or a municipal OVI ordinance as defined in section 4511.181 [4511.18.1] of the Revised Code. Any educational standards prescribed by rule under authority of this division shall be for the purpose of assisting mayors of municipal corporations who conduct a mayor's court and who wish to exercise the jurisdiction granted by section 1905.01 of the Revised Code over such a prosecution or cause in the handling of such a prosecution or cause, and shall include, but shall not be limited to, all of the following:

(1) Provisions for basic training in the general principles of law that apply to the hearing and determination of such prosecutions and causes and provisions for periodic continuing education in those general principles;

(2) Provisions for basic training in the laws of this state that apply relative to persons who are convicted of or plead guilty to any such violation, particularly as those laws apply relative to a person who is convicted of or pleads guilty to any such violation in a prosecution or cause that is within the jurisdiction of a mayor's court as specified in section 1905.01 of the Revised Code, and provisions for periodic continuing education in those laws;

(3) Provisions specifying whether periodic continuing education for a mayor who conducts a mayor's court, who wishes to exercise the jurisdiction granted by section 1905.01 of the Revised Code over such a prosecution or

cause, and who has received basic training in the principles and laws described in divisions (A)(1) and (2) of this section will be required on an annual or biennial basis;

(4) Provisions specifying the number of hours of basic training that a mayor who conducts a mayor's court and who wishes to exercise the jurisdiction granted by section 1905.01 of the Revised Code over such a prosecution or cause will have to obtain to comply with the educational standards and provisions specifying the number of hours of periodic continuing education that such a mayor will have to obtain within each time period specified under authority of division (A)(3) of this section to comply with the educational standards;

(5) Provisions establishing an exemption, for a reasonable period of time, from the basic training requirements for mayors who initially take office on or after July 1, 1991, and who wish to conduct a mayor's court and exercise the jurisdiction granted by section 1905.01 of the Revised Code over such a prosecution or cause.

(B) If the supreme court adopts rules under authority of division (A) of this section prescribing educational standards for mayors of municipal corporations who conduct a mayor's court and who wish to exercise the jurisdiction granted by section 1905.01 of the Revised Code over a prosecution or criminal cause involving a violation described in division (A) of this section, the court may formulate a basic training course and a periodic continuing education course that such a mayor may complete to satisfy those educational standards, and may offer or provide for the offering of the basic training course and the periodic continuing education course to mayors of municipal corporations.

If the supreme court offers or provides for the offering of a basic training course and a periodic continuing education course formulated under this division, the court may prescribe a reasonable fee to cover the cost associated with formulating, offering, and teaching the particular course, which fee would have to be paid by each mayor who attends the particular course or the municipal corporation served by the mayor.

If the supreme court offers or provides for the offering of a basic training course and a periodic continuing education course formulated under this division, the court or other entity that offers either course shall issue to each mayor who successfully completes the particular course a certificate attesting to the mayor's satisfactory completion of the particular course.

(C) Notwithstanding section 1905.01 of the Revised Code, if the supreme court adopts rules under authority of division (A) of this section, if the supreme court formulates a basic training course and a periodic continuing education course under division (B) of this section, and if the supreme court offers or provides for the offering of the basic training course and the periodic continuing education course to mayors, a mayor shall not hear or determine, on or after July 1, 1991, any prosecution or criminal cause involving a violation described in division (A) of this section unless the exemption under the provisions described in division (A)(5) of this section applies to the mayor, or unless, prior to hearing the prosecution or criminal cause, the mayor successfully has completed the basic training course offered or provided for by the supreme court and has been issued a certificate attesting to satisfactory completion of the basic training course and also successfully has completed any periodic continuing education course offered or provided for by the supreme court that is applicable to the mayor under the rules and has been issued a certificate attesting to satisfactory completion of the periodic continuing education course.

This division does not affect and shall not be construed as affecting the authority of a mayor to appoint a mayor's court magistrate under section 1905.05 of the Revised Code. If a mayor is prohibited from hearing or determining a prosecution or criminal cause involving a violation described in division (A) of this section due to the operation of this division, the prohibition against the mayor hearing or determining the prosecution or cause does not affect and shall not be construed as affecting the jurisdiction or authority of a mayor's court magistrate appointed under that section to hear and determine the prosecution or cause in accordance with that section.

**HISTORY: 143 v S 131 (Eff 7-25-90); 143 v H 211 (Eff 4-11-91); 146 v H 670. Eff 12-2-96; 151 v S 8, § 1, eff. 8-17-06.**

**Not analogous to former RC § 1905.03 (RS § 1818; Bates § 1536-779; 66 v 169, § 114; 69 v 192, § 117; GC § 4530; Bureau of Code Revision, 10-1-53; 128 v 823(835)), repealed 130 v 1675, § 2, eff 10-14-63.**

## § 1905.031 Rules providing standards for exercise of jurisdiction in prosecutions other than OMVI.

(A) The supreme court may adopt rules prescribing educational standards and procedural and operational standards for mayors of municipal corporations who conduct a mayor's court and who wish to exercise the jurisdiction granted by section 1905.01 of the Revised Code over a prosecution or criminal cause other than a prosecution or cause within the scope of the standards described in section 1905.03 of the Revised Code. Any educational standards and procedural and operational standards prescribed by rule under authority of this division shall be for the purpose of assisting mayors of municipal corporations who conduct a mayor's court, and shall include, but shall not be limited to, all of the following:

(1) Provisions for basic training in the general principles of law that apply to the hearing and determination of prosecutions and causes that are within the jurisdiction of a mayor's court as specified in section 1905.01 of the Revised Code, other than prosecutions and causes that are within the scope of the standards described in section 1905.03 of the Revised Code, provisions for basic training in the procedural and operational standards prescribed by the court under this division, and provisions for periodic continuing education in those general principles and in those procedural and operational standards;

(2) Provisions for basic training in the laws of this state that apply relative to persons who are convicted of or plead guilty to any violation of a statute or ordinance, particularly as those laws apply relative to a person who is convicted of or pleads guilty to any such violation in a prosecution or cause that is within the jurisdiction of a mayor's court as specified in section 1905.01 of the Revised Code, other than prosecutions and causes that are within the scope of the standards described in section 1905.03 of the Revised Code, and provisions for periodic continuing education in those laws;

(3) Provisions specifying whether periodic continuing education for a mayor who conducts a mayor's court, who wishes to exercise the jurisdiction granted by section 1905.01 of the Revised Code over a prosecution or cause,

and who has received basic training in the principles and laws described in divisions (A)(1) and (2) of this section will be required on an annual or biennial basis;

(4) Provisions specifying the number of hours of basic training that a mayor who conducts a mayor's court and who wishes to exercise the jurisdiction granted by section 1905.01 of the Revised Code over a prosecution or cause, other than a prosecution or cause that is within the scope of the standards described in section 1905.03 of the Revised Code, will have to obtain to comply with the educational standards and provisions specifying the number of hours of periodic continuing education that such a mayor will have to obtain within each time period specified under authority of division (A)(3) of this section to comply with the educational standards;

(5) Provisions establishing an exemption, for a reasonable period of time, from the basic training requirements for mayors who initially take office on or after July 1, 1992, and who wish to conduct a mayor's court and exercise the jurisdiction granted by section 1905.01 of the Revised Code over a prosecution or cause other than a prosecution or cause within the scope of the standards described in section 1905.03 of the Revised Code;

(6) Provisions establishing procedural and operational standards for mayor's courts.

(B) If the supreme court adopts rules under authority of division (A) of this section prescribing educational standards and procedural and operational standards for mayors of municipal corporations who conduct a mayor's court and who wish to exercise the jurisdiction granted by section 1905.01 of the Revised Code over a prosecution or criminal cause, other than a prosecution or cause that is within the scope of the standards described in section 1905.03 of the Revised Code, the court may formulate a basic training course and a periodic continuing education course that such a mayor may complete to satisfy the basic training and periodic continuing education required relative to those standards, and may offer or provide for the offering of the basic training course and the periodic continuing education course to mayors of municipal corporations.

If the supreme court offers or provides for the offering of a basic training course and a periodic continuing education course formulated under this division, the court may prescribe a reasonable fee to cover the cost associated with formulating, offering, and teaching the particular course, which fee would have to be paid by each mayor who attends the particular course or the municipal corporation served by the mayor.

If the supreme court offers or provides for the offering of a basic training course and a periodic continuing education course formulated under this division, the court or other entity that offers either course shall issue to each mayor who successfully completes the particular course a certificate attesting to the mayor's satisfactory completion of the particular course.

(C) Notwithstanding section 1905.01 of the Revised Code, if the supreme court adopts rules under authority of division (A) of this section on or before July 1, 1991, if the supreme court formulates a basic training course and a periodic continuing education course under division (B) of this section, and if the supreme court offers or provides for the offering of the basic training course and the periodic continuing education course to mayors within a reasonable period of time after the adoption of the rules, a mayor shall not hear or determine, on or after July 1, 1992, any prosecution or criminal cause involving a violation described in division (A) of this section unless the exemption under the provisions described in division (A)(5) of this section applies to the mayor, or unless, prior to hearing the prosecution or criminal cause, the mayor has successfully completed the basic training course offered or provided for by the supreme court and has been issued a certificate attesting to satisfactory completion of the basic training course and also has successfully completed any periodic continuing education course offered or provided for by the supreme court that is applicable to the mayor under the rules and has been issued a certificate attesting to satisfactory completion of the periodic continuing education course.

This division does not affect and shall not be construed as affecting the authority of a mayor to appoint a mayor's court magistrate under section 1905.05 of the Revised Code. If a mayor is prohibited from hearing or determining a prosecution or criminal cause involving a violation described in division (A) of this section due to the operation of this division, the prohibition against the mayor hearing or determining the prosecution or cause does not affect and shall not be construed as affecting the jurisdiction or authority of a mayor's court magistrate appointed under that section to hear and determine the prosecution or cause in accordance with that section.

**HISTORY: 143 v S 131 (Eff 7-25-90); 143 v H 837 (Eff 7-25-90); 143 v H 211 (Eff 4-11-91); 146 v H 670. Eff 12-2-96.**

## § 1905.032 Transfer of prosecution to another court; recognizance.

(A) If a person who is charged with a violation of a law or an ordinance is brought before a mayor's court and the violation charged is not within the jurisdiction of the court, as set forth in section 1905.01 of the Revised Code, the mayor promptly shall transfer the case to the municipal court, county court, or court of common pleas with jurisdiction over the alleged violation and shall require the person to enter into a recognizance to appear before that court.

If a person who is charged with a violation of a law or an ordinance is brought before a mayor's court and the violation charged is within the jurisdiction of the court, as set forth in section 1905.01 of the Revised Code, the mayor, at any time prior to the final disposition of the case, may transfer it to the municipal court, county court, or court of common pleas with concurrent jurisdiction over the alleged violation. If a mayor transfers a case under this provision, the mayor shall require the person charged to enter into a recognizance to appear before the court to which the case is transferred.

(B) Upon the transfer of a case by a mayor under division (A) of this section, all of the following apply:

(1) The mayor shall certify all papers filed in the case, together with a transcript of all proceedings, accrued costs to date, and the recognizance given, to the court to which the case is transferred.

(2) All further proceedings under the charge, complaint, information, or indictment in the transferred case shall be discontinued in the mayor's court and shall be conducted in the court to which the case is transferred, in accordance with the provisions governing proceedings in that court.

(3) If the case is transferred to a municipal court that has an environmental division and the case is within the jurisdiction of the environmental division, as set forth in division (A)(1) of section 1901.181 [1901.18.1] of the

Revised Code, the case thereafter shall be within the exclusive jurisdiction of the environmental division of the municipal court to which it is transferred. In all other situations, the case thereafter shall be within the exclusive jurisdiction of the court to which it is transferred.

**HISTORY: 143 v S 131 (Eff 7-25-90); 144 v S 105 (Eff 3-24-92); 146 v H 350, § 1 (Eff 1-27-97); 146 v H 350, § 13 (Eff 7-1-97); 146 v H 438. Eff 7-1-97.**

The effective date is set by section 3 of HB 438.

See provisions, § 2.02(B) and § 3(B)(1) of SB 108 (149 v —), following RC § 1901.04.1.

## § 1905.033 Annual registration with supreme court; reports.

(A) The mayor of a municipal corporation who conducts a mayor's court shall register annually with the supreme court as provided in this division. The mayor shall file the registration on a form prescribed by the supreme court and not later than the fifteenth day of January in any year in which the mayor conducts a mayor's court or at least fifteen days before the mayor first conducts a mayor's court in a particular year, whichever is later. The registration shall include the name of the mayor, the name of any magistrate appointed by the mayor pursuant to section 1905.05 of the Revised Code, and the dates on which the mayor and magistrate last received the training required by section 1905.031 [1905.03.1] of the Revised Code.

(B) The mayor of any municipal corporation who conducts a mayor's court shall make the following reports:

(1) A report to the supreme court of all cases filed, pending, or terminated in the mayor's court in the reporting period covered by the report, and any financial, dispositional, and other information that the supreme court prescribes by rule. The mayor shall make the report under division (B)(1) of this section on a form prescribed by the supreme court and not later than the fifteenth day of January, April, July, and October of each year. The report shall cover all cases filed, pending, or terminated in the mayor's court for the calendar quarter preceding the appropriate filing date.

(2) A report to the bureau of criminal identification and investigation of every conviction in the mayor's court for an offense that is a misdemeanor on a first offense and a felony on any subsequent offense. The mayor shall make the report under division (B)(2) of this section upon entry of the judgment of conviction for the offense.

(C) A mayor of a municipal corporation who fails to comply with the general law on registering and reporting under this section shall not conduct a mayor's court.

**HISTORY: 149 v H 490, § 1, eff. 1-1-2004; 150 v S 57, § 1, eff. 1-1-2004.**

The effective date is set by section 4 of S.B. 57.

The provisions of § 5 of S.B. 57 (150 v —) read as follows:

SECTION 5. This act is hereby declared to be an emergency measure necessary for the immediate preservation of the public peace, health, and safety. The reason for such necessity is that Am. Sub. H.B. 490 of the 124th General Assembly, which made numerous changes to the law governing misdemeanor sentencing that are scheduled to take effect January 1, 2004, requires certain technical corrections and clarifications to ensure the proper administration of justice. Therefore, this act shall go into immediate effect.

## § 1905.04 Clerk, deputy and magistrate of mayor's court must be disinterested.

Neither the clerk of a mayor's court, nor his deputy, nor a mayor's court magistrate shall be concerned as counsel or agent in the prosecution or defense of any case before the mayor's court.

**HISTORY: RS § 1817a; Bates § 1536-778; 78 v 50; GC § 4529; Bureau of Code Revision, 10-1-53; 143 v S 131. Eff 7-25-90.**

## § 1905.05 Appointment of mayor's court magistrate.

(A) A mayor of a municipal corporation that has a mayor's court may appoint a person as mayor's court magistrate to hear and determine prosecutions and criminal causes in the mayor's court that are within the jurisdiction of the mayor's court, as set forth in section 1905.01 of the Revised Code. No person shall be appointed as a mayor's court magistrate unless the person has been admitted to the practice of law in this state and, for a total of at least three years preceding the person's appointment or the commencement of the person's service as magistrate, has been engaged in the practice of law in this state or served as a judge of a court of record in any jurisdiction in the United States, or both.

A person appointed as a mayor's court magistrate under this division is entitled to hear and determine prosecutions and criminal causes in the mayor's court that are within the jurisdiction of the mayor's court, as set forth in section 1905.01 of the Revised Code. If a mayor is prohibited from hearing or determining a prosecution or cause that charges a person with a violation of section 4511.19 of the Revised Code or with a violation of a municipal OVI ordinance as defined in section 4511.181 [4511.18.1] of the Revised Code due to the operation of division (C) of section 1905.03 of the Revised Code, or is prohibited from hearing or determining any other prosecution or cause due to the operation of division (C) of section 1905.031 [1905.03.1] of the Revised Code, the prohibition against the mayor hearing or determining the prosecution or cause does not affect and shall not be construed as affecting the jurisdiction or authority of a person appointed as a mayor's court magistrate under this division to hear and determine the prosecution or cause in accordance with this section. In hearing and determining such prosecutions and causes, the magistrate has the same powers, duties, and authority as does a mayor who conducts a mayor's court to hear and determine prosecutions and causes in general, including, but not limited to, the power and authority to decide the prosecution or cause, enter judgment, and impose sentence; the powers, duties, and authority granted to mayors of mayor's courts by this chapter, in relation to the hearing and determination of prosecutions and causes in mayor's courts; and the powers, duties, and authority granted to mayors of mayor's courts by any other provision of the Revised Code, in relation to the hearing and determination of prosecutions and causes in mayor's courts. A judgment entered and a sentence imposed by a mayor's court magistrate do not have to be reviewed or approved by the mayor who appointed the magistrate, and have the same force and effect as if they had been entered or imposed by the mayor.

A person appointed as a mayor's court magistrate under this division is not entitled to hear or determine any prosecution or criminal cause other than prosecutions and causes that are within the jurisdiction of the mayor's court, as set forth in section 1905.01 of the Revised Code.

A municipal corporation that a mayor's court magistrate serves shall pay the compensation for the services of the magistrate, which shall be either a fixed annual salary set by the legislative authority of the municipal corporation or a fixed annual amount or fees for services rendered set under a contract the magistrate and the municipal corporation enter into.

(B) The appointment of a person as a mayor's court magistrate under division (A) of this section does not preclude the mayor that appointed the magistrate, subject to the limitation contained in section 1905.03 and the limitation contained in section 1905.031 [1905.03.1] of the Revised Code, from also hearing and determining prosecutions and criminal causes in the mayor's court that are within the jurisdiction of the mayor's court, as set forth in section 1905.01 of the Revised Code.

**HISTORY: 143 v S 131 (Eff 7-25-90); 146 v H 670 (Eff 12-2-96); 147 v S 201. Eff 12-21-98; 151 v S 8, § 1, eff. 8-17-06.**

**Not analogous to former RC § 1905.05 (RS § 1819; Bates § 1536-780; 66 v 169, § 114; 69 v 192, § 117; GC § 4531; Bureau of Code Revision, 10-1-53), repealed 129 v S 367, § 2, eff 10-19-61.**

## § 1905.08 Duties of police chief or marshal; fees.

The chief of police of the city or village or a police officer of the city or village designated by him, or the marshal of a village shall attend the sittings of the mayor's court to execute the orders and process of the court, and to preserve order in it. The chief of police, other police officer, or marshal shall execute and return all writs and process directed to him by the mayor. The jurisdiction of the chief of police, other police officer, or marshal in the execution of such writs and process is coextensive with the county in criminal cases and in cases of violations of ordinances of the municipal corporation. In serving such writs and process and taxing costs on them, the chief of police, other police officer, or marshal shall be governed by the laws pertaining to constables. The fees of the mayor are the same as those allowed in the municipal or county court within whose jurisdiction the municipal corporation is located. There shall be allowed and taxed for services of the chief of police, other police officer, or marshal, the same fees and expense as those allowed constables.

**HISTORY: RS § 1822; Bates § 1536-783; 66 v 169, § 114; 69 v 192, § 117; GC § 4534; 102 v 476; 108 v PtII, 1203; Bureau of Code Revision, 10-1-53; 128 v 823 (Eff 11-6-59); 130 v 609 (Eff 10-14-63); 141 v H 158. Eff 3-17-87.**

## § 1905.17 Boundary line between villages adjoining each other.

When two villages adjoin each other on opposite sides of the line of any railroad, the boundary line between such villages, except where otherwise established by law is along the middle of the right of way of such railroad.

**HISTORY: RS § 1830-1; Bates § 1536-883; 78 v 93; 88 v 242; GC § 4543; Bureau of Code Revision. Eff 10-1-53.**

## § 1905.20 Powers of mayors and magistrates in criminal matters.

(A) The mayor of a municipal corporation has, within the corporate limits, all the powers conferred upon sheriffs to suppress disorder and keep the peace.

(B) The mayor of a municipal corporation shall award and issue all writs and process that are necessary to enforce the administration of justice throughout the municipal corporation. The mayor shall subscribe his name and affix his official seal to all writs, process, transcripts, and other official papers. A mayor's court magistrate, in hearing and determining prosecutions and criminal causes that are within the scope of his authority under section 1905.05 of the Revised Code, has the same powers and duties as are granted to or imposed upon a mayor under this division.

(C) The mayor of a municipal corporation shall be disqualified in any criminal case in which he was the arresting officer, assisted in the arrest, or was present at the time of arrest, and shall not hear the case.

**HISTORY: RS § 1837; Bates § 1536-773a; 66 v 169, § 118; GC § 4549; Bureau of Code Revision, 10-1-53; 125 v 297; 128 v 823(836) (Eff 11-6-59); 141 v H 158 (Eff 3-17-87); 143 v S 131. Eff 7-25-90.**

## § 1905.201 License suspension in OVI cases.

The mayor of a municipal corporation that has a mayor's court, and a mayor's court magistrate, are entitled to suspend, and shall suspend, in accordance with sections 4510.02, 4510.07, and 4511.19 of the Revised Code, the driver's or commercial driver's license or permit or nonresident operating privilege of any person who is convicted of or pleads guilty to a violation of division (A) of section 4511.19 of the Revised Code, of a municipal ordinance relating to operating a vehicle while under the influence of alcohol, a drug of abuse, or a combination of them, or of a municipal ordinance relating to operating a vehicle with a prohibited concentration of alcohol, a controlled substance, or a metabolite of a controlled substance in the whole blood, blood serum or plasma, breath, or urine that is substantially equivalent to division (A) of section 4511.19 of the Revised Code. The mayor of a municipal corporation that has a mayor's court, and a mayor's court magistrate, are entitled to suspend, and shall suspend, in accordance with sections 4510.02, 4510.07, and 4511.19 of the Revised Code, the driver's, or commercial driver's license or permit or nonresident operating privilege of any person who is convicted of or pleads guilty to a violation of division (B) of section 4511.19 of the Revised Code or of a municipal ordinance relating to operating a vehicle with a prohibited concentration of alcohol in the whole blood, blood serum or plasma, breath, or urine that is substantially equivalent to division (B) of section 4511.19 of the Revised Code.

Suspension of a commercial driver's license under this section shall be concurrent with any period of disqualification or suspension under section 3123.58 or 4506.16 of the Revised Code. No person who is disqualified for life from holding a commercial driver's license under section 4506.16 of the Revised Code shall be issued a driver's license under Chapter 4507. of the Revised Code during the period for which the commercial driver's license was suspended under this section, and no person whose commercial driver's license is suspended under this section shall be issued a driver's license under Chapter 4507. of the Revised Code during the period of the suspension.

**HISTORY: 142 v H 303 (Eff 10-20-87); 143 v H 381 (Eff 7-1-89); 143 v S 131 (Eff 7-25-90); 144 v S 275 (Eff 9-1-93 †); 145 v S 62, §§ 4, 5 (9-1-93); 145 v S 82 (Eff 5-4-94); 146 v H**

**167 (Eff 5-15-97); 148 v S 180. Eff 3-22-2001; 149 v S 123, § 1, eff. 1-1-04; 151 v S 8, § 1, eff. 8-17-06.**

The effective date is set by section 4 of S.B. 123.

See provisions, § 5 of S.B. 123 (149 v —), following RC § 1905.01.

The provisions of §§ 4, 5 of SB 62 (145 v —) read as follows:

SECTION 4. That Section 3 of Sub. S.B. 275 of the 119th General Assembly be amended to read as follows:

"Sec. 3. Sections 1 and 2 of this act shall take effect September 1, 1993."

SECTION 5. That existing Section 3 of Sub. S.B. 275 of the 119th General Assembly is hereby repealed.

## § 1905.21 Docket; disposition of receipts; salary; office; seal.

The mayor of a municipal corporation and a mayor's court magistrate shall keep a docket. Neither the mayor of a municipal corporation nor a mayor's court magistrate shall retain or receive for his own use any of the fines, forfeitures, fees, or costs he collects. A mayor's court magistrate shall account for all such fines, forfeitures, fees, and costs he collects and transfer them to the mayor. The mayor shall account for and dispose of all such fines, forfeitures, fees, and costs he collects, including all such fines, forfeitures, fees, and costs that are transferred to him by a mayor's court magistrate, as provided in section 733.40 of the Revised Code.

The mayor of a municipal corporation shall be paid such fixed annual salary as the legislative authority of the municipal corporation provides under sections 731.08 and 731.13 of the Revised Code, and a mayor's court magistrate shall receive compensation as provided in section 1905.05 of the Revised Code.

The mayor of a municipal corporation shall keep an office, provided by the legislative authority of the municipal corporation, at a convenient place in the municipal corporation, and shall be furnished by the legislative authority with the corporate seal of the municipal corporation. In the center of such seal shall be the words, "Mayor of the city of ............," or "Mayor of the village of ............"

**HISTORY: RS § 1745; Bates § 1536-774; 66 v 169, § 115; GC § 4550; Bureau of Code Revision, 10-1-53; 125 v 297 (Eff 10-13-53); 143 v S 131. Eff 7-25-90.**

## § 1905.22 Appeals.

Appeals from a mayor's court may be taken to the municipal court or county court having jurisdiction within the municipal corporation.

**HISTORY: 133 v S 530. Eff 6-12-70.**

**Analogous in part to former RC § 1905.22 (RS § 1752; Bates § 1536-775; 66 v 170; 72 v 42; GC § 4551; 116 v 122; Bureau of Code Revision, 10-1-53; 128 v 836; 129 v 425) repealed 133 v S 530, § 2, eff 6-12-70.**

## § 1905.23 Notice of appeal.

Within ten days from the time a mayor renders judgment, the appellant shall file with the mayor's court a written notice of appeal designating the order or judgment appealed from and the court to which the appeal is taken.

All further proceedings in the mayor's court shall be stayed from the time of filing the notice of appeal with the mayor's court.

**HISTORY: 133 v S 530. Eff 6-12-70.**

**Not analogous to former RC § 1905.23 (RS § 1839; Bates § 1536-786; 66 v 180; GC § 4552; Bureau of Code Revision, 10-1-53) repealed 130 v 1675, § 2, eff 10-14-63.**

## § 1905.24 Transcript for appeal.

Upon the filing of the notice of appeal, the clerk of the mayor's court shall make a certified transcript of the proceedings and deliver such transcript together with the original papers used on the trial, to the court to which the appeal is taken, within fifteen days from the rendition of the judgment appealed from.

Upon receipt of the transcript and the papers mentioned in this section, the clerk of the court to which the appeal is taken shall file them and docket the appeal.

**HISTORY: 133 v S 530. Eff 6-12-70.**

**Not analogous to former RC § 1905.24 (RS § 1840; Bates § 1536-787; 66 v 180; GC § 4553; Bureau of Code Revision, 10-1-53) repealed 130 v 1675, § 2, eff 10-14-63.**

## § 1905.25 Appeal; trial de novo.

An appeal from the mayor's court to the municipal court or county court shall proceed as a trial de novo.

**HISTORY: 133 v S 530. Eff 6-12-70.**

**Not analogous to former RC § 1905.25 (RS § 1841; Bates § 1536-788; 66 v 180; GC § 4554; 108 v PtII, 1203; 109 v 174; Bureau of Code Revision, 10-1-53) repealed 130 v 1675, § 2, eff 10-14-63.**

## § 1905.26 Fees and mileage of witnesses.

In cases for the violation of ordinances, the fees of witnesses shall be paid, on the certificate of the officer presiding at the trial, from the treasury of the municipal corporation. Witnesses shall be paid the fees and mileage provided for under section 1901.26 of the Revised Code.

**HISTORY: RS § 1842; Bates § 1536-789; 66 v 180, § 196; GC § 4555; Bureau of Code Revision, 10-1-53; 128 v 823(837). Eff 11-6-59; 152 v H 525, § 1, eff. 7-1-09.**

The effective date is set by § 3 of 152 v H 525.

## § 1905.28 Contempts; rules.

The mayor or mayor's court magistrate presiding at any trial under this chapter may punish contempts, compel the attendance of jurors and witnesses, and establish rules for the examination and trial of all cases brought before him, in the same manner as judges of county courts.

**HISTORY: RS § 1844; Bates § 1536-791; 66 v 180, § 198; GC § 4557; Bureau of Code Revision, 10-1-53; 128 v 823(837) (Eff 11-6-59); 143 v S 131. Eff 7-25-90.**

## § 1905.29 Temporary use of municipal prison by neighboring township.

The mayor of a municipal corporation, and in his absence, the president of the legislative authority of the municipal corporation, may grant to officials of adjoining or contiguous townships the temporary use of the municipal corporation prison, station house, or watchhouse to confine criminals or other persons dangerous to the peace of the community, until they can be safely removed to the county jail, or other place of security.

**HISTORY: RS § 1845; Bates § 1536-792; 66 v 170, § 120; GC § 4558; Bureau of Code Revision, 10-1-53; 143 v S 131. Eff 7-25-90.**

## § 1905.30 Offender may be confined until fine paid.

When a fine is the whole or part of a sentence, the mayor's court may order the person sentenced to remain confined in the county jail, workhouse, or prison of the municipal corporation, until the fine is paid or secured to be paid, or the offender is legally discharged.

**HISTORY: RS § 1846; Bates § 1536-793; S&S 610; 60 v 66; 66 v 314, § 180; GC § 4559; Bureau of Code Revision, 10-1-53; 133 v S 460. Eff 9-3-70.**

## § 1905.31 Jurisdiction over railroad forming part of boundary line.

When the line of a railroad adjoins or forms a part of the boundary line of a municipal corporation, such municipal corporation has jurisdiction over the entire width of the right of way of the line of such railroad for the punishment of the violation of the ordinances of such municipal corporation.

**HISTORY: RS § 1830-2; Bates § 1536-884; 92 v 428; GC § 4560; Bureau of Code Revision. Eff 10-1-53.**

## § 1905.32 Fines and forfeitures recovered.

Fines, penalties, and forfeitures may, in all cases, and in addition to any other mode provided, be recovered by action before any judge of a county court, or other court of competent jurisdiction, in the name of the proper municipal corporation, and for its use. In any action in which a pleading is necessary, it is sufficient if the petition sets forth generally the amount claimed to be due in respect to the violation of the ordinance of the municipal corporation. Such petition shall refer to the title of such ordinance, state the date of its adoption or passage, and show, as near as is practicable, the true time of the alleged violation.

**HISTORY: RS § 1864; Bates § 1536-627; 66 v 167, § 108; GC § 4561; Bureau of Code Revision, 10-1-53; 128 v 823 (837). Eff 11-6-59.**

## § 1905.34 Party committed in default of payment.

When a fine imposed for the violation of an ordinance of a municipal corporation is not paid, the party convicted may, by order of the mayor of the municipal corporation, or other proper authority, or on process issued for the purpose, be committed until such fine and the costs of prosecution are paid, or until the party convicted is legally discharged.

**HISTORY: RS § 1866; Bates § 1536-629; 66 v 168, § 110; GC § 4563; Bureau of Code Revision, 10-1-53; 136 v H 205. Eff 8-19-75.**

## § 1905.35 Imprisonment.

Imprisonment under the ordinances of a municipal corporation shall be in the workhouse or other jail of the municipal corporation. Any municipal corporation not provided with a workhouse, or other jail, may, for the purpose of imprisonment, use the county jail, at the expense of the municipal corporation, until the municipal corporation is provided with a prison, house of correction, or workhouse. Persons so imprisoned in the county jail are under the charge of the sheriff. Such sheriff shall receive and hold such persons in the manner prescribed by the ordinances of the municipal corporation, until such persons are legally discharged.

**HISTORY: RS § 1867; Bates § 1536-630; 66 v 168, § 111; GC § 4564; Bureau of Code Revision. Eff 10-1-53.**

## § 1905.36 Use of county jail prohibited.

The board of county commissioners, at such board's discretion, on giving ninety days' written notice to the legislative authority of any municipal corporation, may prohibit the use of the county jail for the purpose authorized in section 1905.35 of the Revised Code.

**HISTORY: RS § 1868; Bates § 1536-631; 66 v 168, § 112; GC § 4565; Bureau of Code Revision. Eff 10-1-53.**

## § 1905.37 Limit of prohibition.

If, within ninety days after the notice mentioned in section 1905.36 of the Revised Code is given, the legislative authority of the municipal corporation provides by ordinance and the necessary contracts for the immediate erection of a prison, workhouse, or house of correction, the municipal corporation, notwithstanding the notice and prohibition provided for in such section, shall continue to have the use of the county jail for the purpose of imprisonment, until such prison, workhouse, or house of correction is erected and ready for use.

**HISTORY: RS § 1869; Bates § 1536-632; 66 v 168, § 113; GC § 4566; Bureau of Code Revision. Eff 10-1-53.**

# TITLE 21: COURTS — PROBATE — JUVENILE

## CHAPTER 2108: REVISED UNIFORM ANATOMICAL GIFT ACT



### § 2108.18 (UAGA 16) Sale or purchase of parts prohibited.

(A) Except as otherwise provided in division (B) of this section, no person shall, for valuable consideration, knowingly purchase or sell a part for transplantation or therapy if removal of a part from an individual is intended to occur after the individual's death.

(B) A person may charge a reasonable amount for the removal, processing, preservation, quality control, storage, transportation, implantation, or disposal of a part.

**HISTORY: 152 v H 529, § 1, eff. 4-7-09.**

**Not analogous to former RC § 2108.18, amended and renumbered to RC § 2108.23 by 152 v H 529, eff 4-7-09.**

### § 2108.40 Death defined.

An individual is dead if the individual has sustained either irreversible cessation of circulatory and respiratory functions or irreversible cessation of all functions of the brain, including the brain stem, as determined in accordance with accepted medical standards. If the respiratory and circulatory functions of a person are being artificially sustained, under accepted medical standards a determination that death has occurred is made by a physician by observing and conducting a test to determine that the irreversible cessation of all functions of the brain has occurred.

A physician who makes a determination of death in accordance with this section and accepted medical standards is not liable for damages in any civil action or subject to prosecution in any criminal proceeding for the physician's acts or the acts of others based on that determination.

Any person who acts in good faith in reliance on a determination of death made by a physician in accordance with this section and accepted medical standards is not liable for damages in any civil action or subject to prosecution in any criminal proceeding for the person's actions.

**HISTORY: 139 v S 98. Eff 3-15-82; 152 v H 529, § 1, eff. 4-7-09.**

**Publisher's Note:**

This section was amended and renumbered from RC § 2108.30 by 152 v H 529, effective April 7, 2009.

### § 2108.99 Penalty.

Whoever violates division (A) of section 2108.18 or section 2108.19 of the Revised Code is guilty of a felony of the third degree.

**HISTORY: 143 v H 21 (Eff 3-27-91); 146 v S 2. Eff 7-1-96; 152 v H 529, § 1, eff. 4-7-09.**

The effective date is set by section 6 of SB 2.

## CHAPTER 2151: JUVENILE COURT

## § 2151.01 Construction; purpose.

The sections in Chapter 2151. of the Revised Code, with the exception of those sections providing for the criminal prosecution of adults, shall be liberally interpreted and construed so as to effectuate the following purposes:

(A) To provide for the care, protection, and mental and physical development of children subject to Chapter 2151. of the Revised Code, whenever possible, in a family environment, separating the child from the child's parents only when necessary for the child's welfare or in the interests of public safety;

(B) To provide judicial procedures through which Chapters 2151. and 2152. of the Revised Code are executed and enforced, and in which the parties are assured of a fair hearing, and their constitutional and other legal rights are recognized and enforced.

**HISTORY: 133 v H 320 (Eff 11-19-69); 148 v S 179, § 3. Eff 1-1-2002.**

**Not analogous to former RC § 2151.01 (GC § 1639-1; 117 v 520; 121 v 557; Bureau of Code Revision, 10-1-53), repealed, 133 v H 320. For an analogous provision to former RC § 2151.01, see now RC § 2151.01.1.**

The effective date is set by section 5 of SB 179.

## § 2151.011 Definitions.

(A) As used in the Revised Code:

(1) "Juvenile court" means whichever of the following is applicable that has jurisdiction under this chapter and Chapter 2152. of the Revised Code:

(a) The division of the court of common pleas specified in section 2101.022 or 2301.03 of the Revised Code as having jurisdiction under this chapter and Chapter 2152. of the Revised Code or as being the juvenile division or the juvenile division combined with one or more other divisions;

(b) The juvenile court of Cuyahoga county or Hamilton county that is separately and independently created by section 2151.08 or Chapter 2153. of the Revised Code and that has jurisdiction under this chapter and Chapter 2152. of the Revised Code;

(c) If division (A)(1)(a) or (b) of this section does not apply, the probate division of the court of common pleas.

(2) "Juvenile judge" means a judge of a court having jurisdiction under this chapter.

(3) "Private child placing agency" means any association, as defined in section 5103.02 of the Revised Code, that is certified under section 5103.03 of the Revised Code to accept temporary, permanent, or legal custody of children and place the children for either foster care or adoption.

(4) "Private noncustodial agency" means any person, organization, association, or society certified by the department of job and family services that does not accept temporary or permanent legal custody of children, that is privately operated in this state, and that does one or more of the following:

(a) Receives and cares for children for two or more consecutive weeks;

(b) Participates in the placement of children in certified foster homes;

(c) Provides adoption services in conjunction with a public children services agency or private child placing agency.

(B) As used in this chapter:

(1) "Adequate parental care" means the provision by a child's parent or parents, guardian, or custodian of adequate food, clothing, and shelter to ensure the child's health and physical safety and the provision by a child's parent or parents of specialized services warranted by the child's physical or mental needs.

(2) "Adult" means an individual who is eighteen years of age or older.

(3) "Agreement for temporary custody" means a voluntary agreement authorized by section 5103.15 of the Revised Code that transfers the temporary custody of a child to a public children services agency or a private child placing agency.

(4) "Alternative response" means the public children services agency's response to a report of child abuse or neglect that engages the family in a comprehensive evaluation of child safety, risk of subsequent harm, and family strengths and needs and that does not include a determination as to whether child abuse or neglect occurred.

(5) "Certified foster home" means a foster home, as defined in section 5103.02 of the Revised Code, certified under section 5103.03 of the Revised Code.

(6) "Child" means a person who is under eighteen years of age, except that the juvenile court has jurisdiction over any person who is adjudicated an unruly child prior to attaining eighteen years of age until the person attains twenty-one years of age, and, for purposes of that jurisdiction related to that adjudication, a person who is so adjudicated an unruly child shall be deemed a "child" until the person attains twenty-one years of age.

(7) "Child day camp," "child care," "child day-care center," "part-time child day-care center," "type A family day-care home," "certified type B family day-care home," "type B home," "administrator of a child day-care center," "administrator of a type A family day-care home," "in-home aide," and "authorized provider" have the same meanings as in section 5104.01 of the Revised Code.

(8) "Child care provider" means an individual who is a child-care staff member or administrator of a child day-care center, a type A family day-care home, or a type B family day-care home, or an in-home aide or an individual who is licensed, is regulated, is approved, operates under the direction of, or otherwise is certified by the department of job and family services, department of developmental disabilities, or the early childhood programs of the department of education.

(9) "Chronic truant" has the same meaning as in section 2152.02 of the Revised Code.

(10) "Commit" means to vest custody as ordered by the court.

(11) "Counseling" includes both of the following:

(a) General counseling services performed by a public children services agency or shelter for victims of domestic violence to assist a child, a child's parents, and a child's siblings in alleviating identified problems that may cause or have caused the child to be an abused, neglected, or dependent child.

(b) Psychiatric or psychological therapeutic counseling services provided to correct or alleviate any mental or emotional illness or disorder and performed by a licensed psychiatrist, licensed psychologist, or a person licensed under Chapter 4757. of the Revised Code to engage in social work or professional counseling.

(12) "Custodian" means a person who has legal custody of a child or a public children services agency or private child placing agency that has permanent, temporary, or legal custody of a child.

(13) "Delinquent child" has the same meaning as in section 2152.02 of the Revised Code.

(14) "Detention" means the temporary care of children pending court adjudication or disposition, or execution of a court order, in a public or private facility designed to physically restrict the movement and activities of children.

(15) "Developmental disability" has the same meaning as in section 5123.01 of the Revised Code.

(16) "Differential response approach" means an approach that a public children services agency may use to respond to accepted reports of child abuse or neglect with either an alternative response or a traditional response.

(17) "Foster caregiver" has the same meaning as in section 5103.02 of the Revised Code.

(18) "Guardian" means a person, association, or corporation that is granted authority by a probate court pursuant to Chapter 2111. of the Revised Code to exercise parental rights over a child to the extent provided in the court's order and subject to the residual parental rights of the child's parents.

(19) "Habitual truant" means any child of compulsory school age who is absent without legitimate excuse for absence from the public school the child is supposed to attend for five or more consecutive school days, seven or more school days in one school month, or twelve or more school days in a school year.

(20) "Juvenile traffic offender" has the same meaning as in section 2152.02 of the Revised Code.

(21) "Legal custody" means a legal status that vests in the custodian the right to have physical care and control of the child and to determine where and with whom the child shall live, and the right and duty to protect, train, and discipline the child and to provide the child with food, shelter, education, and medical care, all subject to any residual parental rights, privileges, and responsibilities. An individual granted legal custody shall exercise the rights and responsibilities personally unless otherwise authorized by any section of the Revised Code or by the court.

(22) A "legitimate excuse for absence from the public school the child is supposed to attend" includes, but is not limited to, any of the following:

(a) The fact that the child in question has enrolled in and is attending another public or nonpublic school in this or another state;

(b) The fact that the child in question is excused from attendance at school for any of the reasons specified in section 3321.04 of the Revised Code;

(c) The fact that the child in question has received an age and schooling certificate in accordance with section 3331.01 of the Revised Code.

(23) "Mental illness" and "mentally ill person subject to hospitalization by court order" have the same meanings as in section 5122.01 of the Revised Code.

(24) "Mental injury" means any behavioral, cognitive, emotional, or mental disorder in a child caused by an act or omission that is described in section 2919.22 of the Revised Code and is committed by the parent or other person responsible for the child's care.

(25) "Mentally retarded person" has the same meaning as in section 5123.01 of the Revised Code.

(26) "Nonsecure care, supervision, or training" means care, supervision, or training of a child in a facility that

does not confine or prevent movement of the child within the facility or from the facility.

(27) "Of compulsory school age" has the same meaning as in section 3321.01 of the Revised Code.

(28) "Organization" means any institution, public, semipublic, or private, and any private association, society, or agency located or operating in the state, incorporated or unincorporated, having among its functions the furnishing of protective services or care for children, or the placement of children in certified foster homes or elsewhere.

(29) "Out-of-home care" means detention facilities, shelter facilities, certified children's crisis care facilities, certified foster homes, placement in a prospective adoptive home prior to the issuance of a final decree of adoption, organizations, certified organizations, child day-care centers, type A family day-care homes, child care provided by type B family day-care home providers and by in-home aides, group home providers, group homes, institutions, state institutions, residential facilities, residential care facilities, residential camps, day camps, public schools, chartered nonpublic schools, educational service centers, hospitals, and medical clinics that are responsible for the care, physical custody, or control of children.

(30) "Out-of-home care child abuse" means any of the following when committed by a person responsible for the care of a child in out-of-home care:

(a) Engaging in sexual activity with a child in the person's care;

(b) Denial to a child, as a means of punishment, of proper or necessary subsistence, education, medical care, or other care necessary for a child's health;

(c) Use of restraint procedures on a child that cause injury or pain;

(d) Administration of prescription drugs or psychotropic medication to the child without the written approval and ongoing supervision of a licensed physician;

(e) Commission of any act, other than by accidental means, that results in any injury to or death of the child in out-of-home care or commission of any act by accidental means that results in an injury to or death of a child in out-of-home care and that is at variance with the history given of the injury or death.

(31) "Out-of-home care child neglect" means any of the following when committed by a person responsible for the care of a child in out-of-home care:

(a) Failure to provide reasonable supervision according to the standards of care appropriate to the age, mental and physical condition, or other special needs of the child;

(b) Failure to provide reasonable supervision according to the standards of care appropriate to the age, mental and physical condition, or other special needs of the child, that results in sexual or physical abuse of the child by any person;

(c) Failure to develop a process for all of the following:

(i) Administration of prescription drugs or psychotropic drugs for the child;

(ii) Assuring that the instructions of the licensed physician who prescribed a drug for the child are followed;

(iii) Reporting to the licensed physician who prescribed the drug all unfavorable or dangerous side effects from the use of the drug.

(d) Failure to provide proper or necessary subsistence, education, medical care, or other individualized care necessary for the health or well-being of the child;

(e) Confinement of the child to a locked room without monitoring by staff;

(f) Failure to provide ongoing security for all prescription and nonprescription medication;

(g) Isolation of a child for a period of time when there is substantial risk that the isolation, if continued, will impair or retard the mental health or physical well-being of the child.

(32) "Permanent custody" means a legal status that vests in a public children services agency or a private child placing agency, all parental rights, duties, and obligations, including the right to consent to adoption, and divests the natural parents or adoptive parents of all parental rights, privileges, and obligations, including all residual rights and obligations.

(33) "Permanent surrender" means the act of the parents or, if a child has only one parent, of the parent of a child, by a voluntary agreement authorized by section 5103.15 of the Revised Code, to transfer the permanent custody of the child to a public children services agency or a private child placing agency.

(34) "Person" means an individual, association, corporation, or partnership and the state or any of its political subdivisions, departments, or agencies.

(35) "Person responsible for a child's care in out-of-home care" means any of the following:

(a) Any foster caregiver, in-home aide, or provider;

(b) Any administrator, employee, or agent of any of the following: a public or private detention facility; shelter facility; certified children's crisis care facility; organization; certified organization; child day-care center; type A family day-care home; certified type B family day-care home; group home; institution; state institution; residential facility; residential care facility; residential camp; day camp; school district; community school; chartered nonpublic school; educational service center; hospital; or medical clinic;

(c) Any person who supervises or coaches children as part of an extracurricular activity sponsored by a school district, public school, or chartered nonpublic school;

(d) Any other person who performs a similar function with respect to, or has a similar relationship to, children.

(36) "Physically impaired" means having one or more of the following conditions that substantially limit one or more of an individual's major life activities, including self-care, receptive and expressive language, learning, mobility, and self-direction:

(a) A substantial impairment of vision, speech, or hearing;

(b) A congenital orthopedic impairment;

(c) An orthopedic impairment caused by disease, rheumatic fever or any other similar chronic or acute health problem, or amputation or another similar cause.

(37) "Placement for adoption" means the arrangement by a public children services agency or a private child placing agency with a person for the care and adoption by that person of a child of whom the agency has permanent custody.

(38) "Placement in foster care" means the arrangement by a public children services agency or a private child placing agency for the out-of-home care of a child of whom the agency has temporary custody or permanent custody.

(39) "Planned permanent living arrangement" means an order of a juvenile court pursuant to which both of the following apply:

(a) The court gives legal custody of a child to a public children services agency or a private child placing agency without the termination of parental rights.

(b) The order permits the agency to make an appropriate placement of the child and to enter into a written agreement with a foster care provider or with another person or agency with whom the child is placed.

(40) "Practice of social work" and "practice of professional counseling" have the same meanings as in section 4757.01 of the Revised Code.

(41) "Sanction, service, or condition" means a sanction, service, or condition created by court order following an adjudication that a child is an unruly child that is described in division (A)(4) of section 2152.19 of the Revised Code.

(42) "Protective supervision" means an order of disposition pursuant to which the court permits an abused, neglected, dependent, or unruly child to remain in the custody of the child's parents, guardian, or custodian and stay in the child's home, subject to any conditions and limitations upon the child, the child's parents, guardian, or custodian, or any other person that the court prescribes, including supervision as directed by the court for the protection of the child.

(43) "Psychiatrist" has the same meaning as in section 5122.01 of the Revised Code.

(44) "Psychologist" has the same meaning as in section 4732.01 of the Revised Code.

(45) "Residential camp" means a program in which the care, physical custody, or control of children is accepted overnight for recreational or recreational and educational purposes.

(46) "Residential care facility" means an institution, residence, or facility that is licensed by the department of mental health under section 5119.22 of the Revised Code and that provides care for a child.

(47) "Residential facility" means a home or facility that is licensed by the department of developmental disabilities under section 5123.19 of the Revised Code and in which a child with a developmental disability resides.

(48) "Residual parental rights, privileges, and responsibilities" means those rights, privileges, and responsibilities remaining with the natural parent after the transfer of legal custody of the child, including, but not necessarily limited to, the privilege of reasonable visitation, consent to adoption, the privilege to determine the child's religious affiliation, and the responsibility for support.

(49) "School day" means the school day established by the state board of education pursuant to section 3313.48 of the Revised Code.

(50) "School month" and "school year" have the same meanings as in section 3313.62 of the Revised Code.

(51) "Secure correctional facility" means a facility under the direction of the department of youth services that is designed to physically restrict the movement and activities of children and used for the placement of children after adjudication and disposition.

(52) "Sexual activity" has the same meaning as in section 2907.01 of the Revised Code.

(53) "Shelter" means the temporary care of children in physically unrestricted facilities pending court adjudication or disposition.

(54) "Shelter for victims of domestic violence" has the same meaning as in section 3113.33 of the Revised Code.

(55) "Temporary custody" means legal custody of a child who is removed from the child's home, which custody may be terminated at any time at the discretion of the court or, if the legal custody is granted in an agreement for temporary custody, by the person who executed the agreement.

(56) "Traditional response" means a public children services agency's response to a report of child abuse or neglect that encourages engagement of the family in a comprehensive evaluation of the child's current and future safety needs and a fact-finding process to determine whether child abuse or neglect occurred and the circumstances surrounding the alleged harm or risk of harm.

(C) For the purposes of this chapter, a child shall be presumed abandoned when the parents of the child have failed to visit or maintain contact with the child for more than ninety days, regardless of whether the parents resume contact with the child after that period of ninety days.

**HISTORY: 142 v H 403 (Eff 1-1-89); 143 v H 257 (Eff 8-3-89); 143 v H 38 (Eff 7-10-90); 144 v H 155 (Eff 7-22-91); 144 v H 356 (Eff 3-15-93); 145 v H 152 (Eff 7-1-93); 145 v S 21 (Eff 10-29-93); 145 v H 715 (Eff 7-22-94); 146 v H 1 (Eff 1-1-96); 146 v S 2 (Eff 7-1-96); 146 v H 274, §§ 1, 4 (Eff 8-8-96); 146 v H 265 (Eff 3-3-97); 146 v S 223 (Eff 3-18-97); 146 v H 124 (Eff 3-31-97); 147 v H 408 (Eff 10-1-97); 147 v S 212 (Eff 9-30-98); 147 v H 484 (Eff 3-18-99); 148 v H 470 (Eff 7-1-2000); 148 v S 181 (Eff 9-4-2000); 148 v H 448 (Eff 10-5-2000); 148 v H 332 (Eff 1-1-2001); 148 v S 179, § 3 (Eff 1-1-2002); 149 v H 400. Eff 4-3-2003; 150 v H 106, § 1, eff. 9-16-04; 150 v H 11, § 1, eff. 5-18-05; 151 v S 238, § 1, eff. 9-21-06; 153 v S 79, § 1, eff. 10-6-09; 2011 HB 153, § 101.01, eff. Sept. 29, 2011.**

The provisions of § 7 of 151 v S 238 read as follows:

SECTION 7. Section 2151.011 of the Revised Code is presented in this act as a composite of the section as amended by both Am. Sub. * * * The General Assembly, applying the principle stated in division (B) of section 1.52 of the Revised Code that amendments are to be harmonized if reasonably capable of simultaneous operation, finds that the composites are the resulting version of the sections in effect prior to the effective dates of the sections as presented in this act.

**Publisher's Note:**

The amendment of (B)(47) and (48) of RC § 2151.011 by 151 v S 311 was disapproved by the Governor.

## § 2151.02 Repealed, 148 v S 179, § 4 [GC § 1639-2; 117 v 520; Bureau of Code Revision, 10-1-53; 127 v 547; 133 v H 320; 146 v H 4; 147 v H 25; 148 v S 181; 148 v S 218]. Eff 1-1-2002.

This section concerned delinquent child defined.
The effective date is set by section 5 of SB 179.

## § 2151.021 Repealed, 148 v S 179, § 4 [127 v 547; 133 v H 320; 139 v H 707]. Eff 1-1-2002.

This section concerned juvenile traffic offender defined.
The effective date is set by section 5 of SB 179.

## § 2151.022 Unruly child defined.

As used in this chapter, "unruly child" includes any of the following:

(A) Any child who does not submit to the reasonable control of the child's parents, teachers, guardian, or custodian, by reason of being wayward or habitually disobedient;

(B) Any child who is an habitual truant from school and who previously has not been adjudicated an unruly child for being an habitual truant;

(C) Any child who behaves in a manner as to injure or endanger the child's own health or morals or the health or morals of others;

(D) Any child who violates a law, other than division (C) of section 2907.39, division (A) of section 2923.211 [2923.21.1], division (C)(1) or (D) of section 2925.55, or section 2151.87 of the Revised Code, that is applicable only to a child.

**HISTORY: 133 v H 320 (Eff 11-19-69); 146 v H 4 (Eff 11-9-95); 148 v S 181 (Eff 9-4-2000); 148 v S 218 (Eff 3-15-2001); 148 v S 179, § 3. Eff 1-1-2002; 151 v S 53, § 1, eff. 5-17-06; 151 v H 23, § 1, eff. 8-17-06.**

The provisions of § 4 of 151 v H 23 read as follows:

SECTION 4. Section 303.02 of the Revised Code is presented in this act as a composite of the section as amended by both Sub. H.B. 411 and Am. Sub. S.B. 18 of the 125th General Assembly. Section 519.02 of the Revised Code is presented in this act as a composite of the section as amended by both Sub. H.B. 411 and Am. Sub. S.B. 18 of the 125th General Assembly. Section 2151.022 of the Revised Code is presented in this act as a composite of the section as amended by both Am. Sub. S.B. 179 and Sub. S.B. 218 of the 123rd General Assembly. The General Assembly, applying the principle stated in division (B) of section 1.52 of the Revised Code that amendments are to be harmonized if reasonably capable of simultaneous operation, finds that the composite is the resulting version of the section in effect prior to the effective date of the section as presented in this act.

The provisions of § 3 of 151 v S 53 read as follows:

SECTION 3. Section 2151.022 of the Revised Code is presented in this act as a composite of the section as amended by both Am. Sub. S.B. 179 and Sub. S.B. 218 of the 123rd General Assembly. The General Assembly, applying the principle stated in division (B) of section 1.52 of the Revised Code that amendments are to be harmonized if reasonably capable of simultaneous operation, finds that the composite is the resulting version of the section in effect prior to the effective date of the section as presented in this act.

The effective date is set by section 5 of SB 179.

**Comment, Legislative Service Commission**

Section 2151.022 of the Revised Code is amended by Am. Sub. H.B. 23 and Am. Sub. S.B. 53 of the 126th General Assembly. Comparison of these amendments in pursuance of section 1.52 of the Revised Code discloses that they are not irreconcilable so that they are required by that section to be harmonized to give effect to each amendment.

Sections * * * and 2151.36 of the Revised Code are amended by this act [Am. Sub. S.B. 179] and also by Am. Sub. S.B. 180, both of the 123rd General Assembly. Sections 2151.022, 2151.27, and 2151.28 of the Revised Code are amended by this act [Am. Sub. S.B. 179] and also by Sub. S.B. 218, both of the 123rd General Assembly. Section 2151.35 (versions effective April 9, 2001 and January 1, 2002) of the Revised Code is amended by this act [Am. Sub. S.B. 179] and also by Sub. S.B. 218, both of the 123rd General Assembly. Section 2151.141 of the Revised Code is amended by this act [Am. Sub. S.B. 179] and also by Sub. H.B. 412, both of the 123rd General Assembly. Section 2151.23 (effective January 1, 2001) of the Revised Code is amended by this act [Am. Sub. S.B. 179] and also by Am. Sub. S.B. 180 and Sub. S.B. 218, all of the 123rd General Assembly. * * * Comparison of these amendments in pursuance of section 1.52 of the Revised Code discloses that they are not irreconcilable so that they are required by that section to be harmonized to give effect to each amendment.

## § 2151.03 Neglected child defined; failure to provide medical care for religious reasons; duty to report child abuse.

(A) As used in this chapter, "neglected child" includes any child:

(1) Who is abandoned by the child's parents, guardian, or custodian;

(2) Who lacks adequate parental care because of the faults or habits of the child's parents, guardian, or custodian;

(3) Whose parents, guardian, or custodian neglects the child or refuses to provide proper or necessary subsistence, education, medical or surgical care or treatment, or other care necessary for the child's health, morals, or well being;

(4) Whose parents, guardian, or custodian neglects the child or refuses to provide the special care made necessary by the child's mental condition;

(5) Whose parents, legal guardian, or custodian have placed or attempted to place the child in violation of sections 5103.16 and 5103.17 of the Revised Code;

(6) Who, because of the omission of the child's parents, guardian, or custodian, suffers physical or mental injury that harms or threatens to harm the child's health or welfare;

(7) Who is subjected to out-of-home care child neglect.

(B) Nothing in this chapter shall be construed as subjecting a parent, guardian, or custodian of a child to criminal liability when, solely in the practice of religious beliefs, the parent, guardian, or custodian fails to provide adequate medical or surgical care or treatment for the child. This division does not abrogate or limit any person's responsibility under section 2151.421 [2151.42.1] of the Revised Code to report child abuse that is known or reasonably suspected or believed to have occurred, child neglect that is known or reasonably suspected or believed to have occurred, and children who are known to face or are reasonably suspected or believed to be facing a threat of suffering abuse or neglect and does not preclude any exercise of the authority of the state, any political subdivision, or any court to ensure that medical or surgical care or treatment is provided to a child when the child's health requires the provision of medical or surgical care or treatment.

**HISTORY: GC § 1639-3; 117 v 520; Bureau of Code Revision, 10-1-53; 133 v H 320 (Eff 11-19-69); 143 v H 257 (Eff 8-3-89); 146 v H 274. Eff 8-8-96; 151 v S 17, § 1, eff. 8-3-06.**

## § 2151.031 Abused child defined.

As used in this chapter, an "abused child" includes any child who:

(A) Is the victim of "sexual activity" as defined under Chapter 2907. of the Revised Code, where such activity would constitute an offense under that chapter, except that the court need not find that any person has been convicted of the offense in order to find that the child is an abused child;

(B) Is endangered as defined in section 2919.22 of the Revised Code, except that the court need not find that any person has been convicted under that section in order to find that the child is an abused child;

(C) Exhibits evidence of any physical or mental injury or death, inflicted other than by accidental means, or an injury or death which is at variance with the history given of it. Except as provided in division (D) of this section, a child exhibiting evidence of corporal punishment or other physical disciplinary measure by a parent, guardian, custodian, person having custody or control, or person in loco parentis of a child is not an abused child under this division if the measure is not prohibited under section 2919.22 of the Revised Code.

(D) Because of the acts of his parents, guardian, or custodian, suffers physical or mental injury that harms or threatens to harm the child's health or welfare.

(E) Is subjected to out-of-home care child abuse.

**HISTORY: 136 v H 85 (Eff 11-28-75); 142 v S 89 (Eff 1-1-89); 143 v H 257. Eff 8-3-89.**

## § 2151.04 Dependent child defined.

As used in this chapter, "dependent child" means any child:

(A) Who is homeless or destitute or without adequate parental care, through no fault of the child's parents, guardian, or custodian;

(B) Who lacks adequate parental care by reason of the mental or physical condition of the child's parents, guardian, or custodian;

(C) Whose condition or environment is such as to warrant the state, in the interests of the child, in assuming the child's guardianship;

(D) To whom both of the following apply:

(1) The child is residing in a household in which a parent, guardian, custodian, or other member of the household committed an act that was the basis for an adjudication that a sibling of the child or any other child who resides in the household is an abused, neglected, or dependent child.

(2) Because of the circumstances surrounding the abuse, neglect, or dependency of the sibling or other child and the other conditions in the household of the child, the child is in danger of being abused or neglected by that parent, guardian, custodian, or member of the household.

**HISTORY: GC § 1639-4; 117 v 520; Bureau of Code Revision, 10-1-53; 129 v 1778 (Eff 10-27-61); 133 v H 320 (Eff 11-19-69); 142 v S 89 (Eff 1-1-89); 146 v H 274. Eff 8-8-96.**

## § 2151.05 Child without proper parental care.

Under sections 2151.01 to 2151.54 of the Revised Code, a child whose home is filthy and unsanitary; whose parents, stepparents, guardian, or custodian permit him to become dependent, neglected, abused, or delinquent; whose parents, stepparents, guardian, or custodian, when able, refuse or neglect to provide him with necessary care, support, medical attention, and educational facilities; or whose parents, stepparents, guardian, or custodian fail to subject such child to necessary discipline is without proper parental care or guardianship.

**HISTORY: GC § 1639-5; 117 v 520; Bureau of Code Revision, 10-1-53; 136 v H 85. Eff 11-28-75.**

## § 2151.06 Residence or legal settlement.

Under sections 2151.01 to 2151.54, inclusive, of the Revised Code, a child has the same residence or legal settlement as his parents, legal guardian of his person, or his custodian who stands in the relation of loco parentis.

**HISTORY: GC § 1639-6; 117 v 520; 121 v 557; Bureau of Code Revision. Eff 10-1-53.**

## [ESTABLISHMENT AND JURISDICTION]

## § 2151.07 Creation and powers of juvenile court; assignment of judges.

The juvenile court is a court of record within the court of common pleas. The juvenile court has and shall exercise the powers and jurisdiction conferred in Chapters 2151. and 2152. of the Revised Code.

Whenever the juvenile judge of the juvenile court is sick, is absent from the county, or is unable to attend court, or the volume of cases pending in court necessitates it, upon the request of the administrative juvenile judge, the presiding judge of the court of common pleas pursuant to division (EE) of section 2301.03 of the Revised Code shall assign a judge of any division of the court of common pleas of the county to act in the juvenile judge's place or in conjunction with the juvenile judge. If no judge of the court of common pleas is available for that purpose, the chief justice of the supreme court shall assign a judge of the court of common pleas, a juvenile judge, or a probate judge from a different county to act in the place of that juvenile judge or in conjunction with that juvenile judge. The assigned judge shall receive the compensation and expenses for so serving that is provided by law for judges assigned to hold court in courts of common pleas.

**HISTORY: GC § 1639-7; 117 v 520; 122 v 390; Bureau of Code Revision, 10-1-53; 127 v 847 (Eff 9-16-57); 133 v H 320 (Eff 11-19-69); 134 v H 574 (Eff 6-29-72); 148 v S 179, § 3 (Eff 1-1-2002); 149 v H 11, § 3. Eff 1-1-2002; 150 v H 26, § 1, eff. 8-8-03; 150 v H 86, § 1, eff. 11-13-03; 152 v S 155, § 1, eff. 12-21-07.**

## § 2151.08 Juvenile court in Hamilton county.

In Hamilton county, the powers and jurisdiction of the juvenile court as conferred by Chapters 2151. and 2152. of the Revised Code shall be exercised by the judge of the court of common pleas whose term begins on January 1, 1957, and that judge's successors and by the judge of the court of common pleas whose term begins on February 14, 1967, and that judge's successors as provided by section 2301.03 of the Revised Code. This conferral of powers and jurisdiction on the specified judges shall be deemed a creation of a separately and independently created and established juvenile court in Hamilton county, Ohio. The specified judges shall serve in each and every position where the statutes permit or require a juvenile judge to serve.

**HISTORY: GC § 1639-8; 117 v 520; Bureau of Code Revision, 10-1-53; 127 v 847 (Eff 9-16-57); 131 v 631 (Eff 11-16-65); 148 v S 179, § 3. Eff 1-1-2002.**

## § 2151.09 Separate building and site may be purchased or leased.

Upon the advice and recommendation of the juvenile judge, the board of county commissioners may provide by purchase, lease, or otherwise a separate building and site to be known as "the juvenile court" at a convenient location within the county which shall be appropriately constructed, arranged, furnished, and maintained for the convenient and efficient transaction of the business of the court and all parts thereof and its employees, including adequate facilities to be used as laboratories, dispensaries, or clinics for the use of scientific specialists connected with the court.

**HISTORY: GC § 1639-15; 117 v 520; Bureau of Code Revision. Eff 10-1-53.**

## § 2151.10 Appropriation for court expenses and care of children.

The juvenile judge shall annually submit a written request for an appropriation to the board of county commissioners that shall set forth estimated administrative expenses of the juvenile court that the judge considers reasonably necessary for the operation of the court, including reasonably necessary expenses of the judge and such officers and employees as the judge may designate in attending conferences at which juvenile or welfare problems are discussed, and such sum each year as will provide for the maintenance and operation of the detention facility, the care, maintenance, education, and support of neglected, abused, dependent, and delinquent children, other than children eligible to participate in the Ohio works first program established under Chapter 5107. of the Revised Code, and for necessary orthopedic, surgical, and medical treatment, and special care as may be ordered by the court for any neglected, abused, dependent, or delinquent children. The board shall conduct a public hearing with respect to the written request submitted by the judge and shall appropriate such sum of money each year as it determines, after conducting the public hearing and considering the written request of the judge, is reasonably necessary to meet all the administrative expenses of the court. All disbursements from such appropriations shall be upon specifically itemized vouchers, certified to by the judge.

If the judge considers the appropriation made by the board pursuant to this section insufficient to meet all the administrative expenses of the court, the judge shall commence an action under Chapter 2731. of the Revised Code in the court of appeals for the judicial district for a determination of the duty of the board of county commissioners to appropriate the amount of money in dispute. The court of appeals shall give priority to the action filed by the juvenile judge over all cases pending on its docket. The burden shall be on the juvenile judge to prove that the appropriation requested is reasonably necessary to meet all administrative expenses of the court. If, prior to the filing of an action under Chapter 2731. of the Revised Code or during the pendency of the action, the judge exercises the judge's contempt power in order to obtain the sum of money in dispute, the judge shall not order the imprisonment of any member of the board of county commissioners notwithstanding sections 2705.02 to 2705.06 of the Revised Code.

**HISTORY: GC § 1639-57; 117 v 520; 119 v 731; 121 v 557; Bureau of Code Revision, 10-1-53; 136 v H 85 (Eff 11-28-75); 138 v S 63 (Eff 7-26-79); 147 v H 408 (Eff 10-1-97); 148 v S 179, § 3. Eff 1-1-2002.**

## § 2151.11 Amended and renumbered RC § 2152.73 in 148 v S 179. Eff 1-1-2002.

## § 2151.12 Clerk; bond; judge as clerk.

(A) Except as otherwise provided in this division, whenever a court of common pleas, division of domestic relations, exercises the powers and jurisdictions conferred in Chapters 2151. and 2152. of the Revised Code, the judge or judges of that division or, if applicable, the judge of that division who specifically is designated by section 2301.03 of the Revised Code as being responsible for administering sections 2151.13, 2151.16, 2151.17, 2151.18, and 2152.71 of the Revised Code shall be the clerk of the court for all records filed with the court pursuant to Chapter 2151. or 2152. of the Revised Code or pursuant to any other section of the Revised Code that requires documents to be filed with a juvenile judge or a juvenile court. If, in a division of domestic relations of a court of common pleas that exercises the powers and jurisdiction conferred in Chapters 2151. and 2152. of the Revised Code, the judge of the division, both judges in a two-judge division, or a majority of the judges in a division with three or more judges and the clerk of the court of common pleas agree in an agreement that is signed by the agreeing judge or judges and the clerk and entered into formally in the journal of the court, the clerk of courts of common pleas shall keep the records filed with the court pursuant to Chapter 2151. or 2152. of the Revised Code or pursuant to any other section of the Revised Code that requires documents to be filed with a juvenile judge or a juvenile court.

Whenever the juvenile judge, or a majority of the juvenile judges of a multi-judge juvenile division, of a court of common pleas, juvenile division, and the clerk of the court of common pleas agree in an agreement that is signed by the judge and the clerk and entered formally in the journal of the court, the clerks of courts of common pleas shall keep the records of those courts. In all other cases, the juvenile judge shall be the clerk of the judge's own court.

(B) In counties in which the juvenile judge is clerk of the judge's own court, before entering upon the duties of office as the clerk, the judge shall execute and file with the county treasurer a bond in a sum to be determined by the board of county commissioners, with sufficient surety to be approved by the board, conditioned for the faithful performance of duties as clerk. The bond shall be given for the benefit of the county, the state, or any person who may suffer loss by reason of a default in any of the conditions of the bond.

**HISTORY: GC § 1639-17; 117 v 520; Bureau of Code Revision, 10-1-53; 137 v S 336 (Eff 3-3-78); 146 v H 423 (Eff 10-31-96); 148 v S 179, § 3. Eff 1-1-2002.**

## § 2151.13 Employees; compensation; bond.

The juvenile judge may appoint such bailiffs, probation officers, and other employees as are necessary and may designate their titles and fix their duties, compensation, and expense allowances. The juvenile court may by entry on its journal authorize any deputy clerk to administer oaths when necessary in the discharge of his duties. Such employees shall serve during the pleasure of the judge.

The compensation and expenses of all employees and the salary and expenses of the judge shall be paid in semimonthly installments by the county treasurer from the money appropriated for the operation of the court, upon the warrant of the county auditor, certified to by the judge.

The judge may require any employee to give bond in the sum of not less than one thousand dollars, conditioned for the honest and faithful performance of his duties. The sureties on such bonds shall be approved in the manner provided by section 2151.12 of the Revised Code. The judge shall not be personally liable for the default, misfeasance, or nonfeasance of any employee from whom a bond has been required.

**HISTORY: GC § 1639-18; 117 v 520; 121 v 557; Bureau of Code Revision. Eff 10-1-53.**

## § 2151.14 Duties and powers of probation department; records; command assistance.

(A) The chief probation officer, under the direction of the juvenile judge, shall have charge of the work of the probation department. The department shall make any investigations that the judge directs, keep a written record of the investigations, and submit the record to the judge or deal with them as the judge directs. The department shall furnish to any person placed on community control a statement of the conditions of community control and shall instruct the person regarding them. The department shall keep informed concerning the conduct and condition of each person under its supervision and shall report on their conduct and condition to the judge as the judge directs. Each probation officer shall use all suitable methods to aid persons on community control and to bring about improvement in their conduct and condition. The department shall keep full records of its work, keep accurate and complete accounts of money collected from persons under its supervision, give receipts for the money, and make reports on the money as the judge directs.

(B) Except as provided in this division or in division (C) or (D) of this section, the reports and records of the department shall be considered confidential information and shall not be made public. If an officer is preparing pursuant to section 2947.06 or 2951.03 of the Revised Code or Criminal Rule 32.2 a presentence investigation report pertaining to a person, the department shall make available to the officer, for use in preparing the report, any reports and records it possesses regarding any adjudications of that person as a delinquent child or regarding the dispositions made relative to those adjudications. A probation officer may serve the process of the court within or without the county, make arrests without warrant upon reasonable information or upon view of the violation of this chapter or Chapter 2152. of the Revised Code, detain the person arrested pending the issuance of a warrant, and perform any other duties, incident to the office, that the judge directs. All sheriffs, deputy sheriffs, constables, marshals, deputy marshals, chiefs of police, municipal corporation and township police officers, and other peace officers shall render assistance to probation officers in the performance of their duties when requested to do so by any probation officer.

(C) When a complaint has been filed alleging that a child is delinquent by reason of having committed an act that would constitute a violation of section 2907.02, 2907.03, 2907.05, or 2907.06 of the Revised Code if committed by an adult and the arresting authority, a court, or a probation officer discovers that the child or a person whom the child caused to engage in sexual activity, as defined in section 2907.01 of the Revised Code, has a communicable disease, the arresting authority, court, or probation officer immediately shall notify the victim of the delinquent act of the nature of the disease.

(D)(1) In accordance with division (D)(2) of this section, subject to the limitation specified in division (D)(4) of this section, and in connection with a disposition pursuant to section 2151.354 [2151.35.4] of the Revised Code when a child has been found to be an unruly child, a disposition pursuant to sections 2152.19 and 2152.20 of the Revised Code when a child has been found to be a delinquent child, or a disposition pursuant to sections 2152.20 and 2152.21 of the Revised Code when a child has been found to be a juvenile traffic offender, the court may issue an order requiring boards of education, governing bodies of chartered nonpublic schools, public children services agencies, private child placing agencies, probation departments, law enforcement agencies, and prosecuting attorneys that have records related to the child in question to provide copies of one or more specified records, or specified information in one or more specified records, that the individual or entity has with respect to the child to any of the following individuals or entities that request the records in accordance with division (D)(3)(a) of this section:

(a) The child;

(b) The attorney or guardian ad litem of the child;

(c) A parent, guardian, or custodian of the child;

(d) A prosecuting attorney;

(e) A board of education of a public school district;

(f) A probation department of a juvenile court;

(g) A public children services agency or private child placing agency that has custody of the child, is providing services to the child or the child's family, or is preparing a social history or performing any other function for the juvenile court;

(h) The department of youth services when the department has custody of the child or is performing any services for the child that are required by the juvenile court or by statute;

(i) The individual in control of a juvenile detention or rehabilitation facility to which the child has been committed;

(j) An employee of the juvenile court that found the child to be an unruly child, a delinquent child, or a juvenile traffic offender;

(k) Any other entity that has custody of the child or is providing treatment, rehabilitation, or other services for the child pursuant to a court order, statutory requirement, or other arrangement.

(2) Any individual or entity listed in divisions (D)(1)(a) to (k) of this section may file a motion with the court that requests the court to issue an order as described in division (D)(1) of this section. If such a motion is filed, the court shall conduct a hearing on it. If at the hearing the movant demonstrates a need for one or more specified records, or for information in one or more specified records, related to the child in question and additionally demonstrates the relevance of the information sought to be obtained from those records, and if the court determines that the limitation specified in division (D)(4) of this section does not preclude the provision of a specified record or specified information to the movant, then the court may issue an order to a designated individual or entity to provide the movant with copies of one or more specified records or with specified information contained in one or more specified records.

(3)(a) Any individual or entity that is authorized by an order issued pursuant to division (D)(1) of this section to obtain copies of one or more specified records, or specified information, related to a particular child may file a written request for copies of the records or for the information with any individual or entity required by the order to provide copies of the records or the information. The request shall be in writing, describe the type of records or the information requested, explain the need for the records or the information, and be accompanied by a copy of the order.

(b) If an individual or entity that is required by an order issued pursuant to division (D)(1) of this section to provide one or more specified records, or specified information, related to a child receives a written request for the records or information in accordance with division (D)(3)(a) of this section, the individual or entity immediately shall comply with the request to the extent it is able to do so, unless the individual or entity determines that it is unable to comply with the request because it is prohibited by law from doing so, or unless the requesting individual or entity does not have authority to obtain the requested records or information. If the individual or entity determines that it is unable to comply with the request, it shall file a motion with the court that issued the order requesting the court to determine the extent to which it is required to comply with the request for records or information. Upon the filing of the motion, the court immediately shall hold a hearing on the motion, determine the extent to which the movant is required to comply with the request for records or information, and issue findings of fact and conclusions of law in support of its determination. The determination of the court shall be final. If the court determines that the movant is required to comply with the request for records or information, it shall identify the specific records or information that must be supplied to the individual or entity that requested the records or information.

(c) If an individual or entity is required to provide copies of one or more specified records pursuant to division (D) of this section, the individual or entity may charge a fee for the copies that does not exceed the cost of supplying them.

(4) Division (D) of this section does not require, authorize, or permit the dissemination of any records or any information contained in any records if the dissemination of the records or information generally is prohibited by any provision of the Revised Code and a specific provision of the Revised Code does not specifically authorize or permit the dissemination of the records or information pursuant to division (D) of this section.

**HISTORY: GC § 1639-19; 117 v 520; Bureau of Code Revision, 10-1-53; 141 v H 468 (Eff 9-17-86); 143 v S 258 (Eff 8-22-90); 146 v H 445 (Eff 9-3-96); 148 v H 442 (Eff 10-17-2000); 148 v S 179, § 3 (Eff 1-1-2002); 149 v H 247. Eff 5-30-2002.**

## § 2151.141 Request for copies of records concerning child alleged to be abused, neglected or dependent.

(A) If a complaint filed with respect to a child pursuant to section 2151.27 of the Revised Code alleges that a child is an abused, neglected, or dependent child, any individual or entity that is listed in divisions (D)(1)(a) to (k) of section 2151.14 of the Revised Code and that is investigating whether the child is an abused, neglected, or dependent child, has custody of the child, is preparing a social history for the child, or is providing any services for the child may request any board of education, governing body of a chartered nonpublic school, public children services agency, private child placing agency, probation department, law enforcement agency, or prosecuting attorney that has any records related to the child to provide the individual or entity with a copy of the records. The request shall be in writing, describe the type of records requested, explain the need for the records, be accompanied by a copy of the complaint, and describe the relationship of the requesting individual or entity to the child. The individual or entity shall provide a copy of the request to the child in question, the attorney or guardian ad litem of the child, and the parent, guardian, or custodian of the child.

(B)(1) Any board of education, governing body of a chartered nonpublic school, public children services agency, private child placing agency, probation department, law enforcement agency, or prosecuting attorney that has any records related to a child who is the subject of a complaint as described in division (A) of this section and that receives a request for a copy of the records pursuant to division (A) of this section shall comply with the request, unless the individual or entity determines that it is unable to do so because it is prohibited by law from complying with the request, the request does not comply with division (A) of this section, or a complaint as described in division (A) of this section has not been filed with respect to the child who is the subject of the requested records. If the individual or entity determines that it is unable to comply with the request, it shall file a motion with the court in which the complaint as described in division (A) of this section was filed or was alleged to have been filed requesting the court to determine the extent to which it is required to comply with the request for records. Upon the filing of the motion, the court immediately shall hold a hearing on the motion, determine the extent to which the movant is required to comply with the request for records, and issue findings of fact and conclusions of law in support of its determination. The determination of the court shall be final. If the court determines that the movant is required to comply with the request for records, it shall identify the specific records that must be supplied to the individual or entity that requested them.

(2) In addition to or in lieu of the motion described in division (B)(1) of this section, a law enforcement agency or prosecuting attorney that receives a request for a copy of records pursuant to division (A) of this section may file a motion for a protective order as described in this division with the court in which the complaint as described in division (A) of this section was filed or alleged to have been filed. Upon the filing of a motion of that nature, the court shall conduct a hearing on the motion. If at the hearing the law enforcement agency or prosecuting attorney demonstrates that any of the following applies and if, after considering the purposes for which the records were requested pursuant to division (A) of this section, the best interest of the child, and any demonstrated need to prevent specific information in the records from being disclosed, the court determines that the issuance of a protective order is necessary, then the court shall issue a protective order that appropriately limits the disclosure of one or more specified records or specified information in one or more specified records:

(a) The records or information in the records relate to a case in which the child is alleged to be a delinquent child or a case in which a child is transferred for trial as an adult pursuant to section 2152.12 of the Revised Code and Juvenile Rule 30, and the adjudication hearing in the case, the trial in the case, or other disposition of the case has not been concluded.

(b) The records in question, or the records containing the information in question, are confidential law enforcement investigatory records, as defined in section 149.43 of the Revised Code.

(c) The records or information in the records relate to a case in which the child is or was alleged to be a delinquent child or to a case in which a child is or was transferred for trial as an adult pursuant to section 2152.12 of the Revised Code and Juvenile Rule 30; another case is pending against any child or any adult in which the child is alleged to be a delinquent child, the child is so transferred for trial as an adult, or the adult is alleged to be a criminal offender; the allegations in the case to which the records or information relate and the allegations in the other case are based on the same act or transaction, are based on two or more connected transactions or constitute parts of a common scheme or plan, or are part of a course of criminal conduct; and the adjudication hearing in, trial in, or other disposition of the other case has not been concluded.

(C) If an individual or entity is required to provide copies of records pursuant to this section, the individual or entity may charge a fee for the copies that does not exceed the cost of supplying them.

(D) This section does not require, authorize, or permit, the dissemination of any records or any information contained in any records if the dissemination of the records or information generally is prohibited by section 2151.142 [2151.14.2] or another section of the Revised Code and a waiver as described in division (B)(1) of section 2151.142 [2151.14.2] of the Revised Code or a specific provision of the Revised Code does not specifically authorize or permit the dissemination of the records or information pursuant to this section.

**HISTORY: 143 v S 258 (Eff 8-22-90); 148 v H 412 (Eff 4-10-2001); 148 v S 179, § 3. Eff 1-1-2002.**

The effective date is set by section 5 of SB 179.

See Comment, Legislative Service Commission following RC § 2151.022.

## § 2151.142 Confidentiality of residential addresses of public children services agency or private child placing agency personnel.

(A) As used in this section, "public record" and "journalist" have the same meanings as in section 149.43 of the Revised Code.

(B) Both of the following apply to the residential address of each officer or employee of a public children services agency or a private child placing agency who performs official responsibilities or duties described in section 2151.14, 2151.141 [2151.14.1], 2151.33, 2151.353 [2151.35.3], 2151.412 [2151.41.2], 2151.413 [2151.41.3], 2151.414 [2151.41.4], 2151.415 [2151.41.5], 2151.416 [2151.41.6], 2151.417 [2151.41.7], or 2151.421 [2151.42.1] or another section of the Revised Code and to the residential address of persons related to that officer or employee by consanguinity or affinity:

(1) Other officers and employees of a public children services agency, private child placing agency, juvenile court, or law enforcement agency shall consider those residential addresses to be confidential information. The officer or employee of the public children services agency or private child placing agency may waive the confidentiality of those residential addresses by giving express permission for their disclosure to other officers or employees of a public children services agency, private child placing agency, juvenile court, or law enforcement agency.

(2) To the extent that those residential addresses are contained in public records kept by a public children services agency, private child placing agency, juvenile court, or law enforcement agency, they shall not be considered to be information that is subject to inspection or copying as part of a public record under section 149.43 of the Revised Code.

(C) Except as provided in division (D) of this section, in the absence of a waiver as described in division (B)(1) of this section, no officer or employee of a public children services agency, private child placing agency, juvenile court, or law enforcement agency shall disclose the residential address of an officer or employee of a public children services agency or private child placing agency, or the residential address of a person related to that officer or employee by consanguinity or affinity, that is confidential information under division (B)(1) of this section to any person, when the disclosing officer or employee knows that the person is or may be a subject of an investigation, interview, examination, criminal case, other case, or other matter with which the officer or employee to whom the residential address relates currently is or has been associated.

(D) If, on or after the effective date of this section, a journalist requests a public children services agency, private child placing agency, juvenile court, or law enforcement agency to disclose a residential address that is confidential information under division (B)(1) of this section, the agency or juvenile court shall disclose to the journalist the residential address if all of the following apply:

(1) The request is in writing, is signed by the journalist, includes the journalist's name and title, and includes the name and address of the journalist's employer.

(2) The request states that disclosure of the residential address would be in the public interest.

(3) The request adequately identifies the person whose residential address is requested.

(4) The public children services agency, private child placing agency, juvenile court, or law enforcement agency receiving the request is one of the following:

(a) The agency or juvenile court with which the official in question serves or with which the employee in question is employed;

(b) The agency or juvenile court that has custody of the records of the agency with which the official in question serves or with which the employee in question is employed.

**HISTORY: 148 v H 412. Eff 4-10-2001.**

## § 2151.15 Powers and duties vested in county department of probation.

When a county department of probation has been established in the county and the juvenile judge does not establish a probation department within the juvenile court as provided in section 2151.14 of the Revised Code, all powers and duties of the probation department provided for in sections 2151.01 to 2151.54, inclusive, of the Revised Code, shall vest in and be imposed upon such county department of probation.

In counties in which a county department of probation has been or is hereafter established the judge may transfer to such department all or any part of the powers and duties of his own probation department; provided that all juvenile cases shall be handled within a county department of probation exclusively by an officer or division separate and distinct from the officers or division handling adult cases.

**HISTORY: GC § 1639-20; 117 v 520; 121 v 557; Bureau of Code Revision. Eff 10-1-53.**

## § 2151.151 Contract for services for children on probation.

(A) The juvenile judge may contract with any agency, association, or organization, which may be of a public or private, or profit or nonprofit nature, or with any individual for the provision of supervisory or other services to children placed on probation who are under the custody and supervision of the juvenile court.

(B) The juvenile judges of two or more adjoining or neighboring counties may join together for purposes of contracting with any agency, association, or organization, which may be of a public or private, or profit or nonprofit nature, or with any individual for the provision of supervisory or other services to children placed on probation who are under the custody and supervision of the juvenile court of any of the counties that joins [join] together.

**HISTORY: 139 v H 440. Eff 11-23-81.**

## § 2151.152 Reimbursement of court for costs of children in custody of court.

The juvenile judge may enter into an agreement with the department of job and family services pursuant to section 5101.11 of the Revised Code for the purpose of reimbursing the court for foster care maintenance costs and associated administrative and training costs incurred on behalf of a child who is either of the following:

(A) Eligible for payments under Title IV-E of the "Social Security Act," 94 Stat. 501 (1980), 42 U.S.C.A. 670, and who is in the temporary or permanent custody of the court or subject to a disposition issued under division (A)(5) of section 2151.354 [2151.35.4] or division (A)(7)(a)(ii) or (A)(8) of section 2152.19 of the Revised Code;

(B) Determined to be at serious risk of removal from the home and for whom the court has undertaken a plan of reasonable efforts to prevent such removal.

The agreement shall govern the responsibilities and duties the court shall perform in providing services to the child.

**HISTORY: 146 v H 274 (Eff 8-8-96); 148 v H 471 (Eff 7-1-2000); 149 v H 57 (Eff 2-19-2002†); 149 v H 400. Eff 4-3-2003; 152 v H 214, § 1, eff. 5-14-08.**

† The effective date of sections 1 and 2 of Sub. H.B. 57 (149 v —) differs from the effective date set for the sections by section 3 of the Act. See provisions of OConst art II, §§ 1c and d.

## § 2151.16 Referees; powers and duties.

The juvenile judge may appoint and fix the compensation of referees who shall have the usual power of masters in chancery cases, provided, in all such cases submitted to them by the juvenile court, they shall hear the testimony of witnesses and certify to the judge their findings upon the case submitted to them, together with their recommendation as to the judgment or order to be made in the case in question. The court, after notice to the parties in the case of the presentation of such findings and recommendation, may make the order recommended by the referee, or any other order in the judgment of the court required by the findings of the referee, or may hear additional testimony, or may set aside said findings and hear the case anew. In appointing a referee for the trial of females, a female referee shall be appointed where possible.

**HISTORY: GC § 1639-21; 117 v 520; Bureau of Code Revision. Eff 10-1-53.**

## § 2151.17 Rules governing practice and procedure.

Except as otherwise provided by rules promulgated by the supreme court, the juvenile court may prescribe rules regulating the docketing and hearing of causes, motions, and demurrers, and such other matters as are necessary for the orderly conduct of its business and the prevention of delay, and for the government of its officers and employees, including their conduct, duties, hours, expenses, leaves of absence, and vacations.

**HISTORY: GC § 1639-11; 117 v 520; 121 v 557; Bureau of Code Revision, 10-1-53; 133 v H 320. Eff 11-19-69.**

## § 2151.18 Court records generally; annual report.

(A) The juvenile court shall maintain records of all official cases brought before it, including, but not limited to, an appearance docket, a journal, and records of the type required by division (A)(2) of section 2151.35 of the Revised Code. The parents, guardian, or other custodian of any child affected, if living, or the nearest of kin of the child, if the parents would be entitled to inspect the records but are deceased, may inspect these records, either in person or by counsel, during the hours in which the court is open.

(B) Not later than June of each year, the court shall prepare an annual report covering the preceding calendar year showing the number and kinds of cases that have come before it, the disposition of the cases, and any other data pertaining to the work of the court that the juvenile judge directs. The court shall file copies of the report with the board of county commissioners. With the approval of the board, the court may print or cause to be printed copies of the report for distribution to persons and agencies interested in the court or community program for dependent, neglected, abused, or delinquent children and juvenile traffic offenders. The court shall include the number of copies ordered printed and the estimated cost of each printed copy on each copy of the report printed for distribution.

**HISTORY: 148 v S 179, § 3 (Eff 1-1-2002); 149 v H 393. Eff 7-5-2002.**

**Analogous to former RC § 2151.18, amended and renumbered RC § 2152.71 in 148 v S 179, eff 1-1-2002.**

## § 2151.19 Summons; expense.

The summons, warrants, citations, subpoenas, and other writs of the juvenile court may issue to a probation officer of any such court or to the sheriff of any county or any marshal, constable, or police officer, and the provisions of law relating to the subpoenaing of witnesses in other cases shall apply in so far as they are applicable.

When a summons, warrant, citation, subpoena, or other writ is issued to any such officer, other than a probation officer, the expense in serving the same shall be paid by the county, township, or municipal corporation in the manner prescribed for the payment of sheriffs, deputies, assistants, and other employees.

**HISTORY: GC §§ 1639-52, 1639-53; 117 v 520; Bureau of Code Revision. Eff 10-1-53.**

## § 2151.20 Seal of court; dimensions.

Juvenile courts within the probate court shall have a seal which shall consist of the coat of arms of the state within a circle one and one-fourth inches in diameter and shall be surrounded by the words "juvenile court... county."

The seal of other courts exercising the powers and jurisdiction conferred in sections 2151.01 to 2151.54, inclusive, of the Revised Code, shall be attached to all writs and processes.

**HISTORY: GC § 1639-9; 117 v 520; Bureau of Code Revision, 10-1-53; 132 v H 164. Eff 12-15-67.**

## § 2151.21 Jurisdiction in contempt.

The juvenile court has the same jurisdiction in contempt as courts of common pleas.

**HISTORY: GC § 1639-10; 117 v 520; Bureau of Code Revision. Eff 10-1-53.**

## § 2151.211 Employee may not be penalized for being subpoenaed.

No employer shall discharge or terminate from employment, threaten to discharge or terminate from employment, or otherwise punish or penalize any employee because of time lost from regular employment as a result of the employee's attendance at any proceeding pursuant to a subpoena under this chapter or Chapter 2152. of the Revised Code. This section generally does not require and shall not be construed to require an employer to pay an employee for time lost as a result of attendance at any proceeding under either chapter. However, if an employee is subpoenaed to appear at a proceeding under either chapter and the proceeding pertains to an offense against the employer or an offense involving the employee during the course of the employee's employment, the employer shall not decrease or withhold the employee's pay for any time lost as a result of compliance with the subpoena. Any employer who knowingly violates this section is in contempt of court.

**HISTORY: 140 v S 172 (Eff 9-26-84); 148 v S 179, § 3. Eff 1-1-2002.**

The effective date is set by section 5 of SB 179.

## § 2151.22 Terms of court; sessions.

The term of any juvenile or domestic relations court, whether a division of the court of common pleas or an independent court, is one calendar year. All actions and other business pending at the expiration of any term of court is automatically continued without further order. The judge may adjourn court or continue any case whenever, in his opinion, such continuance is warranted.

Sessions of the court may be held at such places throughout the county as the judge shall from time to time determine.

**HISTORY: GC § 1639-12; 117 v 520; Bureau of Code Revision, 10-1-53; 136 v H 390. Eff 8-6-76.**

## § 2151.23 Jurisdiction of juvenile court.

(A) The juvenile court has exclusive original jurisdiction under the Revised Code as follows:

(1) Concerning any child who on or about the date specified in the complaint, indictment, or information is alleged to have violated section 2151.87 of the Revised Code or an order issued under that section or to be a juvenile traffic offender or a delinquent, unruly, abused, neglected, or dependent child and, based on and in relation to the allegation pertaining to the child, concerning the parent, guardian, or other person having care of a child who is alleged to be an unruly or delinquent child for being an habitual or chronic truant;

(2) Subject to divisions (G), (K), and (V) of section 2301.03 of the Revised Code, to determine the custody of any child not a ward of another court of this state;

(3) To hear and determine any application for a writ of habeas corpus involving the custody of a child;

(4) To exercise the powers and jurisdiction given the probate division of the court of common pleas in Chapter 5122. of the Revised Code, if the court has probable cause to believe that a child otherwise within the jurisdiction of the court is a mentally ill person subject to hospitalization by court order, as defined in section 5122.01 of the Revised Code;

(5) To hear and determine all criminal cases charging adults with the violation of any section of this chapter;

(6) To hear and determine all criminal cases in which an adult is charged with a violation of division (C) of section 2919.21, division (B)(1) of section 2919.22, section 2919.222, division (B) of section 2919.23, or section 2919.24 of the Revised Code, provided the charge is not included in an indictment that also charges the alleged adult offender with the commission of a felony arising out of the same actions that are the basis of the alleged violation of division (C) of section 2919.21, division (B)(1) of section 2919.22, section 2919.222, division (B) of section 2919.23, or section 2919.24 of the Revised Code;

(7) Under the interstate compact on juveniles in section 2151.56 of the Revised Code;

(8) Concerning any child who is to be taken into custody pursuant to section 2151.31 of the Revised Code, upon being notified of the intent to take the child into custody and the reasons for taking the child into custody;

(9) To hear and determine requests for the extension of temporary custody agreements, and requests for court approval of permanent custody agreements, that are filed pursuant to section 5103.15 of the Revised Code;

(10) To hear and determine applications for consent to marry pursuant to section 3101.04 of the Revised Code;

(11) Subject to divisions (G), (K), and (V) of section 2301.03 of the Revised Code, to hear and determine a request for an order for the support of any child if the request is not ancillary to an action for divorce, dissolution of marriage, annulment, or legal separation, a criminal or civil action involving an allegation of domestic violence, or an action for support brought under Chapter 3115. of the Revised Code;

(12) Concerning an action commenced under section 121.38 of the Revised Code;

(13) To hear and determine violations of section 3321.38 of the Revised Code;

(14) To exercise jurisdiction and authority over the parent, guardian, or other person having care of a child alleged to be a delinquent child, unruly child, or juvenile traffic offender, based on and in relation to the allegation pertaining to the child;

(15) To conduct the hearings, and to make the determinations, adjudications, and orders authorized or required under sections 2152.82 to 2152.86 and Chapter 2950. of the Revised Code regarding a child who has been adjudicated a delinquent child and to refer the duties conferred upon the juvenile court judge under sections 2152.82 to 2152.86 and Chapter 2950. of the Revised Code to magistrates appointed by the juvenile court judge in accordance with Juvenile Rule 40;

(16) To hear and determine a petition for a protection order against a child under section 2151.34 or 3113.31 of the Revised Code and to enforce a protection order issued or a consent agreement approved under either section against a child until a date certain but not later than the date the child attains nineteen years of age.

(B) Except as provided in divisions (G) and (I) of section 2301.03 of the Revised Code, the juvenile court has original jurisdiction under the Revised Code:

(1) To hear and determine all cases of misdemeanors charging adults with any act or omission with respect to any child, which act or omission is a violation of any state law or any municipal ordinance;

(2) To determine the paternity of any child alleged to have been born out of wedlock pursuant to sections 3111.01 to 3111.18 of the Revised Code;

(3) Under the uniform interstate family support act in Chapter 3115. of the Revised Code;

(4) To hear and determine an application for an order for the support of any child, if the child is not a ward of another court of this state;

(5) To hear and determine an action commenced under section 3111.28 of the Revised Code;

(6) To hear and determine a motion filed under section 3119.961 of the Revised Code;

(7) To receive filings under section 3109.74 of the Revised Code, and to hear and determine actions arising under sections 3109.51 to 3109.80 of the Revised Code.

(8) To enforce an order for the return of a child made under the Hague Convention on the Civil Aspects of International Child Abduction pursuant to section 3127.32 of the Revised Code;

(9) To grant any relief normally available under the laws of this state to enforce a child custody determination made by a court of another state and registered in accordance with section 3127.35 of the Revised Code.

(C) The juvenile court, except as to juvenile courts that are a separate division of the court of common pleas or a separate and independent juvenile court, has jurisdiction to hear, determine, and make a record of any action for divorce or legal separation that involves the custody or care of children and that is filed in the court of common pleas and certified by the court of common pleas with all the papers filed in the action to the juvenile court for trial, provided that no certification of that nature shall be made to any juvenile court unless the consent of the juvenile judge first is obtained. After a certification of that nature is made and consent is obtained, the juvenile court shall proceed as if the action originally had been begun in that court, except as to awards for spousal support or support due and unpaid at the time of certification, over which the juvenile court has no jurisdiction.

(D) The juvenile court, except as provided in divisions (G) and (I) of section 2301.03 of the Revised Code, has jurisdiction to hear and determine all matters as to custody and support of children duly certified by the court of common pleas to the juvenile court after a divorce decree has been granted, including jurisdiction to modify the judgment and decree of the court of common pleas as the same relate to the custody and support of children.

(E) The juvenile court, except as provided in divisions (G) and (I) of section 2301.03 of the Revised Code, has jurisdiction to hear and determine the case of any child certified to the court by any court of competent jurisdiction if the child comes within the jurisdiction of the juvenile court as defined by this section.

(F)(1) The juvenile court shall exercise its jurisdiction in child custody matters in accordance with sections 3109.04 and 3127.01 to 3127.53 of the Revised Code and, as applicable, sections 5103.20 to 5103.22 or 5103.23 to 5103.237 of the Revised Code.

(2) The juvenile court shall exercise its jurisdiction in child support matters in accordance with section 3109.05 of the Revised Code.

(G) Any juvenile court that makes or modifies an order for child support shall comply with Chapters 3119., 3121., 3123., and 3125. of the Revised Code. If any person required to pay child support under an order made by a juvenile court on or after April 15, 1985, or modified on or after December 1, 1986, is found in contempt of court for failure to make support payments under the order, the court that makes the finding, in addition to any other penalty or remedy imposed, shall assess all court costs arising out of the contempt proceeding against the person and require the person to pay any reasonable attorney's fees of any adverse party, as determined by the court, that arose in relation to the act of contempt.

(H) If a child who is charged with an act that would be an offense if committed by an adult was fourteen years of age or older and under eighteen years of age at the time of the alleged act and if the case is transferred for criminal prosecution pursuant to section 2152.12 of the Revised Code, except as provided in section 2152.121 of the Revised Code, the juvenile court does not have jurisdiction to hear or determine the case subsequent to the transfer. The court to which the case is transferred for criminal prosecution pursuant to that section has jurisdiction subsequent to the transfer to hear and determine the case in the same manner as if the case originally had been commenced in that court, subject to section 2152.121 of the Revised Code, including, but not limited to, jurisdiction to accept a plea of guilty or another plea authorized by Criminal Rule 11 or another section of the Revised Code and jurisdiction to accept a verdict and to enter a judgment of conviction pursuant to the Rules of Criminal Procedure against the child for the commission of the offense that was the basis of the transfer of the case for criminal prosecution, whether the conviction is for the same degree or a lesser degree of the offense charged, for the commission of a lesser-included offense, or for the commission of another offense that is different from the offense charged.

(I) If a person under eighteen years of age allegedly commits an act that would be a felony if committed by an adult and if the person is not taken into custody or apprehended for that act until after the person attains twenty-one years of age, the juvenile court does not have jurisdiction to hear or determine any portion of the case charging the person with committing that act. In those circumstances, divisions (A) and (B) of section 2152.12 of the Revised Code do not apply regarding the act, and the case charging the person with committing the act shall be a criminal prosecution commenced and heard in the appropriate court having jurisdiction of the offense as if the person had been eighteen years of age or older when the person committed the act. All proceedings pertaining to the act shall be within the jurisdiction of the court having jurisdiction of the offense, and that court has all the authority and duties in the case that it has in other criminal cases in that court.

(J) In exercising its exclusive original jurisdiction under division (A)(16) of this section with respect to any proceedings brought under section 2151.34 or 3113.31 of the

Revised Code in which the respondent is a child, the juvenile court retains all dispositionary powers consistent with existing rules of juvenile procedure and may also exercise its discretion to adjudicate proceedings as provided in sections 2151.34 and 3113.31 of the Revised Code, including the issuance of protection orders or the approval of consent agreements under those sections.

**HISTORY: 133 v H 320 (Eff 11-19-69); 133 v H 931 (Eff 8-27-70); 136 v H 85 (Eff 11-28-75); 136 v H 244 (Eff 8-26-76); 137 v S 135 (Eff 10-25-77); 139 v H 1 (Eff 8-5-81); 139 v H 515 (Eff 6-1-82); 140 v H 93 (Eff 3-19-84); 140 v H 614 (Eff 4-10-85); 141 v H 509 (Eff 12-1-86); 141 v H 476 (Eff 9-24-86); 141 v H 428 (Eff 12-23-86); 142 v S 89 (Eff 1-1-89); 143 v H 591 (Eff 4-12-90); 143 v H 514 (Eff 1-1-91); 143 v S 258 (Eff 8-22-90); 143 v S 3 (Eff 4-11-91); 144 v S 10 (Eff 7-15-92); 145 v S 21 (Eff 10-29-93); 145 v H 173 (Eff 12-31-93); 146 v H 1 (Eff 1-1-96); 146 v S 269 (Eff 7-1-96); 146 v H 274 (Eff 8-8-96); 146 v H 377 (Eff 10-17-96); 146 v H 124 (Eff 3-31-97); 147 v H 215 (Eff 6-30-97); 147 v H 352 (Eff 1-1-98); 148 v H 583 (Eff 6-14-2000); 148 v S 181 (Eff 9-4-2000); 148 v S 218 (Eff 3-15-2001); 148 v S 180 (Eff 3-22-2001); 148 v S 179, § 3 (Eff 1-1-2002); 149 v S 3. Eff 1-1-2002; 150 v H 38, § 1, eff. 6-17-04; 150 v S 185, § 1, eff. 4-11-05; 151 v S 238, § 1, eff. 9-21-06; 152 v S 10, § 1, eff. 1-1-08; 152 v H 214, § 5, eff. 5-14-08; 153 v H 10, § 1, eff. 6-17-10; 2011 HB 86, § 1, eff. Sept. 30, 2011.**

The provisions of § 3 of 153 v H 10 read as follows:

SECTION 3. Sections 2151.23, 2151.358, 2152.02, 2743.191, 2903.214, 2919.25, 2919.27, 3113.31, and 3113.33 of the Revised Code, as amended by this act, and section 2151.34 of the Revised Code, as enacted by this act, shall be named the "Shynerra Grant Law."

The provisions of § 4 of 153 v H 10 read in part as follows:

SECTION 4. * * * Section 2151.23 of the Revised Code is presented in this act as a composite of the section as amended by both Am. Sub. H.B. 214 and Am. Sub. S.B. 10 of the 127th General Assembly. * * * The General Assembly, applying the principle stated in division (B) of section 1.52 of the Revised Code that amendments are to be harmonized if reasonably capable of simultaneous operation, finds that the composites are the resulting versions of the sections in effect prior to the effective date of the sections as presented in this act.

The provisions of § 7 of 152 v H 214 read as follows:

SECTION 7. Sections 5103.23 to 5103.237 and the amendments to sections 2151.23, 2151.39, 3313.64, and 5103.16 of the Revised Code shall continue in effect until the Interstate Compact for the Placement of Children contained in sections 5103.20 to 5103.22 of the Revised Code becomes effective as described in Article XIV of that Compact, at which time sections 5103.23 to 5103.237 and the amendments made by this act to sections 2151.23, 2151.39, 3313.64, and 5103.16 of the Revised Code regarding the Interstate Compact on the Placement of Children no longer apply.

The provisions of § 8 of 152 v H 214 read as follows:

SECTION 8. The enactment of the Interstate Compact on the Placement of Children in Section 9 of this act is a continuation of the interstate compact of the same name that was repealed in Am. Sub. S.B. 238 of the 126th General Assembly but remains in effect according to Article IX of that Compact.

The effective date is set by § 3 of 152 v S 10.

The provisions of § 3 of SB 3 (149 v —) read as follows:

SECTION 3. Sections 1 and 2 of this act shall take effect on January 1, 2002, or the earliest date permitted by law, whichever is later.

The provisions of § 4 of SB 3 (149 v —) read, in part, as follows:

SECTION 4. Section 2151.23 of the Revised Code is presented in this act as a composite of the section as amended by Am. Sub. S.B. 179, Am. Sub. S.B. 180, and Sub. S.B. 218 of the 123rd General Assembly. The General Assembly, applying the principle stated in division (B) of section 1.52 of the Revised Code that amendments are to be harmonized if reasonably capable of simultaneous operation, finds that the composite is the resulting version of the section in effect prior to the effective date of the section as presented in this act.

## § 2151.231 Child support order without regard to marital status of parents.

The parent, guardian, or custodian of a child, the person with whom a child resides, or the child support enforcement agency of the county in which the child, parent, guardian, or custodian of the child resides may bring an action in a juvenile court or other court with jurisdiction under section 2101.022 [2101.02.2] or 2301.03 of the Revised Code under this section requesting the court to issue an order requiring a parent of the child to pay an amount for the support of the child without regard to the marital status of the child's parents. No action may be brought under this section against a person presumed to be the parent of a child based on an acknowledgment of paternity that has not yet become final under former section 3111.211 [3111.21.1] or 5101.314 [5101.31.4] or section 2151.232 [2151.23.2], 3111.25, or 3111.821 [3111.82.1] of the Revised Code.

The parties to an action under this section may raise the issue of the existence or nonexistence of a parent-child relationship, unless a final and enforceable determination of the issue has been made with respect to the parties pursuant to Chapter 3111. of the Revised Code or an acknowledgment of paternity signed by the child's parents has become final pursuant to former section 3111.211 [3111.21.1] or 5101.314 [5101.31.4] or section 2151.232 [2151.23.2], 3111.25, or 3111.821 [3111.82.1] of the Revised Code. If a complaint is filed under this section and an issue concerning the existence or nonexistence of a parent-child relationship is raised, the court shall treat the action as an action pursuant to sections 3111.01 to 3111.18 of the Revised Code. An order issued in an action under this section does not preclude a party to the action from bringing a subsequent action pursuant to sections 3111.01 to 3111.18 of the Revised Code if the issue concerning the existence or nonexistence of the parent-child relationship was not determined with respect to the party pursuant to a proceeding under this section, a proceeding under Chapter 3111. of the Revised Code, or an acknowledgment of paternity that has become final under former section 3111.211 [3111.21.1] or 5101.314 [5101.31.4] or section 2151.232 [2151.23.2], 3111.25, or 3111.821 [3111.82.1] of the Revised Code. An order issued pursuant to this section shall remain effective until an order is issued pursuant to sections 3111.01 to 3111.18 of the Revised Code that a parent-child relationship does not exist between the alleged father of the child and the child or until the occurrence of an event described in section 3119.88 of the Revised Code that would require the order to terminate.

The court, in accordance with sections 3119.29 to 3119.56 of the Revised Code, shall include in each support order made under this section the requirement that one or both of the parents provide for the health care needs of the child to the satisfaction of the court.

**HISTORY: 144 v S 10 (Eff 7-15-92); 146 v H 167† (Eff 6-11-96); 147 v H 352 (Eff 1-1-98); 148 v S 180 (Eff 3-22-2001); 149 v H 657. Eff 12-13-2002.**

† The effective date of HB 167 (146 v —) for this section was changed from 11-15-96 to 6-11-96 by § 7 of HB 710 (146 v —), effective 6-11-96.

## § 2151.232 Action for child support where acknowledgment is not yet final.

If an acknowledgment has been filed and entered into the birth registry pursuant to section 3111.24 of the Revised Code but has not yet become final, either parent who signed the acknowledgment may bring an action in the juvenile court or other court with jurisdiction under section 2101.022 [2101.02.2] or 2301.03 of the Revised Code under this section requesting that the court issue an order requiring a parent of the child to pay an amount for the support of the child in accordance with Chapters 3119., 3121., 3123., and 3125. of the Revised Code.

The parties to an action under this section may raise the issue of the existence or nonexistence of a parent-child relationship. If an action is commenced pursuant to this section and the issue of the existence or nonexistence of a parent-child relationship is raised, the court shall treat the action as an action commenced pursuant to sections 3111.01 to 3111.18 of the Revised Code. If the issue is raised, the court shall promptly notify the office of child support in the department of job and family services that it is conducting proceedings in compliance with sections 3111.01 to 3111.18 of the Revised Code. On receipt of the notice by the office, the acknowledgment of paternity signed by the parties and filed pursuant to section 3111.23 of the Revised Code shall be considered rescinded.

If the parties do not raise the issue of the existence or nonexistence of a parent-child relationship in the action and an order is issued pursuant to this section prior to the date the acknowledgment filed and entered on the birth registry becomes final, the acknowledgment shall be considered final as of the date of the issuance of the order. An order issued pursuant to this section shall not affect an acknowledgment that becomes final pursuant to section 3111.25 of the Revised Code prior to the issuance of the order.

**HISTORY: 147 v H 352 (Eff 1-1-98); 148 v H 471 (Eff 7-1-2000); 148 v S 180. Eff 3-22-2001.**

## § 2151.24 Separate room for hearings.

(A) Except as provided in division (B) of this section, the board of county commissioners shall provide a special room not used for the trial of criminal or adult cases, when available, for the hearing of the cases of dependent, neglected, abused, and delinquent children.

(B) Division (A) of this section does not apply to the case of an alleged delinquent child when the case is one in which the prosecuting attorney seeks a serious youthful offender disposition under section 2152.13 of the Revised Code.

**HISTORY: GC § 1639-14; 117 v 520; Bureau of Code Revision, 10-1-53; 136 v H 85 (Eff 11-28-75); 148 v S 179, § 3. Eff 1-1-2002.**

The effective date is set by section 5 of SB 179.

## [PROCEDURE IN CHILDREN'S CASES]

**§ 2151.25** Amended and renumbered RC § 2152.03 in 148 v S 179. Eff 1-1-2002.

The effective date is set by section 5 of SB 179.

**§ 2151.26** Amended and renumbered RC § 2152.12 in 148 v S 179. Eff 1-1-2002.

The effective date is set by section 5 of SB 179.

## § 2151.27 Complaint.

(A)(1) Subject to division (A)(2) of this section, any person having knowledge of a child who appears to have violated section 2151.87 of the Revised Code or to be a juvenile traffic offender or to be an unruly, abused, neglected, or dependent child may file a sworn complaint with respect to that child in the juvenile court of the county in which the child has a residence or legal settlement or in which the violation, unruliness, abuse, neglect, or dependency allegedly occurred. If an alleged abused, neglected, or dependent child is taken into custody pursuant to division (D) of section 2151.31 of the Revised Code or is taken into custody pursuant to division (A) of section 2151.31 of the Revised Code without the filing of a complaint and placed into shelter care pursuant to division (C) of that section, a sworn complaint shall be filed with respect to the child before the end of the next day after the day on which the child was taken into custody. The sworn complaint may be upon information and belief, and, in addition to the allegation that the child committed the violation or is an unruly, abused, neglected, or dependent child, the complaint shall allege the particular facts upon which the allegation that the child committed the violation or is an unruly, abused, neglected, or dependent child is based.

(2) Any person having knowledge of a child who appears to be an unruly child for being an habitual truant may file a sworn complaint with respect to that child and the parent, guardian, or other person having care of the child in the juvenile court of the county in which the child has a residence or legal settlement or in which the child is supposed to attend public school. The sworn complaint may be upon information and belief and shall contain the following allegations:

(a) That the child is an unruly child for being an habitual truant and, in addition, the particular facts upon which that allegation is based;

(b) That the parent, guardian, or other person having care of the child has failed to cause the child's attendance at school in violation of section 3321.38 of the Revised Code and, in addition, the particular facts upon which that allegation is based.

(B) If a child, before arriving at the age of eighteen years, allegedly commits an act for which the child may be adjudicated an unruly child and if the specific complaint alleging the act is not filed or a hearing on that specific complaint is not held until after the child arrives at the age of eighteen years, the court has jurisdiction to hear and dispose of the complaint as if the complaint were filed and the hearing held before the child arrived at the age of eighteen years.

(C) If the complainant in a case in which a child is alleged to be an abused, neglected, or dependent child desires permanent custody of the child or children, temporary custody of the child or children, whether as the preferred or an alternative disposition, or the placement of the child in a planned permanent living arrangement, the complaint shall contain a prayer specifically requesting permanent custody, temporary custody, or the placement of the child in a planned permanent living arrangement.

(D) Any person with standing under applicable law may file a complaint for the determination of any other matter over which the juvenile court is given jurisdiction by section 2151.23 of the Revised Code. The complaint shall be filed in the county in which the child who is the subject of the complaint is found or was last known to be found.

(E) A public children services agency, acting pursuant to a complaint or an action on a complaint filed under this section, is not subject to the requirements of section 3127.23 of the Revised Code.

(F) Upon the filing of a complaint alleging that a child is an unruly child, the court may hold the complaint in abeyance pending the child's successful completion of actions that constitute a method to divert the child from the juvenile court system. The method may be adopted by a county pursuant to divisions (D) and (E) of section 121.37 of the Revised Code or it may be another method that the court considers satisfactory. If the child completes the actions to the court's satisfaction, the court may dismiss the complaint. If the child fails to complete the actions to the court's satisfaction, the court may consider the complaint.

**HISTORY: 133 v H 320 (Eff 11-19-69); 136 v H 85 (Eff 11-28-75); 140 v S 5 (Eff 9-26-84); 142 v S 89 (Eff 1-1-89); 144 v H 154 (Eff 7-31-92); 146 v S 2 (Eff 7-1-96); 146 v H 274, §§ 1, 4 (Eff 8-8-96); 146 v H 445 (Eff 9-3-96); 147 v H 484 (Eff 3-18-99); 148 v S 181 (Eff 9-4-2000); 148 v S 218 (Eff 3-15-2001); 148 v S 179, § 3 (Eff 1-1-2002); 149 v H 57. Eff 2-19-2002†; 150 v S 185, § 1, eff. 4-11-05.**

† The effective date of sections 1 and 2 of Sub. H.B. 57 (149 v —) differs from the effective date set for the sections by section 3 of the Act. See provisions of OConst art II, §§ 1c and d.

**Analogous in part to former RC § 2151.27 (GC § 1639-23; 117 v 520; 121 v 557; Bureau of Code Revision, 10-1-53; 127 v 547), repealed 133 v H 320, eff 11-19-69.**

The provisions of § 3 of HB 57 (149 v —) read as follows:

SECTION 3. Sections 1 and 2 of this act shall take effect January 1, 2002.

The provisions of § 6 of HB 57 (149 v —) read as follows:

SECTION 6. Section 2151.27 of the Revised Code is presented in this act as a composite of the section as amended by both Am. Sub. S.B. 179 and Sub. S.B. 218 of the 123rd General Assembly. The General Assembly, applying the principle stated in division (B) of section 1.52 of the Revised Code that amendments are to be harmonized if reasonably capable of simultaneous operation, finds that the composite is the resulting version of the section in effect on January 1, 2002.

## § 2151.271 Transfer to juvenile court of another county.

Except in a case in which the child is alleged to be a serious youthful offender under section 2152.13 of the Revised Code, if the child resides in a county of the state and the proceeding is commenced in a juvenile court of another county, that court, on its own motion or a motion of a party, may transfer the proceeding to the county of the child's residence upon the filing of the complaint or after the adjudicatory, or dispositional hearing, for such further proceeding as required. The court of the child's residence shall then proceed as if the original complaint had been filed in that court. Transfer may also be made if the residence of the child changes. The proceeding shall be so transferred if other proceedings involving the child are pending in the juvenile court of the county of the child's residence.

Whenever a case is transferred to the county of the child's residence and it appears to the court of that county that the interests of justice and the convenience of the parties requires that the adjudicatory hearing be had in the county in which the complaint was filed, the court may return the proceeding to the county in which the complaint was filed for the purpose of the adjudicatory hearing. The court may thereafter proceed as to the transfer to the county of the child's legal residence as provided in this section.

Certified copies of all legal and social records pertaining to the case shall accompany the transfer.

**HISTORY: 133 v H 320 (Eff 11-19-69); 148 v S 179, § 3. Eff 1-1-2002.**

The effective date is set by section 5 of SB 179.

## § 2151.28 Adjudicatory hearing; shelter care determination; summons.

(A) No later than seventy-two hours after the complaint is filed, the court shall fix a time for an adjudicatory hearing. The court shall conduct the adjudicatory hearing within one of the following periods of time:

(1) Subject to division (C) of section 2152.13 of the Revised Code and division (A)(3) of this section, if the complaint alleged that the child violated section 2151.87 of the Revised Code or is a delinquent or unruly child or a juvenile traffic offender, the adjudicatory hearing shall be held and may be continued in accordance with the Juvenile Rules.

(2) If the complaint alleged that the child is an abused, neglected, or dependent child, the adjudicatory hearing shall be held no later than thirty days after the complaint is filed, except that, for good cause shown, the court may continue the adjudicatory hearing for either of the following periods of time:

(a) For ten days beyond the thirty-day deadline to allow any party to obtain counsel;

(b) For a reasonable period of time beyond the thirty-day deadline to obtain service on all parties or any necessary evaluation, except that the adjudicatory hearing shall not be held later than sixty days after the date on which the complaint was filed.

(3) If the child who is the subject of the complaint is in detention and is charged with violating a section of the Revised Code that may be violated by an adult, the hearing shall be held not later than fifteen days after the filing of the complaint. Upon a showing of good cause, the adjudicatory hearing may be continued and detention extended.

(B) At an adjudicatory hearing held pursuant to division (A)(2) of this section, the court, in addition to determining whether the child is an abused, neglected, or dependent child, shall determine whether the child should remain or be placed in shelter care until the dispositional hearing. When the court makes the shelter care determination, all of the following apply:

(1) The court shall determine whether there are any relatives of the child who are willing to be temporary custodians of the child. If any relative is willing to be a temporary custodian, the child otherwise would remain or be placed in shelter care, and the appointment is appropriate, the court shall appoint the relative as temporary custodian of the child, unless the court appoints another relative as custodian. If it determines that the appointment of a relative as custodian would not be appropriate, it shall issue a written opinion setting forth the reasons for its determination and give a copy of the opinion to all parties and the guardian ad litem of the child.

The court's consideration of a relative for appointment as a temporary custodian does not make that relative a party to the proceedings.

(2) The court shall comply with section 2151.419 [2151.41.9] of the Revised Code.

(3) The court shall schedule the date for the dispositional hearing to be held pursuant to section 2151.35 of the Revised Code. The parents of the child have a right to be represented by counsel; however, in no case shall the dispositional hearing be held later than ninety days after the date on which the complaint was filed.

(C)(1) The court shall direct the issuance of a summons directed to the child except as provided by this section, the parents, guardian, custodian, or other person with whom the child may be, and any other persons that appear to the court to be proper or necessary parties to the proceedings, requiring them to appear before the court at the time fixed to answer the allegations of the complaint. The summons shall contain the name and telephone number of the court employee designated by the court pursuant to section 2151.314 [2151.31.4] of the Revised Code to arrange for the prompt appointment of counsel for indigent persons. A child alleged to be an abused, neglected, or dependent child shall not be summoned unless the court so directs. A summons issued for a child who is under fourteen years of age and who is alleged to be a delinquent child, unruly child, or a juvenile traffic offender shall be served on the parent, guardian, or custodian of the child in the child's behalf.

If the person who has physical custody of the child, or with whom the child resides, is other than the parent or guardian, then the parents and guardian also shall be summoned. A copy of the complaint shall accompany the summons.

(2) In lieu of appearing before the court at the time fixed in the summons and prior to the date fixed for appearance in the summons, a child who is alleged to have violated section 2151.87 of the Revised Code and that child's parent, guardian, or custodian may sign a waiver of appearance before the clerk of the juvenile court and pay a fine of one hundred dollars. If the child and that child's parent, guardian, or custodian do not waive the court appearance, the court shall proceed with the adjudicatory hearing as provided in this section.

(D) If the complaint contains a prayer for permanent custody, temporary custody, whether as the preferred or an alternative disposition, or a planned permanent living arrangement in a case involving an alleged abused, neglected, or dependent child, the summons served on the parents shall contain as is appropriate an explanation that the granting of permanent custody permanently divests the parents of their parental rights and privileges, an explanation that an adjudication that the child is an abused, neglected, or dependent child may result in an order of temporary custody that will cause the removal of the child from their legal custody until the court terminates the order of temporary custody or permanently divests the parents of their parental rights, or an explanation that the issuance of an order for a planned permanent living arrangement will cause the removal of the child from the legal custody of the parents if any of the conditions listed in divisions (A)(5)(a) to (c) of section 2151.353 [2151.35.3] of the Revised Code are found to exist.

(E)(1) Except as otherwise provided in division (E)(2) of this section, the court may endorse upon the summons an order directing the parents, guardian, or other person with whom the child may be to appear personally at the hearing and directing the person having the physical custody or control of the child to bring the child to the hearing.

(2) In cases in which the complaint alleges that a child is an unruly or delinquent child for being an habitual or chronic truant and that the parent, guardian, or other person having care of the child has failed to cause the child's attendance at school, the court shall endorse upon the summons an order directing the parent, guardian, or other person having care of the child to appear personally at the hearing and directing the person having the physical custody or control of the child to bring the child to the hearing.

(F)(1) The summons shall contain a statement advising that any party is entitled to counsel in the proceedings and that the court will appoint counsel or designate a county public defender or joint county public defender to provide legal representation if the party is indigent.

(2) In cases in which the complaint alleges a child to be an abused, neglected, or dependent child and no hearing has been conducted pursuant to division (A) of section 2151.314 [2151.31.4] of the Revised Code with respect to the child or a parent, guardian, or custodian of the child does not attend the hearing, the summons also shall contain a statement advising that a case plan may be prepared for the child, the general requirements usually contained in case plans, and the possible consequences of failure to comply with a journalized case plan.

(G) If it appears from an affidavit filed or from sworn testimony before the court that the conduct, condition, or surroundings of the child are endangering the child's health or welfare or those of others, that the child may abscond or be removed from the jurisdiction of the court, or that the child will not be brought to the court, notwithstanding the service of the summons, the court may endorse upon the summons an order that a law enforcement officer serve the summons and take the child into immediate custody and bring the child forthwith to the court.

(H) A party, other than the child, may waive service of summons by written stipulation.

(I) Before any temporary commitment is made permanent, the court shall fix a time for hearing in accordance with section 2151.414 [2151.41.4] of the Revised Code and shall cause notice by summons to be served upon the parent or guardian of the child and the guardian ad litem of the child, or published, as provided in section 2151.29 of the Revised Code. The summons shall contain an explanation that the granting of permanent custody permanently divests the parents of their parental rights and privileges.

(J) Any person whose presence is considered necessary and who is not summoned may be subpoenaed to appear and testify at the hearing. Anyone summoned or subpoenaed to appear who fails to do so may be punished, as in other cases in the court of common pleas, for contempt of court. Persons subpoenaed shall be paid the same witness fees as are allowed in the court of common pleas.

(K) The failure of the court to hold an adjudicatory hearing within any time period set forth in division (A)(2) of this section does not affect the ability of the court to issue any order under this chapter and does not provide any basis for attacking the jurisdiction of the court or the validity of any order of the court.

(L) If the court, at an adjudicatory hearing held pursuant to division (A) of this section upon a complaint alleging that a child is an abused, neglected, dependent, delinquent, or unruly child or a juvenile traffic offender, determines that the child is a dependent child, the court shall incorporate that determination into written findings of fact and conclusions of law and enter those findings of fact and conclusions of law in the record of the case. The court shall include in those findings of fact and conclusions of law specific findings as to the existence of any danger to the child and any underlying family problems that are the basis for the court's determination that the child is a dependent child.

**HISTORY: 133 v H 320 (Eff 11-19-69); 136 v H 85 (Eff 11-28-75); 136 v H 164 (Eff 1-13-76); 142 v S 89 (Eff 1-1-89); 146 v H 274 (Eff 8-8-96); 146 v H 419 (Eff 9-18-96); 147 v H 484 (Eff 3-18-99); 148 v S 181 (Eff 9-4-2000); 148 v S 218 (Eff 3-15-2001); 148 v S 179, § 3 (Eff 1-1-2002); 149 v H 180 (Eff 5-16-2002); 149 v H 393. Eff 7-5-2002.**

**Analogous in part to former RC § 2151.28 (GC § 1639-24; 117 v 520; 121 v 557; Bureau of Code Revision, 10-1-53), repealed 133 v H 320, eff 11-19-69.**

The provisions of § 3 of HB 180 (149 v —) read as follows:

SECTION 3. The General Assembly hereby requests the Supreme Court to promptly modify Rule 29 of the Rules of Juvenile Procedure pursuant to its authority under the Ohio Constitution to make that rule consistent with the amendments of this act to section 2151.28 of the Revised Code.

The General Assembly further requests the Supreme Court to promptly modify Rule 7 of the Rules of Juvenile Procedure pursuant to its authority under the Ohio Constitution to make that rule consistent with the amendments of this act to section 2151.31 of the Revised Code.

## § 2151.281 Guardian ad litem.

(A) The court shall appoint a guardian ad litem, subject to rules adopted by the supreme court, to protect the interest of a child in any proceeding concerning an alleged or adjudicated delinquent child or unruly child when either of the following applies:

(1) The child has no parent, guardian, or legal custodian.

(2) The court finds that there is a conflict of interest between the child and the child's parent, guardian, or legal custodian.

(B)(1) The court shall appoint a guardian ad litem, subject to rules adopted by the supreme court, to protect the interest of a child in any proceeding concerning an alleged abused or neglected child and in any proceeding held pursuant to section 2151.414 [2151.41.4] of the Revised Code. The guardian ad litem so appointed shall not be the attorney responsible for presenting the evidence alleging that the child is an abused or neglected child and shall not be an employee of any party in the proceeding.

(2) The guardian ad litem appointed for an alleged or adjudicated abused or neglected child may bring a civil action against any person who is required by division (A)(1) or (4) of section 2151.421 [2151.42.1] of the Revised Code to file a report of child abuse or child neglect that is known or reasonably suspected or believed to have occurred if that person knows, or has reasonable cause to suspect or believe based on facts that would cause a reasonable person in a similar position to suspect or believe, as applicable, that the child for whom the guardian ad litem is appointed is the subject of child abuse or child neglect and does not file the required report and if the child suffers any injury or harm as a result of the child abuse or child neglect that is known or reasonably suspected or believed to have occurred or suffers additional injury or harm after the failure to file the report.

(C) In any proceeding concerning an alleged or adjudicated delinquent, unruly, abused, neglected, or dependent child in which the parent appears to be mentally incompetent or is under eighteen years of age, the court shall appoint a guardian ad litem to protect the interest of that parent.

(D) The court shall require the guardian ad litem to faithfully discharge the guardian ad litem's duties and, upon the guardian ad litem's failure to faithfully discharge the guardian ad litem's duties, shall discharge the guardian ad litem and appoint another guardian ad litem. The court may fix the compensation for the service of the guardian ad litem, which compensation shall be paid from the treasury of the county, subject to rules adopted by the supreme court.

(E) A parent who is eighteen years of age or older and not mentally incompetent shall be deemed sui juris for the purpose of any proceeding relative to a child of the parent who is alleged or adjudicated to be an abused, neglected, or dependent child.

(F) In any case in which a parent of a child alleged or adjudicated to be an abused, neglected, or dependent child is under eighteen years of age, the parents of that parent shall be summoned to appear at any hearing respecting the child, who is alleged or adjudicated to be an abused, neglected, or dependent child.

(G) In any case involving an alleged or adjudicated abused or neglected child or an agreement for the voluntary surrender of temporary or permanent custody of a child that is made in accordance with section 5103.15 of the Revised Code, the court shall appoint the guardian ad litem in each case as soon as possible after the complaint is filed, the request for an extension of the temporary custody agreement is filed with the court, or the request for court approval of the permanent custody agreement is filed. In any case involving an alleged dependent child in which the parent of the child appears to be mentally incompetent or is under eighteen years of age, there is a conflict of interest between the child and the child's parents, guardian, or custodian, or the court believes that the parent of the child is not capable of representing the best interest of the child, the court shall appoint a guardian ad litem for the child. The guardian ad litem or the guardian ad litem's replacement shall continue to serve until any of the following occur:

(1) The complaint is dismissed or the request for an extension of a temporary custody agreement or for court approval of the permanent custody agreement is withdrawn or denied;

(2) All dispositional orders relative to the child have terminated;

(3) The legal custody of the child is granted to a relative of the child, or to another person;

(4) The child is placed in an adoptive home or, at the court's discretion, a final decree of adoption is issued with respect to the child;

(5) The child reaches the age of eighteen if the child is not mentally retarded, developmentally disabled, or physically impaired or the child reaches the age of twenty-one if the child is mentally retarded, developmentally disabled, or physically impaired;

(6) The guardian ad litem resigns or is removed by the court and a replacement is appointed by the court.

If a guardian ad litem ceases to serve a child pursuant to division (G)(4) of this section and the petition for adoption with respect to the child is denied or withdrawn prior to the issuance of a final decree of adoption or prior to the date an interlocutory order of adoption becomes final, the juvenile court shall reappoint a guardian ad litem for that child. The public children services agency or private child placing agency with permanent custody of the child shall notify the juvenile court if the petition for adoption is denied or withdrawn.

(H) If the guardian ad litem for an alleged or adjudicated abused, neglected, or dependent child is an attorney admitted to the practice of law in this state, the guardian ad litem also may serve as counsel to the ward. Until the supreme court adopts rules regarding service as a guardian ad litem that regulate conflicts between a person's role as guardian ad litem and as counsel, if a person is serving as guardian ad litem and counsel for a child and either that person or the court finds that a conflict may exist between the person's roles as guardian ad litem and as counsel, the court shall relieve the person of duties as guardian ad litem and appoint someone else as guardian ad litem for the child. If the court appoints a person who is not an attorney admitted to the practice of law in this state to be a guardian ad litem, the court also may appoint an attorney admitted to the practice of law in this state to serve as counsel for the guardian ad litem.

(I) The guardian ad litem for an alleged or adjudicated abused, neglected, or dependent child shall perform whatever functions are necessary to protect the best interest of the child, including, but not limited to, investigation, mediation, monitoring court proceedings, and monitoring the services provided the child by the public children services agency or private child placing agency that has temporary or permanent custody of the child, and shall file any motions and other court papers that are in the best interest of the child.

The guardian ad litem shall be given notice of all hearings, administrative reviews, and other proceedings in the same manner as notice is given to parties to the action.

(J)(1) When the court appoints a guardian ad litem pursuant to this section, it shall appoint a qualified volunteer or court appointed special advocate whenever one is available and the appointment is appropriate.

(2) Upon request, the department of job and family services shall provide for the training of volunteer guardians ad litem.

**HISTORY: 133 v H 320 (Eff 11-19-69); 136 v H 85 (Eff 11-28-75); 138 v H 695 (Eff 10-24-80); 140 v S 321 (Eff 4-9-85); 141 v H 529 (Eff 3-11-87); 142 v S 89 (Eff 1-1-89); 146 v H 274 (Eff 8-8-96); 146 v H 419 (Eff 9-18-96); 148 v H 471. Eff 7-1-2000; 151 v S 17, § 1, eff. 8-3-06; 151 v S 238, § 1, eff. 9-21-06.**

The provisions of § 4 of 151 v S 238 read as follows:

SECTION 4. The General Assembly hereby respectfully requests that the Supreme Court adopt rules regarding the standards, qualifications, and service of guardians ad litem.

The effective date is set by section 12(A) of HB 471.

**Comment, Legislative Service Commission**

Section 2151.281 of the Revised Code is amended by Am. Sub. S.B. 238 and Am. Sub. S.B. 17 of the 126th General Assembly. Comparison of these amendments in pursuance of section 1.52 of the Revised Code discloses that they are not irreconcilable so that they are required by that section to be harmonized to give effect to each amendment.

## § 2151.282 CASA/GAL study committee [Repealed].

Repealed by 2011 SB 171, § 2, effective June 30, 2011.

**HISTORY: 151 v H 66, § 101.01, eff. 9-29-05.**

## § 2151.29 Service of summons and other documents.

Service of summons, notices, and subpoenas, prescribed by section 2151.28 of the Revised Code, shall be made by delivering a copy to the person summoned, notified, or subpoenaed, or by leaving a copy at the person's usual place of residence. If the juvenile judge is satisfied that such service is impracticable, the juvenile judge may order service by registered or certified mail. If the person to be served is without the state but the person can be found or the person's address is known, or the person's whereabouts or address can with reasonable diligence be ascertained, service of the summons may be made by delivering a copy to the person personally or mailing a copy to the person by registered or certified mail.

Whenever it appears by affidavit that after reasonable effort the person to be served with summons cannot be found or the person's post-office address ascertained, whether the person is within or without a state, the clerk shall publish such summons once in a newspaper of general circulation throughout the county. The summons shall state the substance and the time and place of the hearing, which shall be held at least one week later than the date of the publication. A copy of the summons and the complaint, indictment, or information shall be sent by registered or certified mail to the last known address of the person summoned unless it is shown by affidavit that a reasonable effort has been made, without success, to obtain such address.

A copy of the advertisement, the summons, and the complaint, indictment, or information, accompanied by the certificate of the clerk that such publication has been made and that the summons and the complaint, indictment, or information have been mailed as required by this section, is sufficient evidence of publication and mailing. When a period of one week from the time of publication has elapsed, the juvenile court shall have full jurisdiction to deal with such child as provided by sections 2151.01 to 2151.99 of the Revised Code.

**HISTORY: 133 v H 320 (Eff 11-19-69); 148 v S 179, § 3. Eff 1-1-2002.**

**Analogous in part to former RC § 2151.29 (GC § 1639-25; 121 v 557; Bureau of Code Revision, 10-1-53), repealed 133 v H 320, eff 11-19-69.**

The effective date is set by section 5 of SB 179.

## § 2151.30 Issuance of warrant.

In any case when it is made to appear to the juvenile judge that the service of a citation under section 2151.29 of the Revised Code will be ineffectual or the welfare of the child requires that he be brought forthwith into the custody of the juvenile court, a warrant may be issued against the parent, custodian, or guardian, or against the child himself.

**HISTORY: GC § 1639-26; 117 v 520; Bureau of Code Revision. Eff 10-1-53.**

## § 2151.31 Apprehension, custody, and detention.

(A) A child may be taken into custody in any of the following ways:

(1) Pursuant to an order of the court under this chapter or pursuant to an order of the court upon a motion filed

pursuant to division (B) of section 2930.05 of the Revised Code;

(2) Pursuant to the laws of arrest;

(3) By a law enforcement officer or duly authorized officer of the court when any of the following conditions are present:

(a) There are reasonable grounds to believe that the child is suffering from illness or injury and is not receiving proper care, as described in section 2151.03 of the Revised Code, and the child's removal is necessary to prevent immediate or threatened physical or emotional harm;

(b) There are reasonable grounds to believe that the child is in immediate danger from the child's surroundings and that the child's removal is necessary to prevent immediate or threatened physical or emotional harm;

(c) There are reasonable grounds to believe that a parent, guardian, custodian, or other household member of the child's household has abused or neglected another child in the household and to believe that the child is in danger of immediate or threatened physical or emotional harm from that person.

(4) By an enforcement official, as defined in section 4109.01 of the Revised Code, under the circumstances set forth in section 4109.08 of the Revised Code;

(5) By a law enforcement officer or duly authorized officer of the court when there are reasonable grounds to believe that the child has run away from the child's parents, guardian, or other custodian;

(6) By a law enforcement officer or duly authorized officer of the court when any of the following apply:

(a) There are reasonable grounds to believe that the conduct, conditions, or surroundings of the child are endangering the health, welfare, or safety of the child.

(b) A complaint has been filed with respect to the child under section 2151.27 or 2152.021 [2152.02.1] of the Revised Code or the child has been indicted under division (A) of section 2152.13 of the Revised Code or charged by information as described in that section and there are reasonable grounds to believe that the child may abscond or be removed from the jurisdiction of the court.

(c) The child is required to appear in court and there are reasonable grounds to believe that the child will not be brought before the court when required.

(d) There are reasonable grounds to believe that the child committed a delinquent act and that taking the child into custody is necessary to protect the public interest and safety.

(B)(1) The taking of a child into custody is not and shall not be deemed an arrest except for the purpose of determining its validity under the constitution of this state or of the United States.

(2) Except as provided in division (C) of section 2151.311 [2151.31.1] of the Revised Code, a child taken into custody shall not be held in any state correctional institution, county, multicounty, or municipal jail or workhouse, or any other place where any adult convicted of crime, under arrest, or charged with crime is held.

(C)(1) Except as provided in division (C)(2) of this section, a child taken into custody shall not be confined in a place of juvenile detention or placed in shelter care prior to the implementation of the court's final order of disposition, unless detention or shelter care is required to protect the child from immediate or threatened physical or emotional harm, because the child is a danger or threat to one or more other persons and is charged with violating a section of the Revised Code that may be violated by an adult, because the child may abscond or be removed from the jurisdiction of the court, because the child has no parents, guardian, or custodian or other person able to provide supervision and care for the child and return the child to the court when required, or because an order for placement of the child in detention or shelter care has been made by the court pursuant to this chapter.

(2) A child alleged to be a delinquent child who is taken into custody may be confined in a place of juvenile detention prior to the implementation of the court's final order of disposition if the confinement is authorized under section 2152.04 of the Revised Code or if the child is alleged to be a serious youthful offender under section 2152.13 of the Revised Code and is not released on bond.

(D) Upon receipt of notice from a person that the person intends to take an alleged abused, neglected, or dependent child into custody pursuant to division (A)(3) of this section, a juvenile judge or a designated referee may grant by telephone an ex parte emergency order authorizing the taking of the child into custody if there is probable cause to believe that any of the conditions set forth in divisions (A)(3)(a) to (c) of this section are present. The judge or referee shall journalize any ex parte emergency order issued pursuant to this division. If an order is issued pursuant to this division and the child is taken into custody pursuant to the order, a sworn complaint shall be filed with respect to the child before the end of the next business day after the day on which the child is taken into custody and a hearing shall be held pursuant to division (E) of this section and the Juvenile Rules. A juvenile judge or referee shall not grant an emergency order by telephone pursuant to this division until after the judge or referee determines that reasonable efforts have been made to notify the parents, guardian, or custodian of the child that the child may be placed into shelter care and of the reasons for placing the child into shelter care, except that, if the requirement for notification would jeopardize the physical or emotional safety of the child or result in the child being removed from the court's jurisdiction, the judge or referee may issue the order for taking the child into custody and placing the child into shelter care prior to giving notice to the parents, guardian, or custodian of the child.

(E) If a judge or referee pursuant to division (D) of this section issues an ex parte emergency order for taking a child into custody, the court shall hold a hearing to determine whether there is probable cause for the emergency order. The hearing shall be held before the end of the next business day after the day on which the emergency order is issued, except that it shall not be held later than seventy-two hours after the emergency order is issued.

If the court determines at the hearing that there is not probable cause for the issuance of the emergency order issued pursuant to division (D) of this section, it shall order the child released to the custody of the child's parents, guardian, or custodian. If the court determines at the hearing that there is probable cause for the issuance of the emergency order issued pursuant to division (D) of this section, the court shall do all of the following:

(1) Ensure that a complaint is filed or has been filed;

(2) Comply with section 2151.419 [2151.41.9] of the Revised Code;

(3) Hold a hearing pursuant to section 2151.314 [2151.31.4] of the Revised Code to determine if the child should remain in shelter care.

(F) If the court determines at the hearing held pursuant to division (E) of this section that there is probable cause to believe that the child is an abused child, as defined in division (A) of section 2151.031 [2151.03.1] of the Revised Code, the court may do any of the following:

(1) Upon the motion of any party, the guardian ad litem, the prosecuting attorney, or an employee of the public children services agency, or its own motion, issue reasonable protective orders with respect to the interviewing or deposition of the child;

(2) Order that the child's testimony be videotaped for preservation of the testimony for possible use in any other proceedings in the case;

(3) Set any additional conditions with respect to the child or the case involving the child that are in the best interest of the child.

(G) This section is not intended, and shall not be construed, to prevent any person from taking a child into custody, if taking the child into custody is necessary in an emergency to prevent the physical injury, emotional harm, or neglect of the child.

**HISTORY: 133 v H 320 (Eff 11-19-69); 137 v H 883 (Eff 1-12-79); 142 v S 89 (Eff 1-1-89); 143 v H 166 (Eff 2-14-90); 145 v H 571 (Eff 10-6-94); 147 v H 408 (Eff 10-1-97); 147 v H 484 (Eff 3-18-99); 148 v H 176 (Eff 10-29-99); 148 v H 3 (Eff 11-22-99); 148 v S 179, § 3 (Eff 1-1-2002); 149 v H 180. Eff 5-16-2002.**

**Analogous in part to former RC § 2151.31 (GC § 1639-27; 117 v 520; 121 v 557; Bureau of Code Revision, 10-1-53), repealed, 133 v H 320, eff 11-19-69.**

See provisions, § 3 of HB 180 (149 v —), following RC § 2151.28.

## § 2151.311 Procedure upon apprehension.

(A) A person taking a child into custody shall, with all reasonable speed and in accordance with division (C) of this section, either:

(1) Release the child to the child's parents, guardian, or other custodian, unless the child's detention or shelter care appears to be warranted or required as provided in section 2151.31 of the Revised Code;

(2) Bring the child to the court or deliver the child to a place of detention or shelter care designated by the court and promptly give notice thereof, together with a statement of the reason for taking the child into custody, to a parent, guardian, or other custodian and to the court.

(B) If a parent, guardian, or other custodian fails, when requested by the court, to bring the child before the court as provided by this section, the court may issue its warrant directing that the child be taken into custody and brought before the court.

(C)(1) Before taking any action required by division (A) of this section, a person taking a child into custody may hold the child for processing purposes in a county, multicounty, or municipal jail or workhouse, or other place where an adult convicted of crime, under arrest, or charged with crime is held for either of the following periods of time:

(a) For a period not to exceed six hours, if all of the following apply:

(i) The child is alleged to be a delinquent child for the commission of an act that would be a felony if committed by an adult;

(ii) The child remains beyond the range of touch of all adult detainees;

(iii) The child is visually supervised by jail or workhouse personnel at all times during the detention;

(iv) The child is not handcuffed or otherwise physically secured to a stationary object during the detention.

(b) For a period not to exceed three hours, if all of the following apply:

(i) The child is alleged to be a delinquent child for the commission of an act that would be a misdemeanor if committed by an adult, is alleged to be a delinquent child for being a chronic truant or an habitual truant who previously has been adjudicated an unruly child for being an habitual truant, or is alleged to be an unruly child or a juvenile traffic offender;

(ii) The child remains beyond the range of touch of all adult detainees;

(iii) The child is visually supervised by jail or workhouse personnel at all times during the detention;

(iv) The child is not handcuffed or otherwise physically secured to a stationary object during the detention.

(2) If a child has been transferred to an adult court for prosecution for the alleged commission of a criminal offense, subsequent to the transfer, the child may be held as described in division (F) of section 2152.26 or division (B) of section 5120.16 of the Revised Code.

(D) As used in division (C)(1) of this section, "processing purposes" means all of the following:

(1) Fingerprinting, photographing, or fingerprinting and photographing the child in a secure area of the facility;

(2) Interrogating the child, contacting the child's parent or guardian, arranging for placement of the child, or arranging for transfer or transferring the child, while holding the child in a nonsecure area of the facility.

**HISTORY: 133 v H 320 (Eff 11-19-69); 133 v H 931 (Eff 8-27-70); 134 v S 445 (Eff 6-29-72); 143 v H 166 (Eff 2-14-90); 145 v H 571 (Eff 10-6-94); 146 v H 480 (Eff 10-16-96); 146 v H 124 (Eff 3-31-97); 148 v S 181 (Eff 9-4-2000); 148 v S 179, § 3. Eff 1-1-2002.**

The effective date is set by section 5 of SB 179.

## § 2151.312 Places where neglected, abused, dependent or unruly child may or may not be held.

(A) A child alleged to be or adjudicated an unruly child may be held only in the following places:

(1) A certified family foster home or a home approved by the court;

(2) A facility operated by a certified child welfare agency;

(3) Any other suitable place designated by the court.

(B)(1) Except as provided under division (C)(1) of section 2151.311 of the Revised Code, a child alleged to be or adjudicated a neglected child, an abused child, a dependent child, or an unruly child may not be held in any of the following facilities:

(a) A state correctional institution, county, multicounty, or municipal jail or workhouse, or other place in which an adult convicted of a crime, under arrest, or charged with a crime is held;

(b) A secure correctional facility.

(2) Except as provided under sections 2151.27 to 2151.59 of the Revised Code and division (B)(3) of this section and except when a case is transferred under section 2152.12 of the Revised Code, a child alleged to be or adjudicated an unruly child may not be held for more than twenty-four hours in a detention facility. A child alleged to be or adjudicated a neglected child, an abused child, or a dependent child shall not be held in a detention facility.

(3) A child who is alleged to be or adjudicated an unruly child and who is taken into custody on a Saturday, Sunday,

or legal holiday, as listed in section 1.14 of the Revised Code, may be held in a detention facility until the next succeeding day that is not a Saturday, Sunday, or legal holiday.

**HISTORY: 148 v S 179, § 3. Eff 1-1-2002; 2011 SB 122, § 1, eff. June 30, 2011.**

Acts 2011, SB 122, § 4 provides: "This act is hereby declared to be an emergency measure necessary for the immediate preservation of the public peace, health, and safety. The reason for such necessity is that Ohio is one of only five states that have not yet enacted the Interstate Compact for Juveniles, which in most states has replaced the Interstate Compact on Juveniles. The rule that allows Ohio to cooperate with the member states of the new compact in the supervision of delinquent youth and the return of escapees, absconders, and runaways will expire on June 30, 2011. It is imperative that this act take effect by that date. Therefore, this act shall go into immediate effect."

**Not analogous to former RC § 2151.31.2, amended and renumbered RC § 2152.26 in 148 v S 179, eff 1-1-2002.**

The effective date is set by section 5 of SB 179.

The provisions of § 11 of SB 179 (148 v —) read, in part, as follows:

SECTION 11. * * * Section 2151.312 of the Revised Code is presented in this act as a composite of the section as amended by Sub. H.B. 332, Sub. H.B. 448, and Am. Sub. S.B. 181, all of the 123rd General Assembly, with the new language of none of the acts shown in capital letters. * * * This is in recognition of the principle stated in division (B) of section 1.52 of the Revised Code that such amendments are to be harmonized where not substantively irreconcilable and constitutes a legislative finding that such is the resulting version in effect prior to the effective date of this act.

## § 2151.313 Fingerprints, photographs, and related arrest or custody records.

(A)(1) Except as provided in division (A)(2) of this section and in sections 109.57, 109.60, and 109.61 of the Revised Code, no child shall be fingerprinted or photographed in the investigation of any violation of law without the consent of the juvenile judge.

(2) Subject to division (A)(3) of this section, a law enforcement officer may fingerprint and photograph a child without the consent of the juvenile judge when the child is arrested or otherwise taken into custody for the commission of an act that would be an offense, other than a traffic offense or a minor misdemeanor, if committed by an adult, and there is probable cause to believe that the child may have been involved in the commission of the act. A law enforcement officer who takes fingerprints or photographs of a child under division (A)(2) of this section immediately shall inform the juvenile court that the fingerprints or photographs were taken and shall provide the court with the identity of the child, the number of fingerprints and photographs taken, and the name and address of each person who has custody and control of the fingerprints or photographs or copies of the fingerprints or photographs.

(3) This section does not apply to a child to whom either of the following applies:

(a) The child has been arrested or otherwise taken into custody for committing, or has been adjudicated a delinquent child for committing, an act that would be a felony if committed by an adult or has been convicted of or pleaded guilty to committing a felony.

(b) There is probable cause to believe that the child may have committed an act that would be a felony if committed by an adult.

(B)(1) Subject to divisions (B)(4), (5), and (6) of this section, all fingerprints and photographs of a child obtained or taken under division (A)(1) or (2) of this section, and any records of the arrest or custody of the child that was the basis for the taking of the fingerprints or photographs, initially may be retained only until the expiration of thirty days after the date taken, except that the court may limit the initial retention of fingerprints and photographs of a child obtained under division (A)(1) of this section to a shorter period of time and except that, if the child is adjudicated a delinquent child for the commission of an act described in division (B)(3) of this section or is convicted of or pleads guilty to a criminal offense for the commission of an act described in division (B)(3) of this section, the fingerprints and photographs, and the records of the arrest or custody of the child that was the basis for the taking of the fingerprints and photographs, shall be retained in accordance with division (B)(3) of this section. During the initial period of retention, the fingerprints and photographs of a child, copies of the fingerprints and photographs, and records of the arrest or custody of the child shall be used or released only in accordance with division (C) of this section. At the expiration of the initial period for which fingerprints and photographs of a child, copies of fingerprints and photographs of a child, and records of the arrest or custody of a child may be retained under this division, if no complaint, indictment, or information is pending against the child in relation to the act for which the fingerprints and photographs originally were obtained or taken and if the child has neither been adjudicated a delinquent child for the commission of that act nor been convicted of or pleaded guilty to a criminal offense based on that act subsequent to a transfer of the child's case for criminal prosecution pursuant to section 2152.12 of the Revised Code, the fingerprints and photographs of the child, all copies of the fingerprints and photographs, and all records of the arrest or custody of the child that was the basis of the taking of the fingerprints and photographs shall be removed from the file and delivered to the juvenile court.

(2) If, at the expiration of the initial period of retention set forth in division (B)(1) of this section, a complaint, indictment, or information is pending against the child in relation to the act for which the fingerprints and photographs originally were obtained or the child either has been adjudicated a delinquent child for the commission of an act other than an act described in division (B)(3) of this section or has been convicted of or pleaded guilty to a criminal offense for the commission of an act other than an act described in division (B)(3) of this section subsequent to transfer of the child's case, the fingerprints and photographs of the child, copies of the fingerprints and photographs, and the records of the arrest or custody of the child that was the basis of the taking of the fingerprints and photographs may further be retained, subject to division (B)(4) of this section, until the earlier of the expiration of two years after the date on which the fingerprints or photographs were taken or the child attains eighteen years of age, except that, if the child is adjudicated a delinquent child for the commission of an act described in division (B)(3) of this section or is convicted of or pleads guilty to a criminal offense for the commission of an act described in division (B)(3) of this section, the fingerprints and photographs, and the records of the arrest or custody of the child that was the basis for the taking of the fingerprints and photographs, shall be retained in accordance with division (B)(3) of this section.

Except as otherwise provided in division (B)(3) of this section, during this additional period of retention, the fingerprints and photographs of a child, copies of the fingerprints and photographs of a child, and records of the arrest or custody of a child shall be used or released only in accordance with division (C) of this section. At the expiration of the additional period, if no complaint, indictment, or information is pending against the child in relation to the act for which the fingerprints originally were obtained or taken or in relation to another act for which the fingerprints were used as authorized by division (C) of this section and that would be a felony if committed by an adult, the fingerprints of the child, all copies of the fingerprints, and all records of the arrest or custody of the child that was the basis of the taking of the fingerprints shall be removed from the file and delivered to the juvenile court, and, if no complaint, indictment, or information is pending against the child concerning the act for which the photographs originally were obtained or taken or concerning an act that would be a felony if committed by an adult, the photographs and all copies of the photographs, and, if no fingerprints were taken at the time the photographs were taken, all records of the arrest or custody that was the basis of the taking of the photographs shall be removed from the file and delivered to the juvenile court. In either case, if, at the expiration of the applicable additional period, such a complaint, indictment, or information is pending against the child, the photographs and copies of the photographs of the child, or the fingerprints and copies of the fingerprints of the child, whichever is applicable, and the records of the arrest or custody of the child may be retained, subject to division (B)(4) of this section, until final disposition of the complaint, indictment, or information, and, upon final disposition of the complaint, indictment, or information, they shall be removed from the file and delivered to the juvenile court, except that, if the child is adjudicated a delinquent child for the commission of an act described in division (B)(3) of this section or is convicted of or pleads guilty to a criminal offense for the commission of an act described in division (B)(3) of this section, the fingerprints and photographs, and the records of the arrest or custody of the child that was the basis for the taking of the fingerprints and photographs, shall be retained in accordance with division (B)(3) of this section.

(3) If a child is adjudicated a delinquent child for violating section 2923.42 of the Revised Code or for committing an act that would be a misdemeanor offense of violence if committed by an adult, or is convicted of or pleads guilty to a violation of section 2923.42 of the Revised Code, a misdemeanor offense of violence, or a violation of an existing or former municipal ordinance or law of this state, another state, or the United States that is substantially equivalent to section 2923.42 of the Revised Code or any misdemeanor offense of violence, both of the following apply:

(a) Originals and copies of fingerprints and photographs of the child obtained or taken under division (A)(1) of this section, and any records of the arrest or custody that was the basis for the taking of the fingerprints or photographs, may be retained for the period of time specified by the juvenile judge in that judge's grant of consent for the taking of the fingerprints or photographs. Upon the expiration of the specified period, all originals and copies of the fingerprints, photographs, and records shall be delivered to the juvenile court or otherwise disposed of in accordance with any instructions specified by the juvenile judge in that judge's grant of consent. During the period of retention of the photographs and records, all originals and copies of them shall be retained in a file separate and apart from all photographs taken of adults. During the period of retention of the fingerprints, all originals and copies of them may be maintained in the files of fingerprints taken of adults. If the juvenile judge who grants consent for the taking of fingerprints and photographs under division (A)(1) of this section does not specify a period of retention in that judge's grant of consent, originals and copies of the fingerprints, photographs, and records may be retained in accordance with this section as if the fingerprints and photographs had been taken under division (A)(2) of this section.

(b) Originals and copies of fingerprints and photographs taken under division (A)(2) of this section, and any records of the arrest or custody that was the basis for the taking of the fingerprints or photographs, may be retained for the period of time and in the manner specified in division (B)(3)(b) of this section. Prior to the child's attainment of eighteen years of age, all originals and copies of the photographs and records shall be retained and shall be kept in a file separate and apart from all photographs taken of adults. During the period of retention of the fingerprints, all originals and copies of them may be maintained in the files of fingerprints taken of adults. Upon the child's attainment of eighteen years of age, all originals and copies of the fingerprints, photographs, and records shall be disposed of as follows:

(i) If the juvenile judge issues or previously has issued an order that specifies a manner of disposition of the originals and copies of the fingerprints, photographs, and records, they shall be delivered to the juvenile court or otherwise disposed of in accordance with the order.

(ii) If the juvenile judge does not issue and has not previously issued an order that specifies a manner of disposition of the originals and copies of the fingerprints not maintained in adult files, photographs, and records, the law enforcement agency, in its discretion, either shall remove all originals and copies of them from the file in which they had been maintained and transfer them to the files that are used for the retention of fingerprints and photographs taken of adults who are arrested for, otherwise taken into custody for, or under investigation for the commission of a criminal offense or shall remove them from the file in which they had been maintained and deliver them to the juvenile court. If the originals and copies of any fingerprints of a child who attains eighteen years of age are maintained in the files of fingerprints taken of adults or if pursuant to division (B)(3)(b)(ii) of this section the agency transfers the originals and copies of any fingerprints not maintained in adult files, photographs, or records to the files that are used for the retention of fingerprints and photographs taken of adults who are arrested for, otherwise taken into custody for, or under investigation for the commission of a criminal offense, the originals and copies of the fingerprints, photographs, and records may be maintained, used, and released after they are maintained in the adult files or after the transfer as if the fingerprints and photographs had been taken of, and as if the records pertained to, an adult who was arrested for, otherwise taken into custody for, or under investigation for the commission of a criminal offense.

(4) If a sealing or expungement order issued under sections 2151.356 [2151.35.6] to 2151.358 [2151.35.8] of the Revised Code requires the sealing or destruction of any fingerprints or photographs of a child obtained or taken under division (A)(1) or (2) of this section or of the records of an arrest or custody of a child that was the basis

of the taking of the fingerprints or photographs prior to the expiration of any period for which they otherwise could be retained under division (B)(1), (2), or (3) of this section, the fingerprints, photographs, and arrest or custody records that are subject to the order and all copies of the fingerprints, photographs, and arrest or custody records shall be sealed or destroyed in accordance with the order.

(5) All fingerprints of a child, photographs of a child, records of an arrest or custody of a child, and copies delivered to a juvenile court in accordance with division (B)(1), (2), or (3) of this section shall be destroyed by the court, provided that, if a complaint is filed against the child in relation to any act to which the records pertain, the court shall maintain all records of an arrest or custody of a child so delivered for at least three years after the final disposition of the case or after the case becomes inactive.

(6)(a) All photographs of a child and records of an arrest or custody of a child retained pursuant to division (B) of this section and not delivered to a juvenile court shall be kept in a file separate and apart from fingerprints, photographs, and records of an arrest or custody of an adult. All fingerprints of a child retained pursuant to division (B) of this section and not delivered to a juvenile court may be maintained in the files of fingerprints taken of adults.

(b) If a child who is the subject of photographs or fingerprints is adjudicated a delinquent child for the commission of an act that would be an offense, other than a traffic offense or a minor misdemeanor, if committed by an adult or is convicted of or pleads guilty to a criminal offense, other than a traffic offense or a minor misdemeanor, all fingerprints not maintained in the files of fingerprints taken of adults and all photographs of the child, and all records of the arrest or custody of the child that is the basis of the taking of the fingerprints or photographs, that are retained pursuant to division (B) of this section and not delivered to a juvenile court shall be kept in a file separate and apart from fingerprints, photographs, and arrest and custody records of children who have not been adjudicated a delinquent child for the commission of an act that would be an offense, other than a traffic offense or a minor misdemeanor, if committed by an adult and have not been convicted of or pleaded guilty to a criminal offense other than a traffic offense or a minor misdemeanor.

(C) Until they are delivered to the juvenile court or sealed, transferred in accordance with division (B)(3)(b) of this section, or destroyed pursuant to a sealing or expungement order, the originals and copies of fingerprints and photographs of a child that are obtained or taken pursuant to division (A)(1) or (2) of this section, and the records of the arrest or custody of the child that was the basis of the taking of the fingerprints or photographs, shall be used or released only as follows:

(1) During the initial thirty-day period of retention, originals and copies of fingerprints and photographs of a child, and records of the arrest or custody of a child, shall be used, prior to the filing of a complaint or information against or the obtaining of an indictment of the child in relation to the act for which the fingerprints and photographs were originally obtained or taken, only for the investigation of that act and shall be released, prior to the filing of the complaint, only to a court that would have jurisdiction of the child's case under this chapter. Subsequent to the filing of a complaint or information or the obtaining of an indictment, originals and copies of fingerprints and photographs of a child, and records of the arrest or custody of a child, shall be used or released during the initial thirty-day period of retention only as provided in division (C)(2)(a), (b), or (c) of this section.

(2) Originals and copies of fingerprints and photographs of a child, and records of the arrest or custody of a child, that are retained beyond the initial thirty-day period of retention subsequent to the filing of a complaint or information or the obtaining of an indictment, a delinquent child adjudication, or a conviction of or guilty plea to a criminal offense shall be used or released only as follows:

(a) Originals and copies of photographs of a child, and, if no fingerprints were taken at the time the photographs were taken, records of the arrest or custody of the child that was the basis of the taking of the photographs, may be used only as follows:

(i) They may be used for the investigation of the act for which they originally were obtained or taken; if the child who is the subject of the photographs is a suspect in the investigation, for the investigation of any act that would be an offense if committed by an adult; and for arresting or bringing the child into custody.

(ii) If the child who is the subject of the photographs is adjudicated a delinquent child for the commission of an act that would be a felony if committed by an adult or is convicted of or pleads guilty to a criminal offense that is a felony as a result of the arrest or custody that was the basis of the taking of the photographs, a law enforcement officer may use the photographs for a photo line-up conducted as part of the investigation of any act that would be a felony if committed by an adult, whether or not the child who is the subject of the photographs is a suspect in the investigation.

(b) Originals and copies of fingerprints of a child, and records of the arrest or custody of the child that was the basis of the taking of the fingerprints, may be used only for the investigation of the act for which they originally were obtained or taken; if a child is a suspect in the investigation, for the investigation of another act that would be an offense if committed by an adult; and for arresting or bringing the child into custody.

(c) Originals and copies of fingerprints, photographs, and records of the arrest or custody that was the basis of the taking of the fingerprints or photographs shall be released only to the following:

(i) Law enforcement officers of this state or a political subdivision of this state, upon notification to the juvenile court of the name and address of the law enforcement officer or agency to whom or to which they will be released;

(ii) A court that has jurisdiction of the child's case under Chapters 2151. and 2152. of the Revised Code or subsequent to a transfer of the child's case for criminal prosecution pursuant to section 2152.12 of the Revised Code.

(D) No person shall knowingly do any of the following:

(1) Fingerprint or photograph a child in the investigation of any violation of law other than as provided in division (A)(1) or (2) of this section or in sections 109.57, 109.60, and 109.61 of the Revised Code;

(2) Retain fingerprints or photographs of a child obtained or taken under division (A)(1) or (2) of this section, copies of fingerprints or photographs of that nature, or records of the arrest or custody that was the basis of the taking of fingerprints or photographs of that nature other than in accordance with division (B) of this section;

(3) Use or release fingerprints or photographs of a child obtained or taken under division (A)(1) or (2) of this section, copies of fingerprints or photographs of that nature, or records of the arrest or custody that was the basis of the taking of fingerprints or photographs of that nature other than in accordance with division (B) or (C) of this section.

**HISTORY: 133 v H 320 (Eff 11-19-69); 135 v S 1 (Eff 1-1-74); 137 v H 315 (Eff 3-15-78); 140 v H 258 (Eff 9-26-84); 144 v H 198 (Eff 10-6-92); 146 v H 1 (Eff 1-1-96); 146 v H 445 (Eff 9-3-96); 146 v H 124 (Eff 3-31-97); 147 v H 2 (Eff 1-1-99); 148 v S 181 (Eff 9-4-2000); 148 v S 179, § 3. Eff 1-1-2002; 151 v H 137, § 1, eff. 10-9-06.**

The effective date is set by § 6 of 151 v H 137.
The effective date is set by section 5 of SB 179.

## § 2151.314 Detention or shelter care hearing.

(A) When a child is brought before the court or delivered to a place of detention or shelter care designated by the court, the intake or other authorized officer of the court shall immediately make an investigation and shall release the child unless it appears that the child's detention or shelter care is warranted or required under section 2151.31 of the Revised Code.

If the child is not so released, a complaint under section 2151.27 or 2152.021 [2152.02.1] or an information under section 2152.13 of the Revised Code shall be filed or an indictment under division (B) of section 2152.13 of the Revised Code shall be sought and an informal detention or shelter care hearing held promptly, not later than seventy-two hours after the child is placed in detention or shelter care, to determine whether detention or shelter care is required. Reasonable oral or written notice of the time, place, and purpose of the detention or shelter care hearing shall be given to the child and, if they can be found, to the child's parents, guardian, or custodian. In cases in which the complaint alleges a child to be an abused, neglected, or dependent child, the notice given the parents, guardian, or custodian shall inform them that a case plan may be prepared for the child, the general requirements usually contained in case plans, and the possible consequences of the failure to comply with a journalized case plan.

Prior to the hearing, the court shall inform the parties of their right to counsel and to appointed counsel or to the services of the county public defender or joint county public defender, if they are indigent, of the child's right to remain silent with respect to any allegation of delinquency, and of the name and telephone number of a court employee who can be contacted during the normal business hours of the court to arrange for the prompt appointment of counsel for any party who is indigent. Unless it appears from the hearing that the child's detention or shelter care is required under the provisions of section 2151.31 of the Revised Code, the court shall order the child's release as provided by section 2151.311 [2151.31.1] of the Revised Code. If a parent, guardian, or custodian has not been so notified and did not appear or waive appearance at the hearing, upon the filing of an affidavit stating these facts, the court shall rehear the matter without unnecessary delay.

(B) When the court conducts a hearing pursuant to division (A) of this section, all of the following apply:

(1) The court shall determine whether an alleged abused, neglected, or dependent child should remain or be placed in shelter care;

(2) The court shall determine whether there are any relatives of the child who are willing to be temporary custodians of the child. If any relative is willing to be a temporary custodian, the child would otherwise be placed or retained in shelter care, and the appointment is appropriate, the court shall appoint the relative as temporary custodian of the child, unless the court appoints another relative as temporary custodian. If it determines that the appointment of a relative as custodian would not be appropriate, it shall issue a written opinion setting forth the reasons for its determination and give a copy of the opinion to all parties and to the guardian ad litem of the child.

The court's consideration of a relative for appointment as a temporary custodian does not make that relative a party to the proceedings.

(3) The court shall comply with section 2151.419 [2151.41.9] of the Revised Code.

(C) If a child is in shelter care following the filing of a complaint pursuant to section 2151.27 or 2152.021 [2152.02.1] of the Revised Code, the filing of an information, or the obtaining of an indictment or following a hearing held pursuant to division (A) of this section, any party, including the public children services agency, and the guardian ad litem of the child may file a motion with the court requesting that the child be released from shelter care. The motion shall state the reasons why the child should be released from shelter care and, if a hearing has been held pursuant to division (A) of this section, any changes in the situation of the child or the parents, guardian, or custodian of the child that have occurred since that hearing and that justify the release of the child from shelter care. Upon the filing of the motion, the court shall hold a hearing in the same manner as under division (A) of this section.

(D) Each juvenile court shall designate at least one court employee to assist persons who are indigent in obtaining appointed counsel. The court shall include in each notice given pursuant to division (A) or (C) of this section and in each summons served upon a party pursuant to this chapter, the name and telephone number at which each designated employee can be contacted during the normal business hours of the court to arrange for prompt appointment of counsel for indigent persons.

**HISTORY: 133 v H 320 (Eff 11-19-69); 136 v H 164 (Eff 1-13-76); 142 v S 89 (Eff 1-1-89); 146 v H 274 (Eff 8-8-96); 147 v H 484 (Eff 3-18-99); 148 v H 176 (Eff 10-29-99); 148 v S 179, § 3 (Eff 1-1-2002); 149 v H 393. Eff 7-5-2002.**

## § 2151.315 Amended and renumbered RC § 2152.74 in 148 v S 179. Eff 1-1-2002.

The effective date is set by section 5 of SB 179.

## § 2151.32 Selection of custodian.

In placing a child under any guardianship or custody other than that of its parent, the juvenile court shall, when practicable, select a person or an institution or agency governed by persons of like religious faith as that of the parents of such child, or in case of a difference in the religious faith of the parents, then of the religious faith of the child, or if the religious faith of the child is not ascertained, then of either of the parents.

**HISTORY: GC § 1639-33; 117 v 520(531); Bureau of Code Revision. Eff 10-1-53.**

**§ 2151.33 Temporary care; emergency medical treatment; reimbursement.**

(A) Pending hearing of a complaint filed under section 2151.27 of the Revised Code or a motion filed or made under division (B) of this section and the service of citations, the juvenile court may make any temporary disposition of any child that it considers necessary to protect the best interest of the child and that can be made pursuant to division (B) of this section. Upon the certificate of one or more reputable practicing physicians, the court may summarily provide for emergency medical and surgical treatment that appears to be immediately necessary to preserve the health and well-being of any child concerning whom a complaint or an application for care has been filed, pending the service of a citation upon the child's parents, guardian, or custodian. The court may order the parents, guardian, or custodian, if the court finds the parents, guardian, or custodian able to do so, to reimburse the court for the expense involved in providing the emergency medical or surgical treatment. Any person who disobeys the order for reimbursement may be adjudged in contempt of court and punished accordingly.

If the emergency medical or surgical treatment is furnished to a child who is found at the hearing to be a nonresident of the county in which the court is located and if the expense of the medical or surgical treatment cannot be recovered from the parents, legal guardian, or custodian of the child, the board of county commissioners of the county in which the child has a legal settlement shall reimburse the court for the reasonable cost of the emergency medical or surgical treatment out of its general fund.

(B)(1) After a complaint, petition, writ, or other document initiating a case dealing with an alleged or adjudicated abused, neglected, or dependent child is filed and upon the filing or making of a motion pursuant to division (C) of this section, the court, prior to the final disposition of the case, may issue any of the following temporary orders to protect the best interest of the child:

(a) An order granting temporary custody of the child to a particular party;

(b) An order for the taking of the child into custody pursuant to section 2151.31 of the Revised Code pending the outcome of the adjudicatory and dispositional hearings;

(c) An order granting, limiting, or eliminating parenting time or visitation rights with respect to the child;

(d) An order requiring a party to vacate a residence that will be lawfully occupied by the child;

(e) An order requiring a party to attend an appropriate counseling program that is reasonably available to that party;

(f) Any other order that restrains or otherwise controls the conduct of any party which conduct would not be in the best interest of the child.

(2) Prior to the final disposition of a case subject to division (B)(1) of this section, the court shall do both of the following:

(a) Issue an order pursuant to Chapters 3119. to 3125. of the Revised Code requiring the parents, guardian, or person charged with the child's support to pay support for the child.

(b) Issue an order requiring the parents, guardian, or person charged with the child's support to continue to maintain any health insurance coverage for the child that existed at the time of the filing of the complaint, petition, writ, or other document, or to obtain health insurance coverage in accordance with sections 3119.29 to 3119.56 of the Revised Code.

(C)(1) A court may issue an order pursuant to division (B) of this section upon its own motion or if a party files a written motion or makes an oral motion requesting the issuance of the order and stating the reasons for it. Any notice sent by the court as a result of a motion pursuant to this division shall contain a notice that any party to a juvenile proceeding has the right to be represented by counsel and to have appointed counsel if the person is indigent.

(2) If a child is taken into custody pursuant to section 2151.31 of the Revised Code and placed in shelter care, the public children services agency or private child placing agency with which the child is placed in shelter care shall file or make a motion as described in division (C)(1) of this section before the end of the next day immediately after the date on which the child was taken into custody and, at a minimum, shall request an order for temporary custody under division (B)(1)(a) of this section.

(3) A court that issues an order pursuant to division (B)(1)(b) of this section shall comply with section 2151.419 [2151.41.9] of the Revised Code.

(D) The court may grant an ex parte order upon its own motion or a motion filed or made pursuant to division (C) of this section requesting such an order if it appears to the court that the best interest and the welfare of the child require that the court issue the order immediately. The court, if acting on its own motion, or the person requesting the granting of an ex parte order, to the extent possible, shall give notice of its intent or of the request to the parents, guardian, or custodian of the child who is the subject of the request. If the court issues an ex parte order, the court shall hold a hearing to review the order within seventy-two hours after it is issued or before the end of the next day after the day on which it is issued, whichever occurs first. The court shall give written notice of the hearing to all parties to the action and shall appoint a guardian ad litem for the child prior to the hearing.

The written notice shall be given by all means that are reasonably likely to result in the party receiving actual notice and shall include all of the following:

(1) The date, time, and location of the hearing;

(2) The issues to be addressed at the hearing;

(3) A statement that every party to the hearing has a right to counsel and to court-appointed counsel, if the party is indigent;

(4) The name, telephone number, and address of the person requesting the order;

(5) A copy of the order, except when it is not possible to obtain it because of the exigent circumstances in the case.

If the court does not grant an ex parte order pursuant to a motion filed or made pursuant to division (C) of this section or its own motion, the court shall hold a shelter care hearing on the motion within ten days after the motion is filed. The court shall give notice of the hearing to all affected parties in the same manner as set forth in the Juvenile Rules.

(E) The court, pending the outcome of the adjudicatory and dispositional hearings, shall not issue an order granting temporary custody of a child to a public children services agency or private child placing agency pursuant to this section, unless the court determines and specifically states in the order that the continued residence of the child in the child's current home will be contrary to the child's best interest and welfare and the court complies with section 2151.419 [2151.41.9] of the Revised Code.

(F) Each public children services agency and private child placing agency that receives temporary custody of a child pursuant to this section shall maintain in the child's case record written documentation that it has placed the child, to the extent that it is consistent with the best interest, welfare, and special needs of the child, in the most family-like setting available and in close proximity to the home of the parents, custodian, or guardian of the child.

(G) For good cause shown, any court order that is issued pursuant to this section may be reviewed by the court at any time upon motion of any party to the action or upon the motion of the court.

**HISTORY: GC § 1639-28; 117 v 520; 119 v 731; 121 v 557; Bureau of Code Revision, 10-1-53; 142 v S 89 (Eff 1-1-89); 146 v H 274 (Eff 8-8-96); 147 v H 352 (Eff 1-1-98); 147 v H 484 (Eff 3-18-99); 148 v H 176 (Eff 10-29-99); 148 v S 180 (Eff 3-22-2001); 149 v H 657. Eff 12-13-2002.**

## § 2151.331 Placement options for alleged or adjudicated abused, neglected, dependent or unruly child.

A child alleged to be or adjudicated an abused, neglected, dependent, or unruly child or a juvenile traffic offender may be detained after a complaint is filed in a certified foster home for a period not exceeding sixty days or until the final disposition of the case, whichever comes first. The court also may arrange with a public children services agency or private child placing agency to receive, or with a private noncustodial agency for temporary care of, the child within the jurisdiction of the court. A child alleged to be or adjudicated an unruly child also may be assigned to an alternative diversion program established by the court for a period not exceeding sixty days after a complaint is filed or until final disposition of the case, whichever comes first.

If the court arranges for the board of a child temporarily detained in a certified foster home or arranges for the board of a child through a private child placing agency, the board of county commissioners shall pay a reasonable sum, which the court shall fix, for the board of the child. In order to have certified foster homes available for service, an agreed monthly subsidy may be paid in addition to a fixed rate per day for care of a child actually residing in the certified foster home.†

**HISTORY: 146 v H 265 (Eff 3-3-97); 148 v H 448 (Eff 10-5-2000); 148 v H 332. Eff 1-1-2001.**

† The amendments made by HB 448 (148 v —), effective 10-5-2000 and HB 332 (148 v —), effective 1-1-2001 are the same. The word "family" before "foster home" is deleted in both amendments.

The effective date is set by section 5 of HB 332.

## [DISTRICT DETENTION HOMES]

## § 2151.34 Procedure for obtaining criminal protection order against person under 18 years of age.

(A) As used in this section:

(1) "Court" means the juvenile division of the court of common pleas of the county in which the person to be protected by the protection order resides.

(2) "Victim advocate" means a person who provides support and assistance for a person who files a petition under this section.

(3) "Family or household member" has the same meaning as in section 3113.31 of the Revised Code.

(4) "Protection order issued by a court of another state" has the same meaning as in section 2919.27 of the Revised Code.

(5) "Petitioner" means a person who files a petition under this section and includes a person on whose behalf a petition under this section is filed.

(6) "Respondent" means a person who is under eighteen years of age and against whom a petition is filed under this section.

(7) "Sexually oriented offense" has the same meaning as in section 2950.01 of the Revised Code.

(8) "Electronic monitoring" has the same meaning as in section 2929.01 of the Revised Code.

(B) The court has jurisdiction over all proceedings under this section.

(C)(1) Any of the following persons may seek relief under this section by filing a petition with the court:

(a) Any person on behalf of that person;

(b) Any parent or adult family or household member on behalf of any other family or household member;

(c) Any person who is determined by the court in its discretion as an appropriate person to seek relief under this section on behalf of any child.

(2) The petition shall contain or state all of the following:

(a) An allegation that the respondent engaged in a violation of section 2903.11, 2903.12, 2903.13, 2903.21, 2903.211 [2903.21.1], 2903.22, or 2911.211 [2911.21.1] of the Revised Code, committed a sexually oriented offense, or engaged in a violation of any municipal ordinance that is substantially equivalent to any of those offenses against the person to be protected by the protection order, including a description of the nature and extent of the violation;

(b) If the petitioner seeks relief in the form of electronic monitoring of the respondent, an allegation that at any time preceding the filing of the petition the respondent engaged in conduct that would cause a reasonable person to believe that the health, welfare, or safety of the person to be protected was at risk, a description of the nature and extent of that conduct, and an allegation that the respondent presents a continuing danger to the person to be protected;

(c) A request for relief under this section.

(3) The court in its discretion may determine whether or not to give notice that a petition has been filed under division (C)(1) of this section on behalf of a child to any of the following:

(a) A parent of the child if the petition was filed by any person other than a parent of the child;

(b) Any person who is determined by the court to be an appropriate person to receive notice of the filing of the petition.

(D)(1) If a person who files a petition pursuant to this section requests an ex parte order, the court shall hold an ex parte hearing as soon as possible after the petition is filed, but not later than the next day after the court is in session after the petition is filed. The court, for good cause shown at the ex parte hearing, may enter any temporary orders, with or without bond, that the court finds necessary for the safety and protection of the person to be protected by the order. Immediate and present danger to the person to be protected by the protection order constitutes good cause for purposes of this section. Immediate and present danger includes, but is not limited to, situations in which the respondent has threatened the person to be protected by the protection order with bodily harm or in which the respondent previously has been convicted of, pleaded guilty to, or been adjudicated a delinquent child for committing a violation of section 2903.11, 2903.12, 2903.13, 2903.21, 2903.211 [2903.21.1], 2903.22, or 2911.211 [2911.21.1] of the Revised Code, a sexually oriented offense, or a violation of any municipal ordinance that is substantially equivalent to any of those offenses against the person to be protected by the protection order.

(2)(a) If the court, after an ex parte hearing, issues a protection order described in division (E) of this section, the court shall schedule a full hearing for a date that is within ten court days after the ex parte hearing. The court shall give the respondent notice of, and an opportunity to be heard at, the full hearing. The court also shall give notice of the full hearing to the parent, guardian, or legal custodian of the respondent. The court shall hold the full hearing on the date scheduled under this division unless the court grants a continuance of the hearing in accordance with this division. Under any of the following circumstances or for any of the following reasons, the court may grant a continuance of the full hearing to a reasonable time determined by the court:

(i) Prior to the date scheduled for the full hearing under this division, the respondent has not been served with the petition filed pursuant to this section and notice of the full hearing.

(ii) The parties consent to the continuance.

(iii) The continuance is needed to allow a party to obtain counsel.

(iv) The continuance is needed for other good cause.

(b) An ex parte order issued under this section does not expire because of a failure to serve notice of the full hearing upon the respondent before the date set for the full hearing under division (D)(2)(a) of this section or because the court grants a continuance under that division.

(3) If a person who files a petition pursuant to this section does not request an ex parte order, or if a person requests an ex parte order but the court does not issue an ex parte order after an ex parte hearing, the court shall proceed as in a normal civil action and grant a full hearing on the matter.

(E)(1)(a) After an ex parte or full hearing, the court may issue any protection order, with or without bond, that contains terms designed to ensure the safety and protection of the person to be protected by the protection order.

(b) After a full hearing, if the court considering a petition that includes an allegation of the type described in division (C)(2)(b) of this section or the court, upon its own motion, finds upon clear and convincing evidence that the petitioner reasonably believed that the respondent's conduct at any time preceding the filing of the petition endangered the health, welfare, or safety of the person to be protected and that the respondent presents a continuing danger to the person to be protected and if division (N) of this section does not prohibit the issuance of an order that the respondent be electronically monitored, the court may order that the respondent be electronically monitored for a period of time and under the terms and conditions that the court determines are appropriate. Electronic monitoring shall be in addition to any other relief granted to the petitioner.

(2)(a) Any protection order issued pursuant to this section shall be valid until a date certain but not later than the date the respondent attains nineteen years of age.

(b) Any protection order issued pursuant to this section may be renewed in the same manner as the original order was issued.

(3) A court may not issue a protection order that requires a petitioner to do or to refrain from doing an act that the court may require a respondent to do or to refrain from doing under division (E)(1) of this section unless all of the following apply:

(a) The respondent files a separate petition for a protection order in accordance with this section.

(b) The petitioner is served with notice of the respondent's petition at least forty-eight hours before the court holds a hearing with respect to the respondent's petition, or the petitioner waives the right to receive this notice.

(c) If the petitioner has requested an ex parte order pursuant to division (D) of this section, the court does not delay any hearing required by that division beyond the time specified in that division in order to consolidate the hearing with a hearing on the petition filed by the respondent.

(d) After a full hearing at which the respondent presents evidence in support of the request for a protection order and the petitioner is afforded an opportunity to defend against that evidence, the court determines that the petitioner has committed a violation of section 2903.11, 2903.12, 2903.13, 2903.21, 2903.211 [2903.21.1], 2903.22, or 2911.211 [2911.21.1] of the Revised Code, a sexually oriented offense, or a violation of any municipal ordinance that is substantially equivalent to any of those offenses against the person to be protected by the protection order issued pursuant to division (E)(3) of this section, or has violated a protection order issued pursuant to this section or section 2903.213 [2903.21.3] of the Revised Code relative to the person to be protected by the protection order issued pursuant to division (E)(3) of this section.

(4) No protection order issued pursuant to this section shall in any manner affect title to any real property.

(5)(a) A protection order issued under this section shall clearly state that the person to be protected by the order cannot waive or nullify by invitation or consent any requirement in the order.

(b) Division (E)(5)(a) of this section does not limit any discretion of a court to determine that a respondent alleged to have violated section 2919.27 of the Revised Code, violated a municipal ordinance substantially equivalent to that section, or committed contempt of court, which allegation is based on an alleged violation of a protection order issued under this section, did not commit the violation or was not in contempt of court.

(6) Any protection order issued pursuant to this section shall include a provision that the court will automatically seal all of the records of the proceeding in which the order is issued on the date the respondent attains the age of nineteen years unless the petitioner provides the court with evidence that the respondent has not complied with all of the terms of the protection order. The protection order shall specify the date when the respondent attains the age of nineteen years.

(F)(1) The court shall cause the delivery of a copy of any protection order that is issued under this section to the petitioner, to the respondent, and to all law enforcement agencies that have jurisdiction to enforce the order. The court shall direct that a copy of the order be delivered to the respondent and the parent, guardian, or legal custodian of the respondent on the same day that the order is entered.

(2) Upon the issuance of a protection order under this section, the court shall provide the parties to the order with the following notice orally or by form:

"NOTICE

As a result of this order, it may be unlawful for you to possess or purchase a firearm, including a rifle, pistol, or revolver, or ammunition pursuant to federal law under 18 U.S.C. 922(g)(8). If you have any questions whether this law makes it illegal for you to possess or purchase a firearm or ammunition, you should consult an attorney."

(3) All law enforcement agencies shall establish and maintain an index for the protection orders delivered to the agencies pursuant to division (F)(1) of this section. With respect to each order delivered, each agency shall note on the index the date and time that it received the order.

(4) Regardless of whether the petitioner has registered the protection order in the county in which the officer's agency has jurisdiction pursuant to division (M) of this section, any officer of a law enforcement agency shall enforce a protection order issued pursuant to this section by any court in this state in accordance with the provisions of the order, including removing the respondent from the premises, if appropriate.

(G) Any proceeding under this section shall be conducted in accordance with the Rules of Civil Procedure, except that a protection order may be obtained under this section with or without bond. An order issued under this section, other than an ex parte order, that grants a protection order, or that refuses to grant a protection order, is a final, appealable order. The remedies and procedures provided in this section are in addition to, and not in lieu of, any other available civil or criminal remedies or any other available remedies under Chapter 2151. or 2152. of the Revised Code.

(H) The filing of proceedings under this section does not excuse a person from filing any report or giving any notice required by section 2151.421 [2151.42.1] of the Revised Code or by any other law.

(I) Any law enforcement agency that investigates an alleged violation of section 2903.11, 2903.12, 2903.13, 2903.21, 2903.211 [2903.21.1], 2903.22, or 2911.211 [2911.21.1] of the Revised Code, an alleged commission of a sexually oriented offense, or an alleged violation of a municipal ordinance that is substantially equivalent to any of those offenses shall provide information to the victim and the family or household members of the victim regarding the relief available under this section.

(J) Notwithstanding any provision of law to the contrary and regardless of whether a protection order is issued or a consent agreement is approved by a court of another county or by a court of another state, no court or unit of state or local government shall charge any fee, cost, deposit, or money in connection with the filing of a petition pursuant to this section, in connection with the filing, issuance, registration, or service of a protection order or consent agreement, or for obtaining a certified copy of a protection order or consent agreement.

(K)(1) A person who violates a protection order issued under this section is subject to the following sanctions:

(a) A delinquent child proceeding or a criminal prosecution for a violation of section 2919.27 of the Revised Code, if the violation of the protection order constitutes a violation of that section;

(b) Punishment for contempt of court.

(2) The punishment of a person for contempt of court for violation of a protection order issued under this section does not bar criminal prosecution of the person or a delinquent child proceeding concerning the person for a violation of section 2919.27 of the Revised Code. However, a person punished for contempt of court is entitled to credit for the punishment imposed upon conviction of or adjudication as a delinquent child for a violation of that section, and a person convicted of or adjudicated a delinquent child for a violation of that section shall not subsequently be punished for contempt of court arising out of the same activity.

(L) In all stages of a proceeding under this section, a petitioner may be accompanied by a victim advocate.

(M)(1) A petitioner who obtains a protection order under this section may provide notice of the issuance or approval of the order to the judicial and law enforcement officials in any county other than the county in which the order is issued by registering that order in the other county pursuant to division (M)(2) of this section and filing a copy of the registered order with a law enforcement agency in the other county in accordance with that division. A person who obtains a protection order issued by a court of another state may provide notice of the issuance of the order to the judicial and law enforcement officials in any county of this state by registering the order in that county pursuant to section 2919.272 [2919.27.2] of the Revised Code and filing a copy of the registered order with a law enforcement agency in that county.

(2) A petitioner may register a protection order issued pursuant to this section in a county other than the county in which the court that issued the order is located in the following manner:

(a) The petitioner shall obtain a certified copy of the order from the clerk of the court that issued the order and present that certified copy to the clerk of the court of common pleas or the clerk of a municipal court or county court in the county in which the order is to be registered.

(b) Upon accepting the certified copy of the order for registration, the clerk of the court of common pleas, municipal court, or county court shall place an endorsement of registration on the order and give the petitioner a copy of the order that bears that proof of registration.

(3) The clerk of each court of common pleas, municipal court, or county court shall maintain a registry of certified copies of protection orders that have been issued by courts in other counties pursuant to this section and that have been registered with the clerk.

(N) If the court orders electronic monitoring of the respondent under this section, the court shall direct the sheriff's office or any other appropriate law enforcement agency to install the electronic monitoring device and to monitor the respondent. Unless the court determines that the respondent is indigent, the court shall order the respondent to pay the cost of the installation and monitoring of the electronic monitoring device. If the court determines that the respondent is indigent and subject to the maximum amount allowable to be paid in any year from the fund and the rules promulgated by the attorney general under section 2903.214 [2903.21.4] of the Revised Code, the cost of the installation and monitoring of the electronic monitoring device may be paid out of funds from the reparations fund created pursuant to section 2743.191 [2743.19.1] of the Revised Code. The total amount paid from the reparations fund created pursuant to section 2743.191 of the Revised Code for electronic monitoring under this section and sections 2903.214 [2903.21.4] and 2919.27 of the Revised Code shall not exceed three hundred thousand dollars per year. When the total amount paid from the reparations fund in any year for electronic monitoring under those sections equals or exceeds three hundred thousand dollars, the court shall not order pursuant to this section that an indigent respondent be electronically monitored.

(O) The court, in its discretion, may determine if the respondent is entitled to court-appointed counsel in a proceeding under this section.

**HISTORY: 153 v H 10, § 1, eff. 6-17-10.**

**Not analogous to former RC § 2151.34, amended and renumbered to RC § 2152.41 by 148 v S 179, eff 1-1-02.**

**§ 2151.341** Amended and renumbered RC § 2152.43 in 148 v S 179. Eff 1-1-2002.

The effective date is set by section 5 of SB 179.

**§ 2151.342** Repealed, 148 v S 179, § 4 [128 v 1211]. Eff 1-1-2002.

This section concerned district detention home may receive donations and bequests.
The effective date is set by section 5 of SB 179.

**§ 2151.343** Amended and renumbered RC § 2152.44 in 148 v S 179. Eff 1-1-2002.

The effective date is set by section 5 of SB 179.

**§ 2151.344** Repealed, 148 v S 179, § 4 [128 v 1211]. Eff 1-1-2002.

This section concerned meetings.
The effective date is set by section 5 of SB 179.

**§ 2151.345** Repealed, 148 v S 179, § 4 [128 v 1211]. Eff 1-1-2002.

This section concerned superintendent of district detention home; duties.
The effective date is set by section 5 of SB 179.

**§ 2151.346** Repealed, 148 v S 179, § 4 [128 v 1211]. Eff 1-1-2002.

This section concerned district detention homes operated in same manner as county detention homes.
The effective date is set by section 5 of SB 179.

**§ 2151.347** Repealed, 148 v S 179, § 4 [128 v 1211]. Eff 1-1-2002.

This section concerned selection of site.
The effective date is set by section 5 of SB 179.

**§ 2151.348** Repealed, 148 v S 179, § 4 [128 v 1211]. Eff 1-1-2002.

This section concerned each county shall be represented on board of trustees.
The effective date is set by section 5 of SB 179.

**§ 2151.349** Repealed, 148 v S 179, § 4 [128 v 1211]. Eff 1-1-2002.

This section concerned removal of trustees.
The effective date is set by section 5 of SB 179.

**§ 2151.3410** Repealed, 148 v S 179, § 4 [128 v 1211; 129 v 582(738)]. Eff 1-1-2002.

This section concerned interim powers of board of trustees.
The effective date is set by section 5 of SB 179.

**§ 2151.3411** Repealed, 148 v S 179, § 4 [128 v 1211]. Eff 1-1-2002.

This section concerned joint board of county commissioners; powers and duties.
The effective date is set by section 5 of SB 179.

**§ 2151.3412** Repealed, 148 v S 179, § 4 [128 v 1211; 134 v H 258; 136 v H 1196; 142 v H 365]. Eff 1-1-2002.

This section concerned appraisal of district detention home's site and buildings; funding of expenses.
The effective date is set by section 5 of SB 179.

**§ 2151.3413** Repealed, 148 v S 179, § 4 [128 v 1211; 134 v H 258]. Eff 1-1-2002.

This section concerned withdrawal by county from detention home district; continuity of district tax levy.
The effective date is set by section 5 of SB 179.

**§ 2151.3414** Repealed, 148 v S 179, § 4 [128 v 1211; 134 v H 258; 135 v H 1033]. Eff 1-1-2002.

This section concerned designation of fiscal officer of detention home district; adjustment of accounts.
The effective date is set by section 5 of SB 179.

**§ 2151.3415** Repealed, 148 v S 179, § 4 [128 v 1211]. Eff 1-1-2002.

This section concerned board of county commissioners; expenses.
The effective date is set by section 5 of SB 179.

**§ 2151.3416** Repealed, 148 v S 179, § 4 [133 v H 1135; 139 v H 440]. Eff 1-1-2002.

This section concerned financial assistance for home.
The effective date is set by section 5 of SB 179.

**§ 2151.35 Hearing procedure; recording of proceedings; dispositional hearing.**

(A)(1) Except as otherwise provided by division (A)(3) of this section or in section 2152.13 of the Revised Code, the juvenile court may conduct its hearings in an informal manner and may adjourn its hearings from time to time. The court may exclude the general public from its hearings in a particular case if the court holds a separate hearing to determine whether that exclusion is appropriate. If the court decides that exclusion of the general public is appropriate, the court still may admit to a particular hearing or all of the hearings relating to a particular case those persons who have a direct interest in the case and those who demonstrate that their need for access outweighs the interest in keeping the hearing closed.

Except cases involving children who are alleged to be unruly or delinquent children for being habitual or chronic truants and except as otherwise provided in section 2152.13 of the Revised Code, all cases involving children shall be heard separately and apart from the trial of cases against adults. The court may excuse the attendance of the child at the hearing in cases involving abused, neglected, or dependent children. The court shall hear and determine all cases of children without a jury, except cases involving serious youthful offenders under section 2152.13 of the Revised Code.

If a complaint alleges a child to be a delinquent child, unruly child, or juvenile traffic offender, the court shall require the parent, guardian, or custodian of the child to attend all proceedings of the court regarding the child. If a parent, guardian, or custodian fails to so attend, the court may find the parent, guardian, or custodian in contempt.

If the court finds from clear and convincing evidence that the child violated section 2151.87 of the Revised Code, the court shall proceed in accordance with divisions (F) and (G) of that section.

If the court at the adjudicatory hearing finds from clear and convincing evidence that the child is an abused, neglected, or dependent child, the court shall proceed, in accordance with division (B) of this section, to hold a dispositional hearing and hear the evidence as to the proper disposition to be made under section 2151.353 [2151.35.3] of the Revised Code. If the court at the adjudicatory hearing finds beyond a reasonable doubt that the child is a delinquent or unruly child or a juvenile traffic offender, the court shall proceed immediately, or at a postponed hearing, to hear the evidence as to the proper disposition to be made under section 2151.354 [2151.35.4] or Chapter 2152. of the Revised Code. If the court at the adjudicatory hearing finds beyond a reasonable doubt that the child is an unruly child for being an habitual truant, or that the child is an unruly child for being an habitual truant and that the parent, guardian, or other person having care of the child has failed to cause the child's attendance at school in violation of section 3321.38 of the Revised Code, the court shall proceed to hold a hearing to hear the evidence as to the proper disposition to be made in regard to the child under division (C)(1) of section 2151.354 [2151.35.4] of the Revised Code and the proper action to take in regard to the parent, guardian, or other person having care of the child under division (C)(2) of section 2151.354 [2151.35.4] of the Revised Code. If the court at the adjudicatory hearing finds beyond a reasonable doubt that the child is a delinquent child for being a chronic truant or for being an habitual truant who previously has been adjudicated an unruly child for being an habitual truant, or that the child is a delinquent child for either of those reasons and the parent, guardian, or other person having care of the child has failed to cause the child's attendance at school in violation of section 3321.38 of the Revised Code, the court shall proceed to hold a hearing to hear the evidence as to the proper disposition to be made in regard to the child under division (A)(7)(a) of section 2152.19 of the Revised Code and the proper action to take in regard to the parent, guardian, or other person having care of the child under division (A)(7)(b) of section 2152.19 of the Revised Code.

If the court does not find the child to have violated section 2151.87 of the Revised Code or to be an abused, neglected, dependent, delinquent, or unruly child or a juvenile traffic offender, it shall order that the case be dismissed and that the child be discharged from any detention or restriction theretofore ordered.

(2) A record of all testimony and other oral proceedings in juvenile court shall be made in all proceedings that are held pursuant to section 2151.414 [2151.41.4] of the Revised Code or in which an order of disposition may be made pursuant to division (A)(4) of section 2151.353 [2151.35.3] of the Revised Code, and shall be made upon request in any other proceedings. The record shall be made as provided in section 2301.20 of the Revised Code.

(3) The authority of a juvenile court to exclude the general public from its hearings that is provided by division (A)(1) of this section does not limit or affect any right of a victim of a crime or delinquent act, or of a victim's representative, under Chapter 2930. of the Revised Code.

(B)(1) If the court at an adjudicatory hearing determines that a child is an abused, neglected, or dependent child, the court shall not issue a dispositional order until after the court holds a separate dispositional hearing. The court may hold the dispositional hearing for an adjudicated abused, neglected, or dependent child immediately after the adjudicatory hearing if all parties were served prior to the adjudicatory hearing with all documents required for the dispositional hearing. The dispositional hearing may not be held more than thirty days after the adjudicatory hearing is held. The court, upon the request of any party or the guardian ad litem of the child, may continue a dispositional hearing for a reasonable time not to exceed the time limits set forth in this division to enable a party to obtain or consult counsel. The dispositional hearing shall not be held more than ninety days after the date on which the complaint in the case was filed.

If the dispositional hearing is not held within the period of time required by this division, the court, on its own motion or the motion of any party or the guardian ad litem of the child, shall dismiss the complaint without prejudice.

(2) The dispositional hearing shall be conducted in accordance with all of the following:

(a) The judge or referee who presided at the adjudicatory hearing shall preside, if possible, at the dispositional hearing;

(b) The court may admit any evidence that is material and relevant, including, but not limited to, hearsay, opinion, and documentary evidence;

(c) Medical examiners and each investigator who prepared a social history shall not be cross-examined, except upon consent of the parties, for good cause shown, or as the court in its discretion may direct. Any party may offer evidence supplementing, explaining, or disputing any information contained in the social history or other reports that may be used by the court in determining disposition.

(3) After the conclusion of the dispositional hearing, the court shall enter an appropriate judgment within seven days and shall schedule the date for the hearing to be held pursuant to section 2151.415 [2151.41.5] of the Revised Code. The court may make any order of disposition that is

set forth in section 2151.353 [2151.35.3] of the Revised Code. A copy of the judgment shall be given to each party and to the child's guardian ad litem. If the judgment is conditional, the order shall state the conditions of the judgment. If the child is not returned to the child's own home, the court shall determine which school district shall bear the cost of the child's education and shall comply with section 2151.36 of the Revised Code.

(4) As part of its dispositional order, the court may issue any order described in division (B) of section 2151.33 of the Revised Code.

(C) The court shall give all parties to the action and the child's guardian ad litem notice of the adjudicatory and dispositional hearings in accordance with the Juvenile Rules.

(D) If the court issues an order pursuant to division (A)(4) of section 2151.353 [2151.35.3] of the Revised Code committing a child to the permanent custody of a public children services agency or a private child placing agency, the parents of the child whose parental rights were terminated cease to be parties to the action upon the issuance of the order. This division is not intended to eliminate or restrict any right of the parents to appeal the permanent custody order issued pursuant to division (A)(4) of section 2151.353 [2151.35.3] of the Revised Code.

(E) Each juvenile court shall schedule its hearings in accordance with the time requirements of this chapter.

(F) In cases regarding abused, neglected, or dependent children, the court may admit any statement of a child that the court determines to be excluded by the hearsay rule if the proponent of the statement informs the adverse party of the proponent's intention to offer the statement and of the particulars of the statement, including the name of the declarant, sufficiently in advance of the hearing to provide the party with a fair opportunity to prepare to challenge, respond to, or defend against the statement, and the court determines all of the following:

(1) The statement has circumstantial guarantees of trustworthiness;

(2) The statement is offered as evidence of a material fact;

(3) The statement is more probative on the point for which it is offered than any other evidence that the proponent can procure through reasonable efforts;

(4) The general purposes of the evidence rules and the interests of justice will best be served by the admission of the statement into evidence.

(G) If a child is alleged to be an abused child, the court may order that the testimony of the child be taken by deposition. On motion of the prosecuting attorney, guardian ad litem, or any party, or in its own discretion, the court may order that the deposition be videotaped. Any deposition taken under this division shall be taken with a judge or referee present.

If a deposition taken under this division is intended to be offered as evidence at the hearing, it shall be filed with the court. Part or all of the deposition is admissible in evidence if counsel for all parties had an opportunity and similar motive at the time of the taking of the deposition to develop the testimony by direct, cross, or redirect examination and the judge determines that there is reasonable cause to believe that if the child were to testify in person at the hearing, the child would experience emotional trauma as a result of participating at the hearing.

**HISTORY: 133 v H 320 (Eff 11-19-69); 136 v H 85 (Eff 11-28-75); 138 v H 695 (Eff 10-24-80); 142 v S 89 (Eff 1-1-89); 146 v H 1 (Eff 1-1-96); 146 v H 274 (Eff 8-8-96); 146 v H 124 (Eff 3-31-97); 148 v S 181 (Eff 9-4-2000); 148 v S 218 (Eff 3-15-2001); 148 v S 179, § 1 (Eff 4-9-2001); 148 v S 179, § 3 (Eff 1-1-2002); 149 v H 400. Eff 4-3-2003.**

**Analogous in part to former RC § 2151.35 (GC § 1639-30; 117 v 520; 119 v 731; 121 v 557; Bureau of Code Revision, 10-1-53; 125 v 324; 127 v 547; 130 v 621; 130 v 623; 132 v S 278; 133 v S 49 (eff 8-13-69)) repealed in 133 v H 320, § 2, eff 11-19-69.**

The provisions of § 3 of HB 400 (149 v —) read as follows:

SECTION 3. Section 2151.35 of the Revised Code is presented in Section 1 of this act as a composite of the section as amended by both Am. Sub. S.B. 179 and Sub. S.B. 218 of the 123rd General Assembly. Section 2152.19 of the Revised Code is presented in Section 1 of this act as a composite of the section as amended by both Sub. H.B. 247 and Sub. H.B. 393 of the 124th General Assembly. The General Assembly, applying the principle stated in division (B) of section 1.52 of the Revised Code that amendments are to be harmonized if reasonably capable of simultaneous operation, finds that the composites are the resulting versions of the sections in effect prior to the effective date of the sections as presented in Section 1 of this act.

## § 2151.351 Repealed, 146 v H 265, § 2 [139 v H 440]. Eff 3-3-97.

This section concerned confinement of non-delinquent children. See now RC §§ 2151.33.1, 2151.35.3 and 2151.35.4.

## § 2151.352 Right to counsel.

A child, the child's parents or custodian, or any other person in loco parentis of the child is entitled to representation by legal counsel at all stages of the proceedings under this chapter or Chapter 2152. of the Revised Code. If, as an indigent person, a party is unable to employ counsel, the party is entitled to have counsel provided for the person pursuant to Chapter 120. of the Revised Code except in civil matters in which the juvenile court is exercising jurisdiction pursuant to division (A)(2), (3), (9), (10), (11), (12), or (13); (B)(2), (3), (4), (5), or (6); (C); (D); or (F)(1) or (2) of section 2151.23 of the Revised Code. If a party appears without counsel, the court shall ascertain whether the party knows of the party's right to counsel and of the party's right to be provided with counsel if the party is an indigent person. The court may continue the case to enable a party to obtain counsel, to be represented by the county public defender or the joint county public defender, or to be appointed counsel upon request pursuant to Chapter 120. of the Revised Code. Counsel must be provided for a child not represented by the child's parent, guardian, or custodian. If the interests of two or more such parties conflict, separate counsel shall be provided for each of them.

Section 2935.14 of the Revised Code applies to any child taken into custody. The parents, custodian, or guardian of a child taken into custody, and any attorney at law representing them or the child, shall be entitled to visit the child at any reasonable time, be present at any hearing involving the child, and be given reasonable notice of the hearing.

Any report or part of a report concerning the child, which is used in the hearing and is pertinent to the hearing, shall for good cause shown be made available to any attorney at law representing the child and to any attorney at law representing the parents, custodian, or guardian of the child, upon written request prior to any hearing involving the child.

**HISTORY: 133 v H 320 (Eff 11-19-69); 136 v H 164 (Eff 1-13-76); 148 v S 179, § 3. Eff 1-1-2002; 150 v H 95, § 1, eff. 9-26-03; 151 v H 66, § 101.01, eff. 9-29-05.**

The effective date is set by § 612.03 of 151 v H 66.
The effective date is set by section 179 of H.B. 95 (150 v —).

## § 2151.353 Disposition of abused, neglected or dependent child.

(A) If a child is adjudicated an abused, neglected, or dependent child, the court may make any of the following orders of disposition:

(1) Place the child in protective supervision;

(2) Commit the child to the temporary custody of a public children services agency, a private child placing agency, either parent, a relative residing within or outside the state, or a probation officer for placement in a certified foster home, or in any other home approved by the court;

(3) Award legal custody of the child to either parent or to any other person who, prior to the dispositional hearing, files a motion requesting legal custody of the child or is identified as a proposed legal custodian in a complaint or motion filed prior to the dispositional hearing by any party to the proceedings. A person identified in a complaint or motion filed by a party to the proceedings as a proposed legal custodian shall be awarded legal custody of the child only if the person identified signs a statement of understanding for legal custody that contains at least the following provisions:

(a) That it is the intent of the person to become the legal custodian of the child and the person is able to assume legal responsibility for the care and supervision of the child;

(b) That the person understands that legal custody of the child in question is intended to be permanent in nature and that the person will be responsible as the custodian for the child until the child reaches the age of majority. Responsibility as custodian for the child shall continue beyond the age of majority if, at the time the child reaches the age of majority, the child is pursuing a diploma granted by the board of education or other governing authority, successful completion of the curriculum of any high school, successful completion of an individualized education program developed for the student by any high school, or an age and schooling certificate. Responsibility beyond the age of majority shall terminate when the child ceases to continuously pursue such an education, completes such an education, or is excused from such an education under standards adopted by the state board of education, whichever occurs first.

(c) That the parents of the child have residual parental rights, privileges, and responsibilities, including, but not limited to, the privilege of reasonable visitation, consent to adoption, the privilege to determine the child's religious affiliation, and the responsibility for support;

(d) That the person understands that the person must be present in court for the dispositional hearing in order to affirm the person's intention to become legal custodian, to affirm that the person understands the effect of the custodianship before the court, and to answer any questions that the court or any parties to the case may have.

(4) Commit the child to the permanent custody of a public children services agency or private child placing agency, if the court determines in accordance with division (E) of section 2151.414 [2151.41.4] of the Revised Code that the child cannot be placed with one of the child's parents within a reasonable time or should not be placed with either parent and determines in accordance with division (D)(1) of section 2151.414 [2151.41.4] of the Revised Code that the permanent commitment is in the best interest of the child. If the court grants permanent custody under this division, the court, upon the request of any party, shall file a written opinion setting forth its findings of fact and conclusions of law in relation to the proceeding.

(5) Place the child in a planned permanent living arrangement with a public children services agency or private child placing agency, if a public children services agency or private child placing agency requests the court to place the child in a planned permanent living arrangement and if the court finds, by clear and convincing evidence, that a planned permanent living arrangement is in the best interest of the child and that one of the following exists:

(a) The child, because of physical, mental, or psychological problems or needs, is unable to function in a family-like setting and must remain in residential or institutional care now and for the foreseeable future beyond the date of the dispositional hearing held pursuant to section 2151.35 of the Revised Code.

(b) The parents of the child have significant physical, mental, or psychological problems and are unable to care for the child because of those problems, adoption is not in the best interest of the child, as determined in accordance with division (D)(1) of section 2151.414 [2151.41.4] of the Revised Code, and the child retains a significant and positive relationship with a parent or relative.

(c) The child is sixteen years of age or older, has been counseled on the permanent placement options available to the child, is unwilling to accept or unable to adapt to a permanent placement, and is in an agency program preparing the child for independent living.

(6) Order the removal from the child's home until further order of the court of the person who committed abuse as described in section 2151.031 [2151.03.1] of the Revised Code against the child, who caused or allowed the child to suffer neglect as described in section 2151.03 of the Revised Code, or who is the parent, guardian, or custodian of a child who is adjudicated a dependent child and order any person not to have contact with the child or the child's siblings.

(B) No order for permanent custody or temporary custody of a child or the placement of a child in a planned permanent living arrangement shall be made pursuant to this section unless the complaint alleging the abuse, neglect, or dependency contains a prayer requesting permanent custody, temporary custody, or the placement of the child in a planned permanent living arrangement as desired, the summons served on the parents of the child contains as is appropriate a full explanation that the granting of an order for permanent custody permanently divests them of their parental rights, a full explanation that an adjudication that the child is an abused, neglected, or dependent child may result in an order of temporary custody that will cause the removal of the child from their legal custody until the court terminates the order of temporary custody or permanently divests the parents of their parental rights, or a full explanation that the granting of an order for a planned permanent living arrangement will result in the removal of the child from their legal custody if any of the conditions listed in divisions (A)(5)(a) to (c) of this section are found to exist, and the summons served on the parents contains a full explanation of their right to be represented by counsel and to have counsel appointed pursuant to Chapter 120. of the Revised Code if they are indigent.

If after making disposition as authorized by division (A)(2) of this section, a motion is filed that requests permanent custody of the child, the court may grant permanent custody of the child to the movant in accordance with section 2151.414 [2151.41.4] of the Revised Code.

(C) If the court issues an order for protective supervision pursuant to division (A)(1) of this section, the court may place any reasonable restrictions upon the child, the child's parents, guardian, or custodian, or any other person, including, but not limited to, any of the following:

(1) Order a party, within forty-eight hours after the issuance of the order, to vacate the child's home indefinitely or for a specified period of time;

(2) Order a party, a parent of the child, or a physical custodian of the child to prevent any particular person from having contact with the child;

(3) Issue an order restraining or otherwise controlling the conduct of any person which conduct would not be in the best interest of the child.

(D) As part of its dispositional order, the court shall journalize a case plan for the child. The journalized case plan shall not be changed except as provided in section 2151.412 [2151.41.2] of the Revised Code.

(E)(1) The court shall retain jurisdiction over any child for whom the court issues an order of disposition pursuant to division (A) of this section or pursuant to section 2151.414 [2151.41.4] or 2151.415 [2151.41.5] of the Revised Code until the child attains the age of eighteen years if the child is not mentally retarded, developmentally disabled, or physically impaired, the child attains the age of twenty-one years if the child is mentally retarded, developmentally disabled, or physically impaired, or the child is adopted and a final decree of adoption is issued, except that the court may retain jurisdiction over the child and continue any order of disposition under division (A) of this section or under section 2151.414 [2151.41.4] or 2151.415 [2151.41.5] of the Revised Code for a specified period of time to enable the child to graduate from high school or vocational school. The court shall make an entry continuing its jurisdiction under this division in the journal.

(2) Any public children services agency, any private child placing agency, the department of job and family services, or any party, other than any parent whose parental rights with respect to the child have been terminated pursuant to an order issued under division (A)(4) of this section, by filing a motion with the court, may at any time request the court to modify or terminate any order of disposition issued pursuant to division (A) of this section or section 2151.414 [2151.41.4] or 2151.415 [2151.41.5] of the Revised Code. The court shall hold a hearing upon the motion as if the hearing were the original dispositional hearing and shall give all parties to the action and the guardian ad litem notice of the hearing pursuant to the Juvenile Rules. If applicable, the court shall comply with section 2151.42 of the Revised Code.

(F) Any temporary custody order issued pursuant to division (A) of this section shall terminate one year after the earlier of the date on which the complaint in the case was filed or the child was first placed into shelter care, except that, upon the filing of a motion pursuant to section 2151.415 [2151.41.5] of the Revised Code, the temporary custody order shall continue and not terminate until the court issues a dispositional order under that section. In resolving the motion, the court shall not order an existing temporary custody order to continue beyond two years after the date on which the complaint was filed or the child was first placed into shelter care, whichever date is earlier, regardless of whether any extensions have been previously ordered pursuant to division (D) of section 2151.415 [2151.41.5] of the Revised Code.

(G)(1) No later than one year after the earlier of the date the complaint in the case was filed or the child was first placed in shelter care, a party may ask the court to extend an order for protective supervision for six months or to terminate the order. A party requesting extension or termination of the order shall file a written request for the extension or termination with the court and give notice of the proposed extension or termination in writing before the end of the day after the day of filing it to all parties and the child's guardian ad litem. If a public children services agency or private child placing agency requests termination of the order, the agency shall file a written status report setting out the facts supporting termination of the order at the time it files the request with the court. If no party requests extension or termination of the order, the court shall notify the parties that the court will extend the order for six months or terminate it and that it may do so without a hearing unless one of the parties requests a hearing. All parties and the guardian ad litem shall have seven days from the date a notice is sent pursuant to this division to object to and request a hearing on the proposed extension or termination.

(a) If it receives a timely request for a hearing, the court shall schedule a hearing to be held no later than thirty days after the request is received by the court. The court shall give notice of the date, time, and location of the hearing to all parties and the guardian ad litem. At the hearing, the court shall determine whether extension or termination of the order is in the child's best interest. If termination is in the child's best interest, the court shall terminate the order. If extension is in the child's best interest, the court shall extend the order for six months.

(b) If it does not receive a timely request for a hearing, the court may extend the order for six months or terminate it without a hearing and shall journalize the order of extension or termination not later than fourteen days after receiving the request for extension or termination or after the date the court notifies the parties that it will extend or terminate the order. If the court does not extend or terminate the order, it shall schedule a hearing to be held no later than thirty days after the expiration of the applicable fourteen-day time period and give notice of the date, time, and location of the hearing to all parties and the child's guardian ad litem. At the hearing, the court shall determine whether extension or termination of the order is in the child's best interest. If termination is in the child's best interest, the court shall terminate the order. If extension is in the child's best interest, the court shall issue an order extending the order for protective supervision six months.

(2) If the court grants an extension of the order for protective supervision pursuant to division (G)(1) of this section, a party may, prior to termination of the extension, file with the court a request for an additional extension of six months or for termination of the order. The court and the parties shall comply with division (G)(1) of this section with respect to extending or terminating the order.

(3) If a court grants an extension pursuant to division (G)(2) of this section, the court shall terminate the order for protective supervision at the end of the extension.

(H) The court shall not issue a dispositional order pursuant to division (A) of this section that removes a child from the child's home unless the court complies with section 2151.419 [2151.41.9] of the Revised Code and includes in the dispositional order the findings of fact required by that section.

(I) If a motion or application for an order described in division (A)(6) of this section is made, the court shall not issue the order unless, prior to the issuance of the order, it provides to the person all of the following:

(1) Notice and a copy of the motion or application;

(2) The grounds for the motion or application;

(3) An opportunity to present evidence and witnesses at a hearing regarding the motion or application;

(4) An opportunity to be represented by counsel at the hearing.

(J) The jurisdiction of the court shall terminate one year after the date of the award or, if the court takes any further action in the matter subsequent to the award, the date of the latest further action subsequent to the award, if the court awards legal custody of a child to either of the following:

(1) A legal custodian who, at the time of the award of legal custody, resides in a county of this state other than the county in which the court is located;

(2) A legal custodian who resides in the county in which the court is located at the time of the award of legal custody, but moves to a different county of this state prior to one year after the date of the award or, if the court takes any further action in the matter subsequent to the award, one year after the date of the latest further action subsequent to the award.

The court in the county in which the legal custodian resides then shall have jurisdiction in the matter.†

**HISTORY: 133 v H 320 (Eff 11-19-69); 136 v H 85 (Eff 11-28-75); 138 v H 695 (Eff 10-24-80); 139 v H 440 (Eff 11-23-81); 141 v H 428 (Eff 12-23-86); 142 v S 89 (Eff 1-1-89); 145 v H 152 (Eff 7-1-93); 146 v H 274 (Eff 8-8-96); 146 v H 419 (Eff 9-18-96); 146 v H 265 (Eff 3-3-97); 147 v H 484 (Eff 3-18-99); 148 v H 471 (Eff 7-1-2000); 148 v H 448 (Eff 10-5-2000); 148 v H 332. Eff 1-1-2001; 150 v S 185, § 1, eff. 4-11-05; 151 v S 238, § 1, eff. 9-21-06; 152 v H 7, § 1, eff. 4-7-09.**

## § 2151.354 Disposition of unruly child.

(A) If the child is adjudicated an unruly child, the court may:

(1) Make any of the dispositions authorized under section 2151.353 of the Revised Code;

(2) Place the child on community control under any sanctions, services, and conditions that the court prescribes, as described in division (A)(4) of section 2152.19 of the Revised Code, provided that, if the court imposes a period of community service upon the child, the period of community service shall not exceed one hundred seventy-five hours;

(3) Suspend the driver's license, probationary driver's license, or temporary instruction permit issued to the child for a period of time prescribed by the court and suspend the registration of all motor vehicles registered in the name of the child for a period of time prescribed by the court. A child whose license or permit is so suspended is ineligible for issuance of a license or permit during the period of suspension. At the end of the period of suspension, the child shall not be reissued a license or permit until the child has paid any applicable reinstatement fee and complied with all requirements governing license reinstatement.

(4) Commit the child to the temporary or permanent custody of the court;

(5) Make any further disposition the court finds proper that is consistent with sections 2151.312 and 2151.56 to 2151.59 of the Revised Code;

(6) If, after making a disposition under division (A)(1), (2), or (3) of this section, the court finds upon further hearing that the child is not amenable to treatment or rehabilitation under that disposition, make a disposition otherwise authorized under divisions (A)(1), (4), (5), and (8) of section 2152.19 of the Revised Code that is consistent with sections 2151.312 and 2151.56 to 2151.59 of the Revised Code.

(B) If a child is adjudicated an unruly child for committing any act that, if committed by an adult, would be a drug abuse offense, as defined in section 2925.01 of the Revised Code, or a violation of division (B) of section 2917.11 of the Revised Code, in addition to imposing, in its discretion, any other order of disposition authorized by this section, the court shall do both of the following:

(1) Require the child to participate in a drug abuse or alcohol abuse counseling program;

(2) Suspend the temporary instruction permit, probationary driver's license, or driver's license issued to the child for a period of time prescribed by the court. The court, in its discretion, may terminate the suspension if the child attends and satisfactorily completes a drug abuse or alcohol abuse education, intervention, or treatment program specified by the court. During the time the child is attending a program as described in this division, the court shall retain the child's temporary instruction permit, probationary driver's license, or driver's license, and the court shall return the permit or license if it terminates the suspension.

(C)(1) If a child is adjudicated an unruly child for being an habitual truant, in addition to or in lieu of imposing any other order of disposition authorized by this section, the court may do any of the following:

(a) Order the board of education of the child's school district or the governing board of the educational service center in the child's school district to require the child to attend an alternative school if an alternative school has been established pursuant to section 3313.533 of the Revised Code in the school district in which the child is entitled to attend school;

(b) Require the child to participate in any academic program or community service program;

(c) Require the child to participate in a drug abuse or alcohol abuse counseling program;

(d) Require that the child receive appropriate medical or psychological treatment or counseling;

(e) Make any other order that the court finds proper to address the child's habitual truancy, including an order requiring the child to not be absent without legitimate excuse from the public school the child is supposed to attend for five or more consecutive days, seven or more school days in one school month, or twelve or more school days in a school year and including an order requiring the child to participate in a truancy prevention mediation program.

(2) If a child is adjudicated an unruly child for being an habitual truant and the court determines that the parent, guardian, or other person having care of the child has failed to cause the child's attendance at school in violation of section 3321.38 of the Revised Code, in addition to any

order of disposition authorized by this section, all of the following apply:

(a) The court may require the parent, guardian, or other person having care of the child to participate in any community service program, preferably a community service program that requires the involvement of the parent, guardian, or other person having care of the child in the school attended by the child.

(b) The court may require the parent, guardian, or other person having care of the child to participate in a truancy prevention mediation program.

(c) The court shall warn the parent, guardian, or other person having care of the child that any subsequent adjudication of the child as an unruly or delinquent child for being an habitual or chronic truant may result in a criminal charge against the parent, guardian, or other person having care of the child for a violation of division (C) of section 2919.21 or section 2919.24 of the Revised Code.

**HISTORY: 133 v H 320 (Eff 11-19-69); 142 v H 643 (Eff 3-17-89); 143 v H 330 (Eff 6-30-89); 143 v H 381 (Eff 7-1-89); 143 v S 131 (Eff 7-25-90); 143 v S 258 (Eff 8-22-90); 144 v H 154 (Eff 7-31-92); 146 v H 274 (Eff 8-8-96); 146 v H 265 (Eff 3-3-97); 147 v S 35 (Eff 1-1-99); 148 v S 181 (Eff 9-4-2000); 148 v S 179, § 3 (Eff 1-1-2002); 149 v H 57 (Eff 2-19-2002†); 149 v H 393 (Eff 7-5-2002); 149 v H 400, § 1. Eff 4-3-2003; 149 v S 123, § 1, eff. 1-1-04; 2011 SB 122, § 1, eff. June 30, 2011.**

Acts 2011, SB 122, § 4 provides: "This act is hereby declared to be an emergency measure necessary for the immediate preservation of the public peace, health, and safety. The reason for such necessity is that Ohio is one of only five states that have not yet enacted the Interstate Compact for Juveniles, which in most states has replaced the Interstate Compact on Juveniles. The rule that allows Ohio to cooperate with the member states of the new compact in the supervision of delinquent youth and the return of escapees, absconders, and runaways will expire on June 30, 2011. It is imperative that this act take effect by that date. Therefore, this act shall go into immediate effect."

The effective date is set by section 4 of S.B. 123.

The provisions of § 5 of S.B. 123 (149 v —), as amended by § 3 of H.B. 163 (150 v —), read as follows:

SECTION 5. (A) Notwithstanding division (B) of section 1.58 of the Revised Code, the provisions of the Revised Code amended or enacted in Sections 1 and 2 of Am. Sub. S.B. 123 of the 124th General Assembly shall apply only in relation to conduct and offenses committed on or after January 1, 2004. Conduct and offenses committed prior to January 1, 2004, shall be governed by the law in effect on the date the conduct or offense was committed.

° ° °

† The effective date of sections 1 and 2 of Sub. H.B. 57 (149 v —) differs from the effective date set for the sections by section 3 of the Act. See provisions of OConst art II, §§ 1c and d.

## [SEALING AND EXPUNGEMENT OF RECORDS CONCERNING DELINQUENT AND UNRULY CHILDREN AND JUVENILE TRAFFIC OFFENDERS]

### § 2151.355 Definitions.

As used in sections 2151.356 [2151.35.6] to 2151.358 [2151.35.8] of the Revised Code:

(A) "Expunge" means to destroy, delete, and erase a record, as appropriate for the record's physical or electronic form or characteristic, so that the record is permanently irretrievable.

(B) "Seal a record" means to remove a record from the main file of similar records and to secure it in a separate file that contains only sealed records accessible only to the juvenile court.

**HISTORY: 151 v H 137, § 1, eff. 10-9-06.**

The effective date is set by § 6 of 151 v H 137.

**Not analogous to former RC § 2151.355 (133 v H 320; 133 v H 931; 134 v H 494; 135 v S 324; 135 v H 1067; 136 v H 1196; 137 v H 1; 137 v S 119; 137 v H 565; 139 v H 440; 139 v H 209; 140 v S 210; 142 v H 643; 143 v H 330; 143 v H 381; 143 v H 166; 143 v H 513; 143 v S 131; 143 v H 266; 143 v H 51; 143 v S 258; 144 v H 154; 144 v S 331; 144 v H 725; 145 v H 571; 146 v H 4; 146 v H 1; 146 v S 2; 146 v S 269; 146 v H 274, §§ 1, 4; 146 v H 445; 146 v H 124; 147 v H 215, § 1; 147 v H 215, § 7; 147 v H 1; 147 v H 526, § 1; 147 v S 35; 147 v H 2; 147 v H 526, § 4; 148 v H 3; 148 v S 181; 148 v S 222), repealed 148 v S 179, § 4, eff 1-1-02.**

### § 2151.356 Procedure for sealing records of alleged and adjudicated delinquent and unruly children and adjudicated juvenile traffic offenders.

(A) The records of a case in which a person was adjudicated a delinquent child for committing a violation of section 2903.01, 2903.02, 2907.02, 2907.03, or 2907.05 of the Revised Code shall not be sealed under this section.

(B)(1) The juvenile court shall promptly order the immediate sealing of records pertaining to a juvenile in any of the following circumstances:

(a) If the court receives a record from a public office or agency under division (B)(2) of this section;

(b) If a person was brought before or referred to the court for allegedly committing a delinquent or unruly act and the case was resolved without the filing of a complaint against the person with respect to that act pursuant to section 2151.27 of the Revised Code;

(c) If a person was charged with violating division (E)(1) of section 4301.69 of the Revised Code and the person has successfully completed a diversion program under division (E)(2)(a) of section 4301.69 of the Revised Code with respect to that charge;

(d) If a complaint was filed against a person alleging that the person was a delinquent child, an unruly child, or a juvenile traffic offender and the court dismisses the complaint after a trial on the merits of the case or finds the person not to be a delinquent child, an unruly child, or a juvenile traffic offender;

(e) Notwithstanding division (C) of this section and subject to section 2151.358 [2151.35.8] of the Revised Code, if a person has been adjudicated an unruly child, that person has attained eighteen years of age, and the person is not under the jurisdiction of the court in relation to a complaint alleging the person to be a delinquent child.

(2) The appropriate public office or agency shall immediately deliver all original records at that public office or agency pertaining to a juvenile to the court, if the person was arrested or taken into custody for allegedly committing a delinquent or unruly act, no complaint was filed against the person with respect to the commission of the act pursuant to section 2151.27 of the Revised Code, and the person was not brought before or referred to the court for the commission of the act. The records delivered to the court as required under this division shall not include fingerprints, DNA specimens, and DNA records described under division (A)(3) of section 2151.357 [2151.35.7] of the Revised Code.

(C)(1) The juvenile court shall consider the sealing of records pertaining to a juvenile upon the court's own motion or upon the application of a person if the person has been adjudicated a delinquent child for committing an act other than a violation of section 2903.01, 2903.02, 2907.02, 2907.03, or 2907.05 of the Revised Code, an unruly child, or a juvenile traffic offender and if, at the time of the motion or application, the person is not under the jurisdiction of the court in relation to a complaint alleging the person to be a delinquent child. The motion or application may be made at any time after two years after the later of the following:

(a) The termination of any order made by the court in relation to the adjudication;

(b) The unconditional discharge of the person from the department of youth services with respect to a dispositional order made in relation to the adjudication or from an institution or facility to which the person was committed pursuant to a dispositional order made in relation to the adjudication.

(2) In making the determination whether to seal records pursuant to division (C)(1) of this section, all of the following apply:

(a) The court may require a person filing an application under division (C)(1) of this section to submit any relevant documentation to support the application.

(b) The court may cause an investigation to be made to determine if the person who is the subject of the proceedings has been rehabilitated to a satisfactory degree.

(c) The court shall promptly notify the prosecuting attorney of any proceedings to seal records initiated pursuant to division (C)(1) of this section.

(d)(i) The prosecuting attorney may file a response with the court within thirty days of receiving notice of the sealing proceedings.

(ii) If the prosecuting attorney does not file a response with the court or if the prosecuting attorney files a response but indicates that the prosecuting attorney does not object to the sealing of the records, the court may order the records of the person that are under consideration to be sealed without conducting a hearing on the motion or application. If the court decides in its discretion to conduct a hearing on the motion or application, the court shall conduct the hearing within thirty days after making that decision and shall give notice, by regular mail, of the date, time, and location of the hearing to the prosecuting attorney and to the person who is the subject of the records under consideration.

(iii) If the prosecuting attorney files a response with the court that indicates that the prosecuting attorney objects to the sealing of the records, the court shall conduct a hearing on the motion or application within thirty days after the court receives the response. The court shall give notice, by regular mail, of the date, time, and location of the hearing to the prosecuting attorney and to the person who is the subject of the records under consideration.

(e) After conducting a hearing in accordance with division (C)(2)(d) of this section or after due consideration when a hearing is not conducted, except as provided in division (B)(1)(c) of this section, the court may order the records of the person that are the subject of the motion or application to be sealed if it finds that the person has been rehabilitated to a satisfactory degree. In determining whether the person has been rehabilitated to a satisfactory degree, the court may consider all of the following:

(i) The age of the person;

(ii) The nature of the case;

(iii) The cessation or continuation of delinquent, unruly, or criminal behavior;

(iv) The education and employment history of the person;

(v) Any other circumstances that may relate to the rehabilitation of the person who is the subject of the records under consideration.

(D)(1)(a) The juvenile court shall provide verbal notice to a person whose records are sealed under division (B) of this section, if that person is present in the court at the time the court issues a sealing order, that explains what sealing a record means, states that the person may apply to have those records expunged under section 2151.358 [2151.35.8] of the Revised Code, and explains what expunging a record means.

(b) The juvenile court shall provide written notice to a person whose records are sealed under division (B) of this section by regular mail to the person's last known address, if that person is not present in the court at the time the court issues a sealing order and if the court does not seal the person's record upon the court's own motion, that explains what sealing a record means, states that the person may apply to have those records expunged under section 2151.358 [2151.35.8] of the Revised Code, and explains what expunging a record means.

(2) Upon final disposition of a case in which a person has been adjudicated a delinquent child for committing an act other than a violation of section 2903.01, 2903.02, 2907.02, 2907.03, or 2907.05 of the Revised Code, an unruly child, or a juvenile traffic offender, the juvenile court shall provide written notice to the person that does all of the following:

(a) States that the person may apply to the court for an order to seal the record;

(b) Explains what sealing a record means;

(c) States that the person may apply to the court for an order to expunge the record under section 2151.358 [2151.35.8] of the Revised Code;

(d) Explains what expunging a record means.

(3) The department of youth services and any other institution or facility that unconditionally discharges a person who has been adjudicated a delinquent child, an unruly child, or a juvenile traffic offender shall immediately give notice of the discharge to the court that committed the person. The court shall note the date of discharge on a separate record of discharges of those natures.

**HISTORY: 151 v H 137, § 1, eff. 10-9-06.**

The effective date is set by § 6 of 151 v H 137.

**Not analogous to former RC § 2151.356, amended and renumbered to RC § 2152.21 by 148 v S 179, eff 1-1-02.**

## § 2151.357 Effects of order sealing records; index of sealed records; inspection of sealed records.

(A) If the court orders the records of a person sealed pursuant to section 2151.356 [2151.35.6] of the Revised Code, the person who is subject of the order properly may, and the court shall, reply that no record exists with respect to the person upon any inquiry in the matter, and the court, except as provided in division (D) of this section, shall do all of the following:

(1) Order that the proceedings in a case described in divisions (B) and (C) of section 2151.356 [2151.35.6] of the Revised Code be deemed never to have occurred;

(2) Except as provided in division (C) of this section, delete all index references to the case and the person so that the references are permanently irretrievable;

(3) Order that all original records of the case maintained by any public office or agency, except fingerprints held by a law enforcement agency, DNA specimens collected pursuant to section 2152.74 of the Revised Code, and DNA records derived from DNA specimens pursuant to section 109.573 [109.57.3] of the Revised Code, be delivered to the court;

(4) Order each public office or agency, upon the delivering of records to the court under division (A)(3) of this section, to expunge remaining records of the case that are the subject of the sealing order that are maintained by that public office or agency, except fingerprints, DNA specimens, and DNA records described under division (A)(3) of this section;

(5) Send notice of the order to seal to any public office or agency that the court has reason to believe may have a record of the sealed record;

(6) Seal all of the records delivered to the court under division (A)(3) of this section, in a separate file in which only sealed records are maintained.

(B) Except as provided in division (D) of this section, an order to seal under section 2151.356 [2151.35.6] of the Revised Code applies to every public office or agency that has a record relating to the case, regardless of whether it receives notice of the hearing on the sealing of the record or a copy of the order. Except as provided in division (D) of this section, upon the written request of a person whose record has been sealed and the presentation of a copy of the order and compliance with division (A)(3) of this section, a public office or agency shall expunge its record relating to the case, except a record of the adjudication or arrest or taking into custody that is maintained for compiling statistical data and that does not contain any reference to the person who is the subject of the order.

(C) The court that maintains sealed records pursuant to this section may maintain a manual or computerized index of the sealed records and shall make the index available only for the purposes set forth in division (E) of this section.

(1) Each entry regarding a sealed record in the index of sealed records shall contain all of the following:

(a) The name of the person who is the subject of the sealed record;

(b) An alphanumeric identifier relating to the person who is the subject of the sealed record;

(c) The word "sealed";

(d) The name of the court that has custody of the sealed record.

(2) Any entry regarding a sealed record in the index of sealed records shall not contain either of the following:

(a) The social security number of the person who is subject of the sealed record;

(b) The name or a description of the act committed.

(D) Notwithstanding any provision of this section that requires otherwise, a board of education of a city, local, exempted village, or joint vocational school district that maintains records of an individual who has been permanently excluded under sections 3301.121 [3301.12.1] and 3313.662 [3313.66.2] of the Revised Code is permitted to maintain records regarding an adjudication that the individual is a delinquent child that was used as the basis for the individual's permanent exclusion, regardless of a court order to seal the record. An order issued under section 2151.356 [2151.35.6] of the Revised Code to seal the record of an adjudication that an individual is a delinquent child does not revoke the adjudication order of the superintendent of public instruction to permanently exclude the individual who is the subject of the sealing order. An order to seal the record of an adjudication that an individual is a delinquent child may be presented to a district superintendent as evidence to support the contention that the superintendent should recommend that the permanent exclusion of the individual who is the subject of the sealing order be revoked. Except as otherwise authorized by this division and sections 3301.121 [3301.12.1] and 3313.662 [3313.66.2] of the Revised Code, any school employee in possession of or having access to the sealed adjudication records of an individual that were the basis of a permanent exclusion of the individual is subject to division (F) of this section.

(E) Inspection of records that have been ordered sealed under section 2151.356 [2151.35.6] of the Revised Code may be made only by the following persons or for the following purposes:

(1) By the court;

(2) If the records in question pertain to an act that would be an offense of violence that would be a felony if committed by an adult, by any law enforcement officer or any prosecutor, or the assistants of a law enforcement officer or prosecutor, for any valid law enforcement or prosecutorial purpose;

(3) Upon application by the person who is the subject of the sealed records, by the person that is named in that application;

(4) If the records in question pertain to an alleged violation of division (E)(1) of section 4301.69 of the Revised Code, by any law enforcement officer or any prosecutor, or the assistants of a law enforcement officer or prosecutor, for the purpose of determining whether the person is eligible for diversion under division (E)(2) of section 4301.69 of the Revised Code;

(5) At the request of a party in a civil action that is based on a case the records for which are the subject of a sealing order issued under section 2151.356 [2151.35.6] of the Revised Code, as needed for the civil action. The party also may copy the records as needed for the civil action. The sealed records shall be used solely in the civil action and are otherwise confidential and subject to the provisions of this section;

(6) By the attorney general or an authorized employee of the attorney general or the court for purposes of determining whether a child is a public registry-qualified juvenile offender registrant, as defined in section 2950.01 of the Revised Code, for purposes of Chapter 2950. of the Revised Code.

(F) No officer or employee of the state or any of its political subdivisions shall knowingly release, disseminate, or make available for any purpose involving employment, bonding, licensing, or education to any person or to any department, agency, or other instrumentality of the state or of any of its political subdivisions any information or other data concerning any arrest, taking into custody, complaint, indictment, information, trial, hearing, adjudication, or correctional supervision, the records of which have been sealed pursuant to section 2151.356 [2151.35.6] of the Revised Code and the release, dissemination, or making available of which is not expressly permitted by this section. Whoever violates this division is guilty of divulging confidential information, a misdemeanor of the fourth degree.

(G) In any application for employment, license, or other right or privilege, any appearance as a witness, or any other inquiry, a person may not be questioned with respect to any arrest or taking into custody for which the records were sealed. If an inquiry is made in violation of this division, the person may respond as if the sealed arrest or taking into custody did not occur, and the person shall not be subject to any adverse action because of the arrest or taking into custody or the response.

(H) The judgment rendered by the court under this chapter shall not impose any of the civil disabilities ordinarily imposed by conviction of a crime in that the child is not a criminal by reason of the adjudication, and no child shall be charged with or convicted of a crime in any court except as provided by this chapter. The disposition of a child under the judgment rendered or any evidence given in court shall not operate to disqualify a child in any future civil service examination, appointment, or application. Evidence of a judgment rendered and the disposition of a child under the judgment is not admissible to impeach the credibility of the child in any action or proceeding. Otherwise, the disposition of a child under the judgment rendered or any evidence given in court is admissible as evidence for or against the child in any action or proceeding in any court in accordance with the Rules of Evidence and also may be considered by any court as to the matter of sentence or to the granting of probation, and a court may consider the judgment rendered and the disposition of a child under that judgment for purposes of determining whether the child, for a future criminal conviction or guilty plea, is a repeat violent offender, as defined in section 2929.01 of the Revised Code.

**HISTORY: 151 v H 137, § 1, eff. 10-9-06; 152 v S 10, § 1, eff. 7-1-07.**

The effective date is set by § 3 of 152 v S 10.
The effective date is set by § 6 of 151 v H 137.
**Not analogous to former RC § 2151.357, renumbered to RC § 2151.362 by 151 v H 137, eff 10-9-06.**

## § 2151.358 Expungement of records.

(A) The juvenile court shall expunge all records sealed under section 2151.356 [2151.35.6] of the Revised Code five years after the court issues a sealing order or upon the twenty-third birthday of the person who is the subject of the sealing order, whichever date is earlier.

(B) Notwithstanding division (A) of this section, upon application by the person who has had a record sealed under section 2151.356 [2151.35.6] of the Revised Code, the juvenile court may expunge a record sealed under section 2151.356 [2151.35.6] of the Revised Code. In making the determination whether to expunge records, all of the following apply:

(1) The court may require a person filing an application for expungement to submit any relevant documentation to support the application.

(2) The court may cause an investigation to be made to determine if the person who is the subject of the proceedings has been rehabilitated to a satisfactory degree.

(3) The court shall promptly notify the prosecuting attorney of any proceedings to expunge records.

(4)(a) The prosecuting attorney may file a response with the court within thirty days of receiving notice of the expungement proceedings.

(b) If the prosecuting attorney does not file a response with the court or if the prosecuting attorney files a response but indicates that the prosecuting attorney does not object to the expungement of the records, the court may order the records of the person that are under consideration to be expunged without conducting a hearing on the application. If the court decides in its discretion to conduct a hearing on the application, the court shall conduct the hearing within thirty days after making that decision and shall give notice, by regular mail, of the date, time, and location of the hearing to the prosecuting attorney and to the person who is the subject of the records under consideration.

(c) If the prosecuting attorney files a response with the court that indicates that the prosecuting attorney objects to the expungement of the records, the court shall conduct a hearing on the application within thirty days after the court receives the response. The court shall give notice, by regular mail, of the date, time, and location of the hearing to the prosecuting attorney and to the person who is the subject of the records under consideration.

(5) After conducting a hearing in accordance with division (B)(4) of this section or after due consideration when a hearing is not conducted, the court may order the records of the person that are the subject of the application to be expunged if it finds that the person has been rehabilitated to a satisfactory degree. In determining whether the person has been rehabilitated to a satisfactory degree, the court may consider all of the following:

(a) The age of the person;

(b) The nature of the case;

(c) The cessation or continuation of delinquent, unruly, or criminal behavior;

(d) The education and employment history of the person;

(e) Any other circumstances that may relate to the rehabilitation of the person who is the subject of the records under consideration.

(C) If the juvenile court is notified by any party in a civil action that a civil action has been filed based on a case the records for which are the subject of a sealing order, the juvenile court shall not expunge a record sealed under section 2151.356 [2151.35.6] of the Revised Code until the civil action has been resolved and is not subject to further appellate review, at which time the records shall be expunged pursuant to division (A) of this section.

(D)(1) A juvenile court that issues a protection order or approves a consent agreement under section 2151.34 or 3113.31 of the Revised Code shall automatically seal all of the records of the proceeding in which the order was issued or agreement approved on the date the person against whom the protection order was issued or the consent agreement approved attains the age of nineteen years if the court determines that the person has complied with all of the terms of the protection order or consent agreement.

(2) In a proceeding under section 2151.34 of the Revised Code, if the juvenile court does not issue any protection order under division (E) of that section, the court shall automatically seal all of the records in that proceeding. In a proceeding under section 3113.31 of the Revised Code, if the juvenile court does not issue any protection order or approve any consent agreement under division (E) of that section, the court shall automatically seal all of the records in that proceeding.

(3)(a) If a juvenile court that issues a protection order or approves a consent agreement under section 2151.34 or 3113.31 of the Revised Code determines that the person against whom the protection order was issued or the consent agreement approved has not complied with all of the terms of the protection order or consent agreement, the court shall consider sealing all of the records of the proceeding in which the order was issued or agreement approved upon the court's own motion or upon the application of a person. The court may make the motion or the person who is the subject of the records under consideration may apply for an order sealing the records of the proceeding at any time after two years after the expiration of the protection order or consent agreement.

(b) In making a determination whether to seal records pursuant to division (D)(3) of this section, all of the following apply:

(i) The court may require a person filing an application under division (D)(3) of this section to submit any relevant documentation to support the application.

(ii) The court shall promptly notify the victim or the victim's attorney of any proceedings to seal records initiated pursuant to division (D)(3) of this section.

(iii) The victim or the victim's attorney may file a response with the court within thirty days of receiving notice of the sealing proceedings.

If the victim or the victim's attorney does not file a response with the court or if the victim or the victim's attorney files a response but indicates that the victim or the victim's attorney does not object to the sealing of the records, the court may order the records of the person that are under consideration to be sealed without conducting a hearing on the motion or application. If the court decides in its discretion to conduct a hearing on the motion or application, the court shall conduct the hearing within thirty days after making that decision and shall give notice, by regular mail, of the date, time, and location of the hearing to the victim or the victim's attorney and to the person who is the subject of the records under consideration.

If the victim or the victim's attorney files a response with the court that indicates that the victim or the victim's attorney objects to the sealing of the records, the court shall conduct a hearing on the motion or application within thirty days after the court receives the response. The court shall give notice, by regular mail, of the date, time, and location of the hearing to the victim or the victim's attorney and to the person who is the subject of the records under consideration.

(iv) After conducting a hearing in accordance with division (D)(3)(b)(iii) of this section or after due consideration when a hearing is not conducted, the court may order the records of the person that are the subject of the motion or application to be sealed.

(4) Inspection of the records sealed pursuant to division (D)(1), (2), or (3) of this section may be made only by the following persons or for the following purposes:

(a) By a law enforcement officer or prosecutor, or the assistants of either, to determine whether the nature and character of the offense with which a person is to be charged would be affected by virtue of the person's previously having been convicted of a crime;

(b) By the parole or probation officer of the person who is the subject of the records, for the exclusive use of the officer in supervising the person while on parole or under a community control sanction or a post-release control sanction, and in making inquiries and written reports as requested by the court or adult parole authority;

(c) Upon application by the person who is the subject of the records, by the persons named in the application;

(d) By a law enforcement officer who was involved in the case, for use in the officer's defense of a civil action arising out of the officer's involvement in that case;

(e) By a prosecuting attorney or the prosecuting attorney's assistants, to determine a defendant's eligibility to enter a pre-trial diversion program established pursuant to section 2935.36 of the Revised Code;

(f) By any law enforcement agency or any authorized employee of a law enforcement agency or by the department of rehabilitation and correction as part of a background investigation of a person who applies for employment with the agency as a law enforcement officer or with the department as a corrections officer;

(g) By any law enforcement agency or any authorized employee of a law enforcement agency, for the purposes set forth in, and in the manner provided in, section 2953.321 [2953.32.1] of the Revised Code;

(h) By the bureau of criminal identification and investigation or any authorized employee of the bureau for the purpose of providing information to a board or person pursuant to division (F) or (G) of section 109.57 of the Revised Code;

(i) By the bureau of criminal identification and investigation or any authorized employee of the bureau for the purpose of performing a criminal history records check on a person to whom a certificate as prescribed in section 109.77 of the Revised Code is to be awarded;

(j) By the bureau of criminal identification and investigation or any authorized employee of the bureau for the purpose of conducting a criminal records check of an individual pursuant to division (B) of section 109.572 [109.57.2] of the Revised Code that was requested pursuant to any of the sections identified in division (B)(1) of that section;

(k) By the bureau of criminal identification and investigation, an authorized employee of the bureau, a sheriff, or an authorized employee of a sheriff in connection with a criminal records check described in section 311.41 of the Revised Code;

(l) By the attorney general or an authorized employee of the attorney general or a court for purposes of determining a person's classification pursuant to Chapter 2950. of the Revised Code.

When the nature and character of the offense with which a person is to be charged would be affected by the information, it may be used for the purpose of charging the person with an offense.

(E) After the records have been expunged under this section, the person who is the subject of the expunged records properly may, and the court shall, reply that no record exists with respect to the person upon any inquiry in the matter.

**HISTORY: 151 v H 137, § 1, eff. 10-9-06; 153 v H 10, § 1, eff. 6-17-10.**

See provisions of § 3 of 153 v H 10 following RC § 2151.23.
The effective date is set by § 6 of 151 v H 137.

**Analogous in part to former RC § 2151.358 (133 v H 320 (Eff 11-19-69); 137 v H 315 (Eff 3-15-78); 139 v H 440 (Eff 11-23-81); 140 v H 37 (Eff 6-22-84); 144 v H 27 (Eff 10-10-91); 144 v H 154 (Eff 7-31-92); 146 v H 1 (Eff 1-1-96); 146 v S 2 (Eff 7-1-96); 148 v S 181 (Eff 9-4-2000); 148 v S 179, § 3 (Eff 1-1-2002); 149 v H 17. Eff 10-11-2002), repealed 151 v H 137, § 2, eff 10-9-06.**

## § 2151.359 Control of conduct of parent, guardian, or custodian.

(A)(1) In any proceeding in which a child has been adjudicated an unruly, abused, neglected, or dependent child, on the application of a party, or on the court's own motion, the court may make an order restraining or otherwise controlling the conduct of any parent, guardian, or other custodian in the relationship of that individual to the child if the court finds that an order of that type is necessary to do either of the following:

(a) Control any conduct or relationship that will be detrimental or harmful to the child.

(b) Control any conduct or relationship that will tend to defeat the execution of the order of disposition made or to be made.

(2) The court shall give due notice of the application or motion under division (A) of this section, the grounds for the application or motion, and an opportunity to be heard to the person against whom an order under this division is directed. The order may include a requirement that the child's parent, guardian, or other custodian enter into a recognizance with sufficient surety, conditioned upon the faithful discharge of any conditions or control required by the court.

(B) The authority to make an order under division (A) of this section and any order made under that authority is in addition to the authority to make an order pursuant to division (C)(2) of section 2151.354 [2151.35.4] or division (A)(7)(b) of section 2152.19 of the Revised Code and to any order made under either division.

(C) A person's failure to comply with any order made by the court under this section is contempt of court under Chapter 2705. of the Revised Code.

**HISTORY: 133 v H 320 (Eff 11-19-69); 136 v H 85 (Eff 11-28-75); 148 v S 181 (Eff 9-4-2000); 148 v S 179, § 3 (Eff 1-1-2002); 149 v H 400. Eff 4-3-2003.**

## § 2151.3510 Notice of intended commitment order.

Before a juvenile court issues an order of disposition pursuant to division (A)(1) of section 2151.354 [2151.35.4] or 2152.19 of the Revised Code committing an unruly or delinquent child to the custody of a public children services agency, it shall give the agency notice in the manner prescribed by the Juvenile Rules of the intended dispositional order.

**HISTORY: 144 v H 298 (Eff 7-26-91); 146 v H 274 (Eff 8-8-96); 148 v S 179, § 3. Eff 1-1-2002.**

The effective date is set by section 5 of SB 179.

## § 2151.3511 Amended and renumbered RC § 2152.81 in 148 v S 179. Eff 1-1-2002.

The effective date is set by section 5 of SB 179.

## § 2151.3512 Repealed, 148 v S 179, § 4 [146 v H 1; 146 v S 269; 148 v S 181]. Eff 1-1-2002.

This section concerned schedule of fines and costs.
The effective date is set by section 5 of SB 179.

## § 2151.3514 Alcohol or other drug testing and treatment of parent or other caregiver.

(A) As used in this section:

(1) "Alcohol and drug addiction program" has the same meaning as in section 3793.01 of the Revised Code;

(2) "Chemical dependency" means either of the following:

(a) The chronic and habitual use of alcoholic beverages to the extent that the user no longer can control the use of alcohol or endangers the user's health, safety, or welfare or that of others;

(b) The use of a drug of abuse to the extent that the user becomes physically or psychologically dependent on the drug or endangers the user's health, safety, or welfare or that of others.

(3) "Drug of abuse" has the same meaning as in section 3719.011 [3719.01.1] of the Revised Code.

(4) "Medicaid" means the program established under Chapter 5111. of the Revised Code.

(B) If the juvenile court issues an order of temporary custody or protective supervision under division (A) of section 2151.353 [2151.35.3] of the Revised Code with respect to a child adjudicated to be an abused, neglected, or dependent child and the alcohol or other drug addiction of a parent or other caregiver of the child was the basis for the adjudication of abuse, neglect, or dependency, the court shall issue an order requiring the parent or other caregiver to submit to an assessment and, if needed, treatment from an alcohol and drug addiction program certified by the department of alcohol and drug addiction services. The court may order the parent or other caregiver to submit to alcohol or other drug testing during, after, or both during and after, the treatment. The court shall send any order issued pursuant to this division to the public children services agency that serves the county in which the court is located for use as described in section 340.15 of the Revised Code.

(C) Any order requiring alcohol or other drug testing that is issued pursuant to division (B) of this section shall require one alcohol or other drug test to be conducted each month during a period of twelve consecutive months beginning the month immediately following the month in which the order for alcohol or other drug testing is issued. Arrangements for administering the alcohol or other drug tests, as well as funding the costs of the tests, shall be locally determined in accordance with sections 340.033 [340.03.3] and 340.15 of the Revised Code. If a parent or other caregiver required to submit to alcohol or other drug tests under this section is not a recipient of medicaid, the agency that refers the parent or caregiver for the tests may require the parent or caregiver to reimburse the agency for the cost of conducting the tests.

(D) The certified alcohol and drug addiction program that conducts any alcohol or other drug tests ordered in accordance with divisions (B) and (C) of this section shall send the results of the tests, along with the program's recommendations as to the benefits of continued treatment, to the court and to the public children services agency providing services to the involved family, according to federal regulations set forth in 42 C.F.R. Part 2, and division (B) of section 340.15 of the Revised Code. The court shall consider the results and the recommendations sent to it under this division in any adjudication or review by the court, according to section 2151.353 [2151.35.3], 2151.414 [2151.41.4], or 2151.419 [2151.41.9] of the Revised Code.

**HISTORY: 147 v H 484. Eff 3-18-99.**

[SAFE HAVENS LAW]

## § 2151.3515 Definitions.

As used in sections 2151.3515 to 2151.3530 of the Revised Code:

(A) "Deserted child" means a child whose parent has voluntarily delivered the child to an emergency medical service worker, peace officer, or hospital employee without expressing an intent to return for the child.

(B) "Emergency medical service organization," "emergency medical technician-basic," "emergency medical technician-intermediate," "first responder," and "paramedic" have the same meanings as in section 4765.01 of the Revised Code.

(C) "Emergency medical service worker" means a first responder, emergency medical technician-basic, emergency medical technician-intermediate, or paramedic.

(D) "Hospital" has the same meaning as in section 3727.01 of the Revised Code.

(E) "Hospital employee" means any of the following persons:

(1) A physician who has been granted privileges to practice at the hospital;

(2) A nurse, physician assistant, or nursing assistant employed by the hospital;

(3) An authorized person employed by the hospital who is acting under the direction of a physician described in division (E)(1) of this section.

(F) "Law enforcement agency" means an organization or entity made up of peace officers.

(G) "Nurse" means a person who is licensed under Chapter 4723. of the Revised Code to practice as a registered nurse or licensed practical nurse.

(H) "Nursing assistant" means a person designated by a hospital as a nurse aide or nursing assistant whose job is to aid nurses, physicians, and physician assistants in the performance of their duties.

(I) "Peace officer" means a sheriff, deputy sheriff, constable, police officer of a township or joint police district, marshal, deputy marshal, municipal police officer, or a state highway patrol trooper.

(J) "Physician" and "physician assistant" have the same meanings as in section 4730.01 of the Revised Code.

**HISTORY: 148 v H 660. Eff 4-9-2001; 2011 HB 153, § 101.01, eff. Sept. 29, 2011.**

## § 2151.3516 Persons authorized to take possession of deserted child.

The following persons, while acting in an official capacity, shall take possession of a child who is thirty days old or younger if that child's parent has voluntarily delivered the child to that person without the parent expressing an intent to return for the child.

(A) A peace officer on behalf of the law enforcement agency that employs the officer;

(B) A hospital employee on behalf of the hospital that has granted the person privilege to practice at the hospital or that employs the person;

(C) An emergency medical service worker on behalf of the emergency medical service organization that employs the worker or for which the worker provides services.

**HISTORY: 148 v H 660. Eff 4-9-2001; 152 v S 304, § 1, eff. 3-24-09.**

## § 2151.3517 Duties of entity or worker taking possession of deserted child.

(A) On taking possession of a child pursuant to section 2151.3516 [2151.35.16] of the Revised Code, a law enforcement agency, hospital, or emergency medical service organization shall do all the following:

(1) Perform any act necessary to protect the child's health or safety;

(2) Notify the public children services agency of the county in which the agency, hospital, or organization is located that the child has been taken into possession;

(3) If possible, make available to the parent who delivered the child forms developed under section 2151.3529 [2151.35.29] of the Revised Code that are designed to gather medical information concerning the child and the child's parents;

(4) If possible, make available to the parent who delivered the child written materials developed under section 2151.3529 [2151.35.29] of the Revised Code that describe services available to assist parents and newborns;

(5) If the child has suffered a physical or mental wound, injury, disability, or condition of a nature that reasonably indicates abuse or neglect of the child, attempt to identify and pursue the person who delivered the child.

(B) An emergency medical service worker who takes possession of a child shall, in addition to any act performed under division (A)(1) of this section, perform any medical service the worker is authorized to perform that is necessary to protect the physical health or safety of the child.

**HISTORY: 148 v H 660. Eff 4-9-2001.**

## § 2151.3518 Duties of public children services agency upon receiving notice of deserted child.

On receipt of a notice given pursuant to section 2151.3517 [2151.35.17] of the Revised Code that an emergency medical service organization, a law enforcement agency, or hospital has taken possession of a child and in accordance with rules of the department of job and family services, a public children services agency shall do all of the following:

(A) Consider the child to be in need of public care and protective services;

(B) Accept and take emergency temporary custody of the child;

(C) Provide temporary emergency care for the child, without agreement or commitment;

(D) Make an investigation concerning the child;

(E) File a motion with the juvenile court of the county in which the agency is located requesting that the court grant temporary custody of the child to the agency or to a private child placing agency;

(F) Provide any care for the child that the public children services agency considers to be in the best interest of the child, including placing the child in shelter care;

(G) Provide any care and perform any duties that are required of public children services agencies under section 5153.16 of the Revised Code;

(H) Prepare and keep written records of the investigation of the child, of the care and treatment afforded the child, and any other records required by the department of job and family services.

**HISTORY: 148 v H 660. Eff 4-9-2001.**

## § 2151.3519 Emergency hearing on motion for temporary custody.

When a public children services agency files a motion pursuant to division (E) of section 2151.3518 [2151.35.18] of the Revised Code, the juvenile court shall hold an emergency hearing as soon as possible to determine whether the child is a deserted child. The court is required to give notice to the parents of the child only if the court has knowledge of the names of the parents. If the court determines at the initial hearing or at any other hearing that a child is a deserted child, the court shall adjudicate the child a deserted child and enter its findings in the record of the case.

**HISTORY: 148 v H 660. Eff 4-9-2001.**

## § 2151.3520 Temporary custody order.

If a juvenile court adjudicates a child a deserted child, the court shall commit the child to the temporary custody of a public children services agency or a private child placing agency. The court shall consider the order committing the child to the temporary custody of the agency to be an order of disposition issued under division (A)(2) of section 2151.353 [2151.35.3] of the Revised Code with respect to a child adjudicated a neglected child.

**HISTORY: 148 v H 660. Eff 4-9-2001.**

## § 2151.3521 Court to treat deserted child as neglected child; exception.

A court that issues an order pursuant to section 2151.3520 [2151.35.20] of the Revised Code shall treat the child who is the subject of the order the same as a child adjudicated a neglected child when performing duties under Chapter 2151. of the Revised Code with respect to the child, except that there is a rebuttable presumption that it is not in the child's best interest to return the child to the natural parents.

**HISTORY: 148 v H 660. Eff 4-9-2001.**

## § 2151.3522 Agency granted temporary custody to treat deserted child or neglected child.

A public children services agency or private child placing agency that receives temporary custody of a child adjudicated a deserted child shall prepare case plans, conduct investigations, conduct periodic administrative reviews of case plans, and provide services for the deserted child as if the child were adjudicated a neglected child and shall follow the same procedures under this chapter in performing those functions as if the deserted child was a neglected child.

**HISTORY: 148 v H 660. Eff 4-9-2001.**

## § 2151.3523 Civil and criminal immunity of parent and of person or entity taking possession of deserted child.

(A) A parent does not commit a criminal offense under the laws of this state and shall not be subject to criminal prosecution in this state for the act of voluntarily delivering a child under section 2151.3516 [2151.35.16] of the Revised Code.

(B) A person who delivers or attempts to deliver a child who has suffered any physical or mental wound, injury, disability, or condition of a nature that reasonably indicates abuse or neglect of the child is not immune from civil or criminal liability for abuse or neglect.

(C) A person or governmental entity that takes possession of a child pursuant to section 2151.3516 [2151.35.16] of the Revised Code or takes emergency temporary custody of and provides temporary emergency care for a child pursuant to section 2151.3518 [2151.35.18] of the Revised Code is immune from any civil liability that might otherwise be incurred or imposed as a result of these actions, unless the person or entity has acted in bad faith or with malicious purpose. The immunity provided by this division does not apply if the person or governmental entity has immunity from civil liability under section 9.86, 2744.02, or 2744.03 of the Revised Code for the action in question.

(D) A person or governmental entity that takes possession of a child pursuant to section 2151.3516 [2151.35.16] of the Revised Code or takes emergency temporary custody of and provides temporary emergency care for a child pursuant to section 2151.3518 [2151.35.18] of the Revised Code is immune from any criminal liability that might otherwise be incurred or imposed as a result of these actions, unless the person or entity has acted in bad faith or with malicious purpose.

(E) Divisions (C) and (D) of this section do not create a new cause of action or substantive legal right against a person or governmental entity, and do not affect any immunities from civil liability or defenses established by another section of the Revised Code or available at common law, to which a person or governmental entity may be entitled under circumstances not covered by this section.

**HISTORY: 148 v H 660. Eff 4-9-2001.**

## § 2151.3524 Parent's right to anonymity.

(A) A parent who voluntarily delivers a child under section 2151.3516 [2151.35.16] of the Revised Code has the absolute right to remain anonymous. The anonymity of a parent who voluntarily delivers a child does not affect any duty imposed under sections 2151.3516 [2151.35.16] or 2151.3517 [2151.35.17] of the Revised Code. A parent who voluntarily delivers a child may leave the place at which the parent delivers the child at any time after the delivery of the child.

(B) Notwithstanding division (A) of this section, a parent who delivers or attempts to deliver a child who has suffered any physical or mental wound, injury, disability, or condition of a nature that reasonably indicates abuse or neglect of the child does not have the right to remain anonymous and may be subject to arrest pursuant to Chapter 2935. of the Revised Code.

**HISTORY: 148 v H 660. Eff 4-9-2001.**

## § 2151.3525 Parent may complete medical information forms.

A parent who voluntarily delivers a child under section 2151.3516 [2151.35.16] of the Revised Code may complete all or any part of the medical information forms the parent receives under division (A)(3) of section 2151.3517 [2151.35.17] of the Revised Code. The parent may deliver the fully or partially completed forms at the same time as delivering the child or at a later time. The parent is not required to complete all or any part of the forms.

**HISTORY: 148 v H 660. Eff 4-9-2001.**

## § 2151.3526 Parent may decline informational materials.

A parent who voluntarily delivers a child under section 2151.3516 [2151.35.16] of the Revised Code may refuse to accept the materials made available under division (A)(4) of section 2151.3517 [2151.35.17] of the Revised Code.

**HISTORY: 148 v H 660. Eff 4-9-2001.**

## § 2151.3527 Prohibited activities by person taking possession of deserted child.

(A) No person described in section 2151.3516 [2151.35.16] of the Revised Code shall do the following with respect to a parent who voluntarily delivers a child under that section:

(1) Coerce or otherwise try to force the parent into revealing the identity of the child's parents;

(2) Pursue or follow the parent after the parent leaves the place at which the child was delivered;

(3) Coerce or otherwise try to force the parent not to desert the child;

(4) Coerce or otherwise try to force the parent to complete all or any part of the medical information forms received under division (A)(3) of section 2151.3517 [2151.35.17] of the Revised Code;

(5) Coerce or otherwise try to force the parent to accept the materials made available under division (A)(4) of section 2151.3517 [2151.35.17] of the Revised Code.

(B) Divisions (A)(1) and (2) of this section do not apply to a person who delivers or attempts to deliver a child who has suffered any physical or mental wound, injury, disability, or condition of a nature that reasonably indicates abuse or neglect of the child.

**HISTORY: 148 v H 660. Eff 4-9-2001.**

## § 2151.3528 DNA testing of person seeking reunification with child.

If a child is adjudicated a deserted child and a person indicates to the court that the person is the parent of the child and that the person seeks to be reunited with the child, the court that adjudicated the child shall require the person, at the person's expense, to submit to a DNA test to verify that the person is a parent of the child.

**HISTORY: 148 v H 660. Eff 4-9-2001.**

## § 2151.3529 Forms requesting medical information concerning child; information materials to be given parents.

(A) The director of job and family services shall promulgate forms designed to gather pertinent medical information concerning a deserted child and the child's parents. The forms shall clearly and unambiguously state on each page that the information requested is to facilitate medical care for the child, that the forms may be fully or partially completed or left blank, that completing the forms or parts of the forms is completely voluntary, and that no adverse legal consequence will result from failure to complete any part of the forms.

(B) The director shall promulgate written materials to be given to the parents of a child delivered pursuant to section 2151.3516 [2151.35.16] of the Revised Code. The materials shall describe services available to assist parents and newborns and shall include information directly relevant to situations that might cause parents to desert a child and information on the procedures for a person to follow in order to reunite with a child the person delivered under section 2151.3516 [2151.35.16] of the Revised Code, including notice that the person will be required to submit to a DNA test, at that person's expense, to prove that the person is the parent of the child.

(C) If the department of job and family services determines that money in the putative father registry fund created under section 2101.16 of the Revised Code is more than is needed for its duties related to the putative father registry, the department may use surplus moneys in the fund for costs related to the development and publication of forms and materials promulgated pursuant to divisions (A) and (B) of this section.

**HISTORY: 148 v H 660. Eff 4-9-2001; 150 v H 95, § 1, eff. 6-26-03.**

The effective date is set by section 182 of H.B. 95 (150 v —).

## § 2151.3530 Distribution of forms and informational materials; educational plan for informing at-risk populations.

(A) The director of job and family services shall distribute the medical information forms and written materials promulgated under section 2151.3529 [2151.35.29] of the Revised Code to entities permitted to receive a deserted child, to public children services agencies, and to other public or private agencies that, in the discretion of the director, are best able to disseminate the forms and materials to the persons who are most in need of the forms and materials.

The department of job and family services shall develop an educational plan, in collaboration with the Ohio family and children first cabinet council, for informing at-risk populations who are most likely to voluntarily deliver a child under section 2151.3516 [2151.35.16] of the Revised Code concerning the provisions of sections 2151.3516 [2151.35.16] to 2151.3530 [2151.35.30] of the Revised Code.

(B) If the department of job and family services determines that money in the putative father registry fund created under section 2101.16 of the Revised Code is more than is needed to perform its duties related to the putative father registry, the department may use surplus moneys in the fund for costs related to the distribution of forms and materials pursuant to this section.

**HISTORY: 148 v H 660. Eff 4-9-2001; 150 v H 95, § 1, eff. 6-26-03; 152 v S 304, § 1, eff. 3-24-09.**

The effective date is set by section 182 of H.B. 95 (150 v —).

## § 2151.36 Support of child.

Except as provided in section 2151.361 [2151.36.1] of the Revised Code, when a child has been committed as provided by this chapter or Chapter 2152. of the Revised Code, the juvenile court shall issue an order pursuant to Chapters 3119., 3121., 3123., and 3125. of the Revised Code requiring that the parent, guardian, or person charged with the child's support pay for the care, support, maintenance, and education of the child. The juvenile court shall order that the parents, guardian, or person pay for the expenses involved in providing orthopedic, medical, or surgical treatment for, or for special care of, the child, enter a judgment for the amount due, and enforce the judgment by execution as in the court of common pleas.

Any expenses incurred for the care, support, maintenance, education, orthopedic, medical, or surgical treatment, and special care of a child who has a legal settlement in another county shall be at the expense of the county of legal settlement if the consent of the juvenile judge of the county of legal settlement is first obtained. When the consent is obtained, the board of county commissioners of the county in which the child has a legal settlement shall reimburse the committing court for the expenses out of its general fund. If the department of job and family services considers it to be in the best interest of any delinquent, dependent, unruly, abused, or neglected child who has a legal settlement in a foreign state or country that the child be returned to the state or country of legal settlement, the juvenile court may commit the child to the department for the child's return to that state or country.

Any expenses ordered by the court for the care, support, maintenance, education, orthopedic, medical, or surgical treatment, or special care of a dependent, neglected, abused, unruly, or delinquent child or of a juvenile traffic offender under this chapter or Chapter 2152. of the Revised Code, except the part of the expense that may be paid by the state or federal government or paid by the parents, guardians, or person charged with the child's support pursuant to this section, shall be paid from the county treasury upon specifically itemized vouchers, certified to by the judge. The court shall not be responsible for any expenses resulting from the commitment of children to any home, public children services agency, private child placing agency, or other institution, association, or agency, unless the court authorized the expenses at the time of commitment.

**HISTORY: GC § 1639-34; 117 v 520; 119 v 731; 121 v 557; Bureau of Code Revision, 10-1-53; 133 v S 49 (Eff 8-13-69); 133 v H 320 (Eff 11-19-69); 136 v H 85 (Eff 11-28-75); 141 v H 428 (Eff 12-23-86); 142 v S 89 (Eff 1-1-89); 146 v H 274 (Eff 8-8-96); 148 v H 471 (Eff 7-1-2000); 148 v S 180 (Eff 3-22-2001); 148 v S 179, § 3 (Eff 1-1-2002); 149 v S 27, §§ 1, 3. Eff 3-15-2002.†.**

† The effective date for RC § 2151.36, § 3, differs from the effective date set for the section by section 5(A) of SB 27 (149 v —). See provisions of OConst Art II, §§ 1c and d.

The provisions of §§ 5(A) and 8(C) of SB 27 (149 v —) read as follows:

SECTION 5. (A) Sections 3 and 4 of this act shall take effect January 1, 2002.

* * *

SECTION 8.

* * *

(C) Section 2151.36 of the Revised Code is presented in Section 3 of this act as a composite of the section as amended by both Am. Sub. S.B. 179 and Am. Sub. S.B. 180 of the 123rd General Assembly. The General Assembly, applying the principle stated in division (B) of section 1.52 of the Revised Code that amendments are to be harmonized if reasonably capable of simultaneous operation, finds that the composite is the resulting version of the section in effect prior to the effective date of the section as presented in Section 3 of this act.

## § 2151.361 Order where adopted child is placed into temporary custody or committed.

(A) If the parents of a child enter into an agreement with a public children services agency or private child placing agency to place the child into the temporary custody of the agency or the child is committed as provided by this chapter, the juvenile court, at its discretion, may issue an order pursuant to Chapters 3119., 3121., 3123., and 3125. of the Revised Code requiring that the parents pay for the care, support, maintenance, and education of the child if the parents adopted the child.

(B) When determining whether to issue an order under division (A) of this section, the juvenile court shall consider all pertinent issues, including, but not limited to, all of the following:

(1) The ability of the parents to pay for the care, support, maintenance, and education of the child;

(2) The chances for reunification of the parents and child;

(3) Whether issuing the order will encourage the reunification of the parents and child or undermine that reunification;

(4) Whether the problem underlying the agreement to place the child into temporary custody existed prior to the parents' adoption of the child and whether the parents were informed of the problem prior to that adoption;

(5) Whether the problem underlying the agreement to place the child into temporary custody began after the parents' adoption of the child;

(6) Whether the parents have contributed to the child's problems;

(7) Whether the parents are part of the solution to the child's problems;

(8) The ability of the parents to meet the needs of all other children residing in the home.

**HISTORY: 149 v S 27. Eff 3-15-2002; 152 v H 7, § 1, eff. 4-7-09.**

## § 2151.362 School district liability for cost of education; state subsidy where placement is in private facility.

(A)(1) In the manner prescribed by division (C)(1) or (2) of section 3313.64 of the Revised Code, as applicable, the court, at the time of making any order that removes a child from the child's own home or that vests legal or permanent custody of the child in a person other than the child's parent or a government agency, shall determine the school district that is to bear the cost of educating the child. The court shall make the determination a part of the order that provides for the child's placement or commitment. That school district shall bear the cost of educating the child unless and until the department of education determines that a different district shall be responsible for bearing that cost pursuant to division (A)(2) of this section. The court's order shall state that the determination of which school district is responsible to bear the cost of educating the child is subject to re-determination by the department pursuant to that division.

(2) If, while the child is in the custody of a person other than the child's parent or a government agency, the department of education determines that the place of residence of the child's parent has changed since the court issued its initial order, the department may name a different school district to bear the cost of educating the child. The department shall make this new determination, and any future determinations, based on evidence received from the school district currently responsible to bear the cost of educating the child. If the department finds that the evidence demonstrates to its satisfaction that the residence of the child's parent has changed since the court issued its initial order under division (A)(1) of this section, or since the department last made a determination under division (A)(2) of this section, the department shall

name the district in which the child's parent currently resides or, if the parent's residence is not known, the district in which the parent's last known residence is located. If the department cannot determine any Ohio district in which the parent currently resides or has resided, the school district designated in the initial court order under division (A)(1) of this section, or in the most recent determination made by the department under division (A)(2) of this section, shall continue to bear the cost of educating the child.

(B) Whenever a child is placed in a detention facility established under section 2152.41 of the Revised Code or a juvenile facility established under section 2151.65 of the Revised Code, the child's school district as determined by the court or the department, in the same manner as prescribed in division (A) of this section, shall pay the cost of educating the child based on the per capita cost of the educational facility within the detention home or juvenile facility.

(C) Whenever a child is placed by the court in a private institution, school, or residential treatment center or any other private facility, the state shall pay to the court a subsidy to help defray the expense of educating the child in an amount equal to the product of the daily per capita educational cost of the private facility, as determined pursuant to this section, and the number of days the child resides at the private facility, provided that the subsidy shall not exceed twenty-five hundred dollars per year per child. The daily per capita educational cost of a private facility shall be determined by dividing the actual program cost of the private facility or twenty-five hundred dollars, whichever is less, by three hundred sixty-five days or by three hundred sixty-six days for years that include February twenty-ninth. The state shall pay seventy-five per cent of the total subsidy for each year quarterly to the court. The state may adjust the remaining twenty-five per cent of the total subsidy to be paid to the court for each year to an amount that is less than twenty-five per cent of the total subsidy for that year based upon the availability of funds appropriated to the department of education for the purpose of subsidizing courts that place a child in a private institution, school, or residential treatment center or any other private facility and shall pay that adjusted amount to the court at the end of the year.

**HISTORY: 133 v H 320 (Eff 11-19-69); 133 v S 518 (Eff 7-16-70); 139 v S 140 (Eff 7-1-81); 146 v H 117 (Eff 6-30-95); 148 v S 179, § 3. Eff 1-1-2002; 151 v H 530, § 101.01, eff. 6-30-06; 151 v H 137, § 1, eff. 10-9-06; 152 v H 119, § 101.01, eff. 9-29-07.**

The effective date is set by § 812.03 of 152 v H 119.
The effective date is set by § 6 of 151 v H 137.
The effective date is set by § 812.03 of 151 v H 530.
The effective date is set by section 5 of SB 179.

**Publisher's Note:**

This section was renumbered from RC § 2151.357 by 151 v H 137, effective October 9, 2006.

## § 2151.37 Institution receiving children required to make report.

At any time the juvenile judge may require from an association receiving or desiring to receive children, such reports, information, and statements as he deems necessary. He may at any time require from an association or institution reports, information, or statements concerning any child committed to it by such judge under sections 2151.01 to 2151.54, inclusive, of the Revised Code.

**HISTORY: GC § 1639-36; 117 v 520(532); Bureau of Code Revision. Eff 10-1-53.**

## § 2151.38 Duration of dispositional order.

Subject to sections 2151.353 [2151.35.3] and 2151.412 [2151.41.2] to 2151.421 [2151.42.1] of the Revised Code, and any other provision of law that specifies a different duration for a dispositional order, all dispositional orders made by the court under this chapter shall be temporary and shall continue for a period that is designated by the court in its order, until terminated or modified by the court or until the child attains twenty-one years of age.

**HISTORY: GC § 1639-35; 117 v 520; 121 v 557; Bureau of Code Revision, 10-1-53; 130 v 625 (Eff 10-7-63); 133 v S 49 (Eff 8-13-69); 133 v H 320 (Eff 11-19-69); 138 v H 695 (Eff 10-24-80); 139 v H 1 (Eff 8-5-81); 139 v H 440 (Eff 11-23-81); 140 v H 291 (Eff 7-1-83); 141 v H 428 (Eff 12-23-86); 142 v S 89 (Eff 1-1-89); 144 v S 241 (Eff 4-9-93); 145 v H 152 (Eff 7-1-93); 145 v H 715 (Eff 7-22-94); 145 v H 314 (Eff 9-29-94); 146 v H 1 (Eff 1-1-96); 146 v H 124 (Eff 3-31-97); 147 v H 1 (Eff 7-1-98); 147 v H 526 (Eff 9-1-98); 148 v H 3 (Eff 11-22-99); 148 v S 179, § 3 (Eff 1-1-2002); 149 v H 393. Eff 7-5-2002.**

## § 2151.39 Placement of children from other states.

No person, association or agency, public or private, of another state, incorporated or otherwise, shall place a child in a family home or with an agency or institution within the boundaries of this state, either for temporary or permanent care or custody or for adoption, unless such person or association has furnished the department of job and family services with a medical and social history of the child, pertinent information about the family, agency, association, or institution in this state with whom the sending party desires to place the child, and any other information or financial guaranty required by the department to determine whether the proposed placement will meet the needs of the child. The department may require the party desiring the placement to agree to promptly receive and remove from the state a child brought into the state whose placement has not proven satisfactorily responsive to the needs of the child at any time until the child is adopted, reaches majority, becomes self-supporting or is discharged with the concurrence of the department. All placements proposed to be made in this state by a party located in a state which is a party to the interstate compact on the placement of children shall be made according to the provisions of sections 5103.20 to 5103.22 of the Revised Code, or, if the interstate compact on the placement of children is in effect in this state, all placements proposed to be made in this state by a party located in a state that is a party to that compact shall be made according to the provisions of sections 5103.23 to 5103.237 [5103.23.7] of the Revised Code.

**HISTORY: GC § 1639-37; 117 v 520; Bureau of Code Revision, 10-1-53; 126 v 1165 (Eff 10-17-55); 136 v H 247 (Eff 1-1-76); 141 v H 428 (Eff 12-23-86); 148 v H 471. Eff 7-1-2000; 151 v S 238, § 1, eff. 9-21-06; 152 v H 214, § 5, eff. 5-14-08.**

See provisions of §§ 7 and 8 of 152 v H 214 following RC § 2151.23.
The effective date is set by section 12(A) of HB 471.

## § 2151.40 Cooperation with court.

Every county, township, or municipal official or department, including the prosecuting attorney, shall render all assistance and co-operation within his jurisdictional power which may further the objects of sections 2151.01 to 2151.54 of the Revised Code. All institutions or agencies to which the juvenile court sends any child shall give to the court or to any officer appointed by it such information concerning such child as said court or officer requires. The court may seek the co-operation of all societies or organizations having for their object the protection or aid of children.

On the request of the judge, when the child is represented by an attorney, or when a trial is requested the prosecuting attorney shall assist the court in presenting the evidence at any hearing or proceeding concerning an alleged or adjudicated delinquent, unruly, abused, neglected, or dependent child or juvenile traffic offender.

**HISTORY: GC § 1639-55; 117 v 520; Bureau of Code Revision, 10-1-53; 133 v H 320 (Eff 11-19-69); 136 v H 85. Eff 11-28-75.**

## § 2151.41 Repealed, 141 v H 349, § 2 [GC § 1639-45; 117 v 520; Bureau of Code Revision, 10-1-53; 133 v H 320]. Eff 3-6-86.

This section concerned abusing or contributing to delinquency of a child. See now RC § 2919.24.

## § 2151.411 Repealed, 148 v S 179, § 4 [127 v 21; 143 v S 258; 143 v S 3; 146 v H 4; 146 v H 124; 148 v H 448]. Eff 1-1-2002.

This section concerned parent or custodian charged with control of child; liability and searches during probation period; order to exercise control.

The effective date is set by section 5 of SB 179.

## § 2151.412 Case plan for each child; changes; priorities.

(A) Each public children services agency and private child placing agency shall prepare and maintain a case plan for any child to whom the agency is providing services and to whom any of the following applies:

(1) The agency filed a complaint pursuant to section 2151.27 of the Revised Code alleging that the child is an abused, neglected, or dependent child;

(2) The agency has temporary or permanent custody of the child;

(3) The child is living at home subject to an order for protective supervision;

(4) The child is in a planned permanent living arrangement.

Except as provided by division (A)(2) of section 5103.153 of the Revised Code, a private child placing agency providing services to a child who is the subject of a voluntary permanent custody surrender agreement entered into under division (B)(2) of section 5103.15 of the Revised Code is not required to prepare and maintain a case plan for that child.

(B) Each public children services agency shall prepare and maintain a case plan or a family service plan for any child for whom the agency is providing in-home services pursuant to an alternative response.

(C)(1) The director of job and family services shall adopt rules pursuant to Chapter 119. of the Revised Code setting forth the content and format of case plans required by division (A) of this section and establishing procedures for developing, implementing, and changing the case plans. The rules shall at a minimum comply with the requirements of Title IV-E of the "Social Security Act," 94 Stat. 501, 42 U.S.C. 671 (1980), as amended.

(2) The director of job and family services shall adopt rules pursuant to Chapter 119. of the Revised Code requiring public children services agencies and private child placing agencies to maintain case plans for children and their families who are receiving services in their homes from the agencies and for whom case plans are not required by division (A) of this section. The rules for public children services agencies shall include the requirements for case plans or family service plans maintained for children and their families who are receiving services in their homes from public children services agencies pursuant to an alternative response. The agencies shall maintain case plans and family service plans as required by those rules; however, the case plans and family service plans shall not be subject to any other provision of this section except as specifically required by the rules.

(D) Each public children services agency and private child placing agency that is required by division (A) of this section to maintain a case plan shall file the case plan with the court prior to the child's adjudicatory hearing but no later than thirty days after the earlier of the date on which the complaint in the case was filed or the child was first placed into shelter care. If the agency does not have sufficient information prior to the adjudicatory hearing to complete any part of the case plan, the agency shall specify in the case plan the additional information necessary to complete each part of the case plan and the steps that will be taken to obtain that information. All parts of the case plan shall be completed by the earlier of thirty days after the adjudicatory hearing or the date of the dispositional hearing for the child.

(E) Any agency that is required by division (A) of this section to prepare a case plan shall attempt to obtain an agreement among all parties, including, but not limited to, the parents, guardian, or custodian of the child and the guardian ad litem of the child regarding the content of the case plan. If all parties agree to the content of the case plan and the court approves it, the court shall journalize it as part of its dispositional order. If the agency cannot obtain an agreement upon the contents of the case plan or the court does not approve it, the parties shall present evidence on the contents of the case plan at the dispositional hearing. The court, based upon the evidence presented at the dispositional hearing and the best interest of the child, shall determine the contents of the case plan and journalize it as part of the dispositional order for the child.

(F)(1) All parties, including the parents, guardian, or custodian of the child, are bound by the terms of the journalized case plan. A party that fails to comply with the terms of the journalized case plan may be held in contempt of court.

(2) Any party may propose a change to a substantive part of the case plan, including, but not limited to, the child's placement and the visitation rights of any party. A party proposing a change to the case plan shall file the proposed change with the court and give notice of the proposed change in writing before the end of the day after the day of filing it to all parties and the child's guardian ad litem. All parties and the guardian ad litem shall have

seven days from the date the notice is sent to object to and request a hearing on the proposed change.

(a) If it receives a timely request for a hearing, the court shall schedule a hearing pursuant to section 2151.417 of the Revised Code to be held no later than thirty days after the request is received by the court. The court shall give notice of the date, time, and location of the hearing to all parties and the guardian ad litem. The agency may implement the proposed change after the hearing, if the court approves it. The agency shall not implement the proposed change unless it is approved by the court.

(b) If it does not receive a timely request for a hearing, the court may approve the proposed change without a hearing. If the court approves the proposed change without a hearing, it shall journalize the case plan with the change not later than fourteen days after the change is filed with the court. If the court does not approve the proposed change to the case plan, it shall schedule a hearing to be held pursuant to section 2151.417 of the Revised Code no later than thirty days after the expiration of the fourteen-day time period and give notice of the date, time, and location of the hearing to all parties and the guardian ad litem of the child. If, despite the requirements of division (F)(2) of this section, the court neither approves and journalizes the proposed change nor conducts a hearing, the agency may implement the proposed change not earlier than fifteen days after it is submitted to the court.

(3) If an agency has reasonable cause to believe that a child is suffering from illness or injury and is not receiving proper care and that an appropriate change in the child's case plan is necessary to prevent immediate or threatened physical or emotional harm, to believe that a child is in immediate danger from the child's surroundings and that an immediate change in the child's case plan is necessary to prevent immediate or threatened physical or emotional harm to the child, or to believe that a parent, guardian, custodian, or other member of the child's household has abused or neglected the child and that the child is in danger of immediate or threatened physical or emotional harm from that person unless the agency makes an appropriate change in the child's case plan, it may implement the change without prior agreement or a court hearing and, before the end of the next day after the change is made, give all parties, the guardian ad litem of the child, and the court notice of the change. Before the end of the third day after implementing the change in the case plan, the agency shall file a statement of the change with the court and give notice of the filing accompanied by a copy of the statement to all parties and the guardian ad litem. All parties and the guardian ad litem shall have ten days from the date the notice is sent to object to and request a hearing on the change.

(a) If it receives a timely request for a hearing, the court shall schedule a hearing pursuant to section 2151.417 of the Revised Code to be held no later than thirty days after the request is received by the court. The court shall give notice of the date, time, and location of the hearing to all parties and the guardian ad litem. The agency shall continue to administer the case plan with the change after the hearing, if the court approves the change. If the court does not approve the change, the court shall make appropriate changes to the case plan and shall journalize the case plan.

(b) If it does not receive a timely request for a hearing, the court may approve the change without a hearing. If the court approves the change without a hearing, it shall journalize the case plan with the change within fourteen days after receipt of the change. If the court does not approve the change to the case plan, it shall schedule a hearing under section 2151.417 of the Revised Code to be held no later than thirty days after the expiration of the fourteen-day time period and give notice of the date, time, and location of the hearing to all parties and the guardian ad litem of the child.

(G)(1) All case plans for children in temporary custody shall have the following general goals:

(a) Consistent with the best interest and special needs of the child, to achieve a safe out-of-home placement in the least restrictive, most family-like setting available and in close proximity to the home from which the child was removed or the home in which the child will be permanently placed;

(b) To eliminate with all due speed the need for the out-of-home placement so that the child can safely return home.

(2) The director of job and family services shall adopt rules pursuant to Chapter 119. of the Revised Code setting forth the general goals of case plans for children subject to dispositional orders for protective supervision, a planned permanent living arrangement, or permanent custody.

(H) In the agency's development of a case plan and the court's review of the case plan, the child's health and safety shall be the paramount concern. The agency and the court shall be guided by the following general priorities:

(1) A child who is residing with or can be placed with the child's parents within a reasonable time should remain in their legal custody even if an order of protective supervision is required for a reasonable period of time;

(2) If both parents of the child have abandoned the child, have relinquished custody of the child, have become incapable of supporting or caring for the child even with reasonable assistance, or have a detrimental effect on the health, safety, and best interest of the child, the child should be placed in the legal custody of a suitable member of the child's extended family;

(3) If a child described in division (H)(2) of this section has no suitable member of the child's extended family to accept legal custody, the child should be placed in the legal custody of a suitable nonrelative who shall be made a party to the proceedings after being given legal custody of the child;

(4) If the child has no suitable member of the child's extended family to accept legal custody of the child and no suitable nonrelative is available to accept legal custody of the child and, if the child temporarily cannot or should not be placed with the child's parents, guardian, or custodian, the child should be placed in the temporary custody of a public children services agency or a private child placing agency;

(5) If the child cannot be placed with either of the child's parents within a reasonable period of time or should not be placed with either, if no suitable member of the child's extended family or suitable nonrelative is available to accept legal custody of the child, and if the agency has a reasonable expectation of placing the child for adoption, the child should be committed to the permanent custody of the public children services agency or private child placing agency;

(6) If the child is to be placed for adoption or foster care, the placement shall not be delayed or denied on the basis of the child's or adoptive or foster family's race, color, or national origin.

(I) The case plan for a child in temporary custody shall include at a minimum the following requirements if the child is or has been the victim of abuse or neglect or if the child witnessed the commission in the child's household of abuse or neglect against a sibling of the child, a parent of the child, or any other person in the child's household:

(1) A requirement that the child's parents, guardian, or custodian participate in mandatory counseling;

(2) A requirement that the child's parents, guardian, or custodian participate in any supportive services that are required by or provided pursuant to the child's case plan.

(J) A case plan may include, as a supplement, a plan for locating a permanent family placement. The supplement shall not be considered part of the case plan for purposes of division (E) of this section.

**HISTORY: 142 v H 403 (Eff 1-1-89); 146 v H 274 (Eff 8-8-96); 146 v H 419 (Eff 9-18-96); 147 v H 484 (Eff 3-18-99); 148 v H 471. Eff 7-1-2000; 2011 HB 153, § 101.01, eff. Sept. 29, 2011.**

**Analogous to former RC § 2151.41.2 (138 v H 695; 141 v H 428; 142 v H 399; 142 v S 89), repealed, 142, v H 403, § 2, eff 1-1-89.**

The effective date is set by section 12(A) of HB 471.

## § 2151.413 Agency may file motion requesting permanent custody.

(A) A public children services agency or private child placing agency that, pursuant to an order of disposition under division (A)(2) of section 2151.353 [2151.35.3] of the Revised Code or under any version of section 2151.353 [2151.35.3] of the Revised Code that existed prior to January 1, 1989, is granted temporary custody of a child who is not abandoned or orphaned may file a motion in the court that made the disposition of the child requesting permanent custody of the child.

(B) A public children services agency or private child placing agency that, pursuant to an order of disposition under division (A)(2) of section 2151.353 [2151.35.3] of the Revised Code or under any version of section 2151.353 [2151.35.3] of the Revised Code that existed prior to January 1, 1989, is granted temporary custody of a child who is orphaned may file a motion in the court that made the disposition of the child requesting permanent custody of the child whenever it can show that no relative of the child is able to take legal custody of the child.

(C) A public children services agency or private child placing agency that, pursuant to an order of disposition under division (A)(5) of section 2151.353 [2151.35.3] of the Revised Code, places a child in a planned permanent living arrangement may file a motion in the court that made the disposition of the child requesting permanent custody of the child.

(D)(1) Except as provided in division (D)(3) of this section, if a child has been in the temporary custody of one or more public children services agencies or private child placing agencies for twelve or more months of a consecutive twenty-two-month period, the agency with custody shall file a motion requesting permanent custody of the child. If the child has been in the temporary custody of one or more public children services agencies or private child placing agencies and the child was previously in the temporary custody of an equivalent agency in another state, the agency with custody of the child shall apply the time in temporary custody in the other state to the time in temporary custody in this state and, except as provided in division (D)(3) of this section, if the time spent in temporary custody equals twelve or more months of a consecutive twenty-two-month period, the agency with custody may file a motion requesting permanent custody of the child. The motion shall be filed in the court that issued the current order of temporary custody. For the purposes of this division, a child shall be considered to have entered the temporary custody of an agency on the earlier of the date the child is adjudicated pursuant to section 2151.28 of the Revised Code or the date that is sixty days after the removal of the child from home.

(2) Except as provided in division (D)(3) of this section, if a court makes a determination pursuant to division (A)(2) of section 2151.419 [2151.41.9] of the Revised Code, the public children services agency or private child placing agency required to develop the permanency plan for the child under division (K) of section 2151.417 [2151.41.7] of the Revised Code shall file a motion in the court that made the determination requesting permanent custody of the child.

(3) An agency shall not file a motion for permanent custody under division (D)(1) or (2) of this section if any of the following apply:

(a) The agency documents in the case plan or permanency plan a compelling reason that permanent custody is not in the best interest of the child.

(b) If reasonable efforts to return the child to the child's home are required under section 2151.419 [2151.41.9] of the Revised Code, the agency has not provided the services required by the case plan to the parents of the child or the child to ensure the safe return of the child to the child's home.

(c) The agency has been granted permanent custody of the child.

(d) The child has been returned home pursuant to court order in accordance with division (A)(3) of section 2151.419 [2151.41.9] of the Revised Code.

(E) Any agency that files a motion for permanent custody under this section shall include in the case plan of the child who is the subject of the motion, a specific plan of the agency's actions to seek an adoptive family for the child and to prepare the child for adoption.

(F) The department of job and family services may adopt rules pursuant to Chapter 119. of the Revised Code that set forth the time frames for case reviews and for filing a motion requesting permanent custody under division (D)(1) of this section.

**HISTORY: 138 v H 695 (Eff 10-24-80); 142 v S 89 (Eff 1-1-89); 146 v H 419 (Eff 9-18-96); 147 v H 484 (Eff 3-18-99); 148 v H 176 (Eff 10-29-99); 148 v H 471. Eff 7-1-2000; 152 v S 163, § 1, eff. 8-14-08.**

The effective date is set by section 12(A) of HB 471.

## § 2151.414 Hearing on motion for permanent custody; notice; determinations necessary for granting motion.

(A)(1) Upon the filing of a motion pursuant to section 2151.413 [2151.41.3] of the Revised Code for permanent custody of a child, the court shall schedule a hearing and give notice of the filing of the motion and of the hearing, in accordance with section 2151.29 of the Revised Code, to all parties to the action and to the child's guardian ad litem. The notice also shall contain a full explanation that the granting of permanent custody permanently divests the parents of their parental rights, a full explanation of their right to be represented by counsel and to have counsel appointed pursuant to Chapter 120. of the Revised Code if they are indigent, and the name and telephone number of the court employee designated by the court pursuant to section 2151.314 [2151.31.4] of the Revised Code to arrange for the prompt appointment of counsel for indigent persons.

The court shall conduct a hearing in accordance with section 2151.35 of the Revised Code to determine if it is in the best interest of the child to permanently terminate parental rights and grant permanent custody to the agency that filed the motion. The adjudication that the child is an abused, neglected, or dependent child and any dispositional order that has been issued in the case under section 2151.353 [2151.35.3] of the Revised Code pursuant to the adjudication shall not be readjudicated at the hearing and shall not be affected by a denial of the motion for permanent custody.

(2) The court shall hold the hearing scheduled pursuant to division (A)(1) of this section not later than one hundred twenty days after the agency files the motion for permanent custody, except that, for good cause shown, the court may continue the hearing for a reasonable period of time beyond the one-hundred-twenty-day deadline. The court shall issue an order that grants, denies, or otherwise disposes of the motion for permanent custody, and journalize the order, not later than two hundred days after the agency files the motion.

If a motion is made under division (D)(2) of section 2151.413 [2151.41.3] of the Revised Code and no dispositional hearing has been held in the case, the court may hear the motion in the dispositional hearing required by division (B) of section 2151.35 of the Revised Code. If the court issues an order pursuant to section 2151.353 [2151.35.3] of the Revised Code granting permanent custody of the child to the agency, the court shall immediately dismiss the motion made under division (D)(2) of section 2151.413 [2151.41.3] of the Revised Code.

The failure of the court to comply with the time periods set forth in division (A)(2) of this section does not affect the authority of the court to issue any order under this chapter and does not provide any basis for attacking the jurisdiction of the court or the validity of any order of the court.

(B)(1) Except as provided in division (B)(2) of this section, the court may grant permanent custody of a child to a movant if the court determines at the hearing held pursuant to division (A) of this section, by clear and convincing evidence, that it is in the best interest of the child to grant permanent custody of the child to the agency that filed the motion for permanent custody and that any of the following apply:

(a) The child is not abandoned or orphaned, has not been in the temporary custody of one or more public children services agencies or private child placing agencies for twelve or more months of a consecutive twenty-two-month period, or has not been in the temporary custody of one or more public children services agencies or private child placing agencies for twelve or more months of a consecutive twenty-two-month period if, as described in division (D)(1) of section 2151.413 [2151.41.3] of the Revised Code, the child was previously in the temporary custody of an equivalent agency in another state, and the child cannot be placed with either of the child's parents within a reasonable time or should not be placed with the child's parents.

(b) The child is abandoned.

(c) The child is orphaned, and there are no relatives of the child who are able to take permanent custody.

(d) The child has been in the temporary custody of one or more public children services agencies or private child placing agencies for twelve or more months of a consecutive twenty-two-month period or the child has been in the temporary custody of one or more public children services agencies or private child placing agencies for twelve or more months of a consecutive twenty-two-month period and, as described in division (D)(1) of section 2151.413 [2151.41.3] of the Revised Code, the child was previously in the temporary custody of an equivalent agency in another state.

For the purposes of division (B)(1) of this section, a child shall be considered to have entered the temporary custody of an agency on the earlier of the date the child is adjudicated pursuant to section 2151.28 of the Revised Code or the date that is sixty days after the removal of the child from home.

(2) With respect to a motion made pursuant to division (D)(2) of section 2151.413 [2151.41.3] of the Revised Code, the court shall grant permanent custody of the child to the movant if the court determines in accordance with division (E) of this section that the child cannot be placed with one of the child's parents within a reasonable time or should not be placed with either parent and determines in accordance with division (D) of this section that permanent custody is in the child's best interest.

(C) In making the determinations required by this section or division (A)(4) of section 2151.353 [2151.35.3] of the Revised Code, a court shall not consider the effect the granting of permanent custody to the agency would have upon any parent of the child. A written report of the guardian ad litem of the child shall be submitted to the court prior to or at the time of the hearing held pursuant to division (A) of this section or section 2151.35 of the Revised Code but shall not be submitted under oath.

If the court grants permanent custody of a child to a movant under this division, the court, upon the request of any party, shall file a written opinion setting forth its findings of fact and conclusions of law in relation to the proceeding. The court shall not deny an agency's motion for permanent custody solely because the agency failed to implement any particular aspect of the child's case plan.

(D)(1) In determining the best interest of a child at a hearing held pursuant to division (A) of this section or for the purposes of division (A)(4) or (5) of section 2151.353 [2151.35.3] or division (C) of section 2151.415 [2151.41.5] of the Revised Code, the court shall consider all relevant factors, including, but not limited to, the following:

(a) The interaction and interrelationship of the child with the child's parents, siblings, relatives, foster caregivers and out-of-home providers, and any other person who may significantly affect the child;

(b) The wishes of the child, as expressed directly by the child or through the child's guardian ad litem, with due regard for the maturity of the child;

(c) The custodial history of the child, including whether the child has been in the temporary custody of one or more public children services agencies or private child placing agencies for twelve or more months of a consecutive twenty-two-month period or the child has been in the temporary custody of one or more public children services agencies or private child placing agencies for twelve or more months of a consecutive twenty-two-month period and, as described in division (D)(1) of section 2151.413 [2151.41.3] of the Revised Code, the child was previously in the temporary custody of an equivalent agency in another state;

(d) The child's need for a legally secure permanent placement and whether that type of placement can be achieved without a grant of permanent custody to the agency;

(e) Whether any of the factors in divisions (E)(7) to (11) of this section apply in relation to the parents and child.

For the purposes of division (D)(1) of this section, a child shall be considered to have entered the temporary custody of an agency on the earlier of the date the child is adjudicated pursuant to section 2151.28 of the Revised Code or the date that is sixty days after the removal of the child from home.

(2) If all of the following apply, permanent custody is in the best interest of the child and the court shall commit the child to the permanent custody of a public children services agency or private child placing agency:

(a) The court determines by clear and convincing evidence that one or more of the factors in division (E) of this section exist and the child cannot be placed with one of the child's parents within a reasonable time or should not be placed with either parent.

(b) The child has been in an agency's custody for two years or longer, and no longer qualifies for temporary custody pursuant to division (D) of section 2151.415 [2151.41.5] of the Revised Code.

(c) The child does not meet the requirements for a planned permanent living arrangement pursuant to division (A)(5) of section 2151.353 [2151.35.3] of the Revised Code.

(d) Prior to the dispositional hearing, no relative or other interested person has filed, or has been identified in, a motion for legal custody of the child.

(E) In determining at a hearing held pursuant to division (A) of this section or for the purposes of division (A)(4) of section 2151.353 [2151.35.3] of the Revised Code whether a child cannot be placed with either parent within a reasonable period of time or should not be placed with the parents, the court shall consider all relevant evidence. If the court determines, by clear and convincing evidence, at a hearing held pursuant to division (A) of this section or for the purposes of division (A)(4) of section 2151.353 [2151.35.3] of the Revised Code that one or more of the following exist as to each of the child's parents, the court shall enter a finding that the child cannot be placed with either parent within a reasonable time or should not be placed with either parent:

(1) Following the placement of the child outside the child's home and notwithstanding reasonable case planning and diligent efforts by the agency to assist the parents to remedy the problems that initially caused the child to be placed outside the home, the parent has failed continuously and repeatedly to substantially remedy the conditions causing the child to be placed outside the child's home. In determining whether the parents have substantially remedied those conditions, the court shall consider parental utilization of medical, psychiatric, psychological, and other social and rehabilitative services and material resources that were made available to the parents for the purpose of changing parental conduct to allow them to resume and maintain parental duties.

(2) Chronic mental illness, chronic emotional illness, mental retardation, physical disability, or chemical dependency of the parent that is so severe that it makes the parent unable to provide an adequate permanent home for the child at the present time and, as anticipated, within one year after the court holds the hearing pursuant to division (A) of this section or for the purposes of division (A)(4) of section 2151.353 [2151.35.3] of the Revised Code;

(3) The parent committed any abuse as described in section 2151.031 [2151.03.1] of the Revised Code against the child, caused the child to suffer any neglect as described in section 2151.03 of the Revised Code, or allowed the child to suffer any neglect as described in section 2151.03 of the Revised Code between the date that the original complaint alleging abuse or neglect was filed and the date of the filing of the motion for permanent custody;

(4) The parent has demonstrated a lack of commitment toward the child by failing to regularly support, visit, or communicate with the child when able to do so, or by other actions showing an unwillingness to provide an adequate permanent home for the child;

(5) The parent is incarcerated for an offense committed against the child or a sibling of the child;

(6) The parent has been convicted of or pleaded guilty to an offense under division (A) or (C) of section 2919.22 or under section 2903.16, 2903.21, 2903.34, 2905.01, 2905.02, 2905.03, 2905.04†, 2905.05, 2907.07, 2907.08, 2907.09, 2907.12††, 2907.21, 2907.22, 2907.23, 2907.25, 2907.31, 2907.32, 2907.321 [2907.32.1], 2907.322 [2907.32.2], 2907.323 [2907.32.3], 2911.01, 2911.02, 2911.11, 2911.12, 2919.12, 2919.24, 2919.25, 2923.12, 2923.13, 2923.161 [2923.16.1], 2925.02, or 3716.11 of the Revised Code and the child or a sibling of the child was a victim of the offense or the parent has been convicted of or pleaded guilty to an offense under section 2903.04 of the Revised Code, a sibling of the child was the victim of the offense, and the parent who committed the offense poses an ongoing danger to the child or a sibling of the child.

(7) The parent has been convicted of or pleaded guilty to one of the following:

(a) An offense under section 2903.01, 2903.02, or 2903.03 of the Revised Code or under an existing or former law of this state, any other state, or the United States that is substantially equivalent to an offense described in those sections and the victim of the offense was a sibling of the child or the victim was another child who lived in the parent's household at the time of the offense;

(b) An offense under section 2903.11, 2903.12, or 2903.13 of the Revised Code or under an existing or former law of this state, any other state, or the United States that is substantially equivalent to an offense described in those sections and the victim of the offense is the child, a sibling of the child, or another child who lived in the parent's household at the time of the offense;

(c) An offense under division (B)(2) of section 2919.22 of the Revised Code or under an existing or former law of this state, any other state, or the United States that is substantially equivalent to the offense described in that section and the child, a sibling of the child, or another child who lived in the parent's household at the time of the offense is the victim of the offense;

(d) An offense under section 2907.02, 2907.03, 2907.04, 2907.05, or 2907.06 of the Revised Code or under an existing or former law of this state, any other state, or the United States that is substantially equivalent to an offense described in those sections and the victim of the offense is the child, a sibling of the child, or another child who lived in the parent's household at the time of the offense;

(e) A conspiracy or attempt to commit, or complicity in committing, an offense described in division (E)(7)(a) or (d) of this section.

(8) The parent has repeatedly withheld medical treatment or food from the child when the parent has the means to provide the treatment or food, and, in the case of withheld medical treatment, the parent withheld it for a purpose other than to treat the physical or mental illness or defect of the child by spiritual means through prayer alone in accordance with the tenets of a recognized religious body.

(9) The parent has placed the child at substantial risk of harm two or more times due to alcohol or drug abuse and has rejected treatment two or more times or refused to participate in further treatment two or more times after a case plan issued pursuant to section 2151.412 [2151.41.2] of the Revised Code requiring treatment of the parent was journalized as part of a dispositional order issued with respect to the child or an order was issued by any other court requiring treatment of the parent.

(10) The parent has abandoned the child.

(11) The parent has had parental rights involuntarily terminated with respect to a sibling of the child pursuant to this section or section 2151.353 [2151.35.3] or 2151.415 [2151.41.5] of the Revised Code, or under an existing or former law of this state, any other state, or the United States that is substantially equivalent to those sections, and the parent has failed to provide clear and convincing evidence to prove that, notwithstanding the prior termination, the parent can provide a legally secure permanent placement and adequate care for the health, welfare, and safety of the child.

(12) The parent is incarcerated at the time of the filing of the motion for permanent custody or the dispositional hearing of the child and will not be available to care for the child for at least eighteen months after the filing of the motion for permanent custody or the dispositional hearing.

(13) The parent is repeatedly incarcerated, and the repeated incarceration prevents the parent from providing care for the child.

(14) The parent for any reason is unwilling to provide food, clothing, shelter, and other basic necessities for the child or to prevent the child from suffering physical, emotional, or sexual abuse or physical, emotional, or mental neglect.

(15) The parent has committed abuse as described in section 2151.031 [2151.03.1] of the Revised Code against the child or caused or allowed the child to suffer neglect as described in section 2151.03 of the Revised Code, and the court determines that the seriousness, nature, or likelihood of recurrence of the abuse or neglect makes the child's placement with the child's parent a threat to the child's safety.

(16) Any other factor the court considers relevant.

(F) The parents of a child for whom the court has issued an order granting permanent custody pursuant to this section, upon the issuance of the order, cease to be parties to the action. This division is not intended to eliminate or restrict any right of the parents to appeal the granting of permanent custody of their child to a movant pursuant to this section.

**HISTORY: 138 v H 695 (Eff 10-24-80); 142 v S 89 (Eff 1-1-89); 146 v H 274 (Eff 8-8-96); 146 v H 419 (Eff 9-18-96); 147 v H 484 (Eff 3-18-99); 148 v H 176 (Eff 10-29-99); 148 v H 448. Eff 10-5-2000; 152 v S 163, § 1, eff. 8-14-08; 152 v H 7, § 1, eff. 4-7-09.**

† Repealed 7-1-96, division (E)(6).
†† Repealed 9-3-96, division (E)(6).

## § 2151.415 Motion requesting disposition order upon expiration of temporary custody order; extension.

(A) Except for cases in which a motion for permanent custody described in division (D)(1) of section 2151.413 [2151.41.3] of the Revised Code is required to be made, a public children services agency or private child placing agency that has been given temporary custody of a child pursuant to section 2151.353 [2151.35.3] of the Revised Code, not later than thirty days prior to the earlier of the date for the termination of the custody order pursuant to division (G) of section 2151.353 [2151.35.3] of the Revised Code or the date set at the dispositional hearing for the hearing to be held pursuant to this section, shall file a motion with the court that issued the order of disposition requesting that any of the following orders of disposition of the child be issued by the court:

(1) An order that the child be returned home and† the custody of the child's parents, guardian, or custodian without any restrictions;

(2) An order for protective supervision;

(3) An order that the child be placed in the legal custody of a relative or other interested individual;

(4) An order permanently terminating the parental rights of the child's parents;

(5) An order that the child be placed in a planned permanent living arrangement;

(6) In accordance with division (D) of this section, an order for the extension of temporary custody.

(B) Upon the filing of a motion pursuant to division (A) of this section, the court shall hold a dispositional hearing on the date set at the dispositional hearing held pursuant to section 2151.35 of the Revised Code, with notice to all parties to the action in accordance with the Juvenile Rules. After the dispositional hearing or at a date after the dispositional hearing that is not later than one year after the earlier of the date on which the complaint in the case was filed or the child was first placed into shelter care, the court, in accordance with the best interest of the child as supported by the evidence presented at the dispositional hearing, shall issue an order of disposition as set forth in division (A) of this section, except that all orders for permanent custody shall be made in accordance with sections 2151.413 [2151.41.3] and 2151.414 [2151.41.4] of the Revised Code. In issuing an order of disposition under this section, the court shall comply with section 2151.42 of the Revised Code.

(C)(1) If an agency pursuant to division (A) of this section requests the court to place a child into a planned permanent living arrangement, the agency shall present evidence to indicate why a planned permanent living arrangement is appropriate for the child, including, but not limited to, evidence that the agency has tried or considered all other possible dispositions for the child. A court shall not place a child in a planned permanent living arrangement, unless it finds, by clear and convincing evidence, that a planned permanent living arrangement is in the best interest of the child and that one of the following exists:

(a) The child, because of physical, mental, or psychological problems or needs, is unable to function in a family-like setting and must remain in residential or institutional care.

(b) The parents of the child have significant physical, mental, or psychological problems and are unable to care for the child because of those problems, adoption is not in the best interest of the child, as determined in accordance with division (D)(1) of section 2151.414 [2151.41.4] of the Revised Code, and the child retains a significant and positive relationship with a parent or relative;

(c) The child is sixteen years of age or older, has been counseled on the permanent placement options available, is unwilling to accept or unable to adapt to a permanent placement, and is in an agency program preparing for independent living.

(2) If the court issues an order placing a child in a planned permanent living arrangement, both of the following apply:

(a) The court shall issue a finding of fact setting forth the reasons for its finding;

(b) The agency may make any appropriate placement for the child and shall develop a case plan for the child that is designed to assist the child in finding a permanent home outside of the home of the parents.

(D)(1) If an agency pursuant to division (A) of this section requests the court to grant an extension of temporary custody for a period of up to six months, the agency shall include in the motion an explanation of the progress on the case plan of the child and of its expectations of reunifying the child with the child's family, or placing the child in a permanent placement, within the extension period. The court shall schedule a hearing on the motion, give notice of its date, time, and location to all parties and the guardian ad litem of the child, and at the hearing consider the evidence presented by the parties and the guardian ad litem. The court may extend the temporary custody order of the child for a period of up to six months, if it determines at the hearing, by clear and convincing evidence, that the extension is in the best interest of the child, there has been significant progress on the case plan of the child, and there is reasonable cause to believe that the child will be reunified with one of the parents or otherwise permanently placed within the period of extension. In determining whether to extend the temporary custody of the child pursuant to this division, the court shall comply with section 2151.42 of the Revised Code. If the court extends the temporary custody of the child pursuant to this division, upon request it shall issue findings of fact.

(2) Prior to the end of the extension granted pursuant to division (D)(1) of this section, the agency that received the extension shall file a motion with the court requesting the issuance of one of the orders of disposition set forth in divisions (A)(1) to (5) of this section or requesting the court to extend the temporary custody order of the child for an additional period of up to six months. If the agency requests the issuance of an order of disposition under divisions (A)(1) to (5) of this section or does not file any motion prior to the expiration of the extension period, the court shall conduct a hearing in accordance with division (B) of this section and issue an appropriate order of disposition. In issuing an order of disposition, the court shall comply with section 2151.42 of the Revised Code.

If the agency requests an additional extension of up to six months of the temporary custody order of the child, the court shall schedule and conduct a hearing in the manner set forth in division (D)(1) of this section. The court may extend the temporary custody order of the child for an additional period of up to six months if it determines at the hearing, by clear and convincing evidence, that the additional extension is in the best interest of the child, there has been substantial additional progress since the original extension of temporary custody in the case plan of the child, there has been substantial additional progress since the original extension of temporary custody toward reunifying the child with one of the parents or otherwise permanently placing the child, and there is reasonable cause to believe that the child will be reunified with one of the parents or otherwise placed in a permanent setting before the expiration of the additional extension period. In determining whether to grant an additional extension, the court shall comply with section 2151.42 of the Revised Code. If the court extends the temporary custody of the child for an additional period pursuant to this division, upon request it shall issue findings of fact.

(3) Prior to the end of the extension of a temporary custody order granted pursuant to division (D)(2) of this section, the agency that received the extension shall file a motion with the court requesting the issuance of one of the orders of disposition set forth in divisions (A)(1) to (5) of this section. Upon the filing of the motion by the agency or, if the agency does not file the motion prior to the expiration of the extension period, upon its own motion, the court, prior to the expiration of the extension period, shall conduct a hearing in accordance with division (B) of this section and issue an appropriate order of disposition. In issuing an order of disposition, the court shall comply with section 2151.42 of the Revised Code.

(4) No court shall grant an agency more than two extensions of temporary custody pursuant to division (D) of this section and the court shall not order an existing temporary custody order to continue beyond two years after the date on which the complaint was filed or the child was first placed into shelter care, whichever date is earlier, regardless of whether any extensions have been previously ordered pursuant to division (D) of this section.

(E) After the issuance of an order pursuant to division (B) of this section, the court shall retain jurisdiction over the child until the child attains the age of eighteen if the child is not mentally retarded, developmentally disabled, or physically impaired, the child attains the age of twenty-one if the child is mentally retarded, developmentally disabled, or physically impaired, or the child is adopted and a final decree of adoption is issued, unless the court's jurisdiction over the child is extended pursuant to division (E) of section 2151.353 [2151.35.3] of the Revised Code.

(F) The court, on its own motion or the motion of the agency or person with legal custody of the child, the child's guardian ad litem, or any other party to the action, may conduct a hearing with notice to all parties to determine whether any order issued pursuant to this section should be modified or terminated or whether any other dispositional order set forth in divisions (A)(1) to (5) of this section should be issued. After the hearing and consideration of all the evidence presented, the court, in accordance with the best interest of the child, may modify or terminate any order issued pursuant to this section or issue any dispositional order set forth in divisions (A)(1) to (5) of this section. In rendering a decision under this division, the court shall comply with section 2151.42 of the Revised Code.

(G) If the court places a child in a planned permanent living arrangement with a public children services agency or a private child placing agency pursuant to this section, the agency with which the child is placed in a planned permanent living arrangement shall not remove the child from the residential placement in which the child is originally placed pursuant to the case plan for the child or in which the child is placed with court approval pursuant to this division, unless the court and the guardian ad litem are given notice of the intended removal and the court issues an order approving the removal or unless the removal is necessary to protect the child from physical or emotional harm and the agency gives the court notice of the removal and of the reasons why the removal is necessary to protect the child from physical or emotional harm immediately after the removal of the child from the prior setting.

(H) If the hearing held under this section takes the place of an administrative review that otherwise would have been held under section 2151.416 [2151.41.6] of the Revised Code, the court at the hearing held under this section shall do all of the following in addition to any other requirements of this section:

(1) Determine the continued necessity for and the appropriateness of the child's placement;

(2) Determine the extent of compliance with the child's case plan;

(3) Determine the extent of progress that has been made toward alleviating or mitigating the causes necessitating the child's placement in foster care;

(4) Project a likely date by which the child may be returned to the child's home or placed for adoption or legal guardianship;

(5) Approve the permanency plan for the child consistent with section 2151.417 [2151.41.7] of the Revised Code.

**HISTORY: 142 v S 89 (Eff 1-1-89); 146 v H 274 (Eff 8-8-96); 147 v H 484 (Eff 3-18-99); 148 v H 176. Eff 10-29-99; 152 v H 7, § 1, eff. 4-7-09.**

† So in enrolled bill, division (A)(1). But see the HB 274 (146 v —) version, in which the preposition "to" was inadvertently deleted.

## § 2151.416 Administrative reviews of case plan; annual report.

(A) Each agency that is required by section 2151.412 [2151.41.2] of the Revised Code to prepare a case plan for a child shall complete a semiannual administrative review of the case plan no later than six months after the earlier of the date on which the complaint in the case was filed or the child was first placed in shelter care. After the first administrative review, the agency shall complete semiannual administrative reviews no later than every six months. If the court issues an order pursuant to section 2151.414 [2151.41.4] or 2151.415 [2151.41.5] of the Revised Code, the agency shall complete an administrative review no later than six months after the court's order and continue to complete administrative reviews no later than every six months after the first review, except that the court hearing held pursuant to section 2151.417 [2151.41.7] of the Revised Code may take the place of any administrative review that would otherwise be held at the time of the court hearing. When conducting a review, the child's health and safety shall be the paramount concern.

(B) Each administrative review required by division (A) of this section shall be conducted by a review panel of at least three persons, including, but not limited to, both of the following:

(1) A caseworker with day-to-day responsibility for, or familiarity with, the management of the child's case plan;

(2) A person who is not responsible for the management of the child's case plan or for the delivery of services to the child or the parents, guardian, or custodian of the child.

(C) Each semiannual administrative review shall include, but not be limited to, a joint meeting by the review panel with the parents, guardian, or custodian of the child, the guardian ad litem of the child, and the child's foster care provider and shall include an opportunity for those persons to submit any written materials to be included in the case record of the child. If a parent, guardian, custodian, guardian ad litem, or foster care provider of the child cannot be located after reasonable efforts to do so or declines to participate in the administrative review after being contacted, the agency does not have to include them in the joint meeting.

(D) The agency shall prepare a written summary of the semiannual administrative review that shall include, but not be limited to, all of the following:

(1) A conclusion regarding the safety and appropriateness of the child's foster care placement;

(2) The extent of the compliance with the case plan of all parties;

(3) The extent of progress that has been made toward alleviating the circumstances that required the agency to assume temporary custody of the child;

(4) An estimated date by which the child may be returned to and safely maintained in the child's home or placed for adoption or legal custody;

(5) An updated case plan that includes any changes that the agency is proposing in the case plan;

(6) The recommendation of the agency as to which agency or person should be given custodial rights over the child for the six-month period after the administrative review;

(7) The names of all persons who participated in the administrative review.

(E) The agency shall file the summary with the court no later than seven days after the completion of the administrative review. If the agency proposes a change to the case plan as a result of the administrative review, the agency shall file the proposed change with the court at the time it files the summary. The agency shall give notice of the summary and proposed change in writing before the end of the next day after filing them to all parties and the child's guardian ad litem. All parties and the guardian ad litem shall have seven days after the date the notice is sent to object to and request a hearing on the proposed change.

(1) If the court receives a timely request for a hearing, the court shall schedule a hearing pursuant to section 2151.417 [2151.41.7] of the Revised Code to be held not later than thirty days after the court receives the request. The court shall give notice of the date, time, and location of the hearing to all parties and the guardian ad litem. The agency may implement the proposed change after the hearing, if the court approves it. The agency shall not implement the proposed change unless it is approved by the court.

(2) If the court does not receive a timely request for a hearing, the court may approve the proposed change without a hearing. If the court approves the proposed change without a hearing, it shall journalize the case plan with the change not later than fourteen days after the change is filed with the court. If the court does not approve the proposed change to the case plan, it shall schedule a review hearing to be held pursuant to section 2151.417 [2151.41.7] of the Revised Code no later than

thirty days after the expiration of the fourteen-day time period and give notice of the date, time, and location of the hearing to all parties and the guardian ad litem of the child. If, despite the requirements of this division and division (D) of section 2151.417 [2151.41.7] of the Revised Code, the court neither approves and journalizes the proposed change nor conducts a hearing, the agency may implement the proposed change not earlier than fifteen days after it is submitted to the court.

(F) The director of job and family services may adopt rules pursuant to Chapter 119. of the Revised Code for procedures and standard forms for conducting administrative reviews pursuant to this section.

(G) The juvenile court that receives the written summary of the administrative review, upon determining, either from the written summary, case plan, or otherwise, that the custody or care arrangement is not in the best interest of the child, may terminate the custody of an agency and place the child in the custody of another institution or association certified by the department of job and family services under section 5103.03 of the Revised Code.

**HISTORY: RC § 5103.15.1, 136 v H 156 (Eff 1-1-77); 137 v H 832 (Eff 3-13-79); 138 v H 695 (Eff 10-24-80); 141 v H 428 (Eff 12-23-86); RC § 2151.41.6, 142 v S 89 (Eff 1-1-89); 146 v H 274 (Eff 8-8-96); 146 v H 419 (Eff 9-18-96); 147 v H 484 (Eff 3-18-99); 148 v H 471. Eff 7-1-2000; 151 v H 66, § 101.01, eff. 6-30-05; 151 v S 238, § 1, eff. 9-21-06.**

The effective date is set by § 612.12 of 151 v H 66.
The effective date is set by section 12(A) of HB 471.

## § 2151.417 Court review of child's placement or custody arrangement; continuing jurisdiction; citizen's review board.

(A) Any court that issues a dispositional order pursuant to section 2151.353 [2151.35.3], 2151.414 [2151.41.4], or 2151.415 [2151.41.5] of the Revised Code may review at any time the child's placement or custody arrangement, the case plan prepared for the child pursuant to section 2151.412 [2151.41.2] of the Revised Code, the actions of the public children services agency or private child placing agency in implementing that case plan, the child's permanency plan if the child's permanency plan has been approved, and any other aspects of the child's placement or custody arrangement. In conducting the review, the court shall determine the appropriateness of any agency actions, the safety and appropriateness of continuing the child's placement or custody arrangement, and whether any changes should be made with respect to the child's permanency plan or placement or custody arrangement or with respect to the actions of the agency under the child's placement or custody arrangement. Based upon the evidence presented at a hearing held after notice to all parties and the guardian ad litem of the child, the court may require the agency, the parents, guardian, or custodian of the child, and the physical custodians of the child to take any reasonable action that the court determines is necessary and in the best interest of the child or to discontinue any action that it determines is not in the best interest of the child.

(B) If a court issues a dispositional order pursuant to section 2151.353 [2151.35.3], 2151.414 [2151.41.4], or 2151.415 [2151.41.5] of the Revised Code, the court has continuing jurisdiction over the child as set forth in division (E)(1) of section 2151.353 [2151.35.3] of the Revised Code. The court may amend a dispositional order in accordance with division (E)(2) of section 2151.353 [2151.35.3] of the Revised Code at any time upon its own motion or upon the motion of any interested party. The court shall comply with section 2151.42 of the Revised Code in amending any dispositional order pursuant to this division.

(C) Any court that issues a dispositional order pursuant to section 2151.353 [2151.35.3], 2151.414 [2151.41.4], or 2151.415 [2151.41.5] of the Revised Code shall hold a review hearing one year after the earlier of the date on which the complaint in the case was filed or the child was first placed into shelter care to review the case plan prepared pursuant to section 2151.412 [2151.41.2] of the Revised Code and the child's placement or custody arrangement, to approve or review the permanency plan for the child, and to make changes to the case plan and placement or custody arrangement consistent with the permanency plan. The court shall schedule the review hearing at the time that it holds the dispositional hearing pursuant to section 2151.35 of the Revised Code.

The court shall hold a similar review hearing no later than every twelve months after the initial review hearing until the child is adopted, returned to the parents, or the court otherwise terminates the child's placement or custody arrangement, except that the dispositional hearing held pursuant to section 2151.415 [2151.41.5] of the Revised Code shall take the place of the first review hearing to be held under this section. The court shall schedule each subsequent review hearing at the conclusion of the review hearing immediately preceding the review hearing to be scheduled.

(D) If, within fourteen days after a written summary of an administrative review is filed with the court pursuant to section 2151.416 [2151.41.6] of the Revised Code, the court does not approve the proposed change to the case plan filed pursuant to division (E) of section 2151.416 [2151.41.6] of the Revised Code or a party or the guardian ad litem requests a review hearing pursuant to division (E) of that section, the court shall hold a review hearing in the same manner that it holds review hearings pursuant to division (C) of this section, except that if a review hearing is required by this division and if a hearing is to be held pursuant to division (C) of this section or section 2151.415 [2151.41.5] of the Revised Code, the hearing held pursuant to division (C) of this section or section 2151.415 [2151.41.5] of the Revised Code shall take the place of the review hearing required by this division.

(E) If a court determines pursuant to section 2151.419 [2151.41.9] of the Revised Code that a public children services agency or private child placing agency is not required to make reasonable efforts to prevent the removal of a child from the child's home, eliminate the continued removal of a child from the child's home, and return the child to the child's home, and the court does not return the child to the child's home pursuant to division (A)(3) of section 2151.419 [2151.41.9] of the revised code, the court shall hold a review hearing to approve the permanency plan for the child and, if appropriate, to make changes to the child's case plan and the child's placement or custody arrangement consistent with the permanency plan. The court may hold the hearing immediately following the determination under section 2151.419 [2151.41.9] of the Revised Code and shall hold it no later than thirty days after making that determination.

(F) The court shall give notice of the review hearings held pursuant to this section to every interested party, including, but not limited to, the appropriate agency employees who are responsible for the child's care and planning, the child's parents, any person who had guardianship or legal custody of the child prior to the custody order, the child's guardian ad litem, and the child. The court shall summon every interested party to appear at the review hearing and give them an opportunity to testify and to present other evidence with respect to the child's custody arrangement, including, but not limited to, the following: the case plan for the child† the permanency plan, if one exists; the actions taken by the child's custodian; the need for a change in the child's custodian or caseworker; and the need for any specific action to be taken with respect to the child. The court shall require any interested party to testify or present other evidence when necessary to a proper determination of the issues presented at the review hearing. In any review hearing that pertains to a permanency plan for a child who will not be returned to the parent, the court shall consider in-state and out-of-state placement options and the court shall determine whether the in-state or the out-of-state placement continues to be appropriate and in the best interests of the child. In any review hearing that pertains to a permanency plan for a child, the court or a citizens board appointed by the court pursuant to division (H) of this section shall consult with the child, in an age-appropriate manner, regarding the proposed permanency plan for the child.

(G) After the review hearing, the court shall take the following actions based upon the evidence presented:

(1) If an administrative review has been conducted, determine whether the conclusions of the review are supported by a preponderance of the evidence and approve or modify the case plan based upon that evidence;

(2) If the hearing was held under division (C) or (E) of this section, approve a permanency plan for the child that specifies whether and, if applicable, when the child will be safely returned home or placed for adoption, for legal custody, or in a planned permanent living arrangement. A permanency plan approved after a hearing under division (E) of this section shall not include any provision requiring the child to be returned to the child's home.

(3) If the child is in temporary custody, do all of the following:

(a) Determine whether the child can and should be returned home with or without an order for protective supervision;

(b) If the child can and should be returned home with or without an order for protective supervision, terminate the order for temporary custody;

(c) If the child cannot or should not be returned home with an order for protective supervision, determine whether the agency currently with custody of the child should retain custody or whether another public children services agency, private child placing agency, or an individual should be given custody of the child.

The court shall comply with section 2151.42 of the Revised Code in taking any action under this division.

(4) If the child is in permanent custody, determine what actions are required by the custodial agency and of any other organizations or persons in order to facilitate an adoption of the child and make any appropriate orders with respect to the custody arrangement or conditions of the child, including, but not limited to, a transfer of permanent custody to another public children services agency or private child placing agency;

(5) Journalize the terms of the updated case plan for the child.

(H) The court may appoint a referee or a citizens review board to conduct the review hearings that the court is required by this section to conduct, subject to the review and approval by the court of any determinations made by the referee or citizens review board. If the court appoints a citizens review board to conduct the review hearings, the board shall consist of one member representing the general public and four members who are trained or experienced in the care or placement of children and have training or experience in the fields of medicine, psychology, social work, education, or any related field. Of the initial appointments to the board, two shall be for a term of one year, two shall be for a term of two years, and one shall be for a term of three years, with all the terms ending one year after the date on which the appointment was made. Thereafter, all terms of the board members shall be for three years and shall end on the same day of the same month of the year as did the term that they succeed. Any member appointed to fill a vacancy occurring prior to the expiration of the term for which the member's predecessor was appointed shall hold office for the remainder of the term.

(I) A copy of the court's determination following any review hearing held pursuant to this section shall be sent to the custodial agency, the guardian ad litem of the child who is the subject of the review hearing, and, if that child is not the subject of a permanent commitment hearing, the parents of the child.

(J) If the hearing held under this section takes the place of an administrative review that otherwise would have been held under section 2151.416 [2151.41.6] of the Revised Code, the court at the hearing held under this section shall do all of the following in addition to any other requirements of this section:

(1) Determine the continued necessity for and the safety and appropriateness of the child's placement;

(2) Determine the extent of compliance with the child's case plan;

(3) Determine the extent of progress that has been made toward alleviating or mitigating the causes necessitating the child's placement in foster care;

(4) Project a likely date by which the child may be safely returned home or placed for adoption or legal custody.

(K)(1) Whenever the court is required to approve a permanency plan under this section or section 2151.415 [2151.41.5] of the Revised Code, the public children services agency or private child placing agency that filed the complaint in the case, has custody of the child, or will be given custody of the child shall develop a permanency plan for the child. The agency must file the plan with the court prior to the hearing under this section or section 2151.415 [2151.41.5] of the Revised Code.

(2) The permanency plan developed by the agency must specify whether and, if applicable, when the child will be safely returned home or placed for adoption or legal custody. If the agency determines that there is a compelling reason why returning the child home or placing the child for adoption or legal custody is not in the best interest of the child, the plan shall provide that the child will be placed in a planned permanent living arrangement. A permanency plan developed as a result of a determination made under division (A)(2) of section 2151.419 [2151.41.9] of the Revised Code may not include any provision requiring the child to be returned home.

**HISTORY: 142 v S 89 (Eff 1-1-89); 146 v H 274 (Eff 8-8-96); 147 v H 484. Eff 3-18-99; 152 v S 163, § 1, eff. 8-14-08.**

† So in enrolled bill, division (F).

## § 2151.418 Amended and renumbered RC § 5103.03.18 in HB 332 (148 v —), eff 1-1-2001.

## § 2151.419 Determination as to whether agency made reasonable efforts to prevent removal or to return child to home.

(A)(1) Except as provided in division (A)(2) of this section, at any hearing held pursuant to section 2151.28, division (E) of section 2151.31, or section 2151.314 [2151.31.4], 2151.33, or 2151.353 [2151.35.3] of the Revised Code at which the court removes a child from the child's home or continues the removal of a child from the child's home, the court shall determine whether the public children services agency or private child placing agency that filed the complaint in the case, removed the child from home, has custody of the child, or will be given custody of the child has made reasonable efforts to prevent the removal of the child from the child's home, to eliminate the continued removal of the child from the child's home, or to make it possible for the child to return safely home. The agency shall have the burden of proving that it has made those reasonable efforts. If the agency removed the child from home during an emergency in which the child could not safely remain at home and the agency did not have prior contact with the child, the court is not prohibited, solely because the agency did not make reasonable efforts during the emergency to prevent the removal of the child, from determining that the agency made those reasonable efforts. In determining whether reasonable efforts were made, the child's health and safety shall be paramount.

(2) If any of the following apply, the court shall make a determination that the agency is not required to make reasonable efforts to prevent the removal of the child from the child's home, eliminate the continued removal of the child from the child's home, and return the child to the child's home:

(a) The parent from whom the child was removed has been convicted of or pleaded guilty to one of the following:

(i) An offense under section 2903.01, 2903.02, or 2903.03 of the Revised Code or under an existing or former law of this state, any other state, or the United States that is substantially equivalent to an offense described in those sections and the victim of the offense was a sibling of the child or the victim was another child who lived in the parent's household at the time of the offense;

(ii) An offense under section 2903.11, 2903.12, or 2903.13 of the Revised Code or under an existing or former law of this state, any other state, or the United States that is substantially equivalent to an offense described in those sections and the victim of the offense is the child, a sibling of the child, or another child who lived in the parent's household at the time of the offense;

(iii) An offense under division (B)(2) of section 2919.22 of the Revised Code or under an existing or former law of this state, any other state, or the United States that is substantially equivalent to the offense described in that section and the child, a sibling of the child, or another child who lived in the parent's household at the time of the offense is the victim of the offense;

(iv) An offense under section 2907.02, 2907.03, 2907.04, 2907.05, or 2907.06 of the Revised Code or under an existing or former law of this state, any other state, or the United States that is substantially equivalent to an offense described in those sections and the victim of the offense is the child, a sibling of the child, or another child who lived in the parent's household at the time of the offense;

(v) A conspiracy or attempt to commit, or complicity in committing, an offense described in division (A)(2)(a)(i) or (iv) of this section.

(b) The parent from whom the child was removed has repeatedly withheld medical treatment or food from the child when the parent has the means to provide the treatment or food. If the parent has withheld medical treatment in order to treat the physical or mental illness or defect of the child by spiritual means through prayer alone, in accordance with the tenets of a recognized religious body, the court or agency shall comply with the requirements of division (A)(1) of this section.

(c) The parent from whom the child was removed has placed the child at substantial risk of harm two or more times due to alcohol or drug abuse and has rejected treatment two or more times or refused to participate in further treatment two or more times after a case plan issued pursuant to section 2151.412 [2151.41.2] of the Revised Code requiring treatment of the parent was journalized as part of a dispositional order issued with respect to the child or an order was issued by any other court requiring such treatment of the parent.

(d) The parent from whom the child was removed has abandoned the child.

(e) The parent from whom the child was removed has had parental rights involuntarily terminated with respect to a sibling of the child pursuant to section 2151.353 [2151.35.3], 2151.414 [2151.41.4], or 2151.415 [2151.41.5] of the Revised Code or under an existing or former law of this state, any other state, or the United States that is substantially equivalent to those sections.

(3) At any hearing in which the court determines whether to return a child to the child's home, the court may issue an order that returns the child in situations in which the conditions described in divisions (A)(2)(a) to (e) of this section are present.

(B)(1) A court that is required to make a determination as described in division (A)(1) or (2) of this section shall issue written findings of fact setting forth the reasons supporting its determination. If the court makes a written determination under division (A)(1) of this section, it shall briefly describe in the findings of fact the relevant services provided by the agency to the family of the child and why those services did not prevent the removal of the child from the child's home or enable the child to return safely home.

(2) If a court issues an order that returns the child to the child's home in situations in which division (A)(2)(a), (b), (c), (d), or (e) of this section applies, the court shall issue written findings of fact setting forth the reasons supporting its determination.

(C) If the court makes a determination pursuant to division (A)(2) of this section, the court shall conduct a review hearing pursuant to section 2151.417 [2151.41.7] of the Revised Code to approve a permanency plan with respect to the child, unless the court issues an order returning the child home pursuant to division (A)(3) of this section. The hearing to approve the permanency plan may be held immediately following the court's determination pursuant to division (A)(2) of this section and shall be held no later than thirty days following that determination.

**HISTORY: 142 v S 89 (Eff 1-1-89); 147 v H 484 (Eff 3-18-99); 148 v H 176. Eff 10-29-99; 152 v S 163, § 1, eff. 8-14-08.**

## § 2151.42 Consideration of whether return to parents is in best interest of child; certain orders granting legal custody intended to be permanent.

(A) At any hearing in which a court is asked to modify or terminate an order of disposition issued under section 2151.353 [2151.35.3], 2151.415 [2151.41.5], or 2151.417 [2151.41.7] of the Revised Code, the court, in determining whether to return the child to the child's parents, shall consider whether it is in the best interest of the child.

(B) An order of disposition issued under division (A)(3) of section 2151.353 [2151.35.3], division (A)(3) of section 2151.415 [2151.41.5], or section 2151.417 [2151.41.7] of the Revised Code granting legal custody of a child to a person is intended to be permanent in nature. A court shall not modify or terminate an order granting legal custody of a child unless it finds, based on facts that have arisen since the order was issued or that were unknown to the court at that time, that a change has occurred in the circumstances of the child or the person who was granted legal custody, and that modification or termination of the order is necessary to serve the best interest of the child.

**HISTORY: 147 v H 484 (Eff 3-18-99); 148 v H 176. Eff 10-29-99.**

**Not analogous to former RC § 2151.42 (GC § 1639-46; 117 v 520; 119 v 731; 121 v 557; Bureau of Code Revision, 10-1-53; 130 v 625), repealed 134 v H 511, § 2, eff 1-1-74.**

## § 2151.421 Duty to report child abuse or neglect; investigation and followup procedures.

(A)(1)(a) No person described in division (A)(1)(b) of this section who is acting in an official or professional capacity and knows, or has reasonable cause to suspect based on facts that would cause a reasonable person in a similar position to suspect, that a child under eighteen years of age or a mentally retarded, developmentally disabled, or physically impaired child under twenty-one years of age has suffered or faces a threat of suffering any physical or mental wound, injury, disability, or condition of a nature that reasonably indicates abuse or neglect of the child shall fail to immediately report that knowledge or reasonable cause to suspect to the entity or persons specified in this division. Except as provided in section 5120.173 of the Revised Code, the person making the report shall make it to the public children services agency or a municipal or county peace officer in the county in which the child resides or in which the abuse or neglect is occurring or has occurred. In the circumstances described in section 5120.173 of the Revised Code, the person making the report shall make it to the entity specified in that section.

(b) Division (A)(1)(a) of this section applies to any person who is an attorney; physician, including a hospital intern or resident; dentist; podiatrist; practitioner of a limited branch of medicine as specified in section 4731.15 of the Revised Code; registered nurse; licensed practical nurse; visiting nurse; other health care professional; licensed psychologist; licensed school psychologist; independent marriage and family therapist or marriage and family therapist; speech pathologist or audiologist; coroner; administrator or employee of a child day-care center; administrator or employee of a residential camp or child day camp; administrator or employee of a certified child care agency or other public or private children services agency; school teacher; school employee; school authority; person engaged in social work or the practice of professional counseling; agent of a county humane society; person, other than a cleric, rendering spiritual treatment through prayer in accordance with the tenets of a well-recognized religion; employee of a county department of job and family services who is a professional and who works with children and families; superintendent, board member, or employee of a county board of developmental disabilities; investigative agent contracted with by a county board of developmental disabilities; employee of the department of developmental disabilities; employee of a facility or home that provides respite care in accordance with section 5123.171 of the Revised Code; employee of a home health agency; employee of an entity that provides homemaker services; a person performing the duties of an assessor pursuant to Chapter 3107. or 5103. of the Revised Code; or third party employed by a public children services agency to assist in providing child or family related services.

(2) Except as provided in division (A)(3) of this section, an attorney or a physician is not required to make a report pursuant to division (A)(1) of this section concerning any communication the attorney or physician receives from a client or patient in an attorney-client or physician-patient relationship, if, in accordance with division (A) or (B) of section 2317.02 of the Revised Code, the attorney or physician could not testify with respect to that communication in a civil or criminal proceeding.

(3) The client or patient in an attorney-client or physician-patient relationship described in division (A)(2) of this section is deemed to have waived any testimonial privilege under division (A) or (B) of section 2317.02 of the Revised Code with respect to any communication the attorney or physician receives from the client or patient in that attorney-client or physician-patient relationship, and the attorney or physician shall make a report pursuant to division (A)(1) of this section with respect to that communication, if all of the following apply:

(a) The client or patient, at the time of the communication, is either a child under eighteen years of age or a mentally retarded, developmentally disabled, or physically impaired person under twenty-one years of age.

(b) The attorney or physician knows, or has reasonable cause to suspect based on facts that would cause a reasonable person in similar position to suspect, as a result of the communication or any observations made during that communication, that the client or patient has suffered or faces a threat of suffering any physical or mental wound, injury, disability, or condition of a nature that reasonably indicates abuse or neglect of the client or patient.

(c) The abuse or neglect does not arise out of the client's or patient's attempt to have an abortion without the notification of her parents, guardian, or custodian in accordance with section 2151.85 of the Revised Code.

(4)(a) No cleric and no person, other than a volunteer, designated by any church, religious society, or faith acting as a leader, official, or delegate on behalf of the church, religious society, or faith who is acting in an official or professional capacity, who knows, or has reasonable cause to believe based on facts that would cause a reasonable person in a similar position to believe, that a child under eighteen years of age or a mentally retarded, developmentally disabled, or physically impaired child under twenty-one years of age has suffered or faces a threat of suffering any physical or mental wound, injury, disability, or condition of a nature that reasonably indicates abuse or neglect of the child, and who knows, or has reasonable cause to believe based on facts that would cause a reasonable person in a similar position to believe, that another cleric or another person, other than a volunteer, designated by a church, religious society, or faith acting as a leader, official, or delegate on behalf of the church, religious society, or faith caused, or poses the threat of causing, the wound, injury, disability, or condition that reasonably indicates abuse or neglect shall fail to immediately report that knowledge or reasonable cause to believe to the entity or persons specified in this division. Except as provided in section 5120.173 of the Revised Code, the person making the report shall make it to the public children services agency or a municipal or county peace officer in the county in which the child resides or in which the abuse or neglect is occurring or has occurred. In the circumstances described in section 5120.173 of the Revised Code, the person making the report shall make it to the entity specified in that section.

(b) Except as provided in division (A)(4)(c) of this section, a cleric is not required to make a report pursuant to division (A)(4)(a) of this section concerning any communication the cleric receives from a penitent in a cleric-penitent relationship, if, in accordance with division (C) of section 2317.02 of the Revised Code, the cleric could not testify with respect to that communication in a civil or criminal proceeding.

(c) The penitent in a cleric-penitent relationship described in division (A)(4)(b) of this section is deemed to have waived any testimonial privilege under division (C) of section 2317.02 of the Revised Code with respect to any communication the cleric receives from the penitent in that cleric-penitent relationship, and the cleric shall make a report pursuant to division (A)(4)(a) of this section with respect to that communication, if all of the following apply:

(i) The penitent, at the time of the communication, is either a child under eighteen years of age or a mentally retarded, developmentally disabled, or physically impaired person under twenty-one years of age.

(ii) The cleric knows, or has reasonable cause to believe based on facts that would cause a reasonable person in a similar position to believe, as a result of the communication or any observations made during that communication, the penitent has suffered or faces a threat of suffering any physical or mental wound, injury, disability, or condition of a nature that reasonably indicates abuse or neglect of the penitent.

(iii) The abuse or neglect does not arise out of the penitent's attempt to have an abortion performed upon a child under eighteen years of age or upon a mentally retarded, developmentally disabled, or physically impaired person under twenty-one years of age without the notification of her parents, guardian, or custodian in accordance with section 2151.85 of the Revised Code.

(d) Divisions (A)(4)(a) and (c) of this section do not apply in a cleric-penitent relationship when the disclosure of any communication the cleric receives from the penitent is in violation of the sacred trust.

(e) As used in divisions (A)(1) and (4) of this section, "cleric" and "sacred trust" have the same meanings as in section 2317.02 of the Revised Code.

(B) Anyone who knows, or has reasonable cause to suspect based on facts that would cause a reasonable person in similar circumstances to suspect, that a child under eighteen years of age or a mentally retarded, developmentally disabled, or physically impaired person under twenty-one years of age has suffered or faces a threat of suffering any physical or mental wound, injury, disability, or other condition of a nature that reasonably indicates abuse or neglect of the child may report or cause reports to be made of that knowledge or reasonable cause to suspect to the entity or persons specified in this division. Except as provided in section 5120.173 of the Revised Code, a person making a report or causing a report to be made under this division shall make it or cause it to be made to the public children services agency or to a municipal or county peace officer. In the circumstances described in section 5120.173 of the Revised Code, a person making a report or causing a report to be made under this division shall make it or cause it to be made to the entity specified in that section.

(C) Any report made pursuant to division (A) or (B) of this section shall be made forthwith either by telephone or in person and shall be followed by a written report, if requested by the receiving agency or officer. The written report shall contain:

(1) The names and addresses of the child and the child's parents or the person or persons having custody of the child, if known;

(2) The child's age and the nature and extent of the child's injuries, abuse, or neglect that is known or reasonably suspected or believed, as applicable, to have occurred or of the threat of injury, abuse, or neglect that is known or reasonably suspected or believed, as applicable, to exist, including any evidence of previous injuries, abuse, or neglect;

(3) Any other information that might be helpful in establishing the cause of the injury, abuse, or neglect that is known or reasonably suspected or believed, as applicable, to have occurred or of the threat of injury, abuse, or neglect that is known or reasonably suspected or believed, as applicable, to exist.

Any person, who is required by division (A) of this section to report child abuse or child neglect that is known or reasonably suspected or believed to have occurred, may take or cause to be taken color photographs of areas of trauma visible on a child and, if medically indicated, cause to be performed radiological examinations of the child.

(D) As used in this division, "children's advocacy center" and "sexual abuse of a child" have the same meanings as in section 2151.425 of the Revised Code.

(1) When a municipal or county peace officer receives a report concerning the possible abuse or neglect of a child or the possible threat of abuse or neglect of a child, upon receipt of the report, the municipal or county peace officer who receives the report shall refer the report to the appropriate public children services agency.

(2) When a public children services agency receives a report pursuant to this division or division (A) or (B) of this section, upon receipt of the report, the public children services agency shall do both of the following:

(a) Comply with section 2151.422 of the Revised Code;

(b) If the county served by the agency is also served by a children's advocacy center and the report alleges sexual abuse of a child or another type of abuse of a child that is specified in the memorandum of understanding that creates the center as being within the center's jurisdiction, comply regarding the report with the protocol and procedures for referrals and investigations, with the coordinating activities, and with the authority or responsibility for performing or providing functions, activities, and services stipulated in the interagency agreement entered into under section 2151.428 of the Revised Code relative to that center.

(E) No township, municipal, or county peace officer shall remove a child about whom a report is made pursuant to this section from the child's parents, stepparents, or guardian or any other persons having custody of the child without consultation with the public children services agency, unless, in the judgment of the officer, and, if the report was made by physician, the physician, immediate removal is considered essential to protect the child from further abuse or neglect. The agency that must be consulted shall be the agency conducting the investigation of the report as determined pursuant to section 2151.422 of the Revised Code.

(F)(1) Except as provided in section 2151.422 of the Revised Code or in an interagency agreement entered into under section 2151.428 of the Revised Code that applies to the particular report, the public children services agency shall investigate, within twenty-four hours, each report of child abuse or child neglect that is known or reasonably suspected or believed to have occurred and of a threat of child abuse or child neglect that is known or reasonably suspected or believed to exist that is referred to it under this section to determine the circumstances surrounding the injuries, abuse, or neglect or the threat of injury, abuse, or neglect, the cause of the injuries, abuse, neglect, or threat, and the person or persons responsible. The investigation shall be made in cooperation with the law enforcement agency and in accordance with the memorandum of understanding prepared under division (J) of this section. A representative of the public children services agency shall, at the time of initial contact with the person subject to the investigation, inform the person of the specific complaints or allegations made against the person. The information shall be given in a manner that is consistent with division (H)(1) of this section and protects the rights of the person making the report under this section.

A failure to make the investigation in accordance with the memorandum is not grounds for, and shall not result in, the dismissal of any charges or complaint arising from the report or the suppression of any evidence obtained as a result of the report and does not give, and shall not be construed as giving, any rights or any grounds for appeal or post-conviction relief to any person. The public children services agency shall report each case to the uniform statewide automated child welfare information system that the department of job and family services shall maintain in accordance with section 5101.13 of the Revised Code. The public children services agency shall submit a report of its investigation, in writing, to the law enforcement agency.

(2) The public children services agency shall make any recommendations to the county prosecuting attorney or city director of law that it considers necessary to protect any children that are brought to its attention.

(G)(1)(a) Except as provided in division (H)(3) of this section, anyone or any hospital, institution, school, health department, or agency participating in the making of reports under division (A) of this section, anyone or any hospital, institution, school, health department, or agency participating in good faith in the making of reports under division (B) of this section, and anyone participating in good faith in a judicial proceeding resulting from the reports, shall be immune from any civil or criminal liability for injury, death, or loss to person or property that otherwise might be incurred or imposed as a result of the making of the reports or the participation in the judicial proceeding.

(b) Notwithstanding section 4731.22 of the Revised Code, the physician-patient privilege shall not be a ground for excluding evidence regarding a child's injuries, abuse, or neglect, or the cause of the injuries, abuse, or neglect in any judicial proceeding resulting from a report submitted pursuant to this section.

(2) In any civil or criminal action or proceeding in which it is alleged and proved that participation in the making of a report under this section was not in good faith or participation in a judicial proceeding resulting from a report made under this section was not in good faith, the court shall award the prevailing party reasonable attorney's fees and costs and, if a civil action or proceeding is voluntarily dismissed, may award reasonable attorney's fees and costs to the party against whom the civil action or proceeding is brought.

(H)(1) Except as provided in divisions (H)(4) and (N) of this section, a report made under this section is confidential. The information provided in a report made pursuant to this section and the name of the person who made the report shall not be released for use, and shall not be used, as evidence in any civil action or proceeding brought against the person who made the report. Nothing in this division shall preclude the use of reports of other incidents of known or suspected abuse or neglect in a civil action or proceeding brought pursuant to division (M) of this section against a person who is alleged to have violated division (A)(1) of this section, provided that any information in a report that would identify the child who is the subject of the report or the maker of the report, if the maker of the report is not the defendant or an agent or employee of the defendant, has been redacted. In a criminal proceeding, the report is admissible in evidence in accordance with the Rules of Evidence and is subject to discovery in accordance with the Rules of Criminal Procedure.

(2) No person shall permit or encourage the unauthorized dissemination of the contents of any report made under this section.

(3) A person who knowingly makes or causes another person to make a false report under division (B) of this section that alleges that any person has committed an act or omission that resulted in a child being an abused child or a neglected child is guilty of a violation of section 2921.14 of the Revised Code.

(4) If a report is made pursuant to division (A) or (B) of this section and the child who is the subject of the report dies for any reason at any time after the report is made, but before the child attains eighteen years of age, the public children services agency or municipal or county peace officer to which the report was made or referred, on the request of the child fatality review board, shall submit a summary sheet of information providing a summary of the report to the review board of the county in which the deceased child resided at the time of death. On the request of the review board, the agency or peace officer may, at its discretion, make the report available to the review board. If the county served by the public children services agency is also served by a children's advocacy center and the report of alleged sexual abuse of a child or another type of abuse of a child is specified in the memorandum of understanding that creates the center as

being within the center's jurisdiction, the agency or center shall perform the duties and functions specified in this division in accordance with the interagency agreement entered into under section 2151.428 of the Revised Code relative to that advocacy center.

(5) A public children services agency shall advise a person alleged to have inflicted abuse or neglect on a child who is the subject of a report made pursuant to this section, including a report alleging sexual abuse of a child or another type of abuse of a child referred to a children's advocacy center pursuant to an interagency agreement entered into under section 2151.428 of the Revised Code, in writing of the disposition of the investigation. The agency shall not provide to the person any information that identifies the person who made the report, statements of witnesses, or police or other investigative reports.

(I) Any report that is required by this section, other than a report that is made to the state highway patrol as described in section 5120.173 of the Revised Code, shall result in protective services and emergency supportive services being made available by the public children services agency on behalf of the children about whom the report is made, in an effort to prevent further neglect or abuse, to enhance their welfare, and, whenever possible, to preserve the family unit intact. The agency required to provide the services shall be the agency conducting the investigation of the report pursuant to section 2151.422 of the Revised Code.

(J)(1) Each public children services agency shall prepare a memorandum of understanding that is signed by all of the following:

(a) If there is only one juvenile judge in the county, the juvenile judge of the county or the juvenile judge's representative;

(b) If there is more than one juvenile judge in the county, a juvenile judge or the juvenile judges' representative selected by the juvenile judges or, if they are unable to do so for any reason, the juvenile judge who is senior in point of service or the senior juvenile judge's representative;

(c) The county peace officer;

(d) All chief municipal peace officers within the county;

(e) Other law enforcement officers handling child abuse and neglect cases in the county;

(f) The prosecuting attorney of the county;

(g) If the public children services agency is not the county department of job and family services, the county department of job and family services;

(h) The county humane society;

(i) If the public children services agency participated in the execution of a memorandum of understanding under section 2151.426 of the Revised Code establishing a children's advocacy center, each participating member of the children's advocacy center established by the memorandum.

(2) A memorandum of understanding shall set forth the normal operating procedure to be employed by all concerned officials in the execution of their respective responsibilities under this section and division (C) of section 2919.21, division (B)(1) of section 2919.22, division (B) of section 2919.23, and section 2919.24 of the Revised Code and shall have as two of its primary goals the elimination of all unnecessary interviews of children who are the subject of reports made pursuant to division (A) or (B) of this section and, when feasible, providing for only one interview of a child who is the subject of any report made pursuant to division (A) or (B) of this section. A failure to follow the procedure set forth in the memorandum by the concerned officials is not grounds for, and shall not result in, the dismissal of any charges or complaint arising from any reported case of abuse or neglect or the suppression of any evidence obtained as a result of any reported child abuse or child neglect and does not give, and shall not be construed as giving, any rights or any grounds for appeal or post-conviction relief to any person.

(3) A memorandum of understanding shall include all of the following:

(a) The roles and responsibilities for handling emergency and nonemergency cases of abuse and neglect;

(b) Standards and procedures to be used in handling and coordinating investigations of reported cases of child abuse and reported cases of child neglect, methods to be used in interviewing the child who is the subject of the report and who allegedly was abused or neglected, and standards and procedures addressing the categories of persons who may interview the child who is the subject of the report and who allegedly was abused or neglected.

(4) If a public children services agency participated in the execution of a memorandum of understanding under section 2151.426 of the Revised Code establishing a children's advocacy center, the agency shall incorporate the contents of that memorandum in the memorandum prepared pursuant to this section.

(5) The clerk of the court of common pleas in the county may sign the memorandum of understanding prepared under division (J)(1) of this section. If the clerk signs the memorandum of understanding, the clerk shall execute all relevant responsibilities as required of officials specified in the memorandum.

(K)(1) Except as provided in division (K)(4) of this section, a person who is required to make a report pursuant to division (A) of this section may make a reasonable number of requests of the public children services agency that receives or is referred the report, or of the children's advocacy center that is referred the report if the report is referred to a children's advocacy center pursuant to an interagency agreement entered into under section 2151.428 of the Revised Code, to be provided with the following information:

(a) Whether the agency or center has initiated an investigation of the report;

(b) Whether the agency or center is continuing to investigate the report;

(c) Whether the agency or center is otherwise involved with the child who is the subject of the report;

(d) The general status of the health and safety of the child who is the subject of the report;

(e) Whether the report has resulted in the filing of a complaint in juvenile court or of criminal charges in another court.

(2) A person may request the information specified in division (K)(1) of this section only if, at the time the report is made, the person's name, address, and telephone number are provided to the person who receives the report.

When a municipal or county peace officer or employee of a public children services agency receives a report pursuant to division (A) or (B) of this section the recipient of the report shall inform the person of the right to request the information described in division (K)(1) of this section. The recipient of the report shall include in the initial child abuse or child neglect report that the person making the report was so informed and, if provided at the time of the making of the report, shall include the person's name, address, and telephone number in the report.

Each request is subject to verification of the identity of the person making the report. If that person's identity is verified, the agency shall provide the person with the information described in division (K)(1) of this section a reasonable number of times, except that the agency shall not disclose any confidential information regarding the child who is the subject of the report other than the information described in those divisions.

(3) A request made pursuant to division (K)(1) of this section is not a substitute for any report required to be made pursuant to division (A) of this section.

(4) If an agency other than the agency that received or was referred the report is conducting the investigation of the report pursuant to section 2151.422 of the Revised Code, the agency conducting the investigation shall comply with the requirements of division (K) of this section.

(L) The director of job and family services shall adopt rules in accordance with Chapter 119. of the Revised Code to implement this section. The department of job and family services may enter into a plan of cooperation with any other governmental entity to aid in ensuring that children are protected from abuse and neglect. The department shall make recommendations to the attorney general that the department determines are necessary to protect children from child abuse and child neglect.

(M) Whoever violates division (A) of this section is liable for compensatory and exemplary damages to the child who would have been the subject of the report that was not made. A person who brings a civil action or proceeding pursuant to this division against a person who is alleged to have violated division (A)(1) of this section may use in the action or proceeding reports of other incidents of known or suspected abuse or neglect, provided that any information in a report that would identify the child who is the subject of the report or the maker of the report, if the maker is not the defendant or an agent or employee of the defendant, has been redacted.

(N)(1) As used in this division:

(a) "Out-of-home care" includes a nonchartered nonpublic school if the alleged child abuse or child neglect, or alleged threat of child abuse or child neglect, described in a report received by a public children services agency allegedly occurred in or involved the nonchartered nonpublic school and the alleged perpetrator named in the report holds a certificate, permit, or license issued by the state board of education under section 3301.071 or Chapter 3319. of the Revised Code.

(b) "Administrator, director, or other chief administrative officer" means the superintendent of the school district if the out-of-home care entity subject to a report made pursuant to this section is a school operated by the district.

(2) No later than the end of the day following the day on which a public children services agency receives a report of alleged child abuse or child neglect, or a report of an alleged threat of child abuse or child neglect, that allegedly occurred in or involved an out-of-home care entity, the agency shall provide written notice of the allegations contained in and the person named as the alleged perpetrator in the report to the administrator, director, or other chief administrative officer of the out-of-home care entity that is the subject of the report unless the administrator, director, or other chief administrative officer is named as an alleged perpetrator in the report. If the administrator, director, or other chief administrative officer of an out-of-home care entity is named as an alleged perpetrator in a report of alleged child abuse or child neglect, or a report of an alleged threat of child abuse or child neglect, that allegedly occurred in or involved the out-of-home care entity, the agency shall provide the written notice to the owner or governing board of the out-of-home care entity that is the subject of the report. The agency shall not provide witness statements or police or other investigative reports.

(3) No later than three days after the day on which a public children services agency that conducted the investigation as determined pursuant to section 2151.422 of the Revised Code makes a disposition of an investigation involving a report of alleged child abuse or child neglect, or a report of an alleged threat of child abuse or child neglect, that allegedly occurred in or involved an out-of-home care entity, the agency shall send written notice of the disposition of the investigation to the administrator, director, or other chief administrative officer and the owner or governing board of the out-of-home care entity. The agency shall not provide witness statements or police or other investigative reports.

(O) As used in this section, "investigation" means the public children services agency's response to an accepted report of child abuse or neglect through either an alternative response or a traditional response.

**HISTORY: 130 v 625 (Eff 10-10-63); 131 v 632 (Eff 11-11-65); 133 v S 49 (Eff 8-13-69); 133 v H 338 (Eff 11-25-69); 136 v H 85 (Eff 11-28-75); 137 v H 219 (Eff 11-1-77); 140 v S 321 (Eff 4-9-85); 141 v H 349 (Eff 3-6-86); 141 v H 528 (Eff 7-9-86); 141 v H 529 (Eff 3-11-87); 143 v H 257 (Eff 8-3-89); 143 v H 44 (Eff 7-24-90); 143 v S 3 (Eff 4-11-91); 144 v H 154 (Eff 7-31-92); 146 v S 269 (Eff 7-1-96); 146 v H 274 (Eff 8-8-96); 146 v S 223 (Eff 3-18-97); 147 v H 215 (6-30-97); 147 v H 408 (Eff 10-1-97); 147 v S 212 (Eff 9-30-98); 147 v H 606 (Eff 3-9-99); 148 v H 471 (Eff 7-1-2000); 148 v H 448 (Eff 10-5-2000); 149 v H 510 (Eff 3-31-2003); 149 v H 374 (Eff 4-7-2003); 149 v S 221. Eff 4-9-2003; 150 v S 178, § 1, eff. 1-30-04; 150 v H 106, § 1, eff. 9-16-04; 150 v S 185, § 1, eff. 4-11-05; 150 v S 66, § 1, eff. 5-6-05; 151 v S 17, § 1, eff. 8-3-06; 151 v S 238, § 1, eff. 9-21-06; 152 v H 314, § 1, eff. 6-20-08; 152 v S 163, § 1, eff. 8-14-08; 152 v H 280, § 1, eff. 4-7-09; 153 v S 79, § 1, eff. 10-6-09; 2011 HB 153, § 101.01, eff. Sept. 29, 2011.**

The provisions of § 4 of 152 v H 280 read as follows:

SECTION 4. Section 2151.421 of the Revised Code, as amended by this act, applies to civil actions filed on or after the effective date of this act and to civil actions that are pending on the effective date of this act.

The provisions of § 5 of 152 v H 280 read in part as follows:

SECTION 5. Section 2151.421 of the Revised Code is presented in this act as a composite of the section as amended by both Am. H.B. 314 and Sub. S.B. 163 of the 127th General Assembly. The General Assembly, applying the principle stated in division (B) of section 1.52 of the Revised Code that amendments are to be harmonized if reasonably capable of simultaneous operation, finds that the composite is the resulting version of the section in effect prior to the effective date of the section as presented in this act.

* * *

The provisions of § 3 of 151 v S 238 read as follows:

SECTION 3. The Department of Job and Family Services shall develop, implement, oversee, and evaluate, on a pilot basis, an "Alternative Response" approach to reports of child abuse, neglect, and dependency. The pilot program shall be implemented in not more than ten counties that are selected by the Department and that agree to participate in the pilot program.

The pilot program shall last eighteen months, not including time expended in preparation for the implementation of the pilot program and any post-pilot program evaluation activity.

The Department shall assure that the Alternative Response pilot is independently evaluated with respect to outcomes for children and families, costs, worker satisfaction, and any other criteria the Department determines will be useful in the consideration of statewide implementation of an Alternative Response approach to child protection. The measure associated with the eighteen-month pilot program shall, for the purposes of the evaluation, be compared with those same measures in the pilot counties during the eighteen-month period immediately preceding the beginning of the pilot-program period.

The Department may adopt rules in accordance with section 111.15 of the Revised Code, as if they were internal management rules, as necessary to carry out the purposes of this section.

The provisions of § 6 of 151 v S 17 read as follows:

SECTION 6. Section 2151.421 of the Revised Code is presented in this act as a composite of the section as amended by both Sub. S.B. 66 and Sub. S.B. 185 of the 125th General Assembly. The General Assembly, applying the principle stated in division (B) of section 1.52 of the Revised Code that amendments are to be harmonized if reasonably capable of simultaneous operation, finds that the composites are the resulting versions of the sections in effect prior to the effective date of the sections as presented in this act.

The provisions of § 4 of S.B. 178 (150 v —) read as follows:

Section 4. Section 2151.421 of the Revised Code is presented in this act as a composite of the section as amended by Am. Sub. H.B. 374, Sub. H.B. 510, and Am. Sub. S.B. 221 all of the 124th General Assembly. Section 5126.28 of the Revised Code is presented in this act as a composite of the section as amended by both Sub. H.B. 538 and Sub. S.B. 171 of the 123rd General Assembly. The General Assembly, applying the principle stated in division (B) of section 1.52 of the Revised Code that amendments are to be harmonized if reasonably capable of simultaneous operation, finds that the composites are the resulting versions of the sections in effect prior to the effective date of the sections as presented in this act.

## § 2151.422 Procedure where child is living in domestic violence or homeless shelter; homeless shelter to obtain last known residence information.

(A) As used in this section, "homeless shelter" means a facility that provides accommodations to homeless individuals.

(B) On receipt of a notice pursuant to division (A), (B), or (D) of section 2151.421 [2151.42.1] of the Revised Code, the public children services agency shall determine whether the child subject to the report is living in a shelter for victims of domestic violence or a homeless shelter and whether the child was brought to that shelter pursuant to an agreement with a shelter in another county. If the child is living in a shelter and was brought there from another county, the agency shall immediately notify the public children services agency of the county from which the child was brought of the report and all the information contained in the report. On receipt of the notice pursuant to this division, the agency of the county from which the child was brought shall conduct the investigation of the report required pursuant to section 2151.421 [2151.42.1] of the Revised Code and shall perform all duties required of the agency under this chapter with respect to the child who is the subject of the report. If the child is not living in a shelter or the child was not brought to the shelter from another county, the agency that received the report pursuant to division (A), (B), or (D) of section 2151.421 [2151.42.1] of the Revised Code shall conduct the investigation required pursuant to section 2151.421 [2151.42.1] of the Revised Code and shall perform all duties required of the agency under this chapter with respect to the child who is the subject of the report. The agency of the county in which the shelter is located in which the child is living and the agency of the county from which the child was brought may ask the shelter to provide information concerning the child's residence address and county of residence to the agency.

(C) If a child is living in a shelter for victims of domestic violence or a homeless shelter and the child was brought to that shelter pursuant to an agreement with a shelter in another county, the public children services agency of the county from which the child was brought shall provide services to or take custody of the child if services or custody are needed or required under this chapter or section 5153.16 of the Revised Code.

(D) When a homeless shelter provides accommodations to a person, the shelter, on admitting the person to the shelter, shall determine, if possible, the person's last known residential address and county of residence. The information concerning the address and county of residence is confidential and may only be released to a public children services agency pursuant to this section.

**HISTORY: 147 v H 215. Eff 6-30-97.**

**Not analogous to former RC § 2151.42.2 (132 v S 316), repealed 137 v H 565, § 2, eff 11-1-78.**

## § 2151.423 Disclosure of confidential information to agencies responsible for protecting children from abuse or neglect.

A public children services agency shall disclose confidential information discovered during an investigation conducted pursuant to section 2151.421 [2151.42.1] or 2151.422 [2151.42.2] of the Revised Code to any federal, state, or local government entity that needs the information to carry out its responsibilities to protect children from abuse or neglect.

Information disclosed pursuant to this section is confidential and is not subject to disclosure pursuant to section 149.43 or 1347.08 of the Revised Code by the agency to whom the information was disclosed. The agency receiving the information shall maintain the confidentiality of information disclosed pursuant to this section.

**HISTORY: 151 v S 238, § 1, eff. 9-21-06.**

## § 2151.424 Rights of foster caregiver, relative, or prospective adoptive parent; criminal records check.

(A) If a child has been placed in a certified foster home or is in the custody of a relative of the child, other than a parent of the child, a court, prior to conducting any hearing pursuant to division (F)(2) or (3) of section 2151.412 or section 2151.28, 2151.33, 2151.35, 2151.414, 2151.415, 2151.416, or 2151.417 of the Revised Code with respect to the child, shall notify the foster caregiver or relative of the date, time, and place of the hearing. At the hearing, the foster caregiver or relative shall have the right to present evidence.

(B) If a public children services agency or private child placing agency has permanent custody of a child and a petition to adopt the child has been filed under Chapter 3107. of the Revised Code, the agency, prior to conducting a review under section 2151.416 of the Revised Code, or a court, prior to conducting a hearing under division (F)(2) or (3) of section 2151.412 or section 2151.416 or 2151.417 of the Revised Code, shall notify the prospective adoptive parent of the date, time, and place of the review or hearing. At the review or hearing, the prospective adoptive parent shall have the right to present evidence.

(C) The notice and the opportunity to present evidence do not make the foster caregiver, relative, or prospective adoptive parent a party in the action or proceeding pursuant to which the review or hearing is conducted.

**HISTORY: 147 v H 484 (Eff 3-18-99); 148 v H 448. Eff 10-5-2000; 152 v S 163, § 1, eff. 8-14-08; 2011 HB 153, § 101.01, eff. Sept. 29, 2011.**

## [CHILDREN'S ADVOCACY CENTERS]

### § 2151.425 Definitions.

As used in sections 2151.426 [2151.42.6] to 2151.428 [2151.42.8] of the Revised Code:

(A) "Children's advocacy center" means a center operated by participating entities within a county or two or more contiguous counties to perform functions and activities and provide services, in accordance with the interagency agreement entered into under section 2151.428 [2151.42.8] of the Revised Code, regarding reports received under section 2151.421 [2151.42.1] of the Revised Code of alleged sexual abuse of a child or another type of abuse of a child that is specified in the memorandum of understanding that creates the center as being within the center's jurisdiction and regarding the children who are the subjects of the report.

(B) "Sexual abuse of a child" means unlawful sexual conduct or sexual contact, as those terms are defined in section 2907.01 of the Revised Code, with a person under eighteen years of age or a mentally retarded, developmentally disabled, or physically impaired person under twenty-one years of age.

**HISTORY: 150 v S 66, § 1, eff. 5-6-05.**

### § 2151.426 Establishment of children's advocacy center.

(A)(1) A children's advocacy center may be established to serve a single county by execution of a memorandum of understanding regarding the participation in the operation of the center by any of the following entities in the county to be served by the center:

(a) The public children services agency;

(b) Representatives of any county or municipal law enforcement agencies serving the county that investigate any of the types of abuse specified in the memorandum of understanding creating the center as being within the center's jurisdiction;

(c) The prosecuting attorney of the county or a village solicitor, city director of law, or similar chief legal officer of a municipal corporation in the county who prosecutes any of the types of abuse specified in the memorandum of understanding creating the center as being within the center's jurisdiction in the area to be served by the center;

(d) Any other entity considered appropriate by all of the other entities executing the memorandum.

(2) A children's advocacy center may be established to serve two or more contiguous counties if a memorandum of understanding regarding the participation in the operation of the center is executed by any of the entities described in division (A)(1) of this section in each county to be served by the center.

(3) Any memorandum of understanding executed under this section may include a provision that specifies types of abuse of a child, in addition to sexual abuse of a child, that are to be within the jurisdiction of the children's advocacy center created as a result of the execution of the memorandum. If a memorandum of understanding executed under this section does not include any provision of that nature, the children's advocacy center created as a result of the execution of the memorandum has jurisdiction only in relation to reports of alleged sexual abuse of a child.

(B) Each entity that participates in the execution of a memorandum of understanding under this section shall cooperate in all of the following:

(1) Developing a multidisciplinary team pursuant to section 2151.427 [2151.42.7] of the Revised Code to perform the functions and activities and provide the services specified in the interagency agreement entered into under section 2151.428 [2151.42.8] of the Revised Code, regarding reports received under section 2151.421 [2151.42.1] of the Revised Code of alleged sexual abuse of a child and reports of allegations of another type of abuse of a child that is specified in the memorandum of understanding that creates the center as being within the center's jurisdiction, and regarding the children who are the subjects of the reports;

(2) Participating in the operation of the center in compliance with standards for full membership established by the national children's alliance;

(3) Employing the center's staff.

(C) A center shall do both of the following:

(1) Operate in accordance with sections 2151.427 [2151.42.7] and 2151.428 [2151.42.8] of the Revised Code, the interagency agreement entered into under section 2151.428 [2151.42.8] of the Revised Code relative to the center, and the standards for full membership established by the national children's alliance;

(2) Register annually with the attorney general.

**HISTORY: 150 v S 66, § 1, eff. 5-6-05.**

### § 2151.427 Assembling of multidisciplinary team.

(A) The entities that participate in a memorandum of understanding executed under section 2151.426 [2151.42.6] of the Revised Code establishing a children's advocacy center shall assemble the center's multidisciplinary team.

(B)(1) The multidisciplinary team for a single county center shall consist of the following members who serve the county:

(a) Any county or municipal law enforcement officer;

(b) The executive director of the public children services agency or a designee of the executive director;

(c) The prosecuting attorney of the county or the prosecuting attorney's designee;

(d) A mental health professional;

(e) A medical health professional;

(f) A victim advocate;

(g) A center staff member;

(h) Any other person considered appropriate by all of the entities that executed the memorandum.

(2) If the center serves two or more contiguous counties, the multidisciplinary team shall consist of the members described in division (B)(1) of this section from the counties to be served by the center, with each county to be served by the center being represented on the multidisciplinary team by at least one member described in that division.

(C) The multidisciplinary team shall perform the functions and activities and provide the services specified in the interagency agreement entered into under section 2151.428 [2151.42.8] of the Revised Code, regarding reports received under section 2151.421 [2151.42.1] of the Revised Code of alleged sexual abuse of a child and reports of allegations of another type of abuse of a child that is specified in the memorandum of understanding that creates the center as being within the center's jurisdiction and regarding the children who are the subjects of the reports.

**HISTORY: 150 v S 66, § 1, eff. 5-6-05.**

## § 2151.428 Interagency agreement regarding reports of alleged child abuse; obligations of public official or agency unaffected.

(A) If a children's advocacy center is established under section 2151.426 [2151.42.6] of the Revised Code, in addition to the memorandum of understanding executed under that section, each public children services agency that participates in the execution of the memorandum of understanding, the children's advocacy center, and the children's advocacy center's multidisciplinary team assembled under section 2151.427 [2151.42.7] of the Revised Code shall enter into an interagency agreement that stipulates all of the following regarding reports received under section 2151.421 [2151.42.1] of the Revised Code of alleged sexual abuse of a child and reports of allegations of another type of abuse of a child that is specified in the memorandum of understanding that creates the center as being within the center's jurisdiction:

(1) The protocol and procedures for any and all referrals and investigations of the reports;

(2) Any and all coordinating activities between the parties that enter into the agreement;

(3) The authority or responsibility for performing any and all functions and activities, and providing any and all services, regarding the reports and the children who are the subjects of the reports.

(B) The parties that enter into an interagency agreement under division (A) of this section shall comply with the agreement in referring the reports, investigating the reports, coordinating the activities between the parties, and performing and providing the functions, activities, and services relative to the reports and the children who are the subjects of the reports.

(C) Nothing in this section, section 2151.421 [2151.42.1], or sections 2151.425 [2151.42.5] to 2151.427 [2151.42.7] of the Revised Code pertaining to the operation of a children's advocacy center shall relieve any public official or agency from any legal obligation or responsibility.

**HISTORY: 150 v S 66, § 1, eff. 5-6-05.**

## § 2151.429 Differential response approach; traditional response pathway and alternative response pathway; criteria for assignment to pathway.

(A) The differential response approach, as defined in section 2151.011 of the Revised Code, pursued by a public children services agency shall include two response pathways, the traditional response pathway and the alternative response pathway. The director of job and family services shall adopt rules pursuant to Chapter 119. of the Revised Code setting forth the procedures and criteria for public children services agencies to assign and reassign response pathways.

(B) The agency shall use the traditional response for the following types of accepted reports:

(1) Physical abuse resulting in serious injury or that creates a serious and immediate risk to a child's health and safety.

(2) Sexual abuse.

(3) Child fatality.

(4) Reports requiring a specialized assessment as identified by rule adopted by the department.

(5) Reports requiring a third party investigative procedure as identified by rule adopted by the department.

(C) For all other child abuse and neglect reports, an alternative response shall be the preferred response, whenever appropriate and in accordance with rules adopted by the department.

**HISTORY: 2011 HB 153, § 101.01, eff. Sept. 29, 2011.**

### [PROCEDURE IN ADULT CASES]

## § 2151.43 Charges against adults; defendant bound over to grand jury.

In cases against an adult under sections 2151.01 to 2151.54 of the Revised Code, any person may file an affidavit with the clerk of the juvenile court setting forth briefly, in plain and ordinary language, the charges against the accused who shall be tried thereon. When the child is a recipient of aid pursuant to Chapter 5107. or 5115. of the Revised Code, the county department of job and family services shall file charges against any person who fails to provide support to a child in violation of section 2919.21 of the Revised Code, unless the department files charges under section 3113.06 of the Revised Code, or unless charges of nonsupport are filed by a relative or guardian of the child, or unless action to enforce support is brought under Chapter 3115. of the Revised Code.

In such prosecution an indictment by the grand jury or information by the prosecuting attorney shall not be required. The clerk shall issue a warrant for the arrest of the accused, who, when arrested, shall be taken before the juvenile judge and tried according to such sections.

The affidavit may be amended at any time before or during the trial.

The judge may bind such adult over to the grand jury, where the act complained of constitutes a felony.

**HISTORY: GC § 1639-39; 117 v 520(533); 119 v 731; Bureau of Code Revision, 10-1-53; 127 v 847 (Eff 9-16-57); 132 v H 390 (Eff 11-7-67); 133 v H 361 (Eff 9-23-69); 134 v H 511 (Eff 1-1-74); 141 v H 428 (Eff 12-23-86); 144 v H 298 (Eff 7-26-91); 146 v H 249 (Eff 7-17-95); 148 v H 471. Eff 7-1-2000.**

The effective date is set by section 12(A) of HB 471.

## § 2151.44 Complaint after hearing.

If it appears at the hearing of a child that any person has abused or has aided, induced, caused, encouraged, or contributed to the dependency, neglect, or delinquency of a child or acted in a way tending to cause delinquency in such child, or that a person charged with the care, support, education, or maintenance of any child has failed to support or sufficiently contribute toward the support, education, and maintenance of such child, the juvenile judge may order a complaint filed against such person and proceed to hear and dispose of the case as provided in sections 2151.01 to 2151.54, inclusive, of the Revised Code.

On the request of the judge, the prosecuting attorney shall prosecute all adults charged with violating such sections.

**HISTORY: GC §§ 1639-40, 1639-42; 117 v 520(533, 534); Bureau of Code Revision. Eff 10-1-53.**

## § 2151.45 Repealed, 148 v S 179, § 4 [GC § 1639-41; 117 v 520(533); Bureau of Code Revision, 10-1-53]. Eff 1-1-2002.

This section concerned expense of extradition.
The effective date is set by section 5 of SB 179.

## § 2151.46 Repealed, 148 v S 179, § 4 [GC § 1639-43; 117 v 520(534); Bureau of Code Revision, 10-1-53]. Eff 1-1-2002.

This section concerned bail.
The effective date is set by section 5 of SB 179.

## § 2151.47 Renumbered RC § 2152.67 in 148 v S 179. Eff 1-1-2002.

The effective date is set by section 5 of SB 179.

## § 2151.48 Repealed, 148 v S 179, § 4 [GC § 1639-48; 117 v 520(535); Bureau of Code Revision, 10-1-53; 145 v H 571]. Eff 1-1-2002.

This section concerned commitment of adult females.
The effective date is set by section 5 of SB 179.

## § 2151.49 Suspension of sentence.

In every case of conviction under sections 2151.01 to 2151.54 of the Revised Code, where imprisonment is imposed as part of the punishment, the juvenile judge may suspend sentence, before or during commitment, upon such condition as the juvenile judge imposes. In the case of conviction for nonsupport of a child who is receiving aid under Chapter 5107. or 5115. of the Revised Code, if the juvenile judge suspends sentence on condition that the person make payments for support, the payment shall be made to the county department of job and family services rather than to the child or custodian of the child.

The court, in accordance with sections 3119.29 to 3119.56 of the Revised Code, shall include in each support order made under this section the requirement that one or both of the parents provide for the health care needs of the child to the satisfaction of the court.

**HISTORY: GC § 1639-49; 117 v 520(535); Bureau of Code Revision, 10-1-53; 132 v H 390 (Eff 11-7-67); 141 v H 428 (Eff 12-23-86); 144 v H 298 (Eff 7-26-91); 146 v H 249 (Eff 7-17-95); 147 v H 352 (Eff 1-1-98); 148 v H 471 (Eff 7-1-2000); 148 v S 180 (Eff 3-22-2001); 149 v H 657. Eff 12-13-2002.**

## § 2151.50 Forfeiture of bond.

When, as a condition of suspension of sentence under section 2151.49 of the Revised Code, bond is required and given, upon the failure of a person giving such bond to comply with the conditions thereof, such bond may be forfeited, the suspension terminated by the juvenile judge, the original sentence executed as though it had not been suspended, and the term of any sentence imposed in such case shall commence from the date of imprisonment of such person after such forfeiture and termination of suspension. Any part of such sentence which may have been served shall be deducted from any such period of imprisonment. When such bond is forfeited the judge may issue execution thereon without further proceedings.

**HISTORY: GC § 1639-50; 117 v 520(535); Bureau of Code Revision. Eff 10-1-53.**

## § 2151.51 Repealed, 148 v S 179, § 4 [GC § 1639-47; 117 v 520(535); Bureau of Code Revision, 10-1-53; 136 v H 1]. Eff 1-1-2002.

This section concerned provision for dependent children of person sentenced to workhouse or jail.
The effective date is set by section 5 of SB 179.

## § 2151.52 Appeals on questions of law.

The sections of the Revised Code and rules relating to appeals on questions of law from the court of common pleas shall apply to prosecutions of adults under this chapter, and from such prosecutions an appeal on a question of law may be taken to the court of appeals of the county under laws or rules governing appeals in other criminal cases to such court of appeals.

**HISTORY: GC § 1639-51; 117 v 520(536); Bureau of Code Revision, 10-1-53; 129 v 290 (Eff 10-2-61); 141 v H 412. Eff 3-17-87.**

### [GENERAL PROVISIONS]

## § 2151.53 Physical and mental examinations; records of examination; expenses.

Any person coming within sections 2151.01 to 2151.54 of the Revised Code may be subjected to a physical examination by competent physicians, physician assistants, clinical nurse specialists, and certified nurse practitioners, and a mental examination by competent psychologists, psychiatrists, and clinical nurse specialists that practice the specialty of mental health or psychiatric mental health to be appointed by the juvenile court. Whenever any child is committed to any institution by virtue of such sections, a record of such examinations shall be sent with the commitment to such institution. The compensation of such physicians, physician assistants, clinical nurse specialists, certified nurse practitioners, psychologists, and psychiatrists and the expenses of such examinations shall be paid by the county treasurer upon specifically itemized vouchers, certified by the juvenile judge.

**HISTORY: GC § 1639-54; 117 v 520(536); Bureau of Code Revision (10-1-53); 149 v S 245. Eff 3-31-2003.**

## § 2151.54 Fees and costs.

The juvenile court shall tax and collect the same fees and costs as are allowed the clerk of the court of common pleas for similar services. No fees or costs shall be taxed in cases of delinquent, unruly, dependent, abused, or neglected children except as required by section 2743.70 or 2949.091 [2949.09.1] of the Revised Code or when specifically ordered by the court. The expense of transportation of children to places to which they have been committed, and the transportation of children to and from another state by police or other officers, acting upon order of the court, shall be paid from the county treasury upon specifically itemized vouchers certified to by the judge.

If a child is adjudicated to be a delinquent child or a juvenile traffic offender and the juvenile court specifically is required, by section 2743.70 or 2949.091 [2949.09.1] of the Revised Code or any other section of the Revised Code, to impose a specified sum of money as court costs in addition to any other court costs that the court is required or permitted by law to impose, the court shall not waive the payment of the specified additional court costs that the section of the Revised Code specifically requires the court to impose unless the court determines that the child is indigent and the court either waives the payment of all court costs or enters an order in its journal stating that no court costs are to be taxed in the case.

**HISTORY: GC § 1639-56; 117 v 520(537); 119 v 731; Bureau of Code Revision, 10-1-53; 133 v H 931 (Eff 8-27-70); 136 v H 85 (Eff 11-28-75); 138 v H 238 (Eff 8-8-80); 143 v S 131. Eff 7-25-90.**

### § 2151.541 Additional fees to pay for computerizing court or office of clerk or for computerized legal research services.

(A)(1) The juvenile judge may determine that, for the efficient operation of the juvenile court, additional funds are required to computerize the court, to make available computerized legal research services, or both. Upon making a determination that additional funds are required for either or both of those purposes, the judge shall do one of the following:

(a) If the judge is clerk of the court, charge one additional fee not to exceed three dollars on the filing of each cause of action or appeal under division (A), (Q), or (U) of section 2303.20 of the Revised Code;

(b) If the clerk of the court of common pleas serves as the clerk of the juvenile court pursuant to section 2151.12 of the Revised Code, authorize and direct the clerk to charge one additional fee not to exceed three dollars on the filing of each cause of action or appeal under division (A), (Q), or (U) of section 2303.20 of the Revised Code.

(2) All moneys collected under division (A)(1) of this section shall be paid to the county treasurer. The treasurer shall place the moneys from the fees in a separate fund to be disbursed either upon an order of the juvenile judge, subject to an appropriation by the board of county commissioners, or upon an order of the juvenile judge, subject to the court making an annual report available to the public listing the use of all such funds, in an amount no greater than the actual cost to the court of procuring and maintaining computerization of the court, computerized legal research services, or both.

(3) If the court determines that the funds in the fund described in division (A)(2) of this section are more than sufficient to satisfy the purpose for which the additional fee described in division (A)(1) of this section was imposed, the court may declare a surplus in the fund and, subject to an appropriation by the board of county commissioners, expend those surplus funds, or upon an order of the court, subject to the court making an annual report available to the public listing the use of all such funds, expend those surplus funds, for other appropriate technological expenses of the court.

(B)(1) If the juvenile judge is the clerk of the juvenile court, the judge may determine that, for the efficient operation of the juvenile court, additional funds are required to computerize the clerk's office and, upon that determination, may charge an additional fee, not to exceed ten dollars, on the filing of each cause of action or appeal, on the filing, docketing, and endorsing of each certificate of judgment, or on the docketing and indexing of each aid in execution or petition to vacate, revive, or modify a judgment under divisions (A), (P), (Q), (T), and (U) of section 2303.20 of the Revised Code. Subject to division (B)(2) of this section, all moneys collected under this division shall be paid to the county treasurer to be disbursed, upon an order of the juvenile judge and subject to appropriation by the board of county commissioners, in an amount no greater than the actual cost to the juvenile court of procuring and maintaining computer systems for the clerk's office.

(2) If the juvenile judge makes the determination described in division (B)(1) of this section, the board of county commissioners may issue one or more general obligation bonds for the purpose of procuring and maintaining the computer systems for the office of the clerk of the juvenile court. In addition to the purposes stated in division (B)(1) of this section for which the moneys collected under that division may be expended, the moneys additionally may be expended to pay debt charges on and financing costs related to any general obligation bonds issued pursuant to this division as they become due. General obligation bonds issued pursuant to this division are Chapter 133. securities.

**HISTORY: 144 v H 405 (Eff 1-1-93); 144 v S 246. Eff 3-24-93; 2011 HB 153, § 101.01, eff. Sept. 29, 2011.**

### § 2151.542 Repealed, 149 v S 108, § 2.02(C) [146 v H 350]. Eff 7-6-2001.

This section concerned dispute resolution procedures; fees.

## [FOSTER HOME PLACEMENT OUTSIDE COUNTY]

### § 2151.55 Required communication upon placement in foster home in another county.

When a private or governmental entity intends to place a child in a certified foster home in a county other than the county in which the child resided at the time of being removed from home, a representative of the placing entity shall orally communicate the intended placement to the foster caregiver with whom the child is to be placed and, if the child will attend the schools of the district in which the certified foster home is located, a representative of the school district's board of education.†

**HISTORY: 148 v H 283 (Eff 9-29-99); 148 v H 448 (Eff 10-5-2000); 148 v H 332. Eff 1-1-2001.**

† The amendments made by HB 448 (148 v —), effective 10-5-2000 and HB 332 (148 v —), effective 1-1-2001 are the same. The word "certified" is added before "foster home" by each amendment.

**Analogous to former RC § 2151.55 (147 v H 215), repealed 148 v H 283, § 2, eff 9-29-99.**

**Not analogous to former RC § 2151.55 (GC § 1639-59;**

**117 v 520 (537); Bureau of Code Revision, 1-1-53), repealed 130 v 1682, § 2, eff 10-7-63.**

The effective date is set by section 5 of HB 332.

## § 2151.551 Contents of communications.

During the oral communication described in section 2151.55 of the Revised Code, the representative of the placing entity shall do the following:

(A) Discuss safety and well-being concerns regarding the child and, if the child attends school, the students, teachers, and personnel of the school;

(B) Provide the following information:

(1) A brief description of the reasons the child was removed from home;

(2) Services the child is receiving;

(3) The name of the contact person for the placing entity that is directly responsible for monitoring the child's placement;

(4) The telephone number of the placing entity and, if the child is in the temporary, permanent, or legal custody of a private or government entity other than the placing entity, the telephone number of the entity with custody;

(5) The previous school district attended by the child;

(6) The last known address of the child's parents.

**HISTORY: 148 v H 283. Eff 9-29-99.**

The effective date is set by section 162 of HB 283.

## § 2151.552 Information required to be provided in writing.

No later than five days after a child described in section 2151.55 of the Revised Code is enrolled in school in the district described in that section, the placing entity shall provide in writing the information described in division (B) of section 2151.551 [2151.55.1] of the Revised Code to the school district and the child's foster caregiver.

**HISTORY: 148 v H 283. Eff 9-29-99.**

The effective date is set by section 162 of HB 283.

## § 2151.553 School district procedure.

Each school district board of education shall implement a procedure for receiving the information described in section 2151.552 [2151.55.2] of the Revised Code.

**HISTORY: 148 v H 283. Eff 9-29-99.**

The effective date is set by section 162 of HB 283.

## § 2151.554 Notification of juvenile court concerning unruly or delinquent child.

When a private or governmental entity places a child who has been adjudicated to be an unruly or delinquent child in a certified foster home in a county other than the county in which the child resided at the time of being removed from home, the placing entity shall provide the following information in writing to the juvenile court of the county in which the certified foster home is located:

(A) The information listed in divisions (B)(2) to (4) of section 2151.551 [2151.55.1] of the Revised Code;

(B) A brief description of the facts supporting the adjudication that the child is unruly or delinquent;

(C) The name and address of the foster caregiver;

(D) Safety and well-being concerns with respect to the child and community.†

**HISTORY: 148 v H 283 (Eff 9-29-99); 148 v H 448 (Eff 10-5-2000); 148 v H 332. Eff 1-1-2001.**

† The amendments made by HB 448 (148 v —), effective 10-5-2000 and HB 332 (148 v —), effective 1-1-2001 are the same. The word "certified" is added before "foster home" by each amendment.

The effective date is set by section 5 of HB 332.

# [INTERSTATE COMPACT ON JUVENILES]

## § 2151.56 Interstate Compact for Juveniles.

The "interstate compact for juveniles" is hereby ratified, enacted into law, and entered into by the state of Ohio as a party to the compact with any other state that has legally joined in the compact as follows:

### INTERSTATE COMPACT FOR JUVENILES

### Article I — Purpose

The compacting states to this interstate compact for juveniles recognize that each state is responsible for the proper supervision or return of juveniles, delinquents, and status offenders who are on probation or parole and who have absconded, escaped, or run away from supervision and control and in so doing have endangered their own safety and the safety of others. The compacting states also recognize that each state is responsible for the safe return of juveniles who have run away from home and in doing so have left their state of residence. The compacting states also recognize that congress, by enacting the Crime Control Act, 4 U.S.C. Section 112 (1965), has authorized and encouraged compacts for cooperative efforts and mutual assistance in the prevention of crime.

It is the policy of the compacting states that the activities conducted by the interstate commission for juveniles created by this compact are the formation of public policies and therefore are public business. Furthermore, the compacting states shall cooperate and observe their individual and collective duties and responsibilities for the prompt return and acceptance of juveniles subject to the provisions of this compact. The provisions of this compact shall be reasonably and liberally construed to accomplish the purposes and policies of the compact.

It is the purpose of this compact, through means of joint and cooperative action among the compacting states, to do all of the following:

(A) Ensure that the adjudicated juveniles and status offenders subject to this compact are provided adequate supervision and services in the receiving state as ordered by the adjudicating judge or parole authority in the sending state;

(B) Ensure that the public safety interests of the citizens, including the victims of juvenile offenders, in both the sending and receiving states are adequately protected;

(C) Return juveniles who have run away, absconded, or escaped from supervision or control or have been accused of an offense to the state requesting their return;

(D) Make contracts for the cooperative institutionalization in public facilities in member states for delinquent youth needing special services;

(E) Provide for the effective tracking and supervision of juveniles;

(F) Equitably allocate the costs, benefits, and obligations of the compacting states;

(G) Establish procedures to manage the movement between states of juvenile offenders released to the community under the jurisdiction of courts, juvenile departments, or any other criminal or juvenile justice agency that has jurisdiction over juvenile offenders;

(H) Ensure immediate notice to jurisdictions where defined offenders are authorized to travel or to relocate across state lines;

(I) Establish procedures to resolve pending charges, such as detainers, against juvenile offenders prior to transfer or release to the community under the terms of this compact;

(J) Establish a system of uniform data collection on information pertaining to juveniles subject to this compact that allows access by authorized juvenile justice and criminal justice officials and regular reporting of compact activities to heads of state executive, judicial, and legislative branches and juvenile justice and criminal justice administrators;

(K) Monitor compliance with rules governing interstate movement of juveniles and initiate interventions to address and correct noncompliance;

(L) Coordinate training and education regarding the regulation of interstate movement of juveniles for officials involved in such activity;

(M) Coordinate the implementation and operation of this compact with the interstate compact for the placement of children, the interstate compact for adult offender supervision, and other compacts affecting juveniles, particularly in those cases where concurrent or overlapping supervision issues arise.

## Article II — Definitions

As used in this compact, unless the context clearly requires a different construction:

(A) "Bylaws" means those bylaws established by the interstate commission for its governance or for directing or controlling its actions or conduct.

(B) "Compact administrator" means the individual in each compacting state appointed pursuant to the terms of this compact who is responsible for the administration and management of the state's supervision and transfer of juveniles subject to the terms of this compact, the rules adopted by the interstate commission under this compact, and policies adopted by the state council under this compact.

(C) "Compacting state" means any state that has enacted the enabling legislation for this compact.

(D) "Commissioner" means the voting representative of each compacting state appointed pursuant to Article III of this compact.

(E) "Court" means any court having jurisdiction over delinquent, neglected, or dependent children.

(F) "Interstate commission for juveniles" or "interstate commission" means the interstate commission for juveniles created by Article III of this compact.

(G) "Juvenile" means any person defined as a juvenile in any member state or by the rules of the interstate commission, including any of the following:

(1) An "accused delinquent," which means a person charged with a violation of a law or municipal ordinance that, if committed by an adult, would be a criminal offense;

(2) An "adjudicated delinquent," which means a person found to have committed a violation of a law or municipal ordinance that, if committed by an adult, would be a criminal offense;

(3) An "accused status offender," which means a person charged with a violation of a law or municipal ordinance that would not be a criminal offense if committed by an adult;

(4) An "adjudicated status offender," which means a person found to have committed a violation of a law or municipal ordinance that would not be a criminal offense if committed by an adult;

(5) A "nonoffender," which means a person in need of supervision who is not an accused or adjudicated status offender or delinquent.

(H) "Noncompacting state" means any state that has not enacted the enabling legislation for this compact.

(I) "Probation or parole" means any kind of supervision or conditional release of juveniles authorized under the laws of the compacting states.

(J) "Rule" means a written statement by the interstate commission promulgated pursuant to Article VI of this compact that is of general applicability, that implements, interprets, or prescribes a policy or provision of the compact, or an organizational, procedural, or practice requirement of the interstate commission, and that has the force and effect of statutory law in a compacting state, and includes the amendment, repeal, or suspension of an existing rule.

(K) "State" means a state of the United States, the District of Columbia or its designee, the Commonwealth of Puerto Rico, the U.S. Virgin Islands, Guam, American Samoa, and the Northern Marianas Islands.

## Article III — Interstate Commission for Juveniles

(A) The compacting states hereby create the "interstate commission for juveniles." The commission shall be a body corporate and joint agency of the compacting states. The commission shall have all the responsibilities, powers, and duties set forth in this compact, and any additional powers that may be conferred upon it by subsequent action of the respective legislatures of the compacting states in accordance with the terms of this compact.

(B) The interstate commission shall consist of commissioners appointed by the appropriate appointing authority in each state pursuant to the rules and requirements of each compacting state and in consultation with the state council for interstate juvenile supervision created in the state in accordance with this compact. The commissioners are the voting representatives of each state. The commissioner for a state shall be the compact administrator or designee from that state who shall serve on the interstate commission in such capacity under or pursuant to the applicable law of the compacting state.

(C) In addition to the commissioners, the interstate commission also shall include individuals who are not commissioners but who are members of interested organizations. The noncommissioner members shall include a member of the national organizations of governors, legislators, state chief justices, attorneys general, interstate compact for adult offender supervision, interstate compact for the placement of children, juvenile justice and juvenile corrections officials, and crime victims. All noncommissioner members of the interstate commission shall be ex officio, nonvoting members. The interstate commission may provide in its bylaws for such additional ex officio, nonvoting members, including members of other national organizations, in such numbers as shall be determined by the commission.

(D) Each compacting state represented at any meeting of the interstate commission is entitled to one vote. A majority of the compacting states shall constitute a quorum for the transaction of business, unless a larger quorum is required by the bylaws of the interstate commission.

(E) The interstate commission shall meet at least once each calendar year. The chairperson may call additional meetings and, upon the request of a simple majority of the compacting states, shall call additional meetings. Public notice shall be given of all meetings, and all meetings, shall be open to the public.

(F) The interstate commission shall establish an executive committee, which shall include commission officers, members, and others as determined by the interstate commission's bylaws. The executive committee shall have the power to act on behalf of the interstate commission during periods when the interstate commission is not in session, with the exception of any rulemaking or amendment to the compact. The executive committee shall do all of the following:

(1) Oversee the day-to-day activities of the administration of the compact, managed by an executive director and interstate commission staff;

(2) Administer enforcement and compliance with the provisions of this compact and the interstate commission's bylaws and rules;

(3) Perform any other duties as directed by the interstate commission or set forth in its bylaws.

(G) Each member of the interstate commission shall have the right and power to cast a vote to which that compacting state is entitled and to participate in the business and affairs of the interstate commission. A member shall vote in person and shall not delegate a vote to another compacting state. However, a commissioner, in consultation with the state council for interstate juvenile supervision for the state, shall appoint another authorized representative, in the absence of the commissioner from that state, to cast a vote on behalf of the compacting state at a specified meeting. The interstate commission's bylaws may provide for members' participation in meetings by telephone or other means of telecommunication or electronic communication.

(H) The interstate commission's bylaws shall establish conditions and procedures under which the interstate commission shall make its information and official records available to the public for inspection or copying. The interstate commission may exempt from disclosure any information or official records to the extent the information or official records would adversely affect personal privacy rights or proprietary interests.

(I) Public notice shall be given of all meetings of the interstate commission, and all of its meetings shall be open to the public, except as set forth in the commission's rules or as otherwise provided in this compact. The interstate commission and any of its committees may close a meeting to the public when it determines by two-thirds vote that an open meeting would be likely to do any of the following:

(1) Relate solely to the interstate commission's internal personnel practices and procedures;

(2) Disclose matters specifically exempted from disclosure by statute;

(3) Disclose trade secrets or commercial or financial information that is privileged or confidential;

(4) Involve accusing any person of a crime or formally censuring any person;

(5) Disclose information of a personal nature where disclosure would constitute a clearly unwarranted invasion of personal privacy;

(6) Disclose investigative records compiled for law enforcement purposes;

(7) Disclose information contained in or related to examination, operating, or condition reports prepared by, or on behalf of or for the use of, the interstate commission with respect to a regulated person or entity for the purpose of regulation or supervision of such person or entity;

(8) Disclose information, the premature disclosure of which would significantly endanger the stability of a regulated person or entity;

(9) Specifically relate to the interstate commission's issuance of a subpoena or its participation in a civil action or other legal proceeding.

(J) For every meeting closed pursuant to division (I) of this Article of this compact, the interstate commission's legal counsel shall publicly certify that, in the legal counsel's opinion, the meeting may be closed to the public and shall reference each relevant exemptive provision. The interstate commission shall keep minutes that fully and clearly describe all matters discussed in any meeting and that provide a full and accurate summary of any actions taken, and the reasons for the actions, including a description of each of the views expressed on any item and the record of any roll call vote (reflected in the vote of each member on the question). All documents considered in connection with any action shall be identified in those minutes.

(K) The interstate commission shall collect standardized data concerning the interstate movement of juveniles as directed through its rules, which shall specify the data to be collected, the means of collection and data exchange, and reporting requirements. Such methods of data collection, exchange, and reporting shall insofar as is reasonably possible conform to up-to-date technology and coordinate the interstate commission's information functions with the appropriate repository of records.

### Article IV — Powers and Duties of the Interstate Commission

The interstate commission shall maintain its corporate books and records in accordance with its bylaws.

The interstate commission shall have all of the following powers and duties:

(A) To provide for dispute resolution among compacting states;

(B) To promulgate rules to affect the purposes and obligations as enumerated in this compact, which rules shall have the force and effect of statutory law and shall be binding in the compacting states to the extent and in the manner provided in this compact;

(C) To oversee, supervise, and coordinate the interstate movement of juveniles, subject to the terms of this compact and any bylaws adopted and rules promulgated by the interstate commission;

(D) To enforce compliance with the provisions of this compact, the rules promulgated by the interstate commission, and the interstate commission's bylaws, using all necessary and proper means, including but not limited to the use of judicial process;

(E) To establish and maintain offices, which shall be located within one or more of the compacting states;

(F) To purchase and maintain insurance and bonds;

(G) To borrow, accept, hire, or contract for services of personnel;

(H) To establish and appoint committees and hire staff that it considers necessary for the carrying out of its functions, including, but not limited to, an executive committee as required by Article III of this compact, which executive committee shall have the power to act on behalf of the interstate commission in carrying out its powers and duties under this compact;

(I) To elect or appoint officers, attorneys, employees, agents, or consultants, to fix their compensation, define their duties, and determine their qualifications, and to establish the interstate commission's personnel policies and programs relating to, inter alia, conflicts of interest, rates of compensation, and qualifications of personnel;

(J) To accept any and all donations and grants of money, equipment, supplies, materials, and services and to receive, utilize, and dispose of same;

(K) To lease, purchase, accept contributions or donations of, or otherwise to own, hold, improve, or use any real property, personal property, or mixed real and personal property;

(L) To sell, convey, mortgage, pledge, lease, exchange, abandon, or otherwise dispose of any real property, personal property, or mixed real and personal property;

(M) To establish a budget and make expenditures and levy dues as provided in Article VIII of this compact;

(N) To sue and be sued;

(O) To adopt a seal and bylaws governing the management and operation of the interstate commission;

(P) To perform any functions that may be necessary or appropriate to achieve the purposes of this compact;

(Q) To report annually to the legislatures, governors, judiciary, and state councils for interstate juvenile supervision of the compacting states concerning the activities of the interstate commission during the preceding year, and with the annual reports also including any recommendations that may have been adopted by the interstate commission.

(R) To coordinate education, training, and public awareness regarding the interstate movement of juveniles for officials involved in such activity.

(S) To establish uniform standards of the reporting, collecting and exchanging of data.

## Article V — Organization and Operation of the Interstate Commission

Section A. Bylaws

The interstate commission, by a majority of the members present and voting and within twelve months after the first interstate commission meeting, shall adopt bylaws to govern its conduct as may be necessary or appropriate to carry out the purposes of this compact, including, but not limited to, bylaws that do all of the following:

(1) Establish the fiscal year of the interstate commission;

(2) Establish an executive committee and any other committees that may be necessary;

(3) Provide for the establishment of committees governing any general or specific delegation of any authority or function of the interstate commission;

(4) Provide reasonable procedures for calling and conducting meetings of the interstate commission and ensuring reasonable notice of each such meeting;

(5) Establish the titles and responsibilities of the officers of the interstate commission;

(6) Provide a mechanism for concluding the operations of the interstate commission and the return of any surplus funds that may exist upon the termination of this compact after the payment or reserving of all of its debts and obligations, or both;

(7) Provide start-up rules for initial administration of this compact;

(8) Establish standards and procedures for compliance and technical assistance in carrying out this compact.

Section B. Officers and Staff

(1) The interstate commission, by a majority of the members, shall elect annually from among its members a chairperson and a vice chairperson, each of whom shall have such authority and duties as may be specified in the interstate commission's bylaws. The chairperson or, in the chairperson's absence or disability, the vice chairperson shall preside at all meetings of the interstate commission. The officers so elected shall serve without compensation or remuneration from the interstate commission; provided that, subject to the availability of budgeted funds, the officers shall be reimbursed for any ordinary and necessary costs and expenses incurred by them in the performance of their duties and responsibilities as officers of the interstate commission.

(2) The interstate commission, through its executive committee, shall appoint or retain an executive director for such period, upon such terms and conditions, and for such compensation as the interstate commission considers appropriate. The executive director shall serve as secretary to the interstate commission but shall not be a member of the interstate commission. The executive director shall hire and supervise such other staff as may be authorized by the interstate commission.

Section C. Qualified Immunity, Defense, and Indemnification

(1) Except as otherwise provided in this subsection, the interstate commission's executive director and each of its employees shall be immune from suit and liability, either personally or in the executive director's or employee's official capacity, for any claim for damage to or loss of property or personal injury or other civil liability caused or arising out of or relating to any actual or alleged act, error, or omission that occurred, or that the executive director or employee had a reasonable basis for believing occurred, within the scope of commission employment, duties, or responsibilities. The executive director or an employee shall not be protected from suit or liability for any damage, loss, injury, or liability caused by the executive director's or employee's willful and wanton misconduct of any such person.

(2) The liability of any commissioner, or the employee or agent of a commissioner, acting within the scope of such person's employment or duties for acts, errors, or omissions occurring within such person's state may not exceed the limits of liability set forth under the constitution and laws of that state for state officials, employees, and agents. Nothing in this subsection shall be construed to protect any such person from suit or liability for any damage, loss, injury, or liability caused by the intentional or willful and wanton misconduct of any such person.

(3) Except as otherwise provided in this subsection, the interstate commission shall defend the executive director or the employees or representatives of the interstate commission and, subject to the approval of the attorney general of the state represented by any commissioner of a compacting state, shall defend such commissioner or the commissioner's representatives or employees in any civil

action seeking to impose liability arising out of any actual or alleged act, error, or omission that occurred within the scope of interstate commission employment, duties, or responsibilities, or that the defendant had a reasonable basis for believing occurred within the scope of interstate commission employment, duties, or responsibilities. The duty to defend described in this division does not apply if the actual or alleged act, error, or omission in question resulted from intentional or willful and wanton misconduct on the part of the executive director, employee, or representative of the interstate commission or the commissioner of a compacting state or the commissioner's representatives or employees.

(4) Except as otherwise provided in this subsection, the interstate commission shall indemnify and hold the commissioner of a compacting state, or the commissioner's representatives or employees, or the interstate commission's representatives or employees, harmless in the amount of any settlement or judgment obtained against such persons arising out of any actual or alleged act, error, or omission that occurred within the scope of interstate commission employment, duties, or responsibilities, or that such persons had a reasonable basis for believing occurred within the scope of interstate commission employment, duties, or responsibilities. The duty to indemnify and hold harmless described in this division does not apply if the actual or alleged act, error, or omission in question resulted from intentional or willful and wanton misconduct on the part of the commissioner of a compacting state or the commissioner's representatives or employees or the interstate commission's representatives or employees.

## Article VI — Rulemaking Functions of the Interstate Commission

(A) The interstate commission shall promulgate and publish rules in order to effectively and efficiently achieve the purposes of this compact.

(B) Rulemaking shall occur pursuant to the criteria set forth in this Article and the bylaws and rules adopted pursuant thereto. The rulemaking shall substantially conform to the principles of the "Model State Administrative Procedures Act," 1981 Act, Uniform Laws Annotated, Vol. 15, p. 1 (2000), or another administrative procedures act, as the interstate commission determines appropriate consistent with due process requirements under the United States Constitution as now or hereafter interpreted by the United States Supreme Court. All rules and amendments shall become binding as of the date specified, as published with the final version of the rule as approved by the interstate commission.

(C) When promulgating a rule, the interstate commission, at a minimum, shall do all of the following:

(1) Publish the proposed rule's entire text stating the reason or reasons for that proposed rule;

(2) Allow and invite any and all persons to submit written data, facts, opinions, and arguments, which information shall be added to the record and be made publicly available;

(3) Provide an opportunity for an informal hearing, if petitioned by ten or more persons;

(4) Promulgate a final rule and its effective date, if appropriate, based on input from state or local officials, or interested parties.

(D) When the interstate commission promulgates a rule, not later than sixty days after the rule is promulgated, any interested person may file a petition in the United States district court for the District of Columbia or in the federal district court where the interstate commission's principal office is located, for judicial review of the rule. If the court finds that the interstate commission's action is not supported by substantial evidence in the rulemaking record, the court shall hold the rule unlawful and set it aside. For purposes of this division, evidence is substantial if it would be considered substantial evidence under the "Model State Administrative Procedures Act," 1981 Act, Uniform Laws Annotated, Vol. 15, p. 1 (2000).

(E) If a majority of the legislatures of the compacting states rejects a rule, those states, by enactment of a statute or resolution in the same manner used to adopt the compact, may cause that such rule shall have no further force and effect in any compacting state.

(F) The existing rules governing the operation of the interstate compact on juveniles that is superseded by this compact shall be null and void twelve months after the first meeting of the interstate commission created under this compact.

(G) Upon determination by the interstate commission that a state of emergency exists, it may promulgate an emergency rule. An emergency rule so promulgated shall become effective immediately upon adoption, provided that the usual rulemaking procedures specified in this Article shall be retroactively applied to the emergency rule as soon as reasonably possible, but not later than ninety days after the effective date of the emergency rule.

## Article VII — Oversight, Enforcement, and Dispute Resolution by the Interstate Commission

A Oversight and Enforcement

(1) The interstate commission shall oversee the administration and operations of the interstate movement of juveniles subject to this compact in the compacting states and shall monitor such activities being administered in noncompacting states that may significantly affect compacting states.

(2) The courts and executive agencies in each compacting state shall enforce this compact and shall take all actions necessary and appropriate to effectuate this compact's purposes and intent. The provisions of this compact and the rules promulgated under it shall be received by all the judges, public officers, commissions, and departments of the state government as evidence of the authorized statute and administrative rules. All courts shall take judicial notice of the compact and the rules. In any judicial or administrative proceeding in a compacting state pertaining to the subject matter of this compact that may affect the powers, responsibilities, or actions of the interstate commission, the interstate commission shall be entitled to receive all service of process in the proceeding and shall have standing to intervene in the proceeding for all purposes.

Section B. Dispute Resolution

(1) The compacting states shall report to the interstate commission on all issues and activities necessary for the administration of this compact and on all issues and activities pertaining to compliance with the provisions of this compact and the interstate commission's bylaws and rules.

(2) The interstate commission, upon the request of a compacting state, shall attempt to resolve any disputes or other issues that are subject to this compact and that may arise among compacting states and between compacting and non-compacting states. The interstate commission shall promulgate a rule providing for both mediation and

binding dispute resolution for disputes among the compacting states.

(3) The interstate commission, in the reasonable exercise of its discretion, shall enforce the provisions and rules of this compact using any or all means set forth in Article XI of this compact.

### Article VIII — Finance

(A) The interstate commission shall pay or provide for the payment of the reasonable expenses of its establishment, organization, and ongoing activities.

(B) The interstate commission shall levy on and collect an annual assessment from each compacting state to cover the cost of the internal operations and activities of the interstate commission and its staff. The annual assessment shall be in a total amount sufficient to cover the interstate commission's annual budget as approved each year. The aggregate annual assessment amount shall be allocated based upon a formula to be determined by the interstate commission, taking into consideration the population of each compacting state and the volume of interstate movement of juveniles in each compacting state. The interstate commission shall promulgate a rule binding upon all compacting states that governs the assessment.

(C) The interstate commission shall not incur any obligations of any kind prior to securing the funds adequate to meet the obligations. The interstate commission shall not pledge the credit of any of the compacting states, except by and with the authority of the compacting state.

(D) The interstate commission shall keep accurate accounts of all receipts and disbursements. The receipts and disbursements of the interstate commission shall be subject to the audit and accounting procedures established under its bylaws. However, all receipts and disbursements of funds handled by the interstate commission shall be audited yearly by a certified or licensed public accountant and the report of the audit shall be included in and become part of the annual report of the interstate commission.

### Article IX — The State Council

Each compacting state shall create a state council for interstate juvenile supervision. While each compacting state may determine the membership of its own state council, its membership must include at least one representative from the legislative, judicial, and executive branches of government, victims groups, and the compact administrator or designee. Each compacting state retains the right to determine the qualifications of the compact administrator for the state. Each state council shall advise and may exercise oversight and advocacy concerning that state's participation in interstate commission activities and other duties as may be determined by that state, including but not limited to, development of policy concerning operations and procedures of the compact within that state.

### Article X — Compacting States, Effective Date, and Amendment

(A) Any state, as defined in Article II of this compact, is eligible to become a compacting state.

(B) This compact shall become effective and binding upon legislative enactment of the compact into law by no less than thirty-five of the states. The initial effective date shall be the later of July 1, 2004, or upon enactment into law by the thirty-fifth jurisdiction. Thereafter, this compact shall become effective and binding as to any other compacting state upon enactment of this compact into law by that state. The governors of non-compacting states or their designees shall be invited to participate in the activities of the interstate commission on a non-voting basis prior to adoption of this compact by all states.

(C) The interstate commission may propose amendments to this compact for enactment by the compacting states. No amendment shall become effective and binding upon the interstate commission and the compacting states unless and until it is enacted into law by unanimous consent of the compacting states.

### Article XI — Withdrawal, Default, Termination, and Judicial Enforcement

Section A. Withdrawal

(1) Once effective, this compact shall continue in force and remain binding upon each and every compacting state, provided that a compacting state may withdraw from this compact by specifically repealing the statute that enacted this compact into law.

(2) The effective date of withdrawal of a compacting state is the effective date of the state's repeal of the statute that enacted this compact into law.

(3) A compacting state that withdraws from this compact shall immediately notify the chairperson of the interstate commission in writing upon the introduction of legislation repealing this compact in the withdrawing state. The interstate commission shall notify the other compacting states of the withdrawing state's intent to withdraw within sixty days of the interstate commission's receipt of the notice from the withdrawing state.

(4) A compacting state that withdraws from this compact is responsible for all assessments, obligations, and liabilities incurred through the effective date of withdrawal, including any obligations, the performance of which extend beyond the effective date of withdrawal.

(5) If a compacting state withdraws from this compact, reinstatement of the withdrawing state following withdrawal shall occur upon the withdrawing state reenacting this compact or upon such later date as determined by the interstate commission.

Section B. Technical Assistance, Fines, Suspension, Termination, and Default

(1) If the interstate commission determines that any compacting state has at any time defaulted in the performance of any of its obligations or responsibilities under this compact, or under the interstate commission's bylaws or duly promulgated rules, the interstate commission may impose one or more of the following penalties:

(a) Remedial training and technical assistance as directed by the interstate commission;

(b) Alternative dispute resolution;

(c) Fines, fees, and costs in such amounts as are deemed to be reasonable as fixed by the interstate commission;

(d) Suspension or termination of membership in this compact, provided that suspension or termination of membership shall be imposed only after all other reasonable means of securing compliance under the bylaws and rules have been exhausted and the interstate commission has therefore determined that the offending state is in default. Immediate notice of suspension shall be given by the interstate commission to the governor of the defaulting state, its chief justice or the chief judicial officer, the majority and minority leaders of its state legislature, and the state council for interstate juvenile supervision. The grounds for default include, but are not limited to, failure of a compacting state to perform such obligations or responsibilities imposed upon it by this compact, by the interstate commission's bylaws, or by its duly promulgated rules, and any other grounds designated in commission bylaws and rules. The interstate commission shall immediately notify the defaulting state in writing of the penalty imposed by the interstate commission and of the default pending a cure of the default. The interstate commission shall stipulate the conditions and the time period within which the defaulting state must cure its default. If the defaulting state fails to cure the default within the time period specified by the interstate commission, the defaulting state shall be terminated from this compact upon an affirmative vote of a majority of the compacting states and all rights, privileges, and benefits conferred by this compact shall be terminated from the effective date of termination.

(2) Within sixty days of the effective date of termination of a defaulting compacting state, the interstate commission shall notify the defaulting state's governor, its chief justice or chief judicial officer, the majority and minority leaders of its state legislature, and the state council for interstate juvenile supervision of the termination.

(3) A defaulting compacting state is responsible for all assessments, obligations, and liabilities incurred through the effective date of termination, including any obligations the performance of which extends beyond the effective date of termination.

(4) The interstate commission shall not bear any costs relating to a defaulting compacting state unless otherwise mutually agreed upon in writing between the interstate commission and the defaulting state.

(5) If a defaulting compacting state is terminated, reinstatement of the defaulting state following termination requires both a reenactment of the compact by the defaulting state and the approval of the interstate commission pursuant to its rules.

Section C. Judicial Enforcement

The interstate commission, by majority vote of the members, may initiate legal action against any compacting state to enforce compliance with the provisions of this compact, and the interstate commission's duly promulgated rules and bylaws. Any such action, if initiated, shall be initiated in the United States district court for the District of Columbia or, at the discretion of the interstate commission, in the federal district where the interstate commission has its offices. In the event judicial enforcement is necessary, the prevailing party shall be awarded all costs of the litigation including reasonable attorney's fees.

D Dissolution of Compact

(1) This compact dissolves effective upon the date of the withdrawal or default of the compacting state, which reduces membership in this compact to one compacting state.

(2) Upon the dissolution of this compact, the compact becomes null and void and shall be of no further force or effect, the business and affairs of the interstate commission shall be concluded, and any surplus funds shall be distributed in accordance with the interstate commission's bylaws.

## Article XII — Severability and Construction

(A) The provisions of this compact shall be severable, and if any phrase, clause, sentence, or provision is deemed unenforceable, the remaining provisions of the compact shall be enforceable.

(B) The provisions of this compact shall be liberally construed to effectuate its purposes.

## Article XIII — Binding Effect of Compact and Other Laws

Section A. Other Laws

(1) Nothing in this compact prevents the enforcement of any other law of a compacting state that is not inconsistent with this compact.

(2) All compacting states' laws, other than state constitutions and other interstate compacts, conflicting with this compact are superseded to the extent of the conflict.

Section B. Binding Effect of the Compact

(1) All lawful actions of the interstate commission, including all rules and bylaws promulgated by the interstate commission, are binding upon the compacting states.

(2) All agreements between the interstate commission and the compacting states are binding in accordance with their terms.

(3) Upon the request of a party to a conflict over the meaning or interpretation of interstate commission actions, and upon a majority vote of the compacting states, the interstate commission may issue advisory opinions regarding that meaning or interpretation.

(4) In the event any provision of this compact exceeds the constitutional limits imposed on the legislature of any compacting state, the obligations, duties, powers, or jurisdiction sought to be conferred by that provision upon the interstate commission shall be ineffective and such obligations, duties, powers, or jurisdiction shall remain in the compacting state and shall be exercised by the agency of that state to which such obligations, duties, powers, or jurisdiction are delegated by law in effect at the time this compact becomes effective.

## Article XIV — Financial Reimbursement

The state agency responsible for administering this compact shall have the legal authority to recoup fines, fees and costs imposed by the interstate commission as stated in Article XI, Section B, Subsection (1)(c) of this compact when the default in performance is the result of a decision made by an entity outside the jurisdiction of the agency administering this compact.

**HISTORY: 2011 SB 122, § 1, eff. June 30, 2011.**

A former section 2151.56 (127 v 530, eff. 9-17-57; 142 v H 790, eff. 3-16-89) was repealed by s. 2, 2011 SB 122, eff. June 30, 2011.

Acts 2011, SB 122, § 3 provides: "Upon the effective date of this act, the versions of sections 2151.56, 2151.57, 2151.58, and 2151.59 of the Revised Code enacted in Section 1 of this act will replace the versions of those sections, and the versions of sections 2151.60 and 2151.61 of the Revised Code, in effect on the day immediately preceding the effective date of this act."

Acts 2011, SB 122, § 4 provides: "This act is hereby declared to be an emergency measure necessary for the immediate preservation of the public peace, health, and safety. The reason for such necessity is that Ohio is one of only five states that have not yet enacted the Interstate Compact for Juveniles, which in most states has replaced the Interstate Compact on Juveniles. The rule that allows Ohio to cooperate with the member states of the new compact in the supervision of delinquent youth and the return of escapees, absconders, and runaways will expire on June 30, 2011. It is imperative that this act take effect by that date. Therefore, this act shall go into immediate effect."

The effective date is set by section 4 of HB 790.

## § 2151.57 State council for interstate juvenile supervision.

(A) As used in sections 2151.57 to 2151.59 of the Revised Code:

(1) "Interstate compact for juveniles" means the interstate compact for juveniles ratified, enacted into law, and entered into by this state pursuant to section 2151.56 of the Revised Code.

(2) "Bylaws," "commissioner," "compact administrator," and "interstate commission for juveniles" have the same meanings as in section 2151.56 of the Revised Code.

(B) The state council for interstate juvenile supervision is hereby established within the department of youth services. The council shall consist of the following members:

(1) One member who is the compact administrator or the designee of the compact administrator;

(2) One member of the house of representatives appointed by the speaker of the house of representatives;

(3) One member of the senate appointed by the president of the senate;

(4) One member who is a representative of the executive branch of state government, in addition to the member described in division (B)(1) of this section, appointed by the governor;

(5) One member who is a representative of the judiciary, who shall be a juvenile court judge appointed by the chief justice of the supreme court;

(6) One member who is a person who represents an organization that advocates for the rights of victims of crime or a delinquent act, appointed by the governor.

(C) The state council for interstate juvenile supervision shall advise and may exercise oversight and advocacy concerning this state's participation in activities of the interstate commission for juveniles, shall develop policy for this state concerning operations and procedures of the interstate compact for juveniles within this state, and shall perform other duties assigned to state councils under that compact.

**HISTORY: 2011 SB 122, § 1, eff. June 30, 2011.**

A former section 2151.57 (127 v 530, eff. 9-17-57) was repealed by s. 2, 2011 SB 122, eff. June 30, 2011.

Acts 2011, SB 122, § 3 provides: "Upon the effective date of this act, the versions of sections 2151.56, 2151.57, 2151.58, and 2151.59 of the Revised Code enacted in Section 1 of this act will replace the versions of those sections, and the versions of sections 2151.60 and 2151.61 of the Revised Code, in effect on the day immediately preceding the effective date of this act."

Acts 2011, SB 122, § 4 provides: "This act is hereby declared to be an emergency measure necessary for the immediate preservation of the public peace, health, and safety. The reason for such necessity is that Ohio is one of only five states that have not yet enacted the Interstate Compact for Juveniles, which in most states has replaced the Interstate Compact on Juveniles. The rule that allows Ohio to cooperate with the member states of the new compact in the supervision of delinquent youth and the return of escapees, absconders, and runaways will expire on June 30, 2011. It is imperative that this act take effect by that date. Therefore, this act shall go into immediate effect."

## § 2151.58 Appointment of compact administrator; commissioner on interstate commission for juveniles.

(A) The governor shall appoint the director of youth services as the compact administrator for the interstate compact for juveniles.

(B) The governor shall appoint the compact administrator or shall allow the compact administrator to appoint a designee to serve as the commissioner from this state on the interstate commission for juveniles.

**HISTORY: 2011 SB 122, § 1, eff. June 30, 2011.**

A former section 2151.58 (127 v 530, eff. 9-17-57) was repealed by s. 2, 2011 SB 122, eff. June 30, 2011.

Acts 2011, SB 122, § 3 provides: "Upon the effective date of this act, the versions of sections 2151.56, 2151.57, 2151.58, and 2151.59 of the Revised Code enacted in Section 1 of this act will replace the versions of those sections, and the versions of sections 2151.60 and 2151.61 of the Revised Code, in effect on the day immediately preceding the effective date of this act."

Acts 2011, SB 122, § 4 provides: "This act is hereby declared to be an emergency measure necessary for the immediate preservation of the public peace, health, and safety. The reason for such necessity is that Ohio is one of only five states that have not yet enacted the Interstate Compact for Juveniles, which in most states has replaced the Interstate Compact on Juveniles. The rule that allows Ohio to cooperate with the member states of the new compact in the supervision of delinquent youth and the return of escapees, absconders, and runaways will expire on June 30, 2011. It is imperative that this act take effect by that date. Therefore, this act shall go into immediate effect."

## § 2151.59 Department of youth services to administer compact.

(A) The department of youth services is the state agency responsible for administering the interstate compact for juveniles in this state.

(B) The department of youth services shall pay all of the following:

(1) The annual assessment charged to this state for participating in the interstate compact for juveniles;

(2) All fines, fees, or costs assessed against this state by the interstate commission for juveniles for any default in the performance of this state's obligations or responsibilities under the compact, the bylaws, or rules duly promulgated under the compact.

**HISTORY: 2011 SB 122, § 1, eff. June 30, 2011.**

A former section 2151.59 (127 v 530 (Eff 9-17-57); 141 v H 201. Eff 7-1-85) was repealed by s. 2, 2011 SB 122, eff. June 30, 2011.

Acts 2011, SB 122, § 3 provides: "Upon the effective date of this act, the versions of sections 2151.56, 2151.57, 2151.58, and 2151.59 of the Revised Code enacted in Section 1 of this act will replace the versions of those sections, and the versions of sections 2151.60 and 2151.61 of the Revised Code, in effect on the day immediately preceding the effective date of this act."

Acts 2011, SB 122, § 4 provides: "This act is hereby declared to be an emergency measure necessary for the immediate preservation of the public peace, health, and safety. The reason for such necessity is that Ohio is one of only five states that have not yet enacted the Interstate Compact for Juveniles, which in most states has replaced the Interstate Compact on Juveniles. The rule that allows Ohio to cooperate with the member states of the new compact in the supervision of delinquent youth and the return of escapees, absconders, and runaways will expire on June 30, 2011. It is imperative that this act take effect by that date. Therefore, this act shall go into immediate effect."

## § 2151.60 Enforcement by agencies of state and subdivisions [Repealed].

Repealed by 2011 SB 122, § 2, effective June 30, 2011.

**HISTORY: 127 v 530. Eff 9-17-57.**

## § 2151.61 Additional article [Repealed].

Repealed by 2011 SB 122, § 2, effective June 30, 2011.

**HISTORY: 127 v 530 (Eff 9-17-57); 144 v H 154. Eff 7-31-92.**

## § 2151.62 Amended and renumbered RC § 2152.72 in 148 v S 179. Eff 1-1-2002.

The effective date is set by section 5 of SB 179.

### [TRAINING AND REHABILITATION]

## § 2151.65 Single-county and joint-county juvenile facilities.

Upon the advice and recommendation of the juvenile judge, the board of county commissioners may provide by purchase, lease, construction, or otherwise a school, forestry camp, or other facility or facilities where delinquent children, as defined in section 2152.02 of the Revised Code, dependent children, abused children, unruly children, as defined in section 2151.022 [2151.02.2] of the Revised Code, or neglected children or juvenile traffic offenders may be held for training, treatment, and rehabilitation. Upon the joint advice and recommendation of the juvenile judges of two or more adjoining or neighboring counties, the boards of county commissioners of such counties may form themselves into a joint board and proceed to organize a district for the establishment and support of a school, forestry camp, or other facility or facilities for the use of the juvenile courts of such counties, where delinquent, dependent, abused, unruly, or neglected children, or juvenile traffic offenders may be held for treatment, training, and rehabilitation, by using a site or buildings already established in one such county, or by providing for the purchase of a site and the erection of the necessary buildings thereon. Such county or district school, forestry camp, or other facility or facilities shall be maintained as provided in Chapters 2151. and 2152. of the Revised Code. Children who are adjudged to be delinquent, dependent, neglected, abused, unruly, or juvenile traffic offenders may be committed to and held in any such school, forestry camp, or other facility or facilities for training, treatment, and rehabilitation.

The juvenile court shall determine:

(A) The children to be admitted to any school, forestry camp, or other facility maintained under this section;

(B) The period such children shall be trained, treated, and rehabilitated at such facility;

(C) The removal and transfer of children from such facility.

**HISTORY: 130 v 626 (Eff 10-14-63); 136 v H 85 (Eff 11-28-75); 138 v S 168 (Eff 10-2-80); 148 v S 179, § 3. Eff 1-1-2002.**

The effective date is set by section 5 of SB 179.

## § 2151.651 State assistance for juvenile facilities.

The board of county commissioners of a county which, either separately or as part of a district, is planning to establish a school, forestry camp, or other facility under section 2151.65 of the Revised Code, to be used exclusively for the rehabilitation of children between the ages of twelve to eighteen years, other than psychotic or mentally retarded children, who are designated delinquent children, as defined in section 2152.02 of the Revised Code, or unruly children, as defined in section 2151.022 [2151.02.2] of the Revised Code, by order of a juvenile court, may make application to the department of youth services, created under section 5139.01 of the Revised Code, for financial assistance in defraying the county's share of the cost of acquisition or construction of such school, camp, or other facility, as provided in section 5139.27 of the Revised Code. Such application shall be made on forms prescribed and furnished by the department.

**HISTORY: 131 v 633 (Eff 8-10-65); 138 v S 168 (Eff 10-2-80); 139 v H 440 (Eff 11-23-81); 148 v S 179, § 3. Eff 1-1-2002.**

The effective date is set by section 5 of SB 179.

## § 2151.652 Repealed, 149 v H 94, §§ 2, 4a [131 v 633; 138 v S 168; 139 v H 440; 148 v S 179]. Eff 9-5-2001; 1-1-2002.

This section concerned state assistance for operation and maintenance. The version of this statute as amended by SB 179 (148 v —), was to become effective 1-1-2002.

The effective date is set by section 5 and section 205 of HB 94.

## § 2151.653 Education of youths.

The board of county commissioners of a county or the board of trustees of a district maintaining a school, forestry camp, or other facility established under section 2151.65 of the Revised Code, shall provide a program of education for the youths admitted to such school, forestry camp, or other facility. Either of such boards and the board of education of any school district may enter into an agreement whereby such board of education provides teachers for such school, forestry camp, or other facility, or permits youths admitted to such school, forestry camp, or other facility to attend a school or schools within such school district, or both. Either of such boards may enter into an agreement with the appropriate authority of any university, college, or vocational institution to assist in providing a program of education for the youths admitted to such school, forestry camp, or other facility.

**HISTORY: 131 v 634. Eff 8-10-65.**

## § 2151.654 Nonresident admission.

The board of county commissioners of a county or the board of trustees of a district maintaining a school, forestry camp, or other facility established under section 2151.65 of the Revised Code, may enter into an agreement with the board of county commissioners of a county which does not maintain such a school, forestry camp, or other facility, to admit to such school, forestry camp, or other facility a child from the county not maintaining such a school, forestry camp, or other facility.

**HISTORY: 131 v 634. Eff 8-10-65.**

## § 2151.655 Taxing authority of county may issue general obligation securities to pay cost of acquiring or acquiring sites for schools, detention facilities, forestry camps, or other facilities; agreements for financing of permanent improvements.

(A) The taxing authority of a county may issue general obligation securities of the county under Chapter 133. of the Revised Code to pay such county's share, either separately or as a part of a district, of the cost of acquiring schools, detention facilities, forestry camps, or other facilities, or any combination thereof, under section 2152.41 or 2151.65 of the Revised Code, or of acquiring sites for and constructing, enlarging, or otherwise improving such schools, detention facilities, forestry camps, other facilities, or combinations thereof.

(B) The joint board of county commissioners, as the taxing authority of a detention facility district, or a district organized under section 2151.65 of the Revised Code, or of a combined district organized under sections 2152.41 and 2151.65 of the Revised Code, may submit to the electors of the district the question of issuing general obligation bonds of the district to pay the cost of acquiring, constructing, enlarging, or otherwise improving sites, buildings, and facilities for any purposes for which the district was organized. The election on such question shall be submitted and held under section 133.18 of the Revised Code.

(C)(1) To pay the cost of permanent improvements of the district, the board of trustees of a detention facility district, of a district organized under section 2151.65 of the Revised Code, or of a combined district organized under sections 2152.41 and 2151.65 of the Revised Code may enter into an agreement with the several boards of county commissioners constituting the joint board of county commissioners. The agreement shall provide for each such board of county commissioners to pay the district a share of such costs for a stated term from the proceeds of a tax levied by the board under division (F) or (R) of section 5705.19 of the Revised Code or from funds of the county otherwise lawfully available to pay the county's share of the costs of the district's permanent improvements. County shares shall be allocated on the basis prescribed in the agreement, which may include an allocation in proportion to the taxable value of each county or in proportion to the number of children from each county who are maintained in district facilities.

More than one agreement may be entered into under this division with respect to a district, and more than one agreement may exist at the same time with respect to a district. An agreement entered into under this division may be amended if the amendment is mutually agreed to by the board of trustees of the district and the several boards of county commissioners constituting the joint board of county commissioners.

If a board of county commissioners withdraws from the district before the end of the term of the agreement, the board shall be required to make payments as required in the agreement until all debt charges or loan repayments for which such payments are pledged are paid in full, unless the board of trustees agrees otherwise.

(2) In any such district where the board of trustees has entered into an agreement under division (C)(1) of this section, the joint board of county commissioners, as the taxing authority of a district, may issue self-supporting securities of the district under section 133.152 [133.15.2] of the Revised Code for the purpose of paying the cost of permanent improvements of the district. If such securities are issued, the term of an agreement shall be for no fewer years than the maximum maturity of securities secured by a pledge of payments made under the agreement.

(3) In any such district where the board of trustees has entered into an agreement under division (C)(1) of this section, the joint board of county commissioners, as the taxing authority of a district, may obtain loans from a financial institution to be repaid from amounts to be paid to the district under the agreement by the boards of county commissioners constituting the joint board of county commissioners.

**HISTORY: RC § 133.15.1, 131 v 74 (Eff 8-10-65); 133 v H 1135 (Eff 9-16-70); 134 v H 258 (Eff 1-27-72); RC § 2151.65.5, 143 v H 230 (Eff 10-30-89); 148 v S 179, § 3. Eff 1-1-2002; 151 v S 125, § 1, eff. 7-20-06.**

The effective date is set by section 5 of SB 179.

## § 2151.66 District tax levies.

The joint boards of county commissioners of district schools, forestry camps, or other facility or facilities created under section 2151.65 of the Revised Code, shall make annual assessments of taxes sufficient to support and defray all necessary expenses of such school, forestry camp, or other facility or facilities.

**HISTORY: 130 v 627. Eff 10-14-63.**

## § 2151.67 Gifts and bequests.

The board of county commissioners of a county or the board of trustees of a district maintaining a school, forestry camp, or other facility established or to be established under section 2151.65 of the Revised Code may receive gifts, grants, devises, and bequests, either absolutely or in trust, and may receive any public moneys made available to it. Each of such boards shall use such gifts, grants, devises, bequests, and public moneys in whatever manner it determines is most likely to carry out the purposes for which such school, forestry camp, or other facility was or is to be established.

**HISTORY: 131 v 635 (Eff 8-10-65); 132 v H 1. Eff 2-21-67.**

**Analogous to former RC § 2151.67 (130 v 627), repealed in 131 v 2019, § 2, eff 8-10-65.**

## § 2151.68 Appointment of district boards of trustees.

Immediately upon the organization of the joint board of county commissioners as provided by section 2151.65 of the Revised Code, or so soon thereafter as practicable, such joint board of county commissioners shall appoint a board of not less than five trustees, which shall hold office and perform its duties until the first annual meeting after the choice of an established site and buildings, or after the selection and purchase of a building site, at which time such joint board of county commissioners shall appoint a board of not less than five trustees, one of whom shall hold office for a term of one year, one for the term of two years, one for the term of three years, half of the remaining number for the term of four years, and the remainder for the term of five years. Annually thereafter, the joint board of county commissioners shall appoint one or more trustees, each of whom shall hold office for the term of five years, to succeed any trustee whose term of office expires. A trustee may be appointed to succeed himself upon such board of trustees, and all appointments to such board of trustees shall be made from persons who are recommended and approved by the juvenile court judge or judges of the county of which such person is a resident. The annual meeting of the board of trustees shall be held on the first Tuesday in May in each year.

**HISTORY: 130 v 627. Eff 10-14-63.**

## § 2151.69 Procedures of district boards of trustees.

A majority of the trustees appointed under section 2151.68 of the Revised Code constitutes a quorum. Board meetings shall be held at least quarterly. The presiding juvenile court judge of each of the counties of the district organized pursuant to section 2151.65 of the Revised Code shall attend such meetings, or shall designate a member of his staff to do so. The members of the board shall receive no compensation for their services, except their actual traveling expenses, which, when properly certified, shall be allowed and paid by the treasurer.

**HISTORY: 130 v 628. Eff 10-14-63.**

## § 2151.70 Employees of juvenile facilities.

The judge, in a county maintaining a school, forestry camp, or other facility or facilities created under section 2151.65 of the Revised Code, shall appoint the superintendent of any such facility. In the case of a district facility created under such section, the board of trustees shall appoint the superintendent. A superintendent, before entering upon his duties, shall give bond with sufficient surety to the judge or to the board, as the case may be, in such amount as may be fixed by the judge or the board, such bond being conditioned upon the full and faithful accounting of the funds and properties coming into his hands.

Compensation of the superintendent and other necessary employees of a school, forestry camp, or other facility or facilities shall be fixed by the judge in the case of a county facility, or by the board of trustees in the case of a district facility. Such compensation and other expenses of maintaining the facility shall be paid in the manner prescribed in section 2151.13 of the Revised Code in the case of a county facility, or in accordance with rules and regulations provided for in section 2151.77 of the Revised Code in the case of a district facility.

The superintendent of a facility shall appoint all employees of such facility. All such employees, except the superintendent, shall be in the classified civil service.

The superintendent of a school, forestry camp, or other facility shall have entire executive charge of such facility, under supervision of the judge, in the case of a county facility, or under supervision of the board of trustees, in the case of a district facility. The superintendent shall control, manage, and operate the facility, and shall have custody of its property, files, and records.

**HISTORY: 130 v 628. Eff 10-14-63.**

## § 2151.71 Manner of operating facilities.

District schools, forestry camps, or other facilities created under section 2151.65 of the Revised Code shall be established, operated, maintained, and managed in the same manner, so far as applicable, as county schools, forestry camps, or other facilities.

**HISTORY: 130 v 629. Eff 10-14-63.**

## § 2151.72 Selection of site for district facility.

When the board of trustees appointed under section 2151.68 of the Revised Code does not choose an established institution in one of the counties of the district, it may select a suitable site for the erection of a district school, forestry camp, or other facility or facilities created under section 2151.65 of the Revised Code.

**HISTORY: 130 v 629. Eff 10-14-63.**

## § 2151.73 Apportionment of board of trustees posts; executive committee.

Each county in the district, organized under section 2151.65 of the Revised Code, shall be entitled to one trustee, and in districts composed of but two counties, each county shall be entitled to not less than two trustees. In districts composed of more than four counties, the number of trustees shall be sufficiently increased so that there shall always be an uneven number of trustees constituting such board. The county in which a district school, forestry camp, or other facility created under section 2151.65 of the Revised Code is located shall have not less than two trustees, who, in the interim period between the regular meetings of the board of trustees, shall act as an executive committee in the discharge of all business pertaining to the school, forestry camp, or other facility.

**HISTORY: 130 v 629. Eff 10-14-63.**

## § 2151.74 Removal of trustees.

The joint board of county commissioners organized under section 2151.65 of the Revised Code may remove any trustee appointed under section 2151.68 of the Revised Code, but no such removal shall be made on account of the religious or political convictions of such trustee. The trustee appointed to fill any vacancy shall hold his office for the unexpired term of his predecessor.

**HISTORY: 130 v 630. Eff 10-14-63.**

## § 2151.75 Interim duties of trustees; trustees' fund; reports.

In the interim, between the selection and purchase of a site, and the erection and occupancy of a district school, forestry camp, or other facility or facilities created under section 2151.65 of the Revised Code, the joint board of county commissioners provided by section 2151.65 of the Revised Code may delegate to a board of trustees appointed under section 2151.68 of the Revised Code, such powers and duties as, in its judgment, will be of general interest or aid to the institution. Such joint board of county commissioners may appropriate a trustees' fund, to be expended by the board of trustees in payment of such contracts, purchases, or other expenses necessary to the wants or requirements of the school, forestry camp, or other facility or facilities which are not otherwise provided for. The board of trustees shall make a complete settlement with the joint board of county commissioners once each six months, or quarterly if required, and shall make a full report of the condition of the school, forestry camp, or other facility or facilities and inmates, to the board of county commissioners, and to the juvenile court of each of the counties.

**HISTORY: 130 v 630. Eff 10-14-63.**

## § 2151.76 Authority for choice, construction, and furnishing of district facility.

The choice of an established site and buildings, or the purchase of a site, stock, implements, and general farm equipment, should there be a farm, the erection of buildings, and the completion and furnishing of the district school, forestry camp, or other facility or facilities for occupancy, shall be in the hands of the joint board of county commissioners organized under section 2151.65 of the Revised Code. Such joint board of county commissioners may delegate all or a portion of these duties to the board of trustees provided for under section 2151.68 of the Revised Code, under such restrictions and regulations as the joint board of county commissioners imposes.

**HISTORY: 130 v 630. Eff 10-14-63.**

## § 2151.77 Capital and current expenses of district.

When an established site and buildings are used for a district school, forestry camp, or other facility or facilities created under section 2151.65 of the Revised Code the joint board of county commissioners organized under section 2151.65 of the Revised Code shall cause the value of such site and buildings to be properly appraised. This appraisal value, or in case of the purchase of a site, the purchase price and the cost of all betterments and additions thereto, shall be paid by the counties comprising the district, in proportion to the taxable property of each county, as shown by its tax duplicate. The current expenses of maintaining the school, forestry camp, or other facility or facilities and the cost of ordinary repairs thereto shall be paid by each such county in accordance with one of the following methods as approved by the joint board of county commissioners:

(A) In proportion to the number of children from such county who are maintained in the school, forestry camp, or other facility or facilities during the year;

(B) By a levy submitted by the joint board of county commissioners under division (A) of section 5705.19 of the Revised Code and approved by the electors of the district;

(C) In proportion to the taxable property of each county, as shown by its tax duplicate;

(D) In any combination of the methods for payment described in division (A), (B), or (C) of this section.

The board of trustees shall, with the approval of the joint board of county commissioners, adopt rules for the management of funds used for the current expenses of maintaining the school, forestry camp, or other facility or facilities.

**HISTORY: 130 v 631 (Eff 10-14-63); 134 v H 258 (Eff 1-27-72); 142 v H 365. Eff 6-14-88.**

## § 2151.78 Withdrawal of county from district; continuity of district tax levy.

The board of county commissioners of any county within a school, forestry camp, or other facility or facilities district may, upon the recommendation of the juvenile court of such county, withdraw from such district and dispose of its interest in such school, forestry camp, or other facility or facilities selling or leasing its right, title, and interest in the site, buildings, furniture, and equipment to any counties in the district, at such price and upon such terms as are agreed upon among the boards of county commissioners of the counties concerned. Section 307.10 of the Revised Code does not apply to this section. The net proceeds of any such sale or lease shall be paid into the treasury of the withdrawing county.

Any county withdrawing from such district or from a combined district organized under sections 2152.41 and 2151.65 of the Revised Code shall continue to have levied against its tax duplicate any tax levied by the district during the period in which the county was a member of the district for current operating expenses, permanent improvements, or the retirement of bonded indebtedness. Such levy shall continue to be a levy against such duplicate of the county until such time that it expires or is renewed.

Members of the board of trustees of a district school, forestry camp, or other facility or facilities who are residents of a county withdrawing from such district are deemed to have resigned their positions upon the completion of the withdrawal procedure provided by this section. Vacancies then created shall be filled according to sections 2151.68 and 2151.74 of the Revised Code.

**HISTORY: 130 v 631 (Eff 10-14-63); 134 v H 258 (Eff 1-27-72); 148 v S 179, § 3. Eff 1-1-2002.**

The effective date is set by section 5 of SB 179.

## § 2151.79 Designation of fiscal officer of district; duties of county auditors in district.

The county auditor of the county having the greatest population, or, with the unanimous concurrence of the county auditors of the counties composing a facilities district, the auditor of the county wherein the facility is located, shall be the fiscal officer of a district organized under section 2151.65 of the Revised Code or a combined district organized under sections 2152.41 and 2151.65 of the Revised Code. The county auditors of the several counties composing a school, forestry camp, or other facility or facilities district, shall meet at the district school, forestry camp, or other facility or facilities not less than once in each six months, to review accounts and to transact such other duties in connection with the institution as pertain to the business of their office.

**HISTORY: 130 v 631 (Eff 10-14-63); 134 v H 258 (Eff 1-27-72); 135 v H 1033 (Eff 10-2-74); 148 v S 179, § 3. Eff 1-1-2002.**

The effective date is set by section 5 of SB 179.

## § 2151.80 Expenses of members of boards of county commissioners.

Each member of the board of county commissioners who meets by appointment to consider the organization of a district school, forestry camp, or other facility or facilities shall, upon presentation of properly certified accounts, be paid his necessary expenses upon a warrant drawn by the county auditor of his county.

**HISTORY: 130 v 632. Eff 10-14-63.**

[INDEPENDENT LIVING SERVICES]

## § 2151.81 Definitions.

As used in sections 2151.82 to 2151.84 of the Revised Code:

(A) "Independent living services" means services and other forms of support designed to aid children and young adults to successfully make the transition to independent adult living and to achieve emotional and economic self-sufficiency. "Independent living services" may include the following:

(1) Providing housing;

(2) Teaching decision-making skills;

(3) Teaching daily living skills such as securing and maintaining a residence, money management, utilization of community services and systems, personal health care, hygiene and safety, and time management;

(4) Assisting in obtaining education, training, and employment skills;

(5) Assisting in developing positive adult relationships and community supports.

(B) "Young adult" means a person eighteen years of age or older but under twenty-one years of age who was in the temporary or permanent custody of, or was provided care in a planned permanent living arrangement by, a public children services agency or private child placing agency on the date the person attained age eighteen.

**HISTORY: 149 v H 38. Eff 11-1-2002.**

## § 2151.82 Agency duty to provide independent living services.

A public children services agency or private child placing agency, that has temporary or permanent custody of, or is providing care in a planned permanent living arrangement to, a child who is sixteen or seventeen years of age, shall provide independent living services to the child. The services to be provided shall be determined based on an evaluation of the strengths and weaknesses of the child, completed or obtained by the agency. If housing is provided as part of the services, the child shall be placed in housing that is supervised or semi-supervised by an adult.

The services shall be included as part of the case plan established for the child pursuant to section 2151.412 [2151.41.2] of the Revised Code.

**HISTORY: 149 v H 38. Eff 11-1-2002.**

## § 2151.83 Agreement with young adult to provide independent living services; addendum.

(A) A public children services agency or private child placing agency, on the request of a young adult, shall enter into a jointly prepared written agreement with the young adult that obligates the agency to ensure that independent living services are provided to the young adult and sets forth the responsibilities of the young adult regarding the services. The agreement shall be developed based on the young adult's strengths, needs, and circumstances. The agreement shall be designed to promote the young adult's successful transition to independent adult living and emotional and economic self-sufficiency.

(B) If the young adult appears to be eligible for services from one or more of the following entities, the agency must contact the appropriate entity to determine eligibility:

(1) An entity, other than the agency, that is represented on a county family and children first council established pursuant to section 121.37 of the Revised Code. If the entity is a board of alcohol, drug addiction, and mental health services, an alcohol and drug addiction services board, or a community mental health board, the agency shall contact the provider of alcohol, drug addiction, or mental health services that has been designated by the board to determine the young adult's eligibility for services.

(2) The rehabilitation services commission;

(3) A metropolitan housing authority established pursuant to section 3735.27 of the Revised Code.

If an entity described in this division determines that the young adult qualifies for services from the entity, that entity, the young adult, and the agency to which the young adult made the request for independent living services shall enter into a written addendum to the jointly prepared agreement entered into under division (A) of this section. The addendum shall indicate how services under the agreement and addendum are to be coordinated and allocate the service responsibilities among the entities and agency that signed the addendum.

**HISTORY: 149 v H 38. Eff 11-1-2002; 150 v H 95, § 1, eff. 9-26-03.**

The effective date is set by section 179 of H.B. 95 (150 v —).

## § 2151.84 Model agreements.

The department of job and family services shall establish model agreements that may be used by public children services agencies and private child placing agencies required to provide services under an agreement with a young adult pursuant to section 2151.83 of the Revised Code. The model agreements shall include provisions describing the specific independent living services to be provided, the duration of the services and the agreement, the duties and responsibilities of each party under the agreement, and grievance procedures regarding disputes that arise regarding the agreement or services provided under it.

**HISTORY: 149 v H 38. Eff 11-1-2002; 150 v H 95, § 1, eff. 9-26-03.**

The effective date is set by section 179 of H.B. 95 (150 v —).

## § 2151.85 Unmarried minor may seek abortion without notice to parent, guardian or custodian.

(A) A woman who is pregnant, unmarried, under eighteen years of age, and unemancipated and who wishes to have an abortion without the notification of her parents, guardian, or custodian may file a complaint in the juvenile court of the county in which she has a residence or legal settlement, in the juvenile court of any county that borders to any extent the county in which she has a residence or legal settlement, or in the juvenile court of the county in which the hospital, clinic, or other facility in which the abortion would be performed or induced is located, requesting the issuance of an order authorizing her to consent to the performance or inducement of an abortion without the notification of her parents, guardian, or custodian.

The complaint shall be made under oath and shall include all of the following:

(1) A statement that the complainant is pregnant;

(2) A statement that the complainant is unmarried, under eighteen years of age, and unemancipated;

(3) A statement that the complainant wishes to have an abortion without the notification of her parents, guardian, or custodian;

(4) An allegation of either or both of the following:

(a) That the complainant is sufficiently mature and well enough informed to intelligently decide whether to have an abortion without the notification of her parents, guardian, or custodian;

(b) That one or both of her parents, her guardian, or her custodian was engaged in a pattern of physical, sexual, or emotional abuse against her, or that the notification of her parents, guardian, or custodian otherwise is not in her best interest.

(5) A statement as to whether the complainant has retained an attorney and, if she has retained an attorney, the name, address, and telephone number of her attorney.

(B)(1) The court shall fix a time for a hearing on any complaint filed pursuant to division (A) of this section and shall keep a record of all testimony and other oral proceedings in the action. The court shall hear and determine the action and shall not refer any portion of it to a referee. The hearing shall be held at the earliest possible time, but not later than the fifth business day after the day that the complaint is filed. The court shall enter judgment on the complaint immediately after the hearing is concluded. If the hearing required by this division is not held by the fifth business day after the complaint is filed, the failure to hold the hearing shall be considered to be a constructive order of the court authorizing the complainant to consent to the performance or inducement of an abortion without the notification of her parent, guardian, or custodian, and the complainant and any other person may rely on the constructive order to the same extent as if the court actually had issued an order under this section authorizing the complainant to consent to the performance or inducement of an abortion without such notification.

(2) The court shall appoint a guardian ad litem to protect the interests of the complainant at the hearing that is held pursuant to this section. If the complainant has not retained an attorney, the court shall appoint an attorney to represent her. If the guardian ad litem is an attorney admitted to the practice of law in this state, the court also may appoint him to serve as the complainant's attorney.

(C)(1) If the complainant makes only the allegation set forth in division (A)(4)(a) of this section and if the court finds, by clear and convincing evidence, that the complainant is sufficiently mature and well enough informed to decide intelligently whether to have an abortion, the court shall issue an order authorizing the complainant to consent to the performance or inducement of an abortion without the notification of her parents, guardian, or custodian. If the court does not make the finding specified in this division, it shall dismiss the complaint.

(2) If the complainant makes only the allegation set forth in division (A)(4)(b) of this section and if the court finds, by clear and convincing evidence, that there is evidence of a pattern of physical, sexual, or emotional abuse of the complainant by one or both of her parents, her guardian, or her custodian, or that the notification of the parents, guardian, or custodian of the complainant otherwise is not in the best interest of the complainant, the court shall issue an order authorizing the complainant to consent to the performance or inducement of an abortion without the notification of her parents, guardian, or custodian. If the court does not make the finding specified in this division, it shall dismiss the complaint.

(3) If the complainant makes both of the allegations set forth in divisions (A)(4)(a) and (b) of this section, the court shall proceed as follows:

(a) The court first shall determine whether it can make the finding specified in division (C)(1) of this section and, if so, shall issue an order pursuant to that division. If the court issues such an order, it shall not proceed pursuant to division (C)(3)(b) of this section. If the court does not make the finding specified in division (C)(1) of this section, it shall proceed pursuant to division (C)(3)(b) of this section.

(b) If the court pursuant to division (C)(3)(a) of this section does not make the finding specified in division (C)(1) of this section, it shall proceed to determine whether it can make the finding specified in division (C)(2) of this section and, if so, shall issue an order pursuant to that division. If the court does not make the finding specified in division (C)(2) of this section, it shall dismiss the complaint.

(D) The court shall not notify the parents, guardian, or custodian of the complainant that she is pregnant or that she wants to have an abortion.

(E) If the court dismisses the complaint, it immediately shall notify the complainant that she has a right to appeal under section 2505.073 [2505.07.3] of the Revised Code.

(F) Each hearing under this section shall be conducted in a manner that will preserve the anonymity of the complainant. The complaint and all other papers and records that pertain to an action commenced under this section shall be kept confidential and are not public records under section 149.43 of the Revised Code.

(G) The clerk of the supreme court shall prescribe complaint and notice of appeal forms that shall be used by a complainant filing a complaint under this section and by an appellant filing an appeal under section 2505.073 [2505.07.3] of the Revised Code. The clerk of each juvenile court shall furnish blank copies of the forms, without charge, to any person who requests them.

(H) No filing fee shall be required of, and no court costs shall be assessed against, a complainant filing a complaint under this section or an appellant filing an appeal under section 2505.073 [2505.07.3] of the Revised Code.

(I) As used in this section, "unemancipated" means that a woman who is unmarried and under eighteen years of age has not entered the armed services of the United States, has not become employed and self-subsisting, or has not otherwise become independent from the care and control of her parent, guardian, or custodian.

**HISTORY: 141 v H 319. Eff 3-24-86.**

## § 2151.86 Criminal records check and fingerprinting of employees responsible for out-of-home child care and prospective adoptive or foster caregivers or adults residing with them.

(A)(1) The appointing or hiring officer of any entity that appoints or employs any person responsible for a child's care in out-of-home care shall request the superintendent of BCII to conduct a criminal records check with respect to any person who is under final consideration for appointment or employment as a person responsible for a child's care in out-of-home care, except that section 3319.39 of the Revised Code shall apply instead of this section if the out-of-home care entity is a public school, educational service center, or chartered nonpublic school.

(2) At the times specified in this division, the administrative director of an agency, or attorney, who arranges an adoption for a prospective adoptive parent shall request the superintendent of BCII to conduct a criminal records check with respect to that prospective adoptive parent and a criminal records check with respect to all persons

eighteen years of age or older who reside with the prospective adoptive parent. The administrative director or attorney shall request a criminal records check pursuant to this division at the time of the initial home study, every four years after the initial home study at the time of an update, and at the time that an adoptive home study is completed as a new home study.

(3) Before a recommending agency submits a recommendation to the department of job and family services on whether the department should issue a certificate to a foster home under section 5103.03 of the Revised Code, and every four years thereafter prior to a recertification under that section, the administrative director of the agency shall request that the superintendent of BCII conduct a criminal records check with respect to the prospective foster caregiver and a criminal records check with respect to all other persons eighteen years of age or older who reside with the foster caregiver.

(B)(1) If a person subject to a criminal records check under division (A)(1) of this section does not present proof that the person has been a resident of this state for the five-year period immediately prior to the date upon which the criminal records check is requested or does not provide evidence that within that five-year period the superintendent of BCII has requested information about the person from the federal bureau of investigation in a criminal records check, the appointing or hiring officer shall request that the superintendent of BCII obtain information from the federal bureau of investigation as a part of the criminal records check, including fingerprint based checks of national crime information databases as described in 42 U.S.C. 671. If a person subject to a criminal records check under division (A)(1) of this section presents proof that the person has been a resident of this state for that five-year period, the appointing or hiring officer or attorney may request that the superintendent of BCII include information from the federal bureau of investigation in the criminal records check, including fingerprint based checks of national crime information databases as described in 42 U.S.C. 671.

When the administrative director of an agency, or attorney, who arranges an adoption for a prospective parent requests, at the time of the initial home study, a criminal records check for a person pursuant to division (A)(2) of this section, the administrative director or attorney shall request that the superintendent of BCII obtain information from the federal bureau of investigation as part of the criminal records check, including fingerprint based checks of national crime information databases as described in 42 U.S.C. 671, for the person subject to the criminal records check. In all other cases in which the administrative director of an agency, or attorney, who arranges an adoption for a prospective parent requests a criminal records check for a person pursuant to division (A)(2) of this section, the administrative director or attorney may request that the superintendent of BCII include information from the federal bureau of investigation in the criminal records check, including fingerprint based checks of national crime information databases as described in 42 U.S.C. 671.

When the administrative director of a recommending agency requests, before submitting a recommendation to the department of job and family services on whether the department should issue a certificate to a foster home under section 5103.03 of the Revised Code, a criminal records check for a person pursuant to division (A)(3) of this section, the administrative director shall request that the superintendent of BCII obtain information from the federal bureau of investigation as part of a criminal records check, including fingerprint based checks of national crime information databases as described in 42 U.S.C. 671, for the person subject to the criminal records check. In all other cases in which the administrative director of a recommending agency requests a criminal records check for a person pursuant to division (A)(3) of this section, the administrative director may request that the superintendent of BCII include information from the federal bureau of investigation in the criminal records check, including fingerprint based checks of national crime information databases as described in 42 U.S.C. 671.

Prior to a hearing on a final decree of adoption or interlocutory order of adoption by a probate court, the administrative director of an agency, or an attorney, who arranges an adoption for a prospective parent shall provide to the clerk of the probate court either of the following:

(a) Any information received pursuant to a request made under this division from the superintendent of BCII or the federal bureau of investigation as part of the criminal records check, including fingerprint-based checks of national crime information databases as described in 42 U.S.C. 671, for the person subject to the criminal records check;

(b) Written notification that the person subject to a criminal records check pursuant to this division failed upon request to provide the information necessary to complete the form or failed to provide impressions of the person's fingerprints as required under division (B)(2) of this section.

(2) An appointing or hiring officer, administrative director, or attorney required by division (A) of this section to request a criminal records check shall provide to each person subject to a criminal records check a copy of the form prescribed pursuant to division (C)(1) of section 109.572 [109.57.2] of the Revised Code and a standard impression sheet to obtain fingerprint impressions prescribed pursuant to division (C)(2) of section 109.572 [109.57.2] of the Revised Code, obtain the completed form and impression sheet from the person, and forward the completed form and impression sheet to the superintendent of BCII at the time the criminal records check is requested.

Any person subject to a criminal records check who receives pursuant to this division a copy of the form prescribed pursuant to division (C)(1) of section 109.572 [109.57.2] of the Revised Code and a copy of an impression sheet prescribed pursuant to division (C)(2) of that section and who is requested to complete the form and provide a set of fingerprint impressions shall complete the form or provide all the information necessary to complete the form and shall provide the impression sheet with the impressions of the person's fingerprints. If a person subject to a criminal records check, upon request, fails to provide the information necessary to complete the form or fails to provide impressions of the person's fingerprints, the appointing or hiring officer shall not appoint or employ the person as a person responsible for a child's care in out-of-home care, a probate court may not issue a final decree of adoption or an interlocutory order of adoption making the person an adoptive parent, and the department of job and family services shall not issue a certificate authorizing the prospective foster caregiver to operate a foster home.

(C)(1) No appointing or hiring officer shall appoint or employ a person as a person responsible for a child's care in out-of-home care, the department of job and family services shall not issue a certificate under section 5103.03 of the Revised Code authorizing a prospective foster caregiver to operate a foster home, and no probate court shall issue a final decree of adoption or an interlocutory order of adoption making a person an adoptive parent if the person or, in the case of a prospective foster caregiver or prospective adoptive parent, any person eighteen years of age or older who resides with the prospective foster caregiver or prospective adoptive parent previously has been convicted of or pleaded guilty to any of the violations described in division (A)(8) of section 109.572 [109.57.2] of the Revised Code, unless the person meets rehabilitation standards established in rules adopted under division (F) of this section.

(2) The appointing or hiring officer may appoint or employ a person as a person responsible for a child's care in out-of-home care conditionally until the criminal records check required by this section is completed and the officer receives the results of the criminal records check. If the results of the criminal records check indicate that, pursuant to division (C)(1) of this section, the person subject to the criminal records check does not qualify for appointment or employment, the officer shall release the person from appointment or employment.

(3) Prior to certification or recertification under section 5103.03 of the Revised Code, the prospective foster caregiver subject to a criminal records check under division (A)(3) of this section shall notify the recommending agency of the revocation of any foster home license, certificate, or other similar authorization in another state occurring within the five years prior to the date of application to become a foster caregiver in this state. The failure of a prospective foster caregiver to notify the recommending agency of any revocation of that type in another state that occurred within that five-year period shall be grounds for denial of the person's foster home application or the revocation of the person's foster home certification, whichever is applicable. If a person has had a revocation in another state within the five years prior to the date of the application, the department of job and family services shall not issue a foster home certificate to the prospective foster caregiver.

(D) The appointing or hiring officer, administrative director, or attorney shall pay to the bureau of criminal identification and investigation the fee prescribed pursuant to division (C)(3) of section 109.572 [109.57.2] of the Revised Code for each criminal records check conducted in accordance with that section upon a request pursuant to division (A) of this section. The officer, director, or attorney may charge the person subject to the criminal records check a fee for the costs the officer, director, or attorney incurs in obtaining the criminal records check. A fee charged under this division shall not exceed the amount of fees the officer, director, or attorney pays for the criminal records check. If a fee is charged under this division, the officer, director, or attorney shall notify the person who is the applicant at the time of the person's initial application for appointment or employment, an adoption to be arranged, or a certificate to operate a foster home of the amount of the fee and that, unless the fee is paid, the person who is the applicant will not be considered for appointment or employment or as an adoptive parent or foster caregiver.

(E) The report of any criminal records check conducted by the bureau of criminal identification and investigation in accordance with section 109.572 [109.57.2] of the Revised Code and pursuant to a request made under division (A) of this section is not a public record for the purposes of section 149.43 of the Revised Code and shall not be made available to any person other than the following:

(1) The person who is the subject of the criminal records check or the person's representative;

(2) The appointing or hiring officer, administrative director, or attorney requesting the criminal records check or the officer's, director's, or attorney's representative;

(3) The department of job and family services, a county department of job and family services, or a public children services agency;

(4) Any court, hearing officer, or other necessary individual involved in a case dealing with the denial of employment, a final decree of adoption or interlocutory order of adoption, or a foster home certificate.

(F) The director of job and family services shall adopt rules in accordance with Chapter 119. of the Revised Code to implement this section. The rules shall include rehabilitation standards a person who has been convicted of or pleaded guilty to an offense listed in division (A)(8) of section 109.572 [109.57.2] of the Revised Code must meet for an appointing or hiring officer to appoint or employ the person as a person responsible for a child's care in out-of-home care, a probate court to issue a final decree of adoption or interlocutory order of adoption making the person an adoptive parent, or the department to issue a certificate authorizing the prospective foster caregiver to operate a foster home or not revoke a foster home certificate for a violation specified in section 5103.0328 [5103.03.28] of the Revised Code.

(G) An appointing or hiring officer, administrative director, or attorney required by division (A) of this section to request a criminal records check shall inform each person who is the applicant, at the time of the person's initial application for appointment or employment, an adoption to be arranged, or a foster home certificate, that the person subject to the criminal records check is required to provide a set of impressions of the person's fingerprints and that a criminal records check is required to be conducted and satisfactorily completed in accordance with section 109.572 [109.57.2] of the Revised Code.

(H) The department of job and family services may waive the requirement that a criminal records check based on fingerprints be conducted for an adult resident of a prospective adoptive or foster home or the home of a foster caregiver if the recommending agency documents to the department's satisfaction that the adult resident is physically unable to comply with the fingerprinting requirement and poses no danger to foster children or adoptive children who may be placed in the home. In such cases, the recommending or approving agency shall request that the bureau of criminal identification and investigation conduct a criminal records check using the person's name and social security number.

(I) As used in this section:

(1) "Children's hospital" means any of the following:

(a) A hospital registered under section 3701.07 of the Revised Code that provides general pediatric medical and surgical care, and in which at least seventy-five per cent of annual inpatient discharges for the preceding two calendar years were individuals less than eighteen years of age;

(b) A distinct portion of a hospital registered under section 3701.07 of the Revised Code that provides general pediatric medical and surgical care, has a total of at least one hundred fifty registered pediatric special care and pediatric acute care beds, and in which at least seventy-five per cent of annual inpatient discharges for the preceding two calendar years were individuals less than eighteen years of age;

(c) A distinct portion of a hospital, if the hospital is registered under section 3701.07 of the Revised Code as a children's hospital and the children's hospital meets all the requirements of division (I)(1)(a) of this section.

(2) "Criminal records check" has the same meaning as in section 109.572 [109.57.2] of the Revised Code.

(3) "Person responsible for a child's care in out-of-home care" has the same meaning as in section 2151.011 [2151.01.1] of the Revised Code, except that it does not include a prospective employee of the department of youth services or a person responsible for a child's care in a hospital or medical clinic other than a children's hospital.

(4) "Person subject to a criminal records check" means the following:

(a) A person who is under final consideration for appointment or employment as a person responsible for a child's care in out-of-home care;

(b) A prospective adoptive parent;

(c) A prospective foster caregiver;

(d) A person eighteen years old or older who resides with a prospective foster caregiver or a prospective adoptive parent.

(5) "Recommending agency" means a public children services agency, private child placing agency, or private noncustodial agency to which the department of job and family services has delegated a duty to inspect and approve foster homes.

(6) "Superintendent of BCII" means the superintendent of the bureau of criminal identification and investigation.

**HISTORY: 145 v S 38 (Eff 10-29-93); 146 v S 2 (Eff 7-1-96); 146 v S 269 (Eff 7-1-96); 146 v H 445 (Eff 9-3-96); 147 v H 446 (Eff 8-5-98); 148 v H 471 (Eff 7-1-2000); 148 v H 448. Eff 10-5-2000; 150 v H 117, § 1, eff. 9-3-04; 150 v H 106, § 1, eff. 9-16-04; 152 v S 163, § 1, eff. 8-14-08.**

The provisions of § 3 of SB 38 (145 v —) read as follows:

SECTION 3. Sections 3301.54, 5104.09, and 5126.28 of the Revised Code, as amended by this act, and sections 109.572, 2151.86, 3301.32, 3301.541, 3319.311 [now 3319.39], 3701.881, 5104.012, 5104.013, and 5153.111 of the Revised Code, as enacted by this act, apply only to persons who apply for employment for a position on or after the effective date of this act.

**Comment, Legislative Service Commission**

Section 2151.86 of the Revised Code is amended by Am. Sub. H.B. 106 and Am. Sub. H.B. 117 of the 125th General Assembly. Comparison of these amendments in pursuance of section 1.52 of the Revised Code discloses that they are not irreconcilable so that they are required by that section to be harmonized to give effect to each amendment.

## § 2151.861 Compliance by child day camps with criminal background check provisions†.

(A) The department of job and family services may periodically conduct a random sampling of registered child day camps to determine compliance with section 2151.86 of the Revised Code.

(B)(1) No child day camp shall fail to comply with section 2151.86 of the Revised Code in regards to a person it appoints or employs.

(2) If the department determines that a child day camp has violated division (B)(1) of this section, the department shall do both of the following:

(a) Consider imposing a civil penalty on the child day camp in an amount that shall not exceed ten per cent of the camp's gross revenues for the full month immediately preceding the month in which the violation occurred. If the camp was not operating for the entire calendar month preceding the month in which the violation occurred, the penalty shall be five hundred dollars.

(b) Order the child day camp to initiate a criminal records check of the person who is the subject of the violation within a specified period of time.

(3) If, within the specified period of time, the child day camp fails to comply with an order to initiate a criminal records check of the person who is the subject of the violation or to release the person from the appointment or employment, the department shall do both of the following:

(a) Impose a civil penalty in an amount not less than the amount previously imposed and that shall not exceed twice the amount permitted by division (B)(2)(a) of this section;

(b) Order the child day camp to initiate a criminal records check of the person who is the subject of the violation within a specified period of time.

(C) If the department determines that a child day camp has violated division (B)(1) of this section, the department may post a notice at a prominent place at the camp that states that the camp has failed to conduct criminal records checks of its appointees or employees as required by section 2151.86 of the Revised Code. Once the camp demonstrates to the department that the camp is in compliance with that section, the department shall permit the camp to remove the notice.

(D) The department shall include on the department's web site a list of child day camps that the department has determined from a random sample to be not in compliance with the criminal records check requirements of section 2151.86 of the Revised Code. The department shall remove a camp's name from the list when the camp demonstrates to the department that the camp is in compliance with that section.

(E) For the purposes of divisions (C) and (D) of this section, a child day camp will be considered to be in compliance with section 2151.86 of the Revised Code by doing any of the following:

(1) Requesting that the bureau of criminal identification and investigation conduct a criminal records check regarding the person who is the subject of the violation of division (B)(1) of this section and, if the person does not qualify for the appointment or employment, releasing the person from the appointment or employment;

(2) Releasing the person who is the subject of the violation from the appointment or employment.

(F) The attorney general shall commence and prosecute to judgment a civil action in a court of competent jurisdiction to collect any civil penalty imposed under this section that remains unpaid.

(G) A child day camp may appeal any action the department takes under divisions (B) to (D) of this section to the court of common pleas of the county in which the camp is located.

**HISTORY: 150 v H 11, § 1, eff. 5-18-05.**

† This section was inadvertently repealed by § 2, 150 v H 11.

## § 2151.87 Child prohibited from possessing, using, purchasing or receiving cigarettes or other tobacco products.

(A) As used in this section:

(1) "Cigarette" and "tobacco product" have the same meanings as in section 2927.02 of the Revised Code.

(2) "Youth smoking education program" means a private or public agency program that is related to tobacco use, prevention, and cessation, that is carried out or funded by the department of health pursuant to section 3701.84 of the Revised Code, that utilizes educational methods focusing on the negative health effects of smoking and using tobacco products, and that is not more than twelve hours in duration.

(B) No child shall do any of the following unless accompanied by a parent, spouse who is eighteen years of age or older, or legal guardian of the child:

(1) Use, consume, or possess cigarettes, other tobacco products, or papers used to roll cigarettes;

(2) Purchase or attempt to purchase cigarettes, other tobacco products, or papers used to roll cigarettes;

(3) Order, pay for, or share the cost of cigarettes, other tobacco products, or papers used to roll cigarettes;

(4) Except as provided in division (E) of this section, accept or receive cigarettes, other tobacco products, or papers used to roll cigarettes.

(C) No child shall knowingly furnish false information concerning that child's name, age, or other identification for the purpose of obtaining cigarettes, other tobacco products, or papers used to roll cigarettes.

(D) A juvenile court shall not adjudicate a child a delinquent or unruly child for a violation of division (B)(1), (2), (3), or (4) or (C) of this section.

(E)(1) It is not a violation of division (B)(4) of this section for a child to accept or receive cigarettes, other tobacco products, or papers used to roll cigarettes if the child is required to do so in the performance of the child's duties as an employee of that child's employer and the child's acceptance or receipt of cigarettes, other tobacco products, or papers used to roll cigarettes occurs exclusively within the scope of the child's employment.

(2) It is not a violation of division (B)(1), (2), (3), or (4) of this section if the child possesses, purchases or attempts to purchase, orders, pays for, shares the cost of, or accepts or receives cigarettes, other tobacco products, or papers used to roll cigarettes while participating in an inspection or compliance check conducted by a federal, state, local, or corporate entity at a location at which cigarettes, other tobacco products, or papers used to roll cigarettes are sold or distributed.

(3) It is not a violation of division (B)(1) or (4) of this section for a child to accept, receive, use, consume, or possess cigarettes, other tobacco products, or papers used to roll cigarettes while participating in a research protocol if all of the following apply:

(a) The parent, guardian, or legal custodian of the child has consented in writing to the child participating in the research protocol.

(b) An institutional human subjects protection review board, or an equivalent entity, has approved the research protocol.

(c) The child is participating in the research protocol at the facility or location specified in the research protocol.

(F) If a juvenile court finds that a child violated division (B)(1), (2), (3), or (4) or (C) of this section, the court may do either or both of the following:

(1) Require the child to attend a youth smoking education program or other smoking treatment program approved by the court, if one is available;

(2) Impose a fine of not more than one hundred dollars.

(G) If a child disobeys a juvenile court order issued pursuant to division (F) of this section, the court may do any or all of the following:

(1) Increase the fine imposed upon the child under division (F)(2) of this section;

(2) Require the child to perform not more than twenty hours of community service;

(3) Suspend for a period of thirty days the temporary instruction permit, probationary driver's license, or driver's license issued to the child.

(H) A child alleged or found to have violated division (B) or (C) of this section shall not be detained under any provision of this chapter or any other provision of the Revised Code.

**HISTORY: 148 v S 218 (Eff 3-15-2001); 149 v H 393. Eff 7-5-2002; 152 v H 544, § 1, eff. 5-6-08.**

The effective date is set by § 11 of 152 v H 544.

## § 2151.99 Penalties.

(A)(1) Except as otherwise provided in division (A)(2) of this section, whoever violates division (D)(2) or (3) of section 2151.313 [2151.31.3] or division (A)(4),† or (H)(2) of section 2151.421 [2151.42.1] of the Revised Code is guilty of a misdemeanor of the fourth degree.

(2) Whoever violates division (A)(4) of section 2151.421 [2151.42.1] of the Revised Code knowing that a child has been abused or neglected and knowing that the person who committed the abuse or neglect was a cleric or another person, other than a volunteer, designated by a church, religious society, or faith acting as a leader, official, or delegate on behalf of the church, religious society, or faith, is guilty of a misdemeanor of the first degree if the person who violates division (A)(4) of this section and the person who committed the abuse or neglect belong to the same church, religious society, or faith.

(B) Whoever violates division (D)(1) of section 2151.313 [2151.31.3] of the Revised Code is guilty of a minor misdemeanor.

(C) Whoever violates division (A)(1) of section 2151.421 [2151.42.1] of the Revised Code shall be punished as follows:

(1) Except as otherwise provided in division (C)(2) of this section, the offender is guilty of a misdemeanor of the fourth degree.

(2) The offender is guilty of a misdemeanor of the first degree if the child who is the subject of the required report that the offender fails to make suffers or faces the threat of suffering the physical or mental wound, injury, disability, or condition that would be the basis of the required report when the child is under the direct care or supervision of the offender who is then acting in the offender's official or professional capacity or when the child is under the direct care or supervision of another person over whom the offender while acting in the offender's official or professional capacity has supervisory control.

**HISTORY: Bureau of Code Revision, 10-1-53; 130 v 632 (Eff 10-10-63); 133 v H 320 (Eff 11-19-69); 134 v H 511 (Eff 1-1-74); 140 v H 258 (Eff 9-26-84); 141 v H 349 (Eff 3-6-86); 141 v H 529 (Eff 3-11-87); 143 v H 257 (Eff 8-3-89); 147 v H 173 (Eff 7-29-98); 148 v S 179, § 3. Eff 1-1-2002; 151 v S 17, § 1, eff. 8-3-06; 151 v S 137, § 1, eff. 3-30-07.**

† As amended by 151 v S 137.

The effective date is set by section 5 of SB 179.

**Comment, Legislative Service Commission**

Section 2151.99 of the Revised Code is amended by Sub. S.B. 137 and Am. Sub. S.B. 17 of the 126th General Assembly. Comparison of these amendments in pursuance of section 1.52 of the Revised Code discloses that they are not irreconcilable so that they are required by that section to be harmonized to give effect to each amendment.

# CHAPTER 2152: DELINQUENT CHILDREN; JUVENILE TRAFFIC OFFENDERS

Section



Section



## § 2152.01 Purposes of dispositions under chapter; application of Chapter 2151.

(A) The overriding purposes for dispositions under this chapter are to provide for the care, protection, and mental and physical development of children subject to this chapter, protect the public interest and safety, hold the offender accountable for the offender's actions, restore the victim, and rehabilitate the offender. These purposes shall be achieved by a system of graduated sanctions and services.

(B) Dispositions under this chapter shall be reasonably calculated to achieve the overriding purposes set forth in this section, commensurate with and not demeaning to the seriousness of the delinquent child's or the juvenile traffic offender's conduct and its impact on the victim, and consistent with dispositions for similar acts committed by similar delinquent children and juvenile traffic offenders. The court shall not base the disposition on the race, ethnic background, gender, or religion of the delinquent child or juvenile traffic offender.

(C) To the extent they do not conflict with this chapter, the provisions of Chapter 2151. of the Revised Code apply to the proceedings under this chapter.

**HISTORY: 148 v S 179. Eff 1-1-2002.**

The effective date is set by section 5 of SB 179.

## § 2152.02 Definitions.

As used in this chapter:

(A) "Act charged" means the act that is identified in a complaint, indictment, or information alleging that a child is a delinquent child.

(B) "Admitted to a department of youth services facility" includes admission to a facility operated, or contracted for, by the department and admission to a comparable facility outside this state by another state or the United States.

(C)(1) "Child" means a person who is under eighteen years of age, except as otherwise provided in divisions (C)(2) to (7) of this section.

(2) Subject to division (C)(3) of this section, any person who violates a federal or state law or a municipal ordinance prior to attaining eighteen years of age shall be deemed a "child" irrespective of that person's age at the time the complaint with respect to that violation is filed or the hearing on the complaint is held.

(3) Any person who, while under eighteen years of age, commits an act that would be a felony if committed by an adult and who is not taken into custody or apprehended for that act until after the person attains twenty-one years of age is not a child in relation to that act.

(4) Except as otherwise provided in division (C)(5) of this section, any person whose case is transferred for criminal prosecution pursuant to section 2152.12 of the Revised Code shall be deemed after the transfer not to be a child in the transferred case.

(5) Any person whose case is transferred for criminal prosecution pursuant to section 2152.12 of the Revised Code and who subsequently is convicted of or pleads guilty to a felony in that case, unless a serious youthful offender dispositional sentence is imposed on the child for that offense under division (B)(2) or (3) of section 2152.121 of the Revised Code and the adult portion of that sentence is not invoked pursuant to section 2152.14 of the Revised Code, and any person who is adjudicated a delinquent child for the commission of an act, who has a serious youthful offender dispositional sentence imposed for the act pursuant to section 2152.13 of the Revised Code, and whose adult portion of the dispositional sentence is invoked pursuant to section 2152.14 of the Revised Code, shall be deemed after the transfer or invocation not to be a child in any case in which a complaint is filed against the person.

(6) The juvenile court has jurisdiction over a person who is adjudicated a delinquent child or juvenile traffic offender prior to attaining eighteen years of age until the person attains twenty-one years of age, and, for purposes of that jurisdiction related to that adjudication, except as otherwise provided in this division, a person who is so adjudicated a delinquent child or juvenile traffic offender shall be deemed a "child" until the person attains twenty-one years of age. If a person is so adjudicated a delinquent child or juvenile traffic offender and the court makes a disposition of the person under this chapter, at any time after the person attains eighteen years of age, the places at which the person may be held under that disposition are not limited to places authorized under this chapter solely for confinement of children, and the person may be confined under that disposition, in accordance with division (F)(2) of section 2152.26 of the Revised Code, in places other than those authorized under this chapter solely for confinement of children.

(7) Any person who, while eighteen years of age, violates division (A)(1) or (2) of section 2919.27 of the Revised Code by violating a protection order issued or consent agreement approved under section 2151.34 or 3113.31 of the Revised Code shall be considered a child for the purposes of that violation of section 2919.27 of the Revised Code.

(D) "Chronic truant" means any child of compulsory school age who is absent without legitimate excuse for absence from the public school the child is supposed to attend for seven or more consecutive school days, ten or more school days in one school month, or fifteen or more school days in a school year.

(E) "Community corrections facility," "public safety beds," "release authority," and "supervised release" have the same meanings as in section 5139.01 of the Revised Code.

(F) "Delinquent child" includes any of the following:

(1) Any child, except a juvenile traffic offender, who violates any law of this state or the United States, or any ordinance of a political subdivision of the state, that would be an offense if committed by an adult;

(2) Any child who violates any lawful order of the court made under this chapter or under Chapter 2151. of the Revised Code other than an order issued under section 2151.87 of the Revised Code;

(3) Any child who violates division (C) of section 2907.39, division (A) of section 2923.211, or division (C)(1) or (D) of section 2925.55 of the Revised Code;

(4) Any child who is a habitual truant and who previously has been adjudicated an unruly child for being a habitual truant;

(5) Any child who is a chronic truant.

(G) "Discretionary serious youthful offender" means a person who is eligible for a discretionary SYO and who is not transferred to adult court under a mandatory or discretionary transfer.

(H) "Discretionary SYO" means a case in which the juvenile court, in the juvenile court's discretion, may impose a serious youthful offender disposition under section 2152.13 of the Revised Code.

(I) "Discretionary transfer" means that the juvenile court has discretion to transfer a case for criminal prosecution under division (B) of section 2152.12 of the Revised Code.

(J) "Drug abuse offense," "felony drug abuse offense," and "minor drug possession offense" have the same meanings as in section 2925.01 of the Revised Code.

(K) "Electronic monitoring" and "electronic monitoring device" have the same meanings as in section 2929.01 of the Revised Code.

(L) "Economic loss" means any economic detriment suffered by a victim of a delinquent act or juvenile traffic offense as a direct and proximate result of the delinquent act or juvenile traffic offense and includes any loss of income due to lost time at work because of any injury caused to the victim and any property loss, medical cost, or funeral expense incurred as a result of the delinquent act or juvenile traffic offense. "Economic loss" does not include non-economic loss or any punitive or exemplary damages.

(M) "Firearm" has the same meaning as in section 2923.11 of the Revised Code.

(N) "Juvenile traffic offender" means any child who violates any traffic law, traffic ordinance, or traffic regulation of this state, the United States, or any political subdivision of this state, other than a resolution, ordinance, or regulation of a political subdivision of this state the violation of which is required to be handled by a parking violations bureau or a joint parking violations bureau pursuant to Chapter 4521. of the Revised Code.

(O) A "legitimate excuse for absence from the public school the child is supposed to attend" has the same meaning as in section 2151.011 of the Revised Code.

(P) "Mandatory serious youthful offender" means a person who is eligible for a mandatory SYO and who is not transferred to adult court under a mandatory or discretionary transfer and also includes, for purposes of imposition of a mandatory serious youthful dispositional sentence under section 2152.13 of the Revised Code, a person upon whom a juvenile court is required to impose such a sentence under division (B)(3) of section 2152.121 of the Revised Code.

(Q) "Mandatory SYO" means a case in which the juvenile court is required to impose a mandatory serious youthful offender disposition under section 2152.13 of the Revised Code.

(R) "Mandatory transfer" means that a case is required to be transferred for criminal prosecution under division (A) of section 2152.12 of the Revised Code.

(S) "Mental illness" has the same meaning as in section 5122.01 of the Revised Code.

(T) "Mentally retarded person" has the same meaning as in section 5123.01 of the Revised Code.

(U) "Monitored time" and "repeat violent offender" have the same meanings as in section 2929.01 of the Revised Code.

(V) "Of compulsory school age" has the same meaning as in section 3321.01 of the Revised Code.

(W) "Public record" has the same meaning as in section 149.43 of the Revised Code.

(X) "Serious youthful offender" means a person who is eligible for a mandatory SYO or discretionary SYO but who is not transferred to adult court under a mandatory or discretionary transfer and also includes, for purposes of imposition of a mandatory serious youthful dispositional sentence under section 2152.13 of the Revised Code, a person upon whom a juvenile court is required to impose such a sentence under division (B)(3) of section 2152.121 of the Revised Code.

(Y) "Sexually oriented offense," "juvenile offender registrant," "child-victim oriented offense," "tier I sex offender/child-victim offender," "tier II sex offender/child-victim offender," "tier III sex offender/child-victim offender," and "public registry-qualified juvenile offender registrant" have the same meanings as in section 2950.01 of the Revised Code.

(Z) "Traditional juvenile" means a case that is not transferred to adult court under a mandatory or discretionary transfer, that is eligible for a disposition under sections 2152.16, 2152.17, 2152.19, and 2152.20 of the Revised Code, and that is not eligible for a disposition under section 2152.13 of the Revised Code.

(AA) "Transfer" means the transfer for criminal prosecution of a case involving the alleged commission by a child of an act that would be an offense if committed by an adult from the juvenile court to the appropriate court that has jurisdiction of the offense.

(BB) "Category one offense" means any of the following:

(1) A violation of section 2903.01 or 2903.02 of the Revised Code;

(2) A violation of section 2923.02 of the Revised Code involving an attempt to commit aggravated murder or murder.

(CC) "Category two offense" means any of the following:

(1) A violation of section 2903.03, 2905.01, 2907.02, 2909.02, 2911.01, or 2911.11 of the Revised Code;

(2) A violation of section 2903.04 of the Revised Code that is a felony of the first degree;

(3) A violation of section 2907.12 of the Revised Code as it existed prior to September 3, 1996.

(DD) "Non-economic loss" means nonpecuniary harm suffered by a victim of a delinquent act or juvenile traffic offense as a result of or related to the delinquent act or juvenile traffic offense, including, but not limited to, pain and suffering; loss of society, consortium, companionship, care, assistance, attention, protection, advice, guidance, counsel, instruction, training, or education; mental anguish; and any other intangible loss.

**HISTORY: 148 v S 179, § 3 (Eff 1-1-2002); 149 v S 3 (Eff 1-1-2002); 149 v H 400. Eff 4-3-2003; 149 v H 490, § 1, eff. 1-1-04; 150 v S 5, § 1, eff. 7-31-03; 150 v S 5, § 3, eff. 1-1-04; 150 v H 52, § 1, eff. 6-1-04; 151 v S 53, § 1, eff. 5-17-06; 151 v H 23, § 1, eff. 8-17-06; 152 v S 10, § 1, eff. 1-1-08; 153 v H 10, § 1, eff. 6-17-10; 2011 HB 86, § 1, eff. Sept. 30, 2011.**

See provisions of § 3 of 153 v H 10 following RC § 2151.23.

The effective date is set by § 3 of 152 v S 10.

The effective date is set by section 5 of S.B. 5.

The provisions of section 7 of S.B. 5 (150 v —) read as follows:

SECTION 7. * * * (B) Section 2152.02 of the Revised Code, effective January 1, 2004, is presented in Section 3 of this act as a composite of the section as amended by both Am. Sub. H.B. 400 and Am. Sub. H.B. 490 of the 124th General Assembly. The General Assembly, applying the principle stated in division (B) of section 1.52 of the Revised Code that amendments are to be harmonized if reasonably capable of simultaneous operation, finds that the composites are the resulting versions of the sections in effect prior to the effective date of the sections as presented in Section 3 of this act.

**Comment, Legislative Service Commission**

Section 2152.02 of the Revised Code is amended by Am. Sub. H.B. 23 and Am. Sub. S.B. 53 of the 126th General Assembly. Comparison of these amendments in pursuance of section 1.52 of the Revised Code discloses that they are not irreconcilable so that they are required by that section to be harmonized to give effect to each amendment.

## § 2152.021 Complaint alleging that child is delinquent child or juvenile traffic offender; initiation of serious youthful offender proceedings.

(A)(1) Subject to division (A)(2) of this section, any person having knowledge of a child who appears to be a juvenile traffic offender or to be a delinquent child may file a sworn complaint with respect to that child in the juvenile court of the county in which the child has a residence or legal settlement or in which the traffic offense or delinquent act allegedly occurred. The sworn complaint may be upon information and belief, and, in addition to the allegation that the child is a delinquent child or a juvenile traffic offender, the complaint shall allege the particular facts upon which the allegation that the child is a delinquent child or a juvenile traffic offender is based.

If a child appears to be a delinquent child who is eligible for a serious youthful offender dispositional sentence under section 2152.11 of the Revised Code and if the prosecuting attorney desires to seek a serious youthful offender dispositional sentence under section 2152.13 of the Revised Code in regard to the child, the prosecuting attorney of the county in which the alleged delinquency occurs may initiate a case in the juvenile court of the county by presenting the case to a grand jury for indictment, by charging the child in a bill of information as a serious youthful offender pursuant to section 2152.13 of the Revised Code, by requesting a serious youthful offender dispositional sentence in the original complaint alleging that the child is a delinquent child, or by filing with the juvenile court a written notice of intent to seek a serious youthful offender dispositional sentence. This paragraph does not apply regarding the imposition of a serious youthful offender dispositional sentence pursuant to section 2152.121 of the Revised Code.

(2) Any person having knowledge of a child who appears to be a delinquent child for being an habitual or chronic truant may file a sworn complaint with respect to that child, or with respect to that child and the parent, guardian, or other person having care of the child, in the juvenile court of the county in which the child has a residence or legal settlement or in which the child is supposed to attend public school. The sworn complaint may be upon information and belief and shall allege that the child is a delinquent child for being a chronic truant or an habitual truant who previously has been adjudicated an unruly child for being a habitual truant and, in addition, the particular facts upon which that allegation is based. If the complaint contains allegations regarding the child's parent, guardian, or other person having care of the child, the complaint additionally shall allege that the parent, guardian, or other person having care of the child has failed to cause the child's attendance at school in violation of section 3321.38 of the Revised Code and, in addition, the particular facts upon which that allegation is based.

(B) Any person with standing under applicable law may file a complaint for the determination of any other matter over which the juvenile court is given jurisdiction by section 2151.23 of the Revised Code. The complaint shall be filed in the county in which the child who is the subject of the complaint is found or was last known to be found.

(C) Within ten days after the filing of a complaint or the issuance of an indictment, the court shall give written notice of the filing of the complaint or the issuance of an indictment and of the substance of the complaint or indictment to the superintendent of a city, local, exempted village, or joint vocational school district if the complaint or indictment alleges that a child committed an act that would be a criminal offense if committed by an adult, that the child was sixteen years of age or older at the time of the commission of the alleged act, and that the alleged act is any of the following:

(1) A violation of section 2923.122 of the Revised Code that relates to property owned or controlled by, or to an activity held under the auspices of, the board of education of that school district;

(2) A violation of section 2923.12 of the Revised Code, of a substantially similar municipal ordinance, or of section 2925.03 of the Revised Code that was committed on property owned or controlled by, or at an activity held under the auspices of, the board of education of that school district;

(3) A violation of section 2925.11 of the Revised Code that was committed on property owned or controlled by, or at an activity held under the auspices of, the board of education of that school district, other than a violation of that section that would be a minor drug possession offense if committed by an adult;

(4) A violation of section 2903.01, 2903.02, 2903.03, 2903.04, 2903.11, 2903.12, 2907.02, or 2907.05 of the Revised Code, or a violation of former section 2907.12 of the Revised Code, that was committed on property owned or controlled by, or at an activity held under the auspices of, the board of education of that school district, if the victim at the time of the commission of the alleged act was an employee of the board of education of that school district;

(5) Complicity in any violation described in division (C)(1), (2), (3), or (4) of this section that was alleged to have been committed in the manner described in division (C)(1), (2), (3), or (4) of this section, regardless of whether the act of complicity was committed on property owned or controlled by, or at an activity held under the auspices of, the board of education of that school district.

(D) A public children services agency, acting pursuant to a complaint or an action on a complaint filed under this section, is not subject to the requirements of section 3127.23 of the Revised Code.

(E) For purposes of the record to be maintained by the clerk under division (B) of section 2152.71 of the Revised Code, when a complaint is filed that alleges that a child is a delinquent child, the court shall determine if the victim of the alleged delinquent act was sixty-five years of age or older or permanently and totally disabled at the time of the alleged commission of the act.

**HISTORY: 148 v S 179, § 3. Eff 1-1-2002; 150 v S 185, § 1, eff. 4-11-05; 2011 HB 86, § 1, eff. Sept. 30, 2011.**

The effective date is set by section 5 of SB 179.

## § 2152.03 Case to be initiated in or transferred to juvenile court.

When a child is arrested under any charge, complaint, affidavit, or indictment for a felony or a misdemeanor, proceedings regarding the child initially shall be in the juvenile court in accordance with this chapter. If the child is taken before a judge of a county court, a mayor, a judge of a municipal court, or a judge of a court of common pleas other than a juvenile court, the judge of the county court, mayor, judge of the municipal court, or judge of the court of common pleas shall transfer the case to the juvenile court, and, upon the transfer, the proceedings shall be in accordance with this chapter. Upon the transfer, all further proceedings under the charge, complaint, information, or indictment shall be discontinued in the court of the judge of the county court, mayor, municipal judge, or judge of the court of common pleas other than a juvenile court subject to section 2152.12 of the Revised Code. The case relating to the child then shall be within the exclusive jurisdiction of the juvenile court, subject to section 2152.12 of the Revised Code.

**HISTORY: GC § 1639-29; 117 v 520; 121 v 557; Bureau of Code Revision, RC § 2151.25, 10-1-53; 129 v 582(738) (Eff 1-10-61); 133 v H 320 (Eff 11-19-69); 136 v H 205 (Eff 1-1-76); 146 v H 1 (Eff 1-1-96); RC § 2152.03, 148 v S 179, § 3. Eff 1-1-2002.**

The effective date is set by section 5 of SB 179.

## § 2152.04 Confinement of delinquent child for purposes of preparing social history.

A child who is alleged to be, or who is adjudicated, a delinquent child may be confined in a place of juvenile detention provided under section 2152.41 of the Revised Code for a period not to exceed ninety days, during which time a social history may be prepared to include court record, family history, personal history, school and attendance records, and any other pertinent studies and material that will be of assistance to the juvenile court in its disposition of the charges against that alleged or adjudicated delinquent child.

**HISTORY: 148 v S 179, § 3. Eff 1-1-2002.**

The effective date is set by section 5 of SB 179.

## § 2152.10 Children eligible for mandatory or discretionary transfer; order of disposition when child not transferred.

(A) A child who is alleged to be a delinquent child is eligible for mandatory transfer and shall be transferred as provided in section 2152.12 of the Revised Code in any of the following circumstances:

(1) The child is charged with a category one offense and either of the following apply:

(a) The child was sixteen years of age or older at the time of the act charged.

(b) The child was fourteen or fifteen years of age at the time of the act charged and previously was adjudicated a delinquent child for committing an act that is a category one or category two offense and was committed to the legal custody of the department of youth services upon the basis of that adjudication.

(2) The child is charged with a category two offense, other than a violation of section 2905.01 of the Revised Code, the child was sixteen years of age or older at the time of the commission of the act charged, and either or both of the following apply:

(a) The child previously was adjudicated a delinquent child for committing an act that is a category one or a category two offense and was committed to the legal custody of the department of youth services on the basis of that adjudication.

(b) The child is alleged to have had a firearm on or about the child's person or under the child's control while committing the act charged and to have displayed the firearm, brandished the firearm, indicated possession of the firearm, or used the firearm to facilitate the commission of the act charged.

(3) Division (A)(2) of section 2152.12 of the Revised Code applies.

(B) Unless the child is subject to mandatory transfer, if a child is fourteen years of age or older at the time of the act charged and if the child is charged with an act that would be a felony if committed by an adult, the child is eligible for discretionary transfer to the appropriate court for criminal prosecution. In determining whether to transfer the child for criminal prosecution, the juvenile court shall follow the procedures in section 2152.12 of the Revised Code. If the court does not transfer the child and if the court adjudicates the child to be a delinquent child for the act charged, the court shall issue an order of disposition in accordance with section 2152.11 of the Revised Code.

**HISTORY: 148 v S 179, § 3 (Eff 1-1-2002); 149 v H 393. Eff 7-5-2002.**

## § 2152.11 Range of dispositions of child adjudicated to be delinquent.

(A) A child who is adjudicated a delinquent child for committing an act that would be a felony if committed by an adult is eligible for a particular type of disposition under this section if the child was not transferred under section 2152.12 of the Revised Code. If the complaint, indictment, or information charging the act includes one or more of the following factors, the act is considered to be enhanced, and the child is eligible for a more restrictive disposition under this section;

(1) The act charged against the child would be an offense of violence if committed by an adult.

(2) During the commission of the act charged, the child used a firearm, displayed a firearm, brandished a firearm, or indicated that the child possessed a firearm and actually possessed a firearm.

(3) The child previously was admitted to a department of youth services facility for the commission of an act that would have been aggravated murder, murder, a felony of the first or second degree if committed by an adult, or an act that would have been a felony of the third degree and an offense of violence if committed by an adult.

(B) If a child is adjudicated a delinquent child for committing an act that would be aggravated murder or murder if committed by an adult, the child is eligible for whichever of the following is appropriate:

(1) Mandatory SYO, if the act allegedly was committed when the child was fourteen or fifteen years of age;

(2) Discretionary SYO, if the act was committed when the child was ten, eleven, twelve, or thirteen years of age;

(3) Traditional juvenile, if divisions (B)(1) and (2) of this section do not apply.

(C) If a child is adjudicated a delinquent child for committing an act that would be attempted aggravated murder or attempted murder if committed by an adult, the child is eligible for whichever of the following is appropriate:

(1) Mandatory SYO, if the act allegedly was committed when the child was fourteen or fifteen years of age;

(2) Discretionary SYO, if the act was committed when the child was ten, eleven, twelve, or thirteen years of age;

(3) Traditional juvenile, if divisions (C)(1) and (2) of this section do not apply.

(D) If a child is adjudicated a delinquent child for committing an act that would be a felony of the first degree if committed by an adult, the child is eligible for whichever of the following is appropriate:

(1) Mandatory SYO, if the act allegedly was committed when the child was sixteen or seventeen years of age, and the act is enhanced by the factors described in division (A)(1) and either division (A)(2) or (3) of this section;

(2) Discretionary SYO, if any of the following applies:

(a) The act was committed when the child was sixteen or seventeen years of age, and division (D)(1) of this section does not apply.

(b) The act was committed when the child was fourteen or fifteen years of age.

(c) The act was committed when the child was twelve or thirteen years of age, and the act is enhanced by any factor described in division (A)(1), (2), or (3) of this section.

(d) The act was committed when the child was ten or eleven years of age, and the act is enhanced by the factors described in division (A)(1) and either division (A)(2) or (3) of this section.

(3) Traditional juvenile, if divisions (D)(1) and (2) of this section do not apply.

(E) If a child is adjudicated a delinquent child for committing an act that would be a felony of the second degree if committed by an adult, the child is eligible for whichever of the following is appropriate:

(1) Discretionary SYO, if the act was committed when the child was fourteen, fifteen, sixteen, or seventeen years of age;

(2) Discretionary SYO, if the act was committed when the child was twelve or thirteen years of age, and the act is enhanced by any factor described in division (A)(1), (2), or (3) of this section;

(3) Traditional juvenile, if divisions (E)(1) and (2) of this section do not apply.

(F) If a child is adjudicated a delinquent child for committing an act that would be a felony of the third degree if committed by an adult, the child is eligible for whichever of the following is appropriate:

(1) Discretionary SYO, if the act was committed when the child was sixteen or seventeen years of age;

(2) Discretionary SYO, if the act was committed when the child was fourteen or fifteen years of age, and the act is enhanced by any factor described in division (A)(1), (2), or (3) of this section;

(3) Traditional juvenile, if divisions (F)(1) and (2) of this section do not apply.

(G) If a child is adjudicated a delinquent child for committing an act that would be a felony of the fourth or fifth degree if committed by an adult, the child is eligible for whichever of the following dispositions is appropriate:

(1) Discretionary SYO, if the act was committed when the child was sixteen or seventeen years of age, and the act is enhanced by any factor described in division (A)(1), (2), or (3) of this section;

(2) Traditional juvenile, if division (G)(1) of this section does not apply.

(H) The following table describes the dispositions that a juvenile court may impose on a delinquent child:

| OFFENSE CATEGORY (Enhancement Factors) | AGE 16 & 17 | AGE 14 & 15 | AGE 12 & 13 | AGE 10 & 11 |
|---|---|---|---|---|
| Murder/Aggravated Murder | N/A | MSYO, TJ | DSYO, TJ | DSYO, TJ |
| Attempted Murder/Attempted Aggravated Murder | N/A | MSYO, TJ | DSYO, TJ | DSYO, TJ |
| F1 (Enhanced by Offense of Violence Factor and Either Disposition Firearm Factor or Previous DYS Admission Factor) | MSYO, | DSYO, TJ | DSYO, TJ | DSYO, TJ |
| F1 (Enhanced by Any Single or Other Combination of Enhancement Factors) | DSYO, TJ | DSYO, TJ | DSYO, TJ | TJ |
| F1 (Not Enhanced) | DSYO, TJ | DSYO, TJ | TJ | TJ |
| F2 (Enhanced by Any Enhancement Factor) | DSYO, TJ | DSYO, TJ | DSYO, TJ | TJ |
| F2 (Not Enhanced) | DSYO, TJ | DSYO, TJ | TJ | TJ |
| F3 (Enhanced by Any Enhancement Factor) | DSYO, TJ | DSYO TJ | TJ | TJ |
| F3 (Not Enhanced) | DSYO, TJ | TJ | TJ | TJ |
| F4 (Enhanced by Any Enhancement Factor) | DSYO, TJ | TJ | TJ | TJ |
| F4 (Not Enhanced) | TJ | TJ | TJ | TJ |
| F5 (Enhanced by Any Enhancement Factor) | DSYO, TJ | TJ | TJ | TJ |
| F5 (Not Enhanced) | TJ | TJ | TJ | TJ |

(I) The table in division (H) of this section is for illustrative purposes only. If the table conflicts with any provision of divisions (A) to (G) of this section, divisions (A) to (G) of this section shall control.

(J) Key for table in division (H) of this section:

(1) "Any enhancement factor" applies when the criteria described in division (A)(1), (2), or (3) of this section apply.

(2) The "disposition firearm factor" applies when the criteria described in division (A)(2) of this section apply.

(3) "DSYO" refers to discretionary serious youthful offender disposition.

(4) "F1" refers to an act that would be a felony of the first degree if committed by an adult.

(5) "F2" refers to an act that would be a felony of the second degree if committed by an adult.

(6) "F3" refers to an act that would be a felony of the third degree if committed by an adult.

(7) "F4" refers to an act that would be a felony of the fourth degree if committed by an adult.

(8) "F5" refers to an act that would be a felony of the fifth degree if committed by an adult.

(9) "MSYO" refers to mandatory serious youthful offender disposition.

(10) The "offense of violence factor" applies when the criteria described in division (A)(1) of this section apply.

(11) The "previous DYS admission factor" applies when the criteria described in division (A)(3) of this section apply.

(12) "TJ" refers to traditional juvenile.

**HISTORY: 148 v S 179, § 3. Eff 1-1-2002.**

The effective date is set by section 5 of SB 179.

## § 2152.12 Transfer of case; prosecution of child nullity in absence of transfer; juvenile court loses jurisdiction if child is not taken into custody or apprehended prior to attaining age twenty-one.

(A)(1)(a) After a complaint has been filed alleging that a child is a delinquent child for committing an act that would be aggravated murder, murder, attempted aggravated murder, or attempted murder if committed by an adult, the juvenile court at a hearing shall transfer the case if either of the following applies:

(i) The child was sixteen or seventeen years of age at the time of the act charged and there is probable cause to believe that the child committed the act charged.

(ii) The child was fourteen or fifteen years of age at the time of the act charged, section 2152.10 of the Revised Code provides that the child is eligible for mandatory transfer, and there is probable cause to believe that the child committed the act charged.

(b) After a complaint has been filed alleging that a child is a delinquent child by reason of committing a category two offense, the juvenile court at a hearing shall transfer the case if the child was sixteen or seventeen years of age at the time of the act charged and either of the following applies:

(i) Division (A)(2)(a) of section 2152.10 of the Revised Code requires the mandatory transfer of the case, and there is probable cause to believe that the child committed the act charged.

(ii) Division (A)(2)(b) of section 2152.10 of the Revised Code requires the mandatory transfer of the case, and there is probable cause to believe that the child committed the act charged.

(2) The juvenile court also shall transfer a case in the circumstances described in division (C)(5) of section 2152.02 of the Revised Code or if either of the following applies:

(a) A complaint is filed against a child who is eligible for a discretionary transfer under section 2152.10 of the Revised Code and who previously was convicted of or pleaded guilty to a felony in a case that was transferred to a criminal court.

(b) A complaint is filed against a child who is domiciled in another state alleging that the child is a delinquent child for committing an act that would be a felony if committed by an adult, and, if the act charged had been committed in that other state, the child would be subject to criminal prosecution as an adult under the law of that other state without the need for a transfer of jurisdiction from a juvenile, family, or similar noncriminal court to a criminal court.

(3) If a complaint is filed against a child alleging that the child is a delinquent child and the case is transferred pursuant to division (A)(1)(a)(i) or (A)(1)(b)(ii) of this section and if the child subsequently is convicted of or pleads guilty to an offense in that case, the sentence to be imposed or disposition to be made of the child shall be determined in accordance with section 2152.121 of the Revised Code.

(B) Except as provided in division (A) of this section, after a complaint has been filed alleging that a child is a delinquent child for committing an act that would be a felony if committed by an adult, the juvenile court at a hearing may transfer the case if the court finds all of the following:

(1) The child was fourteen years of age or older at the time of the act charged.

(2) There is probable cause to believe that the child committed the act charged.

(3) The child is not amenable to care or rehabilitation within the juvenile system, and the safety of the community may require that the child be subject to adult sanctions. In making its decision under this division, the court shall consider whether the applicable factors under division (D) of this section indicating that the case should be transferred outweigh the applicable factors under division (E) of this section indicating that the case should not be transferred. The record shall indicate the specific factors that were applicable and that the court weighed.

(C) Before considering a transfer under division (B) of this section, the juvenile court shall order an investigation, including a mental examination of the child by a public or private agency or a person qualified to make the examination. The child may waive the examination required by this division if the court finds that the waiver is competently and intelligently made. Refusal to submit to a mental examination by the child constitutes a waiver of the examination.

(D) In considering whether to transfer a child under division (B) of this section, the juvenile court shall consider the following relevant factors, and any other relevant factors, in favor of a transfer under that division:

(1) The victim of the act charged suffered physical or psychological harm, or serious economic harm, as a result of the alleged act.

(2) The physical or psychological harm suffered by the victim due to the alleged act of the child was exacerbated because of the physical or psychological vulnerability or the age of the victim.

(3) The child's relationship with the victim facilitated the act charged.

(4) The child allegedly committed the act charged for hire or as a part of a gang or other organized criminal activity.

(5) The child had a firearm on or about the child's person or under the child's control at the time of the act charged, the act charged is not a violation of section 2923.12 of the Revised Code, and the child, during the commission of the act charged, allegedly used or displayed the firearm, brandished the firearm, or indicated that the child possessed a firearm.

(6) At the time of the act charged, the child was awaiting adjudication or disposition as a delinquent child, was under a community control sanction, or was on parole for a prior delinquent child adjudication or conviction.

(7) The results of any previous juvenile sanctions and programs indicate that rehabilitation of the child will not occur in the juvenile system.

(8) The child is emotionally, physically, or psychologically mature enough for the transfer.

(9) There is not sufficient time to rehabilitate the child within the juvenile system.

(E) In considering whether to transfer a child under division (B) of this section, the juvenile court shall consider the following relevant factors, and any other relevant factors, against a transfer under that division:

(1) The victim induced or facilitated the act charged.

(2) The child acted under provocation in allegedly committing the act charged.

(3) The child was not the principal actor in the act charged, or, at the time of the act charged, the child was under the negative influence or coercion of another person.

(4) The child did not cause physical harm to any person or property, or have reasonable cause to believe that harm of that nature would occur, in allegedly committing the act charged.

(5) The child previously has not been adjudicated a delinquent child.

(6) The child is not emotionally, physically, or psychologically mature enough for the transfer.

(7) The child has a mental illness or is a mentally retarded person.

(8) There is sufficient time to rehabilitate the child within the juvenile system and the level of security available in the juvenile system provides a reasonable assurance of public safety.

(F) If one or more complaints are filed alleging that a child is a delinquent child for committing two or more acts that would be offenses if committed by an adult, if a motion is made alleging that division (A) of this section applies and requires that the case or cases involving one or more of the acts charged be transferred for, and if a motion also is made requesting that the case or cases involving one or more of the acts charged be transferred pursuant to division (B) of this section, the juvenile court, in deciding the motions, shall proceed in the following manner:

(1) Initially, the court shall decide the motion alleging that division (A) of this section applies and requires that the case or cases involving one or more of the acts charged be transferred.

(2) If the court determines that division (A) of this section applies and requires that the case or cases involving one or more of the acts charged be transferred, the court shall transfer the case or cases in accordance with that division. After the transfer pursuant to division (A) of this section, the court shall decide, in accordance with division (B) of this section, whether to grant the motion requesting that the case or cases involving one or more of the acts charged be transferred pursuant to that division. Notwithstanding division (B) of this section, prior to transferring a case pursuant to division (A) of this section, the court is not required to consider any factor specified in division (D) or (E) of this section or to conduct an investigation under division (C) of this section.

(3) If the court determines that division (A) of this section does not require that the case or cases involving one or more of the acts charged be transferred, the court shall decide in accordance with division (B) of this section whether to grant the motion requesting that the case or cases involving one or more of the acts charged be transferred pursuant to that division.

(G) The court shall give notice in writing of the time, place, and purpose of any hearing held pursuant to division (A) or (B) of this section to the child's parents, guardian, or other custodian and to the child's counsel at least three days prior to the hearing.

(H) No person, either before or after reaching eighteen years of age, shall be prosecuted as an adult for an offense committed prior to becoming eighteen years of age, unless the person has been transferred as provided in division (A) or (B) of this section or unless division (J) of this section applies. Any prosecution that is had in a criminal court on the mistaken belief that the person who is the subject of the case was eighteen years of age or older at the time of the commission of the offense shall be deemed a nullity, and the person shall not be considered to have been in jeopardy on the offense.

(I) Upon the transfer of a case under division (A) or (B) of this section, the juvenile court shall state the reasons for the transfer on the record, and shall order the child to enter into a recognizance with good and sufficient surety for the child's appearance before the appropriate court for any disposition that the court is authorized to make for a similar act committed by an adult. The transfer abates the jurisdiction of the juvenile court with respect to the delinquent acts alleged in the complaint, and, upon the transfer, all further proceedings pertaining to the act charged shall be discontinued in the juvenile court, and the case then shall be within the jurisdiction of the court to which it is transferred as described in division (H) of section 2151.23 of the Revised Code.

(J) If a person under eighteen years of age allegedly commits an act that would be a felony if committed by an adult and if the person is not taken into custody or apprehended for that act until after the person attains twenty-one years of age, the juvenile court does not have jurisdiction to hear or determine any portion of the case charging the person with committing that act. In those circumstances, divisions (A) and (B) of this section do not apply regarding the act, and the case charging the person with committing the act shall be a criminal prosecution commenced and heard in the appropriate court having jurisdiction of the offense as if the person had been eighteen years of age or older when the person committed the act. All proceedings pertaining to the act shall be within the jurisdiction of the court having jurisdiction of the offense, and that court has all the authority and duties in the case as it has in other criminal cases in that court.

**HISTORY: RC § 2151.26, 133 v H 320 (Eff 11-19-69); 134 v S 325 (Eff 1-14-72); 137 v S 119 (Eff 8-30-78); 139 v H 440 (Eff 11-23-81); 140 v S 210 (Eff 7-1-83); 141 v H 499 (Eff 3-11-87); 144 v H 27 (Eff 10-10-91); 146 v H 1 (Eff 1-1-96); 146 v S 2 (Eff 7-1-96); 146 v S 269 (Eff 7-1-96); 146 v H 124 (Eff 3-31-97); RC § 2152.12, 148 v S 179, § 3. Eff 1-1-2002; 2011 HB 86, § 1, eff. Sept. 30, 2011.**

**Analogous in part to former RC § 2151.26 (GC § 1639-32; 117 v 520; Bureau of Code Revision, 10-1-53; 132 v H 343), repealed 133 v H 320, eff 11-19-69.**

The effective date is set by section 5 of SB 179.

## § 2152.121 When jurisdiction retained by juvenile court for disposition of child where juvenile case transferred pursuant to section 2152.12 of the Revised Code; determination of sentence or disposition.

(A) If a complaint is filed against a child alleging that the child is a delinquent child and the case is transferred pursuant to division (A)(1)(a)(i) or (A)(1)(b)(ii) of section 2152.12 of the Revised Code, the juvenile court that transferred the case shall retain jurisdiction for purposes of making disposition of the child when required under division (B) of this section.

(B) If a complaint is filed against a child alleging that the child is a delinquent child, if the case is transferred pursuant to division (A)(1)(a)(i) or (A)(1)(b)(ii) of section 2152.12 of the Revised Code, and if the child subsequently is convicted of or pleads guilty to an offense in that case, the sentence to be imposed or disposition to be made of the child shall be determined as follows:

(1) The court in which the child is convicted of or pleads guilty to the offense shall determine whether, had a complaint been filed in juvenile court alleging that the child was a delinquent child for committing an act that would be that offense if committed by an adult, division (A) of section 2152.12 of the Revised Code would have required mandatory transfer of the case or division (B) of that section would have allowed discretionary transfer of the case. The court shall not consider the factor specified in division (B)(3) of section 2152.12 of the Revised Code in making its determination under this division.

(2) If the court in which the child is convicted of or pleads guilty to the offense determines under division (B)(1) of this section that, had a complaint been filed in juvenile court alleging that the child was a delinquent child for committing an act that would be that offense if committed by an adult, division (A) of section 2152.12 of the Revised Code would not have required mandatory transfer of the case, and division (B) of that section would not have allowed discretionary transfer of the case, the court shall transfer jurisdiction of the case back to the juvenile court that initially transferred the case, and the juvenile court shall impose one or more traditional juvenile dispositions upon the child under sections 2152.19 and 2152.20 of the Revised Code.

(3) If the court in which the child is convicted of or pleads guilty to the offense determines under division (B)(1) of this section that, had a complaint been filed in juvenile court alleging that the child was a delinquent child for committing an act that would be that offense if committed by an adult, division (A) of section 2152.12 of the Revised Code would not have required mandatory transfer of the case but division (B) of that section would have allowed discretionary transfer of the case, the court shall determine the sentence it believes should be imposed upon the child under Chapter 2929. of the Revised Code, shall impose that sentence upon the child, and shall stay that sentence pending completion of the procedures specified in this division. Upon imposition and staying of the sentence, the court shall transfer jurisdiction of the case back to the juvenile court that initially transferred the case and the juvenile court shall proceed in accordance with this division. In no case may the child waive a right to a hearing of the type described in division (B)(3)(b) of this section, regarding a motion filed as described in that division by the prosecuting attorney in the case. Upon transfer of jurisdiction of the case back to the juvenile court, both of the following apply:

(a) Except as otherwise provided in division (B)(3)(b) of this section, the juvenile court shall impose a serious youthful offender dispositional sentence upon the child under division (D)(1) of section 2152.13 of the Revised Code. In imposing the adult portion of that sentence, the juvenile court shall consider and give preference to the sentence imposed upon the child by the court in which the child was convicted of or pleaded guilty to the offense. Upon imposing a serious youthful offender dispositional sentence upon the child as described in this division, the juvenile court shall notify the court in which the child was convicted of or pleaded guilty to the offense, the sentence imposed upon the child by that court shall terminate, the court and all other agencies that have any record of the conviction of the child shall expunge the conviction or guilty plea and all records of it, the conviction or guilty plea shall be considered and treated for all purposes other than as provided in this section to have never occurred, and the conviction or guilty plea shall be considered and treated for all purposes other than as provided in this section to have been a delinquent child adjudication of the child.

(b) Upon the transfer, the prosecuting attorney in the case may file a motion in the juvenile court that objects to the imposition of a serious youthful offender dispositional sentence upon the child and requests that the sentence imposed upon the child by the court in which the child was convicted of or pleaded guilty to the offense be invoked. Upon the filing of a motion under this division, the juvenile court shall hold a hearing to determine whether the child is not amenable to care or rehabilitation within the juvenile system and whether the safety of the community may require that the child be subject solely to adult sanctions. If the juvenile court at the hearing finds that the child is not amenable to care or rehabilitation within the juvenile system or that the safety of the community may require that the child be subject solely to adult sanctions, the court shall grant the motion. Absent such a finding, the juvenile court shall deny the motion. In making its decision under this division, the juvenile court shall consider the factors listed in division (D) of section 2152.12 of the Revised Code as factors indicating that the motion should be granted, shall consider the factors listed in division (E) of that section as factors indicating that the motion should not be granted, and shall consider whether the applicable factors listed in division (D) of that section outweigh the applicable factors listed in division (E) of that section.

If the juvenile court grants the motion of the prosecuting attorney under this division, the juvenile court shall transfer jurisdiction of the case back to the court in which the child was convicted of or pleaded guilty to the offense, and the sentence imposed by that court shall be invoked. If the juvenile court denies the motion of the prosecuting attorney under this section, the juvenile court shall impose a serious youthful offender dispositional sentence upon the child in accordance with division (B)(3)(a) of this section.

(4) If the court in which the child is convicted of or pleads guilty to the offense determines under division (B)(1) of this section that, had a complaint been filed in juvenile court alleging that the child was a delinquent child for committing an act that would be that offense if committed by an adult, division (A) of section 2152.12 of the Revised Code would have required mandatory transfer of the case, the court shall impose sentence upon the child under Chapter 2929. of the Revised Code.

**HISTORY: 2011 HB 86, § 1, eff. Sept. 30, 2011.**

## § 2152.13 Serious youthful offender dispositional sentence.

(A) A juvenile court shall impose a serious youthful dispositional sentence on a child when required under division (B)(3) of section 2152.121 of the Revised Code. In such a case, the remaining provisions of this division and divisions (B) and (C) do not apply to the child, and the court shall impose the mandatory serious youthful dispositional sentence under division (D)(1) of this section.

In all other cases, a juvenile court may impose a serious youthful offender dispositional sentence on a child only if the prosecuting attorney of the county in which the delinquent act allegedly occurred initiates the process against the child in accordance with this division, and the child is an alleged delinquent child who is eligible for the dispositional sentence. The prosecuting attorney may initiate the process in any of the following ways:

(1) Obtaining an indictment of the child as a serious youthful offender;

(2) The child waives the right to indictment, charging the child in a bill of information as a serious youthful offender;

(3) Until an indictment or information is obtained, requesting a serious youthful offender dispositional sentence in the original complaint alleging that the child is a delinquent child;

(4) Until an indictment or information is obtained, if the original complaint does not request a serious youthful offender dispositional sentence, filing with the juvenile court a written notice of intent to seek a serious youthful offender dispositional sentence within twenty days after the later of the following, unless the time is extended by the juvenile court for good cause shown:

(a) The date of the child's first juvenile court hearing regarding the complaint;

(b) The date the juvenile court determines not to transfer the case under section 2152.12 of the Revised Code.

After a written notice is filed under division (A)(4) of this section, the juvenile court shall serve a copy of the notice on the child and advise the child of the prosecuting attorney's intent to seek a serious youthful offender dispositional sentence in the case.

(B) If an alleged delinquent child is not indicted or charged by information as described in division (A)(1) or (2) of this section and if a notice or complaint as described in division (A)(3) or (4) of this section indicates that the prosecuting attorney intends to pursue a serious youthful offender dispositional sentence in the case, the juvenile court shall hold a preliminary hearing to determine if there is probable cause that the child committed the act charged and is by age eligible for, or required to receive, a serious youthful offender dispositional sentence.

(C)(1) A child for whom a serious youthful offender dispositional sentence is sought by a prosecuting attorney has the right to a grand jury determination of probable cause that the child committed the act charged and that the child is eligible by age for a serious youthful offender dispositional sentence. The grand jury may be impaneled by the court of common pleas or the juvenile court.

Once a child is indicted, or charged by information or the juvenile court determines that the child is eligible for a serious youthful offender dispositional sentence, the child is entitled to an open and speedy trial by jury in juvenile court and to be provided with a transcript of the proceedings. The time within which the trial is to be held under Title XXIX of the Revised Code commences on whichever of the following dates is applicable:

(a) If the child is indicted or charged by information, on the date of the filing of the indictment or information.

(b) If the child is charged by an original complaint that requests a serious youthful offender dispositional sentence, on the date of the filing of the complaint.

(c) If the child is not charged by an original complaint that requests a serious youthful offender dispositional sentence, on the date that the prosecuting attorney files the written notice of intent to seek a serious youthful offender dispositional sentence.

(2) If the child is detained awaiting adjudication, upon indictment or being charged by information, the child has the same right to bail as an adult charged with the offense the alleged delinquent act would be if committed by an adult. Except as provided in division (D) of section 2152.14 of the Revised Code, all provisions of Title XXIX of the Revised Code and the Criminal Rules shall apply in the case and to the child. The juvenile court shall afford the child all rights afforded a person who is prosecuted for committing a crime including the right to counsel and the right to raise the issue of competency. The child may not waive the right to counsel.

(D)(1) If a child is adjudicated a delinquent child for committing an act under circumstances that require the juvenile court to impose upon the child a serious youthful offender dispositional sentence under section 2152.11 of the Revised Code, all of the following apply:

(a) The juvenile court shall impose upon the child a sentence available for the violation, as if the child were an adult, under Chapter 2929. of the Revised Code, except that the juvenile court shall not impose on the child a sentence of death or life imprisonment without parole.

(b) The juvenile court also shall impose upon the child one or more traditional juvenile dispositions under sections 2152.16, 2152.19, and 2152.20, and, if applicable, section 2152.17 of the Revised Code.

(c) The juvenile court shall stay the adult portion of the serious youthful offender dispositional sentence pending the successful completion of the traditional juvenile dispositions imposed.

(2)(a) If a child is adjudicated a delinquent child for committing an act under circumstances that allow, but do not require, the juvenile court to impose on the child a serious youthful offender dispositional sentence under section 2152.11 of the Revised Code, all of the following apply:

(i) If the juvenile court on the record makes a finding that, given the nature and circumstances of the violation and the history of the child, the length of time, level of security, and types of programming and resources available in the juvenile system alone are not adequate to provide the juvenile court with a reasonable expectation that the purposes set forth in section 2152.01 of the Revised Code will be met, the juvenile court may impose upon the child a sentence available for the violation, as if the child were an adult, under Chapter 2929. of the Revised Code, except that the juvenile court shall not impose on the child a sentence of death or life imprisonment without parole.

(ii) If a sentence is imposed under division (D)(2)(a)(i) of this section, the juvenile court also shall impose upon the child one or more traditional juvenile dispositions under sections 2152.16, 2152.19, and 2152.20 and, if applicable, section 2152.17 of the Revised Code.

(iii) The juvenile court shall stay the adult portion of the serious youthful offender dispositional sentence pending the successful completion of the traditional juvenile dispositions imposed.

(b) If the juvenile court does not find that a sentence should be imposed under division (D)(2)(a)(i) of this section, the juvenile court may impose one or more traditional juvenile dispositions under sections 2152.16, 2152.19, 2152.20, and, if applicable, section 2152.17 of the Revised Code.

(3) A child upon whom a serious youthful offender dispositional sentence is imposed under division (D)(1) or (2) of this section has a right to appeal under division (A)(1), (3), (4), or (5) of section 2953.08 of the Revised Code the adult portion of the serious youthful offender dispositional sentence when any of those divisions apply. The child may appeal the adult portion, and the court shall consider the appeal as if the adult portion were not stayed.

**HISTORY: 148 v S 179, § 3 (Eff 1-1-2002); 149 v H 393. Eff 7-5-2002; 2011 HB 86, § 1, eff. Sept. 30, 2011.**

## § 2152.14 Motion to invoke adult portion of dispositional sentence.

(A)(1) The director of youth services may request the prosecuting attorney of the county in which is located the juvenile court that imposed a serious youthful offender dispositional sentence upon a person under section 2152.121 or 2152.13 of the Revised Code to file a motion with that juvenile court to invoke the adult portion of the dispositional sentence if all of the following apply to the person:

(a) The person is at least fourteen years of age.

(b) The person is in the institutional custody, or an escapee from the custody, of the department of youth services.

(c) The person is serving the juvenile portion of the serious youthful offender dispositional sentence.

(2) The motion shall state that there is reasonable cause to believe that either of the following misconduct has occurred and shall state that at least one incident of

misconduct of that nature occurred after the person reached fourteen years of age:

(a) The person committed an act that is a violation of the rules of the institution and that could be charged as any felony or as a first degree misdemeanor offense of violence if committed by an adult.

(b) The person has engaged in conduct that creates a substantial risk to the safety or security of the institution, the community, or the victim.

(B) If a person is at least fourteen years of age, is serving the juvenile portion of a serious youthful offender dispositional sentence imposed under section 2152.121 or 2152.13 of the Revised Code, and is on parole or aftercare from a department of youth services facility, or on community control, the director of youth services, the juvenile court that imposed the serious youthful offender dispositional sentence on the person, or the probation department supervising the person may request the prosecuting attorney of the county in which is located the juvenile court to file a motion with the juvenile court to invoke the adult portion of the dispositional sentence. The prosecuting attorney may file a motion to invoke the adult portion of the dispositional sentence even if no request is made. The motion shall state that there is reasonable cause to believe that either of the following occurred and shall state that at least one incident of misconduct of that nature occurred after the person reached fourteen years of age:

(1) The person committed an act that is a violation of the conditions of supervision and that could be charged as any felony or as a first degree misdemeanor offense of violence if committed by an adult.

(2) The person has engaged in conduct that creates a substantial risk to the safety or security of the community or of the victim.

(C) If the prosecuting attorney declines a request to file a motion that was made by the department of youth services or the supervising probation department under division (A) or (B) of this section or fails to act on a request made under either division by the department within a reasonable time, the department of youth services or the supervising probation department may file a motion of the type described in division (A) or (B) of this section with the juvenile court to invoke the adult portion of the serious youthful offender dispositional sentence. If the prosecuting attorney declines a request to file a motion that was made by the juvenile court under division (B) of this section or fails to act on a request from the court under that division within a reasonable time, the juvenile court may hold the hearing described in division (D) of this section on its own motion.

(D) Upon the filing of a motion described in division (A), (B), or (C) of this section, the juvenile court may hold a hearing to determine whether to invoke the adult portion of a person's serious juvenile offender dispositional sentence. The juvenile court shall not invoke the adult portion of the dispositional sentence without a hearing. At the hearing the person who is the subject of the serious youthful offender disposition has the right to be present, to receive notice of the grounds upon which the adult sentence portion is sought to be invoked, to be represented by counsel including counsel appointed under Juvenile Rule 4(A), to be advised on the procedures and protections set forth in the Juvenile Rules, and to present evidence on the person's own behalf, including evidence that the person has a mental illness or is a mentally retarded person. The person may not waive the right to counsel. The hearing shall be open to the public. If the person presents evidence that the person has a mental illness or is a mentally retarded person, the juvenile court shall consider that evidence in determining whether to invoke the adult portion of the serious youthful offender dispositional sentence.

(E)(1) The juvenile court may invoke the adult portion of a person's serious youthful offender dispositional sentence if the juvenile court finds all of the following on the record by clear and convincing evidence:

(a) The person is serving the juvenile portion of a serious youthful offender dispositional sentence.

(b) The person is at least fourteen years of age and has been admitted to a department of youth services facility, or criminal charges are pending against the person.

(c) The person engaged in the conduct or acts charged under division (A), (B), or (C) of this section, and the person's conduct demonstrates that the person is unlikely to be rehabilitated during the remaining period of juvenile jurisdiction.

(2) The court may modify the adult sentence the court invokes to consist of any lesser prison term that could be imposed for the offense and, in addition to the prison term or in lieu of the prison term if the prison term was not mandatory, any community control sanction that the offender was eligible to receive at sentencing.

(F) If a juvenile court issues an order invoking the adult portion of a serious youthful offender dispositional sentence under division (E) of this section, the juvenile portion of the dispositional sentence shall terminate, and the department of youth services shall transfer the person to the department of rehabilitation and correction or place the person under another sanction imposed as part of the sentence. The juvenile court shall state in its order the total number of days that the person has been held in detention or in a facility operated by, or under contract with, the department of youth services under the juvenile portion of the dispositional sentence. The time the person must serve on a prison term imposed under the adult portion of the dispositional sentence shall be reduced by the total number of days specified in the order plus any additional days the person is held in a juvenile facility or in detention after the order is issued and before the person is transferred to the custody of the department of rehabilitation and correction. In no case shall the total prison term as calculated under this division exceed the maximum prison term available for an adult who is convicted of violating the same sections of the Revised Code.

Any community control imposed as part of the adult sentence or as a condition of a judicial release from prison shall be under the supervision of the entity that provides adult probation services in the county. Any post-release control imposed after the offender otherwise is released from prison shall be supervised by the adult parole authority.

**HISTORY: 148 v S 179, § 3 (Eff 1-1-2002); 149 v H 393. Eff 7-5-2002; 2011 HB 86, § 1, eff. Sept. 30, 2011.**

## § 2152.16 Commitment to youth services department for secure confinement; release by department; effect of prior delinquency adjudication.

(A)(1) If a child is adjudicated a delinquent child for committing an act that would be a felony if committed by an adult, the juvenile court may commit the child to the legal custody of the department of youth services for secure confinement as follows:

(a) For an act that would be aggravated murder or murder if committed by an adult, until the offender attains twenty-one years of age;

(b) For a violation of section 2923.02 of the Revised Code that involves an attempt to commit an act that would be aggravated murder or murder if committed by an adult, a minimum period of six to seven years as prescribed by the court and a maximum period not to exceed the child's attainment of twenty-one years of age;

(c) For a violation of section 2903.03, 2905.01, 2909.02, or 2911.01 or division (A) of section 2903.04 of the Revised Code or for a violation of any provision of section 2907.02 of the Revised Code other than division (A)(1)(b) of that section when the sexual conduct or insertion involved was consensual and when the victim of the violation of division (A)(1)(b) of that section was older than the delinquent child, was the same age as the delinquent child, or was less than three years younger than the delinquent child, for an indefinite term consisting of a minimum period of one to three years, as prescribed by the court, and a maximum period not to exceed the child's attainment of twenty-one years of age;

(d) If the child is adjudicated a delinquent child for committing an act that is not described in division (A)(1)(b) or (c) of this section and that would be a felony of the first or second degree if committed by an adult, for an indefinite term consisting of a minimum period of one year and a maximum period not to exceed the child's attainment of twenty-one years of age.

(e) For committing an act that would be a felony of the third, fourth, or fifth degree if committed by an adult or for a violation of division (A) of section 2923.211 [2923.21.1] of the Revised Code, for an indefinite term consisting of a minimum period of six months and a maximum period not to exceed the child's attainment of twenty-one years of age.

(2) In each case in which a court makes a disposition under this section, the court retains control over the commitment for the minimum period specified by the court in divisions (A)(1)(a) to (e) of this section. During the minimum period, the department of youth services shall not move the child to a nonsecure setting without the permission of the court that imposed the disposition.

(B)(1) Subject to division (B)(2) of this section, if a delinquent child is committed to the department of youth services under this section, the department may release the child at any time after the minimum period specified by the court in division (A)(1) of this section ends.

(2) A commitment under this section is subject to a supervised release or to a discharge of the child from the custody of the department for medical reasons pursuant to section 5139.54 of the Revised Code, but, during the minimum period specified by the court in division (A)(1) of this section, the department shall obtain court approval of a supervised release or discharge under that section.

(C) If a child is adjudicated a delinquent child, at the dispositional hearing and prior to making any disposition pursuant to this section, the court shall determine whether the delinquent child previously has been adjudicated a delinquent child for a violation of a law or ordinance. If the delinquent child previously has been adjudicated a delinquent child for a violation of a law or ordinance, the court, for purposes of entering an order of disposition of the delinquent child under this section, shall consider the previous delinquent child adjudication as a conviction of a violation of the law or ordinance in determining the degree of the offense the current act would be had it been committed by an adult. This division also shall apply in relation to the imposition of any financial sanction under section 2152.19 of the Revised Code.

**HISTORY: 148 v S 179, § 3 (Eff 1-1-2002); 149 v H 393. Eff 7-5-2002.**

## § 2152.17 Commitment for specification; consecutive periods of commitment.

(A) Subject to division (D) of this section, if a child is adjudicated a delinquent child for committing an act, other than a violation of section 2923.12 of the Revised Code, that would be a felony if committed by an adult and if the court determines that, if the child was an adult, the child would be guilty of a specification of the type set forth in section 2941.141, 2941.144, 2941.145, 2941.146, 2941.1412, 2941.1414, or 2941.1415 of the Revised Code, in addition to any commitment or other disposition the court imposes for the underlying delinquent act, all of the following apply:

(1) If the court determines that the child would be guilty of a specification of the type set forth in section 2941.141 of the Revised Code, the court may commit the child to the department of youth services for the specification for a definite period of up to one year.

(2) If the court determines that the child would be guilty of a specification of the type set forth in section 2941.145 of the Revised Code or if the delinquent act is a violation of division (A)(1) or (2) of section 2903.06 of the Revised Code and the court determines that the child would be guilty of a specification of the type set forth in section 2941.1415 of the Revised Code, the court shall commit the child to the department of youth services for the specification for a definite period of not less than one and not more than three years, and the court also shall commit the child to the department for the underlying delinquent act under sections 2152.11 to 2152.16 of the Revised Code.

(3) If the court determines that the child would be guilty of a specification of the type set forth in section 2941.144, 2941.146, or 2941.1412 of the Revised Code or if the delinquent act is a violation of division (A)(1) or (2) of section 2903.06 of the Revised Code and the court determines that the child would be guilty of a specification of the type set forth in section 2941.1414 of the Revised Code, the court shall commit the child to the department of youth services for the specification for a definite period of not less than one and not more than five years, and the court also shall commit the child to the department for the underlying delinquent act under sections 2152.11 to 2152.16 of the Revised Code.

(B)(1) If a child is adjudicated a delinquent child for committing an act, other than a violation of section 2923.12 of the Revised Code, that would be a felony if committed by an adult, if the court determines that the child is complicit in another person's conduct that is of such a nature that the other person would be guilty of a specification of the type set forth in section 2941.141, 2941.144, 2941.145, or 2941.146 of the Revised Code if the other person was an adult, if the other person's conduct relates to the child's underlying delinquent act, and if the child did not furnish, use, or dispose of any firearm that was involved with the underlying delinquent act or with the other person's specification-related conduct, in addition to any other disposition the court imposes for the underlying delinquent act, the court may commit the child to the department of youth services for the specification for a definite period of not more than one year, subject to division (D)(2) of this section.

(2) Except as provided in division (B)(1) of this section, division (A) of this section also applies to a child who is an accomplice regarding a firearm specification of the type set forth in section 2941.1412, 2941.1414, or 2941.1415 of the Revised Code to the same extent the firearm specifications would apply to an adult accomplice in a criminal proceeding.

(C) If a child is adjudicated a delinquent child for committing an act that would be aggravated murder, murder, or a first, second, or third degree felony offense of violence if committed by an adult and if the court determines that, if the child was an adult, the child would be guilty of a specification of the type set forth in section 2941.142 of the Revised Code in relation to the act for which the child was adjudicated a delinquent child, the court shall commit the child for the specification to the legal custody of the department of youth services for institutionalization in a secure facility for a definite period of not less than one and not more than three years, subject to division (D)(2) of this section, and the court also shall commit the child to the department for the underlying delinquent act.

(D)(1) If the child is adjudicated a delinquent child for committing an act that would be an offense of violence that is a felony if committed by an adult and is committed to the legal custody of the department of youth services pursuant to division (A)(1) of section 2152.16 of the Revised Code and if the court determines that the child, if the child was an adult, would be guilty of a specification of the type set forth in section 2941.1411 of the Revised Code in relation to the act for which the child was adjudicated a delinquent child, the court may commit the child to the custody of the department of youth services for institutionalization in a secure facility for up to two years, subject to division (D)(2) of this section.

(2) A court that imposes a period of commitment under division (A) of this section is not precluded from imposing an additional period of commitment under division (C) or (D)(1) of this section, a court that imposes a period of commitment under division (C) of this section is not precluded from imposing an additional period of commitment under division (A) or (D)(1) of this section, and a court that imposes a period of commitment under division (D)(1) of this section is not precluded from imposing an additional period of commitment under division (A) or (C) of this section.

(E) The court shall not commit a child to the legal custody of the department of youth services for a specification pursuant to this section for a period that exceeds five years for any one delinquent act. Any commitment imposed pursuant to division (A), (B), (C), or (D)(1) of this section shall be in addition to, and shall be served consecutively with and prior to, a period of commitment ordered under this chapter for the underlying delinquent act, and each commitment imposed pursuant to division (A), (B), (C), or (D)(1) of this section shall be in addition to, and shall be served consecutively with, any other period of commitment imposed under those divisions. If a commitment is imposed under division (A) or (B) of this section and a commitment also is imposed under division (C) of this section, the period imposed under division (A) or (B) of this section shall be served prior to the period imposed under division (C) of this section.

In each case in which a court makes a disposition under this section, the court retains control over the commitment for the entire period of the commitment.

The total of all the periods of commitment imposed for any specification under this section and for the underlying offense shall not exceed the child's attainment of twenty-one years of age.

(F) If a child is adjudicated a delinquent child for committing two or more acts that would be felonies if committed by an adult and if the court entering the delinquent child adjudication orders the commitment of the child for two or more of those acts to the legal custody of the department of youth services for institutionalization in a secure facility pursuant to section 2152.13 or 2152.16 of the Revised Code, the court may order that all of the periods of commitment imposed under those sections for those acts be served consecutively in the legal custody of the department of youth services, provided that those periods of commitment shall be in addition to and commence immediately following the expiration of a period of commitment that the court imposes pursuant to division (A), (B), (C), or (D)(1) of this section. A court shall not commit a delinquent child to the legal custody of the department of youth services under this division for a period that exceeds the child's attainment of twenty-one years of age.

**HISTORY: 148 v S 179, § 3 (Eff 1-1-2002); 149 v H 393 (Eff 7-5-2002); 149 v H 130. Eff 4-7-2003.†; 150 v H 52, § 1, eff. 6-1-04; 151 v H 95, § 1, eff. 8-3-06; 2011 HB 86, § 1, eff. Sept. 30, 2011.**

† The effective date differs from that specified in section 3 of the Act. See provisions of OConst art II, § 1c.

The provisions of § 3, H.B. 52 (150 v —), read as follows:

SECTION 3. Section 2152.17 of the Revised Code is presented in this act as a composite of the section as amended by both Sub. H.B. 130 and Sub. H.B. 393 of the 124th General Assembly. Section 4511.01 of the Revised Code is presented in this act as a composite of the section as amended by Am. Sub. S.B. 123 and Am. Sub. S.B. 231, both of the 124th General Assembly. The General Assembly, applying the principle stated in division (B) of section 1.52 of the Revised Code that amendments are to be harmonized if reasonably capable of simultaneous operation, finds that the composites are the resulting versions of the sections in effect prior to the effective date of the sections as presented in this act.

The provisions of §§ 3, 4, 5 of HB 130 (149 v —) read as follows:

SECTION 3. Section 2152.17 of the Revised Code, as amended by this act, shall take effect January 1, 2002.

SECTION 4. The amendment of section 2151.355 of the Revised Code is not intended to supersede the earlier repeal, with delayed effective date, of that section.

SECTION 5. (A) Section 2151.355 of the Revised Code is presented in this act as a composite of the section as amended by both Am. Sub. S.B. 181 and Am. Sub. S.B. 222 of the 123rd General Assembly. The General Assembly, applying the principle stated in division (B) of section 1.52 of the Revised Code that amendments are to be harmonized if reasonably capable of simultaneous operation, finds that the composite is the resulting version of the section in effect prior to the effective date of the section as presented in this act.

(B) Section 2152.17 of the Revised Code, as presented in this act, includes matter that was amended into former section 2151.355 of the Revised Code by Am. Sub. S.B. 222 of the 123rd General Assembly. Paragraphs of former section 2151.355 of the Revised Code containing Am. Sub. S.B. 222 amendments were transferred to section 2152.17 of the Revised Code by Am. Sub. S.B. 179 of the 123rd General Assembly as part of its general revision of the juvenile sentencing laws. The General Assembly, applying the principle stated in division (B) of section 1.52 of the Revised Code that amendments are to be harmonized if reasonably capable of simultaneous operation, finds that the version of section 2152.17 of the Revised Code presented in this act is the resulting version of the section in effect prior to the effective date of the section as presented in this act.

**§ 2152.18 Court not to designate institution; reduction due to days held in detention; documents to be provided to department; notice to school district and principal; notice to victims concerning recovery.**

(A) When a juvenile court commits a delinquent child to the custody of the department of youth services pursuant to this chapter, the court shall not designate the specific institution in which the department is to place the child but instead shall specify that the child is to be institutionalized in a secure facility.

(B) When a juvenile court commits a delinquent child to the custody of the department of youth services pursuant to this chapter, the court shall state in the order of commitment the total number of days that the child has been held in detention in connection with the delinquent child complaint upon which the order of commitment is based. The department shall reduce the minimum period of institutionalization that was ordered by both the total number of days that the child has been so held in detention as stated by the court in the order of commitment and the total number of any additional days that the child has been held in detention subsequent to the order of commitment but prior to the transfer of physical custody of the child to the department.

(C)(1) When a juvenile court commits a delinquent child to the custody of the department of youth services pursuant to this chapter, the court shall provide the department with the child's medical records, a copy of the report of any mental examination of the child ordered by the court, the Revised Code section or sections the child violated and the degree of each violation, the warrant to convey the child to the department, a copy of the court's journal entry ordering the commitment of the child to the legal custody of the department, a copy of the arrest record pertaining to the act for which the child was adjudicated a delinquent child, a copy of any victim impact statement pertaining to the act, and any other information concerning the child that the department reasonably requests. The court also shall complete the form for the standard predisposition investigation report that the department furnishes pursuant to section 5139.04 of the Revised Code and provide the department with the completed form.

The department may refuse to accept physical custody of a delinquent child who is committed to the legal custody of the department until the court provides to the department the documents specified in this division. No officer or employee of the department who refuses to accept physical custody of a delinquent child who is committed to the legal custody of the department shall be subject to prosecution or contempt of court for the refusal if the court fails to provide the documents specified in this division at the time the court transfers the physical custody of the child to the department.

(2) Within twenty working days after the department of youth services receives physical custody of a delinquent child from a juvenile court, the court shall provide the department with a certified copy of the child's birth certificate and the child's social security number or, if the court made all reasonable efforts to obtain the information but was unsuccessful, with documentation of the efforts it made to obtain the information.

(3) If an officer is preparing pursuant to section 2947.06 or 2951.03 of the Revised Code or Criminal Rule 32.2 a presentence investigation report pertaining to a person, the department shall make available to the officer, for use in preparing the report, any records or reports it possesses regarding that person that it received from a juvenile court pursuant to division (C)(1) of this section or that pertain to the treatment of that person after the person was committed to the custody of the department as a delinquent child.

(D)(1) Within ten days after an adjudication that a child is a delinquent child, the court shall give written notice of the adjudication to the superintendent of a city, local, exempted village, or joint vocational school district, and to the principal of the school the child attends, if the basis of the adjudication was the commission of an act that would be a criminal offense if committed by an adult, if the act was committed by the delinquent child when the child was fourteen years of age or older, and if the act is any of the following:

(a) An act that would be a felony or an offense of violence if committed by an adult, an act in the commission of which the child used or brandished a firearm, or an act that is a violation of section 2907.06, 2907.07, 2907.08, 2907.09, 2907.24, or 2907.241 [2907.24.1] of the Revised Code and that would be a misdemeanor if committed by an adult;

(b) A violation of section 2923.12 of the Revised Code or of a substantially similar municipal ordinance that would be a misdemeanor if committed by an adult and that was committed on property owned or controlled by, or at an activity held under the auspices of, the board of education of that school district;

(c) A violation of division (A) of section 2925.03 or 2925.11 of the Revised Code that would be a misdemeanor if committed by an adult, that was committed on property owned or controlled by, or at an activity held under the auspices of, the board of education of that school district, and that is not a minor drug possession offense;

(d) An act that would be a criminal offense if committed by an adult and that results in serious physical harm to persons or serious physical harm to property while the child is at school, on any other property owned or controlled by the board, or at an interscholastic competition, an extracurricular event, or any other school program or activity;

(e) Complicity in any violation described in division (D)(1)(a), (b), (c), or (d) of this section that was alleged to have been committed in the manner described in division (D)(1)(a), (b), (c), or (d) of this section, regardless of whether the act of complicity was committed on property owned or controlled by, or at an activity held under the auspices of, the board of education of that school district.

(2) The notice given pursuant to division (D)(1) of this section shall include the name of the child who was adjudicated to be a delinquent child, the child's age at the time the child committed the act that was the basis of the adjudication, and identification of the violation of the law or ordinance that was the basis of the adjudication.

(3) Within fourteen days after committing a delinquent child to the custody of the department of youth services, the court shall give notice to the school attended by the child of the child's commitment by sending to that school a copy of the court's journal entry ordering the commitment. As soon as possible after receipt of the notice described in this division, the school shall provide the department with the child's school transcript. However, the department shall not refuse to accept a child committed to it, and a child committed to it shall not be held in

a county or district detention facility, because of a school's failure to provide the school transcript that it is required to provide under this division.

(4) Within fourteen days after discharging or releasing a child from an institution under its control, the department of youth services shall provide the court and the superintendent of the school district in which the child is entitled to attend school under section 3313.64 or 3313.65 of the Revised Code with the following:

(a) An updated copy of the child's school transcript;

(b) A report outlining the child's behavior in school while in the custody of the department;

(c) The child's current individualized education program, as defined in section 3323.01 of the Revised Code, if such a program has been developed for the child;

(d) A summary of the institutional record of the child's behavior.

The department also shall provide the court with a copy of any portion of the child's institutional record that the court specifically requests, within five working days of the request.

(E) At any hearing at which a child is adjudicated a delinquent child or as soon as possible after the hearing, the court shall notify all victims of the delinquent act who may be entitled to a recovery under any of the following sections of the right of the victims to recover, pursuant to section 3109.09 of the Revised Code, compensatory damages from the child's parents; of the right of the victims to recover, pursuant to section 3109.10 of the Revised Code, compensatory damages from the child's parents for willful and malicious assaults committed by the child; and of the right of the victims to recover an award of reparations pursuant to sections 2743.51 to 2743.72 of the Revised Code.

**HISTORY: 148 v S 179, § 3 (Eff 1-1-2002); 149 v H 247 (Eff 5-30-2002); 149 v H 393. Eff 7-5-2002; 150 v H 106, § 1, eff. 9-16-04.**

The provisions of § 7, H.B. 106 (150 v —) read as follows:

SECTION 7. Section 2152.18 of the Revised Code is presented in this act as a composite of the section as amended by both Sub. H.B. 247 and Sub. H.B. 393 of the 124th General Assembly. The General Assembly, applying the principle stated in division (B) of section 1.52 of the Revised Code that amendments are to be harmonized if reasonably capable of simultaneous operation, finds that the composite is the resulting version of the section in effect prior to the effective date of the section as presented in this act.

## § 2152.19 Additional orders of disposition; motor vehicle license suspension; victim restitution, impact statement; truancy warnings; searches.

(A) If a child is adjudicated a delinquent child, the court may make any of the following orders of disposition, in addition to any other disposition authorized or required by this chapter:

(1) Any order that is authorized by section 2151.353 [2151.35.3] of the Revised Code for the care and protection of an abused, neglected, or dependent child;

(2) Commit the child to the temporary custody of any school, camp, institution, or other facility operated for the care of delinquent children by the county, by a district organized under section 2152.41 or 2151.65 of the Revised Code, or by a private agency or organization, within or without the state, that is authorized and qualified to provide the care, treatment, or placement required, including, but not limited to, a school, camp, or facility operated under section 2151.65 of the Revised Code;

(3) Place the child in a detention facility or district detention facility operated under section 2152.41 of the Revised Code, for up to ninety days;

(4) Place the child on community control under any sanctions, services, and conditions that the court prescribes. As a condition of community control in every case and in addition to any other condition that it imposes upon the child, the court shall require the child to abide by the law during the period of community control. As referred to in this division, community control includes, but is not limited to, the following sanctions and conditions:

(a) A period of basic probation supervision in which the child is required to maintain contact with a person appointed to supervise the child in accordance with sanctions imposed by the court;

(b) A period of intensive probation supervision in which the child is required to maintain frequent contact with a person appointed by the court to supervise the child while the child is seeking or maintaining employment and participating in training, education, and treatment programs as the order of disposition;

(c) A period of day reporting in which the child is required each day to report to and leave a center or another approved reporting location at specified times in order to participate in work, education or training, treatment, and other approved programs at the center or outside the center;

(d) A period of community service of up to five hundred hours for an act that would be a felony or a misdemeanor of the first degree if committed by an adult, up to two hundred hours for an act that would be a misdemeanor of the second, third, or fourth degree if committed by an adult, or up to thirty hours for an act that would be a minor misdemeanor if committed by an adult;

(e) A requirement that the child obtain a high school diploma, a certificate of high school equivalence, vocational training, or employment;

(f) A period of drug and alcohol use monitoring;

(g) A requirement of alcohol or drug assessment or counseling, or a period in an alcohol or drug treatment program with a level of security for the child as determined necessary by the court;

(h) A period in which the court orders the child to observe a curfew that may involve daytime or evening hours;

(i) A requirement that the child serve monitored time;

(j) A period of house arrest without electronic monitoring or continuous alcohol monitoring;

(k) A period of electronic monitoring or continuous alcohol monitoring without house arrest, or house arrest with electronic monitoring or continuous alcohol monitoring or both electronic monitoring and continuous alcohol monitoring, that does not exceed the maximum sentence of imprisonment that could be imposed upon an adult who commits the same act.

A period of house arrest with electronic monitoring or continuous alcohol monitoring or both electronic monitoring and continuous alcohol monitoring, imposed under this division shall not extend beyond the child's twenty-first birthday. If a court imposes a period of house arrest with electronic monitoring or continuous alcohol monitoring or both electronic monitoring and continuous alcohol monitoring, upon a child under this division, it shall require the child: to remain in the child's home or other specified premises for the entire period of house arrest with electronic monitoring or continuous alcohol monitoring or both except when the court permits the child to leave those premises to go to school or to other specified premises. Regarding electronic monitoring, the court also shall require the child to be monitored by a central system that can determine the child's location at designated times; to report periodically to a person designated by the court; and to enter into a written contract with the court agreeing to comply with all requirements imposed by the court, agreeing to pay any fee imposed by the court for the costs of the house arrest with electronic monitoring, and agreeing to waive the right to receive credit for any time served on house arrest with electronic monitoring toward the period of any other dispositional order imposed upon the child if the child violates any of the requirements of the dispositional order of house arrest with electronic monitoring. The court also may impose other reasonable requirements upon the child.

Unless ordered by the court, a child shall not receive credit for any time served on house arrest with electronic monitoring or continuous alcohol monitoring or both toward any other dispositional order imposed upon the child for the act for which was imposed the dispositional order of house arrest with electronic monitoring or continuous alcohol monitoring. As used in this division and division (A)(4)(l) of this section, "continuous alcohol monitoring" has the same meaning as in section 2929.01 of the Revised Code.

(l) A suspension of the driver's license, probationary driver's license, or temporary instruction permit issued to the child for a period of time prescribed by the court, or a suspension of the registration of all motor vehicles registered in the name of the child for a period of time prescribed by the court. A child whose license or permit is so suspended is ineligible for issuance of a license or permit during the period of suspension. At the end of the period of suspension, the child shall not be reissued a license or permit until the child has paid any applicable reinstatement fee and complied with all requirements governing license reinstatement.

(5) Commit the child to the custody of the court;

(6) Require the child to not be absent without legitimate excuse from the public school the child is supposed to attend for five or more consecutive days, seven or more school days in one school month, or twelve or more school days in a school year;

(7)(a) If a child is adjudicated a delinquent child for being a chronic truant or an habitual truant who previously has been adjudicated an unruly child for being a habitual truant, do either or both of the following:

(i) Require the child to participate in a truancy prevention mediation program;

(ii) Make any order of disposition as authorized by this section, except that the court shall not commit the child to a facility described in division (A)(2) or (3) of this section unless the court determines that the child violated a lawful court order made pursuant to division (C)(1)(e) of section 2151.354 [2151.35.4] of the Revised Code or division (A)(6) of this section.

(b) If a child is adjudicated a delinquent child for being a chronic truant or a habitual truant who previously has been adjudicated an unruly child for being a habitual truant and the court determines that the parent, guardian, or other person having care of the child has failed to cause the child's attendance at school in violation of section 3321.38 of the Revised Code, do either or both of the following:

(i) Require the parent, guardian, or other person having care of the child to participate in a truancy prevention mediation program;

(ii) Require the parent, guardian, or other person having care of the child to participate in any community service program, preferably a community service program that requires the involvement of the parent, guardian, or other person having care of the child in the school attended by the child.

(8) Make any further disposition that the court finds proper, except that the child shall not be placed in any of the following:

(a) A state correctional institution, a county, multicounty, or municipal jail or workhouse, or another place in which an adult convicted of a crime, under arrest, or charged with a crime is held;

(b) A community corrections facility, if the child would be covered by the definition of public safety beds for purposes of sections 5139.41 to 5139.43 of the Revised Code if the court exercised its authority to commit the child to the legal custody of the department of youth services for institutionalization or institutionalization in a secure facility pursuant to this chapter.

(B) If a child is adjudicated a delinquent child, in addition to any order of disposition made under division (A) of this section, the court, in the following situations and for the specified periods of time, shall suspend the child's temporary instruction permit, restricted license, probationary driver's license, or nonresident operating privilege, or suspend the child's ability to obtain such a permit:

(1) If the child is adjudicated a delinquent child for violating section 2923.122 [2923.12.2] of the Revised Code, impose a class four suspension of the child's license, permit, or privilege from the range specified in division (A)(4) of section 4510.02 of the Revised Code or deny the child the issuance of a license or permit in accordance with division (F)(1) of section 2923.122 [2923.12.2] of the Revised Code.

(2) If the child is adjudicated a delinquent child for committing an act that if committed by an adult would be a drug abuse offense or for violating division (B) of section 2917.11 of the Revised Code, suspend the child's license, permit, or privilege for a period of time prescribed by the court. The court, in its discretion, may terminate the suspension if the child attends and satisfactorily completes a drug abuse or alcohol abuse education, intervention, or treatment program specified by the court. During the time the child is attending a program described in this division, the court shall retain the child's temporary instruction permit, probationary driver's license, or driver's license, and the court shall return the permit or license if it terminates the suspension as described in this division.

(C) The court may establish a victim-offender mediation program in which victims and their offenders meet to discuss the offense and suggest possible restitution. If the court obtains the assent of the victim of the delinquent act committed by the child, the court may require the child to participate in the program.

(D)(1) If a child is adjudicated a delinquent child for committing an act that would be a felony if committed by an adult and if the child caused, attempted to cause, threatened to cause, or created a risk of physical harm to the victim of the act, the court, prior to issuing an order of disposition under this section, shall order the preparation of a victim impact statement by the probation department of the county in which the victim of the act resides, by the court's own probation department, or by a victim assistance program that is operated by the state, a county, a municipal corporation, or another governmental entity.

The court shall consider the victim impact statement in determining the order of disposition to issue for the child.

(2) Each victim impact statement shall identify the victim of the act for which the child was adjudicated a delinquent child, itemize any economic loss suffered by the victim as a result of the act, identify any physical injury suffered by the victim as a result of the act and the seriousness and permanence of the injury, identify any change in the victim's personal welfare or familial relationships as a result of the act and any psychological impact experienced by the victim or the victim's family as a result of the act, and contain any other information related to the impact of the act upon the victim that the court requires.

(3) A victim impact statement shall be kept confidential and is not a public record. However, the court may furnish copies of the statement to the department of youth services if the delinquent child is committed to the department or to both the adjudicated delinquent child or the adjudicated delinquent child's counsel and the prosecuting attorney. The copy of a victim impact statement furnished by the court to the department pursuant to this section shall be kept confidential and is not a public record. If an officer is preparing pursuant to section 2947.06 or 2951.03 of the Revised Code or Criminal Rule 32.2 a presentence investigation report pertaining to a person, the court shall make available to the officer, for use in preparing the report, a copy of any victim impact statement regarding that person. The copies of a victim impact statement that are made available to the adjudicated delinquent child or the adjudicated delinquent child's counsel and the prosecuting attorney pursuant to this division shall be returned to the court by the person to whom they were made available immediately following the imposition of an order of disposition for the child under this chapter.

The copy of a victim impact statement that is made available pursuant to this division to an officer preparing a criminal presentence investigation report shall be returned to the court by the officer immediately following its use in preparing the report.

(4) The department of youth services shall work with local probation departments and victim assistance programs to develop a standard victim impact statement.

(E) If a child is adjudicated a delinquent child for being a chronic truant or a habitual truant who previously has been adjudicated an unruly child for being a habitual truant and the court determines that the parent, guardian, or other person having care of the child has failed to cause the child's attendance at school in violation of section 3321.38 of the Revised Code, in addition to any order of disposition it makes under this section, the court shall warn the parent, guardian, or other person having care of the child that any subsequent adjudication of the child as an unruly or delinquent child for being a habitual or chronic truant may result in a criminal charge against the parent, guardian, or other person having care of the child for a violation of division (C) of section 2919.21 or section 2919.24 of the Revised Code.

(F)(1) During the period of a delinquent child's community control granted under this section, authorized probation officers who are engaged within the scope of their supervisory duties or responsibilities may search, with or without a warrant, the person of the delinquent child, the place of residence of the delinquent child, and a motor vehicle, another item of tangible or intangible personal property, or other real property in which the delinquent child has a right, title, or interest or for which the delinquent child has the express or implied permission of a person with a right, title, or interest to use, occupy, or possess if the probation officers have reasonable grounds to believe that the delinquent child is not abiding by the law or otherwise is not complying with the conditions of the delinquent child's community control. The court that places a delinquent child on community control under this section shall provide the delinquent child with a written notice that informs the delinquent child that authorized probation officers who are engaged within the scope of their supervisory duties or responsibilities may conduct those types of searches during the period of community control if they have reasonable grounds to believe that the delinquent child is not abiding by the law or otherwise is not complying with the conditions of the delinquent child's community control. The court also shall provide the written notice described in division (E)(2) of this section to each parent, guardian, or custodian of the delinquent child who is described in that division.

(2) The court that places a child on community control under this section shall provide the child's parent, guardian, or other custodian with a written notice that informs them that authorized probation officers may conduct searches pursuant to division (E)(1) of this section. The notice shall specifically state that a permissible search might extend to a motor vehicle, another item of tangible or intangible personal property, or a place of residence or other real property in which a notified parent, guardian, or custodian has a right, title, or interest and that the parent, guardian, or custodian expressly or impliedly permits the child to use, occupy, or possess.

(G) If a juvenile court commits a delinquent child to the custody of any person, organization, or entity pursuant to this section and if the delinquent act for which the child is so committed is a sexually oriented offense or is a child-victim oriented offense, the court in the order of disposition shall do one of the following:

(1) Require that the child be provided treatment as described in division (A)(2) of section 5139.13 of the Revised Code;

(2) Inform the person, organization, or entity that it is the preferred course of action in this state that the child be provided treatment as described in division (A)(2) of section 5139.13 of the Revised Code and encourage the person, organization, or entity to provide that treatment.

**HISTORY: 148 v S 179, § 3 (Eff 1-1-2002); 149 v S 3 (Eff 1-1-2002); 149 v H 247 (Eff 5-30-2002); 149 v H 393 (Eff 7-5-2002); 149 v H 400, § 1. Eff 4-3-2003; 149 v S 123, § 1, eff. 1-1-04; 149 v H 490, § 1, eff. 1-1-04; 150 v S 5, § 1, eff. 7-31-03; 150 v H 95, § 1, eff. 9-26-03; 150 v H 95, § 3.13, eff. 1-1-04; 150 v S 5, § 3, eff. 1-1-04; 150 v H 163, § 1, eff. 9-23-04; 152 v S 10, § 1, eff. 1-1-08.**

The effective date is set by § 3 of 152 v S 10.

The provisions of § 5, H.B. 163 (150 v —), read as follows:

SECTION 5. * * * (B) Section 2152.19 of the Revised Code is presented in this act as a composite of the section as amended by Am. Sub. H.B. 400, Am. Sub. H.B. 490, and Am. Sub. S.B. 123, all of the 124th General Assembly, and Am. Sub. H.B. 95 and Am. Sub. S.B. 5, both of the 125th General Assembly. The General Assembly, applying the principle stated in division (B) of section 1.52 of the Revised Code that amendments are to be harmonized if reasonably capable of simultaneous operation, finds that the composite is the resulting version of the section in effect prior to the effective date of the section as presented in this act. * * *

The provisions of § 5 of S.B. 123 (149 v —), as amended by § 3 of H.B. 163 (150 v —), read as follows:

SECTION 5. (A) Notwithstanding division (B) of section 1.58 of the Revised Code, the provisions of the Revised Code amended or enacted in Sections 1 and 2 of Am. Sub. S.B. 123 of the 124th

General Assembly shall apply only in relation to conduct and offenses committed on or after January 1, 2004. Conduct and offenses committed prior to January 1, 2004, shall be governed by the law in effect on the date the conduct or offense was committed. * * *

## § 2152.191 Children subject to sex offender registration and notification law.

If a child is adjudicated a delinquent child for committing a sexually oriented offense or a child-victim oriented offense, if the child is fourteen years of age or older at the time of committing the offense, and if the child committed the offense on or after January 1, 2002, both of the following apply:

(A) Sections 2152.82 to 2152.86 and Chapter 2950. of the Revised Code apply to the child and the adjudication.

(B) In addition to any order of disposition it makes of the child under this chapter, the court may make any determination, adjudication, or order authorized under sections 2152.82 to 2152.86 and Chapter 2950. of the Revised Code and shall make any determination, adjudication, or order required under those sections and that chapter.

**HISTORY: 149 v S 3. Eff 1-1-2002; 150 v S 5, § 1, eff. 7-31-03; 152 v S 10, § 1, eff. 1-1-08.**

The effective date is set by § 3 of 152 v S 10.

The provisions of § 3 of SB 3 (149 v —) read as follows:

SECTION 3. Sections 1 and 2 of this act shall take effect on January 1, 2002, or the earliest date permitted by law, whichever is later.

## § 2152.192 Notice to institution or association and county sheriff that child has been adjudicated delinquent for sexually oriented offense.

If a court or child welfare agency places a delinquent child in an institution or association, as defined in section 5103.02 of the Revised Code, that is certified by the department of job and family services pursuant to section 5103.03 of the Revised Code and if that child has been adjudicated delinquent for committing an act that is a sexually oriented offense in either a prior delinquency adjudication or in the most recent delinquency adjudication, the court or child welfare agency shall notify the operator of the institution or association and the sheriff of the county in which the institution or association is located that the child has been adjudicated delinquent for committing an act that is a sexually oriented offense.

**HISTORY: 151 v H 95, § 1, eff. 8-3-06.**

## § 2152.20 Fines; costs; restitution; order of criminal forfeiture; community service.

(A) If a child is adjudicated a delinquent child or a juvenile traffic offender, the court may order any of the following dispositions, in addition to any other disposition authorized or required by this chapter:

(1) Impose a fine in accordance with the following schedule:

(a) For an act that would be a minor misdemeanor or an unclassified misdemeanor if committed by an adult, a fine not to exceed fifty dollars;

(b) For an act that would be a misdemeanor of the fourth degree if committed by an adult, a fine not to exceed one hundred dollars;

(c) For an act that would be a misdemeanor of the third degree if committed by an adult, a fine not to exceed one hundred fifty dollars;

(d) For an act that would be a misdemeanor of the second degree if committed by an adult, a fine not to exceed two hundred dollars;

(e) For an act that would be a misdemeanor of the first degree if committed by an adult, a fine not to exceed two hundred fifty dollars;

(f) For an act that would be a felony of the fifth degree or an unclassified felony if committed by an adult, a fine not to exceed three hundred dollars;

(g) For an act that would be a felony of the fourth degree if committed by an adult, a fine not to exceed four hundred dollars;

(h) For an act that would be a felony of the third degree if committed by an adult, a fine not to exceed seven hundred fifty dollars;

(i) For an act that would be a felony of the second degree if committed by an adult, a fine not to exceed one thousand dollars;

(j) For an act that would be a felony of the first degree if committed by an adult, a fine not to exceed one thousand five hundred dollars;

(k) For an act that would be aggravated murder or murder if committed by an adult, a fine not to exceed two thousand dollars.

(2) Require the child to pay costs;

(3) Unless the child's delinquent act or juvenile traffic offense would be a minor misdemeanor if committed by an adult or could be disposed of by the juvenile traffic violations bureau serving the court under Traffic Rule 13.1 if the court has established a juvenile traffic violations bureau, require the child to make restitution to the victim of the child's delinquent act or juvenile traffic offense or, if the victim is deceased, to a survivor of the victim in an amount based upon the victim's economic loss caused by or related to the delinquent act or juvenile traffic offense. The court may not require a child to make restitution pursuant to this division if the child's delinquent act or juvenile traffic offense would be a minor misdemeanor if committed by an adult or could be disposed of by the juvenile traffic violations bureau serving the court under Traffic Rule 13.1 if the court has established a juvenile traffic violations bureau. If the court requires restitution under this division, the restitution shall be made directly to the victim in open court or to the probation department that serves the jurisdiction or the clerk of courts on behalf of the victim.

If the court requires restitution under this division, the restitution may be in the form of a cash reimbursement paid in a lump sum or in installments, the performance of repair work to restore any damaged property to its original condition, the performance of a reasonable amount of labor for the victim or survivor of the victim, the performance of community service work, any other form of restitution devised by the court, or any combination of the previously described forms of restitution.

If the court requires restitution under this division, the court may base the restitution order on an amount recommended by the victim or survivor of the victim, the delinquent child, the juvenile traffic offender, a presentence investigation report, estimates or receipts indicating the cost of repairing or replacing property, and any other information, provided that the amount the court orders as restitution shall not exceed the amount of the economic loss suffered by the victim as a direct and proximate result of the delinquent act or juvenile traffic offense. If the court decides to order restitution under this division and the amount of the restitution is disputed by the victim or survivor or by the delinquent child or juvenile traffic offender, the court shall hold a hearing on the restitution. If the court requires restitution under this division, the court shall determine, or order the determination of, the amount of restitution to be paid by the delinquent child or juvenile traffic offender. All restitution payments shall be credited against any recovery of economic loss in a civil action brought by or on behalf of the victim against the delinquent child or juvenile traffic offender or the delinquent child's or juvenile traffic offender's parent, guardian, or other custodian.

If the court requires restitution under this division, the court may order that the delinquent child or juvenile traffic offender pay a surcharge, in an amount not exceeding five per cent of the amount of restitution otherwise ordered under this division, to the entity responsible for collecting and processing the restitution payments.

The victim or the survivor of the victim may request that the prosecuting authority file a motion, or the delinquent child or juvenile traffic offender may file a motion, for modification of the payment terms of any restitution ordered under this division. If the court grants the motion, it may modify the payment terms as it determines appropriate.

(4) Require the child to reimburse any or all of the costs incurred for services or sanctions provided or imposed, including, but not limited to, the following:

(a) All or part of the costs of implementing any community control imposed as a disposition under section 2152.19 of the Revised Code, including a supervision fee;

(b) All or part of the costs of confinement in a residential facility described in section 2152.19 of the Revised Code or in a department of youth services institution, including, but not limited to, a per diem fee for room and board, the costs of medical and dental treatment provided, and the costs of repairing property the delinquent child damaged while so confined. The amount of reimbursement ordered for a child under this division shall not exceed the total amount of reimbursement the child is able to pay as determined at a hearing and shall not exceed the actual cost of the confinement. The court may collect any reimbursement ordered under this division. If the court does not order reimbursement under this division, confinement costs may be assessed pursuant to a repayment policy adopted under section 2929.37 of the Revised Code and division (D) of section 307.93, division (A) of section 341.19, division (C) of section 341.23 or 753.16, division (C) of section 2301.56, or division (B) of section 341.14, 753.02, 753.04, or 2947.19 of the Revised Code.

(B) Chapter 2981. of the Revised Code applies to a child who is adjudicated a delinquent child for violating section 2923.32 or 2923.42 of the Revised Code or for committing an act that, if committed by an adult, would be a felony drug abuse offense.

(C) The court may hold a hearing if necessary to determine whether a child is able to pay a sanction under this section.

(D) If a child who is adjudicated a delinquent child is indigent, the court shall consider imposing a term of community service under division (A) of section 2152.19 of the Revised Code in lieu of imposing a financial sanction under this section. If a child who is adjudicated a delinquent child is not indigent, the court may impose a term of community service under that division in lieu of, or in addition to, imposing a financial sanction under this section. The court may order community service for an act that if committed by an adult would be a minor misdemeanor.

If a child fails to pay a financial sanction imposed under this section, the court may impose a term of community service in lieu of the sanction.

(E) The clerk of the court, or another person authorized by law or by the court to collect a financial sanction imposed under this section, may do any of the following:

(1) Enter into contracts with one or more public agencies or private vendors for the collection of the amounts due under the financial sanction, which amounts may include interest from the date of imposition of the financial sanction;

(2) Permit payment of all, or any portion of, the financial sanction in installments, by credit or debit card, by another type of electronic transfer, or by any other reasonable method, within any period of time, and on any terms that the court considers just, except that the maximum time permitted for payment shall not exceed five years. The clerk may pay any fee associated with processing an electronic transfer out of public money and may charge the fee to the delinquent child.

(3) To defray administrative costs, charge a reasonable fee to a child who elects a payment plan rather than a lump sum payment of a financial sanction.

**HISTORY: 148 v S 179, § 3 (Eff 1-1-2002); 149 v H 170. Eff 9-6-2002; 149 v H 490, § 1, eff. 1-1-04; 150 v H 52, § 1, eff. 6-1-04; 151 v H 162, § 1, eff. 10-12-06; 151 v H 241, § 1, eff. 7-1-07; 152 v H 120, § 1, eff. 7-1-07.**

The effective date is set by § 3 of 152 v H 120.

The provisions of § 4 of 151 v H 241 read as follows:

SECTION 4. Sections 1, 2, and 3 of this act shall take effect on July 1, 2007. If a criminal or civil forfeiture action relating to misconduct under Title XXIX of the Revised Code was or is commenced before July 1, 2007, and is still pending on that date, the court in which the case is pending shall, to the extent practical, apply the provisions of Chapter 2981. of the Revised Code in the case.

The effective date is set by section 4 of HB 490.

## § 2152.201 Reimbursement of investigation, prosecution, and response costs concerning act of terrorism.

(A) In addition to any other dispositions authorized or required by this chapter, the juvenile court making disposition of a child adjudicated a delinquent child for committing a violation of section 2909.22, 2909.23, or 2909.24 of the Revised Code or a violation of section 2921.32 of the Revised Code when the offense or act committed by the person aided or to be aided as described in that section is an act of terrorism may order the child to pay to the state, municipal, or county law enforcement agencies that handled the investigation and prosecution all of the costs that the state, municipal corporation, or county reasonably incurred in the investigation and prosecution of the violation. The court shall hold a hearing to determine the amount of costs to be imposed under this section. The court may hold the hearing as part of the dispositional hearing for the child.

(B) If a child is adjudicated a delinquent child for committing a violation of section 2909.23 or 2909.24 of the Revised Code and if any political subdivision incurred any response costs as a result of, or in making any response to, the threat of the specified offense involved in the violation of section 2909.23 of the Revised Code or the actual specified offense involved in the violation of section 2909.24 of the Revised Code, in addition to any other dispositions authorized or required by this chapter, the juvenile court making disposition of the child for the violation may order the child to reimburse the involved political subdivision for the response costs it so incurred.

(C) As used in this section, "response costs" and "act of terrorism" have the same meanings as in section 2909.21 of the Revised Code.

**HISTORY: 149 v S 184. Eff 5-15-2002.**

### § 2152.202 Reimbursement of costs of drug tests confirming that substance contained controlled substance.

(A) In addition to the dispositions authorized or required under section 2152.20 of the Revised Code and to any costs otherwise authorized or required under any provision of law, the juvenile court making disposition of a child adjudicated a delinquent child for committing an act that would be a drug abuse offense if committed by an adult may order the child to pay to the state, municipal, or county law enforcement agencies that handled the investigation and prosecution all of the costs that the state, municipal corporation, or county reasonably incurred in having tests performed under section 2925.51 of the Revised Code or in any other manner on any substance that was the basis of, or involved in, the delinquent act to determine whether the substance contained any amount of a controlled substance if the results of the tests indicate that the substance tested contained any controlled substance. No court shall order a delinquent child under this section to pay the costs of tests performed on a substance if the results of the tests do not indicate that the substance tested contained any controlled substance.

The court shall hold a hearing to determine the amount of costs to be imposed under this section. The court may hold the hearing as part of the dispositional hearing for the child.

(B) As used in this section, "controlled substance" has the same meaning as in section 3719.01 of the Revised Code.

**HISTORY: 151 v H 163, § 1, eff. 10-12-06.**

### § 2152.21 Disposition of juvenile traffic offender.

(A) Unless division (C) of this section applies, if a child is adjudicated a juvenile traffic offender, the court may make any of the following orders of disposition:

(1) Impose costs and one or more financial sanctions in accordance with section 2152.20 of the Revised Code;

(2) Suspend the child's driver's license, probationary driver's license, or temporary instruction permit for a definite period not exceeding two years or suspend the registration of all motor vehicles registered in the name of the child for a definite period not exceeding two years. A child whose license or permit is so suspended is ineligible for issuance of a license or permit during the period of suspension. At the end of the period of suspension, the child shall not be reissued a license or permit until the child has paid any applicable reinstatement fee and complied with all requirements governing license reinstatement.

(3) Place the child on community control;

(4) If the child is adjudicated a juvenile traffic offender for an act other than an act that would be a minor misdemeanor if committed by an adult and other than an act that could be disposed of by the juvenile traffic violations bureau serving the court under Traffic Rule 13.1 if the court has established a juvenile traffic violations bureau, require the child to make restitution pursuant to division (A)(3) of section 2152.20 of the Revised Code;

(5)(a) If the child is adjudicated a juvenile traffic offender for committing a violation of division (A) of section 4511.19 of the Revised Code or of a municipal ordinance that is substantially equivalent to that division, commit the child, for not longer than five days, to either of the following:

(i) The temporary custody of a detention facility or district detention facility established under section 2152.41 of the Revised Code;

(ii) The temporary custody of any school, camp, institution, or other facility for children operated in whole or in part for the care of juvenile traffic offenders of that nature by the county, by a district organized under section 2151.65 or 2152.41 of the Revised Code, or by a private agency or organization within the state that is authorized and qualified to provide the care, treatment, or placement required.

(b) If an order of disposition committing a child to the temporary custody of a home, school, camp, institution, or other facility of that nature is made under division (A)(5)(a) of this section, the length of the commitment shall not be reduced or diminished as a credit for any time that the child was held in a place of detention or shelter care, or otherwise was detained, prior to entry of the order of disposition.

(6) If, after making a disposition under divisions (A)(1) to (5) of this section, the court finds upon further hearing that the child has failed to comply with the orders of the court and the child's operation of a motor vehicle constitutes the child a danger to the child and to others, the court may make any disposition authorized by divisions (A)(1), (3), (4), and (7) of section 2152.19 of the Revised Code, except that the child may not be committed to or placed in a secure correctional facility unless authorized by division (A) (5) of this section, and commitment to or placement in a detention facility may not exceed twenty-four hours.

(B) If a child is adjudicated a juvenile traffic offender for violating division (A) or (B) of section 4511.19 of the Revised Code, in addition to any order of disposition made under division (A) of this section, the court shall impose a class six suspension of the temporary instruction permit, probationary driver's license, or driver's license issued to the child from the range specified in Division (A)(6) of section 4510.02 of the revised code. The court, in its discretion, may terminate the suspension if, the child attends and satisfactorily completes a drug abuse or alcohol abuse education, intervention, or treatment program specified by the court. During the time the child is attending a program as described in this division, the court shall retain the child's temporary instruction permit, probationary driver's license, or driver's license issued, and the court shall return the permit or license if it terminated the suspension as descried in this division.

(C) If a child is adjudicated a juvenile traffic offender for violating division (B)(1) of section 4513.263 [4513.26.3] of the Revised Code, the court shall impose the appropriate fine set forth in division (G) of that section. If a child is adjudicated a juvenile traffic offender for violating division (B)(3) of section 4513.263 [4513.26.3] of the Revised Code and if the child is sixteen years of age or older, the court shall impose the fine set forth in division (G)(2) of that section. If a child is adjudicated a juvenile traffic offender for violating division (B)(3) of section 4513.263 [4513.26.3] of the Revised Code and if the child is under sixteen years of age, the court shall not impose a fine but may place the child on probation or community control.

(D) A juvenile traffic offender is subject to sections 4509.01 to 4509.78 of the Revised Code.

**HISTORY: RC § 2151.35.6, 133 v H 320 (Eff 11-19-69); 133 v H 931 (Eff 8-27-70); 137 v H 1 (Eff 8-26-77); 137 v H 222 (Eff 10-4-77); 141 v S 54 (Eff 5-6-86); 141 v H 428 (Eff 12-23-86); 142 v H 643 (Eff 3-17-89); 143 v H 330 (Eff 6-30-89); 143 v H 381 (Eff 7-1-89); 143 v S 131 (Eff 7-25-90); 144 v H 118 (Eff 6-1-92); 144 v H 154 (Eff 7-31-92); 144 v S 98 (Eff 11-12-92); 146 v H 1 (Eff 1-1-96); 146 v H 265 (Eff 3-3-97); 147 v S 35 (Eff 1-1-99); 147 v H 2 (Eff 1-1-99); 148 v S 181 (Eff 9-4-2000); RC § 2152.21, 148 v S 179, § 3 (Eff 1-1-2002); 149 v H 400, § 1. Eff 4-3-2003; 149 v S 123, § 1, eff. 1-1-04; 150 v H 52, § 1, eff. 6-1-04.**

See provisions, § 5 of S.B. 123 (149 v —), following RC § 2152.19.

## § 2152.22 Court control of child following commitment to department; judicial release.

(A) When a child is committed to the legal custody of the department of youth services under this chapter, the juvenile court relinquishes control with respect to the child so committed, except as provided in divisions (B), (C), (D), and (H) of this section or in sections 2152.82 to 2152.86 of the Revised Code. Subject to divisions (B), (C), and (D) of this section, sections 2151.353 and 2151.412 to 2151.421 of the Revised Code, sections 2152.82 to 2152.86 of the Revised Code, and any other provision of law that specifies a different duration for a dispositional order, all other dispositional orders made by the court under this chapter shall be temporary and shall continue for a period that is designated by the court in its order, until terminated or modified by the court or until the child attains twenty-one years of age.

The department shall not release the child from a department facility and as a result shall not discharge the child or order the child's release on supervised release prior to the expiration of the minimum period specified by the court in division (A)(1) of section 2152.16 of the Revised Code and any term of commitment imposed under section 2152.17 of the Revised Code or prior to the child's attainment of twenty-one years of age, except upon the order of a court pursuant to division (B), (C), or (D) of this section or in accordance with section 5139.54 of the Revised Code.

(B)(1) The court that commits a delinquent child to the department of youth services may grant judicial release of the child to court supervision under this division during the first half of the prescribed minimum term for which the child was committed to the department or, if the child was committed to the department until the child attains twenty-one years of age, during the first half of the prescribed period of commitment that begins on the first day of commitment and ends on the child's twenty-first birthday, provided any commitment imposed under division (A), (B), (C), or (D) of section 2152.17 of the Revised Code has ended.

(2) If the department desires to release a child during a period specified in division (B)(1) of this section, it shall request the court that committed the child to grant a judicial release of the child to court supervision under this division. During whichever of those periods is applicable, the child or the parents of the child also may request that court to grant a judicial release of the child to court supervision. Upon receipt of a request for a judicial release to court supervision under this division from the department, the child, or the child's parent, or upon its own motion, the court that committed the child shall do one of the following: approve the release by journal entry; schedule within thirty days after the request is received a time for a hearing on whether the child is to be released; or reject the request by journal entry without conducting a hearing.

If the court rejects an initial request for a release under this division by the child or the child's parent, the child or the child's parent may make one additional request for a judicial release to court supervision within the applicable period. The additional request may be made no earlier than thirty days after the filing of the prior request for a judicial release to court supervision. Upon the filing of a second request for a judicial release to court supervision, the court shall either approve or disapprove the release by journal entry or schedule within thirty days after the request is received a time for a hearing on whether the child is to be released.

(3) If a court schedules a hearing under division (B)(2) of this section, it may order the department to deliver the child to the court on the date set for the hearing and may order the department to present to the court a report on the child's progress in the institution to which the child was committed and recommendations for conditions of supervision of the child by the court after release. The court may conduct the hearing without the child being present. The court shall determine at the hearing whether the child should be granted a judicial release to court supervision.

If the court approves the release under this division, it shall order its staff to prepare a written treatment and rehabilitation plan for the child that may include any conditions of the child's release that were recommended by the department and approved by the court. The committing court shall send the juvenile court of the county in which the child is placed a copy of the recommended plan. The court of the county in which the child is placed may adopt the recommended conditions set by the committing court as an order of the court and may add any additional consistent conditions it considers appropriate. If a child is granted a judicial release to court supervision, the release discharges the child from the custody of the department of youth services.

(C)(1) The court that commits a delinquent child to the department of youth services may grant judicial release of the child to department of youth services supervision under this division during the second half of the prescribed minimum term for which the child was committed to the department or, if the child was committed to the department until the child attains twenty-one years of age, during the second half of the prescribed period of commitment that begins on the first day of commitment and ends on the child's twenty-first birthday, provided any commitment imposed under division (A), (B), (C), or (D) of section 2152.17 of the Revised Code has ended.

(2) If the department desires to release a child during a period specified in division (C)(1) of this section, it shall

request the court that committed the child to grant a judicial release to department of youth services supervision. During whichever of those periods is applicable, the child or the child's parent also may request the court that committed the child to grant a judicial release to department of youth services supervision. Upon receipt of a request for judicial release to department of youth services supervision, the child, or the child's parent, or upon its own motion at any time during that period, the court shall do one of the following: approve the release by journal entry; schedule a time within thirty days after receipt of the request for a hearing on whether the child is to be released; or reject the request by journal entry without conducting a hearing.

If the court rejects an initial request for release under this division by the child or the child's parent, the child or the child's parent may make one or more subsequent requests for a release within the applicable period, but may make no more than one request during each period of ninety days that the child is in a secure department facility after the filing of a prior request for early release. Upon the filing of a request for release under this division subsequent to an initial request, the court shall either approve or disapprove the release by journal entry or schedule a time within thirty days after receipt of the request for a hearing on whether the child is to be released.

(3) If a court schedules a hearing under division (C)(2) of this section, it may order the department to deliver the child to the court on the date set for the hearing and shall order the department to present to the court at that time a treatment plan for the child's post-institutional care. The court may conduct the hearing without the child being present. The court shall determine at the hearing whether the child should be granted a judicial release to department of youth services supervision.

If the court approves the judicial release to department of youth services supervision, the department shall prepare a written treatment and rehabilitation plan for the child pursuant to division (F) of this section that shall include the conditions of the child's release. It shall send the committing court and the juvenile court of the county in which the child is placed a copy of the plan. The court of the county in which the child is placed may adopt the conditions set by the department as an order of the court and may add any additional consistent conditions it considers appropriate, provided that the court may not add any condition that decreases the level or degree of supervision specified by the department in its plan, that substantially increases the financial burden of supervision that will be experienced by the department, or that alters the placement specified by the department in its plan. If the court of the county in which the child is placed adds to the department's plan any additional conditions, it shall enter those additional conditions in its journal and shall send to the department a copy of the journal entry of the additional conditions.

If the court approves the judicial release to department of youth services supervision, the actual date on which the department shall release the child is contingent upon the department finding a suitable placement for the child. If the child is to be returned to the child's home, the department shall return the child on the date that the court schedules for the child's release or shall bear the expense of any additional time that the child remains in a department facility. If the child is unable to return to the child's home, the department shall exercise reasonable diligence in finding a suitable placement for the child, and the child shall remain in a department facility while the department finds the suitable placement.

(D)(1) Subject to division (D)(3) of this section, the court that commits a delinquent child to the department of youth services may grant judicial release of the child under this division at any time after the expiration of one of the following periods of time:

(a) Except as otherwise provided in division (D)(1)(b) of this section, if the child was committed to the department for a prescribed minimum period and a maximum period not to exceed the child's attainment of twenty-one years, the court may grant judicial release of the child at any time after the expiration of the prescribed minimum term for which the child was committed to the department.

(b) If the child was committed to the department for both one or more definite periods under division (A), (B), (C), or (D) of section 2152.17 of the Revised Code and a period of the type described in division (D)(1)(a) of this section, all of the prescribed minimum periods of commitment imposed under division (A), (B), (C), or (D) of section 2152.17 of the Revised Code and the prescribed period of commitment of the type described in division (D)(1)(a) of this section shall be aggregated for purposes of this division, and the court may grant judicial release of the child at any time after the expiration of one year after the child begins serving the aggregate period of commitment.

(2) If a court grants a judicial release of a child under division (D)(1) of this section, the release shall be a judicial release to department of youth services supervision, if the release is granted during a period described in division (C)(1) of this section, and the second and third paragraphs of division (C)(3) of this section apply regarding the release. In all other cases, the release shall be a judicial release to court supervision, and the second paragraph of division (B)(3) of this section applies regarding the release.

(3) A court at the time of making the disposition of a child shall provide notice in the order of disposition that the judge is retaining jurisdiction over the child for the purpose of a possible grant of judicial release of the child under division (D)(1) of this section. The failure of a court to provide this notice does not affect the authority of the court to grant a judicial release under that division and does not constitute grounds for setting aside the child's delinquent child adjudication or disposition or for granting any post-adjudication relief to the child.

(4) The department of youth services, a child committed to the department, or the parents of the child, during a period specified in division (D)(1) of this section, may request the court that committed the child to grant a judicial release of the child under that division. Upon receipt of a request for judicial release of a child under this division from the department, the child, or the child's parent, or upon its own motion, the court that committed the child shall do one of the following:

(a) Approve the request by journal entry;

(b) Schedule within thirty days after the request is received a time for a hearing on whether the child is to be released;

(c) Reject the request by journal entry without conducting a hearing.

If the court rejects an initial request for a release under this division by the child or the child's parent, division (C)(2) of this section applies regarding the making of additional requests.

If the court schedules a hearing under this division to consider the judicial release, the first paragraph of division (B)(3) of this section applies regarding the hearing.

(E) If a child is released under division (B), (C), or (D) of this section and the court of the county in which the child is placed has reason to believe that the child's deportment is not in accordance with the conditions of the child's judicial release, the court of the county in which the child is placed shall schedule a time for a hearing to determine whether the child violated any of the post-release conditions, and, if the child was released under division (C) of this section or under division (D) of this section under department supervision, divisions (A) to (E) of section 5139.52 of the Revised Code apply regarding the child.

If that court determines at the hearing that the child violated any of the post-release conditions, the court, if it determines that the violation was a serious violation, may order the child to be returned to the department for institutionalization, consistent with the original order of commitment of the child, or in any case may make any other disposition of the child authorized by law that the court considers proper. If the court of the county in which the child is placed orders the child to be returned to a department of youth services institution, the time during which the child was held in a secure department facility prior to the child's judicial release shall be considered as time served in fulfilling the prescribed period of institutionalization that is applicable to the child under the child's original order of commitment. If the court orders the child returned to a department institution, the child shall remain in institutional care for a minimum of three months or until the child successfully completes a revocation program of a duration of not less than thirty days operated either by the department or by an entity with which the department has contracted to provide a revocation program.

(F) The department of youth services, prior to the release of a child pursuant to division (C) of this section or pursuant to division (D) of this section on department supervision, shall do all of the following:

(1) After reviewing the child's rehabilitative progress history and medical and educational records, prepare a written treatment and rehabilitation plan for the child that includes conditions of the release;

(2) Completely discuss the conditions of the plan prepared pursuant to division (F)(1) of this section and the possible penalties for violation of the plan with the child and the child's parents, guardian, or legal custodian;

(3) Have the plan prepared pursuant to division (F)(1) of this section signed by the child, the child's parents, legal guardian, or custodian, and any authority or person that is to supervise, control, and provide supportive assistance to the child at the time of the child's release pursuant to division (C) or (D) of this section;

(4) Prior to the child's release, file a copy of the treatment plan prepared pursuant to division (F)(1) of this section with the committing court and the juvenile court of the county in which the child is to be placed.

(G) The department of youth services shall file a written progress report with the committing court regarding each child released pursuant to division (C) of this section or released pursuant to division (D) of this section on judicial release to department supervision at least once every thirty days unless specifically directed otherwise by the court. The report shall indicate the treatment and rehabilitative progress of the child and the child's family, if applicable, and shall include any suggestions for altering the program, custody, living arrangements, or treatment. The department shall retain legal custody of a child so released until it discharges the child or until the custody is terminated as otherwise provided by law.

(H) When a child is committed to the legal custody of the department of youth services, the court retains jurisdiction to perform the functions specified in section 5139.51 of the Revised Code with respect to the granting of supervised release by the release authority and to perform the functions specified in section 5139.52 of the Revised Code with respect to violations of the conditions of supervised release granted by the release authority and to the revocation of supervised release granted by the release authority.

**HISTORY: 148 v S 179, § 3 (Eff 1-1-2002); 149 v S 3 (Eff 1-1-2002); 149 v H 393. Eff 7-5-2002; 152 v S 10, § 1, eff. 1-1-08; 2011 HB 86, § 1, eff. Sept. 30, 2011.**

The effective date is set by § 3 of 152 v S 10.

## § 2152.26 Place of detention.

(A) Except as provided in divisions (B) and (F) of this section, a child alleged to be or adjudicated a delinquent child or a juvenile traffic offender may be held only in the following places:

(1) A certified foster home or a home approved by the court;

(2) A facility operated by a certified child welfare agency;

(3) Any other suitable place designated by the court.

(B) In addition to the places listed in division (A) of this section, a child alleged to be or adjudicated a delinquent child may be held in a detention facility for delinquent children that is under the direction or supervision of the court or other public authority or of a private agency and approved by the court and a child adjudicated a delinquent child may be held in accordance with division (F)(2) of this section in a facility of a type specified in that division. Division (B) of this section does not apply to a child alleged to be or adjudicated a delinquent child for chronic truancy, unless the child violated a lawful court order made pursuant to division (A)(6) of section 2152.19 of the Revised Code. Division (B) of this section also does not apply to a child alleged to be or adjudicated a delinquent child for being an habitual truant who previously has been adjudicated an unruly child for being an habitual truant, unless the child violated a lawful court order made pursuant to division (C)(1)(e) of section 2151.354 of the Revised Code.

(C)(1) Except as provided under division (C)(1) of section 2151.311 of the Revised Code or division (A)(5) of section 2152.21 of the Revised Code, a child alleged to be or adjudicated a juvenile traffic offender may not be held in any of the following facilities:

(a) A state correctional institution, county, multicounty, or municipal jail or workhouse, or other place in which an adult convicted of crime, under arrest, or charged with a crime is held.

(b) A secure correctional facility.

(2) Except as provided under this section, sections 2151.56 to 2151.59, and divisions (A)(5) and (6) of section 2152.21 of the Revised Code, a child alleged to be or adjudicated a juvenile traffic offender may not be held for more than twenty-four hours in a detention facility.

(D) Except as provided in division (F) of this section or in division (C) of section 2151.311, in division (C)(2) of section 5139.06 and section 5120.162, or in division (B) of section 5120.16 of the Revised Code, a child who is alleged to be or is adjudicated a delinquent child may not be held in a state correctional institution, county, multicounty, or municipal jail or workhouse, or other place where an adult convicted of crime, under arrest, or charged with crime is held.

(E) Unless the detention is pursuant to division (F) of this section or division (C) of section 2151.311, division (C)(2) of section 5139.06 and section 5120.162, or division (B) of section 5120.16 of the Revised Code, the official in charge of the institution, jail, workhouse, or other facility shall inform the court immediately when a child, who is or appears to be under the age of eighteen years, is received at the facility, and shall deliver the child to the court upon request or transfer the child to a detention facility designated by the court.

(F)(1) If a case is transferred to another court for criminal prosecution pursuant to section 2152.12 of the Revised Code, the child may be transferred for detention pending the criminal prosecution in a jail or other facility in accordance with the law governing the detention of persons charged with crime. Any child so held shall be confined in a manner that keeps the child beyond the range of touch of all adult detainees. The child shall be supervised at all times during the detention.

(2) If a person is adjudicated a delinquent child or juvenile traffic offender and the court makes a disposition of the person under this chapter, at any time after the person attains eighteen years of age, the person may be held under that disposition in places other than those specified in division (A) of this section, including, but not limited to, a county, multicounty, or municipal jail or workhouse, or other place where an adult convicted of crime, under arrest, or charged with crime is held.

(3)(a) A person alleged to be a delinquent child may be held in places other than those specified in division (A) of this section, including, but not limited to, a county, multicounty, or municipal jail, if the delinquent act that the child allegedly committed would be a felony if committed by an adult, and if either of the following applies:

(i) The person attains eighteen years of age before the person is arrested or apprehended for that act.

(ii) The person is arrested or apprehended for that act before the person attains eighteen years of age, but the person attains eighteen years of age before the court orders a disposition in the case.

(b) If, pursuant to division (F)(3)(a) of this section, a person is held in a place other than a place specified in division (A) of this section, the person has the same rights to bail as an adult charged with the same offense who is confined in a jail pending trial.

**HISTORY: RC § 2151.31.2, 133 v H 320 (Eff 11-19-69); 136 v H 85 (Eff 11-28-75); 139 v H 440 (Eff 11-23-81); 143 v H 166 (Eff 2-14-90); 144 v S 331 (Eff 11-13-92); 145 v H 152 (Eff 7-1-93); 145 v H 571 (Eff 10-6-94); 146 v H 265 (Eff 3-3-97); 146 v H 124 (Eff 3-31-97); 147 v H 1 (Eff 7-1-98); 148 v S 181 (Eff 9-4-2000); 148 v H 448 (Eff 10-5-2000); 148 v H 332 (Eff 1-1-2001); RC § 2152.26, 148 v S 179, § 3 (Eff 1-1-2002); 149 v H 400. Eff 4-3-2003; 2011 SB 122, § 1, eff. June 30, 2011.**

Acts 2011, SB 122, § 4 provides: "This act is hereby declared to be an emergency measure necessary for the immediate preservation of the public peace, health, and safety. The reason for such necessity is that Ohio is one of only five states that have not yet enacted the Interstate Compact for Juveniles, which in most states has replaced the Interstate Compact on Juveniles. The rule that allows Ohio to cooperate with the member states of the new compact in the supervision of delinquent youth and the return of escapees, absconders, and runaways will expire on June 30, 2011. It is imperative that this act take effect by that date. Therefore, this act shall go into immediate effect."

## § 2152.41 County or district detention facility; temporary boarding in private homes.

(A) Upon the recommendation of the judge, the board of county commissioners shall provide, by purchase, lease, construction, or otherwise, a detention facility that shall be within a convenient distance of the juvenile court. The facility shall not be used for the confinement of adults charged with criminal offenses. The facility may be used to detain alleged delinquent children until final disposition for evaluation pursuant to section 2152.04 of the Revised Code, to confine children who are adjudicated delinquent children and placed in the facility pursuant to division (A)(3) of section 2152.19 of the Revised Code, and to confine children who are adjudicated juvenile traffic offenders and committed to the facility under division (A)(5) or (6) of section 2152.21 of the Revised Code.

(B) Upon the joint recommendation of the juvenile judges of two or more neighboring counties, the boards of county commissioners of the counties shall form themselves into a joint board and proceed to organize a district for the establishment and support of a detention facility for the use of the juvenile courts of those counties, in which alleged delinquent children may be detained as provided in division (A) of this section, by using a site or buildings already established in one of the counties or by providing for the purchase of a site and the erection of the necessary buildings on the site.

A child who is adjudicated to be a juvenile traffic offender for having committed a violation of division (A) of section 4511.19 of the Revised Code or of a municipal ordinance that is substantially comparable to that division may be confined in a detention facility or district detention facility pursuant to division (A)(5) of section 2152.21 of the Revised Code, provided the child is kept separate and apart from alleged delinquent children.

Except as otherwise provided by law, district detention facilities shall be established, operated, maintained, and managed in the same manner so far as applicable as county detention facilities.

Members of the board of county commissioners who meet by appointment to consider the organization of a district detention home, upon presentation of properly certified accounts, shall be paid their necessary expenses upon a warrant drawn by the county auditor of their county.

The county auditor of the county having the greatest population or, with the unanimous concurrence of the county auditors of the counties composing a district, the auditor of the county in which the detention facility is located shall be the fiscal officer of a detention facility district. The county auditors of the several counties composing a detention facility district shall meet at the district detention facility, not less than once in six months, to review accounts and to transact any other duties in connection with the institution that pertain to the business of their office.

(C) In any county in which there is no detention facility or that is not served by a district detention facility, the juvenile court may enter into a contract, subject to the approval of the board of county commissioners, with another juvenile court, another county's detention facility, or a joint county detention facility. Alternately, the board of county commissioners shall provide funds for the boarding of children, who would be eligible for detention under division (A) of this section, temporarily in private homes or in certified foster homes approved by the court for a period not exceeding sixty days or until final disposition of their cases, whichever comes first. The court also may arrange with any public children services agency or private child placing agency to receive, or private noncustodial agency for temporary care of, children within the jurisdiction of the court.

If the court arranges for the board of children temporarily detained in certified foster homes or through any private child placing agency, the county shall pay a reasonable sum to be fixed by the court for the board of those children. In order to have certified foster homes available for service, an agreed monthly subsidy may be paid and a fixed rate per day for care of children actually residing in the certified foster home.

(D) The board of county commissioners of any county within a detention facility district, upon the recommendation of the juvenile court of that county, may withdraw from the district and sell or lease its right, title, and interest in the site, buildings, furniture, and equipment of the facility to any counties in the district, at any price and upon any such terms that are agreed upon among the boards of county commissioners of the counties concerned. Section 307.10 of the Revised Code does not apply to this division. The net proceeds of any sale or lease under this division shall be paid into the treasury of the withdrawing county.

The members of the board of trustees of a district detention facility who are residents of a county withdrawing from the district are deemed to have resigned their positions upon the completion of the withdrawal procedure provided by this division. The vacancies then created shall be filled as provided in this section.

(E) The children to be admitted for care in a county or district detention facility established under this section, the period during which they shall be cared for in the facility, and the removal and transfer of children from the facility shall be determined by the juvenile court that ordered the child's detention.

**HISTORY: GC § 1639-22; 117 v 520; 121 v 557; Bureau of Code Revision, RC § 2151.34, 10-1-53; 128 v 1211 (Eff 11-2-59); 133 v S 49 (Eff 8-13-69); 133 v H 320 (Eff 11-19-69); 133 v H 931 (Eff 8-27-70); 136 v H 85 (Eff 11-28-75); 136 v H 1196 (Eff 8-9-76); 139 v H 440 (Eff 11-23-81); 141 v H 428 (Eff 12-23-86); 142 v S 89 (Eff 1-1-89); 143 v H 166 (Eff 2-14-90); 143 v S 131 (Eff 7-25-90); 143 v H 837 (Eff 7-25-90); 145 v H 152 (Eff 7-1-93); 146 v H 265 (Eff 3-3-97); 148 v H 448 (Eff 10-5-2000); 148 v H 332 (Eff 1-1-2001); RC § 2152.41, 148 v S 179, § 3 (Eff 1-1-2002); 149 v H 400. Eff 4-3-2003.**

## § 2152.42 Superintendent of facility; employees; educational and recreational programs; medical and mental health services.

(A) Any detention facility established under section 2152.41 of the Revised Code shall be under the direction of a superintendent. The superintendent shall be appointed by, and under the direction of, the judge or judges or, for a district facility, the board of trustees of the facility. The superintendent serves at the pleasure of the juvenile court or, in a district detention facility, at the pleasure of the board of trustees.

Before commencing work as superintendent, the person appointed shall obtain a bond, with sufficient surety, conditioned upon the full and faithful accounting of the funds and properties under the superintendent's control.

The superintendent, under the supervision and subject to the rules and regulations of the board, shall control, manage, operate, and have general charge of the facility and shall have the custody of its property, files, and records.

(B) For a county facility, the superintendent shall appoint all employees of the facility, who shall be in the unclassified civil service. The salaries shall be paid as provided by section 2151.13 of the Revised Code for other employees of the court, and the necessary expenses incurred in maintaining the facility shall be paid by the county.

For a district facility, the superintendent shall appoint other employees of the facility and fix their compensation, subject to approval of the board of trustees. Employees of a district facility, except for the superintendent, shall be in the classified civil service.

(C) During the school year, when possible, a comparable educational program with competent and trained staff shall be provided for children of school age who are in the facility. A sufficient number of trained recreational personnel shall be included among the staff. Medical and mental health services shall be made available.

**HISTORY: 148 v S 179, § 3. Eff 1-1-2002.**

The effective date is set by section 5 of SB 179.

## § 2152.43 Application to department for assistance; funding of facility through taxes, gifts or other means.

(A) A board of county commissioners that provides a detention facility and the board of trustees of a district detention facility may apply to the department of youth services under section 5139.281 [5139.28.1] of the Revised Code for assistance in defraying the cost of operating and maintaining the facility. The application shall be made on forms prescribed and furnished by the department.

The board of county commissioners of each county that participates in a district detention facility may apply to the department of youth services for assistance in defraying the county's share of the cost of acquisition or construction of the facility, as provided in section 5139.271 [5139.27.1] of the Revised Code. Application shall be made in accordance with rules adopted by the department. No county shall be reimbursed for expenses incurred in the acquisition or construction of a district detention facility that serves a district having a population of less than one hundred thousand.

(B)(1) The joint boards of county commissioners of district detention facilities shall defray all necessary expenses of the facility not paid from funds made available under section 5139.281 [5139.28.1] of the Revised Code, through annual assessments of taxes, through gifts, or through other means.

If any county withdraws from a district under division (D) of section 2152.41 of the Revised Code, it shall continue to have levied against its tax duplicate any tax levied by the district during the period in which the county was a member of the district for current operating expenses, permanent improvements, or the retirement of bonded indebtedness. The levy shall continue to be a levy against the tax duplicate of the county until the time that it expires or is renewed.

(2) The current expenses of maintaining the facility not paid from funds made available under section 5139.281 [5139.28.1] of the Revised Code or division (C) of this section, and the cost of ordinary repairs to the facility, shall be paid by each county in accordance with one of the following methods as approved by the joint board of county commissioners:

(a) In proportion to the number of children from that county who are maintained in the facility during the year;

(b) By a levy submitted by the joint board of county commissioners under division (A) of section 5705.19 of the Revised Code and approved by the electors of the district;

(c) In proportion to the taxable property of each county, as shown by its tax duplicate;

(d) In any other method agreed upon by unanimous vote of the joint board of county commissioners.

(C) When any person donates or bequeaths any real or personal property to a county or district detention facility, the juvenile court or the trustees of the facility may accept and use the gift, consistent with the best interest of the institution and the conditions of the gift.

**HISTORY: RC § 2151.34.1, 128 v 1211 (Eff 11-2-59); 136 v H 1196 (Eff 8-9-76); 137 v S 221 (Eff 11-23-77); 139 v H 440 (Eff 11-23-81); RC § 2152.43, 148 v S 179, § 3. Eff 1-1-2002; 151 v H 66, § 101.01, eff. 9-29-05.**

The effective date is set by § 612.03 of 151 v H 66.
The effective date is set by section 5 of SB 179.

## § 2152.44 Trustees of district detention facility.

(A) As soon as practical after the organization of the joint board of county commissioners as provided by section 2152.41 of the Revised Code, the joint board shall appoint a board of not less than five trustees. The board shall hold office until the first annual meeting after the choice of an established site and buildings, or after the selection and purchase of a building site. At that time, the joint board of county commissioners shall appoint a board of not less than five trustees, one of whom shall hold office for a term of one year, one for a term of two years, one for a term of three years, half of the remaining number for a term of four years, and the remainder for a term of five years. Annually thereafter, the joint board of county commissioners shall appoint one or more trustees, each of whom shall hold office for a term of five years, to succeed the trustee or trustees whose term of office expires. A trustee may be appointed to successive terms. Any person appointed as a trustee shall be recommended and approved by the juvenile court judge or judges of the county of which the person resides.

At least one trustee shall reside in each county in the district. In districts composed of two counties, each county shall be entitled to not less than two trustees. In districts composed of more than four counties, the number of trustees shall be sufficiently increased, provided that there shall always be an uneven number of trustees on the board. The county in which a district detention facility is located shall have not less than two trustees, who, in the interim period between the regular meetings of the trustees, shall act as an executive committee in the discharge of all business pertaining to the facility.

The joint board of county commissioners may remove any trustee for good cause. The trustee appointed to fill any vacancy shall hold the office for the unexpired term of the predecessor trustee.

(B) The annual meeting of the board of trustees shall be held on the first Tuesday in May in each year.

A majority of the board constitutes a quorum. Other board meetings shall be held at least quarterly. The juvenile court judge of each county of the district, or the judge's designee, shall attend the meetings. The members of the board shall receive no compensation for their services, except their actual and necessary expenses. The treasurer shall pay the member's traveling expenses when properly certified.

(C) When the board of trustees does not choose an established institution in one of the counties of the district, it may select a suitable site for the erection of a district detention facility. The site must be easily accessible, conducive to health, economy in purchasing or in building, and the general interest of the facility and its residents, and be as near as practicable to the geographical center of the district.

In the interim between the selection and purchase of a site, and the erection and occupancy of the district detention facility, the joint board of county commissioners provided under section 2152.41 of the Revised Code may delegate to the board of trustees any powers and duties that, in its judgment, will be of general interest or aid to the institution. The joint board of county commissioners may appropriate a trustees' fund, to be expended by the trustees for contracts, purchases, or other necessary expenses of the facility. The trustees shall make a complete settlement with the joint board of county commissioners once each six months, or quarterly if required, and shall make to the board of county commissioners and to the juvenile court of each of the counties a full report of the condition of the facility and residents.

(D) The choice of an established site and buildings, or the purchase of a site, stock, implements, and general farm equipment, should there be a farm, the erection of buildings, and the completion and furnishing of the district detention facility for occupancy, shall be in the hands of the joint board of county commissioners organized under section 2152.41 of the Revised Code. The joint board of county commissioners may delegate all or a portion of these duties to the board of trustees, under any restrictions that the joint board of county commissioners imposes.

When an established site and buildings are used for a district detention facility, the joint board of county commissioners shall cause the value of that site and those buildings to be properly appraised. This appraisal value, or in case of the purchase of a site, the purchase price and the cost of all improvements thereto, shall be paid by the counties comprising the district, in proportion to the taxable property of each county, as shown by its tax duplicate.

(E) Once a district is established, the trustees shall operate, maintain, and manage the facility as provided in sections 2152.41 to 2152.43 of the Revised Code and, on and after the effective date of this amendment and notwithstanding any provision of the Revised Code to the contrary, may adopt bylaws regarding the daily operation, maintenance, and management of the facility. No bylaw adopted pursuant to this division may supersede any provision of the Revised Code.

**HISTORY: RC § 2151.34.3, 128 v 1211 (Eff 11-2-59); RC § 2152.44, 148 v S 179, § 3. Eff 1-1-2002; 151 v H 530, § 101.01, eff. 6-30-06.**

The effective date is set by § 812.03 of 151 v H 530.
The effective date is set by section 5 of SB 179.

## § 2152.51 Definitions; adoption of rules to expedite proceedings; representation of juvenile by attorney required at competency-related hearing.

(A) As used in sections 2152.51 to 2152.59 of the Revised Code:

(1) "Competent" and "competency" refer to a child's ability to understand the nature and objectives of a proceeding against the child and to assist in the child's defense. A child is incompetent if, due to mental illness, intellectual disability, or developmental disability, or otherwise due to a lack of mental capacity, the child is presently incapable of understanding the nature and objective of proceedings against the child or of assisting in the child's defense.

(2) "Delinquent child proceeding" means any proceeding under this chapter.

(3) "A person who is at least moderately intellectually disabled" means "a person who is at least moderately mentally retarded," as defined in section 5123.01 of the Revised Code.

(4) "Person with intellectual disability" has the same meaning as in section 2951.041 of the Revised Code.

(B) Each juvenile court shall adopt rules to expedite proceedings under sections 2152.51 to 2152.59 of the Revised Code. The rules shall include provisions for giving notice of any hearings held under those sections and for staying any proceedings on the underlying complaint pending the determinations under those sections.

(C) At a competency-related hearing held under section 2152.53 or 2152.58 of the Revised Code, the child shall be represented by an attorney. If the child is indigent and cannot obtain counsel, the court shall appoint an attorney under Chapter 120. of the Revised Code or the Rules of Juvenile Procedure.

**HISTORY: 2011 HB 86, § 1, eff. Sept. 30, 2011.**

## § 2152.52 Qualifications of evaluator for child competency determination.

(A)(1) In any proceeding under this chapter other than a proceeding alleging that a child is a juvenile traffic offender, any party or the court may move for a determination regarding the child's competency to participate in the proceeding.

(2) In any proceeding under this chapter other than a proceeding alleging that a child is a juvenile traffic offender, if the child who is the subject of the proceeding is fourteen years of age or older and if the child is not otherwise found to be mentally ill, intellectually disabled, or developmentally disabled, it is rebuttably presumed that the child does not have a lack of mental capacity. This presumption applies only in making a determination as to whether the child has a lack of mental capacity and shall not be used or applicable for any other purpose.

(B) The court may find a child incompetent to proceed without ordering an evaluation of the child's competency or holding a hearing to determine the child's competency if either of the following applies:

(1) The prosecuting attorney, the child's attorney, and at least one of the child's parents, guardians, or custodians agree to the determination.

(2) The court relies on a prior court determination that the child was incompetent and could not attain competency even if the child were to participate in competency attainment services.

**HISTORY: 2011 HB 86, § 1, eff. Sept. 30, 2011.**

## § 2152.53 Proceedings on motion to determine child's competency.

(A) Within fifteen business days after a motion is made under section 2152.52 of the Revised Code, the court shall do one of the following:

(1) Make a determination of incompetency under division (B) of section 2152.52 of the Revised Code;

(2) Determine, without holding a hearing, whether there is a reasonable basis to conduct a competency evaluation;

(3) Hold a hearing to determine whether there is a reasonable basis to conduct a competency evaluation.

(B) If the court holds a hearing, it shall make its determination within ten business days after the conclusion of the hearing. If the court determines that there is a reasonable basis for a competency evaluation or if the prosecuting attorney and the child's attorney agree to an evaluation, the court shall order a competency evaluation and appoint an evaluator.

**HISTORY: 2011 HB 86, § 1, eff. Sept. 30, 2011.**

## § 2152.54 Determination of child's competency to participate in proceeding.

(A) An evaluation of a child who does not appear to the court to be a person who is at least moderately intellectually disabled shall be made by an evaluator who is one of the following:

(1) A professional employed by a psychiatric facility or center certified by the department of mental health to provide forensic services and appointed by the director of the facility or center to conduct the evaluation;

(2) A psychiatrist or a licensed clinical psychologist who satisfies the criteria of division (I)(1) of section 5122.01 of the Revised Code and has specialized education, training, or experience in forensic evaluations of children or adolescents.

(B) An evaluation of a child who appears to the court to be a person who is at least moderately intellectually disabled shall be made by a psychiatrist or licensed clinical psychologist who satisfies the criteria of division (I)(1) of section 5122.01 of the Revised Code and has specialized education, training, or experience in forensic evaluations of children or adolescents who have intellectual disability.

(C) If an evaluation is conducted by an evaluator of the type described in division (A)(1) or (2) of this section and the evaluator concludes that the child is a person who is at least moderately intellectually disabled, the evaluator shall discontinue the evaluation and notify the court within one business day after reaching the conclusion. Within two business days after receiving notification, the court shall order the child to undergo an evaluation by an evaluator of the type described in division (B) of this section. Within two business days after the appointment of the new evaluator, the original evaluator shall deliver to the new evaluator all information relating to the child obtained during the original evaluation.

**HISTORY: 2011 HB 86, § 1, eff. Sept. 30, 2011.**

## § 2152.55 Performance of competency evaluation.

(A) If a court orders a child to receive an evaluation under section 2152.53 of the Revised Code, the child and the child's parents, guardians, or custodians shall be available at the times and places established by the evaluator who conducts the evaluation. The evaluation shall be performed in the least restrictive setting available that will both facilitate an evaluation and maintain the safety of the child and community. If the child has been released on temporary or interim orders and refuses or fails to submit to the evaluation, the court may amend the conditions of the orders in whatever manner necessary to facilitate an evaluation.

(B) The court shall provide in its evaluation order that the evaluator shall have access to all relevant private and public records related to the child, including competency evaluations and reports conducted in prior delinquent child proceedings. The court may include an order for all relevant private and public records related to the child in the journal entry ordering the evaluation.

(C) Within ten business days after the court appoints an evaluator, the prosecuting attorney shall deliver to the evaluator copies of relevant police reports and other background information that pertain to the child and that are in the prosecuting attorney's possession, except for any information that the prosecuting attorney determines would, if released, interfere with the effective prosecution of any person or create a substantial risk of harm to any person.

(D) Within ten business days after the court appoints an evaluator, the child's attorney shall deliver to the evaluator copies of relevant police reports and other background information that pertain to the child and that are in the attorney's possession and that is not protected by attorney-client privilege.

**HISTORY: 2011 HB 86, § 1, eff. Sept. 30, 2011.**

## § 2152.56 Written competency assessment report.

(A) Upon completing an evaluation ordered pursuant to section 2152.53 of the Revised Code, an evaluator shall submit to the court a written competency assessment report. The report shall include the evaluator's opinion as to whether the child, due to mental illness, intellectual disability, or developmental disability, or otherwise due to a lack of mental capacity, is presently incapable of understanding the nature and objective of the proceedings against the child or of assisting in the child's defense. The report shall not include any opinion as to the child's sanity at the time of the alleged offense, details of the alleged offense as reported by the child, or an opinion as to whether the child actually committed the offense or could have been culpable for committing the offense.

(B) A competency assessment report shall address the child's capacity to do all of the following:

(1) Comprehend and appreciate the charges or allegations against the child;

(2) Understand the adversarial nature of the proceedings, including the role of the judge, defense counsel, prosecuting attorney, guardian ad litem or court-appointed special assistant, and witnesses;

(3) Assist in the child's defense and communicate with counsel;

(4) Comprehend and appreciate the consequences that may be imposed or result from the proceedings.

(C) A competency assessment report shall include the evaluator's opinion regarding the extent to which the child's competency may be impaired by the child's failure to meet one or more of the criteria listed in division (B) of this section. If the evaluator concludes that the child's competency is impaired but that the child may be enabled to understand the nature and objectives of the proceeding against the child and to assist in the child's defense with reasonable accommodations, the report shall include recommendations for those reasonable accommodations that the court might make. If the evaluator concludes that the child's competency is so impaired that the child would not be able to understand the nature and objectives of the proceeding against the child and to assist in the child's defense, the report shall include an opinion as to the likelihood that the child could attain competency within the periods set forth in division (D)(2) of section 2152.59 of the Revised Code.

(D) If the evaluator concludes that the child could likely attain competency within the periods set forth in division (D)(2) of section 2152.59 of the Revised Code, the competency assessment report shall include both of the following:

(1) A recommendation as to the least restrictive setting for child competency attainment services that is consistent with the child's ability to attain competency and the safety of both the child and the community;

(2) A list of the providers of child competency attainment services known to the evaluator that are located most closely to the child's current residence.

(E) If the evaluator is unable, within the maximum allowable time for submission of a competency assessment report under division (A) of section 2152.57 of the Revised Code, to form an opinion regarding the extent to which the child's competency may be impaired by the child's failure to meet one or more of the criteria listed in division (B) of this section, the evaluator shall so state in the report. The evaluator shall also include recommendations for services to support the safety of the child or the community.

**HISTORY: 2011 HB 86, § 1, eff. Sept. 30, 2011.**

## § 2152.57 When independent competency report may be submitted into evidence; objection to court-ordered competency report and request for additional evaluation.

(A) An evaluator appointed by the court under section 2152.53 of the Revised Code shall submit a competency assessment report to the court as soon as possible but not more than forty-five calendar days after the order appointing the evaluator is issued. The court may grant one extension for a reasonable length of time if doing so would aid the evaluator in completing the evaluation.

(B) No competency assessment report obtained independently by the child may be admitted into evidence unless it is submitted to the court within the time allowed for submission of a report by a court-appointed evaluator under division (A) of this section and meets all the criteria that apply to a court-ordered report.

(C) The court shall provide a copy of each competency assessment report it receives to the prosecuting attorney, the child's attorney, and the child's parents, guardian, or custodian. Counsel shall not disseminate the report except as necessary to receive clarification of the contents of the report.

(D) The expenses of obtaining an evaluation ordered by the court may not be recovered from the child or the child's parents or guardians. However, expenses associated with missed appointments may be assessed to the child's parents or guardians.

(E)(1) Before a hearing is held under section 2152.58 of the Revised Code, any party may object to the contents of a competency assessment report and by motion request an additional evaluation. If the court determines that an additional evaluation is appropriate and grants the motion, the evaluator shall complete an additional evaluation as soon as possible but not more than forty-five calendar days after the order allowing the additional evaluation is issued. An additional evaluation shall meet all the criteria that apply to a court-ordered evaluation.

(2) An additional evaluation allowed under division (E)(1) of this section shall be made at the moving party's expense unless the child is indigent. If the child is indigent, the county shall pay the costs of the additional evaluation. However, the county shall not be required to pay costs exceeding that which the county would normally pay for a competency evaluation conducted by a provider with which the court or county has contracted to conduct competency evaluations.

**HISTORY: 2011 HB 86, § 1, eff. Sept. 30, 2011.**

## § 2152.58 Hearing to determine child's competency; admission of competency assessment reports.

(A) Not less than fifteen nor more than thirty business days after receiving an evaluation under division (A) of section 2152.57 of the Revised Code or not less than fifteen nor more than thirty business days after receiving an additional evaluation under division (E) of that section, the court shall hold a hearing to determine the child's competency to participate in the proceeding.

(B) At a hearing held under this section, a competency assessment report may be admitted into evidence by stipulation. If the court contacts the evaluator to obtain clarification of the report contents, the court shall promptly inform all parties and allow each party to participate in each contact.

(C) In determining the competency of the child to participate in the proceeding, the court shall consider the content of all competency assessment reports admitted as evidence. The court may consider additional evidence, including the court's own observations of the child's conduct and demeanor in the courtroom.

(D)(1) Except as otherwise provided in this division, the court shall make a written determination as to the child's competency or incompetency based on a preponderance of the evidence within fifteen business days after completion of the hearing. The court, by journal entry, may extend the period for making the determination for not more than fifteen additional days. If the court extends the period for making the determination, it shall make the written determination within the period as extended.

(2) The court shall not find a child incompetent to proceed solely because the child is receiving or has received treatment as a voluntary or involuntary mentally ill patient under Chapter 5122. of the Revised Code, is or has been institutionalized under Chapter 5123. of the Revised Code, or is receiving or has received psychotropic or other medication, even if the child might become incompetent to proceed without that medication.

**HISTORY: 2011 HB 86, § 1, eff. Sept. 30, 2011.**

## § 2152.59 Proceedings where child determined competent; disposition of child determined not competent; competency attainment services.

(A) If after a hearing held pursuant to section 2152.58 of the Revised Code the court determines that a child is competent, the court shall proceed with the delinquent child's proceeding as provided by law. No statement that a child makes during an evaluation or hearing conducted under sections 2152.51 through 2152.59 of the Revised Code shall be used against the child on the issue of responsibility or guilt in any child or adult proceeding.

(B) If after a hearing held pursuant to section 2152.58 of the Revised Code the court determines that the child is not competent and cannot attain competency within the period of time applicable under division (D)(2) of this section, the court shall dismiss the charges without prejudice, except that the court may delay dismissal for up to ninety calendar days and do either of the following:

(1) Refer the matter to a public children services agency and request that agency determine whether to file an action in accordance with section 2151.27 of the Revised Code alleging that the child is a dependent, neglected, or abused child;

(2) Assign court staff to refer the child or the child's family to the local family and children first council or an agency funded by the department of mental health or department of developmental disabilities or otherwise secure services to reduce the potential that the child would engage in behavior that could result in delinquent child or other criminal charges.

(C) If after a hearing held pursuant to section 2152.58 of the Revised Code the court determines that a child is not competent but could likely attain competency by participating in services specifically designed to help the child develop competency, the court may order the child to participate in services specifically designed to help the child develop competency at county expense. The court shall name a reliable provider to deliver the competency attainment services and shall order the child's parent, guardian, or custodian to contact that provider by a specified date to arrange for services.

(D) The competency attainment services provided to a child shall be based on a competency attainment plan described in division (E)(2) of this section and approved by the court. Services are subject to the following conditions and time periods measured from the date the court approves the plan:

(1) Services shall be provided in the least restrictive setting that is consistent with the child's ability to attain competency and the safety of both the child and the community. If the child has been released on temporary or interim orders and refuses or fails to cooperate with the service provider, the court may reassess the orders and amend them to require a more appropriate setting.

(2) No child shall be required to participate in competency attainment services for longer than is required for

the child to attain competency. The following maximum periods of participation apply:

(a) If a child is ordered to participate in competency attainment services that are provided outside of a residential setting, the child shall not participate in those services for a period exceeding three months if the child is charged with an act that would be a misdemeanor if committed by an adult, six months if the child is charged with an act that would be a felony of the third, fourth, or fifth degree if committed by an adult, or one year if the child is charged with an act that would be a felony of the first or second degree, aggravated murder or murder if committed by an adult.

(b) If a child is ordered to receive competency attainment services that are provided in a residential setting that is operated solely or in part for the purpose of providing competency attainment services, the child shall not participate in those services for a period exceeding forty-five calendar days if the child is charged with an act that would be a misdemeanor if committed by an adult, three months if the child is charged with an act that would be a felony of the third, fourth, or fifth degree if committed by an adult, six months if the child is charged with an act that would be a felony of the first or second degree if committed by an adult, or one year if the child is charged with an act that would be aggravated murder or murder if committed by an adult.

(c) If a child is ordered into a residential, detention, or other secured setting for reasons other than to participate in competency attainment services and is also ordered to participate in competency attainment services concurrently, the child shall participate in the competency attainment services for not longer than the relevant period set forth in division (D)(2)(a) of this section.

(d) If a child is ordered to participate in competency attainment services that require the child to live for some but not all of the duration of the services in a residential setting that is operated solely or in part for the purpose of providing competency attainment services, the child shall participate in the competency attainment services for not longer than the relevant period set forth in division (D)(2)(b) of this section. For the purpose of calculating a time period under division (D)(2)(d) of this section, two days of participation in a nonresidential setting shall equal one day of participation in a residential setting.

(3) A child who receives competency attainment services in a residential setting that is operated solely or partly for the purpose of providing competency attainment services is in detention for purposes of section 2921.34 and division (B) of section 2152.18 of the Revised Code during the time that the child resides in the residential setting.

(E)(1) Within ten business days after the court names the provider responsible for the child's competency attainment services under division (D) of this section, the court shall deliver to that provider a copy of each competency assessment report it has received for review. The provider shall return the copies of the reports to the court upon the termination of the services.

(2) Not later than thirty calendar days after the child contacts the competency attainment services provider under division (C) of this section, the provider shall submit to the court a plan for the child to attain competency. The court shall provide copies of the plan to the prosecuting attorney, the child's attorney, the child's guardian ad litem, if any, and the child's parents, guardian, or custodian.

(F) The provider that provides the child's competency attainment services pursuant to the competency attainment plan shall submit reports to the court on the following schedule:

(1) A report on the child's progress every thirty calendar days and on the termination of services;

(2) If the provider determines that the child is not cooperating to a degree that would allow the services to be effective to help the child attain competency, a report informing the court of the determination within three business days after making the determination;

(3) If the provider determines that the current setting is no longer the least restrictive setting that is consistent with the child's ability to attain competency and the safety of both the child and the community, a report informing the court of the determination within three business days after making the determination;

(4) If the provider determines that the child has achieved the goals of the plan and would be able to understand the nature and objectives of the proceeding against the child and to assist in the child's defense, with or without reasonable accommodations to meet the criteria set forth in division (B) of section 2152.56 of the Revised Code, a report informing the court of that determination within three business days after making the determination. If the provider believes that accommodations would be necessary or desirable, the report shall include recommendations for accommodations.

(5) If the provider determines that the child will not achieve the goals of the plan within the applicable period of time under division (D)(2) of this section, a report informing the court of the determination within three business days after making the determination. The report shall include recommendations for services for the child that would support the safety of the child or the community.

(G) The court shall provide copies of any report made under division (F) of this section to the prosecuting attorney, the child's attorney, and the child's guardian ad litem, if any. The court shall provide copies of any report made under division (F) of this section to the child's parents, guardian, or custodian unless the court finds that doing so is not in the best interest of the child.

(H)(1) Within fifteen business days after receiving a report under division (F) of this section, the court may hold a hearing to determine if a new order is necessary. To assist in making a determination under division (H) of this section, the court may order a new competency evaluation in accordance with section 2152.53 of the Revised Code. Until a new order is issued or the required period of participation expires, the child shall continue to participate in competency attainment services.

(2) If after a hearing held under division (H)(1) of this section the court determines that the child is not making progress toward competency or is so uncooperative that attainment services cannot be effective, the court may order a change in setting or services that would help the child attain competency within the relevant period of time under division (D)(2) of this section.

(3) If after a hearing held under division (H)(1) of this section the court determines that the child has not or will not attain competency within the relevant period of time under division (D)(2) of this section, the court shall dismiss the delinquency complaint without prejudice, except that the court may delay dismissal for up to ninety calendar days and do either of the following:

(a) Refer the matter to a public children services agency and request that agency determine whether to file an action in accordance with section 2151.27 of the

Revised Code alleging that the child is a dependent, neglected, or abused child;

(b) Assign court staff to refer the child or the child's family to the local family and children first council or an agency funded by the department of mental health or department of developmental disabilities or otherwise secure services to reduce the potential that the child would engage in behavior that could result in delinquency or other criminal charges.

(4) A dismissal under division (H)(3) of this section does not preclude a future delinquent child proceeding or criminal prosecution as provided under section 2151.23 of the Revised Code if the child eventually attains competency.

(5) If after a hearing held under division (H)(1) of this section the court determines that the child has attained competency, the court shall proceed with the delinquent child's proceeding in accordance with division (A) of this section.

(6) A dismissal under this section does not bar a civil action based on the acts or omissions that formed the basis of the complaint.

**HISTORY: 2011 HB 86, § 1, eff. Sept. 30, 2011.**

## § 2152.61 Orders controlling conduct of parent, guardian or other custodian.

(A) In any proceeding in which a child has been adjudicated a delinquent child or a juvenile traffic offender, on the application of a party or the court's own motion, the court may make an order restraining or otherwise controlling the conduct of any parent, guardian, or other custodian in the relationship of the individual to the child if the court finds that an order of that type necessary to do either of the following:

(1) Control any conduct or relationship that will be detrimental or harmful to the child;

(2) Control any conduct or relationship that will tend to defeat the execution of the order of disposition made or to be made.

(B) Due notice of the application or motion and the grounds for the application or motion under division (A) of this section, and an opportunity to be heard, shall be given to the person against whom the order under that division is directed. The order may include a requirement that the child's parent, guardian, or other custodian enter into a recognizance with sufficient surety, conditioned upon the faithful discharge of any conditions or control required by the court.

(C) A person's failure to comply with any order made by the court under this section is contempt of court under Chapter 2705. of the Revised Code.

**HISTORY: 148 v S 179, § 3. Eff 1-1-2002.**

The effective date is set by section 5 of SB 179.

## § 2152.67 Jury trial; procedure.

Any adult who is arrested or charged under any provision in this chapter and who is charged with a crime may demand a trial by jury, or the juvenile judge upon the judge's own motion may call a jury. A demand for a jury trial shall be made in writing in not less than three days before the date set for trial, or within three days after counsel has been retained, whichever is later. Sections 2945.17 and 2945.23 to 2945.36 of the Revised Code, relating to the drawing and impaneling of jurors in criminal cases in the court of common pleas, other than in capital cases, shall apply to a jury trial under this section. The compensation of jurors and costs of the clerk and sheriff shall be taxed and paid in the same manner as in criminal cases in the court of common pleas.

**HISTORY: GC § 1639-44; 117 v 520(534); Bureau of Code Revision, RC § 2151.47, 10-1-53; 132 v S 55 (Eff 10-24-67); 133 v H 1 (Eff 3-18-69); 148 v S 181 (Eff 9-4-2000); RC § 2152.67, 148 v S 179, § 3. Eff 1-1-2002.**

The effective date is set by section 5 of SB 179.

## § 2152.71 Records; weekly report of case summaries; annual summary and report.

(A)(1) The juvenile court shall maintain records of all official cases brought before it, including, but not limited to, an appearance docket, a journal, and, in cases pertaining to an alleged delinquent child, arrest and custody records, complaints, journal entries, and hearing summaries. The court shall maintain a separate docket for traffic cases and shall record all traffic cases on the separate docket instead of on the general appearance docket. The parents, guardian, or other custodian of any child affected, if they are living, or the nearest of kin of the child, if the parents are deceased, may inspect these records, either in person or by counsel, during the hours in which the court is open. Division (A)(1) of this section does not require the release or authorize the inspection of arrest or incident reports, law enforcement investigatory reports or records, or witness statements.

(2) The juvenile court shall send to the superintendent of the bureau of criminal identification and investigation, pursuant to section 109.57 of the Revised Code, a weekly report containing a summary of each case that has come before it and that involves the disposition of a child who is a delinquent child for committing an act that would be a felony or an offense of violence if committed by an adult.

(B) The clerk of the court shall maintain a statistical record that includes all of the following:

(1) The number of complaints that are filed with, or indictments or information made to, the court that allege that a child is a delinquent child, in relation to which the court determines under division (D) of section 2151.27 of the Revised Code that the victim of the alleged delinquent act was sixty-five years of age or older or permanently and totally disabled at the time of the alleged commission of the act;

(2) The number of complaints, indictments, or information described in division (B)(1) of this section that result in the child being adjudicated a delinquent child;

(3) The number of complaints, indictments, or information described in division (B)(2) of this section in which the act upon which the delinquent child adjudication is based caused property damage or would be a theft offense, as defined in division (K) of section 2913.01 of the Revised Code, if committed by an adult;

(4) The number of complaints, indictments, or information described in division (B)(3) of this section that result in the delinquent child being required as an order of disposition made under division (A) of section 2152.20 of the Revised Code to make restitution for all or part of the property damage caused by the child's delinquent act or for all or part of the value of the property that was the subject of the delinquent act that would be a theft offense if committed by an adult;

(5) The number of complaints, indictments, or information described in division (B)(2) of this section in which the act upon which the delinquent child adjudication is based would have been an offense of violence if committed by an adult;

(6) The number of complaints, indictments, or information described in division (B)(5) of this section that result in the delinquent child being committed as an order of disposition made under section 2152.16, divisions (A) and (B) of section 2152.17, or division (A)(2) of section 2152.19 of the Revised Code to any facility for delinquent children operated by the county, a district, or a private agency or organization or to the department of youth services;

(7) The number of complaints, indictments, or information described in division (B)(1) of this section that result in the case being transferred for criminal prosecution to an appropriate court having jurisdiction of the offense under section 2152.12 of the Revised Code.

(C) The clerk of the court shall compile an annual summary covering the preceding calendar year showing all of the information for that year contained in the statistical record maintained under division (B) of this section. The statistical record and the annual summary shall be public records open for inspection. Neither the statistical record nor the annual summary shall include the identity of any party to a case.

(D) Not later than June of each year, the court shall prepare an annual report covering the preceding calendar year showing the number and kinds of cases that have come before it, the disposition of the cases, and any other data pertaining to the work of the court that the juvenile judge directs. The court shall file copies of the report with the board of county commissioners. With the approval of the board, the court may print or cause to be printed copies of the report for distribution to persons and agencies interested in the court or community program for dependent, neglected, abused, or delinquent children and juvenile traffic offenders. The court shall include the number of copies ordered printed and the estimated cost of each printed copy on each copy of the report printed for distribution.

(E) If an officer is preparing pursuant to section 2947.06 or 2951.03 of the Revised Code or Criminal Rule 32.2 a presentence investigation report pertaining to a person, the court shall make available to the officer, for use in preparing the report, any records it possesses regarding any adjudications of that person as a delinquent child or regarding the dispositions made relative to those adjudications. The records to be made available pursuant to this division include, but are not limited to, any social history or report of a mental or physical examination regarding the person that was prepared pursuant to Juvenile Rule 32.

**HISTORY: GC § 1639-13; 117 v 520; 121 v 557; 123 v 367; Bureau of Code Revision, RC § 2151.18, 10-1-53; 127 v 547 (Eff 9-14-57); 136 v H 85 (Eff 11-28-75); 138 v H 394 (Eff 9-26-79); 139 v H 440 (Eff 11-23-81); 140 v S 5 (Eff 9-26-84); 143 v S 268 (Eff 6-28-90); 145 v H 152 (Eff 7-1-93); 146 v H 1 (Eff 1-1-96); 146 v H 124 (Eff 3-31-97); 147 v H 2 (Eff 1-1-99); 148 v H 3 (Eff 11-22-99); 148 v S 181 (Eff 9-4-2000); RC § 2152.71, 148 v S 179, § 3 (Eff 1-1-2002); 149 v H 247 (Eff 5-30-2002); 149 v H 393. Eff 7-5-2002.**

**Comment, Legislative Service Commission**

Section 2152.71 of the Revised Code is amended by this act [Sub. H.B. 247] and also by Sub. H.B. 393, both of the 124th General Assembly. Comparison of these amendments in pursuance of section 1.52 of the Revised Code discloses that they are not irreconcilable so that they are required by that section to be harmonized to give effect to each amendment.

## § 2152.72 Foster caregivers or prospective adoptive parents to receive information concerning certain delinquent children; psychological examination of child.

(A) This section applies only to a child who is or previously has been adjudicated a delinquent child for an act to which any of the following applies:

(1) The act is a violation of section 2903.01, 2903.02, 2903.03, 2903.04, 2903.11, 2903.12, 2903.13, 2907.02, 2907.03, or 2907.05 of the Revised Code.

(2) The act is a violation of section 2923.01 of the Revised Code and involved an attempt to commit aggravated murder or murder.

(3) The act would be a felony if committed by an adult, and the court determined that the child, if an adult, would be guilty of a specification found in section 2941.141, 2941.144, or 2941.145 of the Revised Code or in another section of the Revised Code that relates to the possession or use of a firearm during the commission of the act for which the child was adjudicated a delinquent child.

(4) The act would be an offense of violence that is a felony if committed by an adult, and the court determined that the child, if an adult, would be guilty of a specification found in section 2941.1411 of the Revised Code or in another section of the Revised Code that relates to the wearing or carrying of body armor during the commission of the act for which the child was adjudicated a delinquent child.

(B)(1) Except as provided in division (E) of this section, a public children services agency, private child placing agency, private noncustodial agency, or court, the department of youth services, or another private or government entity shall not place a child in a certified foster home or for adoption until it provides the foster caregivers or prospective adoptive parents with all of the following:

(a) A written report describing the child's social history;

(b) A written report describing all the acts committed by the child the entity knows of that resulted in the child being adjudicated a delinquent child and the disposition made by the court, unless the records pertaining to the acts have been sealed pursuant to section 2151.356 of the Revised Code;

(c) A written report describing any other violent act committed by the child of which the entity is aware;

(d) The substantial and material conclusions and recommendations of any psychiatric or psychological examination conducted on the child or, if no psychological or psychiatric examination of the child is available, the substantial and material conclusions and recommendations of an examination to detect mental and emotional disorders conducted in compliance with the requirements of Chapter 4757. of the Revised Code by an independent social worker, social worker, professional clinical counselor, or professional counselor licensed under that chapter. The entity shall not provide any part of a psychological, psychiatric, or mental and emotional disorder examination to the foster caregivers or prospective adoptive parents other than the substantial and material conclusions.

(2) Notwithstanding sections 2151.356 to 2151.358 of the Revised Code, if records of an adjudication that a child is a delinquent child have been sealed pursuant to those sections and an entity knows the records have been sealed, the entity shall provide the foster caregivers or prospective

adoptive parents a written statement that the records of a prior adjudication have been sealed.

(C)(1) The entity that places the child in a certified foster home or for adoption shall conduct a psychological examination of the child unless either of the following applies:

(a) An entity is not required to conduct the examination if an examination was conducted no more than one year prior to the child's placement, and division (C)(1)(b) of this section does not apply.

(b) An entity is not required to conduct the examination if a foster caregiver seeks to adopt the foster caregiver's foster child, and an examination was conducted no more than two years prior to the date the foster caregiver seeks to adopt the child.

(2) No later than sixty days after placing the child, the entity shall provide the foster caregiver or prospective adoptive parents a written report detailing the substantial and material conclusions and recommendations of the examination conducted pursuant to this division.

(D)(1) Except as provided in divisions (D)(2) and (3) of this section, the expenses of conducting the examinations and preparing the reports and assessment required by division (B) or (C) of this section shall be paid by the entity that places the child in the certified foster home or for adoption.

(2) When a juvenile court grants temporary or permanent custody of a child pursuant to any section of the Revised Code, including section 2151.33, 2151.353, 2151.354, or 2152.19 of the Revised Code, to a public children services agency or private child placing agency, the court shall provide the agency the information described in division (B) of this section, pay the expenses of preparing that information, and, if a new examination is required to be conducted, pay the expenses of conducting the examination described in division (C) of this section. On receipt of the information described in division (B) of this section, the agency shall provide to the court written acknowledgment that the agency received the information. The court shall keep the acknowledgment and provide a copy to the agency. On the motion of the agency, the court may terminate the order granting temporary or permanent custody of the child to that agency, if the court does not provide the information described in division (B) of this section.

(3) If one of the following entities is placing a child in a certified foster home or for adoption with the assistance of or by contracting with a public children services agency, private child placing agency, or a private noncustodial agency, the entity shall provide the agency with the information described in division (B) of this section, pay the expenses of preparing that information, and, if a new examination is required to be conducted, pay the expenses of conducting the examination described in division (C) of this section:

(a) The department of youth services if the placement is pursuant to any section of the Revised Code including section 2152.22, 5139.06, 5139.07, 5139.38, or 5139.39 of the Revised Code;

(b) A juvenile court with temporary or permanent custody of a child pursuant to section 2151.354 or 2152.19 of the Revised Code;

(c) A public children services agency or private child placing agency with temporary or permanent custody of the child.

The agency receiving the information described in division (B) of this section shall provide the entity described in division (D)(3)(a) to (c) of this section that sent the information written acknowledgment that the agency received the information and provided it to the foster caregivers or prospective adoptive parents. The entity shall keep the acknowledgment and provide a copy to the agency. An entity that places a child in a certified foster home or for adoption with the assistance of or by contracting with an agency remains responsible to provide the information described in division (B) of this section to the foster caregivers or prospective adoptive parents unless the entity receives written acknowledgment that the agency provided the information.

(E) If a child is placed in a certified foster home as a result of an emergency removal of the child from home pursuant to division (D) of section 2151.31 of the Revised Code, an emergency change in the child's case plan pursuant to division (F)(3) of section 2151.412 of the Revised Code, or an emergency placement by the department of youth services pursuant to this chapter or Chapter 5139. of the Revised Code, the entity that places the child in the certified foster home shall provide the information described in division (B) of this section no later than ninety-six hours after the child is placed in the certified foster home.

(F) On receipt of the information described in divisions (B) and (C) of this section, the foster caregiver or prospective adoptive parents shall provide to the entity that places the child in the foster caregiver's or prospective adoptive parents' home a written acknowledgment that the foster caregiver or prospective adoptive parents received the information. The entity shall keep the acknowledgment and provide a copy to the foster caregiver or prospective adoptive parents.

(G) No person employed by an entity subject to this section and made responsible by that entity for the child's placement in a certified foster home or for adoption shall fail to provide the foster caregivers or prospective adoptive parents with the information required by divisions (B) and (C) of this section.

(H) It is not a violation of any duty of confidentiality provided for in the Revised Code or a code of professional responsibility for a person or government entity to provide the substantial and material conclusions and recommendations of a psychiatric or psychological examination, or an examination to detect mental and emotional disorders, in accordance with division (B)(1)(d) or (C) of this section.

(I) As used in this section:

(1) "Body armor" has the same meaning as in section 2941.1411 of the Revised Code.

(2) "Firearm" has the same meaning as in section 2923.11 of the Revised Code.

**HISTORY: RC § 2151.62, 147 v H 173 (Eff 7-29-98); 148 v H 448 (Eff 10-5-2000); 148 v H 332 (Eff 1-1-2001); 148 v S 222 (Eff 3-22-2001); 149 v S 27 (Eff 3-14-2002); RC § 2152.72, 148 v S 179, § 3 (Eff 1-1-2002); 149 v S 27. Eff 3-15-2002; 151 v H 137, § 1, eff. 10-9-06; 2011 HB 153, § 101.01, eff. Sept. 29, 2011.**

The effective date is set by § 6 of 151 v H 137.

The provisions of §§ 5(B), 7, and 8(B) of SB 27 (149 v —) read as follows:

SECTION 5.

* * *

(B) Section 2152.72 of the Revised Code, as amended by this act, shall take effect January 1, 2002.

SECTION 7. The amendment of section 2151.62 of the Revised Code is not intended to supersede its amendment and renumbering by Am. Sub. S.B. 179 of the 123rd General Assembly.

Paragraphs of section 2151.62 of the Revised Code that are amended by this act were moved to section 2152.72 of the Revised Code by Am. Sub. S.B. 179, effective January 1, 2002, as part of its revision of the juvenile sentencing laws. Therefore, section 2152.72 of the Revised Code is amended by this act to continue, on and after January 1, 2002, the amendments this act is making to section 2151.62 of the Revised Code; section 2151.62 of the Revised Code as amended by this act is superseded on January 1, 2002, by the section as it results from its amendment and renumbering by Am. Sub. S.B. 179; and section 2152.72 of the Revised Code as amended by this act takes effect on January 1, 2002.

SECTION 8.

* * *

(B) Section 2152.72 of the Revised Code is presented in this act as a composite of the section as amended by Sub. H.B. 448, Am. Sub. S.B. 222, and Am. Sub. S.B. 179 of the 123rd General Assembly. The General Assembly, applying the principle stated in division (B) of section 1.52 of the Revised Code that amendments are to be harmonized if reasonably capable of simultaneous operation, finds that the composite is the resulting version of the section in effect prior to the effective date of the section as presented in this act.

## § 2152.73 Assignment of court employees to combat juvenile delinquency; administration of donations.

A juvenile court may participate with other public or private agencies of the county served by the court in programs that have as their objective the prevention and control of juvenile delinquency. The juvenile judge may assign employees of the court, as part of their regular duties, to work with organizations concerned with combatting conditions known to contribute to delinquency, providing adult sponsors for children who have been found to be delinquent children, and developing wholesome youth programs.

The juvenile judge may accept and administer on behalf of the court gifts, grants, bequests, and devises made to the court for the purpose of preventing delinquency.

**HISTORY: RC § 2151.11, 131 v 631 (Eff 11-11-65); RC § 2152.73, 148 v S 179, § 3. Eff 1-1-2002.**

**Not analogous to former RC § 2151.11 (GC § 1639-7a; 122 v 390; 123 v 3; Bureau of Code Revision, 10-1-53) repealed, in 129 v 1072, eff 2-8-61.**

The effective date is set by section 5 of SB 179.

## § 2152.74 DNA testing of adjudicated delinquents.

(A) As used in this section, "DNA analysis" and "DNA specimen" have the same meanings as in section 109.573 [109.57.3] of the Revised Code.

(B)(1) A child who is adjudicated a delinquent child for committing an act listed in division (D) of this section and who is committed to the custody of the department of youth services, placed in a detention facility or district detention facility pursuant to division (A)(3) of section 2152.19 of the Revised Code, or placed in a school, camp, institution, or other facility for delinquent children described in division (A)(2) of section 2152.19 of the Revised Code shall submit to a DNA specimen collection procedure administered by the director of youth services if committed to the department or by the chief administrative officer of the detention facility, district detention facility, school, camp, institution, or other facility for delinquent children to which the child was committed or in which the child was placed. If the court commits the child to the department of youth services, the director of youth services shall cause the DNA specimen to be collected from the child during the intake process at an institution operated by or under the control of the department. If the court commits the child to or places the child in a detention facility, district detention facility, school, camp, institution, or other facility for delinquent children, the chief administrative officer of the detention facility, district detention facility, school, camp, institution, or facility to which the child is committed or in which the child is placed shall cause the DNA specimen to be collected from the child during the intake process for the detention facility, district detention facility, school, camp, institution, or facility. The DNA specimen shall be collected from the child in accordance with division (C) of this section.

(2) If a child is adjudicated a delinquent child for committing an act listed in division (D) of this section, is committed to or placed in the department of youth services, a detention facility or district detention facility, or a school, camp, institution, or other facility for delinquent children, and does not submit to a DNA specimen collection procedure pursuant to division (B)(1) of this section, prior to the child's release from the custody of the department of youth services, from the custody of the detention facility or district detention facility, or from the custody of the school, camp, institution, or facility, the child shall submit to, and the director of youth services or the chief administrator† of the detention facility, district detention facility, school, camp, institution, or facility to which the child is committed or in which the child was placed shall administer, a DNA specimen collection procedure at the institution operated by or under the control of the department of youth services or at the detention facility, district detention facility, school, camp, institution, or facility to which the child is committed or in which the child was placed. The DNA specimen shall be collected in accordance with division (C) of this section.

(3) If a child is adjudicated a delinquent child for committing an act listed in division (D) of this section, is not committed to or placed in the department of youth services, a detention facility or district detention facility, or a school, camp, institution, or other facility for delinquent children described in division (A)(2) or (3) of section 2152.19 of the Revised Code, and does not provide a DNA specimen pursuant to division (B)(1) or (2) of this section, the juvenile court shall order the child to report to the county probation department immediately after disposition to submit to a DNA specimen collection procedure administered by the chief administrative officer of the county probation department. The DNA specimen shall be collected from the child in accordance with division (C) of this section.

(C) If the DNA specimen is collected by withdrawing blood from the child or a similarly invasive procedure, a physician, registered nurse, licensed practical nurse, duly licensed clinical laboratory technician, or other qualified medical practitioner shall collect in a medically approved manner the DNA specimen required to be collected pursuant to division (B) of this section. If the DNA specimen is collected by swabbing for buccal cells or a similarly noninvasive procedure, this section does not require that the DNA specimen be collected by a qualified medical practitioner of that nature. No later than fifteen days after the date of the collection of the DNA specimen, the director of youth services or the chief administrative officer of the detention facility, district detention facility, school, camp, institution, or other facility for delinquent children to which the child is committed or in which the child was placed shall cause the DNA specimen to be forwarded to the bureau of criminal identification and investigation in accordance with procedures established by the superintendent of the bureau under division (H) of section 109.573 [109.57.3] of the Revised Code. The bureau shall provide the specimen vials, mailing tubes, labels, postage, and instruction needed for the collection and forwarding of the DNA specimen to the bureau.

(D) The director of youth services and the chief administrative officer of a detention facility, district detention facility, school, camp, institution, or other facility for delinquent children shall cause a DNA specimen to be collected in accordance with divisions (B) and (C) of this section from each child in its custody who is adjudicated a delinquent child for committing any of the following acts:

(1) An act that would be a felony if committed by an adult;

(2) A violation of any law that would be a misdemeanor if committed by an adult and that arose out of the same facts and circumstances and same act as did a charge against the child of a violation of section 2903.01, 2903.02, 2905.01, 2907.02, 2907.03, 2907.05, or 2911.11 of the Revised Code that previously was dismissed or amended or as did a charge against the child of a violation of section 2907.12 of the Revised Code as it existed prior to September 3, 1996, that previously was dismissed or amended;

(3) A violation of section 2919.23 of the Revised Code that would be a misdemeanor if committed by an adult and that would have been a violation of section 2905.04 of the Revised Code as it existed prior to July 1, 1996, had the violation been committed prior to that date;

(4) A violation of section 2923.03 of the Revised Code involving complicity in committing a violation of section 2907.04 of the Revised Code that would be a misdemeanor if committed by an adult.

**HISTORY: RC § 2151.31.5, 146 v H 5 (Eff 8-30-95); 146 v S 269 (Eff 7-1-96); 146 v H 124 (Eff 3-31-97); 147 v H 526 (Eff 9-1-98); 148 v H 442 (Eff 10-17-2000); RC § 2152.74, 148 v S 179, § 3 (Eff 1-1-2002); 149 v H 427 (Eff 8-29-2002); 149 v H 400. Eff 4-3-2003; 150 v H 525, § 1, eff. 5-18-05; 151 v H 66, § 101.01, eff. 6-30-05.**

† So in enrolled bill, division (B)(2). Elsewhere, herein, see "chief administrative officer."

The effective date is set by § 612.12 of 151 v H 66.

**Comment, Legislative Service Commission**

Section 2152.74 of the Revised Code is amended by Sub. H.B. 525 of the 125th General Assembly and Am. Sub. H.B. 66 of the 126th General Assembly. The amendment by H.B. 66 is ineffective. The amendment by H.B. 525 resulted in repealing the language H.B. 66 attempted to amend. The cross-reference did not exist and therefore could not be amended.

## § 2152.81 Deposition of child victim; videotaping; testimony taken outside courtroom and televised into it or replayed in courtroom.

(A)(1) As used in this section, "victim" includes any of the following persons:

(a) A person who was a victim of a violation identified in division (A)(2) of this section or an act that would be an offense of violence if committed by an adult;

(b) A person against whom was directed any conduct that constitutes, or that is an element of, a violation identified in division (A)(2) of this section or an act that would be an offense of violence if committed by an adult.

(2) In any proceeding in juvenile court involving a complaint, indictment, or information in which a child is charged with a violation of section 2905.03, 2905.05, 2907.02, 2907.03, 2907.05, 2907.06, 2907.07, 2907.09, 2907.21, 2907.23, 2907.24, 2907.31, 2907.32, 2907.321 [2907.32.1], 2907.322 [2907.32.2], 2907.323 [2907.32.3], or 2919.22 of the Revised Code or an act that would be an offense of violence if committed by an adult and in which an alleged victim of the violation or act was a child who was less than thirteen years of age when the complaint or information was filed or the indictment was returned, the juvenile judge, upon motion of an attorney for the prosecution, shall order that the testimony of the child victim be taken by deposition. The prosecution also may request that the deposition be videotaped in accordance with division (A)(3) of this section. The judge shall notify the child victim whose deposition is to be taken, the prosecution, and the attorney for the child who is charged with the violation or act of the date, time, and place for taking the deposition. The notice shall identify the child victim who is to be examined and shall indicate whether a request that the deposition be videotaped has been made. The child who is charged with the violation or act shall have the right to attend the deposition and the right to be represented by counsel. Depositions shall be taken in the manner provided in civil cases, except that the judge in the proceeding shall preside at the taking of the deposition and shall rule at that time on any objections of the prosecution or the attorney for the child charged with the violation or act. The prosecution and the attorney for the child charged with the violation or act shall have the right, as at an adjudication hearing, to full examination and cross-examination of the child victim whose deposition is to be taken. If a deposition taken under this division is intended to be offered as evidence in the proceeding, it shall be filed in the juvenile court in which the action is pending and is admissible in the manner described in division (B) of this section. If a deposition of a child victim taken under this division is admitted as evidence at the proceeding under division (B) of this section, the child victim shall not be required to testify in person at the proceeding. However, at any time before the conclusion of the proceeding, the attorney for the child charged with the violation or act may file a motion with the judge requesting that another deposition of the child victim be taken because new evidence material to the defense of the child charged has been discovered that the attorney for the child charged could not with reasonable diligence have discovered prior to the taking of the admitted deposition. Any motion requesting another deposition shall be accompanied by supporting affidavits. Upon the filing of the motion and affidavits, the court may order that additional testimony of the child victim relative to the new evidence be taken by another deposition. If the court orders the taking of another deposition under this provision, the deposition shall be taken in accordance with this division; if the admitted deposition was a videotaped deposition taken in accordance with division (A)(3) of this section, the new deposition also shall be videotaped in accordance with that division, and, in other cases, the new deposition may be videotaped in accordance with that division.

(3) If the prosecution requests that a deposition to be taken under division (A)(2) of this section be videotaped, the juvenile judge shall order that the deposition be videotaped in accordance with this division. If a juvenile

judge issues an order to video tape† the deposition, the judge shall exclude from the room in which the deposition is to be taken every person except the child victim giving the testimony, the judge, one or more interpreters if needed, the attorneys for the prosecution and the child who is charged with the violation or act, any person needed to operate the equipment to be used, one person chosen by the child victim giving the deposition, and any person whose presence the judge determines would contribute to the welfare and well-being of the child victim giving the deposition. The person chosen by the child victim shall not be a witness in the proceeding and, both before and during the deposition, shall not discuss the testimony of the child victim with any other witness in the proceeding. To the extent feasible, any person operating the recording equipment shall be restricted to a room adjacent to the room in which the deposition is being taken, or to a location in the room in which the deposition is being taken that is behind a screen or mirror so that the person operating the recording equipment can see and hear, but cannot be seen or heard by, the child victim giving the deposition during the deposition. The child who is charged with the violation or act shall be permitted to observe and hear the testimony of the child victim giving the deposition on a monitor, shall be provided with an electronic means of immediate communication with the attorney of the child who is charged with the violation or act during the testimony, and shall be restricted to a location from which the child who is charged with the violation or act cannot be seen or heard by the child victim giving the deposition, except on a monitor provided for that purpose. The child victim giving the deposition shall be provided with a monitor on which the child victim can observe, while giving testimony, the child who is charged with the violation or act. The judge, at the judge's discretion, may preside at the deposition by electronic means from outside the room in which the deposition is to be taken; if the judge presides by electronic means, the judge shall be provided with monitors on which the judge can see each person in the room in which the deposition is to be taken and with an electronic means of communication with each person in that room, and each person in the room shall be provided with a monitor on which that person can see the judge and with an electronic means of communication with the judge. A deposition that is videotaped under this division shall be taken and filed in the manner described in division (A)(2) of this section and is admissible in the manner described in this division and division (B) of this section, and, if a deposition that is videotaped under this division is admitted as evidence at the proceeding, the child victim shall not be required to testify in person at the proceeding. No deposition videotaped under this division shall be admitted as evidence at any proceeding unless division (B) of this section is satisfied relative to the deposition and all of the following apply relative to the recording:

(a) The recording is both aural and visual and is recorded on film or videotape, or by other electronic means.

(b) The recording is authenticated under the Rules of Evidence and the Rules of Criminal Procedure as a fair and accurate representation of what occurred, and the recording is not altered other than at the direction and under the supervision of the judge in the proceeding.

(c) Each voice on the recording that is material to the testimony on the recording or the making of the recording, as determined by the judge, is identified.

(d) Both the prosecution and the child who is charged with the violation or act are afforded an opportunity to view the recording before it is shown in the proceeding.

(B)(1) At any proceeding in relation to which a deposition was taken under division (A) of this section, the deposition or a part of it is admissible in evidence upon motion of the prosecution if the testimony in the deposition or the part to be admitted is not excluded by the hearsay rule and if the deposition or the part to be admitted otherwise is admissible under the Rules of Evidence. For purposes of this division, testimony is not excluded by the hearsay rule if the testimony is not hearsay under Evidence Rule 801; if the testimony is within an exception to the hearsay rule set forth in Evidence Rule 803; if the child victim who gave the testimony is unavailable as a witness, as defined in Evidence Rule 804, and the testimony is admissible under that rule; or if both of the following apply:

(a) The child who is charged with the violation or act had an opportunity and similar motive at the time of the taking of the deposition to develop the testimony by direct, cross, or redirect examination.

(b) The judge determines that there is reasonable cause to believe that, if the child victim who gave the testimony in the deposition were to testify in person at the proceeding, the child victim would experience serious emotional trauma as a result of the child victim's participation at the proceeding.

(2) Objections to receiving in evidence a deposition or a part of it under division (B) of this section shall be made as provided in civil actions.

(3) The provisions of divisions (A) and (B) of this section are in addition to any other provisions of the Revised Code, the Rules of Juvenile Procedure, the Rules of Criminal Procedure, or the Rules of Evidence that pertain to the taking or admission of depositions in a juvenile court proceeding and do not limit the admissibility under any of those other provisions of any deposition taken under division (A) of this section or otherwise taken.

(C) In any proceeding in juvenile court involving a complaint, indictment, or information in which a child is charged with a violation listed in division (A)(2) of this section or an act that would be an offense of violence if committed by an adult and in which an alleged victim of the violation or offense was a child who was less than thirteen years of age when the complaint or information was filed or indictment was returned, the prosecution may file a motion with the juvenile judge requesting the judge to order the testimony of the child victim to be taken in a room other than the room in which the proceeding is being conducted and be televised, by closed circuit equipment, into the room in which the proceeding is being conducted to be viewed by the child who is charged with the violation or act and any other persons who are not permitted in the room in which the testimony is to be taken but who would have been present during the testimony of the child victim had it been given in the room in which the proceeding is being conducted. Except for good cause shown, the prosecution shall file a motion under this division at least seven days before the date of the proceeding. The juvenile judge may issue the order upon the motion of the prosecution filed under this division, if the judge determines that the child victim is unavailable to testify in the room in which the proceeding is being conducted in the physical presence of the child charged with the violation or act, due to one or more of the reasons set forth in division (E) of this section. If a juvenile judge issues an order of that nature, the judge shall exclude from the room in which the testimony is to be taken every person except a person described in division (A)(3) of this section. The judge, at the judge's discretion, may preside during the giving of the testimony by electronic means from outside the room in which it is being given, subject to the limitations set forth in division (A)(3) of this section. To the extent feasible, any person operating the televising equipment shall be hidden from the sight and hearing of the child victim giving the testimony, in a manner similar to that described in division (A)(3) of this section. The child who is charged with the violation or act shall be permitted to observe and hear the testimony of the child victim giving the testimony on a monitor, shall be provided with an electronic means of immediate communication with the attorney of the child who is charged with the violation or act during the testimony, and shall be restricted to a location from which the child who is charged with the violation or act cannot be seen or heard by the child victim giving the testimony, except on a monitor provided for that purpose. The child victim giving the testimony shall be provided with a monitor on which the child victim can observe, while giving testimony, the child who is charged with the violation or act.

(D) In any proceeding in juvenile court involving a complaint, indictment, or information in which a child is charged with a violation listed in division (A)(2) of this section or an act that would be an offense of violence if committed by an adult and in which an alleged victim of the violation or offense was a child who was less than thirteen years of age when the complaint or information was filed or the indictment was returned, the prosecution may file a motion with the juvenile judge requesting the judge to order the testimony of the child victim to be taken outside of the room in which the proceeding is being conducted and be recorded for showing in the room in which the proceeding is being conducted before the judge, the child who is charged with the violation or act, and any other persons who would have been present during the testimony of the child victim had it been given in the room in which the proceeding is being conducted. Except for good cause shown, the prosecution shall file a motion under this division at least seven days before the date of the proceeding. The juvenile judge may issue the order upon the motion of the prosecution filed under this division, if the judge determines that the child victim is unavailable to testify in the room in which the proceeding is being conducted in the physical presence of the child charged with the violation or act, due to one or more of the reasons set forth in division (E) of this section. If a juvenile judge issues an order of that nature, the judge shall exclude from the room in which the testimony is to be taken every person except a person described in division (A)(3) of this section. To the extent feasible, any person operating the recording equipment shall be hidden from the sight and hearing of the child victim giving the testimony, in a manner similar to that described in division (A)(3) of this section. The child who is charged with the violation or act shall be permitted to observe and hear the testimony of the child victim giving the testimony on a monitor, shall be provided with an electronic means of immediate communication with the attorney of the child who is charged with the violation or act during the testimony, and shall be restricted to a location from which the child who is charged with the violation or act cannot be seen or heard by the child victim giving the testimony, except on a monitor provided for that purpose. The child victim giving the testimony shall be provided with a monitor on which the child victim can observe, while giving testimony, the child who is charged with the violation or act. No order for the taking of testimony by recording shall be issued under this division unless the provisions set forth in divisions (A)(3)(a), (b), (c), and (d) of this section apply to the recording of the testimony.

(E) For purposes of divisions (C) and (D) of this section, a juvenile judge may order the testimony of a child victim to be taken outside of the room in which a proceeding is being conducted if the judge determines that the child victim is unavailable to testify in the room in the physical presence of the child charged with the violation or act due to one or more of the following circumstances:

(1) The persistent refusal of the child victim to testify despite judicial requests to do so;

(2) The inability of the child victim to communicate about the alleged violation or offense because of extreme fear, failure of memory, or another similar reason;

(3) The substantial likelihood that the child victim will suffer serious emotional trauma from so testifying.

(F)(1) If a juvenile judge issues an order pursuant to division (C) or (D) of this section that requires the testimony of a child victim in a juvenile court proceeding to be taken outside of the room in which the proceeding is being conducted, the order shall specifically identify the child victim to whose testimony it applies, the order applies only during the testimony of the specified child victim, and the child victim giving the testimony shall not be required to testify at the proceeding other than in accordance with the order. The authority of a judge to close the taking of a deposition under division (A)(3) of this section or a proceeding under division (C) or (D) of this section is in addition to the authority of a judge to close a hearing pursuant to section 2151.35 of the Revised Code.

(2) A juvenile judge who makes any determination regarding the admissibility of a deposition under divisions (A) and (B) of this section, the videotaping of a deposition under division (A)(3) of this section, or the taking of testimony outside of the room in which a proceeding is being conducted under division (C) or (D) of this section, shall enter the determination and findings on the record in the proceeding.

**HISTORY: RC § 2151.35.11, 141 v H 108 (Eff 10-14-86); 146 v H 445 (Eff 9-3-96); 147 v S 53 (Eff 10-14-97); 148 v H 442 (Eff 10-17-2000); RC § 2152.81, 148 v S 179, § 3. Eff 1-1-2002.**

† So in enrolled bill, division (A)(3).

The effective date is set by section 5 of SB 179.

## § 2152.811 Deposition of mentally retarded or developmentally disabled victim; taking of testimony outside room where proceeding is being conducted.

(A) As used in this section:

(1) "Mentally retarded person" and "developmentally disabled person" have the same meanings as in section 5123.01 of the Revised Code.

(2) "Mentally retarded or developmentally disabled victim" includes any of the following persons:

(a) A mentally retarded person or developmentally disabled person who was a victim of a violation identified in division (B)(1) of this section or an act that would be an offense of violence if committed by an adult;

(b) A mentally retarded person or developmentally disabled person against whom was directed any conduct that constitutes, or that is an element of, a violation identified in division (B)(1) of this section or an act that would be an offense of violence if committed by an adult.

(B)(1) In any proceeding in juvenile court involving a complaint, indictment, or information in which a child is charged with a violation of section 2903.16, 2903.34, 2903.341 [2903.34.1], 2907.02, 2907.03, 2907.05, 2907.21, 2907.23, 2907.24, 2907.32, 2907.321 [2907.32.1], 2907.322 [2907.32.2], or 2907.323 [2907.32.3] of the Revised Code or an act that would be an offense of violence if committed by an adult and in which an alleged victim of the violation or act was a mentally retarded person or developmentally disabled person, the juvenile judge, upon motion of the prosecution, shall order that the testimony of the mentally retarded or developmentally disabled victim be taken by deposition. The prosecution also may request that the deposition be videotaped in accordance with division (B)(2) of this section. The judge shall notify the mentally retarded or developmentally disabled victim whose deposition is to be taken, the prosecution, and the attorney for the child who is charged with the violation or act of the date, time, and place for taking the deposition. The notice shall identify the mentally retarded or developmentally disabled victim who is to be examined and shall indicate whether a request that the deposition be videotaped has been made. The child who is charged with the violation or act shall have the right to attend the deposition and the right to be represented by counsel. Depositions shall be taken in the manner provided in civil cases, except that the judge in the proceeding shall preside at the taking of the deposition and shall rule at that time on any objections of the prosecution or the attorney for the child charged with the violation or act. The prosecution and the attorney for the child charged with the violation or act shall have the right, as at an adjudication hearing, to full examination and cross-examination of the mentally retarded or developmentally disabled victim whose deposition is to be taken.

If a deposition taken under this division is intended to be offered as evidence in the proceeding, it shall be filed in the juvenile court in which the action is pending and is admissible in the manner described in division (C) of this section. If a deposition of a mentally retarded or developmentally disabled victim taken under this division is admitted as evidence at the proceeding under division (C) of this section, the mentally retarded or developmentally disabled victim shall not be required to testify in person at the proceeding.

At any time before the conclusion of the proceeding, the attorney for the child charged with the violation or act may file a motion with the judge requesting that another deposition of the mentally retarded or developmentally disabled victim be taken because new evidence material to the defense of the child charged has been discovered that the attorney for the child charged could not with reasonable diligence have discovered prior to the taking of the admitted deposition. Any motion requesting another deposition shall be accompanied by supporting affidavits. Upon the filing of the motion and affidavits, the court may order that additional testimony of the mentally retarded or developmentally disabled victim relative to the new evidence be taken by another deposition. If the court orders the taking of another deposition under this provision, the deposition shall be taken in accordance with this division. If the admitted deposition was a videotaped deposition taken in accordance with division (B)(2) of this section, the new deposition also shall be videotaped in accordance with that division. In other cases, the new deposition may be videotaped in accordance with that division.

(2) If the prosecution requests that a deposition to be taken under division (B)(1) of this section be videotaped, the juvenile judge shall order that the deposition be videotaped in accordance with this division. If a juvenile judge issues an order to video tape the deposition, the judge shall exclude from the room in which the deposition is to be taken every person except the mentally retarded or developmentally disabled victim giving the testimony, the judge, one or more interpreters if needed, the attorneys for the prosecution and the child who is charged with the violation or act, any person needed to operate the equipment to be used, one person chosen by the mentally retarded or developmentally disabled victim giving the deposition, and any person whose presence the judge determines would contribute to the welfare and well-being of the mentally retarded or developmentally disabled victim giving the deposition. The person chosen by the mentally retarded or developmentally disabled victim shall not be a witness in the proceeding and, both before and during the deposition, shall not discuss the testimony of the victim with any other witness in the proceeding. To the extent feasible, any person operating the recording equipment shall be restricted to a room adjacent to the room in which the deposition is being taken, or to a location in the room in which the deposition is being taken that is behind a screen or mirror so that the person operating the recording equipment can see and hear, but cannot be seen or heard by, the mentally retarded or developmentally disabled victim giving the deposition during the deposition.

The child who is charged with the violation or act shall be permitted to observe and hear the testimony of the mentally retarded or developmentally disabled victim giving the deposition on a monitor, shall be provided with an electronic means of immediate communication with the attorney of the child who is charged with the violation or act during the testimony, and shall be restricted to a location from which the child who is charged with the violation or act cannot be seen or heard by the mentally retarded or developmentally disabled victim giving the deposition, except on a monitor provided for that purpose. The mentally retarded or developmentally disabled victim giving the deposition shall be provided with a monitor on which the mentally retarded or developmentally disabled victim can observe, while giving testimony, the child who is charged with the violation or act. The judge, at the judge's discretion, may preside at the deposition by electronic means from outside the room in which the deposition is to be taken; if the judge presides by electronic means, the judge shall be provided with monitors on which the judge can see each person in the room in which the deposition is to be taken and with an electronic means of communication with each person in that room, and each person in the room shall be provided with a monitor on which that person can see the judge and with an electronic means of communication with the judge. A deposition that is videotaped under this division shall be taken and filed in the manner described in division (B)(1) of this section and is admissible in the manner described in this division and division (C) of this section. If a deposition that is videotaped under this division is admitted as evidence at the proceeding, the mentally retarded or developmentally disabled victim shall not be required to testify in person at the proceeding. No deposition videotaped under this division shall be admitted as evidence at any proceeding unless division (C) of this section is satisfied relative to the deposition and all of the following apply relative to the recording:

(a) The recording is both aural and visual and is recorded on film or videotape, or by other electronic means.

(b) The recording is authenticated under the Rules of Evidence and the Rules of Criminal Procedure as a fair and accurate representation of what occurred, and the recording is not altered other than at the direction and under the supervision of the judge in the proceeding.

(c) Each voice on the recording that is material to the testimony on the recording or the making of the recording, as determined by the judge, is identified.

(d) Both the prosecution and the child who is charged with the violation or act are afforded an opportunity to view the recording before it is shown in the proceeding.

(C)(1) At any proceeding in relation to which a deposition was taken under division (B) of this section, the deposition or a part of it is admissible in evidence upon motion of the prosecution if the testimony in the deposition or the part to be admitted is not excluded by the hearsay rule and if the deposition or the part to be admitted otherwise is admissible under the Rules of Evidence. For purposes of this division, testimony is not excluded by the hearsay rule if the testimony is not hearsay under Evidence Rule 801; the testimony is within an exception to the hearsay rule set forth in Evidence Rule 803; the mentally retarded or developmentally disabled victim who gave the testimony is unavailable as a witness, as defined in Evidence Rule 804, and the testimony is admissible under that rule; or both of the following apply:

(a) The child who is charged with the violation or act had an opportunity and similar motive at the time of the taking of the deposition to develop the testimony by direct, cross, or redirect examination.

(b) The judge determines that there is reasonable cause to believe that, if the mentally retarded or developmentally disabled victim who gave the testimony in the deposition were to testify in person at the proceeding, the mentally retarded or developmentally disabled victim would experience serious emotional trauma as a result of the mentally retarded or developmentally disabled victim's participation at the proceeding.

(2) Objections to receiving in evidence a deposition or a part of it under division (C) of this section shall be made as provided in civil actions.

(3) The provisions of divisions (B) and (C) of this section are in addition to any other provisions of the Revised Code, the Rules of Juvenile Procedure, the Rules of Criminal Procedure, or the Rules of Evidence that pertain to the taking or admission of depositions in a juvenile court proceeding and do not limit the admissibility under any of those other provisions of any deposition taken under division (B) of this section or otherwise taken.

(D) In any proceeding in juvenile court involving a complaint, indictment, or information in which a child is charged with a violation listed in division (B)(1) of this section or an act that would be an offense of violence if committed by an adult and in which an alleged victim of the violation or offense was a mentally retarded or developmentally disabled person, the prosecution may file a motion with the juvenile judge requesting the judge to order the testimony of the mentally retarded or developmentally disabled victim to be taken in a room other than the room in which the proceeding is being conducted and be televised, by closed circuit equipment, into the room in which the proceeding is being conducted to be viewed by the child who is charged with the violation or act and any other persons who are not permitted in the room in which the testimony is to be taken but who would have been present during the testimony of the mentally retarded or developmentally disabled victim had it been given in the room in which the proceeding is being conducted. Except for good cause shown, the prosecution shall file a motion under this division at least seven days before the date of the proceeding. The juvenile judge may issue the order upon the motion of the prosecution filed under this division, if the judge determines that the mentally retarded or developmentally disabled victim is unavailable to testify in the room in which the proceeding is being conducted in the physical presence of the child charged with the violation or act for one or more of the reasons set forth in division (F) of this section. If a juvenile judge issues an order of that nature, the judge shall exclude from the room in which the testimony is to be taken every person except a person described in division (B)(2) of this section. The judge, at the judge's discretion, may preside during the giving of the testimony by electronic means from outside the room in which it is being given, subject to the limitations set forth in division (B)(2) of this section. To the extent feasible, any person operating the televising equipment shall be hidden from the sight and hearing of the mentally retarded or developmentally disabled victim giving the testimony, in a manner similar to that described in division (B)(2) of this section. The child who is charged with the violation or act shall be permitted to observe and hear the testimony of the mentally retarded or developmentally disabled victim giving the testimony on a monitor, shall be provided with an electronic means of immediate communication with the attorney of the child who is charged with the violation or act during the testimony, and shall be restricted to a location from which the child who is charged with the violation or act cannot be seen or heard by the mentally retarded or developmentally disabled victim giving the testimony, except on a monitor provided for that purpose. The mentally retarded or developmentally disabled victim giving the testimony shall be provided with a monitor on which the mentally retarded or developmentally disabled victim can observe, while giving testimony, the child who is charged with the violation or act.

(E) In any proceeding in juvenile court involving a complaint, indictment, or information in which a child is charged with a violation listed in division (B)(1) of this section or an act that would be an offense of violence if committed by an adult and in which an alleged victim of the violation or offense was a mentally retarded or developmentally disabled person, the prosecution may file a motion with the juvenile judge requesting the judge to order the testimony of the mentally retarded or developmentally disabled victim to be taken outside of the room in which the proceeding is being conducted and be recorded for showing in the room in which the proceeding is being conducted before the judge, the child who is charged with the violation or act, and any other persons who would have been present during the testimony of the mentally retarded or developmentally disabled victim had it been given in the room in which the proceeding is being conducted. Except for good cause shown, the prosecution shall file a motion under this division at least seven days before the date of the proceeding. The juvenile judge may issue the order upon the motion of the prosecution filed under this division, if the judge determines that the mentally retarded or developmentally disabled victim is unavailable to testify in the room in which the proceeding is being conducted in the physical presence of the child charged with the violation or act, due to one or more of the reasons set forth in division (F) of this section. If a juvenile judge issues an order of that nature, the judge shall exclude from the room in which the testimony is to be taken every person except a person described in division (B)(2) of this section. To the extent feasible, any person operating the recording equipment shall be hidden from the sight and hearing of the mentally retarded or developmentally disabled victim giving the testimony, in a manner similar to that described in division (B)(2) of this section. The child who is charged with the violation or act shall be permitted to observe and hear the testimony of the mentally retarded or developmentally disabled victim giving the testimony on a monitor, shall be provided with an electronic means of immediate communication with the attorney of the child who is charged with the violation or act during the testimony, and shall be restricted to a location from which the child who is charged with the violation or act cannot be seen or heard by the mentally retarded or developmentally disabled victim giving the testimony, except on a monitor provided for that purpose. The mentally retarded or developmentally disabled victim giving the testimony shall be provided with a monitor on which the mentally retarded or developmentally disabled victim can observe, while giving testimony, the child who is charged with the violation or act. No order for the taking of testimony by recording shall be issued under this division unless the provisions set forth in divisions (B)(2)(a), (b), (c), and (d) of this section apply to the recording of the testimony.

(F) For purposes of divisions (D) and (E) of this section, a juvenile judge may order the testimony of a mentally retarded or developmentally disabled victim to be taken outside of the room in which a proceeding is being conducted if the judge determines that the mentally retarded or developmentally disabled victim is unavailable to testify in the room in the physical presence of the child charged with the violation or act due to one or more of the following circumstances:

(1) The persistent refusal of the mentally retarded or developmentally disabled victim to testify despite judicial requests to do so;

(2) The inability of the mentally retarded or developmentally disabled victim to communicate about the alleged violation or offense because of extreme fear, failure of memory, or another similar reason;

(3) The substantial likelihood that the mentally retarded or developmentally disabled victim will suffer serious emotional trauma from so testifying.

(G)(1) If a juvenile judge issues an order pursuant to division (D) or (E) of this section that requires the testimony of a mentally retarded or developmentally disabled victim in a juvenile court proceeding to be taken outside of the room in which the proceeding is being conducted, the order shall specifically identify the mentally retarded or developmentally disabled victim to whose testimony it applies, the order applies only during the testimony of the specified mentally retarded or developmentally disabled victim, and the mentally retarded or developmentally disabled victim giving the testimony shall not be required to testify at the proceeding other than in accordance with the order. The authority of a judge to close the taking of a deposition under division (B)(2) of this section or a proceeding under division (D) or (E) of this section is in addition to the authority of a judge to close a hearing pursuant to section 2151.35 of the Revised Code.

(2) A juvenile judge who makes any determination regarding the admissibility of a deposition under divisions (B) and (C) of this section, the videotaping of a deposition under division (B)(2) of this section, or the taking of testimony outside of the room in which a proceeding is being conducted under division (D) or (E) of this section shall enter the determination and findings on the record in the proceeding.

**HISTORY: 150 v S 178, § 1, eff. 1-30-04; 152 v S 10, § 1, eff. 1-1-08.**

**Not analogous to former RC § 2152.811, repealed by 152 v S 10, eff 1-1-08.**

The effective date is set by § 3 of 152 v S 10.

This section was renumbered from RC § 2152.821 by 152 v S 10, effective January 1, 2008.

## [JUVENILE SEX OFFENDER REGISTRATION AND NOTIFICATION LAW]

### § 2152.82 Classification of child as juvenile offender registrant; compliance with sex offender registration and notification law; determination of tier classification.

(A) The court that adjudicates a child a delinquent child shall issue as part of the dispositional order an order that classifies the child a juvenile offender registrant and specifies that the child has a duty to comply with sections 2950.04, 2950.041 [2950.04.1], 2950.05, and 2950.06 of the Revised Code if all of the following apply:

(1) The act for which the child is adjudicated a delinquent child is a sexually oriented offense or a child-victim oriented offense that the child committed on or after January 1, 2002.

(2) The child was fourteen, fifteen, sixteen, or seventeen years of age at the time of committing the offense.

(3) The court has determined that the child previously was adjudicated a delinquent child for committing any sexually oriented offense or child-victim oriented offense, regardless of when the prior offense was committed and regardless of the child's age at the time of committing the offense.

(4) The court is not required to classify the child as both a juvenile offender registrant and a public registry-qualified juvenile offender registrant under section 2152.86 of the Revised Code.

(B) An order required under division (A) of this section shall be issued at the time the judge makes the order of disposition for the delinquent child. Prior to issuing the order required by division (A) of this section, the judge shall conduct a hearing under section 2152.831 [2152.83.1] of the Revised Code to determine whether the child is a tier I sex offender/child-victim offender, a tier II sex offender/child-victim offender, or a tier III sex offender/child-victim offender. If the court determines that the delinquent child to whom the order applies is a tier III sex offender/child-victim offender and the child is not a public registry-qualified juvenile offender registrant, the judge may impose a requirement subjecting the child to the victim and community notification provisions of sections 2950.10 and 2950.11 of the Revised Code. When a judge issues an order under division (A) of this section, all of the following apply:

(1) The judge shall include in the order a statement that, upon completion of the disposition of the delinquent child that was made for the sexually oriented offense or child-victim oriented offense upon which the order is based, a hearing will be conducted, and the order and any determinations included in the order are subject to modification or termination pursuant to sections 2152.84 and 2152.85 of the Revised Code.

(2) The judge shall provide to the delinquent child and to the delinquent child's parent, guardian, or custodian the notice required under divisions (A) and (B) of section 2950.03 of the Revised Code and shall provide as part of that notice a copy of the order.

(3) The judge shall include the order in the delinquent child's dispositional order and shall specify in the dispositional order that the order issued under division (A) of this section was made pursuant to this section.

(4) If the court determines that the delinquent child to whom the order applies is a tier III sex offender/child-victim offender, if the child is not a public registry-qualified juvenile offender registrant, and if the judge imposes a requirement subjecting the child to the victim and community notification provisions of sections 2950.10 and 2950.11 of the Revised Code, the judge shall include the requirement in the order.

(5) The court shall include in the order its determination made at the hearing held under section 2151.831 [2151.83.1] of the Revised Code as to whether the delinquent child is a tier I sex offender/child-victim offender, a tier II sex offender/child-victim offender, or a tier III sex offender/child-victim offender.

(C) Except as provided in division (D) of this section, an order issued under division (A) of this section and any determinations included in the order shall remain in effect for the period of time specified in section 2950.07 of the Revised Code, subject to a modification or termination of the order under section 2152.84 or 2152.85 of the Revised Code, and section 2152.851 [2152.85.1] of the Revised Code applies regarding the order and the determinations. If an order is issued under division (A) of this section, the child's attainment of eighteen or twenty-one years of age does not affect or terminate the order, and the order remains in effect for the period of time described in this division.

(D) If a court issues an order under division (A) of this section before January 1, 2008, not later than February 1, 2008, the court shall terminate the order and issue a new order that reclassifies the child as both a juvenile offender registrant and a public registry-qualified juvenile offender registrant pursuant to section 2152.86 of the Revised Code if the court imposed on the child a serious youthful offender dispositional sentence under section 2152.13 of the Revised Code and if the act that was the basis of the classification of the delinquent child as a juvenile offender registrant and is the basis of the serious youthful offender dispositional sentence is any of the following:

(1) Committing, attempting to commit, conspiring to commit, or complicity in committing a violation of section 2907.02 of the Revised Code, division (B) of section 2907.05 of the Revised Code, or section 2907.03 of the Revised Code if the victim of the violation was less than twelve years of age;

(2) Committing, attempting to commit, conspiring to commit, or complicity in committing a violation of section 2903.01, 2903.02, or 2905.01 of the Revised Code that was committed with a purpose to gratify the sexual needs or desires of the child.

**HISTORY: 149 v S 3 (Eff 1-1-2002); 149 v H 393. Eff 7-5-2002; 150 v S 5, § 1, eff. 7-31-03; 152 v S 10, § 1, eff. 1-1-08.**

The effective date is set by § 3 of 152 v S 10.

## § 2152.821 Renumbered.

Renumbered RC § 2152.811 by 152 v S 10. Eff 1-1-08

The effective date is set by § 3 of 152 v S 10.

## § 2152.83 Classification at time of disposition or release from secure facility; determination of tier classification.

(A)(1) The court that adjudicates a child a delinquent child shall issue as part of the dispositional order or, if the court commits the child for the delinquent act to the custody of a secure facility, shall issue at the time of the child's release from the secure facility, an order that classifies the child a juvenile offender registrant and specifies that the child has a duty to comply with sections 2950.04, 2950.041 [2950.04.1], 2950.05, and 2950.06 of the Revised Code if all of the following apply:

(a) The act for which the child is or was adjudicated a delinquent child is a sexually oriented offense or a child-victim oriented offense that the child committed on or after January 1, 2002.

(b) The child was sixteen or seventeen years of age at the time of committing the offense.

(c) The court was not required to classify the child a juvenile offender registrant under section 2152.82 of the Revised Code or as both a juvenile offender registrant and a public registry-qualified juvenile offender registrant under section 2152.86 of the Revised Code.

(2) Prior to issuing the order required by division (A)(2) of this section, the judge shall conduct a hearing under section 2152.831 [2152.83.1] of the Revised Code, except as otherwise provided in that section, to determine whether the child is a tier I sex offender/child-victim offender, a tier II sex offender/child-victim offender, or a tier III sex offender/child-victim offender. When a judge issues an order under division (A)(1) of this section, the judge shall include in the order the determinations identified in division (B)(5) of section 2152.82 of the Revised Code.

(B)(1) The court that adjudicates a child a delinquent child, on the judge's own motion, may conduct at the time of disposition of the child or, if the court commits the child for the delinquent act to the custody of a secure facility, may conduct at the time of the child's release from the secure facility a hearing for the purposes described in division (B)(2) of this section if all of the following apply:

(a) The act for which the child is adjudicated a delinquent child is a sexually oriented offense or a child-victim oriented offense that the child committed on or after January 1, 2002.

(b) The child was fourteen or fifteen years of age at the time of committing the offense.

(c) The court was not required to classify the child a juvenile offender registrant under section 2152.82 of the

Revised Code or as both a juvenile offender registrant and a public registry-qualified juvenile offender registrant under section 2152.86 of the Revised Code.

(2) A judge shall conduct a hearing under division (B)(1) of this section to review the effectiveness of the disposition made of the child and of any treatment provided for the child placed in a secure setting and to determine whether the child should be classified a juvenile offender registrant. The judge may conduct the hearing on the judge's own initiative or based upon a recommendation of an officer or employee of the department of youth services, a probation officer, an employee of the court, or a prosecutor or law enforcement officer. If the judge conducts the hearing, upon completion of the hearing, the judge, in the judge's discretion and after consideration of the factors listed in division (E) of this section, shall do either of the following:

(a) Decline to issue an order that classifies the child a juvenile offender registrant and specifies that the child has a duty to comply with sections 2950.04, 2950.041 [2950.04.1], 2950.05, and 2950.06 of the Revised Code;

(b) Issue an order that classifies the child a juvenile offender registrant and specifies that the child has a duty to comply with sections 2950.04, 2950.041 [2950.04.1], 2950.05, and 2950.06 of the Revised Code and that states the determination that the judge makes at the hearing held pursuant to section 2152.831 [2152.83.1] of the Revised Code as to whether the child is a tier I sex offender/child-victim offender, a tier II sex offender/child-victim offender, or a tier III sex offender/child-victim offender.

(C)(1) Prior to issuing an order under division (B)(2)(b) of this section, the judge shall conduct a hearing under section 2152.831 [2152.83.1] of the Revised Code to determine whether the child is a tier I sex offender/child-victim offender, a tier II sex offender/child-victim offender, or a tier III sex offender/child-victim offender. The judge may hold the hearing at the same time as the hearing under division (B) of this section.

(2) If a judge issues an order under division (A) or (B) of this section and the court determines that the delinquent child to whom the order applies is a tier III sex offender/child-victim offender and the child is not a public registry-qualified juvenile offender registrant, the judge may impose a requirement subjecting the child to the victim and community notification provisions of sections 2950.10 and 2950.11 of the Revised Code. If the judge imposes a requirement subjecting the child to the victim and community notification provisions of sections 2950.10 and 2950.11 of the Revised Code, the judge shall include the requirement in the order.

(3) If a judge issues an order under division (A) or (B) of this section, the judge shall provide to the delinquent child and to the delinquent child's parent, guardian, or custodian a copy of the order and a notice containing the information described in divisions (A) and (B) of section 2950.03 of the Revised Code. The judge shall provide the notice at the time of the issuance of the order and shall comply with divisions (B) and (C) of that section regarding that notice and the provision of it.

The judge also shall include in the order a statement that, upon completion of the disposition of the delinquent child that was made for the sexually oriented offense or child-victim oriented offense upon which the order is based, a hearing will be conducted and the order is subject to modification or termination pursuant to section 2152.84 of the Revised Code.

(D) In making a decision under division (B) of this section as to whether a delinquent child should be classified a juvenile offender registrant, a judge shall consider all relevant factors, including, but not limited to, all of the following:

(1) The nature of the sexually oriented offense or the child-victim oriented offense committed by the child;

(2) Whether the child has shown any genuine remorse or compunction for the offense;

(3) The public interest and safety;

(4) The factors set forth in division (K) of section 2950.11 of the Revised Code, provided that references in the factors as set forth in that division to "the offender" shall be construed for purposes of this division to be references to "the delinquent child;"

(5) The factors set forth in divisions (B) and (C) of section 2929.12 of the Revised Code as those factors apply regarding the delinquent child, the offense, and the victim;

(6) The results of any treatment provided to the child and of any follow-up professional assessment of the child.

(E) An order issued under division (A) or (B) of this section and any determinations included in the order shall remain in effect for the period of time specified in section 2950.07 of the Revised Code, subject to a modification or termination of the order under section 2152.84 of the Revised Code, and section 2152.851 [2152.85.1] of the Revised Code applies regarding the order and the determinations. The child's attainment of eighteen or twenty-one years of age does not affect or terminate the order, and the order remains in effect for the period of time described in this division.

(F) If a court issues an order under division (A) or (B) of this section before January 1, 2008, not later than February 1, 2008, the court shall terminate the order and issue a new order that reclassifies the child as both a juvenile offender registrant and a public registry-qualified juvenile offender registrant pursuant to section 2152.86 of the Revised Code if the court imposed on the child a serious youthful offender dispositional sentence under section 2152.13 of the Revised Code and if the act that was the basis of the classification of the delinquent child as a juvenile offender registrant and is the basis of the serious youthful offender dispositional sentence is any of the following:

(1) Committing, attempting to commit, conspiring to commit, or complicity in committing a violation of section 2907.02 of the Revised Code, division (B) of section 2907.05 of the Revised Code, or section 2907.03 of the Revised Code if the victim of the violation was less than twelve years of age;

(2) Committing, attempting to commit, conspiring to commit, or complicity in committing a violation of section 2903.01, 2903.02, or 2905.01 of the Revised Code that was committed with a purpose to gratify the sexual needs or desires of the child.

(G) As used in this section, "secure facility" has the same meaning as in section 2950.01 of the Revised Code.

**HISTORY: 149 v S 3 (Eff 1-1-2002); 149 v H 393. Eff 7-5-2002; 150 v S 5, § 1, eff. 7-31-03; 152 v S 10, § 1, eff. 1-1-08.**

The effective date is set by § 3 of 152 v S 10.

## § 2152.831 Hearing to determine tier classification; order; reclassification.

(A) If, on or after January 1, 2008, a juvenile court adjudicates a child a delinquent child and classifies the child a juvenile offender registrant pursuant to section 2152.82 or 2152.83 of the Revised Code, before issuing the order that classifies the child a juvenile offender registrant the court shall conduct a hearing to determine whether to classify the child a tier I sex offender/child-victim offender, a tier II sex offender/child-victim offender, or a tier III sex offender/ child-victim offender.

(B) When a judge issues an order under section 2152.82 or 2152.83 of the Revised Code that classifies a delinquent child a juvenile offender registrant, in addition to the other statements and information required by the section under which the order is issued, the judge shall include in the order its determination made under division (A) of this section as to whether the child is a tier I sex offender/child-victim offender, a tier II sex offender/child-victim offender, or a tier III sex offender/child-victim offender. When a judge issues an order under section 2152.84 or 2152.85 of the Revised Code that reclassifies a delinquent child from one tier of sex offender/child-victim offender to a different tier of sex offender/child-victim offender, in addition to the other statements and information required by the section under which the order is issued, the judge shall include in the order its determination as to the reclassification of the child and the tier to which the child is reclassified.

(C) The provisions of this section do not apply to a delinquent child if the court is required to classify the child as both a juvenile offender registrant and a public registry-qualified juvenile offender registrant pursuant to section 2152.86 of the Revised Code.

**HISTORY: 152 v S 10, § 1, eff. 1-1-08.**

The effective date is set by § 3 of 152 v S 10.

## § 2152.84 Hearing upon completion of disposition on whether to continue classification or determination; reclassification.

(A)(1) When a juvenile court judge issues an order under section 2152.82 or division (A) or (B) of section 2152.83 of the Revised Code that classifies a delinquent child a juvenile offender registrant and specifies that the child has a duty to comply with sections 2950.04, 2950.041 [2950.04.1], 2950.05, and 2950.06 of the Revised Code, upon completion of the disposition of that child made for the sexually oriented offense or the child-victim oriented offense on which the juvenile offender registrant order was based, the judge or the judge's successor in office shall conduct a hearing to review the effectiveness of the disposition and of any treatment provided for the child, to determine the risks that the child might re-offend, to determine whether the prior classification of the child as a juvenile offender registrant should be continued or terminated as provided under division (A)(2) of this section, and to determine whether its prior determination made at the hearing held pursuant to section 2152.831 [2152.83.1] of the Revised Code as to whether the child is a tier I sex offender/child-victim offender, a tier II sex offender/child-victim offender, or a tier III sex offender/child-victim offender should be continued or modified as provided under division (A)(2) of this section.

(2) Upon completion of a hearing under division (A)(1) of this section, the judge, in the judge's discretion and after consideration of all relevant factors, including but not limited to, the factors listed in division (D) of section 2152.83 of the Revised Code, shall do one of the following as applicable:

(a) Enter an order that continues the classification of the delinquent child as a juvenile offender registrant made in the prior order issued under section 2152.82 or division (A) or (B) of section 2152.83 of the Revised Code and the prior determination included in the order that the child is a tier I sex offender/child-victim offender, a tier II sex offender/child-victim offender, or a tier III sex offender/child-victim offender, whichever is applicable;

(b) If the prior order was issued under division (B) of section 2152.83 of the Revised Code, enter an order that contains a determination that the delinquent child no longer is a juvenile offender registrant and no longer has a duty to comply with sections 2950.04, 2950.041 [2950.04.1], 2950.05, and 2950.06 of the Revised Code. An order issued under division (A)(2)(b) of this section also terminates all prior determinations that the child is a tier I sex offender/child-victim offender, a tier II sex offender/child-victim offender, or a tier III sex offender/child-victim offender, whichever is applicable. Division (A)(2)(b) of this section does not apply to a prior order issued under section 2152.82 or division (A) of section 2152.83 of the Revised Code.

(c) If the prior order was issued under section 2152.82 or division (A) or (B) of section 2152.83 of the Revised Code, enter an order that continues the classification of the delinquent child as a juvenile offender registrant made in the prior order issued under section 2152.82 or division (A) or (B) of section 2152.83 of the Revised Code, and that modifies the prior determination made at the hearing held pursuant to section 2152.831 [2152.83.1] of the Revised Code that the child is a tier I sex offender/child-victim offender, a tier II sex offender/child-victim offender, or a tier III sex offender/child-victim offender, whichever is applicable. An order issued under division (A)(2)(c) of this section shall not include a determination that increases to a higher tier the tier classification of the delinquent child. An order issued under division (A)(2)(c) of this section shall specify the new determination made by the court at a hearing held pursuant to division (A)(1) of this section as to whether the child is a tier I sex offender/child-victim offender, a tier II sex offender/child-victim offender, or a tier III sex offender/child-victim offender, whichever is applicable.

(B)(1) If a judge issues an order under division (A)(2)(a) of this section that continues the prior classification of the delinquent child as a juvenile offender registrant and the prior determination included in the order that the child is a tier I sex offender/child-victim offender, a tier II sex offender/child-victim offender, or a tier III sex offender/child-victim offender, whichever is applicable, the prior classification and the prior determination shall remain in effect.

(2) A judge may issue an order under division (A)(2)(c) of this section that contains a determination that reclassifies a child from a tier III sex offender/child-victim offender classification to a tier II sex offender/child-victim offender classification or to a tier I sex offender/child-victim offender classification.

A judge may issue an order under division (A)(2)(c) of this section that contains a determination that reclassifies a child from a tier II sex offender/child-victim offender classification. A judge may not issue an order under that division that contains a determination that reclassifies a child from a tier II sex offender/child-victim offender classification to a tier III sex offender/child-victim offender classification.

A judge may not issue an order under division (A)(2)(c) of this section that contains a determination that reclassifies a child from a tier I sex offender/child-victim offender classification to a tier II sex offender/child-victim offender classification or to a tier III sex offender/child-victim offender classification.

If a judge issues an order under this division that contains a determination that reclassifies a child, the judge shall provide a copy of the order to the delinquent child and the bureau of criminal identification and investigation, and the bureau, upon receipt of the copy of the order, promptly shall notify the sheriff with whom the child most recently registered under section 2950.04 or 2950.041 [2950.04.1] of the Revised Code of the determination and reclassification.

(3) If a judge issues an order under division (A)(2)(b) of this section that declassifies the delinquent child as a juvenile offender registrant, the judge shall provide a copy of the order to the bureau of criminal identification and investigation, and the bureau, upon receipt of the copy of the order, promptly shall notify the sheriff with whom the child most recently registered under section 2950.04 or 2950.041 [2950.04.1] of the Revised Code of the declassification.

(C) If a judge issues an order under division (A)(2)(a), (b), or (c) of this section, the judge shall provide to the delinquent child and to the delinquent child's parent, guardian, or custodian a copy of the order and, if applicable, a notice containing the information described in divisions (A) and (B) of section 2950.03 of the Revised Code. The judge shall provide the notice at the time of the issuance of the order and shall comply with divisions (B) and (C) of that section regarding that notice and the provision of it.

(D) An order issued under division (A)(2)(a) or (c) of this section and any determinations included in the order shall remain in effect for the period of time specified in section 2950.07 of the Revised Code, subject to a modification or termination of the order under section 2152.85 of the Revised Code, and section 2152.851 [2152.85.1] of the Revised Code applies regarding the order and the determinations. If an order is issued under division (A)(2)(a) or (c) of this section, the child's attainment of eighteen or twenty-one years of age does not affect or terminate the order, and the order remains in effect for the period of time described in this division.

(E) The provisions of this section do not apply to a delinquent child who is classified as both a juvenile offender registrant and a public registry-qualified juvenile offender registrant pursuant to section 2152.86 of the Revised Code.

**HISTORY: 149 v S 3 (Eff 1-1-2002); 149 v H 393. Eff 7-5-2002; 150 v S 5, § 1, eff. 7-31-03; 152 v S 10, § 1, eff. 1-1-08.**

The effective date is set by § 3 of 152 v S 10.

## § 2152.85 Petition requesting reclassification or declassification.

(A) Regardless of when the delinquent child was classified a juvenile offender registrant, upon the expiration of the applicable period of time specified in division (B)(1), (2), or (3) of this section, a delinquent child who has been classified pursuant to this section or section 2152.82 or 2152.83 of the Revised Code a juvenile offender registrant may petition the judge who made the classification, or that judge's successor in office, to do one of the following:

(1) If the order containing the juvenile offender registrant classification also includes a determination by the juvenile court judge that the delinquent child is a tier III sex offender/child-victim offender, to enter, as applicable, an order that contains a determination that reclassifies the child as either a tier II sex offender/child-victim offender or a tier I sex offender/child-victim offender, the reason or reasons for that reclassification, and a determination that the child remains a juvenile offender registrant, or an order that contains a determination that the child no longer is a juvenile offender registrant and no longer has a duty to comply with sections 2950.04, 2950.041 [2950.04.1], 2950.05, and 2950.06 of the Revised Code;

(2) If the order containing the juvenile offender registrant classification also includes a determination by the juvenile court judge that the delinquent child is a tier II sex offender/child-victim offender, to enter, as applicable, an order that contains a determination that reclassifies the child as a tier I sex offender/child-victim offender, the reason or reasons for that reclassification, and a determination that the child remains a juvenile offender registrant, or an order that contains a determination that the child no longer is a juvenile offender registrant and no longer has a duty to comply with sections 2950.04, 2950.041 [2950.04.1], 2950.05, and 2950.06 of the Revised Code;

(3) If the order containing the juvenile offender registrant classification also includes a determination by the juvenile court judge that the delinquent child is a tier I sex offender/child-victim offender, to enter an order that contains a determination that the child no longer is a juvenile offender registrant and no longer has a duty to comply with sections 2950.04, 2950.041 [2950.04.1], 2950.05, and 2950.06 of the Revised Code.

(B) A delinquent child who has been adjudicated a delinquent child for committing on or after January 1, 2002, a sexually oriented offense or a child-victim oriented offense and who has been classified a juvenile offender registrant relative to that offense may file a petition under division (A) of this section requesting reclassification or declassification as described in that division after the expiration of one of the following periods of time:

(1) The delinquent child initially may file a petition not earlier than three years after the entry of the juvenile court judge's order after the mandatory hearing conducted under section 2152.84 of the Revised Code.

(2) After the delinquent child's initial filing of a petition under division (B)(1) of this section, the child may file a second petition not earlier than three years after the judge has entered an order deciding the petition under division (B)(1) of this section.

(3) After the delinquent child's filing of a petition under division (B)(2) of this section, thereafter, the delinquent child may file a petition under this division upon the expiration of five years after the judge has entered an order deciding the petition under division (B)(2) of this section or the most recent petition the delinquent child has filed under this division.

(C) Upon the filing of a petition under division (A) of this section, the judge may review the prior classification or determination in question and, upon consideration of all relevant factors and information, including, but not limited to the factors listed in division (D) of section 2152.83 of the Revised Code, the judge, in the judge's discretion, shall do one of the following:

(1) Enter an order denying the petition;

(2) Issue an order that reclassifies or declassifies the delinquent child in the requested manner.

(D) If a judge issues an order under division (C)(1) of this section that denies a petition, the prior classification of the delinquent child as a juvenile offender registrant, and the prior determination that the child is a tier I sex offender/child-victim offender, a tier II sex offender/child-victim offender, or a tier III sex offender/child-victim offender, whichever is applicable, shall remain in effect.

A judge may issue an order under division (C)(2) of this section that contains a determination that reclassifies a child from a tier III sex offender/child-victim offender classification to a tier II sex offender/child-victim offender classification or to a tier I sex offender/child-victim offender classification.

A judge may issue an order under division (C)(2) of this section that contains a determination that reclassifies a child from a tier II sex offender/child-victim offender classification to a tier I sex offender/child-victim offender classification.

If a judge issues an order under this division that contains a determination that reclassifies a child, the judge shall provide a copy of the order to the delinquent child and the bureau of criminal identification and investigation, and the bureau, upon receipt of the copy of the order, promptly shall notify the sheriff with whom the child most recently registered under section 2950.04 or 2950.041 [2950.04.1] of the Revised Code of the determination and reclassification.

If a judge issues an order under division (C)(2) of this section that declassifies the delinquent child, the order also terminates all prior determinations that the child is a tier I sex offender/child-victim offender, a tier II sex offender/child-victim offender, or a tier III sex offender/child-victim offender, whichever is applicable. If a judge issues an order under division (C)(2) of this section that declassifies the delinquent child, the judge shall provide a copy of the order to the bureau of criminal identification and investigation, and the bureau, upon receipt of a copy of the order, promptly shall notify the sheriff with whom the child most recently registered under section 2950.04 or 2950.041 [2950.04.1] of the Revised Code of the declassification.

(E) If a judge issues an order under division (C)(1) or (2) of this section, the judge shall provide to the delinquent child and to the delinquent child's parent, guardian, or custodian a copy of the order and, if applicable, a notice containing the information described in divisions (A) and (B) of section 2950.03 of the Revised Code. The judge shall provide the notice at the time of the issuance of the order and shall comply with divisions (B) and (C) of that section regarding that notice and the provision of it.

(F) An order issued under division (C) of this section shall remain in effect for the period of time specified in section 2950.07 of the Revised Code, subject to a further modification or future termination of the order under this section. If an order is issued under division (C) of this section, the child's attainment of eighteen or twenty-one years of age does not affect or terminate the order, and the order remains in effect for the period of time described in this division.

(G) The provisions of this section do not apply to a delinquent child who is classified as both a juvenile offender registrant and a public registry-qualified juvenile offender registrant pursuant to section 2152.86 of the Revised Code.

**HISTORY: 149 v S 3. Eff 1-1-2002; 150 v S 5, § 1, eff. 7-31-03; 152 v S 10, § 1, eff. 1-1-08.**

The effective date is set by § 3 of 152 v S 10.

The provisions of § 3 of SB 3 (149 v —) read as follows:

SECTION 3. Sections 1 and 2 of this act shall take effect on January 1, 2002, or the earliest date permitted by law, whichever is later.

## § 2152.851 Continuation of duty imposed on child prior to 1-1-08.

If, prior to January 1, 2008, a judge issues an order under section 2152.82, 2152.83, 2152.84, or 2152.85 of the Revised Code that classifies a delinquent child a juvenile offender registrant based on an adjudication for a sexually oriented offense or a child-victim oriented offense as those terms were defined in section 2950.01 of the Revised Code prior to January 1, 2008, and if, on and after January 1, 2008, the offense upon which the order was based is a sexually oriented offense or a child-victim oriented offense as those terms are defined in section 2950.01 of the Revised Code on and after January 1, 2008, notwithstanding the changes to sections 2152.82, 2152.83, 2152.84, and 2152.85 of the Revised Code made on January 1, 2008, on and after that date, the order shall remain in effect for the period described in the section under which it was issued as that section exists on and after January 1, 2008, subject to subsequent modification or termination under section 2152.84, 2152.85, or 2950.15 of the Revised Code, or, if division (A)(3) of section 2152.86 of the Revised Code applies regarding the child, for the period described in division (C) of that section subject to modification or termination under section 2152.84, 2152.85, or 2950.15 of the Revised Code, whichever is applicable, and the duty to comply with sections 2950.04, 2950.041 [2950.04.1], 2950.05, and 2950.06 of the Revised Code on and after January 1, 2008, shall be considered, for purposes of section 2950.07 of the Revised Code and for all other purposes, to be a continuation of the duty imposed upon the child prior to January 1, 2008, under the order issued under section 2152.82, 2152.83, 2152.84, or 2152.85 and Chapter 2950. of the Revised Code.

**HISTORY: 150 v S 5, § 1, eff. 7-31-03; 152 v S 10, § 1, eff. 1-1-08.**

The effective date is set by § 3 of 152 v S 10.

## § 2152.86 Court's duty on or after January 1, 2008 to classify child as juvenile offender registrant, specify compliance with SORN law, and additionally classify child as public registry-qualified juvenile offender registrant; reclassification.

(A)(1) The court that, on or after January 1, 2008, adjudicates a child a delinquent child for committing an act shall issue as part of the dispositional order an order that classifies the child a juvenile offender registrant, specifies that the child has a duty to comply with sections 2950.04, 2950.041 [2950.04.1], 2950.05, and 2950.06 of the Revised Code, and additionally classifies the child a public registry-qualified juvenile offender registrant if the child was fourteen, fifteen, sixteen, or seventeen years of age at the time of committing the act, the court imposed on the child a serious youthful offender dispositional sentence under section 2152.13 of the Revised Code, and the child is adjudicated a delinquent child for committing, attempting to commit, conspiring to commit, or complicity in committing any of the following acts:

(a) A violation of section 2907.02 of the Revised Code, division (B) of section 2907.05 of the Revised Code, or section 2907.03 of the Revised Code if the victim of the violation was less than twelve years of age;

(b) A violation of section 2903.01, 2903.02, or 2905.01 of the Revised Code that was committed with a purpose to gratify the sexual needs or desires of the child.

(2) Upon a child's release, on or after January 1, 2008, from the department of youth services, the court shall issue an order that classifies the child a juvenile offender registrant, specifies that the child has a duty to comply with sections 2950.04, 2950.041 [2950.04.1], 2950.05, and 2950.06 of the Revised Code, and additionally classifies the child a public registry-qualified juvenile offender registrant if all of the following apply:

(a) The child was adjudicated a delinquent child, and a juvenile court imposed on the child a serious youthful offender dispositional sentence under section 2152.13 of the Revised Code for committing one of the acts described in division (A)(1)(a) or (b) of this section.

(b) The child was fourteen, fifteen, sixteen, or seventeen years of age at the time of committing the act.

(c) The court did not issue an order classifying the child as both a juvenile offender registrant and a public registry-qualified juvenile offender registrant pursuant to division (A)(1) of this section.

(3) If a court issued an order classifying a child a juvenile offender registrant pursuant to section 2152.82 or 2152.83 of the Revised Code prior to January 1, 2008, not later than February 1, 2008, the court shall issue a new order that reclassifies the child as a juvenile offender registrant, specifies that the child has a duty to comply with sections 2950.04, 2950.041 [2950.04.1], 2950.05, and 2950.06 of the Revised Code, and additionally classifies the child a public registry-qualified juvenile offender registrant if all of the following apply:

(a) The sexually oriented offense that was the basis of the previous order that classified the child a juvenile offender registrant was an act described in division (A)(1)(a) or (b) of this section.

(b) The child was fourteen, fifteen, sixteen, or seventeen years of age at the time of committing the act.

(c) The court imposed on the child a serious youthful offender dispositional sentence under section 2152.13 of the Revised Code for the act described in division (A)(1)(a) or (b) of this section.

(B)(1) If an order is issued under division (A)(1), (2), or (3) of this section, the classification of tier III sex offender/child-victim offender automatically applies to the delinquent child based on the sexually oriented offense the child committed, subject to a possible reclassification pursuant to division (D) of this section for a child whose delinquent act was committed prior to January 1, 2008. If an order is issued under division (A)(2) of this section regarding a child whose delinquent act described in division (A)(1)(a) or (b) of this section was committed prior to January 1, 2008, or if an order is issued under division (A)(3) of this section regarding a delinquent child, the order shall inform the child and the child's parent, guardian, or custodian, that the child has a right to a hearing as described in division (D) of this section and inform the child and the child's parent, guardian, or custodian of the procedures for requesting the hearing and the period of time within which the request for the hearing must be made. Section 2152.831 [2152.83.1] of the Revised Code does not apply regarding an order issued under division (A)(1), (2), or (3) of this section.

(2) The judge that issues an order under division (A)(1), (2), or (3) of this section shall provide to the delinquent child who is the subject of the order and to the delinquent child's parent, guardian, or custodian the notice required under divisions (A) and (B) of section 2950.03 of the Revised Code and shall provide as part of that notice a copy of the order required under division (A)(1), (2), or (3) of this section. The judge shall include the order in the delinquent child's dispositional order and shall specify in the dispositional order that the order issued under division (A)(1), (2), or (3) of this section was made pursuant to this section.

(C) An order issued under division (A)(1), (2), or (3) of this section shall remain in effect for the period of time specified in section 2950.07 of the Revised Code as it exists on and after January 1, 2008, subject to a judicial termination of that period of time as provided in section 2950.15 of the Revised Code, subject to a possible reclassification of the child pursuant to division (D) of this section if the child's delinquent act was committed prior to January 1, 2008. If an order is issued under division (A)(1), (2), or (3) of this section, the child's attainment of eighteen or twenty-one years of age does not affect or terminate the order, and the order remains in effect for the period of time described in this division. If an order is issued under division (A)(3) of this section, the duty to comply with sections 2950.04, 2950.041 [2950.04.1], 2950.05, and 2950.06 of the Revised Code based upon that order shall be considered, for purposes of section 2950.07 of the Revised Code and for all other purposes, to be a continuation of the duty to comply with those sections imposed upon the child prior to January 1, 2008, under the order issued under section 2152.82, 2152.83, 2152.84, or 2152.85 and Chapter 2950. of the Revised Code.

(D)(1) If an order is issued under division (A)(2) of this section regarding a delinquent child whose delinquent act described in division (A)(1)(a) or (b) of this section was committed prior to January 1, 2008, or if an order is issued under division (A)(3) of this section regarding a delinquent child, except as otherwise provided in this division, the child may request as a matter of right a court hearing to contest the court's classification in the order of the child as a public registry-qualified juvenile offender registrant. To request the hearing, not later than the date that is sixty days after the delinquent child is provided with the copy of the order, the delinquent child shall file a petition with the juvenile court that issued the order.

If the delinquent child requests a hearing by timely filing a petition with the juvenile court, the delinquent child shall serve a copy of the petition on the prosecutor who handled the case in which the delinquent child was adjudicated a delinquent child for committing the sexually oriented offense or child-victim oriented offense that resulted in the delinquent child's registration duty under section 2950.04 or 2950.041 [2950.04.1] of the Revised Code. The prosecutor shall represent the interest of the state in the hearing. In any hearing under this division, the Rules of Juvenile Procedure apply except to the extent that those Rules would by their nature be clearly inapplicable. The court shall schedule a hearing and shall provide notice to the delinquent child and the delinquent child's parent, guardian, or custodian and to the prosecutor of the date, time, and place of the hearing.

If the delinquent child requests a hearing in accordance with this division, until the court issues its decision at or subsequent to the hearing, the delinquent child shall comply with Chapter 2950. of the Revised Code as it exists on and after January 1, 2008. If a delinquent child requests a hearing in accordance with this division, at the hearing, all parties are entitled to be heard, and the court shall consider all relevant information and testimony presented relative to the issue of whether the child should be classified a public registry-qualified juvenile offender registrant. Notwithstanding the court's classification of the delinquent child as a public registry-qualified juvenile offender registrant, the court may terminate that classification if it determines by clear and convincing evidence that the classification is in error.

If the court decides to terminate the court's classification of the delinquent child as a public registry-qualified juvenile offender registrant, the court shall issue an order that specifies that it has determined that the child is not a public registry-qualified juvenile offender registrant and that it has terminated the court's classification of the delinquent child as a public registry-qualified juvenile offender registrant. The court promptly shall serve a copy of the order upon the sheriff with whom the delinquent child most recently registered under section 2950.04 or 2950.041 [2950.04.1] of the Revised Code and upon the bureau of criminal identification and investigation. The delinquent child and the prosecutor have the right to appeal the decision of the court issued under this division.

If the delinquent child fails to request a hearing in accordance with this division within the applicable sixty-day period specified in this division, the failure constitutes a waiver by the delinquent child of the delinquent child's right to a hearing under this division, and the delinquent child is bound by the court's classification of the delinquent child as a public registry-qualified juvenile offender registrant.

(2) An order issued under division (D)(1) of this section is independent of any order of a type described in division (F) of section 2950.031 [2950.03.1] of the Revised Code or division (E) of section 2950.032 [2950.03.2] of the Revised Code, and the court may issue an order under both division (D)(1) of this section and an order of a type described in division (F) of section 2950.031 [2950.03.1] of the Revised Code or division (E) of section 2950.032 [2950.03.2] of the Revised Code. A court that conducts a hearing under division (D)(1) of this section may consolidate that hearing with a hearing conducted for the same delinquent child under division (F) of section 2950.031 [2950.03.1] of the Revised Code or division (E) of section 2950.032 [2950.03.2] of the Revised Code.

**HISTORY: 152 v S 10, § 1, eff. 1-1-08.**

The effective date is set by § 3 of 152 v S 10.

## § 2152.99 Penalty for failing to provide information to foster caregiver.

Whoever violates division (G) of section 2152.72 of the Revised Code is guilty of a minor misdemeanor.

**HISTORY: 148 v S 179, § 3. Eff 1-1-2002.**

The effective date is set by section 5 of SB 179.

# TITLE 23: COURTS — COMMON PLEAS

## CHAPTER 2301: ORGANIZATION



[BAILIFF]

### § 2301.15 Duties of criminal bailiff; costs.

The criminal bailiff shall act for the sheriff in criminal cases and matters of a criminal nature in the court of common pleas and the probate court of the county. Under the direction of the sheriff, he shall be present during trials of criminal cases in those courts and during such trials perform all the duties as are performed by the sheriff. The criminal bailiff shall conduct prisoners to and from the jail of the county and for that purpose shall have access to the jail and to the courtroom, whenever ordered by such courts, and have care and charge of such prisoners when so doing. Under the direction of the sheriff, the criminal bailiff shall convey to state correctional institutions all persons sentenced thereto. He shall receive and collect from the treasurer of state all costs in such criminal cases in the same manner as the sheriff is required to do, and pay the amount so collected to the sheriff of such county.

**HISTORY: RS § 474-2; 76 v 54, § 2; GC § 1543; Bureau of Code Revision, 10-1-53; 145 v H 571. Eff 10-6-94.**

### § 2301.16 Bailiff shall give bond.

Before entering upon the discharge of his duties, the criminal bailiff shall give a bond to the sheriff in the sum of five thousand dollars, with good and sufficient sureties, conditioned for the faithful discharge of his duties. The judges of the court of common pleas shall fix a compensation for his services, payable monthly from the fee fund, upon the warrant of the county auditor.

**HISTORY: RS § 474-4; 76 v 54; 90 v 162, § 4; GC § 1545; Bureau of Code Revision. Eff 10-1-53.**

### § 2301.17 Additional temporary bailiff.

On the application of the sheriff, in a criminal case, if the court of common pleas is satisfied that the administration of justice requires an additional criminal bailiff to execute process, it may appoint such additional bailiff, whose powers and duties shall cease when such case is determined.

**HISTORY: RS § 474-3; 76 v 54, § 3; GC § 1544; Bureau of Code Revision. Eff 10-1-53.**

[DEPARTMENT OF PROBATION]

### § 2301.27 County or multicounty department of probation or contract for probation and supervisory services.

(A)(1)(a) The court of common pleas may establish a county department of probation. The establishment of the department shall be entered upon the journal of the court, and the clerk of the court of common pleas shall certify a copy of the journal entry establishing the department to each elective officer and board of the county. The department shall consist of a chief probation officer and the number of other probation officers and employees, clerks, and stenographers that is fixed from time to time by the court. The court shall appoint those individuals, fix their salaries, and supervise their work.

(b) When appointing a chief probation officer, the court shall do all of the following:

(i) Publicly advertise the position on the court's web site, including, but not limited to, the job description, qualifications for the position, and the application requirements;

(ii) Conduct a competitive hiring process that adheres to state and federal equal employment opportunity laws;

(iii) Review applicants who meet the posted qualifications and comply with the application requirements.

(c) The court shall not appoint as a probation officer any person who does not possess the training, experience, and other qualifications prescribed by the adult parole authority created by section 5149.02 of the Revised Code. Probation officers have all the powers of regular police officers and shall perform any duties that are designated by the judge or judges of the court. All positions within the department of probation shall be in the classified service of the civil service of the county.

(2) If two or more counties desire to jointly establish a probation department for those counties, the judges of the courts of common pleas of those counties may establish a probation department for those counties. If a probation department is established pursuant to division (A)(2) of this section to serve more than one county, the judges of the courts of common pleas that established the department shall designate the county treasurer of one of the counties served by the department as the treasurer to whom probation fees paid under section 2951.021 of the Revised Code are to be appropriated and transferred under division (A)(2) of section 321.44 of the Revised Code for deposit into the multicounty probation services fund established under division (B) of section 321.44 of the Revised Code.

The cost of the administration and operation of a probation department established for two or more counties shall be prorated to the respective counties on the basis of population.

(3) Probation officers shall receive, in addition to their respective salaries, their necessary and reasonable travel and other expenses incurred in the performance of their duties. Their salaries and expenses shall be paid monthly from the county treasury in the manner provided for the payment of the compensation of other appointees of the court.

(4) Probation officers shall be trained in accordance with a set of minimum standards that are established by the adult parole authority of the department of rehabilitation and correction.

(B)(1) In lieu of establishing a county department of probation under division (A) of this section and in lieu of entering into an agreement with the adult parole authority as described in division (B) of section 2301.32 of the Revised Code, the court of common pleas may request the board of county commissioners to contract with, and upon that request the board may contract with, any nonprofit, public or private agency, association, or organization for the provision of probation services and supervisory services for persons placed under community control sanctions. The contract shall specify that each individual providing the probation services and supervisory services shall possess the training, experience, and other qualifications prescribed by the adult parole authority. The individuals who provide the probation services and supervisory services shall not be included in the classified or unclassified civil service of the county.

(2) In lieu of establishing a county department of probation under division (A) of this section and in lieu of entering into an agreement with the adult parole authority as described in division (B) of section 2301.32 of the Revised Code, the courts of common pleas of two or more adjoining counties jointly may request the boards of county commissioners of those counties to contract with, and upon that request the boards of county commissioners of two or more adjoining counties jointly may contract with, any nonprofit, public or private agency, association, or organization for the provision of probation services and supervisory services for persons placed under community control sanctions for those counties. The contract shall specify that each individual providing the probation services and supervisory services shall possess the training, experience, and other qualifications prescribed by the adult parole authority. The individuals who provide the probation services and supervisory services shall not be included in the classified or unclassified civil service of any of those counties.

(C) The chief probation officer may grant permission to a probation officer to carry firearms when required in the discharge of official duties if the probation officer has successfully completed a basic firearm training program that is approved by the executive director of the Ohio peace officer training commission. A probation officer who has been granted permission to carry a firearm in the discharge of official duties, annually shall successfully complete a firearms requalification program in accordance with section 109.801 of the Revised Code.

(D) As used in this section and sections 2301.28 to 2301.32 of the Revised Code, "community control sanction" has the same meaning as in section 2929.01 of the Revised Code.

**HISTORY: GC § 1554-1; 111 v 423; Bureau of Code Revision, 10-1-53; 125 v 327 (Eff 10-13-53); 129 v 481 (Eff 10-18-61); 130 v 647 (Eff 1-23-63); 130 v PtII, 138 (Eff 3-18-65); 145 v H 152 (Eff 7-1-93); 145 v H 406 (Eff 11-11-94); 146 v S 269 (Eff 7-1-96); 146 v H 670 (Eff 12-2-96); 149 v H 510. Eff 3-31-2003; 149 v H 490, § 1, eff. 1-1-04; 2011 HB 86, § 1, eff. Sept. 30, 2011.**

Acts 2011, HB 86, § 12 provides: "Section 1716.99 of the Revised Code is presented in this act as a composite of the section as amended by both Am. Sub. H.B. 59 and Sub. S.B. 2 of the 123rd General Assembly. The General Assembly, applying the principle stated in division (B) of section 1.52 of the Revised Code that amendments are to be harmonized if reasonably capable of simultaneous operation, finds that the composites are the resulting versions of the sections in effect prior to the effective date of the sections as presented in this act."

The effective date is set by section 4 of HB 490.

**Comment, Legislative Service Commission**

Sections 2301.27, 2301.56, and 2967.26 of the Revised Code are amended by this act [Am. Sub. H.B. 490] (effective January 1, 2004) and also by Sub. H.B. 510, both of the 124th General Assembly. * * * Comparison of these amendments in pursuance of section 1.52 of the Revised Code discloses that they are not irreconcilable so that they are required by that section to be harmonized to give effect to each amendment.

## § 2301.271 Development of minimum standards for training of probation officers.

(A) The adult parole authority of the department of rehabilitation and correction shall develop minimum standards for the training of probation officers as provided by section 2301.27 of the Revised Code. The adult parole authority shall consult and collaborate with the supreme court in developing the standards.

(B) Within six months after the effective date of this section, the department of rehabilitation and correction shall make available a copy of the minimum standards to the following entities:

(1) Every municipal court, county court, and court of common pleas;

(2) Every probation department.

**HISTORY: 2011 HB 86, § 1, eff. Sept. 30, 2011.**

## § 2301.28 Supervision over persons on probation, conditionally pardoned, or paroled.

The court of common pleas of a county in which a county department of probation has been established under division (A) of section 2301.27 of the Revised Code, in addition to employing the department in investigation and in the administration of its own orders imposing community control sanctions, shall receive into the legal control or supervision of the department any person who is a resident of the county and who has been placed under a community control sanction by order of any other court exercising criminal jurisdiction in this state, whether within or without the county in which the department of probation is located, upon the request of the other court and subject to its continuing jurisdiction. The court of common pleas also shall receive into the legal custody or supervision of the department any person who is paroled, released under a post-release control sanction, or conditionally pardoned from a state correctional institution and who resides or remains in the county, if requested by the adult parole authority created by section 5149.02 of the Revised Code or any other authority having power to parole or release from any institution of that nature.

As used in this section and section 2301.30 of the Revised Code, "post-release control sanction" has the same meaning as in section 2967.01 of the Revised Code.

**HISTORY: GC § 1554-2; 111 v 424; Bureau of Code Revision, 10-1-53; 129 v 481 (Eff 10-18-61); 130 v PtII, 139 (Eff 3-18-65); 145 v H 152 (Eff 7-1-93); 145 v H 571. Eff 10-6-94; 149 v H 490, § 1, eff. 1-1-04.**

The effective date is set by section 4 of HB 490.

## § 2301.29 Rules of adult parole authority to govern; local court rules.

In all cases in which the county department of probation provided for in division (A) of section 2301.27 of the Revised Code acquires legal custody of or supervision over a person who is granted a conditional pardon or a parole from a state correctional institution, the court of common pleas and the department shall be governed by the rules of the adult parole authority created by section 5149.02 of the Revised Code that are applicable to those cases and by the laws of the state applicable to those cases. In the case of other persons placed in its legal control or under its supervision, the department shall administer the orders and conditions of the authority so placing those persons. The court may exercise supervision over the department by adopting rules that are not inconsistent with law or with the rules of the adult parole authority and that shall be observed and enforced by the probation officers of the department.

As used in this section "pardon," "parole," and "state correctional institution" have the same meanings as in section 2967.01 of the Revised Code.

**HISTORY: GC § 1554-3; 111 v 424; 118 v 288(300), § 25; Bureau of Code Revision, 10-1-53; 130 v PtII, 140 (Eff 3-18-65); 145 v H 152 (Eff 7-1-93); 145 v H 571. Eff 10-6-94.**

## § 2301.30 Duties of probation department.

The court of common pleas of a county in which a county department of probation is established under division (A) of section 2301.27 of the Revised Code shall require the department, in the rules through which the supervision of the department is exercised or otherwise, to do all of the following:

(A) Furnish to each person under a community control sanction or post-release control sanction or on parole under its supervision or in its custody, a written statement of the conditions of the community control sanction, post-release control sanction, or parole and instruct the person regarding the conditions;

(B) Keep informed concerning the conduct and condition of each person in its custody or under its supervision by visiting, the requiring of reports, and otherwise;

(C) Use all suitable methods, not inconsistent with the conditions of the community control sanction, post-release control sanction, or parole, to aid and encourage the persons under its supervision or in its custody and to bring about improvement in their conduct and condition;

(D) Establish policies regarding the supervision of probationers that shall include, but not be limited to, all of the following:

(1) The minimum number of supervision contacts required for probationers, based on each probationer's risk to reoffend as determined by the single validated risk assessment tool selected by the department of rehabilitation and correction under section 5120.114 of the Revised Code, under which higher risk probationers receive the greatest amount of supervision;

(2) A graduated response policy to govern which types of violations a probation officer may respond to administratively and which type require a violation hearing by the court.

(E) Keep detailed records of the work of the department, keep accurate and complete accounts of all moneys collected from persons under its supervision or in its custody, and keep or give receipts for those moneys;

(F) Make reports to the adult parole authority created by section 5149.02 of the Revised Code that it requires.

**HISTORY: GC § 1554-5; 111 v 425; Bureau of Code Revision, 10-1-53; 130 v PtII, 140 (Eff 3-18-65); 145 v H 152. Eff 7-1-93; 149 v H 490, § 1, eff. 1-1-04; 2011 HB 86, § 1, eff. Sept. 30, 2011.**

The effective date is set by section 4 of HB 490.

## § 2301.31 Arrest of parolees.

(A) If a person on parole is in the custody of a county department of probation provided for in division (A) of section 2301.27 of the Revised Code, any probation officer of that department may arrest the person without a warrant for any violation of any condition of parole, as defined in section 2967.01 of the Revised Code, or of any rule governing persons on parole. If a person on parole is in the custody of a county department of probation provided for in division (A) of section 2301.27 of the Revised Code, any probation officer or peace officer shall arrest the person without a warrant for any violation of any condition of parole or any rule governing persons on parole upon the written order of the chief probation officer of that department. Any peace officer may arrest the person without a warrant, in accordance with section 2941.46 of the Revised Code, if the peace officer has reasonable ground to believe that the person has violated or is violating any of the following that is a condition of the person's parole:

(1) A condition that prohibits ownership, possession, or use of a firearm, deadly weapon, ammunition, or dangerous ordnance;

(2) A condition that prohibits the person from being within a specified structure or geographic area;

(3) A condition that confines the person to a residence, facility, or other structure;

(4) A condition that prohibits the person from contacting or communicating with any specified individual;

(5) A condition that prohibits the person from associating with a specified individual.

(B) A person who is arrested as provided in this section may be confined in the jail or juvenile detention facility, as the case may be, of the county in which the person is arrested, until released or removed to the proper institution. Upon making an arrest under this section, the arresting probation officer or peace officer or the arresting officer's department or agency promptly shall notify the chief probation officer of the county department of probation with custody of the person or the chief probation officer's designee that the person has been arrested.

Upon the written order of the chief probation officer of the county department with custody of the person, the person may be released on parole or reimprisoned or recommitted to the proper institution. An appeal from an order of reimprisonment or recommitment may be taken to the adult parole authority created by section 5149.02 of the Revised Code, and the decision of the authority on the appeal shall be final. The manner of taking an appeal of that nature and the disposition of the appellant pending the making and determination of the appeal shall be governed by the rules and orders of the adult parole authority.

(C) Nothing in this section limits the powers of arrest granted to certain law enforcement officers and citizens under sections 2935.03 and 2935.04 of the Revised Code.

(D) As used in this section:

(1) "Peace officer" has the same meaning as in section 2935.01 of the Revised Code.

(2) "Firearm," "deadly weapon," and "dangerous ordnance" have the same meanings as in section 2923.11 of the Revised Code.

**HISTORY: GC § 1554-6; 111 v 425; 118 v 288(300), § 25; Bureau of Code Revision, 10-1-53; 130 v PtII, 141 (Eff 3-12-65); 144 v S 49 (Eff 7-21-92); 145 v H 152 (Eff 7-1-93); 148 v S 179, § 3. Eff 1-1-2002.**

The effective date is set by section 5 of SB 179.

## § 2301.32 Agreements with adult parole authority to provide services.

(A) In any county in which a county department of probation has been established under division (A) of section 2301.27 of the Revised Code and complies with standards and conditions prescribed by the adult parole authority created by section 5149.02 of the Revised Code, an agreement may be entered into between the court of common pleas and the authority under which the county department of probation may receive supplemental investigation or supervisory services from the authority.

(B) In any county in which a county department of probation has not been established under division (A) of section 2301.27 of the Revised Code, an agreement may be entered into between the court of common pleas of that county and the adult parole authority under which the court of common pleas may place defendants under a community control sanction in charge of the authority, and, in consideration of those placements, the county shall pay to the state from time to time the amounts that are provided for in the agreement.

**HISTORY: GC § 1554-7; 121 v 381; Bureau of Code Revision, 10-1-53; 128 v 959 (Eff 10-1-59); 129 v 481 (Eff 10-18-61); 130 v PtII, 141 (Eff 3-18-65); 145 v H 152 (Eff 7-1-93); 145 v H 571 (Eff 10-6-94); 145 v H 406. Eff 11-11-94; 149 v H 490, § 1, eff. 1-1-04.**

The effective date is set by section 4 of HB 490.

The provisions of § 5 of HB 490 (149 v —) read as follows:

SECTION 5. Section 2301.32 of the Revised Code is presented in this act as a composite of the section as amended by both Am. Sub. H.B. 571 and Am. Sub. H.B. 406 of the 120th General Assembly. The General Assembly, applying the principle stated in division (B) of section 1.52 of the Revised Code that amendments are to be harmonized if reasonably capable of simultaneous operation, finds that the specified composite is the resulting version of the specified sections in effect prior to the effective date of the section as presented in this act.

# CHAPTER 2305: JURISDICTION; LIMITATION OF ACTIONS

Section

[INDEMNITY]



[UNIFORM DUTIES TO DISABLED PERSONS]



[INDEMNITY]

## § 2305.40 Immunity of owner, lessee or renter of real property as to self-defense or defense of others.

(A) As used in this section:

(1) "Firearm" has the same meaning as in section 2923.11 of the Revised Code.

(2) "Tort action" means a civil action for damages for injury, death, or loss to person or property other than a civil action for damages for a breach of contract or another agreement between persons.

(3) "Vehicle" has the same meaning as in section 4501.01 of the Revised Code.

(B)(1) The owner, lessee, or renter of real property or a member of the owner's, lessee's, or renter's family who resides on the property is not liable in damages to a trespasser on the property, to a member of the family of the trespasser, or to any other person in a tort action for injury, death, or loss to person or property of the trespasser that allegedly is caused by the owner, lessee, renter, or family member if, at the time the injury, death, or loss to person or property allegedly is caused, all of the following apply:

(a) The owner, lessee, renter, or family member is inside a building or other structure on the property that is maintained as a permanent or temporary dwelling;

(b) The trespasser has made, is making, or is attempting to make an unlawful entry into the building or other structure described in division (B)(1)(a) of this section;

(c) The owner, lessee, renter, or family member uses reasonably necessary force to repel the trespasser from the building or other structure described in division (B)(1)(a) of this section or to prevent the trespasser from making the unlawful entry into that building or other structure.

(2) For purposes of the immunity created by division (B)(1) of this section, reasonably necessary force to repel a trespasser from a building or other structure that is maintained as a permanent or temporary dwelling or to prevent a trespasser from making an unlawful entry into a building or other structure of that nature may include the taking of or attempting to take the trespasser's life, or causing or attempting to cause physical harm or serious physical harm to the person of the trespasser, if the owner, lessee, or renter of real property or a member of the

owner's, lessee's, or renter's family who resides on the property has a reasonable good faith belief that the owner, lessee, or renter or a member of the owner's, lessee's, or renter's family is in imminent danger of death or serious physical harm to person and that the only means to escape from the imminent danger is to use deadly force or other force that likely will cause physical harm or serious physical harm to the person of the trespasser, even if the owner, lessee, renter, or family member is mistaken as to the existence or imminence of the danger of death or serious physical harm to person.

(3) In order to qualify for the immunity created by division (B)(1) of this section, an owner, lessee, or renter of real property or a member of the owner's, lessee's, or renter's family who resides on the property is not required to retreat from a building or other structure that is maintained as a permanent or temporary dwelling prior to using reasonably necessary force to repel a trespasser from the building or other structure or to prevent a trespasser from making an unlawful entry into the building or other structure.

(C) The owner, lessee, or renter of real property or a member of the owner's, lessee's, or renter's family who resides on the property is not liable in damages to a trespasser on the property, to a member of the family of the trespasser, or to any other person in a tort action for injury, death, or loss to person or property of the trespasser that allegedly is caused by the owner, lessee, renter, or family member under circumstances not covered by division (B)(1) of this section if, at the time the injury, death, or loss to person or property allegedly is caused, none of the following applies:

(1) The injury, death, or loss to person or property is caused by a physical assault of the owner, lessee, renter, or family member upon the trespasser other than in self-defense or defense of a third person.

(2) Self-defense or defense of a third person is not involved, and the injury, death, or loss to person or property is caused by a vehicle driven or otherwise set in motion, a firearm shot, or any other item of tangible personal property held, driven, set in motion, projected, or thrown by the owner, lessee, renter, or family member with the intent to cause injury, death, or loss to person or property of the trespasser or with the intent to cause the trespasser to believe that the owner, lessee, renter, or family member would cause injury, death, or loss to person or property of the trespasser.

(3) Under circumstances not described in division (C)(1) or (2) of this section, self-defense or defense of a third person is not involved, and the owner, lessee, renter, or family member intends to create a risk of injury, death, or loss to person or property of any trespasser by direct or indirect means, including, but not limited to, the use of spring guns, traps, or other dangerous instrumentalities.

(D)(1) This section does not create a new cause of action or substantive legal right against the owner, lessee, or renter of real property or a member of the owner's, lessee's, or renter's family who resides on the property.

(2) This section does not affect any civil liability under another section of the Revised Code or the common law of this state of an owner, lessee, or renter of real property or a member of the owner's, lessee's, or renter's family who resides on the property with respect to individuals other than trespassers, including, but not limited to, civil liability to invitees or licensees.

(3) This section does not affect any immunities from or defenses to civil liability established by another section of the Revised Code or available at common law to which the owner, lessee, or renter of real property or a member of the owner's, lessee's, or renter's family who resides on the property may be entitled with respect to individuals other than trespassers, including, but not limited to, immunities from or defenses to civil liability to invitees or licensees.

(4) This section does not affect any criminal liability that the owner, lessee, or renter of real property or a member of the owner's, lessee's, or renter's family who resides on the property may have for injury, death, or loss to person or property of a trespasser, invitee, or licensee on the property.

(5) This section does not affect any immunities from or defenses to civil liability established by another section of the Revised Code or available at common law to which an individual other than the owner, lessee, or renter of real property or a member of the owner's, lessee's, or renter's family who resides on the property may be entitled in connection with injury, death, or loss to person or property of a trespasser on real property owned, leased, or rented by another person, including, but not limited to, self-defense or defense of third persons.

**HISTORY: 146 v H 447. Eff 3-18-97.**

The provisions of § 2 of HB 447 (146 v —) read as follows: SECTION 2. The immunities from tort liability that are contained in section 2305.40 of the Revised Code, as enacted by this act, shall apply only to causes of action for injury, death, or loss to person or property allegedly caused to a trespasser on or after the effective date of this act by the owner, lessee, or renter of real property or a member of the owner's, lessee's, or renter's family who resides on the property. With respect to causes of action for injury, death, or loss to person or property allegedly caused to a trespasser prior to the effective date of this act by the owner, lessee, or renter of real property or a member of the owner's, lessee's, or renter's family who resides on the property, the liability or immunity from liability of, and any defenses available to, the owner, lessee, renter, or family member shall be determined as if this act had not been enacted.

## § 2305.401 Immunity of members of firearms industry from civil liability and injunctive relief.

(A) As used in this section:

(1) "Ammunition" means any projectile capable of being expelled or propelled from a firearm by the action of an explosive or combustible propellant.

(2) "Firearm" has the same meaning as in section 2923.11 of the Revised Code.

(3) Except as provided in division (C)(2) of this section, "harm" means injury, death, or loss to person or property.

(4) "Member of the firearms industry" means any manufacturer, dealer, or importer of firearms, firearms components, or firearms ammunition or any trade association the members of which, in whole or in part, are manufacturers, dealers, or importers of firearms, firearms components, or firearms ammunition.

(5) "Person" has the same meaning as in section 1.59 of the Revised Code and additionally includes all governmental entities.

(6) "Tort action" means a civil action for damages for injury, death, or loss to person or property other than a civil action for damages for a breach of contract or another agreement between persons.

(B)(1) Except as provided in divisions (B)(2) and (3) of this section and subject to division (C) of this section, a member of the firearms industry is not liable in damages in, and is not subject to a grant of injunctive relief in, a tort or other civil action for harm allegedly sustained by any person as a result of the operation or discharge of a firearm. Except as provided in divisions (B)(2) and (3) of this section and subject to division (C) of this section, a person who allegedly sustains harm as a result of the operation or discharge of a firearm or that person's personal representative does not have a claim for relief against, and may not recover damages or injunctive relief in a tort or other civil action against, a member of the firearms industry based upon that harm.

(2) A member of the firearms industry forfeits the immunity from civil liability and injunctive relief conferred by division (B)(1) of this section if the member of the firearms industry operates or discharges the firearm that results in the harm that is the basis of the claim for relief in the tort or other civil action in a manner that constitutes negligence, willful or wanton misconduct, or intentionally tortious conduct or that constitutes a criminal violation of law.

(3) A member of the firearms industry forfeits the immunity from civil liability and injunctive relief conferred by division (B)(1) of this section if the member of the firearms industry sells, lends, gives, or furnishes to any person, in violation of section 2923.20 or 2923.21 or another section of the Revised Code or in violation of federal law, the firearm that results in the harm that is the basis of the claim for relief in the tort or other civil action.

(C)(1) This section does not create a new cause of action or substantive legal right against a member of the firearms industry.

(2) This section does not limit the availability against a member of the firearms industry of a civil action that seeks damages for harm and that is based on a product liability claim authorized by Chapter 2307. of the Revised Code. As used in this division, "harm" and "product liability claim" have the same meanings as in section 2307.71 of the Revised Code.

(3) This section does not limit the availability against a member of the firearms industry of a civil action for a breach of an express provision of a contract or of another agreement between persons, or a civil action for a breach of an express warranty, pertaining to firearms, firearms components, or firearms ammunition.

(D) This section applies to tort or other civil actions commenced on or after the effective date of this section, or commenced prior to and pending on the effective date of this section, for damages or injunctive relief based upon harm allegedly sustained by any person as a result of the operation or discharge of a firearm prior to, on, or after the effective date of this section.

**HISTORY: 149 v H 192. Eff 10-8-2001.**

The provisions of § 2 of HB 192 (149 v —) read as follows:

SECTION 2. It is the intent of the General Assembly in enacting division (D) of section 2305.401 of the Revised Code in this act to provide for both the prospective and retroactive application of the qualified immunity from civil liability and injunctive relief provisions of section 2305.401 of the Revised Code, as enacted by this act as a general law. If, however, the Ohio Supreme Court determines, in any litigation that may be commenced to contest the constitutionality of the qualified immunity from civil liability and injunctive relief provisions of section 2305.401 of the Revised Code, that the retroactive application of those provisions would be violative of either the United States Constitution or the Ohio Constitution, it is the intent of the General Assembly that the severability provision of section 1.50 of the Revised Code be applied, that the qualified immunity from civil liability and injunctive relief provisions of divisions (A), (B), and (C) of section 2305.401 of the Revised Code be severed from the unconstitutional provisions of division (D) of that section, and that the qualified immunity from civil liability and injunctive relief provisions of divisions (A), (B), and (C) of section 2305.401 of the Revised Code be given prospective application consistent with section 1.48 of the Revised Code.

## [UNIFORM DUTIES TO DISABLED PERSONS]

### § 2305.41 Definitions.

As used in sections 2305.41 to 2305.49 of the Revised Code:

(A) "Disabled condition" means the condition of being unconscious, semiconscious, incoherent, or otherwise incapacitated to communicate.

(B) "Disabled person" means a person in a disabled condition.

(C) "Emergency symbol" means the caduceus inscribed within a six-barred cross used by the American medical association to denote emergency information.

(D) "Identifying device" means an identifying bracelet, necklace, metal tag, or similar device bearing the emergency symbol and the information needed in an emergency.

(E) "Identification card" means any card containing the holder's name, type of medical condition, physician's name, and other medical information. "Identification card" does not include any license or permit issued pursuant to Chapter 4507. of the Revised Code.

(F) "Medical practitioner" means an individual who holds a current valid certificate issued under Chapter 4731. of the Revised Code authorizing the practice of medicine and surgery or osteopathic medicine and surgery.

(G) "Paramedic" has the meaning given in section 4765.01 of the Revised Code.

**HISTORY: 136 v H 1217 (Eff 9-30-76); 144 v S 98. Eff 11-12-92.**

### § 2305.42 Disabled person to wear identifying device.

(A) A person who suffers from epilepsy, diabetes, a cardiac condition, or any other type of illness that causes temporary blackouts, semiconscious periods, or complete unconsciousness, or who suffers from a condition requiring specific medication or medical treatment, is allergic to certain medications or items used in medical treatment, wears contact lenses, has religious objections to certain forms of medication or medical treatment, or is unable to communicate coherently or effectively in the English language, is authorized and encouraged to wear an identifying device.

(B) Any person may carry an identification card.

(C) By wearing an identifying device a person gives his consent for any law enforcement officer or medical practitioner who finds him in a disabled condition to make a reasonable search of his clothing or other effects for an identification card.

**HISTORY: 136 v H 1217. Eff 9-30-76.**

### § 2305.43 Law enforcement officer's duties to disabled person.

(A) A law enforcement officer shall make a diligent effort to determine whether any disabled person he finds is an epileptic or a diabetic, or suffers from some other type of illness that would cause the condition. Whenever feasible, this effort shall be made before the person is charged with a crime or taken to a place of detention.

(B) In seeking to determine whether a disabled person suffers from an illness, a law enforcement officer may make a reasonable search for an identifying device and an identification card and examine them for emergency information. The law enforcement officer may not search for an identifying device or an identification card in a manner or to an extent that would appear to a reasonable person in the circumstances to cause an unreasonable risk of worsening the disabled person's condition.

(C) A law enforcement officer who finds a disabled person without an identifying device or identification card is not relieved of his duty to that person to make a diligent effort to ascertain the existence of any illness causing the disabled condition.

(D) A cause of action against a law enforcement officer does not arise from his making a reasonable search of the disabled person to locate an identifying device or identification card, even though the person is not wearing an identifying device or carrying an identification card.

(E) A law enforcement officer who determines or has reason to believe that a disabled person is suffering from an illness causing his condition shall promptly notify the person's physician, if practicable. If the officer is unable to ascertain the physician's identity or to communicate with him, the officer shall make a reasonable effort to cause the disabled person to be transported immediately to a medical practitioner or to a facility where medical treatment is available. If the officer believes it unduly dangerous to move the disabled person, he shall make a reasonable effort to obtain the assistance of a medical practitioner.

**HISTORY: 136 v H 1217. Eff 9-30-76.**

## § 2305.44 Medical practitioner's duty re search for device.

(A) A medical practitioner or a trained paramedic, in discharging his duty to a disabled person whom he has undertaken to examine or treat, shall make a reasonable search for an identifying device or identification card and examine them for emergency information.

(B) A cause of action against a medical practitioner or a trained paramedic does not arise from his making a reasonable search of a disabled person to locate an identifying device or identification card, even though the person is not wearing an identifying device or carrying an identification card.

**HISTORY: 136 v H 1217. Eff 9-30-76.**

## § 2305.45 Search by unauthorized person.

(A) A person, other than a law enforcement officer, medical practitioner, or a trained paramedic, who finds a disabled person shall make a reasonable effort to notify a law enforcement officer or medical practitioner. If a law enforcement officer or medical practitioner is not present, a person who finds a disabled person may:

(1) Make a reasonable search for an identifying device;

(2) If the identifying device is found, make a reasonable search for an identification card.

If a device or card is located, the person making the search shall attempt promptly to bring its contents to the attention of a law enforcement officer or medical practitioner.

(B) A cause of action does not arise from a reasonable search to locate an identifying device or identification card as authorized by division (A) of this section.

**HISTORY: 136 v H 1217. Eff 9-30-76.**

## § 2305.46 False identification prohibited.

(A) No person, with purpose to deceive, shall provide, wear, use, or possess a false identifying device or identification card.

(B) Whoever violates division (A) of this section is guilty of a misdemeanor of the third degree.

**HISTORY: 136 v H 1217. Eff 9-30-76.**

## § 2305.47 Duties.

The duties imposed by sections 2305.41 to 2305.49 of the Revised Code are in addition to, and not in limitation of, other duties existing under the law of this state.

**HISTORY: 136 v H 1217. Eff 9-30-76.**

## § 2305.48 Construction.

Sections 2305.41 to 2305.49 of the Revised Code shall be so applied and construed as to effectuate its [their] general purpose to make uniform among the states the law with respect to duties to disabled persons.

**HISTORY: 136 v H 1217. Eff 9-30-76.**

## § 2305.49 Cite of uniform act.

Sections 2305.41 to 2305.49 of the Revised Code may be cited as the "uniform duties to disabled persons act."

**HISTORY: 136 v H 1217. Eff 9-30-76.**

# CHAPTER 2307: CIVIL ACTIONS

[CHILD STEALING]

## § 2307.52 Civil liability for terminating or attempting termination of pregnancy after viability.

(A) As used in this section:

(1) "Frivolous conduct" has the same meaning as in section 2323.51 of the Revised Code.

(2) "Viable" has the same meaning as in section 2919.16 of the Revised Code.

(B) A woman upon whom an abortion is purposely performed or induced or attempted to be performed or induced in violation of division (A) of section 2919.17 of the Revised Code has and may commence a civil action for compensatory damages, punitive or exemplary damages if authorized by section 2315.21 of the Revised Code, and court costs and reasonable attorney's fees against the person who purposely performed or induced or attempted to perform or induce the abortion in violation of division (A) of section 2919.17 of the Revised Code.

(C) If a judgment is rendered in favor of the defendant in a civil action commenced pursuant to division (B) of this section and the court finds, upon the filing of a motion under section 2323.51 of the Revised Code, that the commencement of the civil action constitutes frivolous conduct and that the defendant was adversely affected by the frivolous conduct, the court shall award in accordance with section 2323.51 of the Revised Code reasonable attorney's fees to the defendant.

**HISTORY: 146 v H 135. Eff 11-15-95; 2011 HB 78, § 1, eff. Oct. 20, 2011.**

## § 2307.53 Civil action for partial birth feticide; sanction for frivolous conduct.

(A) As used in this section:

(1) "Frivolous conduct" has the same meaning as in section 2323.51 of the Revised Code.

(2) "Partial birth procedure" has the same meaning as in section 2919.151 [2919.15.1] of the Revised Code.

(B) A woman upon whom a partial birth procedure is performed in violation of division (B) or (C) of section 2919.151 [2919.15.1] of the Revised Code, the father of the child if the child was not conceived by rape, or the parent of the woman if the woman is not eighteen years of age or older at the time of the violation has and may commence a civil action for compensatory damages, punitive or exemplary damages if authorized by section 2315.21 of the Revised Code, and court costs and reasonable attorney's fees against the person who committed the violation.

(C) If a judgment is rendered in favor of the defendant in a civil action commenced pursuant to division (B) of this section and the court finds, upon the filing of a motion under section 2323.51 of the Revised Code, that the commencement of the civil action constitutes frivolous conduct and that the defendant was adversely affected by the frivolous conduct, the court shall award in accordance with section 2323.51 of the Revised Code reasonable attorney's fees to the defendant.

**HISTORY: 148 v H 351. Eff 8-18-2000.**

The provisions of § 3 of HB 351 (148 v —) read as follows:

SECTION 3. The General Assembly declares all of the following:

(A) In enacting sections 2307.53 and 2919.151 of the Revised Code, its intent is to prevent the unnecessary death of fetuses when they are substantially outside the body of the mother.

(B) This intent is based in part on a state interest in maintaining a strong public policy against infanticide, regardless of the life expectancy or stage of development of the child.

(C) The right to abortion established in *Roe v. Wade* (1973), 410 U.S. 113, was never intended to legitimize infanticide or to deprive the state of all ability to protect fetuses who are substantially outside the body of the mother.

(D) The act also furthers the state interest in preventing unnecessary cruelty. This interest is not necessarily based solely on the ability of the fetus or child to experience pain. The indignity of being partly delivered before being deliberately killed is also a form of cruelty that should not be unnecessarily inflicted upon any being of human origin. Therefore, there are legitimate reasons for deterring the unnecessary use of the partial birth procedure, even though other abortion procedures that may cause pain remain available.

[CRIMINAL ACTS]

## § 2307.60 Civil recovery for criminal act; record of conviction as evidence; when offender barred from recovering in tort action.

(A)(1) Anyone injured in person or property by a criminal act has, and may recover full damages in, a civil action unless specifically excepted by law, may recover the costs of maintaining the civil action and attorney's fees if authorized by any provision of the Rules of Civil Procedure or another section of the Revised Code or under the common law of this state, and may recover punitive or exemplary damages if authorized by section 2315.21 or another section of the Revised Code.

(2) A final judgment of a trial court that has not been reversed on appeal or otherwise set aside, nullified, or vacated, entered after a trial or upon a plea of guilty, but not upon a plea of no contest or the equivalent plea from another jurisdiction, that adjudges an offender guilty of an offense of violence punishable by death or imprisonment in excess of one year, when entered as evidence in any subsequent civil proceeding based on the criminal act, shall preclude the offender from denying in the subsequent civil proceeding any fact essential to sustaining that judgment, unless the offender can demonstrate that extraordinary circumstances prevented the offender from having a full and fair opportunity to litigate the issue in the criminal proceeding or other extraordinary circumstances justify affording the offender an opportunity to relitigate the issue. The offender may introduce evidence of the offender's pending appeal of the final judgment of the trial court, if applicable, and the court may consider that evidence in determining the liability of the offender.

(B)(1) As used in division (B) of this section:

(a) "Tort action" means a civil action for damages for injury, death, or loss to person or property other than a civil action for damages for a breach of contract or another agreement between persons. "Tort action" includes, but is not limited to, a product liability claim, as defined in section 2307.71 of the Revised Code, and an asbestos claim, as defined in section 2307.91 of the Revised Code, an action for wrongful death under Chapter 2125. of the Revised Code, and an action based on derivative claims for relief.

(b) "Residence" has the same meaning as in section 2901.05 of the Revised Code.

(2) Recovery on a claim for relief in a tort action is barred to any person or the person's legal representative if any of the following apply:

(a) The person has been convicted of or has pleaded guilty to a felony, or to a misdemeanor that is an offense of violence, arising out of criminal conduct that was a proximate cause of the injury or loss for which relief is claimed in the tort action.

(b) The person engaged in conduct that, if prosecuted, would constitute a felony, a misdemeanor that is an offense of violence, an attempt to commit a felony, or an attempt to commit a misdemeanor that is an offense of violence and that conduct was a proximate cause of the injury or loss for which relief is claimed in the tort action, regardless of whether the person has been convicted of or pleaded guilty to or has been charged with committing the felony, the misdemeanor, or the attempt to commit the felony or misdemeanor.

(c) The person suffered the injury or loss for which relief is claimed in the tort action as a proximate result of the victim of conduct that, if prosecuted, would constitute a felony, a misdemeanor that is an offense of violence, an attempt to commit a felony, or an attempt to commit a misdemeanor that is an offense of violence acting against the person in self-defense, defense of another, or defense of the victim's residence, regardless of whether the person has been convicted of or pleaded guilty to or has been charged with committing the felony, the misdemeanor, or the attempt to commit the felony or misdemeanor. Division (B)(2)(c) of this section does not apply if the person who suffered the injury or loss, at the time of the victim's act of self-defense, defense of another, or defense of residence, was an innocent bystander who had no connection with the underlying conduct that prompted the victim's exercise of self-defense, defense of another, or defense of residence.

(3) Recovery against a victim of conduct that, if prosecuted, would constitute a felony, a misdemeanor that is an offense of violence, an attempt to commit a felony, or an attempt to commit a misdemeanor that is an offense of violence, on a claim for relief in a tort action is barred to any person or the person's legal representative if conduct the person engaged in against that victim was a proximate cause of the injury or loss for which relief is claimed in the tort action and that conduct, if prosecuted, would constitute a felony, a misdemeanor that is an offense of violence, an attempt to commit a felony, or an attempt to commit a misdemeanor that is an offense of violence, regardless of whether the person has been convicted of or pleaded guilty to or has been charged with committing the felony, the misdemeanor, or the attempt to commit the felony or misdemeanor.

(4) Divisions (B)(1) to (3) of this section do not apply to civil claims based upon alleged intentionally tortious conduct, alleged violations of the United States Constitution, or alleged violations of statutes of the United States pertaining to civil rights. For purposes of division (B)(4) of this section, a person's act of self-defense, defense of another, or defense of the person's residence does not constitute intentionally tortious conduct.

**HISTORY: RS § 6803; 74 v 243, § 10; GC § 12379; Bureau of Code Revision, RC § 1.16, 10-1-53; RC § 2307.60, 140 v H 426 (Eff 4-4-85); 142 v H 1 (Eff 1-5-88); 146 v H 350 (Eff 1-27-97); 147 v H 547 (Eff 8-5-98); 149 v S 108, § 2.01 (Eff 7-6-2001); 149 v S 107. Eff 6-28-2002; 150 v S 80, § 1, eff. 4-7-05; 151 v S 117, § 1, eff. 10-31-07†; 152 v S 184, § 1, eff. 9-9-08.**

† This date is provided by the Ohio Secretary of State. The effective date was determined in State ex rel. Ohio General Assembly v. Brunner (2007 Ohio LEXIS 1954, 2007 Ohio 4460, 115 Ohio St. 3d 103, 873 NE2d 1232) subject to the filing of a referendum petition.

## § 2307.601 When there is no duty to retreat before using force in self-defense, defense of another, or defense of residence.

(A) As used in this section:

(1) "Residence" and "vehicle" have the same meanings as in section 2901.05 of the Revised Code.

(2) "Tort action" has the same meaning as in section 2307.60 of the Revised Code.

(B) For purposes of determining the potential liability of a person in a tort action related to the person's use of force alleged to be in self-defense, defense of another, or defense of the person's residence, if the person lawfully is in that person's residence, the person has no duty to retreat before using force in self-defense, defense of another, or defense of that person's residence, and, if the person lawfully is an occupant of that person's vehicle or lawfully is an occupant in a vehicle owned by an immediate family member of the person, the person has no duty to retreat before using force in self-defense or defense of another.

**HISTORY: 152 v S 184, § 1, eff. 9-9-08.**

[DAMAGE OR THEFT]

## § 2307.61 Property owner may recover for willful damage or theft; written demand for payment.

(A) If a property owner brings a civil action pursuant to division (A) of section 2307.60 of the Revised Code to recover damages from any person who willfully damages the owner's property or who commits a theft offense, as defined in section 2913.01 of the Revised Code, involving the owner's property, the property owner may recover as follows:

(1) In the civil action, the property owner may elect to recover moneys as described in division (A)(1)(a) or (b) of this section:

(a) Compensatory damages that may include, but are not limited to, the value of the property and liquidated damages in whichever of the following amounts applies:

(i) Fifty dollars, if the value of the property was fifty dollars or less at the time it was willfully damaged or was the subject of a theft offense;

(ii) One hundred dollars, if the value of the property was more than fifty dollars, but not more than one hundred dollars, at the time it was willfully damaged or was the subject of a theft offense;

(iii) One hundred fifty dollars, if the value of the property was more than one hundred dollars at the time it was willfully damaged or was the subject of a theft offense.

(b) Liquidated damages in whichever of the following amounts is greater:

(i) Two hundred dollars;

(ii) Three times the value of the property at the time it was willfully damaged or was the subject of a theft offense, irrespective of whether the property is recovered by way of replevin or otherwise, is destroyed or otherwise damaged, is modified or otherwise altered, or is resalable at its full market price. This division does not apply to a check, negotiable order of withdrawal, share draft, or other negotiable instrument that was returned or dishonored for insufficient funds by a financial institution if the check, negotiable order of withdrawal, share draft, or other negotiable instrument was presented by an individual borrower to a licensee under sections 1321.35 to 1321.48 of the Revised Code for a loan transaction.

(2) In a civil action in which the value of the property that was willfully damaged or was the subject of a theft offense is less than five thousand dollars, the property owner may recover damages as described in division (A)(1)(a) or (b) of this section and additionally may recover the reasonable administrative costs, if any, of the property owner that were incurred in connection with actions taken pursuant to division (A)(2) of this section, the cost of maintaining the civil action, and reasonable attorney's fees, if all of the following apply:

(a) The property owner, at least thirty days prior to the filing of the civil action, serves a written demand for payment of moneys as described in division (A)(1)(a) of this section and the reasonable administrative costs, if any, of the property owner that have been incurred in connection with actions taken pursuant to division (A)(2) of this section, upon the person who willfully damaged the property or committed the theft offense.

(b) The demand conforms to the requirements of division (C) of this section and is sent by certified mail, return receipt requested.

(c) Either the person who willfully damaged the property or committed the theft offense does not make payment to the property owner of the amount specified in the demand within thirty days after the date of its service upon that person and does not enter into an agreement with the property owner during that thirty-day period for that payment or the person who willfully damaged the property or committed the theft offense enters into an agreement with the property owner during that thirty-day period for that payment but does not make that payment in accordance with the agreement.

(B) If a property owner who brings a civil action pursuant to division (A) of section 2307.60 of the Revised Code to recover damages for willful damage to property or for a theft offense attempts to collect the reasonable administrative costs, if any, of the property owner that have been incurred in connection with actions taken pursuant to division (A)(2) of this section, the cost of maintaining the civil action, and reasonable attorney's fees under authority of that division and if the defendant prevails in the civil action, the defendant may recover from the property owner reasonable attorney's fees, the cost of defending the civil action, and any compensatory damages that may be proven.

(C) For purposes of division (A)(2) of this section, a written demand for payment shall include a conspicuous notice to the person upon whom the demand is to be served that indicates all of the following:

(1) The willful property damage or theft offense that the person allegedly committed;

(2) That, if the person makes payment of the amount specified in the demand within thirty days after its service upon the person or enters into an agreement with the property owner during that thirty-day period for that payment and makes that payment in accordance with the agreement, the person cannot be sued by the property owner in a civil action in relation to the willful property damage or theft offense;

(3) That, if the person fails to make payment of the amount specified in the demand within thirty days after the date of its service upon the person and fails to enter into an agreement for that payment with the property owner during that thirty-day period or enters into an agreement for that payment with the property owner during that thirty-day period but does not make that payment in accordance with the agreement, the person may be sued in a civil action in relation to the willful property damage or theft offense;

(4) The potential judgment that the person may be required to pay if the person is sued in a civil action in relation to the willful property damage or theft offense and judgment is rendered against the person in that civil action;

(5) That, if the person is sued in a civil action by the property owner in relation to the willful property damage or theft offense, if the civil action requests that the person be required to pay the reasonable administrative costs, if any, of the property owner that have been incurred in connection with actions taken pursuant to division (A)(2) of this section, the cost of maintaining the action, and reasonable attorney's fees, and if the person prevails in the civil action, the person may recover from the property owner reasonable attorney's fees, the cost of defending the action, and any compensatory damages that can be proved.

(D) If a property owner whose property was willfully damaged or was the subject of a theft offense serves a written demand for payment upon a person who willfully damaged the property or committed the theft offense and if the person makes payment of the amount specified in the demand within thirty days after the date of its service upon the person or the person enters into an agreement with the property owner during that thirty-day period for that payment and makes payment in accordance with the agreement, the property owner shall not file a civil action against the person in relation to the willful property damage or theft offense.

(E) If a property owner whose property was willfully damaged or was the subject of a theft offense serves a written demand for payment upon a person who willfully damaged the property or committed the theft offense and if the person, within thirty days after the date of service of the demand upon the person, enters into an agreement with the property owner for the payment of the amount specified in the demand but does not make that payment in accordance with the agreement, the time between the entering of the agreement and the failure to make that payment shall not be computed as any part of the period within which a civil action based on the willful property damage or theft offense must be brought under the Revised Code.

(F) A civil action to recover damages for willful property damage or for a theft offense may be joined with a civil action that is brought pursuant to Chapter 2737. of the Revised Code to recover the property. If the two actions are joined, any compensatory damages recoverable by the property owner shall be limited to the value of the property.

(G)(1) In a civil action to recover damages for willful property damage or for a theft offense, the trier of fact may determine that an owner's property was willfully damaged or that a theft offense involving the owner's property has been committed, whether or not any person has pleaded guilty to or has been convicted of any criminal offense or has been adjudicated a delinquent child in relation to any act involving the owner's property.

(2) This section does not affect the prosecution of any criminal action or proceeding or any action to obtain a delinquent child adjudication in connection with willful property damage or a theft offense.

(H) As used in this section:

(1) "Administrative costs" includes the costs of written demands for payment and associated postage under division (A)(2) of this section.

(2) "Value of the property" means one of the following:

(a) The retail value of any property that is offered for sale by a mercantile establishment, irrespective of whether the property is destroyed or otherwise damaged, is modified or otherwise altered, or otherwise is not resalable at its full market price;

(b) The face value of any check or other negotiable instrument that is not honored due to insufficient funds in the drawer's account, the absence of any drawer's account, or another reason, and all charges imposed by a bank, savings and loan association, credit union, or other financial institution upon the holder of the check or other negotiable instrument;

(c) The replacement value of any property not described in division (H)(1) or (2) of this section.

**HISTORY: 140 v H 426 (Eff 4-4-85); 144 v S 105 (Eff 6-23-92); 146 v H 350 (Eff 1-27-97); 148 v H 294 (Eff 8-29-2000); 149 v S 108, § 2.01 (Eff 7-6-2001); 149 v S 107. Eff 6-28-2002; 152 v H 545, § 1, eff. 9-1-08.**

## § 2307.62 Action by cable television owner or operator to recover damages.

(A) As used in this section:

(1) "Cable service" and "cable system" have the same meanings as in section 2913.04 of the Revised Code.

(2) "Trier of fact" means the jury or, in a nonjury trial, the court.

(3) "Profits" derived from a violation of division (B) of section 2913.04 or division (A) or (B) of section 2913.041 [2913.04.1] of the Revised Code are equal to whichever of the following applies:

(a) The gross revenue derived from the violation by the persons who violated division (B) of section 2913.04 or division (A) or (B) of section 2913.041 [2913.04.1] of the Revised Code, as established by a preponderance of the evidence by the owner or operator of the cable service, cable system, cable television system, or other similar closed circuit coaxial cable communications system who is aggrieved by the violation;

(b) The gross revenue derived from the violation by the persons who violated division (B) of section 2913.04 or division (A) or (B) of section 2913.041 [2913.04.1] of the Revised Code, as established by a preponderance of the evidence by the owner or operator of the cable service, cable system, cable television system, or other similar closed circuit coaxial cable communications system who is aggrieved by the violation, minus deductible expenses and other elements of profit that are not attributable to the violation of division (B) of section 2913.04 or division (A) or (B) of section 2913.041 [2913.04.1] of the Revised Code, as established by a preponderance of the evidence by the persons who violated either or both of those divisions.

(B)(1) An owner or operator of a cable service, cable system, cable television system, or other similar closed circuit coaxial cable communications system who is aggrieved by conduct that is prohibited by division (B) of section 2913.04 or division (A) or (B) of section 2913.041 [2913.04.1] of the Revised Code may elect to commence a civil action for damages in accordance with division (A) of section 2307.60 or section 2307.61 of the Revised Code or to commence a civil action under this section in the appropriate municipal court, county court, or court of common pleas to recover damages and other specified moneys described in division (B)(1)(a), (b), or (c) of this section and, if applicable, damages described in division (B)(2) of this section from the persons who violated division (B) of section 2913.04 or division (A) or (B) of section 2913.041 [2913.04.1] of the Revised Code. If the owner or operator elects to commence a civil action for damages and other specified moneys under this section, the owner or operator shall specify in its complaint which of the following categories of damages and other specified moneys the owner or operator seeks to recover from the persons who violated division (B) of section 2913.04 or division (A) or (B) of section 2913.041 [2913.04.1] of the Revised Code:

(a) Full compensatory damages, punitive or exemplary damages if authorized by section 2315.21 of the Revised Code, and the reasonable attorney's fees, court costs, and other reasonable expenses incurred in maintaining the civil action under this section.

(b) Damages equal to the actual loss suffered by the owner or operator as a proximate result of the conduct that violated division (B) of section 2913.04 or division (A) or (B) of section 2913.041 [2913.04.1] of the Revised Code and, in addition, damages equal to the profits derived by the persons who violated one or more of those divisions as a proximate result of the prohibited conduct.

(c) Regarding a violation of division (A) or (B) of section 2913.041 [2913.04.1] of the Revised Code, liquidated damages in an amount of not less than two hundred fifty dollars and not more than ten thousand dollars, as determined by the trier of fact, for each separate violation of division (A) or (B) of section 2913.041 [2913.04.1] of the Revised Code as described in division (D) of that section. Division (B)(1)(c) of this section does not apply regarding a violation of division (B) of section 2913.04 of the Revised Code.

(2) The trier of fact shall determine the amount of any compensatory damages to be awarded pursuant to division (B)(1)(a) of this section, and the court shall determine the amount of any punitive or exemplary damages authorized by section 2315.21 of the Revised Code and the amount of reasonable attorney's fees, court costs, and other reasonable expenses to be awarded pursuant to division (B)(1)(a) of this section. The trier of fact shall determine the amount of damages to be awarded to the owner or operator under division (B)(1)(b) of this section.

(3) In a civil action under this section, if an owner or operator of a cable service, cable system, cable television system, or other similar closed circuit coaxial cable communications system establishes by a preponderance of the evidence that the persons who violated division (B) of section 2913.04 or division (A) or (B) of section 2913.041 [2913.04.1] of the Revised Code engaged in the prohibited conduct for the purpose of direct or indirect commercial advantage or private financial gain, the trier of fact may award to the owner or operator damages in an amount not to exceed fifty thousand dollars in addition to any amount recovered pursuant to division (B)(1)(a), (b), or (c) of this section, whichever of those divisions applies to the owner or operator.

(C) A person may join a civil action under this section with a civil action under Chapter 2737. of the Revised Code to recover any property of the owner or operator of a cable service, cable system, cable television system, or other similar closed circuit coaxial cable communications system that was the subject of the violation of division (B) of section 2913.04 or division (A) or (B) of section 2913.041 [2913.04.1] of the Revised Code. A person may commence a civil action under this section regardless of whether any person who allegedly violated one or more of those divisions has pleaded guilty to or has been convicted of a violation of one or more of those divisions or has been adjudicated a delinquent child for the commission of any act that constitutes a violation of one or more of those divisions.

**HISTORY: 146 v S 2 (Eff 7-1-96); 149 v S 107 (Eff 6-28-2002); 149 v H 327. Eff 7-8-2002.**

**Comment, Legislative Service Commission**

Section 2307.62 of the Revised Code is amended by this act [Sub. S.B. 107] and also by Am. Sub. H.B. 327, both of the 124th General Assembly. Comparison of these amendments in pursuance of section 1.52 of the Revised Code discloses that they are not irreconcilable so that they are required by that section to be harmonized to give effect to each amendment.

# CHAPTER 2313: COMMISSIONERS OF JURORS

Section



## [COMMISSIONERS]

### § 2313.01 Commissioners of jurors.

The judges of the courts of common pleas shall appoint two suitable persons, neither of whom shall be an attorney at law nor more than one of whom shall be of the same political party, to be commissioners of jurors for the county. The appointments shall be made in writing, by the judge or a majority of all the judges in those counties where there is more than one judge, and shall be filed in the office of the clerk of the court of common pleas of the county and entered upon the journal of the court. The commissioners shall hold office at the pleasure of the judges of the court of common pleas in the county of their appointment. The judges may at any time for good cause shown and by a vote of a majority of all their number, remove any commissioner and appoint a successor. Upon a vacancy occurring in the office of commissioners of jurors, for any cause, the said judges shall, as soon as practicable, in like manner appoint a successor. The successor so appointed shall be of the same political party as the commissioner whose place is to be filled.

The said commissioners shall be officers of the courts of record in such county and shall attend upon each term of such courts for which a jury is drawn.

**HISTORY: GC §§ 11419-3, 11419-2; 114 v 193; Bureau of Code Revision. Eff 10-1-53.**

## [CHALLENGE OF JURORS]

### § 2313.41 Array may be set aside.

A challenge to the array may be made and the whole array set aside by the court when the jury, grand or petit, was not selected, drawn, or summoned, or when the officer who executed the venire did not proceed as prescribed by law. No challenge to the array shall be made or the whole array set aside by the court, by reason of the misnomer of a juror; but on challenge, a juror may be set aside by reason of a misnomer in his name; but such challenge shall only be made before the jury is impaneled and sworn, and no indictment shall be quashed or verdict set aside for any such irregularity or misnomer if the jurors who formed the same possessed the requisite qualifications to act as jurors.

**HISTORY: GC § 11419-50; 114 v 193(207); Bureau of Code Revision. Eff 10-1-53.**

### § 2313.42 Causes for challenge of persons called as jurors; examination under oath.

Any person called as a juror for the trial of any cause shall be examined under oath or upon affirmation as to his qualifications. A person is qualified to serve as a juror if he is an elector of the county and has been certified by the board of elections pursuant to section 2313.06 of the Revised Code. A person also is qualified to serve as a juror if he is eighteen years of age or older, is a resident of the county, would be an elector if he were registered to vote, regardless of whether he actually is registered to vote, and has been certified by the registrar of motor vehicles pursuant to section 2313.06 of the Revised Code or otherwise as having a valid and current driver's or commercial driver's license.

The following are good causes for challenge to any person called as a juror:

(A) That he has been convicted of a crime which by law renders him disqualified to serve on a jury;

(B) That he has an interest in the cause;

(C) That he has an action pending between him and either party;

(D) That he formerly was a juror in the same cause;

(E) That he is the employer, the employee, or the spouse, parent, son, or daughter of the employer or employee, counselor, agent, steward, or attorney of either party;

(F) That he is subpoenaed in good faith as a witness in the cause;

(G) That he is akin by consanguinity or affinity within the fourth degree, to either party, or to the attorney of either party;

(H) That he or his spouse, parent, son, or daughter is a party to another action then pending in any court in which an attorney in the cause then on trial is an attorney, either for or against him;

(I) That he, not being a regular juror of the term, has already served as a talesman in the trial of any cause, in any court of record in the county within the preceding twelve months;

(J) That he discloses by his answers that he cannot be a fair and impartial juror or will not follow the law as given to him by the court.

Each challenge listed in this section shall be considered as a principal challenge, and its validity tried by the court.

**HISTORY: GC § 11419-51; 114 v 193(207); 117 v 72; Bureau of Code Revision, 10-1-53; 127 v 419 (Eff 9-9-57); 133 v H 104 (Eff 9-12-69); 140 v H 183 (Eff 10-1-84); 143 v H 381. Eff 7-1-89.**

## § 2313.43 Challenge of petit juror.

In addition to the causes listed under section 2313.42 of the Revised Code, any petit juror may be challenged on suspicion of prejudice against or partiality for either party, or for want of a competent knowledge of the English language, or other cause that may render him at the time an unsuitable juror. The validity of such challenge shall be determined by the court and be sustained if the court has any doubt as to the juror's being entirely unbiased.

**HISTORY: GC § 11419-52; 114 v 193(208); Bureau of Code Revision. Eff 10-1-53.**

# CHAPTER 2317: EVIDENCE



### [COMPETENCY OF WITNESS AND EVIDENCE]

## § 2317.01 Competent witnesses.

All persons are competent witnesses except those of unsound mind and children under ten years of age who appear incapable of receiving just impressions of the facts and transactions respecting which they are examined, or of relating them truly.

In a hearing in an abuse, neglect, or dependency case, any examination made by the court to determine whether a child is a competent witness shall be conducted by the court in an office or room other than a courtroom or hearing room, shall be conducted in the presence of only those individuals considered necessary by the court for the conduct of the examination or the well-being of the child, and shall be conducted with a court reporter present. The court may allow the prosecutor, guardian ad litem, or attorney for any party to submit questions for use by the court in determining whether the child is a competent witness.

**HISTORY: RS § 5240; S&C 1035; 51 v 57, § 310; 67 v 113, § 314; GC § 11493; Bureau of Code Revision, 10-1-53; 142 v S 89. Eff 1-1-89.**

The effective date is set by section 9 of SB 89.

## § 2317.02 Privileged communications.

The following persons shall not testify in certain respects:

(A)(1) An attorney, concerning a communication made to the attorney by a client in that relation or the attorney's advice to a client, except that the attorney may testify by express consent of the client or, if the client is deceased, by the express consent of the surviving spouse or the executor or administrator of the estate of the deceased client. However, if the client voluntarily testifies or is deemed by section 2151.421 of the Revised Code to have waived any testimonial privilege under this division, the attorney may be compelled to testify on the same subject.

The testimonial privilege established under this division does not apply concerning a communication between a client who has since died and the deceased client's attorney if the communication is relevant to a dispute between parties who claim through that deceased client, regardless of whether the claims are by testate or intestate succession or by inter vivos transaction, and the dispute addresses the competency of the deceased client when the deceased client executed a document that is the basis of the dispute or whether the deceased client was a victim of fraud, undue influence, or duress when the deceased client executed a document that is the basis of the dispute.

(2) An attorney, concerning a communication made to the attorney by a client in that relationship or the attorney's advice to a client, except that if the client is an insurance company, the attorney may be compelled to testify, subject to an in camera inspection by a court, about communications made by the client to the attorney or by the attorney to the client that are related to the attorney's aiding or furthering an ongoing or future commission of bad faith by the client, if the party seeking disclosure of the communications has made a prima facie showing of bad faith, fraud, or criminal misconduct by the client.

(B)(1) A physician or a dentist concerning a communication made to the physician or dentist by a patient in that relation or the physician's or dentist's advice to a patient, except as otherwise provided in this division, division (B)(2), and division (B)(3) of this section, and except that, if the patient is deemed by section 2151.421 of the Revised Code to have waived any testimonial privilege under this division, the physician may be compelled to testify on the same subject.

The testimonial privilege established under this division does not apply, and a physician or dentist may testify or may be compelled to testify, in any of the following circumstances:

(a) In any civil action, in accordance with the discovery provisions of the Rules of Civil Procedure in connection with a civil action, or in connection with a claim under Chapter 4123. of the Revised Code, under any of the following circumstances:

(i) If the patient or the guardian or other legal representative of the patient gives express consent;

(ii) If the patient is deceased, the spouse of the patient or the executor or administrator of the patient's estate gives express consent;

(iii) If a medical claim, dental claim, chiropractic claim, or optometric claim, as defined in section 2305.113 of the Revised Code, an action for wrongful death, any other type of civil action, or a claim under Chapter 4123. of the Revised Code is filed by the patient, the personal representative of the estate of the patient if deceased, or the patient's guardian or other legal representative.

(b) In any civil action concerning court-ordered treatment or services received by a patient, if the court-ordered treatment or services were ordered as part of a case plan journalized under section 2151.412 of the Revised Code or the court-ordered treatment or services are necessary or relevant to dependency, neglect, or abuse or temporary or permanent custody proceedings under Chapter 2151. of the Revised Code.

(c) In any criminal action concerning any test or the results of any test that determines the presence or concentration of alcohol, a drug of abuse, a combination of them, a controlled substance, or a metabolite of a controlled substance in the patient's whole blood, blood serum or plasma, breath, urine, or other bodily substance at any time relevant to the criminal offense in question.

(d) In any criminal action against a physician or dentist. In such an action, the testimonial privilege established under this division does not prohibit the admission into evidence, in accordance with the Rules of Evidence, of a patient's medical or dental records or other communications between a patient and the physician or dentist that are related to the action and obtained by subpoena, search warrant, or other lawful means. A court that permits or compels a physician or dentist to testify in such an action or permits the introduction into evidence of patient records or other communications in such an action shall require that appropriate measures be taken to ensure that the confidentiality of any patient named or otherwise identified in the records is maintained. Measures to ensure confidentiality that may be taken by the court include sealing its records or deleting specific information from its records.

(e)(i) If the communication was between a patient who has since died and the deceased patient's physician or dentist, the communication is relevant to a dispute between parties who claim through that deceased patient, regardless of whether the claims are by testate or intestate succession or by inter vivos transaction, and the dispute addresses the competency of the deceased patient when the deceased patient executed a document that is the basis of the dispute or whether the deceased patient was a victim of fraud, undue influence, or duress when the deceased patient executed a document that is the basis of the dispute.

(ii) If neither the spouse of a patient nor the executor or administrator of that patient's estate gives consent under division (B)(1)(a)(ii) of this section, testimony or the disclosure of the patient's medical records by a physician, dentist, or other health care provider under division (B)(1)(e)(i) of this section is a permitted use or disclosure of protected health information, as defined in 45 C.F.R. 160.103, and an authorization or opportunity to be heard shall not be required.

(iii) Division (B)(1)(e)(i) of this section does not require a mental health professional to disclose psychotherapy notes, as defined in 45 C.F.R. 164.501.

(iv) An interested person who objects to testimony or disclosure under division (B)(1)(e)(i) of this section may seek a protective order pursuant to Civil Rule 26.

(v) A person to whom protected health information is disclosed under division (B)(1)(e)(i) of this section shall not use or disclose the protected health information for any purpose other than the litigation or proceeding for which the information was requested and shall return the protected health information to the covered entity or destroy the protected health information, including all copies made, at the conclusion of the litigation or proceeding.

(2)(a) If any law enforcement officer submits a written statement to a health care provider that states that an official criminal investigation has begun regarding a specified person or that a criminal action or proceeding has been commenced against a specified person, that requests the provider to supply to the officer copies of any records the provider possesses that pertain to any test or the results of any test administered to the specified person to determine the presence or concentration of alcohol, a drug of abuse, a combination of them, a controlled substance, or a metabolite of a controlled substance in the person's whole blood, blood serum or plasma, breath, or urine at any time relevant to the criminal offense in question, and that conforms to section 2317.022 of the Revised Code, the provider, except to the extent specifically prohibited by any law of this state or of the United States, shall supply to the officer a copy of any of the requested records the provider possesses. If the health care provider does not possess any of the requested records, the provider shall give the officer a written statement that indicates that the provider does not possess any of the requested records.

(b) If a health care provider possesses any records of the type described in division (B)(2)(a) of this section regarding the person in question at any time relevant to the criminal offense in question, in lieu of personally testifying as to the results of the test in question, the custodian of the records may submit a certified copy of the records, and, upon its submission, the certified copy is qualified as authentic evidence and may be admitted as evidence in accordance with the Rules of Evidence. Division (A) of section 2317.422 of the Revised Code does not apply to any certified copy of records submitted in accordance with this division. Nothing in this division shall be construed to limit the right of any party to call as a witness the person who administered the test to which the records pertain, the person under whose supervision the test was administered, the custodian of the records, the person who made the records, or the person under whose supervision the records were made.

(3)(a) If the testimonial privilege described in division (B)(1) of this section does not apply as provided in division (B)(1)(a)(iii) of this section, a physician or dentist may be compelled to testify or to submit to discovery under the Rules of Civil Procedure only as to a communication made to the physician or dentist by the patient in question in that relation, or the physician's or dentist's advice to the patient in question, that related causally or historically to physical or mental injuries that are relevant to issues in the medical claim, dental claim, chiropractic claim, or optometric claim, action for wrongful death, other civil action, or claim under Chapter 4123. of the Revised Code.

(b) If the testimonial privilege described in division (B)(1) of this section does not apply to a physician or dentist as provided in division (B)(1)(c) of this section, the physician or dentist, in lieu of personally testifying as to the results of the test in question, may submit a certified copy of those results, and, upon its submission, the certified copy is qualified as authentic evidence and may be admitted as evidence in accordance with the Rules of Evidence. Division (A) of section 2317.422 of the Revised Code does not apply to any certified copy of results submitted in accordance with this division. Nothing in this division shall be construed to limit the right of any party to call as a witness the person who administered the test in question, the person under whose supervision the test was administered, the custodian of the results of the test, the person who compiled the results, or the person under whose supervision the results were compiled.

(4) The testimonial privilege described in division (B)(1) of this section is not waived when a communication is made by a physician to a pharmacist or when there is communication between a patient and a pharmacist in furtherance of the physician-patient relation.

(5)(a) As used in divisions (B)(1) to (4) of this section, "communication" means acquiring, recording, or transmitting any information, in any manner, concerning any facts, opinions, or statements necessary to enable a physician or dentist to diagnose, treat, prescribe, or act for a patient. A "communication" may include, but is not limited to, any medical or dental, office, or hospital communication such as a record, chart, letter, memorandum, laboratory test and results, x-ray, photograph, financial statement, diagnosis, or prognosis.

(b) As used in division (B)(2) of this section, "health care provider" means a hospital, ambulatory care facility, long-term care facility, pharmacy, emergency facility, or health care practitioner.

(c) As used in division (B)(5)(b) of this section:

(i) "Ambulatory care facility" means a facility that provides medical, diagnostic, or surgical treatment to patients who do not require hospitalization, including a dialysis center, ambulatory surgical facility, cardiac catheterization facility, diagnostic imaging center, extracorporeal shock wave lithotripsy center, home health agency, inpatient hospice, birthing center, radiation therapy center, emergency facility, and an urgent care center. "Ambulatory health care facility" does not include the private office of a physician or dentist, whether the office is for an individual or group practice.

(ii) "Emergency facility" means a hospital emergency department or any other facility that provides emergency medical services.

(iii) "Health care practitioner" has the same meaning as in section 4769.01 of the Revised Code.

(iv) "Hospital" has the same meaning as in section 3727.01 of the Revised Code.

(v) "Long-term care facility" means a nursing home, residential care facility, or home for the aging, as those terms are defined in section 3721.01 of the Revised Code; an adult care facility, as defined in section 5119.70 of the Revised Code; a nursing facility or intermediate care facility for the mentally retarded, as those terms are defined in section 5111.20 of the Revised Code; a facility or portion of a facility certified as a skilled nursing facility under Title XVIII of the "Social Security Act," 49 Stat. 286 (1965), 42 U.S.C.A. 1395, as amended.

(vi) "Pharmacy" has the same meaning as in section 4729.01 of the Revised Code.

(d) As used in divisions (B)(1) and (2) of this section, "drug of abuse" has the same meaning as in section 4506.01 of the Revised Code.

(6) Divisions (B)(1), (2), (3), (4), and (5) of this section apply to doctors of medicine, doctors of osteopathic medicine, doctors of podiatry, and dentists.

(7) Nothing in divisions (B)(1) to (6) of this section affects, or shall be construed as affecting, the immunity from civil liability conferred by section 307.628 of the Revised Code or the immunity from civil liability conferred by section 2305.33 of the Revised Code upon physicians who report an employee's use of a drug of abuse, or a condition of an employee other than one involving the use of a drug of abuse, to the employer of the employee in accordance with division (B) of that section. As used in division (B)(7) of this section, "employee," "employer," and "physician" have the same meanings as in section 2305.33 of the Revised Code.

(C)(1) A cleric, when the cleric remains accountable to the authority of that cleric's church, denomination, or sect, concerning a confession made, or any information confidentially communicated, to the cleric for a religious counseling purpose in the cleric's professional character. The cleric may testify by express consent of the person making the communication, except when the disclosure of the information is in violation of a sacred trust and except that, if the person voluntarily testifies or is deemed by division (A)(4)(c) of section 2151.421 of the Revised Code to have waived any testimonial privilege under this division, the cleric may be compelled to testify on the same subject except when disclosure of the information is in violation of a sacred trust.

(2) As used in division (C) of this section:

(a) "Cleric" means a member of the clergy, rabbi, priest, Christian Science practitioner, or regularly ordained, accredited, or licensed minister of an established and legally cognizable church, denomination, or sect.

(b) "Sacred trust" means a confession or confidential communication made to a cleric in the cleric's ecclesiastical capacity in the course of discipline enjoined by the church to which the cleric belongs, including, but not limited to, the Catholic Church, if both of the following apply:

(i) The confession or confidential communication was made directly to the cleric.

(ii) The confession or confidential communication was made in the manner and context that places the cleric specifically and strictly under a level of confidentiality that is considered inviolate by canon law or church doctrine.

(D) Husband or wife, concerning any communication made by one to the other, or an act done by either in the presence of the other, during coverture, unless the communication was made, or act done, in the known presence or hearing of a third person competent to be a witness; and such rule is the same if the marital relation has ceased to exist;

(E) A person who assigns a claim or interest, concerning any matter in respect to which the person would not, if a party, be permitted to testify;

(F) A person who, if a party, would be restricted under section 2317.03 of the Revised Code, when the property or thing is sold or transferred by an executor, administrator, guardian, trustee, heir, devisee, or legatee, shall be restricted in the same manner in any action or proceeding concerning the property or thing.

(G)(1) A school guidance counselor who holds a valid educator license from the state board of education as provided for in section 3319.22 of the Revised Code, a person licensed under Chapter 4757. of the Revised Code as a professional clinical counselor, professional counselor, social worker, independent social worker, marriage and family therapist or independent marriage and family therapist, or registered under Chapter 4757. of the Revised Code as a social work assistant concerning a confidential communication received from a client in that relation or the person's advice to a client unless any of the following applies:

(a) The communication or advice indicates clear and present danger to the client or other persons. For the purposes of this division, cases in which there are indications of present or past child abuse or neglect of the client constitute a clear and present danger.

(b) The client gives express consent to the testimony.

(c) If the client is deceased, the surviving spouse or the executor or administrator of the estate of the deceased client gives express consent.

(d) The client voluntarily testifies, in which case the school guidance counselor or person licensed or registered under Chapter 4757. of the Revised Code may be compelled to testify on the same subject.

(e) The court in camera determines that the information communicated by the client is not germane to the counselor-client, marriage and family therapist-client, or social worker-client relationship.

(f) A court, in an action brought against a school, its administration, or any of its personnel by the client, rules after an in-camera inspection that the testimony of the school guidance counselor is relevant to that action.

(g) The testimony is sought in a civil action and concerns court-ordered treatment or services received by a patient as part of a case plan journalized under section 2151.412 of the Revised Code or the court-ordered treatment or services are necessary or relevant to dependency, neglect, or abuse or temporary or permanent custody proceedings under Chapter 2151. of the Revised Code.

(2) Nothing in division (G)(1) of this section shall relieve a school guidance counselor or a person licensed or registered under Chapter 4757. of the Revised Code from the requirement to report information concerning child abuse or neglect under section 2151.421 of the Revised Code.

(H) A mediator acting under a mediation order issued under division (A) of section 3109.052 of the Revised Code or otherwise issued in any proceeding for divorce, dissolution, legal separation, annulment, or the allocation of parental rights and responsibilities for the care of children, in any action or proceeding, other than a criminal, delinquency, child abuse, child neglect, or dependent child action or proceeding, that is brought by or against either parent who takes part in mediation in accordance with the order and that pertains to the mediation process, to any information discussed or presented in the mediation process, to the allocation of parental rights and responsibilities for the care of the parents' children, or to the awarding of parenting time rights in relation to their children;

(I) A communications assistant, acting within the scope of the communication assistant's authority, when providing telecommunications relay service pursuant to section 4931.06 of the Revised Code or Title II of the "Communications Act of 1934," 104 Stat. 366 (1990), 47 U.S.C. 225, concerning a communication made through a telecommunications relay service. Nothing in this section shall limit the obligation of a communications assistant to divulge information or testify when mandated by federal law or regulation or pursuant to subpoena in a criminal proceeding.

Nothing in this section shall limit any immunity or privilege granted under federal law or regulation.

(J)(1) A chiropractor in a civil proceeding concerning a communication made to the chiropractor by a patient in that relation or the chiropractor's advice to a patient, except as otherwise provided in this division. The testimonial privilege established under this division does not apply, and a chiropractor may testify or may be compelled to testify, in any civil action, in accordance with the discovery provisions of the Rules of Civil Procedure in connection with a civil action, or in connection with a claim under Chapter 4123. of the Revised Code, under any of the following circumstances:

(a) If the patient or the guardian or other legal representative of the patient gives express consent.

(b) If the patient is deceased, the spouse of the patient or the executor or administrator of the patient's estate gives express consent.

(c) If a medical claim, dental claim, chiropractic claim, or optometric claim, as defined in section 2305.113 of the Revised Code, an action for wrongful death, any other type of civil action, or a claim under Chapter 4123. of the Revised Code is filed by the patient, the personal representative of the estate of the patient if deceased, or the patient's guardian or other legal representative.

(2) If the testimonial privilege described in division (J)(1) of this section does not apply as provided in division (J)(1)(c) of this section, a chiropractor may be compelled to testify or to submit to discovery under the Rules of Civil Procedure only as to a communication made to the chiropractor by the patient in question in that relation, or the chiropractor's advice to the patient in question, that related causally or historically to physical or mental injuries that are relevant to issues in the medical claim, dental claim, chiropractic claim, or optometric claim, action for wrongful death, other civil action, or claim under Chapter 4123. of the Revised Code.

(3) The testimonial privilege established under this division does not apply, and a chiropractor may testify or be compelled to testify, in any criminal action or administrative proceeding.

(4) As used in this division, "communication" means acquiring, recording, or transmitting any information, in any manner, concerning any facts, opinions, or statements necessary to enable a chiropractor to diagnose, treat, or act for a patient. A communication may include, but is not limited to, any chiropractic, office, or hospital communication such as a record, chart, letter, memorandum, laboratory test and results, x-ray, photograph, financial statement, diagnosis, or prognosis.

(K)(1) Except as provided under division (K)(2) of this section, a critical incident stress management team member concerning a communication received from an individual who receives crisis response services from the team member, or the team member's advice to the individual, during a debriefing session.

(2) The testimonial privilege established under division (K)(1) of this section does not apply if any of the following are true:

(a) The communication or advice indicates clear and present danger to the individual who receives crisis response services or to other persons. For purposes of this division, cases in which there are indications of present or past child abuse or neglect of the individual constitute a clear and present danger.

(b) The individual who received crisis response services gives express consent to the testimony.

(c) If the individual who received crisis response services is deceased, the surviving spouse or the executor or administrator of the estate of the deceased individual gives express consent.

(d) The individual who received crisis response services voluntarily testifies, in which case the team member may be compelled to testify on the same subject.

(e) The court in camera determines that the information communicated by the individual who received crisis response services is not germane to the relationship between the individual and the team member.

(f) The communication or advice pertains or is related to any criminal act.

(3) As used in division (K) of this section:

(a) "Crisis response services" means consultation, risk assessment, referral, and on-site crisis intervention services provided by a critical incident stress management team to individuals affected by crisis or disaster.

(b) "Critical incident stress management team member" or "team member" means an individual specially trained to provide crisis response services as a member of an organized community or local crisis response team that holds membership in the Ohio critical incident stress management network.

(c) "Debriefing session" means a session at which crisis response services are rendered by a critical incident stress management team member during or after a crisis or disaster.

(L)(1) Subject to division (L)(2) of this section and except as provided in division (L)(3) of this section, an employee assistance professional, concerning a communication made to the employee assistance professional by a client in the employee assistance professional's official capacity as an employee assistance professional.

(2) Division (L)(1) of this section applies to an employee assistance professional who meets either or both of the following requirements:

(a) Is certified by the employee assistance certification commission to engage in the employee assistance profession;

(b) Has education, training, and experience in all of the following:

(i) Providing workplace-based services designed to address employer and employee productivity issues;

(ii) Providing assistance to employees and employees' dependents in identifying and finding the means to resolve personal problems that affect the employees or the employees' performance;

(iii) Identifying and resolving productivity problems associated with an employee's concerns about any of the following matters: health, marriage, family, finances, substance abuse or other addiction, workplace, law, and emotional issues;

(iv) Selecting and evaluating available community resources;

(v) Making appropriate referrals;

(vi) Local and national employee assistance agreements;

(vii) Client confidentiality.

(3) Division (L)(1) of this section does not apply to any of the following:

(a) A criminal action or proceeding involving an offense under sections 2903.01 to 2903.06 of the Revised Code if the employee assistance professional's disclosure or testimony relates directly to the facts or immediate circumstances of the offense;

(b) A communication made by a client to an employee assistance professional that reveals the contemplation or commission of a crime or serious, harmful act;

(c) A communication that is made by a client who is an unemancipated minor or an adult adjudicated to be incompetent and indicates that the client was the victim of a crime or abuse;

(d) A civil proceeding to determine an individual's mental competency or a criminal action in which a plea of not guilty by reason of insanity is entered;

(e) A civil or criminal malpractice action brought against the employee assistance professional;

(f) When the employee assistance professional has the express consent of the client or, if the client is deceased or disabled, the client's legal representative;

(g) When the testimonial privilege otherwise provided by division (L)(1) of this section is abrogated under law.

**HISTORY: RS § 5241; S&S 558; S&C 1038; 51 v 57, § 315; 67 v 113, § 314; GC § 11494; Bureau of Code Revision, 10-1-53; 125 v 313 (Eff 10-13-53); 136 v H 682 (Eff 7-28-75); 136 v H 1426 (Eff 7-1-76); 138 v H 284 (Eff 10-22-80); 140 v H 205 (Eff 10-10-84); 141 v H 528 (Eff 7-9-86); 141 v H 529 (Eff 3-11-87); 142 v H 1 (Eff 1-5-88); 143 v S 2 (Eff 11-1-89); 143 v H 615 (Eff 3-27-91); 143 v S 3 (Eff 4-11-91); 144 v S 343 (Eff 3-24-93); 145 v S 121 (Eff 10-29-93); 145 v H 335 (Eff 12-9-94); 146 v S 230 (Eff 10-29-96); 146 v S 223 (Eff 3-18-97); 147 v H 606 (Eff 3-9-99); 148 v H 448 (Eff 10-5-2000); 148 v S 172 (Eff 2-12-2001); 148 v S 180 (Eff 3-22-2001); 148 v H 506 (Eff 4-10-2001); 149 v H 94 (Eff 9-5-2001); 149 v H 533 (Eff 3-31-2003); 149 v H 374 (Eff 4-7-2003); 149 v S 281. Eff 4-11-2003; 151 v S 19, § 1, eff. 1-27-06; 151 v H 144, § 1, eff. 6-15-06; 151 v S 17, § 1, eff. 8-3-06; 151 v S 8, § 1, eff. 8-17-06; 151 v S 117, § 1, eff. 10-31-07†; 153 v S 162, § 1, eff. 9-13-10; 2011 HB 153, § 101.01, eff. July 1, 2011.**

† This date is provided by the Ohio Secretary of State. The effective date was determined in State ex rel. Ohio General Assembly v. Brunner (2007 Ohio LEXIS 1954, 2007 Ohio 4460, 115 Ohio St. 3d 103, 873 NE2d 1232) subject to the filing of a referendum petition.

The provisions of §§ 6 and 7 of 151 v S 117 read as follows:

SECTION 6. The General Assembly declares that the attorney-client privilege is a substantial right and that it is the public policy of Ohio that all communications between an attorney and a client in that relation are worthy of the protection of privilege, and further that where it is alleged that the attorney aided or furthered an ongoing or future commission of insurance bad faith by the client, that the party seeking waiver of the privilege must make a prima facie showing that the privilege should be waived and the court should conduct an in camera inspection of disputed communications. The common law established in *Boone v. Vanliner Ins. Co.* (2001), 91 Ohio St.3d 209, *Moskovitz v. Mt. Sinai Med. Ctr.* (1994), 69 Ohio St.3d 638, and *Peyko v. Frederick* (1986), 25 Ohio St.3d 164, is modified accordingly to provide for judicial review regarding the privilege.

SECTION 7. Section 2317.02 of the Revised Code is presented in this act as a composite of the section as amended by Sub. H.B. 144, Sub. S.B. 8, and Am. Sub. S.B. 17 of the 126th General Assembly. The General Assembly, applying the principle stated in division (B) of section 1.52 of the Revised Code that amendments are to be harmonized if reasonably capable of simultaneous operation, finds that the composite is the resulting version of the section in effect prior to the effective date of the section as presented in this act.

The provisions of § 3 of 151 v S 19 read as follows:

SECTION 3. Section 2317.02 of the Revised Code is presented in this act as a composite of the section as amended by Am. Sub. H.B. 374, Am. H.B. 533, and Am. Sub. S.B. 281, all of the 124th General Assembly. The General Assembly, applying the principle stated in division (B) of section 1.52 of the Revised Code that amendments are to be harmonized if reasonably capable of simultaneous operation, finds that the composite is the resulting version of the section in effect prior to the effective date of the section as presented in this act.

## § 2317.021 "Client" defined; application of attorney-client privilege to dissolved corporation or association; "incompetent person" defined.

(A) As used in division (A) of section 2317.02 of the Revised Code:

"Client" means a person, firm, partnership, corporation, or other association that, directly or through any representative, consults an attorney for the purpose of retaining the attorney or securing legal service or advice from the attorney in the attorney's professional capacity, or consults an attorney employee for legal service or advice, and who communicates, either directly or through an agent, employee, or other representative, with such attorney; and includes an incompetent person whose guardian so consults the attorney in behalf of the incompetent person.

Where a corporation or association is a client having the privilege and it has been dissolved, the privilege shall extend to the last board of directors, their successors or assigns, or to the trustees, their successors or assigns.

This section shall be construed as in addition to, and not in limitation of, other laws affording protection to communications under the attorney-client privilege.

(B) As used in this section and in sections 2317.02 and 2317.03 of the Revised Code, "incompetent" or "incompetent person" means a person who is so mentally impaired as a result of a mental or physical illness or disability, or mental retardation, or as a result of chronic substance abuse, that the person is incapable of taking proper care of the person's self or property or fails to provide for the person's family or other persons for whom the person is charged by law to provide.

**HISTORY: 130 v 649, § 1. Eff 10-14-63; 152 v H 53, § 1, eff. 8-7-07.**

See provisions of § 3 of 152 v H 53 following RC § 2307.14.

## § 2317.022 Request to health care provider for results of alcohol or drug tests for use in criminal proceedings.

(A) As used in this section:

(1) "Health care provider" has the same meaning as in section 2317.02 of the Revised Code.

(2) "Drug of abuse" has the same meaning as in section 4506.01 of the Revised Code.

(B) If an official criminal investigation has begun regarding a person or if a criminal action or proceeding is commenced against a person, any law enforcement officer who wishes to obtain from any health care provider a copy of any records the provider possesses that pertain to any test or the result of any test administered to the person to determine the presence or concentration of alcohol, a drug of abuse, or alcohol and a drug of abuse in the person's blood, breath, or urine at any time relevant to the criminal offense in question shall submit to the health care facility a written statement in the following form:

WRITTEN STATEMENT REQUESTING THE RELEASE OF RECORDS

To: ......... (insert the name of the health care provider in question).

I hereby state that an official criminal investigation has begun regarding, or a criminal action or proceeding has been commenced against, ......... (insert the name of the person in question), and that I believe that one or more tests has been administered to that person by this health care provider to determine the presence or concentration of alcohol, a drug of abuse, a combination of them, a controlled substance, or a metabolite of a controlled substance in that person's whole blood, blood serum or plasma, breath, or urine at a time relevant to the criminal offense in question. Therefore, I hereby request that, pursuant to division (B)(2) of section 2317.02 of the Revised Code, this health care provider supply me with copies of any records the provider possesses that pertain to any test or the results of any test administered to the person specified above to determine the presence or concentration of alcohol, a drug of abuse, a combination of them, a controlled substance, or a metabolite of a controlled substance in that person's whole blood, blood serum or plasma, breath, or urine at any time relevant to the criminal offense in question.

..........................................................

(Name of officer)

..........................................................

(Officer's title)

..........................................................

(Officer's employing agency)

..........................................................

(Officer's telephone number)

..........................................................

..........................................................

..........................................................

(Agency's address)

..........................................................

(Date written statement submitted)"

(C) A health care provider that receives a written statement of the type described in division (B) of this section shall comply with division (B)(2) of section 2317.02 of the Revised Code relative to the written statement.

**HISTORY: 145 v H 335 (Eff 12-9-94); 149 v H 94. Eff 9-5-2001; 151 v S 8, § 1, eff. 8-17-06.**

The effective date is set by section 204 of HB 94.

## § 2317.023 Repealed, 150 v H 303, § 2 [146 v H 438. Eff 7-1-97; 146 v H 350, § 14. Eff 1-27-97]. Eff 10-29-05.

The effective date is set by section 5 of H.B. 303 (150 v —). This section concerned disclosure of mediation communication.

## § 2317.03 Cases in which a party shall not testify.

A party shall not testify when the adverse party is the guardian or trustee of an incompetent person, or of a child of a deceased person, or is an executor or administrator, or claims or defends as heir, grantee, assignee, devisee, or legatee of a deceased person except:

(A) As to facts which occurred after the appointment of the guardian or trustee of an incompetent person, and, in the other cases, after the time the decedent, grantor, assignor, or testator died;

(B) When the action or proceeding relates to a contract made through an agent by a person since deceased, and the agent is competent to testify as a witness, a party may testify on the same subject;

(C) If a party, or one having a direct interest, testifies to transactions or conversations with another party, the latter may testify as to the same transactions or conversations;

(D) If a party offers evidence of conversations or admissions of the opposite party, the latter may testify concerning the same conversations or admissions; and, if evidence or declarations against interest made by an incompetent or deceased person has been admitted, then any oral or written declaration made by such incompetent or deceased person concerning the same subject to which any such admitted evidence relates, and which but for this provision would be excluded as self-serving, shall be admitted in evidence if it be proved to the satisfaction of the trial judge that the declaration was made at a time when the declarant was competent to testify, concerning a subject matter in issue, and, when no apparent motive to misrepresent appears;

(E) In an action or proceeding by or against a partner or joint contractor, the adverse party shall not testify to transactions with, or admissions by, a partner or joint contractor since deceased, unless they were made in the presence of the surviving partner or joint contractor, and this rule applies without regard to the character in which the parties sue or are sued;

(F) If the claim or defense is founded on a book account, a party may testify that the book is the party's account book, that it is a book of original entries, that the entries therein were made in the regular course of business by the party personally, a person since deceased, or a disinterested person, and the book is then competent evidence in any case, without regard to the parties, upon like proof by any competent witness;

(G) If after testifying orally, a party dies, the evidence may be proved by either party on a further trial of the case, whereupon the opposite party may testify to the same matters;

(H) If a party dies and the party's deposition is offered in evidence, the opposite party may testify as to all competent matters therein.

This section does not apply to actions for causing death, or actions or proceedings involving the validity of a deed, will or codicil. When a case is plainly within the reason and spirit of this section and sections 2317.01 and 2317.02 of the Revised Code, though not within the strict letter, their principles shall be applied.

**HISTORY: RS § 5242; S&S 557; S&C 1037; 51 v 374; 74 v 161, § 313; 82 v 125; GC § 11495; 111 v 33; Bureau of Code Revision, 10-1-53; 126 v 39. Eff 10-4-55; 152 v H 53, § 1, eff. 8-7-07.**

See provisions of § 3 of 152 v H 53 following RC § 2307.14.

## § 2317.04 Impartial report of proceedings privileged.

The publication of a fair and impartial report of the proceedings before state or municipal legislative bodies, or before state or municipal executive bodies, boards, or officers, or the whole or a fair synopsis of any bill, ordinance, report, resolution, bulletin, notice, petition, or other document presented, filed, or issued in any proceeding before such legislative or executive body, board, or officer, shall be privileged, unless it is proved that such publication was made maliciously.

**HISTORY: GC § 11343-1; 102 v 95; Bureau of Code Revision. Eff 10-1-53.**

## § 2317.05 Impartial report of indictment, warrant, affidavit, or arrest privileged.

The publication of a fair and impartial report of the return of any indictment, the issuing of any warrant, the arrest of any person accused of crime, or the filing of any affidavit, pleading, or other document in any criminal or civil cause in any court of competent jurisdiction, or of a fair and impartial report of the contents thereof, is privileged, unless it is proved that the same was published maliciously, or that defendant has refused or neglected to publish in the same manner in which the publication complained of appeared, a reasonable written explanation or contradiction thereof by the plaintiff, or that the publisher has refused, upon request of the plaintiff, to publish the subsequent determination of such suit or action. This section and section 2317.04 of the Revised

Code do not authorize the publication of blasphemous or indecent matter.

**HISTORY: GC § 11343-2; 102 v 95; Bureau of Code Revision. Eff 10-1-53.**

## § 2317.06 Proving testimony of absent witness.

(A) If a party or witness, after testifying orally, dies, is beyond the jurisdiction of the court, cannot be found after diligent search, is unable to testify because of any physical or mental infirmity, or has been summoned but appears to have been kept away by the adverse party and if the evidence of the party or witness has been taken down by an official stenographer, the evidence so taken may be read in evidence by either party on the further trial of the case and shall be prima-facie evidence of what the deceased party or witness testified to orally on the former trial. If the evidence has not been taken by an official stenographer, it may be proved by witnesses who were present at the former trial, having knowledge of the testimony. All testimony so offered shall be open to all objections that might be taken if the witness was personally present.

(B)(1) If it is necessary in a civil action before the court to procure the testimony of a person who is imprisoned in a workhouse, juvenile detention facility, jail, or state correctional institution within this state, or who is in the custody of the department of youth services, the court shall require that the person's testimony be taken by deposition pursuant to the Civil Rules at the place of the person's confinement, unless the court determines that the interests of justice demand that the person be brought before the court for the presentation of the person's testimony.

(2) If the court determines that the interests of justice demand that a person specified in division (B)(1) of this section be brought before the court for the presentation of the person's testimony, the court shall order the person to be brought before it under the procedures set forth in division (B) or (C) of section 2945.47 of the Revised Code.

(C) When a person's deposition is taken pursuant to division (B)(1) of this section, the person shall remain in the custody of the officer who is in charge of the person, and the officer shall provide reasonable facilities for the taking of the deposition.

(D) The person requesting the testimony of the person whose deposition is taken pursuant to division (B)(1) of this section shall pay the expense of taking the deposition, except that the court may tax the expense as court costs in appropriate cases.

**HISTORY: RS § 5242a; 89 v 143; GC § 11496; Bureau of Code Revision, 10-1-53; 139 v H 145 (Eff 5-28-81); 139 v H 440 (Eff 11-23-81); 145 v H 571. Eff 10-6-94; 152 v H 53, § 1, eff. 8-7-07.**

See provisions of § 3 of 152 v H 53 following RC § 2307.14.

## § 2317.07 Examination of parties.

At the instance of the adverse party, a party may be examined as if under cross-examination, orally, by way of deposition, like any other witness, by way of written interrogatories filed in the action or proceeding, or by any one or more of such methods. The party calling for such examination shall not thereby be concluded but may rebut it by evidence.

**HISTORY: RS § 5243; S&C 1037; 51 v 57, § 312; 91 v 86; GC § 11497; 101 v 139; Bureau of Code Revision, 10-1-53; 125 v 35 (Eff 10-2-53); 131 v 658 (Eff 9-28-65); 132 v S 25 (Eff 7-24-67); 133 v H 1 (Eff 3-18-69); 133 v H 1201 (Eff 7-1-71); 134 v H 602, §§ 1, 2. Eff 6-30-71.**

[MEANS OF SECURING ATTENDANCE]

## § 2317.21 Attachment of witness who disobeys subpoena.

When a witness, except a witness who has demanded and has not been paid his traveling fees and fee for one day's attendance when a subpoena is served upon him, as authorized by the provisions of section 2317.18 † of the Revised Code, fails to obey a subpoena personally served, the court or officer, before whom his attendance is required, may issue to the sheriff or a constable of the county, a writ of attachment, commanding him to arrest and bring the person named in the writ before such court or officer at the time and place the writ fixes, to give his testimony and answer for the contempt. If such writ does not require the witness to be immediately brought, he may give bond for a sum fixed by the court of common pleas or the court which issued the subpoena, with surety, for his appearance, which sum shall be endorsed on the back of the writ, except that, if no sum is so endorsed, it shall be one hundred dollars. When the witness was not personally served, the court, by a rule, may order him to show cause why such writ should not issue against him.

**HISTORY: RS § 5253; S&C 1039; 51 v 57, § 323; GC § 11511; Bureau of Code Revision, 10-1-53; 129 v 325 (Eff 10-2-61); 139 v S 114. Eff 10-27-81.**

† Repealed, 133 v H 1201. See now CivR 45(B).

## § 2317.22 Punishment for contempt.

Punishment for the acts of contempt specified in section 2317.20 † of the Revised Code shall be as follows: When the witness fails to attend in obedience to a subpoena, the court or officer may fine him not more than fifty dollars; in other cases, not more than fifty dollars nor less than five dollars; or the court or officer may imprison such witness in the county jail, there to remain until he submits to be sworn, testifies, or gives his deposition.

**HISTORY: RS § 5254; S&C 1039; 77 v 42, 45; GC § 11512; Bureau of Code Revision. Eff 10-1-53.**

† Repealed, 133 v H 1201. See now CivR 45(E).

## § 2317.23 Disposition of fines.

A fine imposed under section 2317.22 of the Revised Code by the court shall be paid into the county treasury; that imposed by an officer shall be for the use of the party for whom the witness was subpoenaed. The witness also shall be liable to the party injured for any damages occasioned by his failure to attend, or refusal to be sworn, to testify, or to give his deposition.

**HISTORY: RS § 5254; S&C 1039; 77 v 42, 45; GC § 11513; Bureau of Code Revision. Eff 10-1-53.**

## § 2317.24 Release of witness from imprisonment.

A witness imprisoned by an officer under section 2317.22 of the Revised Code may apply to a judge of the supreme court, court of appeals, court of common pleas, or probate court, who may discharge him if it appears that such imprisonment is illegal.

**HISTORY: RS § 5255; S&C 1040; 51 v 57, § 325; 82 v 16, 33; GC § 11514; 103 v 405(426); Bureau of Code Revision. Eff 10-1-53.**

## § 2317.25 Contents of attachment or order to commit.

Every attachment for the arrest or order to commit a witness to prison by a court or officer, pursuant to sections 2317.21 and 2317.22 of the Revised Code, must be under seal of the court or official seal of the officer, if he has one, and must particularly specify the cause of the arrest or commitment. When committed for a refusal to answer a question, the question must be stated in the order.

**HISTORY: RS § 5256; S&C 1040; 51 v 57, § 326; GC § 11515; Bureau of Code Revision. Eff 10-1-53.**

## § 2317.26 Order of commitment.

The order of commitment mentioned in section 2317.25 of the Revised Code may be directed to the sheriff or a constable of the county where the witness resides, or is at the time, and shall be executed by committing him to the jail of such county, and delivering a copy of it to the jailer.

**HISTORY: RS § 5256; S&C 1040; 51 v 57, § 326; GC § 11516; Bureau of Code Revision, 10-1-53; 139 v S 114. Eff 10-27-81.**

## § 2317.29 May not sue or serve witness out of his county.

A witness shall not be liable to be sued, in a county in which he does not reside, by being served with a summons in such county while going, returning or attending in obedience to a subpoena.

**HISTORY: RS § 5259; S&C 1040; 51 v 57, § 329; GC § 11519; Bureau of Code Revision. Eff 10-1-53.**

## § 2317.30 Oath of witness.

Before testifying, a witness shall be sworn to testify the truth, the whole truth, and nothing but the truth.

**HISTORY: RS § 5260; S&C 1040; 51 v 57, § 331; GC § 11520; Bureau of Code Revision. Eff 10-1-53.**

# [COMPOSITE REPORTS]

## § 2317.36 Admissible reports.

A written report or finding of facts prepared by an expert who is not a party to the cause, nor an employee of a party, except for the purpose of making such report or finding, nor financially interested in the result of the controversy, and containing the conclusions resulting wholly or partly from written information furnished by the co-operation of several persons acting for a common purpose, shall, in so far as the same is relevant, be admissible when testified to by the person, or one of the persons, making such report or finding without calling as witnesses the persons furnishing the information, and without producing the books or other writings on which the report for finding is based, if, in the opinion of the court, no substantial injustice will be done the opposite party.

**HISTORY: GC § 12102-17; 118 v 663; Bureau of Code Revision. Eff 10-1-53.**

## § 2317.37 Cross-examination by adverse party.

Any person who has furnished information on which a report or finding mentioned in section 2317.36 of the Revised Code is based may be cross-examined by the adverse party, but the fact that his testimony is not obtainable shall not render the report or finding inadmissible, unless the trial court finds that substantial injustice would be done to the adverse party by its admission.

**HISTORY: GC § 12102-18; 118 v 663, § 2; Bureau of Code Revision. Eff 10-1-53.**

## § 2317.38 Notice of intention to offer report.

The report or finding mentioned in section 2317.36 of the Revised Code is not admissible unless the party offering it has given notice to the adverse party a reasonable time before trial of his intention to offer it, together with a copy of the report or finding, or so much thereof as relates to the controversy, and has afforded him a reasonable opportunity to inspect and copy any records or other documents in the offering party's possession or control, on which the report or finding was based, and also the names of all persons furnishing facts upon which the report or finding was based.

This section and sections 2317.36 and 2317.37 of the Revised Code shall be so interpreted and construed as to effectuate their general purpose to make the law of this state uniform with those states which enact similar legislation.

**HISTORY: GC §§ 12102-19, 12102-20; 118 v 663, §§ 3, 4; Bureau of Code Revision. Eff 10-1-53.**

## § 2317.39 Report of investigations conducted by court made available to all parties.

Whenever an investigation into the facts of any case, civil or criminal, pending at the time of such investigation in any court, is made, conducted, or participated in, directly or indirectly, by any court or any department thereof, through public employees, paid private investigators, social workers, friends of the court, or any other persons, and a report of such investigation is prepared for submission to the court, the contents of such report shall not be considered by any judge of the court wherein such case is pending either before the trial of the case or at any stage of the proceedings prior to final disposition thereof, unless the full contents of such report have been made readily available and accessible to all parties to the case or their counsel. The parties or their counsel shall be notified in writing of the fact that an investigation has been made, that a report has been submitted, and that the contents of the report are available for examination. Such notice shall be given at least five days prior to the time the contents of any report are to be considered by any judge of the court wherein the case is pending. In the event that a report following any investigation is prepared for submission orally, such oral report shall be reduced to writing prior to the issuance of notice of the availability of such report for examination.

This section does not apply only to the utilization of the contents of such reports as testimony, but shall prevent any judge from familiarizing himself with such contents in any manner unless this section has been fully complied with.

**HISTORY: GC § 11521-1; 124 v 412; Bureau of Code Revision. Eff 10-1-53.**

[BUSINESS RECORDS]

## § 2317.40 Records as evidence.

As used in this section "business" includes every kind of business, profession, occupation, calling, or operation of institutions, whether carried on for profit or not.

A record of an act, condition, or event, in so far as relevant, is competent evidence if the custodian or the person who made such record or under whose supervision such record was made testifies to its identity and the mode of its preparation, and if it was made in the regular course of business, at or near the time of the act, condition, or event, and if, in the opinion of the court, the sources of information, method, and time of preparation were such as to justify its admission.

This section shall be so interpreted and construed as to effectuate its general purpose to make the law of this state uniform with those states which enact similar legislation.

**HISTORY: GC §§ 12102-22-12102-24; 118 v 662, §§ 1, 2; Bureau of Code Revision, 10-1-53; 127 v 847. Eff 9-16-57.**

## § 2317.41 Photographic copies of records admissible in evidence.

"Photograph" as used in this section includes but is not limited to microphotograph, a roll or strip of film, a roll or strip of microfilm, a photostatic copy, or an optically-imaged copy.

To the extent that a record would be competent evidence under section 2317.40 of the Revised Code, a photograph of such record shall be competent evidence if the custodian of the photograph or the person who made such photograph or under whose supervision such photograph was made testifies to the identity of and the mode of making such photograph, and if, in the opinion of the trial court, the record has been destroyed or otherwise disposed of in good faith in the regular course of business, and the mode of making such photograph was such as to justify its admission. If a photograph is admissible under this section, the court may admit the whole or a part thereof.

Such photograph shall be admissible only if the party offering it has delivered a copy of it, or so much thereof as relates to the controversy, to the adverse party a reasonable time before trial, unless in the opinion of the court the adverse party has not been unfairly surprised by the failure to deliver such copy. No such photograph need be submitted to the adverse party as prescribed in this section unless the original instrument would be required to be so submitted.

**HISTORY: GC § 12102-23a; 122 v 290; Bureau of Code Revision, Eff 10-1-53; 146 v H 495. Eff 10-4-96.**

[OFFICIAL REPORTS]

## § 2317.42 Reports or certified copies to be admitted.

Official reports made by officers of this state, or certified copies of the same, on a matter within the scope of their duty as defined by statute, shall, in so far as relevant, be admitted as evidence of the matters stated therein.

**HISTORY: GC §§ 12102-26, 12102-27; 118 v 665, §§ 1, 2; Bureau of Code Revision, 10-1-53; 133 v H 1201 (Eff 7-1-71); 134 v H 602, §§ 1, 2. Eff 6-30-71.**

[MEDICAL BILLS AND RECORDS]

## § 2317.421 Personal injury or wrongful death action.

In an action for damages arising from personal injury or wrongful death, a written bill or statement, or any relevant portion thereof, itemized by date, type of service rendered, and charge, shall, if otherwise admissible, be prima-facie evidence of the reasonableness of any charges and fees stated therein for medication and prosthetic devices furnished, or medical, dental, hospital, and funeral services rendered by the person, firm, or corporation issuing such bill or statement, provided, that such bill or statement shall be prima-facie evidence of reasonableness only if the party offering it delivers a copy of it, or the relevant portion thereof, to the attorney of record for each adverse party not less than five days before trial.

**HISTORY: 133 v S 352. Eff 6-1-70.**

## § 2317.422 Qualification of nursing, rest and adult care facilities records.

(A) Notwithstanding sections 2317.40 and 2317.41 of the Revised Code but subject to division (B) of this section, the records, or copies or photographs of the records, of a hospital, homes required to be licensed pursuant to section 3721.01 of the Revised Code, and adult care facilities required to be licensed pursuant to Chapter 5119. of the Revised Code, in lieu of the testimony in open court of their custodian, person who made them, or person under whose supervision they were made, may be qualified as authentic evidence if any such person endorses thereon the person's verified certification identifying such records, giving the mode and time of their preparation, and stating that they were prepared in the usual course of the business of the institution. Such records, copies, or photographs may not be qualified by certification as provided in this section unless the party intending to offer them delivers a copy of them, or of their relevant portions, to the attorney of record for each adverse party not less than five days before trial. Nothing in this section shall be construed to limit the right of any party to call the custodian, person who made such records, or person under whose supervision they were made, as a witness.

(B) Division (A) of this section does not apply to any certified copy of the results of any test given to determine the presence or concentration of alcohol, a drug of abuse, a combination of them, a controlled substance, or a metabolite of a controlled substance in a patient's whole blood, blood serum or plasma, breath, or urine at any time relevant to a criminal offense that is submitted in a criminal action or proceeding in accordance with division (B)(2)(b) or (B)(3)(b) of section 2317.02 of the Revised Code.

**HISTORY: 135 v H 614 (Eff 9-30-74); 143 v S 2 (Eff 11-1-89); 143 v H 253 (Eff 11-15-90); 145 v H 335. Eff 12-9-94; 151 v S 8, § 1, eff. 8-17-06; 153 v H 1, § 101.01, eff. 10-16-09; 2011 HB 153, § 101.01, eff. July 1, 2011.**

The effective date is set by § 812.10 of 153 v H 1.

## § 2317.43 Use of defendant's statement of sympathy as evidence in medical liability action prohibited.

(A) In any civil action brought by an alleged victim of an unanticipated outcome of medical care or in any arbitration proceeding related to such a civil action, any and all statements, affirmations, gestures, or conduct expressing apology, sympathy, commiseration, condolence, compassion, or a general sense of benevolence that are made by a health care provider or an employee of a health care provider to the alleged victim, a relative of the alleged victim, or a representative of the alleged victim, and that relate to the discomfort, pain, suffering, injury, or death of the alleged victim as the result of the unanticipated outcome of medical care are inadmissible as evidence of an admission of liability or as evidence of an admission against interest.

(B) For purposes of this section, unless the context otherwise requires:

(1) "Health care provider" has the same meaning as in division (B)(5) of section 2317.02 of the Revised Code.

(2) "Relative" means a victim's spouse, parent, grandparent, stepfather, stepmother, child, grandchild, brother, sister, half brother, half sister, or spouse's parents. The term includes said relationships that are created as a result of adoption. In addition, "relative" includes any person who has a family-type relationship with a victim.

(3) "Representative" means a legal guardian, attorney, person designated to make decisions on behalf of a patient under a medical power of attorney, or any person recognized in law or custom as a patient's agent.

(4) "Unanticipated outcome" means the outcome of a medical treatment or procedure that differs from an expected result.

**HISTORY: 150 v H 215, § 1, eff. 9-13-04.**

**Not analogous to former RC § 2317.43 (GC §§ 12102-28, 12102-29, 12102-31-12102-33; 118 v 665, §§ 3, 4; 118 v 678, §§ 1-3; Bureau of Code Revision, 10-1-53; 132 v S 26), repealed 133 v H 1201, § 1, eff 7-1-71.**

### [BLOOD TESTS]

## § 2317.47 Blood tests by court order.

Whenever it is relevant in a civil or criminal action or proceeding to determine the paternity or identity of any person, the trial court on motion shall order any party to the action and any person involved in the controversy or proceeding to submit to one or more blood-grouping tests, to be made by qualified physicians or other qualified persons not to exceed three, to be selected by the court and under such restrictions or directions as the court or judge deems proper. In cases where exclusion is established, the results of the tests together with the findings of the experts of the fact of nonpaternity are receivable in evidence. Such experts shall be subject to cross-examination by both parties after the court has caused them to disclose their findings to the court or to the court and jury. Whenever the court orders such blood-grouping tests to be taken and one of the parties refuses to submit to such test, such fact shall be disclosed upon the trial unless good cause is shown to the contrary. The court shall determine how and by whom the costs of such examination shall be paid.

**HISTORY: GC § 12122-2; 118 v 570; Bureau of Code Revision. Eff 10-1-53.**

### [DISCOVERY]

## § 2317.48 Action for discovery.

When a person claiming to have a cause of action or a defense to an action commenced against him, without the discovery of a fact from the adverse party, is unable to file his complaint or answer, he may bring an action for discovery, setting forth in his complaint in the action for discovery the necessity and the grounds for the action, with any interrogatories relating to the subject matter of the discovery that are necessary to procure the discovery sought. Unless a motion to dismiss the action is filed under Civil Rule 12, the complaint shall be fully and directly answered under oath by the defendant. Upon the final disposition of the action, the costs of the action shall be taxed in the manner the court deems equitable.

**HISTORY: RS § 5293; S&C 1151; 64 v 23, § 3; GC § 11555; Bureau of Code Revision, 10-1-53; 140 v S 47. Eff 4-4-85.**

### [AGENTS]

## § 2317.52 Cross-examination of agents.

When the action or proceeding relates to a transaction or occurrence in which it has been shown or it is admitted that the adverse party acted either in whole or in part through an agent or employee, such agent or employee of the adverse party may be called as a witness and examined as if under cross-examination upon any matters at issue between the parties which are shown or admitted to have been within the scope of such agent's or employee's authority or employment.

The party calling for such examination shall not thereby be concluded but may rebut such agent's or employee's testimony by counter testimony.

The party whose agent or employee is called as a witness by the adverse party and whose agent or employee is examined as if under cross-examination shall not thereby be concluded but may rebut such agent's or employee's testimony by counter testimony.

**HISTORY: 127 v 95, § 1. Eff 9-13-57.**

### [PATIENT'S INFORMED CONSENT]

## § 2317.54 Consent to surgical or medical procedure; requirements.

No hospital, home health agency, ambulatory surgical facility, or provider of a hospice care program shall be held liable for a physician's failure to obtain an informed consent from the physician's patient prior to a surgical or medical procedure or course of procedures, unless the physician is an employee of the hospital, home health agency, ambulatory surgical facility, or provider of a hospice care program.

Written consent to a surgical or medical procedure or course of procedures shall, to the extent that it fulfills all the requirements in divisions (A), (B), and (C) of this section, be presumed to be valid and effective, in the absence of proof by a preponderance of the evidence that the person who sought such consent was not acting in good faith, or that the execution of the consent was induced by fraudulent misrepresentation of material facts, or that the person executing the consent was not able to communicate effectively in spoken and written English or any other language in which the consent is written. Except as herein provided, no evidence shall be admissible to impeach, modify, or limit the authorization for performance of the procedure or procedures set forth in such written consent.

(A) The consent sets forth in general terms the nature and purpose of the procedure or procedures, and what the procedures are expected to accomplish, together with the reasonably known risks, and, except in emergency situations, sets forth the names of the physicians who shall perform the intended surgical procedures.

(B) The person making the consent acknowledges that such disclosure of information has been made and that all questions asked about the procedure or procedures have been answered in a satisfactory manner.

(C) The consent is signed by the patient for whom the procedure is to be performed, or, if the patient for any reason including, but not limited to, competence, minority, or the fact that, at the latest time that the consent is needed, the patient is under the influence of alcohol, hallucinogens, or drugs, lacks legal capacity to consent, by a person who has legal authority to consent on behalf of such patient in such circumstances, including either of the following:

(1) The parent, whether the parent is an adult or a minor, of the parent's minor child;

(2) An adult whom the parent of the minor child has given written authorization to consent to a surgical or medical procedure or course of procedures for the parent's minor child.

Any use of a consent form that fulfills the requirements stated in divisions (A), (B), and (C) of this section has no effect on the common law rights and liabilities, including the right of a physician to obtain the oral or implied consent of a patient to a medical procedure, that may exist as between physicians and patients on July 28, 1975.

As used in this section the term "hospital" has the same meaning as in section 2305.113 [2305.11.3] of the Revised Code; "home health agency" has the same meaning as in section 5101.61 of the Revised Code; "ambulatory surgical facility" has the meaning as in division (A) of section 3702.30 of the Revised Code; and "hospice care program" has the same meaning as in section 3712.01 of the Revised Code. The provisions of this division apply to hospitals, doctors of medicine, doctors of osteopathic medicine, and doctors of podiatric medicine.

**HISTORY: 136 v H 682 (Eff 7-28-75); 136 v H 1426 (Eff 7-1-76); 137 v H 213 (Eff 11-24-77); 141 v S 22 (Eff 3-1-87); 149 v S 124 (Eff 9-17-2002); 149 v S 281. Eff 4-11-2003; 152 v H 125, § 1, eff. 6-25-08.**

See provisions, § 6 of SB 281 (149 v —) following RC § 2323.43.

## § 2317.56 Information to be provided to woman prior to abortion; consent form; medical emergency or necessity; liability of noncomplying physician and employer; publication of informational materials.

(A) As used in this section:

(1) "Medical emergency" means a condition of a pregnant woman that, in the reasonable judgment of the physician who is attending the woman, creates an immediate threat of serious risk to the life or physical health of the woman from the continuation of the pregnancy necessitating the immediate performance or inducement of an abortion.

(2) "Medical necessity" means a medical condition of a pregnant woman that, in the reasonable judgment of the physician who is attending the woman, so complicates the pregnancy that it necessitates the immediate performance or inducement of an abortion.

(3) "Probable gestational age of the embryo or fetus" means the gestational age that, in the judgment of a physician, is, with reasonable probability, the gestational age of the embryo or fetus at the time that the physician informs a pregnant woman pursuant to division (B)(1)(b) of this section.

(B) Except when there is a medical emergency or medical necessity, an abortion shall be performed or induced only if all of the following conditions are satisfied:

(1) At least twenty-four hours prior to the performance or inducement of the abortion, a physician meets with the pregnant woman in person in an individual, private setting and gives her an adequate opportunity to ask questions about the abortion that will be performed or induced. At this meeting, the physician shall inform the pregnant woman, verbally or, if she is hearing impaired, by other means of communication, of all of the following:

(a) The nature and purpose of the particular abortion procedure to be used and the medical risks associated with that procedure;

(b) The probable gestational age of the embryo or fetus;

(c) The medical risks associated with the pregnant woman carrying the pregnancy to term.

The meeting need not occur at the facility where the abortion is to be performed or induced, and the physician involved in the meeting need not be affiliated with that facility or with the physician who is scheduled to perform or induce the abortion.

(2) At least twenty-four hours prior to the performance or inducement of the abortion, one or more physicians or one or more agents of one or more physicians do each of the following in person, by telephone, by certified mail, return receipt requested, or by regular mail evidenced by a certificate of mailing:

(a) Inform the pregnant woman of the name of the physician who is scheduled to perform or induce the abortion;

(b) Give the pregnant woman copies of the published materials described in division (C) of this section;

(c) Inform the pregnant woman that the materials given pursuant to division (B)(2)(b) of this section are provided by the state and that they describe the embryo or fetus and list agencies that offer alternatives to abortion. The pregnant woman may choose to examine or not to examine the materials. A physician or an agent of a physician may choose to be disassociated from the materials and may choose to comment or not comment on the materials.

(3) Prior to the performance or inducement of the abortion, the pregnant woman signs a form consenting to the abortion and certifies both of the following on that form:

(a) She has received the information and materials described in divisions (B)(1) and (2) of this section, and her questions about the abortion that will be performed or induced have been answered in a satisfactory manner.

(b) She consents to the particular abortion voluntarily, knowingly, intelligently, and without coercion by any person, and she is not under the influence of any drug of abuse or alcohol.

(4) Prior to the performance or inducement of the abortion, the physician who is scheduled to perform or induce the abortion or the physician's agent receives a copy of the pregnant woman's signed form on which she consents to the abortion and that includes the certification required by division (B)(3) of this section.

(C) The department of health shall cause to be published in English and in Spanish, in a typeface large enough to be clearly legible, and in an easily comprehensible format, the following materials:

(1) Materials that inform the pregnant woman about family planning information, of publicly funded agencies that are available to assist in family planning, and of public and private agencies and services that are available to assist her through the pregnancy, upon childbirth, and while the child is dependent, including, but not limited to, adoption agencies. The materials shall be geographically indexed; include a comprehensive list of the available agencies, a description of the services offered by the agencies, and the telephone numbers and addresses of the agencies; and inform the pregnant woman about available medical assistance benefits for prenatal care, childbirth, and neonatal care and about the support obligations of the father of a child who is born alive. The department shall ensure that the materials described in division (C)(1) of this section are comprehensive and do not directly or indirectly promote, exclude, or discourage the use of any agency or service described in this division.

(2) Materials that inform the pregnant woman of the probable anatomical and physiological characteristics of the zygote, blastocyte, embryo, or fetus at two-week gestational increments for the first sixteen weeks of pregnancy and at four-week gestational increments from the seventeenth week of pregnancy to full term, including any relevant information regarding the time at which the fetus possibly would be viable. The department shall cause these materials to be published only after it consults with the Ohio state medical association and the Ohio section of the American college of obstetricians and gynecologists relative to the probable anatomical and physiological characteristics of a zygote, blastocyte, embryo, or fetus at the various gestational increments. The materials shall use language that is understandable by the average person who is not medically trained, shall be objective and nonjudgmental, and shall include only accurate scientific information about the zygote, blastocyte, embryo, or fetus at the various gestational increments. If the materials use a pictorial, photographic, or other depiction to provide information regarding the zygote, blastocyte, embryo, or fetus, the materials shall include, in a conspicuous manner, a scale or other explanation that is understandable by the average person and that can be used to determine the actual size of the zygote, blastocyte, embryo, or fetus at a particular gestational increment as contrasted with the depicted size of the zygote, blastocyte, embryo, or fetus at that gestational increment.

(D) Upon the submission of a request to the department of health by any person, hospital, physician, or medical facility for one or more copies of the materials published in accordance with division (C) of this section, the department shall make the requested number of copies of the materials available to the person, hospital, physician, or medical facility that requested the copies.

(E) If a medical emergency or medical necessity compels the performance or inducement of an abortion, the physician who will perform or induce the abortion, prior to its performance or inducement if possible, shall inform the pregnant woman of the medical indications supporting the physician's judgment that an immediate abortion is necessary. Any physician who performs or induces an abortion without the prior satisfaction of the conditions specified in division (B) of this section because of a medical emergency or medical necessity shall enter the reasons for the conclusion that a medical emergency or medical necessity exists in the medical record of the pregnant woman.

(F) If the conditions specified in division (B) of this section are satisfied, consent to an abortion shall be presumed to be valid and effective.

(G) The performance or inducement of an abortion without the prior satisfaction of the conditions specified in division (B) of this section does not constitute, and shall not be construed as constituting, a violation of division (A) of section 2919.12 of the Revised Code. The failure of a physician to satisfy the conditions of division (B) of this section prior to performing or inducing an abortion upon a pregnant woman may be the basis of both of the following:

(1) A civil action for compensatory and exemplary damages as described in division (H) of this section;

(2) Disciplinary action under section 4731.22 of the Revised Code.

(H)(1) Subject to divisions (H)(2) and (3) of this section, any physician who performs or induces an abortion with actual knowledge that the conditions specified in division (B) of this section have not been satisfied or with a heedless indifference as to whether those conditions have been satisfied is liable in compensatory and exemplary damages in a civil action to any person, or the representative of the estate of any person, who sustains injury, death, or loss to person or property as a result of the failure to satisfy those conditions. In the civil action, the court additionally may enter any injunctive or other equitable relief that it considers appropriate.

(2) The following shall be affirmative defenses in a civil action authorized by division (H)(1) of this section:

(a) The physician performed or induced the abortion under the circumstances described in division (E) of this section.

(b) The physician made a good faith effort to satisfy the conditions specified in division (B) of this section.

(c) The physician or an agent of the physician requested copies of the materials published in accordance with division (C) of this section from the department of health, but the physician was not able to give a pregnant woman copies of the materials pursuant to division (B)(2) of this section and to obtain a certification as described in divisions (B)(3) and (4) of this section because the department failed to make the requested number of copies available to the physician or agent in accordance with division (D) of this section.

(3) An employer or other principal is not liable in damages in a civil action authorized by division (H)(1) of this section on the basis of the doctrine of respondeat superior unless either of the following applies:

(a) The employer or other principal had actual knowledge or, by the exercise of reasonable diligence, should have known that an employee or agent performed or induced an abortion with actual knowledge that the conditions specified in division (B) of this section had not been satisfied or with a heedless indifference as to whether those conditions had been satisfied.

(b) The employer or other principal negligently failed to secure the compliance of an employee or agent with division (B) of this section.

(4) Notwithstanding division (E) of section 2919.12 of the Revised Code, the civil action authorized by division (H)(1) of this section shall be the exclusive civil remedy for persons, or the representatives of estates of persons, who allegedly sustain injury, death, or loss to person or property as a result of a failure to satisfy the conditions specified in division (B) of this section.

(I) The department of job and family services shall prepare and conduct a public information program to inform women of all available governmental programs and agencies that provide services or assistance for family planning, prenatal care, child care, or alternatives to abortion.

**HISTORY: 144 v H 108 (Eff 5-28-92); 145 v H 715 (Eff 7-22-94); 147 v H 421 (Eff 5-6-98); 148 v H 471. Eff 7-1-2000.**

The effective date is set by section 12(A) of HB 471.

## § 2317.561 Physician's duties where obstetric ultrasound examination performed prior to abortion.

In addition to the requirements in section 2317.56 of the Revised Code, if an obstetric ultrasound examination is performed at any time prior to the performance or inducement of an abortion or the physician performing or inducing the abortion determines that an ultrasound examination will be performed as part of the abortion procedure, the physician shall do both of the following prior to the performance or inducement of the abortion:

(A) Provide the pregnant woman receiving the abortion the opportunity to view the active ultrasound image of the embryo or fetus;

(B) Offer to provide the pregnant woman with a physical picture of the ultrasound image of the embryo or fetus.

The requirements of division (A) of this section shall be performed at no additional charge to the pregnant woman.

**HISTORY: 152 v H 314, § 1, eff. 6-20-08.**

## § 2317.62 Evidence of cost of annuity as to future damages in tort actions.

(A) As used in this section:

(1) "Annuity" means an annuity that would be purchased from either of the following types of insurance companies:

(a) An insurance company that the A.M. Best Company, in its most recently published rating guide of life insurance companies, has rated A or better and has rated XII or higher as to financial size or strength;

(b)(i) An insurance company that the superintendent of insurance, under rules adopted pursuant to Chapter 119. of the Revised Code for purposes of implementing this division, determines is licensed to do business in this state and, considering the factors described in division (A)(1)(b)(ii) of this section, is a stable insurance company that issues annuities that are safe and desirable;

(ii) In making determinations as described in division (A)(1)(b)(i) of this section, the superintendent shall be guided by the principle that the trier of fact in a tort action should be presented only with evidence as to the cost of annuities that are safe and desirable for the plaintiffs in such an action who are awarded damages. In making such determinations, the superintendent shall consider the financial condition, general standing, operating results, profitability, leverage, liquidity, amount and soundness of reinsurance, adequacy of reserves, and the management of any insurance company in question and also may consider ratings, grades, and classifications of any nationally recognized rating services of insurance companies and any other factors relevant to the making of such determinations.

(2) "Future damages" means damages that result from an injury or loss to person or property that is a subject of a tort action and that will accrue after the verdict or determination of liability by the trier of fact is rendered in that tort action.

(3) "Tort action" means a civil action for damages for injury or loss to person or property. "Tort action" includes a product liability claim that is subject to sections 2307.71 to 2307.80 of the Revised Code, but does not include a civil action for damages for a breach of contract or another agreement between persons.

(4) "Trier of fact" means the jury or, in a nonjury action, the court.

(B) Consistent with the Rules of Evidence, any party to a tort action may present evidence of the cost of an annuity in connection with any issue of recoverable future damages. If such evidence is presented, then the trier of fact may consider that evidence in determining the future damages suffered by reason of an injury or loss to person or property that is a subject of the tort action. If such evidence is presented, the present value in dollars of any annuity is its cost.

**HISTORY: 142 v H 1 (Eff 1-5-88); 146 v H 350 (Eff 1-27-97); 149 v S 108, § 2.01. Eff 7-6-2001.**

**Publisher's Note:**

Section 2.02(B) of SB 108 (149 v —) repeals the HB 350 (146 v —) version and section 3(A)(4) revives the former version.

# CHAPTER 2335: FEES; COSTS

Section



## § 2335.061 Notice to subpoena coroner or deputy coroner to provide expert testimony; fee for testimony.

(A) As used in this section:

(1) "Coroner" has the same meaning as in section 313.01 of the Revised Code, and includes the following:

(a) The coroner of a county other than a county in which the death occurred or the dead human body was found if the coroner of that other county performed services for the county in which the death occurred or the dead human body was found;

(b) A medical examiner appointed by the governing authority of a county to perform the duties of a coroner set forth in Chapter 313. of the Revised Code.

(2) "Deposition fee" means the amount derived by multiplying the hourly rate by the number of hours a coroner or deputy coroner spent preparing for and giving expert testimony at a deposition in a civil action pursuant to this section.

(3) "Deputy coroner" means a pathologist serving as a deputy coroner.

(4) "Expert testimony" means testimony given by a coroner or deputy coroner as an expert witness pursuant to this section and the Rules of Evidence.

(5) "Fact testimony" means testimony given by a coroner or deputy coroner regarding the performance of the duties of the coroner as set forth in Chapter 313. of the Revised Code. "Fact testimony" does not include expert testimony.

(6) "Hourly rate" means the compensation established in sections 325.15 and 325.18 of the Revised Code for a coroner without a private practice of medicine at the class 8 level for calendar year 2001 and thereafter, divided by two thousand eighty.

(7) "Testimonial fee" means the amount derived by multiplying the hourly rate by six and multiplying the product by the number of hours that a coroner or deputy coroner spent preparing for and giving expert testimony at a trial or hearing in a civil action pursuant to this section.

(B)(1) A party may subpoena a coroner or deputy coroner to give expert testimony at a trial, hearing, or deposition in a civil action only upon filing with the court a notice that includes all of the following:

(a) The name of the coroner or deputy coroner whose testimony is sought;

(b) A brief statement of the issues upon which the party seeks expert testimony from the coroner or deputy coroner;

(c) An acknowledgment by the party that the giving of expert testimony by the coroner or deputy coroner at the trial, hearing, or deposition is governed by this section and that the party will comply with all of the requirements of this section;

(d) A statement of the obligations of the coroner or deputy coroner under division (C) of this section.

(2) The notice under division (B)(1) of this section shall be served together with the subpoena.

(C) A party that obtains the expert testimony of a coroner or deputy coroner at a trial, hearing, or deposition in a civil action pursuant to division (B) or (D) of this section shall pay to the treasury of the county in which the coroner or deputy coroner holds office or is appointed or employed a testimonial fee or deposition fee, whichever is applicable, within thirty days after receiving the statement described in this division. Upon the conclusion of the coroner's or deputy coroner's expert testimony, the coroner or deputy coroner shall file a statement with the court on behalf of the county in which the coroner or deputy coroner holds office or is appointed or employed showing the fee due and how the coroner or deputy coroner calculated the fee. The coroner or deputy coroner shall serve a copy of the statement on each of the parties.

(D) For good cause shown, the court may permit a coroner or deputy coroner who has not been served with a subpoena under division (B) of this section to give expert testimony at a trial, hearing, or deposition in a civil action. Unless good cause is shown, the failure of a party to file with the court the notice described in division (B)(1) of this section prohibits the party from having a coroner or deputy coroner subpoenaed to give expert testimony at a trial, hearing, or deposition in a civil action or from otherwise calling the coroner or a deputy coroner to give expert testimony at a trial, hearing, or deposition in a civil action.

(E) In the event of a dispute as to the contents of the notice filed by a party under division (B) of this section or as to the nature of the testimony sought from or given by a coroner or a deputy coroner at a trial, hearing, or deposition in a civil action, the court shall determine whether the testimony sought from or given by the coroner or deputy coroner is expert testimony or fact testimony. In making this determination, the court shall consider all of the following:

(1) The definitions of "expert testimony" and "fact testimony" set forth in this section;

(2) All applicable rules of evidence;

(3) Any other information that the court considers relevant.

(F) Nothing in this section shall be construed to alter, amend, or supersede the requirements of the Rules of Civil Procedure or the Rules of Evidence.

**HISTORY: 2011 HB 153, § 101.01, eff. Sept. 29, 2011.**

## § 2335.08 Witness fees and mileage in criminal cases.

Each witness attending, under recognizance or subpoena issued by order of the prosecuting attorney or defendant, before the grand jury or the common pleas court, any division of the common pleas court, a county court, or a county-operated municipal court, in criminal causes, shall be allowed the same fees as provided by section 2335.06 of the Revised Code in civil causes, to be taxed in only one cause when such witness is attending in more causes than one on the same days, unless otherwise directed by special order of the court. When certified to the county auditor by the clerk of the court, such fees shall be paid from the county treasury, and except as to the grand jury, taxed in the bill of costs. In state cases such fees shall be paid out of the county treasury, and in ordinance cases they shall be paid out of the treasury of the municipal corporation, upon the certificates of the judge or magistrate, and they shall be taxed in the bill of costs.

When the fees enumerated by this section have been collected from the judgment debtor, they shall be paid to the public treasury from which such fees were advanced.

**HISTORY: RS § 1302; S&C 631; 73 v 95, § 2; 73 v 127, § 25; 81 v 58, 59; GC § 3014; 108 v PtII, 1203; Bureau of Code Revision, 10-1-53; 127 v 1039 (Eff 1-1-58); 136 v H 205. Eff 1-1-76; 152 v H 525, § 1, eff. 7-1-09.**

The effective date is set by § 3 of 152 v H 525.
The effective date of HB 205 is set by § 4 of the act.

## § 2335.11 Payment of fees and costs in felonies and minor state cases.

In felony cases in which the defendant is convicted, the fees of the various magistrates and their officers, the witness fees, and interpreter's fees shall be inserted in the judgment of conviction and, when collected shall be disbursed by the clerk of the court of common pleas to the persons entitled thereto. In minor state cases, which have come to the court of common pleas through such magistrate's courts, the fees enumerated by this section shall be inserted in the judgment of conviction and, when collected shall be disbursed by the clerk to the persons entitled thereto. In both felonies and minor state cases, such clerk shall pay the witness and interpreter's fees into the county treasury, monthly.

In all cases in which recognizances are taken, forfeited, and collected, the amount recovered shall be paid into the county treasury, and if no conviction is had, such costs shall be paid by the county upon the allowance of the county auditor.

**HISTORY: RS § 1306; 75 v 50, § 1; 78 v 201; 97 v 11; GC § 3016; 109 v 173; Bureau of Code Revision. Eff 10-1-53.**

# TITLE 27: COURTS — GENERAL PROVISIONS — SPECIAL REMEDIES

## CHAPTER 2701: COURTS OF RECORD — GENERAL PROVISIONS



### § 2701.031 Disqualification of municipal or county court judge.

(A) If a judge of a municipal or county court allegedly is interested in a proceeding pending before the judge, allegedly is related to or has a bias or prejudice for or against a party to a proceeding pending before the judge or to a party's counsel, or allegedly otherwise is disqualified to preside in a proceeding pending before the judge, any party to the proceeding or the party's counsel may file an affidavit of disqualification with the clerk of the court in which the proceeding is pending.

(B) An affidavit of disqualification shall be filed under this section with the clerk of the court in which the proceeding is pending not less than seven calendar days before the day on which the next hearing in the proceeding is scheduled and shall include all of the following:

(1) The specific allegations on which the claim of interest, bias, prejudice, or disqualification is based and the facts to support each of those allegations;

(2) The jurat of a notary public or another person authorized to administer oaths or affirmations;

(3) A certificate indicating that a copy of the affidavit has been served on the judge of the municipal or county court against whom the affidavit is filed and on all other parties or their counsel;

(4) The date of the next scheduled hearing in the proceeding or, if there is no hearing scheduled, a statement that there is no hearing scheduled.

(C)(1) Except as provided in division (C)(2) of this section, when an affidavit of disqualification is presented to the clerk of a municipal or county court for filing under division (B) of this section, the clerk shall enter the fact of the filing on the docket in that proceeding and shall provide notice of the filing of the affidavit to one of the following:

(a) The presiding judge of the court of common pleas of the county;

(b) If there is no presiding judge of the court of common pleas of the county, a judge of the court of common pleas of the county.

(2) The clerk of the municipal or county court in which a proceeding is pending shall not accept an affidavit of disqualification presented for filing under division (B) of this section if it is not timely presented for filing or does not satisfy the requirements of divisions (B)(2), (3), and (4) of this section.

(D)(1) Except as provided in divisions (D)(2) to (4) of this section, if the clerk of the municipal or county court in which a proceeding is pending accepts an affidavit of disqualification for filing under divisions (B) and (C) of this section, the affidavit deprives the judge of a municipal or county court against whom the affidavit was filed of any authority to preside in the proceeding until the judge who was notified pursuant to division (C)(1) of this section rules on the affidavit pursuant to division (E) of this section.

(2) A judge of a municipal or county court against whom an affidavit of disqualification has been filed under divisions (B) and (C) of this section may preside in the proceeding if, based on the scheduled hearing date, the affidavit was not timely filed.

(3) A judge of a municipal or county court against whom an affidavit of disqualification has been filed under divisions (B) and (C) of this section may determine a matter that does not affect a substantive right of any of the parties.

(4) If the clerk of a municipal or county court accepts an affidavit of disqualification for filing under divisions (B) and (C) of this section, if the judge who is notified pursuant to division (C)(1) of this section of the filing of the affidavit of disqualification denies the affidavit pursuant to division (E) of this section, and if, after the denial, a second or subsequent affidavit of disqualification regarding the same judge and the same proceeding is filed by the same party who filed or on whose behalf was filed the affidavit that was denied or by counsel for the same party who filed or on whose behalf was filed the affidavit that was denied, the judge of a municipal or county court against whom the second or subsequent affidavit is filed may preside in the proceeding prior to the ruling, by the judge who is notified pursuant to division (C)(1) of this section, on the second or subsequent affidavit pursuant to division (E) of this section.

(E) If the clerk of a municipal or county court accepts an affidavit of disqualification for filing under division (B) and (C) of this section and if the judge who is notified pursuant to division (C)(1) of this section of the filing of the affidavit determines that the interest, bias, prejudice, or disqualification alleged in the affidavit does not exist, the judge who is so notified shall issue an entry denying the affidavit of disqualification. If the judge who is notified pursuant to division (C)(1) of this section of the filing of the affidavit determines that the interest, bias, prejudice, or disqualification alleged in the affidavit exists, the judge who is so notified shall issue an entry that disqualifies the judge against whom the affidavit was filed from presiding in the proceeding and designate another judge of the municipal or county court, or of the court of common pleas, to preside in the proceeding in place of the disqualified judge.

**HISTORY: GC § 13433-19; 113 v 123(148), ch 12, § 9; Bureau of Code Revision, RC § 2937.20, 10-1-53; 127 v 423 (Eff 8-27-57); 146 v H 151 (Eff 12-4-95); RC § 2701.03.1, 146 v S 263. Eff 11-20-96.**

# CHAPTER 2705: CONTEMPT OF COURT



[DIRECT]

## § 2705.01 Summary punishment for contempt.

A court, or judge at chambers, may summarily punish a person guilty of misbehavior in the presence of or so near the court or judge as to obstruct the administration of justice.

**HISTORY: RS § 5639; S&C 258; 32 v 17; GC § 12136; Bureau of Code Revision. Eff 10-1-53.**

[INDIRECT]

## § 2705.02 Acts in contempt of court.

A person guilty of any of the following acts may be punished as for a contempt:

(A) Disobedience of, or resistance to, a lawful writ, process, order, rule, judgment, or command of a court or officer;

(B) Misbehavior of an officer of the court in the performance of official duties, or in official transactions;

(C) A failure to obey a subpoena duly served, or a refusal to be sworn or to answer as a witness, when lawfully required;

(D) The rescue, or attempted rescue, of a person or of property in the custody of an officer by virtue of an order or process of court held by the officer;

(E) A failure upon the part of a person recognized to appear as a witness in a court to appear in compliance with the terms of the person's recognizance;

(F) A failure to comply with an order issued pursuant to section 3109.19 or 3111.81 of the Revised Code;

(G) A failure to obey a subpoena issued by the department of job and family services or a child support enforcement agency pursuant to section 5101.37 of the Revised Code;

(H) A willful failure to submit to genetic testing, or a willful failure to submit a child to genetic testing, as required by an order for genetic testing issued under section 3111.41 of the Revised Code.

**HISTORY: RS § 5640; S&S 97; S&C 258; 32 v 17; 59 v 31; GC § 12137; Bureau of Code Revision, 10-1-53; 146 v H 167 (Eff 6-11-96);† 147 v H 352 (Eff 1-1-98); 148 v H 470 (Eff 7-1-2000); 148 v S 180. Eff 3-22-2001.**

† The effective date of RC § 2705.02 has been changed from 11-15-96 to 6-11-96 by Section 7 of Sub. H.B. 710 (146 v —), effective 6-11-96.

## § 2705.03 Hearing.

In cases under section 2705.02 of the Revised Code, a charge in writing shall be filed with the clerk of the court, an entry thereof made upon the journal, and an opportunity given to the accused to be heard, by himself or counsel. This section does not prevent the court from issuing process to bring the accused into court, or from holding him in custody, pending such proceedings.

**HISTORY: RS § 5641; 75 v 745, § 3; GC § 12138; Bureau of Code Revision. Eff 10-1-53.**

## § 2705.031 Contempt action for failure to pay support or comply with parenting time or visitation order.

(A) As used in this section, "Title IV-D case" has the same meaning as in section 3125.01 of the Revised Code.

(B)(1) Any party who has a legal claim to any support ordered for a child, spouse, or former spouse may initiate a contempt action for failure to pay the support. In Title IV-D cases, the contempt action for failure to pay support also may be initiated by an attorney retained by the party who has the legal claim, the prosecuting attorney, or an attorney of the department of job and family services or the child support enforcement agency.

(2) Any parent who is granted parenting time rights under a parenting time order or decree issued pursuant to section 3109.051 [3109.05.1] or 3109.12 of the Revised Code, any person who is granted visitation rights under a visitation order or decree issued pursuant to section 3109.051 [3109.05.1], 3109.11, or 3109.12 of the Revised Code or pursuant to any other provision of the Revised Code, or any other person who is subject to any parenting time or visitation order or decree, may initiate a contempt action for a failure to comply with, or an interference with, the order or decree.

(C) In any contempt action initiated pursuant to division (B) of this section, the accused shall appear upon the summons and order to appear that is issued by the court. The summons shall include all of the following:

(1) Notice that failure to appear may result in the issuance of an order of arrest, and in cases involving alleged failure to pay support, the issuance of an order for the payment of support by withholding an amount from the personal earnings of the accused or by withholding or deducting an amount from some other asset of the accused;

(2) Notice that the accused has a right to counsel, and that if indigent, the accused must apply for a public

defender or court appointed counsel within three business days after receipt of the summons;

(3) Notice that the court may refuse to grant a continuance at the time of the hearing for the purpose of the accused obtaining counsel, if the accused fails to make a good faith effort to retain counsel or to obtain a public defender;

(4) Notice of the potential penalties that could be imposed upon the accused, if the accused is found guilty of contempt for failure to pay support or for a failure to comply with, or an interference with, a parenting time or visitation order or decree.

(D) If the accused is served as required by the Rules of Civil Procedure or by any special statutory proceedings that are relevant to the case, the court may order the attachment of the person of the accused upon failure to appear as ordered by the court.

(E) The imposition of any penalty for contempt under section 2705.05 of the Revised Code shall not eliminate any obligation of the accused to pay any past, present, or future support obligation or any obligation of the accused to comply with or refrain from interfering with the parenting time or visitation order or decree. The court shall have jurisdiction to make a finding of contempt for the failure to pay support and to impose the penalties set forth in section 2705.05 of the Revised Code in all cases in which past due support is at issue even if the duty to pay support has terminated, and shall have jurisdiction to make a finding of contempt for a failure to comply with, or an interference with, a parenting time or visitation order or decree and to impose the penalties set forth in section 2705.05 of the Revised Code in all cases in which the failure or interference is at issue even if the parenting time or visitation order or decree no longer is in effect.

**HISTORY: 141 v H 509 (Eff 12-1-86); 142 v H 231 (Eff 10-5-87); 142 v H 708 (Eff 4-19-88); 143 v S 3 (Eff 4-11-91); 148 v H 471 (Eff 7-1-2000); 148 v S 180. Eff 3-22-2001.**

## § 2705.04 Right of accused to bail.

In proceedings under section 2705.02 of the Revised Code, if the writ is not returnable forthwith, the court may fix the amount of a bond to be given by the accused, with surety to the satisfaction of the sheriff. Upon the return of a writ, when it is not convenient to hear the charge without delay, the court shall fix the amount of a bond to be given, with surety to the satisfaction of the clerk of the court, for the appearance of the accused to answer the charge.

On the execution of such bond, the accused shall be released from custody.

**HISTORY: RS §§ 5642, 5643; 75 v 746, §§ 4, 5; GC §§ 12139, 12140; Bureau of Code Revision. Eff 10-1-53.**

### [TRIAL; PUNISHMENT]

## § 2705.05 Hearing; penalties; duty of garnishee under support order.

(A) In all contempt proceedings, the court shall conduct a hearing. At the hearing, the court shall investigate the charge and hear any answer or testimony that the accused makes or offers and shall determine whether the accused is guilty of the contempt charge. If the accused is found guilty, the court may impose any of the following penalties:

(1) For a first offense, a fine of not more than two hundred fifty dollars, a definite term of imprisonment of not more than thirty days in jail, or both;

(2) For a second offense, a fine of not more than five hundred dollars, a definite term of imprisonment of not more than sixty days in jail, or both;

(3) For a third or subsequent offense, a fine of not more than one thousand dollars, a definite term of imprisonment of not more than ninety days in jail, or both.

(B) In all contempt proceedings initiated pursuant to section 2705.031 [2705.03.1] of the Revised Code against an employer, the bureau of workers' compensation, an employer that is paying workers' compensation benefits, a board, board of trustees, or other governing entity of a retirement system, person paying or distributing income to an obligor under a support order, or financial institution that is ordered to withhold or deduct an amount of money from the income or other assets of a person required to pay support and that fails to withhold or deduct the amount of money as ordered by the support order, the court also may require the employer, the bureau of workers' compensation, an employer that is paying workers' compensation benefits, a board, board of trustees, or other governing entity of a retirement system, person paying or distributing income to an obligor under a support order, or financial institution to pay the accumulated support arrearages.

**HISTORY: RS §§ 5644, 5645; 75 v 746, §§ 6, 7; GC §§ 12141, 12142; Bureau of Code Revision, 10-1-53; 141 v H 509. Eff 12-1-86.**

The effective date is set by section 6 of HB 509.

## § 2705.06 Imprisonment until order obeyed.

When the contempt consists of the omission to do an act which the accused yet can perform, he may be imprisoned until he performs it.

**HISTORY: RS § 5646; 75 v 746, § 8; GC § 12143; Bureau of Code Revision. Eff 10-1-53.**

## § 2705.07 Proceedings when party released on bail fails to appear.

If the party released on bail under section 2705.04 of the Revised Code fails to appear upon the day named, the court may issue another order of arrest, or order the bond for his appearance to be prosecuted, or both. If the bond is prosecuted, the measure of damages in the action is the extent of loss or injury sustained by the aggrieved party by reason of the misconduct for which the contempt was prosecuted, and the costs of the proceeding. Such recovery is for the benefit of the party injured.

**HISTORY: RS § 5647; 75 v 746, § 9; GC § 12144; Bureau of Code Revision. Eff 10-1-53.**

## § 2705.08 Release of prisoner committed for contempt.

When a person is committed to jail for contempt, the court or judge who made the order may discharge him from imprisonment when it appears that the public interest will not suffer thereby.

**HISTORY: RS § 5648; 75 v 746, § 10; GC § 12145; Bureau of Code Revision. Eff 10-1-53.**

[APPEAL]

### § 2705.09 Judgment final.

The judgment and orders of a court or officer made in cases of contempt may be reviewed on appeal. Appeal proceedings shall not suspend execution of the order or judgment until the person in contempt files a bond in the court rendering the judgment, or in the court or before the officer making the order, payable to the state, with sureties to the acceptance of the clerk of that court, in an amount fixed by the reviewing court, or a judge thereof, conditioned that if judgment is rendered against such person he will abide by and perform the order or judgment.

**HISTORY: RS § 5649; 75 v 746, § 11; GC § 12146; Bureau of Code Revision. Eff 10-1-53.**

### § 2705.10 Alternative remedy.

This chapter furnishes a remedy in cases not provided for by another section of the Revised Code.

**HISTORY: RS § 5650; 75 v 746, § 12; GC § 12147; Bureau of Code Revision, 10-1-53; 141 v H 158. Eff 3-17-87.**

## CHAPTER 2725: HABEAS CORPUS

Section



### § 2725.01 Persons entitled to writ of habeas corpus.

Whoever is unlawfully restrained of his liberty, or entitled to the custody of another, of which custody such person is unlawfully deprived, may prosecute a writ of habeas corpus, to inquire into the cause of such imprisonment, restraint, or deprivation.

**HISTORY: RS § 5726; S&C 681; 29 v 164; GC § 12161; Bureau of Code Revision. Eff 10-1-53.**

### § 2725.02 Courts authorized to grant writ.

The writ of habeas corpus may be granted by the supreme court, court of appeals, court of common pleas, probate court, or by a judge of any such court.

**HISTORY: RS § 5727; S&C 681, 1213; 29 v 164; 51 v 167, § 3; 82 v 16, 36; GC § 12162; 103 v 405(429); Bureau of Code Revision. Eff 10-1-53.**

### § 2725.03 Territorial jurisdiction of courts.

If a person restrained of his liberty is an inmate of a state benevolent or correctional institution, the location of which is fixed by statute and at the time is in the custody of the officers of the institution, no court or judge other than the courts or judges of the county in which the institution is located has jurisdiction to issue or determine a writ of habeas corpus for his production or discharge. Any writ issued by a court or judge of another county to an officer or person in charge at the state institution to compel the production or discharge of an inmate thereof is void.

**HISTORY: RS § 5727a; 97 v 318; GC § 12163; Bureau of Code Revision, 10-1-53; 145 v H 571. Eff 10-6-94.**

### § 2725.04 Application for writ.

Application for the writ of habeas corpus shall be by petition, signed and verified either by the party for whose relief it is intended, or by some person for him, and shall specify:

(A) That the person in whose behalf the application is made is imprisoned, or restrained of his liberty;

(B) The officer, or name of the person by whom the prisoner is so confined or restrained; or, if both are unknown or uncertain, such officer or person may be described by an assumed appellation and the person who is served with the writ is deemed the person intended;

(C) The place where the prisoner is so imprisoned or restrained, if known;

(D) A copy of the commitment or cause of detention of such person shall be exhibited, if it can be procured without impairing the efficiency of the remedy; or, if the imprisonment or detention is without legal authority, such fact must appear.

**HISTORY: RS § 5728; S&C 681, 684, 685; 29 v 164; 45 v 45, §§ 4, 5; GC § 12164; Bureau of Code Revision. Eff 10-1-53.**

### § 2725.05 Writ not allowed.

If it appears that a person alleged to be restrained of his liberty is in the custody of an officer under process issued by a court or magistrate, or by virtue of the judgment or order of a court of record, and that the court or magistrate had jurisdiction to issue the process, render the judgment, or make the order, the writ of habeas corpus shall not be allowed. If the jurisdiction appears after the writ is allowed, the person shall not be discharged by reason of any informality or defect in the process, judgment, or order.

**HISTORY: RS § 5729; S&C 681, 684; 29 v 164; 32 v 23; GC § 12165; Bureau of Code Revision. Eff 10-1-53.**

## § 2725.06 Writ must be granted.

When a petition for a writ of habeas corpus is presented, if it appears that the writ ought to issue, a court or judge authorized to grant the writ must grant it forthwith.

**HISTORY: RS § 5730; S&C 681; 29 v 164; GC § 12166; Bureau of Code Revision. Eff 10-1-53.**

## § 2725.07 Clerk shall issue writ.

When a writ of habeas corpus is granted, the clerk of the court which granted the writ shall forthwith issue said writ under the seal of such court. In case of emergency, the judge who allowed the writ may issue it under his own hand, and depute any officer or other person to serve it.

**HISTORY: RS § 5731; S&C 681; 29 v 164; GC § 12167; Bureau of Code Revision. Eff 10-1-53.**

## § 2725.08 Designation of prisoner.

The person to be produced upon a writ of habeas corpus shall be designated by his name, if known, and if his name is not known, or is uncertain, such person may be described in any other way so as to make known who is intended.

**HISTORY: RS § 5732; S&C 685; 45 v 45, § 5; GC § 12168; Bureau of Code Revision. Eff 10-1-53.**

## § 2725.09 Requisites of writ.

In case of confinement, imprisonment, or detention of a person by an officer, a writ of habeas corpus shall be directed to him, and command him to have such person before the court or judge designated in the writ, at a time and place therein specified.

**HISTORY: RS § 5733; S&C 684; 45 v 45; GC § 12169; Bureau of Code Revision. Eff 10-1-53.**

## § 2725.10 Form of writ when prisoner not in custody of an officer.

In case of confinement, imprisonment, or detention by a person not an officer, the writ of habeas corpus shall be in the following form:

The State of Ohio, ................. County, ss.:

To the sheriff of our several counties, greeting:

We command you that the body of .......... of by ..................... of .........., imprisoned and restrained of his liberty, as it is said, you take and have before ............., a judge of our ............... court, or, in case of his absence or disability, before some other judge of the same court, at ........... , forthwith to do and receive what our said judge shall then and there consider ................. concerning him in his behalf; and summon the said ............... then and there to appear before our said judge, to show the cause of the taking and detention of the said ..........................

(Seal) Witness ........................ , at ...................... , this ........ day of ............. , in the year ....... .

**HISTORY: RS § 5734; S&C 684; 45 v 45; GC § 12170; Bureau of Code Revision. Eff 10-1-53.**

## § 2725.11 Service of writ.

The writ of habeas corpus may be served in any county by the sheriff of that or any other county or by a person deputed by the court or judge issuing the writ.

**HISTORY: RS § 5735; S&C 684; 45 v 45, § 2; GC § 12171; Bureau of Code Revision. Eff 10-1-53.**

[RETURN]

## § 2725.12 Execution and return of writ.

The officer or person to whom a writ of habeas corpus is directed shall convey the person imprisoned or detained, and named in the writ, before the judge granting the writ, or, in case of his absence or disability, before some other judge of the same court, on the day specified in the writ. Said officer or person shall make due return of the writ, together with the day and the cause of the caption and detention of such person, according to its command.

**HISTORY: RS § 5736; S&C 682; 29 v 164, § 2; GC § 12172; Bureau of Code Revision. Eff 10-1-53.**

## § 2725.13 Return of writ to another judge.

When a writ of habeas corpus is issued by a court in session, if the court has adjourned when the writ is returned, it shall be returned before any judge of the same court. When the writ is returned before one judge, at a time when the court is in session, he may adjourn the case into the court, there to be heard and determined.

**HISTORY: RS § 5737; S&C 684; 45 v 45, § 3; GC § 12173; Bureau of Code Revision. Eff 10-1-53.**

## § 2725.14 Contents of the return.

When the person to be produced under a writ of habeas corpus is imprisoned or restrained by an officer, the person who makes the return shall state therein, and in other cases the person in whose custody the prisoner is found shall state, in writing, to the court or judge before whom the writ is returnable, plainly and unequivocally:

(A) Whether or not he has the prisoner in his custody or power or under restraint.

(B) If the prisoner is in his custody or power or under restraint, he shall set forth, at large, the authority, and the true and whole cause, of such imprisonment and restraint, with a copy of the writ, warrant, or other process upon which the prisoner is detained.

(C) If such prisoner was in his custody or power or under restraint, and such custody or restraint was transferred to another, he shall state particularly to whom, at what time, for what cause, and by what authority such transfer was made.

**HISTORY: RS § 5738; S&C 685; 45 v 45, § 6; GC § 12174; Bureau of Code Revision. Eff 10-1-53.**

## § 2725.15 Return must be signed and sworn to.

The return or statement referred to in section 2725.14 of the Revised Code shall be signed by the person who makes it, and shall be sworn to by him, unless he is a sworn public officer and makes the return in his official capacity.

**HISTORY: RS § 5739; S&C 685; 45 v 45, § 7; GC § 12175; Bureau of Code Revision. Eff 10-1-53.**

## § 2725.16 Continuance of cause.

The court or judge to whom a writ of habeas corpus is returned, or the court into which it is adjourned, for good cause shown, may continue the cause, and, in that event, shall make such order for the safekeeping of the person imprisoned or detained as the nature of the case requires.

**HISTORY: RS § 5740; S&C 685; 45 v 45, § 9; GC § 12176; Bureau of Code Revision. Eff 10-1-53.**

## § 2725.17 Discharge of prisoner.

When the judge has examined the cause of caption and detention of a person brought before him as provided in section 2725.12 of the Revised Code, and is satisfied that such person is unlawfully imprisoned or detained, he shall forthwith discharge such person from confinement. On such examination, the judge may disregard matters of form or technicalities in any mittimus or order of commitment by a court or officer authorized by law to commit.

**HISTORY: RS § 5741; S&C 682; 29 v 164, § 3; 78 v 113; GC § 12177; Bureau of Code Revision. Eff 10-1-53.**

## § 2725.18 Prisoner may be committed or let to bail.

When the person brought before a judge under section 2725.12 of the Revised Code is confined or detained in a legal manner on a charge of having committed a crime or offense which is bailable, the judge may recommit him or let him to bail. If such person is let to bail, the judge shall require him to enter into a recognizance, with sufficient surety, in such sum as the judge finds reasonable, after considering the circumstances of the prisoner and the nature of the offense charged, and conditioned for his appearance at the court where the offense is properly cognizable. The judge forthwith shall certify his proceedings, together with any recognizance, to the proper court. If the person charged fails to give such recognizance, he shall be committed to prison by the judge.

**HISTORY: RS § 5742; S&C 682; 29 v 164, § 3; GC § 12178; Bureau of Code Revision. Eff 10-1-53.**

## § 2725.19 Mandatory commitment for capital offense.

If a prisoner brought before a judge under section 2725.12 of the Revised Code was committed by a judge, and is plainly and specifically charged in the warrant of commitment with a felony the punishment for which is capital, he shall not be removed, discharged, or let to bail.

**HISTORY: RS § 5743; S&C 683; 29 v 164, § 8; GC § 12179; Bureau of Code Revision, 10-1-53; 129 v 582(745). Eff 1-10-61.**

## § 2725.20 Return as evidence or plea.

If a prisoner brought before a judge under section 2725.12 of the Revised Code is in custody under a warrant or commitment in pursuance of law, the return of the writ of habeas corpus is prima-facie evidence of the cause of detention. If such prisoner is restrained of his liberty by alleged private authority, the return is only a plea of the facts therein set forth, and the party claiming the custody shall be held to make proof of such facts. Upon the final disposition of a case, the court or judge shall make such order as to costs as it requires.

**HISTORY: RS § 5744; S&C 685; 45 v 45, § 8; GC § 12180; Bureau of Code Revision. Eff 10-1-53.**

## § 2725.21 Forfeiture by clerk for refusal to issue writ.

A clerk of a court who refuses to issue a writ of habeas corpus, after an allowance of such writ and a demand therefor, shall forfeit to the party aggrieved the sum of five hundred dollars.

**HISTORY: RS § 5745; S&C 682; 29 v 164, § 5; GC § 12181; Bureau of Code Revision. Eff 10-1-53.**

## § 2725.22 Failure to obey writ.

No person to whom a writ of habeas corpus is directed shall neglect or refuse to obey or make return of it according to the command thereof, or make a false return, or upon demand made by the prisoner, or by any person on his behalf, refuse to deliver to the person demanding, within six hours after demand therefor, a true copy of the warrant of commitment and detainer of the prisoner.

Whoever violates this section shall forfeit to the party aggrieved two hundred dollars for a first offense; for a second offense such person shall forfeit four hundred dollars, and, if an officer, shall be incapable of holding his office.

**HISTORY: RS § 5746; S&C 682; 29 v 164, § 4; GC § 12182; Bureau of Code Revision. Eff 10-1-53.**

## § 2725.23 Persons at large upon writ not to be again imprisoned.

A person who is set at large upon a writ of habeas corpus shall not be imprisoned again for the same offense, unless by the legal order or process of the court in which he is bound by recognizance to appear, or other court having jurisdiction of the cause or offense.

No person shall knowingly, contrary to sections 2725.01 to 2725.28, inclusive, of the Revised Code, recommit, imprison, or cause to be recommitted or imprisoned, for the same offense, or pretended offense, a person so set at large, or knowingly aid or assist therein.

Whoever violates this section shall forfeit to the party aggrieved five hundred dollars, notwithstanding any colorable pretense or variation in the warrant or commitment.

**HISTORY: RS § 5747; S&C 682; 29 v 164, § 6; GC § 12183; Bureau of Code Revision. Eff 10-1-53.**

## § 2725.24 Prisoner shall not be removed from custody of one officer to another.

A person committed to prison, or in the custody of an officer for a criminal matter, shall not be removed therefrom into the custody of another officer, unless by legal process, or unless the prisoner is delivered to an inferior officer to be taken to jail, or, by order of the proper court, is removed from one place to another within this state for trial, or in case of fire, infection, or other necessity.

A person who, after such commitment, makes, signs, or countersigns a warrant for such removal contrary to this section shall forfeit to the party aggrieved five hundred dollars.

**HISTORY: RS § 5748; S&C 683; 29 v 164, § 7; GC § 12184; Bureau of Code Revision. Eff 10-1-53.**

## § 2725.25 Repealed, 152 v H 215, § 2 [RS §§ 5749, 5750; S 387; S 683; 65 v 165, § 9; GC §§ 12185, 12186; Bureau of Code Revision. Eff 10-1-53.]. Eff 4-7-09.

This section prohibited prisoners from being sent out of state.

## § 2725.26 Record of writs.

The proceedings upon a writ of habeas corpus must be recorded by the clerk of the court in which such proceedings were had, and may be reviewed on appeal as in other cases.

**HISTORY: RS § 5751; S&C 685; 45 v 45, § 10; GC § 12187; Bureau of Code Revision. Eff 10-1-53.**

## § 2725.27 Recovery of forfeitures; limitations.

The forfeitures mentioned in sections 2725.21 to 2725.24 of the Revised Code may be recovered by the party aggrieved or the executors or administrators of the party aggrieved against the offender or the offender's executors or administrators by civil action in a court having cognizance thereof.

Actions for violations of sections 2725.21 to 2725.24 of the Revised Code shall be brought within two years after the offense is committed, except in cases of imprisonment of the party aggrieved, when action may be brought within two years after the delivery of the party aggrieved out of prison, or after death if the party aggrieved dies in prison.

**HISTORY: RS § 5752; S&C 683; 29 v 164, § 10; GC § 12188; Bureau of Code Revision. Eff 10-1-53; 152 v H 215, § 1, eff. 4-7-09.**

## § 2725.28 Fees and costs.

The fees of officers and witnesses shall be taxed by the judge, on return of the proceedings on a writ of habeas corpus, and collected as a part of the original costs in the case. When the prisoner is discharged, the costs shall be taxed to the state, and paid out of the county treasury, upon the warrant of the county auditor. No officer or person shall demand payment in advance for any fees to which he is entitled by virtue of the proceedings, when the writ is demanded or issued for the discharge from custody of a person confined under color of proceedings in a criminal case. When a person in custody by virtue or under color of proceedings in a civil case is discharged, costs shall be taxed against the party at whose instance he was so in custody. If he is remanded to custody, costs shall be taxed against him.

**HISTORY: RS § 5753; S&C 685; 45 v 45, § 11; GC § 12189; Bureau of Code Revision. Eff 10-1-53.**

# CHAPTER 2743: COURT OF CLAIMS

Section

[STATE LIABILITY]



[STATE LIABILITY]

## § 2743.191 Reparations fund.

(A)(1) There is hereby created in the state treasury the reparations fund, which shall be used only for the following purposes:

(a) The payment of awards of reparations that are granted by the attorney general;

(b) The compensation of any personnel needed by the attorney general to administer sections 2743.51 to 2743.72 of the Revised Code;

(c) The compensation of witnesses as provided in division (J) of section 2743.65 of the Revised Code;

(d) Other administrative costs of hearing and determining claims for an award of reparations by the attorney general;

(e) The costs of administering sections 2907.28 and 2969.01 to 2969.06 of the Revised Code;

(f) The costs of investigation and decision-making as certified by the attorney general;

(g) The provision of state financial assistance to victim assistance programs in accordance with sections 109.91 and 109.92 of the Revised Code;

(h) The costs of paying the expenses of sex offense-related examinations and antibiotics pursuant to section 2907.28 of the Revised Code;

(i) The cost of printing and distributing the pamphlet prepared by the attorney general pursuant to section 109.42 of the Revised Code;

(j) Subject to division (D) of section 2743.71 of the Revised Code, the costs associated with the printing and providing of information cards or other printed materials to law enforcement agencies and prosecuting authorities and with publicizing the availability of awards of reparations pursuant to section 2743.71 of the Revised Code;

(k) The payment of costs of administering a DNA specimen collection procedure pursuant to sections 2152.74 and 2901.07 of the Revised Code, of performing DNA analysis of those DNA specimens, and of entering the resulting DNA records regarding those analyses into the DNA database pursuant to section 109.573 [109.57.3] of the Revised Code;

(l) The payment of actual costs associated with initiatives by the attorney general for the apprehension, prosecution, and accountability of offenders, and the enhancing of services to crime victims. The amount of payments made pursuant to division (A)(1)(l) of this section during any given fiscal year shall not exceed five per cent of the balance of the reparations fund at the close of the immediately previous fiscal year;

(m) The costs of administering the adult parole authority's supervision pursuant to division (E) of section 2971.05

of the Revised Code of sexually violent predators who are sentenced to a prison term pursuant to division (A)(3) of section 2971.03 of the Revised Code and of offenders who are sentenced to a prison term pursuant to division (B)(1)(a), (b), or (c), (B)(2)(a), (b), or (c), or (B)(3)(a), (b), (c), or (d) of that section;

(n) Subject to the limit set forth in those sections, the costs of the installation and monitoring of an electronic monitoring device used in the monitoring of a respondent pursuant to an electronic monitoring order issued by a court under division (E)(1)(b) of section 2151.34 or division (E)(1)(b) of section 2903.214 [2903.21.4] of the Revised Code if the court determines that the respondent is indigent or used in the monitoring of an offender pursuant to an electronic monitoring order issued under division (B)(5) of section 2919.27 of the Revised Code if the court determines that the offender is indigent.

(2) All costs paid pursuant to section 2743.70 of the Revised Code, the portions of license reinstatement fees mandated by division (F)(2)(b) of section 4511.191 [4511.19.1] of the Revised Code to be credited to the fund, the portions of the proceeds of the sale of a forfeited vehicle specified in division (C)(2) of section 4503.234 [4503.23.4] of the Revised Code, payments collected by the department of rehabilitation and correction from prisoners who voluntarily participate in an approved work and training program pursuant to division (C)(8)(b)(ii) of section 5145.16 of the Revised Code, and all moneys collected by the state pursuant to its right of subrogation provided in section 2743.72 of the Revised Code shall be deposited in the fund.

(B) In making an award of reparations, the attorney general shall render the award against the state. The award shall be accomplished only through the following procedure, and the following procedure may be enforced by writ of mandamus directed to the appropriate official:

(1) The attorney general shall provide for payment of the claimant or providers in the amount of the award only if the amount of the award is fifty dollars or more.

(2) The expense shall be charged against all available unencumbered moneys in the fund.

(3) If sufficient unencumbered moneys do not exist in the fund, the attorney general shall make application for payment of the award out of the emergency purposes account or any other appropriation for emergencies or contingencies, and payment out of this account or other appropriation shall be authorized if there are sufficient moneys greater than the sum total of then pending emergency purposes account requests or requests for releases from the other appropriations.

(4) If sufficient moneys do not exist in the account or any other appropriation for emergencies or contingencies to pay the award, the attorney general shall request the general assembly to make an appropriation sufficient to pay the award, and no payment shall be made until the appropriation has been made. The attorney general shall make this appropriation request during the current biennium and during each succeeding biennium until a sufficient appropriation is made. If, prior to the time that an appropriation is made by the general assembly pursuant to this division, the fund has sufficient unencumbered funds to pay the award or part of the award, the available funds shall be used to pay the award or part of the award, and the appropriation request shall be amended to request only sufficient funds to pay that part of the award that is unpaid.

(C) The attorney general shall not make payment on a decision or order granting an award until all appeals have been determined and all rights to appeal exhausted, except as otherwise provided in this section. If any party to a claim for an award of reparations appeals from only a portion of an award, and a remaining portion provides for the payment of money by the state, that part of the award calling for the payment of money by the state and not a subject of the appeal shall be processed for payment as described in this section.

(D) The attorney general shall prepare itemized bills for the costs of printing and distributing the pamphlet the attorney general prepares pursuant to section 109.42 of the Revised Code. The itemized bills shall set forth the name and address of the persons owed the amounts set forth in them.

(E) As used in this section, "DNA analysis" and "DNA specimen" have the same meanings as in section 109.573 [109.57.3] of the Revised Code.

**HISTORY: 136 v H 82 (Eff 9-29-76); 137 v S 221 (Eff 11-23-77); 138 v H 238 (Eff 8-8-80); 139 v S 30 (Eff 3-18-83); 140 v S 172 (Eff 9-26-84); 141 v H 201 (Eff 7-1-85); 141 v H 657 (Eff 9-12-86); 142 v S 308 (Eff 3-14-89); 143 v H 111 (Eff 7-1-89); 144 v S 275 (Eff 7-1-93); 145 v H 152 (Eff 7-1-93); 145 v S 62, §§ 4, 5 (Eff 9-1-93); 146 v H 117 (Eff 6-30-95); 146 v H 353 (Eff 9-17-96); 148 v S 153 (Eff 7-1-2000); 149 v H 427. Eff 8-29-2002; 149 v S 123, § 1, eff. 1-1-04; 150 v H 95, § 1, eff. 6-26-03; 150 v S 5, § 1, eff. 7-31-03; 150 v H 95, § 3.13, eff. 1-1-04; 150 v S 5, § 3, eff. 1-1-04; 150 v H 525, § 1, eff. 5-18-05; 151 v H 66, § 101.01, eff. 9-29-05; 151 v S 260, § 1, eff. 1-2-07; 152 v S 10, § 1, eff. 1-1-08; 152 v H 471, § 1, eff. 4-7-09; 153 v H 10, § 1, eff. 6-17-10.**

The provisions of § 3 of 153 v H 10 read as follows:

SECTION 3. Sections 2151.23, 2151.358, 2152.02, 2743.191, 2903.214, 2919.25, 2919.27, 3113.31, and 3113.33 of the Revised Code, as amended by this act, and section 2151.34 of the Revised Code, as enacted by this act, shall be named the "Shynerra Grant Law."

The effective date is set by § 3 of 152 v S 10.

The effective date is set by § 612.03 of 151 v H 66.

The provisions of § 4 of H.B. 525 (150 v —) read as follows:

SECTION 4. Section 2743.191 of the Revised Code is presented in this act as a composite of the section as amended by both Am. Sub. H.B. 95 and Am. Sub. S.B. 5 of the 125th General Assembly. The General Assembly, applying the principle stated in division (B) of section 1.52 of the Revised Code that amendments are to be harmonized if reasonably capable of simultaneous operation, finds that the composite is the resulting version of the section in effect prior to the effective date of the section as presented in this act.

The provisions of § 222 of H.B. 95 (150 v —) and § 7 of S.B. 5 (150 v —) both read as follows:

SECTION 222 [SECTION 7]. * * * Section 2743.191 of the Revised Code is presented in Section 3 of this act as a composite of the section as amended by both Sub. H.B. 427 and Am. Sub. S.B. 123 of the 124th General Assembly. The General Assembly, applying the principle stated in division (B) of section 1.52 of the Revised Code that amendments are to be harmonized if reasonably capable of simultaneous operation, finds that the composites are the resulting versions of the sections in effect prior to the effective date of the sections as presented in Section 3 of this act.

The provisions of § 5 of S.B. 123 (149 v —), as amended by § 3 of H.B. 163 (150 v —), read as follows:

SECTION 5. (A) Notwithstanding division (B) of section 1.58 of the Revised Code, the provisions of the Revised Code amended or enacted in Sections 1 and 2 of Am. Sub. S.B. 123 of the 124th General Assembly shall apply only in relation to conduct and offenses committed on or after January 1, 2004. Conduct and offenses committed prior to January 1, 2004, shall be governed by the law in effect on the date the conduct or offense was committed. * * *

# TITLE 31: DOMESTIC RELATIONS — CHILDREN

## CHAPTER 3107: ADOPTION



[PUTATIVE FATHERS]

### § 3107.17 Hearings to be closed; confidentiality of information; indexing of proceedings.

(A) All hearings held under sections 3107.01 to 3107.19 of the Revised Code shall be held in closed court without the admittance of any person other than essential officers of the court, the parties, the witnesses of the parties, counsel, persons who have not previously consented to an adoption but who are required to consent, and representatives of the agencies present to perform their official duties.

(B)(1) Except as provided in divisions (B)(2) and (D) of this section and sections 3107.39 to 3107.44 and 3107.60 to 3107.68 of the Revised Code, no person or governmental entity shall knowingly reveal any information contained in a paper, book, or record pertaining to an adoption that is part of the permanent record of a court or maintained by the department of job and family services, an agency, or attorney without the consent of a court.

(2) An agency or attorney may examine the agency's or attorney's own papers, books, and records pertaining to an adoption without a court's consent for official administrative purposes. The department of job and family services may examine its own papers, books, and records pertaining to an adoption, or such papers, books, and records of an agency, without a court's consent for official administrative, certification, and eligibility determination purposes.

(C) The petition, the interlocutory order, the final decree of adoption, and other adoption proceedings shall be recorded in a book kept for such purposes and shall be separately indexed. The book shall be a part of the records of the court, and all consents, affidavits, and other papers shall be properly filed.

(D) All forms that pertain to the social or medical histories of the biological parents of an adopted person and that were completed pursuant to section 3107.09 or 3107.091 [3107.09.1] of the Revised Code shall be filed only in the permanent record kept by the court. During the minority of the adopted person, only the adoptive parents of the person may inspect the forms. When an adopted person reaches majority, only the adopted person may inspect the forms. Under the circumstances described in this division, an adopted person or the adoptive parents are entitled to inspect the forms upon requesting the clerk of the court to produce them.

(E)(1) The department of job and family services shall prescribe a form that permits any person who is authorized by division (D) of this section to inspect forms that pertain to the social or medical histories of the biological parents and that were completed pursuant to section 3107.09 or 3107.091 [3107.09.1] of the Revised Code to request notice if any correction or expansion of either such history, made pursuant to division (D) of section 3107.09 of the Revised Code, is made a part of the permanent record kept by the court. The form shall be designed to facilitate the provision of the information and statements described in division (E)(3) of this section. The department shall provide copies of the form to each court. A court shall provide a copy of the request form to each adoptive parent when a final decree of adoption is entered and shall explain to each adoptive parent at that time that an adoptive parent who completes and files the form will be notified of any correction or expansion of either the social or medical history of the biological parents of the adopted person made during the minority of the adopted person that is made a part of the permanent record kept by the court, and that, during the adopted person's minority, the adopted person may inspect the forms that pertain to those histories. Upon request, the court also shall provide a copy of the request form to any adoptive parent during the minority of the adopted person and to an adopted person who has reached the age of majority.

(2) Any person who is authorized to inspect forms pursuant to division (D) of this section who wishes to be notified of corrections or expansions pursuant to division (D) of section 3107.09 of the Revised Code that are made a part of the permanent record kept by the court shall file with the court, on a copy of the form prescribed by the department of job and family services pursuant to division (E)(1) of this section, a request for such notification that contains the information and statements required by division (E)(3) of this section. A request may be filed at any time if the person who files the request is authorized at that time to inspect forms that pertain to the social or medical histories.

(3) A request for notification as described in division (E)(2) of this section shall contain all of the following information:

(a) The adopted person's name and mailing address at that time;

(b) The name of each adoptive parent, and if the adoptive person is a minor at the time of the filing of the request, the mailing address of each adoptive parent at that time;

(c) The adopted person's date of birth;

(d) The date of entry of the final decree of adoption;

(e) A statement requesting the court to notify the person who files the request, at the address provided in the request, if any correction or expansion of either the social or medical history of the biological parents is made a part of the permanent record kept by the court;

(f) A statement that the person who files the request is authorized, at the time of the filing, to inspect the forms that pertain to the social and medical histories of the biological parents;

(g) The signature of the person who files the request.

(4) Upon the filing of a request for notification in accordance with division (E)(2) of this section, the clerk of the court in which it is filed immediately shall insert the

request in the permanent record of the case. A person who has filed the request and who wishes to update it with respect to a new mailing address may inform the court in writing of the new address. Upon its receipt, the court promptly shall insert the new address into the permanent record by attaching it to the request. Thereafter, any notification described in this division shall be sent to the new address.

(5) Whenever a social or medical history of a biological parent is corrected or expanded and the correction or expansion is made a part of the permanent record kept by the court, the court shall ascertain whether a request for notification has been filed in accordance with division (E)(2) of this section. If such a request has been filed, the court shall determine whether, at that time, the person who filed the request is authorized, under division (D) of this section, to inspect the forms that pertain to the social or medical history of the biological parents. If the court determines that the person who filed the request is so authorized, it immediately shall notify the person that the social or medical history has been corrected or expanded, that it has been made a part of the permanent record kept by the court, and that the forms that pertain to the records may be inspected in accordance with division (D) of this section.

**HISTORY: 136 v H 156 (Eff 1-1-77); 137 v S 340 (Eff 8-29-78); 137 v H 832 (Eff 3-13-79); 140 v H 84 (Eff 3-19-85); 146 v H 419 (Eff 9-18-96); 148 v H 471. Eff 7-1-2000; 151 v S 238, § 1, eff. 9-21-06.**

**Analogous to former RC § 3107.14, repealed 136 v H 156.**
The effective date is set by section 12(A) of HB 471.

## [PENALTIES]

### § 3107.99 Penalty.

Whoever violates division (B)(1) of section 3107.17 of the Revised Code is guilty of a misdemeanor of the third degree.

**HISTORY: 146 v H 419. Eff 9-18-96.**

The effective date is set by section 3 of HB 419.

# CHAPTER 3109: CHILDREN

Section



### § 3109.09 Liability of parents for destructive acts or theft by their children.

(A) As used in this section, "parent" means one of the following:

(1) Both parents unless division (A)(2) or (3) of this section applies;

(2) The parent designated the residential parent and legal custodian pursuant to an order issued under section 3109.04 of the Revised Code that is not a shared parenting order;

(3) The custodial parent of a child born out of wedlock with respect to whom no custody order has been issued.

(B) Any owner of property, including any board of education of a city, local, exempted village, or joint vocational school district, may maintain a civil action to recover compensatory damages not exceeding ten thousand dollars and court costs from the parent of a minor if the minor willfully damages property belonging to the owner or commits acts cognizable as a "theft offense," as defined in section 2913.01 of the Revised Code, involving the property of the owner. The action may be joined with an action under Chapter 2737. of the Revised Code against the minor, or the minor and the minor's parent, to recover the property regardless of value, but any additional damages recovered from the parent pursuant to this section shall be limited to compensatory damages not exceeding ten thousand dollars, as authorized by this section. A finding of willful destruction of property or of committing acts cognizable as a theft offense is not dependent upon a prior finding that the child is a delinquent child or upon the child's conviction of any criminal offense.

(C)(1) If a court renders a judgment in favor of a board of education of a city, local, exempted village, or joint vocational school district in an action brought pursuant to division (B) of this section, if the board of education agrees to the parent's performance of community service in lieu of full payment of the judgment, and if the parent who is responsible for the payment of the judgment agrees to voluntarily participate in the performance of community service in lieu of full payment of the judgment, the court may order the parent to perform community service in lieu of providing full payment of the judgment.

(2) If a court, pursuant to division (C)(1) of this section, orders a parent to perform community service in lieu of providing full payment of a judgment, the court shall specify in its order the amount of the judgment, if any, to be paid by the parent, the type and number of hours of community service to be performed by the parent, and any other conditions necessary to carry out the order.

(D) This section shall not apply to a parent of a minor if the minor was married at the time of the commission of the acts or violations that would otherwise give rise to a civil action commenced under this section.

(E) Any action brought pursuant to this section shall be commenced and heard as in other civil actions.

(F) The monetary limitation upon compensatory damages set forth in this section does not apply to a civil action brought pursuant to section 2307.70 of the Revised Code.

**HISTORY: 131 v 689 (Eff 10-6-65); 132 v H 257 (Eff 10-24-67); 133 v S 10 (Eff 9-15-69); 137 v H 456 (Eff 5-23-78); 141 v H 158 (Eff 3-17-87); 141 v S 316 (Eff 3-19-87); 142 v H 708 (Eff 4-19-88); 143 v S 3 (Eff 4-11-91); 144 v H 154 (Eff 7-31-92); 146 v H 601. Eff 10-29-96.**

### § 3109.10 Liability of parents for assaults by their children.

As used in this section, "parent" has the same meaning as in section 3109.09 of the Revised Code.

Any person is entitled to maintain an action to recover compensatory damages in a civil action, in an amount not to exceed ten thousand dollars and costs of suit in a court of competent jurisdiction, from the parent of a child under the age of eighteen if the child willfully and maliciously assaults the person by a means or force likely to produce great bodily harm. A finding of willful and malicious assault by a means or force likely to produce great bodily harm is not dependent upon a prior finding that the child is a delinquent child.

Any action brought pursuant to this section shall be commenced and heard as in other civil actions for damages.

The monetary limitation upon compensatory damages set forth in this section does not apply to a civil action brought pursuant to section 2307.70 of the Revised Code.

**HISTORY: 133 v S 11 (Eff 9-15-69); 141 v S 316 (Eff 3-19-87); 143 v S 3 (Eff 4-11-91); 146 v H 18 (Eff 11-24-95); 146 v H 601. Eff 10-29-96.**

## CHAPTER 3111: PARENTAGE



### § 3111.19 Interference with establishment of paternity.

No person, by using physical harassment or threats of violence against another person, shall interfere with the other person's initiation or continuance of, or attempt to prevent the other person from initiating or continuing, an action under sections 3111.01 to 3111.18 of the Revised Code.

**HISTORY: RC § 3111.29, 144 v S 10 (Eff 7-15-92); RC § 3111.19, 148 v S 180. Eff 3-22-2001.**

**Not analogous to former RC § 3111.19 (139 v H 245; 145 v S 115), repealed 148 v S 180, § 2, eff 3-22-2001.**

**Not analogous to former RC § 3111.19 (RS § 5631; S&S 38; 70 v 113; GC § 8006-19; 124 v 178; Bureau of Code Revision, 10-1-53; 127 v 1039); repealed 139 v H 245, § 2, eff 6-29-82.**

[PENALTIES]

### § 3111.99 Penalty.

Whoever violates section 3111.19 of the Revised Code is guilty of interfering with the establishment of paternity, a misdemeanor of the first degree.

**HISTORY: 144 v S 10 (Eff 7-15-92); 146 v S 2 (Eff 7-1-96); 146 v H 167 (Eff 6-11-96)†; 147 v H 352 (Eff 1-1-98); 148 v H 471 (Eff 7-1-2000); 148 v S 180. Eff 3-22-2001.**

† The effective date of HB 167 (146 v —) was changed from 11-15-96 to 6-11-96 by § 7 of HB 710 (146 v —).

## CHAPTER 3113: NEGLECT, ABANDONMENT, OR DOMESTIC VIOLENCE



### § 3113.04 Suspension of nonsupport sentence on posting bond conditioned on providing support; sanctions for contempt.

(A) Sentence may be suspended if a person, after conviction under section 2919.21 of the Revised Code and before sentence under that section, appears before the court of common pleas in which the conviction took place and enters into bond to the state in a sum fixed by the court at not less than five hundred nor more than one thousand dollars, with sureties approved by the court, conditioned that the person will furnish the child or other dependent with necessary or proper home, care, food, and clothing, or will pay promptly each week for such purpose to the office of child support in the department of job and family services, a sum to be fixed by the agency. The child support enforcement agency shall comply with Chapter 3119. of the Revised Code when it fixes the sum to be paid to the division.

(B) If any person required to pay child support under an order made under this section on or after April 15, 1985, or modified on or after December 1, 1986, is found in contempt of court for failure to make support payments under the order, the court that makes the finding, in addition to any other penalty or remedy imposed, shall assess all court costs arising out of the contempt proceeding against the person and require the person to pay any reasonable attorney's fees of any adverse party, as determined by the court, that arose in relation to the act of contempt.

**HISTORY: GC § 13010; 99 v 228; Bureau of Code Revision, 10-1-53; 134 v H 511 (Eff 1-1-74); 137 v S 87 (Eff 1-1-79); 140 v H 614 (Eff 4-10-85); 141 v H 509 (Eff 12-1-86); 142 v H 231 (Eff 10-5-87); 142 v H 708 (Eff 4-19-88); 143 v H 591 (Eff 4-12-90); 144 v S 10 (Eff 7-15-92); 145 v H 173 (Eff 12-31-93); 147 v H 352 (Eff 1-1-98); 148 v H 471 (Eff 7-1-2000); 148 v S 180. Eff 3-22-2001.**

## § 3113.06 Failure to pay maintenance cost.

No father, or mother when she is charged with the maintenance, of a child under eighteen years of age, or a mentally or physically handicapped child under age twenty-one, who is legally a ward of a public children services agency or is the recipient of aid pursuant to Chapter 5107. or 5115. of the Revised Code, shall neglect or refuse to pay such agency the reasonable cost of maintaining such child when such father or mother is able to do so by reason of property, labor, or earnings.

An offense under this section shall be held committed in the county in which the agency is located. The agency shall file charges against any parent who violates this section, unless the agency files charges under section 2919.21 of the Revised Code, or unless charges of nonsupport are filed by a relative or guardian of the child, or unless an action to enforce support is brought under Chapter 3115. of the Revised Code.

**HISTORY: GC §§ 13012, 13014; 99 v 228; 121 v 538; Bureau of Code Revision, 10-1-53; 132 v H 390 (Eff 11-7-67); 133 v S 49 (Eff 8-13-69); 133 v H 361 (Eff 9-23-69); 134 v H 511 (Eff 1-1-74); 141 v H 428 (Eff 12-23-86); 144 v H 298 (Eff 7-26-91); 146 v H 249 (Eff 7-17-95); 146 v H 274 (Eff 8-8-96); 147 v H 408. Eff 10-1-97; 152 v H 562, § 101.01, eff. 9-23-08; 2011 HB 153, § 101.01, eff. Oct. 1, 2011.**

The effective date is set by § 812.10 of 152 v H 562.
The effective date is set by section 26 of HB 408.

## § 3113.07 Suspension of sentence conditioned on payment of public maintenance cost.

As used in this section, "executive director" has the same meaning as in section 5153.01 of the Revised Code.

Sentence may be suspended, if a person, after conviction under section 3113.06 of the Revised Code and before sentence thereunder, appears before the court of common pleas in which such conviction took place and enters into bond to the state in a sum fixed by the court at not less than five hundred dollars, with sureties approved by such court, conditioned that such person will pay, so long as the child remains a ward of the public children services agency or a recipient of aid pursuant to Chapter 5107. or 5115. of the Revised Code, to the executive director thereof or to a trustee to be named by the court, for the benefit of such agency or if the child is a recipient of aid pursuant to Chapter 5107. or 5115. of the Revised Code, to the county department of job and family services, the reasonable cost of keeping such child. The amount of such costs and the time of payment shall be fixed by the court.

The court, in accordance with sections 3119.29 to 3119.56 of the Revised Code, shall include in each support order made under this section the requirement that one or both of the parents provide for the health care needs of the child to the satisfaction of the court.

**HISTORY: GC § 13013; 99 v 228; 121 v 538; Bureau of Code Revision, 10-1-53; 132 v H 390 (Eff 11-7-67); 133 v S 49 (Eff 8-13-69); 141 v H 428 (Eff 12-23-86); 144 v H 82 (Eff 9-10-91); 144 v H 298 (Eff 7-26-91); 146 v H 249 (Eff 7-17-95); 147 v H 408 (Eff 10-1-97); 147 v H 352 (Eff 1-1-98); 148 v H 471 (Eff 7-1-2000); 148 v S 180 (Eff 3-22-2001); 149 v H 657. Eff 12-13-2002.**

## § 3113.08 Failure to give bond; arrest.

Upon failure of the father or mother of a child under eighteen years of age, or of a physically or mentally handicapped child under twenty-one years of age, or the husband of a pregnant woman to comply with any order and undertaking provided for in sections 3113.01 to 3113.14, inclusive, of the Revised Code, such person may be arrested by the sheriff or other officer, on a warrant issued on the praecipe of the prosecuting attorney, and brought before the court of common pleas for sentence. Thereupon the court may pass sentence, or for good cause shown, may modify the order as to the time and amount of payments, or take a new undertaking and further suspend sentence, whichever is for the best interests of such child or pregnant woman and of the public.

**HISTORY: GC § 13015; 99 v 229, § 5; Bureau of Code Revision, 10-1-53; 146 v H 274. Eff 8-8-96.**

## § 3113.09 Duties of trustee.

The trustee appointed by the court of common pleas under sections 3113.04 and 3113.07 of the Revised Code, shall make quarterly reports of the receipts and expenditures of all moneys coming into his hands as provided in sections 3113.01 to 3113.14 of the Revised Code, such reports to be made to the board of county commissioners of the county from which the person described in section 3113.01 of the Revised Code was sentenced, or to the department of job and family services. The court may require such trustee to enter into a good and sufficient bond for the faithful performance of the duties imposed on him.

**HISTORY: GC § 13016; 99 v 229, § 7; Bureau of Code Revision, 10-1-53; 141 v H 428 (Eff 12-23-86); 148 v H 471. Eff 7-1-2000.**

The effective date is set by section 12(A) of HB 471.

## § 3113.10 Humane society may act as trustee.

A humane society, incorporated and existing under the laws of this state, and willing to render its services without compensation, may be appointed by the court of common pleas as trustee under sections 3113.04 and 3113.07 of the Revised Code.

**HISTORY: GC § 13017; 99 v 229, § 6; Bureau of Code Revision. Eff 10-1-53.**

## § 3113.11 Amount credited convict paid to trustee.

When a person is convicted, sentenced, and confined in a workhouse, under sections 3113.01 to 3113.14, inclusive, of the Revised Code, the county from which he is so convicted, sentenced, and confined upon the warrant of the county auditor of such county, and out of the general revenue fund thereof, shall pay monthly fifty cents for each day he is so confined, to the trustee appointed by the court under such sections, to be expended by such trustee for the maintenance of the child under sixteen years of age.

**HISTORY: GC § 13018: 99 v 229, § 7; 103 v 864(913); Bureau of Code Revision. Eff 10-1-53.**

## § 3113.13 Trustee to be named in mittimus.

When a person is imprisoned in a workhouse or state correctional institution under sections 3113.01 to 3113.14 of the Revised Code, the name and post-office address of the trustee appointed by the court of common pleas under sections 3113.04 and 3113.07 of the Revised Code shall appear in the mittimus.

**HISTORY: GC § 13020; 99 v 229, § 7; Bureau of Code Revision, 10-1-53; 145 v H 571. Eff 10-6-94.**

## § 3113.14 Continuance of citizenship.

Citizenship once acquired in this state by a father or mother of a child living in this state, for the purpose of sections 3113.01 to 3113.14 of the Revised Code, shall continue until the child has arrived at the age of sixteen years, provided the child continues to live in this state.

**HISTORY: GC § 13021; 99 v 229, § 4; Bureau of Code Revision, 10-1-53; 146 v H 274. Eff 8-8-96.**

### [DOMESTIC VIOLENCE]

## § 3113.31 Definitions; jurisdiction; petition; hearing; protection orders; consent agreements.

(A) As used in this section:

(1) "Domestic violence" means the occurrence of one or more of the following acts against a family or household member:

(a) Attempting to cause or recklessly causing bodily injury;

(b) Placing another person by the threat of force in fear of imminent serious physical harm or committing a violation of section 2903.211 [2903.21.1] or 2911.211 [2911.21.1] of the Revised Code;

(c) Committing any act with respect to a child that would result in the child being an abused child, as defined in section 2151.031 [2151.03.1] of the Revised Code;

(d) Committing a sexually oriented offense.

(2) "Court" means the domestic relations division of the court of common pleas in counties that have a domestic relations division and the court of common pleas in counties that do not have a domestic relations division, or the juvenile division of the court of common pleas of the county in which the person to be protected by a protection order issued or a consent agreement approved under this section resides if the respondent is less than eighteen years of age.

(3) "Family or household member" means any of the following:

(a) Any of the following who is residing with or has resided with the respondent:

(i) A spouse, a person living as a spouse, or a former spouse of the respondent;

(ii) A parent, a foster parent, or a child of the respondent, or another person related by consanguinity or affinity to the respondent;

(iii) A parent or a child of a spouse, person living as a spouse, or former spouse of the respondent, or another person related by consanguinity or affinity to a spouse, person living as a spouse, or former spouse of the respondent.

(b) The natural parent of any child of whom the respondent is the other natural parent or is the putative other natural parent.

(4) "Person living as a spouse" means a person who is living or has lived with the respondent in a common law marital relationship, who otherwise is cohabiting with the respondent, or who otherwise has cohabited with the respondent within five years prior to the date of the alleged occurrence of the act in question.

(5) "Victim advocate" means a person who provides support and assistance for a person who files a petition under this section.

(6) "Sexually oriented offense" has the same meaning as in section 2950.01 of the Revised Code.

(B) The court has jurisdiction over all proceedings under this section. The petitioner's right to relief under this section is not affected by the petitioner's leaving the residence or household to avoid further domestic violence.

(C) A person may seek relief under this section on the person's own behalf, or any parent or adult household member may seek relief under this section on behalf of any other family or household member, by filing a petition with the court. The petition shall contain or state:

(1) An allegation that the respondent engaged in domestic violence against a family or household member of the respondent, including a description of the nature and extent of the domestic violence;

(2) The relationship of the respondent to the petitioner, and to the victim if other than the petitioner;

(3) A request for relief under this section.

(D)(1) If a person who files a petition pursuant to this section requests an ex parte order, the court shall hold an ex parte hearing on the same day that the petition is filed. The court, for good cause shown at the ex parte hearing, may enter any temporary orders, with or without bond, including, but not limited to, an order described in division (E)(1)(a), (b), or (c) of this section, that the court finds necessary to protect the family or household member from domestic violence. Immediate and present danger of domestic violence to the family or household member constitutes good cause for purposes of this section. Immediate and present danger includes, but is not limited to, situations in which the respondent has threatened the family or household member with bodily harm, in which the respondent has threatened the family or household member with a sexually oriented offense, or in which the respondent previously has been convicted of, pleaded guilty to, or been adjudicated a delinquent child for an offense that constitutes domestic violence against the family or household member.

(2)(a) If the court, after an ex parte hearing, issues an order described in division (E)(1)(b) or (c) of this section, the court shall schedule a full hearing for a date that is within seven court days after the ex parte hearing. If any other type of protection order that is authorized under division (E) of this section is issued by the court after an ex parte hearing, the court shall schedule a full hearing for a date that is within ten court days after the ex parte hearing. The court shall give the respondent notice of, and an opportunity to be heard at, the full hearing. The court shall hold the full hearing on the date scheduled under this division unless the court grants a continuance of the hearing in accordance with this division. Under any of the following circumstances or for any of the following reasons, the court may grant a continuance of the full hearing to a reasonable time determined by the court:

(i) Prior to the date scheduled for the full hearing under this division, the respondent has not been served with the petition filed pursuant to this section and notice of the full hearing.

(ii) The parties consent to the continuance.

(iii) The continuance is needed to allow a party to obtain counsel.

(iv) The continuance is needed for other good cause.

(b) An ex parte order issued under this section does not expire because of a failure to serve notice of the full hearing upon the respondent before the date set for the full hearing under division (D)(2)(a) of this section or because the court grants a continuance under that division.

(3) If a person who files a petition pursuant to this section does not request an ex parte order, or if a person requests an ex parte order but the court does not issue an ex parte order after an ex parte hearing, the court shall proceed as in a normal civil action and grant a full hearing on the matter.

(E)(1) After an ex parte or full hearing, the court may grant any protection order, with or without bond, or approve any consent agreement to bring about a cessation of domestic violence against the family or household members. The order or agreement may:

(a) Direct the respondent to refrain from abusing or from committing sexually oriented offenses against the family or household members;

(b) Grant possession of the residence or household to the petitioner or other family or household member, to the exclusion of the respondent, by evicting the respondent, when the residence or household is owned or leased solely by the petitioner or other family or household member, or by ordering the respondent to vacate the premises, when the residence or household is jointly owned or leased by the respondent, and the petitioner or other family or household member;

(c) When the respondent has a duty to support the petitioner or other family or household member living in the residence or household and the respondent is the sole owner or lessee of the residence or household, grant possession of the residence or household to the petitioner or other family or household member, to the exclusion of the respondent, by ordering the respondent to vacate the premises, or, in the case of a consent agreement, allow the respondent to provide suitable, alternative housing;

(d) Temporarily allocate parental rights and responsibilities for the care of, or establish temporary parenting time rights with regard to, minor children, if no other court has determined, or is determining, the allocation of parental rights and responsibilities for the minor children or parenting time rights;

(e) Require the respondent to maintain support, if the respondent customarily provides for or contributes to the support of the family or household member, or if the respondent has a duty to support the petitioner or family or household member;

(f) Require the respondent, petitioner, victim of domestic violence, or any combination of those persons, to seek counseling;

(g) Require the respondent to refrain from entering the residence, school, business, or place of employment of the petitioner or family or household member;

(h) Grant other relief that the court considers equitable and fair, including, but not limited to, ordering the respondent to permit the use of a motor vehicle by the petitioner or other family or household member and the apportionment of household and family personal property.

(2) If a protection order has been issued pursuant to this section in a prior action involving the respondent and the petitioner or one or more of the family or household members or victims, the court may include in a protection order that it issues a prohibition against the respondent returning to the residence or household. If it includes a prohibition against the respondent returning to the residence or household in the order, it also shall include in the order provisions of the type described in division (E)(7) of this section. This division does not preclude the court from including in a protection order or consent agreement, in circumstances other than those described in this division, a requirement that the respondent be evicted from or vacate the residence or household or refrain from entering the residence, school, business, or place of employment of the petitioner or a family or household member, and, if the court includes any requirement of that type in an order or agreement, the court also shall include in the order provisions of the type described in division (E)(7) of this section.

(3)(a) Any protection order issued or consent agreement approved under this section shall be valid until a date certain, but not later than five years from the date of its issuance or approval, or not later than the date a respondent who is less than eighteen years of age attains nineteen years of age, unless modified or terminated as provided in division (E)(8) of this section.

(b) Subject to the limitation on the duration of an order or agreement set forth in division (E)(3)(a) of this section, any order under division (E)(1)(d) of this section shall terminate on the date that a court in an action for divorce, dissolution of marriage, or legal separation brought by the petitioner or respondent issues an order allocating parental rights and responsibilities for the care of children or on the date that a juvenile court in an action brought by the petitioner or respondent issues an order awarding legal custody of minor children. Subject to the limitation on the duration of an order or agreement set forth in division (E)(3)(a) of this section, any order under division (E)(1)(e) of this section shall terminate on the date that a court in an action for divorce, dissolution of marriage, or legal separation brought by the petitioner or respondent issues a support order or on the date that a juvenile court in an action brought by the petitioner or respondent issues a support order.

(c) Any protection order issued or consent agreement approved pursuant to this section may be renewed in the same manner as the original order or agreement was issued or approved.

(4) A court may not issue a protection order that requires a petitioner to do or to refrain from doing an act that the court may require a respondent to do or to refrain from doing under division (E)(1)(a), (b), (c), (d), (e), (g), or (h) of this section unless all of the following apply:

(a) The respondent files a separate petition for a protection order in accordance with this section.

(b) The petitioner is served notice of the respondent's petition at least forty-eight hours before the court holds a hearing with respect to the respondent's petition, or the petitioner waives the right to receive this notice.

(c) If the petitioner has requested an ex parte order pursuant to division (D) of this section, the court does not delay any hearing required by that division beyond the time specified in that division in order to consolidate the hearing with a hearing on the petition filed by the respondent.

(d) After a full hearing at which the respondent presents evidence in support of the request for a protection order and the petitioner is afforded an opportunity to defend against that evidence, the court determines that the petitioner has committed an act of domestic violence or has violated a temporary protection order issued pursuant to section 2919.26 of the Revised Code, that both the petitioner and the respondent acted primarily as aggressors, and that neither the petitioner nor the respondent acted primarily in self-defense.

(5) No protection order issued or consent agreement approved under this section shall in any manner affect title to any real property.

(6)(a) If a petitioner, or the child of a petitioner, who obtains a protection order or consent agreement pursuant to division (E)(1) of this section or a temporary protection order pursuant to section 2919.26 of the Revised Code and is the subject of a parenting time order issued pursuant to section 3109.051 [3109.05.1] or 3109.12 of the Revised Code or a visitation or companionship order issued pursuant to section 3109.051 [3109.05.1], 3109.11, or 3109.12 of the Revised Code or division (E)(1)(d) of this section granting parenting time rights to the respondent, the court may require the public children services agency of the county in which the court is located to provide supervision of the respondent's exercise of parenting time or visitation or companionship rights with respect to the child for a period not to exceed nine months, if the court makes the following findings of fact:

(i) The child is in danger from the respondent;

(ii) No other person or agency is available to provide the supervision.

(b) A court that requires an agency to provide supervision pursuant to division (E)(6)(a) of this section shall order the respondent to reimburse the agency for the cost of providing the supervision, if it determines that the respondent has sufficient income or resources to pay that cost.

(7)(a) If a protection order issued or consent agreement approved under this section includes a requirement that the respondent be evicted from or vacate the residence or household or refrain from entering the residence, school, business, or place of employment of the petitioner or a family or household member, the order or agreement shall state clearly that the order or agreement cannot be waived or nullified by an invitation to the respondent from the petitioner or other family or household member to enter the residence, school, business, or place of employment or by the respondent's entry into one of those places otherwise upon the consent of the petitioner or other family or household member.

(b) Division (E)(7)(a) of this section does not limit any discretion of a court to determine that a respondent charged with a violation of section 2919.27 of the Revised Code, with a violation of a municipal ordinance substantially equivalent to that section, or with contempt of court, which charge is based on an alleged violation of a protection order issued or consent agreement approved under this section, did not commit the violation or was not in contempt of court.

(8)(a) The court may modify or terminate as provided in division (E)(8) of this section a protection order or consent agreement that was issued after a full hearing under this section. The court that issued the protection order or approved the consent agreement shall hear a motion for modification or termination of the protection order or consent agreement pursuant to division (E)(8) of this section.

(b) Either the petitioner or the respondent of the original protection order or consent agreement may bring a motion for modification or termination of a protection order or consent agreement that was issued or approved after a full hearing. The court shall require notice of the motion to be made as provided by the Rules of Civil Procedure. If the petitioner for the original protection order or consent agreement has requested that the petitioner's address be kept confidential, the court shall not disclose the address to the respondent of the original protection order or consent agreement or any other person, except as otherwise required by law. The moving party has the burden of proof to show, by a preponderance of the evidence, that modification or termination of the protection order or consent agreement is appropriate because either the protection order or consent agreement is no longer needed or because the terms of the original protection order or consent agreement are no longer appropriate.

(c) In considering whether to modify or terminate a protection order or consent agreement issued or approved under this section, the court shall consider all relevant factors, including, but not limited to, the following:

(i) Whether the petitioner consents to modification or termination of the protection order or consent agreement;

(ii) Whether the petitioner fears the respondent;

(iii) The current nature of the relationship between the petitioner and the respondent;

(iv) The circumstances of the petitioner and respondent, including the relative proximity of the petitioner's and respondent's workplaces and residences and whether the petitioner and respondent have minor children together;

(v) Whether the respondent has complied with the terms and conditions of the original protection order or consent agreement;

(vi) Whether the respondent has a continuing involvement with illegal drugs or alcohol;

(vii) Whether the respondent has been convicted of, pleaded guilty to, or been adjudicated a delinquent child for an offense of violence since the issuance of the protection order or approval of the consent agreement;

(viii) Whether any other protection orders, consent agreements, restraining orders, or no contact orders have been issued against the respondent pursuant to this section, section 2919.26 of the Revised Code, any other provision of state law, or the law of any other state;

(ix) Whether the respondent has participated in any domestic violence treatment, intervention program, or other counseling addressing domestic violence and whether the respondent has completed the treatment, program, or counseling;

(x) The time that has elapsed since the protection order was issued or since the consent agreement was approved;

(xi) The age and health of the respondent;

(xii) When the last incident of abuse, threat of harm, or commission of a sexually oriented offense occurred or other relevant information concerning the safety and protection of the petitioner or other protected parties.

(d) If a protection order or consent agreement is modified or terminated as provided in division (E)(8) of this section, the court shall issue copies of the modified or terminated order or agreement as provided in division (F) of this section. A petitioner may also provide notice of the modification or termination to the judicial and law enforcement officials in any county other than the county in which the order or agreement is modified or terminated as provided in division (N) of this section.

(e) If the respondent moves for modification or termination of a protection order or consent agreement pursuant to this section, the court may assess costs against the respondent for the filing of the motion.

(9) Any protection order issued or any consent agreement approved pursuant to this section shall include a provision that the court will automatically seal all of the records of the proceeding in which the order is issued or agreement approved on the date the respondent attains the age of nineteen years unless the petitioner provides the court with evidence that the respondent has not complied with all of the terms of the protection order or consent agreement. The protection order or consent agreement shall specify the date when the respondent attains the age of nineteen years.

(F)(1) A copy of any protection order, or consent agreement, that is issued, approved, modified, or terminated under this section shall be issued by the court to the petitioner, to the respondent, and to all law enforcement agencies that have jurisdiction to enforce the order or agreement. The court shall direct that a copy of an order be delivered to the respondent on the same day that the order is entered.

(2) Upon the issuance of a protection order or the approval of a consent agreement under this section, the court shall provide the parties to the order or agreement with the following notice orally or by form:

"NOTICE

As a result of this order or consent agreement, it may be unlawful for you to possess or purchase a firearm, including a rifle, pistol, or revolver, or ammunition pursuant to federal law under 18 U.S.C. 922(g)(8). If you have any questions whether this law makes it illegal for you to possess or purchase a firearm or ammunition, you should consult an attorney."

(3) All law enforcement agencies shall establish and maintain an index for the protection orders and the approved consent agreements delivered to the agencies pursuant to division (F)(1) of this section. With respect to each order and consent agreement delivered, each agency shall note on the index the date and time that it received the order or consent agreement.

(4) Regardless of whether the petitioner has registered the order or agreement in the county in which the officer's agency has jurisdiction pursuant to division (N) of this section, any officer of a law enforcement agency shall enforce a protection order issued or consent agreement approved by any court in this state in accordance with the provisions of the order or agreement, including removing the respondent from the premises, if appropriate.

(G) Any proceeding under this section shall be conducted in accordance with the Rules of Civil Procedure, except that an order under this section may be obtained with or without bond. An order issued under this section, other than an ex parte order, that grants a protection order or approves a consent agreement that modifies or terminates a protection order or consent agreement, or that refuses to modify or terminate a protection order or consent agreement, that refuses to grant a protection order or approve a consent agreement, is a final, appealable order. The remedies and procedures provided in this section are in addition to, and not in lieu of, any other available civil or criminal remedies.

(H) The filing of proceedings under this section does not excuse a person from filing any report or giving any notice required by section 2151.421 [2151.42.1] of the Revised Code or by any other law. When a petition under this section alleges domestic violence against minor children, the court shall report the fact, or cause reports to be made, to a county, township, or municipal peace officer under section 2151.421 [2151.42.1] of the Revised Code.

(I) Any law enforcement agency that investigates a domestic dispute shall provide information to the family or household members involved regarding the relief available under this section and section 2919.26 of the Revised Code.

(J) Notwithstanding any provision of law to the contrary and regardless of whether a protection order is issued or a consent agreement is approved by a court of another county or a court of another state, no court or unit of state or local government shall charge any fee, cost, deposit, or money in connection with the filing of a petition pursuant to this section or in connection with the filing, issuance, registration, or service of a protection order or consent agreement, or for obtaining a certified copy of a protection order or consent agreement.

(K)(1) The court shall comply with Chapters 3119., 3121., 3123., and 3125. of the Revised Code when it makes or modifies an order for child support under this section.

(2) If any person required to pay child support under an order made under this section on or after April 15, 1985, or modified under this section on or after December 31, 1986, is found in contempt of court for failure to make support payments under the order, the court that makes the finding, in addition to any other penalty or remedy imposed, shall assess all court costs arising out of the contempt proceeding against the person and require the person to pay any reasonable attorney's fees of any adverse party, as determined by the court, that arose in relation to the act of contempt.

(L)(1) A person who violates a protection order issued or a consent agreement approved under this section is subject to the following sanctions:

(a) Criminal prosecution or a delinquent child proceeding for a violation of section 2919.27 of the Revised Code, if the violation of the protection order or consent agreement constitutes a violation of that section;

(b) Punishment for contempt of court.

(2) The punishment of a person for contempt of court for violation of a protection order issued or a consent agreement approved under this section does not bar criminal prosecution of the person or a delinquent child proceeding concerning the person for a violation of section 2919.27 of the Revised Code. However, a person punished for contempt of court is entitled to credit for the punishment imposed upon conviction of or adjudication as a delinquent child for a violation of that section, and a person convicted of or adjudicated a delinquent child for a violation of that section shall not subsequently be punished for contempt of court arising out of the same activity.

(M) In all stages of a proceeding under this section, a petitioner may be accompanied by a victim advocate.

(N)(1) A petitioner who obtains a protection order or consent agreement under this section or a temporary protection order under section 2919.26 of the Revised Code may provide notice of the issuance or approval of the order or agreement to the judicial and law enforcement officials in any county other than the county in which the order is issued or the agreement is approved by registering that order or agreement in the other county pursuant to division (N)(2) of this section and filing a copy of the registered order or registered agreement with a law enforcement agency in the other county in accordance with that division. A person who obtains a protection order issued by a court of another state may provide notice of the issuance of the order to the judicial and law enforcement officials in any county of this state by registering the order in that county pursuant to section 2919.272 [2919.27.2] of the Revised Code and filing a copy of the registered order with a law enforcement agency in that county.

(2) A petitioner may register a temporary protection order, protection order, or consent agreement in a county other than the county in which the court that issued the order or approved the agreement is located in the following manner:

(a) The petitioner shall obtain a certified copy of the order or agreement from the clerk of the court that issued the order or approved the agreement and present that certified copy to the clerk of the court of common pleas or the clerk of a municipal court or county court in the county in which the order or agreement is to be registered.

(b) Upon accepting the certified copy of the order or agreement for registration, the clerk of the court of common pleas, municipal court, or county court shall place an endorsement of registration on the order or agreement and give the petitioner a copy of the order or agreement that bears that proof of registration.

(3) The clerk of each court of common pleas, the clerk of each municipal court, and the clerk of each county court shall maintain a registry of certified copies of temporary protection orders, protection orders, or consent agreements that have been issued or approved by courts in other counties and that have been registered with the clerk.

(O) Nothing in this section prohibits the domestic relations division of a court of common pleas in counties that have a domestic relations division or a court of common pleas in counties that do not have a domestic relations division from designating a minor child as a protected party on a protection order or consent agreement.

**HISTORY: 137 v H 835 (Eff 3-27-79); 138 v H 920 (Eff 4-9-81); 140 v H 587 (Eff 9-25-84); 140 v H 614 (Eff 4-10-85); 140 v H 113 (Eff 1-8-85); 141 v H 509 (Eff 12-1-86); 141 v H 428 (Eff 12-23-86); 142 v H 231 (Eff 10-5-87); 142 v H 708 (Eff 4-19-88); 142 v H 172 (Eff 3-17-89); 143 v H 591 (Eff 4-12-90); 143 v S 3 (Eff 4-11-91); 144 v S 10 (Eff 7-15-92); 144 v H 536 (Eff 11-5-92); 145 v H 173 (Eff 12-31-93); 145 v H 335 (Eff 12-9-94); 146 v H 274 (Eff 8-8-96); 146 v H 438 (Eff 7-1-97); 147 v S 1 (Eff 10-21-97); 147 v H 352 (Eff 1-1-98); 148 v S 180 (Eff 3-22-2001); 149 v H 548. Eff 3-31-2003; 151 v S 17, § 1, eff. 8-3-06; 151 v H 95, § 1, eff. 8-3-06; 151 v S 260, § 1, eff. 1-2-07; 152 v H 562, § 101.01, eff. 6-24-08; 153 v H 10, § 1, eff. 6-17-10.**

The provisions of § 3 of 153 v H 10 read as follows:

SECTION 3. Sections 2151.23, 2151.358, 2152.02, 2743.191, 2903.214, 2919.25, 2919.27, 3113.31, and 3113.33 of the Revised Code, as amended by this act, and section 2151.34 of the Revised Code, as enacted by this act, shall be named the "Shynerra Grant Law."

The effective date is set by § 812.20 of 152 v H 562.

**Comment, Legislative Service Commission**

Section 3113.31 of the Revised Code is amended by Am. Sub. S.B. 17 and Am. Sub. H.B. 95 of the 126th General Assembly. Comparison of these amendments in pursuance of section 1.52 of the Revised Code discloses that they are identical, and that S.B. 17 is the later amendment concurred by the General Assembly.

## § 3113.32 Records of domestic dispute and violence problems; annual statistical report.

(A) The sheriff of a county, constable or chief of police of a township, and chief of police of a city or village shall keep a separate record of domestic dispute and domestic violence problems on a form prepared and distributed by the superintendent of the bureau of criminal identification and investigation. The forms shall contain spaces for the reporting of all information that the superintendent determines to be relevant to domestic dispute and domestic violence problems, including, but not limited to, the number of domestic dispute and domestic violence problems reported to the law enforcement agency for which the record is kept, the relationship of the complainant and the person allegedly the victim of the domestic violence, if different, to the alleged offender, and the relationship of all other persons involved in the domestic dispute or domestic violence problem, and the action taken by the law enforcement officers who handled the domestic dispute or domestic violence problem. A copy of the record shall be submitted to the bureau each month.

(B) The superintendent of the bureau of criminal identification and investigation shall receive copies of monthly records of domestic dispute and domestic violence problems kept by local law enforcement agencies and submitted to him under division (A) of this section. The superintendent shall compile the data and annually produce a statistical public report on the incidence of domestic disputes and violence in this state and its political subdivisions. The report shall be prepared in such a manner that there is no identifying data, including the names and addresses of the persons involved in the domestic dispute and domestic violence problems, that would enable any person to determine the identity of any of the persons involved.

(C) The attorney general shall oversee the statistical reporting required pursuant to this section to ensure that it is complete and accurate.

**HISTORY: 140 v H 587. Eff 9-25-84.**

**Analogous to former RC § 3113.32 (137 v H 835), repealed 137 v H 835, § 3, eff 3-27-83.**

## [SHELTERS FOR DOMESTIC VIOLENCE VICTIMS]

## § 3113.33 Definitions.

As used in sections 3113.33 to 3113.40 of the Revised Code:

(A) "Domestic violence" means attempting to cause or causing bodily injury to a family or household member, or placing a family or household member by threat of force in fear of imminent physical harm.

(B) "Family or household member" means any of the following:

(1) Any of the following who is residing or has resided with the person committing the domestic violence:

(a) A spouse, a person living as a spouse, or a former spouse of the person committing the domestic violence;

(b) A parent, foster parent, or child of the person committing the domestic violence, or another person related by consanguinity or affinity to the person committing the domestic violence;

(c) A parent or a child of a spouse, person living as a spouse, or former spouse of the person committing the domestic violence, or another person related by consanguinity or affinity to a spouse, person living as a spouse, or former spouse of the person committing the domestic violence;

(d) The dependents of any person listed in division (B)(1)(a), (b), or (c) of this section.

(2) The natural parent of any child of whom the person committing the domestic violence is the other natural parent or is the putative other natural parent.

(C) "Shelter for victims of domestic violence" or "shelter" means a facility that provides temporary residential service or facilities to family or household members who are victims of domestic violence.

(D) "Person living as a spouse" means a person who is living or has lived with the person committing the domestic violence in a common law marital relationship, who otherwise is cohabiting with the person committing the domestic violence, or who otherwise has cohabited with the person committing the domestic violence within five years prior to the date of the alleged occurrence of the act in question.

**HISTORY: 138 v S 46 (Eff 1-18-80); 138 v H 920 (Eff 4-9-81); 140 v H 587 (Eff 9-25-84); 142 v H 172 (Eff 3-17-89); 145 v H 335 (Eff 12-9-94); 147 v H 215 (Eff 6-30-97); 147 v S 1. Eff 10-21-97; 153 v H 10, § 1, eff. 6-17-10.**

See provisions of § 3 of 153 v H 10 following RC § 3113.31.

The provisions of § 4 of 153 v H 10 read in part as follows:

SECTION 4. * * * Section 3113.33 of the Revised Code is presented in this act as a composite of the section as amended by both Am. Sub. H.B. 215 and Am. Sub. S.B. 1 of the 122nd General Assembly. The General Assembly, applying the principle stated in division (B) of section 1.52 of the Revised Code that amendments are to be harmonized if reasonably capable of simultaneous operation, finds that the composites are the resulting versions of the sections in effect prior to the effective date of the sections as presented in this act.

## § 3113.34 Additional fee for marriage license; fees to assist shelters for domestic violence victims.

In addition to any fee established under section 2101.16 of the Revised Code for the issuance of a marriage license, the probate court shall collect and deposit in the county treasury a fee of seventeen dollars for each marriage license issued. This fee, plus the thirty-two-dollar fee collected under division (D) of section 2303.201 [2303.20.1] of the Revised Code as additional costs in each new action or proceeding for annulment, divorce, or dissolution of marriage, shall be retained in a special fund and shall be expended only to provide financial assistance to shelters for victims of domestic violence and only as provided in sections 3113.35 to 3113.39 of the Revised Code.

**HISTORY: 138 v S 46 (Eff 1-18-80); 140 v H 319 (Eff 12-26-84); 145 v H 335. Eff 12-9-94.**

## § 3113.35 Shelter may apply to county for release of fees collected for marriage licenses and as additional costs in certain actions.

(A) A shelter for victims of domestic violence may apply to the board of county commissioners of the county in which it is located or of an adjoining county, the population of which is or will be served by the shelter, for the release of funds to be collected as fees for the issuance of marriage licenses pursuant to section 3113.34 or fees as additional costs in annulment, divorce, or dissolution of marriage actions and proceedings pursuant to division (D) of section 2303.201 [2303.20.1] of the Revised Code and that are to be used for the funding of the shelter. All applications for funds shall be submitted by the first day of October of the year preceding the calendar year for which the funding is desired, and shall include all of the following:

(1) Evidence that the shelter is incorporated in this state as a nonprofit corporation;

(2) A list of the trustees of the corporation, and a list of the trustees of the shelter, if different;

(3) The proposed budget of the shelter for the following calendar year;

(4) A summary of the services proposed to be offered in the following calendar year;

(5) An estimate of the number of persons to be served during the following calendar year.

(B) Upon receipt of an application for funds from a shelter that meets the criteria set forth in section 3113.36 of the Revised Code, the board of county commissioners shall, on or before the fifteenth day of November of the year in which the application is filed, notify the shelter, in writing, whether it is eligible for funds, and if the shelter is eligible, estimate the amount available for that shelter from the fees to be collected under section 3113.34 or division (D) of section 2303.201 [2303.20.1] of the Revised Code.

(C) Funds collected as fees for the issuance of marriage licenses pursuant to section 3113.34 or fees as additional costs in annulment, divorce, or dissolution of marriage actions and proceedings pursuant to division (D) of section 2303.201 [2303.20.1] of the Revised Code that are allocated to shelters under this section shall be paid to the shelters twice annually. Funds collected from the first day of January through the thirtieth day of June of the calendar year following the year in which the application is filed shall be allocated to the shelters by the fifteenth day of July of the year following the year in which the application is filed. Funds collected from the first day of July through the thirty-first day of December of the calendar year following the year in which the application is filed shall be allocated to the shelters by the fifteenth day of January of the year following the end of the collection period.

**HISTORY: 138 v S 46 (Eff 1-18-80); 138 v H 736 (Eff 10-16-80); 141 v H 569 (Eff 4-15-86); 145 v H 335. Eff 12-9-94.**

## § 3113.36 Requirements for qualifying for funds; disqualification.

(A) To qualify for funds under section 3113.35 of the Revised Code, a shelter for victims of domestic violence shall meet all of the following requirements:

(1) Be incorporated in this state as a nonprofit corporation;

(2) Have trustees who represent the racial, ethnic, and socioeconomic diversity of the community to be served, including at least one person who is or has been a victim of domestic violence;

(3) Receive at least twenty-five per cent of its funds from sources other than funds distributed pursuant to section 3113.35 of the Revised Code. These other sources may be public or private, and may include funds distributed pursuant to section 3113.37 of the Revised Code, and contributions of goods or services, including materials, commodities, transportation, office space, or other types of facilities or personal services.

(4) Provide residential service or facilities for children when accompanied by a parent, guardian, or custodian who is a victim of domestic violence and who is receiving temporary residential service at the shelter;

(5) Require persons employed by or volunteering services to the shelter to maintain the confidentiality of any information that would identify individuals served by the shelter.

(B) A shelter for victims of domestic violence does not qualify for funds if it discriminates in its admissions or provision of services on the basis of race, religion, color, age, marital status, national origin, or ancestry. A shelter does not qualify for funds in the second half of any year if its application projects the provision of residential service and such service has not been provided in the first half of that year; such a shelter does not qualify for funds in the following year.

**HISTORY: 138 v S 46. Eff 1-18-80.**

## § 3113.37 Deposit of unallocated funds in state treasury to credit of domestic violence shelters fund.

(A) If in any calendar year a board of county commissioners does not allocate all of the funds collected that year under section 3113.34 or division (D) of section 2303.201 [2303.20.1] of the Revised Code to a shelter for victims of domestic violence that applied for them, or if a board receives no application in that year from a shelter that is qualified to receive funds as determined under section 3113.36 of the Revised Code, the funds shall be deposited, on or before the thirty-first day of December of that year, in the state treasury to the credit of the domestic violence shelters fund, which is hereby created. The fund shall be administered by the attorney general for the purpose of providing financial assistance to shelters.

(B) A shelter located in this state may apply to the attorney general for funds. All applications for funds shall be submitted by the first day of February of the year for which the funds are requested and shall contain all of the information set forth in division (A) of section 3113.35 of the Revised Code.

(C) Upon receipt of an application for funds from a shelter that meets the criteria set forth in section 3113.36 of the Revised Code, the attorney general, on or before the fifteenth day of March of the year in which the application is received, shall notify the shelter, in writing, whether it is eligible for funds and, if the shelter is eligible, specify the amount available for that shelter.

(D) Funds allocated under this section shall be paid once annually, on or before the thirtieth day of April of the year in which the application is received.

**HISTORY: 138 v S 46 (Eff 1-18-80); 141 v H 201 (Eff 7-1-85); 145 v H 335. Eff 12-9-94.**

## § 3113.38 Priorities for allocating funds.

If a board of county commissioners or the attorney general receives applications from more than one qualified shelter for victims of domestic violence, and the requests for funds exceed the amount of funds available, funds shall be allocated on the basis of the following priorities:

(A) To shelters in existence on the effective date of this section;

(B) The shelters offering or proposing to offer the broadest range of services and referrals to the community served, including medical, psychological, financial, educational, vocational, child care services, and legal services;

(C) To other qualified shelters.

**HISTORY: 138 v S 46. Eff 1-18-80.**

## § 3113.39 Annual report by shelter; attorney general to compile reports.

(A) A shelter for victims of domestic violence that receives funds pursuant to section 3113.35 or 3113.37 of the Revised Code shall file an annual report with the board of county commissioners of the county in which it is located and of the county from which it is receiving funds, if different, and with the attorney general on or before the thirty- first day of March of the year following the year in which funds were received. The annual report shall include statistics on the number of persons served by the shelter, the relationship of the victim of domestic violence to the abuser, the number of referrals made for medical, psychological, financial, educational, vocational, child care services, or legal services, and shall include a compilation report of an independent accountant. No information contained in the report shall identify any person served by the shelter, or enable any person to determine the identity of any such person.

(B) The attorney general shall compile the reports filed pursuant to division (A) of this section annually.

**HISTORY: 138 v S 46 (Eff 1-18-80); 140 v H 587. Eff 9-25-84.**

## § 3113.40 Shelter to obtain last known residence information.

When a shelter for victims of domestic violence provides accommodations to a person, the shelter, on admitting the person, shall determine, if possible, the person's last known residential address and county of residence. The information concerning the address and county of residence is confidential and may be released only to a public children services agency pursuant to section 2151.422 [2151.42.2] of the Revised Code.

**HISTORY: 147 v H 215. Eff 6-30-97.**

## § 3113.99 Penalties.

Whoever violates section 3113.06 of the Revised Code is guilty of a misdemeanor of the first degree. If the offender previously has been convicted of or pleaded guilty to a violation of section 3113.06 of the Revised Code or if the court finds that the offender has failed to pay the cost of child maintenance under section 3113.06 of the Revised

Code for a total accumulated period of twenty-six weeks out of one hundred four consecutive weeks, whether or not the twenty-six weeks were consecutive, a violation of section 3113.06 of the Revised Code is a felony of the fifth degree.

**HISTORY: Bureau of Code Revision, 10-1-53; 134 v H 511 (Eff 1-1-74); 146 v S 2 (Eff 7-1-96); 146 v H 167 (Eff 6-11-96)†; 147 v H 352 (Eff 1-1-98); 148 v H 471 (Eff 7-1-2000); 148 v S 180. Eff 3-22-2001.**

† The effective date of HB 167 (146 v —) was changed from 11-15-96 to 6-11-96 by § 7 of HB 710 (146 v —).

# CHAPTER 3121: COLLECTION AND DISBURSEMENT OF CHILD SUPPORT



## § 3121.08 Earnings of prisoners.

(A) As used in this section, "prison," "prison term," and "jail" have the same meanings as in section 2929.01 of the Revised Code.

(B) Notwithstanding any other section of the Revised Code, including sections 5145.16 and 5147.30 of the Revised Code, twenty-five per cent of any money earned pursuant to section 5145.16 or 5147.30 of the Revised Code by a prisoner in a prison or jail who has a dependent child receiving assistance under Chapter 5107. of the Revised Code, shall be paid to the state department of job and family services.

**HISTORY: RC § 3113.16, 147 v S 52 (Eff 9-3-97); 148 v H 471 (Eff 7-1-2000); RC § 3121.08, 148 v S 180. Eff 3-22-2001.**

# TITLE 33: EDUCATION — LIBRARIES

## CHAPTER 3301: DEPARTMENT OF EDUCATION



### [SUPERINTENDENT OF PUBLIC INSTRUCTION]

### § 3301.121 Adjudication procedure to determine whether to permanently exclude pupil.

(A) In addition to the duties and responsibilities of the superintendent of public instruction set forth in section 3301.12 of the Revised Code, the superintendent, in accordance with this section and section 3313.662 [3313.66.2] of the Revised Code, shall conduct an adjudication procedure to determine whether to permanently exclude from attending any of the public schools of this state any pupil who is the subject of a resolution forwarded to the superintendent by a board of education pursuant to division (D) of section 3313.662 [3313.66.2] of the Revised Code.

(B)(1) Except as provided in division (B)(3) of this section, within fourteen days after receipt of a resolution forwarded by a board of education pursuant to division (D) of section 3313.662 [3313.66.2] of the Revised Code, the superintendent of public instruction or the superintendent's designee shall provide the pupil who is the subject of the resolution and that pupil's parent, guardian, or custodian with a notice of an opportunity for an adjudication hearing on the proposed permanent exclusion of the pupil from attending any of the public schools of this state. The notice shall include all of the following:

(a) The date, time, and place of the permanent exclusion adjudication hearing;

(b) A statement informing the pupil and the pupil's parent, guardian, or custodian that the pupil may attend the adjudication hearing at the date, time, and place set forth in the notice, that the failure of the pupil or the pupil's parent, guardian, or custodian to attend the adjudication hearing will result in a waiver of the pupil's right to present evidence, testimony, and factors in mitigation of the pupil's permanent exclusion at an adjudication hearing on the proposed permanent exclusion, and that the pupil shall be accorded all of the following rights:

(i) The right to testify, to present evidence and the testimony of witnesses, and to confront, cross-examine, and compel the attendance of witnesses;

(ii) The right to a record of the hearing;

(iii) The right to written findings.

(c) A statement informing the pupil and the pupil's parent, guardian, or custodian that the pupil has the right to be represented by counsel at the adjudication hearing.

(d) A statement informing the pupil and the pupil's parent, guardian, or custodian that, if the pupil by failing to attend the hearing waives the pupil's right to present evidence, testimony, and factors in mitigation of the pupil's permanent exclusion at an adjudication hearing on the proposed permanent exclusion, the superintendent is required to review the information relevant to the permanent exclusion that is available to the superintendent and is permitted to enter an order requiring the pupil's permanent exclusion from attending any of the public schools of this state at any time within seven days after the conclusion of the adjudication hearing.

(2) The superintendent or the superintendent's designee shall provide the notice required by division (B)(1) of this section to the pupil and to the pupil's parent, guardian, or custodian by certified mail or personal service.

(3)(a) If a pupil who is the subject of a resolution forwarded to the superintendent of public instruction by a board of education pursuant to section 3313.662 [3313.66.2] of the Revised Code is in the custody of the department of youth services pursuant to a disposition under any provision of Chapter 2152. of the Revised Code, other than division (A)(1)(a) of section 2152.16 of the Revised Code, at the time the resolution is forwarded, the department shall notify in writing the superintendent of public instruction and the board of education that forwarded the resolution of that fact. Upon receipt of the notice, the superintendent shall delay providing the notice required by division (B)(1) of this section and the adjudication of the request for permanent exclusion until the superintendent receives further notice from the department pursuant to division (B)(3)(b) of this section.

(b) At least sixty days before a pupil described in division (B)(3)(a) of this section will be released from institutionalization or institutionalization in a secure facility by the department of youth services, the department shall notify in writing the superintendent of public instruction and the board of education that forwarded the resolution pursuant to section 3313.662 [3313.66.2] of the Revised Code of the impending release and shall provide in that notice information regarding the extent of the education the pupil received while in the custody of the department, including whether the pupil has obtained a certificate of high school equivalence.

If the pupil has not obtained a certificate of high school equivalence while in the custody of the department of youth services, the superintendent of public instruction shall provide the notice required by division (B)(1) of this section and, at least thirty days before the pupil is to be released from institutionalization or institutionalization in a secure facility, conduct an adjudication procedure to determine whether to permanently exclude the pupil from attending the public schools of this state in accordance with this section. If the pupil has obtained a certificate of high school equivalence while in the custody of the department, the superintendent, in the superintendent's discretion, may conduct the adjudication.

(C)(1) Except as provided in division (B)(3) of this section, the date of the adjudication hearing set forth in the notice required by division (B)(1) of this section shall be a date no less than fourteen days nor more than twenty-one days from the date the superintendent sends the notice by certified mail or initiates personal service of the notice.

(2) The superintendent, for good cause shown on the written request of the pupil or the pupil's parent, guardian, or custodian, or on the superintendent's own motion, may grant reasonable continuances of any adjudication hearing held under this section but shall not grant either party total continuances in excess of ten days.

(3) If a pupil or the pupil's parent, guardian, or custodian does not appear at the adjudication hearing on a proposed permanent exclusion, the superintendent or the referee appointed by the superintendent shall proceed to conduct an adjudication hearing on the proposed permanent exclusion on the date for the adjudication hearing that is set forth in the notice provided pursuant to division (B)(1) of this section or on the date to which the hearing was continued pursuant to division (C)(2) of this section.

(D)(1) The superintendent or a referee appointed by the superintendent may conduct an adjudication hearing to determine whether to permanently exclude a pupil in one of the following counties:

(a) The county in which the superintendent holds the superintendent's office;

(b) Upon the request of the pupil or the pupil's parent, guardian, custodian, or attorney, in the county in which the board of education that forwarded the resolution requesting the permanent exclusion is located if the superintendent, in the superintendent's discretion and upon consideration of evidence of hardship presented on behalf of the requesting pupil, determines that the hearing should be conducted in that county.

(2) The superintendent of public instruction or a referee appointed by the superintendent shall conduct an adjudication hearing on a proposed permanent exclusion of a pupil. The referee may be an attorney admitted to the practice of law in this state but shall not be an attorney that represents the board of education that forwarded the resolution requesting the permanent exclusion.

(3) The superintendent or referee who conducts an adjudication hearing under this section may administer oaths, issue subpoenas to compel the attendance of witnesses and evidence, and enforce the subpoenas by a contempt proceeding in the court of common pleas as provided by law. The superintendent or referee may require the separation of witnesses and may bar from the proceedings any person whose presence is not essential to the proceedings.

(4) The superintendent of public instruction shall request the department of rehabilitation and correction, the sheriff, the department of youth services, or any publicly funded out-of-home care entity that has legal custody of a pupil who is the subject of an adjudication hearing held pursuant to this section to transport the pupil to the place of the adjudication hearing at the time and date set for the hearing. The department, sheriff, or publicly funded out-of-home care entity that receives the request shall provide transportation for the pupil who is the subject of the adjudication hearing to the place of the hearing at the time and date set for the hearing. The department, sheriff, or entity shall pay the cost of transporting the pupil to and from the hearing.

(E)(1) An adjudication hearing held pursuant to this section shall be adversary in nature, shall be conducted fairly and impartially, and may be conducted without the formalities of a criminal proceeding. A pupil whose permanent exclusion is being adjudicated has the right to be represented by counsel at the adjudication hearing. If the pupil has the financial capacity to retain counsel, the superintendent or the referee is not required to provide counsel for the pupil. At the adjudication hearing, the pupil also has the right to cross-examine witnesses against the pupil, to testify, to present evidence and the testimony of witnesses on the pupil's behalf, and to raise factors in mitigation of the pupil's being permanently excluded.

(2) In an adjudication hearing held pursuant to this section and section 3313.662 [3313.66.2] of the Revised Code, a representative of the school district of the board of education that adopted and forwarded the resolution requesting the permanent exclusion of the pupil shall present the case for permanent exclusion to the superintendent or the referee. The representative of the school district may be an attorney admitted to the practice of law in this state. At the adjudication hearing, the representative of the school district shall present evidence in support of the requested permanent exclusion. The superintendent or the superintendent's designee shall consider the entire school record of the pupil who is the subject of the adjudication and shall consider any of the following information that is available:

(a) The academic record of the pupil and a record of any extracurricular activities in which the pupil previously was involved;

(b) The disciplinary record of the pupil and any available records of the pupil's prior behavioral problems other than the behavioral problems contained in the disciplinary record;

(c) The social history of the pupil;

(d) The pupil's response to the imposition of prior discipline and sanctions imposed for behavioral problems;

(e) Evidence regarding the seriousness of and any aggravating factors related to the offense that is the basis of the resolution seeking permanent exclusion;

(f) Any mitigating circumstances surrounding the offense that gave rise to the request for permanent exclusion;

(g) Evidence regarding the probable danger posed to the health and safety of other pupils or of school employees by the continued presence of the pupil in a public school setting;

(h) Evidence regarding the probable disruption of the teaching of any school district's graded course of study by the continued presence of the pupil in a public school setting;

(i) Evidence regarding the availability of alternative sanctions of a less serious nature than permanent exclusion that would enable the pupil to remain in a public school setting without posing a significant danger to the health and safety of other pupils or of school employees and without posing a threat of the disruption of the teaching of any district's graded course of study.

(3) In any adjudication hearing conducted pursuant to this section and section 3313.662 [3313.66.2] of the Revised Code, a court order that proves the adjudication or conviction that is the basis for the resolution of the board of education seeking permanent exclusion is suffi-

cient evidence to prove that the pupil committed a violation as specified in division (F)(1) of this section.

(4) The superintendent or the referee shall make or cause to be made a record of any adjudication hearing conducted pursuant to this section.

(5) A referee who conducts an adjudication hearing pursuant to this section shall promptly report the referee's findings in writing to the superintendent at the conclusion of the adjudication hearing.

(F) If an adjudication hearing is conducted or a determination is made pursuant to this section and section 3313.662 [3313.66.2] of the Revised Code, the superintendent shall review and consider the evidence presented, the entire school record of the pupil, and any available information described in divisions (E)(2)(a) to (i) of this section and shall not enter an order of permanent exclusion unless the superintendent or the superintendent's appointed referee finds, by a preponderance of the evidence, both of the following:

(1) That the pupil was convicted of or adjudicated a delinquent child for committing a violation listed in division (A) of section 3313.662 [3313.66.2] of the Revised Code and that the violation was committed when the child was sixteen years of age or older;

(2) That the pupil's continued attendance in the public school system may endanger the health and safety of other pupils or school employees.

(G)(1) Within seven days after the conclusion of an adjudication hearing that is conducted pursuant to this section, the superintendent of public instruction shall enter an order in relation to the permanent exclusion of the pupil who is the subject of the hearing or determination.

(2) If the superintendent or a referee makes the findings described in divisions (F)(1) and (2) of this section, the superintendent shall issue a written order that permanently excludes the pupil from attending any of the public schools of this state and immediately shall send a written notice of the order to the board of education that forwarded the resolution, to the pupil who was the subject of the resolution, to that pupil's parent, guardian, or custodian, and to that pupil's attorney, that includes all of the following:

(a) A copy of the order of permanent exclusion;

(b) A statement informing the pupil and the pupil's parent, guardian, or custodian of the pupil's right to appeal the order of permanent exclusion pursuant to division (H) of this section and of the possible revocation of the permanent exclusion pursuant to division (I) of this section if a final judicial determination reverses the conviction or adjudication that was the basis for the permanent exclusion;

(c) A statement informing the pupil and the pupil's parent, guardian, or custodian of the provisions of divisions (F), (G), and (H) of section 3313.662 [3313.66.2] of the Revised Code.

(3) If the superintendent or a referee does not make the findings described in divisions (F)(1) and (2) of this section, the superintendent shall issue a written order that rejects the resolution of the board of education and immediately shall send written notice of that fact to the board of education that forwarded the resolution, to the pupil who was the subject of the proposed resolution, and to that pupil's parent, guardian, or custodian.

(H) A pupil may appeal an order of permanent exclusion made by the superintendent of public instruction pursuant to this section and section 3313.662 [3313.66.2] of the Revised Code to the court of common pleas of the county in which the board of education that forwarded the resolution requesting the permanent exclusion is located. The appeal shall be conducted in accordance with Chapter 2505. of the Revised Code.

(I) If a final judicial determination reverses the conviction or adjudication that is the basis of a permanent exclusion ordered under this section, the superintendent of public instruction, upon receipt of a certified copy of an order reflecting that final determination from the pupil or that pupil's parent, guardian, custodian, or attorney, shall revoke the order of permanent exclusion.

(J) As used in this section:

(1) "Permanently exclude" and "permanent exclusion" have the same meanings as in section 3313.662 [3313.66.2] of the Revised Code.

(2) "Out-of-home care" and "legal custody" have the same meanings as in section 2151.011 [2151.01.1] of the Revised Code.

(3) "Certificate of high school equivalence" has the same meaning as in section 4109.06 of the Revised Code.

**HISTORY: 144 v H 154 (Eff 7-31-92); 146 v H 1 (Eff 1-1-96); 148 v S 179, § 3. Eff 1-1-2002.**

The effective date is set by section 5 of SB 179.

## [HEAD START PROGRAM]

### § 3301.32 Criminal records check for head start employees responsible for children; employment of certain offenders prohibited.

(A)(1) The chief administrator of any head start agency shall request the superintendent of the bureau of criminal identification and investigation to conduct a criminal records check with respect to any applicant who has applied to the head start agency for employment as a person responsible for the care, custody, or control of a child. If the applicant does not present proof that the applicant has been a resident of this state for the five-year period immediately prior to the date upon which the criminal records check is requested or does not provide evidence that within that five-year period the superintendent has requested information about the applicant from the federal bureau of investigation in a criminal records check, the chief administrator shall request that the superintendent obtain information from the federal bureau of investigation as a part of the criminal records check for the applicant. If the applicant presents proof that the applicant has been a resident of this state for that five-year period, the chief administrator may request that the superintendent include information from the federal bureau of investigation in the criminal records check.

(2) Any person required by division (A)(1) of this section to request a criminal records check shall provide to each applicant a copy of the form prescribed pursuant to division (C)(1) of section 109.572 [109.57.2] of the Revised Code, provide to each applicant a standard impression sheet to obtain fingerprint impressions prescribed pursuant to division (C)(2) of section 109.572 [109.57.2] of the Revised Code, obtain the completed form and impression sheet from each applicant, and forward the completed form and impression sheet to the superintendent of the bureau of criminal identification and investigation at the time the chief administrator requests a criminal records check pursuant to division (A)(1) of this section.

(3) Any applicant who receives pursuant to division (A)(2) of this section a copy of the form prescribed pursuant to division (C)(1) of section 109.572 [109.57.2] of the Revised Code and a copy of an impression sheet prescribed pursuant to division (C)(2) of that section and who is requested to complete the form and provide a set of fingerprint impressions shall complete the form or provide all the information necessary to complete the form and shall provide the impression sheets with the impressions of the applicant's fingerprints. If an applicant, upon request, fails to provide the information necessary to complete the form or fails to provide impressions of the applicant's fingerprints, the head start agency shall not employ that applicant for any position for which a criminal records check is required by division (A)(1) of this section.

(B)(1) Except as provided in rules adopted by the director of job and family services in accordance with division (E) of this section, no head start agency shall employ a person as a person responsible for the care, custody, or control of a child if the person previously has been convicted of or pleaded guilty to any of the following:

(a) A violation of section 2903.01, 2903.02, 2903.03, 2903.04, 2903.11, 2903.12, 2903.13, 2903.16, 2903.21, 2903.34, 2905.01, 2905.02, 2905.05, 2907.02, 2907.03, 2907.04, 2907.05, 2907.06, 2907.07, 2907.08, 2907.09, 2907.21, 2907.22, 2907.23, 2907.25, 2907.31, 2907.32, 2907.321 [2907.32.1], 2907.322 [2907.32.2], 2907.323 [2907.32.3], 2911.01, 2911.02, 2911.11, 2911.12, 2919.12, 2919.22, 2919.24, 2919.25, 2923.12, 2923.13, 2923.161 [2923.16.1], 2925.02, 2925.03, 2925.04, 2925.05, 2925.06, or 3716.11 of the Revised Code, a violation of section 2905.04 of the Revised Code as it existed prior to July 1, 1996, a violation of section 2919.23 of the Revised Code that would have been a violation of section 2905.04 of the Revised Code as it existed prior to July 1, 1996, had the violation occurred prior to that date, a violation of section 2925.11 of the Revised Code that is not a minor drug possession offense, or felonious sexual penetration in violation of former section 2907.12 of the Revised Code;

(b) A violation of an existing or former law of this state, any other state, or the United States that is substantially equivalent to any of the offenses or violations described in division (B)(1)(a) of this section.

(2) A head start agency may employ an applicant conditionally until the criminal records check required by this section is completed and the agency receives the results of the criminal records check. If the results of the criminal records check indicate that, pursuant to division (B)(1) of this section, the applicant does not qualify for employment, the agency shall release the applicant from employment.

(C)(1) Each head start agency shall pay to the bureau of criminal identification and investigation the fee prescribed pursuant to division (C)(3) of section 109.572 [109.57.2] of the Revised Code for each criminal records check conducted in accordance with that section upon the request pursuant to division (A)(1) of this section of the chief administrator of the head start agency.

(2) A head start agency may charge an applicant a fee for the costs it incurs in obtaining a criminal records check under this section. A fee charged under this division shall not exceed the amount of fees the agency pays under division (C)(1) of this section. If a fee is charged under this division, the agency shall notify the applicant at the time of the applicant's initial application for employment of the amount of the fee and that, unless the fee is paid, the head start agency will not consider the applicant for employment.

(D) The report of any criminal records check conducted by the bureau of criminal identification and investigation in accordance with section 109.572 [109.57.2] of the Revised Code and pursuant to a request made under division (A)(1) of this section is not a public record for the purposes of section 149.43 of the Revised Code and shall not be made available to any person other than the applicant who is the subject of the criminal records check or the applicant's representative, the head start agency requesting the criminal records check or its representative, and any court, hearing officer, or other necessary individual involved in a case dealing with the denial of employment to the applicant.

(E) The director of job and family services shall adopt rules pursuant to Chapter 119. of the Revised Code to implement this section, including rules specifying circumstances under which a head start agency may hire a person who has been convicted of an offense listed in division (B)(1) of this section but who meets standards in regard to rehabilitation set by the director.

(F) Any person required by division (A)(1) of this section to request a criminal records check shall inform each person, at the time of the person's initial application for employment, that the person is required to provide a set of impressions of the person's fingerprints and that a criminal records check is required to be conducted and satisfactorily completed in accordance with section 109.572 [109.57.2] of the Revised Code if the person comes under final consideration for appointment or employment as a precondition to employment for that position.

(G) As used in this section:

(1) "Applicant" means a person who is under final consideration for appointment or employment in a position with a head start agency as a person responsible for the care, custody, or control of a child.

(2) "Head start agency" means an entity in this state that has been approved to be an agency for purposes of the "Head Start Act," 95 State 489 (1981), 42 U.S.C. 9831, as amended.

(3) "Criminal records check" has the same meaning as in section 109.572 [109.57.2] of the Revised Code.

(4) "Minor drug possession offense" has the same meaning as in section 2925.01 of the Revised Code.

**HISTORY: 145 v S 38 (Eff 10-29-93); 145 v H 694 (Eff 11-11-94); 146 v S 2 (Eff 7-1-96); 146 v S 269 (Eff 7-1-96); 146 v H 445 (Eff 9-3-96); 148 v H 471. Eff 7-1-2000; 151 v H 66, § 101.01, eff. 6-30-05.**

The effective date is set by § 612.12 of 151 v H 66.

The effective date is set by section 12(A) of HB 471.

The provisions of § 10 of HB 471 (148 v —) read in part as follows:

SECTION 10. * * * Section 3301.32 of the Revised Code is presented in this act as a composite of the section as amended by both Am. Sub. H.B. 445 and Am. Sub. S.B. 269 of the 121st General Assembly, with the new language of neither of the acts shown in capital letters. * * * This is in recognition of the principle stated in division (B) of section 1.52 of the Revised Code that such amendments are to be harmonized where not substantively irreconcilable and constitutes a legislative finding that such is the resulting version in effect prior to the effective date of this act.

See provisions, § 3 of SB 38 (145 v —) following RC § 3301.54.

[PRESCHOOL, SCHOOL CHILD PROGRAMS]

## § 3301.541 Criminal records check for preschool employees responsible for children; employment of certain offenders prohibited.

(A)(1) The director, head teacher, elementary principal, or site administrator of a preschool program shall request the superintendent of the bureau of criminal identification and investigation to conduct a criminal records check with respect to any applicant who has applied to the preschool program for employment as a person responsible for the care, custody, or control of a child. If the applicant does not present proof that the applicant has been a resident of this state for the five-year period immediately prior to the date upon which the criminal records check is requested or does not provide evidence that within that five-year period the superintendent has requested information about the applicant from the federal bureau of investigation in a criminal records check, the director, head teacher, or elementary principal shall request that the superintendent obtain information from the federal bureau of investigation as a part of the criminal records check for the applicant. If the applicant presents proof that the applicant has been a resident of this state for that five-year period, the director, head teacher, or elementary principal may request that the superintendent include information from the federal bureau of investigation in the criminal records check.

(2) Any director, head teacher, elementary principal, or site administrator required by division (A)(1) of this section to request a criminal records check shall provide to each applicant a copy of the form prescribed pursuant to division (C)(1) of section 109.572 [109.57.2] of the Revised Code, provide to each applicant a standard impression sheet to obtain fingerprint impressions prescribed pursuant to division (C)(2) of section 109.572 [109.57.2] of the Revised Code, obtain the completed form and impression sheet from each applicant, and forward the completed form and impression sheet to the superintendent of the bureau of criminal identification and investigation at the time the person requests a criminal records check pursuant to division (A)(1) of this section.

(3) Any applicant who receives pursuant to division (A)(2) of this section a copy of the form prescribed pursuant to division (C)(1) of section 109.572 [109.57.2] of the Revised Code and a copy of an impression sheet prescribed pursuant to division (C)(2) of that section and who is requested to complete the form and provide a set of fingerprint impressions shall complete the form or provide all the information necessary to complete the form and provide the impression sheet with the impressions of the applicant's fingerprints. If an applicant, upon request, fails to provide the information necessary to complete the form or fails to provide impressions of the applicant's fingerprints, the preschool program shall not employ that applicant for any position for which a criminal records check is required by division (A)(1) of this section.

(B)(1) Except as provided in rules adopted by the department of education in accordance with division (E) of this section, no preschool program shall employ a person as a person responsible for the care, custody, or control of a child if the person previously has been convicted of or pleaded guilty to any of the following:

(a) A violation of section 2903.01, 2903.02, 2903.03, 2903.04, 2903.11, 2903.12, 2903.13, 2903.16, 2903.21, 2903.34, 2905.01, 2905.02, 2905.05, 2907.02, 2907.03, 2907.04, 2907.05, 2907.06, 2907.07, 2907.08, 2907.09, 2907.21, 2907.22, 2907.23, 2907.25, 2907.31, 2907.32, 2907.321 [2907.32.1], 2907.322 [2907.32.2], 2907.323 [2907.32.3], 2911.01, 2911.02, 2911.11, 2911.12, 2919.12, 2919.22, 2919.24, 2919.25, 2923.12, 2923.13, 2923.161 [2923.16.1], 2925.02, 2925.03, 2925.04, 2925.05, 2925.06, or 3716.11 of the Revised Code, a violation of section 2905.04 of the Revised Code as it existed prior to July 1, 1996, a violation of section 2919.23 of the Revised Code that would have been a violation of section 2905.04 of the Revised Code as it existed prior to July 1, 1996, had the violation occurred prior to that date, a violation of section 2925.11 of the Revised Code that is not a minor drug possession offense, or felonious sexual penetration in violation of former section 2907.12 of the Revised Code;

(b) A violation of an existing or former law of this state, any other state, or the United States that is substantially equivalent to any of the offenses or violations described in division (B)(1)(a) of this section.

(2) A preschool program may employ an applicant conditionally until the criminal records check required by this section is completed and the preschool program receives the results of the criminal records check. If the results of the criminal records check indicate that, pursuant to division (B)(1) of this section, the applicant does not qualify for employment, the preschool program shall release the applicant from employment.

(C)(1) Each preschool program shall pay to the bureau of criminal identification and investigation the fee prescribed pursuant to division (C)(3) of section 109.572 [109.57.2] of the Revised Code for each criminal records check conducted in accordance with that section upon the request pursuant to division (A)(1) of this section of the director, head teacher, elementary principal, or site administrator of the preschool program.

(2) A preschool program may charge an applicant a fee for the costs it incurs in obtaining a criminal records check under this section. A fee charged under this division shall not exceed the amount of fees the preschool program pays under division (C)(1) of this section. If a fee is charged under this division, the preschool program shall notify the applicant at the time of the applicant's initial application for employment of the amount of the fee and that, unless the fee is paid, the applicant will not be considered for employment.

(D) The report of any criminal records check conducted by the bureau of criminal identification and investigation in accordance with section 109.572 [109.57.2] of the Revised Code and pursuant to a request under division (A)(1) of this section is not a public record for the purposes of section 149.43 of the Revised Code and shall not be made available to any person other than the applicant who is the subject of the criminal records check or the applicant's representative, the preschool program requesting the criminal records check or its representative, and any court, hearing officer, or other necessary individual in a case dealing with the denial of employment to the applicant.

(E) The department of education shall adopt rules pursuant to Chapter 119. of the Revised Code to implement this section, including rules specifying circumstances under which a preschool program may hire a person who has been convicted of an offense listed in division (B)(1) of this section but who meets standards in regard to rehabilitation set by the department.

(F) Any person required by division (A)(1) of this section to request a criminal records check shall inform each person, at the time of the person's initial application for employment, that the person is required to provide a set of impressions of the person's fingerprints and that a criminal records check is required to be conducted and satisfactorily completed in accordance with section 109.572 [109.57.2] of the Revised Code if the person comes under final consideration for appointment or employment as a precondition to employment for that position.

(G) As used in this section:

(1) "Applicant" means a person who is under final consideration for appointment or employment in a position with a preschool program as a person responsible for the care, custody, or control of a child, except that "applicant" does not include a person already employed by a board of education or chartered nonpublic school in a position of care, custody, or control of a child who is under consideration for a different position with such board or school.

(2) "Criminal records check" has the same meaning as in section 109.572 [109.57.2] of the Revised Code.

(3) "Minor drug possession offense" has the same meaning as in section 2925.01 of the Revised Code.

(H) If the board of education of a local school district adopts a resolution requesting the assistance of the educational service center in which the local district has territory in conducting criminal records checks of substitute teachers under this section, the appointing or hiring officer of such educational service center governing board shall serve for purposes of this section as the appointing or hiring officer of the local board in the case of hiring substitute teachers for employment in the local district.

**HISTORY: 145 v S 38 (Eff 10-29-93); 145 v H 694 (Eff 11-11-94); 146 v H 117 (Eff 9-29-95); 146 v S 2 (Eff 7-1-96); 146 v S 269 (Eff 7-1-96); 146 v H 445 (Eff 9-3-96); 147 v H 396. Eff 1-30-98.**

See provisions, § 3 of SB 38 (145 v —) following RC § 3301.54.

# CHAPTER 3313: BOARDS OF EDUCATION



## [POWERS; REGULATIONS]

### § 3313.20 Rules; locker searches; employee attendance at professional meetings.

(A) The board of education of a school district or the governing board of an educational service center shall make any rules that are necessary for its government and the government of its employees, pupils of its schools, and all other persons entering upon its school grounds or premises. Rules regarding entry of persons other than students, staff, and faculty upon school grounds or premises shall be posted conspicuously at or near the entrance to the school grounds or premises, or near the perimeter of the school grounds or premises, if there are no formal entrances, and at the main entrance to each school building.

(B)(1) The board of education of each city, local, exempted village, or joint vocational school district may adopt a written policy that authorizes principals of public schools within the district or their designees to do one or both of the following:

(a) Search any pupil's locker and the contents of the locker that is searched if the principal reasonably suspects that the locker or its contents contains evidence of a pupil's violation of a criminal statute or of a school rule;

(b) Search any pupil's locker and the contents of any pupil's locker at any time if the board of education posts in a conspicuous place in each school building that has lockers available for use by pupils a notice that the lockers are the property of the board of education and that the lockers and the contents of all the lockers are subject to random search at any time without regard to whether there is a reasonable suspicion that any locker or its contents contains evidence of a violation of a criminal statute or a school rule.

(2) A board of education's adoption of or failure to adopt a written policy pursuant to division (B)(1) of this section does not prevent the principal of any school from searching at any time the locker of any pupil and the contents of any locker of any pupil in the school if an emergency situation exists or appears to exist that immediately threatens the health or safety of any person, or threatens to damage or destroy any property, under the control of the board of education and if a search of lockers and the contents of the lockers is reasonably necessary to avert that threat or apparent threat.

(C) Any employee may receive compensation and expenses for days on which he is excused, in accordance with the policy statement of the board, by the superintendent of such board or by a responsible administrative official designated by the superintendent for the purpose of attending professional meetings as defined by the board policy, and the board may provide and pay the salary of a substitute for such days. The expenses thus incurred by an employee shall be paid by the board from the appropriate fund of the school district or the educational service center governing board fund provided that statements of expenses are furnished in accordance with the policy statement of the board.

(D) Each city, local, and exempted village school district shall adopt a written policy governing the attendance of employees at professional meetings.

**HISTORY: GC § 4834-5; 120 v 475 (519); 123 v 659; Bureau of Code Revision, 10-1-53; 125 v 903 (989); 127 v 552 (Eff 9-16-57); 131 v S 21 (Eff 9-1-65); 135 v S 436 (Eff 9-23-74); 140 v S 385 (Eff 4-10-85); 144 v H 154 (Eff 7-31-92); 145 v S 29 (Eff 9-1-94); 146 v H 117. Eff 9-29-95.**

The effective date is set by section 197 of HB 117.

## [MISCELLANEOUS]

### § 3313.66 Suspension, expulsion or permanent exclusion; removal from curricular or extracurricular activities.

(A) Except as provided under division (B)(2) of this section, the superintendent of schools of a city, exempted village, or local school district, or the principal of a public school may suspend a pupil from school for not more than ten school days. The board of education of a city, exempted village, or local school district may adopt a policy granting assistant principals and other administrators the authority to suspend a pupil from school for a period of time as specified in the policy of the board of education, not to exceed ten school days. If at the time a suspension is imposed there are fewer than ten school days remaining in the school year in which the incident that gives rise to the suspension takes place, the superintendent may apply any remaining part or all of the period of the suspension to the following school year. Except in the case of a pupil given an in-school suspension, no pupil shall be suspended unless prior to the suspension such superintendent or principal does both of the following:

(1) Gives the pupil written notice of the intention to suspend the pupil and the reasons for the intended suspension and, if the proposed suspension is based on a violation listed in division (A) of section 3313.662 [3313.66.2] of the Revised Code and if the pupil is sixteen years of age or older, includes in the notice a statement that the superintendent may seek to permanently exclude the pupil if the pupil is convicted of or adjudicated a delinquent child for that violation;

(2) Provides the pupil an opportunity to appear at an informal hearing before the principal, assistant principal, superintendent, or superintendent's designee and challenge the reason for the intended suspension or otherwise to explain the pupil's actions.

(B)(1) Except as provided under division (B)(2), (3), or (4) of this section, the superintendent of schools of a city, exempted village, or local school district may expel a pupil from school for a period not to exceed the greater of eighty school days or the number of school days remaining in the semester or term in which the incident that gives rise to the expulsion takes place, unless the expulsion is extended pursuant to division (F) of this section. If at the time an expulsion is imposed there are fewer than eighty school days remaining in the school year in which the incident that gives rise to the expulsion takes place, the superintendent may apply any remaining part or all of the period of the expulsion to the following school year.

(2)(a) Unless a pupil is permanently excluded pursuant to section 3313.662 [3313.66.2] of the Revised Code, the superintendent of schools of a city, exempted village, or local school district shall expel a pupil from school for a period of one year for bringing a firearm to a school operated by the board of education of the district or onto any other property owned or controlled by the board, except that the superintendent may reduce this requirement on a case-by-case basis in accordance with the policy adopted by the board under section 3313.661 [3313.66.1] of the Revised Code.

(b) The superintendent of schools of a city, exempted village, or local school district may expel a pupil from school for a period of one year for bringing a firearm to an interscholastic competition, an extracurricular event, or any other school program or activity that is not located in a school or on property that is owned or controlled by the district. The superintendent may reduce this disciplinary action on a case-by-case basis in accordance with the policy adopted by the board under section 3313.661 [3313.66.1] of the Revised Code.

(c) Any expulsion pursuant to division (B)(2) of this section shall extend, as necessary, into the school year following the school year in which the incident that gives rise to the expulsion takes place. As used in this division, "firearm" has the same meaning as provided pursuant to the "Gun-Free Schools Act," 115 Stat. 1762, 20 U.S.C. 7151.

(3) The board of education of a city, exempted village, or local school district may adopt a resolution authorizing the superintendent of schools to expel a pupil from school for a period not to exceed one year for bringing a knife to a school operated by the board, onto any other property owned or controlled by the board, or to an interscholastic competition, an extracurricular event, or any other program or activity sponsored by the school district or in which the district is a participant, or for possessing a firearm or knife at a school, on any other property owned or controlled by the board, or at an interscholastic competition, an extracurricular event, or any other school program or activity, which firearm or knife was initially brought onto school board property by another person. The resolution may authorize the superintendent to extend such an expulsion, as necessary, into the school year following the school year in which the incident that gives rise to the expulsion takes place.

(4) The board of education of a city, exempted village, or local school district may adopt a resolution establishing a policy under section 3313.661 [3313.66.1] of the Revised Code that authorizes the superintendent of schools to expel a pupil from school for a period not to exceed one year for committing an act that is a criminal offense when committed by an adult and that results in serious physical harm to persons as defined in division (A)(5) of section 2901.01 of the Revised Code or serious physical harm to property as defined in division (A)(6) of section 2901.01 of the Revised Code while the pupil is at school, on any other property owned or controlled by the board, or at an interscholastic competition, an extracurricular event, or any other school program or activity. Any expulsion under this division shall extend, as necessary, into the school year following the school year in which the incident that gives rise to the expulsion takes place.

(5) The board of education of any city, exempted village, or local school district may adopt a resolution establishing a policy under section 3313.661 [3313.66.1] of the Revised Code that authorizes the superintendent of schools to expel a pupil from school for a period not to exceed one year for making a bomb threat to a school building or to any premises at which a school activity is occurring at the time of the threat. Any expulsion under this division shall extend, as necessary, into the school year following the school year in which the incident that gives rise to the expulsion takes place.

(6) No pupil shall be expelled under division (B)(1), (2), (3), (4) or (5) of this section unless, prior to the pupil's expulsion, the superintendent does both of the following:

(a) Gives the pupil and the pupil's parent, guardian, or custodian written notice of the intention to expel the pupil;

(b) Provides the pupil and the pupil's parent, guardian, custodian, or representative an opportunity to appear in person before the superintendent or the superintendent's designee to challenge the reasons for the intended expulsion or otherwise to explain the pupil's actions.

The notice required in this division shall include the reasons for the intended expulsion, notification of the opportunity of the pupil and the pupil's parent, guardian, custodian, or representative to appear before the superintendent or the superintendent's designee to challenge the reasons for the intended expulsion or otherwise to explain the pupil's action, and notification of the time and place to appear. The time to appear shall not be earlier than three nor later than five school days after the notice is given, unless the superintendent grants an extension of time at the request of the pupil or the pupil's parent, guardian, custodian, or representative. If an extension is granted after giving the original notice, the superintendent shall notify the pupil and the pupil's parent, guardian, custodian, or representative of the new time and place to appear. If the proposed expulsion is based on a violation listed in division (A) of section 3313.662 [3313.66.2] of the Revised Code and if the pupil is sixteen years of age or older, the notice shall include a statement that the superintendent may seek to permanently exclude the pupil if the pupil is convicted of or adjudicated a delinquent child for that violation.

(7) A superintendent of schools of a city, exempted village, or local school district shall initiate expulsion proceedings pursuant to this section with respect to any pupil who has committed an act warranting expulsion under the district's policy regarding expulsion even if the pupil has withdrawn from school for any reason after the incident that gives rise to the hearing but prior to the hearing or decision to impose the expulsion. If, following the hearing, the pupil would have been expelled for a period of time had the pupil still been enrolled in the school, the expulsion shall be imposed for the same length of time as on a pupil who has not withdrawn from the school.

(C) If a pupil's presence poses a continuing danger to persons or property or an ongoing threat of disrupting the academic process taking place either within a classroom or elsewhere on the school premises, the superintendent or a principal or assistant principal may remove a pupil from curricular activities or from the school premises, and a teacher may remove a pupil from curricular activities under the teacher's supervision, without the notice and hearing requirements of division (A) or (B) of this section. As soon as practicable after making such a removal, the teacher shall submit in writing to the principal the reasons for such removal.

If a pupil is removed under this division from a curricular activity or from the school premises, written notice of the hearing and of the reason for the removal shall be given to the pupil as soon as practicable prior to the hearing, which shall be held within three school days from the time the initial removal is ordered. The hearing shall be held in accordance with division (A) of this section unless it is probable that the pupil may be subject to expulsion, in which case a hearing in accordance with division (B) of this section shall be held, except that the hearing shall be held within three school days of the initial removal. The individual who ordered, caused, or requested the removal to be made shall be present at the hearing.

If the superintendent or the principal reinstates a pupil in a curricular activity under the teacher's supervision prior to the hearing following a removal under this division, the teacher, upon request, shall be given in writing the reasons for such reinstatement.

(D) The superintendent or principal, within one school day after the time of a pupil's expulsion or suspension, shall notify in writing the parent, guardian, or custodian of the pupil and the treasurer of the board of education of the expulsion or suspension. The notice shall include the reasons for the expulsion or suspension, notification of the right of the pupil or the pupil's parent, guardian, or custodian to appeal the expulsion or suspension to the board of education or to its designee, to be represented in all appeal proceedings, to be granted a hearing before the board or its designee in order to be heard against the suspension or expulsion, and to request that the hearing be held in executive session, notification that the expulsion may be subject to extension pursuant to division (F) of this section if the pupil is sixteen years of age or older, and notification that the superintendent may seek the pupil's permanent exclusion if the suspension or expulsion was based on a violation listed in division (A) of section 3313.662 [3313.66.2] of the Revised Code that was committed when the child was sixteen years of age or older and if the pupil is convicted of or adjudicated a delinquent child for that violation.

In accordance with the policy adopted by the board of education under section 3313.661 [3313.66.1] of the Revised Code, the notice provided under this division shall specify the manner and date by which the pupil or the pupil's parent, guardian, or custodian shall notify the board of the pupil's, parent's, guardian's, or custodian's intent to appeal the expulsion or suspension to the board or its designee.

Any superintendent expelling a pupil under this section for more than twenty school days or for any period of time if the expulsion will extend into the following semester or school year shall, in the notice required under this division, provide the pupil and the pupil's parent, guardian, or custodian with information about services or programs offered by public and private agencies that work toward improving those aspects of the pupil's attitudes and behavior that contributed to the incident that gave rise to the pupil's expulsion. The information shall include the names, addresses, and phone numbers of the appropriate public and private agencies.

(E) A pupil or the pupil's parent, guardian, or custodian may appeal the pupil's expulsion by a superintendent or suspension by a superintendent, principal, assistant principal, or other administrator to the board of education or to its designee. If the pupil or the pupil's parent, guardian, or custodian intends to appeal the expulsion or suspension to the board or its designee, the pupil or the pupil's parent, guardian, or custodian shall notify the board in the manner and by the date specified in the notice provided under division (D) of this section. The pupil or the pupil's parent, guardian, or custodian may be represented in all appeal proceedings and shall be granted a hearing before the board or its designee in order to be heard against the suspension or expulsion. At the request of the pupil or of the pupil's parent, guardian, custodian, or attorney, the board or its designee may hold the hearing in executive session but shall act upon the suspension or expulsion only at a public meeting. The board, by a majority vote of its full membership or by the action of its designee, may affirm the order of suspension or expulsion, reinstate the pupil, or otherwise reverse, vacate, or modify the order of suspension or expulsion.

The board or its designee shall make a verbatim record of hearings held under this division. The decisions of the board or its designee may be appealed under Chapter 2506. of the Revised Code.

This section shall not be construed to require notice and hearing in accordance with division (A), (B), or (C) of this section in the case of normal disciplinary procedures in which a pupil is removed from a curricular activity for a period of less than one school day and is not subject to suspension or expulsion.

(F)(1) If a pupil is expelled pursuant to division (B) of this section for committing any violation listed in division (A) of section 3313.662 [3313.66.2] of the Revised Code and the pupil was sixteen years of age or older at the time of committing the violation, if a complaint, indictment, or information is filed alleging that the pupil is a delinquent child based upon the commission of the violation or the pupil is prosecuted as an adult for the commission of the violation, and if the resultant juvenile court or criminal proceeding is pending at the time that the expulsion terminates, the superintendent of schools that expelled the pupil may file a motion with the court in which the proceeding is pending requesting an order extending the expulsion for the lesser of an additional eighty days or the number of school days remaining in the school year. Upon the filing of the motion, the court immediately shall schedule a hearing and give written notice of the time, date, and location of the hearing to the superintendent and to the pupil and the pupil's parent, guardian, or custodian. At the hearing, the court shall determine whether there is reasonable cause to believe that the pupil committed the alleged violation that is the basis of the expulsion and, upon determining that reasonable cause to believe the pupil committed the violation does exist, shall grant the requested extension.

(2) If a pupil has been convicted of or adjudicated a delinquent child for a violation listed in division (A) of section 3313.662 [3313.66.2] of the Revised Code for an act that was committed when the child was sixteen years of age or older, if the pupil has been expelled pursuant to division (B) of this section for that violation, and if the board of education of the school district of the school from which the pupil was expelled has adopted a resolution seeking the pupil's permanent exclusion, the superintendent may file a motion with the court that convicted the pupil or adjudicated the pupil a delinquent child requesting an order to extend the expulsion until an adjudication order or other determination regarding permanent exclusion is issued by the superintendent of public instruction pursuant to section 3301.121 [3301.12.1] and division (D) of section 3313.662 [3313.66.2] of the Revised Code. Upon the filing of the motion, the court immediately shall schedule a hearing and give written notice of the time, date, and location of the hearing to the superintendent of the school district, the pupil, and the pupil's parent, guardian, or custodian. At the hearing, the court shall determine whether there is reasonable cause to believe the pupil's continued attendance in the public school system may endanger the health and safety of other pupils or school employees and, upon making that determination, shall grant the requested extension.

(G) The failure of the superintendent or the board of education to provide the information regarding the possibility of permanent exclusion in the notice required by divisions (A), (B), and (D) of this section is not jurisdictional, and the failure shall not affect the validity of any suspension or expulsion procedure that is conducted in accordance with this section or the validity of a permanent exclusion procedure that is conducted in accordance with sections 3301.121 [3301.12.1] and 3313.662 [3313.66.2] of the Revised Code.

(H) With regard to suspensions and expulsions pursuant to divisions (A) and (B) of this section by the board of education of any city, exempted village, or local school district, this section shall apply to any student, whether or not the student is enrolled in the district, attending or otherwise participating in any curricular program provided in a school operated by the board or provided on any other property owned or controlled by the board.

(I) Whenever a student is expelled under this section, the expulsion shall result in removal of the student from the student's regular school setting. However, during the period of the expulsion, the board of education of the school district that expelled the student or any board of education admitting the student during that expulsion period may provide educational services to the student in an alternative setting.

(J)(1) Notwithstanding sections 3109.51 to 3109.80, 3313.64, and 3313.65 of the Revised Code, any school district, after offering an opportunity for a hearing, may temporarily deny admittance to any pupil if one of the following applies:

(a) The pupil has been suspended from the schools of another district under division (A) of this section and the period of suspension, as established under that division, has not expired;

(b) The pupil has been expelled from the schools of another district under division (B) of this section and the period of the expulsion, as established under that division or as extended under division (F) of this section, has not expired.

If a pupil is temporarily denied admission under this division, the pupil shall be admitted to school in accordance with sections 3109.51 to 3109.80, 3313.64, or 3313.65 of the Revised Code no later than upon expiration of the suspension or expulsion period, as applicable.

(2) Notwithstanding sections 3109.51 to 3109.80, 3313.64, and 3313.65 of the Revised Code, any school district, after offering an opportunity for a hearing, may temporarily deny admittance to any pupil if the pupil has been expelled or otherwise removed for disciplinary purposes from a public school in another state and the period of expulsion or removal has not expired. If a pupil is temporarily denied admission under this division, the pupil shall be admitted to school in accordance with sections 3109.51 to 3109.80, 3313.64, or 3313.65 of the Revised Code no later than the earlier of the following:

(a) Upon expiration of the expulsion or removal period imposed by the out-of-state school;

(b) Upon expiration of a period established by the district, beginning with the date of expulsion or removal from the out-of-state school, that is no greater than the period of expulsion that the pupil would have received under the policy adopted by the district under section 3313.661 [3313.66.1] of the Revised Code had the offense that gave rise to the expulsion or removal by the out-of-state school been committed while the pupil was enrolled in the district.

(K) As used in this section:

(1) "Permanently exclude" and "permanent exclusion" have the same meanings as in section 3313.662 [3313.66.2] of the Revised Code.

(2) "In-school suspension" means the pupil will serve all of the suspension in a school setting.

**HISTORY: GC § 4838-4; 120 v 475 (530); Bureau of Code Revision, 10-1-53; 127 v 104 (Eff 9-9-57); 129 v 239 (Eff 7-28-61); 136 v H 421 (Eff 6-4-76); 138 v H 1 (Eff 5-16-79); 141 v H 666 (Eff 3-25-87); 144 v S 51 (Eff 10-29-91); 144 v H 154 (Eff 7-31-92); 145 v H 152 (Eff 7-1-93); 146 v H 64 (Eff 9-14-95); 146 v H 81 (Eff 6-5-96); 148 v S 1 (Eff 8-6-99); 148 v H 620 (Eff 3-12-2001); 148 v S 179, § 3. Eff 1-1-2002; 150 v H 130, § 1, eff. 7-20-04; 152 v H 119, § 101.01, eff. 9-29-07.**

The effective date is set by § 812.03 of 152 v H 119.

The provisions of § 3 of H.B. 130 (150 v —) read as follows:

SECTION 3. Section 3313.66 of the Revised Code is presented in this act as a composite of the section as amended by both H.B. 620 and Am. Sub. S.B. 179 of the 123rd General Assembly. The General Assembly, applying the principle stated in division (B) of section 1.52 of the Revised Code that amendments are to be harmonized if reasonably capable of simultaneous operation, finds that the composite is the resulting version of the section in effect prior to the effective date of the section as presented in this act.

The effective date is set by section 5 of SB 179.

## § 3313.661 Policy regarding suspension, expulsion, removal and permanent exclusion; community service.

(A) The board of education of each city, exempted village, and local school district shall adopt a policy regarding suspension, expulsion, removal, and permanent exclusion that specifies the types of misconduct for which a pupil may be suspended, expelled, or removed. The types of misconduct may include misconduct by a pupil that occurs off of property owned or controlled by the district but that is connected to activities or incidents that have occurred on property owned or controlled by that district and misconduct by a pupil that, regardless of where it occurs, is directed at a district official or employee, or the property of such official or employee. The policy shall specify the reasons for which the superintendent of the district may reduce the expulsion requirement in division (B)(2) of section 3313.66 of the Revised Code. If a board of education adopts a resolution pursuant to division (B)(3) of section 3313.66 of the Revised Code, the policy shall define the term "knife" or "firearm," as applicable, for purposes of expulsion under that resolution and shall specify any reasons for which the superintendent of the district may reduce any required expulsion period on a case-by-case basis. If a board of education adopts a resolution pursuant to division (B)(4) or (5) of section 3313.66 of the Revised Code, the policy shall specify any reasons for which the superintendent of the district may reduce any required expulsion period on a case-by-case basis. The policy also shall set forth the acts listed in section 3313.662 [3313.66.2] of the Revised Code for which a pupil may be permanently excluded.

The policy adopted under this division shall specify the date and manner by which a pupil or a pupil's parent, guardian, or custodian may notify the board of the pupil's, parent's, guardian's, or custodian's intent to appeal an expulsion or suspension to the board or its designee pursuant to division (E) of section 3313.66 of the Revised Code. In the case of any expulsion, the policy shall not specify a date that is less than fourteen days after the date of the notice provided to the pupil or the pupil's parent, guardian, or custodian under division (D) of that section.

A copy of the policy shall be posted in a central location in the school and made available to pupils upon request. No pupil shall be suspended, expelled, or removed except in accordance with the policy adopted by the board of education of the school district in which the pupil attends school, and no pupil shall be permanently excluded except in accordance with sections 3301.121 [3301.12.1] and 3313.662 [3313.66.2] of the Revised Code.

(B) A board of education may establish a program and adopt guidelines under which a superintendent may require a pupil to perform community service in conjunction with a suspension or expulsion imposed under section 3313.66 of the Revised Code or in place of a suspension or expulsion imposed under section 3313.66 of the Revised Code except for an expulsion imposed pursuant to division (B)(2) of that section. If a board adopts guidelines under this division, they shall permit, except with regard to an expulsion pursuant to division (B)(2) of section 3313.66 of the Revised Code, a superintendent to impose a community service requirement beyond the end of the school year in lieu of applying the suspension or expulsion into the following school year. Any guidelines adopted shall be included in the policy adopted under this section.

(C) The written policy of each board of education that is adopted pursuant to section 3313.20 of the Revised Code shall be posted in a central location in each school that is subject to the policy and shall be made available to pupils upon request.

(D) Any policy, program, or guideline adopted by a board of education under this section with regard to suspensions or expulsions pursuant to division (A) or (B) of section 3313.66 of the Revised Code shall apply to any student, whether or not the student is enrolled in the district, attending or otherwise participating in any curricular program provided in a school operated by the board or provided on any other property owned or controlled by the board.

(E) As used in this section, "permanently exclude" and "permanent exclusion" have the same meanings as in section 3313.662 [3313.66.2] of the Revised Code.

**HISTORY: 136 v H 421 (Eff 6-4-76); 144 v S 51 (Eff 10-29-91); 144 v H 154 (Eff 7-31-92); 145 v H 152 (Eff 7-1-93); 146 v H 64 (Eff 9-14-95); 146 v H 81 (Eff 6-5-96); 148 v S 1 (Eff 8-6-99); 148 v H 620. Eff 3-12-2001; 152 v H 119, § 101.01, eff. 9-29-07.**

The effective date is set by § 812.03 of 152 v H 119.

## § 3313.662 Adjudication order permanently excluding pupil from public schools; board of education resolution requesting permanent exclusion; revocation; probationary admission.

(A) The superintendent of public instruction, pursuant to this section and the adjudication procedures of section 3301.121 [3301.12.1] of the Revised Code, may issue an adjudication order that permanently excludes a pupil from attending any of the public schools of this state if the pupil is convicted of, or adjudicated a delinquent child for, committing, when the pupil was sixteen years of age or older, an act that would be a criminal offense if committed by an adult and if the act is any of the following:

(1) A violation of section 2923.122 [2923.12.2] of the Revised Code;

(2) A violation of section 2923.12 of the Revised Code, of a substantially similar municipal ordinance, or of section 2925.03 of the Revised Code that was committed on property owned or controlled by, or at an activity held under the auspices of, a board of education of a city, local, exempted village, or joint vocational school district;

(3) A violation of section 2925.11 of the Revised Code, other than a violation of that section that would be a minor drug possession offense, that was committed on property owned or controlled by, or at an activity held under the auspices of, the board of education of a city, local, exempted village, or joint vocational school district;

(4) A violation of section 2903.01, 2903.02, 2903.03, 2903.04, 2903.11, 2903.12, 2907.02, or 2907.05 or of former section 2907.12 of the Revised Code that was committed on property owned or controlled by, or at an activity held under the auspices of, a board of education of a city, local, exempted village, or joint vocational school district, if the victim at the time of the commission of the act was an employee of that board of education.

(5) Complicity in any violation described in division (A)(1), (2), (3), or (4) of this section that was alleged to have been committed in the manner described in division (A)(1), (2), (3), or (4) of this section, regardless of whether the act of complicity was committed on property owned or controlled by, or at an activity held under the auspices of, a board of education of a city, local, exempted village, or joint vocational school district.

(B) A pupil may be suspended or expelled in accordance with section 3313.66 of the Revised Code prior to being permanently excluded from public school attendance under this section and section 3301.121 [3301.12.1] of the Revised Code.

(C)(1) If the superintendent of a city, local, exempted village, or joint vocational school district in which a pupil attends school obtains or receives proof that the pupil has been convicted of committing when the pupil was sixteen years of age or older a violation listed in division (A) of this section or adjudicated a delinquent child for the commission when the pupil was sixteen years of age or older of a violation listed in division (A) of this section, the superintendent may issue to the board of education of the school district a request that the pupil be permanently excluded from public school attendance, if both of the following apply:

(a) After obtaining or receiving proof of the conviction or adjudication, the superintendent or the superintendent's designee determines that the pupil's continued attendance in school may endanger the health and safety of other pupils or school employees and gives the pupil and the pupil's parent, guardian, or custodian written notice that the superintendent intends to recommend to the board of education that the board adopt a resolution requesting the superintendent of public instruction to permanently exclude the pupil from public school attendance.

(b) The superintendent or the superintendent's designee forwards to the board of education the superintendent's written recommendation that includes the determinations the superintendent or designee made pursuant to division (C)(1)(a) of this section and a copy of the proof the superintendent received showing that the pupil has been convicted of or adjudicated a delinquent child for a violation listed in division (A) of this section that was committed when the pupil was sixteen years of age or older.

(2) Within fourteen days after receipt of a recommendation from the superintendent pursuant to division (C)(1)(b) of this section that a pupil be permanently excluded from public school attendance, the board of education of a city, local, exempted village, or joint vocational school district, after review and consideration of all of the following available information, may adopt a resolution requesting the superintendent of public instruction to permanently exclude the pupil who is the subject of the recommendation from public school attendance:

(a) The academic record of the pupil and a record of any extracurricular activities in which the pupil previously was involved;

(b) The disciplinary record of the pupil and any available records of the pupil's prior behavioral problems other than the behavioral problems contained in the disciplinary record;

(c) The social history of the pupil;

(d) The pupil's response to the imposition of prior discipline and sanctions imposed for behavioral problems;

(e) Evidence regarding the seriousness of and any aggravating factors related to the offense that is the basis of the resolution seeking permanent exclusion;

(f) Any mitigating circumstances surrounding the offense that gave rise to the request for permanent exclusion;

(g) Evidence regarding the probable danger posed to the health and safety of other pupils or of school employees by the continued presence of the pupil in a public school setting;

(h) Evidence regarding the probable disruption of the teaching of any school district's graded course of study by the continued presence of the pupil in a public school setting;

(i) Evidence regarding the availability of alternative sanctions of a less serious nature than permanent exclusion that would enable the pupil to remain in a public school setting without posing a significant danger to the health and safety of other pupils or of school employees and without posing a threat of the disruption of the teaching of any district's graded course of study.

(3) If the board does not adopt a resolution requesting the superintendent of public instruction to permanently exclude the pupil, it immediately shall send written notice of that fact to the superintendent who sought the resolution, to the pupil who was the subject of the proposed resolution, and to that pupil's parent, guardian, or custodian.

(D)(1) Upon adoption of a resolution under division (C) of this section, the board of education immediately shall forward to the superintendent of public instruction the written resolution, proof of the conviction or adjudication that is the basis of the resolution, a copy of the pupil's entire school record, and any other relevant information and shall forward a copy of the resolution to the pupil who is the subject of the recommendation and to that pupil's parent, guardian, or custodian.

(2) The board of education that adopted and forwarded the resolution requesting the permanent exclusion of the pupil to the superintendent of public instruction promptly shall designate a representative of the school district to present the case for permanent exclusion to the superintendent or the referee appointed by the superintendent. The representative of the school district may be an attorney admitted to the practice of law in this state. At the adjudication hearing held pursuant to section 3301.121 [3301.12.1] of the Revised Code, the representative of the

school district shall present evidence in support of the requested permanent exclusion.

(3) Upon receipt of a board of education's resolution requesting the permanent exclusion of a pupil from public school attendance, the superintendent of public instruction, in accordance with the adjudication procedures of section 3301.121 [3301.12.1] of the Revised Code, promptly shall issue an adjudication order that either permanently excludes the pupil from attending any of the public schools of this state or that rejects the resolution of the board of education.

(E) Notwithstanding any provision of section 3313.64 of the Revised Code or an order of any court of this state that otherwise requires the admission of the pupil to a school, no school official in a city, local, exempted village, or joint vocational school district knowingly shall admit to any school in the school district a pupil who has been permanently excluded from public school attendance by the superintendent of public instruction.

(F)(1)(a) Upon determining that the school attendance of a pupil who has been permanently excluded from public school attendance no longer will endanger the health and safety of other students or school employees, the superintendent of any city, local, exempted village, or joint vocational school district in which the pupil desires to attend school may issue to the board of education of the school district a recommendation, including the reasons for the recommendation, that the permanent exclusion of a pupil be revoked and the pupil be allowed to return to the public schools of the state.

If any violation which in whole or in part gave rise to the permanent exclusion of any pupil involved the pupil's bringing a firearm to a school operated by the board of education of a school district or onto any other property owned or operated by such a board, no superintendent shall recommend under this division an effective date for the revocation of the pupil's permanent exclusion that is less than one year after the date on which the last such firearm incident occurred. However, on a case-by-case basis, a superintendent may recommend an earlier effective date for such a revocation for any of the reasons for which the superintendent may reduce the one-year expulsion requirement in division (B)(2) of section 3313.66 of the Revised Code.

(b) Upon receipt of the recommendation of the superintendent that a permanent exclusion of a pupil be revoked, the board of education of a city, local, exempted village, or joint vocational school district may adopt a resolution by a majority vote of its members requesting the superintendent of public instruction to revoke the permanent exclusion of the pupil. Upon adoption of the resolution, the board of education shall forward a copy of the resolution, the reasons for the resolution, and any other relevant information to the superintendent of public instruction.

(c) Upon receipt of a resolution of a board of education requesting the revocation of a permanent exclusion of a pupil, the superintendent of public instruction, in accordance with the adjudication procedures of Chapter 119. of the Revised Code, shall issue an adjudication order that revokes the permanent exclusion of the pupil from public school attendance or that rejects the resolution of the board of education.

(2)(a) A pupil who has been permanently excluded pursuant to this section and section 3301.121 [3301.12.1] of the Revised Code may request the superintendent of any city, local, exempted village, or joint vocational school district in which the pupil desires to attend school to admit the pupil on a probationary basis for a period not to exceed ninety school days. Upon receiving the request, the superintendent may enter into discussions with the pupil and with the pupil's parent, guardian, or custodian or a person designated by the pupil's parent, guardian, or custodian to develop a probationary admission plan designed to assist the pupil's probationary admission to the school. The plan may include a treatment program, a behavioral modification program, or any other program reasonably designed to meet the educational needs of the child and the disciplinary requirements of the school.

If any violation which in whole or in part gave rise to the permanent exclusion of the pupil involved the pupil's bringing a firearm to a school operated by the board of education of any school district or onto any other property owned or operated by such a board, no plan developed under this division for the pupil shall include an effective date for the probationary admission of the pupil that is less than one year after the date on which the last such firearm incident occurred except that on a case-by-case basis, a plan may include an earlier effective date for such an admission for any of the reasons for which the superintendent of the district may reduce the one-year expulsion requirement in division (B)(2) of section 3313.66 of the Revised Code.

(b) If the superintendent of a school district, a pupil, and the pupil's parent, guardian, or custodian or a person designated by the pupil's parent, guardian, or custodian agree upon a probationary admission plan prepared pursuant to division (F)(2)(a) of this section, the superintendent of the school district shall issue to the board of education of the school district a recommendation that the pupil be allowed to attend school within the school district under probationary admission, the reasons for the recommendation, and a copy of the agreed upon probationary admission plan. Within fourteen days after the board of education receives the recommendation, reasons, and plan, the board may adopt the recommendation by a majority vote of its members. If the board adopts the recommendation, the pupil may attend school under probationary admission within that school district for a period not to exceed ninety days or any additional probationary period permitted under divisions (F)(2)(d) and (e) of this section in accordance with the probationary admission plan prepared pursuant to division (F)(2)(a) of this section.

(c) If a pupil who is permitted to attend school under probationary admission pursuant to division (F)(2)(b) of this section fails to comply with the probationary admission plan prepared pursuant to division (F)(2)(a) of this section, the superintendent of the school district immediately may remove the pupil from the school and issue to the board of education of the school district a recommendation that the probationary admission be revoked. Within five days after the board of education receives the recommendation, the board may adopt the recommendation to revoke the pupil's probationary admission by a majority vote of its members. If a majority of the board does not adopt the recommendation to revoke the pupil's probationary admission, the pupil shall continue to attend school in compliance with the pupil's probationary admission plan.

(d) If a pupil who is permitted to attend school under probationary admission pursuant to division (F)(2)(b) of this section complies with the probationary admission plan prepared pursuant to division (F)(2)(a) of this section, the pupil or the pupil's parent, guardian, or custodian, at any time before the expiration of the ninety-day probationary admission period, may request the superintendent of the school district to extend the terms and period of the pupil's probationary admission for a period not to exceed ninety days or to issue a recommendation pursuant to division (F)(1) of this section that the pupil's permanent exclusion be revoked and the pupil be allowed to return to the public schools of this state.

(e) If a pupil is granted an extension of the pupil's probationary admission pursuant to division (F)(2)(d) of this section, the pupil or the pupil's parent, guardian, or custodian, in the manner described in that division, may request, and the superintendent and board, in the manner described in that division, may recommend and grant, subsequent probationary admission periods not to exceed ninety days each. If a pupil who is permitted to attend school under an extension of a probationary admission plan complies with the probationary admission plan prepared pursuant to the extension, the pupil or the pupil's parent, guardian, or custodian may request a revocation of the pupil's permanent exclusion in the manner described in division (F)(2)(d) of this section.

(f) Any extension of a probationary admission requested by a pupil or a pupil's parent, guardian, or custodian pursuant to divisions (F)(2)(d) or (e) of this section shall be subject to the adoption and approval of a probationary admission plan in the manner described in divisions (F)(2)(a) and (b) of this section and may be terminated as provided in division (F)(2)(c) of this section.

(g) If the pupil has complied with any probationary admission plan and the superintendent issues a recommendation that seeks revocation of the pupil's permanent exclusion pursuant to division (F)(1) of this section, the pupil's compliance with any probationary admission plan may be considered along with other relevant factors in any determination or adjudication conducted pursuant to division (F)(1) of this section.

(G)(1) Except as provided in division (G)(2) of this section, any information regarding the permanent exclusion of a pupil shall be included in the pupil's official records and shall be included in any records sent to any school district that requests the pupil's records.

(2) When a pupil who has been permanently excluded from public school attendance reaches the age of twenty-two or when the permanent exclusion of a pupil has been revoked, all school districts that maintain records regarding the pupil's permanent exclusion shall remove all references to the exclusion from the pupil's file and shall destroy them.

A pupil who has reached the age of twenty-two or whose permanent exclusion has been revoked may send a written notice to the superintendent of any school district maintaining records of the pupil's permanent exclusion requesting the superintendent to ensure that the records are removed from the pupil's file and destroyed. Upon receipt of the request and a determination that the pupil is twenty-two years of age or older or that the pupil's permanent exclusion has been revoked, the superintendent shall ensure that the records are removed from the pupil's file and destroyed.

(H)(1) This section does not apply to any of the following:

(a) An institution that is a residential facility, that receives and cares for children, that is maintained by the department of youth services, and that operates a school chartered by the state board of education under section 3301.16 of the Revised Code;

(b) Any on-premises school operated by an out-of-home care entity, other than a school district, that is chartered by the state board of education under section 3301.16 of the Revised Code;

(c) Any school operated in connection with an out-of-home care entity or a nonresidential youth treatment program that enters into a contract or agreement with a school district for the provision of educational services in a setting other than a setting that is a building or structure owned or controlled by the board of education of the school district during normal school hours.

(2) This section does not prohibit any person who has been permanently excluded pursuant to this section and section 3301.121 [3301.12.1] of the Revised Code from seeking a certificate of high school equivalence. A person who has been permanently excluded may be permitted to participate in a course of study in preparation for the tests of general educational development, except that the person shall not participate during normal school hours in that course of study in any building or structure owned or controlled by the board of education of a school district.

(3) This section does not relieve any school district from any requirement under section 2151.362 [2151.36.2] or 3313.64 of the Revised Code to pay for the cost of educating any child who has been permanently excluded pursuant to this section and section 3301.121 [3301.12.1] of the Revised Code.

(I) As used in this section:

(1) "Permanently exclude" means to forever prohibit an individual from attending any public school in this state that is operated by a city, local, exempted village, or joint vocational school district.

(2) "Permanent exclusion" means the prohibition of a pupil forever from attending any public school in this state that is operated by a city, local, exempted village, or joint vocational school district.

(3) "Out-of-home care" has the same meaning as in section 2151.011 [2151.01.1] of the Revised Code.

(4) "Certificate of high school equivalence" has the same meaning as in section 4109.06 of the Revised Code.

(5) "Nonresidential youth treatment program" means a program designed to provide services to persons under the age of eighteen in a setting that does not regularly provide long-term overnight care, including settlement houses, diversion and prevention programs, run-away centers, and alternative education programs.

(6) "Firearm" has the same meaning as provided pursuant to the "Gun-Free Schools Act of 1994," 108 Stat. 270, 20 U.S.C. 8001(a)(2).

(7) "Minor drug possession offense" has the same meaning as in section 2925.01 of the Revised Code.

**HISTORY: 144 v H 154 (Eff 7-31-92); 146 v H 64 (Eff 9-14-95); 146 v S 2 (Eff 7-1-96); 146 v H 445. Eff 9-3-96; 150 v H 106, § 1, eff. 9-16-04; 151 v H 137, § 1, eff. 10-9-06.**

The effective date is set by § 6 of 151 v H 137.

[USE OF SCHOOLHOUSES]

## § 3313.752 Posting of warning concerning anabolic steroids.

As used in this section, "anabolic steroid" has the same meaning as in section 3719.41 of the Revised Code.

The board of education of each city, local, exempted village, and joint vocational school district shall require the following warning to be conspicuously posted in the locker rooms of each of the district's school buildings that includes any grade higher than sixth grade:

"Warning: Improper use of anabolic steroids may cause serious or fatal health problems, such as heart disease, stroke, cancer, growth deformities, infertility, personality changes, severe acne, and baldness. Possession, sale, or use of anabolic steroids without a valid prescription is a crime punishable by a fine and imprisonment."

**HISTORY: 144 v H 62. Eff 5-21-91.**

# CHAPTER 3319: SCHOOLS — SUPERINTENDENT; TEACHERS; EMPLOYEES

Section



[TEACHERS]

## § 3319.20 Prosecutor to notify board of nonlicensed employee's guilty plea or conviction of certain offenses or eligibility for intervention in lieu of conviction or diversion program.

(A) Whenever an employee of a board of education, other than an employee who is a license holder to whom section 3319.52 of the Revised Code applies, is convicted of or pleads guilty to a felony, a violation of section 2907.04 or 2907.06 or of division (A) or (B) of section 2907.07 of the Revised Code, an offense of violence, theft offense, or drug abuse offense that is not a minor misdemeanor, or a violation of an ordinance of a municipal corporation that is substantively comparable to a felony or to a violation or offense of that nature, or if the employee has been found to be eligible for intervention in lieu of conviction or has agreed to participate in a pre-trial diversion program for one of those offenses, the prosecutor in the case, on forms prescribed and furnished by the state board of education, shall notify the employing board of education of the employee's name and residence address, the fact that the employee was convicted of, pleaded guilty to, has been found eligible for intervention in lieu of conviction for, or has agreed to a diversion program for the specified offense, the section of the Revised Code or the municipal ordinance violated, and the sentence imposed by the court.

(B) In the case of a conviction or guilty plea, the prosecutor shall give the notification required by this section no earlier than the fifth day following the expiration of the period within which the employee may file a notice of appeal from the judgment of the trial court under Appellate Rule 4(B) and no later than the eighth day following the expiration of that period. The notification also shall indicate whether the employee appealed the conviction, and, if applicable, the court in which the appeal will be heard. If the employee is permitted, by leave of court pursuant to Appellate Rule 5, to appeal the judgment of the trial court subsequent to the expiration of the period for filing a notice of appeal under Appellate Rule 4(B), the prosecutor promptly shall notify the employing board of education of the appeal and the court in which the appeal will be heard.

(C) In the case of a finding of eligibility for intervention in lieu of conviction or an agreement to participate in a pre-trial diversion program, the prosecutor shall give the notification required by this section by a deadline prescribed by the state board.

(D) As used in this section:

(1) "Drug abuse offense" has the same meaning as in section 2925.01 of the Revised Code.

(2) "Intervention in lieu of conviction" means intervention in lieu of conviction under section 2951.041 [2951.04.1] of the Revised Code.

(3) "Pre-trial diversion program" means a pre-trial diversion program under section 2935.36 of the Revised Code or a similar diversion program under rules of a court.

(4) "Prosecutor" has the same meaning as in section 2935.01 of the Revised Code.

(5) "Theft offense" has the same meaning as in section 2913.01 of the Revised Code.

**HISTORY: 140 v H 109 (Eff 9-27-83); 145 v H 152 (Eff 7-1-93); 146 v S 2 (Eff 7-1-96); 146 v S 230. Eff 10-29-96; 150 v S 5, § 1, eff. 7-31-03; 152 v H 428, § 1, eff. 9-12-08.**

**Not analogous to former RC § 3319.20 (GC § 4857; 120 v 475(587); Bureau of Code Revision, 10-1-53), repealed 126 v 655(697), § 2, eff 1-3-56.**

# CHAPTER 3321: SCHOOL ATTENDANCE



## [FAILURE TO SEND CHILD TO SCHOOL]

### § 3321.38 Violation of compulsory attendance laws; bond.

(A) No parent, guardian, or other person having care of a child of compulsory school age shall violate any provision of section 3321.01, 3321.03, 3321.04, 3321.07, 3321.10, 3321.19, 3321.20, or 3331.14 of the Revised Code. The juvenile court, which has exclusive original jurisdiction over any violation of this section pursuant to section 2151.23 of the Revised Code, may require a person convicted of violating this division to give bond in a sum of not more than five hundred dollars with sureties to the approval of the court, conditioned that the person will cause the child under the person's charge to attend upon instruction as provided by law, and remain as a pupil in the school or class during the term prescribed by law. If the juvenile court adjudicates the child as an unruly or delinquent child for being an habitual or chronic truant pursuant to section 2151.35 of the Revised Code, the court shall warn the parent, guardian, or other person having care of the child that any subsequent adjudication of that nature involving the child may result in a criminal charge against the parent, guardian, or other person having care of the child for a violation of division (C) of section 2919.21 or section 2919.24 of the Revised Code.

(B) This section does not relieve from prosecution and conviction any parent, guardian, or other person upon further violation of any provision in any of the sections specified in division (A) of this section, any provision of section 2919.222 [2919.22.2] or 2919.24 of the Revised Code, or division (C) of section 2919.21 of the Revised Code. A forfeiture of the bond shall not relieve that parent, guardian, or other person from prosecution and conviction upon further violation of any provision in any of those sections or that division.

(C) Section 4109.13 of the Revised Code applies to this section.

(D) No parent, guardian, or other person having care of a child of compulsary school age shall fail to give bond as required by division (A) of this section in the sum of one hundred dollars with sureties as required by the court.

**HISTORY: RS §§ 4022-1, 4022-2; 86 v 333, 334; 87 v 143; 87 v 316; 89 v 389; 90 v 285; 95 v 615; 97 v 365; GC §§ 12974, 12975; Bureau of Code Revision, 10-1-53; 126 v 655(684) (Eff 1-3-56); 129 v 582(781) (Eff 1-10-61); 137 v H 883 (Eff 1-12-79); 143 v S 140 (Eff 10-2-89); 146 v S 2 (Eff 7-1-96); 148 v S 181. Eff 9-4-2000; 149 v H 490, § 1, eff. 1-1-04.**

The effective date is set by section 4 of H.B. 490.

While GC § 12975 as enacted in 109 v 376 purports to amend former GC § 12975, it is not, in fact, an amendment thereof.

### § 3321.99 Penalty.

Whoever violates division (A) of section 3321.38 of the Revised Code may be fined not more than five hundred dollars or may be ordered to perform not more than seventy hours of community service work.

**HISTORY: Bureau of Code Revision, 10-1-53; 132 v S 191 (Eff 11-14-67); 146 v S 2 (Eff 7-1-96); 148 v S 181. Eff 9-4-2000.**

# CHAPTER 3327: TRANSPORTATION; TUITION



### § 3327.10 Qualifications of drivers.

(A) No person shall be employed as driver of a school bus or motor van, owned and operated by any school district or educational service center or privately owned and operated under contract with any school district or service center in this state, who has not received a certificate from the educational service center governing board in case such person is employed by a service center or by a local school district under the supervision of the service center governing board, or by the superintendent of schools, in case such person is employed by the board of a city or exempted village school district, certifying that such person is at least eighteen years of age and is of good moral character and is qualified physically and otherwise for such position. The service center governing board or the superintendent, as the case may be, shall provide for an annual physical examination that conforms with rules adopted by the state board of education of each driver to ascertain the driver's physical fitness for such employment. Any certificate may be revoked by the authority granting the same on proof that the holder has been guilty of failing to comply with division (D)(1) of this section, or upon a conviction or a guilty plea for a violation, or any other action, that results in a loss or suspension of driving rights. Failure to comply with such division may be cause for disciplinary action or termination of employment under division (C) of section 3319.081 [3319.08.1], or section 124.34 of the Revised Code.

(B) No person shall be employed as driver of a school bus or motor van not subject to the rules of the department of education pursuant to division (A) of this section who has not received a certificate from the school administrator or contractor certifying that such person is at least eighteen years of age, is of good moral character, and is qualified physically and otherwise for such position. Each driver shall have an annual physical examination which conforms to the state highway patrol rules, ascertaining the driver's physical fitness for such employment. The examination shall be performed by one of the following:

(1) A person licensed under Chapter 4731. of the Revised Code or by another state to practice medicine and surgery or osteopathic medicine and surgery;

(2) A physician assistant;

(3) A certified nurse practitioner;

(4) A clinical nurse specialist;

(5) A certified nurse-midwife.

Any written documentation of the physical examination shall be completed by the individual who performed the examination.

Any certificate may be revoked by the authority granting the same on proof that the holder has been guilty of failing to comply with division (D)(2) of this section.

(C) Any person who drives a school bus or motor van must give satisfactory and sufficient bond except a driver who is an employee of a school district and who drives a bus or motor van owned by the school district.

(D) No person employed as driver of a school bus or motor van under this section who is convicted of a traffic violation or who has had the person's commercial driver's license suspended shall drive a school bus or motor van until the person has filed a written notice of the conviction or suspension, as follows:

(1) If the person is employed under division (A) of this section, the person shall file the notice with the superintendent, or a person designated by the superintendent, of the school district for which the person drives a school bus or motor van as an employee or drives a privately owned and operated school bus or motor van under contract.

(2) If employed under division (B) of this section, the person shall file the notice with the employing school administrator or contractor, or a person designated by the administrator or contractor.

(E) In addition to resulting in possible revocation of a certificate as authorized by divisions (A) and (B) of this section, violation of division (D) of this section is a minor misdemeanor.

(F)(1) Not later than thirty days after June 30, 2007, each owner of a school bus or motor van shall obtain the complete driving record for each person who is currently employed or otherwise authorized to drive the school bus or motor van. An owner of a school bus or motor van shall not permit a person to operate the school bus or motor van for the first time before the owner has obtained the person's complete driving record. Thereafter, the owner of a school bus or motor van shall obtain the person's driving record not less frequently than semiannually if the person remains employed or otherwise authorized to drive the school bus or motor van. An owner of a school bus or motor van shall not permit a person to resume operating a school bus or motor van, after an interruption of one year or longer, before the owner has obtained the person's complete driving record.

(2) The owner of a school bus or motor van shall not permit a person to operate the school bus or motor van for six years after the date on which the person pleads guilty to or is convicted of a violation of section 4511.19 of the Revised Code or a substantially equivalent municipal ordinance.

(3) An owner of a school bus or motor van shall not permit any person to operate such a vehicle unless the person meets all other requirements contained in rules adopted by the state board of education prescribing qualifications of drivers of school buses and other student transportation.

(G) No superintendent of a school district, educational service center, community school, or public or private employer shall permit the operation of a vehicle used for pupil transportation within this state by an individual unless both of the following apply:

(1) Information pertaining to that driver has been submitted to the department of education, pursuant to procedures adopted by that department. Information to be reported shall include the name of the employer or school district, name of the driver, driver license number, date of birth, date of hire, status of physical evaluation, and status of training.

(2) The most recent criminal records check required by division (J) of this section has been completed and received by the superintendent or public or private employer.

(H) A person, school district, educational service center, community school, nonpublic school, or other public or nonpublic entity that owns a school bus or motor van, or that contracts with another entity to operate a school bus or motor van, may impose more stringent restrictions on drivers than those prescribed in this section, in any other section of the Revised Code, and in rules adopted by the state board.

(I) For qualified drivers who, on July 1, 2007, are employed by the owner of a school bus or motor van to drive the school bus or motor van, any instance in which the driver was convicted of or pleaded guilty to a violation of section 4511.19 of the Revised Code or a substantially equivalent municipal ordinance prior to two years prior to July 1, 2007, shall not be considered a disqualifying event with respect to division (F) of this section.

(J)(1) This division applies to persons hired by a school district, educational service center, community school, chartered nonpublic school, or science, technology, engineering, and mathematics school established under Chapter 3326. of the Revised Code to operate a vehicle used for pupil transportation.

For each person to whom this division applies who is hired on or after November 14, 2007, the employer shall request a criminal records check in accordance with section 3319.39 of the Revised Code and every six years thereafter. For each person to whom this division applies who is hired prior to that date, the employer shall request a criminal records check by a date prescribed by the department of education and every six years thereafter.

(2) This division applies to persons hired by a public or private employer not described in division (J)(1) of this section to operate a vehicle used for pupil transportation.

For each person to whom this division applies who is hired on or after November 14, 2007, the employer shall request a criminal records check prior to the person's hiring and every six years thereafter. For each person to whom this division applies who is hired prior to that date, the employer shall request a criminal records check by a date prescribed by the department and every six years thereafter.

(3) Each request for a criminal records check under division (J) of this section shall be made to the superintendent of the bureau of criminal identification and investigation in the manner prescribed in section 3319.39 of the Revised Code, except that if both of the following conditions apply to the person subject to the records check, the employer shall request the superintendent only to obtain any criminal records that the federal bureau of investigation has on the person:

(a) The employer previously requested the superintendent to determine whether the bureau of criminal identification and investigation has any information, gathered pursuant to division (A) of section 109.57 of the Revised Code, on the person in conjunction with a criminal records check requested under section 3319.39 of the Revised Code or under division (J) of this section.

(b) The person presents proof that the person has been a resident of this state for the five-year period immediately prior to the date upon which the person becomes subject to a criminal records check under this section.

Upon receipt of a request, the superintendent shall conduct the criminal records check in accordance with section 109.572 [109.57.2] of the Revised Code as if the request had been made under section 3319.39 of the Revised Code. However, as specified in division (B)(2) of section 109.572 [109.57.2] of the Revised Code, if the employer requests the superintendent only to obtain any criminal records that the federal bureau of investigation has on the person for whom the request is made, the superintendent shall not conduct the review prescribed by division (B)(1) of that section.

(K)(1) Until the effective date of the amendments to rule 3301-83-23 of the Ohio Administrative Code required by the second paragraph of division (E) of section 3319.39 of the Revised Code, any person who is the subject of a criminal records check under division (J) of this section and has been convicted of or pleaded guilty to any offense described in division (B)(1) of section 3319.39 of the Revised Code shall not be hired or shall be released from employment, as applicable, unless the person meets the rehabilitation standards prescribed for nonlicensed school personnel by rule 3301-20-03 of the Ohio Administrative Code.

(2) Beginning on the effective date of the amendments to rule 3301-83-23 of the Ohio Administrative Code required by the second paragraph of division (E) of section 3319.39 of the Revised Code, any person who is the subject of a criminal records check under division (J) of this section and has been convicted of or pleaded guilty to any offense that, under the rule, disqualifies a person for employment to operate a vehicle used for pupil transportation shall not be hired or shall be released from employment, as applicable, unless the person meets the rehabilitation standards prescribed by the rule.

**HISTORY: GC § 4855-7; 120 v 475(587); Bureau of Code Revision, 10-1-53; 129 v 1003 (Eff 7-19-61); 130 v 764 (Eff 10-14-63); 135 v S 1 (Eff 1-1-74); 140 v H 295 (Eff 6-28-84); 143 v H 381 (Eff 7-1-89); 146 v H 117 (Eff 9-29-95); 149 v H 94 (Eff 9-5-2001); 149 v S 245, § 1. Eff 3-31-2003; 149 v S 123, § 1, eff. 1-1-04; 151 v S 154, § 1, eff. 5-17-06; 152 v H 67, § 101.01, eff. 6-30-07; 152 v S 97, § 1, eff. 7-1-07; 152 v H 190, § 1, eff. 11-14-07; 152 v H 428, § 1, eff. 9-12-08; 153 v H 1, § 101.01, eff. 1-1-10; 153 v H 19, § 1, eff. 3-29-10.**

The effective date is set by § 812.10 of 153 v H 1.

The effective date is set by § 3 of 152 v S 97.

The provisions of § 5 of 152 v S 97 read as follows:

SECTION 5. This act is hereby declared to be an emergency measure necessary for the immediate preservation of the public peace, health, and safety. The reason for such necessity is that the changes to the state's Sex Offender Registration and Notification Law made by this act are crucially needed to provide increased protection and security for the state's residents from persons who have been convicted of, or found to be delinquent for committing, a sexually oriented offense or a child-victim oriented offense and to conform that Law by July 1, 2007, to recently enacted requirements of federal law. Therefore, this act shall go into immediate effect.

The effective date is set by § 609.10 of 152 v H 67.

The effective date is set by section 4 of S.B. 123.

The provisions of § 5 of S.B. 123 (149 v —), as amended by § 3 of H.B. 163 (150 v —), read as follows:

SECTION 5. (A) Notwithstanding division (B) of section 1.58 of the Revised Code, the provisions of the Revised Code amended or enacted in Sections 1 and 2 of Am. Sub. S.B. 123 of the 124th General Assembly shall apply only in relation to conduct and offenses committed on or after January 1, 2004. Conduct and offenses committed prior to January 1, 2004, shall be governed by the law in effect on the date the conduct or offense was committed.

° ° °

# CHAPTER 3345: STATE UNIVERSITIES — GENERAL POWERS

Section



## § 3345.13 Duplication of keys.

No person shall knowingly make or cause to be made any key for any building, laboratory, facility, or room of any college or university which is supported wholly or in part by the state of Ohio, contrary to any regulation respecting duplication of keys adopted by the board of trustees of such college or university.

**HISTORY: 129 v 1666. Eff 9-9-61.**

## § 3345.34 Student trustee not to receive special benefits.

(A) No student trustee of a state university or the northeast Ohio medical university shall use the trusteeship to influence any grade or other evaluation of the student trustee's performance made by a member of the faculty or other employee of the university.

(B) No member of the faculty or other employee of a state university or the northeast Ohio medical university shall confer any favor, advantage, preference, or other benefit on a student trustee because of the student's trusteeship.

**HISTORY: 142 v H 34. Eff 7-26-88; 152 v H 562, § 101.01, eff. 9-23-08; 2011 HB 139, § 1, eff. Apr. 29, 2011.**

The effective date is set by § 812.10 of 152 v H 562.

## § 3345.41 Posting of warning concerning anabolic steroids.

(A) As used in this section:

(1) "Anabolic steroid" has the same meaning as in section 3719.41 of the Revised Code.

(2) "State university or college" has the same meaning as in section 3345.32 of the Revised Code.

(B) The board of trustees of each state university or college shall require the following warning to be conspicuously posted in locker rooms of recreational and athletic facilities operated by the state university or college for use by students:

"Warning: Improper use of anabolic steroids may cause serious or fatal health problems, such as heart disease, stroke, cancer, growth deformities, infertility, personality changes, severe acne, and baldness. Possession, sale, or use of anabolic steroids without a valid prescription is a crime punishable by a fine and imprisonment."

**HISTORY: 144 v H 62. Eff 5-21-91.**

[FISCAL WATCHES]

## § 3345.78 Duties of employees and officers of institution.

No current or former employee or current or former officer of a state university or college shall knowingly conceal any information from, withhold any information requested by, falsify any information to, or impede the work of any of the following:

(A) A conservator, governance authority, or executive director appointed for the institution under section 3345.74 or 3345.75 of the Revised Code;

(B) Any personnel appointed by the conservator or executive director under division (F) of section 3345.74 or division (B)(1) of section 3345.75 of the Revised Code.

**HISTORY: 147 v S 6. Eff 6-20-97.**

The effective date is set by section 6 of SB 6.

## § 3345.99 Penalties.

(A) Whoever violates section 3345.13 of the Revised Code shall be fined not less than fifty nor more than one hundred fifty dollars.

(B) Whoever violates division (A) or (B) of section 3345.34 of the Revised Code is guilty of a misdemeanor of the first degree.

(C) Whoever violates section 3345.78 of the Revised Code is guilty of a felony of the fourth degree.

**HISTORY: 129 v 1666 (Eff 9-9-61); 142 v H 34 (Eff 7-26-88); 147 v S 6. Eff 6-20-97.**

The effective date is set by section 6 of SB 6.

# TITLE 35: ELECTIONS

## CHAPTER 3599: OFFENSES AND PENALTIES



### § 3599.01 Bribery.

(A) No person shall before, during, or after any primary, convention, or election:

(1) Give, lend, offer, or procure or promise to give, lend, offer, or procure any money, office, position, place or employment, influence, or any other valuable consideration to or for a delegate, elector, or other person;

(2) Attempt by intimidation, coercion, or other unlawful means to induce such delegate or elector to register or refrain from registering or to vote or refrain from voting at a primary, convention, or election for a particular person, question, or issue;

(3) Advance, pay, or cause to be paid or procure or offer to procure money or other valuable thing to or for the use of another, with the intent that it or part thereof shall be used to induce such person to vote or to refrain from voting.

(B) Whoever violates this section is guilty of bribery, a felony of the fourth degree; and if he is a candidate he shall forfeit the nomination he received, or if elected to any office he shall forfeit the office to which he was elected at the election with reference to which such offense was committed.

**HISTORY: GC § 4785-190; 113 v 307(399), § 190; Bureau of Code Revision, 10-1-53; 126 v 575 (Eff 10-6-55); 139 v S 199. Eff 1-1-83.**

The effective date of SB 199 is set by section 11 of the act.

### § 3599.02 Bribery offenses concerning voters or potential voters.

No person shall before, during, or after any primary, general, or special election or convention solicit, request, demand, receive, or contract for any money, gift, loan, property, influence, position, employment, or other thing of value for that person or for another person for doing any of the following:

(A) Registering or refraining from registering to vote;

(B) Agreeing to register or to refrain from registering to vote;

(C) Agreeing to vote or to refrain from voting;

(D) Voting or refraining from voting at any primary, general, or special election or convention for a particular person, question, or issue;

(E) Registering or voting, or refraining from registering or voting, or voting or refraining from voting for a particular person, question, or issue.

Whoever violates this section is guilty of bribery, a felony of the fourth degree, and shall be disfranchised and excluded from holding any public office for five years immediately following such conviction.

**HISTORY: GC § 4785-191; 113 v 307(399), § 191; Bureau of Code Revision, Eff 10-1-53; 147 v S 116. Eff 12-9-97.**

## § 3599.03 Limitations on use of corporate or union funds or property for political purposes [Contingent amendment — see Editor's note].

(A)(1) Except to carry on activities specified in sections 3517.082 [3517.08.2] and 3517.1011 [3517.10.11], division (A)(2) of section 3517.1012 [3517.10.12], division (B) of section 3517.1013 [3517.10.13], division (C)(1) of section 3517.1014 [3517.10.14], and section 3599.031 [3599.03.1] of the Revised Code and except as provided in divisions (D), (E), and (F) of this section, no corporation, no nonprofit corporation, and no labor organization, directly or indirectly, shall pay or use, or offer, advise, consent, or agree to pay or use, the corporation's money or property, or the labor organization's money, including dues, initiation fees, or other assessments paid by members, or property, for or in aid of or opposition to a political party, a candidate for election or nomination to public office, a political action committee including a political action committee of the corporation or labor organization, a legislative campaign fund, or any organization that supports or opposes any such candidate, or for any partisan political purpose, shall violate any law requiring the filing of an affidavit or statement respecting such use of those funds, or shall pay or use the corporation's or labor organization's money for the expenses of a social fundraising event for its political action committee if an employee's or labor organization member's right to attend such an event is predicated on the employee's or member's contribution to the corporation's or labor organization's political action committee.

(2) Whoever violates division (A)(1) of this section shall be fined not less than five hundred nor more than five thousand dollars.

(B)(1) No officer, stockholder, attorney, or agent of a corporation or nonprofit corporation, no member, including an officer, attorney, or agent, of a labor organization, and no candidate, political party official, or other individual shall knowingly aid, advise, solicit, or receive money or other property in violation of division (A)(1) of this section.

(2) Whoever violates division (B)(1) of this section shall be fined not more than one thousand dollars, or imprisoned not more than one year, or both.

(C) A corporation, a nonprofit corporation, or a labor organization may use its funds or property for or in aid of or opposition to a proposed or certified ballot issue. Such use of funds or property shall be reported on a form prescribed by the secretary of state. Reports of contributions in connection with statewide ballot issues shall be filed with the secretary of state. Reports of contributions in connection with local issues shall be filed with the board of elections of the most populous county of the district in which the issue is submitted or to be submitted to the electors. Reports made pursuant to this division shall be filed by the times specified in divisions (A)(1) and (2) of section 3517.10 of the Revised Code.

(D)(1) Any gift made pursuant to section 3517.101 [3517.10.1] of the Revised Code does not constitute a violation of this section or of any other section of the Revised Code.

(2) Any gift made pursuant to division (A)(2) of section 3517.1012 [3517.10.12] of the Revised Code does not constitute a violation of this section.

(3) Any gift made pursuant to division (B) of section 3517.1013 [3517.10.13] of the Revised Code does not constitute a violation of this section.

(4) Any donation made pursuant to division (C)(1) of section 3517.1014 [3517.10.14] of the Revised Code does not constitute a violation of this section.

(E) Any compensation or fees paid by a financial institution to a state political party for services rendered pursuant to division (B) of section 3517.19 of the Revised Code do not constitute a violation of this section or of any other section of the Revised Code.

(F)(1) The use by a nonprofit corporation of its money or property for communicating information for a purpose specified in division (A) of this section is not a violation of that division if the stockholders, members, donors, trustees, or officers of the nonprofit corporation are the predominant recipients of the communication.

(2) The placement of a campaign sign on the property of a corporation, nonprofit corporation, or labor organization is not a use of property in violation of division (A) of this section by that corporation, nonprofit corporation, or labor organization.

(3) The use by a corporation or labor organization of its money or property for communicating information for a purpose specified in division (A) of this section is not a violation of that division if it is not a communication made by mass broadcast such as radio or television or made by advertising in a newspaper of general circulation but is a communication sent exclusively to members, employees, officers, or trustees of that labor organization or shareholders, employees, officers, or directors of that corporation or to members of the immediate families of any such individuals or if the communication intended to be so sent exclusively is unintentionally sent as well to a de minimis number of other individuals.

(G) In addition to the laws listed in division (A) of section 4117.10 of the Revised Code that prevail over conflicting agreements between employee organizations and public employers, this section prevails over any conflicting provisions of agreements between labor organizations and public employers that are entered into on or after March 31, 2005, pursuant to Chapter 4117. of the Revised Code.

(H) As used in this section, "labor organization" has the same meaning as in section 3517.01 of the Revised Code.

**HISTORY: 150 v H 1, § 1, eff. 3-31-05; 153 v H 5, § 1, eff. 9-10-10.**

This section was amended by House Bill 194 of the 2011 legislative session. However, referendum petitions were filed to prevent House Bill 194 from taking effect as scheduled on September 30, 2011. This version of the section will remain in effect at least until the referendum election.

The provisions of § 3 of 151 v S 115 read as follows:

SECTION 3. This act is hereby declared to be an emergency measure necessary for the immediate preservation of the public peace, health, and safety. The reason for the necessity is that the Court of Common Pleas of Franklin County has issued a preliminary injunction prohibiting the enforcement of section 3599.03 of the Revised Code, as enacted by Am. Sub. H.B. 1 of the 125th General Assembly, Special Session, in *United Auto Workers Local Union 1112 v. Blackwell* (March 30, 2005), Case No. O5CVH-03-2553. Therefore, this act shall go into immediate effect.

**Analogous to former RC § 3599.03 (GC § 4785-192; 113 v 307(400), § 192; Bureau of Code Revision, 10-1-53; 138 v H 1062 (Eff 3-23-81); 142 v H 354 (Eff 9-22-87); 143 v S 6 (Eff 10-30-89); 146 v S 8. Eff 8-23-95), repealed 150 v H 1 (special session), § 2, eff 3-31-05.**

## § 3599.03 Limitations on use of corporate or union funds or property for political purposes [Contingent amendment — see Editor's note].

(A)(1)(a) Subject to division (A)(1)(b) of this section, no corporation, no nonprofit corporation, and no labor organization, directly or indirectly, shall pay or use, or offer, advise, consent, or agree to pay or use, the corporation's money or property, or the labor organization's money, including dues, initiation fees, or other assessments paid by members, or property, to make a contribution to a political party, a candidate for election or nomination to public office, a political action committee including a political action committee of the corporation or labor organization, a legislative campaign fund, or any organization that supports or opposes any such candidate, shall violate any law requiring the filing of an affidavit or statement respecting such use of those funds, or shall pay or use the corporation's or labor organization's money for the expenses of a social fund-raising event for its political action committee if an employee's or labor organization member's right to attend such an event is predicated on the employee's or member's contribution to the corporation's or labor organization's political action committee.

(b) Nothing in this section prohibits a labor organization from making a contribution to a candidate's campaign committee or to another political entity or from making an independent expenditure.

(2) Whoever violates division (A)(1)(a) of this section shall be fined not less than five hundred nor more than five thousand dollars.

(B)(1) No officer, stockholder, attorney, or agent of a corporation or nonprofit corporation, no member, including an officer, attorney, or agent, of a labor organization, and no candidate, political party official, or other individual shall knowingly aid, advise, solicit, or receive money or other property in violation of division (A)(1)(a) of this section.

(2) Whoever violates division (B)(1) of this section shall be fined not more than one thousand dollars, or imprisoned not more than one year, or both.

(C) A corporation, a nonprofit corporation, or a labor organization may use its funds or property for or in aid of or opposition to a proposed or certified ballot issue. Such use of funds or property shall be reported on a form prescribed by the secretary of state. Reports of contributions in connection with statewide ballot issues shall be filed with the secretary of state. Reports of contributions in connection with local issues shall be filed with the board of elections of the most populous county of the district in which the issue is submitted or to be submitted to the electors. Reports made pursuant to this division shall be filed by the times specified in divisions (A)(1) and (2) of section 3517.10 of the Revised Code.

(D)(1) Any gift made pursuant to section 3517.101 of the Revised Code does not constitute a violation of this section or of any other section of the Revised Code.

(2) Any gift made pursuant to division (A)(2) of section 3517.1012 of the Revised Code does not constitute a violation of this section.

(3) Any gift made pursuant to division (B) of section 3517.1013 of the Revised Code does not constitute a violation of this section.

(4) Any donation made pursuant to division (C)(1) of section 3517.1014 of the Revised Code does not constitute a violation of this section.

(E) Any compensation or fees paid by a financial institution to a state political party for services rendered pursuant to division (B) of section 3517.19 of the Revised Code do not constitute a violation of this section or of any other section of the Revised Code.

(F)(1) The use by a nonprofit corporation of its money or property for communicating information for a purpose specified in division (A) of this section is not a violation of that division if the stockholders, members, donors, trustees, or officers of the nonprofit corporation are the predominant recipients of the communication.

(2) The placement of a campaign sign on the property of a corporation, nonprofit corporation, or labor organization is not a use of property in violation of division (A) of this section by that corporation, nonprofit corporation, or labor organization.

(3) The use by a corporation or labor organization of its money or property for communicating information for a purpose specified in division (A) of this section is not a violation of that division if it is not a communication made by mass broadcast such as radio or television or made by advertising in a newspaper of general circulation but is a communication sent exclusively to members, employees, officers, or trustees of that labor organization or shareholders, employees, officers, or directors of that corporation or to members of the immediate families of any such individuals or if the communication intended to be so sent exclusively is unintentionally sent as well to a de minimis number of other individuals.

(G) In addition to the laws listed in division (A) of section 4117.10 of the Revised Code that prevail over conflicting agreements between employee organizations and public employers, this section prevails over any conflicting provisions of agreements between labor organizations and public employers that are entered into on or after March 31, 2005, pursuant to Chapter 4117. of the Revised Code.

(H) As used in this section, "labor organization" has the same meaning as in section 3517.01 of the Revised Code.

**HISTORY: 150 v H 1, § 1, eff. 3-31-05; 153 v H 5, § 1, eff. 9-10-10; 2011 HB 194, § 1, eff. Sept. 30, 2011.**

This section was amended by House Bill 194 of the 2011 legislative session. However, referendum petitions were filed to prevent House Bill 194 from taking effect as scheduled on September 30, 2011. This version of the section will take effect if approved at the referendum election.

The provisions of § 3 of 151 v S 115 read as follows:

SECTION 3. This act is hereby declared to be an emergency measure necessary for the immediate preservation of the public peace, health, and safety. The reason for the necessity is that the Court of Common Pleas of Franklin County has issued a preliminary injunction prohibiting the enforcement of section 3599.03 of the Revised Code, as enacted by Am. Sub. H.B. 1 of the 125th General Assembly, Special Session, in *United Auto Workers Local Union 1112 v. Blackwell* (March 30, 2005), Case No. O5CVH-03-2553. Therefore, this act shall go into immediate effect.

**Analogous to former RC § 3599.03 (GC § 4785-192; 113 v 307(400), § 192; Bureau of Code Revision, 10-1-53; 138 v H 1062 (Eff 3-23-81); 142 v H 354 (Eff 9-22-87); 143 v S 6 (Eff 10-30-89); 146 v S 8. Eff 8-23-95), repealed 150 v H 1 (special session), § 2, eff 3-31-05.**

## § 3599.031 Payroll deduction of political contributions.

(A) Notwithstanding any provision of the Revised Code to the contrary and subject to division (C) of section 3517.09 of the Revised Code and division (B) of this section, any employer may deduct from the wages and salaries of its employees amounts for an account described in division (B) of this section, a separate segregated fund, a political action committee of the employer, a political action committee of a labor organization of the employer's employees, a political action committee of an association of which the employer is a member, a political party, a person making disbursements to pay the direct costs of producing or airing electioneering communications, or a ballot issue that the employee by written authorization may designate and shall transmit any amounts so deducted as a separate written authorization described in division (B) of this section shall direct. Any authorization authorizing a deduction from an employee's wages or salary may be on a form that is used to apply for or authorize membership in or authorize payment of dues or fees to any organization, but the authorization for a deduction shall be stated and signed separately from the application for membership or the authorization for the payment of dues or fees. The employer either may deduct from the amount to be so transmitted a uniform amount determined by the employer to be necessary to defray the actual cost of making such deduction and transmittal, or may utilize its own funds in an amount it determines is necessary to defray the actual administrative cost, including making the deduction and transmittal.

(B) If an employer establishes a separate account in the name of an employee for the purpose of depositing into the account amounts deducted from the wages and salary of the employee pursuant to division (A) of this section or amounts directly given by the employee to the employer for the support of a candidate, a separate segregated fund, a political action committee of the employer, a political action committee of a labor organization of the employer's employees, a political action committee of an association of which the employer is a member, a political party, a legislative campaign fund, a person making disbursements to pay the direct costs of producing or airing electioneering communications, or a ballot issue, the employee shall sign a written authorization designating the recipient of a disbursement from that account. The written authorization required under this division is separate and distinct from a written authorization required under division (A) of this section. The authorization required under this division shall clearly identify and designate the candidate, separate segregated fund, political action committee of the employer, political action committee of a labor organization of the employer's employees, political action committee of an association of which the employer is a member, political party, legislative campaign fund, person making disbursements to pay the direct costs of producing or airing electioneering communications, or ballot issue that is to receive any disbursement from the account established pursuant to this division. No person shall designate the recipient of a disbursement from the account except the employee from whose account the disbursement is made. No employer shall make a disbursement from the account of an employee established under this division unless the employer has received the written authorization required under this division.

(C) An employer shall furnish the recipient of any amount transmitted pursuant to this section with the employer's full name and the full name of the labor organization of which the employee whose amount is being transmitted is a member, if any. An employer shall keep and maintain the authorization forms of all its employees from whose wages and salaries any amounts were deducted pursuant to division (A) of this section and the authorizations of disbursements from accounts established under division (B) of this section for a period of at least six years after the year in which the deductions and disbursements were made.

(D) An employee who has made an authorization pursuant to division (A) or (B) of this section may revoke that authorization at any time. A revocation of the authorization does not affect any deduction already made from an employee's wages and salary or any amounts already transmitted or disbursed under this section.

(E) For purposes of this section and for the purpose of the information required to be filed under division (B)(4)(b)(iii) of section 3517.10 of the Revised Code:

(1) If an employer is a corporation, each subsidiary of a parent corporation shall be considered an entity separate and distinct from any other subsidiary and separate and distinct from the parent corporation.

(2) Each national, regional, state, and local affiliate of a labor organization shall be considered a distinct entity.

(F) Whoever violates division (B) of this section shall be fined not less than fifty nor more than five hundred dollars for each disbursement made in violation of that division.

(G) In addition to the laws listed in division (A) of section 4117.10 of the Revised Code that prevail over conflicting agreements between employee organizations and public employers, this section prevails over any conflicting provisions of agreements between labor organizations and public employers that are entered into on or after the effective date of this amendment pursuant to Chapter 4117. of the Revised Code.

(H) As used in this section:

(1) " Electioneering communication," "legislative campaign fund," "labor organization," "political action committee," and "separate segregated fund" have the same meanings as in section 3517.01 of the Revised Code.

(2) "Public employer" means an employer that is the state or a state agency, authority, commission, or board, a political subdivision of the state, a school district or state institution of higher learning, a public or special district, or any other public employer.

(3) "Employee" includes only an employee who is a resident of or is employed in this state.

**HISTORY: 135 v S 46 (Eff 7-23-74); 136 v H 1379 (Eff 6-23-76); 142 v H 354 (Eff 9-22-87); 146 v S 8. Eff 8-23-95; 150 v H 1, § 1, eff. 3-31-05.**

## § 3599.04 Contributions for illegal purposes.

No person shall, directly or indirectly, in connection with any election, pay, lend, or contribute or offer or promise to pay, lend, or contribute any money or other valuable consideration in the election or defeat of any candidate or the adoption or defeat of any question or issue for any purposes other than those enumerated in sections 3517.08 and 3517.12 of the Revised Code.

Whoever violates this section is guilty of corrupt practices and shall be fined not less than twenty-five nor more than five hundred dollars.

**HISTORY: GC § 4785-193; 133 v 307(400), § 193; Bureau of Code Revision. Eff 10-1-53.**

## § 3599.05 Employer shall not influence political action of employee.

No employer or his agent or a corporation shall print or authorize to be printed upon any pay envelopes any statements intended or calculated to influence the political action of his or its employees; or post or exhibit in the establishment or anywhere in or about the establishment any posters, placards, or hand bills containing any threat, notice, or information that if any particular candidate is elected or defeated work in the establishment will cease in whole or in part, or other threats expressed or implied, intended to influence the political opinions or votes of his or its employees.

Whoever violates this section is guilty of corrupt practices, and shall be punished by a fine of not less than five hundred nor more than one thousand dollars.

**HISTORY: GC § 4785-194; 113 v 307(400), § 194; Bureau of Code Revision. Eff 10-1-53.**

## § 3599.06 Employer shall not interfere with employee on election day.

No employer, his officer or agent, shall discharge or threaten to discharge an elector for taking a reasonable amount of time to vote on election day; or require or order an elector to accompany him to a voting place upon such day; or refuse to permit such elector to serve as an election official on any registration or election day; or indirectly use any force or restraint or threaten to inflict any injury, harm, or loss; or in any other manner practice intimidation in order to induce or compel such person to vote or refrain from voting for or against any person or question or issue submitted to the voters.

Whoever violates this section shall be fined not less than fifty nor more than five hundred dollars.

**HISTORY: GC § 4785-195; 113 v 307(400), § 195; Bureau of Code Revision. Eff 10-1-53.**

## § 3599.07 Unlawful possession of ballots [Contingent amendment — see Editor's note].

No judge of elections, observer, or police officer admitted into the polling rooms at the election, at any time while the polls are open, shall have in the individual's possession, distribute, or give out any ballot or ticket to any person on any pretense during the receiving, counting, or certifying of the votes, or have any ballot or ticket in the individual's possession or control, except in the proper discharge of the individual's official duty in receiving, counting, or canvassing the votes. This section does not prevent the lawful exercise by a judge of elections or observer of the individual right to vote at such election.

**HISTORY: GC § 4785-133; 113 v 307(369), § 133; Bureau of Code Revision. Eff 10-1-53; RC § 3505.25, 151 v H 3, § 1, eff. 5-2-06; RC § 3599.07, 152 v S 286, § 1, eff. 2-27-08.**

This section was amended by House Bill 194 of the 2011 legislative session. However, referendum petitions were filed to prevent House Bill 194 from taking effect as scheduled on September 30, 2011. This version of the section will remain in effect at least until the referendum election.

**Not analogous to former RC § 3599.07 (GC § 4785-196; 113 v 307(401); Bureau of Code Revision, 10-1-53), repealed 135 v S 46, § 2, eff 7-23-74.**

**Publisher's Note:**

This section was renumbered from RC § 3505.25 by 152 v S 286, effective February 27, 2008.

## § 3599.07 Unlawful possession of ballots [Contingent amendment — see Editor's note].

No precinct election official, observer, or police officer admitted into the polling rooms at the election, at any time while the polls are open, shall have in the individual's possession, distribute, or give out any ballot or ticket to any person on any pretense during the receiving, counting, or certifying of the votes, or have any ballot or ticket in the individual's possession or control, except in the proper discharge of the individual's official duty in receiving, counting, or canvassing the votes. This section does not prevent the lawful exercise by a precinct election official or observer of the individual right to vote at such election.

**HISTORY: GC § 4785-133; 113 v 307(369), § 133; Bureau of Code Revision. Eff 10-1-53; RC § 3505.25, 151 v H 3, § 1, eff. 5-2-06; RC § 3599.07, 152 v S 286, § 1, eff. 2-27-08; 2011 HB 194, § 1, eff. Sept. 30, 2011.**

This section was amended by House Bill 194 of the 2011 legislative session. However, referendum petitions were filed to prevent House Bill 194 from taking effect as scheduled on September 30, 2011. This version of the section will take effect if approved at the referendum election.

**Not analogous to former RC § 3599.07 (GC § 4785-196; 113 v 307(401); Bureau of Code Revision, 10-1-53), repealed 135 v S 46, § 2, eff 7-23-74.**

**Publisher's Note:**

This section was renumbered from RC § 3505.25 by 152 v S 286, effective February 27, 2008.

## § 3599.08 Influencing candidates and voters by publications.

No owner, editor, writer, or employee of any newspaper, magazine, or other publication of any description, whether published regularly or irregularly, shall use the columns of any such publication for the printing of any threats, direct or implied, in the columns of any such publication for the purpose of controlling or intimidating candidates for public office. Such person shall not directly or indirectly solicit, receive, or accept any payment, promise, or compensation for influencing or attempting to influence votes through any printing matter, except through matter inserted in such publication as "paid advertisement" and so designated.

Whoever violates this section is guilty of a corrupt practice and shall be fined not less than five hundred nor more than one thousand dollars.

**HISTORY: GC § 4785-197; 113 v 307(401), § 197; Bureau of Code Revision. Eff 10-1-53.**

## § 3599.09 Fine for unlawfully seeking multiple offices.

Whoever knowingly violates division (A) of section 3513.052 [3513.05.2] is guilty of seeking nomination or election to more than one prohibited office at the same election and shall be fined not more than five hundred dollars.

**HISTORY: 149 v H 445. Eff 12-23-2002.**

**Not analogous to former RC § 3599.09, amended and renumbered RC § 3517.21 in 146 v S 9, eff 8-24-95.**

## § 3599.10 Candidate for general assembly shall not be asked to pledge vote on legislation.

No person, firm, or corporation shall demand of any candidate for the general assembly any pledge concerning his vote on any legislation, question, or proposition that may come before the general assembly; provided that this shall not be understood to prohibit a reasonable inquiry as to such candidate's views on such question or legislation.

Whoever violates this section is guilty of a corrupt practice and shall be fined not less than five hundred nor more than one thousand dollars.

**HISTORY: GC § 4785-200; 113 v 307(402), § 200; Bureau of Code Revision. Eff 10-1-53.**

## § 3599.11 False registration; election falsification.

(A) No person shall knowingly register or make application or attempt to register in a precinct in which the person is not a qualified voter; or knowingly aid or abet any person to so register; or attempt to register or knowingly induce or attempt to induce any person to so register; or knowingly impersonate another or write or assume the name of another, real or fictitious, in registering or attempting to register; or by false statement or other unlawful means procure, aid, or attempt to procure the erasure or striking out on the register or duplicate list of the name of a qualified elector therein; or knowingly induce or attempt to induce a registrar or other election authority to refuse registration in a precinct to an elector thereof; or knowingly swear or affirm falsely upon a lawful examination by or before any registering officer; or make, print, or issue any false or counterfeit certificate of registration or knowingly alter any certificate of registration.

No person shall knowingly register under more than one name or knowingly induce any person to so register.

No person shall knowingly make any false statement on any form for registration or change of registration or upon any application or return envelope for an absent voter's ballot.

Whoever violates this division is guilty of a felony of the fifth degree.

(B)(1) No person who helps another person register outside an official voter registration place shall knowingly destroy, or knowingly help another person to destroy, any completed registration form.

Whoever violates this division is guilty of election falsification, a felony of the fifth degree.

(2)(a) No person who helps another person register outside an official voter registration place shall knowingly fail to return any registration form entrusted to that person to any board of elections or the office of the secretary of state within ten days after that regsitration† form is completed, or on or before the thirtieth day before the election, whichever day is earlier, unless the registration form is received by the person within twenty-four hours of the thirtieth day before the election, in which case the person shall return the registration form to any board of elections or the office of the secretary of state within ten days of its receipt.

Whoever violates this division is guilty of election falsification, a felony of the fifth degree, unless the person has not previously been convicted of a violation of division (B)(2)(a), (B)(2)(b), (C)(1), or (C)(2) of this section, the violation of this division does not cause any person to miss any voter registration deadline with regard to any election, and the number of voter registration forms that the violator has failed to properly return does not exceed forty-nine, in which case the violator is guilty of a misdemeanor of the first degree.

(b) Subject to division (C)(2) of this section, no person who helps another person register outside an official registration place shall knowingly return any registration form entrusted to that person to any location other than any board of elections or the office of the secretary of state.

Whoever violates this division is guilty of election falsification, a felony of the fifth degree, unless the person has not previously been convicted of a violation of division (B)(2)(a), (B)(2)(b), (C)(1), or (C)(2) of this section, the violation of this division does not cause any person to miss any voter registration deadline with regard to any election, and the number of voter registration forms that the violator has failed to properly return does not exceed forty-nine, in which case the violator is guilty of a misdemeanor of the first degree.

(C)(1) No person who receives compensation for registering a voter shall knowingly fail to return any registration form entrusted to that person to any board of elections or the office of the secretary of state within ten days after that voter registration form is completed, or on or before the thirtieth day before the election, whichever is earlier, unless the registration form is received by the person within twenty-four hours of the thirtieth day before the election, in which case the person shall return the registration form to any board of elections or the office of the secrtary†† of state within ten days of its receipt.

Whoever violates this division is guilty of election falsification, a felony of the fifth degree, unless the person has not previously been convicted of a violation of division (B)(2)(a), (B)(2)(b), (C)(1), or (C)(2) of this section, the violation of this division does not cause any person to miss any voter registration deadline with regard to any election, and the number of voter registration forms that the violator has failed to properly return does not exceed forty-nine, in which case the violator is guilty of a misdemeanor of the first degree.

(2) No person who receives compensation for registering a voter shall knowingly return any registration form entrusted to that person to any location other than any board of elections or the office of the secretary of state.

Whoever violates this division is guilty of election falsification, a felony of the fifth degree, unless the person has not previously been convicted of a violation of division (B)(2)(a), (B)(2)(b), (C)(1), or (C)(2) of this section, the violation of this division does not cause any person to miss any voter registration deadline with regard to any election, and the number of voter registration forms that the violator has failed to properly return does not exceed forty-nine, in which case the violator is guilty of a misdemeanor of the first degree.

(D) As used in division (C) of this section, "registering a voter" includes any effort, for compensation, to provide voter registration forms or to assist persons in completing or returning those forms.

**HISTORY: GC § 4785-201; 113 v 307(402), § 201; Bureau of Code Revision, 10-1-53; 134 v S 460 (Eff 3-23-72); 137 v S 125 (Eff 5-27-77); 137 v H 1209 (Eff 11-3-78); 146 v S 2 (Eff 7-1-96); 147 v S 116. Eff 12-9-97; 151 v H 3, § 1, eff. 5-2-06.**

† As enrolled, subsection (B)(2)(a), 151 v H 3.
†† As enrolled, subsection (C)(1), 151 v H 3.

## § 3599.111 Receiving or paying improper compensation for circulating petition or registering voter.

(A) As used in this section, "registering a voter" or "registering voters" includes any effort, for compensation, to provide voter registration forms or to assist persons in completing or returning those forms.

(B) No person shall receive compensation on a fee per signature or fee per volume basis for circulating any declaration of candidacy, nominating petition, initiative petition, referendum petition, recall petition, or any other election-related petition that is filed with or transmitted to a board of elections, the office of the secretary of state, or other appropriate public office.

(C) No person shall receive compensation on a fee per registration or fee per volume basis for registering a voter.

(D) No person shall pay any other person for collecting signatures on election-related petitions or for registering voters except on the basis of time worked.

(E)(1) Whoever violates division (B) of this section is guilty of receiving improper compensation for circulating a petition, a felony of the fifth degree.

(2) Whoever violates division (C) of this section is guilty of receiving improper compensation for registering a voter, a felony of the fifth degree.

(3) Whoever violates division (D) of this section is guilty of paying improper compensation for circulating a petition or registering a voter, a felony of the fifth degree.

**HISTORY: 150 v H 1, § 1, eff. 3-31-05; 151 v H 3, § 1, eff. 5-2-06.**

## § 3599.12 Illegal voting.

(A) No person shall do any of the following:

(1) Vote or attempt to vote in any primary, special, or general election in a precinct in which that person is not a legally qualified elector;

(2) Vote or attempt to vote more than once at the same election by any means, including voting or attempting to vote both by absent voter's ballots under division (G) of section 3503.16 of the Revised Code and by regular ballot at the polls at the same election, or voting or attempting to vote both by absent voter's ballots under division (G) of section 3503.16 of the Revised Code and by absent voter's ballots under Chapter 3509. or armed service absent voter's ballots under Chapter 3511. of the Revised Code at the same election;

(3) Impersonate or sign the name of another person, real or fictitious, living or dead, and vote or attempt to vote as that other person in any such election;

(4) Cast a ballot at any such election after objection has been made and sustained to that person's vote;

(5) Knowingly vote or attempt to vote a ballot other than the official ballot.

(B) Whoever violates division (A) of this section is guilty of a felony of the fourth degree.

**HISTORY: GC § 4785-202; 113 v 307(403), § 202; Bureau of Code Revision, 10-1-53; 139 v S 199 (Eff 1-1-83); 147 v S 116. Eff 12-9-97; 151 v H 234, § 1, eff. 1-27-06.**

## § 3599.13 Prohibitions concerning signatures on petition or declaration of candidacy.

(A) No person shall do any of the following:

(1) Sign an initiative, supplementary, referendum, recall, or nominating petition knowing that the person is not at the time qualified to sign it;

(2) Knowingly sign such a petition more than once;

(3) Except as otherwise provided in section 3501.382 [3501.38.2] of the Revised Code, sign a name other than the person's own on such a petition;

(4) Accept anything of value for signing such a petition;

(5) Seek by intimidation or threats to influence any person to sign or refrain from signing such a petition, or from circulating or abstaining from circulating such a petition;

(6) Sign a declaration of candidacy and petition for a candidate of a party with which the person is not affiliated, as required by section 3513.05 of the Revised Code;

(7) Make a false affidavit or statement concerning the signatures on any such petition.

(B) Whoever violates division (A) of this section shall be fined not less than fifty or more than five hundred dollars, or imprisoned not less than three or more than six months, or both.

**HISTORY: GC § 4785-203; 113 v 307(403), § 203; Bureau of Code Revision, 10-1-53; 138 v H 1062. Eff 3-23-81; 151 v H 3, § 1, eff. 5-2-06.**

## § 3599.14 Prohibitions relating to petitions or declarations.

(A) No person shall knowingly, directly or indirectly, do any of the following in connection with any declaration of candidacy and petition, declaration of intent to be a write-in candidate, nominating petition, or other petition presented to or filed with the secretary of state, a board of elections, or any other public office for the purpose of becoming a candidate for any elective office, including the office of a political party, for the purpose of submitting a question or issue to the electors at an election, or for the purpose of forming a political party:

(1) Misrepresent the contents, purpose, or effect of the petition or declaration for the purpose of persuading a person to sign or refrain from signing the petition or declaration;

(2) Pay or offer to pay anything of value for signing or refraining from signing the petition or declaration;

(3) Promise to assist any person to obtain appointment to an office or position as a consideration for obtaining or preventing signatures to the petition or declaration;

(4) Obtain or prevent signatures to the petition or declaration as a consideration for the assistance or promise of assistance of a person in securing appointment to an office or position;

(5) Circulate or cause to be circulated the petition or declaration knowing it to contain false, forged, or fictitious names;

(6) Except as otherwise provided in section 3501.382 [3501.38.2] of the Revised Code, add signatures or names except the person's own name on the petition or declaration;

(7) Make a false certification or statement concerning the petition or declaration;

(8) File with the election authorities the petition or declaration knowing it to contain false, forged, or fictitious names;

(9) Fail to fill out truthfully and file all itemized statements required by law in connection with the petition or declaration.

(B) Whoever violates division (A) of this section is guilty of a felony of the fifth degree.

**HISTORY: GC § 4785-204; 113 v 307(403), § 204; Bureau of Code Revision, 10-1-53; 138 v H 1062 (Eff 3-23-81); 143 v H 405 (Eff 4-11-91); 146 v S 2 (Eff 7-1-96); 147 v S 116. Eff 12-9-97; 151 v H 3, § 1, eff. 5-2-06.**

## § 3599.15 Sale, theft, destruction, or mutilation of petitions.

No person shall purchase, steal, attempt to steal, sell, attempt to sell, or willfully destroy or mutilate any initiative, supplementary, referendum, recall, or nominating petition, or any part of a petition, that is being or has been lawfully circulated; provided that the words "purchase" and "sell" do not apply to persons paying or receiving pay for soliciting signatures to or circulating a petition or petition paper.

Whoever violates this section is guilty of a felony of the fifth degree.

**HISTORY: GC § 4785-205; 113 v 307(404), § 205; Bureau of Code Revision, 10-1-53; 139 v S 199 (Eff 1-1-83); 146 v S 2. Eff 7-1-96.**

The effective date is set by section 6 of SB 2.

## § 3599.16 Misconduct of members or employees of board of elections.

No member, director, or employee of a board of elections shall:

(A) Willfully or negligently violate or neglect to perform any duty imposed upon him by law, or willfully perform or neglect to perform it in such a way as to hinder the objects of the law, or willfully disobey any law incumbent upon him so to do;

(B) Willfully or knowingly report as genuine a false or fraudulent signature on a petition or registration form, or willfully or knowingly report as false or fraudulent any such genuine signature;

(C) Willfully add to or subtract from the votes actually cast at an election in any official returns, or add to or take away or attempt to add to or take away any ballot from those legally polled at such election;

(D) Carry away, destroy, or mutilate any registration cards or forms, pollbooks, or other records of any election;

(E) Act as an election official in any capacity in an election, except as specifically authorized in his official capacity;

(F) In any other way willfully and knowingly or unlawfully violate or seek to prevent the enforcement of any other provisions of the election laws.

Whoever violates this section shall be dismissed from his position as a member or employee of the board and is guilty of a felony of the fourth degree.

**HISTORY: GC § 4785-206; 113 v 307(404), § 206; Bureau of Code Revision, 10-1-53; 138 v H 1062 (Eff 3-23-81); 139 v S 199. Eff 1-1-83.**

The effective date of SB 199 is set by section 11 of the act.

## § 3599.161 Prohibiting inspection of election records.

(A) The director of elections, deputy director of elections, or an employee of the board of elections designated by the director or deputy director shall be available during normal office hours to provide any person with access to the public records filed in the office of the board of elections.

(B) No director of elections, deputy director of elections, or employee of the board of elections designated by the director or deputy director shall knowingly prevent or prohibit any person from inspecting, under reasonable regulations established and posted by the board of elections, the public records filed in the office of the board of elections. Records relating to the declination of a person to register to vote and to the identity of a voter registration agency through which any particular person registered to vote are not public records for purposes of this section.

(C) Whoever violates division (B) of this section is guilty of prohibiting inspection of election records, a minor misdemeanor, and shall, upon conviction, be dismissed from his position as director of elections, deputy director of elections, or employee of the board of elections.

**HISTORY: 137 v H 86 (Eff 8-26-77); 145 v S 300. Eff 1-1-95.**

The effective date is set by section 3 of SB 300.

## § 3599.17 Violations by elections officials [Contingent amendment — see Editor's note].

(A) No elections official serving as a registrar or judge of elections shall do any of the following:

(1) Fail to appear before the board of elections, or its representative, after notice has been served personally upon the official or left at the official's usual place of residence, for examination as to the official's qualifications;

(2) Fail to appear at the polling place to which the official is assigned at the hour and during the hours set for the registration or election;

(3) Fail to take the oath prescribed by section 3501.31 of the Revised Code, unless excused by such board;

(4) Refuse or sanction the refusal of another registrar or judge of elections to administer an oath required by law;

(5) Fail to send notice to the board of the appointment of a judge to fill a vacancy;

(6) Act as registrar or judge without having been appointed and having received a certificate of appointment, except a judge appointed to fill a vacancy caused by absence or removal;

(7) Fail in any other way to perform any duty imposed by law.

(B) Whoever violates division (A) of this section is guilty of a misdemeanor of the first degree.

**HISTORY: GC § 4785-207; 113 v 307(405), § 207; Bureau of Code Revision, 10-1-53; 147 v S 116. Eff 12-9-97; 152 v H 119, § 101.01, eff. 9-29-07.**

This section was amended by House Bill 194 of the 2011 legislative session. However, referendum petitions were filed to prevent House Bill 194 from taking effect as scheduled on September 30, 2011. This version of the section will remain in effect at least until the referendum election.

The effective date is set by § 812.03 of 152 v H 119.

## § 3599.17 Violations by elections officials [Contingent amendment — see Editor's note].

(A) No elections official serving as a registrar or precinct election official shall do any of the following:

(1) Fail to appear before the board of elections, or its representative, after notice has been served personally upon the official or left at the official's usual place of residence, for examination as to the official's qualifications;

(2) Fail to appear at the polling place to which the official is assigned at the hour and during the hours set for the registration or election;

(3) Fail to take the oath prescribed by section 3501.31 of the Revised Code, unless excused by such board;

(4) Refuse or sanction the refusal of another registrar or precinct election official to administer an oath required by law;

(5) Fail to send notice to the board of the appointment of a precinct election official to fill a vacancy;

(6) Act as registrar or precinct election official without having been appointed and having received a certificate of appointment, except a precinct election official appointed to fill a vacancy caused by absence or removal;

(7) Fail in any other way to perform any duty imposed by law.

(B) Whoever violates division (A) of this section is guilty of a misdemeanor of the first degree.

**HISTORY: GC § 4785-207; 113 v 307(405), § 207; Bureau of Code Revision, 10-1-53; 147 v S 116. Eff 12-9-97; 152 v H 119, § 101.01, eff. 9-29-07; 2011 HB 194, § 1, eff. Sept. 30, 2011.**

This section was amended by House Bill 194 of the 2011 legislative session. However, referendum petitions were filed to prevent House Bill 194 from taking effect as scheduled on September 30, 2011. This version of the section will take effect if approved at the referendum election.

The effective date is set by § 812.03 of 152 v H 119.

## § 3599.18 Misconduct in connection with registration of electors.

(A) No election official, person assisting in the registration of electors, or police officer shall knowingly do any of the following:

(1) Refuse, neglect, or unnecessarily delay, hinder, or prevent the registration of a qualified elector, who in a lawful manner applies for registration;

(2) Enter or consent to the entry of a fictitious name on a voter registration list;

(3) Alter the name on or remove or destroy the registration card or form of any qualified elector;

(4) Neglect, unlawfully execute, or fail to execute any duty enjoined upon that person as an election official, person assisting in the registration of electors, or police officer.

(B) Whoever violates division (A) of this section is guilty of a misdemeanor of the first degree.

**HISTORY: GC § 4785-208; 113 v 307(405), § 208; Bureau of Code Revision, 10-1-53; 136 v H 1 (Eff 6-13-75); 147 v S 116. Eff 12-9-97.**

## § 3599.19 Misconduct of judges of elections in polling place [Contingent amendment — see Editor's note].

(A) No judge of elections shall knowingly do any of the following:

(1) Unlawfully open or permit to be opened the sealed package containing registration lists, ballots, blanks, pollbooks, and other papers and material to be used in an election;

(2) Unlawfully misplace, carry away, negligently lose or permit to be taken from the judge, fail to deliver, or destroy any such packages, papers, or material;

(3) Receive or sanction the reception of a ballot from a person not a qualified elector or from a person who refused to answer a question in accordance with the election law;

(4) Refuse to receive or sanction the rejection of a ballot from a person, knowing that person to be a qualified elector;

(5) Permit a fraudulent ballot to be placed in the ballot box;

(6) Place or permit to be placed in any ballot box any ballot known by the judge to be improperly or falsely marked;

(7) Count or permit to be counted any illegal or fraudulent ballot;

(8) Mislead an elector who is physically unable to prepare the elector's ballot, mark a ballot for such elector otherwise than as directed by that elector, or disclose to any person, except when legally required to do so, how such elector voted;

(9) Alter or mark or permit any alteration or marking on any ballot when counting the ballots;

(10) Unlawfully count or tally or sanction the wrongful counting or tallying of votes;

(11) After the counting of votes commences, as required by law, postpone or sanction the postponement of the counting of votes, adjourn at any time or to any place, or remove the ballot box from the place of voting, or from the custody or presence of all the judges of such elections;

(12) Permit any ballot to remain or to be in the ballot box at the opening of the polls, or to be put in the box during the counting of the ballots, or to be left in the box without being counted;

(13) Admit or sanction the admission to the polling room at an election during the receiving, counting, and certifying of votes of any person not qualified by law to be so admitted;

(14) Refuse to admit or sanction the refusal to admit any person, upon lawful request for admission, who is legally qualified to be present;

(15) Permit or sanction the counting of the ballots contrary to the manner prescribed by law;

(16) Neglect or unlawfully execute any duty enjoined upon the judge by law.

(B) Whoever violates division (A) of this section is guilty of a misdemeanor of the first degree.

**HISTORY: GC § 4785-209; 113 v 307(405), § 209; Bureau of Code Revision, 10-1-53; 147 v S 116. Eff 12-9-97; 152 v H 119, § 101.01, eff. 9-29-07.**

This section was amended by House Bill 194 of the 2011 legislative session. However, referendum petitions were filed to prevent House Bill 194 from taking effect as scheduled on September 30, 2011. This version of the section will remain in effect at least until the referendum election.

The effective date is set by § 812.03 of 152 v H 119.

## § 3599.19 Misconduct of judges of elections in polling place [Contingent amendment — see Editor's note].

(A) No precinct election official shall knowingly do any of the following:

(1) Unlawfully open or permit to be opened the sealed package containing registration lists, ballots, blanks, pollbooks, and other papers and material to be used in an election;

(2) Unlawfully misplace, carry away, negligently lose or permit to be taken from the precinct election official, fail to deliver, or destroy any such packages, papers, or material;

(3) Receive or sanction the reception of a ballot from a person not a qualified elector or from a person who refused to answer a question in accordance with the election law;

(4) Refuse to receive or sanction the rejection of a ballot from a person, knowing that person to be a qualified elector;

(5) Permit a fraudulent ballot to be placed in the ballot box;

(6) Place or permit to be placed in any ballot box any ballot known by the precinct election official to be improperly or falsely marked;

(7) Count or permit to be counted any illegal or fraudulent ballot;

(8) Mislead an elector who is physically unable to prepare the elector's ballot, mark a ballot for such elector otherwise than as directed by that elector, or disclose to any person, except when legally required to do so, how such elector voted;

(9) Alter or mark or permit any alteration or marking on any ballot when counting the ballots;

(10) Unlawfully count or tally or sanction the wrongful counting or tallying of votes;

(11) After the counting of votes commences, as required by law, postpone or sanction the postponement of the counting of votes, adjourn at any time or to any place, or remove the ballot box from the place of voting, or from the custody or presence of all the precinct election officials;

(12) Permit any ballot to remain or to be in the ballot box at the opening of the polls, or to be put in the box during the counting of the ballots, or to be left in the box without being counted;

(13) Admit or sanction the admission to the polling room at an election during the receiving, counting, and certifying of votes of any person not qualified by law to be so admitted;

(14) Refuse to admit or sanction the refusal to admit any person, upon lawful request for admission, who is legally qualified to be present;

(15) Permit or sanction the counting of the ballots contrary to the manner prescribed by law;

(16) Neglect or unlawfully execute any duty enjoined upon the precinct election official by law.

(B) Whoever violates division (A) of this section is guilty of a misdemeanor of the first degree.

**HISTORY: GC § 4785-209; 113 v 307(405), § 209; Bureau of Code Revision, 10-1-53; 147 v S 116. Eff 12-9-97; 152 v H 119, § 101.01, eff. 9-29-07; 2011 HB 194, § 1, eff. Sept. 30, 2011.**

This section was amended by House Bill 194 of the 2011 legislative session. However, referendum petitions were filed to prevent House Bill 194 from taking effect as scheduled on September 30, 2011. This version of the section will take effect if approved at the referendum election.

The effective date is set by § 812.03 of 152 v H 119.

## § 3599.20 Offenses concerning ballots generally.

No person shall attempt to induce an elector to show how the elector marked the elector's ballot at an election; or, being an elector, allow the elector's ballot to be seen by another, except as provided by section 3505.24 of the Revised Code, with the apparent intention of letting it be known how the elector is about to vote; or make a false statement as to the elector's ability to mark the ballot; or knowingly mark the ballot so it may be identified after it has been cast; or attempt to interfere with an elector in the voting booth when marking the elector's ballot; or knowingly destroy or mutilate a lawful ballot; or remove from the polling place or be found in unlawful possession of a lawful ballot outside the enclosure provided for voting; or knowingly hinder or delay the delivery of a lawful ballot to a person entitled to receive it; or give to an elector a ballot printed or written contrary to law; or forge or falsely make an official indorsement on a ballot.

Whoever violates this section is guilty of a felony of the fifth degree.

**HISTORY: GC § 4785-210; 113 v 307(406), § 210; Bureau of Code Revision, 10-1-53; 147 v S 116. Eff 12-9-97.**

## § 3599.21 Absent voter's ballot.

(A) No person shall knowingly do any of the following:

(1) Impersonate another, or make a false representation in order to obtain an absent voter's ballot;

(2) Aid or abet a person to vote an absent voter's ballot illegally;

(3) If the person is an election official, open, destroy, steal, mark, or mutilate any absent voter's ballot;

(4) Aid or abet another person to open, destroy, steal, mark, or mutilate any absent voter's ballot after the ballot has been voted;

(5) Delay the delivery of any absent voter's ballot with a view to preventing its arrival in time to be counted;

(6) Hinder or attempt to hinder the delivery or counting of such absent voter's ballot;

(7) Fail to forward to the appropriate election official an absent voter's ballot application entrusted to that person to so forward;

(8) Fail to forward to the appropriate election official an absent voter's ballot application entrusted to that person to so forward within ten days after that application is completed or within such a time period that the failure to so forward the application disenfranchises the voter with respect to a particular election, whichever is earlier;

(9) Except as authorized under Chapters 3509. and 3511. of the Revised Code, possess the absent voter's ballot of another.

(B)(1) Subject to division (B)(2) of this section, no person who receives compensation for soliciting persons to apply to vote by absent voter's ballots shall fail to forward to the appropriate election official an absent voter's ballot application entrusted to that person to so forward within ten days after that application is completed.

(2) No person who receives compensation for soliciting persons to apply to vote by absent voter's ballots shall fail to forward to the appropriate election official an absent voter's ballot application entrusted to that person to so forward within such a time period that the failure to so forward the application disenfranchises the voter with respect to a particular election.

(C) Whoever violates division (A) of this section is guilty of a felony of the fourth degree.

(D) As used in this section, "person who receives compensation for soliciting persons to apply to vote by absent voter's ballots" includes any effort, for compensation, to provide absent voter's ballot applications or to assist persons in completing those applications or returning them to the director of the board of elections of the county in which the applicant's voting residence is located.

**HISTORY: GC § 4785-211; 113 v 307(406), § 211; Bureau of Code Revision, 10-1-53; 139 v S 199 (Eff 1-1-83); 147 v S 116. Eff 12-9-97; 151 v H 234, § 1, eff. 1-27-06; 151 v H 3, § 1, eff. 5-2-06.**

## § 3599.22 Printing of ballots.

(A) No person employed to print or engage in printing the official ballots shall knowingly do any of the following:

(1) Print or cause or permit to be printed an official ballot other than the official ballot furnished by the board of elections;

(2) Print or permit to be printed more ballots than are delivered to the board;

(3) Appropriate, give, deliver, or knowingly permit to be taken away any of such ballots by a person other than the person authorized by law to do so;

(4) Print such ballots on paper other than that provided in the contract with the board;

(5) Package or deliver to the board fewer ballots than the number the board directed to be printed.

(B) Whoever violates division (A) of this section is guilty of a misdemeanor of the first degree.

**HISTORY: GC § 4785-212; 113 v 307(407), § 212; Bureau of Code Revision, 10-1-53; 147 v S 116. Eff 12-9-97.**

## § 3599.23 Offenses concerning election materials or papers.

(A) No printer or other person entrusted with the printing, custody, or delivery of registration cards or forms, ballots, blanks, pollbooks, cards of instruction, or other required papers shall do any of the following:

(1) Knowingly and unlawfully open or permit to be opened a sealed package containing ballots or other printed forms;

(2) Knowingly give or deliver to another not lawfully entitled to them, or unlawfully misplace or carry away, or knowingly fail to deliver, or knowingly destroy any such forms or packages of ballots, or a ballot, pollbooks, cards of instruction, or other required papers;

(3) Negligently lose or permit to be taken from the printer or other entrusted person any of the materials described in division (A)(2) of this section.

(B) No person entrusted with the preparation, custody, or delivery of marking devices shall do either of the following:

(1) Unlawfully open or permit to be opened a sealed package containing marking devices, or give or deliver to another not lawfully entitled to them any such marking devices;

(2) Unlawfully or carelessly use or negligently lose or permit to be taken from the printer or other entrusted person and fail to deliver or destroy any such marking devices.

(C) Whoever violates division (A)(1) or (2) or (B) of this section is guilty of a misdemeanor of the first degree. Whoever violates division (A)(3) of this section is guilty of a misdemeanor of the second degree.

**HISTORY: GC § 4785-213; 113 v 307(407), § 213; Bureau of Code Revision, 10-1-53; 129 v 1653 (Eff 6-29-61); 147 v S 116. Eff 12-9-97.**

## § 3599.24 Interference with elections.

(A) No person shall do any of the following:

(1) By force, fraud, or other improper means, obtain or attempt to obtain possession of the ballots, ballot boxes, or pollbooks;

(2) Recklessly destroy any property used in the conduct of elections;

(3) Attempt to intimidate an election officer, or prevent an election official from performing the official's duties;

(4) Knowingly tear down, remove, or destroy any of the registration lists or sample ballots furnished by the board of elections at the polling place;

(5) Loiter in or about a registration or polling place during registration or the casting and counting of ballots so as to hinder, delay, or interfere with the conduct of the registration or election;

(6) Remove from the voting place the pencils, cards of instruction, supplies, or other conveniences furnished to enable the voter to mark the voter's ballot.

(B) Whoever violates division (A)(1) or (2) of this section is guilty of a felony of the fifth degree. Whoever violates division (A)(3), (4), (5), or (6) of this section is guilty of a misdemeanor of the first degree.

**HISTORY: GC § 4785-214; 113 v 307(407), § 214; Bureau of Code Revision, 10-1-53; 138 v H 1062 (Eff 3-23-81); 146 v S 2. Eff 7-1-96; 151 v H 3, § 1, eff. 5-2-06.**

The effective date is set by section 6 of SB 2.

## § 3599.25 Inducing illegal voting.

(A) No person shall knowingly do any of the following:

(1) Counsel or advise another to vote at an election, knowing that the person is not a qualified voter;

(2) Advise, aid, or assist another person to go or come into a precinct for the purpose of voting in it, knowing that such person is not qualified to vote in it;

(3) Counsel, advise, or attempt to induce an election officer to permit a person to vote, knowing such person is not a qualified elector.

(B) Whoever violates division (A) of this section is guilty of a felony of the fourth degree.

**HISTORY: GC § 4785-215; 113 v 307(408), § 215; Bureau of Code Revision, 10-1-53; 147 v S 116. Eff 12-9-97.**

## § 3599.26 Tampering with ballots.

No person shall fraudulently put a ballot or ticket into a ballot box; or knowingly and willfully vote a ballot other than an official ballot lawfully obtained by the person from the precinct election authorities; or fraudulently or deceitfully change a ballot of an elector, by which such elector is prevented from voting for such candidates or on an issue as the elector intends to do; or mark a ballot of an elector except as authorized by section 3505.24 of the Revised Code; or hand a marked ballot to an elector to vote, with intent to ascertain how the elector voted; or furnish a ballot to an elector who cannot read, knowingly informing the elector that it contains a name different from the one that is printed or written thereon, to induce the elector to vote contrary to the elector's intentions; or unduly delay or hinder an elector from applying for registration, registering, or from attempting to vote or voting; or knowingly print or distribute a ballot contrary to law.

Whoever violates this section is guilty of a felony of the fifth degree.

**HISTORY: GC § 4785-216; 113 v 307(408), § 216; 124 v 478; Bureau of Code Revision, 10-1-53; 139 v S 199 (Eff 1-1-83); 146 v S 2. Eff 7-1-96.**

The effective date is set by section 6 of SB 2.

## § 3599.27 Possession of voting machine, tabulating equipment, or marking device prohibited; tampering; penalty.

No unauthorized person shall have in the person's possession any voting machine that may be owned or leased by any county or any of the parts or the keys thereof. No person shall tamper or attempt to tamper with, deface, impair the use of, destroy, or otherwise injure in any manner any voting machine.

No unauthorized person shall have in the person's possession any marking device, automatic tabulating equipment, or any of the parts, appurtenances, or accessories thereof. No person shall tamper or attempt to tamper with, deface, impair the use of, destroy, or otherwise change or injure in any manner any marking device, automatic tabulating equipment, or any appurtenances or accessories thereof.

Whoever violates this section is guilty of a felony of the fifth degree.

**HISTORY: GC § 4785-217; 113 v 307(408), § 217; Bureau of Code Revision, 10-1-53; 126 v 575 (Eff 10-6-55); 129 v 1653 (Eff 6-29-61); 139 v S 199 (Eff 1-1-83); 146 v S 2. Eff 7-1-96.**

The effective date is set by section 6 of SB 2.

## § 3599.28 False signatures.

No person, with intent to defraud or deceive, shall write or sign the name of another person to any document, petition, registration card, or other book or record authorized or required by Title XXXV [35] of the Revised Code.

Whoever violates this section is guilty of a felony of the fifth degree.

**HISTORY: GC § 4785-219; 113 v 307(409), § 219; Bureau of Code Revision, 10-1-53; 139 v S 199 (Eff 1-1-83); 146 v S 2. Eff 7-1-96.**

The effective date is set by section 6 of SB 2.

## § 3599.29 Possession of false records.

No person shall have in the person's possession a falsely made, altered, forged, or counterfeited registration card, form, or list, pollbook, tally sheet, or list of election returns of an election, knowing it to be such, with intent to hinder, defeat, or prevent a fair expression of the popular will at such election.

Whoever violates this section is guilty of a felony of the fifth degree.

**HISTORY: GC § 4785-220; 113 v 307(409), § 220; Bureau of Code Revision, 10-1-53; 139 v S 199 (Eff 1-1-83); 146 v S 2. Eff 7-1-96.**

The effective date is set by section 6 of SB 2.

## § 3599.30 Schools providing transportation for students to polling places prohibited [Contingent enactment — see Editor's note].

No school operated by a school district, no community school established under Chapter 3314. of the Revised Code, no STEM school established under Chapter 3326. of the Revised Code, and no chartered nonpublic school shall, during the regular school day, transport one or more students to a polling place or board of elections for the purpose of casting a ballot.

**HISTORY: 2011 HB 194, § 1, eff. Sept. 30, 2011.**

This section was enacted by House Bill 194 of the 2011 legislative session. However, referendum petitions were filed to prevent House Bill 194 from taking effect as scheduled on September 30, 2011. This section will take effect if approved at the referendum election.

Former § 3599.30 [GC § 4785-222; 113 v 307 (410), § 222; Bureau of Code Revision, 10-1-53], concerning congregating at polls to hinder registering or voting, was repealed by 147 v S 116, § 2, effective December 9, 1997.

## § 3599.31 Failure of officer of law to assist election officers [Contingent amendment — see Editor's note].

No officer of the law shall fail to obey forthwith an order of the presiding judge and aid in enforcing a lawful order of the presiding judges at an election, against persons unlawfully congregating or loitering within one hundred feet of a polling place, hindering or delaying an elector from reaching or leaving the polling place, soliciting or attempting, within one hundred feet of the polling place, to influence an elector in casting the elector's vote, or interfering with the registration of voters or casting and counting of the ballots.

Whoever violates this section is guilty of a misdemeanor of the first degree.

**HISTORY: GC § 4785-218; 113 v 307(408), § 218; Bureau of Code Revision, 10-1-53; 147 v S 116. Eff 12-9-97.**

This section was amended by House Bill 194 of the 2011 legislative session. However, referendum petitions were filed to prevent House Bill 194 from taking effect as scheduled on September 30, 2011. This version of the section will remain in effect at least until the referendum election.

## § 3599.31 Failure of officer of law to assist election officers [Contingent amendment — see Editor's note].

No officer of the law shall fail to obey forthwith an order of the voting location manager and aid in enforcing a lawful order of the voting location manager at an election, against persons unlawfully congregating or loitering within one hundred feet of a polling place, hindering or delaying an elector from reaching or leaving the polling place, soliciting or attempting, within one hundred feet of the polling place, to influence an elector in casting the elector's vote, or interfering with the registration of voters or casting and counting of the ballots.

Whoever violates this section is guilty of a misdemeanor of the first degree.

**HISTORY: GC § 4785-218; 113 v 307(408), § 218; Bureau of Code Revision, 10-1-53; 147 v S 116. Eff 12-9-97; 2011 HB 194, § 1, eff. Sept. 30, 2011.**

This section was amended by House Bill 194 of the 2011 legislative session. However, referendum petitions were filed to prevent House Bill 194 from taking effect as scheduled on September 30, 2011. This version of the section will take effect if approved at the referendum election.

## § 3599.32 Violations by election official not otherwise specified.

No official upon whom a duty is imposed by an election law for the violation of which no penalty is otherwise provided shall knowingly disobey such election law.

Whoever violates this section is guilty of a misdemeanor of the first degree.

**HISTORY: GC § 4785-222; 113 v 307(410), § 222; Bureau of Code Revision, 10-1-53; 147 v S 116. Eff 12-9-97.**

## § 3599.33 Fraudulent writing on ballots or election records.

No person, from the time ballots are cast or counted until the time has expired for using them as evidence in a recount or contest of election, shall willfully and with fraudulent intent make any mark or alteration on any ballot; or inscribe, write, or cause to be inscribed or written in or upon a registration form or list, pollbook, tally sheet, or list, lawfully made or kept at an election, or in or upon a book or paper purporting to be such, or upon an election return, or upon a book or paper containing such return the name of a person not entitled to vote at such election or not voting thereat, or a fictitious name, or, within such time, wrongfully change, alter, erase, or tamper with a name, word, or figure contained in such pollbook, tally sheet, list, book, or paper; or falsify, mark, or write thereon with intent to defeat, hinder, or prevent a fair expression of the will of the people at such election.

Whoever violates this section is guilty of a felony of the fifth degree.

**HISTORY: GC § 4785-223; 113 v 307(410), § 223; Bureau of Code Revision, 10-1-53; 139 v S 199 (Eff 1-1-83); 146 v S 2. Eff 7-1-96.**

The effective date is set by section 6 of SB 2.

## § 3599.34 Destruction of election records before expiration of time for contest.

No person, from the time ballots are cast or voted until the time has expired for using them in a recount or as evidence in a contest of election, shall unlawfully destroy or attempt to destroy the ballots, or permit such ballots or a ballot box or pollbook used at an election to be destroyed; or destroy, falsify, mark, or write in a name on any such ballot that has been voted.

Whoever violates this section is guilty of a felony of the fifth degree.

**HISTORY: GC § 4785-224; 113 v 307(410), § 224; Bureau of Code Revision, 10-1-53; 139 v S 199 (Eff 1-1-83); 146 v S 2. Eff 7-1-96.**

The effective date is set by section 6 of SB 2.

## § 3599.35 Proxies not to be given by party representatives; impersonation of representatives.

No party committeeperson or party delegate or alternate chosen at an election, or a delegate or alternate appointed to a convention provided by law, shall give or issue a proxy or authority to another person to act or vote in that person's stead.

No person shall knowingly or fraudulently act or vote or attempt to impersonate, act, or vote in place of that committeeperson, delegate, or alternate.

Whoever violates this section is guilty of a misdemeanor of the first degree.

**HISTORY: GC § 4785-225; 113 v 307(410), § 225; Bureau of Code Revision, 10-1-53; 147 v S 116. Eff 12-9-97.**

## § 3599.36 Election falsification.

No person, either orally or in writing, on oath lawfully administered or in a statement made under penalty of election falsification, shall knowingly state a falsehood as to a material matter relating to an election in a proceeding before a court, tribunal, or election official, or in a matter in relation to which an oath or statement under penalty of election falsification is authorized by law, including a statement required for verifying or filing any declaration of candidacy, declaration of intent to be a write-in candidate, nominating petition, or other petition presented to or filed with the secretary of state, a board of elections, or any other public office for the purpose of becoming a candidate for any elective office, including the office of a political party, for the purpose of submitting a question or issue to the electors at an election, or for the purpose of forming a political party.

Whoever violates this section is guilty of election falsification, a felony of the fifth degree.

Every paper, card, or other document relating to any election matter that calls for a statement to be made under penalty of election falsification shall be accompanied by the following statement in bold face capital letters: "Whoever commits election falsification is guilty of a felony of the fifth degree."

**HISTORY: GC § 4785-226; 113 v 307(411), § 226; Bureau of Code Revision, 10-1-53; 128 v S 204 (Eff 8-28-59); 135 v S 429 (Eff 7-26-74); 135 v H 662 (Eff 9-27-74); 138 v H 1062 (Eff 3-23-81); 147 v S 116. Eff 12-9-97.**

## § 3599.37 Disobedience of subpoena concerning violation of election laws.

(A) No person having been subpoenaed or ordered to appear before a grand jury, court, board, or officer in a proceeding or prosecution upon a complaint, information, affidavit, or indictment for an offense under an election law shall do either of the following:

(1) Fail to appear or, having appeared, refuse to answer a question pertinent to the matter under inquiry or investigation;

(2) Refuse to produce, upon reasonable notice, any material, books, papers, documents, or records in that person's possession or under that person's control.

(B) Whoever violates division (A) of this section, unless the violator personally appears before the grand jury, court, board, or officer and asserts the protection of the violator's constitutional rights, is guilty of a misdemeanor of the first degree.

**HISTORY: GC § 4785-227; 113 v 307(411), § 227; 114 v 679(713); Bureau of Code Revision, 10-1-53; 147 v S 116. Eff 12-9-97; 152 v H 119, § 101.01, eff. 9-29-07.**

The effective date is set by § 812.03 of 152 v H 119.

## § 3599.38 Illegally influencing voters.

(A) No election official, observer, deputy sheriff, special deputy sheriff, or police officer, while performing that person's duties related to the casting of votes, shall do either of the following:

(1) Wear any badge, sign, or other insignia or thing indicating that person's preference for any candidate or for any question submitted at an election;

(2) Influence or attempt to influence any voter to cast the voter's ballot for or against any candidate or issue submitted at an election.

(B) Whoever violates division (A) of this section is guilty of a misdemeanor of the first degree.

**HISTORY: GC § 4785-228; 113 v 307(411), § 228; Bureau of Code Revision, 10-1-53; 147 v S 116. Eff 12-9-97; 151 v H 3, § 1, eff. 5-2-06.**

See provisions of § 5 of 151 v H 3 following RC § 3501.26.

## § 3599.39 Second conviction under election laws.

Any person convicted of a violation of any provision of Title XXXV [35] of the Revised Code, who is again convicted of a violation of any such provision, whether such conviction is for the same offense or not, is on such second conviction guilty of a felony of the fourth degree, and in addition, shall be disfranchised.

**HISTORY: GC § 4785-230; 113 v 307(412), § 230; Bureau of Code Revision, 10-1-53; 126 v 575 (Eff 10-6-55); 147 v S 116. Eff 12-9-97.**

## § 3599.40 General penalty.

Except as otherwise provided in section 3599.39 of the Revised Code, whoever violates any provision of Title XXXV [35] of the Revised Code, unless otherwise provided in such title, is guilty of a misdemeanor of the first degree.

**HISTORY: GC § 4785-232; 113 v 307(412), § 232; Bureau of Code Revision, 10-1-53; 134 v H 511 (Eff 1-1-74); 147 v S 116. Eff 12-9-97.**

## § 3599.41 Person violating election laws may testify against other violators.

A person violating any provision of Title XXXV [35] of the Revised Code is a competent witness against another person so offending, and may attend and testify at a trial, hearing, or investigation thereof.

**HISTORY: GC § 4785-229; 113 v 307(411), § 229; 114 v 679(713); Bureau of Code Revision. Eff 10-1-53.**

## § 3599.42 Prima-facie case of fraud.

A violation of any provision of Title XXXV [35] of the Revised Code constitutes a prima-facie case of fraud within the purview of such title.

**HISTORY: GC § 4785-231; 113 v 307(412), § 231; Bureau of Code Revision. Eff 10-1-53.**

## § 3599.43 Communications purporting to be from boards of elections; penalty.

No person, not authorized by a board of elections, shall send or transmit to any other person any written or oral communication which purports to be a communication from a board of elections, or which reasonably construed appears to be a communication from such a board and which was intended to be so construed.

Whoever violates this section shall be fined not less than one hundred nor more than one thousand dollars or imprisoned not more than six months or both.

**HISTORY: 130 v 845. Eff 9-16-63.**

## § 3599.45 Accepting contributions from medicaid providers prohibited.

(A) No candidate for the office of attorney general or county prosecutor or such a candidate's campaign committee shall knowingly accept any contribution from a provider of services or goods under contract with the department of job and family services pursuant to the medicaid program of Title XIX of the "Social Security Act," 49 Stat. 620 (1935), 42 U.S.C. 301, as amended, or from any person having an ownership interest in the provider.

As used in this section "candidate," "campaign committee," and "contribution" have the same meaning as in section 3517.01 of the Revised Code.

(B) Whoever violates this section is guilty of a misdemeanor of the first degree.

**HISTORY: 137 v S 159 (Eff 4-24-78); 141 v H 428 (Eff 12-23-86); 148 v H 471. Eff 7-1-2000.**

The effective date is set by section 12(A) of HB 471.

# TITLE 37: HEALTH — SAFETY — MORALS

## CHAPTER 3707: BOARD OF HEALTH



### [MISCELLANEOUS]

### § 3707.50 Posting of warning concerning anabolic steroids in athletic facility locker rooms.

(A) As used in this section:

(1) "Anabolic steroid" has the same meaning as in section 3719.41 of the Revised Code.

(2) "Athletic facility" means both of the following:

(a) A privately owned athletic training, exercise, or sports facility or stadium that is open to the public;

(b) A publicly owned sports facility or stadium.

(B) The following warning shall be conspicuously posted in each locker room of every athletic facility:

"Warning: Improper use of anabolic steroids may cause serious or fatal health problems, such as heart disease, stroke, cancer, growth deformities, infertility, personality changes, severe acne, and baldness. Possession, sale, or use of anabolic steroids without a valid prescription is a crime punishable by a fine and imprisonment."

(C) No privately owned athletic facility shall fail to post the warning required by this section.

(D) Any person who violates division (C) of this section is guilty of a misdemeanor of the fourth degree.

**HISTORY: 144 v H 62. Eff 5-21-91.**

**Not analogous to former RC § 3707.50 (Bureau of Code Revision, 10-1-53), repealed 134 v H 511, § 2, eff 1-1-74.**

## CHAPTER 3712: HOSPICE CARE



### § 3712.09 Criminal records check for prospective employees providing direct care to older adult.

(A) As used in this section:

(1) "Applicant" means a person who is under final consideration for employment with a hospice care program in a full-time, part-time, or temporary position that involves providing direct care to an older adult. "Applicant" does not include a person who provides direct care as a volunteer without receiving or expecting to receive any form of remuneration other than reimbursement for actual expenses.

(2) "Criminal records check" and "older adult" have the same meanings as in section 109.572 [109.57.2] of the Revised Code.

(B)(1) Except as provided in division (I) of this section, the chief administrator of a hospice care program shall request that the superintendent of the bureau of criminal identification and investigation conduct a criminal records check with respect to each applicant. If an applicant for whom a criminal records check request is required under this division does not present proof of having been a resident of this state for the five-year period immediately prior to the date the criminal records check is requested or provide evidence that within that five-year period the superintendent has requested information about the applicant from the federal bureau of investigation in a criminal records check, the chief administrator shall request that the superintendent obtain information from the federal bureau of investigation as part of the criminal records check of the applicant. Even if an applicant for whom a criminal records check request is required under this division presents proof of having been a resident of this state for the five-year period, the chief administrator may request that the superintendent include information from the federal bureau of investigation in the criminal records check.

(2) A person required by division (B)(1) of this section to request a criminal records check shall do both of the following:

(a) Provide to each applicant for whom a criminal records check request is required under that division a copy of the form prescribed pursuant to division (C)(1) of section 109.572 [109.57.2] of the Revised Code and a standard fingerprint impression sheet prescribed pursuant to division (C)(2) of that section, and obtain the completed form and impression sheet from the applicant;

(b) Forward the completed form and impression sheet to the superintendent of the bureau of criminal identification and investigation.

(3) An applicant provided the form and fingerprint impression sheet under division (B)(2)(a) of this section who fails to complete the form or provide fingerprint impressions shall not be employed in any position for which a criminal records check is required by this section.

(C)(1) Except as provided in rules adopted by the public health council in accordance with division (F) of this section and subject to division (C)(2) of this section, no hospice care program shall employ a person in a position that involves providing direct care to an older adult if the person has been convicted of or pleaded guilty to any of the following:

(a) A violation of section 2903.01, 2903.02, 2903.03, 2903.04, 2903.11, 2903.12, 2903.13, 2903.16, 2903.21, 2903.34, 2905.01, 2905.02, 2905.11, 2905.12, 2907.02, 2907.03, 2907.05, 2907.06, 2907.07, 2907.08, 2907.09, 2907.12, 2907.25, 2907.31, 2907.32, 2907.321 [2907.32.1], 2907.322 [2907.32.2], 2907.323 [2907.32.3], 2911.01, 2911.02, 2911.11, 2911.12, 2911.13, 2913.02, 2913.03, 2913.04, 2913.11, 2913.21, 2913.31, 2913.40, 2913.43,

2913.47, 2913.51, 2919.25, 2921.36, 2923.12, 2923.13, 2923.161 [2923.16.1], 2925.02, 2925.03, 2925.11, 2925.13, 2925.22, 2925.23, or 3716.11 of the Revised Code.

(b) A violation of an existing or former law of this state, any other state, or the United States that is substantially equivalent to any of the offenses listed in division (C)(1)(a) of this section.

(2)(a) A hospice care program may employ conditionally an applicant for whom a criminal records check request is required under division (B) of this section prior to obtaining the results of a criminal records check regarding the individual, provided that the program shall request a criminal records check regarding the individual in accordance with division (B)(1) of this section not later than five business days after the individual begins conditional employment. In the circumstances described in division (I)(2) of this section, a hospice care program may employ conditionally an applicant who has been referred to the hospice care program by an employment service that supplies full-time, part-time, or temporary staff for positions involving the direct care of older adults and for whom, pursuant to that division, a criminal records check is not required under division (B) of this section.

(b) A hospice care program that employs an individual conditionally under authority of division (C)(2)(a) of this section shall terminate the individual's employment if the results of the criminal records check requested under division (B) of this section or described in division (I)(2) of this section, other than the results of any request for information from the federal bureau of investigation, are not obtained within the period ending thirty days after the date the request is made. Regardless of when the results of the criminal records check are obtained, if the results indicate that the individual has been convicted of or pleaded guilty to any of the offenses listed or described in division (C)(1) of this section, the program shall terminate the individual's employment unless the program chooses to employ the individual pursuant to division (F) of this section. Termination of employment under this division shall be considered just cause for discharge for purposes of division (D)(2) of section 4141.29 of the Revised Code if the individual makes any attempt to deceive the program about the individual's criminal record.

(D)(1) Each hospice care program shall pay to the bureau of criminal identification and investigation the fee prescribed pursuant to division (C)(3) of section 109.572 [109.57.2] of the Revised Code for each criminal records check conducted pursuant to a request made under division (B) of this section.

(2) A hospice care program may charge an applicant a fee not exceeding the amount the program pays under division (D)(1) of this section. A program may collect a fee only if both of the following apply:

(a) The program notifies the person at the time of initial application for employment of the amount of the fee and that, unless the fee is paid, the person will not be considered for employment;

(b) The medical assistance program established under Chapter 5111. of the Revised Code does not reimburse the program the fee it pays under division (D)(1) of this section.

(E) The report of a criminal records check conducted pursuant to a request made under this section is not a public record for the purposes of section 149.43 of the Revised Code and shall not be made available to any person other than the following:

(1) The individual who is the subject of the criminal records check or the individual's representative;

(2) The chief administrator of the program requesting the criminal records check or the administrator's representative;

(3) The administrator of any other facility, agency, or program that provides direct care to older adults that is owned or operated by the same entity that owns or operates the hospice care program;

(4) A court, hearing officer, or other necessary individual involved in a case dealing with a denial of employment of the applicant or dealing with employment or unemployment benefits of the applicant;

(5) Any person to whom the report is provided pursuant to, and in accordance with, division (I)(1) or (2) of this section.

(F) The public health council shall adopt rules in accordance with Chapter 119. of the Revised Code to implement this section. The rules shall specify circumstances under which a hospice care program may employ a person who has been convicted of or pleaded guilty to an offense listed or described in division (C)(1) of this section but meets personal character standards set by the council.

(G) The chief administrator of a hospice care program shall inform each individual, at the time of initial application for a position that involves providing direct care to an older adult, that the individual is required to provide a set of fingerprint impressions and that a criminal records check is required to be conducted if the individual comes under final consideration for employment.

(H) In a tort or other civil action for damages that is brought as the result of an injury, death, or loss to person or property caused by an individual who a hospice care program employs in a position that involves providing direct care to older adults, all of the following shall apply:

(1) If the program employed the individual in good faith and reasonable reliance on the report of a criminal records check requested under this section, the program shall not be found negligent solely because of its reliance on the report, even if the information in the report is determined later to have been incomplete or inaccurate;

(2) If the program employed the individual in good faith on a conditional basis pursuant to division (C)(2) of this section, the program shall not be found negligent solely because it employed the individual prior to receiving the report of a criminal records check requested under this section;

(3) If the program in good faith employed the individual according to the personal character standards established in rules adopted under division (F) of this section, the program shall not be found negligent solely because the individual prior to being employed had been convicted of or pleaded guilty to an offense listed or described in division (C)(1) of this section.

(I)(1) The chief administrator of a hospice care program is not required to request that the superintendent of the bureau of criminal identification and investigation conduct a criminal records check of an applicant if the applicant has been referred to the program by an employment service that supplies full-time, part-time, or temporary staff for positions involving the direct care of older adults and both of the following apply:

(a) The chief administrator receives from the employment service or the applicant a report of the results of a criminal records check regarding the applicant that has been conducted by the superintendent within the one-year period immediately preceding the applicant's referral;

(b) The report of the criminal records check demonstrates that the person has not been convicted of or pleaded guilty to an offense listed or described in division (C)(1) of this section, or the report demonstrates that the person has been convicted of or pleaded guilty to one or more of those offenses, but the hospice care program chooses to employ the individual pursuant to division (F) of this section.

(2) The chief administrator of a hospice care program is not required to request that the superintendent of the bureau of criminal identification and investigation conduct a criminal records check of an applicant and may employ the applicant conditionally as described in this division, if the applicant has been referred to the program by an employment service that supplies full-time, part-time, or temporary staff for positions involving the direct care of older adults and if the chief administrator receives from the employment service or the applicant a letter from the employment service that is on the letterhead of the employment service, dated, and signed by a supervisor or another designated official of the employment service and that states that the employment service has requested the superintendent to conduct a criminal records check regarding the applicant, that the requested criminal records check will include a determination of whether the applicant has been convicted of or pleaded guilty to any offense listed or described in division (C)(1) of this section, that, as of the date set forth on the letter, the employment service had not received the results of the criminal records check, and that, when the employment service receives the results of the criminal records check, it promptly will send a copy of the results to the hospice care program. If a hospice care program employs an applicant conditionally in accordance with this division, the employment service, upon its receipt of the results of the criminal records check, promptly shall send a copy of the results to the hospice care program, and division (C)(2)(b) of this section applies regarding the conditional employment.

**HISTORY: 146 v S 160 (Eff 1-27-97); 147 v S 96 (Eff 6-11-97); 147 v H 18. Eff 1-30-98; 150 v S 189, § 1, eff. 6-29-04.**

The effective date is set by section 78 of S.B. 189 (150 v —).

See provisions, § 8 of SB 96 (147 v —) following RC § 3701.88.1.

See provisions, § 3 of SB 160 (146 v —) following RC § 3701.88.1.

# CHAPTER 3715: PURE FOOD AND DRUG LAW

Section

[PSEUDOEPHEDRINE PRODUCTS]



## [PSEUDOEPHEDRINE PRODUCTS]

### § 3715.05 Sales of pseudoephedrine products; log book.

(A) As used in this section and section 3715.06 of the Revised Code:

(1) "Consumer product" means any food or drink that is consumed or used by humans and any drug, including a drug that may be provided legally only pursuant to a prescription, that is intended to be consumed or used by humans.

(2) "Drug," "licensed health professional authorized to prescribe drugs," "pharmacy," "prescriber," "prescription," and "terminal distributor of dangerous drugs" have the same meanings as in section 4729.01 of the Revised Code.

(3) "Pharmacist" means a person licensed under Chapter 4729. of the Revised Code to engage in the practice of pharmacy.

(4) "Proof of age" means a driver's license, a commercial driver's license, a military identification card, a passport, or an identification card issued under sections 4507.50 to 4507.52 of the Revised Code that shows a person is eighteen years of age or older.

(5) "Pseudoephedrine" means any material, compound, mixture, or preparation that contains any quantity of pseudoephedrine, any of its salts, optical isomers, or salts of optical isomers.

(6) "Pseudoephedrine product" means a consumer product consisting of a single-ingredient preparation of pseudoephedrine in which pseudoephedrine is the active ingredient. "Pseudoephedrine product" does not include either of the following:

(a) A consumer product containing pseudoephedrine that is in a liquid, liquid capsule, or gel capsule form;

(b) A consumer product primarily intended for administration to children under twelve years of age, according to the label instructions, in solid dosage form, including chewable tablets, when individual dosage units do not exceed fifteen milligrams of pseudoephedrine.

(7) "Retailer" means a place of business that offers consumer products for sale to the general public.

(8) "Single-ingredient preparation" means a compound, mixture, preparation, or substance that contains a single active ingredient.

(9) "Wholesaler" has the same meaning as in section 3719.01 of the Revised Code.

(B) A retailer or terminal distributor of dangerous drugs that sells, offers to sell, holds for sale, delivers, or otherwise provides a pseudoephedrine product to the public shall do all of the following:

(1) Segregate pseudoephedrine products from other merchandise so that no member of the public may procure or purchase such products without the direct assistance of a pharmacist or other authorized employee of the retailer or terminal distributor of dangerous drugs;

(2) With regard to each time a pseudoephedrine product is sold or otherwise provided:

(a) Determine, by examination of a valid proof of age, that the purchaser or recipient is at least eighteen years of age;

(b) Make a reasonable attempt to ensure that no individual purchases or receives more than nine grams of pseudoephedrine products within a period of thirty consecutive days;

(3) Maintain a log book of pseudoephedrine product purchases, in accordance with division (C) of this section.

(C)(1) As used in division (C) of this section, "law enforcement official" means an officer or employee of any agency or authority of the United States, a state, a territory, a political division of a state or territory, or an Indian tribe, who is empowered by the law to investigate or conduct an official inquiry into a potential violation of law or prosecute or otherwise conduct a criminal, civil, or administrative proceeding arising from an alleged violation of law.

(2) A retailer or terminal distributor of dangerous drugs that sells, offers to sell, holds for sale, delivers, or otherwise provides a pseudoephedrine product to the public shall maintain a log book of all purchases of pseudoephedrine products. The log book may be maintained in a tangible format, in an electronic format, or in both a tangible format and an electronic format. As part of this requirement, the retailer or terminal distributor of dangerous drugs shall do all of the following:

(a) Require each purchaser to sign an entry in the log book that is maintained in the electronic or tangible format;

(b) Determine whether the name signed in the entry in the log book corresponds with the name on a government-issued identification card;

(c) Retain the log book in a tangible format, in an electronic format, or in both a tangible format and an electronic format for a minimum of one year after the date of the last purchase recorded in the log book;

(d) Include in the log book in the manner described in division (C)(5) of this section or, in the alternative, post, in a conspicuous location, the following statement: "Ohio law prohibits the over-the-counter purchase within any period of thirty consecutive days of more than nine grams of any consumer product in which pseudoephedrine is the only active ingredient. If you purchase a consumer product in which pseudoephedrine is the only active ingredient, you are required to sign a log book that may be accessible to law enforcement officers and to provide a government-issued identification card to verify your identity. Except in limited circumstances, the purchase within any period of thirty consecutive days of more than nine grams of any consumer product in which pseudoephedrine is the only active ingredient, and the purchase by any individual under eighteen years of age of any consumer product in which pseudoephedrine is the only active ingredient, are subject to criminal prosecution or delinquency proceedings in accordance with Ohio law. Also, the provision of false information concerning an individual's name, age, or other identification for the purpose of acquiring any consumer product in which pseudoephedrine is the only active ingredient is subject to criminal prosecution or delinquency proceedings in accordance with Ohio law."

(3) Each purchaser of a pseudoephedrine product shall do all of the following:

(a) Sign and print the purchaser's name and address in the log book;

(b) Provide a government-issued identification card to the retailer or terminal distributor of dangerous drugs to verify the purchaser's identity.

(4) Information contained in the log book may not be used or disclosed except in the following circumstances:

(a) In response to a court order or subpoena;

(b) In response to a request from a law enforcement official to be used for law enforcement purposes.

(5) If a retailer or terminal distributor of dangerous drugs chooses to include the statement set forth in division (C)(2)(d) of this section in the log book maintained under division (C)(2) of this section, the statement shall be set forth in the following manner:

(a) If the log book is maintained in an electronic format, the statement shall be set forth in such a manner that it is presented on the viewing screen to each purchaser who is signing an entry in the log book before the purchaser may sign the entry.

(b) If the log book is maintained in a tangible format, the statement shall be set forth on the cover of the log book and on each page of the log book.

(D) Prescriptions, orders, and records maintained pursuant to this section and stocks of pseudoephedrine products shall be open for inspection to federal, state, county, and municipal officers, and employees of the state board of pharmacy whose duty it is to enforce the laws of this state or of the United States relating to controlled substances. Such prescriptions, orders, records, and stocks shall be open for inspection by the state medical board and its employees for purposes of enforcing Chapter 4731. of the Revised Code.

**HISTORY: 151 v S 53, § 1, eff. 5-17-06.**

**Not analogous to former RC § 3715.06 (GC §§ 5777, 5779, 5784; 99 v 258; 100 v 105; 103 v 137; 108 v PtI, 15; 112 v 135; 117 v 156; 120 v 255; Bureau of Code Revision, 10-1-53), repealed 127 v 819(835), § 2, eff 9-13-57.**

## § 3715.06 Duty to report theft or loss of pseudoephedrine product.

(A) Each retailer, terminal distributor of dangerous drugs, pharmacy, prescriber, or wholesaler that sells, offers to sell, holds for sale, delivers, or otherwise provides any pseudoephedrine product and that discovers the theft or loss of any pseudoephedrine product in an amount of more than nine grams per incident of theft or loss shall notify all of the following upon discovery of the theft or loss:

(1) The state board of pharmacy, by telephone immediately upon discovery of the theft or loss;

(2) Law enforcement authorities. If the incident is a theft and the theft constitutes a felony, the retailer, terminal distributor of dangerous drugs, pharmacy, prescriber, or wholesaler shall report the theft to the law enforcement authorities in accordance with section 2921.22 of the Revised Code.

(B) Within thirty days after making a report by telephone to the state board of pharmacy pursuant to division (A)(1) of this section, a retailer, terminal distributor of dangerous drugs, pharmacy, prescriber, or wholesaler shall send a written report to the state board of pharmacy.

(C) The reports required under this section shall identify the product that was stolen or lost, the amount of the product stolen or lost, and the date and time of discovery of the theft or loss.

**HISTORY: 151 v S 53, § 1, eff. 5-17-06.**

**Not analogous to former RC § 3715.06 (GC §§ 5777, 5779, 5784; 99 v 258; 100 v 105; 103 v 137; 108 v PtI, 15; 112 v 135; 117 v 156; 120 v 255; Bureau of Code Revision, 10-1-53), repealed 127 v 819(835), § 2, eff 9-13-57.**

# CHAPTER 3716: LABELING OF HAZARDOUS SUBSTANCES

Section



## § 3716.11 Placing harmful objects in food or confection.

No person shall do either of the following, knowing or having reasonable cause to believe that any person may suffer physical harm or be seriously inconvenienced or annoyed thereby:

(A) Place a pin, needle, razor blade, glass, laxative, drug of abuse, or other harmful or hazardous object or substance in any food or confection;

(B) Furnish to any person any food or confection which has been adulterated in violation of division (A) of this section.

**HISTORY: 135 v H 716. Eff 1-1-74.**

The effective date is set by section 1 of HB 716.

## § 3716.99 Penalties.

(A) Whoever violates section 3716.02 of the Revised Code is guilty of a misdemeanor of the third degree on a first offense. On each subsequent offense such person is guilty of a misdemeanor of the second degree.

(B) No person is subject to prosecution for a violation of division (A) of section 3716.02 of the Revised Code with respect to any hazardous substance shipped or delivered for shipment for export to any foreign country, in a package marked for export and branded in accordance with the specifications of the foreign purchaser and in accordance with the laws of the foreign country.

(C) Whoever violates section 3716.11 of the Revised Code is guilty of a misdemeanor of the first degree.

**HISTORY: 128 v 484 (Eff 11-4-59); 129 v 582(816) (Eff 1-10-61); 135 v H 716. Eff 1-1-74.**

The effective date is set by section 1 of HB 716.

# CHAPTER 3719: CONTROLLED SUBSTANCES

Section



## § 3719.01 Definitions.

As used in this chapter:

(A) "Administer" means the direct application of a drug, whether by injection, inhalation, ingestion, or any other means to a person or an animal.

(B) "Drug enforcement administration" means the drug enforcement administration of the United States department of justice or its successor agency.

(C) "Controlled substance" means a drug, compound, mixture, preparation, or substance included in schedule I, II, III, IV, or V.

(D) "Dangerous drug" has the same meaning as in section 4729.01 of the Revised Code.

(E) "Dispense" means to sell, leave with, give away, dispose of, or deliver.

(F) "Distribute" means to deal in, ship, transport, or deliver but does not include administering or dispensing a drug.

(G) "Drug" has the same meaning as in section 4729.01 of the Revised Code.

(H) "Drug abuse offense," "felony drug abuse offense," "cocaine," and "hashish" have the same meanings as in section 2925.01 of the Revised Code.

(I) "Federal drug abuse control laws" means the "Comprehensive Drug Abuse Prevention and Control Act of 1970," 84 Stat. 1242, 21 U.S.C. 801, as amended.

(J) "Hospital" means an institution for the care and treatment of the sick and injured that is certified by the department of health and approved by the state board of pharmacy as proper to be entrusted with the custody of controlled substances and the professional use of controlled substances.

(K) "Hypodermic" means a hypodermic syringe or needle, or other instrument or device for the injection of medication.

(L) "Isomer," except as otherwise expressly stated, means the optical isomer.

(M) "Laboratory" means a laboratory approved by the state board of pharmacy as proper to be entrusted with the custody of controlled substances and the use of controlled substances for scientific and clinical purposes and for purposes of instruction.

(N) "Manufacturer" means a person who manufactures a controlled substance, as "manufacture" is defined in section 3715.01 of the Revised Code.

(O) "Marihuana" means all parts of a plant of the genus cannabis, whether growing or not; the seeds of a plant of that type; the resin extracted from a part of a plant of that type; and every compound, manufacture, salt, derivative, mixture, or preparation of a plant of that type or of its seeds or resin. "Marihuana" does not include the mature stalks of the plant, fiber produced from the stalks, oils or cake made from the seeds of the plant, or any other compound, manufacture, salt, derivative, mixture, or preparation of the mature stalks, except the resin extracted from the mature stalks, fiber, oil or cake, or the sterilized seed of the plant that is incapable of germination.

(P) "Narcotic drugs" means coca leaves, opium, isonipecaine, amidone, isoamidone, ketobemidone, as defined in this division, and every substance not chemically distinguished from them and every drug, other than cannabis, that may be included in the meaning of "narcotic drug" under the federal drug abuse control laws. As used in this division:

(1) "Coca leaves" includes cocaine and any compound, manufacture, salt, derivative, mixture, or preparation of coca leaves, except derivatives of coca leaves, that does not contain cocaine, ecgonine, or substances from which cocaine or ecgonine may be synthesized or made.

(2) "Isonipecaine" means any substance identified chemically as 1-methyl-4-phenyl-piperidine-4-carboxylic acid ethyl ester, or any salt thereof, by whatever trade name designated.

(3) "Amidone" means any substance identified chemically as 4-4-diphenyl-6-dimethylamino-heptanone-3, or any salt thereof, by whatever trade name designated.

(4) "Isoamidone" means any substance identified chemically as 4-4-diphenyl-5-methyl-6-dimethylaminohexanone-3, or any salt thereof, by whatever trade name designated.

(5) "Ketobemidone" means any substance identified chemically as 4-(3-hydroxyphenyl)-1-methyl-4-piperidyl ethyl ketone hydrochloride, or any salt thereof, by whatever trade name designated.

(Q) "Official written order" means an order written on a form provided for that purpose by the director of the United States drug enforcement administration, under any laws of the United States making provision for the order, if the order forms are authorized and required by federal law.

(R) "Opiate" means any substance having an addiction-forming or addiction-sustaining liability similar to morphine or being capable of conversion into a drug having addiction-forming or addiction-sustaining liability. "Opiate" does not include, unless specifically designated as controlled under section 3719.41 of the Revised Code, the dextrorotatory isomer of 3-methoxy-N-methylmorphinan and its salts (dextro-methorphan). "Opiate" does include its racemic and levoratory forms.

(S) "Opium poppy" means the plant of the species papaver somniferum L., except its seeds.

(T) "Person" means any individual, corporation, government, governmental subdivision or agency, business trust, estate, trust, partnership, association, or other legal entity.

(U) "Pharmacist" means a person licensed under Chapter 4729. of the Revised Code to engage in the practice of pharmacy.

(V) "Pharmacy" has the same meaning as in section 4729.01 of the Revised Code.

(W) "Poison" means any drug, chemical, or preparation likely to be deleterious or destructive to adult human life in quantities of four grams or less.

(X) "Poppy straw" means all parts, except the seeds, of the opium poppy, after mowing.

(Y) "Licensed health professional authorized to prescribe drugs," "prescriber," and "prescription" have the same meanings as in section 4729.01 of the Revised Code.

(Z) "Registry number" means the number assigned to each person registered under the federal drug abuse control laws.

(AA) "Sale" includes delivery, barter, exchange, transfer, or gift, or offer thereof, and each transaction of those natures made by any person, whether as principal, proprietor, agent, servant, or employee.

(BB) "Schedule I," "schedule II," "schedule III," "schedule IV," and "schedule V" mean controlled substance schedules I, II, III, IV, and V, respectively, established pursuant to section 3719.41 of the Revised Code, as amended pursuant to section 3719.43 or 3719.44 of the Revised Code.

(CC) "Wholesaler" means a person who, on official written orders other than prescriptions, supplies controlled substances that the person has not manufactured, produced, or prepared personally and includes a "wholesale distributor of dangerous drugs" as defined in section 4729.01 of the Revised Code.

(DD) "Animal shelter" means a facility operated by a humane society or any society organized under Chapter 1717. of the Revised Code or a dog pound operated pursuant to Chapter 955. of the Revised Code.

(EE) "Terminal distributor of dangerous drugs" has the same meaning as in section 4729.01 of the Revised Code.

(FF) "Category III license" means a license issued to a terminal distributor of dangerous drugs as set forth in section 4729.54 of the Revised Code.

(GG) "Prosecutor" has the same meaning as in section 2935.01 of the Revised Code.

(HH)(1) "Controlled substance analog" means, except as provided in division (HH)(2) of this section, a substance to which both of the following apply:

(a) The chemical structure of the substance is substantially similar to the structure of a controlled substance in schedule I or II.

(b) One of the following applies regarding the substance:

(i) The substance has a stimulant, depressant, or hallucinogenic effect on the central nervous system that is substantially similar to or greater than the stimulant, depressant, or hallucinogenic effect on the central nervous system of a controlled substance in schedule I or II.

(ii) With respect to a particular person, that person represents or intends the substance to have a stimulant, depressant, or hallucinogenic effect on the central nervous system that is substantially similar to or greater than the stimulant, depressant, or hallucinogenic effect on the central nervous system of a controlled substance in schedule I or II.

(2) "Controlled substance analog" does not include any of the following:

(a) A controlled substance;

(b) Any substance for which there is an approved new drug application;

(c) With respect to a particular person, any substance if an exemption is in effect for investigational use for that person pursuant to federal law to the extent that conduct with respect to that substance is pursuant to that exemption;

(d) Any substance to the extent it is not intended for human consumption before the exemption described in division (HH)(2)(b) of this section takes effect with respect to that substance.

**HISTORY: 136 v H 300 (Eff 7-1-76); 136 v S 414 (Eff 9-22-76); 137 v H 1 (Eff 8-26-77); 145 v H 88 (Eff 6-29-94); 145 v H 391 (Eff 7-21-94); 146 v S 2 (Eff 7-1-96); 146 v S 269 (Eff 7-1-96); 146 v H 162 (Eff 1-1-97); 147 v S 66. Eff 7-22-98; 2011 HB 64, § 1, eff. Oct. 17, 2011.**

**Analogous to former RC § 3719.01 (GC § 12672-1; 116 v 491, § 1; 123 v 266; Bureau of Code Revision, 10-1-53; 126 v 178; 133 v H 874; 134 v H 924), repealed 136 v H 300, eff 7-1-76.**

## § 3719.011 Definitions.

As used in the Revised Code:

(A) "Drug of abuse" means any controlled substance as defined in section 3719.01 of the Revised Code, any harmful intoxicant as defined in section 2925.01 of the Revised Code, and any dangerous drug as defined in section 4729.01 of the Revised Code.

(B) "Drug dependent person" means any person who, by reason of the use of any drug of abuse, is physically, psychologically, or physically and psychologically dependent upon the use of such drug, to the detriment of the person's health or welfare.

(C) "Person in danger of becoming a drug dependent person" means any person who, by reason of the person's habitual or incontinent use of any drug of abuse, is in imminent danger of becoming a drug dependent person.

**HISTORY: 133 v H 874 (Eff 9-16-70); 134 v S 141 (Eff 12-31-71); 136 v H 300 (Eff 7-1-76); 147 v S 66. Eff 7-22-98.**

## § 3719.012 Minor may give consent to treatment for condition caused by drug or alcohol abuse.

(A) Notwithstanding any other provision of law, a minor may give consent for the diagnosis or treatment by a physician licensed to practice in this state of any condition which it is reasonable to believe is caused by a drug of abuse, beer, or intoxicating liquor. Such consent shall not be subject to disaffirmance because of minority.

(B) A physician licensed to practice in this state, or any person acting at his direction, who in good faith renders medical or surgical services to a minor giving consent under division (A) of this section, shall not be subject to any civil or criminal liability for assault, battery, or assault and battery.

(C) The parent or legal guardian of a minor giving consent under division (A) of this section is not liable for the payment of any charges made for medical or surgical services rendered such minor, unless the parent or legal guardian has also given consent for the diagnosis or treatment.

**HISTORY: 134 v S 406 (Eff 2-9-72); 139 v H 357. Eff 10-1-82.**

## § 3719.013 Controlled substance analog.

A controlled substance analog, to the extent intended for human consumption, shall be treated for purposes of any provision of the Revised Code as a controlled substance in schedule I.

**HISTORY: 2011 HB 64, § 1, eff. Oct. 17, 2011.**

## § 3719.02 Manufacturer of controlled substances; license.

A person may cultivate, grow, or by other process produce or manufacture, and a person on land owned, occupied, or controlled by such person may knowingly allow to be cultivated, grown, or produced, any controlled substance if the person first obtains a license as a manufacturer of controlled substances from the state board of pharmacy.

All licenses issued pursuant to this section shall be for a period of one year from the last day of June and may be renewed for a like period annually according to the standard renewal procedure of sections 4745.01 to 4745.03 of the Revised Code.

The annual license fee shall be thirty-seven dollars and fifty cents and shall accompany each application for a license or renewal thereof. A license that has not been renewed by the first day of August in any year may be reinstated upon payment of the renewal fee and a penalty of fifty-five dollars.

The state board of pharmacy, subject to the approval of the controlling board, may establish a fee in excess of the amount provided in this section, provided that the fee does not exceed the amount established by this section by more than fifty per cent.

**HISTORY: GC § 12672-2; 116 v 491, § 2; Bureau of Code Revision, 10-1-53; 126 v 178 (Eff 9-16-55); 132 v H 911 (Eff 6-11-68); 133 v H 742 (Eff 11-21-69); 136 v H 300 (Eff 7-1-76); 143 v H 111 (Eff 7-1-89); 146 v H 117 (Eff 6-30-95); 147 v H 215. Eff 6-30-97.**

## § 3719.021 License as wholesaler of controlled substances.

Persons other than a licensed manufacturer, pharmacist, or owner of a pharmacy who possess for sale, sell, or dispense controlled substances at wholesale shall first obtain a license as a wholesaler of controlled substances from the state board of pharmacy.

All licenses issued pursuant to this section shall be for a period of one year from the thirtieth day of June and may be renewed for a like period annually according to the standard renewal procedure of sections 4745.01 to 4745.03 of the Revised Code.

The annual license fee shall be thirty-seven dollars and fifty cents and shall accompany each application for such license or renewal thereof. All such renewal fees shall be paid in advance by the renewal applicant to the treasurer of state, and entered by the treasurer of state on the records of the state board of pharmacy. A license that has not been renewed by the first day of August in any year may be reinstated upon payment of the renewal fee and a penalty of fifty-five dollars.

The state board of pharmacy, subject to the approval of the controlling board, may establish a fee in excess of the amount provided in this section, provided that the fee does not exceed the amount established by this section by more than fifty per cent.

**HISTORY: 126 v 178 (Eff 9-16-55); 132 v H 911 (Eff 6-11-68); 133 v H 742 (Eff 11-21-69); 136 v H 300 (Eff 7-1-76); 143 v H 111 (Eff 7-1-89); 146 v H 117 (Eff 6-30-95); 147 v H 215. Eff 6-30-97.**

## § 3719.03 Qualification of applicant for license; revocation.

No license shall be issued under section 3719.02 or 3719.021 [3719.02.1] of the Revised Code unless and until the applicant therefor has furnished proof satisfactory to the state board of pharmacy:

(A) That the applicant is of good moral character or, if the applicant be an association or corporation, that the managing officers are of good moral character;

(B) That the applicant is equipped as to land, buildings, and paraphernalia properly to carry on the business described in his application;

(C) That the applicant's trade connections are such that there is a reasonable probability that he will apply all controlled substances grown, cultivated, processed, produced, or possessed by him to scientific, experimental, medicinal, or instructive purposes;

(D) That the applicant is in sufficiently good financial condition to carry out his obligation;

(E) That the applicant has satisfactorily shown that the granting of such license is in the public interest.

No license shall be granted to any person who has, within five years, been convicted of a drug abuse offense as defined in section 3719.01 of the Revised Code, or to any person who is a drug dependent person.

The board may suspend or revoke, for cause, any license issued under section 3719.02 or 3719.021 [3719.02.1] of the Revised Code.

**HISTORY: GC § 12672-3; 116 v 491, § 3; Bureau of Code Revision, 10-1-53; 126 v 178 (Eff 9-16-55); 136 v H 300. Eff 7-1-76.**

The effective date is set by section 4 of HB 300.

## § 3719.031 Suspension of wholesaler's license.

If the state board of pharmacy determines that there is clear and convincing evidence that the method used by a wholesaler of controlled substances licensed under section 3719.021 of the Revised Code to distribute controlled substances presents a danger of immediate and serious harm to others, the board may suspend the wholesaler's license without a hearing. The board shall follow the procedure for suspension without a prior hearing in section 119.07 of the Revised Code. The suspension shall remain in effect, unless removed by the board, until the board's final adjudication order becomes effective, except that if the board does not issue its final adjudication order within ninety days after the hearing, the suspension shall be void on the ninety-first day after the suspension.

**HISTORY: 2011 HB 93, § 1, eff. May 20, 2011.**

Acts 2011, HB 93, § 8 provides: "(A) Not later than one year after the effective date of this section, and annually each year for four years thereafter, the State Board of Pharmacy shall prepare a report on all of the following:

"(1) The total number of applications received by the Board for a terminal distributor of dangerous drugs license with a pain management clinic classification;

"(2) The total number of licenses with a pain management clinic classification granted or denied by the Board;

"(3) Any disciplinary actions taken by the Board against holders of licenses with a pain management clinic classification;

"(4) Total revenues generated from fees for licenses with a pain management clinic classification, fines and penalties paid by license holders, or other disciplinary actions taken against license holders;

"(5) Any other relevant information regarding the implementation of this act.

"(B) On completion of each report, the Board shall submit a copy of the report to the Governor and, in accordance with section 101.68 of the Revised Code, the General Assembly. In accordance with that section, the Board shall display the report on the Board's internet web site."

## § 3719.04 Sale of Schedule II substances by manufacturer or wholesaler.

(A) A licensed manufacturer or wholesaler of controlled substances may sell at wholesale controlled substances to any of the following persons and subject to the following conditions:

(1) To a licensed manufacturer or wholesaler of controlled substances, or a terminal distributor of dangerous drugs having a category III license;

(2) To a person in the employ of the United States government or of any state, territorial, district, county, municipal, or insular government, purchasing, receiving, possessing, or dispensing controlled substances by reason of his official duties;

(3) To a master of a ship or a person in charge of any aircraft upon which no physician is regularly employed, for the actual medical needs of persons on board the ship or aircraft, when not in port; provided such controlled substances shall be sold to the master of the ship or person in charge of the aircraft only in pursuance of a special official written order approved by a commissioned medical officer or acting assistant surgeon of the United States public health service;

(4) To a person in a foreign country, if the federal drug abuse control laws are complied with.

(B) An official written order for any schedule II controlled substances shall be signed in triplicate by the person giving the order or by his authorized agent. The original shall be presented to the person who sells or dispenses the schedule II controlled substances named in the order and, if that person accepts the order, each party to the transaction shall preserve his copy of the order for a period of two years in such a way as to be readily accessible for inspection by any public officer or employee engaged in the enforcement of Chapter 3719. of the Revised Code. Compliance with the federal drug abuse control laws, respecting the requirements governing the use of a special official written order constitutes compliance with this division.

**HISTORY: GC § 12672-4; 116 v 491, § 4; Bureau of Code Revision, 10-1-53; 126 v 178 (Eff 9-16-55); 134 v H 924 (Eff 10-26-71); 137 v H 1 (Eff 8-26-77); 145 v H 88. Eff 6-29-94.**

## § 3719.05 Dispensing by pharmacist; sale of stock.

(A) A pharmacist may dispense controlled substances to any person upon a prescription issued in accordance with section 3719.06 of the Revised Code. When dispensing controlled substances, a pharmacist shall act in accordance with rules adopted by the state board of pharmacy and in accordance with the following:

(1) The prescription shall be retained on file by the owner of the pharmacy in which it is filled for a period of three years, so as to be readily accessible for inspection by any public officer or employee engaged in the enforcement of Chapter 2925., 3719., or 4729. of the Revised Code.

(2) Each oral prescription shall be recorded by the pharmacist and the record shall show the name and address of the patient for whom, or of the owner of the animal for which the controlled substance is dispensed, the full name, address, and registry number under the federal drug abuse control laws of the prescriber, the name of the controlled substance dispensed, the amount dispensed, and the date when dispensed. The record shall be retained on file by the owner of the pharmacy in which it is filled for a period of three years.

(3) A schedule II controlled substance shall be dispensed only upon a written prescription, except that it may be dispensed upon an oral prescription in emergency situations as provided in the federal drug abuse control laws.

(4) A prescription for a schedule II controlled substance shall not be refilled.

(5) Prescriptions for schedule III and IV controlled substances may be refilled not more than five times in a six-month period from the date the prescription is given by a prescriber.

(B) The legal owner of any stock of schedule II controlled substances in a pharmacy, upon discontinuance of dealing in those drugs, may sell the stock to a manufacturer, wholesaler, or owner of a pharmacy registered under the federal drug abuse control laws pursuant to an official written order.

**HISTORY: GC § 12672-5; 116 v 491, § 5; Bureau of Code Revision, 10-1-53; 126 v 178 (Eff 9-16-55); 134 v H 924 (Eff 10-26-71); 136 v H 300 (Eff 7-1-76); 145 v H 391 (Eff 7-21-94); 147 v S 66. Eff 7-22-98.**

## § 3719.06 Authority of licensed health professional; contents of prescription.

(A)(1) A licensed health professional authorized to prescribe drugs, if acting in the course of professional practice, in accordance with the laws regulating the professional's practice, and in accordance with rules adopted by the state board of pharmacy, may, except as provided in division (A)(2) or (3) of this section, do the following:

(a) Prescribe schedule II, III, IV, and V controlled substances;

(b) Administer or personally furnish to patients schedule II, III, IV, and V controlled substances;

(c) Cause schedule II, III, IV, and V controlled substances to be administered under the prescriber's direction and supervision.

(2) A licensed health professional authorized to prescribe drugs who is a clinical nurse specialist, certified nurse-midwife, or certified nurse practitioner is subject to both of the following:

(a) A schedule II controlled substance may be prescribed only for a patient with a terminal condition, as defined in section 2133.01 of the Revised Code, only if the nurse's collaborating physician initially prescribed the substance for the patient, and only in an amount that does not exceed the amount necessary for the patient's use in a single, twenty-four-hour period.

(b) No schedule II controlled substance shall be personally furnished to any patient.

(3) A licensed health professional authorized to prescribe drugs who is a physician assistant shall not prescribe or personally furnish to patients any controlled substance that is not included in the physician-delegated prescriptive authority granted to the physician assistant in accordance with Chapter 4730. of the Revised Code.

(B) No licensed health professional authorized to prescribe drugs shall prescribe, administer, or personally furnish a schedule III anabolic steroid for the purpose of human muscle building or enhancing human athletic performance and no pharmacist shall dispense a schedule III anabolic steroid for either purpose, unless it has been approved for that purpose under the "Federal Food, Drug, and Cosmetic Act," 52 Stat. 1040 (1938), 21 U.S.C.A. 301, as amended.

(C) Each written prescription shall be properly executed, dated, and signed by the prescriber on the day when issued and shall bear the full name and address of the person for whom, or the owner of the animal for which, the controlled substance is prescribed and the full name, address, and registry number under the federal drug abuse control laws of the prescriber. If the prescription is for an animal, it shall state the species of the animal for which the controlled substance is prescribed.

**HISTORY: GC § 12672-6; 116 v 491, § 6; Bureau of Code Revision, 10-1-53; 126 v 178 (Eff 9-16-55); 134 v H 924 (Eff 10-26-71); 136 v H 300 (Eff 7-1-76); 144 v H 62 (Eff 5-21-91); 145 v H 391 (Eff 7-21-94); 147 v S 66 (Eff 7-22-98); 148 v H 241. Eff 5-17-2000; 151 v S 154, § 1, eff. 5-17-06.**

## § 3719.07 Records of controlled substances.

(A) As used in this section, "description" means the dosage form, strength, and quantity, and the brand name, if any, or the generic name, of a drug or controlled substance.

(B)(1) Every licensed health professional authorized to prescribe drugs shall keep a record of all controlled substances received and a record of all controlled substances administered, dispensed, or used other than by prescription. Every other person, except a pharmacist, manufacturer, or wholesaler, who is authorized to purchase and use controlled substances shall keep a record of all controlled substances purchased and used other than by prescription. The records shall be kept in accordance with division (C)(1) of this section.

(2) Manufacturers and wholesalers shall keep records of all controlled substances compounded, mixed, cultivated, grown, or by any other process produced or prepared by them, and of all controlled substances received or sold by them. The records shall be kept in accordance with division (C)(2) of this section.

(3) Every category III terminal distributor of dangerous drugs shall keep records of all controlled substances received or sold. The records shall be kept in accordance with division (C)(3) of this section.

(4) Every person who sells or purchases for resale schedule V controlled substances exempted by section 3719.15 of the Revised Code shall keep a record showing the quantities and kinds thereof received or sold. The records shall be kept in accordance with divisions (C)(1), (2), and (3) of this section.

(C)(1) The records required by divisions (B)(1) and (4) of this section shall contain the following:

(a) The description of all controlled substances received, the name and address of the person from whom received, and the date of receipt;

(b) The description of controlled substances administered, dispensed, purchased, sold, or used; the date of administering, dispensing, purchasing, selling, or using; the name and address of the person to whom, or for whose use, or the owner and species of the animal for which the controlled substance was administered, dispensed, purchased, sold, or used.

(2) The records required by divisions (B)(2) and (4) of this section shall contain the following:

(a) The description of all controlled substances produced or prepared, the name and address of the person from whom received, and the date of receipt;

(b) The description of controlled substances sold, the name and address of each person to whom a controlled substance is sold, the amount of the controlled substance sold to each person, and the date it was sold.

(3) The records required by divisions (B)(3) and (4) of this section shall contain the following:

(a) The description of controlled substances received, the name and address of the person from whom controlled substances are received, and the date of receipt;

(b) The name and place of residence of each person to whom controlled substances, including those otherwise exempted by section 3719.15 of the Revised Code, are sold, the description of the controlled substances sold to each person, and the date the controlled substances are sold to each person.

(D) Every record required by this section shall be kept for a period of two years.

The keeping of a record required by or under the federal drug abuse control laws, containing substantially the same information as specified in this section, constitutes compliance with this section.

Every person who purchases for resale or who sells controlled substance preparations exempted by section 3719.15 of the Revised Code shall keep the record required by or under the federal drug abuse control laws.

**HISTORY: GC § 12672-8; 116 v 491, § 8; Bureau of Code Revision, 10-1-53; 126 v 178; 127 v 290; 128 v 1044 (Eff 10-22-59); 129 v 1796 (Eff 10-13-61); 134 v H 924 (Eff 10-26-71); 136 v H 300 (Eff 7-1-76); 140 v H 208 (Eff 9-20-84); 145 v H 88 (Eff 6-29-94); 147 v S 66. Eff 7-22-98.**

## § 3719.08 Labeling.

(A) Whenever a manufacturer sells a controlled substance, and whenever a wholesaler sells a controlled substance in a package the wholesaler has prepared, the manufacturer or wholesaler shall securely affix to each package in which the controlled substance is contained a label showing in legible English the name and address of the vendor and the quantity, kind, and form of controlled substance contained therein. No person, except a pharmacist for the purpose of dispensing a controlled substance upon a prescription shall alter, deface, or remove any label so affixed.

(B) Except as provided in division (C) of this section, when a pharmacist dispenses any controlled substance on a prescription for use by a patient, or supplies a controlled substance to a licensed health professional authorized to prescribe drugs for use by the professional in personally furnishing patients with controlled substances, the pharmacist shall affix to the container in which the controlled substance is dispensed or supplied a label showing the following:

(1) The name and address of the pharmacy dispensing or supplying the controlled substance;

(2) The name of the patient for whom the controlled substance is prescribed and, if the patient is an animal, the name of the owner and the species of the animal;

(3) The name of the prescriber;

(4) All directions for use stated on the prescription or provided by the prescriber;

(5) The date on which the controlled substance was dispensed or supplied;

(6) The name, quantity, and strength of the controlled substance and, if applicable, the name of the distributor or manufacturer.

(C) The requirements of division (B) of this section do not apply when a controlled substance is prescribed or supplied for administration to an ultimate user who is institutionalized.

(D) A licensed health professional authorized to prescribe drugs who personally furnishes a controlled substance to a patient shall comply with division (A) of section 4729.291 of the Revised Code with respect to labeling and packaging of the controlled substance.

(E) No person shall alter, deface, or remove any label affixed pursuant to this section as long as any of the original contents remain.

(F) Every label for a schedule II, III, or IV controlled substance shall contain the following warning:

"Caution: federal law prohibits the transfer of this drug to any person other than the patient for whom it was prescribed."

**HISTORY: GC § 12672-9; 116 v 491, § 9; Bureau of Code Revision, 10-1-53; 126 v 178 (Eff 9-16-55); 134 v H 924 (Eff 10-26-71); 136 v H 300 (Eff 7-1-76); 147 v S 66. Eff 7-22-98; 2011 HB 93, § 1, eff. May 20, 2011.**

Acts 2011, HB 93, § 8 provides: "(A) Not later than one year after the effective date of this section, and annually each year for four years thereafter, the State Board of Pharmacy shall prepare a report on all of the following:

"(1) The total number of applications received by the Board for a terminal distributor of dangerous drugs license with a pain management clinic classification;

"(2) The total number of licenses with a pain management clinic classification granted or denied by the Board;

"(3) Any disciplinary actions taken by the Board against holders of licenses with a pain management clinic classification;

"(4) Total revenues generated from fees for licenses with a pain management clinic classification, fines and penalties paid by license holders, or other disciplinary actions taken against license holders;

"(5) Any other relevant information regarding the implementation of this act.

"(B) On completion of each report, the Board shall submit a copy of the report to the Governor and, in accordance with section 101.68 of the Revised Code, the General Assembly. In accordance with that section, the Board shall display the report on the Board's internet web site."

## § 3719.09 When possession of controlled substances is authorized.

Possession or control of controlled substances is authorized in the following instances and subject to the following conditions:

(A) Possession of controlled substances in the course of business by a manufacturer, wholesaler, licensed health professional authorized to prescribe drugs, pharmacist, category III terminal distributor of dangerous drugs, or other person authorized to possess controlled substances under this chapter or Chapter 4729. of the Revised Code;

(B) Possession by any person of any schedule V narcotic drug exempted under section 3719.15 of the Revised Code, where the quantity of the drug does not exceed one hundred thirty milligrams of opium, thirty-two and five-tenths milligrams of morphine or any of its salts, two hundred sixty milligrams of codeine or any of its salts, one hundred thirty milligrams of dihydrocodeine or any of its salts, or thirty-two and five-tenths milligrams of ethylmorphine or any of its salts, or, in the case of any other schedule V controlled substance or any combination of narcotic drugs, where the quantity does not exceed in pharmacologic potency any one of the drugs named above in the quantity stated;

(C) Possession by any person of any controlled substance that the person obtained pursuant to a prescription issued by a licensed health professional authorized to prescribe drugs or that was obtained for the person pursuant to a prescription issued by a prescriber, when the drug is in a container regardless of whether the container is the original container in which the drug was dispensed to that person directly or indirectly by a pharmacist or personally furnished to that person by the prescriber;

(D) Possession in the course of business of combination drugs that contain pentobarbital and at least one noncontrolled substance active ingredient, in a manufactured dosage form, the only indication of which is for euthanizing animals, or other substance that the state veterinary medical licensing board and the state board of pharmacy both approve under division (A) of section 4729.532 [4729.53.2] of the Revised Code, by an agent or employee of an animal shelter who is authorized by the licensure of the animal shelter with the state board of pharmacy to purchase and possess the drug solely for use as specified in that section. As used in this division, "in the course of business" means possession or use at an establishment described in a license issued under section 4729.54 of the Revised Code, or outside that establishment when necessary because of a risk to the health or safety of any person, provided that the substance is in a quantity no greater than reasonably could be used to alleviate the risk, is in the original manufacturer's container, and is returned to the establishment as soon as possible after the risk has passed.

**HISTORY: 138 v S 184, § 5 (Eff 6-20-84); 145 v H 88 (Eff 6-29-94); 146 v S 2 (Eff 7-1-96); 147 v S 66. Eff 7-22-98.**

**Analogous to former RC § 3719.09 (GC § 12672-10, 116 v 491, § 10; Bureau of Code Revision, 10-1-53; 126 v 178; 128 v 1044; 129 v 1796; 133 v H 874; 136 v H 300; 138 v S 184), repealed 138 v S 184, § 4, eff 6-20-84.**

## § 3719.10 Nuisance.

Premises or real estate, including vacant land, on which a felony violation of Chapter 2925. or 3719. of the Revised Code occurs constitute a nuisance subject to abatement pursuant to Chapter 3767. of the Revised Code.

**HISTORY: 136 v H 300. Eff 7-1-76.**

**Analogous to former RC § 3719.10 (GC § 12672-12; 116 v 491; Bureau of Code Revision, 10-1-53), repealed 136 v H 300, eff 7-1-76.**

The effective date is set by section 4 of HB 300.

## § 3719.11 Forfeiture and disposition of controlled substances.

All controlled substances, the lawful possession of which is not established or the title to which cannot be ascertained, that have come into the custody of a peace officer, shall be forfeited pursuant to Chapter 2981. of the Revised Code, and, unless any such section provides for a different manner of disposition, shall be disposed of as follows:

(A) The court or magistrate having jurisdiction shall order the controlled substances forfeited and destroyed. The agency served by the peace officer who obtained or took custody of the controlled substances may destroy them or may send them to the bureau of criminal identification and investigation for destruction by it. A record of the place where the controlled substances were seized, of the kinds and quantities of controlled substances so destroyed, and of the time, place, and manner of destruction, shall be kept, and a return under oath, reporting the destruction, shall be made by the officer who destroys them to the court or magistrate and to the United States director, bureau of narcotics and dangerous drugs.

(B) Upon written application by the department of health, the court or magistrate that ordered the forfeiture of the controlled substances may order the delivery of any of them, except heroin and its salts and derivatives, to the department for distribution or destruction as provided in this section.

(C) Upon application by any hospital within this state that is not operated for private gain, the department of health may deliver any controlled substances that have come into its custody pursuant to this section to the applicant for medicinal use. The department may deliver excess stocks of the controlled substances to the United States director, bureau of narcotics and dangerous drugs, or may destroy the excess stocks.

(D) The department of health shall keep a complete record of all controlled substances received pursuant to this section and of all controlled substances disposed of pursuant to this section, showing all of the following:

(1) The exact kinds, quantities, and forms of the controlled substances;

(2) The persons from whom they were received and to whom they were delivered;

(3) By whose authority they were received, delivered, or destroyed;

(4) The dates of their receipt, delivery, or destruction.

(E) The record required by this section shall be open to inspection by all federal and state officers charged with the enforcement of federal and state narcotic and drug abuse control laws.

**HISTORY: GC § 12672-13; 116 v 491, § 13; Bureau of Code Revision, 10-1-53; 134 v H 924 (Eff 10-26-71); 136 v H 300 (Eff 7-1-76); 141 v S 69 (Eff 9-3-86); 143 v H 215 (Eff**

**4-11-90); 143 v S 258 (Eff 11-20-90); 147 v H 2. Eff 1-1-99; 151 v H 241, § 1, eff. 7-1-07.**

The provisions of § 4 of 151 v H 241 read as follows:

SECTION 4. Sections 1, 2, and 3 of this act shall take effect on July 1, 2007. If a criminal or civil forfeiture action relating to misconduct under Title XXIX of the Revised Code was or is commenced before July 1, 2007, and is still pending on that date, the court in which the case is pending shall, to the extent practical, apply the provisions of Chapter 2981. of the Revised Code in the case.

The effective date is set by section 4 of HB 2.

## § 3719.12 Report of conviction to licensing or registration board.

Unless a report has been made pursuant to section 2929.42 of the Revised Code, on the conviction of a manufacturer, wholesaler, terminal distributor of dangerous drugs, pharmacist, pharmacy intern, dentist, chiropractor, physician, podiatrist, registered nurse, licensed practical nurse, physician assistant, optometrist, or veterinarian of the violation of this chapter or Chapter 2925. of the Revised Code, the prosecutor in the case promptly shall report the conviction to the board that licensed, certified, or registered the person to practice or to carry on business. The responsible board shall provide forms to the prosecutor. Within thirty days of the receipt of this information, the board shall initiate action in accordance with Chapter 119. of the Revised Code to determine whether to suspend or revoke the person's license, certificate, or registration.

**HISTORY: GC § 12672-14; 116 v 491, § 14; Bureau of Code Revision, 10-1-53; 126 v 178 (Eff 9-16-55); 134 v H 924 (Eff 10-26-71); 136 v H 300 (Eff 7-1-76); 143 v H 615 (Eff 3-27-91); 146 v S 2 (Eff 7-1-96); 146 v S 143, § 1 (Eff 3-5-96); 146 v S 143, § 5 (Eff 7-1-96); 147 v S 66 (Eff 7-22-98); 148 v H 506. Eff 4-10-2001; 149 v H 490, § 1, eff. 1-1-04.**

The effective date is set by section 4 of H.B. 490.

## § 3719.121 Suspension of licensed or registered person addicted to or improperly distributing controlled substances.

(A) Except as otherwise provided in section 4723.28, 4723.35, 4730.25, 4731.22, 4734.39, or 4734.41 of the Revised Code, the license, certificate, or registration of any dentist, chiropractor, physician, podiatrist, registered nurse, licensed practical nurse, physician assistant, pharmacist, pharmacy intern, optometrist, or veterinarian who is or becomes addicted to the use of controlled substances shall be suspended by the board that authorized the person's license, certificate, or registration until the person offers satisfactory proof to the board that the person no longer is addicted to the use of controlled substances.

(B) If the board under which a person has been issued a license, certificate, or evidence of registration determines that there is clear and convincing evidence that continuation of the person's professional practice or method of prescribing or personally furnishing controlled substances presents a danger of immediate and serious harm to others, the board may suspend the person's license, certificate, or registration without a hearing. Except as otherwise provided in sections 4715.30, 4723.281 [4723.28.1], 4729.16, 4730.25, 4731.22, and 4734.36 of the Revised Code, the board shall follow the procedure for suspension without a prior hearing in section 119.07 of the Revised Code. The suspension shall remain in effect, unless removed by the board, until the board's final adjudication order becomes effective, except that if the board does not issue its final adjudication order within ninety days after the hearing, the suspension shall be void on the ninety-first day after the hearing.

(C) On receiving notification pursuant to section 2929.42 or 3719.12 of the Revised Code, the board under which a person has been issued a license, certificate, or evidence of registration immediately shall suspend the license, certificate, or registration of that person on a plea of guilty to, a finding by a jury or court of the person's guilt of, or conviction of a felony drug abuse offense; a finding by a court of the person's eligibility for intervention in lieu of conviction; a plea of guilty to, or a finding by a jury or court of the person's guilt of, or the person's conviction of an offense in another jurisdiction that is essentially the same as a felony drug abuse offense; or a finding by a court of the person's eligibility for treatment or intervention in lieu of conviction in another jurisdiction. The board shall notify the holder of the license, certificate, or registration of the suspension, which shall remain in effect until the board holds an adjudicatory hearing under Chapter 119. of the Revised Code.

**HISTORY: 126 v 178 (Eff 9-16-55); 129 v 582(816) (Eff 1-10-61); 136 v H 300 (Eff 7-1-76); 143 v H 615 (Eff 3-27-91); 146 v S 2 (Eff 7-1-96); 146 v S 143, § 1 (Eff 3-5-96); 146 v S 143, § 5 (Eff 7-1-96); 147 v S 66 (Eff 7-22-98); 148 v S 107 (Eff 3-23-2000); 148 v S 172 (Eff 2-12-2001); 148 v H 506. Eff 4-10-2001; 149 v H 490, § 1, eff. 1-1-04.**

The effective date is set by section 4 of H.B. 490.

## § 3719.13 Inspection of prescriptions, orders, records, and stock.

Prescriptions, orders, and records, required by Chapter 3719. of the Revised Code, and stocks of dangerous drugs and controlled substances, shall be open for inspection only to federal, state, county, and municipal officers, and employees of the state board of pharmacy whose duty it is to enforce the laws of this state or of the United States relating to controlled substances. Such prescriptions, orders, records, and stocks shall be open for inspection by employees of the state medical board for purposes of enforcing Chapters 4730. and 4731. of the Revised Code and employees of the board of nursing for purposes of enforcing Chapter 4723. of the Revised Code. No person having knowledge of any such prescription, order, or record shall divulge such knowledge, except in connection with a prosecution or proceeding in court or before a licensing or registration board or officer, to which prosecution or proceeding the person to whom such prescriptions, orders, or records relate is a party.

**HISTORY: GC § 12672-15; 116 v 491, § 15; Bureau of Code Revision, 10-1-53; 136 v H 300 (Eff 7-1-76); 140 v H 208 (Eff 9-20-84); 141 v H 769 (Eff 3-17-87); 148 v H 511. Eff 4-10-2001; 152 v S 175, § 1, eff. 9-12-08.**

## § 3719.14 Exemptions.

(A) A common carrier or warehouse while engaged in lawfully transporting or storing any controlled substance or an employee of a common carrier or warehouse of that nature who is acting within the scope of the employee's employment may control and possess any controlled substance.

(B) Any law enforcement official may purchase, collect, or possess any controlled substance or may offer to sell any controlled substance, or any counterfeit controlled substance as defined in section 2925.01 of the Revised Code, when the purchase, collection, possession, or offer to sell is necessary to do so in the performance of the official's official duties. This division does not permit a law enforcement official to sell any controlled substance in the performance of the official's official duties. A peace officer, as defined in section 3719.141 [3719.14.1] of the Revised Code, may sell a controlled substance in the performance of the officer's official duties only as provided in that section.

(C) Any employee or agent of a person who is entitled to possession of a controlled substance or whose possession of a controlled substance is for the purpose of aiding any law enforcement official in the official's official duties temporarily may possess any controlled substance.

**HISTORY: 136 v H 300 (Eff 7-1-76); 143 v H 215 (Eff 4-11-90); 146 v H 125. Eff 7-1-96; 2011 HB 9, § 1, eff. June 29, 2011.**

Acts 2011, HB 9, § 3 provides: "This act applies to transactions entered into on or after the effective date of this act."

**Analogous to former RC § 3719.14 (GC § 12672-11; 116 v 491; Bureau of Code Revision, 10-1-53), repealed 136 v H 300, eff 7-1-76.**

The effective date is set by section 3 of HB 125.

## § 3719.141 Sales of controlled substances by peace officers.

(A) A peace officer may sell any controlled substance in the performance of the officer's official duties only if either of the following applies:

(1) A peace officer may sell any controlled substance in the performance of the officer's official duties if all of the following apply:

(a) Prior approval for the sale has been given by the prosecuting attorney of the county in which the sale takes place, in any manner described in division (B) of this section;

(b) The peace officer who makes the sale determines that the sale is necessary in the performance of the officer's official duties;

(c) Any of the following applies:

(i) The person to whom the sale is made or any other person who is involved in the sale does not know that the officer who makes the sale is a peace officer, and the peace officer who makes the sale determines that the sale is necessary to prevent the person from determining or suspecting that the officer who makes the sale is a peace officer.

(ii) The peace officer who makes the sale determines that the sale is necessary to preserve an identity that the peace officer who makes the sale has assumed in the performance of the officer's official duties.

(iii) The sale involves a controlled substance that, during the course of another sale, was intercepted by the peace officer who makes the sale or any other peace officer who serves the same agency served by the peace officer who makes the sale; the intended recipient of the controlled substance in the other sale does not know that the controlled substance has been so intercepted; the sale in question is made to the intended recipient of the controlled substance in the other sale and is undertaken with the intent of obtaining evidence of a drug abuse offense against the intended recipient of the controlled substance; and the sale in question does not involve the transfer of any money or other thing of value to the peace officer who makes the sale or any other peace officer who serves the same agency served by the peace officer who makes the sale in exchange for the controlled substance.

(d) If the sale is made under the circumstances described in division (A)(1)(c)(i) or (ii) of this section, no person is charged with any criminal offense or any delinquent act based upon the sale unless both of the following apply:

(i) The person also is charged with a criminal offense or a delinquent act that is based upon an act or omission that is independent of the sale but that either is connected together with the sale, or constitutes a part of a common scheme or plan with the sale, or is part of a course of criminal conduct involving the sale.

(ii) The criminal offense or delinquent act based upon the sale and the other criminal offense or delinquent act are charged in the same indictment, information, or complaint.

(e) The sale is not part of a continuing course of conduct involving the sale of controlled substances by the peace officer who makes the sale.

(f) The amount of the controlled substance sold and the scope of the sale of the controlled substance is as limited as possible under the circumstances.

(g) Prior to the sale, the law enforcement agency served by the peace officer who makes the sale has adopted a written internal control policy that does all of the following:

(i) Addresses the keeping of detailed records as to the amount of money or other things of value obtained in the sale in exchange for the controlled substance;

(ii) Addresses the delivery of all moneys or things of value so obtained to the prosecuting attorney pursuant to division (D) of this section;

(iii) Addresses the agency's use and disposition of all such moneys or things of value that are deposited in the law enforcement trust fund of the sheriff, municipal corporation, or township, pursuant to division (D) of this section, and that are used by the sheriff, are allocated to the police department of the municipal corporation by its legislative authority, or are allocated by the board of township trustees to the township police department, township or joint police district police force, or office of the constable;

(iv) Provides for the keeping of detailed financial records of the receipts of the proceeds, the general types of expenditures made out of the proceeds received, and the specific amount of each general type of expenditure. The policy shall not provide for or permit the identification of any peace officer involved in the sale, any information that is or may be needed in an ongoing investigation, or any specific expenditure that is made in an ongoing investigation.

(2) A peace officer may sell any controlled substance in the performance of the officer's official duties if all of the following apply:

(a) Prior approval for the sale has been given by the prosecuting attorney of the county in which the sale takes place, in any manner described in division (B) of this section;

(b) Prior to the sale, the law enforcement agency served by the peace officer has adopted a written internal control policy that does the things listed in divisions (A)(1)(g)(i) to (iv) of this section;

(c) The purchaser of the controlled substance acquires possession of it in the presence of the peace officer who makes the sale.

(d) Upon the consummation of the sale, either of the following occurs:

(i) The peace officer arrests the purchaser of the controlled substance, recovers it and the proceeds of the sale, and secures it and the proceeds as evidence to be used in a subsequent prosecution.

(ii) The peace officer makes a reasonable, good faith effort to arrest the purchaser of the controlled substance and to recover the controlled substance and the proceeds of the sale, but the officer is unable to make the arrest and recover all of the controlled substance and proceeds for reasons beyond the officer's control, and the peace officer secures all of the controlled substance recovered and all of the proceeds recovered as evidence to be used in a subsequent prosecution.

(B) The approval of a prosecuting attorney required by division (A)(1)(a) or (2)(a) of this section may be in either of the following forms:

(1) A general approval that is given by the prosecuting attorney to the peace officer who makes the sale or to the law enforcement agency served by that peace officer, that grants approval only to that peace officer, and that grants approval for any such sale that may be necessary, after the approval has been granted, under the standards described in division (A)(1) or (2) of this section;

(2) A specific approval that is given by the prosecuting attorney to the peace officer who makes the sale or to the law enforcement agency served by that peace officer, and that grants approval only to that peace officer and only for the particular sale in question, under the standards described in division (A)(1) or (2) of this section.

(C) If a peace officer sells a controlled substance in the performance of the officer's official duties under division (A)(1) or (2) of this section, the peace officer, within a reasonable time after the sale, shall provide the prosecuting attorney who granted approval for the sale with a written summary that identifies the amount and type of controlled substance sold, the circumstances of the sale, and the amount of any money or other thing of value obtained in the sale in exchange for the controlled substance. The summary shall not identify or enable the identification of any peace officer involved in the sale and shall not contain any information that is or may be needed in an ongoing investigation.

(D)(1) Except as provided in division (D)(2) of this section, if a peace officer sells a controlled substance in the performance of the officer's official duties under division (A)(1) or (2) of this section, the peace officer, as soon as possible after the sale, shall deliver all money or other things of value obtained in the sale in exchange for the controlled substance to the prosecuting attorney who granted approval for the sale. The prosecuting attorney shall safely keep all money and other things of value the prosecuting attorney receives under this division for use as evidence in any criminal action or delinquency proceeding based upon the sale. All money so received by a prosecuting attorney that no longer is needed as evidence in any criminal action or delinquency proceeding shall be deposited by the prosecuting attorney in the law enforcement trust fund of the sheriff if the peace officer who made the sale is the sheriff or a deputy sheriff or the law enforcement trust fund of a municipal corporation or township if it is served by the peace officer who made the sale, as established pursuant to section 2981.13 of the Revised Code, and upon deposit shall be expended only as provided in that section. All other things of value so received by a prosecuting attorney that no longer are needed as evidence in any criminal action or delinquency proceeding shall be disposed of, without appraisal, at a public auction to the highest bidder for cash; the proceeds of the sale shall be deposited by the prosecuting attorney in the law enforcement trust fund of the sheriff if the peace officer who made the sale is the sheriff or a deputy sheriff or the law enforcement trust fund of a municipal corporation or township if it is served by the peace officer who made the sale, as established pursuant to section 2981.13 of the Revised Code, and upon deposit shall be expended only as provided in that section. Each law enforcement agency that uses any money that was deposited in a law enforcement trust fund pursuant to this division shall comply with the written internal control policy adopted by the agency, as required by division (A)(1)(g) or (2)(b) of this section, in its use of the money.

(2) Division (D)(1) of this section does not apply in relation to a peace officer who sells a controlled substance in the performance of the officer's official duties under division (A)(1) of this section in any of the following circumstances:

(a) The person to whom the sale is made or any other person who is involved in the sale does not know that the officer is a peace officer, and, if the officer were to retain and deliver the money or other things of value to the prosecuting attorney, the person would determine or suspect that the officer is a peace officer.

(b) If the officer were to retain and deliver the money or other things of value to the prosecuting attorney, an identity that has been assumed in the performance of the officer's official duties would not be preserved.

(c) The sale is made under the circumstances described in division (A)(1)(c)(iii) of this section.

(3) If division (D)(1) of this section does not apply in relation to a peace officer who sells a controlled substance in the performance of the officer's official duties under division (A)(1) of this section due to the operation of division (D)(2) of this section, the peace officer, as soon as possible after the sale, shall deliver to the prosecuting attorney who granted approval for the sale a written summary that describes the circumstances of the sale and the reason for which division (D)(1) of this section does not apply. The summary shall not identify or enable the identification of any peace officer involved in the sale and shall not contain any information that is or may be needed in an ongoing investigation.

(E)(1) A written internal control policy adopted by a law enforcement agency that is served by a peace officer who sells a controlled substance under division (A)(1) or (2) of this section, as required by division (A)(1)(g) or (2)(b) of this section, is a public record open for inspection under section 149.43 of the Revised Code. Each law enforcement agency that adopts a written internal control policy of that nature shall comply with it in relation to any sale of a controlled substance under division (A)(1) or (2) of this section. All records as to the amount of money or things of value obtained in the sale of a controlled substance, in exchange for the controlled substance, and all financial records of the receipts of the proceeds, the general types of expenditures made out of the proceeds received, and the specific amounts of each general type of expenditure by a law enforcement agency in relation to any sale of a controlled substance under division (A)(1) or

(2) of this section are public records open for inspection under section 149.43 of the Revised Code.

(2) A summary required by division (C) or (D)(3) of this section is a public record open for inspection under section 149.43 of the Revised Code.

(F)(1) Each prosecuting attorney who grants approval for a sale of controlled substances by a peace officer and who receives in any calendar year one or more summaries under division (C) of this section relative to the sale of a controlled substance by a peace officer shall prepare a report covering the calendar year that cumulates all of the information contained in each of the summaries so received in the calendar year and shall send the cumulative report, no later than the first day of March in the calendar year following the calendar year covered by the report, to the attorney general.

(2) Each prosecuting attorney who receives any money or any other thing of value under division (D)(1) of this section shall keep detailed financial records of the receipts and dispositions of all such moneys or things of value so received. No record of that nature shall identify, or enable the identification of, any person from whom money or another thing of value was received as a result of the sale of a controlled substance under division (A)(1) or (2) of this section or contain any information that is or may be needed in an ongoing investigation. Each record of that nature is a public record open for inspection under section 149.43 of the Revised Code and shall include, but is not limited to, all of the following information:

(a) The identity of each law enforcement agency that has so delivered any money or other thing of value to the prosecuting attorney;

(b) The total amount of money or other things of value so received from each law enforcement agency;

(c) The disposition made under this section of all money or other things of value so received.

(G) Divisions (A) to (F) of this section do not apply to any peace officer, or to any officer, agent, or employee of the United States, who is operating under the management and direction of the United States department of justice. Any peace officer, or any officer, agent, or employee of the United States, who is operating under the management and direction of the United States department of justice may sell a controlled substance in the performance of the officer's, agent's, or employee's official duties if the sale is made in accordance with federal statutes and regulations.

(H) As used in this section, "peace officer" has the same meaning as in section 2935.01 of the Revised Code and also includes a special agent of the bureau of criminal identification and investigation.

**HISTORY: 143 v H 215 (Eff 4-11-90); 143 v H 588 (Eff 10-31-90); 143 v S 258 (Eff 11-20-90); 146 v S 2 (Eff 7-1-96); 146 v H 125. Eff 7-1-96; 151 v H 241, § 1, eff. 7-1-07; 2011 HB 153, § 101.01, eff. Sept. 29, 2011.**

See provisions of § 4 of 151 v H 241 following RC § 3719.11. The effective date is set by section 3 of HB 125.

## § 3719.15 Exempted preparations.

This chapter and Chapter 2925. of the Revised Code shall not apply, except as specifically provided otherwise in those chapters, to the following cases:

(A) Where a licensed health professional authorized to prescribe drugs administers or personally furnishes, or where a pharmacist sells at retail, any medicinal preparation that contains in thirty milliliters, or if a solid or semisolid preparation, in thirty grams, of any of the following:

(1) Not more than one hundred thirty milligrams of opium;

(2) Not more than sixteen and twenty-five one hundreths milligrams of morphine or of any of its salts;

(3) Not more than sixty-five milligrams of codeine or of any of its salts;

(4) Not more than thirty-two and five-tenths milligrams of dihydrocodeine or any of its salts;

(5) Not more than sixteen and twenty-five one hundreths milligrams of ethylmorphine or any of its salts.

Each preparation specified in divisions (A)(1), (2), (3), (4), and (5) of this section shall in addition contain one or more non-narcotic active medicinal ingredients in sufficient proportion to confer upon the preparation valuable medicinal qualities other than those possessed by the narcotic drug alone.

(6) Pharmaceutical preparations in solid form containing not more than two and five-tenths milligrams diphenoxylate and not less than twenty-five micrograms atropine sulfate per dosage unit.

(B) Where a licensed health professional authorized to prescribe drugs administers or personally furnishes, or where a pharmacist sells at retail, liniments, ointments, and other preparations, that are susceptible of external use only and that contain narcotic drugs in a combination that prevents the drugs from being readily extracted from the liniments, ointments, or preparations, except that this chapter and Chapter 2925. of the Revised Code shall apply to all liniments, ointments, and other preparations that contain coca leaves in any quantity or combination.

The medicinal preparation, or the liniment, ointment, or other preparation susceptible of external use only, prescribed, personally furnished, administered, dispensed, or sold, shall contain, in addition to the narcotic drug in it, some drug or drugs conferring upon it medicinal qualities other than those possessed by the narcotic drug alone. The preparation shall be prescribed, personally furnished, administered, compounded, dispensed, and sold in good faith as a medicine, and not for the purpose of evading this chapter or Chapter 2925. of the Revised Code.

**HISTORY: GC § 12672-7; 116 v 491, § 7; Bureau of Code Revision, 10-1-53; 126 v 178 (Eff 9-16-55); 129 v 1796 (Eff 10-13-61); 134 v H 924 (Eff 10-26-71); 136 v H 300 (Eff 7-1-76); 147 v S 66. Eff 7-22-98.**

## § 3719.16 Dispensing of excepted substances.

No person shall dispense or sell, under the exemptions of section 3719.15 of the Revised Code to any one person, or for the use of any one person or animal, any preparation included within such section, when he knows, or can by reasonable diligence ascertain, that such dispensing or selling will provide the person to whom or for whose use, or the owner of the animal for the use of which, such preparation is dispensed or sold, within any forty-eight consecutive hours, with more than two grains of opium, or more than one-half of a grain of morphine or any of its salts, or more than four grains of codeine or any of its salts, or more than two grains of dihydrocodeine or any of its salts, or more than one-half grain of ethylmorphine or any of its salts, or will provide such person or the owner of such animal, within forty-eight consecutive hours, with more than one preparation exempted by the provisions of section 3719.15 of the Revised Code.

No person shall obtain or attempt to obtain, under the exemptions of section 3719.15e of the Revised Code, more than one preparation exempted by the provisions of that section within forty-eight consecutive hours.

**HISTORY: GC § 12672-7; 116 v 491, § 7; Bureau of Code Revision, 10-1-53; 126 v 178; 127 v 290; 128 v 1044 (Eff 10-22-59); 129 v 1796 (Eff 10-13-61); 134 v H 924. Eff 10-26-71.**

## § 3719.161 Alteration to increase concentration prohibited.

No person shall alter any controlled substance from the original compounded form by evaporation or other means to increase the concentration of narcotic drug contained therein. Altered preparations having a greater concentration of schedule V narcotic drug content than specified under provisions of section 3719.15 of the Revised Code, shall be classified as a schedule III narcotic drug.

**HISTORY: 128 v 1044 (Eff 10-22-59); 134 v H 924 (Eff 10-26-71); 136 v H 300. Eff 7-1-76.**

The effective date is set by section 4 of HB 300.

## § 3719.172 Possession, sale, and disposal of hypodermics.

(A) Possession of a hypodermic is authorized for the following:

(1) A manufacturer or distributor of, or dealer in, hypodermics or medication packaged in hypodermics, and any authorized agent or employee of that manufacturer, distributor, or dealer, in the regular course of business;

(2) A terminal distributor of dangerous drugs, in the regular course of business;

(3) A person authorized to administer injections, in the regular course of the person's profession or employment;

(4) A person, when the hypodermic was lawfully obtained and is kept and used for the purpose of self-administration of insulin or other drug prescribed for the treatment of disease by a licensed health professional authorized to prescribe drugs;

(5) A person whose use of a hypodermic is for legal research, clinical, educational, or medicinal purposes;

(6) A farmer, for the lawful administration of a drug to an animal;

(7) A person whose use of a hypodermic is for lawful professional, mechanical, trade, or craft purposes.

(B) No manufacturer or distributor of, or dealer in, hypodermics or medication packaged in hypodermics, or their authorized agents or employees, and no terminal distributor of dangerous drugs, shall display any hypodermic for sale. No person authorized to possess a hypodermic pursuant to division (A) of this section shall negligently fail to take reasonable precautions to prevent any hypodermic in the person's possession from theft or acquisition by any unauthorized person.

(C) No person other than one of the following shall sell or furnish a hypodermic to another person:

(1) A manufacturer or distributor of, or dealer in, hypodermics or medication packaged in hypodermics, or their authorized agents or employees;

(2) A terminal distributor of dangerous drugs;

(3) A person under the direct supervision of a pharmacist;

(4) A licensed health professional authorized to prescribe drugs, acting in the regular course of business and as permitted by law;

(5) An individual who holds a current license, certificate, or registration issued under Title 47 of the Revised Code and has been certified to conduct diabetes education by a national certifying body specified in rules adopted by the state board of pharmacy under section 4729.68 of the Revised Code, but only if diabetes education is within the individual's scope of practice under statutes and rules regulating the individual's profession.

(D) No person shall sell or furnish a hypodermic to another whom the person knows or has reasonable cause to believe is not authorized by division (A) of this section to possess a hypodermic.

**HISTORY: 134 v H 521 (Eff 10-19-72); 136 v H 300 (Eff 7-1-76); 146 v S 246 (Eff 11-6-96); 147 v S 66. Eff 7-22-98.**

**Not analogous to former RC § 3719.17.2 (126 v 178), repealed 134 v H 521, eff 10-19-72.**

## § 3719.18 Enforcement officers; co-operation with agencies.

(A) The state board of pharmacy, its officers, agents, inspectors, and representatives, and all officers within the state, and all prosecuting attorneys, shall enforce Chapters 2925. and 3719. of the Revised Code, except those specifically delegated, and cooperate with all agencies charged with the enforcement of the laws of the United States, of this state, and of all other states, relating to controlled substances.

(B) Nothing in this chapter shall be construed to require the state board of pharmacy to enforce minor violations of Chapters 2925. and 3719. of the Revised Code if the board determines that the public interest is adequately served by a notice or warning to the alleged offender.

**HISTORY: GC § 12672-18; 116 v 491, § 18; Bureau of Code Revision, 10-1-53; 136 v H 300 (Eff 7-1-76); 140 v H 208. Eff 9-20-84.**

## § 3719.19 Effect of federal prosecution.

No person shall be prosecuted for a violation of this chapter if the person has been acquitted or convicted under the federal drug abuse control laws of the same act or omission which, it is alleged, constitutes a violation of this chapter.

**HISTORY: GC § 12672-20; 116 v 491, § 20; Bureau of Code Revision, 10-1-53; 136 v H 300 (Eff 7-1-76); 147 v S 66. Eff 7-22-98.**

## § 3719.21 Disposition of fines and forfeited bail.

Except as provided in division (C) of section 2923.42, division (B) of section 2923.44, divisions (D)(1), (F), and (H) of section 2925.03, division (D)(1) of section 2925.02, 2925.04, or 2925.05, division (E)(1) of section 2925.11, division (F) of section 2925.13, division (F) of section 2925.36, division (D) of section 2925.22, division (H) of section 2925.23, division (M) of section 2925.37, division (B) of section 2925.42, division (B) of section 2929.18, division (D) of section 3719.99, division (B)(1) of section 4729.65, division (E)(3) of section 4729.99, and division

(I)(4) of section 4729.99 of the Revised Code, the clerk of the court shall pay all fines or forfeited bail assessed and collected under prosecutions or prosecutions commenced for violations of this chapter, section 2923.42 of the Revised Code, or Chapter 2925. of the Revised Code, within thirty days, to the executive director of the state board of pharmacy, and the executive director shall deposit the fines into the state treasury to the credit of the occupational licensing and regulatory fund.

**HISTORY: GC § 12672-19; 116 v 491, § 19; Bureau of Code Revision, 10-1-53; 136 v H 300 (Eff 7-1-76); 138 v H 204 (Eff 7-30-79); 143 v H 266 (Eff 9-6-90); 143 v S 258 (Eff 11-20-90); 145 v H 715 (Eff 7-22-94); 146 v S 2 (Eff 7-1-96); 146 v S 269 (Eff 7-1-96); 146 v S 166 (Eff 10-17-96); 147 v H 2 (Eff 1-1-99); 149 v H 327. Eff 7-8-2002; 151 v H 241, § 1, eff. 7-1-07; 152 v S 203, § 1, eff. 4-8-09; 153 v H 2, § 101.01, eff. 4-1-09.**

The effective date is set by §§ 901.10 and 901.11 of 153 v H 2.
See provisions of § 4 of 151 v H 241 following RC § 3719.11.
The provisions of § 4 of SB 166 (146 v —) read as follows:

SECTION 4. The amendments made by this act to sections 309.08, 2925.03, 2929.18, 3719.21, 3793.06, and 3793.11 of the Revised Code apply to offenses that are committed on or after the effective date of this act.

## § 3719.27 Inspection and checking of files and records.

Persons required, by Chapter 3719. of the Revised Code, to keep files or records shall, upon the written request of an officer or employee designated by the state board of pharmacy, make such files or records available to such officer or employee, at all reasonable hours, for inspection and copying, and accord to such officer or employee full opportunity to check the correctness of such files or records, including opportunity to make inventory of all stocks of controlled substances on hand. No person shall fail to make such files or records available or to accord such opportunity to check their correctness.

**HISTORY: GC § 12673-4; 123 v 174, § 5; Bureau of Code Revision, 10-1-53; 133 v H 90 (Eff 11-19-69); 136 v H 300. Eff 7-1-76.**

The effective date is set by section 4 of HB 300.

## § 3719.28 Rules for administration and enforcement.

(A) The state board of pharmacy, pursuant to Chapter 119. of the Revised Code, shall adopt rules for administration and enforcement of Chapter 3719. of the Revised Code and prescribing the manner of keeping and the form and content of records to be kept by persons authorized to manufacture, distribute, dispense, conduct research in, prescribe, administer, or otherwise deal with controlled substances. Such rules shall be designed to:

(1) Facilitate surveillance of traffic in drugs, to prevent the improper acquisition or use of controlled substances or their diversion into illicit channels;

(2) Aid the state board of pharmacy and state, local, and federal law enforcement officers in enforcing the laws of this state and the federal government dealing with drug abuse and control of drug traffic.

(B) Rules adopted pursuant to this section shall not provide any less stringent requirements with respect to records than the requirements of the federal drug abuse control laws and regulations adopted thereunder. To the extent that records kept under the federal drug abuse control laws and regulations adopted thereunder fulfill requirements for similar records under rules adopted pursuant to this section, compliance with the federal law and regulations shall constitute compliance with the law and rules of this state with respect to such records.

**HISTORY: 136 v H 300. Eff 7-1-76.**

**Analogous to former RC § 3719.28 (GC § 12673-5; 123 v 174, § 6; Bureau of Code Revision, 10-1-53; 126 v 178), repealed 136 v H 300, eff 7-1-76.**

The effective date is set by section 4 of HB 300.

### [POISON]

## § 3719.30 Leaving or depositing dangerous drug or poison.

No person shall leave or deposit dangerous drugs, poisons, or substances containing dangerous drugs or poisons in a common, street, alley, lane, or thoroughfare, or a yard or enclosure occupied by another.

Whoever violates this section shall be liable to the person injured for all damages sustained as a result of leaving or depositing the dangerous drugs, poisons, or other substances.

**HISTORY: RS § 6958; 74 v 13; GC § 12663; Bureau of Code Revision, 10-1-53; 147 v S 66. Eff 7-22-98.**

## § 3719.31 Prohibition against careless distribution of samples containing drug or poison.

No person shall leave, throw, or deposit upon the doorstep or premises owned or occupied by another, or hand, give, or deliver to any person, except in a place where it is kept for sale, a patent or proprietary medicine, preparation, pill, tablet, powder, cosmetic, disinfectant, or antiseptic, or a drug or medicine that contains poison or any ingredient that is deleterious to health, as a sample or for the purpose of advertising.

As used in this section "drug," "medicine," "patent or proprietary medicine," "pill," "tablet," "powder," "cosmetic," "disinfectant," or "antiseptic" includes all remedies for internal or external use.

**HISTORY: RS §§ 4238-34, 4238-35, 4238-36; 95 v 146, §§ 1, 2, 3; GC §§ 12664, 12665; 102 v 87; Bureau of Code Revision. Eff 10-1-53.**

## § 3719.32 Regulating the sale of poisons.

No person shall knowingly sell or deliver to any person otherwise than in the manner prescribed by laws, or sell or deliver to a minor under sixteen years of age in the manner prescribed by law but without the written order of an adult, any of the following substances or any poisonous compounds, combinations, or preparations thereof: the compounds and salts of antimony, arsenic, chromium, copper, lead, mercury, and zinc; the concentrated mineral acids; oxalic and hydrocyanic acids and their salts, and carbolic acid; yellow phosphorus; the essential oils of almonds, pennyroyal, tansy, and savin, croton oil, creosote, chloroform, chloral hydrate, and cantharides; aconite, belladonna, bitter almonds, colchicum, cotton root, cocculus indicus, conium, digitalis, hyoscyamus, ignatia, lobelia, nux vomica, opium, physostigma, phytolacca, strophanthus, stramonium, veratum viride, or any of the poisonous alkaloids or alkaloidal salts or other poisonous principles derived from such alkaloids, or other poisonous alkaloids or their salts; or other virulent poison.

**HISTORY: RS §§ 4238-29, 4238-32; 95 v 280; 95 v 282, § 4; GC § 12666; Bureau of Code Revision, 10-1-53; 125 v 903; 130 v Pt. 2, 194 (Eff 12-16-64); 136 v H 300. Eff 7-1-76.**

The effective date is set by section 4 of HB 300.

## § 3719.33 Labeling poisons.

No person shall sell or deliver to another a substance named in section 3719.32 of the Revised Code without having first learned by due inquiry that such person is aware of the poisonous character of such substance and that it is desired for a lawful purpose; or without plainly labeling "poison," and the names of two or more antidotes therefor, upon the box, bottle, or package containing it; or deliver such substance without recording in a book kept for the purpose, the name thereof, the quantity delivered, the purpose for which it is alleged to be used, the date of its delivery, the name and address of the purchaser, and the name of the dispenser; or fail to preserve said book for five years and submit it at all times for inspection to proper officers of the law.

**HISTORY: RS §§ 4238-29, 4238-32; 95 v 280, 282, §§ 1, 4; GC § 12667; Bureau of Code Revision. Eff 10-1-53.**

## § 3719.34 Good faith sale or delivery.

Sections 3719.32 and 3719.33 of the Revised Code do not apply to substances sold or delivered upon the order or prescription of a person believed by the seller or deliverer to be a licensed health professional authorized to prescribe drugs.

**HISTORY: RS § 4238-30; 95 v 281, § 2; GC § 12668; Bureau of Code Revision, 10-1-53; 147 v S 66. Eff 7-22-98.**

## § 3719.35 Exceptions to labeling and recording of delivery provisions.

It is not necessary to place a poison label upon, nor record the delivery of, any of the following:

(A) Preparations containing substances named in section 3719.32 of the Revised Code when a single box, bottle, or other package of the bulk of fifteen milliliters or the weight of fifteen grams does not contain more than one adult medicinal dose of any of those substances;

(B) The sulphide of antimony, the oxide or carbonate of zinc, or colors ground in oil and intended for use as paints;

(C) Preparations recommended in good faith for diarrhea or cholera, when each bottle or package is accompanied by specific directions for use and a caution against the habitual use of the preparations;

(D) Liniments or ointments when plainly labeled "for external use only";

(E) Preparations put up and sold in the form of pills, tablets, or lozenges and intended for internal use, when the dose recommended does not contain more than one fourth of an adult medicinal dose of any of the substances named in section 3719.35 of the Revised Code.

**HISTORY: RS § 4238-30; 95 v 281, § 2; GC §§ 12669, 12670, 12671; Bureau of Code Revision, 10-1-53; 147 v S 66. Eff 7-22-98.**

## § 3719.36 Board of pharmacy to enforce poison laws.

The state board of pharmacy shall enforce sections 3719.30 to 3719.35 of the Revised Code. If the board has information that any of those sections has been violated, it shall investigate, and upon probable cause appearing, shall file a complaint and prosecute the offender.

Fines assessed and collected under prosecutions commenced by the board shall be paid to the executive director of the state board of pharmacy, and by the executive director paid into the state treasury to the credit of the board of pharmacy drug law enforcement fund created by section 4729.65 of the Revised Code.

**HISTORY: GC § 12671-1; 109 v 100; 122 v 70; Bureau of Code Revision, 10-1-53; 145 v H 715 (Eff 7-22-94); 147 v S 66. Eff 7-22-98.**

# [REGULATIONS; NAMES]

## § 3719.40 Controlled substances included by designated name.

The controlled substances included or to be included in the schedules in section 3719.41 of the Revised Code are included by whatever official, common, usual, chemical, or trade name designated.

**HISTORY: 136 v H 300. Eff 7-1-76.**

**Not analogous to former RC § 3719.40 (132 v S 74; 133 v H 874), repealed 136 v H 300, eff 7-1-76.**

The effective date is set by section 4 of HB 300.

## § 3719.41 Schedules.

Controlled substance schedules I, II, III, IV, and V are hereby established, which schedules include the following, subject to amendment pursuant to section 3719.43 or 3719.44 of the Revised Code.

### SCHEDULE I

(A) Narcotics-opiates

Any of the following opiates, including their isomers, esters, ethers, salts, and salts of isomers, esters, and ethers, unless specifically excepted under federal drug abuse control laws, whenever the existence of these isomers, esters, ethers, and salts is possible within the specific chemical designation:

(1) Acetyl-alpha-methylfentanyl (N-[1-(1-methyl-2-phenethyl)-4-piperidinyl]-N-phenylacetamide);

(2) Acetylmethadol;

(3) Allylprodine;

(4) Alphacetylmethadol (except levo-alphacetylmethadol, also known as levo-alpha-acetylmethadol, levomethadyl acetate, or LAAM);

(5) Alphameprodine;

(6) Alphamethadol;

(7) Alpha-methylfentanyl (N-[1-(alpha-methyl-beta-phenyl)ethyl-4-piperidyl] propionanilide; 1-(1-methyl-2-phenylethyl)-4-(N-propanilido) piperidine);

(8) Alpha-methylthiofentanyl (N-[1-methyl-2-(2-thienyl)ethyl-4-piperidinyl]-N- phenylpropanamide);

(9) Benzethidine;

(10) Betacetylmethadol;

(11) Beta-hydroxyfentanyl (N-[1-(2-hydroxy-2-phenethyl-4-piperidinyl]-N- phenylpropanamide);

(12) Beta-hydroxy-3-methylfentanyl (other name: N-[1-(2-hydroxy-2-phenethyl)-3-methyl-4-piperidinyl]-N-phenylpropanamide);
(13) Betameprodine;
(14) Betamethadol;
(15) Betaprodine;
(16) Clonitazene;
(17) Dextromoramide;
(18) Diampromide;
(19) Diethylthiambutene;
(20) Difenoxin;
(21) Dimenoxadol;
(22) Dimepheptanol;
(23) Dimethylthiambutene;
(24) Dioxaphetyl butyrate;
(25) Dipipanone;
(26) Ethylmethylthiambutene;
(27) Etonitazene;
(28) Etoxeridine;
(29) Furethidine;
(30) Hydroxypethidine;
(31) Ketobemidone;
(32) Levomoramide;
(33) Levophenacylmorphan;
(34) 3-methylfentanyl (N-[3-methyl-1-(2-phenylethyl)-4-piperidyl]-N- phenylpropanamide);
(35) 3-methylthiofentanyl (N-[3-methyl-1-[2-(thienyl)ethyl]-4-piperidinyl]-N- phenylpropanamide);
(36) Morpheridine;
(37) MPPP (1-methyl-4-phenyl-4-propionoxypiperidine);
(38) Noracymethadol;
(39) Norlevorphanol;
(40) Normethadone;
(41) Norpipanone;
(42) Para-fluorofentanyl (N-(4-fluorophenyl)-N-[1-(2-phenethyl)-4-piperidinyl]propanamide;
(43) PEPAP (1-(2-phenethyl)-4-phenyl-4-acetoxypiperidine;
(44) Phenadoxone;
(45) Phenampromide;
(46) Phenomorphan;
(47) Phenoperidine;
(48) Piritramide;
(49) Proheptazine;
(50) Properidine;
(51) Propiram;
(52) Racemoramide;
(53) Thiofentanyl (N-phenyl-N-[1-(2-thienyl)ethyl-4-piperidinyl]-propanamide;
(54) Tilidine;
(55) Trimeperidine.

(B) Narcotics-opium derivatives

Any of the following opium derivatives, including their salts, isomers, and salts of isomers, unless specifically excepted under federal drug abuse control laws, whenever the existence of these salts, isomers, and salts of isomers is possible within the specific chemical designation:
(1) Acetorphine;
(2) Acetyldihydrocodeine;
(3) Benzylmorphine;
(4) Codeine methylbromide;
(5) Codeine-n-oxide;
(6) Cyprenorphine;
(7) Desomorphine;
(8) Dihydromorphine;
(9) Drotebanol;
(10) Etorphine (except hydrochloride salt);
(11) Heroin;
(12) Hydromorphinol;
(13) Methyldesorphine;
(14) Methyldihydromorphine;
(15) Morphine methylbromide;
(16) Morphine methylsulfonate;
(17) Morphine-n-oxide;
(18) Myrophine;
(19) Nicocodeine;
(20) Nicomorphine;
(21) Normorphine;
(22) Pholcodine;
(23) Thebacon.

(C) Hallucinogens

Any material, compound, mixture, or preparation that contains any quantity of the following hallucinogenic substances, including their salts, isomers, and salts of isomers, unless specifically excepted under federal drug abuse control laws, whenever the existence of these salts, isomers, and salts of isomers is possible within the specific chemical designation. For the purposes of this division only, "isomer" includes the optical isomers, position isomers, and geometric isomers.

(1) Alpha-ethyltryptamine (some trade or other names: etryptamine; Monase; alpha-ethyl-1H-indole-3-ethanamine; 3-(2-aminobutyl) indole; alpha-ET; and AET);

(2) 4-bromo-2,5-dimethoxyamphetamine (some trade or other names: 4-bromo-2,5-dimethoxy-alpha-methyphenethylamine; 4-bromo-2,5-DMA);

(3) 4-bromo-2,5-dimethoxyphenethylamine (some trade or other names: 2-(4-bromo-2,5-dimethoxyphenyl)-1-aminoethane; alpha-desmethyl DOB; 2C-B, Nexus);

(4) 2,5-dimethoxyamphetamine (some trade or other names: 2,5-dimethoxy-alpha-methylphenethylamine; 2,5-DMA);

(5) 2,5-dimethoxy-4-ethylamphetamine (some trade or other names: DOET);

(6) 4-methoxyamphetamine (some trade or other names: 4-methoxy-alpha-methylphenethylamine; paramethoxyamphetamine; PMA);

(7) 5-methoxy-3,4-methylenedioxy-amphetamine;

(8) 4-methyl-2,5-dimethoxy-amphetamine (some trade or other names: 4-methyl-2,5-dimethoxy-alpha-methylphenethylamine; "DOM" and "STP");

(9) 3,4-methylenedioxy amphetamine;

(10) 3,4-methylenedioxymethamphetamine (MDMA);

(11) 3,4-methylenedioxy-N-ethylamphetamine (also known as N-ethyl-alpha-methyl-3,4(methylenedioxy)phenethylamine, N-ethyl MDA, MDE, MDEA);

(12) N-hydroxy-3,4-methylenedioxyamphetamine (also known as N-hydroxy-alpha-methyl-3,4(methylenedioxy)phenethylamine and N-hydroxy MDA);

(13) 3,4,5-trimethoxy amphetamine;

(14) Bufotenine (some trade or other names: 3-(beta-dimethylaminoethyl)-5-hydroxyindole; 3-(2-dimethylaminoethyl)-5-indolol; N, N-dimethylserotonin; 5-hydroxy-N, N-dimethyltryptamine; mappine);

(15) Diethyltryptamine (some trade or other names: N, N-diethyltryptamine; DET);

(16) Dimethyltryptamine (some trade or other names: DMT);

(17) Ibogaine (some trade or other names: 7-ethyl-6,6beta,7,8,9,10,12,13-octahydro-2-methoxy-6,9-methano-

5H-pyrido[1',2':1,2] azepino [5, 4-b] indole; tabernanthe iboga);

(18) Lysergic acid diethylamide;

(19) Marihuana;

(20) Mescaline;

(21) Parahexyl (some trade or other names: 3-hexyl-1-hydroxy-7,8,9,10-tetrahydro-6,6,9-trimethyl-6H-dibenzo[b,d]pyra n; synhexyl);

(22) Peyote (meaning all parts of the plant presently classified botanically as "Lophophora williamsii Lemaire," whether growing or not, the seeds of that plant, any extract from any part of that plant, and every compound, manufacture, salts, derivative, mixture, or preparation of that plant, its seeds, or its extracts);

(23) N-ethyl-3-piperidyl benzilate;

(24) N-methyl-3-piperidyl benzilate;

(25) Psilocybin;

(26) Psilocyn;

(27) Tetrahydrocannabinols (synthetic equivalents of the substances contained in the plant, or in the resinous extractives of Cannabis, sp. and/or synthetic substances, derivatives, and their isomers with similar chemical structure and pharmacological activity such as the following: delta-1-cis or trans tetrahydrocannabinol, and their optical isomers; delta-6-cis or trans tetrahydrocannabinol, and their optical isomers; delta-3,4-cis or trans tetrahydrocannabinol, and its optical isomers. (Since nomenclature of these substances is not internationally standardized, compounds of these structures, regardless of numerical designation of atomic positions, are covered.));

(28) Ethylamine analog of phencyclidine (some trade or other names: N-ethyl-1-phenylcyclohexylamine; (1-phenylcyclohexyl)ethylamine; N-(1-phenylcyclohexyl)ethylamine; cyclohexamine; PCE);

(29) Pyrrolidine analog of phencyclidine (some trade or other names: 1-(1-phenylcyclohexyl)pyrrolidine; PCPy; PHP);

(30) Thiophene analog of phencyclidine (some trade or other names: 1-[1-(2-thienyl)-cyclohexyl]-piperidine; 2-thienyl analog of phencyclidine; TPCP; TCP);

(31) 1-[1-(2-thienyl)cyclohexyl]pyrrolidine;

(32) Hashish;

(33) Salvia divinorum;

(34) Salvinorin A;

(35) 1-Pentyl-3-(1-naphthoyl)indole (some trade or other names: JWH-018);

(36) 1-Butyl-3-(1-naphthoyl)indole (some trade or other names: JWH-073);

(37) 1-[2-(4-morpholinyl)ethyl]-3-(1-naphthoyl)indole (some trade or other names: JWH-200);

(38) 5-(1,1-dimethylheptyl)-2-[(1R,3S)-3-hydroxycyclohexyl]-phenol (some trade or other names: CP-47,497);

(39) 5-(1,1-dimethyloctyl)-2-[(1R,3S)-3-hydroxycyclohexyl]-phenol (some trade or other names: cannabicyclohexanol; CP-47,497 C8 homologue);

(40) Methylone (3,4-methylenedioxymethcathinone);

(41) MDPV (3,4-methyenedioxypyrovalerone);

(42) Mephedrone (4-methylmethcathinone);

(43) 4-methoxymethcathinone;

(44) 4-fluoromethcathinone;

(45) 3-fluoromethcathinone.

(D) Depressants

Any material, compound, mixture, or preparation that contains any quantity of the following substances having a depressant effect on the central nervous system, including their salts, isomers, and salts of isomers, unless specifically excepted under federal drug abuse control laws, whenever the existence of these salts, isomers, and salts of isomers is possible within the specific chemical designation:

(1) Mecloqualone;

(2) Methaqualone.

(E) Stimulants

Unless specifically excepted or unless listed in another schedule, any material, compound, mixture, or preparation that contains any quantity of the following substances having a stimulant effect on the central nervous system, including their salts, isomers, and salts of isomers:

(1) Aminorex (some other names: aminoxaphen; 2-amino-5-phenyl-2-oxazoline; or 4,5-dihydro-5-phenyl-2-oxazolamine);

(2) Cathinone (some trade or other names: 2-amino-1-phenyl-1-propanone, alpha-aminopropiophenone, 2-aminopropiophenone, and norephedrone);

(3) Fenethylline;

(4) Methcathinone (some other names: 2-(methylamino)-propiophenone; alpha-(methylamino)propiophenone; 2-methylamino)-1-phenylpropan-1-one; alpha-N-methylaminopropiophenone; monomethylpropion; ephedrone; N-methylcathinone; methylcathinone; AL-464; AL-422; AL-463; and UR1432, its salts, optical isomers, and salts of optical isomers;

(5) (+—)cis-4-methylaminorex ((+—)cis-4,5-dihydro-4-methyl-5-phenyl-2-oxazolamine);

(6) N-ethylamphetamine;

(7) N,N-dimethylamphetamine (also known as N,N-alpha-trimethyl-benzeneethanamine; N,N-alpha-trimethylphenethylamine).

## SCHEDULE II

(A) Narcotics-opium and opium derivatives

Unless specifically excepted under federal drug abuse control laws or unless listed in another schedule, any of the following substances whether produced directly or indirectly by extraction from substances of vegetable origin, independently by means of chemical synthesis, or by a combination of extraction and chemical synthesis:

(1) Opium and opiate, and any salt, compound, derivative, or preparation of opium or opiate, excluding apomorphine, thebaine-derived butorphanol, dextrorphan, nalbuphine, nalmefene, naloxone, and naltrexone, and their respective salts, but including the following:

(a) Raw opium;

(b) Opium extracts;

(c) Opium fluid extracts;

(d) Powdered opium;

(e) Granulated opium;

(f) Tincture of opium;

(g) Codeine;

(h) Ethylmorphine;

(i) Etorphine hydrochloride;

(j) Hydrocodone;

(k) Hydromorphone;

(l) Metopon;

(m) Morphine;

(n) Oxycodone;

(o) Oxymorphone;

(p) Thebaine.

(2) Any salt, compound, derivative, or preparation thereof that is chemically equivalent to or identical with any of the substances referred to in division (A)(1) of this schedule, except that these substances shall not include the isoquinoline alkaloids of opium;

(3) Opium poppy and poppy straw;

(4) Coca leaves and any salt, compound, derivative, or preparation of coca leaves (including cocaine and ecgonine, their salts, isomers, and derivatives, and salts of those isomers and derivatives), and any salt, compound, derivative, or preparation thereof that is chemically equivalent to or identical with any of these substances, except that the substances shall not include decocainized coca leaves or extraction of coca leaves, which extractions do not contain cocaine or ecgonine;

(5) Concentrate of poppy straw (the crude extract of poppy straw in either liquid, solid, or powder form that contains the phenanthrene alkaloids of the opium poppy).

(B) Narcotics-opiates

Unless specifically excepted under federal drug abuse control laws or unless listed in another schedule, any of the following opiates, including their isomers, esters, ethers, salts, and salts of isomers, esters, and ethers, whenever the existence of these isomers, esters, ethers, and salts is possible within the specific chemical designation, but excluding dextrorphan and levopropoxyphene:

(1) Alfentanil;
(2) Alphaprodine;
(3) Anileridine;
(4) Bezitramide;
(5) Bulk dextropropoxyphene (non-dosage forms);
(6) Carfentanil;
(7) Dihydrocodeine;
(8) Diphenoxylate;
(9) Fentanyl;
(10) Isomethadone;
(11) Levo-alphacetylmethadol (some other names: levo-alpha-acetylmethadol; levomethadyl acetate; LAAM);
(12) Levomethorphan;
(13) Levorphanol;
(14) Metazocine;
(15) Methadone;
(16) Methadone-intermediate, 4-cyano-2-dimethylamino-4,4-diphenyl butane;
(17) Moramide-intermediate, 2-methyl-3-morpholino-1,1-diphenylpropane-carboxylic acid;
(18) Pethidine (meperidine);
(19) Pethidine-intermediate-A, 4-cyano-1-methyl-4-phenylpiperidine;
(20) Pethidine-intermediate-B, ethyl-4-phenylpiperidine-4-carboxylate;
(21) Pethidine-intermediate-C, 1-methyl-4-phenylpiperidine-4-carboxylic acid;
(22) Phenazocine;
(23) Piminodine;
(24) Racemethorphan;
(25) Racemorphan;
(26) Remifentanil;
(27) Sufentanil.

(C) Stimulants

Unless specifically excepted under federal drug abuse control laws or unless listed in another schedule, any material, compound, mixture, or preparation that contains any quantity of the following substances having a stimulant effect on the central nervous system:

(1) Amphetamine, its salts, its optical isomers, and salts of its optical isomers;
(2) Methamphetamine, its salts, its isomers, and salts of its isomers;
(3) Methylphenidate;
(4) Phenmetrazine and its salts.

(D) Depressants

Unless specifically excepted under federal drug abuse control laws or unless listed in another schedule, any material, compound, mixture, or preparation that contains any quantity of the following substances having a depressant effect on the central nervous system, including their salts, isomers, and salts of isomers, whenever the existence of these salts, isomers, and salts of isomers is possible within the specific chemical designation:

(1) Amobarbital;
(2) Gamma-hydroxy-butyrate;
(3) Glutethimide;
(4) Pentobarbital;
(5) Phencyclidine (some trade or other names: 1-(1-phenylcyclohexyl)piperidine; PCP);
(6) Secobarbital;
(7) 1-aminophenylcyclohexane and all N-mono-substituted and/or all N-N-disubstituted analogs including, but not limited to, the following:
(a) 1-phenylcyclohexylamine;
(b) (1-phenylcyclohexyl) methylamine;
(c) (1-phenylcyclohexyl) dimethylamine;
(d) (1-phenylcyclohexyl) methylethylamine;
(e) (1-phenylcyclohexyl) isopropylamine;
(f) 1-(1-phenylcyclohexyl) morpholine.

(E) Hallucinogenic substances

(1) Nabilone (another name for nabilone: (+)-trans-3-(1,1-dimethylheptyl)-6,6a,7,8,10,10a-hexahydro-1-hydroxy-6,6-dimethyl-9H-dibenzo[b,d]pyran-9-one).

(F) Immediate precursors

Unless specifically excepted under federal drug abuse control laws or unless listed in another schedule, any material, compound, mixture, or preparation that contains any quantity of the following substances:

(1) Immediate precursor to amphetamine and methamphetamine:
(a) Phenylacetone (some trade or other names: phenyl-2-propanone; P2P; benzyl methyl ketone; methyl benzyl ketone);
(2) Immediate precursors to phencyclidine (PCP):
(a) 1-phenylcyclohexylamine;
(b) 1-piperidinocyclohexanecarbonitrile (PCC).

## SCHEDULE III

(A) Stimulants

Unless specifically excepted under federal drug abuse control laws or unless listed in another schedule, any material, compound, mixture, or preparation that contains any quantity of the following substances having a stimulant effect on the central nervous system, including their salts, their optical isomers, position isomers, or geometric isomers, and salts of these isomers, whenever the existence of these salts, isomers, and salts of isomers is possible within the specific chemical designation:

(1) All stimulant compounds, mixtures, and preparations included in schedule III pursuant to the federal drug abuse control laws and regulations adopted under those laws;
(2) Benzphetamine;
(3) Chlorphentermine;
(4) Clortermine;
(5) Phendimetrazine.

(B) Depressants

Unless specifically excepted under federal drug abuse control laws or unless listed in another schedule, any material, compound, mixture, or preparation that contains any quantity of the following substances having a depressant effect on the central nervous system:

(1) Any compound, mixture, or preparation containing amobarbital, secobarbital, pentobarbital, or any salt of any of these drugs, and one or more other active medicinal ingredients that are not listed in any schedule;

(2) Any suppository dosage form containing amobarbital, secobarbital, pentobarbital, or any salt of any of these drugs and approved by the food and drug administration for marketing only as a suppository;

(3) Any substance that contains any quantity of a derivative of barbituric acid or any salt of a derivative of barbituric acid;

(4) Chlorhexadol;

(5) Ketamine, its salts, isomers, and salts of isomers (some other names for ketamine: (+—)-2-(2-chlorophenyl)-2-(methylamino)-cyclohexanone);

(6) Lysergic acid;

(7) Lysergic acid amide;

(8) Methyprylon;

(9) Sulfondiethylmethane;

(10) Sulfonethylmethane;

(11) Sulfonmethane;

(12) Tiletamine, zolazepam, or any salt of tiletamine or zolazepam (some trade or other names for a tiletamine-zolazepam combination product: Telazol); (some trade or other names for tiletamine: 2-(ethylamino)-2-(2-thienyl)-cyclohexanone); (some trade or other names for zolazepam: 4-(2-fluorophenyl)-6,8- dihydro-1,3,8-trimethylpyrazolo-[3, 4-e][1,4]-diazepin-7(1H)-one; flupyrazapon).

(C) Narcotic antidotes

(1) Nalorphine.

(D) Narcotics-narcotic preparations

Unless specifically excepted under federal drug abuse control laws or unless listed in another schedule, any material, compound, mixture, or preparation that contains any of the following narcotic drugs, or their salts calculated as the free anhydrous base or alkaloid, in limited quantities as set forth below:

(1) Not more than 1.8 grams of codeine per 100 milliliters or not more than 90 milligrams per dosage unit, with an equal or greater quantity of an isoquinoline alkaloid of opium;

(2) Not more than 1.8 grams of codeine per 100 milliliters or not more than 90 milligrams per dosage unit, with one or more active, nonnarcotic ingredients in recognized therapeutic amounts;

(3) Not more than 300 milligrams of dihydrocodeinone per 100 milliliters or not more than 15 milligrams per dosage unit, with a fourfold or greater quantity of an isoquinoline alkaloid of opium;

(4) Not more than 300 milligrams of dihydrocodeinone per 100 milliliters or not more than 15 milligrams per dosage unit, with one or more active, nonnarcotic ingredients in recognized therapeutic amounts;

(5) Not more than 1.8 grams of dihydrocodeine per 100 milliliters or not more than 90 milligrams per dosage unit, with one or more active, nonnarcotic ingredients in recognized therapeutic amounts;

(6) Not more than 300 milligrams of ethylmorphine per 100 milliliters or not more than 15 milligrams per dosage unit, with one or more active, nonnarcotic ingredients in recognized therapeutic amounts;

(7) Not more than 500 milligrams of opium per 100 milliliters or per 100 grams or not more than 25 milligrams per dosage unit, with one or more active, nonnarcotic ingredients in recognized therapeutic amounts;

(8) Not more than 50 milligrams of morphine per 100 milliliters or per 100 grams, with one or more active, nonnarcotic ingredients in recognized therapeutic amounts.

(E) Anabolic steroids

Unless specifically excepted under federal drug abuse control laws or unless listed in another schedule, any material, compound, mixture, or preparation that contains any quantity of the following substances, including their salts, esters, isomers, and salts of esters and isomers, whenever the existence of these salts, esters, and isomers is possible within the specific chemical designation:

(1) Anabolic steroids. Except as otherwise provided in division (E)(1) of schedule III, "anabolic steroids" means any drug or hormonal substance that is chemically and pharmacologically related to testosterone (other than estrogens, progestins, and corticosteroids) and that promotes muscle growth. "Anabolic steroids" does not include an anabolic steroid that is expressly intended for administration through implants to cattle or other nonhuman species and that has been approved by the United States secretary of health and human services for that administration, unless a person prescribes, dispenses, or distributes this type of anabolic steroid for human use. "Anabolic steroid" includes, but is not limited to, the following:

(a) Boldenone;

(b) Chlorotestosterone (4-chlortestosterone);

(c) Clostebol;

(d) Dehydrochlormethyltestosterone;

(e) Dihydrotestosterone (4-dihydrotestosterone);

(f) Drostanolone;

(g) Ethylestrenol;

(h) Fluoxymesterone;

(i) Formebulone (formebolone);

(j) Mesterolone;

(k) Methandienone;

(l) Methandranone;

(m) Methandriol;

(n) Methandrostenolone;

(o) Methenolone;

(p) Methyltestosterone;

(q) Mibolerone;

(r) Nandrolone;

(s) Norethandrolone;

(t) Oxandrolone;

(u) Oxymesterone;

(v) Oxymetholone;

(w) Stanolone;

(x) Stanozolol;

(y) Testolactone;

(z) Testosterone;

(aa) Trenbolone;

(bb) Any salt, ester, isomer, or salt of an ester or isomer of a drug or hormonal substance described or listed in division (E)(1) of schedule III if the salt, ester, or isomer promotes muscle growth.

(F) Hallucinogenic substances

(1) Dronabinol (synthetic) in sesame oil and encapsulated in a soft gelatin capsule in a United States food and drug administration approved drug product (some other names for dronabinol: (6aR-trans)-6a,7,8,10a-tetrahydro-6,6,9-trimethyl-3-pentyl-6H-dibenzo[b,d]pyran-1-ol, or (-)-delta-9-(trans)-tetrahydrocannabinol).

## SCHEDULE IV

(A) Narcotic drugs

Unless specifically excepted by federal drug abuse control laws or unless listed in another schedule, any material, compound, mixture, or preparation that contains any of the following narcotic drugs, or their salts calculated as the free anhydrous base or alkaloid, in limited quantities as set forth below:

(1) Not more than one milligram of difenoxin and not less than 25 micrograms of atropine sulfate per dosage unit;

(2) Dextropropoxyphene (alpha-(+)-4-dimethylamino-1,2-diphenyl-3-methyl-2- propionoxybutane)[final dosage forms].

(B) Depressants

Unless specifically excepted under federal drug abuse control laws or unless listed in another schedule, any material, compound, mixture, or preparation that contains any quantity of the following substances, including their salts, isomers, and salts of isomers, whenever the existence of these salts, isomers, and salts of isomers is possible within the specific chemical designation:

(1) Alprazolam;
(2) Barbital;
(3) Bromazepam;
(4) Camazepam;
(5) Chloral betaine;
(6) Chloral hydrate;
(7) Chlordiazepoxide;
(8) Clobazam;
(9) Clonazepam;
(10) Clorazepate;
(11) Clotiazepam;
(12) Cloxazolam;
(13) Delorazepam;
(14) Diazepam;
(15) Estazolam;
(16) Ethchlorvynol;
(17) Ethinamate;
(18) Ethyl loflazepate;
(19) Fludiazepam;
(20) Flunitrazepam;
(21) Flurazepam;
(22) Halazepam;
(23) Haloxazolam;
(24) Ketazolam;
(25) Loprazolam;
(26) Lorazepam;
(27) Lormetazepam;
(28) Mebutamate;
(29) Medazepam;
(30) Meprobamate;
(31) Methohexital;
(32) Methylphenobarbital (mephobarbital);
(33) Midazolam;
(34) Nimetazepam;
(35) Nitrazepam;
(36) Nordiazepam;
(37) Oxazepam;
(38) Oxazolam;
(39) Paraldehyde;
(40) Petrichloral;
(41) Phenobarbital;
(42) Pinazepam;
(43) Prazepam;
(44) Quazepam;
(45) Temazepam;
(46) Tetrazepam;
(47) Triazolam;
(48) Zaleplon;
(49) Zolpidem.

(C) Fenfluramine

Any material, compound, mixture, or preparation that contains any quantity of the following substances, including their salts, their optical isomers, position isomers, or geometric isomers, and salts of these isomers, whenever the existence of these salts, isomers, and salts of isomers is possible within the specific chemical designation:

(1) Fenfluramine.

(D) Stimulants

Unless specifically excepted under federal drug abuse control laws or unless listed in another schedule, any material, compound, mixture, or preparation that contains any quantity of the following substances having a stimulant effect on the central nervous system, including their salts, their optical isomers, position isomers, or geometric isomers, and salts of these isomers, whenever the existence of these salts, isomers, and salts of isomers is possible within the specific chemical designation:

(1) Cathine ((+)-norpseudoephedrine);
(2) Diethylpropion;
(3) Fencamfamin;
(4) Fenproporex;
(5) Mazindol;
(6) Mefenorex;
(7) Modafinil;
(8) Pemoline (including organometallic complexes and chelates thereof);
(9) Phentermine;
(10) Pipradrol;
(11) Sibutramine;
(12) SPA [(-)-1-dimethylamino-1,2-diphenylethane].

(E) Other substances

Unless specifically excepted under federal drug abuse control laws or unless listed in another schedule, any material, compound, mixture, or preparation that contains any quantity of the following substances, including their salts:

(1) Pentazocine;
(2) Butorphanol (including its optical isomers).

## SCHEDULE V

(A) Narcotic drugs

Unless specifically excepted under federal drug abuse control laws or unless listed in another schedule, any material, compound, mixture, or preparation that contains any of the following narcotic drugs, and their salts, as set forth below:

(1) Buprenorphine.

(B) Narcotics-narcotic preparations

Narcotic drugs containing non-narcotic active medicinal ingredients. Any compound, mixture, or preparation that contains any of the following narcotic drugs, or their salts calculated as the free anhydrous base or alkaloid, in limited quantities as set forth below, and that includes one or more nonnarcotic active medicinal ingredients in sufficient proportion to confer upon the compound, mixture, or preparation valuable medicinal qualities other than those possessed by narcotic drugs alone:

(1) Not more than 200 milligrams of codeine per 100 milliliters or per 100 grams;

(2) Not more than 100 milligrams of dihydrocodeine per 100 milliliters or per 100 grams;

(3) Not more than 100 milligrams of ethylmorphine per 100 milliliters or per 100 grams;

(4) Not more than 2.5 milligrams of diphenoxylate and not less than 25 micrograms of atropine sulfate per dosage unit;

(5) Not more than 100 milligrams of opium per 100 milliliters or per 100 grams;

(6) Not more than 0.5 milligram of difenoxin and not less than 25 micrograms of atropine sulfate per dosage unit.

(C) Stimulants

Unless specifically exempted or excluded under federal drug abuse control laws or unless listed in another schedule, any material, compound, mixture, or preparation that contains any quantity of the following substances having a stimulant effect on the central nervous system, including their salts, isomers, and salts of isomers:

(1) Ephedrine, except as provided in division (K) of section 3719.44 of the Revised Code;

(2) Pyrovalerone.

**HISTORY: 136 v H 300 (Eff 7-1-76); 144 v H 62 (Eff 5-21-91); 145 v H 156 (Eff 5-19-93); 145 v H 391 (Eff 7-21-94); 146 v S 269 (Eff 7-1-96); 148 v H 428. Eff 5-17-2000; 152 v H 215, § 1, eff. 4-7-09; 2011 HB 153, § 101.01, eff. Sept. 29, 2011; 2011 HB 64, § 1, eff. Oct. 17, 2011.**

**Not analogous to former RC § 3719.41 (132 v S 74), repealed 136 v H 300, eff 7-1-76.**

The provisions of §§ 3, 9 of HB 156 (145 v —) read as follows:

SECTION 3. (A) In amending section 3719.41 of the Revised Code in this act, it is the intent of the General Assembly to codify the following in controlled substances Schedules I to V:

(1) The automatic addition of various compounds, mixtures, preparations, or substances to those schedules pursuant to section 3719.43 of the Revised Code following action taken by the United States Attorney General on or after July 1, 1976, and the addition of various compounds, mixtures, preparations, or substances to those schedules on or after July 1, 1976, by the State Board of Pharmacy pursuant to section 3719.44 of the Revised Code;

(2) The automatic transfer of various compounds, mixtures, preparations, or substances within those schedules, and the automatic removal of various compounds, mixtures, preparations, or substances from those schedules, pursuant to section 3719.43 of the Revised Code following action taken by the United States Attorney General on or after July 1, 1976;

(3) The transfer of various compounds, mixtures, preparations, or substances within those schedules, and the removal of various compounds, mixtures, preparations, or substances from those schedules on or after July 1, 1976, by the State Board of Pharmacy pursuant to section 3719.44 of the Revised Code.

(B) The General Assembly hereby declares that, in amending section 3719.41 of the Revised Code in Am. Sub. H.B. 62 of the 119th General Assembly, it solely intended to legislatively add anabolic steroids to controlled substances Schedule III and did not intend to affect controlled substances Schedules I to V insofar as, prior to May 21, 1991, various compounds, mixtures, preparations, or substances had been added to, transferred within, or removed from those schedules pursuant to sections 3719.43 and 3719.44 of the Revised Code.

SECTION 9. This act is hereby declared to be an emergency measure necessary for the immediate preservation of the public peace, health, and safety. The primary reason for the necessity is that the version of section 3719.41 of the Revised Code amended by Am. Sub. H.B. 62 of the 119th General Assembly and effective May 21, 1991, did not include certain compounds, mixtures, preparations, or substances that automatically had been added to controlled substances Schedules I to V pursuant to section 3719.43 of the Revised Code following action taken by the United States Attorney General on or after July 1, 1976, and did not reflect the automatic transfer of various compounds, mixtures, preparations, or substances within those schedules pursuant to section 3719.43 of the Revised Code following action taken by the United States Attorney General on or after July 1, 1976. The clarification of the status of controlled substances Schedules I to V is necessary to eliminate any uncertainty as to the nature of the controlled substances that may be the subject of offenses under Chapters 2925. and 3719. of the Revised Code. Therefore, this act shall go into immediate effect.

## § 3719.42 Annual meeting of state pharmacy board.

The state board of pharmacy shall meet in Columbus at least once each fiscal year for the purpose of carrying out its duties under this chapter.

**HISTORY: 136 v H 300 (Eff 7-1-76); 147 v S 66. Eff 7-22-98.**

**Not analogous to former RC § 3719.42 (132 v S 74), repealed 136 v H 300, eff 7-1-76.**

## § 3719.43 Addition, transfer, removal of substance by attorney general of United States; effect.

When pursuant to the federal drug abuse control laws the attorney general of the United States adds a compound, mixture, preparation, or substance to a schedule of the laws, transfers any of the same between one schedule of the laws to another, or removes a compound, mixture, preparation, or substance from the schedules of the laws then such addition, transfer, or removal is automatically effected in the corresponding schedule or schedules in section 3719.41 of the Revised Code, subject to amendment pursuant to section 3719.44 of the Revised Code.

**HISTORY: 136 v H 300. Eff 7-1-76.**

**Not analogous to former RC § 3719.43 (132 v S 74), repealed 136 v H 300, eff 7-1-76.**

The effective date is set by section 4 of HB 300.

See provisions, §§ 3, 9 of HB 156 (145 v —) following RC § 3719.41.

## § 3719.44 Authority of board of pharmacy to change schedules.

(A) Pursuant to this section, and by rule adopted in accordance with Chapter 119. of the Revised Code, the state board of pharmacy may do any of the following with respect to schedules I, II, III, IV, and V established in section 3719.41 of the Revised Code:

(1) Add a previously unscheduled compound, mixture, preparation, or substance to any schedule;

(2) Transfer a compound, mixture, preparation, or substance from one schedule to another, provided the transfer does not have the effect under this chapter of providing less stringent control of the compound, mixture, preparation, or substance than is provided under the federal drug abuse control laws;

(3) Remove a compound, mixture, preparation, or substance from the schedules where the board had previously added the compound, mixture, preparation, or substance to the schedules, provided that the removal shall not have the effect under this chapter of providing less stringent control of the compound, mixture, preparation, or substance than is provided under the federal drug abuse control laws.

(B) In making a determination to add, remove, or transfer pursuant to division (A) of this section, the board shall consider the following:

(1) The actual or relative potential for abuse;

(2) The scientific evidence of the pharmacological effect of the substance, if known;

(3) The state of current scientific knowledge regarding the substance;

(4) The history and current pattern of abuse;

(5) The scope, duration, and significance of abuse;

(6) The risk to the public health;

(7) The potential of the substance to produce psychic or physiological dependence liability;

(8) Whether the substance is an immediate precursor.

(C) The board may add or transfer a compound, mixture, preparation, or substance to schedule I when it appears that there is a high potential for abuse, that it has no accepted medical use in treatment in this state, or that it lacks accepted safety for use in treatment under medical supervision.

(D) The board may add or transfer a compound, mixture, preparation, or substance to schedule II when it appears that there is a high potential for abuse, that it has a currently accepted medical use in treatment in this state, or currently accepted medical use in treatment with severe restrictions, and that its abuse may lead to severe physical or severe psychological dependence.

(E) The board may add or transfer a compound, mixture, preparation, or substance to schedule III when it appears that there is a potential for abuse less than the substances included in schedules I and II, that it has a currently accepted medical use in treatment in this state, and that its abuse may lead to moderate or low physical or high psychological dependence.

(F) The board may add or transfer a compound, mixture, preparation, or substance to schedule IV when it appears that it has a low potential for abuse relative to substances included in schedule III, that it has a currently accepted medical use in treatment in this state, and that its abuse may lead to limited physical or psychological dependence relative to the substances included in schedule III.

(G) The board may add or transfer a compound, mixture, preparation, or substance to schedule V when it appears that it has lower potential for abuse than substances included in schedule IV, that it has currently accepted medical use in treatment in this state, and that its abuse may lead to limited physical or psychological dependence relative to substances included in schedule IV.

(H) Even though a compound, mixture, preparation, or substance does not otherwise meet the criteria in this section for adding or transferring it to a schedule, the board may nevertheless add or transfer it to a schedule as an immediate precursor when all of the following apply:

(1) It is the principal compound used, or produced primarily for use, in the manufacture of a controlled substance.

(2) It is an immediate chemical intermediary used or likely to be used in the manufacture of such a controlled substance.

(3) Its control is necessary to prevent, curtail, or limit the manufacture of the scheduled compound, mixture, preparation, or substance of which it is the immediate precursor.

(I) Authority to control under this section does not extend to distilled spirits, wine, or beer, as those terms are defined or used in Chapter 4301. of the Revised Code.

(J) Authority to control under this section does not extend to any nonnarcotic substance if the substance may, under the Federal Food, Drug, and Cosmetic Act and the laws of this state, be lawfully sold over the counter without a prescription. If a pattern of abuse develops for any nonnarcotic drug sold over the counter, the board may, by rule adopted in accordance with Chapter 119. of the Revised Code, after a public hearing and a documented study to determine that the substance actually meets the criteria listed in division (B) of this section, place the abused substance on a controlled substance schedule.

(K)(1) A drug product containing ephedrine that is known as one of the following and is in the form specified shall not be considered a schedule V controlled substance:

(a) Amesec capsules;

(b) Bronitin tablets;

(c) Bronkotabs;

(d) Bronkolixir;

(e) Bronkaid tablets;

(f) Efedron nasal jelly;

(g) Guiaphed elixir;

(h) Haysma;

(i) Pazo hemorrhoid ointment and suppositories;

(j) Primatene "M" formula tablets;

(k) Primatene "P" formula tablets;

(l) Tedrigen tablets;

(m) Tedral tablets, suspension and elixir;

(n) T.E.P.;

(o) Vatronol nose drops.

(2)(a) A product containing ephedrine shall not be considered a controlled substance if the product is a food product or dietary supplement that meets all of the following criteria:

(i) It contains, per dosage unit or serving, not more than the lesser of twenty-five milligrams of ephedrine alkaloids or the maximum amount of ephedrine alkaloids provided in applicable regulations adopted by the United States food and drug administration, and no other controlled substance.

(ii) It contains no hydrochloride or sulfate salts of ephedrine alkaloids.

(iii) It is packaged with a prominent label securely affixed to each package that states all of the following: the amount in milligrams of ephedrine in a serving or dosage unit; the amount of the food product or dietary supplement that constitutes a serving or dosage unit; that the maximum recommended dosage of ephedrine for a healthy adult human is the lesser of one hundred milligrams in a twenty-four-hour period for not more than twelve weeks or the maximum recommended dosage or period of use provided in applicable regulations adopted by the United States food and drug administration; and that improper use of the product may be hazardous to a person's health.

(b)(i) Subject to division (K)(2)(b)(ii) of this section, no person shall dispense, sell, or otherwise give a product described in division (K)(2)(a) of this section to any individual under eighteen years of age.

(ii) Division (K)(2)(b)(i) of this section does not apply to a physician or pharmacist who dispenses, sells, or otherwise gives a product described in division (K)(2)(a) of this section to an individual under eighteen years of age, to a parent or guardian of an individual under eighteen years of age who dispenses, sells, or otherwise gives a product of that nature to the individual under eighteen years of age, or to a person who, as authorized by the individual's parent or legal guardian, dispenses, sells, or otherwise gives a product of that nature to an individual under eighteen years of age.

(c) No person in the course of selling, offering for sale, or otherwise distributing a product described in division (K)(2)(a) of this section shall advertise or represent in any manner that the product causes euphoria, ecstasy, a "buzz" or "high," or an altered mental state; heightens sexual performance; or, because it contains ephedrine alkaloids, increased muscle mass.

(3) A drug product that contains the isomer pseudoephedrine, or any of its salts, optical isomers, or salts of optical isomers, shall not be considered a controlled substance if the drug product is labeled in a manner consistent with federal law or with the product's over-the-counter tentative final monograph or final monograph issued by the United States food and drug administration.

(4) At the request of any person, the board may except any product containing ephedrine not described in division (K)(1) or (2) of this section or any class of products containing ephedrine from being included as a schedule V controlled substance if it determines that the product or class of products does not contain any other controlled substance. The board shall make the determination in accordance with this section and by rule adopted in accordance with Chapter 119. of the Revised Code.

(L) As used in this section:

(1) "Food" has the same meaning as in section 3715.01 of the Revised Code.

(2) "Dietary supplement" has the same meaning as in the "Federal Food, Drug, and Cosmetic Act," 108 Stat. 4327 (1994), 21 U.S.C.A. 321(ff), as amended.

(3) "Ephedrine alkaloids" means ephedrine, pseudoephedrine, norephedrine, norpseudoephedrine, methylephedrine, and methylpseudoephedrine.

**HISTORY: 136 v H 300 (Eff 7-1-76); 145 v H 391 (Eff 7-21-94); 146 v H 523 (Eff 3-31-97); 147 v S 66 (Eff 7-22-98); 149 v H 371. Eff 10-11-2002.**

**Not analogous to former RC § 3719.44 (132 v S 74; 133 v H 1), repealed 136 v H 300, eff 7-1-76.**

See provisions, §§ 3, 9 of HB 156 (145 v —) following RC § 3719.41.

## § 3719.61 Methadone maintenance.

Nothing in the laws dealing with drugs of abuse shall be construed to prohibit treatment of narcotic drug dependent persons by the continuing maintenance of their dependence through the administration of methadone in accordance with the rules adopted by the department of alcohol and drug addiction services under section 3793.11 of the Revised Code, when all of the following apply:

(A) The likelihood that any person undergoing maintenance treatment will be cured of dependence on narcotic drugs is remote, the treatment is prescribed for the purpose of alleviating or controlling the patient's drug dependence, and the patient's prognosis while undergoing treatment is at least a partial improvement in the patient's asocial or antisocial behavior patterns;

(B) In the case of an inpatient in a hospital or clinic, the amount of the maintenance drug dispensed at any one time does not exceed the quantity necessary for a single dose, and the dose is administered to the patient immediately;

(C) In the case of an outpatient, the amount of the maintenance drug dispensed at any one time shall be determined by the patient's treatment provider taking into account the patient's progress in the treatment program and the patient's needs for gainful employment, education, and responsible homemaking, except that in no event shall the dosage be greater than the amount permitted by federal law and rules adopted by the department pursuant to section 3793.11 of the Revised Code;

(D) The drug is not dispensed in any case to replace or supplement any part of a supply of the drug previously dispensed, or when there is reasonable cause to believe it will be used or disposed of unlawfully;

(E) The drug is dispensed through a program licensed and operated in accordance with section 3793.11 of the Revised Code.

**HISTORY: 133 v H 874 (Eff 9-16-70); 134 v H 494 (Eff 7-12-72); 134 v H 521 (Eff 10-19-72); 136 v H 300 (Eff 7-1-76); 138 v H 900 (Eff 7-1-80); 143 v H 317 (Eff 10-10-89); 145 v H 385 (Eff 7-19-94); 147 v S 66. Eff 7-22-98.**

## § 3719.70 Grant of immunity or sentencing consideration to person providing information.

(A) When testimony, information, or other evidence in the possession of a person who uses, possesses, or trafficks in any drug of abuse appears necessary to an investigation by law enforcement authorities into illicit sources of any drug of abuse, or appears necessary to successfully institute, maintain, or conclude a prosecution for any drug abuse offense, as defined in section 2925.01 of the Revised Code, a judge of the court of common pleas may grant to that person immunity from prosecution for any offense based upon the testimony, information, or other evidence furnished by that person, other than a prosecution of that person for giving false testimony, information, or other evidence.

(B)(1) When a person is convicted of any misdemeanor drug abuse offense, the court, in determining whether to place the person under a community control sanction pursuant to section 2929.25 of the Revised Code, shall take into consideration whether the person truthfully has revealed all information within the person's knowledge concerning illicit traffic in or use of drugs of abuse and, when required, has testified as to that information in any proceeding to obtain a search or arrest warrant against another or to prosecute another for any offense involving a drug of abuse. The information shall include, but is not limited to, the identity and whereabouts of accomplices, accessories, aiders, and abettors, if any, of the person or persons from whom any drug of abuse was obtained or to whom any drug of abuse was distributed, and of persons known or believed to be drug dependent persons, together with the location of any place or places where and the manner in which any drug of abuse is illegally cultivated, manufactured, sold, possessed, or used. The information also shall include all facts and circumstances surrounding any illicit traffic in or use of drugs of abuse of that nature.

(2) If a person otherwise is eligible for intervention in lieu of conviction and being ordered to a period of rehabilitation under section 2951.041 [2951.04.1] of the Revised Code but the person has failed to cooperate with law enforcement authorities by providing them with the types of information described in division (B)(1) of this section, the person's lack of cooperation may be considered by the court under section 2951.041 [2951.04.1] of the Revised Code in determining whether to stay all criminal proceedings and order the person to a requested period of intervention.

(C) In the absence of a competent and voluntary waiver of the right against self-incrimination, no information or testimony furnished pursuant to division (B) of this section shall be used in a prosecution of the person furnishing it for any offense other than a prosecution of that person for giving false testimony, information, or other evidence.

**HISTORY: 133 v H 874 (Eff 9-16-70); 136 v H 300 (Eff 7-1-76); 146 v S 2 (Eff 7-1-96); 146 v S 269 (Eff 7-1-96); 148 v S 107. Eff 3-23-2000; 149 v H 490, § 1, eff. 1-1-04.**

The effective date is set by section 4 of H.B. 490.

[SAMPLE DRUGS]

## § 3719.81 Furnishing of sample drugs free of charge.

(A) As used in this section, "sample drug" has the same meaning as in section 2925.01 of the Revised Code.

(B) A person may furnish another a sample drug, if all of the following apply:

(1) The sample drug is furnished free of charge by a manufacturer, manufacturer's representative, or wholesale dealer in pharmaceuticals to a licensed health professional authorized to prescribe drugs, or is furnished free of charge by such a professional to a patient for use as medication;

(2) The sample drug is in the original container in which it was placed by the manufacturer, and the container is plainly marked as a sample;

(3) Prior to its being furnished, the sample drug has been stored under the proper conditions to prevent its deterioration or contamination;

(4) If the sample drug is of a type which deteriorates with time, the sample container is plainly marked with the date beyond which the sample drug is unsafe to use, and the date has not expired on the sample furnished. Compliance with the labeling requirements of the "Federal Food, Drug, and Cosmetic Act," 52 Stat. 1040 (1938), 21 U.S.C.A. 301, as amended, shall be deemed compliance with this section.

(5) The sample drug is distributed, stored, or discarded in such a way that the sample drug may not be acquired or used by any unauthorized person, or by any person, including a child, for whom it may present a health or safety hazard.

(C) Division (B) of this section does not do any of the following:

(1) Apply to or restrict the furnishing of any sample of a nonnarcotic substance if the substance may, under the "Federal Food, Drug, and Cosmetic Act" and under the laws of this state, otherwise be lawfully sold over the counter without a prescription;

(2) Authorize a licensed health professional authorized to prescribe drugs who is a clinical nurse specialist, certified nurse-midwife, certified nurse practitioner, optometrist, or physician assistant to furnish a sample drug that is not a drug the professional is authorized to prescribe.

(3) Prohibit a licensed health professional authorized to prescribe drugs, manufacturer of dangerous drugs, wholesale distributor of dangerous drugs, or representative of a manufacturer of dangerous drugs from furnishing a sample drug to a charitable pharmacy in accordance with section 3719.811 [3719.81.1] of the Revised Code.

(4) Prohibit a pharmacist working, whether or not for compensation, in a charitable pharmacy from dispensing a sample drug to a person in accordance with section 3719.811 [3719.81.1] of the Revised Code.

(D) The state board of pharmacy shall, in accordance with Chapter 119. of the Revised Code, adopt rules as necessary to give effect to this section.

**HISTORY: 134 v H 521 (Eff 10-19-72); 136 v H 300 (Eff 7-1-76); 147 v S 66 (Eff 7-22-98); 148 v H 241. Eff 5-17-2000; 150 v S 80, § 1, eff. 4-7-05; 150 v H 454, § 1, eff. 4-15-05; 151 v S 154, § 1, eff. 5-17-06.**

The provisions of § 6 of 151 v S 154 read as follows:

SECTION 6. Section 3719.81 of the Revised Code is presented in this act as a composite of the section as amended by both Am. Sub. H.B. 454 and Am. Sub. S.B. 80 of the 125th General Assembly. The General Assembly, applying the principle stated in division (B) of section 1.52 of the Revised Code that amendments are to be harmonized if reasonably capable of simultaneous operation, finds that the composite is the resulting version of the section in effect prior to the effective date of the section as presented in this act.

**Comment, Legislative Service Commission**

Section 3719.81 of the Revised Code is amended by Am. Sub. S.B. 80 and Am. Sub. H.B. 454 of the 125th General Assembly. Comparison of these amendments in pursuance of section 1.52 of the Revised Code discloses that they are not irreconcilable so that they are required by that section to be harmonized to give effect to each amendment.

## § 3719.811 Distribution of sample drugs by and to charitable pharmacy.

(A) As used in this section:

(1) "Charitable pharmacy" means a pharmacy that meets all of the following requirements:

(a) Holds a terminal distributor of dangerous drugs license under section 4729.54 of the Revised Code.

(b) Is exempt from federal taxation pursuant to 26 U.S.C. 501(a) and (c)(3).

(c) Is not a hospital as defined in section 3727.01 of the Revised Code.

(2) "Prescription" has the same meaning as in section 4729.01 of the Revised Code.

(3) "Sample drug" has the same meaning as in section 2925.01 of the Revised Code.

(B) A manufacturer of dangerous drugs or wholesale distributor of dangerous drugs may furnish a sample drug to a charitable pharmacy if all of the following apply:

(1) The sample drug is in the original container in which it was placed by its manufacturer and the container is plainly marked as a sample.

(2) Prior to its being furnished, the sample drug has been stored under the proper conditions to prevent its deterioration or contamination.

(3) If the sample drug is of a type that deteriorates with time, the container in which the sample drug is stored is plainly marked with the date beyond which the sample drug is unsafe to use, and the date has not expired on the sample drug furnished. Compliance with the labeling requirements of the "Federal Food, Drug, and Cosmetic Act," 52 Stat. 1040 (1938), 21 U.S.C. 301, as amended, constitutes compliance with division (B)(3) of this section.

(4) The sample drug is distributed, stored, or discarded in such a way that the sample drug may not be acquired or used by any unauthorized person, or by any person, including a child, for whom it may present a health or safety hazard.

(5) The sample drug is furnished free of charge.

(6) The sample drug is not a controlled substance.

(C) A representative of a manufacturer of dangerous drugs or a licensed health professional authorized to prescribe drugs may furnish a sample drug to a charitable pharmacy if all of the following apply:

(1) The state board of pharmacy has adopted rules under division (F) of this section to permit such a representative or health professional to furnish a sample drug to a charitable pharmacy.

(2) The representative or health professional complies with standards and procedures established in rules adopted under division (F) of this section.

(3) The requirements in divisions (B)(1) to (6) of this section are satisfied.

(D) A pharmacist working, whether or not for compensation, in a charitable pharmacy may dispense a sample drug to a person if all of the following apply:

(1) The person to whom the sample drug is dispensed is eligible for the sample drug under standards established by the body responsible for the charitable pharmacy's general management.

(2) The person to whom the sample is dispensed presents to the pharmacist a valid prescription for the sample drug.

(3) The sample drug is dispensed free of charge.

(4) The requirements in divisions (B)(1) to (4) and (6) of this section are satisfied.

(E) Divisions (B), (C), and (D) of this section do not do either of the following:

(1) Apply to or restrict the furnishing of any sample of a nonnarcotic substance if the substance may, under the "Federal Food, Drug, and Cosmetic Act" and under the law of this state, otherwise be lawfully sold over the counter without a prescription.

(2) Authorize a pharmacist working, whether or not for compensation, in a charitable pharmacy to dispense a sample drug that the charitable pharmacy is unauthorized to possess, have custody or control of, or distribute.

(F) The state board of pharmacy shall, in accordance with Chapter 119. of the Revised Code, adopt rules as necessary to give effect to this section. The rules may permit representatives of manufacturers of dangerous drugs or licensed health professionals authorized to prescribe drugs to furnish sample drugs to charitable pharmacies under this section. If they do so, the rules shall establish standards and procedures for the representatives or health professionals to furnish the sample drugs.

**HISTORY: 150 v H 454, § 1, eff. 4-15-05.**

## § 3719.812 Immunity.

The state board of pharmacy; any person that donates a sample drug as permitted under section 3719.811 [3719.81.1] of the Revised Code; any charitable pharmacy or pharmacist working in a charitable pharmacy that accepts or dispenses sample drugs as permitted under section 3719.811 [3719.81.1] of the Revised Code; and any licensed health professional authorized to prescribe drugs who accepts delivery of a sample drug on behalf of a charitable pharmacy as permitted under section 3719.811 [3719.81.1] of the Revised Code shall not, in the absence of bad faith, be subject to any of the following for matters related to donating, accepting, or dispensing sample drugs under section 3719.811 [3719.81.1] of the Revised Code: criminal prosecution; liability in tort or other civil action for injury, death, or loss to person or property; or professional disciplinary action.

**HISTORY: 150 v H 454, § 1, eff. 4-15-05.**

## § 3719.813 Immunity of drug manufacturer.

A drug manufacturer shall not, in the absence of bad faith, be subject to criminal prosecution or liability in tort or other civil action for injury, death, or loss to person or property for matters related to the donation, acceptance, or dispensing of a drug manufactured by the drug manufacturer that is donated by any person as permitted under section 3719.811 [3719.81.1] of the Revised Code, including but not limited to liability for failure to transfer or communicate product or consumer information or the expiration date of the donated drug.

**HISTORY: 150 v H 454, § 1, eff. 4-15-05.**

[PENALTIES]

## § 3719.99 Penalties.

(A) Whoever violates section 3719.16 or 3719.161 of the Revised Code is guilty of a felony of the fifth degree. If the offender previously has been convicted of a violation of section 3719.16 or 3719.161 of the Revised Code or a drug abuse offense, a violation of section 3719.16 or 3719.161 of the Revised Code is a felony of the fourth degree. If the violation involves the sale, offer to sell, or possession of a schedule I or II controlled substance, with the exception of marihuana, and if the offender, as a result of the violation, is a major drug offender, division (D) of this section applies.

(B) Whoever violates division (C) or (D) of section 3719.172 of the Revised Code is guilty of a felony of the fifth degree. If the offender previously has been convicted of a violation of division (C) or (D) of section 3719.172 of the Revised Code or a drug abuse offense, a violation of division (C) or (D) of section 3719.172 of the Revised Code is a felony of the fourth degree. If the violation involves the sale, offer to sell, or possession of a schedule I or II controlled substance, with the exception of marihuana, and if the offender, as a result of the violation, is a major drug offender, division (D) of this section applies.

(C) Whoever violates section 3719.07 or 3719.08 of the Revised Code is guilty of a misdemeanor of the first degree. If the offender previously has been convicted of a violation of section 3719.07 or 3719.08 of the Revised Code or a drug abuse offense, a violation of section 3719.07 or 3719.08 of the Revised Code is a felony of the fifth degree. If the violation involves the sale, offer to sell, or possession of a schedule I or II controlled substance, with the exception of marihuana, and if the offender, as a result of the violation, is a major drug offender, division (D) of this section applies.

(D)(1) If an offender is convicted of or pleads guilty to a felony violation of section 3719.07, 3719.08, 3719.16, or 3719.161 or of division (C) or (D) of section 3719.172 of the Revised Code, if the violation involves the sale, offer to sell, or possession of a schedule I or II controlled substance, with the exception of marihuana, and if the court imposing sentence upon the offender finds that the offender as a result of the violation is a major drug offender and is guilty of a specification of the type described in section 2941.1410 of the Revised Code, the court, in lieu of the prison term authorized or required by division (A), (B), or (C) of this section and sections 2929.13 and 2929.14 of the Revised Code and in addition to any other sanction imposed for the offense under sections 2929.11 to 2929.18 of the Revised Code, shall impose upon the offender, in accordance with division (B)(3)(a) of section 2929.14 of the Revised Code, the mandatory prison term specified in that division and may impose an additional prison term under division (B)(3)(b) of that section.

(2) Notwithstanding any contrary provision of section 3719.21 of the Revised Code, the clerk of the court shall pay any fine imposed for a felony violation of section 3719.07, 3719.08, 3719.16, or 3719.161 or of division (C) or (D) of section 3719.172 of the Revised Code pursuant to division (A) of section 2929.18 of the Revised Code in accordance with and subject to the requirements of division (F) of section 2925.03 of the Revised Code. The agency that receives the fine shall use the fine as specified in division (F) of section 2925.03 of the Revised Code.

(E) Whoever violates section 3719.05, 3719.06, 3719.13, or 3719.31 or division (B) of section 3719.172 of the Revised Code is guilty of a misdemeanor of the third degree. If the offender previously has been convicted of a violation of section 3719.05, 3719.06, 3719.13, or 3719.31 or division (B) of section 3719.172 of the Revised Code or a drug abuse offense, a violation of section 3719.05, 3719.06, 3719.13, or 3719.31 or division (B) of section 3719.172 of the Revised Code is a misdemeanor of the first degree.

(F) Whoever violates section 3719.30 of the Revised Code is guilty of a misdemeanor of the fourth degree. If the offender previously has been convicted of a violation of section 3719.30 of the Revised Code or a drug abuse offense, a violation of section 3719.30 of the Revised Code is a misdemeanor of the third degree.

(G) Whoever violates section 3719.32 or 3719.33 of the Revised Code is guilty of a minor misdemeanor.

(H) Whoever violates division (K)(2)(b) of section 3719.44 of the Revised Code is guilty of a felony of the fifth degree.

(I) Whoever violates division (K)(2)(c) of section 3719.44 of the Revised Code is guilty of a misdemeanor of the second degree.

(J) As used in this section, "major drug offender" has the same meaning as in section 2929.01 of the Revised Code.

**HISTORY: 136 v H 300 (Eff 7-1-76); 146 v S 2 (Eff 7-1-96); 146 v S 269 (Eff 7-1-96); 146 v H 523 (Eff 3-31-97); 147 v S 66 (Eff 7-22-98); 148 v S 107. Eff 3-23-2000; 2011 HB 86, § 1, eff. Sept. 30, 2011.**

**Analogous to former RC § 3719.99 (Bureau of Code Revision, 10-1-53; 126 v 178; 128 v 1044; 132 v S 74; 133 v H 1; 133 v H 90; 133 v H 874; 134 v H 924; 134 v H 521), repealed, 136 v H 300, eff 7-1-76.**

## CHAPTER 3722: ADULT CARE FACILITIES

Section



### § 3722.151 Criminal records check for prospective employees providing direct care to older adult [Renumbered].

This section was renumbered as RC § 5119.85 by 2011 HB 153, § 101.01, eff. July 1, 2011.

## CHAPTER 3737: FIRE MARSHAL; FIRE SAFETY

Section



### § 3737.28 Power to administer oaths; failure to cooperate.

The fire marshal or an assistant fire marshal may administer an oath to any person appearing as a witness before the fire marshal or assistant fire marshal. No witness shall refuse to be sworn, refuse to testify, disobey an order of the fire marshal or an assistant fire marshal, or fail or refuse to produce a book, paper, document, or record, regardless of physical form or characteristic, concerning a matter under examination, or be guilty of contemptuous conduct after being summoned by the fire marshal or an assistant fire marshal to appear before the fire marshal or assistant fire marshal to give testimony in relation to a matter or subject under investigation.

**HISTORY: 137 v H 590 (Eff 7-1-79); 149 v S 115. Eff 3-19-2003.**

**Not analogous to former RC § 3737.28 (GC § 836-2; 102 v 430; 122 v 718; Bureau of Code Revision, 10-1-53), repealed 137 v H 590, § 2, eff 7-1-79. That section has been substantially incorporated into RC § 3737.45 (137 v H 590), eff 7-1-79.**

## § 3737.51 Violations of fire code or order prohibited; civil penalties.

(A) No person shall knowingly violate any provision of the state fire code or any order made pursuant to it.

(B) Any person who has received a citation for a serious violation of the fire code or any order issued pursuant to it, shall be assessed a civil penalty of not more than one thousand dollars for each such violation.

(C) Any person who has received a citation for a violation of the fire code or any order issued pursuant to it, and such violation is specifically determined not to be of a serious nature, may be assessed a civil penalty of not more than one thousand dollars for each such violation.

(D) Any person who fails to correct a violation for which a citation has been issued within the period permitted for its correction, may be assessed a civil penalty of not more than one thousand dollars for each day during which such failure or violation continues.

(E) Any person who violates any of the posting requirements, as prescribed by division (C) of section 3737.42 of the Revised Code, shall be assessed a civil penalty of not more than one thousand dollars for each violation.

(F) Due consideration to the appropriateness of the penalty with respect to the gravity of the violation, the good faith of the person being charged, and the history of previous violations shall be given whenever a penalty is assessed under this chapter.

(G) For purposes of this section, a serious violation shall be considered to exist if there is a substantial probability that an occurrence causing death or serious physical harm to persons could result from a condition which exists, or from one or more practices, means, methods, operations or processes which have been adopted or are in use, unless the person did not and could not with the exercise of reasonable diligence, know of the presence of the violation.

(H) Civil penalties imposed by this chapter shall be paid to the fire marshal for deposit into the general revenue fund. Such penalties may be recovered in a civil action in the name of the state brought in the court of common pleas of the county where the violation is alleged to have occurred.

**HISTORY: 137 v H 590. Eff 7-1-79.**

The effective date is set by section 3 of HB 590.

## § 3737.61 Posting of arson laws.

The owner, operator, or lessee of any transient residential building shall post the provisions of sections 2909.02 and 2909.03 of the Revised Code in a conspicuous place in each room occupied by guests in such building. The owner, operator, or lessee of any nontransient residential building, institution, school, or place of assembly shall post the provisions of such sections in conspicuous places upon such premises. No person shall fail to comply with this section.

**HISTORY: 137 v H 590. Eff 7-1-79.**

The effective date is set by section 3 of HB 590.

## § 3737.62 Spreading of fires through negligence.

No person shall set, kindle, or cause to be set or kindled any fire, which through his negligence, spreads beyond its immediate confines to any structure, field, or wood lot.

**HISTORY: 137 v H 590. Eff 7-1-79.**

The effective date is set by section 3 of HB 590.

## § 3737.63 Duty upon discovery of unfriendly fire.

(A) The owner, operator, or lessee, an employee of any owner, operator, or lessee, an occupant, and any person in direct control of any building regulated under the Ohio building code, upon the discovery of an unfriendly fire, or upon receiving information that there is an unfriendly fire on the premises, shall immediately, and with all reasonable dispatch and diligence, call or otherwise notify the fire department concerning the fire, and shall spread an alarm immediately to all occupants of the building.

(B) For the purposes of this section, "unfriendly fire" means a fire of a destructive nature as distinguished from a controlled fire intended for a beneficial purpose.

(C) No person shall fail to comply with this section.

**HISTORY: 137 v H 590. Eff 7-1-79.**

The effective date is set by section 3 of HB 590.

## § 3737.64 Duty to disclose purpose of non-official inspection.

No person who is not a certified fire safety inspector shall act as such or hold himself out to be such, unless prior to commencing any inspection function, he discloses the purpose for which he is making such inspection and the fact that he is not employed by any state or local fire service or agency, and that he is not acting in an official capacity for any governmental subdivision or agency.

**HISTORY: 137 v H 590. Eff 7-1-79.**

The effective date is set by section 3 of HB 590.

## § 3737.65 Prohibitions concerning sale, use or servicing of fire protection equipment.

(A) No person shall sell, offer for sale, or use any fire protection or fire fighting equipment that does not meet the minimum standards established by the fire marshal in the state fire code.

(B) Except for public and private mobile fire trucks, no person shall service, test, repair, or install for profit any fire protection or fire fighting equipment without a certificate or a provisional certificate issued by the fire marshal.

(C) The fire marshal shall not issue a provisional certificate pursuant to division (B) of this section to any individual who is not enrolled in a bona fide apprenticeship training program registered with the apprenticeship council pursuant to section 4139.05 of the Revised Code or with the bureau of apprenticeship and training of the United States department of labor. A provisional certificate issued pursuant to this section authorizes an individual to engage in the activities permitted under division (B) of this section only if the individual:

(1) Remains enrolled in such an apprenticeship training program; and

(2) Is directly supervised by an individual who possesses a valid and current certificate issued pursuant to division (B) of this section for the activities in which the individual issued the provisional certificate is engaged and the certified individual directly supervising the individual issued the provisional certificate only supervises one provisional certificate holder.

**HISTORY: 137 v H 590 (Eff 7-1-79); 143 v H 677 (Eff 11-7-90); 146 v S 162 (Eff 10-29-95); 148 v H 471. Eff 7-1-2000.**

The effective date is set by section 12(A) of HB 471.

## § 3737.66 Qualifications for claiming to be or acting as firefighter or fire official.

(A) As used in this section, "firefighting agency" and "private fire company" have the same meanings as in section 9.60 of the Revised Code.

(B) No person shall claim to the public to be or act as a firefighter, volunteer firefighter, member of a fire department, chief of a fire department, or fire prevention officer unless the person is recognized as a firefighter, volunteer firefighter, member of a fire department, member of a private fire company, chief of a fire department, or fire prevention officer by the fire marshal or has received a certificate issued under former section 3303.07 or section 4765.55 of the Revised Code evidencing satisfactory completion of a firefighter training program and has been appointed by the governing board of a firefighting agency or, in the case of a volunteer firefighter, receives such a certificate within one year after appointment by the governing board of a firefighting agency.

**HISTORY: 141 v H 552 (Eff 9-17-86); 144 v S 98 (Eff 11-12-92); 148 v H 138. Eff 11-3-2000; 151 v H 401, § 1, eff. 4-5-07.**

## § 3737.73 Safety drills or rapid dismissals; tornado safety precautions; inspections, warnings.

(A) No principal or person in charge of a public or private school or educational institution having an average daily attendance of twenty or more pupils, and no person in charge of any children's home or orphanage housing twenty or more minor persons, shall willfully neglect to instruct and train such children by means of drills or rapid dismissals, so that such children in a sudden emergency may leave the building in the shortest possible time without confusion. The principal or person in charge of a school or educational institution shall conduct drills or rapid dismissals at least nine times during the school year, which shall be at the times and frequency prescribed in rules adopted by the fire marshal. However, no drill or rapid dismissal under this division need be conducted in any month that a school safety drill required under division (D) of this section is conducted as long as a total of nine drills or rapid dismissals under this division are conducted in the school year. The principal or person in charge of a children's home or orphanage shall conduct drills or rapid dismissals at least once each month while the home is in operation. In the case of schools, no principal or person in charge of a school shall willfully neglect to keep the doors and exits of such building unlocked during school hours. The fire marshal may order the immediate installation of necessary fire gongs or signals in such schools, institutions, or children's homes and enforce this division and divisions (B) and (C)(3) of this section.

(B) In conjunction with the drills or rapid dismissals required by division (A) of this section, principals or persons in charge of public or private primary and secondary schools, or educational institutions, shall instruct pupils in safety precautions to be taken in case of a tornado alert or warning. Such principals or persons in charge of such schools or institutions shall designate, in accordance with standards prescribed by the fire marshal, appropriate locations to be used to shelter pupils in case of a tornado, tornado alert, or warning.

(C)(1) The fire marshal or the fire marshal's designee shall annually inspect each school, institution, home, or orphanage subject to division (A) of this section to determine compliance with that division, and each school or institution subject to division (B) of this section to ascertain whether the locations comply with the standards prescribed under that division. Nothing in this section shall require a school or institution to construct or improve a facility or location for use as a shelter area.

(2) The fire marshal or the fire marshal's designee shall issue a warning to any person found in violation of division (A) or (B) of this section. The warning shall indicate the specific violation and a date by which such violation shall be corrected.

(3) No person shall fail to correct violations by the date indicated on a warning issued under division (C)(2) of this section.

(D)(1) On or before April 1, 2007, and on or before each first day of December thereafter, the principal or person in charge of each public or private school or educational institution shall conduct a school safety drill to provide pupils with instruction in the procedures to follow in situations where pupils must be secured in the school building, such as a threat to the school involving an act of terrorism; a person possessing a deadly weapon or dangerous ordnance, as defined in section 2923.11 of the Revised Code, on school property; or other act of violence.

(2)(a) The principal or person in charge of each public or private school or educational institution shall provide to the police chief or other similar chief law enforcement officer of the municipal corporation, township, or township or joint police district in which the school or institution is located, or, in absence of any such person, the county sheriff of the county in which the school or institution is located advance written notice of each school safety drill required under division (D)(1) of this section and shall keep a written record of the date and time of each drill conducted. The advance notice shall be provided not later than seventy-two hours prior to the date the drill will be conducted and shall include the date and time the drill will be conducted and the address of the school or educational institution. The notice shall be provided by mail, facsimile, or electronic submission.

(b) Not later than April 5, 2007, and not later than the fifth day of December each year thereafter, the principal or person in charge of each public or private school or educational institution shall provide written certification by mail of the date and time each school safety drill required under division (D)(1) of this section was conducted to the police chief or other similar chief law enforcement officer of the municipal corporation, township, or township or joint police district in which the school or institution is located, or, in the absence of any such person, the county sheriff of the county in which the school or institution is located. If such certification is not provided, the principal or person in charge of the school or institution shall be considered to have failed to conduct the drill and shall be subject to division (D)(4) of this section.

(3) The principal or person in charge of each public or private school or educational institution shall hold annual training sessions for employees of the school or institution regarding the conduct of school safety drills.

(4) The police chief or other similar chief law enforcement officer of a municipal corporation, township, or township or joint police district, or, in the absence of any such person, the county sheriff shall issue a warning to any person found in violation of division (D)(1) of this section. Each warning issued for a violation of division (D)(1) of this section shall require the principal or person in charge of the school or institution to correct the violation by conducting the school safety drill not later than the thirtieth day after the date the warning is issued. The violation shall not be considered corrected unless, not later than forty days after the date the warning is issued, the principal or person in charge of the school or institution provides written certification of the date and time the drill was conducted to the police chief or other similar chief law enforcement officer or county sheriff who issued the warning.

(5) No person shall fail to correct violations by the date indicated on a warning issued under division (D)(4) of this section.

**HISTORY: GC § 12900; 99 v 231; 109 v 253; Bureau of Code Revision, RC § 3737.29, 10-1-53; 136 v H 427 (Eff 1-30-76); RC § 3737.73, 137 v H 590 (Eff 7-1-79); 138 v S 18. Eff 7-1-79; 151 v H 422, § 1, eff. 9-28-06; 2011 HB 153, § 101.01, eff. Sept. 29, 2011.**

The provisions of § 3 of 151 v H 422 read as follows:

SECTION 3. It is the intent of the General Assembly to encourage the United States Congress and the United States Department of Homeland Security to broaden the definition of "critical infrastructure" enacted in the "Homeland Security Act of 2002," 6 U.S.C. 101 et seq., to include school buildings as they are a potential target of terrorist attacks. Including school buildings as critical infrastructure would enable the Department to prioritize the security of school buildings by integrating them into its risk assessments and plans for protecting the national safety and welfare.

The effective date is set by section 3 of SB 18.

## [UNDERGROUND STORAGE TANKS]

### § 3737.88 Underground storage tank and corrective action programs.

(A)(1) The fire marshal shall have responsibility for implementation of the underground storage tank program and corrective action program for releases of petroleum from underground storage tanks established by the "Resource Conservation and Recovery Act of 1976," 90 Stat. 2795, 42 U.S.C.A. 6901, as amended. To implement the programs, the fire marshal may adopt, amend, and rescind such rules, conduct such inspections, require annual registration of underground storage tanks, issue such citations and orders to enforce those rules, enter into environmental covenants in accordance with sections 5301.80 to 5301.92 of the Revised Code, and perform such other duties, as are consistent with those programs. The fire marshal, by rule, may delegate the authority to conduct inspections of underground storage tanks to certified fire safety inspectors.

(2) In the place of any rules regarding release containment and release detection for underground storage tanks adopted under division (A)(1) of this section, the fire marshal, by rule, shall designate areas as being sensitive for the protection of human health and the environment and adopt alternative rules regarding release containment and release detection methods for new and upgraded underground storage tank systems located in those areas. In designating such areas, the fire marshal shall take into consideration such factors as soil conditions, hydrogeology, water use, and the location of public and private water supplies. Not later than July 11, 1990, the fire marshal shall file the rules required under this division with the secretary of state, director of the legislative service commission, and joint committee on agency rule review in accordance with divisions (B) and (H) of section 119.03 of the Revised Code.

(3) Notwithstanding sections 3737.87 to 3737.89 of the Revised Code, a person who is not a responsible person may conduct a voluntary action in accordance with Chapter 3746. of the Revised Code and rules adopted under it for a class C release. The director of environmental protection, pursuant to section 3746.12 of the Revised Code, may issue a covenant not to sue to any person who properly completes a voluntary action with respect to a class C release in accordance with Chapter 3746. of the Revised Code and rules adopted under it.

(B) Before adopting any rule under this section or section 3737.881 or 3737.882 of the Revised Code, the fire marshal shall file written notice of the proposed rule with the chairperson of the state fire council, and, within sixty days after notice is filed, the council may file responses to or comments on and may recommend alternative or supplementary rules to the fire marshal. At the end of the sixty-day period or upon the filing of responses, comments, or recommendations by the council, the fire marshal may adopt the rule filed with the council or any alternative or supplementary rule recommended by the council.

(C) The state fire council may recommend courses of action to be taken by the fire marshal in carrying out the fire marshal's duties under this section. The council shall file its recommendations in the office of the fire marshal, and, within sixty days after the recommendations are filed, the fire marshal shall file with the chairperson of the council comments on, and proposed action in response to, the recommendations.

(D) For the purpose of sections 3737.87 to 3737.89 of the Revised Code, the fire marshal shall adopt, and may amend and rescind, rules identifying or listing hazardous substances. The rules shall be consistent with and equivalent in scope, coverage, and content to regulations identifying or listing hazardous substances adopted under the "Comprehensive Environmental Response, Compensation, and Liability Act of 1980," 94 Stat. 2779, 42 U.S.C.A. 9602, as amended, except that the fire marshal shall not identify or list as a hazardous substance any hazardous waste identified or listed in rules adopted under division (A) of section 3734.12 of the Revised Code.

(E) Except as provided in division (A)(3) of this section, the fire marshal shall have exclusive jurisdiction to regulate the storage, treatment, and disposal of petroleum contaminated soil generated from corrective actions undertaken in response to releases of petroleum from underground storage tank systems. The fire marshal may adopt, amend, or rescind such rules as the fire marshal considers to be necessary or appropriate to regulate the storage, treatment, or disposal of petroleum contaminated soil so generated.

(F) The fire marshal shall adopt, amend, and rescind rules under sections 3737.88 to 3737.882 of the Revised Code in accordance with Chapter 119. of the Revised Code.

**HISTORY: RC § 3737.87, 137 v H 590 (Eff 11-1-78); 141 v H 552 (Eff 9-17-86); 142 v H 171 (Eff 7-1-87); RC § 3737.88, 143 v H 421 (Eff 7-11-89); 145 v H 152. Eff 7-1-93; 150 v H 516, § 1, eff. 12-30-04; 2011 SB 171, § 1, eff. June 30, 2011; 2011 HB 153, § 101.01, eff. Sept. 29, 2011.**

The effective date is set by section 10 of H.B. 516 (150 v —).

## § 3737.881 Certification of underground storage tank systems installers; training programs.

(A) The fire marshal shall certify underground storage tank systems installers who meet the standards for certification established in rules adopted under division (D)(1) of this section, pass the certification examination required by this division, and pay the certificate fee established in rules adopted under division (D)(5) of this section. Any individual who wishes to obtain certification as an installer shall apply to the fire marshal on a form prescribed by the fire marshal. The application shall be accompanied by the application and examination fees established in rules adopted under division (D)(5) of this section.

The fire marshal shall prescribe an examination designed to test the knowledge of applicants for certification as underground storage tank system[s] installers in the installation, repair, abandonment, and removal of those systems. The examination shall also test the applicants' knowledge and understanding of the requirements and standards established in rules adopted under sections 3737.88 and 3737.882 [3737.88.2] of the Revised Code pertaining to the installation, repair, abandonment, and removal of those systems.

Installer certifications issued under this division shall be renewed annually, upon submission of a certification renewal form prescribed by the fire marshal, provision of proof of successful completion of continuing education requirements, and payment of the certification renewal fee established in rules adopted under division (D)(5) of this section. In addition, the fire marshal may from time to time prescribe an examination for certification renewal and may require applicants to pass the examination and pay the fee established for it in rules adopted under division (D)(5) of this section.

The fire marshal may, in accordance with Chapter 119. of the Revised Code, deny, suspend, revoke, or refuse to renew an installer's certification or renewal thereof if he finds that any of the following applies:

(1) The applicant for certification or certificate holder fails to meet the standards for certification or renewal thereof under this section and rules adopted under it;

(2) The certification was obtained through fraud or misrepresentation;

(3) The certificate holder recklessly caused or permitted a person under his supervision to install, perform major repairs on site to, abandon, or remove an underground storage tank system in violation of the performance standards set forth in rules adopted under section 3737.88 or 3737.882 [3737.88.2] of the Revised Code.

As used in division (A)(3) of this section, "recklessly" has the same meaning as in section 2901.22 of the Revised Code.

(B) The fire marshal shall certify persons who sponsor training programs for underground storage tank system[s] installers who meet the criteria for certification established in rules adopted by the fire marshal under division (D)(4) of this section and pay the certificate fee established in rules adopted under division (D)(5) of this section. Any person who wishes to obtain certification to sponsor such a training program shall apply to the fire marshal on a form prescribed by him. Training program certificates issued under this division shall expire annually. Upon submission of a certification renewal application form prescribed by the fire marshal and payment of the application and certification renewal fees established in rules adopted under division (D)(5) of this section, the fire marshal shall issue a training program renewal certificate to the applicant.

The fire marshal may, in accordance with Chapter 119. of the Revised Code, deny an application for, suspend, or revoke a training program certificate or renewal thereof if he finds that the training program does not or will not meet the standards for certification established in rules adopted under division (D)(4) of this section.

(C) The fire marshal may conduct or cause to be conducted training programs for underground storage tank systems installers as he considers to be necessary or appropriate. The fire marshal is not subject to division (B) of this section with respect to training programs conducted by employees of the office of the fire marshal.

(D) The fire marshal shall adopt, and may amend and rescind, rules doing all of the following:

(1) Defining the activities that constitute supervision over the installation, performance of major repairs on site to, abandonment of, and removal of underground storage tank systems;

(2) Establishing standards and procedures for certification of underground storage tank systems installers;

(3) Establishing standards and procedures for continuing education for certification renewal;

(4) Establishing standards and procedures for certification of training programs for installers;

(5) Establishing fees for applications for certifications under this section, the examinations prescribed under division (A) of this section, the issuance and renewal of certificates under divisions (A) and (B) of this section, and attendance at training programs conducted by the fire marshal under division (C) of this section. Fees received under this section shall be credited to the underground storage tank administration fund created in section 3737.02 of the Revised Code and shall be used to defray the costs of implementing, administering, and enforcing this section and the rules adopted thereunder, conducting training sessions, and facilitating prevention of releases.

(6) That are necessary or appropriate for the implementation, administration, and enforcement of this section.

(E) Nothing in this section or the rules adopted under it prohibits an owner or operator of an underground storage tank system from installing, making major repairs on site to, abandoning, or removing an underground storage tank system under the supervision of an installer certified under division (A) of this section who is a full-time or part-time employee of the owner or operator.

(F) On and after the date one hundred eighty days after the effective date of this section, no person shall do any of the following:

(1) Install, make major repairs on site to, abandon, or remove an underground storage tank system unless the activity is performed under the supervision of a qualified individual who holds a valid installer certificate issued under division (A) of this section;

(2) Act in the capacity of providing supervision for the installation of, performance of major repairs on site to, abandonment of, or removal of an underground storage tank system unless the person holds a valid installer certificate issued under division (A) of this section;

(3) Except as provided in division (C) of this section, sponsor a training program for underground storage tank systems installers unless the person holds a valid training program certificate issued under division (B) of this section.

**HISTORY: 143 v H 421. Eff 7-11-89.**

## § 3737.882 Action to confirm or disprove suspected petroleum release; corrective actions; violations.

(A) If, after an examination or inspection, the fire marshal or an assistant fire marshal finds that a release of petroleum is suspected, the fire marshal shall take such action as the fire marshal considers necessary to ensure that a suspected release is confirmed or disproved and, if the occurrence of a release is confirmed, to correct the release. These actions may include one or more of the following:

(1) Issuance of a citation and order requiring the responsible person to undertake, in a manner consistent with the requirements of section 9003 of the "Resource Conservation and Recovery Act of 1976," 98 Stat. 3279, 42 U.S.C.A. 6991b, as amended, applicable regulations adopted thereunder, and rules adopted under division (B) of this section, such actions as are necessary to protect human health and the environment, including, without limitation, the investigation of a suspected release;

(2) Requesting the attorney general to bring a civil action for appropriate relief, including a temporary restraining order or preliminary or permanent injunction, in the court of common pleas of the county in which a suspected release is located or in which the release occurred, to obtain the corrective action necessary to protect human health and the environment. In granting any such relief, the court shall ensure that the terms of the temporary restraining order or injunction are sufficient to provide comprehensive corrective action to protect human health and the environment.

(3) Entry onto premises and undertaking corrective action with respect to a release of petroleum if, in the fire marshal's judgment, such action is necessary to protect human health and the environment. Any corrective action undertaken by the fire marshal or assistant fire marshal under division (A)(3) of this section shall be consistent with the requirements of sections 9003 and 9005 of the "Resource Conservation and Recovery Act of 1976," 98 Stat. 3279, 42 U.S.C.A. 6991b, and 98 Stat. 3284, 42 U.S.C.A. 6991e, respectively, as amended, applicable regulations adopted thereunder, and rules adopted under division (B) of this section.

(B) The fire marshal shall adopt, and may amend and rescind, such rules as the fire marshal considers necessary to establish standards for corrective actions for suspected and confirmed releases of petroleum and standards for the recovery of costs incurred for undertaking corrective or enforcement actions with respect to such releases. The rules also shall include requirements for financial responsibility for the cost of corrective actions for and compensation of bodily injury and property damage incurred by third parties that are caused by releases of petroleum. Rules regarding financial responsibility shall, without limitation, require responsible persons to provide evidence that the parties guaranteeing payment of the deductible amount established under division (E) or (F) of section 3737.91 of the Revised Code are, at a minimum, secondarily liable for all corrective action and third-party liability costs incurred within the scope of the deductible amount. The rules shall be consistent with sections 9003 and 9005 of the "Resource Conservation and Recovery Act of 1976," 98 Stat. 3279, 42 U.S.C.A. 6991b, and 98 Stat. 3284, 42 U.S.C.A. 6991e, respectively, as amended, and applicable regulations adopted thereunder.

(C)(1) No person shall violate or fail to comply with a rule adopted under division (A) of section 3737.88 of the Revised Code or division (B) of this section, and no person shall violate or fail to comply with the terms of any order issued under division (A) of section 3737.88 of the Revised Code or division (A)(1) of this section.

(2) Whoever violates division (C)(1) of this section or division (F) of section 3737.881 [3737.88.1] of the Revised Code shall pay a civil penalty of not more than ten thousand dollars for each day that the violation continues. The fire marshal may, by order, assess a civil penalty under this division, or the fire marshal may request the attorney general to bring a civil action for imposition of the civil penalty in the court of common pleas of the county in which the violation occurred. If the fire marshal determines that a responsible person is in violation of division (C)(1) of this section or division (F) of section 3737.881 [3737.88.1] of the Revised Code, the fire marshal may request the attorney general to bring a civil action for appropriate relief, including a temporary restraining order or preliminary or permanent injunction, in the court of common pleas of the county in which the underground storage tank or, in the case of a violation of division (F)(3) of section 3737.881 [3737.88.1] of the Revised Code, the training program that is the subject of the violation is located. The court shall issue a temporary restraining order or an injunction upon a demonstration that a violation of division (C)(1) of this section or division (F) of section 3737.881 [3737.88.1] of the Revised Code has occurred or is occurring.

Any action brought by the attorney general under this division is a civil action, governed by the Rules of Civil Procedure and other rules of practice and procedure applicable to civil actions.

(D) Orders issued under division (A) of section 3737.88 of the Revised Code and divisions (A)(1) and (C) of this section, and appeals thereof, are subject to and governed by Chapter 3745. of the Revised Code. Such orders shall be issued without the necessity for issuance of a proposed action under that chapter. For purposes of appeals of any such orders, the term "director" as used in Chapter 3745. of the Revised Code includes the fire marshal and an assistant fire marshal.

(E) Any restrictions on the use of real property for the purpose of the achievement by an owner or operator of applicable standards pursuant to rules adopted under division (B) of this section shall be contained in a deed or in another instrument that is signed and acknowledged by the property owner in the same manner as a deed or an environmental covenant that is entered into in accordance with sections 5301.80 to 5301.92 of the Revised Code. The deed, other instrument containing the restrictions, or environmental covenant shall be filed and recorded in the office of the county recorder of the county in which the property is located. Pursuant to Chapter 5309. of the Revised Code, if the use restrictions or environmental covenant are connected with registered land, as defined in section 5309.01 of the Revised Code, the restrictions or environmental covenant shall be entered as a memorial on the page of the register where the title of the owner is registered.

(F) Any restrictions on the use of real property for the purpose of the achievement by a person that is not a responsible person, or by a person undertaking a voluntary action of applicable standards pursuant to rules adopted under division (B) of this section shall be contained in an environmental covenant that is entered into in accordance with sections 5301.80 to 5301.92 of the Revised Code. The environmental covenant shall be filed and recorded in the office of the county recorder of the county in which the property is located. Pursuant to Chapter 5309. of the Revised Code, if the environmental covenant is connected with registered land, as defined in section 5309.01 of the Revised Code, the environmental covenant shall be entered as a memorial on the page of the register where the title of the owner is registered.

**HISTORY: RC § 3737.88, 142 v H 171 (Eff 7-1-87); RC § 3737.88.2, 143 v H 421 (Eff 7-11-89); 149 v H 338. Eff 10-1-2002; 150 v H 516, § 1, eff. 12-30-04.**

The effective date is set by section 10 of H.B. 516 (150 v —).

## § 3737.91 Financial assurance fund; fees; certificate of coverage.

(A) There is hereby created the petroleum underground storage tank financial assurance fund, which shall be in the custody of the treasurer of state, but is not a part of the state treasury. The fund shall consist of moneys from the following sources:

(1) All fees collected under divisions (B) and (F) of this section and all supplemental fees collected under division (C) of this section;

(2) Interest earned on moneys in the fund;

(3) Appropriations to the fund from the general revenue fund;

(4) The proceeds of revenue bonds issued under sections 3737.90 to 3737.948 [3737.94.8] of the Revised Code, provided that upon resolution of the petroleum underground storage tank release compensation board created in section 3737.90 of the Revised Code, all or part of those proceeds may be deposited into a separate account of the fund. Chapters 131. and 135. of the Revised Code do not apply to the establishment, deposit, investment, application, and safeguard of any such account and moneys in any such account.

(B) For the purposes of paying the costs of implementing and administering this section and sections 3737.90 and 3737.92 of the Revised Code and rules adopted under them; payment or reimbursement of corrective action costs under section 3737.92 of the Revised Code; compensating third parties for bodily injury or property damage under that section; and payment of principal and interest on revenue bonds issued under sections 3737.90 to 3737.948 [3737.94.8] of the Revised Code to raise capital for the fund, there is hereby assessed an annual petroleum underground storage tank financial assurance fee on each tank comprising an underground storage tank or an underground storage tank system that contains or has contained petroleum and for which a responsible person is required to demonstrate financial responsibility by rules adopted by the fire marshal under division (B) of section 3737.882 [3737.88.2] of the Revised Code. The fee assessed by this division shall be paid to the board by a responsible person for each tank that is subject to the fee. The fee shall be paid not later than the first day of July of each year, except that in 1989 the fee shall be paid by either the first day of September or ninety days after July 11, 1989, whichever is later. The fee is in addition to any fee established by the fire marshal under section 3737.88 of the Revised Code.

The amount of the annual fee due in 1989 and 1990 is one hundred fifty dollars per tank per year. In 1991 and subsequent years the board shall establish the amount of the annual fee in accordance with this division. Not later than the first day of April of 1991 and each subsequent year, the board, in consultation with the administrative agent of the fund with whom the board has entered into a contract under division (B)(3) of section 3737.90 of the Revised Code, if any, shall determine the amount of the annual fee to be assessed in that year and shall adopt rules in accordance with Chapter 119. of the Revised Code to establish the fee at that amount. The fee shall be established at an amount calculated to maintain the continued financial soundness of the fund, provided that if the unobligated balance of the fund exceeds forty-five million dollars on the date that an annual determination is made, the board may assess a fee in the year to which the determination applies only to the extent required in or by, or necessary to comply with covenants or other requirements in, revenue bonds issued under sections 3737.90 to 3737.948 [3737.94.8] of the Revised Code or in proceedings or other covenants or agreements related to such bonds. Not later than the first day of May of 1991 and each subsequent year, the board shall notify each responsible person by certified mail of the amount of the annual fee per tank due in that year. As used in this paragraph, "proceedings" has the same meaning as in section 133.01 of the Revised Code.

If a responsible person is both the owner and operator of a tank, the responsible person shall pay any annual fee assessed under this division in compliance with this division and the rules adopted thereunder. If the owner of the tank and the operator of the tank are not the same person, any annual fee assessed under this division in compliance with this division and the rules adopted thereunder shall be paid by one of the responsible persons; however, all such responsible persons are liable for noncompliance with this division.

(C) As necessary to maintain the financial soundness of the fund, the board, by rules adopted in accordance with Chapter 119. of the Revised Code, may at any time assess a supplemental petroleum underground storage tank financial assurance fee on tanks subject to the fee assessed under division (B) or (F) of this section in any fiscal year in which the board finds that the unobligated balance in the fund is less than fifteen million dollars. The board, in consultation with the fund's administrative agent, if any, shall establish the amount of the supplemental fee at an amount that will ensure an unobligated balance in the fund of at least fifteen million dollars at the end of the fiscal year in which the supplemental fee is assessed. Not less than thirty days before the date on which payment of the supplemental fee is due under the board's rules, the board shall notify each responsible person by certified mail of the amount of the supplemental fee and the date on which payment of the supplemental fee to the board is due.

If a responsible person is both the owner and operator of a tank, the responsible person shall pay any supplemental fee assessed under this division in compliance with this division and the rules adopted thereunder. If the owner of the tank and the operator of the tank are not the same person, any supplemental fee assessed under this division in compliance with this division and the rules adopted thereunder shall be paid by one of the responsible persons; however, all such responsible persons are liable for noncompliance with this division.

(D)(1) The board shall issue a certificate of coverage to any responsible person who has complied with all of the following:

(a) Paid the fee assessed under division (B) or (F) of this section;

(b) Demonstrated to the board financial responsibility in compliance with the rules adopted by the fire marshal under division (B) of section 3737.882 [3737.88.2] of the Revised Code for the deductible amount established under division (E) of this section or, when appropriate, the reduced deductible amount established under division (F) of this section. If the responsible person utilizes self-insurance as a financial responsibility mechanism, the responsible person shall provide the board with an affidavit in which the responsible party certifies that all documentation submitted to the board is true and accurate;

(c) Certified to the board that for each petroleum underground storage tank system for which a certificate of coverage is sought, the responsible person is in compliance with applicable rules for petroleum underground storage tank systems that have been adopted by the fire marshal under section 3737.88 of the Revised Code.

The certificate of coverage shall state the amount of coverage to which the responsible person is entitled from the fund pursuant to division (D)(3) of this section and the time period for which the certificate provides that coverage. An issued certificate of coverage is subject to the condition that the holder timely pay any supplemental fee assessed under division (C) of this section during the time that the certificate is in effect.

(2) The board shall not issue a certificate of coverage to any responsible person who fails to comply with divisions (D)(1)(a), (b), and (c) of this section.

(3) The maximum disbursement from the fund for any single release of petroleum is the difference between the deductible amount established under division (E) of this section or, when appropriate, the reduced deductible amount established under division (F) of this section and one million dollars. The maximum disbursement from the fund during any fiscal year on behalf of any responsible person shall not exceed in the aggregate one million dollars less the deductible amount if the responsible person owns or operates not more than one hundred tanks comprising underground petroleum storage tanks or underground petroleum storage tank systems, shall not exceed in the aggregate two million dollars less the deductible amount if the responsible person owns or operates not more than two hundred such tanks, shall not exceed in the aggregate three million dollars less the deductible amount if the responsible person owns or operates not more than three hundred such tanks, and shall not exceed in the aggregate four million dollars less the deductible amount if the responsible person owns or operates more than three hundred such tanks. The maximum disbursement from the fund for any single release or for any fiscal year under this division does not in any manner limit the liability of a responsible person for a release of petroleum.

(E)(1) Except as otherwise provided in division (F) of this section, no responsible person is eligible to receive moneys from the fund under section 3737.92 of the Revised Code until the responsible person demonstrates to the board financial responsibility for the first fifty thousand dollars of the cost for corrective action for, and compensating third parties for bodily injury and property damage caused by, accidental releases of petroleum from an underground storage tank owned or operated by the responsible party. The fifty thousand dollar amount is the deductible amount for the purposes of this section and section 3737.92 of the Revised Code.

(2) The board, in consultation with the fund's administrative agent, if any, may, by rules adopted in accordance with Chapter 119. of the Revised Code, establish for any fiscal year a deductible amount that differs from fifty thousand dollars. The deductible amount established by the board shall be such an amount as to maintain the financial soundness of the fund. Any action of the board to establish a differing deductible amount or to alter a deductible amount previously established by it shall be taken concurrently with the establishment under division (B) of this section of the annual fee due on the first day of the fiscal year in which the deductible amount will apply. If the deductible amount established under this division differs from that in effect at the time of the board's action, the board shall notify each responsible person of the change by certified mail not later than the first day of May preceding the effective date of the change.

(F)(1) Any responsible person owning, or owning or operating, a total of six or fewer petroleum underground storage tanks may elect in calendar years 1989 and 1990 to pay twice the amount of the per tank annual fee for each tank assessed under division (B) of this section in order to reduce the amount of the deductible established in division (E) of this section to the total amount of ten thousand dollars. The election shall be available only at the time of the payment of the annual fee and any supplemental fee. The election shall not be retroactively applied.

(2) Any responsible person owning, or owning or operating, a total of six or fewer petroleum underground storage tanks may elect in calendar year 1991 and in each subsequent year to pay an additional fee at an amount established by the board in addition to the per tank annual fee assessed under division (B) of this section in order to reduce the deductible amount established under division (E) of this section. In calendar year 1991 and in each subsequent year, the board shall establish the amount of the additional fee and the reduced deductible amount. In determining the amount of the additional fee and the reduced deductible amount, the board shall take into consideration the effect of the additional claims paid under section 3737.92 of the Revised Code to responsible persons making an election under division (F)(2) of this section and balance that consideration with such factors as the availability of liability insurance, the difficulty of proving financial responsibility pursuant to the rules adopted by the fire marshal under division (B) of section 3737.882 [3737.88.2] of the Revised Code, and the hardship created on small owners and operators of petroleum underground storage tanks by an increase in either the additional fee or the reduced deductible amount.

(3) Any responsible person owning, or owning or operating, a total of six or fewer petroleum underground storage tanks who elects to pay the additional fee under divisions (F)(1) and (2) of this section shall pay any per tank supplemental fee assessed under division (C) of this section.

(G) If the director of the fund determines that a responsible person has failed to comply with division (B), (C), or (F) of this section, the director of the fund shall notify each responsible person for the petroleum underground storage tank of the noncompliance. If, within thirty days after the notification, the responsible person fails to pay the applicable fee or any fee previously assessed upon the responsible person under this section, the director of the fund shall issue an order requiring the responsible person to pay all of the fees the responsible person owes to the fund and an additional late payment fee in the amount of one thousand dollars to the fund.

If a responsible person fails to comply with any order of the director of the fund within thirty days after the issuance of the order, the director shall notify the fire marshal of that noncompliance. Upon the request of the director of the fund, the attorney general may bring a civil action for appropriate relief, including a temporary restraining order or preliminary or permanent injunction, in the court of common pleas of the county in which the petroleum underground storage tank that is the subject of the order is located. The court shall issue an injunction upon a demonstration that a failure to comply with the director's order has occurred or is occurring.

Any orders issued by the director of the fund under this division may be appealed by the responsible person under division (F) of section 3737.92 of the Revised Code. For the purpose of an appeal of any order of the director of the fund, "determination" as used in that division includes any order of the director of the fund. The filing of a notice of appeal under this division does not operate as a stay of any order of the director of the fund.

**HISTORY: 143 v H 421 (Eff 7-11-89); 144 v S 359 (Eff 12-22-92); 147 v S 46. Eff 12-18-97.**

## § 3737.93 Transferor of petroleum to give notice of registration requirements.

During the period commencing ninety days after the effective date of this section and ending on January 1, 1991, a person who transfers title to petroleum that is placed by the person directly into an underground storage tank of the transferee shall provide written notice to the transferee of the requirements for the registration of underground storage tanks established by rules adopted under sections 3737.88 and 3737.882 [3737.88.2] of the Revised Code.

No person shall fail to comply with this section.

**HISTORY: 143 v H 421. Eff 7-11-89.**

## § 3737.99 Penalties.

(A) Whoever violates section 3737.28 of the Revised Code may be summarily punished, by the officer concerned, by a fine of not more than one hundred dollars or commitment to the county jail until that person is willing to comply with the order of such officer.

(B) Except as a violation of section 2923.17 of the Revised Code involves subject matter covered by the state fire code and except as such a violation is covered by division (G) of this section, whoever violates division (A) of section 3737.51 of the Revised Code is guilty of a misdemeanor of the first degree.

(C) Whoever violates section 3737.61 of the Revised Code is guilty of a minor misdemeanor.

(D) Whoever violates section 3737.62 or 3737.64 of the Revised Code is guilty of a misdemeanor of the fourth degree.

(E) Whoever violates section 3737.63 or division (A) or (B) of section 3737.65 of the Revised Code is guilty of a misdemeanor of the third degree.

(F) Whoever violates division (C)(3) or (D)(5) of section 3737.73 of the Revised Code shall be fined one thousand dollars.

(G) Whoever violates section 3737.66 of the Revised Code is guilty of a misdemeanor of the first degree.

(H) Whoever knowingly violates division (C) of section 3737.882 [3737.88.2] of the Revised Code is guilty of an unclassified felony and shall be fined not more than twenty-five thousand dollars or imprisoned for not more than fourteen months, or both. Whoever recklessly violates division (C) of section 3737.882 [3737.88.2] of the Revised Code is guilty of a misdemeanor of the first degree.

(I) Whoever knowingly violates division (F)(1), (2), or (3) of section 3737.881 [3737.88.1] or section 3737.93 of the Revised Code is guilty of a misdemeanor of the fourth degree.

(J) Whoever knowingly violates division (B) or (C) of section 3737.91 of the Revised Code is guilty of a misdemeanor of the second degree.

**HISTORY: 137 v H 590 (Eff 7-1-79); 138 v S 18 (Eff 7-1-79); 141 v S 61 (Eff 5-30-86); 141 v H 552 (Eff 9-17-86); 141 v H 428 (Eff 12-23-86); 142 v H 171 (Eff 7-1-87); 143 v H 421 (Eff 7-11-89); 146 v S 2. Eff 7-1-96; 151 v H 422, § 1, eff. 9-28-06.**

**Analogous to former RC § 3737.99 (Bureau of Code Revision, 10-1-53; 125 v 903; 130 v 863; 133 v S 180; 136 v S 462; 136 v H 837; 137 v H 1), repealed 137 v H 590, § 2, eff 7-1-79.**

The effective date is set by section 6 of SB 2.

# CHAPTER 3743: FIREWORKS

## § 3743.01 Definitions.

As used in this chapter:

(A) "Beer" and "intoxicating liquor" have the same meanings as in section 4301.01 of the Revised Code.

(B) "Booby trap" means a small tube that has a string protruding from both ends, that has a friction-sensitive composition, and that is ignited by pulling the ends of the string.

(C) "Cigarette load" means a small wooden peg that is coated with a small quantity of explosive composition and that is ignited in a cigarette.

(D)(1) "1.3G fireworks" means display fireworks consistent with regulations of the United States department of transportation as expressed using the designation "division 1.3" in Title 49, Code of Federal Regulations.

(2) "1.4G fireworks" means consumer fireworks consistent with regulations of the United States department of transportation as expressed using the designation "division 1.4" in Title 49, Code of Federal Regulations.

(E) "Controlled substance" has the same meaning as in section 3719.01 of the Revised Code.

(F) "Fireworks" means any composition or device prepared for the purpose of producing a visible or an audible effect by combustion, deflagration, or detonation, except ordinary matches and except as provided in section 3743.80 of the Revised Code.

(G) "Fireworks plant" means all buildings and other structures in which the manufacturing of fireworks, or the storage or sale of manufactured fireworks by a manufacturer, takes place.

(H) "Highway" means any public street, road, alley, way, lane, or other public thoroughfare.

(I) "Licensed exhibitor of fireworks" or "licensed exhibitor" means a person licensed pursuant to sections 3743.50 to 3743.55 of the Revised Code.

(J) "Licensed manufacturer of fireworks" or "licensed manufacturer" means a person licensed pursuant to sections 3743.02 to 3743.08 of the Revised Code.

(K) "Licensed wholesaler of fireworks" or "licensed wholesaler" means a person licensed pursuant to sections 3743.15 to 3743.21 of the Revised Code.

(L) "List of licensed exhibitors" means the list required by division (C) of section 3743.51 of the Revised Code.

(M) "List of licensed manufacturers" means the list required by division (C) of section 3743.03 of the Revised Code.

(N) "List of licensed wholesalers" means the list required by division (C) of section 3743.16 of the Revised Code.

(O) "Manufacturing of fireworks" means the making of fireworks from raw materials, none of which in and of themselves constitute a fireworks, or the processing of fireworks.

(P) "Navigable waters" means any body of water susceptible of being used in its ordinary condition as a highway of commerce over which trade and travel is or may be conducted in the customary modes, but does not include a body of water that is not capable of navigation by barges, tugboats, and other large vessels.

(Q) "Novelties and trick noisemakers" include the following items:

(1) Devices that produce a small report intended to surprise the user, including, but not limited to, booby traps, cigarette loads, party poppers, and snappers;

(2) Snakes or glow worms;

(3) Smoke devices;

(4) Trick matches.

(R) "Party popper" means a small plastic or paper item that contains not more than sixteen milligrams of friction-sensitive explosive composition, that is ignited by pulling a string protruding from the item, and from which paper streamers are expelled when the item is ignited.

(S) "Processing of fireworks" means the making of fireworks from materials all or part of which in and of themselves constitute a fireworks, but does not include the mere packaging or repackaging of fireworks.

(T) "Railroad" means any railway or railroad that carries freight or passengers for hire, but does not include auxiliary tracks, spurs, and sidings installed and primarily used in serving a mine, quarry, or plant.

(U) "Retail sale" or "sell at retail" means a sale of fireworks to a purchaser who intends to use the fireworks, and not resell them.

(V) "Smoke device" means a tube or sphere that contains pyrotechnic composition that, upon ignition, produces white or colored smoke as the primary effect.

(W) "Snake or glow worm" means a device that consists of a pressed pellet of pyrotechnic composition that produces a large, snake-like ash upon burning, which ash expands in length as the pellet burns.

(X) "Snapper" means a small, paper-wrapped item that contains a minute quantity of explosive composition coated on small bits of sand, and that, when dropped, implodes.

(Y) "Trick match" means a kitchen or book match that is coated with a small quantity of explosive composition and that, upon ignition, produces a small report or a shower of sparks.

(Z) "Wire sparkler" means a sparkler consisting of a wire or stick coated with a nonexplosive pyrotechnic mixture that produces a shower of sparks upon ignition and that contains no more than one hundred grams of this mixture.

(AA) "Wholesale sale" or "sell at wholesale" means a sale of fireworks to a purchaser who intends to resell the fireworks so purchased.

(BB) "Licensed premises" means the real estate upon which a licensed manufacturer or wholesaler of fireworks conducts business.

(CC) "Licensed building" means a building on the licensed premises of a licensed manufacturer or wholesaler of fireworks that is approved for occupancy by the building official having jurisdiction.

(DD) "Fireworks incident" means any action or omission that occurs at a fireworks exhibition, that results in injury or death, or a substantial risk of injury or death, to any person, and that involves either of the following:

(1) The handling or other use, or the results of the handling or other use, of fireworks or associated equipment or other materials;

(2) The failure of any person to comply with any applicable requirement imposed by this chapter or any applicable rule adopted under this chapter.

(EE) "Discharge site" means an area immediately surrounding the mortars used to fire aerial shells.

(FF) "Fireworks incident site" means a discharge site or other location at a fireworks exhibition where a fireworks incident occurs, a location where an injury or death associated with a fireworks incident occurs, or a location where evidence of a fireworks incident or an injury or death associated with a fireworks incident is found.

(GG) "Storage location" means a single parcel or contiguous parcels of real estate approved by the fire marshal pursuant to division (I) of section 3743.04 of the Revised Code or division (G) of section 3743.17 of the Revised Code that are separate from a licensed premises containing a retail showroom, and which parcel or parcels a licensed manufacturer or wholesaler of fireworks may use only for the distribution, possession, and storage of fireworks in accordance with this chapter.

**HISTORY: 141 v S 61 (Eff 5-30-86); 147 v H 215 (Eff 6-30-97); 149 v H 161, §§ 1, 3. Eff 6-29-2001; 151 v H 66, § 101.01, eff. 9-29-05.**

The effective date is set by § 612.03 of 151 v H 66.

**Somewhat analogous to former RC § 3743.01 (GC § 5903-1; 108 v PtI, 334; Bureau of Code Revision, 10-1-53), repealed 137 v H 590, § 2, eff 7-1-79.**

The provisions of § 6 of HB 161 (149 v —) read as follows:

SECTION 6. (A) The intent of the General Assembly in amending sections 3743.01, 3743.02, 3743.03, 3743.04, 3743.05, 3743.06, 3743.07, 3743.08, 3743.15, 3743.16, 3743.17, 3743.18, 3743.19, 3743.20, 3743.21, 3743.40, 3743.44, 3743.45, 3743.50, 3743.51, 3743.52, 3743.53, 3743.54, 3743.58, 3743.59, 3743.60, 3743.61, 3743.64, 3743.65, 3743.66, 3743.68, 3743.80, and 3743.99 and in enacting sections 3743.25, 3743.56, and 3743.70 of the Revised Code in Section 1 of this act is to reenact the amendments to, or the enactment of, those sections by Am. Sub. H.B. 215 of the 122nd General Assembly to protect those sections against a challenge that their amendment or enactment was invalid because it violated the prohibition contained in Section 15 of Article II of the Constitution of Ohio against a bill containing more than one subject. For purposes of this act, all references in those sections to "the effective date of this section" or to "the effective date of this amendment" shall be construed to mean the effective date of a section or of an amendment to a section by Am. Sub. H.B. 215 of the 122nd General Assembly.

(B) The intent of the General Assembly in further amending sections 3743.01, 3743.50, 3743.52, 3743.53, 3743.54, 3743.64, and 3743.99, in amending sections 3743.56 and 3743.57, and in enacting sections 3743.541 and 3743.75 of the Revised Code in Section 3 of this act is to:

(1) Recognize the versions of sections 3743.01, 3743.50, 3743.52, 3743.53, 3743.54, 3743.64, and 3743.99 of the Revised Code that result from Am. Sub. H.B. 215 of the 122nd General Assembly and Sub. H.B. 405 of the 123rd General Assembly; and

(2) Further amend sections 3743.01, 3743.50, 3743.52, 3743.53, 3743.54, 3743.64, and 3743.99, amend sections 3743.56 and 3743.57, and enact sections 3743.541 and 3743.75 of the Revised Code to make changes pertaining to fireworks incidents and their investigation, to the fees charged for fireworks exhibitor licenses, to the authority of fireworks exhibitor assistants to work for any fireworks exhibitor, to the maximum balance allowed in the Fire Marshal's Training and Education Fund, and to the extension until December 15, 2005, of the general moratorium on the issuance of new licenses to manufacturers and wholesalers of fireworks and on approvals of the transfer of their licenses to other locations.

## § 3743.60 Unlicensed manufacturing prohibited; prohibited activities by manufacturer; prohibitions concerning fireworks plant.

(A) No person shall manufacture fireworks in this state unless it is a licensed manufacturer of fireworks, and no person shall operate a fireworks plant in this state unless it has been issued a license as a manufacturer of fireworks for the particular fireworks plant.

(B) No person shall operate a fireworks plant in this state after its license as a manufacturer of fireworks for the particular fireworks plant has expired, been denied renewal, or been revoked, unless a new license has been obtained.

(C) No licensed manufacturer of fireworks, during the effective period of its licensure, shall construct, locate, or relocate any buildings or other structures on the premises of its fireworks plant, make any structural change or renovation in any building or other structure on the premises of its fireworks plant, or change the nature of its manufacturing of fireworks so as to include the processing of fireworks without first obtaining a written authorization from the fire marshal pursuant to division (B) of section 3743.04 of the Revised Code.

(D) No licensed manufacturer of fireworks shall manufacture fireworks, possess fireworks for sale at wholesale or retail, or sell fireworks at wholesale or retail, in a manner not authorized by division (C) of section 3743.04 of the Revised Code.

(E) No licensed manufacturer of fireworks shall knowingly fail to comply with the rules adopted by the fire marshal pursuant to section 3743.05 of the Revised Code or the requirements of section 3743.06 of the Revised Code.

(F) No licensed manufacturer of fireworks shall fail to maintain complete inventory, wholesale sale, and retail records as required by section 3743.07 of the Revised Code, or to permit inspection of these records or the premises of a fireworks plant pursuant to section 3743.08 of the Revised Code.

(G) No licensed manufacturer of fireworks shall fail to comply with an order of the fire marshal issued pursuant to division (B)(1) of section 3743.08 of the Revised Code, within the specified period of time.

(H) No licensed manufacturer of fireworks shall fail to comply with an order of the fire marshal issued pursuant to division (B)(2) of section 3743.08 of the Revised Code until the nonconformities are eliminated, corrected, or otherwise remedied or the seventy-two hour period specified in that division has expired, whichever first occurs.

(I) No person shall smoke or shall carry a pipe, cigarette, or cigar, or a match, lighter, other flame-producing item, or open flame on, or shall carry a concealed source of ignition into, the premises of a fireworks plant, except as smoking is authorized in specified lunchrooms or restrooms by a manufacturer pursuant to division (C) of section 3743.06 of the Revised Code.

(J) No person shall have possession or control of, or be under the influence of, any intoxicating liquor, beer, or controlled substance, while on the premises of a fireworks plant.

**HISTORY: 141 v S 61 (Eff 5-30-86); 147 v H 215 (Eff 6-30-97); 149 v H 161. Eff 6-29-2001.**

See provisions, § 6(A) of HB 161 (149 v —) following RC § 3743.01.

## § 3743.61 Restrictions on operation as wholesaler.

(A) No person, except a licensed manufacturer of fireworks engaging in the wholesale sale of fireworks as authorized by division (C)(2) of section 3743.04 of the Revised Code, shall operate as a wholesaler of fireworks in this state unless it is a licensed wholesaler of fireworks, or shall operate as a wholesaler of fireworks at any location in this state unless it has been issued a license as a wholesaler of fireworks for the particular location.

(B) No person shall operate as a wholesaler of fireworks at a particular location in this state after its license as a wholesaler of fireworks for the particular location has expired, been denied renewal, or been revoked, unless a new license has been obtained.

(C) No licensed wholesaler of fireworks, during the effective period of its licensure, shall perform any construction, or make any structural change or renovation, on the premises on which the fireworks are sold without first obtaining a written authorization from the fire marshal pursuant to division (B) of section 3743.17 of the Revised Code.

(D) No licensed wholesaler of fireworks shall possess fireworks for sale at wholesale or retail, or sell fireworks at wholesale or retail, in a manner not authorized by division (C) of section 3743.17 of the Revised Code.

(E) No licensed wholesaler of fireworks shall knowingly fail to comply with the rules adopted by the fire marshal pursuant to section 3743.18 or the requirements of section 3743.19 of the Revised Code.

(F) No licensed wholesaler of fireworks shall fail to maintain complete inventory, wholesale sale, and retail records as required by section 3743.20 of the Revised Code, or to permit inspection of these records or the premises of the wholesaler pursuant to section 3743.21 of the Revised Code.

(G) No licensed wholesaler of fireworks shall fail to comply with an order of the fire marshal issued pursuant to division (B)(1) of section 3743.21 of the Revised Code, within the specified period of time.

(H) No licensed wholesaler of fireworks shall fail to comply with an order of the fire marshal issued pursuant to division (B)(2) of section 3743.21 of the Revised Code until the nonconformities are eliminated, corrected, or otherwise remedied or the seventy-two hour period specified in that division has expired, whichever first occurs.

(I) No person shall smoke or shall carry a pipe, cigarette, or cigar, or a match, lighter, other flame-producing item, or open flame on, or shall carry a concealed source of ignition into, the premises of a wholesaler of fireworks, except as smoking is authorized in specified lunchrooms or restrooms by a wholesaler pursuant to division (D) of section 3743.19 of the Revised Code.

(J) No person shall have possession or control of, or be under the influence of, any intoxicating liquor, beer, or controlled substance, while on the premises of a wholesaler of fireworks.

**HISTORY: 141 v S 61 (Eff 5-30-86); 147 v H 215 (Eff 6-30-97); 149 v H 161. Eff 6-29-2001.**

See provisions, § 6(A) of HB 161 (149 v —) following RC § 3743.01.

## § 3743.63 Restrictions on purchasers.

(A) No person who resides in another state and purchases fireworks in this state shall obtain possession of the fireworks in this state unless the person complies with section 3743.44 of the Revised Code, provided that knowingly making a false statement on the fireworks purchaser form is not a violation of this section but is a violation of section 2921.13 of the Revised Code.

(B) No person who resides in another state and who purchases fireworks in this state shall obtain possession of fireworks in this state other than from a licensed manufacturer or wholesaler, or fail, when transporting the fireworks, to transport them directly out of this state within seventy-two hours after the time of their purchase. No such person shall give or sell to any other person in this state fireworks that the person has acquired in this state.

(C) No person who resides in this state and purchases fireworks in this state shall obtain possession of the fireworks in this state unless the person complies with section 3743.45 of the Revised Code, provided that knowingly making a false statement on the fireworks purchaser form is not a violation of this section but is a violation of section 2921.13 of the Revised Code.

(D) No person who resides in this state and who purchases fireworks in this state under section 3743.45 of the Revised Code shall obtain possession of fireworks in this state other than from a licensed manufacturer or licensed wholesaler, or fail, when transporting the fireworks, to transport them directly out of this state within forty-eight hours after the time of their purchase. No such person shall give or sell to any other person in this state fireworks that the person has acquired in this state.

**HISTORY: 141 v S 61 (Eff 5-30-86); 146 v S 2. Eff 7-1-96.**

The effective date is set by section 6 of SB 2.

## § 3743.64 Prohibitions concerning exhibitors and fireworks incident sites.

(A) No person shall conduct a fireworks exhibition in this state or act as an exhibitor of fireworks in this state unless the person is a licensed exhibitor of fireworks.

(B) No person shall conduct a fireworks exhibition in this state or act as an exhibitor of fireworks in this state after the person's license as an exhibitor of fireworks has expired, been denied renewal, or been revoked, unless a new license has been obtained.

(C) No licensed exhibitor of fireworks shall fail to comply with the applicable requirements of the rules adopted by the fire marshal pursuant to divisions (B) and (E) of section 3743.53 of the Revised Code or to comply with divisions (C) and (D) of that section.

(D) No licensed exhibitor of fireworks shall conduct a fireworks exhibition unless a permit has been secured for the exhibition pursuant to section 3743.54 of the Revised Code or if a permit so secured is revoked by a fire chief or fire prevention officer, in consultation with a police chief or other similar chief law enforcement officer of a municipal corporation, township, or township or joint police district or with a designee of such a police chief or other similar chief law enforcement officer, pursuant to that section.

(E) No licensed exhibitor of fireworks shall acquire fireworks for use at a fireworks exhibition other than in accordance with sections 3743.54 and 3743.55 of the Revised Code.

(F) No licensed exhibitor of fireworks or other person associated with the conduct of a fireworks exhibition shall have possession or control of, or be under the influence of, any intoxicating liquor, beer, or controlled substance while on the premises on which the exhibition is being conducted.

(G) No licensed exhibitor of fireworks shall permit an employee to assist the licensed exhibitor in conducting fireworks exhibitions unless the employee is registered with the fire marshal under section 3743.56 of the Revised Code.

(H) Except as provided in division (C) of section 3743.541 of the Revised Code, no person shall knowingly, or knowingly permit another person to, dismantle, reposition, or otherwise disturb any fireworks, associated equipment or materials, or other items within a fireworks incident site, or any evidence related to a fireworks incident, at any time after that person has reason to believe a fireworks incident has occurred, before the state fire marshal, the state fire marshal's designee, a member of the state fire marshal's staff, or other appropriate state or local law enforcement authorities permit in accordance with section 3743.541 of the Revised Code the dismantling, repositioning, or other disturbance of the fireworks, equipment, materials, or items within the fireworks incident site or of any evidence related to the fireworks incident.

**HISTORY: 141 v S 61 (Eff 5-30-86); 147 v H 215 (Eff 6-30-97); 148 v H 405 (Eff 10-19-2000); 149 v H 161, §§ 1, 3. Eff 6-29-2001; 2011 HB 153, § 101.01, eff. Sept. 29, 2011.**

See provisions, § 6(A), (B) of HB 161 (149 v —) following RC § 3743.01.

## § 3743.65 Restrictions on possession, sale and use; persons under age 18; ejection of disruptive persons; disabling fire suppression system.

(A) No person shall possess fireworks in this state or shall possess for sale or sell fireworks in this state, except a licensed manufacturer of fireworks as authorized by sections 3743.02 to 3743.08 of the Revised Code, a licensed wholesaler of fireworks as authorized by sections 3743.15 to 3743.21 of the Revised Code, a shipping permit holder as authorized by section 3743.40 of the Revised Code, an out-of-state resident as authorized by section 3743.44 of the Revised Code, a resident of this state as authorized by section 3743.45 of the Revised Code, or a licensed exhibitor of fireworks as authorized by sections 3743.50 to 3743.55 of the Revised Code, and except as provided in section 3743.80 of the Revised Code.

(B) Except as provided in section 3743.80 of the Revised Code and except for licensed exhibitors of fireworks authorized to conduct a fireworks exhibition pursuant to sections 3743.50 to 3743.55 of the Revised Code, no person shall discharge, ignite, or explode any fireworks in this state.

(C) No person shall use in a theater or public hall, what is technically known as fireworks showers, or a mixture containing potassium chlorate and sulphur.

(D) No person shall sell fireworks of any kind to a person under eighteen years of age. No person under eighteen years of age shall enter a fireworks sales showroom unless that person is accompanied by a parent, legal guardian, or other responsible adult. No person under eighteen years of age shall touch or possess fireworks on a licensed premises without the consent of the licensee. A licensee may eject any person from a licensed premises that is in any way disruptive to the safe operation of the premises.

(E) No person, other than a licensed manufacturer, licensed wholesaler, licensed exhibitor, or shipping permit holder, shall possess 1.3G fireworks in this state.

(F) Except as otherwise provided in division (J) of section 3743.06 and division (K) of section 3743.19 of the Revised Code, no person shall knowingly disable a fire suppression system as defined in section 3781.108 [3781.10.8] of the Revised Code on the premises of a fireworks plant of a licensed manufacturer of fireworks or on the premises of the business operations of a licensed wholesaler of fireworks.

**HISTORY: 141 v S 61 (Eff 5-30-86); 142 v H 436 (Eff 6-14-88); 143 v H 111 (Eff 7-1-89); 146 v S 2 (Eff 7-1-96); 147 v H 215 (Eff 6-30-97); 149 v H 161. Eff 6-29-2001; 151 v H 66, § 101.01, eff. 9-29-05; 152 v H 562, § 101.01, eff. 9-23-08.**

The effective date is set by § 812.10 of 152 v H 562.
The effective date is set by § 612.03 of 151 v H 66.
See provisions, § 6(A) of HB 161 (149 v —) following RC § 3743.01.

## § 3743.66 Limitations on shipping or transporting.

(A) No person shall transport fireworks in this state except in accordance with rules adopted by the fire marshal pursuant to section 3743.58 of the Revised Code.

(B) As used in this division, "fireworks" includes only 1.3G and 1.4G fireworks. No person shall ship fireworks into this state by mail, parcel post, or common carrier unless the person possesses a valid shipping permit issued under section 3743.40 of the Revised Code, and the fireworks are shipped directly to the holder of a license issued under section 3743.03, 3743.16, or 3743.51 of the Revised Code.

No person shall ship fireworks within this state by mail, parcel post, or common carrier unless the fireworks are shipped directly to the holder of a license issued under section 3743.03, 3743.16, or 3743.51 of the Revised Code.

**HISTORY: 141 v S 61 (Eff 5-30-86); 147 v H 215 (Eff 6-30-97); 149 v H 161. Eff 6-29-2001.**

See provisions, § 6(A) of HB 161 (149 v —) following RC § 3743.01.

## § 3743.68 Arrest of violators; seizure; forfeiture; distribution of fines.

(A) The fire marshal, an assistant fire marshal, or a certified fire safety inspector may arrest, or may cause the arrest of, any person whom the fire marshal, assistant fire marshal, or certified fire safety inspector finds in the act of violating, or who the fire marshal, assistant fire marshal, or certified fire safety inspector has reasonable cause to believe has violated, sections 3743.60 to 3743.66 of the Revised Code. Any arrest shall be made in accordance with statutory and constitutional provisions governing arrests by law enforcement officers.

(B) If the fire marshal, an assistant fire marshal, or certified fire safety inspector has probable cause to believe that fireworks are being manufactured, sold, possessed, transported, or used in violation of this chapter, the fire marshal, assistant fire marshal, or certified fire safety inspector may seize the fireworks. Any seizure of fireworks shall be made in accordance with statutory and constitutional provisions governing searches and seizures by law enforcement officers. The fire marshal's or certified fire safety inspector's office shall impound at the site or safely keep seized fireworks pending the time they are no longer needed as evidence. A sample of the seized fireworks is sufficient for evidentiary purposes. The remainder of the seized fireworks may be disposed of pursuant to an order from a court of competent jurisdiction after notice and a hearing.

Fireworks manufactured, sold, possessed, transported, or used in violation of this chapter shall be forfeited by the violator. The fire marshal's or certified fire safety inspector's office shall dispose of seized fireworks pursuant to the procedures specified in sections 2981.11 to 2981.13 of the Revised Code for the disposal of forfeited property by law enforcement agencies, and the fire marshal or that office is not liable for claims for the loss of or damages to the seized fireworks.

(C) This section does not affect the authority of a peace officer, as defined in section 2935.01 of the Revised Code, to make arrests for violations of this chapter or to seize fireworks manufactured, sold, possessed, transported, or used in violation of this chapter.

(D) Any fines imposed for a violation of this chapter relating to the sale, purchase, possession, or discharge of fireworks shall be distributed in the following manner if a municipal corporation, county, or township either filed or enforced the complaint regarding the violation. One-half of the amount of the fine shall be distributed to the municipal corporation, county, or township which filed the complaint regarding the violation and one-half of the amount of the fine shall be distributed to the municipal corporation, county, or township which enforced the complaint. If the same municipal corporation, county, or township both filed the complaint regarding the violation and enforced the complaint, the entire amount of the fine shall be distributed to that municipal corporation, county, or township.

**HISTORY: 141 v S 61 (Eff 5-30-86); 147 v H 215 (Eff 6-30-97); 149 v H 161. Eff 6-29-2001; 151 v H 241, § 1, eff. 7-1-07.**

See provisions of § 4 of 151 v H 241 following RC § 3719.11.

See provisions, § 6(A) of HB 161 (149 v —) following RC § 3743.01.

## § 3743.70 Felony precludes license or permit.

The fire marshal shall not issue an initial or a renewal of a license, permit, or registration under this chapter on or after June 30, 1997, if the applicant for the license or permit, or any individual holding, owning, or controlling a five per cent or greater beneficial or equity interest in the applicant for the license or permit, has been convicted of or pleaded guilty to a felony under the laws of this state, another state, or the United States. The fire marshal shall revoke or deny renewal of a license or permit first issued under this chapter on or after June 30, 1997, if the holder of the license or permit, or any individual holding, owning, or controlling a five per cent or greater beneficial or equity interest in the holder of the license or permit, is convicted of or pleads guilty to a felony under the laws of this state, another state, or the United States.

The state fire marshal may adopt rules under Chapter 119. of the Revised Code specifying the method to be used by the applicants subject to this section to provide the fingerprint or similar identifying information, fees to be assessed by the fire marshal to conduct such background checks, and the procedures to be used by the state fire marshal to verify compliance with this section. Such rules may include provisions establishing rules for conducting background checks and prohibiting licensure, permitting or registration under this chapter for persons convicted of a felony or similar offense in another country, the frequency that license renewal applicants must update background check information filed by the applicant with previous license applications, provisions describing alternative forms of background check information that may be accepted by the fire marshal to verify compliance with this section, and provisions that permit the state fire marshal to waive the applicability of this section if the applicant produces verified documentation that demonstrates that this state, another state, the United States, or another country has determined that applicant is appropriate for licensure, permitting, or registration under this chapter.

**HISTORY: 147 v H 215 (Eff 6-30-97); 149 v H 161. Eff 6-29-2001; 152 v H 562, § 101.01, eff. 9-23-08.**

The effective date is set by § 812.10 of 152 v H 562.

See provisions, § 6(A) of HB 161 (149 v —) following RC § 3743.01.

The provisions of § 167 of HB 215 (147 v —) read as follows:

SECTION 167. The Fire Marshal shall not revoke or deny the renewal of a license or permit that was issued under Chapter 3743. of the Revised Code before the effective date of this act solely on the basis that the license or permit holder, or any individual holding, owning, or controlling a five per cent or greater beneficial or equity interest in the license or permit holder has been convicted of or pled guilty to a felony under the laws of this state, another state, or the United States before the effective date of this act, provided that there is no cause for revocation or denial of renewal pursuant to sections 3743.08, 3743.21, 3743.52, or 3743.54 of the Revised Code.

## § 3743.75 Moratorium concerning manufacturer and wholesaler licenses.

(A) During the period beginning on June 29, 2001, and ending on December 15, 2015, the state fire marshal shall not do any of the following:

(1) Issue a license as a manufacturer of fireworks under sections 3743.02 and 3743.03 of the Revised Code to a person for a particular fireworks plant unless that person possessed such a license for that fireworks plant immediately prior to June 29, 2001;

(2) Issue a license as a wholesaler of fireworks under sections 3743.15 and 3743.16 of the Revised Code to a person for a particular location unless that person possessed such a license for that location immediately prior to June 29, 2001;

(3) Except as provided in division (B) of this section, approve the geographic transfer of a license as a manufacturer or wholesaler of fireworks issued under this chapter to any location other than a location for which a license was issued under this chapter immediately prior to June 29, 2001.

(B) Division (A)(3) of this section does not apply to a transfer that the state fire marshal approves under division (F) of section 3743.17 of the Revised Code.

(C) Notwithstanding section 3743.59 of the Revised Code, the prohibited activities established in divisions (A)(1) and (2) of this section, geographic transfers approved pursuant to division (F) of section 3743.17 of the Revised Code, and storage locations allowed pursuant to division (I) of section 3743.04 of the Revised Code or division (G) of section 3743.17 of the Revised Code are not subject to any variance, waiver, or exclusion.

(D) As used in division (A) of this section:

(1) "Person" includes any person or entity, in whatever form or name, that acquires possession of a manufacturer or wholesaler of fireworks license issued pursuant to this chapter by transfer of possession of a license, whether that transfer occurs by purchase, assignment, inheritance, bequest, stock transfer, or any other type of transfer, on the condition that the transfer is in accordance with division (D) of section 3743.04 of the Revised Code or division (D) of section 3743.17 of the Revised Code and is approved by the fire marshal.

(2) "Particular location" includes a licensed premises and, regardless of when approved, any storage location approved in accordance with section 3743.04 or 3743.17 of the Revised Code.

(3) "Such a license" includes a wholesaler of fireworks license that was issued in place of a manufacturer of fireworks license that existed prior to June 29, 2001, and was requested to be canceled by the license holder pursuant to division (D) of section 3743.03 of the Revised Code.

**HISTORY: 149 v H 161, § 3. Eff 6-29-2001; 150 v H 255, § 1, eff. 3-31-05; 151 v H 66, § 101.01, eff. 9-29-05; 152 v H 119, § 101.01, eff. 9-29-07; 2011 HB 128, § 1, eff. Sept. 23, 2011.**

The effective date is set by § 812.03 of 152 v H 119.

The effective date is set by § 612.03 of 151 v H 66.

See provisions, § 6(B) of HB 161 (149 v —) following RC § 3743.01.

## § 3743.80 Exemptions from provisions.

This chapter does not prohibit or apply to the following:

(A) The manufacture, sale, possession, transportation, storage, or use in emergency situations, of pyrotechnic signaling devices and distress signals for marine, aviation, or highway use;

(B) The manufacture, sale, possession, transportation, storage, or use of fusees, torpedoes, or other signals necessary for the safe operation of railroads;

(C) The manufacture, sale, possession, transportation, storage, or use of blank cartridges in connection with theaters or shows, or in connection with athletics as signals or for ceremonial purposes;

(D) The manufacture for, the transportation, storage, possession, or use by, or sale to the armed forces of the United States and the militia of this state of pyrotechnic devices;

(E) The manufacture, sale, possession, transportation, storage, or use of toy pistols, toy canes, toy guns, or other devices in which paper or plastic caps containing twenty-five hundredths grains or less of explosive material are used, provided that they are constructed so that a hand cannot come into contact with a cap when it is in place for explosion, or apply to the manufacture, sale, possession, transportation, storage, or use of those caps;

(F) The manufacture, sale, possession, transportation, storage, or use of novelties and trick noisemakers, auto burglar alarms, or model rockets and model rocket motors designed, sold, and used for the purpose of propelling recoverable aero models;

(G) The manufacture, sale, possession, transportation, storage, or use of wire sparklers.

(H) The conduct of radio-controlled special effect exhibitions that use an explosive black powder charge of not more than one-quarter pound per charge, and that are not connected in any manner to propellant charges, provided that the exhibition complies with all of following:

(1) No explosive aerial display is conducted in the exhibition;

(2) The exhibition is separated from spectators by not less than two hundred feet;

(3) The person conducting the exhibition complies with regulations of the bureau of alcohol, tobacco, and firearms of the United States department of the treasury and the United States department of transportation with respect to the storage and transport of the explosive black powder used in the exhibition.

**HISTORY: 141 v S 61 (Eff 5-30-86); 147 v H 215 (Eff 6-30-97); 149 v H 161. Eff 6-29-2001.**

See provisions, § 6(A) of HB 161 (149 v —) following RC § 3743.01.

## § 3743.99 Penalties.

(A) Whoever violates division (A) or (B) of section 3743.60 or division (H) of section 3743.64 of the Revised Code is guilty of a felony of the third degree.

(B) Whoever violates division (C) or (D) of section 3743.60, division (A), (B), (C), or (D) of section 3743.61, or division (A) or (B) of section 3743.64 of the Revised Code is guilty of a felony of the fourth degree.

(C) Whoever violates division (E), (F), (G), (H), (I), or (J) of section 3743.60, division (E), (F), (G), (H), (I), or (J) of section 3743.61, section 3743.63, division (D), (E), (F), or (G) of section 3743.64, division (A), (B), (C), (D), or (E) of section 3743.65, or section 3743.66 of the Revised Code is guilty of a misdemeanor of the first degree. If the offender previously has been convicted of or pleaded guilty to a violation of division (I) of section 3743.60 or 3743.61 of the Revised Code, a violation of either of these divisions is a felony of the fifth degree.

(D) Whoever violates division (C) of section 3743.64 of the Revised Code is guilty of a misdemeanor of the first degree. In addition to any other penalties that may be imposed on a licensed exhibitor of fireworks under this division and unless the third sentence of this division applies, the person's license as an exhibitor of fireworks or as an assistant exhibitor of fireworks shall be suspended, and the person is ineligible to apply for either type of license, for a period of five years. If the violation of division (C) of section 3743.64 of the Revised Code results in serious physical harm to persons or serious physical harm to property, the person's license as an exhibitor of fireworks or as an assistant exhibitor of fireworks shall be revoked, and that person is ineligible to apply for a license as or to be licensed as an exhibitor of fireworks or as an assistant exhibitor of fireworks in this state.

(E) Whoever violates division (F) of section 3743.65 of the Revised Code is guilty of a felony of the fifth degree.

**HISTORY: 141 v S 61 (Eff 5-30-86); 142 v H 436 (Eff 6-14-88); 146 v S 2 (Eff 7-1-96); 147 v H 215 (Eff 6-30-97); 148 v H 405 (Eff 10-19-2000); 149 v H 161, §§ 1, 3. Eff 6-29-2001; 152 v H 562, § 101.01, eff. 9-23-08.**

The effective date is set by § 812.10 of 152 v H 562.

See provisions, § 6(A), (B) of HB 161 (149 v —) following RC § 3743.01.

# CHAPTER 3761: ASSEMBLIES; MOBS



## § 3761.12 Prohibition against conspiracy while wearing disguise.

No person shall unite with two or more others to commit a misdemeanor while wearing white caps, masks, or other disguise.

**HISTORY: RS § 6895-1; 86 v 169; GC § 12810; Bureau of Code Revision. Eff 10-1-53.**

## § 3761.16 Cordoning-off riot areas.

The chief administrative officer of a political subdivision with police powers, when engaged in suppressing a riot or when there is a clear and present danger of a riot, may cordon off any area or areas threatened by the riot and prohibit persons from entering the cordoned off area or areas except when carrying on necessary and legitimate pursuits and may prohibit the sale, offering for sale, dispensing, or transportation of firearms or other dangerous weapons, ammunition, dynamite, or other dangerous explosives in, to, or from the cordoned off areas.

**HISTORY: 132 v H 753 (Eff 9-8-67); 146 v S 2. Eff 7-1-96.**

The effective date is set by section 6 of SB 2.

## § 3761.99 Penalty.

Whoever violates section 3761.12 of the Revised Code is guilty of a felony of the fourth degree.

**HISTORY: Bureau of Code Revision, 10-1-53; 131 v 897 (Eff 11-11-65); 132 v H 753 (Eff 9-8-67); 132 v H 996 (Eff 6-13-68); 136 v H 1 (Eff 6-13-75); 139 v S 199 (Eff 1-1-83); 146 v S 2. Eff 7-1-96.**

The effective date is set by section 6 of SB 2.

# CHAPTER 3767: NUISANCES



### [DISORDERLY HOUSES]

## § 3767.01 Definitions.

As used in all sections of the Revised Code relating to nuisances:

(A) "Place" includes any building, erection, or place or any separate part or portion thereof or the ground itself;

(B) "Person" includes any individual, corporation, association, partnership, trustee, lessee, agent, or assignee;

(C) "Nuisance" means any of the following:

(1) That which is defined and declared by statutes to be a nuisance;

(2) Any place in or upon which lewdness, assignation, or prostitution is conducted, permitted, continued, or exists, or any place, in or upon which lewd, indecent, lascivious, or obscene films or plate negatives, film or plate positives, films designed to be projected on a screen for exhibition films, or glass slides either in negative or positive form designed for exhibition by projection on a screen, are photographed, manufactured, developed, screened, exhibited, or otherwise prepared or shown, and the personal property and contents used in conducting and

maintaining any such place for any such purpose. This chapter shall not affect any newspaper, magazine, or other publication entered as second class matter by the post-office department.

(3) Any room, house, building, boat, vehicle, structure, or place where beer or intoxicating liquor is manufactured, sold, bartered, possessed, or kept in violation of law and all property kept and used in maintaining the same, and all property designed for the unlawful manufacture of beer or intoxicating liquor and beer or intoxicating liquor contained in the room, house, building, boat, structure, or place, or the operation of such a room, house, building, boat, structure, or place as described in division (C)(3) of this section where the operation of that place substantially interferes with public decency, sobriety, peace, and good order. "Violation of law" includes, but is not limited to, sales to any person under the legal drinking age as prohibited in division (A) of section 4301.22 or division (A) of section 4301.69 of the Revised Code and any violation of section 2913.46 or 2925.03 of the Revised Code.

**HISTORY: GC § 6212-1; 107 v 514; 120 v 230; Bureau of Code Revision, 10-1-53; 129 v 1400 (Eff 10-11-61); 147 v H 402. Eff 3-30-99.**

## § 3767.02 Nuisance.

(A) Any person, who uses, occupies, establishes, or conducts a nuisance, or aids or abets in the use, occupancy, establishment, or conduct of a nuisance; the owner, agent, or lessee of an interest in any such nuisance; any person who is employed in that nuisance by that owner, agent, or lessee; and any person who is in control of that nuisance is guilty of maintaining a nuisance and shall be enjoined as provided in sections 3767.03 to 3767.11 of the Revised Code.

(B) A criminal gang that uses or occupies any building, premises, or real estate, including vacant land, on more than two occasions within a one-year period to engage in a pattern of criminal gang activity is guilty of maintaining a nuisance and shall be enjoined as provided in sections 3767.03 to 3767.11 of the Revised Code. As used in this division, "criminal gang" and "pattern of criminal gang activity" have the same meanings as in section 2923.41 of the Revised Code.

**HISTORY: GC § 6212-2; 107 v 514, § 2; Bureau of Code Revision, 10-1-53; 147 v H 2. Eff 1-1-99.**

The effective date is set by section 4 of HB 2.

## § 3767.03 Abatement of nuisance; bond.

Whenever a nuisance exists, the attorney general; the village solicitor, city director of law, or other similar chief legal officer of the municipal corporation in which the nuisance exists; the prosecuting attorney of the county in which the nuisance exists; the law director of a township that has adopted a limited home rule government under Chapter 504. of the Revised Code; or any person who is a citizen of the county in which the nuisance exists may bring an action in equity in the name of the state, upon the relation of the attorney general; the village solicitor, city director of law, or other similar chief legal officer of the municipal corporation; the prosecuting attorney; the township law director; or the person, to abate the nuisance and to perpetually enjoin the person maintaining the nuisance from further maintaining it. If an action is instituted under this section by a person other than the prosecuting attorney; the village solicitor, city director of law, or other similar chief legal officer of the municipal corporation; the attorney general; or the township law director, the complainant shall execute a bond in the sum of not less than five hundred dollars, to the defendant, with good and sufficient surety to be approved by the court or clerk of the court, to secure to the defendant any damages the defendant may sustain and the reasonable attorney's fees the defendant may incur in defending the action if the action is wrongfully brought, not prosecuted to final judgment, is dismissed, or is not maintained, or if it is finally decided that an injunction should not have been granted. If it is finally decided that an injunction should not have been granted or if the action was wrongfully brought, not prosecuted to final judgment, dismissed, or not maintained, the defendant shall have recourse against the bond for all damages suffered, including damages to the defendant's property, person, or character, and for the reasonable attorney's fees incurred by the defendant in defending the action.

Any agency, officer, or other person bringing an action under this section against the holder of a liquor permit issued under Chapter 4303. of the Revised Code shall notify the division of liquor control, the liquor control commission, and the liquor enforcement division of the department of public safety regarding the action at the time of bringing the action.

**HISTORY: GC § 6212-3; 107 v 514, § 3; Bureau of Code Revision, 10-1-53; 144 v H 343 (Eff 6-1-92); 146 v H 501 (Eff 11-6-96); 147 v H 402 (Eff 3-30-99); 148 v H 187. Eff 9-20-99.**

## § 3767.04 Procedure in injunction action.

(A) The civil action provided for in section 3767.03 of the Revised Code shall be commenced in the court of common pleas of the county in which the nuisance is located. At the commencement of the action, a complaint alleging the facts constituting the nuisance shall be filed in the office of the clerk of the court of common pleas.

(B)(1) After the filing of the complaint, an application for a temporary injunction may be filed with the court or a judge of the court. A hearing shall be held on the application within ten days after the filing.

(2) If an application for a temporary injunction is filed, the court or a judge of the court, on application of the complainant, may issue an ex parte restraining order restraining the defendant and all other persons from removing or in any manner interfering with the personal property and contents of the place where the nuisance is alleged to exist until the decision of the court or judge granting or refusing the requested temporary injunction and until the further order of the court. The restraining order may be served by handing it to and leaving a copy of it with any person who is in charge of the place where the nuisance is alleged to exist or who resides in that place, by posting a copy of it in a conspicuous place at or upon one or more of the principal doors or entrances to that place, or by both delivery and posting. The officer serving the restraining order forthwith shall make and return into court an inventory of the personal property and contents situated in and used in conducting or maintaining the nuisance. Any violation of the restraining order is a contempt of court, and, if the order is posted, its mutilation or removal while it remains in force is a contempt of court, provided the posted order contains a notice to that effect.

(3) A copy of the complaint, a copy of the application for the temporary injunction, and a notice of the time and place of the hearing on the application shall be served upon the defendant at least five days before the hearing. If the hearing then is continued on the motion of any defendant, the requested temporary injunction shall be granted as a matter of course. If, upon hearing, the allegations of the complaint are sustained to the satisfaction of the court or judge, the court or judge shall issue a temporary injunction without additional bond restraining the defendant and any other person from continuing the nuisance. Except as provided in division (C) of this section, if at the time of granting the temporary injunction it further appears that the person owning, in control, or in charge of the nuisance so enjoined had received five days' notice of the hearing and unless that person shows to the satisfaction of the court or judge that the nuisance complained of is abated or that he proceeded forthwith to enforce his rights under section 3767.10 of the Revised Code, the court or judge forthwith shall issue an order closing the place against its use for any purpose of lewdness, assignation, prostitution, or other prohibited conduct until a final decision is rendered on the complaint for the requested permanent injunction. Except as provided in division (C) of this section, the order closing the place also shall continue in effect for that further period any restraining order already issued under division (B)(2) of this section, or, if a restraining order was not so issued, the order closing the place shall include an order restraining for that further period the removal or interference with the personal property and contents located in the place. The order closing the place shall be served and an inventory of the personal property and contents situated in the place shall be made and filed as provided in division (B)(2) of this section for restraining orders.

(C) The owner of any real or personal property closed or restrained or to be closed or restrained may appear in the court of common pleas between the time of the filing of the complaint for the permanent injunction described in division (A) of this section and the hearing on the complaint, and, if all costs incurred are paid and if the owner of the real property files a bond with sureties approved by the clerk, in the full value of the real property as ascertained by the court or, in vacation, by the judge, and conditioned that the owner of the real property immediately will abate the nuisance and prevent it from being established or kept until the decision of the court or judge is rendered on the complaint for the permanent injunction, the court or judge in vacation, if satisfied of the good faith of the owner of the real property and of innocence on the part of any owner of the personal property of any knowledge of the use of the personal property as a nuisance and that, with reasonable care and diligence, the owner of the personal property could not have known of its use as a nuisance, shall deliver the real or personal property, or both, to the respective owners and discharge or refrain from issuing at the time of the hearing on the application for the temporary injunction any order closing the real property or restraining the removal or interference with the personal property. The release of any real or personal property under this division shall not release it from any judgment, lien, penalty, or liability to which it may be subjected.

**HISTORY: GC § 6212-4; 107 v 514, § 4; Bureau of Code Revision, 10-1-53; 144 v H 343. Eff 6-1-92.**

## § 3767.05 Priority of action; evidence; dismissal of citizen's complaint; costs; permanent injunction; abatement orders concerning beer or intoxicating liquor.

(A) The civil action provided for in section 3767.03 of the Revised Code shall be set down for trial at the earliest possible time and shall have precedence over all other cases except those involving crimes, election contests, or injunctions regardless of the position of the proceedings on the calendar of the court. In the civil action, evidence of the general reputation of the place where the nuisance is alleged to exist or an admission or finding of guilt of any person under the criminal laws against prostitution, lewdness, assignation, or other prohibited conduct at the place is admissible for the purpose of proving the existence of the nuisance and is prima-facie evidence of the nuisance and of knowledge of and of acquiescence and participation in the nuisance on the part of the person charged with maintaining it.

(B) If the complaint for the permanent injunction is filed by a person who is a citizen of the county, it shall not be dismissed unless the complainant and the complainant's attorney submit a sworn statement setting forth the reasons why the civil action should be dismissed and the dismissal is approved by the prosecuting attorney in writing or in open court. If the person who files the complaint for the permanent injunction is a citizen of the county, if that person refuses or otherwise fails to prosecute the complaint to judgment, and if the civil action is not dismissed pursuant to this division, then, with the approval of the court, the attorney general, the prosecuting attorney of the county in which the nuisance exists, or the village solicitor, city director of law, or other similar chief legal officer of the municipal corporation in which the nuisance exists, may be substituted for the complainant and prosecute the civil action to judgment.

(C) If the civil action is commenced by a person who is a citizen of the county where the nuisance is alleged to exist and the court finds that there were no reasonable grounds or cause for the civil action, the costs may be taxed to that person.

(D) If the existence of the nuisance is established upon the trial of the civil action, a judgment shall be entered that perpetually enjoins the defendant and any other person from further maintaining the nuisance at the place complained of and the defendant from maintaining the nuisance elsewhere.

(E) If the court finds that a nuisance described in division (C)(3) of section 3767.01 of the Revised Code exists, the court shall order the nuisance to be abated, and, in entering judgment for nuisance, the court shall do all of the following:

(1) Specify that judgment is entered pursuant to division (E) of this section;

(2) Order that no beer or intoxicating liquor may be manufactured, sold, bartered, possessed, kept, or stored in the room, house, building, structure, place, boat, or vehicle or any part thereof. The court need not find that the property was being unlawfully used at the time of the

hearing on the matter if the court finds there existed a nuisance as described in division (C)(3) of section 3767.01 of the Revised Code.

(3) Order that the room, house, building, boat, vehicle, structure, or place not be occupied or used for one year after the judgment is rendered. The court may permit the premises to be occupied by a person other than the defendant or a business affiliate of the defendant in the nuisance action, or an agent of, or entity owned in whole or part by, the defendant, if the person, lessee, tenant, or occupant of the location posts a bond with sufficient surety, to be approved by the court issuing the order, in the sum of not less than one thousand nor more than five thousand dollars, payable to the state of Ohio, on the condition that no beer or intoxicating liquor thereafter shall be manufactured, sold, bartered, possessed, kept, stored, transported, or otherwise disposed of on the premises, and the person agrees to pay all fines, costs, and damages that may be assessed for a violation. A reasonable sum shall be allowed an officer by the issuing court for the cost of closing and keeping closed the premises that is the subject of the nuisance action.

(4) Send notice of the judgment entered to the division of liquor control, the liquor control commission, and the liquor enforcement division of the department of public safety.

(F) A defendant found to have maintained a nuisance as described in division (C)(3) of section 3767.01 of the Revised Code also is subject to liability and penalties under sections 4301.74 and 4399.09 of the Revised Code. The abatement of a nuisance under section 4399.09 of the Revised Code is in addition to and does not prevent the abatement of a nuisance under division (D) or (E) of this section.

(G) If a court enters judgment pursuant to division (D) or (E) of this section finding that a nuisance exists at a liquor permit premises or as a result of the operation of a liquor permit premises, except in the case of a nuisance found as a result of a violation of a local zoning ordinance or resolution, the certified copy of the judgment required under division (A) of section 4301.331 [4301.33.1] of the Revised Code shall be filed with the board of elections in the county in which the nuisance exists, not later than four p.m. of the ninetieth day before the day of the next general or primary election. However, no election shall be conducted on sales at the liquor permit premises under section 4301.352 [4301.35.2] of the Revised Code until all appeals on the judgment are resolved. The court of appeals shall render a decision on any appeal of the judgment within six months after the date of the filing of the appeal of the judgment with the clerk of the court of appeals, and the supreme court shall render a decision on any appeal of the judgment within six months after the date of the filing of the appeal of the judgment with the clerk of the supreme court.

**HISTORY: GC § 6212-5; 107 v 514, § 5; Bureau of Code Revision, 10-1-53; 144 v H 343 (Eff 6-1-92); 147 v H 402. Eff 3-30-99; 153 v H 48, § 1, eff. 7-2-10.**

## § 3767.06 Order of abatement; removal of personal property and contents; attorney general nuisance abatement fund.

(A) If the existence of a nuisance is admitted or established in the civil action provided for in section 3767.03 of the Revised Code or in a criminal action, an order of abatement shall be included in the judgment entry under division (D) of section 3767.05 of the Revised Code. The order shall direct the removal from the place where the nuisance is found to exist of all personal property and contents used in conducting or maintaining the nuisance and not already released under authority of the court as provided in division (C) of section 3767.04 of the Revised Code and shall direct that the personal property or contents that belong to the defendants notified or appearing be sold, without appraisal, at a public auction to the highest bidder for cash. The order also shall require the renewal for one year of any bond furnished by the owner of the real property under section 3767.04 of the Revised Code; if a bond was not so furnished, shall continue for one year any closing order issued at the time of granting the temporary injunction; or, if a closing order was not then issued, shall include an order directing the effectual closing of the place where the nuisance is found to exist against its use for any purpose and keeping it closed for a period of one year unless sooner released. The owner of any place closed and not released under bond may appear and obtain a release in the manner and upon fulfilling the requirements provided in section 3767.04 of the Revised Code. The release of property under this division shall not release it from any judgment, lien, penalty, or liability to which it may be subject.

(B) Owners of unsold personal property or contents seized pursuant to division (A) of this section shall appear and claim the personal property or contents within ten days after the order of abatement is issued and prove to the satisfaction of the court their lack of any actual knowledge of the use of the personal property or contents in the conduct or maintenance of the nuisance and that with reasonable care and diligence they could not have known of that use. Every defendant in the action shall be presumed to have had knowledge of the general reputation of the place where the nuisance is found to exist. If an owner establishes the lack of actual or constructive knowledge of the use of his personal property or contents in the conduct or maintenance of the nuisance, the unsold personal property and contents shall be delivered to the owner. If an owner does not so establish, the personal property or contents shall be sold or otherwise disposed of as provided in division (A) of this section. For removing and selling the personal property and contents, the officer involved shall be entitled to charge and receive the same fees as he would for levying upon and selling similar property on execution. For closing the place where the nuisance is found to exist and keeping it closed, a reasonable sum shall be allowed by the court.

(C) There is hereby established in the state treasury the attorney general nuisance abatement fund. Except as otherwise provided in sections 3767.07 to 3767.11 of the Revised Code, all proceeds from the sale of personal property or contents seized pursuant to a civil action commenced or otherwise prosecuted by the attorney general under sections 3767.03 to 3767.11 of the Revised Code shall be deposited into the state treasury and credited to the fund. The attorney general shall use the fund solely to defray expenses and costs associated with those types of civil actions.

(D) All proceeds from the sale of personal property or contents seized pursuant to a civil action commenced or otherwise prosecuted under sections 3767.03 to 3767.11 of the Revised Code by a village solicitor, city director of law, or other similar chief legal officer of a municipal corporation initially shall be applied to the payment of the costs incurred in the prosecution of the civil action and the costs associated with the abatement and sale ordered pursuant to division (A) of this section, including, but not limited to, court costs, reasonable attorney's fees, and other litigation expenses incurred by the complainant. Except as otherwise provided in sections 3767.07 to 3767.11 of the Revised Code, any proceeds remaining after that initial application shall be deposited into the city or village treasury and credited to the general fund.

(E) All proceeds from the sale of personal property or contents seized pursuant to a civil action commenced or otherwise prosecuted under sections 3767.03 to 3767.11 of the Revised Code by a prosecuting attorney initially shall be applied to the payment of the costs incurred in the prosecution of the civil action and the costs associated with the abatement and sale ordered pursuant to division (A) of this section, including, but not limited to, court costs, reasonable attorney's fees, and other litigation expenses incurred by the complainant. Except as otherwise provided in sections 3767.07 to 3767.11 of the Revised Code, any proceeds remaining after that initial application shall be deposited into the county treasury and credited to the general fund.

(F) All proceeds from the sale of personal property or contents seized pursuant to a civil action commenced under sections 3767.03 to 3767.11 of the Revised Code by a person who is a citizen of the county where the nuisance is found to exist initially shall be applied to the payment of the costs incurred in the prosecution of the civil action and the costs associated with the abatement and sale ordered pursuant to division (A) of this section, including, but not limited to, court costs, reasonable attorney's fees, and other litigation expenses incurred by the complainant. Except as otherwise provided in sections 3767.07 to 3767.11 of the Revised Code, any proceeds remaining after that initial application shall be deposited into the county treasury and credited to the general fund.

**HISTORY: GC § 6212-6; 107 v 514, § 6; Bureau of Code Revision, 10-1-53; 144 v H 343. Eff 6-1-92.**

## § 3767.07 Court shall punish offender for violation of injunction or order.

In case of the violation of any injunction or closing order, granted under sections 3767.01 to 3767.11, inclusive, of the Revised Code, or of a restraining order or the commission of any contempt of court in proceedings under such sections, the court or, in vacation, a judge thereof, may summarily try and punish the offender. The trial may be had upon affidavits or either party may demand the production and oral examination of the witnesses.

**HISTORY: GC § 6212-8; 107 v 514, § 8; Bureau of Code Revision. Eff 10-1-53.**

## § 3767.08 Tax on nuisance.

Whenever a permanent injunction issues against any person for maintaining a nuisance, there shall be imposed upon said nuisance and against the person maintaining the same a tax of three hundred dollars. Such tax may not be imposed upon the personal property or against the owner thereof who has proved innocence as provided in section 3767.06 of the Revised Code, or upon the real property or against the owner thereof who shows to the satisfaction of the court or judge thereof at the time of the granting of the permanent injunction, that he has, in good faith, permanently abated the nuisance complained of. The imposition of said tax shall be made by the court as a part of the proceeding and the clerk of said court shall make and certify a return of the imposition of said tax thereon to the county auditor, who shall enter the same as a tax upon the property and against the persons upon which or whom the lien was imposed as and when other taxes are entered, and the same shall be and remain a perpetual lien upon all property, both personal and real, used for the purpose of maintaining said nuisance except as excepted in this section until fully paid. Any such lien imposed while the tax books are in the hands of the auditor shall be immediately entered therein. The payment of said tax shall not relieve the persons or property from any other taxes. The provisions of the laws relating to the collection of taxes in this state, the delinquency thereof, and sale of property for taxes shall govern in the collection of the tax prescribed in this section in so far as the same are applicable, and the said tax collected shall be applied in payment of any deficiency in the costs of the action and abatement on behalf of the state to the extent of such deficiency after the application thereto of the proceeds of the sale of personal property.

**HISTORY: GC § 6212-9; 107 v 514, § 9; Bureau of Code Revision, 10-1-53; 134 v H 511. Eff 1-1-74.**

## § 3767.09 Tax shall be imposed against owner of property.

When a nuisance is found to exist in any proceeding under sections 3767.01 to 3767.11, inclusive, of the Revised Code, and the owner or agent of such place whereon the same has been found to exist was not a party to such proceeding, and did not appear therein, the tax of three hundred dollars, imposed under section 3767.08 of the Revised Code, shall, nevertheless, be imposed against the persons served or appearing and against the property as set forth in this section. Before such tax is enforced against such property, the owner or agent thereof shall have appeared therein or shall be served with summons therein, and existing laws, regarding the service of process, shall apply to service in proceedings under sections 3767.01 to 3767.11, inclusive, of the Revised Code. The person in whose name the real estate affected by the action stands on the books of the county auditor for purposes of taxation is presumed to be the owner thereof, and in case of unknown persons having or claiming any ownership, right, title, or interest in property affected by the action, such may be made parties to the action by designating them in the petition as "all other persons unknown claiming any ownership, right, title, or interest in the property affected by the action." Service thereon may be had by publication in the manner prescribed in sections 2703.14 to 2703.19, inclusive, of the Revised Code. Any person having or claiming such ownership, right, title, or interest, and any owner or agent in behalf of himself and such owner may make defense thereto and have trial of his rights in the premises by the court; and if said cause has already proceeded to trial or to findings and judgment, the court shall, by order, fix the time and place of such further trial and shall modify, add to, or confirm such findings and judgment. Other parties to said action shall not be affected thereby.

**HISTORY: GC § 6212-10; 107 v 514, § 10; Bureau of Code Revision. Eff 10-1-53.**

## § 3767.10 Lease void if building used for lewd purposes.

If a tenant or occupant of a building or tenement, under a lawful title, uses such place for the purposes of lewdness, assignation, or prostitution, such use makes void the lease or other title under which he holds, at the option of the owner, and, without any act of the owner, causes the right of possession to revert and vest in such owner, who may without process of law make immediate entry upon the premises.

**HISTORY: GC § 6212-12; 107 v 514, § 12; Bureau of Code Revision. Eff 10-1-53.**

## § 3767.11 Procedure when nuisance established in criminal proceeding.

(A) If a nuisance is established in a criminal action, the prosecuting attorney, village solicitor, city director of law, or other similar chief legal officer shall proceed promptly under sections 3767.03 to 3767.11 of the Revised Code to enforce those sections. The finding of the defendant guilty in the criminal action, unless reversed or set aside, shall be conclusive against the defendant as to the existence of the nuisance in the civil action under those sections.

(B) Except for proceeds described in divisions (C) to (F) of section 3767.06 of the Revised Code, all moneys collected under sections 3767.03 to 3767.11 of the Revised Code shall be paid to the county treasurer.

**HISTORY: GC § 6212-7; 107 v 514, § 7; Bureau of Code Revision, 10-1-53; 144 v H 343. Eff 6-1-92.**

[OTHER NUISANCES]

## § 3767.12 Habitual resort for thieves, burglars, robbers or persons involved in felonious conduct.

(A) As used in this section, "felonious conduct" means an offense that is a felony or a delinquent act that would be a felony if committed by an adult.

(B) A house or building used or occupied as a habitual resort for thieves, burglars, or robbers, or for persons who are conspiring or planning to commit, who are fleeing after having committed or after attempting to commit, or who are in hiding after having committed or after attempting to commit, felonious conduct is a public nuisance, and the court may order the public nuisance abated.

No person shall keep a house that is a habitual resort for thieves, burglars, or robbers, or for persons who are conspiring or planning to commit, who are fleeing after having committed or after attempting to commit, or who are in hiding after having committed or after attempting to commit, felonious conduct. No person shall let a house to be so kept, or knowingly permit a house that the person has let to be so kept.

**HISTORY: RS § 6858a; 85 v 6; GC §§ 12453, 12454; Bureau of Code Revision, 10-1-53; 148 v S 107. Eff 3-23-2000.**

## § 3767.13 Prohibitions.

(A) No person shall erect, continue, use, or maintain a building, structure, or place for the exercise of a trade, employment, or business, or for the keeping or feeding of an animal which, by occasioning noxious exhalations or noisome or offensive smells, becomes injurious to the health, comfort, or property of individuals or of the public.

(B) No person shall cause or allow offal, filth, or noisome substances to be collected or remain in any place to the damage or prejudice of others or of the public.

(C) No person shall unlawfully obstruct or impede the passage of a navigable river, harbor, or collection of water, or corrupt or render unwholesome or impure, a watercourse, stream, or water, or unlawfully divert such watercourse from its natural course or state to the injury or prejudice of others.

(D) Persons who are engaged in agriculture-related activities, as "agriculture" is defined in section 519.01 of the Revised Code, and who are conducting those activities outside a municipal corporation, in accordance with generally accepted agricultural practices, and in such a manner so as not to have a substantial, adverse effect on the public health, safety, or welfare are exempt from divisions (A) and (B) of this section, from any similar ordinances, resolutions, rules, or other enactments of a state agency or political subdivision, and from any ordinances, resolutions, rules, or other enactments of a state agency or political subdivision that prohibit excessive noise.

**HISTORY: RS § 6921; S&C 441, 878, 880; 30 v 22, §§ 1, 2; 32 v 38; 54 v 130, §§ 1, 2; 72 v 112; GC § 12646; Bureau of Code Revision, 10-1-53; 139 v S 78. Eff 6-29-82.**

## § 3767.14 Prohibition against throwing refuse, oil, or filth into lakes, streams, or drains.

No person shall intentionally throw, deposit, or permit to be thrown or deposited, coal dirt, coal slack, coal screenings, or coal refuse from coal mines, refuse or filth from a coal oil refinery or gasworks, or whey or filthy drainage from a cheese factory, into a river, lake, pond, or stream, or a place from which it may wash therein. No person shall cause or permit petroleum, crude oil, refined oil, or a compound, mixture, residuum of oil or filth from an oil well, oil tank, oil vat, or place of deposit of crude or refined oil, to run into or be poured, emptied, or thrown into a river, ditch, drain, or watercourse, or into a place from which it may run or wash therein. Prosecution for a violation of this section must be brought in the county in which such coal mine, coal oil refinery, gasworks, cheese factory, oil well, oil tank, oil vat, or place of deposit of crude or refined oil is situated.

**HISTORY: RS § 6925; 73 v 87; 85 v 286; 87 v 351; 92 v 287; GC § 12647; Bureau of Code Revision. Eff 10-1-53.**

## § 3767.15 Fine and costs are a lien.

The fine and costs imposed in division (D)[A]† of section 3767.99 of the Revised Code shall be a lien on such oil well, oil tank, oil refinery, oil vat, or place of deposit and the contents thereof until paid, and such oil well, oil tank, oil refinery, oil vat, or place of deposit and the contents thereof, may be sold for the payment of such fine and costs upon execution issued for that purpose.

**HISTORY: RS § 6925; 73 v 87; 85 v 286; 87 v 351; 92 v 287; GC § 12648; Bureau of Code Revision. Eff 10-1-53.**

† RC § 3767.99 was revised (136 v S 71) effective 8-18-76 placing the penalty for violating RC § 3767.14 in division (A), but RC § 3767.15 has not been amended to refer to the appropriate division of the penalty section.

## § 3767.16 Prohibition against deposit of dead animals and offal upon land or water.

No person shall put the carcass of a dead animal or the offal from a slaughterhouse, butcher's establishment, packing house, or fish house, or spoiled meat, spoiled fish, or other putrid substance or the contents of a privy vault, upon or into a lake, river, bay, creek, pond, canal, road, street, alley, lot, field, meadow, public ground, market place or common. No owner or occupant of such place, shall knowingly permit such thing to remain therein to the annoyance of any citizen or neglect to remove or abate the nuisance occasioned thereby within twenty-four hours after knowledge of the existence thereof, or after notice thereof in writing from a township trustee or township highway superintendent, constable, or health commissioner of a city or general health district in which such nuisance exists or from a county commissioner of such county.

**HISTORY: RS § 6923; S&S 500; S&C 878, 879; 30 v 22, § 3; 63 v 102; 85 v 268; 87 v 349; 93 v 298; 98 v 339; GC § 12649; Bureau of Code Revision. Eff 10-1-53.**

## § 3767.17 Prohibition against obstructing township or county ditch.

No person shall willfully obstruct a ditch, drain, or watercourse constructed by order of a board of county commissioners or by a board of township trustees, or divert the water therefrom.

**HISTORY: RS § 6926; 68 v 67, § 24; 72 v 150, §§ 1, 2; GC § 12653; Bureau of Code Revision. Eff 10-1-53.**

## § 3767.18 Prohibition against defiling spring or well.

No person shall maliciously put a dead animal, carcass, or part thereof, or other putrid, nauseous, or offensive substance into, or befoul, a well, spring, brook, or branch of running water, or a reservoir of a water works, of which use is or may be made for domestic purposes.

**HISTORY: RS § 6927; S&C 877; 70 v 12, § 2; GC § 12654; Bureau of Code Revision. Eff 10-1-53.**

## § 3767.19 Prohibition against nuisances when near state institutions.

No person shall carry on the business of slaughtering, tallow chandlery, or the manufacturing of glue, soap, starch, or other article, the manufacture of which is productive of unwholesome or noxious odors in a building or place within one mile of a benevolent or correctional institution supported wholly or in part by the state. No person shall erect or operate, within one hundred twenty rods of such benevolent institution, a rolling mill, blast furnace, nail factory, copper-smelting works, petroleum oil refinery, or other works which may generate unwholesome or noxious odors or make loud noises, or which may annoy or endanger the health or prevent the recovery of the inmates of such institution. Each week such business is conducted, or works operated, constitutes a separate offense.

All property, real or personal, which is used with the knowledge of the owner thereof in violation of this section, shall be liable, without exemption, for the fines and costs assessed for such violation.

**HISTORY: RS § 6924; S&S 53, 54; 62 v 137, §§ 1, 2, 3; 63 v 57; 63 v 96, §§ 1, 2; 95 v 592; GC §§ 12655, 12656; Bureau of Code Revision, 10-1-53; 125 v 903(1008) (Eff 10-1-53); 145 v H 571. Eff 10-6-94.**

## § 3767.201 Destruction or removal of barriers along limited access highways prohibited; vehicles to enter and leave at designated intersections.

No person, firm or corporation shall cut, injure, remove, or destroy any fence or other barrier designed and erected to prevent traffic from entering or leaving a limited access highway without the permission of the director of transportation, except in a case of emergency where life or property is in danger. No person, firm, or corporation shall cause a vehicle of any character to enter or leave a limited access highway at any point other than intersections designated by the director for such purpose, except in a case of emergency where life or property is in danger.

**HISTORY: 128 v 1217 (Eff 11-2-59); 135 v H 200. Eff 9-28-73.**

## § 3767.22 Exceptions.

Section 3767.16 of the Revised Code does not prohibit the deposit of the contents of privy vaults and catch basins into trenches or pits not less than three feet deep excavated in a lot, field, or meadow, with the consent of the owner, outside of the limits of a municipal corporation and not less than thirty rods distant from a dwelling, well or spring of water, lake, bay, pond, canal, run, creek, brook or stream of water, public road or highway, provided that such contents so deposited are forthwith covered with at least twelve inches of dry earth; nor prohibit the deposit of such contents in furrows, as specified for such trenches or pits, to be forthwith covered with dry earth by plowing or otherwise, and with the consent of the owner or occupant of the land in which such furrows are plowed.

The board of health of a city or a general health district may allow the contents of privy vaults and catch basins to be deposited within corporate limits into such trenches, pits, or furrows.

**HISTORY: RS § 6923; S&S 500; S&C 878, 879; 30 v 22, § 3; 63 v 102; 85 v 268; 87 v 349; 93 v 298; 98 v 339; GC §§ 12650, 12651; Bureau of Code Revision. Eff 10-1-53.**

## § 3767.23 Prosecution of corporations for nuisances; abatement.

Corporations may be prosecuted by indictment for violation of sections 3767.13 to 3767.29, inclusive, of the Revised Code, and in every case of conviction under such sections, the court shall adjudge that the nuisance described in the indictment be abated or removed within a time fixed, and, if it is of a recurring character, the defendant shall keep such nuisance abated.

**HISTORY: RS § 6919; S&S 53; S&C 881; 54 v 130, § 3; 97 v 310; GC § 12657; Bureau of Code Revision, 10-1-53; 126 v 374. Eff 8-1-55.**

## § 3767.24 Contempt proceedings.

If the defendant, convicted of a violation of sections 3767.13 to 3767.29, inclusive, of the Revised Code, fails, neglects, or refuses to abate the nuisance described in the indictment, as ordered by the court, or, if the nuisance is of a recurring character, and such defendant fails, neglects, or refuses to keep it abated, proceedings in contempt of court may be instituted against him and all others assisting in or conniving at the violation of such order, and the court may direct the sheriff to execute the order of abatement at the cost and expense of the defendant.

**HISTORY: RS § 6919; S&S 53; S&C 881; 54 v 130, § 3; 97 v 310; GC § 12658; Bureau of Code Revision, 10-1-53; 126 v 374. Eff 8-1-55.**

## § 3767.25 Venue.

An offense charged under sections 3767.13 to 3767.29, inclusive, of the Revised Code, shall be held to be committed in any county whose inhabitants are, or have been, aggrieved thereby. The continuance of such nuisance for five days after the prosecution thereof is begun is an additional offense.

**HISTORY: RS § 6920; S&S 500; S&C 878; 30 v 22, §§ 1, 2, 3; 63 v 102; GC § 12659; Bureau of Code Revision, 10-1-53; 126 v 374. Eff 8-1-55.**

## § 3767.26 Judgment for fine and costs.

A judgment for fine and costs rendered against a person or corporation for the violation of sections 3767.13 to 3767.29, inclusive, of the Revised Code, when the defendant has no property or has not a sufficient amount within the county upon which to levy to satisfy such judgment and costs, may be enforced and collected in the manner in which judgments are collected in civil cases.

**HISTORY: RS § 6920c; 87 v 351; GC § 12660; Bureau of Code Revision, 10-1-53; 126 v 374. Eff 8-1-55.**

## § 3767.27 Inspector of nuisances.

The board of county commissioners, whenever there is a violation of sections 3767.13 to 3767.29, inclusive, of the Revised Code, may employ and reasonably compensate one inspector of nuisances who shall be vested with police powers and authorized to examine all cases of violation of such sections.

**HISTORY: RS § 6920a; 87 v 350; GC § 12661; Bureau of Code Revision, 10-1-53; 126 v 374. Eff 8-1-55.**

## § 3767.28 Powers and duties of inspector.

For the purpose of examining cases of violations of sections 3767.13 to 3767.29, inclusive, of the Revised Code, and for obtaining evidence thereof, an inspector of nuisances may enter upon any premises in any county, and shall make a complaint, and institute prosecution, against any one violating such sections. The inspector shall not be required to give security for costs. The prosecuting attorney shall be the legal advisor of such inspector and the attorney in all such prosecutions.

**HISTORY: RS §§ 6920a, 6920b; 87 v 350, 351; GC § 12662; Bureau of Code Revision, 10-1-53; 126 v 374. Eff 8-1-55.**

## § 3767.29 Abandoned refrigerators.

No person shall abandon, discard, or knowingly permit to remain on premises under the person's control, in a place accessible to children, any abandoned or discarded icebox, refrigerator, or other airtight or semi-airtight container which has a capacity of one and one-half cubic feet or more and an opening of fifty square inches or more and which has a door or lid equipped with hinge, latch, or other fastening device capable of securing such door or lid, without rendering said equipment harmless to human life by removing such hinges, latches, or other hardware which may cause a person to be confined therein. This section shall not apply to an icebox, refrigerator, or other airtight or semi-airtight container located in that part of a building occupied by a dealer, warehouse, or repairer.

**HISTORY: 126 v 374. Eff 8-1-55; 2011 HB 9, § 1, eff. June 29, 2011.**

Acts 2011, HB 9, § 3 provides: "This act applies to transactions entered into on or after the effective date of this act."

## § 3767.30 Protest activities near funeral or burial service or funeral procession.

Every citizen may freely speak, write, and publish the person's sentiments on all subjects, being responsible for the abuse of the right, but no person shall picket or engage in other protest activities, nor shall any association or corporation cause picketing or other protest activities to occur, within three hundred feet of any residence, cemetery, funeral home, church, synagogue, or other establishment during or within one hour before or one hour after the conducting of an actual funeral or burial service at that place. No person shall picket or engage in other protest activities, nor shall any association or corporation cause picketing or other protest activities to occur, within three hundred feet of any funeral procession.

As used in this section, "other protest activities" means any action that is disruptive or undertaken to disrupt or disturb a funeral or burial service or a funeral procession.

**HISTORY: 127 v 242 (Eff 9-13-57); 129 v 582(818). Eff 1-10-61; 151 v H 484, § 1, eff. 9-4-06.**

## § 3767.32 Restrictions on depositing litter on public property, on private property owned by others and in state waters.

(A) No person, regardless of intent, shall deposit litter or cause litter to be deposited on any public property, on private property not owned by the person, or in or on waters of the state unless one of the following applies:

(1) The person is directed to do so by a public official as part of a litter collection drive;

(2) Except as provided in division (B) of this section, the person deposits the litter in a litter receptacle in a manner that prevents its being carried away by the elements;

(3) The person is issued a permit or license covering the litter pursuant to Chapter 3734. or 6111. of the Revised Code.

(B) No person, without privilege to do so, shall knowingly deposit litter, or cause it to be deposited, in a litter receptacle located on any public property or on any private property not owned by the person unless one of the following applies:

(1) The litter was generated or located on the property on which the litter receptacle is located;

(2) The person is directed to do so by a public official as part of a litter collection drive;

(3) The person is directed to do so by a person whom the person reasonably believes to have the privilege to use the litter receptacle;

(4) The litter consists of any of the following:

(a) The contents of a litter bag or container of a type and size customarily carried and used in a motor vehicle;

(b) The contents of an ash tray of a type customarily installed or carried and used in a motor vehicle;

(c) Beverage containers and food sacks, wrappings, and containers of a type and in an amount that reasonably may be expected to be generated during routine commuting or business or recreational travel by a motor vehicle;

(d) Beverage containers, food sacks, wrappings, containers, and other materials of a type and in an amount that reasonably may be expected to be generated during a routine day by a person and deposited in a litter receptacle by a casual passerby.

(C)(1) As used in division (B)(1) of this section, "public property" includes any private property open to the public for the conduct of business, the provision of a service, or upon the payment of a fee, but does not include any private property to which the public otherwise does not have a right of access.

(2) As used in division (B)(4) of this section, "casual passerby" means a person who does not have depositing litter in a litter receptacle as the person's primary reason for traveling to or by the property on which the litter receptacle is located.

(D) As used in this section:

(1) "Litter" means garbage, trash, waste, rubbish, ashes, cans, bottles, wire, paper, cartons, boxes, automobile parts, furniture, glass, or anything else of an unsightly or unsanitary nature.

(2) "Deposit" means to throw, drop, discard, or place.

(3) "Litter receptacle" means a dumpster, trash can, trash bin, garbage can, or similar container in which litter is deposited for removal.

(E) This section may be enforced by any sheriff, deputy sheriff, police officer of a municipal corporation, police constable or officer of a township, or township or joint police district, wildlife officer, park officer, forest officer, preserve officer, conservancy district police officer, inspector of nuisances of a county, or any other law enforcement officer within the law enforcement officer's jurisdiction.

**HISTORY: 132 v H 152 (Eff 9-21-67); 138 v H 361 (Eff 7-14-80); 142 v H 333 (Eff 10-20-87); 145 v H 114 (Eff 9-27-93); 145 v S 182. Eff 10-20-94; 2011 HB 153, § 101.01, eff. Sept. 29, 2011.**

## § 3767.33 Authorization for disposal of materials; injunction against disposal.

No zoning commission, municipal corporation, or other governmental authority, except the director of environmental protection acting pursuant to the powers granted to him in sections 6111.01 to 6111.08 of the Revised Code, may authorize the placing or disposal of materials in or upon the banks of a ditch, stream, river, or other watercourse after January 1, 1968, where such placing or disposal would be prohibited under the provisions of section 3767.32 of the Revised Code. Such placing or disposal may be enjoined by the common pleas court in the county in which the placing or disposal occurs, upon application by the prosecuting attorney of the county, the director of environmental protection, the director of health, or the attorney general.

**HISTORY: 132 v H 152 (Eff 9-21-67); 134 v S 397. Eff 10-23-72.**

## § 3767.34 Free rest room facilities.

(A) No person shall make available any rest room facility intended for multiple occupancy and which requires payment of money or any other thing of value for entry into the rest room facility, or for use of a toilet within, unless said person also makes available for use by the same sex, at the same location, an equal number of the same kind of rest room facilities, toilets, urinals, and washbowls free of charge.

(B) Rest room facilities having no more than one toilet and a washbowl, or having no more than one toilet, one urinal, and one washbowl, shall be exempt from the provisions of division (A) of this section if a key is made available immediately, or other means of access made available immediately, for any customer who requests use of the rest room facility or the toilet, urinal, or washbowl within.

(C) As used in divisions (A) and (B) of this section, "rest room facility" means any room or area containing one or more toilets, washbowls, or urinals; "multiple occupancy" means a rest room facility containing more than one toilet and one washbowl, or containing more than one toilet, one urinal, and one washbowl used for the purpose of eliminating human biological waste materials and commonly referred to as "lavatory," "toilet," "urinal," or "water closet."

**HISTORY: 136 v S 71. Eff 8-18-76.**

## § 3767.41 Buildings constituting public nuisance; action to enforce regulations; receivership.

(A) As used in this section:

(1) "Building" means, except as otherwise provided in this division, any building or structure that is used or intended to be used for residential purposes. "Building" includes, but is not limited to, a building or structure in which any floor is used for retail stores, shops, salesrooms, markets, or similar commercial uses, or for offices, banks, civic administration activities, professional services, or similar business or civic uses, and in which the other floors are used, or designed and intended to be used, for residential purposes. "Building" does not include any building or structure that is occupied by its owner and that contains three or fewer residential units.

(2)(a) "Public nuisance" means a building that is a menace to the public health, welfare, or safety; that is structurally unsafe, unsanitary, or not provided with adequate safe egress; that constitutes a fire hazard, is otherwise dangerous to human life, or is otherwise no longer fit and habitable; or that, in relation to its existing use, constitutes a hazard to the public health, welfare, or safety by reason of inadequate maintenance, dilapidation, obsolescence, or abandonment.

(b) "Public nuisance" as it applies to subsidized housing means subsidized housing that fails to meet the following standards as specified in the federal rules governing each standard:

(i) Each building on the site is structurally sound, secure, habitable, and in good repair, as defined in 24 C.F.R. 5.703(b);

(ii) Each building's domestic water, electrical system, elevators, emergency power, fire protection, HVAC, and sanitary system is free of health and safety hazards, functionally adequate, operable, and in good repair, as defined in 24 C.F.R. 5.703(c);

(iii) Each dwelling unit within the building is structurally sound, habitable, and in good repair, and all areas and aspects of the dwelling unit are free of health and safety hazards, functionally adequate, operable, and in good repair, as defined in 24 C.F.R. 5.703(d)(1);

(iv) Where applicable, the dwelling unit has hot and cold running water, including an adequate source of potable water, as defined in 24 C.F.R. 5.703(d)(2);

(v) If the dwelling unit includes its own sanitary facility, it is in proper operating condition, usable in privacy, and adequate for personal hygiene, and the disposal of human waste, as defined in 24 C.F.R. 5.703(d)(3);

(vi) The common areas are structurally sound, secure, and functionally adequate for the purposes intended. The basement, garage, carport, restrooms, closets, utility, mechanical, community rooms, daycare, halls, corridors, stairs, kitchens, laundry rooms, office, porch, patio, balcony, and trash collection areas are free of health and safety hazards, operable, and in good repair. All common area ceilings, doors, floors, HVAC, lighting, smoke detectors, stairs, walls, and windows, to the extent applicable, are free of health and safety hazards, operable, and in good repair, as defined in 24 C.F.R. 5.703(e);

(vii) All areas and components of the housing are free of health and safety hazards. These areas include, but are not limited to, air quality, electrical hazards, elevators, emergency/fire exits, flammable materials, garbage and debris, handrail hazards, infestation, and lead-based paint, as defined in 24 C.F.R. 5.703(f).

(3) "Abate" or "abatement" in connection with any building means the removal or correction of any conditions that constitute a public nuisance and the making of any other improvements that are needed to effect a rehabilitation of the building that is consistent with maintaining safe and habitable conditions over its remaining useful life. "Abatement" does not include the closing or boarding up of any building that is found to be a public nuisance.

(4) "Interested party" means any owner, mortgagee, lienholder, tenant, or person that possesses an interest of record in any property that becomes subject to the jurisdiction of a court pursuant to this section, and any applicant for the appointment of a receiver pursuant to this section.

(5) "Neighbor" means any owner of property, including, but not limited to, any person who is purchasing property by land installment contract or under a duly executed purchase contract, that is located within five hundred feet of any property that becomes subject to the jurisdiction of a court pursuant to this section, and any occupant of a building that is so located.

(6) "Tenant" has the same meaning as in section 5321.01 of the Revised Code.

(7) "Subsidized housing" means a property consisting of more than four dwelling units that, in whole or in part, receives project-based assistance pursuant to a contract under any of the following federal housing programs:

(a) The new construction or substantial rehabilitation program under section 8(b)(2) of the "United States Housing Act of 1937," Pub. L. No. 75-412, 50 Stat. 888, 42 U.S.C. 1437f(b)(2) as that program was in effect immediately before the first day of October, 1983;

(b) The moderate rehabilitation program under section 8(e)(2) of the "United States Housing Act of 1937," Pub. L. No. 75-412, 50 Stat. 888, 42 U.S.C. 1437f(e)(2);

(c) The loan management assistance program under section 8 of the "United States Housing Act of 1937," Pub. L. No. 75-412, 50 Stat. 888, 42 U.S.C. 1437f;

(d) The rent supplement program under section 101 of the "Housing and Urban Development Act of 1965," Pub. L. No. 89-174, 79 Stat. 667, 12 U.S.C. 1701s;

(e) Section 8 of the "United States Housing Act of 1937," Pub. L. No. 75-412, 50 Stat. 888, 42 U.S.C. 1437f, following conversion from assistance under section 101 of the "Housing and Urban Development Act of 1965," Pub. L. No. 89-174, 79 Stat. 667, 12 U.S.C. 1701s;

(f) The program of supportive housing for the elderly under section 202 of the "Housing Act of 1959," Pub. L. No. 86-372, 73 Stat. 654, 12 U.S.C. 1701q;

(g) The program of supportive housing for persons with disabilities under section 811 of the "National Affordable Housing Act of 1990," Pub. L. No. 101-625, 104 Stat. 4313, 42 U.S.C. 8013;

(h) The rental assistance program under section 521 of the "United States Housing Act of 1949," Pub. L. No. 90-448, 82 Stat. 551, as amended by Pub. L. No. 93-383, 88 Stat. 696, 42 U.S.C. 1490a.

(8) "Project-based assistance" means the assistance is attached to the property and provides rental assistance only on behalf of tenants who reside in that property.

(9) "Landlord" has the same meaning as in section 5321.01 of the Revised Code.

(B)(1)(a) In any civil action to enforce any local building, housing, air pollution, sanitation, health, fire, zoning, or safety code, ordinance, resolution, or regulation applicable to buildings, that is commenced in a court of common pleas, municipal court, housing or environmental division of a municipal court, or county court, or in any civil action for abatement commenced in a court of common pleas, municipal court, housing or environmental division of a municipal court, or county court, by a municipal corporation or township in which the building involved is located, by any neighbor, tenant, or by a nonprofit corporation that is duly organized and has as one of its goals the improvement of housing conditions in the county or municipal corporation in which the building involved is located, if a building is alleged to be a public nuisance, the municipal corporation, township, neighbor, tenant, or nonprofit corporation may apply in its complaint for an injunction or other order as described in division (C)(1) of this section, or for the relief described in division (C)(2) of this section, including, if necessary, the appointment of a receiver as described in divisions (C)(2) and (3) of this section, or for both such an injunction or other order and such relief. The municipal corporation, township, neighbor, tenant, or nonprofit corporation commencing the action is not liable for the costs, expenses, and fees of any receiver appointed pursuant to divisions (C)(2) and (3) of this section.

(b) Prior to commencing a civil action for abatement when the property alleged to be a public nuisance is subsidized housing, the municipal corporation, township, neighbor, tenant, or nonprofit corporation commencing the action shall provide the landlord of that property with written notice that specifies one or more defective conditions that constitute a public nuisance as that term applies to subsidized housing and states that if the landlord fails to remedy the condition within sixty days of the service of the notice, a claim pursuant to this section may be brought on the basis that the property constitutes a public nuisance in subsidized housing. Any party authorized to bring an action against the landlord shall make reasonable attempts to serve the notice in the manner prescribed in the Rules of Civil Procedure to the landlord or the landlord's agent for the property at the property's management office, or at the place where the tenants normally pay or send rent. If the landlord is not the owner of record, the party bringing the action shall make a reasonable attempt to serve the owner. If the owner does not receive service the person bringing the action shall certify the attempts to serve the owner.

(2)(a) In a civil action described in division (B)(1) of this section, a copy of the complaint and a notice of the date and time of a hearing on the complaint shall be served upon the owner of the building and all other interested parties in accordance with the Rules of Civil Procedure. If certified mail service, personal service, or residence service of the complaint and notice is refused or certified mail service of the complaint and notice is not claimed, and if the municipal corporation, township, neighbor, tenant, or nonprofit corporation commencing the action makes a written request for ordinary mail service of the complaint and notice, or uses publication service, in accordance with the Rules of Civil Procedure, then a copy of the complaint and notice shall be posted in a conspicuous place on the building.

(b) The judge in a civil action described in division (B)(1) of this section shall conduct a hearing at least twenty-eight days after the owner of the building and the other interested parties have been served with a copy of the complaint and the notice of the date and time of the hearing in accordance with division (B)(2)(a) of this section.

(c) In considering whether subsidized housing is a public nuisance, the judge shall construe the standards set forth in division (A)(2)(b) of this section in a manner consistent with department of housing and urban development and judicial interpretations of those standards. The judge shall deem that the property is not a public nuisance if during the twelve months prior to the service of the notice that division (B)(1)(b) of this section requires, the department of housing and urban development's real estate assessment center issued a score of seventy-five or higher out of a possible one hundred points pursuant to its regulations governing the physical condition of multifamily properties pursuant to 24 C.F.R. part 200, subpart P, and since the most recent inspection, there has been no significant change in the property's conditions that would create a serious threat to the health, safety, or welfare of the property's tenants.

(C)(1) If the judge in a civil action described in division (B)(1) of this section finds at the hearing required by division (B)(2) of this section that the building involved is a public nuisance, if the judge additionally determines that the owner of the building previously has not been afforded a reasonable opportunity to abate the public nuisance or has been afforded such an opportunity and has not refused or failed to abate the public nuisance, and if the complaint of the municipal corporation, township, neighbor, tenant, or nonprofit corporation commencing the action requested the issuance of an injunction as described in this division, then the judge may issue an injunction requiring the owner of the building to abate the public nuisance or issue any other order that the judge considers necessary or appropriate to cause the abatement of the public nuisance. If an injunction is issued pursuant to this division, the owner of the building involved shall be given no more than thirty days from the date of the entry of the judge's order to comply with the injunction, unless the judge, for good cause shown, extends the time for compliance.

(2) If the judge in a civil action described in division (B)(1) of this section finds at the hearing required by division (B)(2) of this section that the building involved is a public nuisance, if the judge additionally determines that the owner of the building previously has been afforded a reasonable opportunity to abate the public nuisance and has refused or failed to do so, and if the complaint of the municipal corporation, township, neighbor, tenant, or nonprofit corporation commencing the action requested relief as described in this division, then the judge shall offer any mortgagee, lienholder, or other interested party associated with the property on which the building is located, in the order of the priority of interest in title, the opportunity to undertake the work and to furnish the materials necessary to abate the public nuisance. Prior to selecting any interested party, the judge shall require the interested party to demonstrate the ability to promptly undertake the work and furnish the materials required, to provide the judge with a viable financial and construction plan for the rehabilitation of the building as described in division (D) of this section, and to post security for the performance of the work and the furnishing of the materials.

If the judge determines, at the hearing, that no interested party is willing or able to undertake the work and to furnish the materials necessary to abate the public nuisance, or if the judge determines, at any time after the hearing, that any party who is undertaking corrective work pursuant to this division cannot or will not proceed, or has not proceeded with due diligence, the judge may appoint a receiver pursuant to division (C)(3) of this section to take possession and control of the building.

(3)(a) The judge in a civil action described in division (B)(1) of this section shall not appoint any person as a receiver unless the person first has provided the judge with a viable financial and construction plan for the rehabilitation of the building involved as described in division (D) of this section and has demonstrated the capacity and expertise to perform the required work and to furnish the required materials in a satisfactory manner. An appointed receiver may be a financial institution that possesses an interest of record in the building or the property on which it is located, a nonprofit corporation as described in divisions (B)(1) and (C)(3)(b) of this section, including, but not limited to, a nonprofit corporation that commenced the action described in division (B)(1) of this section, or any other qualified property manager.

(b) To be eligible for appointment as a receiver, no part of the net earnings of a nonprofit corporation shall inure to the benefit of any private shareholder or individual. Membership on the board of trustees of a nonprofit corporation appointed as a receiver does not constitute the holding of a public office or employment within the meaning of sections 731.02 and 731.12 or any other section of the Revised Code and does not constitute a direct or indirect interest in a contract or expenditure of money by any municipal corporation. A member of a board of trustees of a nonprofit corporation appointed as a receiver shall not be disqualified from holding any public office or employment, and shall not forfeit any public office or employment, by reason of membership on the board of trustees, notwithstanding any law to the contrary.

(D) Prior to ordering any work to be undertaken, or the furnishing of any materials, to abate a public nuisance under this section, the judge in a civil action described in division (B)(1) of this section shall review the submitted financial and construction plan for the rehabilitation of the building involved and, if it specifies all of the following, shall approve that plan:

(1) The estimated cost of the labor, materials, and any other development costs that are required to abate the public nuisance;

(2) The estimated income and expenses of the building and the property on which it is located after the furnishing of the materials and the completion of the repairs and improvements;

(3) The terms, conditions, and availability of any financing that is necessary to perform the work and to furnish the materials;

(4) If repair and rehabilitation of the building are found not to be feasible, the cost of demolition of the building or of the portions of the building that constitute the public nuisance.

(E) Upon the written request of any of the interested parties to have a building, or portions of a building, that constitute a public nuisance demolished because repair and rehabilitation of the building are found not to be feasible, the judge may order the demolition. However, the demolition shall not be ordered unless the requesting interested parties have paid the costs of demolition and, if any, of the receivership, and, if any, all notes, certificates, mortgages, and fees of the receivership.

(F) Before proceeding with the duties of receiver, any receiver appointed by the judge in a civil action described in division (B)(1) of this section may be required by the judge to post a bond in an amount fixed by the judge, but not exceeding the value of the building involved as determined by the judge.

The judge may empower the receiver to do any or all of the following:

(1) Take possession and control of the building and the property on which it is located, operate and manage the building and the property, establish and collect rents and income, lease and rent the building and the property, and evict tenants;

(2) Pay all expenses of operating and conserving the building and the property, including, but not limited to, the cost of electricity, gas, water, sewerage, heating fuel, repairs and supplies, custodian services, taxes and assessments, and insurance premiums, and hire and pay reasonable compensation to a managing agent;

(3) Pay pre-receivership mortgages or installments of them and other liens;

(4) Perform or enter into contracts for the performance of all work and the furnishing of materials necessary to abate, and obtain financing for the abatement of, the public nuisance;

(5) Pursuant to court order, remove and dispose of any personal property abandoned, stored, or otherwise located in or on the building and the property that creates a dangerous or unsafe condition or that constitutes a violation of any local building, housing, air pollution, sanitation, health, fire, zoning, or safety code, ordinance, or regulation;

(6) Obtain mortgage insurance for any receiver's mortgage from any agency of the federal government;

(7) Enter into any agreement and do those things necessary to maintain and preserve the building and the property and comply with all local building, housing, air pollution, sanitation, health, fire, zoning, or safety codes, ordinances, resolutions, and regulations;

(8) Give the custody of the building and the property, and the opportunity to abate the nuisance and operate the property, to its owner or any mortgagee or lienholder of record;

(9) Issue notes and secure them by a mortgage bearing interest, and upon terms and conditions, that the judge approves. When sold or transferred by the receiver in return for valuable consideration in money, material, labor, or services, the notes or certificates shall be freely transferable. Any mortgages granted by the receiver shall be superior to any claims of the receiver. Priority among the receiver's mortgages shall be determined by the order in which they are recorded.

(G) A receiver appointed pursuant to this section is not personally liable except for misfeasance, malfeasance, or nonfeasance in the performance of the functions of the office of receiver.

(H)(1) The judge in a civil action described in division (B)(1) of this section may assess as court costs, the expenses described in division (F)(2) of this section, and may approve receiver's fees to the extent that they are not covered by the income from the property. Subject to that limitation, a receiver appointed pursuant to divisions (C)(2) and (3) of this section is entitled to receive fees in the same manner and to the same extent as receivers appointed in actions to foreclose mortgages.

(2)(a) Pursuant to the police powers vested in the state, all expenditures of a mortgagee, lienholder, or other interested party that has been selected pursuant to division (C)(2) of this section to undertake the work and to furnish the materials necessary to abate a public nuisance, and any expenditures in connection with the foreclosure of the lien created by this division, is a first lien upon the building involved and the property on which it is located and is superior to all prior and subsequent liens or other encumbrances associated with the building or the property, including, but not limited to, those for taxes and assessments, upon the occurrence of both of the following:

(i) The prior approval of the expenditures by, and the entry of a judgment to that effect by, the judge in the civil action described in division (B)(1) of this section;

(ii) The recordation of a certified copy of the judgment entry and a sufficient description of the property on which the building is located with the county recorder in the county in which the property is located within sixty days after the date of the entry of the judgment.

(b) Pursuant to the police powers vested in the state, all expenses and other amounts paid in accordance with division (F) of this section by a receiver appointed pursuant to divisions (C)(2) and (3) of this section, the amounts of any notes issued by the receiver in accordance with division (F) of this section, all mortgages granted by the receiver in accordance with that division, the fees of the receiver approved pursuant to division (H)(1) of this section, and any amounts expended in connection with the foreclosure of a mortgage granted by the receiver in accordance with division (F) of this section or with the foreclosure of the lien created by this division, are a first lien upon the building involved and the property on which it is located and are superior to all prior and subsequent liens or other encumbrances associated with the building or the property, including, but not limited to, those for taxes and assessments, upon the occurrence of both of the following:

(i) The approval of the expenses, amounts, or fees by, and the entry of a judgment to that effect by, the judge in the civil action described in division (B)(1) of this section;

or the approval of the mortgages in accordance with division (F)(9) of this section by, and the entry of a judgment to that effect by, that judge;

(ii) The recordation of a certified copy of the judgment entry and a sufficient description of the property on which the building is located, or, in the case of a mortgage, the recordation of the mortgage, a certified copy of the judgment entry, and such a description, with the county recorder of the county in which the property is located within sixty days after the date of the entry of the judgment.

(c) Priority among the liens described in divisions (H)(2)(a) and (b) of this section shall be determined as described in division (I) of this section. Additionally, the creation pursuant to this section of a mortgage lien that is prior to or superior to any mortgage of record at the time the mortgage lien is so created, does not disqualify the mortgage of record as a legal investment under Chapter 1107. or 1151. or any other chapter of the Revised Code.

(I)(1) If a receiver appointed pursuant to divisions (C)(2) and (3) of this section files with the judge in the civil action described in division (B)(1) of this section a report indicating that the public nuisance has been abated, if the judge confirms that the receiver has abated the public nuisance, and if the receiver or any interested party requests the judge to enter an order directing the receiver to sell the building and the property on which it is located, the judge may enter that order after holding a hearing as described in division (I)(2) of this section and otherwise complying with that division.

(2)(a) The receiver or interested party requesting an order as described in division (I)(1) of this section shall cause a notice of the date and time of a hearing on the request to be served on the owner of the building involved and all other interested parties in accordance with division (B)(2)(a) of this section. The judge in the civil action described in division (B)(1) of this section shall conduct the scheduled hearing. At the hearing, if the owner or any interested party objects to the sale of the building and the property, the burden of proof shall be upon the objecting person to establish, by a preponderance of the evidence, that the benefits of not selling the building and the property outweigh the benefits of selling them. If the judge determines that there is no objecting person, or if the judge determines that there is one or more objecting persons but no objecting person has sustained the burden of proof specified in this division, the judge may enter an order directing the receiver to offer the building and the property for sale upon terms and conditions that the judge shall specify.

(b) In any sale of subsidized housing that is ordered pursuant to this section, the judge shall specify that the subsidized housing not be conveyed unless that conveyance complies with applicable federal law and applicable program contracts for that housing. Any such conveyance shall be subject to the condition that the purchaser enter into a contract with the department of housing and urban development or the rural housing service of the federal department of agriculture under which the property continues to be subsidized housing and the owner continues to operate that property as subsidized housing unless the secretary of housing and urban development or the administrator of the rural housing service terminates that property's contract prior to or upon the conveyance of the property.

(3) If a sale of a building and the property on which it is located is ordered pursuant to divisions (I)(1) and (2) of this section and if the sale occurs in accordance with the terms and conditions specified by the judge in the judge's order of sale, then the receiver shall distribute the proceeds of the sale and the balance of any funds that the receiver may possess, after the payment of the costs of the sale, in the following order of priority and in the described manner:

(a) First, in satisfaction of any notes issued by the receiver pursuant to division (F) of this section, in their order of priority;

(b) Second, any unreimbursed expenses and other amounts paid in accordance with division (F) of this section by the receiver, and the fees of the receiver approved pursuant to division (H)(1) of this section;

(c) Third, all expenditures of a mortgagee, lienholder, or other interested party that has been selected pursuant to division (C)(2) of this section to undertake the work and to furnish the materials necessary to abate a public nuisance, provided that the expenditures were approved as described in division (H)(2)(a) of this section and provided that, if any such interested party subsequently became the receiver, its expenditures shall be paid prior to the expenditures of any of the other interested parties so selected;

(d) Fourth, the amount due for delinquent taxes, assessments, charges, penalties, and interest owed to this state or a political subdivision of this state, provided that, if the amount available for distribution pursuant to division (I)(3)(d) of this section is insufficient to pay the entire amount of those taxes, assessments, charges, penalties, and interest, the proceeds and remaining funds shall be paid to each claimant in proportion to the amount of those taxes, assessments, charges, penalties, and interest that each is due.

(e) The amount of any pre-receivership mortgages, liens, or other encumbrances, in their order of priority.

(4) Following a distribution in accordance with division (I)(3) of this section, the receiver shall request the judge in the civil action described in division (B)(1) of this section to enter an order terminating the receivership. If the judge determines that the sale of the building and the property on which it is located occurred in accordance with the terms and conditions specified by the judge in the judge's order of sale under division (I)(2) of this section and that the receiver distributed the proceeds of the sale and the balance of any funds that the receiver possessed, after the payment of the costs of the sale, in accordance with division (I)(3) of this section, and if the judge approves any final accounting required of the receiver, the judge may terminate the receivership.

(J)(1) A receiver appointed pursuant to divisions (C)(2) and (3) of this section may be discharged at any time in the discretion of the judge in the civil action described in division (B)(1) of this section. The receiver shall be discharged by the judge as provided in division (I)(4) of this section, or when all of the following have occurred:

(a) The public nuisance has been abated;

(b) All costs, expenses, and approved fees of the receivership have been paid;

(c) Either all receiver's notes issued and mortgages granted pursuant to this section have been paid, or all the holders of the notes and mortgages request that the receiver be discharged.

(2) If a judge in a civil action described in division (B)(1) of this section determines that, and enters of record a declaration that, a public nuisance has been abated by a receiver, and if, within three days after the entry of the declaration, all costs, expenses, and approved fees of the

receivership have not been paid in full, then, in addition to the circumstances specified in division (I) of this section for the entry of such an order, the judge may enter an order directing the receiver to sell the building involved and the property on which it is located. Any such order shall be entered, and the sale shall occur, only in compliance with division (I) of this section.

(K) The title in any building, and in the property on which it is located, that is sold at a sale ordered under division (I) or (J)(2) of this section shall be incontestable in the purchaser and shall be free and clear of all liens for delinquent taxes, assessments, charges, penalties, and interest owed to this state or any political subdivision of this state, that could not be satisfied from the proceeds of the sale and the remaining funds in the receiver's possession pursuant to the distribution under division (I)(3) of this section. All other liens and encumbrances with respect to the building and the property shall survive the sale, including, but not limited to, a federal tax lien notice properly filed in accordance with section 317.09 of the Revised Code prior to the time of the sale, and the easements and covenants of record running with the property that were created prior to the time of the sale.

(L)(1) Nothing in this section shall be construed as a limitation upon the powers granted to a court of common pleas, a municipal court or a housing or environmental division of a municipal court under Chapter 1901. of the Revised Code, or a county court under Chapter 1907. of the Revised Code.

(2) The monetary and other limitations specified in Chapters 1901. and 1907. of the Revised Code upon the jurisdiction of municipal and county courts, and of housing or environmental divisions of municipal courts, in civil actions do not operate as limitations upon any of the following:

(a) Expenditures of a mortgagee, lienholder, or other interested party that has been selected pursuant to division (C)(2) of this section to undertake the work and to furnish the materials necessary to abate a public nuisance;

(b) Any notes issued by a receiver pursuant to division (F) of this section;

(c) Any mortgage granted by a receiver in accordance with division (F) of this section;

(d) Expenditures in connection with the foreclosure of a mortgage granted by a receiver in accordance with division (F) of this section;

(e) The enforcement of an order of a judge entered pursuant to this section;

(f) The actions that may be taken pursuant to this section by a receiver or a mortgagee, lienholder, or other interested party that has been selected pursuant to division (C)(2) of this section to undertake the work and to furnish the materials necessary to abate a public nuisance.

(3) A judge in a civil action described in division (B)(1) of this section, or the judge's successor in office, has continuing jurisdiction to review the condition of any building that was determined to be a public nuisance pursuant to this section.

(4) Nothing in this section shall be construed to limit or prohibit a municipal corporation or township that has filed with the superintendent of insurance a certified copy of an adopted resolution, ordinance, or regulation authorizing the procedures described in divisions (C) and (D) of section 3929.86 of the Revised Code from receiving insurance proceeds under section 3929.86 of the Revised Code.

**HISTORY: 140 v H 706 (Eff 12-17-84); 143 v H 387 (Eff 7-18-90); 144 v H 200 (Eff 7-8-91); 146 v H 538. Eff 1-1-97; 152 v H 119, § 101.01, eff. 9-29-07; 153 v H 1, § 101.01, eff. 10-16-09.**

The effective date is set by § 812.10 of 153 v H 1.
The effective date is set by § 812.03 of 152 v H 119.
The effective date is set by section 10 of HB 538.

## § 3767.99 Penalties.

(A) Whoever is guilty of contempt under sections 3767.01 to 3767.11 or violates section 3767.14 of the Revised Code is guilty of a misdemeanor of the first degree.

(B) Whoever violates section 3767.12 or 3767.29, or, being an association, violates section 3767.30 of the Revised Code is guilty of a misdemeanor of the fourth degree.

(C) Whoever violates section 3767.13, 3767.19, or 3767.32 or, being a natural person, violates section 3767.30 of the Revised Code is guilty of a misdemeanor of the third degree. The sentencing court may, in addition to or in lieu of the penalty provided in this division, require a person who violates section 3767.32 of the Revised Code to remove litter from any public or private property, or in or on waters of the state.

(D) Whoever violates section 3767.16, 3767.17, 3767.18, 3767.201 [3767.20.1], or 3767.34 of the Revised Code is guilty of a minor misdemeanor.

**HISTORY: Bureau of Code Revision, 10-1-53; 127 v 242; 128 v 1217 (Eff 11-2-59); 129 v 1075 (Eff 9-25-61); 130 v 866 (Eff 1-23-63); 130 v 867 (Eff 9-30-63); 132 v H 152 (Eff 9-21-67); 133 v S 460 (Eff 9-3-70); 136 v S 71 (Eff 8-18-76); 138 v H 361. Eff 7-14-80.**

# CHAPTER 3770: STATE LOTTERY

Section



## § 3770.08 Prohibitions.

(A) No person shall sell a lottery ticket at a price greater than that fixed by rule of the state lottery commission.

(B) No person other than a licensed lottery sales agent shall sell lottery tickets, but nothing in this section shall be construed to prevent any person from giving lottery tickets to another as a gift. A transfer of lottery tickets by any person which is made in connection with a marketing, promotional, or advertising program shall be deemed to be a gift for the purposes of this chapter.

(C) No person shall sell a lottery ticket to any person under eighteen years of age, and no person under eighteen years of age shall attempt to purchase a lottery ticket.

(D) No person, directly or indirectly, on behalf of self, or another, nor any organization, shall invite, solicit, demand, offer, or accept any payment, contribution, favor, or other consideration to influence the award, renewal, or retention of a lottery sales agent license.

(E) Except as otherwise provided in this division, no person shall sell lottery tickets on any fairgrounds during any annual exhibition conducted in accordance with Chapter 991. or 1711. of the Revised Code. "Fairgrounds" includes any land or property under the control or management of any agricultural society or of the Ohio expositions commission. This division does not apply to the sale of lottery tickets by the commission at the state fairground during the state fair.

**HISTORY: 135 v H 990 (Eff 11-21-73); 137 v H 395 (Eff 11-28-77); 140 v H 665 (Eff 4-4-85); 146 v S 211. Eff 9-26-96.**

[PENALTIES]

## § 3770.99 Penalties.

(A) Whoever is prohibited from claiming a lottery prize award under division (E) of section 3770.07 of the Revised Code and attempts to claim or is paid a lottery prize award is guilty of a minor misdemeanor, and shall provide restitution to the state lottery commission of any moneys erroneously paid as a lottery prize award to that person.

(B) Whoever violates division (C) of section 3770.071 [3770.07.1] or section 3770.08 of the Revised Code is guilty of a misdemeanor of the third degree.

**HISTORY: 135 v H 990 (Eff 11-21-73); 146 v S 211. Eff 9-26-96; 150 v H 95, § 1, eff. 9-26-03.**

The effective date is set by section 179 of H.B. 95 (150 v —).

# CHAPTER 3772: CASINO CONTROL COMMISSION

Section



## § 3772.031 Exclusion or ejection from casino facility.

(A) The general assembly finds that the exclusion or ejection of certain persons from casino facilities is necessary to effectuate the intents and purposes of this chapter and to maintain strict and effective regulation of casino gaming. The commission, by rule, shall provide for a list of persons who are to be excluded or ejected from a casino facility. Persons included on the exclusion list shall be identified by name and physical description. The commission shall publish the exclusion list on its web site, and shall transmit a copy of the exclusion list periodically to casino operators, as it is initially issued and thereafter as it is revised from time to time. A casino operator shall take steps necessary to ensure that all its key employees and casino gaming employees are aware of and understand the exclusion list and its function, and that all its key employees and casino gaming employees are kept aware of the content of the exclusion list as it is issued and thereafter revised from time to time.

(B) The exclusion list may include any person whose presence in a casino facility is determined by the commission to pose a threat to the interests of the state, to achieving the intents and purposes of this chapter, or to the strict and effective regulation of casino gaming. In determining whether to include a person on the exclusion list, the commission may consider:

(1) Any prior conviction of a crime that is a felony under the laws of this state, another state, or the United States, a crime involving moral turpitude, or a violation of the gaming laws of this state, another state, or the United States; and

(2) A violation, or a conspiracy to violate, any provision of this chapter that consists of:

(a) A failure to disclose an interest in a gaming facility for which the person must obtain a license;

(b) Purposeful evasion of taxes or fees;

(c) A notorious or unsavory reputation that would adversely affect public confidence and trust that casino gaming is free from criminal or corruptive elements; or

(d) A violation of an order of the commission or of any other governmental agency that warrants exclusion or ejection of the person from a casino facility.

(3) If the person has pending charges or indictments for a gaming or gambling crime or a crime related to the integrity of gaming operations in any state;

(4) If the person's conduct or reputation is such that the person's presence within a casino facility may call into question the honesty and integrity of the casino gaming operations or interfere with the orderly conduct of the casino gaming operations;

(5) If the person is a career or professional offender whose presence in a casino facility would be adverse to the interest of licensed gaming in this state;

(6) If the person has a known relationship or connection with a career or professional offender whose presence in a casino facility would be adverse to the interest of licensed gaming in this state;

(7) If the commission has suspended the person's gaming privileges;

(8) If the commission has revoked the person's licenses related to this chapter;

(9) If the commission determines that the person poses a threat to the safety of patrons or employees of a casino facility;

(10) If the person has a history of conduct involving the disruption of gaming operations within a casino facility.

Race, color, creed, national origin or ancestry, or sex are not grounds for placing a person on the exclusion list.

(C) The commission shall notify a person of the commission's intent to include such person on the exclusion list. The notice shall be provided by personal service, by certified mail to the person's last known address, or, if service cannot be accomplished by personal service or certified mail, by publication daily for two weeks in a newspaper of general circulation within the county in which the person resides and in a newspaper of general circulation within each county in which a casino facility is located.

(D) A person who receives notice of intent to include the person on the exclusion list is entitled to an adjudication hearing under Chapter 119. of the Revised Code, except as provided in this section, in which the person may demonstrate why the person should not be included on the exclusion list. The person shall request such an adjudication hearing not later than thirty days after the person receives the notice by personal service or certified mail, or not later than thirty days after the last newspaper publication of the notice. If the adjudication hearing or any appeal under Chapter 119. of the Revised Code results in an order that the person should not be included on the exclusion list, the commission shall publish a revised exclusion list that does not include the person. The commission also shall notify casino operators that the person has been removed from the exclusion list. A casino operator shall take all steps necessary to ensure its key employees and casino gaming employees are made aware that the person has been removed from the exclusion list.

(E) This section does not apply to the voluntary exclusion list created as part of the voluntary exclusion program.

**HISTORY: 153 v H 519, § 1, eff. 9-10-10.**

## § 3772.99 Civil and criminal penalties.

(A) The commission shall levy and collect penalties for noncriminal violations of this chapter. Moneys collected from such penalty levies shall be credited to the general revenue fund.

(B) If a licensed casino operator, management company, holding company, gaming-related vendor, or key employee violates this chapter or engages in a fraudulent act, the commission may suspend or revoke the license and may do either or both of the following:

(1) Suspend, revoke, or restrict the casino gaming operations of a casino operator;

(2) Require the removal of a management company, key employee, or discontinuance of services from a gaming-related vendor.

(C) The commission shall impose civil penalties against a person who violates this chapter under the penalties adopted by commission rule and reviewed by the joint committee on gaming and wagering.

(D) A person who knowingly or intentionally does any of the following commits a misdemeanor of the first degree on the first offense and a felony of the fifth degree for a subsequent offense:

(1) Makes a false statement on an application submitted under this chapter;

(2) Permits a person less than twenty-one years of age to make a wager;

(3) Aids, induces, or causes a person less than twenty-one years of age who is not an employee of the casino gaming operation to enter or attempt to enter a casino facility;

(4) Enters or attempts to enter a casino facility while under twenty-one years of age, unless the person enters a designated area as described in section 3772.24 of the Revised Code;

(5) Wagers or accepts a wager at a location other than a casino facility;

(6) Is a casino operator or employee and participates in casino gaming other than as part of operation or employment.

(E) A person who knowingly or intentionally does any of the following commits a felony of the fifth degree on a first offense and a felony of the fourth degree for a subsequent offense. If the person is a licensee under this chapter, the commission shall revoke the person's license after the first offense.

(1) Offers, promises, or gives anything of value or benefit to a person who is connected with the casino operator, management company, holding company, or gaming-related vendor, including their officers and employees, under an agreement to influence or with the intent to influence the actions of the person to whom the offer, promise, or gift was made in order to affect or attempt to affect the outcome of a casino game or an official action of a commission member;

(2) Solicits, accepts, or receives a promise of anything of value or benefit while the person is connected with a casino, including an officer or employee of a casino operator, management company, or gaming-related vendor, under an agreement to influence or with the intent to influence the actions of the person to affect or attempt to affect the outcome of a casino game or an official action of a commission member;

(3) Uses or possesses with the intent to use a device to assist in projecting the outcome of the game, keeping track of the cards played, analyzing the probability of the occurrence of an event relating to the casino game, or analyzing the strategy for playing or betting to be used in the game, except as permitted by the commission;

(4) Cheats at a casino game;

(5) Manufactures, sells, or distributes any cards, chips, dice, game, or device that is intended to be used to violate this chapter;

(6) Alters or misrepresents the outcome of a casino game on which wagers have been made after the outcome is made sure but before the outcome is revealed to the players;

(7) Places a wager on the outcome of a casino game after acquiring knowledge that is not available to all players and concerns the outcome of the casino game that is the subject of the wager;

(8) Aids a person in acquiring the knowledge described in division (E)(7) of this section for the purpose of placing a wager contingent on the outcome of a casino game;

(9) Claims, collects, takes, or attempts to claim, collect, or take money or anything of value in or from a casino game with the intent to defraud or without having made a wager contingent on winning a casino game;

(10) Claims, collects, or takes an amount of money or thing of value of greater value than the amount won in a casino game;

(11) Uses or possesses counterfeit chips or tokens in or for use in a casino game;

(12) Possesses a key or device designed for opening, entering, or affecting the operation of a casino game, drop box, or an electronic or a mechanical device connected with the casino game or removing coins, tokens, chips, or other contents of a casino game. This division does not apply to a casino operator, management company, or gaming-related vendor or their agents and employees in the course of agency or employment.

(13) Possesses materials used to manufacture a slug or device intended to be used in a manner that violates this chapter;

(14) Operates a casino gaming operation in which wagering is conducted or is to be conducted in a manner other than the manner required under this chapter.

(F) The possession of more than one of the devices described in division (E)(11), (12), or (13) of this section creates a rebuttable presumption that the possessor intended to use the devices for cheating.

(G) A person who is convicted of a felony described in this chapter may be barred for life from entering a casino facility by the commission.

**HISTORY: 153 v H 519, § 1, eff. 9-10-10.**

# CHAPTER 3773: BOXING; DISCHARGING FIREARMS; DUELING



## [HUNTING OR SHOOTING GAME NEAR TOWNSHIP PARK]

### § 3773.06 Hunting or shooting game near township park.

No person shall hunt, shoot, or kill game within one-half mile of a township park.

The board of township park commissioners may grant permission to kill game not desired within the limits prohibited by this section.

**HISTORY: RS § 6986-5; 90 v 175; GC § 12820; Bureau of Code Revision, 10-1-53; 135 v H 295. Eff 7-22-74.**

## [SUPPRESSION OF PRIZE FIGHT]

### § 3773.13 Suppression of prize fight.

When a sheriff has reason to believe that a fight or contention is about to take place in his county, he shall forthwith summon sufficient citizens of the county, suppress such fight or contention, and arrest all persons found at such prize fight violating the law and take them before a judge of the court of common pleas or magistrate.

**HISTORY: GC § 13429-4; 113 v 123 (135), ch. 8, § 4; Bureau of Code Revision. Eff 10-1-53.**

## [PENALTIES]

### § 3773.99 Penalties.

(A) Whoever violates section 3773.06 or 3773.50 of the Revised Code is guilty of a misdemeanor of the fourth degree.

(B) Whoever violates section 3773.32, 3773.40, 3773.44, 3773.45, 3773.46, or 3773.47, division (A) of section 3773.54, or division (B) of section 3773.33 of the Revised Code is guilty of a misdemeanor of the first degree.

(C) Whoever violates section 3773.48 or 3773.49 of the Revised Code is guilty of a minor misdemeanor.

**HISTORY: Bureau of Code Revision, 10-1-53; 126 v 392(404); 128 v 862 (Eff 10-1-59); 129 v 1625 (Eff 10-18-61); 134 v H 511 (Eff 1-1-74); 135 v H 59 (Eff 11-21-73); 135 v H 1041 (Eff 3-20-74); 136 v H 1 (Eff 6-13-75); 139 v S 60 (Eff 7-27-81); 140 v H 133 (Eff 9-27-83); 146 v S 240 (Eff 9-3-96); 148 v S 107. Eff 3-23-2000.**

# TITLE 39: INSURANCE

## CHAPTER 3904: INSURANCE INFORMATION PRACTICES



### § 3904.14 Obtaining information under false pretenses.

(A) No person shall knowingly obtain information under false pretenses about an individual from an insurance institution, agent, or insurance support organization.

(B) Whoever violates division (A) of this section is guilty of a felony of the fourth degree.

**HISTORY: 145 v H 329. Eff 6-29-95.**

The effective date is set by section 2 of HB 329.

## CHAPTER 3937: CASUALTY INSURANCE; MOTOR VEHICLE INSURANCE



[MISCELLANEOUS]

### § 3937.42 Duty to cooperate in investigation of fraudulent claims; use of information.

(A) The chief or head law enforcement officer of any federal, state, or local law enforcement agency or a prosecuting attorney of any county may request any insurance company, or agent authorized by the company to act on its behalf, that has investigated or is investigating a claim involving motor vehicle insurance or vessel insurance to release any information in its possession relevant to the claim. The company or agent shall release the information that is requested in writing by the law enforcement officer.

(B) If an insurance company, or agent authorized by the company to act on its behalf, has reason to suspect that a loss involving a motor vehicle or vessel that is insured by the company is part of a fraudulent scheme to obtain control of insurance proceeds, the company or agent shall notify a law enforcement officer or a prosecuting attorney of any county having jurisdiction over the alleged fraud.

(C) An insurance company, or agent authorized by the company to act on its behalf, shall release any information requested in writing pursuant to division (A) of this section and cooperate with the officer or a prosecuting attorney of any county authorized to request the information. The company or agent shall take such action as may be reasonably requested of it by the officer or a prosecuting attorney of any county and shall permit any other person ordered by a court to inspect any information that is specifically requested by the court.

The information that may be requested pursuant to this section may include, but is not limited to, the following:

(1) Any insurance policy relevant to the claim under investigation and any application for such a policy;

(2) Policy premium payment records;

(3) History of previous claims involving a motor vehicle or vessel made by the insured;

(4) Material relating to the investigation of the claim, including statements of any person, proof of loss, and any other relevant evidence.

(D) If the law enforcement officer or a prosecuting attorney of any county mentioned in division (A) of this section has received information pursuant to this section from an insurance company, or agent authorized by the company to act on its behalf, the officer or a prosecuting attorney of any county may release to, and share with, the insurance company or agent any information in the officer's or prosecuting attorney's possession relative to the claim, upon the written request of the insurance company or agent.

(E) In the absence of fraud, recklessness, or malice, no insurance company, or agent authorized by the company to act on its behalf, is liable for damages in any civil action, including any action brought pursuant to section 1347.10 of the Revised Code for any oral or written statement made or any other action taken that is necessary to supply information required pursuant to this section.

(F) Except as otherwise provided in division (D) of this section, any officer or a prosecuting attorney of any county receiving any information furnished pursuant to this section shall hold the information in confidence and shall not disclose it to anyone except other law enforcement officers or agencies until its release is required pursuant to a criminal or civil proceeding.

(G) Any officer or a prosecuting attorney of any county referred to in division (A) of this section may testify as to any information in the officer's or prosecuting attorney's possession regarding the claim referred to in that division in any civil action in which any person seeks recovery under a policy against an insurance company.

(H) As used in this section:

(1) "Motor vehicle" has the same meaning as in section 4501.01 of the Revised Code.

(2) "Vessel" has the same meaning as in section 1547.01 of the Revised Code.

(I)(1) No person shall purposely refuse to release any information requested pursuant to this section by an officer or a prosecuting attorney of any county authorized by division (A) of this section to request the information.

(2) No person shall purposely refuse to notify an appropriate law enforcement officer or a prosecuting

attorney of any county of a loss required to be reported pursuant to division (B) of this section.

(3) No person shall purposely fail to hold in confidence information required to be held in confidence by division (F) of this section.

**HISTORY: 140 v S 2 (Eff 9-26-84); 147 v S 187. Eff 3-18-99.**

### § 3937.99 Penalties.

(A) Whoever purposely violates sections 3937.01 to 3937.17 of the Revised Code shall be fined not more than five hundred dollars.

(B) Whoever violates division (I) of section 3937.42 of the Revised Code is guilty of a misdemeanor of the fourth degree.

**HISTORY: Bureau of Code Revision, 10-1-53; 140 v S 2. Eff 9-26-84.**

## CHAPTER 3999: CRIMES RELATING TO INSURANCE

Section



### § 3999.02 False statement by medical examiner of insurance company.

No medical examiner for a life insurance company or for an applicant for insurance therein shall knowingly make a false statement or report to such company or to an officer thereof concerning the health or physical condition of an applicant for insurance, or other matter or thing affecting the granting of such insurance.

**HISTORY: RS § 7078; 69 v 159, § 31; GC § 13132; Bureau of Code Revision. Eff 10-1-53.**

### § 3999.03 Life insurance; official or agent issuing fraudulent policies.

No trustee, officer, agent, or employee of a corporation, company, or association organized to transact the business of life or accident or life and accident insurance on the assessment plan shall knowingly insure a person, or permit him to be insured without that person's knowledge or consent, or insure a fictitious person, a person over sixty-five or under fifteen years of age, or a sickly or infirm person.

No physician or other person shall knowingly aid or abet any person in effecting insurance described in this section, or in effecting insurance of his own life.

**HISTORY: RS § 3630g; 80 v 179; 82 v 138; GC §§ 13134, 13135; Bureau of Code Revision. Eff 10-1-53.**

### § 3999.04 Changing life insurance policy.

No life insurance company doing business in this state, or an agent thereof, shall make a contract of insurance, or an agreement as to such contract, other than is plainly expressed in the policy issued thereon.

**HISTORY: RS § 3631-6; 90 v 345, § 3; GC § 13136; Bureau of Code Revision. Eff 10-1-53.**

### § 3999.05 Rebates and other inducements from life insurance companies.

No life insurance company doing business in this state, or an officer, agent, solicitor, or representative thereof, shall pay, allow, or give, or offer to pay, allow, or give, directly or indirectly, as an inducement to insurance, a rebate of the premium payable on a policy, or a special favor or advantage in the dividends or other benefits to accrue thereon, or a paid employment or contract for services of any kind, or any valuable consideration or inducement not specified in the policy of insurance, or give, sell, or purchase, or offer to give, sell, or purchase, as an inducement for insurance, any stocks, bonds, or securities of an insurance company or other corporation, association, or partnership, or any dividends or profits to accrue thereon, or anything of value not specified in the policy.

**HISTORY: RS § 3631-6; 90 v 345, § 3; GC § 13137; Bureau of Code Revision. Eff 10-1-53.**

### § 3999.07 Sale or assignment of premium note before delivery of policy.

No person, having accepted a premium note in payment of the purchase price of a policy of insurance, shall sell or assign such note prior to the delivery and acceptance of such policy.

**HISTORY: GC § 13149-1; 101 v 120; Bureau of Code Revision. Eff 10-1-53.**

## § 3999.08 Misrepresentations in soliciting insurance.

No person for himself or as an officer, director, agent, solicitor, or representative of any insurance company, except fire insurance companies or associations or fraternal benefit societies, doing business in this state, shall issue, circulate, or cause or permit to be issued or circulated any estimate, illustration, circular, or statement of any sort misrepresenting the terms of the policy issued or to be issued by such company or the benefits or advantages promised thereby or the dividends or shares or surplus to be received thereon. No person shall use any name or title of any policy or class of policies misrepresenting the true nature thereof, or make, circulate, use, or cause to be made, circulated, or used, any illustration, circular, or statement, whether written or oral, misrepresenting the terms of any policy issued by any such corporation, or the benefits or advantages promised thereby, or any misleading estimate of the dividends or shares of surplus to be received therefrom. No person shall make any misleading representations or incomplete comparison of policies or certificates of insurance to any person insured in any such corporation for the purpose of inducing or tending to induce such person to lapse, forfeit, or surrender his said insurance. Fines collected for violations of this section shall be paid to the county treasurer for the use of the schools as provided in sections 3315.31 and 3315.32 of the Revised Code.

Upon any such conviction the superintendent of insurance shall revoke, for not more than one year, the license of the person, firm, corporation, or association so offending. The superintendent, when he is of the opinion that any company or association writing life insurance in this state, on any plan, is knowingly permitting any of its agents to violate this section, shall give such company or association reasonable notice of a hearing upon the charge of knowingly permitting this section to be violated, and if he finds said company or association guilty of the offense, he shall revoke its license.

**HISTORY: GC § 13171; 99 v 176, § 3; 102 v 509; 106 v 235; 110 v 112; 120 v 358(403), § 2; Bureau of Code Revision. Eff 10-1-53.**

## § 3999.09 False or malicious statements about insurance company.

No company doing business in this state, or any officer, director, clerk, employee, or agent thereof, shall make, orally or otherwise, publish, print, distribute, or circulate, or cause the same to be done, or aid, abet, or encourage the making, printing, publishing, distributing, or circulating of, any pamphlet, circular, article, literature, or statement of any kind which is defamatory of any insurance company doing business in this state, or which contains any false and malicious criticism or false and malicious statement calculated to injure such company in its reputation or business. No officer, director, clerk, employee, or agent of any company shall violate this section.

**HISTORY: GC § 13171-1; 115 v 345, § 2; Bureau of Code Revision. Eff 10-1-53.**

## § 3999.13 Unlawful reinsurance.

No officer, director, or stockholder of a company organized under the laws of this state to do the business of life, accident, or health insurance, either on the stock, mutual, stipulated premiums, assessment, or fraternal plan, shall violate or consent to a violation of any law governing or forbidding the reinsurance of the risks, or any part thereof, or the consolidation of such company with any other company or association, or the assumption of reinsurance of the whole or any portion of the risks of another company by such company.

**HISTORY: RS § 3597; S&S 218; 69 v 150, § 2; 77 v 267; 94 v 103; GC § 13416; Bureau of Code Revision. Eff 10-1-53.**

## § 3999.14 Foreign life insurance companies on the assessment plan.

No officer or agent of a corporation, company, or association organized under the laws of any other state of the United States to transact the business of life or accident insurance or life and accident insurance on the assessment plan, shall violate or fail to comply with any law relating to such corporation, company, or association.

**HISTORY: RS §§ 3630e, 3630g; 77 v 181; 80 v 179; 80 v 180; 82 v 138; 88 v 252; 97 v 144; GC § 13417; Bureau of Code Revision. Eff 10-1-53.**

## § 3999.15 Violations by accident insurance companies and officers thereof.

No company organized under the laws of this state for the special purpose of insuring against accidental personal injury and loss of life sustained while traveling by railroad, steamboat, or other mode of conveyance, against accidental personal injury and loss of life sustained by accident of every description, and against expenses and loss of time occasioned by injury or sickness, on such terms, and for such periods of time, and confined to such countries and localities and to such persons as from time to time may be provided in the bylaws of such company, or any officer of such company, shall violate any law relating to such company.

**HISTORY: RS § 3630i; 84 v 130; 91 v 332; 97 v 435; GC § 13418; Bureau of Code Revision. Eff 10-1-53.**

[FALSE HEALTH INSURANCE CLAIMS]

## § 3999.22 Prohibitions relating to health insurance referrals.

(A) As used in this section:

(1) "Claim" means any attempt to cause a health care insurer to make payment of a health care benefit.

(2) "Health care benefit" means the right under a contract or a certificate or policy of insurance to have a payment made by a health care insurer for a specified health care service.

(3) "Health care insurer" means any person that is authorized to do the business of sickness and accident insurance, any health insuring corporation, and any legal entity that is self-insured and provides health care benefits to its employees or members.

(B) No person shall knowingly solicit, offer, pay, or receive any kickback, bribe, or rebate, directly or indirectly, overtly or covertly, in cash or in kind, in return for referring an individual for the furnishing of health care services or goods for which whole or partial reimbursement is or may be made by a health care insurer, except as authorized by the health care or health insurance contract, policy, or plan. This division does not apply to any of the following:

(1) Deductibles, copayments, or similar amounts owed by the person covered by the health care or health insurance contract, policy, or plan;

(2) Discounts or similar reductions in prices;

(3) Any amount paid within a bona fide legal entity, or within legal entities under common ownership or control, including any amount paid to an employee in a bona fide employment relationship;

(4) Any amount paid as part of a bona fide lease, management, or other business contract.

(C) Nothing in this section shall be construed to apply to any of the following:

(1) A provider who provides goods or services requested by an individual that are not covered by the individual's health care or health insurance contract, policy, or plan;

(2) A provider who, in good faith, provides goods or services ordered by another health care provider;

(3) A provider who, in good faith, resubmits a claim previously submitted that has not been paid or denied within thirty days of the original submission, if the provider notifies the payor or returns any duplicate payment within sixty days after receipt of the duplicate payment;

(4) A provider who, in good faith, makes a diagnosis that differs from the interpretation of a diagnosis reached by a health care insurer in the payment of claims.

(D) Whoever violates this section is guilty of a felony of the fifth degree on a first offense and a felony of the fourth degree on each subsequent offense.

**HISTORY: 146 v S 269 (Eff 7-1-96); 147 v H 698. Eff 3-22-99.**

**Analogous to former RC § 3999.22 (141 v S 18; 143 v H 347), repealed, 146 v S 2, § 2, eff 7-1-96.**

## § 3999.32 Group policy or contract holder and health insurer to give notice of failure to pay premium.

(A) As used in this section:

(1) "Certificate holder" means any person whose employment or retirement status is the basis of eligibility for coverage under a group policy of sickness and accident insurance or for enrollment under a group contract of a health insuring corporation.

(2) "Health insurer" means any sickness and accident insurer or health insuring corporation.

(B) Each person to whom a group policy or contract of sickness and accident insurance or other health care coverage has been delivered or issued for delivery in this state by a health insurer shall make a reasonable effort to notify every certificate holder, or certificate holder's designee, who is covered under that policy or contract whenever the person fails to make a required premium payment or contribution on behalf of the certificate holder and that failure results in the termination of coverage. The person shall mail or present the notice to the certificate holder or certificate holder's designee no later than five days after the date on which the person receives the notice from the health insurer as required under division (D) of this section. If a person other than the policyholder or contract holder is obligated to make the required premium payment or contribution on behalf of the certificate holder, that person shall mail or present the notice as required by this section.

(C) The notice required by division (B) of this section shall be in writing and shall clearly state that the person failed to make the required premium payment or contribution, the reasons for the failure, and the effect of the failure on the coverage of the certificate holder under the policy or contract.

(D) If a person described in division (B) of this section fails to make a required premium payment or contribution on behalf of a certificate holder and that failure results in the termination of the coverage, the health insurer providing the coverage shall notify the person in writing of that person's duties as described in divisions (B) and (C) of this section. If a person other than the policyholder or contract holder is obligated to make the required premium payment or contribution on behalf of the certificate holder, the insurer shall notify the person in writing of that person's duties as described in divisions (B) and (C) of this section.

(E) A certificate holder may designate any person to receive on the certificate holder's behalf the notice required by division (B) of this section. The certificate holder shall furnish the name and address of the person so designated to the person to whom the group policy or contract has been delivered or issued for delivery.

(F) No person shall knowingly fail to comply with division (B) or (C) of this section.

**HISTORY: 144 v H 11 (Eff 5-14-92); 147 v S 67. Eff 6-4-97.**

### [IMPAIRED INSURERS]

## § 3999.36 Chief executive officer of insurer to give notice of impairment.

(A) As used in this section and sections 3999.37 and 3999.38 of the Revised Code:

(1) "Insurer" means any person that is authorized to engage in the business of insurance in this state under Title XXXIX [39] of the Revised Code, any health insuring corporation, or any other person engaging either directly or indirectly in this state in the business of insurance or entering into contracts substantially amounting to insurance under section 3905.42 of the Revised Code.

(2) "Impaired" or "impairment" means a financial situation in which the insurer's assets are less than the sum of the insurer's minimum required capital, minimum required surplus, and all liabilities, as determined in accordance with the requirements for the preparation and filing of the insurer's annual financial statement.

(3) "Chief executive officer" means the person, irrespective of the person's title, designated by the board of directors or trustees of an insurer as the person charged with the responsibility of administering and implementing the insurer's policies and procedures.

(B) Whenever a chief executive officer of an insurer knows or has reason to know that the insurer is impaired, the chief executive officer shall provide written notice of the impairment to the superintendent of insurance and to each member of the board of directors or trustees of the insurer. The chief executive officer shall provide the notice as soon as reasonably possible, but no later than thirty days after the chief executive officer knows or has reason to know of the impairment. No chief executive officer shall fail to provide notice in compliance with this division.

(C) The notice received by the superintendent under division (B) of this section is confidential and is not a public record under section 149.43 of the Revised Code.

(D) Notwithstanding division (C) of this section, the superintendent may do any of the following:

(1) Disclose the notice upon obtaining prior written consent from the insurer to which the notice pertains;

(2) Share the notice that is the subject of this section with the chief deputy rehabilitator, the chief deputy liquidator, other deputy rehabilitators and liquidators, and any other person employed by, or acting on behalf of, the superintendent pursuant to Chapter 3901. or 3903. of the Revised Code, with other local, state, federal, and international regulatory and law enforcement agencies, with local, state, and federal prosecutors, and with the national association of insurance commissioners and its affiliates and subsidiaries, provided that the recipient agrees to maintain the confidential status of the notice and has authority to do so;

(3) Disclose the notice in the furtherance of any regulatory or legal action brought by or on behalf of the superintendent or the state, resulting from the exercise of the superintendent's official duties.

(E) Notwithstanding divisions (C) and (D) of this section, the superintendent may authorize the national association of insurance commissioners and its affiliates and subsidiaries by agreement to share confidential notices received pursuant to division (D)(2) of this section with local, state, federal, and international regulatory and law enforcement agencies and with local, state, and federal prosecutors, provided that the recipient agrees to maintain the confidential status of the notice and has authority to do so.

(F) Notwithstanding divisions (C) and (D) of this section, the chief deputy rehabilitator, the chief deputy liquidator and other deputy rehabilitators and liquidators may disclose notices in the furtherance of any regulatory or legal action brought by or on behalf of the superintendent, the rehabilitator, the liquidator, or the state resulting from the exercise of the superintendent's official duties in any capacity.

(G) Nothing in this section shall prohibit the superintendent from receiving notices in accordance with section 3901.045 [3901.04.5] of the Revised Code.

(H) The superintendent may enter into agreements governing the sharing and use of notices consistent with the requirements of this section.

(I)(1) No waiver of any applicable privilege or claim of confidentiality in the notices that are the subject of this section shall occur as a result of sharing or receiving notices as authorized in divisions (D)(2), (E), and (G) of this section.

(2) The disclosure of a notice in connection with a regulatory or legal action pursuant to divisions (D)(3) and (F) of this section does not prohibit an insurer or any other person from taking steps to limit the dissemination of the notice to persons not involved in or the subject of the regulatory or legal action on the basis of any recognized privilege arising under any other section of the Revised Code or the common law.

**HISTORY: 144 v S 137 (Eff 8-8-91); 147 v S 67 (Eff 6-4-97); 149 v S 138. Eff 6-18-2002.**

## § 3999.37 Fraudulent acts concerning impairment or insolvency of insurer.

No person shall do any of the following:

(A) Conceal any property belonging to an insurer;

(B) Transfer or conceal his own property or property belonging to an insurer in contemplation of a proceeding under Chapter 3903. of the Revised Code;

(C) Conceal, destroy, mutilate, alter, or make a false entry in any document that affects or relates to the property of an insurer;

(D) Withhold any document that affects or relates to the property of an insurer from a receiver, trustee, or other officer of a court entitled to its possession;

(E) Give, obtain, or receive anything of value for acting or forbearing to act in any judicial proceeding, if the act results in or contributes to the impairment or insolvency of any insurer.

**HISTORY: 144 v S 137. Eff 8-8-91.**

## § 3999.38 Dividend prohibited while impaired.

No insurer shall knowingly declare or pay any dividend whenever the insurer is impaired. For purposes of this section, "insurer" also includes any person doing the business of insurance in this state.

**HISTORY: 144 v S 137. Eff 8-8-91.**

## § 3999.99 Penalties.

(A) Whoever violates section 3999.02 of the Revised Code is guilty of a misdemeanor of the second degree.

(B) Whoever violates section 3999.03, 3999.07, 3999.13, 3999.14, or 3999.15 of the Revised Code is guilty of a misdemeanor of the first degree.

(C) Whoever violates section 3999.04, 3999.05, 3999.08, or 3999.09 of the Revised Code is guilty of a misdemeanor of the fourth degree.

(D) Whoever violates section 3999.10 or 3999.11 of the Revised Code shall be fined five hundred dollars for a first offense and shall be fined one thousand dollars for each subsequent offense.

(E) Whoever violates section 3999.12 of the Revised Code shall be fined not less than ten nor more than one thousand dollars.

(F) Whoever violates division (F) of section 3999.32, division (B) of section 3999.36, or section 3999.37 or 3999.38 of the Revised Code is guilty of a felony of the fourth degree.

(G) Whoever violates division (A) of section 3999.18 of the Revised Code is guilty of a felony of the fourth degree.

(H) Whoever violates division (B) of section 3999.18 of the Revised Code is guilty of a misdemeanor of the first degree on a first offense and a felony of the fifth degree on each subsequent offense.

(I) If a person is found guilty under this section, the court may award restitution in accordance with section 2929.18 of the Revised Code.

**HISTORY: Bureau of Code Revision, 10-1-53; 126 v 575 (Eff 10-6-55); 134 v H 511 (Eff 1-1-74); 140 v S 4 (Eff 9-26-84); 144 v S 137 (Eff 8-8-91); 144 v H 11 (Eff 5-14-92); 146 v S 2. Eff 7-1-96; 150 v H 281, § 1, eff. 7-2-04.**

The effective date is set by section 6 of SB 2.

# TITLE 41: LABOR AND INDUSTRY

## CHAPTER 4112: CIVIL RIGHTS COMMISSION



### § 4112.01 Definitions; pregnancy, childbirth, related medical conditions; abortion.

(A) As used in this chapter:

(1) "Person" includes one or more individuals, partnerships, associations, organizations, corporations, legal representatives, trustees, trustees in bankruptcy, receivers, and other organized groups of persons. "Person" also includes, but is not limited to, any owner, lessor, assignor, builder, manager, broker, salesperson, appraiser, agent, employee, lending institution, and the state and all political subdivisions, authorities, agencies, boards, and commissions of the state.

(2) "Employer" includes the state, any political subdivision of the state, any person employing four or more persons within the state, and any person acting directly or indirectly in the interest of an employer.

(3) "Employee" means an individual employed by any employer but does not include any individual employed in the domestic service of any person.

(4) "Labor organization" includes any organization that exists, in whole or in part, for the purpose of collective bargaining or of dealing with employers concerning grievances, terms or conditions of employment, or other mutual aid or protection in relation to employment.

(5) "Employment agency" includes any person regularly undertaking, with or without compensation, to procure opportunities to work or to procure, recruit, refer, or place employees.

(6) "Commission" means the Ohio civil rights commission created by section 4112.03 of the Revised Code.

(7) "Discriminate" includes segregate or separate.

(8) "Unlawful discriminatory practice" means any act prohibited by section 4112.02, 4112.021 [4112.02.1], or 4112.022 [4112.02.2] of the Revised Code.

(9) "Place of public accommodation" means any inn, restaurant, eating house, barbershop, public conveyance by air, land, or water, theater, store, other place for the sale of merchandise, or any other place of public accommodation or amusement of which the accommodations, advantages, facilities, or privileges are available to the public.

(10) "Housing accommodations" includes any building or structure, or portion of a building or structure, that is used or occupied or is intended, arranged, or designed to be used or occupied as the home residence, dwelling, dwelling unit, or sleeping place of one or more individuals, groups, or families whether or not living independently of each other; and any vacant land offered for sale or lease. "Housing accommodations" also includes any housing accommodations held or offered for sale or rent by a real estate broker, salesperson, or agent, by any other person pursuant to authorization of the owner, by the owner, or by the owner's legal representative.

(11) "Restrictive covenant" means any specification limiting the transfer, rental, lease, or other use of any housing accommodations because of race, color, religion, sex, military status, familial status, national origin, disability, or ancestry, or any limitation based upon affiliation with or approval by any person, directly or indirectly, employing race, color, religion, sex, military status, familial status, national origin, disability, or ancestry as a condition of affiliation or approval.

(12) "Burial lot" means any lot for the burial of deceased persons within any public burial ground or cemetery, including, but not limited to, cemeteries owned and operated by municipal corporations, townships, or companies or associations incorporated for cemetery purposes.

(13) "Disability" means a physical or mental impairment that substantially limits one or more major life activities, including the functions of caring for one's self, performing manual tasks, walking, seeing, hearing, speaking, breathing, learning, and working; a record of a physical or mental impairment; or being regarded as having a physical or mental impairment.

(14) Except as otherwise provided in section 4112.021 [4112.02.1] of the Revised Code, "age" means at least forty years old.

(15) "Familial status" means either of the following:

(a) One or more individuals who are under eighteen years of age and who are domiciled with a parent or guardian having legal custody of the individual or domiciled, with the written permission of the parent or guardian having legal custody, with a designee of the parent or guardian;

(b) Any person who is pregnant or in the process of securing legal custody of any individual who is under eighteen years of age.

(16)(a) Except as provided in division (A)(16)(b) of this section, "physical or mental impairment" includes any of the following:

(i) Any physiological disorder or condition, cosmetic disfigurement, or anatomical loss affecting one or more of the following body systems: neurological; musculoskeletal; special sense organs; respiratory, including speech organs; cardiovascular; reproductive; digestive; genito-urinary; hemic and lymphatic; skin; and endocrine;

(ii) Any mental or psychological disorder, including, but not limited to, mental retardation, organic brain syndrome, emotional or mental illness, and specific learning disabilities;

(iii) Diseases and conditions, including, but not limited to, orthopedic, visual, speech, and hearing impairments, cerebral palsy, autism, epilepsy, muscular dystrophy, multiple sclerosis, cancer, heart disease, diabetes, human immunodeficiency virus infection, mental retardation, emotional illness, drug addiction, and alcoholism.

(b) "Physical or mental impairment" does not include any of the following:

(i) Homosexuality and bisexuality;

(ii) Transvestism, transsexualism, pedophilia, exhibitionism, voyeurism, gender identity disorders not resulting from physical impairments, or other sexual behavior disorders;

(iii) Compulsive gambling, kleptomania, or pyromania;

(iv) Psychoactive substance use disorders resulting from the current illegal use of a controlled substance or the current use of alcoholic beverages.

(17) "Dwelling unit" means a single unit of residence for a family of one or more persons.

(18) "Common use areas" means rooms, spaces, or elements inside or outside a building that are made available for the use of residents of the building or their guests, and includes, but is not limited to, hallways, lounges, lobbies, laundry rooms, refuse rooms, mail rooms, recreational areas, and passageways among and between buildings.

(19) "Public use areas" means interior or exterior rooms or spaces of a privately or publicly owned building that are made available to the general public.

(20) "Controlled substance" has the same meaning as in section 3719.01 of the Revised Code.

(21) "Disabled tenant" means a tenant or prospective tenant who is a person with a disability.

(22) "Military status" means a person's status in "service in the uniformed services" as defined in section 5923.05 of the Revised Code.

(23) "Aggrieved person" includes both of the following:

(a) Any person who claims to have been injured by any unlawful discriminatory practice described in division (H) of section 4112.02 of the Revised Code;

(b) Any person who believes that the person will be injured by, any unlawful discriminatory practice described in division (H) of section 4112.02 of the Revised Code that is about to occur.

(B) For the purposes of divisions (A) to (F) of section 4112.02 of the Revised Code, the terms "because of sex" and "on the basis of sex" include, but are not limited to, because of or on the basis of pregnancy, any illness arising out of and occurring during the course of a pregnancy, childbirth, or related medical conditions. Women affected by pregnancy, childbirth, or related medical conditions shall be treated the same for all employment-related purposes, including receipt of benefits under fringe benefit programs, as other persons not so affected but similar in their ability or inability to work, and nothing in division (B) of section 4111.17 of the Revised Code shall be interpreted to permit otherwise. This division shall not be construed to require an employer to pay for health insurance benefits for abortion, except where the life of the mother would be endangered if the fetus were carried to term or except where medical complications have arisen from the abortion, provided that nothing in this division precludes an employer from providing abortion benefits or otherwise affects bargaining agreements in regard to abortion.

**HISTORY: 128 v 12 (Eff 7-29-59); 129 v 582 (860) (Eff 1-10-61); 129 v 1694 (Eff 10-24-61); 131 v 980 (Eff 10-30-65); 133 v H 47 (Eff 10-24-69); 133 v H 432 (Eff 11-12-69); 135 v H 610 (Eff 12-19-73); 136 v S 162 (Eff 7-23-76); 138 v H 230 (Eff 11-13-79); 138 v H 19 (Eff 1-10-80); 143 v H 314 (Eff 5-31-90); 144 v H 321 (Eff 6-30-92); 148 v H 264. Eff 3-17-2000; 151 v H 187, § 1, eff. 7-1-07; 152 v H 372, § 1, eff. 3-24-08; 152 v S 289, § 1, eff. 8-22-08; 153 v H 1, § 101.01, eff. 10-16-09.**

The effective date is set by § 812.10 of 153 v H 1.
The effective date is set by § 7 of 151 v H 187.

# CHAPTER 4117: PUBLIC EMPLOYEES' COLLECTIVE BARGAINING

Section



## § 4117.10 Terms of agreement; grievance arbitration, procedure; approval by legislative body; office of collective bargaining.

(A) An agreement between a public employer and an exclusive representative entered into pursuant to this chapter governs the wages, hours, and terms and conditions of public employment covered by the agreement. If the agreement provides for a final and binding arbitration of grievances, public employers, employees, and employee organizations are subject solely to that grievance procedure and the state personnel board of review or civil service commissions have no jurisdiction to receive and determine any appeals relating to matters that were the subject of a final and binding grievance procedure. Where no agreement exists or where an agreement makes no specification about a matter, the public employer and public employees are subject to all applicable state or local laws or ordinances pertaining to the wages, hours, and terms and conditions of employment for public employees. Laws pertaining to civil rights, affirmative action, unemployment compensation, workers' compensation, the retirement of public employees, and residency requirements, the minimum educational requirements contained in the Revised Code pertaining to public education including the requirement of a certificate by the fiscal officer of a school district pursuant to section 5705.41 of the Revised Code, the provisions of division (A) of section 124.34 of the Revised Code governing the disciplining of officers and employees who have been convicted of a felony, and the minimum standards promulgated by the state board of education pursuant to division (D) of section 3301.07 of the Revised Code prevail over conflicting provisions of agreements between employee organizations and public employers. The law pertaining to the leave of absence and compensation provided under section 5923.05 of the Revised Code prevails over any conflicting provisions of such agreements if the terms of the agreement contain benefits which are less than those contained in that section or the agreement contains no such terms and the public authority is the state or any agency, authority, commission, or board of the state or if the public authority is another entity listed in division (B) of section 4117.01 of the Revised Code that elects to provide leave of absence and compensation as provided in section 5923.05 of the Revised Code. The law pertaining to the leave established under section 5906.02 of the Revised Code prevails over any conflicting provision of an agreement between an employee organization and public employer if the terms of the agreement contain benefits that are less than those contained in section 5906.02 of the Revised Code. Except for sections 306.08, 306.12, 306.35, and 4981.22 of the Revised Code and arrangements entered into thereunder, and section 4981.21 of the Revised Code as necessary to comply with section 13(c) of the "Urban Mass Transportation Act of 1964," 87 Stat. 295, 49 U.S.C.A. 1609(c), as amended, and arrangements entered into thereunder, this chapter prevails over any and all other conflicting laws, resolutions, provisions, present or future, except as otherwise specified in this chapter or as otherwise specified by the general assembly. Nothing in this section prohibits or shall be construed to invalidate the provisions of an agreement establishing supplemental workers' compensation or unemployment compensation benefits or exceeding minimum requirements contained in the Revised Code pertaining to public education or the minimum standards promulgated by the state board of education pursuant to division (D) of section 3301.07 of the Revised Code.

(B) The public employer shall submit a request for funds necessary to implement an agreement and for approval of any other matter requiring the approval of the appropriate legislative body to the legislative body within fourteen days of the date on which the parties finalize the agreement, unless otherwise specified, but if the appropriate legislative body is not in session at the time, then within fourteen days after it convenes. The legislative body must approve or reject the submission as a whole, and the submission is deemed approved if the legislative body fails to act within thirty days after the public employer submits the agreement. The parties may specify that those provisions of the agreement not requiring action by a legislative body are effective and operative in accordance with the terms of the agreement, provided there has been compliance with division (C) of this section. If the legislative body rejects the submission of the public employer, either party may reopen all or part of the entire agreement.

As used in this section, "legislative body" includes the governing board of a municipal corporation, school district, college or university, village, township, or board of county commissioners or any other body that has authority to approve the budget of their public jurisdiction and, with regard to the state, "legislative body" means the controlling board.

(C) The chief executive officer, or the chief executive officer's representative, of each municipal corporation, the designated representative of the board of education of each school district, college or university, or any other body that has authority to approve the budget of their public jurisdiction, the designated representative of the board of county commissioners and of each elected officeholder of the county whose employees are covered by the collective negotiations, and the designated representative of the village or the board of township trustees of each township is responsible for negotiations in the collective bargaining process; except that the legislative body may accept or reject a proposed collective bargaining agreement. When the matters about which there is agreement are reduced to writing and approved by the employee organization and the legislative body, the agreement is binding upon the legislative body, the employer, and the employee organization and employees covered by the agreement.

(D) There is hereby established an office of collective bargaining in the department of administrative services for the purpose of negotiating with and entering into written agreements between state agencies, departments, boards, and commissions and the exclusive representative on matters of wages, hours, terms and other conditions of employment and the continuation, modification, or deletion of an existing provision of a collective bargaining agreement. Nothing in any provision of law to the contrary shall be interpreted as excluding the bureau of workers' compensation and the industrial commission from the preceding sentence. This office shall not negotiate on behalf of other statewide elected officials or boards of trustees of state institutions of higher education who shall be considered as separate public employers for the purposes of this chapter; however, the office may negotiate on behalf of these officials or trustees where authorized by the officials or trustees. The staff of the office of collective bargaining are in the unclassified service. The director of administrative services shall fix the compensation of the staff.

The office of collective bargaining shall:

(1) Assist the director in formulating management's philosophy for public collective bargaining as well as planning bargaining strategies;

(2) Conduct negotiations with the exclusive representatives of each employee organization;

(3) Coordinate the state's resources in all mediation, fact-finding, and arbitration cases as well as in all labor disputes;

(4) Conduct systematic reviews of collective bargaining agreements for the purpose of contract negotiations;

(5) Coordinate the systematic compilation of data by all agencies that is required for negotiating purposes;

(6) Prepare and submit an annual report and other reports as requested to the governor and the general assembly on the implementation of this chapter and its impact upon state government.

**HISTORY: 140 v S 133 (Eff 10-6-83); 140 v S 86 (Eff 9-20-84); 144 v S 3 (Eff 4-17-91); 145 v H 107; (Eff 10-20 93); 147 v H 348. Eff 3-22-99; 151 v H 66, § 101.01, eff. 9-29-05; 153 v H 48, § 1, eff. 7-2-10.**

This section was amended by Senate Bill 5 of the 2011 legislative session. However, referendum petitions were filed to prevent SB 5 from taking effect as scheduled on July 1, 2011. The provisions of SB 5 were rejected by the voters at the referendum election on November 8, 2011.

The effective date is set by § 612.03 of 151 v H 66.

# CHAPTER 4163: ATOMIC ENERGY

Section



## § 4163.07 Notification prior to shipment of nuclear materials within, into, or through the state.

(A)(1) Prior to transporting any high-level radioactive waste, spent nuclear fuel, transuranic waste, or any quantity of special nuclear material or by-product material that meets or exceeds the highway route controlled quantity, within, into, or through the state, the shipper of the material shall notify the executive director of the emergency management agency established under section 5502.22 of the Revised Code of the shipment. The notice shall be in writing and be sent by certified mail and shall include the name of the shipper; the name of the carrier; the type and quantity of the material; the transportation mode of the shipment; the proposed date and time of shipment of the material within, into, or through the state; and the starting point, termination or exit point, scheduled route, and each alternate route, if any, of the shipment. In order to constitute effective notification under division

(A)(1) of this section, notification shall be received by the executive director at least four days prior to shipment within, into, or through the state.

(2) The carrier or shipper of any shipment subject to division (A)(1) of this section shall immediately notify the executive director of any change in the date and time of the shipment or in the route of the shipment within, into, or through the state.

(B) Upon receipt of a notice of any shipment of material that is subject to division (A)(1) of this section within, into, or through the state, the executive director of the emergency management agency shall immediately notify the director of public safety, the director of environmental protection, the director of health, the chairperson of the public utilities commission, and the county emergency management agency and sheriff of each county along the proposed route, or any alternate route, of the shipment.

(C) The executive director of the emergency management agency shall not disclose to any person other than those persons enumerated in division (B) of this section any information pertaining to any shipment of special nuclear material or by-product material prior to the time that the shipment is completed.

(D) This section does not apply to radioactive materials, other than by-products, shipped by or for the United States department of defense and United States department of energy for military or national defense purposes. Nothing in this section requires the disclosure of any defense information or restricted data as defined in the "Atomic Energy Act of 1954," 68 Stat. 919, 42 U.S.C. 2011, as amended.

(E) No person shall transport or cause to be transported within, into, or through the state any material that is subject to division (A)(1) of this section without first providing the notice required in that division.

(F) Whoever violates division (E) of this section, in addition to any penalty imposed under section 4163.99 of the Revised Code, is liable for a civil penalty in an amount not to exceed the following, as applicable:

(1) Twenty-five thousand dollars for a motor carrier;

(2) Forty-five thousand dollars for the first cask designated for transport by rail and thirty thousand dollars for each additional cask designated for transport by rail that is shipped by the same person or entity in the same shipment.

The attorney general, upon the request of the executive director of the emergency management agency, shall bring a civil action to collect the penalty. Fines collected pursuant to this section shall be deposited into the state treasury to the credit of the radioactive waste transportation fund created in section 4905.801 of the Revised Code.

**HISTORY: 138 v S 208 (Eff 7-14-80); 142 v H 131 (Eff 6-29-88); 144 v S 98 (Eff 11-12-92); 146 v S 162 (Eff 10-29-95); 148 v H 283. Eff 9-29-99; 153 v H 2, § 101.01, eff. 7-1-09; 2011 HB 114, § 101.01, eff. June 29, 2011.**

Acts 2011, HB 114, § 806.10 provides: "The items of law contained in this act, and their applications, are severable. If any item of law contained in this act, or if any application of any item of law contained in this act, is held invalid, the invalidity does not affect other items of law contained in this act and their applications that can be given effect without the invalid item or application."

The effective date is set by § 812.10 of 153 v H 2.

The effective date is set by section 162 of HB 283.

## § 4163.99 Penalty.

Whoever violates division (E) of section 4163.07 of the Revised Code is guilty of a felony of the fourth degree. Each shipment made in violation of that division is a separate offense.

**HISTORY: 138 v S 208 (Eff 7-14-80); 146 v S 2. Eff 7-1-96.**

The effective date is set by section 6 of SB 2.

# TITLE 43: LIQUOR

## CHAPTER 4301: LIQUOR CONTROL LAW



### § 4301.01 Definitions.

(A) As used in the Revised Code:

(1) "Intoxicating liquor" and "liquor" include all liquids and compounds, other than beer, containing one-half of one per cent or more of alcohol by volume which are fit to use for beverage purposes, from whatever source and by whatever process produced, by whatever name called, and whether they are medicated, proprietary, or patented. "Intoxicating liquor" and "liquor" include wine even if it contains less than four per cent of alcohol by volume, mixed beverages even if they contain less than four per cent of alcohol by volume, cider, alcohol, and all solids and confections which contain any alcohol.

(2) Except as used in sections 4301.01 to 4301.20, 4301.22 to 4301.52, 4301.56, 4301.70, 4301.72, and 4303.01 to 4303.36 of the Revised Code, "sale" and "sell" include exchange, barter, gift, offer for sale, sale, distribution and delivery of any kind, and the transfer of title or possession of beer and intoxicating liquor either by constructive or actual delivery by any means or devices whatever, including the sale of beer or intoxicating liquor by means of a controlled access alcohol and beverage cabinet pursuant to section 4301.21 of the Revised Code. "Sale" and "sell" do not include the mere solicitation of orders for beer or intoxicating liquor from the holders of permits issued by the division of liquor control authorizing the sale of the beer or intoxicating liquor, but no solicitor shall solicit any such orders until the solicitor has been registered with the division pursuant to section 4303.25 of the Revised Code.

(3) "Vehicle" includes all means of transportation by land, by water, or by air, and everything made use of in any way for such transportation.

(B) As used in this chapter:

(1) "Alcohol" means ethyl alcohol, whether rectified or diluted with water or not, whatever its origin may be, and includes synthetic ethyl alcohol. "Alcohol" does not include denatured alcohol and wood alcohol.

(2) "Beer" includes all beverages brewed or fermented wholly or in part from malt products and containing one-half of one per cent or more, but not more than twelve per cent, of alcohol by volume.

(3) "Wine" includes all liquids fit to use for beverage purposes containing not less than one-half of one per cent of alcohol by volume and not more than twenty-one per cent of alcohol by volume, which is made from the fermented juices of grapes, fruits, or other agricultural products, except that as used in sections 4301.13, 4301.421 [4301.42.1], 4301.422 [4301.42.2], 4301.432 [4301.43.2], and 4301.44 of the Revised Code, and, for purposes of determining the rate of the tax that applies, division (B) of section 4301.43 of the Revised Code, "wine" does not include cider.

(4) "Mixed beverages," such as bottled and prepared cordials, cocktails, and highballs, are products obtained by mixing any type of whiskey, neutral spirits, brandy, gin, or other distilled spirits with, or over, carbonated or plain water, pure juices from flowers and plants, and other flavoring materials. The completed product shall contain not less than one-half of one per cent of alcohol by volume and not more than twenty-one per cent of alcohol by volume.

(5) "Spirituous liquor" includes all intoxicating liquors containing more than twenty-one per cent of alcohol by volume.

(6) "Sealed container" means any container having a capacity of not more than one hundred twenty-eight fluid ounces, the opening of which is closed to prevent the entrance of air.

(7) "Person" includes firms and corporations.

(8) "Manufacture" includes all processes by which beer or intoxicating liquor is produced, whether by distillation, rectifying, fortifying, blending, fermentation, or brewing, or in any other manner.

(9) "Manufacturer" means any person engaged in the business of manufacturing beer or intoxicating liquor.

(10) "Wholesale distributor" and "distributor" means a person engaged in the business of selling to retail dealers for purposes of resale.

(11) "Hotel" has the same meaning as in section 3731.01 of the Revised Code, subject to the exceptions mentioned in section 3731.03 of the Revised Code.

(12) "Restaurant" means a place located in a permanent building provided with space and accommodations wherein, in consideration of the payment of money, hot meals are habitually prepared, sold, and served at noon and evening, as the principal business of the place. "Restaurant" does not include pharmacies, confectionery stores, lunch stands, night clubs, and filling stations.

(13) "Club" means a corporation or association of individuals organized in good faith for social, recreational, benevolent, charitable, fraternal, political, patriotic, or athletic purposes, which is the owner, lessor, or occupant of a permanent building or part of a permanent building operated solely for those purposes, membership in which entails the prepayment of regular dues, and includes the place so operated.

(14) "Night club" means a place operated for profit, where food is served for consumption on the premises and one or more forms of amusement are provided or permitted for a consideration that may be in the form of a cover charge or may be included in the price of the food and beverages, or both, purchased by patrons.

(15) "At retail" means for use or consumption by the purchaser and not for resale.

(16) "Pharmacy" means an establishment, as defined in section 4729.01 of the Revised Code, that is under the management or control of a licensed pharmacist in accordance with section 4729.27 of the Revised Code.

(17) "Enclosed shopping center" means a group of retail sales and service business establishments that face into an enclosed mall, share common ingress, egress, and parking facilities, and are situated on a tract of land that contains an area of not less than five hundred thousand square feet. "Enclosed shopping center" also includes not more than one business establishment that is located within a free-standing building on such a tract of land, so long as the sale of beer and intoxicating liquor on the tract of land was approved in an election held under former section 4301.353 [4301.35.3] of the Revised Code.

(18) "Controlled access alcohol and beverage cabinet" means a closed container, either refrigerated, in whole or in part, or nonrefrigerated, access to the interior of which is restricted by means of a device that requires the use of a key, magnetic card, or similar device and from which beer, intoxicating liquor, other beverages, or food may be sold.

(19) "Community facility" means either of the following:

(a) Any convention, sports, or entertainment facility or complex, or any combination of these, that is used by or accessible to the general public and that is owned or operated in whole or in part by the state, a state agency, or a political subdivision of the state or that is leased from, or located on property owned by or leased from, the state, a state agency, a political subdivision of the state, or a convention facilities authority created pursuant to section 351.02 of the Revised Code;

(b) An area designated as a community entertainment district pursuant to section 4301.80 of the Revised Code.

(20) "Low-alcohol beverage" means any brewed or fermented malt product, or any product made from the fermented juices of grapes, fruits, or other agricultural products, that contains either no alcohol or less than one-half of one per cent of alcohol by volume. The beverages described in division (B)(20) of this section do not include a soft drink such as root beer, birch beer, or ginger beer.

(21) "Cider" means all liquids fit to use for beverage purposes that contain one-half of one per cent of alcohol by volume, but not more than six per cent of alcohol by weight, and that are made through the normal alcoholic fermentation of the juice of sound, ripe apples, including, without limitation, flavored, sparkling, or carbonated cider and cider made from pure condensed apple must.

(22) "Sales area or territory" means an exclusive geographic area or territory that is assigned to a particular A or B permit holder and that either has one or more political subdivisions as its boundaries or consists of an area of land with readily identifiable geographic boundaries. "Sales area or territory" does not include, however, any particular retail location in an exclusive geographic area or territory that had been assigned to another A or B permit holder before April 9, 2001.

**HISTORY: 141 v H 428 (Eff 12-23-86); 142 v H 419 (Eff 7-31-87); 142 v H 562 (Eff 6-29-88); 143 v H 481 (Eff 7-1-89); 143 v S 131 (Eff 7-25-90); 143 v H 405 (Eff 4-11-91); 144 v H 340 (Eff 4-24-92); 145 v S 167 (Eff 11-1-94); 145 v S 209 (Eff 11-9-94); 146 v S 149 (Eff 11-21-95); 146 v H 239 (Eff 11-24-95); 146 v S 162 (Eff 7-1-97); 147 v H 390 (Eff 7-19-97); 147 v S 66 (Eff 7-22-98); 147 v H 402 (Eff 3-30-99); 148 v S 262 (Eff 4-9-2001); 149 v H 371. Eff 10-11-2002; 151 v H 530, § 101.01, eff. 6-30-06.**

The effective date is set by § 812.03 of 151 v H 530.

**Analogous to former RC § 4301.01 (GC § 6064-1; 115 v PtII, 118; 116 v 511; 117 v 628; Bureau of Code Revision, 10-1-53; 135 v S 339; 136 v H 928; 139 v H 357; 140 v S 74; 140 v H 37; 141 v H 39), repealed 141 v H 428, § 2, eff 12-23-86.**

## [POWERS AND DUTIES OF DIVISION]

### § 4301.14 Rationing of liquor; purchase at retail by permit holder for resale prohibited.

(A) When the supply of spirituous liquor in this state is insufficient to meet the demands of ordinary trade, due to causes beyond the control of the superintendent of liquor control, the superintendent may establish rules which will insure the equitable distribution of such supplies of spirituous liquor as are available. The superintendent may institute and terminate such rules as conditions demand, and also make changes and alterations therein in accordance with specific needs.

(B) No permit holder or his employee or agent shall purchase at retail any spirituous liquor for resale or in the permit premises possess such liquor. The permit of any person, firm, partnership, or corporation violating this section, or employing an employee, or authorizing an agent who violates this section shall be suspended or revoked.

**HISTORY: GC § 6064-8a; 120 v 66; Bureau of Code Revision, 10-1-53; 135 v H 496 (Eff 9-30-74); 146 v S 162. Eff 7-1-97.**

The effective date is set by section 10 of SB 162.

## § 4301.15 Violation of rationing prohibited.

No person shall violate any rule issued by the superintendent of liquor control in pursuance of section 4301.14 of the Revised Code.

**HISTORY: GC § 6064-8a; 120 v 66; Bureau of Code Revision, 10-1-53; 146 v S 162. Eff 7-1-97.**

The effective date is set by section 10 of SB 162.

## § 4301.21 Restrictions on sale of beer or intoxicating liquor for consumption on premises.

The sale of beer or intoxicating liquor for consumption on the premises is subject to the following restrictions, in addition to those imposed by the rules and orders of the division of liquor control:

(A) Except as otherwise provided in this chapter, beer or intoxicating liquor may be served to a person not seated at a table unless there is reason to believe that the beer or intoxicating liquor so served will be consumed by a person under twenty-one years of age.

(B) Beer or intoxicating liquor may be served by a hotel in the room of a bona fide guest, and may be sold by a hotel holding a D-5a permit, or a hotel holding a D-3 or D-5 permit that otherwise meets all of the requirements for holding a D-5a permit, by means of a controlled access alcohol and beverage cabinet that shall be located only in the hotel room of a registered guest. A hotel may sell beer or intoxicating liquor as authorized by its permit to a registered guest by means of a controlled access alcohol and beverage cabinet in accordance with the following requirements:

(1) Only a person twenty-one years of age or older who is a guest registered to stay in a guestroom shall be provided a key, magnetic card, or other similar device necessary to obtain access to the contents of a controlled access alcohol and beverage cabinet in that guestroom.

(2) The hotel shall comply with section 4301.22 of the Revised Code in connection with the handling, restocking, and replenishing of the beer and intoxicating liquor in the controlled access alcohol and beverage cabinet.

(3) The hotel shall replenish or restock beer and intoxicating liquor in any controlled access alcohol and beverage cabinet only during the hours during which the hotel may serve or sell beer and intoxicating liquor.

(4) The registered guest shall verify in writing that the guest has read and understands the language that shall be posted on the controlled access alcohol and beverage cabinet as required by division (B)(5) of this section.

(5) A hotel authorized to sell beer and intoxicating liquor pursuant to division (B) of this section shall post on the controlled access alcohol and beverage cabinet, in conspicuous language, the following notice:

"The alcoholic beverages contained in this cabinet shall not be removed from the premises."

(6) The hotel shall maintain a record of each sale of beer or intoxicating liquor made by the hotel by means of a controlled access alcohol and beverage cabinet for any period in which the permit holder is authorized to hold the permit pursuant to sections 4303.26 and 4303.27 of the Revised Code and any additional period during which an applicant exercises its right to appeal a rejection by the department or division of liquor control to renew a permit pursuant to section 4303.271 [4303.27.1] of the Revised Code. The records maintained by the hotel shall comply with both of the following:

(a) Include the name, address, age, and signature of each hotel guest who is provided access by the hotel to a controlled access alcohol and beverage cabinet pursuant to division (B)(1) of this section;

(b) Be made available during business hours to authorized agents of the division of liquor control pursuant to division (A)(6) of section 4301.10 of the Revised Code or to enforcement agents of the department of public safety pursuant to sections 5502.13 to 5502.19 of the Revised Code.

(7) The hotel shall observe all other applicable rules adopted by the division of liquor control and the liquor control commission.

(C) Neither the seller nor the liquor control commission by its regulations shall require the purchase of food with the purchase of beer or intoxicating liquor; nor shall the seller of beer or intoxicating liquor give away food of any kind in connection with the sale of beer or intoxicating liquor, except as authorized by rule of the liquor control commission.

(D) The seller shall not permit the purchaser to remove beer or intoxicating liquor so sold from the premises.

(E) A hotel authorized to sell beer and intoxicating liquor pursuant to division (B) of this section shall provide a registered guest with the opportunity to refuse to accept a key, magnetic card, or other similar device necessary to obtain access to the contents of a controlled access alcohol and beverage cabinet in that guest room. If a registered guest refuses to accept such key, magnetic card, or other similar device, the hotel shall not assess any charges on the registered guest for use of the controlled access alcohol and beverage cabinet in that guest room.

**HISTORY: GC § 6064-21; 115 v PtII, 118(139), § 21; Bureau of Code Revision, 10-1-53; 133 v H 558 (Eff 11-21-69); 135 v H 294 (Eff 11-21-73); 139 v H 357 (Eff 8-19-82); 142 v H 419 (Eff 7-31-87); 142 v H 562 (Eff 6-29-88); 146 v S 162 (Eff 10-29-95); 148 v H 163. Eff 6-30-99.**

## § 4301.22 Restrictions on sale of beer and liquor.

Sales of beer and intoxicating liquor under all classes of permits and from state liquor stores are subject to the following restrictions, in addition to those imposed by the rules or orders of the division of liquor control:

(A)(1) Except as otherwise provided in this chapter, no beer or intoxicating liquor shall be sold to any person under twenty-one years of age.

(2) No low-alcohol beverage shall be sold to any person under eighteen years of age. No permit issued by the division shall be suspended, revoked, or canceled because of a violation of division (A)(2) of this section.

(3) No intoxicating liquor shall be handled by any person under twenty-one years of age, except that a person eighteen years of age or older employed by a permit holder may handle or sell beer or intoxicating liquor in sealed containers in connection with wholesale or retail sales, and any person nineteen years of age or older employed by a permit holder may handle intoxicating liquor in open containers when acting in the capacity of a server in a hotel, restaurant, club, or night club, as defined in division (B) of section 4301.01 of the Revised Code, or in the premises of a D-7 permit holder. This section does not authorize persons under twenty-one years of age to sell intoxicating liquor across a bar. Any person employed by a permit holder may handle beer or intoxicating liquor in sealed containers in connection with manufacturing, storage, warehousing, placement, stocking, bagging, loading, or unloading, and may handle beer or intoxicating liquor in open containers in connection with cleaning tables or handling empty bottles or glasses.

(B) No permit holder and no agent or employee of a permit holder shall sell or furnish beer or intoxicating liquor to an intoxicated person.

(C) No sales of intoxicating liquor shall be made after two-thirty a.m. on Sunday except under either of the following circumstances:

(1) Intoxicating liquor may be sold on Sunday under authority of a permit that authorizes Sunday sale.

(2) Spirituous liquor may be sold on Sunday by any person awarded an agency contract under section 4301.17 of the Revised Code if the sale of spirituous liquor is authorized in the applicable precinct as the result of an election on question (B)(1) or (2) of section 4301.351 [4301.35.1] of the Revised Code and if the agency contract authorizes the sale of spirituous liquor on Sunday.

This section does not prevent a municipal corporation from adopting a closing hour for the sale of intoxicating liquor earlier than two-thirty a.m. on Sunday or to provide that no intoxicating liquor may be sold prior to that hour on Sunday.

(D) No holder of a permit shall give away any beer or intoxicating liquor of any kind at any time in connection with the permit holder's business.

(E) Except as otherwise provided in this division, no retail permit holder shall display or permit the display on the outside of any licensed retail premises, or on any lot of ground on which the licensed premises are situated, or on the exterior of any building of which the licensed premises are a part, any sign, illustration, or advertisement bearing the name, brand name, trade name, trade-mark, designation, or other emblem of or indicating the manufacturer, producer, distributor, place of manufacture, production, or distribution of any beer or intoxicating liquor. Signs, illustrations, or advertisements bearing the name, brand name, trade name, trade-mark, designation, or other emblem of or indicating the manufacturer, producer, distributor, place of manufacture, production, or distribution of beer or intoxicating liquor may be displayed and permitted to be displayed on the interior or in the show windows of any licensed premises, if the particular brand or type of product so advertised is actually available for sale on the premises at the time of such display. The liquor control commission shall determine by rule the size and character of such signs, illustrations, or advertisements.

(F) No retail permit holder shall possess on the licensed premises any barrel or other container from which beer is drawn, unless there is attached to the spigot or other dispensing apparatus the name of the manufacturer of the product contained in the barrel or other container, provided that if the beer is served at a bar the manufacturer's name or brand shall appear in full view of the purchaser. The commission shall regulate the size and character of the devices provided for in this section.

(G) Except as otherwise provided in this division, no sale of any gift certificate shall be permitted whereby beer or intoxicating liquor of any kind is to be exchanged for the certificate, unless the gift certificate can be exchanged only for food, and beer or intoxicating liquor, for on-premises consumption and the value of the beer or intoxicating liquor for which the certificate can be exchanged does not exceed more than thirty per cent of the total value of the gift certificate. The sale of gift certificates for the purchase of beer, wine, or mixed beverages shall be permitted for the purchase of beer, wine, or mixed beverages for off-premises consumption. Limitations on the use of a gift certificate for the purchase of beer, wine, or mixed beverages for off-premises consumption may be expressed by clearly stamping or typing on the face of the certificate that the certificate may not be used for the purchase of beer, wine, or mixed beverages.

**HISTORY: GC § 6064-22; 115 v PtII, 118(140), § 22; 116 v 511(535); 117 v 628(644); Bureau of Code Revision, 10-1-53; 128 v 1282 (Eff 10-23-59); 129 v 1211 (Eff 10-7-61); 133 v H 616 (Eff 11-17-69); 134 v H 859 (Eff 4-28-72); 136 v H 158 (Eff 8-13-76); 139 v H 357 (Eff 8-19-82); 140 v S 74 (Eff 7-4-84); 142 v H 419 (Eff 7-31-87); 145 v S 82 (Eff 5-4-94); 145 v S 167 (Eff 11-1-94); 145 v S 209 (Eff 11-9-94); 146 v H 511, § 1 (Eff 8-20-96); 146 v S 162 (Eff 7-1-97); 146 v H 511, § 3. Eff 7-1-97; 150 v H 306, § 1, eff. 7-23-04; 150 v S 164, §§ 1, 3, eff. 9-16-04.**

The effective date is set by section 3 of S.B. 164 (150 v —).

## [SUSPENSION OR CANCELLATION OF PERMIT]

## § 4301.251 Emergency suspension of retail permits and retail sales.

When so ordered by the governor, the director or, beginning on July 1, 1997, the superintendent of liquor control shall immediately and without a hearing suspend, for a period of not less than twenty-four hours nor more than seventy-two hours, any retail beer or liquor permit issued under Chapters 4301. and 4303. of the Revised Code and the retail sales of spirituous liquor by any state liquor store or agency for premises within any area where the director or superintendent designates that civil disorder, looting, or rioting exists.

Such order of emergency suspension shall contain an identifiable description of the area in which such retail permits and sales by stores and agencies are suspended and shall specify the calendar date and hour of the beginning and the calendar date and hour of the ending of such suspension period. A written copy of such order shall be served upon the owner, operator, manager, agent, bartender, or clerk of such beer or liquor permit premises, upon the manager or clerk of a state liquor store, or upon the agent, manager, or clerk of a state liquor agency by any law enforcement agency or officer designated by the director or superintendent.

The law enforcement officer, upon serving such emergency suspension order, shall forthwith fill in and sign a return of service form provided by the director or superintendent of liquor control, on which the officer shall write the name and address of the permit premises or the state liquor store or agency, the name and title of the person on whom such suspension order was served, and the day, hour, and address at which such service was made.

Upon receipt of such copy of the emergency suspension order by the owner, operator, manager, agent, bartender, or clerk of such retail beer or liquor permit premises or the state liquor store or agency, no beer, intoxicating liquor, or spirituous liquor shall be permitted to be consumed or sold at or upon such permit premises or the state liquor store or agency.

Upon completion of the return of service form, the law enforcement officer shall cause it to be transmitted immediately to the nearest district office of the department or, beginning on July 1, 1997, the division of liquor control, where it shall be filed, recorded, and reported forthwith by telephone or teletype to the central office of the department or division of liquor control.

Any subsequent order by the governor, to cancel or continue such order of emergency suspension or to diminish or expand the area of the last issued emergency suspension order, shall be processed and carried out in the same manner as that required for the issuance of the original order of emergency suspension.

**HISTORY: 132 v H 345 (Eff 7-20-67); 146 v S 162 (Eff 10-29-95); 146 v H 60. Eff 3-4-98.**

## [SEIZURE AND SALE OF CONVEYANCES]

### § 4301.45 Seizure of illegally transported beer or intoxicating liquor and arrest of violator.

When any law enforcement officer discovers any person in the act of transporting in violation of law beer or intoxicating liquors in any wagon, buggy, automobile, watercraft, aircraft, or other vehicle, the officer shall seize all beer or intoxicating liquors found therein being transported contrary to law. Whenever beer or intoxicating liquors transported or possessed illegally are seized by a law enforcement officer, the officer shall take possession of the vehicle and team, or automobile, boat, watercraft, aircraft, or any other conveyance, and shall arrest any person in charge thereof. The law enforcement officer shall at once proceed against the person arrested under Chapters 4301. and 4303. of the Revised Code, in any court having jurisdiction of offenses under those chapters, but the vehicle or conveyance shall be returned to the owner upon execution by the owner of a valid bond with sufficient sureties, in a sum equal to the value of the property, which bond shall be approved by the law enforcement officer and shall be conditioned to return said property to the custody of said officer on the day of trial to abide by the judgment of the court. The court, upon conviction of the person so arrested, shall order the beer or intoxicating liquor that was not illegally manufactured to be forfeited to the state and disposed of under sections 2981.11 to 2981.13 of the Revised Code, and unless good cause to the contrary is shown by the owner, shall order a sale at public auction of the property seized, and the officer making the sale, after deducting the expenses of keeping the property, the fee for the seizure, and the cost of the sale, shall pay all liens, according to their priorities, which are established, by intervention or otherwise at said hearing or in other proceeding brought for said purpose, as being bona fide and as having been created without the lienor having any notice that the carrying vehicle was being used or was to be used for illegal transportation of beer or intoxicating liquor, and shall distribute the balance as money arising from fines and forfeited bonds under such chapters is distributed. The court, upon conviction of the person so arrested, shall order the beer or intoxicating liquor that was illegally manufactured to be destroyed.

All liens against property sold under this section shall be transferred from the property to the proceeds of the sale of the property. If no claimant is found for the team, vehicle, watercraft, aircraft, automobile, or other conveyance, the taking of the same, with its description, shall be advertised in some newspaper published in the city or county where taken, or if there is no newspaper published in such city or county, in a newspaper having circulation in the county, once a week for four weeks and by handbills posted in three public places near the place of seizure, and if no claimant appears within ten days after the last publication of the advertisement, the property shall be sold and the proceeds after deducting the expense and costs shall be distributed as if there were a claimant for said vehicle or conveyance.

**HISTORY: GC § 6212-43; 108 v PtI, 401, § 32; 109 v 95; 115 v PtII, 118(158), § 62; Bureau of Code Revision, 10-1-53; 138 v S 50 (Eff 5-29-80); 146 v S 162. Eff 10-29-95; 151 v H 241, § 1, eff. 7-1-07.**

See provisions of § 4 of 151 v H 241 following RC § 4301.29.

## [PROHIBITIONS]

### § 4301.47 Records required.

Every class A-1, A-2, and A-4 permit holder and each class B or S permit holder shall maintain and keep for a period of three years a record of the beer, wine, and mixed beverages purchased, distributed, or sold within this state by the permit holder, together with invoices, records, receipts, bills of lading, and other pertinent papers required by the tax commissioner and, upon demand by the tax commissioner, shall produce these records for a three-year period prior to the demand unless upon satisfactory proof it is shown that the nonproduction is due to causes beyond the permit holder's control.

**HISTORY: GC § 6064-45; 115 v PtII, 118(153), § 45; 116 v PtII, 89; Bureau of Code Revision, 10-1-53; 130 v 998 (Eff 1-1-64); 142 v H 231 (Eff 10-5-87); 149 v H 371. Eff 10-11-2002; 152 v S 150, § 1, eff. 9-1-08.**

### § 4301.48 False entry upon invoice prohibited.

No person shall make any false entry upon an invoice or upon a container of beer, wine, or mixed beverages required to be made under this chapter and Chapters 4303. and 4307. of the Revised Code, or present any such false entry for the inspection of the tax commissioner.

**HISTORY: GC § 6064-46; 115 v PtII, 118(153), § 46; 116 v PtII, 89; Bureau of Code Revision, 10-1-53; 139 v H 357 (Eff 10-1-82); 143 v S 188. Eff 3-20-90.**

## § 4301.49 Interference with inspection prohibited.

No person shall prevent or hinder the tax commissioner from making a full inspection of any place where beer, wine, or mixed beverages subject to the tax imposed by section 4301.42, 4301.421 [4301.42.1], 4301.424 [4301.42.4], or 4301.43 of the Revised Code is manufactured, sold, or stored. No person shall prevent or hinder the full inspection of invoices, books, records, or papers required to be kept under this chapter and Chapters 4305. and 4307. of the Revised Code.

**HISTORY: GC § 6064-47; 115 v PtII, 118(153), § 47; 116 v PtII, 89; Bureau of Code Revision, 10-1-53; 139 v H 357 (Eff 10-1-82); 143 v S 188 (Eff 3-20-90); 146 v S 188. Eff 7-19-95.**

## § 4301.53 Search warrants; seizure and disposition of property.

The judge of a court of record may issue warrants to search a house, building, place, vehicle, watercraft, aircraft, or conveyance for beer, alcohol, or intoxicating liquor manufactured, possessed, stored, concealed, sold, furnished, given away, or transported in violation of Chapters 4301. and 4303. of the Revised Code, and the containers in which the same is found, or machinery, tools, implements, equipment, supplies, and materials used or kept for use in manufacturing beer or intoxicating liquor in violation of those chapters, and to seize any of that property and things found in it, together with the vehicle, watercraft, aircraft, or conveyance in which the same is found. The issuance of those warrants is subject in all respects to sections 2933.22 to 2933.27 of the Revised Code; except that any such vehicle, watercraft, aircraft, or other conveyance shall be returned to its owner upon execution by the owner of a bond with surety to the satisfaction of the enforcement agent of the department of public safety or other law enforcement officer making the seizure in an equal amount to its value, conditioned upon its return to the custody of such agent or officer on the day of trial to abide by the judgment of the court. Upon conviction of any violation of Chapters 4301. and 4303. of the Revised Code, any property found in the possession of the person convicted or the person's agent or employee shall be disposed of as provided in section 4301.45 of the Revised Code. If the accused is discharged by the judge or magistrate, such vehicle, watercraft, aircraft, or other conveyance shall be returned to its owner, and any bond given pursuant to this section shall be canceled. If the accused is the holder of a permit issued under Chapters 4301. and 4303. of the Revised Code, any beer, intoxicating liquor, or alcohol seized shall be disposed of as provided in section 4301.29 of the Revised Code, and any other property seized shall be returned to its owner by the officer having the custody or possession of such property. If the accused is not the holder of such a permit in force at the time, any beer, intoxicating liquor, or alcohol that was not illegally manufactured shall be forfeited to the state and shall forthwith be disposed of under sections 2981.11 to 2981.13 of the Revised Code. Illegally manufactured beer, intoxicating liquor, or alcohol, and other property, except as provided in this section, shall be destroyed, and any such beer, intoxicating liquor, or alcohol, or other property is hereby declared to be a public nuisance.

**HISTORY: GC § 6064-61; 115 v PtII, 118(157), § 61; Bureau of Code Revision, 10-1-53; 138 v S 50 (Eff 5-29-80); 146 v S 162 (Eff 10-29-95); 148 v H 163. Eff 6-30-99; 151 v H 241, § 1, eff. 7-1-07.**

See provisions of § 4 of 151 v H 241 following RC § 4301.29.

### [ADDITIONAL PROHIBITIONS]

## § 4301.58 Actions prohibited without permit; unauthorized source of liquor.

(A) No person, personally or by the person's clerk, agent, or employee, who is not the holder of an A permit issued by the division of liquor control, in force at the time, and authorizing the manufacture of beer or intoxicating liquor, or who is not an agent or employee of the division authorized to manufacture such beer or intoxicating liquor, shall manufacture any beer or intoxicating liquor for sale, or shall manufacture spirituous liquor.

(B) No person, personally or by the person's clerk, agent, or employee, who is not the holder of an A, B, C, D, E, F, G, I, or S permit issued by the division, in force at the time, and authorizing the sale of beer, intoxicating liquor, or alcohol, or who is not an agent or employee of the division or the tax commissioner authorized to sell such beer, intoxicating liquor, or alcohol, shall sell, keep, or possess beer, intoxicating liquor, or alcohol for sale to any persons other than those authorized by Chapters 4301. and 4303. of the Revised Code to purchase any beer or intoxicating liquor, or sell any alcohol at retail. This division does not apply to or affect the sale or possession for sale of any low-alcohol beverage.

(C) No person, personally or by the person's clerk, agent, or employee, who is the holder of a permit issued by the division, shall sell, keep, or possess for sale any intoxicating liquor not purchased from the division or from the holder of a permit issued by the division authorizing the sale of such intoxicating liquor unless the same has been purchased with the special consent of the division. The division shall revoke the permit of any person convicted of a violation of division (C) of this section.

**HISTORY: GC § 6064-54; 115 v PtII, 118(155), § 54; 116 v 511(540); 117 v 628(651); Bureau of Code Revision, 10-1-53; 145 v S 209 (Eff 11-9-94); 146 v S 162. Eff 7-1-97; 152 v S 150, § 1, eff. 9-1-08.**

The effective date is set by section 10 of SB 162.

## § 4301.59 Fraudulent misrepresentation prohibited.

No person, or his clerk, agent, or employee, shall make or issue any false or fraudulent statement, either orally or in writing, concerning the future value or use of any bonded warehouse receipt for spirituous liquor, or concerning the age, quality, quantity, ingredients, source, future value, or use of the spirituous liquor represented by such receipt for the purpose of promoting or inducing the sale or purchase of such receipt in this state.

**HISTORY: GC § 6064-54a; 116 v 511(541); Bureau of Code Revision. Eff 10-1-53.**

## § 4301.60 Illegal transportation prohibited.

No person, who is not the holder of an H permit, shall transport beer, intoxicating liquor, or alcohol in this state. This section does not apply to the transportation and delivery of beer, alcohol, or intoxicating liquor purchased or to be purchased from the holder of a permit issued by the division of liquor control, in force at the time, and authorizing the sale and delivery of the beer, alcohol, or intoxicating liquor so transported, or to the transportation and delivery of beer, intoxicating liquor, or alcohol purchased from the division or the tax commissioner, or purchased by the holder of an A or B permit outside this state and transported within this state by them in their own trucks for the purpose of sale under their permits.

**HISTORY: GC § 6064-55; 115 v PtII, 118(155), § 55; 117 v 628(651); Bureau of Code Revision, 10-1-53; 146 v S 162. Eff 7-1-97.**

The effective date is set by section 10 of SB 162.

## § 4301.61 Transaction scan in connection with sale or allowing admission to permit premises.

(A) As used in this section and section 4301.611 [4301.61.1] of the Revised Code:

(1) "Card holder" means any person who presents a driver's or commercial driver's license or an identification card to a permit holder, or an agent or employee of a permit holder, for either of the purposes listed in division (A)(4)(a) or (b) of this section.

(2) "Identification card" means an identification card issued under sections 4507.50 to 4507.52 of the Revised Code.

(3) "Permit holder" means the holder of a permit issued under Chapter 4303. of the Revised Code.

(4) "Transaction scan" means the process by which a permit holder or an agent or employee of a permit holder checks, by means of a transaction scan device, the validity of a driver's or commercial driver's license or an identification card that is presented as a condition for doing either of the following:

(a) Purchasing any beer, intoxicating liquor, or low-alcohol beverage;

(b) Gaining admission to a premises that has been issued a liquor permit authorizing the sale of beer or intoxicating liquor for consumption on the premises where sold, and where admission is restricted to persons twenty-one years of age or older.

(5) "Transaction scan device" means any commercial device or combination of devices used at a point of sale that is capable of deciphering in an electronically readable format the information encoded on the magnetic strip or bar code of a driver's or commercial driver's license or an identification card.

(B)(1) A permit holder or an agent or employee of a permit holder may perform a transaction scan by means of a transaction scan device to check the validity of a driver's or commercial driver's license or identification card presented by a card holder for either of the purposes listed in division (A)(4)(a) or (b) of this section.

(2) If the information deciphered by the transaction scan performed under division (B)(1) of this section fails to match the information printed on the driver's or commercial driver's license or identification card presented by the card holder, or if the transaction scan indicates that the information so printed is false or fraudulent, neither the permit holder nor any agent or employee of the permit holder shall sell any beer, intoxicating liquor, or low-alcohol beverage to the card holder.

(3) Division (B)(1) of this section does not preclude a permit holder or an agent or employee of a permit holder from using a transaction scan device to check the validity of a document other than a driver's or commercial driver's license or an identification card, if the document includes a bar code or magnetic strip that may be scanned by the device, as a condition of a sale of beer, intoxicating liquor, or a low-alcohol beverage or of granting admission to a premises described in division (A)(4) of this section.

(C) The registrar of motor vehicles, with the approval of the liquor control commission, shall adopt, and may amend or rescind, rules in accordance with Chapter 119. of the Revised Code that do both of the following:

(1) Govern the recording and maintenance of information described in divisions (D)(1)(a) and (b) of this section, divisions (D)(1)(a) and (b) of section 2927.021 [2927.02.1] of the Revised Code, and divisions (D)(1)(a) and (b) of section 2925.57 of the Revised Code;

(2) Ensure quality control in the use of transaction scan devices under this section and sections 2927.021 [2927.02.1], 2927.022 [2927.02.2], 2925.57, 2925.58, and 4301.611 [4301.61.1] of the Revised Code.

(D)(1) No permit holder or agent or employee of a permit holder shall electronically or mechanically record or maintain any information derived from a transaction scan, except the following:

(a) The name and date of birth of the person listed on the driver's or commercial driver's license or identification card presented by a card holder;

(b) The expiration date and identification number of the driver's or commercial driver's license or identification card presented by a card holder.

(2) No permit holder or agent or employee of a permit holder shall use the information that is derived from a transaction scan or that is permitted to be recorded and maintained by division (D)(1) of this section, except for purposes of section 4301.611 [4301.61.1] of the Revised Code.

(3) No permit holder or agent or employee of a permit holder shall use a transaction scan device for a purpose other than a purpose listed in division (A)(4)(a) or (b) of this section.

(4) No permit holder or agent or employee of a permit holder shall sell or otherwise disseminate the information derived from a transaction scan to any third party, including, but not limited to, selling or otherwise disseminating that information for any marketing, advertising, or promotional activities, but a permit holder or agent or employee of a permit holder may release that information pursuant to a court order or as specifically authorized by section 4301.611 [4301.61.1] or another section of the Revised Code.

(E) Nothing in this section or section 4301.611 [4301.61.1] of the Revised Code relieves a permit holder or an agent or employee of a permit holder of any responsibility to comply with any other applicable state or federal laws or rules governing the sale of beer, intoxicating liquor, or low-alcohol beverages.

(F) Whoever violates division (B)(2) or (D) of this section is guilty of an illegal liquor transaction scan, and the court may impose upon the offender a civil penalty of up to one thousand dollars for each violation. The clerk of the court shall pay each collected civil penalty to the county treasurer for deposit into the county treasury.

**HISTORY: 148 v S 200. Eff 9-21-2000; 151 v S 53, § 1, eff. 5-17-06.**

**Not analogous to former RC § 4301.61 (GC § 6064-56; 115 v PtII, 118(156), § 56; 116 v 511 (541); Bureau of Code**

**Revision, 10-1-53; 140 v H 37), repealed 146 v S 2, § 2, eff 7-1-96.**

## § 4301.611 Transaction scan as affirmative defense.

(A) A permit holder or an agent or employee of a permit holder may not be found guilty of a charge of a violation of this chapter or any rule of the liquor control commission in which the age of a purchaser of any beer, intoxicating liquor, or low-alcohol beverage is an element of the alleged violation, if the permit holder, agent, or employee raises and proves as an affirmative defense that all of the following occurred:

(1) The card holder attempting to purchase any beer, intoxicating liquor, or low-alcohol beverage presented a driver's or commercial driver's license or an identification card.

(2) A transaction scan of the driver's or commercial driver's license or identification card that the card holder presented indicated that the license or card was valid.

(3) The beer, intoxicating liquor, or low-alcohol beverage was sold to the card holder in reasonable reliance upon the identification presented and the completed transaction scan.

(B) In determining whether a permit holder or an agent or employee of a permit holder has proven the affirmative defense provided by division (A) of this section, the liquor control commission or the trier of fact in a court of record shall consider any written policy that the permit holder has adopted and implemented and that is intended to prevent violations of division (A)(1) or (2) of section 4301.22 and of sections 4301.63 to 4301.636 [4301.63.6], 4301.69, and 4301.691 [4301.69.1] of the Revised Code. For purposes of division (A)(3) of this section, the commission or trier of fact shall consider that reasonable reliance upon the identification presented and the completed transaction scan may require a permit holder or an agent or employee of a permit holder to exercise reasonable diligence to determine, and that the use of a transaction scan device does not excuse a permit holder or an agent or employee of a permit holder from exercising reasonable diligence to determine, the following:

(1) Whether a person to whom the permit holder or agent or employee of a permit holder sells any beer or intoxicating liquor is twenty-one years of age or older or sells any low-alcohol beverage is eighteen years of age or older;

(2) Whether the description and picture appearing on the driver's or commercial driver's license or identification card presented by a card holder is that of the card holder.

(C) The affirmative defense provided by division (A) of this section is in addition to the defense provided by section 4301.639 [4301.63.9] of the Revised Code.

(D) In any hearing before the liquor control commission and in any criminal action in which the affirmative defense provided by division (A) of this section is raised, the registrar of motor vehicles or a deputy registrar who issued an identification card under sections 4507.50 to 4507.52 of the Revised Code shall be permitted to submit certified copies of the records of that issuance in lieu of the testimony of the personnel of or contractors with the bureau of motor vehicles in the hearing or action.

**HISTORY: 148 v S 200. Eff 9-21-2000.**

## § 4301.62 Open container law.

(A) As used in this section:

(1) "Chauffeured limousine" means a vehicle registered under section 4503.24 of the Revised Code.

(2) "Street," "highway," and "motor vehicle" have the same meanings as in section 4511.01 of the Revised Code.

(B) No person shall have in the person's possession an opened container of beer or intoxicating liquor in any of the following circumstances:

(1) In a state liquor store;

(2) Except as provided in division (C) of this section, on the premises of the holder of any permit issued by the division of liquor control;

(3) In any other public place;

(4) Except as provided in division (D) or (E) of this section, while operating or being a passenger in or on a motor vehicle on any street, highway, or other public or private property open to the public for purposes of vehicular travel or parking;

(5) Except as provided in division (D) or (E) of this section, while being in or on a stationary motor vehicle on any street, highway, or other public or private property open to the public for purposes of vehicular travel or parking.

(C)(1) A person may have in the person's possession an opened container of any of the following:

(a) Beer or intoxicating liquor that has been lawfully purchased for consumption on the premises where bought from the holder of an A-1-A, A-2, A-3a, D-1, D-2, D-3, D-3a, D-4, D-4a, D-5, D-5a, D-5b, D-5c, D-5d, D-5e, D-5f, D-5g, D-5h, D-5i, D-5j, D-5k, D-5l, D-5m, D-5n, D-5o, D-7, D-8, E, F, F-2, F-5, F-7, or F-8 permit;

(b) Beer, wine, or mixed beverages served for consumption on the premises by the holder of an F-3 permit or wine served for consumption on the premises by the holder of an F-4 or F-6 permit;

(c) Beer or intoxicating liquor consumed on the premises of a convention facility as provided in section 4303.201 [4303.20.1] of the Revised Code;

(d) Beer or intoxicating liquor to be consumed during tastings and samplings approved by rule of the liquor control commission.

(2) A person may have in the person's possession on an F liquor permit premises an opened container of beer or intoxicating liquor that was not purchased from the holder of the F permit if the premises for which the F permit is issued is a music festival and the holder of the F permit grants permission for that possession on the premises during the period for which the F permit is issued. As used in this division, "music festival" means a series of outdoor live musical performances, extending for a period of at least three consecutive days and located on an area of land of at least forty acres.

(3)(a) A person may have in the person's possession on a D-2 liquor permit premises an opened or unopened container of wine that was not purchased from the holder of the D-2 permit if the premises for which the D-2 permit is issued is an outdoor performing arts center, the person is attending an orchestral performance, and the holder of the D-2 permit grants permission for the possession and consumption of wine in certain predesignated areas of the premises during the period for which the D-2 permit is issued.

(b) As used in division (C)(3)(a) of this section:

(i) "Orchestral performance" means a concert comprised of a group of not fewer than forty musicians playing various musical instruments.

(ii) "Outdoor performing arts center" means an outdoor performing arts center that is located on not less than one hundred fifty acres of land and that is open for performances from the first day of April to the last day of October of each year.

(4) A person may have in the person's possession an opened or unopened container of beer or intoxicating liquor at an outdoor location at which the person is attending an orchestral performance as defined in division (C)(3)(b)(i) of this section if the person with supervision and control over the performance grants permission for the possession and consumption of beer or intoxicating liquor in certain predesignated areas of that outdoor location.

(D) This section does not apply to a person who pays all or a portion of the fee imposed for the use of a chauffeured limousine pursuant to a prearranged contract, or the guest of the person, when all of the following apply:

(1) The person or guest is a passenger in the limousine.

(2) The person or guest is located in the limousine, but is not occupying a seat in the front compartment of the limousine where the operator of the limousine is located.

(3) The limousine is located on any street, highway, or other public or private property open to the public for purposes of vehicular travel or parking.

(E) An opened bottle of wine that was purchased from the holder of a permit that authorizes the sale of wine for consumption on the premises where sold is not an opened container for the purposes of this section if both of the following apply:

(1) The opened bottle of wine is securely resealed by the permit holder or an employee of the permit holder before the bottle is removed from the premises. The bottle shall be secured in such a manner that it is visibly apparent if the bottle has been subsequently opened or tampered with.

(2) The opened bottle of wine that is resealed in accordance with division (E)(1) of this section is stored in the trunk of a motor vehicle or, if the motor vehicle does not have a trunk, behind the last upright seat or in an area not normally occupied by the driver or passengers and not easily accessible by the driver.

**HISTORY: 145 v H 281 (Eff 7-2-93); 146 v S 39 (Eff 7-14-95); 146 v S 162 (Eff 7-1-97); 147 v S 85 (Eff 5-15-97); 148 v H 283 (Eff 9-29-99); 148 v S 200 (Eff 9-21-2000); 148 v S 262 (Eff 4-9-2001); 149 v H 371. Eff 10-11-2002; 150 v S 23, § 1, eff. 4-7-04; 151 v S 131, § 1, eff. 9-21-06; 152 v S 150, § 1, eff. 9-1-08; 152 v H 562, § 101.01, eff. 9-23-08; 153 v H 519, § 1, eff. 9-10-10; 2011 HB 114, § 101.01, eff. June 29, 2011; 2011 HB 153, § 101.01, eff. Sept. 29, 2011.**

Acts 2011, HB 114, § 806.10 provides: "The items of law contained in this act, and their applications, are severable. If any item of law contained in this act, or if any application of any item of law contained in this act, is held invalid, the invalidity does not affect other items of law contained in this act and their applications that can be given effect without the invalid item or application."

The provisions of § 6 of 153 v H 519 read in part as follows:

SECTION 6. The General Assembly, applying the principle stated in division (B) of section 1.52 of the Revised Code that amendments are to be harmonized if reasonably capable of simultaneous operation, finds that the following sections, presented in this act as composites of the sections as amended by the acts indicated, are the resulting versions of the sections in effect before the effective date of the sections as presented in this act:

° ° °

Section 4301.62 of the Revised Code as amended by both Am. Sub. H.B. 562 and Sub. S.B. 150 of the 127th General Assembly.

The effective date is set by § 812.10 of 152 v H 562.

**Analogous to former RC § 4301.62 (GC § 6064-57; 115 v PtII 118(156), § 57; 116 v. 511(541); 117 v 628(652); Bureau of Code Revision, 10-1-53; 133 v H 150; 136 v H 613; 139 v H 357; 140 v H 502; 140 v H 711; 141 v H 359; 142 v H 562; 143 v S 131; 143 v H 405; 145 v H 152), repealed 145 v H 281, § 2, eff 7-2-93.**

## § 4301.63 Persons under twenty-one not to purchase beer or intoxicating liquor.

Except as otherwise provided in this chapter, no person under the age of twenty-one years shall purchase beer or intoxicating liquor.

**HISTORY: GC § 6064-57a; 118 v 691; Bureau of Code Revision, 10-1-53; 125 v 113 (Eff 10-2-53); 136 v H 315 (Eff 4-25-75); 139 v H 357 (Eff 8-19-82); 142 v H 419. Eff 7-31-87.**

## § 4301.631 Underage person not to purchase or consume low-alcohol beverage.

(A) As used in this section, "underage person" means a person under eighteen years of age.

(B) No underage person shall purchase any low-alcohol beverage.

(C) No underage person shall order, pay for, share the cost of, or attempt to purchase any low-alcohol beverage.

(D) No person shall knowingly furnish any false information as to the name, age, or other identification of any underage person for the purpose of obtaining or with the intent to obtain any low-alcohol beverage for an underage person, by purchase or as a gift.

(E) No underage person shall knowingly show or give false information concerning the person's name, age, or other identification for the purpose of purchasing or otherwise obtaining any low-alcohol beverage in any place in this state.

(F) No person shall sell or furnish any low-alcohol beverage to, or buy any low-alcohol beverage for, an underage person, unless given by a physician in the regular line of his practice or given for established religious purposes, or unless the underage person is accompanied by a parent, spouse who is not an underage person, or legal guardian.

No permit issued by the division of liquor control shall be suspended, revoked, or canceled because of a violation of this division or division (G) of this section.

(G) No person who is the owner or occupant of any public or private place shall knowingly allow any underage person to remain in or on the place while possessing or consuming any low-alcohol beverage, unless the low-alcohol beverage is given to the person possessing or consuming it by that person's parent, spouse who is not an underage person, or legal guardian, and the parent, spouse who is not an underage person, or legal guardian is present when the person possesses or consumes the low-alcohol beverage.

An owner of a public or private place is not liable for acts or omissions in violation of this division that are committed by a lessee of that place, unless the owner authorizes or acquiesces in the lessee's acts or omissions.

(H) No underage person shall knowingly possess or consume any low-alcohol beverage in any public or private place, unless accompanied by a parent, spouse who is not an underage person, or legal guardian, or unless the low-alcohol beverage is given by a physician in the regular line of the physician's practice or given for established religious purposes.

(I) No parent, spouse who is not an underage person, or legal guardian of an underage person shall knowingly permit the underage person to violate this section.

**HISTORY: 145 v S 209 (Eff 11-9-94); 146 v S 162. Eff 7-1-97.**

**Not analogous to former RC § 4301.631 (130 v 998; 139 v H 357), repealed 142 v H 419, § 2, eff 7-31-87.**

The effective date is set by section 10 of SB 162.

## § 4301.632 Repealed, 149 v H 17, § 2 [130 v 998; 142 v H 419; 143 v H 22]. Eff 10-11-2002.

This section stated that no person under twenty-one shall purchase or consume beer or intoxicating liquor except as otherwise provided by Chapter 4301. See now RC § 4301.69.

## § 4301.633 Misrepresentation to obtain beer or intoxicating liquor for person under twenty-one.

Except as otherwise provided in this chapter, no person shall knowingly furnish any false information as to the name, age, or other identification of any person under twenty-one years of age for the purpose of obtaining or with the intent to obtain, beer or intoxicating liquor for a person under twenty-one years of age, by purchase, or as a gift.

**HISTORY: 130 v 999 (Eff 9-20-63); 139 v H 357 (Eff 8-19-82); 142 v H 419. Eff 7-31-87.**

## § 4301.634 Misrepresentation by person under twenty-one.

Except as otherwise provided in this chapter, no person under the age of twenty-one years shall knowingly show or give false information concerning the person's name, age, or other identification for the purpose of purchasing or otherwise obtaining beer or intoxicating liquor in any place in this state where beer or intoxicating liquor is sold under a permit issued by the division of liquor control or sold by the division.

**HISTORY: 130 v 999 (Eff 9-20-63); 139 v H 357 (Eff 8-19-82); 142 v H 419 (Eff 7-31-87); 146 v S 162. Eff 7-1-97.**

The effective date is set by section 10 of SB 162.

## § 4301.635 Notice to permit holder after compliance check.

(A) As used in this section:

(1) "Compliance check" means an attempt on behalf of a law enforcement agency or the division of liquor control to purchase any beer, wine, mixed beverages, or intoxicating liquor in the enforcement of any section of this chapter or any rule of the liquor control commission in which the age of the purchaser is an element of the offense.

(2) "Confidential informant" means a person who is under twenty-one years of age and who is engaged in conducting compliance checks.

(3) "Law enforcement agency" means an organization or unit made up of law enforcement officers authorized to enforce this chapter and also includes the investigative unit of the department of public safety described in section 5502.13 of the Revised Code.

(B) Within a reasonable period of time after the conduct of a compliance check, the law enforcement agency that conducted the compliance check, or the division of liquor control if the division conducted the compliance check, shall send written notification of it to the permit holder that was its subject. If the confidential informant who participated in the compliance check was able to purchase beer, wine, mixed beverages, or intoxicating liquor, the citation issued for the violation constitutes that notification. If the confidential informant who participated in the compliance check was unable to purchase beer, wine, mixed beverages, or intoxicating liquor, the notification shall indicate the date and time of the compliance check, the law enforcement agency that conducted the compliance check or, when applicable, that the division of liquor control conducted the compliance check, and the permit holder or a general description of the employee of the permit holder who refused to make the sale.

**HISTORY: 150 v S 23, § 1, eff. 4-7-04.**

**Not analogous to former § 4301.635, repealed 142 v H 419, § 2 [130 v 999], eff 7-31-87.**

## § 4301.636 Furnishing false identification card or driver's license.

(A)(1) No person shall manufacture, transfer, or distribute in any manner any identification card issued for the purpose of establishing a person's age that displays the great seal of the state of Ohio, the word "Ohio," "state," or "official," or any other designation that represents the card as the official identification card of Ohio, except for those cards issued pursuant to section 4507.50 of the Revised Code.

(2) No person shall manufacture, sell, or distribute in any manner for any compensation any identification card issued for the purpose of establishing a person's age that displays the great seal of the state of Ohio, the word "Ohio," "state," or "official," or any other designation that represents the card as the official identification card of Ohio, except for those cards issued pursuant to section 4507.50 of the Revised Code.

(B)(1) No person, other than the registrar of motor vehicles or a deputy registrar, shall manufacture, transfer, or distribute in any manner any card that displays the great seal of the state of Ohio, the word "Ohio," "state," "official," "chauffeur," "chauffeur's," "commercial driver," "commercial driver's," "driver," "driver's," "operator," or "operator's," or any other designation that represents the card as the official driver's license of the state.

(2) No person, other than the registrar of motor vehicles or a deputy registrar, shall manufacture, sell, or distribute in any manner for any compensation any card that displays the great seal of the state of Ohio, the word "Ohio," "state," "official," "chauffeur," "chauffeur's," "commercial driver," "commercial driver's," "driver," "driver's," or any other designation that represents the card as the official driver's license of the state.

**HISTORY: 142 v H 419 (Eff 7-31-87); 143 v S 131. Eff 7-25-90.**

**Not analogous to former RC § 4301.63.6 (130 v 999), repealed 134 v H 109, eff 9-8-71.**

## § 4301.637 Posting of warning cards as to underage persons and firearms.

(A) Except as otherwise provided in section 4301.691 [4301.69.1] of the Revised Code, every place in this state where beer, intoxicating liquor, or any low-alcohol beverage is sold for beverage purposes shall display at all times, in a prominent place on the premises thereof, a printed card, which shall be furnished by the division of liquor control and which shall read substantially as follows:

"WARNING TO PERSONS UNDER AGE

If you are under the age of 21

Under the statutes of the state of Ohio, if you order, pay for, share the cost of, or attempt to purchase, or possess or consume beer or intoxicating liquor in any public place, or furnish false information as to name, age, or other identification, you are subject to a fine of up to one thousand dollars, or imprisonment up to six months, or both.

If you are under the age of 18

Under the statutes of the state of Ohio, if you order, pay for, share the cost of, or attempt to purchase, or possess or consume, any type of beer or wine that contains either no alcohol or less than one-half of one per cent of alcohol by volume in any public place, or furnish false information as to name, age, or other identification, you are subject to a fine of up to two hundred fifty dollars or to imprisonment up to thirty days, or both."

No person shall be subject to any criminal prosecution or any proceedings before the division or the liquor control commission for failing to display this card. No permit issued by the division shall be suspended, revoked, or canceled because of the failure of the permit holder to display this card.

(B) Every place in this state for which a D permit has been issued under Chapter 4303. of the Revised Code shall be issued a printed card by the division that shall read substantially as follows:

"WARNING

If you are carrying a firearm

Under the statutes of Ohio, if you possess a firearm in any room in which liquor is being dispensed in premises for which a D permit has been issued under Chapter 4303. of the Revised Code, you may be guilty of a felony and are subject to a term of actual incarceration of one or two years."

No person shall be subject to any criminal prosecution or any proceedings before the division or the liquor control commission for failing to display this card. No permit issued by the division shall be suspended, revoked, or canceled because of the failure of the permit holder to display this card.

**HISTORY: 130 v 999 (Eff 9-20-63); 131 v 1047 (Eff 11-3-65); 132 v H 1 (Eff 2-21-67); 137 v S 49 (Eff 11-14-77); 139 v H 357 (Eff 8-19-82); 141 v H 51 (Eff 7-30-86); 141 v H 39 (Eff 2-21-87); 142 v H 419 (Eff 7-31-87); 145 v S 209 (Eff 11-9-94); 146 v S 2 (Eff 7-1-96); 146 v S 162. Eff 7-1-97.**

The effective date is set by section 10 of SB 162.

See **Comment, Legislative Service Commission** following RC § 4301.26.

## § 4301.638 No modification of other sections intended.

Sections 4301.633 [4301.63.3] to 4301.637 [4301.63.7] of the Revised Code shall not be deemed to modify or affect division (A) of section 4301.22 or section 4301.69 of the Revised Code.

**HISTORY: 130 v 1000 (Eff 9-20-63); 142 v H 419 (Eff 7-31-87); 149 v H 17. Eff 10-11-2002.**

## § 4301.639 Good faith acceptance of false identification.

(A) No permit holder, agent or employee of a permit holder, or any other person may be found guilty of a violation of any section of this chapter or any rule of the liquor control commission in which age is an element of the offense, if the liquor control commission or any court of record finds all of the following:

(1) That the person buying, at the time of so doing, exhibited to the permit holder, the agent or employee of the permit holder, or the other person a driver's or commercial driver's license, an identification card issued under sections 4507.50 to 4507.52 of the Revised Code, or a military identification card issued by the United States department of defense, that displays a picture of the individual for whom the license or card was issued and shows that the person buying was then at least twenty-one years of age, if the person was buying beer as defined in section 4301.01 of the Revised Code or intoxicating liquor, or that the person was then at least eighteen years of age, if the person was buying any low-alcohol beverage;

(2) That the permit holder, the agent or employee of the permit holder, or the other person made a bona fide effort to ascertain the true age of the person buying by checking the identification presented, at the time of the purchase, to ascertain that the description on the identification compared with the appearance of the buyer and that the identification presented had not been altered in any way;

(3) That the permit holder, the agent or employee of the permit holder, or the other person had reason to believe that the person buying was of legal age.

(B) In any hearing before the liquor control commission and in any action or proceeding before a court of record in which a defense is raised under division (A) of this section, the registrar of motor vehicles or deputy registrar who issued an identification card under sections 4507.50 to 4507.52 of the Revised Code shall be permitted to submit certified copies of the records, in the registrar's or deputy's possession, of that issuance in lieu of the testimony of the personnel of or contractors with the bureau of motor vehicles at the hearing, action, or proceeding.

(C) The defense provided by division (A) of this section is in addition to the affirmative defense provided by section 4301.611 [4301.61.1] of the Revised Code.

**HISTORY: 134 v H 453 (Eff 9-28-72); 137 v H 90 (Eff 1-17-78); 143 v H 381 (Eff 7-1-89); 145 v S 209 (Eff 11-9-94); 148 v S 200. Eff 9-21-2000; 152 v S 150, § 1, eff. 9-1-08.**

## § 4301.64 Prohibition against consumption in motor vehicle.

No person shall consume any beer or intoxicating liquor in a motor vehicle. This section does not apply to persons described in division (D) of section 4301.62 of the Revised Code.

**HISTORY: GC § 6064-58; 115 v PtII, 118(156), § 58; Bureau of Code Revision, 10-1-53; 130 v 1000 (Eff 7-11-63); 146 v S 39. Eff 7-14-95.**

## § 4301.65 Alcohol vaporizing devices.

(A) As used in this section, "alcohol vaporizing device" means a machine or other device that mixes beer or intoxicating liquor with pure oxygen or any other gas to produce a vaporized product for the purpose of consumption by inhalation.

(B) No person shall sell or offer for sale an alcohol vaporizing device.

(C) No person shall purchase or use an alcohol vaporizing device.

**HISTORY: 151 v S 131, § 1, eff. 9-21-06.**

**Not analogous to former RC § 4301.65 (GC § 6064-60; 115 v PtII, 118; 116 v 511; Bureau of Code Revision, 10-1-53), repealed 136 v H 158, § 2, eff 8-13-76.**

## § 4301.66 Obstructing search of premises prohibited.

No person shall hinder or obstruct any agent or employee of the division of liquor control, any enforcement agent of the department of public safety, or any officer of the law, from making inspection or search of any place, other than a bona fide private residence, where beer or intoxicating liquor is possessed, kept, sold, or given away.

**HISTORY: GC § 6064-63; 116 v 511(542); Bureau of Code Revision, 10-1-53; 139 v H 357 (Eff 10-1-82); 146 v S 162 (Eff 10-29-95); 148 v H 163. Eff 6-30-99.**

## § 4301.67 Illegal possession of intoxicating liquor prohibited.

No person shall have that person's possession of † any spirituous liquor, in excess of one liter, in one or more containers, which was not purchased at wholesale or retail from the division of liquor control or otherwise lawfully acquired pursuant to Chapters 4301. and 4303. of the Revised Code, or any other intoxicating liquor or beer, in one or more containers, which was not lawfully acquired pursuant to Chapters 4301. and 4303. of the Revised Code.

**HISTORY: GC § 6064-64; 116 v 511(542); Bureau of Code Revision, 10-1-53; 128 v 1282 (Eff 10-23-59); 133 v H 638 (Eff 10-22-69); 139 v H 357 (Eff 10-1-82); 146 v S 149 (Eff 11-21-95); 146 v S 162. Eff 7-1-97.**

† The wording is the result of combining SB 149 (146 v —) and SB 162 (146 v —).

The effective date is set by section 10 of SB 162.

**Publisher's Note:**

The amendments made by SB 149 (146 v —) and SB 162 (146 v —) have been combined. See provisions of RC § 1.52.

## § 4301.68 Prohibition against sale or possession of diluted liquor and refilled containers.

No person shall sell, offer for sale, or possess intoxicating liquor in any original container which has been diluted, refilled, or partly refilled.

**HISTORY: GC § 6064-68; 119 v 217; Bureau of Code Revision. Eff 10-1-53.**

## § 4301.69 Offenses involving underage persons.

(A) Except as otherwise provided in this chapter, no person shall sell beer or intoxicating liquor to an underage person, shall buy beer or intoxicating liquor for an underage person, or shall furnish it to an underage person, unless given by a physician in the regular line of the physician's practice or given for established religious purposes or unless the underage person is supervised by a parent, spouse who is not an underage person, or legal guardian.

In proceedings before the liquor control commission, no permit holder, or no employee or agent of a permit holder, charged with a violation of this division shall be charged, for the same offense, with a violation of division (A)(1) of section 4301.22 of the Revised Code.

(B) No person who is the owner or occupant of any public or private place shall knowingly allow any underage person to remain in or on the place while possessing or consuming beer or intoxicating liquor, unless the intoxicating liquor or beer is given to the person possessing or consuming it by that person's parent, spouse who is not an underage person, or legal guardian and the parent, spouse who is not an underage person, or legal guardian is present at the time of the person's possession or consumption of the beer or intoxicating liquor.

An owner of a public or private place is not liable for acts or omissions in violation of this division that are committed by a lessee of that place, unless the owner authorizes or acquiesces in the lessee's acts or omissions.

(C) No person shall engage or use accommodations at a hotel, inn, cabin, campground, or restaurant when the person knows or has reason to know either of the following:

(1) That beer or intoxicating liquor will be consumed by an underage person on the premises of the accommodations that the person engages or uses, unless the person engaging or using the accommodations is the spouse of the underage person and is not an underage person, or is the parent or legal guardian of all of the underage persons, who consume beer or intoxicating liquor on the premises and that person is on the premises at all times when beer or intoxicating liquor is being consumed by an underage person;

(2) That a drug of abuse will be consumed on the premises of the accommodations by any person, except a person who obtained the drug of abuse pursuant to a prescription issued by a licensed health professional authorized to prescribe drugs and has the drug of abuse in the original container in which it was dispensed to the person.

(D)(1) No person is required to permit the engagement of accommodations at any hotel, inn, cabin, or campground by an underage person or for an underage person, if the person engaging the accommodations knows or has reason to know that the underage person is intoxicated, or that the underage person possesses any beer or intoxicating liquor and is not supervised by a parent, spouse who is not an underage person, or legal guardian who is or will be present at all times when the beer or intoxicating liquor is being consumed by the underage person.

(2) No underage person shall knowingly engage or attempt to engage accommodations at any hotel, inn, cabin, or campground by presenting identification that falsely indicates that the underage person is twenty-one years of age or older for the purpose of violating this section.

(E)(1) No underage person shall knowingly order, pay for, share the cost of, attempt to purchase, possess, or consume any beer or intoxicating liquor in any public or private place. No underage person shall knowingly be under the influence of any beer or intoxicating liquor in any public place. The prohibitions set forth in division (E)(1) of this section against an underage person knowingly possessing, consuming, or being under the influence of any beer or intoxicating liquor shall not apply if the underage person is supervised by a parent, spouse who is not an underage person, or legal guardian, or the beer or intoxicating liquor is given by a physician in the regular line of the physician's practice or given for established religious purposes.

(2)(a) If a person is charged with violating division (E)(1) of this section in a complaint filed under section 2151.27 of the Revised Code, the court may order the child into a diversion program specified by the court and hold the complaint in abeyance pending successful completion of the diversion program. A child is ineligible to enter into a diversion program under division (E)(2)(a) of this section if the child previously has been diverted pursuant to division (E)(2)(a) of this section. If the child completes the diversion program to the satisfaction of the court, the court shall dismiss the complaint and order the child's record in the case sealed under sections 2151.356 [2151.35.6] to 2151.358 [2151.35.8] of the Revised Code. If the child fails to satisfactorily complete the diversion program, the court shall proceed with the complaint.

(b) If a person is charged in a criminal complaint with violating division (E)(1) of this section, section 2935.36 of the Revised Code shall apply to the offense, except that a person is ineligible for diversion under that section if the person previously has been diverted pursuant to division (E)(2)(a) or (b) of this section. If the person completes the diversion program to the satisfaction of the court, the court shall dismiss the complaint and order the record in the case sealed under section 2953.52 of the Revised Code. If the person fails to satisfactorily complete the diversion program, the court shall proceed with the complaint.

(F) No parent, spouse who is not an underage person, or legal guardian of a minor shall knowingly permit the minor to violate this section or section 4301.63, 4301.633 [4301.63.3], or 4301.634 [4301.63.4] of the Revised Code.

(G) The operator of any hotel, inn, cabin, or campground shall make the provisions of this section available in writing to any person engaging or using accommodations at the hotel, inn, cabin, or campground.

(H) As used in this section:

(1) "Drug of abuse" has the same meaning as in section 3719.011 [3719.01.1] of the Revised Code.

(2) "Hotel" has the same meaning as in section 3731.01 of the Revised Code.

(3) "Licensed health professional authorized to prescribe drugs" and "prescription" have the same meanings as in section 4729.01 of the Revised Code.

(4) "Minor" means a person under the age of eighteen years.

(5) "Underage person" means a person under the age of twenty-one years.

**HISTORY: RS § 6943; 63 v 149, § 2; GC § 12960; 113 v 495; 115 v PtII, 118(161), § 62; 116 v 279; Bureau of Code Revision, 10-1-53; 132 v S 128 (Eff 11-24-67); 136 v H 315 (Eff 4-25-75); 139 v H 357 (Eff 8-19-82); 142 v H 419 (Eff 7-31-87); 142 v H 306 (Eff 6-9-88); 143 v H 22 (Eff 8-1-89); 145 v S 82 (Eff 5-4-94); 147 v S 66 (Eff 7-22-98); 149 v H 17. Eff 10-11-2002; 151 v S 131, § 1, eff. 9-21-06; 151 v H 137, § 1, eff. 10-9-06.**

The effective date is set by § 6 of 151 v H 137.

**Comment, Legislative Service Commission**

Section 4301.69 of the Revised Code is amended by Am. Sub. H.B. 137 and Sub. S.B. 131 of the 126th General Assembly. Comparison of these amendments in pursuance of section 1.52 of the Revised Code discloses that they are not irreconcilable so that they are required by that section to be harmonized to give effect to each amendment.

## § 4301.691 Alternate prohibitions if federal mandate is no longer in force.

If the United States congress repeals the mandate established by the "Surface Transportation Assistance Act of 1982" relating to a national uniform drinking age of twenty-one or if a court of competent jurisdiction declares the mandate to be unconstitutional or otherwise invalid, then upon the certification by the secretary of state that this mandate has been repealed or invalidated, the following shall apply:

(A) Beer or intoxicating liquor may be served to a person not seated at a table unless there is reason to believe that the beer will be consumed by a person under nineteen years of age or that the intoxicating liquor will be consumed by a person under twenty-one years of age.

(B) No person under the age of twenty-one years shall purchase intoxicating liquor, nor shall a person under the age of nineteen years purchase beer.

(C) No person under the age of nineteen years shall order, pay for, share the cost of, or attempt to purchase any beer or intoxicating liquor, or consume any beer or intoxicating liquor, either from a sealed or unsealed container or by the glass or by the drink, in any public or private place, except as provided in section 4301.69 of the Revised Code.

(D) No person under the age of twenty-one years shall order, pay for, share the cost of, or attempt to purchase any intoxicating liquor, or consume any intoxicating liquor, either from a sealed or unsealed container or by the glass or by the drink, except as provided in section 4301.69 of the Revised Code.

(E) No person shall knowingly furnish any false information as to the name, age, or other identification of any person under twenty-one years of age for the purpose of obtaining or with the intent to obtain, beer or intoxicating liquor for a person under nineteen years of age, or intoxicating liquor for a person under twenty-one years of age, by purchase, or as a gift.

(F) No person under the age of nineteen years shall knowingly show or give false information concerning the person's name, age, or other identification for the purpose of purchasing or otherwise obtaining beer or intoxicating liquor in any place in this state where beer or intoxicating liquor is sold under a permit issued by the division of liquor control or sold by the division.

(G) No person under the age of twenty-one years shall knowingly show or give false information concerning the person's name, age, or other identification for the purpose of purchasing or otherwise obtaining intoxicating liquor in any place in this state where intoxicating liquor is sold under a permit issued by the division or sold by the division.

(H) No person shall sell intoxicating liquor to a person under the age of twenty-one years or sell beer to a person under the age of nineteen, or buy intoxicating liquor for, or furnish it to, a person under the age of twenty-one years, or buy beer for or furnish it to a person under the age of nineteen, unless given by a physician in the regular line of his practice, or by a parent or legal guardian.

In proceedings before the liquor control commission, no permit holder or the permit holder's employee or agent charged with a violation of this section shall, for the same offense, be charged with a violation of division (A)(1) of section 4301.22 of the Revised Code.

(I) No person who is the owner or occupant of any public or private place shall knowingly allow any person under the age of twenty-one to remain in or on the place while possessing or consuming intoxicating liquor, or knowingly allow any person under the age of nineteen to remain in or on the place while possessing or consuming beer, unless the intoxicating liquor or beer is given to the person possessing or consuming it by that person's parent or legal guardian and the parent or legal guardian is present at the time of the person's possession or consumption of the intoxicating liquor or beer.

(J) The division shall revise the warning sign required by section 4301.637 [4301.63.7] of the Revised Code so that the sign conforms to this section.

**HISTORY: 142 v H 419 (Eff 7-31-87); 142 v H 306 (Eff 6-9-88); 143 v H 22 (Eff 8-1-89); 145 v S 82 (Eff 5-4-94); 146 v S 162. Eff 7-1-97.**

The effective date is set by section 10 of SB 162.

## § 4301.70 Prohibition against violations not otherwise specified.

Any person who is subject to Chapter 4301., 4303., or 4307. of the Revised Code, in the transportation, possession, or sale of wine or mixed beverage subject to the taxes imposed by sections 4301.43 and 4301.432 [4301.43.2] of the Revised Code, and who violates such chapters or any lawful rule promulgated by the tax commissioner under such chapters, for the violation of which no penalty is otherwise provided, shall be fined as provided in division (A) of section 4301.99 of the Revised Code.

**HISTORY: GC § 6064-50; 115 v PtII, 118(154), § 50; 116 v PtII, 89; Bureau of Code Revision, 10-1-53; 125 v 903(1024) (Eff 10-1-53); 139 v H 694 (Eff 11-15-81); 139 v H 357. Eff 10-1-82.**

The effective date of this section is set by section 6 of HB 357.

[NUISANCE]

## § 4301.74 Procedure when injunction violated.

Any person subject to an injunction, temporary or permanent, granted pursuant to division (D) or (E) of section 3767.05 of the Revised Code involving a condition described in division (C)(3) or (4) of section 3767.01 of the Revised Code shall obey such injunction. If such person violates such injunction, the court or in vacation a judge thereof, may summarily try and punish the violator. The proceedings for punishment for contempt shall be commenced by filing with the clerk of the court from which such injunction issued information under oath setting out the alleged facts constituting the violation, whereupon the court shall forthwith cause a warrant to issue under which the defendant shall be arrested. The trial may be had upon affidavits, or either party may demand the production and oral examination of the witnesses.

**HISTORY: GC § 13195-3; 110 v 34; 115 v PtII, 118(162), § 62; Bureau of Code Revision, 10-1-53; 147 v H 402. Eff 3-30-99.**

## § 4301.77 Sharing of social security numbers with state or local agencies for certain purposes.

The division of liquor control may provide the social security number of an individual that the division possesses to the department of public safety, the department of taxation, the office of the attorney general, or any other state or local law enforcement agency if the department, office, or other state or local law enfocement† agency requests the social security number from the division to conduct an investigation, implement an enforcement action, or collect taxes.

**HISTORY: 150 v H 306, § 1, eff. 7-23-04.**

† As enrolled by 150 v H 306.

[PENALTIES]

## § 4301.99 Penalties.

(A) Whoever violates section 4301.47, 4301.48, 4301.49, 4301.62, or 4301.70 or division (C) of section 4301.65 or division (B) of section 4301.691 [4301.69.1] of the Revised Code is guilty of a minor misdemeanor.

(B) Whoever violates section 4301.15, division (A)(2) or (C) of section 4301.22, division (C), (D), (E), (F), (G), (H), or (I) of section 4301.631 [4301.63.1], or section 4301.64 or 4301.67 of the Revised Code is guilty of a misdemeanor of the fourth degree.

If an offender who violates section 4301.64 of the Revised Code was under the age of eighteen years at the time of the offense, the court, in addition to any other penalties it imposes upon the offender, shall suspend the offender's temporary instruction permit, probationary driver's license, or driver's license for a period of not less than six months and not more than one year. If the offender is fifteen years and six months of age or older and has not been issued a temporary instruction permit or probationary driver's license, the offender shall not be eligible to be issued such a license or permit for a period of six months. If the offender has not attained the age of fifteen years and six months, the offender shall not be eligible to be issued a temporary instruction permit until the offender attains the age of sixteen years.

(C) Whoever violates division (D) of section 4301.21, or section 4301.251 [4301.25.1], 4301.58, 4301.59, 4301.60, 4301.633 [4301.63.3], 4301.66, 4301.68, or 4301.74, division (B), (C), (D), (E)(1), or (F) of section 4301.69, or division (C), (D), (E), (F), (G), or (I) of section 4301.691 [4301.69.1] of the Revised Code is guilty of a misdemeanor of the first degree.

If an offender who violates division (E)(1) of section 4301.69 of the Revised Code was under the age of eighteen years at the time of the offense and the offense occurred while the offender was the operator of or a passenger in a motor vehicle, the court, in addition to any other penalties it imposes upon the offender, shall suspend the offender's temporary instruction permit or probationary driver's license for a period of not less than six months and not more than one year. If the offender is fifteen years and six months of age or older and has not been issued a temporary instruction permit or probationary driver's license, the offender shall not be eligible to be issued such a license or permit for a period of six months. If the offender has not attained the age of fifteen years and six months, the offender shall not be eligible to be issued a temporary instruction permit until the offender attains the age of sixteen years.

(D) Whoever violates division (B) of section 4301.14, or division (A)(1) or (3) or (B) of section 4301.22 of the Revised Code is guilty of a misdemeanor of the third degree.

(E) Whoever violates section 4301.63 or division (B) of section 4301.631 [4301.63.1] of the Revised Code shall be fined not less than twenty-five nor more than one hundred dollars. The court imposing a fine for a violation of section 4301.63 or division (B) of section 4301.631 [4301.63.1] of the Revised Code may order that the fine be paid by the performance of public work at a reasonable hourly rate established by the court. The court shall designate the time within which the public work shall be completed.

(F)(1) Whoever violates section 4301.634 [4301.63.4] of the Revised Code is guilty of a misdemeanor of the first degree. If, in committing a first violation of that section, the offender presented to the permit holder or the permit holder's employee or agent a false, fictitious, or altered identification card, a false or fictitious driver's license purportedly issued by any state, or a driver's license issued by any state that has been altered, the offender is guilty of a misdemeanor of the first degree and shall be fined not less than two hundred fifty and not more than one thousand dollars, and may be sentenced to a term of imprisonment of not more than six months.

(2) On a second violation in which, for the second time, the offender presented to the permit holder or the permit holder's employee or agent a false, fictitious, or altered identification card, a false or fictitious driver's license purportedly issued by any state, or a driver's license issued by any state that has been altered, the offender is guilty of a misdemeanor of the first degree and shall be fined not less than five hundred nor more than one thousand dollars, and may be sentenced to a term of imprisonment of not more than six months. The court also may impose a class seven suspension of the offender's driver's or commercial driver's license or permit or nonresident operating privilege from the range specified in division (A)(7) of section 4510.02 of the Revised Code.

(3) On a third or subsequent violation in which, for the third or subsequent time, the offender presented to the permit holder or the permit holder's employee or agent a false, fictitious, or altered identification card, a false or fictitious driver's license purportedly issued by any state, or a driver's license issued by any state that has been altered, the offender is guilty of a misdemeanor of the first degree and shall be fined not less than five hundred nor more than one thousand dollars, and may be sentenced to a term of imprisonment of not more than six months. The court also shall impose a class six suspension of the offender's driver's or commercial driver's license or permit or nonresident operating privilege from the range specified in division (A)(6) of section 4510.02 of the Revised Code, and the court may order that the suspension or denial remain in effect until the offender attains the age of twenty-one years. The court also may order the offender to perform a determinate number of hours of community service, with the court determining the actual number of hours and the nature of the community service the offender shall perform.

(G) Whoever violates section 4301.636 [4301.63.6] of the Revised Code is guilty of a felony of the fifth degree.

(H) Whoever violates division (A)(1) of section 4301.22 of the Revised Code is guilty of a misdemeanor, shall be fined not less than five hundred and not more than one thousand dollars, and, in addition to the fine, may be imprisoned for a definite term of not more than sixty days.

(I) Whoever violates division (A) of section 4301.69 or division (H) of section 4301.691 [4301.69.1] of the Revised Code is guilty of a misdemeanor, shall be fined not less than five hundred and not more than one thousand dollars, and, in addition to the fine, may be imprisoned for a definite term of not more than six months.

(J) Whoever violates division (B) of section 4301.65 of the Revised Code is guilty of a misdemeanor of the third degree. For a second or subsequent violation occurring within a period of five consecutive years after the first violation, a person is guilty of a misdemeanor of the first degree.

**HISTORY: 135 v H 352 (Eff 9-30-74); 135 v H 496 (Eff 9-30-74); 136 v H 1 (Eff 6-13-75); 136 v H 158 (Eff 8-13-76); 137 v S 49 (Eff 11-14-77); 140 v S 74 (Eff 7-4-84); 142 v H 419 (Eff 7-31-87); 142 v H 562 (Eff 6-29-88); 142 v H 306 (Eff 6-9-88); 143 v S 131 (Eff 7-25-90); 145 v S 82 (Eff 5-4-94); 145 v S 209 (Eff 11-9-94); 146 v S 2 (Eff 7-1-96); 147 v S 35 (Eff 1-1-99); 149 v H 17 (Eff 10-11-2002); 149 v S 123. Eff 1-1-2004; 150 v H 306, § 1, eff. 7-23-04; 151 v S 131, § 1, eff. 9-21-06.**

The provisions of § 3 of H.B. 306 (150 v —) read as follows:

SECTION 3. * * * Section 4301.99 of the Revised Code is presented in this act as a composite of the section as amended by both Am. Sub. H.B. 17 and Am. Sub. S.B. 123 of the 124th General Assembly. The General Assembly, applying the principle stated in division (B) of section 1.52 of the Revised Code that amendments are to be harmonized if reasonably capable of simultaneous operation, finds that the composite versions of these sections are the resulting versions of the sections in effect prior to the effective date of the sections as presented in this act.

**Analogous to former RC § 4301.99 (Bureau of Code Revision, 10-1-53; 125 v 113; 126 v 324; 130 v 1000; 130 v 1003; 130 v 1002; 132 v H 345) repealed 135 v H 352 and H 496, eff 9-30-74.**

The effective date is set by section 4 of SB 123.

The provisions of § 5 of S.B. 123 (149 v —), as amended by § 3 of H.B. 163 (150 v —), read as follows:

SECTION 5. (A) Notwithstanding division (B) of section 1.58 of the Revised Code, the provisions of the Revised Code amended or enacted in Sections 1 and 2 of Am. Sub. S.B. 123 of the 124th General Assembly shall apply only in relation to conduct and offenses committed on or after January 1, 2004. Conduct and offenses committed prior to January 1, 2004, shall be governed by the law in effect on the date the conduct or offense was committed. * * *

**Comment, Legislative Service Commission**

* * * Section 4301.99 of the Revised Code is amended by this act [Am. Sub. S.B. 123] (effective January 1, 2004) and also by Am. Sub. H.B. 17, both of the 124th General Assembly. * * * Comparison of these amendments in pursuance of section 1.52 of the Revised Code discloses that they are not irreconcilable so that they are required by that section to be harmonized to give effect to each amendment.

## § 4301.991 Duty to send notice of conviction or acquittal.

Upon the trial of a permit holder, the permit holder's employee, or the permit holder's agent for a violation of sections 4301.01 to 4301.74 of the Revised Code occurring on the premises for which a permit issued by the department or, beginning on July 1, 1997, the division of liquor control is held by the permit holder, the magistrate or the clerk of the municipal court or of the court of common pleas shall, if the permit holder, the permit holder's employee, or the permit holder's agent is found guilty, within seven days after the sentence has been imposed mail a certified copy of the record of such conviction to the director of public safety, who shall forward a copy of that certified copy to the director or, beginning on July 1, 1997, the superintendent of liquor control.

If the permit holder, the permit holder's employee, or the permit holder's agent is found to be not guilty after a trial on the merits, the magistrate or clerk of the municipal court or of the court of common pleas shall within seven days mail a certified copy of the journal entry to the director or superintendent of liquor control and the permit holder shall not be cited to the liquor control commission for any alleged violations of law or rules based upon specifications contained in the indictment, information, or affidavit in the case.

**HISTORY: 126 v 324 (Eff 10-4-55); 140 v S 72 (Eff 10-14-83); 146 v S 162. Eff 10-29-95.**

# CHAPTER 4399: PROHIBITORY PROVISIONS AND CRIMES

Section



## § 4399.09 Keeping place where beer or intoxicating liquors are furnished in violation of law.

(A) No person shall keep a place where beer or intoxicating liquors are sold, furnished, or given away in violation of law. The court, on conviction for a subsequent violation of this section, shall order the place where the beer or intoxicating liquor is sold, furnished, or given away to be abated as a nuisance or shall order the person so convicted to give bond payable to the state in the sum of one thousand dollars, with sureties to the acceptance of the court, that the person will not sell, furnish, or give away beer or intoxicating liquor in violation of law and will pay all fines, costs, and damages assessed against the person for that subsequent violation of this section. The giving away of beer or intoxicating liquors, or any other device to evade this division, constitutes unlawful selling.

As used in this division, "beer" has the same meaning as in section 4301.01 of the Revised Code.

(B) Division (A) of this section does not apply to any premises for which a permit has been issued under Chapter 4303. of the Revised Code while that permit is in effect.

**HISTORY: RS § 6942; S&C 1431; 52 v 153; 92 v 55; 99 v 470; GC § 13195; Bureau of Code Revision, 10-1-53; 140 v S 74 (Eff 7-4-84); 149 v H 371. Eff 10-11-2002.**

## § 4399.10 Intoxicating liquors shall not be sold in brothels.

No person shall sell, exchange, or give away intoxicating liquor in a brothel.

**HISTORY: RS §§ 6943-5, 6943-6; 88 v 567, § 2; GC § 13199; Bureau of Code Revision. Eff 10-1-53.**

## § 4399.11 Selling intoxicating liquors at certain places prohibited.

If a person is convicted of any violation of Title XLIII [43] of the Revised Code that involves the sale of intoxicating liquors at or within twelve hundred yards of the administration or main central building of the Columbus state hospital, Dayton state hospital, Athens state hospital, or Toledo state hospital, or within two miles of the place at which an agricultural fair is being held, or within one mile of a county children's home situated within one mile of a municipal corporation in which the sale of intoxicating liquors is prohibited by ordinance, the place in which the intoxicating liquors are sold shall be shut up and abated as a nuisance by order of the court upon conviction of its owner or keeper.

**HISTORY: RS § 6946; S&C 68; 53 v 141, § 3; 71 v 82; 82 v 222; 84 v 70; 85 v 19; 88 v 603; 92 v 434; 93 v 341; GC § 13206; Bureau of Code Revision, 10-1-53; 137 v S 420 (Eff 7-24-78); 138 v H 965 (Eff 4-9-81); 146 v H 117 (Eff 9-29-95); 146 v S 2. Eff 7-1-96.**

The effective date is set by section 6 of SB 2.

**Comment, Legislative Service Commission**

° ° ° Section ° ° ° 4399.11 of the Revised Code are [is] amended by this act [Am. Sub. S.B. 2] (effective July 1, 1996) and also by Am. Sub. H.B. 117 of the 121st General Assembly. ° ° ° Section 4399.12 of the Revised Code are [is] amended by this act [Am. Sub. S.B. 2] (effective July 1, 1996) and also by Am. Sub. S.B. 162 of the 121st General Assembly (effective July 1, 1997). ° ° ° Comparison of these amendments in pursuance of section 1.52 of the Revised Code discloses that they are not irreconcilable so that they are required by that section to be harmonized to give effect to each amendment.

## § 4399.12 Permit holders excepted.

No provision contained in Title XLIII [43] of the Revised Code that prohibits the sale of intoxicating liquors in any of the circumstances described in section 4399.11 of the Revised Code extends to or prevents the holder of an A, B, C-2, D-2, D-3, D-3a, D-4, D-4a, D-5, D-5a, D-5b, D-5e, D-5f, D-5g, D-5h, D-5i, D-5j, D-5k, D-5l, D-5m, G, or I permit issued by the division of liquor control from distributing or selling intoxicating liquor at the place of business described in the permit of the holder.

**HISTORY: GC § 13207; 122 v 209; Bureau of Code Revision, 10-1-53; 140 v H 711 (Eff 7-1-85); 142 v H 562 (Eff 6-29-88); 143 v H 405 (Eff 4-11-91); 146 v S 2 (Eff 7-1-96); 146 v S 162 (Eff 7-1-97); 148 v H 283 (Eff 9-29-99); 149 v H 371. Eff 10-11-2002; 152 v S 150, § 1, eff. 9-1-08.**

## § 4399.14 Prohibitions concerning public dance halls.

(A) Except as otherwise provided in division (B) of this section, no person who is the proprietor of or who conducts, manages, or is in charge of any public dance hall shall allow the use of any intoxicating liquor or the presence of intoxicated persons in the public dance hall or on the premises on which it is located.

(B) The prohibition against the use of any intoxicating liquor contained in division (A) of this section does not apply to establishments that are holders of a D-1, D-2, D-3, D-4, or D-5 permit whose principal business consists of conducting a hotel, a restaurant, a club, or a night club, all as defined in section 4301.01 of the Revised Code.

**HISTORY: GC § 13393-1; 111 v 83; 116 v 511(547); Bureau of Code Revision. Eff 10-1-53; 151 v H 368, § 1, eff. 9-21-06.**

## § 4399.15 Poisonously adulterated liquors.

No person, for the purpose of sale, shall adulterate spirituous liquor, alcoholic liquor, or beer used or intended for drink or medicinal or mechanical purposes, with cocculus indicus, vitriol, grains of paradise, opium, alum, capsicum, copperas, laurel water, logwood, Brazilwood, cochineal, sugar of lead, aloes, glucose, tannic acid, or any other substance that is poisonous or injurious to health, or with a substance not a necessary ingredient in the manufacture of the spirituous liquor, alcoholic liquor, or beer, or sell, offer, or keep for sale spirituous liquor, alcoholic liquor, or beer that is so adulterated.

In addition to the penalties provided in division (E) of section 4399.99 of the Revised Code, a person convicted of violating this section shall pay all necessary costs and expenses incurred in inspecting and analyzing spirituous liquor, alcoholic liquor, or beer that is so adulterated, sold, kept, or offered for sale.

**HISTORY: RS § 7082; S&C 729; 52 v 108; 79 v 52; GC §§ 12676, 12677; Bureau of Code Revision, 10-1-53; 146 v S 2 (Eff 7-1-96); 149 v H 371. Eff 10-11-2002.**

## § 4399.16 Tavern keeper permitting rioting or drunkenness.

No tavern keeper shall permit rioting, reveling, intoxication, or drunkenness in his house or on his premises.

**HISTORY: RS § 6997; S&S 749; S&C 1430; 64 v 25; GC § 12813; Bureau of Code Revision. Eff 10-1-53.**

## § 4399.17 Manufacturing or selling poisoned liquors.

No person shall use an active poison in the manufacture or preparation of intoxicating liquor or sell intoxicating liquor so manufactured or prepared.

**HISTORY: RS § 7083; S&C 1436; 54 v 183; GC § 12675; Bureau of Code Revision. Eff 10-1-53.**

## § 4399.18 Limitations on liability for acts of intoxicated person.

Notwithstanding division (A) of section 2307.60 of the Revised Code and except as otherwise provided in this section, no person, and no executor or administrator of the person, who suffers personal injury, death, or property damage as a result of the actions of an intoxicated person has a cause of action against any liquor permit holder or an employee of a liquor permit holder who sold beer or intoxicating liquor to the intoxicated person unless the personal injury, death, or property damage occurred on the permit holder's premises or in a parking lot under the control of the permit holder and was proximately caused by the negligence of the permit holder or an employee of the permit holder. A person has a cause of action against a permit holder or an employee of a permit holder for personal injury, death, or property damage caused by the negligent actions of an intoxicated person occurring off the premises or away from a parking lot under the permit holder's control only when both of the following can be shown by a preponderance of the evidence:

(A) The permit holder or an employee of the permit holder knowingly sold an intoxicating beverage to at least one of the following:

(1) A noticeably intoxicated person in violation of division (B) of section 4301.22 of the Revised Code;

(2) A person in violation of section 4301.69 of the Revised Code.

(B) The person's intoxication proximately caused the personal injury, death, or property damage.

Notwithstanding sections 4399.02 and 4399.05 of the Revised Code, no person, and no executor or administrator of the person, who suffers personal injury, death, or property damage as a result of the actions of an intoxicated person has a cause of action against the owner of a building or premises who rents or leases the building or premises to a liquor permit holder against whom a cause of action may be brought under this section, except when the owner and the permit holder are the same person.

**HISTORY: 141 v H 759 (Eff 7-21-86); 146 v H 350 (Eff 1-27-97); 149 v S 108, § 2.01 (Eff 7-6-2001); 149 v S 107. Eff 6-28-2002; 150 v H 306, § 1, eff. 7-23-04.**

**Publisher's Note:**

Section 2.02(B) of SB 108 (149 v —) repeals the HB 350 (146 v —) version and section 3(A)(3) revives and amends the former version.

## § 4399.99 Penalties.

(A) Whoever violates section 4399.16 of the Revised Code shall be fined not less than five nor more than one hundred dollars.

(B) Whoever violates section 4399.09 of the Revised Code shall be fined not less than one hundred nor more than five hundred dollars on a first offense and shall be fined not less than two hundred nor more than five hundred dollars on each subsequent offense.

(C) Whoever violates section 4399.10 of the Revised Code shall be fined not less than one hundred nor more than five hundred dollars and imprisoned not less than one nor more than six months.

(D) Whoever violates section 4399.14 of the Revised Code shall be fined not less than twenty-five nor more than five hundred dollars, imprisoned not more than six months, or both.

(E) Whoever violates section 4399.15 of the Revised Code shall be fined not less than twenty nor more than one hundred dollars, imprisoned not less than twenty nor more than sixty days, or both.

(F) Whoever violates section 4399.17 of the Revised Code is guilty of a felony of the fourth degree.

**HISTORY: Bureau of Code Revision, 10-1-53; 133 v H 876 (Eff 8-25-70); 139 v S 199 (Eff 1-5-83); 146 v S 2. Eff 7-1-96.**

The effective date is set by section 6 of SB 2.

# TITLE 45: MOTOR VEHICLES — AERONAUTICS — WATERCRAFT

## CHAPTER 4501: MOTOR VEHICLES — DEFINITIONS; GENERAL PROVISIONS



### § 4501.01 Definitions.

As used in this chapter and Chapters 4503., 4505., 4507., 4509., 4510., 4511., 4513., 4515., and 4517. of the Revised Code, and in the penal laws, except as otherwise provided:

(A) "Vehicles" means everything on wheels or runners, including motorized bicycles, but does not mean electric personal assistive mobility devices, vehicles that are operated exclusively on rails or tracks or from overhead electric trolley wires, and vehicles that belong to any police department, municipal fire department, or volunteer fire department, or that are used by such a department in the discharge of its functions.

(B) "Motor vehicle" means any vehicle, including mobile homes and recreational vehicles, that is propelled or drawn by power other than muscular power or power collected from overhead electric trolley wires. "Motor vehicle" does not include utility vehicles as defined in division (VV) of this section, motorized bicycles, road rollers, traction engines, power shovels, power cranes, and other equipment used in construction work and not designed for or employed in general highway transportation, well-drilling machinery, ditch-digging machinery, farm machinery, and trailers that are designed and used exclusively to transport a boat between a place of storage and a marina, or in and around a marina, when drawn or towed on a public road or highway for a distance of no more than ten miles and at a speed of twenty-five miles per hour or less.

(C) "Agricultural tractor" and "traction engine" mean any self-propelling vehicle that is designed or used for drawing other vehicles or wheeled machinery, but has no provisions for carrying loads independently of such other vehicles, and that is used principally for agricultural purposes.

(D) "Commercial tractor," except as defined in division (C) of this section, means any motor vehicle that has motive power and either is designed or used for drawing other motor vehicles, or is designed or used for drawing another motor vehicle while carrying a portion of the other motor vehicle or its load, or both.

(E) "Passenger car" means any motor vehicle that is designed and used for carrying not more than nine persons and includes any motor vehicle that is designed and used for carrying not more than fifteen persons in a ridesharing arrangement.

(F) "Collector's vehicle" means any motor vehicle or agricultural tractor or traction engine that is of special interest, that has a fair market value of one hundred dollars or more, whether operable or not, and that is owned, operated, collected, preserved, restored, maintained, or used essentially as a collector's item, leisure pursuit, or investment, but not as the owner's principal means of transportation. "Licensed collector's vehicle" means a collector's vehicle, other than an agricultural tractor or traction engine, that displays current, valid license tags issued under section 4503.45 of the Revised Code, or a similar type of motor vehicle that displays current, valid license tags issued under substantially equivalent provisions in the laws of other states.

(G) "Historical motor vehicle" means any motor vehicle that is over twenty-five years old and is owned solely as a collector's item and for participation in club activities, exhibitions, tours, parades, and similar uses, but that in no event is used for general transportation.

(H) "Noncommercial motor vehicle" means any motor vehicle, including a farm truck as defined in section 4503.04 of the Revised Code, that is designed by the manufacturer to carry a load of no more than one ton and is used exclusively for purposes other than engaging in business for profit.

(I) "Bus" means any motor vehicle that has motor power and is designed and used for carrying more than nine passengers, except any motor vehicle that is designed and used for carrying not more than fifteen passengers in a ridesharing arrangement.

(J) "Commercial car" or "truck" means any motor vehicle that has motor power and is designed and used for carrying merchandise or freight, or that is used as a commercial tractor.

(K) "Bicycle" means every device, other than a tricycle that is designed solely for use as a play vehicle by a child, that is propelled solely by human power upon which any person may ride, and that has two tandem wheels, or one wheel in front and two wheels in the rear, or two wheels in the front and one wheel in the rear, any of which is more than fourteen inches in diameter.

(L) "Motorized bicycle" means any vehicle that either has two tandem wheels or one wheel in the front and two wheels in the rear, that is capable of being pedaled, and that is equipped with a helper motor of not more than fifty cubic centimeters piston displacement that produces no more than one brake horsepower and is capable of propelling the vehicle at a speed of no greater than twenty miles per hour on a level surface.

(M) "Trailer" means any vehicle without motive power that is designed or used for carrying property or persons wholly on its own structure and for being drawn by a motor vehicle, and includes any such vehicle that is formed by or operated as a combination of a semitrailer and a vehicle of the dolly type such as that commonly known as a trailer dolly, a vehicle used to transport agricultural produce or agricultural production materials between a local place of storage or supply and the farm when drawn or towed on a public road or highway at a speed greater than twenty-five miles per hour, and a vehicle that is designed and used exclusively to transport a boat between a place of storage and a marina, or in and around a marina, when drawn or towed on a public road or highway for a distance of more than ten miles or at a speed of more than twenty-five miles per hour. "Trailer" does not include a manufactured home or travel trailer.

(N) "Noncommercial trailer" means any trailer, except a travel trailer or trailer that is used to transport a boat as described in division (B) of this section, but, where applicable, includes a vehicle that is used to transport a boat as described in division (M) of this section, that has a gross weight of no more than ten thousand pounds, and that is used exclusively for purposes other than engaging in business for a profit, such as the transportation of personal items for personal or recreational purposes.

(O) "Mobile home" means a building unit or assembly of closed construction that is fabricated in an off-site facility, is more than thirty-five body feet in length or, when erected on site, is three hundred twenty or more square feet, is built on a permanent chassis, is transportable in one or more sections, and does not qualify as a manufactured home as defined in division (C)(4) of section 3781.06 of the Revised Code or as an industrialized unit as defined in division (C)(3) of section 3781.06 of the Revised Code.

(P) "Semitrailer" means any vehicle of the trailer type that does not have motive power and is so designed or used with another and separate motor vehicle that in operation a part of its own weight or that of its load, or both, rests upon and is carried by the other vehicle furnishing the motive power for propelling itself and the vehicle referred to in this division, and includes, for the purpose only of registration and taxation under those chapters, any vehicle of the dolly type, such as a trailer dolly, that is designed or used for the conversion of a semitrailer into a trailer.

(Q) "Recreational vehicle" means a vehicular portable structure that meets all of the following conditions:

(1) It is designed for the sole purpose of recreational travel.

(2) It is not used for the purpose of engaging in business for profit.

(3) It is not used for the purpose of engaging in intrastate commerce.

(4) It is not used for the purpose of commerce as defined in 49 C.F.R. 383.5, as amended.

(5) It is not regulated by the public utilities commission pursuant to Chapter 4919., 4921., or 4923. of the Revised Code.

(6) It is classed as one of the following:

(a) "Travel trailer" means a nonself-propelled recreational vehicle that does not exceed an overall length of thirty-five feet, exclusive of bumper and tongue or coupling, and contains less than three hundred twenty square feet of space when erected on site. "Travel trailer" includes a tent-type fold-out camping trailer as defined in section 4517.01 of the Revised Code.

(b) "Motor home" means a self-propelled recreational vehicle that has no fifth wheel and is constructed with permanently installed facilities for cold storage, cooking and consuming of food, and for sleeping.

(c) "Truck camper" means a nonself-propelled recreational vehicle that does not have wheels for road use and is designed to be placed upon and attached to a motor vehicle. "Truck camper" does not include truck covers that consist of walls and a roof, but do not have floors and facilities enabling them to be used as a dwelling.

(d) "Fifth wheel trailer" means a vehicle that is of such size and weight as to be movable without a special highway permit, that has a gross trailer area of four hundred square feet or less, that is constructed with a raised forward section that allows a bi-level floor plan, and that is designed to be towed by a vehicle equipped with a fifth-wheel hitch ordinarily installed in the bed of a truck.

(e) "Park trailer" means a vehicle that is commonly known as a park model recreational vehicle, meets the American national standard institute standard A119.5 (1988) for park trailers, is built on a single chassis, has a gross trailer area of four hundred square feet or less when set up, is designed for seasonal or temporary living quarters, and may be connected to utilities necessary for the operation of installed features and appliances.

(R) "Pneumatic tires" means tires of rubber and fabric or tires of similar material, that are inflated with air.

(S) "Solid tires" means tires of rubber or similar elastic material that are not dependent upon confined air for support of the load.

(T) "Solid tire vehicle" means any vehicle that is equipped with two or more solid tires.

(U) "Farm machinery" means all machines and tools that are used in the production, harvesting, and care of farm products, and includes trailers that are used to transport agricultural produce or agricultural production materials between a local place of storage or supply and the farm, agricultural tractors, threshing machinery, hay-baling machinery, corn shellers, hammermills, and machinery used in the production of horticultural, agricultural, and vegetable products.

(V) "Owner" includes any person or firm, other than a manufacturer or dealer, that has title to a motor vehicle, except that, in sections 4505.01 to 4505.19 of the Revised Code, "owner" includes in addition manufacturers and dealers.

(W) "Manufacturer" and "dealer" include all persons and firms that are regularly engaged in the business of manufacturing, selling, displaying, offering for sale, or dealing in motor vehicles, at an established place of business that is used exclusively for the purpose of manufacturing, selling, displaying, offering for sale, or dealing in motor vehicles. A place of business that is used for manufacturing, selling, displaying, offering for sale, or dealing in motor vehicles shall be deemed to be used exclusively for those purposes even though snowmobiles or all-purpose vehicles are sold or displayed for sale thereat, even though farm machinery is sold or displayed for sale thereat, or even though repair, accessory, gasoline and oil, storage, parts, service, or paint departments are maintained thereat, or, in any county having a population of less than seventy-five thousand at the last federal census, even though a department in a place of business is used to dismantle, salvage, or rebuild motor vehicles by means of used parts, if such departments are operated for the purpose of furthering and assisting in the business of manufacturing, selling, displaying, offering for sale, or dealing in motor vehicles. Places of business or departments in a place of business used to dismantle, salvage, or rebuild motor vehicles by means of using used parts are not considered as being maintained for the purpose of assisting or furthering the manufacturing, selling, displaying, and offering for sale or dealing in motor vehicles.

(X) "Operator" includes any person who drives or operates a motor vehicle upon the public highways.

(Y) "Chauffeur" means any operator who operates a motor vehicle, other than a taxicab, as an employee for hire; or any operator whether or not the owner of a motor vehicle, other than a taxicab, who operates such vehicle for transporting, for gain, compensation, or profit, either persons or property owned by another. Any operator of a motor vehicle who is voluntarily involved in a ridesharing arrangement is not considered an employee for hire or operating such vehicle for gain, compensation, or profit.

(Z) "State" includes the territories and federal districts of the United States, and the provinces of Canada.

(AA) "Public roads and highways" for vehicles includes all public thoroughfares, bridges, and culverts.

(BB) "Manufacturer's number" means the manufacturer's original serial number that is affixed to or imprinted upon the chassis or other part of the motor vehicle.

(CC) "Motor number" means the manufacturer's original number that is affixed to or imprinted upon the engine or motor of the vehicle.

(DD) "Distributor" means any person who is authorized by a motor vehicle manufacturer to distribute new motor vehicles to licensed motor vehicle dealers at an established place of business that is used exclusively for the purpose of distributing new motor vehicles to licensed motor vehicle dealers, except when the distributor also is a new motor vehicle dealer, in which case the distributor may distribute at the location of the distributor's licensed dealership.

(EE) "Ridesharing arrangement" means the transportation of persons in a motor vehicle where the transportation is incidental to another purpose of a volunteer driver and includes ridesharing arrangements known as carpools, vanpools, and buspools.

(FF) "Apportionable vehicle" means any vehicle that is used or intended for use in two or more international registration plan member jurisdictions that allocate or proportionally register vehicles, that is used for the transportation of persons for hire or designed, used, or maintained primarily for the transportation of property, and that meets any of the following qualifications:

(1) Is a power unit having a gross vehicle weight in excess of twenty-six thousand pounds;

(2) Is a power unit having three or more axles, regardless of the gross vehicle weight;

(3) Is a combination vehicle with a gross vehicle weight in excess of twenty-six thousand pounds.

"Apportionable vehicle" does not include recreational vehicles, vehicles displaying restricted plates, city pick-up and delivery vehicles, buses used for the transportation of chartered parties, or vehicles owned and operated by the United States, this state, or any political subdivisions thereof.

(GG) "Chartered party" means a group of persons who contract as a group to acquire the exclusive use of a passenger-carrying motor vehicle at a fixed charge for the vehicle in accordance with the carrier's tariff, lawfully on file with the United States department of transportation, for the purpose of group travel to a specified destination or for a particular itinerary, either agreed upon in advance or modified by the chartered group after having left the place of origin.

(HH) "International registration plan" means a reciprocal agreement of member jurisdictions that is endorsed by the American association of motor vehicle administrators, and that promotes and encourages the fullest possible use of the highway system by authorizing apportioned registration of fleets of vehicles and recognizing registration of vehicles apportioned in member jurisdictions.

(II) "Restricted plate" means a license plate that has a restriction of time, geographic area, mileage, or commodity, and includes license plates issued to farm trucks under division (J) of section 4503.04 of the Revised Code.

(JJ) "Gross vehicle weight," with regard to any commercial car, trailer, semitrailer, or bus that is taxed at the rates established under section 4503.042 or 4503.65 of the Revised Code, means the unladen weight of the vehicle fully equipped plus the maximum weight of the load to be carried on the vehicle.

(KK) "Combined gross vehicle weight" with regard to any combination of a commercial car, trailer, and semi-trailer, that is taxed at the rates established under section 4503.042 or 4503.65 of the Revised Code, means the total unladen weight of the combination of vehicles fully equipped plus the maximum weight of the load to be carried on that combination of vehicles.

(LL) "Chauffeured limousine" means a motor vehicle that is designed to carry nine or fewer passengers and is operated for hire on an hourly basis pursuant to a prearranged contract for the transportation of passengers on public roads and highways along a route under the control of the person hiring the vehicle and not over a defined and regular route. "Prearranged contract" means an agreement, made in advance of boarding, to provide transportation from a specific location in a chauffeured limousine at a fixed rate per hour or trip. "Chauffeured limousine" does not include any vehicle that is used exclusively in the business of funeral directing.

(MM) "Manufactured home" has the same meaning as in division (C)(4) of section 3781.06 of the Revised Code.

(NN) "Acquired situs," with respect to a manufactured home or a mobile home, means to become located in this state by the placement of the home on real property, but does not include the placement of a manufactured home or a mobile home in the inventory of a new motor vehicle dealer or the inventory of a manufacturer, remanufacturer, or distributor of manufactured or mobile homes.

(OO) "Electronic" includes electrical, digital, magnetic, optical, electromagnetic, or any other form of technology that entails capabilities similar to these technologies.

(PP) "Electronic record" means a record generated, communicated, received, or stored by electronic means for use in an information system or for transmission from one information system to another.

(QQ) "Electronic signature" means a signature in electronic form attached to or logically associated with an electronic record.

(RR) "Financial transaction device" has the same meaning as in division (A) of section 113.40 of the Revised Code.

(SS) "Electronic motor vehicle dealer" means a motor vehicle dealer licensed under Chapter 4517. of the Revised Code whom the registrar of motor vehicles determines meets the criteria designated in section 4503.035 of the Revised Code for electronic motor vehicle dealers and designates as an electronic motor vehicle dealer under that section.

(TT) "Electric personal assistive mobility device" means a self-balancing two non-tandem wheeled device that is designed to transport only one person, has an electric propulsion system of an average of seven hundred fifty watts, and when ridden on a paved level surface by an operator who weighs one hundred seventy pounds has a maximum speed of less than twenty miles per hour.

(UU) "Limited driving privileges" means the privilege to operate a motor vehicle that a court grants under section 4510.021 of the Revised Code to a person whose driver's or commercial driver's license or permit or nonresident operating privilege has been suspended.

(VV) "Utility vehicle" means a self-propelled vehicle designed with a bed, principally for the purpose of transporting material or cargo in connection with construction, agricultural, forestry, grounds maintenance, lawn and garden, materials handling, or similar activities. "Utility vehicle" includes a vehicle with a maximum attainable speed of twenty miles per hour or less that is used exclusively within the boundaries of state parks by state park employees or volunteers for the operation or maintenance of state park facilities.

**HISTORY: GC § 6290; 100 v 72; 103 v 763; 106 v 139; 108 v PtII, 1078; 110 v 135; 111 v 239; 114 v 173; 114 v 815; 115 v 454; 115 v PtII, 300; 116 v 286; 116 v 474; 117 v 680(691), § 23; 117 v 726; 123 v 513; 124 v 840; Bureau of Code Revision, 10-1-53; 125 v 268; 126 v 783 (Eff 9-30-55); 128 v 1170 (Eff 11-2-59); 130 v 1031 (Eff 9-16-63); 132 v H 684 (Eff 11-24-67); 133 v S 410 (Eff 11-25-69); 135 v S 108 (Eff 11-21-73); 135 v H 1161 (Eff 9-30-74); 136 v S 52 (Eff 9-15-75); 136 v S 56 (Eff 5-25-76); 136 v S 359 (Eff 8-27-76); 137 v H 1 (Eff 8-26-77); 137 v H 3 (Eff 1-1-79); 137 v S 100 (Eff 4-1-78); 137 v H 166 (Eff 3-7-78); 138 v H 1 (Eff 5-16-79); 138 v H 656 (Eff 1-1-80); 138 v H 1171 (Eff 10-24-80); 139 v H 53 (Eff 7-1-82); 140 v S 231 (Eff 9-20-84); 143 v H 422 (Eff 7-1-91); 143 v H 831 (Eff 7-17-90); 144 v H 282 (Eff 6-23-92); 144 v H 485 (Eff 10-7-92); 145 v S 191 (Eff 10-20-94); 147 v H 210 (Eff 3-31-97); 147 v S 60 (Eff 10-21-97); 147 v S 142 (Eff 3-30-99); 147 v H 611 (Eff 7-1-99); 148 v H 600 (Eff 9-1-2000); 148 v S 242 (Eff 9-14-2000); 148 v H 672 (Eff 4-9-2001); 149 v S 59 (Eff 10-31-2001); 149 v S 231. Eff 10-24-2002; 149 v S 123, § 1, eff. 1-1-04; 150 v H 230, § 1, eff. 9-16-04; 151 v H 66, § 101.01, eff. 9-29-05; 151 v H 443, § 1, eff. 4-6-07; 152 v H 9, § 1, eff. 10-18-07; 153 v H 2, § 101.01, eff. 7-1-09; 2011 HB 114, § 101.01, eff. June 29, 2011.**

Acts 2011, HB 114, § 806.10 provides: "The items of law contained in this act, and their applications, are severable. If any item of law contained in this act, or if any application of any item of law contained in this act, is held invalid, the invalidity does not affect other items of law contained in this act and their applications that can be given effect without the invalid item or application."

The effective date is set by § 812.10 of 153 v H 2.

The effective date is set by § 612.03 of 151 v H 66.

The provisions of § 6 of S.B. 59 (149 v —), as amended by § 6 of H.B. 230 (150 v —), read as follows:

SECTION 6. That Section 6 of Sub. S.B. 59 of the 124th General Assembly be amended to read as follows:

Sec. 6. (A) The Registrar of Motor Vehicles shall implement and have operational all provisions of sections 4501.01, 4503.03, 4503.035, 4503.10, 4503.182, 4505.021, 4505.03, 4505.032, 4505.04, 4505.06, 4505.062, 4505.08, 4505.09, 4505.10, 4505.102, 4505.11, 4505.12, 4505.13, 4505.141, 4505.18, 4505.181, 4505.19, 4505.20, 4505.25, 4519.01, 4519.03, 4519.51, 4519.511, 4519.512, 4519.52, 4519.521, 4519.53, 4519.55, 4519.551, 4519.57, 4519.58, 4519.59, 4519.60, 4519.62, 4519.631, 4519.66, 4519.67, and 4519.68 of the Revised Code as amended or enacted by Sub. S.B. 59 of the 124th General Assembly, including especially all electronic titling provisions, and the provisions of Section 3 of Sub. S.B. 59 of the 124th General Assembly, by no later than December 31, 2005.

° ° °

(B) The Registrar shall prepare a written report describing the efforts of the Bureau of Motor Vehicles to fully implement the electronic titling provisions of Sub. S.B. 59 of the 124th General Assembly. The report shall include specific implementation dates and a timeline of actions the Bureau of Motor Vehicles will undertake to comply with the requirement of division (A) of this section that electronic titling be fully implemented and operational by December 31, 2005. Not later than December 1, 2004, the Registrar shall present the report to the Governor, the President of the Senate, the Speaker of the House of Representatives, and the chair and minority leaders of the standing committees of the Senate and the House of Representatives dealing primarily with motor vehicle issues.

The provisions of § 10, H.B. 230 (150 v —), read as follows:

SECTION 10. Section 4501.01 of the Revised Code is presented in this act as a composite of the section as amended by both Am. Sub. S.B. 123 and Am. Sub. S.B. 231 of the 124th General Assembly. ° ° ° The General Assembly, applying the principle stated in division (B) of section 1.52 of the Revised Code that amendments are to be harmonized if reasonably capable of simultaneous operation, finds that each composite is the resulting version of the section in effect prior to the effective date of the section as presented in this act.

The effective date is set by section 4 of S.B. 123.

The provisions of § 5 of S.B. 123 (149 v —), as amended by § 3 of H.B. 163 (150 v —), read as follows:

SECTION 5. (A) Notwithstanding division (B) of section 1.58 of the Revised Code, the provisions of the Revised Code amended or enacted in Sections 1 and 2 of Am. Sub. S.B. 123 of the 124th General Assembly shall apply only in relation to conduct and offenses committed on or after January 1, 2004. Conduct and offenses committed prior to January 1, 2004, shall be governed by the law in effect on the date the conduct or offense was committed.

° ° °

## § 4501.05 Duty of garage keepers.

Keepers of garages, parking lots, or other places where motor vehicles of any kind are stored or left for repair or for any other purpose, or any employee of any such person, who knows or becomes aware of the fact that any motor vehicle so stored or left has upon it, or in it, bullet marks, gunshot marks, blood stains, or marks or evidence of any crime, shall immediately report the facts to the police of a municipal corporation, a sheriff of the county, or a state highway patrol trooper.

Whoever violates this section shall forfeit not more than one hundred dollars, to be recovered on petition as in civil cases, filed by the prosecuting attorney, in the name of the state of Ohio, in the court of common pleas in the county in which such place is located.

**HISTORY: GC § 13431-2; 113 v 123(139), ch 10, § 2; 117 v 432; Bureau of Code Revision, 10-1-53; 144 v S 144. Eff 8-8-91.**

### [MISCELLANEOUS]

## § 4501.34 Records and proceedings of registrar.

(A) The registrar of motor vehicles may adopt and publish rules to govern the registrar's proceedings. All proceedings of the registrar shall be open to the public, and all documents in the registrar's possession are public records. The registrar shall adopt a seal bearing the inscription: "Motor Vehicle Registrar of Ohio." The seal shall be affixed to all writs and authenticated copies of records, and, when it has been so attached, The copies shall be received in evidence with the same effect as other public records. All courts shall take judicial notice of the seal.

(B) Upon the request of any person accompanied by a nonrefundable fee of five dollars per name, the registrar may furnish lists of names and addresses as they appear upon the applications for driver's licenses, provided that any further information contained in the applications shall not be disclosed. The registrar shall pay two dollars of each fee collected into the state treasury to the credit of the state bureau of motor vehicles fund established in section 4501.25 of the Revised Code. Of the remaining three dollars of each such fee the registrar collects, the registrar shall deposit sixty cents into the state treasury to the credit of the trauma and emergency medical services fund established in section 4513.263 [4513.26.3] of the Revised Code, sixty cents into the state treasury to the credit of the homeland security fund established in section 5502.03 of the Revised Code, thirty cents into the state treasury to the credit of the investigations fund established in section 5502.131 [5502.13.1] of the Revised Code, one dollar and twenty-five cents into the state treasury to the credit of the emergency management agency service and reimbursement fund established in section 5502.39 of the Revised Code, and twenty-five cents into the state treasury to the credit of the justice program services fund established in section 5502.67 of the Revised Code.

This division does not apply to the list of qualified driver licensees required to be compiled and filed pursuant to section 2313.06 of the Revised Code.

**HISTORY: GC § 6296-31; 116 v PtII, 33, § 31; Bureau of Code Revision, 10-1-53; 128 v 1176 (Eff 11-2-59); 129 v 381 (Eff 7-1-62); 139 v H 102 (Eff 7-1-81); 140 v H 183 (Eff 10-1-84); 146 v H 107. Eff 6-30-95; 149 v S 123, § 1, eff. 1-1-04; 153 v H 2, § 101.01, eff. 7-1-09.**

The effective date is set by § 812.10 of 153 v H 2.

The effective date is set by section 4 of S.B. 123.

See provisions, § 5 of S.B. 123 (149 v —), following RC § 4501.01.

**Publisher's Note:**

This section was formerly § 4507.25. It was renumbered by S.B. 123, Acts 2002, effective January 1, 2004.

## § 4501.351 Registrar's order may be reversed, vacated, or modified.

An order, except an order relating to a license as defined in section 119.01 of the Revised Code, made by the registrar of motor vehicles may be reversed, vacated, or modified by the court of common pleas of Franklin county, or by the court of common pleas in the county in which the party affected is a resident, or in which the matter complained of arose.

**HISTORY: GC § 6296-32; 116 v PtII, 33, § 32; 120 v 358(396), § 2; Bureau of Code Revision. Eff 10-1-53; 149 v S 123, § 1, eff. 1-1-04.**

The effective date is set by section 4 of S.B. 123.

See provisions, § 5 of S.B. 123 (149 v —), following RC § 4501.01.

**Publisher's Note:**

This section was formerly § 4507.26. It was renumbered by S.B. 123, Acts 2002, effective January 1, 2004.

## § 4501.36 Appeal seeking reversal, vacation, or modification.

A proceeding to obtain the reversal, vacation, or modification of an order of the registrar of motor vehicles shall be by appeal. Any party to the proceedings before the registrar shall file notice of the appeal in the court of common pleas on or before the expiration of thirty days from date of entry of the order. The court shall set the appeal for hearing and take any testimony as is necessary to decide the matter. The court shall give the registrar at least ten days' notice of the time and place of the hearing.

**HISTORY: GC § 6296-33; 116 v PtII, 33, § 33; Bureau of Code Revision. Eff 10-1-53; 149 v S 123, § 1, eff. 1-1-04.**

The effective date is set by section 4 of S.B. 123.

See provisions, § 5 of S.B. 123 (149 v —), following RC § 4501.01.

**Publisher's Note:**

This section was formerly § 4507.27. It was renumbered by S.B. 123, Acts 2002, effective January 1, 2004.

## § 4501.37 Restrictions against interference of court; deletion of record of conviction.

(A) No court may reverse, suspend, or delay any order made by the registrar of motor vehicles, or enjoin, restrain, or interfere with the registrar or a deputy registrar in the performance of official duties, except as provided in this chapter and Chapter 4507. or 4510. of the Revised Code.

(B) A court shall not order the bureau of motor vehicles to delete a record of conviction unless the court finds that deletion of the record of conviction is necessary to correct an error. The bureau shall not comply with a court order that directs the deletion of a record of conviction unless the order states that the record of conviction is being deleted in order to correct an error.

**HISTORY: GC § 6296-34; 116 v PtII, 33, § 34; Bureau of Code Revision. Eff 10-1-53; 149 v S 123, § 1, eff. 1-1-04; 151 v H 66, § 101.01, eff. 9-29-05.**

The effective date is set by § 612.03 of 151 v H 66.

The effective date is set by section 4 of S.B. 123.

See provisions, § 5 of S.B. 123 (149 v —), following RC § 4501.01.

**Publisher's Note:**

This section was formerly § 4507.28. It was renumbered by S.B. 123, Acts 2002, effective January 1, 2004.

## § 4501.38 Prosecuting attorney to assist registrar.

Upon the request of the registrar of motor vehicles, the prosecuting attorney of the county in which any proceedings are pending shall aid in any investigation, prosecution, hearing, or trial held under this chapter or Chapter 4506., 4507., 4510., or 4511. of the Revised Code and shall institute and prosecute any actions or proceedings for the enforcement of the sections contained in those chapters, and for the punishment of all violations of those sections, as the registrar directs.

**HISTORY: GC § 6296-35; 116 v PtII, 33, § 35; Bureau of Code Revision. Eff 10-1-53; 149 v S 123, § 1, eff. 1-1-04.**

The effective date is set by section 4 of S.B. 123.

See provisions, § 5 of S.B. 123 (149 v —), following RC § 4501.01.

**Publisher's Note:**

This section was formerly § 4507.29. It was renumbered by S.B. 123, Acts 2002, effective January 1, 2004.

# CHAPTER 4503: LICENSING OF MOTOR VEHICLES



## § 4503.05 Noncommercial motor vehicle restricted use.

(A) No person shall use a motor vehicle registered as a noncommercial motor vehicle for other than the purposes set forth in section 4501.01 of the Revised Code.

(B) Whoever violates this section is guilty of a misdemeanor of the fourth degree.

**HISTORY: 137 v H 166. Eff 3-7-78; 149 v S 123, § 1, eff. 1-1-04.**

The effective date is set by section 4 of S.B. 123.

See provisions, § 5 of S.B. 123 (149 v —), following RC § 4501.01.

**Analogous to former RC § 4503.05 (Bureau of Code Revision, 10-1-53; 129 v 1364), repealed 137 v H 166, § 2, eff 3-7-78.**

## [MISCELLANEOUS]

## § 4503.13 Ineligibility due to outstanding municipal, county, or mayor's court arrest warrant.

(A) A municipal court, county court, or mayor's court, at the court's discretion, may order the clerk of the court to send to the registrar of motor vehicles a report containing the name, address, and such other information as the registrar may require by rule, of any person for whom an arrest warrant has been issued by that court and is outstanding.

Upon receipt of such a report, the registrar shall enter the information contained in the report into the records of the bureau of motor vehicles. Neither the registrar nor any deputy registrar shall issue a certificate of registration for a motor vehicle owner or lessee, when a lessee is determinable under procedures established by the registrar under division (E) of this section, who is named in the report until the registrar receives notification from the municipal court, county court, or mayor's court that there are no outstanding arrest warrants in the name of the person. The registrar also shall send a notice to the person who is named in the report, via regular first class mail sent to the person's last known address as shown in the records of the bureau, informing the person that neither the registrar nor any deputy registrar is permitted to issue a certificate of registration for a motor vehicle in the name of the person until the registrar receives notification that there are no outstanding arrest warrants in the name of the person.

(B) A clerk who reports an outstanding arrest warrant in accordance with division (A) of this section immediately shall notify the registrar when the warrant has been executed and returned to the issuing court or has been canceled.

Upon receipt of such notification, the registrar shall charge and collect from the person named in the executed or canceled arrest warrant a processing fee of fifteen dollars to cover the costs of the bureau in administering this section. The registrar shall deposit all such processing fees into the state bureau of motor vehicles fund created by section 4501.25 of the Revised Code.

Upon payment of the processing fee, the registrar shall cause the report of that outstanding arrest warrant to be removed from the records of the bureau and, if there are no other outstanding arrest warrants issued by a municipal court or county court in the name of the person and the person otherwise is eligible to be issued a certificate of registration for a motor vehicle, the registrar or a deputy registrar may issue a certificate of registration for a motor vehicle in the name of the person named in the executed or canceled arrest warrant.

(C) Neither the registrar, any employee of the bureau, a deputy registrar, nor any employee of a deputy registrar is personally liable for damages or injuries resulting from any error made by a clerk in entering information contained in a report submitted to the registrar under this section.

(D) Any information submitted to the registrar by a clerk under this section shall be transmitted by means of an electronic data transfer system.

(E) The registrar shall determine the procedures and information necessary to implement this section in regard to motor vehicle lessees. Division (A) of this section shall not apply to cases involving a motor vehicle lessee until such procedures are established.

**HISTORY: 147 v H 141. Eff 3-3-98; 149 v H 490, § 1, eff. 1-1-04; 150 v H 230, § 1, eff. 9-16-04.**

The effective date is set by section 4 of H.B. 490.

**Not analogous to former RC § 4503.13 (GC § 6294-2; 114 v 851, § 4; 116 v 286, § 6; 116 v 295; Bureau of Code Revision, 10-1-53; 131 v 1073; 135 v H 90), repealed 137 v H 3, § 2, eff 1-1-79.**

## § 4503.182 Temporary licenses.

(A) A purchaser of a motor vehicle, upon application and proof of purchase of the vehicle, may be issued a temporary license placard or windshield sticker for the motor vehicle.

The purchaser of a vehicle applying for a temporary license placard or windshield sticker under this section shall execute an affidavit stating that the purchaser has not been issued previously during the current registration year a license plate that could legally be transferred to the vehicle.

Placards or windshield stickers shall be issued only for the applicant's use of the vehicle to enable the applicant to legally operate the motor vehicle while proper title, license plates, and a certificate of registration are being obtained, and shall be displayed on no other motor vehicle.

Placards or windshield stickers issued under this section are valid for a period of thirty days from date of issuance and are not transferable or renewable.

The fee for the placards or windshield stickers issued under this section is two dollars plus a service fee of three dollars and fifty cents.

(B)(1) The registrar of motor vehicles may issue to a motorized bicycle dealer or a licensed motor vehicle dealer temporary license placards to be issued to purchasers for use on vehicles sold by the dealer, in accordance with rules prescribed by the registrar. The dealer shall notify the registrar, within forty-eight hours, of the issuance of a placard by electronic means via computer equipment purchased and maintained by the dealer or in any other manner prescribed by the registrar.

(2) The fee for each placard issued by the registrar to a dealer is two dollars. The registrar shall charge an additional three dollars and fifty cents for each placard issued to a dealer who notifies the registrar of the issuance of the placards in a manner other than by approved electronic means.

(3) When a dealer issues a temporary license placard to a purchaser, the dealer shall collect and retain the fees established under divisions (A) and (D) of this section.

(C) The registrar of motor vehicles, at the registrar's discretion, may issue a temporary license placard. Such a placard may be issued in the case of extreme hardship encountered by a citizen from this state or another state who has attempted to comply with all registration laws, but for extreme circumstances is unable to properly register the citizen's vehicle.

(D) In addition to the fees charged under divisions (A) and (B) of this section, commencing on October 1, 2003, the registrar and each deputy registrar shall collect a fee of five dollars and commencing on October 1, 2009, a fee of thirteen dollars, for each temporary license placard issued. The additional fee is for the purpose of defraying the department of public safety's costs associated with the administration and enforcement of the motor vehicle and traffic laws of Ohio. At the time and in the manner provided by section 4503.10 of the Revised Code, the deputy registrar shall transmit to the registrar the fees collected under this section. The registrar shall deposit all moneys received under this division into the state highway safety fund established in section 4501.06 of the Revised Code.

(E) The registrar shall adopt rules, in accordance with division (B) of section 111.15 of the Revised Code, to specify the procedures for reporting the information from applications for temporary license placards and windshield stickers and for providing the information from these applications to law enforcement agencies.

(F) Temporary license placards issued under this section shall bear a distinctive combination of seven letters, numerals, or letters and numerals, and shall incorporate a security feature that, to the greatest degree possible, prevents tampering with any of the information that is entered upon a placard when it is issued.

(G) Whoever violates division (A) of this section is guilty of a misdemeanor of the fourth degree. Whoever violates division (B) of this section is guilty of a misdemeanor of the first degree.

(H) As used in this section, "motorized bicycle dealer" means any person engaged in the business of selling at retail, displaying, offering for sale, or dealing in motorized bicycles who is not subject to section 4503.09 of the Revised Code.

**HISTORY: 127 v 256 (Eff 9-4-57); 133 v H 207 (Eff 9-4-69); 134 v S 356 (Eff 1-14-72); 135 v S 471 (Eff 9-23-74); 136 v H 612 (Eff 7-9-76); 137 v H 3 (Eff 1-1-79); 139 v S 242 (Eff 1-1-83); 140 v S 169 (Eff 1-1-85); 140 v H 632 (Eff 3-28-85); 142 v S 1 (Eff 11-28-88); 143 v H 381 (Eff 7-1-89); 145 v H 154 (Eff 6-30-93); 148 v H 476 (Eff 10-27-2000); 149 v H 94 (Eff 6-6-2001); 149 v S 59. Eff 10-31-2001; 150 v H 87, §§ 1, 4, eff. 6-30-03; 149 v S 123, § 1, eff. 1-1-04; 150 v H 230, § 1, eff. 9-16-04; 153 v H 2, § 101.01, eff. 7-1-09; 153 v H 1, § 101.01, eff. 7-17-09.**

The effective date is set by § 812.20 of 153 v H 1.
The effective date is set by § 812.10 of 153 v H 2.
See provisions of § 6 of H.B. 230 (150 v —) following RC § 4501.01.
The effective date is set by section 4 of S.B. 123.
See provisions, § 5 of S.B. 123 (149 v —), following RC § 4501.01.

## § 4503.21 Display of license plates and validation stickers or temporary placard or windshield sticker.

(A) No person who is the owner or operator of a motor vehicle shall fail to display in plain view on the front and rear of the motor vehicle the distinctive number and registration mark, including any county identification sticker and any validation sticker issued under sections 4503.19 and 4503.191 [4503.19.1] of the Revised Code, furnished by the director of public safety, except that a manufacturer of motor vehicles or dealer therein, the holder of an in transit permit, and the owner or operator of a motorcycle, motorized bicycle, manufactured home, mobile home, trailer, or semitrailer shall display on the rear only. A motor vehicle that is issued two license plates shall display the validation sticker only on the rear license plate, except that a commercial tractor that does not receive an apportioned license plate under the international registration plan shall display the validation sticker on the front of the commercial tractor. An apportioned vehicle receiving an apportioned license plate under the international registration plan shall display the license plate only on the front of a commercial tractor and on the rear of all other vehicles. All license plates shall be securely fastened so as not to swing, and shall not be covered by any material that obstructs their visibility.

No person to whom a temporary license placard or windshield sticker has been issued for the use of a motor vehicle under section 4503.182 [4503.18.2] of the Revised Code, and no operator of that motor vehicle, shall fail to display the temporary license placard in plain view from the rear of the vehicle either in the rear window or on an external rear surface of the motor vehicle, or fail to display the windshield sticker in plain view on the rear window of the motor vehicle. No temporary license placard or windshield sticker shall be covered by any material that obstructs its visibility.

(B) Whoever violates this section is guilty of a minor misdemeanor.

**HISTORY: GC § 12613; 99 v 540, § 9; 99 v 543, § 24; 103 v 763; 104 v 248; 115 v 108; 123 v 513; Bureau of Code Revision, 10-1-53; 125 v 127; 125 v 230; 126 v 717 (Eff 9-30-55); 130 v 1047 (Eff 1-23-63); 135 v H 90 (Eff 10-31-73); 140 v S 169 (Eff 1-1-85); 140 v S 231 (Eff 9-20-84); 140 v H 632 (Eff 3-28-85); 141 v H 428 (Eff 12-23-86); 142 v H 158 (Eff 9-10-87); 143 v H 831 (Eff 7-17-90); 143 v S 382 (Eff 12-31-90); 144 v S 98 (Eff 11-12-92); 147 v H 143 (Eff 12-18-97); 147 v S 142. Eff 3-30-99; 149 v S 123, § 1, eff. 1-1-04.**

The effective date is set by section 4 of S.B. 123.

See provisions, § 5 of S.B. 123 (149 v —), following RC § 4501.01.

## § 4503.22 Specifications for license plates.

The identification license plate shall consist of a placard upon the face of which shall appear the distinctive number assigned to the motor vehicle as provided in section 4503.19 of the Revised Code, in Arabic numerals or letters, or both. The dimensions of the numerals or letters and of each stroke shall be determined by the director of public safety. The license placard also shall contain the name of this state and the slogan "BIRTHPLACE OF AVIATION." The placard shall be made of steel and the background shall be treated with a reflective material that shall provide effective and dependable reflective brightness during the service period required of the placard. Specifications for the reflective and other materials and the design of the placard, the county identification stickers as provided by section 4503.19 of the Revised Code, and validation stickers as provided by section 4503.191 [4503.19.1] of the Revised Code, shall be adopted by the director as rules under sections 119.01 to 119.13 of the Revised Code. The identification license plate of motorized bicycles and of motor vehicles of the type commonly called "motorcycles" shall consist of a single placard, the size of which shall be prescribed by the director. The identification plate of a vehicle registered in accordance with the international registration plan shall contain the word "apportioned." The director may prescribe the type of placard, or means of fastening the placard, or both; the placard or means of fastening may be so designed and constructed as to render difficult the removal of the placard after it has been fastened to a motor vehicle.

**HISTORY: GC § 6300; 100 v 73, § 10; 103 v 763; 107 v 546; 115 v 102; 116 v 286, § 9; 116 v 295; Bureau of Code Revision, 10-1-53; 125 v 127; 128 v 1173 (Eff 11-2-59); 131 v 1077 (Eff 9-9-65); 134 v H 727 (Eff 1-1-74); 135 v H 90 (Eff 10-31-73); 136 v H 1 (Eff 6-13-75); 137 v H 1 (Eff 8-26-77); 137 v H 3 (Eff 1-1-79); 139 v S 242 (Eff 1-1-83); 140 v S 169 (Eff 1-1-85); 143 v H 831 (Eff 7-17-90); 144 v S 98 (Eff 11-12-92); 145 v H 154 (Eff 6-30-93); 145 v H 687 (Eff 10-12-94); 146 v S 289. Eff 9-27-96.**

## § 4503.231 Restricted license plates for motor vehicles whose standard plates have been impounded; decal for vehicle registered in another state.

(A) No motor vehicle registered in the name of a person whose certificate of registration and identification license plates have been impounded as provided by division (B)(1) of section 4507.02 of the Revised Code, and no vehicle that may be operated pursuant to an immobilization waiver order issued pursuant to section 4503.235 [4503.23.5] of the Revised Code, shall be operated on any highway in this state unless it displays restricted license plates that are a different color from those regularly issued and carry a special serial number that may be readily identified by law enforcement officers. The registrar of motor vehicles shall designate the color and serial number to be used on restricted license plates, which shall remain the same from year to year and shall not be displayed on any other motor vehicles.

The bureau of motor vehicles shall adopt rules providing for the decentralization of the issuance of restricted license plates under this section. The rules shall provide for the issuance of the restricted license plates by at least one agency in each county.

No person operating a motor vehicle displaying restricted license plates as described in this division shall knowingly disguise or obscure the color of the restricted plate.

(B) If a person has been granted limited driving privileges with a condition of the privileges being that the person must display on the vehicle that is driven under the privileges restricted license plates that are described in this section, the person may operate a motor vehicle that is owned by the person's employer only if the person is required to operate that motor vehicle in the course and scope of the person's employment. Such a person may operate that vehicle without displaying on that vehicle restricted license plates that are issued under this section if the employer has been notified that the person has limited driving privileges and of the nature of the restriction and if the person has proof of the employer's notification in the person's possession while operating the employer's vehicle for normal business duties. A motor vehicle owned by a business that is partly or entirely owned or controlled by the person with the limited driving privileges is not a motor vehicle owned by an employer, for purposes of this division.

(C) Whoever violates this section is guilty of a minor misdemeanor.

**HISTORY: 132 v H 518 (Eff 12-14-67); 140 v H 37 (Eff 6-22-84); 141 v S 356 (Eff 9-24-86); 143 v S 131. Eff 7-25-90; 149 v S 123, § 1, eff. 1-1-04; 150 v H 230, § 1, eff. 9-16-04; 152 v S 17, § 1, eff. 9-30-08.**

The effective date is set by section 4 of S.B. 123.

See provisions, § 5 of S.B. 123 (149 v —), following RC § 4501.01.

### [IMPOUNDMENT, IMMOBILIZATION, FORFEITURE ORDERS]

## § 4503.233 Immobilization orders.

(A)(1) If a court is required to order the immobilization of a vehicle for a specified period of time pursuant to section 4510.11, 4510.14, 4510.16, 4510.161 [4510.16.1], 4510.41, 4511.19, 4511.193 [4511.19.3], or 4511.203 [4511.20.3] of the Revised Code, the court, subject to section 4503.235 [4503.23.5] of the Revised Code, shall issue the immobilization order in accordance with this division and for the period of time specified in the particular section, and the immobilization under the order shall be in accordance with this section. The court, at the time of sentencing the offender for the offense relative to which the immobilization order is issued or as soon thereafter as is practicable, shall give a copy of the order to the offender or the offender's counsel. The court promptly shall send a copy of the order to the registrar on a form prescribed by the registrar and to the person or agency it designates to execute the order.

The order shall indicate the date on which it is issued, shall identify the vehicle that is subject to the order, and shall specify all of the following:

(a) The period of the immobilization;

(b) The place at which the court determines that the immobilization shall be carried out, provided that the court shall not determine and shall not specify that the immobilization is to be carried out at any place other than a commercially operated private storage lot, a place owned by a law enforcement or other government agency, or a place to which one of the following applies:

(i) The place is leased by or otherwise under the control of a law enforcement or other government agency.

(ii) The place is owned by the offender, the offender's spouse, or a parent or child of the offender.

(iii) The place is owned by a private person or entity, and, prior to the issuance of the order, the private entity or person that owns the place, or the authorized agent of that private entity or person, has given express written consent for the immobilization to be carried out at that place.

(iv) The place is a public street or highway on which the vehicle is parked in accordance with the law.

(c) The person or agency designated by the court to execute the order, which shall be either the law enforcement agency that employs the law enforcement officer who seized the vehicle, a bailiff of the court, another person the court determines to be appropriate to execute the order, or the law enforcement agency with jurisdiction over the place of residence of the vehicle owner;

(d) That neither the registrar nor a deputy registrar will be permitted to accept an application for the license plate registration of any motor vehicle in the name of the vehicle owner until the immobilization fee is paid.

(2) The person or agency the court designates to immobilize the vehicle shall seize or retain that vehicle's license plates and forward them to the bureau of motor vehicles.

(3) In all cases, the offender shall be assessed an immobilization fee of one hundred dollars, and the immobilization fee shall be paid to the registrar before the vehicle may be released to the offender. Neither the registrar nor a deputy registrar shall accept an application for the registration of any motor vehicle in the name of the offender until the immobilization fee is paid.

(4) If the vehicle subject to the order is immobilized pursuant to the order and is found being operated upon any street or highway in this state during the immobilization period, it shall be seized, removed from the street or highway, and criminally forfeited and disposed of pursuant to section 4503.234 [4503.23.4] of the Revised Code.

(5) The registrar shall deposit the immobilization fee into the law enforcement reimbursement fund created by section 4501.19 of the Revised Code. Money in the fund shall be expended only as provided in division (A)(5) of this section. If the court designated in the order a court bailiff or another appropriate person other than a law enforcement officer to immobilize the vehicle, the amount of the fee deposited into the law enforcement reimbursement fund shall be paid out to the county treasury if the court that issued the order is a county court, to the treasury of the municipal corporation served by the court if the court that issued the order is a mayor's court, or to the city treasury of the legislative authority of the court, both as defined in section 1901.03 of the Revised Code, if the court that issued the order is a municipal court. If the court designated a law enforcement agency to immobilize the vehicle and if the law enforcement agency immobilizes the vehicle, the amount of the fee deposited into the law enforcement reimbursement fund shall be paid out to the law enforcement agency to reimburse the agency for the costs it incurs in obtaining immobilization equipment and, if required, in sending an officer or other person to search for and locate the vehicle specified in the immobilization order and to immobilize the vehicle.

In addition to the immobilization fee required to be paid under division (A)(3) of this section, the offender may be charged expenses or charges incurred in the removal and storage of the immobilized vehicle.

(B) If a court issues an immobilization order under division (A)(1) of this section, the person or agency designated by the court to execute the immobilization order promptly shall immobilize or continue the immobilization of the vehicle at the place specified by the court in the order. The registrar shall not authorize the release of the vehicle or authorize the issuance of new identification license plates for the vehicle at the end of the immobilization period until the immobilization fee has been paid.

(C) Upon receipt of the license plates for a vehicle under this section, the registrar shall destroy the license plates. At the end of the immobilization period and upon the payment of the immobilization fee that must be paid under this section, the registrar shall authorize the release of the vehicle and authorize the issuance, upon the payment of the same fee as is required for the replacement of lost, mutilated, or destroyed license plates and certificates of registration, of new license plates and, if necessary, a new certificate of registration to the offender for the vehicle in question.

(D)(1) If a court issues an immobilization order under division (A) of this section, the immobilization period commences on the day on which the vehicle in question is immobilized. If the vehicle in question had been seized under section 4510.41 or 4511.195 [4511.19.5] of the Revised Code, the time between the seizure and the beginning of the immobilization period shall be credited against the immobilization period specified in the immobilization order issued under division (A) of this section. No vehicle that is immobilized under this section is eligible to have restricted license plates under section 4503.231 [4503.23.1] of the Revised Code issued for that vehicle.

(2) If a court issues an immobilization order under division (A) of this section, if the vehicle subject to the order is immobilized under the order, and if the vehicle is found being operated upon any street or highway of this state during the immobilization period, it shall be seized, removed from the street or highway, and criminally forfeited, and disposed of pursuant to section 4503.234 [4503.23.4] of the Revised Code. No vehicle that is forfeited under this provision shall be considered contraband for purposes of Chapter 2981. of the Revised Code, but shall be held by the law enforcement agency that employs the officer who seized it for disposal in accordance with section 4503.234 [4503.23.4] of the Revised Code.

(3) If a court issues an immobilization order under division (A) of this section, and if the vehicle is not claimed within seven days after the end of the period of immobilization or if the offender has not paid the immobilization fee, the person or agency that immobilized the vehicle shall send a written notice to the offender at the offender's last known address informing the offender of the date on which the period of immobilization ended, that the offender has twenty days after the date of the notice to pay the immobilization fee and obtain the release of the vehicle, and that if the offender does not pay the fee and obtain the release of the vehicle within that twenty-day period, the vehicle will be forfeited under section 4503.234 [4503.23.4] of the Revised Code to the entity that is entitled to the immobilization fee.

(4) An offender whose motor vehicle is subject to an immobilization order issued under division (A) of this section shall not sell the motor vehicle without approval of the court that issued the order. If such an offender wishes to sell the motor vehicle during the immobilization period, the offender shall apply to the court that issued the immobilization order for permission to assign the title to the vehicle. If the court is satisfied that the sale will be in good faith and not for the purpose of circumventing the provisions of division (A)(1) of this section, it may certify its consent to the offender and to the registrar. Upon receipt of the court's consent, the registrar shall enter the court's notice in the offender's vehicle license plate registration record.

If, during a period of immobilization under an immobilization order issued under division (A) of this section, the title to the immobilized motor vehicle is transferred by the foreclosure of a chattel mortgage, a sale upon execution, the cancellation of a conditional sales contract, or an order of a court, the involved court shall notify the registrar of the action, and the registrar shall enter the court's notice in the offender's vehicle license plate registration record.

Nothing in this section shall be construed as requiring the registrar or the clerk of the court of common pleas to note upon the certificate of title records any prohibition regarding the sale of a motor vehicle.

(5) If the title to a motor vehicle that is subject to an immobilization order under division (A) of this section is assigned or transferred without court approval between the time of arrest of the offender who committed the offense for which such an order is to be issued and the time of the actual immobilization of the vehicle, the court shall order that, for a period of two years from the date of the order, neither the registrar nor any deputy registrar shall accept an application for the registration of any motor vehicle in the name of the offender whose vehicle was assigned or transferred without court approval. The court shall notify the registrar of the order on a form prescribed by the registrar for that purpose.

(6) If the title to a motor vehicle that is subject to an immobilization order under division (A) of this section is assigned or transferred without court approval in violation of division (D)(4) of this section, then, in addition to or independent of any other penalty established by law, the court may fine the offender the value of the vehicle as determined by publications of the national auto dealers association. The proceeds from any fine so imposed shall be distributed in the same manner as the proceeds of the sale of a forfeited vehicle are distributed pursuant to division (C)(2) of section 4503.234 [4503.23.4] of the Revised Code.

(E)(1) The court with jurisdiction over the case, after notice to all interested parties including lienholders, and after an opportunity for them to be heard, if the offender fails to appear in person, without good cause, or if the court finds that the offender does not intend to seek release of the vehicle at the end of the period of immobilization or that the offender is not or will not be able to pay the expenses and charges incurred in its removal and storage, may order that title to the vehicle be transferred, in order of priority, first into the name of the entity entitled to the immobilization fee under division (A)(5) of this section, next into the name of a lienholder, or lastly, into the name of the owner of the place of storage.

A lienholder that receives title under a court order shall do so on the condition that it pay any expenses or charges incurred in the vehicle's removal and storage. If the entity that receives title to the vehicle is the entity that is entitled to the immobilization fee under division (A)(5) of this section, it shall receive title on the condition that it pay any lien on the vehicle. The court shall not order that title be transferred to any person or entity other than the owner of the place of storage if the person or entity refuses to receive the title. Any person or entity that receives title may either keep title to the vehicle or may dispose of the vehicle in any legal manner that it considers appropriate, including assignment of the certificate of title to the motor vehicle to a salvage dealer or a scrap metal processing facility. The person or entity shall not transfer the vehicle to the person who is the vehicle's immediate previous owner.

If the person or entity assigns the motor vehicle to a salvage dealer or scrap metal processing facility, the person or entity shall send the assigned certificate of title to the motor vehicle to the clerk of the court of common pleas of the county in which the salvage dealer or scrap metal processing facility is located. The person or entity shall mark the face of the certificate of title with the words "FOR DESTRUCTION" and shall deliver a photocopy of the certificate of title to the salvage dealer or scrap metal processing facility for its records.

(2) Whenever a court issues an order under division (E)(1) of this section, the court also shall order removal of the license plates from the vehicle and cause them to be sent to the registrar if they have not already been sent to the registrar. Thereafter, no further proceedings shall take place under this section, but the offender remains liable for payment of the immobilization fee described in division (A)(3) of this section if an immobilization order previously had been issued by the court.

(3) Prior to initiating a proceeding under division (E)(1) of this section, and upon payment of the fee under division (B) of section 4505.14 of the Revised Code, any interested party may cause a search to be made of the public records of the bureau of motor vehicles or the clerk of the court of common pleas, to ascertain the identity of any lienholder of the vehicle. The initiating party shall furnish this information to the clerk of the court with jurisdiction over the case, and the clerk shall provide notice to the vehicle owner, the defendant, any lienholder, and any other interested parties listed by the initiating party, at the last known address supplied by the initiating party, by certified mail or, at the option of the initiating party, by personal service or ordinary mail.

As used in this section, "interested party" includes the offender, all lienholders, the owner of the place of storage, the person or entity that caused the vehicle to be removed, and the person or entity, if any, entitled to the immobilization fee under division (A)(5) of this section.

**HISTORY: 144 v S 275 (Eff 9-1-93); 145 v S 62, §§ 1, 4 (Eff 9-1-93); 145 v H 154 (Eff 6-30-93); 145 v S 82 (Eff 5-4-94); 145 v H 236 (Eff 9-29-94); 145 v H 687 (Eff 10-12-94); 146 v H 353 (Eff 9-17-96); 146 v H 676 (Eff 10-4-96); 148 v S 107 (Eff 3-23-2000); 148 v S 22 (Eff 5-17-2000); 148 v H 80. Eff 6-8-2000; 149 v S 123, § 1, eff. 1-1-04; 151 v H 461, § 1, eff. 4-4-07; 151 v H 241, § 1, eff. 7-1-07; 152 v S 17, § 1, eff. 9-30-08.**

The provisions of § 3 of 152 v S 17 read as follows:

SECTION 3. * * * Section 4503.233 of the Revised Code is presented in this act as a composite of the section as amended by both Sub. H.B. 241 and Am. Sub. H.B. 461 of the 126th General Assembly. The General Assembly, applying the principle stated in division (B) of section 1.52 of the Revised Code that amendments are to be harmonized if reasonably capable of simultaneous operation, finds that the composite is the resulting version of the section in effect prior to the effective date of the section as presented in this act.

The provisions of § 4 of 151 v H 241 read as follows:

SECTION 4. Sections 1, 2, and 3 of this act shall take effect on July 1, 2007. If a criminal or civil forfeiture action relating to misconduct under Title XXIX of the Revised Code was or is commenced before July 1, 2007, and is still pending on that date, the court in which the case is pending shall, to the extent practical, apply the provisions of Chapter 2981. of the Revised Code in the case.

The effective date is set by section 4 of S.B. 123.

See provisions, § 5 of S.B. 123 (149 v —), following RC § 4501.01.

**Comment, Legislative Service Commission**

* * * Sections * * * 4503.233, 4507.164, 4511.191, 4511.99, * * * of the Revised Code are amended by this act [Am. Sub. S.B. 22] and also by Am. Sub. S.B. 107 of the 123rd General Assembly. * * * Comparison of these amendments in pursuance of section 1.52 of the Revised Code discloses that they are not irreconcilable so that they are required by that section to be harmonized to give effect to each amendment.

## § 4503.234 Order of criminal forfeiture of vehicle; disposal of vehicle or proceeds of sale; registration of other vehicles in person's name.

(A) If a court orders the criminal forfeiture of a vehicle pursuant to section 4503.233 [4503.23.3], 4503.236 [4503.23.6], 4510.11, 4510.14, 4510.16, 4510.161 [4510.16.1], 4510.41, 4511.19, 4511.193 [4511.19.3], or 4511.203 [4511.20.3] of the Revised Code, the order shall be issued and enforced in accordance with this division, subject to division (B) of this section. An order of criminal forfeiture issued under this division shall authorize an appropriate law enforcement agency to seize the vehicle ordered criminally forfeited upon the terms and conditions that the court determines proper. No vehicle ordered criminally forfeited pursuant to this division shall be considered contraband for purposes of Chapter 2981. of the Revised Code, but the law enforcement agency that employs the officer who seized it shall hold the vehicle for disposal in accordance with this section. A forfeiture order may be issued only after the offender has been provided with an opportunity to be heard. The prosecuting attorney shall give the offender written notice of the possibility of forfeiture by sending a copy of the relevant uniform traffic ticket or other written notice to the offender not less than seven days prior to the date of issuance of the forfeiture order. A vehicle is subject to an order of criminal forfeiture pursuant to this division upon the conviction of the offender of or plea of guilty by the offender to a violation of division (A) of section 4503.236 [4503.23.6], section 4510.11, 4510.14, 4510.16, or 4511.203 [4511.20.3], or division (A) of section 4511.19 of the Revised Code, or a municipal ordinance that is substantially equivalent to any of those sections or divisions.

(B)(1) Prior to the issuance of an order of criminal forfeiture pursuant to this section, the law enforcement agency that employs the law enforcement officer who seized the vehicle shall conduct or cause to be conducted a search of the appropriate public records that relate to the vehicle and shall make or cause to be made reasonably diligent inquiries to identify any lienholder or any person or entity with an ownership interest in the vehicle. The court that is to issue the forfeiture order also shall cause a notice of the potential order relative to the vehicle and of the expected manner of disposition of the vehicle after its forfeiture to be sent to any lienholder or person who is known to the court to have any right, title, or interest in the vehicle. The court shall give the notice by certified mail, return receipt requested, or by personal service.

(2) No order of criminal forfeiture shall be issued pursuant to this section if a lienholder or other person with an ownership interest in the vehicle establishes to the court, by a preponderance of the evidence after filing a motion with the court, that the lienholder or other person neither knew nor should have known after a reasonable inquiry that the vehicle would be used or involved, or likely would be used or involved, in the violation resulting in the issuance of the order of criminal forfeiture or the violation of the order of immobilization issued under section 4503.233 [4503.23.3] of the Revised Code, that the lienholder or other person did not expressly or impliedly consent to the use or involvement of the vehicle in that violation, and that the lien or ownership interest was perfected pursuant to law prior to the seizure of the vehicle under section 4503.236 [4503.23.6], 4510.41, 4511.195 [4511.19.5], or 4511.203 [4511.20.3] of the Revised Code. If the lienholder or holder of the ownership interest satisfies the court that these criteria have been met, the court shall preserve the lienholder's or other person's lien or interest, and the court either shall return the vehicle to the holder, or shall order that the proceeds of any sale held pursuant to division (C)(2) of this section be paid to the lienholder or holder of the interest less the costs of seizure, storage, and maintenance of the vehicle. The court shall not return a vehicle to a lienholder or a holder of an ownership interest unless the lienholder or holder submits an affidavit to the court that states that the lienholder or holder will not return the vehicle to the person from whom the vehicle was seized pursuant to the order of criminal forfeiture or to any member of that person's family and will not otherwise knowingly permit that person or any member of that person's family to obtain possession of the vehicle.

(3) No order of criminal forfeiture shall be issued pursuant to this section if a person with an interest in the vehicle establishes to the court, by a preponderance of the evidence after filing a motion with the court, that the person neither knew nor should have known after a reasonable inquiry that the vehicle had been used or was involved in the violation resulting in the issuance of the order of criminal forfeiture or the violation of the order of immobilization issued under section 4503.233 [4503.23.3] of the Revised Code, that the person did not expressly or impliedly consent to the use or involvement of the vehicle in that violation, that the interest was perfected in good faith and for value pursuant to law between the time of the

arrest of the offender and the final disposition of the criminal charge in question, and that the vehicle was in the possession of the interest holder at the time of the perfection of the interest. If the court is satisfied that the interest holder has met these criteria, the court shall preserve the interest holder's interest, and the court either shall return the vehicle to the interest holder or order that the proceeds of any sale held pursuant to division (C) of this section be paid to the holder of the interest less the costs of seizure, storage, and maintenance of the vehicle. The court shall not return a vehicle to an interest holder unless the holder submits an affidavit to the court stating that the holder will not return the vehicle to the person from whom the holder acquired the holder's interest, nor to any member of that person's family, and the holder will not otherwise knowingly permit that person or any member of that person's family to obtain possession of the vehicle.

(C) A vehicle ordered criminally forfeited to the state pursuant to this section shall be disposed of as follows:

(1) It shall be given to the law enforcement agency that employs the law enforcement officer who seized the vehicle, if that agency desires to have it;

(2) If a vehicle is not disposed of pursuant to division (C)(1) of this section, the vehicle shall be sold, without appraisal, if the value of the vehicle is two thousand dollars or more as determined by publications of the national auto dealer's association, at a public auction to the highest bidder for cash. Prior to the sale, the prosecuting attorney in the case shall cause a notice of the proposed sale to be given in accordance with law. The court shall cause notice of the sale of the vehicle to be published in a newspaper of general circulation in the county in which the court is located at least seven days prior to the date of the sale. The proceeds of a sale under this division or division (F) of this section shall be applied in the following order:

(a) First, they shall be applied to the payment of the costs incurred in connection with the seizure, storage, and maintenance of, and provision of security for, the vehicle, any proceeding arising out of the forfeiture, and if any, the sale.

(b) Second, the remaining proceeds after compliance with division (C)(2)(a) of this section, shall be applied to the payment of the value of any lien or ownership interest in the vehicle preserved under division (B) of this section.

(c) Third, the remaining proceeds, after compliance with divisions (C)(2)(a) and (b) of this section, shall be applied to the appropriate funds in accordance with divisions (B) and (C) of section 2981.13 of the Revised Code, provided that the total of the amount so deposited under this division shall not exceed one thousand dollars. The remaining proceeds deposited under this division shall be used only for the purposes authorized by those divisions and division (D) of that section.

(d) Fourth, the remaining proceeds after compliance with divisions (C)(2)(a) and (b) of this section and after deposit of a total amount of one thousand dollars under division (C)(2)(c) of this section shall be applied so that fifty per cent of those remaining proceeds is paid into the reparation fund established by section 2743.191 [2743.19.1] of the Revised Code, twenty-five per cent is paid into the drug abuse resistance education programs fund created by division (F)(2)(e) of section 4511.191 [4511.19.1] of the Revised Code and shall be used only for the purposes authorized by division (F)(2)(e) of that section, and twenty-five per cent is applied to the appropriate funds in accordance with divisions (B) and (C) of section 2981.13 of the Revised Code. The proceeds deposited into any fund described in section 2981.13 of the Revised Code shall be used only for the purposes authorized by divisions (B)(4)(c), (C), and (D) of that section.

(D) Except as provided in division (E) of section 4511.203 of the Revised Code and notwithstanding any other provision of law, neither the registrar of motor vehicles nor any deputy registrar shall accept an application for the registration of any motor vehicle in the name of any person, or register any motor vehicle in the name of any person, if both of the following apply:

(1) Any vehicle registered in the person's name was criminally forfeited under this section and section 4503.233 [4503.23.3], 4503.236 [4503.23.6], 4510.10, 4510.11, 4510.14, 4510.16, 4510.41, 4511.19, 4511.193 [4511.19.3], or 4511.203 [4511.20.3] of the Revised Code;

(2) Less than five years have expired since the issuance of the most recent order of criminal forfeiture issued in relation to a vehicle registered in the person's name.

(E) If a court orders the criminal forfeiture to the state of a vehicle pursuant to section 4503.233 [4503.23.3], 4503.236 [4503.23.6], 4510.10, 4510.11, 4510.14, 4510.16, 4510.161 [4510.16.1], 4510.41, 4511.19, 4511.193 [4511.19.3], or 4511.203 [4511.20.3] of the Revised Code, the title to the motor vehicle is assigned or transferred, and division (B)(2) or (3) of this section applies, in addition to or independent of any other penalty established by law, the court may fine the offender the value of the vehicle as determined by publications of the national auto dealer's association. The proceeds from any fine imposed under this division shall be distributed in accordance with division (C)(2) of this section.

(F) As used in this section and divisions (B)(4)(c), (C), and (D) of section 2981.13 of the Revised Code in relation to proceeds of the sale of a vehicle under division (C) of this section, "prosecuting attorney" includes the prosecuting attorney, village solicitor, city director of law, or similar chief legal officer of a municipal corporation who prosecutes the case resulting in the conviction or guilty plea in question.

(G) If the vehicle to be forfeited has an average retail value of less than two thousand dollars as determined by publications of the national auto dealer's association, no public auction is required to be held. In such a case, the court may direct that the vehicle be disposed of in any manner that it considers appropriate, including assignment of the certificate of title to the motor vehicle to a salvage dealer or a scrap metal processing facility. The court shall not transfer the vehicle to the person who is the vehicle's immediate previous owner.

If the court assigns the motor vehicle to a salvage dealer or scrap metal processing facility and the court is in possession of the certificate of title to the motor vehicle, it shall send the assigned certificate of title to the motor vehicle to the clerk of the court of common pleas of the county in which the salvage dealer or scrap metal processing facility is located. The court shall mark the face of the certificate of title with the words "FOR DESTRUCTION" and shall deliver a photocopy of the certificate of title to the salvage dealer or scrap metal processing facility for its records.

If the court is not in possession of the certificate of title to the motor vehicle, the court shall issue an order transferring ownership of the motor vehicle to a salvage dealer or scrap metal processing facility, send the order to the clerk of the court of common pleas of the county in which the salvage dealer or scrap metal processing facility is located, and send a photocopy of the order to the salvage dealer or scrap metal processing facility for its records. The clerk shall make the proper notations or entries in the clerk's records concerning the disposition of the motor vehicle.

**HISTORY: 144 v S 275 (Eff 9-1-93); 145 v S 62, §§ 1, 4 (Eff 9-1-93); 145 v S 82 (Eff 5-4-94); 146 v H 353 (Eff 9-17-96); 146 v H 676. Eff 10-4-96; 149 v S 123, § 1, eff. 1-1-04; 151 v H 461, § 1, eff. 4-4-07; 151 v H 241, § 1, eff. 7-1-07.**

See provisions of § 4 of 151 v H 241 following RC § 4503.233.

The effective date is set by section 4 of S.B. 123.

See provisions, § 5 of S.B. 123 (149 v —), following RC § 4501.01.

The provisions of § 8 of S.B. 123 read as follows:

SECTION 8. Section 4503.234 of the Revised Code is presented in this act as a composite of the section as amended by both Am. Sub. H.B. 353 and Am. Sub. H.B. 676 of the 121st General Assembly. The General Assembly, applying the principle stated in division (B) of section 1.52 of the Revised Code that amendments are to be harmonized if reasonably capable of simultaneous operation, finds that the composites are the resulting versions of the sections in effect prior to the effective date of the sections as presented in this act.

**Comment, Legislative Service Commission**

Section 4503.234 of the Revised Code is amended by Sub. H.B. 241 and Am. Sub. H.B. 461 of the 126th General Assembly. Comparison of these amendments in pursuance of section 1.52 of the Revised Code discloses that they are not irreconcilable so that they are required by that section to be harmonized to give effect to each amendment.

## § 4503.235 Immobilization waiver order in favor of family or household member.

(A) If division (G) of section 4511.19 or division (C) of section 4511.193 of the Revised Code requires a court, as part of the sentence of an offender who is convicted of or pleads guilty to a violation of division (A) of section 4511.19 of the Revised Code or as a sanction for an offender who is convicted of or pleaded guilty to a violation of a municipal OVI ordinance, to order the immobilization of a vehicle for a specified period of time, notwithstanding the requirement, the court in its discretion may determine not to order the immobilization of the vehicle if both of the following apply:

(1) Prior to the issuance of the order of immobilization, a family or household member of the offender files a motion with the court identifying the vehicle and requesting that the immobilization order not be issued on the ground that the family or household member is completely dependent on the vehicle for the necessities of life and that the immobilization of the vehicle would be an undue hardship to the family or household member.

(2) The court determines that the family or household member who files the motion is completely dependent on the vehicle for the necessities of life and that the immobilization of the vehicle would be an undue hardship to the family or household member.

(B) If a court pursuant to division (A) of this section determines not to order the immobilization of a vehicle that otherwise would be required pursuant to division (G) of section 4511.19 or division (C) of section 4511.193 of the Revised Code, the court shall issue an order that waives the immobilization that otherwise would be required pursuant to either of those divisions. The immobilization waiver order shall be in effect for the period of time for which the immobilization of the vehicle otherwise would have been required under division (G) of section 4511.19 or division (C) of section 4511.193 of the Revised Code if the immobilization waiver order had not been issued, subject to division (D) of this section. The immobilization waiver order shall specify the period of time for which it is in effect. The court shall provide a copy of an immobilization waiver order to the offender and to the family or household member of the offender who filed the motion requesting that the immobilization order not be issued and shall place a copy of the immobilization waiver order in the record in the case. The court shall impose an immobilization waiver fee in the amount of fifty dollars. The court shall determine whether the fee is to be paid by the offender or by the family or household member. The clerk of the court shall deposit all of the fees collected during a month on or before the twenty-third day of the following month into the county or municipal indigent drivers alcohol treatment fund under the control of that court, as created by the county or municipal corporation under division (F) of section 4511.191 of the Revised Code.

(C) If a court pursuant to division (B) of this section issues an immobilization waiver order, the order shall identify the family or household member who requested the order and the vehicle to which the order applies, shall identify the family or household members who are permitted to operate the vehicle, and shall identify the offender and specify that the offender is not permitted to operate the vehicle. The immobilization waiver order shall require that the family or household member display on the vehicle to which the order applies restricted license plates that are issued under section 4503.231 of the Revised Code for the entire period for which the immobilization of the vehicle otherwise would have been required under division (G) of section 4511.19 or division (C) of section 4511.193 of the Revised Code if the immobilization waiver order had not been issued.

(D) A family or household member who is permitted to operate a vehicle under an immobilization waiver order issued under this section shall not permit the offender to operate the vehicle. If a family or household member who is permitted to operate a vehicle under an immobilization waiver order issued under this section permits the offender to operate the vehicle, both of the following apply:

(1) The court that issued the immobilization waiver order shall terminate that order and shall issue an immobilization order in accordance with section 4503.233 of the Revised Code that applies to the vehicle, and the immobilization order shall be in effect for the remaining period of time for which the immobilization of the vehicle otherwise would have been required under division (G) of section 4511.19 or division (C) of section 4511.193 of the Revised Code if the immobilization waiver order had not been issued.

(2) The conduct of the family or household member in permitting the offender to operate the vehicle is a violation of section 4511.203 of the Revised Code.

(E) No offender shall operate a motor vehicle subject to an immobilization waiver order. Whoever violates this division is guilty of operating a motor vehicle in violation of an immobilization waiver, a misdemeanor of the first degree.

(F) "Family or household member" has the same meaning as in section 2919.25 of the Revised Code, except that the person must be currently residing with the offender.

**HISTORY: 152 v S 17, § 1, eff. 9-30-08; 152 v H 215, § 1, eff. 4-7-09; 153 v H 1, § 101.01, eff. 10-16-09; 2011 HB 153, § 101.01, eff. Sept. 29, 2011.**

The effective date is set by § 812.10 of 153 v H 1.

**Not analogous to former RC § 4503.235 (144 v S 275; 145 v S 62, §§ 1, 4; 145 v S 82; 145 v H 687; 146 v H 353), repealed 149 v S 123, § 2, eff 1-1-04.**

## § 4503.236 Forfeiture for violation of immobilization order.

(A) No person shall operate a motor vehicle or permit the operation of a motor vehicle upon any public or private property used by the public for vehicular travel or parking knowing or having reasonable cause to believe that the motor vehicle has been ordered immobilized pursuant to an immobilization order issued under section 4503.233 of the Revised Code.

(B) A motor vehicle that is operated by a person during a violation of division (A) of this section shall be criminally forfeited to the state in accordance with the procedures contained in section 4503.234 of the Revised Code.

(C) Whoever violates division (A) of this section is guilty of a misdemeanor of the second degree.

**HISTORY: 146 v H 353. Eff 9-17-96; 149 v S 123, § 1, eff. 1-1-04.**

The effective date is set by section 4 of S.B. 123.

See provisions, § 5 of S.B. 123 (149 v —), following RC § 4501.01.

## § 4503.28 Failure to file registration application and pay tax and legal fees.

(A) No person who is a manufacturer of, dealer in, or distributor of motor vehicles shall fail to file an application for registration and to pay the tax for the registration and to apply for and pay the legal fees for as many certified copies of the registration as the law requires.

(B) Whoever violates this section is guilty of a misdemeanor of the fourth degree.

**HISTORY: GC § 12621; 99 v 543, § 24; 100 v 73, § 11; 108 v PtII, 1078; 117 v 680, § 23; Bureau of Code Revision, 10-1-53; 135 v H 1161. Eff 9-30-74; 149 v S 123, § 1, eff. 1-1-04.**

The effective date is set by section 4 of S.B. 123.

See provisions, § 5 of S.B. 123 (149 v —), following RC § 4501.01.

## § 4503.30 Display of placards issued to manufacturers, dealers or distributors.

(A) Any placards issued by the registrar of motor vehicles and bearing the distinctive number assigned to a manufacturer, dealer, or distributor pursuant to section 4503.27 of the Revised Code may be displayed on any motor vehicle, other than commercial cars, or on any motorized bicycle owned by the manufacturer, dealer, or distributor, or lawfully in the possession or control of the manufacturer, or the agent or employee of the manufacturer, the dealer, or the agent or employee of the dealer, the distributor, or the agent or employee of the distributor, and shall be displayed on no other motor vehicle or motorized bicycle. A placard may be displayed on a motor vehicle, other than a commercial car, owned by a dealer when the vehicle is in transit from a dealer to a purchaser, when the vehicle is being demonstrated for sale or lease, or when the vehicle otherwise is being utilized by the dealer. A vehicle bearing a placard issued to a dealer under section 4503.27 of the Revised Code may be operated by the dealer, an agent or employee of the dealer, a prospective purchaser, or a third party operating the vehicle with the permission of the dealer.

Such placards may be displayed on commercial cars only when the cars are in transit from a manufacturer to a dealer, from a distributor to a dealer or distributor, or from a dealer to a purchaser, or when the cars are being demonstrated for sale or lease, and shall not be displayed when the cars are being used for delivery, hauling, transporting, or other commercial purpose.

(B) Whoever violates this section is guilty of a misdemeanor of the third degree.

**HISTORY: GC § 6301-1a; 117 v 680(694), § 25; 118 v 486; Bureau of Code Revision, 10-1-53; 135 v H 1161 (Eff 9-30-74); 140 v S 169 (Eff 1-1-85); 146 v S 182. Eff 12-03-96; 149 v S 123, § 1, eff. 1-1-04.**

The effective date is set by section 4 of S.B. 123.

See provisions, § 5 of S.B. 123 (149 v —), following RC § 4501.01.

## § 4503.301 Demonstration placards.

(A) A manufacturer, dealer, or distributor of motor vehicles may apply for a reasonable number of commercial car demonstration placards. The application shall show the make of commercial cars, commercial tractors, trailers, and semitrailers manufactured, dealt, or distributed in and shall show the taxing district in which the applicant's place of business is located.

Upon the filing of such application and the payment of an annual fee of five hundred dollars and appropriate postage as required by the registrar of motor vehicles, the registrar shall assign to the applicant a distinctive placard and number. Such placards shall be known as "commercial car demonstration placards," and shall expire on a date prescribed by the registrar. Upon the first application by any person for such placards, the registrar shall prorate the annual fee in accordance with section 4503.11 of the Revised Code; for all renewals or replacements of such placards, the registrar shall collect the full amount of the annual fee.

Commercial car demonstration placards may be displayed on commercial cars, commercial tractors, trailers and semitrailers owned by the manufacturer, dealer, or distributor, when those vehicles are operated by or being demonstrated to a prospective purchaser. In addition to the purposes permitted by section 4503.30 of the Revised Code, the placards provided for in this section may be displayed on vehicles operated or used for delivery, hauling, transporting, or any other lawful purpose. When such placards are used, the placards provided for in section 4503.30 of the Revised Code need not be displayed.

The operator of any commercial car, commercial tractor, trailer, or semitrailer displaying the placards provided for in this section, at all times, shall carry with the operator a letter from the manufacturer, dealer, or distributor authorizing the use of such manufacturer's, dealer's, or distributor's commercial car demonstration placards.

When such placards are used on any commercial car or commercial tractor, such power unit shall be considered duly registered and licensed for the purposes of section 4503.38 of the Revised Code.

(B) No manufacturer, dealer, or distributor of motor vehicles shall use the commercial car demonstration placard for purposes other than those authorized by this section.

(C) Whoever violates division (B) of this section is guilty of a misdemeanor of the third degree.

**HISTORY: 132 v S 272 (Eff 11-14-67); 135 v H 1161 (Eff 9-30-74); 147 v S 60. Eff 10-21-97; 149 v S 123, § 1, eff. 1-1-04.**

The effective date is set by section 4 of S.B. 123.

See provisions, § 5 of S.B. 123 (149 v —), following RC § 4501.01.

## [SPECIAL LICENSE PLATES AND STICKERS]

### § 4503.44 Windshield placards, license plates and parking cards for walking-impaired persons; specially equipped vehicles; rehabilitation employment fund.

(A) As used in this section and in section 4511.69 of the Revised Code:

(1) "Person with a disability that limits or impairs the ability to walk" means any person who, as determined by a health care provider, meets any of the following criteria:

(a) Cannot walk two hundred feet without stopping to rest;

(b) Cannot walk without the use of, or assistance from, a brace, cane, crutch, another person, prosthetic device, wheelchair, or other assistive device;

(c) Is restricted by a lung disease to such an extent that the person's forced (respiratory) expiratory volume for one second, when measured by spirometry, is less than one liter, or the arterial oxygen tension is less than sixty millimeters of mercury on room air at rest;

(d) Uses portable oxygen;

(e) Has a cardiac condition to the extent that the person's functional limitations are classified in severity as class III or class IV according to standards set by the American heart association;

(f) Is severely limited in the ability to walk due to an arthritic, neurological, or orthopedic condition;

(g) Is blind.

(2) "Organization" means any private organization or corporation, or any governmental board, agency, department, division, or office, that, as part of its business or program, transports persons with disabilities that limit or impair the ability to walk on a regular basis in a motor vehicle that has not been altered for the purpose of providing it with special equipment for use by handicapped persons. This definition does not apply to division (J) of this section.

(3) "Health care provider" means a physician, physician assistant, advanced practice nurse, or chiropractor as defined in this section.

(4) "Physician" means a person licensed to practice medicine or surgery or osteopathic medicine and surgery under Chapter 4731. of the Revised Code.

(5) "Chiropractor" means a person licensed to practice chiropractic under Chapter 4734. of the Revised Code.

(6) "Advanced practice nurse" means any certified nurse practitioner, clinical nurse specialist, certified registered nurse anesthetist, or certified nurse-midwife who holds a certificate of authority issued by the board of nursing under Chapter 4723. of the Revised Code.

(7) "Physician assistant" means a person who holds a certificate to practice as a physician assistant issued under Chapter 4730. of the Revised Code.

(B) Any organization or person with a disability that limits or impairs the ability to walk may apply to the registrar of motor vehicles for a removable windshield placard or, if the person owns or leases a motor vehicle, the person may apply for the registration of any motor vehicle the person owns or leases. In addition to one or more sets of license plates or one placard, a person with a disability that limits or impairs the ability to walk is entitled to one additional placard, but only if the person applies separately for the additional placard, states the reasons why the additional placard is needed, and the registrar, in the registrar's discretion, determines that good and justifiable cause exists to approve the request for the additional placard. When a motor vehicle has been altered for the purpose of providing it with special equipment for a person with a disability that limits or impairs the ability to walk, but is owned or leased by someone other than such a person, the owner or lessee may apply to the registrar or a deputy registrar for registration under this section. The application for registration of a motor vehicle owned or leased by a person with a disability that limits or impairs the ability to walk shall be accompanied by a signed statement from the applicant's health care provider certifying that the applicant meets at least one of the criteria contained in division (A)(1) of this section and that the disability is expected to continue for more than six consecutive months. The application for a removable windshield placard made by a person with a disability that limits or impairs the ability to walk shall be accompanied by a prescription from the applicant's health care provider prescribing such a placard for the applicant, provided that the applicant meets at least one of the criteria contained in division (A)(1) of this section. The health care provider shall state on the prescription the length of time the health care provider expects the applicant to have the disability that limits or impairs the applicant's ability to walk. The application for a removable windshield placard made by an organization shall be accompanied by such documentary evidence of regular transport of persons with disabilities that limit or impair the ability to walk by the organization as the registrar may require by rule and shall be completed in accordance with procedures that the registrar may require by rule. The application for registration of a motor vehicle that has been altered for the purpose of providing it with special equipment for a person with a disability that limits or impairs the ability to walk but is owned by someone other than such a person shall be accompanied by such documentary evidence of vehicle alterations as the registrar may require by rule.

(C) When an organization, a person with a disability that limits or impairs the ability to walk, or a person who does not have a disability that limits or impairs the ability to walk but owns a motor vehicle that has been altered for the purpose of providing it with special equipment for a person with a disability that limits or impairs the ability to walk first submits an application for registration of a motor vehicle under this section and every fifth year thereafter, the organization or person shall submit a signed statement from the applicant's health care provider, a completed application, and any required documentary evidence of vehicle alterations as provided in division (B) of this section, and also a power of attorney from the owner of the motor vehicle if the applicant leases the vehicle. Upon submission of these items, the registrar or deputy registrar shall issue to the applicant appropriate vehicle registration and a set of license plates and validation stickers, or validation stickers alone when required by section 4503.191 [4503.19.1] of the Revised Code. In addition to the letters and numbers ordinarily inscribed thereon, the license plates shall be imprinted with the international symbol of access. The license plates and validation stickers shall be issued upon payment of the regular license fee as prescribed under section 4503.04 of the Revised Code and any motor vehicle tax levied under Chapter 4504. of the Revised Code, and the payment of a service fee equal to the amount specified in division (D) or (G) of section 4503.10 of the Revised Code.

(D)(1) Upon receipt of a completed and signed application for a removable windshield placard, a prescription as described in division (B) of this section, documentary evidence of regular transport of persons with disabilities that limit or impair the ability to walk, if required, and payment of a service fee equal to the amount specified in division (D) or (G) of section 4503.10 of the Revised Code, the registrar or deputy registrar shall issue to the applicant a removable windshield placard, which shall bear the date of expiration on both sides of the placard and shall be valid until expired, revoked, or surrendered. Every removable windshield placard expires as described in division (D)(2) of this section, but in no case shall a removable windshield placard be valid for a period of less than sixty days. Removable windshield placards shall be renewable upon application as provided in division (B) of this section, and a service fee equal to the amount specified in division (D) or (G) of section 4503.10 of the Revised Code shall be charged for the renewal of a removable windshield placard. The registrar shall provide the application form and shall determine the information to be included thereon. The registrar also shall determine the form and size of the removable windshield placard, the material of which it is to be made, and any other information to be included thereon, and shall adopt rules relating to the issuance, expiration, revocation, surrender, and proper display of such placards. Any placard issued after October 14, 1999, shall be manufactured in a manner that allows the expiration date of the placard to be indicated on it through the punching, drilling, boring, or creation by any other means of holes in the placard.

(2) At the time a removable windshield placard is issued to a person with a disability that limits or impairs the ability to walk, the registrar or deputy registrar shall enter into the records of the bureau of motor vehicles the last date on which the person will have that disability, as indicated on the accompanying prescription. Not less than thirty days prior to that date and all removable windshield placard renewal dates, the bureau shall send a renewal notice to that person at the person's last known address as shown in the records of the bureau, informing the person that the person's removable windshield placard will expire on the indicated date not to exceed five years from the date of issuance, and that the person is required to renew the placard by submitting to the registrar or a deputy registrar another prescription, as described in division (B) of this section, and by complying with the renewal provisions prescribed in division (D)(1) of this section. If such a prescription is not received by the registrar or a deputy registrar by that date, the placard issued to that person expires and no longer is valid, and this fact shall be recorded in the records of the bureau.

(3) At least once every year, on a date determined by the registrar, the bureau shall examine the records of the office of vital statistics, located within the department of health, that pertain to deceased persons, and also the bureau's records of all persons who have been issued removable windshield placards and temporary removable windshield placards. If the records of the office of vital statistics indicate that a person to whom a removable windshield placard or temporary removable windshield placard has been issued is deceased, the bureau shall cancel that placard, and note the cancellation in its records.

The office of vital statistics shall make available to the bureau all information necessary to enable the bureau to comply with division (D)(3) of this section.

(4) Nothing in this section shall be construed to require a person or organization to apply for a removable windshield placard or special license plates if the parking card or special license plates issued to the person or organization under prior law have not expired or been surrendered or revoked.

(E)(1)(a) Any person with a disability that limits or impairs the ability to walk may apply to the registrar or a deputy registrar for a temporary removable windshield placard. The application for a temporary removable windshield placard shall be accompanied by a prescription from the applicant's health care provider prescribing such a placard for the applicant, provided that the applicant meets at least one of the criteria contained in division (A)(1) of this section and that the disability is expected to continue for six consecutive months or less. The health care provider shall state on the prescription the length of time the health care provider expects the applicant to have the disability that limits or impairs the applicant's ability to walk, which cannot exceed six months from the date of the prescription. Upon receipt of an application for a temporary removable windshield placard, presentation of the prescription from the applicant's health care provider, and payment of a service fee equal to the amount specified in division (D) or (G) of section 4503.10 of the Revised Code, the registrar or deputy registrar shall issue to the applicant a temporary removable windshield placard.

(b) Any active-duty member of the armed forces of the United States, including the reserve components of the armed forces and the national guard, who has an illness or injury that limits or impairs the ability to walk may apply to the registrar or a deputy registrar for a temporary removable windshield placard. With the application, the person shall present evidence of the person's active-duty status and the illness or injury. Evidence of the illness or injury may include a current department of defense convalescent leave statement, any department of defense document indicating that the person currently has an ill or injured casualty status or has limited duties, or a prescription from any health care provider prescribing the placard for the applicant. Upon receipt of the application and the necessary evidence, the registrar or deputy registrar shall issue the applicant the temporary removable windshield placard without the payment of any service fee.

(2) The temporary removable windshield placard shall be of the same size and form as the removable windshield placard, shall be printed in white on a red-colored background, and shall bear the word "temporary" in letters of such size as the registrar shall prescribe. A temporary removable windshield placard also shall bear the date of expiration on the front and back of the placard, and shall be valid until expired, surrendered, or revoked, but in no

case shall such a placard be valid for a period of less than sixty days. The registrar shall provide the application form and shall determine the information to be included on it, provided that the registrar shall not require a health care provider's prescription or certification for a person applying under division (E)(1)(b) of this section. The registrar also shall determine the material of which the temporary removable windshield placard is to be made and any other information to be included on the placard and shall adopt rules relating to the issuance, expiration, surrender, revocation, and proper display of those placards. Any temporary removable windshield placard issued after October 14, 1999, shall be manufactured in a manner that allows for the expiration date of the placard to be indicated on it through the punching, drilling, boring, or creation by any other means of holes in the placard.

(F) If an applicant for a removable windshield placard is a veteran of the armed forces of the United States whose disability, as defined in division (A)(1) of this section, is service-connected, the registrar or deputy registrar, upon receipt of the application, presentation of a signed statement from the applicant's health care provider certifying the applicant's disability, and presentation of such documentary evidence from the department of veterans affairs that the disability of the applicant meets at least one of the criteria identified in division (A)(1) of this section and is service-connected as the registrar may require by rule, but without the payment of any service fee, shall issue the applicant a removable windshield placard that is valid until expired, surrendered, or revoked.

(G) Upon a conviction of a violation of division (H), (I), or (J) of this section, the court shall report the conviction, and send the placard or parking card, if available, to the registrar, who thereupon shall revoke the privilege of using the placard or parking card and send notice in writing to the placardholder or cardholder at that holder's last known address as shown in the records of the bureau, and the placardholder or cardholder shall return the placard or card if not previously surrendered to the court, to the registrar within ten days following mailing of the notice.

Whenever a person to whom a removable windshield placard or parking card has been issued moves to another state, the person shall surrender the placard or card to the registrar; and whenever an organization to which a placard or card has been issued changes its place of operation to another state, the organization shall surrender the placard or card to the registrar.

(H) Subject to division (I), (J), or (K) of section 4511.69 of the Revised Code, the operator of a motor vehicle displaying a removable windshield placard, temporary removable windshield placard, parking card, or the special license plates authorized by this section is entitled to park the motor vehicle in any special parking location reserved for persons with disabilities that limit or impair the ability to walk, also known as handicapped parking spaces or disability parking spaces.

(I) No person or organization that is not eligible under division (B) or (E) of this section shall willfully and falsely represent that the person or organization is so eligible.

No person or organization shall display license plates issued under this section unless the license plates have been issued for the vehicle on which they are displayed and are valid.

(J) No person or organization to which a removable windshield placard or temporary removable windshield placard is issued shall do either of the following:

(1) Display or permit the display of the placard on any motor vehicle when having reasonable cause to believe the motor vehicle is being used in connection with an activity that does not include providing transportation for persons with disabilities that limit or impair the ability to walk;

(2) Refuse to return or surrender the placard, when required.

(K)(1) No person or organization to which a parking card is issued shall do either of the following:

(a) Display or permit the display of the parking card on any motor vehicle when having reasonable cause to believe the motor vehicle is being used in connection with an activity that does not include providing transportation for a handicapped person;

(b) Refuse to return or surrender the parking card, when required.

(2) As used in division (K) of this section:

(a) "Handicapped person" means any person who has lost the use of one or both legs or one or both arms, who is blind, deaf, or so severely handicapped as to be unable to move about without the aid of crutches or a wheelchair, or whose mobility is restricted by a permanent cardiovascular, pulmonary, or other handicapping condition.

(b) "Organization" means any private organization or corporation, or any governmental board, agency, department, division, or office, that, as part of its business or program, transports handicapped persons on a regular basis in a motor vehicle that has not been altered for the purposes of providing it with special equipment for use by handicapped persons.

(L) If a removable windshield placard, temporary removable windshield placard, or parking card is lost, destroyed, or mutilated, the placardholder or cardholder may obtain a duplicate by doing both of the following:

(1) Furnishing suitable proof of the loss, destruction, or mutilation to the registrar;

(2) Paying a service fee equal to the amount specified in division (D) or (G) of section 4503.10 of the Revised Code.

Any placardholder or cardholder who loses a placard or card and, after obtaining a duplicate, finds the original, immediately shall surrender the original placard or card to the registrar.

(M) The registrar shall pay all fees received under this section for the issuance of removable windshield placards or temporary removable windshield placards or duplicate removable windshield placards or cards into the state treasury to the credit of the state bureau of motor vehicles fund created in section 4501.25 of the Revised Code.

(N) In addition to the fees collected under this section, the registrar or deputy registrar shall ask each person applying for a removable windshield placard or temporary removable windshield placard or duplicate removable windshield placard or license plate issued under this section, whether the person wishes to make a two-dollar voluntary contribution to support rehabilitation employment services. The registrar shall transmit the contributions received under this division to the treasurer of state for deposit into the rehabilitation employment fund, which is hereby created in the state treasury. A deputy registrar shall transmit the contributions received under this division to the registrar in the time and manner prescribed by the registrar. The contributions in the fund shall be used by the rehabilitation services commission to purchase services related to vocational evaluation, work adjustment, personal adjustment, job placement, job coaching, and community-based assessment from accredited community rehabilitation program facilities.

(O) For purposes of enforcing this section, every peace officer is deemed to be an agent of the registrar. Any peace officer or any authorized employee of the bureau of motor vehicles who, in the performance of duties authorized by law, becomes aware of a person whose placard or parking card has been revoked pursuant to this section, may confiscate that placard or parking card and return it to the registrar. The registrar shall prescribe any forms used by law enforcement agencies in administering this section.

No peace officer, law enforcement agency employing a peace officer, or political subdivision or governmental agency employing a peace officer, and no employee of the bureau is liable in a civil action for damages or loss to persons arising out of the performance of any duty required or authorized by this section. As used in this division, "peace officer" has the same meaning as in division (B) of section 2935.01 of the Revised Code.

(P) All applications for registration of motor vehicles, removable windshield placards, and temporary removable windshield placards issued under this section, all renewal notices for such items, and all other publications issued by the bureau that relate to this section shall set forth the criminal penalties that may be imposed upon a person who violates any provision relating to special license plates issued under this section, the parking of vehicles displaying such license plates, and the issuance, procurement, use, and display of removable windshield placards and temporary removable windshield placards issued under this section.

(Q) Whoever violates this section is guilty of a misdemeanor of the fourth degree.

**HISTORY: 138 v H 736 (Eff 10-16-80); 139 v H 48 (Eff 1-1-83); 140 v H 174 (Eff 9-30-83); 141 v H 201 (Eff 7-1-85); 141 v H 80 (Eff 5-26-86); 142 v H 12 (Eff 9-10-87); 142 v H 419 (Eff 7-1-87); 142 v H 708 (Eff 4-19-88); 143 v H 49 (Eff 2-14-90); 143 v H 737 (Eff 4-11-91); 145 v H 154 (Eff 6-30-93); 145 v H 687 (Eff 1-1-95); 146 v H 107 (Eff 6-30-95); 146 v S 2 (Eff 7-1-96); 146 v H 353 (Eff 9-17-96); 148 v H 148 (Eff 10-14-99); 148 v S 22. Eff 5-17-2000; 149 v S 123, § 1, eff. 1-1-04; 150 v H 230, § 1, eff. 9-16-04; 152 v H 67, § 101.01, eff. 6-30-07; 152 v S 279, § 1, eff. 1-6-09; 153 v H 1, § 101.01, eff. 10-16-09.**

The effective date is set by § 812.10 of 153 v H 1.
The effective date is set by § 609.10 of 152 v H 67.
The effective date is set by section 4 of S.B. 123.
See provisions, § 5 of S.B. 123 (149 v —), following RC § 4501.01.

**Analogous to former RC § 4503.44 (137 v H 3), repealed 138 v H 736, § 2, eff 10-16-80. Former RC § 4503.44 was analogous to former RC § 4503.10.5 (136 v S 162; 137 v H 571), repealed 137 v H 3, § 2, eff 1-1-79.**

**Publisher's Note:**

The amendments made by HB 148 (148 v —) and SB 22 (148 v —) have been combined. See provisions of RC § 1.52.

## [MISCELLANEOUS]

**§ 4503.99** Repealed, 149 v S 123, § 2 [Bureau of Code Revision, 10-1-53; 127 v 256; 127 v 725; 129 v 1030; 130 v 1050; 132 v S 272; 133 v H 207; 136 v S 162; 136 v H 837; 137 v H 3; 137 v S 441; 138 v H 736; 138 v H 553; 139 v S 242; 141 v H 500; 141 v H 182; 143 v S 382; 145 v H 285; 146 v H 353; 147 v S 142; 148 v H 225]. Eff. 1-1-04.

This section concerned penalties.
The effective date is set by section 4 of S.B. 123.
See provisions, § 5 of S.B. 123 (149 v —), following RC § 4501.01.

# CHAPTER 4505: CERTIFICATE OF MOTOR VEHICLE TITLE LAW

Section



## § 4505.01 Definitions; forms.

(A) As used in this chapter:

(1) "Lien" includes, unless the context requires a different meaning, a security interest in a motor vehicle.

(2) "Motor vehicle" includes manufactured homes, mobile homes, recreational vehicles, and trailers and semitrailers whose weight exceeds four thousand pounds.

(3) "Manufactured home" has the same meaning as section 3781.06 of the Revised Code.

(4) "Mobile home" has the same meaning as in section 4501.01 of the Revised Code.

(5) "Manufactured housing dealer," "manufactured housing broker," and "manufactured housing salesperson" have the same meanings as in section 4781.01 of the Revised Code.

(6) "Motor vehicle dealer" includes manufactured housing dealers.

(7) "Motor vehicle salesperson" includes manufactured housing salespersons.

(B) The various certificates, applications, and assignments necessary to provide certificates of title for manufactured homes, mobile homes, recreational vehicles, and trailers and semitrailers whose weight exceeds four thousand pounds, shall be made upon forms prescribed by the registrar of motor vehicles.

**HISTORY: GC § 6290-2a; 120 v 313; 124 v 217; Bureau of Code Revision, 10-1-53; 136 v S 359 (Eff 8-27-76); 140 v H 218 (Eff 5-24-84); 140 v S 231 (Eff 9-20-84); 141 v H 428 (Eff 12-23-86); 143 v H 381 (Eff 7-1-89); 147 v S 142. Eff 3-30-99; 153 v H 1, § 101.01, eff. 10-16-09.**

The effective date is set by § 812.10 of 153 v H 1.

## § 4505.11 Surrender and cancellation of certificate of title; issuance of salvage or rebuilt salvage certificate of title.

(A) Each owner of a motor vehicle and each person mentioned as owner in the last certificate of title, when the motor vehicle is dismantled, destroyed, or changed in such manner that it loses its character as a motor vehicle, or changed in such manner that it is not the motor vehicle described in the certificate of title, shall surrender the certificate of title to that motor vehicle to a clerk of a court of common pleas, and the clerk, with the consent of any holders of any liens noted on the certificate of title, then shall enter a cancellation upon the clerk's records and shall notify the registrar of motor vehicles of the cancellation.

Upon the cancellation of a certificate of title in the manner prescribed by this section, any clerk and the registrar of motor vehicles may cancel and destroy all certificates and all memorandum certificates in that chain of title.

(B) If an Ohio certificate of title or salvage certificate of title to a motor vehicle is assigned to a salvage dealer, the dealer is not required to obtain an Ohio certificate of title or a salvage certificate of title to the motor vehicle in the dealer's own name if the dealer dismantles or destroys the motor vehicle, indicates the number of the dealer's motor vehicle salvage dealer's license on it, marks "FOR DESTRUCTION" across the face of the certificate of title or salvage certificate of title, and surrenders the certificate of title or salvage certificate of title to a clerk of a court of common pleas as provided in division (A) of this section. If the salvage dealer retains the motor vehicle for resale, the dealer shall make application for a salvage certificate of title to the motor vehicle in the dealer's own name as provided in division (C)(1) of this section.

(C)(1) When an insurance company declares it economically impractical to repair such a motor vehicle and has paid an agreed price for the purchase of the motor vehicle to any insured or claimant owner, the insurance company shall receive the certificate of title and the motor vehicle and proceed as follows. Within thirty days, the insurance company shall deliver the certificate of title to a clerk of a court of common pleas and shall make application for a salvage certificate of title. The clerk shall issue the salvage certificate of title on a form, prescribed by the registrar, that shall be easily distinguishable from the original certificate of title and shall bear the same information as the original certificate of title except that it may bear a different number than that of the original certificate of title. Except as provided in division (C)(2) of this section, the salvage certificate of title shall be assigned by the insurance company to a salvage dealer or any other person for use as evidence of ownership upon the sale or other disposition of the motor vehicle, and the salvage certificate of title shall be transferrable to any other person. The clerk shall charge a fee of four dollars for the cost of processing each salvage certificate of title.

(2) If an insurance company considers a motor vehicle as described in division (C)(1) of this section to be impossible to restore for highway operation, the insurance company may assign the certificate of title to the motor vehicle to a salvage dealer or scrap metal processing facility and send the assigned certificate of title to the clerk of the court of common pleas of any county. The insurance company shall mark the face of the certificate of title "FOR DESTRUCTION" and shall deliver a photocopy of the certificate of title to the salvage dealer or scrap metal processing facility for its records.

(3) If an insurance company declares it economically impractical to repair a motor vehicle, agrees to pay to the insured or claimant owner an amount in settlement of a claim against a policy of motor vehicle insurance covering the motor vehicle, and agrees to permit the insured or claimant owner to retain possession of the motor vehicle, the insurance company shall not pay the insured or claimant owner any amount in settlement of the insurance claim until the owner obtains a salvage certificate of title to the vehicle and furnishes a copy of the salvage certificate of title to the insurance company.

(D) When a self-insured organization, rental or leasing company, or secured creditor becomes the owner of a motor vehicle that is burned, damaged, or dismantled and is determined to be economically impractical to repair, the self-insured organization, rental or leasing company, or secured creditor shall do one of the following:

(1) Mark the face of the certificate of title to the motor vehicle "FOR DESTRUCTION" and surrender the certificate of title to a clerk of a court of common pleas for cancellation as described in division (A) of this section. The self-insured organization, rental or leasing company, or secured creditor then shall deliver the motor vehicle, together with a photocopy of the certificate of title, to a salvage dealer or scrap metal processing facility and shall cause the motor vehicle to be dismantled, flattened, crushed, or destroyed.

(2) Obtain a salvage certificate of title to the motor vehicle in the name of the self-insured organization, rental or leasing company, or secured creditor, as provided in division (C)(1) of this section, and then sell or otherwise dispose of the motor vehicle. If the motor vehicle is sold, the self-insured organization, rental or leasing company, or secured creditor shall obtain a salvage certificate of title to the motor vehicle in the name of the purchaser from a clerk of a court of common pleas.

(E) If a motor vehicle titled with a salvage certificate of title is restored for operation upon the highways, application shall be made to a clerk of a court of common pleas for a certificate of title. Upon inspection by the state highway patrol, which shall include establishing proof of ownership and an inspection of the motor number and vehicle identification number of the motor vehicle and of documentation or receipts for the materials used in restoration by the owner of the motor vehicle being inspected, which documentation or receipts shall be presented at the time of inspection, the clerk, upon surrender of the salvage certificate of title, shall issue a certificate of title for a fee prescribed by the registrar. The certificate of title shall be in the same form as the original certificate of title and shall bear the words "REBUILT SALVAGE" in black boldface letters on its face. Every subsequent certificate of title, memorandum certificate of title, or duplicate certificate of title issued for the motor vehicle also shall bear the words "REBUILT SALVAGE" in black boldface letters on its face. The exact location on the face of the certificate of title of the words "REBUILT SALVAGE" shall be determined by the registrar, who shall develop an automated procedure within the automated title processing system to comply with this division. The clerk shall use reasonable care in performing the duties imposed on the clerk by this division in issuing a certificate of title pursuant to this division, but the clerk is not liable for any of the clerk's errors or omissions or those of the clerk's deputies, or the automated title processing system in the performance of those duties. A fee of fifty dollars shall be assessed by the state highway patrol for each inspection made pursuant to this division and shall be deposited into the state highway safety fund established by section 4501.06 of the Revised Code.

(F) No person shall operate upon the highways in this state a motor vehicle, title to which is evidenced by a salvage certificate of title, except to deliver the motor vehicle pursuant to an appointment for an inspection under this section.

(G) No motor vehicle the certificate of title to which has been marked "FOR DESTRUCTION" and surrendered to a clerk of a court of common pleas shall be used for anything except parts and scrap metal.

(H)(1) Except as otherwise provided in this division, an owner of a manufactured or mobile home that will be taxed as real property pursuant to division (B) of section 4503.06 of the Revised Code shall surrender the certificate of title to the auditor of the county containing the taxing district in which the home is located. An owner whose home qualifies for real property taxation under divisions (B)(1)(a) and (b) of section 4503.06 of the Revised Code shall surrender the certificate within fifteen days after the home meets the conditions specified in those divisions. The auditor shall deliver the certificate of title to the clerk of the court of common pleas who issued it.

(2) If the certificate of title for a manufactured or mobile home that is to be taxed as real property is held by a lienholder, the lienholder shall surrender the certificate of title to the auditor of the county containing the taxing district in which the home is located, and the auditor shall deliver the certificate of title to the clerk of the court of common pleas who issued it. The lienholder shall surrender the certificate within thirty days after both of the following have occurred:

(a) The homeowner has provided written notice to the lienholder requesting that the certificate of title be surrendered to the auditor of the county containing the taxing district in which the home is located.

(b) The homeowner has either paid the lienholder the remaining balance owed to the lienholder, or, with the lienholder's consent, executed and delivered to the lienholder a mortgage on the home and land on which the home is sited in the amount of the remaining balance owed to the lienholder.

(3) Upon the delivery of a certificate of title by the county auditor to the clerk, the clerk shall inactivate it and maintain it in the automated title processing system for a period of thirty years.

(4) Upon application by the owner of a manufactured or mobile home that is taxed as real property pursuant to division (B) of section 4503.06 of the Revised Code and that no longer satisfies divisions (B)(1)(a) and (b) or divisions (B)(2)(a) and (b) of that section, the clerk shall reactivate the record of the certificate of title that was inactivated under division (H)(3) of this section and shall issue a new certificate of title, but only if the application contains or has attached to it all of the following:

(a) An endorsement of the county treasurer that all real property taxes charged against the home under Title LVII of the Revised Code and division (B) of section 4503.06 of the Revised Code for all preceding tax years have been paid;

(b) An endorsement of the county auditor that the home will be removed from the real property tax list;

(c) Proof that there are no outstanding mortgages or other liens on the home or, if there are such mortgages or other liens, that the mortgagee or lienholder has consented to the reactivation of the certificate of title.

(I)(1) Whoever violates division (F) of this section shall be fined not more than two thousand dollars, imprisoned not more than one year, or both.

(2) Whoever violates division (G) of this section shall be fined not more than one thousand dollars, imprisoned not more than six months, or both.

**HISTORY: GC § 6290-12; 117 v 373; Bureau of Code Revision, 10-1-53; 132 v H 741 (Eff 11-24-67); 134 v H 85 (Eff 9-22-72); 139 v H 694 (Eff 11-15-81); 142 v S 10 (Eff 8-13-87); 143 v H 381 (Eff 7-1-89); 145 v H 206 (Eff 10-1-93); 145 v H 154, § 11 (Eff 10-1-93); 146 v H 353 (Eff 9-17-96); 147 v H 210 (Eff 6-30-97); 147 v S 60 (Eff 10-21-97); 147 v S 142 (Eff 3-30-99); 148 v H 672 (Eff 4-9-2001); 149 v S 59. Eff 10-31-2001; 149 v S 123, § 1, eff. 1-1-04; 150 v H 230, § 1, eff. 9-16-04.**

See provisions of § 6 of H.B. 230 (150 v —) following RC § 4501.01.
The effective date is set by section 4 of S.B. 123.
See provisions, § 5 of S.B. 123 (149 v —), following RC § 4501.01.

## § 4505.111 Inspection of vehicle assembled by person other than manufacturer.

(A) Every motor vehicle, other than a manufactured home, a mobile home, or a motor vehicle as provided in divisions (C), (D), and (E) of section 4505.11 of the Revised Code, that is assembled from component parts by a person other than the manufacturer, shall be inspected by the state highway patrol prior to issuance of title to the motor vehicle. The inspection shall include establishing proof of ownership and an inspection of the motor number and vehicle identification number of the motor vehicle, and any items of equipment the director of public safety considers advisable and requires to be inspected by rule. A fee of forty dollars in fiscal year 1998 and fifty dollars in fiscal year 1999 and thereafter shall be assessed by the state highway patrol for each inspection made pursuant to this section, and shall be deposited in the state highway safety fund established by section 4501.06 of the Revised Code.

(B) Whoever violates this section shall be fined not more than two thousand dollars, imprisoned not more than one year, or both.

**HISTORY: 139 v H 102 (Eff 7-1-81); 139 v H 1 (Eff 8-5-81); 139 v H 694 (Eff 11-15-81); 142 v S 10 (Eff 8-13-87); 144 v S 98 (Eff 11-12-92); 147 v H 210. Eff 6-30-97; 149 v S 123, § 1, eff. 1-1-04; 153 v H 1, § 101.01, eff. 10-16-09.**

The effective date is set by § 812.10 of 153 v H 1.
The effective date is set by section 4 of S.B. 123.
See provisions, § 5 of S.B. 123 (149 v —), following RC § 4501.01.

## § 4505.18 Prohibitions.

(A) No person shall do any of the following:

(1) Operate in this state a motor vehicle for which a certificate of title is required without having that certificate in accordance with this chapter or, if a physical certificate of title has not been issued for a motor vehicle, operate the motor vehicle in this state knowing that the ownership information relating to the vehicle has not been entered into the automated title processing system by a clerk of a court of common pleas;

(2) Display or display for sale or sell as a dealer or acting on behalf of a dealer, a motor vehicle without having obtained a manufacturer's or importer's certificate, a certificate of title, or an assignment of a certificate of title for it as provided in this chapter;

(3) Fail to surrender any certificate of title or any certificate of registration or license plates upon cancellation of the same by the registrar of motor vehicles and notice of the cancellation as prescribed in this chapter;

(4) Fail to surrender the certificate of title to a clerk of a court of common pleas as provided in this chapter in case of the destruction or dismantling or change of a motor vehicle in such respect that it is not the motor vehicle described in the certificate of title;

(5) Violate any rules adopted pursuant to this chapter;

(6) Except as otherwise provided in this chapter and Chapter 4517. of the Revised Code, sell at wholesale a motor vehicle the ownership of which is not evidenced by an Ohio certificate of title, or the current certificate of title issued for the motor vehicle, or the manufacturer's certificate of origin, and all title assignments that evidence the seller's ownership of the motor vehicle, and an odometer disclosure statement that complies with section 4505.06 of the Revised Code and subchapter IV of the "Motor Vehicle Information and Cost Savings Act," 86 Stat. 961 (1972), *15 U.S.C. 1981;*

(7) Operate in this state a motor vehicle knowing that the certificate of title to the vehicle or ownership of the vehicle as otherwise reflected in the automated title processing system has been canceled.

(B) This section does not apply to persons engaged in the business of warehousing or transporting motor vehicles for the purpose of salvage disposition.

(C) Whoever violates this section shall be fined not more than two hundred dollars, imprisoned not more than ninety days, or both.

**HISTORY: GC § 6290-17; 117 v 373(387); 121 v 142; Bureau of Code Revision, 10-1-53; 129 v 1027 (Eff 9-18-61); 130 v 1052 (Eff 1-23-63); 130 v 1052 (Eff 8-19-63); 130 v PtII, H 5 (Eff 12-16-64); 141 v H 382 (Eff 3-19-87); 142 v S 10 (Eff 8-13-87); 149 v S 59. Eff 10-31-2001; 149 v S 123, § 1, eff. 1-1-04.**

See provisions of § 6 of H.B. 230 (150 v —) following RC § 4501.01.

The effective date is set by section 4 of S.B. 123.

See provisions, § 5 of S.B. 123 (149 v —), following RC § 4501.01.

## § 4505.19 Offenses.

(A) No person shall do any of the following:

(1) Procure or attempt to procure a certificate of title or a salvage certificate of title to a motor vehicle, or pass or attempt to pass a certificate of title, a salvage certificate of title, or any assignment of a certificate of title or salvage certificate of title to a motor vehicle, or in any other manner gain or attempt to gain ownership to a motor vehicle, knowing or having reason to believe that the motor vehicle or any part of the motor vehicle has been acquired through commission of a theft offense as defined in section 2913.01 of the Revised Code;

(2) Purport to sell or transfer a motor vehicle without delivering to the purchaser or transferee of it a certificate of title, a salvage certificate of title, or a manufacturer's or importer's certificate to it, assigned to the purchaser as provided for in this chapter, except as otherwise provided in this chapter;

(3) With intent to defraud, possess, sell, offer to sell, counterfeit, or supply a blank, forged, fictitious, counterfeit, stolen, or fraudulently or unlawfully obtained certificate of title, registration, bill of sale, or other instruments of ownership of a motor vehicle, or conspire to do any of the foregoing;

(4) Knowingly obtain goods, services, credit, or money by means of an invalid, fictitious, forged, counterfeit, stolen, or unlawfully obtained original or duplicate certificate of title, registration, bill of sale, or other instrument of ownership of a motor vehicle;

(5) Knowingly obtain goods, services, credit, or money by means of a certificate of title to a motor vehicle, which is required to be surrendered to the registrar of motor vehicles or the clerk of the court of common pleas as provided in this chapter.

(B) Whoever violates this section shall be fined not more than five thousand dollars or imprisoned in the county jail or workhouse not less than six months nor more than one year, or both, or in a state correctional institution not less than one year nor more than five years.

**HISTORY: GC § 6290-16; 117 v 373(387); Bureau of Code Revision, 10-1-53; 134 v H 84 (Eff 2-3-72); 134 v H 85 (Eff 9-22-72); 134 v H 511 (Eff 1-1-74); 140 v H 632 (Eff 3-28-85); 145 v H 687 (Eff 10-12-94); 146 v H 353 (Eff 9-17-96); 149 v S 59. Eff 10-31-2001; 149 v S 123, § 1, eff. 1-1-04.**

See provisions of § 6 of H.B. 230 (150 v —) following RC § 4501.01.

The effective date is set by section 4 of S.B. 123.

See provisions, § 5 of S.B. 123 (149 v —), following RC § 4501.01.

**For provisions analogous to material deleted by HB 511 amendment, see now RC §§ 2913.31, 2921.13.**

## § 4505.21 Duties of owner upon temporary or permanent export of vehicle outside United States.

(A) As used in this section:

(1) "Certified receipt of title cancellation" means a form prescribed by the registrar of motor vehicles for use under this section that shall include all of the following:

(a) The name of the owner who surrenders a certificate of title to a vehicle intended to be exported;

(b) A description of the motor vehicle that shall include the year, make, model, style, vehicle identification number, color, license registration number, and the state of registration;

(c) The destination of the motor vehicle;

(d) Whether the purpose of the export is for sale, lease, personal use, or other specified use;

(e) Such other information as the registrar determines to be appropriate.

(2) A "declaration of temporary export" means a form prescribed by the registrar that includes all of the following:

(a) The items specified in divisions (A) (1) (a) to (e) of this section;

(b) A statement that the vehicle will not be permanently located outside of the United States and that the owner intends to return the vehicle to the United States;

(c) The period of time for which it is anticipated that the motor vehicle will be located outside of the United States.

(3) "Export" means the shipping or transportation of a motor vehicle from any point inside the United States to a point outside of the United States. "Export" does not include operating the motor vehicle by means of its own power or that of a motor vehicle drawing or towing it unless the purpose of the owner is to avoid compliance with division (B) or (C) of this section.

(4) "Owner" means the person named on a certificate of title issued by this state as the owner or assignee of the owner of the motor vehicle for which the certificate of title has been issued and includes any person who is lawfully entitled to the issuance of a new certificate of title to the

motor vehicle naming the person as owner of the vehicle or who is lawfully entitled to surrender the certificate of title under this section. "Owner" includes a secured party who exports or permits the export of a motor vehicle in the exercise of the secured party's rights and powers under the security agreement.

(B) No owner of a motor vehicle who exports or permits the export of the motor vehicle for permanent location outside of the United States shall do any of the following:

(1) Fail to surrender the certificate of title to the motor vehicle to the registrar prior to the date that the motor vehicle is delivered to any person for export;

(2) Knowingly fail to surrender the certificate of title to the motor vehicle to the registrar prior to the date that the motor vehicle is delivered to any person for export.

(C) No owner of a motor vehicle who exports or permits the export of the motor vehicle for temporary location outside of the United States shall do any of the following:

(1) Fail to file a declaration of temporary export with the registrar prior to the date that the motor vehicle is delivered to any person for export;

(2) Purposely fail to file a declaration of temporary export with the registrar prior to the date that the motor vehicle is delivered to any person for export in order to facilitate the commission of a conspiracy, attempt, complicity, or theft offense related to the title of a motor vehicle or the proceeds of a motor vehicle insurance policy.

(D)(1) Proof that the defendant acted in good faith and surrendered the certificate of title to the registrar within a reasonable time after delivery of the motor vehicle for export is an affirmative defense to a prosecution under division (B) (1) of this section.

(2) Proof that the defendant acted in good faith and filed a declaration of temporary export with the registrar within a reasonable time after delivery of the motor vehicle for export is an affirmative defense to a prosecution under division (C) (1) of this section.

(E) The registrar shall prescribe forms to be signed by the owner who surrenders a certificate of title for cancellation under this section and by all secured parties whose uncanceled security interests are noted on the certificate. The form shall indicate the person to whom a certified receipt of title cancellation is to be delivered and any security interests that are to be noted on the certified receipt of title cancellation. The registrar shall inspect the title surrender form and the certificate of title to determine whether any uncanceled security interests have been noted on the title under section 4505.13 of the Revised Code and whether the person exporting the vehicle is the lawful owner. If the registrar determines that the certificate is in proper order and that all secured parties having uncanceled security interests noted on the certificate have consented to the surrender of the certificate, the registrar shall issue a certified receipt of title to the owner with such notation of security interests as shall be requested upon the title surrender form.

(F) The registrar shall record a declaration of temporary export filed under division (B) (2) of this section and retain it with the records of the certificate of title until the owner notifies the registrar, on a form prescribed by the registrar, that the motor vehicle has been returned to the United States.

(G)(1) Whoever violates division (B)(1) or (C)(1) of this section is guilty of a misdemeanor of the first degree.

(2) Whoever violates division (B)(2) or (C)(2) of this section is guilty of a felony of the fifth degree.

**HISTORY: 140 v H 632 (Eff 3-28-85); 146 v H 353. Eff 9-17-96; 149 v S 123, § 1, eff. 1-1-04.**

The effective date is set by section 4 of S.B. 123.

See provisions, § 5 of S.B. 123 (149 v —), following RC § 4501.01.

## § 4505.99 Penalties.

Whoever violates any provision of sections 4505.01 to 4505.21 of the Revised Code for which no penalty otherwise is provided in the section that contains the provision violated shall be fined not more than two hundred dollars, imprisoned not more than ninety days, or both.

**HISTORY: Bureau of Code Revision, 10-1-53; 126 v 575 (Eff 10-6-65); 132 v H 555 (Eff 11-7-67); 134 v H 85 (Eff 9-22-72); 139 v H 102 (Eff 7-1-81); 139 v H 275 (Eff 8-1-81); 139 v H 671 (Eff 12-9-81); 140 v H 632 (Eff 3-28-85); 142 v S 10 (Eff 8-13-87); 145 v H 571 (Eff 10-6-94); 146 v S 2. Eff 7-1-96; 149 v S 123, § 1, eff. 1-1-04.**

The effective date is set by section 4 of S.B. 123.

See provisions, § 5 of S.B. 123 (149 v —), following RC § 4501.01.

# CHAPTER 4506: COMMERCIAL DRIVER'S LICENSING

Section



Section

## § 4506.01 Definitions.

As used in this chapter:

(A) "Alcohol concentration" means the concentration of alcohol in a person's blood, breath, or urine. When expressed as a percentage, it means grams of alcohol per the following:

(1) One hundred milliliters of whole blood, blood serum, or blood plasma;

(2) Two hundred ten liters of breath;

(3) One hundred milliliters of urine.

(B) "Commercial driver's license" means a license issued in accordance with this chapter that authorizes an individual to drive a commercial motor vehicle.

(C) "Commercial driver license information system" means the information system established pursuant to the requirements of the "Commercial Motor Vehicle Safety Act of 1986," 100 Stat. 3207-171, 49 U.S.C.A. App. 2701.

(D) Except when used in section 4506.25 of the Revised Code, "commercial motor vehicle" means any motor vehicle designed or used to transport persons or property that meets any of the following qualifications:

(1) Any combination of vehicles with a combined gross vehicle weight rating of twenty-six thousand one pounds or more, provided the gross vehicle weight rating of the vehicle or vehicles being towed is in excess of ten thousand pounds;

(2) Any single vehicle with a gross vehicle weight rating of twenty-six thousand one pounds or more, or any such vehicle towing a vehicle having a gross vehicle weight rating that is not in excess of ten thousand pounds;

(3) Any single vehicle or combination of vehicles that is not a class A or class B vehicle, but is designed to transport sixteen or more passengers including the driver;

(4) Any school bus with a gross vehicle weight rating of less than twenty-six thousand one pounds that is designed to transport fewer than sixteen passengers including the driver;

(5) Is transporting hazardous materials for which placarding is required under subpart F of 49 C.F.R. part 172, as amended;

(6) Any single vehicle or combination of vehicles that is designed to be operated and to travel on a public street or highway and is considered by the federal motor carrier safety administration to be a commercial motor vehicle, including, but not limited to, a motorized crane, a vehicle whose function is to pump cement, a rig for drilling wells, and a portable crane.

(E) "Controlled substance" means all of the following:

(1) Any substance classified as a controlled substance under the "Controlled Substances Act," 80 Stat. 1242 (1970), 21 U.S.C.A. 802(6), as amended;

(2) Any substance included in schedules I through V of 21 C.F.R. part 1308, as amended;

(3) Any drug of abuse.

(F) "Conviction" means an unvacated adjudication of guilt or a determination that a person has violated or failed to comply with the law in a court of original jurisdiction or an authorized administrative tribunal, an unvacated forfeiture of bail or collateral deposited to secure the person's appearance in court, a plea of guilty or nolo contendere accepted by the court, the payment of a fine or court cost, or violation of a condition of release without bail, regardless of whether or not the penalty is rebated, suspended, or probated.

(G) "Disqualification" means any of the following:

(1) The suspension, revocation, or cancellation of a person's privileges to operate a commercial motor vehicle;

(2) Any withdrawal of a person's privileges to operate a commercial motor vehicle as the result of a violation of state or local law relating to motor vehicle traffic control other than parking, vehicle weight, or vehicle defect violations;

(3) A determination by the federal motor carrier safety administration that a person is not qualified to operate a commercial motor vehicle under 49 C.F.R. 391.

(H) "Drive" means to drive, operate, or be in physical control of a motor vehicle.

(I) "Driver" means any person who drives, operates, or is in physical control of a commercial motor vehicle or is required to have a commercial driver's license.

(J) "Driver's license" means a license issued by the bureau of motor vehicles that authorizes an individual to drive.

(K) "Drug of abuse" means any controlled substance, dangerous drug as defined in section 4729.01 of the Revised Code, or over-the-counter medication that, when taken in quantities exceeding the recommended dosage, can result in impairment of judgment or reflexes.

(L) "Eligible unit of local government" means a village, township, or county that has a population of not more than three thousand persons according to the most recent federal census.

(M) "Employer" means any person, including the federal government, any state, and a political subdivision of any state, that owns or leases a commercial motor vehicle or assigns a person to drive such a motor vehicle.

(N) "Endorsement" means an authorization on a person's commercial driver's license that is required to permit the person to operate a specified type of commercial motor vehicle.

(O) "Farm truck" means a truck controlled and operated by a farmer for use in the transportation to or from a farm, for a distance of not more than one hundred fifty miles, of products of the farm, including livestock and its products, poultry and its products, floricultural and horticultural products, and in the transportation to the farm, from a distance of not more than one hundred fifty miles, of supplies for the farm, including tile, fence, and every other thing or commodity used in agricultural, floricultural, horticultural, livestock, and poultry production, and livestock, poultry, and other animals and things used for breeding, feeding, or other purposes connected with the operation of the farm, when the truck is operated in accordance with this division and is not used in the operations of a motor transportation company or private motor carrier.

(P) "Fatality" means the death of a person as the result of a motor vehicle accident occurring not more than three hundred sixty-five days prior to the date of death.

(Q) "Felony" means any offense under federal or state law that is punishable by death or specifically classified as a felony under the law of this state, regardless of the penalty that may be imposed.

(R) "Foreign jurisdiction" means any jurisdiction other than a state.

(S) "Gross vehicle weight rating" means the value specified by the manufacturer as the maximum loaded weight of a single or a combination vehicle. The gross vehicle weight rating of a combination vehicle is the gross vehicle weight rating of the power unit plus the gross vehicle weight rating of each towed unit.

(T) "Hazardous materials" means any material that has been designated as hazardous under 49 U.S.C. 5103 and is required to be placarded under subpart F of 49 C.F.R. part 172 or any quantity of a material listed as a select agent or toxin in 42 C.F.R. part 73, as amended.

(U) "Imminent hazard" means the existence of a condition that presents a substantial likelihood that death, serious illness, severe personal injury, or a substantial endangerment to health, property, or the environment may occur before the reasonably foreseeable completion date of a formal proceeding begun to lessen the risk of that death, illness, injury, or endangerment.

(V) "Motor vehicle" means a vehicle, machine, tractor, trailer, or semitrailer propelled or drawn by mechanical power used on highways, except that such term does not include a vehicle, machine, tractor, trailer, or semitrailer operated exclusively on a rail.

(W) "Out-of-service order" means a declaration by an authorized enforcement officer of a federal, state, local, Canadian, or Mexican jurisdiction declaring that a driver, commercial motor vehicle, or commercial motor carrier operation is out of service as defined in 49 C.F.R. 390.5.

(X) "Peace officer" has the same meaning as in section 2935.01 of the Revised Code.

(Y) "Portable tank" means a liquid or gaseous packaging designed primarily to be loaded onto or temporarily attached to a vehicle and equipped with skids, mountings, or accessories to facilitate handling of the tank by mechanical means.

(Z) "Public safety vehicle" has the same meaning as in divisions (E)(1) and (3) of section 4511.01 of the Revised Code.

(AA) "Recreational vehicle" includes every vehicle that is defined as a recreational vehicle in section 4501.01 of the Revised Code and is used exclusively for purposes other than engaging in business for profit.

(BB) "Residence" means any person's residence determined in accordance with standards prescribed in rules adopted by the registrar.

(CC) "School bus" has the same meaning as in section 4511.01 of the Revised Code.

(DD) "Serious traffic violation" means a conviction arising from a single charge of operating a commercial motor vehicle in violation of any provision of section 4506.03 of the Revised Code or a conviction arising from the operation of any motor vehicle that involves any of the following:

(1) A single charge of any speed in excess of the posted speed limit by fifteen miles per hour or more;

(2) Violation of section 4511.20 or 4511.201 [4511.20.1] of the Revised Code or any similar ordinance or resolution, or of any similar law of another state or political subdivision of another state;

(3) Violation of a law of this state or an ordinance or resolution relating to traffic control, other than a parking violation, or of any similar law of another state or political subdivision of another state, that results in a fatal accident;

(4) Violation of section 4506.03 of the Revised Code or a substantially similar municipal ordinance or county or township resolution, or of any similar law of another state or political subdivision of another state, that involves the operation of a commercial motor vehicle without a valid commercial driver's license with the proper class or endorsement for the specific vehicle group being operated or for the passengers or type of cargo being transported;

(5) Violation of section 4506.03 of the Revised Code or a substantially similar municipal ordinance or county or township resolution, or of any similar law of another state or political subdivision of another state, that involves the operation of a commercial motor vehicle without a valid commercial driver's license being in the person's possession;

(6) Violation of section 4511.33 or 4511.34 of the Revised Code, or any municipal ordinance or county or township resolution substantially similar to either of those sections, or any substantially similar law of another state or political subdivision of another state;

(7) Violation of any other law of this state or an ordinance or resolution relating to traffic control, other than a parking violation, that is determined to be a serious traffic violation by the United States secretary of transportation and the director designates as such by rule.

(EE) "State" means a state of the United States and includes the District of Columbia.

(FF) "Tank vehicle" means any commercial motor vehicle that is designed to transport any liquid and has a maximum capacity greater than one hundred nineteen gallons or is designed to transport gaseous materials and has a water capacity greater than one thousand pounds within a tank that is either permanently or temporarily attached to the vehicle or its chassis. "Tank vehicle" does not include any of the following:

(1) Any portable tank having a rated capacity of less than one thousand gallons;

(2) Tanks used exclusively as a fuel tank for the motor vehicle to which it is attached;

(3) An empty storage container tank that is not designed for transportation and that is readily distinguishable from a transportation tank;

(4) Ready-mix concrete mixers.

(GG) "Tester" means a person or entity acting pursuant to a valid agreement entered into pursuant to division (B) of section 4506.09 of the Revised Code.

(HH) "United States" means the fifty states and the District of Columbia.

(II) "Vehicle" has the same meaning as in section 4511.01 of the Revised Code.

**HISTORY: 143 v H 381 (Eff 7-1-89); 143 v H 88 (Eff 3-13-90); 143 v H 831 (Eff 7-17-90); 144 v S 98 (Eff 11-12-92); 145 v H 687 (Eff 10-12-94); 146 v S 2 (Eff 7-1-96); 146 v H 353 (Eff 9-17-96); 147 v S 60 (Eff 10-21-97); 147 v S 66 (Eff 7-22-98); 147 v S 213 (Eff 7-29-98); 148 v S 245 (Eff 6-30-2000); 148 v H 600. Eff 9-1-2000; 149 v S 123, § 1, eff. 1-1-04; 150 v H 230, § 1, eff. 9-16-04; 151 v H 68, § 101.01, eff. 6-29-05.**

The effective date is set by § 612.03 of 151 v H 68.
The effective date is set by section 4 of S.B. 123.
See provisions, § 5 of S.B. 123 (149 v —), following RC § 4501.01.

**§ 4506.02** Repealed, 151 v H 68, § 105.01 [143 v H 381 (Eff 7-1-89); 143 v H 831 (Eff 7-17-90); 146 v S 121 (Eff 11-19-96); 147 v S 130 (Eff 9-18-97); 147 v S 213. Eff 7-29-98; 149 v S 123, § 1, eff. 1-1-04]. Eff 3-29-05.

The effective date is set by § 612.18 of 151 v H 68.
This section concerned exceptions to the chapter.

## § 4506.03 Commercial driver's license or permit required; exceptions.

(A) Except as provided in divisions (B) and (C) of this section, the following shall apply:

(1) No person shall drive a commercial motor vehicle on a highway in this state unless the person holds, and has in the person's possession, a valid commercial driver's license with proper endorsements for the motor vehicle being driven, issued by the registrar of motor vehicles, a valid examiner's commercial driving permit issued under section 4506.13 of the Revised Code, a valid restricted commercial driver's license and waiver for farm-related service industries issued under section 4506.24 of the Revised Code, or a valid commercial driver's license temporary instruction permit issued by the registrar and is accompanied by an authorized state driver's license examiner or tester or a person who has been issued and has in the person's immediate possession a current, valid commercial driver's license with proper endorsements for the motor vehicle being driven.

(2) No person shall be issued a commercial driver's license until the person surrenders to the registrar of motor vehicles all valid licenses issued to the person by another jurisdiction recognized by this state. The registrar shall report the surrender of a license to the issuing authority, together with information that a license is now issued in this state. The registrar shall destroy any such license that is not returned to the issuing authority.

(3) No person who has been a resident of this state for thirty days or longer shall drive a commercial motor vehicle under the authority of a commercial driver's license issued by another jurisdiction.

(B) Nothing in division (A) of this section applies to any qualified person when engaged in the operation of any of the following:

(1) A farm truck;

(2) Fire equipment for a fire department, volunteer or nonvolunteer fire company, fire district, or joint fire district;

(3) A public safety vehicle used to provide transportation or emergency medical service for ill or injured persons;

(4) A recreational vehicle;

(5) A commercial motor vehicle within the boundaries of an eligible unit of local government, if the person is employed by the eligible unit of local government and is operating the commercial motor vehicle for the purpose of removing snow or ice from a roadway by plowing, sanding, or salting, but only if either the employee who holds a commercial driver's license issued under this chapter and ordinarily operates a commercial motor vehicle for these purposes is unable to operate the vehicle, or the employing eligible unit of local government determines that a snow or ice emergency exists that requires additional assistance;

(6) A vehicle operated for military purposes by any member or uniformed employee of the armed forces of the United States or their reserve components, including the Ohio national guard. This exception does not apply to United States reserve technicians.

(7) A commercial motor vehicle that is operated for nonbusiness purposes. "Operated for nonbusiness purposes" means that the commercial motor vehicle is not used in commerce as "commerce" is defined in 49 C.F.R. 383.5, as amended, and is not regulated by the public utilities commission pursuant to Chapter 4919., 4921., or 4923. of the Revised Code.

(8) A motor vehicle that is designed primarily for the transportation of goods and not persons, while that motor vehicle is being used for the occasional transportation of personal property by individuals not for compensation and not in the furtherance of a commercial enterprise;

(9) A police SWAT team vehicle;

(10) A police vehicle used to transport prisoners.

(C) Nothing contained in division (B)(5) of this section shall be construed as preempting or superseding any law, rule, or regulation of this state concerning the safe operation of commercial motor vehicles.

(D) Whoever violates this section is guilty of a misdemeanor of the first degree.

**HISTORY: 143 v H 381 (Eff 7-1-89); 144 v H 485. Eff 7-8-92; 149 v S 123, § 1, eff. 1-1-04; 151 v H 68, § 101.01, eff. 6-29-05; 151 v H 66, § 101.01, eff. 9-29-05; 152 v H 215, § 1, eff. 4-7-09.**

The effective date is set by § 612.03 of 151 v H 66.
The effective date is set by section 4 of S.B. 123.
See provisions, § 5 of S.B. 123 (149 v —), following RC § 4501.01.

## § 4506.04 Prohibitions.

(A) No person shall do any of the following:

(1) Drive a commercial motor vehicle while having in the person's possession or otherwise under the person's control more than one valid driver's license issued by this state, any other state, or by a foreign jurisdiction;

(2) Drive a commercial motor vehicle on a highway in this state in violation of an out-of-service order, while the person's driving privilege is suspended, revoked, or canceled, or while the person is subject to disqualification;

(3) Drive a motor vehicle on a highway in this state under authority of a commercial driver's license issued by another state or a foreign jurisdiction, after having been a resident of this state for thirty days or longer;

(4) Knowingly give false information in any application or certification required by section 4506.07 of the Revised Code.

(B) The department of public safety shall give every conviction occurring out of this state and notice of which is received after December 31, 1989, full faith and credit and treat it for sanctioning purposes under this chapter as though the conviction had occurred in this state.

(C)(1) Whoever violates division (A)(1), (2), or (3) of this section is guilty of a misdemeanor of the first degree.

(2) Whoever violates division (A)(4) of this section is guilty of falsification, a misdemeanor of the first degree. In addition, the provisions of section 4507.19 of the Revised Code apply.

**HISTORY: 143 v H 381 (Eff 7-1-89); 144 v S 98. Eff 11-12-92; 149 v S 123, § 1, eff. 1-1-04.**

The effective date is set by section 4 of S.B. 123.
See provisions, § 5 of S.B. 123 (149 v —), following RC § 4501.01.

## § 4506.05 Conditions for driving commercial motor vehicle.

(A) Notwithstanding any other provision of law, a person may drive a commercial motor vehicle on a highway in this state if all of the following conditions are met:

(1) The person has a valid commercial driver's license or commercial driver's license temporary instruction permit issued by any state or jurisdiction in accordance with

the minimum standards adopted by the federal motor carrier safety administration under the "Commercial Motor Vehicle Safety Act of 1986," 100 Stat. 3207-171, 49 U.S.C.A. App. for issuance of commercial drivers' licenses;

(2) The person's commercial driver's license or permit is not suspended, revoked, or canceled;

(3) The person is not disqualified from driving a commercial motor vehicle;

(4) The person is not subject to an out-of-service order.

(B) Whoever violates this section is guilty of a misdemeanor of the first degree.

**HISTORY: 143 v H 381. Eff 7-1-89; 149 v S 123, § 1, eff. 1-1-04; 151 v H 68, § 101.01, eff. 6-29-05.**

The effective date is set by § 612.03 of 151 v H 68.
The effective date is set by section 4 of S.B. 123.
See provisions, § 5 of S.B. 123 (149 v —), following RC § 4501.01.

## § 4506.06 Issuance of temporary instruction permit; effect.

(A) The registrar of motor vehicles, upon receiving an application for a commercial driver's temporary instruction permit, may issue the permit to any person who is at least eighteen years of age and holds a valid driver's license, other than a restricted license, issued under Chapter 4507. of the Revised Code. A commercial driver's temporary instruction permit shall not be issued for a period exceeding six months and only one renewal of a permit shall be granted in a two-year period.

The holder of a commercial driver's temporary instruction permit, unless otherwise disqualified, may drive a commercial motor vehicle when having the permit in the holder's actual possession and accompanied by a person who holds a valid commercial driver's license valid for the type of vehicle being driven and who occupies a seat beside the permit holder for the purpose of giving instruction in driving the motor vehicle.

(B) Whoever violates this section is guilty of a misdemeanor of the first degree.

**HISTORY: 143 v H 381 (Eff 7-1-89); 143 v H 88 (Eff 3-13-90); 146 v H 353. Eff 9-17-96; 149 v S 123, § 1, eff. 1-1-04.**

The effective date is set by section 4 of S.B. 123.
See provisions, § 5 of S.B. 123 (149 v —), following RC § 4501.01.

## § 4506.07 Form of application for license or permit; registration as elector or change of voting residence.

(A) Every application for a commercial driver's license, restricted commercial driver's license, or a commercial driver's temporary instruction permit, or a duplicate of such a license, shall be made upon a form approved and furnished by the registrar of motor vehicles. Except as provided in section 4506.24 of the Revised Code in regard to a restricted commercial driver's license, the application shall be signed by the applicant and shall contain the following information:

(1) The applicant's name, date of birth, social security account number, sex, general description including height, weight, and color of hair and eyes, current residence, duration of residence in this state, country of citizenship, and occupation;

(2) Whether the applicant previously has been licensed to operate a commercial motor vehicle or any other type of motor vehicle in another state or a foreign jurisdiction and, if so, when, by what state, and whether the license or driving privileges currently are suspended or revoked in any jurisdiction, or the applicant otherwise has been disqualified from operating a commercial motor vehicle, or is subject to an out-of-service order issued under this chapter or any similar law of another state or a foreign jurisdiction and, if so, the date of, locations involved, and reason for the suspension, revocation, disqualification, or out-of-service order;

(3) Whether the applicant is afflicted with or suffering from any physical or mental disability or disease that prevents the applicant from exercising reasonable and ordinary control over a motor vehicle while operating it upon a highway or is or has been subject to any condition resulting in episodic impairment of consciousness or loss of muscular control and, if so, the nature and extent of the disability, disease, or condition, and the names and addresses of the physicians attending the applicant;

(4) Whether the applicant has obtained a medical examiner's certificate as required by this chapter;

(5) Whether the applicant has pending a citation for violation of any motor vehicle law or ordinance except a parking violation and, if so, a description of the citation, the court having jurisdiction of the offense, and the date when the offense occurred;

(6) Whether the applicant wishes to certify willingness to make an anatomical gift under section 2108.05 of the Revised Code, which shall be given no consideration in the issuance of a license;

(7) On and after May 1, 1993, whether the applicant has executed a valid durable power of attorney for health care pursuant to sections 1337.11 to 1337.17 of the Revised Code or has executed a declaration governing the use or continuation, or the withholding or withdrawal, of life-sustaining treatment pursuant to sections 2133.01 to 2133.15 of the Revised Code and, if the applicant has executed either type of instrument, whether the applicant wishes the license issued to indicate that the applicant has executed the instrument;

(8) On and after October 7, 2009, whether the applicant is a veteran, active duty, or reservist of the armed forces of the United States and, if the applicant is such, whether the applicant wishes the license issued to indicate that the applicant is a veteran, active duty, or reservist of the armed forces of the United States by a military designation on the license.

(B) Every applicant shall certify, on a form approved and furnished by the registrar, all of the following:

(1) That the motor vehicle in which the applicant intends to take the driving skills test is representative of the type of motor vehicle that the applicant expects to operate as a driver;

(2) That the applicant is not subject to any disqualification or out-of-service order, or license suspension, revocation, or cancellation, under the laws of this state, of another state, or of a foreign jurisdiction and does not have more than one driver's license issued by this or another state or a foreign jurisdiction;

(3) Any additional information, certification, or evidence that the registrar requires by rule in order to ensure that the issuance of a commercial driver's license to the applicant is in compliance with the law of this state and with federal law.

(C) Every applicant shall execute a form, approved and furnished by the registrar, under which the applicant consents to the release by the registrar of information from the applicant's driving record.

(D) The registrar or a deputy registrar, in accordance with section 3503.11 of the Revised Code, shall register as an elector any applicant for a commercial driver's license or for a renewal or duplicate of such a license under this chapter, if the applicant is eligible and wishes to be registered as an elector. The decision of an applicant whether to register as an elector shall be given no consideration in the decision of whether to issue the applicant a license or a renewal or duplicate.

(E) The registrar or a deputy registrar, in accordance with section 3503.11 of the Revised Code, shall offer the opportunity of completing a notice of change of residence or change of name to any applicant for a commercial driver's license or for a renewal or duplicate of such a license who is a resident of this state, if the applicant is a registered elector who has changed the applicant's residence or name and has not filed such a notice.

(F) In considering any application submitted pursuant to this section, the bureau of motor vehicles may conduct any inquiries necessary to ensure that issuance or renewal of a commercial driver's license would not violate any provision of the Revised Code or federal law.

(G) In addition to any other information it contains, on and after October 7, 2009, the form approved and furnished by the registrar of motor vehicles for an application for a commercial driver's license, restricted commercial driver's license, or a commercial driver's temporary instruction permit or an application for a duplicate of such a license shall inform applicants that the applicant must present a copy of the applicant's DD-214 or an equivalent document in order to qualify to have the license or duplicate indicate that the applicant is a veteran, active duty, or reservist of the armed forces of the United States based on a request made pursuant to division (A)(8) of this section.

**HISTORY: 143 v H 381 (Eff 7-1-89); 144 v H 427 (Eff 10-8-92); 144 v H 485 (Eff 7-8-92); 145 v S 300 (Eff 1-1-95); 147 v H 354. Eff 7-9-98; 151 v H 66, § 101.01, eff. 9-29-05; 152 v H 450, § 1, eff. 4-7-09; 152 v H 529, § 1, eff. 4-7-09; 153 v H 2, § 101.01, eff. 7-1-09.**

The effective date is set by § 812.10 of 153 v H 2.

The provisions of § 815.20 of 153 v H 2 read in part as follows:

SECTION 815.20. The General Assembly, applying the principle stated in division (B) of section 1.52 of the Revised Code that amendments are to be harmonized if reasonably capable of simultaneous operation, finds that the following sections, presented in this act as composites of the sections as amended by the acts indicated, are the resulting versions of the sections in effect prior to the effective date of the sections as presented in this act:

* * *

Section 4506.07 of the Revised Code as amended by both Am. Sub. H.B. 450 and Sub. H.B. 529 of the 127th General Assembly.

* * *

The effective date is set by § 612.03 of 151 v H 66.

## § 4506.08 Fees for applications; furnishing information on driving record.

(A)(1) Each application for a commercial driver's license temporary instruction permit shall be accompanied by a fee of ten dollars. Each application for a commercial driver's license, restricted commercial driver's license, renewal of such a license, or waiver for farm-related service industries shall be accompanied by a fee of twenty-five dollars, except that an application for a commercial driver's license or restricted commercial driver's license received pursuant to division (A)(3) of section 4506.14 of the Revised Code shall be accompanied by a fee of eighteen dollars and seventy-five cents if the license will expire on the licensee's birthday three years after the date of issuance, a fee of twelve dollars and fifty cents if the license will expire on the licensee's birthday two years after the date of issuance, and a fee of six dollars and twenty-five cents if the license will expire on the licensee's birthday one year after the date of issuance. Each application for a duplicate commercial driver's license shall be accompanied by a fee of ten dollars.

(2) In addition, the registrar of motor vehicles or deputy registrar may collect and retain an additional fee of no more than three dollars and fifty cents for each application for a commercial driver's license temporary instruction permit, commercial driver's license, renewal of a commercial driver's license, or duplicate commercial driver's license received by the registrar or deputy.

(B) In addition to the fees imposed under division (A) of this section, the registrar of motor vehicles or deputy registrar shall collect a fee of twelve dollars for each application for a commercial driver's license temporary instruction permit, commercial driver's license, or duplicate commercial driver's license and for each application for renewal of a commercial driver's license. The additional fee is for the purpose of defraying the department of public safety's costs associated with the administration and enforcement of the motor vehicle and traffic laws of Ohio.

(C) Each deputy registrar shall transmit the fees collected under divisions (A)(1) and (B) of this section in the time and manner prescribed by the registrar. The registrar shall deposit all moneys received under division (C) of this section into the state highway safety fund established in section 4501.06 of the Revised Code.

(D) Information regarding the driving record of any person holding a commercial driver's license issued by this state shall be furnished by the registrar, upon request and payment of a fee of five dollars, to the employer or prospective employer of such a person and to any insurer.

Of each five-dollar fee the registrar collects under this division, the registrar shall pay two dollars into the state treasury to the credit of the state bureau of motor vehicles fund established in section 4501.25 of the Revised Code, sixty cents into the state treasury to the credit of the trauma and emergency medical services fund established in section 4513.263 [4513.26.3] of the Revised Code, sixty cents into the state treasury to the credit of the homeland security fund established in section 5502.03 of the Revised Code, thirty cents into the state treasury to the credit of the investigations fund established in section 5502.131 [5502.13.1] of the Revised Code, one dollar and twenty-five cents into the state treasury to the credit of the emergency management agency service and reimbursement fund established in section 5502.39 of the Revised Code, and twenty-five cents into the state treasury to the credit of the justice program services fund established in section 5502.67 of the Revised Code.

**HISTORY: 143 v H 381 (Eff 7-1-89); 144 v H 134 (Eff 10-10-91); 144 v H 485 (Eff 7-8-92); 145 v H 154 (Eff 6-30-93); 146 v H 107 (Eff 6-30-95); 147 v S 60 (Eff 10-21-97); 149 v H 94. Eff 6-6-2001; 150 v H 87, § 1, eff. 3-31-03; 150 v H 230, § 1, eff. 9-16-04; 151 v H 68, § 101.01, eff. 6-29-05; 153 v H 2, § 101.01, eff. 7-1-09; 2011 HB 114, § 101.01, eff. June 29, 2011.**

Acts 2011, HB 114, § 806.10 provides: "The items of law contained in this act, and their applications, are severable. If any item of law contained in this act, or if any application of any item of law contained in this act, is held invalid, the invalidity does not affect other items of law contained in this act and their applications that can be given effect without the invalid item or application."

The effective date is set by § 812.10 of 153 v H 2.

The effective date is set by § 612.03 of 151 v H 68.

The effective date is set by section 26 of H.B. 87.

## § 4506.081 Request for donations to second chance trust fund.

In addition to the fees collected under section 4506.08 of the Revised Code, the registrar or deputy registrar of motor vehicles shall ask each person applying for or renewing a commercial driver's license, restricted commercial driver's license, or duplicate whether the person wishes to make a one-dollar voluntary contribution to the second chance trust fund established under section 2108.34 of the Revised Code. The registrar or deputy registrar shall also make available to the person informational material provided by the department of health on the importance of organ, tissue, and eye donation.

All donations collected under this section during each month shall be forwarded by the registrar or deputy registrar not later than the fifth day of the immediately following month to the treasurer of state, who shall deposit them in the second chance trust fund.

**HISTORY: 146 v S 300. Eff 7-1-97; 152 v H 529, § 1, eff. 4-7-09.**

The effective date is set by section 3 of SB 300.

## § 4506.09 Rules for qualification and testing of applicants.

(A) The registrar of motor vehicles, subject to approval by the director of public safety, shall adopt rules conforming with applicable standards adopted by the federal motor carrier safety administration as regulations under Pub. L. No. 103-272, 108 Stat. 1014 to 1029 (1994), 49 U.S.C.A. 31301 to 31317. The rules shall establish requirements for the qualification and testing of persons applying for a commercial driver's license, which shall be in addition to other requirements established by this chapter. Except as provided in division (B) of this section, the highway patrol or any other employee of the department of public safety the registrar authorizes shall supervise and conduct the testing of persons applying for a commercial driver's license.

(B) The director may adopt rules, in accordance with Chapter 119. of the Revised Code and applicable requirements of the federal motor carrier safety administration, authorizing the skills test specified in this section to be administered by any person, by an agency of this or another state, or by an agency, department, or instrumentality of local government. Each party authorized under this division to administer the skills test may charge a maximum divisible fee of eighty-five dollars for each skills test given as part of a commercial driver's license examination. The fee shall consist of not more than twenty dollars for the pre-trip inspection portion of the test, not more than twenty dollars for the off-road maneuvering portion of the test, and not more than forty-five dollars for the on-road portion of the test. Each such party may require an appointment fee in the same manner provided in division (E)(2) of this section, except that the maximum amount such a party may require as an appointment fee is eighty-five dollars. The skills test administered by another party under this division shall be the same as otherwise would be administered by this state. The other party shall enter into an agreement with the director that, without limitation, does all of the following:

(1) Allows the director or the director's representative and the federal motor carrier safety administration or its representative to conduct random examinations, inspections, and audits of the other party without prior notice;

(2) Requires the director or the director's representative to conduct on-site inspections of the other party at least annually;

(3) Requires that all examiners of the other party meet the same qualification and training standards as examiners of the department of public safety, to the extent necessary to conduct skills tests in the manner required by 49 C.F.R. 383.110 through 383.135;

(4) Requires either that state employees take, at least annually and as though the employees were test applicants, the tests actually administered by the other party, that the director test a sample of drivers who were examined by the other party to compare the test results, or that state employees accompany a test applicant during an actual test;

(5) Reserves to this state the right to take prompt and appropriate remedial action against testers of the other party if the other party fails to comply with standards of this state or federal standards for the testing program or with any other terms of the contract.

(C) The director shall enter into an agreement with the department of education authorizing the skills test specified in this section to be administered by the department at any location operated by the department for purposes of training and testing school bus drivers, provided that the agreement between the director and the department complies with the requirements of division (B) of this section. Skills tests administered by the department shall be limited to persons applying for a commercial driver's license with a school bus endorsement.

(D) The director shall adopt rules, in accordance with Chapter 119. of the Revised Code, authorizing waiver of the skills test specified in this section for any applicant for a commercial driver's license who meets all of the following requirements:

(1) Certifies that, during the two-year period immediately preceding application for a commercial driver's license, all of the following apply:

(a) The applicant has not had more than one license.

(b) The applicant has not had any license suspended, revoked, or canceled.

(c) The applicant has not had any convictions for any type of motor vehicle for the offenses for which disqualification is prescribed in section 4506.16 of the Revised Code.

(d) The applicant has not had any violation of a state or local law relating to motor vehicle traffic control other than a parking violation arising in connection with any traffic accident and has no record of an accident in which the applicant was at fault.

(e) The applicant has previously taken and passed a skills test given by a state with a classified licensing and testing system in which the test was behind-the-wheel in a representative vehicle for the applicant's commercial driver's license classification.

(2) Certifies and also provides evidence that the applicant is regularly employed in a job requiring operation of

a commercial motor vehicle and that one of the following applies:

(a) The applicant has previously taken and passed a skills test given by a state with a classified licensing and testing system in which the test was behind-the-wheel in a representative vehicle for the applicant's commercial driver's license classification.

(b) The applicant has regularly operated, for at least two years immediately preceding application for a commercial driver's license, a vehicle representative of the commercial motor vehicle the applicant operates or expects to operate.

(E)(1) The department of public safety may charge and collect a divisible fee of fifty dollars for each skills test given as part of a commercial driver's license examination. The fee shall consist of ten dollars for the pre-trip inspection portion of the test, ten dollars for the off-road maneuvering portion of the test, and thirty dollars for the on-road portion of the test.

(2) The director may require an applicant for a commercial driver's license who schedules an appointment with the highway patrol or other authorized employee of the department of public safety to take all portions of the skills test, to pay an appointment fee of fifty dollars at the time of scheduling the appointment. If the applicant appears at the time and location specified for the appointment and takes all portions of the skills test during that appointment, the appointment fee shall serve as the skills test fee. If the applicant schedules an appointment to take all portions of the skills test and fails to appear at the time and location specified for the appointment, no portion of the appointment fee shall be refunded. If the applicant schedules an appointment to take all portions of the skills test and appears at the time and location specified for the appointment, but declines or is unable to take all portions of the skills test, no portion of the appointment fee shall be refunded. If the applicant cancels a scheduled appointment forty-eight hours or more prior to the time of the appointment time, the applicant shall not forfeit the appointment fee.

An applicant for a commercial driver's license who schedules an appointment to take one or more, but not all, portions of the skills test shall be required to pay an appointment fee equal to the costs of each test scheduled, as prescribed in division (E)(1) of this section, when scheduling such an appointment. If the applicant appears at the time and location specified for the appointment and takes all the portions of the skills test during that appointment that the applicant was scheduled to take, the appointment fee shall serve as the skills test fee. If the applicant schedules an appointment to take one or more, but not all, portions of the skills test and fails to appear at the time and location specified for the appointment, no portion of the appointment fee shall be refunded. If the applicant schedules an appointment to take one or more, but not all, portions of the skills test and appears at the time and location specified for the appointment, but declines or is unable to take all portions of the skills test that the applicant was scheduled to take, no portion of the appointment fee shall be refunded. If the applicant cancels a scheduled appointment forty-eight hours or more prior to the time of the appointment time, the applicant shall not forfeit the appointment fee.

(3) The department of public safety shall deposit all fees it collects under division (E) of this section in the state highway safety fund.

(F) As used in this section, "skills test" means a test of an applicant's ability to drive the type of commercial motor vehicle for which the applicant seeks a commercial driver's license by having the applicant drive such a motor vehicle while under the supervision of an authorized state driver's license examiner or tester.

**HISTORY: 143 v H 381 (Eff 7-1-89); 143 v H 88 (Eff 3-13-90); 144 v S 98 (Eff 11-12-92); 145 v H 687 (Eff 10-12-94); 148 v H 600. Eff 9-1-2000; 150 v H 230, § 1, eff. 9-16-04; 151 v H 68, § 101.01, eff. 6-29-05.**

The effective date is set by § 612.03 of 151 v H 68.
The effective date is set by section 8 of HB 600.

## § 4506.10 Driver to be physically qualified; medical examination; restrictions on license.

(A) No person who holds a valid commercial driver's license shall drive a commercial motor vehicle unless the person is physically qualified to do so. Each person who drives or expects to drive a commercial motor vehicle in interstate or foreign commerce or is otherwise subject to 49 C.F.R. 391, et seq., as amended, shall certify to the registrar of motor vehicles at the time of application for a commercial driver's license that the person is in compliance with these standards. Any person who is not subject to 49 C.F.R. 391, et seq., as amended, also shall certify at the time of application that the person is not subject to these standards.

(B) A person is qualified to drive a school bus if the person holds a valid commercial driver's license along with the proper endorsements, and if the person has been certified as medically qualified in accordance with rules adopted by the department of education.

(C)(1) Except as provided in division (C)(2) of this section, any medical examination required by this section shall be performed only by one of the following:

(a) A person licensed under Chapter 4731. of the Revised Code to practice medicine or surgery or osteopathic medicine and surgery in this state, or licensed under any similar law of another state;

(b) A person licensed as a physician assistant under Chapter 4730. of the Revised Code who practices under the supervision and direction of a physician as required under that chapter and who is authorized by the supervising physician to perform such a medical examination;

(c) A person who is a certified nurse practitioner or a clinical nurse specialist licensed under Chapter 4723. of the Revised Code who is practicing in accordance with a standard care arrangement pursuant to section 4723.431 [4723.43.1] of the Revised Code;

(d) A doctor of chiropractic.

(2) Any part of an examination required by this section that pertains to visual acuity, field of vision, and the ability to recognize colors may be performed by a person licensed under Chapter 4725. of the Revised Code to practice optometry in this state, or licensed under any similar law of another state.

(D) Whenever good cause appears, the registrar, upon issuing a commercial driver's license under this chapter, may impose restrictions suitable to the licensee's driving ability with respect to the type of motor vehicle or special mechanical control devices required on a motor vehicle that the licensee may operate, or such other restrictions applicable to the licensee as the registrar determines to be necessary.

The registrar may either issue a special restricted license or may set forth upon the usual license form the restrictions imposed.

The registrar, upon receiving satisfactory evidence of any violation of the restrictions of the license, may impose a class D license suspension of the license for the period of time specified in division (B)(4) of section 4510.02 of the Revised Code.

The registrar, upon receiving satisfactory evidence that an applicant or holder of a commercial driver's license has violated division (A)(4) of section 4506.04 of the Revised Code and knowingly given false information in any application or certification required by section 4506.07 of the Revised Code, shall cancel the commercial driver's license of the person or any pending application from the person for a commercial driver's license or class D driver's license for a period of at least sixty days, during which time no application for a commercial driver's license or class D driver's license shall be received from the person.

(E) Whoever violates this section is guilty of a misdemeanor of the first degree.

**HISTORY: 143 v H 381 (Eff 7-1-89); 143 v H 88 (Eff 3-13-90); 149 v H 73 (Eff 6-29-2001); 149 v S 245, § 1. Eff 3-31-2003; 149 v S 123, § 1, eff. 1-1-04; 151 v H 68, § 101.01, eff. 6-29-05.**

The effective date is set by § 612.03 of 151 v H 68.
The effective date is set by section 4 of S.B. 123.
See provisions, § 5 of S.B. 123 (149 v —), following RC § 4501.01.

## § 4506.101 Violation of federal law prohibited.

Notwithstanding any provision of the Revised Code, the bureau of motor vehicles shall not issue or renew a commercial driver's license if issuance or renewal of the license would violate federal law.

**HISTORY: 151 v H 66, § 101.01, eff. 9-29-05.**

The effective date is set by § 612.03 of 151 v H 66.

## § 4506.11 Form and material of license; file of negatives.

(A) Every commercial driver's license shall be marked "commercial driver's license" or "CDL" and shall be of such material and so designed as to prevent its reproduction or alteration without ready detection, and, to this end, shall be laminated with a transparent plastic material. The commercial driver's license for licensees under twenty-one years of age shall have characteristics prescribed by the registrar of motor vehicles distinguishing it from that issued to a licensee who is twenty-one years of age or older. Every commercial driver's license shall display all of the following information:

(1) The name and residence address of the licensee;

(2) A color photograph of the licensee showing the licensee's uncovered face;

(3) A physical description of the licensee, including sex, height, weight, and color of eyes and hair;

(4) The licensee's date of birth;

(5) The licensee's social security number if the person has requested that the number be displayed in accordance with section 4501.31 of the Revised Code or if federal law requires the social security number to be displayed and any number or other identifier the director of public safety considers appropriate and establishes by rules adopted under Chapter 119. of the Revised Code and in compliance with federal law;

(6) The licensee's signature;

(7) The classes of commercial motor vehicles the licensee is authorized to drive and any endorsements or restrictions relating to the licensee's driving of those vehicles;

(8) The name of this state;

(9) The dates of issuance and of expiration of the license;

(10) If the licensee has certified willingness to make an anatomical gift under section 2108.05 of the Revised Code, any symbol chosen by the registrar of motor vehicles to indicate that the licensee has certified that willingness;

(11) If the licensee has executed a durable power of attorney for health care or a declaration governing the use or continuation, or the withholding or withdrawal, of life-sustaining treatment and has specified that the licensee wishes the license to indicate that the licensee has executed either type of instrument, any symbol chosen by the registrar to indicate that the licensee has executed either type of instrument;

(12) On and after October 7, 2009, if the licensee has specified that the licensee wishes the license to indicate that the licensee is a veteran, active duty, or reservist of the armed forces of the United States and has presented a copy of the licensee's DD-214 form or an equivalent document, any symbol chosen by the registrar to indicate that the licensee is a veteran, active duty, or reservist of the armed forces of the United States;

(13) Any other information the registrar considers advisable and requires by rule.

(B) The registrar may establish and maintain a file of negatives of photographs taken for the purposes of this section.

(C) Neither the registrar nor any deputy registrar shall issue a commercial driver's license to anyone under twenty-one years of age that does not have the characteristics prescribed by the registrar distinguishing it from the commercial driver's license issued to persons who are twenty-one years of age or older.

(D) Whoever violates division (C) of this section is guilty of a minor misdemeanor.

**HISTORY: 143 v H 381 (Eff 7-1-89); 143 v S 131 (Eff 7-25-90); 144 v H 134 (Eff 10-10-91); 144 v H 427 (Eff 10-8-92); 144 v S 98 (Eff 11-12-92); 145 v H 580 (Eff 12-9-94); 147 v S 213 (Eff 7-29-98); 149 v H 46. Eff 2-1-2002; 149 v S 123, § 1, eff. 1-1-04; 150 v H 230, § 1, eff. 9-16-04; 151 v H 68, § 101.01, eff. 6-29-05; 152 v H 450, § 1, eff. 4-7-09; 152 v H 529, § 1, eff. 4-7-09; 153 v H 2, § 101.01, eff. 7-1-09.**

The effective date is set by § 812.10 of 153 v H 2.
The provisions of § 815.20 of 153 v H 2 read in part as follows:
SECTION 815.20. The General Assembly, applying the principle stated in division (B) of section 1.52 of the Revised Code that amendments are to be harmonized if reasonably capable of simultaneous operation, finds that the following sections, presented in this act as composites of the sections as amended by the acts indicated, are the resulting versions of the sections in effect prior to the effective date of the sections as presented in this act:

° ° °

Section 4506.11 of the Revised Code as amended by both Am. Sub. H.B. 450 and Sub. H.B. 529 of the 127th General Assembly.

° ° °

The effective date is set by § 612.03 of 151 v H 68.
The effective date is set by section 4 of S.B. 123.
See provisions, § 5 of S.B. 123 (149 v —), following RC § 4501.01.

## § 4506.12 Classes of licenses; endorsements; restrictions.

(A) Commercial drivers' licenses shall be issued in the following classes and shall include any endorsements and restrictions that are applicable. Subject to any such endorsements and restrictions, the holder of a valid commercial driver's license may drive all commercial motor vehicles in the class for which that license is issued and all lesser classes of vehicles, except that the holder shall not operate a motorcycle unless the holder is licensed to do so under Chapter 4507. of the Revised Code.

(B) The classes of commercial drivers' licenses and the commercial motor vehicles that they authorize the operation of are as follows:

(1) Class A—any combination of vehicles with a combined gross vehicle weight rating of twenty-six thousand one pounds or more, if the gross vehicle weight rating of the vehicle or vehicles being towed is in excess of ten thousand pounds.

(2) Class B—any single vehicle with a gross vehicle weight rating of twenty-six thousand one pounds or more or any such vehicle towing a vehicle having a gross vehicle weight rating that is not in excess of ten thousand pounds.

(3) Class C—any single vehicle, or combination of vehicles, that is not a class A or class B vehicle, but that is designed to transport sixteen or more passengers, including the driver, or is transporting hazardous materials in an amount requiring placarding, or any school bus with a gross vehicle weight rating of less than twenty-six thousand one pounds that is designed to transport fewer than sixteen passengers including the driver.

(C) The following endorsements and restrictions apply to commercial drivers' licenses:

(1) H—authorizes the driver to drive a vehicle transporting hazardous materials in an amount requiring placarding;

(2) K—restricts the driver to only intrastate operation;

(3) L—restricts the driver to vehicles not equipped with air brakes;

(4) T—authorizes the driver to drive a vehicle configured with double or triple trailers that create more than one articulation point for the combination;

(5) P—authorizes the driver to drive vehicles designed to transport sixteen or more passengers, including the driver;

(6) P1—authorizes the driver to drive class A vehicles designed for fewer than sixteen passengers, including the driver, and all lesser classes of vehicles without restriction as to the designed passenger capacity of the vehicle;

(7) P2—authorizes the driver to drive class A or B vehicles designed for fewer than sixteen passengers, including the driver, and all lesser classes of vehicles without restriction as to the designed passenger capacity of the vehicle;

(8) P4—Restricts the driver to driving class C school buses designed to transport fewer than sixteen passengers including the driver.

(9) N—authorizes the driver to drive tank vehicles;

(10) S—authorizes the driver to drive school buses transporting children;

(11) X—authorizes the driver to drive tank vehicles transporting hazardous materials in a quantity requiring placarding;

(12) W—restricts the driver to the operation of commercial motor vehicles in accordance with a waiver for farm-related service industries issued under section 4506.24 of the Revised Code.

(D) In addition to any endorsement that otherwise may apply, a person who is engaged in the towing of a disabled or wrecked motor vehicle shall hold a commercial driver's license bearing any endorsement required to drive the towed vehicle except the driver is not required to have either of the following:

(1) A passenger endorsement to tow an unoccupied passenger vehicle;

(2) Any endorsement required for the wrecked or disabled vehicle when the driver initially removes a vehicle from the site of the emergency where the vehicle became wrecked or disabled to the nearest appropriate repair, disposal, or storage facility, as applicable.

(E) No person shall drive any commercial motor vehicle for which an endorsement is required under this section unless the proper endorsement appears on the person's commercial driver's license.

(F) Whoever violates this section is guilty of a misdemeanor of the first degree.

**HISTORY: 143 v H 381 (Eff 7-1-89); 143 v H 88 (Eff 3-13-90); 143 v H 831 (Eff 7-17-90); 144 v H 485. Eff 7-8-92; 149 v S 123, § 1, eff. 1-1-04; 150 v H 230, § 1, eff. 9-16-04; 151 v H 68, § 101.01, eff. 6-29-05.**

The effective date is set by § 612.03 of 151 v H 68.
The effective date is set by section 4 of S.B. 123.
See provisions, § 5 of S.B. 123 (149 v —), following RC § 4501.01.

## § 4506.13 Examinations passed form; commercial driver license information system.

(A) The registrar may authorize the highway patrol or any other employee of the department of public safety to issue an examiner's commercial examinations passed form to an applicant who has passed the required examinations. The examiner's commercial examinations passed form shall be used, once it has been validated, to indicate the examinations taken and passed by the commercial driver's license applicant.

(B) Before issuing a commercial driver's license, the registrar of motor vehicles shall obtain information about the applicant's driving record through the commercial driver license information system, when available, and the national driver register. If the record check reveals information that the applicant claims is outdated, contested, or invalid, the registrar shall deny the application until the applicant can resolve the conflict.

Within ten days after issuing a commercial driver's license, the registrar shall notify the commercial driver license information system, when available, of that fact and shall provide all information required to ensure identification of the licensee.

**HISTORY: 143 v H 381 (Eff 7-1-89); 143 v H 88 (Eff 3-13-90); 143 v H 831 (Eff 7-17-90); 148 v H 600. Eff 9-1-2000.**

The effective date is set by section 8 of HB 600.

## § 4506.14 Expiration, renewal of license; notice of change of address.

(A) Commercial driver's licenses shall expire as follows:

(1) Except as provided in division (A)(3) or (4) of this section, each such license issued to replace an operator's or chauffeur's license shall expire on the original expiration date of the operator's or chauffeur's license and, upon

renewal, shall expire on the licensee's birthday in the fourth year after the date of issuance.

(2) Except as provided in division (A)(3) or (4) of this section, each such license issued as an original license to a person whose residence is in this state shall expire on the licensee's birthday in the fourth year after the date of issuance, and each such license issued to a person whose temporary residence is in this state shall expire in accordance with rules adopted by the registrar of motor vehicles. A license issued to a person with a temporary residence in this state is nonrenewable, but may be replaced with a new license within ninety days prior to its expiration upon the applicant's compliance with all applicable requirements.

(3) The registrar or a deputy registrar may issue a license that expires on a date earlier than the licensee's birthday in the fourth year after the date of issuance if the licensee has undergone a security threat assessment required by federal law to obtain a hazardous materials endorsement and the assessment will expire before that date.

(4) Each such license issued to replace the operator's or chauffeur's license of a person who is less than twenty-one years of age, and each such license issued as an original license to a person who is less than twenty-one years of age, shall expire on the licensee's twenty-first birthday.

(B) No commercial driver's license shall be issued for a period longer than four years and one hundred eighty days. Except as provided in section 4507.12 of the Revised Code, the registrar may waive the examination of any person applying for the renewal of a commercial driver's license issued under this chapter, provided that the applicant presents either an unexpired commercial driver's license or a commercial driver's license that has expired not more than six months prior to the date of application.

(C) Subject to the requirements of this chapter and except as provided in division (A)(2) of this section in regard to a person whose temporary residence is in this state, every commercial driver's license shall be renewable one hundred eighty days before its expiration upon payment of the fees required by section 4506.08 of the Revised Code. Each person applying for renewal or transfer of a commercial driver's license shall complete the application form prescribed by section 4506.07 of the Revised Code and shall provide all certifications required. If the person wishes to retain an endorsement authorizing the person to transport hazardous materials, the person shall take and successfully complete the written test for the endorsement and shall submit to any background check required by federal law.

(D) Each person licensed as a driver under this chapter shall notify the registrar of any change in the person's address within ten days following that change. The notification shall be in writing on a form provided by the registrar and shall include the full name, date of birth, license number, county of residence, social security number, and new address of the person.

(E) Whoever violates division (D) of this section is guilty of a minor misdemeanor.

**HISTORY: 143 v H 381 (Eff 7-1-89); 143 v H 88 (Eff 3-13-90); 143 v S 382 (Eff 12-31-90); 144 v H 134 (Eff 10-10-91); 144 v S 98 (Eff 11-12-92); 145 v H 687 (Eff 10-12-94); 147 v S 60. Eff 10-21-97; 149 v S 123, § 1, eff. 1-1-04; 150 v H 95, § 1, eff. 9-26-03; 150 v H 95, § 3.13, eff. 1-1-04; 151 v H 68, § 101.01, eff. 6-29-05.**

The effective date is set by § 612.03 of 151 v H 68.

See provisions, § 5 of S.B. 123 (149 v —), following RC § 4501.01.

## § 4506.15 Alcohol and other prohibitions.

(A) No person shall do any of the following:

(1) Drive a commercial motor vehicle while having a measurable or detectable amount of alcohol or of a controlled substance in the person's blood, breath, or urine;

(2) Drive a commercial motor vehicle while having an alcohol concentration of four-hundredths of one per cent or more by whole blood or breath;

(3) Drive a commercial motor vehicle while having an alcohol concentration of forty-eight-thousandths of one per cent or more by blood serum or blood plasma;

(4) Drive a commercial motor vehicle while having an alcohol concentration of fifty-six-thousandths of one per cent or more by urine;

(5) Drive a motor vehicle while under the influence of a controlled substance;

(6) Use a motor vehicle in the commission of a felony;

(7) Refuse to submit to a test under section 4506.17 of the Revised Code;

(8) Operate a commercial motor vehicle while the person's commercial driving privileges are revoked, suspended, canceled, or disqualified;

(9) Cause a fatality though the negligent operation of a commercial motor vehicle, including, but not limited to, the offenses of aggravated vehicular homicide, vehicular homicide, and vehicular manslaughter;

(10) Use a motor vehicle in the commission of a felony involving the manufacture, distribution, or dispensing of a controlled substance as defined in section 3719.01 of the Revised Code or the possession with intent to manufacture, distribute, or dispense a controlled substance;

(11) Drive a commercial motor vehicle in violation of any provision of sections 4511.61 to 4511.63 of the Revised Code or any federal or local law or ordinance pertaining to railroad-highway grade crossings;

(12) Violate any prohibition described in divisions (A)(2) to (11) of this section while transporting hazardous materials.

(B) Whoever violates this section is guilty of a misdemeanor of the first degree.

**HISTORY: 143 v H 381 (Eff 7-1-89); 143 v H 88. Eff 3-13-90; 149 v S 123, § 1, eff. 1-1-04; 150 v H 95, § 1, eff. 9-26-03; 150 v H 95, § 3.13, eff. 1-1-04; 151 v H 68, § 101.01, eff. 6-29-05.**

The effective date is set by § 612.03 of 151 v H 68.

See provisions, § 5 of S.B. 123 (149 v —), following RC § 4501.01.

## § 4506.16 Disqualification of driver and placement out of service.

(A) Any person who is found to have been convicted of a violation of an out-of-service order shall be disqualified by the registrar of motor vehicles as follows:

(1) If the person has not been convicted previously of a violation of an out-of-service order, the period of disqualification is ninety days.

(2) If, during any ten-year period, the driver is convicted of a second violation of an out-of-service order in an incident separate from the incident that resulted in the first violation, the period of disqualification is one year.

(3) If, during any ten-year period, the driver is convicted of a third or subsequent violation of an out-of-service order in an incident separate from the incidents that resulted in the previous violations during that ten-year period, the period of disqualification is three years.

(B)(1) A driver is disqualified for one hundred eighty days if the driver is convicted of a first violation of an out-of-service order while transporting hazardous materials required to be placarded under the "Hazardous Materials Transportation Act," 88 Stat. 2156 (1975), 49 U.S.C.A. 1801, as amended, or while operating a motor vehicle designed to transport sixteen or more passengers, including the driver.

(2) A driver is disqualified for a period of three years if, during any ten-year period, the driver is convicted of a second or subsequent violation, in an incident separate from the incident that resulted in a previous violation during that ten-year period, of an out-of-service order while transporting hazardous materials required to be placarded under that act, or while operating a motor vehicle designed to transport sixteen or more passengers, including the driver.

(C) Whoever violates division (A)(1) of section 4506.15 of the Revised Code or a similar law of another state or a foreign jurisdiction, immediately shall be placed out-of-service for twenty-four hours, in addition to any disqualification required by this section and any other penalty imposed by the Revised Code.

(D) The registrar of motor vehicles shall disqualify any holder of a commercial driver's license, or any operator of a commercial motor vehicle for which a commercial driver's license is required, from operating a commercial motor vehicle as follows:

(1) Upon a first conviction for a violation of any provision of divisions (A)(2) to (9) of section 4506.15 of the Revised Code, or of section 4511.19 or sections 4549.02 to 4549.03 of the Revised Code, or a similar law of another state or a foreign jurisdiction, one year;

(2) Upon a second conviction for a violation of any provision of divisions (A)(2) to (9) of section 4506.15 of the Revised Code, or of section 4511.19 or sections 4549.02 to 4549.03 of the Revised Code, or a similar law of another state or a foreign jurisdiction, or any combination of such violations arising from two or more separate incidents, the person shall be disqualified for life or for any other period of time as determined by the United States secretary of transportation and designated by the director of public safety by rule;

(3) Upon a first conviction for a violation of division (A)(12) of section 4506.15 of the Revised Code or a similar law of another state or a foreign jurisdiction, three years;

(4) Upon conviction of a violation of division (A)(10) of section 4506.15 of the Revised Code or a similar law of another state or a foreign jurisdiction, the person shall be disqualified for life;

(5) Upon conviction of two serious traffic violations involving the operation of a motor vehicle by the person and arising from separate incidents occurring in a three-year period, the person shall be disqualified for sixty days if the conviction results in the suspension, cancellation, or revocation of the holder's commercial driver's license or noncommercial motor vehicle driving privileges;

(6) Upon conviction of three serious traffic violations involving the operation of a motor vehicle by the person and arising from separate incidents occurring in a three-year period, the person shall be disqualified for one hundred twenty days if the conviction results in the suspension, cancellation, or revocation of the holder's commercial driver's license or noncommercial motor vehicle driving privileges.

(7) Upon a first conviction involving the operation of a commercial motor vehicle in violation of any provisions of sections 4511.61 to 4511.63 of the Revised Code or a similar law of another state or foreign jurisdiction, not less than sixty days;

(8) Upon a second conviction involving the operation of a commercial motor vehicle in violation of any provisions of sections 4511.61 to 4511.63 of the Revised Code or a similar law of another state or foreign jurisdiction within three years of the first such conviction, not less than one hundred twenty days;

(9) Upon a third or subsequent conviction involving the operation of a commercial motor vehicle in violation of any provisions of sections 4511.61 to 4511.63 of the Revised Code or a similar law of another state or foreign jurisdiction within three years of the first such conviction, not less than one year;

(10) Upon receiving notification from the federal motor carrier safety administration, the registrar shall disqualify any commercial motor vehicle driver whose driving is determined to constitute an imminent hazard as defined under federal motor carrier safety regulation 49 C.F.R. 383.52.

(E) For the purposes of this section, conviction of a violation for which disqualification is required may be evidenced by any of the following:

(1) A judgment entry of a court of competent jurisdiction in this or any other state;

(2) An administrative order of a state agency of this or any other state having statutory jurisdiction over commercial drivers;

(3) A computer record obtained from or through the commercial driver's license information system;

(4) A computer record obtained from or through a state agency of this or any other state having statutory jurisdiction over commercial drivers or the records of commercial drivers.

(F) For purposes of this section, conviction of disqualifying offenses committed in a noncommercial motor vehicle are included if either of the following applies:

(1) The offense occurred after the person obtained the person's commercial driver's license.

(2) The offense occurs on or after September 30, 2005.

(G) If a person commits a serious traffic violation by operating a commercial motor vehicle without having a commercial driver's license in the person's possession as described in division (DD)(7) of section 4506.01 of the Revised Code and the person then submits proof to either the enforcement agency that issued the citation for the violation or to the court with jurisdiction over the case before the date of the person's initial appearance that shows that the person held a valid commercial driver's license at the time of the violation, the violation shall not be deemed to be a serious traffic violation.

(H) Any record described in division (C) of this section shall be deemed to be self-authenticating when it is received by the bureau of motor vehicles.

(I) When disqualifying a driver, the registrar shall cause the records of the bureau to be updated to reflect that action within ten days after it occurs.

(J) The registrar immediately shall notify a driver who is finally convicted of any offense described in section 4506.15 of the Revised Code or division (B)(4), (5), or (6) of this section and thereby is subject to disqualification, of the offense or offenses involved, of the length of time for which disqualification is to be imposed, and that the driver may request a hearing within thirty days of the mailing of the notice to show cause why the driver should not be disqualified from operating a commercial motor vehicle. If a request for such a hearing is not made within thirty days of the mailing of the notice, the order of disqualification is final. The registrar may designate hearing examiners who, after affording all parties reasonable notice, shall conduct a hearing to determine whether the disqualification order is supported by reliable evidence. The registrar shall adopt rules to implement this division.

(K) Any person who is disqualified from operating a commercial motor vehicle under this section may apply to the registrar for a driver's license to operate a motor vehicle other than a commercial motor vehicle, provided the person's commercial driver's license is not otherwise suspended. A person whose commercial driver's license is suspended shall not apply to the registrar for or receive a driver's license under Chapter 4507. of the Revised Code during the period of suspension.

(L) The disqualifications imposed under this section are in addition to any other penalty imposed by the Revised Code.

**HISTORY: 143 v H 381 (Eff 7-1-89); 144 v S 98 (Eff 11-12-92); 144 v S 275 (Eff 9-1-93); 145 v S 62, § 4 (Eff 9-1-93); 147 v S 60 (Eff 10-21-97); 148 v H 600. Eff 9-1-2000; 149 v S 123, § 1, eff. 1-1-04; 150 v H 95, § 1, eff. 9-26-03; 150 v H 95, § 3.13, eff. 1-1-04; 151 v H 68, § 101.01, eff. 6-29-05.**

The effective date is set by § 612.03 of 151 v H 68.

See provisions, § 5 of S.B. 123 (149 v —), following RC § 4501.01.

## § 4506.161 Restrictions on granting limited driving privileges.

No court shall issue an order granting limited driving privileges for operation of a commercial motor vehicle to any person whose driver's license or commercial driver's license has been suspended or who has been disqualified from operating a commercial motor vehicle.

**HISTORY: 151 v H 66, § 101.01, eff. 9-29-05.**

The effective date is set by § 612.03 of 151 v H 66.

## § 4506.17 Implied consent to test; effect of refusal; immediate surrender of license; disqualification procedure.

(A) Any person who holds a commercial driver's license or operates a commercial motor vehicle requiring a commercial driver's license within this state shall be deemed to have given consent to a test or tests of the person's whole blood, blood serum or plasma, breath, or urine for the purpose of determining the person's alcohol concentration or the presence of any controlled substance or a metabolite of a controlled substance.

(B) A test or tests as provided in division (A) of this section may be administered at the direction of a peace officer having reasonable ground to stop or detain the person and, after investigating the circumstances surrounding the operation of the commercial motor vehicle, also having reasonable ground to believe the person was driving the commercial vehicle while having a measurable or detectable amount of alcohol or of a controlled substance or a metabolite of a controlled substance in the person's whole blood, blood serum or plasma, breath, or urine. Any such test shall be given within two hours of the time of the alleged violation.

(C) A person requested to submit to a test under division (A) of this section shall be advised by the peace officer requesting the test that a refusal to submit to the test will result in the person immediately being placed out-of-service for a period of twenty-four hours and being disqualified from operating a commercial motor vehicle for a period of not less than one year, and that the person is required to surrender the person's commercial driver's license to the peace officer.

(D) If a person refuses to submit to a test after being warned as provided in division (C) of this section or submits to a test that discloses the presence of a controlled substance or a metabolite of a controlled substance, an alcohol concentration of four-hundredths of one per cent or more by whole blood or breath, an alcohol concentration of forty-eight-thousandths of one per cent or more by blood serum or blood plasma, or an alcohol concentration of fifty-six-thousandths of one per cent or more by urine, the person immediately shall surrender the person's commercial driver's license to the peace officer. The peace officer shall forward the license, together with a sworn report, to the registrar of motor vehicles certifying that the test was requested pursuant to division (A) of this section and that the person either refused to submit to testing or submitted to a test that disclosed the presence of a controlled substance or a metabolite of a controlled substance or a prohibited alcohol concentration. The form and contents of the report required by this section shall be established by the registrar by rule, but shall contain the advice to be read to the driver and a statement to be signed by the driver acknowledging that the driver has been read the advice and that the form was shown to the driver.

(E) Upon receipt of a sworn report from a peace officer as provided in division (D) of this section, the registrar shall disqualify the person named in the report from driving a commercial motor vehicle for the period described below:

(1) Upon a first incident, one year;

(2) Upon an incident of refusal or of a prohibited concentration of alcohol, a controlled substance, or a metabolite of a controlled substance after one or more previous incidents of either refusal or of a prohibited concentration of alcohol, a controlled substance, or a metabolite of a controlled substance, the person shall be disqualified for life or such lesser period as prescribed by rule by the registrar.

(F) A test of a person's whole blood or a person's blood serum or plasma given under this section shall comply with the applicable provisions of division (D) of section 4511.19 of the Revised Code and any physician, registered nurse, emergency medical technician-intermediate, emergency medical technician-paramedic, or qualified technician, chemist, or phlebotomist who withdraws whole blood or blood serum or plasma from a person under this section, and any hospital, first-aid station, clinic, or other facility at which whole blood or blood serum or plasma is withdrawn from a person pursuant to this section, is immune from criminal liability, and from civil liability that is based upon a claim of assault and battery or based upon any other claim of malpractice, for any act performed in withdrawing whole blood or blood serum or plasma from the person. The immunity provided in this division also extends to an emergency medical service organization that employs an emergency medical technician-intermediate or emergency medical technician-paramedic who withdraws blood under this section.

(G) When a person submits to a test under this section, the results of the test, at the person's request, shall be made available to the person, the person's attorney, or the person's agent, immediately upon completion of the chemical test analysis. The person also may have an additional test administered by a physician, a registered nurse, or a qualified technician, chemist, or phlebotomist of the person's own choosing as provided in division (D) of section 4511.19 of the Revised Code for tests administered under that section, and the failure to obtain such a test has the same effect as in that division.

(H) No person shall refuse to immediately surrender the person's commercial driver's license to a peace officer when required to do so by this section.

(I) A peace officer issuing an out-of-service order or receiving a commercial driver's license surrendered under this section may remove or arrange for the removal of any commercial motor vehicle affected by the issuance of that order or the surrender of that license.

(J)(1) Except for civil actions arising out of the operation of a motor vehicle and civil actions in which the state is a plaintiff, no peace officer of any law enforcement agency within this state is liable in compensatory damages in any civil action that arises under the Revised Code or common law of this state for an injury, death, or loss to person or property caused in the performance of official duties under this section and rules adopted under this section, unless the officer's actions were manifestly outside the scope of the officer's employment or official responsibilities, or unless the officer acted with malicious purpose, in bad faith, or in a wanton or reckless manner.

(2) Except for civil actions that arise out of the operation of a motor vehicle and civil actions in which the state is a plaintiff, no peace officer of any law enforcement agency within this state is liable in punitive or exemplary damages in any civil action that arises under the Revised Code or common law of this state for any injury, death, or loss to person or property caused in the performance of official duties under this section of the Revised Code and rules adopted under this section, unless the officer's actions were manifestly outside the scope of the officer's employment or official responsibilities, or unless the officer acted with malicious purpose, in bad faith, or in a wanton or reckless manner.

(K) When disqualifying a driver, the registrar shall cause the records of the bureau of motor vehicles to be updated to reflect the disqualification within ten days after it occurs.

(L) The registrar immediately shall notify a driver who is subject to disqualification of the disqualification, of the length of the disqualification, and that the driver may request a hearing within thirty days of the mailing of the notice to show cause why the driver should not be disqualified from operating a commercial motor vehicle. If a request for such a hearing is not made within thirty days of the mailing of the notice, the order of disqualification is final. The registrar may designate hearing examiners who, after affording all parties reasonable notice, shall conduct a hearing to determine whether the disqualification order is supported by reliable evidence. The registrar shall adopt rules to implement this division.

(M) Any person who is disqualified from operating a commercial motor vehicle under this section may apply to the registrar for a driver's license to operate a motor vehicle other than a commercial motor vehicle, provided the person's commercial driver's license is not otherwise suspended. A person whose commercial driver's license is suspended shall not apply to the registrar for or receive a driver's license under Chapter 4507. of the Revised Code during the period of suspension.

(N) Whoever violates division (H) of this section is guilty of a misdemeanor of the first degree.

(O) As used in this section, "emergency medical technician-intermediate" and "emergency medical technician-paramedic" have the same meanings as in section 4765.01 of the Revised Code.

**HISTORY: 143 v H 381 (Eff 7-1-89); 143 v H 88 (Eff 3-13-90); 145 v S 82 (Eff 5-4-94); 147 v S 60. Eff 10-21-97; 149 v S 123, § 1, eff. 1-1-04; 151 v H 68, § 101.01, eff. 6-29-05; 151 v S 8, § 1, eff. 8-17-06; 153 v S 58, § 1, eff. 9-17-10.**

The effective date is set by § 612.03 of 151 v H 68.
The effective date is set by section 4 of S.B. 123.
See provisions, § 5 of S.B. 123 (149 v —), following RC § 4501.01.

## § 4506.18 Driver to give notice of out-of-state conviction.

(A) Any driver who holds a commercial driver's license issued by this state and is convicted in another state or a foreign jurisdiction of violating any law or ordinance relating to motor vehicle traffic control, other than a parking violation, shall provide written notice of that conviction within thirty days after the date of conviction to the bureau of motor vehicles and to the driver's employer in accordance with the provisions of 49 C.F.R. 383, subpart C, as amended.

(B) Whoever violates this section is guilty of a misdemeanor of the first degree.

**HISTORY: 143 v H 381. Eff 7-1-89; 149 v S 123, § 1, eff. 1-1-04.**

The effective date is set by section 4 of S.B. 123.
See provisions, § 5 of S.B. 123 (149 v —), following RC § 4501.01.

## § 4506.19 Provisions of 49 C.F.R. 383, subpart C.

(A) The provisions of 49 C.F.R. 383, subpart C, as amended, shall apply to all commercial drivers or persons who apply for employment as commercial drivers. No person shall fail to make a report to the person's employer as required by this section.

(B) Whoever violates this section is guilty of a misdemeanor of the first degree.

**HISTORY: 143 v H 381. Eff 7-1-89; 149 v S 123, § 1, eff. 1-1-04.**

The effective date is set by section 4 of S.B. 123.
See provisions, § 5 of S.B. 123 (149 v —), following RC § 4501.01.

## § 4506.20 Duties of employer of driver.

(A) Each employer shall require every applicant for employment as a driver of a commercial motor vehicle to provide the applicant's employment history for the ten years preceding the date the employment application is submitted to the prospective employer. The following information shall be submitted:

(1) A list of the names and addresses of the applicant's previous employers for which the applicant was the operator of a commercial motor vehicle;

(2) The dates the applicant was employed by these employers;

(3) The reason for leaving each of these employers.

(B) No employer shall knowingly permit or authorize any driver employed by the employer to drive a commercial motor vehicle during any period in which any of the following apply:

(1) The driver's commercial driver's license is suspended, revoked, or canceled by any state or a foreign jurisdiction;

(2) The driver has lost the privilege to drive, or currently is disqualified from driving, a commercial motor vehicle in any state or foreign jurisdiction;

(3) The driver, the commercial motor vehicle the driver is driving, or the motor carrier operation is subject to an out-of-service order in any state or foreign jurisdiction;

(4) The driver has more than one driver's license.

(C) No employer shall knowingly permit or authorize a driver to operate a commercial motor vehicle in violation of section 4506.15 of the Revised Code.

(D)(1) Whoever violates division (A) or (B) of this section is guilty of a misdemeanor of the first degree.

(2) Whoever violates division (C) of this section may be assessed a fine not to exceed ten thousand dollars.

**HISTORY: 143 v H 381. Eff 7-1-89; 149 v S 123, § 1, eff. 1-1-04; 150 v H 95, § 1, eff. 9-26-03; 150 v H 95, § 3.13, eff. 1-1-04; 151 v H 68, § 101.01, eff. 6-29-05.**

The effective date is set by § 612.03 of 151 v H 68.

See provisions, § 5 of S.B. 123 (149 v —), following RC § 4501.01.

## § 4506.21 Notice of conviction of nonresident licensee.

Within ten days after receiving a report of conviction of any nonresident holder of a commercial driver's license for a violation of a state law or local ordinance or resolution relating to traffic control, other than parking violations, committed in a commercial motor vehicle, the registrar of motor vehicles shall notify the driver licensing authority in the state that issued the nonresident's commercial driver's license of the conviction.

**HISTORY: 143 v H 381. Eff 7-1-89.**

## § 4506.22 Rules to carry out chapter; authority of public safety department, public utilities commission.

(A) The director of public safety and the registrar of motor vehicles, subject to approval by the director, may, in accordance with Chapter 119. of the Revised Code, adopt any rules necessary to carry out this chapter.

(B) The department of public safety may do all of the following:

(1) Enter into or make any agreements, arrangements, or declarations necessary to carry out this chapter;

(2) Charge a fee for all publications that is equal to the cost of printing the publications.

(C) Nothing in this chapter shall be construed to restrict the authority of the public utilities commission specified in Chapters 4921. and 4923. of the Revised Code regarding safety rules applicable to motor carriers.

**HISTORY: 143 v H 381 (Eff 7-1-89): 144 v S 98 (Eff 11-12-92); 146 v S 162. Eff 10-29-95.**

## § 4506.23 Duties of peace officer as to alcohol or drug offenders.

Within the jurisdictional limits of the appointing authority, any peace officer shall stop and detain any person found violating section 4506.15 of the Revised Code, without obtaining a warrant. When there is reasonable ground to believe that a violation of section 4506.15 of the Revised Code has been committed and a test or tests of the person's whole blood, blood plasma or blood serum, breath, or urine is necessary, the peace officer shall take the person to an appropriate place for testing. If a person refuses to submit to a test after being warned as provided in division (C) of section 4506.17 of the Revised Code or submits to a test that discloses the presence of a controlled substance or an alcohol concentration of four-hundredths of one per cent or more by whole blood or breath, an alcohol concentration of forty-eight-thousandths of one per cent or more by blood serum or blood plasma, or an alcohol concentration of fifty-six-thousandths of one per cent or more by urine, the peace officer shall require that the person immediately surrender the person's commercial driver's license to the peace officer.

As used in this section, "jurisdictional limits" means the limits within which a peace officer may arrest and detain a person without a warrant under section 2935.03 of the Revised Code, except that the superintendent and the troopers of the state highway patrol may stop and detain, without warrant, any person who, in the presence of the superintendent or any trooper, is engaged in the violation of this chapter.

**HISTORY: 143 v H 381 (Eff 7-1-89); 143 v H 88 (Eff 3-13-90); 144 v S 144. Eff 8-8-91; 151 v H 68, § 101.01, eff. 6-29-05.**

The effective date is set by § 612.03 of 151 v H 68.

## § 4506.24 Restricted license and waiver for farm-related service industries.

(A) A restricted commercial driver's license and waiver for farm-related service industries may be issued by the registrar of motor vehicles to allow a person to operate a commercial motor vehicle during seasonal periods determined by the registrar and subject to the restrictions set forth in this section.

(B) Upon receiving an application for a restricted commercial driver's license under section 4506.07 of the Revised Code and payment of a fee as provided in section 4506.08 of the Revised Code, the registrar may issue such license to any person who meets all of the following requirements:

(1) Has at least one year of driving experience in any type of vehicle;

(2) Holds a valid driver's license, other than a restricted license, issued under Chapter 4507. of the Revised Code;

(3) Certifies that during the two-year period immediately preceding application, all of the following apply:

(a) The person has not had more than one license;

(b) The person has not had any license suspended, revoked, or canceled;

(c) The person has not had any convictions for any type of motor vehicle for the offenses for which disqualification is prescribed in section 4506.16 of the Revised Code;

(d) The person has not had any violation of a state or local law relating to motor vehicle traffic control other than a parking violation arising in connection with any traffic accident and has no record of an accident in which the person was at fault.

(4) Certifies and also provides evidence that the person is employed in one or more of the following farm-related service industries requiring the person to operate a commercial motor vehicle:

(a) Custom harvesters;

(b) Farm retail outlets and suppliers;

(c) Agri-chemical business;

(d) Livestock feeders.

(C) An annual waiver for farm-related service industries may be issued to authorize the holder of a restricted commercial driver's license to operate a commercial motor vehicle during seasonal periods designated by the registrar. The registrar shall determine the format of the waiver. The total number of days that a person may operate a commercial motor vehicle pursuant to a waiver for farm-related service industries shall not exceed one hundred eighty days in any twelve-month period. Each time the holder of a restricted commercial driver's license applies for a waiver for farm-related service industries, the registrar shall verify that the person meets all of the requirements set forth in division (B) of this section. The restricted commercial driver's license and waiver shall be carried at all times when a commercial motor vehicle is being operated by the holder of the license and waiver.

(D) The holder of a restricted commercial driver's license and valid waiver for farm-related service industries may operate a class B or C commercial motor vehicle subject to all of the following restrictions:

(1) The commercial motor vehicle is operated within a distance of no more than one hundred fifty miles of the employer's place of business or the farm currently being served;

(2) The operation of the commercial motor vehicle does not involve transporting hazardous materials for which placarding is required, except as follows:

(a) Diesel fuel in quantities of one thousand gallons or less;

(b) Liquid fertilizers in vehicles or implements of husbandry with total capacities of three thousand gallons or less;

(c) Solid fertilizers that are not transported with any organic substance.

(E) Except as otherwise provided in this section an applicant for or holder of a restricted commercial driver's license and waiver for farm-related service industries is subject to the provisions of this chapter. Divisions (A)(4) and (B)(1) of section 4506.07 and sections 4506.09 and 4506.10 of the Revised Code do not apply to an applicant for a restricted commercial driver's license and waiver.

**HISTORY: 144 v H 485 (Eff 7-8-92); 147 v H 210. Eff 3-31-97; 150 v H 95, § 1, eff. 9-26-03.**

The effective date is set by section 179 of H.B. 95 (150 v —).

## § 4506.25 Disqualification for violating out-of-service order.

(A) As used in this section, "commercial motor vehicle" means any self-propelled or towed vehicle used on public highways in intrastate or interstate commerce to transport passengers or property that meets any of the following specifications:

(1) The vehicle has a gross vehicle weight rating or gross combination weight rating of ten thousand one pounds or more.

(2) The vehicle is designed to transport sixteen or more passengers, including the driver.

(3) The vehicle is used in the transportation of hazardous materials in a quantity requiring placarding under the regulations issued by the United States secretary of transportation under the "Hazardous Materials Transportation Act," 88 Stat. 2156 (1975), 49 U.S.C.A. 1801, as amended.

(B) The registrar of motor vehicles shall disqualify any person from operating a commercial motor vehicle who receives a notice of a conviction for violation of an out-of-service order issued under rules of the public utilities commission adopted pursuant to section 4919.79, 4921.04, or 4923.20 of the Revised Code, or a conviction for a violation of the same or similar laws of another state or jurisdiction applicable to vehicles in regulated commerce.

**HISTORY: 147 v S 213. Eff 7-29-98; 151 v H 68, § 101.01, eff. 6-29-05.**

The effective date is set by § 612.03 of 151 v H 68.

## § 4506.26 Repealed, 151 v H 68, § 105.01 [147 v S 213. Eff 7-29-98]. Eff 3-29-05.

The effective date is set by § 612.18 of 151 v H 68.
This section concerned a period of disqualification.

## § 4506.99 Penalties.

Whoever violates any provision of sections 4506.03 to 4506.20 of the Revised Code for which no penalty otherwise is provided in the section that contains the provision violated is guilty of a misdemeanor of the first degree.

**HISTORY: 143 v H 381 (Eff 7-1-89); 143 v H 88 (Eff 3-13-90); 144 v H 134. Eff 10-10-91; 149 v S 123, § 1, eff. 1-1-04.**

The effective date is set by section 4 of S.B. 123.
See provisions, § 5 of S.B. 123 (149 v —), following RC § 4501.01.

# CHAPTER 4507: DRIVER'S LICENSE LAW

Section

## § 4507.01 Definitions; deputy registrars; laminating equipment, materials.

(A) As used in this chapter, "motor vehicle," "motorized bicycle," "state," "owner," "operator," "chauffeur," and "highways" have the same meanings as in section 4501.01 of the Revised Code.

"Driver's license" means a class D license issued to any person to operate a motor vehicle or motor-driven cycle, other than a commercial motor vehicle, and includes "probationary license," "restricted license," and any operator's or chauffeur's license issued before January 1, 1990.

"Probationary license" means the license issued to any person between sixteen and eighteen years of age to operate a motor vehicle.

"Restricted license" means the license issued to any person to operate a motor vehicle subject to conditions or restrictions imposed by the registrar of motor vehicles.

"Commercial driver's license" means the license issued to a person under Chapter 4506. of the Revised Code to operate a commercial motor vehicle.

"Commercial motor vehicle" has the same meaning as in section 4506.01 of the Revised Code.

"Motorized bicycle license" means the license issued under section 4511.521 [4511.52.1] of the Revised Code to any person to operate a motorized bicycle including a "probationary motorized bicycle license."

"Probationary motorized bicycle license" means the license issued under section 4511.521 [4511.52.1] of the Revised Code to any person between fourteen and sixteen years of age to operate a motorized bicycle.

"Identification card" means a card issued under sections 4507.50 and 4507.51 of the Revised Code.

"Resident" means a person who, in accordance with standards prescribed in rules adopted by the registrar, resides in this state on a permanent basis.

"Temporary resident" means a person who, in accordance with standards prescribed in rules adopted by the registrar, resides in this state on a temporary basis.

(B) In the administration of this chapter and Chapter 4506. of the Revised Code, the registrar has the same authority as is conferred on the registrar by section 4501.02 of the Revised Code. Any act of an authorized deputy registrar of motor vehicles under direction of the registrar is deemed the act of the registrar.

To carry out this chapter, the registrar shall appoint such deputy registrars in each county as are necessary.

The registrar also shall provide at each place where an application for a driver's or commercial driver's license or identification card may be made the necessary equipment to take a color photograph of the applicant for such license or card as required under section 4506.11 or 4507.06 of the Revised Code, and to conduct the vision screenings required by section 4507.12 of the Revised Code, and equipment to laminate licenses, motorized bicycle licenses, and identification cards as required by sections 4507.13, 4507.52, and 4511.521 [4511.52.1] of the Revised Code.

The registrar shall assign one or more deputy registrars to any driver's license examining station operated under the supervision of the state highway patrol, whenever the registrar considers such assignment possible. Space shall be provided in the driver's license examining station for any such deputy registrar so assigned. The deputy registrars shall not exercise the powers conferred by such sections upon the registrar, unless they are specifically authorized to exercise such powers by such sections.

(C) No agent for any insurance company, writing automobile insurance, shall be appointed deputy registrar, and any such appointment is void. No deputy registrar shall in any manner solicit any form of automobile insurance, nor in any manner advise, suggest, or influence any licensee or applicant for license for or against any kind or type of automobile insurance, insurance company, or agent, nor have the deputy registrar's office directly connected with the office of any automobile insurance agent, nor impart any information furnished by any applicant for a license or identification card to any person, except the registrar. This division shall not apply to any nonprofit corporation appointed deputy registrar.

(D) The registrar shall immediately remove a deputy registrar who violates the requirements of this chapter.

(E) The registrar shall periodically solicit bids and enter into a contract for the provision of laminating equipment and laminating materials to the registrar and all deputy registrars. The registrar shall not consider any bid that does not provide for the supplying of both laminating equipment and laminating materials. The laminating materials selected shall contain a security feature so that any tampering with the laminating material covering a license or identification card is readily apparent. In soliciting bids and entering into a contract for the provision of laminating equipment and laminating materials, the registrar shall observe all procedures required by law.

**HISTORY: GC § 6296-2; 116 v PtII, 33, § 2; Bureau of Code Revision, 10-1-53; 127 v 839 (Eff 9-16-57); 129 v 421 (Eff 10-19-61); 130 v 1053 (Eff 9-27-63); 132 v H 380 (Eff 1-1-68); 132 v S 43 (Eff 1-1-69); 135 v S 1 (Eff 1-1-74); 135 v S 313 (Eff 7-26-74); 136 v S 435 (Eff 8-24-76); 137 v S 100 (Eff 4-1-78); 140 v S 169 (Eff 1-1-85); 140 v H 58 (Eff 3-1-85); 141 v H 428 (Eff 12-23-86); 142 v S 1 (Eff 11-28-88); 143 v H 381 (Eff 7-1-89); 143 v S 131 (Eff 7-25-90); 147 v S 60. Eff 10-21-97.**

## § 4507.011 Each deputy registrar to pay rental fee; registrar rental fund.

(A) Each deputy registrar assigned to a driver's license examining station by the registrar of motor vehicles as provided in section 4507.01 of the Revised Code shall remit to the superintendent of the state highway patrol a rental fee equal to the percentage of space occupied by the deputy registrar in the driver's license examining station multiplied by the rental fee paid for the entire driver's license examining station plus a pro rata share of all utility costs. All such moneys received by the superintendent shall be deposited in the state treasury to the credit of the registrar rental fund, which is hereby created. The moneys in the fund shall be used by the state highway patrol only to pay the rent and expenses of the driver's license examining stations. All investment earnings of the fund shall be credited to the fund.

(B) Each deputy registrar assigned to a bureau of motor vehicles' location shall reimburse the registrar a monthly building rental fee, including applicable utility charges. All such moneys received by the registrar shall be deposited into the state bureau of motor vehicles fund created in section 4501.25 of the Revised Code.

**HISTORY: 140 v H 58, § 1 (Eff 10-1-84); 140 v H 58, § 4 (Eff 3-1-85); 141 v H 201 (Eff 7-1-85); 141 v S 269 (Eff 3-13-86); 145 v H 154 (Eff 6-30-93); 148 v H 163. Eff 6-30-99.**

## § 4507.012 Repealed, 149 v S 123, § 2 [147 v S 60]. Eff. 1-1-04.

This section concerned definitions for "suspension" and "revocation".

The effective date is set by section 4 of S.B. 123.

See provisions, § 5 of S.B. 123 (149 v —), following RC § 4501.01.

## § 4507.02 Permitting operation without valid license prohibited; multiple licenses; impoundment of plates; restricted plates.

(A)(1) No person shall permit the operation of a motor vehicle upon any public or private property used by the public for purposes of vehicular travel or parking knowing the operator does not have a valid driver's license issued to the operator by the registrar of motor vehicles under this chapter or a valid commercial driver's license issued under Chapter 4506. of the Revised Code. Except as otherwise provided in this division, whoever violates this division is guilty of an unclassified misdemeanor. When the offense is an unclassified misdemeanor, the offender shall be sentenced pursuant to sections 2929.21 to 2929.28 of the Revised Code, except that the offender shall not be sentenced to a jail term; the offender shall not be sentenced to a community residential sanction pursuant to section 2929.26 of the Revised Code; notwithstanding division (A)(2)(a) of section 2929.28 of the Revised Code, the offender may be fined up to one thousand dollars; and, notwithstanding division (A)(3) of section 2929.27 of the Revised Code, the offender may be ordered pursuant to division (C) of that section to serve a term of community service of up to five hundred hours. The failure of an offender to complete a term of community service imposed by the court may be punished as indirect criminal contempt under division (A) of section 2705.02 of the Revised Code that may be filed in the underlying case.

If, within three years of the offense, the offender previously has been convicted of or pleaded guilty to two or more violations of this section or a substantially equivalent municipal ordinance, the offense is a misdemeanor of the first degree.

(2) No person shall receive a driver's license, or a motorcycle operator's endorsement of a driver's or commercial driver's license, unless and until the person surrenders to the registrar all valid licenses issued to the person by another jurisdiction recognized by this state. The registrar shall report the surrender of a license to the issuing authority, together with information that a license is now issued in this state. The registrar shall destroy any such license that is not returned to the issuing authority. No person shall be permitted to have more than one valid license at any time.

(B)(1) If a person is convicted of a violation of section 4510.11, 4510.14, 4510.16 when division (G)(2) and (3) of that section applies, or 4510.21 of the Revised Code or if division (F) of section 4507.164 of the Revised Code applies, the trial judge of any court, in addition to or independent of any other penalties provided by law or ordinance, may impound the identification license plates of any motor vehicle registered in the name of the person. If a person is convicted of a violation of section 4510.16 of the Revised Code and division (G)(1) of that section applies, the trial judge of any court, in addition to or independent of any other penalties provided by law or ordinance, may impound the identification license plates of any motor vehicle registered in the name of the person. The court shall send the impounded license plates to the registrar, who may retain the license plates until the driver's or commercial driver's license of the owner has been reinstated or destroy them pursuant to section 4503.232 of the Revised Code.

If the license plates of a person convicted of a violation of any provision of those sections have been impounded in accordance with the provisions of this division, the court shall notify the registrar of that action. The notice shall contain the name and address of the driver, the serial number of the driver's or commercial driver's license, the serial numbers of the license plates of the motor vehicle, and the length of time for which the license plates have been impounded. The registrar shall record the data in the notice as part of the driver's permanent record.

(2) Any motor vehicle owner who has had the license plates of a motor vehicle impounded pursuant to division (B)(1) of this section may apply to the registrar, or to a deputy registrar, for restricted license plates that shall conform to the requirements of section 4503.231 of the Revised Code. The registrar or deputy registrar forthwith shall notify the court of the application and, upon approval of the court, shall issue restricted license plates to the applicant. Until the driver's or commercial driver's license of the owner is reinstated, any new license plates issued to the owner also shall conform to the requirements of section 4503.231 of the Revised Code.

The registrar or deputy registrar shall charge the owner of a vehicle the fees provided in section 4503.19 of the Revised Code for restricted license plates that are issued in accordance with this division, except upon renewal as specified in section 4503.10 of the Revised Code, when the regular fee as provided in section 4503.04 of the Revised Code shall be charged. The registrar or deputy registrar shall charge the owner of a vehicle the fees provided in section 4503.19 of the Revised Code whenever restricted license plates are exchanged, by reason of the reinstatement of the driver's or commercial driver's license of the owner, for those ordinarily issued.

(3) If an owner wishes to sell a motor vehicle during the time the restricted license plates provided under division (B)(2) of this section are in use, the owner may apply to the court that impounded the license plates of the motor vehicle for permission to transfer title to the motor vehicle. If the court is satisfied that the sale will be made in good faith and not for the purpose of circumventing the provisions of this section, it may certify its consent to the owner and to the registrar of motor vehicles who shall enter notice of the transfer of the title of the motor vehicle in the vehicle registration record.

If, during the time the restricted license plates provided under division (B)(2) of this section are in use, the title to a motor vehicle is transferred by the foreclosure of a chattel mortgage, a sale upon execution, the cancellation of a conditional sales contract, or by order of a court, the court shall notify the registrar of the action and the registrar shall enter notice of the transfer of the title to the motor vehicle in the vehicle registration record.

(C) This section is not intended to change or modify any provision of Chapter 4503. of the Revised Code with respect to the taxation of motor vehicles or the time within which the taxes on motor vehicles shall be paid.

**HISTORY: GC § 6296-29; 116 v PtII, 33, § 29; Bureau of Code Revision, RC § 4507.38, 10-1-53; 130 v 1060 (Eff 10-10-63); 131 v 1087 (Eff 10-30-65); 132 v H 518 (Eff 12-14-67); 132 v S 451 (Eff 2-29-68); 139 v S 432 (Eff 3-16-83); RC § 4507.02, 141 v S 356 (Eff 9-24-86); 141 v S 262 (Eff 3-20-87); 142 v H 419 (Eff 7-1-87); 143 v H 381 (Eff 7-1-89); 143 v S 131 (Eff 7-25-90); 144 v S 275 (Eff 9-1-93); 145 v S 62, §§ 1, 4 (Eff 9-1-93); 145 v H 687 (Eff 10-12-94); 145 v S 20 (Eff 4-20-95); 147 v S 60 (Eff 10-21-97); 148 v H 163. Eff 6-30-99; 149 v S 123, § 1, eff. 1-1-04; 150 v H 163, § 1, eff. 9-23-04; 151 v H 68, § 101.01, eff. 6-29-05; 151 v H 461, § 1, eff. 4-4-07; 153 v H 1, § 101.01, eff. 10-16-09; 153 v H 338, § 1, eff. 9-17-10; 2011 HB 5, § 1, eff. Sept. 23, 2011.**

The effective date is set by § 812.10 of 153 v H 1.

The effective date is set by § 612.03 of 151 v H 68.

The effective date is set by section 4 of S.B. 123.

See provisions, § 5 of S.B. 123 (149 v —), following RC § 4501.01.

**Analogous in part to former RC § 4507.02 (GC § 6296-4; 116 v PtII, 33, § 4; Bureau of Code Revision, 10-1-53; 131 v 1081; 132 v H 380; 133 v H 636), repealed 141 v S 356, § 2, eff 9-24-86.**

## § 4507.021 Repealed, 149 v S 123, § 2 [RC § 4507.40, 127 v 525; 128 v 469; 130 v 1061; 130 v 1064; 132 v S 37; 132 v H 380; 134 v H 1010; 135 v S 325; 135 v S 313; 136 v S 65; 136 v H 451; 137 v H 219; 139 v S 432; 141 v S 54; RC § 4507.02.1, 141 v S 356; 141 v S 262; 142 v H 493; 142 v H 643; 143 v H 329; 143 v H 330; 143 v H 381; 143 v S 49; 143 v S 131; 144 v S 98; 144 v S 331; 144 v S 275; 145 v S 62, §§ 1, 49-1-93); 145 v S 82; 145 v H 687; 146 v H 107; 146 v H 353; 146 v H 438; 147 v S 60; 148 v S 107]. Eff. 1-1-04.

This section concerned the point system for license suspension. See now RC § 4510.036.

The effective date is set by section 4 of S.B. 123.

See provisions, § 5 of S.B. 123 (149 v —), following RC § 4501.01.

## § 4507.022 Amended and renumbered RC § 4510.038 in 149 v SB 123. Eff 1-1-04.

See provisions, § 5 of S.B. 123 (149 v —), following RC § 4501.01.

**Publisher's Note:**

This section was renumbered to § 4510.038 by S.B. 123, Acts 2002, effective January 1, 2004.

## § 4507.023 Information furnished to tax commissioner to discover address.

The registrar of motor vehicles may furnish the name and social security number of any person whose driver's license or commercial driver's license has been suspended or canceled, or of any person whose certificate of registration and license plates are subject to impoundment, to the tax commissioner. The tax commissioner may return to the registrar the address of any such person as shown on the most recent return filed by that person under section 5747.08 of the Revised Code.

**HISTORY: 143 v H 381. Eff 7-1-89; 149 v S 123, § 1, eff. 1-1-04.**

The effective date is set by section 4 of S.B. 123.

See provisions, § 5 of S.B. 123 (149 v —), following RC § 4501.01.

## § 4507.03 Exemptions.

(A)(1) No person shall be required to obtain a driver's or commercial driver's license for the purpose of temporarily driving, operating, drawing, moving, or propelling a road roller or road machinery upon a street or highway.

(2) No person shall be required to obtain a driver's or commercial driver's license for the purpose of temporarily driving, operating, drawing, moving, or propelling any agricultural tractor or implement of husbandry upon a street or highway at a speed of twenty-five miles per hour or less.

(3) No person shall drive, operate, draw, move, or propel any agricultural tractor or implement of husbandry upon a street or highway at a speed greater than twenty-five miles per hour unless the person has a current, valid driver's or commercial driver's license.

(4) No person having a valid driver's or commercial driver's license shall be required to have a motorcycle operator's endorsement to operate a motorcycle having three wheels with a motor of not more than fifty cubic centimeters piston displacement.

(B) Every person on active duty in the armed forces of the United States, when furnished with a driver's permit and when operating an official motor vehicle in connection with such duty, is exempt from the license requirements of Chapters 4506. and 4507. of the Revised Code.

Every person on active duty in the armed forces of the United States or in service with the peace corps, volunteers in service to America, or the foreign service of the United States is exempt from the license requirements of those chapters for the period of the person's active duty or service and for six months thereafter, provided the person was a licensee under those chapters at the time the person commenced the person's active duty or service. The spouse or a dependent of any such person on active duty or in service also is exempt from the license requirements of those chapters for the period of the person's active duty or service and for six months thereafter, provided the spouse or dependent was a licensee under those chapters at the time the person commenced the active duty or service, and provided further that the person's active duty or service causes the spouse or dependent to relocate outside of this state during the period of the active duty or service.

This section does not prevent such a person or the person's spouse or dependent from making an application, as provided in division (C) of section 4507.10 of the Revised Code, for the renewal of a driver's license or motorcycle operator's endorsement or as provided in section 4506.14 of the Revised Code for the renewal of a commercial driver's license during the period of the person's active duty or service.

(C) Whoever violates division (A)(3) of this section is guilty of a misdemeanor of the first degree.

**HISTORY: GC § 6296-5; 116 v PtII, 33, § 5; 120 v 289; 124 v 42; Bureau of Code Revision, 10-1-53; 132 v H 57 (Eff 3-28-67); 134 v S 546 (Eff 10-16-72); 141 v H 165 (Eff 8-1-86); 142 v H 614 (Eff 3-17-89); 143 v H 381 (Eff 7-1-89); 145 v S 96. Eff 5-10-94; 152 v H 9, § 1, eff. 10-18-07; 153 v H 1, § 101.01, eff. 10-16-09.**

The effective date is set by § 812.10 of 153 v H 1.

The provisions of 815.10 of 153 v H 1 read as follows:

SECTION 815.10. The General Assembly, applying the principle stated in division (B) of section 1.52 of the Revised Code that amendments are to be harmonized if reasonably capable of simultaneous operation, finds that the following sections, presented in this act as composites of the sections as amended by the acts indicated, are the resulting versions of the sections in effect prior to the effective date of the sections as presented in this act:

° ° °

Section 4507.03 of the Revised Code as amended by Sub. S.B. 96 of the 120th General Assembly and Sub. H.B. 9 of the 127th General Assembly.

° ° °

**Publisher's Note:**

The version of this section amended in 152 v H 9 did not include the amendments made by 145 v S 96. Please see RC § 1.52 concerning harmonization of amendments.

**Comment, Legislative Service Commission**

Section 4507.03 of the Revised Code is amended by Sub. H.B. 9 of the 127th General Assembly and S.B. 96 of the 120th General Assembly. Comparison of these amendments in pursuance of section 1.52 of the Revised Code discloses that they are not irreconcilable so that they are required by that section to be harmonized to give effect to each amendment.

## § 4507.04 Nonresident exemption.

Nonresidents, permitted to drive upon the highways of their own states, may operate any motor vehicle upon any highway in this state without examination or license under sections 4507.01 to 4507.39, inclusive, of the Revised Code, upon condition that such nonresidents may be required at any time or place to prove lawful possession, or their right to operate, such motor vehicle, and to establish proper identity.

**HISTORY: GC § 6296-6; 116 v PtII 33, § 6; 119 v 701; Bureau of Code Revision. Eff 10-1-53.**

## § 4507.05 Temporary instruction permit and identification card.

(A) The registrar of motor vehicles, or a deputy registrar, upon receiving an application for a temporary instruction permit and a temporary instruction permit identification card for a driver's license from any person who is at least fifteen years six months of age, may issue such a permit and identification card entitling the applicant to drive a motor vehicle, other than a commercial motor vehicle, upon the highways under the following conditions:

(1) If the permit is issued to a person who is at least fifteen years six months of age, but less than sixteen years of age:

(a) The permit and identification card are in the holder's immediate possession;

(b) The holder is accompanied by an eligible adult who actually occupies the seat beside the permit holder and does not have a prohibited concentration of alcohol in the whole blood, blood serum or plasma, breath, or urine as provided in division (A) of section 4511.19 of the Revised Code;

(c) The total number of occupants of the vehicle does not exceed the total number of occupant restraining devices originally installed in the motor vehicle by its manufacturer, and each occupant of the vehicle is wearing all of the available elements of a properly adjusted occupant restraining device.

(2) If the permit is issued to a person who is at least sixteen years of age:

(a) The permit and identification card are in the holder's immediate possession;

(b) The holder is accompanied by a licensed operator who is at least twenty-one years of age, is actually occupying a seat beside the driver, and does not have a prohibited concentration of alcohol in the whole blood, blood serum or plasma, breath, or urine as provided in division (A) of section 4511.19 of the Revised Code;

(c) The total number of occupants of the vehicle does not exceed the total number of occupant restraining devices originally installed in the motor vehicle by its manufacturer, and each occupant of the vehicle is wearing all of the available elements of a properly adjusted occupant restraining device.

(B) The registrar or a deputy registrar, upon receiving from any person an application for a temporary instruction permit and temporary instruction permit identification card to operate a motorcycle or motorized bicycle, may issue such a permit and identification card entitling the applicant, while having the permit and identification card in the applicant's immediate possession, to drive a motorcycle under the restrictions prescribed in section 4511.53 of the Revised Code, or to drive a motorized bicycle under restrictions determined by the registrar. A temporary instruction permit and temporary instruction permit identification card to operate a motorized bicycle may be issued to a person fourteen or fifteen years old.

(C) Any permit and identification card issued under this section shall be issued in the same manner as a driver's license, upon a form to be furnished by the registrar. A temporary instruction permit to drive a motor vehicle other than a commercial motor vehicle shall be valid for a period of one year.

(D) Any person having in the person's possession a valid and current driver's license or motorcycle operator's license or endorsement issued to the person by another jurisdiction recognized by this state is exempt from obtaining a temporary instruction permit for a driver's license, but shall submit to the regular examination in obtaining a driver's license or motorcycle operator's endorsement in this state.

(E) The registrar may adopt rules governing the use of temporary instruction permits and temporary instruction permit identification cards.

(F)(1) No holder of a permit issued under division (A) of this section shall operate a motor vehicle upon a highway or any public or private property used by the public for purposes of vehicular travel or parking in violation of the conditions established under division (A) of this section.

(2) Except as provided in division (F)(2) of this section, no holder of a permit that is issued under division (A) of this section and that is issued on or after July 1, 1998, and who has not attained the age of eighteen years, shall operate a motor vehicle upon a highway or any public or private property used by the public for purposes of vehicular travel or parking between the hours of midnight and six a.m.

The holder of a permit issued under division (A) of this section on or after July 1, 1998, who has not attained the age of eighteen years, may operate a motor vehicle upon a highway or any public or private property used by the public for purposes of vehicular travel or parking between the hours of midnight and six a.m. if, at the time of such operation, the holder is accompanied by the holder's parent, guardian, or custodian, and the parent, guardian, or custodian holds a current valid driver's or commercial driver's license issued by this state, is actually occupying a seat beside the permit holder, and does not have a prohibited concentration of alcohol in the whole blood, blood serum or plasma, breath, or urine as provided in division (A) of section 4511.19 of the Revised Code.

(G)(1) Notwithstanding any other provision of law to the contrary, no law enforcement officer shall cause the operator of a motor vehicle being operated on any street or highway to stop the motor vehicle for the sole purpose of determining whether each occupant of the motor vehicle is wearing all of the available elements of a properly adjusted occupant restraining device as required by division (A) of this section, or for the sole purpose of issuing a ticket, citation, or summons if the requirement in that division has been or is being violated, or for causing the arrest of or commencing a prosecution of a person for a violation of that requirement.

(2) Notwithstanding any other provision of law to the contrary, no law enforcement officer shall cause the operator of a motor vehicle being operated on any street or highway to stop the motor vehicle for the sole purpose of determining whether a violation of division (F)(2) of this section has been or is being committed or for the sole purpose of issuing a ticket, citation, or summons for such a violation or for causing the arrest of or commencing a prosecution of a person for such violation.

(H) As used in this section:

(1) "Eligible adult" means any of the following:

(a) An instructor of a driver education course approved by the department of education or a driver training course approved by the department of public safety;

(b) Any of the following persons who holds a current valid driver's or commercial driver's license issued by this state:

(i) A parent, guardian, or custodian of the permit holder;

(ii) A person twenty-one years of age or older who acts in loco parentis of the permit holder.

(2) "Occupant restraining device" has the same meaning as in section 4513.263 [4513.26.3] of the Revised Code.

(I) Whoever violates division (F)(1) or (2) of this section is guilty of a minor misdemeanor.

**HISTORY: GC § 6296-8; 116 v PtII, 33, § 8; 119 v 701; 123 v 246; Bureau of Code Revision, 10-1-53; 128 v 1169 (Eff 11-2-59); 129 v 1490 (Eff 9-18-61); 131 v 1081 (Eff 10-30-65); 132 v H 380 (Eff 1-1-68); 132 v S 43 (Eff 1-1-69); 133 v H 1 (Eff 3-18-69); 140 v S 169 (Eff 1-1-85); 143 v H 381 (Eff 7-1-89); 147 v S 35 (Eff 7-1-98); 149 v H 407. Eff 10-11-2002; 149 v S 123, § 1, eff. 1-1-04; 150 v H 163, § 1, eff. 9-23-04;**

**151 v H 343, § 1, eff. 4-6-07; 2011 HB 114, § 101.01, eff. June 29, 2011.**

Acts 2011, HB 114, § 806.10 provides: "The items of law contained in this act, and their applications, are severable. If any item of law contained in this act, or if any application of any item of law contained in this act, is held invalid, the invalidity does not affect other items of law contained in this act and their applications that can be given effect without the invalid item or application."

The provisions of § 5, H.B. 163 (150 v —), read as follows:

SECTION 5. * * * (C) Section 4507.05 of the Revised Code is presented in this act as a composite of the section as amended by both Am. Sub. H.B. 407 and Am. Sub. S.B. 123 of the 124th General Assembly. The General Assembly, applying the principle stated in division (B) of section 1.52 of the Revised Code that amendments are to be harmonized if reasonably capable of simultaneous operation, finds that the composite is the resulting version of the section in effect prior to the effective date of the section as presented in this act. * * *

The effective date is set by section 4 of S.B. 123.

See provisions, § 5 of S.B. 123 (149 v —), following RC § 4501.01.

## § 4507.06 Application for license; voter registration.

(A)(1) Every application for a driver's license or motorcycle operator's license or endorsement, or duplicate of any such license or endorsement, shall be made upon the approved form furnished by the registrar of motor vehicles and shall be signed by the applicant.

Every application shall state the following:

(a) The applicant's name, date of birth, social security number if such has been assigned, sex, general description, including height, weight, color of hair, and eyes, residence address, including county of residence, duration of residence in this state, and country of citizenship;

(b) Whether the applicant previously has been licensed as an operator, chauffeur, driver, commercial driver, or motorcycle operator and, if so, when, by what state, and whether such license is suspended or canceled at the present time and, if so, the date of and reason for the suspension or cancellation;

(c) Whether the applicant is now or ever has been afflicted with epilepsy, or whether the applicant now is suffering from any physical or mental disability or disease and, if so, the nature and extent of the disability or disease, giving the names and addresses of physicians then or previously in attendance upon the applicant;

(d) Whether an applicant for a duplicate driver's license, or duplicate license containing a motorcycle operator endorsement has pending a citation for violation of any motor vehicle law or ordinance, a description of any such citation pending, and the date of the citation;

(e) Whether the applicant wishes to certify willingness to make an anatomical gift under section 2108.05 of the Revised Code, which shall be given no consideration in the issuance of a license or endorsement;

(f) Whether the applicant has executed a valid durable power of attorney for health care pursuant to sections 1337.11 to 1337.17 of the Revised Code or has executed a declaration governing the use or continuation, or the withholding or withdrawal, of life-sustaining treatment pursuant to sections 2133.01 to 2133.15 of the Revised Code and, if the applicant has executed either type of instrument, whether the applicant wishes the applicant's license to indicate that the applicant has executed the instrument;

(g) On and after October 7, 2009, whether the applicant is a veteran, active duty, or reservist of the armed forces of the United States and, if the applicant is such, whether the applicant wishes the applicant's license to indicate that the applicant is a veteran, active duty, or reservist of the armed forces of the United States by a military designation on the license.

(2) Every applicant for a driver's license shall be photographed in color at the time the application for the license is made. The application shall state any additional information that the registrar requires.

(B) The registrar or a deputy registrar, in accordance with section 3503.11 of the Revised Code, shall register as an elector any person who applies for a driver's license or motorcycle operator's license or endorsement under division (A) of this section, or for a renewal or duplicate of the license or endorsement, if the applicant is eligible and wishes to be registered as an elector. The decision of an applicant whether to register as an elector shall be given no consideration in the decision of whether to issue the applicant a license or endorsement, or a renewal or duplicate.

(C) The registrar or a deputy registrar, in accordance with section 3503.11 of the Revised Code, shall offer the opportunity of completing a notice of change of residence or change of name to any applicant for a driver's license or endorsement under division (A) of this section, or for a renewal or duplicate of the license or endorsement, if the applicant is a registered elector who has changed the applicant's residence or name and has not filed such a notice.

(D) In addition to any other information it contains, on and after October 7, 2009, the approved form furnished by the registrar of motor vehicles for an application for a driver's license or motorcycle operator's license or endorsement or an application for a duplicate of any such license or endorsement shall inform applicants that the applicant must present a copy of the applicant's DD-214 or an equivalent document in order to qualify to have the license or duplicate indicate that the applicant is a veteran, active duty, or reservist of the armed forces of the United States based on a request made pursuant to division (A)(1)(g) of this section.

**HISTORY: 141 v H 428 (Eff 12-23-86); 143 v H 381 (Eff 7-1-89); 143 v H 21 (Eff 3-27-91); 144 v H 427 (Eff 10-8-92); 145 v S 300 (Eff 1-1-95); 146 v H 353 (Eff 9-17-96); 147 v H 354. Eff 7-9-98; 149 v S 123, § 1, eff. 1-1-04; 152 v H 450, § 1, eff. 4-7-09; 152 v H 529, § 1, eff. 4-7-09; 153 v H 2, § 101.01, eff. 7-1-09.**

The effective date is set by § 812.10 of 153 v H 2.

The provisions of § 815.20 of 153 v H 2 read in part as follows:

SECTION 815.20. The General Assembly, applying the principle stated in division (B) of section 1.52 of the Revised Code that amendments are to be harmonized if reasonably capable of simultaneous operation, finds that the following sections, presented in this act as composites of the sections as amended by the acts indicated, are the resulting versions of the sections in effect prior to the effective date of the sections as presented in this act:

* * *

Section 4507.06 of the Revised Code as amended by both Am. Sub. H.B. 450 and Sub. H.B. 529 of the 127th General Assembly.

* * *

The effective date is set by section 4 of S.B. 123.

See provisions, § 5 of S.B. 123 (149 v —), following RC § 4501.01.

**Analogous to former RC § 4507.06 (GC § 6296-9; 116 v PtII, 33, § 9; 120 v 289; 123 v 246; Bureau of Code Revision, 10-1-53; 126 v 253; 132 v S 259; 132 v H 193; 132 v H 380; 132 v S 43; 132 v S 452; 132 v H 1007; 135 v S 313; 136 H 650;**

**137 v S 125; 140 v H 183), repealed 141 v H 428, § 2, eff 12-23-86.**

## § 4507.061 Amended and renumbered RC § 4510.32 in 149 v SB 123. Eff 1-1-04.

**HISTORY: 143 v H 204 (Eff 5-2-90); 145 v H 687 (Eff 10-12-94); 148 v S 1. Eff 8-6-99; 149 v S 123, § 1, eff. 1-1-04.**

See provisions, § 5 of S.B. 123 (149 v —), following RC § 4501.01.

## § 4507.07 Minor's application for license or permit; liability of signing adult.

(A) The registrar of motor vehicles shall not grant the application of any minor under eighteen years of age for a probationary license, a restricted license, or a temporary instruction permit, unless the application is signed by one of the minor's parents, the minor's guardian, another person having custody of the applicant, or, if there is no parent or guardian, a responsible person who is willing to assume the obligation imposed under this section.

At the time a minor under eighteen years of age submits an application for a license or permit at a driver's license examining station, the adult who signs the application shall present identification establishing that the adult is the individual whose signature appears on the application. The registrar shall prescribe, by rule, the types of identification that are suitable for the purposes of this paragraph. If the adult who signs the application does not provide identification as required by this paragraph, the application shall not be accepted.

When a minor under eighteen years of age applies for a probationary license, a restricted license, or a temporary instruction permit, the registrar shall give the adult who signs the application notice of the potential liability that may be imputed to the adult pursuant to division (B) of this section and notice of how the adult may prevent any liability from being imputed to the adult pursuant to that division.

(B) Any negligence, or willful or wanton misconduct, that is committed by a minor under eighteen years of age when driving a motor vehicle upon a highway shall be imputed to the person who has signed the application of the minor for a probationary license, restricted license, or temporary instruction permit, which person shall be jointly and severally liable with the minor for any damages caused by the negligence or the willful or wanton misconduct. This joint and several liability is not subject to section 2307.22 or 2315.36 of the Revised Code with respect to a tort claim that otherwise is subject to that section.

There shall be no imputed liability imposed under this division if a minor under eighteen years of age has proof of financial responsibility with respect to the operation of a motor vehicle owned by the minor or, if the minor is not the owner of a motor vehicle, with respect to the minor's operation of any motor vehicle, in the form and in the amounts required under Chapter 4509. of the Revised Code.

(C) Any person who has signed the application of a minor under eighteen years of age for a license or permit subsequently may surrender to the registrar the license or temporary instruction permit of the minor and request that the license or permit be canceled. The registrar then shall cancel the license or temporary instruction permit, and the person who signed the application of the minor shall be relieved from the liability imposed by division (B) of this section.

(D) Any minor under eighteen years of age whose probationary license, restricted license, or temporary instruction permit is surrendered to the registrar by the person who signed the application for the license or permit and whose license or temporary instruction permit subsequently is canceled by the registrar may obtain a new license or temporary instruction permit without having to undergo the examinations otherwise required by sections 4507.11 and 4507.12 of the Revised Code and without having to tender the fee for that license or temporary instruction permit, if the minor is able to produce another parent, guardian, other person having custody of the minor, or other adult, and that adult is willing to assume the liability imposed under division (B) of this section. That adult shall comply with the procedures contained in division (A) of this section.

**HISTORY: GC § 6296-10; 116 v PtII, 33, § 10; 119 v 701; 120 v 289; Bureau of Code Revision, 10-1-53; 127 v 839 (Eff 9-16-57); 130 v 1054 (Eff 9-27-63); 132 v S 95 (Eff 11-24-67); 138 v H 522 (Eff 10-29-79); 142 v H 1 (Eff 1-5-88); 143 v H 71 (Eff 9-22-89); 146 v H 350 (Eff 1-27-97); 147 v S 35 (Eff 1-1-99); 149 v S 108, § 2.01 (Eff 7-6-2001); 149 v S 120. Eff 4-9-2003; 150 v S 80, § 1, eff. 4-7-05.**

The provisions of § 3 of SB 120 (149 v —) read as follows:

SECTION 3. Sections 1775.14, 2307.011, 2307.22, 2307.23, 2307.24, 2307.25, 2307.26, 2307.27, 2307.28, 2307.29, 2315.32, 2315.33, 2315.34, 2315.35, 2315.36, 2315.41, 2315.42, 2315.43, 2315.44, 2315.45, 2315.46, 4171.10, 4507.07, and 5703.54 of the Revised Code, as amended or enacted, by this act, apply only to causes of action that accrue on or after the effective date of this act. Any cause of action that accrues prior to the effective date of this act is governed by the law in effect when the cause of action accrued.

## § 4507.071 Probationary license for minor; restricted license for fourteen or fifteen-year-old; restrictions on stops for violations.

(A) No driver's license shall be issued to any person under eighteen years of age, except that a probationary license may be issued to a person who is at least sixteen years of age and has held a temporary instruction permit for a period of at least six months.

(B)(1)(a) No holder of a probationary driver's license who has not attained the age of seventeen years shall operate a motor vehicle upon a highway or any public or private property used by the public for purposes of vehicular travel or parking between the hours of midnight and six a.m. unless the holder is accompanied by the holder's parent or guardian.

(b) No holder of a probationary driver's license who has attained the age of seventeen years but has not attained the age of eighteen years shall operate a motor vehicle upon a highway or any public or private property used by the public for purposes of vehicular travel or parking between the hours of one a.m. and five a.m. unless the holder is accompanied by the holder's parent or guardian.

(2)(a) Subject to division (D)(1)(a) of this section, division (B)(1)(a) of this section does not apply to the holder of a probationary driver's license who is traveling to or from work between the hours of midnight and six a.m. and has in the holder's immediate possession written documentation from the holder's employer.

(b) Division (B)(1)(b) of this section does not apply to the holder of a probationary driver's license who is traveling to or from work between the hours of one a.m. and five a.m. and has in the holder's immediate possession written documentation from the holder's employer.

(3) An employer is not liable in damages in a civil action for any injury, death, or loss to person or property that allegedly arises from, or is related to, the fact that the employer provided an employee who is the holder of a probationary driver's license with the written documentation described in division (B)(2) of this section.

The registrar of motor vehicles shall make available at no cost a form to serve as the written documentation described in division (B)(2) of this section, and employers and holders of probationary driver's licenses may utilize that form or may choose to utilize any other written documentation to meet the requirements of that division.

(4) No holder of a probationary driver's license who is less than seventeen years of age shall operate a motor vehicle upon a highway or any public or private property used by the public for purposes of vehicular travel or parking with more than one person who is not a family member occupying the vehicle unless the probationary license holder is accompanied by the probationary license holder's parent, guardian, or custodian.

(C) It is an affirmative defense to a violation of division (B)(1)(a) or (b) of this section if, at the time of the violation, the holder of the probationary driver's license was traveling to or from an official function sponsored by the school the holder attends, or an emergency existed that required the holder to operate a motor vehicle in violation of division (B)(1)(a) or (b) of this section, or the holder was an emancipated minor.

(D)(1)(a) Except as otherwise provided in division (D)(2) of this section, if a person is issued a probationary driver's license prior to attaining the age of seventeen years and the person pleads guilty to, is convicted of, or is adjudicated in juvenile court of having committed a moving violation during the six-month period commencing on the date on which the person is issued the probationary driver's license, the holder must be accompanied by the holder's parent or guardian whenever the holder is operating a motor vehicle upon a highway or any public or private property used by the public for purposes of vehicular travel or parking during whichever of the following time periods applies:

(i) If, on the date the holder of the probationary driver's license pleads guilty to, is convicted of, or is adjudicated in juvenile court of having committed the moving violation, the holder has not attained the age of sixteen years six months, during the six-month period commencing on that date;

(ii) If, on the date the holder pleads guilty to, is convicted of, or is adjudicated in juvenile court of having committed the moving violation, the holder has attained the age of sixteen years six months but not seventeen years, until the person attains the age of seventeen years.

(b) If the holder of a probationary driver's license commits a moving violation during the six-month period after the person is issued the probationary driver's license and before the person attains the age of seventeen years and on the date the person pleads guilty to, is convicted of, or is adjudicated in juvenile court of having committed the moving violation the person has attained the age of seventeen years, or if the person commits the moving violation during the six-month period after the person is issued the probationary driver's license and after the person attains the age of seventeen years, the holder is not subject to the restriction described in divisions (D)(1)(a)(i) and (ii) of this section unless the court or juvenile court imposes such a restriction upon the holder.

(2) Any person who is subject to the operating restrictions established under division (D)(1) of this section as a result of a first moving violation may petition the court for occupational or educational driving privileges without being accompanied by the holder's parent or guardian during the period of time specified in that division. The court may grant the person such driving privileges if the court finds reasonable cause to believe that the restrictions established in division (D)(1) will seriously affect the person's ability to continue in employment or educational training or will cause undue hardship on the license holder or a family member of the license holder. In granting the driving privileges, the court shall specify the purposes, times, and places of the privileges and shall issue the person appropriate forms setting forth the privileges granted. Occupational or educational driving privileges under this division shall not be granted to the same person more than once. If a person is convicted of, pleads guilty to, or is adjudicated in juvenile court of having committed a second or subsequent moving violation, any driving privileges previously granted under this division are terminated upon the subsequent conviction, plea, or adjudication.

(3) No person shall violate division (D)(1)(a) of this section.

(E) No holder of a probationary license shall operate a motor vehicle upon a highway or any public or private property used by the public for purposes of vehicular travel or parking unless the total number of occupants of the vehicle does not exceed the total number of occupant restraining devices originally installed in the motor vehicle by its manufacturer, and each occupant of the vehicle is wearing all of the available elements of a properly adjusted occupant restraining device.

(F) A restricted license may be issued to a person who is fourteen or fifteen years of age upon proof of hardship satisfactory to the registrar of motor vehicles.

(G) Notwithstanding any other provision of law to the contrary, no law enforcement officer shall cause the operator of a motor vehicle being operated on any street or highway to stop the motor vehicle for the sole purpose of determining whether each occupant of the motor vehicle is wearing all of the available elements of a properly adjusted occupant restraining device as required by division (E) of this section, or for the sole purpose of issuing a ticket, citation, or summons if the requirement in that division has been or is being violated, or for causing the arrest of or commencing a prosecution of a person for a violation of that requirement.

(H) Notwithstanding any other provision of law to the contrary, no law enforcement officer shall cause the operator of a motor vehicle being operated on any street or highway to stop the motor vehicle for the sole purpose of determining whether a violation of division (B)(1)(a) or (b) of this section has been or is being committed or for the sole purpose of issuing a ticket, citation, or summons for such a violation or for causing the arrest of or commencing a prosecution of a person for such violation.

(I) As used in this section:

(1) "Occupant restraining device" has the same meaning as in section 4513.263 [4513.26.3] of the Revised Code.

(2) "Family member" of a probationary license holder includes any of the following:

(a) A spouse;

(b) A child or stepchild;

(c) A parent, stepparent, grandparent, or parent-in-law;

(d) An aunt or uncle;

(e) A sibling, whether of the whole or half blood or by adoption, a brother-in-law, or a sister-in-law;

(f) A son or daughter of the probationary license holder's stepparent if the stepparent has not adopted the probationary license holder;

(g) An eligible adult, as defined in section 4507.05 of the Revised Code.

(3) "Moving violation" means any violation of any statute or ordinance that regulates the operation of vehicles, streetcars, or trackless trolleys on the highways or streets. "Moving violation" does not include a violation of section 4513.263 [4513.26.3] of the Revised Code or a substantially equivalent municipal ordinance, or a violation of any statute or ordinance regulating pedestrians or the parking of vehicles, vehicle size or load limitations, vehicle fitness requirements, or vehicle registration.

(J) Whoever violates division (B)(1) or (4), (D)(3), or (E) of this section is guilty of a minor misdemeanor.

**HISTORY: 147 v S 35. Eff 1-1-99; 149 v S 123, § 1, eff. 1-1-04; 151 v H 343, § 1, eff. 4-6-07; 152 v H 320, § 1, eff. 4-7-09.**

The effective date is set by § 4 of 152 v H 320.

The effective date is set by section 4 of S.B. 123.

See provisions, § 5 of S.B. 123 (149 v —), following RC § 4501.01.

## § 4507.08 Restrictions on issuance of license or temporary instruction permit; reinstatement prohibited for person subject to active arrest warrant.

(A) No probationary license shall be issued to any person under the age of eighteen who has been adjudicated an unruly or delinquent child or a juvenile traffic offender for having committed any act that if committed by an adult would be a drug abuse offense, as defined in section 2925.01 of the Revised Code, a violation of division (B) of section 2917.11, or a violation of division (A) of section 4511.19 of the Revised Code, unless the person has been required by the court to attend a drug abuse or alcohol abuse education, intervention, or treatment program specified by the court and has satisfactorily completed the program.

(B) No temporary instruction permit or driver's license shall be issued to any person whose license has been suspended, during the period for which the license was suspended, nor to any person whose license has been canceled, under Chapter 4510. or any other provision of the Revised Code.

(C) No temporary instruction permit or driver's license shall be issued to any person whose commercial driver's license is suspended under Chapter 4510. or any other provision of the Revised Code during the period of the suspension.

No temporary instruction permit or driver's license shall be issued to any person when issuance is prohibited by division (A) of section 4507.091 of the Revised Code.

(D) No temporary instruction permit or driver's license shall be issued to, or retained by, any of the following persons:

(1) Any person who is an alcoholic, or is addicted to the use of controlled substances to the extent that the use constitutes an impairment to the person's ability to operate a motor vehicle with the required degree of safety;

(2) Any person who is under the age of eighteen and has been adjudicated an unruly or delinquent child or a juvenile traffic offender for having committed any act that if committed by an adult would be a drug abuse offense, as defined in section 2925.01 of the Revised Code, a violation of division (B) of section 2917.11, or a violation of division (A) of section 4511.19 of the Revised Code, unless the person has been required by the court to attend a drug abuse or alcohol abuse education, intervention, or treatment program specified by the court and has satisfactorily completed the program;

(3) Any person who, in the opinion of the registrar, is afflicted with or suffering from a physical or mental disability or disease that prevents the person from exercising reasonable and ordinary control over a motor vehicle while operating the vehicle upon the highways, except that a restricted license effective for six months may be issued to any person otherwise qualified who is or has been subject to any condition resulting in episodic impairment of consciousness or loss of muscular control and whose condition, in the opinion of the registrar, is dormant or is sufficiently under medical control that the person is capable of exercising reasonable and ordinary control over a motor vehicle. A restricted license effective for six months shall be issued to any person who otherwise is qualified and who is subject to any condition that causes episodic impairment of consciousness or a loss of muscular control if the person presents a statement from a licensed physician that the person's condition is under effective medical control and the period of time for which the control has been continuously maintained, unless, thereafter, a medical examination is ordered and, pursuant thereto, cause for denial is found.

A person to whom a six-month restricted license has been issued shall give notice of the person's medical condition to the registrar on forms provided by the registrar and signed by the licensee's physician. The notice shall be sent to the registrar six months after the issuance of the license. Subsequent restricted licenses issued to the same individual shall be effective for six months.

(4) Any person who is unable to understand highway warnings or traffic signs or directions given in the English language;

(5) Any person making an application whose driver's license or driving privileges are under cancellation, revocation, or suspension in the jurisdiction where issued or any other jurisdiction, until the expiration of one year after the license was canceled or revoked or until the period of suspension ends. Any person whose application is denied under this division may file a petition in the municipal court or county court in whose jurisdiction the person resides agreeing to pay the cost of the proceedings and alleging that the conduct involved in the offense that resulted in suspension, cancellation, or revocation in the foreign jurisdiction would not have resulted in a suspension, cancellation, or revocation had the offense occurred in this state. If the petition is granted, the petitioner shall notify the registrar by a certified copy of the court's findings and a license shall not be denied under this division.

(6) Any person who is under a class one or two suspension imposed for a violation of section 2903.01, 2903.02, 2903.04, 2903.06, 2903.08, 2903.11, 2921.331 [2921.33.1], or 2923.02 of the Revised Code or whose driver's or commercial driver's license or permit was permanently revoked prior to January 1, 2004, for a

substantially equivalent violation pursuant to section 4507.16 of the Revised Code;

(7) Any person who is not a resident or temporary resident of this state.

(E) No person whose driver's license or permit has been suspended under Chapter 4510. of the Revised Code or any other provision of the Revised Code shall have driving privileges reinstated if the registrar determines that a warrant has been issued in this state or any other state for the person's arrest and that warrant is an active warrant.

**HISTORY: GC § 6296-7; 116 v PtII, 33, § 7; 119 v 701; 120 v 289; 123 v 246; Bureau of Code Revision, 10-1-53; 127 v 839 (Eff 9-16-57); 127 v 789 (Eff 9-17-57); 128 v 539 (Eff 11-2-59); 129 v 582(896) (Eff 1-10-61); 129 v 1448 (Eff 10-25-61); 130 v 1057 (Eff 9-27-63); 130 v 1055 (Eff 10-10-63); 131 v 1084 (Eff 10-30-65); 131 v 1082 (Eff 11-9-65); 135 v S 1 (Eff 1-1-74); 135 v S 313 (Eff 7-26-74); 136 v H 300 (Eff 7-1-76); 137 v H 71 (Eff 8-26-77); 138 v H 328 (Eff 9-13-79); 138 v H 965 (Eff 4-9-81); 141 v S 262 (Eff 3-20-87); 142 v H 643 (Eff 3-17-89); 143 v H 329 (Eff 6-30-89); 143 v H 330 (Eff 6-30-89); 143 v H 381 (Eff 7-1-89); 144 v S 275 (Eff 9-1-93); 145 v S 62, §§ 1, 4 (Eff 9-1-93); 145 v S 82 (Eff 5-4-94); 146 v H 167 (Eff 5-15-97); 147 v S 60 (Eff 10-21-97); 147 v H 141 (Eff 3-3-98); 147 v S 35 (Eff 1-1-99); 148 v S 180. Eff 3-22-2001; 149 v S 123, § 1, eff. 1-1-04; 151 v S 9, § 1, eff. 4-14-06; 151 v H 461, § 1, eff. 4-4-07.**

The effective date is set by section 4 of S.B. 123.

See provisions, § 5 of S.B. 123 (149 v —), following RC § 4501.01.

## § 4507.081 Driver's license replacing restricted license; renewal; revocation.

(A) Upon the expiration of a restricted license issued under division (D) (3) of section 4507.08 of the Revised Code and submission of a statement as provided in division (C) of this section, the registrar of motor vehicles may issue a driver's license to the person to whom the restricted license was issued. A driver's license issued under this section, unless otherwise suspended or canceled, shall be effective for one year.

(B) A driver's license issued under this section may be renewed annually, for no more than three consecutive years, whenever the person to whom the license has been issued submits to the registrar, by certified mail and no sooner than thirty days prior to the expiration date of the license or renewal thereof, a statement as provided in division (C) of this section. A renewal of a driver's license, unless the license is otherwise suspended or canceled, shall be effective for one year following the expiration date of the license or renewal thereof, and shall be evidenced by a validation sticker. The renewal validation sticker shall be in a form prescribed by the registrar and shall be affixed to the license.

(C) No person may be issued a driver's license under this section, and no such driver's license may be renewed, unless the person presents a signed statement from a licensed physician that the person's condition either is dormant or is under effective medical control, that the control has been maintained continuously for at least one year prior to the date on which application for the license is made, and that, if continued medication is prescribed to control the condition, the person may be depended upon to take the medication.

The statement shall be made on a form provided by the registrar, shall be in not less than duplicate, and shall contain any other information the registrar considers necessary. The duplicate copy of the statement may be retained by the person requesting the license renewal and, when in the person's immediate possession and used in conjunction with the original license, shall entitle the person to operate a motor vehicle during a period of no more than thirty days following the date of submission of the statement to the registrar, except when the registrar denies the request for the license renewal and so notifies the person.

(D) Whenever the registrar receives a statement indicating that the condition of a person to whom a driver's license has been issued under this section no longer is dormant or under effective medical control, the registrar shall cancel the person's driver's license.

(E) Nothing in this section shall require a person submitting a signed statement from a licensed physician to obtain a medical examination prior to the submission of the statement.

(F) Any person whose driver's license has been canceled under this section may apply for a subsequent restricted license according to the provisions of section 4507.08 of the Revised Code.

**HISTORY: 137 v H 71 (Eff 8-26-77); 138 v H 328 (Eff 9-13-79); 140 v H 37 (Eff 6-22-84); 142 v H 643 (Eff 3-17-89); 143 v H 329 (Eff 6-30-89); 143 v H 381 (Eff 7-1-89); 147 v S 35. Eff 1-1-99; 149 v S 123, § 1, eff. 1-1-04.**

The effective date is set by section 4 of S.B. 123.

See provisions, § 5 of S.B. 123 (149 v —), following RC § 4501.01.

## § 4507.09 Expiration, renewal of license; notice of change of address; nonrenewable license for temporary resident.

(A) Except as provided in division (B) of this section, every driver's license issued to a resident of this state expires on the birthday of the applicant in the fourth year after the date it is issued and every driver's license issued to a temporary resident expires in accordance with rules adopted by the registrar of motor vehicles. In no event shall any license be issued for a period longer than four years and ninety days.

Subject to the requirements of section 4507.12 of the Revised Code, every driver's license issued to a resident is renewable at any time prior to its expiration and any license of a temporary resident is nonrenewable. A nonrenewable license may be replaced with a new license within ninety days prior to its expiration in accordance with division (E) of this section. No refund shall be made or credit given for the unexpired portion of the driver's license that is renewed. The registrar of motor vehicles shall notify each person whose driver's license has expired within forty-five days after the date of expiration. Notification shall be made by regular mail sent to the person's last known address as shown in the records of the bureau of motor vehicles. Failure to provide such notification shall not be construed as a renewal or extension of any license. For the purposes of this section, the date of birth of any applicant born on the twenty-ninth day of February shall be deemed to be the first day of March in any year in which there is no twenty-ninth day of February.

(B) Every driver's license or renewal of a driver's license issued to an applicant who is sixteen years of age or older, but less than twenty-one years of age, expires on the twenty-first birthday of the applicant, except that an applicant who applies no more than thirty days before the applicant's twenty-first birthday shall be issued a license in accordance with division (A) of this section.

(C) Each person licensed as a driver under this chapter shall notify the registrar of any change in the person's address within ten days following that change. The notification shall be in writing on a form provided by the registrar and shall include the full name, date of birth, license number, county of residence, social security number, and new address of the person.

(D) No driver's license shall be renewed when renewal is prohibited by division (A) of section 4507.091 [4507.09.1] of the Revised Code.

(E) A nonrenewable license may be replaced with a new license within ninety days prior to its expiration upon the applicant's presentation of documentation verifying the applicant's legal presence in the United States. A nonrenewable license expires on the same date listed on the legal presence documentation, or on the same date in the fourth year after the date the nonrenewable license is issued, whichever comes first. A nonrenewable license is not transferable, and the applicant may not rely on it to obtain a driver's license in another state.

In accordance with Chapter 119. of the Revised Code, the registrar of motor vehicles shall adopt rules governing nonrenewable licenses for temporary residents. At a minimum, the rules shall include provisions specifying all of the following:

(1) That no nonrenewable license may extend beyond the duration of the applicant's temporary residence in this state;

(2) That no nonrenewable license may be replaced by a new license unless the applicant provides acceptable documentation of the person's identity and of the applicant's continued temporary residence in this state;

(3) That no nonrenewable license is valid to apply for a driver's license in any other state;

(4) That every nonrenewable license may contain any security features that the registrar prescribes.

**HISTORY: GC § 6296-15; 116 v PtII, 33, § 15; 119 v 701; 123 v 246; Bureau of Code Revision, 10-1-53; 133 v H 113 (Eff 9-12-69); 136 v H 1337 (Eff 8-31-76); 137 v H 215 (Eff 12-12-78); 140 v H 58 (Eff 3-1-85); 143 v H 381 (Eff 7-1-89); 143 v H 88 (Eff 3-13-90); 144 v H 134 (Eff 10-10-91); 145 v S 96 (Eff 5-10-94); 146 v H 353 (Eff 9-17-96); 147 v S 60 (Eff 10-21-97); 147 v H 141 (Eff 3-3-98); 149 v S 184. Eff 5-15-2002.**

The provisions of § 3 of SB 184 (149 v —) read as follows:

SECTION 3. Section 4507.09 of the Revised Code is presented in this act as a composite of the section as amended by both Am. H.B. 141 and Am. Sub. S.B. 60 of the 122nd General Assembly. The General Assembly, applying the principle stated in division (B) of section 1.52 of the Revised Code that amendments are to be harmonized if reasonably capable of simultaneous operation, finds that the composite is the resulting version of the section in effect prior to the effective date of the section as presented in this act.

## § 4507.091 Ineligibility due to outstanding municipal, county, or mayor's court arrest warrant.

(A) A municipal court, county court, or mayor's court, at the court's discretion, may order the clerk of the court to send to the registrar of motor vehicles a report containing the name, address, and such other information as the registrar may require by rule, of any person for whom an arrest warrant has been issued by that court and is outstanding.

Upon receipt of such a report, the registrar shall enter the information contained in the report into the records of the bureau of motor vehicles. Neither the registrar nor any deputy registrar shall issue a temporary instruction permit or driver's or commercial driver's license to the person named in the report, or renew the driver's or commercial driver's license of such person, until the registrar receives notification from the municipal court, county court, or mayor's court that there are no outstanding arrest warrants in the name of the person. The registrar also shall send a notice to the person who is named in the report, via regular first class mail sent to the person's last known address as shown in the records of the bureau, informing the person that neither the registrar nor any deputy registrar is permitted to issue a temporary instruction permit or driver's or commercial driver's license to the person, or renew the driver's or commercial driver's license of the person, until the registrar receives notification that there are no outstanding arrest warrants in the name of the person.

(B) A clerk who reports an outstanding arrest warrant in accordance with division (A) of this section immediately shall notify the registrar when the warrant has been executed and returned to the issuing court or has been canceled. The clerk shall charge and collect from the person named in the executed or canceled arrest warrant a processing fee of fifteen dollars to cover the costs of the bureau in administering this section. The clerk shall transmit monthly all such processing fees to the registrar for deposit into the state bureau of motor vehicles fund created by section 4501.25 of the Revised Code.

Upon receipt of such notification, the registrar shall cause the report of that outstanding arrest warrant to be removed from the records of the bureau and, if there are no other outstanding arrest warrants issued by a municipal court, county court, or mayor's court in the name of the person and the person otherwise is eligible to be issued a driver's or commercial driver's license or to have such a license renewed, the registrar or a deputy registrar may issue a driver's license or commercial driver's license to the person named in the executed or canceled arrest warrant, or renew the driver's or commercial driver's license of such person.

(C) Neither the registrar, any employee of the bureau, a deputy registrar, nor any employee of a deputy registrar is personally liable for damages or injuries resulting from any error made by a clerk in entering information contained in a report submitted to the registrar under this section.

(D) Any information submitted to the registrar by a clerk under this section shall be transmitted by means of an electronic data transfer system.

**HISTORY: 147 v H 141. Eff 3-3-98; 149 v H 490, § 1, eff. 1-1-04.**

The effective date is set by section 4 of H.B. 490.

### [EXAMINATION]

## § 4507.10 Examination for license, permit or endorsement; exceptions.

(A) Except as provided in section 4507.11 of the Revised Code, the registrar of motor vehicles shall examine every applicant for a temporary instruction permit, driver's license, or motorcycle operator's endorsement before issuing any such permit, license, or endorsement.

(B) Except as provided in section 4507.12 of the Revised Code, the registrar may waive the examination of any person applying for the renewal of a driver's license or motorcycle operator's endorsement issued under this chapter, provided that the applicant presents either an unexpired license or endorsement or a license or endorsement which has expired not more than six months prior to the date of application.

(C) The registrar may waive the examination of any person applying for the renewal of such a license or endorsement who is on active duty in the armed forces of the United States or in service with the peace corps, volunteers in service to America, or the foreign service of the United States if the applicant has no physical or mental disabilities that would affect the applicant's driving ability, had a valid Ohio driver's or commercial driver's license at the time the applicant commenced such active duty or service, and the applicant's license is not under suspension or revocation by this state or any other jurisdiction. The registrar also may waive the examination of the spouse or a dependent of any such person on active duty or in service if the applicant has no physical or mental disabilities that would affect the applicant's driving ability, was an Ohio licensee at the time the person commenced the active duty or service, and if the person's active duty caused the spouse or dependent to relocate outside of this state during the period of the active duty or service.

(D) Except as provided in section 4507.12 of the Revised Code, the registrar may waive the examination of any person applying for such a license or endorsement who meets any of the following sets of qualifications:

(1) Has been on active duty in the armed forces of the United States, presents an honorable discharge certificate showing that the applicant has no physical or mental disabilities that would affect the applicant's driving ability, had a valid Ohio driver's or commercial driver's license at the time the applicant commenced the applicant's active duty, is not under a license suspension or revocation by this state or any other jurisdiction, and makes the application not more than six months after the date of discharge or separation;

(2) Was in service with the peace corps, volunteers in service to America, or the foreign service of the United States; presents such evidence of the applicant's service as the registrar prescribes showing that the applicant has no physical or mental disabilities that would affect the applicant's driving ability; had a valid Ohio driver's or commercial driver's license at the time the applicant commenced the applicant's service, is not under a license suspension or revocation by this state or any other jurisdiction, and makes the application no more than six months after leaving the peace corps, volunteers, or foreign service.

(3) Is the spouse or a dependent of a person on active duty in the armed forces of the United States, or in service with the peace corps, volunteers in service to America, or the foreign service of the United States; presents such evidence as the registrar prescribes showing that the applicant has no physical or mental disabilities that would affect his driving ability; presents such evidence as the registrar prescribes showing that the applicant relocated outside of Ohio as a result of the person's active duty or service; was an Ohio licensee at the time of the relocation; and makes the application not more than six months after returning to Ohio.

**HISTORY: GC § 6296-11; 116 v Pt II, 33, § 11; 119 v 701; 120 v 289; Bureau of Code Revision, 10-1-53; 132 v H 57 (Eff 3-28-67); 132 v H 380 (Eff 1-1-68); 134 v S 546 (Eff 10-16-72); 140 v H 58 (Eff 3-1-85); 142 v H 614 (Eff 3-17-89); 143 v H 381 (Eff 7-1-89); 145 v S 96 (Eff 5-10-94); 147 v S 60 (Eff 10-21-97); 147 v S 35 (Eff 1-1-99); 148 v H 600 (Eff 9-1-2000); 148 v S 271. Eff 1-1-2001.**

The effective date is set by section 3 of SB 271.

The provisions of § 4 of SB 271 (148 v —) read as follows:

SECTION 4. Section 4507.10 of the Revised Code is presented in this act as a composite of the section as amended by Am. Sub. S.B. 35 of the 122nd General Assembly and Sub. S.B. 96 of the 120th General Assembly, with the new language of neither of the acts shown in capital letters. This is in recognition of the principle stated in division (B) of section 1.52 of the Revised Code that such amendments are to be harmonized where not substantively irreconcilable and constitutes a legislative finding that such is the resulting version in effect prior to the effective date of this act.

**Comment, Legislative Service Commission**

Sections 4507.10 and 4507.11 of the Revised Code are amended by this act [S.B. 271] and also by Am. Sub. H.B. 600 of the 123rd General Assembly. Comparison of these amendments in pursuance of section 1.52 of the Revised Code discloses that they are not irreconcilable so that they are required by that section to be harmonized to give effect to each amendment.

## § 4507.11 Examination for permit, license or endorsement; examiner's permit.

(A) The registrar of motor vehicles shall conduct all necessary examinations of applicants for temporary instruction permits, drivers' licenses, or motorcycle operators' endorsements. The examination shall include a test of the applicant's knowledge of motor vehicle laws, including the laws on stopping for school buses, a test of the applicant's physical fitness to drive, and a test of the applicant's ability to understand highway traffic control devices. The examination may be conducted in such a manner that applicants who are illiterate or limited in their knowledge of the English language may be tested by methods that would indicate to the examining officer that the applicant has a reasonable knowledge of motor vehicle laws and understands highway traffic control devices. An applicant for a driver's license shall give an actual demonstration of the ability to exercise ordinary and reasonable control in the operation of a motor vehicle by driving the same under the supervision of an examining officer. Except as provided in division (B) of this section, an applicant for a motorcycle operator's endorsement or a restricted license that permits only the operation of a motorcycle shall give an actual demonstration of the ability to exercise ordinary and reasonable control in the operation of a motorcycle by driving the same under the supervision of an examining officer. Except as provided in section 4507.12 of the Revised Code, the registrar shall designate the highway patrol, any law enforcement body, or any other employee of the department of public safety to supervise and conduct examinations for temporary instruction permits, drivers' licenses, and motorcycle operators' endorsements and shall provide the necessary rules and forms to properly conduct the examinations. The records of the examinations, together with the application for a temporary instruction permit, driver's license, or motorcycle operator's endorsement, shall be forwarded to the registrar by the deputy registrar, and, if in the opinion of the registrar the applicant is qualified to operate a motor vehicle, the registrar shall issue the permit, license, or endorsement.

The registrar may authorize the highway patrol, other designated law enforcement body, or other designated employee of the department of public safety to issue an examiner's driving permit to an applicant who has passed the required examination, authorizing that applicant to operate a motor vehicle while the registrar is completing an investigation relative to that applicant's qualifications to receive a temporary instruction permit, driver's license, or motorcycle operator's endorsement. The examiner's driving permit shall be in the immediate possession of the applicant while operating a motor vehicle and shall be effective until final action and notification has been given by the registrar, but in no event longer than sixty days from its date of issuance.

(B)(1) An applicant for a motorcycle operator's endorsement or a restricted license that permits only the operation of a motorcycle who presents to the registrar of motor vehicles or a deputy registrar a form approved by the director of public safety attesting to the applicant's successful completion within the preceding sixty days of a course of basic instruction provided by the motorcycle safety and education program approved by the director pursuant to section 4508.08 of the Revised Code shall not be required to give an actual demonstration of the ability to operate a motorcycle by driving a motorcycle under the supervision of an examining officer, as described in division (A) of this section. Upon presentation of the form described in division (B)(1) of this section and compliance with all other requirements relating to the issuance of a motorcycle operator's endorsement or a restricted license that permits only the operation of a motorcycle, the registrar or deputy registrar shall issue to the applicant the endorsement or restricted license, as the case may be.

(2) A person who has not attained eighteen years of age and presents an application for a motorcycle operator's endorsement or a restricted license under division (B)(1) of this section also shall comply with the requirements of section 4507.21 of the Revised Code.

**HISTORY: GC § 6296-12; 116 v PtII, 33, § 12; 119 v 701; Bureau of Code Revision, 10-1-53; 129 v 1618 (Eff 10-25-61); 132 v H 380 (Eff 1-1-68); 133 v H 362 (Eff 6-23-70); 137 v S 389 (Eff 3-15-79); 140 v H 58 (Eff 3-1-85); 143 v H 381 (Eff 7-1-89); 147 v S 35 (Eff 1-1-99); 148 v H 600 (Eff 9-1-2000); 148 v S 271. Eff 1-1-2001.**

The effective date is set by section 3 of SB 271.

See Comment, Legislative Service Commission, following RC § 4507.10.

## § 4507.111 Effect of child support default.

On receipt of a notice pursuant to section 3123.54 of the Revised Code, the registrar of motor vehicles shall comply with sections 3123.53 to 3123.60 of the Revised Code and any applicable rules adopted under section 3123.63 of the Revised Code with respect to any driver's or commercial license or permit, motorcycle operator's license or endorsement, or temporary instruction permit or commercial driver's temporary instruction permit issued by this state that is the subject of the notice.

**HISTORY: 146 v H 167 (Eff 5-15-97); 148 v S 180. Eff 3-22-2001; 149 v S 123, § 1, eff. 1-1-04; 2011 HB 153, § 101.01, eff. Sept. 29, 2011.**

The effective date is set by section 4 of S.B. 123.

See provisions, § 5 of S.B. 123 (149 v —), following RC § 4501.01.

[LICENSE]

## § 4507.12 Vision screening prior to license renewal; retention of license upon failure.

(A) Except as provided in division (C) of section 4507.10 of the Revised Code, each person applying for the renewal of a driver's license shall submit to a screening of the person's vision before the license may be renewed. The vision screening shall be conducted at the office of the deputy registrar receiving the application for license renewal.

(B) When the results of a vision screening given under division (A) of this section indicate that the vision of the person examined meets the standards required for licensing, the deputy registrar may renew the person's driver's license at that time.

(C) When the results of a vision screening given under division (A) of this section indicate that the vision of the person screened may not meet the standards required for licensing, the deputy registrar shall not renew the person's driver's license at that time but shall refer the person to a driver's license examiner appointed by the superintendent of the state highway patrol under section 5503.21 of the Revised Code for a further examination of the person's vision. When a person referred to a driver's license examiner by a deputy registrar does not meet the vision standards required for licensing, the driver's license examiner shall retain the person's operator's or chauffeur's license and shall immediately notify the registrar of motor vehicles of that fact. No driver's license shall be issued to any such person, until the person's vision is corrected to meet the standards required for licensing and the person passes the vision screening required by this section. Any person who operates a motor vehicle on a highway, or on any public or private property used by the public for purposes of vehicular travel or parking, during the time the person's driver's license is held by a driver's license examiner under this division, shall be deemed to be operating a motor vehicle in violation of division (A) of section 4510.12 of the Revised Code.

(D) The registrar shall adopt rules and shall provide any forms necessary to properly conduct vision screenings at the office of a deputy registrar.

(E) No person conducting vision screenings under this section shall be personally liable for damages for injury or loss to persons or property and for death caused by the operation of a motor vehicle by any person whose driver's license was renewed by the deputy registrar under division (B) of this section.

**HISTORY: 140 v H 58 (Eff 3-1-85); 141 v S 356 (Eff 9-24-86); 142 v S 1 (Eff 11-28-88); 143 v H 381. Eff 7-1-89; 149 v S 123, § 1, eff. 1-1-04.**

The effective date is set by section 4 of S.B. 123.

See provisions, § 5 of S.B. 123 (149 v —), following RC § 4501.01.

**Not analogous to former RC § 4507.12 (GC § 6296-14; 116 v PtII, 33; 120 v 289; Bureau of Code Revision, 10-1-53), repealed 132 v S 43, § 2, eff 1-1-69.**

## § 4507.13 Contents and characteristics of license; lamination.

(A) The registrar of motor vehicles shall issue a driver's license to every person licensed as an operator of motor vehicles other than commercial motor vehicles. No person licensed as a commercial motor vehicle driver under Chapter 4506. of the Revised Code need procure a driver's license, but no person shall drive any commercial motor vehicle unless licensed as a commercial motor vehicle driver.

Every driver's license shall display on it the distinguishing number assigned to the licensee and shall display the licensee's name and date of birth; the licensee's residence address and county of residence; a color photograph of the licensee; a brief description of the licensee for the purpose of identification; a facsimile of the signature of the licensee as it appears on the application for the license; a notation, in a manner prescribed by the registrar, indicating any condition described in division (D)(3) of section 4507.08 of the Revised Code to which the licensee is subject; if the licensee has executed a durable power of attorney for health care or a declaration governing the use or continuation, or the withholding or withdrawal, of life-sustaining treatment and has specified that the licensee wishes the license to indicate that the licensee has executed either type of instrument, any symbol chosen by the registrar to indicate that the licensee has executed either type of instrument; on and after October 7, 2009, if the licensee has specified that the licensee wishes the license to indicate that the licensee is a veteran, active duty, or reservist of the armed forces of the United States and has presented a copy of the licensee's DD-214 form or an equivalent document, any symbol chosen by the registrar to indicate that the licensee is a veteran, active duty, or reservist of the armed forces of the United States; and any additional information that the registrar requires by rule. No license shall display the licensee's social security number unless the licensee specifically requests that the licensee's social security number be displayed on the license. If federal law requires the licensee's social security number to be displayed on the license, the social security number shall be displayed on the license notwithstanding this section.

The driver's license for licensees under twenty-one years of age shall have characteristics prescribed by the registrar distinguishing it from that issued to a licensee who is twenty-one years of age or older, except that a driver's license issued to a person who applies no more than thirty days before the applicant's twenty-first birthday shall have the characteristics of a license issued to a person who is twenty-one years of age or older.

The driver's license issued to a temporary resident shall contain the word "nonrenewable" and shall have any additional characteristics prescribed by the registrar distinguishing it from a license issued to a resident.

Every driver's or commercial driver's license displaying a motorcycle operator's endorsement and every restricted license to operate a motor vehicle also shall display the designation "novice," if the endorsement or license is issued to a person who is eighteen years of age or older and previously has not been licensed to operate a motorcycle by this state or another jurisdiction recognized by this state. The "novice" designation shall be effective for one year after the date of issuance of the motorcycle operator's endorsement or license.

Each license issued under this section shall be of such material and so designed as to prevent its reproduction or alteration without ready detection and, to this end, shall be laminated with a transparent plastic material.

(B) Except in regard to a driver's license issued to a person who applies no more than thirty days before the applicant's twenty-first birthday, neither the registrar nor any deputy registrar shall issue a driver's license to anyone under twenty-one years of age that does not have the characteristics prescribed by the registrar distinguishing it from the driver's license issued to persons who are twenty-one years of age or older.

(C) Whoever violates division (B) of this section is guilty of a minor misdemeanor.

**HISTORY: GC § 6296-13; 116 v Pt II, 33, § 13; 119 v 701; 120 v 289; 123 v 246; Bureau of Code Revision, 10-1-53; 131 v 1087 (Eff 9-1-66); 132 v H 193 (Eff 12-11-67); 132 v S 43 (Eff 1-1-69); 132 v S 452 (Eff 1-1-69); 136 v H 650 (Eff 1-5-76); 137 v H 71 (Eff 8-26-77); 137 v H 115 (Eff 7-10-78); 138 v H 328 (Eff 9-13-79); 140 v H 183 (Eff 10-1-84); 142 v H 643 (Eff 3-17-89); 143 v H 329 (Eff 6-30-89); 143 v H 381 (Eff 7-1-89); 143 v S 131 (Eff 7-25-90); 144 v H 134 (Eff 10-10-91); 144 v H 427 (Eff 10-8-92); 145 v H 580 (Eff 12-9-94); 147 v S 60 (Eff 10-21-97); 147 v S 213, § 1 (Eff 7-29-98); 147 v S 35 (Eff 1-1-99); 147 v S 213, § 4 (Eff 1-1-99); 149 v H 46. Eff 2-1-2002; 149 v S 123, § 1, eff. 1-1-04; 150 v H 230, § 1, eff. 9-16-04; 152 v H 450, § 1, eff. 4-7-09; 153 v H 2, § 101.01, eff. 7-1-09.**

The effective date is set by § 812.10 of 153 v H 2.

The effective date is set by section 4 of S.B. 123.

See provisions, § 5 of S.B. 123 (149 v —), following RC § 4501.01.

The provisions of § 199 of HB 94 (149 v —) read as follows:

SECTION 199. (A) In prescribing distinguishing characteristics for a driver's license issued to a person who is under twenty-one years of age, the Registrar of Motor Vehicles shall consider both of the following:

(1) Formatting the license vertically;

(2) Conspicuously indicating the month, day, and years on which the licensee becomes eighteen and twenty-one years of age.

(B) In accordance with section 4507.13 of the Revised Code, the Registrar may prescribe either or both of the distinguishing driver's license characteristics considered under this section.

## § 4507.14 Restrictions relating to driving ability.

The registrar of motor vehicles upon issuing a driver's license, a motorcycle operator's endorsement, a driver's license renewal, or the renewal of any other license issued under this chapter, whenever good cause appears, may impose restrictions suitable to the licensee's driving ability with respect to the type of or special mechanical control devices required on a motor vehicle that the licensee may operate, or any other restrictions applicable to the licensee that the registrar determines to be necessary.

When issuing a license to a person with impaired hearing, the registrar shall require that a motor vehicle operated by the person be equipped with two outside rear vision mirrors, one on the left side and the other on the right side.

The registrar either may issue a special restricted license or may set forth any restrictions applicable to the license upon the usual license form.

The registrar, upon receiving satisfactory evidence of any violation of the restrictions of any license, after an opportunity for a hearing in accordance with Chapter 119. of the Revised Code, may impose upon the offender a class D suspension of the license from the range specified in division (B)(4) of section 4510.02 of the Revised Code.

**HISTORY: GC § 6296-14a; 119 v 701; Bureau of Code Revision, 10-1-53; 132 v H 380 (Eff 1-1-68); 143 v H 381 (Eff 7-1-89); 147 v S 60. Eff 10-21-97; 149 v S 123, § 1, eff. 1-1-04.**

The effective date is set by section 4 of S.B. 123.

See provisions, § 5 of S.B. 123 (149 v —), following RC § 4501.01.

## § 4507.141 Sun visor identification card for hearing-impaired persons.

(A) Any hearing-impaired person may apply to the registrar of motor vehicles for an identification card identifying the person as hearing-impaired. The application for a hearing-impaired identification card shall be accompanied by a signed statement from the applicant's personal physician certifying that the applicant is hearing-impaired. Upon receipt of the application for the identification card and the signed statement from the applicant's personal physician, and upon presentation by the applicant of the applicant's driver's or commercial driver's license or motorcycle operator's license, the registrar shall issue the applicant an identification card. A hearing-impaired person may also apply for a hearing-impaired identification card at the time the person applies for a driver's or commercial driver's license or motorcycle operator's license or endorsement. Every hearing-impaired identification card shall expire on the same date that the cardholder's driver's or commercial driver's license or motorcycle operator's license expires.

(B) The hearing-impaired identification card shall be rectangular in shape, approximately the same size as an average motor vehicle sun visor, as determined by the registrar, to enable the identification card to be attached to a sun visor in a motor vehicle. The identification card shall contain the heading "Identification Card for the Hearing-impaired Driver" in boldface type, the name and signature of the hearing-impaired person to whom it is issued, an identifying number, and instructions on the actions the hearing-impaired person should take and the actions the person should refrain from taking in the event the person is stopped by a law enforcement officer while operating the motor vehicle. The registrar shall determine the preferred manner in which a hearing-impaired motorcycle operator should carry or display the hearing-impaired identification card, and the color and composition of, and any other information to be included on, the identification card.

(C) As used in this section, "hearing-impaired" means a hearing loss of forty decibels or more in one or both ears.

**HISTORY: 143 v H 581. Eff 7-13-90; 150 v H 230, § 1, eff. 9-16-04.**

## § 4507.15 Courts of record; reports of convictions and forfeitures.

For the purpose of enforcing this chapter and Chapter 4510. of the Revised Code, any court of record having criminal jurisdiction shall have county-wide jurisdiction within the county in which it is located to hear and finally determine cases arising under this chapter and Chapter 4510. of the Revised Code. An action arising under this section shall be commenced by the filing of an affidavit, and the right of trial by jury is preserved, but indictments are not required in misdemeanor cases arising under this chapter and Chapter 4510. of the Revised Code. The registrar shall prepare and furnish blanks for the use of the court in making reports of convictions and bond forfeitures arising under this chapter and Chapter 4510. of the Revised Code.

**HISTORY: GC § 6296-16; 116 v PtII, 33, § 16; 119 v 701; Bureau of Code Revision, 10-1-53; 127 v 525. Eff 6-22-57; 149 v S 123, § 1, eff. 1-1-04.**

The effective date is set by section 4 of S.B. 123.

See provisions, § 5 of S.B. 123 (149 v —), following RC § 4501.01.

## [SUSPENSION OR REVOCATION]

## § 4507.16 Suspension of license by trial judge; prohibitions concerning registration of vehicle.

(A) The trial judge of any court of record, in addition to or independent of all other penalties provided by law or by ordinance, shall impose upon any person who is convicted of or pleads guilty to perjury or the making of a false affidavit under this chapter, or any other law of this state requiring the registration of motor vehicles or regulating their operation on the highway, a class six suspension of the offender's driver's license, commercial driver's license, temporary instruction permit, probationary license, or nonresident operating privilege from the range specified in division (A)(6) of section 4510.02 of the Revised Code. No judge shall suspend the first three months of suspension of an offender's license, permit, or privilege required by this division.

(B) If the trial judge of any court of record suspends the driver's or commercial driver's license or permit or nonresident operating privilege of a person who is convicted of or pleads guilty to any offense for which a suspension of that type is provided by law or ordinance, in addition to all other penalties provided by law or ordinance, the judge may issue an order prohibiting the offender from registering, renewing, or transferring the registration of any vehicle during the period that the offender's license, permit, or privilege is suspended. The court promptly shall send a copy of the order to the registrar of motor vehicles.

Upon receipt of the order from the court, neither the registrar nor any deputy registrar shall accept any application for the registration, registration renewal, or transfer of registration of any motor vehicle owned or leased by the person named in the order during the period that the person's license, permit, or privilege is suspended, unless the registrar is properly notified by the court that the order of suspension has been canceled. When the period of suspension expires or the order is canceled, the registrar or deputy registrar shall accept the application for registration, registration renewal, or transfer of registration of the person named in the order.

**HISTORY: GC § 6296-17; 116 v PtII, 33, § 17; Bureau of Code Revision, 10-1-53; 125 v 367 (Eff 10-15-53); 132 v S 37 (Eff 11-14-67); 132 v H 380 (Eff 1-1-68); 133 v H 1 (Eff 3-18-69); 136 v H 300 (Eff 7-1-76); 137 v S 141 (Eff 11-11-77); 137 v H 469 (Eff 10-25-78); 139 v S 432 (Eff 3-16-83); 141 v S 262 (Eff 3-20-87); 142 v H 303 (Eff 10-20-87); 142 v H 429 (Eff 6-20-88); 143 v H 381 (Eff 7-1-89); 143 v S 131 (Eff 7-25-90); 143 v H 837 (Eff 7-25-90); 143 v S 258 (Eff 11-20-90); 144 v S 275 (Eff 9-1-93); 145 v S 62, §§ 1, 4 (Eff 9-1-93); 145 v H 377 (Eff 9-30-93); 145 v S 82 (Eff 5-4-94); 145 v H 236 (Eff 9-29-94); 146 v H 107 (Eff 6-30-95); 146 v S 2 (Eff 7-1-96); 146 v S 269, § 1 (Eff 7-1-96); 146 v H 353, § 1 (Eff 9-17-96); 146 v H 676, § 1 (Eff 10-4-96); 146 v S 166, § 1 (Eff 10-17-96); 146 v H 353, § 4 (Eff 5-15-97); 146 v S 269, § 8 (Eff 5-15-97); 146 v H 676, § 3 (Eff 5-15-97); 146 v S 166, § 6 (Eff 5-15-97); 147 v S 60 (Eff 10-21-97); 148 v S 107 (Eff 3-23-2000); 148 v S 180 (Eff 3-22-2001); 149 v H 7. Eff 8-7-2001; 150 v H 50, § 1, eff. 10-21-03; 149 v S 123, § 1, eff. 1-1-04.**

The effective date is set by section 4 of S.B. 123.

The provisions of § 2 of H.B. 50 (150 v —) read as follows:

SECTION 3. The amendment by this act of section 4507.16 of the Revised Code has interim effect and does not supersede the earlier amendment, with delayed effective date, of the section by Am. Sub. S.B. 123 of the 124th General Assembly.

See provisions, § 5 of S.B. 123 (149 v —), following RC § 4501.01.

**§ 4507.161** Amended and renumbered RC § 4510.23 in 149 v SB 123. Eff 1-1-04.

See provisions, § 5 of S.B. 123 (149 v —), following RC § 4501.01.

**§ 4507.162** Amended and renumbered RC § 4510.31 in 149 v SB 123. Eff 1-1-04.

See provisions, § 5 of S.B. 123 (149 v —), following RC § 4501.01.

**§ 4507.163** Amended and renumbered RC § 4510.33 in 149 v SB 123. Eff 1-1-04.

See provisions, § 5 of S.B. 123 (149 v —), following RC § 4501.01.

**§ 4507.164 Impoundment of license plates upon suspension of license; immobilization or criminal forfeiture of vehicle.**

(A) Except as provided in divisions (C) to (E) of this section, when the license of any person is suspended pursuant to any provision of the Revised Code other than division (G) of section 4511.19 of the Revised Code and other than section 4510.07 of the Revised Code for a violation of a municipal OVI ordinance, the trial judge may impound the identification license plates of any motor vehicle registered in the name of the person.

(B)(1) When the license of any person is suspended pursuant to division (G)(1)(a) of section 4511.19 of the Revised Code, or pursuant to section 4510.07 of the Revised Code for a municipal OVI offense when the suspension is equivalent in length to the suspension under division (G) of section 4511.19 of the Revised Code that is specified in this division, the trial judge of the court of record or the mayor of the mayor's court that suspended the license may impound the identification license plates of any motor vehicle registered in the name of the person.

(2) When the license of any person is suspended pursuant to division (G)(1)(b) of section 4511.19 of the Revised Code, or pursuant to section 4510.07 of the Revised Code for a municipal OVI offense when the suspension is equivalent in length to the suspension under division (G) of section 4511.19 of the Revised Code that is specified in this division, the trial judge of the court of record that suspended the license shall order the impoundment of the identification license plates of the motor vehicle the offender was operating at the time of the offense and the immobilization of that vehicle in accordance with section 4503.233 and division (G)(1)(b) of section 4511.19 or division (C)(2)(a) of section 4511.193 of the Revised Code and may impound the identification license plates of any other motor vehicle registered in the name of the person whose license is suspended.

(3) When the license of any person is suspended pursuant to division (G)(1)(c), (d), or (e) of section 4511.19 of the Revised Code, or pursuant to section 4510.07 of the Revised Code for a municipal OVI offense when the suspension is equivalent in length to the suspension under division (G) of section 4511.19 of the Revised Code that is specified in this division, the trial judge of the court of record that suspended the license shall order the criminal forfeiture to the state of the motor vehicle the offender was operating at the time of the offense in accordance with section 4503.234 and division (G)(1)(c), (d), or (e) of section 4511.19 or division (C)(2)(b) of section 4511.193 of the Revised Code and may impound the identification license plates of any other motor vehicle registered in the name of the person whose license is suspended.

(C)(1) When a person is convicted of or pleads guilty to a violation of section 4510.14 of the Revised Code or a substantially equivalent municipal ordinance and division (B)(1) or (2) of section 4510.14 or division (C)(1) or (2) of section 4510.161 of the Revised Code applies, the trial judge of the court of record or the mayor of the mayor's court that imposes sentence shall order the immobilization of the vehicle the person was operating at the time of the offense and the impoundment of its identification license plates in accordance with section 4503.233 and division (B)(1) or (2) of section 4510.14 or division (C)(1) or (2) of section 4510.161 of the Revised Code and may impound the identification license plates of any other vehicle registered in the name of that person.

(2) When a person is convicted of or pleads guilty to a violation of section 4510.14 of the Revised Code or a substantially equivalent municipal ordinance and division (B)(3) of section 4510.14 or division (C)(3) of section 4510.161 of the Revised Code applies, the trial judge of the court of record that imposes sentence shall order the criminal forfeiture to the state of the vehicle the person was operating at the time of the offense in accordance with section 4503.234 and division (B)(3) of section 4510.14 or division (C)(3) of section 4510.161 of the Revised Code and may impound the identification license plates of any other vehicle registered in the name of that person.

(D) When a person is convicted of or pleads guilty to a violation of division (A) of section 4510.16 of the Revised Code or a substantially equivalent municipal ordinance, division (D) or (G) of section 4510.16 or division (B) of section 4510.161 of the Revised Code applies in determining whether the immobilization of the vehicle the person was operating at the time of the offense and the impoundment of its identification license plates or the criminal forfeiture to the state of the vehicle the person was operating at the time of the offense is authorized or required. The trial judge of the court of record or the mayor of the mayor's court that imposes sentence may impound the identification license plates of any other vehicle registered in the name of that person.

(E)(1) When a person is convicted of or pleads guilty to a violation of section 4511.203 of the Revised Code and the person is sentenced pursuant to division (C)(3)(a) or (b) of section 4511.203 of the Revised Code, the trial judge of the court of record or the mayor of the mayor's court that imposes sentence shall order the immobilization of the vehicle that was involved in the commission of the offense and the impoundment of its identification license plates in accordance with division (C)(3)(a) or (b) of section 4511.203 and section 4503.233 of the Revised Code and may impound the identification license plates of any other vehicle registered in the name of that person.

(2) When a person is convicted of or pleads guilty to a violation of section 4511.203 of the Revised Code and the

person is sentenced pursuant to division (C)(3)(c) of section 4511.203 of the Revised Code, the trial judge of the court of record or the mayor of the mayor's court that imposes sentence shall order the criminal forfeiture to the state of the vehicle that was involved in the commission of the offense in accordance with division (C)(3)(c) of section 4511.203 and section 4503.234 of the Revised Code and may impound the identification license plates of any other vehicle registered in the name of that person.

(F) Except as provided in section 4503.233 or 4503.234 of the Revised Code, when the certificate of registration, the identification license plates, or both have been impounded, division (B) of section 4507.02 of the Revised Code is applicable.

(G) As used in this section, "municipal OVI offense" has the same meaning as in section 4511.181 of the Revised Code.

**HISTORY: 132 v H 518 (Eff 12-14-67); 135 v S 313 (Eff 7-26-74); 140 v H 37 (Eff 6-22-84); 141 v S 356 (Eff 9-24-86); 142 v H 303 (Eff 10-20-87); 144 v S 275 (Eff 9-1-93); 145 v S 62, §§ 1, 4 (Eff 9-1-93); 148 v S 107 (Eff 3-23-2000); 148 v S 22 (Eff 5-17-2000); 148 v H 80. Eff 6-8-2000; 149 v S 123, § 1, eff. 1-1-04; 151 v H 461, § 1, eff. 4-4-07; 2011 HB 5, § 1, eff. Sept. 23, 2011; 2011 HB 153, § 101.01, eff. Sept. 29, 2011.**

The effective date is set by section 4 of S.B. 123.

See provisions, § 5 of S.B. 123 (149 v —), following RC § 4501.01.

The provisions of § 8 of S.B. 123 read as follows:

SECTION 8. Sections 4503.233 and 4507.164 of the Revised Code are presented in this act as a composite of the sections as amended by Am. H.B. 80, Am. Sub. S.B. 22 and Am. Sub. S.B. 107 of the 123rd General Assembly. The General Assembly, applying the principle stated in division (B) of section 1.52 of the Revised Code that amendments are to be harmonized if reasonably capable of simultaneous operation, finds that the composites are the resulting versions of the sections in effect prior to the effective date of the sections as presented in this act.

See Comment, Legislative Service Commission following RC § 4503.23.3.

## § 4507.165 Repealed, 149 v S 123, § 2 [137 v S 389; 143 v H 381]. Eff. 1-1-04.

This section concerned suspension for passing a stopped school bus.

The effective date is set by section 4 of S.B. 123.

See provisions, § 5 of S.B. 123 (149 v —), following RC § 4501.01.

## § 4507.166 Repealed, 149 v S 123, § 2 [138 v H 116; 141 v H 428; 143 v H 381]. Eff. 1-1-04.

This section concerned suspension for causing death while fleeing an officer.

The effective date is set by section 4 of S.B. 123.

See provisions, § 5 of S.B. 123 (149 v —), following RC § 4501.01.

## § 4507.167 Amended and renumbered RC § 4510.34 in 149 v SB 1236. Eff 1-1-04.

See provisions, § 5 of S.B. 123 (149 v —), following RC § 4501.01.

## § 4507.168 Amended and renumbered RC § 4510.22 in 149 v SB 123. Eff 1-1-04.

See provisions, § 5 of S.B. 123 (149 v —), following RC § 4501.01.

## § 4507.169 Amended and renumbered RC § 4510.17 in 149 v SB 123. Eff 1-1-04.

See provisions, § 5 of S.B. 123 (149 v —), following RC § 4501.01.

## § 4507.1610 Amended and renumbered RC § 4510.06 in 149 v SB 123. Eff 1-1-04.

See provisions, § 5 of S.B. 123 (149 v —), following RC § 4501.01.

## § 4507.1611 Amended and renumbered RC § 4510.05 in 149 v SB 123. Eff 1-1-04.

See provisions, § 5 of S.B. 123 (149 v —), following RC § 4501.01.

## § 4507.1612 Reinstatement fee after illegally conveying or possessing deadly weapon or dangerous ordnance on school premises.

The registrar of motor vehicles shall not restore any operating privileges or reissue a probationary driver's license, restricted license, driver's license, or probationary commercial driver's license suspended under section 2923.122 of the Revised Code until the person whose license was suspended pays a reinstatement fee of thirty dollars to the registrar or an eligible deputy registrar. In addition, each deputy registrar shall collect a service fee of ten dollars to compensate the deputy registrar for services performed under this section. The deputy registrar shall retain eight dollars of the service fee and shall transmit the reinstatement fee, plus two dollars of the service fee, to the registrar in the manner the registrar shall determine. The bureau of motor vehicles shall pay all fees collected under this section into the state treasury to the credit of the state bureau of motor vehicles fund created by section 4501.25 of the Revised Code.

**HISTORY: 146 v H 124. Eff 3-31-97; 2011 HB 114, § 101.01, eff. June 29, 2011.**

Acts 2011, HB 114, § 806.10 provides: "The items of law contained in this act, and their applications, are severable. If any item of law contained in this act, or if any application of any item of law contained in this act, is held invalid, the invalidity does not affect other items of law contained in this act and their applications that can be given effect without the invalid item or application."

The effective date is set by section 3 of HB 124.

## § 4507.1613 Amended and renumbered RC § 4510.07 in 149 v SB 123. Eff 1-1-04.

See provisions, § 5 of S.B. 123 (149 v —), following RC § 4501.01.

## § 4507.1614 Suspension based on juvenile court disposition.

The registrar shall suspend the person's license or permit under division (A) of section 4507.162 [4507.16.2]† of the Revised Code regardless of whether the disposition of the case in juvenile court occurred after the person's eighteenth birthday.

**HISTORY: 150 v H 230, § 1, eff. 9-16-04.**

† RC § 4507.162 was renumbered to RC § 4510.31.

## § 4507.17 Suspension or cancellation bars new license.

Any person whose license is suspended or canceled is not entitled to apply for or receive a new license during the effective dates of the suspension or cancellation.

**HISTORY: GC § 6296-21; 116 v PtII, 33, § 21; Bureau of Code Revision, 10-1-53; 125 v 367. Eff 10-15-53; 149 v S 123, § 1, eff. 1-1-04.**

The effective date is set by section 4 of S.B. 123.

See provisions, § 5 of S.B. 123 (149 v —), following RC § 4501.01.

## § 4507.18 Repealed, 149 v S 123, § 2 [GC § 6296-18; 116 v PtII, 33, § 18; Bureau of Code Revision, 10-1-53; 142 v H 303; 143 v H 381]. Eff 1-1-04.

This section concerned disposition of license while appeal proceedings are pending.

The effective date is set by section 4 of S.B. 123.

See provisions, § 5 of S.B. 123 (149 v —), following RC § 4501.01.

## § 4507.19 Grounds for cancellation of license or identification card.

The registrar of motor vehicles may cancel any driver's or commercial driver's license or identification card that was obtained fraudulently or unlawfully, was issued in error, or has been altered or willfully destroyed.

**HISTORY: GC § 6296-18a; 119 v 701; Bureau of Code Revision, 10-1-53; 130 v 1060 (Eff 8-9-63); 143 v H 381. Eff 7-1-89; 149 v S 123, § 1, eff. 1-1-04; 150 v H 230, § 1, eff. 9-16-04.**

The effective date is set by section 4 of S.B. 123.

See provisions, § 5 of S.B. 123 (149 v —), following RC § 4501.01.

## § 4507.20 Examination of licensee's competency.

The registrar of motor vehicles, when the registrar has good cause to believe that the holder of a driver's or commercial driver's license is incompetent or otherwise not qualified to be licensed, shall send a written notice to the licensee's last known address, requiring the licensee to submit to a driver's license examination, a physical examination, or both, or a commercial driver's license examination within the time indicated on the notice. The physical examination may be conducted by any individual authorized by the Revised Code to do so, including a physician assistant, a clinical nurse specialist, a certified nurse practitioner, or a certified nurse-midwife. Any written documentation of the physical examination shall be completed by the individual who conducted the examination.

Upon the conclusion of the examination, the registrar may suspend the license of the person, may permit the licensee to retain the license, or may issue the licensee a restricted license. Refusal or neglect of the licensee to submit to the examination is ground for suspension of the licensee's license.

A physician licensed under Chapter 4731. of the Revised Code may submit a report to the registrar stating that in the physician's professional opinion the holder of a driver's or commercial driver's license may be incompetent or otherwise not qualified to operate safely a motor vehicle due to medical reasons. Any such report submitted to the registrar is confidential, is not a public record, and is not subject to disclosure under section 149.43 of the Revised Code.

**HISTORY: GC § 6296-18b; 119 v 701; Bureau of Code Revision, 10-1-53; 129 v 1493 (Eff 9-9-61); 132 v H 135 (Eff 12-9-67); 141 v S 356 (Eff 9-24-86); 143 v H 381 (Eff 7-1-89); 144 v S 331 (Eff 11-13-92); 149 v S 245, § 1. Eff 3-31-2003; 149 v S 123, § 1, eff. 1-1-04; 150 v H 230, § 1, eff. 9-16-04.**

The effective date is set by section 4 of S.B. 123.

See provisions, § 5 of S.B. 123 (149 v —), following RC § 4501.01.

### [APPLICATION]

## § 4507.21 Application for and issuance of license.

(A) Each applicant for a driver's license shall file an application in the office of the registrar of motor vehicles or of a deputy registrar.

(B)(1) Each person under eighteen years of age applying for a driver's license issued in this state shall present satisfactory evidence of having successfully completed any one of the following:

(a) A driver education course approved by the state department of education.

(b) A driver training course approved by the director of public safety.

(c) A driver training course comparable to a driver education or driver training course described in division (B) (1) (a) or (b) of this section and administered by a branch of the armed forces of the United States and completed by the applicant while residing outside this state for the purpose of being with or near any person serving in the armed forces of the United States.

(2) Each person under eighteen years of age applying for a driver's license also shall present, on a form prescribed by the registrar, an affidavit signed by an eligible adult attesting that the person has acquired at least fifty hours of actual driving experience, with at least ten of those hours being at night.

(C) If the registrar or deputy registrar determines that the applicant is entitled to the driver's license, it shall be issued. If the application shows that the applicant's license has been previously canceled or suspended, the deputy registrar shall forward the application to the registrar, who shall determine whether the license shall be granted.

(D) All applications shall be filed in duplicate, and the deputy registrar issuing the license shall immediately forward to the office of the registrar the original copy of the application, together with the duplicate copy of the certificate, if issued. The registrar shall prescribe rules as to the manner in which the deputy registrar files and maintains the applications and other records. The registrar shall file every application for a driver's or commercial driver's license and index them by name and number, and shall maintain a suitable record of all licenses issued, all convictions and bond forfeitures, all applications for licenses denied, and all licenses that have been suspended or canceled.

(E) For purposes of section 2313.06 of the Revised Code, the registrar shall maintain accurate and current lists of the residents of each county who are eighteen years of age or older, have been issued, on and after January 1, 1984, driver's or commercial driver's licenses that are valid and current, and would be electors if they were registered to vote, regardless of whether they actually are registered to vote. The lists shall contain the names, addresses, dates of birth, duration of residence in this state, citizenship status, and social security numbers, if the numbers are available, of the licensees, and may contain any other information that the registrar considers suitable.

(F) Each person under eighteen years of age applying for a motorcycle operator's endorsement or a restricted license enabling the applicant to operate a motorcycle shall present satisfactory evidence of having completed the courses of instruction in the motorcycle safety and education program described in section 4508.08 of the Revised Code or a comparable course of instruction administered by a branch of the armed forces of the United States and completed by the applicant while residing outside this state for the purpose of being with or near any person serving in the armed forces of the United States. If the registrar or deputy registrar then determines that the applicant is entitled to the endorsement or restricted license, it shall be issued.

(G) No person shall knowingly make a false statement in an affidavit presented in accordance with division (B)(2) of this section.

(H) As used in this section, "eligible adult" means any of the following persons:

(1) A parent, guardian, or custodian of the applicant;

(2) A person over the age of twenty-one who acts in loco parentis of the applicant and who maintains proof of financial responsibility with respect to the operation of a motor vehicle owned by the applicant or with respect to the applicant's operation of any motor vehicle.

(I) Whoever violates division (G) of this section is guilty of a minor misdemeanor and shall be fined one hundred dollars.

**HISTORY: GC § 6296-19; 116 v PtII, 33, § 19; 119 v 701; Bureau of Code Revision, 10-1-53; 132 v H 380 (Eff 1-1-68); 135 v S 313 (Eff 7-26-74); 140 v H 183 (Eff 10-1-84); 141 v H 291 (Eff 3-11-87); 143 v H 381 (Eff 7-1-89); 144 v S 98 (Eff 11-12-92); 145 v S 96 (Eff 5-10-94); 147 v S 35 (Eff 1-1-99); 149 v H 407. Eff 10-11-2002; 149 v S 123, § 1, eff. 1-1-04.**

The effective date is set by section 4 of S.B. 123.

See provisions, § 5 of S.B. 123 (149 v —), following RC § 4501.01.

## § 4507.212 Statement of proof of financial responsibility; warning form.

(A) As used in this section, "motor vehicle" has the same meaning as in section 4509.01 of the Revised Code.

(B) An application for a driver's, commercial driver's, restricted, or probationary license, or renewal of such license shall contain a statement, to be signed by the applicant, that does all of the following:

(1) States that the applicant maintains, or has maintained on his behalf, proof of financial responsibility at the time of application, and will not operate a motor vehicle in this state, unless he maintains, or has maintained on his behalf, proof of financial responsibility;

(2) Contains a brief summary of the purposes and operation of section 4509.101 [4509.10.1] of the Revised Code, the rights and duties of the applicant under that section, and the penalties for violation of that section;

(3) Warns the applicant that the financial responsibility law does not prevent the possibility that the applicant may be involved in an accident with an owner or operator of a motor vehicle who is without proof of financial responsibility.

(C) The registrar of motor vehicles shall prescribe the form of the statement, and the manner in which the statement shall be presented to the applicant. The statement shall be designed to enable the applicant to retain a copy of it.

(D) Nothing within this section shall be construed to excuse a violation of section 4509.101 [4509.10.1] of the Revised Code.

(E) At the time a person submits an application for a driver's, commercial driver's, restricted, or probationary license, or renewal of such a license, the applicant also shall be furnished with a form that lists in plain language all the possible penalties to which the applicant could be subject for a violation of the financial responsibility law, including driver's license suspensions; all fees, including nonvoluntary compliance and reinstatement fees; and vehicle immobilization or impoundment. The applicant shall sign the form, which shall be submitted along with the application. The form shall be retained by the registrar or deputy registrar who issues the license or renewal or his successor for a period of two years from the date of issuance of the license or renewal. The registrar shall prescribe the manner in which the form shall be presented to the applicant, and the format of the form, which shall be such that the applicant can retain a copy of it.

**HISTORY: 139 v S 250 (Eff 1-1-84); 140 v H 767 (Eff 8-1-84); 143 v H 381 (Eff 7-1-89); 145 v S 20. Eff 10-20-94.**

## § 4507.22 Transmission of application with report of findings to registrar.

If the deputy registrar finds that an applicant is not entitled to an identification card or a driver's license, he shall transmit to the registrar of motor vehicles the original of the application together with the written report of his findings and recommendations in connection with such application. Upon receipt thereof, the registrar shall review the findings and recommendations and determine whether the application shall be granted, and report his findings to the deputy registrar and the applicant. If the registrar determines that the application should be granted, he shall thereupon notify the deputy registrar, who shall forthwith issue the license or card.

**HISTORY: GC § 6296-20; 116 v PtII, 33, § 20; Bureau of Code Revision, 10-1-53; 136 v S 435 (Eff 8-24-76); 143 v H 381. Eff 7-1-89.**

### [FEES; ORDERS]

## § 4507.23 License fees; lamination fees.

(A) Except as provided in division (I) of this section, each application for a temporary instruction permit and examination shall be accompanied by a fee of five dollars.

(B) Except as provided in division (I) of this section, each application for a driver's license made by a person who previously held such a license and whose license has expired not more than two years prior to the date of application, and who is required under this chapter to give an actual demonstration of the person's ability to drive, shall be accompanied by a fee of three dollars in addition to any other fees.

(C)(1) Except as provided in divisions (E) and (I) of this section, each application for a driver's license, or motorcycle operator's endorsement, or renewal of a driver's license shall be accompanied by a fee of six dollars.

(2) Except as provided in division (I) of this section, each application for a duplicate driver's license shall be accompanied by a fee of seven dollars and fifty cents. The duplicate driver's licenses issued under this section shall be distributed by the deputy registrar in accordance with rules adopted by the registrar of motor vehicles.

(D) Except as provided in division (I) of this section, each application for a motorized bicycle license or duplicate thereof shall be accompanied by a fee of two dollars and fifty cents.

(E) Except as provided in division (I) of this section, each application for a driver's license or renewal of a driver's license that will be issued to a person who is less than twenty-one years of age shall be accompanied by whichever of the following fees is applicable:

(1) If the person is sixteen years of age or older, but less than seventeen years of age, a fee of seven dollars and twenty-five cents;

(2) If the person is seventeen years of age or older, but less than eighteen years of age, a fee of six dollars;

(3) If the person is eighteen years of age or older, but less than nineteen years of age, a fee of four dollars and seventy-five cents;

(4) If the person is nineteen years of age or older, but less than twenty years of age, a fee of three dollars and fifty cents;

(5) If the person is twenty years of age or older, but less than twenty-one years of age, a fee of two dollars and twenty-five cents.

(F) Neither the registrar nor any deputy registrar shall charge a fee in excess of one dollar and fifty cents for laminating a driver's license, motorized bicycle license, or temporary instruction permit identification cards as required by sections 4507.13 and 4511.521 [4511.52.1] of the Revised Code. A deputy registrar laminating a driver's license, motorized bicycle license, or temporary instruction permit identification cards shall retain the entire amount of the fee charged for lamination, less the actual cost to the registrar of the laminating materials used for that lamination, as specified in the contract executed by the bureau for the laminating materials and laminating equipment. The deputy registrar shall forward the amount of the cost of the laminating materials to the registrar for deposit as provided in this section.

(G) Except as provided in division (I) of this section, each transaction described in divisions (A), (B), (C), (D), and (E) of this section shall be accompanied by an additional fee of twelve dollars. The additional fee is for the purpose of defraying the department of public safety's costs associated with the administration and enforcement of the motor vehicle and traffic laws of Ohio.

(H) At the time and in the manner provided by section 4503.10 of the Revised Code, the deputy registrar shall transmit the fees collected under divisions (A), (B), (C), (D), and (E), those portions of the fees specified in and collected under division (F), and the additional fee under division (G) of this section to the registrar. The registrar shall pay two dollars and fifty cents of each fee collected under divisions (A), (B), (C)(1) and (2), (D), and (E)(1) to (4) of this section, and the entire fee collected under division (E)(5) of this section, into the state highway safety fund established in section 4501.06 of the Revised Code, and such fees shall be used for the sole purpose of supporting driver licensing activities. The registrar also shall pay five dollars of each fee collected under division (C)(2) of this section and the entire fee collected under division (G) of this section into the state highway safety fund created in section 4501.06 of the Revised Code. The remaining fees collected by the registrar under this section shall be paid into the state bureau of motor vehicles fund established in section 4501.25 of the Revised Code.

(I) A disabled veteran who has a service-connected disability rated at one hundred per cent by the veterans' administration may apply to the registrar or a deputy registrar for the issuance to that veteran, without the payment of any fee prescribed in this section, of any of the following items:

(1) A temporary instruction permit and examination;

(2) A new, renewal, or duplicate driver's or commercial driver's license;

(3) A motorcycle operator's endorsement;

(4) A motorized bicycle license or duplicate thereof;

(5) Lamination of a driver's license, motorized bicycle license, or temporary instruction permit identification card as provided in division (F) of this section.

An application made under division (I) of this section shall be accompanied by such documentary evidence of disability as the registrar may require by rule.

**HISTORY: GC § 6296-22; 116 v PtII, 33, § 22; 117 v 393; 119 v 701; 123 v 246; Bureau of Code Revision, 10-1-53; 125 v 1135; 129 v 381 (Eff 7-1-62); 132 v H 380 (Eff 1-1-68); 133 v H 113 (Eff 9-12-69); 137 v S 100 (Eff 4-1-78); 137 v S 393 (Eff 5-12-78); 137 v H 215 (Eff 12-12-78); 138 v H 204 (Eff 7-30-79); 140 v H 373 (Eff 9-19-83); 142 v H 171 (Eff 7-1-87); 142 v S 1 (Eff 11-28-88); 143 v H 381 (Eff 7-1-89); 143 v S 131 (Eff 7-25-90); 144 v H 134 (Eff 10-10-91); 145 v H 154 (Eff 6-30-93); 146 v H 107 (Eff 6-30-95); 146 v H 353 (Eff 9-17-96); 147 v H 144 (Eff 10-14-97); 149 v H 94. Eff 9-5-2001; 150 v H 87, § 1, eff. 6-30-03; 150 v H 54, § 1, eff. 4-7-04; 153 v H 2, § 101.01, eff. 7-1-09; 153 v H 1, § 101.01, eff. 7-17-09; 2011 HB 114, § 101.01, eff. June 29, 2011.**

Acts 2011, HB 114, § 806.10 provides: "The items of law contained in this act, and their applications, are severable. If any item of law contained in this act, or if any application of any item of law contained in this act, is held invalid, the invalidity does not affect other items of law contained in this act and their applications that can be given effect without the invalid item or application."

The effective date is set by § 812.20 of 153 v H 1.

The effective date is set by § 812.10 of 153 v H 2.

The effective date is set by section 26 of H.B. 87.

## § 4507.231 Request for donations to second chance trust fund.

In addition to the fees collected under section 4507.23 of the Revised Code, the registrar or deputy registrar of motor vehicles shall ask each person applying for or renewing a driver's license, motorcycle operator's endorsement, or duplicate whether the person wishes to make a one-dollar voluntary contribution to the second chance trust fund established under section 2108.34 of the Revised Code. The registrar or deputy registrar shall also make available to the person informational material provided by the department of health on the importance of organ, tissue, and eye donation.

All donations collected under this section during each month shall be forwarded by the registrar or deputy registrar not later than the fifth day of the immediately following month to the treasurer of state, who shall deposit them in the second chance trust fund.

**HISTORY: 146 v S 300. Eff 7-1-97; 152 v H 529, § 1, eff. 4-7-09.**

The effective date is set by section 3 of SB 300.

## § 4507.232 "Student driver" sticker or banner.

When the registrar of motor vehicles or a deputy registrar issues a temporary instruction permit under this chapter, the registrar or deputy registrar also shall issue to the applicant a sticker or banner that reads "student driver." When the holder of the temporary instruction permit operates a motor vehicle, the sticker or banner may be displayed on the motor vehicle to inform other motor vehicle operators that the motor vehicle is being operated by a holder of a temporary instruction permit, but such display is not required.

The sticker or banner may be displayed on a side window or the rear window of the motor vehicle notwithstanding section 4513.24 and division (F) of section 4513.241 [4513.24.1] of the Revised Code or any rule adopted thereunder.

The registrar shall determine the size of the sticker or banner, which shall not exceed four inches in height by twelve inches in length, and the material and all other properties of the sticker or banner, but shall select a material so that the sticker or banner can be transferred readily from one motor vehicle to another.

**HISTORY: 150 v H 54, § 1, eff. 4-7-04.**

## § 4507.24 Fees collected by registrar or deputy registrar; portions paid to bureau of motor vehicles fund and highway safety fund.

(A) Except as provided in division (C) of this section, the registrar of motor vehicles or a deputy registrar may collect a fee not to exceed the following:

(1) Four dollars and fifty cents commencing on January 1, 2004, and six dollars and twenty-five cents commencing on October 1, 2009, for each application for renewal of a driver's license received by the deputy registrar, when the applicant is required to submit to a screening of the applicant's vision under section 4507.12 of the Revised Code;

(2) Three dollars and fifty cents commencing on January 1, 2004, for each application for a driver's license, or motorized bicycle license, or for renewal of such a license, received by the deputy registrar, when the applicant is not required to submit to a screening of the applicant's vision under section 4507.12 of the Revised Code.

(B) The fees prescribed by division (A) of this section shall be in addition to the fee for a temporary instruction permit and examination, a driver's license, a motorized bicycle license, or duplicates thereof. The fees retained by a deputy registrar shall compensate the deputy registrar for the deputy registrar's services, for office and rental expense, and for costs as provided in division (D) of this section, as are necessary for the proper discharge of the deputy registrar's duties under sections 4507.01 to 4507.39 of the Revised Code.

(C) A disabled veteran who has a service-connected disability rated at one hundred per cent by the veterans' administration is required to pay the applicable fee prescribed in division (A) of this section if the disabled veteran submits an application for a driver's license or motorized bicycle license or a renewal of either of these licenses to a deputy registrar who is acting as a deputy registrar pursuant to a contract with the registrar that is in effect on the effective date of this amendment. The disabled veteran also is required to submit with the disabled veteran's application such documentary evidence of disability as the registrar may require by rule.

A disabled veteran who submits an application described in this division is not required to pay either of the fees prescribed in division (A) of this section if the disabled veteran submits the application to a deputy registrar who is acting as a deputy registrar pursuant to a contract with the registrar that is executed after the effective date of this amendment. The disabled veteran still is required to submit with the disabled veteran's application such documentary evidence of disability as the registrar may require by rule.

A disabled veteran who submits an application described in this division directly to the registrar is not required to pay either of the fees prescribed in division (A) of this section if the disabled veteran submits with the disabled veteran's application such documentary evidence of disability as the registrar may require by rule.

(D)(1) Each deputy registrar shall transmit to the registrar of motor vehicles, at such time and in such manner as the registrar shall require by rule, an amount of each fee collected under division (A)(1) of this section as shall be determined by the registrar. The registrar shall pay all such moneys so received into the state bureau of motor vehicles fund created in section 4501.25 of the Revised Code.

(2) Commencing on October 1, 2009, each deputy registrar shall transmit one dollar and seventy-five cents of each fee collected under division (A)(1) of this section to the registrar at the time and in the manner provided by section 4503.10 of the Revised Code. The registrar shall deposit all moneys received under division (D)(2) of this section into the state highway safety fund established in section 4501.06 of the Revised Code.

**HISTORY: GC § 6296-23; 116 v PtII, 33, § 23; 119 v 701; 123 v 246; Bureau of Code Revision, 10-1-53; 132 v S 484 (Eff 6-11-68); 137 v H 3 (Eff 1-1-79); 137 v S 393 (Eff 5-12-78); 138 v H 656 (Eff 1-1-80); 139 v H 457 (Eff 2-11-82); 140 v H 58 (Eff 3-1-85); 141 v H 201 (Eff 7-1-85); 141 v S 269 (Eff 3-13-86); 142 v H 419 (Eff 7-1-87); 142 v S 1 (Eff 11-28-88); 143 v H 381 (Eff 7-1-89); 145 v H 154 (Eff 6-30-93); 146 v H 107 (Eff 6-30-95); 147 v H 144 (Eff 10-14-97); 149 v H 94. Eff 6-6-2001; 153 v H 2, § 101.01, eff. 7-1-09; 153 v H 1, § 101.01, eff. 10-16-09.**

The effective date is set by § 812.10 of 153 v H 1.

The effective date is set by § 812.10 of 153 v H 2.
The effective date is set by section 206 of HB 94.

### § 4507.25 Amended and renumbered RC § 4501.34 in 150 v S 123. Eff 1-1-04.

See provisions, § 5 of S.B. 123 (149 v —), following RC § 4501.01.

### § 4507.26 Amended and renumbered RC § 4501.351 in 150 v S 123. Eff 1-1-04.

### § 4507.27 Amended and renumbered RC § 4501.36 in 150 v S 123. Eff 1-1-04.

See provisions, § 5 of S.B. 123 (149 v —), following RC § 4501.01.

### § 4507.28 Amended and renumbered RC § 4501.37 in 150 v S 123. Eff 1-1-04.

See provisions, § 5 of S.B. 123 (149 v —), following RC § 4501.01.

### § 4507.29 Amended and renumbered RC § 4501.38 in 150 v S 123. Eff 1-1-04.

See provisions, § 5 of S.B. 123 (149 v —), following RC § 4501.01.

## [PROHIBITIONS]

### § 4507.30 Prohibited acts.

No person shall do any of the following:

(A) Display, or cause or permit to be displayed, or possess any identification card, driver's or commercial driver's license, temporary instruction permit, or commercial driver's license temporary instruction permit knowing the same to be fictitious, or to have been canceled, suspended, or altered;

(B) Lend to a person not entitled thereto, or knowingly permit a person not entitled thereto to use any identification card, driver's or commercial driver's license, temporary instruction permit, or commercial driver's license temporary instruction permit issued to the person so lending or permitting the use thereof;

(C) Display, or represent as one's own, any identification card, driver's or commercial driver's license, temporary instruction permit, or commercial driver's license temporary instruction permit not issued to the person so displaying the same;

(D) Fail to surrender to the registrar of motor vehicles, upon the registrar's demand, any identification card, driver's or commercial driver's license, temporary instruction permit, or commercial driver's license temporary instruction permit that has been suspended or canceled;

(E) In any application for an identification card, driver's or commercial driver's license, temporary instruction permit, or commercial driver's license temporary instruction permit, or any renewal or duplicate thereof, knowingly conceal a material fact, or present any physician's statement required under section 4507.08 or 4507.081 of the Revised Code when knowing the same to be false or fictitious.

(F) Whoever violates any division of this section is guilty of a misdemeanor of the first degree.

**HISTORY: GC § 6296-24; 116 v PtII, 33, § 24; Bureau of Code Revision, 10-1-53; 129 v 1491 (Eff 9-9-61); 136 v S 435 (Eff 8-24-76); 137 v H 71 (Eff 8-26-77); 143 v H 381. Eff 7-1-89; 149 v S 123, § 1, eff. 1-1-04.**

The effective date is set by section 4 of S.B. 123.
See provisions, § 5 of S.B. 123 (149 v —), following RC § 4501.01.

### § 4507.31 Prohibition against permitting minor to drive vehicle.

(A) No person shall cause or knowingly permit any minor to drive a motor vehicle upon a highway as an operator, unless the minor has first obtained a license or permit to drive a motor vehicle under this chapter.

(B) Whoever violates this section is guilty of a misdemeanor of the first degree.

**HISTORY: GC § 6296-26; 116 v PtII, 33, § 26; Bureau of Code Revision. Eff 10-1-53; 149 v S 123, § 1, eff. 1-1-04.**

The effective date is set by section 4 of S.B. 123.
See provisions, § 5 of S.B. 123 (149 v —), following RC § 4501.01.

### § 4507.321 Employment of a minor to operate taxicab prohibited.

(A) Notwithstanding the definition of "chauffeur" in section 4501.01 of the Revised Code, no person shall employ any minor for the purpose of operating a taxicab.

(B) Whoever violates this section is guilty of a misdemeanor of the first degree.

**HISTORY: 133 v S 410 (Eff 11-25-69); 140 v H 37. Eff 6-22-84; 149 v S 123, § 1, eff. 1-1-04.**

The effective date is set by section 4 of S.B. 123.
See provisions, § 5 of S.B. 123 (149 v —), following RC § 4501.01.

### § 4507.33 Amended and renumbered RC § 4511.203 in 149 v SB 123. Eff 1-1-04.

See provisions, § 5 of S.B. 123 (149 v —), following RC § 4501.01.

### § 4507.34 Amended and renumbered RC § 4510.15 in 149 v SB 123. Eff 1-1-04.

See provisions, § 5 of S.B. 123 (149 v —), following RC § 4501.01.

### § 4507.35 Duty to display license or furnish satisfactory proof of license.

(A) The operator of a motor vehicle shall display the operator's driver's license, or furnish satisfactory proof that the operator has a driver's license, upon demand of any peace officer or of any person damaged or injured in any collision in which the licensee may be involved. When a demand is properly made and the operator has the operator's driver's license on or about the operator's person, the operator shall not refuse to display the license. A person's failure to furnish satisfactory evidence that the person is licensed under this chapter when the person does not have the person's license on or about the person's person shall be prima-facie evidence of the person's not having obtained a driver's license.

(B)(1) Except as provided in division (B)(2) of this section, whoever violates this section is guilty of an unclassified misdemeanor. When the offense is an unclassified misdemeanor, the offender shall be sentenced pursuant to sections 2929.21 to 2929.28 of the Revised Code, except that the offender shall not be sentenced to a jail term; the offender shall not be sentenced to a community residential sanction pursuant to section 2929.26 of the Revised Code; notwithstanding division (A)(2)(a) of section 2929.28 of the Revised Code, the offender may be fined up to one thousand dollars; and, notwithstanding division (A)(3) of section 2929.27 of the Revised Code, the offender may be ordered pursuant to division (C) of that section to serve a term of community service of up to five hundred hours. The failure of an offender to complete a term of community service imposed by the court may be punished as indirect criminal contempt under division (A) of section 2705.02 of the Revised Code that may be filed in the underlying case.

(2) If, within three years of the offense, the offender previously has been convicted of or pleaded guilty to two or more violations of this section or a substantially equivalent municipal ordinance, the offense is a misdemeanor of the first degree.

**HISTORY: Bureau of Code Revision, 10-1-53; 143 v H 381. Eff 7-1-89; 149 v S 123, § 1, eff. 1-1-04; 2011 HB 5, § 1, eff. Sept. 23, 2011.**

The effective date is set by section 4 of S.B. 123.

See provisions, § 5 of S.B. 123 (149 v —), following RC § 4501.01.

## § 4507.36 Prohibition against false statements.

(A) No person shall knowingly make a false statement to any matter or thing required by this chapter.

(B) Whoever violates this section is guilty of a misdemeanor of the first degree.

**HISTORY: GC § 6296-25; 116 v PtII, 33, § 25; 119 v 701; Bureau of Code Revision, 10-1-53; 126 v 253. Eff 9-13-55; 149 v S 123, § 1, eff. 1-1-04.**

The effective date is set by section 4 of S.B. 123.

See provisions, § 5 of S.B. 123 (149 v —), following RC § 4501.01.

## § 4507.361 Amended and renumbered RC § 4510.161 in 149 v SB 123. Eff 1-1-04.

See provisions, § 5 of S.B. 123 (149 v —), following RC § 4501.01.

## § 4507.38 Amended and renumbered RC § 4510.41 in 149 v SB 123. Eff 1-1-04.

See provisions, § 5 of S.B. 123 (149 v —), following RC § 4501.01.

## § 4507.45 Reinstatement fee in certain cases.

If a person's driver's license, commercial driver's license, or nonresident operating privilege is suspended, disqualified, or canceled for an indefinite period of time or for a period of at least ninety days, and if at the end of the period of suspension, disqualification, or cancellation the person is eligible to have the license or privilege reinstated, the registrar of motor vehicles or an eligible deputy registrar shall collect a reinstatement fee of forty dollars when the person requests reinstatement. In addition, each deputy registrar shall collect a service fee of ten dollars to compensate the deputy registrar for services performed under this section. The deputy registrar shall retain eight dollars of the service fee and shall transmit the reinstatement fee, plus two dollars of the service fee, to the registrar in the manner the registrar shall determine. However, the registrar or an eligible deputy registrar shall not collect the fee prescribed by this section if a different driver's license, commercial driver's license, or nonresident operating privilege reinstatement fee is prescribed by law.

The registrar shall deposit ten dollars of each forty-dollar fee into the state treasury to the credit of the indigent defense support fund created by section 120.08 of the Revised Code and thirty dollars of each fee into the state treasury to the credit of the state bureau of motor vehicles fund created by section 4501.25 of the Revised Code.

**HISTORY: 147 v H 210. Eff 3-31-97; 149 v S 123, § 1, eff. 1-1-04; 153 v H 1, § 101.01, eff. 10-16-09; 2011 HB 114, § 101.01, eff. June 29, 2011.**

Acts 2011, HB 114, § 806.10 provides: "The items of law contained in this act, and their applications, are severable. If any item of law contained in this act, or if any application of any item of law contained in this act, is held invalid, the invalidity does not affect other items of law contained in this act and their applications that can be given effect without the invalid item or application."

The effective date is set by § 812.10 of 153 v H 1.

The effective date is set by section 4 of S.B. 123.

See provisions, § 5 of S.B. 123 (149 v —), following RC § 4501.01.

### [IDENTIFICATION CARD]

## § 4507.50 Issuance of identification card or temporary card.

(A) The registrar of motor vehicles or a deputy registrar, upon receipt of an application filed in compliance with section 4507.51 of the Revised Code by any person who is a resident or a temporary resident of this state and, except as otherwise provided in this section, is not licensed as an operator of a motor vehicle in this state or another licensing jurisdiction, and, except as provided in division (B) of this section, upon receipt of a fee of three dollars and fifty cents, shall issue an identification card to that person.

Any person who is a resident or temporary resident of this state whose Ohio driver's or commercial driver's license has been suspended or canceled, upon application in compliance with section 4507.51 of the Revised Code and, except as provided in division (B) of this section, payment of a fee of three dollars and fifty cents, may be issued a temporary identification card. The temporary identification card shall be identical to an identification card, except that it shall be printed on its face with a statement that the card is valid during the effective dates of the suspension or cancellation of the cardholder's license, or until the birthday of the cardholder in the fourth year after the date on which it is issued, whichever is shorter. The cardholder shall surrender the identification card to the registrar or any deputy registrar before the cardholder's driver's or commercial driver's license is restored or reissued.

Except as provided in division (B) of this section, the deputy registrar shall be allowed a fee of two dollars and seventy-five cents commencing on July 1, 2001, three dollars and twenty-five cents commencing on January 1, 2003, and three dollars and fifty cents commencing on January 1, 2004, for each identification card issued under this section. The fee allowed to the deputy registrar shall be in addition to the fee for issuing an identification card.

Neither the registrar nor any deputy registrar shall charge a fee in excess of one dollar and fifty cents for laminating an identification card or temporary identification card. A deputy registrar laminating such a card shall retain the entire amount of the fee charged for lamination, less the actual cost to the registrar of the laminating materials used for that lamination, as specified in the contract executed by the bureau for the laminating materials and laminating equipment. The deputy registrar shall forward the amount of the cost of the laminating materials to the registrar for deposit as provided in this section.

The fee collected for issuing an identification card under this section, except the fee allowed to the deputy registrar, shall be paid into the state treasury to the credit of the state bureau of motor vehicles fund created in section 4501.25 of the Revised Code.

(B) A disabled veteran who has a service-connected disability rated at one hundred per cent by the veterans' administration may apply to the registrar or a deputy registrar for the issuance to that veteran of an identification card or a temporary identification card under this section without payment of any fee prescribed in division (A) of this section, including any lamination fee.

An application made under division (B) of this section shall be accompanied by such documentary evidence of disability as the registrar may require by rule.

**HISTORY: 136 v S 435 (Eff 8-24-76); 137 v H 3 (Eff 1-1-79); 137 v S 221 (Eff 11-23-77); 137 v H 90 (Eff 1-17-78); 138 v H 656 (Eff 1-1-80); 139 v H 457 (Eff 2-11-82); 141 v H 201 (Eff 7-1-85); 141 v S 269 (Eff 3-13-86); 141 v H 165 (Eff 8-1-86); 142 v H 419 (Eff 7-1-87); 142 v H 165 (Eff 6-29-88); 142 v S 1 (Eff 11-28-88); 143 v H 381 (Eff 7-1-89); 143 v S 131 (Eff 7-25-90); 145 v H 154 (Eff 6-30-93); 146 v H 107 (Eff 6-30-95); 147 v S 60 (Eff 10-21-97); 147 v S 213 (Eff 7-29-98); 149 v H 94. Eff 6-6-2001; 149 v S 123, § 1, eff. 1-1-04; 150 v H 230, § 1, eff. 9-16-04.**

The effective date is set by section 4 of S.B. 123.

See provisions, § 5 of S.B. 123 (149 v —), following RC § 4501.01.

## § 4507.501 Request for donation to second chance trust fund.

In addition to the fees collected under section 4507.50 of the Revised Code, the registrar or deputy registrar of motor vehicles shall ask each applicant for an identification card or duplicate under section 4507.51 of the Revised Code whether the person wishes to make a one-dollar voluntary contribution to the second chance trust fund established under section 2108.34 of the Revised Code. The registrar or deputy registrar shall also make available to the person informational material provided by the department of health on the importance of organ, tissue, and eye donation.

All donations collected under this section during each month shall be forwarded by the registrar or deputy registrar not later than the fifth day of the immediately following month to the treasurer of state, who shall deposit them in the second chance trust fund.

**HISTORY: 146 v S 300. Eff 7-1-97; 152 v H 529, § 1, eff. 4-7-09.**

The effective date is set by section 3 of SB 300.

## § 4507.51 Application for identification card.

(A)(1) Every application for an identification card or duplicate shall be made on a form furnished by the registrar of motor vehicles, shall be signed by the applicant, and by the applicant's parent or guardian if the applicant is under eighteen years of age, and shall contain the following information pertaining to the applicant: name, date of birth, sex, general description including the applicant's height, weight, hair color, and eye color, address, and social security number. The application also shall state whether an applicant wishes to certify willingness to make an anatomical gift under section 2108.05 of the Revised Code and shall include information about the requirements of sections 2108.01 to 2108.29 of the Revised Code that apply to persons who are less than eighteen years of age. The statement regarding willingness to make such a donation shall be given no consideration in the decision of whether to issue an identification card. Each applicant shall be photographed in color at the time of making application.

(2)(a) The application also shall state whether the applicant has executed a valid durable power of attorney for health care pursuant to sections 1337.11 to 1337.17 of the Revised Code or has executed a declaration governing the use or continuation, or the withholding or withdrawal, of life-sustaining treatment pursuant to sections 2133.01 to 2133.15 of the Revised Code and, if the applicant has executed either type of instrument, whether the applicant wishes the identification card issued to indicate that the applicant has executed the instrument.

(b) On and after October 7, 2009, the application also shall state whether the applicant is a veteran, active duty, or reservist of the armed forces of the United States and, if the applicant is such, whether the applicant wishes the identification card issued to indicate that the applicant is a veteran, active duty, or reservist of the armed forces of the United States by a military designation on the identification card.

(3) The registrar or deputy registrar, in accordance with section 3503.11 of the Revised Code, shall register as an elector any person who applies for an identification card or duplicate if the applicant is eligible and wishes to be registered as an elector. The decision of an applicant whether to register as an elector shall be given no consideration in the decision of whether to issue the applicant an identification card or duplicate.

(B) The application for an identification card or duplicate shall be filed in the office of the registrar or deputy registrar. Each applicant shall present documentary evidence as required by the registrar of the applicant's age and identity, and the applicant shall swear that all information given is true. An identification card issued by the department of rehabilitation and correction under section 5120.59 of the Revised Code shall be sufficient documentary evidence under this division upon verification of the applicant's social security number by the registrar or a deputy registrar. Upon issuing an identification card under this section for a person who has been issued an identification card under section 5120.59 of the Revised Code, the registrar or deputy registrar shall destroy the identification card issued under section 5120.59 of the Revised Code.

All applications for an identification card or duplicate shall be filed in duplicate, and if submitted to a deputy registrar, a copy shall be forwarded to the registrar. The registrar shall prescribe rules for the manner in which a deputy registrar is to file and maintain applications and other records. The registrar shall maintain a suitable, indexed record of all applications denied and cards issued or canceled.

(C) In addition to any other information it contains, on and after the date that is fifteen months after the effective date of this amendment, the form furnished by the registrar of motor vehicles for an application for an identification card or duplicate shall inform applicants that the applicant must present a copy of the applicant's DD-214 or an equivalent document in order to qualify to have the card or duplicate indicate that the applicant is an honorably discharged veteran of the armed forces of the United States based on a request made pursuant to division (A)(2)(b) of this section.

**HISTORY: 136 v S 435 (Eff 8-24-76); 137 v H 90 (Eff 1-17-78); 140 v S 302 (Eff 10-1-84); 142 v H 165 (Eff 6-29-88); 143 v H 381 (Eff 7-1-89); 143 v H 529 Eff (10-30-89); 143 v H 21 (Eff 3-27-91); 144 v H 427 (Eff 10-8-92); 145 v S 300 (Eff 1-1-95); 147 v H 354 (Eff 7-9-98); 147 v S 213. Eff 7-29-98; 150 v H 230, § 1, eff. 9-16-04; 152 v H 450, § 1, eff. 4-7-09; 152 v H 529, § 1, eff. 4-7-09; 152 v H 130, § 1, eff. 4-7-09; 153 v H 2, § 101.01, eff. 7-1-09; 2011 HB 86, § 1, eff. Sept. 30, 2011.**

The effective date is set by § 812.10 of 153 v H 2.

The provisions of § 815.20 of 153 v H 2 read in part as follows:

SECTION 815.20. The General Assembly, applying the principle stated in division (B) of section 1.52 of the Revised Code that amendments are to be harmonized if reasonably capable of simultaneous operation, finds that the following sections, presented in this act as composites of the sections as amended by the acts indicated, are the resulting versions of the sections in effect prior to the effective date of the sections as presented in this act:

° ° °

Section 4507.51 of the Revised Code as amended by Am. Sub. H.B. 130, Am. Sub. H.B. 450, and Sub. H.B. 529 of the 127th General Assembly.

° ° °

The provisions of § 10, H.B. 230 (150 v —), read as follows:

SECTION 10. ° ° ° Section 4507.51 of the Revised Code is presented in this act as a composite of the section as amended by both Sub. H.B. 354 and Am. Sub. S.B. 213 of the 122nd General Assembly. ° ° ° The General Assembly, applying the principle stated in division (B) of section 1.52 of the Revised Code that amendments are to be harmonized if reasonably capable of simultaneous operation, finds that each composite is the resulting version of the section in effect prior to the effective date of the section as presented in this act.

## § 4507.52 Contents and characteristics; expiration; renewal; surrender; duplicate or replacement; cancellation; card not to be required.

(A) Each identification card issued by the registrar of motor vehicles or a deputy registrar shall display a distinguishing number assigned to the cardholder, and shall display the following inscription:

"STATE OF OHIO IDENTIFICATION CARD

This card is not valid for the purpose of operating a motor vehicle. It is provided solely for the purpose of establishing the identity of the bearer described on the card, who currently is not licensed to operate a motor vehicle in the state of Ohio."

The identification card shall display substantially the same information as contained in the application and as described in division (A)(1) of section 4507.51 of the Revised Code, but shall not display the cardholder's social security number unless the cardholder specifically requests that the cardholder's social security number be displayed on the card. If federal law requires the cardholder's social security number to be displayed on the identification card, the social security number shall be displayed on the card notwithstanding this section. The identification card also shall display the color photograph of the cardholder. If the cardholder has executed a durable power of attorney for health care or a declaration governing the use or continuation, or the withholding or withdrawal, of life-sustaining treatment and has specified that the cardholder wishes the identification card to indicate that the cardholder has executed either type of instrument, the card also shall display any symbol chosen by the registrar to indicate that the cardholder has executed either type of instrument. On and after October 7, 2009, if the cardholder has specified that the cardholder wishes the identification card to indicate that the cardholder is a veteran, active duty, or reservist of the armed forces of the United States and has presented a copy of the cardholder's DD-214 form or an equivalent document, the card also shall display any symbol chosen by the registrar to indicate that the cardholder is a veteran, active duty, or reservist of the armed forces of the United States. The card shall be sealed in transparent plastic or similar material and shall be so designed as to prevent its reproduction or alteration without ready detection.

The identification card for persons under twenty-one years of age shall have characteristics prescribed by the registrar distinguishing it from that issued to a person who is twenty-one years of age or older, except that an identification card issued to a person who applies no more than thirty days before the applicant's twenty-first birthday shall have the characteristics of an identification card issued to a person who is twenty-one years of age or older.

Every identification card issued to a resident of this state shall expire, unless canceled or surrendered earlier, on the birthday of the cardholder in the fourth year after the date on which it is issued. Every identification card issued to a temporary resident shall expire in accordance with rules adopted by the registrar and is nonrenewable, but may be replaced with a new identification card upon the applicant's compliance with all applicable requirements. A cardholder may renew the cardholder's identification card within ninety days prior to the day on which it expires by filing an application and paying the prescribed fee in accordance with section 4507.50 of the Revised Code.

If a cardholder applies for a driver's or commercial driver's license in this state or another licensing jurisdiction, the cardholder shall surrender the cardholder's identification card to the registrar or any deputy registrar before the license is issued.

(B) If a card is lost, destroyed, or mutilated, the person to whom the card was issued may obtain a duplicate by doing both of the following:

(1) Furnishing suitable proof of the loss, destruction, or mutilation to the registrar or a deputy registrar;

(2) Filing an application and presenting documentary evidence under section 4507.51 of the Revised Code.

Any person who loses a card and, after obtaining a duplicate, finds the original, immediately shall surrender the original to the registrar or a deputy registrar.

A cardholder may obtain a replacement identification card that reflects any change of the cardholder's name by furnishing suitable proof of the change to the registrar or a deputy registrar and surrendering the cardholder's existing card.

When a cardholder applies for a duplicate or obtains a replacement identification card, the cardholder shall pay a fee of two dollars and fifty cents. A deputy registrar shall be allowed an additional fee of two dollars and seventy-five cents commencing on July 1, 2001, three dollars and twenty-five cents commencing on January 1, 2003, and three dollars and fifty cents commencing on January 1, 2004, for issuing a duplicate or replacement identification card. A disabled veteran who is a cardholder and has a service-connected disability rated at one hundred per cent by the veterans' administration may apply to the registrar or a deputy registrar for the issuance of a duplicate or replacement identification card without payment of any fee prescribed in this section, and without payment of any lamination fee if the disabled veteran would not be required to pay a lamination fee in connection with the issuance of an identification card or temporary identification card as provided in division (B) of section 4507.50 of the Revised Code.

A duplicate or replacement identification card shall expire on the same date as the card it replaces.

(C) The registrar shall cancel any card upon determining that the card was obtained unlawfully, issued in error, or was altered. The registrar also shall cancel any card that is surrendered to the registrar or to a deputy registrar after the holder has obtained a duplicate, replacement, or driver's or commercial driver's license.

(D)(1) No agent of the state or its political subdivisions shall condition the granting of any benefit, service, right, or privilege upon the possession by any person of an identification card. Nothing in this section shall preclude any publicly operated or franchised transit system from using an identification card for the purpose of granting benefits or services of the system.

(2) No person shall be required to apply for, carry, or possess an identification card.

(E) Except in regard to an identification card issued to a person who applies no more than thirty days before the applicant's twenty-first birthday, neither the registrar nor any deputy registrar shall issue an identification card to a person under twenty-one years of age that does not have the characteristics prescribed by the registrar distinguishing it from the identification card issued to persons who are twenty-one years of age or older.

(F) Whoever violates division (E) of this section is guilty of a minor misdemeanor.

**HISTORY: 136 v S 435 (Eff 8-24-76); 137 v H 90 (Eff 1-17-78); 142 v H 165 (Eff 6-29-88); 143 v H 381 (Eff 7-1-89); 143 v S 131 (Eff 7-25-90); 144 v H 134 (Eff 10-10-91); 144 v H 427 (Eff 10-8-92); 145 v H 580 (Eff 12-9-94); 146 v H 353 (Eff 9-17-96); 147 v S 60 (Eff 10-21-97); 147 v S 213 (Eff 7-29-98); 149 v H 94 (Eff 6-6-2001); 149 v H 299 (Eff 6-29-2001); 149 v H 46. Eff 2-1-2002; 149 v S 123, § 1, eff. 1-1-04; 152 v H 450, § 1, eff. 4-7-09; 153 v H 2, § 101.01, eff. 7-1-09.**

The effective date is set by § 812.10 of 153 v H 2.
The effective date is set by section 4 of S.B. 123.
See provisions, § 5 of S.B. 123 (149 v —), following RC § 4501.01.

## § 4507.53 Release of digitalized photographic records.

Digitalized photographic records of the department of public safety may be released only to state, local, or federal governmental agencies for criminal justice purposes and to any court.

**HISTORY: 145 v H 154. Eff 6-30-93; 150 v H 230, § 1, eff. 9-16-04.**

**Not analogous to former RC § 4507.53 (143 v S 71), repealed 143 v S 71, § 2, eff 11-2-91.**

## § 4507.54 Amended and renumbered RC § 4510.52 in 149 v SB 123. Eff 1-1-04.

See provisions, § 5 of S.B. 123 (149 v —), following RC § 4501.01.

## § 4507.55 Amended and renumbered RC § 4510.53 in 149 v SB 123. Eff 1-1-04.

See provisions, § 5 of S.B. 123 (149 v —), following RC § 4501.01.

### [DRIVER LICENSE COMPACT]

## § 4507.60 Amended and renumbered RC § 4510.61 in 149 v SB 123. Eff 1-1-04.

## § 4507.61 Amended and renumbered RC § 4510.62 in 149 v SB 123. Eff 1-1-04.

See provisions, § 5 of S.B. 123 (149 v —), following RC § 4501.01.

## § 4507.62 Amended and renumbered RC § 4510.63 in 149 v SB 123. Eff 1-1-04.

See provisions, § 5 of S.B. 123 (149 v —), following RC § 4501.01.

## § 4507.63 Amended and renumbered RC § 4510.64 in 149 v SB 123. Eff 1-1-04.

See provisions, § 5 of S.B. 123 (149 v —), following RC § 4501.01.

## § 4507.99 Penalty.

Unless another penalty is provided by the section that contains the provision violated or otherwise is provided by the laws of this state, whoever violates any provision of sections 4507.01 to 4507.081 [4507.08.1] or 4507.10 to

4507.37 of the Revised Code is guilty of a misdemeanor of the first degree.

**HISTORY: Bureau of Code Revision, 10-1-53; 125 v 903(1025) (Eff 10-1-53); 131 v 1088 (Eff 9-1-65); 139 v S 432 (Eff 3-16-83); 140 v H 767 (Eff 8-1-84); 140 v H 252 (Eff 4-4-85); 141 v S 356 (Eff 9-24-86); 142 v H 643 (Eff 3-17-89); 143 v H 329 (Eff 6-30-89); 143 v S 102 (Eff 9-15-89); 143 v H 381 (Eff 7-1-89); 143 v H 88 (Eff 3-13-90); 143 v S 131 (Eff 7-25-90); 143 v H 837 (Eff 7-25-90); 144 v H 134 (Eff 10-10-91); 144 v H 725 (Eff 4-16-93); 144 v S 275 (Eff 9-1-93); 145 v S 62, §§ 1, 4 (Eff 9-1-93); 145 v S 82 (Eff 5-4-94); 145 v S 20 (Eff 10-20-94); 146 v S 2 (Eff 7-1-96); 146 v H 676, § 1 (Eff 10-4-96); 146 v H 676, § 6 (Eff 5-15-97); 146 v H 438 (Eff 7-1-97); 147 v S 35 (Eff 7-1-98); 148 v S 180. Eff 3-22-2001; 149 v S 123, § 1, eff. 1-1-04; 150 v H 230, § 1, eff. 9-16-04.**

The effective date is set by section 4 of S.B. 123.

See provisions, § 5 of S.B. 123 (149 v —), following RC § 4501.01.

# CHAPTER 4509: FINANCIAL RESPONSIBILITY

Section



## [ACCIDENT REPORT]

### § 4509.06 Accident report concerning uninsured driver or owner.

(A) The driver of any motor vehicle which is in any manner involved in a motor vehicle accident within six months of the accident may forward a written report of the accident to the registrar of motor vehicles on a form prescribed by the registrar alleging that a driver or owner of any other vehicle involved in the accident was uninsured at the time of the accident.

(B) Upon receipt of the accident report, the registrar shall send a notice by regular mail to the driver and owner alleged to be uninsured requiring the person to give evidence that the person had proof of financial responsibility in effect at the time of the accident.

(C) Within thirty days after the mailing of the notice by the registrar, the driver of the vehicle alleged to be uninsured shall forward a report together with acceptable proof of financial responsibility to the registrar in a form prescribed by the registrar. The forwarding of the report by the owner of the motor vehicle involved in the accident is deemed compliance with this section by the driver. This section does not change or modify the duties of the driver or operator of a motor vehicle as set forth in section 4549.02 of the Revised Code.

(D) In accordance with sections 4509.01 to 4509.78 of the Revised Code, the registrar shall suspend the license of any person who fails to give acceptable proof of financial responsibility as required in this section.

**HISTORY: GC § 6298-17; 124 v 563; Bureau of Code Revision, 10-1-53; 133 v H 131 (Eff 7-25-69); 147 v H 210. Eff 3-31-97.**

The effective date is set by section 20 of HB 210.

### § 4509.07 Contents of accident report.

The report prescribed by the registrar of motor vehicles shall request only information sufficient to enable the registrar to administer and enforce the provisions of sections 4509.01 to 4509.78, inclusive of the Revised Code.

The driver or owner of a motor vehicle involved in an accident shall furnish such additional relevant information as the registrar requires.

**HISTORY: GC §§ 6298-18, 6298-19; 124 v 563; Bureau of Code Revision, 10-1-53; 125 v 383. Eff 10-15-53.**

### § 4509.08 Exception to report requirement.

A driver involved in a motor vehicle accident is not subject to section 4509.06 of the Revised Code if, during the time provided in such section, the driver is physically incapable of making a report, but in such event, the owner, if he were not the driver of the motor vehicle involved in the accident, shall within thirty days after learning of the accident make the report.

**HISTORY: GC § 6298-20; 124 v 563; Bureau of Code Revision, 10-1-53; 133 v H 131. Eff 7-25-69.**

### § 4509.10 Use of report.

The accident reports submitted pursuant to sections 4509.01 to 4509.78 of the Revised Code, shall be without prejudice to the person reporting and shall be for the confidential use of the registrar of motor vehicles, except that the registrar shall furnish a copy of such report to any person claiming to have been injured or damaged in a motor vehicle accident, or to his attorney, upon the receipt of a fee of one dollar and fifty cents for each search or report.

Motor vehicle accident reports shall not be subject to subpoena or be used as evidence in any trial, civil or criminal, arising out of the accident, except that in order to prove compliance or failure to comply with the accident reporting requirement the registrar shall furnish, upon demand of a court or any person who claims to have made an accident report, a certificate stating that a specified accident report has or has not been made to the registrar.

**HISTORY: GC § 6298-22; 124 v 563; Bureau of Code Revision, 10-1-53; 125 v 383 (Eff 10-15-53); 139 v H 102. Eff 7-1-81.**

## § 4509.101 Operation of motor vehicle without proof of financial responsibility prohibited; compliance fund; accident report.

(A)(1) No person shall operate, or permit the operation of, a motor vehicle in this state, unless proof of financial responsibility is maintained continuously throughout the registration period with respect to that vehicle, or, in the case of a driver who is not the owner, with respect to that driver's operation of that vehicle.

(2) Whoever violates division (A)(1) of this section shall be subject to the following civil penalties:

(a) Subject to divisions (A)(2)(b) and (c) of this section, a class E suspension of the person's driver's license, commercial driver's license, temporary instruction permit, probationary license, or nonresident operating privilege for the period of time specified in division (B)(5) of section 4510.02 of the Revised Code and impoundment of the person's license until the person complies with division (A)(5) of this section. The court may grant limited driving privileges to the person only if the person presents proof of financial responsibility and has complied with division (A)(5) of this section.

(b) If, within five years of the violation, the person's operating privileges are again suspended and the person's license again is impounded for a violation of division (A)(1) of this section, a class C suspension of the person's driver's license, commercial driver's license, temporary instruction permit, probationary license, or nonresident operating privilege for the period of time specified in division (B)(3) of section 4510.02 of the Revised Code. The court may grant limited driving privileges to the person only if the person presents proof of financial responsibility and has complied with division (A)(5) of this section, and no court may grant limited driving privileges for the first fifteen days of the suspension.

(c) If, within five years of the violation, the person's operating privileges are suspended and the person's license is impounded two or more times for a violation of division (A)(1) of this section, a class B suspension of the person's driver's license, commercial driver's license, temporary instruction permit, probationary license, or nonresident operating privilege for the period of time specified in division (B)(2) of section 4510.02 of the Revised Code. No court may grant limited driving privileges during the suspension.

(d) In addition to the suspension of an owner's license under division (A)(2)(a), (b), or (c) of this section, the suspension of the rights of the owner to register the motor vehicle and the impoundment of the owner's certificate of registration and license plates until the owner complies with division (A)(5) of this section.

(3) A person to whom this state has issued a certificate of registration for a motor vehicle or a license to operate a motor vehicle or who is determined to have operated any motor vehicle or permitted the operation in this state of a motor vehicle owned by the person shall be required to verify the existence of proof of financial responsibility covering the operation of the motor vehicle or the person's operation of the motor vehicle under any of the following circumstances:

(a) The person or a motor vehicle owned by the person is involved in a traffic accident that requires the filing of an accident report under section 4509.06 of the Revised Code.

(b) The person receives a traffic ticket indicating that proof of the maintenance of financial responsibility was not produced upon the request of a peace officer or state highway patrol trooper made in accordance with division (D)(2) of this section.

(c) Whenever, in accordance with rules adopted by the registrar, the person is randomly selected by the registrar and requested to provide such verification.

(4) An order of the registrar that suspends and impounds a license or registration, or both, shall state the date on or before which the person is required to surrender the person's license or certificate of registration and license plates. The person is deemed to have surrendered the license or certificate of registration and license plates, in compliance with the order, if the person does either of the following:

(a) On or before the date specified in the order, personally delivers the license or certificate of registration and license plates, or causes the delivery of the items, to the registrar;

(b) Mails the license or certificate of registration and license plates to the registrar in an envelope or container bearing a postmark showing a date no later than the date specified in the order.

(5) Except as provided in division (A)(6) or (L) of this section, the registrar shall not restore any operating privileges or registration rights suspended under this section, return any license, certificate of registration, or license plates impounded under this section, or reissue license plates under section 4503.232 [4503.23.2] of the Revised Code, if the registrar destroyed the impounded license plates under that section, or reissue a license under section 4510.52 of the Revised Code, if the registrar destroyed the suspended license under that section, unless the rights are not subject to suspension or revocation under any other law and unless the person, in addition to complying with all other conditions required by law for reinstatement of the operating privileges or registration rights, complies with all of the following:

(a) Pays to the registrar or an eligible deputy registrar a financial responsibility reinstatement fee of one hundred dollars for the first violation of division (A)(1) of this section, three hundred dollars for a second violation of that division, and six hundred dollars for a third or subsequent violation of that division;

(b) If the person has not voluntarily surrendered the license, certificate, or license plates in compliance with the order, pays to the registrar or an eligible deputy registrar a financial responsibility nonvoluntary compliance fee in an amount, not to exceed fifty dollars, determined by the registrar;

(c) Files and continuously maintains proof of financial responsibility under sections 4509.44 to 4509.65 of the Revised Code;

(d) Pays a deputy registrar a service fee of ten dollars to compensate the deputy registrar for services performed under this section. The deputy registrar shall retain eight dollars of the service fee and shall transmit the reinstatement fee, any nonvoluntary compliance fee, and two dollars of the service fee to the registrar in the manner the registrar shall determine.

(6) If the registrar issues an order under division (A)(2) of this section resulting from the failure of a person to respond to a financial responsibility random verification request under division (A)(3)(c) of this section and the person successfully maintains an affirmative defense to a violation of section 4510.16 of the Revised Code or is determined by the registrar or a deputy registrar to have been in compliance with division (A)(1) of this section at the time of the initial financial responsibility random verification request, the registrar shall do both of the following:

(a) Terminate the order of suspension or impoundment;

(b) Restore the operating privileges and registration rights of the person without payment of the fees established in divisions (A)(5)(a) and (b) of this section and without a requirement to file proof of financial responsibility.

(B)(1) Every party required to file an accident report under section 4509.06 of the Revised Code also shall include with the report a document described in division (G)(1) of this section.

If the registrar determines, within forty-five days after the report is filed, that an operator or owner has violated division (A)(1) of this section, the registrar shall do all of the following:

(a) Order the impoundment, with respect to the motor vehicle involved, required under division (A)(2)(d) of this section, of the certificate of registration and license plates of any owner who has violated division (A)(1) of this section;

(b) Order the suspension required under division (A)(2)(a), (b), or (c) of this section of the license of any operator or owner who has violated division (A)(1) of this section;

(c) Record the name and address of the person whose certificate of registration and license plates have been impounded or are under an order of impoundment, or whose license has been suspended or is under an order of suspension; the serial number of the person's license; the serial numbers of the person's certificate of registration and license plates; and the person's social security account number, if assigned, or, where the motor vehicle is used for hire or principally in connection with any established business, the person's federal taxpayer identification number. The information shall be recorded in such a manner that it becomes a part of the person's permanent record, and assists the registrar in monitoring compliance with the orders of suspension or impoundment.

(d) Send written notification to every person to whom the order pertains, at the person's last known address as shown on the records of the bureau. The person, within ten days after the date of the mailing of the notification, shall surrender to the registrar, in a manner set forth in division (A)(4) of this section, any certificate of registration and registration plates under an order of impoundment, or any license under an order of suspension.

(2) The registrar shall issue any order under division (B)(1) of this section without a hearing. Any person adversely affected by the order, within ten days after the issuance of the order, may request an administrative hearing before the registrar, who shall provide the person with an opportunity for a hearing in accordance with this paragraph. A request for a hearing does not operate as a suspension of the order. The scope of the hearing shall be limited to whether the person in fact demonstrated to the registrar proof of financial responsibility in accordance with this section. The registrar shall determine the date, time, and place of any hearing, provided that the hearing shall be held, and an order issued or findings made, within thirty days after the registrar receives a request for a hearing. If requested by the person in writing, the registrar may designate as the place of hearing the county seat of the county in which the person resides or a place within fifty miles of the person's residence. The person shall pay the cost of the hearing before the registrar, if the registrar's order of suspension or impoundment is upheld.

(C) Any order of suspension or impoundment issued under this section or division (B) of section 4509.37 of the Revised Code may be terminated at any time if the registrar determines upon a showing of proof of financial responsibility that the operator or owner of the motor vehicle was in compliance with division (A)(1) of this section at the time of the traffic offense, motor vehicle inspection, or accident that resulted in the order against the person. A determination may be made without a hearing. This division does not apply unless the person shows good cause for the person's failure to present satisfactory proof of financial responsibility to the registrar prior to the issuance of the order.

(D)(1) For the purpose of enforcing this section, every peace officer is deemed an agent of the registrar.

(a) Except as provided in division (D)(1)(b) of this section, any peace officer who, in the performance of the peace officer's duties as authorized by law, becomes aware of a person whose license is under an order of suspension, or whose certificate of registration and license plates are under an order of impoundment, pursuant to this section, may confiscate the license, certificate of registration, and license plates, and return them to the registrar.

(b) Any peace officer who, in the performance of the peace officer's duties as authorized by law, becomes aware of a person whose license is under an order of suspension, or whose certificate of registration and license plates are under an order of impoundment resulting from failure to respond to a financial responsibility random verification, shall not, for that reason, arrest the owner or operator or seize the vehicle or license plates. Instead, the peace officer shall issue a citation for a violation of section 4510.16 of the Revised Code specifying the circumstances as failure to respond to a financial responsibility random verification.

(2) A peace officer shall request the owner or operator of a motor vehicle to produce proof of financial responsibility in a manner described in division (G) of this section at the time the peace officer acts to enforce the traffic laws of this state and during motor vehicle inspections conducted pursuant to section 4513.02 of the Revised Code.

(3) A peace officer shall indicate on every traffic ticket whether the person receiving the traffic ticket produced proof of the maintenance of financial responsibility in response to the officer's request under division (D)(2) of this section. The peace officer shall inform every person who receives a traffic ticket and who has failed to produce

proof of the maintenance of financial responsibility that the person must submit proof to the traffic violations bureau with any payment of a fine and costs for the ticketed violation or, if the person is to appear in court for the violation, the person must submit proof to the court.

(4)(a) If a person who has failed to produce proof of the maintenance of financial responsibility appears in court for a ticketed violation, the court may permit the defendant to present evidence of proof of financial responsibility to the court at such time and in such manner as the court determines to be necessary or appropriate. In a manner prescribed by the registrar, the clerk of courts shall provide the registrar with the identity of any person who fails to submit proof of the maintenance of financial responsibility pursuant to division (D)(3) of this section.

(b) If a person who has failed to produce proof of the maintenance of financial responsibility also fails to submit that proof to the traffic violations bureau with payment of a fine and costs for the ticketed violation, the traffic violations bureau, in a manner prescribed by the registrar, shall notify the registrar of the identity of that person.

(5)(a) Upon receiving notice from a clerk of courts or traffic violations bureau pursuant to division (D)(4) of this section, the registrar shall order the suspension of the license of the person required under division (A)(2)(a), (b), or (c) of this section and the impoundment of the person's certificate of registration and license plates required under division (A)(2)(d) of this section, effective thirty days after the date of the mailing of notification. The registrar also shall notify the person that the person must present the registrar with proof of financial responsibility in accordance with this section, surrender to the registrar the person's certificate of registration, license plates, and license, or submit a statement subject to section 2921.13 of the Revised Code that the person did not operate or permit the operation of the motor vehicle at the time of the offense. Notification shall be in writing and shall be sent to the person at the person's last known address as shown on the records of the bureau of motor vehicles. The person, within fifteen days after the date of the mailing of notification, shall present proof of financial responsibility, surrender the certificate of registration, license plates, and license to the registrar in a manner set forth in division (A)(4) of this section, or submit the statement required under this section together with other information the person considers appropriate.

If the registrar does not receive proof or the person does not surrender the certificate of registration, license plates, and license, in accordance with this division, the registrar shall permit the order for the suspension of the license of the person and the impoundment of the person's certificate of registration and license plates to take effect.

(b) In the case of a person who presents, within the fifteen-day period, documents to show proof of financial responsibility, the registrar shall terminate the order of suspension and the impoundment of the registration and license plates required under division (A)(2)(d) of this section and shall send written notification to the person, at the person's last known address as shown on the records of the bureau.

(c) Any person adversely affected by the order of the registrar under division (D)(5)(a) or (b) of this section, within ten days after the issuance of the order, may request an administrative hearing before the registrar, who shall provide the person with an opportunity for a hearing in accordance with this paragraph. A request for a hearing does not operate as a suspension of the order. The scope of the hearing shall be limited to whether, at the time of the hearing, the person presents proof of financial responsibility covering the vehicle and whether the person is eligible for an exemption in accordance with this section or any rule adopted under it. The registrar shall determine the date, time, and place of any hearing; provided, that the hearing shall be held, and an order issued or findings made, within thirty days after the registrar receives a request for a hearing. If requested by the person in writing, the registrar may designate as the place of hearing the county seat of the county in which the person resides or a place within fifty miles of the person's residence. Such person shall pay the cost of the hearing before the registrar, if the registrar's order of suspension or impoundment under division (D)(5)(a) or (b) of this section is upheld.

(6) A peace officer may charge an owner or operator of a motor vehicle with a violation of section 4510.16 of the Revised Code when the owner or operator fails to show proof of the maintenance of financial responsibility pursuant to a peace officer's request under division (D)(2) of this section, if a check of the owner or operator's driving record indicates that the owner or operator, at the time of the operation of the motor vehicle, is required to file and maintain proof of financial responsibility under section 4509.45 of the Revised Code for a previous violation of this chapter.

(7) Any forms used by law enforcement agencies in administering this section shall be prescribed, supplied, and paid for by the registrar.

(8) No peace officer, law enforcement agency employing a peace officer, or political subdivision or governmental agency that employs a peace officer shall be liable in a civil action for damages or loss to persons arising out of the performance of any duty required or authorized by this section.

(9) As used in this division and divisions (E) and (G) of this section, "peace officer" has the meaning set forth in section 2935.01 of the Revised Code.

(E) All fees, except court costs, fees paid to a deputy registrar, and those portions of the financial responsibility reinstatement fees as otherwise specified in this division, collected under this section shall be paid into the state treasury to the credit of the financial responsibility compliance fund. The financial responsibility compliance fund shall be used exclusively to cover costs incurred by the bureau in the administration of this section and sections 4503.20, 4507.212 [4507.21.2], and 4509.81 of the Revised Code, and by any law enforcement agency employing any peace officer who returns any license, certificate of registration, and license plates to the registrar pursuant to division (C) of this section, except that the director of budget and management may transfer excess money from the financial responsibility compliance fund to the state bureau of motor vehicles fund if the registrar determines that the amount of money in the financial responsibility compliance fund exceeds the amount required to cover such costs incurred by the bureau or a law enforcement agency and requests the director to make the transfer.

Of each financial responsibility reinstatement fee the registrar collects pursuant to division (A)(5)(a) of this sectionor receives from a deputy registrar under division (A)(5)(d) of this section, the registrar shall deposit twenty-five dollars of each one-hundred-dollar reinstatement fee, fifty dollars of each three-hundred-dollar reinstatement fee, and one hundred dollars of each six-hundred-dollar reinstatement fee into the state treasury to the credit of the indigent defense support fund created by section 120.08 of the Revised Code.

All investment earnings of the financial responsibility compliance fund shall be credited to the fund.

(F) Chapter 119. of the Revised Code applies to this section only to the extent that any provision in that chapter is not clearly inconsistent with this section.

(G)(1) The registrar, court, traffic violations bureau, or peace officer may require proof of financial responsibility to be demonstrated by use of a standard form prescribed by the registrar. If the use of a standard form is not required, a person may demonstrate proof of financial responsibility under this section by presenting to the traffic violations bureau, court, registrar, or peace officer any of the following documents or a copy of the documents:

(a) A financial responsibility identification card as provided in section 4509.103 [4509.10.3] of the Revised Code;

(b) A certificate of proof of financial responsibility on a form provided and approved by the registrar for the filing of an accident report required to be filed under section 4509.06 of the Revised Code;

(c) A policy of liability insurance, a declaration page of a policy of liability insurance, or liability bond, if the policy or bond complies with section 4509.20 or sections 4509.49 to 4509.61 of the Revised Code;

(d) A bond or certification of the issuance of a bond as provided in section 4509.59 of the Revised Code;

(e) A certificate of deposit of money or securities as provided in section 4509.62 of the Revised Code;

(f) A certificate of self-insurance as provided in section 4509.72 of the Revised Code.

(2) If a person fails to demonstrate proof of financial responsibility in a manner described in division (G)(1) of this section, the person may demonstrate proof of financial responsibility under this section by any other method that the court or the bureau, by reason of circumstances in a particular case, may consider appropriate.

(3) A motor carrier certificated by the interstate commerce commission or by the public utilities commission may demonstrate proof of financial responsibility by providing a statement designating the motor carrier's operating authority and averring that the insurance coverage required by the certificating authority is in full force and effect.

(4)(a) A finding by the registrar or court that a person is covered by proof of financial responsibility in the form of an insurance policy or surety bond is not binding upon the named insurer or surety or any of its officers, employees, agents, or representatives and has no legal effect except for the purpose of administering this section.

(b) The preparation and delivery of a financial responsibility identification card or any other document authorized to be used as proof of financial responsibility under this division does not do any of the following:

(i) Create any liability or estoppel against an insurer or surety, or any of its officers, employees, agents, or representatives;

(ii) Constitute an admission of the existence of, or of any liability or coverage under, any policy or bond;

(iii) Waive any defenses or counterclaims available to an insurer, surety, agent, employee, or representative in an action commenced by an insured or third-party claimant upon a cause of action alleged to have arisen under an insurance policy or surety bond or by reason of the preparation and delivery of a document for use as proof of financial responsibility.

(c) Whenever it is determined by a final judgment in a judicial proceeding that an insurer or surety, which has been named on a document accepted by a court or the registrar as proof of financial responsibility covering the operation of a motor vehicle at the time of an accident or offense, is not liable to pay a judgment for injuries or damages resulting from such operation, the registrar, notwithstanding any previous contrary finding, shall forthwith suspend the operating privileges and registration rights of the person against whom the judgment was rendered as provided in division (A)(2) of this section.

(H) In order for any document described in division (G)(1)(b) of this section to be used for the demonstration of proof of financial responsibility under this section, the document shall state the name of the insured or obligor, the name of the insurer or surety company, and the effective and expiration dates of the financial responsibility, and designate by explicit description or by appropriate reference all motor vehicles covered which may include a reference to fleet insurance coverage.

(I) For purposes of this section, "owner" does not include a licensed motor vehicle leasing dealer as defined in section 4517.01 of the Revised Code, but does include a motor vehicle renting dealer as defined in section 4549.65 of the Revised Code. Nothing in this section or in section 4509.51 of the Revised Code shall be construed to prohibit a motor vehicle renting dealer from entering into a contractual agreement with a person whereby the person renting the motor vehicle agrees to be solely responsible for maintaining proof of financial responsibility, in accordance with this section, with respect to the operation, maintenance, or use of the motor vehicle during the period of the motor vehicle's rental.

(J) The purpose of this section is to require the maintenance of proof of financial responsibility with respect to the operation of motor vehicles on the highways of this state, so as to minimize those situations in which persons are not compensated for injuries and damages sustained in motor vehicle accidents. The general assembly finds that this section contains reasonable civil penalties and procedures for achieving this purpose.

(K) Nothing in this section shall be construed to be subject to section 4509.78 of the Revised Code.

(L)(1) The registrar may terminate any suspension imposed under this section and not require the owner to comply with divisions (A)(5)(a), (b), and (c) of this section if the registrar with or without a hearing determines that the owner of the vehicle has established by clear and convincing evidence that all of the following apply:

(a) The owner customarily maintains proof of financial responsibility.

(b) Proof of financial responsibility was not in effect for the vehicle on the date in question for one of the following reasons:

(i) The vehicle was inoperable.

(ii) The vehicle is operated only seasonally, and the date in question was outside the season of operation.

(iii) A person other than the vehicle owner or driver was at fault for the lapse of proof of financial responsibility through no fault of the owner or driver.

(iv) The lapse of proof of financial responsibility was caused by excusable neglect under circumstances that are not likely to recur and do not suggest a purpose to evade the requirements of this chapter.

(2) The registrar may grant an owner or driver relief for a reason specified in division (L)(1)(b)(i) or (ii) of this section whenever the owner or driver is randomly selected to verify the existence of proof of financial responsibility for such a vehicle. However, the registrar may grant an owner or driver relief for a reason specified in division (L)(1)(b)(iii) or (iv) of this section only if the owner or driver has not previously been granted relief under division (L)(1)(b)(iii) or (iv) of this section.

(M) The registrar shall adopt rules in accordance with Chapter 119. of the Revised Code that are necessary to administer and enforce this section. The rules shall include procedures for the surrender of license plates upon failure to maintain proof of financial responsibility and provisions relating to reinstatement of registration rights, acceptable forms of proof of financial responsibility, and verification of the existence of financial responsibility during the period of registration.

**HISTORY: 139 v S 250 (Eff 1-1-84); 140 v H 767 (Eff 8-1-84); 141 v H 201 (Eff 7-1-85); 141 v S 269 (Eff 3-13-86); 142 v H 419 (Eff 7-1-87); 143 v H 422 (Eff 7-1-91); 144 v S 331 (Eff 11-13-92); 144 v S 275 (Eff 9-1-93); 145 v S 62, § 4 (Eff 9-1-93); 145 v H 687 (Eff 10-12-94); 145 v S 20 (Eff 4-20-95); 146 v H 107 (Eff 6-30-95); 146 v H 353 (Eff 9-17-96); 146 v H 438 (Eff 7-1-97); 147 v H 215 (Eff 6-30-97); 147 v H 261 (Eff 9-3-97); 148 v H 163. Eff 6-30-99; 149 v S 123, § 1, eff. 1-1-04; 150 v H 230, § 1, eff. 9-16-04; 153 v H 1, § 101.01, eff. 10-16-09; 2011 HB 114, § 101.01, eff. June 29, 2011.**

Acts 2011, HB 114, § 806.10 provides: "The items of law contained in this act, and their applications, are severable. If any item of law contained in this act, or if any application of any item of law contained in this act, is held invalid, the invalidity does not affect other items of law contained in this act and their applications that can be given effect without the invalid item or application."

The effective date is set by § 812.10 of 153 v H 1.

The effective date is set by section 4 of S.B. 123.

See provisions, § 5 of S.B. 123 (149 v —), following RC § 4501.01.

The provisions of § 30 of HB 163 (148 v —) read as follows:

SECTION 30. Section 4509.101 of the Revised Code is presented in this act as a composite of the section as amended by both Am. Sub. H.B. 215 and Am. Sub. H.B. 261 of the 122nd General Assembly, with the new language of neither of the acts shown in capital letters. This is in recognition of the principle stated in division (B) of section 1.52 of the Revised Code that such amendments are to be harmonized where not substantively irreconcilable and constitutes a legislative finding that such is the resulting version in effect prior to the effective date of this act.

## § 4509.102 Falsification.

No person who has knowingly failed to maintain proof of financial responsibility in accordance with section 4509.101 [4509.10.1] of the Revised Code shall produce any document with the purpose to mislead a peace officer upon the request of a peace officer for proof of financial responsibility made in accordance with division (D)(2) of section 4509.101 [4509.10.1] of the Revised Code. Any person who violates this division is guilty of falsification under section 2921.13 of the Revised Code.

**HISTORY: 145 v S 20 (Eff 4-20-95); 146 v H 438. Eff 7-1-97.**

The effective date is set by section 3 of HB 438.

## § 4509.103 Insurer to provide identification cards.

(A) Each insurer writing motor vehicle liability insurance in this state shall provide financial responsibility identification cards to every policyholder in this state to whom it has delivered or issued for delivery a motor vehicle liability insurance policy. A minimum of one financial responsibility identification card shall be issued for every motor vehicle insured under a motor vehicle liability insurance policy.

(B) A financial responsibility identification card shall be valid only for the policy period. The card shall be in a form prescribed by the registrar of motor vehicles. It shall disclose the policy period and shall contain such other information as required by the registrar.

**HISTORY: 145 v S 20. Eff 10-20-95; 146 v H 248, § 1. Eff 10-20-95.**

## § 4509.104 Warning that policy does not meet minimum amounts.

Any automobile insurance policy that does not provide liability coverage at the time of issuance of at least the minimum amounts provided under division (K) of section 4509.01 of the Revised Code for proof of financial responsibility shall contain a clear and conspicuous warning on the face of the policy stating the policy does not constitute proof of financial responsibility as required for the operation of a motor vehicle under division (A)(1) of section 4509.101 [4509.10.1] of the Revised Code.

**HISTORY: 145 v S 20. Eff 4-20-95.**

## § 4509.105 Repealed, 149 v S 123, § 2 [147 v H 261]. Eff. 1-1-04.

This section concerned occupational driving privileges for first time violators.

The effective date is set by section 4 of S.B. 123.

See provisions, § 5 of S.B. 123 (149 v —), following RC § 4501.01.

# [USE OF REPORT OR FINDINGS AT TRIAL]

## § 4509.30 Accident report and findings of registrar prohibited at trial.

The report required following a motor vehicle accident, the action taken by the registrar of motor vehicles pursuant to sections 4509.11 to 4509.291 [4509.29.1], inclusive, of the Revised Code, the findings of the registrar upon which such action is based, and the security filed as provided in such sections, shall not be referred to in any way and shall not be evidence of the negligence or due care of either party at the trial of any action to recover damages.

**HISTORY: GC § 6298-41; 124 v 563; Bureau of Code Revision, 10-1-53; 128 v 1221. Eff 7-1-60.**

# [SUSPENSION OF REGISTRATION AND LICENSE; JUDGMENT]

## § 4509.31 Repealed, 149 v S 123, § 2 [GC § 6298-42; 124 v 563; Bureau of Code Revision, 10-1-53; 125 v 381; 128 v 1221; 133 v H 236; 139 v S 432; 141 v S 262; 142 v H 303; 143 v H 381; 144 v S 275; 145 v S 62, § 4; 146 v H 353; 147 v S 60]. Eff. 1-1-04.

This section concerned suspension of license and registration upon conviction, a plea of guilty, and forfeiture of bail or collateral.
The effective date is set by section 4 of S.B. 123.
See provisions, § 5 of S.B. 123 (149 v —), following RC § 4501.01.

## § 4509.32 Repealed, 149 v S 123, § 2 [GC § 6298-44; 124 v 563; Bureau of Code Revision, 10-1-53; 128 v 1221; 131 v 1089; 142 v H 303]. Eff. 1-1-04.

This section concerned the withholding of a registration or license.
The effective date is set by section 4 of S.B. 123.
See provisions, § 5 of S.B. 123 (149 v —), following RC § 4501.01.

## § 4509.33 Suspension of nonresidents' operating privilege and registration.

If a nonresident by final order or judgment of a court of record or mayor's court is convicted of, or forfeits bail or collateral deposited to secure an appearance for trial for, any offense for which the suspension of a license is provided, the registrar of motor vehicles shall impose a suspension of the privilege of the nonresident to operate a motor vehicle for the same period for which suspension of a license by a court of record is authorized by the applicable section of the Revised Code. The suspension shall remain in effect until the expiration of the period so ordered and thereafter until the nonresident gives and thereafter maintains proof of financial responsibility in accordance with section 4509.45 of the Revised Code.

The registrar shall also suspend the privilege of the use in this state of every motor vehicle owned by the nonresident, except that the registrar shall not suspend the privilege if the owner has given or immediately gives and thereafter maintains proof of financial responsibility with respect to all motor vehicles owned by the nonresident. The registrar shall restore such privilege of a nonresident owner when the owner gives and thereafter maintains proof of financial responsibility in accordance with section 4509.45 of the Revised Code.

**HISTORY: GC § 6298-45; 124 v 563; Bureau of Code Revision, 10-1-53; 128 v 1221 (Eff 7-1-60); 131 v 1090 (Eff 10-30-65); 142 v H 303. Eff 10-20-87; 149 v S 123, § 1, eff. 1-1-04.**

The effective date is set by section 4 of S.B. 123.
See provisions, § 5 of S.B. 123 (149 v —), following RC § 4501.01.

## § 4509.34 Period of suspension.

(A) The suspension of a license referred to in section 4509.291 of the Revised Code shall remain in effect and the registrar of motor vehicles shall not issue to any person whose license is so suspended any new or renewal license until permitted under the motor vehicle laws, and not then until such person gives and thereafter maintains proof of financial responsibility in accordance with section 4509.45 of the Revised Code.

(B) The suspension of registration referred to in such sections shall remain in effect and the registrar shall not register or reregister in the name of any person whose registration is so suspended as owner of any motor vehicle, nor return or re-issue license plates for such vehicle, until such person gives and thereafter maintains proof of financial responsibility in accordance with section 4509.45 of the Revised Code.

**HISTORY: GC § 6298-43; 124 v 563; Bureau of Code Revision, 10-1-53; 128 v 1221 (Eff 7-1-60); 131 v 1090. Eff 10-30-65; 149 v S 123, § 1, eff. 1-1-04.**

The effective date is set by section 4 of S.B. 123.
See provisions, § 5 of S.B. 123 (149 v —), following RC § 4501.01.

## [PROOF OF FINANCIAL RESPONSIBILITY]

## § 4509.44 Proof of financial responsibility required for registration.

No motor vehicle shall be or continue to be registered in the name of any person required to file proof of financial responsibility unless such proof is furnished and maintained in accordance with section 4509.45 of the Revised Code.

**HISTORY: GC § 6298-58; 124 v 563(577); Bureau of Code Revision, 10-1-53; 131 v 1093. Eff 10-30-65.**

## § 4509.45 Filing of proof of financial responsibility.

(A) Proof of financial responsibility when required under section 4509.101, 4509.33, 4509.34, 4509.38, 4509.40, 4509.42, 4509.44, or 4510.038 of the Revised Code may be given by filing any of the following:

(1) A financial responsibility identification card as provided in section 4509.104 of the Revised Code;

(2) A certificate of insurance as provided in section 4509.46 or 4509.47 of the Revised Code;

(3) A bond as provided in section 4509.59 of the Revised Code;

(4) A certificate of deposit of money or securities as provided in section 4509.62 of the Revised Code;

(5) A certificate of self-insurance, as provided in section 4509.72 of the Revised Code, supplemented by an agreement by the self-insurer that, with respect to accidents occurring while the certificate is in force, the self-insurer will pay the same amounts that an insurer would have been obligated to pay under an owner's motor vehicle liability policy if it had issued such a policy to the self-insurer.

(B) Proof under division (A) of this section shall be filed and maintained for five years from the date of the registrar's imposition of a class A, B, or C suspension of operating privileges and shall be filed and maintained for three years from the date of the registrar's imposition of a class D, E, or F suspension of operating privileges.

**HISTORY: GC § 6298-59; 124 v 563(577); Bureau of Code Revision, 10-1-53; 131 v 1093 (Eff 10-30-65); 139 v S 250 (Eff 1-1-84); 141 v S 356 (Eff 9-24-86); 145 v S 20. Eff 4-20-95; 149 v S 123, § 1, eff. 1-1-04.**

The effective date is set by section 4 of S.B. 123.
See provisions, § 5 of S.B. 123 (149 v —), following RC § 4501.01.

## [PROHIBITIONS]

## § 4509.74 Prohibition against failure to report accident.

(A) No person shall fail to report a motor vehicle accident as required under the laws of this state.

(B) Whoever violates this section is guilty of a minor misdemeanor.

**HISTORY: GC § 6298-85; 124 v 563(583); Bureau of Code Revision. Eff 10-1-53; 149 v S 123, § 1, eff. 1-1-04.**

The effective date is set by section 4 of S.B. 123.
See provisions, § 5 of S.B. 123 (149 v —), following RC § 4501.01.

## § 4509.77 Prohibition against failure to return license.

(A) No person shall willfully fail to return a license or registration as required in section 4509.69 of the Revised Code.

(B) Whoever violates this section shall be fined not more than five hundred dollars, imprisoned, for not more than thirty days, or both.

**HISTORY: GC § 6298-88; 124 v 563(584); Bureau of Code Revision. Eff 10-1-53; 149 v S 123, § 1, eff. 1-1-04.**

The effective date is set by section 4 of S.B. 123.
See provisions, § 5 of S.B. 123 (149 v —), following RC § 4501.01.

## § 4509.78 General prohibition.

(A) No person shall violate section 4509.01 to 4509.78 of the Revised Code for which no penalty is otherwise provided.

(B) Whoever violates this section shall be fined not more than five hundred dollars, imprisoned not more than ninety days, or both.

**HISTORY: GC § 6298-89; 124 v 563(584); Bureau of Code Revision. Eff 10-1-53; 149 v S 123, § 1, eff. 1-1-04.**

The effective date is set by section 4 of S.B. 123.
See provisions, § 5 of S.B. 123 (149 v —), following RC § 4501.01.

## § 4509.79 Liability insurance for motor vehicles used in a ridesharing arrangement.

(A) As used in this section, "ridesharing arrangement" means the transportation of persons in a motor vehicle where such transportation is incidental to another purpose of a volunteer driver and includes ridesharing arrangements known as carpools, vanpools, and buspools.

(B) Every owner registering as a passenger car a motor vehicle designed and used for carrying more than nine but not more than fifteen passengers or registering a bus under division (G) of section 4503.04 of the Revised Code shall have in effect, whenever the motor vehicle is used in a ridesharing arrangement, a policy of liability insurance with respect to the motor vehicle in amounts and coverage no less than:

(1) One hundred thousand dollars because of bodily injury to or death of one person in any one accident;

(2) Three hundred thousand dollars because of bodily injury to or death of two or more persons in any one accident;

(3) Fifty thousand dollars because of injury to property of others in any one accident.

(C) Whoever violates this section shall be fined not more than five thousand dollars.

**HISTORY: 139 v H 53 (Eff 7-1-82); 139 v S 331. Eff 5-21-82; 149 v S 123, § 1, eff. 1-1-04; 150 v H 230, § 1, eff. 9-16-04.**

The effective date is set by section 4 of S.B. 123.
See provisions, § 5 of S.B. 123 (149 v —), following RC § 4501.01.

## § 4509.80 Requirements for chauffeured limousines.

(A) Every owner registering a chauffeured limousine shall furnish and maintain proof of financial responsibility with respect to the limousine by filing with the registrar of motor vehicles any of the following:

(1) A certificate of insurance as provided in section 4509.46 or 4509.47 of the Revised Code;

(2) A policy of liability insurance, a declaration page of a policy of liability insurance, or liability bond, if the policy or bond provides coverage in accordance with division (B) of this section and otherwise complies with sections 4509.49 to 4509.61 of the Revised Code, and if the policy or bond provides that such policy or bond shall not be canceled or terminated prior to not less than ten days after a written notice of cancellation or termination is filed with the registrar;

(3) A bond or certification of the issuance of a bond if the bond provides coverage in the amount of three hundred thousand dollars and otherwise complies with section 4509.59 of the Revised Code;

(4) A certificate of deposit of money or securities if the certificate of deposit provides coverage in the amount of three hundred thousand dollars and otherwise complies with section 4509.62 of the Revised Code;

(5) A certificate of self-insurance as provided in section 4509.72 of the Revised Code.

(B) As used in this section and section 4509.81 of the Revised Code, "proof of financial responsibility" means proof of ability to respond in damages for liability, on account of accidents occurring subsequent to the effective date of such proof, arising out of the ownership, maintenance, or use of a chauffeured limousine in the amount of one hundred thousand dollars because of bodily injury to or death of one person in any one accident, three hundred thousand dollars because of bodily injury to or death of two or more persons in any one accident, and fifty thousand dollars because of injury to property of others in any one accident.

(C) Upon the request of a law enforcement officer, the operator of any chauffeured limousine shall produce proof of compliance with this section. The law enforcement officer requesting such proof shall notify the registrar of any violation of this section. The notice to the registrar shall be on a form prescribed by the registrar and supplied by the registrar at the registrar's expense, and shall include the license plate number of the chauffeured limousine and any other information the registrar requires.

(D) The owner, or the owner's designee, shall provide written notice to the registrar of cancellation or termination of the coverage required by this section not less than ten days prior to the effective date of cancellation, and, on or before the effective date of cancellation, shall voluntarily surrender the livery license plate sticker for the vehicle or vehicles for which the cancellation is effective. If the livery license plate sticker is timely and voluntarily surrendered, the registrar shall, upon the filing of proof of financial responsibility as required by this section, reinstate the livery registration of the vehicle and issue a current livery license plate sticker for the vehicle.

(E) Whoever violates this section is guilty of a misdemeanor of the first degree.

**HISTORY: 143 v H 422. Eff 7-1-91; 149 v S 123, § 1, eff. 1-1-04.**

The effective date is set by section 4 of S.B. 123.
See provisions, § 5 of S.B. 123 (149 v —), following RC § 4501.01.

## § 4509.81 Suspension of rights of owner of chauffeured limousine; impoundment.

(A) Upon receipt of a notification of violation as provided in division (C) of section 4509.80 of the Revised Code; upon failure of a timely surrender of the livery license plate sticker as required by division (D) of section 4509.80 of the Revised Code; or if the registrar of motor vehicles, upon receipt of notification from an insurer of the imminent cancellation or termination of coverage required by section 4509.80 of the Revised Code, fails to receive evidence of a continuation or substitution of coverage prior to the cancellation or termination date, the registrar shall order the immediate suspension of the rights of the owner of the chauffeured limousine described in the notice to register the limousine and the impoundment of the certificate of registration and registration plates for the limousine. The registrar shall notify the owner that the owner must surrender the certificate of registration and registration plates to the registrar. The notification shall be in writing and sent to the owner at the owner's last known address as shown in the records of the bureau of motor vehicles. Proceedings under this section are deemed special, summary statutory proceedings.

(B) The order of suspension and impoundment of a registration shall state the date on or before which the owner of the chauffeured limousine involved is required to surrender the certificate of registration and registration plates to the registrar. The owner shall be deemed to have surrendered the certificate of registration and registration plates if the owner causes the items to be delivered to the registrar on or before the date specified in the order or mails the items to the registrar in an envelope or container bearing a postmark showing a date no later than the date specified in the order.

(C) The registrar shall not restore any registration rights suspended under this section, return any certificate of registration or registration plates impounded under this section, or reissue registration plates under section 4503.232 of the Revised Code, if the registrar destroyed the impounded registration plates under that section, unless those rights are not subject to suspension under any other law and unless the owner complies with both of the following:

(1) Pays to the registrar or an eligible deputy registrar a financial responsibility reinstatement fee of thirty dollars. The reinstatement fee may be increased, upon approval of the controlling board, up to an amount not exceeding fifty dollars. In addition, pays a service fee of ten dollars to each deputy registrar to compensate the deputy registrar for services performed under this section. The deputy registrar shall retain eight dollars of the service fee and shall transmit the reinstatement fee and two dollars of the service fee to the registrar in the manner the registrar shall determine.

(2) Files and maintains proof of financial responsibility under section 4509.80 of the Revised Code.

(D) Any owner adversely affected by the order of the registrar under this section may, within ten days after the issuance of the order, request an administrative hearing before the registrar, who shall provide the owner with an opportunity for a hearing in accordance with this division. A request for a hearing does not operate as a suspension of the order unless the owner establishes to the satisfaction of the registrar that the operation of the owner's chauffeured limousine will be covered by proof of financial responsibility during the pendency of the appeal. The scope of the hearing shall be limited to whether the owner in fact demonstrated to the registrar proof of financial responsibility in accordance with section 4509.80 of the Revised Code. The registrar shall determine the date, time, and place of any hearing, provided that the hearing shall be held and an order issued or findings made within thirty days after the registrar receives a request for a hearing. If requested by the owner in writing, the registrar may designate as the place of hearing the county seat of the county in which the owner resides or a place within fifty miles of the owner's residence. The owner shall pay the cost of the hearing before the registrar, if the registrar's order of suspension or impoundment is upheld.

(E) Any order of suspension or impoundment issued under this section may be terminated at any time if the registrar determines upon a showing of proof of financial responsibility that the owner of the limousine was in compliance with section 4509.80 of the Revised Code at the time of the incident that resulted in the order against the owner. Such a determination may be made without a hearing.

(F) All fees except the two dollar service fee transmitted to the registrar by a deputy registrar, that are collected by the registrar or transmitted to the registrar under this section shall be paid into the state treasury to the credit of the financial responsibility compliance fund created by section 4509.101 of the Revised Code.

(G) Chapter 119. of the Revised Code applies to this section only to the extent that any provision in that chapter is not clearly inconsistent with this section.

(H)(1) Proof of financial responsibility may be demonstrated by any of the methods authorized in section 4509.80 of the Revised Code.

(2) Divisions (G) (4) (a) and (b) of section 4509.101 of the Revised Code apply to any finding by the registrar under this section that an owner is covered by proof of financial responsibility.

**HISTORY: 143 v H 422 (Eff 7-1-91); 144 v S 331 (Eff 11-13-92); 144 v S 275 (Eff 9-1-93); 145 v S 62, § 4 (Eff 9-1-93); 145 v H 687 (Eff 10-12-94); 146 v H 438. Eff 7-1-97; 149 v S 123, § 1, eff. 1-1-04; 2011 HB 114, § 101.01, eff. June 29, 2011.**

Acts 2011, HB 114, § 806.10 provides: "The items of law contained in this act, and their applications, are severable. If any item of law contained in this act, or if any application of any item of law contained in this act, is held invalid, the invalidity does not affect other items of law contained in this act and their applications that can be given effect without the invalid item or application."
The effective date is set by section 4 of S.B. 123.
See provisions, § 5 of S.B. 123 (149 v —), following RC § 4501.01.

## § 4509.99 Repealed, 149 v S 123, § 2 [Bureau of Code Revision, 10-1-53; 139 v H 53; 141 v S 356; 143 v H 422; 146 v S 2]. Eff. 1-1-04.

This section concerned penalties.
The effective date is set by section 4 of S.B. 123.
See provisions, § 5 of S.B. 123 (149 v —), following RC § 4501.01.

# CHAPTER 4510: DRIVER'S LICENSE SUSPENSION, CANCELLATION, REVOCATION

Section



Section



## § 4510.01 Definitions.

As used in this title and in Title XXIX of the Revised Code:

(A) "Cancel" or "cancellation" means the annulment or termination by the bureau of motor vehicles of a driver's license, commercial driver's license, temporary instruction permit, probationary license, or nonresident operating privilege because it was obtained unlawfully, issued in error, altered, or willfully destroyed, or because the holder no longer is entitled to the license, permit, or privilege.

(B) "Drug abuse offense," "cocaine," and "L.S.D." have the same meanings as in section 2925.01 of the Revised Code.

(C) "Ignition interlock device" means a device approved by the director of public safety that connects a breath analyzer to a motor vehicle's ignition system, that is constantly available to monitor the concentration by weight of alcohol in the breath of any person attempting to start that motor vehicle by using its ignition system, and that deters starting the motor vehicle by use of its ignition system unless the person attempting to start the vehicle provides an appropriate breath sample for the device and the device determines that the concentration by weight of alcohol in the person's breath is below a preset level.

(D) "Immobilizing or disabling device" means a device approved by the director of public safety that may be ordered by a court to be used by an offender as a condition of limited driving privileges. "Immobilizing or disabling device" includes an ignition interlock device, and any prototype device that is used according to protocols designed to ensure efficient and effective monitoring of limited driving privileges granted by a court to an offender.

(E) "Moving violation" means any violation of any statute or ordinance that regulates the operation of vehicles, streetcars, or trackless trolleys on the highways or streets. "Moving violation" does not include a violation of section 4513.263 [4513.26.3] of the Revised Code or a substantially equivalent municipal ordinance, a violation of any statute or ordinance regulating pedestrians or the parking of vehicles, vehicle size or load limitations, vehicle fitness requirements, or vehicle registration.

(F) "Municipal OVI ordinance" and "municipal OVI offense" have the same meanings as in section 4511.181 of the Revised Code.

(G) "Prototype device" means any testing device to monitor limited driving privileges that has not yet been approved or disapproved by the director of public safety.

(H) "Suspend" or "suspension" means the permanent or temporary withdrawal, by action of a court or the bureau of motor vehicles, of a driver's license, commercial driver's license, temporary instruction permit, probationary license, or nonresident operating privilege for the period of the suspension or the permanent or temporary withdrawal of the privilege to obtain a license, permit, or privilege of that type for the period of the suspension.

(I) "Controlled substance" and "marihuana" have the same meanings as in section 3719.01 of the Revised Code.

**HISTORY: 149 v S 123, § 1, eff. 1-1-04; 151 v S 8, § 1, eff. 8-17-06.**

The effective date is set by section 4 of S.B. 123.

See provisions, § 5 of S.B. 123 (149 v —), following RC § 4501.01.

## § 4510.011 Drug of abuse defined.

As used in this chapter, "drug of abuse" has the same meaning as in section 4506.01 of the Revised Code.

**HISTORY: 151 v S 8, § 1, eff. 8-17-06.**

## § 4510.02 Definite periods of suspension; remedial driving course; suspension subject to chapter.

(A) When a court elects or is required to suspend the driver's license, commercial driver's license, temporary instruction permit, probationary license, or nonresident operating privilege of any offender from a specified suspension class, for each of the following suspension classes, the court shall impose a definite period of suspension from the range specified for the suspension class:

(1) For a class one suspension, a definite period for the life of the person subject to the suspension;

(2) For a class two suspension, a definite period of three years to life;

(3) For a class three suspension, a definite period of two to ten years;

(4) For a class four suspension, a definite period of one to five years;

(5) For a class five suspension, a definite period of six months to three years;

(6) For a class six suspension, a definite period of three months to two years;

(7) For a class seven suspension, a definite period not to exceed one year.

(B) When the bureau of motor vehicles elects or is required to suspend the driver's license, commercial driver's license, temporary instruction permit, probationary license, or nonresident operating privilege of any person from a specified suspension class, for each of the following suspension classes, the period of suspension shall be as follows:

(1) For a class A suspension, three years;

(2) For a class B suspension, two years;

(3) For a class C suspension, one year;

(4) For a class D suspension, six months;

(5) For a class E suspension, three months;

(6) For a class F suspension, until conditions are met.

(C) The court may require a person to successfully complete a remedial driving course as a condition for the return of full driving privileges after a suspension period imposed from any range in division (A) of this section or otherwise imposed by the court pursuant to any other provision of law ends.

(D) When a court or the bureau suspends the driver's license, commercial driver's license, temporary instruction permit, probationary license, or nonresident operating privilege of any offender or person pursuant to any provision of law that does not provide for the suspension to be from a class set forth in division (A) or (B) of this section, except as otherwise provided in the provision that authorizes or requires the suspension, the suspension shall be subject to and governed by this chapter.

**HISTORY: 149 v S 123, § 1, eff. 1-1-04.**

The effective date is set by section 4 of S.B. 123.

See provisions, § 5 of S.B. 123 (149 v —), following RC § 4501.01.

## § 4510.021 Limited driving privileges.

(A) Unless expressly prohibited by section 2919.22, section 4510.13, or any other section of the Revised Code, a court may grant limited driving privileges for any purpose described in division (A)(1), (2), or (3) of this section during any suspension imposed by the court. In granting the privileges, the court shall specify the purposes, times, and places of the privileges and may impose any other reasonable conditions on the person's driving of a motor vehicle. The privileges shall be for any of the following limited purposes:

(1) Occupational, educational, vocational, or medical purposes;

(2) Taking the driver's or commercial driver's license examination;

(3) Attending court-ordered treatment.

(B) Unless expressly authorized by a section of the Revised Code, a court may not grant limited driving privileges during any suspension imposed by the bureau of motor vehicles. To obtain limited driving privileges during a suspension imposed by the bureau, the person under suspension may file a petition in a court of record in the county in which the person resides. A person who is not a resident of this state shall file any petition for privileges either in the Franklin county municipal court or in the municipal or county court located in the county where the offense occurred. If the person who is not a resident of this state is a minor, the person may file the petition either in the Franklin county juvenile court or in the juvenile court with jurisdiction over the offense. If a court grants limited driving privileges as described in this division, the privileges shall be for any of the limited purposes identified in division (A) of this section.

(C) When the use of an immobilizing or disabling device is not otherwise required by law, the court, as a condition of granting limited driving privileges, may require that the person's vehicle be equipped with an immobilizing or disabling device, except as provided in division (C) of section 4510.43 of the Revised Code. When the use of restricted license plates issued under section 4503.231 [4503.23.1] of the Revised Code is not otherwise required by law, the court, as a condition of granting limited driving privileges, may require that the person's vehicle be equipped with restricted license plates of that nature, except as provided in division (B) of that section.

(D) When the court grants limited driving privileges under section 4510.31 of the Revised Code or any other provision of law during the suspension of the temporary instruction permit or probationary driver's license of a person who is under eighteen years of age, the court may include as a purpose of the privilege the person's practicing of driving with the person's parent, guardian, or other custodian during the period of the suspension. If the court grants limited driving privileges for this purpose, the court, in addition to all other conditions it imposes, shall impose as a condition that the person exercise the privilege only when a parent, guardian, or custodian of the person who holds a current valid driver's or commercial driver's license issued by this state actually occupies the seat beside the person in the vehicle the person is operating.

(E) Before granting limited driving privileges under this section, the court shall require the offender to provide proof of financial responsibility pursuant to section 4509.45 of the Revised Code.

**HISTORY: 149 v S 123, § 1, eff. 1-1-04; 150 v H 52, § 1, eff. 6-1-04.**

The effective date is set by section 4 of S.B. 123.

The provisions of § 5 of S.B. 123 (149 v —), as amended by § 3 of H.B. 163 (150 v —), read as follows:

SECTION 5. * * * (B)(1) Notwithstanding division (A) of this section, all of the following apply to conduct or an offense committed prior to January 1, 2004:

(a) A person whose driver's or commercial driver's license, temporary instruction permit, probationary license, or nonresident operating privilege was suspended by a court may apply to the sentencing court for limited driving privileges under division (A) of section 4510.021 of the Revised Code;

(b) A person whose license, permit, or privilege was suspended by the Registrar of Motor Vehicles may apply for limited driving privileges under division (B) of section 4510.021 of the Revised Code if limited driving privileges are expressly authorized by a section of the Revised Code for the type of conduct or offense that caused the suspension;

(c) A person whose license, permit, or privilege was suspended, canceled, or revoked for life may file a motion for modification or termination of the suspension, cancellation, or revocation in accordance with section 4510.54 of the Revised Code.

(2) The terms and conditions of any limited driving privileges granted under this section shall be governed by the law in effect on and after January 1, 2004.

## § 4510.03 Court records of traffic violation charges; abstract of conviction or bail forfeiture forwarded to BMV.

(A) Every county court judge, mayor of a mayor's court, and clerk of a court of record shall keep a full record of every case in which a person is charged with any violation of any provision of sections 4511.01 to 4511.771 or 4513.01 to 4513.36 of the Revised Code or of any other law or ordinance regulating the operation of vehicles, streetcars, and trackless trolleys on highways or streets.

(B) If a person is convicted of or forfeits bail in relation to a violation of any section listed in division (A) of this section or a violation of any other law or ordinance regulating the operation of vehicles, streetcars, and trackless trolleys on highways or streets, the county court judge, mayor of a mayor's court, or clerk, within ten days after the conviction or bail forfeiture, shall prepare and immediately forward to the bureau of motor vehicles an abstract, certified by the preparer to be true and correct, of the court record covering the case in which the person was convicted or forfeited bail. Every court of record also shall forward to the bureau of motor vehicles an abstract of the court record as described in division (C) of this section upon the conviction of any person of aggravated vehicular homicide or vehicular homicide or of a felony in the commission of which a vehicle was used.

(C) Each abstract required by this section shall be made upon a form approved and furnished by the bureau and shall include the name and address of the person charged, the number of the person's driver's or commercial driver's license, probationary driver's license, or temporary instruction permit, the registration number of the vehicle involved, the nature of the offense, the date of the offense, the date of hearing, the plea, the judgment, or whether bail was forfeited, and the amount of the fine or forfeiture.

**HISTORY: 149 v S 123, § 1, eff. 1-1-04.**

The effective date is set by section 4 of S.B. 123.

See provisions, § 5 of S.B. 123 (149 v —), following RC § 4501.01.

## § 4510.031 Authority of United States district court.

(A) A United States district court that has jurisdiction within this state may utilize the provisions of section 4510.03 of the Revised Code in regard to any case in which a person is charged with any violation of any provision of sections 4511.01 to 4511.771 or 4513.01 to 4513.36 of the Revised Code or of any other law or ordinance regulating the operation of vehicles, streetcars, and trackless trolleys on highways or streets located on federal property within this state. The court also may forward to the bureau an abstract upon the conviction of any person of aggravated vehicular homicide or vehicular homicide or of a felony in the commission of which a vehicle was used.

(B) If a United States district court acts under this section, it shall follow the procedures established in section 4510.03 of the Revised Code.

(C) The bureau of motor vehicles shall accept and process an abstract received from a United States district court under this section in the same manner as it accepts and processes an abstract received from a county court judge, mayor of a mayor's court, or clerk of a court of record.

**HISTORY: 149 v S 123, § 1, eff. 1-1-04.**

The effective date is set by section 4 of S.B. 123.

See provisions, § 5 of S.B. 123 (149 v —), following RC § 4501.01.

## § 4510.032 Abstract where certain charges are dismissed or reduced or there is a conviction or bail forfeiture on related charges; abstract of juvenile court proceedings.

(A) If a person is charged with a violation of section 4511.19 of the Revised Code or a violation of any municipal OVI ordinance; if that charge is dismissed or reduced; if the person is convicted of or forfeits bail in relation to a violation of any other section of the Revised Code or of any ordinance that regulates the operation of vehicles, streetcars, and trackless trolleys on highways and streets but that does not relate to operating a vehicle while under the influence of alcohol, a drug of abuse, or a combination of them or to operating a vehicle with a prohibited concentration of alcohol, a controlled substance, or a metabolite of a controlled substance in the whole blood, blood serum or plasma, breath, or urine; and if the violation of which the person was convicted or in relation to which the person forfeited bail arose out of the same facts and circumstances and the same act as did the charge that was dismissed or reduced, the abstract prepared under section 4510.03 of the Revised Code also shall set forth the charge that was dismissed or reduced, indicate that it was dismissed or reduced, and indicate that the violation resulting in the conviction or bail forfeiture arose out of the same facts and circumstances and the same act as did the charge that was dismissed or reduced.

(B) If a charge against a person of a violation of division (A) of section 4510.11, division (A) of section 4510.14, or division (A) of section 4510.16 of the Revised Code or any municipal ordinance that is substantially equivalent to any of those divisions is dismissed or reduced and if the person is convicted of or forfeits bail in relation to a violation of any other section of the Revised Code or any other ordinance that regulates the operation of vehicles, streetcars, and trackless trolleys on highways and streets that arose out of the same facts and circumstances as did the charge that was dismissed or reduced, the abstract also shall set forth the charge that was dismissed or reduced, indicate that it was dismissed or reduced, and indicate that the violation resulting in the conviction or bail forfeiture arose out of the same facts and circumstances and the same act as did the charge that was dismissed or reduced.

(C)(1) If a child has been adjudicated an unruly or delinquent child or a juvenile traffic offender for having committed any act that if committed by an adult would be a drug abuse offense or any violation of division (B) of section 2917.11 or of section 4511.19 of the Revised Code, the court shall notify the bureau, by means of an abstract of the court record as described in divisions (B) and (C) of section 4510.03 of the Revised Code, within ten days after the adjudication.

(2) If a court requires a child to attend a drug abuse or alcohol abuse education, intervention, or treatment program, the abstract required by division (C)(1) of this section and forwarded to the bureau also shall include the name and address of the operator of the program and the date that the child entered the program. If the child satisfactorily completes the program, the court, immediately upon receipt of the information, shall send to the bureau an updated abstract that also shall contain the date on which the child satisfactorily completed the program.

**HISTORY: 149 v S 123, § 1, eff. 1-1-04; 151 v S 8, § 1, eff. 8-17-06.**

The effective date is set by section 4 of S.B. 123.

See provisions, § 5 of S.B. 123 (149 v —), following RC § 4501.01.

## § 4510.034 When abstract to include ineligibility for registration of vehicle.

(A) Division (B) of this section applies in relation to persons who are convicted of or plead guilty to any of the following:

(1) A violation of division (A) of section 4510.11, division (A) of section 4510.14, or division (A) of section 4510.16 of the Revised Code;

(2) A violation of a municipal ordinance substantially equivalent to any division set forth in division (A)(1) of this section;

(3) A violation of division (A) of section 4511.19 of the Revised Code or a violation of section 4511.203 of the Revised Code;

(4) A violation of a municipal OVI ordinance.

(B) If a person is convicted of or pleads guilty to any violation set forth in division (A) of this section and if division (D) of section 4503.234 of the Revised Code prohibits the registrar of motor vehicles and all deputy registrars from accepting an application for the registration of, or registering, any motor vehicle in the name of that person, the abstract prepared pursuant to section 4510.03, 4510.031, or 4510.032 of the Revised Code shall specifically set forth these facts and clearly indicate the date on which the order of criminal forfeiture was issued or would have been issued but for the operation of section 4503.234 of the Revised Code. If the registrar receives an abstract containing this information relating to a person, the registrar, in accordance with sections 4503.12 and 4503.234 of the Revised Code, shall take all necessary measures to prevent the registrar's office or any deputy registrar from accepting from the person, for the period of time ending five years after the date on which the order was issued or would have been issued and as described in section 4503.234 of the Revised Code, any new application for the registration of any motor vehicle in the name of the person.

**HISTORY: 149 v S 123, § 1, eff. 1-1-04.**

The effective date is set by section 4 of S.B. 123.

See provisions, § 5 of S.B. 123 (149 v —), following RC § 4501.01.

## § 4510.035 Official's failure or refusal to comply.

The purposeful failure or refusal of any person to comply with any provision of section 4510.03, 4510.032, 4510.034, 4510.036, or 4510.037 of the Revised Code constitutes misconduct in office and is a ground for removal of the person from the office.

**HISTORY: 149 v S 123, § 1, eff. 1-1-04.**

The effective date is set by section 4 of S.B. 123.

See provisions, § 5 of S.B. 123 (149 v —), following RC § 4501.01.

## § 4510.036 Bureau records; points assessed for offense.

(A) The bureau of motor vehicles shall record within ten days, after receipt, and shall keep at its main office, all abstracts received under this section or section 4510.03, 4510.031, 4510.032, or 4510.034 of the Revised Code and shall maintain records of convictions and bond forfeitures for any violation of a state law or a municipal ordinance regulating the operation of vehicles, streetcars, and trackless trolleys on highways and streets, except a violation related to parking a motor vehicle.

(B) Every court of record or mayor's court before which a person is charged with a violation for which points are chargeable by this section shall assess and transcribe to the abstract of conviction that is furnished by the bureau to the court the number of points chargeable by this section in the correct space assigned on the reporting form. A

United States district court that has jurisdiction within this state and before which a person is charged with a violation for which points are chargeable by this section may assess and transcribe to the abstract of conviction report that is furnished by the bureau the number of points chargeable by this section in the correct space assigned on the reporting form. If the federal court so assesses and transcribes the points chargeable for the offense and furnishes the report to the bureau, the bureau shall record the points in the same manner as those assessed and transcribed by a court of record or mayor's court.

(C) A court shall assess the following points for an offense based on the following formula:

(1) Aggravated vehicular homicide, vehicular homicide, vehicular manslaughter, aggravated vehicular assault, or vehicular assault when the offense involves the operation of a vehicle, streetcar, or trackless trolley on a highway or street ........ 6 points

(2) A violation of section 2921.331 of the Revised Code or any ordinance prohibiting the willful fleeing or eluding of a law enforcement officer ........ 6 points

(3) A violation of section 4549.02 or 4549.021 of the Revised Code or any ordinance requiring the driver of a vehicle to stop and disclose identity at the scene of an accident ........ 6 points

(4) A violation of section 4511.251 of the Revised Code or any ordinance prohibiting street racing ........ 6 points

(5) A violation of section 4510.037 of the Revised Code or any ordinance prohibiting the operation of a motor vehicle while the driver's or commercial driver's license is under a twelve-point suspension ........ 6 points

(6) A violation of section 4510.14 of the Revised Code, or any ordinance prohibiting the operation of a motor vehicle upon the public roads or highways within this state while the driver's or commercial driver's license of the person is under suspension and the suspension was imposed under section 4511.19, 4511.191, or 4511.196 of the Revised Code or section 4510.07 of the Revised Code due to a conviction for a violation of a municipal OVI ordinance or any ordinance prohibiting the operation of a motor vehicle while the driver's or commercial driver's license is under suspension for an OVI offense ........ 6 points

(7) A violation of division (A) of section 4511.19 of the Revised Code, any ordinance prohibiting the operation of a vehicle while under the influence of alcohol, a drug of abuse, or a combination of them, or any ordinance substantially equivalent to division (A) of section 4511.19 of the Revised Code prohibiting the operation of a vehicle with a prohibited concentration of alcohol, a controlled substance, or a metabolite of a controlled substance in the whole blood, blood serum or plasma, breath, or urine ........ 6 points

(8) A violation of section 2913.03 of the Revised Code that does not involve an aircraft or motorboat or any ordinance prohibiting the operation of a vehicle without the consent of the owner ........ 6 points

(9) Any offense under the motor vehicle laws of this state that is a felony, or any other felony in the commission of which a motor vehicle was used ........ 6 points

(10) A violation of division (B) of section 4511.19 of the Revised Code or any ordinance substantially equivalent to that division prohibiting the operation of a vehicle with a prohibited concentration of alcohol in the whole blood, blood serum or plasma, breath, or urine ........ 4 points

(11) A violation of section 4511.20 of the Revised Code or any ordinance prohibiting the operation of a motor vehicle in willful or wanton disregard of the safety of persons or property ........ 4 points

(12) A violation of any law or ordinance pertaining to speed:

(a) Notwithstanding divisions (C)(12)(b) and (c) of this section, when the speed exceeds the lawful speed limit by thirty miles per hour or more ........ 4 points

(b) When the speed exceeds the lawful speed limit of fifty-five miles per hour or more by more than ten miles per hour ........ 2 points

(c) When the speed exceeds the lawful speed limit of less than fifty-five miles per hour by more than five miles per hour ........ 2 points

(d) When the speed does not exceed the amounts set forth in divisions (C)(12)(a), (b), or (c) of this section ........ 0 points

(13) Operating a motor vehicle in violation of a restriction imposed by the registrar ........ 2 points

(14) A violation of section 4510.11, 4510.111, 4510.16, or 4510.21 of the Revised Code or any ordinance prohibiting the operation of a motor vehicle while the driver's or commercial driver's license is under suspension ........ 2 points

(15) With the exception of violations under section 4510.12 of the Revised Code where no points shall be assessed, all other moving violations reported under this section ........ 2 points

(D) Upon receiving notification from the proper court, including a United States district court that has jurisdiction within this state, the bureau shall delete any points entered for a bond forfeiture if the driver is acquitted of the offense for which bond was posted.

(E) If a person is convicted of or forfeits bail for two or more offenses arising out of the same facts and points are chargeable for each of the offenses, points shall be charged for only the conviction or bond forfeiture for which the greater number of points is chargeable, and, if the number of points chargeable for each offense is equal, only one offense shall be recorded, and points shall be charged only for that offense.

**HISTORY: 149 v S 123, § 1, eff. 1-1-04; 151 v S 8, § 1, eff. 8-17-06; 2011 HB 5, § 1, eff. Sept. 23, 2011.**

The effective date is set by section 4 of S.B. 123.

See provisions, § 5 of S.B. 123 (149 v —), following RC § 4501.01.

## § 4510.037 Warning letter; notice of suspension; remedial driving course.

(A) When the registrar of motor vehicles determines that the total points charged against any person under section 4510.036 of the Revised Code exceed five, the registrar shall send a warning letter to the person at the person's last known address by regular mail. The warning letter shall list the reported violations that are the basis of the points charged, list the number of points charged for each violation, and outline the suspension provisions of this section.

(B) When the registrar determines that the total points charged against any person under section 4510.036 of the Revised Code within any two-year period beginning on the date of the first conviction within the two-year period is equal to twelve or more, the registrar shall send a written notice to the person at the person's last known address by regular mail. The notice shall list the reported violations that are the basis of the points charged, list the number of points charged for each violation, and state that, because the total number of points charged against the person within the applicable two-year period is equal to twelve or more, the registrar is imposing a class D suspension of the person's driver's or commercial driver's license or permit or nonresident operating privileges for the period of time specified in division (B)(4) of section 4510.02 of the Revised Code. The notice also shall state that the suspension is effective on the twentieth day after the mailing of the notice, unless the person files a petition appealing the determination and suspension in the municipal court, county court, or, if the person is under the age of eighteen, the juvenile division of the court of common pleas in whose jurisdiction the person resides or, if the person is not a resident of this state, in the Franklin county municipal court or juvenile division of the Franklin county court of common pleas. By filing the appeal of the determination and suspension, the person agrees to pay the cost of the proceedings in the appeal of the determination and suspension and alleges that the person can show cause why the person's driver's or commercial driver's license or permit or nonresident operating privileges should not be suspended.

(C)(1) Any person against whom at least two but less than twelve points have been charged under section 4510.036 of the Revised Code may enroll in a course of remedial driving instruction that is approved by the director of public safety. Upon the person's completion of an approved course of remedial driving instruction, the person may apply to the registrar on a form prescribed by the registrar for a credit of two points on the person's driving record. Upon receipt of the application and proof of completion of the approved remedial driving course, the registrar shall approve the two-point credit. The registrar shall not approve any credits for a person who completes an approved course of remedial driving instruction pursuant to a judge's order under section 4510.02 of the Revised Code.

(2) In any three-year period, the registrar shall approve only one two-point credit on a person's driving record under division (C)(1) of this section. The registrar shall approve not more than five two-point credits on a person's driving record under division (C)(1) of this section during that person's lifetime.

(D) When a judge of a court of record suspends a person's driver's or commercial driver's license or permit or nonresident operating privilege and charges points against the person under section 4510.036 of the Revised Code for the offense that resulted in the suspension, the registrar shall credit that period of suspension against the time of any subsequent suspension imposed under this section for which those points were used to impose the subsequent suspension. When a United States district court that has jurisdiction within this state suspends a person's driver's or commercial driver's license or permit or nonresident operating privileges pursuant to the "Assimilative Crimes Act," 102 Stat. 4381 (1988), 18 U.S.C.A. 13, as amended, the district court prepares an abstract pursuant to section 4510.031 of the Revised Code, and the district court charges points against the person under section 4510.036 of the Revised Code for the offense that resulted in the suspension, the registrar shall credit the period of suspension imposed by the district court against the time of any subsequent suspension imposed under this section for which the points were used to impose the subsequent suspension.

(E) The registrar, upon the written request of a licensee who files a petition under division (B) of this section, shall furnish the licensee a certified copy of the registrar's record of the convictions and bond forfeitures of the person. This record shall include the name, address, and date of birth of the licensee; the name of the court in which each conviction or bail forfeiture took place; the nature of the offense that was the basis of the conviction or bond forfeiture; and any other information that the registrar considers necessary. If the record indicates that twelve points or more have been charged against the person within a two-year period, it is prima-facie evidence that the person is a repeat traffic offender, and the registrar shall suspend the person's driver's or commercial driver's license or permit or nonresident operating privilege pursuant to division (B) of this section.

In hearing the petition and determining whether the person filing the petition has shown cause why the person's driver's or commercial driver's license or permit or nonresident operating privilege should not be suspended, the court shall decide the issue on the record certified by the registrar and any additional relevant, competent, and material evidence that either the registrar or the person whose license is sought to be suspended submits.

(F) If a petition is filed under division (B) of this section in a county court, the prosecuting attorney of the county in which the case is pending shall represent the registrar in the proceedings, except that, if the petitioner resides in a municipal corporation within the jurisdiction of the county court, the city director of law, village solicitor, or other chief legal officer of the municipal corporation shall represent the registrar in the proceedings. If a petition is filed under division (B) of this section in a municipal court, the registrar shall be represented in the resulting proceedings as provided in section 1901.34 of the Revised Code.

(G) If the court determines from the evidence submitted that a person who filed a petition under division (B) of this section has failed to show cause why the person's driver's or commercial driver's license or permit or nonresident operating privileges should not be suspended, the court shall assess against the person the cost of the proceedings in the appeal of the determination and suspension and shall impose the applicable suspension under this section or suspend all or a portion of the suspension and impose any conditions upon the person that the court considers proper or impose upon the person a community control sanction pursuant to section 2929.15 or 2929.25 of the Revised Code. If the court determines from the evidence submitted that a person who filed a petition under division (B) of this section has shown cause why the person's driver's or commercial driver's license or permit or nonresident operating privileges should not be suspended, the costs of the appeal proceeding shall be paid out of the county treasury of the county in which the proceedings were held.

(H) Any person whose driver's or commercial driver's license or permit or nonresident operating privileges are suspended under this section is not entitled to apply for or receive a new driver's or commercial driver's license or permit or to request or be granted nonresident operating privileges during the effective period of the suspension.

(I) Upon the termination of any suspension or other penalty imposed under this section involving the surrender of license or permit and upon the request of the person whose license or permit was suspended or surrendered, the registrar shall return the license or permit to the person upon determining that the person has complied with all provisions of section 4510.038 of the Revised Code or, if the registrar destroyed the license or permit pursuant to section 4510.52 of the Revised Code, shall reissue the person's license or permit.

(J) Any person whose driver's or commercial driver's license or permit or nonresident operating privileges are suspended as a repeat traffic offender under this section and who, during the suspension, operates any motor vehicle upon any public roads and highways is guilty of driving under a twelve-point suspension, a misdemeanor of the first degree. The court shall sentence the offender to a minimum term of three days in jail. No court shall suspend the first three days of jail time imposed pursuant to this division.

(K) The registrar, in accordance with specific statutory authority, may suspend the privilege of driving a motor vehicle on the public roads and highways of this state that is granted to nonresidents by section 4507.04 of the Revised Code.

(L) Any course of remedial driving instruction the director of public safety approves under this section shall require its students to attend at least fifty per cent of the course in person. The director shall not approve any course of remedial driving instruction that permits its students to take more than fifty per cent of the course in any other manner, including via video teleconferencing or the internet.

**HISTORY: 149 v S 123, § 1, eff. 1-1-04; 149 v H 490, § 1, eff. 1-1-04; 152 v H 67, § 101.01, eff. 6-30-07; 2011 HB 5, § 1, eff. Sept. 23, 2011.**

The effective date is set by § 609.10 of 152 v H 67.

The effective date is set by section 4 of S.B. 123.

See provisions, § 5 of S.B. 123 (149 v —), following RC § 4501.01.

## § 4510.038 Conditions for return of full driving privileges.

(A) Any person whose driver's or commercial driver's license or permit is suspended, or who is granted limited driving privileges, under section 4510.037, under division (H) of section 4511.19, or under section 4510.07 of the Revised Code for a violation of a municipal ordinance that is substantially equivalent to division (B) of section 4511.19 of the Revised Code, is not eligible to retain the license, or to have the driving privileges reinstated, until each of the following has occurred:

(1) The person successfully completes a course of remedial driving instruction approved by the director of public safety, provided the person commences taking the course after the person's driver's or commercial driver's license or permit is suspended under section 4507.021 or division (E) of section 4507.16 of the Revised Code. A minimum of twenty-five per cent of the number of hours of instruction included in the course shall be devoted to instruction on driver attitude.

The course also shall devote a number of hours to instruction in the area of alcohol and drugs and the operation of vehicles. The instruction shall include, but not be limited to, a review of the laws governing the operation of a motor vehicle while under the influence of alcohol, drugs, or a combination of them, the dangers of operating a motor vehicle while under the influence of alcohol, drugs, or a combination of them, and other information relating to the operation of motor vehicles and the consumption of alcoholic beverages and use of drugs. The director, in consultation with the director of alcohol and drug addiction services, shall prescribe the content of the instruction. The number of hours devoted to the area of alcohol and drugs and the operation of motor vehicles shall comprise a minimum of twenty-five per cent of the number of hours of instruction included in the course.

(2) The person is examined in the manner provided for in section 4507.20 of the Revised Code, and found by the registrar of motor vehicles to be qualified to operate a motor vehicle;

(3) The person gives and maintains proof of financial responsibility, in accordance with section 4509.45 of the Revised Code.

(B) Any course of remedial driving instruction the director of public safety approves under this section shall require its students to attend at least fifty per cent of the course in person. The director shall not approve any course of remedial driving instruction that permits its students to take more than fifty per cent of the course in any other manner, including via video teleconferencing or the internet.

**HISTORY: RC § 4507.41, 129 v 238 (Eff 9-14-61); 131 v 1087 (Eff 10-30-65); 140 v H 278 (Eff 7-26-84); RC § 4507.02.2, 141 v S 356 (Eff 9-24-86); 143 v H 381 (Eff 7-1-89); 144 v S 98 (Eff 11-12-92); 145 v S 82 (Eff 5-4-94); 146 v H 353 (Eff 9-17-96); 147 v S 60. Eff 10-21-97; 149 v S 123, § 1, eff. 1-1-04; 149 v S 123, § 1, eff. 1-1-04; 152 v H 67, § 101.01, eff. 6-30-07.**

The effective date is set by § 609.10 of 152 v H 67.

The effective date is set by section 4 of S.B. 123.

See provisions, § 5 of S.B. 123 (149 v —), following RC § 4501.01.

**Publisher's Note:**

This section was formerly § 4507.022. It was renumbered by S.B. 123, Acts 2002, effective January 1, 2004.

## § 4510.04 Affirmative defenses to driving under suspension and financial responsibility charges.

It is an affirmative defense to any prosecution brought under section 4510.11, 4510.14, 4510.16, or 4510.21 of the Revised Code or under any substantially equivalent municipal ordinance that the alleged offender drove under suspension, without a valid permit or driver's or commercial driver's license, or in violation of a restriction because of a substantial emergency, and because no other person was reasonably available to drive in response to the emergency.

It is an affirmative defense to any prosecution brought under section 4510.16 of the Revised Code that the order of suspension resulted from the failure of the alleged offender to respond to a financial responsibility random verification request under division (A)(3)(c) of section 4509.101 of the Revised Code and that, at the time of the initial financial responsibility random verification request, the alleged offender was in compliance with division (A)(1) of section 4509.101 of the Revised Code as shown by proof of financial responsibility that was in effect at the time of that request.

**HISTORY: 149 v S 123, § 1, eff. 1-1-04.**

The effective date is set by section 4 of S.B. 123.

See provisions, § 5 of S.B. 123 (149 v —), following RC § 4501.01.

## § 4510.05 Suspension for violation of ordinance substantially similar to statute.

Except as otherwise provided in section 4510.07 or in any other provision of the Revised Code, whenever an offender is convicted of or pleads guilty to a violation of a municipal ordinance that is substantially similar to a provision of the Revised Code, and a court is permitted or required to suspend a person's driver's or commercial driver's license or permit for a violation of that provision, a court, in addition to any other penalties authorized by law to impose upon the offender, may suspend the offender's driver's or commercial driver's license or permit or nonresident operating privileges for the period of time the court determines appropriate, but in no case shall the period of suspension imposed for the violation of the municipal ordinance shall not exceed the period of suspension that is permitted or required to be imposed for the violation of the provision of the Revised Code to which the municipal ordinance is substantially similar.

**HISTORY: 146 v H 510. Eff 9-19-96; 149 v S 123, § 1, eff. 1-1-04.**

The effective date is set by section 4 of S.B. 123.

See provisions, § 5 of S.B. 123 (149 v —), following RC § 4501.01.

**Publisher's Note:**

This section was formerly § 4507.1611. It was renumbered by S.B. 123, Acts 2002, effective January 1, 2004.

## § 4510.06 Suspension or cancellation by federal court.

If a United States district court whose jurisdiction lies within this state suspends or cancels the driver's or commercial driver's license, permit, or nonresident operating privileges of any person pursuant to the "Assimilative Crimes Act," 102 Stat. 4381 (1988), 18 U.S.C.A. 13, as amended, that suspension or cancellation is deemed to have the same effect throughout this state as if it were imposed under the laws of this state. In that type of case, if the United States district court observes the procedures prescribed by the Revised Code and utilizes the forms prescribed by the registrar of motor vehicles, the bureau of motor vehicles shall make the appropriate notation or record and shall take any other action that is prescribed or permitted by the Revised Code.

**HISTORY: 146 v H 353. Eff 9-17-96; 149 v S 123, § 1, eff. 1-1-04.**

The effective date is set by section 4 of S.B. 123.

See provisions, § 5 of S.B. 123 (149 v —), following RC § 4501.01.

**Not analogous to former RC § 4507.16.10, amended and renumbered to RC § 4507.55 in 145 v H 687, eff 10-12-94.**

**Publisher's Note:**

This section was formerly § 4507.1610. It was renumbered by S.B. 123, Acts 2002, effective January 1, 2004.

## § 4510.07 Violation of ordinance equivalent to vehicular homicide or manslaughter or solicitation offense.

The court imposing a sentence upon an offender for any violation of a municipal ordinance that is substantially equivalent to a violation of section 2903.06 or 2907.24 of the Revised Code or for any violation of a municipal OVI ordinance also shall impose a suspension of the offender's driver's license, commercial driver's license, temporary instruction permit, probationary license, or nonresident operating privilege from the range specified in division (B) of section 4510.02 of the Revised Code that is equivalent in length to the suspension required for a violation of section 2903.06 or 2907.24 or division (A) or (B) of section 4511.19 of the Revised Code under similar circumstances.

**HISTORY: 148 v S 107. Eff 3-23-2000; 149 v S 123, § 1, eff. 1-1-04.**

The effective date is set by section 4 of S.B. 123.

See provisions, § 5 of S.B. 123 (149 v —), following RC § 4501.01.

**Publisher's Note:**

This section was formerly § 4507.1613. It was renumbered by S.B. 123, Acts 2002, effective January 1, 2004.

## § 4510.10 Payment plan or extension where offender cannot reasonably pay reinstatement fees.

(A) As used in this section, "reinstatement fees" means the fees that are required under section 4507.1612, 4507.45, 4509.101, 4509.81, 4511.191, 4511.951, or any other provision of the Revised Code, or under a schedule established by the bureau of motor vehicles, in order to reinstate a driver's or commercial driver's license or permit or nonresident operating privilege of an offender under a suspension.

(B) Reinstatement fees are those fees that compensate the bureau of motor vehicles for suspensions, cancellations, or disqualifications of a person's driving privileges and to compensate the bureau and other agencies in their administration of programs intended to reduce and eliminate threats to public safety through education, treatment, and other activities. The registrar of motor vehicles shall not reinstate a driver's or commercial driver's license or permit or nonresident operating privilege of a person until the person has paid all reinstatement fees and has complied with all conditions for each suspension, cancellation, or disqualification incurred by that person.

(C) When a municipal court or county court determines in a pending case involving an offender that the offender cannot reasonably pay reinstatement fees due and owing by the offender relative to one or more suspensions that have been or will be imposed by the bureau of motor vehicles or by a court of this state, the court, by order, may undertake an installment payment plan or a payment extension plan for the payment of reinstatement fees due and owing to the bureau in that pending case. The court shall establish an installment payment plan or a payment extension plan under this division in accordance with the requirements of divisions (D)(1) and (2) of this section.

(D) Independent of the provisions of division (C) of this section, an offender who cannot reasonably pay reinstatement fees due and owing by the offender relative to a suspension that has been imposed on the offender may file a petition in the municipal court, county court, or, if the person is under the age of eighteen, the juvenile division of the court of common pleas in whose jurisdiction the person resides or, if the person is not a resident of this state, in the Franklin county municipal court or juvenile division of the Franklin county court of common pleas for an order that does either of the following, in order of preference:

(1) Establishes a reasonable payment plan of not less than fifty dollars per month, to be paid by the offender to the registrar of motor vehicles or an eligible deputy registrar, in all succeeding months until all reinstatement fees required of the offender are paid in full. If the person is making payments to a deputy registrar, the deputy registrar shall collect a service fee of ten dollars each time the deputy registrar collects a payment to compensate the deputy registrar for services performed under this section. The deputy registrar shall retain eight dollars of the service fee and shall transmit the reinstatement payments, plus two dollars of each service fee, to the registrar in the manner the registrar shall determine.

(2) If the offender, but for the payment of the reinstatement fees, otherwise would be entitled to operate a vehicle in this state or to obtain reinstatement of the offender's operating privileges, permits the offender to operate a motor vehicle, as authorized by the court, until a future date upon which date all reinstatement fees must be paid in full. A payment extension granted under this division shall not exceed one hundred eighty days, and any operating privileges granted under this division shall be solely for the purpose of permitting the offender occupational or 'family necessity' privileges in order to enable the offender to reasonably acquire the delinquent reinstatement fees due and owing.

(E) If a municipal court, county court, or juvenile division enters an order of the type described in division (C) or division (D)(1) or (2) of this section, the court, at any time after the issuance of the order, may determine that a change of circumstances has occurred and may amend the order as justice requires, provided that the amended order also shall be an order that is permitted under division (C) or division (D)(1) or (2) of this section.

(F) If a court enters an order of the type described in division (C), (D)(1), (D)(2), or (E) of this section, during the pendency of the order, the offender in relation to whom it applies is not subject to prosecution for failing to pay the reinstatement fees covered by the order.

(G) Reinstatement fees are debts that may be discharged in bankruptcy.

**HISTORY: 149 v S 123, § 1, eff. 1-1-04; 150 v H 230, § 1, eff. 9-16-04; 151 v H 461, § 1, eff. 4-4-07; 152 v H 562, § 101.01, eff. 9-23-08; 2011 HB 114, § 101.01, eff. June 29, 2011.**

Acts 2011, HB 114, § 806.10 provides: "The items of law contained in this act, and their applications, are severable. If any item of law contained in this act, or if any application of any item of law contained in this act, is held invalid, the invalidity does not affect other items of law contained in this act and their applications that can be given effect without the invalid item or application."

The effective date is set by § 812.10 of 152 v H 562.

The effective date is set by section 4 of S.B. 123.

See provisions, § 5 of S.B. 123 (149 v —), following RC § 4501.01.

## § 4510.11 Driving under suspension.

(A) Except as provided in division (B) of this section, no person whose driver's or commercial driver's license or permit or nonresident operating privilege has been suspended under any provision of the Revised Code, other than Chapter 4509. of the Revised Code, or under any applicable law in any other jurisdiction in which the person's license or permit was issued shall operate any motor vehicle upon the public roads and highways or upon any public or private property used by the public for purposes of vehicular travel or parking within this state during the period of suspension unless the person is granted limited driving privileges and is operating the vehicle in accordance with the terms of the limited driving privileges.

(B) No person shall operate any motor vehicle upon a highway or any public or private property used by the public for purposes of vehicular travel or parking in this state in violation of any restriction of the person's driver's or commercial driver's license or permit imposed under division (D) of section 4506.10 or under section 4507.14 of the Revised Code.

(C) Upon the request or motion of the prosecuting authority, a noncertified copy of the law enforcement automated data system report or a noncertified copy of a record of the registrar of motor vehicles that shows the name, date of birth, and social security number of a person charged with a violation of division (A) or (B) of this section may be admitted into evidence as prima-facie evidence that the license of the person was under suspension at the time of the alleged violation of division (A) of this section or the person operated a motor vehicle in violation of a restriction at the time of the alleged violation of division (B) of this section. The person charged with a violation of division (A) or (B) of this section may offer evidence to rebut this prima-facie evidence.

(D)(1) Whoever violates division (A) or (B) of this section is guilty of a misdemeanor of the first degree. The court may impose upon the offender a class seven suspension of the offender's driver's license, commercial driver's license, temporary instruction permit, probationary license, or nonresident operating privilege from the range specified in division (A)(7) of section 4510.02 of the Revised Code.

(2)(a) Except as provided in division (D)(2)(b) or (c) of this section, the court, in addition to any other penalty that it imposes on the offender and if the vehicle is registered in the offender's name and if, within three years of the offense, the offender previously has been convicted of or pleaded guilty to one violation of this section or section 4510.111 or 4510.16 of the Revised Code, or a substantially equivalent municipal ordinance, the court, in addition to or independent of any other sentence that it imposes upon the offender, may order the immobilization of the vehicle involved in the offense for thirty days and the impoundment of that vehicle's license plates for thirty days in accordance with section 4503.233 of the Revised Code.

(b) If the vehicle is registered in the offender's name and if, within three years of the offense, the offender previously has been convicted of or pleaded guilty to two violations of this section, or any combination of two violations of this section or section 4510.111 or 4510.16 of the Revised Code, or of a substantially similar municipal ordinance, the court, in addition to any other sentence that it imposes on the offender, may order the immobilization of the vehicle involved in the offense for sixty days and the impoundment of that vehicle's license plates for sixty days in accordance with section 4503.233 of the Revised Code.

(c) If the vehicle is registered in the offender's name and if, within three years of the offense, the offender previously has been convicted of or pleaded guilty to three or more violations of this section, or any combination of three or more violations of this section or section 4510.111 or 4510.16 of the Revised Code, or of a substantially similar municipal ordinance, the court, in addition to any other sentence that it imposes on the offender, may order the criminal forfeiture of the vehicle involved in the offense to the state.

(E) Any order for immobilization and impoundment under this section shall be issued and enforced under sections 4503.233 and 4507.02 of the Revised Code, as applicable. The court shall not release a vehicle from immobilization ordered under this section unless the court is presented with current proof of financial responsibility with respect to that vehicle.

(F) Any order of criminal forfeiture under this section shall be issued and enforced under section 4503.234 of the Revised Code. Upon receipt of the copy of the order from the court, neither the registrar of motor vehicles nor a deputy registrar shall accept any application for the registration or transfer of registration of any motor vehicle owned or leased by the person named in the declaration of forfeiture. The period of registration denial shall be five years after the date of the order, unless, during that period, the court having jurisdiction of the offense that led to the order terminates the forfeiture and notifies the registrar of the termination. The registrar then shall take necessary measures to permit the person to register a vehicle owned or leased by the person or to transfer registration of the vehicle.

(G) The offender shall provide the court with proof of financial responsibility as defined in section 4509.01 of the Revised Code. If the offender fails to provide that proof of financial responsibility, then, in addition to any other penalties provided by law, the court may order restitution pursuant to section 2929.28 of the Revised Code in an amount not exceeding five thousand dollars for any economic loss arising from an accident or collision that was the direct and proximate result of the offender's operation of the vehicle before, during, or after committing the offense for which the offender is sentenced under this section.

**HISTORY: 149 v S 123, § 1, eff. 1-1-04; 153 v H 1, § 101.01, eff. 10-16-09; 153 v H 338, § 1, eff. 9-17-10; 2011 HB 5, § 1, eff. Sept. 23, 2011.**

The effective date is set by § 812.10 of 153 v H 1.

The effective date is set by section 4 of S.B. 123.

See provisions, § 5 of S.B. 123 (149 v —), following RC § 4501.01.

## § 4510.111 Operating a motor vehicle with a suspended license prohibited; prima facie evidence; penalty; order for immobilization and impoundment; order for criminal forfeiture.

(A) No person shall operate any motor vehicle upon a highway or any public or private property used by the public for purposes of vehicular travel or parking in this state whose driver's or commercial driver's license has been suspended pursuant to section 4510.22 of the Revised Code for failing to appear in court or to pay a fine, resulting in license forfeiture.

(B) No person shall operate any motor vehicle upon a highway or any public or private property used by the public for purposes of vehicular travel or parking in this state whose driver's or commercial driver's license has been suspended pursuant to section 3123.58 of the Revised Code for being in default in payment of child support.

(C) Upon the request or motion of the prosecuting authority, a noncertified copy of the law enforcement automated data system report or a noncertified copy of a record of the registrar of motor vehicles that shows the name, date of birth, and social security number of a person charged with a violation of division (A) or (B) of this section may be admitted into evidence as prima-facie evidence that the license of the person was under suspension at the time of the alleged violation of division (A) or (B) of this section. The person charged with a violation of division (A) or (B) of this section may offer evidence to rebut this prima-facie evidence.

(D) Whoever violates division (A) or (B) of this section is guilty of driving under suspension and shall be punished as provided in division (D) of this section.

(1) Except as otherwise provided in division (D)(2) of this section, the offense is an unclassified misdemeanor. The offender shall be sentenced pursuant to sections 2929.21 to 2929.28 of the Revised Code, except that the offender shall not be sentenced to a jail term; the offender shall not be sentenced to a community residential sanction pursuant to section 2929.26 of the Revised Code; notwithstanding division (A)(2)(a) of section 2929.28 of the Revised Code, the offender may be fined up to one thousand dollars; and, notwithstanding division (A)(3) of section 2929.27 of the Revised Code, the offender may be ordered pursuant to division (C) of that section to serve a term of community service of up to five hundred hours. The failure of an offender to complete a term of community service imposed by the court may be punished as indirect criminal contempt under division (A) of section 2705.02 of the Revised Code that may be filed in the underlying case.

(2) If, within three years of the offense, the offender previously was convicted of or pleaded guilty to two or more violations of division (A) or (B) of this section, or any combination of two or more violations of division (A) or (B) of this section or section 4510.11 or 4510.16 of the Revised Code, or a substantially equivalent municipal ordinance, the offense is a misdemeanor of the first degree. The offender shall provide the court with proof of financial responsibility as defined in section 4509.01 of the Revised Code. If the offender fails to provide that proof of financial responsibility, then, in addition to any penalties provided by law, the court may order restitution pursuant to section 2929.28 of the Revised Code in an amount not exceeding five thousand dollars for any economic loss arising from an accident or collision that was the direct and proximate result of the offender's operation of the vehicle before, during, or after committing the offense for which the offender is sentenced under this section.

(3) In all cases, the court may impose a class seven suspension of the offender's driver's or commercial driver's license or permit or nonresident operating privilege from the range of time specified in division (A)(7) of section 4507.02 of the Revised Code.

(4)(a) In all cases, if the vehicle is registered in the offender's name and if, within three years of the offense, the offender previously has been convicted of or pleaded guilty to one violation of division (A) or (B) of this section or section 4510.11 or 4510.16 of the Revised Code, or a substantially equivalent municipal ordinance, the court, in addition to any other sentence that it imposes upon the offender, may order the immobilization of the vehicle involved in the offense for thirty days and the impoundment of that vehicle's license plates for thirty days in accordance with section 4503.233 of the Revised Code.

(b) In all cases, if the vehicle is registered in the offender's name and if, within three years of the offense, the offender previously has been convicted of or pleaded guilty to two violations of division (A) or (B) of this section, or any combination of two violations of division (A) or (B) of this section or section 4510.11 or 4510.16 of the Revised Code, or a substantially equivalent municipal ordinance, the court, in addition to any other sentence that it imposes upon the offender, may order the immobilization of the vehicle involved in the offense for sixty days and the impoundment of that vehicle's license plates for sixty days in accordance with section 4503.233 of the Revised Code.

(c) In all cases, if the vehicle is registered in the offender's name and if, within three years of the offense, the offender previously has been convicted of or pleaded guilty to three or more violations of this section, or any combination of three or more violations of this section or section 4510.11 or 4510.16 of the Revised Code, or a substantially equivalent municipal ordinance, the court, in addition to any other sentence that it imposes upon the offender, may order the criminal forfeiture of the vehicle involved in the offense to the state.

(E) An order for immobilization and impoundment under this section shall be issued and enforced under sections 4503.233 and 4507.02 of the Revised Code, as applicable. The court shall not release a motor vehicle from immobilization ordered under this section unless the court is presented with current proof of financial responsibility with respect to that motor vehicle.

(F) An order for criminal forfeiture under this section shall be issued and enforced under section 4503.234 of the Revised Code. Upon receipt of a copy of the order from the court, neither the registrar of motor vehicles nor a deputy registrar shall accept any application for the registration or transfer of registration of any motor vehicle owned or leased by the person named in the declaration of forfeiture. The period of registration denial shall be five years after the date of the order unless, during that period, the court having jurisdiction of the offense that led to the order terminates the forfeiture and notifies the registrar of the termination. The registrar then shall take the necessary measures to permit the person to register a vehicle owned or leased by the person or to transfer registration of the vehicle.

**HISTORY: 2011 HB 5, § 1, eff. Sept. 23, 2011.**

## § 4510.12 Operating motor vehicle without valid license.

(A)(1) No person, except those expressly exempted under sections 4507.03, 4507.04, and 4507.05 of the Revised Code, shall operate any motor vehicle upon a public road or highway or any public or private property used by the public for purposes of vehicular travel or parking in this state unless the person has a valid driver's license issued under Chapter 4507. of the Revised Code or a commercial driver's license issued under Chapter 4506. of the Revised Code.

(2) No person, except a person expressly exempted under sections 4507.03, 4507.04, and 4507.05 of the Revised Code, shall operate any motorcycle upon a public road or highway or any public or private property used by the public for purposes of vehicular travel or parking in this state unless the person has a valid license as a motorcycle operator that was issued upon application by the registrar of motor vehicles under Chapter 4507. of the Revised Code. The license shall be in the form of an endorsement, as determined by the registrar, upon a driver's or commercial driver's license, if the person has a valid license to operate a motor vehicle or commercial motor vehicle, or in the form of a restricted license as provided in section 4507.14 of the Revised Code, if the person does not have a valid license to operate a motor vehicle or commercial motor vehicle.

(B) Upon the request or motion of the prosecuting authority, a noncertified copy of the law enforcement automated data system report or a noncertified copy of a record of the registrar of motor vehicles that shows the name, date of birth, and social security number of a person charged with a violation of division (A)(1) or (2) of this section may be admitted into evidence as prima-facie evidence that the person did not have either a valid driver's or commercial driver's license at the time of the alleged violation of division (A)(1) of this section or a valid license as a motorcycle operator either in the form of an endorsement upon a driver's or commercial driver's license or a restricted license at the time of the alleged violation of division (A)(2) of this section. The person charged with a violation of division (A)(1) or (2) of this section may offer evidence to rebut this prima-facie evidence.

(C) Whoever violates this section is guilty of operating a motor vehicle or motorcycle without a valid license and shall be punished as follows:

(1) If the trier of fact finds that the offender never has held a valid driver's or commercial driver's license issued by this state or any other jurisdiction, or, in a case involving the operation of a motorcycle by the offender, if the offender has never held a valid license as a motorcycle operator, either in the form of an endorsement upon a driver's or commercial driver's license or in the form of a restricted license, except as otherwise provided in this division, the offense is an unclassified misdemeanor. When the offense is an unclassified misdemeanor, the offender shall be sentenced pursuant to sections 2929.21 to 2929.28 of the Revised Code, except that the offender shall not be sentenced to a jail term; the offender shall not be sentenced to a community residential sanction pursuant to section 2929.26 of the Revised Code; notwithstanding division (A)(2)(a) of section 2929.28 of the Revised Code, the offender may be fined up to one thousand dollars; and, notwithstanding division (A)(3) of section 2929.27 of the Revised Code, the offender may be ordered pursuant to division (C) of that section to serve a term of community service of up to five hundred hours. The failure of an offender to complete a term of community service imposed by the court may be punished as indirect criminal contempt under division (A) of section 2705.02 of the Revised Code that may be filed in the underlying case. If the offender previously has been convicted of or pleaded guilty to any violation of this section or a substantially equivalent municipal ordinance, the offense is a misdemeanor of the first degree.

(2) If the offender's driver's or commercial driver's license or permit or, in a case involving the operation of a motorcycle by the offender, the offender's driver's or commercial driver's license bearing the motorcycle endorsement or the offender's restricted license was expired at the time of the offense, except as otherwise provided in this division, the offense is a minor misdemeanor. If, within three years of the offense, the offender previously has been convicted of or pleaded guilty to two or more violations of this section or a substantially equivalent municipal ordinance, the offense is a misdemeanor of the first degree.

(D) The court shall not impose a license suspension for a first violation of this section or if more than three years have passed since the offender's last violation of this section or a substantially equivalent municipal ordinance.

(E) If the offender is sentenced under division (C)(2) of this section, if within three years of the offense the offender previously was convicted of or pleaded guilty to one or more violations of this section or a substantially equivalent municipal ordinance, and if the offender's license was expired for more than six months at the time of the offense, the court may impose a class seven suspension of the offender's driver's license, commercial driver's license, temporary instruction permit, probationary license, or nonresident operating privilege from the range specified in division (A)(7) of section 4510.02 of the Revised Code.

**HISTORY: 149 v S 123, § 1, eff. 1-1-04; 150 v H 52, § 1, eff. 6-1-04; 153 v H 1, § 101.01, eff. 10-16-09; 153 v H 338, § 1, eff. 9-17-10; 2011 HB 5, § 1, eff. Sept. 23, 2011.**

The effective date is set by § 812.10 of 153 v H 1.
The effective date is set by section 4 of S.B. 123.
See provisions, § 5 of S.B. 123 (149 v —), following RC § 4501.01.

## § 4510.13 Restrictions on suspending suspension or granting limited driving privileges; surrender of license or permit in certain cases; immobilizing or disabling device order.

(A)(1) Divisions (A)(2) to (9) of this section apply to a judge or mayor regarding the suspension of, or the grant of limited driving privileges during a suspension of, an offender's driver's or commercial driver's license or permit or nonresident operating privilege imposed under division (G) or (H) of section 4511.19 of the Revised Code, under division (B) or (C) of section 4511.191 [4511.19.1] of the Revised Code, or under section 4510.07 of the Revised Code for a conviction of a violation of a municipal OVI ordinance.

(2) No judge or mayor shall suspend the following portions of the suspension of an offender's driver's or commercial driver's license or permit or nonresident operating privilege imposed under division (G) or (H) of section 4511.19 of the Revised Code or under section 4510.07 of the Revised Code for a conviction of a violation of a municipal OVI ordinance, provided that division (A)(2) of this section does not limit a court or mayor in crediting any period of suspension imposed pursuant to division (B) or (C) of section 4511.191 [4511.19.1] of the Revised Code against any time of judicial suspension imposed pursuant to section 4511.19 or 4510.07 of the Revised Code, as described in divisions (B)(2) and (C)(2) of section 4511.191 [4511.19.1] of the Revised Code:

(a) The first six months of a suspension imposed under division (G)(1)(a) of section 4511.19 of the Revised Code or of a comparable length suspension imposed under section 4510.07 of the Revised Code;

(b) The first year of a suspension imposed under division (G)(1)(b) or (c) of section 4511.19 of the Revised Code or of a comparable length suspension imposed under section 4510.07 of the Revised Code;

(c) The first three years of a suspension imposed under division (G)(1)(d) or (e) of section 4511.19 of the Revised Code or of a comparable length suspension imposed under section 4510.07 of the Revised Code;

(d) The first sixty days of a suspension imposed under division (H) of section 4511.19 of the Revised Code or of a comparable length suspension imposed under section 4510.07 of the Revised Code.

(3) No judge or mayor shall grant limited driving privileges to an offender whose driver's or commercial driver's license or permit or nonresident operating privilege has been suspended under division (G) or (H) of section 4511.19 of the Revised Code, under division (C) of section 4511.191 [4511.19.1] of the Revised Code, or under section 4510.07 of the Revised Code for a municipal OVI conviction if the offender, within the preceding six years, has been convicted of or pleaded guilty to three or more violations of one or more of the Revised Code sections, municipal ordinances, statutes of the United States or another state, or municipal ordinances of a municipal corporation of another state that are identified in divisions (G)(2)(b) to (h) of section 2919.22 of the Revised Code.

Additionally, no judge or mayor shall grant limited driving privileges to an offender whose driver's or commercial driver's license or permit or nonresident operating privilege has been suspended under division (B) of section 4511.191 [4511.19.1] of the Revised Code if the offender, within the preceding six years, has refused three previous requests to consent to a chemical test of the person's whole blood, blood serum or plasma, breath, or urine to determine its alcohol content.

(4) No judge or mayor shall grant limited driving privileges for employment as a driver of commercial motor vehicles to an offender whose driver's or commercial driver's license or permit or nonresident operating privilege has been suspended under division (G) or (H) of section 4511.19 of the Revised Code, under division (B) or (C) of section 4511.191 [4511.19.1] of the Revised Code, or under section 4510.07 of the Revised Code for a municipal OVI conviction if the offender is disqualified from operating a commercial motor vehicle, or whose license or permit has been suspended, under section 3123.58 or 4506.16 of the Revised Code.

(5) No judge or mayor shall grant limited driving privileges to an offender whose driver's or commercial driver's license or permit or nonresident operating privilege has been suspended under division (G) or (H) of section 4511.19 of the Revised Code, under division (C) of section 4511.191 [4511.19.1] of the Revised Code, or under section 4510.07 of the Revised Code for a conviction of a violation of a municipal OVI ordinance during any of the following periods of time:

(a) The first fifteen days of a suspension imposed under division (G)(1)(a) of section 4511.19 of the Revised Code or a comparable length suspension imposed under section 4510.07 of the Revised Code, or of a suspension imposed under division (C)(1)(a) of section 4511.191 [4511.19.1] of the Revised Code. On or after the sixteenth day of the suspension, the court may grant limited driving privileges, but the court may require that the offender shall not exercise the privileges unless the vehicles the offender operates are equipped with immobilizing or disabling devices that monitor the offender's alcohol consumption or any other type of immobilizing or disabling devices, except as provided in division (C) of section 4510.43 of the Revised Code.

(b) The first forty-five days of a suspension imposed under division (C)(1)(b) of section 4511.191 [4511.19.1] of the Revised Code. On or after the forty-sixth day of suspension, the court may grant limited driving privileges, but the court may require that the offender shall not exercise the privileges unless the vehicles the offender operates are equipped with immobilizing or disabling devices that monitor the offender's alcohol consumption or any other type of immobilizing or disabling devices, except as provided in division (C) of section 4510.43 of the Revised Code.

(c) The first sixty days of a suspension imposed under division (H) of section 4511.19 of the Revised Code or a comparable length suspension imposed under section 4510.07 of the Revised Code.

(d) The first one hundred eighty days of a suspension imposed under division (C)(1)(c) of section 4511.191 [4511.19.1] of the Revised Code. On or after the one hundred eighty-first day of suspension, the court may grant limited driving privileges, and either of the following applies:

(i) If the underlying arrest is alcohol-related, the court shall issue an order that, except as provided in division (C) of section 4510.43 of the Revised Code, for the remainder of the period of suspension the offender shall not exercise the privileges unless the vehicles the offender operates are equipped with a certified ignition interlock device.

(ii) If the underlying arrest is drug-related, the court in its discretion may issue an order that, except as provided in division (C) of section 4510.43 of the Revised Code, for the remainder of the period of suspension the offender shall not exercise the privileges unless the vehicles the offender operates are equipped with a certified ignition interlock device.

(e) The first forty-five days of a suspension imposed under division (G)(1)(b) of section 4511.19 of the Revised Code or a comparable length suspension imposed under section 4510.07 of the Revised Code. On or after the forty-sixth day of the suspension, the court may grant limited driving privileges, and either of the following applies:

(i) If the underlying conviction is alcohol-related, the court shall issue an order that, except as provided in division (C) of section 4510.43 of the Revised Code, for the remainder of the period of suspension the offender shall not exercise the privileges unless the vehicles the offender operates are equipped with a certified ignition interlock device.

(ii) If the underlying conviction is drug-related, the court in its discretion may issue an order that, except as provided in division (C) of section 4510.43 of the Revised Code, for the remainder of the period of suspension the offender shall not exercise the privileges unless the vehicles the offender operates are equipped with a certified ignition interlock device.

(f) The first one hundred eighty days of a suspension imposed under division (G)(1)(c) of section 4511.19 of the Revised Code or a comparable length suspension imposed under section 4510.07 of the Revised Code. On or after the one hundred eighty-first day of the suspension, the court may grant limited driving privileges, and either of the following applies:

(i) If the underlying conviction is alcohol-related, the court shall issue an order that, except as provided in division (C) of section 4510.43 of the Revised Code, for the remainder of the period of suspension the offender shall not exercise the privileges unless the vehicles the offender operates are equipped with a certified ignition interlock device.

(ii) If the underlying conviction is drug-related, the court in its discretion may issue an order that, except as provided in division (C) of section 4510.43 of the Revised Code, for the remainder of the period of suspension the offender shall not exercise the privileges unless the vehicles the offender operates are equipped with a certified ignition interlock device.

(g) The first three years of a suspension imposed under division (G)(1)(d) or (e) of section 4511.19 of the Revised Code or a comparable length suspension imposed under section 4510.07 of the Revised Code, or of a suspension imposed under division (C)(1)(d) of section 4511.191 [4511.19.1] of the Revised Code. On or after the first three years of suspension, the court may grant limited driving privileges, and either of the following applies:

(i) If the underlying conviction is alcohol-related, the court shall issue an order that, except as provided in division (C) of section 4510.43 of the Revised Code, for the remainder of the period of suspension the offender shall not exercise the privileges unless the vehicles the offender operates are equipped with a certified ignition interlock device.

(ii) If the underlying conviction is drug-related, the court in its discretion may issue an order that, except as provided in division (C) of section 4510.43 of the Revised Code, for the remainder of the period of suspension the offender shall not exercise the privileges unless the vehicles the offender operates are equipped with a certified ignition interlock device.

(6) No judge or mayor shall grant limited driving privileges to an offender whose driver's or commercial driver's license or permit or nonresident operating privilege has been suspended under division (B) of section 4511.191 [4511.19.1] of the Revised Code during any of the following periods of time:

(a) The first thirty days of suspension imposed under division (B)(1)(a) of section 4511.191 [4511.19.1] of the Revised Code;

(b) The first ninety days of suspension imposed under division (B)(1)(b) of section 4511.191 [4511.19.1] of the Revised Code;

(c) The first year of suspension imposed under division (B)(1)(c) of section 4511.191 [4511.19.1] of the Revised Code;

(d) The first three years of suspension imposed under division (B)(1)(d) of section 4511.191 [4511.19.1] of the Revised Code.

(7) In any case in which a judge or mayor grants limited driving privileges to an offender whose driver's or commercial driver's license or permit or nonresident operating privilege has been suspended under division (G)(1)(b), (c), (d), or (e) of section 4511.19 of the Revised Code, under division (G)(1)(a) of section 4511.19 of the Revised Code for a violation of division (A)(1)(f), (g), (h), or (i) of that section, or under section 4510.07 of the Revised Code for a municipal OVI conviction for which sentence would have been imposed under division (G)(1)(a)(ii) or (G)(1)(b), (c), (d), or (e) of section 4511.19 of the Revised Code had the offender been charged with and convicted of a violation of section 4511.19 of the Revised Code instead of a violation of the municipal OVI ordinance, the judge or mayor shall impose as a condition of the privileges that the offender must display on the vehicle that is driven subject to the privileges restricted license plates that are issued under section 4503.231 [4503.23.1] of the Revised Code, except as provided in division (B) of that section.

(8) In any case in which the offender operates a motor vehicle that is not equipped with an ignition interlock device, circumvents the device, or tampers with the device or in any case in which the court receives notice pursuant to section 4510.46 of the Revised Code that a certified

ignition interlock device required by an order issued under division (A)(5)(e), (f), or (g) of this section prevented an offender from starting a motor vehicle, the following applies:

(a) If the offender was sentenced under division (G)(1)(b) of section 4511.19 of the Revised Code, on a first instance the court may require the offender to wear a monitor that provides continuous alcohol monitoring that is remote. On a second instance, the court shall require the offender to wear a monitor that provides continuous alcohol monitoring that is remote for a minimum of forty days. On a third instance or more, the court shall require the offender to wear a monitor that provides continuous alcohol monitoring that is remote for a minimum of sixty days.

(b) If the offender was sentenced under division (G)(1)(c), (d), or (e) of section 4511.19 of the Revised Code, on a first instance the court shall require the offender to wear a monitor that provides continuous alcohol monitoring that is remote for a minimum of forty days. On a second instance or more, the court shall require the offender to wear a monitor that provides continuous alcohol monitoring that is remote for a minimum of sixty days.

(9) In any case in which the court issues an order under this section prohibiting an offender from exercising limited driving privileges unless the vehicles the offender operates are equipped with an immobilizing or disabling device, including a certified ignition interlock device, or requires an offender to wear a monitor that provides continuous alcohol monitoring that is remote, the court shall impose an additional court cost of two dollars and fifty cents upon the offender. The court shall not waive the payment of the two dollars and fifty cents unless the court determines that the offender is indigent and waives the payment of all court costs imposed upon the indigent offender. The clerk of court shall transmit one hundred per cent of this mandatory court cost collected during a month on or before the twenty-third day of the following month to the state treasury to be credited to the state highway safety fund created under section 4501.06 of the Revised Code, to be used by the department of public safety to cover costs associated with maintaining the habitual OVI/OMWI offender registry created under section 5502.10 of the Revised Code. In its discretion the court may impose an additional court cost of two dollars and fifty cents upon the offender. The clerk of court shall retain this discretionary two dollar and fifty cent court cost, if imposed, and shall deposit it in the court's special projects fund that is established under division (E)(1) of section 2303.201 [2303.20.1], division (B)(1) of section 1901.26, or division (B)(1) of section 1907.24 of the Revised Code.

(10) In any case in which the court issues an order under this section prohibiting an offender from exercising limited driving privileges unless the vehicles the offender operates are equipped with an immobilizing or disabling device, including a certified ignition interlock device, the court shall notify the offender at the time the offender is granted limited driving privileges that, in accordance with section 4510.46 of the Revised Code, if the court receives notice that the device prevented the offender from starting the motor vehicle because the device was tampered with or circumvented or because the analysis of the deep-lung breath sample or other method employed by the device to measure the concentration by weight of alcohol in the offender's breath indicated the presence of alcohol in the offender's breath in a concentration sufficient to prevent the device from permitting the motor vehicle to be started, the court may increase the period of suspension of the offender's driver's or commercial driver's license or permit or nonresident operating privilege from that originally imposed by the court by a factor of two and may increase the period of time during which the offender will be prohibited from exercising any limited driving privileges granted to the offender unless the vehicles the offender operates are equipped with a certified ignition interlock device by a factor of two.

(B) Any person whose driver's or commercial driver's license or permit or nonresident operating privilege has been suspended pursuant to section 4511.19 or 4511.191 [4511.19.1] of the Revised Code or under section 4510.07 of the Revised Code for a violation of a municipal OVI ordinance may file a petition for limited driving privileges during the suspension. The person shall file the petition in the court that has jurisdiction over the place of arrest. Subject to division (A) of this section, the court may grant the person limited driving privileges during the period during which the suspension otherwise would be imposed. However, the court shall not grant the privileges for employment as a driver of a commercial motor vehicle to any person who is disqualified from operating a commercial motor vehicle under section 4506.16 of the Revised Code or during any of the periods prescribed by division (A) of this section.

(C)(1) After a driver's or commercial driver's license or permit or nonresident operating privilege has been suspended pursuant to section 2903.06, 2903.08, 2903.11, 2907.24, 2921.331 [2921.33.1], 2923.02, 2929.02, 4511.19, 4511.251 [4511.25.1], 4549.02, 4549.021 [4549.02.1], or 5743.99 of the Revised Code, any provision of Chapter 2925. of the Revised Code, or section 4510.07 of the Revised Code for a violation of a municipal OVI ordinance, the judge of the court or mayor of the mayor's court that suspended the license, permit, or privilege shall cause the offender to deliver to the court the license or permit. The judge, mayor, or clerk of the court or mayor's court shall forward to the registrar the license or permit together with notice of the action of the court.

(2) A suspension of a commercial driver's license under any section or chapter identified in division (C)(1) of this section shall be concurrent with any period of suspension or disqualification under section 3123.58 or 4506.16 of the Revised Code. No person who is disqualified for life from holding a commercial driver's license under section 4506.16 of the Revised Code shall be issued a driver's license under this chapter during the period for which the commercial driver's license was suspended under this section, and no person whose commercial driver's license is suspended under any section or chapter identified in division (C)(1) of this section shall be issued a driver's license under Chapter 4507. of the Revised Code during the period of the suspension.

(3) No judge or mayor shall suspend any class one suspension, or any portion of any class one suspension, imposed under section 2903.04, 2903.06, 2903.08, or 2921.331 [2921.33.1] of the Revised Code. No judge or mayor shall suspend the first thirty days of any class two, class three, class four, class five, or class six suspension imposed under section 2903.06, 2903.08, 2903.11, 2923.02, or 2929.02 of the Revised Code.

(D) The judge of the court or mayor of the mayor's court shall credit any time during which an offender was subject to an administrative suspension of the offender's driver's or commercial driver's license or permit or nonresident operating privilege imposed pursuant to section 4511.191 [4511.19.1] or 4511.192 [4511.19.2] of the Revised Code or a suspension imposed by a judge, referee, or mayor pursuant to division (B)(1) or (2) of section 4511.196 [4511.19.6] of the Revised Code against the time to be served under a related suspension imposed pursuant to any section or chapter identified in division (C)(1) of this section.

(E) The judge or mayor shall notify the bureau of motor vehicles of any determinations made pursuant to this section and of any suspension imposed pursuant to any section or chapter identified in division (C)(1) of this section.

(F)(1) If a court issues an immobilizing or disabling device order under section 4510.43 of the Revised Code, the order shall authorize the offender during the specified period to operate a motor vehicle only if it is equipped with an immobilizing or disabling device, except as provided in division (C) of that section. The court shall provide the offender with a copy of an immobilizing or disabling device order issued under section 4510.43 of the Revised Code, and the offender shall use the copy of the order in lieu of an Ohio driver's or commercial driver's license or permit until the registrar or a deputy registrar issues the offender a restricted license.

An order issued under section 4510.43 of the Revised Code does not authorize or permit the offender to whom it has been issued to operate a vehicle during any time that the offender's driver's or commercial driver's license or permit is suspended under any other provision of law.

(2) An offender may present an immobilizing or disabling device order to the registrar or to a deputy registrar. Upon presentation of the order to the registrar or a deputy registrar, the registrar or deputy registrar shall issue the offender a restricted license. A restricted license issued under this division shall be identical to an Ohio driver's license, except that it shall have printed on its face a statement that the offender is prohibited during the period specified in the court order from operating any motor vehicle that is not equipped with an immobilizing or disabling device. The date of commencement and the date of termination of the period of suspension shall be indicated conspicuously upon the face of the license.

**HISTORY: 149 v S 123, § 1, eff. 1-1-04; 150 v H 163, § 1, eff. 9-23-04; 151 v H 461, § 1, eff. 4-4-07; 152 v S 17, § 1, eff. 9-30-08; 152 v H 215, § 1, eff. 4-7-09.**

The effective date is set by section 4 of S.B. 123.

See provisions, § 5 of S.B. 123 (149 v —), following RC § 4501.01.

## § 4510.14 Driving under OVI suspension.

(A) No person whose driver's or commercial driver's license or permit or nonresident operating privilege has been suspended under section 4511.19, 4511.191, or 4511.196 of the Revised Code or under section 4510.07 of the Revised Code for a conviction of a violation of a municipal OVI ordinance shall operate any motor vehicle upon the public roads or highways within this state during the period of the suspension.

(B) Whoever violates this section is guilty of driving under OVI suspension. The court shall sentence the offender under Chapter 2929. of the Revised Code, subject to the differences authorized or required by this section.

(1) Except as otherwise provided in division (B)(2) or (3) of this section, driving under OVI suspension is a misdemeanor of the first degree. The court shall sentence the offender to all of the following:

(a) A mandatory jail term of three consecutive days. The three-day term shall be imposed, unless, subject to division (C) of this section, the court instead imposes a sentence of not less than thirty consecutive days of house arrest with electronic monitoring. A period of house arrest with electronic monitoring imposed under this division shall not exceed six months. If the court imposes a mandatory three-day jail term under this division, the court may impose a jail term in addition to that term, provided that in no case shall the cumulative jail term imposed for the offense exceed six months.

(b) A fine of not less than two hundred fifty and not more than one thousand dollars;

(c) A license suspension under division (E) of this section;

(d) If the vehicle the offender was operating at the time of the offense is registered in the offender's name, immobilization for thirty days of the offender's vehicle and impoundment for thirty days of the identification license plates of that vehicle. The order for immobilization and impoundment shall be issued and enforced in accordance with section 4503.233 of the Revised Code.

(2) If, within six years of the offense, the offender previously has been convicted of or pleaded guilty to one violation of this section or one equivalent offense, driving under OVI suspension is a misdemeanor of the first degree. The court shall sentence the offender to all of the following:

(a) A mandatory jail term of ten consecutive days. Notwithstanding the jail terms provided in sections 2929.21 to 2929.28 of the Revised Code, the court may sentence the offender to a longer jail term of not more than one year. The ten-day mandatory jail term shall be imposed unless, subject to division (C) of this section, the court instead imposes a sentence of not less than ninety consecutive days of house arrest with electronic monitoring. The period of house arrest with electronic monitoring shall not exceed one year.

(b) Notwithstanding the fines provided for in Chapter 2929. of the Revised Code, a fine of not less than five hundred and not more than two thousand five hundred dollars;

(c) A license suspension under division (E) of this section;

(d) If the vehicle the offender was operating at the time of the offense is registered in the offender's name, immobilization of the offender's vehicle for sixty days and the impoundment for sixty days of the identification license plates of that vehicle. The order for immobilization and impoundment shall be issued and enforced in accordance with section 4503.233 of the Revised Code.

(3) If, within six years of the offense, the offender previously has been convicted of or pleaded guilty to two or more violations of this section or two or more equivalent offenses, driving under OVI suspension is a misdemeanor. The court shall sentence the offender to all of the following:

(a) A mandatory jail term of thirty consecutive days. Notwithstanding the jail terms provided in sections 2929.21 to 2929.28 of the Revised Code, the court may sentence the offender to a longer jail term of not more than one year. The court shall not sentence the offender to a term of house arrest with electronic monitoring in lieu of the mandatory portion of the jail term.

(b) Notwithstanding the fines set forth in Chapter 2929. of the Revised Code, a fine of not less than five hundred and not more than two thousand five hundred dollars;

(c) A license suspension under division (E) of this section;

(d) If the vehicle the offender was operating at the time of the offense is registered in the offender's name, criminal forfeiture to the state of the offender's vehicle. The order of criminal forfeiture shall be issued and enforced in accordance with section 4503.234 of the Revised Code. If title to a motor vehicle that is subject to an order for criminal forfeiture under this division is assigned or transferred and division (B)(2) or (3) of section 4503.234 of the Revised Code applies, the court may fine the offender the value of the vehicle as determined by publications of the national automobile dealers association. The proceeds from any fine so imposed shall be distributed in accordance with division (C)(2) of section 4503.234 of the Revised Code.

(C) No court shall impose an alternative sentence of house arrest with electronic monitoring under division (B)(1) or (2) of this section unless, within sixty days of the date of sentencing, the court issues a written finding on the record that, due to the unavailability of space at the jail where the offender is required to serve the jail term imposed, the offender will not be able to begin serving that term within the sixty-day period following the date of sentencing.

An offender sentenced under this section to a period of house arrest with electronic monitoring shall be permitted work release during that period.

(D) Fifty per cent of any fine imposed by a court under division (B)(1), (2), or (3) of this section shall be deposited into the county indigent drivers alcohol treatment fund or municipal indigent drivers alcohol treatment fund under the control of that court, as created by the county or municipal corporation pursuant to division (H) of section 4511.191 of the Revised Code.

(E) In addition to or independent of all other penalties provided by law or ordinance, the trial judge of any court of record or the mayor of a mayor's court shall impose on an offender who is convicted of or pleads guilty to a violation of this section a class seven suspension of the offender's driver's or commercial driver's license or permit or nonresident operating privilege from the range specified in division (A)(7) of section 4510.02 of the Revised Code.

When permitted as specified in section 4510.021 of the Revised Code, if the court grants limited driving privileges during a suspension imposed under this section, the privileges shall be granted on the additional condition that the offender must display restricted license plates, issued under section 4503.231 of the Revised Code, on the vehicle driven subject to the privileges, except as provided in division (B) of that section.

A suspension of a commercial driver's license under this section shall be concurrent with any period of suspension or disqualification under section 3123.58 or 4506.16 of the Revised Code. No person who is disqualified for life from holding a commercial driver's license under section 4506.16 of the Revised Code shall be issued a driver's license under Chapter 4507. of the Revised Code during the period for which the commercial driver's license was suspended under this section, and no person whose commercial driver's license is suspended under this section shall be issued a driver's license under Chapter 4507. of the Revised Code during the period of the suspension.

(F) The offender shall provide the court with proof of financial responsibility as defined in section 4509.01 of the Revised Code. If the offender fails to provide that proof of financial responsibility, then, in addition to any other penalties provided by law, the court may order restitution pursuant to section 2929.28 of the Revised Code in an amount not exceeding five thousand dollars for any economic loss arising from an accident or collision that was the direct and proximate result of the offender's operation of the vehicle before, during, or after committing the offense that is a misdemeanor of the first degree under this section for which the offender is sentenced.

(G) As used in this section:

(1) "Electronic monitoring" has the same meaning as in section 2929.01 of the Revised Code.

(2) "Equivalent offense" means any of the following:

(a) A violation of a municipal ordinance, law of another state, or law of the United States that is substantially equivalent to division (A) of this section;

(b) A violation of a former law of this state that was substantially equivalent to division (A) of this section.

(3) "Jail" has the same meaning as in section 2929.01 of the Revised Code.

(4) "Mandatory jail term" means the mandatory term in jail of three, ten, or thirty consecutive days that must be imposed under division (B)(1), (2), or (3) of this section upon an offender convicted of a violation of division (A) of this section and in relation to which all of the following apply:

(a) Except as specifically authorized under this section, the term must be served in a jail.

(b) Except as specifically authorized under this section, the term cannot be suspended, reduced, or otherwise modified pursuant to any provision of the Revised Code.

**HISTORY: 149 v S 123, § 1, eff. 1-1-04; 149 v H 490, § 1, eff. 1-1-04; 2011 HB 5, § 1, eff. Sept. 23, 2011.**

The effective date is set by section 4 of H.B. 490.

See provisions, § 5 of S.B. 123 (149 v —), following RC § 4501.01.

## § 4510.15 Suspension or revocation of license for reckless operation violation.

Whenever a person is found guilty under the laws of this state, or under any ordinance of any political subdivision of this state, of operating a motor vehicle in violation of any such law or ordinance relating to reckless operation, the trial court of any court of record, in addition to or independent of all other penalties provided by law, may impose a class five suspension of the offender's driver's or commercial driver's license or permit or nonresident operating privilege from the range specified in division (A)(5) of section 4510.02 of the Revised Code.

Suspension of a commercial driver's license under this section shall be concurrent with any period of suspension disqualification under section 3123.58 or 4506.16 of the Revised Code. No person who is disqualified for life from holding a commercial driver's license under section 4506.16 of the Revised Code shall be issued a driver's license under chapter 4507. of the Revised Code during the period for which the commercial driver's license was suspended under this section, and no person whose commercial driver's license is suspended under this section shall be issued a driver's license under chapter 4507. of the Revised Code during the period of the suspension.

**HISTORY: GC § 6296-30; 116 v PtII, 33, § 30; Bureau of Code Revision, 10-1-53; 143 v H 381 (Eff 7-1-89); 144 v S 275 (Eff 9-1-93); 145 v S 62, § 4 (Eff 9-1-93); 146 v H 167 (Eff 5-15-97); 148 v S 180. Eff 3-22-2001; 149 v S 123, § 1, eff. 1-1-04; 150 v H 52, § 1, eff. 6-1-04.**

The effective date is set by section 4 of S.B. 123.The effective date is set by section 4 of S.B. 123.

See provisions, § 5 of S.B. 123 (149 v —), following RC § 4501.01.

**Publisher's Note:**

This section was formerly § 4507.34. It was renumbered by S.B. 123, Acts 2002, effective January 1, 2004.

## § 4510.16 Driving under financial responsibility law suspension or cancellation.

(A) No person, whose driver's or commercial driver's license or temporary instruction permit or nonresident's operating privilege has been suspended or canceled pursuant to Chapter 4509. of the Revised Code, shall operate any motor vehicle within this state, or knowingly permit any motor vehicle owned by the person to be operated by another person in the state, during the period of the suspension or cancellation, except as specifically authorized by Chapter 4509. of the Revised Code. No person shall operate a motor vehicle within this state, or knowingly permit any motor vehicle owned by the person to be operated by another person in the state, during the period in which the person is required by section 4509.45 of the Revised Code to file and maintain proof of financial responsibility for a violation of section 4509.101 of the Revised Code, unless proof of financial responsibility is maintained with respect to that vehicle.

(B) No person shall operate any motor vehicle upon a highway or any public or private property used by the public for purposes of vehicular travel or parking in this state if the person's driver's or commercial driver's license or temporary instruction permit or nonresident operating privilege has been suspended pursuant to section 4509.37 or 4509.40 of the Revised Code for nonpayment of a judgment.

(C) Upon the request or motion of the prosecuting authority, a noncertified copy of the law enforcement automated data system report or a noncertified copy of a record of the registrar of motor vehicles that shows the name, date of birth, and social security number of a person charged with a violation of division (A) or (B) of this section may be admitted into evidence as prima-facie evidence that the license of the person was under either a financial responsibility law suspension at the time of the alleged violation of division (A) of this section or a nonpayment of judgment suspension at the time of the alleged violation of division (B) of this section. The person charged with a violation of division (A) or (B) of this section may offer evidence to rebut this prima-facie evidence.

(D) Whoever violates division (A) of this section is guilty of driving under financial responsibility law suspension or cancellation and shall be punished as provided in divisions (D) to (I) of this section. Whoever violates division (B) of this section is guilty of driving under a nonpayment of judgment suspension and shall be punished as provided in divisions (D) to (I) of this section.

(1) Except as otherwise provided in division (D)(2) of this section, the offense is an unclassified misdemeanor. When the offense is an unclassified misdemeanor, the offender shall be sentenced pursuant to sections 2929.21 to 2929.28 of the Revised Code, except that the offender shall not be sentenced to a jail term; the offender shall not be sentenced to a community residential sanction pursuant to section 2929.26 of the Revised Code; notwithstanding division (A)(2)(a) of section 2929.28 of the Revised Code, the offender may be fined up to one thousand dollars; and, notwithstanding division (A)(3) of section 2929.27 of the Revised Code, the offender may be ordered pursuant to division (C) of that section to serve a term of community service of up to five hundred hours. The failure of an offender to complete a term of community service imposed by the court may be punished as indirect criminal contempt under division (A) of section 2705.02 of the Revised Code that may be filed in the underlying case.

(2) If, within three years of the offense, the offender previously was convicted of or pleaded guilty to two or more violations of this section, or any combination of two violations of this section or section 4510.11 or 4510.111 of the Revised Code, or a substantially equivalent municipal ordinance, the offense is a misdemeanor of the first degree.

(E) The offender shall provide the court with proof of financial responsibility as defined in section 4509.01 of the Revised Code. If the offender fails to provide that proof of financial responsibility, then, in addition to any other penalties provided by law, the court may order restitution pursuant to section 2929.28 of the Revised Code in an amount not exceeding five thousand dollars for any economic loss arising from an accident or collision that was the direct and proximate result of the offender's operation of the vehicle before, during, or after committing the offense for which the offender is sentenced under this section.

(F) The court may impose a class seven suspension of the offender's driver's or commercial driver's license or permit or nonresident operating privilege from the range of time specified in division (A)(7) of section 4510.02 of the Revised Code.

(G)(1) If the vehicle is registered in the offender's name and if, within three years of the offense, the offender previously has been convicted of or pleaded guilty to one violation of division (A) or (B) of this section or section 4510.11 or 4510.111 of the Revised Code or a substantially equivalent municipal ordinance, the court, in addition to or independent of any other sentence that it imposes upon the offender, may order the immobilization for thirty days of the vehicle involved in the offense and the impoundment for thirty days of the license plates of that vehicle in accordance with section 4503.233 of the Revised Code.

(2) If the vehicle is registered in the offender's name and if, within three years of the offense, the offender has been convicted of or pleaded guilty to two violations of division (A) or (B) of this section or section 4510.11 or 4510.111 of the Revised Code, or any combination of two violations of this section or section 4510.11 or 4510.111 of the Revised Code, or a substantially similar municipal ordinance, the court, in addition to or independent of any other sentence that it imposes on the offender, may order the immobilization for sixty days of the vehicle involved in the offense and the impoundment for sixty days of the license plates of that vehicle in accordance with section 4503.233 of the Revised Code.

(3) If the vehicle is registered in the offender's name and if, within three years of the offense, the offender has been convicted of or pleaded guilty to three or more violations of this section or section 4510.11 or 4510.111 of the Revised Code, or any combination of three or more violations of this section or section 4510.11 or 4510.111 of the Revised Code, or a substantially similar municipal ordinance, the court, in addition to or independent of any other sentence that it imposes upon the offender, may order the criminal forfeiture to the state of the vehicle involved in the offense. If title to a motor vehicle that is subject to an order for criminal forfeiture under this division is assigned or transferred and division (B)(2) or (3) of section 4503.234 of the Revised Code applies, in addition to or independent of any other penalty established by law, the court may fine the offender the value of the vehicle as determined by publications of the national automobile dealers association. The proceeds from any fine so imposed shall be distributed in accordance with division (C)(2) of that section.

(H) Any order for immobilization and impoundment under this section shall be issued and enforced in accordance with sections 4503.233 and 4507.02 of the Revised Code, as applicable. The court shall not release a vehicle from immobilization ordered under this section unless the court is presented with current proof of financial responsibility with respect to that vehicle.

(I) An order for criminal forfeiture under this section shall be issued and enforced under section 4503.234 of the Revised Code. Upon receipt of a copy of the order from the court, neither the registrar of motor vehicles nor a deputy registrar shall accept any application for the registration or transfer of registration of any motor vehicle owned or leased by the person named in the declaration of forfeiture. The period of registration denial shall be five years after the date of the order unless, during that period, the court having jurisdiction of the offense that led to the order terminates the forfeiture and notifies the registrar of the termination. The registrar then shall take the necessary measures to permit the person to register a vehicle owned or leased by the person or to transfer registration of the vehicle.

**HISTORY: 149 v S 123, § 1, eff. 1-1-04; 150 v H 52, § 1, eff. 6-1-04; 151 v H 461, § 1, eff. 4-4-07; 153 v H 1, § 101.01, eff. 10-16-09; 153 v H 338, § 1, eff. 9-17-10; 2011 HB 5, § 1, eff. Sept. 23, 2011.**

The effective date is set by § 812.10 of 153 v H 1.

The effective date is set by section 4 of S.B. 123.

See provisions, § 5 of S.B. 123 (149 v —), following RC § 4501.01.

## § 4510.161 Additional sanctions for violating municipal ordinance concerning financial responsibility or OVI suspension.

(A) The requirements and sanctions imposed by divisions (B) and (C) of this section are an adjunct to and derive from the state's exclusive authority over the registration and titling of motor vehicles and do not comprise a part of the criminal sentence to be imposed upon a person who violates a municipal ordinance that is substantially equivalent to section 4510.14 or to division (A) of section 4510.16 of the Revised Code.

(B) If a person is convicted of or pleads guilty to a violation of a municipal ordinance that is substantially equivalent to division (A) of section 4510.16 of the Revised Code or former division (B)(1) of section 4507.02 of the Revised Code or a municipal ordinance that is substantially equivalent to either of those divisions, the court, in addition to or independent of any sentence that it imposes upon the offender for the offense, may do whichever of the following is applicable:

(1) If the vehicle is registered in the offender's name and if, within three years of the current offense, the offender previously has been convicted of or pleaded guilty to one violation of this section or section 4510.11, 4510.111, or 4510.16 of the Revised Code or a substantially equivalent municipal ordinance, the court, in addition to or independent of any other sentence that it imposes upon the offender, may order the immobilization of the vehicle involved in the offense for thirty days and the impoundment of that vehicle's license plates for thirty days in accordance with section 4503.233 of the Revised Code.

(2) If the vehicle is registered in the offender's name and if, within three years of the current offense, the offender previously has been convicted of or pleaded guilty to two violations of this section or any combination of two violations of this section or section 4510.11, 4510.111, or 4510.16 of the Revised Code, or a substantially equivalent municipal ordinance, the court, in addition to or independent of any other sentence that it imposes upon the offender, may order the immobilization for sixty days of the vehicle involved in the offense and the impoundment of that vehicle's license plates for sixty days in accordance with section 4503.233 of the Revised Code.

(3) If the vehicle is registered in the offender's name and if, within three years of the current offense, the offender previously has been convicted of or pleaded guilty to three or more violations of this section or any combination of three or more violations of this section or section 4510.11, 4510.111, or 4510.16 of the Revised Code, or a substantially equivalent municipal ordinance, the court may order the criminal forfeiture to the state of the vehicle the offender was operating at the time of the offense. If title to a motor vehicle that is subject to an order for criminal forfeiture under this division is assigned or transferred and division (B)(2) or (3) of section 4503.234 of the Revised Code applies, in addition to or independent of any other penalty established by law, the court may fine the offender the value of the motor vehicle as determined by publications of the national automobile dealers association. The proceeds from any fine so imposed shall be distributed in accordance with division (C)(2) of that section.

(C) If a person is convicted of or pleads guilty to a violation of a municipal ordinance that is substantially equivalent to section 4510.14 of the Revised Code, the court, in addition to and independent of any sentence that it imposes upon the offender for the offense, if the vehicle the offender was operating at the time of the offense is registered in the offender's name, shall do whichever of the following is applicable:

(1) If, within six years of the current offense, the offender has not been convicted of or pleaded guilty to a violation of section 4510.14 or former division (D)(2) of section 4507.02 of the Revised Code or a municipal ordinance that is substantially equivalent to that section or former division, the court shall order the immobilization for thirty days of the vehicle involved in the offense and the impoundment for thirty days of the license plates of that vehicle in accordance with section 4503.233 of the Revised Code.

(2) If, within six years of the current offense, the offender has been convicted of or pleaded guilty to one violation of section 4510.14 or former division (D)(2) of section 4507.02 of the Revised Code or a municipal ordinance that is substantially equivalent to that section or former division, the court shall order the immobilization for sixty days of the vehicle involved in the offense and the impoundment for sixty days of the license plates of that vehicle in accordance with section 4503.233 of the Revised Code.

(3) If, within six years of the current offense, the offender has been convicted of or pleaded guilty to two or more violations of section 4510.14 or former division (D)(2) of section 4507.02 of the Revised Code or a municipal ordinance that is substantially equivalent to that section or former division, the court shall order the criminal forfeiture to the state of the vehicle the offender was operating at the time of the offense.

(D) An order for immobilization and impoundment of a vehicle under this section shall be issued and enforced in accordance with sections 4503.233 and 4507.02 of the Revised Code, as applicable. The court shall not release a vehicle from immobilization ordered under this section unless the court is presented with current proof of financial responsibility with respect to that vehicle.

(E) An order for criminal forfeiture of a vehicle under this section shall be issued and enforced under section 4503.234 of the Revised Code. Upon receipt of a copy of the order from the court, neither the registrar of motor vehicles nor a deputy registrar shall accept any application for the registration or transfer of registration of any motor vehicle owned or leased by the person named in the declaration of forfeiture. The period of registration denial shall be five years after the date of the order unless, during that period, the court having jurisdiction of the offense that led to the order terminates the forfeiture and notifies the registrar of the termination. The registrar then shall take the necessary measures to permit the person to register a vehicle owned or leased by the person or to transfer registration of the vehicle.

**HISTORY: 145 v S 62. Eff 9-1-93; 149 v S 123, § 1, eff. 1-1-04; 151 v H 461, § 1, eff. 4-4-07; 2011 HB 5, § 1, eff. Sept. 23, 2011.**

The effective date is set by section 4 of S.B. 123.

See provisions, § 5 of S.B. 123 (149 v —), following RC § 4501.01.

**Publisher's Note:**

This section was formerly § 4507.361. It was renumbered by S.B. 123, Acts 2002, effective January 1, 2004.

## § 4510.17 Suspension upon drug offense conviction under federal law or in another state or for OVI offense in another state; application to minors; limited driving privileges.

(A) The registrar of motor vehicles shall impose a class D suspension of the person's driver's license, commercial driver's license, temporary instruction permit, probationary license, or nonresident operating privilege for the period of time specified in division (B)(4) of section 4510.02 of the Revised Code on any person who is a resident of this state and is convicted of or pleads guilty to a violation of a statute of any other state or any federal statute that is substantially similar to section 2925.02, 2925.03, 2925.04, 2925.041 [2925.04.1], 2925.05, 2925.06, 2925.11, 2925.12, 2925.13, 2925.14, 2925.22, 2925.23, 2925.31, 2925.32, 2925.36, or 2925.37 of the Revised Code. Upon receipt of a report from a court, court clerk, or other official of any other state or from any federal authority that a resident of this state was convicted of or pleaded guilty to an offense described in this division, the registrar shall send a notice by regular first class mail to the person, at the person's last known address as shown in the records of the bureau of motor vehicles, informing the person of the suspension, that the suspension will take effect twenty-one days from the date of the notice, and that, if the person wishes to appeal the suspension or denial, the person must file a notice of appeal within twenty-one days of the date of the notice requesting a hearing on the matter. If the person requests a hearing, the registrar shall hold the hearing not more than forty days after receipt by the registrar of the notice of appeal. The filing of a notice of appeal does not stay the operation of the suspension that must be imposed pursuant to this division. The scope of the hearing shall be limited to whether the person actually was convicted of or pleaded guilty to the offense for which the suspension is to be imposed.

The suspension the registrar is required to impose under this division shall end either on the last day of the class D suspension period or of the suspension of the person's nonresident operating privilege imposed by the state or federal court, whichever is earlier.

The registrar shall subscribe to or otherwise participate in any information system or register, or enter into reciprocal and mutual agreements with other states and federal authorities, in order to facilitate the exchange of information with other states and the United States government regarding persons who plead guilty to or are convicted of offenses described in this division and therefore are subject to the suspension or denial described in this division.

(B) The registrar shall impose a class D suspension of the person's driver's license, commercial driver's license, or temporary instruction permit, probationary license, or nonresident operating privilege for the period of time specified in division (B)(4) of section 4510.02 of the Revised Code on any person who is a resident of this state and is convicted of or pleads guilty to a violation of a statute of any other state or a municipal ordinance of a municipal corporation located in any other state that is substantially similar to section 4511.19 of the Revised Code. Upon receipt of a report from another state made pursuant to section 4510.61 of the Revised Code indicating that a resident of this state was convicted of or pleaded guilty to an offense described in this division, the registrar shall send a notice by regular first class mail to the person, at the person's last known address as shown in the records of the bureau of motor vehicles, informing the person of the suspension, that the suspension or denial will take effect twenty-one days from the date of the notice, and that, if the person wishes to appeal the suspension, the person must file a notice of appeal within twenty-one days of the date of the notice requesting a hearing on the matter. If the person requests a hearing, the registrar shall hold the hearing not more than forty days after receipt by the registrar of the notice of appeal. The filing of a notice of appeal does not stay the operation of the suspension that must be imposed pursuant to this division. The scope of the hearing shall be limited to whether the person actually was convicted of or pleaded guilty to the offense for which the suspension is to be imposed.

The suspension the registrar is required to impose under this division shall end either on the last day of the class D suspension period or of the suspension of the person's nonresident operating privilege imposed by the state or federal court, whichever is earlier.

(C) The registrar shall impose a class D suspension of the child's driver's license, commercial driver's license, temporary instruction permit, or nonresident operating privilege for the period of time specified in division (B)(4) of section 4510.02 of the Revised Code on any child who is a resident of this state and is convicted of or pleads guilty to a violation of a statute of any other state or any federal statute that is substantially similar to section 2925.02, 2925.03, 2925.04, 2925.041 [2925.04.1], 2925.05, 2925.06, 2925.11, 2925.12, 2925.13, 2925.14, 2925.22, 2925.23, 2925.31, 2925.32, 2925.36, or 2925.37 of the Revised Code. Upon receipt of a report from a court, court clerk, or other official of any other state or from any federal authority that a child who is a resident of this state was convicted of or pleaded guilty to an offense described in this division, the registrar shall send a notice by regular first class mail to the child, at the child's last known address as shown in the records of the bureau of motor vehicles, informing the child of the suspension, that the suspension or denial will take effect twenty-one days from the date of the notice, and that, if the child wishes to appeal the suspension, the child must file a notice of appeal within twenty-one days of the date of the notice requesting a hearing on the matter. If the child requests a hearing, the registrar shall hold the hearing not more than forty days after receipt by the registrar of the notice of appeal. The filing of a notice of appeal does not stay the operation of the suspension that must be imposed pursuant to this division. The scope of the hearing shall be limited to whether the child actually was convicted of or pleaded guilty to the offense for which the suspension is to be imposed.

The suspension the registrar is required to impose under this division shall end either on the last day of the class D suspension period or of the suspension of the child's nonresident operating privilege imposed by the state or federal court, whichever is earlier. If the child is a resident of this state who is sixteen years of age or older and does not have a current, valid Ohio driver's or commercial driver's license or permit, the notice shall inform the child that the child will be denied issuance of a driver's or commercial driver's license or permit for six months beginning on the date of the notice. If the child has not attained the age of sixteen years on the date of the notice, the notice shall inform the child that the period of denial of six months shall commence on the date the child attains the age of sixteen years.

The registrar shall subscribe to or otherwise participate in any information system or register, or enter into reciprocal and mutual agreements with other states and federal authorities, in order to facilitate the exchange of information with other states and the United States government regarding children who are residents of this state and plead guilty to or are convicted of offenses described in this division and therefore are subject to the suspension or denial described in this division.

(D) The registrar shall impose a class D suspension of the child's driver's license, commercial driver's license, temporary instruction permit, probationary license, or nonresident operating privilege for the period of time specified in division (B)(4) of section 4510.02 of the Revised Code on any child who is a resident of this state and is convicted of or pleads guilty to a violation of a statute of any other state or a municipal ordinance of a municipal corporation located in any other state that is substantially similar to section 4511.19 of the Revised Code. Upon receipt of a report from another state made pursuant to section 4510.61 of the Revised Code indicating that a child who is a resident of this state was convicted of or pleaded guilty to an offense described in this division, the registrar shall send a notice by regular first class mail to the child, at the child's last known address as shown in the records of the bureau of motor vehicles, informing the child of the suspension, that the suspension will take effect twenty-one days from the date of the notice, and that, if the child wishes to appeal the suspension, the child must file a notice of appeal within twenty-one days of the date of the notice requesting a hearing on the matter. If the child requests a hearing, the registrar shall hold the hearing not more than forty days after receipt by the registrar of the notice of appeal. The filing of a notice of appeal does not stay the operation of the suspension that must be imposed pursuant to this division. The scope of the hearing shall be limited to whether the child actually was convicted of or pleaded guilty to the offense for which the suspension is to be imposed.

The suspension the registrar is required to impose under this division shall end either on the last day of the class D suspension period or of the suspension of the child's nonresident operating privilege imposed by the state or federal court, whichever is earlier. If the child is a resident of this state who is sixteen years of age or older and does not have a current, valid Ohio driver's or commercial driver's license or permit, the notice shall inform the child that the child will be denied issuance of a driver's or commercial driver's license or permit for six months beginning on the date of the notice. If the child has not attained the age of sixteen years on the date of the notice, the notice shall inform the child that the period of denial of six months shall commence on the date the child attains the age of sixteen years.

(E) Any person whose license or permit has been suspended pursuant to this section may file a petition in the municipal or county court, or in case the person is under eighteen years of age, the juvenile court, in whose jurisdiction the person resides, agreeing to pay the cost of the proceedings and alleging that the suspension would seriously affect the person's ability to continue the person's employment. Upon satisfactory proof that there is reasonable cause to believe that the suspension would seriously affect the person's ability to continue the person's employment, the judge may grant the person limited driving privileges during the period during which the suspension otherwise would be imposed, except that the judge shall not grant limited driving privileges for employment as a driver of a commercial motor vehicle to any person who would be disqualified from operating a commercial motor vehicle under section 4506.16 of the Revised Code if the violation had occurred in this state, or during any of the following periods of time:

(1) The first fifteen days of a suspension under division (B) or (D) of this section, if the person has not been convicted within six years of the date of the offense giving rise to the suspension under this section of a violation of any of the following:

(a) Section 4511.19 of the Revised Code, or a municipal ordinance relating to operating a vehicle while under the influence of alcohol, a drug of abuse, or alcohol and a drug of abuse;

(b) A municipal ordinance relating to operating a motor vehicle with a prohibited concentration of alcohol, a controlled substance, or a metabolite of a controlled substance in the whole blood, blood serum or plasma breath, or urine;

(c) Section 2903.04 of the Revised Code in a case in which the person was subject to the sanctions described in division (D) of that section;

(d) Division (A) (1) of section 2903.06 or division (A)(1) of section 2903.08 of the Revised Code or a municipal ordinance that is substantially similar to either of those divisions;

(e) Division (A)(2), (3), or (4) of section 2903.06, division (A)(2) of section 2903.08, or as it existed prior to March 23, 2000 section 2903.07 of the Revised Code, or a municipal ordinance that is substantially similar to any of those divisions or that former section, in a case in which the jury or judge found that the person was under the influence of alcohol, a drug of abuse, or alcohol and a drug of abuse.

(2) The first thirty days of a suspension under division (B) or (D) of this section, if the person has been convicted one time within six years of the date of the offense giving rise to the suspension under this section of any violation identified in division (E)(1) of this section.

(3) The first one hundred eighty days of a suspension under division (B) or (D) of this section, if the person has been convicted two times within six years of the date of the offense giving rise to the suspension under this section of any violation identified in division (E)(1) of this section.

(4) No limited driving privileges may be granted if the person has been convicted three or more times within five years of the date of the offense giving rise to a suspension under division (B) or (D) of this section of any violation identified in division (E)(1) of this section.

If a person petitions for limited driving privileges under division (E) of this section, the registrar shall be represented by the county prosecutor of the county in which the person resides if the petition is filed in a juvenile court or county court, except that if the person resides within a city or village that is located within the jurisdiction of the county in which the petition is filed, the city director of law or village solicitor of that city or village shall represent the registrar. If the petition is filed in a municipal court, the registrar shall be represented as provided in section 1901.34 of the Revised Code.

In granting limited driving privileges under division (E) of this section, the court may impose any condition it considers reasonable and necessary to limit the use of a vehicle by the person. The court shall deliver to the person a permit card, in a form to be prescribed by the court, setting forth the time, place, and other conditions limiting the person's use of a motor vehicle. The grant of limited driving privileges shall be conditioned upon the person's having the permit in the person's possession at all times during which the person is operating a vehicle.

A person granted limited driving privileges who operates a vehicle for other than limited purposes, in violation of any condition imposed by the court or without having the permit in the person's possession, is guilty of a violation of section 4510.11 of the Revised Code.

(F) As used in divisions (C) and (D) of this section:

(1) "Child" means a person who is under the age of eighteen years, except that any person who violates a statute or ordinance described in division (C) or (D) of this section prior to attaining eighteen years of age shall be deemed a "child" irrespective of the person's age at the time the complaint or other equivalent document is filed in the other state or a hearing, trial, or other proceeding is held in the other state on the complaint or other equivalent document, and irrespective of the person's age when the period of license suspension or denial prescribed in division (C) or (D) of this section is imposed.

(2) "Is convicted of or pleads guilty to" means, as it relates to a child who is a resident of this state, that in a proceeding conducted in a state or federal court located in another state for a violation of a statute or ordinance described in division (C) or (D) of this section, the result of the proceeding is any of the following:

(a) Under the laws that govern the proceedings of the court, the child is adjudicated to be or admits to being a delinquent child or a juvenile traffic offender for a violation described in division (C) or (D) of this section that would be a crime if committed by an adult;

(b) Under the laws that govern the proceedings of the court, the child is convicted of or pleads guilty to a violation described in division (C) or (D) of this section;

(c) Under the laws that govern the proceedings of the court, irrespective of the terminology utilized in those laws, the result of the court's proceedings is the functional equivalent of division (F)(2)(a) or (b) of this section.

**HISTORY: 145 v H 377 (Eff 9-30-93); 146 v S 2 (Eff 7-1-96); 146 v H 353 (Eff 9-17-96); 147 v S 60 (Eff 10-21-97); 148 v S 107 (Eff 3-23-2000); 149 v H 7. Eff 8-7-2001; 149 v S 123, § 1, eff. 1-1-04; 150 v H 163, § 1, eff. 9-23-04; 151 v S 8, § 1, eff. 8-17-06.**

The effective date is set by section 4 of S.B. 123.

See provisions, § 5 of S.B. 123 (149 v —), following RC § 4501.01.

**Publisher's Note:**

This section was formerly § 4507.169. It was renumbered by S.B. 123, Acts 2002, effective January 1, 2004.

## § 4510.18 Driving under specified lifetime suspension.

(A) No person whose driver's or commercial driver's license or permit or nonresident operating privilege has been suspended for life under a class one suspension imposed under division (B)(3) of section 2903.06 or section 2903.08 of the Revised Code shall operate any motor vehicle upon the public roads or highways within this state during the remaining life of the person.

(B) Whoever violates this section is guilty of driving under specified lifetime suspension, a felony of the third degree.

**HISTORY: 151 v H 461, § 1, eff. 4-4-07.**

## § 4510.21 Failure to reinstate license.

(A) No person whose driver's license, commercial driver's license, temporary instruction permit, or nonresident's operating privilege has been suspended shall operate any motor vehicle upon a public road or highway or any public or private property after the suspension has expired unless the person has complied with all license reinstatement requirements imposed by the court, the bureau of motor vehicles, or another provision of the Revised Code.

(B) Upon the request or motion of the prosecuting authority, a noncertified copy of the law enforcement automated data system report or a noncertified copy of a record of the registrar of motor vehicles that shows the name, date of birth, and social security number of a person charged with a violation of division (A) of this section may be admitted into evidence as prima-facie evidence that the license of the person had not been reinstated by the person at the time of the alleged violation of division (A) of this section. The person charged with a violation of division (A) of this section may offer evidence to rebut this prima-facie evidence.

(C) Whoever violates this section is guilty of failure to reinstate a license and shall be punished as follows:

(1) Except as provided in division (C)(2) of this section, whoever violates division (A) of this section is guilty of an unclassified misdemeanor. When the offense is an unclassified misdemeanor, the offender shall be sentenced pursuant to sections 2929.21 to 2929.28 of the Revised Code, except that the offender shall not be sentenced to a jail term; the offender shall not be sentenced to a community residential sanction pursuant to section 2929.26 of the Revised Code; notwithstanding division (A)(2)(a) of section 2929.28 of the Revised Code, the offender may be fined up to one thousand dollars; and, notwithstanding division (A)(3) of section 2929.27 of the Revised Code, the offender may be ordered pursuant to division (C) of that section to serve a term of community service of up to five hundred hours. The failure of an offender to complete a term of community service imposed by the court may be punished as indirect criminal contempt under division (A) of section 2705.02 of the Revised Code that may be filed in the underlying case.

(2) If, within three years of a violation of division (A) of this section, the offender previously has pleaded guilty to or been convicted of two or more violations of division (A) of this section or a substantially equivalent municipal ordinance, the offender is guilty of a misdemeanor of the first degree.

(3) In all cases, the court may impose upon the offender a class seven suspension of the offender's driver's license, commercial driver's license, temporary instruction permit, probationary driver's license, or nonresident operating privilege from the range specified in division (A)(7) of section 4510.02 of the Revised Code.

**HISTORY: 149 v S 123, § 1, eff. 1-1-04; 2011 HB 5, § 1, eff. Sept. 23, 2011.**

The effective date is set by section 4 of S.B. 123.
See provisions, § 5 of S.B. 123 (149 v —), following RC § 4501.01.

## § 4510.22 Forfeiture for failure to appear or pay fine; denial of vehicle registration.

(A) If a person who has a current valid Ohio driver's, commercial driver's license, or temporary instruction permit is charged with a violation of any provision in sections 4503.11, 4503.12, 4503.182, 4503.21, 4507.02, 4507.05, 4507.35, 4510.11, 4510.111, 4510.12, 4510.16, 4510.21, 4511.01 to 4511.76, 4511.81, 4511.82, 4511.84, 4513.01 to 4513.65, or 4549.01 to 4549.65 of the Revised Code or with a violation of any substantially equivalent municipal ordinance and if the person either fails to appear in court at the required time and place to answer the charge or pleads guilty to or is found guilty of the violation and fails within the time allowed by the court to pay the fine imposed by the court, the court may declare the forfeiture of the person's license. Thirty days after such a declaration of forfeiture, the court shall inform the registrar of motor vehicles of the forfeiture by entering information relative to the forfeiture on a form approved and furnished by the registrar and sending the form to the registrar. The court also shall forward the person's license, if it is in the possession of the court, to the registrar.

The registrar shall impose a class F suspension of the person's driver's or commercial driver's license, or temporary instruction permit for the period of time specified in division (B)(6) of section 4510.02 of the Revised Code on any person who is named in a declaration received by the registrar under this section. The registrar shall send written notification of the suspension to the person at the person's last known address and, if the person is in possession of the license, order the person to surrender the person's license or permit to the registrar within forty-eight hours.

No valid driver's or commercial driver's license shall be granted to the person after the suspension, unless the court having jurisdiction of the offense that led to the suspension orders that the forfeiture be terminated. The court shall order the termination of the forfeiture if the person thereafter appears to answer the charge and pays any fine imposed by the court or pays the fine originally imposed by the court. The court shall inform the registrar of the termination of the forfeiture by entering information relative to the termination on a form approved and furnished by the registrar and sending the form to the registrar. The person shall pay to the registrar of motor vehicles or an eligible deputy registrar a twenty-five-dollar reinstatement fee. In addition, each deputy registrar shall collect a service fee of ten dollars to compensate the deputy registrar for services performed under this section. The deputy registrar shall retain eight dollars of the service fee and shall transmit the reinstatement fee, plus two dollars of the service fee, to the registrar in the manner the registrar shall determine. The registrar shall deposit fifteen dollars of the reinstatement fee into the state treasury to the credit of the state bureau of motor vehicles fund created by section 4501.25 of the Revised Code to cover the costs of the bureau in administering this section and shall deposit ten dollars of the fee into the state treasury to the credit of the indigent defense support fund created by section 120.08 of the Revised Code.

(B) In addition to suspending the driver's or commercial driver's license or permit of the person named in a declaration of forfeiture, the registrar, upon receipt from the court of the copy of the declaration of forfeiture, shall take any measures that may be necessary to ensure that neither the registrar nor any deputy registrar accepts any application for the registration or transfer of registration of any motor vehicle owned or leased by the person named in the declaration of forfeiture. However, for a motor vehicle leased by a person named in a declaration of forfeiture, the registrar shall not implement the preceding sentence until the registrar adopts procedures for that implementation under section 4503.39 of the Revised Code. The period of denial of registration or transfer shall continue until such time as the court having jurisdiction of the offense that led to the suspension orders the forfeiture be terminated. Upon receipt by the registrar of an order terminating the forfeiture, the registrar also shall take any measures that may be necessary to permit the person to register a motor vehicle owned or leased by the person or to transfer the registration of such a motor vehicle, if the person later makes application to take such action and otherwise is eligible to register the motor vehicle or to transfer its registration.

The registrar shall not be required to give effect to any declaration of forfeiture or order terminating a forfeiture provided by a court under this section unless the information contained in the declaration or order is transmitted to the registrar by means of an electronic transfer system. The registrar shall not restore the person's driving or vehicle registration privileges until the person pays the reinstatement fee as provided in this section.

The period of denial relating to the issuance or transfer of a certificate of registration for a motor vehicle imposed pursuant to this division remains in effect until the person pays any fine imposed by the court relative to the offense.

**HISTORY: 143 v S 338 (Eff 11-28-90); 143 v S 285 (Eff 4-10-91); 144 v S 331 (Eff 11-13-92); 144 v S 275 (Eff 9-1-93); 145 v S 62, § 4 (Eff 9-1-93); 145 v H 687 (Eff 10-12-94); 146 v H 353 (Eff 9-17-96); 146 v S 121 (Eff 11-19-96); 147 v S 85. Eff 5-15-97; 149 v S 123, § 1, eff. 1-1-04; 150 v H 230, § 1, eff. 9-16-04; 153 v H 1, § 101.01, eff. 10-16-09; 2011 HB 114, § 101.01, eff. June 29, 2011; 2011 HB 5, § 1, eff. Sept. 23, 2011.**

Acts 2011, HB 114, § 806.10 provides: "The items of law contained in this act, and their applications, are severable. If any item of law contained in this act, or if any application of any item of law contained in this act, is held invalid, the invalidity does not affect other items of law contained in this act and their applications that can be given effect without the invalid item or application."

The effective date is set by § 812.10 of 153 v H 1.

The effective date is set by section 4 of S.B. 123.

See provisions, § 5 of S.B. 123 (149 v —), following RC § 4501.01.

**Publisher's Note:**

This section was formerly § 4507.168. It was renumbered by S.B. 123, Acts 2002, effective January 1, 2004.

## § 4510.23 Suspension of license of mentally ill person.

When any person having a driver's or commercial driver's license is adjudicated incompetent for the purpose of holding the license, as provided in section 5122.301 of the Revised Code, the probate judge shall order the license of the person delivered to the court. The court shall forward the license with notice of the adjudication to the registrar of motor vehicles. The registrar shall impose a class F suspension of the person's driver's or commercial driver's license for the period of time specified in division (B)(6) of section 4510.02 of the Revised Code. The suspension shall remain in effect until receipt of written notice by the head of the hospital, or other agency which has or had custody of such person, that such person's mental illness is not an impairment to such person's ability to operate a motor vehicle, or upon receipt of notice from the adjudicating court that such person has been restored to competency by court decree.

**HISTORY: 126 v 600 (Eff 9-30-55); 129 v 1448 (Eff 10-25-61); 130 v 1059 (Eff 10-10-63); 137 v H 725 (Eff 3-16-78); 143 v H 381. Eff 7-1-89; 149 v S 123, § 1, eff. 1-1-04.**

The effective date is set by section 4 of S.B. 123.

See provisions, § 5 of S.B. 123 (149 v —), following RC § 4501.01.

**Publisher's Note:**

This section was formerly § 4507.161. It was renumbered by S.B. 123, Acts 2002, effective January 1, 2004.

## § 4510.31 Suspension of probationary or restricted license or temporary instruction permit; juvenile driver improvement programs.

(A)(1) Except as provided in division (C) of this section, the registrar of motor vehicles shall suspend the probationary driver's license, restricted license, or temporary instruction permit issued to any person when the person has been convicted of, pleaded guilty to, or been adjudicated in juvenile court of having committed, prior to the person's eighteenth birthday, any of the following:

(a) Three separate violations of section 2903.06, 2903.08, 2921.331 [2921.33.1], 4511.12, 4511.13, 4511.15, 4511.191 [4511.19.1], 4511.20, 4511.201 [4511.20.1], 4511.202 [4511.20.2], 4511.21, 4511.22, 4511.23, 4511.25 to 4511.48, 4511.57 to 4511.65, 4511.75, 4549.02, 4549.021 [4549.02.1], or 4549.03 of the Revised Code, section 4510.14 of the Revised Code involving a suspension imposed under section 4511.191 [4511.19.1] or 4511.196 [4511.19.1] of the Revised Code, section 2903.04 of the Revised Code in a case in which the person would have been subject to the sanctions described in division (D) of that section had the person been convicted of the violation of that section, former section 2903.07 of the Revised Code, or any municipal ordinances similarly relating to the offenses referred to in those sections;

(b) One violation of section 4511.19 of the Revised Code or a substantially similar municipal ordinance;

(c) Two separate violations of any of the Revised Code sections referred to in division (A)(1)(a) of this section, or any municipal ordinance that is substantially similar to any of those sections.

(2) Any person whose license or permit is suspended under division (A)(1)(a), (b), or (c) of this section shall mail or deliver the person's probationary driver's license, restricted license, or temporary instruction permit to the registrar within fourteen days of notification of the suspension. The registrar shall retain the license or permit during the period of the suspension. A suspension pursuant to division (A)(1)(a) of this section shall be a class C suspension, a suspension pursuant to division (A)(1)(b) of this section shall be a class D suspension, and a suspension pursuant to division (A)(1)(c) of this section shall be a class E suspension, all for the periods of time specified in division (B) of section 4510.02 of the Revised Code. If the person's probationary driver's license, restricted license, or temporary instruction permit is under suspension on the date the court imposes sentence upon the person for a violation described in division (A)(1)(b) of this section, the suspension shall take effect on the next day immediately following the end of that period of suspension. If the person is sixteen years of age or older and pleads guilty to or is convicted of a violation described in division (A)(1)(b) of this section and the person does not have a current, valid probationary driver's license, restricted license, or temporary instruction permit, the registrar shall deny the issuance to the person of a probationary driver's license, restricted license, driver's license, commercial driver's license, or temporary instruction permit, as the case may be, for six months beginning on the date the court imposes sentence upon the person for the violation. If the person has not attained the age of sixteen years on the date the court imposes sentence upon the person for the violation, the period of denial shall commence on the date the person attains the age of sixteen years.

(3) The registrar shall suspend the person's license or permit under division (A) of this section regardless of

whether the disposition of the case in juvenile court occurred after the person's eighteenth birthday.

(B) The registrar also shall impose a class D suspension for the period of time specified in division (B)(4) of section 4510.02 of the Revised Code of the temporary instruction permit or probationary driver's license of any person under the age of eighteen who has been adjudicated an unruly child, delinquent child, or juvenile traffic offender for having committed any act that if committed by an adult would be a drug abuse offense or a violation of division (B) of section 2917.11 of the Revised Code. The registrar, in the registrar's discretion, may terminate the suspension if the child, at the discretion of the court, attends and satisfactorily completes a drug abuse or alcohol abuse education, intervention, or treatment program specified by the court. Any person whose temporary instruction permit or probationary driver's license is suspended under this division shall mail or deliver the person's permit or license to the registrar within fourteen days of notification of the suspension. The registrar shall retain the permit or license during the period of the suspension.

(C)(1) Except as provided in division (C)(3) of this section, for any person who is convicted of, pleads guilty to, or is adjudicated in juvenile court of having committed a second or third violation of section 4511.12, 4511.13, 4511.15, 4511.20 to 4511.23, 4511.25, 4511.26 to 4511.48, 4511.57 to 4511.65, or 4511.75 of the Revised Code or any similar municipal ordinances and whose license or permit is suspended under division (A)(1)(a) or (c) of this section, the court in which the second or third conviction, finding, plea, or adjudication resulting in the suspension was made, upon petition of the person, may grant the person limited driving privileges during the period which the suspension otherwise would be imposed under division (A)(1)(a) or (c) of this section if the court finds reasonable cause to believe that the suspension will seriously affect the person's ability to continue in employment, educational training, vocational training, or treatment. In granting the limited driving privileges, the court shall specify the purposes, times, and places of the privileges and may impose any other conditions upon the person's driving a motor vehicle that the court considers reasonable and necessary.

A court that grants limited driving privileges to a person under this division shall retain the person's probationary driver's license, restricted license, or temporary instruction permit during the period the license or permit is suspended and also during the period for which limited driving privileges are granted, and shall deliver to the person a permit card, in a form to be prescribed by the court, setting forth the date on which the limited driving privileges will become effective, the purposes for which the person may drive, the times and places at which the person may drive, and any other conditions imposed upon the person's use of a motor vehicle.

The court immediately shall notify the registrar, in writing, of a grant of limited driving privileges under this division. The notification shall specify the date on which the limited driving privileges will become effective, the purposes for which the person may drive, the times and places at which the person may drive, and any other conditions imposed upon the person's use of a motor vehicle. The registrar shall not suspend the probationary driver's license, restricted license, or temporary instruction permit of any person pursuant to division (A) of this section during any period for which the person has been granted limited driving privileges as provided in this division, if the registrar has received the notification described in this division from the court.

(2) Except as provided in division (C)(3) of this section, in any case in which the temporary instruction permit or probationary driver's license of a person under eighteen years of age has been suspended under division (A) or (B) of this section or any other provision of law, the court may grant the person limited driving privileges for the purpose of the person's practicing of driving with the person's parent, guardian, or other custodian during the period of the suspension. Any grant of limited driving privileges under this division shall comply with division (D) of section 4510.021 [4510.02.1] of the Revised Code.

(3) A court shall not grant limited driving privileges to a person identified in division (C)(1) or (2) of this section if the person, within the preceding six years, has been convicted of, pleaded guilty to, or adjudicated in juvenile court of having committed three or more violations of one or more of the divisions or sections set forth in divisions (G)(2)(b) to (g) of section 2919.22 of the Revised Code.

(D) If a person who has been granted limited driving privileges under division (C) of this section is convicted of, pleads guilty to, or is adjudicated in juvenile court of having committed, a violation of chapter 4510. of the Revised Code, or a subsequent violation of any of the sections of the Revised Code listed in division (A)(1)(a) of this section or any similar municipal ordinance during the period for which the person was granted limited driving privileges, the court that granted the limited driving privileges shall suspend the person's permit card. The court or the clerk of the court immediately shall forward the person's probationary driver's license, restricted license, or temporary instruction permit together with written notification of the court's action to the registrar. Upon receipt of the license or permit and notification, the registrar shall impose a class C suspension of the person's probationary driver's license, restricted license, or temporary instruction permit for the period of time specified in division (B)(3) of section 4510.02 of the Revised Code. The registrar shall retain the license or permit during the period of suspension, and no further limited driving privileges shall be granted during that period.

(E) No application for a driver's or commercial driver's license shall be received from any person whose probationary driver's license, restricted license, or temporary instruction permit has been suspended under this section until each of the following has occurred:

(1) The suspension period has expired;

(2) A temporary instruction permit or commercial driver's license temporary instruction permit has been issued;

(3) The person successfully completes a juvenile driver improvement program approved by the registrar under section 4510.311 [4510.31.1] of the Revised Code;

(4) The applicant has submitted to the examination for a driver's license as provided for in section 4507.11 or a commercial driver's license as provided in Chapter 4506. of the Revised Code.

**HISTORY: 127 v 839 (Eff 9-16-57); 128 v 539 (Eff 11-2-59); 129 v 1599 (Eff 10-11-61); 130 v 1060 (Eff 9-27-63); 132 v H 380 (Eff 1-1-68); 135 v S 1 (Eff 1-1-74); 140 v H 252 (Eff 4-4-85); 142 v H 643 (Eff 3-17-89); 143 v H 329 (Eff 6-30-89); 143 v H 330 (Eff 6-30-89); 143 v H 381 (Eff 7-1-89); 143 v S 49 (Eff 11-3-89); 143 v S 131 (Eff 7-25-90); 144 v S 275 (Eff 9-1-93); 145 v S 62, § 4 (Eff 9-1-93); 145 v H 377 (Eff 9-30-93); 145 v H 236 (Eff 9-29-94); 147 v S 60 (Eff 10-21-97); 147 v S 35 (Eff 1-1-99); 148 v S 107 (Eff 3-23-2000); 149 v H 490, § 6. Eff 4-3-2003; 149 v S 123, § 1, eff. 1-1-04; 150 v H 230, § 1, eff. 9-16-04.**

The effective date is set by section 4 of S.B. 123.

See provisions, § 5 of S.B. 123 (149 v —), following RC § 4501.01.

The provisions of § 8 of HB 490 (149 v ) read as follows:

SECTION 8. The amendments to section 4507.162 of the Revised Code that are made in Sections 6 and 7 of this act are made for the period of time that section 4507.162 of the Revised Code is in existence under that number until, on January 1, 2004, that section is renumbered by Am. Sub. S.B. 123 of the 124th General Assembly to section 4510.31 of the Revised Code and is amended. On and after January 1, 2004, the amendments to section 4507.16 of the Revised Code that are made in Sections 6 and 7 of this act have no meaning and no force and effect, and do not affect or supersede the renumbering and amendment of section 4507.162 of the Revised Code that was done in Am. Sub. S.B. 123 of the 124th General Assembly.

**Publisher's Note:**

This section was formerly § 4507.162. It was renumbered by S.B. 123, Acts 2002, effective January 1, 2004.

## § 4510.311 Juvenile driver improvement programs.

The registrar of motor vehicles shall establish standards for juvenile driver improvement programs and shall approve any programs that meet the established standards. The standards established by the registrar shall require a minimum of five hours of classroom instruction, with at least three hours devoted to driver skill requirements and two hours devoted to juvenile driver information related to the driving records of drivers under eighteen years of age, driver perceptions, and the value of the traffic laws. The standards also shall require a person whose probationary driver's license was suspended under section 4510.31 of the Revised Code to undertake and pass, as successful completion of an approved juvenile driver improvement program, the driver's license examination that a person who holds a temporary instruction permit is required to undertake and pass in order to be issued a probationary driver's license. The person shall pay the applicable fee that is required to accompany an application for a driver's license as prescribed in division (E) of section 4507.23 of the Revised Code. The registrar shall prescribe the requirements for the curriculum to be provided as well as other program directives. Only those programs approved by the registrar shall be acceptable for reinstatement of the driving privileges of a person whose probationary driver's license was suspended under section 4510.31 of the Revised Code.

**HISTORY: 149 v S 123, § 1, eff. 1-1-04.**

The effective date is set by section 4 of S.B. 123.

See provisions, § 5 of S.B. 123 (149 v —), following RC § 4501.01.

## § 4510.32 Restrictions where minor withdraws from school or is habitually absent.

(A) The registrar of motor vehicles shall record within ten days of receipt and keep at the main office of the bureau of motor vehicles all information provided to the registrar by the superintendent of a school district in accordance with division (B) of section 3321.13 of the Revised Code.

(B) Whenever the registrar receives a notice under division (B) of section 3321.13 of the Revised Code, the registrar shall impose a class F suspension of the temporary instruction permit or driver's license of the person who is the subject of the notice for the period of time specified in division (B)(6) of section 4510.02 of the Revised Code, or, if the person has not been issued a temporary instruction permit or driver's license, the registrar shall deny to the person the issuance of a permit or license. The requirements of the second paragraph of section 119.06 of the Revised Code do not apply to a suspension of a person's temporary instruction permit or driver's license or a denial of a person's opportunity to obtain a temporary instruction permit or driver's license by the registrar under this division.

(C) Upon suspending the temporary instruction permit or driver's license of any person or denying any person the opportunity to be issued such a license or permit as provided in division (B) of this section, the registrar immediately shall notify the person in writing of the suspension or denial and inform the person that the person may petition for a hearing as provided in division (E) of this section.

(D) Any person whose permit or license is suspended under this section shall mail or deliver the person's permit or license to the registrar of motor vehicles within twenty days of notification of the suspension; however, the person's permit or license and the person's driving privileges shall be suspended immediately upon receipt of the notification. The registrar may retain the permit or license during the period of the suspension or the registrar may destroy it under section 4510.52 of the Revised Code.

(E) Any person whose temporary instruction permit or driver's license has been suspended, or whose opportunity to obtain such a permit or license has been denied pursuant to this section, may file a petition in the juvenile court in whose jurisdiction the person resides alleging error in the action taken by the registrar under division (B) of this section or alleging one or more of the matters within the scope of the hearing, as described in this division, or both. The petitioner shall notify the registrar and the superintendent of the school district who gave the notice to the registrar and juvenile judge under division (B) of section 3321.13 of the Revised Code of the filing of the petition and send them copies of the petition. The scope of the hearing is limited to the issues of whether the notice given by the superintendent to the registrar was in error and whether the suspension or denial of driving privileges will result in substantial hardship to the petitioner.

The registrar shall furnish the court a copy of the record created in accordance with division (A) of this section. The registrar and the superintendent shall furnish the court with any other relevant information required by the court.

In hearing the matter and determining whether the petitioner has shown that the petitioner's temporary instruction permit or driver's license should not be suspended or that the petitioner's opportunity to obtain such a permit or license should not be denied, the court shall decide the issue upon the information furnished by the registrar and the superintendent and any such additional evidence that the registrar, the superintendent, or the petitioner submits.

If the court finds from the evidence submitted that the petitioner has failed to show error in the action taken by the registrar under division (B) of this section and has failed to prove any of the matters within the scope of the hearing, then the court may assess the cost of the proceeding against the petitioner and shall uphold the suspension of the petitioner's permit or license or the denial of the petitioner's opportunity to obtain a permit or license. If the court finds that the petitioner has shown error in the action taken by the registrar under division (B) of this section or has proved one or more of the matters within the scope of the hearing, or both, the cost of the proceeding shall be paid out of the county treasury of the county in which the proceedings were held, and the suspension of the petitioner's permit or license or the denial of the person's opportunity to obtain a permit or license shall be terminated.

(F) The registrar shall cancel the record created under this section of any person who is the subject of a notice given under division (B) of section 3321.13 of the Revised Code and shall terminate the suspension of the person's permit or license or the denial of the person's opportunity to obtain a permit or license, if any of the following applies:

(1) The person is at least eighteen years of age.

(2) The person provides evidence, as the registrar shall require by rule, of receipt of a high school diploma or a general educational development certificate of high school equivalence.

(3) The superintendent of a school district informs the registrar that the notification of withdrawal, habitual absence without legitimate excuse, suspension, or expulsion concerning the person was in error.

(4) The suspension or denial was imposed subsequent to a notification given under division (B)(3) or (4) of section 3321.13 of the Revised Code, and the superintendent of a school district informs the registrar that the person in question has satisfied any terms or conditions established by the school as necessary to terminate the suspension or denial of driving privileges.

(5) The suspension or denial was imposed subsequent to a notification given under division (B)(1) of section 3321.13 of the Revised Code, and the superintendent of a school district informs the registrar that the person in question is now attending school or enrolled in and attending an approved program to obtain a diploma or its equivalent to the satisfaction of the school superintendent.

(6) The suspension or denial was imposed subsequent to a notification given under division (B)(2) of section 3321.13 of the Revised Code, the person has completed at least one semester or term of school after the one in which the notification was given, the person requests the superintendent of the school district to notify the registrar that the person no longer is habitually absent without legitimate excuse, the superintendent determines that the person has not been absent from school without legitimate excuse in the current semester or term, as determined under that division, for more than ten consecutive school days or for more than fifteen total school days, and the superintendent informs the registrar of that fact. If a person described in division (F)(6) of this section requests the superintendent of the school district to notify the registrar that the person no longer is habitually absent without legitimate excuse and the superintendent makes the determination described in this division, the superintendent shall provide the information described in division (F) (6) of this section to the registrar within five days after receiving the request.

(7) The suspension or denial was imposed subsequent to a notification given under division (B)(2) of section 3321.13 of the Revised Code, and the superintendent of a school district informs the registrar that the person in question has received an age and schooling certificate in accordance with section 3331.01 of the Revised Code.

(8) The person filed a petition in court under division (E) of this section and the court found that the person showed error in the action taken by the registrar under division (B) of this section or proved one or more of the matters within the scope of the hearing on the petition, as set forth in division (E) of this section, or both.

At the end of the suspension period under this section and upon the request of the person whose temporary instruction permit or driver's license was suspended, the registrar shall return the driver's license or permit to the person or reissue the person's license or permit under section 4510.52 of the Revised Code, if the registrar destroyed the suspended license or permit under that section.

**HISTORY: 143 v H 204 (Eff 5-2-90); 145 v H 687 (Eff 10-12-94); 148 v S 1. Eff 8-6-99; 149 v S 123, § 1, eff. 1-1-04.**

The effective date is set by section 4 of S.B. 123.

See provisions, § 5 of S.B. 123 (149 v —), following RC § 4501.01.

**Publisher's Note:**

This section was formerly § 4507.061. It was amended and renumbered by S.B. 123, Acts 2002, effective January 1, 2004.

## § 4510.33 Underage persons using license to purchase liquor or beer.

(A) No person of insufficient age to purchase intoxicating liquor or beer, contrary to division (A) or (C) of section 4507.30 of the Revised Code, shall display as proof that the person is of sufficient age to purchase intoxicating liquor or beer, a driver's or commercial driver's license, knowing the same to be fictitious, altered, or not the person's own. The registrar of motor vehicles shall impose a class C suspension of the person's driver's license, probationary driver's license, commercial driver's license, temporary instruction permit, or commercial driver's license temporary instruction permit for the period of for the period of time specified in division (B)(3) of section 4510.02 of the Revised Code upon the offender and shall not issue or reissue a license or permit of that type to the offender during the suspension period.

(B) In any prosecution, or in any proceeding before the liquor control commission, in which the defense authorized by section 4301.639 of the Revised Code is sustained, the clerk of the court in which the prosecution was had, or the clerk of the liquor control commission, shall certify to the registrar the facts ascertainable from the clerk's records evidencing violation of division (A) or (C) of section 4507.30 of the Revised Code by a person of insufficient age to purchase intoxicating liquor or beer, including in the certification the person's name and residence address.

(C) The registrar, upon receipt of the certification, shall suspend the person's license or permit to drive subject to review as provided in this section, and shall mail to the person, at the person's last known address, a notice of the suspension and of the hearing provided in division (D) of this section.

(D) Any person whose license or permit to drive has been suspended under this section, within twenty days of the mailing of the notice provided above, may file a petition in the municipal court or county court, or in case the person is under the age of eighteen years, in the juvenile court, in whose jurisdiction the person resides, agreeing to pay the cost of the proceedings, and alleging error by the registrar in the suspension of the license or permit to drive, or in one or more of the matters within the scope of the hearing as provided in this section, or both. The petitioner shall notify the registrar of the filing of the petition and send the registrar a copy thereof. The scope of the hearing shall be limited to whether a court of record did in fact find that the petitioner displayed, or, if the original proceedings were before the liquor control commission, whether the petitioner did in fact display, as proof that the person was of sufficient age to purchase intoxicating liquor or beer, a driver's or commercial driver's license knowing the same to be fictitious, altered, or not the person's own, and whether the person was at that time of insufficient age legally to make a purchase of intoxicating liquor or beer.

(E) In any hearing authorized by this section, the registrar shall be represented by the prosecuting attorney of the county where the petitioner resides.

(F) If the court finds from the evidence submitted that the person has failed to show error in the action by the registrar or in one or more of the matters within the scope of the hearing as limited in division (D) of this section, or both, the court shall assess the cost of the proceeding against the person and shall impose the suspension provided in divisions (A) and (C) of this section. If the court finds that the person has shown error in the action taken by the registrar, or in one or more of the matters within the scope of the hearing as limited in division (B) of this section, or both, the cost of the proceeding shall be paid out of the county treasury of the county in which the proceedings were held, and the suspension provided in divisions (A) and (C) of this section shall not be imposed. The court shall inform the registrar in writing of the action taken.

**HISTORY: 134 v H 453 (Eff 9-28-72); 143 v H 381 (Eff 7-1-89); 147 v S 60. Eff 10-21-97; 149 v S 123, § 1, eff. 1-1-04.**

The effective date is set by section 4 of S.B. 123.

See provisions, § 5 of S.B. 123 (149 v —), following RC § 4501.01.

**Publisher's Note:**

This section was formerly § 4507.163. It was amended and renumbered by S.B. 123, Acts 2002, effective January 1, 2004.

## § 4510.34 Suspension of probationary motorized bicycle license.

(A) The registrar of motor vehicles shall impose a class F suspension for the period of time specified in division (B)(6) of section 4510.02 of the Revised Code of the probationary motorized bicycle license issued to any person when the person has been convicted of or has been adjudicated in juvenile court of having committed, a violation of division (A) or (D) of section 4511.521 of the Revised Code, or of any other section of the Revised Code or similar municipal ordinance for which points are chargeable under section 4510.036 of the Revised Code.

(B) Any person whose license is suspended under this section shall mail or deliver the person's probationary motorized bicycle license to the registrar within fourteen days of notification of the suspension. The registrar shall retain the license during the period of suspension.

(C) No application for a motorized bicycle license or probationary motorized bicycle license shall be received from any person whose probationary motorized bicycle license has been suspended under this section until the person reaches sixteen years of age.

**HISTORY: RC § 4507.16.3†, 140 v S 169 (Eff 1-1-85); RC § 4507.16.7, 141 v H 356. Eff 9-24-86; 149 v S 123, § 1, eff. 1-1-04.**

The effective date is set by section 4 of S.B. 123.

See provisions, § 5 of S.B. 123 (149 v —), following RC § 4501.01.

† This section was inadvertently numbered RC § 4507.16.3 in Am. Sub. S.B. 169; it was renumbered to RC § 4507.16.7 by H.B. 356.

**Publisher's Note:**

This section was formerly § 4507.167. It was amended and renumbered by S.B. 123, Acts 2002, effective January 1, 2004.

## § 4510.41 Seizure of vehicle and license plates upon arrest for certain violations; motion for return or release; immobilization or forfeiture orders upon guilty plea or conviction.

(A) As used in this section:

(1) "Arrested person" means a person who is arrested for a violation of section 4510.14, 4510.16, or 4511.203 of the Revised Code, or a municipal ordinance that is substantially equivalent to any of those sections, and whose arrest results in a vehicle being seized under division (B) of this section.

(2) "Vehicle owner" means either of the following:

(a) The person in whose name is registered, at the time of the seizure, a vehicle that is seized under division (B) of this section;

(b) A person to whom the certificate of title to a vehicle that is seized under division (B) of this section has been assigned and who has not obtained a certificate of title to the vehicle in that person's name, but who is deemed by the court as being the owner of the vehicle at the time the vehicle was seized under division (B) of this section.

(3) "Interested party" includes the owner of a vehicle seized under this section, all lienholders, the arrested person, the owner of the place of storage at which a vehicle seized under this section is stored, and the person or entity that caused the vehicle to be removed.

(B)(1) If a person is arrested for a violation of section 4510.14 or 4511.203 of the Revised Code or a municipal ordinance that is substantially equivalent to either of those sections or if a person is arrested for a violation of section 4510.16 of the Revised Code or a municipal ordinance that is substantially equivalent to that section and if division (G)(2) of section 4510.16 or division (B) of section 4510.161 of the Revised Code applies, the arresting officer or another officer of the law enforcement agency that employs the arresting officer, in addition to any action that the arresting officer is required or authorized to take by any other provision of law, shall seize the vehicle that the person was operating at the time of, or that was involved in, the alleged offense if the vehicle is registered in the arrested person's name and its license plates. A law enforcement agency that employs a law enforcement officer who makes an arrest of a type that is described in this division and that involves a rented or leased vehicle that is being rented or leased for a period of thirty days or less shall notify, within twenty-four hours after the officer makes the arrest, the lessor or owner of the vehicle regarding the circumstances of the arrest and the location at which the vehicle may be picked up. At the time of the seizure of the vehicle, the law enforcement officer who made the arrest shall give the arrested person written notice that the vehicle and its license plates have been seized; that the vehicle either will be kept by the officer's law enforcement agency or will be immobilized at least until the person's initial appearance on the charge of the offense for which the arrest was made; that, at the initial appearance, the court in certain circumstances may order that the vehicle and license plates be released to the arrested person until the disposition of that charge; that, if the arrested person is convicted of that charge, the court generally must order the immobilization of the vehicle and the impoundment of its license plates or the forfeiture of the vehicle; and that the arrested person may be charged expenses or charges incurred under this section and section 4503.233 of the Revised Code for the removal and storage of the vehicle.

(2) The arresting officer or a law enforcement officer of the agency that employs the arresting officer shall give written notice of the seizure under division (B)(1) of this section to the court that will conduct the initial appearance of the arrested person on the charges arising out of the arrest. Upon receipt of the notice, the court promptly shall determine whether the arrested person is the vehicle owner. If the court determines that the arrested person is not the vehicle owner, it promptly shall send by regular mail written notice of the seizure to the vehicle's registered owner. The written notice shall contain all of the information required by division (B)(1) of this section to be in a notice to be given to the arrested person and also shall specify the date, time, and place of the arrested person's initial appearance. The notice also shall inform the vehicle owner that if title to a motor vehicle that is subject to an order for criminal forfeiture under this section is assigned or transferred and division (B)(2) or (3) of section 4503.234 of the Revised Code applies, the court may fine the arrested person the value of the vehicle. The notice also shall state that if the vehicle is immobilized under division (A) of section 4503.233 of the Revised Code, seven days after the end of the period of immobilization a law enforcement agency will send the vehicle owner a notice, informing the owner that if the release of the vehicle is not obtained in accordance with division (D)(3) of section 4503.233 of the Revised Code, the vehicle shall be forfeited. The notice also shall inform the vehicle owner that the owner may be charged expenses or charges incurred under this section and section 4503.233 of the Revised Code for the removal and storage of the vehicle.

The written notice that is given to the arrested person also shall state that if the person is convicted of or pleads guilty to the offense and the court issues an immobilization and impoundment order relative to that vehicle, division (D)(4) of section 4503.233 of the Revised Code prohibits the vehicle from being sold during the period of immobilization without the prior approval of the court.

(3) At or before the initial appearance, the vehicle owner may file a motion requesting the court to order that the vehicle and its license plates be released to the vehicle owner. Except as provided in this division and subject to the payment of expenses or charges incurred in the removal and storage of the vehicle, the court, in its discretion, then may issue an order releasing the vehicle and its license plates to the vehicle owner. Such an order may be conditioned upon such terms as the court determines appropriate, including the posting of a bond in an amount determined by the court. If the arrested person is not the vehicle owner and if the vehicle owner is not present at the arrested person's initial appearance, and if the court believes that the vehicle owner was not provided with adequate notice of the initial appearance, the court, in its discretion, may allow the vehicle owner to file a motion within seven days of the initial appearance. If the court allows the vehicle owner to file such a motion after the initial appearance, the extension of time granted by the court does not extend the time within which the initial appearance is to be conducted. If the court issues an order for the release of the vehicle and its license plates, a copy of the order shall be made available to the vehicle owner. If the vehicle owner presents a copy of the order to the law enforcement agency that employs the law enforcement officer who arrested the arrested person, the law enforcement agency promptly shall release the vehicle and its license plates to the vehicle owner upon payment by the vehicle owner of any expenses or charges incurred in the removal or storage of the vehicle.

(4) A vehicle seized under division (B)(1) of this section either shall be towed to a place specified by the law enforcement agency that employs the arresting officer to be safely kept by the agency at that place for the time and in the manner specified in this section or shall be otherwise immobilized for the time and in the manner specified in this section. A law enforcement officer of that agency shall remove the identification license plates of the vehicle, and they shall be safely kept by the agency for the time and in the manner specified in this section. No vehicle that is seized and either towed or immobilized pursuant to this division shall be considered contraband for purposes of Chapter 2981. of the Revised Code. The vehicle shall not be immobilized at any place other than a commercially operated private storage lot, a place owned by a law enforcement or other government agency, or a place to which one of the following applies:

(a) The place is leased by or otherwise under the control of a law enforcement or other government agency.

(b) The place is owned by the arrested person, the arrested person's spouse, or a parent or child of the arrested person.

(c) The place is owned by a private person or entity, and, prior to the immobilization, the private entity or person that owns the place, or the authorized agent of that private entity or person, has given express written consent for the immobilization to be carried out at that place.

(d) The place is a public street or highway on which the vehicle is parked in accordance with the law.

(C)(1) A vehicle seized under division (B)(1) of this section shall be safely kept at the place to which it is towed or otherwise moved by the law enforcement agency that employs the arresting officer until the initial appearance of the arrested person relative to the charge in question. The license plates of the vehicle that are removed pursuant to division (B)(1) of this section shall be safely kept by the law enforcement agency that employs the arresting officer until at least the initial appearance of the arrested person relative to the charge in question.

(2)(a) At the initial appearance or not less than seven days prior to the date of final disposition, the court shall notify the arrested person that, if title to a motor vehicle that is subject to an order for criminal forfeiture under this section is assigned or transferred and division (B)(2) or (3) of section 4503.234 of the Revised Code applies, the court may fine the arrested person the value of the vehicle. If, at the initial appearance, the arrested person pleads guilty to the violation of section 4510.14, 4510.16, or 4511.203 of the Revised Code, or a municipal ordinance that is substantially equivalent to any of those sections or pleads no contest to and is convicted of the violation, the following sentencing provisions apply:

(i) If the person violated section 4510.14 of the Revised Code or a municipal ordinance that is substantially equivalent to that section, the court shall impose sentence upon the person as provided by law or ordinance; the court shall order the immobilization of the vehicle the arrested person was operating at the time of, or that was involved in, the offense if registered in the arrested person's name and the impoundment of its license plates under sections 4503.233 and 4510.14 of the Revised Code or the criminal forfeiture to the state of the vehicle if registered in the arrested person's name under sections 4503.234 and 4510.14 of the Revised Code, whichever is applicable; and the vehicle and its license plates shall not be returned or released to the arrested person.

If the person violated section 4511.203 of the Revised Code or a municipal ordinance that is substantially equivalent to that section, or violated section 4510.16 of the Revised Code or a municipal ordinance that is substantially equivalent to that section and division (G)(2) of section 4510.16 or division (B) of section 4510.161 of the Revised Code applies, the court shall impose sentence upon the person as provided by law or ordinance; the court may order the immobilization of the vehicle the arrested person was operating at the time of, or that was involved in, the offense if registered in the arrested person's name and the impoundment of its license plates under section 4503.233 and section 4510.16, 4510.161, or 4511.203 of the Revised Code or the criminal forfeiture to the state of the vehicle if registered in the arrested person's name under section 4503.234 and section 4510.16, 4510.161, or 4511.203 of the Revised Code, whichever is applicable; and the vehicle and its license plates shall not be returned or released to the arrested person.

(ii) If the person violated section 4510.16 of the Revised Code or a municipal ordinance that is substantially equivalent to that section and division (G)(1) of section 4510.16 or division (B) of section 4510.161 applies, the court shall impose sentence upon the person as provided by law or ordinance and may order the immobilization of the vehicle the person was operating at the time of, or that was involved in, the offense if it is registered in the arrested person's name and the impoundment of its license plates under section 4503.233 and section 4510.16 or 4510.161 of the Revised Code, and the vehicle and its license plates shall not be returned or released to the arrested person.

(b) If, at any time, the charge that the arrested person violated section 4510.14, 4510.16, or 4511.203 of the Revised Code, or a municipal ordinance that is substantially equivalent to any of those sections is dismissed for any reason, the court shall order that the vehicle seized at the time of the arrest and its license plates immediately be released to the person.

(D) If a vehicle and its license plates are seized under division (B)(1) of this section and are not returned or released to the arrested person pursuant to division (C) of this section, the vehicle and its license plates shall be retained until the final disposition of the charge in question. Upon the final disposition of that charge, the court shall do whichever of the following is applicable:

(1) If the arrested person is convicted of or pleads guilty to the violation of section 4510.14 of the Revised Code or a municipal ordinance that is substantially equivalent to that section, the court shall impose sentence upon the person as provided by law or ordinance and shall order the immobilization of the vehicle the person was operating at the time of, or that was involved in, the offense if it is registered in the arrested person's name and the impoundment of its license plates under sections 4503.233 and 4510.14 of the Revised Code or the criminal forfeiture of the vehicle if it is registered in the arrested person's name under sections 4503.234 and 4510.14 of the Revised Code, whichever is applicable.

If the arrested person is convicted of or pleads guilty to the violation of section 4511.203 of the Revised Code, or a municipal ordinance that is substantially equivalent to that section, or to the violation of section 4510.16 of the Revised Code or a municipal ordinance that is substantially equivalent to that section and division (F)(2) of section 4510.16 or division (B) of section 4510.161 of the Revised Code applies, the court shall impose sentence upon the person as provided by law or ordinance and may order the immobilization of the vehicle the person was operating at the time of, or that was involved in, the offense if it is registered in the arrested person's name and the impoundment of its license plates under section 4503.233 and section 4510.16, 4510.161, or 4511.203 of the Revised Code or the criminal forfeiture of the vehicle if it is registered in the arrested person's name under section 4503.234 and section 4510.16, 4510.161, or 4511.203 of the Revised Code, whichever is applicable.

(2) If the person violated section 4510.16 of the Revised Code or a municipal ordinance that is substantially equivalent to that section and division (G)(1) of section 4510.16 or division (B) of section 4510.161 applies, the court shall impose sentence upon the person as provided by law or ordinance and may order the immobilization of the vehicle the person was operating at the time of, or that was involved in, the offense if it is registered in the person's name and the impoundment of its license plates under section 4503.233 and section 4510.16 or 4510.161 of the Revised Code.

(3) If the arrested person is found not guilty of the violation of section 4510.14, 4510.16, or 4511.203 of the Revised Code, or a municipal ordinance that is substantially equivalent to any of those sections, the court shall order that the vehicle and its license plates immediately be released to the arrested person.

(4) If the charge that the arrested person violated section 4510.14, 4510.16, or 4511.203 of the Revised Code, or a municipal ordinance that is substantially equivalent to any of those sections is dismissed for any reason, the court shall order that the vehicle and its license plates immediately be released to the arrested person.

(5) If the impoundment of the vehicle was not authorized under this section, the court shall order that the vehicle and its license plates be returned immediately to the arrested person or, if the arrested person is not the vehicle owner, to the vehicle owner and shall order that the state or political subdivision of the law enforcement agency served by the law enforcement officer who seized the vehicle pay all expenses and charges incurred in its removal and storage.

(E) If a vehicle is seized under division (B)(2) of this section, the time between the seizure of the vehicle and either its release to the arrested person pursuant to division (C) of this section or the issuance of an order of immobilization of the vehicle under section 4503.233 of the Revised Code shall be credited against the period of immobilization ordered by the court.

(F)(1) Except as provided in division (D)(4) of this section, the arrested person may be charged expenses or charges incurred in the removal and storage of the immobilized vehicle. The court with jurisdiction over the case, after notice to all interested parties, including lienholders, and after an opportunity for them to be heard, if the court finds that the arrested person does not intend to seek release of the vehicle at the end of the period of immobilization under section 4503.233 of the Revised Code or that the arrested person is not or will not be able to pay the expenses and charges incurred in its removal and storage, may order that title to the vehicle be transferred, in order of priority, first into the name of the person or entity that removed it, next into the name of a lienholder, or lastly into the name of the owner of the place of storage.

Any lienholder that receives title under a court order shall do so on the condition that it pay any expenses or charges incurred in the vehicle's removal and storage. If the person or entity that receives title to the vehicle is the person or entity that removed it, the person or entity shall receive title on the condition that it pay any lien on the vehicle. The court shall not order that title be transferred to any person or entity other than the owner of the place of storage if the person or entity refuses to receive the title. Any person or entity that receives title either may keep title to the vehicle or may dispose of the vehicle in any legal manner that it considers appropriate, including assignment of the certificate of title to the motor vehicle to a salvage dealer or a scrap metal processing facility. The person or entity shall not transfer the vehicle to the person who is the vehicle's immediate previous owner.

If the person or entity that receives title assigns the motor vehicle to a salvage dealer or scrap metal processing facility, the person or entity shall send the assigned certificate of title to the motor vehicle to the clerk of the court of common pleas of the county in which the salvage dealer or scrap metal processing facility is located. The person or entity shall mark the face of the certificate of title with the words "FOR DESTRUCTION" and shall deliver a photocopy of the certificate of title to the salvage dealer or scrap metal processing facility for its records.

(2) Whenever a court issues an order under division (F)(1) of this section, the court also shall order removal of the license plates from the vehicle and cause them to be sent to the registrar if they have not already been sent to the registrar. Thereafter, no further proceedings shall take place under this section or under section 4503.233 of the Revised Code.

(3) Prior to initiating a proceeding under division (F)(1) of this section, and upon payment of the fee under division (B) of section 4505.14, any interested party may cause a search to be made of the public records of the bureau of motor vehicles or the clerk of the court of common pleas, to ascertain the identity of any lienholder of the vehicle. The initiating party shall furnish this information to the clerk of the court with jurisdiction over the case, and the clerk shall provide notice to the arrested person, any lienholder, and any other interested parties listed by the initiating party, at the last known address supplied by the initiating party, by certified mail, or, at the option of the initiating party, by personal service or ordinary mail.

**HISTORY: 144 v S 275 (Eff 9-1-93); 145 v S 62, §§ 1, 4 (Eff 9-1-93); 145 v H 236 (Eff 9-29-94); 145 v H 687 (Eff 10-12-94); 146 v H 353. Eff 9-17-96; 149 v S 123, § 1, eff. 1-1-04; 151 v H 461, § 1, eff. 4-4-07; 151 v H 241, § 1, eff. 7-1-07; 2011 HB 5, § 1, eff. Sept. 23, 2011.**

See provisions of § 4 of 151 v H 241 following RC § 4503.233.

The effective date is set by section 4 of S.B. 123.

See provisions, § 5 of S.B. 123 (149 v —), following RC § 4501.01.

The provisions of § 8 of S.B. 123 read as follows:

SECTION 8. Section 4507.38 of the Revised Code, renumbered as section 4510.41 of the Revised Code, is presented in this act as a composite of the section as amended by both Am. Sub. H.B. 353 and Am. Sub. H.B. 676 of the 121st General Assembly. The General Assembly, applying the principle stated in division (B) of section 1.52 of the Revised Code that amendments are to be harmonized if reasonably capable of simultaneous operation, finds that the composites are the resulting versions of the sections in effect prior to the effective date of the sections as presented in this act.

**Publisher's Note:**

This section was formerly § 4507.38. It was amended and renumbered by S.B. 123, Acts 2002, effective January 1, 2004.

**Comment, Legislative Service Commission**

Section 4510.41 of the Revised Code is amended by Sub. H.B. 241 and Am. Sub. H.B. 461 of the 126th General Assembly. Comparison of these amendments in pursuance of section 1.52 of the Revised Code discloses that they are not irreconcilable so that they are required by that section to be harmonized to give effect to each amendment.

## § 4510.43 Certification of immobilizing and disabling devices; prototype devices; vehicles owned by employer.

(A)(1) The director of public safety, upon consultation with the director of health and in accordance with Chapter 119. of the Revised Code, shall certify immobilizing and disabling devices and, subject to section 4510.45 of the Revised Code, shall publish and make available to the courts, without charge, a list of licensed manufacturers of ignition interlock devices and approved devices together with information about the manufacturers of the devices and where they may be obtained. The manufacturer of an immobilizing or disabling device shall pay the cost of obtaining the certification of the device to the director of public safety, and the director shall deposit the payment in the indigent drivers alcohol treatment fund established by section 4511.191 of the Revised Code.

(2) The director of public safety, in accordance with Chapter 119. of the Revised Code, shall adopt and publish rules setting forth the requirements for obtaining the certification of an immobilizing or disabling device. The director of public safety shall not certify an immobilizing or disabling device under this section unless it meets the requirements specified and published by the director in the rules adopted pursuant to this division. A certified device may consist of an ignition interlock device, an ignition blocking device initiated by time or magnetic or electronic encoding, an activity monitor, or any other device that reasonably assures compliance with an order granting limited driving privileges. Ignition interlock devices shall be certified annually.

The requirements for an immobilizing or disabling device that is an ignition interlock device shall require that the manufacturer of the device submit to the department of public safety a certificate from an independent testing laboratory indicating that the device meets or exceeds the standards of the national highway traffic safety administration, as defined in section 4511.19 of the Revised Code, that are in effect at the time of the director's decision regarding certification of the device, shall include provisions for setting a minimum and maximum calibration range, and shall include, but shall not be limited to, specifications that the device complies with all of the following:

(a) It does not impede the safe operation of the vehicle.

(b) It has features that make circumvention difficult and that do not interfere with the normal use of the vehicle, and the features are operating and functioning.

(c) It correlates well with established measures of alcohol impairment.

(d) It works accurately and reliably in an unsupervised environment.

(e) It is resistant to tampering and shows evidence of tampering if tampering is attempted.

(f) It is difficult to circumvent and requires premeditation to do so.

(g) It minimizes inconvenience to a sober user.

(h) It requires a proper, deep-lung breath sample or other accurate measure of the concentration by weight of alcohol in the breath.

(i) It operates reliably over the range of automobile environments.

(j) It is made by a manufacturer who is covered by product liability insurance.

(3) The director of public safety may adopt, in whole or in part, the guidelines, rules, regulations, studies, or independent laboratory tests performed and relied upon by other states, or their agencies or commissions, in the certification or approval of immobilizing or disabling devices.

(4) The director of public safety shall adopt rules in accordance with Chapter 119. of the Revised Code for the design of a warning label that shall be affixed to each immobilizing or disabling device upon installation. The label shall contain a warning that any person tampering, circumventing, or otherwise misusing the device is subject to a fine, imprisonment, or both and may be subject to civil liability.

(B) A court considering the use of a prototype device in a pilot program shall advise the director of public safety, thirty days before the use, of the prototype device and its protocol, methodology, manufacturer, and licensor, lessor, other agent, or owner, and the length of the court's pilot program. A prototype device shall not be used for a violation of section 4510.14 or 4511.19 of the Revised Code, a violation of a municipal OVI ordinance, or in relation to a suspension imposed under section 4511.191 of the Revised Code. A court that uses a prototype device in a pilot program, periodically during the existence of the program and within fourteen days after termination of the program, shall report in writing to the director of public safety regarding the effectiveness of the prototype device and the program.

(C) If a person has been granted limited driving privileges with a condition of the privileges being that the motor vehicle that is operated under the privileges must be equipped with an immobilizing or disabling device, the person may operate a motor vehicle that is owned by the person's employer only if the person is required to operate that motor vehicle in the course and scope of the offender's employment. Such a person may operate that vehicle without the installation of an immobilizing or disabling device, provided that the employer has been notified that the person has limited driving privileges and of the nature of the restriction and further provided that the person has proof of the employer's notification in the person's possession while operating the employer's vehicle for normal business duties. A motor vehicle owned by a business that is partly or entirely owned or controlled by a person with limited driving privileges is not a motor vehicle owned by an employer, for purposes of this division.

**HISTORY: 149 v S 123, § 1, eff. 1-1-04; 150 v H 230, § 1, eff. 9-16-04; 152 v S 17, § 1, eff. 9-30-08; 2011 HB 114, § 101.01, eff. June 29, 2011.**

Acts 2011, HB 114, § 806.10 provides: "The items of law contained in this act, and their applications, are severable. If any item of law contained in this act, or if any application of any item of law contained in this act, is held invalid, the invalidity does not affect other items of law contained in this act and their applications that can be given effect without the invalid item or application."

The effective date is set by section 4 of S.B. 123.

See provisions, § 5 of S.B. 123 (149 v —), following RC § 4501.01.

## § 4510.44 Immobilizing or disabling device violation.

(A)(1) No offender with limited driving privileges, during any period that the offender is required to operate only a motor vehicle equipped with an immobilizing or disabling device, shall request or permit any other person to breathe into the device if it is an ignition interlock device or another type of device that monitors the concentration of alcohol in a person's breath or to otherwise start the motor vehicle equipped with the device, for the purpose of providing the offender with an operable motor vehicle.

(2)(a) Except as provided in division (A)(2)(b) of this section, no person shall breathe into an immobilizing or disabling device that is an ignition interlock device or another type of device that monitors the concentration of alcohol in a person's breath or otherwise start a motor vehicle equipped with an immobilizing or disabling device, for the purpose of providing an operable motor vehicle to an offender with limited driving privileges who is permitted to operate only a motor vehicle equipped with an immobilizing or disabling device.

(b) Division (A)(2)(a) of this section does not apply to a person in the following circumstances:

(i) The person is an offender with limited driving privileges.

(ii) The person breathes into an immobilizing or disabling device that is an ignition interlock device or another type of device that monitors the concentration of alcohol in a person's breath or otherwise starts a motor vehicle equipped with an immobilizing or disabling device.

(iii) The person breathes into the device or starts the vehicle for the purpose of providing the person with an operable motor vehicle.

(3) No unauthorized person shall tamper with or circumvent the operation of an immobilizing or disabling device.

(B) Whoever violates this section is guilty of an immobilizing or disabling device violation, a misdemeanor of the first degree.

**HISTORY: 149 v S 123, § 1, eff. 1-1-04.**

The effective date is set by section 4 of S.B. 123.

See provisions, § 5 of S.B. 123 (149 v —), following RC § 4501.01.

## § 4510.45 Licensing of manufacturers of ignition interlock devices.

(A)(1) A manufacturer of ignition interlock devices that desires for its devices to be certified under section 4510.43 of the Revised Code and then to be included on the list of certified devices that the department of public safety compiles and makes available to courts pursuant to that section first shall obtain a license from the department under this section. The department, in accordance with Chapter 119. of the Revised Code, shall adopt any rules that are necessary to implement this licensing requirement.

(2) A manufacturer shall apply to the department for the license and shall include all information the department may require by rule. Each application, including an application for license renewal, shall be accompanied by an application fee of one hundred dollars, which the department shall deposit into the state treasury to the credit of the indigent drivers alcohol treatment fund created by section 4511.191 [4511.19.1] of the Revised Code.

(3) Upon receipt of a completed application, if the department finds that a manufacturer has complied with all application requirements, the department shall issue a license to the manufacturer. A manufacturer that has been issued a license under this section is eligible immediately to have the models of ignition interlock devices it produces certified under section 4510.43 of the Revised Code and then included on the list of certified devices that the department compiles and makes available to courts pursuant to that section.

(4)(a) A license issued under this section shall expire annually on a date selected by the department. The department shall reject the license application of a manufacturer if any of the following apply:

(i) The application is not accompanied by the application fee.

(ii) The department finds that the manufacturer has not complied with all application requirements.

(iii) The license application is a renewal application and the manufacturer failed to file the annual report or failed to pay the fee as required by division (B) of this section.

(b) A manufacturer whose license application is rejected by the department may appeal the decision to the director of public safety. The director or the director's designee shall hold a hearing on the matter not more than thirty days from the date of the manufacturer's appeal. If the director or the director's designee upholds the denial of the manufacturer's application for a license, the manufacturer may appeal the decision to the Franklin county court of common pleas. If the director or the director's designee reverses the denial of the manufacturer's application for a license, the director or the director's designee shall issue a written order directing that the department issue a license to the manufacturer.

(B) Every manufacturer of ignition interlock devices that is issued a license under this section shall file an annual report with the department on a form the department prescribes on or before a date the department prescribes. The annual report shall state the amount of net profit the manufacturer earned during a twelve-month period specified by the department that is attributable to the sales of that manufacturer's certified ignition interlock devices to purchasers in this state. Each manufacturer shall pay a fee equal to five per cent of the amount of the net profit described in this division.

The department may permit annual reports to be filed via electronic means.

(C) The department shall deposit all fees it receives from manufacturers under this section into the state treasury to the credit of the indigent drivers alcohol treatment fund created by section 4511.191 [4511.19.1] of the Revised Code. All money so deposited into that fund that is paid by the department of alcohol and drug addiction services to county indigent drivers alcohol treatment funds, county juvenile indigent drivers alcohol treatment funds, and municipal indigent drivers alcohol treatment funds shall be used only as described in division (H)(3) of section 4511.191 [4511.19.1] of the Revised Code.

(D)(1) The director may make an assessment, based on any information in the director's possession, against any manufacturer that fails to file an annual report or pay the fee required by division (B) of this section. The director, in accordance with Chapter 119. of the Revised Code, shall adopt rules governing assessments and assessment procedures and related provisions. In adopting these rules, the director shall incorporate the provisions of section 5751.09 of the Revised Code to the greatest extent possible, except that the director is not required to incorporate any provisions of that section that by their nature are not applicable, appropriate, or necessary to assessments made by the director under this section.

(2) A manufacturer may appeal the final determination of the director regarding an assessment made by the director under this section. The director, in accordance with Chapter 119. of the Revised Code, shall adopt rules governing such appeals. In adopting these rules, the director shall incorporate the provisions of section 5717.02 of the Revised Code to the greatest extent possible, except that the director is not required to incorporate any provisions of that section that by their nature are not applicable, appropriate, or necessary to appeals of assessments made by the director under this section.

(E) The director, in accordance with Chapter 119. of the Revised Code, shall adopt a penalty schedule setting forth the monetary penalties to be imposed upon a manufacturer that is issued a license under this section and fails to file an annual report or pay the fee required by division (B) of this section in a timely manner. The penalty amounts shall not exceed the maximum penalty amounts established in section 5751.06 of the Revised Code for similar or equivalent facts or circumstances.

(F)(1) No manufacturer of ignition interlock devices that is required by division (B) of this section to file an annual report with the department or to pay a fee shall fail to do so as required by that division.

(2) No manufacturer of ignition interlock devices that is required by division (B) of this section to file an annual report with the department shall file a report that contains incorrect or erroneous information.

(G) Whoever violates division (F)(2) of this section is guilty of a misdemeanor of the first degree. The department shall remove from the list of certified devices described in division (A)(1) of this section the ignition interlock devices manufactured by a manufacturer that violates division (F)(1) or (2) of this section.

**HISTORY: 152 v S 17, § 1, eff. 9-30-08.**

## § 4510.46 Monitoring entity to notify court when ignition interlock device prevents offender from starting vehicle; notice to offender.

(A) A governmental agency, bureau, department, or office, or a private corporation, or any other entity that monitors certified ignition interlock devices for or on behalf of a court shall inform the court whenever such a device that has been installed in a motor vehicle indicates that it has prevented an offender whose driver's or commercial driver's license or permit or nonresident operating privilege has been suspended by a court under division (G)(1)(a), (b), (c), (d), or (e) of section 4511.19 of the Revised Code and who has been granted limited driving privileges under section 4510.13 of the Revised Code from starting the motor vehicle because the device was tampered with or circumvented or because the analysis of the deep-lung breath sample or other method employed by the ignition interlock device to measure the concentration by weight of alcohol in the offender's breath indicated the presence of alcohol in the offender's breath in a concentration sufficient to prevent the ignition interlock device from permitting the motor vehicle to be started.

(B) Upon receipt of such information pertaining to an offender whose driver's or commercial driver's license or permit or nonresident operating privilege has been suspended by a court under division (G)(1)(b), (c), (d), or (e) of section 4511.19 of the Revised Code and who has been granted limited driving privileges under section 4510.13 of the Revised Code, the court shall send a notice to the offender stating that it has received evidence of an instance described in division (A) of this section. If a court pursuant to division (A)(8) of section 4510.13 of the Revised Code requires the offender to wear an alcohol monitor, the notice shall state that because of this instance the offender is required to wear a monitor that provides for continuous alcohol monitoring in accordance with division (A)(8) of section 4510.13 of the Revised Code. The notice shall further state that because of this instance the court may increase the period of suspension of the offender's driver's or commercial driver's license or permit or nonresident operating privilege from that originally imposed by the court by a factor of two and may increase the period of time during which the offender will be prohibited from exercising any limited driving privileges granted to the offender unless the vehicles the offender operates are equipped with a certified ignition interlock device by a factor of two.

The notice shall state whether the court will impose these increases and, if so, that these increases will take effect fourteen days from the date of the notice unless the offender files a timely motion with the court, appealing the increases in the time described in this division and requesting a hearing on the matter. Any such motion that is filed within that fourteen-day period shall be considered to be filed in a timely manner, and any such motion that is filed after that fourteen-day period shall be considered not to be filed in a timely manner. If the offender files a timely motion, the court may hold a hearing on the matter. The scope of the hearing is limited to determining whether the offender in fact was prevented from starting a motor vehicle that is equipped with a certified ignition interlock device because the device was tampered with or circumvented or because the analysis of the deep-lung breath sample or other method employed by the ignition interlock device to measure the concentration by weight of alcohol in the offender's breath indicated the presence of alcohol in the offender's breath in a concentration sufficient to prevent the ignition interlock device from permitting the motor vehicle to be started.

If the court finds by a preponderance of the evidence that this instance as indicated by the ignition interlock device in fact did occur, it may deny the offender's appeal and issue the order increasing the relevant periods of time described in this division. If the court finds by a preponderance of the evidence that this instance as indicated by the ignition interlock device in fact did not occur, it shall grant the offender's appeal and no such order shall be issued.

(C) In no case shall any period of suspension of an offender's driver's or commercial driver's license or permit or nonresident operating privilege that is increased by a factor of two or any period of time during which the offender is prohibited from exercising any limited driving privileges granted to the offender unless the vehicles the offender operates are equipped with a certified ignition interlock device that is increased by a factor of two exceed the maximum period of time for which the court originally was authorized to suspend the offender's driver's or commercial driver's license or permit or nonresident operating privilege under division (G)(1)(a), (b), (c), (d), or (e) of section 4511.19 of the Revised Code.

(D) Nothing in this section shall be construed as prohibiting the court from revoking an individual's driving privileges.

**HISTORY: 152 v S 17, § 1, eff. 9-30-08.**

## § 4510.52 Destruction of license or permit; reissuance.

(A) Upon the receipt of any driver's license or commercial driver's license or permit that has been suspended or canceled under any provision of law, and notwithstanding any other provision of law that requires the registrar of motor vehicles to retain the license or permit, the registrar may destroy the license or permit.

(B) If, as authorized by division (A) of this section, the registrar destroys a license or permit that has been suspended or canceled, the registrar shall reissue or authorize the reissuance of a new license or permit to the person to whom the destroyed license or permit originally was issued upon payment of a fee in the same amount as the fee specified in division (C) of section 4507.23 of the Revised Code for a duplicate license or permit and upon payment of a service fee in the same amount as specified in division (D) of section 4503.10 of the Revised Code if issued by a deputy registrar or in division (G) of that section if issued by the registrar.

This division applies only if the driver's license or commercial driver's license or permit that was destroyed would have been valid at the time the person applies for the duplicate license or permit. A duplicate driver's license or commercial driver's license or permit issued under this section shall bear the same expiration date that appeared on the license or permit it replaces.

**HISTORY: 145 v H 687. Eff 10-12-94; 149 v S 123, § 1, eff. 1-1-04.**

See provisions, § 5 of S.B. 123 (149 v —), following RC § 4501.01.

**Publisher's Note:**

This section was formerly § 4507.54. It was amended and renumbered by S.B. 123, Acts 2002, effective January 1, 2004.

## § 4510.53 Destruction of license or permit after suspension under OVI implied consent law; reissuance.

(A) Upon receipt of any driver's or commercial driver's license or permit that has been suspended under section 4511.19 or 4511.191 of the Revised Code, the registrar of motor vehicles, notwithstanding any other provision of law that purports to require the registrar to retain the license or permit, may destroy the license or permit.

(B)(1) Subject to division (B)(2) of this section, if a driver's or commercial driver's license or permit that has been suspended under section 4511.19 or 4511.191 of the Revised Code is delivered to the registrar and if the registrar destroys the license or permit under authority of division (A) of this section, the registrar shall reissue or authorize the reissuance of a driver's or commercial driver's license to the person, free of payment of any type of fee or charge, if either of the following applies:

(a) The person appeals the suspension of the license or permit at or within thirty days of the person's initial appearance, pursuant to section 4511.197 of the Revised Code, the judge of the court of record or the mayor of the mayor's court who conducts the initial appearance terminates the suspension, and the judge or mayor does not suspend the license or permit under section 4511.196 of the Revised Code;

(b) The person appeals the suspension of the license or permit at or within thirty days of the person's initial appearance, pursuant to section 4511.197 of the Revised Code, the judge of the court of record or the mayor of the mayor's court who conducts the initial appearance does not terminate the suspension, the person appeals the judge's or mayor's decision not to terminate the suspension that is made at the initial appearance, and upon appeal of the decision, the suspension is terminated.

(2) Division (B)(1) of this section applies only if the driver's or commercial driver's license that was destroyed would have been valid at the time in question, if it had not been destroyed as permitted by division (A) of this section.

(C) A driver's or commercial driver's license or permit issued to a person pursuant to division (B)(1) of this section shall bear the same expiration date as the expiration date that appeared on the license it replaces.

**HISTORY: RC § 4507.16.10, 145 v S 62 (Eff 9-1-93); RC § 4507.55, 145 v H 687. Eff 10-12-94; 149 v S 123, § 1, eff. 1-1-04.**

The effective date is set by section 4 of S.B. 123.

See provisions, § 5 of S.B. 123 (149 v —), following RC § 4501.01.

**Publisher's Note:**

This section was formerly § 4507.55. It was amended and renumbered by S.B. 123, Acts 2002, effective January 1, 2004.

## § 4510.54 Motion for modification or termination of suspension for life or for period exceeding fifteen years.

(A) Except as provided in division (F) of this section, a person whose driver's or commercial driver's license has been suspended for life under a class one suspension or as otherwise provided by law or has been suspended for a period in excess of fifteen years under a class two suspension may file a motion with the sentencing court for modification or termination of the suspension. The person filing the motion shall demonstrate all of the following:

(1) At least fifteen years have elapsed since the suspension began.

(2) For the past fifteen years, the person has not been found guilty of any felony, any offense involving a moving violation under federal law, the law of this state, or the law of any of its political subdivisions, or any violation of a suspension under this chapter or a substantially equivalent municipal ordinance.

(3) The person has proof of financial responsibility, a policy of liability insurance in effect that meets the minimum standard set forth in section 4509.51 of the Revised Code, or proof, to the satisfaction of the registrar of motor vehicles, that the person is able to respond in damages in an amount at least equal to the minimum amounts specified in that section.

(4) If the suspension was imposed because the person was under the influence of alcohol, a drug of abuse, or combination of them at the time of the offense or because at the time of the offense the person's whole blood, blood serum or plasma, breath, or urine contained at least the concentration of alcohol specified in division (A)(1)(b), (c), (d), or (e) of section 4511.19 of the Revised Code or at least the concentration of a listed controlled substance or a listed metabolite of a controlled substance specified in division (A)(1)(j) of section 4511.19 of the Revised Code, the person also shall demonstrate all of the following:

(a) The person successfully completed an alcohol, drug, or alcohol and drug treatment program.

(b) The person has not abused alcohol or other drugs for a period satisfactory to the court.

(c) For the past fifteen years, the person has not been found guilty of any alcohol-related or drug-related offense.

(B) Upon receipt of a motion for modification or termination of the suspension under this section, the court may schedule a hearing on the motion. The court may deny the motion without a hearing but shall not grant the motion without a hearing. If the court denies a motion without a hearing, the court may consider a subsequent motion filed under this section by that person. If a court denies the motion after a hearing, the court shall not consider a subsequent motion for that person. The court shall hear only one motion filed by a person under this section. If scheduled, the hearing shall be conducted in open court within ninety days after the date on which the motion is filed.

(C) The court shall notify the person whose license was suspended and the prosecuting attorney of the date, time, and location of the hearing. Upon receipt of the notice from the court, the prosecuting attorney shall notify the victim or the victim's representative of the date, time, and location of the hearing.

(D) At any hearing under this section, the person who seeks modification or termination of the suspension has the burden to demonstrate, under oath, that the person meets the requirements of division (A) of this section. At the hearing, the court shall afford the offender or the offender's counsel an opportunity to present oral or written information relevant to the motion. The court shall afford a similar opportunity to provide relevant information to the prosecuting attorney and the victim or victim's representative.

Before ruling on the motion, the court shall take into account the person's driving record, the nature of the offense that led to the suspension, and the impact of the offense on any victim. In addition, if the offender is eligible for modification or termination of the suspension under division (A)(2) of this section, the court shall consider whether the person committed any other offense while under suspension and determine whether the offense is relevant to a determination under this section. The court may modify or terminate the suspension subject to any considerations it considers proper if it finds that allowing the person to drive is not likely to present a danger to the public. After the court makes a ruling on a motion filed under this section, the prosecuting attorney shall notify the victim or the victim's representative of the court's ruling.

(E) If a court modifies a person's license suspension under this section and the person subsequently is found guilty of any moving violation or of any substantially equivalent municipal ordinance that carries as a possible penalty the suspension of a person's driver's or commercial driver's license, the court may reimpose the class one or other lifetime suspension, or the class two suspension, whichever is applicable.

(F) This section does not apply to any person whose driver's or commercial driver's license or permit or nonresident operating privilege has been suspended for life under a class one suspension imposed under division (B)(3) of section 2903.06 or section 2903.08 of the Revised Code or a class two suspension imposed under division (C) of section 2903.06 or section 2903.11, 2923.02, or 2929.02 of the Revised Code.

**HISTORY: 149 v S 123, § 1, eff. 1-1-04; 150 v H 52, § 1, eff. 6-1-04; 150 v H 163, § 1, eff. 9-23-04; 151 v S 8, § 1, eff. 8-17-06; 151 v H 461, § 1, eff. 4-4-07.**

The provisions of § 3 of 151 v S 8 read as follows:

SECTION 3. Section 4510.54 of the Revised Code is presented in this act as a composite of the section as amended by both Sub. H.B. 52 and Am. Sub. H.B. 163 of the 125th General Assembly. The General Assembly, applying the principle stated in division (B) of section 1.52 of the Revised Code that amendments are to be harmonized if reasonably capable of simultaneous operation, finds that the composite is the resulting version of the section in effect prior to the effective date of the section as presented in this act.

The effective date is set by section 4 of S.B. 123.

See provisions, § 5 of S.B. 123 (149 v —), following RC § 4510.021.

## § 4510.61 Driver license compact enacted.

The driver license compact is hereby enacted into law and entered into with all other jurisdictions legally joining therein in the form substantially as follows:

### ARTICLE I

### Findings and Declaration of Policy

(a) The party states find that:

(1) The safety of their streets and highways is materially affected by the degree of compliance with state and local ordinances relating to the operation of motor vehicles.

(2) Violation of such a law or ordinance is evidence that the violator engages in conduct which is likely to endanger the safety of persons and property.

(3) The continuance in force of a license to drive is predicated upon compliance with laws and ordinances relating to the operation of motor vehicles, in whichever jurisdiction the vehicle is operated.

(b) It is the policy of each of the party states to:

(1) Promote compliance with the laws, ordinances, and administrative rules and regulations relating to the operation of motor vehicles by their operators in each of the jurisdictions where such operators drive motor vehicles.

(2) Make the reciprocal recognition of licenses to drive and eligibility therefor more just and equitable by considering the over-all compliance with motor vehicle laws, ordinances, and administrative rules and regulations as a condition precedent to the continuance or issuance of any license by reason of which the licensee is authorized or permitted to operate a motor vehicle in any of the party states.

### ARTICLE II

### Definitions

As used in this compact:

(a) "State" means a state, territory, or possession of the United States, the District of Columbia, or the Commonwealth of Puerto Rico.

(b) "Home state" means the state that has issued and has the power to suspend or revoke the use of the license or permit to operate a motor vehicle.

(c) "Conviction" means a conviction of any offense related to the use or operation of a motor vehicle that is prohibited by state law, municipal ordinance, or administrative rule or regulation; or a forfeiture of bail, bond, or other security deposited to secure appearance by a person charged with having committed any such offense, and which conviction or forfeiture is required to be reported to the licensing authority.

### ARTICLE III

### Reports of Conviction

The licensing authority of a party state shall report each conviction of a person from another party state occurring within its jurisdiction to the licensing authority of the home state of the licensee. Such report shall clearly identify the person convicted; describe the violation specifying the section of the statute, code, or ordinance violated; identify the court in which action was taken; indicate whether a plea of guilty or not guilty was entered, or the security; and shall include any special findings made in connection therewith.

### ARTICLE IV

### Effect of Conviction

(a) The licensing authority in the home state, for the purpose of suspension, revocation, or limitation of the license to operate a motor vehicle, shall give the same effect to the conduct reported, pursuant to Article III of this compact, as it would if such conduct had occurred in the home state, in the case of convictions for:

(1) Manslaughter or negligent homicide resulting from the operation of a motor vehicle;

(2) Driving a motor vehicle while under the influence of intoxicating liquor or a narcotic drug, or under the influence of any other drug to a degree that renders the driver incapable of safely driving a motor vehicle;

(3) Any felony in the commission of which a motor vehicle is used;

(4) Failure to stop and render aid in the event of a motor vehicle accident resulting in the death or personal injury of another.

(b) As to other convictions, reported pursuant to Article III, the licensing authority in the home state shall give such effect to conduct as is provided by the laws of the home state.

(c) If the laws of a party state do not provide for offenses or violations denominated or described in precisely the words employed in subdivision (a) of this Article, such party state shall construe the denominations and descriptions appearing in subdivision (a) hereof as being applicable to and identifying those offenses or violations of a substantially similar nature, and the laws of such party state shall contain such provisions as may be necessary to ensure that full force and effect is given to this Article.

### ARTICLE V

### Applications for New Licenses

Upon application for a license to drive, the licensing authority in a party state shall ascertain whether the applicant has ever held, or is the holder of, a license to drive issued by any other party state. The licensing authority in the state where application is made shall not issue a license to drive to the applicant if:

(1) The applicant has held such a license, but the same has been suspended by reason, in whole or in part, of a violation and if such suspension period has not terminated.

(2) The applicant has held such a license, but the same has been revoked by reason, in whole or in part, of a violation; and if such revocation has not terminated, except that after the expiration of one year from the date the license was revoked, such person may make application for a new license if permitted by law. The licensing authority may refuse to issue a license to any such applicant if, after investigation, the licensing authority determines that it will not be safe to grant to such person the privilege of driving a motor vehicle on the public highways.

(3) The applicant is the holder of a license to drive issued by another party state and currently in force unless the applicant surrenders such license.

### ARTICLE VI

### Applicability of Other Laws

Except as expressly required by provisions of this compact, nothing contained herein shall be construed to affect the right of any party state to apply any of its other laws relating to licenses to drive to any person or circumstance, nor to invalidate or prevent any driver license agreement or other cooperative arrangement between a party state and a nonparty state.

### ARTICLE VII

### Compact Administrator and Interchange of Information

(a) The head of the licensing authority of each party state shall be the administrator of this compact for his state. The administrators, acting jointly, shall have the power to formulate all necessary and proper procedures for the exchange of information under this compact.

(b) The administrator of each party state shall furnish to the administrator of each other party state any information or documents reasonably necessary to facilitate the administration of this compact.

### ARTICLE VIII

### Entry Into Force and Withdrawal

(a) This compact shall enter into force and become effective as to any state when it has enacted the same into law.

(b) Any party state may withdraw from this compact by enacting a statute repealing the same, but no such withdrawal shall take effect until six months after the executive head of the withdrawing state has given notice of the withdrawal to the executive heads of all other party states. No withdrawal shall affect the validity or applicability by the licensing authorities of states remaining party to the compact of any report of conviction occurring prior to the withdrawal.

### ARTICLE IX

### Construction and Severability

This compact shall be liberally construed so as to effectuate the purposes thereof. The provisions of this compact shall be severable; and if any phrase, clause, sentence, or provision of this compact is declared to be contrary to the constitution of any party state or of the United States or the applicability thereof to any government, agency, person, or circumstance is held invalid, the validity of the remainder of this compact and the applicability thereof to any government, agency, person, or circumstance shall not be affected thereby. If this compact shall be held contrary to the constitution of any state party thereto, the compact shall remain in full force and effect as to the remaining states and in full force and effect as to the state affected as to all severable matters.

**HISTORY: 142 v H 419. Eff 7-1-87; 149 v S 123, § 1, eff. 1-1-04.**

The effective date is set by section 4 of S.B. 123.

See provisions, § 5 of S.B. 123 (149 v —), following RC § 4501.01.

**Publisher's Note:**

This section was formerly § 4507.60. It was renumbered by S.B. 123, Acts 2002, effective January 1, 2004.

According to Ohio Bureau of Motor Vehicles, as of April 1999, the following states are members of the Driver's License Compact: Alabama, Alaska, Arizona, Arkansas, California, Colorado, Connecticut, Delaware, D.C., Florida, Hawaii, Idaho, Illinois, Indiana, Iowa, Kansas, Kentucky, Louisiana, Maine, Maryland, Minnesota, Mississippi, Missouri, Montana, Nebraska, Nevada, New Hampshire, New Jersey, New Mexico, New York, North Carolina, North Dakota, Ohio, Oklahoma, Oregon, Pennsylvania, Rhode Island, South Carolina, South Dakota, Tennessee, Texas, Utah, Vermont, Virginia, Washington, West Virginia, and Wyoming. For more up-to-date information, please call the Bureau of Motor Vehicles at (614) 752-7600.

## § 4510.62 Executive head and licensing authority specified.

(A) "Executive head" as used in article VIII (B) of the compact set forth in section 4510.61 of the Revised Code with reference to this state means the governor.

(B) "Licensing authority" as used in Articles III, IV, V, and VII of the compact set forth in section 4510.61 of the Revised Code with reference to this state means the bureau of motor vehicles within the department of public safety.

**HISTORY: 142 v H 419 (Eff 7-1-87); 144 v S 98. Eff 11-12-92; 149 v S 123, § 1, eff. 1-1-04.**

The effective date is set by section 4 of S.B. 123.

See provisions, § 5 of S.B. 123 (149 v —), following RC § 4501.01.

**Publisher's Note:**

This section was formerly § 4507.61. It was renumbered by S.B. 123, Acts 2002, effective January 1, 2004.

## § 4510.63 Information or documents furnished to other states.

Pursuant to Article VII of the compact set forth in section 4510.61 of the Revised Code the bureau of motor vehicles shall furnish to the appropriate authorities of any other party state any information or documents reasonably necessary to facilitate the administration of Articles III, IV, and V of the compact set forth in section 4510.61 of the Revised Code.

**HISTORY: 142 v H 419. Eff 7-1-87; 149 v S 123, § 1, eff. 1-1-04.**

The effective date is set by section 4 of S.B. 123.

See provisions, § 5 of S.B. 123 (149 v —), following RC § 4501.01.

**Publisher's Note:**

This section was formerly § 4507.62. It was renumbered by S.B. 123, Acts 2002, effective January 1, 2004.

## § 4510.64 Reimbursement for compact administrator.

The compact administrator provided for in Article VII of the compact set forth in section 4510.61 of the Revised Code is not entitled to any additional compensation for serving as administrator of the compact, but shall be reimbursed for travel and other necessary expenses incurred in the performance of official duties thereunder as provided by law for other state officers.

**HISTORY: 142 v H 419. Eff 7-1-87; 149 v S 123, § 1, eff. 1-1-04.**

The effective date is set by section 4 of S.B. 123.

See provisions, § 5 of S.B. 123 (149 v —), following RC § 4501.01.

**Publisher's Note:**

This section was formerly § 4507.63. It was renumbered by S.B. 123, Acts 2002, effective January 1, 2004.

## § 4510.71 Nonresident violator compact.

The nonresident violator compact, hereinafter called "the compact," is hereby enacted into law and entered into with all other jurisdictions legally joining therein in the form substantially as follows:

### "NONRESIDENT VIOLATOR COMPACT

### Article I

### Findings, Declaration of Policy and Purpose

(A) The party jurisdictions find that:

(1) In most instances, a motorist who is cited for a traffic violation in a jurisdiction other than his home jurisdiction:

(a) Must post collateral or bond to secure appearance for trial at a later date; or

(b) If unable to post collateral or bond, is taken into custody until the collateral or bond is posted; or

(c) Is taken directly to court for his trial to be held.

(2) In some instances, the motorist's driver's license may be deposited as collateral to be returned after he has complied with the terms of the citation.

(3) The purpose of the practices described in divisions (A) (1) and (2) of this article is to ensure compliance with the terms of a traffic citation by the motorist who, if permitted to continue on his way after receiving the traffic citation, could return to his home jurisdiction and disregard his duty under the terms of the traffic citation.

(4) A motorist receiving a traffic citation in his home jurisdiction is permitted, except for certain violations, to accept the citation from the officer at the scene of the violation and to immediately continue on his way after promising or being instructed to comply with the terms of the citation.

(5) The practice described in division (A) (1) of this article causes unnecessary inconvenience and, at times, a hardship for the motorist who is unable at the time to post collateral, furnish a bond, stand trial, or pay the fine, and thus is compelled to remain in custody until some arrangement can be made.

(6) The deposit of a driver's license as a bail bond, as described in division (A) (2) of this article, is viewed with disfavor.

(7) The practices described herein consume an undue amount of law enforcement time.

(B) It is the policy of the party jurisdictions to:

(1) Seek compliance with the laws, ordinances, and administrative rules and regulations relating to the operation of motor vehicles in each of the jurisdictions;

(2) Allow motorists to accept a traffic citation for certain violations and proceed on their way without delay whether or not the motorist is a resident of the jurisdiction in which the citation was issued;

(3) Extend cooperation to its fullest extent among the jurisdictions for obtaining compliance with the terms of a traffic citation issued in one jurisdiction to a resident of another jurisdiction;

(4) Maximize effective utilization of law enforcement personnel and assist court systems in the efficient disposition of traffic violations.

(C) The purpose of this compact is to:

(1) Provide a means through which the party jurisdictions may participate in a reciprocal program to effectuate the policies enumerated in division (B) of this article in a uniform and orderly manner;

(2) Provide for the fair and impartial treatment of traffic violators operating within party jurisdictions in recognition of the motorist's right of due process and the sovereign status of a party jurisdiction.

### Article II

### Definitions

(A) In the nonresident violator compact, the following words have the meaning indicated, unless the context requires otherwise.

(B)(1) "Citation" means any summons, ticket, or other official document issued by a police officer for a traffic violation containing an order which requires the motorist to respond.

(2) "Collateral" means any cash or other security deposited to secure an appearance for trial, following the issuance by a police officer of a citation for a traffic violation.

(3) "Court" means a court of law or traffic tribunal.

(4) "Driver's license" means any license or privilege to operate a motor vehicle issued under the laws of the home jurisdiction.

(5) "Home jurisdiction" means the jurisdiction that issued the driver's license of the traffic violator.

(6) "Issuing jurisdiction" means the jurisdiction in which the traffic citation was issued to the motorist.

(7) "Jurisdiction" means a state, territory, or possession of the United States, the District of Columbia, or the Commonwealth of Puerto Rico.

(8) "Motorist" means a driver of a motor vehicle operating in a party jurisdiction other than the home jurisdiction.

(9) "Personal recognizance" means an agreement by a motorist made at the time of issuance of the traffic citation that he will comply with the terms of that traffic citation.

(10) "Police officer" means any individual authorized by the party jurisdiction to issue a citation for a traffic violation.

(11) "Terms of the citation" means those options expressly stated upon the citation.

## Article III

## Procedure for Issuing Jurisdiction

(A) When issuing a citation for a traffic violation, a police officer shall issue the citation to a motorist who possesses a driver's license issued by a party jurisdiction and shall not, subject to the exceptions noted in division (B) of this article, require the motorist to post collateral to secure appearance, if the officer receives the motorist's signed, personal recognizance that he or she will comply with the terms of the citation.

(B) Personal recognizance is acceptable only if not prohibited by law. If mandatory appearance is required, it must take place immediately following issuance of the citation.

(C) Upon failure of a motorist to comply with the terms of a traffic citation, the appropriate official shall report the failure to comply to the licensing authority of the jurisdiction in which the traffic citation was issued. The report shall be made in accordance with procedures specified by the issuing jurisdiction and shall contain information as specified in the compact manual as minimum requirements for effective processing by the home jurisdiction.

(D) Upon receipt of the report, the licensing authority of the issuing jurisdiction shall transmit to the licensing authority in the home jurisdiction of the motorist the information in a form and content as contained in the compact manual.

(E) The licensing authority of the issuing jurisdiction may not suspend the privilege of a motorist for whom a report has been transmitted.

(F) The licensing authority of the issuing jurisdiction shall not transmit a report on any violation if the date of transmission is more than six months after the date on which the traffic citation was issued.

(G) The licensing authority of the issuing jurisdiction shall not transmit a report on any violation where the date of issuance of the citation predates the most recent of the effective dates of entry for the two jurisdictions affected.

## Article IV

## Procedures for Home Jurisdiction

(A) Upon receipt of a report of a failure to comply from the licensing authority of the issuing jurisdiction, the licensing authority of the home jurisdiction shall notify the motorist and initiate a suspension action, in accordance with the home jurisdiction's procedures, to suspend the motorist's driver's license until satisfactory evidence of compliance with the terms of the traffic citation has been furnished to the home jurisdiction licensing authority. Due process safeguards will be accorded.

(B) The licensing authority of the home jurisdiction shall maintain a record of actions taken and make reports to issuing jurisdictions as provided in the compact manual.

## Article V

## Applicability of Other Laws

Except as expressly required by provisions of this compact, nothing contained herein shall be construed to affect the right of any party jurisdiction to apply any of its other laws relating to licenses to drive to any person or circumstance, or to invalidate or prevent any driver license agreement or other cooperative arrangement between a party jurisdiction and nonparty jurisdiction.

## Article VI

## Compact Administrator Procedures

(A) For the purpose of administering the provisions of this compact and to serve as a governing body for the resolution of all matters relating to the operation of this compact, a board of compact administrators is established. The board shall be composed of one representative from each party jurisdiction to be known as the compact administrator. The compact administrator shall be appointed by the jurisdiction executive and will serve and be subject to removal in accordance with the laws of the jurisdiction he represents. A compact administrator may provide for the discharge of his duties and the performance of his functions as a board member by an alternate. An alternate may not be entitled to serve unless written notification of his identity has been given to the board.

(B) Each member of the board of compact administrators shall be entitled to one vote. No action of the board shall be binding unless taken at a meeting at which a majority of the total number of votes on the board are cast in favor. Action by the board shall be only at a meeting at which a majority of the party jurisdictions are represented.

(C) The board shall elect annually, from its membership, a chairman and a vice chairman.

(D) The board shall adopt bylaws, not inconsistent with the provisions of this compact or the laws of a party jurisdiction, for the conduct of its business and shall have the power to amend and rescind its bylaws.

(E) The board may accept for any of its purposes and functions under this compact any and all donations, and grants of money, equipment, supplies, materials, and services, conditional or otherwise, from any jurisdiction, the United States, or any other governmental agency, and may receive, utilize, and dispose of the same.

(F) The board may contract with, or accept services or personnel from, any governmental or intergovernmental agency, person, firm, or corporation, or any private nonprofit organization or institution.

(G) The board shall formulate all necessary procedures and develop uniform forms and documents for administering the provisions of this compact. All procedures and forms adopted pursuant to board action shall be contained in the compact manual.

## Article VII

## Entry into Compact and Withdrawal

(A) This compact shall become effective when it has been adopted by at least two jurisdictions.

(B)(1) Entry into the compact shall be made by a resolution of ratification executed by the authorized officials of the applying jurisdiction and submitted to the chairman of the board.

(2) The resolution shall be in a form and content as provided in the compact manual and shall include statements that in substance are as follows:

(a) A citation of the authority by which the jurisdiction is empowered to become a party to this compact;

(b) Agreement to comply with the terms and provisions of the compact;

(c) That compact entry is with all jurisdictions then party to the compact and with any jurisdiction that legally becomes a party to the compact.

(3) The effective date of entry shall be specified by the applying jurisdiction, but it shall not be less than sixty days after notice has been given by the chairman of the board of compact administrators or by the secretariat of the board to each party jurisdiction that the resolution from the applying jurisdiction has been received.

(C) A party jurisdiction may withdraw from this compact by official written notice to the other party jurisdictions, but a withdrawal shall not take effect until ninety days after notice of withdrawal is given. The notice shall be directed to the compact administrator of each member jurisdiction. No withdrawal shall affect the validity of this compact as to the remaining party jurisdictions.

### Article VIII

### Exceptions

The provisions of this compact shall not apply to parking or standing violations, highway weight limit violations, and violations of law governing the transportation of hazardous materials.

### Article IX

### Amendments to the Compact

(A) This compact may be amended from time to time. Amendments shall be presented in resolution form to the chairman of the board of compact administrators and may be initiated by one or more party jurisdictions.

(B) Adoption of an amendment shall require endorsement of all party jurisdictions and shall become effective thirty days after the date of the last endorsement.

(C) Failure of a party jurisdiction to respond to the compact chairman within one hundred twenty days after receipt of the proposed amendment shall constitute endorsement.

### Article X

### Construction and Severability

This compact shall be liberally construed so as to effectuate the purposes stated herein. The provisions of this compact shall be severable and if any phrase, clause, sentence, or provision of this compact is declared to be contrary to the constitution of any party jurisdiction or of the United States or the applicability thereof to any government, agency, person, or circumstance, the compact shall not be affected thereby. If this compact shall be held contrary to the constitution of any jurisdiction party thereto, the compact shall remain in full force and effect as to the remaining jurisdictions and in full force and effect as to the jurisdiction affected as to all severable matters.

### Article XI

### Title

This compact shall be known as the Nonresident Violator Compact of 1977."

**HISTORY: 149 v S 123, § 1, eff. 1-1-04.**

The effective date is set by section 4 of S.B. 123.

See provisions, § 5 of S.B. 123 (149 v —), following RC § 4501.01.

**Publisher's Note:**

This section was formerly § 4511.95. It was renumbered by S.B. 123, Acts 2002, effective January 1, 2004.

## § 4510.72 License reinstatement fee; compact administrator.

(A) A fee of thirty dollars shall be charged by the registrar of motor vehicles or an eligible deputy registrar for the reinstatement of any driver's license suspended pursuant to division (A) of Article IV of the compact enacted in section 4510.71 of the Revised Code. In addition, each deputy registrar shall collect a service fee of ten dollars to compensate the deputy registrar for services performed under this section. The deputy registrar shall retain eight dollars of the service fee and shall transmit the reinstatement fee, plus two dollars of the service fee, to the registrar in the manner the registrar shall determine.

(B) Pursuant to division (A) of Article VI of the nonresident violator compact of 1977 enacted in section 4510.71 of the Revised Code, the director of public safety shall serve as the compact administrator for Ohio.

**HISTORY: 149 v S 123, § 1, eff. 1-1-04; 2011 HB 114, § 101.01, eff. June 29, 2011.**

Acts 2011, HB 114, § 806.10 provides: "The items of law contained in this act, and their applications, are severable. If any item of law contained in this act, or if any application of any item of law contained in this act, is held invalid, the invalidity does not affect other items of law contained in this act and their applications that can be given effect without the invalid item or application."

The effective date is set by section 4 of S.B. 123.

See provisions, § 5 of S.B. 123 (149 v —), following RC § 4501.01.

**Publisher's Note:**

This section was formerly § 4511.951. It was renumbered by S.B. 123, Acts 2002, effective January 1, 2004.

## § 4510.73 Jurisdiction to adjudicate all issues and appeals involving driver's license matter; procedure for licensee to invoke court's jurisdiction.

(A) It is the intent of this section to allow all issues concerning driver's licenses to be litigated in a single forum, not to eliminate any forum venue in existence on the effective date of this section.

(B) Notwithstanding any provision of the Revised Code to the contrary, any court whose jurisdiction has been invoked under this chapter or any other chapter of the Revised Code regarding a driver's license matter, other than a matter involving a commercial driver's license, is hereby conferred concurrent jurisdiction to adjudicate all issues and appeals regarding that driver's license matter, including issues of validity, suspension, and, with regard to any suspension imposed by the bureau of motor vehicles, driving privileges. Nothing in this section shall be construed as applying to any issue involving a commercial driver's license, except that a court may adjudicate an issue that does not relate to a commercial driver's license but involves a holder of a commercial driver's license so long as the court does not alter the status of that holder's commercial driver's license. In the event that another court has obtained jurisdiction over one or more driver's license suspensions imposed by the bureau involving the same driver's license holder, that jurisdiction may not be divested by an action filed under this section unless that court transfers its jurisdiction over that holder's driver's license issue by issuance of a court order.

(C)(1) The court's jurisdiction over a particular driver's license issue may be invoked by a motion, appeal, or petition filed by a holder of a driver's license. Any such motion, appeal, or petition shall state the issue with respect to which the court's jurisdiction is invoked.

(2) When a court's jurisdiction over a driver's license issue is properly invoked, that court shall adjudicate all issues and appeals brought before the court regarding that issue, unless the motion, appeal, or petition is withdrawn.

(D) Any court whose jurisdiction is invoked under this section shall have the discretionary authority to issue a stay of any suspension pending resolution of the matters before the court. This provision does not alter or eliminate any automatic stay provision provided for elsewhere in the Revised Code.

(E) Any court whose jurisdiction is invoked under this section, in its discretion, may order the bureau to renew the holder's driver's license pending resolution of the matters before the court, provided that the license is not more than six months expired prior to the date of application for renewal. The court, in its discretion, also may order the bureau to renew the holder's driver's license in its final judgment, provided that the license is not more than six months expired prior to the date of application for renewal.

(F) If jurisdiction is invoked under this section in a court of common pleas or county court, the prosecuting attorney of the county in which the case is pending shall represent the registrar in the proceedings; provided, that if the driver's license holder resides in a municipal corporation that lies within the jurisdiction of a county court, the city director of law, village solicitor, or similar chief legal officer of the municipal corporation shall represent the registrar in the proceedings. In a municipal court, the registrar shall be represented in the resulting proceedings as provided in section 1901.34 of the Revised Code. At the election of the registrar, the attorney general may enter the proceedings at any time and henceforth represent the registrar in the case.

(G) Either party may appeal the final judgment of the court. Any such appeal shall be taken as provided in section 1901.30 or 1907.30 of the Revised Code and shall conform with Chapter 2505. of the Revised Code.

**HISTORY: 153 v H 338, § 1, eff. 9-17-10.**

# CHAPTER 4511: TRAFFIC LAWS — OPERATION OF MOTOR VEHICLES

Section



Section

## § 4511.01 Definitions.

As used in this chapter and in Chapter 4513. of the Revised Code:

(A) "Vehicle" means every device, including a motorized bicycle, in, upon, or by which any person or property may be transported or drawn upon a highway, except that "vehicle" does not include any motorized wheelchair, any electric personal assistive mobility device, any device that is moved by power collected from overhead electric trolley wires or that is used exclusively upon stationary rails or tracks, or any device, other than a bicycle, that is moved by human power.

(B) "Motor vehicle" means every vehicle propelled or drawn by power other than muscular power or power collected from overhead electric trolley wires, except motorized bicycles, road rollers, traction engines, power shovels, power cranes, and other equipment used in construction work and not designed for or employed in general highway transportation, hole-digging machinery, well-drilling machinery, ditch-digging machinery, farm machinery, and trailers designed and used exclusively to transport a boat between a place of storage and a marina, or in and around a marina, when drawn or towed on a street or highway for a distance of no more than ten miles and at a speed of twenty-five miles per hour or less.

(C) "Motorcycle" means every motor vehicle, other than a tractor, having a seat or saddle for the use of the operator and designed to travel on not more than three wheels in contact with the ground, including, but not limited to, motor vehicles known as "motor-driven cycle," "motor scooter," or "motorcycle" without regard to weight or brake horsepower.

(D) "Emergency vehicle" means emergency vehicles of municipal, township, or county departments or public utility corporations when identified as such as required by law, the director of public safety, or local authorities, and motor vehicles when commandeered by a police officer.

(E) "Public safety vehicle" means any of the following:

(1) Ambulances, including private ambulance companies under contract to a municipal corporation, township, or county, and private ambulances and nontransport vehicles bearing license plates issued under section 4503.49 of the Revised Code;

(2) Motor vehicles used by public law enforcement officers or other persons sworn to enforce the criminal and traffic laws of the state;

(3) Any motor vehicle when properly identified as required by the director of public safety, when used in response to fire emergency calls or to provide emergency medical service to ill or injured persons, and when operated by a duly qualified person who is a member of a volunteer rescue service or a volunteer fire department, and who is on duty pursuant to the rules or directives of that service. The state fire marshal shall be designated by the director of public safety as the certifying agency for all public safety vehicles described in division (E)(3) of this section.

(4) Vehicles used by fire departments, including motor vehicles when used by volunteer fire fighters responding to emergency calls in the fire department service when identified as required by the director of public safety.

Any vehicle used to transport or provide emergency medical service to an ill or injured person, when certified as a public safety vehicle, shall be considered a public safety vehicle when transporting an ill or injured person to a hospital regardless of whether such vehicle has already passed a hospital.

(5) Vehicles used by the motor carrier enforcement unit for the enforcement of orders and rules of the public utilities commission as specified in section 5503.34 of the Revised Code.

(F) "School bus" means every bus designed for carrying more than nine passengers that is owned by a public, private, or governmental agency or institution of learning and operated for the transportation of children to or from a school session or a school function, or owned by a private person and operated for compensation for the transportation of children to or from a school session or a school function, provided "school bus" does not include a bus operated by a municipally owned transportation system, a mass transit company operating exclusively within the territorial limits of a municipal corporation, or within such limits and the territorial limits of municipal corporations immediately contiguous to such municipal corporation, nor a common passenger carrier certified by the public utilities commission unless such bus is devoted exclusively to the transportation of children to and from a school session or a school function, and "school bus" does not include a van or bus used by a licensed child day-care center or type A family day-care home to transport children from the child day-care center or type A family day-care home to a school if the van or bus does not have more than fifteen children in the van or bus at any time.

(G) "Bicycle" means every device, other than a tricycle designed solely for use as a play vehicle by a child, propelled solely by human power upon which any person may ride having two tandem wheels, or one wheel in the front and two wheels in the rear, or two wheels in the front and one wheel in the rear, any of which is more than fourteen inches in diameter.

(H) "Motorized bicycle" means any vehicle having either two tandem wheels or one wheel in the front and two wheels in the rear, that is capable of being pedaled and is equipped with a helper motor of not more than fifty cubic centimeters piston displacement that produces no more than one brake horsepower and is capable of propelling the vehicle at a speed of no greater than twenty miles per hour on a level surface.

(I) "Commercial tractor" means every motor vehicle having motive power designed or used for drawing other vehicles and not so constructed as to carry any load thereon, or designed or used for drawing other vehicles while carrying a portion of such other vehicles, or load thereon, or both.

(J) "Agricultural tractor" means every self-propelling vehicle designed or used for drawing other vehicles or wheeled machinery but having no provision for carrying loads independently of such other vehicles, and used principally for agricultural purposes.

(K) "Truck" means every motor vehicle, except trailers and semitrailers, designed and used to carry property.

(L) "Bus" means every motor vehicle designed for carrying more than nine passengers and used for the transportation of persons other than in a ridesharing arrangement, and every motor vehicle, automobile for hire, or funeral car, other than a taxicab or motor vehicle used in a ridesharing arrangement, designed and used for the transportation of persons for compensation.

(M) "Trailer" means every vehicle designed or used for carrying persons or property wholly on its own structure and for being drawn by a motor vehicle, including any such vehicle when formed by or operated as a combination of a "semitrailer" and a vehicle of the dolly type, such as that commonly known as a "trailer dolly," a vehicle used to transport agricultural produce or agricultural production materials between a local place of storage or supply and the farm when drawn or towed on a street or highway at a speed greater than twenty-five miles per hour, and a vehicle designed and used exclusively to transport a boat between a place of storage and a marina, or in and around a marina, when drawn or towed on a street or highway for a distance of more than ten miles or at a speed of more than twenty-five miles per hour.

(N) "Semitrailer" means every vehicle designed or used for carrying persons or property with another and separate motor vehicle so that in operation a part of its own weight or that of its load, or both, rests upon and is carried by another vehicle.

(O) "Pole trailer" means every trailer or semitrailer attached to the towing vehicle by means of a reach, pole, or by being boomed or otherwise secured to the towing vehicle, and ordinarily used for transporting long or irregular shaped loads such as poles, pipes, or structural members capable, generally, of sustaining themselves as beams between the supporting connections.

(P) "Railroad" means a carrier of persons or property operating upon rails placed principally on a private right-of-way.

(Q) "Railroad train" means a steam engine or an electric or other motor, with or without cars coupled thereto, operated by a railroad.

(R) "Streetcar" means a car, other than a railroad train, for transporting persons or property, operated upon rails principally within a street or highway.

(S) "Trackless trolley" means every car that collects its power from overhead electric trolley wires and that is not operated upon rails or tracks.

(T) "Explosives" means any chemical compound or mechanical mixture that is intended for the purpose of producing an explosion that contains any oxidizing and combustible units or other ingredients in such proportions, quantities, or packing that an ignition by fire, by friction, by concussion, by percussion, or by a detonator of any part of the compound or mixture may cause such a sudden generation of highly heated gases that the resultant gaseous pressures are capable of producing destructive effects on contiguous objects, or of destroying life or limb. Manufactured articles shall not be held to be explosives when the individual units contain explosives in such limited quantities, of such nature, or in such packing, that it is impossible to procure a simultaneous or a destructive explosion of such units, to the injury of life, limb, or property by fire, by friction, by concussion, by percussion, or by a detonator, such as fixed ammunition for small arms, firecrackers, or safety fuse matches.

(U) "Flammable liquid" means any liquid that has a flash point of seventy degrees fahrenheit, or less, as determined by a tagliabue or equivalent closed cup test device.

(V) "Gross weight" means the weight of a vehicle plus the weight of any load thereon.

(W) "Person" means every natural person, firm, co-partnership, association, or corporation.

(X) "Pedestrian" means any natural person afoot.

(Y) "Driver or operator" means every person who drives or is in actual physical control of a vehicle, trackless trolley, or streetcar.

(Z) "Police officer" means every officer authorized to direct or regulate traffic, or to make arrests for violations of traffic regulations.

(AA) "Local authorities" means every county, municipal, and other local board or body having authority to adopt police regulations under the constitution and laws of this state.

(BB) "Street" or "highway" means the entire width between the boundary lines of every way open to the use of the public as a thoroughfare for purposes of vehicular travel.

(CC) "Controlled-access highway" means every street or highway in respect to which owners or occupants of abutting lands and other persons have no legal right of access to or from the same except at such points only and in such manner as may be determined by the public authority having jurisdiction over such street or highway.

(DD) "Private road or driveway" means every way or place in private ownership used for vehicular travel by the owner and those having express or implied permission from the owner but not by other persons.

(EE) "Roadway" means that portion of a highway improved, designed, or ordinarily used for vehicular travel, except the berm or shoulder. If a highway includes two or more separate roadways the term "roadway" means any such roadway separately but not all such roadways collectively.

(FF) "Sidewalk" means that portion of a street between the curb lines, or the lateral lines of a roadway, and the adjacent property lines, intended for the use of pedestrians.

(GG) "Laned highway" means a highway the roadway of which is divided into two or more clearly marked lanes for vehicular traffic.

(HH) "Through highway" means every street or highway as provided in section 4511.65 of the Revised Code.

(II) "State highway" means a highway under the jurisdiction of the department of transportation, outside the limits of municipal corporations, provided that the authority conferred upon the director of transportation in section 5511.01 of the Revised Code to erect state highway route markers and signs directing traffic shall not be modified by sections 4511.01 to 4511.79 and 4511.99 of the Revised Code.

(JJ) "State route" means every highway that is designated with an official state route number and so marked.

(KK) "Intersection" means:

(1) The area embraced within the prolongation or connection of the lateral curb lines, or, if none, then the lateral boundary lines of the roadways of two highways which join one another at, or approximately at, right angles, or the area within which vehicles traveling upon different highways joining at any other angle may come in conflict.

(2) Where a highway includes two roadways thirty feet or more apart, then every crossing of each roadway of such divided highway by an intersecting highway shall be

regarded as a separate intersection. If an intersecting highway also includes two roadways thirty feet or more apart, then every crossing of two roadways of such highways shall be regarded as a separate intersection.

(3) The junction of an alley with a street or highway, or with another alley, shall not constitute an intersection.

(LL) "Crosswalk" means:

(1) That part of a roadway at intersections ordinarily included within the real or projected prolongation of property lines and curb lines or, in the absence of curbs, the edges of the traversable roadway;

(2) Any portion of a roadway at an intersection or elsewhere, distinctly indicated for pedestrian crossing by lines or other markings on the surface;

(3) Notwithstanding divisions (LL)(1) and (2) of this section, there shall not be a crosswalk where local authorities have placed signs indicating no crossing.

(MM) "Safety zone" means the area or space officially set apart within a roadway for the exclusive use of pedestrians and protected or marked or indicated by adequate signs as to be plainly visible at all times.

(NN) "Business district" means the territory fronting upon a street or highway, including the street or highway, between successive intersections within municipal corporations where fifty per cent or more of the frontage between such successive intersections is occupied by buildings in use for business, or within or outside municipal corporations where fifty per cent or more of the frontage for a distance of three hundred feet or more is occupied by buildings in use for business, and the character of such territory is indicated by official traffic control devices.

(OO) "Residence district" means the territory, not comprising a business district, fronting on a street or highway, including the street or highway, where, for a distance of three hundred feet or more, the frontage is improved with residences or residences and buildings in use for business.

(PP) "Urban district" means the territory contiguous to and including any street or highway which is built up with structures devoted to business, industry, or dwelling houses situated at intervals of less than one hundred feet for a distance of a quarter of a mile or more, and the character of such territory is indicated by official traffic control devices.

(QQ) "Traffic control devices" means all flaggers, signs, signals, markings, and devices placed or erected by authority of a public body or official having jurisdiction, for the purpose of regulating, warning, or guiding traffic, including signs denoting names of streets and highways.

(RR) "Traffic control signal" means any device, whether manually, electrically, or mechanically operated, by which traffic is alternately directed to stop, to proceed, to change direction, or not to change direction.

(SS) "Railroad sign or signal" means any sign, signal, or device erected by authority of a public body or official or by a railroad and intended to give notice of the presence of railroad tracks or the approach of a railroad train.

(TT) "Traffic" means pedestrians, ridden or herded animals, vehicles, streetcars, trackless trolleys, and other devices, either singly or together, while using any highway for purposes of travel.

(UU) "Right-of-way" means either of the following, as the context requires:

(1) The right of a vehicle, streetcar, trackless trolley, or pedestrian to proceed uninterruptedly in a lawful manner in the direction in which it or the individual is moving in preference to another vehicle, streetcar, trackless trolley, or pedestrian approaching from a different direction into its or the individual's path;

(2) A general term denoting land, property, or the interest therein, usually in the configuration of a strip, acquired for or devoted to transportation purposes. When used in this context, right-of-way includes the roadway, shoulders or berm, ditch, and slopes extending to the right-of-way limits under the control of the state or local authority.

(VV) "Rural mail delivery vehicle" means every vehicle used to deliver United States mail on a rural mail delivery route.

(WW) "Funeral escort vehicle" means any motor vehicle, including a funeral hearse, while used to facilitate the movement of a funeral procession.

(XX) "Alley" means a street or highway intended to provide access to the rear or side of lots or buildings in urban districts and not intended for the purpose of through vehicular traffic, and includes any street or highway that has been declared an "alley" by the legislative authority of the municipal corporation in which such street or highway is located.

(YY) "Freeway" means a divided multi-lane highway for through traffic with all crossroads separated in grade and with full control of access.

(ZZ) "Expressway" means a divided arterial highway for through traffic with full or partial control of access with an excess of fifty per cent of all crossroads separated in grade.

(AAA) "Thruway" means a through highway whose entire roadway is reserved for through traffic and on which roadway parking is prohibited.

(BBB) "Stop intersection" means any intersection at one or more entrances of which stop signs are erected.

(CCC) "Arterial street" means any United States or state numbered route, controlled access highway, or other major radial or circumferential street or highway designated by local authorities within their respective jurisdictions as part of a major arterial system of streets or highways.

(DDD) "Ridesharing arrangement" means the transportation of persons in a motor vehicle where such transportation is incidental to another purpose of a volunteer driver and includes ridesharing arrangements known as carpools, vanpools, and buspools.

(EEE) "Motorized wheelchair" means any self-propelled vehicle designed for, and used by, a handicapped person and that is incapable of a speed in excess of eight miles per hour.

(FFF) "Child day-care center" and "type A family day-care home" have the same meanings as in section 5104.01 of the Revised Code.

(GGG) "Multi-wheel agricultural tractor" means a type of agricultural tractor that has two or more wheels or tires on each side of one axle at the rear of the tractor, is designed or used for drawing other vehicles or wheeled machinery, has no provision for carrying loads independently of the drawn vehicles or machinery, and is used principally for agricultural purposes.

(HHH) "Operate" means to cause or have caused movement of a vehicle, streetcar, or trackless trolley.

(III) "Predicate motor vehicle or traffic offense" means any one of the following:

(1) A violation of section 4511.03, 4511.051 [4511.05.1], 4511.12, 4511.132 [4511.13.2], 4511.16, 4511.20, 4511.201 [4511.20.1], 4511.21, 4511.211 [4511.21.1], 4511.213 [4511.21.3], 4511.22, 4511.23, 4511.25, 4511.26, 4511.27, 4511.28, 4511.29, 4511.30,

4511.31, 4511.32, 4511.33, 4511.34, 4511.35, 4511.36, 4511.37, 4511.38, 4511.39, 4511.40, 4511.41, 4511.42, 4511.43, 4511.431 [4511.43.1], 4511.432 [4511.43.2], 4511.44, 4511.441 [4511.44.1], 4511.451 [4511.45.1], 4511.452 [4511.45.2], 4511.46, 4511.47, 4511.48, 4511.481 [4511.48.1], 4511.49, 4511.50, 4511.511 [4511.51.1], 4511.53, 4511.54, 4511.55, 4511.56, 4511.57, 4511.58, 4511.59, 4511.60, 4511.61, 4511.64, 4511.66, 4511.661 [4511.66.1], 4511.68, 4511.70, 4511.701 [4511.70.1], 4511.71, 4511.711 [4511.71.1], 4511.712 [4511.71.2], 4511.713 [4511.71.3], 4511.72, 4511.73, 4511.763 [4511.76.3], 4511.771 [4511.77.1], 4511.78, or 4511.84 of the Revised Code;

(2) A violation of division (A)(2) of section 4511.17, divisions (A) to (D) of section 4511.51, or division (A) of section 4511.74 of the Revised Code;

(3) A violation of any provision of sections 4511.01 TO 4511.76 of the Revised Code for which no penalty otherwise is provided in the section that contains the provision violated;

(4) A violation of a municipal ordinance that is substantially similar to any section or provision set forth or described in division (III)(1), (2), or (3) of this section.

(JJJ) "Road service vehicle" means wreckers, utility repair vehicles, and state, county, and municipal service vehicles equipped with visual signals by means of flashing, rotating, or oscillating lights.

**HISTORY: GC § 6307-2; 119 v 766, § 2; 120 v 221; 124 v 514; Bureau of Code Revision, 10-1-53; 126 v 392(408) (Eff 3-17-55); 126 v 790 (Eff 9-14-55); 126 v 115 (Eff 10-1-56); 127 v 54 (Eff 8-27-57); 128 v 1270 (Eff 11-4-59); 129 v 1273 (Eff 10-26-61); 130 v 1068 (Eff 8-5-63); 130 v 1074 (Eff 10-10-63); 131 v 1094 (Eff 10-15-65); 132 v H 634 (Eff 11-24-67); 132 v H 380 (Eff 1-1-68); 132 v H 878 (Eff 12-14-67); 132 v S 451 (Eff 2-29-68); 135 v H 200 (Eff 9-23-73); 135 v S 108 (Eff 11-21-73); 135 v H 995 (Eff 1-1-75); 136 v H 338 (Eff 1-9-76); 136 v S 56 (Eff 5-25-76); 136 v H 235 (Eff 10-1-76); 137 v S 100 (Eff 4-1-78); 138 v S 9 (Eff 6-20-79); 139 v H 53 (Eff 7-1-82); 143 v H 258 (Eff 11-2-89); 143 v H 319 (Eff 7-2-90); 143 v S 272 (Eff 11-28-90); 143 v S 382 (Eff 12-31-90); 144 v H 485 (Eff 10-7-92); 144 v S 98 (Eff 11-12-92); 144 v H 356 (Eff 12-31-92); 146 v S 293 (Eff 9-26-96); 148 v H 484 (Eff 10-5-2000); 149 v S 231. Eff 10-24-2002; 149 v S 123, § 1, eff. 1-1-04; 150 v H 52, § 1, eff. 6-1-04; 150 v H 230, § 1, eff. 9-16-04; 152 v H 9, § 1, eff. 10-18-07; 152 v H 562, § 101.01, eff. 9-23-08; 153 v H 2, § 101.01, eff. 7-1-09.**

The effective date is set by § 812.10 of 153 v H 2.

The effective date is set by § 812.10 of 152 v H 562.

The provisions of § 3 of 152 v H 9 read as follows:

SECTION 3. Section 4511.01 of the Revised Code is presented in this act as a composite of the section as amended by both Sub. H.B. 52 and Sub. H.B. 230 of the 125th General Assembly. The General Assembly, applying the principle stated in division (B) of section 1.52 of the Revised Code that amendments are to be harmonized if reasonably capable of simultaneous operation, finds that the composite is the resulting version of the section in effect prior to the effective date of the section as presented in this act.

The provisions of § 3, H.B. 52 (150 v —), and § 10, H.B. 230 (150 v —), read as follows:

SECTION 10. * * * Section 4511.01 of the Revised Code is presented in this act as a composite of the section as amended by both Am. Sub. S.B. 123 and Am. Sub. S.B. 231 of the 124th General Assembly. The General Assembly, applying the principle stated in division (B) of section 1.52 of the Revised Code that amendments are to be harmonized if reasonably capable of simultaneous operation, finds that each composite is the resulting version of the section in effect prior to the effective date of the section as presented in this act.

The effective date is set by section 4 of S.B. 123.

See provisions, § 5 of S.B. 123 (149 v —), following RC § 4501.01.

## § 4511.011 Designation of freeway, expressway, and thruway.

The director of transportation, the board of county commissioners of a county, and the legislative authority of a municipality may, for highways under their jurisdiction, designate an existing highway in whole or in part as or included in a "freeway," "expressway," or "thruway."

**HISTORY: 130 v 1080 (Eff 8-5-63); 135 v H 200. Eff 9-28-73.**

## § 4511.03 Emergency vehicles to proceed cautiously past red or stop signal.

(A) The driver of any emergency vehicle or public safety vehicle, when responding to an emergency call, upon approaching a red or stop signal or any stop sign shall slow down as necessary for safety to traffic, but may proceed cautiously past such red or stop sign or signal with due regard for the safety of all persons using the street or highway.

(B) Except as otherwise provided in this division, whoever violates this section is guilty of a minor misdemeanor. If, within one year of the offense, the offender previously has been convicted of or pleaded guilty to one predicate motor vehicle or traffic offense, whoever violates this section is guilty of a misdemeanor of the fourth degree. If, within one year of the offense, the offender previously has been convicted of two or more predicate motor vehicle or traffic offenses, whoever violates this section is guilty of a misdemeanor of the third degree.

**HISTORY: GC § 6307-4; 119 v 766, § 4; Bureau of Code Revision, 10-1-53; 132 v H 378. Eff 12-14-67; 149 v S 123, § 1, eff. 1-1-04.**

The effective date is set by section 4 of S.B. 123.

See provisions, § 5 of S.B. 123 (149 v —), following RC § 4501.01.

## § 4511.031 Portable signal preemption devices.

(A)(1) No person shall possess a portable signal preemption device.

(2) No person shall use a portable signal preemption device to affect the operation of the traffic control signal.

(B) Division (A)(1) of this section does not apply to any of the following persons and division (A)(2) of this section does not apply to any of the following persons when responding to an emergency call:

(1) A peace officer, as defined in division (A)(1), (12), (14), or (19) of section 109.71 of the Revised Code;

(2) A state highway patrol trooper;

(3) A person while occupying a public safety vehicle as defined in division (E)(1), (3), or (4) of section 4511.01 of the Revised Code.

(C) Whoever violates division (A)(1) of this section is guilty of a misdemeanor of the fourth degree. Whoever violates division (A)(2) of this section is guilty of a misdemeanor of the first degree.

(D) As used in this section, "portable signal preemption device" means a device that, if activated by a person, is capable of changing a traffic control signal to green out of sequence.

**HISTORY: 150 v H 406, § 1, eff. 3-23-05.**

The provisions of § 555.19 of 152 v H 67, as amended by § 3 of 152 v H 30, read as follows:

SECTION 3. That Sections 555.07 and 555.19 of Am. Sub. H.B. 67 of the 127th General Assembly be amended to read as follows:

° ° °

Sec. 555.19. In fiscal year 2008, the Department of Transportation shall expend at least $400,000 in the township having the largest population according to the 2000 federal decennial census for a pilot program involving the installation and operation of a system of portable signal preemption devices. Use of the devices in the pilot program shall be in accordance with section 4511.031 of the Revised Code. The Department shall consult with appropriate township officials in implementing the pilot program.

## § 4511.04 Exceptions.

(A) Sections 4511.01 to 4511.18, 4511.20 to 4511.78, 4511.99, and 4513.01 to 4513.37 of the Revised Code do not apply to persons, teams, motor vehicles, and other equipment while actually engaged in work upon the surface of a highway within an area designated by traffic control devices, but apply to such persons and vehicles when traveling to or from such work.

(B) The driver of a highway maintenance vehicle owned by this state or any political subdivision of this state, while the driver is engaged in the performance of official duties upon a street or highway, provided the highway maintenance vehicle is equipped with flashing lights and such other markings as are required by law and such lights are in operation when the driver and vehicle are so engaged, shall be exempt from criminal prosecution for violations of sections 4511.22, 4511.25, 4511.26, 4511.27, 4511.28, 4511.30, 4511.31, 4511.33, 4511.35, 4511.66, 4513.02, and 5577.01 to 5577.09 of the Revised Code.

(C)(1) This section does not exempt a driver of a highway maintenance vehicle from civil liability arising from a violation of section 4511.22, 4511.25, 4511.26, 4511.27, 4511.28, 4511.30, 4511.31, 4511.33, 4511.35, 4511.66, or 4513.02 or sections 5577.01 to 5577.09 of the Revised Code.

(2) This section does not exempt the driver of a vehicle that is engaged in the transport of highway maintenance equipment from criminal liability for a violation of sections 5577.01 to 5577.09 of the Revised Code.

(D) As used in this section, "highway maintenance vehicle" means a vehicle used in snow and ice removal or road surface maintenance, including a snow plow, traffic line striper, road sweeper, mowing machine, asphalt distributing vehicle, or other such vehicle designed for use in specific highway maintenance activities.

**HISTORY: GC § 6307-4; 119 v 766, § 4; Bureau of Code Revision, 10-1-53; 133 v S 77. Eff 11-17-69; 150 v H 87, § 1, eff. 6-30-03.**

The effective date is set by section 26 of H.B. 87.

## § 4511.041 Exceptions for emergency or public safety vehicle responding to emergency call.

Sections 4511.12, 4511.13, 4511.131 [4511.13.1], 4511.132 [4511.13.2], 4511.14, 4511.15, 4511.202 [4511.20.2], 4511.21, 4511.211 [4511.21.1], 4511.22, 4511.23, 4511.25, 4511.26, 4511.27, 4511.28, 4511.29, 4511.30, 4511.31, 4511.32, 4511.33, 4511.34, 4511.35, 4511.36, 4511.37, 4511.38, 4511.39, 4511.40, 4511.41, 4511.42, 4511.43, 4511.431 [4511.43.1], 4511.432 [4511.43.2], 4511.44, 4511.441 [4511.44.1], 4511.57, 4511.58, 4511.59, 4511.60, 4511.61, 4511.62, 4511.66, 4511.68, 4511.681 [4511.68.1], and 4511.69 of the Revised Code do not apply to the driver of an emergency vehicle or public safety vehicle if the emergency vehicle or public safety vehicle is responding to an emergency call, is equipped with and displaying at least one flashing, rotating, or oscillating light visible under normal atmospheric conditions from a distance of five hundred feet to the front of the vehicle and if the driver of the vehicle is giving an audible signal by siren, exhaust whistle, or bell. This section does not relieve the driver of an emergency vehicle or public safety vehicle from the duty to drive with due regard for the safety of all persons and property upon the highway.

**HISTORY: 145 v H 149. Eff 5-20-93.**

## § 4511.042 Exception for coroner's vehicles.

Sections 4511.25, 4511.26, 4511.27, 4511.28, 4511.29, 4511.30, 4511.31, 4511.32, 4511.33, 4511.35, 4511.36, 4511.37, 4511.38, and 4511.66 of the Revised Code do not apply to a coroner, deputy coroner, or coroner's investigator operating a motor vehicle in accordance with section 4513.171 [4513.17.1] of the Revised Code. This section does not relieve a coroner, deputy coroner, or coroner's investigator operating a motor vehicle from the duty to drive with due regard for the safety of all persons and property upon the highway.

**HISTORY: 147 v H 282. Eff 11-12-97.**

## § 4511.05 Persons riding or driving animals upon roadways.

Every person riding, driving, or leading an animal upon a roadway is subject to sections 4511.01 to 4511.78, inclusive, 4511.99, and 4513.01 to 4513.37, inclusive, of the Revised Code, applicable to the driver of a vehicle, except those provisions of such sections which by their nature are inapplicable.

**HISTORY: GC § 6307-5; 119 v 766, § 5; Bureau of Code Revision. Eff 10-1-53.**

## § 4511.051 Prohibitions on use of freeways.

(A) No person, unless otherwise directed by a police officer, shall:

(1) As a pedestrian, occupy any space within the limits of the right-of-way of a freeway, except: in a rest area; on a facility that is separated from the roadway and shoulders of the freeway and is designed and appropriately marked for pedestrian use; in the performance of public works or official duties; as a result of an emergency caused by an accident or breakdown of a motor vehicle; or to obtain assistance;

(2) Occupy any space within the limits of the right-of-way of a freeway, with: an animal-drawn vehicle; a ridden or led animal; herded animals; a pushcart; a bicycle, except on a facility that is separated from the roadway and shoulders of the freeway and is designed and appropriately marked for bicycle use; a bicycle with motor attached; a motor driven cycle with a motor which produces not to exceed five brake horsepower; an agricultural tractor; farm machinery; except in the performance of public works or official duties.

(B) Except as otherwise provided in this division, whoever violates this section is guilty of a minor misdemeanor. If, within one year of the offense, the offender previously has been convicted of or pleaded guilty to one predicate motor vehicle or traffic offense, whoever violates this section is guilty of a misdemeanor of the fourth degree. If, within one year of the offense, the offender previously has been convicted of two or more predicate motor vehicle or traffic offenses, whoever violates this section is guilty of a misdemeanor of the third degree.

**HISTORY: 131 v 1099 (Eff 9-1-65); 132 v H 1 (Eff 2-21-67); 143 v H 258. Eff 11-2-89; 149 v S 123, § 1, eff. 1-1-04.**

The effective date is set by section 4 of S.B. 123.

See provisions, § 5 of S.B. 123 (149 v —), following RC § 4501.01.

## § 4511.06 Uniform application and precedence of traffic law.

Sections 4511.01 to 4511.78, 4511.99, and 4513.01 to 4513.37 of the Revised Code shall be applicable and uniform throughout this state and in all political subdivisions and municipal corporations of this state. No local authority shall enact or enforce any rule in conflict with such sections, except that this section does not prevent local authorities from exercising the rights granted them by Chapter 4521. of the Revised Code and does not limit the effect or application of the provisions of that chapter.

**HISTORY: GC § 6307-6; 119 v 766, § 6; Bureau of Code Revision, 10-1-53; 139 v H 707. Eff 1-1-83.**

The effective date is set by section 3 of HB 707.

## § 4511.07 Local traffic regulations.

(A) Sections 4511.01 to 4511.78, 4511.99, and 4513.01 to 4513.37 of the Revised Code do not prevent local authorities from carrying out the following activities with respect to streets and highways under their jurisdiction and within the reasonable exercise of the police power:

(1) Regulating the stopping, standing, or parking of vehicles, trackless trolleys, and streetcars;

(2) Regulating traffic by means of police officers or traffic control devices;

(3) Regulating or prohibiting processions or assemblages on the highways;

(4) Designating particular highways as one-way highways and requiring that all vehicles, trackless trolleys, and streetcars on the one-way highways be moved in one specific direction;

(5) Regulating the speed of vehicles, streetcars, and trackless trolleys in public parks;

(6) Designating any highway as a through highway and requiring that all vehicles, trackless trolleys, and streetcars stop before entering or crossing a through highway, or designating any intersection as a stop intersection and requiring all vehicles, trackless trolleys, and streetcars to stop at one or more entrances to the intersection;

(7) Regulating or prohibiting vehicles and trackless trolleys from passing to the left of safety zones;

(8) Regulating the operation of bicycles; provided that no such regulation shall be fundamentally inconsistent with the uniform rules of the road prescribed by this chapter and that no such regulation shall prohibit the use of bicycles on any public street or highway except as provided in section 4511.051 [4511.05.1] of the Revised Code;

(9) Requiring the registration and licensing of bicycles, including the requirement of a registration fee for residents of the local authority;

(10) Regulating the use of certain streets by vehicles, streetcars, or trackless trolleys.

(B) No ordinance or regulation enacted under division (A)(4), (5), (6), (7), (8), or (10) of this section shall be effective until signs giving notice of the local traffic regulations are posted upon or at the entrance to the highway or part of the highway affected, as may be most appropriate.

(C) Every ordinance, resolution, or regulation enacted under division (A)(1) of this section shall be enforced in compliance with section 4511.071 [4511.07.1] of the Revised Code, unless the local authority that enacted it also enacted an ordinance, resolution, or regulation pursuant to division (A) of section 4521.02 of the Revised Code that specifies that a violation of it shall not be considered a criminal offense, in which case the ordinance, resolution, or regulation shall be enforced in compliance with Chapter 4521. of the Revised Code.

**HISTORY: GC § 6307-7; 119 v 766; Bureau of Code Revision, 10-1-53; 129 v 1037 (Eff 8-11-61); 133 v S 452 (Eff 7-17-70); 135 v H 995 (Eff 1-1-75); 138 v S 257 (Eff 6-25-80); 139 v H 707. Eff 1-1-83; 151 v H 389, § 1, eff. 9-21-06.**

The effective date is set by section 3 of HB 707.

## § 4511.071 Lessor under written lease may establish nonliability for violation.

(A) Except as provided in division (C) of this section, the owner of a vehicle shall be entitled to establish nonliability for prosecution for violation of an ordinance, resolution, or regulation enacted under division (A)(1) of section 4511.07 of the Revised Code by proving the vehicle was in the care, custody, or control of a person other than the owner at the time of the violation pursuant to a written rental or lease agreement or affidavit providing that except for such agreement, no other business relationship with respect to the vehicle in question exists between the operator and owner.

(B) Proof that the vehicle was in the care, custody, or control of a person other than the owner shall be established by sending a copy of such written rental or lease agreement or affidavit to the prosecuting authority within thirty days from the date of receipt by the owner of the notice of violation. The furnishing of a copy of a written rental or lease agreement or affidavit shall be prima-facie evidence that a vehicle was in the care, custody, or control of a person other than the owner.

(C) This section does not apply to a violation of an ordinance, resolution, or regulation enacted under division (A)(1) of section 4511.07 of the Revised Code if the ordinance, resolution, or regulation is one that is required to be enforced in compliance with Chapter 4521 of the Revised Code.

**HISTORY: 138 v S 257 (Eff 6-25-80); 139 v H 707. Eff 1-1-83; 151 v H 389, § 1, eff. 9-21-06.**

The effective date is set by section 3 of HB 707.

## § 4511.08 Use of private property for vehicular travel.

Sections 4511.01 to 4511.78, inclusive, 4511.99, and 4513.01 to 4513.37, inclusive, of the Revised Code do not prevent the owner of real property, used by the public for purposes of vehicular travel by permission of the owner and not as a matter of right, from prohibiting such use or from requiring additional conditions to those specified in such sections, or otherwise regulating such use as may seem best to such owner.

**HISTORY: GC § 6307-8; 119 v 766, § 8; Bureau of Code Revision. Eff 10-1-53.**

## [TRAFFIC CONTROL DEVICES, SIGNS]

### § 4511.09 Uniform system of traffic control devices.

The department of transportation shall adopt a manual and specifications for a uniform system of traffic control devices, including signs denoting names of streets and highways, for use upon highways within this state. Such uniform system shall correlate with, and so far as possible conform to, the system approved by the American Association of State Highway Officials.

**HISTORY: GC § 6307-9; 119 v 766, § 9; Bureau of Code Revision, 10-1-53; 135 v H 200. Eff 9-28-73.**

### § 4511.091 Arrest or citation based on radar, timing device or radio message from another officer.

(A) The driver of any motor vehicle that has been checked by radar, or by any electrical or mechanical timing device to determine the speed of the motor vehicle over a measured distance of a highway or a measured distance of a private road or driveway, and found to be in violation of any of the provisions of section 4511.21 or 4511.211 of the Revised Code, may be arrested until a warrant can be obtained, provided the arresting officer has observed the recording of the speed of the motor vehicle by the radio microwaves, electrical or mechanical timing device, or has received a radio message from the officer who observed the speed of the motor vehicle recorded by the radio microwaves, electrical or mechanical timing device; provided, in case of an arrest based on such a message, the radio message has been dispatched immediately after the speed of the motor vehicle was recorded and the arresting officer is furnished a description of the motor vehicle for proper identification and the recorded speed.

(B) If the driver of a motor vehicle being driven on a public street or highway of this state is observed violating any provision of this chapter other than section 4511.21 or 4511.211 of the Revised Code by a law enforcement officer situated at any location, including in any type of airborne aircraft or airship, that law enforcement officer may send a radio message to another law enforcement officer, and the other law enforcement officer may arrest the driver of the motor vehicle until a warrant can be obtained or may issue the driver a citation for the violation; provided, if an arrest or citation is based on such a message, the radio message is dispatched immediately after the violation is observed and the law enforcement officer who observes the violation furnishes to the law enforcement officer who makes the arrest or issues the citation a description of the alleged violation and the motor vehicle for proper identification.

(C)(1) No person shall be arrested, charged, or convicted of a violation of any provision of divisions (B) to (O) of section 4511.21 or section 4511.211 of the Revised Code or a substantially similar municipal ordinance based on a peace officer's unaided visual estimation of the speed of a motor vehicle, trackless trolley, or streetcar. This division does not do any of the following:

(a) Preclude the use by a peace officer of a stopwatch, radar, laser, or other electrical, mechanical, or digital device to determine the speed of a motor vehicle;

(b) Apply regarding any violation other than a violation of divisions (B) to (O) of section 4511.21 or section 4511.211 of the Revised Code or a substantially similar municipal ordinance;

(c) Preclude a peace officer from testifying that the speed of operation of a motor vehicle, trackless trolley, or streetcar was at a speed greater or less than a speed described in division (A) of section 4511.21 of the Revised Code, the admission into evidence of such testimony, or preclude a conviction of a violation of that division based in whole or in part on such testimony.

(2) As used in this division, "peace officer" has the same meaning as in section 2935.01 of the Revised Code.

**HISTORY: 125 v 396; 129 v 582(898) (Eff 1-10-61); 130 v 1080 (Eff 10-10-63); 132 v H 380 (Eff 1-1-68); 143 v H 171 (Eff 5-31-90); 147 v S 213. Eff 7-29-98; 2011 HB 86, § 1, eff. Sept. 30, 2011.**

### § 4511.092 Leased or rented vehicle traffic law violations detected by photo-monitoring devices.

(A) As used in this section:

(1) "Motor vehicle leasing dealer" has the same meaning as in section 4517.01 of the Revised Code.

(2) "Motor vehicle renting dealer" has the same meaning as in section 4549.65 of the Revised Code.

(3) "Ticket" means any traffic ticket, citation, summons, or other notice of liability issued in response to an alleged traffic law violation detected by a traffic law photo-monitoring device.

(4) "Traffic law photo-monitoring device" means an electronic system consisting of a photographic, video, or electronic camera and a means of sensing the presence of a motor vehicle that automatically produces photographs, videotape, or digital images of the vehicle or its license plate.

(B) A motor vehicle leasing dealer or motor vehicle renting dealer who receives a ticket for an alleged traffic law violation detected by a traffic law photo-monitoring device is not liable for a ticket issued for a vehicle that was in the care, custody, or control of a lessee or renter at the time of the alleged violation. A dealer who receives a ticket for such a violation shall notify whoever issued the ticket of the vehicle lessee's or renter's name and address. In no case shall the dealer pay such a ticket and then attempt to collect a fee or assess the lessee or renter a charge for any payment of such a ticket made on behalf of the lessee or renter.

**HISTORY: 152 v H 67, § 101.01, eff. 6-30-07.**

The effective date is set by § 609.10 of 152 v H 67.

### § 4511.093 Limited secondary traffic offense enforcement at vehicle checkpoints and inspections.

(A)(1) No law enforcement officer who stops the operator of a motor vehicle in the course of an authorized sobriety or other motor vehicle checkpoint operation or a motor vehicle safety inspection shall issue a ticket, citation, or summons for a secondary traffic offense unless in the course of the checkpoint operation or safety inspection the officer first determines that an offense other than a secondary traffic offense has occurred and either places the operator or a vehicle occupant under arrest or issues a ticket, citation, or summons to the operator or a vehicle occupant for an offense other than a secondary offense.

(2) A law enforcement agency that operates a motor vehicle checkpoint for an express purpose related to a secondary traffic offense shall not issue a ticket, citation, or summons for any secondary traffic offense at such a checkpoint, but may use such a checkpoint operation to conduct a public awareness campaign and distribute information.

(B) As used in this section, "secondary traffic offense" means a violation of division (A) or (F)(2) of section 4507.05, division (B)(1)(a) or (b) or (E) of section 4507.071 [4507.07.1], division (C) of section 4511.81, division (A)(3) of section 4513.03, or division (B) of section 4513.263 [4513.26.3] of the Revised Code.

**HISTORY: 152 v H 119, § 101.01, eff. 9-29-07; 152 v H 320, § 1, eff. 10-7-09; 153 v H 2, § 101.01, eff. 7-1-09.**

The effective date is set by § 812.10 of 153 v H 2.
The effective date is set by § 4 of 152 v H 320.
The effective date is set by § 812.03 of 152 v H 119.

## § 4511.094 Signs indicating use of traffic law photo-monitoring devices.

(A) As used in this section:

(1) "Local authority" means a municipal corporation, county, or township.

(2) "Traffic law photo-monitoring device" means an electronic system consisting of a photographic, video, or electronic camera and a means of sensing the presence of a motor vehicle that automatically produces photographs, videotape, or digital images of the vehicle or its license plate.

(B)(1) No local authority shall use traffic law photo-monitoring devices to enforce any traffic law until after it has erected signs on every highway that is not a freeway that is part of the state highway system and that enters that local authority. The signs shall inform inbound traffic that the local authority utilizes traffic law photo-monitoring devices to enforce traffic laws. The signs shall be erected within the first three hundred feet of the boundary of the local authority or, if the signs cannot be located within the first three hundred feet of the boundary of the local authority, as close to that distance as possible, provided that if a particular highway enters and exits the territory of a local authority multiple times, the local authority shall erect the signs as required by this division at the locations in each direction of travel where inbound traffic on the highway first enters the territory of the local authority and is not required to erect additional signs along such highway each time the highway reenters the territory of the local authority. The local authority is responsible for all costs associated with the erection, maintenance, and replacement, if necessary, of the signs. All signs erected under this division shall conform in size, color, location, and content to standards contained in the manual adopted by the department of transportation pursuant to section 4511.09 of the Revised Code and shall remain in place for as long as the local authority utilizes traffic law photo-monitoring devices to enforce any traffic law. Any ticket, citation, or summons issued by or on behalf of the local authority for any traffic law violation based upon evidence gathered by a traffic law photo-monitoring device after the effective date of this section, but before the signs have been erected is invalid; provided that no ticket, citation, or summons is invalid if the local authority is in substantial compliance with the requirement of this division to erect the signs.

(2) A local authority is deemed to be in substantial compliance with the requirement of division (B)(1) of this section to erect the advisory signs if the authority does both of the following:

(a) First erects all signs as required by division (B)(1) of this section and subsequently maintains and replaces the signs as needed so that at all times at least ninety per cent of the required signs are in place and functional;

(b) Annually documents and upon request certifies its compliance with division (B)(2)(a) of this section.

(C) A local authority that uses traffic law photo-monitoring devices to enforce any traffic law at an intersection where traffic is controlled by traffic control signals that exhibit different colored lights or colored lighted arrows shall time the operation of the yellow lights and yellow arrows of those traffic control signals so that the steady yellow indication exceeds by one second the minimum duration for yellow indicators at similar intersections as established by the provisions of the manual adopted by the department of transportation under section 4511.09 of the Revised Code.

**HISTORY: 152 v H 30, § 1, eff. 3-12-09.**

The effective date is set by § 8 of 152 v H 30.

## § 4511.10 Placing and maintaining traffic control devices.

The department of transportation may place and maintain traffic control devices, conforming to its manual and specifications, upon all state highways as are necessary to indicate and to carry out sections 4511.01 to 4511.78 and 4511.99 of the Revised Code, or to regulate, warn, or guide traffic.

No local authority shall place or maintain any traffic control device upon any highway under the jurisdiction of the department except by permission of the director of transportation.

**HISTORY: GC § 6307-10; 119 v 766, § 10; Bureau of Code Revision, 10-1-53; 135 H 200. Eff 9-28-73.**

## § 4511.101 Business logos on directional signs along interstates.

(A) The director of transportation, in accordance with 23 U.S.C.A. 109(d), 131(f), and 315, as amended, shall establish a program for the placement of business logos for identification purposes on state directional signs within the rights-of-way of divided, multi-lane, limited access highways in both rural and urban areas.

(B)(1) The director shall establish, and may revise at any time, a fee for participation in the business logo sign program. All direct and indirect costs of the business logo sign program established pursuant to this section shall be fully paid by the businesses applying for participation in the program. The direct and indirect costs of the program shall include, but not be limited to, the cost of capital, directional signs, blanks, posts, logos, installation, repair, engineering, design, insurance, removal, replacement, and administration.

(2) Money generated from participating businesses in excess of the direct and indirect costs and any reasonable profit earned by a person awarded a contract under division (C) of this section shall be remitted to the department.

(3) Nothing in this chapter shall be construed to prohibit the director from establishing such a program. If the department operates such a program and does not contract with a private person to operate it, all money collected from participating businesses shall be deposited and credited as prescribed in division (B)(2) of this section.

(C) The director, in accordance with rules adopted pursuant to Chapter 119. of the Revised Code, may contract with any private person to operate, maintain, or market the business logo sign program. The contract may allow for a reasonable profit to be earned by the successful applicant. In awarding the contract, the director shall consider the skill, expertise, prior experience, and other qualifications of each applicant.

(D) As used in this section, "urban area" means an area having a population of fifty thousand or more according to the most recent federal census and designated as such on urban maps prepared by the department.

(E) In implementing this section, neither the department nor the director shall do either of the following:

(1) Limit the right of any person to erect, maintain, repair, remove, or utilize any off-premises or on-premises advertising device;

(2) Make participation in the business logo sign program conditional upon a business agreeing to limit, discontinue, withdraw, modify, alter, or change any advertising or sign.

(F) The program shall permit the business logo signs of a seller of motor vehicle fuel to include on the seller's signs a marking or symbol indicating that the seller sells one or more types of alternative fuel so long as the seller in fact sells that fuel.

As used in this division, "alternative fuel" has the same meaning as in section 125.831 [125.83.1] of the Revised Code.

**HISTORY: 143 v H 356 (Eff 11-2-89); 143 v H 737 (Eff 4-11-91); 145 v H 154 (Eff 6-30-93); 146 v H 107 (Eff 6-30-95); 146 v H 353 (Eff 9-17-96); 146 v H 670 (Eff 12-2-96); 147 v H 210 (Eff 6-30-97); 147 v H 462. Eff 3-18-99; 151 v H 245, § 1, eff. 10-12-06; 152 v H 562, § 101.01, eff. 9-23-08.**

The effective date is set by § 812.10 of 152 v H 562.

**Publisher's Note:**

The amendment of (B) of RC § 4311.101 by 152 v H 562 was disapproved in part by the Governor.

## § 4511.102 Definitions.

As used in sections 4511.102 [4511.10.2] to 4511.106 [4511.10.6] of the Revised Code:

(A) "Tourist-oriented activity" includes any lawful cultural, historical, recreational, educational, or commercial activity a major portion of whose income or visitors are derived during the normal business season from motorists not residing in the immediate area of the activity and attendance at which is no less than two thousand visitors in any consecutive twelve-month period.

(B) "Eligible attraction" means any tourist-oriented activity that meets all of the following criteria:

(1) Is not eligible for inclusion in the business logo sign program established under section 4511.101 [4511.10.1] of the Revised Code;

(2) If currently advertised by signs adjacent to a highway on the interstate system or state system, those signs are consistent with Chapter 5516. of the Revised Code and the "National Highway Beautification Act of 1965," 79 Stat. 1028, 23 U.S.C. 131, and the national standards, criteria, and rules adopted pursuant to that act;

(3) Is within ten miles of the highway for which signing is sought under sections 4511.102 [4511.10.2] to 4511.105 [4511.10.5] of the Revised Code;

(4) Meets any additional criteria developed by the director of transportation and adopted by the director as rules in accordance with Chapter 119. of the Revised Code.

(C) "Interstate system" has the same meaning as in section 5516.01 of the Revised Code.

(D) "Commercial activity" means a farm market, winery, bed and breakfast, lodging that is not a franchise or part of a national chain, antiques shop, craft store, or gift store.

**HISTORY: 145 v H 687 (Eff 10-12-94); 146 v H 217 (Eff 11-1-95); 147 v H 210 (Eff 6-30-97); 147 v H 215. Eff 6-30-97.**

## § 4511.103 Rules for placement of tourist-oriented directional signs and trailblazer markers.

(A) The director of transportation, in accordance with 23 U.S.C. 109(d) and 315, with the provisions of the federal manual of uniform traffic control devices relating to tourist-oriented directional signs and trailblazer markers, and with Chapter 119. of the Revised Code, shall adopt rules to carry out a program for the placement of tourist-oriented directional signs and trailblazer markers within the rights-of-way of those portions of rural state highways that are not on the interstate system. The rules shall prohibit the placement of tourist-oriented directional signs and trailblazer markers at interchanges on state system expressways and freeways. The rules shall include, but need not be limited to, all of the following:

(1) The form of the application to participate in the program. The form shall include such necessary information as the director requires to ensure that a tourist-oriented activity for which signing is sought is an eligible attraction.

(2) Provisions for covering or otherwise obscuring signs during off-seasons for eligible attractions that operate on a seasonal basis;

(3) A determination as to the circumstances that justify including on a sign the hours of operation of an eligible attraction;

(4) Criteria for use of the signs at at-grade intersections on expressways.

(B) The program established pursuant to division (A) of this section may be operated, maintained, and marketed either by the department of transportation or by any private person with whom the director, in accordance with rules adopted by the director pursuant to Chapter 119. of the Revised Code, contracts for the operation, maintenance, and marketing. The rules shall describe the terms of the contract and shall allow for a reasonable profit to be made by the successful applicant. In awarding the contract, the director shall consider the skill, expertise, prior experience, and other qualifications of each applicant.

(C) All direct and indirect costs of the program shall be fully paid by the eligible attractions that participate in the program. The director shall develop a fee schedule for participation in the program, and shall charge each program participant the appropriate fee. Direct and indirect costs include, but are not limited to, the cost of all of the following:

(1) Capital;

(2) Insurance;

(3) Directional signs, sign blanks, and posts, and the design, engineering, installation, repair, replacement, and removal of directional signs and posts;

(4) Program administration.

**HISTORY: 145 v H 687 (Eff 10-12-94); 146 v H 217. Eff 11-1-95.**

## § 4511.104 Advertising agreement with tourist-oriented attractions.

(A) The operator of any tourist-oriented activity who wishes to participate in the tourist-oriented directional sign program established under sections 4511.102 [4511.10.2] to 4511.105 [4511.10.5] of the Revised Code shall forward a completed application, as provided in section 4511.103 [4511.10.3] of the Revised Code, to the director of transportation or person holding a contract under division (B) of section 4511.103 [4511.10.3] of the Revised Code. If the director or person finds the application to be complete and determines that the activity constitutes an eligible attraction, the director or person shall so notify the applicant in writing. Upon receipt of the notice, the applicant shall forward to the director or person, in a manner determined by the director, the amount of the fee due and thereupon shall execute an advertising agreement in a form prescribed by the director.

(B) The operator of any eligible attraction for which an advertising agreement is in effect under this section immediately shall forward the advertising agreement to the director or person holding a contract under division (B) of section 4511.103 [4511.10.3] of the Revised Code for cancellation if the eligible attraction ceases to be such an attraction.

(C) The director, when having reasonable cause to believe that an eligible attraction for which an advertising agreement is in effect has ceased to be such an attraction, immediately and without conducting an adjudication shall issue an order canceling the advertising agreement and forward notice of the cancellation in writing to the operator of the attraction together with information that the cancellation may be appealed in accordance with section 119.12 of the Revised Code. If no appeal is entered within the period specified in that section or if an appeal is entered but cancellation of the advertising agreement subsequently is affirmed, the director shall order the removal of the signs relating to the former eligible attraction.

(D) Any person holding a contract under division (B) of section 4511.103 [4511.10.3] of the Revised Code, when having reasonable cause to believe that an eligible attraction for which an advertising agreement is in effect has ceased to be such an attraction, immediately shall notify the director in writing of that fact. Upon receipt of the notice, the director shall proceed in accordance with division (C) of this section.

**HISTORY: 145 v H 687 (Eff 10-12-94); 146 v H 217. Eff 11-1-95.**

## § 4511.105 Signs to conform to federal manual; logos.

Tourist-oriented directional signs shall conform to the specifications contained in the federal manual of uniform traffic control devices.

If more than one eligible attraction requires a sign at the same location, multiple signs may be combined on the same panel in accordance with the federal manual of uniform traffic control devices.

Advance signing may be installed in those situations where sight distance, intersection vehicle maneuvers, or other vehicle operating characteristics require advance notice of an eligible attraction in order to reduce vehicle conflicts and improve highway safety.

The design, arrangement, size, and location of tourist-oriented directional signs, including advance signs and trailblazer markers, authorized under sections 4511.102 [4511.10.2] to 4511.105 [4511.10.5] of the Revised Code shall conform to the applicable specifications contained in the federal manual of uniform traffic control devices.

**HISTORY: 145 v H 687 (Eff 10-12-94); 146 v H 217. Eff 11-1-95.**

## § 4511.106 Local authority programs.

The legislative authority of a local authority may adopt a resolution establishing a program for the placement of tourist-oriented directional signs and trailblazer markers within the rights-of-way of streets and highways under its jurisdiction. Any program established under this section shall conform to the rules and specifications contained in the program established by the director of transportation pursuant to sections 4511.102 [4511.10.2] to 4511.105 [4511.10.5] of the Revised Code and the applicable provisions of the federal manual of uniform traffic control devices. If a local authority establishes a program under this section, the local authority may request guidance from the department of transportation in structuring, implementing, and administering its program, but the local authority is solely responsible for the structure and actual implementation and administration of its program, including, but not limited to, the evaluation and review of applications to participate in the local program and the execution of advertising agreements with eligible attractions.

**HISTORY: 145 v H 687 (Eff 10-12-94); 146 v H 217. Eff 11-1-95.**

## § 4511.107 Acquisition of outdoor advertising devices.

The department of transportation shall not enter into any program to purchase or acquire any outdoor advertising device for which a valid permit has been issued by this state, except in cases of eminent domain involving an appropriation pursuant to Chapter 163. of the Revised Code, unless the purchase or acquisition program is first approved by the general assembly.

**HISTORY: 145 v H 687. Eff 10-12-94.**

## § 4511.108 Traffic generator sign program.

The director of transportation shall adopt rules under Chapter 119. of the Revised Code to establish a traffic generator sign program and shall set forth in the traffic engineering manual the specifications for a uniform system of traffic generator signs and the criteria for participation in the program. The director shall establish, and may revise at any time, an annual fee to be charged for participation in the traffic generator sign program. Money paid by the qualifying program participants shall be deposited into the state treasury to the credit of the highway operating fund.

The director may contract with any person that applies to operate, construct, maintain, or market the traffic generator sign program. The contract may allow for a reasonable profit to be earned by the successful applicant. In awarding the contract, the director may consider the skill, expertise, prior experience, and other qualifications of each applicant.

If the director determines that the department shall operate this program, all money collected from program participants shall be deposited and credited as prescribed in this section.

**HISTORY: 153 v H 2, § 101.01, eff. 7-1-09; 2011 HB 114, § 101.01, eff. June 29, 2011.**

Acts 2011, HB 114, § 806.10 provides: "The items of law contained in this act, and their applications, are severable. If any item of law contained in this act, or if any application of any item of law contained in this act, is held invalid, the invalidity does not affect other items of law contained in this act and their applications that can be given effect without the invalid item or application."

The effective date is set by § 812.10 of 153 v H 2.

**Publisher's Note:**

The enactment of RC § 4511.108 by 153 v H 2 was disapproved in part by the Governor.

## § 4511.11 Uniformity of traffic control devices.

(A) Local authorities in their respective jurisdictions shall place and maintain traffic control devices in accordance with the department of transportation manual and specifications for a uniform system of traffic control devices, adopted under section 4511.09 of the Revised Code, upon highways under their jurisdiction as are necessary to indicate and to carry out sections 4511.01 to 4511.76 and 4511.99 of the Revised Code, local traffic ordinances, or to regulate, warn, or guide traffic.

(B) The director of transportation may require to be removed any traffic control device that does not conform to the manual and specifications for a uniform system of traffic control devices on the extensions of the state highway system within municipal corporations.

(C) No village shall place or maintain any traffic control signal upon an extension of the state highway system within the village without first obtaining the permission of the director. The director may revoke the permission and may require to be removed any traffic control signal that has been erected without the director's permission on an extension of a state highway within a village, or that, if erected under a permit granted by the director, does not conform to the state manual and specifications, or that is not operated in accordance with the terms of the permit.

(D) All traffic control devices erected on a public road, street, or alley, shall conform to the state manual and specifications.

(E) No person, firm, or corporation shall sell or offer for sale to local authorities any traffic control device that does not conform to the state manual and specifications, except by permission of the director.

(F) No local authority shall purchase or manufacture any traffic control device that does not conform to the state manual and specifications, except by permission of the director.

(G) Whoever violates division (E) of this section is guilty of a misdemeanor of the third degree.

**HISTORY: GC § 6307-11; 119 v 766, § 11; 121 v 684; Bureau of Code Revision, 10-1-53; 130 v 1081 (Eff 10-14-63); 130 v PtII, H 5 (Eff 12-16-64); 131 v 1100 (Eff 11-1-65); 135 v H 200 (Eff 9-28-73); 143 v H 258 (Eff 11-2-89); 143 v H 162. Eff 6-28-90; 149 v S 123, § 1, eff. 1-1-04.**

The effective date is set by section 4 of S.B. 123.

See provisions, § 5 of S.B. 123 (149 v —), following RC § 4501.01.

## § 4511.12 Obeying traffic control devices.

(A) No pedestrian, driver of a vehicle, or operator of a streetcar or trackless trolley shall disobey the instructions of any traffic control device placed in accordance with this chapter, unless at the time otherwise directed by a police officer.

No provision of this chapter for which signs are required shall be enforced against an alleged violator if at the time and place of the alleged violation an official sign is not in proper position and sufficiently legible to be seen by an ordinarily observant person. Whenever a particular section of this chapter does not state that signs are required, that section shall be effective even though no signs are erected or in place.

(B) Except as otherwise provided in this division, whoever violates this section is guilty of a minor misdemeanor. If, within one year of the offense, the offender previously has been convicted of or pleaded guilty to one predicate motor vehicle or traffic offense, whoever violates this section is guilty of a misdemeanor of the fourth degree. If, within one year of the offense, the offender previously has been convicted of two or more predicate motor vehicle or traffic offenses, whoever violates this section is guilty of a misdemeanor of the third degree.

**HISTORY: GC § 6307-12; 119 v 766, § 12; 124 v 514; Bureau of Code Revision, 10-1-53; 143 v H 258. Eff 11-2-89; 149 v S 123, § 1, eff. 1-1-04.**

The effective date is set by section 4 of S.B. 123.

See provisions, § 5 of S.B. 123 (149 v —), following RC § 4501.01.

## § 4511.121 Compliance at scale locations by operator of commercial motor vehicle.

(A)(1) Except as provided in division (B) of this section, any operator of a commercial motor vehicle, upon approaching a scale location established for the purpose of determining the weight of the vehicle and its load, shall comply with any traffic control device or the order of a peace officer directing the vehicle to proceed to be weighed or otherwise inspected.

(2) Any operator of a commercial motor vehicle, upon bypassing a scale location in accordance with division (B) of this section, shall comply with an order of a peace officer to stop the vehicle to verify the use and operation of an electronic clearance device.

(B) Any operator of a commercial motor vehicle that is equipped with an electronic clearance device authorized by the superintendent of the state highway patrol under section 4549.081 [4549.08.1] of the Revised Code may bypass a scale location, regardless of the instruction of a traffic control device to enter the scale facility, if either of the following apply:

(1) The in-cab transponder displays a green light or other affirmative visual signal and also sounds an affirmative audible signal;

(2) Any other criterion established by the superintendent by rule is met.

(C) Any peace officer may order the operator of a commercial motor vehicle that bypasses a scale location to stop the vehicle to verify the use and operation of an electronic clearance device.

(D) Whoever violates division (A) of this section is guilty of a minor misdemeanor. If, within one year of the offense, the offender previously has been convicted of or pleaded guilty to a violation of division (A) of this section, whoever violates that division is guilty of a misdemeanor of the fourth degree. If, within one year of the offense, the offender previously has been convicted of or pleaded guilty to two or more violations of division (A) of this section, whoever violates division (A) is guilty of a misdemeanor of the third degree.

(E) As used in this section and in section 4549.081 [4549.08.1] of the Revised Code, "commercial motor vehicle" means any combination of vehicles with a gross vehicle weight rating or an actual gross vehicle weight of more than ten thousand pounds if the vehicle is used in interstate or intrastate commerce to transport property and also means any vehicle that is transporting hazardous materials for which placarding is required pursuant to 49 C.F.R. Parts 100 to 180.

**HISTORY: 150 v H 230, § 1, eff. 9-16-04.**

## § 4511.13 Signal lights.

Whenever traffic is controlled by traffic control signals exhibiting different colored lights, or colored lighted arrows, successively one at a time or in combination, only the colors green, red, and yellow shall be used, except for special pedestrian signals carrying words or symbols, and said lights shall indicate and apply to drivers of vehicles, streetcars, and trackless trolleys, and to pedestrians as follows:

(A) Green indication:

(1) Vehicular traffic, streetcars, and trackless trolleys facing a circular green signal may proceed straight through or turn right or left unless a sign at such place prohibits either such turn. But vehicular traffic, streetcars, and trackless trolleys, including vehicles, streetcars, and trackless trolleys turning right or left, shall yield the right-of-way to other vehicles, streetcars, trackless trolleys, and pedestrians lawfully within the intersection or an adjacent crosswalk at the time such signal is exhibited.

(2) Vehicular traffic, streetcars, and trackless trolleys facing a green arrow signal, shown alone or in combination with another indication, may cautiously enter the intersection only to make the movement indicated by such arrow, or such other movement as is permitted by other indications shown at the same time. Such vehicular traffic, streetcars, and trackless trolleys shall yield the right-of-way to pedestrians lawfully within an adjacent crosswalk and to other traffic lawfully using the intersection.

(3) Unless otherwise directed by a pedestrian-control signal, as provided in section 4511.14 of the Revised Code, pedestrians facing any green signal, except when the sole green signal is a turn arrow, may proceed across the roadway within any marked or unmarked crosswalk.

(B) Steady yellow indication:

(1) Vehicular traffic, streetcars, and trackless trolleys facing a steady circular yellow or yellow arrow signal are thereby warned that the related green movement is being terminated or that a red indication will be exhibited immediately thereafter when vehicular traffic, streetcars, and trackless trolleys shall not enter the intersection.

(2) Pedestrians facing a steady circular yellow or yellow arrow signal, unless otherwise directed by a pedestrian-control signal as provided in section 4511.14 of the Revised Code, are thereby advised that there is insufficient time to cross the roadway before a red indication is shown and no pedestrian shall then start to cross the roadway.

(C) Steady red indication:

(1) Vehicular traffic, streetcars, and trackless trolleys facing a steady red signal alone shall stop at a clearly marked stop line, but if none, before entering the crosswalk on the near side of the intersection, or if none, then before entering the intersection and shall remain standing until an indication to proceed is shown except as provided in divisions (C)(2) and (3) of this section.

(2) Unless a sign is in place prohibiting a right turn as provided in division (C)(5) of this section, vehicular traffic, streetcars, and trackless trolleys facing a steady red signal may cautiously enter the intersection to make a right turn after stopping as required by division (C)(1) of this section. Such vehicular traffic, streetcars, and trackless trolleys shall yield the right-of-way to pedestrians lawfully within an adjacent crosswalk and to other traffic lawfully using the intersection.

(3) Unless a sign is in place prohibiting a left turn as provided in division (C)(5) of this section, vehicular traffic, streetcars, and trackless trolleys facing a steady red signal on a one-way street that intersects another one-way street on which traffic moves to the left may cautiously enter the intersection to make a left turn into the one-way street after stopping as required by division (C)(1) of this section, and yielding the right-of-way to pedestrians lawfully within an adjacent crosswalk and to other traffic lawfully using the intersection.

(4) Unless otherwise directed by a pedestrian-control signal as provided in section 4511.14 of the Revised Code, pedestrians facing a steady red signal alone shall not enter the roadway.

(5) Local authorities may by ordinance, or the director of transportation on state highways may, prohibit a right or a left turn against a steady red signal at any intersection, which shall be effective when signs giving notice thereof are posted at the intersection.

(D) In the event an official traffic-control signal is erected and maintained at a place other than an intersection, the provisions of this section shall be applicable except as to those provisions which by their nature can have no application. Any stop required shall be made at a sign or marking on the pavement indicating where the stop shall be made, but in the absence of any such sign or marking the stop shall be made at the signal.

**HISTORY: GC § 6307-13; 119 v 766, § 13; 124 v 514; Bureau of Code Revision, 10-1-53; 130 v 1081 (Eff 8-9-63); 135 v S 263 (Eff 7-3-74); 135 v H 99 (Eff 7-1-75); 137 v H 171 (Eff 8-26-77); 140 v H 703. Eff 3-28-85.**

## § 4511.131 Signals over reversible lanes.

When lane-use control signals are placed over individual lanes of a street or highway, said signals shall indicate and apply to drivers of vehicles and trackless trolleys as follows:

(A) A steady downward green arrow:
Vehicular traffic and trackless trolleys may travel in any lane over which a green arrow signal is shown.
(B) A steady yellow "X":
Vehicular traffic and trackless trolleys are warned to vacate in a safe manner any lane over which such signal is shown to avoid occupying that lane when a steady red "X" signal is shown.
(C) A flashing yellow "X":
Vehicular traffic and trackless trolleys may use with proper caution any lane over which such signal is shown for only the purpose of making a left turn.
(D) A steady red "X".
Vehicular traffic and trackless trolleys shall not enter or travel in any lane over which such signal is shown.

**HISTORY: 130 v 1083 (Eff 8-9-63); 135 v S 263. Eff 7-3-74.**

## § 4511.132 Malfunctioning traffic signals.

(A) The driver of a vehicle, streetcar, or trackless trolley who approaches an intersection where traffic is controlled by traffic control signals shall do all of the following, if the signal facing the driver either exhibits no colored lights or colored lighted arrows or exhibits a combination of such lights or arrows that fails to clearly indicate the assignment of right-of-way:
(1) Stop at a clearly marked stop line, but if none, stop before entering the crosswalk on the near side of the intersection, or, if none, stop before entering the intersection;
(2) Yield the right-of-way to all vehicles, streetcars, or trackless trolleys in the intersection or approaching on an intersecting road, if the vehicles, streetcars, or trackless trolleys will constitute an immediate hazard during the time the driver is moving across or within the intersection or junction of roadways;
(3) Exercise ordinary care while proceeding through the intersection.
(B) Except as otherwise provided in this division, whoever violates this section is guilty of a minor misdemeanor. If, within one year of the offense, the offender previously has been convicted of or pleaded guilty to one predicate motor vehicle or traffic offense, whoever violates this section is guilty of a misdemeanor of the fourth degree. If, within one year of the offense, the offender previously has been convicted of two or more predicate motor vehicle or traffic offenses, whoever violates this section is guilty of a misdemeanor of the third degree.

**HISTORY: 143 v S 44. Eff 7-25-89; 149 v S 123, § 1, eff. 1-1-04.**

The effective date is set by section 4 of S.B. 123.
See provisions, § 5 of S.B. 123 (149 v —), following RC § 4501.01.

## § 4511.14 Pedestrian control signals.

Whenever special pedestrian control signals exhibiting the words "walk" or "don't walk," or the symbol of a walking person or an upraised palm are in place, such signals shall indicate the following instructions:
(A) "Walk" or the symbol of a walking person: Pedestrians facing such signal may proceed across the roadway in the direction of the signal and shall be given the right of way by the operators of all vehicles, streetcars, and trackless trolleys.
(B) "Don't walk" or the symbol of an upraised palm: No pedestrian shall start to cross the roadway in the direction of the signal.
(C) Nothing in this section shall be construed to invalidate the continued use of pedestrian control signals utilizing the word "wait" if those signals were installed prior to the effective date of this act.

**HISTORY: GC § 6307-14; 119 v 766, § 14; 124 v 514; Bureau of Code Revision, 10-1-53; 140 v H 703. Eff 3-28-85.**

## § 4511.15 Flashing traffic signals.

Whenever an illuminated flashing red or yellow traffic signal is used in a traffic signal or with a traffic sign it shall require obedience as follows:
(A) Flashing red stop signal: Operators of vehicles, trackless trolleys, and streetcars shall stop at a clearly marked stop line, but if none, before entering the crosswalk on the near side of the intersection, or if none, then at the point nearest the intersecting roadway where the driver has a view of approaching traffic on the intersecting roadway before entering it, and the right to proceed shall be subject to the rules applicable after making a stop at a stop sign.
(B) Flashing yellow caution signal: Operators of vehicles, trackless trolleys, and streetcars may proceed through the intersection or past such signal only with caution.
This section shall not apply at railroad grade crossings. Conduct of drivers of vehicles, trackless trolleys, and streetcars approaching railroad grade crossings shall be governed by sections 4511.61 and 4511.62 of the Revised Code.

**HISTORY: GC § 6307-15; 119 v 766, § 15; Bureau of Code Revision, 10-1-53; 135 v H 995. Eff 1-1-75.**

The effective date is set by section 3 of HB 995.

## § 4511.16 Prohibition against unauthorized signs and signals.

(A) No person shall place, maintain, or display upon or in view of any highway any unauthorized sign, signal, marking, or device which purports to be, is an imitation of, or resembles a traffic control device or railroad sign or signal, or which attempts to direct the movement of traffic or hides from view or interferes with the effectiveness of any traffic control device or any railroad sign or signal, and no person shall place or maintain, nor shall any public authority permit, upon any highway any traffic sign or signal bearing thereon any commercial advertising. This section does not prohibit either the erection upon private property adjacent to highways of signs giving useful directional information and of a type that cannot be mistaken for traffic control devices or the erection upon private property of traffic control devices by the owner of real property in accordance with sections 4511.211 and 4511.432 of the Revised Code.
Every such prohibited sign, signal, marking, or device is a public nuisance, and the authority having jurisdiction over the highway may remove it or cause it to be removed.
(B) Except as otherwise provided in this division, whoever violates this section is guilty of a minor misdemeanor. If, within one year of the offense, the offender previously has been convicted of or pleaded guilty to one predicate motor vehicle or traffic offense, whoever violates this

section is guilty of a misdemeanor of the fourth degree. If, within one year of the offense, the offender previously has been convicted of two or more predicate motor vehicle or traffic offenses, whoever violates this section is guilty of a misdemeanor of the third degree.

**HISTORY: GC § 6307-16; 119 v 766, § 16; Bureau of Code Revision, 10-1-53; 143 v H 171. Eff 5-31-90; 149 v S 123, § 1, eff. 1-1-04.**

The effective date is set by section 4 of S.B. 123.
See provisions, § 5 of S.B. 123 (149 v —), following RC § 4501.01.

## § 4511.17 Tampering with sign, device or manhole cover; driving on freshly applied marking material.

(A) No person, without lawful authority, shall do any of the following:
(1) Knowingly move, deface, damage, destroy, or otherwise improperly tamper with any traffic control device, any railroad sign or signal, or any inscription, shield, or insignia on the device, sign, or signal, or any part of the device, sign, or signal;
(2) Knowingly drive upon or over any freshly applied pavement marking material on the surface of a roadway while the marking materiel is in an undried condition and is marked by flags, markers, signs, or other devices intended to protect it;
(3) Knowingly move, damage, destroy, or otherwise improperly tamper with a manhole cover.
(B)(1) Except as otherwise provided in this division, whoever violates division (A)(1) or (3) of this section is guilty of a misdemeanor of the third degree. If a violation of division (A)(1) or (3) of this section creates a risk of physical harm to any person, the offender is guilty of a misdemeanor of the first degree. If a violation of division (A)(1) or (3) of this section causes serious physical harm to property that is owned, leased, or controlled by a state or local authority, the offender is guilty of a felony of the fifth degree.
(2) Except as otherwise provided in this division, whoever violates division (A)(2) of this section is guilty of a minor misdemeanor. If, within one year of the offense, the offender previously has been convicted of or pleaded guilty to one predicate motor vehicle or traffic offense, whoever violates division (A)(2) of this section is guilty of a misdemeanor of the fourth degree. If, within one year of the offense, the offender previously has been convicted of two or more predicate motor vehicle or traffic offenses, whoever violates division (A)(2) of this section is guilty of a misdemeanor of the third degree.

**HISTORY: GC § 6307-17; 119 v 766, § 17; 121 v 684; Bureau of Code Revision, 10-1-53; 143 v H 162. Eff 6-28-90; 149 v S 123, § 1, eff. 1-1-04.**

The effective date is set by section 4 of S.B. 123.
See provisions, § 5 of S.B. 123 (149 v —), following RC § 4501.01.

## § 4511.18 Possession or sale of sign or device prohibited.

(A) As used in this section, "traffic control device" means any sign, traffic control signal, or other device conforming to and placed or erected in accordance with the manual adopted under section 4511.09 of the Revised Code by authority of a public body or official having jurisdiction, for the purpose of regulating, warning, or guiding traffic, including signs denoting the names of streets and highways, but does not mean any pavement marking.
(B) No individual shall buy or otherwise possess, or sell, a traffic control device, except when one of the following applies:
(1) In the course of the individual's employment by the state or a local authority for the express or implied purpose of manufacturing, providing, erecting, moving, or removing such a traffic control device;
(2) In the course of the individual's employment by any manufacturer of traffic control devices other than a state or local authority;
(3) For the purpose of demonstrating the design and function of a traffic control device to state or local officials;
(4) When the traffic control device has been purchased from the state or a local authority at a sale of property that is no longer needed or is unfit for use;
(5) The traffic control device has been properly purchased from a manufacturer for use on private property and the person possessing the device has a sales receipt for the device or other acknowledgment of sale issued by the manufacturer.
(C) This section does not preclude, and shall not be construed as precluding, prosecution for theft in violation of section 2913.02 of the Revised Code or a municipal ordinance relating to theft, or for receiving stolen property in violation of section 2913.51 of the Revised Code or a municipal ordinance relating to receiving stolen property.
(D) Whoever violates this section is guilty of a misdemeanor of the third degree.

**HISTORY: 143 v H 162. Eff 6-28-90; 149 v S 123, § 1, eff. 1-1-04.**

The effective date is set by section 4 of S.B. 123.
See provisions, § 5 of S.B. 123 (149 v —), following RC § 4501.01.
**Not analogous to former RC § 4511.18 (GC § 6307-18; 119 v 766; Bureau of Code Revision, 10-1-53; 132 v S 37), repealed 134 v H 511, § 2, eff 1-1-74.**

### [DRIVING WHILE INTOXICATED]

## § 4511.181 Definitions.

As used in sections 4511.181 [4511.18.1] to 4511.198 [4511.19.8] of the Revised Code:
(A) "Equivalent offense" means any of the following:
(1) A violation of division (A) or (B) of section 4511.19 of the Revised Code;
(2) A violation of a municipal OVI ordinance;
(3) A violation of section 2903.04 of the Revised Code in a case in which the offender was subject to the sanctions described in division (D) of that section;
(4) A violation of division (A)(1) of section 2903.06 or 2903.08 of the Revised Code or a municipal ordinance that is substantially equivalent to either of those divisions;
(5) A violation of division (A)(2), (3), or (4) of section 2903.06, division (A)(2) of section 2903.08, or former section 2903.07 of the Revised Code, or a municipal ordinance that is substantially equivalent to any of those divisions or that former section, in a case in which a judge or jury as the trier of fact found that the offender was under the influence of alcohol, a drug of abuse, or a combination of them;

(6) A violation of division (A) or (B) of section 1547.11 of the Revised Code;

(7) A violation of a municipal ordinance prohibiting a person from operating or being in physical control of any vessel underway or from manipulating any water skis, aquaplane, or similar device on the waters of this state while under the influence of alcohol, a drug of abuse, or a combination of them or prohibiting a person from operating or being in physical control of any vessel underway or from manipulating any water skis, aquaplane, or similar device on the waters of this state with a prohibited concentration of alcohol, a controlled substance, or a metabolite of a controlled substance in the whole blood, blood serum or plasma, breath, or urine;

(8) A violation of an existing or former municipal ordinance, law of another state, or law of the United States that is substantially equivalent to division (A) or (B) of section 4511.19 or division (A) or (B) of section 1547.11 of the Revised Code;

(9) A violation of a former law of this state that was substantially equivalent to division (A) or (B) of section 4511.19 or division (A) or (B) of section 1547.11 of the Revised Code.

(B) "Mandatory jail term" means the mandatory term in jail of three, six, ten, twenty, thirty, or sixty days that must be imposed under division (G)(1)(a), (b), or (c) of section 4511.19 of the Revised Code upon an offender convicted of a violation of division (A) of that section and in relation to which all of the following apply:

(1) Except as specifically authorized under section 4511.19 of the Revised Code, the term must be served in a jail.

(2) Except as specifically authorized under section 4511.19 of the Revised Code, the term cannot be suspended, reduced, or otherwise modified pursuant to sections 2929.21 to 2929.28 or any other provision of the Revised Code.

(C) "Municipal OVI ordinance" and "municipal OVI offense" mean any municipal ordinance prohibiting a person from operating a vehicle while under the influence of alcohol, a drug of abuse, or a combination of them or prohibiting a person from operating a vehicle with a prohibited concentration of alcohol, a controlled substance, or a metabolite of a controlled substance in the whole blood, blood serum or plasma, breath, or urine.

(D) "Community residential sanction," "continuous alcohol monitoring," "jail," "mandatory prison term," "mandatory term of local incarceration," "sanction," and "prison term" have the same meanings as in section 2929.01 of the Revised Code.

(E) "Drug of abuse" has the same meaning as in section 4506.01 of the Revised Code.

(F) "Equivalent offense that is vehicle-related" means an equivalent offense that is any of the following:

(1) A violation described in division (A)(1), (2), (3), (4), or (5) of this section;

(2) A violation of an existing or former municipal ordinance, law of another state, or law of the United States that is substantially equivalent to division (A) or (B) of section 4511.19 of the Revised Code;

(3) A violation of a former law of this state that was substantially equivalent to division (A) or (B) of section 4511.19 of the Revised Code.

**HISTORY: 149 v S 123, § 1, eff. 1-1-04; 149 v H 490, § 1, eff. 1-1-04; 151 v S 8, § 1, eff. 8-17-06; 152 v H 562, § 101.01, eff. 9-23-08; 152 v S 17, § 1, eff. 9-30-08; 153 v H 2, § 101.01, eff. 7-1-09.**

The effective date is set by § 812.10 of 153 v H 2.

The provisions of § 815.20 of 153 v H 2 read in part as follows:

SECTION 815.20. The General Assembly, applying the principle stated in division (B) of section 1.52 of the Revised Code that amendments are to be harmonized if reasonably capable of simultaneous operation, finds that the following sections, presented in this act as composites of the sections as amended by the acts indicated, are the resulting versions of the sections in effect prior to the effective date of the sections as presented in this act:

° ° °

Section 4511.181 of the Revised Code as amended by both Am. Sub. H.B. 562 and Am. Sub. S.B. 17 of the 127th General Assembly.

° ° °

The effective date is set by § 812.10 of 152 v H 562.

The effective date is set by section 4 of H.B. 490.

**Not analogous to former RC § 4511.181 (132 v S 37), repealed 134 v H 511, § 2, eff 1-1-74.**

See provisions, § 5 of S.B. 123 (149 v —), following RC § 4501.01.

This section concerned homicide by vehicle in the first degree. See RC §§ 2903.06 and 2903.07 concerning vehicular homicide.

## § 4511.19 Operation while under the influence of alcohol or drug of abuse or with specified concentration of alcohol or drug in certain bodily substances; chemical test; penalties; underage alcohol consumption.

(A)(1) No person shall operate any vehicle, streetcar, or trackless trolley within this state, if, at the time of the operation, any of the following apply:

(a) The person is under the influence of alcohol, a drug of abuse, or a combination of them.

(b) The person has a concentration of eight-hundredths of one per cent or more but less than seventeen-hundredths of one per cent by weight per unit volume of alcohol in the person's whole blood.

(c) The person has a concentration of ninety-six-thousandths of one per cent or more but less than two hundred four-thousandths of one per cent by weight per unit volume of alcohol in the person's blood serum or plasma.

(d) The person has a concentration of eight-hundredths of one gram or more but less than seventeen-hundredths of one gram by weight of alcohol per two hundred ten liters of the person's breath.

(e) The person has a concentration of eleven-hundredths of one gram or more but less than two hundred thirty-eight-thousandths of one gram by weight of alcohol per one hundred milliliters of the person's urine.

(f) The person has a concentration of seventeen-hundredths of one per cent or more by weight per unit volume of alcohol in the person's whole blood.

(g) The person has a concentration of two hundred four-thousandths of one per cent or more by weight per unit volume of alcohol in the person's blood serum or plasma.

(h) The person has a concentration of seventeen-hundredths of one gram or more by weight of alcohol per two hundred ten liters of the person's breath.

(i) The person has a concentration of two hundred thirty-eight-thousandths of one gram or more by weight of alcohol per one hundred milliliters of the person's urine.

(j) Except as provided in division (K) of this section, the person has a concentration of any of the following controlled substances or metabolites of a controlled substance in the person's whole blood, blood serum or plasma, or urine that equals or exceeds any of the following:

(i) The person has a concentration of amphetamine in the person's urine of at least five hundred nanograms of amphetamine per milliliter of the person's urine or has a concentration of amphetamine in the person's whole blood or blood serum or plasma of at least one hundred nanograms of amphetamine per milliliter of the person's whole blood or blood serum or plasma.

(ii) The person has a concentration of cocaine in the person's urine of at least one hundred fifty nanograms of cocaine per milliliter of the person's urine or has a concentration of cocaine in the person's whole blood or blood serum or plasma of at least fifty nanograms of cocaine per milliliter of the person's whole blood or blood serum or plasma.

(iii) The person has a concentration of cocaine metabolite in the person's urine of at least one hundred fifty nanograms of cocaine metabolite per milliliter of the person's urine or has a concentration of cocaine metabolite in the person's whole blood or blood serum or plasma of at least fifty nanograms of cocaine metabolite per milliliter of the person's whole blood or blood serum or plasma.

(iv) The person has a concentration of heroin in the person's urine of at least two thousand nanograms of heroin per milliliter of the person's urine or has a concentration of heroin in the person's whole blood or blood serum or plasma of at least fifty nanograms of heroin per milliliter of the person's whole blood or blood serum or plasma.

(v) The person has a concentration of heroin metabolite (6-monoacetyl morphine) in the person's urine of at least ten nanograms of heroin metabolite (6-monoacetyl morphine) per milliliter of the person's urine or has a concentration of heroin metabolite (6-monoacetyl morphine) in the person's whole blood or blood serum or plasma of at least ten nanograms of heroin metabolite (6-monoacetyl morphine) per milliliter of the person's whole blood or blood serum or plasma.

(vi) The person has a concentration of L.S.D. in the person's urine of at least twenty-five nanograms of L.S.D. per milliliter of the person's urine or a concentration of L.S.D. in the person's whole blood or blood serum or plasma of at least ten nanograms of L.S.D. per milliliter of the person's whole blood or blood serum or plasma.

(vii) The person has a concentration of marihuana in the person's urine of at least ten nanograms of marihuana per milliliter of the person's urine or has a concentration of marihuana in the person's whole blood or blood serum or plasma of at least two nanograms of marihuana per milliliter of the person's whole blood or blood serum or plasma.

(viii) Either of the following applies:

(I) The person is under the influence of alcohol, a drug of abuse, or a combination of them, and, as measured by gas chromatography mass spectrometry, the person has a concentration of marihuana metabolite in the person's urine of at least fifteen nanograms of marihuana metabolite per milliliter of the person's urine or has a concentration of marihuana metabolite in the person's whole blood or blood serum or plasma of at least five nanograms of marihuana metabolite per milliliter of the person's whole blood or blood serum or plasma.

(II) As measured by gas chromatography mass spectrometry, the person has a concentration of marihuana metabolite in the person's urine of at least thirty-five nanograms of marihuana metabolite per milliliter of the person's urine or has a concentration of marihuana metabolite in the person's whole blood or blood serum or plasma of at least fifty nanograms of marihuana metabolite per milliliter of the person's whole blood or blood serum or plasma.

(ix) The person has a concentration of methamphetamine in the person's urine of at least five hundred nanograms of methamphetamine per milliliter of the person's urine or has a concentration of methamphetamine in the person's whole blood or blood serum or plasma of at least one hundred nanograms of methamphetamine per milliliter of the person's whole blood or blood serum or plasma.

(x) The person has a concentration of phencyclidine in the person's urine of at least twenty-five nanograms of phencyclidine per milliliter of the person's urine or has a concentration of phencyclidine in the person's whole blood or blood serum or plasma of at least ten nanograms of phencyclidine per milliliter of the person's whole blood or blood serum or plasma.

(xi) The state board of pharmacy has adopted a rule pursuant to section 4729.041 of the Revised Code that specifies the amount of salvia divinorum and the amount of salvinorin A that constitute concentrations of salvia divinorum and salvinorin A in a person's urine, in a person's whole blood, or in a person's blood serum or plasma at or above which the person is impaired for purposes of operating any vehicle, streetcar, or trackless trolley within this state, the rule is in effect, and the person has a concentration of salvia divinorum or salvinorin A of at least that amount so specified by rule in the person's urine, in the person's whole blood, or in the person's blood serum or plasma.

(2) No person who, within twenty years of the conduct described in division (A)(2)(a) of this section, previously has been convicted of or pleaded guilty to a violation of this division, a violation of division (A)(1) or (B) of this section, or any other equivalent offense shall do both of the following:

(a) Operate any vehicle, streetcar, or trackless trolley within this state while under the influence of alcohol, a drug of abuse, or a combination of them;

(b) Subsequent to being arrested for operating the vehicle, streetcar, or trackless trolley as described in division (A)(2)(a) of this section, being asked by a law enforcement officer to submit to a chemical test or tests under section 4511.191 of the Revised Code, and being advised by the officer in accordance with section 4511.192 of the Revised Code of the consequences of the person's refusal or submission to the test or tests, refuse to submit to the test or tests.

(B) No person under twenty-one years of age shall operate any vehicle, streetcar, or trackless trolley within this state, if, at the time of the operation, any of the following apply:

(1) The person has a concentration of at least two-hundredths of one per cent but less than eight-hundredths of one per cent by weight per unit volume of alcohol in the person's whole blood.

(2) The person has a concentration of at least three-hundredths of one per cent but less than ninety-six-thousandths of one per cent by weight per unit volume of alcohol in the person's blood serum or plasma.

(3) The person has a concentration of at least two-hundredths of one gram but less than eight-hundredths of one gram by weight of alcohol per two hundred ten liters of the person's breath.

(4) The person has a concentration of at least twenty-eight one-thousandths of one gram but less than eleven-

hundredths of one gram by weight of alcohol per one hundred milliliters of the person's urine.

(C) In any proceeding arising out of one incident, a person may be charged with a violation of division (A)(1)(a) or (A)(2) and a violation of division (B)(1), (2), or (3) of this section, but the person may not be convicted of more than one violation of these divisions.

(D)(1)(a) In any criminal prosecution or juvenile court proceeding for a violation of division (A)(1)(a) of this section or for an equivalent offense that is vehicle-related, the result of any test of any blood or urine withdrawn and analyzed at any health care provider, as defined in section 2317.02 of the Revised Code, may be admitted with expert testimony to be considered with any other relevant and competent evidence in determining the guilt or innocence of the defendant.

(b) In any criminal prosecution or juvenile court proceeding for a violation of division (A) or (B) of this section or for an equivalent offense that is vehicle-related, the court may admit evidence on the concentration of alcohol, drugs of abuse, controlled substances, metabolites of a controlled substance, or a combination of them in the defendant's whole blood, blood serum or plasma, breath, urine, or other bodily substance at the time of the alleged violation as shown by chemical analysis of the substance withdrawn within three hours of the time of the alleged violation. The three-hour time limit specified in this division regarding the admission of evidence does not extend or affect the two-hour time limit specified in division (A) of section 4511.192 of the Revised Code as the maximum period of time during which a person may consent to a chemical test or tests as described in that section. The court may admit evidence on the concentration of alcohol, drugs of abuse, or a combination of them as described in this division when a person submits to a blood, breath, urine, or other bodily substance test at the request of a law enforcement officer under section 4511.191 of the Revised Code or a blood or urine sample is obtained pursuant to a search warrant. Only a physician, a registered nurse, an emergency medical technician-intermediate, an emergency medical technician-paramedic, or a qualified technician, chemist, or phlebotomist shall withdraw a blood sample for the purpose of determining the alcohol, drug, controlled substance, metabolite of a controlled substance, or combination content of the whole blood, blood serum, or blood plasma. This limitation does not apply to the taking of breath or urine specimens. A person authorized to withdraw blood under this division may refuse to withdraw blood under this division, if in that person's opinion, the physical welfare of the person would be endangered by the withdrawing of blood.

The bodily substance withdrawn under division (D)(1)(b) of this section shall be analyzed in accordance with methods approved by the director of health by an individual possessing a valid permit issued by the director pursuant to section 3701.143 of the Revised Code.

(c) As used in division (D)(1)(b) of this section, "emergency medical technician-intermediate" and "emergency medical technician-paramedic" have the same meanings as in section 4765.01 of the Revised Code.

(2) In a criminal prosecution or juvenile court proceeding for a violation of division (A) of this section or for an equivalent offense that is vehicle-related, if there was at the time the bodily substance was withdrawn a concentration of less than the applicable concentration of alcohol specified in divisions (A)(1)(b), (c), (d), and (e) of this section or less than the applicable concentration of a listed controlled substance or a listed metabolite of a controlled substance specified for a violation of division (A)(1)(j) of this section, that fact may be considered with other competent evidence in determining the guilt or innocence of the defendant. This division does not limit or affect a criminal prosecution or juvenile court proceeding for a violation of division (B) of this section or for an equivalent offense that is substantially equivalent to that division.

(3) Upon the request of the person who was tested, the results of the chemical test shall be made available to the person or the person's attorney, immediately upon the completion of the chemical test analysis.

If the chemical test was obtained pursuant to division (D)(1)(b) of this section, the person tested may have a physician, a registered nurse, or a qualified technician, chemist, or phlebotomist of the person's own choosing administer a chemical test or tests, at the person's expense, in addition to any administered at the request of a law enforcement officer. If the person was under arrest as described in division (A)(5) of section 4511.191 of the Revised Code, the arresting officer shall advise the person at the time of the arrest that the person may have an independent chemical test taken at the person's own expense. If the person was under arrest other than described in division (A)(5) of section 4511.191 of the Revised Code, the form to be read to the person to be tested, as required under section 4511.192 of the Revised Code, shall state that the person may have an independent test performed at the person's expense. The failure or inability to obtain an additional chemical test by a person shall not preclude the admission of evidence relating to the chemical test or tests taken at the request of a law enforcement officer.

(4)(a) As used in divisions (D)(4)(b) and (c) of this section, "national highway traffic safety administration" means the national highway traffic safety administration established as an administration of the United States department of transportation under 96 Stat. 2415 (1983), 49 U.S.C.A. 105.

(b) In any criminal prosecution or juvenile court proceeding for a violation of division (A) or (B) of this section, of a municipal ordinance relating to operating a vehicle while under the influence of alcohol, a drug of abuse, or alcohol and a drug of abuse, or of a municipal ordinance relating to operating a vehicle with a prohibited concentration of alcohol, a controlled substance, or a metabolite of a controlled substance in the whole blood, blood serum or plasma, breath, or urine, if a law enforcement officer has administered a field sobriety test to the operator of the vehicle involved in the violation and if it is shown by clear and convincing evidence that the officer administered the test in substantial compliance with the testing standards for any reliable, credible, and generally accepted field sobriety tests that were in effect at the time the tests were administered, including, but not limited to, any testing standards then in effect that were set by the national highway traffic safety administration, all of the following apply:

(i) The officer may testify concerning the results of the field sobriety test so administered.

(ii) The prosecution may introduce the results of the field sobriety test so administered as evidence in any proceedings in the criminal prosecution or juvenile court proceeding.

(iii) If testimony is presented or evidence is introduced under division (D)(4)(b)(i) or (ii) of this section and if the testimony or evidence is admissible under the Rules of Evidence, the court shall admit the testimony or evidence and the trier of fact shall give it whatever weight the trier of fact considers to be appropriate.

(c) Division (D)(4)(b) of this section does not limit or preclude a court, in its determination of whether the arrest of a person was supported by probable cause or its determination of any other matter in a criminal prosecution or juvenile court proceeding of a type described in that division, from considering evidence or testimony that is not otherwise disallowed by division (D)(4)(b) of this section.

(E)(1) Subject to division (E)(3) of this section, in any criminal prosecution or juvenile court proceeding for a violation of division (A)(1)(b), (c), (d), (e), (f), (g), (h), (i), or (j) or (B)(1), (2), (3), or (4) of this section or for an equivalent offense that is substantially equivalent to any of those divisions, a laboratory report from any laboratory personnel issued a permit by the department of health authorizing an analysis as described in this division that contains an analysis of the whole blood, blood serum or plasma, breath, urine, or other bodily substance tested and that contains all of the information specified in this division shall be admitted as prima-facie evidence of the information and statements that the report contains. The laboratory report shall contain all of the following:

(a) The signature, under oath, of any person who performed the analysis;

(b) Any findings as to the identity and quantity of alcohol, a drug of abuse, a controlled substance, a metabolite of a controlled substance, or a combination of them that was found;

(c) A copy of a notarized statement by the laboratory director or a designee of the director that contains the name of each certified analyst or test performer involved with the report, the analyst's or test performer's employment relationship with the laboratory that issued the report, and a notation that performing an analysis of the type involved is part of the analyst's or test performer's regular duties;

(d) An outline of the analyst's or test performer's education, training, and experience in performing the type of analysis involved and a certification that the laboratory satisfies appropriate quality control standards in general and, in this particular analysis, under rules of the department of health.

(2) Notwithstanding any other provision of law regarding the admission of evidence, a report of the type described in division (E)(1) of this section is not admissible against the defendant to whom it pertains in any proceeding, other than a preliminary hearing or a grand jury proceeding, unless the prosecutor has served a copy of the report on the defendant's attorney or, if the defendant has no attorney, on the defendant.

(3) A report of the type described in division (E)(1) of this section shall not be prima-facie evidence of the contents, identity, or amount of any substance if, within seven days after the defendant to whom the report pertains or the defendant's attorney receives a copy of the report, the defendant or the defendant's attorney demands the testimony of the person who signed the report. The judge in the case may extend the seven-day time limit in the interest of justice.

(F) Except as otherwise provided in this division, any physician, registered nurse, emergency medical technician-intermediate, emergency medical technician-paramedic, or qualified technician, chemist, or phlebotomist who withdraws blood from a person pursuant to this section or section 4511.191 or 4511.192 of the Revised Code, and any hospital, first-aid station, or clinic at which blood is withdrawn from a person pursuant to this section or section 4511.191 or 4511.192 of the Revised Code, is immune from criminal liability and civil liability based upon a claim of assault and battery or any other claim that is not a claim of malpractice, for any act performed in withdrawing blood from the person. The immunity provided in this division also extends to an emergency medical service organization that employs an emergency medical technician-intermediate or emergency medical technician-paramedic who withdraws blood under this section. The immunity provided in this division is not available to a person who withdraws blood if the person engages in willful or wanton misconduct.

As used in this division, "emergency medical technician-intermediate" and "emergency medical technician-paramedic" have the same meanings as in section 4765.01 of the Revised Code.

(G)(1) Whoever violates any provision of divisions (A)(1)(a) to (i) or (A)(2) of this section is guilty of operating a vehicle under the influence of alcohol, a drug of abuse, or a combination of them. Whoever violates division (A)(1)(j) of this section is guilty of operating a vehicle while under the influence of a listed controlled substance or a listed metabolite of a controlled substance. The court shall sentence the offender for either offense under Chapter 2929. of the Revised Code, except as otherwise authorized or required by divisions (G)(1)(a) to (e) of this section:

(a) Except as otherwise provided in division (G)(1)(b), (c), (d), or (e) of this section, the offender is guilty of a misdemeanor of the first degree, and the court shall sentence the offender to all of the following:

(i) If the sentence is being imposed for a violation of division (A)(1)(a), (b), (c), (d), (e), or (j) of this section, a mandatory jail term of three consecutive days. As used in this division, three consecutive days means seventy-two consecutive hours. The court may sentence an offender to both an intervention program and a jail term. The court may impose a jail term in addition to the three-day mandatory jail term or intervention program. However, in no case shall the cumulative jail term imposed for the offense exceed six months.

The court may suspend the execution of the three-day jail term under this division if the court, in lieu of that suspended term, places the offender under a community control sanction pursuant to section 2929.25 of the Revised Code and requires the offender to attend, for three consecutive days, a drivers' intervention program certified under section 3793.10 of the Revised Code. The court also may suspend the execution of any part of the three-day jail term under this division if it places the offender under a community control sanction pursuant to section 2929.25 of the Revised Code for part of the three days, requires the offender to attend for the suspended part of the term a drivers' intervention program so certified, and sentences the offender to a jail term equal to the remainder of the three consecutive days that the offender does not spend attending the program. The court may require the offender, as a condition of community control and in addition to the required attendance at a drivers' intervention program, to attend and satisfactorily complete any treatment or education programs that comply with the minimum standards adopted pursuant to Chapter 3793. of the Revised Code by the director of alcohol and drug addiction services that the operators of the drivers' intervention program determine that the offender should attend and to report periodically to the court on the offender's progress in the programs. The court also may impose on the offender any other conditions of community control that it considers necessary.

(ii) If the sentence is being imposed for a violation of division (A)(1)(f), (g), (h), or (i) or division (A)(2) of this section, except as otherwise provided in this division, a mandatory jail term of at least three consecutive days and a requirement that the offender attend, for three consecutive days, a drivers' intervention program that is certified pursuant to section 3793.10 of the Revised Code. As used in this division, three consecutive days means seventy-two consecutive hours. If the court determines that the offender is not conducive to treatment in a drivers' intervention program, if the offender refuses to attend a drivers' intervention program, or if the jail at which the offender is to serve the jail term imposed can provide a driver's intervention program, the court shall sentence the offender to a mandatory jail term of at least six consecutive days.

The court may require the offender, under a community control sanction imposed under section 2929.25 of the Revised Code, to attend and satisfactorily complete any treatment or education programs that comply with the minimum standards adopted pursuant to Chapter 3793. of the Revised Code by the director of alcohol and drug addiction services, in addition to the required attendance at drivers' intervention program, that the operators of the drivers' intervention program determine that the offender should attend and to report periodically to the court on the offender's progress in the programs. The court also may impose any other conditions of community control on the offender that it considers necessary.

(iii) In all cases, a fine of not less than three hundred seventy-five and not more than one thousand seventy-five dollars;

(iv) In all cases, a class five license suspension of the offender's driver's or commercial driver's license or permit or nonresident operating privilege from the range specified in division (A)(5) of section 4510.02 of the Revised Code. The court may grant limited driving privileges relative to the suspension under sections 4510.021 and 4510.13 of the Revised Code.

(b) Except as otherwise provided in division (G)(1)(e) of this section, an offender who, within six years of the offense, previously has been convicted of or pleaded guilty to one violation of division (A) or (B) of this section or one other equivalent offense is guilty of a misdemeanor of the first degree. The court shall sentence the offender to all of the following:

(i) If the sentence is being imposed for a violation of division (A)(1)(a), (b), (c), (d), (e), or (j) of this section, a mandatory jail term of ten consecutive days. The court shall impose the ten-day mandatory jail term under this division unless, subject to division (G)(3) of this section, it instead imposes a sentence under that division consisting of both a jail term and a term of house arrest with electronic monitoring, with continuous alcohol monitoring, or with both electronic monitoring and continuous alcohol monitoring. The court may impose a jail term in addition to the ten-day mandatory jail term. The cumulative jail term imposed for the offense shall not exceed six months.

In addition to the jail term or the term of house arrest with electronic monitoring or continuous alcohol monitoring or both types of monitoring and jail term, the court shall require the offender to be assessed by an alcohol and drug treatment program that is authorized by section 3793.02 of the Revised Code, subject to division (I) of this section, and shall order the offender to follow the treatment recommendations of the program. The purpose of the assessment is to determine the degree of the offender's alcohol usage and to determine whether or not treatment is warranted. Upon the request of the court, the program shall submit the results of the assessment to the court, including all treatment recommendations and clinical diagnoses related to alcohol use.

(ii) If the sentence is being imposed for a violation of division (A)(1)(f), (g), (h), or (i) or division (A)(2) of this section, except as otherwise provided in this division, a mandatory jail term of twenty consecutive days. The court shall impose the twenty-day mandatory jail term under this division unless, subject to division (G)(3) of this section, it instead imposes a sentence under that division consisting of both a jail term and a term of house arrest with electronic monitoring, with continuous alcohol monitoring, or with both electronic monitoring and continuous alcohol monitoring. The court may impose a jail term in addition to the twenty-day mandatory jail term. The cumulative jail term imposed for the offense shall not exceed six months.

In addition to the jail term or the term of house arrest with electronic monitoring or continuous alcohol monitoring or both types of monitoring and jail term, the court shall require the offender to be assessed by an alcohol and drug treatment program that is authorized by section 3793.02 of the Revised Code, subject to division (I) of this section, and shall order the offender to follow the treatment recommendations of the program. The purpose of the assessment is to determine the degree of the offender's alcohol usage and to determine whether or not treatment is warranted. Upon the request of the court, the program shall submit the results of the assessment to the court, including all treatment recommendations and clinical diagnoses related to alcohol use.

(iii) In all cases, notwithstanding the fines set forth in Chapter 2929. of the Revised Code, a fine of not less than five hundred twenty-five and not more than one thousand six hundred twenty-five dollars;

(iv) In all cases, a class four license suspension of the offender's driver's license, commercial driver's license, temporary instruction permit, probationary license, or nonresident operating privilege from the range specified in division (A)(4) of section 4510.02 of the Revised Code. The court may grant limited driving privileges relative to the suspension under sections 4510.021 and 4510.13 of the Revised Code.

(v) In all cases, if the vehicle is registered in the offender's name, immobilization of the vehicle involved in the offense for ninety days in accordance with section 4503.233 of the Revised Code and impoundment of the license plates of that vehicle for ninety days.

(c) Except as otherwise provided in division (G)(1)(e) of this section, an offender who, within six years of the offense, previously has been convicted of or pleaded guilty to two violations of division (A) or (B) of this section or other equivalent offenses is guilty of a misdemeanor. The court shall sentence the offender to all of the following:

(i) If the sentence is being imposed for a violation of division (A)(1)(a), (b), (c), (d), (e), or (j) of this section, a mandatory jail term of thirty consecutive days. The court shall impose the thirty-day mandatory jail term under this division unless, subject to division (G)(3) of this section, it instead imposes a sentence under that division consisting of both a jail term and a term of house arrest with electronic monitoring, with continuous alcohol monitoring, or with both electronic monitoring and continuous alcohol monitoring. The court may impose a jail term in addition to the thirty-day mandatory jail term. Notwithstanding the jail terms set forth in sections 2929.21 to 2929.28 of the Revised Code, the additional jail term shall not exceed one year, and the cumulative jail term imposed for the offense shall not exceed one year.

(ii) If the sentence is being imposed for a violation of division (A)(1)(f), (g), (h), or (i) or division (A)(2) of this section, a mandatory jail term of sixty consecutive days. The court shall impose the sixty-day mandatory jail term under this division unless, subject to division (G)(3) of this section, it instead imposes a sentence under that division consisting of both a jail term and a term of house arrest with electronic monitoring, with continuous alcohol monitoring, or with both electronic monitoring and continuous alcohol monitoring. The court may impose a jail term in addition to the sixty-day mandatory jail term. Notwithstanding the jail terms set forth in sections 2929.21 to 2929.28 of the Revised Code, the additional jail term shall not exceed one year, and the cumulative jail term imposed for the offense shall not exceed one year.

(iii) In all cases, notwithstanding the fines set forth in Chapter 2929. of the Revised Code, a fine of not less than eight hundred fifty and not more than two thousand seven hundred fifty dollars;

(iv) In all cases, a class three license suspension of the offender's driver's license, commercial driver's license, temporary instruction permit, probationary license, or nonresident operating privilege from the range specified in division (A)(3) of section 4510.02 of the Revised Code. The court may grant limited driving privileges relative to the suspension under sections 4510.021 and 4510.13 of the Revised Code.

(v) In all cases, if the vehicle is registered in the offender's name, criminal forfeiture of the vehicle involved in the offense in accordance with section 4503.234 of the Revised Code. Division (G)(6) of this section applies regarding any vehicle that is subject to an order of criminal forfeiture under this division.

(vi) In all cases, the court shall order the offender to participate in an alcohol and drug addiction program authorized by section 3793.02 of the Revised Code, subject to division (I) of this section, and shall order the offender to follow the treatment recommendations of the program. The operator of the program shall determine and assess the degree of the offender's alcohol dependency and shall make recommendations for treatment. Upon the request of the court, the program shall submit the results of the assessment to the court, including all treatment recommendations and clinical diagnoses related to alcohol use.

(d) Except as otherwise provided in division (G)(1)(e) of this section, an offender who, within six years of the offense, previously has been convicted of or pleaded guilty to three or four violations of division (A) or (B) of this section or other equivalent offenses or an offender who, within twenty years of the offense, previously has been convicted of or pleaded guilty to five or more violations of that nature is guilty of a felony of the fourth degree. The court shall sentence the offender to all of the following:

(i) If the sentence is being imposed for a violation of division (A)(1)(a), (b), (c), (d), (e), or (j) of this section, a mandatory prison term of one, two, three, four, or five years as required by and in accordance with division (G)(2) of section 2929.13 of the Revised Code if the offender also is convicted of or also pleads guilty to a specification of the type described in section 2941.1413 of the Revised Code or, in the discretion of the court, either a mandatory term of local incarceration of sixty consecutive days in accordance with division (G)(1) of section 2929.13 of the Revised Code or a mandatory prison term of sixty consecutive days in accordance with division (G)(2) of that section if the offender is not convicted of and does not plead guilty to a specification of that type. If the court imposes a mandatory term of local incarceration, it may impose a jail term in addition to the sixty-day mandatory term, the cumulative total of the mandatory term and the jail term for the offense shall not exceed one year, and, except as provided in division (A)(1) of section 2929.13 of the Revised Code, no prison term is authorized for the offense. If the court imposes a mandatory prison term, notwithstanding division (A)(4) of section 2929.14 of the Revised Code, it also may sentence the offender to a definite prison term that shall be not less than six months and not more than thirty months and the prison terms shall be imposed as described in division (G)(2) of section 2929.13 of the Revised Code. If the court imposes a mandatory prison term or mandatory prison term and additional prison term, in addition to the term or terms so imposed, the court also may sentence the offender to a community control sanction for the offense, but the offender shall serve all of the prison terms so imposed prior to serving the community control sanction.

(ii) If the sentence is being imposed for a violation of division (A)(1)(f), (g), (h), or (i) or division (A)(2) of this section, a mandatory prison term of one, two, three, four, or five years as required by and in accordance with division (G)(2) of section 2929.13 of the Revised Code if the offender also is convicted of or also pleads guilty to a specification of the type described in section 2941.1413 of the Revised Code or, in the discretion of the court, either a mandatory term of local incarceration of one hundred twenty consecutive days in accordance with division (G)(1) of section 2929.13 of the Revised Code or a mandatory prison term of one hundred twenty consecutive days in accordance with division (G)(2) of that section if the offender is not convicted of and does not plead guilty to a specification of that type. If the court imposes a mandatory term of local incarceration, it may impose a jail term in addition to the one hundred twenty-day mandatory term, the cumulative total of the mandatory term and the jail term for the offense shall not exceed one year, and, except as provided in division (A)(1) of section 2929.13 of the Revised Code, no prison term is authorized for the offense. If the court imposes a mandatory prison term, notwithstanding division (A)(4) of section 2929.14 of the Revised Code, it also may sentence the offender to a definite prison term that shall be not less than six months and not more than thirty months and the prison terms shall be imposed as described in division (G)(2) of section 2929.13 of the Revised Code. If the court imposes a mandatory prison term or mandatory prison term and additional prison term, in addition to the term or terms so imposed, the court also may sentence the offender to a community control sanction for the offense, but the offender shall serve all of the prison terms so imposed prior to serving the community control sanction.

(iii) In all cases, notwithstanding section 2929.18 of the Revised Code, a fine of not less than one thousand three hundred fifty nor more than ten thousand five hundred dollars;

(iv) In all cases, a class two license suspension of the offender's driver's license, commercial driver's license, temporary instruction permit, probationary license, or nonresident operating privilege from the range specified in division (A)(2) of section 4510.02 of the Revised Code. The court may grant limited driving privileges relative to the suspension under sections 4510.021 and 4510.13 of the Revised Code.

(v) In all cases, if the vehicle is registered in the offender's name, criminal forfeiture of the vehicle involved in the offense in accordance with section 4503.234 of the Revised Code. Division (G)(6) of this section applies regarding any vehicle that is subject to an order of criminal forfeiture under this division.

(vi) In all cases, the court shall order the offender to participate in an alcohol and drug addiction program authorized by section 3793.02 of the Revised Code, subject to division (I) of this section, and shall order the offender to follow the treatment recommendations of the program. The operator of the program shall determine and assess the degree of the offender's alcohol dependency and shall make recommendations for treatment. Upon the request of the court, the program shall submit the results of the assessment to the court, including all treatment recommendations and clinical diagnoses related to alcohol use.

(vii) In all cases, if the court sentences the offender to a mandatory term of local incarceration, in addition to the mandatory term, the court, pursuant to section 2929.17 of the Revised Code, may impose a term of house arrest with electronic monitoring. The term shall not commence until after the offender has served the mandatory term of local incarceration.

(e) An offender who previously has been convicted of or pleaded guilty to a violation of division (A) of this section that was a felony, regardless of when the violation and the conviction or guilty plea occurred, is guilty of a felony of the third degree. The court shall sentence the offender to all of the following:

(i) If the offender is being sentenced for a violation of division (A)(1)(a), (b), (c), (d), (e), or (j) of this section, a mandatory prison term of one, two, three, four, or five years as required by and in accordance with division (G)(2) of section 2929.13 of the Revised Code if the offender also is convicted of or also pleads guilty to a specification of the type described in section 2941.1413 of the Revised Code or a mandatory prison term of sixty consecutive days in accordance with division (G)(2) of section 2929.13 of the Revised Code if the offender is not convicted of and does not plead guilty to a specification of that type. The court may impose a prison term in addition to the mandatory prison term. The cumulative total of a sixty-day mandatory prison term and the additional prison term for the offense shall not exceed five years. In addition to the mandatory prison term or mandatory prison term and additional prison term the court imposes, the court also may sentence the offender to a community control sanction for the offense, but the offender shall serve all of the prison terms so imposed prior to serving the community control sanction.

(ii) If the sentence is being imposed for a violation of division (A)(1)(f), (g), (h), or (i) or division (A)(2) of this section, a mandatory prison term of one, two, three, four, or five years as required by and in accordance with division (G)(2) of section 2929.13 of the Revised Code if the offender also is convicted of or also pleads guilty to a specification of the type described in section 2941.1413 of the Revised Code or a mandatory prison term of one hundred twenty consecutive days in accordance with division (G)(2) of section 2929.13 of the Revised Code if the offender is not convicted of and does not plead guilty to a specification of that type. The court may impose a prison term in addition to the mandatory prison term. The cumulative total of a one hundred twenty-day mandatory prison term and the additional prison term for the offense shall not exceed five years. In addition to the mandatory prison term or mandatory prison term and additional prison term the court imposes, the court also may sentence the offender to a community control sanction for the offense, but the offender shall serve all of the prison terms so imposed prior to serving the community control sanction.

(iii) In all cases, notwithstanding section 2929.18 of the Revised Code, a fine of not less than one thousand three hundred fifty nor more than ten thousand five hundred dollars;

(iv) In all cases, a class two license suspension of the offender's driver's license, commercial driver's license, temporary instruction permit, probationary license, or nonresident operating privilege from the range specified in division (A)(2) of section 4510.02 of the Revised Code. The court may grant limited driving privileges relative to the suspension under sections 4510.021 and 4510.13 of the Revised Code.

(v) In all cases, if the vehicle is registered in the offender's name, criminal forfeiture of the vehicle involved in the offense in accordance with section 4503.234 of the Revised Code. Division (G)(6) of this section applies regarding any vehicle that is subject to an order of criminal forfeiture under this division.

(vi) In all cases, the court shall order the offender to participate in an alcohol and drug addiction program authorized by section 3793.02 of the Revised Code, subject to division (I) of this section, and shall order the offender to follow the treatment recommendations of the program. The operator of the program shall determine and assess the degree of the offender's alcohol dependency and shall make recommendations for treatment. Upon the request of the court, the program shall submit the results of the assessment to the court, including all treatment recommendations and clinical diagnoses related to alcohol use.

(2) An offender who is convicted of or pleads guilty to a violation of division (A) of this section and who subsequently seeks reinstatement of the driver's or occupational driver's license or permit or nonresident operating privilege suspended under this section as a result of the conviction or guilty plea shall pay a reinstatement fee as provided in division (F)(2) of section 4511.191 of the Revised Code.

(3) If an offender is sentenced to a jail term under division (G)(1)(b)(i) or (ii) or (G)(1)(c)(i) or (ii) of this section and if, within sixty days of sentencing of the offender, the court issues a written finding on the record that, due to the unavailability of space at the jail where the offender is required to serve the term, the offender will not be able to begin serving that term within the sixty-day period following the date of sentencing, the court may impose an alternative sentence under this division that includes a term of house arrest with electronic monitoring, with continuous alcohol monitoring, or with both electronic monitoring and continuous alcohol monitoring.

As an alternative to a mandatory jail term of ten consecutive days required by division (G)(1)(b)(i) of this section, the court, under this division, may sentence the offender to five consecutive days in jail and not less than eighteen consecutive days of house arrest with electronic monitoring, with continuous alcohol monitoring, or with both electronic monitoring and continuous alcohol monitoring. The cumulative total of the five consecutive days in jail and the period of house arrest with electronic monitoring, continuous alcohol monitoring, or both types of monitoring shall not exceed six months. The five consecutive days in jail do not have to be served prior to or consecutively to the period of house arrest.

As an alternative to the mandatory jail term of twenty consecutive days required by division (G)(1)(b)(ii) of this section, the court, under this division, may sentence the offender to ten consecutive days in jail and not less than thirty-six consecutive days of house arrest with electronic monitoring, with continuous alcohol monitoring, or with both electronic monitoring and continuous alcohol monitoring. The cumulative total of the ten consecutive days in jail and the period of house arrest with electronic monitoring, continuous alcohol monitoring, or both types of monitoring shall not exceed six months. The ten consecutive days in jail do not have to be served prior to or consecutively to the period of house arrest.

As an alternative to a mandatory jail term of thirty consecutive days required by division (G)(1)(c)(i) of this section, the court, under this division, may sentence the offender to fifteen consecutive days in jail and not less than fifty-five consecutive days of house arrest with electronic monitoring, with continuous alcohol monitoring, or with both electronic monitoring and continuous alcohol monitoring. The cumulative total of the fifteen consecutive days in jail and the period of house arrest with electronic monitoring, continuous alcohol monitoring, or both types of monitoring shall not exceed one year. The fifteen consecutive days in jail do not have to be served prior to or consecutively to the period of house arrest.

As an alternative to the mandatory jail term of sixty consecutive days required by division (G)(1)(c)(ii) of this section, the court, under this division, may sentence the offender to thirty consecutive days in jail and not less than one hundred ten consecutive days of house arrest with electronic monitoring, with continuous alcohol monitoring, or with both electronic monitoring and continuous alcohol monitoring. The cumulative total of the thirty consecutive days in jail and the period of house arrest with electronic monitoring, continuous alcohol monitoring, or both types of monitoring shall not exceed one year. The thirty consecutive days in jail do not have to be served prior to or consecutively to the period of house arrest.

(4) If an offender's driver's or occupational driver's license or permit or nonresident operating privilege is suspended under division (G) of this section and if section 4510.13 of the Revised Code permits the court to grant limited driving privileges, the court may grant the limited driving privileges in accordance with that section. If division (A)(7) of that section requires that the court impose as a condition of the privileges that the offender must display on the vehicle that is driven subject to the privileges restricted license plates that are issued under section 4503.231 of the Revised Code, except as provided in division (B) of that section, the court shall impose that condition as one of the conditions of the limited driving privileges granted to the offender, except as provided in division (B) of section 4503.231 of the Revised Code.

(5) Fines imposed under this section for a violation of division (A) of this section shall be distributed as follows:

(a) Twenty-five dollars of the fine imposed under division (G)(1)(a)(iii), thirty-five dollars of the fine imposed under division (G)(1)(b)(iii), one hundred twenty-three dollars of the fine imposed under division (G)(1)(c)(iii), and two hundred ten dollars of the fine imposed under division (G)(1)(d)(iii) or (e)(iii) of this section shall be paid to an enforcement and education fund established by the legislative authority of the law enforcement agency in this state that primarily was responsible for the arrest of the offender, as determined by the court that imposes the fine. The agency shall use this share to pay only those costs it incurs in enforcing this section or a municipal OVI ordinance and in informing the public of the laws governing the operation of a vehicle while under the influence of alcohol, the dangers of the operation of a vehicle under the influence of alcohol, and other information relating to the operation of a vehicle under the influence of alcohol and the consumption of alcoholic beverages.

(b) Fifty dollars of the fine imposed under division (G)(1)(a)(iii) of this section shall be paid to the political subdivision that pays the cost of housing the offender during the offender's term of incarceration. If the offender is being sentenced for a violation of division (A)(1)(a), (b), (c), (d), (e), or (j) of this section and was confined as a result of the offense prior to being sentenced for the offense but is not sentenced to a term of incarceration, the fifty dollars shall be paid to the political subdivision that paid the cost of housing the offender during that period of confinement. The political subdivision shall use the share under this division to pay or reimburse incarceration or treatment costs it incurs in housing or providing drug and alcohol treatment to persons who violate this section or a municipal OVI ordinance, costs of any immobilizing or disabling device used on the offender's vehicle, and costs of electronic house arrest equipment needed for persons who violate this section.

(c) Twenty-five dollars of the fine imposed under division (G)(1)(a)(iii) and fifty dollars of the fine imposed under division (G)(1)(b)(iii) of this section shall be deposited into the county or municipal indigent drivers' alcohol treatment fund under the control of that court, as created by the county or municipal corporation under division (F) of section 4511.191 of the Revised Code.

(d) One hundred fifteen dollars of the fine imposed under division (G)(1)(b)(iii), two hundred seventy-seven dollars of the fine imposed under division (G)(1)(c)(iii), and four hundred forty dollars of the fine imposed under division (G)(1)(d)(iii) or (e)(iii) of this section shall be paid to the political subdivision that pays the cost of housing the offender during the offender's term of incarceration. The political subdivision shall use this share to pay or reimburse incarceration or treatment costs it incurs in housing or providing drug and alcohol treatment to persons who violate this section or a municipal OVI ordinance, costs for any immobilizing or disabling device used on the offender's vehicle, and costs of electronic house arrest equipment needed for persons who violate this section.

(e) Fifty dollars of the fine imposed under divisions (G)(1)(a)(iii), (G)(1)(b)(iii), (G)(1)(c)(iii), (G)(1)(d)(iii), and (G)(1)(e)(iii) of this section shall be deposited into the special projects fund of the court in which the offender was convicted and that is established under division (E)(1) of section 2303.201, division (B)(1) of section 1901.26, or division (B)(1) of section 1907.24 of the Revised Code, to be used exclusively to cover the cost of immobilizing or disabling devices, including certified ignition interlock devices, and remote alcohol monitoring devices for indigent offenders who are required by a judge to use either of these devices. If the court in which the offender was convicted does not have a special projects fund that is established under division (E)(1) of section 2303.201, division (B)(1) of section 1901.26, or division (B)(1) of section 1907.24 of the Revised Code, the fifty dollars shall be deposited into the indigent drivers interlock and alcohol monitoring fund under division (I) of section 4511.191 of the Revised Code.

(f) Seventy-five dollars of the fine imposed under division (G)(1)(a)(iii), one hundred twenty-five dollars of the fine imposed under division (G)(1)(b)(iii), two hundred fifty dollars of the fine imposed under division (G)(1)(c)(iii), and five hundred dollars of the fine imposed under division (G)(1)(d)(iii) or (e)(iii) of this section shall be transmitted to the treasurer of state for deposit into the indigent defense support fund established under section 120.08 of the Revised Code.

(g) The balance of the fine imposed under division (G)(1)(a)(iii), (b)(iii), (c)(iii), (d)(iii), or (e)(iii) of this section shall be disbursed as otherwise provided by law.

(6) If title to a motor vehicle that is subject to an order of criminal forfeiture under division (G)(1)(c), (d), or (e) of this section is assigned or transferred and division (B)(2) or (3) of section 4503.234 of the Revised Code applies, in addition to or independent of any other penalty established by law, the court may fine the offender the value of the vehicle as determined by publications of the national automobile dealers association. The proceeds of any fine so imposed shall be distributed in accordance with division (C)(2) of that section.

(7) In all cases in which an offender is sentenced under division (G) of this section, the offender shall provide the court with proof of financial responsibility as defined in section 4509.01 of the Revised Code. If the offender fails to provide that proof of financial responsibility, the court, in addition to any other penalties provided by law, may order restitution pursuant to section 2929.18 or 2929.28 of the Revised Code in an amount not exceeding five thousand dollars for any economic loss arising from an accident or collision that was the direct and proximate result of the offender's operation of the vehicle before, during, or after committing the offense for which the offender is sentenced under division (G) of this section.

(8) As used in division (G) of this section, "electronic monitoring," "mandatory prison term," and "mandatory term of local incarceration" have the same meanings as in section 2929.01 of the Revised Code.

(H) Whoever violates division (B) of this section is guilty of operating a vehicle after underage alcohol consumption and shall be punished as follows:

(1) Except as otherwise provided in division (H)(2) of this section, the offender is guilty of a misdemeanor of the fourth degree. In addition to any other sanction imposed for the offense, the court shall impose a class six suspension of the offender's driver's license, commercial driver's license, temporary instruction permit, probationary license, or nonresident operating privilege from the range specified in division (A)(6) of section 4510.02 of the Revised Code.

(2) If, within one year of the offense, the offender previously has been convicted of or pleaded guilty to one or more violations of division (A) or (B) of this section or other equivalent offenses, the offender is guilty of a misdemeanor of the third degree. In addition to any other sanction imposed for the offense, the court shall impose a class four suspension of the offender's driver's license, commercial driver's license, temporary instruction permit, probationary license, or nonresident operating privilege from the range specified in division (A)(4) of section 4510.02 of the Revised Code.

(3) If the offender also is convicted of or also pleads guilty to a specification of the type described in section 2941.1416 of the Revised Code and if the court imposes a jail term for the violation of division (B) of this section, the court shall impose upon the offender an additional definite jail term pursuant to division (E) of section 2929.24 of the Revised Code.

(4) The offender shall provide the court with proof of financial responsibility as defined in section 4509.01 of the Revised Code. If the offender fails to provide that proof of financial responsibility, then, in addition to any other penalties provided by law, the court may order restitution pursuant to section 2929.28 of the Revised Code in an amount not exceeding five thousand dollars for any economic loss arising from an accident or collision that was the direct and proximate result of the offender's operation of the vehicle before, during, or after committing the violation of division (B) of this section.

(I)(1) No court shall sentence an offender to an alcohol treatment program under this section unless the treatment program complies with the minimum standards for alcohol treatment programs adopted under Chapter 3793. of the Revised Code by the director of alcohol and drug addiction services.

(2) An offender who stays in a drivers' intervention program or in an alcohol treatment program under an order issued under this section shall pay the cost of the stay in the program. However, if the court determines that an offender who stays in an alcohol treatment program under an order issued under this section is unable to pay the cost of the stay in the program, the court may order that the cost be paid from the court's indigent drivers' alcohol treatment fund.

(J) If a person whose driver's or commercial driver's license or permit or nonresident operating privilege is suspended under this section files an appeal regarding any aspect of the person's trial or sentence, the appeal itself does not stay the operation of the suspension.

(K) Division (A)(1)(j) of this section does not apply to a person who operates a vehicle, streetcar, or trackless trolley while the person has a concentration of a listed controlled substance or a listed metabolite of a controlled substance in the person's whole blood, blood serum or plasma, or urine that equals or exceeds the amount specified in that division, if both of the following apply:

(1) The person obtained the controlled substance pursuant to a prescription issued by a licensed health professional authorized to prescribe drugs.

(2) The person injected, ingested, or inhaled the controlled substance in accordance with the health professional's directions.

(L) The prohibited concentrations of a controlled substance or a metabolite of a controlled substance listed in division (A)(1)(j) of this section also apply in a prosecution of a violation of division (D) of section 2923.16 of the Revised Code in the same manner as if the offender is being prosecuted for a prohibited concentration of alcohol.

(M) All terms defined in section 4510.01 of the Revised Code apply to this section. If the meaning of a term defined in section 4510.01 of the Revised Code conflicts with the meaning of the same term as defined in section 4501.01 or 4511.01 of the Revised Code, the term as defined in section 4510.01 of the Revised Code applies to this section.

(N)(1) The Ohio Traffic Rules in effect on January 1, 2004, as adopted by the supreme court under authority of section 2937.46 of the Revised Code, do not apply to felony violations of this section. Subject to division (N)(2) of this section, the Rules of Criminal Procedure apply to felony violations of this section.

(2) If, on or after January 1, 2004, the supreme court modifies the Ohio Traffic Rules to provide procedures to govern felony violations of this section, the modified rules shall apply to felony violations of this section.

**HISTORY: GC § 6307-19; 119 v 766, § 19; Bureau of Code Revision, 10-1-53; 125 v 461; 130 v 1083 (Eff 7-11-63); 132 v H 380 (Eff 1-1-68); 133 v H 874 (Eff 9-16-70); 134 v S 14 (Eff 12-3-71); 135 v H 995 (Eff 1-1-75); 139 v S 432 (Eff 3-16-83); 141 v S 262 (Eff 3-20-87); 143 v S 131 (Eff 7-25-90); 143 v H 837 (Eff 7-25-90); 145 v S 82 (Eff 5-4-94); 148 v S 22 (Eff 5-17-2000); 149 v S 163, § 1. Eff 4-9-2003; 149 v S 123, § 1, eff. 1-1-04; 149 v H 490, § 1, eff. 1-1-04; 149 v S 163, § 3, eff. 1-1-04; 150 v H 87, § 1, eff. 6-30-03; 150 v H 87, § 4, eff. 1-1-04; 150 v H 163, § 1, eff. 9-23-04; 151 v S 8, § 1, eff. 8-17-06; 151 v H 461, § 1, eff. 4-4-07; 152 v S 209, § 1, eff. 3-26-08; 152 v S 17, § 1, eff. 9-30-08; 152 v H 215, § 1, eff. 4-7-09; 153 v S 58, § 1, eff. 9-17-10; 2011 HB 5, § 1, eff. Sept. 23, 2011.**

The effective date is set by § 6 of 152 v S 209.

The provisions of § 5, H.B. 163 (150 v —), read as follows:

SECTION 5. * * * (D) Section 4511.19 of the Revised Code is presented in this act as a composite of the section as amended by Am. Sub. H.B. 87 of the 125th General Assembly and Am. Sub. H.B. 490 and Am. Sub. S.B. 163, both of the 124th General Assembly. The General Assembly, applying the principle stated in division (B) of section 1.52 of the Revised Code that amendments are to be harmonized if reasonably capable of simultaneous operation, finds that the composite is the resulting version of the section in effect prior to the effective date of the section as presented in this act.

The effective date is set by section 26 of H.B. 87.

See provisions, § 5 of S.B. 123 (149 v —), following RC § 4501.01.

## § 4511.191 Implied consent.

(A)(1) As used in this section:

(a) "Physical control" has the same meaning as in section 4511.194 of the Revised Code.

(b) "Alcohol monitoring device" means any device that provides for continuous alcohol monitoring, any ignition interlock device, any immobilizing or disabling device other than an ignition interlock device that is constantly available to monitor the concentration of alcohol in a person's system, or any other device that provides for the automatic testing and periodic reporting of alcohol consumption by a person and that a court orders a person to use as a sanction imposed as a result of the person's conviction of or plea of guilty to an offense.

(2) Any person who operates a vehicle, streetcar, or trackless trolley upon a highway or any public or private property used by the public for vehicular travel or parking within this state or who is in physical control of a vehicle, streetcar, or trackless trolley shall be deemed to have given consent to a chemical test or tests of the person's whole blood, blood serum or plasma, breath, or urine to determine the alcohol, drug of abuse, controlled substance, metabolite of a controlled substance, or combination content of the person's whole blood, blood serum or plasma, breath, or urine if arrested for a violation of division (A) or (B) of section 4511.19 of the Revised Code, section 4511.194 of the Revised Code or a substantially equivalent municipal ordinance, or a municipal OVI ordinance.

(3) The chemical test or tests under division (A)(2) of this section shall be administered at the request of a law enforcement officer having reasonable grounds to believe the person was operating or in physical control of a vehicle, streetcar, or trackless trolley in violation of a division, section, or ordinance identified in division (A)(2) of this section. The law enforcement agency by which the officer is employed shall designate which of the tests shall be administered.

(4) Any person who is dead or unconscious, or who otherwise is in a condition rendering the person incapable of refusal, shall be deemed to have consented as provided in division (A)(2) of this section, and the test or tests may be administered, subject to sections 313.12 to 313.16 of the Revised Code.

(5)(a) If a law enforcement officer arrests a person for a violation of division (A) or (B) of section 4511.19 of the Revised Code, section 4511.194 of the Revised Code or a substantially equivalent municipal ordinance, or a municipal OVI ordinance and if the person if convicted would be required to be sentenced under division (G)(1)(c), (d), or (e) of section 4511.19 of the Revised Code, the law enforcement officer shall request the person to submit, and the person shall submit, to a chemical test or tests of the person's whole blood, blood serum or plasma, breath, or urine for the purpose of determining the alcohol, drug of abuse, controlled substance, metabolite of a controlled substance, or combination content of the person's whole blood, blood serum or plasma, breath, or urine. A law enforcement officer who makes a request pursuant to this division that a person submit to a chemical test or tests is not required to advise the person of the consequences of submitting to, or refusing to submit to, the test or tests and is not required to give the person the form described in division (B) of section 4511.192 of the Revised Code, but the officer shall advise the person at the time of the arrest that if the person refuses to take a chemical test the officer may employ whatever reasonable means are necessary to ensure that the person submits to a chemical test of the person's whole blood or blood serum or plasma. The officer shall also advise the person at the time of the arrest that the person may have an independent chemical test taken at the person's own expense. Divisions (A)(3) and (4) of this section apply to the administration of a chemical test or tests pursuant to this division.

(b) If a person refuses to submit to a chemical test upon a request made pursuant to division (A)(5)(a) of this section, the law enforcement officer who made the request may employ whatever reasonable means are necessary to ensure that the person submits to a chemical test of the person's whole blood or blood serum or plasma. A law enforcement officer who acts pursuant to this division to ensure that a person submits to a chemical test of the person's whole blood or blood serum or plasma is immune from criminal and civil liability based upon a claim for assault and battery or any other claim for the acts, unless the officer so acted with malicious purpose, in bad faith, or in a wanton or reckless manner.

(B)(1) Upon receipt of the sworn report of a law enforcement officer who arrested a person for a violation of division (A) or (B) of section 4511.19 of the Revised Code, section 4511.194 of the Revised Code or a substantially equivalent municipal ordinance, or a municipal OVI ordinance that was completed and sent to the registrar of motor vehicles and a court pursuant to section 4511.192 of the Revised Code in regard to a person who refused to take the designated chemical test, the registrar shall enter into the registrar's records the fact that the person's driver's or commercial driver's license or permit or nonresident operating privilege was suspended by the arresting officer under this division and that section and the period of the suspension, as determined under this section. The suspension shall be subject to appeal as provided in section 4511.197 of the Revised Code. The suspension shall be for whichever of the following periods applies:

(a) Except when division (B)(1)(b), (c), or (d) of this section applies and specifies a different class or length of suspension, the suspension shall be a class C suspension for the period of time specified in division (B)(3) of section 4510.02 of the Revised Code.

(b) If the arrested person, within six years of the date on which the person refused the request to consent to the chemical test, had refused one previous request to consent to a chemical test or had been convicted of or pleaded guilty to one violation of division (A) or (B) of section 4511.19 of the Revised Code or one other equivalent offense, the suspension shall be a class B suspension imposed for the period of time specified in division (B)(2) of section 4510.02 of the Revised Code.

(c) If the arrested person, within six years of the date on which the person refused the request to consent to the chemical test, had refused two previous requests to consent to a chemical test, had been convicted of or pleaded guilty to two violations of division (A) or (B) of section 4511.19 of the Revised Code or other equivalent offenses, or had refused one previous request to consent to a chemical test and also had been convicted of or pleaded guilty to one violation of division (A) or (B) of section 4511.19 of the Revised Code or other equivalent offenses, which violation or offense arose from an incident other than the incident that led to the refusal, the suspension shall be a class A suspension imposed for the period of time specified in division (B)(1) of section 4510.02 of the Revised Code.

(d) If the arrested person, within six years of the date on which the person refused the request to consent to the chemical test, had refused three or more previous requests to consent to a chemical test, had been convicted of or pleaded guilty to three or more violations of division (A) or (B) of section 4511.19 of the Revised Code or other equivalent offenses, or had refused a number of previous requests to consent to a chemical test and also had been convicted of or pleaded guilty to a number of violations of division (A) or (B) of section 4511.19 of the Revised Code or other equivalent offenses that cumulatively total three or more such refusals, convictions, and guilty pleas, the suspension shall be for five years.

(2) The registrar shall terminate a suspension of the driver's or commercial driver's license or permit of a resident or of the operating privilege of a nonresident, or a denial of a driver's or commercial driver's license or permit, imposed pursuant to division (B)(1) of this section upon receipt of notice that the person has entered a plea of guilty to, or that the person has been convicted after entering a plea of no contest to, operating a vehicle in violation of section 4511.19 of the Revised Code or in violation of a municipal OVI ordinance, if the offense for which the conviction is had or the plea is entered arose from the same incident that led to the suspension or denial.

The registrar shall credit against any judicial suspension of a person's driver's or commercial driver's license or permit or nonresident operating privilege imposed pursuant to section 4511.19 of the Revised Code, or pursuant to section 4510.07 of the Revised Code for a violation of a municipal OVI ordinance, any time during which the person serves a related suspension imposed pursuant to division (B)(1) of this section.

(C)(1) Upon receipt of the sworn report of the law enforcement officer who arrested a person for a violation of division (A) or (B) of section 4511.19 of the Revised Code or a municipal OVI ordinance that was completed and sent to the registrar and a court pursuant to section 4511.192 of the Revised Code in regard to a person whose test results indicate that the person's whole blood, blood serum or plasma, breath, or urine contained at least the concentration of alcohol specified in division (A)(1)(b), (c), (d), or (e) of section 4511.19 of the Revised Code or at least the concentration of a listed controlled substance or a listed metabolite of a controlled substance specified in division (A)(1)(j) of section 4511.19 of the Revised Code, the registrar shall enter into the registrar's records the fact that the person's driver's or commercial driver's license or permit or nonresident operating privilege was suspended by the arresting officer under this division and section 4511.192 of the Revised Code and the period of the suspension, as determined under divisions (C)(1)(a) to (d) of this section. The suspension shall be subject to appeal as provided in section 4511.197 of the Revised Code. The suspension described in this division does not apply to, and shall not be imposed upon, a person arrested for a violation of section 4511.194 of the Revised Code or a substantially equivalent municipal ordinance who submits to a designated chemical test. The suspension shall be for whichever of the following periods applies:

(a) Except when division (C)(1)(b), (c), or (d) of this section applies and specifies a different period, the suspension shall be a class E suspension imposed for the period of time specified in division (B)(5) of section 4510.02 of the Revised Code.

(b) The suspension shall be a class C suspension for the period of time specified in division (B)(3) of section 4510.02 of the Revised Code if the person has been convicted of or pleaded guilty to, within six years of the date the test was conducted, one violation of division (A) or (B) of section 4511.19 of the Revised Code or one other equivalent offense.

(c) If, within six years of the date the test was conducted, the person has been convicted of or pleaded guilty to two violations of a statute or ordinance described in division (C)(1)(b) of this section, the suspension shall be a class B suspension imposed for the period of time specified in division (B)(2) of section 4510.02 of the Revised Code.

(d) If, within six years of the date the test was conducted, the person has been convicted of or pleaded guilty to more than two violations of a statute or ordinance described in division (C)(1)(b) of this section, the suspension shall be a class A suspension imposed for the period of time specified in division (B)(1) of section 4510.02 of the Revised Code.

(2) The registrar shall terminate a suspension of the driver's or commercial driver's license or permit of a resident or of the operating privilege of a nonresident, or a denial of a driver's or commercial driver's license or

permit, imposed pursuant to division (C)(1) of this section upon receipt of notice that the person has entered a plea of guilty to, or that the person has been convicted after entering a plea of no contest to, operating a vehicle in violation of section 4511.19 of the Revised Code or in violation of a municipal OVI ordinance, if the offense for which the conviction is had or the plea is entered arose from the same incident that led to the suspension or denial.

The registrar shall credit against any judicial suspension of a person's driver's or commercial driver's license or permit or nonresident operating privilege imposed pursuant to section 4511.19 of the Revised Code, or pursuant to section 4510.07 of the Revised Code for a violation of a municipal OVI ordinance, any time during which the person serves a related suspension imposed pursuant to division (C)(1) of this section.

(D)(1) A suspension of a person's driver's or commercial driver's license or permit or nonresident operating privilege under this section for the time described in division (B) or (C) of this section is effective immediately from the time at which the arresting officer serves the notice of suspension upon the arrested person. Any subsequent finding that the person is not guilty of the charge that resulted in the person being requested to take the chemical test or tests under division (A) of this section does not affect the suspension.

(2) If a person is arrested for operating a vehicle, streetcar, or trackless trolley in violation of division (A) or (B) of section 4511.19 of the Revised Code or a municipal OVI ordinance, or for being in physical control of a vehicle, streetcar, or trackless trolley in violation of section 4511.194 of the Revised Code or a substantially equivalent municipal ordinance, regardless of whether the person's driver's or commercial driver's license or permit or nonresident operating privilege is or is not suspended under division (B) or (C) of this section or Chapter 4510. of the Revised Code, the person's initial appearance on the charge resulting from the arrest shall be held within five days of the person's arrest or the issuance of the citation to the person, subject to any continuance granted by the court pursuant to section 4511.197 of the Revised Code regarding the issues specified in that division.

(E) When it finally has been determined under the procedures of this section and sections 4511.192 to 4511.197 of the Revised Code that a nonresident's privilege to operate a vehicle within this state has been suspended, the registrar shall give information in writing of the action taken to the motor vehicle administrator of the state of the person's residence and of any state in which the person has a license.

(F) At the end of a suspension period under this section, under section 4511.194, section 4511.196, or division (G) of section 4511.19 of the Revised Code, or under section 4510.07 of the Revised Code for a violation of a municipal OVI ordinance and upon the request of the person whose driver's or commercial driver's license or permit was suspended and who is not otherwise subject to suspension, cancellation, or disqualification, the registrar shall return the driver's or commercial driver's license or permit to the person upon the occurrence of all of the conditions specified in divisions (F)(1) and (2) of this section:

(1) A showing that the person has proof of financial responsibility, a policy of liability insurance in effect that meets the minimum standards set forth in section 4509.51 of the Revised Code, or proof, to the satisfaction of the registrar, that the person is able to respond in damages in an amount at least equal to the minimum amounts specified in section 4509.51 of the Revised Code.

(2) Subject to the limitation contained in division (F)(3) of this section, payment by the person to the registrar or an eligible deputy registrar of a license reinstatement fee of four hundred seventy-five dollars, which fee shall be deposited in the state treasury and credited as follows:

(a) One hundred twelve dollars and fifty cents shall be credited to the statewide treatment and prevention fund created by section 4301.30 of the Revised Code. Money credited to the fund under this section shall be used for purposes identified in the comprehensive statewide alcohol and drug addiction services plan developed under section 3793.04 of the Revised Code.

(b) Seventy-five dollars shall be credited to the reparations fund created by section 2743.191 of the Revised Code.

(c) Thirty-seven dollars and fifty cents shall be credited to the indigent drivers alcohol treatment fund, which is hereby established in the state treasury. Except as otherwise provided in division (F)(2)(c) of this section, moneys in the fund shall be distributed by the department of alcohol and drug addiction services to the county indigent drivers alcohol treatment funds, the county juvenile indigent drivers alcohol treatment funds, and the municipal indigent drivers alcohol treatment funds that are required to be established by counties and municipal corporations pursuant to division (H) of this section, and shall be used only to pay the cost of an alcohol and drug addiction treatment program attended by an offender or juvenile traffic offender who is ordered to attend an alcohol and drug addiction treatment program by a county, juvenile, or municipal court judge and who is determined by the county, juvenile, or municipal court judge not to have the means to pay for the person's attendance at the program or to pay the costs specified in division (H)(4) of this section in accordance with that division. In addition, a county, juvenile, or municipal court judge may use moneys in the county indigent drivers alcohol treatment fund, county juvenile indigent drivers alcohol treatment fund, or municipal indigent drivers alcohol treatment fund to pay for the cost of the continued use of an alcohol monitoring device as described in divisions (H)(3) and (4) of this section. Moneys in the fund that are not distributed to a county indigent drivers alcohol treatment fund, a county juvenile indigent drivers alcohol treatment fund, or a municipal indigent drivers alcohol treatment fund under division (H) of this section because the director of alcohol and drug addiction services does not have the information necessary to identify the county or municipal corporation where the offender or juvenile offender was arrested may be transferred by the director of budget and management to the statewide treatment and prevention fund created by section 4301.30 of the Revised Code, upon certification of the amount by the director of alcohol and drug addiction services.

(d) Seventy-five dollars shall be credited to the Ohio rehabilitation services commission established by section 3304.12 of the Revised Code, to the services for rehabilitation fund, which is hereby established. The fund shall be used to match available federal matching funds where appropriate, and for any other purpose or program of the commission to rehabilitate people with disabilities to help them become employed and independent.

(e) Seventy-five dollars shall be deposited into the state treasury and credited to the drug abuse resistance education programs fund, which is hereby established, to be used by the attorney general for the purposes specified in division (F)(4) of this section.

(f) Thirty dollars shall be credited to the state bureau of motor vehicles fund created by section 4501.25 of the Revised Code.

(g) Twenty dollars shall be credited to the trauma and emergency medical services grants fund created by section 4513.263 of the Revised Code.

(h) Fifty dollars shall be credited to the indigent drivers interlock and alcohol monitoring fund, which is hereby established in the state treasury. Moneys in the fund shall be distributed by the department of public safety to the county indigent drivers interlock and alcohol monitoring funds, the county juvenile indigent drivers interlock and alcohol monitoring funds, and the municipal indigent drivers interlock and alcohol monitoring funds that are required to be established by counties and municipal corporations pursuant to this section, and shall be used only to pay the cost of an immobilizing or disabling device, including a certified ignition interlock device, or an alcohol monitoring device used by an offender or juvenile offender who is ordered to use the device by a county, juvenile, or municipal court judge and who is determined by the county, juvenile, or municipal court judge not to have the means to pay for the person's use of the device.

(3) If a person's driver's or commercial driver's license or permit is suspended under this section, under section 4511.196 or division (G) of section 4511.19 of the Revised Code, under section 4510.07 of the Revised Code for a violation of a municipal OVI ordinance or under any combination of the suspensions described in division (F)(3) of this section, and if the suspensions arise from a single incident or a single set of facts and circumstances, the person is liable for payment of, and shall be required to pay to the registrar or an eligible deputy registrar, only one reinstatement fee of four hundred seventy-five dollars. The reinstatement fee shall be distributed by the bureau in accordance with division (F)(2) of this section.

(4) The attorney general shall use amounts in the drug abuse resistance education programs fund to award grants to law enforcement agencies to establish and implement drug abuse resistance education programs in public schools. Grants awarded to a law enforcement agency under this section shall be used by the agency to pay for not more than fifty per cent of the amount of the salaries of law enforcement officers who conduct drug abuse resistance education programs in public schools. The attorney general shall not use more than six per cent of the amounts the attorney general's office receives under division (F)(2)(e) of this section to pay the costs it incurs in administering the grant program established by division (F)(2)(e) of this section and in providing training and materials relating to drug abuse resistance education programs.

The attorney general shall report to the governor and the general assembly each fiscal year on the progress made in establishing and implementing drug abuse resistance education programs. These reports shall include an evaluation of the effectiveness of these programs.

(5) In addition to the reinstatement fee under this section, if the person pays the reinstatement fee to a deputy registrar, the deputy registrar shall collect a service fee of ten dollars to compensate the deputy registrar for services performed under this section. The deputy registrar shall retain eight dollars of the service fee and shall transmit the reinstatement fee, plus two dollars of the service fee, to the registrar in the manner the registrar shall determine.

(G) Suspension of a commercial driver's license under division (B) or (C) of this section shall be concurrent with any period of disqualification under section 3123.611 or 4506.16 of the Revised Code or any period of suspension under section 3123.58 of the Revised Code. No person who is disqualified for life from holding a commercial driver's license under section 4506.16 of the Revised Code shall be issued a driver's license under Chapter 4507. of the Revised Code during the period for which the commercial driver's license was suspended under division (B) or (C) of this section. No person whose commercial driver's license is suspended under division (B) or (C) of this section shall be issued a driver's license under Chapter 4507. of the Revised Code during the period of the suspension.

(H)(1) Each county shall establish an indigent drivers alcohol treatment fund, each county shall establish a juvenile indigent drivers alcohol treatment fund, and each municipal corporation in which there is a municipal court shall establish an indigent drivers alcohol treatment fund. All revenue that the general assembly appropriates to the indigent drivers alcohol treatment fund for transfer to a county indigent drivers alcohol treatment fund, a county juvenile indigent drivers alcohol treatment fund, or a municipal indigent drivers alcohol treatment fund, all portions of fees that are paid under division (F) of this section and that are credited under that division to the indigent drivers alcohol treatment fund in the state treasury for a county indigent drivers alcohol treatment fund, a county juvenile indigent drivers alcohol treatment fund, or a municipal indigent drivers alcohol treatment fund, all portions of additional costs imposed under section 2949.094 of the Revised Code that are specified for deposit into a county, county juvenile, or municipal indigent drivers alcohol treatment fund by that section, and all portions of fines that are specified for deposit into a county or municipal indigent drivers alcohol treatment fund by section 4511.193 of the Revised Code shall be deposited into that county indigent drivers alcohol treatment fund, county juvenile indigent drivers alcohol treatment fund, or municipal indigent drivers alcohol treatment fund. The portions of the fees paid under division (F) of this section that are to be so deposited shall be determined in accordance with division (H)(2) of this section. Additionally, all portions of fines that are paid for a violation of section 4511.19 of the Revised Code or of any prohibition contained in Chapter 4510. of the Revised Code, and that are required under section 4511.19 or any provision of Chapter 4510. of the Revised Code to be deposited into a county indigent drivers alcohol treatment fund or municipal indigent drivers alcohol treatment fund shall be deposited into the appropriate fund in accordance with the applicable division of the section or provision.

(2) That portion of the license reinstatement fee that is paid under division (F) of this section and that is credited under that division to the indigent drivers alcohol treatment fund shall be deposited into a county indigent drivers alcohol treatment fund, a county juvenile indigent drivers alcohol treatment fund, or a municipal indigent drivers alcohol treatment fund as follows:

(a) Regarding a suspension imposed under this section, that portion of the fee shall be deposited as follows:

(i) If the fee is paid by a person who was charged in a county court with the violation that resulted in the suspension or in the imposition of the court costs, the portion shall be deposited into the county indigent drivers alcohol treatment fund under the control of that court;

(ii) If the fee is paid by a person who was charged in a juvenile court with the violation that resulted in the suspension or in the imposition of the court costs, the portion shall be deposited into the county juvenile indigent drivers alcohol treatment fund established in the county served by the court;

(iii) If the fee is paid by a person who was charged in a municipal court with the violation that resulted in the suspension or in the imposition of the court costs, the portion shall be deposited into the municipal indigent drivers alcohol treatment fund under the control of that court.

(b) Regarding a suspension imposed under section 4511.19 of the Revised Code or under section 4510.07 of the Revised Code for a violation of a municipal OVI ordinance, that portion of the fee shall be deposited as follows:

(i) If the fee is paid by a person whose license or permit was suspended by a county court, the portion shall be deposited into the county indigent drivers alcohol treatment fund under the control of that court;

(ii) If the fee is paid by a person whose license or permit was suspended by a municipal court, the portion shall be deposited into the municipal indigent drivers alcohol treatment fund under the control of that court.

(3) Expenditures from a county indigent drivers alcohol treatment fund, a county juvenile indigent drivers alcohol treatment fund, or a municipal indigent drivers alcohol treatment fund shall be made only upon the order of a county, juvenile, or municipal court judge and only for payment of the cost of an assessment or the cost of the attendance at an alcohol and drug addiction treatment program of a person who is convicted of, or found to be a juvenile traffic offender by reason of, a violation of division (A) of section 4511.19 of the Revised Code or a substantially similar municipal ordinance, who is ordered by the court to attend the alcohol and drug addiction treatment program, and who is determined by the court to be unable to pay the cost of the assessment or the cost of attendance at the treatment program or for payment of the costs specified in division (H)(4) of this section in accordance with that division. The alcohol and drug addiction services board or the board of alcohol, drug addiction, and mental health services established pursuant to section 340.02 or 340.021 of the Revised Code and serving the alcohol, drug addiction, and mental health service district in which the court is located shall administer the indigent drivers alcohol treatment program of the court. When a court orders an offender or juvenile traffic offender to obtain an assessment or attend an alcohol and drug addiction treatment program, the board shall determine which program is suitable to meet the needs of the offender or juvenile traffic offender, and when a suitable program is located and space is available at the program, the offender or juvenile traffic offender shall attend the program designated by the board. A reasonable amount not to exceed five per cent of the amounts credited to and deposited into the county indigent drivers alcohol treatment fund, the county juvenile indigent drivers alcohol treatment fund, or the municipal indigent drivers alcohol treatment fund serving every court whose program is administered by that board shall be paid to the board to cover the costs it incurs in administering those indigent drivers alcohol treatment programs.

In addition, upon exhaustion of moneys in the indigent drivers interlock and alcohol monitoring fund for the use of an alcohol monitoring device, a county, juvenile, or municipal court judge may use moneys in the county indigent drivers alcohol treatment fund, county juvenile indigent drivers alcohol treatment fund, or municipal indigent drivers alcohol treatment fund in the following manners:

(a) If the source of the moneys was an appropriation of the general assembly, a portion of a fee that was paid under division (F) of this section, a portion of a fine that was specified for deposit into the fund by section 4511.193 of the Revised Code, or a portion of a fine that was paid for a violation of section 4511.19 of the Revised Code or of a provision contained in Chapter 4510. of the Revised Code that was required to be deposited into the fund, to pay for the continued use of an alcohol monitoring device by an offender or juvenile traffic offender, in conjunction with a treatment program approved by the department of alcohol and drug addiction services, when such use is determined clinically necessary by the treatment program and when the court determines that the offender or juvenile traffic offender is unable to pay all or part of the daily monitoring or cost of the device;

(b) If the source of the moneys was a portion of an additional court cost imposed under section 2949.094 of the Revised Code, to pay for the continued use of an alcohol monitoring device by an offender or juvenile traffic offender when the court determines that the offender or juvenile traffic offender is unable to pay all or part of the daily monitoring or cost of the device. The moneys may be used for a device as described in this division if the use of the device is in conjunction with a treatment program approved by the department of alcohol and drug addiction services, when the use of the device is determined clinically necessary by the treatment program, but the use of a device is not required to be in conjunction with a treatment program approved by the department in order for the moneys to be used for the device as described in this division.

(4) If a county, juvenile, or municipal court determines, in consultation with the alcohol and drug addiction services board or the board of alcohol, drug addiction, and mental health services established pursuant to section 340.02 or 340.021 of the Revised Code and serving the alcohol, drug addiction, and mental health district in which the court is located, that the funds in the county indigent drivers alcohol treatment fund, the county juvenile indigent drivers alcohol treatment fund, or the municipal indigent drivers alcohol treatment fund under the control of the court are more than sufficient to satisfy the purpose for which the fund was established, as specified in divisions (H)(1) to (3) of this section, the court may declare a surplus in the fund. If the court declares a surplus in the fund, the court may expend the amount of the surplus in the fund for:

(a) Alcohol and drug abuse assessment and treatment of persons who are charged in the court with committing a criminal offense or with being a delinquent child or juvenile traffic offender and in relation to whom both of the following apply:

(i) The court determines that substance abuse was a contributing factor leading to the criminal or delinquent activity or the juvenile traffic offense with which the person is charged.

(ii) The court determines that the person is unable to pay the cost of the alcohol and drug abuse assessment and treatment for which the surplus money will be used.

(b) All or part of the cost of purchasing alcohol monitoring devices to be used in conjunction with division (H)(3) of this section, upon exhaustion of moneys in the indigent drivers interlock and alcohol monitoring fund for the use of an alcohol monitoring device.

(5) For the purpose of determining as described in division (F)(2)(c) of this section whether an offender does not have the means to pay for the offender's attendance at an alcohol and drug addiction treatment program or whether an alleged offender or delinquent child is unable to pay the costs specified in division (H)(4) of this section, the court shall use the indigent client eligibility guidelines and the standards of indigency established by the state public defender to make the determination.

(6) The court shall identify and refer any alcohol and drug addiction program that is not certified under section 3793.06 of the Revised Code and that is interested in receiving amounts from the surplus in the fund declared under division (H)(4) of this section to the department of alcohol and drug addiction services in order for the program to become a certified alcohol and drug addiction program. The department shall keep a record of applicant referrals received pursuant to this division and shall submit a report on the referrals each year to the general assembly. If a program interested in becoming certified makes an application to become certified pursuant to section 3793.06 of the Revised Code, the program is eligible to receive surplus funds as long as the application is pending with the department. The department of alcohol and drug addiction services must offer technical assistance to the applicant. If the interested program withdraws the certification application, the department must notify the court, and the court shall not provide the interested program with any further surplus funds.

(7)(a) Each alcohol and drug addiction services board and board of alcohol, drug addiction, and mental health services established pursuant to section 340.02 or 340.021 of the Revised Code shall submit to the department of alcohol and drug addiction services an annual report for each indigent drivers alcohol treatment fund in that board's area.

(b) The report, which shall be submitted not later than sixty days after the end of the state fiscal year, shall provide the total payment that was made from the fund, including the number of indigent consumers that received treatment services and the number of indigent consumers that received an alcohol monitoring device. The report shall identify the treatment program and expenditure for an alcohol monitoring device for which that payment was made. The report shall include the fiscal year balance of each indigent drivers alcohol treatment fund located in that board's area. In the event that a surplus is declared in the fund pursuant to division (H)(4) of this section, the report also shall provide the total payment that was made from the surplus moneys and identify the treatment program and expenditure for an alcohol monitoring device for which that payment was made. The department may require additional information necessary to complete the comprehensive statewide alcohol and drug addiction services plan as required by section 3793.04 of the Revised Code.

(c) If a board is unable to obtain adequate information to develop the report to submit to the department for a particular indigent drivers alcohol treatment fund, the board shall submit a report detailing the effort made in obtaining the information.

(I)(1) Each county shall establish an indigent drivers interlock and alcohol monitoring fund and a juvenile indigent drivers interlock and alcohol treatment fund, and each municipal corporation in which there is a municipal court shall establish an indigent drivers interlock and alcohol monitoring fund. All revenue that the general assembly appropriates to the indigent drivers interlock and alcohol monitoring fund for transfer to a county indigent drivers interlock and alcohol monitoring fund, a county juvenile indigent drivers interlock and alcohol monitoring fund, or a municipal indigent drivers interlock and alcohol monitoring fund, all portions of license reinstatement fees that are paid under division (F)(2) of this section and that are credited under that division to the indigent drivers interlock and alcohol monitoring fund in the state treasury, and all portions of fines that are paid under division (G) of section 4511.19 of the Revised Code and that are credited by division (G)(5)(e) of that section to the indigent drivers interlock and alcohol monitoring fund in the state treasury shall be deposited in the appropriate fund in accordance with division (I)(2) of this section.

(2) That portion of the license reinstatement fee that is paid under division (F) of this section and that portion of the fine paid under division (G) of section 4511.19 of the Revised Code and that is credited under either division to the indigent drivers interlock and alcohol monitoring fund shall be deposited into a county indigent drivers interlock and alcohol monitoring fund, a county juvenile indigent drivers interlock and alcohol monitoring fund, or a municipal indigent drivers interlock and alcohol monitoring fund as follows:

(a) If the fee or fine is paid by a person who was charged in a county court with the violation that resulted in the suspension or fine, the portion shall be deposited into the county indigent drivers interlock and alcohol monitoring fund under the control of that court.

(b) If the fee or fine is paid by a person who was charged in a juvenile court with the violation that resulted in the suspension or fine, the portion shall be deposited into the county juvenile indigent drivers interlock and alcohol monitoring fund established in the county served by the court.

(c) If the fee or fine is paid by a person who was charged in a municipal court with the violation that resulted in the suspension, the portion shall be deposited into the municipal indigent drivers interlock and alcohol monitoring fund under the control of that court.

**HISTORY: 132 v H 380 (Eff 1-1-68); 132 v S 512 (Eff 3-10-68); 133 v H 1 (Eff 3-18-69); 134 v H 792 (Eff 2-3-72); 136 v H 1 (Eff 6-13-75); 136 v H 451 (Eff 1-3-77); 137 v H 219 (Eff 11-1-77); 137 v H 469 (Eff 10-25-78); 139 v S 432 (Eff 3-16-83); 141 v H 201 (Eff 7-1-85); 141 v S 262 (Eff 3-20-87); 142 v H 303 (Eff 10-20-87); 142 v S 308 (Eff 3-14-89); 142 v H 643 (Eff 3-17-89); 143 v H 329 (Eff 6-30-89); 143 v H 381 (Eff 7-1-89); 143 v H 317 (Eff 10-10-89); 143 v S 131 (Eff 7-25-90); 143 v H 837 (Eff 7-25-90); 144 v S 275 (Eff 9-1-93); 145 v H 152 (Eff 7-1-93); 145 v S 62, §§ 1, 4 (Eff 9-1-93); 145 v S 82 (Eff 5-4-94); 145 v H 236 (Eff 9-29-94); 145 v H 687 (Eff 10-12-94); 146 v H 117 (Eff 6-30-95); 146 v S 2 (Eff 7-1-96); 146 v H 353, § 1 (Eff 9-17-96); 146 v S 166, § 1 (Eff 10-17-96); 146 v H 167 (Eff 5-15-97); 146 v H 353, § 4 (Eff 5-15-97); 146 v S 166, § 6 (Eff 5-15-97); 147 v S 85 (Eff 5-15-97); 147 v H 210 (Eff 6-30-97); 147 v S 60 (Eff 10-21-97); 147 v S 80 (Eff 9-16-98); 148 v H 283 (Eff 6-30-99); 148 v S 107 (Eff 3-23-2000); 148 v S 22 (Eff 5-17-2000); 148 v H 138 (Eff 11-3-2000); 148 v S 180. Eff 3-22-2001; 149 v S 123, § 1, eff. 1-1-04; 150 v H 87, § 1, eff. 6-30-03; 150 v H 163, § 1, eff. 9-23-04; 151 v H 66, § 101.01, eff. 9-29-05; 151 v S 8, § 1, eff. 8-17-06; 152 v H 562, § 101.01, eff. 9-23-08; 152 v S 17, § 1, eff. 9-30-08; 152 v H 215, § 1, eff. 4-7-09; 153 v H 2,**

**§ 101.01, eff. 7-1-09; 153 v H 1, § 101.01, eff. 10-16-09; 2011 HB 114, § 101.01, eff. June 29, 2011; 2011 HB 153, § 101.01, eff. June 30, 2011.**

The effective date is set by § 812.10 of 153 v H 1.
The effective date is set by § 812.10 of 153 v H 2.
The provisions of § 3 of 152 v H 215 read as follows:
SECTION 3. Section 4511.191 of the Revised Code is presented in this act as a composite of the section as amended by both Am. Sub. H.B. 562 and Am. Sub. S.B. 17 of the 127th General Assembly. The General Assembly, applying the principle stated in division (B) of section 1.52 of the Revised Code that amendments are to be harmonized if reasonably capable of simultaneous operation, finds that the composite is the resulting version of the section in effect prior to the effective date of the section as presented in this act.
The effective date is set by § 812.10 of 152 v H 562.
The effective date is set by § 612.03 of 151 v H 66.
The provisions of § 7, H.B. 87 (150 v —), read as follows:
SECTION 7. The amendment of section 4511.191 of the Revised Code by this act does not supersede the earlier amendment with delayed effective date of that section by Am. Sub. S.B. 123 of the 124th General Assembly.
The effective date is set by section 26 of H.B. 87.
See provisions, § 5 of S.B. 123 (149 v —), following RC § 4501.01.
Acts 2011, HB 114, § 806.10 provides: "The items of law contained in this act, and their applications, are severable. If any item of law contained in this act, or if any application of any item of law contained in this act, is held invalid, the invalidity does not affect other items of law contained in this act and their applications that can be given effect without the invalid item or application."
Acts 2011, HB 114, § 815.10 provides: "Section 4511.191 of the Revised Code is presented in this act as a composite of the section as amended by both Am. Sub. H.B. 1 and Am. Sub. H.B. 2 of the 128th General Assembly. The General Assembly, applying the principle stated in division (B) of section 1.52 of the Revised Code that amendments are to be harmonized if reasonably capable of simultaneous operation, finds that the composite is the resulting version of the section in effect prior to the effective date of the section as presented in this act."

**Comment, Legislative Service Commission**

Section 4511.191 of the Revised Code is amended by Am. Sub. H.B. 1 and H.B. 2 of the 128th General Assembly. Comparison of these amendments in pursuance of section 1.52 of the Revised Code discloses that they are not irreconcilable so that they are required by that section to be harmonized to give effect to each amendment.

## § 4511.192 Arrestee for OVI or having physical control while under influence to receive written and verbal advice; submission or refusal to submit to test or tests; license suspension or seizure; officer's sworn report.

(A) Except as provided in division (A)(5) of section 4511.191 [4511.19.1] of the Revised Code, the arresting law enforcement officer shall give advice in accordance with this section to any person under arrest for a violation of division (A) or (B) of section 4511.19 of the Revised Code, section 4511.194 [4511.19.4] of the Revised Code or a substantially equivalent municipal ordinance, or a municipal OVI ordinance. The officer shall give that advice in a written form that contains the information described in division (B) of this section and shall read the advice to the person. The form shall contain a statement that the form was shown to the person under arrest and read to the person by the arresting officer. One or more persons shall witness the arresting officer's reading of the form, and the witnesses shall certify to this fact by signing the form. The person must submit to the chemical test or tests, subsequent to the request of the arresting officer, within two hours of the time of the alleged violation and, if the person does not submit to the test or tests within that two-hour time limit, the failure to submit automatically constitutes a refusal to submit to the test or tests.

(B) Except as provided in division (A)(5) of section 4511.191 [4511.19.1] of the Revised Code, if a person is under arrest as described in division (A) of this section, before the person may be requested to submit to a chemical test or tests to determine the alcohol, drug of abuse, controlled substance, metabolite of a controlled substance, or combination content of the person's whole blood, blood serum or plasma, breath, or urine, the arresting officer shall read the following form to the person:

"You now are under arrest for (specifically state the offense under state law or a substantially equivalent municipal ordinance for which the person was arrested — operating a vehicle under the influence of alcohol, a drug, or a combination of them; operating a vehicle while under the influence of a listed controlled substance or a listed metabolite of a controlled substance; operating a vehicle after underage alcohol consumption; or having physical control of a vehicle while under the influence).

If you refuse to take any chemical test required by law, your Ohio driving privileges will be suspended immediately, and you will have to pay a fee to have the privileges reinstated. If you have a prior of OVI, OVUAC, or operating a vehicle while under the influence of a listed controlled substance or a listed metabolite of a controlled substance conviction under state or municipal law within the preceding twenty years, you now are under arrest for state OVI, and, if you refuse to take a chemical test, you will face increased penalties if you subsequently are convicted of the state OVI.

(Read this part unless the person is under arrest for solely having physical control of a vehicle while under the influence.) If you take any chemical test required by law and are found to be at or over the prohibited amount of alcohol, a controlled substance, or a metabolite of a controlled substance in your whole blood, blood serum or plasma, breath, or urine as set by law, your Ohio driving privileges will be suspended immediately, and you will have to pay a fee to have the privileges reinstated.

If you take a chemical test, you may have an independent chemical test taken at your own expense."

(C) If the arresting law enforcement officer does not ask a person under arrest as described in division (A) of this section or division (A)(5) of section 4511.191 [4511.19.1] of the Revised Code to submit to a chemical test or tests under section 4511.191 [4511.19.1] of the Revised Code, the arresting officer shall seize the Ohio or out-of-state driver's or commercial driver's license or permit of the person and immediately forward it to the court in which the arrested person is to appear on the charge. If the arrested person is not in possession of the person's license or permit or it is not in the person's vehicle, the officer shall order the person to surrender it to the law enforcement agency that employs the officer within twenty-four hours after the arrest, and, upon the surrender, the agency immediately shall forward the license or permit to the court in which the person is to appear on the charge. Upon receipt of the license or permit, the court shall retain it pending the arrested person's initial appearance and any action taken under section 4511.196 [4511.19.6] of the Revised Code.

(D)(1) If a law enforcement officer asks a person under arrest as described in division (A)(5) of section 4511.191 [4511.19.1] of the Revised Code to submit to a chemical test or tests under that section and the test results indicate a prohibited concentration of alcohol, a controlled substance, or a metabolite of a controlled substance in the person's whole blood, blood serum or plasma, breath, or urine at the time of the alleged offense, or if a law enforcement officer asks a person under arrest as described in division (A) of this section to submit to a chemical test or tests under section 4511.191 [4511.19.1] of the Revised Code, the officer advises the person in accordance with this section of the consequences of the person's refusal or submission, and either the person refuses to submit to the test or tests or, unless the arrest was for a violation of section 4511.194 [4511.19.4] of the Revised Code or a substantially equivalent municipal ordinance, the person submits to the test or tests and the test results indicate a prohibited concentration of alcohol, a controlled substance, or a metabolite of a controlled substance in the person's whole blood, blood serum or plasma, breath, or urine at the time of the alleged offense, the arresting officer shall do all of the following:

(a) On behalf of the registrar of motor vehicles, notify the person that, independent of any penalties or sanctions imposed upon the person, the person's Ohio driver's or commercial driver's license or permit or nonresident operating privilege is suspended immediately, that the suspension will last at least until the person's initial appearance on the charge, which will be held within five days after the date of the person's arrest or the issuance of a citation to the person, and that the person may appeal the suspension at the initial appearance or during the period of time ending thirty days after that initial appearance;

(b) Seize the driver's or commercial driver's license or permit of the person and immediately forward it to the registrar. If the arrested person is not in possession of the person's license or permit or it is not in the person's vehicle, the officer shall order the person to surrender it to the law enforcement agency that employs the officer within twenty-four hours after the person is given notice of the suspension, and, upon the surrender, the officer's employing agency immediately shall forward the license or permit to the registrar.

(c) Verify the person's current residence and, if it differs from that on the person's driver's or commercial driver's license or permit, notify the registrar of the change;

(d) Send to the registrar, within forty-eight hours after the arrest of the person, a sworn report that includes all of the following statements:

(i) That the officer had reasonable grounds to believe that, at the time of the arrest, the arrested person was operating a vehicle, streetcar, or trackless trolley in violation of division (A) or (B) of section 4511.19 of the Revised Code or a municipal OVI ordinance or for being in physical control of a stationary vehicle, streetcar, or trackless trolley in violation of section 4511.194 [4511.19.4] of the Revised Code or a substantially equivalent municipal ordinance;

(ii) That the person was arrested and charged with a violation of division (A) or (B) of section 4511.19 of the Revised Code, section 4511.194 [4511.19.4] of the Revised Code or a substantially equivalent municipal ordinance, or a municipal OVI ordinance;

(iii) Unless division (D)(1)(d)(v) of this section applies, that the officer asked the person to take the designated chemical test or tests, advised the person in accordance with this section of the consequences of submitting to, or refusing to take, the test or tests, and gave the person the form described in division (B) of this section;

(iv) Unless division (D)(1)(d)(v) of this section applies, that either the person refused to submit to the chemical test or tests or, unless the arrest was for a violation of section 4511.194 [4511.19.4] of the Revised Code or a substantially equivalent municipal ordinance, the person submitted to the chemical test or tests and the test results indicate a prohibited concentration of alcohol, a controlled substance, or a metabolite of a controlled substance in the person's whole blood, blood serum or plasma, breath, or urine at the time of the alleged offense;

(v) If the person was under arrest as described in division (A)(5) of section 4511.191 [4511.19.1] of the Revised Code and the chemical test or tests were performed in accordance with that division, that the person was under arrest as described in that division, that the chemical test or tests were performed in accordance with that division, and that test results indicated a prohibited concentration of alcohol, a controlled substance, or a metabolite of a controlled substance in the person's whole blood, blood serum or plasma, breath, or urine at the time of the alleged offense.

(2) Division (D)(1) of this section does not apply to a person who is arrested for a violation of section 4511.194 [4511.19.4] of the Revised Code or a substantially equivalent municipal ordinance, who is asked by a law enforcement officer to submit to a chemical test or tests under section 4511.191 [4511.19.1] of the Revised Code, and who submits to the test or tests, regardless of the amount of alcohol, a controlled substance, or a metabolite of a controlled substance that the test results indicate is present in the person's whole blood, blood serum or plasma, breath, or urine.

(E) The arresting officer shall give the officer's sworn report that is completed under this section to the arrested person at the time of the arrest, or the registrar of motor vehicles shall send the report to the person by regular first class mail as soon as possible after receipt of the report, but not later than fourteen days after receipt of it. An arresting officer may give an unsworn report to the arrested person at the time of the arrest provided the report is complete when given to the arrested person and subsequently is sworn to by the arresting officer. As soon as possible, but not later than forty-eight hours after the arrest of the person, the arresting officer shall send a copy of the sworn report to the court in which the arrested person is to appear on the charge for which the person was arrested.

(F) The sworn report of an arresting officer completed under this section is prima-facie proof of the information and statements that it contains. It shall be admitted and considered as prima-facie proof of the information and statements that it contains in any appeal under section 4511.197 [4511.19.7] of the Revised Code relative to any suspension of a person's driver's or commercial driver's license or permit or nonresident operating privilege that results from the arrest covered by the report.

**HISTORY: 137 v S 381 (Eff 10-19-78); 139 v S 432 (Eff 3-16-83); 141 v S 262 (Eff 3-20-87); 143 v H 381 (Eff 7-1-89); 145 v S 62. Eff 9-1-93; 149 v S 123, § 1, eff. 1-1-04; 150 v H 163, § 1, eff. 9-23-04; 151 v S 8, § 1, eff. 8-17-06; 152 v S 17, § 1, eff. 9-30-08; 152 v H 215, § 1, eff. 4-7-09.**

The effective date is set by section 4 of S.B. 123.

See provisions, § 5 of S.B. 123 (149 v —), following RC § 4501.01.

## § 4511.193 Deposit of $25 of fine for violating OVI ordinance into indigent drivers alcohol treatment fund; immobilization or forfeiture orders based on prior convictions.

(A) Twenty-five dollars of any fine imposed for a violation of a municipal OVI ordinance shall be deposited into the municipal or county indigent drivers alcohol treatment fund created pursuant to division (H) of section 4511.191 of the Revised Code in accordance with this section and section 733.40, divisions (A) , (B), and (C) of section 1901.024, division (F) of section 1901.31, or division (C) of section 1907.20 of the Revised Code. Regardless of whether the fine is imposed by a municipal court, a mayor's court, or a juvenile court, if the fine was imposed for a violation of an ordinance of a municipal corporation that is within the jurisdiction of a county-operated municipal court or a municipal court that is not a county-operated municipal court, the twenty-five dollars that is subject to this section shall be deposited into the indigent drivers alcohol treatment fund of the county in which that municipal corporation is located if the municipal court that has jurisdiction over that municipal corporation is a county-operated municipal court or of the municipal corporation in which is located the municipal court that has jurisdiction over that municipal corporation if that municipal court is not a county-operated municipal court. Regardless of whether the fine is imposed by a county court, a mayor's court, or a juvenile court, if the fine was imposed for a violation of an ordinance of a municipal corporation that is within the jurisdiction of a county court, the twenty-five dollars that is subject to this section shall be deposited into the indigent drivers alcohol treatment fund of the county in which is located the county court that has jurisdiction over that municipal corporation. The deposit shall be made in accordance with section 733.40, divisions (A) , (B), and (C) of section 1901.024, division (F) of section 1901.31, or division (C) of section 1907.20 of the Revised Code.

(B) Any court cost imposed as a result of a violation of a municipal ordinance that is a moving violation and designated for an indigent drivers alcohol treatment fund established pursuant to division (H) of section 4511.191 of the Revised Code shall be deposited into the municipal or county indigent drivers alcohol treatment fund created pursuant to division (H) of section 4511.191 of the Revised Code in accordance with this section and section 733.40, divisions (A), (B), and (C) of section 1901.024, division (F) of section 1901.31, or division (C) of section 1907.20 of the Revised Code. Regardless of whether the court cost is imposed by a municipal court, a mayor's court, or a juvenile court, if the court cost was imposed for a violation of an ordinance of a municipal corporation that is within the jurisdiction of a county-operated municipal court or a municipal court that is not a county-operated municipal court, the court cost that is subject to this section shall be deposited into the indigent drivers alcohol treatment fund of the county in which that municipal corporation is located if the municipal court that has jurisdiction over that municipal corporation is a county-operated municipal court or of the municipal corporation in which is located the municipal court that has jurisdiction over that municipal corporation if that municipal court is not a county-operated municipal court. Regardless of whether the court cost is imposed by a county court, a mayor's court, or a juvenile court, if the court cost was imposed for a violation of an ordinance of a municipal corporation that is within the jurisdiction of a county court, the court cost that is subject to this section shall be deposited into the indigent drivers alcohol treatment fund of the county in which is located the county court that has jurisdiction over that municipal corporation. The deposit shall be made in accordance with section 733.40, divisions (A), (B), and (C) of section 1901.024, division (F) of section 1901.31, or division (C) of section 1907.20 of the Revised Code.

(C)(1) The requirements and sanctions imposed by divisions (C)(1) and (2) of this section are an adjunct to and derive from the state's exclusive authority over the registration and titling of motor vehicles and do not comprise a part of the criminal sentence to be imposed upon a person who violates a municipal OVI ordinance.

(2) If a person is convicted of or pleads guilty to a violation of a municipal OVI ordinance, if the vehicle the offender was operating at the time of the offense is registered in the offender's name, and if, within six years of the current offense, the offender has been convicted of or pleaded guilty to one or more violations of division (A) or (B) of section 4511.19 of the Revised Code or one or more other equivalent offenses, the court, in addition to and independent of any sentence that it imposes upon the offender for the offense, shall do whichever of the following is applicable:

(a) Except as otherwise provided in division (C)(2)(b) of this section, if, within six years of the current offense, the offender has been convicted of or pleaded guilty to one violation described in division (C)(2) of this section, the court shall order the immobilization for ninety days of that vehicle and the impoundment for ninety days of the license plates of that vehicle. The order for the immobilization and impoundment shall be issued and enforced in accordance with section 4503.233 of the Revised Code.

(b) If, within six years of the current offense, the offender has been convicted of or pleaded guilty to two or more violations described in division (C)(2) of this section, or if the offender previously has been convicted of or pleaded guilty to a violation of division (A) of section 4511.19 of the Revised Code under circumstances in which the violation was a felony and regardless of when the violation and the conviction or guilty plea occurred, the court shall order the criminal forfeiture to the state of that vehicle. The order of criminal forfeiture shall be issued and enforced in accordance with section 4503.234 of the Revised Code.

(D) As used in this section, "county-operated municipal court" has the same meaning as in section 1901.03 of the Revised Code.

**HISTORY: 145 v S 62 (Eff 9-1-93); 146 v H 353 (Eff 9-17-96); 146 v S 166 (Eff 10-17-96); 147 v S 60 (Eff 10-21-97); 148 v S 107. Eff 3-23-2000; 149 v S 123, § 1, eff. 1-1-04; 2011 HB 153, § 101.01, eff. Sept. 29, 2011.**

The effective date is set by section 4 of S.B. 123.

See provisions, § 5 of S.B. 123 (149 v —), following RC § 4501.01.

The provisions of § 8 of S.B. 123 read as follows:

SECTION 8. Section 4511.193 of the Revised Code is presented in this act as a composite of the section as amended by both Am. H.B. 80 and Am. Sub. S.B. 107 of the 123rd General Assembly. The General Assembly, applying the principle stated in division (B) of section 1.52 of the Revised Code that amendments are to be harmonized if reasonably capable of simultaneous operation, finds that the composites are the resulting versions of the sections in effect prior to the effective date of the sections as presented in this act.

**Analogous to former RC § 4511.19.3 (143 v S 131; 143 v H 837), repealed 144 v S 275, § 2, eff 9-1-93.**

## § 4511.194 Having physical control of vehicle while under influence.

(A) As used in this section:

(1) "National highway traffic safety administration" has the same meaning as in section 4511.19 of the Revised Code.

(2) "Physical control" means being in the driver's position of the front seat of a vehicle or in the driver's position of a streetcar or trackless trolley and having possession of the vehicle's, streetcar's, or trackless trolley's ignition key or other ignition device.

(B) No person shall be in physical control of a vehicle, streetcar, or trackless trolley if, at the time of the physical control, any of the following apply:

(1) The person is under the influence of alcohol, a drug of abuse, or a combination of them.

(2) The person's whole blood, blood serum or plasma, breath, or urine contains at least the concentration of alcohol specified in division (A)(1)(b), (c), (d), or (e) of section 4511.19 of the Revised Code.

(3) Except as provided in division (E) of this section, the person has a concentration of a listed controlled substance or a listed metabolite of a controlled substance in the person's whole blood, blood serum or plasma, or urine that equals or exceeds the concentration specified in division (A)(1)(j) of section 4511.19 of the Revised Code.

(C)(1) In any criminal prosecution or juvenile court proceeding for a violation of this section or a substantially equivalent municipal ordinance, if a law enforcement officer has administered a field sobriety test to the person in physical control of the vehicle involved in the violation and if it is shown by clear and convincing evidence that the officer administered the test in substantial compliance with the testing standards for any reliable, credible, and generally accepted field sobriety tests that were in effect at the time the tests were administered, including, but not limited to, any testing standards then in effect that were set by the national highway traffic safety administration, all of the following apply:

(a) The officer may testify concerning the results of the field sobriety test so administered.

(b) The prosecution may introduce the results of the field sobriety test so administered as evidence in any proceedings in the criminal prosecution or juvenile court proceeding.

(c) If testimony is presented or evidence is introduced under division (C)(1)(a) or (b) of this section and if the testimony or evidence is admissible under the Rules of Evidence, the court shall admit the testimony or evidence, and the trier of fact shall give it whatever weight the trier of fact considers to be appropriate.

(2) Division (C)(1) of this section does not limit or preclude a court, in its determination of whether the arrest of a person was supported by probable cause or its determination of any other matter in a criminal prosecution or juvenile court proceeding of a type described in that division, from considering evidence or testimony that is not otherwise disallowed by division (C)(1) of this section.

(D) Whoever violates this section is guilty of having physical control of a vehicle while under the influence, a misdemeanor of the first degree. In addition to other sanctions imposed, the court may impose on the offender a class seven suspension of the offender's driver's license, commercial driver's license, temporary instruction permit, probationary license, or nonresident operating privilege from the range specified in division (A)(7) of section 4510.02 of the Revised Code.

(E) Division (B)(3) of this section does not apply to a person who is in physical control of a vehicle, streetcar, or trackless trolley while the person has a concentration of a listed controlled substance or a listed metabolite of a controlled substance in the person's whole blood, blood serum or plasma, or urine that equals or exceeds the amount specified in division (A)(1)(j) of section 4511.19 of the Revised Code, if both of the following apply:

(1) The person obtained the controlled substance pursuant to a prescription issued by a licensed health professional authorized to prescribe drugs.

(2) The person injected, ingested, or inhaled the controlled substance in accordance with the health professional's directions.

**HISTORY: 149 v S 123, § 1, eff. 1-1-04; 149 v S 163, § 3, eff. 1-1-04; 150 v H 163, § 1, eff. 9-23-04; 151 v S 8, § 1, eff. 8-17-06.**

The effective date is set by section 5 of S.B. 163 (149 v —).

See provisions, § 5 of S.B. 123 (149 v —), following RC § 4501.01.

## § 4511.195 Seizure and detention of vehicle where arrestee has prior conviction; return, immobilization or forfeiture after disposition of charge; rights of vehicle owner.

(A) As used in this section:

(1) "Arrested person" means a person who is arrested for a violation of division (A) of section 4511.19 of the Revised Code or a municipal OVI ordinance and whose arrest results in a vehicle being seized under division (B) of this section.

(2) "Vehicle owner" means either of the following:

(a) The person in whose name is registered, at the time of the seizure, a vehicle that is seized under division (B) of this section;

(b) A person to whom the certificate of title to a vehicle that is seized under division (B) of this section has been assigned and who has not obtained a certificate of title to the vehicle in that person's name, but who is deemed by the court as being the owner of the vehicle at the time the vehicle was seized under division (B) of this section.

(3) "Interested party" includes the owner of a vehicle seized under this section, all lienholders, the defendant arrested person, the owner of the place of storage at which a vehicle seized under this section is stored, and the person or entity that caused the vehicle to be removed.

(B)(1) The arresting officer or another officer of the law enforcement agency that employs the arresting officer, in addition to any action that the arresting officer is required or authorized to take by section 4511.19 or 4511.191 [4511.19.1] of the Revised Code or by any other provision of law, shall seize the vehicle that a person was operating at the time of the alleged offense and its license plates if the vehicle is registered in the arrested person's name and if either of the following applies:

(a) The person is arrested for a violation of division (A) of section 4511.19 of the Revised Code or of a municipal OVI ordinance and, within six years of the alleged violation, the person previously has been convicted of or pleaded guilty to one or more violations of Division (A) or (B) of section 4511.19 of the Revised Code or one of more other equivalent offenses.

(b) The person is arrested for a violation of division (A) of section 4511.19 of the Revised Code or of a municipal OVI ordinance and the person previously has been convicted of or pleaded guilty to a violation of division (A) of section 4511.19 of the Revised Code under circumstances in which the violation was a felony, regardless of when the prior felony violation of division (A) of section 4511.19 of the Revised Code and the conviction or guilty plea occurred.

(2) A law enforcement agency that employs a law enforcement officer who makes an arrest of a type that is described in division (B))(1) of this section and that involves a rented or leased vehicle that is being rented or lease for a period of thirty days or less shall notify, within twenty-four hours after the officer makes the arrest, the lessor or owner of the vehicle regarding the circumstances of the arrest and the location at which the vehicle may be picked up. At the time of the seizure of the vehicle, the law enforcement officer who made the arrest shall give the arrested person written notice that the vehicle and its license plates have been seized; that the vehicle either will be kept by the officer's law enforcement agency or will be immobilized at least until the operator's initial appearance on the charge of the offense for which the arrest was made; that, at the initial appearance, the court in certain circumstances may order that the vehicle and license plates be released to the arrested person until the disposition of that charge; and that, if the arrested person is convicted of that charge, the court generally must order the immobilization of the vehicle and the impoundment of its license plates, or the forfeiture of the vehicle.

(3) The arresting officer or a law enforcement officer of the agency that employs the arresting officer shall give written notice of the seizure to the court that will conduct the initial appearance of the arrested person on the charges arising out of the arrest. Upon receipt of the notice, the court promptly shall determine whether the arrested person is the vehicle owner. If the court determines that the arrested person is not the vehicle owner, it promptly shall send by regular mail written notice of the seizure to the vehicle's registered owner. The written notice shall contain all of the information required by division (B)(2) of this section to be in a notice to be given to the arrested person and also shall specify the date, time, and place of the arrested person's initial appearance. The notice also shall inform the vehicle owner that if title to a motor vehicle that is subject to an order for criminal forfeiture under this section is assigned or transferred and division (B)(2) or (3) of section 4503.234 [4503.23.4] of the Revised Code applies, the court may fine the arrested person the value of the vehicle. The notice also shall state that if the vehicle is immobilized under division (A) of section 4503.233 [4503.23.3] of the Revised Code, seven days after the end of the period of immobilization a law enforcement agency will send the vehicle owner a notice, informing the owner that if the release of the vehicle is not obtained in accordance with division (D)(3) of section 4503.233 [4503.23.3] of the Revised Code, the vehicle shall be forfeited. The notice also shall inform the vehicle owner that the vehicle owner may be charged expenses or charges incurred under this section and section 4503.233 [4503.23.3] of the Revised Code for the removal and storage of the vehicle.

The written notice that is given to the arrested person also shall state that if the person is convicted of or pleads guilty to the offense and the court issues an immobilization and impoundment order relative to that vehicle, division (D)(4) of section 4503.233 [4503.23.3] of the Revised Code prohibits the vehicle from being sold during the period of immobilization without the prior approval of the court.

(4) At or before the initial appearance, the vehicle owner may file a motion requesting the court to order that the vehicle and its license plates be released to the vehicle owner. Except as provided in this division and subject to the payment of expenses or charges incurred in the removal and storage of the vehicle, the court, in its discretion, then may issue an order releasing the vehicle and its license plates to the vehicle owner. Such an order may be conditioned upon such terms as the court determines appropriate, including the posting of a bond in an amount determined by the court. If the arrested person is not the vehicle owner and if the vehicle owner is not present at the arrested person's initial appearance, and if the court believes that the vehicle owner was not provided with adequate notice of the initial appearance, the court, in its discretion, may allow the vehicle owner to file a motion within seven days of the initial appearance. If the court allows the vehicle owner to file such a motion after the initial appearance, the extension of time granted by the court does not extend the time within which the initial appearance is to be conducted. If the court issues an order for the release of the vehicle and its license plates, a copy of the order shall be made available to the vehicle owner. If the vehicle owner presents a copy of the order to the law enforcement agency that employs the law enforcement officer who arrested the arrested person, the law enforcement agency promptly shall release the vehicle and its license plates to the vehicle owner upon payment by the vehicle owner of any expenses or charges incurred in the removal and storage of the vehicle.

(5) A vehicle seized under division (B)(1) of this section either shall be towed to a place specified by the law enforcement agency that employs the arresting officer to be safely kept by the agency at that place for the time and in the manner specified in this section or shall be otherwise immobilized for the time and in the manner specified in this section. A law enforcement officer of that agency shall remove the identification license plates of the vehicle, and they shall be safely kept by the agency for the time and in the manner specified in this section. No vehicle that is seized and either towed or immobilized pursuant to this division shall be considered contraband for purposes of Chapter 2981. of the Revised Code. The vehicle shall not be immobilized at any place other than a commercially operated private storage lot, a place owned by a law enforcement agency or other government agency, or a place to which one of the following applies:

(a) The place is leased by or otherwise under the control of a law enforcement agency or other government agency.

(b) The place is owned by the vehicle operator, the vehicle operator's spouse, or a parent or child of the vehicle operator.

(c) The place is owned by a private person or entity, and, prior to the immobilization, the private entity or person that owns the place, or the authorized agent of that private entity or person, has given express written consent for the immobilization to be carried out at that place.

(d) The place is a street or highway on which the vehicle is parked in accordance with the law.

(C)(1) A vehicle seized under division (B) of this section shall be safely kept at the place to which it is towed or otherwise moved by the law enforcement agency that employs the arresting officer until the initial appearance of the arrested person relative to the charge in question. The license plates of the vehicle that are removed pursuant to division (B) of this section shall be safely kept by the law enforcement agency that employs the arresting officer until the initial appearance of the arrested person relative to the charge in question.

(2)(a) At the initial appearance or not less than seven days prior to the date of final disposition, the court shall notify the arrested person, if title to a motor vehicle that is subject to an order for criminal forfeiture under this section is assigned or transferred and division (B)(2) or (3) of section 4503.234 of the Revised Code applies, the court may fine the arrested person the value of the vehicle. If, at the initial appearance, the arrested person pleads guilty to the violation of division (A) of section 4511.19 of the Revised Code or of the municipal OVI ordinance or pleads no contest to and is convicted of the violation, the court shall impose sentence upon the person as provided by law or ordinance; the court shall order the immobilization of the vehicle the arrested person was operating at the time of the offense if registered in the arrested person's name and the impoundment of its license plates under section 4503.233 [4503.23.3] and section 4511.19 or 4511.193 [4511.19.3] of the Revised Code or the criminal forfeiture to the state of the vehicle if registered in the arrested person's name under section 4503.234 [4503.23.4] and section 4511.19 or 4511.193 [4511.19.3] of the Revised Code, whichever is applicable; and the vehicle and its license plates shall not be returned or released to the arrested person.

(b) If, at any time, the charge that the arrested person violated division (A) of section 4511.19 of the Revised Code or the municipal OVI ordinance is dismissed for any reason, the court shall order that the vehicle seized at the time of the arrest and its license plates immediately be released to the person.

(D) If a vehicle and it license plates are seized under division (B) of this section and are not returned or released to the arrested person pursuant to division (C) of this section, the vehicle and its license plates shall be retained until the final disposition of the charge in question. Upon the final disposition of that charge, the court shall do whichever of the following is applicable:

(1) If the arrested person is convicted of or pleads guilty to the violation of division (A) of section 4511.19 of the Revised Code or of the municipal OVI ordinance, the court shall impose sentence upon the person as provided by law or ordinance and shall order the immobilization of the vehicle the person was operating at the time of the offense if it is registered in the arrested person's name and the impoundment of its license plates under section 4503.233 [4503.23.3] and section 4511.19 or 4511.193 [4511.19.3] of the Revised Code, or the criminal forfeiture of the vehicle if it is registered in the arrested person's name under section 4503.234 [4503.23.4] and section 4511.19 or 4511.193 [4511.19.3] of the Revised Code, whichever is applicable.

(2) If the arrested person is found not guilty of the violation of division (A) of section 4511.19 of the Revised Code or of the municipal OVI ordinance, the court shall order that the vehicle and its license plates immediately be released to the arrested person.

(3) If the charge that the arrested person violated division (A) of section 4511.19 of the Revised Code or the municipal OVI ordinance is dismissed for any reason, the court shall order that the vehicle and its license plates immediately be released to the arrested person.

(4) If the impoundment of the vehicle was not authorized under this section, the court shall order that the vehicle and its license plates be returned immediately to the arrested person or, if the arrested person is not the vehicle owner, to the vehicle owner, and shall order that the state or political subdivision of the law enforcement agency served by the law enforcement officer who seized the vehicle pay all expenses and charges incurred in its removal and storage.

(E) If a vehicle is seized under division (B) of this section, the time between the seizure of the vehicle and either its release to the arrested person under division (C) of this section or the issuance of an order of immobilization of the vehicle under section 4503.233 [4503.23.3] of the Revised Code shall be credited against the period of immobilization ordered by the court.

(F)(1) Except as provided in Division (D)(4) of this section, the arrested person may be charged expenses or charges incurred in the removal and storage of the immobilized vehicle. The court with jurisdiction over the case, after notice to all interested parties, including lienholders, and after an opportunity for them to be heard, if the court finds that the arrested person does not intend to seek release of the vehicle at the end of the period of immobilization under section 4503.233 [4503.23.3] of the Revised Code or that the arrested person is not or will not be able to pay the expenses and charges incurred in its removal and storage, may order that title to the vehicle be transferred, in order of priority, first into the name of the person or entity that removed it, next into the name of a lienholder, or lastly into the name of the owner of the place of storage.

Any lienholder that receives title under a court order shall do so on the condition that it pay any expenses or charges incurred in the vehicle's removal and storage. If the person or entity that receives title to the vehicle is the person or entity that removed it, the person or entity shall receive title on the condition that it pay any lien on the vehicle. The court shall not order that title be transferred to any person or entity other than the owner of the place of storage if the person or entity refuses to receive the title. Any person or entity that receives title either may keep title to the vehicle or may dispose of the vehicle in any legal manner that it considers appropriate, including assignment of the certificate of title to the motor vehicle to a salvage dealer or a scrap metal processing facility. The person or entity shall not transfer the vehicle to the person who is the vehicle's immediate previous owner.

If the person or entity that receives title assigns the motor vehicle to a salvage dealer or scrap metal processing facility, the person or entity shall send the assigned certificate of title to the motor vehicle to the clerk of the court of common pleas of the county in which the salvage dealer or scrap metal processing facility is located. The person or entity shall mark the face of the certificate of title with the words "FOR DESTRUCTION" and shall deliver a photocopy of the certificate of title to the salvage dealer or scrap metal processing facility for its records.

(2) Whenever a court issues an order under division (F)(1) of this section, the court also shall order removal of

the license plates from the vehicle and cause them to be sent to the registrar of motor vehicles if they have not already been sent to the registrar. Thereafter, no further proceedings shall take place under this section or under section 4503.233 [4503.23.3] of the Revised Code.

(3) Prior to initiating a proceeding under division (F)(1) of this section, and upon payment of the fee under division (B) of section 4505.14 of the Revised Code, any interested party may cause a search to be made of the public records of the bureau of motor vehicles or the clerk of the court of common pleas, to ascertain the identity of any lienholder of the vehicle. The initiating party shall furnish this information to the clerk of the court with jurisdiction over the case, and the clerk shall provide notice to the arrested person, any lienholder, and any other interested parties listed by the initiating party, at the last known address supplied by the initiating party, by certified mail or, at the option of the initiating party, by personal service or ordinary mail.

**HISTORY: 144 v S 275 (Eff 9-1-93); 145 v S 62, §§ 1, 4 (Eff 9-1-93); 145 v S 82 (Eff 5-4-94); 145 v H 236 (Eff 9-29-94); 145 v H 687 (Eff 10-12-94); 146 v H 353 (Eff 9-17-96); 146 v H 676 (Eff 10-4-96); 146 v S 166 (Eff 10-17-96); 147 v S 60 (Eff 10-21-97); 147 v S 213 (Eff 7-29-98); 148 v S 107. Eff 3-23-2000; 149 v S 123, § 1, eff. 1-1-04; 151 v H 241, § 1, eff. 7-1-07.**

See provisions of § 4 of 151 v H 241 following RC § 4503.233.

The effective date is set by section 4 of S.B. 123.

See provisions, § 5 of S.B. 123 (149 v —), following RC § 4501.01.

## § 4511.196 Initial appearance; new suspension of license.

(A) If a person is arrested for being in physical control of a vehicle, streetcar, or trackless trolley in violation of section 4511.194 [4511.19.4] of the Revised Code or a substantially equivalent municipal ordinance, or for operating a vehicle, streetcar, or trackless trolley in violation of division (A) or (B) of section 4511.19 of the Revised Code or a municipal OVI ordinance, regardless of whether the person's driver's or commercial driver's license or permit or nonresident operating privilege is or is not suspended under section 4511.191 [4511.19.1] of the Revised Code, the person's initial appearance on the charge resulting from the arrest shall be held within five days of the person's arrest or the issuance of the citation to the person.

(B)(1) If a person is arrested as described in division (A) of this section, if the person's driver's or commercial driver's license or permit or nonresident operating privilege has been suspended under section 4511.191 [4511.19.1] of the Revised Code in relation to that arrest, if the person appeals the suspension in accordance with section 4511.197 [4511.19.7] of the Revised Code, and if the judge, magistrate, or mayor terminates the suspension in accordance with that section, the judge, magistrate, or mayor, at any time prior to adjudication on the merits of the charge resulting from the arrest, may impose a new suspension of the person's license, permit, or nonresident operating privilege, notwithstanding the termination, if the judge, magistrate, or mayor determines that the person's continued driving will be a threat to public safety.

(2) If a person is arrested as described in division (A) of this section and if the person's driver's or commercial driver's license or permit or nonresident operating privilege has not been suspended under section 4511.191 [4511.19.1] of the Revised Code in relation to that arrest, the judge, magistrate, or mayor, at any time prior to the adjudication on the merits of the charge resulting from the arrest, may impose a suspension of the person's license, permit, or nonresident operating privilege if the judge, magistrate, or mayor determines that the person's continued driving will be a threat to public safety.

(C) A suspension under division (B)(1) or (2) of this section shall continue until the complaint on the charge resulting from the arrest is adjudicated on the merits. A court that imposes a suspension under division (B)(2) of this section shall send the person's driver's license or permit to the registrar of motor vehicles. If the court possesses the license or permit of a person in the category described in division (B)(2) of this section and the court does not impose a suspension under that division, the court shall return the license or permit to the person if the license or permit has not otherwise been suspended or cancelled.

Any time during which the person serves a suspension of the person's license, permit, or privilege that is imposed pursuant to division (B)(1) or (2) of this section shall be credited against any period of judicial suspension of the person's license, permit, or privilege that is imposed under division (G) of section 4511.19 of the Revised Code or under section 4510.07 of the Revised Code for a violation of a municipal ordinance substantially equivalent to division (A) section 4511.19 of the Revised Code.

(D) If a person is arrested and charged with a violation of section 2903.08 of the Revised Code or a violation of section 2903.06 of the Revised Code that is a felony offense, the judge at the person's initial appearance, preliminary hearing, or arraignment may suspend the person's driver's or commercial driver's license or permit or nonresident operating privilege if the judge determines at any of those proceedings that the person's continued driving will be a threat to public safety.

A suspension imposed under this division shall continue until the indictment or information alleging the violation specified in this division is adjudicated on the merits. A court that imposes a suspension under this division shall send the person's driver's or commercial driver's license or permit to the registrar.

**HISTORY: 145 v S 62 (Eff 9-1-93); 147 v S 60 (Eff 10-21-97); 148 v H 61 (Eff 8-25-99); 148 v S 107. Eff 3-23-2000; 149 v S 123, § 1, eff. 1-1-04; 150 v H 163, § 1, eff. 9-23-04.**

The effective date is set by section 4 of S.B. 123.

See provisions, § 5 of S.B. 123 (149 v —), following RC § 4501.01.

## § 4511.197 Appeal of suspension under implied consent provisions; length of suspension that is upheld or not appealed; petition for limited driving privileges.

(A) If a person is arrested for operating a vehicle, streetcar, or trackless trolley in violation of division (A) or (B) of section 4511.19 of the Revised Code or a municipal OVI ordinance or for being in physical control of a vehicle, streetcar, or trackless trolley in violation of section 4511.194 [4511.19.4] of the Revised Code or a substantially equivalent municipal ordinance and if the person's driver's or commercial driver's license or permit or nonresident operating privilege is suspended under sections 4511.191 [4511.19.1] and 4511.192 [4511.19.2] of the Revised Code, the person may appeal the suspension at the person's initial appearance on the charge resulting from the arrest or within the period ending thirty days after the person's initial appearance on that charge, in the court in which the person will appear on that charge. If the person appeals the suspension, the appeal itself does not stay the operation of the suspension. If the person appeals the suspension, either the person or the registrar of motor vehicles may request a continuance of the appeal, and the court may grant the continuance. The court also may continue the appeal on its own motion. Neither the request for, nor the granting of, a continuance stays the suspension that is the subject of the appeal, unless the court specifically grants a stay.

(B) A person shall file an appeal under division (A) of this section in the municipal court, county court, juvenile court, mayor's court, or court of common pleas that has jurisdiction over the charge in relation to which the person was arrested.

(C) If a person appeals a suspension under division (A) of this section, the scope of the appeal is limited to determining whether one or more of the following conditions have not been met:

(1) Whether the arresting law enforcement officer had reasonable ground to believe the arrested person was operating a vehicle, streetcar, or trackless trolley in violation of division (A) or (B) of section 4511.19 of the Revised Code or a municipal OVI ordinance or was in physical control of a vehicle, streetcar, or trackless trolley in violation of section 4511.194 [4511.19.4] of the Revised Code or a substantially equivalent municipal ordinance and whether the arrested person was in fact placed under arrest;

(2) Whether the law enforcement officer requested the arrested person to submit to the chemical test or tests designated pursuant to division (A) of section 4511.191 [4511.19.1] of the Revised Code;

(3) If the person was under arrest as described in division (A)(5) of section 4511.191 [4511.19.1] of the Revised Code, whether the arresting officer advised the person at the time of the arrest that if the person refused to take a chemical test, the officer could employ whatever reasonable means were necessary to ensure that the person submitted to a chemical test of the person's whole blood or blood serum or plasma; or if the person was under arrest other than as described in division (A)(5) of section 4511.191 [4511.19.1] of the Revised Code, whether the arresting officer informed the arrested person of the consequences of refusing to be tested or of submitting to the test or tests;

(4) Whichever of the following is applicable:

(a) If the suspension was imposed under division (B) of section 4511.191 [4511.19.1] and section 4511.192 [4511.19.2] of the Revised Code, whether the arrested person refused to submit to the chemical test or tests requested by the officer;

(b) If the suspension was imposed under division (C) of section 4511.191 [4511.19.1] and section 4511.192 [4511.19.2] of the Revised Code, whether the arrest was for a violation of division (A) or (B) of section 4511.19 of the Revised Code or a municipal OVI ordinance and, if it was, whether the chemical test results indicate that at the time of the alleged offense the arrested person's whole blood, blood serum or plasma, breath, or urine contained at least the concentration of alcohol specified in division (A)(1)(b), (c), (d), or (e) of section 4511.19 of the Revised Code or at least the concentration of a listed controlled substance or a listed metabolite of a controlled substance specified in division (A)(1)(j) of section 4511.19 of the Revised Code.

(D) A person who appeals a suspension under division (A) of this section has the burden of proving, by a preponderance of the evidence, that one or more of the conditions specified in division (C) of this section has not been met. If, during the appeal, the judge or magistrate of the court or the mayor of the mayor's court determines that all of those conditions have been met, the judge, magistrate, or mayor shall uphold the suspension, continue the suspension, and notify the registrar of motor vehicles of the decision on a form approved by the registrar.

Except as otherwise provided in this section, if a suspension imposed under section 4511.191 [4511.19.1] of the Revised Code is upheld on appeal or if the subject person does not appeal the suspension under division (A) of this section, the suspension shall continue until the complaint alleging the violation for which the person was arrested and in relation to which the suspension was imposed is adjudicated on the merits or terminated pursuant to law. If the suspension was imposed under division (B)(1) of section 4511.191 [4511.19.1] of the Revised Code and it is continued under this section, any subsequent finding that the person is not guilty of the charge that resulted in the person being requested to take the chemical test or tests under division (A) of section 4511.191 [4511.19.1] of the Revised Code does not terminate or otherwise affect the suspension. If the suspension was imposed under division (C) of section 4511.191 [4511.19.1] of the Revised Code in relation to an alleged misdemeanor violation of division (A) or (B) of section 4511.19 of the Revised Code or of a municipal OVI ordinance and it is continued under this section, the suspension shall terminate if, for any reason, the person subsequently is found not guilty of the charge that resulted in the person taking the chemical test or tests.

If, during the appeal, the judge or magistrate of the trial court or the mayor of the mayor's court determines that one or more of the conditions specified in division (C) of this section have not been met, the judge, magistrate, or mayor shall terminate the suspension, subject to the imposition of a new suspension under division (B) of section 4511.196 [4511.19.6] of the Revised Code; shall notify the registrar of motor vehicles of the decision on a form approved by the registrar; and, except as provided in division (B) of section 4511.196 [4511.19.6] of the Revised Code, shall order the registrar to return the driver's or commercial driver's license or permit to the person or to take any other measures that may be necessary, if the license or permit was destroyed under section 4510.53 of the Revised Code, to permit the person to obtain a replacement driver's or commercial driver's license or permit from the registrar or a deputy registrar in accordance with that section. The court also shall issue to the person a court order, valid for not more than ten days from the date of issuance, granting the person operating privileges for that period.

(E) Any person whose driver's or commercial driver's license or permit or nonresident operating privilege has been suspended pursuant to section 4511.191 [4511.19.1] of the Revised Code may file a petition requesting limited driving privileges in the common pleas court, municipal court, county court, mayor's court, or juvenile court with jurisdiction over the related criminal or delinquency case. The petition may be filed at any time subsequent to the date on which the arresting law enforcement officer serves the notice of suspension upon the arrested person but no later than thirty days after the arrested person's initial appearance or arraignment. Upon the making of the request, limited driving privileges may be granted under sections 4510.021 [4510.02.1] and 4510.13 of the Revised Code, regardless of whether the person appeals the suspension under this section or appeals the decision of the court on the appeal, and, if the person has so appealed the suspension or decision, regardless of whether the matter has been heard or decided by the court. The person shall pay the costs of the proceeding, notify the registrar of the filing of the petition, and send the registrar a copy of the petition.

The court may not grant the person limited driving privileges when prohibited by section 4510.13 or 4511.191 [4511.19.1] of the Revised Code.

(F) Any person whose driver's or commercial driver's license or permit has been suspended under section 4511.19 of the Revised Code or under section 4510.07 of the Revised Code for a conviction of a municipal OVI offense and who desires to retain the license or permit during the pendency of an appeal, at the time sentence is pronounced, shall notify the court of record or mayor's court that suspended the license or permit of the person's intention to appeal. If the person so notifies the court, the court, mayor, or clerk of the court shall retain the license or permit until the appeal is perfected, and, if execution of sentence is stayed, the license or permit shall be returned to the person to be held by the person during the pendency of the appeal. If the appeal is not perfected or is dismissed or terminated in an affirmance of the conviction, then the license or permit shall be taken up by the court, mayor, or clerk, at the time of putting the sentence into execution, and the court shall proceed in the same manner as if no appeal was taken.

(G) Except as otherwise provided in this division, if a person whose driver's or commercial driver's license or permit or nonresident operating privilege was suspended under section 4511.191 [4511.19.1] of the Revised Code appeals the suspension under division (A) of this section, the prosecuting attorney of the county in which the arrest occurred shall represent the registrar of motor vehicles in the appeal. If the arrest occurred within a municipal corporation within the jurisdiction of the court in which the appeal is conducted, the city director of law, village solicitor, or other chief legal officer of that municipal corporation shall represent the registrar. If the appeal is conducted in a municipal court, the registrar shall be represented as provided in section 1901.34 of the Revised Code. If the appeal is conducted in a mayor's court, the city director of law, village solicitor, or other chief legal officer of the municipal corporation that operates that mayor's court shall represent the registrar.

(H) The court shall give information in writing of any action taken under this section to the registrar of motor vehicles.

(I) When it finally has been determined under the procedures of this section that a nonresident's privilege to operate a vehicle within this state has been suspended, the registrar of motor vehicles shall give information in writing of the action taken to the motor vehicle administrator of the state of the nonresident's residence and of any state in which the nonresident has a license.

**HISTORY: 149 v S 123 (Eff 1-1-2004); 150 v H 87. Eff 1-1-2004; 150 v H 87, § 3, eff. 3-31-03; 150 v H 87, § 1, eff. 1-1-04; 150 v H 163, § 1, eff. 9-23-04; 152 v H 215, § 1, eff. 4-7-09.**

The effective date is set by section 3 of H.B. 87.

See provisions, § 5 of S.B. 123 (149 v —), following RC § 4501.01.

## § 4511.198 Court granting limited driving privileges to certain arrestees to prohibit consumption of alcohol and to require wearing of monitor.

(A)(1) If a court grants limited driving privilege to a person who is described in division (B) of this section and who is alleged to have committed a violation of division (A) of section 4511.19 of the Revised Code or of a substantially equivalent municipal ordinance, the court as a condition of granting limited driving privileges may prohibit the person from consuming any beer or intoxicating liquor and may require the person to wear a monitor that provides continuous alcohol monitoring that is remote. If the court imposes the requirement, the court shall require the person to wear the monitor until the person is convicted of, pleads guilty to, or is found not guilty of the alleged violation or the charges in the case are dismissed. Any consumption by the person of beer or intoxicating liquor prior to that time is grounds for revocation by the court of the person's limited driving privilege. The person shall pay all costs associated with the monitor, including the cost of remote monitoring.

(2) If a court grants limited driving privilege to a person who is described in division (C) of this section and who is alleged to have committed a violation of division (A) of section 4511.19 of the Revised Code or of a substantially equivalent municipal ordinance, the court as a condition of granting limited driving privileges, unless the court determines otherwise, shall prohibit the person from consuming any beer or intoxicating liquor and shall require the person to wear a monitor that provides continuous alcohol monitoring that is remote. The court shall require the person to wear the monitor until the person is convicted of, pleads guilty to, or is found not guilty of the alleged violation or the charges in the case are dismissed. Any consumption by the person of beer or intoxicating liquor prior to that time is grounds for revocation by the court of the person's limited driving privilege. The person shall pay all costs associated with the monitor, including the cost of remote monitoring.

(B) Division (A)(1) of this section applies to the following persons:

(1) A person who is alleged to have committed a violation of division (A) of section 4511.19 of the Revised Code and who, if convicted of the alleged violation, is required to be sentenced under division (G)(1)(c) or (d) of section 4511.19 of the Revised Code;

(2) A person who is alleged to have committed a violation of a municipal ordinance that is substantially equivalent to division (A) of section 4511.19 of the Revised Code and who, if the law enforcement officer who arrested and charged the person with the violation of the municipal ordinance instead had charged the person with a violation of division (A) of section 4511.19 of the Revised Code, would be required to be sentenced under division (G)(1)(c) or (d) of section 4511.19 of the Revised Code.

(C) Division (A)(2) of this section applies to the following persons:

(1) A person who is alleged to have committed a violation of division (A) of section 4511.19 of the Revised Code and who, if convicted of the alleged violation, is required to be sentenced under division (G)(1)(e) of section 4511.19 of the Revised Code;

(2) A person who is alleged to have committed a violation of a municipal ordinance that is substantially equivalent to division (A) of section 4511.19 of the Revised Code and who, if the law enforcement officer who arrested and charged the person with the violation of the municipal ordinance instead had charged the person with a violation of division (A) of section 4511.19 of the Revised Code, would be required to be sentenced under division (G)(1)(e) of section 4511.19 of the Revised Code.

**HISTORY: 152 v S 17, § 1, eff. 9-30-08.**

[RECKLESS OPERATION]

## § 4511.20 Willful or wanton operation on street or highway.

(A) No person shall operate a vehicle, trackless trolley, or streetcar on any street or highway in willful or wanton disregard of the safety of persons or property.

(B) Except as otherwise provided in this division, whoever violates this section is guilty of a minor misdemeanor. If, within one year of the offense, the offender previously has been convicted of or pleaded guilty to one predicate motor vehicle or traffic offense, whoever violates this section is guilty of a misdemeanor of the fourth degree. If, within one year of the offense, the offender previously has been convicted of two or more predicate motor vehicle or traffic offenses, whoever violates this section is guilty of a misdemeanor of the third degree.

**HISTORY: GC § 6307-20; 119 v 766, § 20; Bureau of Code Revision, 10-1-53; 132 v S 179 (Eff 12-13-67); 139 v S 432. Eff 3-16-83; 149 v S 123, § 1, eff. 1-1-04.**

The effective date is set by section 4 of S.B. 123.

See provisions, § 5 of S.B. 123 (149 v —), following RC § 4501.01.

## § 4511.201 Willful or wanton operation off street or highway; competitive operation exception.

(A) No person shall operate a vehicle, trackless trolley, or streetcar on any public or private property other than streets or highways, in willful or wanton disregard of the safety of persons or property.

This section does not apply to the competitive operation of vehicles on public or private property when the owner of such property knowingly permits such operation thereon.

(B) Except as otherwise provided in this division, whoever violates this section is guilty of a minor misdemeanor. If, within one year of the offense, the offender previously has been convicted of or pleaded guilty to one predicate motor vehicle or traffic offense, whoever violates this section is guilty of a misdemeanor of the fourth degree. If, within one year of the offense, the offender previously has been convicted of two or more predicate motor vehicle or traffic offenses, whoever violates this section is guilty of a misdemeanor of the third degree.

**HISTORY: 129 v 1637 (Eff 10-2-61); 132 v S 179 (Eff 12-13-67); 139 v S 432. Eff 3-16-83; 149 v S 123, § 1, eff. 1-1-04.**

The effective date is set by section 4 of S.B. 123.

See provisions, § 5 of S.B. 123 (149 v —), following RC § 4501.01.

## § 4511.202 Operating vehicle or agricultural tractor without reasonable control.

(A) No person shall operate a motor vehicle, trackless trolley, streetcar, agricultural tractor, or agricultural tractor that is towing, pulling, or otherwise drawing a unit of farm machinery on any street, highway, or property open to the public for vehicular traffic without being in reasonable control of the vehicle, trolley, streetcar, agricultural tractor, or unit of farm machinery.

(B) Whoever violates this section is guilty of operating a motor vehicle or agricultural tractor without being in control of it, a minor misdemeanor.

**HISTORY: 139 v S 432. Eff 3-16-83; 149 v S 123, § 1, eff. 1-1-04; 152 v H 9, § 1, eff. 10-18-07.**

The effective date is set by section 4 of S.B. 123.

See provisions, § 5 of S.B. 123 (149 v —), following RC § 4501.01.

## § 4511.203 Wrongful entrustment of motor vehicle.

(A) No person shall permit a motor vehicle owned by the person or under the person's control to be driven by another if any of the following apply:

(1) The offender knows or has reasonable cause to believe that the other person does not have a valid driver's or commercial driver's license or permit or valid nonresident driving privileges.

(2) The offender knows or has reasonable cause to believe that the other person's driver's or commercial driver's license or permit or nonresident operating privileges have been suspended or canceled under Chapter 4510. or any other provision of the Revised Code.

(3) The offender knows or has reasonable cause to believe that the other person's act of driving the motor vehicle would violate any prohibition contained in Chapter 4509. of the Revised Code.

(4) The offender knows or has reasonable cause to believe that the other person's act of driving would violate section 4511.19 of the Revised Code or any substantially equivalent municipal ordinance.

(5) The offender knows or has reasonable cause to believe that the vehicle is the subject of an immobilization waiver order issued under section 4503.235 of the Revised Code and the other person is prohibited from operating the vehicle under that order.

(B) Without limiting or precluding the consideration of any other evidence in determining whether a violation of division (A)(1), (2), (3), (4), or (5) of this section has occurred, it shall be prima-facie evidence that the offender knows or has reasonable cause to believe that the operator of the motor vehicle owned by the offender or under the offender's control is in a category described in division (A)(1), (2), (3), (4), or (5) of this section if any of the following applies:

(1) Regarding an operator allegedly in the category described in division (A)(1), (3), or (5) of this section, the offender and the operator of the motor vehicle reside in the same household and are related by consanguinity or affinity.

(2) Regarding an operator allegedly in the category described in division (A)(2) of this section, the offender and the operator of the motor vehicle reside in the same household, and the offender knows or has reasonable cause to believe that the operator has been charged with or convicted of any violation of law or ordinance, or has

committed any other act or omission, that would or could result in the suspension or cancellation of the operator's license, permit, or privilege.

(3) Regarding an operator allegedly in the category described in division (A)(4) of this section, the offender and the operator of the motor vehicle occupied the motor vehicle together at the time of the offense.

(C) Whoever violates this section is guilty of wrongful entrustment of a motor vehicle and shall be punished as provided in divisions (C) to (H) of this section.

(1) Except as provided in division (C)(2) of this section, whoever violates division (A)(1), (2), or (3) of this section is guilty of an unclassified misdemeanor. When the offense is an unclassified misdemeanor, the offender shall be sentenced pursuant to sections 2929.21 to 2929.28 of the Revised Code, except that the offender shall not be sentenced to a jail term; the offender shall not be sentenced to a community residential sanction pursuant to section 2929.26 of the Revised Code; notwithstanding division (A)(2)(a) of section 2929.28 of the Revised Code, the offender may be fined up to one thousand dollars; and, notwithstanding division (A)(3) of section 2929.27 of the Revised Code, the offender may be ordered pursuant to division (C) of that section to serve a term of community service of up to five hundred hours. The failure of an offender to complete a term of community service imposed by the court may be punished as indirect criminal contempt under division (A) of section 2705.02 of the Revised Code that may be filed in the underlying case.

(2)(a) If, within three years of a violation of division (A)(1), (2), or (3) of this section, the offender previously has pleaded guilty to or been convicted of two or more violations of division (A)(1), (2), or (3) of this section or a substantially equivalent municipal ordinance, the offender is guilty of a misdemeanor of the first degree.

(b) Whoever violates division (A)(4) or (5) of this section is guilty of a misdemeanor of the first degree.

(3) For any violation of this section, in addition to the penalties imposed under Chapter 2929. of the Revised Code, the court may impose a class seven suspension of the offender's driver's license, commercial driver's license, temporary instruction permit, probationary license, or nonresident operating privilege from the range specified in division (A)(7) of section 4510.02 of the Revised Code, and, if the vehicle involved in the offense is registered in the name of the offender, the court may order one of the following:

(a) Except as otherwise provided in division (C)(3)(b) or (c) of this section, the court may order, for thirty days, the immobilization of the vehicle involved in the offense and the impoundment of that vehicle's license plates. If issued, the order shall be issued and enforced under section 4503.233 of the Revised Code.

(b) If the offender previously has been convicted of or pleaded guilty to one violation of this section or a substantially equivalent municipal ordinance, the court may order, for sixty days, the immobilization of the vehicle involved in the offense and the impoundment of that vehicle's license plates. If issued, the order shall be issued and enforced under section 4503.233 of the Revised Code.

(c) If the offender previously has been convicted of or pleaded guilty to two or more violations of this section or a substantially equivalent municipal ordinance, the court may order the criminal forfeiture to the state of the vehicle involved in the offense. If issued, the order shall be issued and enforced under section 4503.234 of the Revised Code.

If title to a motor vehicle that is subject to an order for criminal forfeiture under division (C)(3)(c) of this section is assigned or transferred and division (B)(2) or (3) of section 4503.234 of the Revised Code applies, in addition to or independent of any other penalty established by law, the court may fine the offender the value of the vehicle as determined by publications of the national automobile dealers association. The proceeds from any fine imposed under this division shall be distributed in accordance with division (C)(2) of section 4503.234 of the Revised Code.

(D) If a court orders the immobilization of a vehicle under division (C)(3)(a) or (b) of this section, the court shall not release the vehicle from the immobilization before the termination of the period of immobilization ordered unless the court is presented with current proof of financial responsibility with respect to that vehicle.

(E) If a court orders the criminal forfeiture of a vehicle under division (C)(3)(c) of this section, upon receipt of the order from the court, neither the registrar of motor vehicles nor any deputy registrar shall accept any application for the registration or transfer of registration of any motor vehicle owned or leased by the person named in the order. The period of denial shall be five years after the date the order is issued, unless, during that five-year period, the court with jurisdiction of the offense that resulted in the order terminates the forfeiture and notifies the registrar of the termination. If the court terminates the forfeiture and notifies the registrar, the registrar shall take all necessary measures to permit the person to register a vehicle owned or leased by the person or to transfer the registration of the vehicle.

(F) This section does not apply to motor vehicle rental dealers or motor vehicle leasing dealers, as defined in section 4549.65 of the Revised Code.

(G) Evidence of a conviction of, plea of guilty to, or adjudication as a delinquent child for a violation of this section or a substantially similar municipal ordinance shall not be admissible as evidence in any civil action that involves the offender or delinquent child who is the subject of the conviction, plea, or adjudication and that arises from the wrongful entrustment of a motor vehicle.

(H) For purposes of this section, a vehicle is owned by a person if, at the time of a violation of this section, the vehicle is registered in the person's name.

**HISTORY: GC § 6296-28; 116 v PtII, 33, § 28; Bureau of Code Revision, 10-1-53; 144 v S 275 (Eff 9-1-93); 145 v S 62, § 4. Eff 9-1-93; 149 v S 123, § 1, eff. 1-1-04; 152 v S 17, § 1, eff. 9-30-08; 2011 HB 5, § 1, eff. Sept. 23, 2011.**

See provisions, § 5 of S.B. 123 (149 v —), following RC § 4501.01.

## [SPEED REGULATIONS]

## § 4511.21 Speed limits.

(A) No person shall operate a motor vehicle, trackless trolley, or streetcar at a speed greater or less than is reasonable or proper, having due regard to the traffic, surface, and width of the street or highway and any other conditions, and no person shall drive any motor vehicle, trackless trolley, or streetcar in and upon any street or highway at a greater speed than will permit the person to bring it to a stop within the assured clear distance ahead.

(B) It is prima-facie lawful, in the absence of a lower limit declared or established pursuant to this section by the director of transportation or local authorities, for the operator of a motor vehicle, trackless trolley, or streetcar to operate the same at a speed not exceeding the following:

(1)(a) Twenty miles per hour in school zones during school recess and while children are going to or leaving school during the opening or closing hours, and when twenty miles per hour school speed limit signs are erected; except that, on controlled-access highways and expressways, if the right-of-way line fence has been erected without pedestrian opening, the speed shall be governed by division (B)(4) of this section and on freeways, if the right-of-way line fence has been erected without pedestrian opening, the speed shall be governed by divisions (B)(9) and (10) of this section. The end of every school zone may be marked by a sign indicating the end of the zone. Nothing in this section or in the manual and specifications for a uniform system of traffic control devices shall be construed to require school zones to be indicated by signs equipped with flashing or other lights, or giving other special notice of the hours in which the school zone speed limit is in effect.

(b) As used in this section and in section 4511.212 [4511.21.2] of the Revised Code, "school" means any school chartered under section 3301.16 of the Revised Code and any nonchartered school that during the preceding year filed with the department of education in compliance with rule 3301-35-08 of the Ohio Administrative Code, a copy of the school's report for the parents of the school's pupils certifying that the school meets Ohio minimum standards for nonchartered, nontax-supported schools and presents evidence of this filing to the jurisdiction from which it is requesting the establishment of a school zone. "School" also includes a special elementary school that in writing requests the county engineer of the county in which the special elementary school is located to create a school zone at the location of that school. Upon receipt of such a written request, the county engineer shall create a school zone at that location by erecting the appropriate signs.

(c) As used in this section, "school zone" means that portion of a street or highway passing a school fronting upon the street or highway that is encompassed by projecting the school property lines to the fronting street or highway, and also includes that portion of a state highway. Upon request from local authorities for streets and highways under their jurisdiction and that portion of a state highway under the jurisdiction of the director of transportation or a request from a county engineer in the case of a school zone for a special elementary school, the director may extend the traditional school zone boundaries. The distances in divisions (B)(1)(c)(i), (ii), and (iii) of this section shall not exceed three hundred feet per approach per direction and are bounded by whichever of the following distances or combinations thereof the director approves as most appropriate:

(i) The distance encompassed by projecting the school building lines normal to the fronting highway and extending a distance of three hundred feet on each approach direction;

(ii) The distance encompassed by projecting the school property lines intersecting the fronting highway and extending a distance of three hundred feet on each approach direction;

(iii) The distance encompassed by the special marking of the pavement for a principal school pupil crosswalk plus a distance of three hundred feet on each approach direction of the highway.

Nothing in this section shall be construed to invalidate the director's initial action on August 9, 1976, establishing all school zones at the traditional school zone boundaries defined by projecting school property lines, except when those boundaries are extended as provided in divisions (B)(1)(a) and (c) of this section.

(d) As used in this division, "crosswalk" has the meaning given that term in division (LL)(2) of section 4511.01 of the Revised Code.

The director may, upon request by resolution of the legislative authority of a municipal corporation, the board of trustees of a township, or a county board of developmental disabilities created pursuant to Chapter 5126. of the Revised Code, and upon submission by the municipal corporation, township, or county board of such engineering, traffic, and other information as the director considers necessary, designate a school zone on any portion of a state route lying within the municipal corporation, lying within the unincorporated territory of the township, or lying adjacent to the property of a school that is operated by such county board, that includes a crosswalk customarily used by children going to or leaving a school during recess and opening and closing hours, whenever the distance, as measured in a straight line, from the school property line nearest the crosswalk to the nearest point of the crosswalk is no more than one thousand three hundred twenty feet. Such a school zone shall include the distance encompassed by the crosswalk and extending three hundred feet on each approach direction of the state route.

(e) As used in this section, "special elementary school" means a school that meets all of the following criteria:

(i) It is not chartered and does not receive tax revenue from any source.

(ii) It does not educate children beyond the eighth grade.

(iii) It is located outside the limits of a municipal corporation.

(iv) A majority of the total number of students enrolled at the school are not related by blood.

(v) The principal or other person in charge of the special elementary school annually sends a report to the superintendent of the school district in which the special elementary school is located indicating the total number of students enrolled at the school, but otherwise the principal or other person in charge does not report any other information or data to the superintendent.

(2) Twenty-five miles per hour in all other portions of a municipal corporation, except on state routes outside business districts, through highways outside business districts, and alleys;

(3) Thirty-five miles per hour on all state routes or through highways within municipal corporations outside business districts, except as provided in divisions (B)(4) and (6) of this section;

(4) Fifty miles per hour on controlled-access highways and expressways within municipal corporations;

(5) Fifty-five miles per hour on highways outside municipal corporations, other than highways within island jurisdictions as provided in division (B)(8) of this section and freeways as provided in divisions (B)(13) and (14) of this section;

(6) Fifty miles per hour on state routes within municipal corporations outside urban districts unless a lower prima-facie speed is established as further provided in this section;

(7) Fifteen miles per hour on all alleys within the municipal corporation;

(8) Thirty-five miles per hour on highways outside municipal corporations that are within an island jurisdiction;

(9) Fifty-five miles per hour at all times on freeways with paved shoulders inside municipal corporations, other than freeways as provided in divisions (B)(13) and (14) of this section;

(10) Fifty-five miles per hour at all times on freeways outside municipal corporations, other than freeways as provided in divisions (B)(13) and (14) of this section;

(11) Fifty-five miles per hour at all times on all portions of freeways that are part of the interstate system and on all portions of freeways that are not part of the interstate system, but are built to the standards and specifications that are applicable to freeways that are part of the interstate system for operators of any motor vehicle weighing in excess of eight thousand pounds empty weight and any noncommercial bus, except as provided in division (B)(14) of this section;

(12) Fifty-five miles per hour for operators of any motor vehicle weighing eight thousand pounds or less empty weight and any commercial bus at all times on all portions of freeways that are part of the interstate system and that had such a speed limit established prior to October 1, 1995, and freeways that are not part of the interstate system, but are built to the standards and specifications that are applicable to freeways that are part of the interstate system and that had such a speed limit established prior to October 1, 1995, unless a higher speed limit is established under division (L) of this section;

(13) Sixty-five miles per hour for operators of any motor vehicle weighing eight thousand pounds or less empty weight and any commercial bus at all times on all portions of the following:

(a) Freeways that are part of the interstate system and that had such a speed limit established prior to October 1, 1995, and freeways that are not part of the interstate system, but are built to the standards and specifications that are applicable to freeways that are part of the interstate system and that had such a speed limit established prior to October 1, 1995;

(b) Freeways that are part of the interstate system and freeways that are not part of the interstate system but are built to the standards and specifications that are applicable to freeways that are part of the interstate system, and that had such a speed limit established under division (L) of this section;

(c) Rural, divided, multi-lane highways that are designated as part of the national highway system under the "National Highway System Designation Act of 1995," 109 Stat. 568, 23 U.S.C.A. 103, and that had such a speed limit established under division (M) of this section.

(14) Sixty-five miles per hour at all times on all portions of freeways that are part of the interstate system and that had such a speed limit on the effective date of this amendment for operators of any motor vehicle weighing in excess of eight thousand pounds empty weight and any noncommercial bus.

(C) It is prima-facie unlawful for any person to exceed any of the speed limitations in divisions (B)(1)(a), (2), (3), (4), (6), (7), and (8) of this section, or any declared or established pursuant to this section by the director or local authorities and it is unlawful for any person to exceed any of the speed limitations in division (D) of this section. No person shall be convicted of more than one violation of this section for the same conduct, although violations of more than one provision of this section may be charged in the alternative in a single affidavit.

(D) No person shall operate a motor vehicle, trackless trolley, or streetcar upon a street or highway as follows:

(1) At a speed exceeding fifty-five miles per hour, except upon a freeway as provided in divisions (B)(13) and (14) of this section;

(2) At a speed exceeding sixty-five miles per hour upon a freeway as provided in divisions (B)(13) and (14) of this section;

(3) If a motor vehicle weighing in excess of eight thousand pounds empty weight or a noncommercial bus as prescribed in division (B)(11) of this section, at a speed exceeding fifty-five miles per hour upon a freeway as provided in that division;

(4) At a speed exceeding the posted speed limit upon a freeway for which the director has determined and declared a speed limit of not more than sixty-five miles per hour pursuant to division (L)(2) or (M) of this section;

(5) At a speed exceeding sixty-five miles per hour upon a freeway for which such a speed limit has been established through the operation of division (L)(3) of this section;

(6) At a speed exceeding the posted speed limit upon a freeway for which the director has determined and declared a speed limit pursuant to division (I)(2) of this section.

(E) In every charge of violation of this section the affidavit and warrant shall specify the time, place, and speed at which the defendant is alleged to have driven, and in charges made in reliance upon division (C) of this section also the speed which division (B)(1)(a), (2), (3), (4), (6), (7), or (8) of, or a limit declared or established pursuant to, this section declares is prima-facie lawful at the time and place of such alleged violation, except that in affidavits where a person is alleged to have driven at a greater speed than will permit the person to bring the vehicle to a stop within the assured clear distance ahead the affidavit and warrant need not specify the speed at which the defendant is alleged to have driven.

(F) When a speed in excess of both a prima-facie limitation and a limitation in division (D)(1), (2), (3), (4), (5), or (6) of this section is alleged, the defendant shall be charged in a single affidavit, alleging a single act, with a violation indicated of both division (B)(1)(a), (2), (3), (4), (6), (7), or (8) of this section, or of a limit declared or established pursuant to this section by the director or local authorities, and of the limitation in division (D)(1), (2), (3), (4), (5), or (6) of this section. If the court finds a violation of division (B)(1)(a), (2), (3), (4), (6), (7), or (8) of, or a limit declared or established pursuant to, this section has occurred, it shall enter a judgment of conviction under such division and dismiss the charge under division (D)(1), (2), (3), (4), (5), or (6) of this section. If it finds no violation of division (B)(1)(a), (2), (3), (4), (6), (7), or (8) of, or a limit declared or established pursuant to, this section, it shall then consider whether the evidence supports a conviction under division (D)(1), (2), (3), (4), (5), or (6) of this section.

(G) Points shall be assessed for violation of a limitation under division (D) of this section in accordance with section 4510.036 [4510.03.6] of the Revised Code.

(H) Whenever the director determines upon the basis of a geometric and traffic characteristic study that any speed limit set forth in divisions (B)(1)(a) to (D) of this section is greater or less than is reasonable or safe under the conditions found to exist at any portion of a street or highway under the jurisdiction of the director, the director shall determine and declare a reasonable and safe prima-facie speed limit, which shall be effective when appropriate signs giving notice of it are erected at the location.

(I)(1) Except as provided in divisions (I)(2) and (K) of this section, whenever local authorities determine upon the basis of an engineering and traffic investigation that the speed permitted by divisions (B)(1)(a) to (D) of this section, on any part of a highway under their jurisdiction, is greater than is reasonable and safe under the conditions found to exist at such location, the local authorities may by resolution request the director to determine and declare a reasonable and safe prima-facie speed limit. Upon receipt of such request the director may determine and declare a reasonable and safe prima-facie speed limit at such location, and if the director does so, then such declared speed limit shall become effective only when appropriate signs giving notice thereof are erected at such location by the local authorities. The director may withdraw the declaration of a prima-facie speed limit whenever in the director's opinion the altered prima-facie speed becomes unreasonable. Upon such withdrawal, the declared prima-facie speed shall become ineffective and the signs relating thereto shall be immediately removed by the local authorities.

(2) A local authority may determine on the basis of a geometric and traffic characteristic study that the speed limit of sixty-five miles per hour on a portion of a freeway under its jurisdiction that was established through the operation of division (L)(3) of this section is greater than is reasonable or safe under the conditions found to exist at that portion of the freeway. If the local authority makes such a determination, the local authority by resolution may request the director to determine and declare a reasonable and safe speed limit of not less than fifty-five miles per hour for that portion of the freeway. If the director takes such action, the declared speed limit becomes effective only when appropriate signs giving notice of it are erected at such location by the local authority.

(J) Local authorities in their respective jurisdictions may authorize by ordinance higher prima-facie speeds than those stated in this section upon through highways, or upon highways or portions thereof where there are no intersections, or between widely spaced intersections, provided signs are erected giving notice of the authorized speed, but local authorities shall not modify or alter the basic rule set forth in division (A) of this section or in any event authorize by ordinance a speed in excess of fifty miles per hour.

Alteration of prima-facie limits on state routes by local authorities shall not be effective until the alteration has been approved by the director. The director may withdraw approval of any altered prima-facie speed limits whenever in the director's opinion any altered prima-facie speed becomes unreasonable, and upon such withdrawal, the altered prima-facie speed shall become ineffective and the signs relating thereto shall be immediately removed by the local authorities.

(K)(1) As used in divisions (K)(1), (2), (3), and (4) of this section, "unimproved highway" means a highway consisting of any of the following:

(a) Unimproved earth;

(b) Unimproved graded and drained earth;

(c) Gravel.

(2) Except as otherwise provided in divisions (K)(4) and (5) of this section, whenever a board of township trustees determines upon the basis of an engineering and traffic investigation that the speed permitted by division (B)(5) of this section on any part of an unimproved highway under its jurisdiction and in the unincorporated territory of the township is greater than is reasonable or safe under the conditions found to exist at the location, the board may by resolution declare a reasonable and safe prima-facie speed limit of fifty-five but not less than twenty-five miles per hour. An altered speed limit adopted by a board of township trustees under this division becomes effective when appropriate traffic control devices, as prescribed in section 4511.11 of the Revised Code, giving notice thereof are erected at the location, which shall be no sooner than sixty days after adoption of the resolution.

(3)(a) Whenever, in the opinion of a board of township trustees, any altered prima-facie speed limit established by the board under this division becomes unreasonable, the board may adopt a resolution withdrawing the altered prima-facie speed limit. Upon the adoption of such a resolution, the altered prima-facie speed limit becomes ineffective and the traffic control devices relating thereto shall be immediately removed.

(b) Whenever a highway ceases to be an unimproved highway and the board has adopted an altered prima-facie speed limit pursuant to division (K)(2) of this section, the board shall, by resolution, withdraw the altered prima-facie speed limit as soon as the highway ceases to be unimproved. Upon the adoption of such a resolution, the altered prima-facie speed limit becomes ineffective and the traffic control devices relating thereto shall be immediately removed.

(4)(a) If the boundary of two townships rests on the centerline of an unimproved highway in unincorporated territory and both townships have jurisdiction over the highway, neither of the boards of township trustees of such townships may declare an altered prima-facie speed limit pursuant to division (K)(2) of this section on the part of the highway under their joint jurisdiction unless the boards of township trustees of both of the townships determine, upon the basis of an engineering and traffic investigation, that the speed permitted by division (B)(5) of this section is greater than is reasonable or safe under the conditions found to exist at the location and both boards agree upon a reasonable and safe prima-facie speed limit of less than fifty-five but not less than twenty-five miles per hour for that location. If both boards so agree, each shall follow the procedure specified in division (K)(2) of this section for altering the prima-facie speed limit on the highway. Except as otherwise provided in division (K)(4)(b) of this section, no speed limit altered pursuant to division (K)(4)(a) of this section may be withdrawn unless the boards of township trustees of both townships determine that the altered prima-facie speed limit previously adopted becomes unreasonable and each board adopts a resolution withdrawing the altered prima-facie speed limit pursuant to the procedure specified in division (K)(3)(a) of this section.

(b) Whenever a highway described in division (K)(4)(a) of this section ceases to be an unimproved highway and two boards of township trustees have adopted an altered prima-facie speed limit pursuant to division (K)(4)(a) of this section, both boards shall, by resolution, withdraw the altered prima-facie speed limit as soon as the highway ceases to be unimproved. Upon the adoption of the resolution, the altered prima-facie speed limit becomes ineffective and the traffic control devices relating thereto shall be immediately removed.

(5) As used in division (K)(5) of this section:

(a) "Commercial subdivision" means any platted territory outside the limits of a municipal corporation and fronting a highway where, for a distance of three hundred feet or more, the frontage is improved with buildings in use for commercial purposes, or where the entire length of the highway is less than three hundred feet long and the frontage is improved with buildings in use for commercial purposes.

(b) "Residential subdivision" means any platted territory outside the limits of a municipal corporation and fronting a highway, where, for a distance of three hundred feet or more, the frontage is improved with residences or residences and buildings in use for business, or where the entire length of the highway is less than three hundred feet long and the frontage is improved with residences or residences and buildings in use for business.

Whenever a board of township trustees finds upon the basis of an engineering and traffic investigation that the prima-facie speed permitted by division (B)(5) of this section on any part of a highway under its jurisdiction that is located in a commercial or residential subdivision, except on highways or portions thereof at the entrances to which vehicular traffic from the majority of intersecting highways is required to yield the right-of-way to vehicles on such highways in obedience to stop or yield signs or traffic control signals, is greater than is reasonable and safe under the conditions found to exist at the location, the board may by resolution declare a reasonable and safe prima-facie speed limit of less than fifty-five but not less than twenty-five miles per hour at the location. An altered speed limit adopted by a board of township trustees under this division shall become effective when appropriate signs giving notice thereof are erected at the location by the township. Whenever, in the opinion of a board of township trustees, any altered prima-facie speed limit established by it under this division becomes unreasonable, it may adopt a resolution withdrawing the altered prima-facie speed, and upon such withdrawal, the altered prima-facie speed shall become ineffective, and the signs relating thereto shall be immediately removed by the township.

(L)(1) Within one hundred twenty days of February 29, 1996, the director of transportation, based upon a geometric and traffic characteristic study of a freeway that is part of the interstate system or that is not part of the interstate system, but is built to the standards and specifications that are applicable to freeways that are part of the interstate system, in consultation with the director of public safety and, if applicable, the local authority having jurisdiction over a portion of such freeway, may determine and declare that the speed limit of less than sixty-five miles per hour established on such freeway or portion of freeway either is reasonable and safe or is less than that which is reasonable and safe.

(2) If the established speed limit for such a freeway or portion of freeway is determined to be less than that which is reasonable and safe, the director of transportation, in consultation with the director of public safety and, if applicable, the local authority having jurisdiction over the portion of freeway, shall determine and declare a reasonable and safe speed limit of not more than sixty-five miles per hour for that freeway or portion of freeway.

The director of transportation or local authority having jurisdiction over the freeway or portion of freeway shall erect appropriate signs giving notice of the speed limit at such location within one hundred fifty days of February 29, 1996. Such speed limit becomes effective only when such signs are erected at the location.

(3) If, within one hundred twenty days of February 29, 1996, the director of transportation does not make a determination and declaration of a reasonable and safe speed limit for a freeway or portion of freeway that is part of the interstate system or that is not part of the interstate system, but is built to the standards and specifications that are applicable to freeways that are part of the interstate system and that has a speed limit of less than sixty-five miles per hour, the speed limit on that freeway or portion of a freeway shall be sixty-five miles per hour. The director of transportation or local authority having jurisdiction over the freeway or portion of the freeway shall erect appropriate signs giving notice of the speed limit of sixty-five miles per hour at such location within one hundred fifty days of February 29, 1996. Such speed limit becomes effective only when such signs are erected at the location. A speed limit established through the operation of division (L)(3) of this section is subject to reduction under division (I)(2) of this section.

(M) Within three hundred sixty days after February 29, 1996, the director of transportation, based upon a geometric and traffic characteristic study of a rural, divided, multi-lane highway that has been designated as part of the national highway system under the "National Highway System Designation Act of 1995," 109 Stat. 568, 23 U.S.C.A. 103, in consultation with the director of public safety and, if applicable, the local authority having jurisdiction over a portion of the highway, may determine and declare that the speed limit of less than sixty-five miles per hour established on the highway or portion of highway either is reasonable and safe or is less than that which is reasonable and safe.

If the established speed limit for the highway or portion of highway is determined to be less than that which is reasonable and safe, the director of transportation, in consultation with the director of public safety and, if applicable, the local authority having jurisdiction over the portion of highway, shall determine and declare a reasonable and safe speed limit of not more than sixty-five miles per hour for that highway or portion of highway. The director of transportation or local authority having jurisdiction over the highway or portion of highway shall erect appropriate signs giving notice of the speed limit at such location within three hundred ninety days after February 29, 1996. The speed limit becomes effective only when such signs are erected at the location.

(N)(1)(a) If the boundary of two local authorities rests on the centerline of a highway and both authorities have jurisdiction over the highway, the speed limit for the part of the highway within their joint jurisdiction shall be either one of the following as agreed to by both authorities:

(i) Either prima-facie speed limit permitted by division (B) of this section;

(ii) An altered speed limit determined and posted in accordance with this section.

(b) If the local authorities are unable to reach an agreement, the speed limit shall remain as established and posted under this section.

(2) Neither local authority may declare an altered prima-facie speed limit pursuant to this section on the part of the highway under their joint jurisdiction unless both of the local authorities determine, upon the basis of an engineering and traffic investigation, that the speed permitted by this section is greater than is reasonable or safe under the conditions found to exist at the location and

both authorities agree upon a uniform reasonable and safe prima-facie speed limit of less than fifty-five but not less than twenty-five miles per hour for that location. If both authorities so agree, each shall follow the procedure specified in this section for altering the prima-facie speed limit on the highway, and the speed limit for the part of the highway within their joint jurisdiction shall be uniformly altered. No altered speed limit may be withdrawn unless both local authorities determine that the altered prima-facie speed limit previously adopted becomes unreasonable and each adopts a resolution withdrawing the altered prima-facie speed limit pursuant to the procedure specified in this section.

(O) As used in this section:

(1) "Interstate system" has the same meaning as in 23 U.S.C.A. 101.

(2) "Commercial bus" means a motor vehicle designed for carrying more than nine passengers and used for the transportation of persons for compensation.

(3) "Noncommercial bus" includes but is not limited to a school bus or a motor vehicle operated solely for the transportation of persons associated with a charitable or nonprofit organization.

(P)(1) A violation of any provision of this section is one of the following:

(a) Except as otherwise provided in divisions (P)(1)(b), (1)(c), (2), and (3) of this section, a minor misdemeanor;

(b) If, within one year of the offense, the offender previously has been convicted of or pleaded guilty to two violations of any provision of this section or of any provision of a municipal ordinance that is substantially similar to any provision of this section, a misdemeanor of the fourth degree;

(c) If, within one year of the offense, the offender previously has been convicted of or pleaded guilty to three or more violations of any provision of this section or of any provision of a municipal ordinance that is substantially similar to any provision of this section, a misdemeanor of the third degree.

(2) If the offender has not previously been convicted of or pleaded guilty to a violation of any provision of this section or of any provision of a municipal ordinance that is substantially similar to this section and operated a motor vehicle faster than thirty-five miles an hour in a business district of a municipal corporation, faster than fifty miles an hour in other portions of a municipal corporation, or faster than thirty-five miles an hour in a school zone during recess or while children are going to or leaving school during the school's opening or closing hours, a misdemeanor of the fourth degree.

(3) Notwithstanding division (P)(1) of this section, if the offender operated a motor vehicle in a construction zone where a sign was then posted in accordance with section 4511.98 of the Revised Code, the court, in addition to all other penalties provided by law, shall impose upon the offender a fine of two times the usual amount imposed for the violation. No court shall impose a fine of two times the usual amount imposed for the violation upon an offender if the offender alleges, in an affidavit filed with the court prior to the offender's sentencing, that the offender is indigent and is unable to pay the fine imposed pursuant to this division and if the court determines that the offender is an indigent person and unable to pay the fine.

**HISTORY: GC § 6307-21; 119 v 766, § 21; 124 v 514; Bureau of Code Revision, 10-1-53; 126 v 115 (Eff 10-1-56); 127 v 931 (Eff 9-14-57); 128 v 1270 (Eff 11-4-59); 130 v 1083 (Eff 9-30-63); 130 v PtII, H 5 (Eff 12-16-64); 131 v 1101 (Eff 11-4-65); 132 v H 1 (Eff 2-21-67); 135 v H 200 (Eff 9-28-73); 136 v H 632 (Eff 6-27-75); 136 v H 1166 (Eff 8-9-76); 137 v H 587 (Eff 11-3-77); 138 v H 20 (Eff 8-29-79); 138 v H 32 (Eff 8-29-79); 138 v S 14 (Eff 10-25-79); 140 v S 37 (Eff 9-7-83); 141 v H 795 (Eff 8-29-86); 141 v S 356 (Eff 9-24-86); 141 v H 428 (Eff 12-23-86); 141 v H 666 (Eff 3-25-87); 142 v H 43 (Eff 7-31-87); 142 v H 493 (Eff 7-15-87); 143 v H 381 (Eff 7-1-89); 144 v H 96 (Eff 6-18-91); 144 v S 201 (Eff 8-19-92); 144 v S 301 (Eff 3-15-93); 146 v H 565. Eff 2-29-96; 149 v S 123, § 1, eff. 1-1-04; 151 v H 68, § 101.01, eff. 6-29-05; 151 v S 184, § 1, eff. 6-15-06; 152 v H 67, § 101.01, eff. 6-30-07; 153 v H 2, § 101.01, eff. 7-1-09; 153 v S 79, § 1, eff. 10-6-09.**

The effective date is set by § 812.10 of 153 v H 2.

The effective date is set by § 609.10 of 152 v H 67.

The effective date is set by § 612.03 of 151 v H 68.

See provisions, § 5 of S.B. 123 (149 v —), following RC § 4501.01.

The provisions of § 3 of HB 565 (146 v —) read as follows:

SECTION 3. It is the intent of the General Assembly in amending section 4511.21 of the Revised Code to retain the speed limits established by that section at the limits and locations established prior to the repeal of the National Maximum Speed Limit Compliance Program in Pub. L. No. 104-59.

**Publisher's Note:**

The amendment of RC § 4511.21 by 153 v H 2 was disapproved in part by the Governor.

## § 4511.211 Speed limit on private residential road or driveway.

(A) The owner of a private road or driveway located in a private residential area containing twenty or more dwelling units may establish a speed limit on the road or driveway by complying with all of the following requirements:

(1) The speed limit is not less than twenty-five miles per hour and is indicated by a sign that is in a proper position, is sufficiently legible to be seen by an ordinarily observant person, and meets the specifications for the basic speed limit sign included in the manual adopted by the department of transportation pursuant to section 4511.09 of the Revised Code;

(2) The owner has posted a sign at the entrance of the private road or driveway that is in plain view and clearly informs persons entering the road or driveway that they are entering private property, a speed limit has been established for the road or driveway, and the speed limit is enforceable by law enforcement officers under state law.

(B) No person shall operate a vehicle upon a private road or driveway as provided in division (A) of this section at a speed exceeding any speed limit established and posted pursuant to that division.

(C) When a speed limit is established and posted in accordance with division (A) of this section, any law enforcement officer may apprehend a person violating the speed limit of the residential area by utilizing any of the means described in section 4511.091 of the Revised Code or by any other accepted method of determining the speed of a motor vehicle and may stop and charge the person with exceeding the speed limit.

(D) Points shall be assessed for violation of a speed limit established and posted in accordance with division (A) of this section in accordance with section 4510.036 of the Revised Code.

(E) As used in this section:

(1) "Owner" includes but is not limited to a person who holds title to the real property in fee simple, a condomin-

ium owners' association, a property owner's association, the board of directors or trustees of a private community, and a nonprofit corporation governing a private community.

(2) "Private residential area containing twenty or more dwelling units" does not include a Chautauqua assembly as defined in section 4511.90 of the Revised Code.

(F) A violation of division (B) of this section is one of the following:

(1) Except as otherwise provided in divisions (F)(2) and (3) of this section, a minor misdemeanor;

(2) If, within one year of the offense, the offender previously has been convicted of or pleaded guilty to two violations of division (B) of this section or of any municipal ordinance that is substantially similar to division (B) of this section, a misdemeanor of the fourth degree;

(3) If, within one year of the offense, the offender previously has been convicted of or pleaded guilty to three or more violations of division (B) of this section or of any municipal ordinance that is substantially similar to division (B) of this section, a misdemeanor of the third degree.

**HISTORY: 143 v H 171. Eff 5-31-90; 149 v S 123, § 1, eff. 1-1-04.**

The effective date is set by section 4 of S.B. 123.

See provisions, § 5 of S.B. 123 (149 v —), following RC § 4501.01.

**Not analogous to former RC § 4511.21.1 (135 v H 1052), repealed 136 v H 632, § 2, eff 6-27-75.**

## § 4511.212 Complaint that local authority is not complying with school zone sign laws.

(A) As used in this section, "local authority" means the legislative authority of a municipal corporation, the board of trustees of a township, or the board of county commissioners of a county.

(B) The board of education or the chief administrative officer operating or in charge of any school may submit a written complaint to the director of transportation alleging that a local authority is not complying with section 4511.11 or divisions (B)(1)(a) to (d) of section 4511.21 of the Revised Code with regard to school zones. Upon receipt of such a complaint, the director shall review or investigate the facts of the complaint and discuss the complaint with the local authority and the board of education or chief administrative officer submitting the complaint. If the director finds that the local authority is not complying with section 4511.11 or divisions (B)(1)(a) to (d) of section 4511.21 of the Revised Code with regard to school zones, the director shall issue a written order requiring the local authority to comply by a specified date and the local authority shall comply with the order. If the local authority fails to comply with the order, the director shall implement the order and charge the local authority for the cost of the implementation. Any local authority being so charged shall pay to the state the amount charged. Any amounts received under this section shall be deposited into the state treasury to the credit of the highway operating fund created by section 5735.291 [5735.29.1] of the Revised Code.

**HISTORY: 144 v S 201. Eff 8-19-92.**

## § 4511.213 Duties upon approaching stationary public safety, emergency, or road service vehicle displaying flashing lights.

(A) The driver of a motor vehicle, upon approaching a stationary public safety vehicle, an emergency vehicle, or a road service vehicle that is displaying the appropriate visual signals by means of flashing, oscillating, or rotating lights, as prescribed in section 4513.17 of the Revised Code, shall do either of the following:

(1) If the driver of the motor vehicle is traveling on a highway that consists of at least two lanes that carry traffic in the same direction of travel as that of the driver's motor vehicle, the driver shall proceed with due caution and, if possible and with due regard to the road, weather, and traffic conditions, shall change lanes into a lane that is not adjacent to that of the stationary public safety vehicle, an emergency vehicle, or a road service vehicle.

(2) If the driver is not traveling on a highway of a type described in division (A)(1) of this section, or if the driver is traveling on a highway of that type but it is not possible to change lanes or if to do so would be unsafe, the driver shall proceed with due caution, reduce the speed of the motor vehicle, and maintain a safe speed for the road, weather, and traffic conditions.

(B) This section does not relieve the driver of a public safety vehicle, an emergency vehicle, or a road service vehicle from the duty to drive with due regard for the safety of all persons and property upon the highway.

(C) No person shall fail to drive a motor vehicle in compliance with division (A)(1) or (2) of this section when so required by division (A) of this section.

(D)(1) Except as otherwise provided in this division, whoever violates this section is guilty of a minor misdemeanor. If, within one year of the offense, the offender previously has been convicted of or pleaded guilty to one predicate motor vehicle or traffic offense, whoever violates this section is guilty of a misdemeanor of the fourth degree. If, within one year of the offense, the offender previously has been convicted of two or more predicate motor vehicle or traffic offenses, whoever violates this section is guilty of a misdemeanor of the third degree.

(2) Notwithstanding section 2929.28 of the Revised Code, upon a finding that a person operated a motor vehicle in violation of division (C) of this section, the court, in addition to all other penalties provided by law, shall impose a fine of two times the usual amount imposed for the violation.

**HISTORY: 148 v H 86. Eff 9-28-99; 149 v. s 123, §1, eff. 1-1-04; 149 v H 490, § 1, eff. 1-1-04; 153 v H 2, § 101.01, eff. 7-1-09.**

The effective date is set by § 812.10 of 153 v H 2.

The effective date is set by section 4 of H.B. 490.

See provisions, § 5 of S.B. 123 (149 v —), following RC § 4501.01.

## § 4511.22 Stopping or operating vehicle at unreasonably slow speed; minimum speed limit.

(A) No person shall stop or operate a vehicle, trackless trolley, or street car at such an unreasonably slow speed as to impede or block the normal and reasonable movement of traffic, except when stopping or reduced speed is necessary for safe operation or to comply with law.

(B) Whenever the director of transportation or local authorities determine on the basis of an engineering and traffic investigation that slow speeds on any part of a controlled-access highway, expressway, or freeway consistently impede the normal and reasonable movement of traffic, the director or such local authority may declare a minimum speed limit below which no person shall operate a motor vehicle, trackless trolley, or street car except when necessary for safe operation or in compliance with law. No minimum speed limit established hereunder shall be less than thirty miles per hour, greater than fifty miles per hour, nor effective until the provisions of section 4511.21 of the Revised Code, relating to appropriate signs, have been fulfilled and local authorities have obtained the approval of the director.

(C) In a case involving a violation of this section, the trier of fact, in determining whether the vehicle was being operated at an unreasonably slow speed, shall consider the capabilities of the vehicle and its operator.

(D) Except as otherwise provided in this division, whoever violates this section is guilty of a minor misdemeanor. If, within one year of the offense, the offender previously has been convicted of or pleaded guilty to one predicate motor vehicle or traffic offense, whoever violates this section is guilty of a misdemeanor of the fourth degree. If, within one year of the offense, the offender previously has been convicted of two or more predicate motor vehicle or traffic offenses, whoever violates this section is guilty of a misdemeanor of the third degree.

**HISTORY: GC § 6307-22; 119 v 766, § 22; Bureau of Code Revision, 10-1-53; 127 v 51 (Eff 8-23-57); 135 v H 200 (Eff 9-28-73); 136 v H 632 (Eff 6-27-75); 144 v H 96. Eff 6-18-91; 149 v S 123, § 1, eff. 1-1-04; 151 v H 389, § 1, eff. 9-21-06.**

The effective date is set by section 4 of S.B. 123.

See provisions, § 5 of S.B. 123 (149 v —), following RC § 4501.01.

## § 4511.23 Speed regulations on bridges.

(A) No person shall operate a vehicle, trackless trolley, or streetcar over any bridge or other elevated structure constituting a part of a highway at a speed which is greater than the maximum speed that can be maintained with safety to such bridge or structure, when such structure is posted with signs as provided in this section.

The department of transportation upon request from any local authority shall, or upon its own initiative may, conduct an investigation of any bridge or other elevated structure constituting a part of a highway, and if it finds that such structure cannot with safety withstand traffic traveling at the speed otherwise permissible under sections 4511.01 to 4511.85 and 4511.98 of the Revised Code, the department shall determine and declare the maximum speed of traffic which such structure can withstand, and shall cause or permit suitable signs stating such maximum speed to be erected and maintained at a distance of at least one hundred feet before each end of such structure.

Upon the trial of any person charged with a violation of this section, proof of said determination of the maximum speed by the department and the existence of said signs shall constitute prima-facie evidence of the maximum speed which can be maintained with safety to such bridge or structure.

(B) Except as otherwise provided in this division, whoever violates this section is guilty of a minor misdemeanor. If, within one year of the offense, the offender previously has been convicted of or pleaded guilty to one predicate motor vehicle or traffic offense, whoever violates this section is guilty of a misdemeanor of the fourth degree. If, within one year of the offense, the offender previously has been convicted of two or more predicate motor vehicle or traffic offenses, whoever violates this section is guilty of a misdemeanor of the third degree.

**HISTORY: GC § 6307-23; 119 v 766, § 23; Bureau of Code Revision, 10-1-53; 135 v H 200. Eff 9-28-73; 149 v S 123, § 1, eff. 1-1-04.**

The effective date is set by section 4 of S.B. 123.

See provisions, § 5 of S.B. 123 (149 v —), following RC § 4501.01.

## § 4511.24 Emergency vehicles excepted from speed limitations.

The prima-facie speed limitations set forth in section 4511.21 of the Revised Code do not apply to emergency vehicles or public safety vehicles when they are responding to emergency calls and are equipped with and displaying at least one flashing, rotating, or oscillating light visible under normal atmospheric conditions from a distance of five hundred feet to the front of the vehicle and when the drivers thereof sound audible signals by bell, siren, or exhaust whistle. This section does not relieve the driver of an emergency vehicle or public safety vehicle from the duty to drive with due regard for the safety of all persons using the street or highway.

**HISTORY: GC § 6307-24; 119 v 766, § 24; Bureau of Code Revision, 10-1-53; 132 v H 378 (Eff 12-14-67); 135 v H 995. Eff 1-1-75.**

The effective date is set by section 3 of HB 995.

### [TRAFFIC RULES]

## § 4511.25 Lanes of travel upon roadways.

(A) Upon all roadways of sufficient width, a vehicle or trackless trolley shall be driven upon the right half of the roadway, except as follows:

(1) When overtaking and passing another vehicle proceeding in the same direction, or when making a left turn under the rules governing such movements;

(2) When an obstruction exists making it necessary to drive to the left of the center of the highway; provided, any person so doing shall yield the right of way to all vehicles traveling in the proper direction upon the unobstructed portion of the highway within such distance as to constitute an immediate hazard;

(3) When driving upon a roadway divided into three or more marked lanes for traffic under the rules applicable thereon;

(4) When driving upon a roadway designated and posted with signs for one-way traffic;

(5) When otherwise directed by a police officer or traffic control device.

(B)(1) Upon all roadways any vehicle or trackless trolley proceeding at less than the prevailing and lawful speed of traffic at the time and place and under the conditions then existing shall be driven in the right-hand lane then available for traffic, and far enough to the right to allow passing by faster vehicles if such passing is safe and reasonable, except under any of the following circumstances:

(a) When overtaking and passing another vehicle or trackless trolley proceeding in the same direction;

(b) When preparing for a left turn;

(c) When the driver must necessarily drive in a lane other than the right-hand lane to continue on the driver's intended route.

(2) Nothing in division (B)(1) of this section requires a driver of a slower vehicle to compromise the driver's safety to allow overtaking by a faster vehicle.

(C) Upon any roadway having four or more lanes for moving traffic and providing for two-way movement of traffic, no vehicle or trackless trolley shall be driven to the left of the center line of the roadway, except when authorized by official traffic control devices designating certain lanes to the left of the center of the roadway for use by traffic not otherwise permitted to use the lanes, or except as permitted under division (A)(2) of this section.

This division shall not be construed as prohibiting the crossing of the center line in making a left turn into or from an alley, private road, or driveway.

(D) Except as otherwise provided in this division, whoever violates this section is guilty of a minor misdemeanor. If, within one year of the offense, the offender previously has been convicted of or pleaded guilty to one predicate motor vehicle or traffic offense, whoever violates this section is guilty of a misdemeanor of the fourth degree. If, within one year of the offense, the offender previously has been convicted of two or more predicate motor vehicle or traffic offenses, whoever violates this section is guilty of a misdemeanor of the third degree.

**HISTORY: GC § 6307-25; 119 v 766, § 25; Bureau of Code Revision, 10-1-53; 129 v 1032 (Eff 9-9-61); 130 v 1086 (Eff 6-10-63); 135 v H 995. Eff 1-1-75; 149 v S 123, § 1, eff. 1-1-04; 151 v H 389, § 1, eff. 9-21-06.**

The effective date is set by section 4 of S.B. 123.
See provisions, § 5 of S.B. 123 (149 v —), following RC § 4501.01.

## § 4511.251 Street racing.

(A) As used in this section and section 4510.036 [4510.03.6] of the Revised Code, "street racing" means the operation of two or more vehicles from a point side by side at accelerating speeds in a competitive attempt to outdistance each other or the operation of one or more vehicles over a common selected course, from the same point to the same point, wherein timing is made of the participating vehicles involving competitive accelerations or speeds. Persons rendering assistance in any manner to such competitive use of vehicles shall be equally charged as the participants. The operation of two or more vehicles side by side either at speeds in excess of prima-facie lawful speeds established by divisions (B)(1)(a) to (B)(8) of section 4511.21 of the Revised Code or rapidly accelerating from a common starting point to a speed in excess of such prima-facie lawful speeds shall be prima-facie evidence of street racing.

(B) No person shall participate in street racing upon any public road, street, or highway in this state.

(C) Whoever violates this section is guilty of street racing, a misdemeanor of the first degree. In addition to any other sanctions, the court shall suspend the offender's driver's license, commercial driver's license, temporary instruction permit, probationary license, or nonresident operating privilege for not less than thirty days or more than three years. No judge shall suspend the first thirty days of any suspension of an offender's license, permit, or privilege imposed under this division.

**HISTORY: 128 v 469 (Eff 11-10-59); 138 v S 14 (Eff 10-25-79); 146 v H 107. Eff 6-30-95; 149 v S 123, § 1, eff. 1-1-04; 150 v H 52, § 1, eff. 6-1-04; 151 v S 184, § 1, eff. 6-15-06.**

The effective date is set by section 4 of S.B. 123.
See provisions, § 5 of S.B. 123 (149 v —), following RC § 4501.01.

## § 4511.252 Closing of public roads for competitive racing.

In townships in this state composed entirely of islands, the legislative authority of a municipal corporation, the county commissioners of the county wherein such township is located, and the trustees of such township may, by joint consent, cause any road, street, or highway in said township, whether within or without the limits of a municipal corporation, excepting state highways, to be closed to public travel, except in cases of emergency, for periods of not to exceed twenty-four hours, and during such period such roads, streets, or highways so closed may be used for supervised sports car racing;

(A) Any competitive racing event to be held upon a public road, street, or highway shall be sponsored by a recognized responsible organization.

(B) Any race held pursuant to division (A) of this section shall be conducted under the rules and regulations of the Sports Car Clubs of America.

(C) Adequate barricades shall be maintained at all hazardous sections of the racing course, hazardous corners shall be provided with barricades in the form of bales of hay or similar material sufficient to check accidental deviations from the course, and spectators shall be prohibited from entering a designated zone within two hundred feet from such corner extending two hundred feet along the exit outside section of such corner.

(D) The sponsoring organization under division (A) of this section shall furnish public liability insurance in the amount of two hundred fifty thousand dollars because of bodily injury to or death of one person resulting from any one accident, in the amount of one million dollars because of bodily injury to or death of two or more persons in any one accident, and in the amount of fifty thousand dollars because of injury to property of others in any one accident.

**HISTORY: 130 v 1086. Eff 5-1-63.**

## § 4511.26 Vehicles traveling in opposite directions.

(A) Operators of vehicles and trackless trolleys proceeding in opposite directions shall pass each other to the right, and upon roadways having width for not more than one line of traffic in each direction, each operator shall give to the other one-half of the main traveled portion of the roadway or as nearly one-half as is reasonable possible.

(B) Except as otherwise provided in this division, whoever violates this section is guilty of a minor misdemeanor. If, within one year of the offense, the offender previously has been convicted of or pleaded guilty to one predicate motor vehicle or traffic offense, whoever violates this section is guilty of a misdemeanor of the fourth degree. If, within one year of the offense, the offender previously has been convicted of two or more predicate motor vehicle or traffic offenses, whoever violates this section is guilty of a misdemeanor of the third degree.

**HISTORY: GC § 6307-26; 119 v 766(778), § 26; Bureau of Code Revision. Eff 10-1-53; 149 v S 123, § 1, eff. 1-1-04.**

The effective date is set by section 4 of S.B. 123.
See provisions, § 5 of S.B. 123 (149 v —), following RC § 4501.01.

## § 4511.27 Rules governing overtaking and passing of vehicles.

(A) The following rules govern the overtaking and passing of vehicles or trackless trolleys proceeding in the same direction:

(1) The operator of a vehicle or trackless trolley overtaking another vehicle or trackless trolley proceeding in the same direction shall, except as provided in division (A)(3) of this section, signal to the vehicle or trackless trolley to be overtaken, shall pass to the left thereof at a safe distance, and shall not again drive to the right side of the roadway until safely clear of the overtaken vehicle or trackless trolley.

(2) Except when overtaking and passing on the right is permitted, the operator of an overtaken vehicle shall give way to the right in favor of the overtaking vehicle at the latter's audible signal, and the operator shall not increase the speed of the operator's vehicle until completely passed by the overtaking vehicle.

(3) The operator of a vehicle or trackless trolley overtaking and passing another vehicle or trackless trolley proceeding in the same direction on a divided highway as defined in section 4511.35 of the Revised Code, a limited access highway as defined in section 5511.02 of the Revised Code, or a highway with four or more traffic lanes, is not required to signal audibly to the vehicle or trackless trolley being overtaken and passed.

(B) Except as otherwise provided in this division, whoever violates this section is guilty of a minor misdemeanor. If, within one year of the offense, the offender previously has been convicted of or pleaded guilty to one predicate motor vehicle or traffic offense, whoever violates this section is guilty of a misdemeanor of the fourth degree. If, within one year of the offense, the offender previously has been convicted of two or more predicate motor vehicle or traffic offenses, whoever violates this section is guilty of a misdemeanor of the third degree.

**HISTORY: GC § 6307-27; 119 v 766(778), § 27; Bureau of Code Revision, 10-1-53; 133 v S 289. Eff 11-6-69; 149 v S 123, § 1, eff. 1-1-04.**

The effective date is set by section 4 of S.B. 123.

See provisions, § 5 of S.B. 123 (149 v —), following RC § 4501.01.

## § 4511.28 Permission to overtake and pass on the right.

(A) The driver of a vehicle or trackless trolley may overtake and pass upon the right of another vehicle or trackless trolley only under the following conditions:

(1) When the vehicle or trackless trolley overtaken is making or about to make a left turn;

(2) Upon a roadway with unobstructed pavement of sufficient width for two or more lines of vehicles moving lawfully in the direction being traveled by the overtaking vehicle.

(B) The driver of a vehicle or trackless trolley may overtake and pass another vehicle or trackless trolley only under conditions permitting such movement in safety. The movement shall not be made by driving off the roadway.

(C) Except as otherwise provided in this division, whoever violates this section is guilty of a minor misdemeanor. If, within one year of the offense, the offender previously has been convicted of or pleaded guilty to one predicate motor vehicle or traffic offense, whoever violates this section is guilty of a misdemeanor of the fourth degree. If, within one year of the offense, the offender previously has been convicted of two or more predicate motor vehicle or traffic offenses, whoever violates this section is guilty of a misdemeanor of the third degree.

**HISTORY: GC § 6307-28; 119 v 766(778), § 28; Bureau of Code Revision, 10-1-53; 135 v H 995. Eff 1-1-75; 149 v S 123, § 1, eff. 1-1-04.**

The effective date is set by section 4 of S.B. 123.

See provisions, § 5 of S.B. 123 (149 v —), following RC § 4501.01.

## § 4511.29 Driving to left of center line.

(A) No vehicle or trackless trolley shall be driven to the left of the center of the roadway in overtaking and passing traffic proceeding in the same direction, unless such left side is clearly visible and is free of oncoming traffic for a sufficient distance ahead to permit such overtaking and passing to be completely made, without interfering with the safe operation of any traffic approaching from the opposite direction or any traffic overtaken. In every event the overtaking vehicle or trackless trolley must return to an authorized lane of travel as soon as practicable and in the event the passing movement involves the use of a lane authorized for traffic approaching from the opposite direction, before coming within two hundred feet of any approaching vehicle.

(B) Except as otherwise provided in this division, whoever violates this section is guilty of a minor misdemeanor. If, within one year of the offense, the offender previously has been convicted of or pleaded guilty to one predicate motor vehicle or traffic offense, whoever violates this section is guilty of a misdemeanor of the fourth degree. If, within one year of the offense, the offender previously has been convicted of two or more predicate motor vehicle or traffic offenses, whoever violates this section is guilty of a misdemeanor of the third degree.

**HISTORY: GC § 6307-29; 119 v 766(778), § 29; Bureau of Code Revision, 10-1-53; 135 v H 995. Eff 1-1-75; 149 v S 123, § 1, eff. 1-1-04.**

The effective date is set by section 4 of S.B. 123.

See provisions, § 5 of S.B. 123 (149 v —), following RC § 4501.01.

## § 4511.30 Prohibition against driving upon left side of roadway.

(A) No vehicle or trackless trolley shall be driven upon the left side of the roadway under the following conditions:

(1) When approaching the crest of a grade or upon a curve in the highway, where the operator's view is obstructed within such a distance as to create a hazard in the event traffic might approach from the opposite direction;

(2) When the view is obstructed upon approaching within one hundred feet of any bridge, viaduct, or tunnel;

(3) When approaching within one hundred feet of or traversing any intersection or railroad grade crossing.

(B) This section does not apply to vehicles or trackless trolleys upon a one-way roadway, upon a roadway where traffic is lawfully directed to be driven to the left side, or under the conditions described in division (A)(2) of section 4511.25 of the Revised Code.

(C) Except as otherwise provided in this division, whoever violates this section is guilty of a minor misdemeanor. If, within one year of the offense, the offender previously has been convicted of or pleaded guilty to one predicate motor vehicle or traffic offense, whoever violates this section is guilty of a misdemeanor of the fourth degree. If, within one year of the offense, the offender previously has been convicted of two or more predicate motor vehicle or traffic offenses, whoever violates this section is guilty of a misdemeanor of the third degree.

**HISTORY: GC § 6307-30; 119 v 766(779), § 30; 120 v 221; Bureau of Code Revision, 10-1-53; 135 v H 995. Eff 1-1-75; 149 v S 123, § 1, eff. 1-1-04.**

The effective date is set by section 4 of S.B. 123.

See provisions, § 5 of S.B. 123 (149 v —), following RC § 4501.01.

## § 4511.31 Hazardous zones.

(A) The department of transportation may determine those portions of any state highway where overtaking and passing other traffic or driving to the left of the center or center line of the roadway would be especially hazardous and may, by appropriate signs or markings on the highway, indicate the beginning and end of such zones. When such signs or markings are in place and clearly visible, every operator of a vehicle or trackless trolley shall obey the directions of the signs or markings, notwithstanding the distances set out in section 4511.30 of the Revised Code.

(B) Division (A) of this section does not apply when all of the following apply:

(1) The slower vehicle is proceeding at less than half the speed of the speed limit applicable to that location.

(2) The faster vehicle is capable of overtaking and passing the slower vehicle without exceeding the speed limit.

(3) There is sufficient clear sight distance to the left of the center or center line of the roadway to meet the overtaking and passing provisions of section 4511.29 of the Revised Code, considering the speed of the slower vehicle.

(C) Except as otherwise provided in this division, whoever violates this section is guilty of a minor misdemeanor. If, within one year of the offense, the offender previously has been convicted of or pleaded guilty to one predicate motor vehicle or traffic offense, whoever violates this section is guilty of a misdemeanor of the fourth degree. If, within one year of the offense, the offender previously has been convicted of two or more predicate motor vehicle or traffic offenses, whoever violates this section is guilty of a misdemeanor of the third degree.

**HISTORY: GC § 6307-31; 119 v 766(779), § 31; 124 v 514; Bureau of Code Revision, 10-1-53; 135 v H 200. Eff 9-28-73; 149 v S 123, § 1, eff. 1-1-04; 151 v H 389, § 1, eff. 9-21-06.**

The effective date is set by section 4 of S.B. 123.

See provisions, § 5 of S.B. 123 (149 v —), following RC § 4501.01.

## § 4511.32 One-way highways and rotary traffic islands.

(A) The department of transportation may designate any highway or any separate roadway under its jurisdiction for one-way traffic and shall erect appropriate signs giving notice thereof.

Upon a roadway designated and posted with signs for one-way traffic a vehicle shall be driven only in the direction designated.

A vehicle passing around a rotary traffic island shall be driven only to the right of the rotary traffic island.

(B) Except as otherwise provided in this division, whoever violates this section is guilty of a minor misdemeanor. If, within one year of the offense, the offender previously has been convicted of or pleaded guilty to one predicate motor vehicle or traffic offense, whoever violates this section is guilty of a misdemeanor of the fourth degree. If, within one year of the offense, the offender previously has been convicted of two or more predicate motor vehicle or traffic offenses, whoever violates this section is guilty of a misdemeanor of the third degree.

**HISTORY: GC § 6307-32; 119 v 766(779), § 32; Bureau of Code Revision, 10-1-53; 135 v H 200. Eff 9-28-73; 149 v S 123, § 1, eff. 1-1-04.**

The effective date is set by section 4 of S.B. 123.

See provisions, § 5 of S.B. 123 (149 v —), following RC § 4501.01.

## § 4511.33 Rules for driving in marked lanes.

(A) Whenever any roadway has been divided into two or more clearly marked lanes for traffic, or wherever within municipal corporations traffic is lawfully moving in two or more substantially continuous lines in the same direction, the following rules apply:

(1) A vehicle or trackless trolley shall be driven, as nearly as is practicable, entirely within a single lane or line of traffic and shall not be moved from such lane or line until the driver has first ascertained that such movement can be made with safety.

(2) Upon a roadway which is divided into three lanes and provides for two-way movement of traffic, a vehicle or trackless trolley shall not be driven in the center lane except when overtaking and passing another vehicle or trackless trolley where the roadway is clearly visible and such center lane is clear of traffic within a safe distance, or when preparing for a left turn, or where such center lane is at the time allocated exclusively to traffic moving in the direction the vehicle or trackless trolley is proceeding and is posted with signs to give notice of such allocation.

(3) Official signs may be erected directing specified traffic to use a designated lane or designating those lanes to be used by traffic moving in a particular direction regardless of the center of the roadway, or restricting the use of a particular lane to only buses during certain hours or during all hours, and drivers of vehicles and trackless trolleys shall obey the directions of such signs.

(4) Official traffic control devices may be installed prohibiting the changing of lanes on sections of roadway and drivers of vehicles shall obey the directions of every such device.

(B) Except as otherwise provided in this division, whoever violates this section is guilty of a minor misdemeanor. If, within one year of the offense, the offender previously has been convicted of or pleaded guilty to one predicate motor vehicle or traffic offense, whoever violates this section is guilty of a misdemeanor of the fourth degree. If, within one year of the offense, the offender previously has been convicted of two or more predicate motor vehicle or traffic offenses, whoever violates this section is guilty of a misdemeanor of the third degree.

**HISTORY: GC § 6307-33; 119 v 766(779), § 33; Bureau of Code Revision, 10-1-53; 135 v H 995. Eff 1-1-75; 149 v S 123, § 1, eff. 1-1-04; 150 v H 95, § 1, eff. 9-26-03; 150 v H 95, § 3.13, eff. 1-1-04.**

The effective dates are set by sections 3.15 and 179 of H.B. 95 (150 v —).

See provisions, § 5 of S.B. 123 (149 v —), following RC § 4501.01.

## § 4511.34 Space between moving vehicles.

(A) The operator of a motor vehicle, streetcar, or trackless trolley shall not follow another vehicle, streetcar, or trackless trolley more closely than is reasonable and prudent, having due regard for the speed of such vehicle, streetcar, or trackless trolley, and the traffic upon and the condition of the highway.

The driver of any truck, or motor vehicle drawing another vehicle, when traveling upon a roadway outside a business or residence district shall maintain a sufficient space, whenever conditions permit, between such vehicle and another vehicle ahead so an overtaking motor vehicle may enter and occupy such space without danger. This paragraph does not prevent overtaking and passing nor does it apply to any lane specially designated for use by trucks.

Outside a municipal corporation, the driver of any truck, or motor vehicle when drawing another vehicle, while ascending to the crest of a grade beyond which the driver's view of a roadway is obstructed, shall not follow within three hundred feet of another truck, or motor vehicle drawing another vehicle. This paragraph shall not apply to any lane specially designated for use by trucks.

Motor vehicles being driven upon any roadway outside of a business or residence district in a caravan or motorcade, shall maintain a sufficient space between such vehicles so an overtaking vehicle may enter and occupy such space without danger. This paragraph shall not apply to funeral processions.

(B) Except as otherwise provided in this division, whoever violates this section is guilty of a minor misdemeanor. If, within one year of the offense, the offender previously has been convicted of or pleaded guilty to one predicate motor vehicle or traffic offense, whoever violates this section is guilty of a misdemeanor of the fourth degree. If, within one year of the offense, the offender previously has been convicted of two or more predicate motor vehicle or traffic offenses, whoever violates this section is guilty of a misdemeanor of the third degree.

**HISTORY: GC § 6307-34; 119 v 766(789), § 34; Bureau of Code Revision, 10-1-53; 126 v 113. Eff 9-30-55; 149 v S 123, § 1, eff. 1-1-04.**

The effective date is set by section 4 of S.B. 123.

See provisions, § 5 of S.B. 123 (149 v —), following RC § 4501.01.

## § 4511.35 Divided roadways.

(A) Whenever any highway has been divided into two roadways by an intervening space, or by a physical barrier, or clearly indicated dividing section so constructed as to impede vehicular traffic, every vehicle shall be driven only upon the right-hand roadway, and no vehicle shall be driven over, across, or within any such dividing space, barrier, or section, except through an opening, crossover, or intersection established by public authority. This section does not prohibit the occupancy of such dividing space, barrier, or section for the purpose of an emergency stop or in compliance with an order of a police officer.

(B) Except as otherwise provided in this division, whoever violates this section is guilty of a minor misdemeanor. If, within one year of the offense, the offender previously has been convicted of or pleaded guilty to one predicate motor vehicle or traffic offense, whoever violates this section is guilty of a misdemeanor of the fourth degree. If, within one year of the offense, the offender previously has been convicted of two or more predicate motor vehicle or traffic offenses, whoever violates this section is guilty of a misdemeanor of the third degree.

**HISTORY: GC § 6307-34a; 124 v 514; Bureau of Code Revision. Eff 10-1-53; 149 v S 123, § 1, eff. 1-1-04.**

The effective date is set by section 4 of S.B. 123.

See provisions, § 5 of S.B. 123 (149 v —), following RC § 4501.01.

## § 4511.36 Rules for turns at intersections.

(A) The driver of a vehicle intending to turn at an intersection shall be governed by the following rules:

(1) Approach for a right turn and a right turn shall be made as close as practicable to the right-hand curb or edge of the roadway.

(2) At any intersection where traffic is permitted to move in both directions on each roadway entering the intersection, an approach for a left turn shall be made in that portion of the right half of the roadway nearest the center line thereof and by passing to the right of such center line where it enters the intersection and after entering the intersection the left turn shall be made so as to leave the intersection to the right of the center line of the roadway being entered. Whenever practicable the left turn shall be made in that portion of the intersection to the left of the center of the intersection.

(3) At any intersection where traffic is restricted to one direction on one or more of the roadways, the driver of a vehicle intending to turn left at any such intersection shall approach the intersection in the extreme left-hand lane lawfully available to traffic moving in the direction of travel of such vehicle, and after entering the intersection the left turn shall be made so as to leave the intersection, as nearly as practicable, in the left-hand lane of the roadway being entered lawfully available to traffic moving in that lane.

(B) The operator of a trackless trolley shall comply with divisions (A)(1), (2), and (3) of this section wherever practicable.

(C) The department of transportation and local authorities in their respective jurisdictions may cause markers, buttons, or signs to be placed within or adjacent to intersections and thereby require and direct that a different course from that specified in this section be traveled by vehicles, streetcars, or trackless trolleys, turning at an intersection, and when markers, buttons, or signs are so placed, no operator of a vehicle, streetcar, or trackless trolley shall turn such vehicle, streetcar, or trackless trolley at an intersection other than as directed and required by such markers, buttons, or signs.

(D) Except as otherwise provided in this division, whoever violates this section is guilty of a minor misdemeanor. If, within one year of the offense, the offender previously has been convicted of or pleaded guilty to one predicate motor vehicle or traffic offense, whoever violates this section is guilty of a misdemeanor of the fourth degree. If, within one year of the offense, the offender previously has been convicted of two or more predicate motor vehicle or traffic offenses, whoever violates this section is guilty of a misdemeanor of the third degree.

**HISTORY: GC § 6307-35; 119 v 766(780), § 35; 124 v 514; Bureau of Code Revision, 10-1-53; 135 v H 200. Eff 9-28-73; 149 v S 123, § 1, eff. 1-1-04.**

The effective date is set by section 4 of S.B. 123.

See provisions, § 5 of S.B. 123 (149 v —), following RC § 4501.01.

## § 4511.37 Turning in roadway prohibited; exception for emergency or public safety vehicle.

(A) Except as provided in division (B) of this section, no vehicle shall be turned so as to proceed in the opposite direction upon any curve, or upon the approach to or near the crest of a grade, if the vehicle cannot be seen within five hundred feet by the driver of any other vehicle approaching from either direction.

(B) The driver of an emergency vehicle or public safety vehicle, when responding to an emergency call, may turn the vehicle so as to proceed in the opposite direction. This division applies only when the emergency vehicle or public safety vehicle is responding to an emergency call, is equipped with and displaying at least one flashing, rotating, or oscillating light visible under normal atmospheric conditions from a distance of five hundred feet to the front of the vehicle, and when the driver of the vehicle is giving an audible signal by siren, exhaust whistle, or bell. This division does not relieve the driver of an emergency vehicle or public safety vehicle from the duty to drive with due regard for the safety of all persons and property upon the highway.

(C) Except as otherwise provided in this division, whoever violates this section is guilty of a minor misdemeanor. If, within one year of the offense, the offender previously has been convicted of or pleaded guilty to one predicate motor vehicle or traffic offense, whoever violates this section is guilty of a misdemeanor of the fourth degree. If, within one year of the offense, the offender previously has been convicted of two or more predicate motor vehicle or traffic offenses, whoever violates this section is guilty of a misdemeanor of the third degree.

**HISTORY: GC § 6307-36; 119 v 766(781), § 36; Bureau of Code Revision, 10-1-53; 145 v H 149. Eff 5-20-93; 149 v S 123, § 1, eff. 1-1-04.**

The effective date is set by section 4 of S.B. 123.

See provisions, § 5 of S.B. 123 (149 v —), following RC § 4501.01.

## § 4511.38 Rules for starting and backing vehicles.

(A) No person shall start a vehicle, streetcar, or trackless trolley which is stopped, standing, or parked until such movement can be made with reasonable safety.

Before backing, operators of vehicle, streetcars, or trackless trolleys shall give ample warning, and while backing they shall exercise vigilance not to injure person or property on the street or highway.

No person shall back a motor vehicle on a freeway, except: in a rest area; in the performance of public works or official duties; as a result of an emergency caused by an accident or breakdown of a motor vehicle.

(B) Except as otherwise provided in this division, whoever violates this section is guilty of a minor misdemeanor. If, within one year of the offense, the offender previously has been convicted of or pleaded guilty to one predicate motor vehicle or traffic offense, whoever violates this section is guilty of a misdemeanor of the fourth degree. If, within one year of the offense, the offender previously has been convicted of two or more predicate motor vehicle or traffic offenses, whoever violates this section is guilty of a misdemeanor of the third degree.

**HISTORY: GC § 6307-37; 119 v 766(781), § 37; Bureau of Code Revision, 10-1-53; 131 v 1103. Eff 11-4-65; 149 v S 123, § 1, eff. 1-1-04.**

The effective date is set by section 4 of S.B. 123.

See provisions, § 5 of S.B. 123 (149 v —), following RC § 4501.01.

## § 4511.39 Turn and stop signals.

(A) No person shall turn a vehicle or trackless trolley or move right or left upon a highway unless and until such person has exercised due care to ascertain that the movement can be made with reasonable safety nor without giving an appropriate signal in the manner hereinafter provided.

When required, a signal of intention to turn or move right or left shall be given continuously during not less than the last one hundred feet traveled by the vehicle or trackless trolley before turning, except that in the case of a person operating a bicycle, the signal shall be made not less than one time but is not required to be continuous. A bicycle operator is not required to make a signal if the bicycle is in a designated turn lane, and a signal shall not be given when the operator's hands are needed for the safe operation of the bicycle.

No person shall stop or suddenly decrease the speed of a vehicle or trackless trolley without first giving an appropriate signal in the manner provided herein to the driver of any vehicle or trackless trolley immediately to the rear when there is opportunity to give a signal.

Any stop or turn signal required by this section shall be given either by means of the hand and arm, or by signal lights that clearly indicate to both approaching and following traffic intention to turn or move right or left, except that any motor vehicle in use on a highway shall be equipped with, and the required signal shall be given by, signal lights when the distance from the center of the top of the steering post to the left outside limit of the body, cab, or load of such motor vehicle exceeds twenty-four inches, or when the distance from the center of the top of the steering post to the rear limit of the body or load thereof exceeds fourteen feet, whether a single vehicle or a combination of vehicles.

The signal lights required by this section shall not be flashed on one side only on a disabled vehicle or trackless trolley, flashed as a courtesy or "do pass" signal to operators of other vehicles or trackless trolleys approaching from the rear, nor be flashed on one side only of a parked vehicle or trackless trolley except as may be necessary for compliance with this section.

(B) Except as otherwise provided in this division, whoever violates this section is guilty of a minor misdemeanor. If, within one year of the offense, the offender previously has been convicted of or pleaded guilty to one predicate motor vehicle or traffic offense, whoever violates this section is guilty of a misdemeanor of the fourth degree. If, within one year of the offense, the offender previously has been convicted of two or more predicate motor vehicle or traffic offenses, whoever violates this section is guilty of a misdemeanor of the third degree.

**HISTORY: GC § 6307-38; 119 v 766(781), § 38; 124 v 514(533); Bureau of Code Revision, 10-1-53; 125 v 460 (Eff**

**10-19-53); 135 v H 995. Eff 1-1-75; 149 v S 123, § 1, eff. 1-1-04; 151 v H 389, § 1, eff. 9-21-06.**

The effective date is set by section 4 of S.B. 123.

See provisions, § 5 of S.B. 123 (149 v —), following RC § 4501.01.

## § 4511.40 Hand and arm signals.

(A) Except as provided in division (B) of this section, all signals required by sections 4511.01 to 4511.78 of the Revised Code, when given by hand and arm, shall be given from the left side of the vehicle in the following manner, and such signals shall indicate as follows:

(1) Left turn, hand and arm extended horizontally;

(2) Right turn, hand and arm extended upward;

(3) Stop or decrease speed, hand and arm extended downward.

(B) As an alternative to division (A)(2) of this section, a person operating a bicycle may give a right turn signal by extending the right hand and arm horizontally and to the right side of the bicycle.

(C) Except as otherwise provided in this division, whoever violates this section is guilty of a minor misdemeanor. If, within one year of the offense, the offender previously has been convicted of or pleaded guilty to one predicate motor vehicle or traffic offense, whoever violates this section is guilty of a misdemeanor of the fourth degree. If, within one year of the offense, the offender previously has been convicted of two or more predicate motor vehicle or traffic offenses, whoever violates this section is guilty of a misdemeanor of the third degree.

**HISTORY: GC § 6307-39; 119 v 766(782), § 39; Bureau of Code Revision, 10-1-53); 146 v H 461. Eff 9-10-96; 149 v S 123, § 1, eff. 1-1-04.**

The effective date is set by section 4 of S.B. 123.

See provisions, § 5 of S.B. 123 (149 v —), following RC § 4501.01.

[RIGHT OF WAY]

## § 4511.41 Right-of-way at intersections.

(A) When two vehicles, including any trackless trolley or streetcar, approach or enter an intersection from different streets or highways at approximately the same time, the driver of the vehicle on the left shall yield the right-of-way to the vehicle on the right.

(B) The right-of-way rule declared in division (A) of this section is modified at through highways and otherwise as stated in Chapter 4511. of the Revised Code.

(C) Except as otherwise provided in this division, whoever violates this section is guilty of a minor misdemeanor. If, within one year of the offense, the offender previously has been convicted of or pleaded guilty to one predicate motor vehicle or traffic offense, whoever violates this section is guilty of a misdemeanor of the fourth degree. If, within one year of the offense, the offender previously has been convicted of two or more predicate motor vehicle or traffic offenses, whoever violates this section is guilty of a misdemeanor of the third degree.

**HISTORY: 135 v H 995 (Eff 1-1-75); 136 v H 1. Eff 6-13-75; 149 v S 123, § 1, eff. 1-1-04.**

The effective date is set by section 4 of S.B. 123.

See provisions, § 5 of S.B. 123 (149 v —), following RC § 4501.01.

**Analogous to former RC § 4511.41 (GC § 6307-40; 119 v 766(782), § 40; Bureau of Code Revision, 10-1-53; 128 v 1270), repealed 135 v H 995, eff 1-1-75.**

## § 4511.42 Right of way when turning left.

(A) The operator of a vehicle, streetcar, or trackless trolley intending to turn to the left within an intersection or into an alley, private road, or driveway shall yield the right of way to any vehicle, streetcar, or trackless trolley approaching from the opposite direction, whenever the approaching vehicle, streetcar, or trackless trolley is within the intersection or so close to the intersection, alley, private road, or driveway as to constitute an immediate hazard.

(B) Except as otherwise provided in this division, whoever violates this section is guilty of a minor misdemeanor. If, within one year of the offense, the offender previously has been convicted of or pleaded guilty to one predicate motor vehicle or traffic offense, whoever violates this section is guilty of a misdemeanor of the fourth degree. If, within one year of the offense, the offender previously has been convicted of two or more predicate motor vehicle or traffic offenses, whoever violates this section is guilty of a misdemeanor of the third degree.

**HISTORY: GC § 6307-41; 119 v 766(782), § 41; Bureau of Code Revision, 10-1-53; 130 v 1087 (Eff 6-27-63); 135 v H 995 (Eff 1-1-75); 137 v S 62. Eff 7-8-77; 149 v S 123, § 1, eff. 1-1-04.**

The effective date is set by section 4 of S.B. 123.

See provisions, § 5 of S.B. 123 (149 v —), following RC § 4501.01.

## § 4511.43 Right-of-way at through highways; stop signs; yield signs.

(A) Except when directed to proceed by a law enforcement officer, every driver of a vehicle or trackless trolley approaching a stop sign shall stop at a clearly marked stop line, but if none, before entering the crosswalk on the near side of the intersection, or, if none, then at the point nearest the intersecting roadway where the driver has a view of approaching traffic on the intersecting roadway before entering it. After having stopped, the driver shall yield the right-of-way to any vehicle in the intersection or approaching on another roadway so closely as to constitute an immediate hazard during the time the driver is moving across or within the intersection or junction of roadways.

(B) The driver of a vehicle or trackless trolley approaching a yield sign shall slow down to a speed reasonable for the existing conditions and, if required for safety to stop, shall stop at a clearly marked stop line, but if none, before entering the crosswalk on the near side of the intersection, or, if none, then at the point nearest the intersecting roadway where the driver has a view of approaching traffic on the intersecting roadway before entering it. After slowing or stopping, the driver shall yield the right-of-way to any vehicle or trackless trolley in the intersection or approaching on another roadway so closely as to constitute an immediate hazard during the time the driver is moving across or within the intersection or junction of roadways. Whenever a driver is involved in a collision with a vehicle or trackless trolley in the intersection or junction of roadways, after driving past a yield sign without stopping, the collision shall be prima-facie evidence of the driver's failure to yield the right-of-way.

(C) Except as otherwise provided in this division, whoever violates this section is guilty of a minor misdemeanor. If, within one year of the offense, the offender previously has been convicted of or pleaded guilty to one predicate motor vehicle or traffic offense, whoever violates this section is guilty of a misdemeanor of the fourth degree. If, within one year of the offense, the offender previously has been convicted of two or more predicate motor vehicle or traffic offenses, whoever violates this section is guilty of a misdemeanor of the third degree.

**HISTORY: 135 v H 995. Eff 1-1-75; 149 v S 123, § 1, eff. 1-1-04.**

The effective date is set by section 4 of S.B. 123.

See provisions, § 5 of S.B. 123 (149 v —), following RC § 4501.01.

**Analogous to former RC § 4511.43 (GC § 6307-42; 119 v 766(782), § 42; Bureau of Code Revision, 10-1-53; 126 v 1119; 128 v 1270), repealed 135 v H 995, § 2, eff 1-1-75.**

## § 4511.431 Stop at sidewalk area.

(A) The driver of a vehicle or trackless trolley emerging from an alley, building, private road, or driveway within a business or residence district shall stop the vehicle or trackless trolley immediately prior to driving onto a sidewalk or onto the sidewalk area extending across the alley, building entrance, road, or driveway, or in the event there is no sidewalk area, shall stop at the point nearest the street to be entered where the driver has a view of approaching traffic thereon.

(B) Except as otherwise provided in this division, whoever violates this section is guilty of a minor misdemeanor. If, within one year of the offense, the offender previously has been convicted of or pleaded guilty to one predicate motor vehicle or traffic offense, whoever violates this section is guilty of a misdemeanor of the fourth degree. If, within one year of the offense, the offender previously has been convicted of two or more predicate motor vehicle or traffic offenses, whoever violates this section is guilty of a misdemeanor of the third degree.

**HISTORY: 135 v H 995. Eff 1-1-75; 149 v S 123, § 1, eff. 1-1-04.**

The effective date is set by section 4 of S.B. 123.

See provisions, § 5 of S.B. 123 (149 v —), following RC § 4501.01.

## § 4511.432 Stop signs on private residential road or driveway.

(A) The owner of a private road or driveway located in a private residential area containing twenty or more dwelling units may erect stop signs at places where the road or driveway intersects with another private road or driveway in the residential area, in compliance with all of the following requirements:

(1) The stop sign is sufficiently legible to be seen by an ordinarily observant person and meets the specifications of and is placed in accordance with the manual adopted by the department of transportation pursuant to section 4511.09 of the Revised Code.

(2) The owner has posted a sign at the entrance of the private road or driveway that is in plain view and clearly informs persons entering the road or driveway that they are entering private property, stop signs have been posted and must be obeyed, and the signs are enforceable by law enforcement officers under state law. The sign required by division (A)(2) of this section, where appropriate, may be incorporated with the sign required by division (A)(2) of section 4511.211 of the Revised Code.

(B) Division (A) of section 4511.43 and section 4511.46 of the Revised Code shall be deemed to apply to the driver of a vehicle on a private road or driveway where a stop sign is placed in accordance with division (A) of this section and to a pedestrian crossing such a road or driveway at an intersection where a stop sign is in place.

(C) When a stop sign is placed in accordance with division (A) of this section, any law enforcement officer may apprehend a person found violating the stop sign and may stop and charge the person with violating the stop sign.

(D) Except as otherwise provided in this division, whoever violates this section is guilty of a minor misdemeanor. If, within one year of the offense, the offender previously has been convicted of or pleaded guilty to one predicate motor vehicle or traffic offense, whoever violates this section is guilty of a misdemeanor of the fourth degree. If, within one year of the offense, the offender previously has been convicted of two or more predicate motor vehicle or traffic offenses, whoever violates this section is guilty of a misdemeanor of the third degree.

(E) As used in this section, and for the purpose of applying division (A) of section 4511.43 and section 4511.46 of the Revised Code to conduct under this section:

(1) "Intersection" means:

(a) The area embraced within the prolongation or connection of the lateral curb lines, or, if none, then the lateral boundary lines of the roadways of two private roads or driveways which join one another at, or approximately at, right angles, or the area within which vehicles traveling upon different private roads or driveways joining at any other angle may come in conflict.

(b) Where a private road or driveway includes two roadways thirty feet or more apart, then every crossing of two roadways of such private roads or driveways shall be regarded as a separate intersection.

(2) "Roadway" means that portion of a private road or driveway improved, designed, or ordinarily used for vehicular travel, except the berm or shoulder. If a private road or driveway includes two or more separate roadways, the term "roadway" means any such roadway separately but not all such roadways collectively.

(3) "Owner" and "private residential area containing twenty or more dwelling units" have the same meanings as in section 4511.211 of the Revised Code.

**HISTORY: 143 v H 171. Eff 5-31-90; 149 v S 123, § 1, eff. 1-1-04.**

The effective date is set by section 4 of S.B. 123.

See provisions, § 5 of S.B. 123 (149 v —), following RC § 4501.01.

## § 4511.44 Right of way on public highway.

(A) The operator of a vehicle, streetcar, or trackless trolley about to enter or cross a highway from any place other than another roadway shall yield the right of way to all traffic approaching on the roadway to be entered or crossed.

(B) Except as otherwise provided in this division, whoever violates this section is guilty of a minor misdemeanor.

If, within one year of the offense, the offender previously has been convicted of or pleaded guilty to one predicate motor vehicle or traffic offense, whoever violates this section is guilty of a misdemeanor of the fourth degree. If, within one year of the offense, the offender previously has been convicted of two or more predicate motor vehicle or traffic offenses, whoever violates this section is guilty of a misdemeanor of the third degree.

**HISTORY: GC § 6307-43; 119 v 766(782), § 43; Bureau of Code Revision, 10-1-53; 135 v H 995. Eff 1-1-75; 149 v S 123, § 1, eff. 1-1-04.**

The effective date is set by section 4 of S.B. 123.
See provisions, § 5 of S.B. 123 (149 v —), following RC § 4501.01.

## § 4511.441 Pedestrian on sidewalk has right-of-way.

(A) The driver of a vehicle shall yield the right-of-way to any pedestrian on a sidewalk.

(B) Except as otherwise provided in this division, whoever violates this section is guilty of a minor misdemeanor. If, within one year of the offense, the offender previously has been convicted of or pleaded guilty to one predicate motor vehicle or traffic offense, whoever violates this section is guilty of a misdemeanor of the fourth degree. If, within one year of the offense, the offender previously has been convicted of two or more predicate motor vehicle or traffic offenses, whoever violates this section is guilty of a misdemeanor of the third degree.

**HISTORY: 135 v H 995. Eff 1-1-75; 149 v S 123, § 1, eff. 1-1-04.**

The effective date is set by section 4 of S.B. 123.
See provisions, § 5 of S.B. 123 (149 v —), following RC § 4501.01.

## § 4511.45 Right-of-way of public safety or coroner's vehicle.

(A)(1) Upon the approach of a public safety vehicle or coroner's vehicle, equipped with at least one flashing, rotating or oscillating light visible under normal atmospheric conditions from a distance of five hundred feet to the front of the vehicle and the driver is giving an audible signal by siren, exhaust whistle, or bell, no driver of any other vehicle shall fail to yield the right-of-way, immediately drive if practical to a position parallel to, and as close as possible to, the right edge or curb of the highway clear of any intersection, and stop and remain in that position until the public safety vehicle or coroner's vehicle has passed, except when otherwise directed by a police officer.

(2) Upon the approach of a public safety vehicle or coroner's vehicle, as stated in division (A)(1) of this section, no operator of any streetcar or trackless trolley shall fail to immediately stop the streetcar or trackless trolley clear of any intersection and keep it in that position until the public safety vehicle or coroner's vehicle has passed, except when otherwise directed by a police officer.

(B) This section does not relieve the driver of a public safety vehicle or coroner's vehicle from the duty to drive with due regard for the safety of all persons and property upon the highway.

(C) This section applies to a coroner's vehicle only when the vehicle is operated in accordance with section 4513.171 of the Revised Code. As used in this section, "coroner's vehicle" means a vehicle used by a coroner, deputy coroner, or coroner's investigator that is equipped with a flashing, oscillating, or rotating red or blue light and a siren, exhaust whistle, or bell capable of giving an audible signal.

(D) Except as otherwise provided in this division, whoever violates division (A)(1) or (2) of this section is guilty of a misdemeanor of the fourth degree on a first offense. On a second offense within one year after the first offense, the person is guilty of a misdemeanor of the third degree, and, on each subsequent offense within one year after the first offense, the person is guilty of a misdemeanor of the second degree.

**HISTORY: GC § 6307-44; 119 v 766(782), § 44; 124 v 514; Bureau of Code Revision, 10-1-53; 132 v H 878 (Eff 12-14-67); 132 v S 451 (Eff 2-29-68); 145 v H 149 (Eff 5-20-93); 147 v H 282. Eff 11-12-97; 149 v S 123, § 1, eff. 1-1-04.**

The effective date is set by section 4 of S.B. 123.
See provisions, § 5 of S.B. 123 (149 v —), following RC § 4501.01.

## § 4511.451 Funeral procession has right of way.

(A) As used in this section, "funeral procession" means two or more vehicles accompanying the cremated remains or the body of a deceased person in the daytime when each of the vehicles has its headlights lighted and is displaying a purple and white or an orange and white pennant attached to each vehicle in such a manner as to be clearly visible to traffic approaching from any direction.

(B) Excepting public safety vehicles proceeding in accordance with section 4511.45 of the Revised Code or when directed otherwise by a police officer, pedestrians and the operators of all vehicles, street cars, and trackless trolleys shall yield the right of way to each vehicle that is a part of a funeral procession. Whenever the lead vehicle in a funeral procession lawfully enters an intersection, the remainder of the vehicles in the procession may continue to follow the lead vehicle through the intersection notwithstanding any traffic control devices or right of way provisions of the Revised Code, provided that the operator of each vehicle exercises due care to avoid colliding with any other vehicle or pedestrian.

(C) No person shall operate any vehicle as a part of a funeral procession without having the headlights of the vehicle lighted and without displaying a purple and white or an orange and white pennant in such a manner as to be clearly visible to traffic approaching from any direction.

(D) Except as otherwise provided in this division, whoever violates this section is guilty of a minor misdemeanor. If, within one year of the offense, the offender previously has been convicted of or pleaded guilty to one predicate motor vehicle or traffic offense, whoever violates this section is guilty of a misdemeanor of the fourth degree. If, within one year of the offense, the offender previously has been convicted of two or more predicate motor vehicle or traffic offenses, whoever violates this section is guilty of a misdemeanor of the third degree.

**HISTORY: 126 v 632 (Eff 1-1-56); 132 v H 878 (Eff 12-14-67); 149 v H 322. Eff 4-7-2003; 149 v S 123, § 1, eff. 1-1-04; 151 v H 426, § 1, eff. 10-12-06.**

The provisions of § 3 of 151 v H 426 read as follows:
SECTION 3. Section 4511.451 of the Revised Code is presented in this act as a composite of the section as amended by both Sub. H.B. 322 and Am. Sub. S.B. 123 of the 124th General Assembly.

The General Assembly, applying the principle stated in division (B) of section 1.52 of the Revised Code that amendments are to be harmonized if reasonably capable of simultaneous operation, finds that the composite is the resulting version of the section in effect prior to the effective date of the section as presented in this act.

The effective date is set by section 4 of S.B. 123.

See provisions, § 5 of S.B. 123 (149 v —), following RC § 4501.01.

## § 4511.452 Pedestrian to yield right-of-way to public safety vehicle.

(A) Upon the immediate approach of a public safety vehicle, as stated in section 4511.45 of the Revised Code, every pedestrian shall yield the right-of-way to the public safety vehicle.

(B) This section shall not relieve the driver of a public safety vehicle from the duty to exercise due care to avoid colliding with any pedestrian.

(C) Except as otherwise provided in this division, whoever violates this section is guilty of a minor misdemeanor. If, within one year of the offense, the offender previously has been convicted of or pleaded guilty to one predicate motor vehicle or traffic offense, whoever violates this section is guilty of a misdemeanor of the fourth degree. If, within one year of the offense, the offender previously has been convicted of two or more predicate motor vehicle or traffic offenses, whoever violates this section is guilty of a misdemeanor of the third degree.

**HISTORY: 135 v H 995. Eff 1-1-75; 149 v S 123, § 1, eff. 1-1-04.**

The effective date is set by section 4 of S.B. 123.

See provisions, § 5 of S.B. 123 (149 v —), following RC § 4501.01.

## § 4511.453 Immunity in connection with movement of funeral procession.

(A) Neither the owner, the operator, or an employee of a funeral home nor the owner or operator of a funeral escort vehicle is liable in damages in a civil action for injury, death, or loss to person or property that allegedly arises from the movement of a funeral procession if either of the following applies:

(1) The movement of the funeral procession is in accordance with section 4511.451 [4511.45.1] of the Revised Code.

(2) The movement of the funeral procession generally is in accordance with section 4511.451 [4511.45.1] of the Revised Code, but the operator of one or more motor vehicles that are in the procession, that are not owned or operated by the owner, the operator, or an employee of the funeral home, and that are not funeral escort vehicles fails to do either of the following and the injury, death, or loss to person or property allegedly arose from that failure:

(a) Exercise due care as required by division (B) of section 4511.451 [4511.45.1] of the Revised Code;

(b) Comply with division (C) of section 4511.451 [4511.45.1] of the Revised Code, provided that the owner, the operator, or an employee of the funeral home informed the motor vehicle operator of the requirements and made the appropriate pennant available to the motor vehicle operator.

(B)(1) This section does not apply if the injury, death, or loss allegedly arose from any of the following:

(a) The willful, wanton, or intentional acts or omissions of the owner, the operator, or an employee of a funeral home or the owner or the operator of a funeral escort vehicle;

(b) The negligent or reckless acts or omissions in the operation of a motor vehicle by the owner, the operator, or an employee of a funeral home or the owner or the operator of a funeral escort vehicle.

(2) This section does not create a new cause of action or substantive legal right against an owner, operator, or employee of a funeral home or an owner or operator of a funeral escort vehicle.

(3) This section does not affect any immunities from civil liability or defenses established by another section of the Revised Code or any immunities from civil liability or defenses available at common law to which an owner, operator, or employee of a funeral home or an owner or operator of a funeral escort vehicle may be entitled.

(C) As used in this section:

(1) "Funeral home" has the same meaning as in section 4717.01 of the Revised Code.

(2) "Funeral procession" has the same meaning as in section 4511.451 [4511.45.1] of the Revised Code.

**HISTORY: 149 v H 322. Eff 4-7-2003.**

## § 4511.46 Pedestrian on crosswalk has right-of-way.

(A) When traffic control signals are not in place, not in operation, or are not clearly assigning the right-of-way, the driver of a vehicle, trackless trolley, or streetcar shall yield the right of way, slowing down or stopping if need be to so yield or if required by section 4511.132 of the Revised Code, to a pedestrian crossing the roadway within a crosswalk when the pedestrian is upon the half of the roadway upon which the vehicle is traveling, or when the pedestrian is approaching so closely from the opposite half of the roadway as to be in danger.

(B) No pedestrian shall suddenly leave a curb or other place of safety and walk or run into the path of a vehicle, trackless trolley, or streetcar which is so close as to constitute an immediate hazard.

(C) Division (A) of this section does not apply under the conditions stated in division (B) of section 4511.48 of the Revised Code.

(D) Whenever any vehicle, trackless trolley, or streetcar is stopped at a marked crosswalk or at any unmarked crosswalk at an intersection to permit a pedestrian to cross the roadway, the driver of any other vehicle, trackless trolley, or streetcar approaching from the rear shall not overtake and pass the stopped vehicle.

(E) Except as otherwise provided in this division, whoever violates this section is guilty of a minor misdemeanor. If, within one year of the offense, the offender previously has been convicted of or pleaded guilty to one predicate motor vehicle or traffic offense, whoever violates this section is guilty of a misdemeanor of the fourth degree. If, within one year of the offense, the offender previously has been convicted of two or more predicate motor vehicle or traffic offenses, whoever violates this section is guilty of a misdemeanor of the third degree.

**HISTORY: 135 v H 995 (Eff 1-1-75); 143 v S 44. Eff 7-25-89; 149 v S 123, § 1, eff. 1-1-04.**

The effective date is set by section 4 of S.B. 123.

See provisions, § 5 of S.B. 123 (149 v —), following RC § 4501.01.

**Analogous to former RC § 4511.46 (GC § 6307-45; 119 v 766; Bureau of Code Revision, 10-1-53), repealed 135 v H 995, § 2, eff 1-1-75.**

## § 4511.47 Right of way yielded to blind person.

(A) As used in this section "blind person" or "blind pedestrian" means a person having not more than 20/200 visual acuity in the better eye with correcting lenses or visual acuity greater than 20/200 but with a limitation in the fields of vision such that the widest diameter of the visual field subtends an angle no greater than twenty degrees.

The driver of every vehicle shall yield the right of way to every blind pedestrian guided by a guide dog, or carrying a cane which is predominantly white or metallic in color, with or without a red tip.

(B) No person, other than a blind person, while on any public highway, street, alley, or other public thoroughfare shall carry a white or metallic cane with or without a red tip.

(C) Except as otherwise provided in this division, whoever violates this section is guilty of a minor misdemeanor. If, within one year of the offense, the offender previously has been convicted of or pleaded guilty to one predicate motor vehicle or traffic offense, whoever violates this section is guilty of a misdemeanor of the fourth degree. If, within one year of the offense, the offender previously has been convicted of two or more predicate motor vehicle or traffic offenses, whoever violates this section is guilty of a misdemeanor of the third degree.

**HISTORY: GC §§ 6307-45a, 6307-45b, 6307-45c; 124 v 59; Bureau of Code Revision, 10-1-53; 133 v S 514. Eff 7-16-70; 149 v S 123, § 1, eff. 1-1-04.**

The effective date is set by section 4 of S.B. 123.

See provisions, § 5 of S.B. 123 (149 v —), following RC § 4501.01.

## § 4511.48 Right of way yielded by pedestrian.

(A) Every pedestrian crossing a roadway at any point other than within a marked crosswalk or within an unmarked crosswalk at an intersection shall yield the right of way to all vehicles, trackless trolleys, or streetcars upon the roadway.

(B) Any pedestrian crossing a roadway at a point where a pedestrian tunnel or overhead pedestrian crossing has been provided shall yield the right of way to all traffic upon the roadway.

(C) Between adjacent intersections at which traffic control signals are in operation, pedestrians shall not cross at any place except in a marked crosswalk.

(D) No pedestrian shall cross a roadway intersection diagonally unless authorized by official traffic control devices; and, when authorized to cross diagonally, pedestrians shall cross only in accordance with the official traffic control devices pertaining to such crossing movements.

(E) This section does not relieve the operator of a vehicle, streetcar, or trackless trolley from exercising due care to avoid colliding with any pedestrian upon any roadway.

(F) Except as otherwise provided in this division, whoever violates this section is guilty of a minor misdemeanor. If, within one year of the offense, the offender previously has been convicted of or pleaded guilty to one predicate motor vehicle or traffic offense, whoever violates this section is guilty of a misdemeanor of the fourth degree. If, within one year of the offense, the offender previously has been convicted of two or more predicate motor vehicle or traffic offenses, whoever violates this section is guilty of a misdemeanor of the third degree.

**HISTORY: GC § 6307-46; 119 v 766(783), § 46; Bureau of Code Revision, 10-1-53; 135 v H 995. Eff 1-1-75; 149 v S 123, § 1, eff. 1-1-04.**

The effective date is set by section 4 of S.B. 123.

See provisions, § 5 of S.B. 123 (149 v —), following RC § 4501.01.

[PEDESTRIANS]

## § 4511.481 Intoxicated or drugged pedestrian hazard on highway.

(A) A pedestrian who is under the influence of alcohol, any drug of abuse, or any combination of them to a degree that renders the pedestrian a hazard shall not walk or be upon a highway.

(B) Except as otherwise provided in this division, whoever violates this section is guilty of a minor misdemeanor. If, within one year of the offense, the offender previously has been convicted of or pleaded guilty to one predicate motor vehicle or traffic offense, whoever violates this section is guilty of a misdemeanor of the fourth degree. If, within one year of the offense, the offender previously has been convicted of two or more predicate motor vehicle or traffic offenses, whoever violates this section is guilty of a misdemeanor of the third degree.

**HISTORY: 135 v H 995. Eff 1-1-75; 149 v S 123, § 1, eff. 1-1-04.**

The effective date is set by section 4 of S.B. 123.

See provisions, § 5 of S.B. 123 (149 v —), following RC § 4501.01.

## § 4511.49 Pedestrians.

(A) Pedestrians shall move, whenever practicable, upon the right half of crosswalks.

(B) Except as otherwise provided in this division, whoever violates this section is guilty of a minor misdemeanor. If, within one year of the offense, the offender previously has been convicted of or pleaded guilty to one predicate motor vehicle or traffic offense, whoever violates this section is guilty of a misdemeanor of the fourth degree. If, within one year of the offense, the offender previously has been convicted of two or more predicate motor vehicle or traffic offenses, whoever violates this section is guilty of a misdemeanor of the third degree.

**HISTORY: GC § 6307-47; 119 v 766(783), § 47; Bureau of Code Revision, 10-1-53; 135 v H 995. Eff 1-1-75; 149 v S 123, § 1, eff. 1-1-04.**

The effective date is set by section 4 of S.B. 123.

See provisions, § 5 of S.B. 123 (149 v —), following RC § 4501.01.

## § 4511.491 Motorized wheelchair operators.

Every person operating a motorized wheelchair shall have all of the rights and duties applicable to a pedestrian that are contained in this chapter, except those provisions which by their nature can have no application.

**HISTORY: 143 v S 272. Eff 11-28-90.**

## § 4511.50 Pedestrian walking along highway.

(A) Where a sidewalk is provided and its use is practicable, it shall be unlawful for any pedestrian to walk along and upon an adjacent roadway.

(B) Where a sidewalk is not available, any pedestrian walking along and upon a highway shall walk only on a shoulder, as far as practicable from the edge of the roadway.

(C) Where neither a sidewalk nor a shoulder is available, any pedestrian walking along and upon a highway shall walk as near as practicable to an outside edge of the roadway, and, if on a two-way roadway, shall walk only on the left side of the roadway.

(D) Except as otherwise provided in sections 4511.13 and 4511.46 of the Revised Code, any pedestrian upon a roadway shall yield the right-of-way to all vehicles, trackless trolleys, or streetcars upon the roadway.

(E) Except as otherwise provided in this division, whoever violates this section is guilty of a minor misdemeanor. If, within one year of the offense, the offender previously has been convicted of or pleaded guilty to one predicate motor vehicle or traffic offense, whoever violates this section is guilty of a misdemeanor of the fourth degree. If, within one year of the offense, the offender previously has been convicted of two or more predicate motor vehicle or traffic offenses, whoever violates this section is guilty of a misdemeanor of the third degree.

**HISTORY: 135 v H 995. Eff 1-1-75; 149 v S 123, § 1, eff. 1-1-04.**

The effective date is set by section 4 of S.B. 123.

See provisions, § 5 of S.B. 123 (149 v —), following RC § 4501.01.

**Analogous to former RC § 4511.50 (GC § 6307-48; 119 v 776; Bureau of Code Revision, 10-1-53), repealed 135 v H 995, § 2, eff 1-1-75.**

The effective date is set by section 3 of HB 995.

## § 4511.51 Prohibited solicitations by pedestrians; riding on outside of vehicle or in open cargo storage area or on tailgate.

(A) No person while on a roadway outside a safety zone shall solicit a ride from the driver of any vehicle.

(B)(1) Except as provided in division (B)(2) of this section, no person shall stand on a highway for the purpose of soliciting employment, business, or contributions from the occupant of any vehicle.

(2) The legislative authority of a municipal corporation, by ordinance, may authorize the issuance of a permit to a charitable organization to allow a person acting on behalf of the organization to solicit charitable contributions from the occupant of a vehicle by standing on a highway, other than a freeway as provided in division (A)(1) of section 4511.051 of the Revised Code, that is under the jurisdiction of the municipal corporation. The permit shall be valid for only one period of time, which shall be specified in the permit, in any calendar year. The legislative authority also may specify the locations where contributions may be solicited and may impose any other restrictions on or requirements regarding the manner in which the solicitations are to be conducted that the legislative authority considers advisable.

(3) As used in division (B)(2) of this section, "charitable organization" means an organization that has received from the internal revenue service a currently valid ruling or determination letter recognizing the tax-exempt status of the organization pursuant to section 501(c)(3) of the "Internal Revenue Code."

(C) No person shall hang onto or ride on the outside of any motor vehicle, streetcar, or trackless trolley while it is moving upon a roadway, except mechanics or test engineers making repairs or adjustments, or workers performing specialized highway or street maintenance or construction under authority of a public agency.

(D) No operator shall knowingly permit any person to hang onto, or ride on the outside of, any motor vehicle, streetcar, or trackless trolley while it is moving upon a roadway, except mechanics or test engineers making repairs or adjustments, or workers performing specialized highway or street maintenance or construction under authority of a public agency.

(E) No driver of a truck, trailer, or semitrailer shall knowingly permit any person who has not attained the age of sixteen years to ride in the unenclosed or unroofed cargo storage area of the driver's vehicle if the vehicle is traveling faster than twenty-five miles per hour, unless either of the following applies:

(1) The cargo storage area of the vehicle is equipped with a properly secured seat to which is attached a seat safety belt that is in compliance with federal standards for an occupant restraining device as defined in division (A)(2) of section 4513.263 of the Revised Code, the seat and seat safety belt were installed at the time the vehicle was originally assembled, and the person riding in the cargo storage area is in the seat and is wearing the seat safety belt;

(2) An emergency exists that threatens the life of the driver or the person being transported in the cargo storage area of the truck, trailer, or semitrailer.

(F) No driver of a truck, trailer, or semitrailer shall permit any person, except for those workers performing specialized highway or street maintenance or construction under authority of a public agency, to ride in the cargo storage area or on a tailgate of the driver's vehicle while the tailgate is unlatched.

(G)(1) Except as otherwise provided in this division, whoever violates any provision of divisions (A) to (D) of this section is guilty of a minor misdemeanor. If, within one year of the offense, the offender previously has been convicted of or pleaded guilty to one predicate motor vehicle or traffic offense, whoever violates any provision of divisions (A) to (D) of this section is guilty of a misdemeanor of the fourth degree. If, within one year of the offense, the offender previously has been convicted of two or more predicate motor vehicle or traffic offenses, whoever violates any provision of divisions (A) to (D) of this section is guilty of a misdemeanor of the third degree.

(2) Whoever violates division (E) or (F) of this section is guilty of a minor misdemeanor.

**HISTORY: GC § 6307-49; 119 v 776, § 49; 121 v 684; Bureau of Code Revision, 10-1-53; 135 v H 995 (Eff 1-1-75); 143 v H 8 (Eff 9-13-89); 145 v H 331. Eff 7-2-93; 149 v S 123, § 1, eff. 1-1-04.**

The effective date is set by section 4 of S.B. 123.

See provisions, § 5 of S.B. 123 (149 v —), following RC § 4501.01.

## § 4511.511 Pedestrian on bridge or railroad crossing.

(A) No pedestrian shall enter or remain upon any bridge or approach thereto beyond the bridge signal, gate, or barrier after a bridge operation signal indication has been given.

(B) No pedestrian shall pass through, around, over, or under any crossing gate or barrier at a railroad grade crossing or bridge while the gate or barrier is closed or is being opened or closed.

(C) Except as otherwise provided in this division, whoever violates this section is guilty of a minor misdemeanor. If, within one year of the offense, the offender previously has been convicted of or pleaded guilty to one predicate motor vehicle or traffic offense, whoever violates this section is guilty of a misdemeanor of the fourth degree. If, within one year of the offense, the offender previously has been convicted of two or more predicate motor vehicle or traffic offenses, whoever violates this section is guilty of a misdemeanor of the third degree.

**HISTORY: 135 v H 995. Eff 1-1-75; 149 v S 123, § 1, eff. 1-1-04.**

The effective date is set by section 4 of S.B. 123.

See provisions, § 5 of S.B. 123 (149 v —), following RC § 4501.01.

## § 4511.512 Electric personal assistive mobility devices.

(A)(1) Electric personal assistive mobility devices may be operated on the public streets, highways, sidewalks, and paths and portions of roadways set aside for the exclusive use of bicycles in accordance with this section.

(2) Except as otherwise provided in this section, those sections of this chapter that by their nature are applicable to an electric personal assistive mobility device apply to the device and the person operating it whenever it is operated upon any public street, highway, sidewalk, or path or upon any portion of a roadway set aside for the exclusive use of bicycles.

(3) A local authority may regulate or prohibit the operation of electric personal assistive mobility devices on public streets, highways, sidewalks, and paths, and portions of roadways set aside for the exclusive use of bicycles, under its jurisdiction.

(B) No operator of an electric personal assistive mobility device shall do any of the following:

(1) Fail to yield the right-of-way to all pedestrians and human-powered vehicles at all times;

(2) Fail to give an audible signal before overtaking and passing a pedestrian;

(3) Operate the device at night unless the device or its operator is equipped with or wearing both of the following:

(a) A lamp pointing to the front that emits a white light visible from a distance of not less than five hundred feet;

(b) A red reflector facing the rear that is visible from all distances from one hundred feet to six hundred feet when directly in front of lawful lower beams of head lamps on a motor vehicle.

(4) Operate the device on any portion of a street or highway that has an established speed limit of fifty-five miles per hour or more;

(5) Operate the device upon any path set aside for the exclusive use of pedestrians or other specialized use when an appropriate sign giving notice of the specialized use is posted on the path;

(6) If under eighteen years of age, operate the device unless wearing a protective helmet on the person's head with the chin strap properly fastened;

(7) If under sixteen years of age, operate the device unless, during the operation, the person is under the direct visual and audible supervision of another person who is eighteen years of age or older and is responsible for the immediate care of the person under sixteen years of age.

(C) No person who is under fourteen years of age shall operate an electric personal assistive mobility device.

(D) No person shall distribute or sell an electric personal assistive mobility device unless the device is accompanied by a written statement that is substantially equivalent to the following: "WARNING: TO REDUCE THE RISK OF SERIOUS INJURY, USE ONLY WHILE WEARING FULL PROTECTIVE EQUIPMENT — HELMET, WRIST GUARDS, ELBOW PADS, AND KNEE PADS."

(E) Nothing in this section affects or shall be construed to affect any rule of the director of natural resources or a board of park district commissioners governing the operation of vehicles on lands under the control of the director or board, as applicable.

(F)(1) Whoever violates division (B) or (C) of this section is guilty of a minor misdemeanor and shall be punished as follows:

(a) The offender shall be fined ten dollars.

(b) If the offender previously has been convicted of or pleaded guilty to a violation of division (B) or (C) of this section or a substantially similar municipal ordinance, the court, in addition to imposing the fine required under division (F)(1) of this section, shall do one of the following:

(i) Order the impoundment for not less than one day but not more than thirty days of the electric personal assistive mobility device that was involved in the current violation of that division. The court shall order the device to be impounded at a safe indoor location designated by the court and may assess storage fees of not more than five dollars per day, provided the total storage, processing, and release fees assessed against the offender or the device in connection with the device's impoundment or subsequent release shall not exceed fifty dollars.

(ii) If the court does not issue an impoundment order pursuant to division (F)(1)(b)(i) of this section, issue an order prohibiting the offender from operating any electric personal assistive mobility device on the public streets, highways, sidewalks, and paths and portions of roadways set aside for the exclusive use of bicycles for not less than one day but not more than thirty days.

(2) Whoever violates division (D) of this section is guilty of a minor misdemeanor.

**HISTORY: 149 v S 231. Eff 10-24-2002; 149 v H 490, § 1, eff. 1-1-04.**

The effective date is set by section 4 of H.B. 490.

### [BICYCLES, MOTORCYCLES AND SNOWMOBILES]

## § 4511.52 Bicycles.

(A) Sections 4511.01 to 4511.78, 4511.99, and 4513.01 to 4513.37 of the Revised Code that are applicable to bicycles apply whenever a bicycle is operated upon any highway or upon any path set aside for the exclusive use of bicycles.

(B) Except as provided in division (D) of this section, a bicycle operator who violates any section of the Revised Code described in division (A) of this section that is applicable to bicycles may be issued a ticket, citation, or summons by a law enforcement officer for the violation in the same manner as the operator of a motor vehicle would be cited for the same violation. A person who commits any such violation while operating a bicycle shall not have any points assessed against the person's driver's license, commercial driver's license, temporary instruction permit, or probationary license under section 4510.036 [4510.03.6] of the Revised Code.

(C) Except as provided in division (D) of this section, in the case of a violation of any section of the Revised Code described in division (A) of this section by a bicycle operator or by a motor vehicle operator when the trier of fact finds that the violation by the motor vehicle operator endangered the lives of bicycle riders at the time of the violation, the court, notwithstanding any provision of the Revised Code to the contrary, may require the bicycle operator or motor vehicle operator to take and successfully complete a bicycling skills course approved by the court in addition to or in lieu of any penalty otherwise prescribed by the Revised Code for that violation.

(D) Divisions (B) and (C) of this section do not apply to violations of section 4511.19 of the Revised Code.

**HISTORY: GC § 6307-50; 119 v 766(784), § 50; Bureau of Code Revision. Eff 10-1-53; 151 v H 389, § 1, eff. 9-21-06.**

## § 4511.521 Rules governing operation of motorized bicycles.

(A) No person shall operate a motorized bicycle upon a highway or any public or private property used by the public for purposes of vehicular travel or parking, unless all of the following conditions are met:

(1) The person is fourteen or fifteen years of age and holds a valid probationary motorized bicycle license issued after the person has passed the test provided for in this section, or the person is sixteen years of age or older and holds either a valid commercial driver's license issued under Chapter 4506. or a driver's license issued under Chapter 4507. of the Revised Code or a valid motorized bicycle license issued after the person has passed the test provided for in this section, except that if a person is sixteen years of age, has a valid probationary motorized bicycle license and desires a motorized bicycle license, the person is not required to comply with the testing requirements provided for in this section;

(2) The motorized bicycle is equipped in accordance with the rules adopted under division (B) of this section and is in proper working order;

(3) The person, if under eighteen years of age, is wearing a protective helmet on the person's head with the chin strap properly fastened and the motorized bicycle is equipped with a rear-view mirror.

(4) The person operates the motorized bicycle when practicable within three feet of the right edge of the roadway obeying all traffic rules applicable to vehicles.

(B) The director of public safety, subject to sections 119.01 to 119.13 of the Revised Code, shall adopt and promulgate rules concerning protective helmets, the equipment of motorized bicycles, and the testing and qualifications of persons who do not hold a valid driver's or commercial driver's license. The test shall be as near as practicable to the examination required for a motorcycle operator's endorsement under section 4507.11 of the Revised Code. The test shall also require the operator to give an actual demonstration of the operator's ability to operate and control a motorized bicycle by driving one under the supervision of an examining officer.

(C) Every motorized bicycle license expires on the birthday of the applicant in the fourth year after the date it is issued, but in no event shall any motorized bicycle license be issued for a period longer than four years.

(D) No person operating a motorized bicycle shall carry another person upon the motorized bicycle.

(E) The protective helmet and rear-view mirror required by division (A) (3) of this section shall, on and after January 1, 1985, conform with rules adopted by the director under division (B) of this section.

(F) Each probationary motorized bicycle license or motorized bicycle license shall be laminated with a transparent plastic material.

(G) Whoever violates division (A), (D), or (E) of this section is guilty of a minor misdemeanor.

**HISTORY: 137 v S 100 (Eff 4-1-78); 137 v S 393 (Eff 5-12-78); 140 v S 169 (Eff 6-18-84); 140 v S 169, § 6 (Eff 1-1-85); 143 v H 381 (Eff 7-1-89); 143 v S 131 (Eff 7-25-90); 144 v S 98. Eff 11-12-92; 149 v S 123, § 1, eff. 1-1-04.**

The effective date is set by section 4 of S.B. 123.

See provisions, § 5 of S.B. 123 (149 v —), following RC § 4501.01.

## § 4511.53 Rules for bicycles, motorcycles and snowmobiles.

(A) For purposes of this section, "snowmobile" has the same meaning as given that term in section 4519.01 of the Revised Code.

(B) No person operating a bicycle shall ride other than upon or astride the permanent and regular seat attached thereto or carry any other person upon such bicycle other than upon a firmly attached and regular seat thereon, and no person shall ride upon a bicycle other than upon such a firmly attached and regular seat.

No person operating a motorcycle shall ride other than upon or astride the permanent and regular seat or saddle attached thereto, or carry any other person upon such motorcycle other than upon a firmly attached and regular seat or saddle thereon, and no person shall ride upon a motorcycle other than upon such a firmly attached and regular seat or saddle.

No person shall ride upon a motorcycle that is equipped with a saddle other than while sitting astride the saddle, facing forward, with one leg on each side of the motorcycle.

No person shall ride upon a motorcycle that is equipped with a seat other than while sitting upon the seat.

No person operating a bicycle shall carry any package, bundle, or article that prevents the driver from keeping at least one hand upon the handle bars.

No bicycle or motorcycle shall be used to carry more persons at one time than the number for which it is designed and equipped, nor shall any motorcycle be operated on a highway when the handle bars or grips are more than fifteen inches higher than the seat or saddle for the operator.

No person shall operate or be a passenger on a snowmobile or motorcycle without using safety glasses or other protective eye device. No person who is under the age of eighteen years, or who holds a motorcycle operator's endorsement or license bearing a "novice" designation that is currently in effect as provided in section 4507.13 of the Revised Code, shall operate a motorcycle on a highway, or be a passenger on a motorcycle, unless wearing a protective helmet on the person's head, and no other person shall be a passenger on a motorcycle operated by such a person unless similarly wearing a protective helmet. The helmet, safety glasses, or other protective eye device shall conform with rules adopted by the director of public safety. The provisions of this paragraph or a violation thereof shall not be used in the trial of any civil action.

(C)(1) No person shall operate a motorcycle with a valid temporary instruction permit and temporary instruction permit identification card issued by the registrar of motor vehicles pursuant to section 4507.05 of the Revised Code unless the person, at the time of such operation, is wearing on the person's head a protective helmet that conforms with rules adopted by the director.

(2) No person shall operate a motorcycle with a valid temporary instruction permit and temporary instruction permit identification card issued by the registrar pursuant to section 4507.05 of the Revised Code in any of the following circumstances:

(a) At any time when lighted lights are required by division (A)(1) of section 4513.03 of the Revised Code;

(b) While carrying a passenger;

(c) On any limited access highway.

(D) Nothing in this section shall be construed as prohibiting the carrying of a child in a seat or trailer that is designed for carrying children and is firmly attached to the bicycle.

(E) Except as otherwise provided in this division, whoever violates this section is guilty of a minor misdemeanor. If, within one year of the offense, the offender previously has been convicted of or pleaded guilty to one predicate motor vehicle or traffic offense, whoever violates this section is guilty of a misdemeanor of the fourth degree. If, within one year of the offense, the offender previously has been convicted of two or more predicate motor vehicle or traffic offenses, whoever violates this section is guilty of a misdemeanor of the third degree.

**HISTORY: GC § 6307-51; 119 v 766(784); Bureau of Code Revision, 10-1-53; 132 v H 380 (Eff 1-1-68); 134 v H 214 (Eff 3-7-72); 135 v H 995 (Eff 1-1-75); 137 v H 115 (Eff 7-10-78); 144 v S 98. Eff 11-12-92; 149 v S 123, § 1, eff. 1-1-04; 151 v H 389, § 1, eff. 9-21-06; 152 v H 562, § 101.01, eff. 9-23-08; 2011 HB 114, § 101.01, eff. June 29, 2011.**

Acts 2011, HB 114, § 806.10 provides: "The items of law contained in this act, and their applications, are severable. If any item of law contained in this act, or if any application of any item of law contained in this act, is held invalid, the invalidity does not affect other items of law contained in this act and their applications that can be given effect without the invalid item or application."

The effective date is set by § 812.10 of 152 v H 562.

The effective date is set by section 4 of S.B. 123.

See provisions, § 5 of S.B. 123 (149 v —), following RC § 4501.01.

## § 4511.54 Prohibition against attaching bicycles and sleds to vehicles.

(A) No person riding upon any bicycle, coaster, roller skates, sled, or toy vehicle shall attach the same or self to any streetcar, trackless trolley, or vehicle upon a roadway.

No operator shall knowingly permit any person riding upon any bicycle, coaster, roller skates, sled, or toy vehicle to attach the same or self to any streetcar, trackless trolley, or vehicle while it is moving upon a roadway.

This section does not apply to the towing of a disabled vehicle.

(B) Except as otherwise provided in this division, whoever violates this section is guilty of a minor misdemeanor. If, within one year of the offense, the offender previously has been convicted of or pleaded guilty to one predicate motor vehicle or traffic offense, whoever violates this section is guilty of a misdemeanor of the fourth degree. If, within one year of the offense, the offender previously has been convicted of two or more predicate motor vehicle or traffic offenses, whoever violates this section is guilty of a misdemeanor of the third degree.

**HISTORY: GC § 6307-52; 119 v 776, § 52; 121 v 684; Bureau of Code Revision. Eff 10-1-53; 149 v S 123, § 1, eff. 1-1-04.**

The effective date is set by section 4 of S.B. 123.

See provisions, § 5 of S.B. 123 (149 v —), following RC § 4501.01.

## § 4511.55 Bicycle to be ridden near right side of roadway; riding bicycles or motorcycles abreast.

(A) Every person operating a bicycle upon a roadway shall ride as near to the right side of the roadway as practicable obeying all traffic rules applicable to vehicles and exercising due care when passing a standing vehicle or one proceeding in the same direction.

(B) Persons riding bicycles or motorcycles upon a roadway shall ride not more than two abreast in a single lane, except on paths or parts of roadways set aside for the exclusive use of bicycles or motorcycles.

(C) This section does not require a person operating a bicycle to ride at the edge of the roadway when it is unreasonable or unsafe to do so. Conditions that may require riding away from the edge of the roadway include when necessary to avoid fixed or moving objects, parked or moving vehicles, surface hazards, or if it otherwise is unsafe or impracticable to do so, including if the lane is too narrow for the bicycle and an overtaking vehicle to travel safely side by side within the lane.

(D) Except as otherwise provided in this division, whoever violates this section is guilty of a minor misdemeanor. If, within one year of the offense, the offender previously has been convicted of or pleaded guilty to one predicate motor vehicle or traffic offense, whoever violates this section is guilty of a misdemeanor of the fourth degree. If, within one year of the offense, the offender previously has been convicted of two or more predicate motor vehicle or traffic offenses, whoever violates this section is guilty of a misdemeanor of the third degree.

**HISTORY: GC § 6307-53; 119 v 766(784), § 53; Bureau of Code Revision, 10-1-53; 135 v H 995. Eff 1-1-75; 149 v S 123, § 1, eff. 1-1-04; 151 v H 389, § 1, eff. 9-21-06.**

The effective date is set by section 4 of S.B. 123.

See provisions, § 5 of S.B. 123 (149 v —), following RC § 4501.01.

## § 4511.56 Signal devices on bicycle; brake.

(A) Every bicycle when in use at the times specified in section 4513.03 of the Revised Code, shall be equipped with the following:

(1) A lamp mounted on the front of either the bicycle or the operator that shall emit a white light visible from a distance of at least five hundred feet to the front and three hundred feet to the sides. A generator-powered lamp that emits light only when the bicycle is moving may be used to meet this requirement.

(2) A red reflector on the rear that shall be visible from all distances from one hundred feet to six hundred feet to the rear when directly in front of lawful lower beams of head lamps on a motor vehicle;

(3) A lamp emitting either flashing or steady red light visible from a distance of five hundred feet to the rear shall be used in addition to the red reflector. If the red lamp performs as a reflector in that it is visible as specified in division (A)(2) of this section, the red lamp may serve as the reflector and a separate reflector is not required.

(B) Additional lamps and reflectors may be used in addition to those required under division (A) of this section, except that red lamps and red reflectors shall not be used on the front of the bicycle and white lamps and white reflectors shall not be used on the rear of the bicycle.

(C) A bicycle may be equipped with a device capable of giving an audible signal, except that a bicycle shall not be equipped with nor shall any person use upon a bicycle any siren or whistle.

(D) Every bicycle shall be equipped with an adequate brake when used on a street or highway.

(E) Except as otherwise provided in this division, whoever violates this section is guilty of a minor misdemeanor. If, within one year of the offense, the offender previously has been convicted of or pleaded guilty to one predicate motor vehicle or traffic offense, whoever violates this section is guilty of a misdemeanor of the fourth degree. If, within one year of the offense, the offender previously has been convicted of two or more predicate motor vehicle or traffic offenses, whoever violates this section is guilty of a misdemeanor of the third degree.

**HISTORY: 135 v H 995 (Eff 1-1-75); 142 v H 412 (Eff 3-10-88); 144 v S 98. Eff 11-12-92; 149 v S 123, § 1, eff. 1-1-04; 151 v H 389, § 1, eff. 9-21-06.**

The effective date is set by section 4 of S.B. 123.

See provisions, § 5 of S.B. 123 (149 v —), following RC § 4501.01.

**Analogous to former RC § 4511.56 (GC § 6307-54; 119 v 766; Bureau of Code Revision, 10-1-53), repealed 135 v H 995, § 2, eff 1-1-75.**

## [STREETCARS]

## § 4511.57 Passing on left side of streetcar.

(A) The driver of a vehicle shall not overtake and pass upon the left nor drive upon the left side of any streetcar proceeding in the same direction, whether such streetcar is in motion or at rest, except:

(1) When so directed by a police officer or traffic control device;

(2) When upon a one-way street;

(3) When upon a street where the tracks are so located as to prevent compliance with this section;

(4) When authorized by local authorities.

(B) The driver of any vehicle when permitted to overtake and pass upon the left of a streetcar which has stopped for the purpose of receiving or discharging any passenger shall accord pedestrians the right of way.

(C) Except as otherwise provided in this division, whoever violates this section is guilty of a minor misdemeanor. If, within one year of the offense, the offender previously has been convicted of or pleaded guilty to one predicate motor vehicle or traffic offense, whoever violates this section is guilty of a misdemeanor of the fourth degree. If, within one year of the offense, the offender previously has been convicted of two or more predicate motor vehicle or traffic offenses, whoever violates this section is guilty of a misdemeanor of the third degree.

**HISTORY: GC § 6307-55; 119 v 766(785), § 55; Bureau of Code Revision. Eff 10-1-53; 149 v S 123, § 1, eff. 1-1-04.**

The effective date is set by section 4 of S.B. 123.

See provisions, § 5 of S.B. 123 (149 v —), following RC § 4501.01.

## § 4511.58 Vehicle shall not pass streetcar discharging passengers; exception.

(A) The driver of a vehicle overtaking upon the right any streetcar stopped for the purpose of receiving or discharging any passenger shall stop such vehicle at least five feet to the rear of the nearest running board or door of such streetcar and remain standing until all passengers have boarded such streetcar, or upon alighting therefrom have reached a place of safety, except that where a safety zone has been established, a vehicle need not be brought to a stop before passing any such streetcar or any trackless trolley, but may proceed past such streetcar or trackless trolley at a speed not greater than is reasonable and proper considering the safety of pedestrians.

(B) Except as otherwise provided in this division, whoever violates this section is guilty of a minor misdemeanor. If, within one year of the offense, the offender previously has been convicted of or pleaded guilty to one predicate motor vehicle or traffic offense, whoever violates this section is guilty of a misdemeanor of the fourth degree. If, within one year of the offense, the offender previously has been convicted of two or more predicate motor vehicle or traffic offenses, whoever violates this section is guilty of a misdemeanor of the third degree.

**HISTORY: GC § 6307-56; 119 v 766(785), § 56; Bureau of Code Revision. Eff 10-1-53; 149 v S 123, § 1, eff. 1-1-04.**

The effective date is set by section 4 of S.B. 123.

See provisions, § 5 of S.B. 123 (149 v —), following RC § 4501.01.

## § 4511.59 Driving and turning in front of streetcars.

(A) The driver of any vehicle proceeding upon any streetcar tracks in front of a streetcar shall remove such vehicle from the track as soon as practicable after signal from the operator of said streetcar.

The driver of a vehicle upon overtaking and passing a streetcar shall not turn in front of such streetcar unless such movement can be made in safety.

(B) Except as otherwise provided in this division, whoever violates this section is guilty of a minor misdemeanor. If, within one year of the offense, the offender previously has been convicted of or pleaded guilty to one predicate motor vehicle or traffic offense, whoever violates this section is guilty of a misdemeanor of the fourth degree. If, within one year of the offense, the offender previously has been convicted of two or more predicate motor vehicle or traffic offenses, whoever violates this section is guilty of a misdemeanor of the third degree.

**HISTORY: GC § 6307-57; 119 v 766(785), § 57; Bureau of Code Revision. Eff 10-1-53; 149 v S 123, § 1, eff. 1-1-04.**

The effective date is set by section 4 of S.B. 123.

See provisions, § 5 of S.B. 123 (149 v —), following RC § 4501.01.

## § 4511.60 Driving through safety zone.

(A) No vehicle shall at any time be driven through or within a safety zone.

(B) Except as otherwise provided in this division, whoever violates this section is guilty of a minor misdemeanor. If, within one year of the offense, the offender previously has been convicted of or pleaded guilty to one predicate motor vehicle or traffic offense, whoever violates this section is guilty of a misdemeanor of the fourth degree. If, within one year of the offense, the offender previously has been convicted of two or more predicate motor vehicle or traffic offenses, whoever violates this section is guilty of a misdemeanor of the third degree.

**HISTORY: GC § 6307-58; 119 v 766(785), § 58; Bureau of Code Revision. Eff 10-1-53; 149 v S 123, § 1, eff. 1-1-04.**

The effective date is set by section 4 of S.B. 123.

See provisions, § 5 of S.B. 123 (149 v —), following RC § 4501.01.

### [GRADE CROSSINGS]

## § 4511.61 Stop signs at grade crossings.

(A) The department of transportation and local authorities in their respective jurisdictions, with the approval of the department, may designate dangerous highway crossings over railroad tracks whether on state, county, or township highways or on streets or ways within municipal corporations, and erect stop signs thereat. When such stop signs are erected, the operator of any vehicle, streetcar, or trackless trolley shall stop within fifty, but not less than fifteen, feet from the nearest rail of the railroad tracks and shall exercise due care before proceeding across such grade crossing.

(B) Except as otherwise provided in this division, whoever violates this section is guilty of a minor misdemeanor. If, within one year of the offense, the offender previously has been convicted of or pleaded guilty to one predicate motor vehicle or traffic offense, whoever violates this section is guilty of a misdemeanor of the fourth degree. If, within one year of the offense, the offender previously has been convicted of two or more predicate motor vehicle or traffic offenses, whoever violates this section is guilty of a misdemeanor of the third degree.

**HISTORY: GC § 6307-59; 119 v 766(786), § 59; Bureau of Code Revision, 10-1-53; 127 v 887 (Eff 9-16-57); 135 v H 200 (Eff 9-28-73); 135 v S 171. Eff 10-31-73; 149 v S 123, § 1, eff. 1-1-04.**

The effective date is set by section 4 of S.B. 123.

See provisions, § 5 of S.B. 123 (149 v —), following RC § 4501.01.

## § 4511.62 Driver's duties relating to railroad grade crossings.

(A)(1) Whenever any person driving a vehicle or trackless trolley approaches a railroad grade crossing, the person shall stop within fifty feet, but not less than fifteen feet from the nearest rail of the railroad if any of the following circumstances exist at the crossing:

(a) A clearly visible electric or mechanical signal device gives warning of the immediate approach of a train.

(b) A crossing gate is lowered.

(c) A flagperson gives or continues to give a signal of the approach or passage of a train.

(d) There is insufficient space on the other side of the railroad grade crossing to accommodate the vehicle or trackless trolley the person is operating without obstructing the passage of other vehicles, trackless trolleys, pedestrians, or railroad trains, notwithstanding any traffic control signal indication to proceed.

(e) An approaching train is emitting an audible signal or is plainly visible and is in hazardous proximity to the crossing.

(f) There is insufficient undercarriage clearance to safely negotiate the crossing.

(2) A person who is driving a vehicle or trackless trolley and who approaches a railroad grade crossing shall not proceed as long as any of the circumstances described in divisions (A)(1)(a) to (f) of this section exist at the crossing.

(B) No person shall drive any vehicle through, around, or under any crossing gate or barrier at a railroad crossing while the gate or barrier is closed or is being opened or closed unless the person is signaled by a law enforcement officer or flagperson that it is permissible to do so.

(C) Whoever violates this section is guilty of a misdemeanor of the fourth degree.

**HISTORY: GC § 6307-60; 119 v 766(786), § 60; Bureau of Code Revision, 10-1-53; 135 v H 995 (Eff 1-1-75); 147 v S 60. Eff 10-21-97; 149 v S 123, § 1, eff. 1-1-04; 150 v H 95, § 1, eff. 9-26-03; 150 v H 95, § 3.13, eff. 1-1-04.**

The effective dates are set by sections 3.15 and 179 of H.B. 95 (150 v —).

See provisions, § 5 of S.B. 123 (149 v —), following RC § 4501.01.

## § 4511.63 Vehicles required to stop at grade crossings; exempt crossings.

(A) Except as provided in division (B) of this section, the operator of any bus, any school vehicle, or any vehicle transporting a material or materials required to be placarded under 49 C.F.R. Parts 100-185, before crossing at grade any track of a railroad, shall stop the vehicle and, while so stopped, shall listen through an open door or open window and look in both directions along the track for any approaching train, and for signals indicating the approach of a train, and shall proceed only upon exercising due care after stopping, looking, and listening as required by this section. Upon proceeding, the operator of such a vehicle shall cross only in a gear that will ensure there will be no necessity for changing gears while traversing the crossing and shall not shift gears while crossing the tracks.

(B) This section does not apply at grade crossings when the public utilities commission has authorized and approved an exempt crossing as provided in this division.

(1) Any local authority may file an application with the commission requesting the approval of an exempt crossing. Upon receipt of such a request, the commission shall authorize a limited period for the filing of comments by any party regarding the application and then shall conduct a public hearing in the community seeking the exempt crossing designation. The commission shall provide appropriate prior public notice of the comment period and the

public hearing. By registered mail, the commission shall notify each railroad operating over the crossing of the comment period.

(2) After considering any comments or other information received, the commission may approve or reject the application. By order, the commission may establish conditions for the exempt crossing designation, including compliance with division (b) of 49 C.F.R. Part 392.10, when applicable. An exempt crossing designation becomes effective only when appropriate signs giving notice of the exempt designation are erected at the crossing as ordered by the commission and any other conditions ordered by the commission are satisfied.

(3) By order, the commission may rescind any exempt crossing designation made under this section if the commission finds that a condition at the exempt crossing has changed to such an extent that the continuation of the exempt crossing designation compromises public safety. The commission may conduct a public hearing to investigate and determine whether to rescind the exempt crossing designation. If the commission rescinds the designation, it shall order the removal of any exempt crossing signs and may make any other necessary order.

(C) As used in this section:

(1) "School vehicle" means any vehicle used for the transportation of pupils to and from a school or school-related function if the vehicle is owned or operated by, or operated under contract with, a public or nonpublic school.

(2) "Bus" means any vehicle originally designed by its manufacturer to transport sixteen or more passengers, including the driver, or carries sixteen or more passengers, including the driver.

(3) "Exempt crossing" means a highway rail grade crossing authorized and approved by the public utilities commission under division (B) of this section at which vehicles may cross without making the stop otherwise required by this section.

(D) Except as otherwise provided in this division, whoever violates this section is guilty of a minor misdemeanor. If the offender previously has been convicted of or pleaded guilty to one or more violations of this section or section 4511.76, 4511.761 [4511.76.1], 4511.762 [4511.76.2], 4511.764 [4511.76.4], 4511.77, or 4511.79 of the Revised Code or a municipal ordinance that is substantially similar to any of those sections, whoever violates this section is guilty of a misdemeanor of the fourth degree.

**HISTORY: GC § 6307-61; 119 v 766(786), § 61; 124 v 514; Bureau of Code Revision, 10-1-53; 125 v 903(1025) (Eff 10-1-53); 145 v H 154. Eff 6-30-93; 149 v S 123, § 1, eff. 1-1-04; 150 v H 95, § 1, eff. 9-26-03; 150 v H 95, § 3.13, eff. 1-1-04; 150 v S 156, § 1, eff. 5-18-05.**

See provisions, § 5 of S.B. 123 (149 v —), following RC § 4501.01.

## § 4511.64 Slow-moving vehicles or equipment crossing railroad tracks.

(A) No person shall operate or move any crawler-type tractor, steam shovel, derrick, roller, or any equipment or structure having a normal operating speed of six or less miles per hour or a vertical body or load clearance of less than nine inches above the level surface of a roadway, upon or across any tracks at a railroad grade crossing without first complying with divisions (A)(1) and (2) of this section.

(1) Before making any such crossing, the person operating or moving any such vehicle or equipment shall first stop the same, and while stopped the person shall listen and look in both directions along such track for any approaching train and for signals indicating the approach of a train, and shall proceed only upon exercising due care.

(2) No such crossing shall be made when warning is given by automatic signal or crossing gates or a flagperson or otherwise of the immediate approach of a railroad train or car.

(B) If the normal sustained speed of such vehicle, equipment, or structure is not more than three miles per hour, the person owning, operating, or moving the same shall also give notice of such intended crossing to a station agent or superintendent of the railroad, and a reasonable time shall be given to such railroad to provide proper protection for such crossing. Where such vehicles or equipment are being used in constructing or repairing a section of highway lying on both sides of a railroad grade crossing, and in such construction or repair it is necessary to repeatedly move such vehicles or equipment over such crossing, one daily notice specifying when such work will start and stating the hours during which it will be prosecuted is sufficient.

(C) Except as otherwise provided in this division, whoever violates this section is guilty of a minor misdemeanor. If, within one year of the offense, the offender previously has been convicted of or pleaded guilty to one predicate motor vehicle or traffic offense, whoever violates this section is guilty of a misdemeanor of the fourth degree. If, within one year of the offense, the offender previously has been convicted of two or more predicate motor vehicle or traffic offenses, whoever violates this section is guilty of a misdemeanor of the third degree.

**HISTORY: GC § 6307-62; 119 v 766(786), § 62; Bureau of Code Revision. Eff 10-1-53; 149 v S 123, § 1, eff. 1-1-04.**

The effective date is set by section 4 of S.B. 123.

See provisions, § 5 of S.B. 123 (149 v —), following RC § 4501.01.

[THROUGH HIGHWAYS]

## § 4511.65 Through highways.

(A) All state routes are hereby designated as through highways, provided that stop signs, yield signs, or traffic control signals shall be erected at all intersections with such through highways by the department of transportation as to highways under its jurisdiction and by local authorities as to highways under their jurisdiction, except as otherwise provided in this section. Where two or more state routes that are through highways intersect and no traffic control signal is in operation, stop signs or yield signs shall be erected at one or more entrances thereto by the department, except as otherwise provided in this section.

Whenever the director of transportation determines on the basis of an engineering and traffic investigation that stop signs are necessary to stop traffic on a through highway for safe and efficient operation, nothing in this section shall be construed to prevent such installations. When circumstances warrant, the director also may omit stop signs on roadways intersecting through highways under his jurisdiction. Before the director either installs or removes a stop sign under this division, he shall give notice, in writing, of that proposed action to the affected local authority at least thirty days before installing or removing the stop sign.

(B) Other streets or highways, or portions thereof, are hereby designated through highways if they are within a municipal corporation, if they have a continuous length of more than one mile between the limits of said street or highway or portion thereof, and if they have "stop" or "yield" signs or traffic control signals at the entrances of the majority of intersecting streets or highways. For purposes of this section, the limits of said street or highway or portion thereof shall be a municipal corporation line, the physical terminus of the street or highway, or any point on said street or highway at which vehicular traffic thereon is required by regulatory signs to stop or yield to traffic on the intersecting street, provided that in residence districts a municipal corporation may by ordinance designate said street or highway, or portion thereof, not to be a through highway and thereafter the affected residence district shall be indicated by official traffic control devices. Where two or more through highways designated under this division intersect and no traffic control signal is in operation, stop signs or yield signs shall be erected at one or more entrances thereto by the department or by local authorities having jurisdiction, except as otherwise provided in this section.

(C) The department or local authorities having jurisdiction need not erect stop signs at intersections they find to be so constructed as to permit traffic to safely enter a through highway without coming to a stop. Signs shall be erected at such intersections indicating that the operator of a vehicle shall yield the right-of-way to or merge with all traffic proceeding on the through highway.

(D) Local authorities with reference to highways under their jurisdiction may designate additional through highways and shall erect stop signs, yield signs, or traffic control signals at all streets and highways intersecting such through highways, or may designate any intersection as a stop or yield intersection and shall erect like signs at one or more entrances to such intersection.

**HISTORY: GC § 6307-63; 119 v 766(787), § 63; Bureau of Code Revision, 10-1-53; 128 v 1270 (Eff 11-4-59); 131 v 1103 (Eff 10-15-65); 135 v H 200 (Eff 9-28-73); 136 v H 21 (Eff 12-30-75); 138 v H 290 (Eff 1-10-80); 143 v H 258. Eff 11-2-89.**

## [PARKING]

## § 4511.66 Prohibition against parking on highways.

(A) Upon any highway outside a business or residence district, no person shall stop, park, or leave standing any vehicle, whether attended or unattended, upon the paved or main traveled part of the highway if it is practicable to stop, park, or so leave such vehicle off the paved or main traveled part of said highway. In every event a clear and unobstructed portion of the highway opposite such standing vehicle shall be left for the free passage of other vehicles, and a clear view of such stopped vehicle shall be available from a distance of two hundred feet in each direction upon such highway.

This section does not apply to the driver of any vehicle which is disabled while on the paved or improved or main traveled portion of a highway in such manner and to such extent that it is impossible to avoid stopping and temporarily leaving the disabled vehicle in such position.

(B) Except as otherwise provided in this division, whoever violates this section is guilty of a minor misdemeanor. If, within one year of the offense, the offender previously has been convicted of or pleaded guilty to one predicate motor vehicle or traffic offense, whoever violates this section is guilty of a misdemeanor of the fourth degree. If, within one year of the offense, the offender previously has been convicted of two or more predicate motor vehicle or traffic offenses, whoever violates this section is guilty of a misdemeanor of the third degree.

**HISTORY: GC § 6307-64; 119 v 766(788), § 64; Bureau of Code Revision. Eff 10-1-53; 149 v S 123, § 1, eff. 1-1-04.**

The effective date is set by section 4 of S.B. 123.

See provisions, § 5 of S.B. 123 (149 v —), following RC § 4501.01.

## § 4511.661 Condition when motor vehicle left unattended.

(A) No person driving or in charge of a motor vehicle shall permit it to stand unattended without first stopping the engine, locking the ignition, removing the key from the ignition, effectively setting the parking brake, and, when the motor vehicle is standing upon any grade, turning the front wheels to the curb or side of the highway.

The requirements of this section relating to the stopping of the engine, locking of the ignition, and removing the key from the ignition of a motor vehicle shall not apply to an emergency vehicle or a public safety vehicle.

(B) Except as otherwise provided in this division, whoever violates this section is guilty of a minor misdemeanor. If, within one year of the offense, the offender previously has been convicted of or pleaded guilty to one predicate motor vehicle or traffic offense, whoever violates this section is guilty of a misdemeanor of the fourth degree. If, within one year of the offense, the offender previously has been convicted of two or more predicate motor vehicle or traffic offenses, whoever violates this section is guilty of a misdemeanor of the third degree.

**HISTORY: 135 v H 995 (Eff 1-1-75); 136 v H 763. Eff 8-6-76; 149 v S 123, § 1, eff. 1-1-04.**

The effective date is set by section 4 of S.B. 123.

See provisions, § 5 of S.B. 123 (149 v —), following RC § 4501.01.

## § 4511.67 Police may remove illegally parked vehicle.

Whenever any police officer finds a vehicle standing upon a highway in violation of section 4511.66 of the Revised Code, such officer may move such vehicle, or require the driver or other person in charge of the vehicle to move the same, to a position off the paved or improved or main traveled part of such highway.

Whenever any police officer finds a vehicle unattended upon any highway, bridge, or causeway, or in any tunnel, where such vehicle constitutes an obstruction to traffic, such officer may provide for the removal of such vehicle to the nearest garage or other place of safety.

**HISTORY: GC § 6307-65; 119 v 766(788), § 65; 121 v 684; Bureau of Code Revision. Eff 10-1-53.**

## § 4511.68 Parking prohibitions.

(A) No person shall stand or park a trackless trolley or vehicle, except when necessary to avoid conflict with other traffic or to comply with sections 4511.01 to 4511.78, 4511.99, and 4513.01 to 4513.37 of the Revised Code, or while obeying the directions of a police officer or a traffic control device, in any of the following places:

(1) On a sidewalk, except a bicycle;

(2) In front of a public or private driveway;

(3) Within an intersection;

(4) Within ten feet of a fire hydrant;

(5) On a crosswalk;

(6) Within twenty feet of a crosswalk at an intersection;

(7) Within thirty feet of, and upon the approach to, any flashing beacon, stop sign, or traffic control device;

(8) Between a safety zone and the adjacent curb or within thirty feet of points on the curb immediately opposite the ends of a safety zone, unless a different length is indicated by a traffic control device;

(9) Within fifty feet of the nearest rail of a railroad crossing;

(10) Within twenty feet of a driveway entrance to any fire station and, on the side of the street opposite the entrance to any fire station, within seventy-five feet of the entrance when it is properly posted with signs;

(11) Alongside or opposite any street excavation or obstruction when such standing or parking would obstruct traffic;

(12) Alongside any vehicle stopped or parked at the edge or curb of a street;

(13) Upon any bridge or elevated structure upon a highway, or within a highway tunnel;

(14) At any place where signs prohibit stopping;

(15) Within one foot of another parked vehicle;

(16) On the roadway portion of a freeway, expressway, or thruway.

(B) Except as otherwise provided in this division, whoever violates this section is guilty of a minor misdemeanor. If, within one year of the offense, the offender previously has been convicted of or pleaded guilty to one predicate motor vehicle or traffic offense, whoever violates this section is guilty of a misdemeanor of the fourth degree. If, within one year of the offense, the offender previously has been convicted of two or more predicate motor vehicle or traffic offenses, whoever violates this section is guilty of a misdemeanor of the third degree.

**HISTORY: GC § 6307-66; 119 v 766(788), § 66; 124 v 514; Bureau of Code Revision, 10-1-53; 130 v 1087. Eff 8-5-63; 149 v S 123, § 1, eff. 1-1-04.**

The effective date is set by section 4 of S.B. 123.

See provisions, § 5 of S.B. 123 (149 v —), following RC § 4501.01.

## § 4511.681 Parking prohibitions on private property.

(A) If an owner of private property posts on the property, in a conspicuous manner, a prohibition against parking on the property or conditions and regulations under which parking is permitted, no person shall do either of the following:

(1) Park a vehicle on the property without the owner's consent;

(2) Park a vehicle on the property in violation of any condition or regulation posted by the owner.

(B) Whoever violates this section is guilty of a minor misdemeanor.

**HISTORY: 139 v H 707 (Eff 1-1-83); 140 v H 112. Eff 10-4-84; 149 v S 123, § 1, eff. 1-1-04.**

The effective date is set by section 4 of S.B. 123.

See provisions, § 5 of S.B. 123 (149 v —), following RC § 4501.01.

## § 4511.69 Parking near curb, facing direction of travel; locations and privileges for walking-impaired persons.

(A) Every vehicle stopped or parked upon a roadway where there is an adjacent curb shall be stopped or parked with the right-hand wheels of the vehicle parallel with and not more than twelve inches from the right-hand curb, unless it is impossible to approach so close to the curb; in such case the stop shall be made as close to the curb as possible and only for the time necessary to discharge and receive passengers or to load or unload merchandise. Local authorities by ordinance may permit angle parking on any roadway under their jurisdiction, except that angle parking shall not be permitted on a state route within a municipal corporation unless an unoccupied roadway width of not less than twenty-five feet is available for free-moving traffic.

(B) Local authorities by ordinance may permit parking of vehicles with the left-hand wheels adjacent to and within twelve inches of the left-hand curb of a one-way roadway.

(C)(1) Except as provided in division (C) (2) of this section, no vehicle or trackless trolley shall be stopped or parked on a road or highway with the vehicle or trackless trolley facing in a direction other than the direction of travel on that side of the road or highway.

(2) The operator of a motorcycle may back the motorcycle into an angled parking space so that when the motorcycle is parked it is facing in a direction other than the direction of travel on the side of the road or highway.

(D) Notwithstanding any statute or any rule, resolution, or ordinance adopted by any local authority, air compressors, tractors, trucks, and other equipment, while being used in the construction, reconstruction, installation, repair, or removal of facilities near, on, over, or under a street or highway, may stop, stand, or park where necessary in order to perform such work, provided a flagperson is on duty or warning signs or lights are displayed as may be prescribed by the director of transportation.

(E) Special parking locations and privileges for persons with disabilities that limit or impair the ability to walk, also known as handicapped parking spaces or disability parking spaces, shall be provided and designated by all political subdivisions and by the state and all agencies and instrumentalities thereof at all offices and facilities, where parking is provided, whether owned, rented, or leased, and at all publicly owned parking garages. The locations shall be designated through the posting of an elevated sign, whether permanently affixed or movable, imprinted with the international symbol of access and shall be reasonably close to exits, entrances, elevators, and ramps. All elevated signs posted in accordance with this division and division (C) of section 3781.111 of the Revised Code shall be mounted on a fixed or movable post, and the distance from the ground to the top edge of the sign shall measure five feet. If a new sign or a replacement sign designating a special parking location is posted on or after October 14,

1999, there also shall be affixed upon the surface of that sign or affixed next to the designating sign a notice that states the fine applicable for the offense of parking a motor vehicle in the special designated parking location if the motor vehicle is not legally entitled to be parked in that location.

(F)(1) No person shall stop, stand, or park any motor vehicle at special parking locations provided under division (E) of this section or at special clearly marked parking locations provided in or on privately owned parking lots, parking garages, or other parking areas and designated in accordance with that division, unless one of the following applies:

(a) The motor vehicle is being operated by or for the transport of a person with a disability that limits or impairs the ability to walk and is displaying a valid removable windshield placard or special license plates;

(b) The motor vehicle is being operated by or for the transport of a handicapped person and is displaying a parking card or special handicapped license plates.

(2) Any motor vehicle that is parked in a special marked parking location in violation of division (F)(1)(a) or (b) of this section may be towed or otherwise removed from the parking location by the law enforcement agency of the political subdivision in which the parking location is located. A motor vehicle that is so towed or removed shall not be released to its owner until the owner presents proof of ownership of the motor vehicle and pays all towing and storage fees normally imposed by that political subdivision for towing and storing motor vehicles. If the motor vehicle is a leased vehicle, it shall not be released to the lessee until the lessee presents proof that that person is the lessee of the motor vehicle and pays all towing and storage fees normally imposed by that political subdivision for towing and storing motor vehicles.

(3) If a person is charged with a violation of division (F)(1)(a) or (b) of this section, it is an affirmative defense to the charge that the person suffered an injury not more than seventy-two hours prior to the time the person was issued the ticket or citation and that, because of the injury, the person meets at least one of the criteria contained in division (A)(1) of section 4503.44 of the Revised Code.

(G) When a motor vehicle is being operated by or for the transport of a person with a disability that limits or impairs the ability to walk and is displaying a removable windshield placard or a temporary removable windshield placard or special license plates, or when a motor vehicle is being operated by or for the transport of a handicapped person and is displaying a parking card or special handicapped license plates, the motor vehicle is permitted to park for a period of two hours in excess of the legal parking period permitted by local authorities, except where local ordinances or police rules provide otherwise or where the vehicle is parked in such a manner as to be clearly a traffic hazard.

(H) No owner of an office, facility, or parking garage where special parking locations are required to be designated in accordance with division (E) of this section shall fail to properly mark the special parking locations in accordance with that division or fail to maintain the markings of the special locations, including the erection and maintenance of the fixed or movable signs.

(I) Nothing in this section shall be construed to require a person or organization to apply for a removable windshield placard or special license plates if the parking card or special license plates issued to the person or organization under prior law have not expired or been surrendered or revoked.

(J)(1) Whoever violates division (A) or (C) of this section is guilty of a minor misdemeanor.

(2)(a) Whoever violates division (F)(1)(a) or (b) of this section is guilty of a misdemeanor and shall be punished as provided in division (J)(2)(a) and (b) of this section. Except as otherwise provided in division (J)(2)(a) of this section, an offender who violates division (F)(1)(a) or (b) of this section shall be fined not less than two hundred fifty nor more than five hundred dollars. An offender who violates division (F)(1)(a) or (b) of this section shall be fined not more than one hundred dollars if the offender, prior to sentencing, proves either of the following to the satisfaction of the court:

(i) At the time of the violation of division (F)(1)(a) of this section, the offender or the person for whose transport the motor vehicle was being operated had been issued a removable windshield placard that then was valid or special license plates that then were valid but the offender or the person neglected to display the placard or license plates as described in division (F)(1)(a) of this section.

(ii) At the time of the violation of division (F)(1)(b) of this section, the offender or the person for whose transport the motor vehicle was being operated had been issued a parking card that then was valid or special handicapped license plates that then were valid but the offender or the person neglected to display the card or license plates as described in division (F)(1)(b) of this section.

(b) In no case shall an offender who violates division (F)(1)(a) or (b) of this section be sentenced to any term of imprisonment.

An arrest or conviction for a violation of division (F)(1)(a) or (b) of this section does not constitute a criminal record and need not be reported by the person so arrested or convicted in response to any inquiries contained in any application for employment, license, or other right or privilege, or made in connection with the person's appearance as a witness.

The clerk of the court shall pay every fine collected under division (J)(2) of this section to the political subdivision in which the violation occurred. Except as provided in division (J)(2) of this section, the political subdivision shall use the fine moneys it receives under division (J)(2) of this section to pay the expenses it incurs in complying with the signage and notice requirements contained in division (E) of this section. The political subdivision may use up to fifty per cent of each fine it receives under division (J)(2) of this section to pay the costs of educational, advocacy, support, and assistive technology programs for persons with disabilities, and for public improvements within the political subdivision that benefit or assist persons with disabilities, if governmental agencies or nonprofit organizations offer the programs.

(3) Whoever violates division (H) of this section shall be punished as follows:

(a) Except as otherwise provided in division (J)(3) of this section, the offender shall be issued a warning.

(b) If the offender previously has been convicted of or pleaded guilty to a violation of division (H) of this section or of a municipal ordinance that is substantially similar to that division, the offender shall not be issued a warning but shall be fined not more than twenty-five dollars for each parking location that is not properly marked or whose markings are not properly maintained.

(K) As used in this section:

(1) "Handicapped person" means any person who has lost the use of one or both legs or one or both arms, who is blind, deaf, or so severely handicapped as to be unable to move without the aid of crutches or a wheelchair, or whose mobility is restricted by a permanent cardiovascular, pulmonary, or other handicapping condition.

(2) "Person with a disability that limits or impairs the ability to walk" has the same meaning as in section 4503.44 of the Revised Code.

(3) "Special license plates" and "removable windshield placard" mean any license plates or removable windshield placard or temporary removable windshield placard issued under section 4503.41 or 4503.44 of the Revised Code, and also mean any substantially similar license plates or removable windshield placard or temporary removable windshield placard issued by a state, district, country, or sovereignty.

**HISTORY: GC § 6307-67; 119 v 766(789), § 67; 121 v 684; 124 v 514; Bureau of Code Revision, 10-1-53; 135 v H 200 (Eff 9-28-73); 136 v S 162 (Eff 7-23-76); 137 v H 652 (Eff 3-13-78); 139 v H 1 (Eff 8-5-81); 139 v H 48 (Eff 1-1-83); 139 v H 116 (Eff 7-5-82); 140 v H 174 (Eff 9-30-83); 142 v H 111 (Eff 4-27-88); 144 v H 73 (Eff 9-25-91); 144 v S 98 (Eff 11-12-92); 145 v H 687 (Eff 1-1-95); 148 v H 148. Eff 10-14-99; 149 v S 123, § 1, eff. 1-1-04; 149 v H 490, § 1, eff. 1-1-04; 2011 HB 114, § 101.01, eff. June 29, 2011.**

Acts 2011, HB 114, § 806.10 provides: "The items of law contained in this act, and their applications, are severable. If any item of law contained in this act, or if any application of any item of law contained in this act, is held invalid, the invalidity does not affect other items of law contained in this act and their applications that can be given effect without the invalid item or application."

The effective date is set by section 4 of H.B. 490.

See provisions, § 5 of S.B. 123 (149 v —), following RC § 4501.01.

**Publisher's Note:**

The amendment of RC § 4511.69 by 153 v H 1 was disapproved by the Governor.

## [PROHIBITIONS]

## § 4511.70 Obstruction and interference affecting view and control of driver.

(A) No person shall drive a vehicle or trackless trolley when it is so loaded, or when there are in the front seat such number of persons, as to obstruct the view of the driver to the front or sides of the vehicle or to interfere with the driver's control over the driving mechanism of the vehicle.

(B) No passenger in a vehicle or trackless trolley shall ride in such position as to interfere with the driver's view ahead or to the sides, or to interfere with the driver's control over the driving mechanism of the vehicle.

(C) No person shall open the door of a vehicle on the side available to moving traffic unless and until it is reasonably safe to do so, and can be done without interfering with the movement of other traffic, nor shall any person leave a door open on the side of a vehicle available to moving traffic for a period of time longer than necessary to load or unload passengers.

(D) Except as otherwise provided in this division, whoever violates this section is guilty of a minor misdemeanor. If, within one year of the offense, the offender previously has been convicted of or pleaded guilty to one predicate motor vehicle or traffic offense, whoever violates this section is guilty of a misdemeanor of the fourth degree. If, within one year of the offense, the offender previously has been convicted of two or more predicate motor vehicle or traffic offenses, whoever violates this section is guilty of a misdemeanor of the third degree.

**HISTORY: GC § 6307-68; 119 v 766(789), § 68; Bureau of Code Revision, 10-1-53; 135 v H 995. Eff 1-1-75; 149 v S 123, § 1, eff. 1-1-04.**

The effective date is set by section 4 of S.B. 123.

See provisions, § 5 of S.B. 123 (149 v —), following RC § 4501.01.

## § 4511.701 Occupancy while in motion prohibited.

(A) No person shall occupy any travel trailer or manufactured or mobile home while it is being used as a conveyance upon a street or highway.

(B) Except as otherwise provided in this division, whoever violates this section is guilty of a minor misdemeanor. If, within one year of the offense, the offender previously has been convicted of or pleaded guilty to one predicate motor vehicle or traffic offense, whoever violates this section is guilty of a misdemeanor of the fourth degree. If, within one year of the offense, the offender previously has been convicted of two or more predicate motor vehicle or traffic offenses, whoever violates this section is guilty of a misdemeanor of the third degree.

**HISTORY: 135 v S 205 (Eff 11-21-73); 140 v S 231 (Eff 9-20-84); 147 v S 142. Eff 3-30-99; 149 v S 123, § 1, eff. 1-1-04.**

The effective date is set by section 4 of S.B. 123.

See provisions, § 5 of S.B. 123 (149 v —), following RC § 4501.01.

## § 4511.71 Prohibition against driving upon closed highway.

(A) No person shall drive upon, along, or across a street or highway, or any part of a street or highway that has been closed in the process of its construction, reconstruction, or repair, and posted with appropriate signs by the authority having jurisdiction to close such highway.

(B) Except as otherwise provided in this division, whoever violates this section is guilty of a minor misdemeanor. If, within one year of the offense, the offender previously has been convicted of or pleaded guilty to one predicate motor vehicle or traffic offense, whoever violates this section is guilty of a misdemeanor of the fourth degree. If, within one year of the offense, the offender previously has been convicted of two or more predicate motor vehicle or traffic offenses, whoever violates this section is guilty of a misdemeanor of the third degree.

**HISTORY: GC § 6307-69; 119 v 766(789), § 69; Bureau of Code Revision. Eff 10-1-53; 149 v S 123, § 1, eff. 1-1-04.**

The effective date is set by section 4 of S.B. 123.

See provisions, § 5 of S.B. 123 (149 v —), following RC § 4501.01.

## § 4511.711 Driving on sidewalk or sidewalk area.

(A) No person shall drive any vehicle, other than a bicycle, upon a sidewalk or sidewalk area except upon a permanent or duly authorized temporary driveway.

Nothing in this section shall be construed as prohibiting local authorities from regulating the operation of bicycles within their respective jurisdictions, except that no local authority may require that bicycles be operated on sidewalks.

(B) Except as otherwise provided in this division, whoever violates this section is guilty of a minor misdemeanor. If, within one year of the offense, the offender previously has been convicted of or pleaded guilty to one predicate motor vehicle or traffic offense, whoever violates this section is guilty of a misdemeanor of the fourth degree. If, within one year of the offense, the offender previously has been convicted of two or more predicate motor vehicle or traffic offenses, whoever violates this section is guilty of a misdemeanor of the third degree.

**HISTORY: 135 v H 995 (Eff 1-1-75); 136 v S 56. Eff 5-25-76; 149 v S 123, § 1, eff. 1-1-04; 151 v H 389, § 1, eff. 9-21-06.**

The effective date is set by section 4 of S.B. 123.

See provisions, § 5 of S.B. 123 (149 v —), following RC § 4501.01.

## § 4511.712 Obstructing passage of other vehicles.

(A) No driver shall enter an intersection or marked crosswalk or drive onto any railroad grade crossing unless there is sufficient space on the other side of the intersection, crosswalk, or grade crossing to accommodate the vehicle, streetcar, or trackless trolley the driver is operating without obstructing the passage of other vehicles, streetcars, trackless trolleys, pedestrians, or railroad trains, notwithstanding any traffic control signal indication to proceed.

(B) Except as otherwise provided in this division, whoever violates this section is guilty of a minor misdemeanor. If, within one year of the offense, the offender previously has been convicted of or pleaded guilty to one predicate motor vehicle or traffic offense, whoever violates this section is guilty of a misdemeanor of the fourth degree. If, within one year of the offense, the offender previously has been convicted of two or more predicate motor vehicle or traffic offenses, whoever violates this section is guilty of a misdemeanor of the third degree.

**HISTORY: 135 v H 995. Eff 1-1-75; 149 v S 123, § 1, eff. 1-1-04.**

The effective date is set by section 4 of S.B. 123.

See provisions, § 5 of S.B. 123 (149 v —), following RC § 4501.01.

## § 4511.713 Paths exclusively for bicycles.

(A) No person shall operate a motor vehicle, snowmobile, or all-purpose vehicle upon any path set aside for the exclusive use of bicycles, when an appropriate sign giving notice of such use is posted on the path.

Nothing in this section shall be construed to affect any rule of the director of natural resources governing the operation of motor vehicles, snowmobiles, all-purpose vehicles, and bicycles on lands under the director's jurisdiction.

(B) Except as otherwise provided in this division, whoever violates this section is guilty of a minor misdemeanor. If, within one year of the offense, the offender previously has been convicted of or pleaded guilty to one predicate motor vehicle or traffic offense, whoever violates this section is guilty of a misdemeanor of the fourth degree. If, within one year of the offense, the offender previously has been convicted of two or more predicate motor vehicle or traffic offenses, whoever violates this section is guilty of a misdemeanor of the third degree.

**HISTORY: 141 v H 311. Eff 3-11-87; 149 v S 123, § 1, eff. 1-1-04.**

The effective date is set by section 4 of S.B. 123.

See provisions, § 5 of S.B. 123 (149 v —), following RC § 4501.01.

## § 4511.72 Following an emergency or public safety vehicle prohibited.

(A) The driver of any vehicle, other than an emergency vehicle or public safety vehicle on official business, shall not follow any emergency vehicle or public safety vehicle traveling in response to an alarm closer than five hundred feet, or drive into or park such vehicle within the block where fire apparatus has stopped in answer to a fire alarm, unless directed to do so by a police officer or a firefighter.

(B) Except as otherwise provided in this division, whoever violates this section is guilty of a minor misdemeanor. If, within one year of the offense, the offender previously has been convicted of or pleaded guilty to one predicate motor vehicle or traffic offense, whoever violates this section is guilty of a misdemeanor of the fourth degree. If, within one year of the offense, the offender previously has been convicted of two or more predicate motor vehicle or traffic offenses, whoever violates this section is guilty of a misdemeanor of the third degree.

**HISTORY: GC § 6307-70; 119 v 766(790), § 70; 124 v 514 (525); Bureau of Code Revision, 10-1-53; 132 v H 878. Eff 12-14-67; 149 v S 123, § 1, eff. 1-1-04.**

The effective date is set by section 4 of S.B. 123.

See provisions, § 5 of S.B. 123 (149 v —), following RC § 4501.01.

## § 4511.73 Driving over unprotected fire hose.

(A) No streetcar, trackless trolley, or vehicle shall, without the consent of the fire department official in command, be driven over any unprotected hose of a fire department that is laid down on any street, private driveway, or streetcar track to be used at any fire or alarm of fire.

(B) Except as otherwise provided in this division, whoever violates this section is guilty of a minor misdemeanor. If, within one year of the offense, the offender previously has been convicted of or pleaded guilty to one predicate motor vehicle or traffic offense, whoever violates this section is guilty of a misdemeanor of the fourth degree. If, within one year of the offense, the offender previously has been convicted of two or more predicate motor vehicle or traffic offenses, whoever violates this section is guilty of a misdemeanor of the third degree.

**HISTORY: GC § 6307-71; 119 v 766(790), § 71; Bureau of Code Revision. Eff 10-1-53; 149 v S 123, § 1, eff. 1-1-04.**

The effective date is set by section 4 of S.B. 123.

See provisions, § 5 of S.B. 123 (149 v —), following RC § 4501.01.

## § 4511.74 Prohibition against placing injurious material on highway.

(A) No person shall place or knowingly drop upon any part of a highway, lane, road, street, or alley any tacks, bottles, wire, glass, nails, or other articles which may damage or injure any person, vehicle, streetcar, trackless trolley, or animal traveling along or upon such highway, except such substances that may be placed upon the roadway by proper authority for the repair or construction thereof.

Any person who drops or permits to be dropped or thrown upon any highway any destructive or injurious material shall immediately remove the same.

Any person authorized to remove a wrecked or damaged vehicle, streetcar, or trackless trolley from a highway shall remove any glass or other injurious substance dropped upon the highway from such vehicle, streetcar, or trackless trolley.

No person shall place any obstruction in or upon a highway without proper authority.

(B) No person, with intent to cause physical harm to a person or a vehicle, shall place or knowingly drop upon any part of a highway, lane, road, street, or alley any tacks, bottles, wire, glass, nails, or other articles which may damage or injure any person, vehicle, streetcar, trackless trolley, or animal traveling along or upon such highway, except such substances that may be placed upon the roadway by proper authority for the repair or construction thereof.

(C)(1) Except as otherwise provided in this division, whoever violates division (A) of this section is guilty of a minor misdemeanor. If, within one year of the offense, the offender previously has been convicted of or pleaded guilty to one predicate motor vehicle or traffic offense, whoever violates division (A) of this section is guilty of a misdemeanor of the fourth degree. If, within one year of the offense, the offender previously has been convicted of two or more predicate motor vehicle or traffic offenses, whoever violates division (A) of this section is guilty of a misdemeanor of the third degree.

(2) Whoever violates division (B) of this section is guilty of a misdemeanor of the first degree.

**HISTORY: GC § 6307-72; 119 v 766(790), § 72; Bureau of Code Revision, 10-1-53; 140 v H 133. Eff 9-27-83; 149 v S 123, § 1, eff. 1-1-04.**

The effective date is set by section 4 of S.B. 123.

See provisions, § 5 of S.B. 123 (149 v —), following RC § 4501.01.

# [SCHOOL BUSES]

## § 4511.75 Stopping for school bus; signals.

(A) The driver of a vehicle, streetcar, or trackless trolley upon meeting or overtaking from either direction any school bus stopped for the purpose of receiving or discharging any school child, person attending programs offered by community boards of mental health and county boards of developmental disabilities, or child attending a program offered by a head start agency, shall stop at least ten feet from the front or rear of the school bus and shall not proceed until such school bus resumes motion, or until signaled by the school bus driver to proceed.

It is no defense to a charge under this division that the school bus involved failed to display or be equipped with an automatically extended stop warning sign as required by division (B) of this section.

(B) Every school bus shall be equipped with amber and red visual signals meeting the requirements of section 4511.771 [4511.77.1] of the Revised Code, and an automatically extended stop warning sign of a type approved by the state board of education, which shall be actuated by the driver of the bus whenever but only whenever the bus is stopped or stopping on the roadway for the purpose of receiving or discharging school children, persons attending programs offered by community boards of mental health and county boards of developmental disabilities, or children attending programs offered by head start agencies. A school bus driver shall not actuate the visual signals or the stop warning sign in designated school bus loading areas where the bus is entirely off the roadway or at school buildings when children or persons attending programs offered by community boards of mental health and county boards of developmental disabilities are loading or unloading at curbside or at buildings when children attending programs offered by head start agencies are loading or unloading at curbside. The visual signals and stop warning sign shall be synchronized or otherwise operated as required by rule of the board.

(C) Where a highway has been divided into four or more traffic lanes, a driver of a vehicle, streetcar, or trackless trolley need not stop for a school bus approaching from the opposite direction which has stopped for the purpose of receiving or discharging any school child, persons attending programs offered by community boards of mental health and county boards of developmental disabilities, or children attending programs offered by head start agencies. The driver of any vehicle, streetcar, or trackless trolley overtaking the school bus shall comply with division (A) of this section.

(D) School buses operating on divided highways or on highways with four or more traffic lanes shall receive and discharge all school children, persons attending programs offered by community boards of mental health and county boards of developmental disabilities, and children attending programs offered by head start agencies on their residence side of the highway.

(E) No school bus driver shall start the driver's bus until after any child, person attending programs offered by community boards of mental health and county boards of developmental disabilities, or child attending a program offered by a head start agency who may have alighted therefrom has reached a place of safety on the child's or person's residence side of the road.

(F)(1) Whoever violates division (A) of this section may be fined an amount not to exceed five hundred dollars. A person who is issued a citation for a violation of division (A) of this section is not permitted to enter a written plea of guilty and waive the person's right to contest the citation in a trial but instead must appear in person in the proper court to answer the charge.

(2) In addition to and independent of any other penalty provided by law, the court or mayor may impose upon an offender who violates this section a class seven suspension of the offender's driver's license, commercial driver's license, temporary instruction permit, probationary license, or nonresident operating privilege from the range specified in division (A)(7) of section 4510.02 of the Revised Code. When a license is suspended under this section, the court or mayor shall cause the offender to deliver the license to the court, and the court or clerk of the court immediately shall forward the license to the

registrar of motor vehicles, together with notice of the court's action.

(G) As used in this section:

(1) "Head start agency" has the same meaning as in section 3301.32 of the Revised Code.

(2) "School bus," as used in relation to children who attend a program offered by a head start agency, means a bus that is owned and operated by a head start agency, is equipped with an automatically extended stop warning sign of a type approved by the state board of education, is painted the color and displays the markings described in section 4511.77 of the Revised Code, and is equipped with amber and red visual signals meeting the requirements of section 4511.771 [4511.77.1] of the Revised Code, irrespective of whether or not the bus has fifteen or more children aboard at any time. "School bus" does not include a van owned and operated by a head start agency, irrespective of its color, lights, or markings.

**HISTORY: GC § 6307-73; 119 v 766(790), § 73; 123 v 614; Bureau of Code Revision, 10-1-53; 125 v 167 (Eff 10-2-53); 135 v H 995 (Eff 1-1-75); 136 v H 369 (Eff 8-29-75); 137 v S 389 (Eff 3-15-79); 138 v S 160 (Eff 10-31-80); 140 v H 478 (Eff 3-28-85); 147 v H 618. Eff 3-22-99; 149 v S 123, § 1, eff. 1-1-04; 150 v H 95, § 3.13, eff. 7-1-04; 151 v H 66, § 101.01, eff. 6-30-05; 153 v S 79, § 1, eff. 10-6-09.**

The effective date is set by § 612.12 of 151 v H 66.

The effective date is set by section 3.15 of H.B. 95 (150 v —).

The provisions of § 193 of H.B. 95 (150 v —) read as follows:

SECTION 193. The amendment by this act of the version of section 4511.75 of the Revised Code that is scheduled to take effect January 1, 2004, and the items of law of which that amendment is composed, are not subject to the referendum under Ohio Constitution, Article II, Section 1d and section 1.471 of the Revised Code and go into effect on July 1, 2004.

See provisions, § 5 of S.B. 123 (149 v —), following RC § 4501.01.

## § 4511.751 Operator or person with first-hand knowledge to report violation; information furnished upon issuance of plates.

As used in this section, "license plate" includes, but is not limited to, any temporary license placard issued under section 4503.182 of the Revised Code or similar law of another jurisdiction.

When the operator of a school bus believes that a motorist has violated division (A) of section 4511.75 of the Revised Code, the operator shall report the license plate number and a general description of the vehicle and of the operator of the vehicle to the law enforcement agency exercising jurisdiction over the area where the alleged violation occurred. The information contained in the report relating to the license plate number and to the general description of the vehicle and the operator of the vehicle at the time of the alleged violation may be supplied by any person with first-hand knowledge of the information. Information of which the operator of the school bus has first-hand knowledge also may be corroborated by any other person.

Upon receipt of the report of the alleged violation of division (A) of section 4511.75 of the Revised Code, the law enforcement agency shall conduct an investigation to attempt to determine or confirm the identity of the operator of the vehicle at the time of the alleged violation. If the identity of the operator at the time of the alleged violation is established, the reporting of the license plate number of the vehicle shall establish probable cause for the law enforcement agency to issue a citation for the violation of division (A) of section 4511.75 of the Revised Code. However, if the identity of the operator of the vehicle at the time of the alleged violation cannot be established, the law enforcement agency shall issue a warning to the owner of the vehicle at the time of the alleged violation, except in the case of a leased or rented vehicle when the warning shall be issued to the lessee at the time of the alleged violation.

The registrar of motor vehicles and deputy registrars shall, at the time of issuing license plates to any person, include with the license plate a summary of the requirements of division (A) of section 4511.75 of the Revised Code and the procedures of, and penalty in, division (F) of section 4511.75 of the Revised Code.

**HISTORY: 137 v S 389 (Eff 3-15-79); 144 v H 130. Eff 10-10-91; 149 v S 123, § 1, eff. 1-1-04.**

The effective date is set by section 4 of S.B. 123.

See provisions, § 5 of S.B. 123 (149 v —), following RC § 4501.01.

## § 4511.76 School bus construction, design, equipment, operation and licensing rules.

(A) The department of public safety, by and with the advice of the superintendent of public instruction, shall adopt and enforce rules relating to the construction, design, and equipment, including lighting equipment required by section 4511.771 of the Revised Code, of all school buses both publicly and privately owned and operated in this state.

(B) The department of education, by and with the advice of the director of public safety, shall adopt and enforce rules relating to the operation of all vehicles used for pupil transportation.

(C) No person shall operate a vehicle used for pupil transportation within this state in violation of the rules of the department of education or the department of public safety. No person, being the owner thereof or having the supervisory responsibility therefor, shall permit the operation of a vehicle used for pupil transportation within this state in violation of the rules of the department of education or the department of public safety.

(D) The department of public safety shall adopt and enforce rules relating to the issuance of a license under section 4511.763 of the Revised Code. The rules may relate to the moral character of the applicant; the condition of the equipment to be operated; the liability and property damage insurance carried by the applicant; the posting of satisfactory and sufficient bond; and such other rules as the director of public safety determines reasonably necessary for the safety of the pupils to be transported.

(E) As used in this section, "vehicle used for pupil transportation" means any vehicle that is identified as such by the department of education by rule and that is subject to Chapter 3301-83 of the Administrative Code.

(F) Except as otherwise provided in this division, whoever violates this section is guilty of a minor misdemeanor. If the offender previously has been convicted of or pleaded guilty to one or more violations of this section or section 4511.63, 4511.761, 4511.762, 4511.764, 4511.77, or 4511.79 of the Revised Code or a municipal ordinance that is substantially similar to any of those sections, whoever violates this section is guilty of a misdemeanor of the fourth degree.

**HISTORY: GC § 6307-74; 119 v 766(790), § 74; 122 v 284; Bureau of Code Revision, 10-1-53; 126 v 392(412) (Eff**

**3-17-55); 129 v 1273 (Eff 10-26-61); 131 v 1105 (Eff 9-1-65); 132 v H 1 (Eff 2-21-67); 135 v H 995 (Eff 1-1-75); 144 v S 98 (Eff 11-12-92); 147 v S 60 (Eff 10-21-97); 149 v H 73. Eff 6-29-2001; 149 v S 123, § 1, eff. 1-1-04.**

The effective date is set by section 4 of S.B. 123.

See provisions, § 5 of S.B. 123 (149 v —), following RC § 4501.01.

## § 4511.761 School bus inspection.

(A) The state highway patrol shall inspect every school bus to ascertain whether its construction, design, and equipment comply with the regulations adopted pursuant to section 4511.76 of the Revised Code and all other provisions of law.

The superintendent of the state highway patrol shall adopt a distinctive inspection decal not less than twelve inches in size, and bearing the date of the inspection, which shall be affixed to the outside surface of each side of each school bus which upon such inspection is found to comply with the regulations adopted pursuant to section 4511.76 of the Revised Code. The appearance of said decal shall be changed from year to year as to shape and color in order to provide easy visual inspection.

No person shall operate, nor shall any person being the owner thereof or having supervisory responsibility therefor permit the operation of, a school bus within this state unless there are displayed thereon the decals issued by the state highway patrol bearing the proper date of inspection for the calendar year for which the inspection decals were issued.

(B) Except as otherwise provided in this division, whoever violates this section is guilty of a minor misdemeanor. If the offender previously has been convicted of or pleaded guilty to one or more violations of this section or section 4511.63, 4511.76, 4511.762, 4511.764, 4511.77, or 4511.79 of the Revised Code or a municipal ordinance that is substantially similar to any of those sections, whoever violates this section is guilty of a misdemeanor of the fourth degree.

(C) Whenever a person is found guilty in a court of record of a violation of this section, the trial judge, in addition to or independent of all other penalties provided by law, may suspend for any period of time not exceeding three years, or cancel the license of any person, partnership, association, or corporation, issued under section 4511.763 of the Revised Code.

**HISTORY: 129 v 1273 (Eff 10-26-61); 131 v 1106 (Eff 9-1-65); 144 v S 98 (Eff 11-12-92); 145 v H 687. Eff 10-12-94; 149 v S 123, § 1, eff. 1-1-04.**

The effective date is set by section 4 of S.B. 123.

See provisions, § 5 of S.B. 123 (149 v —), following RC § 4501.01.

## § 4511.762 School bus no longer used for school purposes.

(A) Except as provided in division (B) of this section, no person who is the owner of a bus that previously was registered as a school bus that is used or is to be used exclusively for purposes other than the transportation of children, shall operate the bus or permit it to be operated within this state unless the bus has been painted a color different from that prescribed for school buses by section 4511.77 of the Revised Code and painted in such a way that the words "stop" and "school bus" are obliterated.

(B) Any church bus that previously was registered as a school bus and is registered under section 4503.07 of the Revised Code may retain the paint color prescribed for school buses by section 4511.77 of the Revised Code if the bus complies with all of the following:

(1) The words "school bus" required by section 4511.77 of the Revised Code are covered or obliterated and the bus is marked on the front and rear with the words "church bus" painted in black lettering not less than ten inches in height;

(2) The automatically extended stop warning sign required by section 4511.75 of the Revised Code is removed and the word "stop" required by section 4511.77 of the Revised Code is covered or obliterated;

(3) The flashing red and amber lights required by section 4511.771 of the Revised Code are covered or removed;

(4) The inspection decal required by section 4511.761 of the Revised Code is covered or removed;

(5) The identification number assigned under section 4511.764 of the Revised Code and marked in black lettering on the front and rear of the bus is covered or obliterated.

(C) Except as otherwise provided in this division, whoever violates this section is guilty of a minor misdemeanor. If the offender previously has been convicted of or pleaded guilty to one or more violations of this section or section 4511.63, 4511.76, 4511.761, 4511.764, 4511.77, or 4511.79 of the Revised Code or a municipal ordinance that is substantially similar to any of those sections, whoever violates this section is guilty of a misdemeanor of the fourth degree.

(D) Whenever a person is found guilty in a court of record of a violation of this section, the trial judge, in addition to or independent of all other penalties provided by law, may suspend for any period of time not exceeding three years, or cancel the license of any person, partnership, association, or corporation, issued under section 4511.763 of the Revised Code.

**HISTORY: 129 v 1273 (Eff 10-26-61); 147 v S 85. Eff 5-15-97; 149 v S 123, § 1, eff. 1-1-04.**

The effective date is set by section 4 of S.B. 123.

See provisions, § 5 of S.B. 123 (149 v —), following RC § 4501.01.

## § 4511.763 Licensing by department of public safety.

(A) No person, partnership, association, or corporation shall transport pupils to or from school on a school bus or enter into a contract with a board of education of any school district for the transportation of pupils on a school bus, without being licensed by the department of public safety.

(B) Except as otherwise provided in this division, whoever violates this section is guilty of a minor misdemeanor. If, within one year of the offense, the offender previously has been convicted of or pleaded guilty to one predicate motor vehicle or traffic offense, whoever violates this section is guilty of a misdemeanor of the fourth degree. If, within one year of the offense, the offender previously has been convicted of two or more predicate motor vehicle or traffic offenses, whoever violates this section is guilty of a misdemeanor of the third degree.

**HISTORY: 131 v 1106 (Eff 9-1-65); 144 v S 98 (Eff 11-12-92); 145 v H 687. Eff 10-12-94; 149 v S 123, § 1, eff. 1-1-04.**

The effective date is set by section 4 of S.B. 123.

See provisions, § 5 of S.B. 123 (149 v —), following RC § 4501.01.

## § 4511.764 Registration and identification of school buses.

(A) The superintendent of the state highway patrol shall require school buses to be registered, in the name of the owner, with the state highway patrol on forms and in accordance with regulations as the superintendent may adopt.

When the superintendent is satisfied that the registration has been completed, the superintendent shall assign an identifying number to each school bus registered in accordance with this section. The number so assigned shall be marked on the front and rear of the vehicle in black lettering not less than six inches in height and will remain unchanged as long as the ownership of that vehicle remains the same.

No person shall operate, nor shall any person, being the owner thereof or having supervisory responsibility therefor, permit the operation of a school bus within this state unless there is displayed thereon an identifying number in accordance with this section.

(B) Except as otherwise provided in this division, whoever violates this section is guilty of a minor misdemeanor. If the offender previously has been convicted of or pleaded guilty to one or more violations of section 4511.63, 4511.76, 4511.761, 4511.762, 4511.77, or 4511.79 of the Revised Code or a municipal ordinance that is substantially similar to any of those sections, whoever violates this section is guilty of a misdemeanor of the fourth degree.

**HISTORY: 131 v 1106 (Eff 9-22-65); 136 v H 1. Eff 6-13-75; 149 v S 123, § 1, eff. 1-1-04.**

The effective date is set by section 4 of S.B. 123.

See provisions, § 5 of S.B. 123 (149 v —), following RC § 4501.01.

## § 4511.77 School bus marking.

(A) No person shall operate, nor shall any person being the owner thereof or having supervisory responsibility therefor permit the operation of, a school bus within this state unless it is painted national school bus yellow and is marked on both front and rear with the words "school bus" in black lettering not less than eight inches in height and on the rear of the bus with the word "stop" in black lettering not less than ten inches in height.

(B) Except as otherwise provided in this division, whoever violates this section is guilty of a minor misdemeanor. If the offender previously has been convicted of or pleaded guilty to one or more violations of this section or section 4511.63, 4511.76, 4511.761, 4511.762, 4511.764, or 4511.79 of the Revised Code or a municipal ordinance that is substantially similar to any of those sections, whoever violates this section is guilty of a misdemeanor of the fourth degree.

(C) Whenever a person is found guilty in a court of record of a violation of this section, the trial judge, in addition to or independent of all other penalties provided by law, may suspend for any period of time not exceeding three years, or cancel the license of any person, partnership, association, or corporation, issued under section 4511.763 of the Revised Code.

**HISTORY: 129 v 1273 (Eff 10-26-61); 148 v H 600. Eff 9-1-2000; 149 v S 123, § 1, eff. 1-1-04.**

The effective date is set by section 4 of S.B. 123.

See provisions, § 5 of S.B. 123 (149 v —), following RC § 4501.01.

**Not analogous to former RC § 4511.77 (Bureau of Code Revision, 10-1-53; 125 v 903 [1025]), repealed 128 v 469, § 2, eff 11-10-59.**

## § 4511.771 Flashing red and amber lights.

(A) Every school bus shall, in addition to any other equipment and distinctive markings required pursuant to sections 4511.76, 4511.761, 4511.764, and 4511.77 of the Revised Code, be equipped with signal lamps mounted as high as practicable, which shall display to the front two alternately flashing red lights and two alternately flashing amber lights located at the same level and to the rear two alternately flashing red lights and two alternately flashing amber lights located at the same level, and these lights shall be visible at five hundred feet in normal sunlight. The alternately flashing red lights shall be spaced as widely as practicable, and the alternately flashing amber lights shall be located next to them.

(B) Except as otherwise provided in this division, whoever violates this section is guilty of a minor misdemeanor. If, within one year of the offense, the offender previously has been convicted of or pleaded guilty to one predicate motor vehicle or traffic offense, whoever violates this section is guilty of a misdemeanor of the fourth degree. If, within one year of the offense, the offender previously has been convicted of two or more predicate motor vehicle or traffic offenses, whoever violates this section is guilty of a misdemeanor of the third degree.

**HISTORY: 135 v H 995 (Eff 1-1-75); 137 v S 389. Eff 3-15-79; 149 v S 123, § 1, eff. 1-1-04.**

The effective date is set by section 4 of S.B. 123.

See provisions, § 5 of S.B. 123 (149 v —), following RC § 4501.01.

## § 4511.772 Operator's seat belt.

(A) On and after May 6, 1986, no person, school board, or governmental entity shall purchase, lease, or rent a new school bus unless the school bus has an occupant restraining device, as defined in section 4513.263 of the Revised Code, installed for use in its operator's seat.

(B) Whoever violates this section is guilty of a minor misdemeanor.

**HISTORY: 141 v S 54. Eff 5-6-86; 149 v S 123, § 1, eff. 1-1-04.**

The effective date is set by section 4 of S.B. 123.

See provisions, § 5 of S.B. 123 (149 v —), following RC § 4501.01.

## § 4511.78 Transporting school children.

(A) As used in this section:

(1) "Mass transit system" means any county transit system, regional transit authority, regional transit commission, municipally owned transportation system, mass transit company operating exclusively within the territorial limits of a municipal corporation, or within such limits and the territorial limits of municipal corporations immediately contiguous to such municipal corporation, and any

common passenger carrier certified by the public utilities commission, that provides transportation for children to or from a school session or a school function.

(2) "Bus" means every motor vehicle designed for carrying more than nine passengers and used for the transportation of persons, but does not mean any school bus as defined in section 4511.01 of the Revised Code.

(B) Whenever a mass transit system transports children to or from a school session or school function, the mass transit system shall provide for:

(1) Periodic safety inspections of all buses used to provide transportation service. The inspections shall be based on rules adopted by the public utilities commission under Chapters 4921. and 4923. of the Revised Code to ensure the safety of operation of motor transportation companies and private motor carriers.

(2) The safety training of all drivers operating buses used to provide transportation service;

(3) The equipping of every bus with outside rear-view mirrors meeting the motor carrier regulations for bus equipment adopted by the federal highway administration. No exclusions from this requirement granted under the federal regulations shall be considered exclusions for the purposes of this division.

(C) Except as otherwise provided in this division, whoever violates this section is guilty of a minor misdemeanor. If, within one year of the offense, the offender previously has been convicted of or pleaded guilty to one predicate motor vehicle or traffic offense, whoever violates this section is guilty of a misdemeanor of the fourth degree. If, within one year of the offense, the offender previously has been convicted of two or more predicate motor vehicle or traffic offenses, whoever violates this section is guilty of a misdemeanor of the third degree.

**HISTORY: 136 v H 234. Eff 8-25-76; 149 v S 123, § 1, eff. 1-1-04.**

The effective date is set by section 4 of S.B. 123.

See provisions, § 5 of S.B. 123 (149 v —), following RC § 4501.01.

**Not analogous to former RC § 4511.78 (Bureau of Code Revision, 10-1-53), repealed 134 v H 511, § 2, eff 1-1-74. For sections analogous to former RC § 4511.78, see RC §§ 2921.31 and 2921.33.**

## [COMMERCIAL DRIVER PROHIBITIONS]

### § 4511.79 Driving commercial vehicle with impaired alertness or ability; use of drugs.

(A) No person shall drive a "commercial motor vehicle" as defined in section 4506.01 of the Revised Code, or a "commercial car" or "commercial tractor," as defined in section 4501.01 of the Revised Code, while the person's ability or alertness is so impaired by fatigue, illness, or other causes that it is unsafe for the person to drive such vehicle. No driver shall use any drug which would adversely affect the driver's ability or alertness.

(B) No owner, as defined in section 4501.01 of the Revised Code, of a "commercial motor vehicle," "commercial car," or "commercial tractor," or a person employing or otherwise directing the driver of such vehicle, shall require or knowingly permit a driver in any such condition described in division (A) of this section to drive such vehicle upon any street or highway.

(C) Except as otherwise provided in this division, whoever violates this section is guilty of a minor misdemeanor. If the offender previously has been convicted of or pleaded guilty to one or more violations of this section or section 4511.63, 4511.76, 4511.761, 4511.762, 4511.764, or 4511.77 of the Revised Code or a municipal ordinance that is substantially similar to any of those sections, whoever violates this section is guilty of a misdemeanor of the fourth degree.

**HISTORY: 130 v H 391 (Eff 10-10-63); 143 v H 381. Eff 7-1-89; 149 v S 123, § 1, eff. 1-1-04.**

The effective date is set by section 4 of S.B. 123.

See provisions, § 5 of S.B. 123 (149 v —), following RC § 4501.01.

### § 4511.81 Motor vehicle child restraint law; booster seats; child highway safety fund.

(A) When any child who is in either or both of the following categories is being transported in a motor vehicle, other than a taxicab or public safety vehicle as defined in section 4511.01 of the Revised Code, that is required by the United States department of transportation to be equipped with seat belts at the time of manufacture or assembly, the operator of the motor vehicle shall have the child properly secured in accordance with the manufacturer's instructions in a child restraint system that meets federal motor vehicle safety standards:

(1) A child who is less than four years of age;

(2) A child who weighs less than forty pounds.

(B) When any child who is in either or both of the following categories is being transported in a motor vehicle, other than a taxicab, that is owned, leased, or otherwise under the control of a nursery school or day-care center, the operator of the motor vehicle shall have the child properly secured in accordance with the manufacturer's instructions in a child restraint system that meets federal motor vehicle safety standards:

(1) A child who is less than four years of age;

(2) A child who weighs less than forty pounds.

(C) When any child who is less than eight years of age and less than four feet nine inches in height, who is not required by division (A) or (B) of this section to be secured in a child restraint system, is being transported in a motor vehicle, other than a taxicab or public safety vehicle as defined in section 4511.01 of the Revised Code or a vehicle that is regulated under section 5104.011 [5104.01.1] of the Revised Code, that is required by the United States department of transportation to be equipped with seat belts at the time of manufacture or assembly, the operator of the motor vehicle shall have the child properly secured in accordance with the manufacturer's instructions on a booster seat that meets federal motor vehicle safety standards.

(D) When any child who is at least eight years of age but not older than fifteen years of age, and who is not otherwise required by division (A), (B), or (C) of this section to be secured in a child restraint system or booster seat, is being transported in a motor vehicle, other than a taxicab or public safety vehicle as defined in section 4511.01 of the Revised Code, that is required by the United States department of transportation to be equipped with seat belts at the time of manufacture or assembly, the operator of the motor vehicle shall have the child properly restrained either in accordance with the manufacturer's instructions in a child restraint system that meets federal motor vehicle safety standards or in an occupant restraining device as defined in section 4513.263 [4513.26.3] of the Revised Code.

(E) Notwithstanding any provision of law to the contrary, no law enforcement officer shall cause an operator of a motor vehicle being operated on any street or highway to stop the motor vehicle for the sole purpose of determining whether a violation of division (C) or (D) of this section has been or is being committed or for the sole purpose of issuing a ticket, citation, or summons for a violation of division (C) or (D) of this section or causing the arrest of or commencing a prosecution of a person for a violation of division (C) or (D) of this section, and absent another violation of law, a law enforcement officer's view of the interior or visual inspection of a motor vehicle being operated on any street or highway may not be used for the purpose of determining whether a violation of division (C) or (D) of this section has been or is being committed.

(F) The director of public safety shall adopt such rules as are necessary to carry out this section.

(G) The failure of an operator of a motor vehicle to secure a child in a child restraint system, a booster seat, or an occupant restraining device as required by this section is not negligence imputable to the child, is not admissible as evidence in any civil action involving the rights of the child against any other person allegedly liable for injuries to the child, is not to be used as a basis for a criminal prosecution of the operator of the motor vehicle other than a prosecution for a violation of this section, and is not admissible as evidence in any criminal action involving the operator of the motor vehicle other than a prosecution for a violation of this section.

(H) This section does not apply when an emergency exists that threatens the life of any person operating or occupying a motor vehicle that is being used to transport a child who otherwise would be required to be restrained under this section. This section does not apply to a person operating a motor vehicle who has an affidavit signed by a physician licensed to practice in this state under Chapter 4731. of the Revised Code or a chiropractor licensed to practice in this state under Chapter 4734. of the Revised Code that states that the child who otherwise would be required to be restrained under this section has a physical impairment that makes use of a child restraint system, booster seat, or an occupant restraining device impossible or impractical, provided that the person operating the vehicle has safely and appropriately restrained the child in accordance with any recommendations of the physician or chiropractor as noted on the affidavit.

(I) There is hereby created in the state treasury the child highway safety fund, consisting of fines imposed pursuant to division (K)(1) of this section for violations of divisions (A), (B), (C), and (D) of this section. The money in the fund shall be used by the department of health only to defray the cost of designating hospitals as pediatric trauma centers under section 3727.081 [3727.08.1] of the Revised Code and to establish and administer a child highway safety program. The purpose of the program shall be to educate the public about child restraint systems and booster seats and the importance of their proper use. The program also shall include a process for providing child restraint systems and booster seats to persons who meet the eligibility criteria established by the department, and a toll-free telephone number the public may utilize to obtain information about child restraint systems and booster seats, and their proper use.

(J) The director of health, in accordance with Chapter 119. of the Revised Code, shall adopt any rules necessary to carry out this section, including rules establishing the criteria a person must meet in order to receive a child restraint system or booster seat under the department's child highway safety program; provided that rules relating to the verification of pediatric trauma centers shall not be adopted under this section.

(K) Nothing in this section shall be construed to require any person to carry with the person the birth certificate of a child to prove the age of the child, but the production of a valid birth certificate for a child showing that the child was not of an age to which this section applies is a defense against any ticket, citation, or summons issued for violating this section.

(L)(1) Whoever violates division (A), (B), (C), or (D) of this section shall be punished as follows, provided that the failure of an operator of a motor vehicle to secure more than one child in a child restraint system, booster seat, or occupant restraining device as required by this section that occurred at the same time, on the same day, and at the same location is deemed to be a single violation of this section:

(a) Except as otherwise provided in division (L)(1)(b) of this section, the offender is guilty of a minor misdemeanor and shall be fined not less than twenty-five dollars nor more than seventy-five dollars.

(b) If the offender previously has been convicted of or pleaded guilty to a violation of division (A), (B), (C), or (D) of this section or of a municipal ordinance that is substantially similar to any of those divisions, the offender is guilty of a misdemeanor of the fourth degree.

(2) All fines imposed pursuant to division (L)(1) of this section shall be forwarded to the treasurer of state for deposit in the child highway safety fund created by division (I) of this section.

**HISTORY: 139 v H 605 (Eff 3-7-83); 141 v S 54 (Eff 5-6-86); 141 v H 428 (Eff 12-23-86); 142 v S 53 (Eff 10-20-87); 144 v S 98 (Eff 11-12-92); 145 v H 381 (Eff 6-23-94); 148 v H 138 (Eff 11-3-2000); 149 v H 94. Eff 6-6-2001; 149 v S 123, § 1, eff. 1-1-04; 151 v H 343, § 1, eff. 4-6-07; 152 v H 30, § 1, eff. 9-12-08; 152 v H 320, § 1, eff. 10-7-09.**

The provisions of § 3 of 152 v H 320 read as follows:

SECTION 3. Notwithstanding any provision of law to the contrary, during the first six months after the effective date of this section, no person who violates division (C) of section 4511.81 of the Revised Code concerning the use of booster seats, as that division is amended by this act, shall be issued a ticket, citation, or summons in relation to the violation or be arrested for the violation. Instead, the person shall be issued a written warning that states the requirements contained in division (C) of section 4511.81 of the Revised Code, as amended by this act. In addition, the warning shall explain that on or after a date certain, which date shall be six months after the effective date of this section, the law will allow a person to be charged with and prosecuted for such a violation.

The effective date is set by § 4 of 152 v H 320.

The effective date is set by section 4 of S.B. 123.

See provisions, § 5 of S.B. 123 (149 v —), following RC § 4501.01.

## § 4511.82 Littering offenses.

(A) No operator or occupant of a motor vehicle shall, regardless of intent, throw, drop, discard, or deposit litter from any motor vehicle in operation upon any street, road, or highway, except into a litter receptacle in a manner that prevents its being carried away or deposited by the elements.

(B) No operator of a motor vehicle in operation upon any street, road, or highway shall allow litter to be thrown, dropped, discarded, or deposited from the motor vehicle, except into a litter receptacle in a manner that prevents its being carried away or deposited by the elements.

(C) Whoever violates division (A) or (B) of this section is guilty of a minor misdemeanor.

(D) As used in this section, "litter" means garbage, trash, waste, rubbish, ashes, cans, bottles, wire, paper, cartons, boxes, automobile parts, furniture, glass, or anything else of an unsightly or unsanitary nature.

**HISTORY: 142 v H 333. Eff 10-20-87; 149 v S 123, § 1, eff. 1-1-04.**

The effective date is set by section 4 of S.B. 123.

See provisions, § 5 of S.B. 123 (149 v —), following RC § 4501.01.

## § 4511.83 Repealed, 149 v S 123, § 2 [142 v H 429; 143 v S 131; 143 v H 837; 144 v S 98; 145 v S 82; 146 v S 2; 148 v H 283; 148 v H 349]. Eff. 1-1-04.

This section concerned ignition interlock devices.

The effective date is set by section 4 of S.B. 123.

See provisions, § 5 of S.B. 123 (149 v —), following RC § 4501.01.

## § 4511.84 Earphones or earplugs on operator prohibited.

(A) No person shall operate a motor vehicle while wearing earphones over, or earplugs in, both ears. As used in this section, "earphones" means any headset, radio, tape player, or other similar device that provides the listener with radio programs, music, or other recorded information through a device attached to the head and that covers all or a portion of both ears. "Earphones" does not include speakers or other listening devices that are built into protective headgear.

(B) This section does not apply to:

(1) Any person wearing a hearing aid;

(2) Law enforcement personnel while on duty;

(3) Fire department personnel and emergency medical service personnel while on duty;

(4) Any person engaged in the operation of equipment for use in the maintenance or repair of any highway;

(5) Any person engaged in the operation of refuse collection equipment.

(C) Except as otherwise provided in this division, whoever violates this section is guilty of a minor misdemeanor. If, within one year of the offense, the offender previously has been convicted of or pleaded guilty to one predicate motor vehicle or traffic offense, whoever violates this section is guilty of a misdemeanor of the fourth degree. If, within one year of the offense, the offender previously has been convicted of two or more predicate motor vehicle or traffic offenses, whoever violates this section is guilty of a misdemeanor of the third degree.

**HISTORY: 143 v S 6. Eff 10-30-89; 149 v S 123, § 1, eff. 1-1-04.**

The effective date is set by section 4 of S.B. 123.

See provisions, § 5 of S.B. 123 (149 v —), following RC § 4501.01.

## § 4511.85 Chauffeured limousines.

(A) The operator of a chauffeured limousine shall accept passengers only on the basis of prearranged contracts, as defined in division (LL) of section 4501.01 of the Revised Code, and shall not cruise in search of patronage unless the limousine is in compliance with any statute or ordinance governing the operation of taxicabs or other similar vehicles for hire.

(B) No person shall advertise or hold self out as doing business as a limousine service or livery service or other similar designation unless each vehicle used by the person to provide the service is registered in accordance with section 4503.24 of the Revised Code and is in compliance with section 4509.80 of the Revised Code.

(C) Whoever violates this section is guilty of a misdemeanor of the first degree.

**HISTORY: 143 v H 422 (Eff 7-1-91); 147 v H 611. Eff 7-1-99; 149 v S 123, § 1, eff. 1-1-04.**

The effective date is set by section 4 of S.B. 123.

See provisions, § 5 of S.B. 123 (149 v —), following RC § 4501.01.

### [CHAUTAUQUA ASSEMBLY]

## § 4511.90 Application to streets within Chautauqua Assembly.

As used in this section, "Chautauqua assembly" means a corporation that is organized in this state for the purpose of holding Chautauqua assemblies or encouraging religion, art, science, literature, or the general dissemination of knowledge, or two or more of such purposes, and that occupies grounds and holds meetings or entertainments on the grounds for the purposes for which it is organized.

Chapters 4511. and 4513. of the Revised Code are applicable to streets within a Chautauqua assembly. A Chautauqua assembly is a local authority for the purposes of section 4511.07 of the Revised Code.

**HISTORY: 138 v H 316 (Eff 10-26-79); 138 v H 948. Eff 5-22-80.**

### [NONRESIDENT VIOLATOR COMPACT OF 1977]

## § 4511.95 Renumbered RC § 4510.71 in 149 v S 123. Eff 1-1-04

## § 4511.951 Amended and renumbered RC § 4510.72 in 149 v S 123. Eff 1-1-04

See provisions, § 5 of S.B. 123 (149 v —), following RC § 4501.01.

## § 4511.98 Warning signs as to increased penalties in construction zones.

The director of transportation, board of county commissioners, or board of township trustees shall cause signs to be erected advising motorists that increased penalties apply for certain traffic violations occurring on streets or highways in a construction zone. The increased penalties shall be effective only when signs are erected in accordance with the guidelines and design specifications established by the director under section 5501.27 of the

Revised Code, and when a violation occurs during hours of actual work within the construction zone.

**HISTORY: 145 v H 247. Eff 5-1-95; 150 v H 52, § 1, eff. 6-1-04.**

The effective date is set by section 4 of HB 247.

## § 4511.99 Penalties.

Whoever violates any provision of sections 4511.01 to 4511.76 of the Revised Code for which no penalty otherwise is provided in the section violated is guilty of one of the following:

(A) Except as otherwise provided in division (B) or (C) of this section, a minor misdemeanor;

(B) If, within one year of the offense, the offender previously has been convicted of or pleaded guilty to one predicate motor vehicle or traffic offense, a misdemeanor of the fourth degree;

(C) If, within one year of the offense, the offender previously has been convicted of or pleaded guilty to two or more predicate motor vehicle or traffic offenses, a misdemeanor of the third degree.

**HISTORY: Bureau of Code Revision, 10-1-53; 125 v 461; 128 v 469 (Eff 11-10-59); 129 v 1273 (Eff 10-26-61); 130 v 1089 (Eff 10-10-63); 131 v 1109 (Eff 9-1-65); 131 v 1107 (Eff 9-22-65); 132 v H 1 (Eff 2-21-67); 132 v S 37 (Eff 11-14-67); 132 v H 380 (Eff 1-1-68); 134 v H 511 (Eff 1-1-74); 137 v H 652 (Eff 3-13-78); 137 v S 381 (Eff 10-19-78); 137 v S 389 (Eff 3-15-79); 139 v H 707 (Eff 1-1-83); 139 v H 605 (Eff 3-7-83); 139 v S 432 (Eff 3-16-83); 140 v H 133 (Eff 9-27-83); 140 v S 169, § 1 (Eff 6-18-84); 140 v S 169, § 3 (Eff 1-1-85); 140 v H 112 (Eff 10- 4-84); 140 v H 460 (Eff 4-4-85); 141 v S 54 (Eff 5-6-86); 141 v S 262 (Eff 3-20-87); 142 v H 333 (Eff 10-20-87); 142 v S 53 (Eff 10-20-87); 142 v H 429 (Eff 6-20-88); 142 v H 708 (Eff 4-19-88); 143 v H 8 (Eff 9-13-89); 143 v H 381 (Eff 7-1-89); 143 v S 86 (Eff 10-30-89); 143 v S 49 (Eff 11-3-89); 143 v H 317 (Eff 10-10-89); 143 v H 162 (Eff 6-28-90); 143 v H 422 (Eff 7-1-91); 143 v S 131 (Eff 7-25-90); 143 v H 837 (Eff 7-25-90); 143 v S 382 (Eff 12-31-90); 144 v H 73 (Eff 9-25-91); 144 v H 130 (Eff 10-10-91); 144 v H 725 (Eff 4-16-93); 144 v S 275 (Eff 9-1-93); 145 v H 149 (Eff 5-20-93); 145 v S 62, §§ 1, 4 (Eff 9-1-93); 145 v S 82 (Eff 5-4-94); 145 v H 381 (Eff 6-23-94); 145 v H 247 (Eff 5-1-95); 146 v S 2 (Eff 7-1-96); 146 v H 353 (Eff 9-17-96); 146 v H 676 (Eff 10-4-96); 146 v S 166 (Eff 10-17-96); 146 v H 72 (Eff 3-18-97); 147 v S 60 (Eff 10-21-97); 148 v H 86 (Eff 9-28-99); 148 v H 148 (Eff 10-14-99); 148 v S 107 (Eff 3-23-2000); 148 v S 22 (Eff 5-17-2000); 148 v H 80 (Eff 6-8-2000); 148 v H 138 (Eff 11-3-2000); 149 v S 231. Eff 10-24-2002; 149 v S 123, § 1, Eff 1-1-04; 149 v H 490, § 4, Eff 1-1-04.**

The effective date is set by section 4 of H.B. 490.

The provisions of § 5 of H.B. 490 (149 v —) read as follows:

SECTION 5. Section 4511.99 of the Revised Code is presented in this act as a composite of the section as amended by both Am. Sub. S.B. 123 and Am. Sub. S.B. 231 of the 124th General Assembly. The General Assembly, applying the principle stated in division (B) of section 1.52 of the Revised Code that amendments are to be harmonized if reasonably capable of simultaneous operation, finds that the specified composite is the resulting version of the specified sections in effect prior to the effective date of the section as presented in this act.

See provisions, § 5 of S.B. 123 (149 v —), following RC § 4501.01.

## § 4511.991 Repealed, 149 v S 123, § 2 [139 v S 432]. Eff. 1-1-04.

This section defined "three consecutive days".

The effective date is set by section 4 of S.B. 123.

See provisions, § 5 of S.B. 123 (149 v —), following RC § 4501.01.

# CHAPTER 4513: TRAFFIC LAWS — EQUIPMENT; LOADS

## § 4513.01 Definitions.

As provided in section 4511.01 of the Revised Code, the definitions set forth in that section apply to this chapter.

**HISTORY: Bureau of Code Revision, 10-1-53; 148 v H 672 (Eff 4-9-2001); 149 v H 520, Eff 4-3-2003.**

## § 4513.02 Unsafe vehicles, prohibition against operation; inspection by state highway patrol.

(A) No person shall drive or move, or cause or knowingly permit to be driven or moved, on any highway any vehicle or combination of vehicles which is in such unsafe condition as to endanger any person.

(B) When directed by any state highway patrol trooper, the operator of any motor vehicle shall stop and submit such motor vehicle to an inspection under division (B)(1) or (2) of this section, as appropriate, and such tests as are necessary.

(1) Any motor vehicle not subject to inspection by the public utilities commission shall be inspected and tested to determine whether it is unsafe or not equipped as required by law, or that its equipment is not in proper adjustment or repair, or in violation of the equipment provisions of Chapter 4513. of the Revised Code.

Such inspection shall be made with respect to the brakes, lights, turn signals, steering, horns and warning devices, glass, mirrors, exhaust system, windshield wipers, tires, and such other items of equipment as designated by the superintendent of the state highway patrol by rule or regulation adopted pursuant to sections 119.01 to 119.13 of the Revised Code.

Upon determining that a motor vehicle is in safe operating condition and its equipment in conformity with Chapter 4513. of the Revised Code, the inspecting officer shall issue to the operator an official inspection sticker, which shall be in such form as the superintendent prescribes except that its color shall vary from year to year.

(2) Any motor vehicle subject to inspection by the public utilities commission shall be inspected and tested in accordance with rules adopted by the commission. Upon determining that the vehicle and operator are in compliance with rules adopted by the commission, the inspecting officer shall issue to the operator an appropriate official inspection sticker.

(C) The superintendent of the state highway patrol, pursuant to sections 119.01 to 119.13 of the Revised Code, shall determine and promulgate standards for any inspection program conducted by a political subdivision of this state. These standards shall exempt licensed collector's vehicles and historical motor vehicles from inspection. Any motor vehicle bearing a valid certificate of inspection issued by another state or a political subdivision of this state whose inspection program conforms to the superintendent's standards, and any licensed collector's vehicle or historical motor vehicle which is not in a condition which endangers the safety of persons or property, shall be exempt from the tests provided in division (B) of this section.

(D) Every person, firm, association, or corporation that, in the conduct of its business, owns and operates not less than fifteen motor vehicles in this state that are not subject to regulation by the public utilities commission and that, for the purpose of storing, repairing, maintaining, and servicing such motor vehicles, equips and operates one or more service departments within this state, may file with the superintendent of the state highway patrol applications for permits for such service departments as official inspection stations for its own motor vehicles. Upon receiving an application for each such service department, and after determining that it is properly equipped and has competent personnel to perform the inspections referred to in this section, the superintendent shall issue the necessary inspection stickers and permit to operate as an official inspection station. Any such person who has had one or more service departments so designated as official inspection stations may have motor vehicles that are owned and operated by the person and that are not subject to regulation by the public utilities commission, excepting private passenger cars owned by the person or the person's employees, inspected at such service department; and any motor vehicle bearing a valid certificate of inspection issued by such service department shall be exempt from the tests provided in division (B) of this section.

No permit for an official inspection station shall be assigned or transferred or used at any location other than therein designated, and every such permit shall be posted in a conspicuous place at the location designated.

If a person, firm, association, or corporation owns and operates fifteen or more motor vehicles in the conduct of business and is subject to regulation by the public utilities commission, that person, firm, association, or corporation is not eligible to apply to the superintendent for permits to enable any of its service departments to serve as official inspection stations for its own motor vehicles.

(E) When any motor vehicle is found to be unsafe for operation, the inspecting officer may order it removed from the highway and not operated, except for purposes of removal and repair, until it has been repaired pursuant to a repair order as provided in division (F) of this section.

(F) When any motor vehicle is found to be defective or in violation of Chapter 4513. of the Revised Code, the inspecting officer may issue a repair order, in such form and containing such information as the superintendent shall prescribe, to the owner or operator of the motor vehicle. The owner or operator shall thereupon obtain such repairs as are required and shall, as directed by the inspecting officer, return the repair order together with proof of compliance with its provisions. When any motor vehicle or operator subject to rules of the public utilities commission fails the inspection, the inspecting officer shall issue an appropriate order to obtain compliance with such rules.

(G) Sections 4513.01 to 4513.37 of the Revised Code, with respect to equipment on vehicles, do not apply to implements of husbandry, road machinery, road rollers, or agricultural tractors except as made applicable to such articles of machinery.

(H) Except as otherwise provided in this division, whoever violates this section is guilty of a minor misdemeanor. If the offender previously has been convicted of a violation of this section, whoever violates this section is guilty of a misdemeanor of the third degree.

**HISTORY: GC § 6307-75; 119 v 766(791), § 75; Bureau of Code Revision, 10-1-53; 132 v H 380 (Eff 1-1-68); 136 v S 52 (Eff 9-15-75); 144 v S 144 (Eff 8-8-91); 144 v S 351 (Eff 7-1-92); 144 v S 301 (Eff 3-15-93); 148 v H 86. Eff 6-29-99; 149 v S 123, § 1, eff. 1-1-04.**

The effective date is set by section 4 of S.B. 123.

See provisions, § 5 of S.B. 123 (149 v —), following RC § 4501.01.

## § 4513.021 Maximum bumper height; modifying vehicle; disconnecting suspension system.

(A) As used in this section:

(1) "Passenger car" means any motor vehicle with motive power, designed for carrying ten persons or less, except a multipurpose passenger vehicle or motorcycle.

(2) "Multipurpose passenger vehicle" means a motor vehicle with motive power, except a motorcycle, designed to carry ten persons or less, that is constructed either on a truck chassis or with special features for occasional off-road operation.

(3) "Truck" means every motor vehicle, except trailers and semitrailers, designed and used to carry property and having a gross vehicle weight rating of ten thousand pounds or less.

(4) "Manufacturer" has the same meaning as in section 4501.01 of the Revised Code.

(5) "Gross vehicle weight rating" means the manufacturer's gross vehicle weight rating established for that vehicle.

(B) The director of public safety, in accordance with Chapter 119. of the Revised Code, shall adopt rules in conformance with standards of the vehicle equipment safety commission, that shall govern the maximum bumper height or, in the absence of bumpers and in cases where bumper heights have been lowered or modified, the maximum height to the bottom of the frame rail, of any passenger car, multipurpose passenger vehicle, or truck.

(C) No person shall operate upon a street or highway any passenger car, multipurpose passenger vehicle, or truck registered in this state that does not conform to the requirements of this section or to any applicable rule adopted pursuant to this section.

(D) No person shall modify any motor vehicle registered in this state in such a manner as to cause the vehicle body or chassis to come in contact with the ground, expose the fuel tank to damage from collision, or cause the wheels to come in contact with the body under normal operation, and no person shall disconnect any part of the original suspension system of the vehicle to defeat the safe operation of that system.

(E) Nothing contained in this section or in the rules adopted pursuant to this section shall be construed to prohibit either of the following:

(1) The installation upon a passenger car, multipurpose passenger vehicle, or truck registered in this state of heavy duty equipment, including shock absorbers and overload springs;

(2) The operation on a street or highway of a passenger car, multipurpose passenger vehicle, or truck registered in this state with normal wear to the suspension system if the normal wear does not adversely affect the control of the vehicle.

(F) This section and the rules adopted pursuant to it do not apply to any specially designed or modified passenger car, multipurpose passenger vehicle, or truck when operated off a street or highway in races and similar events.

(G) Except as otherwise provided in this division, whoever violates this section is guilty of a minor misdemeanor. If the offender previously has been convicted of a violation of this section, whoever violates this section is guilty of a misdemeanor of the third degree.

**HISTORY: 142 v H 447 (Eff 9-27-88); 144 v S 98. Eff 11-12-92; 149 v S 123, § 1, eff. 1-1-04.**

The effective date is set by section 4 of S.B. 123.

See provisions, § 5 of S.B. 123 (149 v —), following RC § 4501.01.

**Analogous in part to former RC § 4513.02.1 (135 v H 173), repealed 142 v H 447, § 2, eff 9-27-88.**

**Publisher's Note:**

The amendment of RC § 4513.021 by 153 v H 1 was disapproved by the Governor.

## § 4513.022 Trooper may request proof of financial responsibility; indication on ticket; failure to produce proof.

(A) As part of the motor vehicle inspection conducted pursuant to section 4513.02 of the Revised Code, the state highway patrol trooper shall request that the owner or operator of the motor vehicle produce proof that the owner maintains or has maintained on the owner's behalf, proof of financial responsibility as required by section 4509.101 of the Revised Code.

(B) A state highway patrol trooper shall indicate on every traffic ticket issued pursuant to a motor vehicle inspection whether the person receiving the traffic ticket produced proof of the maintenance of financial responsibility in response to the state highway patrol trooper's request. The state highway patrol trooper shall inform every person who receives a traffic ticket and who has failed to produce proof of the maintenance of financial responsibility at the time of the motor vehicle inspection that the person must submit proof to the traffic violations bureau with any payment of a fine and costs for the ticketed violation or, if the person is to appear in court for the violation, the person must submit proof to the court.

(C)(1) If a person who has failed to produce proof of the maintenance of financial responsibility appears in court for a ticketed violation, the court may permit the defendant to present evidence of proof of financial responsibility to the court at such time and in such manner as the court determines to be necessary or appropriate. The clerk of courts shall provide the registrar with the identity of any person who fails to submit proof of the maintenance of financial responsibility pursuant to division (B) of this section.

(2) If a person who has failed to present proof of the maintenance of financial responsibility also fails to submit that proof to the traffic violations bureau, the traffic violations bureau shall notify the registrar of the identity of that person.

(3) Upon receiving notice from a clerk of courts or a traffic violation bureau pursuant to division (C) of this section, the registrar shall proceed against these persons under division (D) of section 4509.101 of the Revised Code in the same manner as the registrar proceeds against persons identified by the clerk of courts under division (D)(4) of section 4509.101 of the Revised Code.

(D) A state highway patrol trooper may charge an owner or operator of a motor vehicle with a violation of section 4510.16 of the Revised Code when the operator fails to produce proof of the maintenance of financial responsibility upon the state highway patrol trooper's request under division (A) of this section, if a check of the owner or operator's driving record indicates that the owner or operator, at the time of the motor vehicle inspection, is required to file and maintain proof of financial responsibility under section 4509.45 of the Revised Code for a previous violation of Chapter 4509. of the Revised Code.

**HISTORY: 145 v S 20 (Eff 10-20-95); 146 v H 248, § 1(Eff 10-20-95); 146 v H 438. Eff 7-1-97; 149 v S 123, § 1, eff. 1-1-04.**

The effective date is set by section 4 of S.B. 123.

See provisions, § 5 of S.B. 123 (149 v —), following RC § 4501.01.

## [EQUIPMENT]

### § 4513.03 Lighted lights and illuminating devices required.

(A) Every vehicle, other than a motorized bicycle, operated upon a street or highway within this state shall display lighted lights and illuminating devices as required by sections 4513.04 to 4513.37 of the Revised Code during all of the following times:

(1) The time from sunset to sunrise;

(2) At any other time when, due to insufficient natural light or unfavorable atmospheric conditions, persons, vehicles, and substantial objects on the highway are not discernible at a distance of one thousand feet ahead;

(3) At any time when the windshield wipers of the vehicle are in use because of precipitation on the windshield.

Every motorized bicycle shall display at such times lighted lights meeting the rules adopted by the director of public safety under section 4511.521 [4511.52.1] of the Revised Code. No motor vehicle, during any time specified in this section, shall be operated upon a street or highway within this state using only parking lights as illumination.

Whenever in such sections a requirement is declared as to the distance from which certain lamps and devices shall render objects visible, or within which such lamps or devices shall be visible, such distance shall be measured upon a straight level unlighted highway under normal atmospheric conditions unless a different condition is expressly stated.

Whenever in such sections a requirement is declared as to the mounted height of lights or devices, it shall mean from the center of such light or device to the level ground upon which the vehicle stands.

(B) Notwithstanding any provision of law to the contrary, no law enforcement officer shall cause the operator of a vehicle being operated upon a street or highway within this state to stop the vehicle solely because the officer observes that a violation of division (A)(3) of this section has been or is being committed or for the sole purpose of issuing a ticket, citation, or summons for a violation of that division, or causing the arrest of or commencing a prosecution of a person for a violation of that division.

(C) Whoever violates this section is guilty of a minor misdemeanor.

**HISTORY: GC § 6307-76; 119 v 766(791), § 76; Bureau of Code Revision, 10-1-53; 129 v 232 (Eff 9-21-61); 135 v H 272 (Eff 11-21-73); 137 v S 100 (Eff 4-1-78); 144 v S 98 (Eff 11-12-92); 148 v H 484. Eff 10-5-2000; 149 v S 123, § 1, eff. 1-1-04; 153 v H 2, § 101.01, eff. 7-1-09; 153 v H 1, § 101.01, eff. 10-16-09.**

The effective date is set by § 812.10 of 153 v H 1.

The provisions of § 756.15 of 153 v H 2 read as follows:

SECTION 756.15. For the six-month period commencing on the effective date of the amendments to section 4513.03 of the Revised Code contained in Section 101.01 of this act, no law enforcement officer shall issue to the operator of any motor vehicle being operated upon a street or highway within this state a ticket, citation, or summons for a violation of division (A)(3) of section 4513.03 of the Revised Code, or cause the arrest of or commence a prosecution of a person for a violation of that division. Instead, during that period of time the law enforcement officer shall issue to such an operator a written warning, informing the operator of the existence of division (A)(3) of section 4513.03 of the Revised Code and that after the date that is six months after the effective date of the amendments to section 4513.03 of the Revised Code contained in Section 101.01 of this act, a law enforcement officer who observes that the operator of a motor vehicle has committed or is committing a violation of division (A)(3) of section 4513.03 of the Revised Code will be authorized to issue a ticket, citation, or summons to that operator for that violation or to cause the arrest of or commence a prosecution of such an operator for a violation of that division.

The effective date is set by § 812.10 of 153 v H 2.

The effective date is set by section 4 of S.B. 123.

See provisions, § 5 of S.B. 123 (149 v —), following RC § 4501.01.

**Comment, Legislative Service Commission**

Section 4513.03 of the Revised Code is amended by Am. Sub. H.B. 1 and H.B. 2 of the 128th General Assembly. Comparison of these amendments in pursuance of section 1.52 of the Revised Code discloses that they are not irreconcilable so that they are required by that section to be harmonized to give effect to each amendment.

## § 4513.04 Headlights.

(A) Every motor vehicle, other than a motorcycle, and every trackless trolley shall be equipped with at least two headlights with at least one near each side of the front of the motor vehicle or trackless trolley.

Every motorcycle shall be equipped with at least one and not more than two headlights.

(B) Whoever violates this section is guilty of a minor misdemeanor.

**HISTORY: GC § 6307-77; 119 v 766(792), § 77; Bureau of Code Revision. Eff 10-1-53; 149 v S 123, § 1, eff. 1-1-04; 153 v H 1, § 101.01, eff. 10-16-09.**

The effective date is set by § 812.10 of 153 v H 1.
The effective date is set by section 4 of S.B. 123.
See provisions, § 5 of S.B. 123 (149 v —), following RC § 4501.01.

## § 4513.05 Tail lights and illumination of rear license plate.

(A) Every motor vehicle, trackless trolley, trailer, semitrailer, pole trailer, or vehicle which is being drawn at the end of a train of vehicles shall be equipped with at least one tail light mounted on the rear which, when lighted, shall emit a red light visible from a distance of five hundred feet to the rear, provided that in the case of a train of vehicles only the tail light on the rearmost vehicle need be visible from the distance specified.

Either a tail light or a separate light shall be so constructed and placed as to illuminate with a white light the rear registration plate, when such registration plate is required, and render it legible from a distance of fifty feet to the rear. Any tail light, together with any separate light for illuminating the rear registration plate, shall be so wired as to be lighted whenever the headlights or auxiliary driving lights are lighted, except where separate lighting systems are provided for trailers for the purpose of illuminating such registration plate.

(B) Whoever violates this section is guilty of a minor misdemeanor.

**HISTORY: GC § 6307-78; 119 v 766(792), § 78; Bureau of Code Revision. Eff 10-1-53; 149 v S 123, § 1, eff. 1-1-04; 153 v H 1, § 101.01, eff. 10-16-09.**

The effective date is set by § 812.10 of 153 v H 1.
The effective date is set by section 4 of S.B. 123.
See provisions, § 5 of S.B. 123 (149 v —), following RC § 4501.01.

## § 4513.06 Red reflectors required.

(A) Every new motor vehicle sold after September 6, 1941, and operated on a highway, other than a commercial tractor, to which a trailer or semitrailer is attached shall carry at the rear, either as a part of the tail lamps or separately, two red reflectors meeting the requirements of this section, except that vehicles of the type mentioned in section 4513.07 of the Revised Code shall be equipped with reflectors as required by the regulations provided for in said section.

Every such reflector shall be of such size and characteristics and so maintained as to be visible at night from all distances within three hundred feet to fifty feet from such vehicle.

(B) Whoever violates this section is guilty of a minor misdemeanor.

**HISTORY: GC § 6307-79; 119 v 766(792), § 79; Bureau of Code Revision. Eff 10-1-53; 149 v S 123, § 1, eff. 1-1-04; 153 v H 1, § 101.01, eff. 10-16-09.**

The effective date is set by § 812.10 of 153 v H 1.
The effective date is set by section 4 of S.B. 123.
See provisions, § 5 of S.B. 123 (149 v —), following RC § 4501.01.

## § 4513.07 Safety lighting of commercial vehicles.

(A) The director of public safety shall prescribe and promulgate regulations relating to clearance lights, marker lights, reflectors, and stop lights on buses, trackless trolleys, trucks, commercial tractors, trailers, semitrailers, and pole trailers, when operated upon any highway, and such vehicles shall be equipped as required by such regulations, and such equipment shall be lighted at all times mentioned in section 4513.03 of the Revised Code, except that clearance lights and side marker lights need not be lighted on any such vehicle when it is operated within a municipal corporation where there is sufficient light to reveal any person or substantial object on the highway at a distance of five hundred feet.

Such equipment shall be in addition to all other lights specifically required by sections 4513.03 to 4513.16 of the Revised Code.

Vehicles operated under the jurisdiction of the public utilities commission are not subject to this section.

(B) Whoever violates this section is guilty of a minor misdemeanor.

**HISTORY: GC § 6307-80; 119 v 766(793), § 80; Bureau of Code Revision, 10-1-53; 129 v 1180 (Eff 11-2-59); 144 v S 98. Eff 11-12-92; 149 v S 123, § 1, eff. 1-1-04; 153 v H 1, § 101.01, eff. 10-16-09.**

The effective date is set by § 812.10 of 153 v H 1.
The effective date is set by section 4 of S.B. 123.
See provisions, § 5 of S.B. 123 (149 v —), following RC § 4501.01.

## § 4513.071 Stop lights.

(A) Every motor vehicle, trailer, semitrailer, and pole trailer when operated upon a highway shall be equipped with two or more stop lights, except that passenger cars manufactured or assembled prior to January 1, 1967, motorcycles, and motor-driven cycles shall be equipped with at least one stop light. Stop lights shall be mounted on the rear of the vehicle, actuated upon application of the service brake, and may be incorporated with other rear lights. Such stop lights when actuated shall emit a red light visible from a distance of five hundred feet to the rear, provided that in the case of a train of vehicles only the stop lights on the rear-most vehicle need be visible from the distance specified.

Such stop lights when actuated shall give a steady warning light to the rear of a vehicle or train of vehicles to indicate the intention of the operator to diminish the speed of or stop a vehicle or train of vehicles.

When stop lights are used as required by this section, they shall be constructed or installed so as to provide adequate and reliable illumination and shall conform to the appropriate rules and regulations established under section 4513.19 of the Revised Code.

Historical motor vehicles as defined in section 4503.181 of the Revised Code, not originally manufactured with stop lights, are not subject to this section.

(B) Whoever violates this section is guilty of a minor misdemeanor.

**HISTORY: 134 v S 227 (Eff 12-17-71); 148 v H 600. Eff 9-1-2000; 149 v S 123, § 1, eff. 1-1-04; 153 v H 1, § 101.01, eff. 10-16-09.**

The effective date is set by § 812.10 of 153 v H 1.
The effective date is set by section 4 of S.B. 123.
See provisions, § 5 of S.B. 123 (149 v —), following RC § 4501.01.

## § 4513.08 Obscured lights on vehicles.

Whenever motor and other vehicles are operated in combination during the time that lights are required, any light, except tail lights, which by reason of its location on a vehicle of the combination would be obscured by another vehicle of the combination need not be lighted, but this section does not affect the requirement that lighted clearance lights be displayed on the front of the foremost vehicle required to have clearance lights or that all lights required on the rear of the rearmost vehicle of any combination shall be lighted.

**HISTORY: GC § 6307-81; 119 v 766(793), § 81; Bureau of Code Revision. Eff 10-1-53.**

## § 4513.09 Red light or flag required.

(A) Whenever the load upon any vehicle extends to the rear four feet or more beyond the bed or body of such vehicle, there shall be displayed at the extreme rear end of the load, at the times specified in section 4513.03 of the Revised Code, a red light or lantern plainly visible from a distance of at least five hundred feet to the sides and rear. The red light or lantern required by this section is in addition to the red rear light required upon every vehicle. At any other time there shall be displayed at the extreme rear end of such load a red flag or cloth not less than sixteen inches square.

(B) Whoever violates this section is guilty of a minor misdemeanor.

**HISTORY: GC § 6307-82; 119 v 766(793), § 82; Bureau of Code Revision. Eff 10-1-53; 149 v S 123, § 1, eff. 1-1-04; 153 v H 1, § 101.01, eff. 10-16-09.**

The effective date is set by § 812.10 of 153 v H 1.
The effective date is set by section 4 of S.B. 123.
See provisions, § 5 of S.B. 123 (149 v —), following RC § 4501.01.

## § 4513.10 Lights on parked vehicles.

(A) Except in case of an emergency, whenever a vehicle is parked or stopped upon a roadway open to traffic or a shoulder adjacent thereto, whether attended or unattended, during the times mentioned in section 4513.03 of the Revised Code, such vehicle shall be equipped with one or more lights which shall exhibit a white or amber light on the roadway side visible from a distance of five hundred feet to the front of such vehicle, and a red light visible from a distance of five hundred feet to the rear. No lights need be displayed upon any such vehicle when it is stopped or parked within a municipal corporation where there is sufficient light to reveal any person or substantial object within a distance of five hundred feet upon such highway. Any lighted headlights upon a parked vehicle shall be depressed or dimmed.

(B) Whoever violates this section shall be punished as provided in section 4513.99 of the Revised Code.

**HISTORY: GC § 6307-83; 119 v 766(793), § 83; Bureau of Code Revision, 10-1-53; 128 v 1167. Eff 10-19-55; 149 v S 123, § 1, eff. 1-1-04.**

The effective date is set by section 4 of S.B. 123.
See provisions, § 5 of S.B. 123 (149 v —), following RC § 4501.01.

## § 4513.11 Lamps, reflectors and emblems for animal-drawn or slow-moving vehicles; speed identification symbol for farm machinery designed to operate at greater than 25 MPH.

(A) All vehicles other than bicycles, including animal-drawn vehicles and vehicles referred to in division (G) of section 4513.02 of the Revised Code, not specifically required to be equipped with lamps or other lighting devices by sections 4513.03 to 4513.10 of the Revised Code, shall, at the times specified in section 4513.03 of the Revised Code, be equipped with at least one lamp displaying a white light visible from a distance of not less than one thousand feet to the front of the vehicle, and also shall be equipped with two lamps displaying red light visible from a distance of not less than one thousand feet to the rear of the vehicle, or as an alternative, one lamp displaying a red light visible from a distance of not less than one thousand feet to the rear and two red reflectors visible from all distances of six hundred feet to one hundred feet to the rear when illuminated by the lawful lower beams of headlamps.

Lamps and reflectors required or authorized by this section shall meet standards adopted by the director of public safety.

(B) All boat trailers, farm machinery, and other machinery, including all road construction machinery, upon a street or highway, except when being used in actual construction and maintenance work in an area guarded by a flagperson, or where flares are used, or when operating or traveling within the limits of a construction area designated by the director of transportation, a city engineer, or the county engineer of the several counties, when such construction area is marked in accordance with requirements of the director and the manual of uniform traffic control devices, as set forth in section 4511.09 of the Revised Code, which is designed for operation at a speed of twenty-five miles per hour or less shall be operated at a speed not exceeding twenty-five miles per hour, and shall display a triangular slow-moving vehicle emblem (SMV). The emblem shall be mounted so as to be visible from a distance of not less than five hundred feet to the rear. The director of public safety shall adopt standards and specifications for the design and position of mounting the SMV emblem. The standards and specifications for SMV emblems referred to in this section shall correlate with and, so far as possible, conform with those approved by the American society of agricultural engineers.

A unit of farm machinery that is designed by its manufacturer to operate at a speed greater than twenty-five miles per hour may be operated on a street or highway at a speed greater than twenty-five miles per hour provided it is operated in accordance with this section.

As used in this division, "machinery" does not include any vehicle designed to be drawn by an animal.

(C) The use of the SMV emblem shall be restricted to animal-drawn vehicles, and to the slow-moving vehicles specified in division (B) of this section operating or traveling within the limits of the highway. Its use on slow-moving vehicles being transported upon other types of vehicles or on any other type of vehicle or stationary object on the highway is prohibited.

(D)(1) No person shall sell, lease, rent, or operate any boat trailer, farm machinery, or other machinery defined as a slow-moving vehicle in division (B) of this section, except those units designed to be completely mounted on a primary power unit, which is manufactured or assembled on or after April 1, 1966, unless the vehicle is equipped with a slow-moving vehicle emblem mounting device as specified in division (B) of this section.

(2) No person shall sell, lease, rent, or operate on a street or highway any unit of farm machinery that is designed by its manufacturer to operate at a speed greater than twenty-five miles per hour unless the unit displays a slow-moving vehicle emblem as specified in division (B) of this section and a speed identification symbol that meets the specifications contained in the American society of agricultural engineers standard ANSI/ASAE S584 JAN2005, agricultural equipment: speed identification symbol (SIS).

(E) Any boat trailer, farm machinery, or other machinery defined as a slow-moving vehicle in division (B) of this section, in addition to the use of the slow-moving vehicle emblem, and any unit of farm machinery that is designed by its manufacturer to operate at a speed greater than twenty-five miles per hour, in addition to the display of a speed identification symbol, may be equipped with a red flashing light that shall be visible from a distance of not less than one thousand feet to the rear at all times specified in section 4513.03 of the Revised Code. When a double-faced light is used, it shall display amber light to the front and red light to the rear.

In addition to the lights described in this division, farm machinery and motor vehicles escorting farm machinery may display a flashing, oscillating, or rotating amber light, as permitted by section 4513.17 of the Revised Code, and also may display simultaneously flashing turn signals or warning lights, as permitted by that section.

(F) Every animal-drawn vehicle upon a street or highway shall at all times be equipped in one of the following ways:

(1) With a slow-moving vehicle emblem complying with division (B) of this section;

(2) With alternate reflective material complying with rules adopted under this division;

(3) With both a slow-moving vehicle emblem and alternate reflective material as specified in this division.

The director of public safety, subject to Chapter 119. of the Revised Code, shall adopt rules establishing standards and specifications for the position of mounting of the alternate reflective material authorized by this division. The rules shall permit, as a minimum, the alternate reflective material to be black, gray, or silver in color. The alternate reflective material shall be mounted on the animal-drawn vehicle so as to be visible, at all times specified in section 4513.03 of the Revised Code, from a distance of not less than five hundred feet to the rear when illuminated by the lawful lower beams of headlamps.

(G) Every unit of farm machinery that is designed by its manufacturer to operate at a speed greater than twenty-five miles per hour shall display a slow-moving vehicle emblem and a speed identification symbol that meets the specifications contained in the American society of agricultural engineers standard ANSI/ASAE S584 JAN2005, agricultural equipment: speed identification symbol (SIS) when the unit is operated upon a street or highway, irrespective of the speed at which the unit is operated on the street or highway. The speed identification symbol shall indicate the maximum speed in miles per hour at which the unit of farm machinery is designed by its manufacturer to operate. The display of the speed identification symbol shall be in accordance with the standard prescribed in this division.

If an agricultural tractor that is designed by its manufacturer to operate at a speed greater than twenty-five miles per hour is being operated on a street or highway at a speed greater than twenty-five miles per hour and is towing, pulling, or otherwise drawing a unit of farm machinery, the unit of farm machinery shall display a slow-moving vehicle emblem and a speed identification symbol that is the same as the speed identification symbol that is displayed on the agricultural tractor.

(H) When an agricultural tractor that is designed by its manufacturer to operate at a speed greater than twenty-five miles per hour is being operated on a street or highway at a speed greater than twenty-five miles per hour, the operator shall possess some documentation published or provided by the manufacturer indicating the maximum speed in miles per hour at which the manufacturer designed the agricultural tractor to operate.

(I) Whoever violates this section is guilty of a minor misdemeanor.

(J) As used in this section, "boat trailer" means any vehicle designed and used exclusively to transport a boat between a place of storage and a marina, or in and around a marina, when drawn or towed on a street or highway for a distance of no more than ten miles and at a speed of twenty-five miles per hour or less.

**HISTORY: GC § 6307-84; 119 v 766(794), § 84; Bureau of Code Revision, 10-1-53; 128 v 591 (Eff 11-2-59); 131 v 1110 (Eff 4-1-66); 132 v H 172 (Eff 9-26-67); 135 v H 200 (Eff 9-28-73); 135 v H 472 (Eff 1-1-75); 135 v H 995 (Eff 1-1-75); 136 v H 1 (Eff 6-13-75); 142 v H 52 (Eff 10-1-87); 142 v H 708 (Eff 4-19-88); 144 v H 485 (Eff 10-7-92); 144 v S 98 (Eff 11-12-92); 146 v S 121 (Eff 11-19-96); 147 v H 282. Eff 11-12-97; 149 v S 123, § 1, eff. 1-1-04; 152 v H 9, § 1, eff. 10-18-07; 153 v H 1, § 101.01, eff. 10-16-09.**

The effective date is set by § 812.10 of 153 v H 1.
The effective date is set by section 4 of S.B. 123.
See provisions, § 5 of S.B. 123 (149 v —), following RC § 4501.01.

## § 4513.111 Lights and reflectors for multi-wheel agricultural tractors and farm machinery units.

(A)(1) Every multi-wheel agricultural tractor whose model year was 2001 or earlier, when being operated or traveling on a street or highway at the times specified in section 4513.03 of the Revised Code, at a minimum shall be equipped with and display reflectors and illuminated amber lamps so that the extreme left and right projections of the tractor are indicated by flashing lamps displaying amber light, visible to the front and the rear, by amber reflectors, all visible to the front, and by red reflectors, all visible to the rear.

(2) The lamps displaying amber light need not flash simultaneously and need not flash in conjunction with any directional signals of the tractor.

(3) The lamps and reflectors required by division (A)(1) of this section and their placement shall meet stan-

dards and specifications contained in rules adopted by the director of public safety in accordance with Chapter 119. of the Revised Code. The rules governing the amber lamps, amber reflectors, and red reflectors and their placement shall correlate with and, as far as possible, conform with paragraphs 4.1.4.1, 4.1.7.1, and 4.1.7.2 respectively of the American society of agricultural engineers standard ANSI/ASAE S279.10 OCT 98, lighting and marking of agricultural equipment on highways.

(B) Every unit of farm machinery whose model year was 2002 or later, when being operated or traveling on a street or highway at the times specified in section 4513.03 of the Revised Code, shall be equipped with and display markings and illuminated lamps that meet or exceed the lighting, illumination, and marking standards and specifications that are applicable to that type of farm machinery for the unit's model year specified in the American society of agricultural engineers standard ANSI/ASAE S279.10 OCT 98, lighting and marking of agricultural equipment on highways.

(C) The lights and reflectors required by division (A) of this section are in addition to the slow-moving vehicle emblem and lights required or permitted by section 4513.11 or 4513.17 of the Revised Code to be displayed on farm machinery being operated or traveling on a street or highway.

(D) No person shall operate any unit of farm machinery on a street or highway or cause any unit of farm machinery to travel on a street or highway in violation of division (A) or (B) of this section.

(E) Whoever violates this section is guilty of a minor misdemeanor.

**HISTORY: 148 v H 48, eff. 10-5-2000; 150 v H 87, §§ 1, 4, eff. 6-30-03; 150 v H 87, § 26, eff. 6-30-03; 149 v S 123, § 1, eff. 1-1-04; 153 v H 1, § 101.01, eff. 10-16-09.**

The effective date is set by § 812.10 of 153 v H 1.
The effective date is set by section 4 of S.B. 123.
See provisions, § 5 of S.B. 123 (149 v —), following RC § 4501.01.
The provisions of § 3 of HB 484 (148 v —) read as follows:
SECTION 3. Sections 1 and 2 of this act shall take effect on the earliest date permitted by law. However, the provisions of division (D) of section 4513.111 of the Revised Code, as enacted by this act, first apply one year after the effective date of this act.

## § 4513.12 Spotlight and auxiliary driving lights.

(A) Any motor vehicle may be equipped with not more than one spotlight and every lighted spotlight shall be so aimed and used upon approaching another vehicle that no part of the high-intensity portion of the beam will be directed to the left of the prolongation of the extreme left side of the vehicle, nor more than one hundred feet ahead of the vehicle.

Any motor vehicle may be equipped with not more than three auxiliary driving lights mounted on the front of the vehicle. The director of public safety shall prescribe specifications for auxiliary driving lights and regulations for their use, and any such lights which do not conform to said specifications and regulations shall not be used.

(B) Whoever violates this section is guilty of a minor misdemeanor.

**HISTORY: GC § 6307-85; 119 v 766(794), § 85; Bureau of Code Revision, 10-1-53; 128 v 1180 (Eff 11-2-59); 144 v S 98. Eff 11-12-92; 149 v S 123, § 1, eff. 1-1-04; 153 v H 1, § 101.01, eff. 10-16-09.**

The effective date is set by § 812.10 of 153 v H 1.
The effective date is set by section 4 of S.B. 123.
See provisions, § 5 of S.B. 123 (149 v —), following RC § 4501.01.

## § 4513.13 Cowl, fender, and back-up lights.

(A) Any motor vehicle may be equipped with side cowl or fender lights which shall emit a white or amber light without glare.

Any motor vehicle may be equipped with lights on each side thereof which shall emit a white or amber light without glare.

Any motor vehicle may be equipped with back-up lights, either separately or in combination with another light. No back-up lights shall be continuously lighted when the motor vehicle is in forward motion.

(B) Whoever violates this section is guilty of a minor misdemeanor.

**HISTORY: GC § 6307-86; 119 v 766(794), § 86; Bureau of Code Revision. Eff 10-1-53; 149 v S 123, § 1, eff. 1-1-04; 153 v H 1, § 101.01, eff. 10-16-09.**

The effective date is set by § 812.10 of 153 v H 1.
The effective date is set by section 4 of S.B. 123.
See provisions, § 5 of S.B. 123 (149 v —), following RC § 4501.01.

## § 4513.14 Two lights displayed.

(A) At all times mentioned in section 4513.03 of the Revised Code at least two lighted lights shall be displayed, one near each side of the front of every motor vehicle and trackless trolley, except when such vehicle or trackless trolley is parked subject to the regulations governing lights on parked vehicles and trackless trolleys.

The director of public safety shall prescribe and promulgate regulations relating to the design and use of such lights and such regulations shall be in accordance with currently recognized standards.

(B) Whoever violates this section is guilty of a minor misdemeanor.

**HISTORY: GC § 6307-87; 119 v 766(794), § 87; Bureau of Code Revision, 10-1-53; 128 v 1180 (Eff 11-2-59); 144 v S 98. Eff 11-12-92; 149 v S 123, § 1, eff. 1-1-04; 153 v H 1, § 101.01, eff. 10-16-09.**

The effective date is set by § 812.10 of 153 v H 1.
The effective date is set by section 4 of S.B. 123.
See provisions, § 5 of S.B. 123 (149 v —), following RC § 4501.01.

## § 4513.15 Headlight illumination requirements; protection of oncoming drivers; high beam indicator.

(A) Whenever a motor vehicle is being operated on a roadway or shoulder adjacent thereto during the times specified in section 4513.03 of the Revised Code, the driver shall use a distribution of light, or composite beam, directed high enough and of sufficient intensity to reveal persons, vehicles, and substantial objects at a safe distance in advance of the vehicle, subject to the following requirements;

(1) Whenever the driver of a vehicle approaches an oncoming vehicle, such driver shall use a distribution of light, or composite beam, so aimed that the glaring rays are not projected into the eyes of the oncoming driver.

(2) Every new motor vehicle registered in this state, which has multiple-beam road lighting equipment shall be equipped with a beam indicator, which shall be lighted whenever the uppermost distribution of light from the headlights is in use, and shall not otherwise be lighted. Said indicator shall be so designed and located that, when lighted, it will be readily visible without glare to the driver of the vehicle.

(B) Whoever violates this section is guilty of a minor misdemeanor.

**HISTORY: GC § 6307-88; 119 v 766(795), § 88; Bureau of Code Revision. Eff 10-1-53; 149 v S 123, § 1, eff. 1-1-04; 153 v H 1, § 101.01, eff. 10-16-09.**

The effective date is set by § 812.10 of 153 v H 1.

The effective date is set by section 4 of S.B. 123.

See provisions, § 5 of S.B. 123 (149 v —), following RC § 4501.01.

## § 4513.16 Lights of less intensity.

(A) Any motor vehicle may be operated under the conditions specified in section 4513.03 of the Revised Code when it is equipped with two lighted lights upon the front thereof capable of revealing persons and substantial objects seventy-five feet ahead, in lieu of lights required in section 4513.14 of the Revised Code, provided that such vehicle shall not be operated at a speed in excess of twenty miles per hour.

(B) Whoever violates this section is guilty of a minor misdemeanor.

**HISTORY: GC § 6307-89; 119 v 766(795), § 89; Bureau of Code Revision. Eff 10-1-53; 149 v S 123, § 1, eff. 1-1-04; 153 v H 1, § 101.01, eff. 10-16-09.**

The effective date is set by § 812.10 of 153 v H 1.

The effective date is set by section 4 of S.B. 123.

See provisions, § 5 of S.B. 123 (149 v —), following RC § 4501.01.

## § 4513.17 Number of lights permitted; direction of beam; flashing, oscillating or rotating lights.

(A) Whenever a motor vehicle equipped with headlights also is equipped with any auxiliary lights or spotlight or any other light on the front thereof projecting a beam of an intensity greater than three hundred candle power, not more than a total of five of any such lights on the front of a vehicle shall be lighted at any one time when the vehicle is upon a highway.

(B) Any lighted light or illuminating device upon a motor vehicle, other than headlights, spotlights, signal lights, or auxiliary driving lights, that projects a beam of light of an intensity greater than three hundred candle power, shall be so directed that no part of the beam will strike the level of the roadway on which the vehicle stands at a distance of more than seventy-five feet from the vehicle.

(C)(1) Flashing lights are prohibited on motor vehicles, except as a means for indicating a right or a left turn, or in the presence of a vehicular traffic hazard requiring unusual care in approaching, or overtaking or passing. This prohibition does not apply to emergency vehicles, road service vehicles servicing or towing a disabled vehicle, traffic line stripers, snow plows, rural mail delivery vehicles, vehicles as provided in section 4513.182 of the Revised Code, department of transportation maintenance vehicles, funeral hearses, funeral escort vehicles, and similar equipment operated by the department or local authorities, which shall be equipped with and display, when used on a street or highway for the special purpose necessitating such lights, a flashing, oscillating, or rotating amber light, but shall not display a flashing, oscillating, or rotating light of any other color, nor to vehicles or machinery permitted by section 4513.11 of the Revised Code to have a flashing red light.

(2) When used on a street or highway, farm machinery and vehicles escorting farm machinery may be equipped with and display a flashing, oscillating, or rotating amber light, and the prohibition contained in division (C)(1) of this section does not apply to such machinery or vehicles. Farm machinery also may display the lights described in section 4513.11 of the Revised Code.

(D) Except a person operating a public safety vehicle, as defined in division (E) of section 4511.01 of the Revised Code, or a school bus, no person shall operate, move, or park upon, or permit to stand within the right-of-way of any public street or highway any vehicle or equipment that is equipped with and displaying a flashing red or a flashing combination red and white light, or an oscillating or rotating red light, or a combination red and white oscillating or rotating light; and except a public law enforcement officer, or other person sworn to enforce the criminal and traffic laws of the state, operating a public safety vehicle when on duty, no person shall operate, move, or park upon, or permit to stand within the right-of-way of any street or highway any vehicle or equipment that is equipped with, or upon which is mounted, and displaying a flashing blue or a flashing combination blue and white light, or an oscillating or rotating blue light, or a combination blue and white oscillating or rotating light.

(E) This section does not prohibit the use of warning lights required by law or the simultaneous flashing of turn signals on disabled vehicles or on vehicles being operated in unfavorable atmospheric conditions in order to enhance their visibility. This section also does not prohibit the simultaneous flashing of turn signals or warning lights either on farm machinery or vehicles escorting farm machinery, when used on a street or highway.

(F) Whoever violates this section is guilty of a minor misdemeanor.

**HISTORY: GC § 6307-90; 119 v 766(795), § 90; Bureau of Code Revision, 10-1-53; 126 v 790 (Eff 9-14-55); 127 v 54 (Eff 8-27-57); 128 v 591 (Eff 11-2-59); 131 v 1112 (Eff 4-1-66); 131 v 1113 (Eff 10-13-65); 132 v H 878 (Eff 12-14-67); 135 v H 956 (Eff 7-26-74); 136 v H 272 (Eff 1-1-76); 146 v S 121 (Eff 11-19-96); 147 v H 282. Eff 11-12-97; 149 v S 123, § 1, eff. 1-1-04; 153 v H 1, § 101.01, eff. 10-16-09.**

The effective date is set by § 812.10 of 153 v H 1.

The effective date is set by section 4 of S.B. 123.

See provisions, § 5 of S.B. 123 (149 v —), following RC § 4501.01.

## § 4513.171 Coroner's vehicles responding to fatality.

(A) Notwithstanding any other provision of law, a motor vehicle operated by a coroner, deputy coroner, or coroner's investigator may be equipped with a flashing, oscillating, or rotating red or blue light and a siren, whistle, or bell capable of emitting sound audible under normal conditions from a distance of not less than five hundred feet. Such a vehicle may display the flashing, oscillating, or rotating red or blue light and may give the audible signal of the siren, exhaust whistle, or bell only when responding to a fatality or a fatal motor vehicle accident on a street or highway and only at those locations where the stoppage of traffic impedes the ability of the coroner, deputy coroner, or coroner's investigator to arrive at the site of the fatality.

This section does not relieve a coroner, deputy coroner, or coroner's investigator operating a motor vehicle from the duty to drive with due regard for the safety of all persons and property upon the highway.

(B) Whoever violates this section is guilty of a minor misdemeanor.

**HISTORY: 147 v H 282. Eff 11-12-97; 149 v S 123, § 1, eff. 1-1-04; 153 v H 1, § 101.01, eff. 10-16-09.**

The effective date is set by § 812.10 of 153 v H 1.

The effective date is set by section 4 of S.B. 123.

See provisions, § 5 of S.B. 123 (149 v —), following RC § 4501.01.

## § 4513.18 Standards for lights on snow removal equipment and oversize vehicles.

(A) The director of transportation shall adopt standards and specifications applicable to headlights, clearance lights, identification, and other lights, on snow removal equipment when operated on the highways, and on vehicles operating under special permits pursuant to section 4513.34 of the Revised Code, in lieu of the lights otherwise required on motor vehicles. Such standards and specifications may permit the use of flashing lights for purposes of identification on snow removal equipment, and oversize vehicles when in service upon the highways. The standards and specifications for lights referred to in this section shall correlate with and, so far as possible, conform with those approved by the American association of state highway officials.

It is unlawful to operate snow removal equipment on a highway unless the lights thereon comply with and are lighted when and as required by the standards and specifications adopted as provided in this section.

(B) Whoever violates this section is guilty of a minor misdemeanor.

**HISTORY: GC § 6307-90a; 124 v 514(525); Bureau of Code Revision, 10-1-53; 131 v 1113 (Eff 10-13-65); 132 v H 1 (Eff 2-21-67); 135 v H 200. Eff 9-28-73; 149 v S 123, § 1, eff. 1-1-04; 153 v H 1, § 101.01, eff. 10-16-09.**

The effective date is set by § 812.10 of 153 v H 1.

The effective date is set by section 4 of S.B. 123.

See provisions, § 5 of S.B. 123 (149 v —), following RC § 4501.01.

## § 4513.181 Standards and specifications for certain types of vehicles.

The director of public safety subject to the provisions of sections 119.01 to 119.13 of the Revised Code shall adopt standards and specifications applicable to rural mail delivery vehicles, state highway survey vehicles, and funeral escort vehicles. Such standards and specifications shall permit rural mail delivery vehicles, state highway survey vehicles, and funeral escort vehicles the use of flashing lights.

**HISTORY: 126 v 790 (Eff 9-14-55); 127 v 54 (Eff 8-27-57); 144 v S 98. Eff 11-12-92.**

## § 4513.182 Lights and sign on transportation for preschool children.

(A) No person shall operate any motor vehicle owned, leased, or hired by a nursery school, kindergarten, or day-care center, while transporting preschool children to or from such an institution unless the motor vehicle is equipped with and displaying two amber flashing lights mounted on a bar attached to the top of the vehicle, and a sign bearing the designation "caution—children," which shall be attached to the bar carrying the amber flashing lights in such a manner as to be legible to persons both in front of and behind the vehicle. The lights and sign shall meet standards and specifications adopted by the director of public safety. The director, subject to Chapter 119. of the Revised Code, shall adopt standards and specifications for the lights and sign, which shall include, but are not limited to, requirements for the color and size of lettering to be used on the sign, the type of material to be used for the sign, and the method of mounting the lights and sign so that they can be removed from a motor vehicle being used for purposes other than those specified in this section.

(B) No person shall operate a motor vehicle displaying the lights and sign required by this section for any purpose other than the transportation of preschool children as provided in this section.

(C) Whoever violates this section shall be punished as provided in section 4513.99 of the Revised Code.

**HISTORY: 136 v H 272 (Eff 1-1-76); 144 v S 98. Eff 11-12-92; 149 v S 123, § 1, eff. 1-1-04.**

The effective date is set by section 4 of S.B. 123.

See provisions, § 5 of S.B. 123 (149 v —), following RC § 4501.01.

## § 4513.19 Focus and aim of headlights.

(A) No person shall use any lights mentioned in sections 4513.03 to 4513.18 of the Revised Code upon any motor vehicle, trailer, or semitrailer unless said lights are equipped, mounted, and adjusted as to focus and aim in accordance with regulations which are prescribed by the director of public safety.

(B) Whoever violates this section is guilty of a minor misdemeanor.

**HISTORY: GC § 6307-91; 118 v 766(796), § 91; Bureau of Code Revision, 10-1-53; 128 v 1180 (Eff 11-2-59); 144 v S 98. Eff 11-12-92; 149 v S 123, § 1, eff. 1-1-04; 153 v H 1, § 101.01, eff. 10-16-09.**

The effective date is set by § 812.10 of 153 v H 1.

The effective date is set by section 4 of S.B. 123.

See provisions, § 5 of S.B. 123 (149 v —), following RC § 4501.01.

## § 4513.20 Brake equipment.

(A) The following requirements govern as to brake equipment on vehicles:

(1) Every trackless trolley and motor vehicle, other than a motorcycle, when operated upon a highway shall be equipped with brakes adequate to control the movement of and to stop and hold such trackless trolley or motor vehicle, including two separate means of applying the brakes, each of which means shall be effective to apply the brakes to at least two wheels. If these two separate means of applying the brakes are connected in any way, then on

such trackless trolleys or motor vehicles manufactured or assembled after January 1, 1942, they shall be so constructed that failure of any one part of the operating mechanism shall not leave the trackless trolley or motor vehicle without brakes on at least two wheels.

(2) Every motorcycle, when operated upon a highway shall be equipped with at least one adequate brake, which may be operated by hand or by foot.

(3) Every motorized bicycle shall be equipped with brakes meeting the rules adopted by the director of public safety under section 4511.521 of the Revised Code.

(4) When operated upon the highways of this state, the following vehicles shall be equipped with brakes adequate to control the movement of and to stop and to hold the vehicle, designed to be applied by the driver of the towing motor vehicle from its cab, and also designed and connected so that, in case of a breakaway of the towed vehicle, the brakes shall be automatically applied:

(a) Except as otherwise provided in this section, every trailer or semitrailer, except a pole trailer, with an empty weight of two thousand pounds or more, manufactured or assembled on or after January 1, 1942;

(b) Every manufactured home or travel trailer with an empty weight of two thousand pounds or more, manufactured or assembled on or after January 1, 2001.

(5) Every watercraft trailer with a gross weight or manufacturer's gross vehicle weight rating of three thousand pounds or more that is manufactured or assembled on or after January 1, 2008, shall have separate brakes equipped with hydraulic surge or electrically operated brakes on two wheels.

(6) In any combination of motor-drawn trailers or semitrailers equipped with brakes, means shall be provided for applying the rearmost brakes in approximate synchronism with the brakes on the towing vehicle, and developing the required braking effort on the rearmost wheels at the fastest rate; or means shall be provided for applying braking effort first on the rearmost brakes; or both of the above means, capable of being used alternatively, may be employed.

(7) Every vehicle and combination of vehicles, except motorcycles and motorized bicycles, and except trailers and semitrailers of a gross weight of less than two thousand pounds, and pole trailers, shall be equipped with parking brakes adequate to hold the vehicle on any grade on which it is operated, under all conditions of loading, on a surface free from snow, ice, or loose material. The parking brakes shall be capable of being applied in conformance with the foregoing requirements by the driver's muscular effort or by spring action or by equivalent means. Their operation may be assisted by the service brakes or other source of power provided that failure of the service brake actuation system or other power assisting mechanism will not prevent the parking brakes from being applied in conformance with the foregoing requirements. The parking brakes shall be so designed that when once applied they shall remain applied with the required effectiveness despite exhaustion of any source of energy or leakage of any kind.

(8) The same brake drums, brake shoes and lining assemblies, brake shoe anchors, and mechanical brake shoe actuation mechanism normally associated with the wheel brake assemblies may be used for both the service brakes and the parking brakes. If the means of applying the parking brakes and the service brakes are connected in any way, they shall be so constructed that failure of any one part shall not leave the vehicle without operative brakes.

(9) Every trackless trolley, motor vehicle, or combination of motor-drawn vehicles shall be capable at all times and under all conditions of loading of being stopped on a dry, smooth, level road free from loose material, upon application of the service or foot brake, within the following specified distances, or shall be capable of being decelerated at a sustained rate corresponding to these distances:

(a) Trackless trolleys, vehicles, or combinations of vehicles having brakes on all wheels shall come to a stop in thirty feet or less from a speed of twenty miles per hour.

(b) Vehicles or combinations of vehicles not having brakes on all wheels shall come to a stop in forty feet or less from a speed of twenty miles per hour.

(10) All brakes shall be maintained in good working order and shall be so adjusted as to operate as equally as practicable with respect to the wheels on opposite sides of the trackless trolley or vehicle.

(B) Whoever violates this section shall be punished as provided in section 4513.99 of the Revised Code.

**HISTORY: GC § 6307-92; 119 v 766(796), § 92; Bureau of Code Revision, 10-1-53; 130 v 1090 (Eff 7-25-63); 131 v 1114 (Eff 11-1-65); 132 v H 1 (Eff 2-21-67); 137 v S 100 (Eff 4-1-78); 138 v H 736 (Eff 10-16-80); 144 v S 98 (Eff 11-12-92); 148 v H 600. Eff 9-1-2000; 149 v S 123, § 1, eff. 1-1-04; 152 v H 67, § 101.01, eff. 6-30-07.**

The effective date is set by § 609.10 of 152 v H 67.

The effective date is set by section 4 of S.B. 123.

See provisions, § 5 of S.B. 123 (149 v —), following RC § 4501.01.

## § 4513.201 Brake fluid.

(A) No hydraulic brake fluid for use in motor vehicles shall be sold in this state if the brake fluid is below the minimum standard of specifications for heavy duty type brake fluid established by the society of automotive engineers and the standard of specifications established by 49 C.F.R. 571.116, as amended.

(B) All manufacturers, packers, or distributors of brake fluid selling such fluid in this state shall state on the containers that the brake fluid therein meets or exceeds the applicable minimum SAE standard of specifications and the standard of specifications established in 49 C.F.R. 571.116, as amended.

(C) Whoever violates this section shall be punished as provided in section 4513.99 of the Revised Code.

**HISTORY: 129 v 1574 (Eff 1-1-62); 144 v S 98 (Eff 11-12-92); 147 v S 60. Eff 10-21-97; 149 v S 123, § 1, eff. 1-1-04.**

The effective date is set by section 4 of S.B. 123.

See provisions, § 5 of S.B. 123 (149 v —), following RC § 4501.01.

## § 4513.202 Minimum standards for brakes and components.

(A) No brake lining, brake lining material, or brake lining assemblies for use as repair and replacement parts in motor vehicles shall be sold in this state if these items do not meet or exceed the minimum standard of specifications established by the society of automotive engineers and the standard of specifications established in 49 C.F.R. 571.105, as amended, and 49 C.F.R. 571.135, as amended.

(B) All manufacturers or distributors of brake lining, brake lining material, or brake lining assemblies selling these items for use as repair and replacement parts in motor vehicles shall state that the items meet or exceed the applicable minimum standard of specifications.

(C) Whoever violates this section shall be punished as provided in section 4513.99 of the Revised Code.

(D) As used in this section, "minimum standard of specifications" means a minimum standard for brake system or brake component performance that meets the need for motor vehicle safety and complies with the applicable SAE standards and recommended practices, and the federal motor vehicle safety standards that cover the same aspect of performance for any brake lining, brake lining material, or brake lining assemblies.

**HISTORY: 134 v H 150 (Eff 9-8-71); 144 v S 98 (Eff 11-12-92); 147 v S 60. Eff 10-21-97; 149 v S 123, § 1, eff. 1-1-04.**

The effective date is set by section 4 of S.B. 123.

See provisions, § 5 of S.B. 123 (149 v —), following RC § 4501.01.

## § 4513.21 Horns, sirens, and warning devices.

(A) Every motor vehicle or trackless trolley when operated upon a highway shall be equipped with a horn which is in good working order and capable of emitting sound audible, under normal conditions, from a distance of not less than two hundred feet.

No motor vehicle or trackless trolley shall be equipped with, nor shall any person use upon a vehicle, any siren, whistle, or bell. Any vehicle may be equipped with a theft alarm signal device which shall be so arranged that it cannot be used as an ordinary warning signal. Every emergency vehicle shall be equipped with a siren, whistle, or bell, capable of emitting sound audible under normal conditions from a distance of not less than five hundred feet and of a type approved by the director of public safety. Such equipment shall not be used except when such vehicle is operated in response to an emergency call or is in the immediate pursuit of an actual or suspected violator of the law, in which case the driver of the emergency vehicle shall sound such equipment when it is necessary to warn pedestrians and other drivers of the approach thereof.

(B) Whoever violates this section is guilty of a minor misdemeanor.

**HISTORY: GC § 6307-93; 119 v 766(797), § 93; Bureau of Code Revision, 10-1-53; 135 v H 200 (Eff 9-28-73); 144 v S 98. Eff 11-12-92; 149 v S 123, § 1, eff. 1-1-04; 153 v H 1, § 101.01, eff. 10-16-09.**

The effective date is set by § 812.10 of 153 v H 1.

The effective date is set by section 4 of S.B. 123.

See provisions, § 5 of S.B. 123 (149 v —), following RC § 4501.01.

## § 4513.22 Mufflers; excessive smoke or gas.

(A) Every motor vehicle and motorcycle with an internal combustion engine shall at all times be equipped with a muffler which is in good working order and in constant operation to prevent excessive or unusual noise, and no person shall use a muffler cutout, by-pass, or similar device upon a motor vehicle on a highway. Every motorcycle muffler shall be equipped with baffle plates.

No person shall own, operate, or have in the person's possession any motor vehicle or motorcycle equipped with a device for producing excessive smoke or gas, or so equipped as to permit oil or any other chemical to flow into or upon the exhaust pipe or muffler of such vehicle, or equipped in any other way to produce or emit smoke or dangerous or annoying gases from any portion of such vehicle, other than the ordinary gases emitted by the exhaust of an internal combustion engine under normal operation.

(B) Whoever violates this section is guilty of a minor misdemeanor.

**HISTORY: GC § 6307-94; 119 v 766(798), § 94; Bureau of Code Revision, 10-1-53; 132 v H 380 (Eff 1-1-68); 137 v H 115. Eff 7-10-78; 149 v S 123, § 1, eff. 1-1-04; 153 v H 1, § 101.01, eff. 10-16-09.**

The effective date is set by § 812.10 of 153 v H 1.

The effective date is set by section 4 of S.B. 123.

See provisions, § 5 of S.B. 123 (149 v —), following RC § 4501.01.

## § 4513.221 Regulation of vehicle and engine noise in unincorporated areas.

(A) The board of county commissioners of any county, and the board of township trustees of any township subject to section 505.17 of the Revised Code, may regulate passenger car and motorcycle noise on streets and highways under their jurisdiction. Such regulations shall include maximum permissible noise limits measured in decibels, subject to the requirements of this section.

(B) Regulations establishing maximum permissible noise limits measured in decibels shall prohibit the operation, within the speed limits specified herein, of a passenger car or motorcycle of a type subject to registration at any time or under any condition of load, acceleration, or deceleration in such manner as to exceed the following maximum noise limits, based on a distance of not less than fifty feet from the center of the line of travel:

(1) For passenger cars:

(a) When operated at a speed of thirty-five miles per hour or less, a maximum noise limit of seventy decibels;

(b) When operated at a speed of more than thirty-five miles per hour, a maximum noise limit of seventy-nine decibels.

(2) For motorcycles:

(a) When operated at a speed of thirty-five miles per hour or less, a maximum noise limit of eighty-two decibels;

(b) When operated at a speed of more than thirty-five miles per hour, a maximum noise limit of eighty-six decibels.

(C) Maximum noise limits established pursuant to division (B) of this section shall be measured on the "A" scale of a standard sound level meter meeting the applicable requirements for a type 2 sound level meter as defined in American national standards institute standard S1.4 — 1983, or the most recent revision thereof. Measurement practices shall be in substantial conformity with standards and recommended practice established by the society of automotive engineers, including SAE standard J 986 A NOV81, SAE standard J 366 MAR85, SAE standard J 331 A, and such other standards and practices as may be approved by the federal government.

(D) No regulation enacted under division (B) of this section shall be effective until signs giving notice of the regulation are posted upon or at the entrance to the highway or part thereof affected, as may be most appropriate.

(E) A board of county commissioners of any county may regulate noise from passenger cars, motorcycles, or other devices using internal combustion engines in the unincorporated area of the county, and a board of township trustees may regulate such noise in the unincorporated area of the township, in any of the following ways:

(1) By prohibiting operating or causing to be operated any motor vehicle, agricultural tractor, motorcycle, all-purpose vehicle, or snowmobile not equipped with a factory-installed muffler or equivalent muffler in good working order and in constant operation;

(2) By prohibiting the removing or rendering inoperative, or causing to be removed or rendered inoperative, other than for purposes of maintenance, repair, or replacement, of any muffler;

(3) By prohibiting the discharge into the open air of exhaust of any stationary or portable internal combustion engine except through a factory-installed muffler or equivalent muffler in good working order and in constant operation;

(4) By prohibiting racing the motor of any vehicle described in division (E)(1) of this section in such a manner that the exhaust system emits a loud, cracking, or chattering noise unusual to its normal operation.

(F) Whoever violates any maximum noise limit established as provided in division (B) of this section or any of the prohibitions authorized in division (E) of this section is guilty of a minor misdemeanor. Fines collected under this section by the county shall be paid into the county general fund, and such fines collected by the township shall be paid into the township general fund.

No regulation adopted under this section shall apply to commercial racetrack operations.

**HISTORY: 141 v H 131. Eff 6-26-86.**

## § 4513.23 Rear view mirrors.

(A) Every motor vehicle, motorcycle, and trackless trolley shall be equipped with a mirror so located as to reflect to the operator a view of the highway to the rear of such vehicle, motorcycle, or trackless trolley. Operators of vehicles, motorcycles, streetcars, and trackless trolleys shall have a clear and unobstructed view to the front and to both sides of their vehicles, motorcycles, streetcars, or trackless trolleys and shall have a clear view to the rear of their vehicles, motorcycles, streetcars, or trackless trolleys by mirror.

(B) Whoever violates this section is guilty of a minor misdemeanor.

**HISTORY: GC § 6307-95; 119 v 766(798), § 95; Bureau of Code Revision, 10-1-53; 132 v H 380. Eff 1-1-68; 149 v S 123, § 1, eff. 1-1-04; 153 v H 1, § 101.01, eff. 10-16-09.**

The effective date is set by § 812.10 of 153 v H 1.

The effective date is set by section 4 of S.B. 123.

See provisions, § 5 of S.B. 123 (149 v —), following RC § 4501.01.

## § 4513.24 Windshields and wipers.

(A) No person shall drive any motor vehicle on a street or highway in this state, other than a motorcycle or motorized bicycle, that is not equipped with a windshield.

(B)(1) No person shall drive any motor vehicle, other than a bus, with any sign, poster, or other nontransparent material upon the front windshield, sidewings, side, or rear windows of such vehicle other than a certificate or other paper required to be displayed by law, except that there may be in the lower left-hand or right-hand corner of the windshield a sign, poster, or decal not to exceed four inches in height by six inches in width. No sign, poster, or decal shall be displayed in the front windshield in such a manner as to conceal the vehicle identification number for the motor vehicle when, in accordance with federal law, that number is located inside the vehicle passenger compartment and so placed as to be readable through the vehicle glazing without moving any part of the vehicle.

(2) Division (B)(1) of this section does not apply to a person who is driving a passenger car with an electronic device, including an antenna, electronic tolling or other transponder, camera, directional navigation device, or other similar electronic device located in the front windshield if the device meets both of the following:

(a) It does not restrict the vehicle operator's sight lines to the road and highway signs and signals.

(b) It does not conceal the vehicle identification number.

(3) Division (B)(1) of this section does not apply to a person who is driving a commercial car with an electronic device, including an antenna, electronic tolling or other transponder, camera, directional navigation device, or other similar electronic device located in the front windshield if the device meets both of the following:

(a) It does not restrict the vehicle operator's sight lines to the road and highway signs and signals.

(b) It is mounted not more than six inches below the upper edge of the windshield and is outside the area swept by the vehicle's windshield wipers.

(C) The windshield on every motor vehicle, streetcar, and trackless trolley shall be equipped with a device for cleaning rain, snow, or other moisture from the windshield. The device shall be maintained in good working order and so constructed as to be controlled or operated by the operator of the vehicle, streetcar, or trackless trolley.

(D) Whoever violates this section is guilty of a minor misdemeanor.

**HISTORY: GC § 6307-96; 119 v 766(798), § 96; Bureau of Code Revision, 10-1-53; 143 v S 117 (Eff 10-26-89); 146 v H 353. Eff 9-17-96; 149 v S 123, § 1, eff. 1-1-04; 153 v H 1, § 101.01, eff. 10-16-09; 2011 HB 114, § 101.01, eff. June 29, 2011.**

Acts 2011, HB 114, § 806.10 provides: "The items of law contained in this act, and their applications, are severable. If any item of law contained in this act, or if any application of any item of law contained in this act, is held invalid, the invalidity does not affect other items of law contained in this act and their applications that can be given effect without the invalid item or application."

The effective date is set by § 812.10 of 153 v H 1.

The effective date is set by section 4 of S.B. 123.

See provisions, § 5 of S.B. 123 (149 v —), following RC § 4501.01.

## § 4513.241 Restrictions on use of tinted glass and other vision obscuring materials.

(A) The director of public safety, in accordance with Chapter 119. of the Revised Code, shall adopt rules governing the use of tinted glass, and the use of transparent, nontransparent, translucent, and reflectorized materials in or on motor vehicle windshields, side windows, sidewings, and rear windows that prevent a person of normal vision looking into the motor vehicle from seeing or identifying persons or objects inside the motor vehicle.

(B) The rules adopted under this section may provide for persons who meet either of the following qualifications:

(1) On November 11, 1994, or the effective date of any rule adopted under this section, own a motor vehicle that does not conform to the requirements of this section or of any rule adopted under this section;

(2) Establish residency in this state and are required to register a motor vehicle that does not conform to the requirements of this section or of any rule adopted under this section.

(C) No person shall operate, on any highway or other public or private property open to the public for vehicular travel or parking, lease, or rent any motor vehicle that is registered in this state unless the motor vehicle conforms to the requirements of this section and of any applicable rule adopted under this section.

(D) No person shall install in or on any motor vehicle, any glass or other material that fails to conform to the requirements of this section or of any rule adopted under this section.

(E) No used motor vehicle dealer or new motor vehicle dealer, as defined in section 4517.01 of the Revised Code, shall sell any motor vehicle that fails to conform to the requirements of this section or of any rule adopted under this section.

(F) No reflectorized materials shall be permitted upon or in any front windshield, side windows, sidewings, or rear window.

(G) This section does not apply to the manufacturer's tinting or glazing of motor vehicle windows or windshields that is otherwise in compliance with or permitted by federal motor vehicle safety standard number two hundred five.

(H) With regard to any side window behind a driver's seat or any rear window other than any window on an emergency door, this section does not apply to any school bus used to transport a child with disabilities pursuant to Chapter 3323. of the Revised Code, whom it is impossible or impractical to transport by regular school bus in the course of regular route transportation provided by a school district. As used in this division, "child with disabilities" has the same meaning as in section 3323.01 of the Revised Code.

(I) This section does not apply to any school bus that is to be sold and operated outside this state.

(J) Whoever violates division (C), (D), (E), or (F) of this section is guilty of a minor misdemeanor.

**HISTORY: 141 v H 291 (Eff 3-11-88); 144 v S 98 (Eff 11-12-92); 145 v S 234. Eff 11-8-94; 149 v S 123, § 1, eff. 1-1-04; 152 v H 119, § 101.01, eff. 9-29-07.**

The effective date is set by § 812.03 of 152 v H 119.
The effective date is set by section 4 of S.B. 123.
See provisions, § 5 of S.B. 123 (149 v —), following RC § 4501.01.

## § 4513.242 Display of security decal on side window or sidewing.

(A) Notwithstanding section 4513.24 and division (F) of section 4513.241 of the Revised Code or any rule adopted thereunder, a decal, whether reflectorized or not, may be displayed upon any side window or sidewing of a motor vehicle if all of the following are met:

(1) The decal is necessary for public or private security arrangements to which the motor vehicle periodically is subjected;

(2) The decal is no larger than is necessary to accomplish the security arrangements;

(3) The decal does not obscure the vision of the motor vehicle operator or prevent a person looking into the motor vehicle from seeing or identifying persons or objects inside the motor vehicle.

(B) Whoever violates this section is guilty of a minor misdemeanor.

**HISTORY: 147 v H 210. Eff 3-31-97; 149 v S 123, § 1, eff. 1-1-04; 153 v H 1, § 101.01, eff. 10-16-09.**

The effective date is set by § 812.10 of 153 v H 1.
The effective date is set by section 4 of S.B. 123.
See provisions, § 5 of S.B. 123 (149 v —), following RC § 4501.01.

## § 4513.25 Solid tire requirements.

(A) Every solid tire, as defined in section 4501.01 of the Revised Code, on a vehicle shall have rubber or other resilient material on its entire traction surface at least one inch thick above the edge of the flange of the entire periphery.

(B) Whoever violates this section shall be punished as provided in section 4513.99 of the Revised Code.

**HISTORY: GC § 6307-97; 119 v 766(798), § 97; Bureau of Code Revision. Eff 10-1-53; 149 v S 123, § 1, eff. 1-1-04.**

The effective date is set by section 4 of S.B. 123.
See provisions, § 5 of S.B. 123 (149 v —), following RC § 4501.01.

## § 4513.26 Safety glass required.

(A) No person shall sell any new motor vehicle nor shall any new motor vehicle be registered, and no person shall operate any motor vehicle, which is registered in this state and which has been manufactured or assembled on or after January 1, 1936, unless the motor vehicle is equipped with safety glass wherever glass is used in the windshields, doors, partitions, rear windows, and windows on each side immediately adjacent to the rear window.

"Safety glass" means any product composed of glass so manufactured, fabricated, or treated as substantially to prevent shattering and flying of the glass when it is struck or broken, or such other or similar product as may be approved by the registrar of motor vehicles.

Glass other than safety glass shall not be offered for sale, or sold for use in, or installed in any door, window, partition, or windshield that is required by this section to be equipped with safety glass.

(B) Whoever violates this section shall be punished as provided in section 4513.99 of the Revised Code.

**HISTORY: GC § 6307-98; 119 v 766(798), § 98; Bureau of Code Revision, 10-1-53; 146 v H 353. Eff 9-17-96; 149 v S 123, § 1, eff. 1-1-04.**

The effective date is set by section 4 of S.B. 123.
See provisions, § 5 of S.B. 123 (149 v —), following RC § 4501.01.

## § 4513.261 Directional signals.

(A)(1) No person shall operate any motor vehicle manufactured or assembled on or after January 1, 1954, unless the vehicle is equipped with electrical or mechanical directional signals.

(2) No person shall operate any motorcycle or motor-driven cycle manufactured or assembled on or after January 1, 1968, unless the vehicle is equipped with electrical or mechanical directional signals.

(B) "Directional signals" means an electrical or mechanical signal device capable of clearly indicating an intention to turn either to the right or to the left and which shall be visible from both the front and rear.

(C) All mechanical signal devices shall be self-illuminating devices when in use at the times mentioned in section 4513.03 of the Revised Code.

(D) Whoever violates this section is guilty of a minor misdemeanor.

**HISTORY: 125 v 456 (Eff 10-19-53); 148 v H 600. Eff 9-1-2000; 149 v S 123, § 1, eff. 1-1-04.**

The effective date is set by section 4 of S.B. 123.

See provisions, § 5 of S.B. 123 (149 v —), following RC § 4501.01.

## § 4513.262 Installation and sale of seat safety belts required; definition.

(A) As used in this section and in section 4513.263 of the Revised Code, the component parts of a "seat safety belt" include a belt, anchor attachment assembly, and a buckle or closing device.

(B) No person shall sell, lease, rent, or operate any passenger car, as defined in division (E) of section 4501.01 of the Revised Code, that is registered or to be registered in this state and that is manufactured or assembled on or after January 1, 1962, unless the passenger car is equipped with sufficient anchorage units at the attachment points for attaching at least two sets of seat safety belts to its front seat. Such anchorage units at the attachment points shall be of such construction, design, and strength to support a loop load pull of not less than four thousand pounds for each belt.

(C) No person shall sell, lease, or rent any passenger car, as defined in division (E) of section 4501.01 of the Revised Code, that is registered or to be registered in this state and that is manufactured or assembled on or after January 1, 1966, unless the passenger car has installed in its front seat at least two seat safety belt assemblies.

(D) After January 1, 1966, neither any seat safety belt for use in a motor vehicle nor any component part of any such seat safety belt shall be sold in this state unless the seat safety belt or the component part satisfies the minimum standard of specifications established by the society of automotive engineers for automotive seat belts and unless the seat safety belt or component part is labeled so as to indicate that it meets those minimum standard specifications.

(E) Each sale, lease, or rental in violation of this section constitutes a separate offense.

(F) Whoever violates this section is guilty of a minor misdemeanor.

**HISTORY: 129 v 1567 (Eff 9-23-61); 131 v 1115 (Eff 8-9-65); 141 v S 54. Eff 5-6-86; 149 v S 123, § 1, eff. 1-1-04.**

The effective date is set by section 4 of S.B. 123.

See provisions, § 5 of S.B. 123 (149 v —), following RC § 4501.01.

## § 4513.263 Occupant restraining devices.

(A) As used in this section and in section 4513.99 of the Revised Code:

(1) "Automobile" means any commercial tractor, passenger car, commercial car, or truck that is required to be factory-equipped with an occupant restraining device for the operator or any passenger by regulations adopted by the United States secretary of transportation pursuant to the "National Traffic and Motor Vehicle Safety Act of 1966," 80 Stat. 719, 15 U.S.C.A. 1392.

(2) "Occupant restraining device" means a seat safety belt, shoulder belt, harness, or other safety device for restraining a person who is an operator of or passenger in an automobile and that satisfies the minimum federal vehicle safety standards established by the United States department of transportation.

(3) "Passenger" means any person in an automobile, other than its operator, who is occupying a seating position for which an occupant restraining device is provided.

(4) "Commercial tractor," "passenger car," and "commercial car" have the same meanings as in section 4501.01 of the Revised Code.

(5) "Vehicle" and "motor vehicle," as used in the definitions of the terms set forth in division (A)(4) of this section, have the same meanings as in section 4511.01 of the Revised Code.

(6) "Tort action" means a civil action for damages for injury, death, or loss to person or property. "Tort action" includes a product liability claim, as defined in section 2307.71 of the Revised Code, and an asbestos claim, as defined in section 2307.91 of the Revised Code, but does not include a civil action for damages for breach of contract or another agreement between persons.

(B) No person shall do any of the following:

(1) Operate an automobile on any street or highway unless that person is wearing all of the available elements of a properly adjusted occupant restraining device, or operate a school bus that has an occupant restraining device installed for use in its operator's seat unless that person is wearing all of the available elements of the device, as properly adjusted;

(2) Operate an automobile on any street or highway unless each passenger in the automobile who is subject to the requirement set forth in division (B)(3) of this section is wearing all of the available elements of a properly adjusted occupant restraining device;

(3) Occupy, as a passenger, a seating position on the front seat of an automobile being operated on any street or highway unless that person is wearing all of the available elements of a properly adjusted occupant restraining device;

(4) Operate a taxicab on any street or highway unless all factory-equipped occupant restraining devices in the taxicab are maintained in usable form.

(C) Division (B)(3) of this section does not apply to a person who is required by section 4511.81 of the Revised Code to be secured in a child restraint device. Division (B)(1) of this section does not apply to a person who is an employee of the United States postal service or of a newspaper home delivery service, during any period in which the person is engaged in the operation of an automobile to deliver mail or newspapers to addressees. Divisions (B)(1) and (3) of this section do not apply to a person who has an affidavit signed by a physician licensed to practice in this state under Chapter 4731. of the Revised Code or a chiropractor licensed to practice in this state under Chapter 4734. of the Revised Code that states that the person has a physical impairment that makes use of an occupant restraining device impossible or impractical.

(D) Notwithstanding any provision of law to the contrary, no law enforcement officer shall cause an operator of an automobile being operated on any street or highway to stop the automobile for the sole purpose of determining whether a violation of division (B) of this section has been or is being committed or for the sole purpose of issuing a ticket, citation, or summons for a violation of that nature or causing the arrest of or commencing a prosecution of a person for a violation of that nature, and no law enforcement officer shall view the interior or visually inspect any automobile being operated on any street or highway for the sole purpose of determining whether a violation of that nature has been or is being committed.

(E) All fines collected for violations of division (B) of this section, or for violations of any ordinance or resolution of a political subdivision that is substantively comparable to that division, shall be forwarded to the treasurer of state for deposit as follows:

(1) Eight per cent shall be deposited into the elementary school program fund, which is hereby created in the state treasury, and shall be used by the department of public safety to establish and administer elementary school programs that encourage seat safety belt use.

(2) Two per cent shall be deposited into the occupational licensing and regulatory fund created by section 4743.05 of the Revised Code.

(3) Thirty-six per cent, plus sixty cents of each fee collected under sections 4501.34, 4503.26, 4506.08, and 4509.05, plus on and after October 1, 2009, sixty cents of each fee collected under sections 4505.14 and 4519.63 of the Revised Code as specified in those sections, shall be deposited into the trauma and emergency medical services fund, which is hereby created in the state treasury, and shall be used by the department of public safety for the administration of the division of emergency medical services and the state board of emergency medical services, except that the director of budget and management may transfer excess money from the trauma and emergency medical services fund to the state highway safety fund if the director of public safety determines that the amount of money in the trauma and emergency medical services fund exceeds the amount required to cover such costs incurred by the emergency medical services agency and requests the director of budget and management to make the transfer.

(4) Fifty-four per cent shall be deposited into the trauma and emergency medical services grants fund, which is hereby created in the state treasury, and shall be used by the state board of emergency medical services to make grants, in accordance with section 4765.07 of the Revised Code and rules the board adopts under section 4765.11 of the Revised Code.

(F)(1) Subject to division (F)(2) of this section, the failure of a person to wear all of the available elements of a properly adjusted occupant restraining device in violation of division (B)(1) or (3) of this section or the failure of a person to ensure that each minor who is a passenger of an automobile being operated by that person is wearing all of the available elements of a properly adjusted occupant restraining device in violation of division (B)(2) of this section shall not be considered or used by the trier of fact in a tort action as evidence of negligence or contributory negligence. But, the trier of fact may determine based on evidence admitted consistent with the Ohio Rules of Evidence that the failure contributed to the harm alleged in the tort action and may diminish a recovery of compensatory damages that represents noneconomic loss, as defined in section 2307.011 of the Revised Code, in a tort action that could have been recovered but for the plaintiff's failure to wear all of the available elements of a properly adjusted occupant restraining device. Evidence of that failure shall not be used as a basis for a criminal prosecution of the person other than a prosecution for a violation of this section; and shall not be admissible as evidence in a criminal action involving the person other than a prosecution for a violation of this section.

(2) If, at the time of an accident involving a passenger car equipped with occupant restraining devices, any occupant of the passenger car who sustained injury or death was not wearing an available occupant restraining device, was not wearing all of the available elements of such a device, or was not wearing such a device as properly adjusted, then, consistent with the Rules of Evidence, the fact that the occupant was not wearing the available occupant restraining device, was not wearing all of the available elements of such a device, or was not wearing such a device as properly adjusted is admissible in evidence in relation to any claim for relief in a tort action to the extent that the claim for relief satisfies all of the following:

(a) It seeks to recover damages for injury or death to the occupant.

(b) The defendant in question is the manufacturer, designer, distributor, or seller of the passenger car.

(c) The claim for relief against the defendant in question is that the injury or death sustained by the occupant was enhanced or aggravated by some design defect in the passenger car or that the passenger car was not crashworthy.

(G)(1) Whoever violates division (B)(1) of this section shall be fined thirty dollars.

(2) Whoever violates division (B)(3) of this section shall be fined twenty dollars.

(3) Except as otherwise provided in this division, whoever violates division (B)(4) of this section is guilty of a minor misdemeanor. If the offender previously has been convicted of or pleaded guilty to a violation of division (B)(4) of this section, whoever violates division (B) (4) of this section is guilty of a misdemeanor of the third degree.

**HISTORY: 141 v S 54 (Eff 5-6-86); 141 v S 262 (Eff 3-20-87); 141 v H 428 (Eff 12-23-86); 142 v H 1 (Eff 1-5-88); 144 v H 118 (Eff 6-1-92); 144 v S 105 (Eff 6-23-92); 144 v S 98 (Eff 11-12-92); 145 v H 154 (Eff 6-30-93); 146 v H 350 (Eff 1-27-97); 147 v H 215 (Eff 6-30-97); 148 v H 138 (Eff 11-3-2000); 149 v S 108, § 2.01. Eff 7-6-2001; 149 v S 123, § 1, eff. 1-1-04; 150 v H 85, §§ 1, 3, eff. 3-9-04; 150 v S 80, § 1, eff. 4-7-05; 152 v H 119, § 101.01, eff. 6-30-07; 152 v H 320, § 1, eff. 10-7-09; 153 v H 2, § 101.01, eff. 7-1-09; 2011 HB 114, § 101.01, eff. June 29, 2011.**

Acts 2011, HB 114, § 806.10 provides: "The items of law contained in this act, and their applications, are severable. If any item of law contained in this act, or if any application of any item of law contained in this act, is held invalid, the invalidity does not affect other items of law contained in this act and their applications that can be given effect without the invalid item or application."

The effective date is set by § 812.10 of 153 v H 2.

The provisions of § 815.10 of 153 v H 2 read as follows:

SECTION 815.10. The amendment by this act to section 4513.263 of the Revised Code does not affect the taking effect of the amendment previously made to that section by Am. Sub. H.B. 320 of the 127th General Assembly. The amendment of Am. Sub. H.B. 320 to that section takes effect as specified in that act.

The effective date is set by § 4 of 152 v H 320.

The effective date is set by § 815.03 of 152 v H 119.

The effective date is set by section 4 of S.B. 123.

See provisions, § 5 of S.B. 123 (149 v —), following RC § 4501.01.

**Analogous to former RC § 4513.26.3 (129 v 1567), repealed, 131 v 1436, § 2, eff 8-9-65.**

**Publisher's Note:**

Section 5 of H 85 purported to amend R.C. § 4513.263 effective January 1, 2004.

Section 2.02(A) of SB 108 (149 v —) repeals the existing version and section 3(A)(1) amends this SB 108 version to remove HB 350 matter or to revive matter removed by HB 350.

## § 4513.27 Requirements for extra signal equipment.

(A) No person shall operate any motor truck, trackless trolley, bus, or commercial tractor upon any highway outside the corporate limits of municipalities at any time from sunset to sunrise unless there is carried in such vehicle and trackless trolley, except as provided in division (B) of this section, the following equipment which shall be of the types approved by the director of transportation:

(1) At least three flares or three red reflectors or three red electric lanterns, each of which is capable of being seen and distinguished at a distance of five hundred feet under normal atmospheric conditions at night time;

(2) At least three red-burning fusees, unless red reflectors or red electric lanterns are carried;

(3) At least two red cloth flags, not less than twelve inches square, with standards to support them;

(4) The type of red reflectors shall comply with such standards and specifications in effect on September 16, 1963 or later established by the interstate commerce commission and must be certified as meeting such standards by underwriter's laboratories.

(B) No person shall operate at the time and under the conditions stated in this section any motor vehicle used in transporting flammable liquids in bulk, or in transporting compressed flammable gases, unless there is carried in such vehicle three red electric lanterns or three red reflectors meeting the requirements stated in division (A) of this section. There shall not be carried in any such vehicle any flare, fusee, or signal produced by a flame.

(C) This section does not apply to any person who operates any motor vehicle in a work area designated by protection equipment devices that are displayed and used in accordance with the manual adopted by the department of transportation under section 4511.09 of the Revised Code.

(D) Whoever violates this section shall be punished as provided in section 4513.99 of the Revised Code.

**HISTORY: GC § 6307-99; 119 v 766(799), § 99; 124 v 514(526); Bureau of Code Revision, 10-1-53; 130 v 1092 (Eff 9-16-63); 130 v PtII, H 5 (Eff 12-16-64); 135 v H 200 (Eff 9-28-73); 143 v H 258 (Eff 11-2-89); 148 v H 484. Eff 10-5-2000; 149 v S 123, § 1, eff. 1-1-04.**

The effective date is set by section 4 of S.B. 123.

See provisions, § 5 of S.B. 123 (149 v —), following RC § 4501.01.

## § 4513.28 Display of warning devices on disabled vehicles.

(A) Whenever any motor truck, trackless trolley, bus, commercial tractor, trailer, semi-trailer, or pole trailer is disabled upon the traveled portion of any highway or the shoulder thereof outside of any municipality, or upon any freeway, expressway, thruway and connecting, entering or exiting ramps within a municipality, at any time when lighted lamps are required on vehicles and trackless trolleys, the operator of such vehicle or trackless trolley shall display the following warning devices upon the highway during the time the vehicle or trackless trolley is so disabled on the highway except as provided in division (B) of this section:

(1) A lighted fusee shall be immediately placed on the roadway at the traffic side of such vehicle or trackless trolley, unless red electric lanterns or red reflectors are displayed.

(2) Within the burning period of the fusee and as promptly as possible, three lighted flares or pot torches, or three red reflectors or three red electric lanterns shall be placed on the roadway as follows:

(a) One at a distance of forty paces or approximately one hundred feet in advance of the vehicle;

(b) One at a distance of forty paces or approximately one hundred feet to the rear of the vehicle or trackless trolley except as provided in this section, each in the center of the lane of traffic occupied by the disabled vehicle or trackless trolley;

(c) One at the traffic side of the vehicle or trackless trolley.

(B) Whenever any vehicle used in transporting flammable liquids in bulk, or in transporting compressed flammable gases, is disabled upon a highway at any time or place mentioned in division (A) of this section, the driver of such vehicle shall display upon the roadway the following warning devices:

(1) One red electric lantern or one red reflector shall be immediately placed on the roadway at the traffic side of the vehicle;

(2) Two other red electric lanterns or two other red reflectors shall be placed to the front and rear of the vehicle in the same manner prescribed for flares in division (A) of this section.

(C) When a vehicle of a type specified in division (B) of this section is disabled, the use of flares, fusees, or any signal produced by flame as warning signals is prohibited.

(D) Whenever any vehicle or trackless trolley of a type referred to in this section is disabled upon the traveled portion of a highway or the shoulder thereof, outside of any municipality, or upon any freeway, expressway, thruway and connecting, entering or exiting ramps within a municipality, at any time when the display of fusees, flares, red reflectors, or electric lanterns is not required, the operator of such vehicle or trackless trolley shall display two red flags upon the roadway in the lane of traffic occupied by the disabled vehicle or trackless trolley, one at a distance of forty paces or approximately one hundred feet in advance of the vehicle or trackless trolley, and one at a distance of forty paces or approximately one hundred feet to the rear of the vehicle or trackless trolley, except as provided in this section.

(E) The flares, fusees, lanterns, red reflectors, and flags to be displayed as required in this section shall conform with the requirements of section 4513.27 of the Revised Code applicable thereto.

(F) In the event the vehicle or trackless trolley is disabled near a curve, crest of a hill, or other obstruction of view, the flare, flag, reflector, or lantern in that direction shall be placed as to afford ample warning to other users of the highway, but in no case shall it be placed less than forty paces or approximately one hundred feet nor more than one hundred twenty paces or approximately three hundred feet from the disabled vehicle or trackless trolley.

(G) This section does not apply to the operator of any vehicle in a work area designated by protection equipment devices that are displayed and used in accordance with the manual adopted by the department of transportation under section 4511.09 of the Revised Code.

(H) Whoever violates this section is guilty of a minor misdemeanor.

**HISTORY: GC § 6307-100; 119 v 766(800), § 100; Bureau of Code Revision, 10-1-53; 130 v 1092 (Eff 9-16-63); 143 v H 258. Eff 11-2-89; 149 v S 123, § 1, eff. 1-1-04; 153 v H 1, § 101.01, eff. 10-16-09.**

The effective date is set by § 812.10 of 153 v H 1.

The effective date is set by section 4 of S.B. 123.

See provisions, § 5 of S.B. 123 (149 v —), following RC § 4501.01.

## § 4513.29 Requirements for vehicles transporting explosives.

(A) Any person operating any vehicle transporting explosives upon a highway shall at all times comply with the following requirements:

(1) Said vehicle shall be marked or placarded on each side and on the rear with the word "explosives" in letters not less than eight inches high, or there shall be displayed on the rear of such vehicle a red flag not less than twenty-four inches square marked with the word "danger" in white letters six inches high, or shall be marked or placarded in accordance with section 177.823 of the United States department of transportation regulations.

(2) Said vehicle shall be equipped with not less than two fire extinguishers, filled and ready for immediate use, and placed at convenient points on such vehicle.

(3) The director of transportation may promulgate such regulations governing the transportation of explosives and other dangerous articles by vehicles upon the highway as are reasonably necessary to enforce sections 4513.01 to 4513.37 of the Revised Code.

(B) Whoever violates this section shall be punished as provided in section 4513.99 of the Revised Code.

**HISTORY: GC § 6307-101; 119 v 766(801), § 101; Bureau of Code Revision, 10-1-53; 133 v H 460 (Eff 10-22-69); 135 v H 200. Eff 9-28-73; 149 v S 123, § 1, eff. 1-1-04.**

The effective date is set by section 4 of S.B. 123.

See provisions, § 5 of S.B. 123 (149 v —), following RC § 4501.01.

# [LOADS]

## § 4513.30 Limitation of load extension on left side of vehicle.

(A) No passenger-type vehicle shall be operated on a highway with any load carried on such vehicle which extends more than six inches beyond the line of the fenders on the vehicle's left side.

(B) Whoever violates this section shall be punished as provided in section 4513.99 of the Revised Code.

**HISTORY: GC § 6307-102; 119 v 766(801), § 102; Bureau of Code Revision. Eff 10-1-53; 149 v S 123, § 1, eff. 1-1-04.**

The effective date is set by section 4 of S.B. 123.

See provisions, § 5 of S.B. 123 (149 v —), following RC § 4501.01.

## § 4513.31 All loads to be properly secured.

(A) No vehicle shall be driven or moved on any highway unless the vehicle is so constructed, loaded, or covered as to prevent any of its load from dropping, sifting, leaking, or otherwise escaping therefrom, except that sand or other substance may be dropped for the purpose of securing traction, or water or other substance may be sprinkled on a roadway in cleaning or maintaining the roadway.

(B) Except for a farm vehicle used to transport agricultural produce or agricultural production materials or a rubbish vehicle in the process of acquiring its load, no vehicle loaded with garbage, swill, cans, bottles, waste paper, ashes, refuse, trash, rubbish, waste, wire, paper, cartons, boxes, glass, solid waste, or any other material of an unsanitary nature that is susceptible to blowing or bouncing from a moving vehicle shall be driven or moved on any highway unless the load is covered with a sufficient cover to prevent the load or any part of the load from spilling onto the highway.

(C) Whoever violates this section shall be punished as provided in section 4513.99 of the Revised Code.

**HISTORY: GC § 6307-103; 119 v 766(801), § 103; Bureau of Code Revision, 10-1-53; 142 v H 514. Eff 2-11-88; 149 v S 123, § 1, eff. 1-1-04.**

The effective date is set by section 4 of S.B. 123.

See provisions, § 5 of S.B. 123 (149 v —), following RC § 4501.01.

## § 4513.32 Towing requirements.

(A) When one vehicle is towing another vehicle, the drawbar or other connection shall be of sufficient strength to pull all the weight towed thereby, and the drawbar or other connection shall not exceed fifteen feet from one vehicle to the other, except the connection between any two vehicles transporting poles, pipe, machinery, or other objects of structural nature which cannot readily be dismembered.

When one vehicle is towing another and the connection consists only of a chain, rope, or cable, there shall be displayed upon such connection a white flag or cloth not less than twelve inches square.

In addition to such drawbar or other connection, each trailer and each semitrailer which is not connected to a commercial tractor by means of a fifth wheel shall be coupled with stay chains or cables to the vehicle by which it is being drawn. The chains or cables shall be of sufficient size and strength to prevent the towed vehicle's parting from the drawing vehicle in case the drawbar or other connection should break or become disengaged. In case of a loaded pole trailer, the connecting pole to the drawing vehicle shall be coupled to the drawing vehicle with stay chains or cables of sufficient size and strength to prevent the towed vehicle's parting from the drawing vehicle.

Every trailer or semitrailer, except pole and cable trailers and pole and cable dollies operated by a public utility as defined in section 5727.01 of the Revised Code, shall be equipped with a coupling device, which shall be so designed and constructed that the trailer will follow substantially in the path of the vehicle drawing it, without whipping or swerving from side to side. Vehicles used to transport agricultural produce or agricultural production materials between a local place of storage and supply and the farm, when drawn or towed on a street or highway at a speed of twenty-five miles per hour or less, and vehicles designed and used exclusively to transport a boat between a place of storage and a marina, or in and around a marina, when drawn or towed on a street or highway for a distance of no more than ten miles and at a speed of twenty-five miles per hour or less, shall have a drawbar or other connection, including the hitch mounted on the towing vehicle, which shall be of sufficient strength to pull all the weight towed thereby. Only one such vehicle used to transport agricultural produce or agricultural production materials as provided in this section may be towed or drawn at one time, except as follows:

(1) An agricultural tractor may tow or draw more than one such vehicle;

(2) A pickup truck or straight truck designed by the manufacturer to carry a load of not less than one-half ton and not more than two tons may tow or draw not more than two such vehicles that are being used to transport agricultural produce from the farm to a local place of storage. No vehicle being so towed by such a pickup truck or straight truck shall be considered to be a motor vehicle.

(B) Whoever violates this section shall be punished as provided in section 4513.99 of the Revised Code.

**HISTORY: GC § 6307-104; 119 v 766(801), § 104; Bureau of Code Revision, 10-1-53; 132 v H 684 (Eff 11-24-67); 132 v H 1002 (Eff 6-3-68); 138 v H 1 (Eff 5-16-79); 144 v H 485 (Eff 10-7-92); 147 v H 425. Eff 7-29-98; 149 v S 123, § 1, eff. 1-1-04.**

The effective date is set by section 4 of S.B. 123.

See provisions, § 5 of S.B. 123 (149 v —), following RC § 4501.01.

## § 4513.33 Weighing vehicle; scales; alteration of weight limits by local authorities.

Any police officer having reason to believe that the weight of a vehicle and its load is unlawful may require the driver of said vehicle to stop and submit to a weighing of it by means of a compact, self-contained, portable, sealed scale specially adapted to determine the wheel loads of vehicles on highways; a sealed scale permanently installed in a fixed location, having a load-receiving element specially adapted to determining the wheel loads of highway vehicles; a sealed scale, permanently installed in a fixed location, having a load-receiving element specially adapted to determining the combined load of all wheels on a single axle or on successive axles of a highway vehicle, or a sealed scale adapted to weighing highway vehicles, loaded or unloaded. The driver of such vehicle shall, if necessary, be directed to proceed to the nearest available of such sealed scales to accomplish the weighing, provided such scales are within three miles of the point where such vehicle is stopped. Any vehicle stopped in accordance with this section may be held by the police officer for a reasonable time only to accomplish the weighing as prescribed by this section. All scales used in determining the lawful weight of a vehicle and its load shall be annually compared by a municipal, county, or state sealer with the state standards or standards approved by the state and such scales shall not be sealed if they do not conform to the state standards or standards approved by the state.

At each end of a permanently installed scale, there shall be a straight approach in the same plane as the platform, of sufficient length and width to insure the level positioning of vehicles during weight determinations.

During determination of weight by compact, self-contained, portable, sealed scales, specially adapted to determining the wheel loads of vehicles on highways, they shall always be used on terrain of sufficient length and width to accommodate the entire vehicle being weighed. Such terrain shall be level, or if not level, it shall be of such elevation that the difference in elevation between the wheels on any one axle does not exceed two inches and the difference in elevation between axles being weighed does not exceed one-fourth inch per foot of the distance between said axles.

In all determination of all weights, except gross weight, by compact, self-contained, portable sealed scales, specially adapted to determining the wheel loads of vehicles on highways, all successive axles, twelve feet or less apart, shall be weighed simultaneously by placing one such scale under the outside wheel of each such axle. In determinations of gross weight by the use of compact, self-contained, portable sealed scales, specially adapted to determining the wheel loads of vehicles on highways, all axles shall be weighed simultaneously by placing one such scale under the outside wheel of each axle.

Whenever such officer upon weighing a vehicle and load determines that the weight is unlawful, he may require the driver to stop the vehicle in a suitable place and remain standing until such portion of the load is removed as is necessary to reduce the weight of such vehicle to the limit permitted under sections 5577.01 to 5577.14 of the Revised Code.

Whenever local authorities determine upon the basis of an engineering and traffic investigation that the weight limits permitted under sections 5577.01 to 5577.14 of the Revised Code, or the weight limits permitted when compact, self-contained, portable, sealed scales, specially adapted to determining the wheel loads of vehicles on highways, are used on any part of a state route under their jurisdiction is greater than is reasonable under the conditions found to exist at such location, the local authorities may, by resolution, request the director of transportation to determine and declare reasonable weight limits. Upon receipt of such request the director may determine and declare reasonable weight limits at such location, and if the director alters the weight limits set by sections 5577.01 to 5577.14 and this section of the Revised Code, then such altered weight limits shall become effective only when appropriate signs giving notice thereof are erected at such location by local authorities.

The director may withdraw his approval of any altered weight limit whenever, in his opinion, any altered weight limit becomes unreasonable, and upon such withdrawal the altered weight limit shall become ineffective, and the signs relating thereto shall be immediately removed by local authorities. Alteration of weight limits on state routes by local authorities is not effective until alteration has been approved by the director.

This section does not derogate or limit the power and authority conferred upon the director or boards of county commissioners by section 5577.07 of the Revised Code.

**HISTORY: GC § 6307-105; 119 v 766(802), § 105; Bureau of Code Revision, 10-1-53; 130 v 1094 (Eff 8-19-63); 131 v 1116 (Eff 11-1-65); 132 v H 1 (Eff 2-21-67); 135 v H 200 (Eff 9-28-73); 136 v H 624. Eff 11-26-75.**

## § 4513.34 Issuance of special permits.

(A) The director of transportation with respect to all highways that are a part of the state highway system and local authorities with respect to highways under their jurisdiction, upon application in writing and for good cause shown, may issue a special permit in writing authorizing the applicant to operate or move a vehicle or combination of vehicles of a size or weight of vehicle or load exceeding the maximum specified in sections 5577.01 to 5577.09 of the Revised Code, or otherwise not in conformity with sections 4513.01 to 4513.37 of the Revised Code, upon any highway under the jurisdiction of the authority granting the permit.

For purposes of this section, the director may designate certain state highways or portions of state highways as special economic development highways. If an application submitted to the director under this section involves travel of a nonconforming vehicle or combination of vehicles upon a special economic development highway, the director, in determining whether good cause has been shown that issuance of a permit is justified, shall consider the effect the travel of the vehicle or combination of vehicles will have on the economic development in the area in which the designated highway or portion of highway is located.

(B) Notwithstanding sections 715.22 and 723.01 of the Revised Code, the holder of a special permit issued by the director under this section may move the vehicle or combination of vehicles described in the special permit on any highway that is a part of the state highway system when the movement is partly within and partly without the corporate limits of a municipal corporation. No local authority shall require any other permit or license or charge any license fee or other charge against the holder of a permit for the movement of a vehicle or combination of vehicles on any highway that is a part of the state highway system. The director shall not require the holder of a permit issued by a local authority to obtain a special permit for the movement of vehicles or combination of vehicles on highways within the jurisdiction of the local authority. Permits may be issued for any period of time not to exceed one year, as the director in the director's discretion or a local authority in its discretion determines advisable, or for the duration of any public construction project.

(C) The application for a permit shall be in the form that the director or local authority prescribes. The director or local authority may prescribe a permit fee to be imposed and collected when any permit described in this section is issued. The permit fee may be in an amount sufficient to reimburse the director or local authority for the administrative costs incurred in issuing the permit, and also to cover the cost of the normal and expected damage caused to the roadway or a street or highway structure as the result of the operation of the nonconforming vehicle or combination of vehicles. The director, in accordance with Chapter 119. of the Revised Code, shall establish a schedule of fees for permits issued by the director under this section.

For the purposes of this section and of rules adopted by the director under this section, milk transported in bulk by vehicle is deemed a nondivisible load.

(D) The director or local authority may issue or withhold a permit. If a permit is to be issued, the director or local authority may limit or prescribe conditions of operation for the vehicle and may require the posting of a bond or other security conditioned upon the sufficiency of the permit fee to compensate for damage caused to the roadway or a street or highway structure. In addition, a local authority, as a condition of issuance of an overweight permit, may require the applicant to develop and enter into a mutual agreement with the local authority to compensate for or to repair excess damage caused to the roadway by travel under the permit.

For a permit that will allow travel of a nonconforming vehicle or combination of vehicles on a special economic development highway, the director, as a condition of issuance, may require the applicant to agree to make periodic payments to the department to compensate for damage caused to the roadway by travel under the permit.

(E) Every permit shall be carried in the vehicle or combination of vehicles to which it refers and shall be open to inspection by any police officer or authorized agent of any authority granting the permit. No person shall violate any of the terms of a permit.

(F) The director may debar an applicant from applying for a special permit under this section upon a finding based on a reasonable belief that the applicant has done any of the following:

(1) Abused the process by repeatedly submitting false information or false travel plans or by using another company or individual's name, insurance, or escrow account without proper authorization;

(2) Failed to comply with or substantially perform under a previously issued special permit according to its terms, conditions, and specifications within specified time limits;

(3) Failed to cooperate in the application process for the special permit or in any other procedures that are related to the issuance of the special permit by refusing to provide information or documents required in a permit or by failing to respond to and correct matters related to the special permit;

(4) Accumulated repeated justified complaints regarding performance under a special permit that was previously issued to the applicant or previously failed to obtain a special permit when such a permit was required;

(5) Attempted to influence a public employee to breach ethical conduct standards;

(6) Been convicted of a criminal offense related to the application for, or performance under, a special permit, including, but not limited to, bribery, falsification, fraud or destruction of records, receiving stolen property, and any other offense that directly reflects on the applicant's integrity or commercial driver's license;

(7) Accumulated repeated convictions under a state or federal safety law governing commercial motor vehicles or a rule or regulation adopted under such a law;

(8) Accumulated repeated convictions under a law, rule, or regulation governing the movement of traffic over the public streets and highways;

(9) Failed to pay any fees associated with any permitted operation or move;

(10) Deliberately or willfully submitted false or misleading information in connection with the application for, or performance under, a special permit issued under this section.

If the applicant is a partnership, association, or corporation, the director also may debar from consideration for special permits any partner of the partnership, or the officers, directors, or employees of the association or corporation being debarred.

The director may adopt rules in accordance with Chapter 119. of the Revised Code governing the debarment of an applicant.

(G) When the director reasonably believes that grounds for debarment exist, the director shall send the person that is subject to debarment a notice of the proposed debarment. A notice of proposed debarment shall indicate the grounds for the debarment of the person and the procedure for requesting a hearing. The notice and hearing shall be in accordance with Chapter 119. of the Revised Code. If the person does not respond with a request for a hearing in the manner specified in that chapter, the director shall issue the debarment decision without a hearing and shall notify the person of the decision by certified mail, return receipt requested. The debarment period may be of any length determined by the director, and the director may modify or rescind the debarment at any time. During the period of debarment, the director shall not issue, or consider issuing, a special permit to any partnership, association, or corporation that is affiliated with a debarred person. After the debarment period expires, the person, and any partnership, association, or corporation affiliated with the person, may reapply for a special permit.

(H) Whoever violates this section shall be punished as provided in section 4513.99 of the Revised Code.

**HISTORY: GC § 6307-106; 119 v 766(802), § 106; Bureau of Code Revision, 10-1-53; 131 v 1118 (Eff 9-28-65); 135 v H 200 (Eff 9-28-73); 142 v H 712 (Eff 9-9-88); 144 v S 223 (Eff 9-30-92); 149 v H 73. Eff 6-29-2001; 149 v S 123, § 1, eff. 1-1-04; 151 v H 68, § 101.01, eff. 6-29-05.**

The provisions of § 555.07 of 152 v H 67, as amended by § 3 of 152 v H 30, read as follows:

SECTION 3. That Sections 555.07 and 555.19 of Am. Sub. H.B. 67 of the 127th General Assembly be amended to read as follows:

SECTION 555.07. From July 1, 2008, through June 30, 2009, three or fewer steel coils are deemed to be a nondivisible load for purposes of special permits issued under section 4513.34 of the Revised Code, provided that the maximum overall gross vehicle weight of the vehicle and load shall not exceed 120,000 pounds.

° ° °

The effective date is set by § 612.03 of 151 v H 68.

The provisions of § 503.03 of 151 v H 68 read as follows:

SECTION 503.03. From July 1, 2005, through June 30, 2007, three or fewer steel coils are deemed to be a nondivisible load for purposes of special permits issued under section 4513.34 of the Revised Code, provided that the maximum overall gross vehicle weight of the vehicle and load shall not exceed 92,000 pounds.

The effective date is set by section 4 of S.B. 123.

See provisions, § 5 of S.B. 123 (149 v —), following RC § 4501.01.

The provisions of § 13 of HB 73 (149 v —) read as follows:

SECTION 13. From July 1, 2001, through June 30, 2003, three or fewer steel coils are deemed to be a nondivisible load for purposes of special permits issued under section 4513.34 of the Revised Code, provided that the maximum overall gross vehicle weight of the vehicle and load shall not exceed ninety-two thousand pounds.

**Publisher's Note:**

The amendment of RC § 4513.34 by 153 v H 2 was disapproved by the Governor.

## § 4513.35 Disposition of moneys collected.

(A) All fines collected under sections 4511.01 to 4511.78, 4511.99, and 4513.01 to 4513.37 of the Revised Code shall be paid into the county treasury and, with the exception of that portion distributed under section 307.515 [307.51.5] of the Revised Code, shall be placed to the credit of the fund for the maintenance and repair of the highways within that county, except that:

(1) All fines for violations of division (B) of section 4513.263 [4513.26.3] shall be delivered to the treasurer of state as provided in division (E) of section 4513.263 [4513.26.3] of the Revised Code.

(2) All fines collected from, or moneys arising from bonds forfeited by, persons apprehended or arrested by state highway patrolmen shall be distributed as provided in section 5503.04 of the Revised Code.

(3)(a) Subject to division (E) of section 4513.263 [4513.26.3] of the Revised Code and except as otherwise provided in division (A)(3)(b) of this section, one-half of all fines collected from, and one-half of all moneys arising from bonds forfeited by, persons apprehended or arrested by a township constable or other township police officer shall be paid to the township treasury to be placed to the credit of the general fund.

(b) All fines collected from, and all moneys arising from bonds forfeited by, persons apprehended or arrested by a township constable or other township police officer pursuant to division (B)(2) of section 4513.39 of the Revised Code for a violation of section 4511.21 of the Revised Code or any other law, ordinance, or regulation pertaining to speed that occurred on a highway included as part of the interstate system, as defined in section 5516.01 of the Revised Code, shall be paid into the county treasury and be credited as provided in the first paragraph of this section.

(B) Notwithstanding any other provision of this section or of any other section of the Revised Code:

(1) All fines collected from, and all moneys arising from bonds forfeited by, persons arrested under division (E)(1) or (2) of section 2935.03 of the Revised Code are deemed to be collected, and to arise, from arrests made within the jurisdiction in which the arresting officer is appointed, elected, or employed, for violations of one of the sections or chapters of the Revised Code listed in division (E)(1) of that section and shall be distributed accordingly.

(2) All fines collected from, and all moneys arising from bonds forfeited by, persons arrested under division (E)(3) of section 2935.03 of the Revised Code are deemed to be collected, and to arise, from arrests made within the jurisdiction in which the arresting officer is appointed, elected, or employed, for violations of municipal ordinances that are substantially equivalent to one of the sections or one of the provisions of one of the chapters of the Revised Code listed in division (E)(1) of that section and for violations of one of the sections or one of the provisions of one of the chapters of the Revised Code listed in division (E)(1) of that section, and shall be distributed accordingly.

**HISTORY: GC § 6307-108; 119 v 766(803), § 108; Bureau of Code Revision, 10-1-53; 126 v 773 (Eff 10-5-55); 132 v H 24 (Eff 8-15-67); 141 v S 54 (Eff 5-6-86); 143 v H 171 (Eff 5-31-90); 143 v H 669 (Eff 1-10-91); 145 v H 687. Eff 10-12-94; 152 v H 119, § 101.01, eff. 9-29-07; 152 v H 420, § 101.01, eff. 1-1-10.**

The provisions of § 503 of 152 v H 420 read in part as follows:

SECTION 503. The amendment, enactment, or repeal by this act of the following sections takes effect on the dates specified below:

° ° °

The amendment of sections 733.40, 1901.024, 1901.31, 1907.20, 2949.111, 3375.50 (307.515), and 4513.35 of the Revised Code, on January 1, 2010;

° ° °

The effective date is set by § 812.03 of 152 v H 119.

### [MISCELLANEOUS PROVISIONS]

## § 4513.36 Prohibition against resisting or interfering with official.

(A) No person shall resist, hinder, obstruct, or abuse any sheriff, constable, or other official while that official is attempting to arrest offenders under any provision of sections 4511.01 to 4511.78, 4511.99, and 4513.01 to 4513.37 of the Revised Code. No person shall interfere with any person charged under any provision of any of those sections with the enforcement of the law relative to public highways.

(B) Whoever violates this section is guilty of a minor misdemeanor.

**HISTORY: GC § 6307-109; 119 v 766(803), § 109; Bureau of Code Revision. Eff 10-1-53; 149 v S 123, § 1, eff. 1-1-04.**

The effective date is set by section 4 of S.B. 123.

See provisions, § 5 of S.B. 123 (149 v —), following RC § 4501.01.

## § 4513.361 Furnishing false information to avoid citation.

(A) No person shall knowingly present, display, or orally communicate a false name, social security number, or date of birth to a law enforcement officer who is in the process of issuing to the person a traffic ticket or complaint.

(B) Whoever violates this section is guilty of a misdemeanor of the first degree.

**HISTORY: 144 v H 96. Eff 6-18-91; 149 v S 123, § 1, eff. 1-1-04.**

The effective date is set by section 4 of S.B. 123.

See provisions, § 5 of S.B. 123 (149 v —), following RC § 4501.01.

## § 4513.37 Record of violations.

Every county court judge, mayor, and clerk of a court of record shall keep a full record of every case in which a person is charged with any violation of sections 4511.01 to 4511.78, section 4511.99, and sections 4513.01 to 4513.37 of the Revised Code, or of any other law or ordinance regulating the operation of vehicles, streetcars, and trackless trolleys on highways.

Within ten days after the conviction or forfeiture of bail of a person upon a charge of violating any of such sections or other law or ordinance regulating the operation of vehicles, streetcars, and trackless trolleys on highways, said judge, mayor, or clerk shall prepare and immediately forward to the department of public safety an abstract of the court record covering the case in which said person was convicted for forfeited bail, which abstract must be certified by the person required to prepare the same to be true and correct.

Said abstract shall be made upon a form approved and furnished by the department and shall include the name and address of the party charged, the number of his driver's or commercial driver's license, the registration number of the vehicle involved, the nature of the offense, the date of hearing, the plea, the judgment, or whether bail forfeited, and the amount of the fine or forfeiture.

Every court of record shall also forward a like report to the department upon the conviction of any person of manslaughter or other felony in the commission of which a vehicle was used.

The failure, refusal, or neglect of such officer to comply with this section constitutes misconduct in office and is ground for removal therefrom.

The department shall keep all abstracts received under this section at its main office.

**HISTORY: GC § 6307-110; 119 v 766(804), § 110; Bureau of Code Revision, 10-1-53; 125 v 127 (140); 127 v 1039(1107) (Eff 1-1-58); 143 v H 381 (Eff 7-1-89); 144 v S 98. Eff 11-12-92.**

## § 4513.38 Collector's or historical motor vehicle test exemptions.

No person shall be prohibited from owning or operating a licensed collector's vehicle or historical motor vehicle that is equipped with a feature of design, type of material, or article of equipment that was not in violation of any motor vehicle equipment law of this state or of its political subdivisions in effect during the calendar year the vehicle was manufactured, and no licensed collector's vehicle or historical motor vehicle shall be prohibited from displaying or using any such feature of design, type of material, or article of equipment.

No person shall be prohibited from owning or operating a licensed collector's vehicle or historical motor vehicle for failing to comply with an equipment provision contained in Chapter 4513. of the Revised Code or in any state rule that was enacted or adopted in a year subsequent to that in which the vehicle was manufactured, and no licensed collector's vehicle or historical motor vehicle shall be required to comply with an equipment provision enacted into Chapter 4513. of the Revised Code or adopted by state rule subsequent to the calendar year in which it was manufactured. No political subdivision shall require an owner of a licensed collector's vehicle or historical motor vehicle to comply with equipment provisions contained in laws or rules that were enacted or adopted subsequent to the calendar year in which the vehicle was manufactured, and no political subdivision shall prohibit the operation of a licensed collector's vehicle or historical motor vehicle for failure to comply with any such equipment laws or rules.

**HISTORY: 136 v S 52. Eff 9-15-75.**

**Not analogous to former RC § 4513.38 (119 v 766 (803)); (GC § 6307-107; Bureau of Code Revision, 10-1-53), repealed 125 v 903(1064), eff 10-1-53.**

## § 4513.39 Power to make arrests on highways.

(A) The state highway patrol and sheriffs or their deputies shall exercise, to the exclusion of all other peace officers except within municipal corporations and except as specified in division (B) of this section and division (E) of section 2935.03 of the Revised Code, the power to make arrests for violations on all state highways, of sections 4503.11, 4503.21, 4511.14 to 4511.16, 4511.20 to 4511.23, 4511.26 to 4511.40, 4511.42 to 4511.48, 4511.58, 4511.59, 4511.62 to 4511.71, 4513.03 to 4513.13, 4513.15 to 4513.22, 4513.24 to 4513.34, 4549.01, 4549.08 to 4549.12, and 4549.62 of the Revised Code.

(B) A member of the police force of a township police district created under section 505.48 of the Revised Code or of a joint police district created under section 505.482 of the Revised Code, and a township constable appointed pursuant to section 509.01 of the Revised Code, who has received a certificate from the Ohio peace officer training commission under section 109.75 of the Revised Code, shall exercise the power to make arrests for violations of those sections listed in division (A) of this section, other than sections 4513.33 and 4513.34 of the Revised Code, as follows:

(1) If the population of the township that created the township or joint police district served by the member's

police force or the township that is served by the township constable is fifty thousand or less, the member or constable shall exercise that power on those portions of all state highways, except those highways included as part of the interstate system, as defined in section 5516.01 of the Revised Code, that are located within the township or joint police district, in the case of a member of a township or joint police district police force, or within the unincorporated territory of the township, in the case of a township constable;

(2) If the population of the township that created the township or joint police district served by the member's police force or the township that is served by the township constable is greater than fifty thousand, the member or constable shall exercise that power on those portions of all state highways and highways included as part of the interstate highway system, as defined in section 5516.01 of the Revised Code, that are located within the township or joint police district, in the case of a member of a township or joint police district police force, or within the unincorporated territory of the township, in the case of a township constable.

**HISTORY: GC § 6297; 119 v 810; Bureau of Code Revision, 10-1-53; 138 v H 207 (Eff 3-13-81); 139 v H 738 (Eff 6-25-82); 140 v H 632 (Eff 3-28-85); 143 v H 171 (Eff 5-31-90); 143 v H 669 (Eff 1-10-91); 145 v H 687. Eff 10-12-94; 150 v H 163, § 1, eff. 9-23-04; 2011 HB 153, § 101.01, eff. Sept. 29, 2011.**

## § 4513.40 Warning sign before safety device at street crossing.

When a safety device has been installed in the traveled portion of a street at a railroad grade crossing for the protection of the traveling public, the municipal corporation shall place a warning sign not less than two hundred feet from the crossing. The driver of any vehicle shall place his vehicle under control at the location of said warning signs so as to be able to bring said vehicle to a complete stop at said safety device. Colliding with such safety device at the crossing is prima-facie evidence that the driver is a reckless driver.

**HISTORY: GC § 591-1; 117 v 655; Bureau of Code Revision, 10-1-53; 125 v 903(1026). Eff 10-1-53.**

## § 4513.41 Collector's agricultural tractor or tractor engine test exemptions.

(A) No owner of a licensed collector's vehicle, a historical motor vehicle, or a collector's vehicle that is an agricultural tractor or traction engine shall be required to comply with an emission, noise control, or fuel usage provision contained in a law or rule of this state or its political subdivisions that was enacted or adopted subsequent to the calendar year in which the vehicle was manufactured.

(B) No person shall be prohibited from operating a licensed collector's vehicle, a historical motor vehicle, or a collector's vehicle that is an agricultural tractor or traction engine for failing to comply with an emission, noise control, or fuel usage law or rule of this state or its political subdivisions that was enacted or adopted subsequent to the calendar year in which his vehicle was manufactured.

(C) Except as provided in section 4505.061 [4505.06.1] of the Revised Code, no person shall be required to submit his collector's vehicle to a physical inspection prior to or in connection with an issuance of title to, or the sale or transfer of ownership of such vehicle, except that a police officer may inspect it to determine ownership.

In accordance with section 1.51 of the Revised Code, this section shall, without exception, prevail over any special or local provision of the Revised Code that requires owners or operators of collector's vehicles to comply with standards of emission, noise, fuel usage, or physical condition in connection with an issuance of title to, or the sale or transfer of ownership of such vehicle or part thereof.

**HISTORY: 136 v S 52. Eff 9-15-75.**

**Not analogous to former RC § 4513.41 (131 v 1119), repealed 134 v H 24, § 2, eff 10-6-71.**

### [BUS SAFETY INSPECTIONS]

## § 4513.50 Definitions.

As used in sections 4513.50 to 4513.53 of the Revised Code:

(A)(1) "Bus" means any vehicle used for the transportation of passengers that meets at least one of the following:

(a) Was originally designed by the manufacturer to transport more than fifteen passengers, including the driver;

(b) Either the gross vehicle weight rating or the gross vehicle weight exceeds ten thousand pounds.

(2) "Bus" does not include a church bus as defined in section 4503.07 of the Revised Code or a school bus unless the church bus or school bus is used in the transportation of passengers for hire by a motor transportation company or a common carrier by motor vehicle or by a private motor carrier or contract carrier by motor vehicle.

(3) "Bus" also does not include any of the following:

(a) Any vehicle operated exclusively on a rail or rails;

(b) A trolley bus operated by electric power derived from a fixed overhead wire furnishing local passenger transportation similar to street-railway service;

(c) Vehicles owned or leased by government agencies or political subdivisions.

(B)(1) "Motor transportation company" and "common carrier by motor vehicle" have the same meanings as in section 4921.02 of the Revised Code.

(2) "Private motor carrier" and "contract carrier by motor vehicle" have the same meanings as in section 4923.02 of the Revised Code.

**HISTORY: 148 v H 600. Eff 9-1-2000.**

The effective date is set by section 8 of HB 600.

## § 4513.51 Safety inspection decal required to operate bus; inspection report required for registration.

(A) Except as provided in division (B) of this section, on and after July 1, 2001, no person shall operate a bus, nor shall any person being the owner of a bus or having supervisory responsibility for a bus permit the operation of any bus, unless the bus displays a valid, current safety inspection decal issued by the state highway patrol under section 4513.52 of the Revised Code.

(B) For the purpose of complying with the requirements of this section and section 4513.52 of the Revised Code, the owner or other operator of a bus may drive the bus directly to an inspection site conducted by the state highway patrol and directly back to the person's place of business without a valid registration and without displaying a safety inspection decal, provided that no passengers may occupy the bus during such operation.

(C) The registrar of motor vehicles shall not accept an application for registration of a bus unless the bus owner presents a valid safety inspection report for the applicable registration year.

(D) Whoever violates division (A) of this section is guilty of a misdemeanor of the first degree.

**HISTORY: 148 v H 600. Eff 9-1-2000; 149 v S 123, § 1, eff. 1-1-04.**

The effective date is set by section 4 of S.B. 123.

See provisions, § 5 of S.B. 123 (149 v —), following RC § 4501.01.

**Not analogous to former RC § 4513.51 (130 v 1095), repealed 146 v H 23, § 1, eff 2-25-97.**

The effective date is set by section 8 of HB 600.

## § 4513.52 Bus safety inspections.

(A) The department of public safety, with the advice of the public utilities commission, shall adopt and enforce rules relating to the inspection of buses to determine whether a bus is safe and lawful, including whether its equipment is in proper adjustment or repair.

(B) The rules shall determine the safety features, items of equipment, and other safety-related conditions subject to inspection. The rules may authorize the state highway patrol to operate safety inspection sites, or to enter in or upon the property of any bus operator to conduct the safety inspections, or both. The rules also shall establish a fee, not to exceed two hundred dollars, for each bus inspected.

(C) The state highway patrol shall conduct the bus safety inspections at least on an annual basis. An inspection conducted under this section is valid for twelve months unless, prior to that time, the bus fails a subsequent inspection or ownership of the bus is transferred.

(D) The state highway patrol shall collect a fee for each bus inspected.

(E) Upon determining that a bus is in safe operating condition, that its equipment is in proper adjustment and repair, and that it is otherwise lawful, the inspecting officer shall do both of the following:

(1) Affix an official safety inspection decal to the outside surface of each side of the bus;

(2) Issue the owner or operator of the bus a safety inspection report, to be presented to the registrar or a deputy registrar upon application for registration of the bus.

**HISTORY: 148 v H 600. Eff 9-1-2000; 150 v H 87, § 1, eff. 6-30-03.**

**Not analogous to former RC § 4513.52 (130 v 1102), repealed 146 v H 23, § 1, eff 2-25-97.**

The effective date is set by section 26 of H.B. 87.

## § 4513.53 Bus inspection staff; decal.

(A) The superintendent of the state highway patrol, with approval of the director of public safety, may appoint and maintain necessary staff to carry out the inspection of buses.

(B) The superintendent of the state highway patrol shall adopt a distinctive annual safety inspection decal bearing the date of inspection. The state highway patrol may remove any decal from a bus that fails any inspection.

(C) Fees collected by the state highway patrol shall be paid into the state treasury to the credit of the general revenue fund. Annually by the first day of June, the director of public safety shall determine the amount of fees collected under section 4513.52 of the Revised Code and shall certify the amount to the director of budget and management for reimbursement. The director of budget and management then may transfer cash up to the amount certified from the general revenue fund to the state highway safety fund.

**HISTORY: 148 v H 600. Eff 6-1-2000; 150 v H 87, § 1, eff. 6-30-03.**

**Not analogous to former RC § 4513.53 (130 v 1102; 144 v S 98), repealed 146 v H 23, § 1, eff 2-25-97.**

The effective date is set by section 26 of H.B. 87.

### [ABANDONED VEHICLES]

## § 4513.60 Sheriff or chief of police may order vehicle left on private property into storage; private tow-away zone.

(A)(1) The sheriff of a county or chief of police of a municipal corporation, township, or township or joint police district, within the sheriff's or chief's respective territorial jurisdiction, upon complaint of any person adversely affected, may order into storage any motor vehicle, other than an abandoned junk motor vehicle as defined in section 4513.63 of the Revised Code, that has been left on private residential or private agricultural property for at least four hours without the permission of the person having the right to the possession of the property. The sheriff or chief of police, upon complaint of the owner of a repair garage or place of storage, may order into storage any motor vehicle, other than an abandoned junk motor vehicle, that has been left at the garage or place of storage for a longer period than that agreed upon. The place of storage shall be designated by the sheriff or chief of police. When ordering a motor vehicle into storage pursuant to this division, a sheriff or chief of police, whenever possible, shall arrange for the removal of the motor vehicle by a private tow truck operator or towing company. Subject to division (C) of this section, the owner of a motor vehicle that has been removed pursuant to this division may recover the vehicle only in accordance with division (E) of this section.

(2) Divisions (A)(1) to (3) of this section do not apply to any private residential or private agricultural property that is established as a private tow-away zone in accordance with division (B) of this section.

(3) As used in divisions (A)(1) and (2) of this section, "private residential property" means private property on which is located one or more structures that are used as a home, residence, or sleeping place by one or more persons, if no more than three separate households are maintained in the structure or structures. "Private residential property" does not include any private property on which is located one or more structures that are used as a home, residence, or sleeping place by two or more persons, if more than three separate households are maintained in the structure or structures.

(B)(1) The owner of private property may establish a private tow-away zone only if all of the following conditions are satisfied:

(a) The owner posts on the owner's property a sign, that is at least eighteen inches by twenty-four inches in size, that is visible from all entrances to the property, and that contains at least all of the following information:

(i) A notice that the property is a private tow-away zone and that vehicles not authorized to park on the property will be towed away;

(ii) The telephone number of the person from whom a towed-away vehicle can be recovered, and the address of the place to which the vehicle will be taken and the place from which it may be recovered;

(iii) A statement that the vehicle may be recovered at any time during the day or night upon the submission of proof of ownership and the payment of a towing charge, in an amount not to exceed ninety dollars, and a storage charge, in an amount not to exceed twelve dollars per twenty-four-hour period; except that the charge for towing shall not exceed one hundred fifty dollars, and the storage charge shall not exceed twenty dollars per twenty-four-hour period, if the vehicle has a manufacturer's gross vehicle weight rating in excess of ten thousand pounds and is a truck, bus, or a combination of a commercial tractor and trailer or semitrailer.

(b) The place to which the towed vehicle is taken and from which it may be recovered is conveniently located, is well lighted, and is on or within a reasonable distance of a regularly scheduled route of one or more modes of public transportation, if any public transportation is available in the municipal corporation or township in which the private tow-away zone is located.

(2) If a vehicle is parked on private property that is established as a private tow-away zone in accordance with division (B)(1) of this section, without the consent of the owner of the property or in violation of any posted parking condition or regulation, the owner or the owner's agent may remove, or cause the removal of, the vehicle, the owner and the operator of the vehicle shall be deemed to have consented to the removal and storage of the vehicle and to the payment of the towing and storage charges specified in division (B)(1)(a)(iii) of this section, and the owner, subject to division (C) of this section, may recover a vehicle that has been so removed only in accordance with division (E) of this section.

(3) If a municipal corporation requires tow trucks and tow truck operators to be licensed, no owner of private property located within the municipal corporation shall remove, or shall cause the removal and storage of, any vehicle pursuant to division (B)(2) of this section by an unlicensed tow truck or unlicensed tow truck operator.

(4) Divisions (B)(1) to (3) of this section do not affect or limit the operation of division (A) of this section or sections 4513.61 to 4513.65 of the Revised Code as they relate to property other than private property that is established as a private tow-away zone under division (B)(1) of this section.

(C) If the owner or operator of a motor vehicle that has been ordered into storage pursuant to division (A)(1) of this section or of a vehicle that is being removed under authority of division (B)(2) of this section arrives after the motor vehicle or vehicle has been prepared for removal, but prior to its actual removal from the property, the owner or operator shall be given the opportunity to pay a fee of not more than one-half of the charge for the removal of motor vehicles under division (A)(1) of this section or of vehicles under division (B)(2) of this section, whichever is applicable, that normally is assessed by the person who has prepared the motor vehicle or vehicle for removal, in order to obtain release of the motor vehicle or vehicle. Upon payment of that fee, the motor vehicle or vehicle shall be released to the owner or operator, and upon its release, the owner or operator immediately shall move it so that:

(1) If the motor vehicle was ordered into storage pursuant to division (A)(1) of this section, it is not on the private residential or private agricultural property without the permission of the person having the right to possession of the property, or is not at the garage or place of storage without the permission of the owner, whichever is applicable.

(2) If the vehicle was being removed under authority of division (B)(2) of this section, it is not parked on the private property established as a private tow-away zone without the consent of the owner or in violation of any posted parking condition or regulation.

(D)(1) If an owner of private property that is established as a private tow-away zone in accordance with division (B)(1) of this section or the authorized agent of such an owner removes or causes the removal of a vehicle from that property under authority of division (B)(2) of this section, the owner or agent promptly shall notify the police department of the municipal corporation, township, or township or joint police district in which the property is located, of the removal, the vehicle's license number, make, model, and color, the location from which it was removed, the date and time of its removal, the telephone number of the person from whom it may be recovered, and the address of the place to which it has been taken and from which it may be recovered.

(2) Each county sheriff and each chief of police of a municipal corporation, township, or township or joint police district shall maintain a record of motor vehicles that the sheriff or chief orders into storage pursuant to division (A)(1) of this section and of vehicles removed from private property in the sheriff's or chief's jurisdiction that is established as a private tow-away zone of which the sheriff or chief has received notice under division (D)(1) of this section. The record shall include an entry for each such motor vehicle or vehicle that identifies the motor vehicle's or vehicle's license number, make, model, and color, the location from which it was removed, the date and time of its removal, the telephone number of the person from whom it may be recovered, and the address of the place to which it has been taken and from which it may be recovered. Any information in the record that pertains to a particular motor vehicle or vehicle shall be provided to any person who, either in person or pursuant to a telephone call, identifies self as the owner or operator of the motor vehicle or vehicle and requests information pertaining to its location.

(3) Any person who registers a complaint that is the basis of a sheriff's or police chief's order for the removal and storage of a motor vehicle under division (A)(1) of this section shall provide the identity of the law enforcement agency with which the complaint was registered to any person who identifies self as the owner or operator of the motor vehicle and requests information pertaining to its location.

(E) The owner of a motor vehicle that is ordered into storage pursuant to division (A)(1) of this section or of a vehicle that is removed under authority of division (B)(2) of this section may reclaim it upon payment of any expenses or charges incurred in its removal, in an amount not to exceed ninety dollars, and storage, in an amount not to exceed twelve dollars per twenty-four-hour period;

except that the charge for towing shall not exceed one hundred fifty dollars, and the storage charge shall not exceed twenty dollars per twenty-four-hour period, if the vehicle has a manufacturer's gross vehicle weight rating in excess of ten thousand pounds and is a truck, bus, or a combination of a commercial tractor and trailer or semi-trailer. Presentation of proof of ownership, which may be evidenced by a certificate of title to the motor vehicle or vehicle also shall be required for reclamation of the vehicle. If a motor vehicle that is ordered into storage pursuant to division (A)(1) of this section remains unclaimed by the owner for thirty days, the procedures established by sections 4513.61 and 4513.62 of the Revised Code shall apply.

(F) No person shall remove, or cause the removal of, any vehicle from private property that is established as a private tow-away zone under division (B)(1) of this section other than in accordance with division (B)(2) of this section, and no person shall remove, or cause the removal of, any motor vehicle from any other private property other than in accordance with division (A)(1) of this section or sections 4513.61 to 4513.65 of the Revised Code.

(G) Whoever violates division (B)(3) or (F) of this section is guilty of a minor misdemeanor.

**HISTORY: 134 v H 24 (Eff 10-6-71); 135 v H 650 (Eff 7-9-74); 138 v S 257 (Eff 6-25-80); 140 v H 112 (Eff 10-4-84); 143 v S 285 (Eff 4-10-91); 148 v H 600. Eff 9-1-2000; 149 v S 123, § 1, eff. 1-1-04; 153 v H 1, § 101.01, eff. 10-16-09; 2011 HB 153, § 101.01, eff. Sept. 29, 2011.**

The effective date is set by § 812.10 of 153 v H 1.

The effective date is set by section 4 of S.B. 123.

See provisions, § 5 of S.B. 123 (149 v —), following RC § 4501.01.

**Analogous in part to former RC § 737.31.1 (131 v 276; 133 v H 13), and RC § 311.30 (131 v 208; 133 v S 218), both repealed 134 v H 24, § 2, eff 10-6-71.**

## § 4513.61 Storage of vehicles in possession of law enforcement officers or left on public property; reclamation or disposal.

The sheriff of a county or chief of police of a municipal corporation, township, or township or joint police district, within the sheriff's or chief's respective territorial jurisdiction, or a state highway patrol trooper, upon notification to the sheriff or chief of police of such action and of the location of the place of storage, may order into storage any motor vehicle, including an abandoned junk motor vehicle as defined in section 4513.63 of the Revised Code, that has come into the possession of the sheriff, chief of police, or state highway patrol trooper as a result of the performance of the sheriff's, chief's, or trooper's duties or that has been left on a public street or other property open to the public for purposes of vehicular travel, or upon or within the right-of-way of any road or highway, for forty-eight hours or longer without notification to the sheriff or chief of police of the reasons for leaving the motor vehicle in such place, except that when such a motor vehicle constitutes an obstruction to traffic it may be ordered into storage immediately. The sheriff or chief of police shall designate the place of storage of any motor vehicle so ordered removed.

The sheriff or chief of police immediately shall cause a search to be made of the records of the bureau of motor vehicles to ascertain the owner and any lienholder of a motor vehicle ordered into storage by the sheriff or chief of police, or by a state highway patrol trooper, and, if known, shall send or cause to be sent notice to the owner or lienholder at the owner's or lienholder's last known address by certified mail with return receipt requested, that the motor vehicle will be declared a nuisance and disposed of if not claimed within ten days of the date of mailing of the notice. The owner or lienholder of the motor vehicle may reclaim it upon payment of any expenses or charges incurred in its removal and storage, and presentation of proof of ownership, which may be evidenced by a certificate of title or memorandum certificate of title to the motor vehicle. If the owner or lienholder of the motor vehicle reclaims it after a search of the records of the bureau has been conducted and after notice has been sent to the owner or lienholder as described in this section, and the search was conducted by the owner of the place of storage or the owner's employee, and the notice was sent to the motor vehicle owner by the owner of the place of storage or the owner's employee, the owner or lienholder shall pay to the place of storage a processing fee of twenty-five dollars, in addition to any expenses or charges incurred in the removal and storage of the vehicle.

If the owner or lienholder makes no claim to the motor vehicle within ten days of the date of mailing of the notice, and if the vehicle is to be disposed of at public auction as provided in section 4513.62 of the Revised Code, the sheriff or chief of police, without charge to any party, shall file with the clerk of courts of the county in which the place of storage is located an affidavit showing compliance with the requirements of this section. Upon presentation of the affidavit, the clerk, without charge, shall issue a salvage certificate of title, free and clear of all liens and encumbrances, to the sheriff or chief of police. If the vehicle is to be disposed of to a motor vehicle salvage dealer or other facility as provided in section 4513.62 of the Revised Code, the sheriff or chief of police shall execute in triplicate an affidavit, as prescribed by the registrar of motor vehicles, describing the motor vehicle and the manner in which it was disposed of, and that all requirements of this section have been complied with. The sheriff or chief of police shall retain the original of the affidavit for the sheriff's or chief's records, and shall furnish two copies to the motor vehicle salvage dealer or other facility. Upon presentation of a copy of the affidavit by the motor vehicle salvage dealer, the clerk of courts, within thirty days of the presentation, shall issue to such owner a salvage certificate of title, free and clear of all liens and encumbrances.

Whenever a motor vehicle salvage dealer or other facility receives an affidavit for the disposal of a motor vehicle as provided in this section, the dealer or facility shall not be required to obtain an Ohio certificate of title to the motor vehicle in the dealer's or facility's own name if the vehicle is dismantled or destroyed and both copies of the affidavit are delivered to the clerk of courts.

**HISTORY: 134 v H 24 (Eff 10-6-71); 135 v H 650 (Eff 7-9-74); 138 v S 257 (Eff 6-25-80); 141 v H 428 (Eff 12-23-86); 142 v S 10 (Eff 8-13-87); 142 v H 373 (Eff 10-9-89); 144 v S 144 (Eff 8-8-91); 146 v S 121 (Eff 11-19-96); 147 v S 60. Eff 10-21-97; 150 v H 230, § 1, eff. 9-16-04; 2011 HB 114, § 101.01, eff. June 29, 2011; 2011 HB 153, § 101.01, eff. Sept. 29, 2011.**

**Analogous in part to former RC §§ 4513.41, 4513.42 (131 v 1119), and RC § 737.33.1 (127 v 285; 130 v 243; 133 v H 13), all repealed 134 v H 24, § 2, eff 10-6-71.**

Acts 2011, HB 114, § 806.10 provides: "The items of law contained in this act, and their applications, are severable. If any item of law contained in this act, or if any application of any item of law contained in this act, is held invalid, the invalidity does not affect other items of law contained in this act and their applications that can be given effect without the invalid item or application."

## § 4513.62 Disposal of unclaimed vehicles.

Unclaimed motor vehicles ordered into storage pursuant to division (A)(1) of section 4513.60 or section 4513.61 of the Revised Code shall be disposed of at the order of the sheriff of the county or the chief of police of the municipal corporation, township, or township or joint police district to a motor vehicle salvage dealer or scrap metal processing facility as defined in section 4737.05 of the Revised Code, or to any other facility owned by or under contract with the county, municipal corporation, or township, for the disposal of such motor vehicles, or shall be sold by the sheriff, chief of police, or licensed auctioneer at public auction, after giving notice thereof by advertisement, published once a week for two successive weeks in a newspaper of general circulation in the county or as provided in section 7.16 of the Revised Code. Any moneys accruing from the disposition of an unclaimed motor vehicle that are in excess of the expenses resulting from the removal and storage of the vehicle shall be credited to the general fund of the county, municipal corporation, township, or joint police district, as the case may be.

**HISTORY: 134 v H 24 (Eff 10-6-71); 138 v S 257 (Eff 6-25-80); 140 v H 112 (Eff 10-4-84); 142 v S 10 (Eff 8-13-87); 142 v H 373. Eff 10-9-89; 2011 HB 153, § 101.01, eff. Sept. 29, 2011.**

**Analogous to former RC § 737.31.2 (133 v H 13), repealed 134 v H 24, § 2, eff 10-6-71.**

## § 4513.63 Photographing and recording information as to abandoned junk vehicles; disposal of vehicle.

"Abandoned junk motor vehicle" means any motor vehicle meeting all of the following requirements:

(A) Left on private property for forty-eight hours or longer without the permission of the person having the right to the possession of the property, on a public street or other property open to the public for purposes of vehicular travel or parking, or upon or within the right-of-way of any road or highway, for forty-eight hours or longer;

(B) Three years old, or older;

(C) Extensively damaged, such damage including but not limited to any of the following: missing wheels, tires, motor, or transmission;

(D) Apparently inoperable;

(E) Having a fair market value of one thousand five hundred dollars or less.

The sheriff of a county or chief of police of a municipal corporation, township, or township or joint police district, within the sheriff's or chief's respective territorial jurisdiction, or a state highway patrol trooper, upon notification to the sheriff or chief of police of such action, shall order any abandoned junk motor vehicle to be photographed by a law enforcement officer. The officer shall record the make of motor vehicle, the serial number when available, and shall also detail the damage or missing equipment to substantiate the value of one thousand five hundred dollars or less. The sheriff or chief of police shall thereupon immediately dispose of the abandoned junk motor vehicle to a motor vehicle salvage dealer as defined in section 4738.01 of the Revised Code or a scrap metal processing facility as defined in section 4737.05 of the Revised Code which is under contract to the county, township, or municipal corporation, or to any other facility owned by or under contract with the county, township, or municipal corporation for the destruction of such motor vehicles. The records and photograph relating to the abandoned junk motor vehicle shall be retained by the law enforcement agency ordering the disposition of such vehicle for a period of at least two years. The law enforcement agency shall execute in quadruplicate an affidavit, as prescribed by the registrar of motor vehicles, describing the motor vehicle and the manner in which it was disposed of, and that all requirements of this section have been complied with, and, within thirty days of disposing of the vehicle, shall sign and file the affidavit with the clerk of courts of the county in which the motor vehicle was abandoned. The clerk of courts shall retain the original of the affidavit for the clerk's files, shall furnish one copy thereof to the registrar, one copy to the motor vehicle salvage dealer or other facility handling the disposal of the vehicle, and one copy to the law enforcement agency ordering the disposal, who shall file such copy with the records and photograph relating to the disposal. Any moneys arising from the disposal of an abandoned junk motor vehicle shall be deposited in the general fund of the county, township, or the municipal corporation, as the case may be.

Notwithstanding section 4513.61 of the Revised Code, any motor vehicle meeting the requirements of divisions (C), (D), and (E) of this section which has remained unclaimed by the owner or lienholder for a period of ten days or longer following notification as provided in section 4513.61 of the Revised Code may be disposed of as provided in this section.

**HISTORY: 134 v H 24 (Eff 10-6-71); 135 v H 650 (Eff 7-9-74); 136 v S 52 (Eff 9-15-75); 137 v H 865 (Eff 12-12-78); 138 v S 257 (Eff 6-25-80); 144 v S 144 (Eff 8-8-91); 144 v S 125 (Eff 4-16-93); 147 v S 60. Eff 10-21-97; 150 v H 230, § 1, eff. 9-16-04; 2011 HB 153, § 101.01, eff. Sept. 29, 2011.**

**Analogous in part to former RC §§ 311.33, 737.31.3 (133 v H 920), 737.31.2 (133 v H 13), 311.30.1 (133 v S 218), repealed 134 v H 24, § 2, eff 10-6-71.**

## § 4513.64 Willfully abandoning junk motor vehicle prohibited.

(A) No person shall willfully leave an abandoned junk motor vehicle as defined in section 4513.63 of the Revised Code on private property for more than seventy-two hours without the permission of the person having the right to the possession of the property, or on a public street or other property open to the public for purposes of vehicular travel or parking, or upon or within the right-of-way of any road or highway, for forty-eight hours or longer without notification to the sheriff of the county or chief of police of the municipal corporation, township, or township or joint police district of the reasons for leaving the motor vehicle in such place.

For purposes of this section, the fact that a motor vehicle has been so left without permission or notification is prima-facie evidence of abandonment.

Nothing contained in sections 4513.60, 4513.61, and 4513.63 of the Revised Code shall invalidate the provisions of municipal ordinances or township resolutions regulating or prohibiting the abandonment of motor vehicles on streets, highways, public property, or private property within municipal corporations or townships.

(B) Whoever violates this section is guilty of a minor misdemeanor and shall also be assessed any costs incurred by the county, township, joint police district, or municipal corporation in disposing of the abandoned junk motor vehicle that is the basis of the violation, less any money accruing to the county, township, joint police district, or municipal corporation from this disposal of the vehicle.

**HISTORY: 134 v H 24 (Eff 10-6-71); 138 v S 257 (Eff 6-25-80); 144 v H 77. Eff 9-17-91; 149 v S 123, § 1, eff. 1-1-04; 2011 HB 153, § 101.01, eff. Sept. 29, 2011.**

The effective date is set by section 4 of S.B. 123.

See provisions, § 5 of S.B. 123 (149 v —), following RC § 4501.01.

**Analogous to former RC §§ 311.34, 737.31.4 (133 v H 920), repealed 134 v H 24, § 2, eff 10-6-71.**

## § 4513.65 Junk motor vehicle; collector's vehicle; storage; notice.

(A) For purposes of this section, "junk motor vehicle" means any motor vehicle meeting the requirements of divisions (B), (C), (D), and (E) of section 4513.63 of the Revised Code that is left uncovered in the open on private property for more than seventy-two hours with the permission of the person having the right to the possession of the property, except if the person is operating a junk yard or scrap metal processing facility licensed under authority of sections 4737.05 to 4737.12 of the Revised Code, or regulated under authority of a political subdivision; or if the property on which the motor vehicle is left is not subject to licensure or regulation by any governmental authority, unless the person having the right to the possession of the property can establish that the motor vehicle is part of a bona fide commercial operation; or if the motor vehicle is a collector's vehicle.

No political subdivision shall prevent a person from storing or keeping, or restrict a person in the method of storing or keeping, any collector's vehicle on private property with the permission of the person having the right to the possession of the property; except that a political subdivision may require a person having such permission to conceal, by means of buildings, fences, vegetation, terrain, or other suitable obstruction, any unlicensed collector's vehicle stored in the open.

The sheriff of a county, or chief of police of a municipal corporation, within the sheriff's or chief's respective territorial jurisdiction, a state highway patrol trooper, a board of township trustees, the legislative authority of a municipal corporation, or the zoning authority of a township or a municipal corporation, may send notice, by certified mail with return receipt requested, to the person having the right to the possession of the property on which a junk motor vehicle is left, that within ten days of receipt of the notice, the junk motor vehicle either shall be covered by being housed in a garage or other suitable structure, or shall be removed from the property.

No person shall willfully leave a junk motor vehicle uncovered in the open for more than ten days after receipt of a notice as provided in this section. The fact that a junk motor vehicle is so left is prima-facie evidence of willful failure to comply with the notice, and each subsequent period of thirty days that a junk motor vehicle continues to be so left constitutes a separate offense.

(B) Whoever violates this section is guilty of a minor misdemeanor.

**HISTORY: 135 v H 635 (Eff 5-7-74); 136 v S 52 (Eff 9-15-75); 144 v S 144. Eff 8-8-91; 149 v S 123, § 1, eff. 1-1-04; 153 v H 1, § 101.01, eff. 10-16-09.**

The effective date is set by § 812.10 of 153 v H 1.

The effective date is set by section 4 of S.B. 123.

See provisions, § 5 of S.B. 123 (149 v —), following RC § 4501.01.

## § 4513.66 Removal of motor vehicle from roadway.

(A) If a motor vehicle accident occurs on any highway, public street, or other property open to the public for purposes of vehicular travel and if any motor vehicle, cargo, or personal property that has been damaged or spilled as a result of the motor vehicle accident is blocking the highway, street, or other property or is otherwise endangering public safety, the sheriff of the county, or the chief of police of the municipal corporation, township, or township or joint police district, in which the accident occurred, a state highway patrol trooper, or the chief of the fire department having jurisdiction where the accident occurred may, without consent of the owner but with the approval of the law enforcement agency conducting any investigation of the accident, remove the motor vehicle if the motor vehicle is unoccupied, cargo, or personal property from the portion of the highway, public street, or property ordinarily used for vehicular travel on the highway, public street, or other property open to the public for purposes of vehicular travel.

(B)(1) Except as provided in division (B)(2) or (3) of this section, no employee of the department of transportation, sheriff, deputy sheriff, chief of police or police officer of a municipal corporation, township, or township or joint police district, state highway patrol trooper, chief of a fire department, or fire fighter who authorizes or participates in the removal of any unoccupied motor vehicle, cargo, or personal property as authorized by division (A) of this section is liable in civil damages for any injury, death, or loss to person or property that results from the removal of that unoccupied motor vehicle, cargo, or personal property. Except as provided in division (B)(2) or (3) of this section, if the department of transportation or a sheriff, chief of police of a municipal corporation, township, or township or joint police district, head of the state highway patrol, or chief of a fire department authorizes, employs, or arranges to have a private tow truck operator or towing company remove any unoccupied motor vehicle, cargo, or personal property as authorized by division (A) of this section, that private tow truck operator or towing company is not liable in civil damages for any injury, death, or loss to person or property that results from the removal of that unoccupied motor vehicle, cargo, or personal property, and the department of transportation, sheriff, chief of police, head of the state highway patrol, or fire department chief is not liable in civil damages for any injury, death, or loss to person or property that results from the private tow truck operator or towing company's removal of that unoccupied motor vehicle, cargo, or personal property.

(2) Division (B)(1) of this section does not apply to any person or entity involved in the removal of an unoccupied motor vehicle, cargo, or personal property pursuant to division (A) of this section if that removal causes or contributes to the release of a hazardous material or to structural damage to the roadway.

(3) Division (B)(1) of this section does not apply to a private tow truck operator or towing company that was not authorized, employed, or arranged by the department of transportation, a sheriff, a chief of police of a municipal corporation, township, or township or joint police district, the head of the state highway patrol, or a chief of a fire department or to a private tow truck operator or towing company that was authorized, employed, or arranged by the department of transportation, a sheriff, a chief of police of a municipal corporation, township, or township or joint police district, the head of the state highway patrol, or a chief of a fire department to perform the removal of the unoccupied motor vehicle, cargo, or personal property and the private tow truck operator or towing company performed the removal in a reckless or willful manner.

(C) As used in this section, "hazardous material" has the same meaning as in section 2305.232 of the Revised Code.

**HISTORY: 152 v S 129, § 1, eff. 12-30-08; 2011 HB 153, § 101.01, eff. Sept. 29, 2011.**

## § 4513.99 Penalties.

(A) Any violation of section 4513.10, 4513.182 [4513.18.2], 4513.20, 4513.201 [4513.20.1], 4513.202 [4513.20.2], 4513.25, 4513.26, 4513.27, 4513.29, 4513.30, 4513.31, 4513.32, or 4513.34 of the Revised Code shall be punished under division (B) of this section.

(B) Whoever violates the sections of this chapter that are specifically required to be punished under this division, or any provision of sections 4513.03 to 4513.262 [4513.26.2] or 4513.27 to 4513.37 of the Revised Code for which violation no penalty is otherwise provided, is guilty of a minor misdemeanor on a first offense; on a second offense within one year after the first offense, the person is guilty of a misdemeanor of the fourth degree; on each subsequent offense within one year after the first offense, the person is guilty of a misdemeanor of the third degree.

**HISTORY: Bureau of Code Revision, 10-1-53; 125 v 903(1026); 125 v 456; 129 v 1567 (Eff 9-23-61); 132 v H 380 (Eff 1-1-68); 134 v H 24 (Eff 10-6-71); 135 v H 90 (Eff 10-31-73); 135 v H 173, § 1, 3 (Eff 1-1-74); 135 v H 635 (Eff 5-7-74); 138 v S 257 (Eff 6-25-80); 140 v H 112 (Eff 10-4-84); 141 v S 54 (Eff 5-6-86); 141 v H 291 (Eff 3-11-88); 144 v H 96 (Eff 6-18-91); 144 v H 118 (Eff 6-1-92); 144 v S 98 (Eff 11-12-92); 148 v H 600 (Eff 9-1-2000); 148 v H 138. Eff 11-3-2000; 149 v S 123, § 1, eff. 1-1-04; 152 v H 9, § 1, eff. 10-18-07; 153 v H 1, § 101.01, eff. 10-16-09.**

The effective date is set by § 812.10 of 153 v H 1.

The effective date is set by section 4 of S.B. 123.

See provisions, § 5 of S.B. 123 (149 v —), following RC § 4501.01.

The provisions of § 8 of S.B. 123 read as follows:

SECTION 8. Section 4513.99 of the Revised Code is presented in this act as a composite of the section as amended by both Am. Sub. H.B. 138 and Am. Sub. H.B. 600 of the 123rd General Assembly. The General Assembly, applying the principle stated in division (B) of section 1.52 of the Revised Code that amendments are to be harmonized if reasonably capable of simultaneous operation, finds that the composites are the resulting versions of the sections in effect prior to the effective date of the sections as presented in this act.

# CHAPTER 4549: MOTOR VEHICLE CRIMES

Section



[ODOMETER ROLLBACK AND DISCLOSURE ACT]



Section



[TAMPERING WITH IDENTIFYING NUMBERS]



## § 4549.01 Stopping motor vehicle when signalled by horse-drawn vehicle or horse rider.

(A) No person while operating a motor vehicle shall fail to slow down and stop the vehicle when signalled to do so upon meeting or overtaking a horse-drawn vehicle or person on horseback and to remain stationary until the vehicle or person has passed, provided the signal to stop is given in good faith, under circumstances of necessity, and only as often and for that length of time as is required for the vehicle or person to pass, whether it is approaching from the front or rear.

(B) Whoever violates this section is guilty of a minor misdemeanor on a first offense and a misdemeanor of the fourth degree on each subsequent offense.

**HISTORY: GC § 12605; 99 v 541, § 16; 99 v 543, § 25; Bureau of Code Revision. Eff 10-1-53; 149 v S 123, § 1, eff. 1-1-04.**

The effective date is set by section 4 of S.B. 123.

See provisions, § 5 of S.B. 123 (149 v —), following RC § 4501.01.

## § 4549.02 Stopping after accident; exchange of identity information and vehicle registration.

(A) In case of accident to or collision with persons or property upon any of the public roads or highways, due to the driving or operation thereon of any motor vehicle, the person driving or operating the motor vehicle, having knowledge of the accident or collision, immediately shall stop the driver's or operator's motor vehicle at the scene of the accident or collision and shall remain at the scene of the accident or collision until the driver or operator has given the driver's or operator's name and address and, if the driver or operator is not the owner, the name and address of the owner of that motor vehicle, together with the registered number of that motor vehicle, to any person injured in the accident or collision or to the operator, occupant, owner, or attendant of any motor vehicle damaged in the accident or collision, or to any police officer at the scene of the accident or collision.

In the event the injured person is unable to comprehend and record the information required to be given by this section, the other driver involved in the accident or collision forthwith shall notify the nearest police authority concerning the location of the accident or collision, and the driver's name, address, and the registered number of the motor vehicle the driver was operating, and then remain at the scene of the accident or collision until a police officer arrives, unless removed from the scene by an emergency vehicle operated by a political subdivision or an ambulance.

If the accident or collision is with an unoccupied or unattended motor vehicle, the operator who collides with the motor vehicle shall securely attach the information required to be given in this section, in writing, to a conspicuous place in or on the unoccupied or unattended motor vehicle.

(B) Whoever violates division (A) of this section is guilty of failure to stop after an accident, a misdemeanor of the first degree. If the accident or collision results in serious physical harm to a person, failure to stop after an accident is a felony of the fifth degree. If the accident or collision results in the death of a person, failure to stop after an accident is a felony of the third degree. The court, in addition to any other penalties provided by law, shall impose upon the offender a class five suspension of the offender's driver's license, commercial driver's license, temporary instruction permit, probationary license, or nonresident operating privilege from the range specified in division (A)(5) of section 4510.02 of the Revised Code. No judge shall suspend the first six months of suspension of an offender's license, permit, or privilege required by this division.

The offender shall provide the court with proof of financial responsibility as defined in section 4509.01 of the Revised Code. If the offender fails to provide that proof of financial responsibility, then, in addition to any other penalties provided by law, the court may order restitution pursuant to section 2929.18 or 2929.28 of the Revised Code in an amount not exceeding five thousand dollars for any economic loss arising from an accident or collision that was the direct and proximate result of the offender's operation of the motor vehicle before, during, or after committing the offense charged under this section.

**HISTORY: GC § 12606; 99 v 541, § 16; 99 v 543, § 25; 113 v 76; Bureau of Code Revision, 10-1-53; 130 v H 180. Eff 8-19-63; 149 v S 123, § 1, eff. 1-1-04; 150 v H 50, § 4, eff. 1-1-04; 153 v H 338, § 1, eff. 9-17-10; 2011 HB 5, § 1, eff. Sept. 23, 2011.**

The effective date is set by section 6 of H.B. 50.

See provisions, § 5 of S.B. 123 (149 v —), following RC § 4501.01.

## § 4549.021 Stopping after accident or collision involving injury to persons or property.

(A) In case of accident or collision resulting in injury or damage to persons or property upon any public or private property other than public roads or highways, due to the driving or operation thereon of any motor vehicle, the person driving or operating the motor vehicle, having knowledge of the accident or collision, shall stop, and, upon request of the person injured or damaged, or any other person, shall give that person the driver's or operator's name and address, and, if the driver or operator is not the owner, the name and address of the owner of that motor vehicle, together with the registered number of that motor vehicle, and, if available, exhibit the driver's or operator's driver's or commercial driver's license.

If the owner or person in charge of the damaged property is not furnished such information, the driver of the motor vehicle involved in the accident or collision, within twenty-four hours after the accident or collision, shall forward to the police department of the city or village in which the accident or collision occurred or if it occurred outside the corporate limits of a city or village to the sheriff of the county in which the accident or collision occurred the same information required to be given to the owner or person in control of the damaged property and give the date, time, and location of the accident or collision.

If the accident or collision is with an unoccupied or unattended motor vehicle, the operator who collides with the motor vehicle shall securely attach the information required to be given in this section, in writing, to a conspicuous place in or on the unoccupied or unattended motor vehicle.

(B) Whoever violates division (A) of this section is guilty of failure to stop after a nonpublic road accident, a misdemeanor of the first degree. If the accident or collision results in serious physical harm to a person, failure to stop after a nonpublic road accident is a felony of the fifth degree. If the accident or collision results in the death of a person, failure to stop after a nonpublic road accident is a felony of the third degree. The court, in addition to any other penalties provided by law, shall impose upon the offender a class five suspension of the offender's driver's license, commercial driver's license, temporary instruction permit, probationary license, or nonresident operating privilege from the range specified in division (A)(5) of section 4510.02 of the Revised Code. No judge shall suspend the first six months of suspension of an offender's license, permit, or privilege required by this division.

The offender shall provide the court with proof of financial responsibility as defined in section 4509.01 of the Revised Code. If the offender fails to provide that proof of financial responsibility, then, in addition to any other penalties provided by law, the court may order restitution pursuant to section 2929.18 or 2929.28 of the Revised Code in an amount not exceeding five thousand dollars for any economic loss arising from an accident or collision that was the direct and proximate result of the offender's operation of the motor vehicle before, during, or after committing the offense charged under this section.

**HISTORY: 130 v S 312 (Eff 9-30-63); 131 v 1132 (Eff 11-5-65); 143 v H 381. Eff 7-1-89; 149 v S 123, § 1, eff. 1-1-04; 150 v H 50, § 4, eff. 1-1-04; 153 v H 338, § 1, eff. 9-17-10; 2011 HB 5, § 1, eff. Sept. 23, 2011.**

The effective date is set by section 6 of H.B. 50.

See provisions, § 5 of S.B. 123 (149 v —), following RC § 4501.01.

## § 4549.03 Failure to stop after accident involving property of others.

(A) The driver of any vehicle involved in an accident resulting in damage to real property, or personal property attached to real property, legally upon or adjacent to a public road or highway immediately shall stop and take reasonable steps to locate and notify the owner or person in charge of the property of that fact, of the driver's name and address, and of the registration number of the vehicle the driver is driving and, upon request and if available, shall exhibit the driver's or commercial driver's license.

If the owner or person in charge of the property cannot be located after reasonable search, the driver of the vehicle involved in the accident resulting in damage to the property, within twenty-four hours after the accident, shall forward to the police department of the city or village in which the accident or collision occurred, or if it occurred outside the corporate limits of a city or village to the sheriff of the county in which the accident or collision occurred, the same information required to be given to the owner or person in control of the property and give the location of the accident and a description of the damage insofar as it is known.

(B) Whoever violates division (A) of this section is guilty of failure to stop after an accident involving the property of others, a misdemeanor of the first degree.

The offender shall provide the court with proof of financial responsibility as defined in section 4509.01 of the Revised Code. If the offender fails to provide that proof of financial responsibility, then, in addition to any other penalties provided by law, the court may order restitution pursuant to section 2929.28 of the Revised Code in an amount not exceeding five thousand dollars for any economic loss arising from an accident or collision that was the direct and proximate result of the offender's operation of the motor vehicle before, during, or after committing the offense charged under this section.

**HISTORY: GC § 12606-1; 124 v 205; Bureau of Code Revision, 10-1-53; 131 v 1132 (Eff 11-5-65); 143 v H 381. Eff 7-1-89; 149 v S 123, § 1, eff. 1-1-04; 2011 HB 5, § 1, eff. Sept. 23, 2011.**

The effective date is set by section 4 of S.B. 123.

See provisions, § 5 of S.B. 123 (149 v —), following RC § 4501.01.

## § 4549.042 Motor vehicle master key violation.

(A)(1) No person shall sell or otherwise dispose of a master key designed to fit more than one motor vehicle, knowing or having reasonable cause to believe the key will be used to commit a crime.

(2) No person shall buy, receive, or have in the person's possession a master key designed to fit more than one motor vehicle, for the purpose of using the key to commit a crime.

(B) Whoever violates division (A)(1) or (2) of this section is guilty of a motor vehicle master key violation, a felony of the fifth degree on a first offense and a felony of the fourth degree on each subsequent offense.

**HISTORY: 132 v H 591. Eff 12-14-67; 149 v S 123, § 1, eff. 1-1-04.**

The effective date is set by section 4 of S.B. 123.

See provisions, § 5 of S.B. 123 (149 v —), following RC § 4501.01.

## § 4549.05 Officer may remove ignition key.

A law enforcement officer may remove the ignition key left in the ignition switch of an unlocked and unattended motor vehicle parked on a street or highway. The officer removing said key shall place notification upon the vehicle detailing his name and badge number, the place where said key may be reclaimed, and the procedure for reclaiming said key. The key shall be returned to the owner of the motor vehicle upon presentation of proof of ownership.

**HISTORY: GC § 12619-1; 103 v 524; Bureau of Code Revision, 10-1-53; 133 v H 386 (Eff 10-30-69); 134 v H 511. Eff 1-1-74.**

**For provisions analogous to material deleted by HB 511 amendment, see now RC §§ 2913.02, 2913.51.**

## § 4549.08 Operating motor vehicle bearing invalid license plate or identification mark.

(A) No person shall operate or drive a motor vehicle upon the public roads and highways in this state if it displays a license plate or a distinctive number or identification mark that meets any of the following criteria:

(1) Is fictitious;

(2) Is a counterfeit or an unlawfully made copy of any distinctive number or identification mark;

(3) Belongs to another motor vehicle, provided that this section does not apply to a motor vehicle that is operated on the public roads and highways in this state when the motor vehicle displays license plates that originally were issued for a motor vehicle that previously was owned by the same person who owns the motor vehicle that is operated on the public roads and highways in this state, during the thirty-day period described in division (A) (4) of section 4503.12 of the Revised Code.

(B) A person who fails to comply with the transfer of registration provisions of section 4503.12 of the Revised Code and is charged with a violation of that section shall not be charged with a violation of this section.

(C) Whoever violates division (A)(1), (2), or (3) of this section is guilty of operating a motor vehicle bearing an invalid license plate or identification mark, a misdemeanor of the fourth degree on a first offense and a misdemeanor of the third degree on each subsequent offense.

**HISTORY: GC § 12618; 99 v 543, § 26; 108 v PtII, 1078; 116 v 286, § 10; 116 v 295, § 3; Bureau of Code Revision, 10-1-53; 129 v 1030 (Eff 9-1-61); 130 v H 1 (Eff 1-23-63); 146 v H 353 (Eff 9-17-96); 149 v H 345. Eff 7-23-2002; 149 v S 123, § 1, eff. 1-1-04.**

The effective date is set by section 4 of S.B. 123.

See provisions, § 5 of S.B. 123 (149 v —), following RC § 4501.01.

## § 4549.081 Electronic clearance device for commercial motor vehicle.

(A) The superintendent of the state highway patrol shall adopt rules governing the use of an electronic clearance device that enables an operator of a commercial motor vehicle, in accordance with division (B) of section 4511.121 [4511.12.1] of the Revised Code, to bypass a scale location established for the purpose of determining the weight of the vehicle and its load. The superintendent shall establish the acceptable types and features of such devices. The rules of the superintendent also shall establish a method for a peace officer to determine that the device and its use are in compliance with this section and the rules of the superintendent.

(B) No person shall use an electronic clearance device if the device or its use is not in compliance with rules of the superintendent.

(C) Whoever violates division (B) of this section is guilty of a misdemeanor of the fourth degree on a first offense and a misdemeanor of the third degree on each subsequent offense.

**HISTORY: 150 v H 230, § 1, eff. 9-16-04.**

## § 4549.10 Illegal operation of manufacturer's or dealer's motor vehicle.

(A) No person shall operate or cause to be operated upon a public road or highway a motor vehicle of a manufacturer or dealer unless the vehicle carries and displays two placards, except as provided in section 4503.21 of the Revised Code, issued by the director of public safety that bear the registration number of its manufacturer or dealer.

(B) Whoever violates division (A) of this section is guilty of illegal operation of a manufacturer's or dealer's motor vehicle, a minor misdemeanor.

**HISTORY: GC § 12622; 99 v 543, § 24; 100 v 73, § 11; 115 v 109; Bureau of Code Revision, 10-1-53; 129 v 1492 (Eff 8-10-61); 144 v S 98. Eff 11-12-92; 149 v S 123, § 1, eff. 1-1-04; 153 v H 1, § 101.01, eff. 10-16-09.**

The effective date is set by § 812.10 of 153 v H 1.

The effective date is set by section 4 of S.B. 123.

See provisions, § 5 of S.B. 123 (149 v —), following RC § 4501.01.

## § 4549.11 Operating with number of former owner.

(A) No person shall operate or drive upon the highways of this state a motor vehicle acquired from a former owner who has registered the motor vehicle, while the motor vehicle displays the distinctive number or identification mark assigned to it upon its original registration.

(B) Whoever violates division (A) of this section is guilty of operation of a motor vehicle bearing license plates or an identification mark issued to another, a minor misdemeanor on a first offense and a misdemeanor of the fourth degree on each subsequent offense.

**HISTORY: GC § 12618-1; 108 v PtII, 1078; Bureau of Code Revision. Eff 10-1-53; 149 v S 123, § 1, eff. 1-1-04.**

The effective date is set by section 4 of S.B. 123.

See provisions, § 5 of S.B. 123 (149 v —), following RC § 4501.01.

## § 4549.12 Resident operating with number issued by foreign state.

(A) No person who is the owner of a motor vehicle and a resident of this state shall operate or drive the motor vehicle upon the highways of this state, while it displays a distinctive number or identification mark issued by or under the authority of another state, without complying with the laws of this state relating to the registration and identification of motor vehicles.

(B) Whoever violates division (A) of this section is guilty of illegal operation by a resident of this state of a motor vehicle bearing the distinctive number or identification mark issued by a foreign jurisdiction, a minor misdemeanor.

**HISTORY: GC § 12618-3; 108 v PtII, 1078; Bureau of Code Revision. Eff 10-1-53; 149 v S 123, § 1, eff. 1-1-04; 153 v H 1, § 101.01, eff. 10-16-09.**

The effective date is set by § 812.10 of 153 v H 1.

The effective date is set by section 4 of S.B. 123.

See provisions, § 5 of S.B. 123 (149 v —), following RC § 4501.01.

## § 4549.13 Motor vehicles used by traffic officers.

Any motor vehicle used by a member of the state highway patrol or by any other peace officer, while said officer is on duty for the exclusive or main purpose of enforcing the motor vehicle or traffic laws of this state, provided the offense is punishable as a misdemeanor, shall be marked in some distinctive manner or color and shall be equipped with, but need not necessarily have in operation at all times, at least one flashing, oscillating, or rotating colored light mounted outside on top of the vehicle. The superintendent of the state highway patrol shall specify what constitutes such a distinctive marking or color for the state highway patrol.

**HISTORY: GC § 12616; 118 v 271; Bureau of Code Revision, 10-1-53; 133 v H 625 (Eff 11-21-69); 138 v S 141. Eff 10-25-79.**

## § 4549.14 Incompetency of officer as witness.

Any officer arresting, or participating or assisting in the arrest of, a person charged with violating the motor vehicle or traffic laws of this state, provided the offense is punishable as a misdemeanor, such officer being on duty exclusively or for the main purpose of enforcing such laws, is incompetent to testify as a witness in any prosecution against such arrested person if such officer at the time of the arrest was using a motor vehicle not marked in accordance with section 4549.13 of the Revised Code.

**HISTORY: GC § 12616-1; 118 v 271, § 2; Bureau of Code Revision. Eff 10-1-53.**

## § 4549.15 Uniform for traffic officers.

Every member of the state highway patrol and every other peace officer, while such officer is on duty for the exclusive or main purpose of enforcing motor vehicle or traffic laws of this state, provided the offense is punishable as a misdemeanor, shall wear a distinctive uniform. The superintendent of the patrol shall specify what constitutes such a distinctive uniform for the state highway patrol.

**HISTORY: GC § 12616-2; 118 v 271, § 3; Bureau of Code Revision, 10-1-53; 133 v H 625 (Eff 11-21-69); 138 v S 141. Eff 10-25-79.**

## § 4549.16 Arresting officer as witness.

Any officer arresting, or participating or assisting in the arrest of, a person charged with violating the motor vehicle or traffic laws of this state, provided the offense is punishable as a misdemeanor, such officer being on duty exclusively or for the main purpose of enforcing such laws is incompetent to testify as a witness in any prosecution against such arrested person if such officer at the time of the arrest was not wearing a distinctive uniform in accordance with section 4549.15 of the Revised Code.

**HISTORY: GC § 12616-3; 118 v 271, § 4; Bureau of Code Revision. Eff 10-1-53.**

## § 4549.17 Restriction on local officers where only small portion of freeway located in their jurisdiction.

(A) No law enforcement officer employed by a law enforcement agency of a municipal corporation, township, or joint police district shall issue any citation, summons, or ticket for a violation of section 4511.21 of the Revised Code or a substantially similar municipal ordinance or for a violation of section 5577.04 of the Revised Code or a substantially similar municipal ordinance, if all of the following apply:

(1) The citation, summons, or ticket would be issued for a violation described in division (A) of this section that occurs on a freeway that is part of the interstate system;

(2) The municipal corporation, township, or joint police district that employs the law enforcement officer has less than eight hundred eighty yards of the freeway that is part of the interstate system within its jurisdiction;

(3) The law enforcement officer must travel outside the boundaries of the municipal corporation, township, or joint police district that employs the officer in order to enter onto the freeway;

(4) The law enforcement officer travels onto the freeway for the primary purpose of issuing citations, summonses, or tickets for violations of section 4511.21 of the Revised Code or a substantially similar municipal ordinance or for violations of section 5577.04 of the Revised Code or a substantially similar municipal ordinance.

(B) As used in this section, "interstate system" has the same meaning as in section 5516.01 of the Revised Code.

**HISTORY: 145 v H 687. Eff 10-12-94; 2011 HB 153, § 101.01, eff. Sept. 29, 2011.**

**Not analogous to former RC § 4549.17 (RS § 4379-40; GC §§ 12626-12628; 99 v 544; Bureau of Code Revision, 10-1-53; 126 v 623), repealed 128 v 97, § 2, eff 1-1-60.**

## § 4549.18 Commercial car certificate of registration violation.

(A) The operator of a "commercial car," as defined in section 4501.01 of the Revised Code, when the commercial car is required to be registered under the Revised Code, shall, when operating the commercial car, trailer, or semitrailer on the streets, roads, or highways of this state, display inside or on the vehicle the certificate of registration for the commercial car, trailer, or semitrailer provided for in section 4503.19 of the Revised Code, or shall carry the certificate on the operator's person and display it upon the demand of any state highway patrol trooper or other peace officer.

Every person operating a commercial car, trailer, or semitrailer required to be registered under the Revised Code shall permit the inspection of the certificate of registration upon demand of the superintendent or any member of the state highway patrol or other peace officer of this state.

(B) Whoever violates division (A) of this section is guilty of a commercial car certificate of registration violation, a minor misdemeanor.

**HISTORY: GC §§ 12630-1, 12630-2; 116 v PtII, 155; Bureau of Code Revision, 10-1-53; 134 v H 1 (Eff 3-26-71); 143 v H 831 (Eff 7-17-90); 144 v S 144. Eff 8-8-91; 149 v S 123, § 1, eff. 1-1-04.**

The effective date is set by section 4 of S.B. 123.

See provisions, § 5 of S.B. 123 (149 v —), following RC § 4501.01.

## § 4549.19 Enforcement of proceedings against violators.

Proceedings to enforce section 4549.18 of the Revised Code shall be brought in any court of record situated in the county in which the violation occurred, and all municipal courts shall have county-wide jurisdiction over such violations. Such actions shall be governed by section 4507.15 of the Revised Code. Commercial cars which are registered under the laws of another state, the owners of which are not residents of this state and which are operated in compliance with the laws of the state of their owner's residence, are not subject to this section and section 4549.18 of the Revised Code.

**HISTORY: GC § 12630-3; 116 v PtII, 155, § 3; Bureau of Code Revision. Eff 10-1-53.**

## § 4549.20 Improper replacement of motor vehicle air bag.

(A) As used in this section, "air bag" has the same meaning as in 49 C.F.R. 579.4, as amended.

(B) No person shall install or reinstall in any motor vehicle any object to fulfill the function of an air bag, including an air bag, other than an air bag that was designed in conformance with or that is regulated by federal motor vehicle safety standard number 208 for the make, model, and model year of the vehicle, knowing that the object is not in accordance with that standard.

(C) Whoever violates division (B) of this section is guilty of improper replacement of a motor vehicle air bag, a misdemeanor of the first degree on a first offense. On each subsequent offense, the person is guilty of a felony of the fifth degree.

**HISTORY: 150 v H 219, § 1, eff. 9-16-04.**

## § 4549.31 Venue.

(A) Any person who as a part of a continuing course of criminal conduct commits auto theft offenses in more than one county may be indicted and tried for all such offenses in any county where one such offense was committed. It is prima-facie evidence of a continuing course of criminal conduct if an offender commits two or more auto theft offenses within a period of six months.

(B) As used in this section, "auto theft offense" means any of the following:

(1) A violation of section 4505.19, 4549.05, 4549.08, or 4549.62 of the Revised Code;

(2) A violation of a law of another state or the United States substantially equivalent to any offense listed in division (B)(1) of this section;

(3) A violation of a law of this or any other state, or of the United States, of which an element is forging or altering a motor vehicle title or registration, or obtaining a motor vehicle or motor vehicle parts or accessories by theft or fraud, or wrongful conversion of a motor vehicle, or taking, operating, or keeping a motor vehicle without the consent of the owner, or receiving or disposing of a motor vehicle or motor vehicle parts or accessories knowing the same to have been unlawfully obtained.

**HISTORY: 134 v H 101 (Eff 3-20-72); 136 v H 837 (Eff 5-25-76); 140 v H 632. Eff 3-28-85.**

## [ODOMETER ROLLBACK AND DISCLOSURE ACT]

## § 4549.41 Definitions.

As used in sections 4549.41 to 4549.51 of the Revised Code:

(A) "Person" includes an individual, corporation, government, governmental subdivision or agency, business trust, estate, trust, partnership, association, or cooperative or any other legal entity, whether acting individually or by their agents, officers, employees, or representatives.

(B) "Motor vehicle" means any vehicle driven or drawn by mechanical power for use on the public streets, roads, or highways.

(C) "Odometer" means an instrument for measuring and recording the total distance that a motor vehicle travels while in operation, including any cable, line, or other part necessary to make the instrument function properly. Odometer does not include any auxiliary odometer designed to be reset by the operator of a motor vehicle for the purpose of recording mileage on trips.

(D) "Transfer" means to change ownership of a motor vehicle by purchase, by gift, or, except as otherwise provided in this division, by any other means. A "transfer" does not include a change of ownership as a result of a bequest, under the laws of intestate succession, as a result of a surviving spouse's actions pursuant to section 2106.18 or 4505.10 of the Revised Code, as a result of the operation of section 2131.12 or 2131.13 of the Revised Code, or in connection with the creation of a security interest.

(E) "Transferor" means the person involved in a transfer, who transfers ownership of a motor vehicle.

(F) "Transferee" means the person involved in a transfer, to whom the ownership of a motor vehicle is transferred.

(G) "Service" means to repair or replace an odometer that is not properly functioning.

**HISTORY: 137 v S 78 (Eff 9-6-77); 140 v S 115 (Eff 10-14-83); 141 v H 382 (Eff 3-19-87); 143 v H 346 (Eff 5-31-90); 145 v H 458 (Eff 7-20-94); 149 v H 345. Eff 7-23-2002.**

The effective date is set by section 6 of HB 345.

## § 4549.42 Tampering with odometer.

(A) No person shall adjust, alter, change, tamper with, advance, set back, disconnect, or fail to connect, an odometer of a motor vehicle, or cause any of the foregoing to occur to an odometer of a motor vehicle with the intent to alter the number of miles registered on the odometer.

(B) Division (A) of this section does not apply to the disconnection of an odometer used for registering the mileage of any new motor vehicle being tested by the manufacturer prior to delivery to a franchise dealer.

(C) Nothing in this section prevents the service of an odometer, provided that after the service a completed form, captioned "notice of odometer repair," shall be attached to the left door frame of the motor vehicle by the person performing the repairs. The notice shall contain, in bold-face type, the following information and statements:

"Notice of Odometer Repair

The odometer of this motor vehicle was repaired or replaced on__________ (date of service).

The mileage registered on the odometer of this motor vehicle before repair was__________ (mileage).

The mileage registered on the odometer of this motor vehicle after repair is__________ (mileage).

..............................

(Repairer's signature)"

(D) No person shall intentionally remove or alter the notice required by division (C) of this section.

(E) If after the service of an odometer, the odometer can be set at the same mileage as before the service, the odometer shall be adjusted to reflect that mileage registered on the odometer of the motor vehicle before the service. If the odometer cannot be set at the same mileage as before the service, the odometer of the motor vehicle shall be adjusted to read "zero. "

(F) Except as otherwise provided in this division, whoever violates this section is guilty of tampering with an odometer, a felony of the fifth degree. If the offender previously has been convicted of or pleaded guilty to a violation of this section or of any provision of sections 4549.43 to 4549.46 of the Revised Code, tampering with an odometer is a felony of the fourth degree.

**HISTORY: 137 v S 78. Eff 9-6-77; 149 v S 123, § 1, eff. 1-1-04.**

The effective date is set by section 4 of S.B. 123.

See provisions, § 5 of S.B. 123 (149 v —), following RC § 4501.01.

## § 4549.43 Selling or installing odometer tampering device.

(A) No person, with intent to defraud, shall advertise for sale, sell, use, or install on any part of any motor vehicle or an odometer in any motor vehicle any device that causes the odometer to register any mileage other than the actual mileage driven by the motor vehicle. For the purpose of this section, the actual mileage driven is that mileage driven by the motor vehicle as registered by an odometer within the manufacturer's designed tolerance.

(B) Except as otherwise provided in this division, whoever violates this section is guilty of selling or installing an odometer tampering device, a felony of the fourth degree. If the offender previously has been convicted of or pleaded guilty to a violation of this section, section

4549.42, or any provision of sections 4549.44 to 4549.46 of the Revised Code, selling or installing an odometer tampering device is a felony of the third degree.

**HISTORY: 137 v S 78. Eff 9-6-77; 149 v S 123, § 1, eff. 1-1-04.**

The effective date is set by section 4 of S.B. 123.

See provisions, § 5 of S.B. 123 (149 v —), following RC § 4501.01.

## § 4549.44 Fraudulent driving without functional odometer.

(A) No person, with intent to defraud, shall operate a motor vehicle on any public street, road, or highway of this state knowing that the odometer of the vehicle is disconnected or nonfunctional.

A person's intent to defraud under this section may be inferred from evidence of the circumstances of the vehicle's operation, including facts pertaining to the length of time or number of miles of operation with a nonfunctioning or disconnected odometer, and the fact that the person subsequently transferred the vehicle without disclosing the inoperative odometer to the transferee in violation of section 4549.45 of the Revised Code.

(B) Except as otherwise provided in this division, whoever violates this section is guilty of fraudulent driving without a functional odometer, a felony of the fourth degree. If the offender previously has been convicted of or pleaded guilty to a violation of this section, section 4549.42 or 4549.43, or any provision of sections 4549.45 to 4549.46 of the Revised Code, fraudulent driving without a functional odometer is a felony of the third degree.

**HISTORY: 137 v S 78 (Eff 9-6-77); 141 v H 382. Eff 3-19-87; 149 v S 123, § 1, eff. 1-1-04.**

The effective date is set by section 4 of S.B. 123.

See provisions, § 5 of S.B. 123 (149 v —), following RC § 4501.01.

## § 4549.45 Transferring motor vehicle with tampered or nonfunctional odometer.

(A) No person shall transfer a motor vehicle if the person knows or recklessly disregards facts indicating that the odometer of the motor vehicle has been changed, tampered with, or disconnected, or has been in any other manner nonfunctional, to reflect a lesser mileage or use, unless that person gives clear and unequivocal notice of the tampering or nonfunction or of the person's reasonable belief of tampering or nonfunction, to the transferee in writing prior to the transfer. In a prosecution for violation of this section, evidence that a transferor or the transferor's agent has changed, tampered with, disconnected, or failed to connect the odometer of the motor vehicle constitutes prima-facie evidence of knowledge of the odometer's altered condition.

(B) Except as otherwise provided in this division, whoever violates this section is guilty of transferring a motor vehicle that has a tampered or nonfunctional odometer, a felony of the fourth degree. If the offender previously has been convicted of or pleaded guilty to a violation of this section, any provision of sections 4549.42 to 4549.44, or any provision of section 4549.451 or 4549.46 of the Revised Code, transferring a motor vehicle that has a tampered or nonfunctional odometer is a felony of the third degree.

**HISTORY: 137 v S 78 (Eff 9-6-77); 141 v H 382. Eff 3-19-87; 149 v S 123, § 1, eff. 1-1-04.**

The effective date is set by section 4 of S.B. 123.

See provisions, § 5 of S.B. 123 (149 v —), following RC § 4501.01.

## § 4549.451 Auctioneer's statement.

(A) No auctioneer licensed under Chapter 4707. of the Revised Code shall advertise for sale by means of any written advertisement, brochure, flyer, or other writing, any motor vehicle the auctioneer knows or has reason to believe has an odometer that has been changed, tampered with, or disconnected, or in any other manner has been nonfunctional, unless the listing or description of the vehicle contained in the written advertisement, brochure, flyer, or other writing contains one of the two following statements:

(1) "This motor vehicle has an odometer that has been changed, tampered with, or disconnected, or otherwise has been nonfunctional."

(2) "Nonactual odometer reading: warning — odometer discrepancy."

(B) The statement selected by the auctioneer shall be printed in type identical in size to the other type used in the listing or description, and shall be located within the listing or description and not located as a footnote to the listing or description.

(C) Except as otherwise provided in this division, whoever violates this section is guilty of a felony of the fourth degree. If the offender previously has been convicted of or pleaded guilty to a violation of this section, any provision of sections 4549.42 to 4549.45, or section 4549.46 of the Revised Code, whoever violates this section is guilty of a felony of the third degree.

**HISTORY: 147 v S 60. Eff 10-21-97; 149 v S 123, § 1, eff. 1-1-04.**

The effective date is set by section 4 of S.B. 123.

See provisions, § 5 of S.B. 123 (149 v —), following RC § 4501.01.

## § 4549.46 Odometer disclosure violation.

(A) No transferor shall fail to provide the true and complete odometer disclosures required by section 4505.06 of the Revised Code. The transferor of a motor vehicle is not in violation of this division requiring a true odometer reading if the odometer reading is incorrect due to a previous owner's violation of any of the provisions contained in sections 4549.42 to 4549.46 of the Revised Code, unless the transferor knows of or recklessly disregards facts indicating the violation.

(B) No dealer or wholesaler who acquires ownership of a motor vehicle shall accept any written odometer disclosure statement unless the statement is completed as required by section 4505.06 of the Revised Code.

(C) A motor vehicle leasing dealer may obtain a written odometer disclosure statement completed as required by section 4505.06 of the Revised Code from a motor vehicle lessee that can be used as prima-facie evidence in any legal action arising under sections 4549.41 to 4549.46 of the Revised Code.

(D) Except as otherwise provided in this division, whoever violates division (A) or (B) of this section is guilty of an odometer disclosure violation, a felony of the fourth degree. If the offender previously has been convicted of or pleaded guilty to a violation of this section or any provision of sections 4549.42 to 4549.451 of the Revised Code, a violation of this section is a felony of the third degree.

**HISTORY: 137 v S 78 (Eff 9-6-77); 140 v S 115 (Eff 10-14-83); 141 v H 382. Eff 3-19-87; 149 v S 123, § 1, eff. 1-1-04.**

The effective date is set by section 4 of S.B. 123.

See provisions, § 5 of S.B. 123 (149 v —), following RC § 4501.01.

## § 4549.47 Attorney general may investigate violations.

(A) If by his own inquiries or as a result of complaints, the attorney general has reason to believe that a person has engaged, is engaging, or is preparing to engage, in a violation of sections 4549.41 to 4549.46 of the Revised Code, he may investigate.

(B) For this purpose the attorney general may administer oaths, subpoena witnesses, adduce evidence, and require the production of relevant matter.

If the matter that the attorney general requires to be produced is located outside the state, he may designate representatives, including officials of the state in which the matter is located, to inspect the matter on his behalf, and he may respond to similar requests from officials of other states. The person subpoenaed may make the matter available to the attorney general at a convenient location within the state or pay the reasonable and necessary expenses for the attorney general or his representative to examine the matter at the place where it is located, provided that expenses shall not be charged to a party not subsequently found to have engaged in a violation of sections 4549.41 to 4549.46 of the Revised Code.

(C) At any time before the return day specified in the subpoena, or within twenty days after the subpoena has been served, whichever period is shorter, a petition to extend the return day, or to modify or quash the subpoena, stating good cause, may be filed in the court of common pleas in Franklin county or in the county where the person served resides or has his principal place of business.

(D) A person subpoenaed under this section shall comply with the terms of the subpoena unless otherwise provided by court order entered prior to the day for return contained in the subpoena or as extended by the court. If a person fails without lawful excuse to obey a subpoena or to produce relevant matter, the attorney general may apply to a court of common pleas and obtain an order doing any of the following:

(1) Adjudging the person in contempt of court;

(2) Granting injunctive relief to restrain the person from engaging in any conduct that violates sections 4549.41 to 4549.46 of the Revised Code;

(3) Granting injunctive relief to preserve or restore the status quo;

(4) Granting such other relief as may be required until the person obeys the subpoena.

If a person violates any order entered by a court under this section, the violation shall be punished as a violation of an injunction issued under division (A) of section 4549.48 of the Revised Code.

(E) The attorney general may request that an individual who refuses to testify or to produce relevant matter on the ground that the testimony or matter may incriminate him be ordered by the court to provide the testimony or matter. With the exception of a prosecution for perjury and an action for damages under section 4549.49 of the Revised Code, an individual who complies with a court order to provide testimony or matter, after asserting a privilege against self-incrimination to which he is entitled by law, shall not be subjected to a criminal proceeding on the basis of the testimony or matter required to be disclosed or testimony or matter discovered through that testimony or matter.

**HISTORY: 137 v S 78. Eff 9-6-77.**

## § 4549.48 Action to enjoin violation; penalty; remedies.

(A) Whenever it appears that a person has violated, is violating, or is about to violate any provision of sections 4549.41 to 4549.46 of the Revised Code, the attorney general may bring an action in the court of common pleas to enjoin the violation. Upon a showing of a violation of sections 4549.41 to 4549.46 of the Revised Code, a temporary restraining order, preliminary injunction, or permanent injunction shall be granted without bond. The court may impose a penalty of not more than five thousand dollars for each day of violation of a temporary restraining order, preliminary injunction, or permanent injunction issued under this section. The court may issue an order requiring the reimbursement of a consumer for any loss that results from a violation of sections 4549.41 to 4549.46 of the Revised Code, for the recovery of any amounts for which a violator is liable pursuant to division (A) of section 4549.49 of the Revised Code, for the appointment of a referee or receiver, for the sequestration of assets, for the rescission of transfers of motor vehicles, or granting any other appropriate relief. The court may award the attorney general all costs together with all expenses of his investigation and reasonable attorneys' fees incurred in the prosecution of the action, which shall be deposited in the consumer protection enforcement fund created by section 1345.51 of the Revised Code.

(B) In addition to the remedies otherwise provided by this section, the attorney general may request and the court shall impose a civil penalty of not less than one thousand nor more than two thousand dollars for each violation. A violation of any provision of sections 4549.41 to 4549.46 of the Revised Code shall, for purposes of this section, constitute a separate violation with respect to each motor vehicle or unlawful device involved, except that the maximum civil penalty shall not exceed one hundred thousand dollars for any related series of violations by a person. Civil penalties ordered pursuant to this division shall be paid as follows: one-fourth of the amount to the treasurer of the county in which the action is brought; three-fourths to the consumer protection enforcement fund created by section 1345.51 of the Revised Code.

(C) The remedies prescribed by this section are cumulative and concurrent with any other remedy, and the existence or exercise of one remedy does not prevent the exercise of any other remedy.

**HISTORY: 137 v S 78 (Eff 9-6-77); 141 v H 382. Eff 3-19-87.**

The effective date is set by section 3 of HB 382.

## § 4549.49 Liability to transferee.

(A) Any person who violates any requirement imposed by sections 4549.41 to 4549.46 of the Revised Code is liable to any transferee of the motor vehicle subsequent to the violation, in an amount equal to:

(1) Three times the amount of actual damages sustained or fifteen hundred dollars, whichever is greater; and

(2) In the case of any successful action to enforce the foregoing liability, the costs of the action together with reasonable attorneys' fees as determined by the court.

(B) An action to enforce any liability created under sections 4549.41 to 4549.46 of the Revised Code may be brought in a court of common pleas without regard to the amount in controversy, or in any other court of competent jurisdiction, within two years from the date on which the liability arises. For the purpose of this section, liability arises when the transferee discovers, or with due diligence should have discovered, the violation.

**HISTORY: 137 v S 78. Eff 9-6-77.**

## § 4549.50 Revocation or denial of license or permit; surety bond.

Violation of sections 4549.41 to 4549.46 of the Revised Code by any person licensed or granted a permit by this state as a dealer, wholesaler, distributor, salesman, or auction owner under Chapter 4517. of the Revised Code, is prima-facie evidence of intent to defraud and constitutes cause for the revocation or denial of the license of such person to sell any motor vehicle in this state. Any person who violates sections 4549.41 to 4549.46 of the Revised Code, upon receiving notice from the registrar of motor vehicles or motor vehicle dealers board of the intent to revoke or suspend a license or permit, shall immediately post a surety bond with the registrar in favor of the state in the amount of twenty-five thousand dollars and shall maintain the bond while the license or permit is in effect. The bond shall be for the use, benefit, and protection of any transferee damaged by the licensee's or permitee's violation of sections 4549.41 to 4549.46 of the Revised Code or for the payment of civil penalties or costs resulting from enforcement actions. Any transferee claiming against the bond or the attorney general may maintain an action against the transferor or the surety, except that the surety is liable only for actual damages. The aggregate liability of the surety shall not exceed twenty-five thousand dollars. Any money unclaimed by transferees after two years from the date of the conviction of or judgment against the transferor shall be deposited in the consumer protection enforcement fund created by section 1345.51 of the Revised Code. The surety bond shall remain in effect until the license or permit is revoked or suspended by the motor vehicle dealers board pursuant to section 4517.33 of the Revised Code. Upon reinstatement of a license or permit that has been suspended, or upon reissuance of a license or permit after the period of revocation, the licensee or permit[t]ee shall post an additional surety bond in accordance with this section. The surety bond shall remain in effect during the period in which the licensee or permitee engages in business in the state.

**HISTORY: 137 v S 78 (Eff 9-6-77); 141 v H 382. Eff 3-19-87.**

The effective date is set by section 3 of HB 382.

## § 4549.51 Additional remedies.

The remedies under sections 4549.41 to 4549.51 of the Revised Code are in addition to remedies otherwise available for the same conduct under federal, state, or local law.

**HISTORY: 137 v S 78. Eff 9-6-77.**

## § 4549.52 Criminal action to enforce provisions.

The prosecuting attorney of the county in which a violation of any provision of sections 4549.41 to 4549.51 of the Revised Code occurs, or the attorney general, may bring a criminal action to enforce the provisions of sections 4549.41 to 4549.51 of the Revised Code. The attorney general and the prosecuting attorney of the county in which a person licensed or granted a permit under Chapter 4517. of the Revised Code is convicted of or pleads guilty to a violation of any provision of sections 4549.41 to 4549.46 of the Revised Code shall report the conviction or guilty plea to the registrar of motor vehicles within five business days of the conviction or plea.

**HISTORY: 149 v S 123, § 1, eff. 1-1-04.**

The effective date is set by section 4 of S.B. 123.
See provisions, § 5 of S.B. 123 (149 v —), following RC § 4501.01.

### [TAMPERING WITH IDENTIFYING NUMBERS]

## § 4549.61 Definitions.

As used in sections 4549.61 to 4549.63 of the Revised Code, "vehicle identification number or derivative thereof" means any number or derivative of such a number that is embossed, engraved, etched, or otherwise marked on any vehicle or vehicle part by the manufacturer. "Vehicle identification number" also includes a duplicate vehicle identification number replaced upon a vehicle under the authority of the registrar of motor vehicles.

**HISTORY: 140 v H 632. Eff 3-28-85.**

## § 4549.62 Offenses involving tampering with identifying numbers to conceal identity of vehicle or part; replacement.

(A) No person, with purpose to conceal or destroy the identity of a vehicle or vehicle part, shall remove, deface, cover, alter, or destroy any vehicle identification number or derivative of a vehicle identification number on a vehicle or vehicle part.

(B) No person, with purpose to conceal or destroy the identity of a vehicle or a vehicle part, shall remove, deface, cover, alter, or destroy any identifying number that has been lawfully placed upon a vehicle or vehicle part by an owner of the vehicle or vehicle part, other than the manufacturer, for the purpose of deterring its theft and facilitating its recovery if stolen.

(C) No person, with purpose to conceal or destroy the identity of a vehicle or vehicle part, shall place a counterfeit vehicle identification number or derivative of a vehicle identification number upon the vehicle or vehicle part.

(D)(1) No person shall buy, offer to buy, sell, offer to sell, receive, dispose of, conceal, or, except as provided in division (D)(4) of this section, possess any vehicle or vehicle part with knowledge that the vehicle identification number or a derivative of the vehicle identification number has been removed, defaced, covered, altered, or destroyed in such a manner that the identity of the vehicle or part cannot be determined by a visual examination of the number at the site where the manufacturer placed the number.

(2)(a) A vehicle or vehicle part from which the vehicle identification number or a derivative of the vehicle identification number has been so removed, defaced, covered, altered, or destroyed shall be seized and forfeited under Chapter 2981. of the Revised Code unless division (D)(3) or (4) of this section applies to the vehicle or part. If a derivative of the vehicle identification number has been removed, defaced, covered, altered, or destroyed in such a manner that the identity of the part cannot be determined, the entire vehicle is subject to seizure pending a determination of the original identity and ownership of the vehicle and parts of the vehicle, and the rights of innocent owners to reclaim the remainder or any part of the vehicle.

(b) The lawful owners of parts upon a vehicle that has been seized under this section and that is subject to forfeiture under Chapter 2981. of the Revised Code are entitled to reclaim their respective parts upon satisfactory proof of all of the following:

(i) That the part is not needed for evidence in pending proceedings involving the vehicle or part and is not subject to forfeiture under Chapter 2981. of the Revised Code;

(ii) That the original identity and ownership of the part can be determined and that the claimant is the lawful owner of the part;

(iii) That no vehicle identification number or derivative of a vehicle identification number on the part has been destroyed or concealed in such a manner that the identity of the part cannot be determined from that number;

(iv) Payment of all costs of removing the part.

(3) Divisions (A), (B), and (D)(1) and (2) of this section do not apply to the good faith acquisition and disposition of vehicles and vehicle parts as junk or scrap in the ordinary course of business by a scrap metal processing facility as defined in division (D) of section 4737.05 of the Revised Code or by a motor vehicle salvage dealer licensed under Chapter 4738. of the Revised Code. This division does not create an element of an offense or an affirmative defense, or affect the burden of proceeding with the evidence or burden of proof in a criminal proceeding.

(4)(a) Divisions (D)(1) and (2) of this section do not apply to the possession of an owner, or the owner's insurer, who provides satisfactory evidence of all of the following:

(i) That the vehicle identification number or derivative thereof on the vehicle or part has been removed, defaced, covered, altered, or destroyed, after the owner acquired such possession, by another person without the consent of the owner, by accident or other casualty not due to the owner's purpose to conceal or destroy the identity of the vehicle or vehicle part, or by ordinary wear and tear;

(ii) That the person is the owner of the vehicle as shown on a valid certificate of title issued by this state or certificate of title or other lawful evidence of title issued in another state, in a clear chain of title beginning with the manufacturer;

(iii) That the original identity of the vehicle can be established in a manner that excludes any reasonable probability that the vehicle has been stolen from another person.

(b) The registrar of motor vehicles shall adopt rules under Chapter 119. of the Revised Code to permit an owner described in division (D)(4)(a) of this section, upon application and submission of satisfactory evidence to the registrar, to obtain authority to replace the vehicle identification number under the supervision of a peace officer, trooper of the state highway patrol, or representative of the registrar. The rules shall be designed to restore the identification of the vehicle in a manner that will deter its theft and facilitate its marketability. Until such rules are adopted, the registrar shall follow the existing procedure for the replacement of vehicle identification numbers that have been established by the registrar, with such modifications as the registrar determines to be necessary or appropriate for the administration of the laws the registrar is required to administer.

The registrar may issue a temporary permit to an owner of a motor vehicle who is described in division (D)(4)(a) of this section to authorize the owner to retain possession of the motor vehicle and to transfer title to the motor vehicle with the consent of the registrar.

(c) No owner described in division (D)(4)(a) of this section shall fail knowingly to apply to the registrar for authority to replace the vehicle identification number, within thirty days after the later of the following dates:

(i) The date of receipt by the applicant of actual knowledge of the concealment or destruction;

(ii) If the property has been stolen, the date thereafter upon which the applicant obtains possession of the vehicle or has been notified by a law enforcement agency that the vehicle has been recovered.

The requirement of division (D)(4)(c) of this section may be excused by the registrar for good cause shown.

(E) Whoever violates division (A), (B), (C), or (D)(1) of this section is guilty of a felony of the fifth degree on a first offense and a felony of the fourth degree on each subsequent offense.

(F) Whoever violates division (D)(4)(c) of this section is guilty of a minor misdemeanor.

**HISTORY: 140 v H 632 (Eff 3-28-85); 144 v S 144. Eff 8-8-91; 149 v S 123, § 1, eff. 1-1-04; 151 v H 241, § 1, eff. 7-1-07.**

See provisions of § 4 of 151 v H 241 following RC § 4503.233. The effective date is set by section 4 of S.B. 123.

See provisions, § 5 of S.B. 123 (149 v —), following RC § 4501.01.

## § 4549.63 Seizure of vehicle or parts.

(A) A law enforcement officer may seize and take possession of a vehicle or vehicle part if the officer has probable cause to believe that any vehicle identification number or derivative thereof on the vehicle or part has been removed, defaced, covered, altered, or destroyed in such a manner that the identity of the vehicle or part cannot be determined by visual examination of the number at the site where the manufacturer placed the number. The seizure shall be pursuant to a warrant, unless the circumstances are within one of the exceptions to the warrant requirement that have been established by the supreme court of the United States or of the supreme court of this state.

(B) A vehicle or vehicle part seized under division (A) of this section shall be held in custody pursuant to section 2981.11 of the Revised Code or any applicable municipal ordinance.

(C) A law enforcement officer who acts in good faith in the belief that the seizure of a vehicle or vehicle part is justified under division (A) of this section is immune from any civil or criminal liability for such seizure.

(D) The lawful owner of a vehicle or vehicle part seized under this section that is not needed as evidence and is not subject to forfeiture under division (D)(2) of section 4549.62 of the Revised Code may reclaim the property by submitting satisfactory proof of ownership to the law enforcement agency or court holding the property.

**HISTORY: 140 v H 632. Eff 3-28-85; 151 v H 241, § 1, eff. 7-1-07.**

See provisions of § 4 of 151 v H 241 following RC § 4503.233.

## § 4549.65 Immunity of leasing or renting dealer believing that vehicle has been converted or stolen.

(A) As used in this section:

(1) "Motor vehicle leasing dealer" has the meaning set forth in division (M) of section 4517.01 of the Revised Code.

(2) "Motor vehicle renting dealer" means any person engaged in the business of regularly making available, offering to make available, or arranging for another person to use a motor vehicle pursuant to a bailment, rental agreement, or other contractual arrangement for a period of less than thirty days under which a charge is made for its use at a periodic rate and the title to the motor vehicle is in a person other than the user, but does not mean a manufacturer or its affiliate renting to its employees or to dealers.

(B) A motor vehicle leasing dealer or a motor vehicle renting dealer and its officers, employees, agents, and representatives are not liable to a lessee or renter for damages or injuries sustained as a result of the lessee's or renter's being stopped, detained, arrested, or charged in connection with a theft offense involving the leased or rented motor vehicle if such dealer, its officers, employees, agents, or representatives act in good faith upon a reasonable belief that the motor vehicle was or is being converted or stolen or if both of the following apply:

(1) The lessee or renter did not return the motor vehicle at the time and place specified in the lease or rental contract;

(2) The lessee or renter failed to return the motor vehicle within twenty-four hours after the dealer, or an officer, employee, agent, or representative of the dealer has served a written notice upon the lessee or renter, requesting the return of the motor vehicle, at the lessee's or renter's address set forth in the lease or rental contract. Service may be by certified mail, return receipt requested, or by personal or residence service.

**HISTORY: 140 v H 632. Eff 3-28-85.**

## § 4549.99 Repealed, 149 v S 123, § 2 [Bureau of Code Revision, 10-1-53; 129 v 366; 130 v S 312; 132 v H 591; 134 v H 101; 134 v H 511; 137 v S 78; 140 v H 632; 141 v H 382; 146 v S 2; 147 v H 618; 150 v H 50.] Eff. 1-1-04.

This section concerned penalties.

The effective date is set by section 4 of S.B. 123.

See provisions, § 5 of S.B. 123 (149 v —), following RC § 4501.01.

# CHAPTER 4561: AERONAUTICS



## § 4561.01 Definitions.

As used in sections 4561.01 to 4561.151 [4561.15.1] of the Revised Code:

(A) "Aviation" means transportation by aircraft; operation of aircraft; the establishment, operation, maintenance, repair, and improvement of airports, landing fields, and other air navigation facilities; and all other activities connected therewith or incidental thereto.

(B) "Aircraft" means any contrivance used or designed for navigation or flight in the air, excepting a parachute or other contrivance for such navigation used primarily as safety equipment.

(C) "Airport" means any location either on land or water which is used for the landing and taking off of aircraft.

(D) "Landing field" means any location either on land or water of such size and nature as to permit the landing or taking off of aircraft with safety, and used for that purpose but not equipped to provide for the shelter, supply, or care of aircraft.

(E) "Air navigation facility" means any facility used, available for use, or designed for use in aid of navigation of aircraft, including airports, landing fields, facilities for the servicing of aircraft or for the comfort and accommodation of air travelers, and any structures, mechanisms, lights, beacons, marks, communicating systems, or other instrumentalities or devices used or useful as an aid to the safe taking off, navigation, and landing of aircraft, or to the safe and efficient operation or maintenance of an airport or landing field, and any combination of such facilities.

(F) "Air navigation hazard" means any structure, object of natural growth, or use of land, that obstructs the air space required for the flight of aircraft in landing or taking off at any airport or landing field, or that otherwise is hazardous to such landing or taking off.

(G) "Air navigation," "navigation of aircraft," or "navigate aircraft" means the operation of aircraft in the air space over this state.

(H) "Airperson" means any individual who, as the person in command, or as pilot, mechanic, or member of the crew, engages in the navigation of aircraft.

(I) "Airway" means a route in the air space over and above the lands or waters of this state, designated by the federal aviation administration as a route suitable for the navigation of aircraft.

(J) "Person" means any individual, firm, partnership, corporation, company, association, joint stock association, or body politic, and includes any trustee, receiver, assignee, or other similar representative thereof.

HISTORY: GC § 6310-38; 121 v 253; Bureau of Code Revision, Eff 10-1-53; 146 v S 2 Eff 7-1-96.

[DIVISION OF AVIATION]

## § 4561.13 Investigation of accidents; enforcement of laws.

Every state, county, and municipal law enforcement officer charged with the enforcement of state or municipal laws may investigate aircraft accidents and enforce sections 4561.14, 4561.15, and 4561.24 of the Revised Code.

The state highway patrol may use any of its personnel and equipment to investigate all aircraft accidents within this state.

**HISTORY: GC §§ 6310-49, 6310-50b; 121 v 253, § 12; 122 v 72; Bureau of Code Revision, 10-1-53; 127 v 349 (Eff 9-17-57); 135 v S 96 (Eff 8-22-73); 146 v S 2 (Eff 7-1-96); 149 v H 73. Eff 6-29-2001.**

The effective date is set by section 16 of HB 73.

## § 4561.14 Prohibitions.

(A) No person shall operate any aircraft in this state unless such person is the holder of a valid aviator's license issued by the United States.

No person operating an aircraft within this state shall fail to exhibit such license for inspection upon the demand of any passenger on such aircraft, or fail to exhibit same for inspection upon the demand of any peace officer, member or employee of the department of transportation, or manager or person in charge of an airport or landing field within this state, prior to taking off or upon landing said aircraft.

No person shall operate an aircraft within this state unless such aircraft is licensed and registered by the United States; this section is inapplicable to the operation of military aircraft of the United States, aircraft of a state, territory, or possession of the United States, or aircraft licensed by a foreign country with which the United States has a reciprocal agreement covering the operation of such aircraft.

No person shall operate an aircraft within this state in violation of any air traffic rules in force under the laws of the United States or under sections 4561.01 to 4561.14 of the Revised Code, and the rules and regulations of the department adopted pursuant thereto.

(B) Whoever violates this section shall be fined not more than five hundred dollars, imprisoned not more than ninety days, or both.

**HISTORY: GC § 6310-50; 121 v 253, § 13; Bureau of Code Revision, 10-1-53; 127 v 349 (Eff 9-17-57); 135 v S 96. Eff 8-22-73; 149 v S 123, § 1, eff. 1-1-04.**

The effective date is set by section 4 of S.B. 123.

See provisions, § 5 of S.B. 123 (149 v —), following RC § 4501.01.

## § 4561.15 Unsafe operation of aircraft.

(A) No person shall commit any of the following acts:

(1) Carry passengers in an aircraft unless the person piloting the aircraft is a holder of a valid airperson's certificate of competency issued by the United States that authorizes the holder to carry passengers and the person is carrying any passenger in accordance with the applicable certificate requirements; this division of this section is inapplicable to the operation of military aircraft of the United States, aircraft of a state, territory, or possession of the United States, or aircraft licensed by a foreign country with which the United States has a reciprocal agreement covering the operation of such aircraft;

(2) Operate an aircraft on the land or water or in the air space over this state in a careless or reckless manner that endangers any person or property, or with willful or wanton disregard for the rights or safety of others;

(3) Operate an aircraft on the land or water or in the air space over this state while under the influence of intoxicating liquor, controlled substances, or other habit-forming drugs;

(4) Tamper with, alter, destroy, remove, carry away, or cause to be carried away any object used for the marking of airports, landing fields, or other aeronautical facilities in this state, or in any way change the position or location of such markings, except by the direction of the proper authorities charged with the maintenance and operation of such facilities, or illegally possess any object used for such markings.

(B) Jurisdiction over any proceedings charging a violation of this section is limited to courts of record.

(C) Whoever violates this section shall be fined not more than five hundred dollars, imprisoned not more than six months, or both.

**HISTORY: GC § 6310-50a; 122 v 72; Bureau of Code Revision, 10-1-53; 136 v H 300 (Eff 7-1-76); 146 v S 2. Eff 7-1-96; 149 v S 123, § 1, eff. 1-1-04; 153 v H 50, § 1, eff. 9-8-10.**

The effective date is set by section 4 of S.B. 123.

See provisions, § 5 of S.B. 123 (149 v —), following RC § 4501.01.

## § 4561.24 Operation of motor vehicles on airport runways prohibited.

(A) No person shall operate a motor vehicle upon any runway of an airport without prior approval of the person in charge of the airport when the airport has been certified as a commercial airport by the office of aviation.

Any person lending assistance to the operator or operation of a vehicle engaged in such activity shall be equally charged as the participants.

(B) Except as otherwise provided in this division, whoever violates this section shall be fined not less than one hundred nor more than five hundred dollars, imprisoned for not more than six months, or both. If the offender previously has committed a violation of this section, whoever violates this section shall be fined not less than two hundred nor more than one thousand dollars, imprisoned for not more than one year, or both.

(C) As used in this section, "motor vehicle" has the same meaning as in section 4501.01 of the Revised Code.

(D) Airport vehicles and emergency and maintenance equipment are exempted from this section.

**HISTORY: 133 v H 266 (Eff 8-28-69); 146 v H 572. Eff 9-17-96; 149 v S 123, § 1, eff. 1-1-04.**

The effective date is set by section 4 of S.B. 123.

See provisions, § 5 of S.B. 123 (149 v —), following RC § 4501.01.

[PENALTIES]

## § 4561.99 Penalties.

Whoever violates any provision of sections 4561.021 to 4561.13 of the Revised Code for which no penalty otherwise is provided in the section that contains the provision violated shall be fined not more than five hundred dollars, imprisoned not more than ninety days, or both.

**HISTORY: Bureau of Code Revision, 10-1-53; 133 v H 266 (Eff 8-28-69); 144 v H 15 (Eff 10-15-91); 145 v H 571 (Eff 10-6-94); 146 v S 2. Eff 7-1-96; 149 v S 123, § 1, eff. 1-1-04.**

The effective date is set by section 4 of S.B. 123.

See provisions, § 5 of S.B. 123 (149 v —), following RC § 4501.01.

# TITLE 47: OCCUPATIONS — PROFESSIONS

## CHAPTER 4712: OHIO CREDIT SERVICES ORGANIZATION ACT

Section



### § 4712.02 Credit services organization to obtain registration certificate; notice of change in information; statutory agent for nonresident.

(A) A credit services organization shall file a registration application with, and receive a certificate of registration from, the division of financial institutions before conducting business in this state. The registration application shall be accompanied by a one-hundred-dollar fee and shall contain all of the following information:

(1) The name and address of the credit services organization;

(2) The name and address of any person that directly or indirectly owns or controls ten per cent or more of the outstanding shares of stock in the organization;

(3) Either of the following:

(a) A full and complete disclosure of any litigation commenced against the organization or unresolved complaint that relates to the operation of the organization and that is filed with the attorney general, the secretary of state, or any other governmental authority of the United States, this state, or any other state of the United States;

(b) A notarized statement stating that no litigation has been commenced and no unresolved complaint relating to the operation of the organization has been filed with the attorney general, the secretary of state, or any other governmental authority of the United States, this state, or any other state of the United States.

(4) Any other information required at any time by the division.

(B)(1) Except as otherwise provided in division (B)(2) of this section, each credit services organization shall notify the division in writing within thirty days after the date of a change in the information required by division (A) of this section.

(2) Each organization shall notify the division in writing no later than thirty days prior to any change in the information required by division (A)(1) or (2) of this section and shall receive approval from the division before making any such change.

(C)(1) A credit services organization shall attach both of the following to the registration application submitted pursuant to division (A) of this section:

(a) A copy of the contract that the organization intends to execute with its customers;

(b) Evidence of the bond required under section 4712.06 of the Revised Code.

(2) Any modification made to the contract described in division (C)(1)(a) of this section shall be filed with the division prior to its use by the organization.

(D) Each credit services organization registering under this section shall maintain a copy of the registration application in its files. The organization shall allow a buyer to inspect the registration application upon request.

(E) Each nonresident credit services organization registering under this section shall designate and maintain a resident of this state as the organization's statutory agent for purposes of receipt of service of process.

(F) If, in order to issue a certificate of registration to a credit services organization, investigation by the division outside this state is necessary, the division may require the organization to advance sufficient funds to pay the actual expenses of the investigation.

(G) Each credit services organization registering under this section shall use no more than one fictitious or trade name.

(H)(1) A certificate of registration issued by the division pursuant to this section shall expire annually on the thirtieth day of April.

(2) A credit services organization may renew its certificate of registration by filing with the division a renewal application accompanied by a one-hundred-dollar renewal fee.

(I) All money collected by the division pursuant to this section shall be deposited by it in the state treasury to the credit of the consumer finance fund.

(J)(1) No credit services organization shall fail to comply with division (A) of this section.

(2) No credit services organization shall fail to comply with division (B), (D), (E), (F), or (G) of this section.

**HISTORY: 144 v S 323 (Eff 4-16-93); 146 v S 293†. Eff 9-26-96.**

† See Publisher's Note following RC § 4707.05.

### § 4712.04 Statement of rights to be provided to buyer prior to executing contract or receiving consideration.

(A) Before executing a contract or agreement with a buyer or receiving money or other valuable consideration, a credit services organization shall provide the buyer with a written statement containing all of the following information:

(1) A complete and detailed description of the services to be performed by the organization for the buyer and the total cost of the services;

(2) A statement explaining the buyer's rights against the surety bond required pursuant to section 4712.06 of the Revised Code;

(3) The name and address of the surety company that issued the surety bond;

(4) A complete and accurate statement of the availability of nonprofit budget and debt counseling services.

(B) The written statement required under division (A) of this section shall be printed in at least ten-point boldface type and shall include the following statement or any alternative statement prescribed by the division of financial institutions:

"Credit Reporting Practices

Rights of Consumers Under

Ohio and Federal Law

Under the federal Fair Credit Reporting Act, you have all of the following legal rights:

You have a right to obtain a copy of your credit report from a consumer reporting agency. You may be charged a reasonable fee. However, there is no fee if you have been turned down within the preceding sixty days for credit, employment, insurance, or a rental dwelling because of information in your credit report. The consumer reporting agency must provide someone to help you interpret the information in your credit file.

You have a right to dispute inaccurate information by contacting the consumer reporting agency directly. However, neither you nor any credit services organization has the right to have accurate, current, and verifiable information removed from your consumer reporting agency report. The consumer reporting agency must remove accurate, negative information from your report only if it is more than seven years old. Bankruptcy information can be reported for ten years. Accurate information cannot be permanently removed from the files of a consumer reporting agency. Credit reporting agencies are required to follow reasonable procedures to ensure that creditors report information accurately. However, mistakes may occur.

You may, on your own, notify a consumer reporting agency in writing that you dispute the accuracy of information in your credit file. The consumer reporting agency then must reinvestigate and modify or remove inaccurate information. The consumer reporting agency must not charge any fee for this service. Any pertinent information and copies of all documents you have concerning an error should be given to the consumer reporting agency.

If reinvestigation does not resolve the dispute to your satisfaction, you may send a brief statement to the consumer reporting agency to keep in your file, explaining why you think the record is inaccurate. The consumer reporting agency must include your statement about disputed information in any reports it issues about you.

Under Ohio law, you have a right to sue a credit services organization that violates the Ohio Credit Services Organization Act. This law prohibits deceptive practices by credit services organizations and gives you a right to cancel your contract for any reason within three business days from the date you signed it."

(C) The credit services organization shall maintain a copy of the statement, signed by the buyer, acknowledging receipt of the statement. The copy shall be maintained in the organization's files for at least two years after the date on which the statement is provided to the buyer.

(D) The credit services organization, in a timely manner, shall notify each buyer of all substantive changes in the "Fair Credit Reporting Act," 84 Stat. 1128, 15 U.S.C.A. 1681a, and shall provide each buyer with copies of those changes.

(E) No credit services organization shall fail to comply with this section.

**HISTORY: 144 v S 323 (Eff 4-16-93); 146 v H 193 (Eff 11-24-95); 146 v S 293†. Eff 9-26-96.**

† See Publisher's Note following RC § 4707.05.

## § 4712.05 Execution and contents of contract; notice of right to cancel; obligations of organization.

(A) Each contract between the buyer and a credit services organization for the purchase of the services of the organization shall be in writing, dated and signed by the buyer, and shall include all of the following:

(1) A statement, in type that is boldfaced, capitalized, underlined, or otherwise conspicuously set out from surrounding written material and that is in immediate proximity to the space reserved for the signature of the buyer, as follows:

"If you, the buyer, have been denied credit within the last sixty days, you may obtain a free copy of the consumer credit report from the consumer reporting agency. You also have the right to dispute inaccurate information in a report.

You may cancel this contract at any time before midnight of the third business day after the date you signed it. See the attached notice of cancellation form for an explanation of this right."

(2) The terms and conditions of payment, including the total of all payments to be made by the buyer, whether to the credit services organization or to another person;

(3) A full and detailed description of the services to be performed for the buyer by the credit services organization, including all guarantees and all promises of full or partial refunds, and the estimated length of time, not exceeding sixty days or any shorter time period prescribed by the superintendent of financial institutions, for performing the services;

(4) The address of the credit services organization's principal place of business and the name and address of its agent in this state authorized to receive service of process;

(5) With respect to the previous calendar year or the time period during which the credit services organization has been in business, whichever is shorter, the percentage of the organization's customers for whom the organization has fully and completely performed the services the organization agreed to perform for the buyer.

(B) The contract shall have attached two easily detachable copies of a notice of cancellation. The notice shall be in boldface type and in the following form:

"Notice of Cancellation

You may cancel this contract, without any penalty or obligation, within three business days after the date the contract is signed.

To cancel this contract, mail or deliver a signed, dated copy of this cancellation notice, or other written notice, to:

______________ at ______________

(Name of Seller) (Address of Seller)
(Place of Business)

Not later than midnight ______________
(Date)

I hereby cancel this transaction.

Dated: ______________ ______________
(Buyer's Signature)"

(C) The credit services organization, at the time of signing, shall give to the buyer a copy of the completed contract and all other documents the organization requires the buyer to sign.

(D) No credit services organization shall breach a contract described in this section or fail to comply with any obligation arising from such a contract.

(E) No credit services organization shall fail to comply with division (A), (B), or (C) of this section.

**HISTORY: 144 v S 323 (Eff 4-16-93); 146 v S 293†. Eff 9-26-96.**

† See Publisher's Note following RC § 4707.05.

## § 4712.06 Surety bond.

(A) No credit services organization shall conduct business in this state unless the organization has obtained a surety bond issued by a surety company authorized to do business in this state and all of the following conditions are met:

(1) A copy of the bond is filed with the division of financial institutions.

(2) The bond is in favor of any person, and of the state for the benefit of any person, that is injured by any violation of sections 4712.01 to 4712.14 of the Revised Code.

(3) The bond is in the amount of fifty thousand dollars.

(4) The bond is maintained and in effect for at least two years after the date on which the credit services organization ceases to conduct business in this state.

(B) Any person claiming against the bond for a violation of sections 4712.01 to 4712.14 of the Revised Code may maintain an action at law against the credit services organization and against the surety company. However, the surety company is liable only for damages awarded under division (A)(2) of section 4712.10 of the Revised Code and not for punitive damages awarded under division (A)(3) of section 4712.10 of the Revised Code. The aggregate liability of the surety company to all persons injured by a credit services organization's violation of sections 4712.01 to 4712.14 of the Revised Code shall not exceed the amount of the bond.

**HISTORY: 144 v S 323 (Eff 4-16-93); 146 v S 293†. Eff 9-26-96.**

† See Publisher's Note following RC § 4707.05.

## § 4712.07 Prohibited sales activities; other prohibitions.

No credit services organization, salesperson, agent, or representative of a credit services organization, or independent contractor that sells or attempts to sell the services of a credit services organization shall do any of the following:

(A) Charge or receive directly or indirectly from a buyer money or other consideration readily convertible into money until all services the organization has agreed to perform for the buyer are completed within the time periods described in division (A)(3) of section 4712.05 of the Revised Code.

(B) Charge or receive directly or indirectly from a buyer money or other consideration readily convertible into money for the referral of the buyer to a person that makes an extension of credit or to a consumer reporting agency, except when credit has actually been extended as a result of that referral;

(C) Make or use a false or misleading representation in the offer or sale of the services of the organization, including either of the following:

(1) Guarantying or otherwise stating that the organization is able to delete an adverse credit history, unless the representation clearly discloses that this can be done only if the credit history is inaccurate or obsolete;

(2) Guarantying or otherwise stating that the organization is able to obtain an extension of credit regardless of the buyer's previous credit problems or credit history, unless the representation clearly discloses the eligibility requirements for obtaining an extension of credit.

(D) Engage, directly or indirectly, in an unconscionable, unfair, or deceptive act or practice, as those terms are used and defined in Chapter 1345. of the Revised Code, in connection with the offer or sale of the services of a credit services organization;

(E)(1) Make or advise a buyer to make a false or misleading statement concerning the buyer's creditworthiness, identification, credit standing, or credit capacity to any of the following:

(a) A consumer reporting agency;

(b) A person that has made an extension of credit to the buyer;

(c) A person to which the buyer is applying for an extension of credit.

(2) Division (E)(1) of this section applies to any statement that the organization, salesperson, agent, representative, or independent contractor knows or should know to be false or misleading through the exercise of reasonable care.

(F) Advertise or cause to be advertised, in any manner, the services of a credit services organization without being registered with the division of financial institutions;

(G) Fail to maintain a statutory agent as required under division (E) of section 4712.02 of the Revised Code;

(H) Transfer or assign a certificate of registration issued by the division pursuant to section 4712.02 of the Revised Code;

(I) Submit the buyer's disputes to a consumer reporting agency without the buyer's knowledge as evidenced by positive identification, including the buyer's correct current residence address, and written authorization personally signed by the buyer;

(J) Fail to maintain, for a period of time as determined by the superintendent of financial institutions, all of the following:

(1) A log of all contracts;

(2) Copies of each contract;

(3) Documentation that substantiates the validity of the representation made pursuant to division (A)(5) of section 4712.05 of the Revised Code;

(4) Any other record specified by the superintendent.

(K) Contact a consumer reporting agency, by telephone or otherwise, for the purpose of submitting or obtaining information relative to any buyer, and state or imply that he or she is the buyer or the buyer's attorney, guardian, or other legal representative;

(L) Engage, directly or indirectly, in any fraudulent or deceptive act, practice, or course of business in connection with the offer or sale of the services of a credit services organization.

**HISTORY: 144 v S 323 (Eff 4-16-93); 146 v S 293†. Eff 9-26-96.**

† See Publisher's Note following RC § 4707.05.

## § 4712.08 Fraudulent activities; notice of fraud conviction.

No credit services organization shall do any of the following:

(A) Obtain a certificate of registration through any false or fraudulent representation or make any substantial misrepresentation in any registration application;

(B) Make false promises through advertising or other means in the conduct of its business or engage in a continued course of misrepresentations in the conduct of its business;

(C) Engage in conduct that constitutes improper, fraudulent, or dishonest dealings in the conduct of its business;

(D) Fail to notify the division of financial institutions if the credit services organization is convicted, in a court of competent jurisdiction of this state or any other state, of a felony or any criminal offense involving fraud.

**HISTORY: 144 v S 323 (Eff 4-16-93); 146 v S 293†. Eff 9-26-96.**

† See Publisher's Note following RC § 4707.05.

## § 4712.09 Waiver of rights.

(A) No credit services organization shall cause or attempt to cause a buyer to waive a right under sections 4712.01 to 4712.14 of the Revised Code.

(B) Any waiver by a buyer of a right under sections 4712.01 to 4712.14 of the Revised Code is void.

**HISTORY: 144 v S 323. Eff 4-16-93.**

## § 4712.99 Penalties.

Whoever violates division (J) of section 4712.02, division (E) of section 4712.04, division (D) or (E) of section 4712.05, division (A) of section 4712.06, section 4712.07 or 4712.08, or division (A) of section 4712.09 of the Revised Code is guilty of a felony of the fifth degree.

**HISTORY: 144 v S 323 (Eff 4-16-93); 146 v S 2. Eff 7-1-96.**

The effective date is set by section 6 of SB 2.

# CHAPTER 4719: TELEPHONE SOLICITORS

Section



## § 4719.02 Certificate of registration or renewal required to act as telephone solicitor; contents of application; notice of change in information; statutory agent.

(A) No person shall act as a telephone solicitor without first having obtained a certificate of registration or registration renewal from the attorney general under section 4719.03 of the Revised Code.

(B) The application for a certificate of registration or registration renewal as a telephone solicitor shall contain all of the following information:

(1) The true name, date of birth, driver's license number, social security number or tax identification number, business address, and home address of the applicant, including each name under which the applicant intends to engage in telephone solicitations;

(2) Each business or occupation engaged in by the applicant during the three years immediately preceding the date of the application, and the location of each such business or occupation;

(3) The previous experience of the applicant as a telephone solicitor or salesperson;

(4) Whether in any jurisdiction the applicant has been arrested for, convicted of, or pleaded guilty to, has entered a plea of no contest for, or is being prosecuted by indictment or information for a felony and, if so, the nature of the felony;

(5) Whether, in a court of competent jurisdiction of this state or any other state or the United States, the applicant has been convicted of or pleaded guilty to, has entered a plea of no contest for, or is being prosecuted by indictment or information for engaging in a pattern of corrupt activity, racketeering, a violation of federal or state securities law, or a theft offense as defined in section 2913.01 of the Revised Code or in similar law of any other state or the United States;

(6) Whether there has ever been a judicial or administrative finding that the applicant has acted as a salesperson without a license, or whether such a license has been refused, revoked, or suspended in any jurisdiction;

(7) Whether the applicant has worked for or been affiliated with a company that has had entered against it an injunction, a temporary restraining order, or a final judgment or order, including an agreed judgment or order, an assurance of voluntary compliance, or any similar instrument, in any civil or administrative action involving racketeering, fraud, theft, embezzlement, fraudulent conversion, or misappropriation of property; the use of any untrue, deceptive, or misleading representation; or the use of any unfair, unlawful, deceptive, or unconscionable trade act or practice;

(8) Whether in any jurisdiction there has been entered against the applicant an injunction, a temporary restraining order, or a final judgment or order, including an agreed judgment or order, an assurance of voluntary compliance, or any similar instrument, in any civil or administrative action involving engaging in a pattern of corrupt activity, racketeering, fraud, theft, embezzlement, fraudulent conversion, or misappropriation of property; the use of any untrue, deceptive, or misleading representation; or the use of any unfair, unlawful, deceptive, or unconscionable trade act or practice; and whether there is any litigation or proceeding pending against the applicant;

(9) Whether the applicant, at any time during the previous seven years, has filed for bankruptcy, been

adjudged bankrupt, or been reorganized because of insolvency;

(10) The name of any parent, affiliate, or other related entity to which either of the following applies:

(a) The entity may engage in a business transaction with a purchaser relating to any telephone solicitation by the applicant.

(b) The entity accepts responsibility or is otherwise held out by the applicant as being responsible for any statement or act of the applicant relating to any telephone solicitation by the applicant.

(11) The complete street address of each location, designating the principal location, from which the applicant will be doing business, including each location at which mail will be received by or on behalf of the applicant, and identifying any such location that is a post office box or mail drop;

(12) A list of all telephone numbers to be used by the applicant, with the street address where each telephone using these numbers will be located;

(13) The true name, current home address, date of birth, social security number, and all other names by which known, or previously known, of each of the following:

(a) Each principal officer, director, trustee, shareholder, owner, or partner of the applicant, and each other person participating in or responsible for the management of the applicant's business;

(b) Each office manager or other person principally responsible for each location from which the applicant will do business;

(c) Each salesperson or other person to be employed by the applicant.

(14) The name and street address of the statutory agent required by division (D) of this section;

(15) For any application containing answers in the affirmative to any information required by divisions (B)(4) to (8) of this section:

(a) The name of the court or administrative agency rendering the conviction, judgment, or order against the person or in which the litigation or proceeding is pending;

(b) The docket number of the matter; the date of the conviction, judgment, or order or the date the pending litigation or proceeding was initiated; and the name of the governmental agency, if any, that brought the action resulting in the conviction, judgment, order, or pending litigation or proceeding.

(16) If the applicant is other than an individual or if any parent, affiliate, or other related entity is identified pursuant to division (B)(10) of this section:

(a) The applicant's place of organization and the place of organization of any such parent, affiliate, or other related entity;

(b) In the case of a partnership on the part of the applicant or such parent, affiliate, or other related entity, a copy of any written partnership agreement;

(c) In the case of a corporation, a copy of the articles of incorporation and bylaws of the applicant and such parent, affiliate, or other related entity.

(17) The identity of any person, identified pursuant to division (B)(13) of this section, that in any jurisdiction:

(a) Has been convicted of or pleaded guilty to, entered a plea of no contest for, or is being prosecuted by indictment or information for a felony, engaging in a pattern of corrupt activity, racketeering, a violation of federal or state securities law, or a theft offense as defined in section 2913.01 of the Revised Code or in similar law of any other state or the United States;

(b) Is involved in pending litigation or proceedings or has had entered against itself an injunction, a temporary restraining order, or a final judgment or order, including a stipulated judgment or order, an assurance of voluntary compliance, or any similar instrument, in any civil or administrative action involving engaging in a pattern of corrupt activity, racketeering, fraud, theft, embezzlement, fraudulent conversion, or misappropriation of property; the use of any untrue, deceptive, or misleading representation; or the use of any unfair, unlawful, deceptive, or unconscionable trade act or practice;

(c) Is or has been subject to any litigation, injunction, temporary restraining order, or final judgment or order, including a stipulated judgment or order, an assurance of voluntary compliance, or any similar instrument, in any civil or administrative action involving engaging in a pattern of corrupt activity, racketeering, fraud, theft, embezzlement, fraudulent conversion, or misappropriation of property; the use of any untrue, deceptive, or misleading representation; or the use of any unfair, unlawful, deceptive, or unconscionable trade act or practice;

(d) At any time during the previous seven years, has filed for bankruptcy, been adjudged bankrupt, or been reorganized because of insolvency;

(e) Has been a principal, director, officer, or trustee of or a general or limited partner in, or had responsibilities as a manager in, any corporation, partnership, joint venture, or other entity that filed for bankruptcy, was adjudged bankrupt, or was reorganized because of insolvency within one year after the person held that position.

(18) For any application containing answers in the affirmative to any information required by division (B)(9) of this section and for any person described in division (B)(17)(d) of this section:

(a) The name of the court or administrative agency rendering the conviction, judgment, or order against the person or in which the litigation is pending;

(b) The docket number of the matter; the date of the conviction, judgment, or order or the date the pending litigation was initiated; and the name of the governmental agency, if any, that brought the action resulting in the conviction, judgment, order or pending litigation.

(19) The name and address of any person identified under division (B)(17)(e) of this section; the date of the action; the name of court that exercised jurisdiction; and the docket number of the matter;

(20) The name, address, and account number of each institution where banking or similar monetary transactions are done by the applicant;

(21) A copy of any script, outline, or presentation the applicant will require or suggest be used by a salesperson when soliciting or, if no such document is to be used, a notarized statement to that effect; sales information or literature to be provided by the applicant to a salesperson; and sales information or literature to be provided by the applicant to a purchaser in connection with any solicitation;

(22) Any other information required at any time by the attorney general.

(C)(1) Except as otherwise provided in divisions (C)(2) and (3) of this section, no telephone solicitor shall fail to notify the attorney general in writing any later than thirty days after the date of a change in the information required by division (B) of this section.

(2) No telephone solicitor shall fail to notify the attorney general in writing any later than thirty days before any

change in the information required by divisions (B)(1), (11), and (12) of this section.

(3) No telephone solicitor shall fail to notify the attorney general in writing of any change in the information required by division (B)(21) of this section prior to its use in a solicitation.

(D) No nonresident telephone solicitor shall fail to maintain a resident of this state as its statutory agent for the purpose of service of process.

(E) Information regarding social security numbers, bank accounts, and solicitation scripts, outlines, or presentations submitted in an application under this section is not a public record under section 149.43 of the Revised Code. The attorney general shall not release information of that nature to the public.

**HISTORY: 146 v S 214. Eff 12-5-96.**

**Not analogous to former RC § 4719.02 (RS § 7068; S&C 859; 29 v 449, § 3; GC § 13110; Bureau of Code Revision, 10-1-53), repealed 133 v H 153, § 1, eff 8-28-69.**

## § 4719.05 Prior submission of representation concerning gift, award or prize.

No telephone solicitor that intends to represent or cause to be represented, expressly or impliedly, to a purchaser that the purchaser is or may be eligible to receive a gift, award, or prize, however denominated, shall fail to submit to the attorney general, any later than fourteen days prior to first making that representation, a statement setting forth all of the following, for each item mentioned:

(A) A description of the item;

(B) The item's verifiable market value and the basis for the valuation;

(C) All terms and conditions a purchaser must satisfy in order to receive the item. The statement shall be accompanied by a copy of the written confirmation provided to purchasers pursuant to section 4719.07 of the Revised Code.

(D) Verification that no payment or purchase of any kind is required to win a prize or to participate in a prize promotion, and a description of the no-purchase or no-payment method of participating in the prize promotion;

(E)(1) If they are ascertainable, the odds, for a given purchaser, of receiving the item;

(2) If the odds are not ascertainable, all the factors and methods used in calculating the odds.

(F) If a purchaser is to receive fewer than all the items described by the seller:

(1) The manner in which the telephone solicitor decides which item a given purchaser is to receive;

(2)(a) If they are ascertainable, the odds, for a given purchaser, of receiving each item described;

(b) If the odds are not ascertainable, all the factors and methods used in calculating the odds.

(3) The name, address, and telephone number of each person that, during the preceding twelve months or any portion of that twelve-month period in which the telephone solicitor has done business, has received each gift, award, or prize.

**HISTORY: 146 v S 214. Eff 12-5-96.**

## § 4719.06 Information to be disclosed by solicitor or salesperson.

(A) Within the first sixty seconds of a telephone call, and before requesting any financial information or conveying to the consumer any substantive information about a prize, product, or service, no telephone solicitor or salesperson shall fail to do all of the following:

(1) State the solicitor's or salesperson's true name and the company on whose behalf the solicitation is being made;

(2) State that the purpose of the telephone call is to effect a sale;

(3) Identify the goods or services being sold.

(B) If a sale or an agreement to purchase is completed during a telephone call, no telephone solicitor or salesperson, before requesting payment, shall fail to inform the purchaser of the rights granted under section 4719.07 of the Revised Code and disclose all of the following information in a clear and conspicuous manner:

(1) The street address and telephone number of the telephone solicitor;

(2) The total costs to purchase, receive, or use, and the quantity of, any goods or services that are the subject of the telephone solicitation;

(3) All material restrictions, limitations, or conditions to purchase, receive, or use the goods or services that are the subject of the telephone solicitation;

(4) All material terms and conditions of the telephone solicitor's policy of making refunds, cancellations, exchanges, or repurchases;

(5) In any prize promotion, a description of the prize; its market value; all material conditions to receive or redeem the prize; the odds of being able to receive the prize and, if the odds are not calculable in advance, the factors and methods used in calculating the odds; that no purchase or payment of any kind is required to win a prize or to participate in a prize promotion; and the no-purchase or no-payment method of participating in the prize promotion, with either instructions on how to participate or an address or local or toll-free telephone number to which customers may write or call for information on how to participate.

(C) No telephone solicitor or salesperson shall fail to make an oral disclosure required by this section in a clear and intelligible manner.

**HISTORY: 146 v S 214. Eff 12-5-96.**

## § 4719.07 Signed, written confirmation to be obtained from purchaser; exemption; cancellation rights.

(A) No verbal agreement, made by a purchaser as a result of a telephone solicitation, to purchase goods or services from a telephone solicitor is valid or legally binding unless the telephone solicitor receives from the purchaser a signed, written confirmation that complies with divisions (F) and (G) of this section and discloses in full the terms of the agreement.

(B) No purchaser is liable for payment for goods or services provided by a telephone solicitor as a result of a telephone solicitation unless the solicitor has first received a signed, written confirmation from the purchaser that complies with divisions (F) and (G) of this section. Any goods sent or services provided without a signed, written confirmation are deemed unsolicited goods or services and become the property of the purchaser free of charge or obligation.

(C) No telephone solicitor or salesperson shall make or submit a charge to a purchaser's account, including, but not limited to, a checking, savings, share, credit card, or other account for which the purchaser may be obligated financially, unless the telephone solicitor has received from the purchaser the original copy of a confirmation that is signed by the purchaser and that complies with divisions (F) and (G) of this section.

(D) No telephone solicitor that causes a written confirmation under this section to be delivered to a purchaser by a courier shall cause the courier to obtain the signed, written confirmation or payment from the purchaser or to transport the signed, written confirmation or payment to the solicitor, or shall request that the purchaser arrange for the transportation of the signed, written confirmation or payment to occur, sooner than seven days following delivery of the written confirmation to the purchaser.

(E) No telephone solicitor who receives payment in any form from a purchaser without also receiving a signed, written confirmation that complies with divisions (F) and (G) of this section shall fail to do all of the following within five business days after the receipt of the payment:

(1) Refund all payments made, including any down payment made under the agreement;

(2) Return any goods traded in to the telephone solicitor on account of or in contemplation of an agreement resulting from the telephone solicitation, in substantially the same condition as when received by the telephone solicitor;

(3) Take any action necessary or appropriate to terminate promptly any security interest created in connection with the agreement.

(F) A confirmation under this section shall include, but not be limited to, all of the following:

(1) The name of the telephone solicitor;

(2) The number of the telephone solicitor's certificate of registration or registration renewal issued under section 4719.03 of the Revised Code;

(3) The address and telephone number at which personal or voice contact with an employee or agent of the telephone solicitor may be made during normal business hours;

(4) An itemized list of all prices or fees being requested, including any handling, shipping, delivery, or other charges;

(5) The date of the transaction;

(6) A detailed description of the goods or services being sold through the telephone solicitation;

(7) All material terms and conditions of the telephone solicitor's policy of making refunds, cancellations, exchanges, or repurchases;

(8) A duplicate copy, with the complete information as presented in the original confirmation, to be retained by the purchaser as proof of the terms of the agreement to purchase;

(9) In any prize promotion, a description of the prize; its market value; all material conditions to receive or redeem the prize; the odds of being able to receive the prize and, if the odds are not calculable in advance, the factors and methods used in calculating the odds; that no purchase or payment of any kind is required to win a prize or to participate in a prize promotion; and the no-purchase or no-payment method of participating in the prize promotion, with either instructions on how to participate or an address or local or toll-free telephone number to which customers may write or call for information on how to participate;

(10) In a type size of a minimum of twelve points, in boldface print, and in a color clearly contrasting with all other text and background on the confirmation, in a space immediately preceding the space allotted for the purchaser's signature, the following statement:

"YOU ARE NOT OBLIGATED TO PAY ANY MONEY UNLESS YOU SIGN THIS CONFIRMATION AND RETURN IT TO THE SELLER."

(G) Except as provided in division (F)(10) of this section, all text of a confirmation under division (A) of this section shall be printed in a type size of a minimum of ten points, in a color clearly contrasting with all background.

(H) A telephone solicitor that meets all of the following requirements is exempt from the provisions of divisions (A) through (G) of this section:

(1) The telephone solicitor does not conduct a prize promotion or offer the sale of an investment opportunity;

(2) The telephone solicitor conducts all telephone solicitation activities according to sections 310.3, 310.4, and 310.5 of the telemarketing sales rules adopted by the federal trade commission in 16 C.F.R. part 310;

(3) The telephone solicitor gives an unconditional full refund to any purchaser for the return of goods or cancellation of services within a period of not fewer than seven days after purchaser's receipt of the goods, agreement to the services, or receipt of two copies of the written notice of cancellation required by division (H)(4) of this section, whichever is later; and provides the refund to the purchaser within thirty days after receiving the goods returned by the purchaser or the written notice of cancellation of services.

(4) The telephone solicitor provides to the purchaser two copies of a written notice of cancellation rights which contains the following printed in a type size of a minimum of ten points, in a color clearly contrasting with all background:

(a) The name of the telephone solicitor;

(b) The number of the telephone solicitor's certificate of registration or registration renewal issued under section 4719.03 of the Revised Code;

(c) The address and telephone number at which personal or voice contact with an employee or agent of the telephone solicitor may be made during normal business hours;

(d) An itemized list of all prices or fees being charged, including any handling, shipping, delivery, or other charges;

(e) The date of the transaction;

(f) A detailed description of the goods or services being sold;

(g) The following language in boldface print:

**"NOTICE OF CANCELLATION RIGHTS**

**Because you agreed to buy these goods (or services or other appropriate description) as a result of a telephone solicitation, Ohio law gives you seven (7) days to cancel your purchase. If you cancel we must provide you a full refund within thirty (30) days. If you want to cancel, you must sign your name below and return a copy of this notice, together with any goods you have received, so they are postmarked no later than midnight of the seventh day following the date you received the goods or agreed to the services, or the seventh day following the date you received this notice, whichever is later. The notice and goods must be addressed as follows:**

**(Name and address of merchant)**

**I want to cancel my agreement to purchase.**

..................................................

**(Signature)**

....................................................

**(Name of purchaser — printed)**

....................................................

**(Address of purchaser — printed)**

....................................................

**(Address — city, state, zip)**

....................................................

**(Date)"**

**HISTORY: 146 v S 214. Eff 12-5-96.**

## § 4719.08 Prohibitions.

No telephone solicitor shall do any of the following:

(A) Obtain a certificate of registration or registration renewal under section 4719.03 of the Revised Code through any false or fraudulent representation or make any material misrepresentation in any registration or registration renewal application;

(B) Fail to maintain a valid certificate of registration or registration renewal;

(C) Advertise that one is registered as a telephone solicitor or represent that registration as a telephone solicitor constitutes approval or endorsement by any government or governmental office or agency;

(D) Provide inaccurate or incomplete information to the attorney general when making an application for a certificate or certificate renewal;

(E) Misrepresent that a person is registered or that the person has a valid certificate number;

(F) Misrepresent, directly or by implication, any of the following information:

(1) The total costs to purchase, receive, or use, and the quantity of, any goods or services that are the subject of a telephone solicitation;

(2) A material restriction, limitation, or condition to purchase, receive, or use goods or services that are the subject of a telephone solicitation;

(3) A material aspect of the performance, efficacy, nature, or characteristics of goods or services that are the subject of a telephone solicitation;

(4) A material aspect of the nature or terms of the telephone solicitor's refund, cancellation, exchange, or repurchase policies;

(5) A material aspect of a prize promotion, including, but not limited to, the odds of being able to receive a prize, the nature or value of a prize, or that a purchase or payment of any kind is required to win a prize or to participate in a prize promotion;

(6) A material aspect of an investment opportunity, including, but not limited to, risk, liquidity, earnings potential, or profitability;

(7) The telephone solicitor's affiliation with, or endorsement by, any government or third-party organization.

(G) Make a false or misleading statement to induce a purchaser to pay for goods or services;

(H) Fail to notify the attorney general within fifteen days if, in a court of competent jurisdiction of this state or any other state or of the United States, the telephone solicitor is convicted of, pleads guilty to, or enters a plea of no contest for a felony, engaging in a pattern of corrupt activity, racketeering, a violation of federal or state securities law, or a theft offense as defined in section 2913.01 of the Revised Code or in similar law of any other state or of the United States;

(I) Intentionally block or intentionally authorize or cause to be blocked the disclosure of the telephone number from which a telephone solicitation is made.

**HISTORY: 146 v S 214 (Eff 12-5-96); 149 v H 312. Eff 4-9-2003.**

## § 4719.09 Purchaser's waiver of right.

(A) No telephone solicitor or salesperson shall cause or attempt to cause a purchaser to waive a right granted under section 4719.07 or 4719.15 of the Revised Code.

(B) Any waiver by a purchaser of a right granted under section 4719.07 or 4719.15 of the Revised Code is contrary to the fundamental public policy of this state and is void and unenforceable.

**HISTORY: 146 v S 214. Eff 12-5-96.**

## § 4719.99 Penalties.

Prior to July 1, 1996, whoever violates section 4719.02, 4719.05, or 4719.06, division (C), (D), or (E) of section 4719.07, section 4719.08, or division (A) of section 4719.09 of the Revised Code is guilty of a felony of the fourth degree. On or after July 1, 1996, whoever violates section 4719.02, 4719.05, or 4719.06, division (C), (D), or (E) of section 4719.07, section 4719.08, or division (A) of section 4719.09 of the Revised Code is guilty of a felony of the fifth degree.

**HISTORY: 146 v S 214. Eff 12-5-96.**

**Not analogous to former RC § 4719.99 (Bureau of Code Revision, 10-1-53), repealed 133 v H 153, § 1, eff 8-28-69.**

# CHAPTER 4723: NURSES



## § 4723.03 Unlicensed practice of nursing; authorized titles and initials.

(A) No person shall engage in the practice of nursing as a registered nurse, represent the person as being a registered nurse, or use the title "registered nurse," the initials "R.N.," or any other title implying that the person is a registered nurse, for a fee, salary, or other consideration, or as a volunteer, without holding a current, valid license as a registered nurse under this chapter.

(B) No person shall engage in the practice of nursing as a licensed practical nurse, represent the person as being a licensed practical nurse, or use the title "licensed practical nurse," the initials "L.P.N.," or any other title implying that the person is a licensed practical nurse, for a fee, salary, or other consideration, or as a volunteer, without holding a current, valid license as a practical nurse under this chapter.

(C) No person shall use the titles or initials "graduate nurse," "G.N.," "professional nurse," "P.N.," "graduate practical nurse," "G.P.N.," "practical nurse," "P.N.," "trained nurse," "T.N.," or any other statement, title, or initials that would imply or represent to the public that the person is authorized to practice nursing in this state, except as follows:

(1) A person licensed under this chapter to practice nursing as a registered nurse may use that title and the initials "R.N.";

(2) A person licensed under this chapter to practice nursing as a licensed practical nurse may use that title and the initials "L.P.N.";

(3) A person authorized under this chapter to practice nursing as a certified registered nurse anesthetist may use that title, the initials "C.R.N.A." or "N.A.," and any other title or initials approved by the board of nursing;

(4) A person authorized under this chapter to practice nursing as a clinical nurse specialist may use that title, the initials "C.N.S.," and any other title or initials approved by the board;

(5) A person authorized under this chapter to practice nursing as a certified nurse-midwife may use that title, the initials "C.N.M.," and any other title or initials approved by the board;

(6) A person authorized under this chapter to practice nursing as a certified nurse practitioner may use that title, the initials "C.N.P.," and any other title or initials approved by the board;

(7) A person authorized under this chapter to practice as a certified registered nurse anesthetist, clinical nurse specialist, certified nurse-midwife, or certified nurse practitioner may use the title "advanced practice nurse" or the initials "A.P.N."

(D) No person shall employ a person not licensed as a registered nurse under this chapter to engage in the practice of nursing as a registered nurse. No person shall employ a person not licensed as a practical nurse under this chapter to engage in the practice of nursing as a licensed practical nurse.

(E) No person shall sell or fraudulently obtain or furnish any nursing diploma, license, certificate, renewal, or record, or aid or abet such acts.

**HISTORY: 142 v H 529 (Eff 6-14-88); 146 v S 154 (Eff 9-10-97); 148 v H 511. Eff 4-10-2001; 150 v S 80, § 1, eff. 4-7-05.**

**Not analogous to former RC § 4723.03 amended and renumbered RC § 4723.05 in 142 v H 529, eff 6-14-88.**

## [NURSE-MIDWIFERY, OTHER SPECIALTIES]

### § 4723.44 Unauthorized practice or use of title or initials; employment without certificate prohibited.

(A) No person shall do any of the following unless the person holds a current, valid certificate of authority to practice nursing as a certified registered nurse anesthetist, clinical nurse specialist, certified nurse-midwife, or certified nurse practitioner issued by the board of nursing under this chapter:

(1) Engage in the practice of nursing as a certified registered nurse anesthetist, clinical nurse specialist, certified nurse-midwife, or certified nurse practitioner for a fee, salary, or other consideration, or as a volunteer;

(2) Represent the person as being a certified registered nurse anesthetist, clinical nurse specialist, certified nurse-midwife, or certified nurse practitioner;

(3) Use any title or initials implying that the person is a certified registered nurse anesthetist, clinical nurse specialist, certified nurse-midwife, or certified nurse practitioner;

(4) Represent the person as being an advanced practice nurse;

(5) Use any title or initials implying that the person is an advanced practice nurse.

(B) No person who is not certified by the national council on certification of nurse anesthetists of the American association of nurse anesthetists, the national council on recertification of nurse anesthetists of the American association of nurse anesthetists, or another national certifying organization approved by the board under section 4723.46 of the Revised Code shall use the title "certified registered nurse anesthetist" or the initials "C.R.N.A.," or any other title or initial implying that the person has been certified by the council or organization.

(C) No certified registered nurse anesthetist, clinical nurse specialist, certified nurse-midwife, or certified nurse practitioner shall do any of the following:

(1) Engage, for a fee, salary, or other consideration, or as a volunteer, in the practice of a nursing specialty other than the specialty designated on the nurse's current, valid certificate of authority issued by the board under this chapter;

(2) Represent the person as being authorized to practice any nursing specialty other than the specialty designated on the current, valid certificate of authority;

(3) Use the title "certified registered nurse anesthetist" or the initials "N.A." or "C.R.N.A.," the title "clinical nurse specialist" or the initials "C.N.S.," the title "certified nurse-midwife" or the initials "C.N.M.," the title "certified nurse practitioner" or the initials "C.N.P.," the title "advanced practice nurse" or the initials "A.P.N.," or any other title or initials implying that the nurse is authorized to practice any nursing specialty other than the specialty designated on the nurse's current, valid certificate of authority;

(4) Enter into a standard care arrangement with a physician or podiatrist whose practice is not the same as or similar to the nurse's nursing specialty;

(5) Prescribe drugs or therapeutic devices unless the nurse holds a current, valid certificate to prescribe issued under section 4723.48 of the Revised Code;

(6) Prescribe drugs or therapeutic devices under a certificate to prescribe in a manner that does not comply with section 4723.481 [4723.48.1] of the Revised Code;

(7) Prescribe any drug or device to perform or induce an abortion, or otherwise perform or induce an abortion.

(D) No person shall knowingly employ a person to engage in the practice of nursing as a certified registered nurse anesthetist, clinical nurse specialist, certified nurse-midwife, or certified nurse practitioner unless the person so employed holds a current, valid certificate of authority to engage in that nursing specialty issued by the board under this chapter.

(E) A certificate certified by the executive director of the board, under the official seal of the board, to the effect that it appears from the records that no certificate of authority to practice nursing as a certified registered nurse anesthetist, clinical nurse specialist, certified nurse-midwife, or certified nurse practitioner has been issued to any person specified therein, or that a certificate, if issued, has been revoked or suspended, shall be received as prima-facie evidence of the record in any court or before any officer of the state.

**HISTORY: GC § 12695; 99 v 502, § 53; 103 v 438; Bureau of Code Revision, RC § 4731.42, 10-1-53; RC § 4723.44, 142 v H 529 (Eff 6-14-88); 146 v S 154 (Eff 9-10-97); 148 v H 241. Eff 5-17-2000; 150 v S 80, § 1, eff. 4-7-05.**

## [DIALYSIS TECHNICIANS]

### § 4723.73 Prohibitions concerning dialysis technicians.

(A) No person shall claim to the public to be a dialysis technician unless the person holds a current, valid certificate issued under section 4723.75 or renewed under section 4723.77 or a current, valid temporary certificate issued under section 4723.76 of the Revised Code.

(B) No person shall use the title "Ohio certified dialysis technician," the initials "OCDT," or any other title or initials to represent that the person is authorized to perform dialysis care as a fully certified dialysis technician, unless the person holds a current, valid certificate issued under section 4723.75 or renewed under section 4723.77 of the Revised Code.

(C) No person shall use any title or initials to represent that the person is authorized to perform dialysis care as a temporarily certified dialysis technician, unless the person holds a current, valid temporary certificate issued under section 4723.76 of the Revised Code.

(D) No dialysis technician shall engage in dialysis care in a manner that is inconsistent with section 4723.72 of the Revised Code.

(E) No person other than a dialysis technician shall engage in the dialysis care that is authorized by section 4723.72 of the Revised Code, unless one of the following applies:

(1) The person is a registered nurse or licensed practical nurse.

(2) The person is a physician.

(3) The person is a student performing dialysis care under the supervision of an instructor as an integral part of a dialysis training program approved by the board of nursing under section 4723.74 of the Revised Code.

(4) The person is a dialysis patient who has been trained to engage in the dialysis care with little or no professional assistance by completing a Medicare-approved self-dialysis or home dialysis training program.

(5) The person is a family member or friend of a dialysis patient who engages in self-dialysis or home dialysis, and the person engages in the dialysis care by assisting the patient in performing the self-dialysis or home dialysis, after the person providing the assistance has completed a Medicare-approved self-dialysis or home dialysis training program for the particular dialysis patient being assisted.

(F) No person shall operate a dialysis training program, unless the program is approved by the board of nursing under section 4723.74 of the Revised Code.

**HISTORY: 148 v S 111. Eff 6-27-2001.**

The effective date is set by section 3 of SB 111.

## [CERTIFICATION OF COMMUNITY HEALTH WORKERS]

### § 4723.99 Penalties.

(A) Except as provided in division (B) of this section, whoever violates section 4723.03, 4723.44, or 4723.73 of the Revised Code is guilty of a felony of the fifth degree on a first offense and a felony of the fourth degree on each subsequent offense.

(B) A registered nurse or licensed practical nurse who violates division (A) or (B) of section 4723.03 of the Revised Code by reason of a license to practice nursing that has lapsed for failure to renew or by practicing nursing after a license has been classified as inactive is guilty of a minor misdemeanor.

**HISTORY: 126 v 122(133) (Eff 1-1-56); 142 v H 529 (Eff 6-14-88); 143 v S 113 (Eff 11-3-89); 148 v H 511, § 1 (Eff 4-10-2001); 148 v S 111 (Eff 6-27-2001); 148 v H 511, § 10. Eff 6-27-2001.**

**Analogous to former RC § 4723.99 (Bureau of Code Revision, 10-1-53), repealed 126 v 122, eff 1-1-56.**

The effective date is set by section 12 of HB 511.

# CHAPTER 4729: PHARMACISTS; DANGEROUS DRUGS

## § 4729.01 Definitions.

As used in this chapter:

(A) "Pharmacy," except when used in a context that refers to the practice of pharmacy, means any area, room, rooms, place of business, department, or portion of any of the foregoing where the practice of pharmacy is conducted.

(B) "Practice of pharmacy" means providing pharmacist care requiring specialized knowledge, judgment, and skill derived from the principles of biological, chemical, behavioral, social, pharmaceutical, and clinical sciences. As used in this division, "pharmacist care" includes the following:

(1) Interpreting prescriptions;

(2) Dispensing drugs and drug therapy related devices;

(3) Compounding drugs;

(4) Counseling individuals with regard to their drug therapy, recommending drug therapy related devices, and assisting in the selection of drugs and appliances for treatment of common diseases and injuries and providing instruction in the proper use of the drugs and appliances;

(5) Performing drug regimen reviews with individuals by discussing all of the drugs that the individual is taking and explaining the interactions of the drugs;

(6) Performing drug utilization reviews with licensed health professionals authorized to prescribe drugs when the pharmacist determines that an individual with a prescription has a drug regimen that warrants additional discussion with the prescriber;

(7) Advising an individual and the health care professionals treating an individual with regard to the individual's drug therapy;

(8) Acting pursuant to a consult agreement with a physician authorized under Chapter 4731. of the Revised Code to practice medicine and surgery or osteopathic medicine and surgery, if an agreement has been established with the physician;

(9) Engaging in the administration of immunizations to the extent authorized by section 4729.41 of the Revised Code.

(C) "Compounding" means the preparation, mixing, assembling, packaging, and labeling of one or more drugs in any of the following circumstances:

(1) Pursuant to a prescription issued by a licensed health professional authorized to prescribe drugs;

(2) Pursuant to the modification of a prescription made in accordance with a consult agreement;

(3) As an incident to research, teaching activities, or chemical analysis;

(4) In anticipation of orders for drugs pursuant to prescriptions, based on routine, regularly observed dispensing patterns;

(5) Pursuant to a request made by a licensed health professional authorized to prescribe drugs for a drug that is to be used by the professional for the purpose of direct administration to patients in the course of the professional's practice, if all of the following apply:

(a) At the time the request is made, the drug is not commercially available regardless of the reason that the drug is not available, including the absence of a manufacturer for the drug or the lack of a readily available supply of the drug from a manufacturer.

(b) A limited quantity of the drug is compounded and provided to the professional.

(c) The drug is compounded and provided to the professional as an occasional exception to the normal practice of dispensing drugs pursuant to patient-specific prescriptions.

(D) "Consult agreement" means an agreement to manage an individual's drug therapy that has been entered into by a pharmacist and a physician authorized under Chapter 4731. of the Revised Code to practice medicine and surgery or osteopathic medicine and surgery.

(E) "Drug" means:

(1) Any article recognized in the United States pharmacopoeia and national formulary, or any supplement to them, intended for use in the diagnosis, cure, mitigation, treatment, or prevention of disease in humans or animals;

(2) Any other article intended for use in the diagnosis, cure, mitigation, treatment, or prevention of disease in humans or animals;

(3) Any article, other than food, intended to affect the structure or any function of the body of humans or animals;

(4) Any article intended for use as a component of any article specified in division (E)(1), (2), or (3) of this section; but does not include devices or their components, parts, or accessories.

(F) "Dangerous drug" means any of the following:

(1) Any drug to which either of the following applies:

(a) Under the "Federal Food, Drug, and Cosmetic Act," 52 Stat. 1040 (1938), 21 U.S.C.A. 301, as amended, the drug is required to bear a label containing the legend "Caution: Federal law prohibits dispensing without prescription" or "Caution: Federal law restricts this drug to use by or on the order of a licensed veterinarian" or any similar restrictive statement, or the drug may be dispensed only upon a prescription;

(b) Under Chapter 3715. or 3719. of the Revised Code, the drug may be dispensed only upon a prescription.

(2) Any drug that contains a schedule V controlled substance and that is exempt from Chapter 3719. of the Revised Code or to which that chapter does not apply;

(3) Any drug intended for administration by injection into the human body other than through a natural orifice of the human body.

(G) "Federal drug abuse control laws" has the same meaning as in section 3719.01 of the Revised Code.

(H) "Prescription" means a written, electronic, or oral order for drugs or combinations or mixtures of drugs to be used by a particular individual or for treating a particular animal, issued by a licensed health professional authorized to prescribe drugs.

(I) "Licensed health professional authorized to prescribe drugs" or "prescriber" means an individual who is authorized by law to prescribe drugs or dangerous drugs or drug therapy related devices in the course of the individual's professional practice, including only the following:

(1) A dentist licensed under Chapter 4715. of the Revised Code;

(2) A clinical nurse specialist, certified nurse-midwife, or certified nurse practitioner who holds a certificate to prescribe issued under section 4723.48 of the Revised Code;

(3) An optometrist licensed under Chapter 4725. of the Revised Code to practice optometry under a therapeutic pharmaceutical agents certificate;

(4) A physician authorized under Chapter 4731. of the Revised Code to practice medicine and surgery, osteopathic medicine and surgery, or podiatric medicine and surgery;

(5) A physician assistant who holds a certificate to prescribe issued under Chapter 4730. of the Revised Code;

(6) A veterinarian licensed under Chapter 4741. of the Revised Code.

(J) "Sale" and "sell" include delivery, transfer, barter, exchange, or gift, or offer therefor, and each such transaction made by any person, whether as principal proprietor, agent, or employee.

(K) "Wholesale sale" and "sale at wholesale" mean any sale in which the purpose of the purchaser is to resell the article purchased or received by the purchaser.

(L) "Retail sale" and "sale at retail" mean any sale other than a wholesale sale or sale at wholesale.

(M) "Retail seller" means any person that sells any dangerous drug to consumers without assuming control over and responsibility for its administration. Mere advice or instructions regarding administration do not constitute control or establish responsibility.

(N) "Price information" means the price charged for a prescription for a particular drug product and, in an easily understandable manner, all of the following:

(1) The proprietary name of the drug product;

(2) The established (generic) name of the drug product;

(3) The strength of the drug product if the product contains a single active ingredient or if the drug product contains more than one active ingredient and a relevant strength can be associated with the product without indicating each active ingredient. The established name and quantity of each active ingredient are required if such a relevant strength cannot be so associated with a drug product containing more than one ingredient.

(4) The dosage form;

(5) The price charged for a specific quantity of the drug product. The stated price shall include all charges to the consumer, including, but not limited to, the cost of the drug product, professional fees, handling fees, if any, and a statement identifying professional services routinely furnished by the pharmacy. Any mailing fees and delivery fees may be stated separately without repetition. The information shall not be false or misleading.

(O) "Wholesale distributor of dangerous drugs" means a person engaged in the sale of dangerous drugs at wholesale and includes any agent or employee of such a person authorized by the person to engage in the sale of dangerous drugs at wholesale.

(P) "Manufacturer of dangerous drugs" means a person, other than a pharmacist, who manufactures dangerous drugs and who is engaged in the sale of those dangerous drugs within this state.

(Q) "Terminal distributor of dangerous drugs" means a person who is engaged in the sale of dangerous drugs at retail, or any person, other than a wholesale distributor or a pharmacist, who has possession, custody, or control of dangerous drugs for any purpose other than for that person's own use and consumption, and includes pharmacies, hospitals, nursing homes, and laboratories and all other persons who procure dangerous drugs for sale or other distribution by or under the supervision of a pharmacist or licensed health professional authorized to prescribe drugs.

(R) "Promote to the public" means disseminating a representation to the public in any manner or by any means, other than by labeling, for the purpose of inducing, or that is likely to induce, directly or indirectly, the purchase of a dangerous drug at retail.

(S) "Person" includes any individual, partnership, association, limited liability company, or corporation, the state, any political subdivision of the state, and any district, department, or agency of the state or its political subdivisions.

(T) "Finished dosage form" has the same meaning as in section 3715.01 of the Revised Code.

(U) "Generically equivalent drug" has the same meaning as in section 3715.01 of the Revised Code.

(V) "Animal shelter" means a facility operated by a humane society or any society organized under Chapter 1717. of the Revised Code or a dog pound operated pursuant to Chapter 955. of the Revised Code.

(W) "Food" has the same meaning as in section 3715.01 of the Revised Code.

(X) "Pain management clinic" has the same meaning as in section 4731.054 of the Revised Code.

**HISTORY: GC § 1296-1; 121 v 681; Bureau of Code Revision, RC § 4729.02, 10-1-53; 130 v 1140 (Eff 10-7-63); 134 v S 141 (Eff 12-31-71); 136 v H 300 (Eff 7-1-76); 136 v H 912 (Eff 10-1-76); 137 v H 1 (Eff 8-26-77); 137 v S 45 (Eff 1-1-78); 139 v S 4 (Eff 10-1-82); 140 v H 208 (Eff 9-20-84); 144 v S 110 (Eff 5-19-92); 145 v H 88 (Eff 6-29-94); 145 v S 74 (Eff 7-1-94); 145 v H 391 (Eff 7-21-94); 146 v H 162 (Eff 1-1-97); RC § 4729.01, 147 v S 66 (Eff 7-22-98); 148 v H 241 (Eff 5-17-2000); 148 v S 248. Eff 3-12-2001; 150 v H 95, § 1, eff. 6-26-03; 150 v S 80, § 1, eff. 4-7-05; 151 v S 18, § 1, eff.**

**8-19-05; 151 v S 154, § 1, eff. 5-17-06; 152 v S 58, § 1, eff. 8-30-07; 2011 HB 93, § 1, eff. May 20, 2011.**

Acts 2011, HB 93, § 8 provides: "(A) Not later than one year after the effective date of this section, and annually each year for four years thereafter, the State Board of Pharmacy shall prepare a report on all of the following:

"(1) The total number of applications received by the Board for a terminal distributor of dangerous drugs license with a pain management clinic classification;

"(2) The total number of licenses with a pain management clinic classification granted or denied by the Board;

"(3) Any disciplinary actions taken by the Board against holders of licenses with a pain management clinic classification;

"(4) Total revenues generated from fees for licenses with a pain management clinic classification, fines and penalties paid by license holders, or other disciplinary actions taken against license holders;

"(5) Any other relevant information regarding the implementation of this act.

"(B) On completion of each report, the Board shall submit a copy of the report to the Governor and, in accordance with section 101.68 of the Revised Code, the General Assembly. In accordance with that section, the Board shall display the report on the Board's internet web site."

**Not analogous to former RC § 4729.01, amended and renumbered RC § 4729.02 in 147 v S 66, eff 7-22-98.**

## § 4729.16 Disciplinary actions.

(A) The state board of pharmacy, after notice and hearing in accordance with Chapter 119. of the Revised Code, may revoke, suspend, limit, place on probation, or refuse to grant or renew an identification card, or may impose a monetary penalty or forfeiture not to exceed in severity any fine designated under the Revised Code for a similar offense, or in the case of a violation of a section of the Revised Code that does not bear a penalty, a monetary penalty or forfeiture of not more than five hundred dollars, if the board finds a pharmacist or pharmacy intern:

(1) Guilty of a felony or gross immorality;

(2) Guilty of dishonesty or unprofessional conduct in the practice of pharmacy;

(3) Addicted to or abusing liquor or drugs or impaired physically or mentally to such a degree as to render the pharmacist or pharmacy intern unfit to practice pharmacy;

(4) Has been convicted of a misdemeanor related to, or committed in, the practice of pharmacy;

(5) Guilty of willfully violating, conspiring to violate, attempting to violate, or aiding and abetting the violation of any of the provisions of this chapter, sections 3715.52 to 3715.72 of the Revised Code, Chapter 2925. or 3719. of the Revised Code, or any rule adopted by the board under those provisions;

(6) Guilty of permitting anyone other than a pharmacist or pharmacy intern to practice pharmacy;

(7) Guilty of knowingly lending the pharmacist's or pharmacy intern's name to an illegal practitioner of pharmacy or having professional connection with an illegal practitioner of pharmacy;

(8) Guilty of dividing or agreeing to divide remuneration made in the practice of pharmacy with any other individual, including, but not limited to, any licensed health professional authorized to prescribe drugs or any owner, manager, or employee of a health care facility, residential care facility, or nursing home;

(9) Has violated the terms of a consult agreement entered into pursuant to section 4729.39 of the Revised Code;

(10) Has committed fraud, misrepresentation, or deception in applying for or securing a license or identification card issued by the board under this chapter or under Chapter 3715. or 3719. of the Revised Code.

(B) Any individual whose identification card is revoked, suspended, or refused, shall return the identification card and license to the offices of the state board of pharmacy within ten days after receipt of notice of such action.

(C) As used in this section:

"Unprofessional conduct in the practice of pharmacy" includes any of the following:

(1) Advertising or displaying signs that promote dangerous drugs to the public in a manner that is false or misleading;

(2) Except as provided in section 4729.281 [4729.28.1] of the Revised Code, the sale of any drug for which a prescription is required, without having received a prescription for the drug;

(3) Knowingly dispensing medication pursuant to false or forged prescriptions;

(4) Knowingly failing to maintain complete and accurate records of all dangerous drugs received or dispensed in compliance with federal laws and regulations and state laws and rules;

(5) Obtaining any remuneration by fraud, misrepresentation, or deception.

(D) The board may suspend a license or identification card under division (B) of section 3719.121 [3719.12.1] of the Revised Code by utilizing a telephone conference call to review the allegations and take a vote.

(E) If, pursuant to an adjudication under Chapter 119. of the Revised Code, the board has reasonable cause to believe that a pharmacist or pharmacy intern is physically or mentally impaired, the board may require the pharmacist or pharmacy intern to submit to a physical or mental examination, or both.

**HISTORY: GC § 1307; 99 v 505, § 71; 103 v 487; 107 v 541; 120 v 358 (381), § 2; Bureau of Code Revision, 10-1-53; 127 v 162; 128 v 867 (Eff 10-19-59); 129 v 582 (918) (Eff 1-10-61); 132 v S 70 (Eff 9-14-67); 133 v H 1 (Eff 3-18-69); 134 v S 141 (Eff 12-31-71); 136 v H 300 (Eff 7-1-76); 140 v H 208 (Eff 9-20-84); 145 v S 279 (Eff 10-20-94); 146 v H 117 (Eff 9-29-95); 147 v S 66 (Eff 7-22-98); 148 v S 172. Eff 2-12-2001.**

## § 4729.162 Licensed prescriber duties; fines for failure to comply.

(A) As used in this section, "drug database" means the database established and maintained by the state board of pharmacy pursuant to section 4729.75 of the Revised Code.

(B) The state board of pharmacy shall adopt rules in accordance with Chapter 119. of the Revised Code that establish standards and procedures to be followed by a pharmacist regarding the review of patient information available through the drug database.

(C) This section and the rules adopted under it do not apply if the board no longer maintains the drug database.

**HISTORY: 2011 HB 93, § 1, eff. May 20, 2011.**

Acts 2011, HB 93, § 8 provides: "(A) Not later than one year after the effective date of this section, and annually each year for four years thereafter, the State Board of Pharmacy shall prepare a report on all of the following:

"(1) The total number of applications received by the Board for a terminal distributor of dangerous drugs license with a pain management clinic classification;

"(2) The total number of licenses with a pain management clinic classification granted or denied by the Board;

"(3) Any disciplinary actions taken by the Board against holders of licenses with a pain management clinic classification;

"(4) Total revenues generated from fees for licenses with a pain management clinic classification, fines and penalties paid by license holders, or other disciplinary actions taken against license holders;

"(5) Any other relevant information regarding the implementation of this act.

"(B) On completion of each report, the Board shall submit a copy of the report to the Governor and, in accordance with section 101.68 of the Revised Code, the General Assembly. In accordance with that section, the Board shall display the report on the Board's internet web site."

## § 4729.25 Enforcement of chapter.

(A) The state board of pharmacy shall enforce, or cause to be enforced, this chapter. If it has information that any provision of this chapter has been violated, it shall investigate the matter, and take such action as it considers appropriate.

(B) Nothing in this chapter shall be construed to require the state board of pharmacy to enforce minor violations of this chapter if the board determines that the public interest is adequately served by a notice or warning to the alleged offender.

**HISTORY: GC § 1313; 99 v 508, § 82; 103 v 304 (340); 107 v 148; 122 v 70; Bureau of Code Revision, 10-1-53; 130 v 1141 (Eff 10-14-63); 134 v S 141 (Eff 12-31-71); 140 v H 208 (Eff 9-20-84); 147 v S 66. Eff 7-22-98; 150 v H 377, § 1, eff. 5-18-05.**

## § 4729.26 Rules; publication and availability to licensees.

The state board of pharmacy may adopt rules in accordance with Chapter 119. of the Revised Code, not inconsistent with the law, as may be necessary to carry out the purposes of and to enforce the provisions of this chapter. The rules shall be published and made available by the board to each pharmacist licensed under this chapter.

**HISTORY: GC § 12705-1; 121 v 681; Bureau of Code Revision, 10-1-53; 134 v S 141 (Eff 12-31-71); 147 v S 66. Eff 7-22-98; 150 v H 377, § 1, eff. 5-18-05.**

[PROHIBITIONS]

## § 4729.27 Pharmacist must be in charge of pharmacy.

A person not a pharmacist, who owns, manages, or conducts a pharmacy, shall employ a pharmacist to be in full and actual charge of such pharmacy. Any pharmacist who owns, manages, or conducts a pharmacy shall be personally in full and actual charge of the pharmacy, or shall employ another pharmacist to be in full and actual charge of the pharmacy.

**HISTORY: GC § 12705; 99 v 507, §§ 77, 78; 102 v 116; 108 v Pt II 1233; 121 v 681; Bureau of Code Revision, 10-1-53; 134 v S 141 (Eff 12-31-71); 147 v S 66. Eff 7-22-98.**

## § 4729.28 Unauthorized practice of pharmacy.

No person who is not a pharmacist or a pharmacy intern under the personal supervision of a pharmacist shall compound, dispense, or sell dangerous drugs or otherwise engage in the practice of pharmacy.

**HISTORY: GC § 12706; 99 v 507, §§ 77, 78; 108 v Pt II 1233; 121 v 681; Bureau of Code Revision, 10-1-53; 134 v S 141 (Eff 12-31-71); 147 v S 66. Eff 7-22-98.**

## § 4729.281 Refilling of prescription without health professional authorization.

(A) A pharmacist may dispense or sell a dangerous drug, other than a schedule II controlled substance as defined in section 3719.01 of the Revised Code, without a written or oral prescription from a licensed health professional authorized to prescribe drugs if all of the following conditions are met:

(1) The pharmacy at which the pharmacist works has a record of a prescription for the drug in the name of the patient who is requesting it, but the prescription does not provide for a refill or the time permitted by rules adopted by the state board of pharmacy for providing refills has elapsed.

(2) The pharmacist is unable to obtain authorization to refill the prescription from the health care professional who issued the prescription or another health professional responsible for the patient's care.

(3) In the exercise of the pharmacist's professional judgment:

(a) The drug is essential to sustain the life of the patient or continue therapy for a chronic condition of the patient.

(b) Failure to dispense or sell the drug to the patient could result in harm to the health of the patient.

(4) The amount of the drug that is dispensed or sold under this section does not exceed a seventy-two hour supply as provided in the prescription.

(B) A pharmacist who dispenses or sells a drug under this section shall do all of the following:

(1) For one year after the date of dispensing or sale, maintain a record in accordance with this chapter of the drug dispensed or sold, including the name and address of the patient and the individual receiving the drug, if the individual receiving the drug is not the patient, the amount dispensed or sold, and the original prescription number;

(2) Notify the health professional who issued the prescription described in division (A)(1) of this section or another health professional responsible for the patient's care not later than seventy-two hours after the drug is sold or dispensed;

(3) If applicable, obtain authorization for additional dispensing from one of the health professionals described in division (B)(2) of this section.

(C) A pharmacist who dispenses or sells a drug under this section may do so once for each prescription described in division (A)(1) of this section.

**HISTORY: 147 v S 66. Eff 7-22-98.**

**Not analogous to former RC § 4729.281 (134 v S 141), repealed 136 v H 300, § 2, eff 7-1-76.**

## § 4729.29 Exceptions to certain provisions.

Divisions (A) and (B) of section 4729.01 and section 4729.28 of the Revised Code do not do any of the following:

(A) Apply to a licensed health professional authorized to prescribe drugs who is acting within the prescriber's scope of professional practice;

(B) Prevent a prescriber from personally furnishing the prescriber's patients with drugs, within the prescriber's scope of professional practice, that seem proper to the prescriber , as long as the drugs are furnished in accordance with section 4729.291 of the Revised Code;

(C) Apply to the sale of oxygen, peritoneal dialysis solutions, or the sale of drugs that are not dangerous drugs by a retail dealer, in original packages when labeled as required by the "Federal Food, Drug, and Cosmetic Act," 52 Stat. 1040 (1938), 21 U.S.C.A. 301, as amended.

**HISTORY: GC § 12707; 99 v 507, § 79; 118 v 682; 121 v 681; Bureau of Code Revision, 10-1-53; 134 v S 141 (Eff 12-31-71); 140 v S 187 (Eff 6-14-84); 145 v H 391 (Eff 7-21-94); 146 v H 595 (Eff 10-16-96); 147 v H 215 (Eff 6-30-97); 147 v S 66 (Eff 7-22-98); 147 v H 553. Eff 3-9-99; 150 v H 126, § 1, eff. 9-23-04; 2011 HB 93, § 1, eff. May 20, 2011.**

Acts 2011, HB 93, § 8 provides: "(A) Not later than one year after the effective date of this section, and annually each year for four years thereafter, the State Board of Pharmacy shall prepare a report on all of the following:

"(1) The total number of applications received by the Board for a terminal distributor of dangerous drugs license with a pain management clinic classification;

"(2) The total number of licenses with a pain management clinic classification granted or denied by the Board;

"(3) Any disciplinary actions taken by the Board against holders of licenses with a pain management clinic classification;

"(4) Total revenues generated from fees for licenses with a pain management clinic classification, fines and penalties paid by license holders, or other disciplinary actions taken against license holders;

"(5) Any other relevant information regarding the implementation of this act.

"(B) On completion of each report, the Board shall submit a copy of the report to the Governor and, in accordance with section 101.68 of the Revised Code, the General Assembly. In accordance with that section, the Board shall display the report on the Board's internet web site."

## § 4729.30 Certain preceding sections do not prohibit sale of Paris green.

Sections 4729.27 and 4729.28 of the Revised Code shall not prohibit a person from selling Paris green and other materials or compounds used exclusively for spraying and disinfecting when put up in bottles or boxes, bearing the name of a licensed pharmacist or wholesale dealer, and labeled as required by section 3719.33 of the Revised Code or apply to or interfere with the exclusively wholesale business of a dealer.

**HISTORY: GC § 12708; 99 v 507, § 79; 108 v PtI 427; Bureau of Code Revision, 10-1-53; 147 v S 66. Eff 7-22-98.**

## § 4729.31 Exceptions.

Sections 4729.27 and 4729.28 of the Revised Code shall not apply to, interfere with, or prohibit any person, firm, or corporation from selling completely denatured alcohol or wood alcohol.

**HISTORY: GC § 12708-1; 110 v 294; Bureau of Code Revision. Eff 10-1-53.**

## § 4729.32 Requirements for sale of denatured or wood alcohol in five gallon lots or more.

No person shall have in his possession, or dispense or sell packages or containers of completely denatured alcohol or wood alcohol containing five wine gallons or more without having marked or stenciled thereon the name and address of the seller, the degree of proof of such alcohol, the formula number, and, in letters of not less than one inch in height, the words, "Completely Denatured Alcohol" or "Wood Alcohol," as the case may be, and the names of two or more antidotes for the same. This section, and sections 4729.33 and 3719.33 of the Revised Code shall not interfere with the transfer of such alcohol from storage tanks to other packages or containers, nor require the placing of such mark or stencil upon transportation tanks, nor the registration or placing of mark or stencil upon fuel tanks, automobile radiators, or similar containers for the final use or consumption of such alcohol and from which no further distribution thereof is made.

**HISTORY: GC § 12708-2; 110 v 294; Bureau of Code Revision. Eff 10-1-53.**

## § 4729.33 Requirements for sale of denatured or wood alcohol in less than five gallon lots.

No person shall dispense or sell completely denatured alcohol or wood alcohol in packages containing less than five wine gallons without having affixed thereto a label on which is printed or stenciled in plain, legible, red letters of equal prominence on a white background the words, "Completely Denatured Alcohol" or "Wood Alcohol," as the case may be, and in addition on the same label in red ink, under the skull and crossbones symbol, the word "POISON" together with the following statement: "Completely denatured alcohol, or wood alcohol is a violent poison. It cannot be applied externally to human or animal tissue without serious injurious results. It cannot be taken internally without inducing blindness and general physical decay ultimately resulting in death," and without having stamped, stenciled, or printed upon such label the name and address of the seller, the degree of proof, and the formula number thereof. Neither the word "pure" nor the single word "alcohol" alone shall appear on any label of completely denatured alcohol or wood alcohol.

**HISTORY: GC § 12708-3; 110 v 294; Bureau of Code Revision. Eff 10-1-53.**

## § 4729.34 Advertising.

No person shall dispense, sell, or offer for sale completely denatured alcohol or wood alcohol, or shall display a sign or use a label or advertise such alcohol having the word "pure" or the single word "alcohol" alone thereon, or shall fail to state the degree of proof of such alcohol, or to have the letters displaying or advertising "Completely Denatured Alcohol" or "Wood Alcohol" plain, legible, and of equal prominence.

**HISTORY: GC § 12708-4; 110 v 294; Bureau of Code Revision. Eff 10-1-53.**

## § 4729.35 Violation of drug laws as public nuisance.

The violation by a pharmacist or other person of any laws of Ohio or of the United States of America or of any rule of the board of pharmacy controlling the distribution of a drug of abuse as defined in section 3719.011 [3719.01.1] of the Revised Code or the commission of any act set forth in division (A) of section 4729.16 of the Revised Code, is hereby declared to be inimical, harmful, and adverse to the public welfare of the citizens of Ohio and to constitute a public nuisance. The attorney general, the prosecuting attorney of any county in which the offense was committed or in which the person committing the offense resides, or the state board of pharmacy may maintain an action in the name of the state to enjoin such person from engaging in such violation. Any action under this section shall be brought in the common pleas court of the county where the offense occurred or the county where the alleged offender resides.

**HISTORY: 134 v S 141 (Eff 12-31-71); 134 v H 511 (Eff 1-1-74); 135 v H 716 (Eff 1-1-74); 140 v H 208. Eff 9-20-84.**

**Not analogous to former RC § 4729.35 (GC § 12709; 99 v 507; Bureau of Code Revision, 10-1-53), repealed 134 v S 141, § 2, eff 12-31-71.**

## § 4729.36 Advertising prohibitions; price information to be included.

(A) No place except a pharmacy licensed as a terminal distributor of dangerous drugs and no person except a licensed pharmacist shall display any sign or advertise in any fashion, using the words "pharmacy," "drugs," "drug store," "drug store supplies," "pharmacist," "druggist," "pharmaceutical chemist," "apothecary," "drug sundries," "medicine," or any of these words or their equivalent, in any manner.

(B) A pharmacy making retail sales may advertise by name or therapeutic class the availability for sale or dispensing of any dangerous drug provided that the advertising includes the price information specified in the definition of that term in section 4729.01 of the Revised Code.

**HISTORY: 130 v 1141 (Eff 10-7-63); 134 v S 141 (Eff 12-31-71); 136 v H 912 (Eff 10-1-76); 137 v H 1 (Eff 8-26-77); 140 v H 208 (Eff 9-20-84); 147 v S 66. Eff 7-22-98.**

## § 4729.361 Retail seller to disclose price information.

(A) A retail seller of dangerous drugs shall disclose price information regarding dangerous drugs to any person requesting such information.

(B) Pursuant to division (A) of this section, a retail seller of dangerous drugs shall disclose price information in the following ways:

(1) By means of verbal disclosure on the premises of the retail seller to all persons requesting such information;

(2) By means of telephone to any person having a valid prescription, who identifies himself and requests such information.

(C) Price disclosure shall not be required for those schedule II controlled substances where lives or property could be endangered by such disclosure.

**HISTORY: 136 v H 912. Eff 10-1-76.**

## § 4729.37 Filling prescriptions; records.

A copy of an original prescription may only be filled in accordance with the rules and regulations adopted by the state board of pharmacy.

Prescriptions received electronically or by word of mouth, telephone, telegraph, or other means of communication shall be recorded in writing by the pharmacist and the record so made by the pharmacist shall constitute the original prescription to be filled by the pharmacist. All prescriptions shall be preserved on file at the pharmacy for a period of three years, subject to inspection by the proper officers of the law.

**HISTORY: 130 v 1142 (Eff 10-7-63); 134 v S 141 (Eff 12-31-71); 147 v S 66. Eff 7-22-98.**

## § 4729.38 Generically equivalent drugs.

(A) Unless instructed otherwise by the person receiving the drug pursuant to the prescription, a pharmacist filling a prescription for a drug prescribed by its brand name may select a generically equivalent drug, as defined in section 3715.01 of the Revised Code, subject to the following conditions:

(1) The pharmacist shall not select a generically equivalent drug if the prescriber handwrites "dispense as written," or "D.A.W.," on the written prescription, or, when ordering a prescription electronically or orally, the prescriber specifies that the prescribed drug is medically necessary. These designations shall not be preprinted or stamped on the prescription. Division (A)(1) of this section does not preclude a reminder of the procedure required to prohibit the selection of a generically equivalent drug from being preprinted on the prescription.

(2) The pharmacist shall not select a generically equivalent drug unless its price to the patient is less than or equal to the price of the prescribed drug.

(3) The pharmacist, or the pharmacist's agent, assistant, or employee shall inform the patient or the patient's agent if a generically equivalent drug is available at a lower or equal cost, and of the person's right to refuse the drug selected. Division (A)(3) of this section does not apply to any:

(a) Prescription that is billed to any agency, division, or department of this state which will reimburse the pharmacy;

(b) Prescriptions for patients of a hospital, nursing home, or similar patient care facility.

(B) Unless the prescriber instructs otherwise, the label for every drug dispensed shall include the drug's brand name, if any, or its generic name and the name of the distributor, using abbreviations if necessary. When dispensing at retail a generically equivalent drug for the brand name drug prescribed, the pharmacist shall indicate on the drug's label or container that a generic substitution was made. The labeling requirements established by this division are in addition to all other labeling requirements of Chapter 3715. of the Revised Code.

(C) A pharmacist who selects a generically equivalent drug pursuant to this section assumes no greater liability for selecting the dispensed drug than would be incurred in filling a prescription for a drug prescribed by its brand name.

(D) The failure of a prescriber to restrict a prescription by specifying "dispense as written," or "D.A.W.," pursuant to division (A)(1) of this section shall not constitute evidence of the prescriber's negligence unless the prescriber had reasonable cause to believe that the health condition of the patient for whom the drug was intended warranted the prescription of a specific brand name drug and no other. No prescriber shall be liable for civil damages or in any criminal prosecution arising from the interchange of a generically equivalent drug for a prescribed brand name drug by a pharmacist, unless the prescribed brand name drug would have reasonably caused the same loss, damage, injury, or death.

**HISTORY: 139 v H 694 (Eff 11-15-81); 147 v S 66. Eff 7-22-98.**

**Analogous to former RC § 4729.38 (137 v S 45), repealed 139 v H 694, eff 11-15-81.**

## § 4729.381 Immunity based on compliance with formulary.

No licensed pharmacist shall be liable for civil damages or in any criminal prosecution arising from the dispensing of a drug based upon a formulary established by a hospital, a health insuring corporation, a long-term care facility, or the department of rehabilitation and corrections and requiring the pharmacist to dispense the particular drug.

**HISTORY: 140 v H 208 (Eff 9-20-84); 147 v S 67 (Eff 6-4-97); 147 v S 66. Eff 7-22-98.**

## § 4729.39 Pharmacist's management of drug therapy under consult agreement with physician.

(A) A pharmacist may enter into a consult agreement with a physician authorized under Chapter 4731. of the Revised Code to practice medicine and surgery or osteopathic medicine and surgery. Under a consult agreement, a pharmacist is authorized to manage an individual's drug therapy, but only to the extent specified in the agreement, this section, and the rules adopted under this section.

(B) All of the following apply to a consult agreement that authorizes a pharmacist to manage the drug therapy of an individual who is not a patient of a hospital, as defined in section 3727.01 of the Revised Code, or a resident in a long-term care facility, as defined in section 3729.01 of the Revised Code:

(1) A separate consult agreement must be entered into for each individual whose drug therapy is to be managed by a pharmacist. A consult agreement applies only to the particular diagnosis for which a physician prescribed an individual's drug therapy. If a different diagnosis is made for the individual, the pharmacist and physician must enter into a new or additional consult agreement.

(2) Management of an individual's drug therapy by a pharmacist under a consult agreement may include monitoring and modifying a prescription that has been issued for the individual. Except as provided in section 4729.38 of the Revised Code for the selection of generically equivalent drugs, management of an individual's drug therapy by a pharmacist under a consult agreement shall not include dispensing a drug that has not been prescribed by the physician.

(3) Each consult agreement shall be in writing, except that a consult agreement may be entered into verbally if it is immediately reduced to writing.

(4) A physician entering into a consult agreement shall specify in the agreement the extent to which the pharmacist is authorized to manage the drug therapy of the individual specified in the agreement.

(5) A physician entering into a consult agreement may specify one other physician who has agreed to serve as an alternate physician in the event that the primary physician is unavailable to consult directly with the pharmacist. The pharmacist may specify one other pharmacist who has agreed to serve as an alternate pharmacist in the event that the primary pharmacist is unavailable to consult directly with the physician.

(6) A consult agreement may not be implemented until it has been signed by the primary pharmacist, the primary physician, and the individual whose drug therapy will be managed or another person who has the authority to provide consent to treatment on behalf of the individual. Once the agreement is signed by all required parties, the physician shall include in the individual's medical record the fact that a consult agreement has been entered into with a pharmacist.

(7) Prior to commencing any action to manage an individual's drug therapy under a consult agreement, the pharmacist shall make reasonable attempts to contact and confer with the physician who entered into the consult agreement with the pharmacist. A pharmacist may commence an action to manage an individual's drug therapy prior to conferring with the physician or the physician's alternate, but shall immediately cease the action that was commenced if the pharmacist has not conferred with either physician within forty-eight hours.

A pharmacist acting under a consult agreement shall maintain a record of each action taken to manage an individual's drug therapy. The pharmacist shall send to the individual's physician a written report of all actions taken to manage the individual's drug therapy at intervals the physician shall specify when entering into the agreement. The physician shall include the pharmacist's report in the medical records the physician maintains for the individual.

(8) A consult agreement may be terminated by either the pharmacist or physician who entered into the agreement. By withdrawing consent, the individual whose drug therapy is being managed or the individual who consented to the treatment on behalf of the individual may terminate a consult agreement. The pharmacist or physician who receives the individual's withdrawal of consent shall provide written notice to the opposite party. A pharmacist or physician who terminates a consult agreement shall provide written notice to the opposite party and to the individual who consented to treatment under the agreement. The termination of a consult agreement shall be recorded by the pharmacist and physician in the records they maintain on the individual being treated.

(9) Except as described in division (B)(5) of this section, the authority of a pharmacist to manage an individual's drug therapy under a consult agreement does not permit the pharmacist to manage drug therapy prescribed by any other physician.

(C) All of the following apply to a consult agreement that authorizes a pharmacist to manage the drug therapy of an individual who is a patient of a hospital, as defined in section 3727.01 of the Revised Code, or a resident in a long-term care facility, as defined in section 3729.01 of the Revised Code:

(1) Before a consult agreement may be entered into and implemented, a hospital or long-term care facility shall adopt a policy for consult agreements. For any period of time during which a pharmacist or physician acting under a consult agreement is not physically present and available at the hospital or facility, the policy shall require that another pharmacist and physician be available at the hospital or facility.

(2) The consult agreement shall be made in writing and shall comply with the hospital's or facility's policy on consult agreements.

(3) The content of the consult agreement shall be communicated to the individual whose drug therapy will be managed in a manner consistent with the hospital's or facility's policy on consult agreements.

(4) A pharmacist acting under a consult agreement shall maintain in the individual's medical record a record of each action taken under the agreement.

(5) Communication between a pharmacist and physician acting under the consult agreement shall take place at regular intervals specified by the primary physician acting under the agreement.

(6) A consult agreement may be terminated by the individual, a person authorized to act on behalf of the individual, the primary physician acting under the agreement, or the primary pharmacist acting under the agreement. When a consult agreement is terminated, all parties to the agreement shall be notified and the termination shall be recorded in the individual's medical record.

(7) The authority of a pharmacist acting under a consult agreement does not permit the pharmacist to act under the agreement in a hospital long-term care facility at which the pharmacist is not authorized to practice.

(D) The state board of pharmacy, in consultation with the state medical board, shall adopt rules to be followed by pharmacists, and the state medical board, in consultation with the state board of pharmacy, shall adopt rules to be followed by physicians, that establish standards and procedures for entering into a consult agreement and managing an individual's drug therapy under a consult agreement. The boards shall specify in the rules any categories of drugs or types of diseases for which a consult agreement may not be established. Either board may adopt any other rules it considers necessary for the implementation and administration of this section. All rules adopted under this division shall be adopted in accordance with Chapter 119. of the Revised Code.

**HISTORY: 147 v S 66 (Eff 7-22-98); 148 v S 172. Eff 2-12-2001.**

## § 4729.42 Unauthorized pharmacy-related drug conduct relative to pharmacy technicians; criminal records check; confidentiality of examination materials.

(A) As used in this section, "qualified pharmacy technician" means a person who is under the personal supervision of a pharmacist and to whom all of the following apply:

(1) The person is eighteen years of age or older.

(2) The person possesses a high school diploma, possesses a certificate of high school equivalence, or was employed prior to April 8, 2009, as a pharmacy technician without a high school diploma or a certificate of high school equivalence.

(3) The person has passed an examination approved by the state board of pharmacy to determine a person's competency to perform services as a pharmacy technician.

(4) Except as otherwise provided in this section, the person has submitted to a criminal records check in accordance with section 4776.02 of the Revised Code as if the person was an applicant for an initial license who is subject to that section, and the results of the criminal records check provided as described in that section and section 4776.04 of the Revised Code do not show that the person previously has been convicted of or pleaded guilty to any felony in this state, any other state, or the United States.

(B) Except as provided in division (F) of this section, no person who is not a pharmacist, pharmacy intern, or qualified pharmacy technician shall do any of the following in a pharmacy or while performing a function of a pharmacy:

(1) Engage in the compounding of any drug;

(2) Package or label any drug;

(3) Prepare or mix any intravenous drug to be injected into a human being.

(C) No pharmacist shall allow any person employed or otherwise under the control of the pharmacist to violate division (B) of this section.

(D) No person who owns, manages, or conducts a pharmacy shall allow any person employed or otherwise under the control of the person who owns, manages, or conducts the pharmacy to violate division (B) of this section.

(E) No person who submits to a criminal records check in accordance with section 4776.02 of the Revised Code for the purpose of satisfying the criterion set forth in division (A)(4) of this section and who obtains a report pursuant to section 4776.02 or 4776.04 of the Revised Code containing the results of the criminal records check and any information provided by the federal bureau of investigation shall modify or alter, or allow any other person to modify or alter, any item, record, or information contained in the report and thereafter use the modified or altered report for the purpose of satisfying the criterion set forth in division (A)(4) of this section or otherwise submit or use it for any purpose or in any manner identified in division (A) of section 2921.13 of the Revised Code.

(F)(1) Division (B) of this section does not prohibit a health care professional authorized to engage in the activities specified in division (B)(1), (2), or (3) of this section while acting in the course of the professional's practice.

(2) Division (B) of this section does not prohibit the activities performed by a student as an integral part of a pharmacy technician training program that is operated by a vocational school district or joint vocational school district, certified by the department of education, or approved by the Ohio board of regents.

(3) In the case of a person employed after April 8, 2009, division (B) of this section does not prohibit the person's activities for the first twelve months following the initial date of employment, if both of the following apply:

(a) The person is participating in or has completed a pharmacy technician training program that meets the board's standards for those programs and is making substantial progress in preparation to take a pharmacy technician examination approved by the board.

(b) The results of the person's criminal records check provided as described in sections 4776.02 and 4776.04 of the Revised Code show that the person previously has not been convicted of or has not pleaded guilty to any felony in this state, any other state, or the United States.

(4) In the case of a person who completes a pharmacy technician training program that is operated by a vocational school district or joint vocational school district, division (B) of this section does not prohibit the person's activities for the first twelve months following the date of completing the program, if both of the following apply:

(a) The person is making substantial progress in preparation to take a pharmacy technician examination approved by the board.

(b) The results of the person's criminal records check show that the person previously has not been convicted of or has not pleaded guilty to any felony in this state, any other state, or the United States.

(5) In the case of a person employed on April 8, 2009, in the capacity of a pharmacy technician, division (B) of this section does not do either of the following:

(a) Require the person to undergo a criminal records check if the person has been employed for five years or longer;

(b) Prohibit the person's activities until the earlier of either of the following:

(i) If the person has not passed an examination described in division (A)(3) of this section, eighteen months after April 8, 2009;

(ii) If a criminal records check is required because the person has not been employed for five years or longer, the date on which the person and the employer receive the results of a criminal records check provided as described in sections 4776.02 and 4776.04 of the Revised Code that show the person previously has been convicted of or pleaded guilty to any felony in this state, any other state, or the United States.

(G) If, pursuant to rules adopted under section 4729.26 of the Revised Code, the board requires a person that develops or administers a pharmacy technician examination to submit examination materials to the board for approval, any examination materials that are submitted shall not be public records for purposes of section 149.43 of the Revised Code.

**HISTORY: 152 v S 203, § 1, eff. 4-8-09; 153 v H 2, § 101.01, eff. 4-1-09; 153 v H 1, § 101.01, eff. 10-16-09.**

The effective date is set by § 812.10 of 153 v H 1.
The effective date is set by §§ 901.10 and 901.11 of 153 v H 2.

## [DANGEROUS DRUGS]

### § 4729.51 Persons who may sell, purchase, distribute, or deliver dangerous drugs.

(A) No person other than a registered wholesale distributor of dangerous drugs shall possess for sale, sell, distribute, or deliver, at wholesale, dangerous drugs, except as follows:

(1) A pharmacist who is a licensed terminal distributor of dangerous drugs or who is employed by a licensed terminal distributor of dangerous drugs may make occasional sales of dangerous drugs at wholesale;

(2) A licensed terminal distributor of dangerous drugs having more than one establishment or place may transfer or deliver dangerous drugs from one establishment or place for which a license has been issued to the terminal distributor to another establishment or place for which a license has been issued to the terminal distributor if the license issued for each establishment or place is in effect at the time of the transfer or delivery.

(B)(1) No registered wholesale distributor of dangerous drugs shall possess for sale, or sell, at wholesale, dangerous drugs to any person other than the following:

(a) Except as provided in division (B)(3) of this section, a licensed health professional authorized to prescribe drugs;

(b) An optometrist licensed under Chapter 4725. of the Revised Code who holds a topical ocular pharmaceutical agents certificate;

(c) A registered wholesale distributor of dangerous drugs;

(d) A manufacturer of dangerous drugs;

(e) Subject to division (B)(3) of this section, a licensed terminal distributor of dangerous drugs;

(f) Carriers or warehouses for the purpose of carriage or storage;

(g) Terminal or wholesale distributors of dangerous drugs who are not engaged in the sale of dangerous drugs within this state;

(h) An individual who holds a current license, certificate, or registration issued under Title 47 of the Revised Code and has been certified to conduct diabetes education by a national certifying body specified in rules adopted by the state board of pharmacy under section 4729.68 of the Revised Code, but only with respect to insulin that will be used for the purpose of diabetes education and only if diabetes education is within the individual's scope of practice under statutes and rules regulating the individual's profession;

(i) An individual who holds a valid certificate issued by a nationally recognized S.C.U.B.A. diving certifying organization approved by the state board of pharmacy in rule, but only with respect to medical oxygen that will be used for the purpose of emergency care or treatment at the scene of a diving emergency;

(j) Except as provided in division (B)(2) of this section, a business entity that is a corporation formed under division (B) of section 1701.03 of the Revised Code, a limited liability company formed under Chapter 1705. of the Revised Code, or a professional association formed under Chapter 1785. of the Revised Code if the entity has a sole shareholder who is a licensed health professional authorized to prescribe drugs and is authorized to provide the professional services being offered by the entity;

(k) Except as provided in division (B)(2) of this section, a business entity that is a corporation formed under division (B) of section 1701.03 of the Revised Code, a limited liability company formed under Chapter 1705. of the Revised Code, a partnership or a limited liability partnership formed under Chapter 1775. of the Revised Code, or a professional association formed under Chapter 1785. of the Revised Code, if, to be a shareholder, member, or partner, an individual is required to be licensed, certified, or otherwise legally authorized under Title XLVII of the Revised Code to perform the professional service provided by the entity and each such individual is a licensed health professional authorized to prescribe drugs.

(2) No registered wholesaler of dangerous drugs shall possess for sale, or sell, at wholesale, dangerous drugs to any of the following:

(a) A prescriber who is employed by a pain management clinic that is not licensed as a terminal distributor of dangerous drugs with a pain management clinic classification issued under section 4729.552 of the Revised Code;

(b) A business entity described in division (B)(1)(j) of this section that is, or is operating, a pain management clinic without a license as a terminal distributor of dangerous drugs with a pain management clinic classification issued under section 4729.552 of the Revised Code;

(c) A business entity described in division (B)(1)(k) of this section that is, or is operating, a pain management clinic without a license as a terminal distributor of dangerous drugs with a pain management clinic classification issued under section 4729.552 of the Revised Code.

(3) No registered wholesale distributor of dangerous drugs shall possess dangerous drugs for sale at wholesale, or sell such drugs at wholesale, to a licensed terminal distributor of dangerous drugs, except as follows:

(a) In the case of a terminal distributor with a category I license, only dangerous drugs described in category I, as defined in division (A)(1) of section 4729.54 of the Revised Code;

(b) In the case of a terminal distributor with a category II license, only dangerous drugs described in category I and category II, as defined in divisions (A)(1) and (2) of section 4729.54 of the Revised Code;

(c) In the case of a terminal distributor with a category III license, dangerous drugs described in category I, category II, and category III, as defined in divisions (A)(1), (2), and (3) of section 4729.54 of the Revised Code;

(d) In the case of a terminal distributor with a limited category I, II, or III license, only the dangerous drugs specified in the certificate furnished by the terminal distributor in accordance with section 4729.60 of the Revised Code.

(C)(1) Except as provided in division (C)(4) of this section, no person shall sell, at retail, dangerous drugs.

(2) Except as provided in division (C)(4) of this section, no person shall possess for sale, at retail, dangerous drugs.

(3) Except as provided in division (C)(4) of this section, no person shall possess dangerous drugs.

(4) Divisions (C)(1), (2), and (3) of this section do not apply to a registered wholesale distributor of dangerous drugs, a licensed terminal distributor of dangerous drugs, or a person who possesses, or possesses for sale or sells, at retail, a dangerous drug in accordance with Chapters 3719., 4715., 4723., 4725., 4729., 4730., 4731., and 4741. of the Revised Code.

Divisions (C)(1), (2), and (3) of this section do not apply to an individual who holds a current license, certificate, or registration issued under Title XLVII of the Revised Code and has been certified to conduct diabetes education by a national certifying body specified in rules adopted by the state board of pharmacy under section 4729.68 of the Revised Code, but only to the extent that the individual possesses insulin or personally supplies insulin solely for the purpose of diabetes education and only if diabetes education is within the individual's scope of practice under statutes and rules regulating the individual's profession.

Divisions (C)(1), (2), and (3) of this section do not apply to an individual who holds a valid certificate issued by a nationally recognized S.C.U.B.A. diving certifying organization approved by the state board of pharmacy in rule, but only to the extent that the individual possesses medical oxygen or personally supplies medical oxygen for the purpose of emergency care or treatment at the scene of a diving emergency.

(D) No licensed terminal distributor of dangerous drugs shall purchase for the purpose of resale dangerous drugs from any person other than a registered wholesale distributor of dangerous drugs, except as follows:

(1) A licensed terminal distributor of dangerous drugs may make occasional purchases of dangerous drugs for resale from a pharmacist who is a licensed terminal distributor of dangerous drugs or who is employed by a licensed terminal distributor of dangerous drugs;

(2) A licensed terminal distributor of dangerous drugs having more than one establishment or place may transfer or receive dangerous drugs from one establishment or place for which a license has been issued to the terminal distributor to another establishment or place for which a license has been issued to the terminal distributor if the license issued for each establishment or place is in effect at the time of the transfer or receipt.

(E) No licensed terminal distributor of dangerous drugs shall engage in the sale or other distribution of dangerous drugs at retail or maintain possession, custody, or control of dangerous drugs for any purpose other than the distributor's personal use or consumption, at any establishment or place other than that or those described in the license issued by the state board of pharmacy to such terminal distributor.

(F) Nothing in this section shall be construed to interfere with the performance of official duties by any law enforcement official authorized by municipal, county, state, or federal law to collect samples of any drug, regardless of its nature or in whose possession it may be.

**HISTORY: 129 v 1376 (Eff 1-1-62); 133 v H 90 (Eff 11-19-69); 139 v S 4 (Eff 10-1-82); 140 v S 187 (Eff 6-14-84); 145 v H 391 (Eff 7-21-94); 146 v S 246 (Eff 11-6-96); 147 v H 215 (Eff 6-30-97); 147 v S 66 (Eff 7-22-98); 147 v H 553 (Eff 3-9-99); 148 v H 241. Eff 5-17-2000; 150 v H 64, § 1, eff. 5-4-04; 151 v S 154, § 1, eff. 5-17-06; 152 v H 283, § 1, eff. 9-12-08; 2011 HB 93, § 1, eff. May 20, 2011; 2011 HB 9, § 1, eff. June 29, 2011.**

Acts 2011, HB 9, § 3 provides: "This act applies to transactions entered into on or after the effective date of this act."

Acts 2011, HB 93, § 8 provides: "(A) Not later than one year after the effective date of this section, and annually each year for four years thereafter, the State Board of Pharmacy shall prepare a report on all of the following:

"(1) The total number of applications received by the Board for a terminal distributor of dangerous drugs license with a pain management clinic classification;

"(2) The total number of licenses with a pain management clinic classification granted or denied by the Board;

"(3) Any disciplinary actions taken by the Board against holders of licenses with a pain management clinic classification;

"(4) Total revenues generated from fees for licenses with a pain management clinic classification, fines and penalties paid by license holders, or other disciplinary actions taken against license holders;

"(5) Any other relevant information regarding the implementation of this act.

"(B) On completion of each report, the Board shall submit a copy of the report to the Governor and, in accordance with section 101.68 of the Revised Code, the General Assembly. In accordance with that section, the Board shall display the report on the Board's internet web site."

## § 4729.52 Registration as wholesale distributor.

(A) A person desiring to be registered as a wholesale distributor of dangerous drugs shall file with the executive director of the state board of pharmacy a verified application containing such information as the board requires of the applicant relative to the qualifications to be registered as a wholesale distributor of dangerous drugs set forth in section 4729.53 of the Revised Code and the rules adopted under that section. The board shall register as a wholesale distributor of dangerous drugs each applicant who has paid the required registration fee, if the board determines that the applicant meets the qualifications to be registered as a wholesale distributor of dangerous drugs set forth in section 4729.53 of the Revised Code and the rules adopted under that section.

(B) The board may register and issue to a person who does not reside in this state a registration certificate as a wholesale distributor of dangerous drugs if the person possesses a current and valid wholesale distributor of dangerous drugs registration certificate or license issued by another state that has qualifications for licensure or registration comparable to the registration requirements in this state and pays the required registration fee.

(C) All registration certificates issued pursuant to this section are effective for a period of twelve months from the first day of July of each year. A registration certificate shall be renewed annually by the board for a like period, pursuant to this section and the standard renewal procedure of Chapter 4745. of the Revised Code. A person desiring to renew a registration certificate shall submit an application for renewal and pay the required renewal fee before the first day of July each year.

(D) Each registration certificate and its application shall describe not more than one establishment or place where the registrant or applicant may engage in the sale of dangerous drugs at wholesale. No registration certificate shall authorize or permit the wholesale distributor of dangerous drugs named therein to engage in the sale of drugs at wholesale or to maintain possession, custody, or control of dangerous drugs for any purpose other than for the registrant's own use and consumption at any establishment or place other than that described in the certificate.

(E)(1) The registration fee is seven hundred fifty dollars and shall accompany each application for registration. The registration renewal fee is seven hundred fifty dollars and shall accompany each renewal application.

A registration certificate that has not been renewed in any year by the first day of August may be reinstated upon payment of the renewal fee and a penalty of one hundred fifty dollars.

(2) Renewal fees and penalties assessed under division (E)(1) of this section shall not be returned if the applicant fails to qualify for renewal.

(F) The registration of any person as a wholesale distributor of dangerous drugs subjects the person and the person's agents and employees to the jurisdiction of the board and to the laws of this state for the purpose of the enforcement of this chapter and the rules of the board. However, the filing of an application for registration as a wholesale distributor of dangerous drugs by, or on behalf of, any person or the registration of any person as a wholesale distributor of dangerous drugs shall not, of itself, constitute evidence that the person is doing business within this state.

**HISTORY: 129 v 1376 (Eff 1-1-62); 132 v S 70 (Eff 9-14-67); 132 v H 911 (Eff 6-11-68); 133 v H 742 (Eff 11-21-69); 139 v H 694 (Eff 11-15-81); 144 v H 298 (Eff 7-26-91); 144 v S 193 (Eff 7-1-92); 146 v H 117 (Eff 6-30-95); 147 v H 215 (Eff 6-30-97); 147 v S 66. Eff 7-22-98; 2011 HB 153, § 101.01, eff. Sept. 29, 2011.**

## § 4729.53 Requirements for registration.

(A) The board of pharmacy shall not register any person as a wholesale distributor of dangerous drugs unless the applicant for registration furnishes satisfactory proof to the board of pharmacy that he meets all of the following:

(1) That if the applicant has been convicted of a violation of any federal, state, or local law relating to drug samples, wholesale or retail drug distribution, or distribution of controlled substances or of a felony, or if a federal, state, or local governmental entity has suspended or revoked any current or prior license or registration of the applicant for the manufacture or sale of any dangerous drugs, including controlled substances, the applicant, to the satisfaction of the board, assures that he has in place adequate safeguards to prevent the recurrence of any such violations;

(2) The applicant's past experience in the manufacture or distribution of dangerous drugs, including controlled substances, is acceptable to the board.

(3) The applicant is equipped as to land, buildings, equipment, and personnel to properly carry on the business of a wholesale distributor of dangerous drugs, including providing adequate security for and proper storage conditions and handling for dangerous drugs, and is complying with the requirements under this chapter and the rules adopted pursuant thereto for maintaining and making available records to properly identified board officials and federal, state, and local law enforcement agencies.

(4) Personnel employed by the applicant have the appropriate education or experience, as determined by the board, to assume responsibility for positions related to compliance with this chapter and the rules adopted pursuant thereto.

(5) The applicant has designated the name and address of a person to whom communications from the board may be directed and upon whom the notices and citations provided for in section 4729.56 of the Revised Code may be served.

(6) Adequate safeguards are assured to prevent the sale of dangerous drugs to any person other than those named in division (B) of section 4729.51 of the Revised Code.

(7) Any other requirement or qualification the board, by rule adopted in accordance with Chapter 119. of the Revised Code, considers relevant to and consistent with the public safety and health.

(B) The board may refuse to register or renew the registration certificate of any person if the board determines that the granting of the registration certificate or its renewal is not in the public interest.

**HISTORY: 129 v 1376 (Eff 1-1-62); 136 v H 300 (Eff 7-1-76); 144 v S 193. Eff 7-1-92.**

## § 4729.54 Licensing of terminal distributors.

(A) As used in this section and section 4729.541 of the Revised Code:

(1) "Category I" means single-dose injections of intravenous fluids, including saline, Ringer's lactate, five per cent dextrose and distilled water, and other intravenous fluids or parenteral solutions included in this category by rule of the state board of pharmacy, that have a volume of one hundred milliliters or more and that contain no added substances, or single-dose injections of epinephrine to be administered pursuant to sections 4765.38 and 4765.39 of the Revised Code.

(2) "Category II" means any dangerous drug that is not included in category I or III.

(3) "Category III" means any controlled substance that is contained in schedule I, II, III, IV, or V.

(4) "Emergency medical service organization" has the same meaning as in section 4765.01 of the Revised Code.

(5) "Person" includes an emergency medical service organization.

(6) "Schedule I, schedule II, schedule III, schedule IV, and schedule V" mean controlled substance schedules I, II, III, IV, and V, respectively, as established pursuant to section 3719.41 of the Revised Code and as amended.

(B)(1) A person who desires to be licensed as a terminal distributor of dangerous drugs shall file with the executive director of the state board of pharmacy a verified application. After it is filed, the application may not be withdrawn without approval of the board.

(2) An application shall contain all the following that apply in the applicant's case :

(a) Information that the board requires relative to the qualifications of a terminal distributor of dangerous drugs set forth in section 4729.55 of the Revised Code;

(b) A statement that the person wishes to be licensed as a category I, category II, category III, limited category I, limited category II, or limited category III terminal distributor of dangerous drugs;

(c) If the person wishes to be licensed as a limited category I, limited category II, or limited category III terminal distributor of dangerous drugs, a notarized list of the dangerous drugs that the person wishes to possess, have custody or control of, and distribute, which list shall also specify the purpose for which those drugs will be used and their source;

(d) If the person is an emergency medical service organization, the information that is specified in division (C)(1) of this section;

(e) Except for an emergency medical service organization, the identity of the one establishment or place at which the person intends to engage in the sale or other distribution of dangerous drugs at retail, and maintain possession, custody, or control of dangerous drugs for purposes other than the person's own use or consumption;

(f) If the application pertains to a pain management clinic, information that demonstrates, to the satisfaction of the board, compliance with division (A) of section 4729.552 of the Revised Code.

(C)(1) An emergency medical service organization that wishes to be licensed as a terminal distributor of dangerous drugs shall list in its application for licensure the following additional information:

(a) The units under its control that the organization determines will possess dangerous drugs for the purpose of administering emergency medical services in accordance with Chapter 4765. of the Revised Code;

(b) With respect to each such unit, whether the dangerous drugs that the organization determines the unit will possess are in category I, II, or III.

(2) An emergency medical service organization that is licensed as a terminal distributor of dangerous drugs shall file a new application for such licensure if there is any change in the number, or location of, any of its units or any change in the category of the dangerous drugs that any unit will possess.

(3) A unit listed in an application for licensure pursuant to division (C)(1) of this section may obtain the dangerous drugs it is authorized to possess from its emergency medical service organization or, on a replacement basis, from a hospital pharmacy. If units will obtain dangerous drugs from a hospital pharmacy, the organization shall file, and maintain in current form, the following items with the pharmacist who is responsible for the hospital's terminal distributor of dangerous drugs license:

(a) A copy of its standing orders or protocol;

(b) A list of the personnel employed or used by the organization to provide emergency medical services in accordance with Chapter 4765. of the Revised Code, who are authorized to possess the drugs, which list also shall indicate the personnel who are authorized to administer the drugs.

(D) Each emergency medical service organization that applies for a terminal distributor of dangerous drugs license shall submit with its application the following:

(1) A notarized copy of its standing orders or protocol, which orders or protocol shall be signed by a physician and specify the dangerous drugs that its units may carry, expressed in standard dose units;

(2) A list of the personnel employed or used by the organization to provide emergency medical services in accordance with Chapter 4765. of the Revised Code.

An emergency medical service organization that is licensed as a terminal distributor shall notify the board immediately of any changes in its standing orders or protocol.

(E) There shall be six categories of terminal distributor of dangerous drugs licenses, which categories shall be as follows:

(1) Category I license. A person who obtains this license may possess, have custody or control of, and distribute only the dangerous drugs described in category I.

(2) Limited category I license. A person who obtains this license may possess, have custody or control of, and distribute only the dangerous drugs described in category I that were listed in the application for licensure.

(3) Category II license. A person who obtains this license may possess, have custody or control of, and distribute only the dangerous drugs described in category I and category II.

(4) Limited category II license. A person who obtains this license may possess, have custody or control of, and distribute only the dangerous drugs described in category I or category II that were listed in the application for licensure.

(5) Category III license, which may include a pain management clinic classification issued under section 4729.552 of the Revised Code. A person who obtains this license may possess, have custody or control of, and distribute the dangerous drugs described in category I, category II, and category III. If the license includes a pain management clinic classification, the person may operate a pain management clinic.

(6) Limited category III license. A person who obtains this license may possess, have custody or control of, and distribute only the dangerous drugs described in category I, category II, or category III that were listed in the application for licensure.

(F) Except for an application made on behalf of an animal shelter, if an applicant for licensure as a limited category I, II, or III terminal distributor of dangerous drugs intends to administer dangerous drugs to a person or animal, the applicant shall submit, with the application, a notarized copy of its protocol or standing orders, which protocol or orders shall be signed by a licensed health professional authorized to prescribe drugs, specify the dangerous drugs to be administered, and list personnel who are authorized to administer the dangerous drugs in accordance with federal law or the law of this state. An application made on behalf of an animal shelter shall include a notarized list of the dangerous drugs to be administered to animals and the personnel who are authorized to administer the drugs to animals in accordance with section 4729.532 of the Revised Code. After obtaining a terminal distributor license, a licensee shall notify the board immediately of any changes in its protocol or standing orders, or in such personnel.

(G)(1) Except as provided in division (G)(2) of this section, each applicant for licensure as a terminal distributor of dangerous drugs shall submit, with the application, a license fee determined as follows:

(a) For a category I or limited category I license, forty-five dollars;

(b) For a category II or limited category II license, one hundred twelve dollars and fifty cents;

(c) For a category III license, including a license with a pain management clinic classification issued under section 4729.552 of the Revised Code, or a limited category III license, one hundred fifty dollars.

(2) For a professional association, corporation, partnership, or limited liability company organized for the purpose of practicing veterinary medicine, the fee shall be forty dollars.

(3) Fees assessed under divisions (G)(1) and (2) of this section shall not be returned if the applicant fails to qualify for registration.

(H)(1) The board shall issue a terminal distributor of dangerous drugs license to each person who submits an application for such licensure in accordance with this section, pays the required license fee, is determined by the board to meet the requirements set forth in section 4729.55 of the Revised Code, and satisfies any other applicable requirements of this section.

(2) The license of a person other than an emergency medical service organization shall describe the one establishment or place at which the licensee may engage in the sale or other distribution of dangerous drugs at retail and maintain possession, custody, or control of dangerous drugs for purposes other than the licensee's own use or consumption. The one establishment or place shall be that which is described in the application for licensure.

No such license shall authorize or permit the terminal distributor of dangerous drugs named in it to engage in the sale or other distribution of dangerous drugs at retail or to maintain possession, custody, or control of dangerous drugs for any purpose other than the distributor's own use or consumption, at any establishment or place other than that described in the license, except that an agent or employee of an animal shelter may possess and use dangerous drugs in the course of business as provided in division (D) of section 4729.532 of the Revised Code.

(3) The license of an emergency medical service organization shall cover and describe all the units of the organization listed in its application for licensure.

(4) The license of every terminal distributor of dangerous drugs shall indicate, on its face, the category of licensure. If the license is a limited category I, II, or III license, it shall specify, and shall authorize the licensee to possess, have custody or control of, and distribute only, the dangerous drugs that were listed in the application for licensure.

(I) All licenses issued pursuant to this section shall be effective for a period of twelve months from the first day of January of each year. A license shall be renewed by the board for a like period, annually, according to the provisions of this section, and the standard renewal procedure of Chapter 4745. of the Revised Code. A person who desires to renew a license shall submit an application for renewal and pay the required fee on or before the thirty-first day of December each year. The fee required for the renewal of a license shall be the same as the fee paid for the license being renewed, and shall accompany the application for renewal.

A license that has not been renewed during December in any year and by the first day of February of the following year may be reinstated only upon payment of the required renewal fee and a penalty fee of fifty-five dollars.

(J)(1) No emergency medical service organization that is licensed as a terminal distributor of dangerous drugs shall fail to comply with division (C)(2) or (3) of this section.

(2) No emergency medical service organization that is licensed as a terminal distributor of dangerous drugs shall fail to comply with division (D) of this section.

(3) No licensed terminal distributor of dangerous drugs shall possess, have custody or control of, or distribute dangerous drugs that the terminal distributor is not entitled to possess, have custody or control of, or distribute by virtue of its category of licensure.

(4) No licensee that is required by division (F) of this section to notify the board of changes in its protocol or standing orders, or in personnel, shall fail to comply with that division.

**HISTORY: 129 v 1376 (Eff 1-1-62); 132 v S 70 (Eff 9-14-67); 132 v H 911 (Eff 6-11-68); 133 v H 742 (Eff 11-21-69); 139 v H 694 (Eff 11-15-81); 139 v S 4 (Eff 10-1-82); 140 v S 19 (Eff 9-18-84); 144 v H 298 (Eff 7-26-91); 144 v S 98 (Eff 11-12-92); 145 v H 88 (Eff 6-29-94); 146 v H 117 (Eff 6-30-95); 147 v H 215 (Eff 6-30-97); 147 v S 66 (Eff 7-22-98); 148 v H 283. Eff 6-30-99; 152 v H 283, § 1, eff. 9-12-08; 2011 HB 93, § 1, eff. May 20, 2011.**

Acts 2011, HB 93, § 8 provides: "(A) Not later than one year after the effective date of this section, and annually each year for four years thereafter, the State Board of Pharmacy shall prepare a report on all of the following:

"(1) The total number of applications received by the Board for a terminal distributor of dangerous drugs license with a pain management clinic classification;

"(2) The total number of licenses with a pain management clinic classification granted or denied by the Board;

"(3) Any disciplinary actions taken by the Board against holders of licenses with a pain management clinic classification;

"(4) Total revenues generated from fees for licenses with a pain management clinic classification, fines and penalties paid by license holders, or other disciplinary actions taken against license holders;

"(5) Any other relevant information regarding the implementation of this act.

"(B) On completion of each report, the Board shall submit a copy of the report to the Governor and, in accordance with section 101.68 of the Revised Code, the General Assembly. In accordance with that section, the Board shall display the report on the Board's internet web site."

The effective date is set by section 164 of HB 283.

## § 4729.541 License exemption for certain professional business entities.

(A) Except as provided in division (B) of this section, a business entity described in division (B)(1)(j) or (k) of section 4729.51 of the Revised Code may possess, have custody or control of, and distribute the dangerous drugs in category I, category II, and category III of section 4729.54 of the Revised Code without holding a terminal distributor of dangerous drugs license issued under that section.

(B) If a business entity described in division (B)(1)(j) or (k) of section 4729.51 of the Revised Code is a pain management clinic or is operating a pain management clinic, the entity shall hold a license as a terminal distributor of dangerous drugs with a pain management clinic classification issued under section 4729.552 of the Revised Code.

**HISTORY: 152 v H 283, § 1, eff. 9-12-08; 2011 HB 93, § 1, eff. May 20, 2011.**

Acts 2011, HB 93, § 8 provides: "(A) Not later than one year after the effective date of this section, and annually each year for four years thereafter, the State Board of Pharmacy shall prepare a report on all of the following:

"(1) The total number of applications received by the Board for a terminal distributor of dangerous drugs license with a pain management clinic classification;

"(2) The total number of licenses with a pain management clinic classification granted or denied by the Board;

"(3) Any disciplinary actions taken by the Board against holders of licenses with a pain management clinic classification;

"(4) Total revenues generated from fees for licenses with a pain management clinic classification, fines and penalties paid by license holders, or other disciplinary actions taken against license holders;

"(5) Any other relevant information regarding the implementation of this act.

"(B) On completion of each report, the Board shall submit a copy of the report to the Governor and, in accordance with section 101.68 of the Revised Code, the General Assembly. In accordance with that section, the Board shall display the report on the Board's internet web site."

## § 4729.55 Requirements for issuance of license.

No license shall be issued to an applicant for licensure as a terminal distributor of dangerous drugs unless the applicant has furnished satisfactory proof to the state board of pharmacy that:

(A) The applicant is equipped as to land, buildings, and equipment to properly carry on the business of a terminal distributor of dangerous drugs within the category of licensure approved by the board.

(B) A pharmacist, licensed health professional authorized to prescribe drugs, animal shelter licensed with the state board of pharmacy under section 4729.531 of the Revised Code, or a laboratory as defined in section 3719.01 of the Revised Code will maintain supervision and control over the possession and custody of dangerous drugs that may be acquired by or on behalf of the applicant.

(C) Adequate safeguards are assured to prevent the sale or other distribution of dangerous drugs by any person other than a pharmacist or licensed health professional authorized to prescribe drugs.

(D) Adequate safeguards are assured that the applicant will carry on the business of a terminal distributor of dangerous drugs in a manner that allows pharmacists and pharmacy interns employed by the terminal distributor to practice pharmacy in a safe and effective manner.

(E) If the applicant, or any agent or employee of the applicant, has been found guilty of violating section 4729.51 of the Revised Code, the "Federal Food, Drug, and Cosmetic Act," 52 Stat. 1040 (1938), 21 U.S.C.A. 301, the federal drug abuse control laws, Chapter 2925., 3715., 3719., or 4729. of the Revised Code, or any rule of the board, adequate safeguards are assured to prevent the recurrence of the violation.

(F) In the case of an applicant who is a food processor or retail seller of food, the applicant will maintain supervision and control over the possession and custody of nitrous oxide.

(G) In the case of an applicant who is a retail seller of oxygen in original packages labeled as required by the "Federal Food, Drug, and Cosmetic Act," the applicant will maintain supervision and control over the possession, custody, and retail sale of the oxygen.

(H) If the application is made on behalf of an animal shelter, at least one of the agents or employees of the animal shelter is certified in compliance with section 4729.532 of the Revised Code.

(I) In the case of an applicant who is a retail seller of peritoneal dialysis solutions in original packages labeled as required by the "Federal Food, Drug, and Cosmetic Act," 52 Stat. 1040 (1938), 21 U.S.C.A. 301, the applicant will maintain supervision and control over the possession, custody, and retail sale of the peritoneal dialysis solutions.

(J) In the case of an applicant who is a pain management clinic, the applicant meets the requirements to receive a license with a pain management clinic classification issued under section 4729.552 of the Revised Code.

**HISTORY: 129 v 1376 (Eff 1-1-62); 136 v H 300 (Eff 7-1-76); 139 v S 4 (Eff 10-1-82); 145 v H 88 (Eff 6-29-94); 145 v H 391 (Eff 7-21-94); 146 v H 595 (Eff 10-16-96); 147 v H 215 (Eff 6-30-97); 147 v S 66 (Eff 7-22-98); 148 v S 172. Eff 2-12-2001; 2011 HB 93, § 1, eff. May 20, 2011.**

Acts 2011, HB 93, § 8 provides: "(A) Not later than one year after the effective date of this section, and annually each year for four years thereafter, the State Board of Pharmacy shall prepare a report on all of the following:

"(1) The total number of applications received by the Board for a terminal distributor of dangerous drugs license with a pain management clinic classification;

"(2) The total number of licenses with a pain management clinic classification granted or denied by the Board;

"(3) Any disciplinary actions taken by the Board against holders of licenses with a pain management clinic classification;

"(4) Total revenues generated from fees for licenses with a pain management clinic classification, fines and penalties paid by license holders, or other disciplinary actions taken against license holders;

"(5) Any other relevant information regarding the implementation of this act.

"(B) On completion of each report, the Board shall submit a copy of the report to the Governor and, in accordance with section 101.68 of the Revised Code, the General Assembly. In accordance with that section, the Board shall display the report on the Board's internet web site."

## § 4729.552 Category III terminal distributor of dangerous drugs; eligibility.

(A) To be eligible to receive a license as a category III terminal distributor of dangerous drugs with a pain management clinic classification, an applicant shall submit evidence satisfactory to the board that the applicant's pain management clinic will be operated in accordance with the requirements specified in division (B) of this section and that the applicant meets any other applicable requirements under this chapter or Chapter 3719. of the Revised Code.

If the board determines that an applicant meets all of the requirements, the board shall issue to the applicant a license as a category III terminal distributor of dangerous drugs and specify on the license that the terminal distributor is classified as a pain management clinic.

(B) The holder of a terminal distributor license with a pain management clinic classification shall do all of the following:

(1) Be in control of a facility that is owned and operated solely by one or more physicians authorized under Chapter 4731. of the Revised Code to practice medicine and surgery or osteopathic medicine and surgery;

(2) Ensure that any person employed by the facility complies with the requirements for the operation of a pain management clinic established by the state medical board in rules adopted under section 4731.054 of the Revised Code;

(3) Require any person with ownership of the facility to submit to a criminal records check in accordance with

section 4776.02 of the Revised Code and send the results of the criminal records check directly to the state board of pharmacy for review and decision under section 4729.071 of the Revised Code;

(4) Require all employees of the facility to submit to a criminal records check in accordance with section 4776.02 of the Revised Code and ensure that no person is employed who has previously been convicted of, or pleaded guilty to, either of the following:

(a) A theft offense, described in division (K)(3) of section 2913.01 of the Revised Code, that would constitute a felony under the laws of this state, any other state, or the United States;

(b) A felony drug abuse offense, as defined in section 2925.01 of the Revised Code.

(5) Maintain a list of each person with ownership of the facility and notify the state board of pharmacy of any change to that list.

(C) No person shall operate a facility that under this chapter is subject to licensure as a category III terminal distributor of dangerous drugs with a pain management clinic classification without obtaining and maintaining the license with the classification.

No person who holds a category III license with a pain management clinic classification shall fail to remain in compliance with the requirements of division (A) of this section and any other applicable requirements under this chapter or Chapter 3719. of the Revised Code.

(D) The board may impose a fine of not more than five thousand dollars on a terminal distributor of dangerous drugs license holder who violates division (C) of this section. A separate fine may be imposed for each day the violation continues. In imposing the fine, the board's actions shall be taken in accordance with Chapter 119. of the Revised Code.

**HISTORY: 2011 HB 93, § 1, eff. May 20, 2011 and June 19, 2011; 2011 HB 153, § 101.01, eff. Sept. 29, 2011.**

Acts 2011, HB 93, § 4 provides: "Division (C) of section 4729.552 of the Revised Code, as enacted by this act, shall take effect thirty days after the effective date of this section."

Acts 2011, HB 93, § 8 provides: "(A) Not later than one year after the effective date of this section, and annually each year for four years thereafter, the State Board of Pharmacy shall prepare a report on all of the following:

"(1) The total number of applications received by the Board for a terminal distributor of dangerous drugs license with a pain management clinic classification;

"(2) The total number of licenses with a pain management clinic classification granted or denied by the Board;

"(3) Any disciplinary actions taken by the Board against holders of licenses with a pain management clinic classification;

"(4) Total revenues generated from fees for licenses with a pain management clinic classification, fines and penalties paid by license holders, or other disciplinary actions taken against license holders;

"(5) Any other relevant information regarding the implementation of this act.

"(B) On completion of each report, the Board shall submit a copy of the report to the Governor and, in accordance with section 101.68 of the Revised Code, the General Assembly. In accordance with that section, the Board shall display the report on the Board's internet web site."

## § 4729.56 Suspension, revocation or refusal to renew registration of wholesale distributor.

(A) In accordance with Chapter 119. of the Revised Code, the board of pharmacy may suspend, revoke, or refuse to renew any registration certificate issued to a wholesale distributor of dangerous drugs pursuant to section 4729.52 of the Revised Code or may impose a monetary penalty or forfeiture not to exceed in severity any fine designated under the Revised Code for a similar offense or one thousand dollars if the acts committed are not classified as an offense by the Revised Code for any of the following causes:

(1) Making any false material statements in an application for registration as a wholesale distributor of dangerous drugs;

(2) Violating any federal, state, or local drug law; any provision of this chapter or Chapter 2925., 3715., or 3719. of the Revised Code; or any rule of the board;

(3) A conviction of a felony;

(4) Ceasing to satisfy the qualifications for registration under section 4729.53 of the Revised Code or the rules of the board.

(B) Upon the suspension or revocation of the registration certificate of any wholesale distributor of dangerous drugs, the distributor shall immediately surrender his registration certificate to the board.

(C) If the board suspends, revokes, or refuses to renew any registration certificate issued to a wholesale distributor of dangerous drugs and determines that there is clear and convincing evidence of a danger of immediate and serious harm to any person, the board may place under seal all dangerous drugs owned by or in the possession, custody, or control of the affected wholesale distributor of dangerous drugs. Except as provided in this division, the board shall not dispose of the dangerous drugs sealed under this division until the wholesale distributor of dangerous drugs exhausts all of his appeal rights under Chapter 119. of the Revised Code. The court involved in such an appeal may order the board, during the pendency of the appeal, to sell sealed dangerous drugs that are perishable. The board shall deposit the proceeds of the sale with the court.

**HISTORY: 129 v 1376 (Eff 1-1-62); 139 v H 135 (Eff 10-6-81); 144 v S 193. Eff 7-1-92.**

## § 4729.57 Disciplinary actions; sealing of drugs.

(A) The state board of pharmacy may suspend, revoke, or refuse to renew any license issued to a terminal distributor of dangerous drugs pursuant to section 4729.54 of the Revised Code, or may impose a monetary penalty or forfeiture not to exceed in severity any fine designated under the Revised Code for a similar offense or one thousand dollars if the acts committed have not been classified as an offense by the Revised Code, for any of the following causes:

(1) Making any false material statements in an application for a license as a terminal distributor of dangerous drugs;

(2) Violating any rule of the board;

(3) Violating any provision of this chapter;

(4) Violating any provision of the "Federal Food, Drug, and Cosmetic Act," 52 Stat. 1040 (1938), 21 U.S.C.A. 301, or Chapter 3715. of the Revised Code;

(5) Violating any provision of the federal drug abuse control laws or Chapter 2925. or 3719. of the Revised Code;

(6) Falsely or fraudulently promoting to the public a dangerous drug, except that nothing in this division prohibits a terminal distributor of dangerous drugs from furnishing information concerning a dangerous drug to a

health care provider or another licensed terminal distributor;

(7) Ceasing to satisfy the qualifications of a terminal distributor of dangerous drugs set forth in section 4729.55 of the Revised Code;

(8) Except as provided in division (B) of this section:

(a) Waiving the payment of all or any part of a deductible or copayment that an individual, pursuant to a health insurance or health care policy, contract, or plan that covers the services provided by a terminal distributor of dangerous drugs, would otherwise be required to pay for the services if the waiver is used as an enticement to a patient or group of patients to receive pharmacy services from that terminal distributor;

(b) Advertising that the terminal distributor will waive the payment of all or any part of a deductible or copayment that an individual, pursuant to a health insurance or health care policy, contract, or plan that covers the pharmaceutical services, would otherwise be required to pay for the services.

(B) Sanctions shall not be imposed under division (A)(8) of this section against any terminal distributor of dangerous drugs that waives deductibles and copayments as follows:

(1) In compliance with a health benefit plan that expressly allows such a practice. Waiver of the deductibles or copayments shall be made only with the full knowledge and consent of the plan purchaser, payer, and third-party administrator. Documentation of the consent shall be made available to the board on request.

(2) For professional services rendered to any other person licensed pursuant to this chapter to the extent allowed by this chapter and the rules of the board.

(C)(1) Upon the suspension or revocation of a license issued to a terminal distributor of dangerous drugs or the refusal by the board to renew such a license, the distributor shall immediately surrender the license to the board.

(2) The board may place under seal all dangerous drugs that are owned by or in the possession, custody, or control of a terminal distributor at the time the license is suspended or revoked or at the time the board refuses to renew the license. Except as otherwise provided in this division, dangerous drugs so sealed shall not be disposed of until appeal rights under Chapter 119. of the Revised Code have expired or an appeal filed pursuant to that chapter has been determined.

The court involved in an appeal filed pursuant to Chapter 119. of the Revised Code may order the board, during the pendency of the appeal, to sell sealed dangerous drugs that are perishable. The proceeds of such a sale shall be deposited with that court.

**HISTORY: 129 v 1376 (Eff 1-1-62); 130 v 1143 (Eff 1-23-63); 134 v S 141 (Eff 12-31-71); 136 v H 300 (Eff 7-1-76); 139 v H 135 (Eff 10-6-81); 139 v S 4 (Eff 10-1-82); 147 v S 66. Eff 7-22-98.**

## § 4729.571 Suspension of terminal distributor's license.

If the state board of pharmacy determines that there is clear and convincing evidence that the method used by a terminal distributor of dangerous drugs to distribute controlled substances presents a danger of immediate and serious harm to others, the board may suspend the terminal distributor's license without a hearing. The board shall follow the procedure for suspension without a prior hearing in section 119.07 of the Revised Code. The suspension shall remain in effect, unless removed by the board, until the board's final adjudication order becomes effective, except that if the board does not issue its final adjudication order within ninety days after the hearing, the suspension shall be void on the ninety-first day after the suspension.

If the terminal distributor holds a license with a pain management clinic classification issued under section 4729.552 of the Revised Code and the person holding the license also holds a certificate issued under Chapter 4731. of the Revised Code to practice medicine and surgery or osteopathic medicine and surgery, prior to suspending the license without a hearing, the board shall consult with the secretary of the state medical board or, if the secretary is unavailable, another physician member of the board.

**HISTORY: 2011 HB 93, § 1, eff. May 20, 2011.**

Acts 2011, HB 93, § 8 provides: "(A) Not later than one year after the effective date of this section, and annually each year for four years thereafter, the State Board of Pharmacy shall prepare a report on all of the following:

"(1) The total number of applications received by the Board for a terminal distributor of dangerous drugs license with a pain management clinic classification;

"(2) The total number of licenses with a pain management clinic classification granted or denied by the Board;

"(3) Any disciplinary actions taken by the Board against holders of licenses with a pain management clinic classification;

"(4) Total revenues generated from fees for licenses with a pain management clinic classification, fines and penalties paid by license holders, or other disciplinary actions taken against license holders;

"(5) Any other relevant information regarding the implementation of this act.

"(B) On completion of each report, the Board shall submit a copy of the report to the Governor and, in accordance with section 101.68 of the Revised Code, the General Assembly. In accordance with that section, the Board shall display the report on the Board's internet web site."

## § 4729.58 Renewal of license or registration.

The board of pharmacy, within thirty days after receipt of an application filed in the form and manner set forth in section 4729.52 or 4729.54 of the Revised Code for the issuance of a new license or registration certificate or the renewal of a license or registration certificate previously issued, shall notify the applicant therefor whether or not such license or registration certificate will be issued or renewed. If the board determines that such license or registration certificate will not be issued or renewed, such notice to the applicant shall set forth the reason or reasons that such license or registration certificate will not be issued or renewed.

**HISTORY: 129 v 1376. Eff 1-1-62.**

## § 4729.59 Register and roster of wholesale and terminal distributors.

The executive director of the state board of pharmacy shall maintain a register of the names, addresses, and the date of registration of those persons to whom a registration certificate has been issued pursuant to section 4729.52 of the Revised Code and those persons to whom a license has been issued pursuant to section 4729.54 of the Revised Code. The register shall be the property of the board and shall be open for public examination and inspection at all reasonable times, as the board may direct.

The board shall publish or make available to registered wholesale distributors and licensed terminal distributors of dangerous drugs, annually, and at such other times and in such manner as the board shall prescribe, a roster setting forth the names and addresses of those persons who have been registered by the board pursuant to section 4729.52 of the Revised Code and those persons who have been licensed pursuant to section 4729.54 of the Revised Code, those persons whose licenses or registration certificates have been suspended, revoked, or surrendered, and those persons whose licenses or registration certificates have not been renewed.

A written statement signed and verified by the executive director of the board in which it is stated that after diligent search of the register no record or entry of the issuance of a license or registration certificate to a person is found is admissible in evidence and constitutes presumptive evidence of the fact that the person is not a licensed terminal distributor or is not a registered wholesale distributor of dangerous drugs.

**HISTORY: 129 v 1376 (Eff 1-1-62); 147 v S 66. Eff 7-22-98.**

## § 4729.60 Wholesale distributor to obtain certificate from certain purchasers; terminal distributor to obtain registration number.

(A) Before a registered wholesale distributor of dangerous drugs may sell dangerous drugs at wholesale to any person, other than the persons specified in divisions (B)(1)(a) to (d) and (B)(1)(f) to (h) of section 4729.51 of the Revised Code, such wholesale distributor shall obtain from the purchaser and the purchaser shall furnish to the wholesale distributor a certificate indicating that the purchaser is a licensed terminal distributor of dangerous drugs. The certificate shall be in the form that the state board of pharmacy shall prescribe, and shall set forth the name of the licensee, the number of the license, a description of the place or establishment or each place or establishment for which the license was issued, the category of licensure, and, if the license is a limited category I, II, or III license, the dangerous drugs that the licensee is authorized to possess, have custody or control of, and distribute.

If no certificate is obtained or furnished before a sale is made, it shall be presumed that the sale of dangerous drugs by the wholesale distributor is in violation of division (B) of section 4729.51 of the Revised Code and the purchase of dangerous drugs by the purchaser is in violation of division (C) of section 4729.51 of the Revised Code. If a registered wholesale distributor of dangerous drugs obtains or is furnished a certificate from a terminal distributor of dangerous drugs and relies on the certificate in selling dangerous drugs at wholesale to the terminal distributor of dangerous drugs, the wholesale distributor of dangerous drugs shall be deemed not to have violated division (B) of section 4729.51 of the Revised Code in making the sale.

(B) Before a licensed terminal distributor of dangerous drugs may purchase dangerous drugs at wholesale, the terminal distributor shall obtain from the seller and the seller shall furnish to the terminal distributor the number of the seller's registration certificate to engage in the sale of dangerous drugs at wholesale.

If no registration number is obtained or furnished before a purchase is made, it shall be presumed that the purchase of dangerous drugs by the terminal distributor is in violation of division (D) of section 4729.51 of the Revised Code and the sale of dangerous drugs by the seller is in violation of division (A) of section 4729.51 of the Revised Code. If a licensed terminal distributor of dangerous drugs obtains or is furnished a registration number from a wholesale distributor of dangerous drugs and relies on the registration number in purchasing dangerous drugs at wholesale from the wholesale distributor of dangerous drugs, the terminal distributor shall be deemed not to have violated division (D) of section 4729.51 of the Revised Code in making the purchase.

**HISTORY: 129 v 1376 (Eff 1-1-62); 139 v S 4 (Eff 10-1-82); 147 v S 66 (Eff 7-22-98); 147 v H 553. Eff 3-9-99.**

## § 4729.61 Fraudulent certificates; prohibition.

(A) No person shall make or cause to be made, or furnish or cause to be furnished to a wholesale distributor of dangerous drugs, a false certificate required to be furnished to a wholesale distributor of dangerous drugs by section 4729.60 of the Revised Code for the purchase of dangerous drugs at wholesale.

(B) No person shall make or cause to be made a false registration certificate of a wholesale distributor of dangerous drugs or a false or fraudulent license of a terminal distributor of dangerous drugs.

**HISTORY: 129 v 1376 (Eff 1-1-62); 136 v H 300 (Eff 7-1-76); 146 v S 2. Eff 7-1-96.**

The effective date is set by section 6 of SB 2.

## § 4729.62 Surrender of license.

If a wholesale distributor of dangerous drugs who has been registered ceases to engage in the sale of dangerous drugs at wholesale, or if a terminal distributor of dangerous drugs to whom a license has been issued ceases to engage in the sale of dangerous drugs at retail, such terminal or wholesale distributor of dangerous drugs shall notify the board of pharmacy of such fact and shall surrender such license or registration certificate to the board; provided, that on dissolution of a partnership by death, the surviving partner may operate under a license or registration certificate issued to the partnership until expiration, revocation, or suspension of such license or registration certificate, and the heirs or legal representatives of deceased persons, and receivers and trustees in bankruptcy appointed by any competent authority, may operate under the license or registration certificate issued to the persons succeeded in possession by such heir, representative, receiver, or trustee in bankruptcy until expiration, revocation, or suspension of such license or registration certificate.

**HISTORY: 129 v 1376. Eff 1-1-62.**

## § 4729.63 Repealed, 150 v H 377, § 2 [129 v 1376 (Eff 1-1-62); 137 v H 219 (Eff 11-1-77); 140 v H 208 (Eff 9-20-84); 147 v S 66. Eff 7-22-98]. Eff 5-18-05.

This section concerned enforcement.

## § 4729.64 Injunctions.

In addition to the remedies provided and irrespective of whether or not there exists an adequate remedy at law, the board of pharmacy may apply to the court of common pleas in the county where any of the provisions of sections 4729.51 to 4729.62 of the Revised Code are being violated or where any violation described in section 4729.35 of the Revised Code is occurring for a temporary or permanent injunction restraining any person from such violation.

**HISTORY: 129 v 1376 (Eff 1-1-62); 140 v H 206. Eff 3-14-85.**

## § 4729.65 Deposit of receipts; vouchers; excess fees.

(A) Except as provided in division (B) of this section, all receipts of the state board of pharmacy, from any source, shall be deposited into the state treasury to the credit of the occupational licensing and regulatory fund. All vouchers of the board shall be approved by the president or executive director of the board, or both, as authorized by the board. All initial issuance fees and renewal fees required by sections 4729.01 to 4729.54 of the Revised Code shall be payable by the applicant at the time of making application.

(B)(1) There is hereby created in the state treasury the board of pharmacy drug law enforcement fund. All moneys that are derived from any fines, mandatory fines, or forfeited bail to which the board may be entitled under Chapter 2925., division (C) of section 2923.42, or division (B) of section 2925.42 of the Revised Code and all moneys that are derived from forfeitures of property to which the board may be entitled pursuant to Chapter 2925. or 2981. of the Revised Code, any other provision of the Revised Code, or federal law shall be deposited into the fund. Subject to division (B)(2) of this section, division (B) of section 2923.44, and divisions (B), (C), and (D) of section 2981.13 of the Revised Code, the moneys in the fund shall be used solely to subsidize the drug law enforcement efforts of the board.

(2) Notwithstanding any contrary provision in the Revised Code, moneys that are derived from forfeitures of property pursuant to federal law and that are deposited into the board of pharmacy drug law enforcement fund in accordance with division (B)(1) of this section shall be used and accounted for in accordance with the applicable federal law, and the board otherwise shall comply with that law in connection with the moneys.

(C) All fines and forfeited bonds assessed and collected under prosecution or prosecution commenced in the enforcement of this chapter shall be paid to the executive director of the board within thirty days and by the executive director paid into the state treasury to the credit of the occupational licensing and regulatory fund. The board, subject to the approval of the controlling board and except for fees required to be established by the board at amounts "adequate" to cover designated expenses, may establish fees in excess of the amounts provided by this chapter, provided that such fees do not exceed the amounts permitted by this chapter by more than fifty per cent.

**HISTORY: 129 v 1376 (Eff 1-1-62); 130 v 1144 (Eff 10-14-63); 132 v H 911 (Eff 6-11-68); 134 v S 141 (Eff 12-31-71); 136 v H 300 (Eff 7-1-76); 138 v H 204 (Eff 7-30-79); 139 v H 694 (Eff 7-1-82); 141 v H 201 (Eff 7-1-85); 142 v S 386 (Eff 3-29-88); 143 v H 266 (Eff 9-6-90); 143 v S 258 (Eff 11-20-90); 144 v S 218 (Eff 10-11-91); 145 v H 715 (Eff 7-22-94); 147 v H 215 (Eff 9-29-97); 147 v H 2. Eff 1-1-99; 151 v H 241, § 1, eff. 7-1-07.**

See provisions of § 4 of 151 v H 241 following RC § 4728.04. The effective date is set by section 4 of HB 2.

## § 4729.66 Repealed, 150 v H 377, § 2 [129 v 1376 (Eff 1-1-62); 147 v S 66. Eff 7-22-98]. Eff 5-18-05.

This section concerned rules.

## § 4729.69 Establishment of drug take-back program.

(A) The state board of pharmacy, in collaboration with the director of alcohol and drug addiction services and attorney general, shall establish and administer a drug take-back program under which drugs are collected from the community for the purpose of destruction or disposal of the drugs.

(B) The program shall be established and administered in such a manner that it does both of the following:

(1) Complies with any state or federal laws regarding the collection, destruction, or disposal of drugs;

(2) Maintains the confidentiality of individuals who submit or otherwise provide drugs under the program.

(C) In consultation with the director of alcohol and drug addiction services and attorney general, the board shall adopt rules governing the program. The rules shall be adopted in accordance with Chapter 119. of the Revised Code. In adopting the rules, the board shall specify all of the following:

(1) The entities that may participate;

(2) Guidelines and responsibilities for accepting drugs by participating entities;

(3) Drugs that may be collected;

(4) Record-keeping requirements;

(5) Proper methods to destroy unused drugs;

(6) Privacy protocols and security standards;

(7) Drug transportation procedures;

(8) The schedule, duration, and frequency of the collections of drugs, except that the first collection shall occur not later than one year after the effective date of this section;

(9) Any other standards and procedures the board considers necessary for purposes of governing the program.

(D) In accordance with state and federal law, the board may adopt rules to allow an entity participating in the program to return any unused drugs to the pharmacy that originally dispensed the drug. The rules shall include procedures to be followed to maintain the confidentiality of the person for whom the drug was dispensed.

(E) Rules adopted under this section may not do any of the following:

(1) Require any entity to establish, fund, or operate a drug take-back program;

(2) Establish any new licensing requirement or fee to participate in the program;

(3) Require any entity to compile data on drugs collected.

(F) The board may compile data on the amount and type of drugs collected under the program. For purposes of this division, the board may cooperate with a public or private entity in obtaining assistance in the compilation of data. An entity providing the assistance shall not be reimbursed under the program for any costs incurred in providing the assistance.

(G) If the board compiles data under division (F) of this section, the board shall submit a report to the governor and, in accordance with section 101.68 of the Revised Code, the general assembly. The report, to the extent possible, shall include the following information:

(1) Total weight of drugs collected, both with and without packaging;

(2) The weight of controlled substances;

(3) The amount of all of the following as a per cent of total drugs collected:

(a) Controlled substances;

(b) Brand name drugs;

(c) Generic drugs;

(d) Prescription drugs;

(e) Non-prescription drugs.

(4) The amount of vitamins, herbal supplements, and personal care products collected;

(5) If provided by the person who submitted or otherwise donated drugs to the program, the reasons why the drugs were returned or unused.

(H) No entity is required to participate in a drug take-back program established under this section, and no entity shall be subject to civil liability or professional disciplinary action for declining to participate.

(I) The board may accept grants, gifts, or donations for purposes of the program. Money received under this division shall be deposited into the drug take-back program fund established under section 109.90 of the Revised Code.

**HISTORY: 2011 HB 93, § 1, eff. May 20, 2011.**

Acts 2011, HB 93, § 8 provides: "(A) Not later than one year after the effective date of this section, and annually each year for four years thereafter, the State Board of Pharmacy shall prepare a report on all of the following:

"(1) The total number of applications received by the Board for a terminal distributor of dangerous drugs license with a pain management clinic classification;

"(2) The total number of licenses with a pain management clinic classification granted or denied by the Board;

"(3) Any disciplinary actions taken by the Board against holders of licenses with a pain management clinic classification;

"(4) Total revenues generated from fees for licenses with a pain management clinic classification, fines and penalties paid by license holders, or other disciplinary actions taken against license holders;

"(5) Any other relevant information regarding the implementation of this act.

"(B) On completion of each report, the Board shall submit a copy of the report to the Governor and, in accordance with section 101.68 of the Revised Code, the General Assembly. In accordance with that section, the Board shall display the report on the Board's internet web site."

## § 4729.70 Medical gases safety program.

(A) As used in this section, "cryogenic vessel" means an insulated metal container in the form of a cylinder or other design used to hold gases that have been liquefied by extreme reductions in temperature.

(B) The state board of pharmacy shall establish and implement a medical gases safety program to ensure that cryogenic vessels containing medical gases meet the requirements of this section and are properly handled. The program applies only to cryogenic vessels that are portable and contain medical gases in a volume intended for use in administering direct treatment to one or more individuals. The program does not apply to cylinders or containers of other designs that contain medical gases that are only compressed.

(C) Each cryogenic vessel subject to this section shall meet the following requirements:

(1) The vessel shall be properly labeled according to the medical gas contained in the vessel.

(2) The vessel shall be color coded as follows:

(a) Air — yellow;

(b) Carbon dioxide — gray;

(c) Cyclopropane — orange;

(d) Helium — brown;

(e) Nitrogen — black;

(f) Nitrous oxide — blue;

(g) Oxygen — green.

The colors specified in this division shall not be used for any medical gas other than those specified in this division.

(3) The color coding specified in division (C)(2) of this section shall be applied to the vessel by doing either of the following:

(a) Applying the appropriate color to the top six inches of the body of the vessel;

(b) Affixing a wrap to the vessel that encircles the vessel completely, has the identity of the contained gas printed completely or continuously around the wrap, and uses the appropriate color as the print or background for the identity of the gas.

(4) The vessel shall not have previously contained a gas that is not a medical gas.

(5) When the vessel is being reused for a medical gas other than the medical gas it previously contained, new labeling and color coding shall be applied to the vessel and all old labeling and color coding shall be completely removed.

(6) The connector between the vessel and the valve through which the medical gas is delivered shall be either of the following:

(a) A threaded or socket connection that is silver brazed or welded to the valve;

(b) A permanent and integral part of the valve.

(D) No person shall remove a connector between a cryogenic vessel subject to this section and the valve through which the medical gas is delivered from the vessel, replace the connector with another connector, or attach an adapter to the vessel or connector unless the person meets standards established by the board in rules adopted under this section. A person who violates this division is guilty of tampering with drugs pursuant to section 2925.24 of the Revised Code.

(E) All employees who are responsible for installing or changing the cryogenic vessels subject to this section shall be trained in the proper handling of medical gases and cryogenic vessels, including training in understanding the labeling of the vessels and recognizing the color coding required by this section.

(F) The board shall adopt rules to implement the medical gases safety program established pursuant to this section. The rules shall be adopted in accordance with Chapter 119. of the Revised Code.

The board's rules shall specify standards and procedures to be followed in ensuring that the individuals who modify existing cryogenic vessels for purposes of bringing the vessels into compliance with this section are qualified individuals. The board's standards for being considered qualified shall include requirements for knowledge in proper safety precautions concerning medical gases, cryogenic vessels that contain medical gases, and devices through which medical gases are delivered from cryogenic vessels.

**HISTORY: 149 v S 117. Eff 3-15-2002.**

[DRUG DATABASE TO MONITOR MISUSE AND DIVERSION]

## § 4729.75 Establishment and maintenance of drug database to monitor misuse and diversion.

The state board of pharmacy may establish and maintain a drug database. The board shall use the drug database to monitor the misuse and diversion of controlled substances, as defined in section 3719.01 of the Revised Code, and other dangerous drugs the board includes in the database pursuant to rules adopted under section 4729.84 of the Revised Code. In establishing and maintaining the database, the board shall electronically collect information pursuant to sections 4729.77 and 4729.79 of the Revised Code and shall disseminate information as authorized or required by sections 4729.80 and 4729.81 of the Revised Code. The board's collection and dissemination of information shall be conducted in accordance with rules adopted under section 4729.84 of the Revised Code.

**HISTORY: 150 v H 377, § 1, eff. 5-18-05; 2011 HB 93, § 1, eff. May 20, 2011.**

Acts 2011, HB 93, § 5 provides: "(A) The State Board of Pharmacy, in consultation with prescribers and pharmacists, shall consider improvements to the state's methods of monitoring, through the drug database established and maintained under section 4729.75 of the Revised Code, the misuse and diversion of controlled substances. Not later than six months after the effective date of this section, the Board shall prepare a report of its findings and recommendations.

"(B) In preparing the report, the Board shall include all of the following:

"(1) Recommendations on the establishment of a real-time drug database that permits information to be immediately submitted to the database and immediately accessible to the individuals authorized to access information in the database;

"(2) Recommendations on potential improvements to the Board's existing drug database, including both of the following:

"(a) Improvements that are necessary to facilitate information exchange between the database and database users;

"(b) Improvements that allow a drug utilization review to occur whereby patient use of controlled substances is monitored.

"(3) The potential cost of upgrading the Board's existing drug database or establishing a new database to monitor the misuse or diversion of controlled substances in this state;

"(4) Information on the availability of, and methods to secure, federal grants necessary to implement the Board's recommendations;

"(5) A description of any other matters the Board considers relevant to the report.

"(C) On completion of the report, the Board shall submit copies to the Speaker of the House of Representatives, President of the Senate, and Governor."

Acts 2011, HB 93, § 8 provides: "(A) Not later than one year after the effective date of this section, and annually each year for four years thereafter, the State Board of Pharmacy shall prepare a report on all of the following:

"(1) The total number of applications received by the Board for a terminal distributor of dangerous drugs license with a pain management clinic classification;

"(2) The total number of licenses with a pain management clinic classification granted or denied by the Board;

"(3) Any disciplinary actions taken by the Board against holders of licenses with a pain management clinic classification;

"(4) Total revenues generated from fees for licenses with a pain management clinic classification, fines and penalties paid by license holders, or other disciplinary actions taken against license holders;

"(5) Any other relevant information regarding the implementation of this act.

"(B) On completion of each report, the Board shall submit a copy of the report to the Governor and, in accordance with section 101.68 of the Revised Code, the General Assembly. In accordance with that section, the Board shall display the report on the Board's internet web site."

## § 4729.76 Administrator and staff.

If the state board of pharmacy establishes and maintains a drug database pursuant to section 4729.75 of the Revised Code, the executive director of the board shall do all of the following:

(A) Employ an administrator to manage and direct the duties of staff employed to operate the drug database. The administrator shall be a person who has had training and experience in areas related to the duties of the database.

(B) Employ such professional, technical, and clerical employees as are necessary, and employ or hire on a consulting basis other technical services required for the operation of the database;

(C) Fix the compensation of the administrator and all other staff employed to operate the database.

**HISTORY: 150 v H 377, § 1, eff. 5-18-05.**

## § 4729.77 Prescription information to be submitted by pharmacies.

(A) If the state board of pharmacy establishes and maintains a drug database pursuant to section 4729.75 of the Revised Code, each pharmacy licensed as a terminal distributor of dangerous drugs that dispenses drugs to patients in this state and is included in the types of pharmacies specified in rules adopted under section 4729.84 of the Revised Code shall submit to the board the following prescription information:

(1) Terminal distributor identification;

(2) Patient identification;

(3) Prescriber identification;

(4) Date prescription was issued by prescriber;

(5) Date drug was dispensed;

(6) Indication of whether the drug dispensed is new or a refill;

(7) Name, strength, and national drug code of the drug dispensed;

(8) Quantity of drug dispensed;

(9) Number of days' supply of drug dispensed;

(10) Serial or prescription number assigned by the terminal distributor;

(11) Source of payment for the drug dispensed.

(B)(1) The information shall be transmitted as specified by the board in rules adopted under section 4729.84 of the Revised Code.

(2) The information shall be submitted electronically in the format specified by the board, except that the board may grant a waiver allowing the distributor to submit the information in another format.

(3) The information shall be submitted in accordance with any time limits specified by the board, except that the board may grant an extension if either of the following occurs:

(a) The distributor suffers a mechanical or electronic failure, or cannot meet the deadline for other reasons beyond the distributor's control.

(b) The board is unable to receive electronic submissions.

(C) This section does not apply to a prescriber personally furnishing or administering dangerous drugs to the prescriber's patient.

**HISTORY: 150 v H 377, § 1, eff. 5-18-05; 2011 HB 93, § 1, eff. May 20, 2011.**

Acts 2011, HB 93, § 8 provides: "(A) Not later than one year after the effective date of this section, and annually each year for four years thereafter, the State Board of Pharmacy shall prepare a report on all of the following:

"(1) The total number of applications received by the Board for a terminal distributor of dangerous drugs license with a pain management clinic classification;

"(2) The total number of licenses with a pain management clinic classification granted or denied by the Board;

"(3) Any disciplinary actions taken by the Board against holders of licenses with a pain management clinic classification;

"(4) Total revenues generated from fees for licenses with a pain management clinic classification, fines and penalties paid by license holders, or other disciplinary actions taken against license holders;

"(5) Any other relevant information regarding the implementation of this act.

"(B) On completion of each report, the Board shall submit a copy of the report to the Governor and, in accordance with section 101.68 of the Revised Code, the General Assembly. In accordance with that section, the Board shall display the report on the Board's internet web site."

## § 4729.78 Purchase information to be submitted by wholesale distributor.

(A) If the state board of pharmacy establishes and maintains a drug database pursuant to section 4729.75 of the Revised Code, each wholesale distributor of dangerous drugs that delivers drugs in this state to prescribers or terminal distributors of dangerous drugs shall submit to the board the following purchase information:

(1) Purchaser identification;

(2) Identification of the drug sold;

(3) Quantity of the drug sold;

(4) Date of sale;

(5) The wholesale distributor's license number issued by the board.

(B)(1) The information shall be transmitted as specified by the board in rules adopted under section 4729.84 of the Revised Code.

(2) The information shall be submitted electronically in the format specified by the board, except that the board may grant a waiver allowing the distributor to submit the information in another format.

(3) The information shall be submitted in accordance with any time limits specified by the board, except that the board may grant an extension if either of the following occurs:

(a) The distributor suffers a mechanical or electronic failure, or cannot meet the deadline for other reasons beyond the distributor's control.

(b) The board is unable to receive electronic submissions.

**HISTORY: 150 v H 377, § 1, eff. 5-18-05; 2011 HB 93, § 1, eff. May 20, 2011.**

Acts 2011, HB 93, § 8 provides: "(A) Not later than one year after the effective date of this section, and annually each year for four years thereafter, the State Board of Pharmacy shall prepare a report on all of the following:

"(1) The total number of applications received by the Board for a terminal distributor of dangerous drugs license with a pain management clinic classification;

"(2) The total number of licenses with a pain management clinic classification granted or denied by the Board;

"(3) Any disciplinary actions taken by the Board against holders of licenses with a pain management clinic classification;

"(4) Total revenues generated from fees for licenses with a pain management clinic classification, fines and penalties paid by license holders, or other disciplinary actions taken against license holders;

"(5) Any other relevant information regarding the implementation of this act.

"(B) On completion of each report, the Board shall submit a copy of the report to the Governor and, in accordance with section 101.68 of the Revised Code, the General Assembly. In accordance with that section, the Board shall display the report on the Board's internet web site."

## § 4729.79 Drug database; submission of required information.

(A) If the state board of pharmacy establishes and maintains a drug database pursuant to section 4729.75 of the Revised Code, each licensed health professional authorized to prescribe drugs, other than a veterinarian, who personally furnishes a controlled substance or other dangerous drug the board includes in the database pursuant to rules adopted under section 4729.84 of the Revised Code to a patient in this state shall submit to the board the following information:

(1) Prescriber identification;

(2) Patient identification;

(3) Date drug was furnished by the prescriber;

(4) Indication of whether the drug furnished is new or a refill;

(5) Name, strength, and national drug code of drug furnished;

(6) Quantity of drug furnished;

(7) Number of days' supply of drug furnished;

(8) Source of payment for the drug furnished.

(B)(1) The information shall be transmitted as specified by the board in rules adopted under section 4729.84 of the Revised Code.

(2) The information shall be submitted electronically in the format specified by the board, except that the board may grant a waiver allowing the prescriber to submit the information in another format.

(3) The information shall be submitted in accordance with any time limits specified by the board, except that the board may grant an extension if either of the following occurs:

(a) The prescriber's transmission system suffers a mechanical or electronic failure, or the prescriber cannot meet the deadline for other reasons beyond the prescriber's control.

(b) The board is unable to receive electronic submissions.

(C) If the board becomes aware of a prescriber's failure to comply with this section, the board shall notify the government entity responsible for licensing the prescriber.

**HISTORY: 2011 HB 93, § 1, eff. May 20, 2011.**

Former § 4729.79 was renumbered as RC § 4729.80 by 2011 HB 93, § 1, effective May 20, 2011.

Acts 2011, HB 93, § 8 provides: "(A) Not later than one year after the effective date of this section, and annually each year for four years thereafter, the State Board of Pharmacy shall prepare a report on all of the following:

"(1) The total number of applications received by the Board for a terminal distributor of dangerous drugs license with a pain management clinic classification;

"(2) The total number of licenses with a pain management clinic classification granted or denied by the Board;

"(3) Any disciplinary actions taken by the Board against holders of licenses with a pain management clinic classification;

"(4) Total revenues generated from fees for licenses with a pain management clinic classification, fines and penalties paid by license holders, or other disciplinary actions taken against license holders;

"(5) Any other relevant information regarding the implementation of this act.

"(B) On completion of each report, the Board shall submit a copy of the report to the Governor and, in accordance with section 101.68 of the Revised Code, the General Assembly. In accordance with that section, the Board shall display the report on the Board's internet web site."

## § 4729.80 Information provided by board; records; immunity.

(A) If the state board of pharmacy establishes and maintains a drug database pursuant to section 4729.75 of the Revised Code, the board is authorized or required to provide information from the database in accordance with the following:

(1) On receipt of a request from a designated representative of a government entity responsible for the licensure, regulation, or discipline of health care professionals with authority to prescribe, administer, or dispense drugs, the board may provide to the representative information from the database relating to the professional who is the subject of an active investigation being conducted by the government entity.

(2) On receipt of a request from a federal officer, or a state or local officer of this or any other state, whose duties include enforcing laws relating to drugs, the board shall provide to the officer information from the database relating to the person who is the subject of an active investigation of a drug abuse offense, as defined in section 2925.01 of the Revised Code, being conducted by the officer's employing government entity.

(3) Pursuant to a subpoena issued by a grand jury, the board shall provide to the grand jury information from the database relating to the person who is the subject of an investigation being conducted by the grand jury.

(4) Pursuant to a subpoena, search warrant, or court order in connection with the investigation or prosecution of a possible or alleged criminal offense, the board shall provide information from the database as necessary to comply with the subpoena, search warrant, or court order.

(5) On receipt of a request from a prescriber or the prescriber's agent registered with the board, the board may provide to the prescriber information from the database relating to a current patient of the prescriber, if the prescriber certifies in a form specified by the board that it is for the purpose of providing medical treatment to the patient who is the subject of the request.

(6) On receipt of a request from a pharmacist, the board may provide to the pharmacist information from the database relating to a current patient of the pharmacist, if the pharmacist certifies in a form specified by the board that it is for the purpose of the pharmacist's practice of pharmacy involving the patient who is the subject of the request.

(7) On receipt of a request from an individual seeking the individual's own database information in accordance with the procedure established in rules adopted under section 4729.84 of the Revised Code, the board may provide to the individual the individual's own database information.

(8) On receipt of a request from the medical director of a managed care organization that has entered into a data security agreement with the board required by section 5111.1710 of the Revised Code, the board may provide to the medical director information from the database relating to a medicaid recipient enrolled in the managed care organization.

(9) On receipt of a request from the director of job and family services, the board may provide to the director information from the database relating to a recipient of a program administered by the department of job and family services.

(10) On receipt of a request from the administrator of workers' compensation, the board may provide to the administrator information from the database relating to a claimant under Chapter 4121., 4123., 4127., or 4131. of the Revised Code.

(11) On receipt of a request from a requestor described in division (A)(1), (2), (5), or (6) of this section who is from or participating with another state's prescription monitoring program, the board may provide to the requestor information from the database, but only if there is a written agreement under which the information is to be used and disseminated according to the laws of this state.

(B) The state board of pharmacy shall maintain a record of each individual or entity that requests information from the database pursuant to this section. In accordance with rules adopted under section 4729.84 of the Revised Code, the board may use the records to document and report statistics and law enforcement outcomes.

The board may provide records of an individual's requests for database information to the following:

(1) A designated representative of a government entity that is responsible for the licensure, regulation, or discipline of health care professionals with authority to prescribe, administer, or dispense drugs who is involved in an active investigation being conducted by the government entity of the individual who submitted the requests for database information;

(2) A federal officer, or a state or local officer of this or any other state, whose duties include enforcing laws relating to drugs and who is involved in an active investigation being conducted by the officer's employing government entity of the individual who submitted the requests for database information.

(C) Information contained in the database and any information obtained from it is not a public record. Information contained in the records of requests for information from the database is not a public record. Information that does not identify a person may be released in summary, statistical, or aggregate form.

(D) A pharmacist or prescriber shall not be held liable in damages to any person in any civil action for injury, death, or loss to person or property on the basis that the pharmacist or prescriber did or did not seek or obtain information from the database.

**HISTORY: 150 v H 377, § 1, eff. 5-18-05; 2011 HB 93, § 1, eff. May 20, 2011.**

This section was renumbered from RC § 4729.79 by 2011, HB 93, § 1, effective May 20, 2011.

Former § 4729.80 was renumbered as RC § 4729.81 by 2011 HB 93, § 1, effective May 20, 2011.

Acts 2011, HB 93, § 8 provides: "(A) Not later than one year after the effective date of this section, and annually each year for four years thereafter, the State Board of Pharmacy shall prepare a report on all of the following:

"(1) The total number of applications received by the Board for a terminal distributor of dangerous drugs license with a pain management clinic classification;

"(2) The total number of licenses with a pain management clinic classification granted or denied by the Board;

"(3) Any disciplinary actions taken by the Board against holders of licenses with a pain management clinic classification;

"(4) Total revenues generated from fees for licenses with a pain management clinic classification, fines and penalties paid by license holders, or other disciplinary actions taken against license holders;

"(5) Any other relevant information regarding the implementation of this act.

"(B) On completion of each report, the Board shall submit a copy of the report to the Governor and, in accordance with section 101.68 of the Revised Code, the General Assembly. In accordance with that section, the Board shall display the report on the Board's internet web site."

## § 4729.81 Board to review information; notice of possible violation.

If the state board of pharmacy establishes and maintains a drug database pursuant to section 4729.75 of the Revised Code, the board shall review the information in the drug database. If the board determines from the review that a violation of law may have occurred, it shall notify the appropriate law enforcement agency or a government entity responsible for the licensure, regulation, or discipline of licensed health professionals authorized to prescribe drugs and supply information required by the agency or entity for an investigation of the violation of law that may have occurred.

**HISTORY: 150 v H 377, § 1, eff. 5-18-05; 2011 HB 93, § 1, eff. May 20, 2011.**

This section was renumbered from RC § 4729.80 by Act 2011, HB 93, § 1, effective May 20, 2011.

Former § 4729.81 was renumbered as RC § 4729.82 by 2011 HB 93, § 1, effective May 20, 2011.

Acts 2011, HB 93, § 8 provides: "(A) Not later than one year after the effective date of this section, and annually each year for four years thereafter, the State Board of Pharmacy shall prepare a report on all of the following:

"(1) The total number of applications received by the Board for a terminal distributor of dangerous drugs license with a pain management clinic classification;

"(2) The total number of licenses with a pain management clinic classification granted or denied by the Board;

"(3) Any disciplinary actions taken by the Board against holders of licenses with a pain management clinic classification;

"(4) Total revenues generated from fees for licenses with a pain management clinic classification, fines and penalties paid by license holders, or other disciplinary actions taken against license holders;

"(5) Any other relevant information regarding the implementation of this act.

"(B) On completion of each report, the Board shall submit a copy of the report to the Governor and, in accordance with section 101.68 of the Revised Code, the General Assembly. In accordance with that section, the Board shall display the report on the Board's internet web site."

## § 4729.82 Retention and destruction of information.

If the state board of pharmacy establishes a drug database pursuant to section 4729.75 of the Revised Code, the information collected for the database shall be retained in the database for at least two years. Any information that identifies a patient shall be destroyed after it has been retained for two years unless a law enforcement agency or a government entity responsible for the licensure, regulation, or discipline of licensed health professionals authorized to prescribe drugs has submitted a written request to the board for retention of the information in accordance with rules adopted by the board under section 4729.84 of the Revised Code.

**HISTORY: 150 v H 377, § 1, eff. 5-18-05; 2011 HB 93, § 1, eff. May 20, 2011.**

This section was renumbered from RC § 4729.81 by Act 2011, HB 93, § 1, effective May 20, 2011.

Former § 4729.82 was renumbered as RC § 4729.83 by 2011 HB 93, § 1, effective May 20, 2011.

Acts 2011, HB 93, § 8 provides: "(A) Not later than one year after the effective date of this section, and annually each year for four years thereafter, the State Board of Pharmacy shall prepare a report on all of the following:

"(1) The total number of applications received by the Board for a terminal distributor of dangerous drugs license with a pain management clinic classification;

"(2) The total number of licenses with a pain management clinic classification granted or denied by the Board;

"(3) Any disciplinary actions taken by the Board against holders of licenses with a pain management clinic classification;

"(4) Total revenues generated from fees for licenses with a pain management clinic classification, fines and penalties paid by license holders, or other disciplinary actions taken against license holders;

"(5) Any other relevant information regarding the implementation of this act.

"(B) On completion of each report, the Board shall submit a copy of the report to the Governor and, in accordance with section 101.68 of the Revised Code, the General Assembly. In accordance with that section, the Board shall display the report on the Board's internet web site."

## § 4729.83 Charges and fees.

(A) If the state board of pharmacy establishes and maintains a drug database pursuant to section 4729.75 of the Revised Code, the board shall not impose any charge on a terminal distributor of dangerous drugs, pharmacist, or prescriber for the establishment or maintenance of the database. The board shall not charge any fees for the transmission of data to the database or for the receipt of information from the database, except that the board may charge a fee in accordance with rules adopted under section 4729.84 of the Revised Code to an individual who requests the individual's own database information under section 4729.80 of the Revised Code.

(B) The board may accept grants, gifts, or donations for purposes of the drug database. Any money received shall be deposited into the state treasury to the credit of the drug database fund, which is hereby created. Money in the fund shall be used solely for purposes of the drug database.

**HISTORY: 150 v H 377, § 1, eff. 5-18-05; 2011 HB 93, § 1, eff. May 20, 2011.**

This section was renumbered from RC § 4729.82 by Act 2011, HB 93, § 1, effective May 20, 2011.

Former § 4729.83 was renumbered as RC § 4729.84 by 2011 HB 93, § 1, effective May 20, 2011.

Acts 2011, HB 93, § 8 provides: "(A) Not later than one year after the effective date of this section, and annually each year for four years thereafter, the State Board of Pharmacy shall prepare a report on all of the following:

"(1) The total number of applications received by the Board for a terminal distributor of dangerous drugs license with a pain management clinic classification;

"(2) The total number of licenses with a pain management clinic classification granted or denied by the Board;

"(3) Any disciplinary actions taken by the Board against holders of licenses with a pain management clinic classification;

"(4) Total revenues generated from fees for licenses with a pain management clinic classification, fines and penalties paid by license holders, or other disciplinary actions taken against license holders;

"(5) Any other relevant information regarding the implementation of this act.

"(B) On completion of each report, the Board shall submit a copy of the report to the Governor and, in accordance with section 101.68 of the Revised Code, the General Assembly. In accordance with that section, the Board shall display the report on the Board's internet web site."

## § 4729.84 Rules.

For purposes of establishing and maintaining a drug database pursuant to section 4729.75 of the Revised Code, the state board of pharmacy shall adopt rules in accordance with Chapter 119. of the Revised Code to carry out and enforce sections 4729.75 to 4729.83 of the Revised Code. The rules shall specify all of the following:

(A) A means of identifying each patient, each terminal distributor of dangerous drugs, and each purchase at wholesale of dangerous drugs about which information is entered into the drug database;

(B) Requirements for the transmission of information from terminal distributors of dangerous drugs, wholesale distributors of dangerous drugs, and prescribers;

(C) An electronic format for the submission of information from terminal distributors, wholesale distributors, and prescribers;

(D) A procedure whereby a terminal distributor, wholesale distributor, or prescriber unable to submit information electronically may obtain a waiver to submit information in another format;

(E) A procedure whereby the board may grant a request from a law enforcement agency or a government entity responsible for the licensure, regulation, or discipline of licensed health professionals authorized to prescribe drugs that information that has been stored for two years be retained when the information pertains to an open investigation being conducted by the agency or entity;

(F) A procedure whereby a terminal distributor, wholesale distributor, or prescriber may apply for an extension to the time by which information must be transmitted to the board;

(G) A procedure whereby a person or government entity to which the board is authorized to provide information may submit a request to the board for the information and the board may verify the identity of the requestor;

(H) A procedure whereby the board can use the database request records required by division (B) of section 4729.80 of the Revised Code to document and report statistics and law enforcement outcomes;

(I) A procedure whereby an individual may request the individual's own database information and the board may verify the identity of the requestor;

(J) A reasonable fee that the board may charge under section 4729.83 of the Revised Code for providing an individual with the individual's own database information pursuant to section 4729.80 of the Revised Code;

(K) The other specific dangerous drugs that, in addition to controlled substances, must be included in the database;

(L) The types of pharmacies licensed as terminal distributors of dangerous drugs that are required to submit prescription information to the board pursuant to section 4729.77 of the Revised Code.

**HISTORY: 150 v H 377, § 1, eff. 5-18-05; 2011 HB 93, § 1, eff. May 20, 2011.**

This section was renumbered from RC § 4729.83 by Act 2011, HB 93, § 1, effective May 20, 2011.

Former § 4729.84 was renumbered as RC § 4729.85 by 2011 HB 93, § 1, effective May 20, 2011.

Acts 2011, HB 93, § 8 provides: "(A) Not later than one year after the effective date of this section, and annually each year for four years thereafter, the State Board of Pharmacy shall prepare a report on all of the following:

"(1) The total number of applications received by the Board for a terminal distributor of dangerous drugs license with a pain management clinic classification;

"(2) The total number of licenses with a pain management clinic classification granted or denied by the Board;

"(3) Any disciplinary actions taken by the Board against holders of licenses with a pain management clinic classification;

"(4) Total revenues generated from fees for licenses with a pain management clinic classification, fines and penalties paid by license holders, or other disciplinary actions taken against license holders;

"(5) Any other relevant information regarding the implementation of this act.

"(B) On completion of each report, the Board shall submit a copy of the report to the Governor and, in accordance with section 101.68 of the Revised Code, the General Assembly. In accordance with that section, the Board shall display the report on the Board's internet web site."

## § 4729.85 Biennial reports to legislative committees.

(A) If the state board of pharmacy establishes and maintains a drug database pursuant to section 4729.75 of the Revised Code, the board shall present a biennial report to the standing committees of the house of representatives and the senate that are primarily responsible for considering health and human services issues. The initial report shall be presented not later than two years after the database is established.

(B) Each report presented under this section shall include all of the following:

(1) The cost to the state of establishing and maintaining the database;

(2) Information from terminal distributors of dangerous drugs, prescribers, and the board regarding the board's effectiveness in providing information from the database;

(3) The board's timeliness in transmitting information from the database.

**HISTORY: 150 v H 377, § 1, eff. 5-18-05; 2011 HB 93, § 1, eff. May 20, 2011.**

This section was renumbered from RC § 4729.84 by Act 2011, HB 93, § 1, effective May 20, 2011.

Acts 2011, HB 93, § 8 provides: "(A) Not later than one year after the effective date of this section, and annually each year for four years thereafter, the State Board of Pharmacy shall prepare a report on all of the following:

"(1) The total number of applications received by the Board for a terminal distributor of dangerous drugs license with a pain management clinic classification;

"(2) The total number of licenses with a pain management clinic classification granted or denied by the Board;

"(3) Any disciplinary actions taken by the Board against holders of licenses with a pain management clinic classification;

"(4) Total revenues generated from fees for licenses with a pain management clinic classification, fines and penalties paid by license holders, or other disciplinary actions taken against license holders;

"(5) Any other relevant information regarding the implementation of this act.

"(B) On completion of each report, the Board shall submit a

copy of the report to the Governor and, in accordance with section 101.68 of the Revised Code, the General Assembly. In accordance with that section, the Board shall display the report on the Board's internet web site."

## § 4729.86 Drug database; regulations.

If the state board of pharmacy establishes and maintains a drug database pursuant to section 4729.75 of the Revised Code, all of the following apply:

(A)(1) No person identified in divisions (A)(1) to (10) or (B) of section 4729.80 of the Revised Code shall disseminate any written or electronic document the person receives from the drug database, except as necessary in the investigation or prosecution of a possible or alleged criminal offense.

(2) No person shall provide false information to the state board of pharmacy with the intent to obtain information contained in the drug database.

(3) No person shall obtain drug database information by any means except as provided under section 4729.80 or 4729.81 of the Revised Code.

(B) A person shall not use a document obtained pursuant to division (A) of section 4729.80 of the Revised Code as evidence in any civil or administrative proceeding.

(C)(1) The board may restrict a person from obtaining further information from the drug database if any of the following is the case:

(a) The person is convicted of or pleads guilty to a violation of division (A)(1), (2), or (3) of this section;

(b) The person is a requestor identified in division (A)(11) of section 4729.80 of the Revised Code and the board determines that the person's actions in another state would have constituted a violation of division (A)(1), (2), or (3) of this section;

(c) The person fails to comply with division (B) of this section, regardless of the jurisdiction in which the failure to comply occurred.

(2) The board shall determine the extent to which the person is restricted from obtaining further information from the database.

**HISTORY: 2011 HB 93, § 1, eff. May 20, 2011.**

Acts 2011, HB 93, § 8 provides: "(A) Not later than one year after the effective date of this section, and annually each year for four years thereafter, the State Board of Pharmacy shall prepare a report on all of the following:

"(1) The total number of applications received by the Board for a terminal distributor of dangerous drugs license with a pain management clinic classification;

"(2) The total number of licenses with a pain management clinic classification granted or denied by the Board;

"(3) Any disciplinary actions taken by the Board against holders of licenses with a pain management clinic classification;

"(4) Total revenues generated from fees for licenses with a pain management clinic classification, fines and penalties paid by license holders, or other disciplinary actions taken against license holders;

"(5) Any other relevant information regarding the implementation of this act.

"(B) On completion of each report, the Board shall submit a copy of the report to the Governor and, in accordance with section 101.68 of the Revised Code, the General Assembly. In accordance with that section, the Board shall display the report on the Board's internet web site."

## § 4729.99 Penalties.

(A) Whoever violates section 4729.16, division (A) or (B) of section 4729.38, or section 4729.57 of the Revised Code is guilty of a minor misdemeanor. Each day's violation constitutes a separate offense.

(B) Whoever violates section 4729.27, 4729.28, or 4729.36 of the Revised Code is guilty of a misdemeanor of the third degree. Each day's violation constitutes a separate offense. If the offender previously has been convicted of or pleaded guilty to a violation of this chapter, that person is guilty of a misdemeanor of the second degree.

(C) Whoever violates section 4729.32, 4729.33, or 4729.34 of the Revised Code is guilty of a misdemeanor.

(D) Whoever violates division (A), (B), (D), or (E) of section 4729.51 of the Revised Code is guilty of a misdemeanor of the first degree.

(E)(1) Whoever violates section 4729.37, division (C)(2) of section 4729.51, division (J) of section 4729.54, or section 4729.61 of the Revised Code is guilty of a felony of the fifth degree. If the offender previously has been convicted of or pleaded guilty to a violation of this chapter or a violation of Chapter 2925. or 3719. of the Revised Code, that person is guilty of a felony of the fourth degree.

(2) If an offender is convicted of or pleads guilty to a violation of section 4729.37, division (C) of section 4729.51, division (J) of section 4729.54, or section 4729.61 of the Revised Code, if the violation involves the sale, offer to sell, or possession of a schedule I or II controlled substance, with the exception of marihuana, and if the court imposing sentence upon the offender finds that the offender as a result of the violation is a major drug offender, as defined in section 2929.01 of the Revised Code, and is guilty of a specification of the type described in section 2941.1410 of the Revised Code, the court, in lieu of the prison term authorized or required by division (E)(1) of this section and sections 2929.13 and 2929.14 of the Revised Code and in addition to any other sanction imposed for the offense under sections 2929.11 to 2929.18 of the Revised Code, shall impose upon the offender, in accordance with division (B)(3) of section 2929.14 of the Revised Code, the mandatory prison term specified in that division.

(3) Notwithstanding any contrary provision of section 3719.21 of the Revised Code, the clerk of court shall pay any fine imposed for a violation of section 4729.37, division (C) of section 4729.51, division (J) of section 4729.54, or section 4729.61 of the Revised Code pursuant to division (A) of section 2929.18 of the Revised Code in accordance with and subject to the requirements of division (F) of section 2925.03 of the Revised Code. The agency that receives the fine shall use the fine as specified in division (F) of section 2925.03 of the Revised Code.

(F) Whoever violates section 4729.531 of the Revised Code or any rule adopted thereunder or section 4729.532 of the Revised Code is guilty of a misdemeanor of the first degree.

(G) Whoever violates division (C)(1) of section 4729.51 of the Revised Code is guilty of a felony of the fourth degree. If the offender has previously been convicted of or pleaded guilty to a violation of this chapter, or of a violation of Chapter 2925. or 3719. of the Revised Code, that person is guilty of a felony of the third degree.

(H) Whoever violates division (C)(3) of section 4729.51 of the Revised Code is guilty of a misdemeanor of the first degree. If the offender has previously been convicted of or pleaded guilty to a violation of this chapter, or of a violation of Chapter 2925. or 3719. of the Revised Code, that person is guilty of a felony of the fifth degree.

(I)(1) Whoever violates division (B) of section 4729.42 of the Revised Code is guilty of unauthorized pharmacy-related drug conduct. Except as otherwise provided in this section, unauthorized pharmacy-related drug conduct is a misdemeanor of the second degree. If the offender previously has been convicted of or pleaded guilty to a violation of division (B), (C), (D), or (E) of that section, unauthorized pharmacy-related drug conduct is a misdemeanor of the first degree on a second offense and a felony of the fifth degree on a third or subsequent offense.

(2) Whoever violates division (C) or (D) of section 4729.42 of the Revised Code is guilty of permitting unauthorized pharmacy-related drug conduct. Except as otherwise provided in this section, permitting unauthorized pharmacy-related drug conduct is a misdemeanor of the second degree. If the offender previously has been convicted of or pleaded guilty to a violation of division (B), (C), (D), or (E) of that section, permitting unauthorized pharmacy-related drug conduct is a misdemeanor of the first degree on a second offense and a felony of the fifth degree on a third or subsequent offense.

(3) Whoever violates division (E) of section 4729.42 of the Revised Code is guilty of the offense of falsification under section 2921.13 of the Revised Code. In addition to any other sanction imposed for the violation, the offender is forever disqualified from engaging in any activity specified in division (B)(1), (2), or (3) of section 4729.42 of the Revised Code and from performing any function as a health care professional or health care worker. As used in this division, "health care professional" and "health care worker" have the same meanings as in section 2305.234 of the Revised Code.

(4) Notwithstanding any contrary provision of section 3719.21 of the Revised Code or any other provision of law that governs the distribution of fines, the clerk of the court shall pay any fine imposed pursuant to division (I)(1), (2), or (3) of this section to the state board of pharmacy if the board has adopted a written internal control policy under division (F)(2) of section 2925.03 of the Revised Code that addresses fine moneys that it receives under Chapter 2925. of the Revised Code and if the policy also addresses fine moneys paid under this division. The state board of pharmacy shall use the fines so paid in accordance with the written internal control policy to subsidize the board's law enforcement efforts that pertain to drug offenses.

(J)(1) Whoever violates division (A)(1) of section 4729.86 of the Revised Code is guilty of a misdemeanor of the third degree. If the offender has previously been convicted of or pleaded guilty to a violation of division (A)(1), (2), or (3) of section 4729.86 of the Revised Code, that person is guilty of a misdemeanor of the first degree.

(2) Whoever violates division (A)(2) of section 4729.86 of the Revised Code is guilty of a misdemeanor of the first degree. If the offender has previously been convicted of or pleaded guilty to a violation of division (A)(1), (2), or (3) of section 4729.86 of the Revised Code, that person is guilty of a felony of the fifth degree.

(3) Whoever violates division (A)(3) of section 4729.86 of the Revised Code is guilty of a felony of the fifth degree. If the offender has previously been convicted of or pleaded guilty to a violation of division (A)(1), (2), or (3) of section 4729.86 of the Revised Code, that person is guilty of a felony of the fourth degree.

(K) A person who violates division (C) of section 4729.552 of the Revised Code is guilty of a misdemeanor of the first degree. If the person previously has been convicted of or pleaded guilty to a violation of division (C) of section 4729.552 of the Revised Code, that person is guilty of a felony of the fifth degree.

**HISTORY: Bureau of Code Revision, 10-1-53; 127 v 162 (Eff 9-16-57); 129 v 1376 (Eff 1-1-62); 130 v 1145 (Eff 3-8-64); 133 v H 874 (Eff 9-16-70); 134 v S 141 (Eff 12-31-71); 136 v H 1 (Eff 6-13-75); 136 v H 300 (Eff 7-1-76); 137 v S 45 (Eff 1-1-78); 139 v H 694 (Eff 11-15-81); 139 v S 4 (Eff 10-1-82); 140 v H 208 (Eff 9-20-84); 145 v H 88 (Eff 6-29-94); 145 v H 391 (Eff 7-21-94); 146 v S 2 (Eff 7-1-96); 146 v S 269 (Eff 7-1-96); 148 v S 107. Eff 3-23-2000; 152 v S 203, § 1, eff. 4-8-09; 153 v H 2, § 101.01, eff. 4-1-09; 153 v H 1, § 101.01, eff. 10-16-09; 2011 HB 93, § 1, eff. May 20, 2011; 2011 HB 86, § 1, eff. Sept. 30, 2011.**

Acts 2011, HB 93, § 8 provides: "(A) Not later than one year after the effective date of this section, and annually each year for four years thereafter, the State Board of Pharmacy shall prepare a report on all of the following:

"(1) The total number of applications received by the Board for a terminal distributor of dangerous drugs license with a pain management clinic classification;

"(2) The total number of licenses with a pain management clinic classification granted or denied by the Board;

"(3) Any disciplinary actions taken by the Board against holders of licenses with a pain management clinic classification;

"(4) Total revenues generated from fees for licenses with a pain management clinic classification, fines and penalties paid by license holders, or other disciplinary actions taken against license holders;

"(5) Any other relevant information regarding the implementation of this act.

"(B) On completion of each report, the Board shall submit a copy of the report to the Governor and, in accordance with section 101.68 of the Revised Code, the General Assembly. In accordance with that section, the Board shall display the report on the Board's internet web site."

The effective date is set by § 812.10 of 153 v H 1.

The effective date is set by §§ 901.10 and 901.11 of 153 v H 2.

# CHAPTER 4731: PHYSICIANS; LIMITED PRACTITIONERS



## § 4731.224 Health care facilities, licensees, professional associations and insurers to report misconduct.

(A) Within sixty days after the imposition of any formal disciplinary action taken by any health care facility, including a hospital, health care facility operated by a health insuring corporation, ambulatory surgical center, or similar facility, against any individual holding a valid certificate to practice issued pursuant to this chapter, the chief administrator or executive officer of the facility shall report to the state medical board the name of the individual, the action taken by the facility, and a summary of the underlying facts leading to the action taken. Upon request, the board shall be provided certified copies of the patient records that were the basis for the facility's action. Prior to release to the board, the summary shall be approved by the peer review committee that reviewed the case or by the governing board of the facility. As used in this division, "formal disciplinary action" means any action resulting in the revocation, restriction, reduction, or termination of clinical privileges for violations of professional ethics, or for reasons of medical incompetence, medical malpractice, or drug or alcohol abuse. "Formal disciplinary action" includes a summary action, an action that takes effect notwithstanding any appeal rights that may exist, and an action that results in an individual surrendering clinical privileges while under investigation and during proceedings regarding the action being taken or in return for not being investigated or having proceedings held. "Formal disciplinary action" does not include any action taken for the sole reason of failure to maintain records on a timely basis or failure to attend staff or section meetings.

The filing or nonfiling of a report with the board, investigation by the board, or any disciplinary action taken by the board, shall not preclude any action by a health care facility to suspend, restrict, or revoke the individual's clinical privileges.

In the absence of fraud or bad faith, no individual or entity that provides patient records to the board shall be liable in damages to any person as a result of providing the records.

(B) If any individual authorized to practice under this chapter or any professional association or society of such individuals believes that a violation of any provision of this chapter, Chapter 4730., 4760., 4762., or 4774. of the Revised Code, or any rule of the board has occurred, the individual, association, or society shall report to the board the information upon which the belief is based. This division does not require any treatment provider approved by the board under section 4731.25 of the Revised Code or any employee, agent, or representative of such a provider to make reports with respect to an impaired practitioner participating in treatment or aftercare for substance abuse as long as the practitioner maintains participation in accordance with the requirements of section 4731.25 of the Revised Code, and as long as the treatment provider or employee, agent, or representative of the provider has no reason to believe that the practitioner has violated any provision of this chapter or any rule adopted under it, other than the provisions of division (B)(26) of section 4731.22 of the Revised Code. This division does not require reporting by any member of an impaired practitioner committee established by a health care facility or by any representative or agent of a committee or program sponsored by a professional association or society of individuals authorized to practice under this chapter to provide peer assistance to practitioners with substance abuse problems with respect to a practitioner who has been referred for examination to a treatment program approved by the board under section 4731.25 of the Revised Code if the practitioner cooperates with the referral for examination and with any determination that the practitioner should enter treatment and as long as the committee member, representative, or agent has no reason to believe that the practitioner has ceased to participate in the treatment program in accordance with section 4731.25 of the Revised Code or has violated any provision of this chapter or any rule adopted under it, other than the provisions of division (B)(26) of section 4731.22 of the Revised Code.

(C) Any professional association or society composed primarily of doctors of medicine and surgery, doctors of osteopathic medicine and surgery, doctors of podiatric medicine and surgery, or practitioners of limited branches of medicine that suspends or revokes an individual's membership for violations of professional ethics, or for reasons of professional incompetence or professional malpractice, within sixty days after a final decision shall report to the board, on forms prescribed and provided by the board, the name of the individual, the action taken by the professional organization, and a summary of the underlying facts leading to the action taken.

The filing of a report with the board or decision not to file a report, investigation by the board, or any disciplinary action taken by the board, does not preclude a professional organization from taking disciplinary action against an individual.

(D) Any insurer providing professional liability insurance to an individual authorized to practice under this chapter, or any other entity that seeks to indemnify the professional liability of such an individual, shall notify the board within thirty days after the final disposition of any written claim for damages where such disposition results in a payment exceeding twenty-five thousand dollars. The notice shall contain the following information:

(1) The name and address of the person submitting the notification;

(2) The name and address of the insured who is the subject of the claim;

(3) The name of the person filing the written claim;

(4) The date of final disposition;

(5) If applicable, the identity of the court in which the final disposition of the claim took place.

(E) The board may investigate possible violations of this chapter or the rules adopted under it that are brought to its attention as a result of the reporting requirements of this section, except that the board shall conduct an investigation if a possible violation involves repeated malpractice. As used in this division, "repeated malpractice" means three or more claims for medical malpractice within the previous five-year period, each resulting in a judgment or settlement in excess of twenty-five thousand dollars in favor of the claimant, and each involving negligent conduct by the practicing individual.

(F) All summaries, reports, and records received and maintained by the board pursuant to this section shall be held in confidence and shall not be subject to discovery or introduction in evidence in any federal or state civil action involving a health care professional or facility arising out of matters that are the subject of the reporting required by this section. The board may use the information obtained only as the basis for an investigation, as evidence in a disciplinary hearing against an individual whose practice is regulated under this chapter, or in any subsequent trial or appeal of a board action or order.

The board may disclose the summaries and reports it receives under this section only to health care facility committees within or outside this state that are involved in credentialing or recredentialing the individual or in reviewing the individual's clinical privileges. The board shall indicate whether or not the information has been verified. Information transmitted by the board shall be subject to the same confidentiality provisions as when maintained by the board.

(G) Except for reports filed by an individual pursuant to division (B) of this section, the board shall send a copy of any reports or summaries it receives pursuant to this section to the individual who is the subject of the reports or summaries. The individual shall have the right to file a statement with the board concerning the correctness or relevance of the information. The statement shall at all times accompany that part of the record in contention.

(H) An individual or entity that, pursuant to this section, reports to the board or refers an impaired practitioner to a treatment provider approved by the board under section 4731.25 of the Revised Code shall not be subject to suit for civil damages as a result of the report, referral, or provision of the information.

(I) In the absence of fraud or bad faith, no professional association or society of individuals authorized to practice under this chapter that sponsors a committee or program to provide peer assistance to practitioners with substance abuse problems, no representative or agent of such a committee or program, and no member of the state medical board shall be held liable in damages to any person by reason of actions taken to refer a practitioner to a treatment provider approved under section 4731.25 of the Revised Code for examination or treatment.

**HISTORY: 141 v H 769 (Eff 3-17-87); 143 v H 332 (Eff 8-5-89); 143 v H 615 (Eff 3-27-91); 146 v S 143 (Eff 3-5-96); 147 v H 606 (Eff 3-9-99); 148 v S 278 (Eff 5-31-2000); 148 v H 341 (Eff 8-10-2000); 148 v H 585. Eff 4-10-2001; 152 v S 229, § 1, eff. 9-11-08.**

## [PROHIBITIONS]

### § 4731.41 Practice of medicine or surgery without certificate.

No person shall practice medicine and surgery, or any of its branches, without the appropriate certificate from the state medical board to engage in the practice. No person shall advertise or claim to the public to be a practitioner of medicine and surgery, or any of its branches, without a certificate from the board. No person shall open or conduct an office or other place for such practice without a certificate from the board. No person shall conduct an office in the name of some person who has a certificate to practice medicine and surgery, or any of its branches. No person shall practice medicine and surgery, or any of its branches, after the person's certificate has been revoked, or, if suspended, during the time of such suspension.

A certificate signed by the secretary of the board to which is affixed the official seal of the board to the effect that it appears from the records of the board that no such certificate to practice medicine and surgery, or any of its branches, in this state has been issued to the person specified therein, or that a certificate to practice, if issued, has been revoked or suspended, shall be received as prima-facie evidence of the record of the board in any court or before any officer of the state.

**HISTORY: GC § 12694; 99 v 502, § 52; 103 v 438; 108 v PtI, 40; Bureau of Code Revision, 10-1-53; 125 v 903 (Eff 10-1-53); 132 v S 258 (Eff 12-13-67); 133 v H 1 (Eff 3-18-69); 147 v H 606. Eff 3-9-99.**

### § 4731.43 Practicing osteopathy without certificate.

No person shall announce or advertise himself as an osteopathic physician and surgeon, or shall practice as such, without a certificate from the state medical board or without complying with all the provisions of law relating to such practice, or shall practice after such certificate has been revoked, or if suspended, during the time of such suspension.

A certificate certified by the secretary, under the official seal of the said board to the effect that it appears from the records of the board that no certificate to practice osteopathic medicine and surgery has been issued to any person specified therein, or that a certificate, if issued, has been revoked or suspended shall be received as prima-facie evidence of the record in any court or before any officer of the state.

**HISTORY: GC § 12696; 99 v 502, § 54; 103 v 438; Bureau of Code Revision, 10-1-53; 139 v H 317. Eff 8-27-82.**

### § 4731.46 Issuing false medical diploma.

No person shall make, issue, publish, or cause to be made, issued, or published, for the purpose of sale, barter, or gift, a diploma, certificate, or writing representing the holder thereof to be a graduate of a medical school, college, or educational institution of medicine, unless such holder has attended a complete course of instruction therein, equal to the average course of instruction in other such schools, colleges, or institutions in good standing in this state.

**HISTORY: GC § 12700; 99 v 503, § 57; Bureau of Code Revision. Eff 10-1-53.**

### § 4731.47 Selling false medical diploma.

No person shall make, issue, or publish, for the purpose of sale, barter, or gift, a certificate, diploma, or other writing or document falsely representing the holder or receiver thereof to be a graduate of a medical school, college, or educational institution of medicine and entitled to the powers, privileges, or degrees thereby pretended to be conferred, or sell or dispose of, or offer to sell or dispose of such diploma, certificate, writing, or document containing such false representation or use his name, or permit it to be used, as a subscriber to such false and fictitious diploma, certificate, writing, or document or engage in the practice of medicine and surgery under and by virtue of such fraudulent diploma, certificate, writing, or document.

**HISTORY: GC § 12701; 99 v 503, § 58; Bureau of Code Revision. Eff 10-1-53.**

### § 4731.48 Physician giving false certificate of disability.

No surgeon or physician shall knowingly give to a person liable to be enrolled in the militia a false certificate of disability.

**HISTORY: RS § 3030; S&S 451; 63 v 70, § 8; GC § 12927; Bureau of Code Revision. Eff 10-1-53.**

### § 4731.481 Falsely enabling person to obtain or retain special parking privileges.

No physician shall do either of the following:

(A) Furnish a person with a prescription in order to enable the person to be issued a removable windshield placard, temporary removable windshield placard, or license plates under section 4503.44 of the Revised Code, knowing that the person does not meet any of the criteria contained in division (A)(1) of that section;

(B) Furnish a person with a prescription described in division (A) of this section and knowingly misstate on the prescription the length of time the physician expects the person to have the disability that limits or impairs the person's ability to walk in order to enable the person to retain a placard issued under section 4503.44 of the Revised Code for a period of time longer than that which would be estimated by a similar practitioner under the same or similar circumstances.

**HISTORY: 148 v H 148. Eff 10-14-99.**

The effective date is set by section 3 of HB 148.

## § 4731.49 Physician making an unlawful prescription for intoxicating liquor.

No physician shall issue a prescription for intoxicating liquor not in writing, or shall issue a written prescription therefor knowing such liquor is to be used as a beverage, or not containing the name and quantity of liquor prescribed, the name of the person for whom prescribed, and the date on which such prescription is written, and direction for the use of such liquor.

**HISTORY: RS § 4364-30zc; 98 v 17, § 16; GC § 13217; Bureau of Code Revision. Eff 10-1-53.**

## § 4731.50 Further punishment of physician so convicted.

No practicing physician who has been convicted of issuing a verbal prescription for intoxicating liquor, or issuing a prescription therefor in a form which does not comply with law, or issuing a prescription, knowing such liquor to be for use as a beverage, shall issue a prescription for intoxicating liquor within two years from the date of such conviction.

**HISTORY: RS § 4364-30zc; 98 v 17, § 16; GC § 13218; Bureau of Code Revision. Eff 10-1-53.**

### [PODIATRIC MEDICINE AND SURGERY]

## § 4731.60 Prohibitions.

No person shall practice podiatric medicine and surgery without a certificate from the state medical board; no person shall advertise or announce as a practitioner of podiatric medicine and surgery without a certificate from the board; no person shall open or conduct an office or other place for such practice without a certificate from the board; no person shall conduct an office in the name of some person who has a certificate to practice podiatric medicine and surgery; and no person shall practice podiatric medicine and surgery after a certificate has been revoked, or if suspended, during the time of such suspension.

A certificate signed by the secretary to which is affixed the official seal of the board to the effect that it appears from the records of the board that no such certificate to practice podiatric medicine and surgery, in the state has been issued to any such person specified therein, or that a certificate, if issued, has been revoked or suspended, shall be received as prima-facie evidence of the record of such board in any court or before any officer of this state.

**HISTORY: 128 v 57 (Eff 8-24-59); 132 v H 662 (Eff 12-14-67); 148 v H 585. Eff 4-10-2001.**

### [MISCELLANEOUS]

## § 4731.81 Administering general anesthetic.

No person shall knowingly administer a general anesthetic to another, unless at the time of administration a competent witness is present.

**HISTORY: 134 v H 511. Eff 1-1-74.**

## § 4731.99 Penalties.

(A) Whoever violates section 4731.41, 4731.43, or 4731.60 of the Revised Code is guilty of a felony of the fifth degree on a first offense and a felony of the fourth degree on each subsequent offense.

(B) Whoever violates section 4731.49, 4731.50, or 4731.81 of the Revised Code is guilty of a misdemeanor of the fourth degree on a first offense and a misdemeanor of the first degree on each subsequent offense.

(C) Whoever violates section 4731.46 or 4731.47 of the Revised Code is guilty of a felony of the fifth degree.

(D) Whoever violates section 4731.48 of the Revised Code is guilty of a misdemeanor of the fourth degree.

(E) Whoever violates division (A), (B), (C), or (D) of section 4731.224 [4731.22.4] of the Revised Code is guilty of a minor misdemeanor on a first offense and a misdemeanor of the fourth degree on each subsequent offense, except that an individual guilty of a subsequent offense shall not be subject to imprisonment, but to a fine alone of up to one thousand dollars for each offense.

(F) Whoever violates section 4731.481 [4731.48.1] of the Revised Code is guilty of a misdemeanor of the first degree.

**HISTORY: Bureau of Code Revision, 10-1-53; 128 v 57 (Eff 8-24-59); 128 v 346 (Eff 10-8-59); 132 v H 418 (Eff 12-1-67); 134 v H 511 (Eff 1-1-74); 135 v H 716 (Eff 1-1-74); 136 v H 832 (Eff 8-31-76); 136 v H 1 (Special) (Eff 9-2-76); 137 v H 209 (Eff 11-21-77); 137 v S 347 (Eff 7-13-78); 137 v H 1092 (Eff 7-21-78); 139 v H 317 (Eff 8-27-82); 141 v H 222 (Eff 5-15-86); 141 v H 769 (Eff 3-17-87); 143 v S 113 (Eff 11-3-89); 146 v S 2 (Eff 7-1-96); 147 v H 606 (Eff 3-9-99); 148 v H 148. Eff 10-14-99.**

The effective date is set by section 3 of HB 148.

# CHAPTER 4749: PRIVATE INVESTIGATORS; SECURITY SERVICES

Section



## § 4749.10 When licensee or employee may carry a firearm.

(A) No class A, B, or C licensee and no registered employee of a class A, B, or C licensee shall carry a firearm, as defined in section 2923.11 of the Revised Code, in the course of engaging in the business of private investigation, the business of security services, or both businesses, unless all of the following apply:

(1) The licensee or employee either has successfully completed a basic firearm training program at a training school approved by the Ohio peace officer training commission, which program includes twenty hours of training in handgun use and, if any firearm other than a handgun is to be used, five hours of training in the use of other firearms, and has received a certificate of satisfactory completion of that program from the executive director of the commission; the licensee or employee has, within three years prior to November 27, 1985, satisfactorily completed firearms training that has been approved by the commission as being equivalent to such a program and has received written evidence of approval of that training from the executive director of the commission; or the licensee or employee is a former peace officer, as defined in section 109.71 of the Revised Code, who previously had successfully completed a firearms training course at a training school approved by the Ohio peace officer training commission and has received a certificate or other evidence of satisfactory completion of that course from the executive director of the commission.

(2) The licensee or employee submits an application to the director of public safety, on a form prescribed by the director, in which the licensee or employee requests registration as a class A, B, or C licensee or employee who may carry a firearm. The application shall be accompanied by a copy of the certificate or the written evidence or other evidence described in division (A)(1) of this section, the identification card issued pursuant to section 4749.03 or 4749.06 of the Revised Code if one has previously been issued, a statement of the duties that will be performed while the licensee or employee is armed, and a fee the director determines, not to exceed fifteen dollars. In the case of a registered employee, the statement shall be prepared by the employing class A, B, or C licensee.

(3) The licensee or employee receives a notation on the licensee's or employee's identification card that the licensee or employee is a firearm-bearer and carries the identification card whenever the licensee or employee carries a firearm in the course of engaging in the business of private investigation, the business of security services, or both businesses.

(4) At any time within the immediately preceding twelve-month period, the licensee or employee has requalified in firearms use on a firearms training range at a firearms requalification program certified by the Ohio peace officer training commission or on a firearms training range under the supervision of an instructor certified by the commission and has received a certificate of satisfactory requalification from the certified program or certified instructor, provided that this division does not apply to any licensee or employee prior to the expiration of eighteen months after the licensee's or employee's completion of the program described in division (A)(1) of this section. A certificate of satisfactory requalification is valid and remains in effect for twelve months from the date of the requalification.

(5) If division (A)(4) of this section applies to the licensee or employee, the licensee or employee carries the certificate of satisfactory requalification that then is in effect or any other evidence of requalification issued or provided by the director.

(B)(1) The director of public safety shall register an applicant under division (A) of this section who satisfies divisions (A)(1) and (2) of this section, and place a notation on the applicant's identification card indicating that the applicant is a firearm-bearer and the date on which the applicant completed the program described in division (A)(1) of this section.

(2) A firearms requalification training program or instructor certified by the commission for the annual requalification of class A, B, or C licensees or employees who are authorized to carry a firearm under section 4749.10 of the Revised Code shall award a certificate of satisfactory requalification to each class A, B, or C licensee or registered employee of a class A, B, or C licensee who satisfactorily requalifies in firearms training. The certificate shall identify the licensee or employee and indicate the date of the requalification. A licensee or employee who receives such a certificate shall submit a copy of it to the director of public safety. A licensee shall submit the copy of the requalification certificate at the same time that the licensee makes application for renewal of the licensee's class A, B, or C license. The director shall keep a record of all copies of requalification certificates the director receives under this division and shall establish a procedure for the updating of identification cards to provide evidence of compliance with the annual requalification requirement. The procedure for the updating of identification cards may provide for the issuance of a new card containing the evidence, the entry of a new notation containing the evidence on the existing card, the issuance of a separate card or paper containing the evidence, or any other procedure determined by the director to be reasonable. Each person who is issued a requalification certificate under this division promptly shall pay to the Ohio peace officer training commission established by section 109.71 of the Revised Code a fee the director determines, not to exceed fifteen dollars, which fee shall be transmitted to the treasurer of state for deposit in the peace officer private security fund established by section 109.78 of the Revised Code.

(C) Nothing in this section prohibits a private investigator or a security guard provider from carrying a concealed handgun if the private investigator or security guard provider complies with sections 2923.124 [2923.12.4] to 2923.1213 [2923.12.13] of the Revised Code.

**HISTORY: 141 v H 402 (Eff 11-27-85); 141 v H 428 (Eff 12-23-86); 146 v H 670. Eff 12-2-96; 150 v H 12, § 1, eff. 4-8-04; 150 v H 230, § 1, eff. 7-1-04; 151 v H 68, § 101.01, eff. 7-1-05.**

The effective date is set by § 612.09 of 151 v H 68.

The provisions of § 6, H.B. 12 (150 v —), read as follows:

SECTION 6. In amending sections 1547.69, 2911.21, 2921.13,

2923.12, 2923.121, 2923.123, 2923.13, 2923.16, 2953.32, and 4749.10 of the Revised Code and in enacting sections 109.69, 109.731, 311.41, 311.42, and 2923.124 to 2923.1213 of the Revised Code in this act, the General Assembly hereby declares its intent to recognize both of the following:

(A) The inalienable and fundamental right of an individual to defend the individual's person and the members of the individual's family;

(B) The fact that the right described in division (A) of this section predates the adoption of the United States Constitution, the adoption of the Ohio Constitution, and the enactment of all statutory laws by the General Assembly and may not be infringed by any enactment of the General Assembly.

The provisions of § 7, H.B. 12 (150 v —), read as follows:

SECTION 7. In enacting sections 109.69, 109.731, 311.41, 311.42, and 2923.124 to 2923.1213 of the Revised Code in this act and in amending sections 1547.69, 2911.21, 2921.13, 2923.12, 2923.121, 2923.123, 2923.13, 2923.16, 2953.32, and 4749.10 of the Revised Code in this act relative to licenses to carry a concealed handgun, the General Assembly hereby declares that it is not its intent to declare or otherwise give the impression that, prior to the effective date of this act, an individual did not have an inalienable and fundamental right, or a right under the Ohio Constitution or the United States Constitution, to carry a concealed handgun or other firearm for the defense of the individual's person or a member of the individual's family while engaged in lawful activity. Further, the General Assembly declares that it is not its intent to invalidate any prior convictions for violating any section of the Revised Code or a municipal ordinance prior to the effective date of this act or to prevent the prosecution of any violation committed prior to the effective date of this act.

The provisions of § 9, H.B. 12 (150 v —), read as follows:

SECTION 9. The General Assembly finds that licenses to carry concealed handguns are a matter of statewide concern and wishes to ensure uniformity throughout the state regarding the qualifications for a person to hold a license to carry a concealed handgun and the authority granted to a person holding a license of that nature. It is the intent of the General Assembly in amending sections 1547.69, 2911.21, 2921.13, 2923.12, 2923.121, 2923.123, 2923.16, 2953.32, and 4749.10 and enacting sections 109.69, 109.731, 311.41, 311.42, and 2923.124 to 2923.1213 of the Revised Code to enact laws of a general nature, and, by enacting those laws of a general nature, the state occupies and preempts the field of issuing licenses to carry a concealed handgun and the validity of licenses of that nature. No municipal corporation may adopt or continue in existence any ordinance, and no township may adopt or continue in existence any resolution, that is in conflict with those sections, including, but not limited to, any ordinance or resolution that attempts to restrict the places where a person possessing a valid license to carry a concealed handgun may carry a handgun concealed.

The provisions of § 10, H.B. 12 (150 v —), read as follows:

SECTION 10. If any provision of sections 1547.69, 2911.21, 2913.02, 2921.13, 2923.12, 2923.121, 2923.123, 2923.16, 2929.14, 2953.32, and 4749.10 of the Revised Code, as amended by this act, any provision of sections 109.69, 109.731, 311.41, 311.42, 2923.124, 2923.125, 2923.126, 2923.127, 2923.128, 2923.129, 2923.1210, 2923.1211, 2923.1212, and 2923.1213 of the Revised Code, as enacted by this act, or the application of any provision of those sections to any person or circumstance is held invalid, the invalidity does not affect other provisions or applications of the particular section or related sections that can be given effect without the invalid provision or application, and to this end the provisions of the particular section are severable.

**Not analogous to former RC § 4749.10 (133 v H 341), amended and renumbered RC § 4749.13, 141 v H 402, eff 11-27-85.**

## § 4749.13 Prohibitions.

(A) No person shall engage in the business of private investigation, the business of security services, or both businesses in this state unless the person is licensed pursuant to this chapter. Each day of continuing violation constitutes a separate offense. Nothing in this chapter shall be construed to require any employee of a class A, B, or C licensee to obtain a class A, B, or C license, provided that an employee shall be registered by a licensee when required by section 4749.06 of the Revised Code. Nothing in this chapter shall be construed to require a partner to be a class A, B, or C licensee except as provided in division (A)(3) of section 4749.03 of the Revised Code. Nothing in this chapter shall be construed to require a director, officer, or qualifying agent of a corporation to individually be a class A, B, or C licensee if the corporation is licensed pursuant to this chapter.

(B) No class A, B, or C licensee, or registered employee of a class A, B, or C licensee shall:

(1) Knowingly violate any provision of this chapter or any rule of the director of public safety adopted for the administration of this chapter;

(2) Knowingly make a false report with respect to any matter with which the licensee or registered employee is employed;

(3) Divulge any information acquired from or for a client to persons other than the client or the client's authorized agent without express authorization to do so or unless required by law;

(4) Knowingly accept employment which includes obtaining information intended for illegal purposes.

(C) No person shall knowingly authorize or permit another person to violate any provision of this chapter or any rule of the director adopted for the administration of this chapter.

(D) No person who is not licensed as a class A, B, or C licensee shall advertise that the person is or otherwise hold self out as a class A, B, or C licensee. This division does not prohibit registered employees from indicating in the course of authorized employment for a class A, B, or C licensee that they are authorized to engage in investigatory, security services activities, or both activities.

**HISTORY: RC § 4749.10, 133 v H 341 (Eff 1-1-70); RC § 4749.13, 141 v H 402. Eff 11-27-85; 150 v H 230, § 1, eff. 7-1-04.**

The effective date is set by section 8 of H.B. 230 (150 v —).

## § 4749.99 Penalties.

(A) Except as otherwise provided in this division, whoever violates division (A) of section 4749.13 of the Revised Code is guilty of a misdemeanor of the first degree. Whoever violates division (A) of section 4749.13 of the Revised Code and previously has been convicted of one or more violations of division (A) of that section is guilty of a felony of the fifth degree. If the offender previously has been convicted of two or more violations of division (A) of that section, the offender shall be fined ten thousand dollars and also may be imprisoned not more than one year.

(B) Whoever violates division (B), (C), or (D) of section 4749.13 of the Revised Code shall be fined not less than one hundred or more than one thousand dollars, imprisoned not more than one year, or both.

**HISTORY: 133 v H 341 (Eff 1-1-70); 141 v H 402 (Eff 11-27-85); 144 v H 536 (Eff 11-5-92); 146 v S 2. Eff 7-1-96.**

The effective date is set by section 6 of SB 2.

# TITLE 49: PUBLIC UTILITIES

## CHAPTER 4931: TELEPHONE COMPANIES



### [DIVULGING MESSAGE]

**§ 4931.26** Repealed, 153 v S 162, § 2 [RS § 3466; S 156; 62 v 72, § 10; 94 v 209; GC § 13388; Bureau of Code Revision. Eff 10-1-53]. Eff 9-13-10.

This section concerned divulging telegraph messages.

**§ 4931.27** Repealed, 153 v S 162, § 2 [RS § 3373-2; 88 v 429, § 3; GC § 13389; Bureau of Code Revision, 10-1-53; 144 v S 343. Eff 3-24-93]. Eff 9-13-10.

This section concerned delaying telegraph messages.

**§ 4931.28** Repealed, 153 v S 162, § 2 [RS § 3467a; 89 v 52; 89 v 100; 90 v 346; 95 v 101; GC § 13402; Bureau of Code Revision, 10-1-53; 141 v S 222. Eff 3-25-87]. Eff 9-13-10.

This section concerned interfering with telegraph or telephone messages.

**§ 4931.29** Repealed, 153 v S 162, § 2 [100 v 10; GC § 13419; Bureau of Code Revision. Eff 10-1-53]. Eff 9-13-10.

This section concerned divulging telephone communication.

**§ 4931.30** Repealed, 153 v S 162, § 2 [126 v 74, § 1 (Eff 6-30-55); 129 v 582(928). Eff 1-10-61]. Eff 9-13-10.

This section concerned party lines to be yielded in emergencies.

**§ 4931.31** Repealed, 153 v S 162, § 2 [128 v 692 (Eff 8-14-59); 129 v 582(929). Eff 1-10-61]. Eff 9-13-10.

This section concerned prohibition of threat or harassment in telephone communication and directory notice.

### [UNIFORM EMERGENCY TELEPHONE NUMBER SYSTEM]

**§ 4931.55** Amended and renumbered RC § 4931.75 in 150 v H 361. Eff 5-6-05

### [WIRELESS ENHANCED 9-1-1]

**§ 4931.75 Restrictions on transmitting advertising by facsimile device.**

(A) As used in this section:

(1) "Advertisement" means a message or material intended to cause the sale of realty, goods, or services.

(2) "Facsimile device" means a device that electronically or telephonically receives and copies onto paper reasonable reproductions or facsimiles of documents and photographs through connection with a telephone network.

(3) "Pre-existing business relationship" does not include transmitting an advertisement to the owner's or lessee's facsimile device.

(B)(1) No person shall transmit an advertisement to a facsimile device unless the person has received prior permission from the owner or, if the device is leased, from the lessee of the device to which the message is to be sent to transmit the advertisement; or the person has a pre-existing business relationship with such owner or lessee. Division (B)(1) of this section does not apply to a person who transmits an advertisement to a facsimile device located on residential premises.

(2) No person shall transmit an advertisement to a facsimile device located on residential premises unless the person has received prior written permission from the owner or, if the device is leased, from the lessee of the device to which the message is to be sent to transmit the advertisement. In addition to any other penalties or remedies, a recipient of an advertisement transmitted in violation of division (B)(2) of this section may bring a civil action against the person who transmitted that advertisement or caused it to be transmitted. In that action, the recipient may recover one thousand dollars for each violation.

(C) When requested by the owner or lessee, the transmission shall occur between seven p.m. and five a.m.

This section applies to all such advertisements intended to be so transmitted within this state.

**HISTORY: 144 v H 233. Eff 1-10-92; 150 v H 361, § 1, eff. 5-6-05.**

**Publisher's Note:**

This section was amended and renumbered from RC § 4931.55 by 150 v H 361, effective May 6, 2005.

## § 4931.99 Penalties.

(A) Whoever violates division (D) of section 4931.49 of the Revised Code is guilty of a misdemeanor of the fourth degree.

(B) Whoever violates division (B) of section 4931.06 of the Revised Code is guilty of a misdemeanor in the first degree.

(C) Whoever violates division (E) or (F) of section 4931.49 or division (B)(2) of section 4931.66 of the Revised Code is guilty of a misdemeanor of the fourth degree on a first offense and a felony of the fifth degree on each subsequent offense.

(D) Whoever violates section 4931.75 of the Revised Code is guilty of a minor misdemeanor for a first offense and a misdemeanor of the first degree on each subsequent offense.

**HISTORY: Bureau of Code Revision, 10-1-53; 126 v 74 (Eff 8-14-59); 129 v 1306 (Eff 9-14-61); 131 v 1197 (Eff 7-20-65); 131 v 1196 (Eff 7-20-65); 139 v S 199 (Eff 1-1-83); 139 v H 269 (Eff 1-5-83); 141 v H 491 (Eff 6-18-85); 144 v H 233 (Eff 1-10-92); 144 v S 343 (Eff 3-24-93); 146 v S 2 (Eff 7-1-96); 148 v H 283. Eff 9-29-99; 150 v H 361, § 1, eff. 5-6-05; 153 v S 162, § 1, eff. 9-13-10.**

# CHAPTER 4933: COMPANIES — GAS; ELECTRIC; WATER; OTHERS



### [TAMPERING WITH EQUIPMENT]

## § 4933.18 Tampering with utility equipment.

(A) In a prosecution for a theft offense, as defined in section 2913.01 of the Revised Code, that involves alleged tampering with a gas, electric, steam, or water meter, conduit, or attachment of a utility that has been disconnected by the utility, proof that a meter, conduit, or attachment of a utility has been tampered with is prima-facie evidence that the person who is obligated to pay for the service rendered through the meter, conduit, or attachment and is in possession or control of the meter, conduit, or attachment at the time the tampering occurred has caused the tampering with intent to commit a theft offense.

In a prosecution for a theft offense, as defined in section 2913.01 of the Revised Code, that involves the alleged reconnection of a gas, electric, steam, or water meter, conduit, or attachment of a utility that has been disconnected by the utility, proof that a meter, conduit, or attachment disconnected by a utility has been reconnected without the consent of the utility is prima-facie evidence that the person in possession or control of the meter, conduit, or attachment at the time of the reconnection has reconnected the meter, conduit, or attachment with intent to commit a theft offense.

(B) As used in this section:

(1) "Utility" means any electric light company, gas company, natural gas company, pipe-line company, water-works company, or heating or cooling company, as defined by division (A)(3), (4), (5), (6), (7), or (8) of section 4905.03 of the Revised Code, its lessees, trustees, or receivers, or any similar utility owned or operated by a political subdivision.

(2) "Tamper" means to interfere with, damage, or by-pass a utility meter, conduit, or attachment with the intent to impede the correct registration of a meter or the proper functions of a conduit or attachment so as to reduce the amount of utility service that is registered on the meter.

**HISTORY: 137 v H 605 (Eff 8-18-78); 146 v S 2. Eff 7-1-96; 153 v S 162, § 1, eff. 9-13-10.**

**Analogous to former RC § 4933.18 (RS § 3560; S&S 160; GC § 9337; 63 v 164, §§ 13, 14; Bureau of Code Revision, 10-1-53), repealed 137 v H 605, § 2, eff 8-18-78.**

The effective date is set by section 6 of SB 2.

## § 4933.19 Notice to customers concerning theft offenses.

Electric light company, gas company, natural gas company, pipe-line company, water-works company, or heating or cooling company, as defined by division (A)(3), (4), (5), (6), (7), or (8) of section 4905.03 of the Revised Code, or its lessees, trustees, or receivers, and each similar utility owned or operated by a political subdivision shall notify its customers, on an annual basis, that tampering with or bypassing a meter constitutes a theft offense that could result in the imposition of criminal sanctions.

**HISTORY: 137 v H 605 (Eff 8-18-78); 146 v S 2. Eff 7-1-96; 153 v S 162, § 1, eff. 9-13-10.**

**Analogous in part to former RC § 4933.19 (RS § 6860-1; 88 v 241, GC §§ 12512, 12513; Bureau of Code Revision, 10-1-53) renumbered RC § 4933.20 in 137 v H 605, eff 8-18-78.**

The effective date is set by section 6 of SB 2.

## § 4933.20 Tampering with gas pipes and apparatus.

No person shall maliciously open, close, adjust, or interfere with a valve, regulator, gauge, gate, disc, curb cock, stopcock, meter, or other regulating, operating, or measuring device or appliance in or attached to the wells, tanks, conduits, pipelines, mains, service pipes, house pipes, display pipes, or other pipes of a gas company or manufacturer or furnisher of gas with intent to cause the escape of gas or to injure or destroy such property. No person shall maliciously enlarge or alter a mixer furnished or approved by a gas company or manufacturer or furnisher of gas to or for a consumer of gas, or maliciously remove from its connection a mixer so furnished or approved. No person shall without express permission, consume for fuel the gas of a gas company or manufacturer or furnisher of gas without the use of a mixer so furnished or approved by such gas company or manufacturer or furnisher of gas, or tap, sever, or open a main or pipe used or intended for the transmission of gas, or connect with such main or pipe any other main or pipe. This section does not apply to an agent or employee, for that purpose, of the owner, manufacturer, or operator of the devices or appliances referred to in this section.

As used in this section, "gas" includes natural and artificial gas used for heating and illuminating purposes.

**HISTORY: RS § 6860-1; 88 v 241; GC §§ 12512, 12513; Bureau of Code Revision, RC § 4933.19, 10-1-53; RC § 4933.20, 137 v H 605. Eff 8-18-78.**

**Not analogous to former RC § 4933.20 (RS § 3467a; 89 v 52; 89 v 100; 90 v 346; 95 v 101; GC § 12508; 111 v 58; Bureau of Code Revision, 10-1-53), repealed 137 v H 605, § 2, eff 8-18-78.**

## § 4933.21 Interfering with electric wires.

No person shall willfully or maliciously injure, destroy, or intentionally permit to be injured or destroyed, disconnect, displace, cut, break, tap, ground, or make a connection with, or willfully or maliciously interfere with any pole, pier, cable, tower, or wire, legally erected, put, or strung, or electrical apparatus, appliance, or machinery used in the construction or operation of an electrical railway, electric light plant, or plant used in generating or transmitting electricity, or any meter, pipe, conduit, wire, line, post, lamp, burner, heater, machine, motor, or other appliance or apparatus used in the construction or operation of any such electrical railway or electrical plant. No person shall willfully or maliciously prevent any electric meter used in the construction or operation of any such electrical railway or electrical plant, from registering the quantity of electricity supplied, interfere with the proper action or just registration by such meter, alter the index in such meter, or, without the consent of the owner of such electrical railway or electrical plant, willfully or maliciously divert electric current from any such wire or otherwise willfully or maliciously use or cause to be used, without the consent of the owner of such electrical railway or electrical plant, electricity manufactured or distributed by any such electrical railway or electrical plant.

**HISTORY: RS § 3467a; 89 v 52; 89 v 100; 90 v 346; 95 v 101; GC § 12507; 111 v 58; Bureau of Code Revision. Eff 10-1-53.**

## § 4933.22 Tampering with hydrant, pipe, or meter.

No person shall maliciously open, close, adjust, or interfere with a fire hydrant, valve, regulator, gauge, gate, disc, curb cock, stopcock, meter, or other regulator, operating or measuring device, or appliance in or attached to the wells, tanks, reservoirs, conduits, pipes, mains, service pipes, house pipes, or other pipes or apparatus of a water company or furnisher of water, with intent to cause the escape of water or to injure or destroy such property. No person shall tap, sever, open, or make unauthorized connections with a main or pipe used or intended for the transmission of water. This section does not apply to the agent or employee for that purpose, of the owner or operator of the appliances referred to in this section, and does not apply to anything done by or under authority of any regularly constituted fire department.

**HISTORY: GC § 12512-1; 108 v PtI, 187; Bureau of Code Revision. 10-1-53.**

## § 4933.23 Interfering with pipes and meters.

No person shall willfully or maliciously injure or destroy, or intentionally permit to be injured or destroyed, cut, break, adjust, or interfere with any pipe, valve, regulator, gauge, gate, stopcock, trap, meter, or other regulating or measuring device or appliance used in the construction or operation of any plant furnishing or distributing hot water or steam for heating purposes. No person shall willfully or maliciously prevent any meter or other measuring device or appliance used in any such heating plant from duly registering the quantity of hot water or steam supplied. No person shall, without the consent of the owner of such heating plant, willfully or maliciously divert any hot water or steam from any pipe or other part of such heating plant or otherwise willfully or maliciously use or cause to be used, without the consent of the owner of such heating plant, hot water or steam supplied by any such heating plant.

**HISTORY: GC § 12512-2; 111 v 59; Bureau of Code Revision. Eff 10-1-53.**

## § 4933.24 Prohibition against interference with apparatus of sewage disposal companies.

No person shall maliciously open, close, adjust, or interfere with a valve, regulator, gauge, gate, disc, curb cock, stopcock, meter, or other regulator, operating or measuring device, or appliance in or attached to the tanks, conduits, pipes, mains, service pipes, house pipes, or other pipes or apparatus of a sewage disposal company, with intent to interfere with the flow of sewage, or to injure or destroy such property. No person shall tap, sever, open, or make unauthorized connections with a main or pipe used or intended for the transmission of sewage.

**HISTORY: 129 v 501. Eff 9-19-61.**

[PENALTIES]

## § 4933.99 Penalties.

(A) Whoever violates section 4933.16 of the Revised Code is guilty of a misdemeanor of the third degree.

(B) Whoever violates section 4933.20, 4933.22, 4933.24, or 4933.25 of the Revised Code is guilty of a misdemeanor of the fourth degree.

(C) Whoever violates section 4933.21 or 4933.23 of the Revised Code is guilty of a misdemeanor of the first degree.

(D) Whoever violates division (E) of section 4933.28 of the Revised Code is guilty of a misdemeanor of the fourth degree. Each day of a violation of that division constitutes a separate offense.

**HISTORY: Bureau of Code Revision, 10-1-53; 129 v 501 (Eff 9-19-61); 137 v H 271 (Eff 10-12-77); 137 v H 605 (Eff 8-18-78); 137 v H 1111 (Eff 1-12-79); 139 v S 199 (Eff 7-1-83); 140 v S 183 (Eff 9-26-84); 146 v S 2. Eff 7-1-96.**

The effective date is set by section 6 of SB 2.

# CHAPTER 4953: TRANSPORTATION TERMINAL COMPANIES



## § 4953.11 Detention of suspect by company officer or agent; arrest by peace officer.

(A) An officer or agent of a union terminal company who has probable cause to believe that a person is a pickpocket, is a thief, has violated the public peace, has violated any rule or regulation posted as provided by section 4953.07 of the Revised Code, or has committed any crime or misdemeanor on the depot grounds may detain the person in a reasonable manner and for a reasonable length of time within the property of the union terminal company, for the purpose of recovering any property involved in the violation, causing an arrest to be made by a peace officer, or obtaining a warrant of arrest.

(B) An officer or agent of a union terminal company acting under division (A) of this section shall not search the person detained, search or seize any property belonging to the person detained without the person's consent, or use undue restraint upon the person detained.

(C) Any peace officer, as defined in section 2935.01 of the Revised Code, may arrest without a warrant any person who the officer has probable cause to believe is a pickpocket, is a thief, has violated any rule or regulation provided by section 4953.07 of the Revised Code that also is a violation of law, or has committed any crime or misdemeanor on the depot grounds and shall make the arrest within a reasonable time after the commission of the act or violation that is the basis of the arrest.

**HISTORY: RS § 3450; S&S 122; 65 v 63, § 3; GC § 9166; Bureau of Code Revision, 10-1-53; 148 v S 107. Eff 3-23-2000.**

# CHAPTER 4955: TRACKS; CROSSINGS



### [HIGHWAY CROSSINGS]

## § 4955.201 Abandonment of track; restoration of roadway.

(A) If the interstate commerce commission approves the abandonment of a railroad track that crosses a road or highway at grade, the railroad that owned the track immediately after the approval of the abandonment shall remove the track at the crossing and fill the space previously occupied by the rails with the same material that comprises the road or highway at the crossing. Upon completion of the work, the surface of the crossing where the rails previously were located shall be the same height as the surface of the road or highway abutting the crossing. The restored portion of the road or highway shall meet the construction standards applicable to the road or highway of which the restored portion is a part.

(B) No railroad shall fail to remove from a crossing the rails that comprise a track whose abandonment has been approved or fail to fill the space previously occupied by the rails as required by division (A) of this section.

**HISTORY: 145 v H 154. Eff 6-30-93.**

# CHAPTER 4999: CRIMES RELATING TO RAILROADS



## § 4999.01 Drawing, driving, or moving vehicle on railroad track.

No person shall draw, drive, or cause to be moved any vehicle on or between the rails or tracks or on or along the graded roadway of a railroad without the knowledge and consent of the owner or controller of such railroad, unless compelled by necessity to do so. Whoever violates this section is guilty of a minor misdemeanor.

**HISTORY: RS § 6872; S&S 268; S&C 419; 46 v 26; 60 v 17; GC § 12542; Bureau of Code Revision, 10-1-53; 144 v H 667. Eff 3-15-93.**

## § 4999.02 Climbing upon railroad cars.

No person shall climb, jump, step, or stand upon, or cling or attach himself to, a locomotive, engine, or car upon the track of a railroad, unless in compliance with law or by permission under the rules of the corporation managing such railroad. Whoever violates this section is guilty of a minor misdemeanor.

**HISTORY: RS § 6982; 74 v 202, §§ 1, 2; GC § 12543; Bureau of Code Revision, 10-1-53; 144 v H 667. Eff 3-15-93.**

## § 4999.03 Riding or driving into enclosures of railroads.

No person shall, at a place other than a private crossing or for a purpose other than crossing a railroad, ride or drive a horse or other domestic animal into an enclosure of a railroad or knowingly permit such animal to go into or remain in such enclosure, or place feed, salt, or other thing within such enclosure to induce such animal to enter into it or upon the track of such railroad, or, while constructing a private crossing or crossing a railroad at a private crossing, permit a fence to remain down or open for a longer time than is necessary to construct or use such crossing. Whoever violates this section shall be fined not more than ten dollars or imprisoned for not less than ten nor more than thirty days.

Each ten hours such animal is knowingly permitted to remain in such enclosure or upon such track is an additional offense. Such animal is not exempt from execution for a fine or costs imposed under this section.

**HISTORY: RS § 6981; S&S 117; 65 v 194, §§ 1, 2; 72 v 32; GC §§ 12544, 12545; Bureau of Code Revision. Eff 10-1-53.**

## § 4999.04 Duties of engineer.

(A) No person in charge of a locomotive shall do the following:

(1) Fail to bring the locomotive to a full stop at least two hundred feet before arriving at a crossing with another track, or proceed through the crossing before signaled to do so or before the way is clear;

(2) When approaching a grade crossing, fail to sound the locomotive whistle at frequent intervals, beginning no less than thirteen hundred twenty feet from such crossing and continuing until the locomotive has passed the crossing.

(B) Whoever violates this section is guilty of a misdemeanor of the fourth degree. If violation of this section causes physical harm to any person, whoever violates this section is guilty of a misdemeanor of the third degree.

**HISTORY: 134 v H 511 (Eff 1-1-74); 137 v S 167. Eff 8-26-77.**

**Analogous to former RC § 4999.04 [RS § 6980; 69 v 49; 71 v 50; 85 v 112; GC §§ 12549, 12550; Bureau of Code Revision, 10-1-53], repealed 134 v H 511, § 2, eff 1-1-74.**

## § 4999.05 Flagmen on railroads.

No person or company owning, operating, or controlling a railroad shall employ as a flagman, hostler, or assistant hostler, a person who cannot read, write, and speak the English language. Whoever violates this section shall be fined not less than five hundred nor more than one thousand dollars. This section does not apply to flagmen at street or highway crossings.

**HISTORY: RS §§ 3365-17a, 3365-17b; 97 v 72, §§ 1, 2; GC § 12551; Bureau of Code Revision. Eff 10-1-53.**

## § 4999.06 Running passenger trains with less than full crew.

No superintendent, trainmaster, or other employee of a railroad shall send or cause to be sent outside of yard limits, a passenger train of not more than five cars, any one of which carries passengers, with a crew consisting of less than one engineer, one fireman, one conductor, and one brakeman. If four of said cars are day coaches carrying passengers, or if in a train of more than five cars, three or more cars are day coaches carrying passengers, or if in a train of more than six cars, four cars carrying passengers, or if in a train of more than seven cars, two or more cars are carrying passengers, of [or] if any train, six or more cars are carrying passengers, such crew shall consist of at least one additional brakeman, regularly employed as such. When such train consists of more than two cars, either of which carries passengers, no such superintendent, trainmaster, or other employee shall require a brakeman to perform the duties of baggage master or express agent. Whoever violates this section shall be fined not less than twenty-five dollars for each offense.

For the purpose of this section, a combination mail or baggage and passenger car is a day coach, but straight dining cars and private cars are not cars carrying passengers.

This section does not apply to trains picking up a car between terminals in this state, or to cars propelled by electricity.

Mayors and county court judges have jurisdiction under this section. The public utilities commission shall enforce this section.

**HISTORY: RS §§ 3365-33, 3365-34; 95 v 343; GC §§ 12553, 12555; 102 v 508; Bureau of Code Revision, 10-1-53; 132 v H 2 (Eff 2-14-67); 136 v H 205. Eff 1-1-76.**

## § 4999.10 Constructing bridges over tracks.

No person, railroad company, private corporation, county, municipal corporation, or township shall violate any law relating to the height of bridges, viaducts, overhead roadways, footbridges, wires, or other structures constructed over the tracks of a railroad. Whoever violates this section shall be fined not less than one hundred nor more than one thousand dollars. Each day such structure or wire is permitted to so remain constitutes a separate offense.

**HISTORY: RS § 3337-19; 91 v 365, § 2; GC § 12546; Bureau of Code Revision. Eff 10-1-53.**

## § 4999.11 Mail cranes; livestock chutes.

No person or company owning, operating, or controlling a railroad shall erect or permit to be erected, place, or maintain along said railroad, a mail crane or livestock chute, any portion of which approaches nearer than eighteen inches to the nearest point of contact with the cab of the widest locomotive used on such railroad.

Whoever violates this section shall be fined not less than five hundred nor more than one thousand dollars.

**HISTORY: RS §§ 3365-19a, 3365-19b; 97 v 274, 275, §§ 1, 2; GC § 12552; Bureau of Code Revision. Eff 10-1-53.**

## § 4999.13 Couplers and brakes on railroads.

No superintendent, conductor, or other officer or employee of a railroad company, shall refuse or neglect, upon receiving notice from the inspector appointed by the public utilities commission, of a defective coupler or brake, to have it repaired forthwith or, on receiving notice from such inspector condemning a car, tender, or engine, shall fail to put it out of service at the first freight division terminal. No superintendent, conductor, or other officer or employee shall violate any other law relating to automatic couplers and air brakes. Whoever violates this section shall be fined not less than twenty-five nor more than five hundred dollars. Such person is also personally liable for any injuries resulting to any employee from such violation.

**HISTORY: RS § 3365-23i; 95 v 660; GC § 12562; Bureau of Code Revision. Eff 10-1-53.**

## § 4999.16 Examination of employee for color blindness.

No railroad company shall contract to employ a person in a position which requires such person to distinguish form or color signals, unless within two years preceding such date he has been examined for color blindness, in the distinct colors in actual use by such company by a competent person employed and paid by such company, and has received a certificate that he is not disqualified for such position by color blindness in the colors used by the company. No such company shall fail to require such person to be re-examined at least once each two years at the expense of such company. This section does not prevent a railroad company from continuing in its employment an employee having defective sight when such defective sight can be fully remedied by the use of glasses or by other means satisfactory to the person making such examination. Whoever violates this section shall be fined one hundred dollars.

**HISTORY: RS §§ 3365-9, 3365-10; 82 v 65; 85 v 58, §§ 1, 2; GC § 12548; Bureau of Code Revision. Eff 10-1-53.**

## § 4999.17 Discipline or discharge of employee without hearing.

No railroad company, or its superintendent, or manager, employing any special agent, detective, or person commonly known as "spotter" for the purpose of investigating, obtaining, and reporting to the employer, its agent, superintendent, or manager, information concerning its employees, shall discipline or discharge any employee in its service, where such act of discipline or the discharge is based upon a report by such special agent, detective, or spotter, which report involves a question of integrity, honesty, or a breach of rules of the employer, unless such employer, its agent, superintendent, or manager, before disciplining or discharging such employee, grants such employee a fair opportunity to be heard in defense or explanation of the complaint against him, at which hearing said employer shall state specific charges on which said act or discharge is based and at which the accused employee has the right to furnish testimony in his defense.

Whoever violates this section shall be fined not less than fifty nor more than three hundred dollars or imprisoned not more than one year, or both. Such imprisonment, when imposed, shall be imposed upon the officers or agents of such company committing such offense.

**HISTORY: GC §§ 12956-1, 12956-2; 107 v 603, §§ 1, 2; Bureau of Code Revision. Eff 10-1-53.**

## § 4999.18 Demanding compensation when telegraph or telephone wires not working.

No officer, agent, or other person acting for or in behalf of a railroad company operating ten or more miles of its railroad for the carrying or transporting of passengers or freight over its railroad within this state which fails to erect and maintain telegraph or telephone wires in complete working order for use and operation along its railroad, with an office and proper means of communication by such wires at each of its principal railway stations, shall order, direct, advise, ask, demand, or receive compensation for transportation of passengers or freight. Whoever violates this section be fined not less than one hundred nor more than five hundred dollars or imprisoned for not less than thirty nor more than ninety days, or both.

**HISTORY: RS § 3354-6; 93 v 89, § 2; GC § 12547; Bureau of Code Revision. Eff 10-1-53.**

## § 4999.19 Diverting freight.

No agent of a railroad company shall knowingly divert or permit freight under his control to be diverted from the railroads over which it is ordered to be conveyed by the shipper of such freight. Whoever violates this section shall be fined not more than one hundred dollars or imprisoned not more than thirty days, or both.

**HISTORY: RS § 3370; S&S 117; 58 v 74, § 3; GC § 13420; Bureau of Code Revision. Eff 10-1-53.**

## § 4999.20 Maintenance of employee rights; penalty.

No railroad employee who has a seniority roster date on the effective date of the repeal of sections 4999.07 and 4999.08 of the Revised Code shall be removed from his employment or have his seniority rights or vacation or other fringe benefits reduced by reason of such repeal.

Any carrier which violates this section shall be fined not less than one hundred nor more than five thousand dollars. The public utilities commission shall enforce this section and prosecute any violations thereof.

**HISTORY: 134 v H 464. Eff 6-15-72.**

# TITLE 51: PUBLIC WELFARE

## CHAPTER 5101: DEPARTMENT OF JOB AND FAMILY SERVICES — GENERAL PROVISIONS



[ADULT PROTECTIVE SERVICES]

### § 5101.61 Duty to report abuse, neglect or exploitation of adult.

(A) As used in this section:

(1) "Senior service provider" means any person who provides care or services to a person who is an adult as defined in division (B) of section 5101.60 of the Revised Code.

(2) "Ambulatory health facility" means a nonprofit, public or proprietary freestanding organization or a unit of such an agency or organization that:

(a) Provides preventive, diagnostic, therapeutic, rehabilitative, or palliative items or services furnished to an outpatient or ambulatory patient, by or under the direction of a physician or dentist in a facility which is not a part of a hospital, but which is organized and operated to provide medical care to outpatients;

(b) Has health and medical care policies which are developed with the advice of, and with the provision of review of such policies, an advisory committee of professional personnel, including one or more physicians, one or more dentists, if dental care is provided, and one or more registered nurses;

(c) Has a medical director, a dental director, if dental care is provided, and a nursing director responsible for the execution of such policies, and has physicians, dentists, nursing, and ancillary staff appropriate to the scope of services provided;

(d) Requires that the health care and medical care of every patient be under the supervision of a physician, provides for medical care in a case of emergency, has in effect a written agreement with one or more hospitals and other centers or clinics, and has an established patient referral system to other resources, and a utilization review plan and program;

(e) Maintains clinical records on all patients;

(f) Provides nursing services and other therapeutic services in accordance with programs and policies, with such services supervised by a registered professional nurse, and has a registered professional nurse on duty at all times of clinical operations;

(g) Provides approved methods and procedures for the dispensing and administration of drugs and biologicals;

(h) Has established an accounting and record keeping system to determine reasonable and allowable costs;

(i) "Ambulatory health facilities" also includes an alcoholism treatment facility approved by the joint commission on accreditation of healthcare organizations as an alcoholism treatment facility or certified by the department of alcohol and drug addiction services, and such facility shall comply with other provisions of this division not inconsistent with such accreditation or certification.

(3) "Community mental health facility" means a facility which provides community mental health services and is included in the comprehensive mental health plan for the alcohol, drug addiction, and mental health service district in which it is located.

(4) "Community mental health service" means services, other than inpatient services, provided by a community mental health facility.

(5) "Home health agency" means an institution or a distinct part of an institution operated in this state which:

(a) Is primarily engaged in providing home health services;

(b) Has home health policies which are established by a group of professional personnel, including one or more duly licensed doctors of medicine or osteopathy and one or more registered professional nurses, to govern the home health services it provides and which includes a requirement that every patient must be under the care of a duly licensed doctor of medicine or osteopathy;

(c) Is under the supervision of a duly licensed doctor of medicine or doctor of osteopathy or a registered professional nurse who is responsible for the execution of such home health policies;

(d) Maintains comprehensive records on all patients;

(e) Is operated by the state, a political subdivision, or an agency of either, or is operated not for profit in this state and is licensed or registered, if required, pursuant to law by the appropriate department of the state, county, or municipality in which it furnishes services; or is operated for profit in this state, meets all the requirements specified in divisions (A)(5)(a) to (d) of this section, and is certified under Title XVIII of the "Social Security Act," 49 Stat. 620 (1935), 42 U.S.C. 301, as amended.

(6) "Home health service" means the following items and services, provided, except as provided in division (A)(6)(g) of this section, on a visiting basis in a place of residence used as the patient's home:

(a) Nursing care provided by or under the supervision of a registered professional nurse;

(b) Physical, occupational, or speech therapy ordered by the patient's attending physician;

(c) Medical social services performed by or under the supervision of a qualified medical or psychiatric social worker and under the direction of the patient's attending physician;

(d) Personal health care of the patient performed by aides in accordance with the orders of a doctor of medicine or osteopathy and under the supervision of a registered professional nurse;

(e) Medical supplies and the use of medical appliances;

(f) Medical services of interns and residents-in-training under an approved teaching program of a nonprofit hospital and under the direction and supervision of the patient's attending physician;

(g) Any of the foregoing items and services which:

(i) Are provided on an outpatient basis under arrangements made by the home health agency at a hospital or skilled nursing facility;

(ii) Involve the use of equipment of such a nature that the items and services cannot readily be made available to the patient in the patient's place of residence, or which are furnished at the hospital or skilled nursing facility while the patient is there to receive any item or service involving the use of such equipment.

Any attorney, physician, osteopath, podiatrist, chiropractor, dentist, psychologist, any employee of a hospital as defined in section 3701.01 of the Revised Code, any nurse licensed under Chapter 4723. of the Revised Code, any employee of an ambulatory health facility, any employee of a home health agency, any employee of an adult care facility as defined in section 5119.70 of the Revised Code, any employee of a nursing home, residential care facility, or home for the aging, as defined in section 3721.01 of the Revised Code, any senior service provider, any peace officer, coroner, clergyman, any employee of a community mental health facility, and any person engaged in social work or counseling having reasonable cause to believe that an adult is being abused, neglected, or exploited, or is in a condition which is the result of abuse, neglect, or exploitation shall immediately report such belief to the county department of job and family services. This section does not apply to employees of any hospital or public hospital as defined in section 5122.01 of the Revised Code.

(B) Any person having reasonable cause to believe that an adult has suffered abuse, neglect, or exploitation may report, or cause reports to be made of such belief to the department.

(C) The reports made under this section shall be made orally or in writing except that oral reports shall be followed by a written report if a written report is requested by the department. Written reports shall include:

(1) The name, address, and approximate age of the adult who is the subject of the report;

(2) The name and address of the individual responsible for the adult's care, if any individual is, and if the individual is known;

(3) The nature and extent of the alleged abuse, neglect, or exploitation of the adult;

(4) The basis of the reporter's belief that the adult has been abused, neglected, or exploited.

(D) Any person with reasonable cause to believe that an adult is suffering abuse, neglect, or exploitation who makes a report pursuant to this section or who testifies in any administrative or judicial proceeding arising from such a report, or any employee of the state or any of its subdivisions who is discharging responsibilities under section 5101.62 of the Revised Code shall be immune from civil or criminal liability on account of such investigation, report, or testimony, except liability for perjury, unless the person has acted in bad faith or with malicious purpose.

(E) No employer or any other person with the authority to do so shall discharge, demote, transfer, prepare a negative work performance evaluation, or reduce benefits, pay, or work privileges, or take any other action detrimental to an employee or in any way retaliate against an employee as a result of the employee's having filed a report under this section.

(F) Neither the written or oral report provided for in this section nor the investigatory report provided for in section 5101.62 of the Revised Code shall be considered a public record as defined in section 149.43 of the Revised Code. Information contained in the report shall upon request be made available to the adult who is the subject of the report, to agencies authorized by the department to receive information contained in the report, and to legal counsel for the adult.

**HISTORY: 139 v H 694 (Eff 11-15-81); 141 v H 66 (Eff 3-6-86); 142 v S 124 (Eff 10-1-87); 143 v S 2 (Eff 11-1-89); 143 v H 253 (Eff 11-15-90); 143 v H 317 (Eff 10-10-89); 146 v H 117 (Eff 9-29-95); 148 v H 471. Eff 7-1-2000; 153 v H 1, § 101.01, eff. 10-16-09; 2011 HB 153, § 101.01, eff. July 1, 2011.**

The effective date is set by § 812.10 of 153 v H 1.
The effective date is set by section 12(A) of HB 471.

## § 5101.99 Penalties.

(A) Whoever violates division (A) or (B) of section 5101.61 of the Revised Code shall be fined not more than five hundred dollars.

(B) Whoever violates division (A) of section 5101.27 of the Revised Code is guilty of a misdemeanor of the first degree.

(C) Whoever violates section 5101.133 [5101.13.3] of the Revised Code is guilty of a misdemeanor of the fourth degree.

**HISTORY: 139 v S 530 (Eff 1-1-83); 140 v H 37 (Eff 6-22-84); 142 v H 231 (Eff 10-5-87); 144 v H 298 (Eff 7-26-91); 146 v H 249 (Eff 7-17-95); 146 v H 167 (Eff 11-15-95); 147 v H 408 (Eff 10-1-97); 147 v H 352 (Eff 1-1-98); 148 v S 180. Eff 3-22-2001; 151 v S 238, § 1, eff. 9-21-06.**

# CHAPTER 5103: PLACEMENT OF CHILDREN



## § 5103.0318 Application of zoning laws to foster homes.

Any certified foster home shall be considered to be a residential use of property for purposes of municipal, county, and township zoning and shall be a permitted use in all zoning districts in which residential uses are permitted. No municipal, county, or township zoning regulation shall require a conditional permit or any other special exception certification for any certified foster home.

**HISTORY: RC § 2151.41.8, 142 v S 89 (Eff 1-1-89); 145 v H 152 (Eff 7-1-93); 148 v H 448 (Eff 10-5-2000); RC § 5103.03.18, 148 v H 332. Eff 1-1-2001.**

The effective date is set by section 5 of HB 332.

**Comment, Legislative Service Commission**

* * * Section 2151.418 (5103.0318) is amended and renumbered by this act [Sub. H.B. 448] and also amended and renumbered as 5103.0318 by Sub. H.B. 332 (effective January 1, 2001) of the 123rd General Assembly. * * * Comparison of these amendments in pursuance of section 1.52 of the Revised Code discloses that they are not irreconcilable so that they are required by that section to be harmonized to give effect to each amendment.

# CHAPTER 5104: CHILD CARE



## § 5104.012 Criminal records check and fingerprinting of prospective employees responsible for child; employment of certain offenders prohibited.

(A)(1) At the times specified in this division, the administrator of a child day-care center or a type A family day-care home shall request the superintendent of the bureau of criminal identification and investigation to conduct a criminal records check with respect to any applicant who has applied to the center or type A home for employment as a person responsible for the care, custody, or control of a child.

The administrator shall request a criminal records check pursuant to this division at the time of the applicant's initial application for employment and every four years thereafter. When the administrator requests pursuant to this division a criminal records check for an applicant at the time of the applicant's initial application for employment, the administrator shall request that the superintendent obtain information from the federal bureau of investigation as a part of the criminal records check for the applicant, including fingerprint - based checks of national crime information databases as described in 42 U.S.C. 671, for the person subject to the criminal records check. In all other cases in which the administrator requests a criminal records check for an applicant pursuant to this division, the administrator may request that the superintendent include information from the federal bureau of investigation in the criminal records check, including fingerprint - based checks of national crime information databases as described in 42 U.S.C. 671.

(2) A person required by division (A)(1) of this section to request a criminal records check shall provide to each applicant a copy of the form prescribed pursuant to division (C)(1) of section 109.572 of the Revised Code, provide to each applicant a standard impression sheet to obtain fingerprint impressions prescribed pursuant to division (C)(2) of section 109.572 of the Revised Code, obtain the completed form and impression sheet from each applicant, and forward the completed form and impression sheet to the superintendent of the bureau of criminal identification and investigation at the time the person requests a criminal records check pursuant to division (A)(1) of this section. On and after August 14, 2008, the administrator of a child day-care center or a type A family day-care home shall review the results of the criminal records check before the applicant has sole responsibility for the care, custody, or control of any child.

(3) An applicant who receives pursuant to division (A)(2) of this section a copy of the form prescribed pursuant to division (C)(1) of section 109.572 of the Revised Code and a copy of an impression sheet prescribed pursuant to division (C)(2) of that section and who is requested to complete the form and provide a set of fingerprint impressions shall complete the form or provide all the information necessary to complete the form and shall provide the impression sheet with the impressions of the applicant's fingerprints. If an applicant, upon request, fails to provide the information necessary to complete the form or fails to provide impressions of the applicant's fingerprints, the center or type A home shall not employ that applicant for any position for which a criminal records check is required by division (A)(1) of this section.

(B)(1) Except as provided in rules adopted under division (E) of this section, no child day-care center or type A family day-care home shall employ or contract with another entity for the services of a person as a person responsible for the care, custody, or control of a child if the person previously has been convicted of or pleaded guilty to any of the violations described in division (A)(9) of section 109.572 of the Revised Code.

(2) A child day-care center or type A family day-care home may employ an applicant conditionally until the criminal records check required by this section is completed and the center or home receives the results of the criminal records check. If the results of the criminal records check indicate that, pursuant to division (B)(1) of this section, the applicant does not qualify for employment, the center or home shall release the applicant from employment.

(C)(1) Each child day-care center and type A family day-care home shall pay to the bureau of criminal identification and investigation the fee prescribed pursuant to division (C)(3) of section 109.572 of the Revised Code for each criminal records check conducted in accordance with that section upon the request pursuant to division (A)(1) of this section of the administrator or provider of the center or home.

(2) A child day-care center and type A family day-care home may charge an applicant a fee for the costs it incurs in obtaining a criminal records check under this section. A fee charged under this division shall not exceed the amount of fees the center or home pays under division (C)(1) of this section. If a fee is charged under this division, the center or home shall notify the applicant at the time of the applicant's initial application for employment of the amount of the fee and that, unless the fee is paid, the center or type A home will not consider the applicant for employment.

(D) The report of any criminal records check conducted by the bureau of criminal identification and investigation in accordance with section 109.572 of the Revised Code and pursuant to a request under division (A)(1) of this section is not a public record for the purposes of section 149.43 of the Revised Code and shall not be made available to any person other than the applicant who is the subject of the criminal records check or the applicant's representative; the center or type A home requesting the criminal records check or its representative; the department of job and family services or a county department of job and family services; and any court, hearing officer, or other necessary individual involved in a case dealing with the denial of employment to the applicant.

(E) The director of job and family services shall adopt rules pursuant to Chapter 119. of the Revised Code to implement this section, including rules specifying circumstances under which a center or home may hire a person who has been convicted of an offense listed in division (B)(1) of this section but who meets standards in regard to rehabilitation set by the department.

(F) Any person required by division (A)(1) of this section to request a criminal records check shall inform each person, at the time of the person's initial application for employment, that the person is required to provide a set of impressions of the person's fingerprints and that a criminal records check is required to be conducted and satisfactorily completed in accordance with section 109.572 of the Revised Code if the person comes under final consideration for appointment or employment as a precondition to employment for that position.

(G) As used in this section:

(1) "Applicant" means a person who is under final consideration for appointment to or employment in a position with a child day-care center or a type A family day-care home as a person responsible for the care, custody, or control of a child; an in-home aide certified pursuant to section 5104.12 of the Revised Code; or any person who would serve in any position with a child day-care center or a type A family day-care home as a person responsible for the care, custody, or control of a child pursuant to a contract with another entity.

(2) "Criminal records check" has the same meaning as in section 109.572 of the Revised Code.

**HISTORY: 145 v S 38 (Eff 10-29-93); 145 v H 694 (Eff 11-11-94); 146 v S 2 (Eff 7-1-96); 146 v S 269 (Eff 7-1-96); 146 v H 445 (Eff 9-3-96); 148 v H 471. Eff 7-1-2000; 152 v S 163, § 1, eff. 8-14-08; 2011 HB 153, § 101.01, eff. Sept. 29, 2011.**

The effective date is set by section 12(A) of HB 471.

## § 5104.013 Criminal records checks and fingerprinting; licensing or certification of certain offenders prohibited.

(A)(1) At the times specified in division (A)(3) of this section, the director of job and family services, as part of the process of licensure of child day-care centers and type A family day-care homes, shall request the superintendent of the bureau of criminal identification and investigation to conduct a criminal records check with respect to the following persons:

(a) Any owner, licensee, or administrator of a child day-care center;

(b) Any owner, licensee, or administrator of a type A family day-care home and any person eighteen years of age or older who resides in a type A family day-care home.

(2) At the times specified in division (A)(3) of this section, the director of a county department of job and family services, as part of the process of certification of type B family day-care homes, shall request the superintendent of the bureau of criminal identification and investigation to conduct a criminal records check with respect to any authorized provider of a certified type B family day-care home and any person eighteen years of age or older who resides in a certified type B family day-care home.

(3) The director of job and family services shall request a criminal records check pursuant to division (A)(1) of this section at the time of the initial application for licensure and every four years thereafter. The director of a county department of job and family services shall request a criminal records check pursuant to division (A)(2) of this section at the time of the initial application for certification and every four years thereafter at the time of a certification renewal. When the director of job and family services or the director of a county department of job and family services requests pursuant to division (A)(1) or (2) of this section a criminal records check for a person at the time of the person's initial application for licensure or certification, the director shall request that the superintendent of the bureau of criminal identification and investigation obtain information from the federal bureau of investigation as a part of the criminal records check for the person, including fingerprint — based checks of national crime information databases as described in 42 U.S.C. 671 for the person subject to the criminal records check. In all other cases in which the director of job and family services or the director of a county department of job and family services requests a criminal records check for an applicant pursuant to division (A)(1) or (2) of this section, the director may request that the superintendent include information from the federal bureau of investigation in the criminal records check, including fingerprint — based checks of national crime information databases as described in 42 U.S.C. 671.

(4) The director of job and family services shall review the results of a criminal records check subsequent to a request made pursuant to divisions (A)(1) and (3) of this section prior to approval of a license. The director of a county department of job and family services shall review the results of a criminal records check subsequent to a request made pursuant to divisions (A)(2) and (3) of this section prior to approval of certification.

(B) The director of job and family services or the director of a county department of job and family services shall provide to each person for whom a criminal records check is required under this section a copy of the form prescribed pursuant to division (C)(1) of section 109.572 of the Revised Code and a standard impression sheet to obtain fingerprint impressions prescribed pursuant to division (C)(2) of that section, obtain the completed form and impression sheet from that person, and forward the completed form and impression sheet to the superintendent of the bureau of criminal identification and investigation.

(C) A person who receives pursuant to division (B) of this section a copy of the form and standard impression sheet described in that division and who is requested to complete the form and provide a set of fingerprint impressions shall complete the form or provide all the information necessary to complete the form and shall provide the impression sheet with the impressions of the person's fingerprints. If the person, upon request, fails to provide the information necessary to complete the form or fails to provide impressions of the person's fingerprints, the director may consider the failure as a reason to deny licensure or certification.

(D) Except as provided in rules adopted under division (G) of this section, the director of job and family services shall not grant a license to a child day-care center or type A family day-care home and a county director of job and family services shall not certify a type B family day-care home if a person for whom a criminal records check was required in connection with the center or home previously has been convicted of or pleaded guilty to any of the violations described in division (A)(9) of section 109.572 of the Revised Code.

(E) Each child day-care center, type A family day-care home, and type B family day-care home shall pay to the bureau of criminal identification and investigation the fee prescribed pursuant to division (C)(3) of section 109.572 of the Revised Code for each criminal records check conducted in accordance with that section upon a request made pursuant to division (A) of this section.

(F) The report of any criminal records check conducted by the bureau of criminal identification and investigation in accordance with section 109.572 of the Revised Code and pursuant to a request made under division (A) of this section is not a public record for the purposes of section 149.43 of the Revised Code and shall not be made available to any person other than the person who is the subject of the criminal records check or the person's representative, the director of job and family services, the director of a county department of job and family services, the center, type A home, or type B home involved, and any court, hearing officer, or other necessary individual involved in a case dealing with a denial of licensure or certification related to the criminal records check.

(G) The director of job and family services shall adopt rules pursuant to Chapter 119. of the Revised Code to implement this section, including rules specifying exceptions to the prohibition in division (D) of this section for persons who have been convicted of an offense listed in that division but who meet standards in regard to rehabilitation set by the department.

(H) As used in this section, "criminal records check" has the same meaning as in section 109.572 of the Revised Code.

**HISTORY: 145 v S 38 (Eff 10-29-93); 145 v H 694 (Eff 11-11-94); 146 v S 2 (Eff 7-1-96); 146 v S 269 (Eff 7-1-96); 146 v H 445 (Eff 9-3-96); 148 v H 471. Eff 7-1-2000; 150 v H 11, § 1, eff. 5-18-05; 152 v S 163, § 1, eff. 8-14-08; 2011 HB 153, § 101.01, eff. Sept. 29, 2011.**

The effective date is set by section 12(A) of HB 471.

## [TYPE B HOMES]

## § 5104.09 Certain offenders disqualified from day-care activities; statements of denial; discrimination in enrollment prohibited.

(A)(1) Except as provided in rules adopted pursuant to division (D) of this section, no individual who has been convicted of or pleaded guilty to a violation described in division (A)(9) of section 109.572 of the Revised Code, a violation of section 2905.11, 2909.02, 2909.03, 2909.04, 2909.05, 2917.01, 2917.02, 2917.03, 2917.31, 2921.03, 2921.34, or 2921.35 of the Revised Code or a violation of an existing or former law or ordinance of any municipal corporation, this state, any other state, or the United States that is substantially equivalent to any of those violations, or two violations of section 4511.19 of the Revised Code during operation of the center or home shall be certified as an in-home aide or be employed in any capacity in or own or operate a child day-care center, type A family day-care home, type B family day-care home, or certified type B family day-care home.

(2) Each employee of a child day-care center and type A home and every person eighteen years of age or older residing in a type A home shall sign a statement on forms prescribed by the director of job and family services attesting to the fact that the employee or resident person has not been convicted of or pleaded guilty to any offense set forth in division (A)(1) of this section and that no child has been removed from the employee's or resident person's home pursuant to section 2151.353 [2151.35.3] of the Revised Code. Each licensee of a type A home shall sign a statement on a form prescribed by the director attesting to the fact that no person who resides at the type A home and who is under the age of eighteen has been adjudicated a delinquent child for committing a violation of any section listed in division (A)(1) of this section. The statements shall be kept on file at the center or type A home.

(3) Each in-home aide and every person eighteen years of age or older residing in a certified type B home shall sign a statement on forms prescribed by the director of job and family services attesting that the aide or resident person has not been convicted of or pleaded guilty to any offense set forth in division (A)(1) of this section and that no child has been removed from the aide's or resident person's home pursuant to section 2151.353 [2151.35.3] of the Revised Code. Each authorized provider shall sign a statement on forms prescribed by the director attesting that the provider has not been convicted of or pleaded guilty to any offense set forth in division (A)(1) of this section and that no child has been removed from the provider's home pursuant to section 2151.353 [2151.35.3] of the Revised Code. Each authorized provider shall sign a statement on a form prescribed by the director attesting to the fact that no person who resides at the certified type B home and who is under the age of eighteen has been adjudicated a delinquent child for committing a violation of any section listed in division (A)(1) of this section. The statements shall be kept on file at the county department of job and family services.

(4) Each administrator and licensee of a center or type A home shall sign a statement on a form prescribed by the director of job and family services attesting that the administrator or licensee has not been convicted of or pleaded guilty to any offense set forth in division (A)(1) of this section and that no child has been removed from the administrator's or licensee's home pursuant to section 2151.353 [2151.35.3] of the Revised Code. The statement shall be kept on file at the center or type A home.

(B) No in-home aide, no administrator, licensee, authorized provider, or employee of a center, type A home, or certified type B home, and no person eighteen years of age or older residing in a type A home or certified type B home shall withhold information from, or falsify information on, any statement required pursuant to division (A)(2), (3), or (4) of this section.

(C) No administrator, licensee, or child-care staff member shall discriminate in the enrollment of children in a child day-care center upon the basis of race, color, religion, sex, or national origin.

(D) The director of job and family services shall adopt rules pursuant to Chapter 119. of the Revised Code to implement this section, including rules specifying exceptions to the prohibition in division (A) of this section for persons who have been convicted of an offense listed in that division but meet rehabilitation standards set by the department.

**HISTORY: 141 v H 435 (Eff 9-1-86); 145 v S 38 (Eff 10-29-93); 146 v S 2 (Eff 7-1-96); 146 v H 445 (Eff 9-3-96); 148 v H 471. Eff 7-1-2000; 150 v H 11, § 1, eff. 5-18-05; 152 v S 163, § 1, eff. 8-14-08.**

The effective date is set by section 12(A) of HB 471.

# CHAPTER 5111: MEDICAID PROGRAM



## § 5111.032 Criminal records check as condition of becoming or continuing to be a provider or affiliated person.

(A) As used in this section:

(1) "Criminal records check" has the same meaning as in section 109.572 [109.57.2] of the Revised Code.

(2) "Department" includes a designee of the department of job and family services.

(3) "Owner" means a person who has an ownership interest in a provider in an amount designated by the department of job and family services in rules adopted under this section.

(4) "Provider" means a person, institution, or entity that has a provider agreement with the department of job and family services pursuant to Title XIX of the "Social Security Act," 49 State. 620 (1965), 42 U.S.C. 1396, as amended.

(B)(1) Except as provided in division (B)(2) of this section, the department of job and family services may require that any provider, applicant to be a provider, employee or prospective employee of a provider, owner or prospective owner of a provider, officer or prospective officer of a provider, or board member or prospective board member of a provider submit to a criminal records check as a condition of obtaining a provider agreement, continuing to hold a provider agreement, being employed by a provider, having an ownership interest in a provider, or being an officer or board member of a provider. The department may designate the categories of persons who are subject to the criminal records check requirement. The department shall designate the times at which the criminal records checks must be conducted.

(2) The section does not apply to providers, applicants to be providers, employees of a provider, or prospective employees of a provider who are subject to criminal records checks under section 5111.033 [5111.03.3] or 5111.034 [5111.03.4] of the Revised Code.

(C)(1) The department shall inform each provider or applicant to be a provider whether the provider or applicant is subject to a criminal records check requirement under division (B) of this section. For providers, the information shall be given at times designated in rules adopted under this section. For applicants to be providers, the information shall be given at the time of initial application. When the information is given, the department shall specify which of the provider's or applicant's employees or prospective employees, owners or prospective owners, officers or prospective officers, or board members or prospective board members are subject to the criminal records check requirement.

(2) At times designated in rules adopted under this section, a provider that is subject to the criminal records check requirement shall inform each person specified by the department under division (C)(1) of this section that the person is required, as applicable, to submit to a criminal records check for final consideration for employment in a full-time, part-time, or temporary position; as a condition of continued employment; or as a condition of becoming or continuing to be an officer, board member or owner of a provider.

(D)(1) If a provider or applicant to be a provider is subject to a criminal records check under this section, the department shall require the conduct of a criminal records check by the superintendent of the bureau of criminal identification and investigation. If a provider or applicant to be a provider for whom a criminal records check is required does not present proof of having been a resident of this state for the five-year period immediately prior to the date the criminal records check is requested or provide evidence that within that five-year period the superintendent has requested information about the individual from the federal bureau of investigation in a criminal records check, the department shall require the provider or applicant to request that the superintendent obtain information from the federal bureau of investigation as part of the criminal records check of the provider or applicant. Even if a provider or applicant for whom a criminal records check request is required presents proof of having been a resident of this state for the five-year period, the department may require that the provider or applicant request that the superintendent obtain information from the federal bureau of investigation and include it in the criminal records check of the provider or applicant.

(2) A provider shall require the conduct of a criminal records check by the superintendent with respect to each of the persons specified by the department under division (C)(1) of this section. If the person for whom a criminal records check is required does not present proof of having been a resident of this state for the five-year period immediately prior to the date the criminal records check is requested or provide evidence that within that five-year period the superintendent of the bureau of criminal identification and investigation has requested information about the individual from the federal bureau of investigation in a criminal records check, the individual shall request that the superintendent obtain information from the federal bureau of investigation as part of the criminal records check of the individual. Even if an individual for whom a criminal records check request is required presents proof of having been a resident of this state for the five-year period, the department may require the provider to request that the superintendent obtain information from the federal bureau of investigation and include it in the criminal records check of the person.

(E)(1) Criminal records checks required under this section for providers or applicants to be providers shall be obtained as follows:

(a) The department shall provide each provider or applicant information about accessing and completing the form prescribed pursuant to division (C)(1) of section 109.572 [109.57.2] of the Revised Code and the standard fingerprint impression sheet prescribed pursuant to division (C)(2) of that section.

(b) The provider or applicant shall submit the required form and one complete set of fingerprint impressions directly to the superintendent for purposes of conducting the criminal records check using the applicable methods prescribed by division (C) of section 109.572 [109.57.2] of the Revised Code. The applicant or provider shall pay all fees associated with obtaining the criminal records check.

(c) The superintendent shall conduct the criminal records check in accordance with section 109.572 [109.57.2] of the Revised Code. The provider or applicant shall instruct the superintendent to submit the report of the criminal records check directly to the director of job and family services.

(2) Criminal records checks required under this section for persons specified by the department under division (C)(1) of this section shall be obtained as follows:

(a) The provider shall give to each person subject to criminal records check requirement information about accessing and completing the form prescribed pursuant to division (C)(1) of section 109.572 [109.57.2] of the Revised Code and the standard fingerprint impression sheet prescribed pursuant to division (C)(2) of that section.

(b) The person shall submit the required form and one complete set of fingerprint impressions directly to the superintendent for purposes of conducting the criminal records check using the applicable methods prescribed by division (C) of section 109.572 [109.57.2] of the Revised Code. The person shall pay all fees associated with obtaining the criminal records check.

(c) The superintendent shall conduct the criminal records check in accordance with section 109.572 [109.57.2] of the Revised Code. The person subject to the criminal records check shall instruct the superintendent to submit the report of the criminal records check directly to the provider. The department may require the provider to submit the report to the department.

(F) If a provider or applicant to be a provider is given the information specified in division (E)(1)(a) of this section but fails to obtain a criminal records check, the department shall, as applicable, terminate the provider agreement or deny the application to be a provider.

If a person is given the information specified in division (E)(2)(a) of this section but fails to obtain a criminal records check, the provider shall not, as applicable, permit the person to be an employee, owner, officer, or board member of the provider.

(G) Except as provided in rules adopted under division (J) of this section, the department shall terminate the provider agreement of a provider or the department shall not issue a provider agreement to an applicant if the provider or applicant is subject to a criminal records check under this section and the provider or applicant has been convicted of, has pleaded guilty to, or has been found eligible for intervention in lieu of conviction for any of the following, regardless of the date of the conviction, the date of entry of the guilty plea, or the date the applicant or provider was found eligible for intervention in lieu of conviction:

(1) A violation of section 959.13, 2903.01, 2903.02, 2903.03, 2903.04, 2903.041 [2903.04.1], 2903.11, 2903.12, 2903.13, 2903.15, 2903.16, 2903.21, 2903.211 [2903.21.1], 2903.22, 2903.34, 2905.01, 2905.02, 2905.05, 2905.11, 2905.12, 2907.02, 2907.03, 2907.04, 2907.05, 2907.06, 2907.07, 2907.08, 2907.09, 2907.21, 2907.22, 2907.23, 2907.24, 2907.25, 2907.31, 2907.32, 2907.321 [2907.32.1], 2907.322 [2907.32.2], 2907.323 [2907.32.3], 2909.02, 2909.03, 2909.04, 2909.05, 2909.22, 2909.23, 2909.24, 2911.01, 2911.02, 2911.11, 2911.12, 2911.13, 2913.02, 2913.03, 2913.04, 2913.05, 2913.11, 2913.21, 2913.31, 2913.32, 2913.40, 2913.41, 2913.42, 2913.43, 2913.44, 2913.441 [2913.44.1], 2913.45, 2913.46, 2913.47, 2913.48, 2913.49, 2913.51, 2917.01, 2917.02, 2917.03, 2917.11, 2917.31, 2919.12, 2919.22, 2919.23, 2919.24, 2919.25, 2921.03, 2921.11, 2921.13, 2921.34, 2921.35, 2921.36, 2923.01, 2923.02, 2923.03, 2923.12, 2923.13, 2923.161 [2923.16.1], 2923.32, 2925.02, 2925.03, 2925.04, 2925.05, 2925.06, 2925.11, 2925.13, 2925.14, 2925.22, 2925.23, 2927.12, or 3716.11 of the Revised Code, felonious sexual penetration in violation of former section 2907.12 of the Revised Code, a violation of section 2905.04 of the Revised Code as it existed prior to July 1, 1996, a violation of section 2919.23 of the Revised Code that would have been a violation of section 2905.04 of the Revised Code as it existed prior to July 1, 1996, had the violation been committed prior to that date;

(2) A violation of an existing or former municipal ordinance or law of this state, any other state, or the United States that is substantially equivalent to any of the offenses listed in division (G)(1) of this section.

(H)(1)(a) Except as provided in rules adopted under division (J) of this section and subject to division (H)(2) of this section, no provider shall permit a person to be an employee, owner, officer, or board member of the provider if the person is subject to a criminal records check under this section and the person has been convicted of, has pleaded guilty to, or has been found eligible for intervention in lieu of conviction for any of the offenses specified in division (G)(1) or (2) of this section.

(b) No provider shall employ a person who has been excluded from participating in the medicaid program, the medicare program operated pursuant to Title XVIII of the "Social Security Act," or any other federal health care program.

(2)(a) A provider may employ conditionally a person for whom a criminal records check is required under this section prior to obtaining the results of a criminal records check regarding the person, but only if the person submits a request for a criminal records check not later than five business days after the individual begins conditional employment.

(b) A provider that employs a person conditionally under authority of division (H)(2)(a) of this section shall terminate the person's employment if the results of the criminal records check request are not obtained within the period ending sixty days after the date the request is made. Regardless of when the results of the criminal records check are obtained, if the results indicate that the individual has been convicted of, has pleaded guilty to, or has been found eligible for intervention in lieu of conviction for any of the offenses specified in division (G)(1) or (2) of this section, the provider shall terminate the person's employment unless the provider chooses to employ the individual pursuant to division (J) of this section.

(I) The report of a criminal records check conducted pursuant to this section is not a public record for the purposes of section 149.43 of the Revised Code and shall not be made available to any person other than the following:

(1) The person who is the subject of the criminal records check or the person's representative;

(2) The director of job and family services and the staff of the department in the administration of the medicaid program;

(3) A court, hearing officer, or other necessary individual involved in a case dealing with the denial or termination of a provider agreement;

(4) A court, hearing officer, or other necessary individual involved in a case dealing with a person's denial of employment, termination of employment, or employment or unemployment benefits.

(J) The department may adopt rules in accordance with Chapter 119. of the Revised Code to implement this section. The rules may specify circumstances under which the department may continue a provider agreement or issue a provider agreement to an applicant when the provider or applicant has been convicted of, has pleaded guilty to, or has been found eligible for intervention in lieu of conviction for any of the offenses specified in division (G)(1) or (2) of this section. The rules may also specify circumstances under which a provider may permit a person to be an employee, owner, officer, or board member of the provider, when the person has been convicted of, has pleaded guilty to, or has been found eligible for intervention in lieu of conviction for any of the offenses specified in division (G)(1) or (2) of this section.

**HISTORY: 152 v H 119, § 101.01, eff. 9-29-07; 152 v H 562, § 101.01, eff. 9-23-08; 153 v H 1, § 101.01, eff. 10-16-09.**

The effective date is set by § 812.10 of 153 v H 1.
The effective date is set by § 812.10 of 152 v H 562.
The effective date is set by § 812.03 of 152 v H 119.

## § 5111.033 Criminal records check of applicant for employment in providing home and community-based waiver services to persons with disabilities; ineligibility due to certain convictions; application to current employees.

(A) As used in this section:

(1) "Applicant" means a person who is under final consideration for employment or, after September 26, 2003, an existing employee with a waiver agency in a full-time, part-time, or temporary position that involves providing home and community-based waiver services to a person with disabilities. "Applicant" also means an existing employee with a waiver agency in a full-time, part-time, or temporary position that involves providing home and community-based waiver services to a person with disabilities after September 26, 2003.

(2) "Criminal records check" has the same meaning as in section 109.572 [109.57.2] of the Revised Code.

(3) "Waiver agency" means a person or government entity that is not certified under the medicare program and is accredited by the community health accreditation program or the joint commission on accreditation of health care organizations or a company that provides home and community-based waiver services to persons with disabilities through department of job and family services administered home and community-based waiver programs.

(4) "Home and community-based waiver services" means services furnished under the provision of 42 C.F.R. 441, subpart G, that permit individuals to live in a home setting rather than a nursing facility or hospital. Home and community-based waiver services are approved by the centers for medicare and medicaid for specific populations and are not otherwise available under the medicaid state plan.

(B)(1) The chief administrator of a waiver agency shall require each applicant to request that the superintendent of the bureau of criminal identification and investigation conduct a criminal records check with respect to the applicant. If an applicant for whom a criminal records check request is required under this division does not present proof of having been a resident of this state for the five-year period immediately prior to the date the criminal records check is requested or provide evidence that within that five-year period the superintendent has requested information about the applicant from the federal bureau of investigation in a criminal records check, the chief administrator shall require the applicant to request that the superintendent obtain information from the federal bureau of investigation as part of the criminal records check of the applicant. Even if an applicant for whom a criminal records check request is required under this division presents proof of having been a resident of this state for the five-year period, the chief administrator may require the applicant to request that the superintendent include information from the federal bureau of investigation in the criminal records check.

(2) The chief administrator shall provide the following to each applicant for whom a criminal records check request is required under division (B)(1) of this section:

(a) Information about accessing, completing, and forwarding to the superintendent of the bureau of criminal identification and investigation the form prescribed pursuant to division (C)(1) of section 109.572 [109.57.2] of the Revised Code and the standard fingerprint impression sheet prescribed pursuant to division (C)(2) of that section;

(b) Written notification that the applicant is to instruct the superintendent to submit the completed report of the criminal records check directly to the chief administrator.

(3) An applicant given information and notification under divisions (B)(2)(a) and (b) of this section who fails to access, complete, and forward to the superintendent the form or the standard fingerprint impression sheet, or who fails to instruct the superintendent to submit the completed report of the criminal records check directly to the chief administrator, shall not be employed in any position in a waiver agency for which a criminal records check is required by this section.

(C)(1) Except as provided in rules adopted by the department of job and family services in accordance with division (F) of this section and subject to division (C)(2) of this section, no waiver agency shall employ a person in a position that involves providing home and community-based waiver services to persons with disabilities if the person has been convicted of, has pleaded guilty to, or has been found eligible for intervention in lieu of conviction for any of the following, regardless of the date of the conviction, the date of entry of the guilty plea, or the date the person was found eligible for intervention in lieu of conviction:

(a) A violation of section 959.13, 2903.01, 2903.02, 2903.03, 2903.04, 2903.041 [2903.04.1], 2903.11, 2903.12, 2903.13, 2903.15, 2903.16, 2903.21, 2903.211 [2903.21.1], 2903.22, 2903.34, 2905.01, 2905.02, 2905.05, 2905.11, 2905.12, 2907.02, 2907.03, 2907.04, 2907.05, 2907.06, 2907.07, 2907.08, 2907.09, 2907.21, 2907.22, 2907.23, 2907.24, 2907.25, 2907.31, 2907.32, 2907.321 [2907.32.1], 2907.322 [2907.32.2], 2907.323 [2907.32.3], 2909.02, 2909.03, 2909.04, 2909.05, 2909.22, 2909.23, 2909.24, 2911.01, 2911.02, 2911.11, 2911.12, 2911.13, 2913.02, 2913.03, 2913.04, 2913.05, 2913.11, 2913.21, 2913.31, 2913.32, 2913.40, 2913.41, 2913.42, 2913.43, 2913.44, 2913.441, 2913.45, 2913.46, 2913.47, 2913.48, 2913.49,

2913.51, 2917.01, 2917.02, 2917.03, 2917.11, 2917.31, 2919.12, 2919.22, 2919.23, 2919.24, 2919.25, 2921.03, 2921.11, 2921.13, 2921.34, 2921.35, 2921.36, 2923.01, 2923.02, 2923.03, 2923.12, 2923.13, 2923.161, 2923.32, 2925.02, 2925.03, 2925.04, 2925.05, 2925.06, 2925.11, 2925.13, 2925.14, 2925.22, 2925.23, 2927.12, or 3716.11 of the Revised Code, felonious sexual penetration in violation of former section 2907.12 of the Revised Code, a violation of section 2905.04 of the Revised Code as it existed prior to July 1, 1996, a violation of section 2919.23 of the Revised Code that would have been a violation of section 2905.04 of the Revised Code as it existed prior to July 1, 1996, had the violation been committed prior to that date;

(b) A violation of an existing or former municipal ordinance or law of this state, any other state, or the United States that is substantially equivalent to any of the offenses listed in division (C)(1)(a) of this section.

(2)(a) A waiver agency may employ conditionally an applicant for whom a criminal records check request is required under division (B) of this section prior to obtaining the results of a criminal records check regarding the individual, provided that the agency shall require the individual to request a criminal records check regarding the individual in accordance with division (B)(1) of this section not later than five business days after the individual begins conditional employment.

(b) A waiver agency that employs an individual conditionally under authority of division (C)(2)(a) of this section shall terminate the individual's employment if the results of the criminal records check request under division (B) of this section, other than the results of any request for information from the federal bureau of investigation, are not obtained within the period ending sixty days after the date the request is made. Regardless of when the results of the criminal records check are obtained, if the results indicate that the individual has been convicted of, has pleaded guilty to, or has been found eligible for intervention in lieu of conviction for any of the offenses listed or described in division (C)(1) of this section, the agency shall terminate the individual's employment unless the agency chooses to employ the individual pursuant to division (F) of this section.

(D)(1) The fee prescribed pursuant to division (C)(3) of section 109.572 [109.57.2] of the Revised Code for each criminal records check conducted pursuant to a request made under division (B) of this section shall be paid to the bureau of criminal identification and investigation by the applicant or the waiver agency.

(2) If a waiver agency pays the fee, it may charge the applicant a fee not exceeding the amount the agency pays under division (D)(1) of this section. An agency may collect a fee only if the agency notifies the person at the time of initial application for employment of the amount of the fee and that, unless the fee is paid, the person will not be considered for employment.

(E) The report of any criminal records check conducted pursuant to a request made under this section is not a public record for the purposes of section 149.43 of the Revised Code and shall not be made available to any person other than the following:

(1) The individual who is the subject of the criminal records check or the individual's representative;

(2) The chief administrator of the agency requesting the criminal records check or the administrator's representative;

(3) An administrator at the department;

(4) A court, hearing officer, or other necessary individual involved in a case dealing with a denial of employment of the applicant or dealing with employment or unemployment benefits of the applicant.

(F) The department shall adopt rules in accordance with Chapter 119. of the Revised Code to implement this section. The rules shall specify circumstances under which a waiver agency may employ a person who has been convicted of, has pleaded guilty to, or has been found eligible for intervention in lieu of conviction for an offense listed or described in division (C)(1) of this section.

(G) The chief administrator of a waiver agency shall inform each person, at the time of initial application for a position that involves providing home and community-based waiver services to a person with a disability, that the person is required to provide a set of fingerprint impressions and that a criminal records check is required to be conducted if the person comes under final consideration for employment.

(H)(1) A person who, on September 26, 2003, is an employee of a waiver agency in a full-time, part-time, or temporary position that involves providing home and community-based waiver services to a person with disabilities shall comply with this section within sixty days after September 26, 2003, unless division (H)(2) of this section applies.

(2) This section shall not apply to a person to whom all of the following apply:

(a) On September 26, 2003, the person is an employee of a waiver agency in a full-time, part-time, or temporary position that involves providing home and community-based waiver services to a person with disabilities.

(b) The person previously had been the subject of a criminal background check relating to that position;

(c) The person has been continuously employed in that position since that criminal background check had been conducted.

**HISTORY: 150 v H 95, § 1, eff. 9-26-03; 152 v H 119, § 101.01, eff. 9-29-07; 153 v H 1, § 101.01, eff. 10-16-09.**

The effective date is set by § 812.10 of 153 v H 1.
The effective date is set by § 812.03 of 152 v H 119.

**Publisher's Note:**

This section was amended and renumbered from RC § 5111.95 by 152 v H 119, effective September 29, 2007.

## § 5111.034 Criminal records check of independent provider; ineligibility due to certain convictions.

(A) As used in this section:

(1) "Anniversary date" means the later of the effective date of the provider agreement relating to the independent provider or sixty days after September 26, 2003.

(2) "Criminal records check" has the same meaning as in section 109.572 [109.57.2] of the Revised Code.

(3) "Department" includes a designee of the department of job and family services.

(4) "Independent provider" means a person who is submitting an application for a provider agreement or who has a provider agreement as an independent provider in a department of job and family services administered home and community-based services program providing home and community-based waiver services to consumers with disabilities.

(5) "Home and community-based waiver services" has the same meaning as in section 5111.033 [5111.03.3] of the Revised Code.

(B)(1) The department of job and family services shall inform each independent provider, at the time of initial application for a provider agreement that involves providing home and community-based waiver services to consumers with disabilities, that the independent provider is required to provide a set of fingerprint impressions and that a criminal records check is required to be conducted if the person is to become an independent provider in a department administered home and community-based waiver program.

(2) Beginning on September 26, 2003, the department shall inform each enrolled medicaid independent provider on or before time of the anniversary date of the provider agreement that involves providing home and community-based waiver services to consumers with disabilities that the independent provider is required to provide a set of fingerprint impressions and that a criminal records check is required to be conducted.

(C)(1) The department shall require the independent provider to complete a criminal records check prior to entering into a provider agreement with the independent provider and at least annually thereafter. If an independent provider for whom a criminal records check is required under this division does not present proof of having been a resident of this state for the five-year period immediately prior to the date the criminal records check is requested or provide evidence that within that five-year period the superintendent of the bureau of criminal identification and investigation has requested information about the independent provider from the federal bureau of investigation in a criminal records check, the department shall request that the independent provider obtain through the superintendent a criminal records request from the federal bureau of investigation as part of the criminal records check of the independent provider. Even if an independent provider for whom a criminal records check request is required under this division presents proof of having been a resident of this state for the five-year period, the department may request that the independent provider obtain information through the superintendent from the federal bureau of investigation in the criminal records check.

(2) The department shall provide the following to each independent provider for whom a criminal records check request is required under division (C)(1) of this section:

(a) Information about accessing, completing, and forwarding to the superintendent of the bureau of criminal identification and investigation the form prescribed pursuant to division (C)(1) of section 109.572 [109.57.2] of the Revised Code and the standard fingerprint impression sheet prescribed pursuant to division (C)(2) of that section;

(b) Written notification that the independent provider is to instruct the superintendent to submit the completed report of the criminal records check directly to the department.

(3) An independent provider given information and notification under divisions (C)(2)(a) and (b) of this section who fails to access, complete, and forward to the superintendent the form or the standard fingerprint impression sheet, or who fails to instruct the superintendent to submit the completed report of the criminal records check directly to the department, shall not be approved as an independent provider.

(D) Except as provided in rules adopted by the department in accordance with division (G) of this section, the department shall not issue a new provider agreement to, and shall terminate an existing provider agreement of, an independent provider if the person has been convicted of, has pleaded guilty to, or has been found eligible for intervention in lieu of conviction for any of the following, regardless of the date of the conviction, the date of entry of the guilty plea, or the date the person was found eligible for intervention in lieu of conviction:

(1) A violation of section 959.13, 2903.01, 2903.02, 2903.03, 2903.04, 2903.041 [2903.04.1], 2903.11, 2903.12, 2903.13, 2903.15, 2903.16, 2903.21, 2903.211 [2903.21.1], 2903.22, 2903.34, 2905.01, 2905.02, 2905.05, 2905.11, 2905.12, 2907.02, 2907.03, 2907.04, 2907.05, 2907.06, 2907.07, 2907.08, 2907.09, 2907.21, 2907.22, 2907.23, 2907.24, 2907.25, 2907.31, 2907.32, 2907.321 [2907.32.1], 2907.322 [2907.32.2], 2907.323 [2907.32.3], 2909.02, 2909.03, 2909.04, 2909.05, 2909.22, 2909.23, 2909.24, 2911.01, 2911.02, 2911.11, 2911.12, 2911.13, 2913.02, 2913.03, 2913.04, 2913.05, 2913.11, 2913.21, 2913.31, 2913.32, 2913.40, 2913.41, 2913.42, 2913.43, 2913.44, 2913.441 [2913.44.1], 2913.45, 2913.46, 2913.47, 2913.48, 2913.49, 2913.51, 2917.01, 2917.02, 2917.03, 2917.11, 2917.31, 2919.12, 2919.22, 2919.23, 2919.24, 2919.25, 2921.03, 2921.11, 2921.13, 2921.34, 2921.35, 2921.36, 2923.01, 2923.02, 2923.03, 2923.12, 2923.13, 2923.161 [2923.16.1], 2923.32, 2925.02, 2925.03, 2925.04, 2925.05, 2925.06, 2925.11, 2925.13, 2925.14, 2925.22, 2925.23, 2927.12, or 3716.11 of the Revised Code, felonious sexual penetration in violation of former section 2907.12 of the Revised Code, a violation of section 2905.04 of the Revised Code as it existed prior to July 1, 1996, a violation of section 2919.23 of the Revised Code that would have been a violation of section 2905.04 of the Revised Code as it existed prior to July 1, 1996, had the violation been committed prior to that date;

(2) A violation of an existing or former municipal ordinance or law of this state, any other state, or the United States that is substantially equivalent to any of the offenses listed in division (D)(1) of this section.

(E) Each independent provider shall pay to the bureau of criminal identification and investigation the fee prescribed pursuant to division (C)(3) of section 109.572 [109.57.2] of the Revised Code for each criminal records check conducted pursuant to a request made under division (C) of this section.

(F) The report of any criminal records check conducted by the bureau of criminal identification and investigation in accordance with section 109.572 [109.57.2] of the Revised Code and pursuant to a request made under division (C) of this section is not a public record for the purposes of section 149.43 of the Revised Code and shall not be made available to any person other than the following:

(1) The person who is the subject of the criminal records check or the person's representative;

(2) An administrator at the department or the administrator's representative;

(3) A court, hearing officer, or other necessary individual involved in a case dealing with a denial or termination of a provider agreement related to the criminal records check.

(G) The department shall adopt rules in accordance with Chapter 119. of the Revised Code to implement this section. The rules shall specify circumstances under which the department may either issue a provider agreement to an independent provider or allow an independent provider to maintain an existing provider agreement when the independent provider has been convicted of, has pleaded guilty to, or has been found eligible for intervention in lieu of conviction for an offense listed or described in division (D)(1) or (2) of this section.

**HISTORY: 150 v H 95, § 1, eff. 9-26-03; 152 v H 119, § 101.01, eff. 9-29-07; 153 v H 1, § 101.01, eff. 10-16-09.**

The effective date is set by § 812.10 of 153 v H 1.
The effective date is set by § 812.03 of 152 v H 119.
The effective date is set by section 179 of H.B. 95 (150 v —).

**Publisher's Note:**

This section was amended and renumbered from RC § 5111.96 by 152 v H 119, effective September 29, 2007.

[ASSISTED LIVING PROGRAM]

**§ 5111.95** Renumbered. Amended and renumbered RC § 5111.033 by 152 v H 119. Eff 9-29-07

The effective date is set by § 812.03 of 152 v H 119.

**§ 5111.96** Renumbered. Amended and renumbered RC § 5111.034 by 152 v H 119. Eff 9-29-07

The effective date is set by § 812.03 of 152 v H 119.

# CHAPTER 5119: DEPARTMENT OF MENTAL HEALTH

Section

[INTERSTATE COMPACT ON MENTAL HEALTH]



## [INTERSTATE COMPACT ON MENTAL HEALTH]

### § 5119.57 System for tracking and monitoring after release of insanity acquittees or defendants found incompetent.

No later than January 1, 1998, the department of mental health, in conjunction with boards of alcohol, drug addiction, and mental health services and community mental health boards, shall develop a coordinated system for tracking and monitoring persons found not guilty by reason of insanity and committed pursuant to section 2945.40 of the Revised Code who have been granted a conditional release and persons found incompetent to stand trial and committed pursuant to section 2945.39 of the Revised Code who have been granted a conditional release. The system shall do all of the following:

(A) Centralize responsibility for the tracking of those persons;

(B) Develop uniformity in monitoring those persons;

(C) Develop a mechanism to allow prompt rehospitalization, reinstitutionalization, or detention when a violation of the conditional release or decompensation occurs.

**HISTORY: 146 v S 285. Eff 7-1-97.**

**Not analogous to former RC § 5119.57 (125 v 859), repealed 184 v H 494, § 2, eff 7-12-72.**
The effective date is set by section 4 of SB 285.

### § 5119.85 Criminal records check for prospective employees providing direct care to older adult.

(A) As used in this section:

(1) "Adult resident" means an individual residing in an adult care facility licensed by the department of mental health.

(2) "Applicant" means a person who is under final consideration for employment with an adult care facility in a full-time, part-time, or temporary position that involves providing direct care to an adult resident. "Applicant" does not include a person who provides direct care as a volunteer without receiving or expecting to receive any form of remuneration other than reimbursement for actual expenses.

(3) "Criminal records check" has the same meaning as in section 109.572 of the Revised Code.

(B)(1) Except as provided in division (I) of this section, the chief administrator of an adult care facility shall request that the superintendent of the bureau of criminal identification and investigation conduct a criminal records check with respect to each applicant. If an applicant for whom a criminal records check request is required under this division does not present proof of having been a resident of this state for the five-year period immediately prior to the date the criminal records check is requested or provide evidence that within that five-year period the superintendent has requested information about the applicant from the federal bureau of investigation in a criminal records check, the chief administrator shall request that the superintendent obtain information from the federal bureau of investigation as part of the criminal records check of the applicant. Even if an applicant for whom a criminal records check request is required under this division presents proof of having been a resident of this state for the five-year period, the chief administrator may request that the superintendent include information from the federal bureau of investigation in the criminal records check.

(2) A person required by division (B)(1) of this section to request a criminal records check shall do both of the following:

(a) Provide to each applicant for whom a criminal records check request is required under that division a copy of the form prescribed pursuant to division (C)(1) of section 109.572 of the Revised Code and a standard fingerprint impression sheet prescribed pursuant to division (C)(2) of that section, and obtain the completed form and impression sheet from the applicant;

(b) Forward the completed form and impression sheet to the superintendent of the bureau of criminal identification and investigation.

(3) An applicant provided the form and fingerprint impression sheet under division (B)(2)(a) of this section

who fails to complete the form or provide fingerprint impressions shall not be employed in any position for which a criminal records check is required by this section.

(C)(1) Except as provided in rules adopted by the department of mental health in accordance with division (F) of this section and subject to division (C)(2) of this section, no adult care facility shall employ a person in a position that involves providing direct care to an adult resident if the person has been convicted of or pleaded guilty to any of the following:

(a) A violation of section 2903.01, 2903.02, 2903.03, 2903.04, 2903.11, 2903.12, 2903.13, 2903.16, 2903.21, 2903.34, 2905.01, 2905.02, 2905.11, 2905.12, 2907.02, 2907.03, 2907.05, 2907.06, 2907.07, 2907.08, 2907.09, 2907.12, 2907.25, 2907.31, 2907.32, 2907.321, 2907.322, 2907.323, 2911.01, 2911.02, 2911.11, 2911.12, 2911.13, 2913.02, 2913.03, 2913.04, 2913.11, 2913.21, 2913.31, 2913.40, 2913.43, 2913.47, 2913.51, 2919.25, 2921.36, 2923.12, 2923.13, 2923.161, 2925.02, 2925.03, 2925.11, 2925.13, 2925.22, 2925.23, or 3716.11 of the Revised Code.

(b) A violation of an existing or former law of this state, any other state, or the United States that is substantially equivalent to any of the offenses listed in division (C)(1)(a) of this section.

(2)(a) An adult care facility may employ conditionally an applicant for whom a criminal records check request is required under division (B) of this section prior to obtaining the results of a criminal records check regarding the individual, provided that the facility shall request a criminal records check regarding the individual in accordance with division (B)(1) of this section not later than five business days after the individual begins conditional employment. In the circumstances described in division (I)(2) of this section, an adult care facility may employ conditionally an applicant who has been referred to the adult care facility by an employment service that supplies full-time, part-time, or temporary staff for positions involving the direct care of adult residents and for whom, pursuant to that division, a criminal records check is not required under division (B) of this section.

(b) An adult care facility that employs an individual conditionally under authority of division (C)(2)(a) of this section shall terminate the individual's employment if the results of the criminal records check requested under division (B) of this section or described in division (I)(2) of this section, other than the results of any request for information from the federal bureau of investigation, are not obtained within the period ending thirty days after the date the request is made. Regardless of when the results of the criminal records check are obtained, if the results indicate that the individual has been convicted of or pleaded guilty to any of the offenses listed or described in division (C)(1) of this section, the facility shall terminate the individual's employment unless the facility chooses to employ the individual pursuant to division (F) of this section. Termination of employment under this division shall be considered just cause for discharge for purposes of division (D)(2) of section 4141.29 of the Revised Code if the individual makes any attempt to deceive the facility about the individual's criminal record.

(D)(1) Each adult care facility shall pay to the bureau of criminal identification and investigation the fee prescribed pursuant to division (C)(3) of section 109.572 of the Revised Code for each criminal records check conducted pursuant to a request made under division (B) of this section.

(2) An adult care facility may charge an applicant a fee not exceeding the amount the facility pays under division (D)(1) of this section. A facility may collect a fee only if it notifies the person at the time of initial application for employment of the amount of the fee and that, unless the fee is paid, the person will not be considered for employment.

(E) The report of any criminal records check conducted pursuant to a request made under this section is not a public record for the purposes of section 149.43 of the Revised Code and shall not be made available to any person other than the following:

(1) The individual who is the subject of the criminal records check or the individual's representative;

(2) The chief administrator of the facility requesting the criminal records check or the administrator's representative;

(3) The administrator of any other facility, agency, or program that provides direct care to adult residents that is owned or operated by the same entity that owns or operates the adult care facility;

(4) A court, hearing officer, or other necessary individual involved in a case dealing with a denial of employment of the applicant or dealing with employment or unemployment benefits of the applicant;

(5) Any person to whom the report is provided pursuant to, and in accordance with, division (I)(1) or (2) of this section.

(F) The department may adopt rules in accordance with Chapter 119. of the Revised Code to implement this section. The rules may specify circumstances under which an adult care facility may employ a person who has been convicted of or pleaded guilty to an offense listed or described in division (C)(1) of this section but meets personal character standards set by the council.

(G) The chief administrator of an adult care facility shall inform each individual, at the time of initial application for a position that involves providing direct care to an adult resident, that the individual is required to provide a set of fingerprint impressions and that a criminal records check is required to be conducted if the individual comes under final consideration for employment.

(H) In a tort or other civil action for damages that is brought as the result of an injury, death, or loss to person or property caused by an individual who an adult care facility employs in a position that involves providing direct care to adult residents, all of the following shall apply:

(1) If the facility employed the individual in good faith and reasonable reliance on the report of a criminal records check requested under this section, the facility shall not be found negligent solely because of its reliance on the report, even if the information in the report is determined later to have been incomplete or inaccurate;

(2) If the facility employed the individual in good faith on a conditional basis pursuant to division (C)(2) of this section, the facility shall not be found negligent solely because it employed the individual prior to receiving the report of a criminal records check requested under this section;

(3) If the facility in good faith employed the individual according to the personal character standards established in rules adopted under division (F) of this section, the facility shall not be found negligent solely because the individual prior to being employed had been convicted of or pleaded guilty to an offense listed or described in division (C)(1) of this section.

(I)(1) The chief administrator of an adult care facility is not required to request that the superintendent of the bureau of criminal identification and investigation conduct a criminal records check of an applicant if the applicant has been referred to the facility by an employment service that supplies full-time, part-time, or temporary staff for positions involving the direct care of adult residents and both of the following apply:

(a) The chief administrator receives from the employment service or the applicant a report of the results of a criminal records check regarding the applicant that has been conducted by the superintendent within the one-year period immediately preceding the applicant's referral;

(b) The report of the criminal records check demonstrates that the person has not been convicted of or pleaded guilty to an offense listed or described in division (C)(1) of this section, or the report demonstrates that the person has been convicted of or pleaded guilty to one or more of those offenses, but the adult care facility chooses to employ the individual pursuant to division (F) of this section.

(2) The chief administrator of an adult care facility is not required to request that the superintendent of the bureau of criminal identification and investigation conduct a criminal records check of an applicant and may employ the applicant conditionally as described in this division, if the applicant has been referred to the facility by an employment service that supplies full-time, part-time, or temporary staff for positions involving the direct care of adult residents and if the chief administrator receives from the employment service or the applicant a letter from the employment service that is on the letterhead of the employment service, dated, and signed by a supervisor or another designated official of the employment service and that states that the employment service has requested the superintendent to conduct a criminal records check regarding the applicant, that the requested criminal records check will include a determination of whether the applicant has been convicted of or pleaded guilty to any offense listed or described in division (C)(1) of this section, that, as of the date set forth on the letter, the employment service had not received the results of the criminal records check, and that, when the employment service receives the results of the criminal records check, it promptly will send a copy of the results to the adult care facility. If an adult care facility employs an applicant conditionally in accordance with this division, the employment service, upon its receipt of the results of the criminal records check, promptly shall send a copy of the results to the adult care facility, and division (C)(2)(b) of this section applies regarding the conditional employment.

**HISTORY: 146 v S 160 (Eff 1-27-97); 147 v S 96 (Eff 6-11-97); 147 v H 18. Eff 1-30-98; 150 v H 95, § 1, eff. 9-26-03; 2011 HB 153, § 101.01, eff. July 1, 2011.**

This section was formerly codified as RC § 3722.151.

A former RC § 5119.85 was amended and renumbered RC §§ 5123.55, 5123.56, 5123.57 in 138 v H 900, eff. July 1, 1980.

The effective date is set by section 179 of H.B. 95 (150 v —).

See provisions, § 8 of SB 96 (147 v —) following RC § 3701.88.1.

See provisions, § 3 of SB 160 (146 v —) following RC § 3701.88.1.

# CHAPTER 5120: DEPARTMENT OF REHABILITATION AND CORRECTION

## § 5120.01 Director of rehabilitation and correction.

The director of rehabilitation and correction is the executive head of the department of rehabilitation and correction. All duties conferred on the various divisions and institutions of the department by law or by order of the director shall be performed under the rules and regulations that the director prescribes and shall be under the director's control. Inmates committed to the department of rehabilitation and correction shall be under the legal custody of the director or the director's designee, and the director or the director's designee shall have power to control transfers of inmates between the several state institutions included under section 5120.05 of the Revised Code.

**HISTORY: 134 v H 494 (Eff 7-12-72); 149 v H 510. Eff 3-31-2003.**

## § 5120.011 Sanctions where inmate's action is found to be frivolous or malicious.

(A) As used in this section, "civil action or appeal against a government entity or employee," "inmate," "political subdivision," and "employee" have the same meanings as in section 2969.21 of the Revised Code.

(B) The director of rehabilitation and correction may adopt rules under section 5120.01 of the Revised Code to implement the procedures described in sections 2323.51, 2969.22, and 2969.23 of the Revised Code.

(C) The director of rehabilitation and correction shall adopt rules that provide that, if an inmate files a civil action or appeal against a government entity or employee or files a civil action against the state, a political subdivision, or an employee in a federal court and if the court in which the action or appeal is filed dismisses the action or appeal pursuant to section 2969.24 of the Revised Code or the federal court finds the action to be frivolous under 28 U.S.C. 1915(d), the inmate shall be subject to one or more of the following sanctions:

(1) Extra work duty, without compensation, for not more than sixty days;

(2) The loss of commissary privileges for not more than sixty days;

(3) The loss of sundry-package privileges for one time in any calendar year;

(4) The loss of television privileges for not more than sixty days;

(5) The loss of radio privileges for not more than sixty days;

(6) The loss of recreational activity privileges for not more than sixty days.

**HISTORY: 146 v H 455. Eff 10-17-96.**

## § 5120.02 Assistant director of the department; powers and duties.

The assistant director of the department of rehabilitation and correction is hereby excepted from section 121.05 of the Revised Code. The assistant director shall exercise the powers and perform the duties which the director of correction may order and shall act as director in the absence or disability of the director, or in case of a vacancy in the position of director.

**HISTORY: 134 v H 494. Eff 7-12-72.**

## § 5120.021 Application of provisions effective 7-1-96 and of prior provisions.

(A) The provisions of Chapter 5120. of the Revised Code, as they existed prior to July 1, 1996, and that address the duration or potential duration of incarceration or parole or other forms of supervised release, apply to all persons upon whom a court imposed a term of imprisonment prior to July 1, 1996, and all persons upon whom a court, on or after July 1, 1996, and in accordance with law existing prior to July 1, 1996, imposed a term of imprisonment for an offense that was committed prior to July 1, 1996.

(B) The provisions of Chapter 5120. of the Revised Code, as they exist on or after July 1, 1996, and that address the duration or potential duration of incarceration or supervised release, apply to all persons upon whom a court imposed a stated prison term for an offense committed on or after July 1, 1996.

(C) Nothing in this section limits or affects the applicability of any provision in Chapter 5120. of the Revised Code, as amended or enacted on or after July 1, 1996, that pertains to an issue other than the duration or potential duration of incarceration or supervised release, to persons in custody or under the supervision of the department of rehabilitation and correction.

**HISTORY: 146 v S 2. Eff 7-1-96; 150 v H 525, § 1, eff. 5-18-05.**

The provisions of § 3 of H.B. 525 (150 v —) read as follows:

SECTION 3. The General Assembly hereby declares that its purpose in amending section 5120.021 of the Revised Code in Sections 1 and 2 of this act is to clarify the applicability of the provisions in Chapter 5120. of the Revised Code that address the duration or potential duration of incarceration and supervision of offenders by the Department of Rehabilitation and Correction, and to clarify the applicability of any other provision in Chapter 5120. of the Revised Code amended or enacted on or after July 1, 1996, to persons in custody or under supervision of the Department. The General Assembly believes that the amendments to section 5120.021 of the Revised Code made in Sections 1 and 2 of this act are not substantive in nature, that these amendments do not affect any substantive right of any offender, and that the version of section 5120.021 of the Revised Code resulting from this act is substantively the same as the version of that section in existence immediately prior to the effective date of this act.

The effective date is set by section 6 of SB 2.

The provisions of § 5 of SB 2 (146 v —) read as follows:

SECTION 5. The provisions of the Revised Code in existence prior to July 1, 1996, shall apply to a person upon whom a court imposed a term of imprisonment prior to that date and to a person upon whom a court, on or after that date and in accordance with the law in existence prior to that date, imposed a term of imprisonment for an offense that was committed prior to that date.

The provisions of the Revised Code in existence on and after July 1, 1996, apply to a person who commits an offense on or after that date.

## § 5120.03 Change of use of institution; penal/reformatory distinction eliminated; privatization of facilities.

(A) Subject to division (C) of this section, the director of rehabilitation and correction may change the purpose for which any institution or place under the control of the department of rehabilitation and correction is being used. The director may designate a new or another use for such institution, if the change of use and new designation has for its objective, improvement in the classification, segregation, care, education, cure, or rehabilitation of persons subject to the control of the department.

(B) The director of rehabilitation and correction, by executive order, issued on or before December 31, 1988, shall eliminate the distinction between penal institutions and reformatory institutions. Notwithstanding any provision of the Revised Code or the Administrative Code to the contrary, upon the issuance of the executive order, any distinction made between the types of prisoners sentenced to or otherwise assigned to the institutions under the control of the department shall be discontinued.

(C) The director shall contract under section 9.06 of the Revised Code for the private operation and management of not less than two facilities under the control of the department, unless the contractor managing and operating a facility is not in substantial compliance with the material terms and conditions of its contract and no other person or entity is willing and able to satisfy the obligations of the contract. All inmates assigned to a facility operated and managed by a private .contractor remain inmates in the care and custody of the department. The statutes, rules, and policies of the department may apply to the private contractor and any inmate assigned to a facility operated and managed by a private contractor as agreed to in the contract entered into under section 9.06 of the Revised Code.

**HISTORY: 134 v H 494 (Eff 7-12-72); 142 v H 261 (Eff 11-1-87); 147 v H 215. Eff 9-29-97; 151 v H 699, § 101.01, eff. 3-29-07.**

The effective date is set by § 612.03 of 151 v H 699.

The effective date is set by section 222 of HB 215.

**§ 5120.031 Pilot program of shock incarceration for eligible offenders.**

(A) As used in this section:

(1) "Certificate of high school equivalence" means a statement that is issued by the state board of education or an equivalent agency of another state and that indicates that its holder has achieved the equivalent of a high school education as measured by scores obtained on the tests of general educational development published by the American council on education.

(2) "Certificate of adult basic education" means a statement that is issued by the department of rehabilitation and correction through the Ohio central school system approved by the state board of education and that indicates that its holder has achieved a 6.0 grade level, or higher, as measured by scores of nationally standardized or recognized tests.

(3) "Deadly weapon" and "firearm" have the same meanings as in section 2923.11 of the Revised Code.

(4) "Eligible offender" means a person, other than one who is ineligible to participate in an intensive program prison under the criteria specified in section 5120.032 of the Revised Code, who has been convicted of or pleaded guilty to, and has been sentenced for, a felony.

(5) "Shock incarceration" means the program of incarceration that is established pursuant to the rules of the department of rehabilitation and correction adopted under this section.

(B)(1) The director of rehabilitation and correction, by rules adopted under Chapter 119. of the Revised Code, shall establish a pilot program of shock incarceration that may be used for offenders who are sentenced to serve a term of imprisonment under the custody of the department of rehabilitation and correction, whom the department determines to be eligible offenders, and whom the department, subject to the approval of the sentencing judge, may permit to serve their sentence as a sentence of shock incarceration in accordance with this section.

(2) The rules for the pilot program shall require that the program be established at an appropriate state correctional institution designated by the director and that the program consist of both of the following for each eligible offender whom the department, with the approval of the sentencing judge, permits to serve the eligible offender's sentence as a sentence of shock incarceration:

(a) A period of imprisonment at that institution of ninety days that shall consist of a military style combination of discipline, physical training, and hard labor and substance abuse education, employment skills training, social skills training, and psychological treatment. During the ninety-day period, the department may permit an eligible offender to participate in a self-help program. Additionally, during the ninety-day period, an eligible offender who holds a high school diploma or a certificate of high school equivalence may be permitted to tutor other eligible offenders in the shock incarceration program. If an eligible offender does not hold a high school diploma or certificate of high school equivalence, the eligible offender may elect to participate in an education program that is designed to award a certificate of adult basic education or an education program that is designed to award a certificate of high school equivalence to those eligible offenders who successfully complete the education program, whether the completion occurs during or subsequent to the ninety-day period. To the extent possible, the department shall use as teachers in the education program persons who have been issued a license pursuant to sections 3319.22 to 3319.31 of the Revised Code, who have volunteered their services to the education program, and who satisfy any other criteria specified in the rules for the pilot project.

(b) Immediately following the ninety-day period of imprisonment, and notwithstanding any other provision governing the early release of a prisoner from imprisonment or the transfer of a prisoner to transitional control, one of the following, as determined by the director:

(i) An intermediate, transitional type of detention for the period of time determined by the director and, immediately following the intermediate, transitional type of detention, a release under a post-release control sanction imposed in accordance with section 2967.28 of the Revised Code. The period of intermediate, transitional type of detention imposed by the director under this division may be in a halfway house, in a community-based correctional facility and program or district community-based correctional facility and program established under sections 2301.51 to 2301.58 of the Revised Code, or in any other facility approved by the director that provides for detention to serve as a transition between imprisonment in a state correctional institution and release from imprisonment.

(ii) A release under a post-release control sanction imposed in accordance with section 2967.28 of the Revised Code.

(3) The rules for the pilot program also shall include, but are not limited to, all of the following:

(a) Rules identifying the locations within the state correctional institution designated by the director that will be used for eligible offenders serving a sentence of shock incarceration;

(b) Rules establishing specific schedules of discipline, physical training, and hard labor for eligible offenders serving a sentence of shock incarceration, based upon the offender's physical condition and needs;

(c) Rules establishing standards and criteria for the department to use in determining which eligible offenders the department will permit to serve their sentence of imprisonment as a sentence of shock incarceration;

(d) Rules establishing guidelines for the selection of post-release control sanctions for eligible offenders;

(e) Rules establishing procedures for notifying sentencing courts of the performance of eligible offenders serving their sentences of imprisonment as a sentence of shock incarceration;

(f) Any other rules that are necessary for the proper conduct of the pilot program.

(C)(1) If an offender is sentenced to a term of imprisonment under the custody of the department, if the sentencing court either recommends the offender for placement in a program of shock incarceration under this section or makes no recommendation on placement of the offender, and if the department determines that the offender is an eligible offender for placement in a program of shock incarceration under this section, the department may permit the eligible offender to serve the sentence in a program of shock incarceration, in accordance with division (I) of section 2929.14 of the Revised Code, with this section, and with the rules adopted under this section. If the sentencing court disapproves placement of the offender in a program of shock incarceration, the department shall not place the offender in any program of shock incarceration.

If the sentencing court recommends the offender for placement in a program of shock incarceration and if the department subsequently places the offender in the recommended program, the department shall notify the court of the offender's placement in the recommended program and shall include with the notice a brief description of the placement.

If the sentencing court recommends placement of the offender in a program of shock incarceration and the department for any reason does not subsequently place the offender in the recommended program, the department shall send a notice to the court indicating why the offender was not placed in the recommended program.

If the sentencing court does not make a recommendation on the placement of an offender in a program of shock incarceration and if the department determines that the offender is an eligible offender for placement in a program of that nature, the department shall screen the offender and determine if the offender is suited for the program of shock incarceration. If the offender is suited for the program of shock incarceration, at least three weeks prior to permitting an eligible offender to serve the sentence in a program of shock incarceration, the department shall notify the sentencing court of the proposed placement of the offender in the program and shall include with the notice a brief description of the placement. The court shall have ten days from receipt of the notice to disapprove the placement. If the sentencing court disapproves of the placement, the department shall not permit the eligible offender to serve the sentence in a program of shock incarceration. If the judge does not timely disapprove of placement of the offender in the program of shock incarceration, the department may proceed with plans for placement of the offender.

If the department determines that the offender is not eligible for placement in a program of shock incarceration, the department shall not place the offender in any program of shock incarceration.

(2) If the department permits an eligible offender to serve the eligible offender's sentence of imprisonment as a sentence of shock incarceration and the eligible offender does not satisfactorily complete the entire period of imprisonment described in division (B)(2)(a) of this section, the offender shall be removed from the pilot program for shock incarceration and shall be required to serve the remainder of the offender's sentence of imprisonment imposed by the sentencing court as a regular term of imprisonment. If the eligible offender commences a period of post-release control described in division (B)(2)(b) of this section and violates the conditions of that post-release control, the eligible offender shall be subject to the provisions of sections 2929.141, 2967.15, and 2967.28 of the Revised Code regarding violation of post-release control sanctions.

(3) If an eligible offender's stated prison term expires at any time during the eligible offender's participation in the shock incarceration program, the adult parole authority shall terminate the eligible offender's participation in the program and shall issue to the eligible offender a certificate of expiration of the stated prison term.

(D) The director shall keep sentencing courts informed of the performance of eligible offenders serving their sentences of imprisonment as a sentence of shock incarceration, including, but not limited to, notice of eligible offenders who fail to satisfactorily complete their entire sentence of shock incarceration or who satisfactorily complete their entire sentence of shock incarceration.

(E) Within a reasonable period of time after November 20, 1990, the director shall appoint a committee to search for one or more suitable sites at which one or more programs of shock incarceration, in addition to the pilot program required by division (B)(1) of this section, may be established. The search committee shall consist of the director or the director's designee, as chairperson; employees of the department of rehabilitation and correction appointed by the director; and any other persons that the director, in the director's discretion, appoints. In searching for such sites, the search committee shall give preference to any site owned by the state or any other governmental entity and to any existing structure that reasonably could be renovated, enlarged, converted, or remodeled for purposes of establishing such a program. The search committee shall prepare a report concerning its activities and, on the earlier of the day that is twelve months after the first day on which an eligible offender began serving a sentence of shock incarceration under the pilot program or January 1, 1992, shall file the report with the president and the minority leader of the senate, the speaker and the minority leader of the house of representatives, the members of the senate who were members of the senate judiciary committee in the 118th general assembly or their successors, and the members of the house of representatives who were members of the select committee to hear drug legislation that was established in the 118th general assembly or their successors. Upon the filing of the report, the search committee shall terminate. The report required by this division shall contain all of the following:

(1) A summary of the process used by the search committee in performing its duties under this division;

(2) A summary of all of the sites reviewed by the search committee in performing its duties under this division, and the benefits and disadvantages it found relative to the establishment of a program of shock incarceration at each such site;

(3) The findings and recommendations of the search committee as to the suitable site or sites, if any, at which a program of shock incarceration, in addition to the pilot program required by division (B)(1) of this section, may be established.

(F) The director periodically shall review the pilot program for shock incarceration required to be established by division (B)(1) of this section. The director shall prepare a report relative to the pilot program and, on the earlier of the day that is twelve months after the first day on which an eligible offender began serving a sentence of shock incarceration under the pilot program or January 1, 1992, shall file the report with the president and the minority leader of the senate, the speaker and the minority leader of the house of representatives, the members of the senate who were members of the senate judiciary committee in the 118th general assembly or their successors, and the members of the house of representatives who were members of the select committee to hear drug legislation that was established in the 118th general assembly or their successors. The pilot program shall not terminate at the time of the filing of the report, but shall continue in operation in accordance with this section. The report required by this division shall include all of the following:

(1) A summary of the pilot program as initially established, a summary of all changes in the pilot program made during the period covered by the report and the reasons for the changes, and a summary of the pilot program as it exists on the date of preparation of the report;

(2) A summary of the effectiveness of the pilot program, in the opinion of the director and employees of the department involved in its operation;

(3) An analysis of the total cost of the pilot program, of its cost per inmate who was permitted to serve a sentence of shock incarceration and who served the entire sentence of shock incarceration, and of its cost per inmate who was permitted to serve a sentence of shock incarceration;

(4) A summary of the standards and criteria used by the department in determining which eligible offenders were permitted to serve their sentence of imprisonment as a sentence of shock incarceration;

(5) A summary of the characteristics of the eligible offenders who were permitted to serve their sentence of imprisonment as a sentence of shock incarceration, which summary shall include, but not be limited to, a listing of every offense of which any such eligible offender was convicted or to which any such eligible offender pleaded guilty and in relation to which the eligible offender served a sentence of shock incarceration, and the total number of such eligible offenders who were convicted of or pleaded guilty to each such offense;

(6) A listing of the number of eligible offenders who were permitted to serve a sentence of shock incarceration and who did not serve the entire sentence of shock incarceration, and, to the extent possible, a summary of the length of the terms of imprisonment served by such eligible offenders after they were removed from the pilot program;

(7) A summary of the effect of the pilot program on overcrowding at state correctional institutions;

(8) To the extent possible, an analysis of the rate of recidivism of eligible offenders who were permitted to serve a sentence of shock incarceration and who served the entire sentence of shock incarceration;

(9) Recommendations as to legislative changes to the pilot program that would assist in its operation or that could further alleviate overcrowding at state correctional institutions, and recommendations as to whether the pilot program should be expanded.

**HISTORY: 143 v S 258 (Eff 11-20-90); 145 v H 314 (Eff 9-29-94); 145 v H 571 (Eff 10-6-94); 146 v S 2 (Eff 7-1-96); 146 v S 269 (Eff 7-1-96); 146 v S 230 (Eff 10-29-96); 147 v S 111 (Eff 3-17-98); 148 v S 107 (Eff 3-23-2000); 149 v H 327. Eff 7-8-2002; 151 v H 162, § 1, eff. 10-12-06; 2011 HB 86, § 1, eff. Sept. 30, 2011.**

## § 5120.032 Intensive program prisons.

(A) No later than January 1, 1998, the department of rehabilitation and correction may develop and implement intensive program prisons for male and female prisoners other than prisoners described in division (B)(2) of this section. The intensive program prisons, if developed and implemented, shall include institutions at which imprisonment of the type described in division (B)(2)(a) of section 5120.031 [5120.03.1] of the Revised Code is provided and prisons that focus on educational achievement, vocational training, alcohol and other drug abuse treatment, community service and conservation work, and other intensive regimens or combinations of intensive regimens.

(B)(1)(a) Except as provided in division (B)(2) of this section, if one or more intensive program prisons are established under this section, if an offender is sentenced to a term of imprisonment under the custody of the department, if the sentencing court either recommends the prisoner for placement in an intensive program prison under this section or makes no recommendation on placement of the prisoner, and if the department determines that the prisoner is eligible for placement in an intensive program prison under this section, the department may place the prisoner in an intensive program prison established pursuant to division (A) of this section. If the sentencing court disapproves placement of the prisoner in an intensive program prison, the department shall not place the prisoner in any intensive program prison.

If the sentencing court recommends a prisoner for placement in an intensive program prison and if the department subsequently places the prisoner in the recommended prison, the department shall notify the court of the prisoner's placement in the recommended intensive program prison and shall include with the notice a brief description of the placement.

If the sentencing court recommends placement of a prisoner in an intensive program prison and the department for any reason does not subsequently place the prisoner in the recommended prison, the department shall send a notice to the court indicating why the prisoner was not placed in the recommended prison.

If the sentencing court does not make a recommendation on the placement of a prisoner in an intensive program prison and if the department determines that the prisoner is eligible for placement in a prison of that nature, the department shall screen the prisoner and determine if the prisoner is suited for the prison. If the prisoner is suited for an intensive program prison, at least three weeks prior to placing the prisoner in the prison, the department shall notify the sentencing court of the proposed placement of the prisoner in the intensive program prison and shall include with the notice a brief description of the placement. The court shall have ten days from receipt of the notice to disapprove the placement. If the sentencing court disapproves the placement, the department shall not proceed with it. If the sentencing court does not timely disapprove of the placement, the department may proceed with plans for it.

If the department determines that a prisoner is not eligible for placement in an intensive program prison, the department shall not place the prisoner in any intensive program prison.

(b) The department may reduce the stated prison term of a prisoner upon the prisoner's successful completion of a ninety-day period in an intensive program prison. A prisoner whose term has been so reduced shall be required to serve an intermediate, transitional type of detention followed by a release under post-release control sanctions or, in the alternative, shall be placed under post-release control sanctions, as described in division (B)(2)(b)(ii) of section 5120.031 [5120.03.1] of the Revised Code. In either case, the placement under post-release control sanctions shall be under terms set by the parole board in accordance with section 2967.28 of the Revised Code and shall be subject to the provisions of that section and section 2929.141 [2929.14.1] of the Revised Code with respect to a violation of any post-release control sanction.

(2) A prisoner who is in any of the following categories is not eligible to participate in an intensive program prison established pursuant to division (A) of this section:

(a) The prisoner is serving a prison term for aggravated murder, murder, or a felony of the first or second degree or a comparable offense under the law in effect prior to July 1, 1996, or the prisoner previously has been imprisoned for aggravated murder, murder, or a felony of the first or second degree or a comparable offense under the law in effect prior to July 1, 1996.

(b) The prisoner is serving a mandatory prison term, as defined in section 2929.01 of the Revised Code.

(c) The prisoner is serving a prison term for a felony of the third, fourth, or fifth degree that either is a sex offense, an offense betraying public trust, or an offense in which the prisoner caused or attempted to cause actual physical harm to a person, the prisoner is serving a prison term for a comparable offense under the law in effect prior to July 1, 1996, or the prisoner previously has been imprisoned for an offense of that type or a comparable offense under the law in effect prior to July 1, 1996.

(d) The prisoner is serving a mandatory prison term in prison for a third or fourth degree felony OVI offense, as defined in section 2929.01 of the Revised Code, that was imposed pursuant to division (G)(2) of section 2929.13 of the Revised Code.

(C) Upon the implementation of intensive program prisons pursuant to division (A) of this section, the department at all times shall maintain intensive program prisons sufficient in number to reduce the prison terms of at least three hundred fifty prisoners who are eligible for reduction of their stated prison terms as a result of their completion of a regimen in an intensive program prison under this section.

**HISTORY: 146 v S 2 (Eff 7-1-96); 146 v S 269 (Eff 7-1-96); 146 v S 166 (Eff 10-17-96); 148 v S 107 (Eff 3-23-2000); 148 v S 22 (Eff 5-17-2000); 149 v H 327. Eff 7-8-2002; 149 v S 123, § 1, eff. 1-1-04; 153 v H 1, § 101.01, eff. 10-16-09.**

The effective date is set by § 812.10 of 153 v H 1.

The effective date is set by section 4 of S.B. 123.

The provisions of § 5 of S.B. 123 (149 v —), as amended by § 3 of H.B. 163 (150 v —), read as follows:

SECTION 5. (A) Notwithstanding division (B) of section 1.58 of the Revised Code, the provisions of the Revised Code amended or enacted in Sections 1 and 2 of Am. Sub. S.B. 123 of the 124th General Assembly shall apply only in relation to conduct and offenses committed on or after January 1, 2004. Conduct and offenses committed prior to January 1, 2004, shall be governed by the law in effect on the date the conduct or offense was committed. * * *

The provisions of § 4 of HB 327 (149 v —) read in part as follows:

SECTION 4. * * * Section 5120.032 of the Revised Code is presented in this act as a composite of the section as amended by both Am. Sub. S.B. 22 and Am. Sub. S.B. 107 of the 123rd General Assembly. The General Assembly, applying the principle stated in division (B) of section 1.52 of the Revised Code that amendments are to be harmonized if reasonably capable of simultaneous operation, finds that the composites are the resulting versions of the sections in effect prior to the effective date of the sections as presented in this act.

## § 5120.033 Intensive program prisons for certain OVI offenders.

(A) As used in this section, "third degree felony OVI offense" and "fourth degree felony OVI offense" have the same meanings as in section 2929.01 of the Revised Code.

(B) Within eighteen months after October 17, 1996, the department of rehabilitation and correction may develop and implement intensive program prisons for male and female prisoners who are sentenced pursuant to division (G)(2) of section 2929.13 of the Revised Code to a mandatory prison term for a third or fourth degree felony OVI offense. If one or more intensive program prisons are established under this section, the department may contract pursuant to section 9.06 of the Revised Code for the private operation and management of the initial intensive program prison established under this section and may contract pursuant to that section for the private operation and management of any other intensive program prison established under this section. The intensive program prisons, if established under this section, shall include prisons that focus on educational achievement, vocational training, alcohol and other drug abuse treatment, community service and conservation work, and other intensive regimens or combinations of intensive regimens.

(C) Except as provided in division (D) of this section, the department may place a prisoner who is sentenced to a mandatory prison term for a third or fourth degree felony OVI offense in an intensive program prison established pursuant to division (B) of this section if the sentencing judge, upon notification by the department of its intent to place the prisoner in an intensive program prison, does not notify the department that the judge disapproves the placement. If the stated prison term imposed on a prisoner who is so placed is longer than the mandatory prison term that is required to be imposed on the prisoner, the department may reduce the stated prison term upon the prisoner's successful completion of the prisoner's mandatory prison term in an intensive program prison. A prisoner whose term has been so reduced shall be required to serve an intermediate, transitional type of detention followed by a release under post-release control sanctions or, in the alternative, shall be placed under post-release control sanctions, as described in division (B)(2)(b)(ii) of section 5120.031 [5120.03.1] of the Revised Code. In either case, the placement under post-release control sanctions shall be under terms set by the parole board in accordance with section 2967.28 of the Revised Code and shall be subject to the provisions of that section and section 2929.141 [2929.14.1] of the Revised Code with respect to a violation of any post-release control sanction. If one or more intensive program prisons are established pursuant to division (B) of this section and if as described in that division the initial intensive program prison is to be privately operated and managed by a contractor pursuant to a contract the department entered into under section 9.06 of the Revised Code, upon the establishment of that initial intensive program prison the department shall comply with divisions (G)(2)(a) and (b) of section 2929.13 of the Revised Code in placing prisoners in intensive program prisons under this section.

(D) A prisoner who is sentenced to a mandatory prison term for a third or fourth degree felony OVI offense is not eligible to participate in an intensive program prison established under division (B) of this section if any of the following applies regarding the prisoner:

(1) In addition to the mandatory prison term for the third or fourth degree felony OVI offense, the prisoner also is serving a prison term of a type described in division (B)(2)(a), (b), or (c) of section 5120.032 [5120.03.2] of the Revised Code.

(2) The prisoner previously has been imprisoned for an offense of a type described in division (B)(2)(a) or (c) of section 5120.032 [5120.03.2] of the Revised Code or a comparable offense under the law in effect prior to July 1, 1996.

(E) Intensive program prisons established under division (B) of this section are not subject to section 5120.032 [5120.03.2] of the Revised Code.

**HISTORY: 146 v S 166 (Eff 10-17-96); 147 v H 293 (Eff 3-17-98); 148 v S 22 (Eff 5-17-2000); 149 v H 327. Eff 7-8-2002; 149 v S 123, § 1, eff. 1-1-04; 153 v H 1, § 101.01, eff. 10-16-09.**

The effective date is set by § 812.10 of 153 v H 1.

The effective date is set by section 4 of S.B. 123.

See provisions, § 5 of S.B. 123 (149 v —), following RC § 5120.032.

## § 5120.034 Reentry services for inmates.

(A)(1) The department of rehabilitation and correction shall permit representatives of all nonprofit faith-based, business, professional, civic, educational, and community organizations that are registered with the department to enter institutions under the control of the department for the purpose of providing reentry services to inmates. Reentry services may include, but are not limited to, counseling, housing, job-placement, and money-management assistance.

(2) The department shall adopt rules pursuant to Chapter 119. of the Revised Code for the screening and registration of nonprofit faith-based, business, professional, civic, educational, and community organizations that apply to provide reentry services in institutions under the department's control.

(B)(1) The department shall post a department telephone number on the department's official internet web site that nonprofit faith-based, business, professional, civic, educational, and community organizations that wish to provide reentry services to inmates may call to obtain information. The internet web site also shall list all of the nonprofit faith-based, business, professional, civic, educational, and community organizations that are registered with the department under this section.

(2) The department shall actively recruit nonprofit faith-based, business, professional, civic, educational, and community organizations to provide reentry services in institutions under the department's control. The department shall recruit nonprofit organizations from all faiths and beliefs.

(C) Annually, the department shall issue a written report on the department's progress in implementing the recommendations of the correctional faith-based initiatives task force. The department shall provide a copy of the written report to each member of the correctional institution inspection committee created under section 103.71 of the Revised Code.

(D) The department shall not endorse or sponsor any faith-based reentry program or endorse any specific religious message. The department may not require an inmate to participate in a faith-based program.

**HISTORY: 152 v H 113, § 1, eff. 6-25-08.**

## § 5120.036 Risk reduction programming and treatment for inmates serving risk reduction sentence; eligibility criteria; conditions for release upon successful completion of assessment and treatment or programming required by department.

(A) The department of rehabilitation and correction shall provide risk reduction programming and treatment for inmates whom a court under section 2929.143 of the Revised Code recommends serve a risk reduction sentence and who meet the eligibility criteria described in division (B) of this section.

(B) If an offender is sentenced to a term of imprisonment in a state correctional institution and the sentencing court recommended that the offender serve a risk reduction sentence, the department of rehabilitation and correction shall conduct a validated and objective assessment of the person's needs and risk of reoffending. If the offender cooperates with the risk assessment and agrees to participate in any programming or treatment ordered by the department, the department shall provide programming and treatment to the offender to address the risks and needs identified in the assessment.

(C) If the department determines that an offender serving a term of incarceration for whom the sentencing court recommended a risk reduction sentence under section 2929.143 of the Revised Code has successfully completed the assessment and treatment or programming required by the department under division (B) of this section, the department shall release the offender to supervised release after the offender has served each mandatory prison term to which the offender was sentenced, if any, and a minimum of eighty per cent of the aggregated nonmandatory prison terms to which the offender was sentenced. No mandatory prison term shall be reduced by, or as a result of, an offender's service of a risk reduction sentence. The department shall notify the sentencing court that the offender has successfully completed the terms of the risk reduction sentence at least thirty days prior to the date upon which the offender is to be released.

(D) As used in this section:

(1) "Mandatory prison term" has the same meaning as in section 2929.01 of the Revised Code.

(2) "Nonmandatory prison term" means a prison term that is not a mandatory prison term.

**HISTORY: 2011 HB 86, § 1, eff. Sept. 30, 2011.**

## § 5120.04 Assignment of prisoner labor.

The department of rehabilitation and correction, with the approval of the governor and in accordance with rules adopted pursuant to division (B) of section 5145.03 of the Revised Code, may assign prisoners who are committed or transferred to institutions under the administration of the department to perform labor on any public work of the state.

**HISTORY: 134 v H 494 (Eff 7-12-72); 138 v H 654. Eff 4-9-82.**

The effective date is set by section 4 of HB 654.

## § 5120.05 Management, naming of institutions; receipt of delinquent juveniles.

The department of rehabilitation and correction may maintain, operate, manage, and govern all state institutions for the custody, control, training, and rehabilitation of persons convicted of crime and sentenced to correctional institutions.

The department may designate correctional institutions by appropriate respective names.

The department may receive from the department of youth services any children in the custody of the department of youth services, committed to the department of rehabilitation and correction by the department of youth services, upon the terms and conditions that are agreed upon by the departments.

**HISTORY: 134 v H 494 (Eff 7-12-72); 139 v H 440 (Eff 11-23-81); 145 v H 571 (Eff 10-6-94); 147 v S 111. Eff 3-17-98.**

## § 5120.051 Mentally ill or retarded inmates.

The department of rehabilitation and correction shall provide for the needs of mentally ill and mentally retarded persons who are incarcerated in state correctional institutions. The department may designate an institution or a unit within an institution for the custody, care, special training, treatment, and rehabilitation of mentally ill or mentally retarded persons.

**HISTORY: RC § 5125.02, 139 v S 550 (Eff 11-26-82); RC § 5120.05.1, 145 v H 571 (Eff 10-6-94); 146 v S 310. Eff 6-20-96.**

The effective date is determined by § 23 of SB 310 (146 v —).

## § 5120.06 Divisions; offices; administrative units.

(A) The following divisions are hereby established in the department of rehabilitation and correction:

(1) The division of business administration;

(2) The division of parole and community services.

(B) The director of rehabilitation and correction may establish offices, divisions in addition to those specified in division (A) of this section, bureaus, and other administrative units within the department of rehabilitation and correction and prescribe their powers and duties.

**HISTORY: 134 v H 494 (Eff 7-12-72); 147 v S 111. Eff 3-17-98.**

## § 5120.07 Ex-offender reentry coalition [Repealed effective December 31, 2014].

(A) There is hereby created the ex-offender reentry coalition consisting of the following seventeen members or their designees:

(1) The director of rehabilitation and correction;

(2) The director of aging;

(3) The director of alcohol and drug addiction services;

(4) The director of development;

(5) The superintendent of public instruction;

(6) The director of health;

(7) The director of job and family services;

(8) The director of mental health;

(9) The director of developmental disabilities;

(10) The director of public safety;

(11) The director of youth services;

(12) The chancellor of the Ohio board of regents;

(13) A representative or member of the governor's staff;

(14) The director of the rehabilitation services commission;

(15) The director of the department of commerce;

(16) The executive director of a health care licensing board created under Title XLVII of the Revised Code, as appointed by the chairperson of the coalition;

(17) The director of veterans services.

(B) The members of the coalition shall serve without compensation. The director of rehabilitation and correction or the director's designee shall be the chairperson of the coalition.

(C) In consultation with persons interested and involved in the reentry of ex-offenders into the community, including but not limited to, service providers, community-based organizations, and local governments, the coalition shall identify and examine social service barriers and other obstacles to the reentry of ex-offenders into the community. Not later than one year after April 7, 2009, and on or before the same date of each year thereafter, the coalition shall submit to the speaker of the house of representatives and the president of the senate a report, including recommendations for legislative action, the activities of the coalition, and the barriers affecting the successful reentry of ex-offenders into the community. The report shall analyze the effects of those barriers on ex-offenders and on their children and other family members in various areas, including but not limited to, the following:

(1) Admission to public and other housing;

(2) Child support obligations and procedures;

(3) Parental incarceration and family reunification;

(4) Social security benefits, veterans' benefits, food stamps, and other forms of public assistance;

(5) Employment;

(6) Education programs and financial assistance;

(7) Substance abuse, mental health, and sex offender treatment programs and financial assistance;

(8) Civic and political participation;

(9) Other collateral consequences under the Revised Code or the Ohio administrative code law that may result from a criminal conviction.

(D)(1) The report shall also include the following information:

(a) Identification of state appropriations for reentry programs;

(b) Identification of other funding sources for reentry programs that are not funded by the state;

(2) The coalition shall gather information about reentry programs in a repository maintained and made available by the coalition. Where available, the information shall include the following:

(a) The amount of funding received;

(b) The number of program participants;

(c) The composition of the program, including program goals, methods for measuring success, and program success rate;

(d) The type of post-program tracking that is utilized;

(e) Information about employment rates and recidivism rates of ex-offenders.

(E) The coalition shall cease to exist on December 31, 2014.

**HISTORY: 152 v H 130, § 1, eff. 4-7-09; 153 v S 79, § 1, eff. 10-6-09; 2011 HB 86, § 1, eff. Sept. 30, 2011.**

This section will be repealed by 2011 HB 86, § 7, effective December 31, 2014.

The provisions of § 14 of 153 v S 79 read as follows:

Section 14. The amendment of section 5120.07 of the Revised Code is not intended to supersede the earlier repeal, with delayed effective date, of that section.

**Not analogous to former RC § 5120.07 (134 v H 494; 137 v H 1), repealed 147 v S 111, § 2, eff 3-17-98.**

The provisions of § 3 of 152 v H 130, as amended by 2011 HB 86 § 7, read as follows:

SECTION 3. Section 5120.07 of the Revised Code is hereby repealed, effective December 31, 2014.

## § 5120.08 Filing of bond of employees.

The department of rehabilitation and correction shall require any of its employees and each officer and employee of every institution under its control who may be charged with custody or control of any money or property belonging to the state or who is required to give bond, to give a surety company bond, properly conditioned, in a sum to be fixed by the department which when approved by the department, shall be filed in the office of the secretary of state. The cost of such bonds, when approved by the department, shall be paid from funds available for the department. The bonds required or authorized by this section may, in the discretion of the director of rehabilitation and correction, be individual, schedule, or blanket bonds.

**HISTORY: 134 v H 494. Eff 7-12-72.**

## § 5120.09 Duties of division of business administration.

Under the supervision and control of the director of rehabilitation and correction, the division of business administration shall do all of the following:

(A) Submit the budgets for the several divisions of the department of rehabilitation and correction, as prepared by the respective chiefs of those divisions, to the director. The director, with the assistance of the chief of the division of business administration, shall compile a departmental budget that contains all proposals submitted by the chiefs of the divisions and shall forward the departmental budget to the governor with comments and recommendations that the director considers necessary.

(B) Maintain accounts and records and compile statistics that the director prescribes;

(C) Under the control of the director, coordinate and make the necessary purchases and requisitions for the department and its divisions, except when goods and services are provided to the department as described in section 5119.16 of the Revised Code;

(D) Administer within this state federal criminal justice acts that the governor requires the department to administer. In order to improve the criminal justice system of this state, the division of business administration shall apply for, allocate, disburse, and account for grants that are made available pursuant to those federal criminal justice acts and grants that are made available from other federal government sources, state government sources, or private sources. As used in this division, "criminal justice system" and "federal criminal justice acts" have the same meanings as in section 5502.61 of the Revised Code.

(E) Audit the activities of governmental entities, persons as defined in section 1.59 of the Revised Code, and other types of nongovernmental entities that are financed in whole or in part by funds that the department allocates or disburses and that are derived from grants described in division (D) of this section;

(F) Enter into contracts, including contracts with federal, state, or local governmental entities, persons as defined in section 1.59 of the Revised Code, foundations, and other types of nongovernmental entities, that are necessary for the department to carry out its duties and that neither the director nor another section of the Revised Code authorizes another division of the department to enter;

(G) Exercise other powers and perform other duties that the director may assign to the division of business administration.

**HISTORY: 134 v H 494 (Eff 7-12-72); 139 v H 1 (Eff 8-5-81); 140 v H 291 (Eff 7-1-83); 147 v H 215. Eff 9-29-97; 151 v H 66, § 101.01, eff. 6-30-05; 153 v H 1, § 101.01, eff. 10-16-09.**

The effective date is set by § 812.10 of 153 v H 1.
The effective date is set by § 612.12 of 151 v H 66.
The effective date is set by section 222 of HB 215.

## § 5120.091 Education services fund.

There is hereby created in the state treasury the education services fund. The department of rehabilitation and correction shall deposit into the fund all state revenues it receives from the Ohio department of education. Any money in the fund shall solely be used to pay educational expenses incurred by the department.

**HISTORY: 145 v H 715. Eff 7-22-94.**

## § 5120.092 Adult and juvenile correctional facilities bond retirement fund.

There is hereby created in the state treasury the adult and juvenile correctional facilities bond retirement fund. The fund shall receive proceeds derived from the sale of state adult or juvenile correctional facilities. Investment income with respect to moneys on deposit in the fund shall be retained by the fund. No investment of moneys in, or transfer of moneys from, the fund shall be made if the effect of the investment or transfer would be to adversely affect the exclusion from gross income of the interest payable on state bonds issued for state adult or juvenile correctional facilities that have been sold under authority of Section 753.10 or 753.30 of the act in which this section was enacted. To the extent necessary to maintain the exclusion from gross income of the interest payable on those bonds, moneys in the fund shall first be used to redeem or defease the outstanding portion of such bonds. To accomplish the redemption or defeasance, the director of budget and management, at the request of the Ohio building authority, may direct that moneys in the fund be transferred to the appropriate trustees under the applicable bond trust agreements. Upon receipt of both (i) one or more opinions of a nationally recognized bond counsel firm appointed by the Ohio building authority stating that the aforementioned bonds have been redeemed or defeased and that the transfer of such moneys will not adversely affect the exclusion from gross income of the interest payable on such bonds, and (ii) a certification by both the director of administrative services and the director of rehabilitation and correction stating either that all sales of state adult and juvenile correctional facilities contemplated by Sections 753.10 and 753.30 of the act in which this section was enacted have been completed or that no further sales of any such facilities will be undertaken, the director of budget and management may direct that any moneys remaining in the fund after the redemption or defeasance of the aforementioned bonds shall be transferred to the general revenue fund. Upon completion of that transfer, the adult and juvenile correctional facilities bond retirement fund shall be abolished.

**HISTORY: 2011 HB 153, § 101.01, eff. June 30, 2011.**

## § 5120.10 Minimum standards for jails; powers and duties of division of parole and community services.

(A)(1) The director of rehabilitation and correction, by rule, shall promulgate minimum standards for jails in Ohio, including minimum security jails dedicated under section 341.34 or 753.21 of the Revised Code. Whenever the director files a rule or an amendment to a rule in final form with both the secretary of state and the director of the legislative service commission pursuant to section 111.15 of the Revised Code, the director of rehabilitation and correction promptly shall send a copy of the rule or amendment, if the rule or amendment pertains to minimum jail standards, by ordinary mail to the political subdivisions or affiliations of political subdivisions that operate jails to which the standards apply.

(2) The rules promulgated in accordance with division (A)(1) of this section shall serve as criteria for the investigative and supervisory powers and duties vested by division (D) of this section in the division of parole and community services of the department of rehabilitation and correction or in another division of the department to which those powers and duties are assigned.

(B) The director may initiate an action in the court of common pleas of the county in which a facility that is subject to the rules promulgated under division (A)(1) of this section is situated to enjoin compliance with the minimum standards for jails or with the minimum standards and minimum renovation, modification, and construction criteria for minimum security jails.

(C) Upon the request of an administrator of a jail facility, the chief executive of a municipal corporation, or a board of county commissioners, the director of rehabilitation and correction or the director's designee shall grant a variance from the minimum standards for jails in Ohio for a facility that is subject to one of those minimum standards when the director determines that strict compliance with the minimum standards would cause unusual, practical difficulties or financial hardship, that existing or alternative practices meet the intent of the minimum standards, and that granting a variance would not seriously affect the security of the facility, the supervision of the inmates, or the safe, healthful operation of the facility. If the director or the director's designee denies a variance, the applicant may appeal the denial pursuant to section 119.12 of the Revised Code.

(D) The following powers and duties shall be exercised by the division of parole and community services unless assigned to another division by the director:

(1) The investigation and supervision of county and municipal jails, workhouses, minimum security jails, and other correctional institutions and agencies;

(2) The review and approval of plans submitted to the department of rehabilitation and correction pursuant to division (E) of this section;

(3) The management and supervision of the adult parole authority created by section 5149.02 of the Revised Code;

(4) The review and approval of proposals for community-based correctional facilities and programs and district community-based correctional facilities and programs that are submitted pursuant to division (B) of section 2301.51 of the Revised Code;

(5) The distribution of funds made available to the division for purposes of assisting in the renovation, maintenance, and operation of community-based correctional facilities and programs and district community-based correctional facilities and programs in accordance with section 5120.112 [5120.11.2] of the Revised Code;

(6) The performance of the duty imposed upon the department of rehabilitation and correction in section 5149.31 of the Revised Code to establish and administer a program of subsidies to eligible municipal corporations, counties, and groups of contiguous counties for the development, implementation, and operation of community-based corrections programs;

(7) Licensing halfway houses and community residential centers for the care and treatment of adult offenders in accordance with section 2967.14 of the Revised Code;

(8) Contracting with a public or private agency or a department or political subdivision of the state that operates a licensed halfway house or community residential center for the provision of housing, supervision, and other services to parolees, releasees, persons placed under a residential sanction, persons under transitional control, and other eligible offenders in accordance with section 2967.14 of the Revised Code.

Other powers and duties may be assigned by the director of rehabilitation and correction to the division of parole and community services. This section does not apply to the department of youth services or its institutions or employees.

(E) No plan for any new jail, workhouse, or lockup, and no plan for a substantial addition or alteration to an existing jail, workhouse, or lockup, shall be adopted unless the officials responsible for adopting the plan have submitted the plan to the department of rehabilitation and correction for approval, and the department has approved the plan as provided in division (D)(2) of this section.

**HISTORY: 134 v H 494 (Eff 7-12-72); 139 v H 440 (Eff 11-23-81); 139 v S 23 (Eff 7-6-82); 143 v S 131 (Eff 7-25-90); 144 v S 351 (Eff 7-1-92); 145 v H 571 (Eff 10-6-94); 146 v H 480 (Eff 10-16-96); 149 v H 269. Eff 7-24-2002; 149 v H 490, § 1, eff. 1-1-04.**

The effective date is set by section 4 of H.B. 490.

See provisions, § 3 of HB 269 (149 v —), following RC § 5149.18.

## [HALFWAY HOUSE FACILITIES]

## § 5120.102 Definitions.

As used in sections 5120.102 [5120.10.2] to 5120.105 [5120.10.5] of the Revised Code:

(A) "Private, nonprofit organization" means a private association, organization, corporation, or other entity that is exempt from federal income taxation under section 501(a) and is described in section 501(c) of the "Internal Revenue Code of 1986," 100 Stat. 2085, 26 U.S.C.A. 501, as amended.

(B) "Governmental agency" means a state agency; a municipal corporation, county, township, other political subdivision or special district in this state established by or pursuant to law, or a combination of those political subdivisions or special districts; the United States or a department, division, or agency of the United States; or an agency, commission, or authority established pursuant to an interstate compact or agreement.

(C) "State agency" means the state or one of its branches, offices, boards, commissions, authorities, departments, divisions, or other units or agencies of the state.

(D) "Halfway house organization" means a private, nonprofit organization or a governmental agency that provides programs or activities in areas directly concerned with housing and monitoring offenders who are under the community supervision of the department of rehabilitation and correction or whom a court places in a halfway house pursuant to section 2929.16 or 2929.26 of the Revised Code.

(E) "Halfway house facility" means a capital facility in this state to which all of the following apply:

(1) The construction of the capital facility is authorized or funded by the general assembly pursuant to division (C) of section 5120.105 [5120.10.5] of the Revised Code.

(2) The state owns or has a sufficient real property interest in the capital facility or in the site of the capital facility for a period of not less than the greater of the useful life of the capital facility, as determined by the director of budget and management using the guidelines for maximum maturities as provided under divisions (B), (C), and (E) of section 133.20 of the Revised Code and certified to the department of rehabilitation and correction and the Ohio building authority, or the final maturity of obligations issued by the Ohio building authority to finance the capital facility.

(3) The capital facility is managed directly by, or by contract with, the department of rehabilitation and correction and is used for housing offenders who are under the community supervision of the department of rehabilitation and correction or whom a court places in a halfway house pursuant to section 2929.16 or 2929.26 of the Revised Code.

(F) "Construction" includes acquisition, demolition, reconstruction, alteration, renovation, remodeling, enlargement, improvement, site improvements, and related equipping and furnishing.

(G) "General building services" means general building services for a halfway house facility that include, but are not limited to, general custodial care, security, maintenance, repair, painting, decoration, cleaning, utilities, fire safety, grounds and site maintenance and upkeep, and plumbing.

(H) "Manage," "operate," or "management" means the provision of, or the exercise of control over the provision of, activities that relate to the housing of offenders in correctional facilities, including, but not limited to, providing for release services for offenders who are under the community supervision of the department of rehabilitation and correction or are placed by a court in a halfway house pursuant to section 2929.16 or 2929.26 of the Revised Code, and who reside in halfway house facilities.

**HISTORY: 146 v H 117 (Eff 6-30-95); 146 v S 269 (Eff 7-1-96); 147 v S 111. Eff 3-17-98; 149 v H 490, § 1, eff. 1-1-04.**

**Not analogous to former RC § 5120.10.2 (144 v H 298), repealed 145 v H 152, § 2, eff 7-1-93.**

The effective date is set by section 4 of H.B. 490.

## § 5120.103 Grants for construction of halfway houses.

(A) To the extent that funds are available, the department of rehabilitation and correction, in accordance with this section and sections 5120.104 [5120.10.4] and 5120.105 [5120.10.5] of the Revised Code, may construct or provide for the construction of halfway house facilities for offenders whom a court places in a halfway house pursuant to section 2929.16 or 2929.26 of the Revised Code or who are eligible for community supervision by the department of rehabilitation and correction.

(B) A halfway house organization that seeks to assist in the program planning of a halfway house facility described in division (A) of this section shall file an application with the director of rehabilitation and correction as set forth in a request for proposal. Upon the submission of an application, the division of parole and community services shall review it and, if the division believes it is appropriate, shall submit a recommendation for its approval to the director. When the division submits a recommendation for approval of an application, the director may approve the application. The director shall not take action or fail to take action, or permit the taking of action or the failure to take action, with respect to halfway house facilities that would adversely affect the exclusion of interest on public obligations or on fractionalized interests in public obligations from gross income for federal income tax purposes, or the classification or qualification of the public obligations or the interest on or fractionalized interests in public obligations for, or their exemption from, other treatment under the Internal Revenue Code.

(C) The director of rehabilitation and correction and the halfway house organization may enter into an agreement establishing terms for the program planning of the halfway house facility. Any terms so established shall conform to the terms of any covenant or agreement pertaining to an obligation from which the funds used for the construction of the halfway house facility are derived.

(D) The director of rehabilitation and correction, in accordance with Chapter 119. of the Revised Code, shall adopt rules that specify procedures by which a halfway house organization may apply for a contract for program planning of a halfway house facility constructed under this section, procedures for the department to follow in considering an application, criteria for granting approval of an application, and any other rules that are necessary for the selection of program planners of a halfway house facility.

**HISTORY: 144 v H 904 (Eff 12-22-92); 146 v H 117 (Eff 9-29-95); 146 v S 2 (Eff 7-1-96); 146 v S 269 (Eff 7-1-96); 147 v S 111. Eff 3-17-98; 149 v H 490, § 1, eff. 1-1-04.**

The effective date is set by section 4 of H.B. 490.

## § 5120.11 Bureau of examination and classification.

Within the department of rehabilitation and correction, there shall be established and maintained a bureau of examination and classification. The bureau shall conduct or provide for sociological, psychological, and psychiatric examination of each inmate of the correctional institutions. The examination shall be made as soon as possible after each inmate is admitted to any of the institutions, and further examinations may be made, if it is advisable. If the inmate is determined to be a mentally retarded or developmentally disabled person, as defined in section 5123.01 of the Revised Code, the bureau shall notify the sentencing court in writing of its determination within forty-five days after sentencing.

The bureau shall collect such social and other information as will aid in the interpretation of its examinations.

Subject to division (C) of section 5120.21 of the Revised Code, the bureau shall keep a record of the health, activities, and behavior of each inmate while the inmate is in the custody of the state. The records, including the findings and recommendations of the bureau, shall be made available to the adult parole authority for use in imposing post-release control sanctions under section 2967.28 of the Revised Code or any other section of the Revised Code, in granting parole, and in making parole, post-release, and rehabilitation plans for the inmate when the inmate leaves the institution, and to the department for its use in approving transfers of inmates from one institution to another.

**HISTORY: 134 v H 494 (Eff 7-12-72); 137 v H 565 (Eff 11-1-78); 138 v S 297 (Eff 4-30-80); 138 v H 965 (Eff 4-9-81); 142 v S 94 (Eff 7-20-88); 143 v H 569 (Eff 7-1-91); 145 v H**

**571 (Eff 10-6-94); 146 v S 2 (Eff 7-1-96); 146 v S 269. Eff 7-1-96.**

## § 5120.111 Rules and forms for community-based correctional facilities and programs.

With respect to community-based correctional facilities and programs and district community-based correctional facilities and programs authorized under section 2301.51 of the Revised Code, the department of rehabilitation and correction shall do all of the following:

(A) Adopt rules, under Chapter 119. of the Revised Code, that serve as criteria for the operation of community-based correctional facilities and programs and district community-based correctional facilities and programs approved in accordance with sections 2301.51 and 5120.10 of the Revised Code;

(B) Adopt rules, under Chapter 119. of the Revised Code, governing the procedures for the submission of proposals for the establishment of community-based correctional facilities and programs and district community-based correctional facilities and programs to the division of parole and community services under division (B) of section 2301.51 of the Revised Code;

(C) Prescribe forms that are to be used by facility governing boards of community-based correctional facilities and programs and district community-based correctional facilities and programs in making application for state financial assistance under section 2301.56 of the Revised Code;

(D) Adopt rules, under Chapter 119. of the Revised Code, that prescribe the standards of operation for the facilities and programs that must be satisfied for community-based correctional facilities and programs and district community-based correctional facilities and programs to be eligible for state financial assistance. The standards adopted by the department shall specify the class of offender whose degree of felony, whose community control sanction revocation history, or whose risk level as assessed by the single validated risk assessment tool described in section 5120.114 of the Revised Code, make the offender suitable for admission to the facility. The rules shall make the level of state financial assistance provided to every facility contingent upon the number of offenders admitted to the facility each fiscal year who satisfy the admission suitability standards established by the department.

(E) Through the division of parole and community services, accept and review proposals for the establishment of community-based correctional facilities and programs and district community-based correctional facilities and programs and approve those proposals that satisfy the minimum requirements contained in section 2301.52 of the Revised Code; and administer the program for state financial assistance to the facilities and programs in accordance with section 5120.112 of the Revised Code.

**HISTORY: 138 v H 1000 (Eff 4-9-81); 145 v H 571. Eff 10-6-94; 151 v H 162, § 1, eff. 10-12-06; 2011 HB 86, § 1, eff. Sept. 30, 2011.**

## § 5120.112 Application for state financial assistance to community-based corrections; agreement.

(A) The division of parole and community services shall accept applications for state financial assistance for the renovation, maintenance, and operation of proposed and approved community-based correctional facilities and programs and district community-based correctional facilities and programs that are filed in accordance with section 2301.56 of the Revised Code. The division, upon receipt of an application for a particular facility and program, shall determine whether the application is in proper form, whether the applicant satisfies the standards of operation that are prescribed by the department of rehabilitation and correction under section 5120.111 [5120.11.1] of the Revised Code, whether the applicant has established the facility and program, and, if the applicant has not at that time established the facility and program, whether the proposal of the applicant sufficiently indicates that the standards will be satisfied upon the establishment of the facility and program. If the division determines that the application is in proper form and that the applicant has satisfied or will satisfy the standards of the department, the division shall notify the applicant that it is qualified to receive state financial assistance for the facility and program under this section from moneys made available to the division for purposes of providing assistance to community-based correctional facilities and programs and district community-based correctional facilities and programs.

(B) The amount of state financial assistance that is awarded to a qualified applicant under this section shall be determined by the division of parole and community services in accordance with this division. In determining the amount of state financial assistance to be awarded to a qualified applicant under this section, the division shall not calculate the cost of an offender incarcerated in a community-based correctional facility and program or district community-based correctional facility program to be greater than the average yearly cost of incarceration per inmate in all state correctional institutions, as defined in section 2967.01 of the Revised Code, as determined by the department of rehabilitation and correction.

The times and manner of distribution of state financial assistance to be awarded to a qualified applicant under this section shall be determined by the division of parole and community services.

(C) Upon approval of a proposal for a community-based correctional facility and program or a district community-based correctional facility and program by the division of parole and community services, the facility governing board, upon the advice of the judicial advisory board, shall enter into an award agreement with the department of rehabilitation and correction that outlines terms and conditions of the agreement on an annual basis. In the award agreement, the facility governing board shall identify a fiscal agent responsible for the deposit of funds and compliance with sections 2301.55 and 2301.56 of the Revised Code.

(D) No state financial assistance shall be distributed to a qualified applicant until an agreement concerning the assistance has been entered into by the director of rehabilitation and correction and the deputy director of the division of parole and community services on the part of the state, and by the chairperson of the facility governing board of the community-based correctional facility and program or district community-based correctional facility and program to receive the financial assistance, whichever is applicable. The agreement shall be effective for a period of one year from the date of the agreement and shall specify all terms and conditions that are applicable to the awarding of the assistance, including, but not limited to:

(1) The total amount of assistance to be awarded for each community-based correctional facility and program or district community-based correctional facility and program, and the times and manner of the payment of the assistance;

(2) How persons who will staff and operate the facility and program are to be utilized during the period for which the assistance is to be granted, including descriptions of their positions and duties, and their salaries and fringe benefits;

(3) A statement that none of the persons who will staff and operate the facility and program, including those who are receiving some or all of their salaries out of funds received by the facility and program as state financial assistance, are employees or are to be considered as being employees of the department of rehabilitation and correction, and a statement that the employees who will staff and operate that facility and program are employees of the facility and program;

(4) A list of the type of expenses, other than salaries of persons who will staff and operate the facility and program, for which the state financial assistance can be used, and a requirement that purchases made with funds received as state financial assistance follow established fiscal guidelines as determined by the division of parole and community services and any applicable sections of the Revised Code, including, but not limited to, sections 125.01 to 125.11 and Chapter 153. of the Revised Code;

(5) The accounting procedures that are to be used by the facility and program in relation to the state financial assistance;

(6) A requirement that the facility and program file reports, during the period that it receives state financial assistance, with the division of parole and community services, which reports shall be statistical in nature and shall contain that information required under a research design agreed upon by all parties to the agreement, for purposes of evaluating the facility and program;

(7) A requirement that the facility and program comply with standards of operation as prescribed by the department under section 5120.111 of the Revised Code, and with all information submitted on its application;

(8) A statement that the facility and program will make a reasonable effort to augment the funding received from the state.

(E)(1) No state financial assistance shall be distributed to a qualified applicant until its proposal for a community-based correctional facility and program or district community-based correctional facility and program has been approved by the division of parole and community services.

(2) State financial assistance may be denied to any applicant if it fails to comply with the terms of any agreement entered into pursuant to division (D) of this section.

**HISTORY: RC § 5149.06.1, 138 v H 1000 (Eff 4-9-81); 145 v H 152 (Eff 7-1-93); RC § 5120.11.2, 145 v H 571 (Eff 10-6-94); 145 v H 335. Eff 12-9-94; 151 v H 162, § 1, eff. 10-12-06.**

## § 5120.113 Requirement of written reentry plan for inmate committed to department of rehabilitation and correction; exceptions; collection of information for preparation of plan; liability of department.

(A) For each inmate committed to the department of rehabilitation and correction, except as provided in division (B) of this section, the department shall prepare a written reentry plan for the inmate to help guide the inmate's rehabilitation program during imprisonment, to assist in the inmate's reentry into the community, and to assess the inmate's needs upon release.

(B) Division (A) of this section does not apply to an inmate who has been sentenced to life imprisonment without parole or who has been sentenced to death. Division (A) of this section does not apply to any inmate who is expected to be imprisoned for thirty days or less, but the department may prepare a written reentry plan of the type described in that division if the department determines that the plan is needed.

(C) The department may collect, if available, any social and other information that will aid in the preparation of reentry plans under this section.

(D) In the event the department does not prepare a written reentry plan as specified in division (A) of this section, or makes a decision to not prepare a written reentry plan under division (B) of this section or to not collect information under division (C) of this section, that fact does not give rise to a claim for damages against the state, the department, the director of the department, or any employee of the department.

**HISTORY: 2011 HB 86, § 1, eff. Sept. 30, 2011.**

## § 5120.114 Single validated risk assessment tool; entities required to use tool; training and certification; policies and protocols required.

(A) The department of rehabilitation and correction shall select a single validated risk assessment tool for adult offenders. This assessment tool shall be used by the following entities:

(1) Municipal courts, when the particular court orders an assessment of an offender for sentencing or another purpose;

(2) Common pleas courts, when the particular court orders an assessment of an offender for sentencing or another purpose;

(3) County courts, when the particular court orders an assessment of an offender for sentencing or another purpose;

(4) Municipal court departments of probation;

(5) County departments of probation;

(6) Probation departments established by two or more counties;

(7) State and local correctional institutions;

(8) Private correctional facilities;

(9) Community-based correctional facilities;

(10) The adult parole authority;

(11) The parole board.

(B) For each entity required to use the assessment tool, every employee of the entity who actually uses the tool shall be trained and certified by a trainer who is certified by the department. Each entity utilizing the assessment tool shall develop policies and protocols regarding all of the following activities:

(1) Application and integration of the assessment tool into operations, supervision, and case planning;

(2) Administrative oversight of the use of the assessment tool;

(3) Staff training;

(4) Quality assurance;

(5) Data collection and sharing as described under section 5120.115 of the Revised Code.

**HISTORY: 2011 HB 86, § 1, eff. Sept. 30, 2011.**

## § 5120.115 Access to reports generated by and data stored in risk assessment tool; confidentiality.

(A) Each authorized user of the single validated risk assessment tool described in section 5120.114 of the Revised Code shall have access to all reports generated by the risk assessment tool and all data stored in the risk assessment tool. An authorized user may disclose any report generated by the risk assessment tool to law enforcement agencies, halfway houses, and medical, mental health, and substance abuse treatment providers for penological and rehabilitative purposes. The user shall make the disclosure in a manner calculated to maintain the report's confidentiality.

(B) All reports generated by or data collected in the risk assessment tool are confidential information and are not a public record. No person shall disclose any report generated by or data collected in the risk assessment tool except as provided in division (A) of this section.

(C) As used in this section, "public record" has the same meaning as in section 149.43 of the Revised Code.

**HISTORY: 2011 HB 86, § 1, eff. Sept. 30, 2011.**

## § 5120.12 Lease of real estate for oil and gas [Repealed].

Repealed by 2011 HB 133, § 2, effective September 30, 2011.

**HISTORY: 134 v H 494 (Eff 7-12-72); 141 v S 312 (Eff 9-24-86); 146 v H 60. Eff 3-4-98.**

Acts 2011, HB 133, § 3 provides: "A lease entered into under division (B) of section 3345.181 or section 123.01, 1531.06, 5119.40, 5120.12, or 5123.23 of the Revised Code as those sections existed prior to their amendment or repeal by this act shall remain in effect until the term of the lease expires as provided in the lease."

## § 5120.13 Acceptance of devise, grant, or bequest by department of rehabilitation and correction; trust funds for inmates.

(A) The department of rehabilitation and correction shall accept and hold on behalf of the state, if it is for the public interest, any grant, gift, devise, or bequest of money or property made to or for the use or benefit of any institution described in section 5120.05 of the Revised Code. The department shall keep such gift, grant, devise, or bequest as a distinct property or fund, and shall invest the same, if in money, in the manner provided by law. The department may deposit in a proper trust company or savings bank any fund left in trust during a specified life or lives, and shall adopt rules governing the deposit, transfer, withdrawal, or investment of such funds and the income thereof. Upon the expiration of any trust according to its terms, the department shall dispose of the funds or property held thereunder in the manner provided in the instrument creating the trust; except that, if the instrument creating the trust failed to make any terms of disposition, or if no trust was in evidence, then the decedent patient's, pupil's, or inmate's moneys, savings or commercial deposits, dividends or distributions, bonds, or any other interest bearing debt certificate or stamp issued by the United States government shall escheat to the state. All such unclaimed intangible personal property of a former inmate shall be retained by the managing officer in such institution for the period of one year during which time every possible effort shall be made to find that former inmate or that former inmate's legal representative. If, after a period of one year from the time such inmate has left such institution or has died, the managing officer is unable to locate the inmate or the inmate's legal representative, upon proper notice of such fact, the director of rehabilitation and correction shall at that time formulate in writing a method of disposition on the minutes of the department authorizing the managing officer of the institution to convert the same to cash to be paid into the treasury of the state to the credit of the general revenue fund. The department shall include in the annual report a statement of all such funds and property and the terms and conditions relating thereto.

Moneys or property deposited with managing officers of institutions by relatives, guardians, conservators, and friends for the special benefit of any inmate shall remain in the hands of such officers for use accordingly. Such funds shall be deposited in a personal deposit fund. Each such managing officer shall keep an itemized book account of the receipt and disposition thereof, which book shall be open at all times to the inspection of the department. The department shall adopt rules governing the deposit, transfer, withdrawal, or investment of such funds and the income thereof.

(B) Whenever an inmate confined in any state institution subject to the jurisdiction of the department dies, escapes, is discharged or paroled from the institution, or is placed on a term of post-release control under any section of the Revised Code and personal funds of the person remain in the hands of the managing officer of the institution and no demand is made upon the managing officer by the owner of the funds or the owner's legally appointed representative, the managing officer shall hold the funds in the personal deposit fund for a period of at least one year during which time the managing officer shall make every effort possible to locate the owner or the owner's legally appointed representative.

If, at the end of this period, no demand has been made for the funds, the managing officer shall dispose of the funds as follows:

(1) All moneys in a personal deposit fund in excess of ten dollars due for the support of an inmate shall be paid into the state's general revenue fund.

(2) All moneys in a personal deposit fund in excess of ten dollars not due for the support of an inmate shall be placed to the credit of the institution's local account designated as "industrial and entertainment" fund.

(3) All moneys less than ten dollars to the credit of an inmate shall be placed to the credit of the institution's local account designated as "industrial and entertainment" fund.

(C) Whenever an inmate in any state institution subject to the jurisdiction of the department dies, escapes, is discharged or paroled from the institution or is placed on a term of post-release control, and personal effects of the person remain in the hands of the managing officer of the institution, and no demand is made upon the managing officer by the owner of the property or the owner's legally appointed representative, the managing officer shall hold and dispose of such property as follows:

All the miscellaneous personal effects shall be held for a period of at least one year, during which time the managing officer shall make every effort possible to locate the owner or the owner's legal representative. If at the end of this period no demand has been made by the owner of the property or the owner's legal representative, the managing officer shall file with the county recorder of the county of commitment of the owner, all deeds, wills, contract mortgages, or assignments. The balance of the personal effects shall be sold at public auction after being duly advertised, and the funds turned over to the treasurer of state for credit to the general revenue fund. If any of the property is not of a type to be filed with the county recorder and is not salable at public auction, then the managing officer of the institution shall destroy the property.

**HISTORY: 134 v H 494 (Eff 7-12-72); 137 v S 221 (Eff 11-23-77); 140 v H 250 (Eff 7-30-84); 146 v S 2. Eff 7-1-96.**

The effective date is set by section 6 of SB 2.

## § 5120.131 Industrial and entertainment fund; commissary fund.

Each managing officer of an institution under the jurisdiction of the department of rehabilitation and correction as described in section 5120.05 of the Revised Code, with the approval of the director of the department of rehabilitation and correction, may establish local institution funds designated as follows:

(A) Industrial and entertainment fund created and maintained for the entertainment and welfare of the inmates of the institutions under the jurisdiction of the department. The director shall establish rules and regulations for the operation of the industrial and entertainment fund.

(B) Commissary fund created and maintained for the benefit of inmates in the institutions under the jurisdiction of the department.

Commissary revenue over and above operating costs and reserve shall be considered profits. All profits from the commissary fund operations shall be paid into the industrial and entertainment fund and used only for the entertainment and welfare of inmates. The director shall establish rules and regulations for the operation of the commissary fund.

**HISTORY: 134 v H 494. Eff 7-12-72.**

## § 5120.132 Prisoner programs fund.

(A) There is hereby created in the state treasury the prisoner programs fund. The director of rehabilitation and correction shall deposit in the fund all moneys received by the department from commissions on telephone systems established for the use of prisoners. The money in the fund shall be used only to pay for the costs of the following:

(1) The purchase of material, supplies, and equipment used in any library program, educational program, religious program, recreational program, or pre-release program operated by the department for the benefit of prisoners;

(2) The construction, alteration, repair, or reconstruction of buildings and structures owned by the department for use in any library program, educational program, religious program, recreational program, or pre-release program operated by the department for the benefit of prisoners;

(3) The payment of salary, wages, and other compensation to employees of the department who are employed in any library program, educational program, religious program, recreational program, or pre-release program operated by the department for the benefit of prisoners;

(4) The compensation to vendors that contract with the department for the provision of services for the benefit of prisoners in any library program, educational program, religious program, recreational program, or pre-release program operated by the department;

(5) The payment of prisoner release payments in an appropriate amount as determined pursuant to rule;

(6) The purchase of other goods and the payment of other services that are determined, in the discretion of the director, to be goods and services that may provide additional benefit to prisoners.

(B) The director shall establish rules for the operation of the prisoner programs fund.

**HISTORY: 144 v S 351. Eff 7-1-92.**

## § 5120.133 Transfer of prisoner's funds to satisfy judgment; exemptions.

(A) The department of rehabilitation and correction, upon receipt of a certified copy of the judgment of a court of record in an action in which a prisoner was a party that orders a prisoner to pay a stated obligation, may apply toward payment of the obligation money that belongs to a prisoner and that is in the account kept for the prisoner by the department. The department may transmit the prisoner's funds directly to the court for disbursement or may make payment in another manner as directed by the court. Except as provided in rules adopted under this section, when an amount is received for the prisoner's account, the department shall use it for the payment of the obligation and shall continue using amounts received for the account until the full amount of the obligation has been paid. No proceedings in aid of execution are necessary for the department to take the action required by this section.

(B) The department may adopt rules specifying a portion of an inmate's earnings or other receipts that the inmate is allowed to retain to make purchases from the commissary and that may not be used to satisfy an obligation pursuant to division (A) of this section. The rules shall not permit the application or disbursement of funds belonging to an inmate if those funds are exempt from execution, garnishment, attachment, or sale to satisfy a judgment or order pursuant to section 2329.66 of the Revised Code or to any other provision of law.

**HISTORY: 145 v H 571. Eff 10-6-94.**

## § 5120.135 Providing of laboratory services.

(A) As used in this section, "laboratory services" includes the performance of medical laboratory analysis; professional laboratory and pathologist consultation; the procurement, storage, and distribution of laboratory supplies; and the performance of phlebotomy services.

(B) The department of rehabilitation and correction may provide laboratory services to the departments of mental health, developmental disabilities, youth services, and rehabilitation and correction. The department of rehabilitation and correction may also provide laboratory services to other state, county, or municipal agencies and to private persons that request laboratory services if the department of rehabilitation and correction determines that the provision of laboratory services is in the public interest and considers it advisable to provide such services. The department of rehabilitation and correction may also provide laboratory services to agencies operated by the United States government and to public and private entities funded in whole or in part by the state if the director of rehabilitation and correction designates them as eligible to receive such services.

The department of rehabilitation and correction shall provide laboratory services from a laboratory that complies with the standards for certification set by the United States department of health and human services under the "Clinical Laboratory Improvement Amendments of 1988," 102 Stat. 293, 42 U.S.C.A. 263a. In addition, the laboratory shall maintain accreditation or certification with an appropriate accrediting or certifying organization as considered necessary by the recipients of its laboratory services and as authorized by the director of rehabilitation and correction.

(C) The cost of administering this section shall be determined by the department of rehabilitation and correction and shall be paid by entities that receive laboratory services to the department for deposit in the state treasury to the credit of the laboratory services fund, which is hereby created. The fund shall be used to pay the costs the department incurs in administering this section.

(D) Whenever a state agency fails to make a payment for laboratory services provided to it by the department of rehabilitation and correction under this section within thirty-one days after the date the payment was due, the office of budget and management may transfer moneys from that state agency to the department of rehabilitation and correction for deposit to the credit of the laboratory services fund. The amount transferred shall not exceed the amount of the overdue payments. Prior to making a transfer under this division, the office shall apply any credits the state agency has accumulated in payment for laboratory services provided under this section.

**HISTORY: 147 v H 850. Eff 3-18-99; 153 v S 79, § 1, eff. 10-6-09; 2011 HB 153, § 101.01, eff. Sept. 29, 2011.**

The effective date is set by section 102 of HB 850.

## § 5120.14 Duty to give notice of escape and of apprehension of escapee.

(A) If a person who was convicted of or pleaded guilty to an offense escapes from a correctional institution in this state under the control of the department of rehabilitation and correction or otherwise escapes from the custody of the department, the department immediately after the escape shall report the escape, by telephone and in writing, to all local law enforcement agencies with jurisdiction in the county in which the institution from which the escape was made or to which the person was sentenced is located, to all local law enforcement agencies with jurisdiction in the county in which the person was convicted or pleaded guilty to the offense for which the escaped person was sentenced, to the state highway patrol, to the prosecuting attorney of the county in which the institution from which the escape was made or to which the person was sentenced is located, to the prosecuting attorney of the county in which the person was convicted or pleaded guilty to the offense for which the escaped person was sentenced, to a newspaper of general circulation in the county in which the institution from which the escape was made or to which the person was sentenced is located, and to a newspaper of general circulation in each county in which the escaped person was indicted for an offense for which, at the time of the escape, the escaped person had been sentenced to that institution. The written notice may be by either facsimile transmission or mail. A failure to comply with this requirement is a violation of section 2921.22 of the Revised Code.

(B) Upon the apprehension of the escaped person, the department shall give notice of the apprehension by telephone and in writing to the persons who were given notice of the escape under division (A) of this section.

**HISTORY: 142 v H 207 (Eff 9-24-87); 145 v H 571 (Eff 10-6-94); 148 v H 283. Eff 6-30-99.**

**Not analogous to former RC § 5120.14 (134 v H 494), repealed 137 v H 565, § 2, eff 11-1-78.**

The effective date is set by section 164 of HB 283.

## § 5120.15 Regulation of admission and discharge of inmates.

The department of rehabilitation and correction shall regulate the admission and discharge of inmates in the institutions described in section 5120.05 of the Revised Code.

**HISTORY: 134 v H 494. Eff 7-12-72.**

## § 5120.16 Examination, observation, and classification; assignment to institution; transfer.

(A) Persons sentenced to any institution, division, or place under the control of the department of rehabilitation and correction are committed to the control, care, and custody of the department. Subject to division (B) of this section, the director of rehabilitation and correction or the director's designee may direct that persons sentenced to the department, or to any institution or place within the department, shall be conveyed initially to an appropriate facility established and maintained by the department for reception, examination, observation, and classification of the persons so sentenced. If a presentence investigation report was not prepared pursuant to section 2947.06 or 2951.03 of the Revised Code or Criminal Rule 32.2 regarding any person sentenced to the department or to any institution or place within the department, the director or the director's designee may order the department's field staff to conduct an offender background investigation and prepare an offender background investigation report regarding the person. The investigation and report shall be conducted in accordance with division (A) of section 2951.03 of the Revised Code and the report shall contain the same information as a presentence investigation report prepared pursuant to that section.

When the examination, observation, and classification of the person have been completed by the facility and a written report of the examination, observation, and classification is filed with the commitment papers, the director or the director's designee, subject to division (B) of this section, shall assign the person to a suitable state institution or place maintained by the state within the director's department or shall designate that the person is to be housed in a county, multicounty, municipal, municipal-county, or multicounty-municipal jail or workhouse, if authorized by section 5120.161 of the Revised Code, there to be confined, cared for, treated, trained, and rehabilitated until paroled, released in accordance with section 2929.20, 2967.26, 2967.28, or 5120.036 of the Revised Code, or otherwise released under the order of the court that imposed the person's sentence. No person committed by a probate court, a trial court pursuant to section 2945.40, 2945.401, or 2945.402 of the Revised Code subsequent to a finding of not guilty by reason of insanity, or a juvenile court shall be assigned to a state correctional institution.

If a person is sentenced, committed, or assigned for the commission of a felony to any one of the institutions or places maintained by the department or to a county, multicounty, municipal, municipal-county, or multicounty-municipal jail or workhouse, the department, by order duly recorded and subject to division (B) of this section, may transfer the person to any other institution, or, if authorized by section 5120.161 of the Revised Code, to a county, multicounty, municipal, municipal-county, or multicounty-municipal jail or workhouse.

(B) If the case of a child who is alleged to be a delinquent child is transferred for criminal prosecution to the appropriate court having jurisdiction of the offense pursuant to section 2152.12 of the Revised Code, if the child is convicted of or pleads guilty to a felony in that case, if the child is sentenced to a prison term, as defined in section 2901.01 of the Revised Code, and if the child is under eighteen years of age when delivered to the custody of the department of rehabilitation and correction, all of the following apply regarding the housing of the child:

(1) Until the child attains eighteen years of age, subject to divisions (B)(2), (3), and (4) of this section, the department shall house the child in a housing unit in a state correctional institution separate from inmates who are eighteen years of age or older.

(2) The department is not required to house the child in the manner described in division (B)(1) of this section if the child does not observe the rules and regulations of the institution or the child otherwise creates a security risk by being housed separately.

(3) If the department receives too few inmates who are under eighteen years of age to fill a housing unit in a state correctional institution separate from inmates who are eighteen years of age or older, as described in division (B)(1) of this section, the department may house the child in a housing unit in a state correctional institution that includes both inmates who are under eighteen years of age and inmates who are eighteen years of age or older and under twenty-one years of age.

(4) Upon the child's attainment of eighteen years of age, the department may house the child with the adult population of the state correctional institution.

(C) The director or the director's designee shall develop a policy for dealing with problems related to infection with the human immunodeficiency virus. The policy shall include methods of identifying individuals committed to the custody of the department who are at high risk of infection with the virus and counseling those individuals.

Arrangements for housing individuals diagnosed as having AIDS or an AIDS-related condition shall be made by the department based on security and medical considerations and in accordance with division (B) of this section, if applicable.

**HISTORY: 134 v H 494 (Eff 7-12-72); 137 v H 565 (Eff 11-1-78); 138 v S 297 (Eff 4-30-80); 138 v H 900 (Eff 7-1-80); 138 v H 965 (Eff 4-9-81); 139 v S 199 (Eff 1-1-83); 142 v H 455 (Eff 7-20-87); 143 v S 2 (Eff 11-1-89); 144 v S 331 (Eff 11-13-92); 145 v H 571 (Eff 10-6-94); 146 v S 310 (Eff 6-20-96); 146 v S 2 (Eff 7-1-96); 146 v H 124 (Eff 3-31-97); 146 v S 285 (Eff 7-1-97); 147 v H 215 (Eff 9-29-97); 147 v S 111 (Eff 3-17-98); 148 v S 179, § 3. Eff 1-1-2002; 2011 HB 86, § 1, eff. Sept. 30, 2011.**

The effective date is set by section 5 of SB 179.

## § 5120.161 Agreements with local authorities for housing of certain state prisoners.

(A) Except as provided in division (C) of this section, the department of rehabilitation and correction may enter into an agreement with any local authority operating a county, multicounty, municipal, municipal-county, or multicounty-municipal jail or workhouse, as described in section 307.93, 341.21, or 753.16 of the Revised Code, for the housing in the jail or workhouse operated by the local authority of persons who are convicted of or plead guilty to a felony of the fourth or fifth degree if the person previously has not been convicted of or pleaded guilty to a felony and if the felony is not an offense of violence. The agreement shall specify a per diem fee that the department shall pay the local authority for each such person housed in the jail or workhouse pursuant to the agreement, shall set forth any other terms and conditions for the housing of such persons in the jail or workhouse, and shall indicate that the department, subject to the relevant terms and conditions set forth, may designate those persons to be housed at the jail or workhouse.

(B) A person designated by the department to be housed in a county, multicounty, municipal, municipal-county, or multicounty-municipal jail or workhouse that is the subject of an agreement entered into under division (A) of this section shall be conveyed by the department to that jail or workhouse and shall be kept at the jail or workhouse until the person's term of imprisonment expires, the person is pardoned, paroled, or placed under a post-release control sanction, or the person is transferred under the laws permitting the transfer of prisoners. The department shall pay the local authority that operates the jail or workhouse the per diem fee specified in the agreement for each such person housed in the jail or workhouse. Each such person housed in the jail or workhouse shall be under the direct supervision and control of the keeper, superintendent, or other person in charge of the jail or workhouse, but shall be considered for all other purposes to be within the custody of the department of rehabilitation and correction. Section 2967.193 [2967.19.3] of the Revised Code and all other provisions of the Revised Code that pertain to persons within the custody of the department that would not by their nature clearly be inapplicable apply to persons housed pursuant to this section.

(C) The department of rehabilitation and correction shall not enter into an agreement pursuant to division (A) of this section with any local authority unless the jail or workhouse operated by the authority complies with the Minimum Standards for Jails in Ohio.

(D) A court that sentences a person for a felony may include as the sentence or part of the sentence, in accordance with division (A) of section 2929.16 of the Revised Code and regardless of whether the jail or workhouse is the subject of an agreement entered into under division (A) of this section, a sanction that consists of a term of up to six months in a jail or workhouse or, if the offense is a fourth degree felony OVI offense and the offender is sentenced under division (G)(1) of section 2929.13 of the Revised Code, a sanction that consists of a term of up to one year in jail less the mandatory term of local incarceration of sixty or one hundred twenty consecutive days imposed pursuant to division (G)(1) of section 2929.13 of the Revised Code.

(E) "Fourth degree felony OVI offense" and "mandatory term of local incarceration" have the same meanings as in section 2929.01 of the Revised Code.

**HISTORY: 139 v S 199 (Eff 1-1-83); 139 v H 269 (Eff 7-1-83); 142 v H 455 (Eff 7-20-87); 146 v S 2 (Eff 7-1-96); 146 v S 269 (Eff 7-1-96); 146 v H 72 (Eff 3-18-97); 148 v S 22. Eff 5-17-2000; 149 v S 123, § 1, eff. 1-1-04.**

The effective date is set by section 4 of S.B. 123.

See provisions, § 5 of S.B. 123 (149 v —), following RC § 5120.032.

## § 5120.162 Agreement for transfer of children in custody of youth services department to correctional medical center.

(A) The department of rehabilitation and correction may enter into an agreement with the department of youth services pursuant to which the department of youth services may transfer to a correctional medical center established by the department of rehabilitation and correction children who are within its custody, who have an illness, physical condition, or other medical problem, and who apparently would benefit from diagnosis or treatment at the center for that illness, condition, or problem. Notwithstanding the fact that portions of the center may be used for the benefit of children in the custody of the department of youth services, the center shall be considered a facility of the department of rehabilitation and correction and shall be controlled and operated in accordance with the agreement and the provisions of this section. A child who is in the custody of the department of youth services and who is transferred to the center shall be considered as remaining in the custody of the department of youth services during the period of his diagnosis, treatment, or housing for diagnosis or treatment in the center.

During the development or renovation of a correctional medical center that is the subject of an agreement under this section, the department of rehabilitation and correction shall confer with the department of youth services to ensure that the center is planned and constructed or renovated to facilitate its use for the diagnosis or treatment of both prisoners in the custody of the department of rehabilitation and correction and children in the custody of the department of youth services who may be transferred to the center.

(B) All children who are in the custody of the department of youth services and who are transferred to a correctional medical center pursuant to an agreement under this section shall be housed in areas of the center that are totally separate and removed by sight and sound from all prisoners who are in the custody of the department of rehabilitation and correction and who are being diagnosed, treated, or housed for diagnosis or treatment in the center or who otherwise are in the center. For purposes of this division, children who are being diagnosed, treated, or housed for diagnosis or treatment in a building or wing of a building in which no prisoners in the custody of the department of rehabilitation and correction are being diagnosed, treated, or housed for diagnosis or treatment or otherwise are present are being housed totally separate from any prisoners who are in the custody of the department of rehabilitation and correction.

**HISTORY: 144 v S 331. Eff 11-13-92.**

## § 5120.163 Testing and treatment for certain diseases.

At the time of reception and at other times the director determines to be appropriate, the department of rehabilitation and correction may examine and test a prisoner for tuberculosis, HIV infection, hepatitis, including but not limited to hepatitis A, B, and C, and other contagious diseases. The department may test and treat involuntarily a prisoner in a state correctional institution who refuses to be tested or treated for tuberculosis, HIV infection, hepatitis, including but not limited to hepatitis A, B, and C, or another contagious disease.

**HISTORY: 147 v S 111. Eff 3-17-98.**

## § 5120.17 Transfer of inmate to psychiatric hospital; discharge; parole; expiration of prison term.

(A) As used in this section:

(1) "Mental illness" means a substantial disorder of thought, mood, perception, orientation, or memory that grossly impairs judgment, behavior, capacity to recognize reality, or ability to meet the ordinary demands of life.

(2) "Mentally ill person subject to hospitalization" means a mentally ill person to whom any of the following applies because of the person's mental illness:

(a) The person represents a substantial risk of physical harm to the person as manifested by evidence of threats of, or attempts at, suicide or serious self-inflicted bodily harm.

(b) The person represents a substantial risk of physical harm to others as manifested by evidence of recent homicidal or other violent behavior, evidence of recent threats that place another in reasonable fear of violent behavior and serious physical harm, or other evidence of present dangerousness.

(c) The person represents a substantial and immediate risk of serious physical impairment or injury to the person as manifested by evidence that the person is unable to provide for and is not providing for the person's basic physical needs because of the person's mental illness and that appropriate provision for those needs cannot be made immediately available in the correctional institution in which the inmate is currently housed.

(d) The person would benefit from treatment in a hospital for the person's mental illness and is in need of treatment in a hospital as manifested by evidence of behavior that creates a grave and imminent risk to substantial rights of others or the person.

(3) "Psychiatric hospital" means all or part of a facility that is operated and managed by the department of mental health to provide psychiatric hospitalization services in accordance with the requirements of this section pursuant to an agreement between the directors of rehabilitation and correction and mental health or, is licensed by the department of mental health pursuant to section 5119.20 of the Revised Code as a psychiatric hospital and is accredited by a healthcare accrediting organization approved by the department of mental health and the psychiatric hospital is any of the following:

(a) Operated and managed by the department of rehabilitation and correction within a facility that is operated by the department of rehabilitation and correction;

(b) Operated and managed by a contractor for the department of rehabilitation and correction within a facility that is operated by the department of rehabilitation and correction;

(c) Operated and managed in the community by an entity that has contracted with the department of rehabilitation and correction to provide psychiatric hospitalization services in accordance with the requirements of this section.

(4) "Inmate patient" means an inmate who is admitted to a psychiatric hospital.

(5) "Admitted" to a psychiatric hospital means being accepted for and staying at least one night at the psychiatric hospital.

(6) "Treatment plan" means a written statement of reasonable objectives and goals for an inmate patient that is based on the needs of the inmate patient and that is established by the treatment team, with the active participation of the inmate patient and with documentation of that participation. "Treatment plan" includes all of the following:

(a) The specific criteria to be used in evaluating progress toward achieving the objectives and goals;

(b) The services to be provided to the inmate patient during the inmate patient's hospitalization;

(c) The services to be provided to the inmate patient after discharge from the hospital, including, but not limited to, housing and mental health services provided at the state correctional institution to which the inmate patient returns after discharge or community mental health services.

(7) "Mentally retarded person subject to institutionalization by court order" has the same meaning as in section 5123.01 of the Revised Code.

(8) "Emergency transfer" means the transfer of a mentally ill inmate to a psychiatric hospital when the inmate presents an immediate danger to self or others and requires hospital-level care.

(9) "Uncontested transfer" means the transfer of a mentally ill inmate to a psychiatric hospital when the inmate has the mental capacity to, and has waived, the hearing required by division (B) of this section.

(10)(a) "Independent decision-maker" means a person who is employed or retained by the department of rehabilitation and correction and is appointed by the chief or chief clinical officer of mental health services as a hospitalization hearing officer to conduct due process hearings.

(b) An independent decision-maker who presides over any hearing or issues any order pursuant to this section shall be a psychiatrist, psychologist, or attorney, shall not be specifically associated with the institution in which the inmate who is the subject of the hearing or order resides at the time of the hearing or order, and previously shall not have had any treatment relationship with nor have represented in any legal proceeding the inmate who is the subject of the order.

(B)(1) Except as provided in division (C) of this section, if the warden of a state correctional institution or the warden's designee believes that an inmate should be transferred from the institution to a psychiatric hospital, the department shall hold a hearing to determine whether the inmate is a mentally ill person subject to hospitalization. The department shall conduct the hearing at the state correctional institution in which the inmate is confined, and the department shall provide qualified independent assistance to the inmate for the hearing. An independent decision-maker provided by the department shall preside at the hearing and determine whether the inmate is a mentally ill person subject to hospitalization.

(2) Except as provided in division (C) of this section, prior to the hearing held pursuant to division (B)(1) of this section, the warden or the warden's designee shall give written notice to the inmate that the department is considering transferring the inmate to a psychiatric hospital, that it will hold a hearing on the proposed transfer at which the inmate may be present, that at the hearing the inmate has the rights described in division (B)(3) of this section, and that the department will provide qualified independent assistance to the inmate with respect to the hearing. The department shall not hold the hearing until the inmate has received written notice of the proposed transfer and has had sufficient time to consult with the person appointed by the department to provide assistance to the inmate and to prepare for a presentation at the hearing.

(3) At the hearing held pursuant to division (B)(1) of this section, the department shall disclose to the inmate the evidence that it relies upon for the transfer and shall give the inmate an opportunity to be heard. Unless the independent decision-maker finds good cause for not permitting it, the inmate may present documentary evidence and the testimony of witnesses at the hearing and may confront and cross-examine witnesses called by the department.

(4) If the independent decision-maker does not find clear and convincing evidence that the inmate is a mentally ill person subject to hospitalization, the department shall not transfer the inmate to a psychiatric hospital but shall continue to confine the inmate in the same state correctional institution or in another state correctional institution that the department considers appropriate. If the independent decision-maker finds clear and convincing evidence that the inmate is a mentally ill person subject to hospitalization, the decision-maker shall order that the inmate be transported to a psychiatric hospital for observation and treatment for a period of not longer than thirty days. After the hearing, the independent decision-maker shall submit to the department a written decision that states one of the findings described in division (B)(4) of this section, the evidence that the decision-maker relied on in reaching that conclusion, and, if the decision is that the inmate should be transferred, the reasons for the transfer.

(C)(1) The department may transfer an inmate to a psychiatric hospital under an emergency transfer order if the chief clinical officer of mental health services of the department or that officer's designee and either a psychiatrist employed or retained by the department or, in the absence of a psychiatrist, a psychologist employed or retained by the department determines that the inmate is mentally ill, presents an immediate danger to self or others, and requires hospital-level care.

(2) The department may transfer an inmate to a psychiatric hospital under an uncontested transfer order if both of the following apply:

(a) A psychiatrist employed or retained by the department determines all of the following apply:

(i) The inmate has a mental illness or is a mentally ill person subject to hospitalization.

(ii) The inmate requires hospital care to address the mental illness.

(iii) The inmate has the mental capacity to make a reasoned choice regarding the inmate's transfer to a hospital.

(b) The inmate agrees to a transfer to a hospital.

(3) The written notice and the hearing required under divisions (B)(1) and (2) of this section are not required for an emergency transfer or uncontested transfer under division (C)(1) or (2) of this section.

(4) After an emergency transfer under division (C)(1) of this section, the department shall hold a hearing for continued hospitalization within five working days after admission of the transferred inmate to the psychiatric hospital. The department shall hold subsequent hearings pursuant to division (F) of this section at the same intervals as required for inmate patients who are transported to a psychiatric hospital under division (B)(4) of this section.

(5) After an uncontested transfer under division (C)(2) of this section, the inmate may withdraw consent to the transfer in writing at any time. Upon the inmate's withdrawal of consent, the hospital shall discharge the inmate, or, within five working days, the department shall hold a hearing for continued hospitalization. The department shall hold subsequent hearings pursuant to division (F) of this section at the same time intervals as required for inmate patients who are transported to a psychiatric hospital under division (B)(4) of this section.

(D)(1) If an independent decision-maker, pursuant to division (B)(4) of this section, orders an inmate transported to a psychiatric hospital or if an inmate is transferred pursuant to division (C)(1) or (2) of this section, the staff of the psychiatric hospital shall examine the inmate patient when admitted to the psychiatric hospital as soon as practicable after the inmate patient arrives at the hospital and no later than twenty-four hours after the time of arrival. The attending physician responsible for the inmate patient's care shall give the inmate patient all information necessary to enable the patient to give a fully informed, intelligent, and knowing consent to the treatment the inmate patient will receive in the hospital. The attending physician shall tell the inmate patient the expected physical and medical consequences of any proposed treatment and shall give the inmate patient the opportunity to consult with another psychiatrist at the hospital and with the inmate advisor.

(2) No inmate patient who is transported or transferred pursuant to division (B)(4) or (C)(1) or (2) of this section to a psychiatric hospital within a facility that is operated by the department of rehabilitation and correction shall be subjected to any of the following procedures:

(a) Convulsive therapy;

(b) Major aversive interventions;

(c) Any unusually hazardous treatment procedures;

(d) Psychosurgery.

(E) The department of rehabilitation and correction shall ensure that an inmate patient hospitalized pursuant to this section receives or has all of the following:

(1) Receives sufficient professional care within twenty days of admission to ensure that an evaluation of the inmate patient's current status, differential diagnosis, probable prognosis, and description of the current treatment plan have been formulated and are stated on the inmate patient's official chart;

(2) Has a written treatment plan consistent with the evaluation, diagnosis, prognosis, and goals of treatment;

(3) Receives treatment consistent with the treatment plan;

(4) Receives periodic reevaluations of the treatment plan by the professional staff at intervals not to exceed thirty days;

(5) Is provided with adequate medical treatment for physical disease or injury;

(6) Receives humane care and treatment, including, without being limited to, the following:

(a) Access to the facilities and personnel required by the treatment plan;

(b) A humane psychological and physical environment;

(c) The right to obtain current information concerning the treatment program, the expected outcomes of treatment, and the expectations for the inmate patient's participation in the treatment program in terms that the inmate patient reasonably can understand;

(d) Opportunity for participation in programs designed to help the inmate patient acquire the skills needed to work toward discharge from the psychiatric hospital;

(e) The right to be free from unnecessary or excessive medication and from unnecessary restraints or isolation;

(f) All other rights afforded inmates in the custody of the department consistent with rules, policy, and procedure of the department.

(F) The department shall hold a hearing for the continued hospitalization of an inmate patient who is transported or transferred to a psychiatric hospital pursuant to division (B)(4) or (C)(1) of this section prior to the expiration of the initial thirty-day period of hospitalization. The department shall hold any subsequent hearings, if necessary, not later than ninety days after the first thirty-day hearing and then not later than each one hundred and eighty days after the immediately prior hearing. An independent decision-maker shall conduct the hearings at the psychiatric hospital in which the inmate patient is confined. The inmate patient shall be afforded all of the rights set forth in this section for the hearing prior to transfer to the psychiatric hospital. The department may not waive a hearing for continued commitment. A hearing for continued commitment is mandatory for an inmate patient transported or transferred to a psychiatric hospital pursuant to division (B)(4) or (C)(1) of this section unless the inmate patient has the capacity to make a reasoned choice to execute a waiver and waives the hearing in writing. An inmate patient who is transferred to a psychiatric hospital pursuant to an uncontested transfer under division (C)(2) of this section and who has scheduled hearings after withdrawal of consent for hospitalization may waive any of the scheduled hearings if the inmate has the capacity to make a reasoned choice and executes a written waiver of the hearing.

If upon completion of the hearing the independent decision-maker does not find by clear and convincing evidence that the inmate patient is a mentally ill person subject to hospitalization, the independent decision-maker shall order the inmate patient's discharge from the psychiatric hospital. If the independent decision-maker finds by clear and convincing evidence that the inmate patient is a mentally ill person subject to hospitalization, the independent decision-maker shall order that the inmate patient remain at the psychiatric hospital for continued hospitalization until the next required hearing.

If at any time prior to the next required hearing for continued hospitalization, the medical director of the hospital or the attending physician determines that the treatment needs of the inmate patient could be met equally well in an available and appropriate less restrictive state correctional institution or unit, the medical director or attending physician may discharge the inmate to that facility.

(G) An inmate patient is entitled to the credits toward the reduction of the inmate patient's stated prison term pursuant to Chapters 2967. and 5120. of the Revised Code under the same terms and conditions as if the inmate patient were in any other institution of the department of rehabilitation and correction.

(H) The adult parole authority may place an inmate patient on parole or under post-release control directly from a psychiatric hospital.

(I) If an inmate patient who is a mentally ill person subject to hospitalization is to be released from a psychiatric hospital because of the expiration of the inmate patient's stated prison term, the director of rehabilitation and correction or the director's designee, at least fourteen days before the expiration date, may file an affidavit under section 5122.11 or 5123.71 of the Revised Code with the probate court in the county where the psychiatric hospital is located or the probate court in the county where the inmate will reside, alleging that the inmate patient is a mentally ill person subject to hospitalization by court order or a mentally retarded person subject to institutionalization by court order, whichever is applicable. The proceedings in the probate court shall be conducted pursuant to Chapter 5122. or 5123. of the Revised Code except as modified by this division.

Upon the request of the inmate patient, the probate court shall grant the inmate patient an initial hearing under section 5122.141 of the Revised Code or a probable cause hearing under section 5123.75 of the Revised Code before the expiration of the stated prison term. After holding a full hearing, the probate court shall make a disposition authorized by section 5122.15 or 5123.76 of the Revised Code before the date of the expiration of the stated prison term. No inmate patient shall be held in the custody of the department of rehabilitation and correction past the date of the expiration of the inmate patient's stated prison term.

(J) The department of rehabilitation and correction shall set standards for treatment provided to inmate patients.

(K) A certificate, application, record, or report that is made in compliance with this section and that directly or indirectly identifies an inmate or former inmate whose hospitalization has been sought under this section is confidential. No person shall disclose the contents of any certificate, application, record, or report of that nature or any other psychiatric or medical record or report regarding a mentally ill inmate unless one of the following applies:

(1) The person identified, or the person's legal guardian, if any, consents to disclosure, and the chief clinical officer or designee of mental health services of the department of rehabilitation and correction determines that disclosure is in the best interests of the person.

(2) Disclosure is required by a court order signed by a judge.

(3) An inmate patient seeks access to the inmate patient's own psychiatric and medical records, unless access is specifically restricted in the treatment plan for clear treatment reasons.

(4) Hospitals and other institutions and facilities within the department of rehabilitation and correction may exchange psychiatric records and other pertinent information with other hospitals, institutions, and facilities of the department, but the information that may be released about an inmate patient is limited to medication history, physical health status and history, summary of course of treatment in the hospital, summary of treatment needs, and a discharge summary, if any.

(5) An inmate patient's family member who is involved in planning, providing, and monitoring services to the inmate patient may receive medication information, a summary of the inmate patient's diagnosis and prognosis, and a list of the services and personnel available to assist the inmate patient and family if the attending physician determines that disclosure would be in the best interest of the inmate patient. No disclosure shall be made under this division unless the inmate patient is notified of the possible disclosure, receives the information to be disclosed, and does not object to the disclosure.

(6) The department of rehabilitation and correction may exchange psychiatric hospitalization records, other mental health treatment records, and other pertinent information with county sheriffs' offices, hospitals, institutions, and facilities of the department of mental health and with community mental health agencies and boards of alcohol, drug addiction, and mental health services with which the department of mental health has a current agreement for patient care or services to ensure continuity of care. Disclosure under this division is limited to records regarding a mentally ill inmate's medication history, physical health status and history, summary of course of treatment, summary of treatment needs, and a discharge summary, if any. No office, department, agency, or board shall disclose the records and other information unless one of the following applies:

(a) The mentally ill inmate is notified of the possible disclosure and consents to the disclosure.

(b) The mentally ill inmate is notified of the possible disclosure, an attempt to gain the consent of the inmate is made, and the office, department, agency, or board documents the attempt to gain consent, the inmate's objections, if any, and the reasons for disclosure in spite of the inmate's objections.

(7) Information may be disclosed to staff members designated by the director of rehabilitation and correction for the purpose of evaluating the quality, effectiveness, and efficiency of services and determining if the services meet minimum standards.

The name of an inmate patient shall not be retained with the information obtained during the evaluations.

(L) The director of rehabilitation and correction may adopt rules setting forth guidelines for the procedures required under divisions (B), (C)(1), and (C)(2) of this section.

**HISTORY: 146 v S 310 (Eff 6-20-96); 147 v S 52 (Eff 9-3-97); 149 v H 355. Eff 7-23-2002; 2011 HB 153, § 101.01, eff. Sept. 29, 2011.**

**Analogous to former RC § 5120.17 (GC § 1890-73; 117 v 550 (572), § 73; 119 v 616 (633); 121 v 423 (437); Bureau of Code Revision, RC § 5125.05, 10-1-53; 125 v 872; 130 v 1203; 134 v H 494; 137 v H 565; 138 v S 297; RC § 5120.17, 138 v H 900; 138 v H 965; 140 v H 37; 142 v S 156; 146 v S 2), repealed 146 v S 310, § 2, eff 6-20-96.**

## § 5120.171 Care and treatment of seriously mentally ill inmates.

(A) The department of rehabilitation and correction shall have exclusive direction and control of the care and treatment of seriously mentally ill inmates who are in the department's custody. The department shall enter into any arrangements it considers desirable on such matters, including but not limited to both of the following:

(1) The monitoring of such services by another state agency or agencies;

(2) Adopting joint standards for the provision and monitoring of mental health services with the department of mental health and other state agencies.

(B) In order to implement its duties imposed by division (A) of this section, the department of rehabilitation and correction may enter into a contract for the provision of the mental health services described in that division.

**HISTORY: 146 v H 117. Eff 6-30-95.**

## § 5120.172 Medical treatment of minor prosecuted as adult.

A minor whose case is transferred for criminal prosecution pursuant to section 2152.12 of the Revised Code, who is prosecuted as an adult and is convicted of or pleads guilty to one or more offenses in that case, and who is sentenced to a prison term or term of imprisonment in a state correctional institution for one or more of those offenses shall be considered emancipated for the purpose of consenting to medical treatment while confined in the state correctional institution.

**HISTORY: 147 v S 111 (Eff 3-17-98); 148 v S 179, § 3. Eff 1-1-2002.**

The effective date is set by section 5 of SB 179.

## § 5120.173 Report of abuse or neglect of child or person with mental retardation or developmental disability.

Any person who is required to report abuse or neglect of a child under eighteen years of age that is reasonably suspected or believed to have occurred or the threat of which is reasonably suspected or believed to exist pursuant to division (A) of section 2151.421 [2151.42.1] of the Revised Code, any person who is permitted to report or cause a report to be made of reasonably suspected abuse or neglect of a child under eighteen years of age pursuant to division (B) of that section, any person who is required to report suspected abuse or neglect of a person with mental retardation or a developmental disability pursuant to division (C) of section 5123.61 of the Revised Code, and any person who is permitted to report suspected abuse or neglect of a person with mental retardation or a developmental disability pursuant to division (F) of that section and who makes or causes the report to be made, shall direct that report to the state highway patrol if the child or the person with mental retardation or a developmental disability is an inmate in the custody of a state correctional institution. If the state highway patrol determines after receipt of the report that it is probable that abuse or neglect of the inmate occurred, the patrol shall report its findings to the department of rehabilitation and correction, to the court that sentenced the inmate for the offense for which the inmate is in the custody of the department, and to the chairperson and vice-chairperson of the correctional institution inspection committee established by section 103.71 of the Revised Code.

**HISTORY: 149 v H 510. Eff 3-31-2003; 150 v S 178, § 1, eff. 1-30-04; 151 v S 17, § 1, eff. 8-3-06.**

## § 5120.18 Classification of public buildings; purchase of articles to be used therein.

The department of rehabilitation and correction shall, with the advice and consent of the department of administrative services, classify public buildings, offices, and institutions and determine the kinds, patterns, designs, and qualities of articles to be manufactured for use therein, which shall be uniform for each class, so far as practicable.

Whenever the department of rehabilitation and correction gives written notice to the superintendent of purchases and printing, or other official having authority to purchase articles, that the department is prepared to supply such articles from any institution under its control, the superintendent or other official shall make any needed purchases of said articles from such institution, unless the chief officer thereof, or the department, having been requested to furnish such articles, gives notice in writing within thirty days from the date of the request, that such articles cannot be furnished.

If the superintendent requires such articles within thirty days from the day of making such request and so states upon the face of such request, the chief officer of such institution or the department of rehabilitation and correction shall forthwith advise the superintendent whether it will be able to furnish such articles within such time, the superintendent may purchase such articles in the open market as in other cases. This section does not apply to any officer, board, or agent of any municipal corporation which maintains an institution that produces or manufactures articles of the kind desired.

**HISTORY: 134 v H 494 (Eff 7-12-72); 137 v H 1. Eff 8-26-77.**

## § 5120.19 Cultivation and use of lands; transactions between institutions.

(A) The department of rehabilitation and correction, in accordance with rules adopted pursuant to division (B) of section 5145.03 of the Revised Code, shall determine and direct what lands belonging to institutions under its control shall be cultivated, the crops to be raised, and the use to be made of the land and crops, and may distribute the products among the different institutions. If the crops are distributed to institutions under the control of the department, the department shall keep records of the distributions and of the fair market value of the crops distributed. The department may sell any crops that are not necessary for the institutions under its control to any person. The money received from the sale of the crops shall be deposited in the services and agricultural fund created pursuant to section 5120.29 of the Revised Code.

The department may require institutions under its control, when they have proper lands and labor, to undertake intensive agriculture, may rent lands for the production of supplies for any of the institutions that have surplus labor, and may rent lands for the production of crops for sale, when it can be done to advantage.

The department shall pay and assign the prisoners who perform any labor pursuant to this division in accordance with the rules adopted pursuant to division (B) of section 5145.03 of the Revised Code.

(B) The department may direct the purchase of any materials, supplies, or other articles for any institution under its control from any other institution under its control at the reasonable market value, which value shall be fixed by the department. Payments for the articles shall be made as between institutions in the manner provided for payment for supplies.

**HISTORY: 134 v H 494 (Eff 7-12-72); 138 v H 654 (Eff 4-9-82); 141 v H 201 (Eff 7-1-85); 142 v H 171. Eff 7-1-87.**

## § 5120.20 Cooperation from agriculture and health departments and Ohio state university.

The department of agriculture, department of health, and Ohio state university shall cooperate with the department of rehabilitation and correction in making such cooperative tests as are necessary to determine the quality, strength, and purity of supplies, the value and use of farm lands, or conditions and needs of mechanical equipment.

**HISTORY: 134 v H 494 (Eff 7-12-72); 136 v H 1. Eff 6-13-75.**

## § 5120.21 Records; report on accident or injury or peculiar death.

(A) The department of rehabilitation and correction shall keep in its office, accessible only to its employees, except by the consent of the department or the order of the judge of a court of record, and except as provided in division (C) of this section, a record showing the name, residence, sex, age, nativity, occupation, condition, and date of entrance or commitment of every inmate in the several institutions governed by it. The record also shall include the date, cause, and terms of discharge and the condition of such person at the time of leaving, a record of all transfers from one institution to another, and, if such inmate is dead, the date and cause of death. These and other facts that the department requires shall be furnished by the managing officer of each institution within ten days after the commitment, entrance, death, or discharge of an inmate.

(B) In case of an accident or injury or peculiar death of an inmate, the managing officer shall make a special report to the department within twenty-four hours thereafter, giving the circumstances as fully as possible.

(C)(1) As used in this division, "medical record" means any document or combination of documents that pertains to the medical history, diagnosis, prognosis, or medical condition of a patient and that is generated and maintained in the process of medical treatment.

(2) A separate medical record of every inmate in an institution governed by the department shall be compiled, maintained, and kept apart from and independently of any other record pertaining to the inmate. Upon the signed written request of the inmate to whom the record pertains together with the written request of either a licensed attorney at law or a licensed physician designated by the inmate, the department shall make the inmate's medical record available to the designated attorney or physician. The record may be inspected or copied by the inmate's designated attorney or physician. The department may establish a reasonable fee for the copying of any medical record. If a physician concludes that presentation of all or any part of the medical record directly to the inmate will result in serious medical harm to the inmate, the physician shall so indicate on the medical record. An inmate's medical record shall be made available to a physician or to an attorney designated in writing by the inmate not more than once every twelve months.

(D) Except as otherwise provided by a law of this state or the United States, the department and the officers of its institutions shall keep confidential and accessible only to its employees, except by the consent of the department or the order of a judge of a court of record, all of the following:

(1) Architectural, engineering, or construction diagrams, drawings, or plans of a correctional institution;

(2) Plans for hostage negotiation, for disturbance control, for the control and location of keys, and for dealing with escapes;

(3) Statements made by inmate informants;

(4) Records that are maintained by the department of youth services, that pertain to children in its custody, and that are released to the department of rehabilitation and correction by the department of youth services pursuant to section 5139.05 of the Revised Code;

(5) Victim impact statements and information provided by victims of crimes that the department considers when determining the security level assignment, program participation, and release eligibility of inmates;

(6) Information and data of any kind or medium pertaining to groups that pose a security threat;

(7) Conversations recorded from the monitored inmate telephones that involve nonprivileged communications.

(E) Except as otherwise provided by a law of this state or the United States, the department of rehabilitation and correction may release inmate records to the department of youth services or a court of record, and the department of youth services or the court of record may use those records for the limited purpose of carrying out the duties of the department of youth services or the court of record. Inmate records released by the department of rehabilitation and correction to the department of youth services or a court of record shall remain confidential and shall not be considered public records as defined in section 149.43 of the Revised Code.

(F) Except as otherwise provided in division (C) of this section, records of inmates committed to the department of rehabilitation and correction as well as records of persons under the supervision of the adult parole authority shall not be considered public records as defined in section 149.43 of the Revised Code.

**HISTORY: 134 v H 494 (Eff 7-12-72); 142 v S 94 (Eff 7-20-88); 145 v H 571 (Eff 10-6-94); 146 v S 269 (Eff 7-1-96); 149 v H 510. Eff 3-31-2003.**

## § 5120.211 Confidentiality of quality assurance records; immunity.

(A) As used in this section:

(1) "Quality assurance committee" means a committee that is appointed in the central office of the department of rehabilitation and correction by the director of rehabilitation and correction, a committee appointed at a state correctional institution by the managing officer of the institution, or a duly authorized subcommittee of a committee of that nature and that is designated to carry out quality assurance program activities.

(2) "Quality assurance program" means a comprehensive program within the department of rehabilitation and correction to systematically review and improve the quality of medical and mental health services within the department and its institutions, the safety and security of persons receiving medical and mental health services within the department and its institutions, and the efficiency and effectiveness of the utilization of staff and resources in the delivery of medical and mental health services within the department and its institutions.

(3) "Quality assurance program activities" includes the activities of the institutional and central office quality assurance committees, of persons who provide, collect, or compile information and reports required by quality assurance committees, and of persons who receive, review, or implement the recommendations made by quality

assurance committees. "Quality assurance program activities" includes credentialing, infection control, utilization review including access to patient care, patient care assessments, medical and mental health records, medical and mental health resource management, mortality and morbidity review, and identification and prevention of medical or mental health incidents and risks, whether performed by a quality assurance committee or by persons who are directed by a quality assurance committee.

(4) "Quality assurance records" means the proceedings, records, minutes, and reports that emanate from quality assurance program activities. "Quality assurance records" does not include aggregate statistical information that does not disclose the identity of persons receiving or providing medical or mental health services in state correctional institutions.

(B)(1) Except as provided in division (E) of this section, quality assurance records are confidential and are not public records under section 149.43 of the Revised Code, and shall be used only in the course of the proper functions of a quality assurance program.

(2) Except as provided in division (E) of this section, no person who possesses or has access to quality assurance records and who knows that the records are quality assurance records shall wilfully disclose the contents of the records to any person or entity.

(C)(1) Except as provided in division (E) of this section, no quality assurance record shall be subject to discovery, and is not admissible in evidence, in any judicial or administrative proceeding.

(2) Except as provided in division (E) of this section, no member of a quality assurance committee or a person who is performing a function that is part of a quality assurance program shall be permitted or required to testify in a judicial or administrative proceeding with respect to quality assurance records or with respect to any finding, recommendation, evaluation, opinion, or other action taken by the committee, member, or person.

(3) Information, documents, or records otherwise available from original sources are not to be construed as being unavailable for discovery or admission in evidence in a judicial or administrative proceeding merely because they were presented to a quality assurance committee. No person testifying before a quality assurance committee or person who is a member of a quality assurance committee shall be prevented from testifying as to matters within the person's knowledge, but the witness cannot be asked about the witness' testimony before the quality assurance committee or about an opinion formed by the person as a result of the quality assurance committee proceedings.

(D)(1) A person who, without malice and in the reasonable belief that the information is warranted by the facts known to the person, provides information to a person engaged in quality assurance program activities is not liable for damages in a civil action for injury, death, or loss to person or property to any person as a result of providing the information.

(2) A member of a quality assurance committee, a person engaged in quality assurance program activities, and an employee of the department of rehabilitation and correction shall not be liable in damages in a civil action for injury, death, or loss to person or property to any person for any acts, omissions, decisions, or other conduct within the scope of the functions of the quality assurance program.

(3) Nothing in this section shall relieve any institution or individual from liability arising from the treatment of a patient.

(E) Quality assurance records may be disclosed, and testimony may be provided concerning quality assurance records, only to the following persons or entities or in the following circumstances:

(1) Persons who are employed or retained by the department of rehabilitation and correction and who have authority to evaluate or implement the recommendations of an institutional or central office quality assurance committee;

(2) Public or private agencies or organizations if needed to perform a licensing or accreditation function related to state correctional institutions or to perform monitoring of state correctional institutions as required by law;

(3) A governmental board or agency, a professional health care society or organization, or a professional standards review organization, if the records or testimony are needed to perform licensing, credentialing, or monitoring of professional standards with respect to medical or mental health professionals employed or retained by the department;

(4) A criminal or civil law enforcement agency or public health agency charged by law with the protection of public health or safety, if a qualified representative of the agency makes a written request stating that the records or testimony is necessary for a purpose authorized by law;

(5) In a judicial or administrative proceeding commenced by an entity described in division (E)(3) or (4) of this section and for a purpose described in that division, but only with respect to the subject of the proceedings.

(F) A disclosure of quality assurance records pursuant to division (E) of this section does not otherwise waive the confidential and privileged status of the disclosed quality assurance records. The names and other identifying information regarding individual patients, employees, or members of a quality assurance committee contained in a quality assurance record shall be deleted from the record prior to the disclosure of the record unless the identity of an individual is necessary to the purpose for which disclosure is being made and does not constitute a clearly unwarranted invasion of personal privacy.

**HISTORY: 147 v S 111. Eff 3-17-98.**

## § 5120.22 Property management duties of division of business administration.

(A) The division of business administration shall examine the conditions of all buildings, grounds, and other property connected with the institutions under the control of the department of rehabilitation and correction, the methods of bookkeeping and storekeeping, and all matters relating to the management of such property. The division shall study and become familiar with the advantages and disadvantages of each as to location, freight rates, and efficiency of farm and equipment, for the purpose of aiding in the determination of the local and general requirements both for maintenance and improvements.

(B) The division, with respect to the various types of state-owned housing under jurisdiction of the department, shall adopt, in accordance with section 111.15 of the Revised Code, rules governing maintenance of the housing and its usage by department personnel. The rules shall include a procedure for determining charges for rent and utilities, which the division shall assess against and collect from department personnel using the housing. All money collected for rent and utilities pursuant to the rules shall be deposited into the property receipts fund, which is hereby created in the state treasury. Money in the fund shall be used for any expenses necessary to provide housing of department employees, including but not limited to expenses for the acquisition, construction, operation, maintenance, repair, reconstruction, or demolition of land and buildings.

(C) The division may enter into a lease or agreement with a state agency, political subdivision of the state, or private entity to use facilities or other property under the jurisdiction of the department that is not being utilized by the department. All money collected for leasing and services performed in accordance with the lease or agreement shall be deposited into the property receipts fund created under division (B) of this section. Money in the fund shall be used for any expenses resulting from the lease or agreement, including, but not limited to, expenses for services performed, construction, maintenance, repair, reconstruction, or demolition of the facilities or other property.

**HISTORY: 134 v H 494 (Eff 7-12-72); 145 v H 152 (Eff 7-1-93); 146 v H 117. Eff 6-30-95; 2011 HB 153, § 101.01, eff. Sept. 29, 2011.**

## § 5120.23 Estimate of needed supplies made by correctional and penal institutions; disposition of money received.

(A) The department of rehabilitation and correction shall require proper officials of the state and its political subdivisions and of the institutions of the state and its political subdivisions, to report estimates for the ensuing year of the amount of supplies required by them, of the kinds that are produced by the state correctional and penal institutions. It may make rules for the reports and provide the manner in which the estimates shall be made.

(B) Any money that is received by the department of rehabilitation and correction from the state and its political subdivisions, any other state and its political subdivisions, the United States, or private persons for products and services produced by the state correctional and penal institutions shall be deposited in the services and agricultural fund or the Ohio penal industries manufacturing fund created pursuant to section 5120.29 of the Revised Code and shall be used and accounted for as provided in that section.

**HISTORY: 134 v H 494 (Eff 7-12-72); 138 v H 654 (Eff 4-9-82); 142 v H 171. Eff 7-1-87.**

## § 5120.24 Purchase of supplies; competitive bidding.

The department of administrative services shall purchase all supplies needed for the proper support and maintenance of the institutions under the control of the department of rehabilitation and correction in accordance with the competitive selection procedures of Chapter 125. of the Revised Code and such rules as the department of administrative services adopts. All bids shall be publicly opened on the day and hour and at the place specified in the advertisement.

Preference shall be given to bidders in localities wherein the institution is located if the price is fair and reasonable and not greater than the usual price. Bids not meeting the specifications shall be rejected.

The department of administrative services may require such security as it considers proper to accompany the bids and shall fix the security to be given by the contractor.

The department of administrative services may reject any or all bids and secure new bids, if for any reason it is considered to be in the best interest of the state to do so, and it may authorize the managing officer of any institution to purchase perishable goods and supplies for use in cases of emergency, in which cases such managing officer shall certify such fact in writing and the department of administrative services shall record the reasons for such purchase.

**HISTORY: 134 v H 494 (Eff 7-12-72); 136 v S 430 (Eff 8-13-76); 142 v H 88 (Eff 1-1-88); 145 v H 152. Eff 7-1-93.**

## § 5120.25 Books and accounts; department to prescribe form and method; audit.

The department of correction shall keep in its office a proper and complete set of books and accounts with each institution, which shall clearly show the nature and amount of every expenditure authorized and made at such institution, and which shall contain an account of all appropriations made by the general assembly and of all other funds, together with the disposition of such funds.

The department shall prescribe the form of vouchers, records, and methods of keeping accounts at each of the institutions, which shall be as nearly uniform as possible. The department may examine the records of each institution, at any time.

The department may authorize any of its bookkeepers, accountants, or employees to examine and check the records, accounts, and vouchers or take an inventory of the property of any institution, or do whatever is necessary, and pay the actual and reasonable expenses incurred in such service when an itemized account is filed and approved.

**HISTORY: 134 v H 494. Eff 7-12-72.**

## § 5120.26 Use, custody, and insurance of funds.

(A) The treasurer of state shall have charge of all funds under the jurisdiction of the department of rehabilitation and correction and shall pay out the funds only in accordance with this chapter.

(B) The department shall cause to be furnished a contract of indemnity to cover all moneys and funds received by it or by its managing officers, employees, or agents while the moneys or funds are in the possession of the managing officers, employees, or agents. The funds are designated as follows:

(1) Funds that are due and payable to the treasurer of state as provided by Chapter 131. of the Revised Code;

(2) Funds that are held in trust by the managing officers, employees, or agents of the institution as local funds or accounts under the jurisdiction of the department.

The contract of indemnity shall be made payable to the state and the premium for the contract of indemnity may be paid from any of the moneys received for the use of the department under this chapter and Chapters 5121., 5123., and 5125.† of the Revised Code.

(C) Moneys collected from various sources, such as the sale of goods, farm products, services, and all miscellaneous articles, shall be transmitted on or before Monday of each week to the treasurer of state and a detailed statement of the collections shall be made to the division of business administration by each managing officer. The receipts from manufacturing and service industries and agricultural products shall be used and accounted for as provided in section 5120.29 of the Revised Code.

**HISTORY: 134 v H 494 (Eff 7-12-72); 137 v S 221 (Eff 11-23-77); 138 v H 654. Eff 4-9-82.**

The effective date is set by section 4 of HB 654.

† As enrolled. RC Chapter 5125 has been completely repealed or renumbered.

## § 5120.27 Industries to be carried on by institutions determined by department.

The department of rehabilitation and correction may assign among the correctional and penal institutions under its control and in accordance with the rules adopted pursuant to division (B) of section 5145.03 of the Revised Code, the industries to be carried on by the institutions, having due regard to the location and convenience of the industries, other institutions to be supplied, to the machinery in the institutions, and to the number and character of prisoners employed in the industries.

**HISTORY: 134 v H 494 (Eff 7-12-72); 138 v H 654. Eff 4-9-82.**

The effective date is set by section 4 of HB 654.

## § 5120.28 Prices fixed for labor, services, products and articles; disposition of money received.

(A) The department of rehabilitation and correction, subject to the approval of the office of budget and management, shall fix the prices at which all labor and services performed, all agricultural products produced, and all articles manufactured in correctional and penal institutions shall be furnished to the state, the political subdivisions of the state, and the public institutions of the state and the political subdivisions, and to private persons. The prices shall be uniform to all and not higher than the usual market price for like labor, products, services, and articles.

(B) Any money received by the department of rehabilitation and correction for labor and services performed shall be deposited into the institutional services fund created pursuant to division (A) of section 5120.29 of the Revised Code and shall be used and accounted for as provided in that section and division (B) of section 5145.03 of the Revised Code.

(C) Any money received by the department of rehabilitation and correction for articles manufactured and agricultural products produced in penal and correctional institutions shall be deposited into the Ohio penal industries manufacturing fund created pursuant to division (B) of section 5120.29 of the Revised Code and shall be used and accounted for as provided in that section and division (B) of section 5145.03 of the Revised Code.

**HISTORY: 134 v H 494 (Eff 7-12-72); 137 v H 1 (Eff 8-26-77); 138 v H 654 (Eff 4-9-82); 142 v H 171. Eff 7-1-87; 2011 HB 153, § 101.01, eff. Sept. 29, 2011.**

## § 5120.29 Services and agricultural fund; penal industries manufacturing fund.

(A) There is hereby created, in the state treasury, the institutional services fund, which shall be used for the:

(1) Purchase of material, supplies, and equipment and the erection and extension of buildings used in services provided between institutions of the department of rehabilitation and correction;

(2) Payment of compensation to employees necessary to carry on institutional services;

(3) Payment of prisoners confined in state correctional institutions a portion of their earnings in accordance with rules adopted pursuant to section 5145.03 of the Revised Code.

(B) There is hereby created, in the state treasury, the Ohio penal industries manufacturing fund, which shall be used for the:

(1) Purchase of material, supplies, and equipment and the erection and extension of buildings used in manufacturing industries and agriculture;

(2) Purchase of lands and buildings necessary to carry on or extend the manufacturing industries and agriculture upon the approval of the governor;

(3) Payment of compensation to employees necessary to carry on the manufacturing industries and agriculture;

(4) Payment of prisoners confined in state correctional institutions a portion of their earnings in accordance with rules adopted pursuant to section 5145.03 of the Revised Code.

(C) The department of rehabilitation and correction shall, in accordance with rules adopted pursuant to section 5145.03 of the Revised Code and subject to any pledge made as provided in division (D) of this section, place to the credit of each prisoner the prisoner's earnings and pay the earnings so credited to the prisoner or the prisoner's family.

(D) Receipts credited to the funds created in divisions (A) and (B) of this section constitute available receipts as defined in section 152.09 of the Revised Code, and may be pledged to the payment of bond service charges on obligations issued by the Ohio building authority pursuant to Chapter 152. of the Revised Code to construct, reconstruct, or otherwise improve capital facilities useful to the department. The authority may, with the consent of the department, provide in the bond proceedings for a pledge of all or such portion of receipts credited to the funds as the authority determines. The authority may provide in the bond proceedings for the transfer of receipts credited to the funds to the appropriate bond service fund or bond service reserve fund as required to pay the bond service charges when due, and any such provision for the transfer of receipts shall be controlling notwithstanding any other provision of law pertaining to such receipts.

All receipts received by the treasurer of state on account of the department and required by the applicable bond proceedings to be deposited, transferred, or credited to the bond service fund or bond service reserve fund established by such bond proceedings shall be transferred by the treasurer of state to such fund, whether or not such fund is in the custody of the treasurer of state, without necessity for further appropriation, upon receipt of notice from the Ohio building authority as prescribed in the bond proceedings. The authority may covenant in the bond proceedings that so long as any obligations are outstanding to which receipts credited to the fund are pledged, the state and the department shall neither reduce the prices charged pursuant to section 5120.28 of the Revised Code nor the level of manpower collectively devoted to the production of goods and services for which prices are set pursuant to section 5120.28 of the Revised Code, which covenant shall be controlling notwithstanding any other provision of law; provided, that no covenant shall require the general assembly to appropriate money derived from the levying of excises or taxes to purchase such goods and services or to pay rent or bond service charges.

**HISTORY: 134 v H 494 (Eff 7-12-72); 138 v H 654 (Eff 4-9-82); 139 v H 530, § 1 (Eff 5-28-82); 139 v H 530, § 3 (Eff 4-9-82); 141 v H 201 (Eff 7-1-85); 142 v H 171 (Eff 7-1-87); 145 v H 571. Eff 10-6-94; 2011 HB 153, § 101.01, eff. Sept. 29, 2011.**

## § 5120.30 Investigations; director to have powers of county court judge; records; witness fees and mileage.

The department of rehabilitation and correction may make any investigations that are necessary in the performance of its duties, and to that end the director of rehabilitation and correction shall have the same power as a judge of a county court to administer oaths and to enforce the attendance and testimony of witnesses and the production of books or papers.

The department shall keep a record of the investigations pursuant to the record retention schedule approved by the department of administrative services.

Witnesses shall be paid the fees and mileage provided for under section 119.094 [119.09.4] of the Revised Code, but no officer or employee of the institution under investigation is entitled to such fees.

Any judge of the probate court or of the court of common pleas, upon application of the department, may compel the attendance of witnesses, the production of books or papers, and the giving of testimony before the department, by a judgment for contempt or otherwise, in the same manner as in cases before courts of common pleas.

**HISTORY: 134 v H 494 (Eff 7-12-72); 136 v H 390 (Eff 8-6-76); 149 v H 510. Eff 3-31-2003; 152 v H 525, § 1, eff. 7-1-09.**

The effective date is set by § 3 of 152 v H 525.

## § 5120.31 Appointment of competent agency or person; content of credentials.

The department of rehabilitation and correction may appoint and commission any competent agency or person, to serve without compensation, as a special agent, investigator, or representative to perform a designated duty for and in behalf of the department. Specific credentials shall be given by the department to each person so designated, and each credential shall state:

(A) The name;

(B) Agency with which such person is connected;

(C) Purpose of appointment;

(D) Date of expiration of appointment;

(E) Such information as the department considers proper.

**HISTORY: 134 v H 494. Eff 7-12-72.**

## § 5120.32 Annual report; content.

In its annual report, the department of rehabilitation and correction shall include a complete financial statement of the various institutions under its control. The report shall state, as to each such institution, whether;

(A) The moneys appropriated have been economically and judiciously expended;

(B) The objects of the several institutions have been accomplished;

(C) The laws in relation to such institutions have been fully complied with;

(D) All parts of the state are equally benefited by said institutions.

Such annual report shall be accompanied by the reports of the managing officers and such other information and recommendations as the department considers proper.

**HISTORY: 134 v H 494. Eff 7-12-72.**

## § 5120.33 List of employees; condition of state institutions; other statistics.

The annual report of the department of rehabilitation and correction shall include a list of the officers and agents employed, and the conditions of the state institutions under its control. Such report may include statistics and information in regard to correctional institutions of this or other states.

**HISTORY: 134 v H 494. Eff 7-12-72.**

## § 5120.331 Report on time served by released inmates.

(A) Not later than the first day of April of each year, the department of rehabilitation and correction shall prepare an annual report covering the preceding calendar year that does all of the following:

(1) Indicates the total number of persons sentenced to any institution, division, or place under its control and management who are delivered within that calendar year to its custody and control;

(2) Indicates the total number of persons who, during that calendar year, were released from a prison term on any of the following bases:

(a) On judicial release under section 2929.20 of the Revised Code;

(b) On transitional control under section 2967.26 of the Revised Code;

(c) As a result of successfully completing a risk reduction sentence under section 5120.036 of the Revised Code;

(d) On parole;

(e) Due to the expiration of the stated prison term imposed;

(f) On any basis not described in divisions (A)(2)(a) to (e) of this section.

(3) Lists each offense, by Revised Code section number and, if applicable, by designated name, for which at least one person who was released from a prison term in that calendar year was serving a prison term at the time of release;

(4) For each offense included in the list described in division (A)(3) of this section, indicates all of the following:

(a) The total number of persons released from a prison term in that calendar year who were serving a prison term for that offense at the time of release;

(b) The shortest, longest, and average prison term that had been imposed for that offense upon the persons described in division (A)(4)(a) of this section and that they were serving at the time of release;

(c) The shortest, longest, and average period of imprisonment actually served by the persons described in division (A)(4)(a) of this section under a prison term that had been imposed for that offense upon them and that they were serving at the time of release;

(d) The total number of persons released from a prison term in that calendar year under each of the bases for release set forth in division (A)(2) of this section who were serving a prison term for that offense at the time of release;

(e) The shortest, longest, and average prison term that had been imposed for that offense upon the persons in each category described in division (A)(4)(d) of this section and that they were serving at the time of release;

(f) The shortest, longest, and average period of imprisonment actually served by the persons in each category described in division (A)(4)(d) of this section under a prison term that had been imposed for that offense upon them and that they were serving at the time of release.

(B) No report prepared under division (A) of this section shall identify or enable the identification of any person released from a prison term in the preceding calendar year.

(C) Each annual report prepared under division (A) of this section shall be distributed to each member of the general assembly.

(D) As used in this section, "prison term" and "stated prison term" have the same meanings as in section 2929.01 of the Revised Code.

**HISTORY: 142 v H 261 (Eff 11-1-87); 146 v S 2 (Eff 7-1-96); 147 v S 111. Eff 3-17-98; 2011 HB 86, § 1, eff. Sept. 30, 2011.**

## § 5120.34 Internal management.

The department of rehabilitation and correction shall make rules for the nonpartisan management of the institutions under its control. Any officer or employee of the department or any officer or employee of any institution under its control, who, by solicitation or otherwise, exerts his influence, directly or indirectly, to induce any other officer or employee of any such institutions to adopt his political views or to favor any particular person, issue, or candidate for office shall be removed from his office or position, by the department in case of an officer or employee and by the governor in case of the director of rehabilitation and correction.

**HISTORY: 134 v H 494 (Eff 7-12-72); 136 v H 617. Eff 11-7-75.**

## § 5120.35 Suggestions of department in annual report.

In its annual report, the department of rehabilitation and correction shall make any suggestions or recommendations it considers wise for the more effectual accomplishment of the general purpose of Chapter 5120. of the Revised Code.

**HISTORY: 134 v H 494. Eff 7-12-72.**

## § 5120.36 Executive, administrative, and fiscal supervision of institutions; powers of department.

The department of rehabilitation and correction, in addition to the powers expressly conferred, shall have all power and authority necessary for the full and efficient exercise of the executive, administrative, and fiscal supervision over the state institutions described in section 5120.05 of the Revised Code.

**HISTORY: 134 v H 494. Eff 7-12-72.**

## § 5120.37 Information exchanges with job and family services department.

The department of rehabilitation and correction shall enter into an agreement with the department of job and family services to exchange or share information monthly concerning persons under the control or supervision of the department of rehabilitation and correction.

**HISTORY: 147 v S 52 (Eff 9-3-97); 148 v H 471. Eff 7-1-2000.**

**Not analogous to former RC § 5120.37 (134 v H 494), repealed 145 v H 571, § 2, eff 10-6-94.**

The effective date is set by section 12(A) of HB 471.

## § 5120.38 Managing officer; duties.

Subject to the rules of the department of rehabilitation and correction, each institution under the department's jurisdiction other than an institution operated pursuant to a contract entered into under section 9.06 of the Revised Code shall be under the control of a managing officer known as a warden or other appropriate title. The managing officer shall be appointed by the director of the department of rehabilitation and correction and shall be in the unclassified service and serve at the pleasure of the director. Appointment to the position of managing officer shall be made from persons who have criminal justice experience.

A person who is appointed to the position of managing officer from a position in the classified service shall retain the right to resume the status that the person held in the classified service immediately prior to the appointment. Upon being relieved of the person's duties as managing officer, the person shall be reinstated to the position in the classified service that the person held immediately prior to the appointment to the position of managing officer or to another position that the director, with approval of the state department of administrative services, certifies as being substantially equal to that prior position. Service as a managing officer shall be counted as service in the position in the classified service held by the person immediately preceding the person's appointment as managing officer. A person who is reinstated to a position in the classified service, as provided in this section, shall be entitled to all rights and emoluments accruing to the position during the time of the person's service as managing officer.

The managing officer, under the director, shall have entire executive charge of the institution for which the managing officer is appointed. Subject to civil service rules and regulations, the managing officer shall appoint the necessary employees and the managing officer or the director may remove such employees for cause. A report of all appointments, resignations, and discharges shall be filed with the director at the close of each month.

**HISTORY: 134 v H 494 (Eff 7-12-72); 147 v H 215 (Eff 9-29-97); 147 v S 111 (Eff 3-17-98); 149 v H 510. Eff 3-31-2003.**

## § 5120.381 Deputy warden for each institution.

Subject to the rules of the department of rehabilitation and correction, the director of rehabilitation and correction may appoint a deputy warden for each institution under the jurisdiction of the department. A deputy warden shall be in the unclassified service and serve at the pleasure of the director. The director shall make an appointment to the position of deputy warden from persons having criminal justice experience. A person who is appointed to a position as deputy warden from a position in the classified service shall retain the right to resume the position and status that the person held in the classified service immediately prior to the appointment. If the person is relieved of the person's duties as deputy warden, the director shall reinstate the person to the position in the classified service that the person held immediately prior to the appointment as deputy warden or to another position that is certified by the director, with approval of the department of administrative services, as being substantially equal to that prior position. Service as deputy warden shall be counted as service in the position in the classified service that the person held immediately preceding the appointment as deputy warden. A person who is reinstated to a position in the classified service as provided in this section is entitled to all rights and emoluments accruing to the position during the time of the person's service as deputy warden.

**HISTORY: 147 v S 111. Eff 3-17-98.**

## § 5120.382 Employees generally.

Except as otherwise provided in this chapter for appointments by division chiefs and managing officers, the director of rehabilitation and correction shall appoint employees who are necessary for the efficient conduct of the department of rehabilitation and correction and prescribe their titles and duties. A person who is appointed to an unclassified position from a position in the classified service shall serve at the pleasure of the director and retain the right to resume the position and status that the person held in the classified service immediately prior to the appointment. If the person is relieved of the person's duties for the unclassified position, the director shall reinstate the person to the position in the classified service that the person held immediately prior to the appointment or to another position that is certified by the director, with approval of the department of administrative services, as being substantially equal to that prior classified position. Service in the unclassified service pursuant to the appointment shall be counted as service in the position in the classified service that the person held immediately preceding the appointment. A person who is reinstated to a position in the classified service as provided in this section is entitled to all rights and emoluments accruing to the position during the time of the person's unclassified service.

**HISTORY: 147 v S 111. Eff 3-17-98.**

## § 5120.39 Superintendent; qualifications; powers and duties.

Each superintendent of an institution under the control of the department of rehabilitation and correction shall be of good moral character and have skill, ability, and experience in his profession. He shall have control of the institution, and be responsible for the management thereof and for the service of all its employees. He shall appoint necessary teachers, attendants, nurses, servants, and other persons, assign their places and duties, and may discharge them, keeping a record thereof and reasons therefor.

**HISTORY: 134 v H 494. Eff 7-12-72.**

## § 5120.40 Teacher qualifications.

All teachers employed in any institution under the jurisdiction of the department of rehabilitation and correction shall possess educator licenses or have the qualifications and approval that the superintendent of the Ohio central school system, after conference with the officers in charge of the several institutions, prescribes for the various particular types of service or service in the particular institutions.

**HISTORY: 134 v H 494 (Eff 7-12-72); 138 v H 900 (Eff 7-1-80); 145 v H 571 (Eff 10-6-94); 146 v S 230. Eff 10-29-96.**

## § 5120.41 Courses of study subject to approval of superintendent of public instruction.

The courses of study for the instruction and training of all persons in the correctional institutions under the control of the department of rehabilitation and correction shall be subject to the approval of the superintendent of public instruction.

**HISTORY: 134 v H 494 (Eff 7-12-72); 145 v H 571. Eff 10-6-94.**

## § 5120.42 Rules for proper execution of powers.

The department of rehabilitation and correction shall make rules for the proper execution of its powers and may require the performance of additional duties by the officers of the several institutions, so as to fully meet the requirements, intents, and purposes of Chapter 5120. of the Revised Code, and particularly those relating to making estimates and furnishing proper proof of the use made of all articles furnished or produced in such institutions. In case of an apparent conflict between the powers conferred upon any managing officer and those conferred by such sections upon the department, the presumption shall be conclusive in favor of the department.

**HISTORY: 134 v H 494. Eff 7-12-72.**

## § 5120.421 Searches of visitors to correctional institutions.

(A) As used in this section:

(1) "Body cavity search" means an inspection of the anal or vaginal cavity of a person that is conducted visually, manually, by means of any instrument, apparatus, or object, or in any other manner.

(2) "Deadly weapon" and "dangerous ordnance" have the same meanings as in section 2923.11 of the Revised Code.

(3) "Drug of abuse" has the same meaning as in section 3719.011 [3719.01.1] of the Revised Code.

(4) "Intoxicating liquor" has the same meaning as in section 4301.01 of the Revised Code.

(5) "Strip search" means an inspection of the genitalia, buttocks, breasts, or undergarments of a person that is preceded by the removal or rearrangement of some or all of the person's clothing that directly covers the person's

genitalia, buttocks, breasts, or undergarments and that is conducted visually, manually, by means of any instrument, apparatus, or object, or in any other manner.

(B) For purposes of determining whether visitors to an institution under the control of the department of rehabilitation and correction are knowingly conveying, or attempting to convey, onto the grounds of the institution any deadly weapon, dangerous ordnance, drug of abuse, intoxicating liquor, or electronic communications device in violation of section 2921.36 of the Revised Code, the department may adopt rules, pursuant to Chapter 119. of the Revised Code, that are consistent with this section.

(C) For the purposes described in division (B) of this section, visitors who are entering or have entered an institution under the control of the department of rehabilitation and correction may be searched by the use of a magnetometer or similar device, by a pat-down of the visitor's person that is conducted by a person of the same sex as that of the visitor, and by an examination of the contents of pockets, bags, purses, packages, and other containers proposed to be conveyed or already conveyed onto the grounds of the institution. Searches of visitors authorized by this division may be conducted without cause, but shall be conducted uniformly or by automatic random selection. Discriminatory or arbitrary selection searches of visitors are prohibited under this division.

(D) For the purposes described in division (B) of this section, visitors who are entering or have entered an institution under the control of the department of rehabilitation and correction may be searched by a strip or body cavity search, but only under the circumstances described in this division. In order for a strip or body cavity search to be conducted of a visitor, the highest officer present in the institution shall expressly authorize the search on the basis of a reasonable suspicion, based on specific objective facts and reasonable inferences drawn from those facts in the light of experience, that a visitor proposed to be so searched possesses, and intends to convey or already has conveyed, a deadly weapon, dangerous ordnance, drug of abuse, intoxicating liquor, or electronic communications device onto the grounds of the institution in violation of section 2921.36 of the Revised Code.

Except as otherwise provided in this division, prior to the conduct of the strip or body cavity search, the highest officer present in the institution shall cause the visitor to be provided with a written statement that sets forth the specific objective facts upon which the proposed search is based. In the case of an emergency under which time constraints make it impossible to prepare the written statement before the conduct of the proposed search, the highest officer in the institution instead shall cause the visitor to be orally informed of the specific objective facts upon which the proposed search is based prior to its conduct, and shall cause the preparation of the written statement and its provision to the visitor within twenty-four hours after the conduct of the search. Both the highest officer present in the institution and the visitor shall retain a copy of a written statement provided in accordance with this division.

Any strip or body cavity search conducted pursuant to this division shall be conducted in a private setting by a person of the same sex as that of the visitor. Any body cavity search conducted under this division additionally shall be conducted by medical personnel.

This division does not preclude, and shall not be construed as precluding, a less intrusive search as authorized by division (C) of this section when reasonable suspicion as described in this division exists for a strip or body cavity search.

**HISTORY: 143 v S 258 (Eff 8-22-90); 149 v H 510. Eff 3-31-2003.**

## § 5120.423 Designation of additional exercise equipment and fighting skills programs to be denied to prisoners.

The department of rehabilitation and correction shall adopt rules in accordance with Chapter 119. of the Revised Code that designate devices and programs that, in addition to free weight exercise equipment as defined in sections 341.41, 753.31, and 5145.30 of the Revised Code and in addition to boxing, wrestling, and martial arts programs, would enable a person who uses a designated device or participates in a designated program to increase muscle mass and physical strength or to improve fighting skills.

**HISTORY: 146 v H 152. Eff 10-4-96.**

### [PRISONER ACCESS TO INFLAMMATORY AND OTHER MATERIALS]

## § 5120.425 Definitions.

As used in sections 5120.425 [5120.42.5] to 5120.428 [5120.42.8] of the Revised Code:

(A) "Head of a state correctional institution," "prisoner," and "state correctional institution" have the same meanings as in section 2967.01 of the Revised Code.

(B) "Material" means a prerecorded magnetic audio or video tape, book, drawing, magazine, newspaper, pamphlet, poster, print, photograph, or other similar printed, written, recorded, or otherwise produced item.

(C) "Prohibited inflammatory material" means a material that, in the determination of the warden or the warden's designee, is detrimental to, or poses a threat to, the rehabilitation of the inmates or the security, good order, or discipline within or on the grounds of the institution for any reason, including, but not limited to, that it is material with a sexually explicit nature.

(D) "Publication review committee" means the committee created by the director of rehabilitation and correction pursuant to division (C) of section 5120.426 [5120.42.6] of the Revised Code.

(E) "Warden" means the head of a state correctional institution.

(F) "Warden's designee" means a person or a panel of persons designated by a warden to perform a responsibility that sections 5120.425 [5120.42.5] to 5120.428 [5120.42.8] of the Revised Code generally otherwise impose upon the warden.

**HISTORY: 148 v H 62. Eff 11-3-99.**

## § 5120.426 Rules and regulations governing prisoner access to materials; prohibited inflammatory materials; publication review committee.

(A) The director of rehabilitation and correction shall adopt rules, and each warden shall adopt regulations that govern the form, medium, and quantity of materials that each prisoner confined in the warden's institution is permitted to receive and retain. Those rules and regulations shall be consistent with sections 5120.425 [5120.42.5] to 5120.428 [5120.42.8] of the Revised Code. The regulations adopted by the warden shall be consistent with the rules that the director of rehabilitation and correction adopts pursuant to this division.

(B) The director of rehabilitation and correction shall adopt a rule establishing a standard for determining whether material is a prohibited inflammatory material. In establishing the standard for determining whether material is a prohibited inflammatory material, the director shall consider all relevant information, including, but not limited to, the standard established for material that is harmful to juveniles in section 2907.01 of the Revised Code; in establishing the standard under this division, the director shall not be governed or limited by the standard established by section 2907.01 of the Revised Code.

(C) The director of rehabilitation and correction shall appoint a publication review committee of one or more persons. The member or members of the committee shall review withholding determinations pursuant to section 5120.428 [5120.42.8] of the Revised Code.

**HISTORY: 148 v H 62. Eff 11-3-99.**

## § 5120.427 Prisoner's right to receive materials; inspections; withholding.

(A) Each prisoner confined in a state correctional institution may receive a reasonable number of materials directly from the publishers or other distributors of those materials. With the prior approval of the warden of the state correctional institution in which a prisoner is confined, each prisoner also may receive a reasonable number of materials from a source other than the publisher or other distributor of those materials.

A prisoner's receipt and retention of materials is subject to security inspections conducted by the institution in which the prisoner is confined and to the rules and regulations adopted pursuant to section 5120.426 [5120.42.6] of the Revised Code. Subject to a contrary decision with respect to a material's nature by the publication review committee following a review pursuant to section 5120.428 [5120.42.8] of the Revised Code, a prisoner is not entitled to receive or retain any material that a warden or the warden's designee determines during the course of a security inspection to be a prohibited inflammatory material.

(B)(1) For each state correctional institution, the warden or the warden's designee shall inspect each incoming material to determine whether the material is a prohibited inflammatory material or another type of material. The warden or the warden's designee shall not determine a material to be a prohibited inflammatory material solely on the basis of its appeal to a particular ethnic, racial, or religious audience.

(2) If the warden or the warden's designee determines that an incoming material is not a prohibited inflammatory material, the warden or the warden's designee shall cause the material to be promptly forwarded to the prisoner who is its intended recipient. If the warden or the warden's designee determines that an incoming material is a prohibited inflammatory material, the warden or the warden's designee shall cause the material to be withheld from the prisoner who is its intended recipient and promptly shall provide that prisoner with a written withholding notice containing all of the following:

(a) A general description of the withheld material;

(b) The reason why the material has not been forwarded to the prisoner;

(c) A statement of the prisoner's right under division (A) of section 5120.428 [5120.42.8] of the Revised Code to have the publication review committee review the withholding decision of the warden or the warden's designee.

(3) Within five working days after a prisoner's receipt of the withholding notice described in division (B)(2) of this section, the prisoner may submit to the warden a written request for a review of the withholding decision. If the prisoner fails to submit a timely written request for a review of that nature, the failure shall constitute the prisoner's acceptance of the withholding decision, and the warden or the warden's designee shall cause the material to be disposed of in the manner that the warden or the warden's designee considered to be most appropriate under the circumstances.

**HISTORY: 148 v H 62. Eff 11-3-99.**

## § 5120.428 Prisoner may request review by committee.

(A) If a prisoner confined in a state correctional institution submits a timely written review request under division (B)(3) of section 5120.427 [5120.42.7] of the Revised Code, the warden of the state correctional institution in which the prisoner is confined or the warden's designee promptly shall forward the withheld material to the publication review committee. As soon as is practicable after receipt of the withheld material, the publication review committee shall review the material to determine whether it is a prohibited inflammatory material or another type of material.

(B) If the publication review committee determines that the withheld material is not a prohibited inflammatory material, the committee shall cause the withheld material to be promptly forwarded to the prisoner who requested the review.

(C) If the publication review committee determines that the withheld material is a prohibited inflammatory material, the committee shall forward the material to the warden or the warden's designee for disposal in the manner considered to be most appropriate under the circumstances.

**HISTORY: 148 v H 62. Eff 11-3-99.**

## § 5120.43 Repealed, 149 v H 510, § 2 [134 v H 494]. Eff 3-31-2003.

This section required the managing officer of an institution to develop occupational therapy programs for inmates.

## § 5120.44 Liberal construction.

Chapter 5120. of the Revised Code attempts:

(A) To provide humane and scientific treatment and care and the highest attainable degree of individual development for the dependent wards of the state;

(B) To provide for the delinquent, conditions of modern education and training that will restore the largest possible portion of them to useful citizenship;

(C) To promote the study of the causes of dependency and delinquency, and of mental, moral, and physical defects, with a view to cure and ultimate prevention;

(D) To secure by uniform and systematic management the highest attainable degree of economy in the administration of the state institutions.

Such sections shall be liberally construed to attain such purposes.

**HISTORY: 134 v H 494. Eff 7-12-72.**

## § 5120.45 Burial or cremation of inmate at state's expense.

The state shall bear the expense of the burial or cremation of an inmate who dies in a state correctional institution, if the body is not claimed for interment or cremation at the expense of friends or relatives, or is not delivered for anatomical purposes or for the study of embalming in accordance with section 1713.34 of the Revised Code. When the expense is borne by the state, interment of the person or the person's cremated remains shall be in the institution cemetery or other place provided by the state. The managing officer of the institution shall provide at the grave of the person or, if the person's cremated remains are buried, at the grave of the person's cremated remains, a metal, stone, or concrete marker on which shall be inscribed the name and age of the person and the date of death.

**HISTORY: 138 v H 900 (Eff 7-1-80); 145 v H 571 (Eff 10-6-94); 147 v S 117. Eff 8-5-98.**

## § 5120.46 Appropriation of property.

When it is necessary for a state correctional institution to acquire any real estate, right-of-way, or easement in real estate in order to accomplish the purposes for which it was organized or is being conducted, and the department of rehabilitation and correction is unable to agree with the owner of the property upon the price to be paid therefor, the property may be appropriated in the manner provided for the appropriation of property for other state purposes.

Any instrument by which real property is acquired pursuant to this section shall identify the agency of the state that has the use and benefit of the real property as specified in section 5301.012 [5301.01.2] of the Revised Code.

**HISTORY: 138 v H 900 (Eff 7-1-80); 145 v H 571 (Eff 10-6-94); 148 v H 19. Eff 10-26-99.**

## § 5120.47 Lease of capital facilities.

The department of rehabilitation and correction shall lease capital facilities constructed, reconstructed, otherwise improved, or financed by the Ohio building authority pursuant to Chapter 152. of the Revised Code for the use of the department, and may enter into any other agreements with the authority ancillary to the construction, reconstruction, improvement, financing, leasing, or operation of such capital facilities, including, but not limited to, any agreements required by the applicable bond proceedings authorized by Chapter 152. of the Revised Code. Such agreements shall not be subject to section 5120.24 of the Revised Code. Any lease of capital facilities authorized by this section shall be governed by division (D) of section 152.24 of the Revised Code.

**HISTORY: 139 v H 530. Eff 5-28-82.**

## § 5120.48 Apprehension of escapee or prisoner mistakenly released.

(A) If a prisoner escapes from a state correctional institution, the managing officer of the institution, after consultation with and upon the advice of appropriate law enforcement officials, shall assign and deploy into the community appropriate staff persons necessary to apprehend the prisoner. Correctional officers and officials may carry firearms when required in the discharge of their duties in apprehending, taking into custody, or transporting to a place of confinement a prisoner who has escaped from a state correctional institution.

(B) If a prisoner is released from a state correctional institution prior to the lawful end of the person's prison term or term of imprisonment, whether by error, inadvertence, fraud, or any other cause except a lawful parole or judicial release granted pursuant to section 2929.20 of the Revised Code or the successful completion of a risk reduction sentence under section 5120.036 of the Revised Code, the managing officer of the institution, after consulting with the bureau of sentence computation, shall notify the chief of the adult parole authority, the office of victim services of the division of parole and community services, and the sentencing court of the mistaken release. Upon the direction of the chief, or the chief's designee, field officers of the authority may arrest the prisoner without a warrant and return the prisoner to the state correctional institution to complete the balance of the prisoner's sentence. The chief of the adult parole authority, or the chief's designee, may require the assistance of any peace officer or law enforcement officer in the apprehension of a prisoner of that nature.

**HISTORY: 145 v H 571 (Eff 10-6-94); 149 v H 510. Eff 3-31-2003; 2011 HB 86, § 1, eff. Sept. 30, 2011.**

## § 5120.49 Rules for termination of parole board's control over certain sexually violent offenders.

The department of rehabilitation and correction, by rule adopted under Chapter 119. of the Revised Code, shall prescribe standards and guidelines to be used by the parole board in determining, pursuant to section 2971.04 of the Revised Code, whether it should terminate its control over an offender's service of a prison term imposed upon the offender under division (A)(3), (B)(1)(a), (b), or (c), (B)(2)(a), (b), or (c), or (B)(3)(a), (b), (c), or (d) of section 2971.03 of the Revised Code. The rules shall include provisions that specify that the parole board may not terminate its control over an offender's service of a prison term imposed upon the offender under any of the specified divisions until after the offender has served the minimum term imposed as part of that prison term and until the parole board has determined that the offender does not represent a substantial risk of physical harm to others.

**HISTORY: 146 v H 180. Eff 1-1-97; 150 v H 473, § 1, eff. 4-29-05; 151 v S 260, § 1, eff. 1-2-07; 152 v S 10, § 1, eff. 1-1-08.**

The effective date is set by § 3 of 152 v S 10.

The effective date is set by section 3 of HB 180.

The provisions of § 4 of HB 180 (146 v —) read in part as follows:

SECTION 4. * * * 5120.49, 5120.61, 5149.03, and 5149.10 of the Revised Code, as amended or enacted in Sections 1 and 2 of this act, shall apply only to persons who commit an offense governed by those amended and enacted sections on or after the effective date of this act.

## § 5120.50 Interstate correction compact.

(A) The party states, desiring by common action to fully utilize and improve their programs for the confinement, treatment, and rehabilitation of various types of offenders, declare that it is the policy of each of the party states to provide institutional facilities and such programs on a basis of cooperation with one another, thereby serving the best interest of such offenders and of society and effecting economies in capital expenditures and operational costs. The purpose of this compact is to provide for the mutual development and execution of such programs of cooperation for the confinement, treatment, and rehabilitation of offenders with the most economical use of human and material resources.

(B) DEFINITIONS

As used in the compact, unless the context clearly requires otherwise:

(1) "State" means a state of the United States; the United States; a territory or possession of the United States; the District of Columbia; the Commonwealth of Puerto Rico.

(2) "Sending state" means a state party to this compact in which conviction or court commitment was had.

(3) "Receiving state" means a state party to this compact to which an inmate is sent for confinement other than a state in which conviction or court commitment was had.

(4) "Inmate" means a male or female offender who is committed, under sentence to or confined in a state penal or state reformatory institution.

(5) "Institution" means any state penal or state reformatory facility, including but not limited to a facility for the mentally ill or mentally defective, in which inmates as defined in division (B)(4) of this section may lawfully be confined.

(C) CONTRACTS

(1) Each party state may make one or more contracts with any one or more of the other party states for the confinement of inmates on behalf of a sending state in institutions situated within receiving states. Any such contract shall provide for:

(a) Its duration;

(b) Payments to be made to the receiving state by the sending state for inmate maintenance, extraordinary medical and dental expenses, and any participation in or receipt by inmates of rehabilitative or correctional services, facilities, programs, or treatment not reasonably included as part of normal maintenance;

(c) Participation in programs of inmate employment, if any; the disposition or crediting of any payments received by inmates on account thereof; and the crediting of proceeds from or disposal of any products resulting therefrom;

(d) Delivery and retaking of inmates;

(e) Such other matters as may be necessary and appropriate to fix the obligations, responsibilities, and rights of the sending and receiving states.

(2) The terms and provisions of this compact shall be a part of any contract entered into by the authority of or pursuant thereto, and nothing in any such contract shall be inconsistent therewith.

(D) PROCEDURES AND RIGHTS

(1) Whenever the duly constituted authorities in a state party to this compact, and which has entered into a contract pursuant to division (C) of this section, shall decide that confinement in, or transfer of an inmate to, an institution within the territory of another party state is necessary or desirable in order to provide adequate quarters and care, or an appropriate program of rehabilitation or treatment, said officials may direct that the confinement be within an institution within the territory of said other party state, the receiving state to act in that regard solely as agent for the sending state.

(2) No transfer shall take place pursuant to this compact unless one of the following has occurred: (a) the inmate has given his written consent to such transfer; (b) in the event the inmate does not consent to such transfer, a hearing shall be held and a record made indicating the reasons for said transfer.

(3) The appropriate officials of any state party to this compact shall have access, at all reasonable times, to any institution in which it has a contractural [contractual] right to confine inmates for the purpose of inspecting the facilities thereof and visiting such of its inmates as may be confined in the institution.

(4) Inmates confined in an institution pursuant to the terms of this compact shall at all times be subject to the jurisdiction of the sending state and may at any time be removed therefrom for transfer to a prison or other institution within the sending state, for transfer to another institution in which the sending state may have a contractual or other right to confine inmates, for release on probation or parole, for discharge, or for any other purpose permitted by the laws of the sending state; provided that the sending state shall continue to be obligated to such payments as may be required pursuant to the terms of any contract entered into under the terms of division (C) of this section.

(5) Each receiving state shall provide regular reports, no less than semiannually, to each sending state on the inmates of that sending state in institutions pursuant to this compact, including a conduct record of each inmate and certify said record to the official designated by the sending state, in order that each inmate may have official review of his or her record in determining and altering the disposition of said inmate in accordance with the law which may obtain in the sending state and in order that the same may be a source of information for the sending state.

(6) All inmates who may be confined in an institution pursuant to the provisions of this compact shall be treated in a reasonable and humane manner and shall be treated equally with such similar inmates of the receiving state as may be confined in the same institution. The fact of confinement in a receiving state shall not deprive any inmate so confined of any legal rights which said inmate would have had if confined in an appropriate institution of the sending state.

(7) Any hearing or hearings to which an inmate confined pursuant to this compact may be entitled by the laws of the sending state may be had before the appropriate authorities of the sending state, or of the receiving state if authorized by the sending state. The receiving state shall provide adequate facilities for such hearings as may be conducted by the appropriate officials of a sending state. In the event such hearing or hearings are had before officials of the receiving state, the governing law shall be that of the sending state and a record of the hearing or hearings as prescribed by the sending state shall be made. Said record together with any recommendations of the hearing officials shall be transmitted forthwith to the official or officials before whom the hearing would have

been had if it had taken place in the sending state. In any and all proceedings had pursuant to the provisions of this division, the officials of the receiving state shall act solely as agents of the sending state and no final determination shall be made in any matter except by the appropriate officials of the sending state.

(8) Any inmate confined pursuant to this compact shall be released within the territory of the sending state unless the inmate, and the sending and receiving states, shall agree upon release in some other place. The sending state shall bear the cost of such return to its territory.

(9) Any inmate confined pursuant to the terms of this compact shall have any and all rights to participate in and derive any benefits, or incur or be relieved of any obligations, or have such obligations modified or his status changed on account of any action or proceeding in which he could have participated if confined in any appropriate institution of the sending state located within such state.

(10) The parent, guardian, trustee, or other person or persons entitled under the laws of the sending state to act for, advise, or otherwise function with respect to any inmate shall not be deprived of or restricted in his exercise of any power in respect of any inmate confined pursuant to the terms of this compact.

(E) ACTS NOT REVIEWABLE IN RECEIVING STATE: EXTRADITION

(1) Any decision of the sending state in respect of any matter over which it retains jurisdiction pursuant to this compact shall be conclusive upon and not reviewable within the receiving state, but if at the time the sending state seeks to remove an inmate from an institution in the receiving state there is pending against the inmate within such state any criminal charge or if the inmate is formally accused of having committed within such state a criminal offense, the inmate shall not be returned without the consent of the receiving state until discharged from prosecution or other form of proceeding, imprisonment or detention for such offense. The duly accredited officers of the sending state shall be permitted to transport inmates pursuant to this compact through any and all states party to this compact without interference.

(2) An inmate who escapes from an institution in which he is confined pursuant to this compact shall be deemed a fugitive from the sending state and from the state in which the institution is situated. In the case of an escape to a jurisdiction other than the sending or receiving state, the responsibility for institution of extradition or rendition proceedings shall be that of the sending state, but nothing contained herein shall be construed to prevent or affect the activities of officers and agencies of any jurisdiction directed toward the apprehension and return of an escapee.

(F) FEDERAL AID

Any state party to this compact may accept federal aid for use in connection with any institution or program, the use of which is or may be affected by this compact or any contract pursuant hereto. Any inmate in a receiving state pursuant to this compact may participate in any such federally aided program or activity for which the sending and receiving states have made contractual provision, provided that if such program or activity is not part of the customary correctional regimen, the express consent of the appropriate official of the sending state shall be required therefor.

(G) ENTRY INTO FORCE

This compact shall enter into force and become effective and binding upon the states so acting when it has been enacted into law by any two states. Thereafter, this compact shall enter into force and become effective and binding as to any other of said states upon similar action by such state.

(H) WITHDRAWAL AND TERMINATION

This compact shall continue in force and remain binding upon a party state until it shall have enacted a statute repealing the same and providing for the sending of formal written notice of withdrawal from the compact to the appropriate officials of all other party states. An actual withdrawal shall not take effect until one year after the notices provided in said statute have been sent. Such withdrawal shall not relieve the withdrawing state from its obligations assumed hereunder prior to the effective date of withdrawal. Before the effective date of withdrawal, a withdrawing state shall remove to its territory, at its own expense, such inmates as it may have confined pursuant to the provisions of this compact.

(I) OTHER ARRANGEMENTS UNAFFECTED

Nothing contained in this compact shall be construed to abrogate or impair any agreement or other arrangement which a party state may have with a nonparty state for the confinement, rehabilitation, or treatment of inmates nor to repeal any other laws of a party state authorizing the making of cooperative institutional arrangements.

(J) CONSTRUCTION AND SEVERABILITY

The provisions of this compact shall be liberally construed and shall be severable. If any phrase, clause, sentence, or provision of this compact is declared to be contrary to the constitution of any participating state or of the United States, or the applicability thereof to any government, agency, person, or circumstance is held invalid, the validity of the remainder of this compact and the applicability thereof to any government, agency, person, or circumstance shall not be affected thereby. If this compact shall be held contrary to the constitution of any state participating therein, the compact shall remain in full force and effect as to the remaining states and in full force and effect as to the state affected as to all severable matters.

(K) POWERS

The director of the department of rehabilitation and correction is hereby authorized and directed to do all things necessary or incidental to the carrying out of the compact in every particular and he may in his discretion delegate this authority to the deputy director of the department of rehabilitation and correction.

**HISTORY: 136 v H 47. Eff 12-28-76.**

## § 5120.51 Population and cost impact statement for bill.

(A)(1) If the director of rehabilitation and correction determines that a bill introduced in the general assembly is likely to have a significant impact on the population of, or the cost of operating, any or all state correctional institutions under the administration of the department of rehabilitation and correction, the department shall prepare a population and cost impact statement for the bill, in accordance with division (A)(2) of this section.

(2) A population and cost impact statement required for a bill shall estimate the increase or decrease in the correctional institution population that likely would result if the bill were enacted, shall estimate, in dollars, the amount by which revenues or expenditures likely would increase or decrease if the bill were enacted, and briefly shall explain each of the estimates.

A population and cost impact statement required for a bill initially shall be prepared after the bill is referred to a committee of the general assembly in the house of origination but before the meeting of the committee at which the committee is scheduled to vote on whether to recommend the bill for passage. A copy of the statement shall be distributed to each member of the committee that is considering the bill and to the member of the general assembly who introduced it. If the bill is recommended for passage by the committee, the department shall update the statement before the bill is taken up for final consideration by the house of origination. A copy of the updated statement shall be distributed to each member of that house and to the member of the general assembly who introduced the bill. If the bill is passed by the house of origination and is introduced in the second house, the provisions of this division concerning the preparation, updating, and distribution of the statement in the house of origination also apply in the second house.

(B) The governor or any member of the general assembly, at any time, may request the department to prepare a population and cost impact statement for any bill introduced in the general assembly. Upon receipt of a request, the department promptly shall prepare a statement that includes the estimates and explanations described in division (A)(2) of this section and present a copy of it to the governor or member who made the request.

(C) In the preparation of a population and cost impact statement required by division (A) or (B) of this section, the department shall use a technologically sophisticated system capable of estimating future state correctional institution populations. The system shall have the capability to adjust its estimates based on actual and proposed changes in sentencing laws and trends, sentence durations, parole rates, crime rates, and any other data that affect state correctional institution populations. The department, in conjunction with the advisory committee appointed under division (E) of this section, shall review and update the data used in the system, not less than once every six months, to improve the accuracy of the system.

(D) At least once every six months, the department shall provide to the correctional institution inspection committee a copy of the estimates of state correctional institution populations obtained through use of the system described in division (C) of this section and a description of the assumptions regarding sentencing laws and trends, sentence durations, parole rates, crime rates, and other relevant data that were made by the department to obtain the estimates. Additionally, a copy of the estimates and a description of the assumptions made to obtain them shall be provided, upon reasonable request, to other legislative staff, including the staff of the legislative service commission, to the office of budget and management, and to the division of criminal justice services in the department of public safety.

(E) The correctional institution inspection committee shall appoint an advisory committee to review the operation of the system for estimating future state correctional institution populations that is used by the department in the preparation of population cost impact statements pursuant to this section and to join with the department in its reviews and updating of the data used in the system under division (C) of this section. The advisory committee shall be comprised of at least one prosecuting attorney, at least one common pleas court judge, at least one public defender, at least one person who is a member or staff employee of the committee, and at least one representative of the division of criminal justice services in the department of public safety.

**HISTORY: 142 v S 94 (Eff 7-20-88); 144 v H 298 (Eff 7-26-91); 145 v H 152 (Eff 7-1-93); 145 v H 571. Eff 10-6-94; 151 v H 66, § 101.01, eff. 6-30-05.**

The effective date is set by § 612.12 of 151 v H 66.

## § 5120.52 Contract with person or political subdivision to provide sewage treatment services.

The department of rehabilitation and correction may enter into a contract with any person or with a political subdivision in which a state correctional institution is located under which an institution will provide water or sewage treatment services for the person or political subdivision if the institution has a water or sewage treatment facility with sufficient excess capacity to provide the services.

Any such contract shall include all of the following:

(A) Limitations on the quantity of sewage that the facility will accept or the quantity of potable water that the facility will provide that are compatible with the needs of the state correctional institution;

(B) The bases for calculating reasonable rates to be charged the person or political subdivision for potable water or for sewage treatment services and for adjusting the rates;

(C) All other provisions the department considers necessary or proper to protect the interests of the state in the facility and the purpose for which it was constructed.

All amounts due the department under the contract shall be paid to the department by the person or political subdivision at the times specified in the contract. The department shall deposit all such amounts in the state treasury to the credit of the correctional institution water and sewage treatment facility services fund, which is hereby created. The fund shall be used by the department to pay costs associated with operating and maintaining the water or sewage treatment facility.

**HISTORY: 143 v S 330 (Eff 7-18-90); 145 v H 571. Eff 10-6-94; 152 v H 130, § 1, eff. 4-7-09.**

## § 5120.53 Transfer or exchange of offender to foreign country pursuant to treaty.

(A) If a treaty between the United States and a foreign country provides for the transfer or exchange, from one of the signatory countries to the other signatory country, of convicted offenders who are citizens or nationals of the other signatory country, the governor, subject to and in accordance with the terms of the treaty, may authorize the director of rehabilitation and correction to allow the transfer or exchange of convicted offenders and to take any action necessary to initiate participation in the treaty. If the governor grants the director the authority described in this division, the director may take the necessary action to initiate participation in the treaty and, subject to and in accordance with division (B) of this section and the terms of the treaty, may allow the transfer or exchange to a foreign country that has signed the treaty of any convicted offender who is a citizen or national of that signatory country.

(B)(1) No convicted offender who is serving a term of imprisonment in this state for aggravated murder, murder, or a felony of the first or second degree, who is serving a mandatory prison term imposed under section 2925.03 or 2925.11 of the Revised Code in circumstances in which the court was required to impose as the mandatory prison term the maximum prison term authorized for the degree of offense committed, who is serving a term of imprisonment in this state imposed for an offense committed prior to the effective date of this amendment that was an aggravated felony of the first or second degree or that was aggravated trafficking in violation of division (A)(9) or (10) of section 2925.03 of the Revised Code, or who has been sentenced to death in this state shall be transferred or exchanged to another country pursuant to a treaty of the type described in division (A) of this section.

(2) If a convicted offender is serving a term of imprisonment in this state and the offender is a citizen or national of a foreign country that has signed a treaty of the type described in division (A) of this section, if the governor has granted the director of rehabilitation and correction the authority described in that division, and if the transfer or exchange of the offender is not barred by division (B)(1) of this section, the director or the director's designee may approve the offender for transfer or exchange pursuant to the treaty if the director or the designee, after consideration of the factors set forth in the rules adopted by the department under division (D) of this section and all other relevant factors, determines that the transfer or exchange of the offender is appropriate.

(C) Notwithstanding any provision of the Revised Code regarding the parole eligibility of, or the duration or calculation of a sentence of imprisonment imposed upon, an offender, if a convicted offender is serving a term of imprisonment in this state and the offender is a citizen or national of a foreign country that has signed a treaty of the type described in division (A) of this section, if the offender is serving an indefinite term of imprisonment, if the offender is barred from being transferred or exchanged pursuant to the treaty due to the indefinite nature of the offender's term of imprisonment, and if in accordance with division (B)(2) of this section the director of rehabilitation and correction or the director's designee approves the offender for transfer or exchange pursuant to the treaty, the parole board, pursuant to rules adopted by the director, shall set a date certain for the release of the offender. To the extent possible, the date certain that is set shall be reasonably proportionate to the indefinite term of imprisonment that the offender is serving. The date certain that is set for the release of the offender shall be considered only for purposes of facilitating the international transfer or exchange of the offender, shall not be viable or actionable for any other purpose, and shall not create any expectation or guarantee of release. If an offender for whom a date certain for release is set under this division is not transferred to or exchanged with the foreign country pursuant to the treaty, the date certain is null and void, and the offender's release shall be determined pursuant to the laws and rules of this state pertaining to parole eligibility and the duration and calculation of an indefinite sentence of imprisonment.

(D) If the governor, pursuant to division (A) of this section, authorizes the director of rehabilitation and correction to allow any transfer or exchange of convicted offenders as described in that division, the director shall adopt rules under Chapter 119. of the Revised Code to implement the provisions of this section. The rules shall include a rule that requires the director or the director's designee, in determining whether to approve a convicted offender who is serving a term of imprisonment in this state for transfer or exchange pursuant to a treaty of the type described in division (A) of this section, to consider all of the following factors:

(1) The nature of the offense for which the offender is serving the term of imprisonment in this state;

(2) The likelihood that, if the offender is transferred or exchanged to a foreign country pursuant to the treaty, the offender will serve a shorter period of time in imprisonment in the foreign country than the offender would serve if the offender is not transferred or exchanged to the foreign country pursuant to the treaty;

(3) The likelihood that, if the offender is transferred or exchanged to a foreign country pursuant to the treaty, the offender will return or attempt to return to this state after the offender has been released from imprisonment in the foreign country;

(4) The degree of any shock to the conscience of justice and society that will be experienced in this state if the offender is transferred or exchanged to a foreign country pursuant to the treaty;

(5) All other factors that the department determines are relevant to the determination.

**HISTORY: 145 v S 242 (Eff 10-6-94); 146 v S 2. Eff 7-1-96.**

The effective date is set by section 6 of SB 2.

## § 5120.55 Licensed health professional recruitment program.

(A) As used in this section, "licensed health professional" means any or all of the following:

(1) A dentist who holds a current, valid license issued under Chapter 4715. of the Revised Code to practice dentistry;

(2) A licensed practical nurse who holds a current, valid license issued under Chapter 4723. of the Revised Code that authorizes the practice of nursing as a licensed practical nurse;

(3) An optometrist who holds a current, valid certificate of licensure issued under Chapter 4725. of the Revised Code that authorizes the holder to engage in the practice of optometry;

(4) A physician who is authorized under Chapter 4731. of the Revised Code to practice medicine and surgery, osteopathic medicine and surgery, or podiatry;

(5) A psychologist who holds a current, valid license issued under Chapter 4732. of the Revised Code that authorizes the practice of psychology as a licensed psychologist;

(6) A registered nurse who holds a current, valid license issued under Chapter 4723. of the Revised Code that authorizes the practice of nursing as a registered nurse regardless of whether the nurse is authorized to practice as an advanced practice nurse as defined in section 4723.01 of the Revised Code.

(B)(1) The department of rehabilitation and correction may establish a recruitment program under which the department, by means of a contract entered into under division (C) of this section, agrees to repay all or part of the principal and interest of a government or other educational loan incurred by a licensed health professional who agrees to provide services to inmates of correctional institutions under the department's administration.

(2)(a) For a physician to be eligible to participate in the program, a physician must have attended a school that was, during the time of attendance, a medical school or osteopathic medical school in this country accredited by the liaison committee on medical education or the American osteopathic association, a college of podiatry in this country recognized as being in good standing under section 4731.53 of the Revised Code, or a medical school, osteopathic medical school, or college of podiatry located outside this country that was acknowledged by the world health organization and verified by a member state of that organization as operating within that state's jurisdiction.

(b) For a nurse to be eligible to participate in the program, the nurse must have attended a school that was, during the time of attendance, a nursing school in this country accredited by the commission on collegiate nursing education or the national league for nursing accrediting commission or a nursing school located outside this country that was acknowledged by the world health organization and verified by a member state of that organization as operating within that state's jurisdiction.

(c) For a dentist to be eligible to participate in the program, the dentist must have attended a school that was, during the time of attendance, a dental college that enabled the dentist to meet the requirements specified in section 4715.10 of the Revised Code to be granted a license to practice dentistry.

(d) For an optometrist to be eligible to participate in the program, the optometrist must have attended a school of optometry that was, during the time of attendance, approved by the state board of optometry.

(e) For a psychologist to be eligible to participate in the program, the psychologist must have attended an educational institution that, during the time of attendance, maintained a specific degree program recognized by the state board of psychology as acceptable for fulfilling the requirement of division (B)(4) of section 4732.10 of the Revised Code.

(C) The department shall enter into a contract with each licensed health professional it recruits under this section. Each contract shall include at least the following terms:

(1) The licensed health professional agrees to provide a specified scope of medical, osteopathic medical, podiatric, optometric, psychological, nursing, or dental services to inmates of one or more specified state correctional institutions for a specified number of hours per week for a specified number of years.

(2) The department agrees to repay all or a specified portion of the principal and interest of a government or other educational loan taken by the licensed health professional for the following expenses to attend, for up to a maximum of four years, a school that qualifies the licensed health professional to participate in the program:

(a) Tuition;

(b) Other educational expenses for specific purposes, including fees, books, and laboratory expenses, in amounts determined to be reasonable in accordance with rules adopted under division (D) of this section;

(c) Room and board, in an amount determined to be reasonable in accordance with rules adopted under division (D) of this section.

(3) The licensed health professional agrees to pay the department a specified amount, which shall be no less than the amount already paid by the department pursuant to its agreement, as damages if the licensed health professional fails to complete the service obligation agreed to or fails to comply with other specified terms of the contract. The contract may vary the amount of damages based on the portion of the service obligation that remains uncompleted.

(4) Other terms agreed upon by the parties.

The licensed health professional's lending institution or the Ohio board of regents, may be a party to the contract. The contract may include an assignment to the department of the licensed health professional's duty to repay the principal and interest of the loan.

(D) If the department elects to implement the recruitment program, it shall adopt rules in accordance with Chapter 119. of the Revised Code that establish all of the following:

(1) Criteria for designating institutions for which licensed health professionals will be recruited;

(2) Criteria for selecting licensed health professionals for participation in the program;

(3) Criteria for determining the portion of a loan which the department will agree to repay;

(4) Criteria for determining reasonable amounts of the expenses described in divisions (C)(2)(b) and (c) of this section;

(5) Procedures for monitoring compliance by a licensed health professional with the terms of the contract the licensed health professional enters into under this section;

(6) Any other criteria or procedures necessary to implement the program.

**HISTORY: 144 v H 478 (Eff 1-14-93); 145 v H 571 (Eff 10-6-94); 146 v S 143 (Eff 3-5-96); 146 v H 627. Eff 12-2-96; 152 v S 147, § 1, eff. 4-7-09.**

## § 5120.56 Recovery of cost of incarceration or supervision from offender; offender financial responsibility fund.

(A) As used in sections 5120.56 to 5120.58 of the Revised Code:

(1) "Ancillary services" means services provided to an offender as necessary for the particular circumstances of the offender's personal supervision, including, but not limited to, specialized counseling, testing, or other services not included in the calculation of residential or supervision costs.

(2) "Cost debt" means a cost of incarceration or supervision that may be assessed against and collected from an offender as a debt to the state as described in division (D) of this section.

(3) "Detention facility" means any place used for the confinement of a person charged with or convicted of any crime.

(4) "Offender" means any inmate, parolee, person placed under a community control sanction, releasee, or other person who has been convicted of or pleaded guilty to any felony or misdemeanor and is sentenced to any of the following:

(a) A term of imprisonment, a prison term, a jail term, or another type of confinement in a detention facility;

(b) Participation in another correctional program in lieu of incarceration.

(5) "Community control sanction," "prison term," and "jail term" have the same meanings as in section 2929.01 of the Revised Code.

(6) "Parolee" and "releasee" have the same meanings as in section 2967.01 of the Revised Code.

(B) The department of rehabilitation and correction may recover from an offender who is in its custody or under its supervision any cost debt described in division (D) of this section. To satisfy a cost debt described in that division that relates to an offender, the department may apply directly assets that are in the department's possession and that are being held for that offender without further proceedings in aid of execution, and, if assets belonging to or subject to the direction of that offender are in the possession of a third party, the department may request the attorney general to initiate proceedings to collect the assets from the third party to satisfy the cost debt.

(C) Except as otherwise provided in division (E) or (G) of this section, all of the following assets of an offender shall be subject to attachment, collection, or application toward the cost debts described in division (D) of this section that are to be recovered under division (B) of this section:

(1) Subject to division (E) of this section, any pay the offender receives from the state;

(2) Subject to division (E) of this section, any funds the offender receives from persons on an approved visitor list;

(3) Any liquid assets belonging to the offender and in the custody of the department;

(4) Any assets the offender acquires or any other income the offender earns subsequent to the offender's commitment.

(D) Costs of incarceration or supervision that may be assessed against and collected from an offender under division (B) of this section as a debt to the state shall include, but are not limited to, all of the following costs that accrue while the offender is in the custody or under the supervision of the department:

(1) Any user fee or copayment for services at a detention facility or housing facility, including, but not limited to, a fee or copayment for sick call visits;

(2) Assessment for damage to or destruction of property in a detention facility subsequent to commitment;

(3) Restitution to an offender or to a staff member of a state correctional institution for theft, loss, or damage to the personal property of the offender or staff member;

(4) The cost of housing and feeding the offender in a detention facility;

(5) The cost of supervision of the offender;

(6) The cost of any ancillary services provided to the offender;

(7) The cost of any medical care provided to the offender.

(E) The cost of housing and feeding an offender in a state correctional institution shall not be collected from a payment made to the offender for performing an activity at a state job or assignment that pays less than the minimum wage or from money the offender receives from visitors, unless the combined assets in the offender's institution personal account exceed, at any time, one hundred dollars. If the combined assets in that account exceed one hundred dollars, the cost of housing and feeding the offender may be collected from the amount in excess of one hundred dollars.

(F)(1) The department shall adopt rules pursuant to section 111.15 of the Revised Code to implement the requirements of this section.

(2) The rules adopted under division (F)(1) of this section shall include, but are not limited to, rules that establish or contain all of the following:

(a) A process for ascertaining the items of cost to be assessed against an offender;

(b) Subject to division (F)(3) of this section, a process by which the offender shall have the opportunity to respond to the assessment of costs under division (B) of this section and to contest any item of cost in the department's calculation or as it applies to the offender;

(c) A requirement that the offender be notified, in writing, of a final decision to collect or apply the offender's assets under division (B) of this section and that the notification be provided after the offender has had an opportunity to contest the application or collection;

(d) Criteria for evaluating an offender's ongoing, permanent injury and evaluating the ability of that type of offender to provide for the offender after incarceration.

(3) The rules adopted under division (F)(1) of this section may allow the collection of a cost debt as a flat fee or over time in installments. If the cost debt is to be collected over time in installments, the rules are not required to permit the offender an opportunity to contest the assessment of each installment. The rules may establish a standard fee to apply to all offenders who receive a particular service.

(G) The department shall not collect cost debts or apply offender assets toward a cost debt under division (B) of this section if, due to an ongoing, permanent injury, the collection or application would unjustly limit the offender's ability to provide for the offender after incarceration.

(H) If an offender acquires assets after the offender is convicted of or pleads guilty to an offense and if the transferor knows of the offender's status as an offender, the transferor shall notify the department in advance of the transfer.

(I) There is hereby created in the state treasury the offender financial responsibility fund. All moneys collected by or on behalf of the department under this section, and all moneys currently in the department's custody that are applied to satisfy an allowable cost debt under this section, shall be deposited into the fund. The department may expend moneys in the fund for goods and services of the same type as those for which offenders are assessed pursuant to this section.

**HISTORY: 147 v S 111 (Eff 3-17-98); 149 v H 170. Eff 9-6-2002; 149 v H 490, § 1, eff. 1-1-04.**

The effective date is set by section 4 of H.B. 490.

## § 5120.57 Reimbursement for health care services rendered to insured offender.

(A) For each offender who is in the custody or under the supervision of the department of rehabilitation and correction, the department may make a determination as to whether the offender is covered under an individual or group sickness and accident insurance policy or an individual or group health insuring corporation policy, contract, or agreement. If the offender has coverage of that type, the department shall familiarize itself with the terms and conditions to receive benefits under the policy, contract, or agreement.

(B) If, pursuant to division (A) of this section, it is determined that the offender is covered under an individual or group sickness and accident insurance policy or an individual or group health insuring corporation policy, contract, or agreement and if, while that coverage is in force, the department renders or arranges for the rendering of health care services to the person in accordance with the terms and conditions of the policy, contract, or agreement, the department or provider of the health care services, as appropriate under the terms and conditions of the policy, contract, or agreement, may submit a claim for payment for the health care services to the appropriate third-party payer. If the policy holder is the offender, the offender shall be required to assign payment of benefits directly to the provider or department, as appropriate. If the policy holder is not the offender, the policy holder shall be asked to voluntarily provide policy information and assign payments directly to the provider or department, as appropriate. The department shall provide the third-party payer with a copy of the assignment of benefits by the policy holder. The policy holder and the third-party payer shall make all arrangements necessary to ensure that payment of any amount due on the claim is made to the provider or department as specified in the assignment. The department shall remain ultimately responsible for payment of all health care services provided to an offender in the custody or under the supervision of the department but shall be the payer of last resort. If the department pays a provider for health care services rendered to an offender and payment subsequently is made for the same services by a third-party payer, the provider shall refund the duplicate payment to the department and, the department shall deposit the refunded payment into the offender financial responsibility fund as described in division (E) of this section.

(C) If, pursuant to division (A) of this section, it is determined that the offender is covered under an individual or group sickness and accident insurance policy or an individual or group health insuring corporation policy, contract, or agreement, the department shall make a determination, after considering security, public safety, and transportation issues, whether or not to render or arrange for the rendering of health care services in accordance with the terms and conditions of the policy, contract, or agreement. The department, based on security, public safety, or transportation concerns or any combination of those concerns, may arrange for the rendering of health care services for the offender at a health care facility, by a provider, or at a health care facility and by a provider not covered by the policy, contract, or agreement and pay the costs of the health care services for the offender.

(D) If the department renders or arranges for the rendering of health care services to an offender and pays for the services, the department reserves the right to seek reimbursement from a third-party payer for the services if it subsequently is determined that the offender was covered under an individual or group sickness and accident insurance policy or an individual or group health insuring corporation policy, contract, or agreement. The department shall submit a claim for reimbursement of the type described in this division within the time frames applicable to claims submitted by a policy holder in accordance with the terms and conditions of the policy, contract, or agreement.

(E) Any payment made to the department pursuant to division (B) of this section shall be deposited into the offender financial responsibility fund created in section 5120.56 of the Revised Code.

(F) If, at the time the department arranges for health care services for an offender and a provider renders those services, the department determines pursuant to division (A) of this section that the offender is covered, or potentially is covered, under an individual or group sickness and accident insurance policy or an individual or group health insuring corporation policy, contract, or agreement, then all of the following apply:

(1) The department is responsible for any cost-sharing, co-payments, or deductibles required under the policy, contract, or agreement.

(2) If the insurer or potential insurer denies the claim for payment, the department remains liable for payment to the provider of services.

(3) If an insurer covers a service, but the amount the insurer pays to the provider is less than the amount negotiated and established by contract then in effect between the department and the provider, the department is liable for reimbursing the difference to the provider.

(G) Nothing in this section requires a third-party payer to reimburse any provider or the department for health care services not covered under the terms or conditions of an individual or group sickness and accident insurance policy, an individual or group health insuring corporation policy, contract, or agreement, or any other policy, contract, or agreement.

**HISTORY: 149 v H 170. Eff 9-6-2002.**

See provisions, § 3 of HB 170 (149 v —) following RC § 5120.58.

## § 5120.58 Health care benefits and preventive services.

The department of rehabilitation and correction shall adopt rules under section 111.15 of the Revised Code to do both of the following:

(A) Establish a schedule of health care benefits that are available to offenders who are in the custody or under the supervision of the department;

(B) Establish a program to encourage the utilization of preventive health care services by offenders.

**HISTORY: 149 v H 170. Eff 9-6-2002.**

The provisions of § 3 of HB 170 (149 v —) read as follows:

SECTION 3. (A) The Department of Rehabilitation and Correction shall examine the feasibility and desirability of purchasing insurance coverage to protect against unpredictable or catastrophic losses that may be incurred by the state in the provision of health care services to offenders who are in the custody or under the supervision of the Department. Not later than six months after the effective date of this act, the Department shall report its findings and any recommendations to the Speaker of the House of Representatives, the President of the Senate, and the chairs of the standing committees of the House of Representatives and the Senate that have primary jurisdiction over issues related to the Department.

(B) The Department of Rehabilitation and Correction shall develop specifications for a utilization review program under which the clinical necessity, appropriateness, efficacy, or efficiency of any outside health care service recommended for an offender may be evaluated by an external utilization review organization. The Department shall request proposals for the provision of services of that nature. The request for proposals shall adequately describe the specifications developed by the Department. Within six months after the effective date of this section, the Department shall report the responses to the request for proposals to the Speaker of the House of Representatives, the President of the Senate, and the chairs of the standing committees of the House of Representatives and the Senate that have primary jurisdiction over issues related to the Department. The Department is not required to enter into a contract for the provision of that nature unless money has been appropriated to the Department adequate to fund the provision of services of that nature.

## § 5120.59 Identification cards for prisoners upon release.

Before a prisoner is released from a state correctional institution, the department of rehabilitation and correction shall attempt to verify the prisoner's identification and social security number. If the department is not able to verify the prisoner's identification and social security number, if the prisoner has no other documentary evidence required by the registrar of motor vehicles for the issuance of an identification card under section 4507.50 of the Revised Code, and if the department determines that the prisoner is legally living in the United States, the department shall issue to the prisoner upon the prisoner's release an identification card that the prisoner may present to the registrar or a deputy registrar of motor vehicles.

**HISTORY: 152 v H 130, § 1, eff. 4-7-09; 2011 HB 86, § 1, eff. Sept. 30, 2011.**

## § 5120.60 Office of victims' services.

(A) There is hereby created in the division of parole and community services the office of victim services.

(B) The office shall provide assistance to victims of crime, victims' representatives designated under section 2930.02 of the Revised Code, and members of the victim's family. The assistance shall include, but not be limited to, providing information about the policies and procedures of the department of rehabilitation and correction and the status of offenders under the department's jurisdiction.

(C) The office shall also make available publications that will assist victims in contacting staff of the department about problems with offenders under the supervision of the adult parole authority or confined in state correctional institutions under the department's jurisdiction.

(D) The office shall employ a victim coordinator who shall administer the office's functions. The victim coordinator shall be in the unclassified civil service and report directly to the chief of the division.

(E) The office shall also employ at least three persons in the unclassified civil service whose primary duties shall be to help parole board hearing officers identify victims' issues and to make recommendations to the parole board in accordance with rules adopted by the department. The member of the parole board appointed pursuant to division (B) of section 5149.10 of the Revised Code shall approve the hiring of the employees of the office.

(F) The office shall coordinate its activities with the member of the parole board appointed pursuant to division (B) of section 5149.10 of the Revised Code. The victim coordinator and other employees of the office shall have full access to records of prisoners under the department's jurisdiction.

(G) Information provided to the office of victim services by victims of crime or a victim representative designated under section 2930.02 of the Revised Code for the purpose of program participation, of receiving services, or to communicate acts of an inmate or person under the supervision of the adult parole authority that threaten the safety and security of the victim shall be confidential and is not a public record under section 149.43 of the Revised Code.

(H)(1) If a person who was convicted of or pleaded guilty to an offense of violence that is a felony escapes from a correctional institution under the control of the department of rehabilitation and correction or otherwise escapes from the custody of the department, the office of victim services shall notify each victim of the offense or offenses committed by that person of that person's escape and, if applicable, of that person's subsequent apprehension. The office shall give this notice as soon as practicable after the escape and the office identifies and locates the victim. The office shall give this notice to each victim of the escaped person, regardless of whether the victim is registered for notification with the office, unless the victim has specifically notified the office that the victim does not wish to be notified regarding the person.

The office may give the notice required by this division by telephone, in person, or by e-mail or other electronic means. If the office cannot locate a victim to whom notice is to be provided under this division, the office shall send the notice in writing to the last known address of that victim.

(2) If a person escapes as described in division (H)(1) of this section, the office of victim services may request assistance from the prosecuting attorney of the county in which the person was convicted of or pleaded guilty to the offense in identifying and locating the victim of the offense.

(I) Any reference in any Revised Code section other than this section to the "office of victims' services" of the division of parole and community services or of the department of rehabilitation and correction shall be construed as being a reference to, and meaning, the office of victim services created by division (A) of this section.

(J) As used in this section, "crime," "member of the victim's family," and "victim" have the meanings given in section 2930.01 of the Revised Code.

**HISTORY: 146 v S 2 (Eff 7-1-96); 149 v H 510. Eff 3-31-2003; 2011 HB 86, § 1, eff. Sept. 30, 2011.**

## § 5120.61 Risk assessment reports for sexually violent predators.

(A)(1) Not later than ninety days after January 1, 1997, the department of rehabilitation and correction shall adopt standards that it will use under this section to assess the following criminal offenders and may periodically revise the standards:

(a) A criminal offender who is convicted of or pleads guilty to a violent sex offense or designated homicide, assault, or kidnapping offense and is adjudicated a sexually violent predator in relation to that offense;

(b) A criminal offender who is convicted of or pleads guilty to a violation of division (A)(1)(b) of section 2907.02 of the Revised Code committed on or after January 2, 2007, and either who is sentenced under section 2971.03 of the Revised Code or upon whom a sentence of life without parole is imposed under division (B) of section 2907.02 of the Revised Code;

(c) A criminal offender who is convicted of or pleads guilty to attempted rape committed on or after January 2, 2007, and a specification of the type described in section 2941.1418 [2941.14.18], 2941.1419 [2941.14.19], or 2941.1420 [2941.14.20] of the Revised Code;

(d) A criminal offender who is convicted of or pleads guilty to a violation of section 2905.01 of the Revised Code and also is convicted of or pleads guilty to a sexual motivation specification that was included in the indictment, count in the indictment, or information charging that offense, and who is sentenced pursuant to section 2971.03 of the Revised Code;

(e) A criminal offender who is convicted of or pleads guilty to aggravated murder and also is convicted of or pleads guilty to a sexual motivation specification that was included in the indictment, count in the indictment, or information charging that offense, and who pursuant to division (A)(2)(b)(ii) of section 2929.022 [2929.02.2], division (A)(1)(e), (C)(1)(a)(v), (C)(2)(a)(ii), (D)(2)(b), (D)(3)(a)(iv), or (E)(1)(d) of section 2929.03, or division

(A) or (B) of section 2929.06 of the Revised Code is sentenced pursuant to division (B)(3) of section 2971.03 of the Revised Code;

(f) A criminal offender who is convicted of or pleads guilty to murder and also is convicted of or pleads guilty to a sexual motivation specification that was included in the indictment, count in the indictment, or information charging that offense, and who pursuant to division (B)(2) of section 2929.02 of the Revised Code is sentenced pursuant to section 2971.03 of the Revised Code.

(2) When the department is requested by the parole board or the court to provide a risk assessment report of the offender under section 2971.04 or 2971.05 of the Revised Code, it shall assess the offender and complete the assessment as soon as possible after the offender has commenced serving the prison term or term of life imprisonment without parole imposed under division (A), (B)(1)(a), (b), or (c), (B)(2)(a), (b), or (c), or (B)(3)(a), (b), (c), or (d) of section 2971.03 of the Revised Code. Thereafter, the department shall update a risk assessment report pertaining to an offender as follows:

(a) Periodically, in the discretion of the department, provided that each report shall be updated no later than two years after its initial preparation or most recent update;

(b) Upon the request of the parole board for use in determining pursuant to section 2971.04 of the Revised Code whether it should terminate its control over an offender's service of a prison term imposed upon the offender under division (A)(3), (B)(1)(a), (b), or (c), (B)(2)(a), (b), or (c), or (B)(3)(a), (b), (c), or (d) of section 2971.03 of the Revised Code;

(c) Upon the request of the court.

(3) After the department of rehabilitation and correction assesses an offender pursuant to division (A)(2) of this section, it shall prepare a report that contains its risk assessment for the offender or, if a risk assessment report previously has been prepared, it shall update the risk assessment report.

(4) The department of rehabilitation and correction shall provide each risk assessment report that it prepares or updates pursuant to this section regarding an offender to all of the following:

(a) The parole board for its use in determining pursuant to section 2971.04 of the Revised Code whether it should terminate its control over an offender's service of a prison term imposed upon the offender under division (A)(3), (B)(1)(a), (b), or (c), (B)(2)(a), (b), or (c), or (B)(3)(a), (b), (c), or (d) of section 2971.03 of the Revised Code, if the parole board has not terminated its control over the offender;

(b) The court for use in determining, pursuant to section 2971.05 of the Revised Code, whether to modify the requirement that the offender serve the entire prison term imposed upon the offender under division (A)(3), (B)(1)(a), (b), or (c), (B)(2)(a), (b), or (c), or (B)(3)(a), (b), (c), or (d) of section 2971.03 of the Revised Code in a state correctional institution, whether to revise any modification previously made, or whether to terminate the prison term;

(c) The prosecuting attorney who prosecuted the case, or the successor in office to that prosecuting attorney;

(d) The offender.

(B) When the department of rehabilitation and correction provides a risk assessment report regarding an offender to the parole board or court pursuant to division (A)(4)(a) or (b) of this section, the department, prior to the parole board's or court's hearing, also shall provide to the offender or to the offender's attorney of record a copy of the report and a copy of any other relevant documents the department possesses regarding the offender that the department does not consider to be confidential.

(C) As used in this section:

(1) "Adjudicated a sexually violent predator" has the same meaning as in section 2929.01 of the Revised Code, and a person is "adjudicated a sexually violent predator" in the same manner and the same circumstances as are described in that section.

(2) "Designated homicide, assault, or kidnapping offense" and "violent sex offense" have the same meanings as in section 2971.01 of the Revised Code.

**HISTORY: 146 v H 180. Eff 1-1-97; 150 v H 473, § 1, eff. 4-29-05; 151 v S 260, § 1, eff. 1-2-07; 152 v S 10, § 1, eff. 1-1-08.**

The effective date is set by § 3 of 152 v S 10.

The effective date is set by section 3 of HB 180.

See provisions, § 4 of HB 180 (146 v —), following RC § 5120.49.

## § 5120.62 Rules for prisoner access to Internet.

The director of rehabilitation and correction shall adopt rules under Chapter 119. of the Revised Code that govern the establishment and operation of a system that provides access to the internet for prisoners who are participating in an approved educational program with direct supervision that requires the use of the internet for training or research purposes. The rules shall include all of the following:

(A) Criteria by which inmates may be screened and approved for access or training involving the internet;

(B) Designation of the authority to approve internet sites for authorized use;

(C) A requirement that only pre-approved sites will be accessible on the computers used by prisoners in the educational program;

(D) A process for the periodic review of the operation of the system, including users of the system and the sites accessed by the system;

(E) Sanctions that must be imposed against prisoners and staff members who violate department rules governing prisoner access to the internet.

**HISTORY: 148 v S 12. Eff 6-8-2000.**

## § 5120.63 Random drug testing of state prisoners.

(A) As used in this section:

(1) "Random drug testing" means a procedure in which blood or urine specimens are collected from individuals chosen by automatic, random selection and without prearrangement or planning, for the purpose of scientifically analyzing the specimens to determine whether the individual ingested or was injected with a drug of abuse.

(2) "State correctional institution" has the same meaning as in section 2967.01 of the Revised Code.

(3) "Stated prison term" has the same meaning as in section 2929.01 of the Revised Code.

(B) The department of rehabilitation and correction shall establish and administer a statewide random drug testing program in which all persons who were convicted of or pleaded guilty to a felony offense and are serving a stated prison term in a state correctional institution shall submit to random drug testing. The department may enter into contracts with laboratories or entities in the state that are accredited by the national institute on drug abuse to perform blood or urine specimen collection, documentation, maintenance, transportation, preservation, storage, and analyses and other duties required under this section in the performance of random drug testing of prisoners in those correctional institutions. The terms of any contract entered into under this division shall include a requirement that the laboratory or entity and its employees, the superintendents, managing officers, and employees of state correctional institutions, all employees of the department, and all other persons comply with the standards for the performance of random drug testing as specified in the policies and procedures established by the department under division (D) of this section. If no laboratory or entity has entered into a contract as specified in this division, the department shall cause a prisoner to submit to random drug testing performed by a reputable public laboratory to determine whether the prisoner ingested or was injected with a drug of abuse.

(C) A prisoner who is subjected to random drug testing under this section and whose test indicates that the prisoner ingested or was injected with a drug of abuse shall pay the fee for that positive test and other subsequent test fees as a sanction specified by the department of rehabilitation and correction pursuant to division (D)(6) of this section.

(D) The department of rehabilitation and correction shall establish policies and procedures to implement the random drug testing program established under this section. The policies and procedures shall include, but are not limited to, provisions that do the following:

(1) Establish standards for the performance of random drug testing that include, but are not limited to, standards governing the following:

(a) The collection by the laboratory or entity described in division (B) of this section of blood or urine specimens of individuals in a scientifically or medically approved manner and under reasonable and sanitary conditions;

(b) The collection and testing by the laboratory or entity described in division (B) of this section of blood or urine specimens with due regard for the privacy of the individual being tested and in a manner reasonably calculated to prevent substitutions or interference with the collection and testing of the specimens;

(c) The documentation of blood or urine specimens collected by the laboratory or entity described in division (B) of this section and documentation procedures that reasonably preclude the possibility of erroneous identification of test results and that provide the individual being tested an opportunity to furnish information identifying any prescription or nonprescription drugs used by the individual in connection with a medical condition;

(d) The collection, maintenance, storage, and transportation by the laboratory or entity described in division (B) of this section of blood or urine specimens in a manner that reasonably precludes the possibility of contamination or adulteration of the specimens;

(e) The testing by the laboratory or entity described in division (B) of this section of blood or urine specimen of an individual to determine whether the individual ingested or was injected with a drug of abuse, in a manner that conforms to scientifically accepted analytical methods and procedures and that may include verification or confirmation of any positive test result by a reliable analytical method;

(f) The analysis of an individual's blood or urine specimen by an employee of the laboratory or entity described in division (B) of this section who is qualified by education, training, and experience to perform that analysis and whose regular duties include the analysis of blood or urine specimens to determine the presence of a drug of abuse and whether the individual who is the subject of the test ingested or was injected with a drug of abuse.

(2) Specify the frequency of performing random drug testing of prisoners in a state correctional institution;

(3) Prescribe procedures for the automatic, random selection of prisoners in a state correctional institution to submit to random drug testing under this section;

(4) Provide for reasonable safeguards for the transmittal from the laboratory or entity described in division (B) of this section to the department of the results of the random drug testing of prisoners in state correctional institutions pursuant to division (F) of this section;

(5) Establish a reasonable fee to cover the costs associated with random drug testing and analyses performed by a laboratory or entity under this section and establish procedures for the collection of those fees from the prisoners subjected to the drug test;

(6) Establish guidelines for imposing sanctions upon a prisoner whose test results indicate that the prisoner ingested or was injected with a drug of abuse.

(E) The warden of each correctional institution, pursuant to the contract entered into under division (B) of this section or, if no contract was entered into under that division, pursuant to the policies and procedures established by the department of rehabilitation and correction under division (D) of this section, shall facilitate the collection, documentation, maintenance, and transportation by the laboratory or entity described in division (B) of this section, of the blood or urine specimens of the prisoners in the state correctional institution who are subject to random drug testing.

(F) A laboratory or entity that performs random drug testing of prisoners and analyses of blood or urine specimens under this section shall transmit the results of each drug test to the department of rehabilitation and correction. The department shall file for record the results of the drug tests that indicate whether or not each prisoner in the state correctional institution who was subjected to the drug test ingested or was injected with a drug of abuse. The department shall send a copy of the results of the drug tests to the warden of the state correctional institution in which the prisoner who was subjected to the drug test is confined. The warden shall give appropriate notice of the drug test results to each prisoner who was subjected to the drug test and whose drug test results indicate that the prisoner ingested or was injected with a drug of abuse. In accordance with institutional disciplinary procedures, the warden shall afford that prisoner an opportunity to be heard regarding the results of the drug test and to present contrary evidence at a hearing held before the warden within thirty days after notification to the prisoner under this division. After the hearing, if a hearing is held, the warden shall make a determination regarding any evidence presented by the prisoner. If the warden rejects the evidence presented by the prisoner at the hearing or if no hearing is held under this division, the warden may subject the prisoner to sanctions that include payment of the fee for the test.

(G) All fees for random drug tests collected from prisoners under this section or collected by the adult parole authority under section 2929.15, 2951.05, or

2967.131 [2967.13.1] of the Revised Code shall be forwarded to the treasurer of state for deposit in the offender financial responsibility fund created in division (I) of section 5120.56 of the Revised Code.

**HISTORY: 148 v H 349. Eff 9-22-2000; 152 v H 130, § 1, eff. 4-7-09.**

## § 5120.64 Contracts for return of Ohio prisoners from outside Ohio.

(A) As used in this section:

(1) "Ohio prisoner" means a person who is charged with or convicted of a crime in this state or who is alleged or found to be a delinquent child in this state.

(2) "Out-of-state prisoner" and "private contractor" have the same meanings as in section 9.07 of the Revised Code.

(B) Not later than nine months after the effective date of this section, the department of rehabilitation and correction, in consultation with the attorney general, the county commissioners association of Ohio, and the buckeye state sheriffs association, shall adopt rules under Chapter 119. of the Revised Code regarding the return of Ohio prisoners from outside of this state into this state by a private person or entity pursuant to a contract entered into with a sheriff under authority of division (E) of section 311.29 of the Revised Code or the adult parole authority under authority of division (B) of section 5149.03 of the Revised Code. The rules shall establish all of the following:

(1) Standards that specify required training of officers and employees of the private person or entity that actually engage in the return of the prisoners, including standards related to the length and nature of the training;

(2) Physical standards for vehicles used in the return of the prisoners;

(3) Standards that govern the responsibility of the private person or entity to do one or more of the following:

(a) Provide an adequate policy of liability insurance to cover all injuries, death, or loss to person or property that arise from or is related to its return of the prisoners;

(b) Indemnify and hold harmless the sheriff, the county, and all county officers and employees regarding a contract for the return of prisoners entered into under division (E) of section 311.29 of the Revised Code or the department of rehabilitation and correction and all state officers and employees regarding a contract for the return of prisoners entered into under division (B) of section 5149.03 of the Revised Code;

(c) File a performance bond or other surety to guarantee performance.

(4) Standards requiring the private person or entity to have criminal records checks and pre-employment drug testing performed for officers and employees of the private person or entity that actually engage in the return of the prisoners and to have a random drug-screening policy and be able to document compliance with the policy;

(5) Standards requiring the private person or entity to have twenty-four-hour operations staff to constantly monitor activities in the field and to have on-board, constant communication ability with vehicles in the field;

(6) Standards requiring the officers and employees of the private person or entity that actually engage in the return of the prisoners to be CPR and first-aid certified.

(C) Upon the effective date of the rules adopted under division (B) of this section, in no case shall a private person or entity return Ohio prisoners from outside of this state into this state for a sheriff or for the adult parole authority unless the private person or entity complies with all applicable standards that are contained in the rules.

(D) This section does not apply regarding any out-of-state prisoner who is brought into this state to be housed pursuant to section 9.07 of the Revised Code in a correctional facility in this state that is managed and operated by a private contractor.

**HISTORY: 148 v H 661. Eff 3-15-2001.**

## [PRISON NURSERY PROGRAM]

## § 5120.65 Prison nursery program may be established.

(A) The department of rehabilitation and correction may establish in one or more of the institutions for women operated by the department a prison nursery program under which eligible inmates and children born to them while in the custody of the department may reside together in the institution. If the department establishes a prison nursery program in one or more institutions under this section, sections 5120.651 [5120.65.1] to 5120.657 [5120.65.7] of the Revised Code apply regarding the program. If the department establishes a prison nursery program and an inmate participates in the program, neither the inmate's participation in the program nor any provision of sections 5120.65 to 5120.657 [5120.65.7] of the Revised Code affects, modifies, or interferes with the inmate's custodial rights of the child or establishes legal custody of the child with the department.

(B) As used in sections 5120.651 [5120.65.1] to 5120.657 [5120.65.7] of the Revised Code:

(1) "Prison nursery program" means the prison nursery program established by the department of rehabilitation and correction under this section, if one is so established.

(2) "Public assistance" has the same meaning as in section 5101.58 of the Revised Code.

(3) "Support" means amounts to be paid under a support order.

(4) "Support order" has the same meaning as in section 3119.01 of the Revised Code.

**HISTORY: 148 v H 661. Eff 3-15-2001; 150 v H 117, § 1, eff. 9-3-04.**

## § 5120.651 Inmate's eligibility for program.

An inmate is eligible to participate in the prison nursery program if she is pregnant at the time she is delivered into the custody of the department of rehabilitation and correction, she gives birth on or after the date the program is implemented, she is subject to a sentence of imprisonment of not more than eighteen months, and she and the child meet any other criteria established by the department.

**HISTORY: 148 v H 661. Eff 3-15-2001.**

## § 5120.652 Duties of inmate.

To participate in the prison nursery program, each eligible inmate selected by the department shall do all the following:

(A) Agree in writing to do all the following:

(1) Comply with any program, educational, counseling, and other requirements established for the program by the department of rehabilitation and correction;

(2) If eligible, have the child participate in the medicaid program or a health insurance program;

(3) Accept the normal risks of childrearing;

(4) Abide by any court decisions regarding the allocation of parental rights and responsibilities with respect to the child.

(B) Assign to the department any rights to support from any other person, excluding support assigned pursuant to section 5107.20 of the Revised Code and medical support assigned pursuant to section 5101.59 of the Revised Code;

(C) Specify with whom the child is to be placed in the event the inmate's participation in the program is terminated for a reason other than release from imprisonment.

**HISTORY: 148 v H 661. Eff 3-15-2001.**

## § 5120.653 Termination of inmate's participation.

An inmate's participation in the prison nursery program may be terminated by the department of rehabilitation and correction if one of the following occurs:

(A) The inmate fails to comply with the agreement entered into under division (A) of section 5120.652 [5120.65.2] of the Revised Code.

(B) The inmate's child becomes seriously ill, cannot meet medical criteria established by the department of rehabilitation and correction for the program, or otherwise cannot safely participate in the program.

(C) A court issues an order that designates a person other than the inmate as the child's residential parent and legal custodian.

(D) A juvenile court, in an action brought pursuant to division (A)(2) of section 2151.23 of the Revised Code, grants custody of the child to a person other than the inmate.

(E) An order is issued pursuant to section 3109.04 of the Revised Code granting shared parenting of the child.

(F) An order of disposition regarding the child is issued pursuant to division (A)(2), (3), or (4) of section 2151.353 [2151.35.3] of the Revised Code granting temporary, permanent, or legal custody of the child to a person, other than the inmate, or to a public children services agency or private child placing agency.

(G) The inmate is released from imprisonment.

**HISTORY: 148 v H 661. Eff 3-15-2001.**

## § 5120.654 Collection of assigned support payments; donations and other funding; deposit of receipts.

(A) The rights to support assigned by an inmate pursuant to section 5120.652 [5120.65.2] of the Revised Code constitute an obligation of the person who is responsible for providing the support to the department of rehabilitation and correction for the support provided the inmate and child pursuant to the prison nursery program. The division of child support in the department of job and family services shall collect support payments made pursuant to the assignment and forward them to the department of rehabilitation and correction.

(B) The department of rehabilitation and correction may receive the following:

(1) Money that is assigned or donated on behalf of, and public assistance provided to, a specific inmate or child participating in the prison nursery program;

(2) Money assigned or donated to establish and maintain the prison nursery program.

(C) The amounts described in division (B)(1) of this section shall be placed in the individual nursery account created and maintained under section 5120.655 [5120.65.5] of the Revised Code for the inmate and child for whom the money was received. The money described in division (B)(2) of this section shall be deposited in the appropriate prison nursery program fund.

**HISTORY: 148 v H 661. Eff 3-15-2001.**

## § 5120.655 Program fund at each institution; individual accounts.

The managing officer of each institution in which a prison nursery program is established pursuant to section 5120.65 of the Revised Code shall do the following:

(A) Create and maintain a prison nursery program fund to pay expenses associated with the prison nursery program;

(B) Create and maintain an individual nursery account for each inmate participating in the prison nursery program at the institution to help pay for the support provided to the inmate and child pursuant to the program.

**HISTORY: 148 v H 661. Eff 3-15-2001.**

## § 5120.656 Involvement of job and family services department.

Notwithstanding any other provision of the Revised Code, neither the prison nursery program nor the department of rehabilitation and correction, with respect to the program, is subject to any regulation, licensing, or oversight by the department of job and family services unless the departments agree to voluntary regulation, licensing, or oversight by the department of job and family services.

**HISTORY: 148 v H 661. Eff 3-15-2001.**

## § 5120.657 Rules.

If the department of rehabilitation and correction establishes the prison nursery program, it shall, in accordance with Chapter 119. of the Revised Code, adopt rules that establish requirements necessary and appropriate to the establishment, implementation, and operation of the program. The department shall adopt the rules prior to implementing the program.

**HISTORY: 148 v H 661. Eff 3-15-2001.**

## § 5120.66 Internet database containing offense, sentence, and release information for each inmate in custody of department; designation as "Laura's Law".

(A) Within ninety days after November 23, 2005, but not before January 1, 2006, the department of rehabilitation and correction shall establish and operate on the internet a database that contains all of the following:

(1) For each inmate in the custody of the department under a sentence imposed for a conviction of or plea of guilty to any offense, all of the following information:

(a) The inmate's name;

(b) For each offense for which the inmate was sentenced to a prison term or term of imprisonment and is in the department's custody, the name of the offense, the Revised Code section of which the offense is a violation, the gender of each victim of the offense if those facts are known, whether each victim of the offense was an adult or child if those facts are known, the range of the possible prison terms or term of imprisonment that could have been imposed for the offense, the actual prison term or term of imprisonment imposed for the offense, the county in which the offense was committed, the date on which the inmate began serving the prison term or term of imprisonment imposed for the offense, and either the date on which the inmate will be eligible for parole relative to the offense if the prison term or term of imprisonment is an indefinite term or life term or the date on which the term ends if the prison term is a definite term;

(c) All of the following information that is applicable regarding the inmate:

(i) If known to the department prior to the conduct of any hearing for judicial release of the defendant pursuant to section 2929.20 of the Revised Code in relation to any prison term or term of imprisonment the inmate is serving for any offense or any hearing for release of the defendant pursuant to section 2967.19 of the Revised Code in relation to any such term, notice of the fact that the inmate will be having a hearing regarding a possible grant of judicial release or release, the date of the hearing, and the right of any person pursuant to division (J) of section 2929.20 or division (H) of section 2967.19 of the Revised Code, whichever is applicable, to submit to the court a written statement regarding the possible judicial release or release. The department also shall post notice of the filing of any petition for release of the inmate pursuant to section 2967.19 of the Revised Code, as required by division (E) of that section.

(ii) If the inmate is serving a prison term pursuant to division (A)(3), (B)(1)(a), (b), or (c), (B)(2)(a), (b), or (c), or (B)(3)(a), (b), (c), or (d) of section 2971.03 of the Revised Code, prior to the conduct of any hearing pursuant to section 2971.05 of the Revised Code to determine whether to modify the requirement that the inmate serve the entire prison term in a state correctional facility in accordance with division (C) of that section, whether to continue, revise, or revoke any existing modification of that requirement, or whether to terminate the prison term in accordance with division (D) of that section, notice of the fact that the inmate will be having a hearing regarding those determinations and of the date of the hearing;

(iii) At least three weeks before the adult parole authority recommends a pardon or commutation of sentence for the inmate or at least three weeks prior to a hearing before the adult parole authority regarding a grant of parole to the inmate in relation to any prison term or term of imprisonment the inmate is serving for any offense, notice of the fact that the inmate might be under consideration for a pardon or commutation of sentence or will be having a hearing regarding a possible grant of parole, of the date of any hearing regarding a possible grant of parole, and of the right of any person to submit a written statement regarding the pending action;

(iv) At least three weeks before the inmate is transferred to transitional control under section 2967.26 of the Revised Code in relation to any prison term or term of imprisonment the inmate is serving for any offense, notice of the pendency of the transfer, of the date of the possible transfer, and of the right of any person to submit a statement regarding the possible transfer;

(v) Prompt notice of the inmate's escape from any facility in which the inmate was incarcerated and of the capture of the inmate after an escape;

(vi) Notice of the inmate's death while in confinement;

(vii) Prior to the release of the inmate from confinement, notice of the fact that the inmate will be released, of the date of the release, and, if applicable, of the standard terms and conditions of the release;

(viii) Notice of the inmate's judicial release pursuant to section 2929.20 of the Revised Code or release pursuant to section 2967.19 of the Revised Code.

(2) Information as to where a person can send written statements of the types referred to in divisions (A)(1)(c)(i), (iii), and (iv) of this section.

(B)(1) The department shall update the database required under division (A) of this section every twenty-four hours to ensure that the information it contains is accurate and current.

(2) The database required under division (A) of this section is a public record open for inspection under section 149.43 of the Revised Code. The department shall make the database searchable by inmate name and by the county and zip code where the offender intends to reside after release from a state correctional institution if this information is known to the department.

(3) The database required under division (A) of this section may contain information regarding inmates who are listed in the database in addition to the information described in that division.

(4) No information included on the database required under division (A) of this section shall identify or enable the identification of any victim of any offense committed by an inmate.

(C) The failure of the department to comply with the requirements of division (A) or (B) of this section does not give any rights or any grounds for appeal or post-conviction relief to any inmate.

(D) This section, and the related provisions of sections 2929.20, 2967.03, 2967.12, and 2967.26 of the Revised Code enacted in the act in which this section was enacted, shall be known as "Laura's Law."

**HISTORY: 151 v H 15, § 1, eff. 11-23-05; 151 v S 260, § 1, eff. 1-2-07; 152 v S 10, § 1, eff. 1-1-08; 152 v H 130, § 1, eff. 4-7-09; 2011 HB 86, § 1, eff. Sept. 30, 2011.**

The effective date is set by § 3 of 152 v S 10.

## § 5120.99 Penalties for disclosing quality assurance records.

A person who violates division (B)(2) of section 5120.211 [5120.21.1] of the Revised Code shall be fined not more than two thousand five hundred dollars on a first offense and not more than twenty thousand dollars on a subsequent offense.

**HISTORY: 147 v S 111. Eff 3-17-98.**

# CHAPTER 5122: HOSPITALIZATION OF MENTALLY ILL

Section



## § 5122.01 Definitions [Effective until October 1, 2012].

As used in this chapter and Chapter 5119. of the Revised Code:

(A) "Mental illness" means a substantial disorder of thought, mood, perception, orientation, or memory that grossly impairs judgment, behavior, capacity to recognize reality, or ability to meet the ordinary demands of life.

(B) "Mentally ill person subject to hospitalization by court order" means a mentally ill person who, because of the person's illness:

(1) Represents a substantial risk of physical harm to self as manifested by evidence of threats of, or attempts at, suicide or serious self-inflicted bodily harm;

(2) Represents a substantial risk of physical harm to others as manifested by evidence of recent homicidal or other violent behavior, evidence of recent threats that place another in reasonable fear of violent behavior and serious physical harm, or other evidence of present dangerousness;

(3) Represents a substantial and immediate risk of serious physical impairment or injury to self as manifested by evidence that the person is unable to provide for and is not providing for the person's basic physical needs because of the person's mental illness and that appropriate provision for those needs cannot be made immediately available in the community; or

(4) Would benefit from treatment in a hospital for the person's mental illness and is in need of such treatment as manifested by evidence of behavior that creates a grave and imminent risk to substantial rights of others or the person.

(C)(1) "Patient" means, subject to division (C)(2) of this section, a person who is admitted either voluntarily or involuntarily to a hospital or other place under section 2945.39, 2945.40, 2945.401, or 2945.402 of the Revised Code subsequent to a finding of not guilty by reason of insanity or incompetence to stand trial or under this chapter, who is under observation or receiving treatment in such place.

(2) "Patient" does not include a person admitted to a hospital or other place under section 2945.39, 2945.40, 2945.401, or 2945.402 of the Revised Code to the extent that the reference in this chapter to patient, or the context in which the reference occurs, is in conflict with any provision of sections 2945.37 to 2945.402 of the Revised Code.

(D) "Licensed physician" means a person licensed under the laws of this state to practice medicine or a medical officer of the government of the United States while in this state in the performance of the person's official duties.

(E) "Psychiatrist" means a licensed physician who has satisfactorily completed a residency training program in psychiatry, as approved by the residency review committee of the American medical association, the committee on post-graduate education of the American osteopathic association, or the American osteopathic board of neurology and psychiatry, or who on July 1, 1989, has been recognized as a psychiatrist by the Ohio state medical association or the Ohio osteopathic association on the basis of formal training and five or more years of medical practice limited to psychiatry.

(F) "Hospital" means a hospital or inpatient unit licensed by the department of mental health under section 5119.20 of the Revised Code, and any institution, hospital, or other place established, controlled, or supervised by the department under Chapter 5119. of the Revised Code.

(G) "Public hospital" means a facility that is tax-supported and under the jurisdiction of the department of mental health.

(H) "Community mental health agency" means an agency that provides community mental health services that are certified by the director of mental health under section 5119.611 of the Revised Code.

(I) "Licensed clinical psychologist" means a person who holds a current valid psychologist license issued under section 4732.12 or 4732.15 of the Revised Code, and in addition, meets either of the following criteria:

(1) Meets the educational requirements set forth in division (B) of section 4732.10 of the Revised Code and has a minimum of two years' full-time professional experience, or the equivalent as determined by rule of the state board of psychology, at least one year of which shall be a predoctoral internship, in clinical psychological work in a public or private hospital or clinic or in private practice, diagnosing and treating problems of mental illness or mental retardation under the supervision of a psychologist who is licensed or who holds a diploma issued by the American board of professional psychology, or whose qualifications are substantially similar to those required for licensure by the state board of psychology when the supervision has occurred prior to enactment of laws governing the practice of psychology;

(2) Meets the educational requirements set forth in division (B) of section 4732.15 of the Revised Code and has a minimum of four years' full-time professional experience, or the equivalent as determined by rule of the state board of psychology, in clinical psychological work in a public or private hospital or clinic or in private practice, diagnosing and treating problems of mental illness or mental retardation under supervision, as set forth in division (I)(1) of this section.

(J) "Health officer" means any public health physician; public health nurse; or other person authorized by or designated by a city health district; a general health district; or a board of alcohol, drug addiction, and mental health services to perform the duties of a health officer under this chapter.

(K) "Chief clinical officer" means the medical director of a hospital, or a community mental health agency, or a board of alcohol, drug addiction, and mental health services, or, if there is no medical director, the licensed physician responsible for the treatment a hospital or community mental health agency provides. The chief clinical officer may delegate to the attending physician responsible for a patient's care the duties imposed on the chief clinical officer by this chapter. Within a community mental health agency, the chief clinical officer shall be designated by the governing body of the agency and shall be a licensed physician or licensed clinical psychologist who supervises diagnostic and treatment services. A licensed physician or licensed clinical psychologist designated by the chief clinical officer may perform the duties and accept the responsibilities of the chief clinical officer in the chief clinical officer's absence.

(L) "Working day" or "court day" means Monday, Tuesday, Wednesday, Thursday, and Friday, except when such day is a holiday.

(M) "Indigent" means unable without deprivation of satisfaction of basic needs to provide for the payment of an attorney and other necessary expenses of legal representation, including expert testimony.

(N) "Respondent" means the person whose detention, commitment, hospitalization, continued hospitalization or commitment, or discharge is being sought in any proceeding under this chapter.

(O) "Legal rights service" means the service established under section 5123.60 of the Revised Code.

(P) "Independent expert evaluation" means an evaluation conducted by a licensed clinical psychologist, psychiatrist, or licensed physician who has been selected by the respondent or the respondent's counsel and who consents to conducting the evaluation.

(Q) "Court" means the probate division of the court of common pleas.

(R) "Expunge" means:

(1) The removal and destruction of court files and records, originals and copies, and the deletion of all index references;

(2) The reporting to the person of the nature and extent of any information about the person transmitted to any other person by the court;

(3) Otherwise insuring that any examination of court files and records in question shall show no record whatever with respect to the person;

(4) That all rights and privileges are restored, and that the person, the court, and any other person may properly reply that no such record exists, as to any matter expunged.

(S) "Residence" means a person's physical presence in a county with intent to remain there, except that:

(1) If a person is receiving a mental health service at a facility that includes nighttime sleeping accommodations, residence means that county in which the person maintained the person's primary place of residence at the time the person entered the facility;

(2) If a person is committed pursuant to section 2945.38, 2945.39, 2945.40, 2945.401, or 2945.402 of the Revised Code, residence means the county where the criminal charges were filed.

When the residence of a person is disputed, the matter of residence shall be referred to the department of mental health for investigation and determination. Residence shall not be a basis for a board's denying services to any person present in the board's service district, and the board shall provide services for a person whose residence is in dispute while residence is being determined and for a person in an emergency situation.

(T) "Admission" to a hospital or other place means that a patient is accepted for and stays at least one night at the hospital or other place.

(U) "Prosecutor" means the prosecuting attorney, village solicitor, city director of law, or similar chief legal officer who prosecuted a criminal case in which a person was found not guilty by reason of insanity, who would have had the authority to prosecute a criminal case against a person if the person had not been found incompetent to stand trial, or who prosecuted a case in which a person was found guilty.

(V) "Treatment plan" means a written statement of reasonable objectives and goals for an individual established by the treatment team, with specific criteria to evaluate progress towards achieving those objectives. The active participation of the patient in establishing the objectives and goals shall be documented. The treatment plan shall be based on patient needs and include services to be provided to the patient while the patient is hospitalized and after the patient is discharged. The treatment plan shall address services to be provided upon discharge, including but not limited to housing, financial, and vocational services.

(W) "Community control sanction" has the same meaning as in section 2929.01 of the Revised Code.

(X) "Post-release control sanction" has the same meaning as in section 2967.01 of the Revised Code.

**HISTORY: 129 v 1448 (1458) (Eff 10-25-61); 130 v 1190 (Eff 10-10-63); 133 v H 874 (Eff 9-16-70); 134 v H 494 (Eff 7-12-72); 136 v H 244 (Eff 8-26-76); 137 v H 1 (Eff 8-26-77); 137 v H 725 (Eff 3-16-78); 138 v S 297 (Eff 4-30-80); 138 v H 900 (Eff 7-1-80); 138 v H 965 (Eff 4-9-81); 142 v S 156 (Eff 7-1-89); 143 v H 317 (Eff 10-10-89); 146 v S 285. Eff 7-1-97; 149 v H 490, § 1, eff. 1-1-04; 152 v H 503, § 1, eff. 4-7-09; 2011 HB 153, § 101.01, eff. Sept. 29, 2011.**

**Analogous to former RC § 5123.01.**
The effective date is set by section 4 of H.B. 490.

## § 5122.01 Definitions [Effective October 1, 2012].

As used in this chapter and Chapter 5119. of the Revised Code:

(A) "Mental illness" means a substantial disorder of thought, mood, perception, orientation, or memory that grossly impairs judgment, behavior, capacity to recognize reality, or ability to meet the ordinary demands of life.

(B) "Mentally ill person subject to hospitalization by court order" means a mentally ill person who, because of the person's illness:

(1) Represents a substantial risk of physical harm to self as manifested by evidence of threats of, or attempts at, suicide or serious self-inflicted bodily harm;

(2) Represents a substantial risk of physical harm to others as manifested by evidence of recent homicidal or other violent behavior, evidence of recent threats that place another in reasonable fear of violent behavior and serious physical harm, or other evidence of present dangerousness;

(3) Represents a substantial and immediate risk of serious physical impairment or injury to self as manifested by evidence that the person is unable to provide for and is not providing for the person's basic physical needs because of the person's mental illness and that appropriate provi-

sion for those needs cannot be made immediately available in the community; or

(4) Would benefit from treatment in a hospital for the person's mental illness and is in need of such treatment as manifested by evidence of behavior that creates a grave and imminent risk to substantial rights of others or the person.

(C)(1) "Patient" means, subject to division (C)(2) of this section, a person who is admitted either voluntarily or involuntarily to a hospital or other place under section 2945.39, 2945.40, 2945.401, or 2945.402 of the Revised Code subsequent to a finding of not guilty by reason of insanity or incompetence to stand trial or under this chapter, who is under observation or receiving treatment in such place.

(2) "Patient" does not include a person admitted to a hospital or other place under section 2945.39, 2945.40, 2945.401, or 2945.402 of the Revised Code to the extent that the reference in this chapter to patient, or the context in which the reference occurs, is in conflict with any provision of sections 2945.37 to 2945.402 of the Revised Code.

(D) "Licensed physician" means a person licensed under the laws of this state to practice medicine or a medical officer of the government of the United States while in this state in the performance of the person's official duties.

(E) "Psychiatrist" means a licensed physician who has satisfactorily completed a residency training program in psychiatry, as approved by the residency review committee of the American medical association, the committee on post-graduate education of the American osteopathic association, or the American osteopathic board of neurology and psychiatry, or who on July 1, 1989, has been recognized as a psychiatrist by the Ohio state medical association or the Ohio osteopathic association on the basis of formal training and five or more years of medical practice limited to psychiatry.

(F) "Hospital" means a hospital or inpatient unit licensed by the department of mental health under section 5119.20 of the Revised Code, and any institution, hospital, or other place established, controlled, or supervised by the department under Chapter 5119. of the Revised Code.

(G) "Public hospital" means a facility that is tax-supported and under the jurisdiction of the department of mental health.

(H) "Community mental health agency" means an agency that provides community mental health services that are certified by the director of mental health under section 5119.611 of the Revised Code.

(I) "Licensed clinical psychologist" means a person who holds a current valid psychologist license issued under section 4732.12 or 4732.15 of the Revised Code, and in addition, meets either of the following criteria:

(1) Meets the educational requirements set forth in division (B) of section 4732.10 of the Revised Code and has a minimum of two years' full-time professional experience, or the equivalent as determined by rule of the state board of psychology, at least one year of which shall be a predoctoral internship, in clinical psychological work in a public or private hospital or clinic or in private practice, diagnosing and treating problems of mental illness or mental retardation under the supervision of a psychologist who is licensed or who holds a diploma issued by the American board of professional psychology, or whose qualifications are substantially similar to those required for licensure by the state board of psychology when the supervision has occurred prior to enactment of laws governing the practice of psychology;

(2) Meets the educational requirements set forth in division (B) of section 4732.15 of the Revised Code and has a minimum of four years' full-time professional experience, or the equivalent as determined by rule of the state board of psychology, in clinical psychological work in a public or private hospital or clinic or in private practice, diagnosing and treating problems of mental illness or mental retardation under supervision, as set forth in division (I)(1) of this section.

(J) "Health officer" means any public health physician; public health nurse; or other person authorized by or designated by a city health district; a general health district; or a board of alcohol, drug addiction, and mental health services to perform the duties of a health officer under this chapter.

(K) "Chief clinical officer" means the medical director of a hospital, or a community mental health agency, or a board of alcohol, drug addiction, and mental health services, or, if there is no medical director, the licensed physician responsible for the treatment a hospital or community mental health agency provides. The chief clinical officer may delegate to the attending physician responsible for a patient's care the duties imposed on the chief clinical officer by this chapter. Within a community mental health agency, the chief clinical officer shall be designated by the governing body of the agency and shall be a licensed physician or licensed clinical psychologist who supervises diagnostic and treatment services. A licensed physician or licensed clinical psychologist designated by the chief clinical officer may perform the duties and accept the responsibilities of the chief clinical officer in the chief clinical officer's absence.

(L) "Working day" or "court day" means Monday, Tuesday, Wednesday, Thursday, and Friday, except when such day is a holiday.

(M) "Indigent" means unable without deprivation of satisfaction of basic needs to provide for the payment of an attorney and other necessary expenses of legal representation, including expert testimony.

(N) "Respondent" means the person whose detention, commitment, hospitalization, continued hospitalization or commitment, or discharge is being sought in any proceeding under this chapter.

(O) "Ohio protection and advocacy system" has the same meaning as in section 5123.60 of the Revised Code.

(P) "Independent expert evaluation" means an evaluation conducted by a licensed clinical psychologist, psychiatrist, or licensed physician who has been selected by the respondent or the respondent's counsel and who consents to conducting the evaluation.

(Q) "Court" means the probate division of the court of common pleas.

(R) "Expunge" means:

(1) The removal and destruction of court files and records, originals and copies, and the deletion of all index references;

(2) The reporting to the person of the nature and extent of any information about the person transmitted to any other person by the court;

(3) Otherwise insuring that any examination of court files and records in question shall show no record whatever with respect to the person;

(4) That all rights and privileges are restored, and that the person, the court, and any other person may properly

reply that no such record exists, as to any matter expunged.

(S) "Residence" means a person's physical presence in a county with intent to remain there, except that:

(1) If a person is receiving a mental health service at a facility that includes nighttime sleeping accommodations, residence means that county in which the person maintained the person's primary place of residence at the time the person entered the facility;

(2) If a person is committed pursuant to section 2945.38, 2945.39, 2945.40, 2945.401, or 2945.402 of the Revised Code, residence means the county where the criminal charges were filed.

When the residence of a person is disputed, the matter of residence shall be referred to the department of mental health for investigation and determination. Residence shall not be a basis for a board's denying services to any person present in the board's service district, and the board shall provide services for a person whose residence is in dispute while residence is being determined and for a person in an emergency situation.

(T) "Admission" to a hospital or other place means that a patient is accepted for and stays at least one night at the hospital or other place.

(U) "Prosecutor" means the prosecuting attorney, village solicitor, city director of law, or similar chief legal officer who prosecuted a criminal case in which a person was found not guilty by reason of insanity, who would have had the authority to prosecute a criminal case against a person if the person had not been found incompetent to stand trial, or who prosecuted a case in which a person was found guilty.

(V) "Treatment plan" means a written statement of reasonable objectives and goals for an individual established by the treatment team, with specific criteria to evaluate progress towards achieving those objectives. The active participation of the patient in establishing the objectives and goals shall be documented. The treatment plan shall be based on patient needs and include services to be provided to the patient while the patient is hospitalized and after the patient is discharged. The treatment plan shall address services to be provided upon discharge, including but not limited to housing, financial, and vocational services.

(W) "Community control sanction" has the same meaning as in section 2929.01 of the Revised Code.

(X) "Post-release control sanction" has the same meaning as in section 2967.01 of the Revised Code.

**HISTORY: 2011 HB 153, § 101.01, eff. Sept. 29, 2011; 2011 HB 153, § 120.20, eff. Oct. 1, 2012.**

## § 5122.011 Application to defendant found incompetent or to insanity acquittee.

The provisions of this chapter regarding hospitalization apply to a person who is found incompetent to stand trial or not guilty by reason of insanity and is committed pursuant to section 2945.39, 2945.40, 2945.401 [2945.40.1], or 2945.402 [2945.40.2] of the Revised Code to the extent that the provisions are not in conflict with any provision of sections 2945.37 to 2945.402 [2945.40.2] of the Revised Code. If a provision of this chapter is in conflict with a provision in sections 2945.37 to 2945.402 [2945.40.2] of the Revised Code regarding a person who has been so committed, the provision in sections 2945.37 to 2945.402 [2945.40.2] of the Revised Code shall control regarding that person.

**HISTORY: 146 v S 285. Eff 7-1-97.**

The effective date is set by section 4 of SB 285.

## § 5122.02 Admission of voluntary patients [Effective until October 1, 2012].

(A) Except as provided in division (D) of this section, any person who is eighteen years of age or older and who is, appears to be, or believes self to be mentally ill may make written application for voluntary admission to the chief medical officer of a hospital.

(B) Except as provided in division (D) of this section, the application also may be made on behalf of a minor by a parent, a guardian of the person, or the person with custody of the minor, and on behalf of an adult incompetent person by the guardian or the person with custody of the incompetent person.

Any person whose admission is applied for under division (A) or (B) of this section may be admitted for observation, diagnosis, care, or treatment, in any hospital unless the chief clinical officer finds that hospitalization is inappropriate, and except that, in the case of a public hospital, no person shall be admitted without the authorization of the board of the person's county of residence.

(C) If a minor or person adjudicated incompetent due to mental illness whose voluntary admission is applied for under division (B) of this section is admitted, the court shall determine, upon petition by the legal rights service, private or otherwise appointed counsel, a relative, or one acting as next friend, whether the admission or continued hospitalization is in the best interest of the minor or incompetent.

The chief clinical officer shall discharge any voluntary patient who has recovered or whose hospitalization the officer determines to be no longer advisable and may discharge any voluntary patient who refuses to accept treatment consistent with the written treatment plan required by section 5122.27 of the Revised Code.

(D) A person who is found incompetent to stand trial or not guilty by reason of insanity and who is committed pursuant to section 2945.39, 2945.40, 2945.401 [2945.40.1], or 2945.402 [2945.40.2] of the Revised Code shall not voluntarily admit himself or herself or be voluntarily admitted to a hospital pursuant to this section until after the final termination of the commitment, as described in division (J) of section 2945.401 [2945.40.1] of the Revised Code.

**HISTORY: 129 v 1448(1459) (Eff 10-25-61); 133 v H 874 (Eff 9-16-70); 134 v H 494 (Eff 7-12-72); 136 v H 244 (Eff 8-26-76); 137 v H 725 (Eff 3-16-78); 138 v S 297 (Eff 4-30-80); 138 v H 965 (Eff 4-9-81); 142 v S 156 (Eff 7-1-89); 146 v S 285. Eff 7-1-97.**

**Analogous to former RC §§ 5123.43, 5123.44, 5123.45.**
The effective date is set by section 4 of SB 285.

## § 5122.02 Admission of voluntary patients [Effective October 1, 2012].

(A) Except as provided in division (D) of this section, any person who is eighteen years of age or older and who is, appears to be, or believes self to be mentally ill may make written application for voluntary admission to the chief medical officer of a hospital.

(B) Except as provided in division (D) of this section, the application also may be made on behalf of a minor by a parent, a guardian of the person, or the person with custody of the minor, and on behalf of an adult incompetent person by the guardian or the person with custody of the incompetent person.

Any person whose admission is applied for under division (A) or (B) of this section may be admitted for observation, diagnosis, care, or treatment, in any hospital unless the chief clinical officer finds that hospitalization is inappropriate, and except that, in the case of a public hospital, no person shall be admitted without the authorization of the board of the person's county of residence.

(C) If a minor or person adjudicated incompetent due to mental illness whose voluntary admission is applied for under division (B) of this section is admitted, the court shall determine, upon petition by private or otherwise appointed counsel, a relative, or one acting as next friend, whether the admission or continued hospitalization is in the best interest of the minor or incompetent.

The chief clinical officer shall discharge any voluntary patient who has recovered or whose hospitalization the officer determines to be no longer advisable and may discharge any voluntary patient who refuses to accept treatment consistent with the written treatment plan required by section 5122.27 of the Revised Code.

(D) A person who is found incompetent to stand trial or not guilty by reason of insanity and who is committed pursuant to section 2945.39, 2945.40, 2945.401, or 2945.402 of the Revised Code shall not voluntarily admit the person or be voluntarily admitted to a hospital pursuant to this section until after the final termination of the commitment, as described in division (J) of section 2945.401 of the Revised Code.

**HISTORY: 2011 HB 153, § 120.20, eff. Oct. 1, 2012.**

## § 5122.05 Admission and rights of involuntary patients.

(A) The chief clinical officer of a hospital may, and the chief clinical officer of a public hospital in all cases of psychiatric medical emergencies, shall receive for observation, diagnosis, care, and treatment any person whose admission is applied for under any of the following procedures:

(1) Emergency procedure, as provided in section 5122.10 of the Revised Code;

(2) Judicial procedure as provided in sections 2945.38, 2945.39, 2945.40, 2945.401 [2945.40.1], 2945.402 [2945.40.2], and 5122.11 to 5122.15 of the Revised Code.

Upon application for such admission, the chief clinical officer of a hospital immediately shall notify the board of the patient's county of residence. To assist the hospital in determining whether the patient is subject to involuntary hospitalization and whether alternative services are available, the board or an agency the board designates promptly shall assess the patient unless the board or agency already has performed such assessment, or unless the commitment is pursuant to section 2945.38, 2945.39, 2945.40, 2945.401 [2945.40.1], or 2945.402 [2945.40.2] of the Revised Code.

(B) No person who is being treated by spiritual means through prayer alone, in accordance with a recognized religious method of healing, may be involuntarily committed unless the court has determined that the person represents a substantial risk of impairment or injury to self or others;

(C) Any person who is involuntarily detained in a hospital or otherwise is in custody under this chapter, immediately upon being taken into custody, shall be informed and provided with a written statement that the person may do any of the following:

(1) Immediately make a reasonable number of telephone calls or use other reasonable means to contact an attorney, a licensed physician, or a licensed clinical psychologist, to contact any other person or persons to secure representation by counsel, or to obtain medical or psychological assistance, and be provided assistance in making calls if the assistance is needed and requested;

(2) Retain counsel and have independent expert evaluation of the person's mental condition and, if the person is unable to obtain an attorney or independent expert evaluation, be represented by court-appointed counsel or have independent expert evaluation of the person's mental condition, or both, at public expense if the person is indigent;

(3) Have a hearing to determine whether or not the person is a mentally ill person subject to hospitalization by court order.

**HISTORY: 129 v 1448(1460) (Eff 10-25-61); 136 v H 244 (Eff 8-26-76); 137 v H 725 (Eff 3-16-78); 138 v S 297 (Eff 4-30-80); 142 v S 156 (Eff 7-1-89); 146 v S 310 (Eff 6-20-96); 146 v S 285. Eff 7-1-97.**

The effective date is set by section 4 of SB 285.

## § 5122.11 Judicial hospitalization; temporary detention order.

Proceedings for the hospitalization of a person pursuant to sections 5122.11 to 5122.15 of the Revised Code shall be commenced by the filing of an affidavit in the manner and form prescribed by the department of mental health, by any person or persons with the court, either on reliable information or actual knowledge, whichever is determined to be proper by the court. This section does not apply to the hospitalization of a person pursuant to section 2945.39, 2945.40, 2945.401 [2945.40.1], or 2945.402 [2945.40.2] of the Revised Code.

The affidavit shall contain an allegation setting forth the specific category or categories under division (B) of section 5122.01 of the Revised Code upon which the jurisdiction of the court is based and a statement of alleged facts sufficient to indicate probable cause to believe that the person is a mentally ill person subject to hospitalization by court order. The affidavit may be accompanied, or the court may require that the affidavit be accompanied, by a certificate of a psychiatrist, or a certificate signed by a licensed clinical psychologist and a certificate signed by a licensed physician stating that the person who issued the certificate has examined the person and is of the opinion that the person is a mentally ill person subject to hospitalization by court order, or shall be accompanied by a written statement by the applicant, under oath, that the person has refused to submit to an examination by a psychiatrist, or by a licensed clinical psychologist and licensed physician.

Upon receipt of the affidavit, if a judge of the court or a referee who is an attorney at law appointed by the court has probable cause to believe that the person named in the affidavit is a mentally ill person subject to hospitalization by court order, the judge or referee may issue a temporary order of detention ordering any health or police officer or sheriff to take into custody and transport the person to a hospital or other place designated in section 5122.17 of the Revised Code, or may set the matter for further hearing.

The person may be observed and treated until the hearing provided for in section 5122.141 [5122.14.1] of the Revised Code. If no such hearing is held, the person may be observed and treated until the hearing provided for in section 5122.15 of the Revised Code.

**HISTORY: 129 v 1448(1462) (Eff 10-25-61); 130 v 1193 (Eff 10-10-63); 134 v H 494 (Eff 7-12-72); 136 v H 244 (Eff 8-26-76); 138 v S 297 (Eff 4-30-80); 138 v H 900 (Eff 7-1-80); 138 v H 965 (Eff 4-9-81); 142 v S 156 (Eff 7-1-89); 146 v S 285. Eff 7-1-97.**

**Analogous to former RC § 5123.18.**
The effective date is set by section 4 of SB 285.

## § 5122.15 Full hearing; disposition; mandatory hearing on continued commitment.

(A) Full hearings shall be conducted in a manner consistent with this chapter and with due process of law. The hearings shall be conducted by a judge of the probate court or a referee designated by a judge of the probate court and may be conducted in or out of the county in which the respondent is held. Any referee designated under this division shall be an attorney.

(1) With the consent of the respondent, the following shall be made available to counsel for the respondent:

(a) All relevant documents, information, and evidence in the custody or control of the state or prosecutor;

(b) All relevant documents, information, and evidence in the custody or control of the hospital in which the respondent currently is held, or in which the respondent has been held pursuant to this chapter;

(c) All relevant documents, information, and evidence in the custody or control of any hospital, facility, or person not included in division (A)(1)(a) or (b) of this section.

(2) The respondent has the right to attend the hearing and to be represented by counsel of the respondent's choice. The right to attend the hearing may be waived only by the respondent or counsel for the respondent after consultation with the respondent.

(3) If the respondent is not represented by counsel, is absent from the hearing, and has not validly waived the right to counsel, the court shall appoint counsel immediately to represent the respondent at the hearing, reserving the right to tax costs of appointed counsel to the respondent, unless it is shown that the respondent is indigent. If the court appoints counsel, or if the court determines that the evidence relevant to the respondent's absence does not justify the absence, the court shall continue the case.

(4) The respondent shall be informed that the respondent may retain counsel and have independent expert evaluation. If the respondent is unable to obtain an attorney, the respondent shall be represented by court-appointed counsel. If the respondent is indigent, court-appointed counsel and independent expert evaluation shall be provided as an expense under section 5122.43 of the Revised Code.

(5) The hearing shall be closed to the public, unless counsel for the respondent, with the permission of the respondent, requests that the hearing be open to the public.

(6) If the hearing is closed to the public, the court, for good cause shown, may admit persons who have a legitimate interest in the proceedings. If the respondent, the respondent's counsel, the designee of the director or of the chief clinical officer objects to the admission of any person, the court shall hear the objection and any opposing argument and shall rule upon the admission of the person to the hearing.

(7) The affiant under section 5122.11 of the Revised Code shall be subject to subpoena by either party.

(8) The court shall examine the sufficiency of all documents filed and shall inform the respondent, if present, and the respondent's counsel of the nature and content of the documents and the reason for which the respondent is being detained, or for which the respondent's placement is being sought.

(9) The court shall receive only reliable, competent, and material evidence.

(10) Unless proceedings are initiated pursuant to section 5120.17 or 5139.08 of the Revised Code or proceedings are initiated regarding a resident of the service district of a board of alcohol, drug addiction, and mental health services that elects under division (C)(2) of section 5119.62 of the Revised Code not to accept the amount allocated to it under that section, an attorney that the board designates shall present the case demonstrating that the respondent is a mentally ill person subject to hospitalization by court order. The attorney shall offer evidence of the diagnosis, prognosis, record of treatment, if any, and less restrictive treatment plans, if any. In proceedings pursuant to section 5120.17 or 5139.08 of the Revised Code and in proceedings in which the respondent is a resident of a service district of a board that elects under division (C)(2) of section 5119.62 of the Revised Code not to accept the amount allocated to it under that section, the attorney general shall designate an attorney who shall present the case demonstrating that the respondent is a mentally ill person subject to hospitalization by court order. The attorney shall offer evidence of the diagnosis, prognosis, record of treatment, if any, and less restrictive treatment plans, if any.

(11) The respondent or the respondent's counsel has the right to subpoena witnesses and documents and to examine and cross-examine witnesses.

(12) The respondent has the right, but shall not be compelled, to testify, and shall be so advised by the court.

(13) On motion of the respondent or the respondent's counsel for good cause shown, or on the court's own motion, the court may order a continuance of the hearing.

(14) If the respondent is represented by counsel and the respondent's counsel requests a transcript and record, or if the respondent is not represented by counsel, the court shall make and maintain a full transcript and record of the proceeding. If the respondent is indigent and the transcript and record is made, a copy shall be provided to the respondent upon request and be treated as an expense under section 5122.43 of the Revised Code.

(15) To the extent not inconsistent with this chapter, the Rules of Civil Procedure are applicable.

(B) Unless, upon completion of the hearing the court finds by clear and convincing evidence that the respondent is a mentally ill person subject to hospitalization by court order, it shall order the respondent's discharge immediately.

(C) If, upon completion of the hearing, the court finds by clear and convincing evidence that the respondent is a mentally ill person subject to hospitalization by court order, the court shall order the respondent for a period not to exceed ninety days to any of the following:

(1) A hospital operated by the department of mental health if the respondent is committed pursuant to section 5139.08 of the Revised Code;

(2) A nonpublic hospital;

(3) The veterans' administration or other agency of the United States government;

(4) A board of alcohol, drug addiction, and mental health services or agency the board designates;

(5) Receive private psychiatric or psychological care and treatment;

(6) Any other suitable facility or person consistent with the diagnosis, prognosis, and treatment needs of the respondent.

(D) Any order made pursuant to division (C)(2), (3), (5), or (6) of this section shall be conditioned upon the receipt by the court of consent by the hospital, facility, agency, or person to accept the respondent.

(E) In determining the place to which, or the person with whom, the respondent is to be committed, the court shall consider the diagnosis, prognosis, preferences of the respondent and the projected treatment plan for the respondent and shall order the implementation of the least restrictive alternative available and consistent with treatment goals. If the court determines that the least restrictive alternative available that is consistent with treatment goals is inpatient hospitalization, the court's order shall so state.

(F) During such ninety-day period the hospital; facility; board of alcohol, drug addiction, and mental health services; agency the board designates; or person shall examine and treat the individual. If, at any time prior to the expiration of the ninety-day period, it is determined by the hospital, facility, board, agency, or person that the respondent's treatment needs could be equally well met in an available and appropriate less restrictive environment, both of the following apply:

(1) The respondent shall be released from the care of the hospital, agency, facility, or person immediately and shall be referred to the court together with a report of the findings and recommendations of the hospital, agency, facility, or person; and

(2) The hospital, agency, facility, or person shall notify the respondent's counsel or the attorney designated by a board of alcohol, drug addiction, and mental health services or, if the respondent was committed to a board or an agency designated by the board, it shall place the respondent in the least restrictive environment available consistent with treatment goals and notify the court and the respondent's counsel of the placement.

The court shall dismiss the case or order placement in the least restrictive environment.

(G)(1) Except as provided in divisions (G)(2) and (3) of this section, any person who has been committed under this section, or for whom proceedings for hospitalization have been commenced pursuant to section 5122.11 of the Revised Code, may apply at any time for voluntary admission to the hospital, facility, agency that the board designates, or person to which the person was committed. Upon admission as a voluntary patient the chief clinical officer of the hospital, agency, or other facility, or the person immediately shall notify the court, the patient's counsel, and the attorney designated by the board, if the attorney has entered the proceedings, in writing of that fact, and, upon receipt of the notice, the court shall dismiss the case.

(2) A person who is found incompetent to stand trial or not guilty by reason of insanity and who is committed pursuant to section 2945.39, 2945.40, 2945.401, or 2945.402 of the Revised Code shall not voluntarily commit the person pursuant to this section until after the final termination of the commitment, as described in division (J) of section 2945.401 of the Revised Code.

(H) If, at the end of the first ninety-day period or any subsequent period of continued commitment, there has been no disposition of the case, either by discharge or voluntary admission, the hospital, facility, board, agency, or person shall discharge the patient immediately, unless at least ten days before the expiration of the period the attorney the board designates or the prosecutor files with the court an application for continued commitment. The application of the attorney or the prosecutor shall include a written report containing the diagnosis, prognosis, past treatment, a list of alternative treatment settings and plans, and identification of the treatment setting that is the least restrictive consistent with treatment needs. The attorney the board designates or the prosecutor shall file the written report at least three days prior to the full hearing. A copy of the application and written report shall be provided to the respondent's counsel immediately.

The court shall hold a full hearing on applications for continued commitment at the expiration of the first ninety-day period and at least every two years after the expiration of the first ninety-day period.

Hearings following any application for continued commitment are mandatory and may not be waived.

Upon request of a person who is involuntarily committed under this section, or the person's counsel, that is made more than one hundred eighty days after the person's last full hearing, mandatory or requested, the court shall hold a full hearing on the person's continued commitment. Upon the application of a person involuntarily committed under this section, supported by an affidavit of a psychiatrist or licensed clinical psychologist, alleging that the person no longer is a mentally ill person subject to hospitalization by court order, the court for good cause shown may hold a full hearing on the person's continued commitment prior to the expiration of one hundred eighty days after the person's last full hearing. Section 5122.12 of the Revised Code applies to all hearings on continued commitment.

If the court, after a hearing for continued commitment finds by clear and convincing evidence that the respondent is a mentally ill person subject to hospitalization by court order, the court may order continued commitment at places specified in division (C) of this section.

(I) Unless the admission is pursuant to section 5120.17 or 5139.08 of the Revised Code, the chief clinical officer of the hospital or agency admitting a respondent pursuant to a judicial proceeding, within ten working days of the admission, shall make a report of the admission to the board of alcohol, drug addiction, and mental health services serving the respondent's county of residence.

(J) A referee appointed by the court may make all orders that a judge may make under this section and sections 5122.11 and 5122.141 of the Revised Code, except an order of contempt of court. The orders of a referee take effect immediately. Within fourteen days of the making of an order by a referee, a party may file written objections to the order with the court. The filed objections shall be considered a motion, shall be specific, and shall state their grounds with particularity. Within ten days of the filing of the objections, a judge of the court shall hold a hearing on the objections and may hear and consider any testimony or other evidence relating to the respondent's mental condition. At the conclusion of the hearing, the judge may ratify, rescind, or modify the referee's order.

(K) An order of the court under division (C), (H), or (J) of this section is a final order.

(L) Before a board, or an agency the board designates, may place an unconsenting respondent in an inpatient setting from a less restrictive placement, the board or agency shall do all of the following:

(1) Determine that the respondent is in immediate need of treatment in an inpatient setting because the respondent represents a substantial risk of physical harm to the respondent or others if allowed to remain in a less restrictive setting;

(2) On the day of placement in the inpatient setting or on the next court day, file with the court a motion for transfer to an inpatient setting or communicate to the court by telephone that the required motion has been mailed;

(3) Ensure that every reasonable and appropriate effort is made to take the respondent to the inpatient setting in the least conspicuous manner possible;

(4) Immediately notify the board's designated attorney and the respondent's attorney.

At the respondent's request, the court shall hold a hearing on the motion and make a determination pursuant to division (E) of this section within five days of the placement.

(M) Before a board, or an agency the board designates, may move a respondent from one residential placement to another, the board or agency shall consult with the respondent about the placement. If the respondent objects to the placement, the proposed placement and the need for it shall be reviewed by a qualified mental health professional who otherwise is not involved in the treatment of the respondent.

**HISTORY: 129 v 1448(1464) (Eff 10-25-61); 130 v 1194 (Eff 10-10-63); 134 v H 494 (Eff 7-12-72); 136 v H 244 (Eff 8-26-76); 137 v H 725 (Eff 3-16-78); 138 v S 297 (Eff 4-30-80); 138 v H 900 (Eff 7-1-80); 138 v H 965 (Eff 4-9-81); 142 v S 156 (Eff 7-1-89); 143 v H 317 (Eff 10-10-89); 146 v S 310 (Eff 6-20-96); 146 v H 567 (Eff 10-29-96); 146 v S 285. Eff 7-1-97; 2011 HB 153, § 101.01, eff. July 1, 2011.**

**Analogous to former RC § 5123.23.**
The effective date is set by section 4 of SB 285.

## § 5122.21 Discharge of involuntary patients.

(A) The chief clinical officer shall as frequently as practicable, and at least once every thirty days, examine or cause to be examined every patient, and, whenever the chief clinical officer determines that the conditions justifying involuntary hospitalization or commitment no longer obtain, shall discharge the patient not under indictment or conviction for crime and immediately make a report of the discharge to the department of mental health. The chief clinical officer may discharge a patient who is under an indictment, a sentence of imprisonment, a community control sanction, or a post-release control sanction or on parole ten days after written notice of intent to discharge the patient has been given by personal service or certified mail, return receipt requested, to the court having criminal jurisdiction over the patient. Except when the patient was found not guilty by reason of insanity and the defendant's commitment is pursuant to section 2945.40 of the Revised Code, the chief clinical officer has final authority to discharge a patient who is under an indictment, a sentence of imprisonment, a community control sanction, or a post-release control sanction or on parole.

(B) After a finding pursuant to section 5122.15 of the Revised Code that a person is a mentally ill person subject to hospitalization by court order, the chief clinical officer of the hospital or agency to which the person is ordered or to which the person is transferred under section 5122.20 of the Revised Code, may grant a discharge without the consent or authorization of any court.

Upon discharge, the chief clinical officer shall notify the court that caused the judicial hospitalization of the discharge from the hospital.

**HISTORY: 129 v 1448(1467) (Eff 10-25-61); 130 v 1197 (Eff 10-10-63); 132 v H 15 (Eff 10-1-67); 133 v H 1 (Eff 3-18-69); 134 v H 494 (Eff 7-12-72); 136 v H 244 (Eff 8-26-76); 137 v H 725 (Eff 3-16-78); 138 v S 297 (Eff 4-30-80); 138 v H 900 (Eff 7-1-80); 138 v H 965 (Eff 4-9-81); 142 v S 156 (Eff 7-1-89); 146 v S 285. Eff 7-1-97; 149 v H 490, § 1, eff. 1-1-04; 2011 HB 153, § 101.01, eff. Sept. 29, 2011.**

The effective date is set by section 4 of H.B. 490.
**Analogous to former RC § 5123.50.**
Division (C), referred to in this section, does not exist.

## § 5122.26 Patient absent without leave.

(A) If a patient is absent without leave, on a verbal or written order issued within five days of the time of the unauthorized absence by the department of mental health, the chief clinical officer of the hospital from which the patient is absent without leave, or the court of either the county from which the patient was committed or in which the patient is found, any health or police officer or sheriff may take the patient into custody and transport the patient to the hospital in which the patient was hospitalized or to a place that is designated in the order. The officer immediately shall report such fact to the agency that issued the order.

The chief clinical officer of a hospital may discharge a patient who is under an indictment, a sentence of imprisonment, a community control sanction, or a post-release control sanction or on parole and who has been absent without leave for more than thirty days but shall give written notice of the discharge to the court with criminal jurisdiction over the patient. The chief clinical officer of a hospital may discharge any other patient who has been absent without leave for more than fourteen days.

The chief clinical officer shall take all proper measures for the apprehension of an escaped patient. The expense of the return of an escaped patient shall be borne by the hospital where the patient is hospitalized.

(B)(1) Subject to division (B)(2) of this section, no patient hospitalized under Chapter 5122. of the Revised Code whose absence without leave was caused or contributed to by the patient's mental illness shall be subject to a charge of escape.

(2) Division (B)(1) of this section does not apply to any person who was hospitalized, institutionalized, or confined in a facility under an order made pursuant to or under authority of section 2945.37, 2945.371 [2945.37.1], 2945.38, 2945.39, 2945.40, 2945.401 [2945.40.1], or 2945.402 [2945.40.2] of the Revised Code and who escapes from the facility, from confinement in a vehicle for transportation to or from the facility, or from supervision by an employee of the facility that is incidental to hospitalization, institutionalization, or confinement in the facility and that occurs outside the facility, in violation of section 2921.34 of the Revised Code.

**HISTORY: 129 v 1448(1469) (Eff 10-25-61); 134 v H 494 (Eff 7-12-72); 136 v H 244 (Eff 8-26-76); 137 v H 725 (Eff**

**3-16-78); 138 v H 900 (Eff 7-1-80); 142 v S 156 (Eff 7-1-89); 145 v H 42 (Eff 2-9-94); 146 v S 285. Eff 7-1-97; 149 v H 490, § 1, eff. 1-1-04.**

**Analogous to former RC § 5123.54.**
The effective date is set by section 4 of H.B. 490.

## § 5122.30 Right to writ of habeas corpus.

Any person detained pursuant to this chapter or section 2945.39, 2945.40, 2945.401 [2945.40.1], or 2945.402 [2945.40.2] of the Revised Code shall be entitled to the writ of habeas corpus upon proper petition by self or by a friend to any court generally empowered to issue the writ of habeas corpus in the county in which the person is detained.

No person may bring a petition for a writ of habeas corpus that alleges that a person involuntarily detained pursuant to this chapter no longer is a mentally ill person subject to hospitalization by court order unless the person shows that the release procedures of division (H) of section 5122.15 of the Revised Code are inadequate or unavailable.

**HISTORY: 129 v 1448(1470) (Eff 10-25-61); 136 v H 244 (Eff 8-26-76); 138 v H 965 (Eff 4-9-81); 146 v S 285. Eff 7-1-97.**

The effective date is set by section 4 of SB 285.

## § 5122.31 Disclosure of information [Effective until October 1, 2012].

(A) All certificates, applications, records, and reports made for the purpose of this chapter and sections 2945.38, 2945.39, 2945.40, 2945.401, and 2945.402 of the Revised Code, other than court journal entries or court docket entries, and directly or indirectly identifying a patient or former patient or person whose hospitalization has been sought under this chapter, shall be kept confidential and shall not be disclosed by any person except:

(1) If the person identified, or the person's legal guardian, if any, or if the person is a minor, the person's parent or legal guardian, consents, and if the disclosure is in the best interests of the person, as may be determined by the court for judicial records and by the chief clinical officer for medical records;

(2) When disclosure is provided for in this chapter or section 5123.60 of the Revised Code;

(3) That hospitals, boards of alcohol, drug addiction, and mental health services, and community mental health agencies may release necessary medical information to insurers and other third-party payers, including government entities responsible for processing and authorizing payment, to obtain payment for goods and services furnished to the patient;

(4) Pursuant to a court order signed by a judge;

(5) That a patient shall be granted access to the patient's own psychiatric and medical records, unless access specifically is restricted in a patient's treatment plan for clear treatment reasons;

(6) That hospitals and other institutions and facilities within the department of mental health may exchange psychiatric records and other pertinent information with other hospitals, institutions, and facilities of the department, and with community mental health agencies and boards of alcohol, drug addiction, and mental health services with which the department has a current agreement for patient care or services. Records and information that may be released pursuant to this division shall be limited to medication history, physical health status and history, financial status, summary of course of treatment in the hospital, summary of treatment needs, and a discharge summary, if any.

(7) That hospitals within the department, other institutions and facilities within the department, hospitals licensed by the department under section 5119.20 of the Revised Code, and community mental health agencies may exchange psychiatric records and other pertinent information with payers and other providers of treatment and health services if the purpose of the exchange is to facilitate continuity of care for a patient;

(8) That a patient's family member who is involved in the provision, planning, and monitoring of services to the patient may receive medication information, a summary of the patient's diagnosis and prognosis, and a list of the services and personnel available to assist the patient and the patient's family, if the patient's treating physician determines that the disclosure would be in the best interests of the patient. No such disclosure shall be made unless the patient is notified first and receives the information and does not object to the disclosure.

(9) That community mental health agencies may exchange psychiatric records and certain other information with the board of alcohol, drug addiction, and mental health services and other agencies in order to provide services to a person involuntarily committed to a board. Release of records under this division shall be limited to medication history, physical health status and history, financial status, summary of course of treatment, summary of treatment needs, and discharge summary, if any.

(10) That information may be disclosed to the executor or the administrator of an estate of a deceased patient when the information is necessary to administer the estate;

(11) That records in the possession of the Ohio historical society may be released to the closest living relative of a deceased patient upon request of that relative;

(12) That information may be disclosed to staff members of the appropriate board or to staff members designated by the director of mental health for the purpose of evaluating the quality, effectiveness, and efficiency of services and determining if the services meet minimum standards. Information obtained during such evaluations shall not be retained with the name of any patient.

(13) That records pertaining to the patient's diagnosis, course of treatment, treatment needs, and prognosis shall be disclosed and released to the appropriate prosecuting attorney if the patient was committed pursuant to section 2945.38, 2945.39, 2945.40, 2945.401, or 2945.402 of the Revised Code, or to the attorney designated by the board for proceedings pursuant to involuntary commitment under this chapter.

(14) That the department of mental health may exchange psychiatric hospitalization records, other mental health treatment records, and other pertinent information with the department of rehabilitation and correction to ensure continuity of care for inmates who are receiving mental health services in an institution of the department of rehabilitation and correction. The department shall not disclose those records unless the inmate is notified, receives the information, and does not object to the disclosure. The release of records under this division is limited to records regarding an inmate's medication history, physical health status and history, summary of course of

treatment, summary of treatment needs, and a discharge summary, if any.

(15) That a community mental health agency that ceases to operate may transfer to either a community mental health agency that assumes its caseload or to the board of alcohol, drug addiction, and mental health services of the service district in which the patient resided at the time services were most recently provided any treatment records that have not been transferred elsewhere at the patient's request.

(B) Before records are disclosed pursuant to divisions (A)(3), (6), (7), and (9) of this section, the custodian of the records shall attempt to obtain the patient's consent for the disclosure. No person shall reveal the contents of a medical record of a patient except as authorized by law.

(C) The managing officer of a hospital who releases necessary medical information under division (A)(3) of this section to allow an insurance carrier or other third party payor to comply with section 5121.43 of the Revised Code shall neither be subject to criminal nor civil liability.

**HISTORY: 129 v 1448(1470) (Eff 10-25-61); 136 v H 244 (Eff 8-26-76); 137 v H 725 (Eff 3-16-78); 138 v H 900 (Eff 7-1-80); 142 v S 156 (Eff 7-1-89); 143 v H 317 (Eff 10-10-89); 146 v S 310 (Eff 6-20-96); 146 v S 285 (Eff 7-1-97); 149 v H 94. Eff 9-5-2001; 151 v H 66, § 101.01, eff. 1-1-06; 153 v H 1, § 101.01, eff. 10-16-09; 2011 HB 153, § 101.01, eff. Sept. 29, 2011.**

The effective date is set by § 812.10 of 153 v H 1.
The effective date is set by § 612.09 of 151 v H 66.
The effective date is set by section 204 of HB 94.

## § 5122.31 Disclosure of information [Effective October 1, 2012].

(A) All certificates, applications, records, and reports made for the purpose of this chapter and sections 2945.38, 2945.39, 2945.40, 2945.401, and 2945.402 of the Revised Code, other than court journal entries or court docket entries, and directly or indirectly identifying a patient or former patient or person whose hospitalization has been sought under this chapter, shall be kept confidential and shall not be disclosed by any person except:

(1) If the person identified, or the person's legal guardian, if any, or if the person is a minor, the person's parent or legal guardian, consents, and if the disclosure is in the best interests of the person, as may be determined by the court for judicial records and by the chief clinical officer for medical records;

(2) When disclosure is provided for in this chapter or section 5123.601 of the Revised Code;

(3) That hospitals, boards of alcohol, drug addiction, and mental health services, and community mental health agencies may release necessary medical information to insurers and other third-party payers, including government entities responsible for processing and authorizing payment, to obtain payment for goods and services furnished to the patient;

(4) Pursuant to a court order signed by a judge;

(5) That a patient shall be granted access to the patient's own psychiatric and medical records, unless access specifically is restricted in a patient's treatment plan for clear treatment reasons;

(6) That hospitals and other institutions and facilities within the department of mental health may exchange psychiatric records and other pertinent information with other hospitals, institutions, and facilities of the department, and with community mental health agencies and boards of alcohol, drug addiction, and mental health services with which the department has a current agreement for patient care or services. Records and information that may be released pursuant to this division shall be limited to medication history, physical health status and history, financial status, summary of course of treatment in the hospital, summary of treatment needs, and a discharge summary, if any.

(7) That hospitals within the department, other institutions and facilities within the department, hospitals licensed by the department under section 5119.20 of the Revised Code, and community mental health agencies may exchange psychiatric records and other pertinent information with payers and other providers of treatment and health services if the purpose of the exchange is to facilitate continuity of care for a patient;

(8) That a patient's family member who is involved in the provision, planning, and monitoring of services to the patient may receive medication information, a summary of the patient's diagnosis and prognosis, and a list of the services and personnel available to assist the patient and the patient's family, if the patient's treating physician determines that the disclosure would be in the best interests of the patient. No such disclosure shall be made unless the patient is notified first and receives the information and does not object to the disclosure.

(9) That community mental health agencies may exchange psychiatric records and certain other information with the board of alcohol, drug addiction, and mental health services and other agencies in order to provide services to a person involuntarily committed to a board. Release of records under this division shall be limited to medication history, physical health status and history, financial status, summary of course of treatment, summary of treatment needs, and discharge summary, if any.

(10) That information may be disclosed to the executor or the administrator of an estate of a deceased patient when the information is necessary to administer the estate;

(11) That records in the possession of the Ohio historical society may be released to the closest living relative of a deceased patient upon request of that relative;

(12) That information may be disclosed to staff members of the appropriate board or to staff members designated by the director of mental health for the purpose of evaluating the quality, effectiveness, and efficiency of services and determining if the services meet minimum standards. Information obtained during such evaluations shall not be retained with the name of any patient.

(13) That records pertaining to the patient's diagnosis, course of treatment, treatment needs, and prognosis shall be disclosed and released to the appropriate prosecuting attorney if the patient was committed pursuant to section 2945.38, 2945.39, 2945.40, 2945.401, or 2945.402 of the Revised Code, or to the attorney designated by the board for proceedings pursuant to involuntary commitment under this chapter.

(14) That the department of mental health may exchange psychiatric hospitalization records, other mental health treatment records, and other pertinent information with the department of rehabilitation and correction to ensure continuity of care for inmates who are receiving mental health services in an institution of the department of rehabilitation and correction. The department shall not disclose those records unless the inmate is notified, receives the information, and does not object to the disclosure. The release of records under this division is limited to records regarding an inmate's medication history, phys-

ical health status and history, summary of course of treatment, summary of treatment needs, and a discharge summary, if any.

(15) That a community mental health agency that ceases to operate may transfer to either a community mental health agency that assumes its caseload or to the board of alcohol, drug addiction, and mental health services of the service district in which the patient resided at the time services were most recently provided any treatment records that have not been transferred elsewhere at the patient's request.

(B) Before records are disclosed pursuant to divisions (A)(3), (6), (7), and (9) of this section, the custodian of the records shall attempt to obtain the patient's consent for the disclosure. No person shall reveal the contents of a medical record of a patient except as authorized by law.

(C) The managing officer of a hospital who releases necessary medical information under division (A)(3) of this section to allow an insurance carrier or other third party payor to comply with section 5121.43 of the Revised Code shall neither be subject to criminal nor civil liability.

**HISTORY: 129 v 1448(1470) (Eff 10-25-61); 136 v H 244 (Eff 8-26-76); 137 v H 725 (Eff 3-16-78); 138 v H 900 (Eff 7-1-80); 142 v S 156 (Eff 7-1-89); 143 v H 317 (Eff 10-10-89); 146 v S 310 (Eff 6-20-96); 146 v S 285 (Eff 7-1-97); 149 v H 94. Eff 9-5-2001; 151 v H 66, § 101.01, eff. 1-1-06; 153 v H 1, § 101.01, eff. 10-16-09; 2011 HB 153, § 101.01, eff. Sept. 29, 2011; 2011 HB 153, § 120.20, eff. Oct. 1, 2012.**

## § 5122.311 Notice for purpose of incompetency records checks in connection with license to carry concealed handgun.

(A) Notwithstanding any provision of the Revised Code to the contrary, if, on or after the effective date of this section, an individual is found by a court to be a mentally ill person subject to hospitalization by court order or becomes an involuntary patient other than one who is a patient only for purposes of observation, the probate judge who made the adjudication or the chief clinical officer of the hospital, agency, or facility in which the person is an involuntary patient shall notify the bureau of criminal identification and investigation, on the form described in division (C) of this section, of the identity of the individual. The notification shall be transmitted by the judge or the chief clinical officer not later than seven days after the adjudication or commitment.

(B) The bureau of criminal identification and investigation shall compile and maintain the notices it receives under division (A) of this section and shall use them for the purpose of conducting incompetency records checks pursuant to section 311.41 of the Revised Code. The notices and the information they contain are confidential, except as provided in this division, and are not public records.

(C) The attorney general, by rule adopted under Chapter 119. of the Revised Code, shall prescribe and make available to all probate judges and all chief clinical officers a form to be used by them for the purpose of making the notifications required by division (A) of this section.

**HISTORY: 150 v H 12, § 1, eff. 4-8-04.**

## § 5122.32 Confidentiality of quality assurance records; immunity [Effective until October 1, 2012].

(A) As used in this section:

(1) "Quality assurance committee" means a committee that is appointed in the central office of the department of mental health by the director of mental health, a committee of a hospital or community setting program, a committee established pursuant to section 5119.47 of the Revised Code of the department of mental health appointed by the managing officer of the hospital or program, or a duly authorized subcommittee of a committee of that nature and that is designated to carry out quality assurance program activities.

(2) "Quality assurance program" means a comprehensive program within the department of mental health to systematically review and improve the quality of medical and mental health services within the department and its hospitals and community setting programs, the safety and security of persons receiving medical and mental health services within the department and its hospitals and community setting programs, and the efficiency and effectiveness of the utilization of staff and resources in the delivery of medical and mental health services within the department and its hospitals and community setting programs. "Quality assurance program" includes the central office quality assurance committees, morbidity and mortality review committees, quality assurance programs of community setting programs, quality assurance committees of hospitals operated by the department of mental health, and the office of licensure and certification of the department.

(3) "Quality assurance program activities" include collecting or compiling information and reports required by a quality assurance committee, receiving, reviewing, or implementing the recommendations made by a quality assurance committee, and credentialing, privileging, infection control, tissue review, peer review, utilization review including access to patient care records, patient care assessment records, and medical and mental health records, medical and mental health resource management, mortality and morbidity review, and identification and prevention of medical or mental health incidents and risks, whether performed by a quality assurance committee or by persons who are directed by a quality assurance committee.

(4) "Quality assurance records" means the proceedings, discussion, records, findings, recommendations, evaluations, opinions, minutes, reports, and other documents or actions that emanate from quality assurance committees, quality assurance programs, or quality assurance program activities. "Quality assurance records" does not include aggregate statistical information that does not disclose the identity of persons receiving or providing medical or mental health services in department of mental health institutions.

(B)(1) Except as provided in division (E) of this section, quality assurance records are confidential and are not public records under section 149.43 of the Revised Code, and shall be used only in the course of the proper functions of a quality assurance program.

(2) Except as provided in division (E) of this section, no person who possesses or has access to quality assurance records and who knows that the records are quality assurance records shall willfully disclose the contents of the records to any person or entity.

(C)(1) Except as provided in division (E) of this section, no quality assurance record shall be subject to discovery in, and is not admissible in evidence, in any judicial or administrative proceeding.

(2) Except as provided in division (E) of this section, no member of a quality assurance committee or a person who is performing a function that is part of a quality assurance program shall be permitted or required to testify in a judicial or administrative proceeding with respect to quality assurance records or with respect to any finding, recommendation, evaluation, opinion, or other action taken by the committee, member, or person.

(3) Information, documents, or records otherwise available from original sources are not to be construed as being unavailable for discovery or admission in evidence in a judicial or administrative proceeding merely because they were presented to a quality assurance committee. No person testifying before a quality assurance committee or person who is a member of a quality assurance committee shall be prevented from testifying as to matters within the person's knowledge, but the witness cannot be asked about the witness' testimony before the quality assurance committee or about an opinion formed by the person as a result of the quality assurance committee proceedings.

(D)(1) A person who, without malice and in the reasonable belief that the information is warranted by the facts known to the person, provides information to a person engaged in quality assurance program activities is not liable for damages in a civil action for injury, death, or loss to person or property to any person as a result of providing the information.

(2) A member of a quality assurance committee, a person engaged in quality assurance program activities, and an employee of the department of mental health shall not be liable in damages in a civil action for injury, death, or loss to person or property to any person for any acts, omissions, decisions, or other conduct within the scope of the functions of the quality assurance program.

(3) Nothing in this section shall relieve any institution or individual from liability arising from the treatment of a patient.

(E) Quality assurance records may be disclosed, and testimony may be provided concerning quality assurance records, only to the following persons or entities:

(1) Persons who are employed or retained by the department of mental health and who have authority to evaluate or implement the recommendations of a state-operated hospital, community setting program, or central office quality assurance committee;

(2) Public or private agencies or organizations if needed to perform a licensing or accreditation function related to department of mental health hospitals or community setting programs, or to perform monitoring of a hospital or program of that nature as required by law.

(F) A disclosure of quality assurance records pursuant to division (E) of this section does not otherwise waive the confidential and privileged status of the disclosed quality assurance records.

(G) Nothing in this section shall limit the access of the legal rights service to records or personnel as set forth in sections 5123.60 to 5123.604 [5123.60.4] of the Revised Code. Nothing in this section shall limit the admissibility of documentary or testimonial evidence in an action brought by the legal rights service in its own name or on behalf of a client.

**HISTORY: 147 v S 111. Eff 3-17-98.**

**Not analogous to former RC § 5122.32 (129 v 1448 (1470)), repealed, 136 v H 244, § 2, eff 8-26-76.**

## § 5122.32 Confidentiality of quality assurance records; immunity [Effective October 1, 2012].

(A) As used in this section:

(1) "Quality assurance committee" means a committee that is appointed in the central office of the department of mental health by the director of mental health, a committee of a hospital or community setting program, a committee established pursuant to section 5119.47 of the Revised Code of the department of mental health appointed by the managing officer of the hospital or program, or a duly authorized subcommittee of a committee of that nature and that is designated to carry out quality assurance program activities.

(2) "Quality assurance program" means a comprehensive program within the department of mental health to systematically review and improve the quality of medical and mental health services within the department and its hospitals and community setting programs, the safety and security of persons receiving medical and mental health services within the department and its hospitals and community setting programs, and the efficiency and effectiveness of the utilization of staff and resources in the delivery of medical and mental health services within the department and its hospitals and community setting programs. "Quality assurance program" includes the central office quality assurance committees, morbidity and mortality review committees, quality assurance programs of community setting programs, quality assurance committees of hospitals operated by the department of mental health, and the office of licensure and certification of the department.

(3) "Quality assurance program activities" include collecting or compiling information and reports required by a quality assurance committee, receiving, reviewing, or implementing the recommendations made by a quality assurance committee, and credentialing, privileging, infection control, tissue review, peer review, utilization review including access to patient care records, patient care assessment records, and medical and mental health records, medical and mental health resource management, mortality and morbidity review, and identification and prevention of medical or mental health incidents and risks, whether performed by a quality assurance committee or by persons who are directed by a quality assurance committee.

(4) "Quality assurance records" means the proceedings, discussion, records, findings, recommendations, evaluations, opinions, minutes, reports, and other documents or actions that emanate from quality assurance committees, quality assurance programs, or quality assurance program activities. "Quality assurance records" does not include aggregate statistical information that does not disclose the identity of persons receiving or providing medical or mental health services in department of mental health institutions.

(B)(1) Except as provided in division (E) of this section, quality assurance records are confidential and are not public records under section 149.43 of the Revised Code, and shall be used only in the course of the proper functions of a quality assurance program.

(2) Except as provided in division (E) of this section, no person who possesses or has access to quality assurance records and who knows that the records are quality assurance records shall willfully disclose the contents of the records to any person or entity.

(C)(1) Except as provided in division (E) of this section, no quality assurance record shall be subject to discovery in, and is not admissible in evidence, in any judicial or administrative proceeding.

(2) Except as provided in division (E) of this section, no member of a quality assurance committee or a person who is performing a function that is part of a quality assurance program shall be permitted or required to testify in a judicial or administrative proceeding with respect to quality assurance records or with respect to any finding, recommendation, evaluation, opinion, or other action taken by the committee, member, or person.

(3) Information, documents, or records otherwise available from original sources are not to be construed as being unavailable for discovery or admission in evidence in a judicial or administrative proceeding merely because they were presented to a quality assurance committee. No person testifying before a quality assurance committee or person who is a member of a quality assurance committee shall be prevented from testifying as to matters within the person's knowledge, but the witness cannot be asked about the witness' testimony before the quality assurance committee or about an opinion formed by the person as a result of the quality assurance committee proceedings.

(D)(1) A person who, without malice and in the reasonable belief that the information is warranted by the facts known to the person, provides information to a person engaged in quality assurance program activities is not liable for damages in a civil action for injury, death, or loss to person or property to any person as a result of providing the information.

(2) A member of a quality assurance committee, a person engaged in quality assurance program activities, and an employee of the department of mental health shall not be liable in damages in a civil action for injury, death, or loss to person or property to any person for any acts, omissions, decisions, or other conduct within the scope of the functions of the quality assurance program.

(3) Nothing in this section shall relieve any institution or individual from liability arising from the treatment of a patient.

(E) Quality assurance records may be disclosed, and testimony may be provided concerning quality assurance records, only to the following persons or entities:

(1) Persons who are employed or retained by the department of mental health and who have authority to evaluate or implement the recommendations of a state-operated hospital, community setting program, or central office quality assurance committee;

(2) Public or private agencies or organizations if needed to perform a licensing or accreditation function related to department of mental health hospitals or community setting programs, or to perform monitoring of a hospital or program of that nature as required by law.

(F) A disclosure of quality assurance records pursuant to division (E) of this section does not otherwise waive the confidential and privileged status of the disclosed quality assurance records.

(G) Nothing in this section shall limit the access of the Ohio protection and advocacy system to records or personnel as required under section 5123.601 of the Revised Code. Nothing in this section shall limit the admissibility of documentary or testimonial evidence in an action brought by the Ohio protection and advocacy system in its own name or on behalf of a client.

**HISTORY: 147 v S 111. Eff 3-17-98; 2011 HB 153, § 120.20, eff. Oct. 1, 2012.**

### § 5122.99 Penalties for disclosing quality assurance records.

A person who violates division (B)(2) of section 5122.32 of the Revised Code shall be fined not more than two thousand five hundred dollars on a first offense and not more than twenty thousand dollars on a subsequent offense.

**HISTORY: 147 v S 111. Eff 3-17-98.**

**Not analogous to former RC § 5122.99, amended and renumbered RC § 3793.99 in 143 v H 317, eff 10-10-89.**

## CHAPTER 5123: DEPARTMENT OF DEVELOPMENTAL DISABILITIES

Section



Section



### § 5123.01 Definitions.

As used in this chapter:

(A) "Chief medical officer" means the licensed physician appointed by the managing officer of an institution for the mentally retarded with the approval of the director of developmental disabilities to provide medical treatment for residents of the institution.

(B) "Chief program director" means a person with special training and experience in the diagnosis and management of the mentally retarded, certified according to division (C) of this section in at least one of the designated fields, and appointed by the managing officer of an institution for the mentally retarded with the approval of the director to provide habilitation and care for residents of the institution.

(C) "Comprehensive evaluation" means a study, including a sequence of observations and examinations, of a person leading to conclusions and recommendations formulated jointly, with dissenting opinions if any, by a group of persons with special training and experience in the diagnosis and management of persons with mental retardation or a developmental disability, which group shall include individuals who are professionally qualified in the fields of medicine, psychology, and social work, together with such other specialists as the individual case may require.

(D) "Education" means the process of formal training and instruction to facilitate the intellectual and emotional development of residents.

(E) "Habilitation" means the process by which the staff of the institution assists the resident in acquiring and maintaining those life skills that enable the resident to cope more effectively with the demands of the resident's own person and of the resident's environment and in raising the level of the resident's physical, mental, social, and vocational efficiency. Habilitation includes but is not limited to programs of formal, structured education and training.

(F) "Health officer" means any public health physician, public health nurse, or other person authorized or designated by a city or general health district.

(G) "Home and community-based services" means medicaid-funded home and community-based services specified in division (B)(1) of section 5111.87 of the Revised Code provided under the medicaid waiver components the department of developmental disabilities administers pursuant to section 5111.871 of the Revised Code. However, home and community-based services provided under the medicaid waiver component known as the transitions developmental disabilities waiver are to be considered to be home and community-based services for the purposes of this chapter only to the extent, if any, provided by the contract required by section 5111.871 of the Revised Code regarding the waiver.

(H) "Indigent person" means a person who is unable, without substantial financial hardship, to provide for the payment of an attorney and for other necessary expenses of legal representation, including expert testimony.

(I) "Institution" means a public or private facility, or a part of a public or private facility, that is licensed by the appropriate state department and is equipped to provide residential habilitation, care, and treatment for the mentally retarded.

(J) "Licensed physician" means a person who holds a valid certificate issued under Chapter 4731. of the Revised Code authorizing the person to practice medicine and surgery or osteopathic medicine and surgery, or a medical officer of the government of the United States while in the performance of the officer's official duties.

(K) "Managing officer" means a person who is appointed by the director of developmental disabilities to be in executive control of an institution for the mentally retarded under the jurisdiction of the department.

(L) "Medicaid" has the same meaning as in section 5111.01 of the Revised Code.

(M) "Medicaid case management services" means case management services provided to an individual with mental retardation or other developmental disability that the state medicaid plan requires.

(N) "Mentally retarded person" means a person having significantly subaverage general intellectual functioning existing concurrently with deficiencies in adaptive behavior, manifested during the developmental period.

(O) "Mentally retarded person subject to institutionalization by court order" means a person eighteen years of age or older who is at least moderately mentally retarded and in relation to whom, because of the person's retardation, either of the following conditions exist:

(1) The person represents a very substantial risk of physical impairment or injury to self as manifested by evidence that the person is unable to provide for and is not providing for the person's most basic physical needs and that provision for those needs is not available in the community;

(2) The person needs and is susceptible to significant habilitation in an institution.

(P) "A person who is at least moderately mentally retarded" means a person who is found, following a comprehensive evaluation, to be impaired in adaptive behavior to a moderate degree and to be functioning at the moderate level of intellectual functioning in accordance with standard measurements as recorded in the most current revision of the manual of terminology and classification in mental retardation published by the American association on mental retardation.

(Q) As used in this division, "substantial functional limitation," "developmental delay," and "established risk" have the meanings established pursuant to section 5123.011 of the Revised Code.

"Developmental disability" means a severe, chronic disability that is characterized by all of the following:

(1) It is attributable to a mental or physical impairment or a combination of mental and physical impairments, other than a mental or physical impairment solely caused by mental illness as defined in division (A) of section 5122.01 of the Revised Code.

(2) It is manifested before age twenty-two.

(3) It is likely to continue indefinitely.

(4) It results in one of the following:

(a) In the case of a person under three years of age, at least one developmental delay or an established risk;

(b) In the case of a person at least three years of age but under six years of age, at least two developmental delays or an established risk;

(c) In the case of a person six years of age or older, a substantial functional limitation in at least three of the following areas of major life activity, as appropriate for the person's age: self-care, receptive and expressive language, learning, mobility, self-direction, capacity for independent living, and, if the person is at least sixteen years of age, capacity for economic self-sufficiency.

(5) It causes the person to need a combination and sequence of special, interdisciplinary, or other type of care, treatment, or provision of services for an extended period of time that is individually planned and coordinated for the person.

(R) "Developmentally disabled person" means a person with a developmental disability.

(S) "State institution" means an institution that is tax-supported and under the jurisdiction of the department.

(T) "Residence" and "legal residence" have the same meaning as "legal settlement," which is acquired by residing in Ohio for a period of one year without receiving general assistance prior to July 17, 1995, under former Chapter 5113. of the Revised Code, financial assistance under Chapter 5115. of the Revised Code, or assistance from a private agency that maintains records of assistance given. A person having a legal settlement in the state shall be considered as having legal settlement in the assistance area in which the person resides. No adult person coming into this state and having a spouse or minor children residing in another state shall obtain a legal settlement in this state as long as the spouse or minor children are receiving public assistance, care, or support at the expense of the other state or its subdivisions. For the purpose of determining the legal settlement of a person who is living in a public or private institution or in a home subject to licensing by the department of job and family services, the department of mental health, or the department of developmental disabilities, the residence of the person shall be considered as though the person were residing in the county in which the person was living prior to the person's entrance into the institution or home. Settlement once acquired shall continue until a person has been continuously absent from Ohio for a period of one year or has acquired a legal residence in another state. A woman who marries a man with legal settlement in any county immediately acquires the settlement of her husband. The legal settlement of a minor is that of the parents, surviving parent, sole parent, parent who is designated the residential parent and legal custodian by a court, other adult having permanent custody awarded by a court, or guardian of the person of the minor, provided that:

(1) A minor female who marries shall be considered to have the legal settlement of her husband and, in the case of death of her husband or divorce, she shall not thereby lose her legal settlement obtained by the marriage.

(2) A minor male who marries, establishes a home, and who has resided in this state for one year without receiving general assistance prior to July 17, 1995, under former Chapter 5113. of the Revised Code, financial assistance under Chapter 5115. of the Revised Code, or assistance from a private agency that maintains records of assistance given shall be considered to have obtained a legal settlement in this state.

(3) The legal settlement of a child under eighteen years of age who is in the care or custody of a public or private child caring agency shall not change if the legal settlement of the parent changes until after the child has been in the home of the parent for a period of one year.

No person, adult or minor, may establish a legal settlement in this state for the purpose of gaining admission to any state institution.

(U)(1) "Resident" means, subject to division (R)(2) of this section, a person who is admitted either voluntarily or involuntarily to an institution or other facility pursuant to section 2945.39, 2945.40, 2945.401, or 2945.402 of the Revised Code subsequent to a finding of not guilty by reason of insanity or incompetence to stand trial or under this chapter who is under observation or receiving habilitation and care in an institution.

(2) "Resident" does not include a person admitted to an institution or other facility under section 2945.39, 2945.40, 2945.401, or 2945.402 of the Revised Code to the extent that the reference in this chapter to resident, or the context in which the reference occurs, is in conflict with any provision of sections 2945.37 to 2945.402 of the Revised Code.

(V) "Respondent" means the person whose detention, commitment, or continued commitment is being sought in any proceeding under this chapter.

(W) "Working day" and "court day" mean Monday, Tuesday, Wednesday, Thursday, and Friday, except when such day is a legal holiday.

(X) "Prosecutor" means the prosecuting attorney, village solicitor, city director of law, or similar chief legal officer who prosecuted a criminal case in which a person was found not guilty by reason of insanity, who would have had the authority to prosecute a criminal case against a person if the person had not been found incompetent to stand trial, or who prosecuted a case in which a person was found guilty.

(Y) "Court" means the probate division of the court of common pleas.

(Z) "Supported living" and "residential services" have the same meanings as in section 5126.01 of the Revised Code.

**HISTORY: RC § 5123.68, 135 v S 336 (Eff 7-1-75); 138 v S 297 (Eff 4-30-80); RC § 5123.01, 138 v H 900 (Eff 7-1-80); 138 v H 965 (Eff 4-9-81); 139 v H 1 (Eff 8-5-81); 142 v H 231 (Eff 10-5-87); 143 v H 569 (Eff 7-1-91); 143 v S 3 (Eff 4-11-91); 144 v H 298 (Eff 7-26-91); 145 v S 21 (Eff 10-29-93); 145 v H 694 (Eff 11-11-94); 146 v H 249 (Eff 7-17-95); 146 v S 285 (Eff 7-1-97); 148 v H 471 (Eff 7-1-2000); 148 v H 538 (Eff 9-22-2000); 149 v H 94. Eff 6-6-2001; 150 v H 95, § 1, eff. 6-26-03; 151 v H 66, § 101.01, eff. 7-1-05; 152 v H 119, § 101.01, eff. 6-30-07; 153 v S 79, § 1, eff. 10-6-09; 2011 HB 153, § 101.01, eff. Sept. 29, 2011.**

The effective date is set by § 815.03 of 152 v H 119.

The effective date is set by § 612.18 of 151 v H 66.

**Not analogous to former RC § 5123.01 (GC § 1890-19; 117 v 550; 121 v 423; Bureau of Code Revision, 10-1-53), repealed 129 v 1448(1483), § 2, eff 10-25-61.**

The effective date is set by section 182 of H.B. 95 (150 v —).

## § 5123.011 Rules establishing certain definitions.

The director of developmental disabilities shall adopt rules in accordance with Chapter 119. of the Revised Code that establish definitions of "substantial functional limitation," "developmental delay," "established risk," "biological risk," and "environmental risk."

**HISTORY: 143 v H 569 (Eff 11-11-91); 144 v S 156. Eff 1-10-92; 153 v S 79, § 1, eff. 10-6-09.**

## § 5123.13 Special police officers for institutions.

(A) As used in this section, "felony" has the same meaning as in section 109.511 [109.51.1] of the Revised Code.

(B)(1) Subject to division (C) of this section, upon the recommendation of the director of developmental disabilities, the managing officer of an institution under the jurisdiction of the department of developmental disabilities may designate one or more employees to be special police officers of the department. The special police officers shall take an oath of office, wear the badge of office, and give bond for the proper and faithful discharge of their duties in an amount that the director requires.

(2) In accordance with section 109.77 of the Revised Code, the special police officers shall be required to complete successfully a peace officer basic training program approved by the Ohio peace officer training commission and to be certified by the commission. The cost of the training shall be paid by the department of developmental disabilities.

(3) Special police officers, on the premises of institutions under the jurisdiction of the department of developmental disabilities and subject to the rules of the depart-

ment, shall protect the property of the institutions and the persons and property of patients in the institutions, suppress riots, disturbances, and breaches of the peace, and enforce the laws of the state and the rules of the department for the preservation of good order. They may arrest any person without a warrant and detain the person until a warrant can be obtained under the circumstances described in division (F) of section 2935.03 of the Revised Code.

(C)(1) The managing officer of an institution under the jurisdiction of the department of developmental disabilities shall not designate an employee as a special police officer of the department pursuant to division (B)(1) of this section on a permanent basis, on a temporary basis, for a probationary term, or on other than a permanent basis if the employee previously has been convicted of or has pleaded guilty to a felony.

(2)(a) The managing officer of an institution under the jurisdiction of the department of developmental disabilities shall terminate the employment as a special police officer of the department of an employee designated as a special police officer under division (B)(1) of this section if that employee does either of the following:

(i) Pleads guilty to a felony;

(ii) Pleads guilty to a misdemeanor pursuant to a negotiated plea agreement as provided in division (D) of section 2929.43 of the Revised Code in which the employee agrees to surrender the certificate awarded to that employee under section 109.77 of the Revised Code.

(b) The managing officer shall suspend from employment as a special police officer of the department an employee designated as a special police officer under division (B)(1) of this section if that employee is convicted, after trial, of a felony. If the special police officer files an appeal from that conviction and the conviction is upheld by the highest court to which the appeal is taken or if the special police officer does not file a timely appeal, the managing officer shall terminate the employment of that special police officer. If the special police officer files an appeal that results in that special police officer's acquittal of the felony or conviction of a misdemeanor, or in the dismissal of the felony charge against that special police officer, the managing officer shall reinstate that special police officer. A special police officer of the department who is reinstated under division (C)(2)(b) of this section shall not receive any back pay unless that special police officer's conviction of the felony was reversed on appeal, or the felony charge was dismissed, because the court found insufficient evidence to convict the special police officer of the felony.

(3) Division (C) of this section does not apply regarding an offense that was committed prior to January 1, 1997.

(4) The suspension from employment, or the termination of the employment, of a special police officer under division (C)(2) of this section shall be in accordance with Chapter 119. of the Revised Code.

**HISTORY: 138 v H 900 (Eff 7-1-80); 139 v H 694 (Eff 11-15-81); 144 v S 49 (Eff 7-21-92); 145 v H 42 (Eff 2-9-94); 146 v H 566 (Eff 10-16-96); 146 v H 670. Eff 12-2-96; 149 v H 490, § 1, eff. 1-1-04; 153 v S 79, § 1, eff. 10-6-09.**

**Not analogous to former RC § 5123.13 (GC § 1890-16; 117 v 550; 119 v 616; 121 v 423; Bureau of Code Revision, 10-1-53; 125 v 864; 129 v 1448(1473); 120 v H 357; 133 v H 1; 134 v H 494) renumbered RC § 5119.25 in 138 v H 900, eff 7-1-80, repealed, eff 9-29-97.**

The effective date is set by section 4 of H.B. 490.

The provisions of § 5 of H.B. 490 (149 v —) read as follows: SECTION 5. Section 5123.13 of the Revised Code is presented in this act as a composite of the section as amended by both Am. Sub. H.B. 566 and Sub. H.B. 670 of the 121st General Assembly. The General Assembly, applying the principle stated in division (B) of section 1.52 of the Revised Code that amendments are to be harmonized if reasonably capable of simultaneous operation, finds that the specified composite is the resulting version of the specified sections in effect prior to the effective date of the section as presented in this act.

## § 5123.14 Investigations by department.

The department of developmental disabilities may make such investigations as are necessary in the performance of its duties and to that end the director of developmental disabilities shall have the same power as a judge of a county court to administer oaths and to enforce the attendance and testimony of witnesses and the production of books or papers.

The department shall keep a record of such investigations stating the time, place, charges or subject, witnesses summoned and examined, and its conclusions.

In matters involving the conduct of an officer, a stenographic report of the evidence shall be taken and a copy of such report, with all documents introduced, kept on file at the office of the department.

Witnesses shall be paid the fees and mileage provided for under section 119.094 [119.09.4] of the Revised Code, but no officer or employee of the institution under investigation is entitled to such fees.

Any judge of the probate court or of the court of common pleas, upon application of the department, may compel the attendance of witnesses, the production of books or papers, and the giving of testimony before the department, by a judgment for contempt or otherwise, in the same manner as in cases before said courts.

**HISTORY: 138 v H 900. Eff 7-1-80; 152 v H 525, § 1, eff. 7-1-09; 153 v S 79, § 1, eff. 10-6-09.**

The effective date is set by § 3 of 152 v H 525.

**Not analogous to former RC § 5123.14 (GC § 1890-17; 117 v 550; 119 v 616; Bureau of Code Revision, 10-1-53; 129 v 1448(1473); 130 v 1201; 134 v H 494), repealed 138 v H 900, § 2, eff 7-1-80.**

The effective date is set by section 3 of HB 900.

### [SUPPORTED LIVING CERTIFICATE]

## § 5123.20 Operation without license or certificate prohibited.

No person or government agency shall operate a residential facility or receive a mentally retarded or developmentally disabled person as a resident of a residential facility unless the facility is licensed under section 5123.19 of the Revised Code, and no person or governmental agency shall operate a respite care home or receive a mentally retarded or developmentally disabled person in a respite care home unless the home is certified under section 5126.05 of the Revised Code.

**HISTORY: RC § 5123.19, 133 v S 367 (Eff 6-8-70); 137 v S 71 (Eff 10-31-77); RC § 5123.20, 138 v H 900 (Eff 7-1-80); 143 v H 257 (Eff 8-3-89); 143 v H 569 (Eff 7-1-91); 145 v S 21 (Eff 10-29-93); 145 v H 694. Eff 11-11-94; 152 v H 119, § 101.01, eff. 6-30-07.**

The effective date is set by § 815.03 of 152 v H 119.

**Not analogous to former RC § 5123.20 (GC § 1890-25;**

**117 v 550; 119 v 616; 121 v 423; Bureau of Code Revision, 10-1-53), repealed 129 v 1448(1483), § 2, eff 10-25-61.**

**Former RC § 5123.20 (137 v H 870) was renumbered RC § 5119.22 in 138 v H 900.**

## [REGISTRY OF EMPLOYEES GUILTY OF ABUSE, NEGLECT OR MISAPPROPRIATION]

### § 5123.50 Definitions.

As used in this section and sections 5123.51, 5123.52, and 5123.541 [5123.54.1] of the Revised Code:

(A) "Abuse" means all of the following:

(1) The use of physical force that can reasonably be expected to result in physical harm or serious physical harm;

(2) Sexual abuse;

(3) Verbal abuse.

(B) "Misappropriation" means depriving, defrauding, or otherwise obtaining the real or personal property of an individual by any means prohibited by the Revised Code, including violations of Chapter 2911. or 2913. of the Revised Code.

(C) "MR/DD employee" means all of the following:

(1) An employee of the department of developmental disabilities;

(2) An employee of a county board of developmental disabilities;

(3) An employee in a position that includes providing specialized services to an individual with mental retardation or another developmental disability.

(D) "Neglect" means, when there is a duty to do so, failing to provide an individual with any treatment, care, goods, or services that are necessary to maintain the health and safety of the individual.

(E) "Physical harm" and "serious physical harm" have the same meanings as in section 2901.01 of the Revised Code.

(F) "Sexual abuse" means unlawful sexual conduct or sexual contact.

(G) "Specialized services" means any program or service designed and operated to serve primarily individuals with mental retardation or a developmental disability, including a program or service provided by an entity licensed or certified by the department of developmental disabilities. A program or service available to the general public is not a specialized service.

(H) "Verbal abuse" means purposely using words to threaten, coerce, intimidate, harass, or humiliate an individual.

(I) "Sexual conduct," "sexual contact," and "spouse" have the same meanings as in section 2907.01 of the Revised Code.

**HISTORY: 148 v S 171 (Eff 11-22-2000); 149 v S 191. Eff 12-31-2003; 150 v S 178, § 1, eff. 1-30-04; 153 v S 79, § 1, eff. 10-6-09.**

**Not analogous to former RC § 5123.50 (GC § 1890-63; 117 v 550(569), § 63; 119 v 616(630); 121 v 423(435); Bureau of Code Revision, 10-1-53; 125 v 122; 125 v 867; 126 v 313; 128 v 522), repealed 129 v 1448 (1483), § 2, eff 10-25-61.**

The effective date is set by section 3 of SB 191.

### § 5123.51 Review of report of abuse, neglect or misappropriation by employee; hearing; inclusion in registry.

(A) In addition to any other action required by sections 5123.61 and 5126.31 of the Revised Code, the department of developmental disabilities shall review each report the department receives of abuse or neglect of an individual with mental retardation or a developmental disability or misappropriation of an individual's property that includes an allegation that an MR/DD employee committed or was responsible for the abuse, neglect, or misappropriation. The department shall review a report it receives from a public children services agency only after the agency completes its investigation pursuant to section 2151.421 [2151.42.1] of the Revised Code. On receipt of a notice under section 2930.061 [2930.06.1] or 5123.541 [5123.54.1] of the Revised Code, the department shall review the notice.

(B) The department shall do both of the following:

(1) Investigate the allegation or adopt the findings of an investigation or review of the allegation conducted by another person or government entity and determine whether there is a reasonable basis for the allegation;

(2) If the department determines that there is a reasonable basis for the allegation, conduct an adjudication pursuant to Chapter 119. of the Revised Code.

(C)(1) The department shall appoint an independent hearing officer to conduct any hearing conducted pursuant to division (B)(2) of this section, except that, if the hearing is regarding an employee of the department who is represented by a union, the department and a representative of the union shall jointly select the hearing officer.

(2)(a) Except as provided in division (C)(2)(b) of this section, no hearing shall be conducted under division (B)(2) of this section until any criminal proceeding or collective bargaining arbitration concerning the same allegation has concluded.

(b) The department may conduct a hearing pursuant to division (B)(2) of this section before a criminal proceeding concerning the same allegation is concluded if both of the following are the case:

(i) The department notifies the prosecutor responsible for the criminal proceeding that the department proposes to conduct a hearing.

(ii) The prosecutor consents to the hearing.

(3) In conducting a hearing pursuant to division (B)(2) of this section, the hearing officer shall do all of the following:

(a) Determine whether there is clear and convincing evidence that the MR/DD employee has done any of the following:

(i) Misappropriated property of one or more individuals with mental retardation or a developmental disability that has a value, either separately or taken together, of one hundred dollars or more;

(ii) Misappropriated property of an individual with mental retardation or a developmental disability that is designed to be used as a check, draft, negotiable instrument, credit card, charge card, or device for initiating an electronic fund transfer at a point of sale terminal, automated teller machine, or cash dispensing machine;

(iii) Knowingly abused such an individual;

(iv) Recklessly abused or neglected such an individual, with resulting physical harm;

(v) Negligently abused or neglected such an individual, with resulting serious physical harm;

(vi) Recklessly neglected such an individual, creating a substantial risk of serious physical harm;

(vii) Engaged in sexual conduct or had sexual contact with an individual with mental retardation or another developmental disability who was not the MR/DD employee's spouse and for whom the MR/DD employee was employed or under a contract to provide care;

(viii) Unreasonably failed to make a report pursuant to division (C) of section 5123.61 of the Revised Code when the employee knew or should have known that the failure would result in a substantial risk of harm to an individual with mental retardation or a developmental disability.

(b) Give weight to the decision in any collective bargaining arbitration regarding the same allegation;

(c) Give weight to any relevant facts presented at the hearing.

(D)(1) Unless the director of developmental disabilities determines that there are extenuating circumstances and except as provided in division (E) of this section, if the director, after considering all of the factors listed in division (C)(3) of this section, finds that there is clear and convincing evidence that an MR/DD employee has done one or more of the things described in division (C)(3)(a) of this section the director shall include the name of the employee in the registry established under section 5123.52 of the Revised Code.

(2) Extenuating circumstances the director must consider include the use of physical force by an MR/DD employee that was necessary as self-defense.

(3) If the director includes an MR/DD employee in the registry established under section 5123.52 of the Revised Code, the director shall notify the employee, the person or government entity that employs or contracts with the employee, the individual with mental retardation or a developmental disability who was the subject of the report and that individual's legal guardian, if any, the attorney general, and the prosecuting attorney or other law enforcement agency. If the MR/DD employee holds a license, certificate, registration, or other authorization to engage in a profession issued pursuant to Title XLVII of the Revised Code, the director shall notify the appropriate agency, board, department, or other entity responsible for regulating the employee's professional practice.

(4) If an individual whose name appears on the registry is involved in a court proceeding or arbitration arising from the same facts as the allegation resulting in the individual's placement on the registry, the disposition of the proceeding or arbitration shall be noted in the registry next to the individual's name.

(E) In the case of an allegation concerning an employee of the department, after the hearing conducted pursuant to division (B)(2) of this section, the director of health or that director's designee shall review the decision of the hearing officer to determine whether the standard described in division (C)(3) of this section has been met. If the director or designee determines that the standard has been met and that no extenuating circumstances exist, the director or designee shall notify the director of developmental disabilities that the MR/DD employee is to be included in the registry established under section 5123.52 of the Revised Code. If the director of developmental disabilities receives such notification, the director shall include the MR/DD employee in the registry and shall provide the notification described in division (D)(3) of this section.

(F) If the department is required by Chapter 119. of the Revised Code to give notice of an opportunity for a hearing and the MR/DD employee subject to the notice does not timely request a hearing in accordance with section 119.07 or 5123.0414 [5123.04.14] of the Revised Code, the department is not required to hold a hearing.

(G) Files and records of investigations conducted pursuant to this section are not public records as defined in section 149.43 of the Revised Code, but, on request, the department shall provide copies of those files and records to the attorney general, a prosecuting attorney, or a law enforcement agency.

**HISTORY: 148 v S 171. Eff 11-22-2000; 150 v S 178, § 1, eff. 1-30-04; 152 v H 119, § 101.01, eff. 6-30-07; 153 v S 79, § 1, eff. 10-6-09.**

This section was amended by Senate Bill 5 of the 2011 legislative session. However, referendum petitions were filed to prevent SB 5 from taking effect as scheduled on July 1, 2011. The provisions of SB 5 were rejected by the voters at the referendum election on November 8, 2011.

The effective date is set by § 815.03 of 152 v H 119.

**Not analogous to former RC § 5123.51 (GC § 1890-63a; 121 v 321, § 1; Bureau of Code Revision, 10-1-53), repealed 129 v 1448 (1483), § 2, eff 10-25-61.**

## § 5123.52 Registry of employees guilty of abuse, neglect or misappropriation.

(A) The department of developmental disabilities shall establish a registry of MR/DD employees consisting of the names of MR/DD employees included in the registry pursuant to section 5123.51 of the Revised Code.

(B) Before a person or government entity hires, contracts with, or employs an individual as an MR/DD employee, the person or government entity shall inquire whether the individual is included in the registry.

(C) When it receives an inquiry regarding whether an individual is included in the registry, the department shall inform the person making the inquiry whether the individual is included in the registry.

(D)(1) Except as otherwise provided in a collective bargaining agreement entered into under Chapter 4117. of the Revised Code that is in effect on November 22, 2000, no person or government entity shall hire, contract with, or employ as an MR/DD employee an individual who is included in the registry. Notwithstanding sections 4117.08 and 4117.10 of the Revised Code, no agreement entered into under Chapter 4117. of the Revised Code after November 22, 2000, may contain any provision that in any way limits the effect or operation of this section.

(2) Neither the department nor any county board of developmental disabilities may enter into a new contract or renew a contract with a person or government entity that fails to comply with division (D)(1) of this section until the department or board is satisfied that the person or government entity will comply.

(3) A person or government entity that fails to hire or retain as an MR/DD employee a person because the person is included in the registry shall not be liable in damages in a civil action brought by the employee or applicant for employment. Termination of employment pursuant to division (D)(1) of this section constitutes a discharge for just cause for the purposes of section 4141.29 of the Revised Code.

(E) Information contained in the registry is a public record for the purposes of section 149.43 of the Revised Code and is subject to inspection and copying under section 1347.08 of the Revised Code.

**HISTORY: 148 v S 171. Eff 11-22-2000; 153 v S 79, § 1, eff. 10-6-09.**

**Not analogous to former RC § 5123.52 (GC § 1890-63b; 121 v 423(435); Bureau of Code Revision, 10-1-53; 125 v 867), repealed 129 v 1448 (1483), § 2, eff 10-25-61.**

## § 5123.53 Petition for removal from registry.

An individual who is included in the registry may petition the director of developmental disabilities for removal from the registry. If the director determines that good cause exists, the director shall remove the individual from the registry and may properly reply to an inquiry that the individual is not included in the registry. Good cause includes meeting rehabilitation standards established in rules adopted under section 5123.54 of the Revised Code.

**HISTORY: 148 v S 171. Eff 11-22-2000; 153 v S 79, § 1, eff. 10-6-09.**

**Not analogous to former RC § 5123.53, amended and renumbered RC § 5123.80.1 in 138 v H 900, eff 7-1-80.**

## § 5123.54 Rules.

The director of developmental disabilities shall adopt rules under Chapter 119. of the Revised Code to implement sections 5123.51, 5123.52, and 5123.53 of the Revised Code. The rules shall establish rehabilitation standards for the purposes of section 5123.53 of the Revised Code and specify circumstances, other than meeting the standards, that constitute good cause for the purposes of that section.

**HISTORY: 148 v S 171. Eff 11-22-2000; 153 v S 79, § 1, eff. 10-6-09.**

**Not analogous to former RC § 5123.54 (GC § 1890-65; 117 v 550(570), § 65; 119 v 616(631); Bureau of Code Revision, 10-1-53; 125 v 123; 125 v 868; 126 v 313), repealed 129 v 1448 (1483), § 2, eff 10-25-61.**

## § 5123.541 Sexual conduct or contact between employee and person to whom care provided prohibited.

(A) No MR/DD employee shall engage in any sexual conduct or have any sexual contact with an individual with mental retardation or another developmental disability for whom the MR/DD employee is employed or under a contract to provide care unless the individual is the MR/DD employee's spouse.

(B) Any MR/DD employee who violates division (A) of this section shall be eligible to be included in the registry regarding misappropriation, abuse, neglect, or other specified misconduct by MR/DD employees established under section 5123.52 of the Revised Code, in addition to any other sanction or penalty authorized or required by law.

(C)(1) Any person listed in division (C)(2) of section 5123.61 of the Revised Code who has reason to believe that an MR/DD employee has violated division (A) of this section shall immediately report that belief to the department of developmental disabilities.

(2) Any person who has reason to believe that an MR/DD employee has violated division (A) of this section may report that belief to the department of developmental disabilities.

**HISTORY: 150 v S 178, § 1, eff. 1-30-04; 153 v S 79, § 1, eff. 10-6-09.**

## § 5123.542 Annual notice to employee explaining conduct for which employee may be included in registry.

(A) Each of the following shall annually provide a written notice to each of its MR/DD employees explaining the conduct for which an MR/DD employee may be included in the registry established under section 5123.52 of the Revised Code:

(1) The department of developmental disabilities;

(2) Each county board of developmental disabilities;

(3) Each contracting entity, as defined in section 5126.281 [5126.28.1] of the Revised Code;

(4) Each owner, operator, or administrator of a residential facility, as defined in section 5123.19 of the Revised Code;

(5) Each owner, operator, or administrator of a program certified by the department to provide supported living.

(B) The notice described in division (A) of this section shall be in a form and provided in a manner prescribed by the department of developmental disabilities. The form shall be the same for all persons and entities required to provide notice under division (A) of this section.

(C) The fact that an MR/DD employee does not receive the notice required by this section does not exempt the employee from inclusion in the registry established under section 5123.52 of the Revised Code.

**HISTORY: 150 v S 178, § 1, eff. 1-30-04; 153 v S 79, § 1, eff. 10-6-09.**

### [LEGAL RIGHTS SERVICES]

## § 5123.61 Duty to report abuse, neglect, and other major unusual incidents [Effective until October 1, 2012].

(A) As used in this section:

(1) "Law enforcement agency" means the state highway patrol, the police department of a municipal corporation, or a county sheriff.

(2) "Abuse" has the same meaning as in section 5123.50 of the Revised Code, except that it includes a misappropriation, as defined in that section.

(3) "Neglect" has the same meaning as in section 5123.50 of the Revised Code.

(B) The department of developmental disabilities shall establish a registry office for the purpose of maintaining reports of abuse, neglect, and other major unusual incidents made to the department under this section and reports received from county boards of developmental disabilities under section 5126.31 of the Revised Code. The department shall establish committees to review reports of abuse, neglect, and other major unusual incidents.

(C)(1) Any person listed in division (C)(2) of this section, having reason to believe that a person with mental retardation or a developmental disability has suffered or faces a substantial risk of suffering any wound, injury, disability, or condition of such a nature as to reasonably indicate abuse or neglect of that person, shall immediately report or cause reports to be made of such information to the entity specified in this division. Except as provided in section 5120.173 [5120.17.3] of the Revised Code or as otherwise provided in this division, the person making the report shall make it to a law enforcement agency or to the county board of developmental disabilities. If the report concerns a resident of a facility operated by the department of developmental disabilities the report shall be made either to a law enforcement agency or to the department. If the report concerns any act or omission of an employee of a county board of developmental disabilities, the report immediately shall be made to the department and to the county board.

(2) All of the following persons are required to make a report under division (C)(1) of this section:

(a) Any physician, including a hospital intern or resident, any dentist, podiatrist, chiropractor, practitioner of a limited branch of medicine as specified in section 4731.15 of the Revised Code, hospital administrator or employee of a hospital, nurse licensed under Chapter 4723. of the Revised Code, employee of an ambulatory health facility as defined in section 5101.61 of the Revised Code, employee of a home health agency, employee of an adult care facility licensed under Chapter 3722. of the Revised Code, or employee of a community mental health facility;

(b) Any school teacher or school authority, social worker, psychologist, attorney, peace officer, coroner, or residents' rights advocate as defined in section 3721.10 of the Revised Code;

(c) A superintendent, board member, or employee of a county board of developmental disabilities; an administrator, board member, or employee of a residential facility licensed under section 5123.19 of the Revised Code; an administrator, board member, or employee of any other public or private provider of services to a person with mental retardation or a developmental disability, or any MR/DD employee, as defined in section 5123.50 of the Revised Code;

(d) A member of a citizen's advisory council established at an institution or branch institution of the department of developmental disabilities under section 5123.092 [5123.09.2] of the Revised Code;

(e) A clergyman who is employed in a position that includes providing specialized services to an individual with mental retardation or another developmental disability, while acting in an official or professional capacity in that position, or a person who is employed in a position that includes providing specialized services to an individual with mental retardation or another developmental disability and who, while acting in an official or professional capacity, renders spiritual treatment through prayer in accordance with the tenets of an organized religion.

(3)(a) The reporting requirements of this division do not apply to members of the legal rights service commission or to employees of the legal rights service.

(b) An attorney or physician is not required to make a report pursuant to division (C)(1) of this section concerning any communication the attorney or physician receives from a client or patient in an attorney-client or physician-patient relationship, if, in accordance with division (A) or (B) of section 2317.02 of the Revised Code, the attorney or physician could not testify with respect to that communication in a civil or criminal proceeding, except that the client or patient is deemed to have waived any testimonial privilege under division (A) or (B) of section 2317.02 of the Revised Code with respect to that communication and the attorney or physician shall make a report pursuant to division (C)(1) of this section, if both of the following apply:

(i) The client or patient, at the time of the communication, is a person with mental retardation or a developmental disability.

(ii) The attorney or physician knows or suspects, as a result of the communication or any observations made during that communication, that the client or patient has suffered or faces a substantial risk of suffering any wound, injury, disability, or condition of a nature that reasonably indicates abuse or neglect of the client or patient.

(4) Any person who fails to make a report required under division (C) of this section and who is an MR/DD employee, as defined in section 5123.50 of the Revised Code, shall be eligible to be included in the registry regarding misappropriation, abuse, neglect, or other specified misconduct by MR/DD employees established under section 5123.52 of the Revised Code.

(D) The reports required under division (C) of this section shall be made forthwith by telephone or in person and shall be followed by a written report. The reports shall contain the following:

(1) The names and addresses of the person with mental retardation or a developmental disability and the person's custodian, if known;

(2) The age of the person with mental retardation or a developmental disability;

(3) Any other information that would assist in the investigation of the report.

(E) When a physician performing services as a member of the staff of a hospital or similar institution has reason to believe that a person with mental retardation or a developmental disability has suffered injury, abuse, or physical neglect, the physician shall notify the person in charge of the institution or that person's designated delegate, who shall make the necessary reports.

(F) Any person having reasonable cause to believe that a person with mental retardation or a developmental disability has suffered or faces a substantial risk of suffering abuse or neglect may report or cause a report to be made of that belief to the entity specified in this division. Except as provided in section 5120.173 [5120.17.3] of the Revised Code or as otherwise provided in this division, the person making the report shall make it to a law enforcement agency or the county board of developmental disabilities. If the person is a resident of a facility operated by the department of developmental disabilities, the report shall be made to a law enforcement agency or to the department. If the report concerns any act or omission of an employee of a county board of developmental disabilities, the report immediately shall be made to the department and to the county board.

(G)(1) Upon the receipt of a report concerning the possible abuse or neglect of a person with mental retardation or a developmental disability, the law enforcement agency shall inform the county board of developmental disabilities or, if the person is a resident of a facility operated by the department of developmental disabilities, the director of the department or the director's designee.

(2) On receipt of a report under this section that includes an allegation of action or inaction that may constitute a crime under federal law or the law of this state, the department of developmental disabilities shall notify the law enforcement agency.

(3) When a county board of developmental disabilities receives a report under this section that includes an allegation of action or inaction that may constitute a crime under federal law or the law of this state, the superintendent of the board or an individual the superintendent designates under division (H) of this section shall notify the law enforcement agency. The superintendent or individual shall notify the department of developmental disabilities when it receives any report under this section.

(4) When a county board of developmental disabilities receives a report under this section and believes that the degree of risk to the person is such that the report is an emergency, the superintendent of the board or an employee of the board the superintendent designates shall

attempt a face-to-face contact with the person with mental retardation or a developmental disability who allegedly is the victim within one hour of the board's receipt of the report.

(H) The superintendent of the board may designate an individual to be responsible for notifying the law enforcement agency and the department when the county board receives a report under this section.

(I) An adult with mental retardation or a developmental disability about whom a report is made may be removed from the adult's place of residence only by law enforcement officers who consider that the adult's immediate removal is essential to protect the adult from further injury or abuse or in accordance with the order of a court made pursuant to section 5126.33 of the Revised Code.

(J) A law enforcement agency shall investigate each report of abuse or neglect it receives under this section. In addition, the department, in cooperation with law enforcement officials, shall investigate each report regarding a resident of a facility operated by the department to determine the circumstances surrounding the injury, the cause of the injury, and the person responsible. The investigation shall be in accordance with the memorandum of understanding prepared under section 5126.058 [5126.05.8] of the Revised Code. The department shall determine, with the registry office which shall be maintained by the department, whether prior reports have been made concerning an adult with mental retardation or a developmental disability or other principals in the case. If the department finds that the report involves action or inaction that may constitute a crime under federal law or the law of this state, it shall submit a report of its investigation, in writing, to the law enforcement agency. If the person with mental retardation or a developmental disability is an adult, with the consent of the adult, the department shall provide such protective services as are necessary to protect the adult. The law enforcement agency shall make a written report of its findings to the department.

If the person is an adult and is not a resident of a facility operated by the department, the county board of developmental disabilities shall review the report of abuse or neglect in accordance with sections 5126.30 to 5126.33 of the Revised Code and the law enforcement agency shall make the written report of its findings to the county board.

(K) Any person or any hospital, institution, school, health department, or agency participating in the making of reports pursuant to this section, any person participating as a witness in an administrative or judicial proceeding resulting from the reports, or any person or governmental entity that discharges responsibilities under sections 5126.31 to 5126.33 of the Revised Code shall be immune from any civil or criminal liability that might otherwise be incurred or imposed as a result of such actions except liability for perjury, unless the person or governmental entity has acted in bad faith or with malicious purpose.

(L) No employer or any person with the authority to do so shall discharge, demote, transfer, prepare a negative work performance evaluation, reduce pay or benefits, terminate work privileges, or take any other action detrimental to an employee or retaliate against an employee as a result of the employee's having made a report under this section. This division does not preclude an employer or person with authority from taking action with regard to an employee who has made a report under this section if there is another reasonable basis for the action.

(M) Reports made under this section are not public records as defined in section 149.43 of the Revised Code. Information contained in the reports on request shall be made available to the person who is the subject of the report, to the person's legal counsel, and to agencies authorized to receive information in the report by the department or by a county board of developmental disabilities.

(N) Notwithstanding section 4731.22 of the Revised Code, the physician-patient privilege shall not be a ground for excluding evidence regarding the injuries or physical neglect of a person with mental retardation or a developmental disability or the cause thereof in any judicial proceeding resulting from a report submitted pursuant to this section.

**HISTORY: RC § 5123.98, 135 v S 336 (Eff 7-1-75); 137 v H 219 (Eff 11-1-77); RC § 5123.61, 138 v H 900 (Eff 7-1-80); 141 v H 66 (Eff 3-6-86); 142 v H 403 (Eff 3-16-89); 143 v H 569 (Eff 7-1-91); 145 v S 21 (Eff 10-29-93); 146 v H 670 (Eff 12-2-96); 147 v H 606 (Eff 3-9-99); 148 v S 171. Eff 11-22-2000; 150 v S 178, § 1, eff. 1-30-04; 153 v S 79, § 1, eff. 10-6-09.**

The provisions of § 3 of S.B. 178 (150 v —) read as follows:

SECTION 3. The Department of Mental Retardation and Developmental Disabilities shall adopt rules pursuant to Chapter 119. of the Revised Code that provide standards for the substantiation by the Department and by county boards of mental retardation of reports of abuse or neglect filed under section 5123.61 of the Revised Code.

**Not analogous to former RC § 5123.61 (GC § 1890-110; 117 v 581; 119 v 638; 121 v 442; Bureau of Code Revision, 10-1-53; 125 v 870), repealed 129 v 1448(1483), § 2, eff 10-25-61.**

## § 5123.61 Duty to report abuse, neglect, and other major unusual incidents [Effective October 1, 2012].

(A) As used in this section:

(1) "Law enforcement agency" means the state highway patrol, the police department of a municipal corporation, or a county sheriff.

(2) "Abuse" has the same meaning as in section 5123.50 of the Revised Code, except that it includes a misappropriation, as defined in that section.

(3) "Neglect" has the same meaning as in section 5123.50 of the Revised Code.

(B) The department of developmental disabilities shall establish a registry office for the purpose of maintaining reports of abuse, neglect, and other major unusual incidents made to the department under this section and reports received from county boards of developmental disabilities under section 5126.31 of the Revised Code. The department shall establish committees to review reports of abuse, neglect, and other major unusual incidents.

(C)(1) Any person listed in division (C)(2) of this section, having reason to believe that a person with mental retardation or a developmental disability has suffered or faces a substantial risk of suffering any wound, injury, disability, or condition of such a nature as to reasonably indicate abuse or neglect of that person, shall immediately report or cause reports to be made of such information to the entity specified in this division. Except as provided in section 5120.173 of the Revised Code or as otherwise provided in this division, the person making the report shall make it to a law enforcement agency or to the county board of developmental disabilities. If the report concerns a resident of a facility operated by the department of developmental disabilities the report shall be made either to a law enforcement agency or to the department. If the report concerns any act or omission of an employee of a county board of developmental disabilities, the report immediately shall be made to the department and to the county board.

(2) All of the following persons are required to make a report under division (C)(1) of this section:

(a) Any physician, including a hospital intern or resident, any dentist, podiatrist, chiropractor, practitioner of a limited branch of medicine as specified in section 4731.15 of the Revised Code, hospital administrator or employee of a hospital, nurse licensed under Chapter 4723. of the Revised Code, employee of an ambulatory health facility as defined in section 5101.61 of the Revised Code, employee of a home health agency, employee of an adult care facility licensed under Chapter 3722. of the Revised Code, or employee of a community mental health facility;

(b) Any school teacher or school authority, social worker, psychologist, attorney, peace officer, coroner, or residents' rights advocate as defined in section 3721.10 of the Revised Code;

(c) A superintendent, board member, or employee of a county board of developmental disabilities; an administrator, board member, or employee of a residential facility licensed under section 5123.19 of the Revised Code; an administrator, board member, or employee of any other public or private provider of services to a person with mental retardation or a developmental disability, or any MR/DD employee, as defined in section 5123.50 of the Revised Code;

(d) A member of a citizen's advisory council established at an institution or branch institution of the department of developmental disabilities under section 5123.092 of the Revised Code;

(e) A clergyman who is employed in a position that includes providing specialized services to an individual with mental retardation or another developmental disability, while acting in an official or professional capacity in that position, or a person who is employed in a position that includes providing specialized services to an individual with mental retardation or another developmental disability and who, while acting in an official or professional capacity, renders spiritual treatment through prayer in accordance with the tenets of an organized religion.

(3)(a) The reporting requirements of this division do not apply to employees of the Ohio protection and advocacy system.

(b) An attorney or physician is not required to make a report pursuant to division (C)(1) of this section concerning any communication the attorney or physician receives from a client or patient in an attorney-client or physician-patient relationship, if, in accordance with division (A) or (B) of section 2317.02 of the Revised Code, the attorney or physician could not testify with respect to that communication in a civil or criminal proceeding, except that the client or patient is deemed to have waived any testimonial privilege under division (A) or (B) of section 2317.02 of the Revised Code with respect to that communication and the attorney or physician shall make a report pursuant to division (C)(1) of this section, if both of the following apply:

(i) The client or patient, at the time of the communication, is a person with mental retardation or a developmental disability.

(ii) The attorney or physician knows or suspects, as a result of the communication or any observations made during that communication, that the client or patient has suffered or faces a substantial risk of suffering any wound, injury, disability, or condition of a nature that reasonably indicates abuse or neglect of the client or patient.

(4) Any person who fails to make a report required under division (C) of this section and who is an MR/DD employee, as defined in section 5123.50 of the Revised Code, shall be eligible to be included in the registry regarding misappropriation, abuse, neglect, or other specified misconduct by MR/DD employees established under section 5123.52 of the Revised Code.

(D) The reports required under division (C) of this section shall be made forthwith by telephone or in person and shall be followed by a written report. The reports shall contain the following:

(1) The names and addresses of the person with mental retardation or a developmental disability and the person's custodian, if known;

(2) The age of the person with mental retardation or a developmental disability;

(3) Any other information that would assist in the investigation of the report.

(E) When a physician performing services as a member of the staff of a hospital or similar institution has reason to believe that a person with mental retardation or a developmental disability has suffered injury, abuse, or physical neglect, the physician shall notify the person in charge of the institution or that person's designated delegate, who shall make the necessary reports.

(F) Any person having reasonable cause to believe that a person with mental retardation or a developmental disability has suffered or faces a substantial risk of suffering abuse or neglect may report or cause a report to be made of that belief to the entity specified in this division. Except as provided in section 5120.173 of the Revised Code or as otherwise provided in this division, the person making the report shall make it to a law enforcement agency or the county board of developmental disabilities. If the person is a resident of a facility operated by the department of developmental disabilities, the report shall be made to a law enforcement agency or to the department. If the report concerns any act or omission of an employee of a county board of developmental disabilities, the report immediately shall be made to the department and to the county board.

(G)(1) Upon the receipt of a report concerning the possible abuse or neglect of a person with mental retardation or a developmental disability, the law enforcement agency shall inform the county board of developmental disabilities or, if the person is a resident of a facility operated by the department of developmental disabilities, the director of the department or the director's designee.

(2) On receipt of a report under this section that includes an allegation of action or inaction that may constitute a crime under federal law or the law of this state, the department of developmental disabilities shall notify the law enforcement agency.

(3) When a county board of developmental disabilities receives a report under this section that includes an allegation of action or inaction that may constitute a crime under federal law or the law of this state, the superintendent of the board or an individual the superintendent designates under division (H) of this section shall notify the law enforcement agency. The superintendent or indi-

vidual shall notify the department of developmental disabilities when it receives any report under this section.

(4) When a county board of developmental disabilities receives a report under this section and believes that the degree of risk to the person is such that the report is an emergency, the superintendent of the board or an employee of the board the superintendent designates shall attempt a face-to-face contact with the person with mental retardation or a developmental disability who allegedly is the victim within one hour of the board's receipt of the report.

(H) The superintendent of the board may designate an individual to be responsible for notifying the law enforcement agency and the department when the county board receives a report under this section.

(I) An adult with mental retardation or a developmental disability about whom a report is made may be removed from the adult's place of residence only by law enforcement officers who consider that the adult's immediate removal is essential to protect the adult from further injury or abuse or in accordance with the order of a court made pursuant to section 5126.33 of the Revised Code.

(J) A law enforcement agency shall investigate each report of abuse or neglect it receives under this section. In addition, the department, in cooperation with law enforcement officials, shall investigate each report regarding a resident of a facility operated by the department to determine the circumstances surrounding the injury, the cause of the injury, and the person responsible. The investigation shall be in accordance with the memorandum of understanding prepared under section 5126.058 of the Revised Code. The department shall determine, with the registry office which shall be maintained by the department, whether prior reports have been made concerning an adult with mental retardation or a developmental disability or other principals in the case. If the department finds that the report involves action or inaction that may constitute a crime under federal law or the law of this state, it shall submit a report of its investigation, in writing, to the law enforcement agency. If the person with mental retardation or a developmental disability is an adult, with the consent of the adult, the department shall provide such protective services as are necessary to protect the adult. The law enforcement agency shall make a written report of its findings to the department.

If the person is an adult and is not a resident of a facility operated by the department, the county board of developmental disabilities shall review the report of abuse or neglect in accordance with sections 5126.30 to 5126.33 of the Revised Code and the law enforcement agency shall make the written report of its findings to the county board.

(K) Any person or any hospital, institution, school, health department, or agency participating in the making of reports pursuant to this section, any person participating as a witness in an administrative or judicial proceeding resulting from the reports, or any person or governmental entity that discharges responsibilities under sections 5126.31 to 5126.33 of the Revised Code shall be immune from any civil or criminal liability that might otherwise be incurred or imposed as a result of such actions except liability for perjury, unless the person or governmental entity has acted in bad faith or with malicious purpose.

(L) No employer or any person with the authority to do so shall discharge, demote, transfer, prepare a negative work performance evaluation, reduce pay or benefits, terminate work privileges, or take any other action detrimental to an employee or retaliate against an employee as a result of the employee's having made a report under this section. This division does not preclude an employer or person with authority from taking action with regard to an employee who has made a report under this section if there is another reasonable basis for the action.

(M) Reports made under this section are not public records as defined in section 149.43 of the Revised Code. Information contained in the reports on request shall be made available to the person who is the subject of the report, to the person's legal counsel, and to agencies authorized to receive information in the report by the department or by a county board of developmental disabilities.

(N) Notwithstanding section 4731.22 of the Revised Code, the physician-patient privilege shall not be a ground for excluding evidence regarding the injuries or physical neglect of a person with mental retardation or a developmental disability or the cause thereof in any judicial proceeding resulting from a report submitted pursuant to this section.

**HISTORY: RC § 5123.98, 135 v S 336 (Eff 7-1-75); 137 v H 219 (Eff 11-1-77); RC § 5123.61, 138 v H 900 (Eff 7-1-80); 141 v H 66 (Eff 3-6-86); 142 v H 403 (Eff 3-16-89); 143 v H 569 (Eff 7-1-91); 145 v S 21 (Eff 10-29-93); 146 v H 670 (Eff 12-2-96); 147 v H 606 (Eff 3-9-99); 148 v S 171. Eff 11-22-2000; 150 v S 178, § 1, eff. 1-30-04; 153 v S 79, § 1, eff. 10-6-09; 2011 HB 153, § 120.20, eff. Oct. 1, 2012.**

## § 5123.614 Independent review or investigation of major unusual incident report.

(A) Subject to division (B) of this section, on receipt of a report of a major unusual incident made pursuant to section 5123.61 or 5126.31 of the Revised Code or rules adopted under section 5123.612 [5123.61.2] of the Revised Code, the department of developmental disabilities may do either of the following:

(1) Conduct an independent review or investigation of the incident;

(2) Request that an independent review or investigation of the incident be conducted by a county board of developmental disabilities that is not implicated in the report, a regional council of government, or any other entity authorized to conduct such investigations.

(B) If a report described in division (A) of this section concerning the health or safety of a person with mental retardation or a developmental disability involves an allegation that an employee of a county board of developmental disabilities has created a substantial risk of serious physical harm to a person with mental retardation or a developmental disability, the department shall do one of the following:

(1) Conduct an independent investigation regarding the incident;

(2) Request that an independent review or investigation of the incident be conducted by a county board of developmental disabilities that is not implicated in the report, a regional council of government, or any other entity authorized to conduct such investigations.

**HISTORY: 150 v S 178, § 1, eff. 1-30-04; 153 v S 79, § 1, eff. 10-6-09.**

### [ADMISSIONS GUIDELINES]

## § 5123.69 Voluntary admission [Effective until October 1, 2012].

(A) Except as provided in division (E) of this section, any person who is eighteen years of age or older and who is or believes self to be mentally retarded may make written application to the managing officer of any institution for voluntary admission. Except as provided in division (E) of this section, the application may be made on behalf of a minor by a parent or guardian, and on behalf of an adult adjudicated mentally incompetent by a guardian.

(B) The managing officer of an institution, with the concurrence of the chief program director, may admit a person applying pursuant to this section only after a comprehensive evaluation has been made of the person and only if the comprehensive evaluation concludes that the person is mentally retarded and would benefit significantly from admission.

(C) If application for voluntary admission of a minor or of a person adjudicated mentally incompetent is made by the parent or guardian of the minor or by the guardian of an incompetent and the minor or incompetent is admitted, the probate division of the court of common pleas shall determine, upon petition by the legal rights service, whether the voluntary admission or continued institutionalization is in the best interest of the minor or incompetent.

(D) The managing officer shall discharge any voluntary resident if, in the judgment of the chief program director, the results of a comprehensive examination indicate that institutionalization no longer is advisable. In light of the results of the comprehensive evaluation, the managing officer also may discharge any voluntary resident if, in the judgment of the chief program director, the discharge would contribute to the most effective use of the institution in the habilitation and care of the mentally retarded.

(E) A person who is found incompetent to stand trial or not guilty by reason of insanity and who is committed pursuant to section 2945.39, 2945.40, 2945.401 [2945.40.1], or 2945.402 [2945.40.2] of the Revised Code shall not voluntarily commit self pursuant to this section until after the final termination of the commitment, as described in division (J) of section 2945.401 [2945.40.1] of the Revised Code.

**HISTORY: 135 v S 336 (Eff 7-1-75); 138 v S 297 (Eff 4-30-80); 146 v S 285. Eff 7-1-97.**

The effective date is set by section 4 of SB 285.

## § 5123.69 Voluntary admission [Effective October 1, 2012].

(A) Except as provided in division (D) of this section, any person who is eighteen years of age or older and who is or believes self to be mentally retarded may make written application to the managing officer of any institution for voluntary admission. Except as provided in division (D) of this section, the application may be made on behalf of a minor by a parent or guardian, and on behalf of an adult adjudicated mentally incompetent by a guardian.

(B) The managing officer of an institution, with the concurrence of the chief program director, may admit a person applying pursuant to this section only after a comprehensive evaluation has been made of the person and only if the comprehensive evaluation concludes that the person is mentally retarded and would benefit significantly from admission.

(C) The managing officer shall discharge any voluntary resident if, in the judgment of the chief program director, the results of a comprehensive examination indicate that institutionalization no longer is advisable. In light of the results of the comprehensive evaluation, the managing officer also may discharge any voluntary resident if, in the judgment of the chief program director, the discharge would contribute to the most effective use of the institution in the habilitation and care of the mentally retarded.

(D) A person who is found incompetent to stand trial or not guilty by reason of insanity and who is committed pursuant to section 2945.39, 2945.40, 2945.401, or 2945.402 of the Revised Code shall not voluntarily commit self pursuant to this section until after the final termination of the commitment, as described in division (J) of section 2945.401 of the Revised Code.

**HISTORY: 2011 HB 153, § 120.20, eff. Oct. 1, 2012.**

## § 5123.701 Application for admission for short-term care [Effective until October 1, 2012].

(A) Except as provided in division (E) of this section, any person in the community who is eighteen years of age or older and who is or believes self to be mentally retarded may make written application to the managing officer of any institution for temporary admission for short-term care. The application may be made on behalf of a minor by a parent or guardian, and on behalf of an adult adjudicated mentally incompetent by a guardian.

(B) For purposes of this section, short-term care shall be defined to mean appropriate services provided to a person with mental retardation for no more than fourteen consecutive days and for no more than forty-two days in a fiscal year. When circumstances warrant, the fourteen-day period may be extended at the discretion of the managing officer. Short-term care is provided in a developmental center to meet the family's or caretaker's needs for separation from the person with mental retardation.

(C) The managing officer of an institution, with the concurrence of the chief program director, may admit a person for short-term care only after a medical examination has been made of the person and only if the managing officer concludes that the person is mentally retarded.

(D) If application for admission for short-term care of a minor or of a person adjudicated mentally incompetent is made by the minor's parent or guardian or by the incompetent's guardian and the minor or incompetent is admitted, the probate division of the court of common pleas shall determine, upon petition by the legal rights service, whether the admission for short-term care is in the best interest of the minor or the incompetent.

(E) A person who is found not guilty by reason of insanity shall not admit self to an institution for short-term care unless a hearing was held regarding the person pursuant to division (A) of section 2945.40 of the Revised Code and either of the following applies:

(1) The person was found at the hearing not to be a mentally retarded person subject to institutionalization by court order;

(2) The person was found at the hearing to be a mentally retarded person subject to institutionalization by court order, was involuntarily committed, and was finally discharged.

(F) The mentally retarded person, liable relatives, and guardians of mentally retarded persons admitted for respite care shall pay support charges in accordance with sections 5121.01 to 5121.21 of the Revised Code.

(G) At the conclusion of each period of short-term care, the person shall return to the person's family or caretaker. Under no circumstances shall a person admitted for short-term care according to this section remain in the institution after the period of short-term care unless the person is admitted according to section 5123.70, sections 5123.71 to 5123.76, or section 2945.38, 2945.39, 2945.40, 2945.401 [2945.40.1], or 2945.402 [2945.40.2] of the Revised Code.

**HISTORY: 139 v H 694 (Eff 11-15-81); 146 v S 285. Eff 7-1-97; 151 v H 66, § 101.01, eff. 1-1-06.**

The effective date is set by § 612.09 of 151 v H 66.
The effective date is set by section 4 of SB 285.

## § 5123.701 Application for admission for short-term care [Effective October 1, 2012].

(A) Except as provided in division (D) of this section, any person in the community who is eighteen years of age or older and who is or believes self to be mentally retarded may make written application to the managing officer of any institution for temporary admission for short-term care. The application may be made on behalf of a minor by a parent or guardian, and on behalf of an adult adjudicated mentally incompetent by a guardian.

(B) For purposes of this section, short-term care shall be defined to mean appropriate services provided to a person with mental retardation for no more than fourteen consecutive days and for no more than forty-two days in a fiscal year. When circumstances warrant, the fourteen-day period may be extended at the discretion of the managing officer. Short-term care is provided in a developmental center to meet the family's or caretaker's needs for separation from the person with mental retardation.

(C) The managing officer of an institution, with the concurrence of the chief program director, may admit a person for short-term care only after a medical examination has been made of the person and only if the managing officer concludes that the person is mentally retarded.

(D) A person who is found not guilty by reason of insanity shall not admit self to an institution for short-term care unless a hearing was held regarding the person pursuant to division (A) of section 2945.40 of the Revised Code and either of the following applies:

(1) The person was found at the hearing not to be a mentally retarded person subject to institutionalization by court order;

(2) The person was found at the hearing to be a mentally retarded person subject to institutionalization by court order, was involuntarily committed, and was finally discharged.

(E) The mentally retarded person, liable relatives, and guardians of mentally retarded persons admitted for respite care shall pay support charges in accordance with sections 5121.01 to 5121.21 of the Revised Code.

(F) At the conclusion of each period of short-term care, the person shall return to the person's family or caretaker. Under no circumstances shall a person admitted for short-term care according to this section remain in the institution after the period of short-term care unless the person is admitted according to section 5123.70, sections 5123.71 to 5123.76, or section 2945.38, 2945.39, 2945.40, 2945.401, or 2945.402 of the Revised Code.

**HISTORY: 139 v H 694 (Eff 11-15-81); 146 v S 285. Eff 7-1-97; 151 v H 66, § 101.01, eff. 1-1-06; 2011 HB 153, § 120.20, eff. Oct. 1, 2012.**

## § 5123.76 Full hearing by probate judge, common pleas judge, or referee; disposition orders or discharge.

(A) The full hearing shall be conducted in a manner consistent with the procedures outlined in this chapter and with due process of law. The hearing shall be held by a judge of the probate division or, upon transfer by the judge of the probate division, by another judge of the court of common pleas, or a referee designated by the judge of the probate division. Any referee designated by the judge of the probate division must be an attorney.

(1) The following shall be made available to counsel for the respondent:

(a) All relevant documents, information, and evidence in the custody or control of the state or prosecutor;

(b) All relevant documents, information, and evidence in the custody or control of the institution, facility, or program in which the respondent currently is held or in which the respondent has been held pursuant to these proceedings;

(c) With the consent of the respondent, all relevant documents, information, and evidence in the custody or control of any institution or person other than the state.

(2) The respondent has the right to be represented by counsel of the respondent's choice and has the right to attend the hearing except if unusual circumstances of compelling medical necessity exist that render the respondent unable to attend and the respondent has not expressed a desire to attend.

(3) If the respondent is not represented by counsel and the court determines that the conditions specified in division (A)(2) of this section justify the respondent's absence and the right to counsel has not been validly waived, the court shall appoint counsel forthwith to represent the respondent at the hearing, reserving the right to tax costs of appointed counsel to the respondent unless it is shown that the respondent is indigent. If the court appoints counsel, or if the court determines that the evidence relevant to the respondent's absence does not justify the absence, the court shall continue the case.

(4) The respondent shall be informed of the right to retain counsel, to have independent expert evaluation, and, if an indigent person, to be represented by court appointed counsel and have expert independent evaluation at court expense.

(5) The hearing may be closed to the public unless counsel for the respondent requests that the hearing be open to the public.

(6) Unless objected to by the respondent, the respondent's counsel, or the designee of the director of developmental disabilities, the court, for good cause shown, may admit persons having a legitimate interest in the proceedings.

(7) The affiant under section 5123.71 of the Revised Code shall be subject to subpoena by either party.

(8) The court shall examine the sufficiency of all documents filed and shall inform the respondent, if present, and the respondent's counsel of the nature of the content of the documents and the reason for which the respondent is being held or for which the respondent's placement is being sought.

(9) The court shall receive only relevant, competent, and material evidence.

(10) The designee of the director shall present the evidence for the state. In proceedings under this chapter, the attorney general shall present the comprehensive evaluation, assessment, diagnosis, prognosis, record of habilitation and care, if any, and less restrictive habilitation plans, if any. The attorney general does not have a similar presentation responsibility in connection with a person who has been found not guilty by reason of insanity and who is the subject of a hearing under section 2945.40 of

the Revised Code to determine whether the person is a mentally retarded person subject to institutionalization by court order.

(11) The respondent has the right to testify and the respondent or the respondent's counsel has the right to subpoena witnesses and documents and to present and cross-examine witnesses.

(12) The respondent shall not be compelled to testify and shall be so advised by the court.

(13) On motion of the respondent or the respondent's counsel for good cause shown, or upon the court's own motion, the court may order a continuance of the hearing.

(14) To an extent not inconsistent with this chapter, the Rules of Civil Procedure shall be applicable.

(B) Unless, upon completion of the hearing, the court finds by clear and convincing evidence that the respondent named in the affidavit is a mentally retarded person subject to institutionalization by court order, it shall order the respondent's discharge forthwith.

(C) If, upon completion of the hearing, the court finds by clear and convincing evidence that the respondent is a mentally retarded person subject to institutionalization by court order, the court may order the respondent's discharge or order the respondent, for a period not to exceed ninety days, to any of the following:

(1) A public institution, provided that commitment of the respondent to the institution will not cause the institution to exceed its licensed capacity determined in accordance with section 5123.19 of the Revised Code and provided that such a placement is indicated by the comprehensive evaluation report filed pursuant to section 5123.71 of the Revised Code;

(2) A private institution;

(3) A county mental retardation program;

(4) Receive private habilitation and care;

(5) Any other suitable facility, program, or the care of any person consistent with the comprehensive evaluation, assessment, diagnosis, prognosis, and habilitation needs of the respondent.

(D) Any order made pursuant to division (C)(2), (4), or (5) of this section shall be conditional upon the receipt by the court of consent by the facility, program, or person to accept the respondent.

(E) In determining the place to which, or the person with whom, the respondent is to be committed, the court shall consider the comprehensive evaluation, assessment, diagnosis, and projected habilitation plan for the respondent, and shall order the implementation of the least restrictive alternative available and consistent with habilitation goals.

(F) If, at any time it is determined by the director of the facility or program to which, or the person to whom, the respondent is committed that the respondent could be equally well habilitated in a less restrictive environment that is available, the following shall occur:

(1) The respondent shall be released by the director of the facility or program or by the person forthwith and referred to the court together with a report of the findings and recommendations of the facility, program, or person.

(2) The director of the facility or program or the person shall notify the respondent's counsel and the designee of the director of developmental disabilities.

(3) The court shall dismiss the case or order placement in the less restrictive environment.

(G)(1) Except as provided in divisions (G)(2) and (3) of this section, any person who has been committed under this section may apply at any time during the ninety-day period for voluntary admission to an institution under section 5123.69 of the Revised Code. Upon admission of a voluntary resident, the managing officer immediately shall notify the court, the respondent's counsel, and the designee of the director in writing of that fact by mail or otherwise, and, upon receipt of the notice, the court shall dismiss the case.

(2) A person who is found incompetent to stand trial or not guilty by reason of insanity and who is committed pursuant to section 2945.39, 2945.40, 2945.401 [2945.40.1], or 2945.402 [2945.40.2] of the Revised Code shall not be voluntarily admitted to an institution pursuant to division (G)(1) of this section until after the termination of the commitment, as described in division (J) of section 2945.401 [2945.40.1] of the Revised Code.

(H) If, at the end of any commitment period, the respondent has not already been discharged or has not requested voluntary admission status, the director of the facility or program, or the person to whose care the respondent has been committed, shall discharge the respondent forthwith, unless at least ten days before the expiration of that period the designee of the director of developmental disabilities or the prosecutor files an application with the court requesting continued commitment.

(1) An application for continued commitment shall include a written report containing a current comprehensive evaluation and assessment, a diagnosis, a prognosis, an account of progress and past habilitation, and a description of alternative habilitation settings and plans, including a habilitation setting that is the least restrictive setting consistent with the need for habilitation. A copy of the application shall be provided to respondent's counsel. The requirements for notice under section 5123.73 of the Revised Code and the provisions of divisions (A) to (E) of this section apply to all hearings on such applications.

(2) A hearing on the first application for continued commitment shall be held at the expiration of the first ninety-day period. The hearing shall be mandatory and may not be waived.

(3) Subsequent periods of commitment not to exceed one hundred eighty days each may be ordered by the court if the designee of the director of developmental disabilities files an application for continued commitment, after a hearing is held on the application or without a hearing if no hearing is requested and no hearing required under division (H)(4) of this section is waived. Upon the application of a person involuntarily committed under this section, supported by an affidavit of a licensed physician alleging that the person is no longer a mentally retarded person subject to institutionalization by court order, the court for good cause shown may hold a full hearing on the person's continued commitment prior to the expiration of any subsequent period of commitment set by the court.

(4) A mandatory hearing shall be held at least every two years after the initial commitment.

(5) If the court, after a hearing upon a request to continue commitment, finds that the respondent is a mentally retarded person subject to institutionalization by court order, the court may make an order pursuant to divisions (C), (D), and (E) of this section.

(I) Notwithstanding the provisions of division (H) of this section, no person who is found to be a mentally retarded person subject to institutionalization by court order pursuant to division (O)(2) of section 5123.01 of the Revised Code shall be held under involuntary commitment for more than five years.

(J) The managing officer admitting a person pursuant to a judicial proceeding, within ten working days of the admission, shall make a report of the admission to the department.

**HISTORY: 135 v S 336 (Eff 7-1-75); 138 v S 297 (Eff 4-30-80); 138 v H 900 (Eff 7-1-80); 138 v H 965 (Eff 4-9-81); 142 v H 231 (Eff 10-5-87); 145 v S 21 (Eff 10-29-93); 146 v H 567 (Eff 10-29-96); 146 v H 629 (Eff 3-13-97); 146 v S 285 (Eff 7-1-97); 149 v H 94. Eff 6-6-2001; 151 v H 66, § 101.01, eff. 7-1-05; 153 v S 79, § 1, eff. 10-6-09.**

The effective date is set by § 612.18 of 151 v H 66.

The effective date is set by section 206 of HB 94.

The provisions of § 247 of HB 94 (149 v —) read as follows:

SECTION 247. Section 5123.76 of the Revised Code is presented in this act as a composite of the section as amended by both Sub. H.B. 629 and Am. Sub. S.B. 285 of the 121st General Assembly. The General Assembly, applying the principle stated in division (B) of section 1.52 of the Revised Code that amendments are to be harmonized if reasonably capable of simultaneous operation, finds that the composite is the resulting version of the section in effect prior to the effective date of the section as presented in this act.

## § 5123.99 Penalties [Effective until October 1, 2012].

(A) Whoever violates section 5123.16 or 5123.20 of the Revised Code is guilty of a misdemeanor of the first degree.

(B) Whoever violates division (C), (E), or (G)(3) of section 5123.61 of the Revised Code is guilty of a misdemeanor of the fourth degree or, if the abuse or neglect constitutes a felony, a misdemeanor of the second degree. In addition to any other sanction or penalty authorized or required by law, if a person who is convicted of or pleads guilty to a violation of division (C), (E), or (G)(3) of section 5123.61 of the Revised Code is an MR/DD employee, as defined in section 5123.50 of the Revised Code, the offender shall be eligible to be included in the registry regarding misappropriation, abuse, neglect, or other specified misconduct by MR/DD employees established under section 5123.52 of the Revised Code.

(C) Whoever violates division (A) of section 5123.604 [5123.60.4] of the Revised Code is guilty of a misdemeanor of the second degree.

(D) Whoever violates division (B) of section 5123.604 [5123.60.4] of the Revised Code shall be fined not more than one thousand dollars. Each violation constitutes a separate offense.

**HISTORY: Bureau of Code Revision, 10-1-53; 129 v 1448(1479) (Eff 10-25-61); 133 v S 367 (Eff 6-8-70); 137 v S 71 (Eff 10-31-77); 137 v H 870 (Eff 9-25-78); 138 v H 900 (Eff 7-1-80); 141 v H 66 (Eff 3-6-86); 141 v S 322 (Eff 4-4-86); 145 v S 21. Eff 10-29-93; 150 v S 178, § 1, eff. 1-30-04; 152 v H 119, § 101.01, eff. 6-30-07.**

The effective date is set by § 815.03 of 152 v H 119.

## § 5123.99 Penalties [Effective October 1, 2012].

(A) Whoever violates section 5123.16 or 5123.20 of the Revised Code is guilty of a misdemeanor of the first degree.

(B) Whoever violates division (C), (E), or (G)(3) of section 5123.61 of the Revised Code is guilty of a misdemeanor of the fourth degree or, if the abuse or neglect constitutes a felony, a misdemeanor of the second degree. In addition to any other sanction or penalty authorized or required by law, if a person who is convicted of or pleads guilty to a violation of division (C), (E), or (G)(3) of section 5123.61 of the Revised Code is an MR/DD employee, as defined in section 5123.50 of the Revised Code, the offender shall be eligible to be included in the registry regarding misappropriation, abuse, neglect, or other specified misconduct by MR/DD employees established under section 5123.52 of the Revised Code.

**HISTORY: Bureau of Code Revision, 10-1-53; 129 v 1448(1479) (Eff 10-25-61); 133 v S 367 (Eff 6-8-70); 137 v S 71 (Eff 10-31-77); 137 v H 870 (Eff 9-25-78); 138 v H 900 (Eff 7-1-80); 141 v H 66 (Eff 3-6-86); 141 v S 322 (Eff 4-4-86); 145 v S 21. Eff 10-29-93; 150 v S 178, § 1, eff. 1-30-04; 152 v H 119, § 101.01, eff. 6-30-07; 2011 HB 153, § 120.20, eff. Oct. 1, 2012.**

# CHAPTER 5126: COUNTY BOARDS OF DEVELOPMENTAL DISABILITIES

Section



## [EMPLOYEES]

## § 5126.28 Criminal records check and fingerprinting of prospective employees; employment of certain offenders prohibited.

(A) As used in this section:

(1) "Applicant" means a person who is under final consideration for appointment to or employment in a position with a county board of developmental disabilities, including, but not limited to, a person who is being transferred to the county board and an employee who is being recalled or reemployed after a layoff.

(2) "Criminal records check" has the same meaning as in section 109.572 [109.57.2] of the Revised Code.

(3) "Minor drug possession offense" has the same meaning as in section 2925.01 of the Revised Code.

(B) The superintendent of a county board of developmental disabilities shall request the superintendent of the bureau of criminal identification and investigation to conduct a criminal records check with respect to any applicant who has applied to the board for employment in any position, except that a county board superintendent is not required to request a criminal records check for an employee of the board who is being considered for a different position or is returning after a leave of absence or seasonal break in employment, as long as the superintendent has no reason to believe that the employee has committed any of the offenses listed or described in division (E) of this section.

If the applicant does not present proof that the applicant has been a resident of this state for the five-year period immediately prior to the date upon which the criminal records check is requested, the county board superintendent shall request that the superintendent of the bureau obtain information from the federal bureau of investigation as a part of the criminal records check for the applicant. If the applicant presents proof that the applicant has been a resident of this state for that five-year period, the county board superintendent may request that the superintendent of the bureau include information from the federal bureau of investigation in the criminal records check. For purposes of this division, an applicant may provide proof of residency in this state by presenting, with a notarized statement asserting that the applicant has been a resident of this state for that five-year period, a valid driver's license, notification of registration as an elector, a copy of an officially filed federal or state tax form identifying the applicant's permanent residence, or any other document the superintendent considers acceptable.

(C) The county board superintendent shall provide to each applicant a copy of the form prescribed pursuant to division (C)(1) of section 109.572 [109.57.2] of the Revised Code, provide to each applicant a standard impression sheet to obtain fingerprint impressions prescribed pursuant to division (C)(2) of section 109.572 [109.57.2] of the Revised Code, obtain the completed form and impression sheet from each applicant, and forward the completed form and impression sheet to the superintendent of the bureau of criminal identification and investigation at the time the criminal records check is requested.

Any applicant who receives pursuant to this division a copy of the form prescribed pursuant to division (C)(1) of section 109.572 [109.57.2] of the Revised Code and a copy of an impression sheet prescribed pursuant to division (C)(2) of that section and who is requested to complete the form and provide a set of fingerprint impressions shall complete the form or provide all the information necessary to complete the form and shall provide the impression sheet with the impressions of the applicant's fingerprints. If an applicant, upon request, fails to provide the information necessary to complete the form or fails to provide impressions of the applicant's fingerprints, the county board superintendent shall not employ that applicant.

(D) A county board superintendent may request any other state or federal agency to supply the board with a written report regarding the criminal record of each applicant. With regard to an applicant who becomes a board employee, if the employee holds an occupational or professional license or other credentials, the superintendent may request that the state or federal agency that regulates the employee's occupation or profession supply the board with a written report of any information pertaining to the employee's criminal record that the agency obtains in the course of conducting an investigation or in the process of renewing the employee's license or other credentials.

(E) Except as provided in division (K)(2) of this section and in rules adopted by the department of developmental disabilities in accordance with division (M) of this section, no county board of developmental disabilities shall employ a person to fill a position with the board who has been convicted of or pleaded guilty to any of the following:

(1) A violation of section 2903.01, 2903.02, 2903.03, 2903.04, 2903.11, 2903.12, 2903.13, 2903.16, 2903.21, 2903.34, 2903.341 [2903.34.1], 2905.01, 2905.02, 2905.05, 2907.02, 2907.03, 2907.04, 2907.05, 2907.06, 2907.07, 2907.08, 2907.09, 2907.21, 2907.22, 2907.23, 2907.25, 2907.31, 2907.32, 2907.321 [2907.32.1], 2907.322 [2907.32.2], 2907.323 [2907.32.3], 2911.01, 2911.02, 2911.11, 2911.12, 2919.12, 2919.22, 2919.24, 2919.25, 2923.12, 2923.13, 2923.161 [2923.16.1], 2925.02, 2925.03, 2925.04, 2925.05, 2925.06, or 3716.11 of the Revised Code, a violation of section 2905.04 of the Revised Code as it existed prior to July 1, 1996, a violation of section 2919.23 of the Revised Code that would have been a violation of section 2905.04 of the Revised Code as it existed prior to July 1, 1996, had the violation occurred prior to that date, a violation of section 2925.11 of the Revised Code that is not a minor drug possession offense, or felonious sexual penetration in violation of former section 2907.12 of the Revised Code;

(2) A felony contained in the Revised Code that is not listed in this division, if the felony bears a direct and substantial relationship to the duties and responsibilities of the position being filled;

(3) Any offense contained in the Revised Code constituting a misdemeanor of the first degree on the first offense and a felony on a subsequent offense, if the offense bears a direct and substantial relationship to the position being filled and the nature of the services being provided by the county board;

(4) A violation of an existing or former municipal ordinance or law of this state, any other state, or the United States, if the offense is substantially equivalent to any of the offenses listed or described in division (E)(1), (2), or (3) of this section.

(F) Prior to employing an applicant, the county board superintendent shall require the applicant to submit a statement with the applicant's signature attesting that the applicant has not been convicted of or pleaded guilty to any of the offenses listed or described in division (E) of this section. The superintendent also shall require the applicant to sign an agreement under which the applicant agrees to notify the superintendent within fourteen calendar days if, while employed by the board, the applicant is ever formally charged with, convicted of, or pleads guilty to any of the offenses listed or described in division (E) of this section. The agreement shall inform the applicant that failure to report formal charges, a conviction, or a guilty plea may result in being dismissed from employment.

(G) A county board of developmental disabilities shall pay to the bureau of criminal identification and investigation the fee prescribed pursuant to division (C)(3) of section 109.572 [109.57.2] of the Revised Code for each criminal records check requested and conducted pursuant to this section.

(H)(1) Any report obtained pursuant to this section is not a public record for purposes of section 149.43 of the Revised Code and shall not be made available to any person, other than the applicant who is the subject of the records check or criminal records check or the applicant's representative, the board requesting the records check or criminal records check or its representative, the department of developmental disabilities, and any court, hearing officer, or other necessary individual involved in a case dealing with the denial of employment to the applicant or the denial, suspension, or revocation of a certificate or evidence of registration under section 5126.25 of the Revised Code.

(2) An individual for whom a county board superintendent has obtained reports under this section may submit a written request to the county board to have copies of the reports sent to any state agency, entity of local government, or private entity. The individual shall specify in the request the agencies or entities to which the copies are to

be sent. On receiving the request, the county board shall send copies of the reports to the agencies or entities specified.

A county board may request that a state agency, entity of local government, or private entity send copies to the board of any report regarding a records check or criminal records check that the agency or entity possesses, if the county board obtains the written consent of the individual who is the subject of the report.

(I) Each county board superintendent shall request the registrar of motor vehicles to supply the superintendent with a certified abstract regarding the record of convictions for violations of motor vehicle laws of each applicant who will be required by the applicant's employment to transport individuals with mental retardation or developmental disabilities or to operate the board's vehicles for any other purpose. For each abstract provided under this section, the board shall pay the amount specified in section 4509.05 of the Revised Code.

(J) The county board superintendent shall provide each applicant with a copy of any report or abstract obtained about the applicant under this section. At the request of the director of developmental disabilities, the superintendent also shall provide the director with a copy of a report or abstract obtained under this section.

(K)(1) The county board superintendent shall inform each person, at the time of the person's initial application for employment, that the person is required to provide a set of impressions of the person's fingerprints and that a criminal records check is required to be conducted and satisfactorily completed in accordance with section 109.572 [109.57.2] of the Revised Code if the person comes under final consideration for appointment or employment as a precondition to employment in a position.

(2) A board may employ an applicant pending receipt of reports requested under this section. The board shall terminate employment of any such applicant if it is determined from the reports that the applicant failed to inform the county board that the applicant had been convicted of or pleaded guilty to any of the offenses listed or described in division (E) of this section.

(L) The board may charge an applicant a fee for costs it incurs in obtaining reports, abstracts, or fingerprint impressions under this section. A fee charged under this division shall not exceed the amount of the fees the board pays under divisions (G) and (I) of this section. If a fee is charged under this division, the board shall notify the applicant of the amount of the fee at the time of the applicant's initial application for employment and that, unless the fee is paid, the board will not consider the applicant for employment.

(M) The department of developmental disabilities shall adopt rules pursuant to Chapter 119. of the Revised Code to implement this section and section 5126.281 [5126.28.1] of the Revised Code, including rules specifying circumstances under which a county board or contracting entity may hire a person who has been convicted of or pleaded guilty to an offense listed or described in division (E) of this section but who meets standards in regard to rehabilitation set by the department. The rules may not authorize a county board or contracting entity to hire an individual who is included in the registry established under section 5123.52 of the Revised Code.

**HISTORY: 144 v H 387 (Eff 5-4-92); 145 v S 38 (Eff 10-29-93); 145 v H 694 (Eff 11-11-94); 146 v S 2 (Eff 7-1-96); 146 v H 445 (Eff 9-3-96); 146 v S 269 (Eff 9-26-96); 146 v H 629 (Eff 3-13-97); 148 v H 538 (Eff 9-22-2000); 148 v S 171. Eff 11-22-2000; 150 v S 178, § 1, eff. 1-30-04; 153 v S 79, § 1, eff. 10-6-09.**

**Comment, Legislative Service Commission**

Section 5126.28 of the Revised Code is amended by this act [Sub. S.B. 171] and also by Sub. H.B. 538 of the 123rd General Assembly. Comparison of these amendments in pursuance of section 1.52 of the Revised Code discloses that they are not irreconcilable so that they are required by that section to be harmonized to give effect to each amendment.

## § 5126.281 Background investigations of prospective employees of contracting entities; restrictions on certain offenders.

(A) As used in this section:

(1) "Contracting entity" means an entity under contract with a county board of developmental disabilities for the provision of specialized services to individuals with mental retardation or a developmental disability.

(2) "Direct services position" means an employment position in which the employee has physical contact with, the opportunity to be alone with, or exercises supervision or control over one or more individuals with mental retardation or a developmental disability.

(3) "Specialized services" means any program or service designed and operated to serve primarily individuals with mental retardation or a developmental disability, including a program or service provided by an entity licensed or certified by the department of developmental disabilities. If there is a question as to whether a contracting entity is providing specialized services, the contracting entity may request that the director of developmental disabilities make a determination. The director's determination is final.

(B)(1) Except as provided in division (B)(2) of this section, each contracting entity shall conduct background investigations in the same manner county boards conduct investigations under section 5126.28 of the Revised Code of all persons under final consideration for employment with the contracting entity in a direct services position. On request, the county board shall assist a contracting entity in obtaining reports from the bureau of criminal identification and investigation or any other state or federal agency and in obtaining abstracts from the registrar of motor vehicles.

(2) A contracting entity is not required to request a criminal records check for either of the following:

(a) An employee of the entity who is in a direct services position and being considered for a different direct services position or is returning after a leave of absence or seasonal break in employment, as long as the contracting entity has no reason to believe that the employee has committed any of the offenses listed or described in division (E) of section 5126.28 of the Revised Code;

(b) A person who will provide only respite care under a family support services program established under section 5126.11 of the Revised Code, if the person is selected by a family member of the individual with mental retardation or a developmental disability who is to receive the respite care.

(C) No contracting entity shall place a person in a direct services position if the person has been convicted of or pleaded guilty to any offense listed or described in division (E) of section 5126.28 of the Revised Code, unless the person meets the standards for rehabilitation established by rules adopted under section 5126.28 of the Revised Code.

(D) A contracting entity may place a person in a direct services position pending receipt of information concerning the person's background investigation from the bureau of criminal identification and investigation, the registrar of motor vehicles, or any other state or federal agency if the person submits to the contracting entity a statement with the person's signature that the person has not been convicted of or pleaded guilty to any of the offenses listed or described in division (E) of section 5126.28 of the Revised Code. No contracting entity shall fail to terminate the placement of such person if the contracting entity is informed that the person has been convicted of or pleaded guilty to any of the offenses listed or described in division (E) of section 5126.28 of the Revised Code.

(E) Prior to employing a person in a direct services position, the contracting entity shall require the person to submit a statement with the applicant's signature attesting that the applicant has not been convicted of or pleaded guilty to any of the offenses listed or described in division (E) of section 5126.28 of the Revised Code. The contracting entity also shall require the person to sign an agreement to notify the contracting entity within fourteen calendar days if, while employed by the entity, the person is ever formally charged with, convicted of, or pleads guilty to any of the offenses listed or described in division (E) of section 5126.28 of the Revised Code. The agreement shall inform the person that failure to report formal charges, a conviction, or a guilty plea may result in being dismissed from employment.

(F) A county board may take appropriate action against a contracting entity that violates this section, including terminating the contracting entity's contract with the board.

**HISTORY: 145 v H 694 (Eff 11-11-94); 146 v H 629 (Eff 3-13-97); 148 v H 538. Eff 9-22-2000; 153 v S 79, § 1, eff. 10-6-09.**

# CHAPTER 5139: YOUTH SERVICES



## § 5139.21 Prohibition.

No person shall influence or attempt to influence any child under supervision of the department of youth services, to leave the institution or home in which he was placed, his home, or place of employment or to violate any of the conditions upon which he was released under supervision.

**HISTORY: 130 v 1228 (Eff 10-7-63); 132 v H 491 (Eff 10-19-67); 139 v H 440. Eff 11-23-81.**

## [RELEASE OR DISCHARGE]

## § 5139.99 Penalty.

Whoever violates section 5139.21 of the Revised Code shall be fined not less than ten nor more than five hundred dollars or imprisoned not more than one year, or both.

**HISTORY: 130 v 1229. Eff 3-10-64.**

# CHAPTER 5145: STATE CORRECTIONAL INSTITUTIONS



## [SENTENCE; TERMINATION]

## § 5145.01 Duration of sentences.

Courts shall impose sentences to a state correctional institution for felonies pursuant to sections 2929.13 and 2929.14 of the Revised Code. All prison terms may be ended in the manner provided by law, but no prison term shall exceed the maximum term provided for the felony of which the prisoner was convicted as extended pursuant to section 2929.141 [2929.14.1] or 2967.28 of the Revised Code.

If a prisoner is sentenced for two or more separate felonies, the prisoner's term of imprisonment shall run as a concurrent sentence, except if the consecutive sentence provisions of sections 2929.14 and 2929.41 of the Revised Code apply. If sentenced consecutively, for the purposes of sections 5145.01 to 5145.27 of the Revised Code, the prisoner shall be held to be serving one continuous term of imprisonment.

If a court imposes a sentence to a state correctional institution for a felony of the fourth or fifth degree, the department of rehabilitation and correction, notwithstanding the court's designation of a state correctional institution as the place of service of the sentence, may designate that the person sentenced is to be housed in a county, multicounty, municipal, municipal-county, or multicounty-municipal jail or workhouse if authorized pursuant to section 5120.161 [5120.16.1] of the Revised Code.

If, through oversight or otherwise, a person is sentenced to a state correctional institution under a definite term for an offense for which a definite term of imprisonment is not provided by statute, the sentence shall not thereby become void, but the person shall be subject to the liabilities of such sections and receive the benefits thereof, as if the person had been sentenced in the manner required by this section.

As used in this section, "prison term" has the same meaning as in section 2929.01 of the Revised Code.

**HISTORY: RS § 7388-6; 81 v 72; 81 v 186; 87 v 164, § 5; GC § 2166; 103 v 29; 109 v 64; 114 v 188; Bureau of Code Revision, 10-1-53; 129 v 1193 (Eff 10-26-61); 139 v S 199 (Eff 1-1-83); 140 v S 210 (Eff 7-1-83); 142 v H 455 (Eff 7-20-87); 145 v H 571 (Eff 10-6-94); 146 v S 2 (Eff 7-1-96); 149 v H 327. Eff 7-8-2002; 152 v H 130, § 1, eff. 4-7-09.**

[MISCELLANEOUS]

### § 5145.21 Escaped convicts to be arrested and returned.

The warden of a state correctional institution shall arrest and again commit to the institution a convict who escapes from the institution and is found at large, whether the term for which he was sentenced to imprisonment has expired.

**HISTORY: RS § 7404; S&C 918; 33 v 14, § 15; GC § 2186; Bureau of Code Revision, 10-1-53; 145 v H 571. Eff 10-6-94.**

**Publisher's Note:**

H.B. 571 (145 v —), effective 10-6-94 also purported to repeal this section. For related provisions, see RC § 5120.48.

## CHAPTER 5149: ADULT PAROLE AUTHORITY

Section



### § 5149.101 Petition for full board hearing on proposed parole or re-parole; who may attend.

(A)(1) A board hearing officer, a board member, or the office of victims' services may petition the board for a full board hearing that relates to the proposed parole or re-parole of a prisoner. At a meeting of the board at which a majority of board members are present, the majority of those present shall determine whether a full board hearing shall be held.

(2) A victim of a violation of section 2903.01 or 2903.02 of the Revised Code, the victim's representative, or any person described in division (B)(5) of this section may request the board hold a full board hearing that relates to the proposed parole or re-parole of the person that committed the violation. If a victim, victim's representative, or other person requests a full board hearing pursuant to this division, the board shall hold a full board hearing.

(B) At a full board hearing that relates to the proposed parole or re-parole of a prisoner and that has been petitioned for or requested in accordance with division (A) of this section, the parole board shall permit the following persons to appear and to give testimony or to submit written statements:

(1) The prosecuting attorney of the county in which the original indictment against the prisoner was found and members of any law enforcement agency that assisted in the prosecution of the original offense;

(2) The judge of the court of common pleas who imposed the original sentence of incarceration upon the prisoner, or the judge's successor;

(3) The victim of the original offense for which the prisoner is serving the sentence or the victim's representative designated pursuant to section 2930.02 of the Revised Code:

(4) The victim of any behavior that resulted in parole being revoked;

(5) With respect to a full board hearing held pursuant to division (A)(2) of this section, all of the following:

(a) The spouse of the victim of the original offense;

(b) The parent or parents of the victim of the original offense;

(c) The sibling of the victim of the original offense;

(d) The child or children of the victim of the original offense.

(6) Counsel or some other person designated by the prisoner as a representative, as described in division (C) of this section.

(C) Except as otherwise provided in this division, a full board hearing of the parole board is not subject to section 121.22 of the Revised Code. The persons who may attend a full board hearing are the persons described in divisions (B)(1) to (6) of this section, and representatives of the press, radio and television stations, and broadcasting networks who are members of a generally recognized professional media organization.

At the request of a person described in division (B)(3) of this section, representatives of the news media described in this division shall be excluded from the hearing while that person is giving testimony at the hearing. The prisoner being considered for parole has no right to be present at the hearing, but may be represented by counsel or some other person designated by the prisoner.

If there is an objection at a full board hearing to a recommendation for the parole of a prisoner, the board may approve or disapprove the recommendation or defer its decision until a subsequent full board hearing. The board may permit interested persons other than those listed in this division and division (B) of this section to attend full board hearings pursuant to rules adopted by the adult parole authority.

(D) The adult parole authority shall adopt rules for the implementation of this section. The rules shall specify reasonable restrictions on the number of media representatives that may attend a hearing, based on considerations of space, and other procedures designed to accomplish an effective, orderly process for full board hearings.

**HISTORY: 146 v S 2. Eff 7-1-96; 150 v H 375, § 1, eff. 4-29-05.**

The effective date is set by section 6 of SB 2.

See provisions, § 5 of SB 2 (146 v —), following RC § 5120.02.1.

# CHAPTER 5153: COUNTY CHILDREN SERVICES



## § 5153.111 Criminal records check and fingerprinting of prospective employees responsible for child; employment of certain offenders prohibited.

(A)(1) The executive director of a public children services agency shall request the superintendent of the bureau of criminal identification and investigation to conduct a criminal records check with respect to any applicant who has applied to the agency for employment as a person responsible for the care, custody, or control of a child. If the applicant does not present proof that the applicant has been a resident of this state for the five-year period immediately prior to the date upon which the criminal records check is requested or does not provide evidence that within that five-year period the superintendent has requested information about the applicant from the federal bureau of investigation in a criminal records check, the executive director shall request that the superintendent obtain information from the federal bureau of investigation as a part of the criminal records check for the applicant. If the applicant presents proof that the applicant has been a resident of this state for that five-year period, the executive director may request that the superintendent include information from the federal bureau of investigation in the criminal records check.

(2) Any person required by division (A)(1) of this section to request a criminal records check shall provide to each applicant a copy of the form prescribed pursuant to division (C)(1) of section 109.572 [109.57.2] of the Revised Code, provide to each applicant a standard impression sheet to obtain fingerprint impressions prescribed pursuant to division (C)(2) of section 109.572 [109.57.2] of the Revised Code, obtain the completed form and impression sheet from each applicant, and forward the completed form and impression sheet to the superintendent of the bureau of criminal identification and investigation at the time the person requests a criminal records check pursuant to division (A)(1) of this section.

(3) Any applicant who receives pursuant to division (A)(2) of this section a copy of the form prescribed pursuant to division (C)(1) of section 109.572 [109.57.2] of the Revised Code and a copy of an impression sheet prescribed pursuant to division (C)(2) of that section and who is requested to complete the form and provide a set of fingerprint impressions shall complete the form or provide all the information necessary to complete the form and shall provide the impression sheet with the impressions of the applicant's fingerprints. If an applicant, upon request, fails to provide the information necessary to complete the form or fails to provide impressions of the applicant's fingerprints, that agency shall not employ that applicant for any position for which a criminal records check is required by division (A)(1) of this section.

(B)(1) Except as provided in rules adopted by the director of job and family services in accordance with division (E) of this section, no public children services agency shall employ a person as a person responsible for the care, custody, or control of a child if the person previously has been convicted of or pleaded guilty to any of the following:

(a) A violation of section 2903.01, 2903.02, 2903.03, 2903.04, 2903.11, 2903.12, 2903.13, 2903.16, 2903.21, 2903.34, 2905.01, 2905.02, 2905.05, 2907.02, 2907.03, 2907.04, 2907.05, 2907.06, 2907.07, 2907.08, 2907.09, 2907.21, 2907.22, 2907.23, 2907.25, 2907.31, 2907.32, 2907.321 [2907.32.1], 2907.322 [2907.32.2], 2907.323 [2907.32.3], 2909.02, 2909.03, 2911.01, 2911.02, 2911.11, 2911.12, 2919.12, 2919.22, 2919.24, 2919.25, 2923.12, 2923.13, 2923.161 [2923.16.1], 2925.02, 2925.03, 2925.04, 2925.05, 2925.06, or 3716.11 of the Revised Code, a violation of section 2905.04 of the Revised Code as it existed prior to July 1, 1996, a violation of section 2919.23 of the Revised Code that would have been a violation of section 2905.04 of the Revised Code as it existed prior to July 1, 1996, had the violation occurred prior to that date, a violation of section 2925.11 of the Revised Code that is not a minor drug possession offense, or felonious sexual penetration in violation of former section 2907.12 of the Revised Code;

(b) A violation of an existing or former law of this state, any other state, or the United States that is substantially equivalent to any of the offenses or violations described in division (B)(1)(a) of this section.

(2) A public children services agency may employ an applicant conditionally until the criminal records check required by this section is completed and the agency receives the results of the criminal records check. If the results of the criminal records check indicate that, pursuant to division (B)(1) of this section, the applicant does not qualify for employment, the agency shall release the applicant from employment.

(C)(1) Each public children services agency shall pay to the bureau of criminal identification and investigation the fee prescribed pursuant to division (C)(3) of section 109.572 [109.57.2] of the Revised Code for each criminal records check conducted in accordance with that section upon the request pursuant to division (A)(1) of this section of the executive director of the agency.

(2) A public children services agency may charge an applicant a fee for the costs it incurs in obtaining a criminal records check under this section. A fee charged under this division shall not exceed the amount of fees the agency pays under division (C)(1) of this section. If a fee is charged under this division, the agency shall notify the applicant at the time of the applicant's initial application for employment of the amount of the fee and that, unless the fee is paid, the agency will not consider the applicant for employment.

(D) The report of any criminal records check conducted by the bureau of criminal identification and investigation in accordance with section 109.572 [109.57.2] of the Revised Code and pursuant to a request under division (A)(1) of this section is not a public record for the purposes of section 149.43 of the Revised Code and shall not be made available to any person other than the applicant who is the subject of the criminal records check or the applicant's representative, the public children services agency requesting the criminal records check or its representative, and any court, hearing officer, or other necessary individual involved in a case dealing with the denial of employment to the applicant.

(E) The director of job and family services shall adopt rules pursuant to Chapter 119. of the Revised Code to implement this section, including rules specifying circumstances under which a public children services agency may hire a person who has been convicted of an offense listed in division (B)(1) of this section but who meets standards in regard to rehabilitation set by the department.

(F) Any person required by division (A)(1) of this section to request a criminal records check shall inform each person, at the time of the person's initial application for employment, that the person is required to provide a set of impressions of the person's fingerprints and that a criminal records check is required to be conducted and satisfactorily completed in accordance with section 109.572 [109.57.2] of the Revised Code if the person comes under final consideration for appointment or employment as a precondition to employment for that position.

(G) As used in this section:

(1) "Applicant" means a person who is under final consideration for appointment or employment in a position with the agency as a person responsible for the care, custody, or control of a child.

(2) "Criminal records check" has the same meaning as in section 109.572 [109.57.2] of the Revised Code.

(3) "Minor drug possession offense" has the same meaning as in section 2925.01 of the Revised Code.

**HISTORY: 145 v S 38 (Eff 10-29-93); 145 v H 694 (Eff 11-11-94); 146 v S 2 (Eff 7-1-96); 146 v H 445 (Eff 9-3-96); 146 v S 269 (Eff 9-26-96); 147 v H 408 (Eff 10-1-97); 148 v H 471. Eff 7-1-2000; 151 v S 238, § 1, eff. 9-21-06.**

The effective date is set by section 12(A) of HB 471.

## [PENALTIES]

### § 5153.99 Penalties.

Whoever violates division (F) of section 5153.176 [5153.17.6] of the Revised Code shall be punished as follows:

(A) Except as otherwise provided in division (B) of this section, the person is guilty of a misdemeanor of the fourth degree.

(B) The person is guilty of a misdemeanor of the first degree if, during the period between the violation and the conviction of or plea of guilty by the person for that violation, the license holder who is the subject of the investigation about which the person fails to provide information inflicts on any child attending a school district, educational service center, public or nonpublic school, or county board of developmental disabilities where the license holder works any physical or mental wound, injury, disability, or condition of a nature that constitutes abuse or neglect of the child.

**HISTORY: 152 v H 428, § 1, eff. 9-12-08; 153 v S 79, § 1, eff. 10-6-09.**

# TITLE 53: REAL PROPERTY

## CHAPTER 5301: CONVEYANCES; ENCUMBRANCES



[MARKETABLE TITLE ACT]

### § 5301.61 Improper removal of improvements from mortgaged realty.

No person having an interest in real property, buyer, lessee, tenant, or occupant of real property, knowing that such real property is mortgaged or the subject of a land contract, shall remove, or cause or permit the removal of any improvement or fixture from such real property without the consent of the mortgagee, vendor under the land contract, or other person authorized to give such consent.

**HISTORY: 134 v H 511. Eff 1-1-74.**

The effective date of H 511 is set by § 4 of the act.

### § 5301.99 Penalties.

(A) Any individual, corporation, or other business entity that violates section 5301.254 [5301.25.4] of the Revised Code shall be fined not less than five thousand dollars nor more than an amount equal to twenty-five per cent of the market value of the real property or mineral or mining rights about which information must be filed with the secretary of state pursuant to section 5301.254 [5301.25.4] of the Revised Code.

(B) Whoever violates section 5301.61 of the Revised Code is guilty of a misdemeanor of the first degree.

**HISTORY: Bureau of Code Revision, 10-1-53; 134 v H 511 (Eff 1-1-74); 137 v S 508. Eff 3-19-79.**

# TITLE 55: ROADS — HIGHWAYS — BRIDGES

## CHAPTER 5502: DEPARTMENT OF PUBLIC SAFETY



### § 5502.01 General duties of department.

(A) The department of public safety shall administer and enforce the laws relating to the registration, licensing, sale, and operation of motor vehicles and the laws pertaining to the licensing of drivers of motor vehicles.

The department shall compile, analyze, and publish statistics relative to motor vehicle accidents and the causes of them, prepare and conduct educational programs for the purpose of promoting safety in the operation of motor vehicles on the highways, and conduct research and studies for the purpose of promoting safety on the highways of this state.

(B) The department shall administer the laws and rules relative to trauma and emergency medical services specified in Chapter 4765. of the Revised Code.

(C) The department shall administer and enforce the laws contained in Chapters 4301. and 4303. of the Revised Code and enforce the rules and orders of the liquor control commission pertaining to retail liquor permit holders.

(D) The department shall administer the laws governing the state emergency management agency and shall enforce all additional duties and responsibilities as prescribed in the Revised Code related to emergency management services.

(E) The department shall conduct investigations pursuant to Chapter 5101. of the Revised Code in support of the duty of the department of job and family services to administer the supplemental nutrition assistance program throughout this state. The department of public safety shall conduct investigations necessary to protect the state's property rights and interests in the supplemental nutrition assistance program.

(F) The department of public safety shall enforce compliance with orders and rules of the public utilities commission and applicable laws in accordance with Chapters 4919., 4921., and 4923. of the Revised Code regarding commercial motor vehicle transportation safety, economic, and hazardous materials requirements.

(G) Notwithstanding Chapter 4117. of the Revised Code, the department of public safety may establish requirements for its enforcement personnel, including its enforcement agents described in section 5502.14 of the Revised Code, that include standards of conduct, work rules and procedures, and criteria for eligibility as law enforcement personnel.

(H) The department shall administer, maintain, and operate the Ohio criminal justice network. The Ohio criminal justice network shall be a computer network that supports state and local criminal justice activities. The network shall be an electronic repository for various data, which may include arrest warrants, notices of persons wanted by law enforcement agencies, criminal records, prison inmate records, stolen vehicle records, vehicle operator's licenses, and vehicle registrations and titles.

(I) The department shall coordinate all homeland security activities of all state agencies and shall be a liaison between state agencies and local entities for those activities and related purposes.

(J) Beginning July 1, 2004, the department shall administer and enforce the laws relative to private investigators and security service providers specified in Chapter 4749. of the Revised Code.

(K) The department shall administer criminal justice services in accordance with sections 5502.61 to 5502.66 of the Revised Code.

**HISTORY: 125 v 127 (Eff 10-2-53); 132 v H 380 (Eff 1-1-68); 144 v S 98 (Eff 11-12-92); 146 v S 162 (Eff 10-29-95); 147 v H 210 (Eff 6-30-97); 148 v H 163 (Eff 6-30-99); 148 v H 471 (Eff 7-1-2000); 148 v H 138 (Eff 11-3-2000); 149 v H 407. Eff 10-11-2002; 150 v H 95, § 1, eff. 9-26-03; 150 v H 230, § 1, eff. 7-1-04; 151 v H 66, § 101.01, eff. 6-30-05; 153 v H 1, § 101.01, eff. 10-16-09.**

The effective date is set by § 812.10 of 153 v H 1.
The effective date is set by § 612.12 of 151 v H 66.
The effective date is set by section 8 of H.B. 230 (150 v —).

### § 5502.03 Division of homeland security created.

(A) There is hereby created in the department of public safety a division of homeland security.

(B) The division shall do all of the following:

(1) Coordinate all homeland security activities of all state agencies and be the liaison between state agencies and local entities for the purposes of communicating homeland security funding and policy initiatives;

(2) Collect, analyze, maintain, and disseminate information to support local, state, and federal law enforcement agencies, other government agencies, and private organizations in detecting, deterring, preventing, preparing for, responding to, and recovering from threatened or actual terrorist events. This information is not a public record pursuant to section 149.43 of the Revised Code.

(3) Coordinate efforts of state and local governments and private organizations to enhance the security and protection of critical infrastructure, including casino facilities, and key assets in this state;

(4) Develop and coordinate policies, protocols, and strategies that may be used to prevent, detect, prepare for, respond to, and recover from terrorist acts or threats;

(5) Develop, update, and coordinate the implementation of an Ohio homeland security strategic plan that will

guide state and local governments in the achievement of homeland security in this state.

(C) The director of public safety shall appoint an executive director, who shall be head of the division of homeland security and who regularly shall advise the governor and the director on matters pertaining to homeland security. The executive director shall serve at the pleasure of the director of public safety. To carry out the duties assigned under this section, the executive director, subject to the direction and control of the director of public safety, may appoint and maintain necessary staff and may enter into any necessary agreements.

(D) Except as otherwise provided by law, nothing in this section shall be construed to give the director of public safety or the executive director of the division of homeland security authority over the incident management structure or responsibilities of local emergency response personnel.

(E) There is hereby created in the state treasury the homeland security fund. The fund shall consist of sixty cents of each fee collected under sections 4501.34, 4503.26, 4506.08, and 4509.05 of the Revised Code as specified in those sections, plus on and after October 1, 2009, sixty cents of each fee collected under sections 4505.14 and 4519.63 of the Revised Code as specified in those sections. The fund shall be used to pay the expenses of administering the law relative to the powers and duties of the executive director of the division of homeland security, except that the director of budget and management may transfer excess money from the homeland security fund to the state highway safety fund if the director of public safety determines that the amount of money in the homeland security fund exceeds the amount required to cover such costs incurred by the division of homeland security and requests the director of budget and management to make the transfer.

**HISTORY: 150 v H 95, § 1, eff. 9-26-03; 151 v S 9, § 1, eff. 4-14-06; 152 v H 67, § 101.01, eff. 6-30-07; 153 v H 2, § 101.01, eff. 7-1-09; 153 v H 519, § 1, eff. 9-10-10.**

The effective date is set by § 812.10 of 153 v H 2.
The effective date is set by § 609.10 of 152 v H 67.
The effective date is set by section 179 of H.B. 95 (150 v —).
**Not analogous to former RC § 5502.03 (145 v H 687, § 2 [142 v H 111; 144 v S 98]), eff 10-12-94.**

**Publisher's Note:**

The amendment of RC § 5502.03 by 151 v H 66 was disapproved by the Governor.

(B)(2) of the enactment of RC § 5502.03 by Am. Sub. H.B. 95 (150 v —) was disapproved by the Governor.

## [DIVISION OF CRIMINAL JUSTICE SERVICES]

## § 5502.61 Definitions.

As used in sections 5502.61 to 5502.66 of the Revised Code:

(A) "Federal criminal justice acts" means any federal law that authorizes financial assistance and other forms of assistance to be given by the federal government to the states to be used for the improvement of the criminal and juvenile justice systems of the states.

(B)(1) "Criminal justice system" includes all of the functions of the following:

(a) The state highway patrol, county sheriff offices, municipal and township police departments, and all other law enforcement agencies;

(b) The courts of appeals, courts of common pleas, municipal courts, county courts, and mayor's courts, when dealing with criminal cases;

(c) The prosecuting attorneys, city directors of law, village solicitors, and other prosecuting authorities when prosecuting or otherwise handling criminal cases, and the county and joint county public defenders and other public defender agencies or offices;

(d) The department of rehabilitation and correction, probation departments, county and municipal jails and workhouses, and any other department, agency, or facility that is concerned with the rehabilitation or correction of criminal offenders;

(e) Any public or private agency whose purposes include the prevention of crime or the diversion, adjudication, detention, or rehabilitation of criminal offenders;

(f) Any public or private agency, the purposes of which include assistance to crime victims or witnesses.

(2) The inclusion of any public or private agency, the purposes of which include assistance to crime victims or witnesses, as part of the criminal justice system pursuant to division (B)(1) of this section does not limit, and shall not be construed as limiting, the discretion or authority of the attorney general with respect to crime victim assistance and criminal justice programs.

(C) "Juvenile justice system" includes all of the functions of the juvenile courts, the department of youth services, any public or private agency whose purposes include the prevention of delinquency or the diversion, adjudication, detention, or rehabilitation of delinquent children, and any of the functions of the criminal justice system that are applicable to children.

(D) "Comprehensive plan" means a document that coordinates, evaluates, and otherwise assists, on an annual or multi-year basis, any of the functions of the criminal and juvenile justice systems of the state or a specified area of the state, that conforms to the priorities of the state with respect to criminal and juvenile justice systems, and that conforms with the requirements of all federal criminal justice acts. These functions may include, but are not limited to, any of the following:

(1) Crime and delinquency prevention;

(2) Identification, detection, apprehension, and detention of persons charged with criminal offenses or delinquent acts;

(3) Assistance to crime victims or witnesses, except that the comprehensive plan does not include the functions of the attorney general pursuant to sections 109.91 and 109.92 of the Revised Code;

(4) Adjudication or diversion of persons charged with criminal offenses or delinquent acts;

(5) Custodial treatment of criminal offenders, delinquent children, or both;

(6) Institutional and noninstitutional rehabilitation of criminal offenders, delinquent children, or both.

(E) "Metropolitan county criminal justice services agency" means an agency that is established pursuant to division (A) of section 5502.64 of the Revised Code.

(F) "Administrative planning district" means a district that is established pursuant to division (A) or (B) of section 5502.66 of the Revised Code.

(G) "Criminal justice coordinating council" means a criminal justice services agency that is established pursuant to division (D) of section 5502.66 of the Revised Code.

(H) "Local elected official" means any person who is a member of a board of county commissioners or township trustees or of a city or village council, judge of the court of common pleas, a municipal court, or a county court, sheriff, county coroner, prosecuting attorney, city director of law, village solicitor, or mayor.

(I) "Juvenile justice coordinating council" means a juvenile justice services agency that is established pursuant to division (D) of section 5502.66 of the Revised Code.

(J) "Mcgruff house program" means a program in which individuals or families volunteer to have their homes or other buildings serve as places of temporary refuge for children and to display the mcgruff house symbol identifying the home or building as that type of place.

(K) "Mcgruff house symbol" means the symbol that is characterized by the image of "mcgruff," the crime dog, and the slogan "take a bite out of crime," and that has been adopted by the national crime prevention council as the symbol of its national citizens' crime prevention campaign.

(L) "Sponsoring agency" means any of the following:

(1) The board of education of any city, local, or exempted village school district;

(2) The governing board of any educational service center;

(3) The governing authority of any chartered nonpublic school;

(4) The police department of any municipal corporation, township, township police district, or joint police district;

(5) The office of any township constable or county sheriff.

**HISTORY: RC § 122.21, 137 v H 1277 (Eff 12-14-78); 139 v H 440 (Eff 11-23-81); RC § 109.93, 142 v H 171 (Eff 7-1-87); RC § 122.21, 142 v H 231 (Eff 10-5-87); 142 v H 708 (Eff 4-19-88); 144 v H 298 (Eff 7-26-91); RC § 181.51, 145 v H 152 (Eff 7-1-93); 149 v H 94. Eff 9-5-2001; 151 v H 66, § 101.01, eff. 6-30-05; 151 v H 374, § 1, eff. 4-1-07; 2011 HB 153, § 101.01, eff. Sept. 29, 2011.**

The effective date is set by § 3(C) of 151 v H 374.

**Not analogous to former RC § 5502.61 (146 v S 162; 146 v H 566), repealed 148 v H 163, § 2, eff 6-30-99.**

The effective date is set by § 612.12 of 151 v H 66.

See provisions of § 4 (B) of 151 v H 374 following RC § 5502.62.

**Publisher's Note:**

This section was amended and renumbered from RC § 181.51 by 151 v H 66, effective June 30, 2005.

## § 5502.62 Division of criminal justice services created.

(A) There is hereby created in the department of public safety a division of criminal justice services. The director of public safety, with the concurrence of the governor, shall appoint an executive director of the division of criminal justice services. The executive director shall be the head of the division. The executive director shall serve at the pleasure of the director of public safety. To carry out the duties assigned under this section and to comply with sections 5502.63 to 5502.66 of the Revised Code, the executive director, subject to the direction and control of the director of public safety, may appoint and maintain any necessary staff and may enter into any necessary contracts and other agreements. The executive director of the division, and all professional and technical personnel employed within the division who are not public employees as defined in section 4117.01 of the Revised Code, shall be in the unclassified civil service, and all other persons employed within the division shall be in the classified civil service.

(B) Subject to division (F) of this section and subject to divisions (D) to (F) of section 5120.09 of the Revised Code insofar as those divisions relate to federal criminal justice acts that the governor requires the department of rehabilitation and correction to administer, the division of criminal justice services shall do all of the following:

(1) Serve as the state criminal justice services agency and perform criminal justice system planning in the state, including any planning that is required by any federal law;

(2) Collect, analyze, and correlate information and data concerning the criminal justice system in the state;

(3) Cooperate with and provide technical assistance to state departments, administrative planning districts, metropolitan county criminal justice services agencies, criminal justice coordinating councils, agencies, offices, and departments of the criminal justice system in the state, and other appropriate organizations and persons;

(4) Encourage and assist agencies, offices, and departments of the criminal justice system in the state and other appropriate organizations and persons to solve problems that relate to the duties of the division;

(5) Administer within the state any federal criminal justice acts that the governor requires it to administer;

(6) Administer funds received under the "Family Violence Prevention and Services Act," 98 Stat. 1757 (1984), 42 U.S.C.A. 10401, as amended, with all powers necessary for the adequate administration of those funds, including the authority to establish a family violence prevention and services program;

(7) Implement the state comprehensive plans;

(8) Audit grant activities of agencies, offices, organizations, and persons that are financed in whole or in part by funds granted through the division;

(9) Monitor or evaluate the performance of criminal justice system projects and programs in the state that are financed in whole or in part by funds granted through the division;

(10) Apply for, allocate, disburse, and account for grants that are made available pursuant to federal criminal justice acts, or made available from other federal, state, or private sources, to improve the criminal justice system in the state. All money from such federal grants that require that the money be deposited into an interest-bearing fund or account, that are intended to provide funding to local criminal justice programs, and that require that investment earnings be distributed for program purposes shall be deposited in the state treasury to the credit of the federal justice programs funds, which are hereby created. A separate fund shall be established each federal fiscal year. All investment earnings of a federal justice programs fund shall be credited to that fund and distributed in accordance with the terms of the grant under which the money is received. If the terms under which the money is received do not require the money to be deposited into an interest-bearing fund or account, all money from such federal grants shall be deposited into the state treasury to the credit of the federal justice grants fund, which is hereby created. Money credited to the fund shall be used or distributed pursuant to the federal grant programs under which the money is received.

(11) Contract with federal, state, and local agencies, foundations, corporations, businesses, and persons when necessary to carry out the duties of the division;

(12) Oversee the activities of metropolitan county criminal justice services agencies, administrative planning districts, and criminal justice coordinating councils in the state;

(13) Advise the director of public safety, general assembly, and governor on legislation and other significant matters that pertain to the improvement and reform of criminal and juvenile justice systems in the state;

(14) Prepare and recommend legislation to the director of public safety, general assembly, and governor for the improvement of the criminal and juvenile justice systems in the state;

(15) Assist, advise, and make any reports that are requested or required by the governor, director of public safety, attorney general, or general assembly;

(16) Develop and maintain the Ohio incident-based reporting system in accordance with division (C) of this section;

(17) Subject to the approval of the director of public safety, adopt rules pursuant to Chapter 119. of the Revised Code.

(18)(a) Not later than June 1, 2007, and subject to the approval of the director of public safety, adopt rules for the establishment and maintenance of a mcgruff house program by any sponsoring agency. The rules shall include the following:

(i) The adoption of the mcgruff house symbol to be used exclusively in all mcgruff house programs in this state;

(ii) The requirements for any sponsoring agency to establish and maintain a mcgruff house program;

(iii) The criteria for the selection of volunteers to participate in a mcgruff house program that shall include, but not be limited to, criminal background checks of those volunteers;

(iv) Any other matters that the division of criminal justice services considers necessary for the establishment and maintenance of mcgruff house programs by sponsoring agencies and the participation of volunteers in those programs.

(b) The division of criminal justice services shall distribute materials and provide technical assistance to any sponsoring agency that establishes and maintains a mcgruff house program, any volunteer group or organization that provides assistance to that sponsoring agency, or any volunteer who participates in a mcgruff house program.

(C) The division of criminal justice services shall develop and maintain the Ohio incident-based reporting system to facilitate the sharing of information with the federal bureau of investigation and participating law enforcement agencies in Ohio. The Ohio incident-based reporting system shall be known as OIBRS. In connection with OIBRS, the division shall do all of the following:

(1) Collect and organize statistical data for reporting to the national incident-based reporting system operated by the federal bureau of investigation for the purpose of securing federal criminal justice grants;

(2) Analyze and highlight mapping data for participating law enforcement agencies;

(3) Distribute data and analyses to participating law enforcement agencies;

(4) Encourage nonparticipating law enforcement agencies to participate in OIBRS by offering demonstrations, training, and technical assistance;

(5) Provide assistance, advice, and reports requested by the governor, the general assembly, or the federal bureau of investigation;

(6) Require every law enforcement agency that receives federal criminal justice grants or state criminal justice information system general revenue funds through the division to participate in OIBRS or in the uniform crime reporting program of the federal bureau of investigation. An agency that submits OIBRS data to the Ohio local law enforcement information sharing network shall be considered to be in compliance with division (C)(6) of this section if both of the following apply:

(a) The Ohio local law enforcement information sharing network is capable of collecting OIBRS data.

(b) The division of criminal justice services has the ability to extract the OIBRS data for reporting to the national incident-based reporting system in the manner required by the federal bureau of investigation.

(D) Upon the request of the director of public safety or governor, the division of criminal justice services may do any of the following:

(1) Collect, analyze, or correlate information and data concerning the juvenile justice system in the state;

(2) Cooperate with and provide technical assistance to state departments, administrative planning districts, metropolitan county criminal justice service agencies, criminal justice coordinating councils, agency offices, and the departments of the juvenile justice system in the state and other appropriate organizations and persons;

(3) Encourage and assist agencies, offices, and departments of the juvenile justice system in the state and other appropriate organizations and persons to solve problems that relate to the duties of the division.

(E) Divisions (B), (C), and (D) of this section do not limit the discretion or authority of the attorney general with respect to crime victim assistance and criminal justice programs.

(F) Nothing in this section is intended to diminish or alter the status of the office of the attorney general as a criminal justice services agency or to diminish or alter the status or discourage the development and use of other law enforcement information systems in Ohio.

**HISTORY: RC § 122.22, 137 v H 1277 (Eff 12-14-78); 139 v H 536 (Eff 8-12-82); RC § 109.94, 142 v H 171 (Eff 7-1-87); RC § 122.22, 142 v H 231 (Eff 10-5-87); 142 v H 708 (Eff 4-19-88); 143 v S 258 (Eff 8-22-90); 144 v H 298 (Eff 7-26-91); RC § 181.52, 145 v H 152 (Eff 7-1-93); 145 v H 715 (Eff 7-22-94); 147 v H 215 (Eff 9-29-97); 148 v H 283 (Eff 9-29-99); 149 v H 94. Eff 6-6-2001; 151 v H 4, § 1, eff. 9-16-05; 151 v H 66, § 101.01, eff. 6-30-05; 151 v H 374, § 1, eff. 4-1-07; 151 v H 699, § 101.01, eff. 12-28-06; 151 v H 699, § 110.07, eff. 4-1-07; 152 v H 67, § 101.01, eff. 6-30-07.**

The effective date is set by § 609.10 of 152 v H 67.

The effective date is set by §§ 110.09 and 615.09 of 151 v H 699.

The effective date is set by § 615.03 of 151 v H 699.

The effective date is set by § 3(C) of 151 v H 374.

The provisions of § 623.03 of 151 v H 699 read in part as follows:

SECTION 623.03. The General Assembly, applying the principle stated in division (B) of section 1.52 of the Revised Code that amendments are to be harmonized if reasonably capable of simultaneous operation, finds that the following sections, presented in this act as composites of the sections as amended by the acts indicated, are the resulting versions of the sections in effect prior to the effective date of the sections as presented in this act:

* * *

Section 181.52 (5502.62) of the Revised Code as amended by both Sub. H.B. 4 and Am. Sub. H.B. 66 of the 126th General Assembly.

The provisions of § 4(B) of 151 v H 374 read as follows:

SECTION 4. * * * (B) On or after April 1, 2007, but not later than June 1, 2007, the Division of Criminal Justice Services in the

Department of Public Safety shall adopt rules for the establishment and maintenance of a McGruff House Program pursuant to sections 5502.61 and 5502.62 of the Revised Code, as amended by this act. The rules adopted by the Division of Criminal Justice Services under this division shall take effect July 1, 2007.

The provisions of § 5 of 151 v H 374 read as follows:

SECTION 5. Section 181.52 (5502.62) of the Revised Code is presented in this act as a composite of the section as amended by both Sub. H.B. 4 and Am. Sub. H.B. 66 of the 126th General Assembly. The General Assembly, applying the principle stated in division (B) of section 1.52 of the Revised Code that amendments are to be harmonized if reasonably capable of simultaneous operation, finds that the composite is the resulting version of the section in effect prior to the effective date of the section as presented in this act.

**Not analogous to former RC § 5502.62, amended and renumbered to RC § 5502.19 by 148 v H 163, eff. 6-30-99.**

The effective date is set by § 612.12 of 151 v H 66.

**Publisher's Note:**

This section was amended and renumbered from RC § 181.52 by 151 v H 66, effective June 30, 2005.

## § 5502.63 Poster and brochure describing safe firearms practices.

The division of criminal justice services in the department of public safety shall prepare a poster and a brochure that describe safe firearms practices. The poster and brochure shall contain typeface that is at least one-quarter inch tall. The division shall furnish copies of the poster and brochure free of charge to each federally licensed firearms dealer in this state.

As used in this section, "federally licensed firearms dealer" means an importer, manufacturer, or dealer having a license to deal in destructive devices or their ammunition, issued and in effect pursuant to the federal "Gun Control Act of 1968," 82 Stat. 1213, 18 U.S.C. 923 et seq., and any amendments or additions to that act or reenactments of that act.

**HISTORY: 150 v H 12, § 1, eff. 4-8-04; 151 v H 66, § 101.01, eff. 6-30-05.**

The effective date is set by § 612.12 of 151 v H 66.

**Publisher's Note:**

This section was amended and renumbered from RC § 181.251 by 151 v H 66, effective June 30, 2005.

## § 5502.64 Metropolitan county criminal justice services agency; formation, powers, duties.

(A) A county may enter into an agreement with the largest city within the county to establish a metropolitan county criminal justice services agency, if the population of the county exceeds five hundred thousand or the population of the city exceeds two hundred fifty thousand.

(B) A metropolitan county criminal justice services agency shall do all of the following:

(1) Accomplish criminal and juvenile justice systems planning within its services area;

(2) Collect, analyze, and correlate information and data concerning the criminal and juvenile justice systems within its services area;

(3) Cooperate with and provide technical assistance to all criminal and juvenile justice agencies and systems and other appropriate organizations and persons within its services area;

(4) Encourage and assist agencies of the criminal and juvenile justice systems and other appropriate organizations and persons to solve problems that relate to its duties;

(5) Administer within its services area any federal criminal justice acts or juvenile justice acts that the division of criminal justice services pursuant to section 5139.11 of the Revised Code or the department of youth services administers within the state;

(6) Implement the comprehensive plans for its services area;

(7) Monitor or evaluate, within its services area, the performance of the criminal and juvenile justice systems projects and programs that are financed in whole or in part by funds granted through it;

(8) Apply for, allocate, and disburse grants that are made available pursuant to any federal criminal justice acts, or pursuant to any other federal, state, or private sources for the purpose of improving the criminal and juvenile justice systems;

(9) Contract with federal, state, and local agencies, foundations, corporations, and other businesses or persons to carry out the duties of the agency.

**HISTORY: RC § 122.25, 137 v H 1277 (Eff 12-14-78); RC § 109.95, 142 v H 171 (Eff 7-1-87); RC § 122.25, 142 v H 231 (Eff 10-5-87); 144 v H 298 (Eff 7-26-91); RC § 181.54, 145 v H 152 (Eff 7-1-93); 149 v H 94. Eff 9-5-2001; 151 v H 66, § 101.01, eff. 6-30-05.**

The effective date is set by § 612.12 of 151 v H 66.

**Publisher's Note:**

This section was amended and renumbered from RC § 181.54 by 151 v H 66, effective June 30, 2005.

## § 5502.65 Funding, comprehensive plan, supervisory board for metropolitan county agency.

(A)(1) When funds are available for criminal justice purposes pursuant to section 5502.64 of the Revised Code, the division of criminal justice services shall provide funds to metropolitan county criminal justice services agencies for the purpose of developing, coordinating, evaluating, and implementing comprehensive plans within their respective counties. The division of criminal justice services shall provide funds to an agency only if it complies with the conditions of division (B) of this section.

(2) When funds are available for juvenile justice purposes pursuant to section 5502.64 of the Revised Code, the department of youth services shall provide funds to metropolitan county criminal justice services agencies for the purpose of developing, coordinating, evaluating, and implementing comprehensive plans within their respective counties. The department shall provide funds to an agency only if it complies with the conditions of division (B) of this section.

(B) A metropolitan county criminal justice services agency shall do all of the following:

(1) Submit, in a form that is acceptable to the division of criminal justice services or the department of youth services pursuant to section 5139.01 of the Revised Code, a comprehensive plan for the county;

(2) Establish a metropolitan county criminal justice services supervisory board whose members shall include a majority of the local elected officials in the county and representatives from law enforcement agencies, courts, prosecuting authorities, public defender agencies, rehabilitation and correction agencies, community organizations,

juvenile justice services agencies, professionals, and private citizens in the county, and that shall have the authority set forth in division (C) of this section;

(3) Organize in the manner provided in sections 167.01 to 167.03, 302.21 to 302.24, or 713.21 to 713.27 of the Revised Code, unless the board created pursuant to division (B)(2) of this section organizes pursuant to these sections.

(C) A metropolitan county criminal justice services supervisory board shall do all of the following:

(1) Exercise leadership in improving the quality of the criminal and juvenile justice systems in the county;

(2) Review, approve, and maintain general oversight of the comprehensive plans for the county and the implementation of the plans;

(3) Review and comment on the overall needs and accomplishments of the criminal and juvenile justice systems in the county;

(4) Establish, as required to comply with this division, task forces, ad hoc committees, and other committees, whose members shall be appointed by the chairperson of the board;

(5) Establish any rules that the board considers necessary and that are consistent with the federal criminal justice acts and section 5502.62 of the Revised Code.

**HISTORY: RC § 122.26, 137 v H 1277 (Eff 12-14-78); 139 v H 536 (Eff 8-12-82); RC § 109.96, 142 v H 171 (Eff 7-1-87); RC § 122.26, 142 v H 231 (Eff 10-5-87); 144 v H 298 (Eff 7-26-91); RC § 181.55, 145 v H 152 (Eff 7-1-93); 149 v H 94. Eff 9-5-2001; 151 v H 66, § 101.01, eff. 6-30-05.**

The effective date is set by § 612.12 of 151 v H 66.

**Publisher's Note:**

This section was amended and renumbered from RC § 181.55 by 151 v H 66, effective June 30, 2005.

## § 5502.66 Administrative planning districts; criminal justice coordinating councils.

(A) In counties in which a metropolitan county criminal justice services agency does not exist, the division of criminal justice services shall discharge the division's duties that the director of public safety requires it to administer by establishing administrative planning districts for criminal justice programs. An administrative planning district shall contain a group of contiguous counties in which no county has a metropolitan county criminal justice services agency.

(B) In counties in which a metropolitan county criminal justice services agency does not exist, the department of youth services shall discharge pursuant to section 5139.11 of the Revised Code the department's duty by establishing administrative planning districts for juvenile justice programs.

(C) All administrative planning districts shall contain a group of contiguous counties in which no county has a metropolitan county criminal justice services agency.

(D) Any county or any combination of contiguous counties within an administrative planning district may form a criminal justice coordinating council or a juvenile justice coordinating council for its respective programs, if the county or the group of counties has a total population in excess of two hundred fifty thousand. The council shall comply with the conditions set forth in divisions (B) and (C) of section 5502.65 of the Revised Code, and exercise within its jurisdiction the powers and duties set forth in division (B) of section 5502.64 of the Revised Code.

**HISTORY: RC § 122.27, 137 v H 1277 (Eff 12-14-78); RC § 109.97, 142 v H 171 (Eff 7-1-87); RC § 122.27, 142 v H 231 (Eff 10-5-87); 142 v H 708 (Eff 4-19-88); RC § 181.56, 145 v H 152 (Eff 7-1-93); 149 v H 94. Eff 9-5-2001; 151 v H 66, § 101.01, eff. 6-30-05.**

The effective date is set by § 612.12 of 151 v H 66.

**Publisher's Note:**

This section was amended and renumbered from RC § 181.56 by 151 v H 66, effective June 30, 2005.

## § 5502.67 Justice program services fund.

There is hereby created in the state treasury the justice program services fund. The fund shall consist of the court costs designated for the fund pursuant to section 2949.094 [2949.09.4] of the Revised Code, twenty-five cents of each fee collected under sections 4501.34, 4503.26, 4506.08, and 4509.05 of the Revised Code as specified in those sections, plus on and after October 1, 2009, twenty-five cents of each fee collected under sections 4505.14 and 4519.63 of the Revised Code as specified in those sections, and all money collected by the division of criminal justice services for nonfederal purposes, including subscription fees for participating in the Ohio incident-based reporting system under division (C) of section 5502.62 of the Revised Code, unless otherwise designated by law. The justice program services fund shall be used to pay costs of administering the operations of the division of criminal justice services, except that the director of budget and management may transfer excess money from the justice program services fund to the state highway safety fund if the director of public safety determines that the amount of money in the justice program services fund exceeds the amount required to cover such costs incurred by the office of criminal justice services and requests the director of budget and management to make the transfer.

**HISTORY: 152 v H 67, § 101.01, eff. 6-30-07; 153 v H 2, § 101.01, eff. 7-1-09.**

The effective date is set by § 812.10 of 153 v H 2.
The effective date is set by § 609.10 of 152 v H 67.

## § 5502.68 Drug law enforcement fund.

(A) There is hereby created in the state treasury the drug law enforcement fund. Ninety-seven per cent of three dollars and fifty cents out of each ten-dollar court cost imposed pursuant to section 2949.094 of the Revised Code shall be credited to the fund. Money in the fund shall be used only in accordance with this section to award grants to counties, municipal corporations, townships, township police districts, and joint police districts to defray the expenses that a drug task force organized in the county, or in the county in which the municipal corporation, township, or district is located, incurs in performing its functions related to the enforcement of the state's drug laws and other state laws related to illegal drug activity.

The division of criminal justice services shall administer all money deposited into the drug law enforcement fund and, by rule adopted under Chapter 119. of the Revised Code, shall establish procedures for a county, municipal corporation, township, township police district, or joint police district to apply for money from the fund to defray the expenses that a drug task force organized in the county, or in the county in which the municipal corporation, township, or district is located, incurs in performing its functions related to the enforcement of the state's drug laws and other state laws related to illegal drug activity, procedures and criteria for determining eligibility of applicants to be provided money from the fund, and procedures and criteria for determining the amount of money to be provided out of the fund to eligible applicants.

(B) The procedures and criteria established under division (A) of this section for applying for money from the fund shall include, but shall not be limited to, a provision requiring a county, municipal corporation, township, township police district, or joint police district that applies for money from the fund to specify in its application the amount of money desired from the fund, provided that the cumulative amount requested in all applications submitted for any single drug task force may not exceed more than two hundred fifty thousand dollars in any calendar year for that task force.

(C) The procedures and criteria established under division (A) of this section for determining eligibility of applicants to be provided money from the fund and for determining the amount of money to be provided out of the fund to eligible applicants shall include, but not be limited to, all of the following:

(1) Provisions requiring that, in order to be eligible to be provided money from the fund, a drug task force that applies for money from the fund must provide evidence that the drug task force will receive a local funding match of at least twenty-five per cent of the task force's projected operating costs in the period of time covered by the grant;

(2) Provisions requiring that money from the fund be allocated and provided to drug task forces that apply for money from the fund in accordance with the following priorities:

(a) Drug task forces that apply, that are in existence on the date of the application, and that are determined to be eligible applicants, and to which either of the following applies shall be given first priority to be provided money from the fund:

(i) Drug task forces that received funding through the division of criminal justice services in calendar year 2007;

(ii) Drug task forces in a county that has a population that exceeds seven hundred fifty thousand.

(b) If any moneys remain in the fund after all drug task forces that apply, that are in existence on the date of the application, that are determined to be eligible applicants, and that satisfy the criteria set forth in division (C)(2)(a)(i) or (ii) of this section are provided money from the fund as described in division (C)(2)(a) of this section, the following categories of drug task forces that apply and that are determined to be eligible applicants shall be given priority to be provided money from the fund in the order in which they apply for money from the fund:

(i) Drug task forces that are not in existence on the date of the application;

(ii) Drug task forces that are in existence on the date of the application but that do not satisfy the criteria set forth in division (C)(2)(a)(i) or (ii) of this section.

(D) The procedures and criteria established under division (A) of this section for determining the amount of money to be provided out of the fund to eligible applicants shall include, but shall not be limited to, a provision specifying that the cumulative amount provided to any single drug task force may not exceed more than two hundred fifty thousand dollars in any calendar year.

(E) As used in this section, "drug task force" means a drug task force organized in any county by the sheriff of the county, the prosecuting attorney of the county, the chief of police of the organized police department of any municipal corporation or township in the county, and the chief of police of the police force of any township police district or joint police district in the county to perform functions related to the enforcement of state drug laws and other state laws related to illegal drug activity.

**HISTORY: 152 v H 562, § 101.01, eff. 9-23-08; 153 v H 2, § 101.01, eff. 7-1-09; 2011 HB 153, § 101.01, eff. Sept. 29, 2011.**

The effective date is set by § 812.10 of 153 v H 2.
The effective date is set by § 812.10 of 152 v H 562.

**Publisher's Note:**

The enactment of RC § 5502.68 by 152 v H 562 was disapproved in part by the Governor.

# CHAPTER 5503: STATE HIGHWAY PATROL

Section



[AUTHORITY ON TURNPIKE PROJECTS]



## § 5503.01 Division of state highway patrol.

There is hereby created in the department of public safety a division of state highway patrol which shall be administered by a superintendent of the state highway patrol.

The superintendent shall be appointed by the director of public safety, and shall serve at the director's pleasure. The superintendent shall give bond for the faithful performance of the superintendent's official duties in such amount and with such security as the director approves.

The superintendent, with the approval of the director, may appoint any number of state highway patrol troopers and radio operators as are necessary to carry out sections 5503.01 to 5503.06 of the Revised Code, but the number of troopers shall not be less than eight hundred eighty. The number of radio operators shall not exceed eighty in number. Except as provided in this section, at the time of appointment, troopers shall be not less than twenty-one years of age, nor have reached thirty-five years of age. A person who is attending a training school for prospective state highway patrol troopers established under section 5503.05 of the Revised Code and attains the age of thirty-five years during the person's period of attendance at that training school shall not be disqualified as over age and shall be permitted to continue to attend the training school as long as the person otherwise is eligible to do so. Such a person also remains eligible to be appointed a trooper. Any other person who attains or will attain the age of thirty-five years prior to the time of appointment shall be disqualified as over age.

At the time of appointment, troopers shall have been legal residents of Ohio for at least one year, except that this residence requirement may be waived by the superintendent.

If any state highway patrol troopers become disabled through accident or illness, the superintendent, with the approval of the director, shall fill any vacancies through the appointment of other troopers from a qualified list to serve during the period of the disability.

The superintendent and state highway patrol troopers shall be vested with the authority of peace officers for the purpose of enforcing the laws of the state that it is the duty of the patrol to enforce and may arrest, without warrant, any person who, in the presence of the superintendent or any trooper, is engaged in the violation of any such laws. The state highway patrol troopers shall never be used as peace officers in connection with any strike or labor dispute.

Each state highway patrol trooper and radio operator, upon appointment and before entering upon official duties, shall take an oath of office for faithful performance of the trooper's or radio operator's official duties and execute a bond in the sum of twenty-five hundred dollars, payable to the state and for the use and benefit of any aggrieved party who may have a cause of action against any trooper or radio operator for misconduct while in the performance of official duties. In no event shall the bond include any claim arising out of negligent operation of a motorcycle or motor vehicle used by a trooper or radio operator in the performance of official duties.

The superintendent shall prescribe a distinguishing uniform and badge which shall be worn by each state highway patrol trooper and radio operator while on duty, unless otherwise designated by the superintendent. No person shall wear the distinguishing uniform of the state highway patrol or the badge or any distinctive part of that uniform, except on order of the superintendent.

The superintendent, with the approval of the director, may appoint necessary clerks, stenographers, and employees.

**HISTORY: GC § 1183; 121 v 455 (518); 123 v 862 (923); 124 v 711; Bureau of Code Revision, 10-1-53; 125 v 127 (142) (Eff 10-2-53); 126 v 621 (Eff 10-5-55); 129 v 1671 (1691); 131 v 1263 (Eff 11-11-65); 132 v H 1 (Eff 2-21-67); 132 v H 658 (Eff 3-20-68); 138 v H 165 (Eff 11-13-79); 144 v S 144 (Eff 8-8-91); 144 v S 98 (Eff 11-12-92); 147 v S 22. Eff 4-22-97.**

## § 5503.02 Duties and powers of state highway patrol.

(A) The state highway patrol shall enforce the laws of the state relating to the titling, registration, and licensing of motor vehicles; enforce on all roads and highways, notwithstanding section 4513.39 of the Revised Code, the laws relating to the operation and use of vehicles on the highways; enforce and prevent the violation of the laws relating to the size, weight, and speed of commercial motor vehicles and all laws designed for the protection of the highway pavements and structures on the highways; investigate and enforce rules and laws of the public utilities commission governing the transportation of persons and property by motor carriers and report violations of such rules and laws to the commission; enforce against any motor transportation company as defined in section 4921.02 of the Revised Code, any contract carrier by motor vehicle as defined in section 4923.02 of the Revised Code, any private motor carrier as defined in section 4923.20 of the Revised Code, and any motor carrier as defined in section 4919.75 of the Revised Code those rules and laws that, if violated, may result in a forfeiture as provided in section 4905.83, 4919.99, 4921.99, or 4923.99 of the Revised Code; investigate and report violations of all laws relating to the collection of excise taxes on motor vehicle fuels; and regulate the movement of traffic on the roads and highways of the state, notwithstanding section 4513.39 of the Revised Code.

The patrol, whenever possible, shall determine the identity of the persons who are causing or who are responsible for the breaking, damaging, or destruction of any improved surfaced roadway, structure, sign, marker, guardrail, or other appurtenance constructed or maintained by the department of transportation and shall arrest the persons who are responsible for the breaking, damaging, or destruction and bring them before the proper officials for prosecution.

State highway patrol troopers shall investigate and report all motor vehicle accidents on all roads and highways outside of municipal corporations. The superintendent of the patrol or any state highway patrol trooper may arrest, without a warrant, any person, who is the driver of or a passenger in any vehicle operated or standing on a state highway, whom the superintendent or trooper has reasonable cause to believe is guilty of a felony, under the same circumstances and with the same power that any peace officer may make such an arrest.

The superintendent or any state highway patrol trooper may enforce the criminal laws on all state properties and state institutions, owned or leased by the state, and, when so ordered by the governor in the event of riot, civil disorder, or insurrection, may, pursuant to sections 2935.03 to 2935.05 of the Revised Code, arrest offenders against the criminal laws wherever they may be found within the state if the violations occurred upon, or resulted in injury to person or property on, state properties or state institutions, or under the conditions described in division (B) of this section.

(B) In the event of riot, civil disorder, or insurrection, or the reasonable threat of riot, civil disorder, or insurrection, and upon request, as provided in this section, of the sheriff of a county or the mayor or other chief executive of a municipal corporation, the governor may order the state highway patrol to enforce the criminal laws within the area threatened by riot, civil disorder, or insurrection, as designated by the governor, upon finding that law enforcement agencies within the counties involved will not be reasonably capable of controlling the riot, civil disorder, or insurrection and that additional assistance is necessary. In cities in which the sheriff is under contract to provide exclusive police services pursuant to section 311.29 of the Revised Code, in villages, and in the unincorporated areas of the county, the sheriff has exclusive authority to request the use of the patrol. In cities in which the sheriff does not exclusively provide police services, the mayor, or other chief executive performing the duties of mayor, has exclusive authority to request the use of the patrol.

The superintendent or any state highway patrol trooper may enforce the criminal laws within the area designated by the governor during the emergency arising out of the riot, civil disorder, or insurrection until released by the governor upon consultation with the requesting authority. State highway patrol troopers shall never be used as peace officers in connection with any strike or labor dispute.

When a request for the use of the patrol is made pursuant to this division, the requesting authority shall notify the law enforcement authorities in contiguous communities and the sheriff of each county within which the threatened area, or any part of the threatened area, lies of the request, but the failure to notify the authorities or a sheriff shall not affect the validity of the request.

(C) Any person who is arrested by the superintendent or a state highway patrol trooper shall be taken before any court or magistrate having jurisdiction of the offense with which the person is charged. Any person who is arrested or apprehended within the limits of a municipal corporation shall be brought before the municipal court or other tribunal of the municipal corporation.

(D)(1) State highway patrol troopers have the same right and power of search and seizure as other peace officers.

No state official shall command, order, or direct any state highway patrol trooper to perform any duty or service that is not authorized by law. The powers and duties conferred on the patrol are supplementary to, and in no way a limitation on, the powers and duties of sheriffs or other peace officers of the state.

(2)(a) A state highway patrol trooper, pursuant to the policy established by the superintendent of the state highway patrol under division (D)(2)(b) of this section, may render emergency assistance to any other peace officer who has arrest authority under section 2935.03 of the Revised Code, if both of the following apply:

(i) There is a threat of imminent physical danger to the peace officer, a threat of physical harm to another person, or any other serious emergency situation;

(ii) Either the peace officer requests emergency assistance or it appears that the peace officer is unable to request emergency assistance and the circumstances observed by the state highway patrol trooper reasonably indicate that emergency assistance is appropriate, or the peace officer requests emergency assistance and in the request the peace officer specifies a particular location and the state highway patrol trooper arrives at that location prior to the time that the peace officer arrives at that location and the circumstances observed by the state highway patrol trooper reasonably indicate that emergency assistance is appropriate.

(b) The superintendent of the state highway patrol shall establish, within sixty days of August 8, 1991, a policy that sets forth the manner and procedures by which a state highway patrol trooper may render emergency assistance to any other peace officer under division (D)(2)(a) of this section. The policy shall include a provision that a state highway patrol trooper never be used as a peace officer in connection with any strike or labor dispute.

(3)(a) A state highway patrol trooper who renders emergency assistance to any other peace officer under the policy established by the superintendent pursuant to division (D)(2)(b) of this section shall be considered to be performing regular employment for the purposes of compensation, pension, indemnity fund rights, workers' compensation, and other rights or benefits to which the trooper may be entitled as incident to regular employment.

(b) A state highway patrol trooper who renders emergency assistance to any other peace officer under the policy established by the superintendent pursuant to division (D)(2)(b) of this section retains personal immunity from liability as specified in section 9.86 of the Revised Code.

(c) A state highway patrol trooper who renders emergency assistance under the policy established by the superintendent pursuant to division (D)(2)(b) of this section has the same authority as the peace officer for or with whom the state highway patrol trooper is providing emergency assistance.

(E)(1) Subject to the availability of funds specifically appropriated by the general assembly for security detail purposes, the state highway patrol shall provide security as follows:

(a) For the governor;

(b) At the direction of the governor, for other officials of the state government of this state; officials of the state governments of other states who are visiting this state; officials of the United States government who are visiting this state; officials of the governments of foreign countries or their political subdivisions who are visiting this state; or other officials or dignitaries who are visiting this state, including, but not limited to, members of trade missions;

(c) For the capitol square, as defined in section 105.41 of the Revised Code;

(d) For other state property.

(2) To carry out the security responsibilities of the patrol listed in division (E)(1) of this section, the superintendent may assign state highway patrol troopers to a separate unit that is responsible for security details. The number of troopers assigned to particular security details shall be determined by the superintendent.

(3) The superintendent and any state highway patrol trooper, when providing security pursuant to division (E)(1)(a) or (b) of this section, have the same arrest powers as other peace officers to apprehend offenders against the criminal laws who endanger or threaten the security of any person being protected, no matter where the offense occurs.

The superintendent, any state highway patrol trooper, and any special police officer designated under section 5503.09 of the Revised Code, when providing security pursuant to division (E)(1)(c) of this section, shall enforce any rules governing capitol square adopted by the capitol square review and advisory board.

(F) The governor may order the state highway patrol to undertake major criminal investigations that involve state property interests. If an investigation undertaken pursuant to this division results in either the issuance of a no bill or the filing of an indictment, the superintendent shall file a complete and accurate report of the investigation with the president of the senate, the speaker of the house of representatives, the minority leader of the senate, and the minority leader of the house of representatives within fifteen days after the issuance of the no bill or the filing of an indictment. If the investigation does not have as its result any prosecutorial action, the superintendent shall, upon reporting this fact to the governor, file a complete and accurate report of the investigation with the president of the senate, the speaker of the house of representatives, the minority leader of the senate, and the minority leader of the house of representatives.

(G) The superintendent may purchase or lease real property and buildings needed by the patrol, negotiate the sale of real property owned by the patrol, rent or lease real property owned or leased by the patrol, and make or cause to be made repairs to all property owned or under the control of the patrol. Any instrument by which real property is acquired pursuant to this division shall identify the agency of the state that has the use and benefit of the real property as specified in section 5301.012 of the Revised Code.

Sections 123.01 and 125.02 of the Revised Code do not limit the powers granted to the superintendent by this division.

**HISTORY: GC § 1183-2; 121 v 455 (520); 122 v 531; Bureau of Code Revision, 10-1-53; 132 v H 996 (Eff 6-13-68); 134 v H 600 (Eff 3-3-72); 135 v H 200 (Eff 9-28-73); 135 v H 323 (Eff 10-31-73); 137 v S 221 (Eff 11-23-77); 138 v H 837 (Eff 3-23-81); 139 v H 694 (Eff 11-15-81); 142 v H 428 (Eff 9-26-88); 144 v S 144 (Eff 8-8-91); 144 v S 351 (Eff 7-1-92); 144 v S 381 (Eff 1-15-93); 145 v H 687 (Eff 10-12-94); 146 v H 117 (Eff 9-29-95); 146 v S 34 (Eff 10-25-95); 148 v H 19. Eff 10-26-99; 2011 HB 114, § 101.01, eff. June 29, 2011.**

Acts 2011, HB 114, § 806.10 provides: "The items of law contained in this act, and their applications, are severable. If any item of law contained in this act, or if any application of any item of law contained in this act, is held invalid, the invalidity does not affect other items of law contained in this act and their applications that can be given effect without the invalid item or application."

SECTION 3. * * * Section 5503.02 of the Revised Code is presented in this act as a composite of the section as amended by both Am. Sub. H.B. 117 and Am. S.B. 34 of the 121st General Assembly, with the new language of neither of the acts shown in capital letters. This is in recognition of the principle stated in division (B) of section 1.52 of the Revised Code that such amendments are to be harmonized where not substantively irreconcilable and constitutes a legislative finding that such is the resulting version in effect prior to the effective date of this act.

## § 5503.03 Equipment; rules; promotions.

The state highway patrol and the superintendent of the state highway patrol shall be furnished by the state with such vehicles, equipment, and supplies as the director of public safety deems necessary, all of which shall remain the property of the state and be strictly accounted for by each member of the patrol.

The patrol may be equipped with standardized and tested devices for weighing vehicles, and may stop and weigh any vehicle which appears to weigh in excess of the amounts permitted by sections 5577.01 to 5577.14 of the Revised Code.

The superintendent, with the approval of the director, shall prescribe rules for instruction and discipline, make all administrative rules, and fix the hours of duty for patrol officers. He shall divide the state into districts and assign members of the patrol to such districts in a manner that he deems proper. He may transfer members of the patrol from one district to another, and classify and rank members of the patrol. All promotions to a higher grade shall be made from the next lower grade. When a patrol officer is promoted by the superintendent, the officer's salary shall be increased to that of the lowest step in the pay range for the new grade which shall increase the officer's salary or wage by at least nine per cent of the base pay wherever possible.

**HISTORY: GC § 1183-3; 121 v 455 (521); Bureau of Code Revision, 10-1-53; 125 v 127 (142) (10-2-53); 139 v H 694 (Eff 11-15-81); 144 v S 98. Eff 11-12-92.**

This section was amended by Senate Bill 5 of the 2011 legislative session. However, referendum petitions were filed to prevent SB 5 from taking effect as scheduled on July 1, 2011. The provisions of SB 5 were rejected by the voters at the referendum election on November 8, 2011.

## § 5503.04 Disposition of fines and moneys arising from bail forfeitures.

Forty-five per cent of the fines collected from or moneys arising from bail forfeited by persons apprehended or arrested by state highway patrol troopers shall be paid into the state treasury to be credited to the general revenue fund, five per cent shall be paid into the state treasury to be credited to the trauma and emergency medical services grants fund created by division (E) of section 4513.263 [4513.26.3] of the Revised Code, and fifty per cent shall be paid into the treasury of the municipal corporation where the case is prosecuted, if in a mayor's court. If the prosecution is in a trial court outside a municipal corporation, or outside the territorial jurisdiction of a municipal court, the fifty per cent of the fines and moneys that is not paid into the state treasury shall be paid into the treasury of the county where the case is prosecuted. The fines and moneys paid into a county treasury and the fines and moneys paid into the treasury of a municipal corporation shall be deposited one-half to the same fund and expended in the same manner as is the revenue received from the registration of motor vehicles, and one-half to the general fund of such county or municipal corporation.

If the prosecution is in a municipal court, forty-five per cent of the fines and moneys shall be paid into the state treasury to be credited to the general revenue fund, five per cent shall be paid into the state treasury to be credited to the trauma and emergency medical services grants fund created by division (E) of section 4513.263 [4513.26.3] of the Revised Code, ten per cent shall be paid into the county treasury to be credited to the general fund of the county, and forty per cent shall be paid into the municipal treasury to be credited to the general fund of the municipal corporation. In the Auglaize county, Clermont county, Crawford county, Hocking county, Jackson county, Lawrence county, Madison county, Miami county, Ottawa county, Portage county, and Wayne county municipal courts, that portion of money otherwise paid into the municipal treasury shall be paid into the county treasury.

The trial court shall make remittance of the fines and moneys as prescribed in this section, and at the same time as the remittance is made of the state's portion to the state treasury, the trial court shall notify the superintendent of the state highway patrol of the case and the amount covered by the remittance.

This section does not apply to fines for violations of division (B) of section 4513.263 [4513.26.3] of the Revised Code, or for violations of any municipal ordinance that is substantively comparable to that division, all of which shall be delivered to the treasurer of state as provided in division (E) of section 4513.263 [4513.26.3] of the Revised Code.

**HISTORY: GC § 1183-4; 121 v 455 (521); Bureau of Code Revision, 10-1-53; 126 v 773 (Eff 10-5-55); 129 v 1011 (Eff 1-1-62); 132 v H 361 (Eff 7-25-67); 136 v H 205 (Eff 1-1-76); 137 v S 221 (Eff 11-23-77); 137 v H 312 (Eff 1-1-78); 138 v H 1 (Eff 5-16-79); 138 v H 961 (Eff 9-29-80); 141 v S 54 (Eff 5-6-86); 142 v H 171 (Eff 7-1-87); 144 v H 200 (Eff 7-8-91); 144 v S 144 (Eff 8-8-91); 145 v H 21 (Eff 2-4-94); 148 v H 138. Eff 11-3-2000.**

## § 5503.07 Misdemeanor arrests.

In addition to the powers and duties of the state highway patrol set forth in section 5503.02 of the Revised Code and subject to the limitations of section 5503.01 of the Revised Code, a state highway patrol trooper shall arrest any person found committing a misdemeanor within the bounds of rest areas or roadside parks within the limits of the right-of-way of interstate highways and other state highways, or in violation of section 5515.07 of the Revised

Code in other areas within the limits of the right-of-way of interstate highways.

**HISTORY: 130 v 1263 (Eff 9-20-63); 144 v S 144. Eff 8-8-91.**

### [AUTHORITY ON TURNPIKE PROJECTS]

### § 5503.31 Authority on turnpike projects.

The state highway patrol shall have the same authority as is conferred upon it by section 5503.02 of the Revised Code with respect to the enforcement of state laws on other roads and highways and on other state properties, to enforce on all turnpike projects the laws of the state and the bylaws, rules, and regulations of the Ohio turnpike commission. The patrol, the superintendent of the patrol, and all state highway patrol troopers shall have the same authority to make arrests on all turnpike projects for violations of state laws and of bylaws, rules, and regulations of the Ohio turnpike commission as is conferred upon them by section 5503.02 of the Revised Code to make arrests on, and in connection with offenses committed on, other roads and highways and on other state properties.

**HISTORY: 126 v 1036 (Eff 6-20-55); 144 v S 144. Eff 8-8-91.**

## CHAPTER 5589: OFFENSES RELATING TO HIGHWAYS

Section



### § 5589.01 Obstructing public grounds, highway, street, or alley.

No person shall obstruct or encumber by fences, buildings, structures, or otherwise, a public ground, highway, street, or alley of a municipal corporation.

**HISTORY: RS § 6921; S&C 441, 878, 880; GC § 13421; 30 v 22, §§ 1, 2; 32 v 38; 54 v 130, §§ 1, 2; 72 v 112; Bureau of Code Revision. Eff 10-1-53.**

### § 5589.02 Altering or injuring marker or monument.

No person shall alter, deface, injure, or destroy any marker or monument placed along, upon, or near a public highway, by the proper authorities, to mark the boundaries thereof, or for any other purpose.

**HISTORY: GC § 13421-4; 106 v 574 (659), § 281; Bureau of Code Revision. Eff 10-1-53.**

### § 5589.03 Refusal or neglect of officials to perform duty.

No county engineer, township trustee, or township highway superintendent shall willfully neglect, fail, or refuse to perform the duties of his office. Conviction for such neglect, failure, or refusal shall operate as a removal from office.

**HISTORY: GC § 13421-5; 106 v 574 (659), § 282; Bureau of Code Revision. Eff 10-1-53.**

### § 5589.05 Interfering with drawbridge on Muskingum improvement.

No person, except a commissioner, engineer, superintendent, lock tender, bridge tender, or collector and without express direction or permission from one of them, shall open or interfere with a drawbridge on the Muskingum improvement.

**HISTORY: RS § 218-216; GC § 12640; 76 v 187, § 12; Bureau of Code Revision. Eff 10-1-53.**

### § 5589.06 Obstructing ditch, drain, or watercourse; duty of superintendent.

No person shall wrongfully obstruct any ditch, drain, or watercourse along, upon or across a public highway, or divert any water from adjacent lands to or upon a public highway. Whenever the township highway superintendent learns of any obstruction of any ditch, drain, or watercourse along, upon, or across a public highway, or diversion of any water from adjacent lands to or upon a public highway, he shall notify the board of township trustees, which shall cause written notice thereof to be personally served upon the person, firm, or corporation, or upon any agent in charge of the property of the person, firm, or corporation causing such obstruction or diversion. Notice may be served by a constable of the proper township or any person authorized and deputed therefor by the board of township trustees, and shall describe and locate said obstruction or diversion and direct its immediate removal.

If the person, company, or corporation does not within five days from the receipt of written notice proceed to remove such obstruction and complete the removal within a reasonable time, the township highway superintendent, upon the order of the board of township trustees, shall remove the obstruction. The expense incurred shall be paid in the first instance out of any money levied, collected, and available for highway purposes and shall then be collected from the person, company, or corporation by civil action by the board of township trustees, and paid into the highway fund of the township.

**HISTORY: GC § 13421-7; 106 v 574 (659), § 284; Bureau of Code Revision. Eff 10-1-53.**

## § 5589.07 Failure to make levy or furnish estimates.

No person charged with the duty of making any levy or furnishing any estimates or budgets requesting any levy or allowance for the construction, improvement, maintenance, or repair of any public highway, bridge, or culvert shall fail to make such levy or allowance, or furnish such estimate, budget, or request.

**HISTORY: GC § 13421-8; 106 v 574 (660), § 285; Bureau of Code Revision. Eff 10-1-53.**

## § 5589.08 Operating traction engines upon improved highways.

No person shall drive over the improved highways of the state, or any political subdivision thereof, a traction engine or tractor with tires or wheels equipped with ice picks, spuds, spikes, chains, or other projections of any kind extending beyond the cleats, or no person shall tow or in any way pull another vehicle over the improved highways of the state, or any political subdivision thereof, which towed or pulled vehicle has tires or wheels equipped with ice picks, spuds, spikes, chains or other projections of any kind. "Traction engine" or "tractor," as used in this section, applies to all self-propelling engines equipped with metal-tired wheels operated or propelled by any form of engine, motor, or mechanical power.

No municipal corporation, county, or township shall adopt, enforce, or maintain any ordinance, rule, or regulation contrary to or inconsistent with this section, or require of any person any license tax upon or registration fee for any traction engine, tractor, or trailer, or any permit or license to operate. Operators of traction engines or tractors shall have the same rights upon the public streets and highways as the drivers of any other vehicles, unless some other safe and convenient way is provided, and no public road open to traffic shall be closed to traction engines or tractors.

**HISTORY: GC § 13421-12; 106 v 574 (660), § 289; 107 v 652; Bureau of Code Revision, 10-1-53; 125 v 401. Eff 10-16-53.**

## § 5589.081 Studded tires; prohibitions.

(A) For purposes of this section, "studded tire" means any tire designed for use on a vehicle, and equipped with metal studs or studs of wear-resisting material that project beyond the tread of the traction surface of the tire; and "motor vehicle," "street or highway," "public safety vehicle," and "school bus" have the same meanings as given those terms in section 4511.01 of the Revised Code.

(B)(1) Except as provided in division (B)(2) of this section, no person shall operate any motor vehicle, other than a public safety vehicle or school bus, that is equipped with studded tires on any street or highway in this state, except during the period extending from the first day of November of each year through the fifteenth day of April of the succeeding year.

(2) A person may operate a motor vehicle that is equipped with retractable studded tires with the studs retracted at any time of the year, but shall operate the motor vehicle with the studs extended only as provided in division (B)(1) of this section.

(C) This section does not apply to the use of tire chains when there is snow or ice on the streets or highways where such chains are being used, or the immediate vicinity thereof.

**HISTORY: 135 v H 398 (Eff 1-1-74); 136 v S 40. Eff 3-12-75; 152 v S 44, § 1, eff. 8-22-08.**

## § 5589.09 Failure or neglect to drag road.

No person, charged with the duty of causing any unimproved or gravel road or part thereof to be dragged, shall willfully fail, neglect, or refuse to cause the same to be done, in such manner and within the time fixed by the sections of the Revised Code applicable thereto, or by the proper authority.

**HISTORY: GC § 13421-13; 106 v 574 (660), § 290; Bureau of Code Revisions. Eff 10-1-53.**

## § 5589.10 Digging, excavating, piling earth, or building fence on highway.

No person shall dig up, remove, excavate, or place any earth or mud upon any portion of any public highway or build a fence upon the same without authority to do so. Each day that such person continues to dig up, remove, or excavate any portion of the public highway constitutes a separate offense.

**HISTORY: GC § 13421-14; 106 v 574 (660), § 291; Bureau of Code Revision. Eff 10-1-53.**

## § 5589.11 Failure or neglect to cut weeds, briers, or bushes.

No person, charged with the duty of cutting, destroying, or removing any weeds, briers, or bushes upon or along a public highway shall willfully fail, neglect, or refuse to cut, destroy, or remove such weeds, briers, or bushes as required in sections 5579.04 and 5579.08 of the Revised Code or on the order of the proper officials.

**HISTORY: GC § 13421-15; 106 v 574 (661), § 292; Bureau of Code Revision, 10-1-53; 140 v S 108. Eff 7-4-84.**

## § 5589.12 Possession of tools belonging to state or county.

No person shall, without being authorized, have in his control or possession any equipment, tools, implements, or other property belonging to the state, county, or township.

**HISTORY: GC § 13421-18; 106 v 574 (661), § 295; Bureau of Code Revision. Eff 10-1-53.**

### § 5589.13 Fines credited to maintenance and repair fund.

All fines collected for violations of sections 5589.02 to 5589.14, inclusive, of the Revised Code, shall be paid into the county treasury and placed to the credit of the fund for the maintenance and repair of the highways within such county.

**HISTORY: GC § 13421-20; 106 v 574 (661), § 297; Bureau of Code Revision. Eff 10-1-53.**

### § 5589.14 Prosecution of offenses.

The prosecuting attorney shall prosecute all offenders under sections 5589.02 to 5589.13, inclusive, of the Revised Code, upon application of any official or individual filing any affidavit before any magistrate of the county charging an offense under such sections. This section shall not prevent the prosecuting attorney or any other official from prosecuting offenders under such sections upon his own initiative.

**HISTORY: GC § 13421-22; 106 v 574 (661), § 299; Bureau of Code Revision. Eff 10-1-53.**

[RAILROADS]

### § 5589.20 Legislative intent concerning obstruction of grade crossings by trains.

The general assembly finds that the improper obstruction of railroad grade crossings by trains is a direct threat to the health, safety, and welfare of the citizens of this state inasmuch as improper obstructions create uniquely different local safety problems by preventing the timely movement of ambulances, the vehicles of law enforcement officers and firefighters, and official and unofficial vehicles transporting health care officials and professionals. It is the intent of the general assembly in amending sections 5589.21, 5589.24, and 5589.99 of the Revised Code that the health, safety, and welfare of the citizens of this state be enhanced through those amendments.

**HISTORY: 148 v S 207. Eff 10-27-2000.**

### § 5589.21 Obstruction of roads by railroads.

(A) No railroad company shall obstruct, or permit or cause to be obstructed a public street, road, or highway, by permitting a railroad car, locomotive, or other obstruction to remain upon or across it for longer than five minutes, to the hindrance or inconvenience of travelers or a person passing along or upon such street, road, or highway.

(B) At the end of each five minute period of obstruction of a public street, road, or highway, each railroad company shall cause such railroad car, locomotive, or other obstruction to be removed for sufficient time, not less than three minutes, to allow the passage of persons and vehicles waiting to cross.

(C) This section does not apply to obstruction of a public street, road, or highway by a continuously moving through train or caused by circumstances wholly beyond the control of the railroad company, but does apply to other obstructions, including without limitation those caused by stopped trains and trains engaged in switching, loading, or unloading operations.

(D) If a railroad car, locomotive, or other obstruction is obstructing a public street, road, or highway in violation of division (A) of this section and the violation occurs in the unincorporated area of one or more counties, or in one or more municipal corporations, the officers and employees of each affected county or municipal corporation may charge the railroad company with only one violation of the law arising from the same facts and circumstances and the same act.

(E) Upon the filing of an affidavit or complaint for violation of division (A) of this section, summons shall be issued to the railroad company pursuant to division (B) of section 2935.10 of the Revised Code, which summons shall be served on the regular ticket or freight agent of the company in the county where the offense occurred.

**HISTORY: RS § 4748; S&S 669; S&C 1311; GC § 7472; 65 v 14, § 31; Bureau of Code Revision, 10-1-53; 133 v S 5 (Eff 9-4-69); 148 v S 207. Eff 10-27-2000.**

### § 5589.211 Obstructing street, road or highway by abandoning locomotive.

No railroad company shall obstruct, or permit or cause to be obstructed, a public street, road, or highway, by permitting any part of a train whose crew has abandoned the locomotive to remain across it for longer than five minutes to the hindrance or inconvenience of travelers or a person passing along or upon the street, road, or highway, unless the safety of the train crew requires them to abandon the locomotive.

Upon the filing of an affidavit or complaint for violation of this section, summons shall be issued to the railroad company pursuant to division (B) of section 2935.10 of the Revised Code, which summons shall be served on the regular ticket or freight agent of the company in the county where the offense occurred.

**HISTORY: 148 v S 207. Eff 10-27-2000.**

### § 5589.22 Damages.

A corporation or person shall be liable for all damages arising to a person from an obstruction or injury to a road or highway as provided by section 5589.21 of the Revised Code, which damage shall be recovered by an action at the suit of the board of township trustees of the township in which the offense is committed, or of any person suing therefor before a judge of a county court or judge of a municipal court having jurisdiction within the county where the offense is committed, or by indictment in the court of common pleas in the proper county. Each twenty-four hours the person or corporation, after being notified, permits such obstruction to remain, shall be an additional offense against such section.

**HISTORY: RS § 4748; S&S 669; S&C 1311; GC § 7473; 65 v 14, § 31; Bureau of Code Revision, 10-1-53; 129 v 582 (949). Eff 1-10-61.**

### § 5589.23 Company liable for fines against employees.

A railroad company or other corporation, the servant, agent, or employee of which, in any manner, obstructs a public road or highway, shall pay all penalties which may be assessed against such servant, agent, or employee for obstructing it. The penalties may be enforced by execution issued against such corporation on the judgment rendered against the servant, agent, or employee.

**HISTORY: RC § 4749; S&S 669; S&C 1311; GC § 7475; 65 v 14, § 32; Bureau of Code Revision. Eff 10-1-53.**

## § 5589.24 Fines paid to railroad grade crossing improvement fund.

(A) All fines collected for a violation of division (A) of section 5589.21 or 5589.211 [5589.21.1] of the Revised Code shall be paid as follows:

(1) To the railroad grade crossing improvement fund of the county if the violation occurred in an unincorporated area of the county;

(2) To the railroad grade crossing improvement fund of the municipal corporation in which the violation occurred if the violation occurred in a municipal corporation.

(B) The board of county commissioners of each county and the legislative authority of each municipal corporation shall establish a railroad grade crossing improvement fund. The fund shall consist of fines paid to the county or municipal corporation under division (A) of this section and any other moneys allocated to the fund by the county or municipal corporation. Except as otherwise provided in this division, a county or municipal corporation shall use its railroad grade crossing improvement fund to pay any part of the cost assigned by the public utilities commission to the county or municipal corporation under section 4907.471 [4907.47.1] of the Revised Code. The county or municipal corporation also may use its railroad grade crossing improvement fund for other improvements to railroad grade crossings, including signs, signals, gates, or other protective devices, as the board of county commissioners or legislative authority of a municipal corporation determines to be appropriate.

If, during any fiscal year, the fines a county collects for violations of division (A) of section 5589.21 and section 5589.211 [5589.21.1] of the Revised Code equal three thousand dollars or less, during the subsequent fiscal year the county may use that amount of money in its railroad grade crossing improvement fund for any purpose that the board of county commissioners determines to be appropriate.

If, during any fiscal year, the fines a county collects for violations of division (A) of section 5589.21 and section 5589.211 [5589.21.1] of the Revised Code exceed three thousand dollars, during the subsequent two fiscal years the county shall use all the money in its railroad grade crossing improvement fund only for those purposes described in this division. In such a case, the amount of money the county collects for violations of division (A) of section 5589.21 and section 5589.211 [5589.21.1] of the Revised Code during the fiscal year immediately following the second of those two fiscal years shall determine the disposition under this division of the money the county collects during that fiscal year.

**HISTORY: RS § 4748; S&S 669; S&C 1311; GC § 7474; 65 v 14, § 31; Bureau of Code Revision, 10-1-53; 148 v S 207. Eff 10-27-2000.**

### [OBSTRUCTIONS; SIGNS]

## § 5589.31 Construction of walk or ditch across highway.

No person, firm, or corporation shall construct a walk or dig a ditch across a public highway outside any municipal corporation without the consent of the director of transportation in the case of an intercounty or a state highway, county engineer in the case of a county road, or board of township trustees in the case of a township road.

**HISTORY: GC § 7202; 106 v 574 (618), § 159; 107 v 69 (116); Bureau of Code Revision, 10-1-53; 135 v H 200. Eff 9-28-73.**

**P&A § 7202 repealed 106 v 574 (664), § 305.**

## § 5589.32 Erection of advertising signs resembling those required of railroad companies.

No person, firm, or corporation shall erect, display, or maintain an advertising or other sign on, along, or near any public highway, in any county of this state, which resembles the highway crossing signs which steam and interurban railroads have erected, in compliance with section 4955.33 of the Revised Code, at the crossings of public roads and railroads.

The public utilities commission shall enforce this section, prosecute any violations thereof, and order the removal of any such prohibited sign.

The attorney general and the prosecuting attorney of any county shall carry into effect the orders of the commission made under this section and shall prosecute any violations of such orders.

Each day that any violation of this section continues constitutes a separate offense. The erection, display, or maintenance of each advertising or other sign referred to in this section, except as provided in section 4955.33 of the Revised Code, constitutes a separate offense.

**HISTORY: GC §§ 7204-1—7204-3; 109 v 358, §§ 1 to 3; Bureau of Code Revision. Eff 10-1-53.**

## § 5589.33 Advertising on public highway.

Except as provided in this section and in section 5515.04 of the Revised Code, no person shall place within the limits of the right-of-way or affix any sign, poster, or advertisement to any tree or utility pole within the right-of-way of any public highway outside of municipal corporations. No person, organization, corporation, or group shall place within the limits of the right-of-way any object as determined by the department of transportation to obscure sight distance.

Nothing in this section shall be construed to prohibit the erection and maintaining of notices of the existence and location of public utility facilities under or upon the highway and warnings against disturbing such facilities, or of notices that emergency or other public telephones are available for users of the highway at specified locations upon or near the highway.

**HISTORY: 129 v 995 (Eff 10-25-61); 130 v 1294 (Eff 1-23-63); 135 v H 200. Eff 9-28-73.**

## § 5589.99 Penalties.

(A) Whoever violates section 5589.01 of the Revised Code is guilty of a misdemeanor of the third degree.

(B) Whoever violates section 5589.02, 5589.03, 5589.05, 5589.06, 5589.08, 5589.081 [5589.08.1], 5589.09, 5589.11, 5589.12, 5589.32, or 5589.33 of the Revised Code is guilty of a minor misdemeanor.

(C) Whoever violates section 5589.07 or 5589.10 of the Revised Code is guilty of a misdemeanor of the fourth degree.

(D) Whoever violates division (A) of section 5589.21 of the Revised Code is guilty of a misdemeanor of the first degree and shall be fined one thousand dollars.

(E) Whoever violates section 5589.211 [5589.21.1] of the Revised Code is guilty of a misdemeanor of the first degree and shall be fined five thousand dollars.

**HISTORY: Bureau of Code Revision, 10-1-53; 129 v 995 (Eff 10-25-61); 133 v S 5 (Eff 9-4-69); 135 v H 398 (Eff 1-1-74); 146 v S 2 (Eff 7-1-96); 148 v S 207. Eff 10-27-2000.**

# CHAPTER 5591: COUNTY BRIDGES

Section

[FERRY; CAPACITY OF BRIDGE]



## [FERRY; CAPACITY OF BRIDGE]

### § 5591.42 Carrying capacity of bridges; warning notice.

The board of county commissioners together with the county engineer or an engineer to be selected by the board, or the director of transportation, may ascertain the safe carrying capacity of the bridges on roads or highways under their jurisdiction. Where the safe carrying capacity of any such bridge is ascertained and found to be less than the load limit prescribed by sections 5577.01 to 5577.12 of the Revised Code, warning notice shall be conspicuously posted near each end of the bridge. The notice shall caution all persons against driving on the bridge a loaded conveyance of greater weight than the bridge's carrying capacity.

**HISTORY: RS § 4944; S&C 193; 66 v 90; GC § 7572; 101 v 220; 119 v 182; Bureau of Code Revision, 10-1-53; 135 v H 200 (Eff 9-28-73); 139 v S 114 (Eff 10-27-81); 143 v H 258. Eff 11-2-89.**

### § 5591.43 Arrest of certain persons on view.

A constable of a township, a marshal of a village, or a police officer of a city may arrest upon view, and without process, a person violating section 5591.42 of the Revised Code.

**HISTORY: RS § 4945; 66 v 90, § 3; GC § 7573; Bureau of Code Revision. Eff 10-1-53.**

### § 5591.44 Prosecutions.

Prosecution under sections 5591.42 and 5591.43 of the Revised Code shall be in the name of the state and be commenced within three months after the offense is committed. Sections 5591.33 to 5591.43 of the Revised Code do not take away from the board of county commissioners a right of action for damages, which it may have against a person for injury done to a bridge.

**HISTORY: RS § 4946; 66 v 90, §§ 4, 5; GC § 7574; Bureau of Code Revision, 10-1-53; 143 v H 111. Eff 7-1-89.**

**Comment, Legislative Service Commission**

This section was amended by Am. Sub. H.B. 111 of the 118th G.A. Its existing version, however, was not repealed by that act, as required by § 15(D) of Art. II, Ohio Constitution. Since the title, amending clause, and body of the act nevertheless indicate an intention to amend the section, it is presented here as having been amended by H.B. 111. The Code Revision Section of the Legislative Service Commission will propose legislation to confirm these amendments.

# TITLE 57: TAXATION

## CHAPTER 5705: TAX LEVY LAW



### § 5705.19 Resolution relative to tax levy in excess of ten-mill limitation.

This section does not apply to school districts or county school financing districts.

The taxing authority of any subdivision at any time and in any year, by vote of two-thirds of all the members of the taxing authority, may declare by resolution and certify the resolution to the board of elections not less than ninety days before the election upon which it will be voted that the amount of taxes that may be raised within the ten-mill limitation will be insufficient to provide for the necessary requirements of the subdivision and that it is necessary to levy a tax in excess of that limitation for any of the following purposes:

(A) For current expenses of the subdivision, except that the total levy for current expenses of a detention facility district or district organized under section 2151.65 of the Revised Code shall not exceed two mills and that the total levy for current expenses of a combined district organized under sections 2151.65 and 2152.41 of the Revised Code shall not exceed four mills;

(B) For the payment of debt charges on certain described bonds, notes, or certificates of indebtedness of the subdivision issued subsequent to January 1, 1925;

(C) For the debt charges on all bonds, notes, and certificates of indebtedness issued and authorized to be issued prior to January 1, 1925;

(D) For a public library of, or supported by, the subdivision under whatever law organized or authorized to be supported;

(E) For a municipal university, not to exceed two mills over the limitation of one mill prescribed in section 3349.13 of the Revised Code;

(F) For the construction or acquisition of any specific permanent improvement or class of improvements that the taxing authority of the subdivision may include in a single bond issue;

(G) For the general construction, reconstruction, resurfacing, and repair of streets, roads, and bridges in municipal corporations, counties, or townships;

(H) For parks and recreational purposes;

(I) For the purpose of providing and maintaining fire apparatus, appliances, buildings, or sites therefor, or sources of water supply and materials therefor, or the establishment and maintenance of lines of fire alarm telegraph, or the payment of firefighting companies or permanent, part-time, or volunteer firefighting, emergency medical service, administrative, or communications personnel to operate the same, including the payment of any employer contributions required for such personnel under section 145.48 or 742.34 of the Revised Code, or the purchase of ambulance equipment, or the provision of ambulance, paramedic, or other emergency medical services operated by a fire department or firefighting company;

(J) For the purpose of providing and maintaining motor vehicles, communications, other equipment, buildings, and sites for such buildings used directly in the operation of a police department, or the payment of salaries of permanent or part-time police, communications, or administrative personnel to operate the same, including the payment of any employer contributions required for such personnel under section 145.48 or 742.33 of the Revised Code, or the payment of the costs incurred by townships as a result of contracts made with other political subdivisions in order to obtain police protection, or the provision of ambulance or emergency medical services operated by a police department;

(K) For the maintenance and operation of a county home or detention facility;

(L) For community mental retardation and developmental disabilities programs and services pursuant to Chapter 5126. of the Revised Code, except that the procedure for such levies shall be as provided in section 5705.222 of the Revised Code;

(M) For regional planning;

(N) For a county's share of the cost of maintaining and operating schools, district detention facilities, forestry camps, or other facilities, or any combination thereof, established under section 2151.65 or 2152.41 of the Revised Code or both of those sections;

(O) For providing for flood defense, providing and maintaining a flood wall or pumps, and other purposes to prevent floods;

(P) For maintaining and operating sewage disposal plants and facilities;

(Q) For the purpose of purchasing, acquiring, constructing, enlarging, improving, equipping, repairing, maintaining, or operating, or any combination of the foregoing, a county transit system pursuant to sections 306.01 to 306.13 of the Revised Code, or of making any payment to a board of county commissioners operating a transit system or a county transit board pursuant to section 306.06 of the Revised Code;

(R) For the subdivision's share of the cost of acquiring or constructing any schools, forestry camps, detention facilities, or other facilities, or any combination thereof, under section 2151.65 or 2152.41 of the Revised Code or both of those sections;

(S) For the prevention, control, and abatement of air pollution;

(T) For maintaining and operating cemeteries;

(U) For providing ambulance service, emergency medical service, or both;

(V) For providing for the collection and disposal of garbage or refuse, including yard waste;

(W) For the payment of the police officer employers' contribution or the firefighter employers' contribution required under sections 742.33 and 742.34 of the Revised Code;

(X) For the construction and maintenance of a drainage improvement pursuant to section 6131.52 of the Revised Code;

(Y) For providing or maintaining senior citizens services or facilities as authorized by section 307.694, 307.85,

505.70, or 505.706 or division (EE) of section 717.01 of the Revised Code;

(Z) For the provision and maintenance of zoological park services and facilities as authorized under section 307.76 of the Revised Code;

(AA) For the maintenance and operation of a free public museum of art, science, or history;

(BB) For the establishment and operation of a 9-1-1 system, as defined in section 4931.40 of the Revised Code;

(CC) For the purpose of acquiring, rehabilitating, or developing rail property or rail service. As used in this division, "rail property" and "rail service" have the same meanings as in section 4981.01 of the Revised Code. This division applies only to a county, township, or municipal corporation.

(DD) For the purpose of acquiring property for, constructing, operating, and maintaining community centers as provided for in section 755.16 of the Revised Code;

(EE) For the creation and operation of an office or joint office of economic development, for any economic development purpose of the office, and to otherwise provide for the establishment and operation of a program of economic development pursuant to sections 307.07 and 307.64 of the Revised Code, or to the extent that the expenses of a county land reutilization corporation organized under Chapter 1724. of the Revised Code are found by the board of county commissioners to constitute the promotion of economic development, for the payment of such operations and expenses;

(FF) For the purpose of acquiring, establishing, constructing, improving, equipping, maintaining, or operating, or any combination of the foregoing, a township airport, landing field, or other air navigation facility pursuant to section 505.15 of the Revised Code;

(GG) For the payment of costs incurred by a township as a result of a contract made with a county pursuant to section 505.263 of the Revised Code in order to pay all or any part of the cost of constructing, maintaining, repairing, or operating a water supply improvement;

(HH) For a board of township trustees to acquire, other than by appropriation, an ownership interest in land, water, or wetlands, or to restore or maintain land, water, or wetlands in which the board has an ownership interest, not for purposes of recreation, but for the purposes of protecting and preserving the natural, scenic, open, or wooded condition of the land, water, or wetlands against modification or encroachment resulting from occupation, development, or other use, which may be styled as protecting or preserving "greenspace" in the resolution, notice of election, or ballot form. Except as otherwise provided in this division, land is not acquired for purposes of recreation, even if the land is used for recreational purposes, so long as no building, structure, or fixture used for recreational purposes is permanently attached or affixed to the land. Except as otherwise provided in this division, land that previously has been acquired in a township for these greenspace purposes may subsequently be used for recreational purposes if the board of township trustees adopts a resolution approving that use and no building, structure, or fixture used for recreational purposes is permanently attached or affixed to the land. The authorization to use greenspace land for recreational use does not apply to land located in a township that had a population, at the time it passed its first greenspace levy, of more than thirty-eight thousand within a county that had a population, at that time, of at least eight hundred sixty thousand.

(II) For the support by a county of a crime victim assistance program that is provided and maintained by a county agency or a private, nonprofit corporation or association under section 307.62 of the Revised Code;

(JJ) For any or all of the purposes set forth in divisions (I) and (J) of this section. This division applies only to a township.

(KK) For a countywide public safety communications system under section 307.63 of the Revised Code. This division applies only to counties.

(LL) For the support by a county of criminal justice services under section 307.45 of the Revised Code;

(MM) For the purpose of maintaining and operating a jail or other detention facility as defined in section 2921.01 of the Revised Code;

(NN) For purchasing, maintaining, or improving, or any combination of the foregoing, real estate on which to hold agricultural fairs. This division applies only to a county.

(OO) For constructing, rehabilitating, repairing, or maintaining sidewalks, walkways, trails, bicycle pathways, or similar improvements, or acquiring ownership interests in land necessary for the foregoing improvements;

(PP) For both of the purposes set forth in divisions (G) and (OO) of this section.

(QQ) For both of the purposes set forth in divisions (H) and (HH) of this section. This division applies only to a township.

(RR) For the legislative authority of a municipal corporation, board of county commissioners of a county, or board of township trustees of a township to acquire agricultural easements, as defined in section 5301.67 of the Revised Code, and to supervise and enforce the easements.

(SS) For both of the purposes set forth in divisions (BB) and (KK) of this section. This division applies only to a county.

(TT) For the maintenance and operation of a facility that is organized in whole or in part to promote the sciences and natural history under section 307.761 of the Revised Code.

(UU) For the creation and operation of a county land reutilization corporation and for any programs or activities of the corporation found by the board of directors of the corporation to be consistent with the purposes for which the corporation is organized;

(VV) For construction and maintenance of improvements and expenses of soil and water conservation district programs under Chapter 1515. of the Revised Code;

(WW) For the Ohio cooperative extension service fund created under section 3335.35 of the Revised Code for the purposes prescribed under section 3335.36 of the Revised Code for the benefit of the citizens of a county. This division applies only to a county.

The resolution shall be confined to the purpose or purposes described in one division of this section, to which the revenue derived therefrom shall be applied. The existence in any other division of this section of authority to levy a tax for any part or all of the same purpose or purposes does not preclude the use of such revenues for any part of the purpose or purposes of the division under which the resolution is adopted.

The resolution shall specify the amount of the increase in rate that it is necessary to levy, the purpose of that increase in rate, and the number of years during which the increase in rate shall be in effect, which may or may not include a levy upon the duplicate of the current year. The number of years may be any number not exceeding five, except as follows:

(1) When the additional rate is for the payment of debt charges, the increased rate shall be for the life of the indebtedness.

(2) When the additional rate is for any of the following, the increased rate shall be for a continuing period of time:

(a) For the current expenses for a detention facility district, a district organized under section 2151.65 of the Revised Code, or a combined district organized under sections 2151.65 and 2152.41 of the Revised Code;

(b) For providing a county's share of the cost of maintaining and operating schools, district detention facilities, forestry camps, or other facilities, or any combination thereof, established under section 2151.65 or 2152.41 of the Revised Code or under both of those sections.

(3) When the additional rate is for either of the following, the increased rate may be for a continuing period of time:

(a) For the purposes set forth in division (I), (J), (U), or (KK) of this section;

(b) For the maintenance and operation of a joint recreation district.

(4) When the increase is for the purpose or purposes set forth in division (D), (G), (H), (CC), or (PP) of this section, the tax levy may be for any specified number of years or for a continuing period of time, as set forth in the resolution.

(5) When the additional rate is for the purpose described in division (Z) of this section, the increased rate shall be for any number of years not exceeding ten.

A levy for one of the purposes set forth in division (G), (I), (J), or (U) of this section may be reduced pursuant to section 5705.261 or 5705.31 of the Revised Code. A levy for one of the purposes set forth in division (G), (I), (J), or (U) of this section may also be terminated or permanently reduced by the taxing authority if it adopts a resolution stating that the continuance of the levy is unnecessary and the levy shall be terminated or that the millage is excessive and the levy shall be decreased by a designated amount.

A resolution of a detention facility district, a district organized under section 2151.65 of the Revised Code, or a combined district organized under both sections 2151.65 and 2152.41 of the Revised Code may include both current expenses and other purposes, provided that the resolution shall apportion the annual rate of levy between the current expenses and the other purpose or purposes. The apportionment need not be the same for each year of the levy, but the respective portions of the rate actually levied each year for the current expenses and the other purpose or purposes shall be limited by the apportionment.

Whenever a board of county commissioners, acting either as the taxing authority of its county or as the taxing authority of a sewer district or subdistrict created under Chapter 6117. of the Revised Code, by resolution declares it necessary to levy a tax in excess of the ten-mill limitation for the purpose of constructing, improving, or extending sewage disposal plants or sewage systems, the tax may be in effect for any number of years not exceeding twenty, and the proceeds of the tax, notwithstanding the general provisions of this section, may be used to pay debt charges on any obligations issued and outstanding on behalf of the subdivision for the purposes enumerated in this paragraph, provided that any such obligations have been specifically described in the resolution.

The resolution shall go into immediate effect upon its passage, and no publication of the resolution is necessary other than that provided for in the notice of election.

When the electors of a subdivision have approved a tax levy under this section, the taxing authority of the subdivision may anticipate a fraction of the proceeds of the levy and issue anticipation notes in accordance with section 5705.191 or 5705.193 of the Revised Code.

**HISTORY: GC § 5625-15; 112 v 391, § 15; 114 v 843; 115 v PtII, 412; 118 v 20; 118 v 248; 121 v 776; 122 v 75; Bureau of Code Revision, 10-1-53; 125 v 104; 125 v 713(799) (Eff 1-1-54); 126 v 882; 126 v 1126; 127 v 519; 128 v 574; 129 v 1209 (Eff 9-5-61); 130 v 1300 (Eff 8-19-63); 130 v PtII, 275 (Eff 12-16-64); 131 v 1316 (Eff 8-10-65); 131 v 1314 (Eff 10-25-65); 132 v H 1 (Eff 2-21-67); 132 v S 169 (Eff 10-25-67); 132 v 478 (Eff 11-14-67); 132 v S 350 (Eff 9-1-67); 133 v H 1 (Eff 3-18-69); 133 v H 769 (Eff 10-24-69); 133 v S 476 (Eff 8-31-70); 133 v H 1135 (Eff 9-16-70); 134 v S 370 (Eff 12-23-71); 134 v H 258 (Eff 1-27-72); 134 v H 1158 (Eff 3-31-73); 135 v S 44 (Eff 9-11-73); 135 v H 1173 (Eff 8-30-74); 136 v H 111 (Eff 8-31-76); 136 v H 920 (Eff 10-11-76); 136 v S 434 (Eff 1-17-77); 137 v H 277 (Eff 11-3-77); 137 v H 617 (Eff 1-13-78); 137 v S 58 (Eff 5-17-78); 137 v S 491 (Eff 7-13-78); 138 v H 36 (Eff 11-13-79); 138 v S 274 (Eff 8-7-80); 138 v H 850 (Eff 8-7-80); 138 v H 873 (Eff 10-6-80); 138 v S 160 (Eff 10-31-80); 138 v H 1062 (Eff 3-23-81); 138 v H 268 (Eff 4-9-81); 139 v H 1 (Eff 8-5-81); 139 v H 694 (Eff 11-15-81); 139 v S 550 (Eff 11-26-82); 140 v H 372 (Eff 11-8-83); 140 v H 56 (Eff 7-20-84); 140 v H 572 (Eff 9-26-84); 141 v H 203 (Eff 5-14-85); 141 v H 491 (Eff 6-18-85); 141 v S 289 (Eff 6-24-86); 142 v H 180 (Eff 6-29-88); 142 v S 318 (Eff 7-20-88); 142 v S 155 (Eff 6-24-88); 142 v H 661 (Eff 12-8-88); 143 v S 140 (Eff 10-2-89); 143 v H 173 (Eff 10-30-89); 143 v S 75 (Eff 3-1-90); 143 v H 717 (Eff 6-28-90); 143 v H 247 (Eff 11-30-90); 144 v S 32 (Eff 7-1-92); 144 v H 416 (Eff 8-3-92); 144 v H 791 (Eff 3-15-93); 144 v S 190 (Eff 4-16-93); 145 v H 184 (Eff 9-20-93); 145 v H 612 (Eff 7-19-94); 145 v H 677 (Eff 4-21-94); 146 v H 61 (Eff 10-25-95); 147 v H 117 (Eff 9-3-97); 147 v H 336 (Eff 11-12-97); 147 v H 368 (Eff 9-30-98); 147 v S 223 (Eff 4-5-99); 148 v H 222 (Eff 11-2-99); 148 v H 417 (Eff 9-21-2000); 149 v H 94, § 1 (Eff 6-6-2001); 148 v S 179, § 3 (Eff 1-1-2002); 149 v H 94, § 4 (Eff 1-1-2002); 149 v H 524 (Eff 6-28-2002); 149 v H 513. Eff 3-31-2003; 150 v H 127, § 1, eff. 3-11-04; 151 v H 530, § 101.01, eff. 3-30-06; 152 v H 385, § 1, eff. 9-12-08; 152 v S 353, § 1, eff. 4-7-09; 153 v H 48, § 1, eff. 7-2-10; 153 v H 313, § 1, eff. 7-7-10; 2011 HB 153, § 101.01, eff. Sept. 29, 2011.**

Acts 2011, HB 153, § 815.20 provides: "The General Assembly, applying the principle stated in division (B) of section 1.52 of the Revised Code that amendments are to be harmonized if reasonably capable of simultaneous operation, finds that the following sections, presented in this act as composites of the sections as amended by the acts indicated, are the resulting versions of the sections in effect prior to the effective date of the sections as presented in this act:

"Section 5705.19 of the Revised Code as amended by Am. Sub. H.B. 48 and Sub. H.B. 313 of the 128th General Assembly."

The effective date is set by § 818.03 of 151 v H 530.

The provisions of § 11, H.B. 127 (150 v—), read as follows:

The amendment by this act of section 5705.19 of the Revised Code applies to resolutions adopted under that section on or after the effective date of this act.

**Comment, Legislative Service Commission**

Section 5705.19 of the Revised Code is enacted by Sub. H.B. 48 and Sub. H.B. 313 of the 128th General Assembly. Comparison of these amendments in pursuance of section 1.52 of the Revised Code discloses that they are not irreconcilable so that they are required by that section to be harmonized to give effect to each amendment.

# TITLE 61: WATER SUPPLY — SANITATION — DITCHES

## CHAPTER 6101: CONSERVANCY DISTRICTS



[CONSTRUCTION AND INTERPRETATION]

### § 6101.83 Fraud by officers prohibited.

No officer of a conservancy district or any other public officer shall make a profit, directly or indirectly, out of any contracts entered into by the district, or, for the purpose of profit, use any money belonging to a district by loaning it or otherwise using it, or by depositing it in any manner, contrary to law, or by removal of any money by any such officer or by his consent and placing it elsewhere than is prescribed either by law or by the official acts of the board of directors of the conservancy district. The officer offending shall be liable personally and upon his official bond for all losses to such district and for all profits realized by such unlawful use of moneys.

**HISTORY: GC § 6828-68; 104 v 13(54), § 68; 117 v 163(215); Bureau of Code Revision. Eff 10-1-53.**

### § 6101.99 Penalties.

(A) Whoever violates division (B) of section 6101.14 of the Revised Code shall be fined not more than fifty dollars.

(B) Whoever violates division (B) of section 6101.19 of the Revised Code shall be fined not more than one thousand dollars.

(C) Whoever violates section 6101.81 of the Revised Code shall be fined not more than one hundred dollars.

(D) Whoever violates division (B) of section 6101.82 of the Revised Code shall be fined not more than five hundred dollars.

(E) Whoever violates section 6101.83 of the Revised Code is guilty of a felony of the fourth degree, and the court may impose an additional fine of not more than two thousand five hundred dollars.

**HISTORY: Bureau of Code Revision, 10-1-53; 126 v 575(586); 128 v 967(984) (Eff 10-12-59); 139 v S 199 (Eff 1-1-83); 146 v S 2. Eff 7-1-96.**

The effective date is set by section 6 of SB 2.

# CONSTITUTION OF THE UNITED STATES

EFFECTIVE 1789
WITH ALL AMENDMENTS TO 1994

---

We the people of the United States, in Order to form a more perfect Union, establish Justice, insure domestic Tranquility, provide for the common defence, promote the general Welfare, and secure the Blessings of Liberty to ourselves and our Posterity, do ordain and establish this Constitution for the United States of America.

## ARTICLE I

SECTION 1. All legislative Powers herein granted shall be vested in a Congress of the United States, which shall consist of a Senate and House of Representatives.

SECTION 2. The House of Representatives shall be composed of Members chosen every second Year by the People of the several States, and the Electors in each State shall have the Qualifications requisite for Electors of the most numerous Branch of the State Legislature.

No person shall be a Representative who shall not have attained to the Age of twenty five Years, and been seven Years a Citizen of the United States, and who shall not, when elected, be an Inhabitant of that State in which he shall be chosen.

Representatives and direct Taxes shall be apportioned among the several States which may be included within this Union, according to their respective Numbers, which shall be determined by adding to the whole Number of free Persons, including those bound to Service for a Term of Years, and excluding Indians not taxed, three fifths of all other Persons. The actual Enumeration shall be made within three Years after the first Meeting of the Congress of the United States, and within every subsequent term of ten Years, in such Manner as they shall by Law direct. The Number of Representatives shall not exceed one for every thirty Thousand, but each State shall have at Least one Representative; and until such enumeration shall be made, the State of New Hampshire shall be entitled to chuse three, Massachusetts eight, Rhode-Island and Providence Plantations one, Connecticut five, New York six, New Jersey four, Pennsylvania eight, Delaware one, Maryland six, Virginia ten, North Carolina five, South Carolina five, and Georgia three.

When vacancies happen in the Representation from any State, the Executive Authority thereof shall issue Writs of Election to fill such Vacancies.

The House of Representatives shall chuse their Speaker and other Officers; and shall have the sole Power of Impeachment.

SECTION 3. The Senate of the United States shall be composed of two Senators from each State, chosen by the Legislature thereof, for six Years; and each Senator shall have one Vote.

Immediately after they shall be assembled in Consequence of the first Election, they shall be divided as equally as may be into three Classes. The Seats of the Senators of the first Class shall be vacated at the Expiration of the second Year, of the second Class at the Expiration of the fourth Year, and of the third Class at the Expiration of the sixth Year, so that one third may be chosen every second Year; and if Vacancies happen by Resignation, or otherwise, during the Recess of the Legislature of any State, the Executive thereof may make temporary Appointments until the next Meeting of the Legislature, which shall then fill such Vacancies.

No Person shall be a Senator who shall not have attained to the Age of thirty Years, and been nine Years a Citizen of the United States, and who shall not, when elected, be an Inhabitant of that State for which he shall be chosen.

The Vice President of the United States shall be President of the Senate, but shall have no Vote, unless they be equally divided.

The Senate shall chuse their other Officers, and also a President pro tempore, in the absence of the Vice President, or when he shall exercise the Office of President of the United States.

The Senate shall have the sole Power to try all Impeachments. When sitting for that Purpose, they shall be on Oath or Affirmation. When the President of the United States is tried, the Chief Justice shall preside: And no Person shall be convicted without the Concurrence of two thirds of the Members present.

Judgment in Cases of Impeachment shall not extend further than to removal from Office, and disqualification to hold and enjoy any Office of honor, Trust or Profit under the United States: but the Party convicted shall nevertheless be liable and subject to Indictment, Trial, Judgment and Punishment, according to Law.

SECTION 4. The Times, Places and Manner of holding Elections for Senators and Representatives, shall be prescribed in each State by the Legislature thereof; but the Congress may at any time by Law make or alter such Regulations, except as to the Places of Chusing Senators.

The Congress shall assemble at least once in every Year, and such Meeting shall be on the first Monday in December, unless they shall by Law appoint a different Day.

SECTION 5. Each House shall be the Judge of the Elections, Returns and Qualifications of its own Members, and a Majority of each shall constitute a Quorum to do Business; but a smaller Number may adjourn from day to day, and may be authorized to compel the Attendance of Absent Members, in such Manner, and under such Penalties as each House may provide.

Each House may determine the Rules of its Proceedings, punish its Members for disorderly Behavior, and, with the Concurrence of two thirds, expel a Member.

Each House shall keep a Journal of its Proceedings, and from time to time publish the same, excepting such Parts as may in their Judgment require Secrecy; and the Yeas and Nays of the Members of either House on any question shall, at the Desire of one fifth of those Present, be entered on the Journal.

Neither House, during the Session of Congress, shall, without the Consent of the other, adjourn for more than three days, nor to any other Place than that in which the two Houses shall be sitting.

SECTION 6. The Senators and Representatives shall receive a Compensation for their Services, to be ascertained by Law, and paid out of the Treasury of the United States. They shall in all Cases, except Treason, Felony and Breach of the Peace, be privileged from Arrest during their Attendance at the Session of their respective Houses, and in going to and returning from the same; and for any Speech or Debate in either House, they shall not be questioned in any other Place.

No Senator or Representative shall, during the Time for which he was elected, be appointed to any civil Office under the Authority of the United States, which shall have been created, or the Emoluments whereof shall have been encreased during such time; and no Person holding any Office under the United States, shall be a Member of either House during his Continuance in Office.

SECTION 7. All Bills for raising Revenue shall originate in the House of Representatives; but the Senate may propose or concur with Amendments as on other Bills.

Every Bill which shall have passed the House of Representatives and the Senate, shall, before it become a Law, be presented to the President of the United States; If he approve he shall sign it, but if not he shall return it, with his Objections to that House in which it shall have originated, who shall enter the Objections at large on their Journal, and proceed to reconsider it. If after such Reconsideration two thirds of that House shall agree to pass the Bill, it shall be sent, together with the Objections, to the other House, by which it shall likewise be reconsidered, and if approved by two thirds of that House, it shall become a Law. But in all such Cases the Votes of both Houses shall be determined by Yeas and Nays, and the Names of the Persons voting for and against the Bill shall be entered on the Journal of each House respectively. If any Bill shall not be returned by the President within ten Days (Sundays excepted) after it shall have been presented to him, the Same shall be a Law, in like Manner as if he had signed it, unless the Congress by their Adjournment prevent its Return, in which Case it shall not be a Law.

Every Order, Resolution, or Vote to which the Concurrence of the Senate and House of Representatives may be necessary (except on a question of Adjournment) shall be presented to the President of the United States; and before the Same shall take Effect, shall be approved by him, or being disapproved by him, shall be repassed by two thirds of the Senate and House of Representatives, according to the Rules and Limitations prescribed in the Case of a Bill.

SECTION 8. The Congress shall have Power To lay and collect Taxes, Duties, Imposts and Excises, to pay the Debts and provide for the common Defence and general Welfare of the United States; but all Duties, Imposts and Excises shall be uniform throughout the United States;

To borrow Money on the Credit of the United States;

To regulate Commerce with foreign Nations, and among the several States, and with the Indian Tribes;

To establish an uniform Rule of Naturalization, and uniform Laws on the subject of Bankruptcies throughout the United States;

To coin Money, regulate the Value thereof, and of foreign Coin, and fix the Standard of Weights and Measures;

To provide for the Punishment of counterfeiting the Securities and current Coin of the United States;

To establish Post Offices and post Roads;

To promote the Progress of Science and useful Arts, by securing for limited Times to Authors and Inventors the exclusive Right to their respective Writings and Discoveries;

To constitute Tribunals inferior to the supreme Court;

To define and punish Piracies and Felonies committed on the high Seas, and Offences against the Law of Nations;

To declare War, grant Letters of Marque and Reprisal, and make Rules concerning Captures on Land and Water;

To raise and support Armies, but no appropriation of Money to that Use shall be for a longer Term than two Years;

To provide and maintain a Navy;

To make Rules for the Government and Regulation of the land and naval Forces;

To provide for calling forth the Militia to execute the Laws of the Union, suppress Insurrections and repel Invasions;

To provide for organizing, arming, and disciplining the Militia, and for governing such Part of them as may be employed in the Service of the United States, reserving to the States, respectively, the Appointment of the Officers, and the Authority of training the Militia according to the discipline prescribed by Congress.

To exercise exclusive Legislation in all Cases whatsoever, over such District (not exceeding ten Miles square) as may be, by Cession of particular States, and the Acceptance of Congress, become the Seat of the Government of the United States, and to exercise like Authority over all Places purchased by the Consent of the Legislature of the State in which the Same shall be, for the Erection of Forts, Magazines, Arsenals, dock-Yards, and other needful Buildings;— And

To make all Laws which shall be necessary and proper for carrying into Execution the foregoing Powers, and all other Powers vested by this Constitution in the Government of the United States, or in any Department or Officer thereof.

SECTION 9. The Migration or Importation of such Persons as any of the States now existing shall think proper to admit, shall not be prohibited by the Congress prior to the Year one thousand eight hundred and eight, but a Tax or duty may be imposed on such Importation, not exceeding ten dollars for each Person.

The privilege of the Writ of Habeas Corpus shall not be suspended, unless when in Cases of Rebellion or Invasion the public Safety may require it.

No Bill of Attainder or ex post facto Law shall be passed.

No capitation, or other direct, Tax shall be laid, unless in Proportion to the Census or Enumeration herein before directed to be taken.

No Tax or Duty shall be laid on Articles exported from any State.

No Preference shall be given by any Regulation of Commerce or Revenue to the Ports of one State over those of another; nor shall Vessels bound to, or from, one State, be obliged to enter, clear, or pay Duties in another.

No Money shall be drawn from the Treasury, but in Consequence of Appropriations made by Law; and a regular Statement and Account of the Receipts and Expenditures of all public Money shall be published from time to time.

No Title of Nobility shall be granted by the United States: And no Person holding any Office of Profit or Trust under them, shall, without the Consent of the Congress, accept of any present, Emolument, Office, or Title, of any kind whatever, from any King, Prince, or foreign State.

SECTION 10. No State shall enter into any Treaty, Alliance, or Confederation; grant Letters of Marque or Reprisal; coin Money; emit Bills of Credit; make any Thing but gold and silver Coin a Tender in Payment of Debts; pass any Bill of Attainder, ex post facto Law, or Law impairing the Obligation of Contracts, or grant any Title of Nobility.

No State shall, without the Consent of the Congress, lay any Imposts or Duties on Imports or Exports, except what may be absolutely necessary for executing its inspection Laws: and the net Produce of all Duties and Imposts, laid by any State on Imports or Exports, shall be for the Use of the Treasury of the United States; and all such Laws shall be subject to the Revision and Control of the Congress.

No State shall, without the Consent of Congress, lay any duty of Tonnage, keep Troops, or Ships of War in time of Peace, enter into any Agreement or Compact with another State, or with a foreign Power, or engage in War, unless actually invaded, or in such imminent Danger as will not admit of delay.

## ARTICLE II

SECTION 1. The executive Power shall be vested in a President of the United States of America. He shall hold his Office during the Term of four Years, and, together with the Vice President, chosen for the same Term, be elected, as follows

Each State shall appoint, in such Manner as the Legislature thereof may direct, a Number of Electors, equal to the whole Number of Senators and Representatives to which the State may be entitled in the Congress; but no Senator or Representative, or Person holding an Office of Trust or Profit under the United States, shall be appointed an Elector.

The Electors shall meet in their respective States, and vote by Ballot for two persons, of whom one at least shall not be an Inhabitant of the same State with themselves. And they shall make a List of all the Persons voted for, and of the Number of Votes for each; which List they shall sign and certify, and transmit sealed to the Seat of the Government of the United States, directed to the President of the Senate. The President of the Senate shall, in the Presence of the Senate and House of Representatives, open all the Certificates, and the Votes shall then be counted. The Person having the greatest Number of Votes shall be the President, if such Number be a Majority of the whole Number of Electors appointed; and if there be more than one who have such Majority, and have an equal Number of Votes, then the House of Representatives shall immediately chuse by Ballot one of them for President; and if no Person have a Majority, then from the five highest on the List the said House shall in like Manner chuse the President. But in chusing the President, the Votes shall be taken by States, the Representation from each State having one Vote; A quorum for this Purpose shall consist of a Member or Members from two thirds of the States, and a Majority of all the States shall be necessary to a Choice. In every Case, after the Choice of the President, the Person having the greatest Number of Votes of the Electors shall be the Vice President. But if there should remain two or more who have equal Votes, the Senate shall chuse from them by Ballot the Vice President.

The Congress may determine the Time of chusing the Electors, and the Day on which they shall give their Votes; which Day shall be the same throughout the United States.

No Person except a natural born Citizen, or a Citizen of the United States, at the time of the Adoption of this Constitution, shall be eligible to the Office of President; neither shall any Person be eligible to that Office who shall not have attained to the Age of thirty five Years, and been fourteen Years a Resident within the United States.

In Case of the Removal of the President from Office, or of his Death, Resignation, or Inability to Discharge the Powers and Duties of the said Office, the same shall devolve on the Vice President, and the Congress may by Law provide for the Case of Removal, Death, Resignation or Inability, both of the President and Vice President, declaring what Officer shall then act as President, and such Officer shall act accordingly, until the Disability be removed, or a President shall be elected.

The President shall, at stated Times, receive for his Services, a Compensation, which shall neither be encreased nor diminished during the Period for which he shall have been elected, and he shall not receive within that Period any other Emolument from the United States, or any of them.

Before he enter on the Execution of his Office, he shall take the following Oath or Affirmation: "I do solemnly swear (or affirm) that I will faithfully execute the Office of President of the United States, and will to the best of my Ability, preserve, protect and defend the Constitution of the United States."

SECTION 2. The President shall be Commander in Chief of the Army and Navy of the United States, and of the Militia of the several States, when called into the actual Service of the United States; he may require the Opinion, in writing, of the principal Officer in each of the executive Departments, upon any Subject relating to the Duties of their respective Offices, and he shall have Power to grant Reprieves and Pardons for Offences against the United States, except in Cases of Impeachment.

He shall have Power, by and with the Advice and Consent of the Senate, to make Treaties, provided two thirds of the Senators present concur; and he shall nominate, and by and with the Advice and Consent of the Senate, shall appoint Ambassadors, other public Ministers and Consuls, Judges of the supreme Court, and all other Officers of the United States, whose Appointments are not herein otherwise provided for, and which shall be established by Law; but the Congress may by Law vest the Appointment of such inferior Officers, as they think proper, in the President alone, in the Courts of Law, or in the Heads of Departments.

The President shall have Power to fill up all Vacancies that may happen during the Recess of the Senate, by granting Commissions which shall expire at the End of their next Session.

SECTION 3. He shall from time to time give to the Congress Information of the State of the Union, and recommend to their Consideration such Measures as he shall judge necessary and expedient; he may, on extraordinary Occasions, convene both Houses, or either of them, and in Case of Disagreement between them, with Respect to the Time of Adjournment, he may adjourn them to such Time as he shall think proper; he shall receive Ambassadors and other public Ministers; he shall take Care that the Laws be faithfully executed, and shall Commission all the Officers of the United States.

SECTION 4. The President, Vice President and all civil Officers of the United States, shall be removed from Office on Impeachment for, and Conviction of, Treason, Bribery, or other high Crimes and Misdemeanors.

## ARTICLE III

SECTION 1. The judicial Power of the United States, shall be vested in one supreme Court, and in such inferior Courts as the Congress may from time to time ordain and establish. The Judges, both of the supreme and inferior Courts, shall hold their offices during good Behaviour, and shall, at stated Times, receive for their Services, a Compensation, which shall not be diminished during their Continuance in Office.

SECTION 2. The judicial Power shall extend to all Cases, in Law and Equity, arising under this Constitution, the Laws of the United States, and Treaties made, or which shall be made, under their authority;—to all Cases affecting Ambassadors, other public Ministers and Consuls;—to all Cases of admiralty and maritime Jurisdiction;—to Controversies to which the United States shall be a Party;—to Controversies between two or more States;—between a State and Citizens of another State;—between Citizens of different States;—between Citizens of the same State claiming Lands under Grants of different States, and between a State, or the Citizens thereof, and foreign States, Citizens or Subjects.

In all Cases affecting Ambassadors, other public Ministers and Consuls, and those in which a State shall be Party, the supreme Court shall have original Jurisdiction. In all the other Cases before mentioned, the supreme Court shall have appellate Jurisdiction, both as to Law and Fact, with such Exceptions, and under such Regulations as the Congress shall make.

The trial of all Crimes, except in Cases of Impeachment, shall be by Jury; and such Trial shall be held in the State where the said Crimes shall have been committed; but when not committed within any State, the Trial shall be at such Place or Places as the Congress may by Law have directed.

SECTION 3. Treason against the United States, shall consist only in levying War against them, or in adhering to their Enemies, giving them Aid and Comfort. No Person shall be convicted of Treason unless on the Testimony of two Witnesses to the same overt Act, or on Confession in open Court.

The Congress shall have Power to declare the Punishment of Treason, but no Attainder of Treason shall work Corruption of Blood, or Forfeiture except during the Life of the Person attainted.

## ARTICLE IV

SECTION 1. Full Faith and Credit shall be given in each State to the public Acts, Records, and judicial Proceedings of every other State. And the Congress may by general Laws prescribe the Manner in which such Acts, Records and Proceedings shall be proved, and the Effect thereof.

SECTION 2. The Citizens of each State shall be entitled to all Privileges and Immunities of Citizens in the several States.

A Person charged in any State with Treason, Felony, or other Crime, who shall flee from Justice, and be found in another State, shall on demand of the executive Authority of the State from which he fled, be delivered up, to be removed to the State having Jurisdiction of the Crime.

No Person held to Service or Labour in one State, under the Laws thereof, escaping into another, shall, in Consequence of any Law or Regulation therein, be discharged from such Service or Labour, but shall be delivered up on Claim of the Party to whom such Service or Labour may be due.

SECTION 3. New States may be admitted by the Congress into this Union; but no new State shall be formed or erected within the Jurisdiction of any other State; nor any State be formed by the Junction of two or more States, or parts of States, without the Consent of the Legislatures of the States concerned as well as of the Congress.

The Congress shall have Power to dispose of and make all needful Rules and Regulations respecting the Territory or other Property belonging to the United States; and nothing in this Constitution shall be so construed as to Prejudice any Claims of the United States, or of any particular State.

SECTION 4. The United States shall guarantee to every State in this Union a Republican Form of Government, and shall protect each of them against Invasion; and on Application of the Legislature, or of the Executive (when the Legislature cannot be convened) against domestic Violence.

## ARTICLE V

The Congress, whenever two thirds of both Houses shall deem it necessary, shall propose Amendments to this Constitution, or, on the Application of the Legislatures of two thirds of the several States, shall call a Convention for proposing Amendments, which, in either Case, shall be valid to all Intents and Purposes, as part of this Constitution, when ratified by the Legislatures of three fourths of the several States, or by Conventions in three fourths thereof, as the one or the other Mode of Ratification may be proposed by the Congress; Provided that no Amendment which may be made prior to the Year One thousand eight hundred and eight shall in any Manner affect the first and fourth Clauses in the Ninth Section of the first Article; and that no State, without its Consent, shall be deprived of its equal Suffrage in the Senate.

## ARTICLE VI

All Debts contracted and Engagements entered into, before the Adoption of this Constitution, shall be as valid against the United States under this Constitution, as under the Confederation.

This Constitution, and the Laws of the United States which shall be made in Pursuance thereof; and all Treaties made, or which shall be made, under the Authority of the United States, shall be the supreme Law of the Land; and the Judges in every State shall be bound thereby, any Thing in the Constitution or Laws of any State to the Contrary notwithstanding.

The Senators and Representatives before mentioned, and the Members of the several State Legislatures, and all executive and judicial Officers, both of the United States and of the several States, shall be bound by Oath or Affirmation, to support this Constitution; but no religious Test shall ever be required as a Qualification to any Office or public Trust under the United States.

## ARTICLE VII

The Ratification of the Conventions of nine States shall be sufficient for the Establishment of this Constitution between the States so ratifying the Same.

Done in Convention by the Unanimous Consent of the States present the Seventeenth Day of September in the Year of our Lord one thousand seven hundred and Eighty seven and of the Independence of the United States of America the Twelfth. IN WITNESS whereof We have hereunto subscribed our Names.

G. WASHINGTON — Presidt.
and Deputy from Virginia

Attest.—WILLIAM JACKSON, Secretary.

**New Hampshire.**—John Langdon, Nicholas Gilman.

**Massachusetts.**—Nathaniel Gorham, Rufus King.

**Connecticut.**—Wm. Saml. Johnson, Roger Sherman.

**New York.**—Alexander Hamilton.

**New Jersey.**—Wil: Livingston, David Brearley, Wm. Paterson, Jona: Dayton.

**Pennsylvania.**—B Franklin, Thomas Mifflin, Robt. Morris, Geo. Clymer, Thos. FitzSimons, Jared Ingersoll, James Wilson, Gouv Morris.

**Delaware.**—Geo: Read, Gunning Bedford Jun, John Dickinson, Richard Bassett, Jaco: Broom.

**Maryland.**—James McHenry, Dan of St Thos. Jenifer, Danl. Carroll.

**Virginia.**—John Blair—James Madison, Jr.

**North Carolina.**—Wm. Blount, Richd. Dobbs Spaight, Hu Williamson.

**South Carolina.**—J. Rutledge, Charles Cotesworth Pinckney, Charles Pinckney, Pierce Butler.

**Georgia.**—William Few, Abr. Baldwin.

# AMENDMENTS TO THE CONSTITUTION OF THE UNITED STATES

*Articles in addition to, and amendments of the Constitution of the United States of America, proposed by Congress, and ratified by the Legislatures of the several States, pursuant to the fifth article of the original Constitution.*

---

## AMENDMENT I

Congress shall make no law respecting an establishment of religion, or prohibiting the free exercise thereof; or abridging the freedom of speech, or of the press; or the right of the people peaceably to assemble, and to petition the Government for a redress of grievances.
(Effective 1791)

## AMENDMENT II

A well regulated Militia, being necessary to the security of a free State, the right of the people to keep and bear Arms, shall not be infringed.
(Effective 1791)

## AMENDMENT III

No Soldier shall, in time of peace be quartered in any house, without the consent of the Owner, nor in time of war, but in a manner to be prescribed by law.
(Effective 1791)

## AMENDMENT IV

The right of the people to be secure in their persons, houses, papers, and effects, against unreasonable searches and seizures, shall not be violated, and no Warrants shall issue, but upon probable cause, supported by Oath or affirmation, and particularly describing the place to be searched, and the persons or things to be seized.
(Effective 1791)

## AMENDMENT V

No person shall be held to answer for a capital, or otherwise infamous crime, unless on a presentment or indictment of a Grand Jury, except in cases arising in the land or naval forces, or in the Militia, when in actual service in time of War or public danger; nor shall any person be subject for the same offence to be twice put in jeopardy of life or limb; nor shall be compelled in any criminal case to be a witness against himself, nor be deprived of life, liberty, or property, without due process of law; nor shall private property be taken for public use, without just compensation.
(Effective 1791)

## AMENDMENT VI

In all criminal prosecutions, the accused shall enjoy the right to a speedy and public trial, by an impartial jury of the State and district wherein the crime shall have been committed, which district shall have been previously ascertained by law, and to be informed of the nature and cause of the accusation; to be confronted with the witnesses against him; to have compulsory process for obtaining witnesses in his favor, and to have the Assistance of Counsel for his defence.
(Effective 1791)

## AMENDMENT VII

In Suits at common law, where the value in controversy shall exceed twenty dollars, the right of trial by jury shall be preserved, and no fact tried by a jury, shall be otherwise reexamined in any Court of the United States, than according to the rules of the common law.
(Effective 1791)

## AMENDMENT VIII

Excessive bail shall not be required, nor excessive fines imposed, nor cruel and unusual punishments inflicted.
(Effective 1791)

## AMENDMENT IX

The enumeration in the Constitution, of certain rights, shall not be construed to deny or disparage others retained by the people.
(Effective 1791)

## AMENDMENT X

The powers not delegated to the United States by the Constitution, nor prohibited by it to the States, are reserved to the States respectively, or to the people.
(Effective 1791)

## AMENDMENT XI

The Judicial power of the United States shall not be construed to extend to any suit in law or equity, commenced or prosecuted against one of the United States by Citizens of another State, or by Citizens or Subjects of any Foreign State.
(Effective 1798)

## AMENDMENT XII

The Electors shall meet in their respective states and vote by ballot for President and Vice President, one of whom, at least, shall not be an inhabitant of the same state with themselves; they shall name in their ballots the person voted for as President, and in distinct ballots the person voted for as Vice President, and they shall make distinct lists of all persons voted for as President, and of all persons voted for as Vice-President, and of the number of votes for each, which lists they shall sign and certify, and transmit sealed to the seat of the government of the United States, directed to the President of the Senate;—The President of the Senate shall, in the presence of the Senate and House of Representatives; open all the certificates and the votes shall then be counted;—The person having the greatest number of votes for President, shall be the President, if such number be a majority of the whole number of Electors appointed; and if no person have such majority, then from the persons having the highest numbers not exceeding three on the list of those voted for as President, the House of Representatives shall choose immediately, by ballot, the President. But in choosing the

President, the votes shall be taken by states, the representation from each state having one vote; a quorum for this purpose shall consist of a member or members from two-thirds of the states, and a majority of all the states shall be necessary to a choice. And if the House of Representatives shall not choose a President whenever the right of choice shall devolve upon them, before the fourth day of March next following, then the Vice President shall act as President, as in the case of the death or other constitutional disability of the President.—The person having the greatest number of votes as Vice President, shall be the Vice President, if such number be a majority of the whole number of Electors appointed, and if no person have a majority, then from the two highest numbers on the list, the Senate shall choose the Vice President; a quorum for the purpose shall consist of two-thirds of the whole number of Senators, and a majority of the whole number shall be necessary to a choice. But no person constitutionally ineligible to the office of President shall be eligible to that of Vice President of the United States.

(Effective 1804)

## AMENDMENT XIII

SECTION 1. Neither slavery nor involuntary servitiude, except as a punishment for crime whereof the party shall have been duly convicted, shall exist within the United States, or any place subject to their jurisdiction.

SECTION 2. Congress shall have power to enforce this article by appropriate legislation.

(Effective 1865)

## AMENDMENT XIV

SECTION 1. All persons born or naturalized in the United States, and subject to the jurisdiction thereof, are citizens of the United States and of the State wherein they reside. No State shall make or enforce any law which shall abridge the privileges or immunities of citizens of the United States; nor shall any State deprive any person of life, liberty, or property, without due process of law; nor deny to any person within its jurisdiction the equal protection of the laws.

**Ohio Constitution**

Due process, OConst art I, § 16
Equal protection, OConst art I, § 2

SECTION 2. Representatives shall be apportioned among the several States according to their respective numbers, counting the whole number of persons in each State, excluding Indians not taxed. But when the right to vote at any election for the choice of electors for President and Vice President of the United States, Representatives in Congress, the Executive and Judicial officers of a State, or the members of the Legislature thereof, is denied to any of the male inhabitants of such State, being twenty-one years of age, and citizens of the United States, or in any way abridged, except for participation in rebellion, or other crime, the basis of representation therein shall be reduced in the proportion which the number of such male citizens shall bear to the whole number of male citizens twenty-one years of age in such State.

**Ohio Constitution**

Apportionment, OConst art XI, §§ 1, 2, 3

SECTION 3. No person shall be a Senator or Representative in Congress, or elector of President and Vice President, or hold any office, civil or military, under the United States, or under any State, who, having previously taken an oath, as a member of Congress, or as an officer of the United States, or as a member of any State legislature, or as an executive or judicial officer of any State, to support the Constitution of the United States, shall have engaged in insurrection or rebellion against the same, or given aid or comfort to the enemies thereof. But Congress may by a vote of two-thirds of each House, remove such disability.

**Ohio Constitution**

Qualification for office, OConst art II, § 5

SECTION 4. The validity of the public debt of the United States, authorized by law, including debts incurred for payment of pensions and bounties for services in suppressing insurrection or rebellion, shall not be questioned. But neither the United States nor any State shall assume or pay any debt or obligation incurred in aid of insurrection or rebellion against the United States, or any claim for the loss or emancipation of any slave; but all such debts, obligations and claims shall be held illegal and void.

**Ohio Constitution**

Public debt, OConst art VIII, §§ 1, 3

SECTION 5. The Congress shall have power to enforce, by appropriate legislation, the provisions of this article.

(Effective 1868)

## AMENDMENT XV

SECTION 1. The right of citizens of the United States to vote shall not be denied or abridged by the United States or by any State on account of race, color, or previous condition of servitude.

(Effective 1870)

SECTION 2. The Congress shall have power to enforce this article by appropriate legislation.

## AMENDMENT XVI

The Congress shall have power to lay and collect taxes on incomes, from whatever source derived, without apportionment among the several States, and without regard to any census or enumeration.

(Effective 1913)

## AMENDMENT XVII

The Senate of the United States shall be composed of two Senators from each State, elected by the people thereof, for six years; and each Senator shall have one vote. The electors in each State shall have the qualifications requisite for electors of the most numerous branch of the State legislatures.

When vacancies happen in the representation of any State in the Senate, the executive authority of such State shall issue writs of election to fill such vacancies: Provided, That the legislature of any State may empower the executive thereof to make temporary appointments until the people fill the vacancies by election as the legislature may direct.

This amendment shall not be so construed as to affect the election or term of any Senator chosen before it becomes valid as part of the Constitution.

(Effective 1913)

## AMENDMENT XVIII

SECTION 1. After one year from the ratification of this article the manufacture, sale, or transportation of intoxicating liquors within, the importation thereof into, or the exportation thereof from the United States and all territory subject to the jurisdiction thereof for beverage purposes is hereby prohibited.

SECTION 2. The Congress and the several States shall have concurrent power to enforce this article by appropriate legislation.

SECTION 3. This article shall be inoperative unless it shall have been ratified as an amendment to the Constitution by the legislatures of the several States, as provided in the Constitution, within seven years from the date of the submission hereof to the States by the Congress.

(Effective 1919)

## AMENDMENT XIX

The right of citizens of the United States to vote shall not be denied or abridged by the United States or by any State on account of sex.

Congress shall have power to enforce this article by appropriate legislation.

(Effective 1920)

## AMENDMENT XX

SECTION 1. The terms of the President and Vice President shall end at noon on the 20th day of January, and the terms of Senators and Representatives at noon on the 3d day of January, of the years in which such terms would have ended if this article had not been ratified; and the terms of their successors shall then begin.

SECTION 2. The Congress shall assemble at least once in every year, and such meeting shall begin at noon on the 3d day of January, unless they shall by law appoint a different day.

SECTION 3. If, at the time fixed for the beginning of the term of the President, the President elect shall have died, the Vice President elect shall become President. If a President shall not have been chosen before the time fixed for the beginning of his term, or if the President elect shall have failed to qualify, then the Vice President elect shall act as President until a President shall have qualified; and the Congress may by law provide for the case wherein neither a President elect nor a Vice President elect shall have qualified, declaring who shall then act as President, or the manner in which one who is to act shall be selected, and such person shall act accordingly until a President or Vice President shall have qualified.

SECTION 4. The Congress may by law provide for the case of the death of any of the persons from whom the House of Representatives may choose a President whenever the right of choice shall have devolved upon them, and for the case of the death of any of the persons from whom the Senate may choose a Vice President whenever the right of choice shall have devolved upon them.

SECTION 5. Sections 1 and 2 shall take effect on the 15th day of October following the ratification of this article.

SECTION 6. This article shall be inoperative unless it shall have been ratified as an amendment to the Constitution by the legislatures of three-fourths of the several States within seven years from the date of its submission.

(Effective 1933)

## AMENDMENT XXI

SECTION 1. The eighteenth article of amendment to the Constitution of the United States is hereby repealed.

SECTION 2. The transportation or importation into any State, Territory, or possession of the United States for delivery or use therein of intoxicating liquors, in violation of the laws thereof, is hereby prohibited.

SECTION 3. This article shall be inoperative unless it shall have been ratified as an amendment to the Constitution by conventions in the several States, as provided in the Constitution, within seven years from the date of the submission hereof to the States by the Congress.

(Effective 1933)

## AMENDMENT XXII

SECTION 1. No person shall be elected to the office of the President more than twice, and no person who has held the office of President, or acted as President, for more than two years of a term to which some other person was elected President shall be elected to the office of the President more than once. But this Article shall not apply to any person holding the office of President when this Article was proposed by the Congress, and shall not prevent any person who may be holding the office of President, or acting as President, during the term within which this Article becomes operative from holding the office of President or acting as President during the remainder of such term.

SECTION 2. This article shall be inoperative unless it shall have been ratified as an amendment to the Constitution by the legislatures of three-fourths of the several States within seven years from the date of its submission to the States by the Congress.

(Effective 1951)

## AMENDMENT XXIII

SECTION 1. The District constituting the seat of Government of the United States shall appoint in such manner as the Congress may direct:

A number of electors of President and Vice President equal to the whole number of Senators and Representatives in Congress to which the District would be entitled if it were a State, but in no event more than the least populous State; they shall be in addition to those appointed by the States, but they shall be considered, for the purposes of the election of President and Vice President, to be electors appointed by a State; and they shall meet in the District and perform such duties as provided by the twelfth article of amendment.

SECTION 2. The Congress shall have power to enforce this article by appropriate legislation.
(Effective 1961)

### AMENDMENT XXIV

SECTION 1. The right of citizens of the United States to vote in any primary or other election for President or Vice President, for electors for President or Vice President, or for Senator or Representative in Congress, shall not be denied or abridged by the United States or any State by reason of failure to pay any poll tax or other tax.

SECTION 2. The Congress shall have power to enforce this article by appropriate legislation.
(Effective 1964)

### AMENDMENT XXV

SECTION 1. In case of the removal of the President from office or of his death or resignation, the Vice President shall become President.

SECTION 2. Whenever there is a vacancy in the office of the Vice President, the President shall nominate a Vice President who shall take office upon confirmation by a majority vote of both Houses of Congress.

SECTION 3. Whenever the President transmits to the President pro tempore of the Senate and the Speaker of the House of Representatives his written declaration that he is unable to discharge the powers and duties of his office, and until he transmits to them a written declaration to the contrary, such powers and duties shall be discharged by the Vice President as Acting President.

SECTION 4. Whenever the Vice President and a majority of either the principal officers of the executive departments or of such other body as Congress may by law provide, transmit to the President pro tempore of the Senate and the Speaker of the House of Representatives their written declaration that the President is unable to discharge the powers and duties of his office, the Vice President shall immediately assume the powers and duties of the office as Acting President.

Thereafter, when the President transmits to the President pro tempore of the Senate and the Speaker of the House of Representatives his written declaration that no inability exists, he shall resume the powers and duties of his office unless the Vice President and a majority of either the principal officers of the executive department or of such other body as Congress may by law provide, transmit within four days to the President pro tempore of the Senate and the Speaker of the House of Representatives their written declaration that the President is unable to discharge the powers and duties of his office. Thereupon Congress shall decide the issue, assembling within forty-eight hours for that purpose if not in session. If the Congress, within twenty-one days after receipt of the latter written declaration, or, if Congress is required to assemble, determines by two-thirds vote of both Houses that the President is unable to discharge the powers and duties of his office, the Vice President shall continue to discharge the same as Acting President; otherwise, the President shall resume the powers and duties of his office.
(Effective 1967)

### AMENDMENT XXVI

SECTION 1. The right of citizens of the United States, who are eighteen years of age or older, to vote shall not be denied or abridged by the United States or by any State on account of age.

SECTION 2. The Congress shall have power to enforce this article by appropriate legislation.

(Effective 1971)

### AMENDMENT XXVII

No law, varying the compensation for the services of the Senators and Representatives, shall take effect, until an election of Representatives shall have intervened.
(Effective 1992)

# CONSTITUTION OF THE STATE OF OHIO

ADOPTED MARCH 10, 1851
WITH AMENDMENTS CURRENT TO OCTOBER 1, 2011

## ARTICLE I: BILL OF RIGHTS

Section



### § 1 Right to freedom and protection of property.

All men are, by nature, free and independent, and have certain inalienable rights, among which are those of enjoying and defending life and liberty, acquiring, possessing, and protecting property, and seeking and obtaining happiness and safety.

### § 2 Right to alter, reform, or abolish government, and repeal special privileges.

All political power is inherent in the people. Government is instituted for their equal protection and benefit, and they have the right to alter, reform, or abolish the same, whenever they may deem it necessary; and no special privileges or immunities shall ever be granted, that may not be altered, revoked, or repealed by the general assembly.

### § 3 Right to assemble together.

The people have the right to assemble together, in a peaceable manner, to consult for their common good; to instruct their representatives; and to petition the general assembly for the redress of grievances.

### § 4 Bearing arms; standing armies; subordination of military power.

The people have the right to bear arms for their defense and security; but standing armies, in time of peace, are dangerous to liberty, and shall not be kept up; and the military shall be in strict subordination to the civil power.

### § 5 Trial by jury; reform in civil jury system.

The right of trial by jury shall be inviolate, except that, in civil cases, laws may be passed to authorize the rendering of a verdict by the concurrence of not less than three-fourths of the jury.

**HISTORY: (As amended September 3, 1912.)**

### § 6 Slavery and involuntary servitude.

There shall be no slavery in this state; nor involuntary servitude, unless for the punishment of crime.

### § 7 Rights of conscience; education; necessity of religion and knowledge.

All men have a natural and indefeasible right to worship Almighty God according to the dictates of their own conscience. No person shall be compelled to attend, erect, or support any place of worship, or maintain any form of worship, against his consent; and no preference shall be given, by law, to any religious society; nor shall any interference with the rights of conscience be permitted. No religious test shall be required, as a qualification for office, nor shall any person be incompetent to be a witness on account of his religious belief; but nothing herein shall be construed to dispense with oaths and affirmations. Religion, morality, and knowledge, however, being essential to good government, it shall be the duty of the general assembly to pass suitable laws to protect every religious denomination in the peaceable enjoyment of its own mode of public worship, and to encourage schools and the means of instruction.

### § 8 Writ of habeas corpus.

The privilege of the writ of habeas corpus shall not be suspended, unless, in cases of rebellion or invasion, the public safety require it.

### § 9 Bail; cruel and unusual punishments.

All persons shall be bailable by sufficient sureties, except for a person who is charged with a capital offense where the proof is evident or the presumption great, and except for a person who is charged with a felony where the proof is evident or the presumption great and where the person poses a substantial risk of serious physical harm to any person or to the community. Where a person is charged with any offense for which the person may be incarcerated, the court may determine at any time the type, amount, and conditions of bail. Excessive bail shall not be required; nor excessive fines imposed; nor cruel and unusual punishments inflicted.

The General Assembly shall fix by law standards to determine whether a person who is charged with a felony where the proof is evident or the presumption great poses a substantial risk of serious physical harm to any person or to the community. Procedures for establishing the amount and conditions of bail shall be established pursuant to Article IV, Section 5(b) of the Constitution of the state of Ohio.

**HISTORY: (As amended January 1, 1998.)**

## § 10 Trial of accused persons and their rights; depositions by state and comment on failure of accused to testify in criminal cases.

Except in cases of impeachment, cases arising in the army and navy, or in the militia when in actual service in time of war or public danger, and cases involving offenses for which the penalty provided is less than imprisonment in the penitentiary, no person shall be held to answer for a capital, or otherwise infamous, crime, unless on presentment or indictment of a grand jury; and the number of persons necessary to constitute such grand jury and the number thereof necessary to concur in finding such indictment shall be determined by law. In any trial, in any court, the party accused shall be allowed to appear and defend in person and with counsel; to demand the nature and cause of the accusation against him, and to have a copy thereof; to meet the witnesses face to face, and to have compulsory process to procure the attendance of witnesses in his behalf, and a speedy public trial by an impartial jury of the county in which the offense is alleged to have been committed; but provision may be made by law for the taking of the deposition by the accused or by the state, to be used for or against the accused, of any witness whose attendance can not be had at the trial, always securing to the accused means and the opportunity to be present in person and with counsel at the taking of such deposition, and to examine the witness face to face as fully and in the same manner as if in court. No person shall be compelled, in any criminal case, to be a witness against himself; but his failure to testify may be considered by the court and jury and may be made the subject of comment by counsel. No person shall be twice put in jeopardy for the same offense.

**HISTORY: (As amended September 3, 1912.)**

## § 10a Rights of victims of crime.

Victims of criminal offenses shall be accorded fairness, dignity, and respect in the criminal justice process, and, as the general assembly shall define and provide by law, shall be accorded rights to reasonable and appropriate notice, information, access, and protection and to a meaningful role in the criminal justice process. This section does not confer upon any person a right to appeal or modify any decision in a criminal proceeding, does not abridge any other right guaranteed by the Constitution of the United States or this constitution, and does not create any cause of action for compensation or damages against the state, any political subdivision of the state, any officer, employee, or agent of the state or of any political subdivision, or any officer of the court.

**HISTORY: (Adopted November 8, 1994).**

## § 11 Freedom of speech and of the press; libel.

Every citizen may freely speak, write, and publish his sentiments on all subjects, being responsible for the abuse of the right; and no law shall be passed to restrain or abridge the liberty of speech, or of the press. In all criminal prosecutions for libel, the truth may be given in evidence to the jury, and if it shall appear to the jury, that the matter charged as libelous is true, and was published with good motives, and for justifiable ends, the party shall be acquitted.

## § 12 Transportation, etc., for crime.

No person shall be transported out of the state, for any offense committed within the same; and no conviction shall work corruption of blood, or forfeiture of estate.

## § 13 Quartering of troops.

No soldier shall, in time of peace, be quartered in any house, without the consent of the owner; nor, in time of war, except in the manner prescribed by law.

## § 14 Search warrants and general warrants.

The right of the people to be secure in their persons, houses, papers, and possessions, against unreasonable searches and seizures shall not be violated; and no warrant shall issue, but upon probable cause, supported by oath or affirmation, particularly describing the place to be searched and the person and things to be seized.

## § 15 No imprisonment for debt.

No person shall be imprisoned for debt in any civil action, on mesne or final process, unless in cases of fraud.

## § 16 Redress in courts.

All courts shall be open, and every person, for an injury done him in his land, goods, person, or reputation, shall have remedy by due course of law, and shall have justice administered without denial or delay.

**[Suits against the state.]** Suits may be brought against the state, in such courts and in such manner, as may be provided by law.

**HISTORY: (As amended September 3, 1912.)**

## § 17 Hereditary privileges, etc.

No hereditary emoluments, honors, or privileges, shall ever be granted or conferred by this state.

## § 18 Suspension of laws.

No power of suspending laws shall ever be exercised, except by the general assembly.

## § 19 Inviolability of private property.

Private property shall ever be held inviolate, but subservient to the public welfare. When taken in time of war or other public exigency, imperatively requiring its immediate seizure or for the purpose of making or repairing roads, which shall be open to the public, without charge, a compensation shall be made to the owner, in money, and in all other cases, where private property shall be taken for public use, a compensation therefor shall first be made in money, or first secured by a deposit of money; and such compensation shall be assessed by a jury, without deduction for benefits to any property of the owner.

The provisions of 151 v S 167 read as follows:

SECTION 1. As used in Sections 2 to 7 of this act:

(A) "Blighted area" has the same meaning as in section 303.26 of the Revised Code, but also includes an area in a municipal corporation.

(B) "Public body" means any entity of the state government, and any county, municipal corporation, township, commission, district, authority, or other political subdivision of the state, that has the power to take private property by eminent domain.

SECTION 2. (A) Notwithstanding any provision of the Revised Code to the contrary, until December 31, 2006, no public body shall use eminent domain to take, without the consent of the owner, private property that is not within a blighted area, as determined by the public body, when the primary purpose for the taking is economic development that will ultimately result in ownership of that property being vested in another private person.

(B)(1) Until December 31, 2006, if any public body uses eminent domain to take, without the consent of the owner, private property that is not within a blighted area, as determined by the public body, when the primary purpose for the taking is economic development that will ultimately result in ownership of that property being vested in another private person, each of the following shall apply:

(a) The Ohio Public Works Commission shall not award or distribute to the public body any funding under a capital improvement program created under Chapter 164. of the Revised Code.

(b) The Department of Development shall not award or distribute to the public body any funding under a shovel ready sites program created under section 122.083 of the Revised Code.

(c) The public body shall not receive any funding designated for capital purposes in any act of the General Assembly.

(2) Until December 31, 2006, any public body seeking to obtain funds described in division (B)(1) of this section, shall certify in writing to the grantor of the funds that the public body has not used its eminent domain authority on or after the effective date of this act to take private property in violation of the moratorium established by this act.

(C) Divisions (A) and (B) of this section do not apply to the use of eminent domain for the taking of private property to be used as follows:

(1) In the construction, maintenance, or repair of streets, roads, or walkways, paths, or other ways open to the public's use, including rights of way immediately adjacent to those public ways, including, but not limited to, such use pursuant to authority granted under Title LV of the Revised Code;

(2) For a public utility purpose;

(3) By a common carrier;

(4) For parks or recreation areas open to the public;

(5) In the construction, maintenance, or repair of buildings and grounds used for governmental purposes.

SECTION 3. (A) There is hereby created the Legislative Task Force to Study Eminent Domain and Its Use and Application in the State. The Task Force shall consist of the following twenty-five members:

(1) Three members of the House of Representatives, appointed by the Speaker of the House of Representatives in consultation with the Minority Leader of the House of Representatives. The Speaker of the House of Representatives shall designate one of the members the Speaker appoints to serve as co-chairperson of the Task Force.

(2) Three members of the Senate, appointed by the President of the Senate in consultation with the Minority Leader of the Senate. The President of the Senate shall designate one of the members the President appoints to serve as co-chairperson of the Task Force.

(3) One member representing the home building industry in the state, appointed jointly by the Speaker of the House of Representatives and the President of the Senate;

(4) One member who shall be a statewide advocate on the issues raised in Kelo v. City of New London (2005), 125 S. Ct. 2655, insofar as they affect eminent domain, appointed jointly by the Speaker of the House of Representatives and the President of the Senate;

(5) One member representing the agricultural industry in the state, appointed jointly by the Speaker of the House of Representatives and the President of the Senate;

(6) One member representing the commercial real estate industry in the state, appointed jointly by the Speaker of the House of Representatives and the President of the Senate;

(7) One member representing licensed realtors in the state, appointed jointly by the Speaker of the House of Representatives and the President of the Senate;

(8) One member representing the Ohio Prosecuting Attorneys Association or the Ohio Association of Probate Judges, appointed jointly by the Speaker of the House of Representatives and the President of the Senate;

(9) One member who shall be an attorney who is knowledgeable on the issues confronting the Task Force and who represents persons who own property and reside within Ohio, appointed jointly by the Speaker of the House of Representatives and the President of the Senate;

(10) One member knowledgeable on the issues confronting the Task Force who represents persons who own property and reside within Ohio, appointed jointly by the Speaker of the House of Representatives and the President of the Senate;

(11) One member representing the planning industry in the state, one member representing an Ohio labor organization, one member representing a statewide historic preservation organization that works within commercial districts, one member representing municipal corporations, one member representing counties, and one member representing townships, each appointed by the Governor;

(12) The Director of Development or the Director's designee;

(13) The Director of Transportation or the Director's designee;

(14) Two members who shall be attorneys with expertise in eminent domain issues, each appointed by the Attorney General;

(15) One member representing small businesses, appointed jointly by the Speaker of the House of Representatives and the President of the Senate.

(B) Appointments to the Task Force shall be made not later than thirty days after the effective date of this section. Any vacancy in the membership of the Task Force shall be filled in the same manner as the original appointment. Members of the Task Force shall serve without compensation.

(C)(1) The Task Force shall study each of the following:

(a) The use of eminent domain and its impact on the state;

(b) How the decision of the United States Supreme Court in *Kelo v. City of New London* (2005), 125 S. Ct. 2655, affects state law governing the use of eminent domain in the state;

(c) The overall impact of state laws governing the use of eminent domain on economic development, residents, and local governments in Ohio.

(2) The Task Force shall prepare and submit to the General Assembly by not later than April 1, 2006, a report that shall include the findings of its study and recommendations concerning the use of eminent domain and its impact on the state, and by not later than August 1, 2006, a report that shall include findings and recommendations regarding the updating of state law governing eminent domain. On submission of the report due not later than August 1, 2006, the Task Force shall cease to exist.

(D) The Legislative Service Commission shall provide any

technical, professional, and clerical employees that are necessary for the Task Force to perform its duties.

(E) All meetings of the Task Force are declared to be public meetings open to the public at all times. A member of the Task Force shall be present in person at a meeting that is open to the public in order to be considered present or to vote at the meeting and for the purposes of determining whether a quorum is present. The Task Force shall promptly prepare and maintain the minutes of its meetings, which shall be public records under section 149.43 of the Revised Code. The Task Force shall give reasonable notice of its meetings so that any person may determine the time and place of all scheduled meetings. The Task Force shall not hold a meeting unless it gives at least twenty-four hours advance notification to the news media organizations that have requested such notification.

SECTION 4. The General Assembly hereby makes the following statements of findings and intent:

(A) On June 23, 2005, the United States Supreme Court rendered its decision in *Kelo v. City of New London* (2005), 125 S. Ct. 2655, which allows the taking of private property that is not within a blighted area by eminent domain for the purpose of economic development even when the ultimate result of the taking is ownership of the property being vested in another private person. As a result of this decision, the General Assembly believes the interpretation and use of the state's eminent domain law could be expanded to allow the taking of private property that is not within a blighted area, ultimately resulting in ownership of that property being vested in another private person in violation of Sections 1 and 19 of Article I, Ohio Constitution, which protect the rights of Ohio citizens to maintain property as inviolate, subservient only to the public welfare. Thus, the General Assembly finds it is necessary to enact a moratorium on any takings of this nature by any public body until further legislative remedies may be considered.

(B) The General Assembly finds that it is a matter of statewide concern to enact the moratorium. The moratorium is necessary to protect the general welfare and the rights of citizens under Sections 1 and 19 of Article I, Ohio Constitution, and to ensure that these rights are not violated due to the *Kelo* decision. In enacting this provision, the General Assembly wishes to ensure uniformity throughout the state.

SECTION 5. Section 2 of this act applies only to taking actions initiated on or after the effective date of this act. As used in this section, "initiated" means the adoption of a resolution or ordinance of necessity by the public body or filing of a court action, but excludes taking actions for which a resolution or ordinance of necessity or other official action of a public body has been taken and public funds have been expended in connection with that taking action prior to the effective date of this act.

SECTION 6. If any item of law that constitutes the whole or part of an uncodified section of law contained in this act, or if any application of any item of law that constitutes the whole or part of an uncodified section of law contained in this act, is held invalid, the invalidity does not affect other items of law or applications of items of law that can be given effect without the invalid item of law or application. To this end, the items of law of which the uncodified sections contained in this act are composed, and their applications, are independent and severable.

SECTION 7. Nothing in this act shall be construed to imply that any public body with eminent domain authority has prior to the enactment of this act abused that authority or engaged in any wrongdoing in the exercise of its eminent domain authority conferred by statute or the Ohio Constitution.

SECTION 8. This act is hereby declared to be an emergency measure necessary for the immediate preservation of the public peace, health, and safety. The reason for the necessity is that the United States Supreme Court decision in *Kelo v. City of New London* (2005), 125 S. Ct. 2655, could allow the taking of private property that is not within a blighted area, ultimately resulting in ownership of that property being vested in another private person in violation of Sections 1 and 19 of Article I, Ohio Constitution, and, as a result, warrants a moratorium on any takings of this type until further legislative remedies may be considered. Therefore, this act shall go into immediate effect.

## § 19a Damage for wrongful death.

The amount of damages recoverable by civil action in the courts for death caused by the wrongful act, neglect, or default of another, shall not be limited by law.

**HISTORY: (Adopted September 3, 1912.)**

## § 19b Private property rights in ground water, lakes and other watercourses.

(A) The protection of the rights of Ohio's property owners, the protection of Ohio's natural resources, and the maintenance of the stability of Ohio's economy require the recognition and protection of property interests in ground water, lakes, and watercourses.

(B) The preservation of private property interests recognized under divisions (C) and (D) of this section shall be held inviolate, but subservient to the public welfare as provided in Section 19 of Article I of the Constitution.

(C) A property owner has a property interest in the reasonable use of the ground water underlying the property owner's land.

(D) An owner of riparian land has a property interest in the reasonable use of the water in a lake or watercourse located on or flowing through the owner's riparian land.

(E) Ground water underlying privately owned land and nonnavigable waters located on or flowing through privately owned land shall not be held in trust by any governmental body. The state, and a political subdivision to the extent authorized by state law, may provide for the regulation of such waters. An owner of land voluntarily may convey to a governmental body the owner's property interest held in the ground water underlying the land or nonnavigable waters located on or flowing through the land.

(F) Nothing in this section affects the application of the public trust doctrine as it applies to Lake Erie or the navigable waters of the state.

(G) Nothing in Section 1e of Article II, Section 36 of Article II, Article VIII, Section 1 of Article X, Section 3 of Article XVIII, or Section 7 of Article XVIII of the Constitution shall impair or limit the rights established in this section.

**HISTORY: (Adopted November 4, 2008, effective December 1, 2008.)**

## § 20 Powers reserved to the people.

This enumeration of rights shall not be construed to impair or deny others retained by the people; and all powers, not herein delegated, remain with the people.

# ARTICLE II: LEGISLATIVE

Section



## § 39 Regulating expert testimony in criminal trials.

Laws may be passed for the regulation of the use of expert witnesses and expert testimony in criminal trials and proceedings.

**HISTORY: (Adopted September 3, 1912.)**

## ARTICLE III: EXECUTIVE



### § 11 May grant reprieves, commutations, and pardons.

The Governor shall have power, after conviction, to grant reprieves, commutations, and pardons, for all crimes and offenses, except treason and cases of impeachment, upon such conditions as the Governor may think proper; subject, however, to such regulations, as to the manner of applying for commutations and pardons, as may be prescribed by law. Upon conviction for treason, the Governor may suspend the execution of the sentence, and report the case to the General Assembly, at its next meeting, when the General Assembly shall either pardon, commute the sentence, direct its execution, or grant a further reprieve. The Governor shall communicate to the general assembly, at every regular session, each case of reprieve, commutation, or pardon granted, stating the name and crime of the convict, the sentence, its date, and the date of the commutation, pardon, or reprieve, with the Governor's reasons therefor.

**HISTORY: (As amended January 1, 1996).**

## ARTICLE IV: JUDICIAL



### § 1 In whom judicial power vested.

The judicial power of the state is vested in a supreme court, courts of appeals, courts of common pleas and divisions thereof, and such other courts inferior to the supreme court as may from time to time be established by law.

**HISTORY: (Amended May 7, 1968; Nov. 6, 1973; SJR No.30.)**

### § 2 The supreme court.

(A) The supreme court shall, until otherwise provided by law, consist of seven judges, who shall be known as the chief justice and justices. In case of the absence or disability of the chief justice, the judge having the period of longest total service upon the court shall be the acting chief justice. If any member of the court shall be unable, by reason of illness, disability or disqualification, to hear, consider and decide a cause or causes, the chief justice or the acting chief justice may direct any judge of any court of appeals to sit with the judges of the supreme court in the place and stead of the absent judge. A majority of the supreme court shall be necessary to constitute a quorum or to render a judgment.

(B)(1) The supreme court shall have original jurisdiction in the following:

(a) Quo warranto;

(b) Mandamus;

(c) Habeas corpus;

(d) Prohibition;

(e) Procedendo;

(f) In any cause on review as may be necessary to its complete determination;

(g) Admission to the practice of law, the discipline of persons so admitted, and all other matters relating to the practice of law.

(2) The supreme court shall have appellate jurisdiction as follows:

(a) In appeals from the courts of appeals as a matter of right in the following:

(i) Cases originating in the courts of appeals;

(ii) Cases involving questions arising under the constitution of the United States or of this state.

(b) In appeals from the courts of appeals in cases of felony on leave first obtained,

(c) In direct appeals from the courts of common pleas or other courts of record inferior to the court of appeals as a matter of right in cases in which the death penalty has been imposed;

(d) Such revisory jurisdiction of the proceedings of administrative officers or agencies as may be conferred by law;

(e) In cases of public or great general interest, the supreme court may direct any court of appeals to certify its record to the supreme court, and may review and affirm, modify, or reverse the judgment of the court of appeals;

(f) The supreme court shall review and affirm, modify, or reverse the judgment in any case certified by any court of appeals pursuant to section 3(B) (4) of this article.

(3) No law shall be passed or rule made whereby any person shall be prevented from invoking the original jurisdiction of the supreme court.

(C) The decisions in all cases in the supreme court shall be reported, together with the reasons therefor.

**HISTORY: (Amended November 8, 1994).**

### § 3 Court of appeals.

(A) The state shall be divided by law into compact appellate districts in each of which there shall be a court of appeals consisting of three judges. Laws may be passed increasing the number of judges in any district wherein the volume of business may require such additional judge or judges. In districts having additional judges, three judges shall participate in the hearing and disposition of each case. The court shall hold sessions in each county of the district as the necessity arises. The county commissioners of each county shall provide a proper and convenient place for the court of appeals to hold court.

(B)(1) The courts of appeals shall have original jurisdiction in the following:

(a) Quo warranto;

(b) Mandamus;

(c) Habeas corpus;

(d) Prohibition;

(e) Procedendo;

(f) In any cause on review as may be necessary to its complete determination.

(2) Courts of appeals shall have such jurisdiction as may be provided by law to review and affirm, modify, or reverse judgments or final orders of the courts of record inferior to the court of appeals within the district, except that courts of appeals shall not have jurisdiction to review on direct appeal a judgment that imposes a sentence of death.

Courts of appeals shall have such appellate jurisdiction as may be provided by law to review and affirm, modify, or reverse final orders or actions of administrative officers or agencies.

(3) A majority of the judges hearing the cause shall be necessary to render a judgment. Judgments of the courts of appeals are final except as provided in section 2(B) (2) of this article. No judgment resulting from a trial by jury shall be reversed on the weight of the evidence except by the concurrence of all three judges hearing the cause.

(4) Whenever the judges of a court of appeals find that a judgment upon which they have agreed is in conflict with a judgment pronounced upon the same question by any other court of appeals of the state, the judges shall certify the record of the case to the supreme court for review and final determination.

(C) Laws may be passed providing for the reporting of cases in the courts of appeals.

**HISTORY: (Amended November 8, 1994).**

**Analogous to former Art. IV, § 6.**

## § 4 Common pleas court.

(A) There shall be a court of common pleas and such divisions thereof as may be established by law serving each county of the state. Any judge of a court of common pleas or a division thereof may temporarily hold court in any county. In the interests of the fair, impartial, speedy, and sure administration of justice, each county shall have one or more resident judges, or two or more counties may be combined into districts having one or more judges resident in the district and serving the common pleas courts of all counties in the district, as may be provided by law. Judges serving a district shall sit in each county in the district as the business of the court requires. In counties or districts having more than one judge of the court of common pleas, the judges shall select one of their number to act as presiding judge, to serve at their pleasure. If the judges are unable because of equal division of the vote to make such selection, the judge having the longest total service on the court of common pleas shall serve as presiding judge until selection is made by vote. The presiding judge shall have such duties and exercise such powers as are prescribed by rule of the supreme court.

(B) The courts of common pleas and divisions thereof shall have such original jurisdiction over all justiciable matters and such powers of review of proceedings of administrative officers and agencies as may be provided by law.

(C) Unless otherwise provided by law, there shall be a probate division and such other divisions of the courts of common pleas as may be provided by law. Judges shall be elected specifically to such probate division and to such other divisions. The judges of the probate division shall be empowered to employ and control the clerks, employees, deputies, and referees of such probate division of the common pleas courts.

**HISTORY: (Amended, effective Nov. 6, 1973; SJR No.30. Adopted May 7, 1968. Former § 4 repealed.)**

## § 5 Additional powers of supreme court; supervision; rule making.

(A)(1) In addition to all other powers vested by this article in the supreme court, the supreme court shall have general superintendence over all courts in the state. Such general superintending power shall be exercised by the chief justice in accordance with rules promulgated by the supreme court.

(2) The supreme court shall appoint an administrative director who shall assist the chief justice and who shall serve at the pleasure of the court. The compensation and duties of the administrative director shall be determined by the court.

(3) The chief justice or acting chief justice, as necessity arises, shall assign any judge of a court of common pleas or a division thereof temporarily to sit or hold court on any other court of common pleas or division thereof or any court of appeals or shall assign any judge of a court of appeals temporarily to sit or hold court on any other court of appeals or any court of common pleas or division thereof and upon such assignment said judge shall serve in such assigned capacity until the termination of the assignment. Rules may be adopted to provide for the temporary assignment of judges to sit and hold court in any court established by law.

(B) The supreme court shall prescribe rules governing practice and procedure in all courts of the state, which rules shall not abridge, enlarge, or modify any substantive right. Proposed rules shall be filed by the court, not later than the fifteenth day of January, with the clerk of each house of the general assembly during a regular session thereof, and amendments to any such proposed rules may be so filed not later than the first day of May in that session. Such rules shall take effect on the following first day of July, unless prior to such day the general assembly adopts a concurrent resolution of disapproval. All laws in conflict with such rules shall be of no further force or effect after such rules have taken effect.

Courts may adopt additional rules concerning local practice in their respective courts which are not inconsistent with the rules promulgated by the supreme court. The supreme court may make rules to require uniform record keeping for all courts of the state, and shall make rules governing the admission to the practice of law and discipline of persons so admitted.

(C) The chief justice of the supreme court or any judge of that court designated by him shall pass upon the disqualification of any judge of the courts of appeals or courts of common pleas or division thereof. Rules may be adopted to provide for the hearing of disqualification matters involving judges of courts established by law.

**HISTORY: (Amended, effective Nov. 6, 1973; SJR No.30. Adopted May 7, 1968.)**

**Not analogous to former § 5, repealed October 9, 1883.**

## § 20 Style of process, prosecution, and indictment.

The style of all process shall be, "The State of Ohio;" all prosecutions shall be carried on, in the name, and by the authority, of the state of Ohio; and all indictments shall conclude, "against the peace and dignity of the state of Ohio."

# ARTICLE V: ELECTIVE FRANCHISE

Section

## § 3 Repealed, June 8, 1976.

This section referred to the privilege from arrest of voters during elections.

## § 4 Forfeiture of elective franchise.

The General Assembly shall have power to exclude from the privilege of voting, or of being eligible to office, any person convicted of a felony.

**HISTORY: (Amended, effective June 8, 1976; SJR No.16.)**

# ARTICLE XVIII: MUNICIPAL CORPORATIONS

Section



## § 3 Powers.

Municipalities shall have authority to exercise all powers of local self-government and to adopt and enforce within their limits such local police, sanitary and other similar regulations, as are not in conflict with general laws.

**HISTORY: (Adopted September 3, 1912.)**

The provisions of § 3 of HB 386 (149 v —) read as follows:

SECTION 3. (A) The provisions of the Revised Code, including, but not limited to, Titles XI, XIII, XVII, and XLVII, relating to the origination, granting, servicing, and collection of loans and other forms of credit prescribe rules of conduct upon citizens generally, comprise a comprehensive regulatory framework intended to operate uniformly throughout the state under the same circumstances and conditions, and constitute general laws within the meaning of Section 3 of Article XVIII of the Ohio Constitution.

(B) The provisions of the Revised Code, including, but not limited to, Titles XI, XIII, XVII, and XLVII, relating to the origination, granting, servicing, and collection of loans and other forms of credit have been enacted in furtherance of the police powers of the state.

(C) Silence in the Revised Code, including, but not limited to, Titles XI, XIII, XVII, and XLVII, with respect to any act or practice in the origination, granting, servicing, or collection of loans or other forms of credit shall not be interpreted to mean that the state has not completely occupied the field or has only set minimum standards in its regulation of lending and other credit activities.

(D) It is the intent of the General Assembly to entirely preempt municipal corporations and other political subdivisions from the regulation and licensing of lending and other credit activities.

## § 7 Home rule.

Any municipality may frame and adopt or amend a charter for its government and may, subject to the provisions of section 3 of this article, exercise thereunder all powers of local self-government.

**HISTORY: (Adopted September 3, 1912.)**

# TIME TABLE IN CRIMINAL CASES

## (Alphabetical Order)

---

**ACQUITTAL — Crim. R. 29**

**Motion for Judgment of**

An oral or written motion for judgment of acquittal is offered by the Defendant or by the court on its own motion:

a. *When* the State rests its case in chief.
b. *When* the Defense rests.
c. *When* all the evidence has been received.
d. After or renewed within *14 days* following a jury's discharge *or* within such further time as the Court may fix during the 14 day period.

The Court *must* rule immediately on the motion offered at the close of the State's case.

The Court *may* reserve ruling on the motion offered at other authorized times and decide the same before or after submission of the case to the jury, after a guilty verdict or after a jury standing in disagreement is discharged.

**ALIBI — Crim. R. 12.1**

**Written Notice Of**

Shall be filed and served upon the Prosecuting Attorney *no later than 7 days before trial.*

**APPEAL (Listed in case progression order)**

**Notice of Appeal—App. R. 4(B)**

*Defendant's notice of appeal* shall be filed with the Trial Court Clerk within *30 days* of the date of the entry of the judgment or order appealed from.

*The Prosecution's Notice of Appeal* in all cases except under Crim. R. 12(K) (a Trial Court order granting a Motion to Suppress Evidence) and Juv. R. 22(F) (a Juvenile Court order granting a Motion to Suppress Evidence) shall be filed *within 30 days* of the date of entry of the judgment or order appealed from. Appeal by the Prosecution from an order granting a Motion to Suppress Evidence is commenced by the filing of the Notice of Appeal with the Trial Court Clerk *within 7 days* from the date of entry of such order.

**Motion For Leave To Appeal—App. R. 5.**

After expiration of the 30-day period for filing a Notice of Appeal as of right, the Defendant may appeal only by leave of the court to which the appeal is taken. A Notice of Appeal must be filed concurrently with the Motion and a copy of the Notice must be filed in the Trial Court, also.

The prosecution may, *within 30 days* from the filing of the Motion for Leave to Appeal, file affidavits, parts of the record and brief or memorandum of law to refute the claims of the Defendant.

The Prosecution must file its Motion for Leave to Appeal *within 30 days* from the entry of the judgment or order appealed from.

The Defendant may *within 30 days thereafter* file affidavits, parts of the record, and a brief or memorandum of law to refute the claims of the Prosecution.

**Application For Release On Bail—App. R. 8(B)**

Application for release on bail and for suspension of execution of sentence after conviction shall be made *in the first instance* in the Trial Court.

**Transcript Of Proceedings—App. R. 9(B)**

*At the time of filing* the notice of appeal, Appellant shall order from the Court Reporter a complete or partial transcript of proceedings. Where appellant orders only a partial transcript of proceedings, he shall, *with his notice of appeal,* file and serve on appellee a description of the parts ordered and a statement of his assignments of error. Appellee, then, *within 10 days after service* of such statement, may serve on appellant a designation of additional parts to be included in the transcript of proceedings.

If the Appellant refuses or fails within *ten days after service* of the Appellee's designation to order such parts, the Appellee *within five days thereafter* shall either order the parts in writing or apply to the Court of Appeals for an order requiring Appellant to do so.

*At the time of ordering,* a party shall arrange for the payment to the reporter of the cost of the transcript.

**Objections Or Amendments To Statement of The Evidence Where A Transcript Of Proceedings Is Not Available—App. R. 9(C)**

Objections or amendments shall be filed by appellee *within 10 days* after he is served with a copy of statement of the evidence.

**Correction Or Modification Of Trial Court Record—App. R. 9(E)**

*Either before or after* the record is transmitted to the Court of Appeals, the parties, by stipulation, or the trial court, may direct that an omission or misstatement be corrected.

**Transmission Of The Record To Court of Appeals—App. R. 10**

The record shall be transmitted to the Court of Appeals when the record is complete for purposes of the appeal, or when *40 days,* or *20 days* in an accelerated calendar case *have elapsed after the filing of the Notice of Appeal* and no extension has been granted. Where leave to appeal must be obtained, all time limits run from the filing of the journal entry granting leave.

**Trial Court Extension—App. R. 10(C)**

The Trial Court may extend the time for transmitting the record, provided the request for extension is filed within the *time originally prescribed* or within an *extension granted previously* except as provided by a local rule.

**When The Record Is Deemed Complete—App. R. 10(B)**

(1) When the transcript of proceedings is filed with the Clerk of the Trial Court.

(2) When a statement of the evidence or proceedings, pursuant to Rule 9(C), is settled and approved by the Trial Court, and filed with the Clerk of the Trial Court.

(3) When an agreed statement in lieu of the record, pursuant to Rule 9(D), is approved by the Trial Court, and filed with the Clerk of the Trial Court.

(4) Where Appellant, pursuant to Rule 9(B), designates that no part of the transcript of proceedings is to be included in the record or that no transcript is necessary for appeal, after the expiration of ten days following service of such designation upon Appellee, unless Appellee has within such time filed a designation of additional parts of the transcript to be included in the record.

(5) When forty days have elapsed after filing of the last Notice of Appeal, in an accelerated calendar case and there is no extension of time for transmission of the record.

(6) When twenty days have elapsed after filing of the last notice of appeal in an accelerated calendar case, and there is no extension of time for transmission of the record.

(7) Where the Appellant fails to file either the docketing statement or the statement required by App. R. 9(B), ten days after filing the Notice of Appeal.

**When Transmission Is Effected—App. R. 10(B)**

Transmission is effected when the Trial Court Clerk mails or otherwise forwards the records to the Clerk of the Court of Appeals. The Trial Court Clerk shall note the date of transmission on the face of the record and shall note the transmission on the appearance docket.

**Notice To Parties When Record Filed—App. R. 11(B)**

The Clerk of the Court of Appeals shall *immediately* give notice to all parties of the date on which the trial court record was filed in the Court of Appeals.

**Response By Appellant To Motion To Dismiss For Failure To File, Within Time, The Trial Court Record In The Court of Appeals—App. R. 11(C)**

Appellant *may* respond to such motion within *10 days of service.*

**Service By Mail—App. R. 13(C)**

Service by mail is complete on mailing.

**Additional Time After Service By Mail—App. R. 14(C)**

Where service by mail is permitted and used, *3 days* shall be added to any prescribed period.

**Computing Time—App. R. 14(A)**

The day of the act, event or default from which the designated period of time begins to run *shall not be included* but the *last day* shall be included unless it is a Saturday, Sunday, or legal holiday, in which event, the period runs until the end of the next day which is not a Saturday, Sunday or legal holiday. But, where the time allowed or prescribed *is less than 7 days,* Saturdays, Sundays, and legal holidays *are not* included.

**Enlargement Or Reduction Of Time—App. R. 14(B)**

Except for the filing of a Notice of Appeal, the Court of Appeals may enlarge or reduce the prescribed time or permit an act to be done *after the expiration of such time.* The court may not enlarge or reduce the time for filing a notice of appeal or motion to certify pursuant to App. R. 25. Enlargement of time to file an application to reconsider pursuant to App. R. 26(A) shall not be granted except on a showing of extraordinary circumstances.

**Serving And Filing Briefs—App. R. 18**

1. *Appellant shall* serve and file his Brief *within 20 days after* the date on which the Clerk has mailed the notice [required by Rule 11(B)] that the record has been filed. For accelerated calendar cases, *within 15 days* thereafter—App. R. 11.1.
2. *Appellee shall* serve and file his Brief *within 20 days after* service of the Brief of Appellant. For accelerated calendar cases, *within 15 days* thereafter—App. R. 11.1.
3. *Appellant may* serve and file a Reply Brief *within 10 days after* service of the Brief of Appellee. For accelerated calendar cases, Reply Briefs are prohibited unless ordered under order by the Court—App. R. 11.1.

**NOTE:** Counsel should be aware of App. R. 18(C)—Consequence of failure to file briefs.

**Brief Of Amicus Curiae—App. R. 17**

A Brief of an Amicus Curiae, unless all parties otherwise consent, shall be filed *within the time allowed* the party whose position the Brief supports, unless the Court extends such time and fixes the period when an opposing party may answer.

**Argument Of Case—App. R. 21(B)**

Each side is allowed 30 minutes for argument which time can be extended or reduced as the Court may order.

**Argument On Motions—App. R. 21(G)**

Oral argument *will not be heard* upon motions unless ordered by the Court.

**Entry Of Judgment—App. R. 22(C)**

*Within 5 days from* the Order, Decree or Judgment, Counsel for the prevailing party shall prepare and submit to opposing Counsel a proper journal entry *and within 5 days after* receipt of such entry, opposing Counsel shall approve or reject the entry and forward the same to Counsel for the prevailing party who shall immediately submit it to the Court.

**NOTE:** *App. R. 22(D)* authorizes the Court, *sua sponte,* to prepare and file its own Entry of Judgment.

**Motion To Certify A Conflict—App. R. 25**

A motion to certify a conflict under Article IV, Section 3(B)(4) of the Ohio Constitution shall be made in writing no later than ten days after the clerk has both mailed to the parties the judgment or order of the court that creates a conflict with a judgment or order of another court of appeals and made note on the docket of the mailing, as required by App. R. 30(A). The filing of a motion to certify a conflict does not extend the time to appeal from the judgment of the court of appeals to the Ohio Supreme Court. A motion under this rule shall specify the issue proposed for certification and shall cite the judgment or judgments alleged to be in conflict with the judgment of the court in which the motion is filed.

Parties opposing the motion shall answer in writing within ten days of service of the motion. The moving party may file a reply brief within seven days after service of the answer brief in opposition. Copies of the motion, answer brief in opposition, and reply brief shall be served as prescribed for the service and filing of briefs in the initial action. Oral argument of a motion to certify a conflict shall not be permitted except at the request of the court.

The court of appeals shall rule upon a motion to certify within sixty days of its filing.

**Application For Reconsideration—App. R. 26**
Application for reconsideration of any cause or motion submitted on appeal shall be made in writing no later than ten days after the clerk has both mailed to the parties the judgment or order in question and made a note on the docket of the mailing as required by App. R. 30(A).

Parties opposing the application shall answer in writing within ten days of service of the application. The party making the application may file a reply brief within seven days of service of the answer brief in opposition. Copies of the application, answer brief in opposition, and reply brief shall be served in the manner prescribed for the service and filing of briefs in the initial action. Oral argument of an application for reconsideration shall not be permitted except at the request of the court.

The application for reconsideration shall be considered by the panel that issued the original decision.

**Supreme Court Of Ohio, Appeal To**

**Institution of Appeal From Court of Appeals—Sup. Ct. R. II**

To perfect an appeal from a court of appeals to the Supreme Court, other than in a certified conflict case (which is addressed in Sup. Ct. R. IV) the appellant shall file a notice of appeal within 45 days from the entry of the judgment being appealed.

**APPEARANCE — Crim. R. 4(E)**

One arrested with or without an arrest warrant having first been issued shall be brought before the Court having jurisdiction *without unnecessary delay.* The court shall proceed according to Crim. R. 5.

**ARRAIGNMENT — Crim. R. 10(A)**

*Before* being called upon to plead, a defendant shall be given a copy of the indictment, information or complaint.

**ARREST — Crim. R. 4(E)(1)**

**With Arrest Warrant**
A defendant shall be brought before the Court which issued the warrant, or before a court of record where the arrest takes place in another county *without unnecessary delay.*

**Without An Arrest Warrant—Crim. R. 4(E)(2)**
A defendant shall be brought before the Court having jurisdiction of the offense *without unnecessary delay.*

**ARREST OF JUDGMENT — Crim. R. 34**

**Motion For**
Shall be filed *within 14 days* after a verdict, or finding of guilty, or after plea of guilty or no contest, *or* within such time as the Court shall fix *within* the 14 day period.

**ASSIGNMENT OF COUNSEL**

**Serious Offenses—Crim. R. 44(A)**
Counsel shall be assigned for a defendant unable to obtain representation *at every stage of the proceedings, from his initial appearance before a court through appeal as of right,* unless Counsel is knowingly, intelligently and voluntarily waived.

**Petty Offenses—Crim. R. 44(B)**
Confinement may not be imposed unless Counsel is assigned for a defendant who desires representation *prior* to trial, unless counsel is knowingly, intelligently, and voluntarily waived.

**BAIL**

**Amendments—Crim. R. 46(E)**
*At any time* the judge who ordered release on bail on any condition may amend his order.

**Where Summons Has Issued—Crim. R. 46(D)**
Where summons has been issued and the defendant has appeared pursuant to the summons, absent good cause, a recognizance bond shall be the preferred type of bail.

**BILL OF PARTICULARS — Crim. R. 7(E)**

**Amendment**
A bill of particulars may be amended *at any time* subject to such conditions as justice requires.

**Motion For—Crim. R. 7(E)**
The written request shall be filed within *21 days after arraignment, but not later than 7 days before trial* or upon court order. But see R.C. § 2941.07, which states that the written request shall be filed *not less than 5 days before trial* or upon Court order.

**CHANGE OF VENUE — Crim. R. 18(B)(1)**

**Motion For**
The written motion shall be filed *within 35 days after arraignment or 7 days before trial whichever is earlier,* or at such later, reasonable time as the Court may permit.

**CLERICAL MISTAKES — Crim. R. 36**

May be corrected at any time.

**COMPLAINT — Crim. R. 4(E)(2)**

One arrested without a warrant having first been issued shall be brought before the Court having jurisdiction of the offense and a complaint shall *without unnecessary delay be filed.*

**COUNSEL,** *See* **Assignment of Counsel**

**DEFENSES AND MOTIONS — Crim. R. 12**

**Defects In Indictment, Information Or Complaint—Crim. R. 12(C)(2)**
Those which show a lack of jurisdiction or the failure to charge an offense, shall be noticed by the Court *at any time.*

**Failure To Raise Defenses Or Objections—Crim. R. 12(H)**
Unless for good cause shown, the Court *extends the time for filing,* a failure to file *prior to trial* constitutes a waiver.

**Mandatory Pre-Trial Motions—Crim. R. 12(C)**
1. Defects in the institution of the prosecution.
2. Defects in the charge, except those which demonstrate that the Court is without jurisdiction or that no crime is charged.
3. Suppression of evidence.
4. Requests for discovery.
5. Requests for severance.

**Pre-Trial Motions—When Made—Crim. R. 12(D)**
All pre-trial motions *except* motions for Bill of Particulars and for Discovery *shall be filed within 35 days after arraignment or 7 days before trial, whichever is earlier*

and, in the interest of justice, the Court may extend the time.

**Ruling On PreTrial Motions—Crim. R. 12(F)**
Except on a Change of Venue Motion, the Court must make a *timely ruling before trial.*

**DEPOSITIONS—Crim. R. 15**

**Notice Of Taking—Crim. R. 15(B)**
*Reasonable* written notice must be given to each opposing party of the time and place of the deposition by the party at whose instance the deposition is taken.

**When Taken—Crim. R. 15(A)**
*At any time* after the filing of the indictment, information or complaint.

**DISABILITY OF JUDGE — Crim. R. 25**

*At any time,* when it appears that the Judge before whom the trial has commenced is unable to proceed, a substitute judge who can adequately familiarize himself with the record may be designated to conclude the trial.

**DISCHARGE — Crim. R. 5(B)(3)**

**Defendant's Motion At Preliminary Hearing**
*At the conclusion of the State's case,* motion for discharge for failure of proof is proper.

**DISCOVERY — Crim. R. 16**

**Defendant's Motion—When Made—Crim. R. 16(M)**
The written motion shall be filed *within 21 days after arraignment or 7 days before trial whichever is earlier,* or at such later, reasonable time as the Court shall permit.

**Failure To Comply—Crim. R. 16(L)(1)**
*At any time* when it comes to the Court's attention that the order for discovery has not been observed, the court may order such party to permit the discovery or inspection, grant a continuance, or prohibit the party from introducing in evidence the material not disclosed, or it may make such other order as it deems just under the circumstances.

**Prosecuting Attorney—Certification of Nondisclosure—Crim. R. 16(D)**
If the prosecuting attorney does not disclose materials or portions of materials under this rule, the prosecuting attorney shall certify to the court that the prosecuting attorney is not disclosing material or portions of material otherwise subject to disclosure under this rule for one or more of the following reasons:

(1) The prosecuting attorney has reasonable, articulable grounds to believe that disclosure will compromise the safety of a witness, victim, or third party, or subject them to intimidation or coercion;
(2) The prosecuting attorney has reasonable, articulable grounds to believe that disclosure will subject a witness, victim, or third party to a substantial risk of serious economic harm;
(3) Disclosure will compromise an ongoing criminal investigation or a confidential law enforcement technique or investigation regardless of whether that investigation involves the pending case or the defendant;
(4) The statement is of a child victim of sexually oriented offense under the age of thirteen;
(5) The interests of justice require non-disclosure.

Reasonable, articulable grounds may include, but are not limited to, the nature of the case, the specific course of conduct of one or more parties, threats or prior instances of witness tampering or intimidation, whether or not those instances resulted in criminal charges, whether the defendant is pro se, and any other relevant information.

The prosecuting attorney's certification shall identify the nondisclosed material.

**Prosecuting Attorney—Designation of "Counsel Only" Materials—Crim. R. 16(C)**
The prosecuting attorney may designate any material subject to disclosure under this rule as "counsel only" by stamping a prominent notice on each page or thing so designated. Except as otherwise provided, "counsel only" material may not be shown to the defendant or any other person, but may be disclosed only to defense counsel, or the agents or employees of defense counsel, and may not otherwise be reproduced, copied or disseminated in any way. Defense counsel may orally communicate the content of the "counsel only" material to the defendant.

**GRAND JURY — Crim. R. 6**

**Challenges—When Made—Crim. R. 6(B)(1)**
The array or an individual juror shall be challenged *before* the administration of the oath to the jurors.

**Summoning Of Grand Juries—Crim. R. 6(A)**
One or more Grand Juries may be summoned *at such time as the public interest requires.*

**Term Of Service, Discharge And Excuse Of Juror—Crim. R. 6(G)**
The Grand Jury shall serve until discharged, for 4 months, but not more than 9 months. A juror may be excused and replaced, temporarily or permanently *at any time* for cause shown.

**INDICTMENT, INFORMATION OR COMPLAINT — Crim. R. 7**

**Amendment—Crim. R. 7(D)**
At any time, before, during or after trial, amendment is proper so long as there is no change in the name or identity of the crime charged.

**Delivery Of Copy To Defendant—Crim. R. 10(A)**
*Before* defendant is called upon to plead he shall receive a copy of the charge.

**Dismissal—Crim. R. 7(A)**
Where an indictment is waived, the offense may be prosecuted by information unless the indictment is filed *within 14 days after the date of the waiver.* Failure to file an information or indictment *within 14 days after the waiver date* operates as a dismissal of the complaint and a discharge of the defendant.

**Secret Indictment—Crim. R. 6(E)**
The Court may direct that an indictment shall be kept secret *until* the defendant is in custody or has been admitted to bail.

**INSTRUCTIONS — Crim. R. 30**

**Action On Written Requests**
*Before* closing argument the Court shall rule on requested instructions.

**Cautionary Instructions**
At the commencement and during the trial the Court may give instructions of law relating to procedure, credibility and weight of the evidence, duty and function of the jury and may acquaint the jury generally with the nature of the case.

**Service Of Copies**
Opposing parties shall receive copies of requests *at the time of making.*

**Time For Filing Written Requests**
At the *close of the evidence,* or at such earlier time during the trial as the Court reasonably directs.

**Time For Objections To Charge**
Objections shall specifically be made before the jury retires to deliberate.

**Writing or Recording of Instructions**
The court shall reduce its final instructions to writing or make an audio, electronic, or other recording of those instructions, provide at least one written copy or recording of those instructions to the jury for use during deliberations, and preserve those instructions for the record.

**JURY — Crim. R. 24**

**Challenge To Array—Crim. R. 24(F)**
Either party may challenge the array of Petit Jurors before the examination commences.

**Demand For—Crim. R. 23(A)**
In petty offenses, where there is a right to trial by jury (R.C. § 2945.17 guarantees the right to trial by jury where the penalty is any possible confinement and/or the possible fine is in excess of $100.00). Written demand shall be filed *not less than 10 days* prior to the date set for trial or on or before the *3rd day* following receipt of notice of the date set for trial, whichever is later.

**Peremptory Challenges—Crim. R. 24(D)**
Challenges without cause (3 for each party in misdemeanor cases, 4 for each party in felony cases and 6 for each party in capital cases) may be exercised after the minimum number of jurors (8 in misdemeanor cases and 12 in felony cases) have been passed for cause.

**Poll—Crim. R. 31(D)**
*After* a verdict is returned and *before* it is accepted, the jury may be polled by any party or the Court.

**LIMITATIONS OF ACTION**

**Statute Of—R.C. § 2901.13**
Prosecution shall be barred unless commenced within the following periods after an offense is committed:

1. a. For a *FELONY, 6 YEARS.*
   b. For *ALL MISDEMEANORS,* other than minor misdemeanors, 2 *YEARS.*
   c. For *MINOR MISDEMEANORS, 6 MONTHS.*
2. For a violation of 2903.01 or 2903.02, there is *NO PERIOD OF LIMITATION.*
3. a. For a violation of 2903.03, 2903.04, 2905.01, 2907.02, 2907.03, 2907.04, 2907.05, 2907.21, 2909.02, 2909.22, 2909.23, 2909.24, 2909.26, 2909.27, 2909.28, 2909.29, 2911.01, 2911.02, 2911.11, 2911.12, or 2917.02, a violation of 2903.11 or 2903.12 if the victim is a peace officer, a violation of 2903.13 that is a felony, or a violation of former 2907.12, *20 YEARS AFTER THE OFFENSE IS COMMITTED.*
   b. For a conspiracy to commit, attempt to commit, or complicity in committing a violation set forth in 3 a. above, *20 YEARS AFTER THE OFFENSE IS COMMITTED.*
4. For a violation of any provision of Title XXIX of the Revised Code that involves a physical or mental wound, injury, disability, or condition of a nature that reasonably indicates abuse or neglect of a child under eighteen years of age or of a mentally retarded, developmentally disabled, or physically impaired child under 21 years of age shall not begin to run until either of the following occurs:
   (1) The victim of the offense reaches the age of majority.
   (2) A public children services agency, or a municipal or county peace officer that is not the parent or guardian of the child, in the county in which the child resides or in which the abuse or neglect is occurring or has occurred has been notified that abuse or neglect is known, suspected, or believed to have occurred.

*But,* where the time has expired and the offense involves either *fraud or breach of a fiduciary duty,* prosecution is not barred until *1 YEAR* after discovery. Where the time has expired and the offense is a violation of 2913.49, prosecution shall be commenced within *5 YEARS* after discovery. *And* where the offense involves misconduct in office by a public servant, prosecution may be commenced at any time while the accused remains in office or *within 2 YEARS after he leaves office.*

**NOTE:** The time during which prosecution must be commenced *DOES NOT BEGIN TO RUN:*

1. Until all the elements of the crime have been committed,
2. Until the Corpus Delicti is discovered, or
3. Where the accused voluntarily avoids prosecution by flight or otherwise.
4. During any time a prosecution against the accused based on the same conduct is pending in this state.

**NEW TRIAL — Crim. R. 33(B)**

**Motion For**
The written New Trial Motion shall be filed within *14 days after verdict or court decision.* Where the Court finds by clear and convincing proof that unavoidable delay prevented a timely filing, the motion shall be filed *within 7 days from the Court finding of unavoidable delay.*

**Newly Discovered Evidence—Crim. R. 33(B)**
The written new trial motion alleging newly discovered evidence shall be filed within *120 days following the day when the verdict or court decision was rendered.* Where the Court finds by clear and convincing proof that unavoidable delay prevented a timely filing, the motion shall be filed *within 7 days from the Court finding of unavoidable delay.*

**PLEA OF GUILTY — Crim. R. 32.1**

**Withdrawal Of Plea**
A motion to withdraw a guilty plea may be made *only before* sentence is imposed or suspended.

**Withdrawal Of No Contest Plea—Crim. R. 32.1**

A motion to withdraw a no contest plea may be made *only before* sentence is imposed or suspended.

*BUT* to correct manifest injustice, the Court, *after sentence,* may permit the withdrawal of either plea.

## PRELIMINARY HEARING — Crim. R. 5

**Docketing—Crim. R. 5(B)(7)**

The Clerk of Court shall, *within 7 days* from the hearing and finding of probable cause, file a transcript of the docket and copies of all original papers, pleading and documents with the Clerk of the Court in which defendant is to appear.

**Extension Of Time For—Crim. R. 5(B)(1)**

With the consent of the defendant and upon a showing of good cause, the time limits may be extended. Without the defendant's consent, time limits may be extended only as required by law, or upon a showing that extraordinary circumstances exist, and that delay is indispensable to the interest of justice.

**Time When Hearing Shall Be Held—Crim. R. 5(B)(1) (See Time)**

A Preliminary Hearing desired by the felony charged defendant shall be held *no later than 10 days following arrest or service of summons* if the defendant is in custody and *no later than 15 consecutive days following arrest or service of summons* if the defendant is not confined.

## PRE-TRIAL CONFERENCE — Crim. R. 17.1

**When Held**

*At any time after* the filing of an indictment, information or complaint a pre-trial conference may be had *after* defendant is represented by Counsel.

**Memorandum Of Agreed Matters**

*At the conclusion of the conference,* the Court shall prepare and file a memorandum of agreed matters.

## PROBATION — Crim. R. 32.2

**Pre-Sentence Investigation—When Made**

*Before* imposing community control sanctions or granting probation in felony cases, a pre-sentence investigation and report *must* be made. *Before* imposing community control sanction or granting probation in misdemeanor cases, the court *may* order a presentence investigation and report.

**Revocation—When—Crim. R. 32.3(A)**

Only *after* a hearing at which defendant is present may probation be revoked or a prison term invoked for violation of a community control sanction.

## SEARCH WARRANT — Crim. R. 41

**Time For Return Of Warrant—Crim. R. 41(D)**

The search warrant shall be returned *promptly* to a designated judge, accompanied by a written inventory of the property taken.

**Time For Execution Of Warrant—Crim. R. 41(C)**

The search warrant shall be executed and served *within 3 days* from the date of issuance, during the daytime (from the hours of 7:00 A.M. to 8:00 P.M.) unless the issuing Court authorizes otherwise.

## SENTENCE — Crim. R. 32

**Time For Imposition—Crim. R. 32(A)**

Sentence shall be imposed *without unnecessary delay, but not before* affording Counsel and the defendant the opportunity to be heard in mitigation.

**Procedure Following Sentence—Crim. R. 32(B)**

*After* imposing sentence in a serious offense in which trial was had on a not guilty plea, the Court shall advise the defendant of all his appellate rights.

## SERVICE — Crim. R. 49

**Time For Filing—Crim. R. 49(C)**

All papers required to be served upon a party shall be filed *simultaneously with or* immediately after service.

**Time For Serving Motions: Affidavits—Crim. R. 45(D)**

A written motion and notice of hearing thereof shall be served *not later than 7 days before the time specfied for the hearing,* unless a different period is fixed by rule or order of the Court.

Opposing affidavits may be served *not less than 1 day before the hearing;* unless the Court permits them to be served at a later time.

## SUBPOENA — Crim. R. 17

**When Available To Indigent Defendant—Crim. R. 17(B)**

At any time the Court shall order that a subpoena be issued for a necessary witness upon ex parte application of the indigent defendant.

## SUMMONS — Crim. R. 4

**When Service Of Summons Shall Be Made—Crim. R. 4(D)(4)**

When the person serving summons is unable to serve a copy of summons *within 28 days of the date of issuance,* he shall endorse that fact and the reasons therefor and return the summons and copies to the clerk.

## SUPPRESSIONS OF EVIDENCE — Crim. R. 12

**Appeal As Of Right By The State—Crim. R. 12(K)**

The State's Notice of Appeal shall be filed *within 7 days* after the date of the order granting the motion to suppress evidence, with the Trial Court Clerk, and any such appeal shall be *diligently prosecuted.*

**Time For Filing Motion For Suppression Of Evidence—Crim. R. 12(D)**

Defendant's motion to suppress evidence and/or to return property shall be filed *within 35 days after arraignment or 7 days before trial,* whichever is earlier. The Court, in the interest of justice, may extend the times.

**Return Of Tangible Property—Crim. R. 12(G)**

An order granting a motion to suppress tangible evidence, where a return of the seized property is also ordered, is *stayed* pending appeal by the State.

## TIME COMPUTATION

**Computation—Crim. R. 45(A)**

In computing time, the date of the act or event from which the designated period of time begins shall not be included. The last day is excluded if it is a Saturday, Sunday or legal holiday, in which event, the period runs until the end of the next day which is not a Saturday, Sunday or legal holiday. If the time prescribed *is less than 7 days,* intermediate Saturdays, Sundays and legal holidays *shall be excluded* in computation.

**Credit For All Confinement—R.C. § 2967.191**
The adult parole authority shall reduce the minimum and maximum sentence or the definite sentence of a prisoner by the total number of days that the prisoner was confined for any reason arising out of the offense for which he was convicted and sentenced, including confinement in lieu of bail while awaiting trial, confinement for examination to determine his competence to stand trial or sanity, confinement in a community based correctional facility and program or district community based correctional facility and program, and confinement while awaiting transportation to the place where he is to serve his sentence.

**Enlargement Of Time—Crim. R. 45(B)**

**A. After the Expiration of Time**
Time may be extended *after* the designated period has expired if the failure to act on time was the result of excusable delay or would result in injustice to the defendant, *EXCEPT:* The Court may not extend the time for:

1. Filing Motion for Acquittal.
2. Filing Motion for New Trial.
3. Filing Motion for Arrest of Judgment.
4. Demand for a Jury Trial.

**B. Before Expiration of Time**
With or without motion, for good cause shown, the Court may order the designated period either as determined by the criminal rule or fixed by the Court, extended.

**TRIAL — R.C. § 2945.71**

**Misdemeanors**

**Minor Misdemeanor.** Trial shall be had *within 30 days after arrest* or service of summons if the Court is *not* of record or if the crime charged is a *minor misdemeanor* pending in a Court of Record.

**Misdemeanor.** Where the crime charged is a *misdemeanor,* other than a minor misdemeanor, pending in a Court of Record, trial shall be had:

1. Within *45 days* after arrest or service of summons, if the misdemeanor charged is of the *3rd* or *4th* degree, *or* where the penalty is *not more* than *60 days* confinement.
2. Within 90 days after arrest or service of summons, if the misdemeanor charged is of the *1st* or *2nd* degree *or* where the penalty is *more* than *60 days* confinement.

**Felony**

1. A preliminary hearing shall be had within 15 days from time of arrest, *but see Crim. R. 5(B)(1)* which provides that a preliminary hearing shall be scheduled within a reasonable time, but, in any event, *no later than 10 days* following arrest or service of summons if defendant is in custody and *no later than 15 consecutive days* following arrest or service of summons if he is not in custody.
2. *Trial* shall be had *within 270 days* following arrest.

**NOTE:** For both misdemeanors and felonies, each day of confinement shall be counted as *3 days.*

**Trial Time Extension—R.C. § 2945.72**

1. *Any period* during which the accused is unavailable for hearing or trial, by reason of other criminal proceedings against him, within or outside the state, by reason of his confinement in another state, or by reason of the pendency of extradition proceedings, provided that the prosecution exercises reasonable diligence to secure his availability;
2. *Any period* during which the accused is mentally incompetent to stand trial, or is physically incapable of standing trial;
3. *Any period* of delay necessitated by the accused's lack of counsel, provided that such delay is not occasioned by any lack of diligence in providing counsel to an indigent accused upon his request as required by law;
4. *Any period* of delay occasioned by the neglect or improper act of the accused;
5. *Any period* of delay necessitated by reason of a plea in bar or abatement, motion, proceeding, or action made or instituted by the accused;
6. *Any period* of delay necessitated by a removal or change of venue pursuant to law;
7. *Any period* during which trial is stayed pursuant to any express statutory requirement, or pursuant to an order of another Court competent to issue such order;
8. The *period of any continuance granted* on the accused's own motion, and the period of any reasonable continuance granted other than upon the accused's own motion.
9. Any period during which an appeal filed pursuant to R.C. § 2945.67 is pending.

**NOTE: For Effect Of Failure To Bring To Trial, See: R.C. § 2945.73**

**Trial, Transfer For—Crim. R. 21**
Within *14 days after* an indictment or information which charges only *misdemeanors* is filed in the Court of Common Pleas, the Administrative Judge of such Court may transfer it to the Court from which the bindover to the Grand Jury was made or to the Court of Record of the jurisdiction in which the offense was committed.

**VENUE** — *See* **Change of Venue**

**WARRANT — Crim. R. 4**

**Appearance After Physical Arrest—Crim. R. 4(E)(1)**
When the accused is physically arrested, he shall be brought before the Court which issued the warrant *without unnecessary delay.*

**Delivery Of Copy Of Warrant—Crim. R. 4(D)(3)**
A copy of the warrant shall be given to the defendant *as soon as possible.*

**Issuance Of Warrant—Crim. R. 4(A)(l)**
No warrant shall issue until it has been determined from the complaint, with or without affidavits attached thereto, that there is probable cause to believe that an offense has been committed and that defendant has committed it.

**Return Of Warrant—Crim. R. 4(D)(4)**

The officer executing a warrant shall make return thereof to the issuing Court before whom the defendant is brought.

# OHIO RULES OF CRIMINAL PROCEDURE

**Complete with amendments through July, 1 2011.**



**APPENDIX OF FORMS**



## RULE 1. Scope of Rules: Applicability; Construction; Exceptions

(A) **Applicability.** These rules prescribe the procedure to be followed in all courts of this state in the exercise of criminal jurisdiction, with the exceptions stated in division (C) of this rule.

(B) **Purpose and construction.** These rules are intended to provide for the just determination of every criminal proceeding. They shall be construed and applied to secure the fair, impartial, speedy, and sure administration of justice, simplicity in procedure, and the elimination of unjustifiable expense and delay.

(C) **Exceptions.** These rules, to the extent that specific procedure is provided by other rules of the Supreme Court or to the extent that they would by their nature be clearly inapplicable, shall not apply to procedure (1) upon appeal to review any judgment, order or ruling, (2) upon extradition and rendition of fugitives, (3) in cases covered by the Uniform Traffic Rules, (4) upon the application and enforcement of peace bonds, (5) in juvenile proceedings against a child as defined in Rule 2(D) of the Rules of Juvenile Procedure, (6) upon forfeiture of property for violation of a statute of this state, or (7) upon the collection of fines and penalties. Where any statute or rule provides for procedure by a general or specific reference to the statutes governing procedure in criminal actions, the procedure shall be in accordance with these rules.

**History:** Amended, eff 7-1-75; 7-1-96.

## RULE 2. Definitions

As used in these rules:

(A) "Felony" means an offense defined by law as a felony.

(B) "Misdemeanor" means an offense defined by law as a misdemeanor.

(C) "Serious offense" means any felony, and any misdemeanor for which the penalty prescribed by law includes confinement for more than six months.

(D) "Petty offense" means a misdemeanor other than a serious offense.

(E) "Judge" means judge of the court of common pleas, juvenile court, municipal court, or county court, or the mayor or mayor's court magistrate of a municipal corporation having a mayor's court.

(F) "Magistrate" means any person appointed by a court pursuant to Crim. R. 19. "Magistrate" does not include an official included within the definition of magistrate contained in section 2931.01 of the Revised Code, or a mayor's court magistrate appointed pursuant to section 1905.05 of the Revised Code.

(G) "Prosecuting attorney" means the attorney general of this state, the prosecuting attorney of a county, the law director, city solicitor, or other officer who prosecutes a criminal case on behalf of the state or a city, village, township, or other political subdivision, and the assistant or assistants of any of them. As used in Crim. R. 6, "prosecuting attorney" means the attorney general of this state, the prosecuting attorney of a county, and the assistant or assistants of either of them.

(H) "State" means this state, a county, city, village, township, other political subdivision, or any other entity of this state that may prosecute a criminal action.

(I) "Clerk of court" means the duly elected or appointed clerk of any court of record or the deputy clerk, and the mayor or mayor's court magistrate of a municipal corporation having a mayor's court.

(J) "Law enforcement officer" means a sheriff, deputy sheriff, constable, municipal police officer, marshal, deputy marshal, or state highway patrolman, and also means any officer, agent, or employee of the state or any of its agencies, instrumentalities, or political subdivisions, upon whom, by statute, the authority to arrest violators is conferred, when the officer, agent, or employee is acting within the limits of statutory authority. The definition of "law enforcement officer" contained in this rule shall not be construed to limit, modify, or expand any statutory definition, to the extent the statutory definition applies to matters not covered by the Rules of Criminal Procedure.

**History:** Amended, eff 7-1-76; 7-1-90.

## RULE 3. Complaint

The complaint is a written statement of the essential facts constituting the offense charged. It shall also state the numerical designation of the applicable statute or ordinance. It shall be made upon oath before any person authorized by law to administer oaths.

## RULE 4. Warrant or Summons; Arrest

(A) **Issuance.**

(1) **Upon complaint.** If it appears from the complaint, or from an affidavit or affidavits filed with the complaint, that there is probable cause to believe that an offense has been committed, and that the defendant has committed it, a warrant for the arrest of the defendant, or a summons in lieu of a warrant, shall be issued by a judge, magistrate, clerk of court, or officer of the court designated by the judge, to any law enforcement officer authorized by law to execute or serve it.

The finding of probable cause may be based upon hearsay in whole or in part, provided there is a substantial basis for believing the source of the hearsay to be credible and for believing that there is a factual basis for the information furnished. Before ruling on a request for a warrant, the issuing authority may require the complainant to appear personally and may examine under oath the complainant and any witnesses. The testimony shall be admissible at a hearing on a motion to suppress, if it was taken down by a court reporter or recording equipment.

The issuing authority shall issue a summons instead of a warrant upon the request of the prosecuting attorney, or when issuance of a summons appears reasonably calculated to ensure the defendant's appearance.

(2) **By law enforcement officer with warrant.** In misdemeanor cases where a warrant has been issued to a law enforcement officer, the officer, unless the issuing authority includes a prohibition against it in the warrant, may issue a summons in lieu of executing the warrant by arrest, when issuance of a summons appears reasonably calculated to ensure the defendant's appearance. The officer issuing the summons shall note on the warrant and the return that the warrant was executed by issuing summons, and shall also note the time and place the defendant shall appear. No alias warrant shall be issued unless the defendant fails to appear in response to the summons, or unless subsequent to the issuance of summons it appears improbable that the defendant will appear in response to the summons.

(3) **By law enforcement officer without a warrant.** In misdemeanor cases where a law enforcement officer is empowered to arrest without a warrant, the officer may issue a summons in lieu of making an arrest, when issuance of a summons appears reasonably calculated to assure the defendant's appearance. The officer issuing the summons shall file, or cause to be filed, a complaint describing the offense. No warrant shall be issued unless the defendant fails to appear in response to the summons, or unless subsequent to the issuance of summons it appears improbable that the defendant will appear in response to the summons.

(B) **Multiple issuance; sanction.** More than one warrant or summons may issue on the same complaint. If the defendant fails to appear in response to summons, a warrant or alias warrant shall issue.

(C) **Warrant and summons: form.**

(1) **Warrant.** The warrant shall contain the name of the defendant or, if that is unknown, any name or description by which the defendant can be identified with reasonable certainty, a description of the offense charged in the complaint, whether the warrant is being issued before the defendant has appeared or was scheduled to appear, and the numerical designation of the applicable statute or ordinance. A copy of the complaint shall be attached to the warrant.

(a) If the warrant is issued after the defendant has made an initial appearance or has failed to appear at an initial appearance, the warrant shall command that the defendant be arrested and either of the following:

(i) That the defendant shall be required to post a sum of cash or secured bail bond with the condition that the defendant appear before the issuing court at a time and date certain;

(ii) That the defendant shall be held without bail until brought before the issuing court without unnecessary delay.

(b) If the warrant is issued before the defendant has appeared or is scheduled to appear, the warrant shall so indicate and the bail provisions of Crim. R. 46 shall apply.

(2) **Summons.** The summons shall be in the same

form as the warrant, except that it shall not command that the defendant be arrested, but shall order the defendant to appear at a stated time and place and inform the defendant that he or she may be arrested if he or she fails to appear at the time and place stated in the summons. A copy of the complaint shall be attached to the summons, except where an officer issues summons in lieu of making an arrest without a warrant, or where an officer issues summons after arrest without a warrant.

(D) **Warrant and summons: execution or service; return.**

(1) **By whom.** Warrants shall be executed and summons served by any officer authorized by law.

(2) **Territorial limits.** Warrants may be executed or summons may be served at any place within this state.

(3) **Manner.** Except as provided in division (A)(2) of this rule, warrants shall be executed by the arrest of the defendant. The officer need not have the warrant in the officer's possession at the time of the arrest. In such case, the officer shall inform the defendant of the offense charged and of the fact that the warrant has been issued. A copy of the warrant shall be given to the defendant as soon as possible.

Summons may be served upon a defendant by delivering a copy to the defendant personally, or by leaving it at the defendant's usual place of residence with some person of suitable age and discretion then residing therein, or, except when the summons is issued in lieu of executing a warrant by arrest, by mailing it to the defendant's last known address by certified mail with a return receipt requested. When service of summons is made by certified mail it shall be served by the clerk in the manner prescribed by Civil Rule 4.1(1). A summons to a corporation shall be served in the manner provided for service upon corporations in Civil Rules 4 through 4.2 and 4.6(A) and (B), except that the waiver provisions of Civil Rule 4(D) shall not apply. Summons issued under division (A)(2) of this rule in lieu of executing a warrant by arrest shall be served by personal or residence service. Summons issued under division (A)(3) of this rule in lieu of arrest and summons issued after arrest under division (F) of this rule shall be served by personal service only.

(4) **Return.** The officer executing a warrant shall make return of the warrant to the issuing court before whom the defendant is brought pursuant to Crim. R. 5. At the request of the prosecuting attorney, any unexecuted warrant shall be returned to the issuing court and cancelled by a judge of that court.

When the copy of the summons has been served, the person serving summons shall endorse that fact on the summons and return it to the clerk, who shall make the appropriate entry on the appearance docket.

When the person serving summons is unable to serve a copy of the summons within twenty-eight days of the date of issuance, the person serving summons shall endorse that fact and the reasons for the failure of service on the summons and return the summons and copies to the clerk, who shall make the appropriate entry on the appearance docket.

At the request of the prosecuting attorney, made while the complaint is pending, a warrant returned unexecuted and not cancelled, or a summons returned unserved, or a copy of either, may be delivered by the court to an authorized officer for execution or service.

(E) **Arrest.**

(1) **Arrest upon warrant.**

(a) Where a person is arrested upon a warrant that states it was issued before a scheduled initial appearance, or the warrant is silent as to when it was issued, the judicial officer before whom the person is brought shall apply Crim. R. 46.

(b) Where a person is arrested upon a warrant that states it was issued after an initial appearance or the failure to appear at an initial appearance and the arrest occurs either in the county from which the warrant issued or in an adjoining county, the arresting officer shall, except as provided in division (F) of this rule, where the warrant provides for the posting of bail, permit the arrested person to post a sum of cash or secured bail bond as contained in the warrant with the requirement that the arrested person appear before the warrant issuing court at a time and date certain, or bring the arrested person without unnecessary delay before the court that issued the warrant.

(c) Where a person is arrested upon a warrant that states it was issued after an initial appearance or the failure to appear at an initial appearance and the arrest occurs in any county other than the county from which the warrant was issued or in an adjoining county, the following sequence of procedures shall be followed:

(i) Where the warrant provides for the posting of bail, the arrested person shall be permitted to post a sum of cash or secured bail bond as contained in the warrant with the requirement that the arrested person appear before the warrant issuing court at a time and date certain.

(ii) The arrested person may in writing waive the procedures in division (E)(1)(c)(iii) of this rule after having been informed in writing and orally by a law enforcement officer of those procedures, and consenting to being removed to the warrant issuing court without further delay. This waiver shall contain a representation by a law enforcement officer that the waiver was read to the arrested person and that the arrested person signed the waiver in the officer's presence.

(iii) Where the warrant is silent as to the posting of bail, requires that the arrested person be held without bail, the arrested person chooses not to post bail, or the arrested person chooses not to waive the procedures contained in division (E)(1) of this rule, the arrested person shall, except as provided in division (F) of this rule, be brought without unnecessary delay before a court of record therein, having jurisdiction over such an offense, and the arrested person shall not be removed from that county until the arrested person has been given a reasonable opportunity to consult with an attorney, or individual of the arrested person's choice, and to post bail to be determined by the judge or magistrate of that court not inconsistent with the directions of the issuing court as contained in the warrant or after consultation with the issuing court. If the warrant is silent as to the posting of bail or holding the arrested person without bail, the court may permit the arrested person to post bail, hold the arrested person without bail, or consult with the warrant issuing court on the issue of bail.

(d) If the arrested person is not released, the arrested person shall then be removed from the county and brought before the court issuing the warrant, without unnecessary delay. If the arrested person is released, the release shall be on condition that the arrested person appear in the issuing court at a time and date certain.

(2) **Arrest without warrant.** Where a person is arrested without a warrant the arresting officer shall, except as provided in division (F), bring the arrested person without unnecessary delay before a court having jurisdiction of the offense, and shall file or cause to be filed

a complaint describing the offense for which the person was arrested. Thereafter the court shall proceed in accordance with Crim. R. 5.

(F) **Release after arrest.** In misdemeanor cases where a person has been arrested with or without a warrant, the arresting officer, the officer in charge of the detention facility to which the person is brought or the superior of either officer, without unnecessary delay, may release the arrested person by issuing a summons when issuance of a summons appears reasonably calculated to assure the person's appearance. The officer issuing such summons shall note on the summons the time and place the person must appear and, if the person was arrested without a warrant, shall file or cause to be filed a complaint describing the offense. No warrant or alias warrant shall be issued unless the person fails to appear in response to the summons.

**History:** Amended, eff 7-1-75; 7-1-90; 7-1-98.

## RULE 4.1. Optional Procedure in Minor Misdemeanor Cases

(A) **Procedure in minor misdemeanor cases.** Notwithstanding Rule 3, Rule 5(A), Rule 10, Rule 11(A), Rule 11(E), Rule 22, Rule 43(A), and Rule 44, a court may establish the following procedure for all or particular minor misdemeanors other than offenses covered by the Uniform Traffic Rules.

(B) **Definition of minor misdemeanor.** A minor misdemeanor is an offense for which the potential penalty does not exceed a fine of one hundred fifty dollars. With respect to offenses committed prior to January 1, 2004, a minor misdemeanor is an offense for which the potential penalty does not exceed a fine of one hundred dollars.

(C) **Form of citation.** In minor misdemeanor cases a law enforcement officer may issue a citation. The citation shall: contain the name and address of the defendant; describe the offense charged; give the numerical designation of the applicable statute or ordinance; state the name of the law enforcement officer who issued the citation; and order the defendant to appear at a stated time and place.

The citation shall inform the defendant that, in lieu of appearing at the time and place stated, he may, within that stated time, appear personally at the office of the clerk of court and upon signing a plea of guilty and a waiver of trial pay a stated fine and stated costs, if any. The citation shall inform the defendant that, in lieu of appearing at the time and place stated, he may, within a stated time, sign the guilty plea and waiver of trial provision of the citation, and mail the citation and a check or money order for the total amount of the fine and costs to the violations bureau. The citation shall inform the defendant that he may be arrested if he fails to appear either at the clerk's office or at the time and place stated in the citation.

(D) **Duty of law enforcement officer.** A law enforcement officer who issues a citation shall complete and sign the citation form, serve a copy of the completed form upon the defendant and, without unnecessary delay, swear to and file the original with the court.

(E) **Fine schedule.** The court shall establish a fine schedule which shall list the fine for each minor misdemeanor, and state the court costs. The fine schedule shall be prominently posted in the place where violation fines are paid.

(F) **Procedure upon failure to appear.** When a defendant fails to appear, the court may issue a supplemental citation, or a summons or warrant under Rule 4. Supplemental citations shall be in the form prescribed by subdivision (C), but shall be issued and signed by the clerk and served in the same manner as a summons under Rule 4.

(G) **Procedure where defendant does not enter a waiver.** Where a defendant appears but does not sign a guilty plea and waiver of trial, the court shall proceed in accordance with Rule 5.

**History:** Amended, eff 7-1-78; 7-1-04.

## RULE 5. Initial Appearance, Preliminary Hearing

(A) **Procedure upon initial appearance.** When a defendant first appears before a judge or magistrate, the judge or magistrate shall permit the accused or his counsel to read the complaint or a copy thereof, and shall inform the defendant:

(1) Of the nature of the charge against him;

(2) That he has a right to counsel and the right to a reasonable continuance in the proceedings to secure counsel, and, pursuant to Crim. R. 44, the right to have counsel assigned without cost to himself if he is unable to employ counsel;

(3) That he need make no statement and any statement made may be used against him;

(4) Of his right to a preliminary hearing in a felony case, when his initial appearance is not pursuant to indictment;

(5) Of his right, where appropriate, to jury trial and the necessity to make demand therefore in petty offense cases.

In addition, if the defendant has not been admitted to bail for a bailable offense, the judge or magistrate shall admit the defendant to bail as provided in these rules.

In felony cases the defendant shall not be called upon to plead either at the initial appearance or at a preliminary hearing.

In misdemeanor cases the defendant may be called upon to plead at the initial appearance. Where the defendant enters a plea the procedure established by Crim. R. 10 and Crim. R. 11 applies.

(B) **Preliminary hearing in felony cases; procedure.**

(1) In felony cases a defendant is entitled to a preliminary hearing unless waived in writing. If the defendant waives preliminary hearing, the judge or magistrate shall forthwith order the defendant bound over to the court of common pleas. If the defendant does not waive the preliminary hearing, the judge or magistrate shall schedule a preliminary hearing within a reasonable time, but in any event not later than ten consecutive days following arrest or service of summons if the defendant is in custody and not later than fifteen consecutive days following arrest or service of summons if he is not in custody. The preliminary hearing shall not be held, however, if the defendant is indicted. With the consent of the defendant and upon a showing of good cause, taking into account the public interest in the prompt disposition of criminal cases, time limits specified in this division may be extended. In the absence of such consent by the defendant, time limits may be extended only as required by law, or upon a showing that extraordinary circumstances exist and that delay is indispensable to the interests of justice.

(2) At the preliminary hearing the prosecuting attorney may state orally the case for the state, and shall then proceed to examine witnesses and introduce exhibits for the state. The defendant and the judge or magistrate have full right of cross-examination, and the defendant has the

right of inspection of exhibits prior to their introduction. The hearing shall be conducted under the rules of evidence prevailing in criminal trial generally.

(3) At the conclusion of the presentation of the state's case, defendant may move for discharge for failure of proof, and may offer evidence on his own behalf. If the defendant is not represented by counsel, the court shall advise him, prior to the offering of evidence on behalf of the defendant:

(a) That any such evidence, if unfavorable to him in any particular, may be used against him at later trial.

(b) That he may make a statement, not under oath, regarding the charge, for the purpose of explaining the facts in evidence.

(c) That he may refuse to make any statement, and such refusal may not be used against him at trial.

(d) That any statement he makes may be used against him at trial.

(4) Upon conclusion of all the evidence and the statement, if any, of the accused, the court shall do one of the following:

(a) Find that there is probable cause to believe the crime alleged or another felony has been committed and that the defendant committed it, and bind the defendant over to the court of common pleas of the county or any other county in which venue appears.

(b) Find that there is probable cause to believe that a misdemeanor was committed and that the defendant committed it, and retain the case for trial or order the defendant to appear for trial before an appropriate court.

(c) Order the accused discharged.

(5) Any finding requiring the accused to stand trial on any charge shall be based solely on the presence of substantial credible evidence thereof. No appeal shall lie from such decision and the discharge of defendant shall not be a bar to further prosecution.

(6) In any case in which the defendant is ordered to appear for trial for any offense other than the one charged the court shall cause a complaint charging such offense to be filed.

(7) Upon the conclusion of the hearing and finding, the court or the clerk of such court, shall, within seven days, complete all notations of appearance, motions, pleas, and findings on the criminal docket of the court, and shall transmit a transcript of the appearance docket entries, together with a copy of the original complaint and affidavits, if any, filed with the complaint, the journal or docket entry of reason for changes in the charge, if any, together with the order setting bail and the bail including any bail deposit, if any, filed, to the clerk of the court in which defendant is to appear. Such transcript shall contain an itemized account of the costs accrued.

**History:** Amended, eff 7-1-75; 7-1-76; 7-1-82; 7-1-90.

## RULE 6. The Grand Jury

(A) **Summoning grand juries.** The judge of the court of common pleas for each county, or the administrative judge of the general division in a multi-judge court of common pleas or a judge designated by him, shall order one or more grand juries to be summoned at such times as the public interest requires. The grand jury shall consist of nine members, including the foreman, plus not more than five alternates.

(B) **Objections to grand jury and to grand jurors.**

(1) **Challenges.** The prosecuting attorney, or the attorney for a defendant who has been held to answer in the court of common pleas, may challenge the array of jurors or an individual juror on the ground that the grand jury or individual juror was not selected, drawn, or summoned in accordance with the statutes of this state. Challenges shall be made before the administration of the oath to the jurors and shall be tried by the court.

(2) **Motion to dismiss.** A motion to dismiss the indictment may be based on objections to the array or on the lack of legal qualification of an individual juror, if not previously determined upon challenge. An indictment shall not be dismissed on the ground that one or more members of the grand jury were not legally qualified, if it appears from the record kept pursuant to subdivision (C) that seven or more jurors, after deducting the number not legally qualified, concurred in finding the indictment.

(C) **Foreman and deputy foreman.** The court may appoint any qualified elector or one of the jurors to be foreman and one of the jurors to be deputy foreman. The foreman shall have power to administer oaths and affirmations and shall sign all indictments. He or another juror designated by him shall keep a record of the number of jurors concurring in the finding of every indictment and shall upon the return of the indictment file the record with the clerk of court, but the record shall not be made public except on order of the court. During the absence or disqualification of the foreman, the deputy foreman shall act as foreman.

(D) **Who may be present.** The prosecuting attorney, the witness under examination, interpreters when needed and, for the purpose of taking the evidence, a stenographer or operator of a recording device may be present while the grand jury is in session, but no person other than the jurors may be present while the grand jury is deliberating or voting.

(E) **Secrecy of proceedings and disclosure.** Deliberations of the grand jury and the vote of any grand juror shall not be disclosed. Disclosure of other matters occurring before the grand jury may be made to the prosecuting attorney for use in the performance of his duties. A grand juror, prosecuting attorney, interpreter, stenographer, operator of a recording device, or typist who transcribes recorded testimony, may disclose matters occurring before the grand jury, other than the deliberations of a grand jury or the vote of a grand juror, but may disclose such matters only when so directed by the court preliminary to or in connection with a judicial proceeding, or when permitted by the court at the request of the defendant upon a showing that grounds may exist for a motion to dismiss the indictment because of matters occurring before the grand jury. No grand juror, officer of the court, or other person shall disclose that an indictment has been found against a person before such indictment is filed and the case docketed. The court may direct that an indictment shall be kept secret until the defendant is in custody or has been released pursuant to Rule 46. In that event the clerk shall seal the indictment, the indictment shall not be docketed by name until after the apprehension of the accused, and no person shall disclose the finding of the indictment except when necessary for the issuance of a warrant or summons. No obligation of secrecy may be imposed upon any person except in accordance with this rule.

(F) **Finding and return of indictment.** An indictment may be found only upon the concurrence of seven or more jurors. When so found the foreman or deputy foreman shall sign the indictment as foreman or deputy foreman. The indictment shall be returned by the foreman or deputy foreman to a judge of the court of common pleas and filed with the clerk who shall endorse thereon the date of filing and enter each case upon the appearance and trial dockets. If the defendant is in custody or has been released pursuant to Rule 46 and seven jurors do not concur in finding an indictment, the foreman shall so report to the court forthwith.

(G) **Discharge and excuse.** A grand jury shall serve until discharged by the court. A grand jury may serve for four months, but the court upon a showing of good cause by the prosecuting attorney may order a grand jury to serve more than four months but not more than nine months. The tenure and powers of a grand jury are not affected by the beginning or expiration of a term of court. At any time for cause shown the court may excuse a juror either temporarily or permanently, and in the latter event the court may impanel another eligible person in place of the juror excused.

(H) **Alternate grand jurors.** The court may order that not more than five grand jurors, in addition to the regular grand jury, be called, impanelled and sit as alternate grand jurors. Alternate grand jurors, in the order in which they are called, shall replace grand jurors who, prior to the time the grand jury votes on an indictment, are found to be unable or disqualified to perform their duties. Alternate grand jurors shall be drawn in the same manner, shall have the same qualifications, shall be subjected to the same examination and challenges, shall take the same oath, and shall have the same functions, powers, facilities, and privileges as the regular grand jurors. Alternate grand jurors may sit with the regular grand jury, but shall not be present when the grand jury deliberates and votes.

## RULE 7. The Indictment and the Information

(A) **Use of indictment or information.** A felony that may be punished by death or life imprisonment shall be prosecuted by indictment. All other felonies shall be prosecuted by indictment, except that after a defendant has been advised by the court of the nature of the charge against the defendant and of the defendant's right to indictment, the defendant may waive that right in writing and in open court.

Where an indictment is waived, the offense may be prosecuted by information, unless an indictment is filed within fourteen days after the date of waiver. If an information or indictment is not filed within fourteen days after the date of waiver, the defendant shall be discharged and the complaint dismissed. This division shall not prevent subsequent prosecution by information or indictment for the same offense.

A misdemeanor may be prosecuted by indictment or information in the court of common pleas, or by complaint in the juvenile court, as defined in the Rules of Juvenile Procedure, and in courts inferior to the court of common pleas. An information may be filed without leave of court.

(B) **Nature and contents.** The indictment shall be signed, in accordance with Crim. R. 6 (C) and (F) and contain a statement that the defendant has committed a public offense specified in the indictment. The information shall be signed by the prosecuting attorney or in the name of the prosecuting attorney by an assistant prosecuting attorney and shall contain a statement that the defendant has committed a public offense specified in the information. The statement may be made in ordinary and concise language without technical averments or allegations not essential to be proved. The statement may be in the words of the applicable section of the statute, provided the words of that statute charge an offense, or in words sufficient to give the defendant notice of all the elements of the offense with which the defendant is charged. It may be alleged in a single count that the means by which the defendant committed the offense are unknown or that the defendant committed it by one or more specified means. Each count of the indictment or information shall state the numerical designation of the statute that the defendant is alleged to have violated. Error in the numerical designation or omission of the numerical designation shall not be ground for dismissal of the indictment or information, or for reversal of a conviction, if the error or omission did not prejudicially mislead the defendant.

(C) **Surplusage.** The court on motion of the defendant or the prosecuting attorney may strike surplusage from the indictment or information.

(D) **Amendment of indictment, information, or complaint.** The court may at any time before, during, or after a trial amend the indictment, information, complaint, or bill of particulars, in respect to any defect, imperfection, or omission in form or substance, or of any variance with the evidence, provided no change is made in the name or identity of the crime charged. If any amendment is made to the substance of the indictment, information, or complaint, or to cure a variance between the indictment, information, or complaint and the proof, the defendant is entitled to a discharge of the jury on the defendant's motion, if a jury has been impanelled, and to a reasonable continuance, unless it clearly appears from the whole proceedings that the defendant has not been misled or prejudiced by the defect or variance in respect to which the amendment is made, or that the defendant's rights will be fully protected by proceeding with the trial, or by a postponement thereof to a later day with the same or another jury. Where a jury is discharged under this division, jeopardy shall not attach to the offense charged in the amended indictment, information, or complaint. No action of the court in refusing a continuance or postponement under this division is reviewable except after motion to grant a new trial therefore is refused by the trial court, and no appeal based upon such action of the court shall be sustained nor reversal had unless, from consideration of the whole proceedings, the reviewing court finds that a failure of justice resulted.

(E) **Bill of particulars.** When the defendant makes a written request within twenty-one days after arraignment but not later than seven days before trial, or upon court order, the prosecuting attorney shall furnish the defendant with a bill of particulars setting up specifically the nature of the offense charge and of the conduct of the defendant alleged to constitute the offense. A bill of particulars may be amended at any time subject to such conditions as justice requires.

**History:** Amended, eff 7-1-93; 7-1-00.

## RULE 8. Joinder of Offenses and Defendants

(A) **Joinder of offenses.** Two or more offenses may be charged in the same indictment, information or complaint in a separate count for each offense if the offenses charged, whether felonies or misdemeanors or both, are of the same or similar character, or are based on the same act or transaction, or are based on two or more acts or transactions connected together or constituting parts of a common scheme or plan, or are part of a course of criminal conduct.

(B) **Joinder of defendants.** Two or more defendants may be charged in the same indictment, information or complaint if they are alleged to have participated in the same act or transaction or in the same series of acts or transactions constituting an offense or offenses, or in the same course of criminal conduct. Such defendants may be charged in one or more counts together or separately, and all of the defendants need not be charged in each count.

## RULE 9. Warrant or Summons Upon Indictment or Information

(A) **Issuance.** Upon the request of the prosecuting attorney the clerk shall forthwith issue a warrant for each defendant named in the indictment or in the information. The clerk shall issue a summons instead of a warrant where the defendant has been released pursuant to Rule 46 and is indicted for the same offense for which he was bound over pursuant to Rule 5. In addition, the clerk shall issue a summons instead of a warrant upon the request of the prosecuting attorney or by direction of the court.

Upon like request or direction, the clerk shall issue more than one warrant or summons for the same defendant. He shall deliver the warrant or summons to any officer authorized by law to execute or serve it. If a defendant fails to appear in response to summons, a warrant shall issue.

(B) **Form of warrant and summons.**

(1) **Warrant.** The form of the warrant shall be as provided in Rule 4(C)(1) except that it shall be signed by the court or clerk. It shall describe the offense charged in the indictment or information. A copy of the indictment or information shall be attached to the warrant which shall command that the defendant be arrested and brought before the court issuing the warrant without unnecessary delay.

(2) **Summons.** The summons shall be in the same form as the warrant, except that it shall not command that the defendant be arrested, but shall order the defendant to appear before the court at a stated time and place and inform him that he may be arrested if he fails to appear at the time and place stated in the summons. A copy of the indictment or information shall be attached to the summons.

(C) **Execution or service; return.**

(1) **Execution or service.** Warrants shall be executed or summons served as provided in Rule 4(D) and the arrested person shall be treated in accordance with Rule 4(E)(1).

(2) **Return.** The officer executing a warrant shall make return thereof to the court.

When the person serving summons is unable to serve a copy of the summons within twenty-eight days of the date of issuance, he shall endorse that fact and the reasons therefore on the summons and return the summons and copies to the clerk, who shall make the appropriate entry on the appearance docket.

At the request of the prosecuting attorney made at any time while the indictment or information is pending, a warrant returned unexecuted and not cancelled, or a summons returned unserved, or a copy thereof, may be delivered by the clerk to the sheriff or other authorized person for execution or service.

**History:** Amended, eff 7-1-75.

## RULE 10. Arraignment

(A) **Arraignment procedure.** Arraignment shall be conducted in open court, and shall consist of reading the indictment, information or complaint to the defendant, or stating to the defendant the substance of the charge, and calling on the defendant to plead thereto. The defendant may in open court waive the reading of the indictment, information, or complaint. The defendant shall be given a copy of the indictment, information, or complaint, or shall acknowledge receipt thereof, before being called upon to plead.

(B) **Presence of defendant.**

(1) The defendant must be present, except that the court, with the written consent of the defendant and the approval of the prosecuting attorney, may permit arraignment without the presence of the defendant, if a plea of not guilty is entered.

(2) In a felony or misdemeanor arraignment or a felony initial appearance, a court may permit the presence and participation of a defendant by remote contemporaneous video provided the use of video complies with the requirements set out in Rule 43(A)(2) of these rules. This division shall not apply to any other felony proceeding.

(C) **Explanation of rights.** When a defendant not represented by counsel is brought before a court and called upon to plead, the judge or magistrate shall cause the defendant to be informed and shall determine that the defendant understands all of the following:

(1) The defendant has a right to retain counsel even if the defendant intends to plead guilty, and has a right to a reasonable continuance in the proceedings to secure counsel.

(2) The defendant has a right to counsel, and the right to a reasonable continuance in the proceeding to secure counsel, and, pursuant to Crim. R. 44, the right to have counsel assigned without cost if the defendant is unable to employ counsel.

(3) The defendant has a right to bail, if the offense is bailable.

(4) The defendant need make no statement at any point in the proceeding, but any statement made can and may be used against the defendant.

(D) **Joint arraignment.** If there are multiple defendants to be arraigned, the judge or magistrate may by general announcement advise them of their rights as prescribed in this rule.

**History:** Amended, eff 7-1-90; 7-1-08.

## RULE 11. Pleas, Rights Upon Plea

(A) **Pleas.** A defendant may plead not guilty, not guilty by reason of insanity, guilty or, with the consent of the court, no contest. A plea of not guilty by reason of insanity shall be made in writing by either the defendant or the defendant's attorney. All other pleas may be made orally. The pleas of not guilty and not guilty by reason of insanity may be joined. If a defendant refuses to plead, the court shall enter a plea of not guilty on behalf of the defendant.

(B) **Effect of guilty or no contest pleas.** With reference to the offense or offenses to which the plea is entered:

(1) The plea of guilty is a complete admission of the defendant's guilt.

(2) The plea of no contest is not an admission of defendant's guilt, but is an admission of the truth of the facts alleged in the indictment, information, or complaint,

and the plea or admission shall not be used against the defendant in any subsequent civil or criminal proceeding.

(3) When a plea of guilty or no contest is accepted pursuant to this rule, the court, except as provided in divisions (C)(3) and (4) of this rule, shall proceed with sentencing under Crim. R. 32.

(C) **Pleas of guilty and no contest in felony cases.**

(1) Where in a felony case the defendant is unrepresented by counsel the court shall not accept a plea of guilty or no contest unless the defendant, after being readvised that he or she has the right to be represented by retained counsel, or pursuant to Crim. R. 44 by appointed counsel, waives this right.

(2) In felony cases the court may refuse to accept a plea of guilty or a plea of no contest, and shall not accept a plea of guilty or no contest without first addressing the defendant personally and doing all of the following:

(a) Determining that the defendant is making the plea voluntarily, with understanding of the nature of the charges and of the maximum penalty involved, and, if applicable, that the defendant is not eligible for probation or for the imposition of community control sanctions at the sentencing hearing.

(b) Informing the defendant of and determining that the defendant understands the effect of the plea of guilty or no contest, and that the court, upon acceptance of the plea, may proceed with judgment and sentence.

(c) Informing the defendant and determining that the defendant understands that by the plea the defendant is waiving the rights to jury trial, to confront witnesses against him or her, to have compulsory process for obtaining witnesses in the defendant's favor, and to require the state to prove the defendant's guilt beyond a reasonable doubt at a trial at which the defendant cannot be compelled to testify against himself or herself.

(3) With respect to aggravated murder committed on and after January 1, 1974, the defendant shall plead separately to the charge and to each specification, if any. A plea of guilty or no contest to the charge waives the defendant's right to a jury trial, and before accepting a plea of guilty or no contest the court shall so advise the defendant and determine that the defendant understands the consequences of the plea.

If the indictment contains no specification, and a plea of guilty or no contest to the charge is accepted, the court shall impose the sentence provided by law.

If the indictment contains one or more specifications, and a plea of guilty or no contest to the charge is accepted, the court may dismiss the specifications and impose sentence accordingly, in the interests of justice.

If the indictment contains one or more specifications that are not dismissed upon acceptance of a plea of guilty or no contest to the charge, or if pleas of guilty or no contest to both the charge and one or more specifications are accepted, a court composed of three judges shall: (a) determine whether the offense was aggravated murder or a lesser offense; and (b) if the offense is determined to have been a lesser offense, impose sentence accordingly; or (c) if the offense is determined to have been aggravated murder, proceed as provided by law to determine the presence or absence of the specified aggravating circumstances and of mitigating circumstances, and impose sentence accordingly.

(4) With respect to all other cases the court need not take testimony upon a plea of guilty or no contest.

(D) **Misdemeanor cases involving serious offenses.** In misdemeanor cases involving serious offenses the court may refuse to accept a plea of guilty or no contest, and shall not accept such plea without first addressing the defendant personally and informing the defendant of the effect of the pleas of guilty, no contest, and not guilty and determining that the defendant is making the plea voluntarily. Where the defendant is unrepresented by counsel the court shall not accept a plea of guilty or no contest unless the defendant, after being readvised that he or she has the right to be represented by retained counsel, or pursuant to Crim. R. 44 by appointed counsel, waives this right.

(E) **Misdemeanor cases involving petty offenses.** In misdemeanor cases involving petty offenses the court may refuse to accept a plea of guilty or no contest, and shall not accept such plea without first informing the defendant of the effect of the pleas of guilty, no contest, and not guilty.

The counsel provisions of Crim. R. 44(B) and (C) apply to division (E) of this rule.

(F) **Negotiated plea in felony cases.** When, in felony cases, a negotiated plea of guilty or no contest to one or more offenses charged or to one or more other or lesser offenses is offered, the underlying agreement upon which the plea is based shall be stated on the record in open court.

(G) **Refusal of court to accept plea.** If the court refuses to accept a plea of guilty or no contest, the court shall enter a plea of not guilty on behalf of the defendant. In such cases neither plea shall be admissible in evidence nor be the subject of comment by the prosecuting attorney or court.

(H) **Defense of insanity.** The defense of not guilty by reason of insanity must be pleaded at the time of arraignment, except that the court for good cause shown shall permit such a plea to be entered at any time before trial.

**History:** Amended, eff 7-1-76; 7-1-80; 7-1-98.

## RULE 12. Pleadings and Motions Before Trial: Defenses and Objections

(A) **Pleadings and motions.** Pleadings in criminal proceedings shall be the complaint, and the indictment or information, and the pleas of not guilty, not guilty by reason of insanity, guilty, and no contest. All other pleas, demurrers, and motions to quash, are abolished. Defenses and objections raised before trial which heretofore could have been raised by one or more of them shall be raised only by motion to dismiss or to grant appropriate relief, as provided in these rules.

(B) **Filing with the court defined.** The filing of documents with the court, as required by these rules, shall be made by filing them with the clerk of court, except that the judge may permit the documents to be filed with the judge, in which event the judge shall note the filing date on the documents and transmit them to the clerk. A court may provide, by local rules adopted pursuant to the Rules of Superintendence, for the filing of documents by electronic means. If the court adopts such local rules, they shall include all of the following:

(1) The complaint, if permitted by local rules to be filed electronically, shall comply with Crim. R. 3.

(2) Any signature on electronically transmitted documents shall be considered that of the attorney or party it purports to be for all purposes. If it is established that the documents were transmitted without authority, the court shall order the filing stricken.

(3) A provision shall specify the days and hours during which electronically transmitted documents will be received by the court, and a provision shall specify when documents received electronically will be considered to have been filed.

(4) Any document filed electronically that requires a filing fee may be rejected by the clerk of court unless the filer has complied with the mechanism established by the court for the payment of filing fees.

(C) **Pretrial motions.** Prior to trial, any party may raise by motion any defense, objection, evidentiary issue, or request that is capable of determination without the trial of the general issue. The following must be raised before trial:

(1) Defenses and objections based on defects in the institution of the prosecution;

(2) Defenses and objections based on defects in the indictment, information, or complaint (other than failure to show jurisdiction in the court or to charge an offense, which objections shall be noticed by the court at any time during the pendency of the proceeding);

(3) Motions to suppress evidence, including but not limited to statements and identification testimony, on the ground that it was illegally obtained. Such motions shall be filed in the trial court only.

(4) Requests for discovery under Crim. R. 16;

(5) Requests for severance of charges or defendants under Crim. R. 14.

(D) **Motion date.** All pretrial motions except as provided in Crim. R. 7(E) and 16(M) shall be made within thirty-five days after arraignment or seven days before trial, whichever is earlier. The court in the interest of justice may extend the time for making pretrial motions.

(E) **Notice by the prosecuting attorney of the intention to use evidence.**

(1) **At the discretion of the prosecuting attorney.** At the arraignment or as soon thereafter as is practicable, the prosecuting attorney may give notice to the defendant of the prosecuting attorney's intention to use specified evidence at trial, in order to afford the defendant an opportunity to raise objections to such evidence prior to trial under division (C)(3) of this rule.

(2) **At the request of the defendant.** At the arraignment or as soon thereafter as is practicable, the defendant, in order to raise objections prior to trial under division (C)(3) of this rule, may request notice of the prosecuting attorney's intention to use evidence in chief at trial, which evidence the defendant is entitled to discover under Crim. R. 16.

(F) **Ruling on motion.** The court may adjudicate a motion based upon briefs, affidavits, the proffer of testimony and exhibits, a hearing, or other appropriate means.

A motion made pursuant to divisions (C)(1) to (C)(5) of this rule shall be determined before trial. Any other motion made pursuant to division (C) of this rule shall be determined before trial whenever possible. Where the court defers ruling on any motion made by the prosecuting attorney before trial and makes a ruling adverse to the prosecuting attorney after the commencement of trial, and the ruling is appealed pursuant to law with the certification required by division (K) of this rule, the court shall stay the proceedings without discharging the jury or dismissing the charges.

Where factual issues are involved in determining a motion, the court shall state its essential findings on the record.

(G) **Return of tangible evidence.** Where a motion to suppress tangible evidence is granted, the court upon request of the defendant shall order the property returned to the defendant if the defendant is entitled to possession of the property. The order shall be stayed pending appeal by the state pursuant to division (K) of this rule.

(H) **Effect of failure to raise defenses or objections.** Failure by the defendant to raise defenses or objections or to make requests that must be made prior to trial, at the time set by the court pursuant to division (D) of this rule, or prior to any extension of time made by the court, shall constitute waiver of the defenses or objections, but the court for good cause shown may grant relief from the waiver.

(I) **Effect of plea of no contest.** The plea of no contest does not preclude a defendant from asserting upon appeal that the trial court prejudicially erred in ruling on a pretrial motion, including a pretrial motion to suppress evidence.

(J) **Effect of determination.** If the court grants a motion to dismiss based on a defect in the institution of the prosecution or in the indictment, information, or complaint, it may also order that the defendant be held in custody or that the defendant's bail be continued for a specified time not exceeding fourteen days, pending the filing of a new indictment, information, or complaint. Nothing in this rule shall affect any statute relating to periods of limitations. Nothing in this rule shall affect the state's right to appeal an adverse ruling on a motion under divisions (C)(1) or (2) of this rule, when the motion raises issues that were formerly raised pursuant to a motion to quash, a plea in abatement, a demurrer, or a motion in arrest of judgment.

(K) **Appeal by state.** When the state takes an appeal as provided by law from an order suppressing or excluding evidence, or from an order directing pretrial disclosure of evidence, the prosecuting attorney shall certify that both of the following apply:

(1) the appeal is not taken for the purpose of delay;

(2) the ruling on the motion or motions has rendered the state's proof with respect to the pending charge so weak in its entirety that any reasonable possibility of effective prosecution has been destroyed, or the pretrial disclosure of evidence ordered by the court will have one of the effects enumerated in Crim. R. 16(D).

The appeal from an order suppressing or excluding evidence shall not be allowed unless the notice of appeal and the certification by the prosecuting attorney are filed with the clerk of the trial court within seven days after the date of the entry of the judgment or order granting the motion. Any appeal taken under this rule shall be prosecuted diligently.

If the defendant previously has not been released, the defendant shall, except in capital cases, be released from custody on the defendant's own recognizance pending appeal when the prosecuting attorney files the notice of appeal and certification.

This appeal shall take precedence over all other appeals.

If an appeal from an order suppressing or excluding evidence pursuant to this division results in an affirmance of the trial court, the state shall be barred from prosecuting the defendant for the same offense or offenses except upon a showing of newly discovered evidence that the state could not, with reasonable diligence, have discovered before filing of the notice of appeal.

**History:** Amended, eff 7-1-75; 7-1-80; 7-1-95; 7-1-98; 7-1-01; 7-1-10; 7-1-11.

## RULE 12.1. Notice of Alibi

Whenever a defendant in a criminal case proposes to offer testimony to establish an alibi on his behalf, he shall, not less than seven days before trial, file and serve upon the prosecuting attorney a notice in writing of his intention to claim alibi. The notice shall include specific information as to the place at which the defendant claims to have been at the time of the alleged offense. If the defendant fails to file such written notice, the court may exclude evidence offered by the defendant for the purpose of proving such alibi, unless the court determines that in the interest of justice such evidence should be admitted.

## RULE 13. Trial Together of Indictments or Informations or Complaints

The court may order two or more indictments or informations or both to be tried together, if the offenses or the defendants could have been joined in a single indictment or information. The procedure shall be the same as if the prosecution were under such single indictment or information.

The court may order two or more complaints to be tried together, if the offenses or the defendants could have been joined in a single complaint. The procedure shall be the same as if the prosecution were under such single complaint.

## RULE 14. Relief from Prejudicial Joinder

If it appears that a defendant or the state is prejudiced by a joinder of offenses or of defendants in an indictment, information, or complaint, or by such joinder for trial together of indictments, informations or complaints, the court shall order an election or separate trial of counts, grant a severance of defendants, or provide such other relief as justice requires. In ruling on a motion by a defendant for severance, the court shall order the prosecuting attorney to deliver to the court for inspection pursuant to Rule 16(B)(1) any statements or confessions made by the defendants which the state intends to introduce in evidence at the trial.

When two or more persons are jointly indicted for a capital offense, each of such persons shall be tried separately, unless the court orders the defendants to be tried jointly, upon application by the prosecuting attorney or one or more of the defendants, and for good cause shown.

**History:** Amended 7-1-11.

## RULE 15. Deposition

(A) **When taken.** If it appears probable that a prospective witness will be unable to attend or will be prevented from attending a trial or hearing, and if it further appears that his testimony is material and that it is necessary to take his deposition in order to prevent a failure of justice, the court at any time after the filing of an indictment, information, or complaint shall upon motion of the defense attorney or the prosecuting attorney and notice to all the parties, order that his testimony be taken by deposition and that any designated books, papers, documents or tangible objects, not privileged, be produced at the same time and place.

If a witness is committed for failure to give bail or to appear to testify at a trial or hearing, the court on written motion of the witness and notice to the parties, may direct that his deposition be taken. After the deposition is completed, the court may discharge the witness.

(B) **Notice of taking.** The party at whose instance a deposition is to be taken shall give to every other party reasonable written notice of the time and place for taking the deposition. The notice shall state the name and address of each person to be examined. On motion of a party upon whom the notice is served, the court for cause shown may extend or shorten the time or fix the place of deposition.

(C) **Attendance of defendant.** The defendant shall have the right to attend the deposition. If he is confined the person having custody of the defendant shall be ordered by the court to take him to the deposition. The defendant may waive his right to attend the deposition, provided he does so in writing and in open court, is represented by counsel, and is fully advised of his right to attend by the court at a recorded proceeding.

(D) **Counsel.** Where a defendant is without counsel the court shall advise him of his right to counsel and assign counsel to represent him unless the defendant waives counsel or is able to obtain counsel. If it appears that a defendant at whose instance a deposition is to be taken cannot bear the expense thereof, the court may direct that all deposition expenses, including but not limited to travel and subsistence of the defendant's attorney for attendance at such examination together with a reasonable attorney fee, in addition to the compensation allowed for defending the defendant, and the expenses of the prosecuting attorney in the taking of such deposition, shall be paid out of public funds upon the certificate of the court making such order. Waiver of counsel shall be as prescribed in Rule 44(C).

(E) **How taken.** Depositions shall be taken in the manner provided in civil cases. The prosecution and defense shall have the right, as at trial, to full examination of witnesses. A deposition taken under this rule shall be filed in the court in which the action is pending.

(F) **Use.** At the trial or upon any hearing, a part or all of a deposition, so far as otherwise admissible under the rules of evidence, may be used if it appears: that the witness is dead; or, that the witness is out of the state, unless it appears that the absence of the witness was procured by the party offering the deposition; or that the witness is unable to attend or testify because of sickness or infirmity; or that the party offering the deposition has been unable to procure the attendance of the witness by subpoena. Any deposition may also be used by any party for the purpose of refreshing the recollection, or contradicting or impeaching the testimony of the deponent as a witness. If only a part of a deposition is offered in evidence by a party, any party may offer other parts.

(G) **Objections to admissibility.** Objections to receiving in evidence a deposition or a part thereof shall be made as provided in civil actions.

## RULE 16. Discovery and Inspection

(A) **Purpose, Scope and Reciprocity.** This rule is to provide all parties in a criminal case with the information necessary for a full and fair adjudication of the facts, to protect the integrity of the justice system and the rights of defendants, and to protect the well-being of witnesses, victims, and society at large. All duties and remedies are subject to a standard of due diligence, apply to the defense and the prosecution equally, and are intended to be reciprocal. Once discovery is initiated by demand of the defendant, all parties have a continuing duty to supplement their disclosures.

(B) **Discovery: Right to Copy or Photograph.** Upon receipt of a written demand for discovery by the defendant, and except as provided in division (C), (D), (E), (F), or (J) of this rule, the prosecuting attorney shall provide copies or photographs, or permit counsel for the defendant to copy or photograph, the following items related to the particular case indictment, information, or complaint, and which are material to the preparation of a defense, or are intended for use by the prosecuting attorney as evidence at the trial, or were obtained from or belong to the defendant, within the possession of, or reasonably available to the state, subject to the provisions of this rule:

(1) Any written or recorded statement by the defendant or a co-defendant, including police summaries of such statements, and including grand jury testimony by either the defendant or co-defendant;

(2) Criminal records of the defendant, a co-defendant, and the record of prior convictions that could be admissible under Rule 609 of the Ohio Rules of Evidence of a witness in the state's case-in-chief, or that it reasonably anticipates calling as a witness in rebuttal;

(3) Subject to divisions (D)(4) and (E) of this rule, all laboratory or hospital reports, books, papers, documents, photographs, tangible objects, buildings, or places;

(4) Subject to division (D)(4) and (E) of this rule, results of physical or mental examinations, experiments or scientific tests;

(5) Any evidence favorable to the defendant and material to guilt or punishment;

(6) All reports from peace officers, the Ohio State Highway Patrol, and federal law enforcement agents, provided however, that a document prepared by a person other than the witness testifying will not be considered to be the witness's prior statement for purposes of the cross examination of that particular witness under the Rules of Evidence unless explicitly adopted by the witness;

(7) Any written or recorded statement by a witness in the state's case-in-chief, or that it reasonably anticipates calling as a witness in rebuttal.

(C) **Prosecuting Attorney's Designation of "Counsel Only" Materials.** The prosecuting attorney may designate any material subject to disclosure under this rule as "counsel only" by stamping a prominent notice on each page or thing so designated. "Counsel only" material also includes materials ordered disclosed under division (F) of this rule. Except as otherwise provided, "counsel only" material may not be shown to the defendant or any other person, but may be disclosed only to defense counsel, or the agents or employees of defense counsel, and may not otherwise be reproduced, copied or disseminated in any way. Defense counsel may orally communicate the content of the "counsel only" material to the defendant.

(D) **Prosecuting Attorney's Certification of Nondisclosure.** If the prosecuting attorney does not disclose materials or portions of materials under this rule, the prosecuting attorney shall certify to the court that the prosecuting attorney is not disclosing material or portions of material otherwise subject to disclosure under this rule for one or more of the following reasons:

(1) The prosecuting attorney has reasonable, articulable grounds to believe that disclosure will compromise the safety of a witness, victim, or third party, or subject them to intimidation or coercion;

(2) The prosecuting attorney has reasonable, articulable grounds to believe that disclosure will subject a witness, victim, or third party to a substantial risk of serious economic harm;

(3) Disclosure will compromise an ongoing criminal investigation or a confidential law enforcement technique or investigation regardless of whether that investigation involves the pending case or the defendant;

(4) The statement is of a child victim of sexually oriented offense under the age of thirteen;

(5) The interests of justice require non-disclosure.

Reasonable, articulable grounds may include, but are not limited to, the nature of the case, the specific course of conduct of one or more parties, threats or prior instances of witness tampering or intimidation, whether or not those instances resulted in criminal charges, whether the defendant is pro se, and any other relevant information.

The prosecuting attorney's certification shall identify the nondisclosed material.

(E) **Right of Inspection in Cases of Sexual Assault.**

(1) In cases of sexual assault, defense counsel, or the agents or employees of defense counsel, shall have the right to inspect photographs, results of physical or mental examinations, or hospital reports, related to the indictment, information, or complaint as described in section (B)(3) or (B)(4) of this rule. Hospital records not related to the information, indictment, or complaint are not subject to inspection or disclosure. Upon motion by defendant, copies of the photographs, results of physical or mental examinations, or hospital reports, shall be provided to defendant's expert under seal and under protection from unauthorized dissemination pursuant to protective order.

(2) In cases involving a victim of a sexually oriented offense less than thirteen years of age, the court, for good cause shown, may order the child's statement be provided, under seal and pursuant to protective order from unauthorized dissemination, to defense counsel and the defendant's expert. Notwithstanding any provision to the contrary, counsel for the defendant shall be permitted to discuss the content of the statement with the expert.

(F) **Review of Prosecuting Attorney's Certification of Non-Disclosure.** Upon motion of the defendant, the trial court shall review the prosecuting attorney's decision of nondisclosure or designation of "counsel only" material for abuse of discretion during an *in camera* hearing conducted seven days prior to trial, with counsel participating.

(1) Upon a finding of an abuse of discretion by the prosecuting attorney, the trial court may order disclosure, grant a continuance, or other appropriate relief.

(2) Upon a finding by the trial court of an abuse of discretion by the prosecuting attorney, the prosecuting attorney may file an interlocutory appeal pursuant to division (K) of Rule 12 of the Rules of Criminal Procedure.

(3) Unless, for good cause shown, the court orders otherwise, any material disclosed by court order under this section shall be deemed to be "counsel only" material, whether or not it is marked as such.

(4) Notwithstanding the provisions of (E)(2), in the case of a statement by a victim of a sexually oriented offense less than thirteen years of age, where the trial court finds no abuse of discretion, and the prosecuting attorney has not certified for nondisclosure under (D)(1) or (D)(2) of this rule, or has filed for nondisclosure under (D)(1) or (D)(2) of this rule and the court has found an abuse of discretion in doing so, the prosecuting attorney shall permit defense counsel, or the agents or employees

of defense counsel to inspect the statement at that time.

(5) If the court finds no abuse of discretion by the prosecuting attorney, a copy of any discoverable material that was not disclosed before trial shall be provided to the defendant no later than commencement of trial. If the court continues the trial after the disclosure, the testimony of any witness shall be perpetuated on motion of the state subject to further cross-examination for good cause shown.

(G) **Perpetuation of Testimony.** Where a court has ordered disclosure of material certified by the prosecuting attorney under division (F) of this rule, the prosecuting attorney may move the court to perpetuate the testimony of relevant witnesses in a hearing before the court, in which hearing the defendant shall have the right of cross-examination. A record of the witness's testimony shall be made and shall be admissible at trial as part of the state's case in chief, in the event the witness has become unavailable through no fault of the state.

(H) **Discovery: Right to Copy or Photograph.** If the defendant serves a written demand for discovery or any other pleading seeking disclosure of evidence on the prosecuting attorney, a reciprocal duty of disclosure by the defendant arises without further demand by the state. The defendant shall provide copies or photographs, or permit the prosecuting attorney to copy or photograph, the following items related to the particular case indictment, information or complaint, and which are material to the innocence or alibi of the defendant, or are intended for use by the defense as evidence at the trial, or were obtained from or belong to the victim, within the possession of, or reasonably available to the defendant, except as provided in division (J) of this rule:

(1) All laboratory or hospital reports, books, papers, documents, photographs, tangible objects, buildings or places;

(2) Results of physical or mental examinations, experiments or scientific tests;

(3) Any evidence that tends to negate the guilt of the defendant, or is material to punishment, or tends to support an alibi. However, nothing in this rule shall be construed to require the defendant to disclose information that would tend to incriminate that defendant;

(4) All investigative reports, except as provided in division (J) of this rule;

(5) Any written or recorded statement by a witness in the defendant's case-in-chief, or any witness that it reasonably anticipates calling as a witness in surrebuttal.

(I) **Witness List.** Each party shall provide to opposing counsel a written witness list, including names and addresses of any witness it intends to call in its case-in-chief, or reasonably anticipates calling in rebuttal or surrebuttal. The content of the witness list may not be commented upon or disclosed to the jury by opposing counsel, but during argument, the presence or absence of the witness may be commented upon.

(J) **Information Not Subject to Disclosure.** The following items are not subject to disclosure under this rule:

(1) Materials subject to the work product protection. Work product includes, but is not limited to, reports, memoranda, or other internal documents made by the prosecuting attorney or defense counsel, or their agents in connection with the investigation or prosecution or defense of the case;

(2) Transcripts of grand jury testimony, other than transcripts of the testimony of a defendant or codefendant. Such transcripts are governed by Crim. R. 6;

(3) Materials that by law are subject to privilege, or confidentiality, or are otherwise prohibited from disclosure.

(K) **Expert Witnesses; Reports.** An expert witness for either side shall prepare a written report summarizing the expert witness's testimony, findings, analysis, conclusions, or opinion, and shall include a summary of the expert's qualifications. The written report and summary of qualifications shall be subject to disclosure under this rule no later than twenty-one days prior to trial, which period may be modified by the court for good cause shown, which does not prejudice any other party. Failure to disclose the written report to opposing counsel shall preclude the expert's testimony at trial.

(L) **Regulation of discovery.**

(1) The trial court may make orders regulating discovery not inconsistent with this rule. If at any time during the course of the proceedings it is brought to the attention of the court that a party has failed to comply with this rule or with an order issued pursuant to this rule, the court may order such party to permit the discovery or inspection, grant a continuance, or prohibit the party from introducing in evidence the material not disclosed, or it may make such other order as it deems just under the circumstances.

(2) The trial court specifically may regulate the time, place, and manner of a *pro se* defendant's access to any discoverable material not to exceed the scope of this rule.

(3) In cases in which the attorney-client relationship is terminated prior to trial for any reason, any material that is designated "counsel only", or limited in dissemination by protective order, must be returned to the state. Any work product derived from said material shall not be provided to the defendant.

(M) **Time of motions.** A defendant shall make his demand for discovery within twenty-one days after arraignment or seven days before the date of trial, whichever is earlier, or at such reasonable time later as the court may permit. A party's motion to compel compliance with this rule shall be made no later than seven days prior to trial, or three days after the opposing party provides discovery, whichever is later. The motion shall include all relief sought under this rule. A subsequent motion may be made only upon showing of cause why such motion would be in the interest of justice.

**History:** Amended, eff 7-1-10.

## RULE 17. Subpoena

(A) **For attendance of witnesses; form; issuance.** Every subpoena issued by the clerk shall be under the seal of the court, shall state the name of the court and the title of the action, and shall command each person to whom it is directed to attend and give testimony at a time and place therein specified. The clerk shall issue a subpoena, or a subpoena for the production of documentary evidence, signed and sealed but otherwise in blank, to a party requesting it, who shall fill it in and file a copy thereof with the clerk before service.

(B) **Defendants unable to pay.** The court shall order at any time that a subpoena be issued for service on a named witness upon an *ex parte* application of a defendant upon a satisfactory showing that the presence of the witness is necessary to an adequate defense and that the defendant is financially unable to pay the witness fees required by subdivision (D). If the court orders the subpoena to be issued the costs incurred by the process and the fees of the witness so subpoenaed shall be taxed as costs.

(C) **For production of documentary evidence.** A subpoena may also command the person to whom it is directed to produce the books, papers, documents or other objects designated therein; but the court, upon motion made promptly and in any event made at or before the time specified in the subpoena for compliance therewith, may quash or modify the subpoena if compliance would be unreasonable or oppressive. The court may direct that the books, papers, documents or other objects designated in the subpoena be produced before the court at a time prior to the trial or prior to the time they are offered in evidence, and may, upon their production, permit them or portions thereof to be inspected by the parties or their attorneys.

(D) **Service.** A subpoena may be served by a sheriff, bailiff, coroner, clerk of court, constable, marshal, or a deputy of any, by a municipal or township policeman, by an attorney at law or by any person designated by order of the court who is not a party and is not less than eighteen years of age. Service of a subpoena upon a person named therein shall be made by delivering a copy thereof to such person or by reading it to him in person or by leaving it at his usual place of residence, and by tendering to him upon demand the fees for one day's attendance and the mileage allowed by law. The person serving the subpoena shall file a return thereof with the clerk. If the witness being subpoenaed resides outside the county in which the court is located, the fees for one day's attendance and mileage shall be tendered without demand. The return may be forwarded through the postal service, or otherwise.

(E) **Subpoena for taking depositions; place of examination.** When the attendance of a witness before an official authorized to take depositions is required, the subpoena shall be issued by such person and shall command the person to whom it is directed to attend and give testimony at a time and place specified therein. The subpoena may command the person to whom it is directed to produce designated books, papers, documents, or tangible objects which constitute or contain evidence relating to any of the matters within the scope of the examination permitted by Rule 16.

A person whose deposition is to be taken may be required to attend an examination in the county wherein he resides or is employed or transacts his business in person, or at such other convenient place as is fixed by an order of court.

(F) **Subpoena for a hearing or trial.** At the request of any party, subpoenas for attendance at a hearing or trial shall be issued by the clerk of the court in which the hearing or trial is held. A subpoena requiring the attendance of a witness at a hearing or trial may be served at any place within this state.

(G) **Contempt.** Failure by any person without adequate excuse to obey a subpoena served upon him may be deemed a contempt of the court or officer issuing the subpoena.

## RULE 17.1. Pretrial Conference

At any time after the filing of an indictment, information or complaint the court may, upon its own motion or the motion of any party, order one or more conferences to consider such matters as will promote a fair and expeditious trial. At the conclusion of a conference the court shall prepare and file a memorandum of the matters agreed upon. No admissions made by the defendant or defendant's counsel at the conference shall be used against the defendant unless the admissions are reduced to writing and signed by the defendant and defendant's counsel. The court shall not conduct pretrial conferences in any case in which a term of imprisonment is a possible penalty unless the defendant is represented by counsel or counsel has been waived pursuant to Crim. R. 44. In any case in which the defendant is not represented by counsel, any pretrial conference shall be conducted in open court and shall be recorded as provided in Crim. R. 22.

**History:** Amended, eff 7-1-00.

## RULE 18. Venue and Change of Venue

(A) **General venue provision.** The venue of a criminal case shall be as provided by law.

(B) **Change of venue; procedure upon change of venue.** Upon the motion of any party or upon its own motion the court may transfer an action to any court having jurisdiction of the subject matter outside the county in which trial would otherwise be held, when it appears that a fair and impartial trial cannot be held in the court in which the action is pending.

(1) **Time of motion.** A motion under this rule shall be made within thirty-five days after arraignment or seven days before trial, whichever is earlier, or at such reasonable time later as the court may permit.

(2) **Clerk's obligations upon change of venue.** Where a change of venue is ordered the clerk of the court in which the cause is pending shall make copies of all of the papers in the action which, with the original complaint, indictment, or information, he shall transmit to the clerk of the court to which the action is sent for trial, and the trial and all subsequent proceedings shall be conducted as if the action had originated in the latter court.

(3) **Additional counsel for prosecuting attorney.** The prosecuting attorney of the political subdivision in which the action originated shall take charge of and try the case. The court to which the action is sent may on application appoint one or more attorneys to assist the prosecuting attorney in the trial, and allow the appointed attorneys reasonable compensation.

(4) **Appearance of defendant, witnesses.** Where a change of venue is ordered and the defendant is in custody, a warrant shall be issued by the clerk of the court in which the action originated, directed to the person having custody of the defendant commanding him to bring the defendant to the jail of the county to which the action is transferred, there to be kept until discharged. If the defendant on the date of the order changing venue is not in custody, the court in the order changing venue shall continue the conditions of release and direct the defendant to appear in the court to which the venue is changed. The court shall recognize the witnesses to appear before the court in which the accused is to be tried.

(5) **Expenses.** The reasonable expenses of the prosecuting attorney incurred in consequence of a change of venue, compensation of counsel appointed pursuant to Rule 44, the fees of the clerk of the court to which the venue is changed, the sheriff or bailiff, and of the jury shall be allowed and paid out of the treasury of the political subdivision in which the action originated.

## RULE 19. Magistrates

(A) **Appointment.** A court other than a mayor's court

may appoint one or more magistrates who shall have been engaged in the practice of law for at least four years and be in good standing with the Supreme Court of Ohio at the time of appointment. A magistrate may serve in more than one county or in two or more courts of the same criminal jurisdiction within the same county.

(B) **Compensation.** The compensation of magistrates shall be fixed by the court, and no part of the compensation shall be taxed as costs.

(C) **Authority.**

(1) **Scope.** To assist courts of record and pursuant to reference under Crim. R. 19(D)(1), magistrates are authorized, subject to the terms of the relevant reference, to do any of the following:

(a) Conduct initial appearances and preliminary hearings pursuant to Crim. R. 5.

(b) Conduct arraignments pursuant to Crim. R. 10.

(c) Receive pleas, in accordance with Crim R. 11, only as follows:

(i) In felony and misdemeanor cases, accept and enter not guilty pleas.

(ii) In misdemeanor cases, accept and enter guilty and no contest pleas, determine guilt or innocence, receive statements in explanation and in mitigation of sentence, and recommend a penalty to be imposed. If imprisonment is a possible penalty for the offense charged, the matter may be referred only with the unanimous consent of the parties, in writing or on the record in open court.

(d) Conduct pretrial conferences pursuant to Crim. R. 17.1.

(e) Conduct proceedings to establish bail pursuant to Crim. R. 46.

(f) Hear and decide the following motions:

(i) Any pretrial or post-judgment motion in any misdemeanor case for which imprisonment is not a possible penalty.

(ii) Upon the unanimous consent of the parties in writing or on the record in open court, any pretrial or post-judgment motion in any misdemeanor case for which imprisonment is a possibility.

(g) Conduct proceedings upon application for the issuance of a temporary protection order as authorized by law.

(h) Conduct the trial of any misdemeanor case that will not be tried to a jury. If the offense charged is an offense for which imprisonment is a possible penalty, the matter may be referred only with unanimous consent of the parties in writing or on the record in open court.

(i) Exercise any other authority specifically vested in magistrates by statute and consistent with this rule.

(2) **Regulation of proceedings.** In performing the responsibilities described in Crim. R. 19(C)(1), magistrates are authorized, subject to the terms of the relevant reference, to regulate all proceedings as if by the court and to do everything necessary for the efficient performance of those responsibilities, including but not limited to, the following:

(a) Issuing subpoenas for the attendance of witnesses and the production of evidence;

(b) Ruling upon the admissibility of evidence in misdemeanor cases in accordance with division (C)(1)(f) of this rule;

(c) Putting witnesses under oath and examining them;

(d) When necessary to obtain the presence of an alleged contemnor in cases involving direct or indirect contempt of court, issuing attachment for the alleged contemnor and setting the type, amount, and any conditions of bail pursuant to Crim. R. 46;

(e) Imposing, subject to Crim. R. 19(D)(8), appropriate sanctions for civil or criminal contempt committed in the presence of the magistrate.

(D) **Proceedings in Matters Referred to Magistrates**

(1) **Reference by court of record.**

(a) **Purpose and method.** A court of record may, for one or more of the purposes described in Crim. R. 19(C)(1), refer a particular case or matter of a category of cases or matters to a magistrate by a specific or general order of reference or by a rule.

(b) **Limitation.** A court of record may limit a reference by specifying or limiting the magistrate's powers, including, but not limited to, directing the magistrate to determine only particular issues, directing the magistrate to perform particular responsibilities, directing the magistrate to receive and report evidence only, fixing the time and place for beginning and closing any hearings, or fixing the time for filing any magistrate's decision on the matter or matters referred.

(2) **Magistrate's order; motion to set aside magistrate's order.**

(a) **Magistrate's order.**

(i) **Nature of order.** Subject to the terms of the relevant reference, a magistrate may enter pretrial orders without judicial approval if necessary to regulate the proceedings and if not dispositive of a claim or defense of a party.

(ii) **Form, filing, and service of magistrate's order.** A magistrate's order shall be in writing, identified as a magistrate's order in the caption, signed by the magistrate, filed with the clerk, and served by the clerk on all parties or their attorneys.

(b) **Motion to set aside magistrate's order.** Any party may file a motion with the court to set aside a magistrate's order. The motion shall state the moving party's reasons with particularity and shall be filed not later than ten days after the magistrate's order is filed. The pendency of a motion to set aside does not stay the effectiveness of the magistrate's order, though the magistrate or the court may by order stay the effectiveness of a magistrate's order.

(3) **Magistrate's decision; objections to magistrate's decision.**

(a) **Magistrate's decision.**

(i) **When required.** Subject to the terms of the relevant reference, a magistrate shall prepare a magistrate's decision respecting any matter referred under Crim. R. 19(D)(1).

(ii) **Findings of fact and conclusions of law.** Subject to the terms of the relevant reference, a magistrate's decision may be general unless findings of fact and conclusions of law are timely requested by a party or otherwise required by law. A request for findings of fact and conclusions of law shall be made before the entry of a magistrate's decision or within seven days after the filing of a magistrate's decision. If a request for findings of fact and conclusions of law is timely made, the magistrate may require any or all of the parties to submit proposed findings of fact and conclusions of law.

(iii) **Form; filing; and service of magistrate's decision.** A magistrate's decision shall be in writing, identified as a magistrate's decision in the caption, signed by the magistrate, filed with the clerk, and served by the clerk on all parties or their attorneys no later than three days after the decision is filed. A magistrate's decision shall indicate conspicuously that a party shall not assign as error on appeal the court's adoption of any factual finding or legal conclusion, whether or not specifically designated as a finding of fact or conclusion of law under Crim. R.19(D)(3)(a)(ii), unless the party timely and specifically objects to that factual finding or legal conclusion as required by Crim. R.19(D)(3)(b).

(b) **Objections to magistrate's decision.**

(i) **Time for filing.** A party may file written objections to a magistrate's decision within fourteen days of the filing of the decision, whether or not the court has adopted the decision during that fourteen-day period as permitted by Crim. R. 19(D)(4)(e)(i). If any party timely files objections, any other party may also file objections not later than ten days after the first objections are filed. If a party makes a timely request for findings of fact and conclusions of law, the time for filing objections begins to run when the magistrate files a decision that includes findings of fact and conclusions of law.

(ii) **Specificity of objection.** An objection to a magistrate's decision shall be specific and state with particularity all grounds for objection.

(iii) **Objection to magistrate's factual finding; transcript or affidavit.** An objection to a factual finding, whether or not specifically designated as a finding of fact under Crim. R. 19(D)(3)(a)(ii), shall be supported by a transcript of all the evidence submitted to the magistrate relevant to that finding or an affidavit of that evidence if a transcript is not available. With leave of court, alternative technology or manner of reviewing the relevant evidence may be considered. The objecting party shall file the transcript or affidavit with the court within thirty days after filing objections unless the court extends the time in writing for preparation of the transcript or other good cause. If a party files timely objections prior to the date on which a transcript is prepared, the party may seek leave of court to supplement the objections.

(iv) **Waiver of right to assign adoption by court as error on appeal.** Except for a claim of plain error, a party shall not assign on appeal the court's adoption of any factual finding or legal conclusion, whether or not specifically designated as a finding of fact or conclusion of law under Crim. R. 19(D)(3)(a)(ii), unless the party has objected to that finding or conclusion as required by Crim. R. 19(D)(3)(b).

(4) **Action of court on magistrate's decision and on any objection to magistrate's decision; entry of judgment or interim order by court.**

(a) **Action of court required.** A magistrate's decision is not effective unless adopted by the court.

(b) **Action on magistrate's decision.** Whether or not objections are timely filed, a court may adopt or reject a magistrate's decision in whole or in part, with or without modification. A court may hear a previously-referred matter, take additional evidence, or return a matter to a magistrate. No sentence recommended by a magistrate shall be enforced until the court has entered judgment.

(c) **If no objections are filed.** If no timely objections are filed, the court may adopt a magistrate's decision, unless it determines that there is an error of law or other defect evident on the face of the magistrate's decision.

(d) **Action on objections.** If one or more objections to a magistrate's decision are timely filed, the court shall rule on those objections. In ruling on objections, the court shall undertake an independent review as to the objected matters to ascertain that the magistrate has properly determined the factual issues and appropriately applied the law. Before so ruling, the court may hear additional evidence but may refuse to do so unless the objecting party demonstrates that the party could not, with reasonable diligence, have produced that evidence for consideration by the magistrate.

(e) **Entry of Judgment or interim order by court.** A court that adopts, rejects, or modifies a magistrate's decision shall also enter a judgment or interim order.

(i) **Judgment.** The court may enter a judgment either during the fourteen days permitted by Crim. R. 19(D)(3)(b)(i) for the filing of objections to a magistrate's decision or after the fourteen days have expired. If the court enters a judgment during the fourteen days permitted by Crim. R. 19(D)(3)(b)(i) for the filing of objections, the timely filing of objections to the magistrate's decision shall operate as an automatic stay of execution of the judgment until the court disposes of those objections and vacates, modifies, or adheres to the judgment previously entered.

(ii) **Interim order.** The court may enter an interim order on the basis of a magistrate's decision without waiting for or ruling on timely objections by the parties where immediate relief is justified. The timely filing of objections does not stay the execution of an interim order, but an interim order shall not extend more than twenty-eight days from the date of entry, subject to extension by the court in increments of twenty-eight additional days for good cause shown. An interim order shall comply with Civ. R. 54(A), be journalized pursuant to Civ. R. 58(A), and be served pursuant to Civ. R. 58(B).

(5) **Extension of time.** For good cause shown, the court shall allow a reasonable extension of time for a party to file a motion to set aside a magistrate's order or file objections to a magistrate's decision. "Good cause" includes, but is not limited to, a failure by the clerk to timely serve the party seeking the extension with the magistrate's order or decision.

(6) **Disqualification of a magistrate.** Disqualification of a magistrate for bias or other cause is within the discretion of the court and may be sought by motion filed with the court.

(7) **Recording of proceedings before a magistrate.** Except as otherwise provided by law, all proceedings before a magistrate shall be recorded in accordance with procedures established by the court.

(8) **Contempt in the presence of a magistrate.**

(a) **Contempt Order.** Contempt sanctions under Crim. R. 19 (C)(2)(e) may be imposed only by a written order that recites the facts and certifies that the magistrate saw or heard the conduct constituting contempt.

(b) **Filing and provision of copies of contempt order.** A contempt order shall be filed and copies provided forthwith by the clerk to the appropriate judge of the court and to the subject of the order.

(c) **Review of contempt order by court; bail.** The subject of a contempt order may by motion obtain immediate review by a judge. A judge or the magistrate entering the contempt order may set bail pending judicial review of the order.

**History:** Effective 7-1-90; amended, eff 7-1-95; 7-1-00; 7-1-06; 7-1-11.

## RULE 20. Reserved

## RULE 21. Transfer From Common Pleas Court for Trial

(A) **When permitted.** Where an indictment or information charging only misdemeanors is filed in the court of common pleas, such court may retain the case for trial or the administrative judge may, within fourteen days after the indictment or information is filed with the clerk of the court of common pleas, transfer it to the court from which the bindover to the grand jury was made or to the court of record of the jurisdiction in which venue appears.

(B) **Proceedings on transfer.** When a transfer is ordered, the clerk of the court of common pleas, within three days, shall transmit to the clerk of the court to which the case is transferred, certified copies of the indictment, information, and all other papers in the case, and any bail taken, and the prosecution shall continue in that court.

**History:** Amended, eff 7-1-04.

## RULE 22. Recording of Proceedings

In serious offense cases all proceedings shall be recorded.

In petty offense cases all waivers of counsel required by Rule 44(B) shall be recorded, and if requested by any party all proceedings shall be recorded.

Proceedings may be recorded in shorthand, or stenotype, or by any other adequate mechanical, electronic or video recording device.

## RULE 23. Trial by Jury or by the Court

(A) **Trial by jury.** In serious offense cases the defendant before commencement of the trial may knowingly, intelligently and voluntarily waive in writing his right to trial by jury. Such waiver may also be made during trial with the approval of the court and the consent of the prosecuting attorney. In petty offense cases, where there is a right of jury trial, the defendant shall be tried by the court unless he demands a jury trial. Such demand must be in writing and filed with the clerk of court not less than ten days prior to the date set for trial, or on or before the third day following receipt of notice of the date set for trial, whichever is later. Failure to demand a jury trial as provided in this subdivision is a complete waiver of the right thereto.

(B) **Number of jurors.** In felony cases juries shall consist of twelve.

In misdemeanor cases juries shall consist of eight.

If a defendant is charged with a felony and with a misdemeanor or, if a felony and a misdemeanor involving different defendants are joined for trial, the jury shall consist of twelve.

(C) **Trial without a jury.** In a case tried without a jury the court shall make a general finding.

**History:** Amended, eff 7-1-80.

## RULE 24. Trial Jurors

(A) **Brief introduction of case.** To assist prospective jurors in understanding the general nature of the case, the court, in consultation with the parties, may give jurors a brief introduction to the case.

(B) **Examination of prospective jurors.** Any person called as a prospective juror for the trial of any cause shall be examined under oath or upon affirmation as to the prospective juror's qualifications. The court may permit the attorney for the defendant, or the defendant if appearing *pro se*, and the attorney for the state to conduct the examination of the prospective jurors or may itself conduct the examination. In the latter event, the court shall permit the state and defense to supplement the examination by further inquiry. Nothing in this rule shall limit the court's discretion, with timely notice to the parties at anytime prior to trial, to allow the examination of all prospective jurors in the array or, in the alternative, to permit individual examination or each prospective juror seated on a panel, prior to any challenges for cause or peremptory challenges.

(C) **Challenge for cause.** A person called as a juror may be challenged for the following causes:

(1) That the juror has been convicted of a crime which by law renders the juror disqualified to serve on a jury.

(2) That the juror is a chronic alcoholic, or drug dependent person.

(3) That the juror was a member of the grand jury that found the indictment in the case.

(4) That the juror served on a petit jury drawn in the same cause against the same defendant, and the petit jury was discharged after hearing the evidence or rendering a verdict on the evidence that was set aside.

(5) That the juror served as a juror in a civil case brought against the defendant for the same act.

(6) That the juror has an action pending between him or her and the State of Ohio or the defendant.

(7) That the juror or the juror's spouse is a party to another action then pending in any court in which an attorney in the cause then on trial is an attorney, either for or against the juror.

(8) That the juror has been subpoenaed in good faith as a witness in the case.

(9) That the juror is possessed of a state of mind evincing enmity or bias toward the defendant or the state; but no person summoned as a juror shall be disqualified by reason of a previously formed or expressed opinion with reference to the guilt or innocence of the accused, if the court is satisfied, from the examination of the juror or from other evidence, that the juror will render an impartial verdict according to the law and the evidence submitted to the jury at the trial.

(10) That the juror is related by consanguinity or affinity within the fifth degree to the person alleged to be injured or attempted to be injured by the offense charged, or to the person on whose complaint the prosecution was instituted; or to the defendant.

(11) That the juror is the person alleged to be injured or attempted to be injured by the offense charged, or the person on whose complaint the prosecution was instituted, or the defendant.

(12) That the juror is the employer or employee, or the spouse, parent, son, or daughter of the employer or employee, or the counselor, agent, or attorney, of any person included in division (B)(11) of this rule.

(13) That English is not the juror's native language, and the juror's knowledge of English is insufficient to permit the juror to understand the facts and the law in the case.

(14) That the juror is otherwise unsuitable for any other cause to serve as a juror.

The validity of each challenge listed in division (B) of this rule shall be determined by the court.

(D) **Peremptory challenges.** In addition to challenges provided in division (C) of this rule, if there is one defendant, each party peremptorily may challenge three prospective jurors in misdemeanor cases, four prospective jurors in felony cases other than capital cases, and six prospective jurors in capital cases. If there is more than one defendant, each defendant peremptorily may challenge the same number of prospective jurors as if the defendant was the sole defendant.

In any case where there are multiple defendants, the prosecuting attorney peremptorily may challenge a number of prospective jurors equal to the total peremptory challenges allowed all defendants. In case of the consolidation of any indictments, informations, or complaints for trial, the consolidated cases shall be considered, for purposes of exercising peremptory challenges, as though the defendants or offenses had been joined in the same indictment, information, or complaint.

(E) **Manner of exercising peremptory challenges.** Peremptory challenges shall be exercised alternately, with the first challenge exercised by the state. The failure of a party to exercise a peremptory challenge constitutes a waiver of that challenge, but does not constitute a waiver of any subsequent challenge. However, if all parties, alternately and in sequence, fail to exercise a peremptory challenge, the joint failure constitutes a waiver of all peremptory challenges.

A prospective juror peremptorily challenged by either party shall be excused.

Nothing in this rule shall limit the court's discretion to allow challenges under this division or division (D) of this rule to be made outside the hearing of prospective jurors.

(F) **Challenge to array.** The prosecuting attorney or the attorney for the defendant may challenge the array of petit jurors on the ground that it was not selected, drawn or summoned in accordance with law. A challenge to the array shall be made before the examination of the jurors pursuant to division (A) of this rule and shall be tried by the court.

No array of petit jurors shall be set aside, nor shall any verdict in any case be set aside because the jury commissioners have returned such jury or any juror in any informal or irregular manner, if in the opinion of the court the irregularity is unimportant and insufficient to vitiate the return.

(G) **Alternate jurors.**

(1) **Non-capital cases.** The court may direct that not more than six jurors in addition to the regular jury be called and impaneled to sit as alternate jurors. Alternate jurors in the order in which they are called shall replace jurors who, prior to the time the jury retires to consider its verdict, become or are found to be unable or disqualified to perform their duties. Alternate jurors shall be drawn in the same manner, have the same qualifications, be subject to the same examination and challenges, take the same oath, and have the same functions, powers, facilities, and privileges as the regular jurors. The court may retain alternate jurors after the jury retires to deliberate. The court must ensure that a retained alternate does not discuss the case with anyone until that alternate replaces a juror or is discharged. If an alternate replaces a juror after deliberations have begun, the court must instruct the jury to begin its deliberations anew. Each party is entitled to one peremptory challenge in addition to those otherwise allowed if one or two alternate jurors are to be impaneled, two peremptory challenges if three or four alternate jurors are to be impaneled, and three peremptory challenges if five or six alternative jurors are to be impaneled. The additional peremptory challenges may be used against an alternate juror only, and the other peremptory challenges allowed by this rule may not be used against an alternate juror.

(2) **Capital cases.** The procedure designated in division (G)(1) of this rule shall be the same in capital cases, except that any alternate juror shall continue to serve if more than one deliberation is required. If an alternate juror replaces a regular juror after a guilty verdict, the court shall instruct the alternate juror that the juror is bound by that verdict.

(H) **Control of juries.**

(1) **Before submission of case to jury.** Before submission of a case to the jury, the court, upon its own motion or the motion of a party, may restrict the separation of jurors or may sequester the jury.

(2) **After submission of case to jury.**

(a) **Misdemeanor cases.** After submission of a misdemeanor case to the jury, the court, after giving cautionary instructions, may permit the separation of jurors.

(b) **Non-capital felony cases.** After submission of a non-capital felony case to the jury, the court, after giving cautionary instructions, may permit the separation of jurors during any period of court adjournment or may require the jury to remain under the supervision of an officer of the court.

(c) **Capital cases.** After submission of a capital case to the jury, the jury shall remain under the supervision of an officer of the court until a verdict is rendered or the jury is discharged by the court.

(3) **Separation in emergency.** Where the jury is sequestered or after a capital case is submitted to the jury, the court may, in an emergency and upon giving cautionary instructions, allow temporary separation of jurors.

(4) **Duties of supervising officer.** Where jurors are required to remain under the supervision of an officer of the court, the court shall make arrangements for their care, maintenance and comfort.

When the jury is in the care of an officer of the court and until the jury is discharged by the court, the officer may inquire whether the jury has reached a verdict, but shall not:

(a) Communicate any matter concerning jury conduct to anyone except the judge or;

(b) Communicate with the jurors or permit communications with jurors, except as allowed by court order.

(I) **Taking of notes by jurors.** The court, after providing appropriate cautionary instructions, may permit jurors who wish to do so to take notes during a trial. If the court permits the taking of notes, notes taken by a juror may be carried into deliberations by that juror. The court shall require that all juror notes be collected and destroyed promptly after the jury renders a verdict.

(J) **Juror questions to witnesses.** The court may permit jurors to propose questions for the court to ask of the witnesses. If the court permits jurors to propose questions, the court shall use procedures that minimize the risk of prejudice, including all of the following:

(1) Require jurors to propose any questions to the court in writing;

(2) Retain a copy of each proposed question for the record;

(3) Instruct the jurors that they shall not display or discuss a proposed question with other jurors;

(4) Before reading a question to a witness, provide counsel with an opportunity to object to each question on the record and outside the hearing of the jury;

(5) Read the question, either as proposed or rephrased, to the witness;

(6) Permit counsel to reexamine the witness regarding a matter addressed by a juror question;

(7) If a question proposed by a juror is not asked, instruct the jurors that they should not draw any adverse inference from the court's refusal to ask any question proposed by a juror.

**History:** Amended, eff 7-1-75; 7-1-02; 7-1-05; 7-1-06; 7-1-08; 7-1-09.

## RULE 25. Disability of a Judge

(A) **During trial.** If for any reason the judge before whom a jury trial has commenced is unable to proceed with the trial, another judge designated by the administrative judge, or, in the case of a single-judge division, by the Chief Justice of the Supreme Court of Ohio, may proceed with and finish the trial, upon certifying in the record that he has familiarized himself with the record of the trial. If such other judge is satisfied that he cannot adequately familiarize himself with the record, he may in his discretion grant a new trial.

(B) **After verdict or finding of guilt.** If for any reason the judge before whom the defendant has been tried is unable to perform the duties of the court after a verdict or finding of guilt, another judge designated by the administrative judge, or, in the case of a single-judge division, by the Chief Justice of the Supreme Court of Ohio, may perform those duties. If such other judge is satisfied that he cannot perform those duties because he did not preside at the trial, he may in his discretion grant a new trial.

## RULE 26. Substitution of Photographs for Physical Evidence

Physical property, other than contraband, as defined by statute, under the control of a Prosecuting Attorney for use as evidence in a hearing or trial should be returned to the owner at the earliest possible time. To facilitate the early return of such property, where appropriate, and by court order, photographs, as defined in Evid. R. 1001(2), may be taken of the property and introduced as evidence in the hearing or trial. The admission of such photographs is subject to the relevancy requirements of Evid. R. 401, Evid. R. 402, Evid. R. 403, the authentication requirements of Evid. R. 901, and the best evidence requirements of Evid. R. 1002.

**History:** Effective, 7-1-81.

## RULE 27. Proof of Official Record; Judicial Notice: Determination of Foreign Law

The proof of official records provisions of Civil Rule 44, and the judicial notice and determination of foreign law provisions of Civil Rule 44.1 apply in criminal cases.

## RULE 28. Reserved

## RULE 29. Motion for Acquittal

(A) **Motion for judgment of acquittal.** The court on motion of a defendant or on its own motion, after the evidence on either side is closed, shall order the entry of a judgment of acquittal of one or more offenses charged in the indictment, information, or complaint, if the evidence is insufficient to sustain a conviction of such offense or offenses. The court may not reserve ruling on a motion for judgment of acquittal made at the close of the state's case.

(B) **Reservation of decision on motion.** If a motion for a judgment of acquittal is made at the close of all the evidence, the court may reserve decision on the motion, submit the case to the jury and decide the motion either before the jury returns a verdict, or after it returns a verdict of guilty, or after it is discharged without having returned a verdict.

(C) **Motion after verdict or discharge of jury.** If a jury returns a verdict of guilty or is discharged without having returned a verdict, a motion for judgment of acquittal may be made or renewed within fourteen days after the jury is discharged or within such further time as the court may fix during the fourteen day period. If a verdict of guilty is returned, the court may on such motion set aside the verdict and enter judgment of acquittal. If no verdict is returned, the court may enter judgment of acquittal. It shall not be a prerequisite to the making of such motion that a similar motion has been made prior to the submission of the case to the jury.

## RULE 30. Instructions

(A) **Instructions; error; record.** At the close of the evidence or at such earlier time during the trial as the court reasonably directs, any party may file written requests that the court instruct the jury on the law as set forth in the requests. Copies shall be furnished to all other parties at the time of making the requests. The court shall inform counsel of its proposed action on the requests prior to counsel's arguments to the jury and shall give the jury complete instructions after the arguments are completed. The court also may give some or all of its instructions to the jury prior to counsel's arguments. The court shall reduce its final instructions to writing or make an audio, electronic, or other recording of those instructions, provide at least one written copy or recording of those instructions to the jury for use during deliberations, and preserve those instructions for the record.

On appeal, a party may not assign as error the giving or the failure to give any instructions unless the party objects before the jury retires to consider its verdict, stating specifically the matter objected to and the grounds of the objection. Opportunity shall be given to make the objection out of the hearing of the jury.

(B) **Cautionary instructions.** At the commencement and during the course of the trial, the court may give the jury cautionary and other instructions of law relating to trial procedure, credibility and weight of the evidence, and the duty and function of the jury and may acquaint the jury generally with the nature of the case.

**History:** Amended, eff 7-1-75; 7-1-82; 7-1-92; 7-1-05.

## RULE 31. Verdict

(A) **Return.** The verdict shall be unanimous. It shall be in writing, signed by all jurors concurring therein, and returned by the jury to the judge in open court.

(B) **Several defendants.** If there are two or more defendants the jury at any time during its deliberations may return a verdict or verdicts with respect to a defendant or defendants as to whom it has agreed. If the jury cannot agree with respect to all, the defendant or defendants as to whom it does not agree may be tried again.

(C) **Conviction of lesser offense.** The defendant may be found not guilty of the offense charged but guilty of an attempt to commit it if such an attempt is an offense at law. When the indictment, information, or complaint charges an offense including degrees, or if lesser offenses are included within the offense charged, the defendant may be found not guilty of the degree charged but guilty of an inferior degree thereof, or of a lesser included offense.

(D) **Poll of jury.** When a verdict is returned and before it is accepted the jury shall be polled at the request of any party or upon the court's own motion. If upon the poll there is not unanimous concurrence, the jury may be directed to retire for further deliberation or may be discharged.

### RULE 32. Sentence

(A) **Imposition of sentence.** Sentence shall be imposed without unnecessary delay. Pending sentence, the court may commit the defendant or continue or alter the bail. At the time of imposing sentence, the court shall do all of the following:

(1) Afford counsel an opportunity to speak on behalf of the defendant and address the defendant personally and ask if he or she wishes to make a statement in his or her own behalf or present any information in mitigation of punishment.

(2) Afford the prosecuting attorney an opportunity to speak;

(3) Afford the victim the rights provided by law;

(4) In serious offenses, state its statutory findings and give reasons supporting those findings, if appropriate.

(B) **Notification of right to appeal.**

(1) After imposing sentence in a serious offense that has gone to trial, the court shall advise the defendant that the defendant has a right to appeal the conviction.

(2) After imposing sentence in a serious offense, the court shall advise the defendant of the defendant's right, where applicable, to appeal or to seek leave to appeal the sentence imposed.

(3) If a right to appeal or a right to seek leave to appeal applies under division (B)(1) or (B)(2) of this rule, the court shall also advise the defendant of all of the following:

(a) That if the defendant is unable to pay the cost of an appeal, the defendant has the right to appeal without payment;

(b) That if the defendant is unable to obtain counsel for an appeal, counsel will be appointed without cost;

(c) That if the defendant is unable to pay the costs of documents necessary to an appeal, the documents will be provided without cost;

(d) That the defendant has a right to have a notice of appeal timely filed on his or her behalf.

Upon defendant's request, the court shall forthwith appoint counsel for appeal.

(C) **Judgment.** A judgment of conviction shall set forth the plea, the verdict, or findings, upon which each conviction is based, and the sentence. Multiple judgments of conviction may be addressed in one judgment entry. If the defendant is found not guilty or for any other reason is entitled to be discharged, the court shall render judgment accordingly. The judge shall sign the judgment and the clerk shall enter it on the journal. A judgment is effective only when entered on the journal by the clerk.

**History:** Amended, eff 7-1-92; 7-1-98; 7-1-04; 7-1-09.

### RULE 32.1. Withdrawal of Guilty Plea

A motion to withdraw a plea of guilty or no contest may be made only before sentence is imposed; but to correct manifest injustice the court after sentence may set aside the judgment of conviction and permit the defendant to withdraw his or her plea.

**History:** Amended, eff 7-1-98.

### RULE 32.2. Presentence Investigation

In felony cases the court shall, and in misdemeanor cases the court may, order a presentence investigation and report before imposing community control sanctions or granting probation.

**History:** Amended, eff 7-1-76; 7-1-98.

### RULE 32.3. Revocation of Probation

(A) **Hearing.** The court shall not impose a prison term for violation of the conditions of a community control sanction or revoke probation except after a hearing at which the defendant shall be present and apprised of the grounds on which action is proposed. The defendant may be admitted to bail pending hearing.

(B) **Counsel.** The defendant shall have the right to be represented by retained counsel and shall be so advised. Where a defendant convicted of a serious offense is unable to obtain counsel, counsel shall be assigned to represent the defendant, unless the defendant after being fully advised of his or her right to assigned counsel, knowingly, intelligently, and voluntarily waives the right to counsel. Where a defendant convicted of a petty offense is unable to obtain counsel, the court may assign counsel to represent the defendant.

(C) **Confinement in petty offense cases.** If confinement after conviction was precluded by Crim. R. 44(B), revocation of probation shall not result in confinement.

If confinement after conviction was not precluded by Crim. R. 44(B), revocation of probation shall not result in confinement unless, at the revocation hearing, there is compliance with Crim. R. 44(B).

(D) **Waiver of counsel.** Waiver of counsel shall be as prescribed in Crim. R. 44(C).

**History:** Amended, eff 7-1-98.

### RULE 33. New Trial

(A) **Grounds.** A new trial may be granted on motion of the defendant for any of the following causes affecting materially his substantial rights:

(1) Irregularity in the proceedings, or in any order or ruling of the court, or abuse of discretion by the court, because of which the defendant was prevented from having a fair trial;

(2) Misconduct of the jury, prosecuting attorney, or the witnesses for the state;

(3) Accident or surprise which ordinary prudence could not have guarded against;

(4) That the verdict is not sustained by sufficient evidence or is contrary to law. If the evidence shows the defendant is not guilty of the degree of crime for which he was convicted, but guilty of a lesser degree thereof, or of a lesser crime included therein, the court may modify the verdict or finding accordingly, without granting or order-

ing a new trial, and shall pass sentence on such verdict or finding as modified;

(5) Error of law occurring at the trial;

(6) When new evidence material to the defense is discovered, which the defendant could not with reasonable diligence have discovered and produced at the trial. When a motion for a new trial is made upon the ground of newly discovered evidence, the defendant must produce at the hearing on the motion, in support thereof, the affidavits of the witnesses by whom such evidence is expected to be given, and if time is required by the defendant to procure such affidavits, the court may postpone the hearing of the motion for such length of time as is reasonable under all the circumstances of the case. The prosecuting attorney may produce affidavits or other evidence to impeach the affidavits of such witnesses.

(B) **Motion for new trial; form, time.** Application for a new trial shall be made by motion which, except for the cause of newly discovered evidence, shall be filed within fourteen days after the verdict was rendered, or the decision of the court where a trial by jury has been waived, unless it is made to appear by clear and convincing proof that the defendant was unavoidably prevented from filing his motion for a new trial, in which case the motion shall be filed within seven days from the order of the court finding that the defendant was unavoidably prevented from filing such motion within the time provided herein.

Motions for new trial on account of newly discovered evidence shall be filed within one hundred twenty days after the day upon which the verdict was rendered, or the decision of the court where trial by jury has been waived. If it is made to appear by clear and convincing proof that the defendant was unavoidably prevented from the discovery of the evidence upon which he must rely, such motion shall be filed within seven days from an order of the court finding that he was unavoidably prevented from discovering the evidence within the one hundred twenty day period.

(C) **Affidavits required.** The causes enumerated in subsection (A)(2) and (3) must be sustained by affidavit showing their truth, and may be controverted by affidavit.

(D) **Procedure when new trial granted.** When a new trial is granted by the trial court, or when a new trial is awarded on appeal, the accused shall stand trial upon the charge or charges of which he was convicted.

(E) **Invalid grounds for new trial.** No motion for a new trial shall be granted or verdict set aside, nor shall any judgment of conviction be reversed in any court because of:

(1) An inaccuracy or imperfection in the indictment, information, or complaint, provided that the charge is sufficient to fairly and reasonably inform the defendant of all the essential elements of the charge against him.

(2) A variance between the allegations and the proof thereof, unless the defendant is misled or prejudiced thereby;

(3) The admission or rejection of any evidence offered against or for the defendant, unless the defendant was or may have been prejudiced thereby;

(4) A misdirection of the jury, unless the defendant was or may have been prejudiced thereby;

(5) Any other cause, unless it affirmatively appears from the record that the defendant was prejudiced thereby or was prevented from having a fair trial.

(F) **Motion for new trial not a condition for appellate review.** A motion for a new trial is not a prerequisite to obtain appellate review.

## RULE 34. Arrest of Judgment

The court on motion of the defendant shall arrest judgment if the indictment, information, or complaint does not charge an offense or if the court was without jurisdiction of the offense charged. The motion shall be made within fourteen days after verdict, or finding of guilty, or after plea of guilty or no contest, or within such further time as the court may fix during the fourteen day period.

When the judgment is arrested, the defendant shall be discharged, and his position with respect to the prosecution is as if the indictment, information, or complaint had not been returned or filed.

## RULE 35. Post-Conviction Petition

(A) A petition for post-conviction relief pursuant to section 2953.21 of the Revised Code shall contain a case history, statement of facts, and separately identified grounds for relief. Each ground for relief shall not exceed three pages in length. (See recommended Form XV in Appendix of Forms.) A petition may be accompanied by an attachment of exhibits or other supporting materials. A trial court may extend the page limits provided in this rule, request further briefing on any ground for relief presented, or direct the petitioner to file a supplemental petition in the recommended form.

(B) The clerk of court immediately shall send a copy of the petition to the prosecuting attorney. Upon order of the trial court, the clerk of court shall duplicate all or any part of the record that the trial court requires.

(C) The trial court shall file its ruling upon a petition for post-conviction relief, including findings of fact and conclusions of law if required by law, not later than one hundred eighty days after the petition is filed.

**History:** Effective 7-1-97.

## RULE 36. Clerical Mistakes

Clerical mistakes in judgments, orders, or other parts of the record, and errors in the record arising from oversight or omission, may be corrected by the court at any time.

## RULE 37. Reserved

## RULE 38. Reserved

## RULE 39. Reserved

## RULE 40. Reserved

## RULE 41. Search and Seizure

(A) **Authority to issue warrant.** A search warrant authorized by this rule may be issued by a judge of a court of record to search and seize property located within the court's territorial jurisdiction, upon the request of a prosecuting attorney or a law enforcement officer.

(B) **Property which may be seized with a warrant.** A warrant may be issued under this rule to search for and seize any: (1) evidence of the commission of a criminal offense; or (2) contraband, the fruits of crime, or things otherwise criminally possessed; or (3) weapons or other things by means of which a crime has been committed or reasonably appears about to be committed.

(C) **Issuance and contents.**

(1) A warrant shall issue on either an affidavit or affidavits sworn to before a judge of a court of record or an affidavit or affidavits communicated to the judge by reliable electronic means establishing the grounds for issuing the warrant. The affidavit shall name or describe the person to be searched or particularly describe the place to be searched, name or describe the property to be searched for and seized, state substantially the offense in relation thereto, and state the factual basis for the affiant's belief that such property is there located. If the affidavit is provided by reliable electronic means, the applicant communicating the affidavit shall be placed under oath and shall swear to or affirm the affidavit communicated.

(2) If the judge is satisfied that probable cause for the search exists, the judge shall issue a warrant identifying the property and naming or describing the person or place to be searched. The warrant may be issued to the requesting prosecuting attorney or other law enforcement officer through reliable electronic means. The finding of probable cause may be based upon hearsay in whole or in part, provided there is a substantial basis for believing the source of the hearsay to be credible and for believing that there is a factual basis for the information furnished. Before ruling on a request for a warrant, the judge may require the affiant to appear personally, and may examine under oath the affiant and any witnesses the affiant may produce. Such testimony shall be admissible at a hearing on a motion to suppress if taken down by a court reporter or recording equipment, transcribed, and made part of the affidavit. The warrant shall be directed to a law enforcement officer. It shall command the officer to search, within three days, the person or place named for the property specified. The warrant shall be served in the daytime, unless the issuing court, by appropriate provision in the warrant, and for reasonable cause shown, authorizes its execution at times other than daytime. The warrant shall designate a judge to whom it shall be returned.

(D) **Execution and return with inventory.** The officer taking property under the warrant shall give to the person from whom or from whose premises the property was taken a copy of the warrant and a receipt for the property taken, or shall leave the copy and receipt at the place from which the property was taken. The return shall be made promptly and shall be accompanied by a written inventory of any property taken. The inventory shall be made in the presence of the applicant for the warrant and the person from whose possession or premises the property was taken, if they are present, or in the presence of at least one credible person other than the applicant for the warrant or the person from whose possession or premises the property was taken, and shall be verified by the officer. The judge shall upon request deliver a copy of the inventory to the person from whom or from whose premises the property was taken and to the applicant for the warrant. Property seized under a warrant shall be kept for use as evidence by the court which issued the warrant or by the law enforcement agency which executed the warrant.

(E) **Return of papers to clerk.** The judge before whom the warrant is returned shall attach to the warrant a copy of the return, inventory, and all other papers in connection therewith and shall file them with the clerk.

(F) **Definition of property and daytime.** The term "property" is used in this rule to include documents, books, papers and any other tangible objects. The term "daytime" is used in this rule to mean the hours from 7:00 a.m. to 8:00 p.m.

**History:** Amended, eff 7-1-10.

## RULE 42. Reserved

## RULE 43. Presence of the Defendant

(A) **Defendant's presence.**

(1) Except as provided in Rule 10 of these rules and division (A)(2) of this rule, the defendant must be physically present at every stage of the criminal proceeding and trial, including the impaneling of the jury, the return of the verdict, and the imposition of sentence, except as otherwise provided by these rules. In all prosecutions, the defendant's voluntary absence after the trial has been commenced in the defendant's presence shall not prevent continuing the trial to and including the verdict. A corporation may appear by counsel for all purposes.

(2) Notwithstanding the provisions of division (A)(1) of this rule, in misdemeanor cases or in felony cases where a waiver has been obtained in accordance with division (A)(3) of this rule, the court may permit the presence and participation of a defendant by remote contemporaneous video for any proceeding if all of the following apply:

(a) The court gives appropriate notice to all the parties;

(b) The video arrangements allow the defendant to hear and see the proceeding;

(c) The video arrangements allow the defendant to speak, and to be seen and heard by the court and all parties;

(d) The court makes provision to allow for private communication between the defendant and counsel. The court shall inform the defendant on the record how to, at any time, communicate privately with counsel. Counsel shall be afforded the opportunity to speak to defendant privately and in person. Counsel shall be permitted to appear with defendant at the remote location if requested.

(e) The proceeding may involve sworn testimony that is subject to cross examination, if counsel is present, participates and consents.

(3) The defendant may waive, in writing or on the record, the defendant's right to be physically present under these rules with leave of court.

(B) **Defendant excluded because of disruptive conduct.** Where a defendant's conduct in the courtroom is so disruptive that the hearing or trial cannot reasonably be conducted with the defendant's continued physical presence, the hearing or trial may proceed in the defendant's absence or by remote contemporaneous video, and judgment and sentence may be pronounced as if the defendant were present. Where the court determines that it may be essential to the preservation of the constitutional rights of the defendant, it may take such steps as are required for the communication of the courtroom proceedings to the defendant.

**History:** Amended, eff. 7-1-08.

## RULE 44. Assignment of Counsel

(A) **Counsel in serious offenses.** Where a defendant charged with a serious offense is unable to obtain counsel, counsel shall be assigned to represent him at every stage of the proceedings from his initial appearance before a court through appeal as of right, unless the defendant, after being fully advised of his right to assigned counsel, knowingly, intelligently, and voluntarily waives his right to counsel.

(B) **Counsel in petty offenses.** Where a defendant charged with a petty offense is unable to obtain counsel, the court may assign counsel to represent him. When a defendant charged with a petty offense is unable to obtain counsel, no sentence of confinement may be imposed upon him, unless after being fully advised by the court, he knowingly, intelligently, and voluntarily waives assignment of counsel.

(C) **Waiver of counsel.** Waiver of counsel shall be in open court and the advice and waiver shall be recorded as provided in Rule 22. In addition, in serious offense cases the waiver shall be in writing.

(D) **Assignment procedure.** The determination of whether a defendant is able or unable to obtain counsel shall be made in a recorded proceeding in open court.

## RULE 45. Time

(A) **Time: computation.** In computing any period of time prescribed or allowed by these rules, by the local rules of any court, by order of court, or by any applicable statute, the date of the act or event from which the designated period of time begins to run shall not be included. The last day of the period so computed shall be included, unless it is a Saturday, Sunday, or legal holiday, in which event the period runs until the end of the next day which is not Saturday, Sunday, or legal holiday. When the period of time prescribed or allowed is less than seven days, intermediate Saturdays, Sundays, and legal holidays shall be excluded in computation.

(B) **Time: enlargement.** When an act is required or allowed to be performed at or within a specified time, the court for cause shown may at any time in its discretion (1) with or without motion or notice, order the period enlarged if application therefore is made before expiration of the period originally prescribed or as extended by a previous order; or (2) upon motion permit the act to be done after expiration of the specified period, if the failure to act on time was the result of excusable neglect or would result in injustice to the defendant. The court may not extend the time for taking any action under Rule 23, Rule 29, Rule 33, and Rule 34 except to the extent and under the conditions stated in them.

(C) **Time: unaffected by expiration of term.** The period of time provided for the doing of any act or the taking of any proceeding is not affected or limited by the expiration of a term of court. The expiration of a term of court in no way affects the power of a court to do any act in a criminal proceeding.

(D) **Time: for motions; affidavits.** A written motion, other than one which may be heard *ex parte*, and notice of the hearing thereof, shall be served not later than seven days before the time specified for the hearing unless a different period is fixed by rule or order of the court. For cause shown such an order may be made on ex parte application. When a motion is supported by affidavit, the affidavit shall be served with the motion. Opposing affidavits may be served not less than one day before the hearing, unless the court permits them to be served at a later time.

(E) **Time: additional time after service by mail.** Whenever a party has the right or is required to do an act within a prescribed period after the service of a notice or other paper upon him, and the notice or other paper is served upon him by mail, three days shall be added to the prescribed period. This subdivision does not apply to responses to service of summons under Rule 4 and Rule 9.

## RULE 46. Bail

(A) **Types and amounts of bail.** Any person who is entitled to release shall be released upon one or more of the following types of bail in the amount set by the court:

(1) The personal recognizance of the accused or an unsecured bail bond;

(2) A bail bond secured by the deposit of ten percent of the amount of the bond in cash. Ninety percent of the deposit shall be returned upon compliance with all conditions of the bond;

(3) A surety bond, a bond secured by real estate or securities as allowed by law, or the deposit of cash, at the option of the defendant.

(B) **Conditions of bail.** The court may impose any of the following conditions of bail:

(1) Place the person in the custody of a designated person or organization agreeing to supervise the person;

(2) Place restrictions on the travel, association, or place of abode of the person during the period of release;

(3) Place the person under a house arrest, electronic monitoring, or work release program;

(4) Regulate or prohibit the person's contact with the victim;

(5) Regulate the person's contact with witnesses or others associated with the case upon proof of the likelihood that the person will threaten, harass, cause injury, or seek to intimidate those persons;

(6) Require a person who is charged with an offense that is alcohol or drug related, and who appears to need treatment, to attend treatment while on bail;

(7) Any other constitutional condition considered reasonably necessary to ensure appearance or public safety.

(C) **Factors.** In determining the types, amounts, and conditions of bail, the court shall consider all relevant information, including but not limited to:

(1) The nature and circumstances of the crime charged, and specifically whether the defendant used or had access to a weapon;

(2) The weight of the evidence against the defendant;

(3) The confirmation of the defendant's identity;

(4) The defendant's family ties, employment, financial resources, character, mental condition, length of residence in the community, jurisdiction of residence, record of convictions, record of appearance at court proceedings or of flight to avoid prosecution;

(5) Whether the defendant is on probation, a community control sanction, parole, post-release control, bail, or under a court protection order.

(D) **Appearance pursuant to summons.** When summons has been issued and the defendant has appeared pursuant to the summons, absent good cause, a recognizance bond shall be the preferred type of bail.

(E) **Amendments.** A court, at any time, may order additional or different types, amounts, or conditions of bail.

(F) **Information need not be admissible.** Information stated in or offered in connection with any order entered pursuant to this rule need not conform to the rules pertaining to the admissibility of evidence in a court of law. Statements or admissions of the defendant made at a bail proceeding shall not be received as substantive evidence in the trial of the case.

(G) **Bond schedule.** Each court shall establish a bail

bond schedule covering all misdemeanors including traffic offenses, either specifically, by type, by potential penalty, or by some other reasonable method of classification. The court also may include requirements for release in consideration of divisions (B) and (C)(5) of this rule. Each municipal or county court shall, by rule, establish a method whereby a person may make bail by use of a credit card. No credit card transaction shall be permitted when a service charge is made against the court or clerk unless allowed by law.

(H) **Continuation of bonds.** Unless otherwise ordered by the court pursuant to division (E) of this rule, or if application is made by the surety for discharge, the same bond shall continue until the return of a verdict or the acceptance of a guilty plea. In the discretion of the court, the same bond may also continue pending sentence or disposition of the case on review. Any provision of a bond or similar instrument that is contrary to this rule is void.

(I) **Failure to appear; breach of conditions.** Any person who fails to appear before any court as required is subject to the punishment provided by the law, and any bail given for the person's release may be forfeited. If there is a breach of condition of bail, the court may amend the bail.

(J) **Justification of sureties.** Every surety, except a corporate surety licensed as provided by law, shall justify by affidavit, and may be required to describe in the affidavit, the property that the surety proposes as security and the encumbrances on it, the number and amount of other bonds and undertakings for bail entered into by the surety and remaining undischarged, and all of the surety's other liabilities. The surety shall provide other evidence of financial responsibility as the court or clerk may require. No bail bond shall be approved unless the surety or sureties appear, in the opinion of the court or clerk, to be financially responsible in at least the amount of the bond. No licensed attorney at law shall be a surety.

**History:** Amended, eff 7-1-90; 7-1-94; 7-1-98; 7-1-06.

## RULE 47. Motions

An application to the court for an order shall be by motion. A motion, other than one made during trial or hearing, shall be in writing unless the court permits it to be made orally. It shall state with particularity the grounds upon which it is made and shall set forth the relief or order sought. It shall be supported by a memorandum containing citations of authority, and may also be supported by an affidavit.

To expedite its business, the court may make provision by rule or order for the submission and determination of motions without oral hearing upon brief written statements of reasons in support and opposition.

## RULE 48. Dismissal

(A) **Dismissal by the state.** The state may by leave of court and in open court file an entry of dismissal of an indictment, information, or complaint and the prosecution shall thereupon terminate.

(B) **Dismissal by the court.** If the court over objection of the state dismisses an indictment, information, or complaint, it shall state on the record its findings of fact and reasons for the dismissal.

## RULE 49. Service and Filing of Papers

(A) **Service: when required.** Written notices, requests for discovery, designation of record on appeal, written motions other than those heard ex parte, and similar papers, shall be served upon each of the parties.

(B) **Service: how made.** Whenever under these rules or by court order service is required or permitted to be made upon a party represented by an attorney, the service shall be made upon the attorney unless service upon the party himself is ordered by the court. Service upon the attorney or upon the party shall be made in the manner provided in Civil Rule 5(B).

(C) **Filing.** All papers required to be served upon a party shall be filed simultaneously with or immediately after service. Papers filed with the court shall not be considered until proof of service is endorsed thereon or separately filed. The proof of service shall state the date and the manner of service and shall be signed and filed in the manner provided in Civil Rule 5(D).

## RULE 50. Calendars

Criminal cases shall be given precedence over civil matters and proceedings.

## RULE 51. Exceptions Unnecessary

An exception, at any stage or step of the case or matter, is unnecessary to lay a foundation for review, whenever a matter has been called to the attention of the court by objection, motion, or otherwise, and the court has ruled thereon.

## RULE 52. Harmless Error and Plain Error

(A) **Harmless error.** Any error, defect, irregularity, or variance which does not affect substantial rights shall be disregarded.

(B) **Plain error.** Plain errors or defects affecting substantial rights may be noticed although they were not brought to the attention of the court.

## RULE 53. Reserved

## RULE 54. Amendment of Incorporated Civil Rules

An amendment to or recision of any provision of the Ohio Rules of Civil Procedure which has been incorporated by reference in these rules, shall, without the necessity of further action, be incorporated by reference in these rules unless the amendment or recision specifies otherwise, effective on the effective date of the amendment or recision.

## RULE 55. Records

(A) **Criminal appearance docket.** The clerk shall keep a criminal appearance docket. Upon the commencement of a criminal action the clerk shall assign each action a number. This number shall be placed on the first page, and every continuation page, of the appearance docket which concerns the particular action. In addition this number and the names of the parties shall be placed on the case file and every paper filed in the action.

At the time the action is commenced the clerk shall enter in the appearance docket the names, except as provided in Rule 6(E), of the parties in full, the names of counsel and index the action by the name of each defendant. Thereafter the clerk shall chronologically note in the appearance docket all: process issued and returns, pleas and motions, papers filed in the action, orders, verdicts and judgments. The notations shall be brief but shall show the date of filing and the substance of each order, verdict and judgment.

An action is commenced for purposes of this rule by the earlier of, (a) the filing of a complaint, uniform traffic ticket, citation, indictment, or information with the clerk, or (b) the receipt by the clerk of the court of common pleas of a bind over order under Rule 5(B)(4)(a).

(B) **Files.** All papers filed in a case shall be filed in a separate file folder and on or after July 1, 1986 shall not exceed 8 1/2 inches x 11 inches in size and without backing or cover.

(C) **Other books and records.** The clerk shall keep such other books and records as required by law and as the supreme court or other court may from time to time require.

(D) **Applicability to courts not of record.** In courts not of record the notations required by subdivision (A) shall be placed on a separate sheet or card kept in the file folder.

**History:** Amended, eff 7-1-85.

## RULE 56. Reserved

## RULE 57. Rule of court; procedure not otherwise specified

(A) **Rule of court.**

(1) The expression "rule of court" as used in these rules means a rule promulgated by the Supreme Court or a rule concerning local practice adopted by another court that is not inconsistent with the rules promulgated by the Supreme Court and is filed with the Supreme Court.

(2) Local rules shall be adopted only after the court gives appropriate notice and an opportunity for comment. If the court determines that there is an immediate need for a rule, the court may adopt the rule without prior notice and opportunity for comment, but promptly shall afford notice and opportunity for comment.

(B) **Procedure not otherwise specified.** If no procedure is specifically prescribed by rule, the court may proceed in any lawful manner not inconsistent with these rules of criminal procedure, and shall look to the rules of civil procedure and to the applicable law if no rule of criminal procedure exists.

**History:** Amended, eff 7-1-94.

## RULE 58. Forms

The forms contained in the Appendix of Forms which the Supreme Court from time to time may approve are sufficient under these rules and shall be accepted for filing by courts of this state. Forms adopted by local courts that are substantially similar to the forms in the Appendix of Forms, may also be accepted for filing. The forms in the Appendix of Forms are intended to indicate the simplicity and brevity of statement which these rules contemplate.

**History:** Amended 7-1-11.

## RULE 59. Effective date

(A) **Effective date of rules.** These rules shall take effect on July 1, 1973, except for rules or portions of rules for which a later date is specified, which shall take effect on such later date. They govern all proceedings in actions brought after they take effect, and also all further proceedings in actions then pending, except to the extent that their application in a particular action pending when the rules take effect would not be feasible or would work injustice, in which event the former procedure applies.

(B) **Effective date of amendments.** The amendments submitted by the supreme court to the general assembly on January 10, 1975, shall take effect on July 1, 1975. They govern all proceedings in actions brought after they take effect and also all further proceedings in actions then pending, except to the extent that their application in a particular action pending when the amendments take effect would not be feasible or would work injustice, in which event the former procedures applies.

(C) **Effective date of amendments.** The amendments submitted by the supreme court to the general assembly on January 9, 1976, shall take effect on July 1, 1976. They govern all proceedings in actions brought after they take effect and also all further proceedings in actions then pending, except to the extent that their application in a particular action pending when the rules take effect would not be feasible or would work injustice, in which event the former procedure applies.

(D) **Effective date of amendments.** The amendments submitted by the Supreme Court to the General Assembly on January 12, 1978, and on April 28, 1978, shall take effect on July 1, 1978. They govern all proceedings in actions brought after they take effect and also all further proceedings in actions then pending, except to the extent that their application in a particular action pending when the amendments take effect would not be feasible or would work injustice, in which event the former procedure applies.

(E) **Effective date of amendments.** The amendments submitted by the Supreme Court to the General Assembly on January 14, 1980, shall take effect on July 1, 1980. They govern all proceedings in actions brought after they take effect and also all further proceedings in actions then pending, except to the extent that their application in a particular action pending when the amendments take effect would not be feasible or would work injustice, in which event the former procedure applies.

(F) **Effective date of amendments.** The amendments submitted by the Supreme Court to the General Assembly on January 14, 1981, and on April 29, 1981, shall take effect on July 1, 1981. They govern all proceedings in actions brought after they take effect and also all further proceedings in actions then pending, except to the extent that their application in a particular action pending when the amendments take effect would not be feasible or would work injustice, in which event the former procedure applies.

(G) **Effective date of amendments.** The amendments submitted by the Supreme Court to the General Assembly on January 14, 1982 shall take effect on July 1, 1982. They govern all proceedings in actions brought after they take effect and also all further proceedings in actions then pending, except to the extent that their application in a particular action pending when the amendments take effect would not be feasible or would work injustice, in which event the former procedure applies.

(H) **Effective date of amendments.** The amendments submitted by the Supreme Court to the General Assembly on December 24, 1984 and January 8, 1985 shall take effect on July 1, 1985. They govern all proceedings in actions brought after they take effect and also all further proceedings in actions then pending, except to the extent that their application in a particular action pending when the amendments take effect would not be feasible or would work injustice, in which event the former procedure applies.

(I) **Effective date of amendments.** The amendments submitted by the Supreme Court to the General Assembly on January 12, 1990 and further revised and submitted on April 16, 1990, shall take effect on July 1, 1990. They govern all proceedings in actions brought after they take effect and also all further proceedings in actions then pending, except to the extent that their application in a particular action pending when the amendments take effect would not be feasible or would work injustice, in which event the former procedure applies.

(J) **Effective date of amendments.** The amendments filed by the Supreme Court with the General Assembly on January 14, 1992 and further revised and filed on April 30, 1992, shall take effect on July 1, 1992. They govern all proceedings in actions brought after they take effect and also all further proceedings in actions then pending, except to the extent that their application in a particular action pending when the amendments take effect would not be feasible or would work injustice, in which event the former procedure applies.

(K) **Effective date of amendments.** The amendments submitted by the Supreme Court to the General Assembly on January 8, 1993 and further filed on April 30, 1993 shall take effect on July 1, 1993. They govern all proceedings in actions brought after they take effect and also all further proceedings in actions then pending, except to the extent that their application in a particular action pending when the amendments take effect would not be feasible or would work injustice, in which event the former procedure applies.

(L) **Effective date of amendments.** The amendments submitted by the Supreme Court to the General Assembly on January 14, 1994 and further filed on April 29, 1994 shall take effect on July 1, 1994. They govern all proceedings in actions brought after they take effect and also all further proceedings in actions then pending, except to the extent that their application in a particular action pending when the amendments take effect would not be feasible or would work injustice, in which event the former procedure applies.

(M) **Effective date of amendments.** The amendments to rules 12 and 19 filed by the Supreme Court with the General Assembly on January 11, 1995 shall take effect on July 1, 1995. They govern all proceedings in actions brought after they take effect and also all further proceedings in actions then pending, except to the extent that their application in a particular action pending when the amendments take effect would not be feasible or would work injustice, in which event the former procedure applies.

(N) **Effective date of amendments.** The amendments to Rule 1 filed by the Supreme Court with the General Assembly on January 5, 1996 and refiled on April 26, 1996 shall take effect on July 1, 1996. They govern all proceedings in actions brought after they take effect and also all further proceedings in actions then pending, except to the extent that their application in a particular action pending when the amendments take effect would not be feasible or would work injustice, in which event the former procedure applies.

(O) **Effective date of amendments.** The amendments to Rule 35 filed by the Supreme Court with the General Assembly on January 10, 1997 and refiled on April 24, 1997 shall take effect on July 1, 1997. They govern all proceedings in actions brought after they take effect and also all further proceedings in actions then pending, except to the extent that their application in a particular action pending when the amendments take effect would not be feasible or would work injustice, in which event the former procedure applies.

(P) **Effective date of amendments.** The amendments to Rules 4, 11, 12, 32, 32.1, 32.2, 32.3, and 46 filed by the Supreme Court with the General Assembly on January 15, 1998 and further revised and refiled on April 30, 1998 shall take effect on July 1, 1998. They govern all proceedings in actions brought after they take effect and also all further proceedings in actions then pending, except to the extent that their application in a particular action pending when the amendments take effect would not be feasible or would work injustice, in which event the former procedure applies.

(Q) **Effective date of amendments.** The amendments to Criminal Rules 7, 17.1, and 19 filed by the Supreme Court with the General Assembly on January 13, 2000 and refiled on April 27, 2000 shall take effect on July 1, 2000. They govern all proceedings in actions brought after they take effect and also all further proceedings in actions then pending, except to the extent that their application in a particular action pending when the amendments take effect would not be feasible or would work injustice, in which event the former procedure applies.

(R) **Effective date of amendments.** The amendments to Criminal Rule 12 filed by the Supreme Court with the General Assembly on January 12, 2001, and refiled on April 26, 2001, shall take effect on July 1, 2001. They govern all proceedings in actions brought after they take effect and also all further proceedings in actions then pending, except to the extent that their application in a particular action pending when the amendments take effect would not be feasible or would work injustice, in which event the former procedure applies.

(S) **Effective date of amendments.** The amendments to Criminal Rule 24 filed by the Supreme Court with the General Assembly on January 11, 2002, and refiled on April 18, 2002, shall take effect on July 1, 2002. They govern all proceedings in actions brought after they take effect and also all further proceedings in actions then pending, except to the extent that their application in a particular action pending when the amendments take effect would not be feasible or would work injustice, in which event the former procedure applies.

(T) **Effective date of amendments.** The amendments to Criminal Rules 4.1, 21, and 32, filed by the Supreme Court with the General Assembly on January 7, 2004 and refiled on April 28, 2004 shall take effect on July 1, 2004. They govern all proceedings in actions brought after they take effect and also all further proceedings in actions then pending, except to the extent that their application in a particular action pending when the amendments take effect would not be feasible or would work injustice, in which event the former procedure applies.

(U) **Effective date of amendments.** The amendments to Criminal Rules 24 and 30 filed by the Supreme

Court with the General Assembly on January 14, 2005 and revised and refiled on April 20, 2005 shall take effect on July 1, 2005. They govern all proceedings in actions brought after they take effect and also all further proceedings in actions then pending, except to the extent that their application in a particular action pending when the amendments take effect would not be feasible or would work injustice, in which event the former procedure applies.

(V) **Effective date of amendments.** The amendments to Criminal Rules 19, 24, and 46 filed by the Supreme Court with the General Assembly on January 12, 2006 shall take effect on July 1, 2006. They govern all proceedings in actions brought after they take effect and also all further proceedings in actions then pending, except to the extent that their application in a particular action pending when the amendments take effect would not be feasible or would work injustice, in which event the former procedure applies.

(W) **Effective date of amendments.** The amendments to Criminal Rules 10, 24, and 43 filed by the Supreme Court with the General Assembly on January 14, 2008 and refiled on April 28, 2008 shall take effect on July 1, 2008. They govern all proceedings in actions brought after they take effect and also all further proceedings in actions then pending, except to the extent that their application in a particular action pending when the amendments take effect would not be feasible or would work injustice, in which event the former procedure applies.

(X) **Effective date of amendments.** The amendments to Criminal Rules 24 and 32 filed by the Supreme Court with the General Assembly on January 14, 2009 and refiled on April 30, 2009 shall take effect on July 1, 2009. They govern all proceedings in actions brought after they take effect and also all further proceedings in actions then pending, except to the extent that their application in a particular action pending when the amendments take effect would not be feasible or would work injustice, in which event the former procedure applies.

(Y) **Effective date of amendments.** The amendments to Criminal Rules 12, 16 and 41 filed by the Supreme Court with the General Assembly on January 14, 2010 and revised and refiled on April 28, 2010 shall take effect on July 1, 2010. They govern all proceedings in actions brought after they take effect and also all further proceedings in actions then pending, except to the extent that their application in a particular action pending when the amendments take effect would not be feasible or would work injustice, in which event the former procedure applies.

(Z) **Effective date of amendments.** The amendments to Criminal Rule 12, 14, 19, and 58 filed by the Supreme Court with the General Assembly on January 5, 2011 and refiled on April 21, 2011 shall take effect on July 1, 2011. They govern all proceedings in actions brought after they take effect and also all further proceedings in actions then pending, except to the extent that their application in a particular action pending when the amendments take effect would not be feasible or would work injustice, in which event the former procedure applies.

**History:** Amended, eff 7-1-75; 7-1-76; 7-1-78; 7-1-80; 7-1-81; 7-1-82; 7-1-85; 7-1-90; 7-1-92; 7-1-93; 7-1-94; 7-1-95; 7-1-96; 7-1-97; 7-1-98; 7-1-00; 7-1-01; 7-1-02; 7-1-04; 7-1-05; 7-1-06; 7-1-08; 7-1-09; 7-1-10; 7-1-11.

## RULE 60. Title

These rules shall be known as the Ohio Rules of Criminal Procedure and may be cited as "Criminal Rules" or "Crim. R. ____."

# APPENDIX OF FORMS

(See Crim. R. 58)

The forms which follow are intended for illustration only. They are limited in number, there being no attempt to furnish a complete manual of forms.

Although the forms are for illustrative purposes, they have been drafted to conform to the policies expressed in the Criminal Rules.

In the illustrations, the Franklin County Court of Common Pleas and the Franklin County Municipal Court identifications have each been used with the forms to show the adjustments required at the two levels of adjudication.

## FORM I

### FRANKLIN COUNTY MUNICIPAL COURT
### FRANKLIN COUNTY, OHIO

| | | |
|---|---|---|
| State of Ohio | ) | |
| /City of Columbus/ | ) | |
| | ) | NO.________________ |
| v. | ) | |
| | ) | COMPLAINT |
| ______________________ | ) | |
| name | ) | (Rule 4) |
| | ) | |
| ______________________ | ) | |
| address | | |

Complainant being duly sworn states that ______________ C.D. ______________
defendant
at ______________, County, Ohio on or about ______________,
place
19____ , ______________________________________________
state the essential facts
______________________________________________

______________________________________________

in violation of ______________________________________________.
state the numerical designation of the applicable statute or ordinance

A.B. ______________________________
Complainant

Sworn to and subscribed before me by ______________________________ on

______________________, 19 ____.

______________________________
/ Judge / Clerk / Deputy Clerk /
Franklin County Municipal Court

or

______________________________
Notary Public,
My Commission expires ______________, 19 ____
/ Franklin County / State of Ohio /

## FORM II

### FRANKLIN COUNTY MUNICIPAL COURT
### FRANKLIN COUNTY, OHIO

| | | |
|---|---|---|
| State of Ohio | ) | |
| /City of Columbus/ | ) | NO.________________ |
| | ) | |
| v. | ) | COMPLAINT BY |
| | ) | PROSECUTING ATTORNEY |
| ________________ | ) | UPON AFFIDAVIT |
| name | ) | |
| | ) | (Rule 4) |
| ________________ | ) | |
| address | ) | |

Complainant prosecuting attorney being duly sworn states that ________________
name of affiant
has filed an affidavit, a copy of which is attached hereto, stating that ________________
C.D.
________________ at ________________, County, Ohio on or
place
about ________________, 19 ____, ________________
state the essential facts
________________

________________

Upon this affidavit complainant states that ________________ on or
C.D.
defendant
about the above date and at the above place did violate ________________
state the numerical designation
________________.
of the applicable statute or ordinance

A.B.
Complainant, Title

Sworn to and subscribed before me by ________________
A.B.
on ________________, 19 ____.

________________
/ Judge / Clerk / Deputy Clerk /
Franklin County Municipal Court

or

________________
Notary Public,
My Commission expires ________________, 19 ____
/ Franklin County / State of Ohio /

**FORM III**

**/ FRANKLIN COUNTY MUNICIPAL COURT /**
**/ COURT OF COMMON PLEAS /**
**FRANKLIN COUNTY, OHIO**

| | | |
|---|---|---|
| State of Ohio | ) | |
| /City of Columbus/ | ) | |
| | ) | NO.______________________ |
| v. | ) | |
| | ) | DIRECTION TO ISSUE SUMMONS |
| ______________________ | ) | |
| name | ) | (Rules 4 and 9) |
| | ) | |
| ______________________ | ) | |
| address | ) | |

TO______________________________________________
/ Clerk / Deputy Clerk /

Issue summons to an appropriate officer and direct him to make / personal service / residence service / certified mail service / upon ______C.D.______ at / the address
defendant

stated in the caption of this direction./ ______________________________________________

______________________________________________/
fill in address if different from caption

Special instructions for server:______________________________________________

______________________________________________

______________________________________________

______________________________________________
/ Judge / Officer Designated by Judge(s) /
Franklin County Municipal Court

or

______________________________________________
Judge
Court of Common Pleas
Franklin County, Ohio

# FORM IV

## FRANKLIN COUNTY MUNICIPAL COURT
## FRANKLIN COUNTY, OHIO

| | | |
|---|---|---|
| State of Ohio | ) | |
| /City of Columbus/ | ) | |
| | ) | NO.____________________ |
| v. | ) | |
| | ) | CLERK'S MEMORANDUM |
| ______________________ | ) | OF DETERMINATION TO ISSUE |
| name | ) | SUMMONS UPON COMPLAINT |
| | ) | (Rule 4) |
| ______________________ | ) | |
| address | ) | |

It appearing that summons will reasonably assure the appearance of ________C.D.________
defendant
summons shall issue:

/ to an appropriate officer and such officer shall be directed to make / personal service / residence service /.

/ by certified mail /

Service shall be at / the address stated in the caption of this notice / ____________________

________________________________________
fill in address if different from caption

Special instructions for server: ______________________________

________________________________________

________________________________________

______________________________
/ Clerk / Deputy Clerk /
Franklin County Municipal Court

**FORM V**

**FRANKLIN COUNTY MUNICIPAL COURT**
**FRANKLIN COUNTY, OHIO**

| | | |
|---|---|---|
| State of Ohio<br>/City of Columbus/<br><br>v.<br>____________________<br>name<br>____________________<br>address | )<br>)<br>)<br>)<br>)<br>)<br>)<br>)<br>) | NO.____________________<br><br>**PROSECUTING ATTORNEY'S REQUEST FOR ISSUANCE OF SUMMONS UPON COMPLAINT**<br><br>**(Rule 4)** |

TO________________________________________
/ Clerk / Deputy Clerk /

A complaint has been filed against ____________C.D.____________
defendant

Issue summons to an appropriate officer and direct him to make / personal service / residence service / certified mail service / upon defendant at / the address stated in the caption of this request. / ________________________________________

________________________________________/
fill in address if different from caption

Special instructions for server: ________________________________________

________________________________________

________________________________________

________________________
Prosecuting Attorney, Title

## FORM VI

### / FRANKLIN COUNTY MUNICIPAL COURT /
### / COURT OF COMMON PLEAS /
### FRANKLIN COUNTY, OHIO

State of Ohio )
/City of Columbus/ ) NO.____________________
)
v. ) SUMMONS UPON / COMPLAINT /
) INDICTMENT / INFORMATION /
____________________ )
name )
)
)
____________________ ) (Rules 4 and 9)
address )
)

TO ____________________ C.D.
defendant

A / complaint / indictment / information /, a copy of which is attached hereto, has been filed in the / Franklin County Municipal Court, 120 West Gay Street, Columbus, Ohio 43215, / Franklin County Court of Common Pleas, 410 South High Street, Columbus, Ohio 43215, / charging that you: ____________________
describe the offense

____________________
and state the numerical designation of the applicable statute or ordinance

____________________.

You are hereby summoned and ordered to appear at ____________________

____________________, / Franklin County Municipal Court, 120 West Gay
time, day, date, room

Street, Columbus, Ohio 43215. / Franklin County Court of Common Pleas, 410 South High Street, Columbus, Ohio 43215. /

If you fail to appear at the time and place stated above you may be arrested.

____________________
/ Judge / Officer Designated by Judge(s) /
/ Clerk / Deputy Clerk /
Franklin County Municipal Court

(or)

____________________
/ Judge / Clerk / Deputy Clerk /
Court of Common Pleas
Franklin County, Ohio

NOTICE TO DEFENDANT: For information regarding your duty to appear call

____________________
fill in phone number(s)

## CLERK'S INSTRUCTIONS TO SERVING OFFICER FOR PERSONAL OR RESIDENCE SERVICE

TO ______________________________________________
officer other than clerk authorized to serve summons

Make / personal service / residence service / upon ______________________________
defendant

at / the address stated in the caption of the summons. / ______________________________

______________________________________________/
fill in address for service if different from caption of summons

Special instructions for server: ______________________________

______________________________________________

______________________________________________

______________________________
/ Clerk / Deputy Clerk /

• • • • • • • • • • •

## CLERK'S INSTRUCTIONS FOR CERTIFIED MAIL SERVICE

TO ______________________________________________
clerk

Make certified mail service upon ______________________________
defendant

at / the address stated in the caption of the summons. / ______________________________

______________________________________________/
fill in address for service if different from caption of summons

Special instructions for server: ______________________________

______________________________________________

______________________________________________.

______________________________
/ Clerk / Deputy Clerk /

## RECEIPT OF SUMMONS BY SERVING AUTHORITY

***First Receipt***

**Received this summons on ________________________________________, 19 _____,**

**at ______________ o'clock ____m.**

______________________________
**Officer**

**By** ______________________________
**Title**

***Subsequent Receipt***

**Received this summons on ________________________________________, 19 _____,**

**at ______________ o'clock ____m.**

______________________________
**Officer**

**By** ______________________________
**Title**

## RETURN OF SERVICE OF SUMMONS
## (PERSONAL)

| Fees | |
|---|---|
| Mileage $ | ____ |
| | ____ |
| | ____ |
| | ____ |
| | ____ |
| Total $ | ____ |

I received this summons on ________________, 19 ______, at ______________ o'clock, _____.m., and made personal service of it upon ______________________________
fill in name
by locating / him/her / and tendering a copy of the summons, a copy of the / complaint / indictment / information / and accompanying documents, on ______________________, 19 ______.

______________________________
Serving Officer, Title

Date return made: ______________________, 19 ______

• • • • • • • • • •

## RETURN OF SERVICE OF SUMMONS
## (RESIDENCE)

| Fees | |
|---|---|
| Mileage $ | ____ |
| | ____ |
| | ____ |
| | ____ |
| | ____ |
| Total $ | ____ |

I received this summons on ________________, 19 ______, at ______________ o'clock, _____.m., and made residence service of it upon ______________________________
fill in name
by leaving, at / his/her / usual place of residence with ______________________________ a person of suitable
fill in name
age and discretion then residing therein, a copy of the summons, a copy of the / complaint / indictment / information / and accompanying documents, on ______________________, 19 ______.

______________________________
Serving Officer, Title

Date return made: ______________________, 19 ______

**RETURN OF SERVICE OF SUMMONS**
**(FAILURE OF SERVICE)**

| |
|---|
| **Fees** |
| **Mileage $** ____ |
| ____ |
| ____ |
| ____ |
| ____ |
| **Total $** ____ |

I received this summons on ______________, 19 ____, at ______________ o'clock, ____m., with instructions to make / personal service / residence service / upon
________________________________________
fill in name
and I was unable to serve a copy of the summons upon / him/her / for the following reasons: ______________
________________________________________
________________________________________
________________________________________

________________________________________
Serving Officer, Title
Date return made: ______________________, 19 ____

• • • • • • • • • •

**RETURN OF SERVICE OF SUMMONS**
**(FAILURE OF SERVICE)**

| |
|---|
| **Fees** |
| **Mileage $** ____ |
| ____ |
| ____ |
| ____ |
| ____ |
| **Total $** ____ |

I received this summons on ______________, 19 ____, at ______________ o'clock, ____m., with instructions to make / personal service / residence service / upon
________________________________________
fill in name
and I was unable to serve a copy of the summons upon / him/her / for the following reasons: ______________
________________________________________
________________________________________
________________________________________

________________________________________
Serving Officer, Title
Date return made: ______________________, 19 ____

## FORM VII

### FRANKLIN COUNTY MUNICIPAL COURT
### FRANKLIN COUNTY, OHIO

State of Ohio )
/City of Columbus/ )
) NO.____________________
v. )
____________________ ) WARRANT ON COMPLAINT
name )
____________________ ) (Rule 4)
address )

TO ________________________________________
officer authorized to execute a warrant

A complaint, a copy of which is attached hereto, has been filed in this court charging ____________

________________________________________
describe the offense and state the numerical designation of the applicable statute or ordinance

________________________________________

You are ordered to arrest ________C.D.________ and bring / him/her / before
defendant
this court without unnecessary delay.

You / may / may not / issue summons in lieu of arrest under Rule 4(A)(2) or issue summons after arrest under Rule 4(F) because ____________________
state specific reasons if issuance of summons
________________________________________
restricted

Special instructions to executing officer: ____________________

________________________________________

________________________________________

______________________________
/ Judge / Officer Designated by Judge(s) /
/ Clerk / Deputy Clerk /
Franklin County Municipal Court

## SUMMONS ENDORSEMENT

*See NOTE: Use only in appropriate case*

This warrant was executed / by arrest and / by issuing the following summons:

TO ______________________ C.D. ______________________
defendant

You are hereby summoned and ordered to appear at ______________________
time, day, date, room

Franklin County Municipal Court, 120 West Gay Street, Columbus, Ohio 43215.

If you fail to appear at the time and place stated above you may be arrested.

______________________
Issuing Officer, Title
*See Rule 4(A)(2), Rule 4(F) and Return Forms*

NOTICE TO DEFENDANT: For information regarding your duty to appear call ______________________

______________________
fill in telephone number(s)

• • • • • • • • • •

## RECEIPT OF WARRANT BY EXECUTING AUTHORITY

*First Receipt*

Received this warrant on ______________________, 19 ____, at ____ o'clock ____.m.

______________________
Officer

By ______________________
Title

*Subsequent Receipt*

Received this / alias / warrant on ______________________, 19 ____, at ____ o'clock ____.m.

______________________
Officer

By ______________________
Title

## RETURN OF EXECUTED WARRANT

| Fees | |
|---|---|
| Mileage $ | ____ |
| | ____ |
| | ____ |
| | ____ |
| | ____ |
| Total $ | ____ |

1. **Execution By Arrest**

I received this warrant on ______________, 19 ____, at ______ o'clock _____.m. On ______________, 19 ____, I arrested ______________ and gave / him/ her / a copy of this warrant with complaint attached and brought / him/her / to ______________
state the place

______________________________
Arresting Officer, Title

| Fees | |
|---|---|
| Mileage $ | ____ |
| | ____ |
| | ____ |
| | ____ |
| | ____ |
| Total $ | ____ |

2. **Execution By Issuance Of Summons Under Rule 4(A)(2) By Executing Officer**

I received this warrant on ______________, 19 ____, at ______ o'clock _____.m. On ______________, 19 ____, I executed this warrant by issuing ______ C.D. ______ a summons by / personal service / residence service / which ordered / him/her / to appear at ______________
time, day, date
______________, Franklin County Municipal Court,
room
120 West Gay Street, Columbus, Ohio, 43215. The summons was endorsed upon the warrant and accompanied by a copy of the complaint.

______________________________
Arresting Officer, Title

| Fees | |
|---|---|
| Mileage $ | ____ |
| | ____ |
| | ____ |
| | ____ |
| | ____ |
| Total $ | ____ |

3. **Execution By Arrest And Issuance Of Summons Under Rule 4(F) By Arresting Officer**

I received this warrant on ______________, 19 ____, at ____ o'clock ____.m. On ______________, 19 ____, I arrested _______ C.D. _______ and after arrest I issued _______ C.D. _______ a summons by personal service which ordered / him/her / to appear at ______________________________, Franklin County Municipal Court, 120 West Gay Street, Columbus, Ohio, 43215. The summons was endorsed upon the warrant and accompanied by a copy of the complaint.

______________________________
Arresting-Issuing Officer, Title

4. **Execution By Arrest And Issuance Of Summons Under Rule 4(F) By Superior Of Arresting Officer**

On ______________, 19 ____, _______ C.D. _______ was arrested by ______________________________
name of arresting officer
and I issued _______ C.D. _______ a summons by personal service which ordered / him/ her / to appear at ______________________________
time, day, date, room
Franklin County Municipal Court, 120 West Gay Street, Columbus, Ohio 43215. The summons was endorsed upon the warrant and accompanied by a copy of the complaint.

______________________________
Arresting-Issuing Officer, Title

## RETURN OF UNEXECUTED WARRANT

| Fees | |
|---|---|
| Mileage $ | ____ |
| | ____ |
| | ____ |
| | ____ |
| | ____ |
| Total $ | ____ |

I received this warrant on ______________, 19 ______, at ______ o'clock, ______.m. On ______________, 19 ______, I attempted to execute this warrant but was unable to to so because ________________________________
state specific reason or reasons and
________________________________
additional information regarding defendant's whereabouts
________________________________

________________________________
Executing Officer, Title

## RETURN OF UNEXECUTED WARRANT

| Fees | |
|---|---|
| Mileage $ | ____ |
| | ____ |
| | ____ |
| | ____ |
| | ____ |
| Total $ | ____ |

I received this warrant on ______________, 19 ______, at ______ o'clock, ______.m. On ______________, 19 ______, I attempted to execute this warrant but was unable to to so because ________________________________
state specific reason or reasons and
________________________________
additional information regarding defendant's whereabouts
________________________________

________________________________
Executing Officer, Title

**FORM VIII**

**COURT OF COMMON PLEAS**
**FRANKLIN COUNTY, OHIO**

| | | |
|---|---|---|
| State of Ohio | ) | |
| | ) | NO.____________________ |
| v. | ) | |
| | ) | CLERK'S MEMORANDUM OF |
| ____________________ | ) | DETERMINATION TO ISSUE |
| name | ) | SUMMONS UPON INDICTMENT |
| | ) | |
| ____________________ | ) | (Rule 9) |
| address | ) | |

It appearing that defendant ____________________ (name) was released pursuant to Rule 46 by the ____________________ (bind-over court) on the same offense for which / he/she / was indicted in this court, summons shall issue: / to an appropriate officer and such officer shall be directed to make / personal service / residence service /.

/ by certified mail service /

Service shall be at / the address stated in the caption of this notice / ____________________

________________________________________

fill in address if different from caption

Special instructions for server: ____________________

________________________________________

________________________________________

____________________________

/ Clerk / Deputy Clerk /
Court of Common Pleas
Franklin County, Ohio

## FORM IX

### COURT OF COMMON PLEAS
### FRANKLIN COUNTY, OHIO

| | | |
|---|---|---|
| State of Ohio | ) | |
| | ) | NO.______________________ |
| v. | ) | |
| | ) | PROSECUTING ATTORNEY'S |
| ______________________ | ) | REQUEST FOR ISSUANCE OF |
| name | ) | SUMMONS UPON/INDICTMENT |
| | ) | /INFORMATION/ |
| ______________________ | ) | (Rule 9) |
| address | ) | |
| | ) | |

TO ______________________________________________

/ Clerk / Deputy Clerk /

C.D.
______________________ has been named a defendant in an / indictment re-
defendant
turned by the grand jury / information filed by the prosecuting attorney. / Issue summons to an appropriate officer and direct him to make / personal service / residence service / certified mail service / upon defendant at / the address stated in the caption of this request./______________________
fill in address if different from caption

Special instructions for server: ______________________________________________

______________________________________________

______________________________________________

______________________
Prosecuting Attorney, Title

## FORM X

## COURT OF COMMON PLEAS
## FRANKLIN COUNTY, OHIO

| | | |
|---|---|---|
| State of Ohio | ) | |
| | ) | NO.____________________ |
| v. | ) | |
| | ) | PROSECUTING ATTORNEY'S |
| ____________________ | ) | REQUEST FOR ISSUANCE OF |
| name | ) | WARRANT UPON |
| ____________________ | ) | /INDICTMENT/INFORMATION/ |
| address | ) | |
| | ) | (Rule 9) |

TO: ________________________________________
/ Clerk / Deputy Clerk /

__________C.D.__________ has been named a defendant in an / indictment re-
defendant
turned by the grand jury / information filed by the prosecuting attorney./

Issue a warrant to an appropriate officer and direct him to execute it upon ________________
__________C.D.__________ / at the address stated in the caption of this request./
defendant
________________________________________ ./
fill in address if different from caption

Special instructions for executing officer: ________________________________
________________________________________
________________________________________

______________________________
Prosecuting Attorney, Title

**FORM XI**

**COURT OF COMMON PLEAS**
**FRANKLIN COUNTY, OHIO**

| | | |
|---|---|---|
| State of Ohio | ) | |
| | ) | |
| v. | ) | NO.____________________ |
| | ) | |
| ____________________ | ) | WARRANT UPON/INDICTMENT/ |
| name | ) | INFORMATION/ |
| | ) | |
| ____________________ | ) | (Rule 9) |
| address | ) | |
| | ) | |

TO ________________________________________
officer authorized to execute warrant

An / indictment / information /, a copy of which is attached hereto has been filed in the Franklin County Court of Common Pleas, 410 South High Street, Columbus, Ohio 43215, charging ________C.D.________ with: ____________________
defendant

________________________________________
describe the offense and state the numerical designation of the applicable statute

________________________________________

You are ordered to arrest ________C.D.________ and bring him before this
defendant

court without unnecessary delay.

Special instructions to executing officer: ____________________

________________________________________

________________________________________

________________________________
/ Judge / Clerk / Deputy Clerk /
Court of Common Pleas
Franklin County, Ohio

## RECEIPT OF WARRANT BY EXECUTING AUTHORITY

*First Receipt*

Received this warrant on ______________________, 19 ____, at ____ o'clock ____.m.

______________________________
Officer

By ______________________________
Title

*Subsequent Receipt*

Received this warrant on ______________________, 19 ____, at ____ o'clock ____.m.

______________________________
Officer

By ______________________________
Title

• • • • • • • • • •

## RETURN OF EXECUTED WARRANT

| |
|---|
| **Fees** |
| **Mileage $** ____ |
| ____ |
| ____ |
| ____ |
| ____ |
| **Total $** ____ |

I received this warrant on ______________, 19 ____, at ____ o'clock ____.m. On ______________, 19 ____, I arrested ______________________, gave / him/her a copy of this warrant with / indictment / information / attached and brought / him/her / to ______________
state the place

______________________________

______________________________
Arresting Officer, Title

## RETURN OF UNEXECUTED WARRANT

| |
|---|
| **Fees** |
| **Mileage $** ____ |
| ____ |
| ____ |
| ____ |
| ____ |
| **Total $** ____ |

I received this warrant on ________________, 19 _____, at _____ o'clock, ____.m. On ______________, 19 _____, I attempted to execute this warrant but was unable to do so because ________________________________

state specific reason or reasons and

______________________________________________

additional information regarding defendant's

______________________________________________

whereabouts

______________________________________________

_____________________________________

Executing Officer, Title

. . . . . . . . . .

## RETURN OF UNEXECUTED WARRANT

| |
|---|
| **Fees** |
| **Mileage $** ____ |
| ____ |
| ____ |
| ____ |
| ____ |
| **Total $** ____ |

I received this warrant on ________________, 19 _____, at _____ o'clock, ____.m. On ______________, 19 _____, I attempted to execute this warrant but was unable to do so because ________________________________

state specific reason or reasons and

______________________________________________

additional information regarding defendant's

______________________________________________

whereabouts

______________________________________________

_____________________________________

Executing Officer, Title

**FORM XII**

**FRANKLIN COUNTY MUNICIPAL COURT**
**FRANKLIN COUNTY, OHIO**

State of Ohio )
/City of Columbus/ ) SUMMONS NO. ____________
)
v. ) CASE NO.____________
)
____________________ )
name of defendant ) SUMMONS IN LIEU OF ARREST WITHOUT WARRANT, AND COMPLAINT UPON SUCH SUMMONS
____________________ )
address )
____________________ ) (Rule 4 (A) (3))
age )

TO DEFENDANT:

SUMMONS

In lieu of immediate arrest upon a misdemeanor you are summoned and ordered to appear / at ____________________
time, day, date, room
Franklin County Municipal Court, 120 West Gay Street, Columbus, Ohio 43215. / before the Franklin County Juvenile Court, 50 East Mound Street, Columbus, Ohio 43215 at the time and place ordered by that court. / If you fail to appear at this time and place you may be arrested.

This summons served personally on the defendant on ____________________, 19 ______.

COMPLAINT

On ____________________, 19______, at ____________________
____________________
place
you ____________________
describe the offense charged and state the numerical
____________________
designation of the applicable statute or ordinance
____________________
____________________
____________________

____________________
Signature of Issuing-Charging
Law Enforcement Officer

Being duly sworn the issuing-charging law enforcement officer states that he has read the above complaint and that it is true.

____________________________________
Issuing-Charging Law Enforcement Officer

Sworn to and subscribed before me by ____________________________________
on ________________________, 19____.

____________________________________
/ Judge / Clerk / Deputy Clerk
Franklin County Municipal Court

or

____________________________________
Notary Public
My Commission Expires ________________, 19____.
/ Franklin County / State of Ohio /

NOTICE TO DEFENDANT: The officer is not required to swear to the complaint upon your copy of the summons and complaint. He swears to the complaint on the copy he files with the court. You may obtain a copy of the sworn complaint before hearing time. You will be given a copy of the sworn complaint before or at the hearing. For information regarding your duty to appear call ____________________________________
fill in telephone number(s)

NOTICE TO DEFENDANT UNDER EIGHTEEN YEARS OF AGE: You must appear before the Franklin County Juvenile Court, 50 East Mound Street, Columbus, Ohio 43215, at the time and place determined by that Court. The Juvenile Court will notify you when and where to appear. This Summons and Complaint will be filed with the Juvenile Court. The Complaint may be used as a juvenile complaint. You may obtain a copy of the sworn complaint from the Juvenile Court before the Juvenile Court hearing. You will be given a copy of the sworn complaint before or at the Juvenile Court hearing. For information regarding your duty to appear at Juvenile Court call ____________________________________
fill in telephone number(s)

**FORM XIII**

**FRANKLIN COUNTY MUNICIPAL COURT**
**FRANKLIN COUNTY, OHIO**

| | | |
|---|---|---|
| State of Ohio<br>/City of Columbus/<br><br>v.<br><br>______________________<br>name of defendant<br>______________________<br>address<br>______________________<br>age | ) | SUMMONS NO. ______________<br><br>CASE NO. ______________<br><br>SUMMONS AFTER ARREST WITHOUT WARRANT, AND COMPLAINT UPON EACH SUCH SUMMONS<br><br>(Rule 4 (F)) |

TO DEFENDANT:

SUMMONS

In lieu of continued custody upon a misdemeanor you are summoned and ordered to appear / at ______________________________
time, day, date, room
Franklin County Municipal Court, 120 West Gay Street, Columbus, Ohio 43215. / before the Franklin County Juvenile Court, 50 East Mound Street, Columbus, Ohio 43215 at the time and place ordered by that court. / If you fail to appear at this time and place you may be rearrested.

This summons served personally on the defendant on ______________________, 19 ____.

COMPLAINT

On ______________________, 19____, at ______________________
place
______________________________________________
you ______________________________________________
describe the offense charged and state the numerical
______________________________________________
designation of the applicable statute or ordinance
______________________________________________
______________________________________________
______________________________________________

______________________
Signature of Issuing-Charging
Law Enforcement Officer

Being duly sworn the issuing-charging law enforcement officer states that he has read the above complaint and that it is true.

______________________________
Issuing-Charging Law Enforcement Officer

Sworn to and subscribed before me by ______________________________
on ______________________, 19____.

______________________________
/ Judge / Clerk / Deputy Clerk
Franklin County Municipal Court

or

______________________________
Notary Public
My Commission Expires ______________, 19____.
/ Franklin County / State of Ohio /

NOTICE TO DEFENDANT: The officer is not required to swear to the complaint upon your copy of the summons and complaint. He swears to the complaint on the copy he files with the court. You may obtain a copy of the sworn complaint before hearing time. You will be given a copy of the sworn complaint before or at the hearing. For information regarding your duty to appear call ______________________________
fill in telephone number(s)

NOTICE TO DEFENDANT UNDER EIGHTEEN YEARS OF AGE: You must appear before the Franklin County Juvenile Court, 50 East Mound Street, Columbus, Ohio 43215, at the time and place determined by that Court. The Juvenile Court will notify you when and where to appear. This Summons and Complaint will be filed with the Juvenile Court. The Complaint may be used as a juvenile complaint. You may obtain a copy of the sworn complaint from the Juvenile Court before the Juvenile Court hearing. You will be given a copy of the sworn complaint before or at the Juvenile Court hearing. For information regarding your duty to appear at Juvenile Court call ______________________________
fill in telephone number(s)

# FORM XIV

## FRANKLIN COUNTY MUNICIPAL COURT
## FRANKLIN COUNTY, OHIO

State of Ohio
/City of Columbus/

v.

______________________
name of defendant

______________________
address

______________________
age

Citation No. ______________

Case No. ______________

MINOR MISDEMEANOR
CITATION

(Rule 4.1)

TO DEFENDANT:

On ______________ , 19____ , at ______________________
date place

______________________________________________

You ______________________________________________
describe the offense charged and state the

______________________________________________
numerical designation of the applicable statute or ordinance

______________________________________________

______________________________________________

______________________________________________

______________________________________________

You are ordered to appear at ______________________________
time, day, date, room

Franklin County Municipal Court, 120 West Gay Street, Columbus, Ohio 43215,/ before the Franklin County Juvenile Court, 50 East Mound Street, Columbus, Ohio 43215, at the time and place ordered by that court. /

If you wish to contest this matter you must appear at the above time and place. In lieu of appearing at the above time and place you may, within the time stated above, appear personally at 120 West Gay Street, Columbus, Ohio 43215, Room 120, sign the guilty plea and waiver of trial which appear in this form, and pay a fine of $ __________ and court costs of $ __________ .

If you fail to appear at the time and place stated above you may be arrested.

This citation was served personally on the defendant.

____________________________________
Signature of Issuing Law Enforcement Officer

Being duly sworn the issuing law enforcement officer states that he has read the citation and that it is true.

____________________________________
Issuing Officer

Sworn to and subscribed before me by ________________________________________
on ____________________, 19_____ .

____________________________________
/ Judge / Clerk / Deputy Clerk /

or

____________________________________
Notary Public,
My Commission expires ____________________, 19_____
Franklin County / State of Ohio /

NOTICE TO DEFENDANT: The officer is not required to swear to your copy of the citation and complaint. He swears to citation in the copy he files with the court. You may obtain a copy of the sworn citation before hearing time. You will be given a copy of the sworn citation before or at the hearing. For information regarding your duty to appear call

______________________________________________________________________________
fill in telephone number(s)

NOTICE TO DEFENDANT UNDER EIGHTEEN YEARS OF AGE: The appearance, guilty plea, waiver and payment provisions of this form do not apply to you. You must appear before the Franklin County Juvenile Court, 50 East Mound Street, Columbus, Ohio 43215, at the time and place determined by that Court. The Juvenile Court will notify you when and where to appear. This citation will be filed with the Juvenile Court. The citation may be used as a juvenile complaint. You may obtain a copy of the sworn citation from the Juvenile Court before the Juvenile Court hearing. You will be given a copy of the sworn citation before or at the Juvenile Court hearing. For information regarding your duty to appear at Juvenile Court call ________

____________________________________________

fill in telephone number(s)

GUILTY PLEA, WAIVER OF TRIAL, PAYMENT OF FINE AND COSTS

I, the undersigned defendant, do hereby enter my written plea of guilty to the offense charged in this citation. I realize that by signing this guilty plea I admit my guilt of the offense charged and waive my right to contest the offense in a trial before the court. I plead guilty to the offense charged in the citation.

FINE ____________________ ____________________
Signature of Defendant

COST ____________________ ____________________
address

TOTAL ____________________ ____________________
Signature And Title Of Person Taking Guilty Plea, Waiver And Payment

RECEIPT NO. ____________________

# FORM XV

## UNIFORM PETITION FORM

IN THE COURT OF COMMON PLEAS
______________ COUNTY, OHIO

CASE NOS.: ______________
______________

JUDGE: ______________

STATE OF OHIO
Plaintiff-Respondent

-vs-

______________
Defendant-Petitioner

POST-CONVICTION PETITION

### I. CASE HISTORY

TRIAL:

Charge (include specifications) Disposition

______________ ______________

______________

Date Sentenced: ______________

Name of Attorney: ______________

Was this conviction the result of a (circle one): **Guilty Plea** **No Contest Plea** **Trial**

If the conviction resulted in a trial, what was the length of the trial?

______________

*Appeal to Court of Appeals*

Number or citation ______________

Disposition ______________

Name of Attorney ______________

*Appeal to Supreme Court of Ohio*

Number or citation ______________

Disposition ______________

Name of Attorney ______________

HAS A POST-CONVICTION PETITION BEEN FILED BEFORE IN THIS CASE?

YES NO

If YES, attach a copy of the Petition and the Judgment Entry showing how it was disposed.

IF THIS IS NOT THE FIRST POST-CONVICTION PETITION, OR IT IS FILED OUTSIDE THE TIME LIMITS PROVIDED BY LAW, STATE THE REASONS WHY THE COURT SHOULD CONSIDER THIS PETITION: ______________

______________

______________

______________

______________

OTHER RELEVANT CASE HISTORY: ______________

## II. STATEMENT OF FACTS

## III. GROUNDS FOR RELIEF

(each ground not to exceed three pages)

Ground for relief 1: ____________________

____________________

____________________

____________________

____________________

Attached exhibit numbers which support ground for relief:

____________________

____________________

Legal authority (constitutional provisions, statutes, cases, rules, etc.) in support of ground for relief: ____________________

____________________

____________________

____________________

____________________
(name)

# OHIO RULES OF EVIDENCE

**Complete with amendments through July 1, 2011.**



## ARTICLE I
## GENERAL PROVISIONS

### RULE 101. Scope of Rules: Applicability; Privileges; Exceptions

(A) **Applicability.** These rules govern proceedings in

the courts of this state, subject to the exceptions stated in division (C) of this rule.

(B) **Privileges.** The rule with respect to privileges applies at all stages of all actions, cases, and proceedings conducted under these rules.

(C) **Exceptions.** These rules (other than with respect to privileges) do not apply in the following situations:

(1) Admissibility determinations. Determinations prerequisite to rulings on the admissibility of evidence when the issue is to be determined by the court under Evid.R. 104.

(2) Grand jury. Proceedings before grand juries.

(3) Miscellaneous criminal proceedings. Proceedings for extradition or rendition of fugitives; sentencing; granting or revoking probation; proceedings with respect to community control sanctions; issuance of warrants for arrest; criminal summonses and search warrants; and proceedings with respect to release on bail or otherwise.

(4) Contempt. Contempt proceedings in which the court may act summarily.

(5) Arbitration. Proceedings for those mandatory arbitrations of civil cases authorized by the rules of superintendence and governed by local rules of court.

(6) Other rules. Proceedings in which other rules prescribed by the Supreme Court govern matters relating to evidence.

(7) Special non-adversary statutory proceedings. Special statutory proceedings of a non-adversary nature in which these rules would by nature be clearly inapplicable.

(8) Small claims division. Proceedings in the small claims division of a county or municipal court.

**History:** Amended, eff 7-1-90; 7-1-96; 7-1-99.

## RULE 102. Purpose and Construction

The purpose of these rules is to provide procedures for the adjudication of causes to the end that the truth may be ascertained and proceedings justly determined. The principles of the common law of Ohio shall supplement the provisions of these rules, and the rules shall be construed to state the principles of the common law of Ohio unless the rule clearly indicates that a change is intended. These rules shall not supersede substantive statutory provisions.

**History:** Amended, eff 7-1-96.

## RULE 103. Rulings on Evidence

(A) **Effect of erroneous ruling.** Error may not be predicated upon a ruling which admits or excludes evidence unless a substantial right of the party is affected, and

(1) **Objection.** In case the ruling is one admitting evidence, timely objection or motion to strike appears of record stating the specific ground of objection, if the specific ground was not apparent from the context; or

(2) **Offer of proof.** In case the ruling is one excluding evidence, the substance of the evidence was made known to the court by offer or was apparent from the context within which questions were asked. Offer of proof is not necessary if evidence is excluded during cross-examination.

(B) **Record of offer and ruling.** At the time of making the ruling, the court may add any other or further statement which shows the character of the evidence, the form in which it was offered, the objection made, and the ruling thereon. It may direct the making of an offer in question and answer form.

(C) **Hearing of jury.** In jury cases, proceedings shall be conducted, to the extent practicable, so as to prevent inadmissible evidence from being suggested to the jury by any means, such as making statements or offers of proof or asking questions in the hearing of the jury.

(D) **Plain error.** Nothing in this rule precludes taking notice of plain errors affecting substantial rights although they were not brought to the attention of the court.

## RULE 104. Preliminary Questions

(A) **Questions of admissibility generally.** Preliminary questions concerning the qualification of a person to be a witness, the existence of a privilege, or the admissibility of evidence shall be determined by the court, subject to the provisions of subdivision (B). In making its determination it is not bound by the rules of evidence except those with respect to privileges.

(B) **Relevancy conditioned on fact.** When the relevancy of evidence depends upon the fulfillment of a condition of fact, the court shall admit it upon, or subject to, the introduction of evidence sufficient to support a finding of the fulfillment of the condition.

(C) **Hearing of jury.** Hearings on the admissibility of confessions shall in all cases be conducted out of the hearing of the jury. Hearings on other preliminary matters shall also be conducted out of the hearing of the jury when the interests of justice require.

(D) **Testimony by accused.** The accused does not, by testifying upon a preliminary matter, become subject to cross-examination as to other issues in the case.

(E) **Weight and credibility.** This rule does not limit the right of a party to introduce before the jury evidence relevant to weight or credibility.

**History:** Amended, eff 7-1-07.

## RULE 105. Limited Admissibility

When evidence which is admissible as to one party or for one purpose but not admissible as to another party or for another purpose is admitted, the court, upon request of a party, shall restrict the evidence to its proper scope and instruct the jury accordingly.

## RULE 106. Remainder of or Related Writings or Recorded Statements

When a writing or recorded statement or part thereof is introduced by a party, an adverse party may require the introduction at that time of any other part or any other writing or recorded statement which is otherwise admissible and which ought in fairness to be considered contemporaneously with it.

**History:** Amended, eff 7-1-07.

# ARTICLE II
# JUDICIAL NOTICE

## RULE 201. Judicial Notice of Adjudicative Facts

(A) **Scope of rule.** This rule governs only judicial notice of adjudicative facts; i.e., the facts of the case.

(B) **Kinds of facts.** A judicially noticed fact must be one not subject to reasonable dispute in that it is either (1) generally known within the territorial jurisdiction of the trial court or (2) capable of accurate and ready determination by resort to sources whose accuracy cannot reasonably be questioned.

(C) **When discretionary.** A court may take judicial notice, whether requested or not.

(D) **When mandatory.** A court shall take judicial notice if requested by a party and supplied with the necessary information.

(E) **Opportunity to be heard.** A party is entitled upon timely request to an opportunity to be heard as to the propriety of taking judicial notice and the tenor of the matter noticed. In the absence of prior notification, the request may be made after judicial notice has been taken.

(F) **Time of taking notice.** Judicial notice may be taken at any stage of the proceeding.

(G) **Instructing jury.** In a civil action or proceeding, the court shall instruct the jury to accept as conclusive any fact judicially noticed. In a criminal case, the court shall instruct the jury that it may, but is not required to, accept as conclusive any fact judicially noticed.

## ARTICLE III PRESUMPTIONS

### RULE 301. Presumptions in General in Civil Actions and Proceedings

In all civil actions and proceedings not otherwise provided for by statute enacted by the General Assembly or by these rules, a presumption imposes on the party against whom it is directed the burden of going forward with evidence to rebut or meet the presumption, but does not shift to such party the burden of proof in the sense of the risk of non-persuasion, which remains throughout the trial upon the party on whom it was originally cast.

### RULE 302. [Reserved]

## ARTICLE IV RELEVANCY AND ITS LIMITS

### RULE 401. Definition of "Relevant Evidence"

"Relevant evidence" means evidence having any tendency to make the existence of any fact that is of consequence to the determination of the action more probable or less probable than it would be without the evidence.

### RULE 402. Relevant Evidence Generally Admissible; Irrelevant Evidence Inadmissible

All relevant evidence is admissible, except as otherwise provided by the Constitution of the United States, by the Constitution of the State of Ohio, by statute enacted by the General Assembly not in conflict with a rule of the Supreme Court of Ohio, by these rules, or by other rules prescribed by the Supreme Court of Ohio. Evidence which is not relevant is not admissible.

### RULE 403. Exclusion of Relevant Evidence on Grounds of Prejudice, Confusion, or Undue Delay

(A) **Exclusion mandatory.** Although relevant, evidence is not admissible if its probative value is substantially outweighed by the danger of unfair prejudice, of confusion of the issues, or of misleading the jury.

(B) **Exclusion discretionary.** Although relevant, evidence may be excluded if its probative value is substantially outweighed by considerations of undue delay, or needless presentation of cumulative evidence.

**History:** Amended, eff 7-1-96.

### RULE 404. Character Evidence Not Admissible to Prove Conduct; Exceptions; Other Crimes

(A) **Character evidence generally.** Evidence of a person's character or a trait of character is not admissible for the purpose of proving action in conformity therewith on a particular occasion, subject to the following exceptions:

(1) Character of accused. Evidence of a pertinent trait of character offered by an accused, or by the prosecution to rebut the same is admissible; however, in prosecutions for rape, gross sexual imposition, and prostitution, the exceptions provided by statute enacted by the General Assembly are applicable.

(2) Character of victim. Evidence of a pertinent trait of character of the victim of the crime offered by an accused, or by the prosecution to rebut the same, or evidence of a character trait of peacefulness of the victim offered by the prosecution in a homicide case to rebut evidence that the victim was the first aggressor is admissible; however, in prosecutions for rape, gross sexual imposition, and prostitution, the exceptions provided by statute enacted by the General Assembly are applicable.

(3) Character of witness. Evidence of the character of a witness on the issue of credibility is admissible as provided in Rules 607, 608, and 609.

(B) **Other crimes, wrongs or acts.** Evidence of other crimes, wrongs, or acts is not admissible to prove the character of a person in order to show action in conformity therewith. It may, however, be admissible for other purposes, such as proof of motive, opportunity, intent, preparation, plan, knowledge, identity, or absence of mistake or accident.

**History:** Amended, eff 7-1-07.

### RULE 405. Methods of Proving Character

(A) **Reputation or opinion.** In all cases in which evidence of character or a trait of character of a person is admissible, proof may be made by testimony as to reputation or by testimony in the form of an opinion. On cross-examination, inquiry is allowable into relevant specific instances of conduct.

(B) **Specific instances of conduct.** In cases in which character or a trait of character of a person is an essential element of a charge, claim, or defense, proof may also be made of specific instances of his conduct.

### RULE 406. Habit; Routine Practice

Evidence of the habit of a person or of the routine

practice of an organization, whether corroborated or not and regardless of the presence of eyewitnesses, is relevant to prove that the conduct of the person or organization on a particular occasion was in conformity with the habit or routine practice.

### RULE 407. Subsequent Remedial Measures

When, after an injury or harm allegedly caused by an event, measures are taken which, if taken previously, would have made the injury or harm less likely to occur, evidence of the subsequent measures is not admissible to prove negligence or culpable conduct in connection with the event. This rule does not require the exclusion of evidence of subsequent measures when offered for another purpose, such as proving ownership, control, or feasibility of precautionary measures, if controverted, or impeachment.

**History:** Amended, eff 7-1-00.

### RULE 408. Compromise and Offers to Compromise

Evidence of (1) furnishing or offering or promising to furnish, or (2) accepting or offering or promising to accept, a valuable consideration in compromising or attempting to compromise a claim which was disputed as to either validity or amount, is not admissible to prove liability for or invalidity of the claim or its amount. Evidence of conduct or statements made in compromise negotiations is likewise not admissible. This rule does not require the exclusion of any evidence otherwise discoverable merely because it is presented in the course of compromise negotiations. This rule also does not require exclusion when the evidence is offered for another purpose, such as proving bias or prejudice of a witness, negativing a contention of undue delay, or proving an effort to obstruct a criminal investigation or prosecution.

### RULE 409. Payment of Medical and Similar Expenses

Evidence of furnishing or offering or promising to pay medical, hospital, or similar expenses occasioned by an injury is not admissible to prove liability for the injury.

### RULE 410. Inadmissibility of Pleas, Offers of Pleas, and Related Statements

(A) Except as provided in division (B) of this rule, evidence of the following is not admissible in any civil or criminal proceeding against the defendant who made the plea or who was a participant personally or through counsel in the plea discussions:

(1) A plea of guilty that later was withdrawn;

(2) A plea of no contest or the equivalent plea from another jurisdiction;

(3) A plea of guilty in a violations bureau;

(4) Any statement made in the course of any proceedings under Rule 11 of the Rules of Criminal Procedure or equivalent procedure from another jurisdiction regarding the foregoing pleas;

(5) Any statement made in the course of plea discussions in which counsel for the prosecuting authority or for the defendant was a participant and that do not result in a plea of guilty or that result in a plea of guilty later withdrawn.

(B) A statement otherwise inadmissible under this rule is admissible in either of the following:

(1) Any proceeding in which another statement made in the course of the same plea or plea discussions has been introduced and the statement should, in fairness, be considered contemporaneously with it;

(2) A criminal proceeding for perjury or false statement if the statement was made by the defendant under oath, on the record, and in the presence of counsel.

**History:** Amended, eff 7-1-91.

### RULE 411. Liability Insurance

Evidence that a person was or was not insured against liability is not admissible upon the issue whether the person acted negligently or otherwise wrongfully. This rule does not require the exclusion of evidence of insurance against liability when offered for another purpose, such as proof of agency, ownership or control, if controverted, or bias or prejudice of a witness.

**History:** Amended, eff 7-1-07.

## ARTICLE V PRIVILEGES

### RULE 501. General Rule

The privilege of a witness, person, state or political subdivision thereof shall be governed by statute enacted by the General Assembly or by principles of common law as interpreted by the courts of this state in the light of reason and experience.

## ARTICLE VI WITNESSES

### RULE 601. General Rule of Competency

Every person is competent to be a witness except:

(A) Those of unsound mind, and children under ten years of age, who appear incapable of receiving just impressions of the facts and transactions respecting which they are examined, or of relating them truly.

(B) A spouse testifying against the other spouse charged with a crime except when either of the following applies:

(1) A crime against the testifying spouse or a child of either spouse is charged;

(2) The testifying spouse elects to testify.

(C) An officer, while on duty for the exclusive or main purpose of enforcing traffic laws, arresting or assisting in the arrest of a person charged with a traffic violation punishable as a misdemeanor where the officer at the time of the arrest was not using a properly marked motor vehicle as defined by statute or was not wearing a legally distinctive uniform as defined by statute.

(D) A person giving expert testimony on the issue of liability in any claim asserted in any civil action against a physician, podiatrist, or hospital arising out of the diagnosis, care, or treatment of any person by a physician or podiatrist, unless the person testifying is licensed to practice medicine and surgery, osteopathic medicine and surgery, or podiatric medicine and surgery by the state medical board or by the licensing authority of any state, and unless the person devotes at least one-half of his or her professional time to the active clinical practice in his or her field of licensure, or to its instruction in an accredited school. This division shall not prohibit other medical professionals who otherwise are competent to testify under these rules from giving expert testimony on the appropriate standard of care in their own profession in any claim asserted in any civil action against a physician, podiatrist, medical professional, or hospital arising out of the diagnosis, care, or treatment of any person.

(E) As otherwise provided in these rules.

**History:** Amended, eff 7-1-91.

## RULE 602. Lack of Personal Knowledge

A witness may not testify to a matter unless evidence is introduced sufficient to support a finding that the witness has personal knowledge of the matter. Evidence to prove personal knowledge may, but need not, consist of the witness' own testimony. This rule is subject to the provisions of Rule 703, relating to opinion testimony by expert witnesses.

**History:** Amended, eff 7-1-07.

## RULE 603. Oath or Affirmation

Before testifying, every witness shall be required to declare that the witness will testify truthfully, by oath or affirmation administered in a form calculated to awaken the witness' conscience and impress the witness' mind with the duty to do so.

**History:** Amended, eff 7-1-07.

## RULE 604. Interpreters

An interpreter is subject to the provisions of these rules relating to qualification as an expert and the administration of an oath or affirmation to make a true translation.

**History:** Amended, eff 7-1-07.

## RULE 605. Competency of Judge as Witness

The judge presiding at the trial may not testify in that trial as a witness. No objection need be made in order to preserve the point.

## RULE 606. Competency of Juror as Witness

(A) **At the trial.** A member of the jury may not testify as a witness before that jury in the trial of the case in which the juror is sitting. If the juror is called so to testify, the opposing party shall be afforded an opportunity to object out of the presence of the jury.

(B) **Inquiry into validity of verdict or indictment.** Upon an inquiry into the validity of a verdict or indictment, a juror may not testify as to any matter or statement occurring during the course of the jury's deliberations or to the effect of anything upon that or any other juror's mind or emotions as influencing the juror to assent to or dissent from the verdict or indictment or concerning the juror's mental processes in connection therewith. A juror may testify on the question whether extraneous prejudicial information was improperly brought to the jury's attention or whether any outside influence was improperly brought to bear on any juror, only after some outside evidence of that act or event has been presented. However a juror may testify without the presentation of any outside evidence concerning any threat, any bribe, any attempted threat or bribe, or any improprieties of any officer of the court. A juror's affidavit or evidence of any statement by the juror concerning a matter about which the juror would be precluded from testifying will not be received for these purposes.

**History:** Amended, eff 7-1-07.

## RULE 607. Impeachment

(A) **Who May Impeach.** The credibility of a witness may be attacked by any party except that the credibility of a witness may be attacked by the party calling the witness by means of a prior inconsistent statement only upon a showing of surprise and affirmative damage. This exception does not apply to statements admitted pursuant to Evid. R. 801(D)(1)(a), 801(D)(2), or 803.

(B) **Impeachment: reasonable basis.** A questioner must have a reasonable basis for asking any question pertaining to impeachment that implies the existence of an impeaching fact.

**History:** Amended, eff 7-1-98.

## RULE 608. Evidence of Character and Conduct of Witness

(A) **Opinion and reputation evidence of character.** The credibility of a witness may be attacked or supported by evidence in the form of opinion or reputation, but subject to these limitations: (1) the evidence may refer only to character for truthfulness or untruthfulness, and (2) evidence of truthful character is admissible only after the character of the witness for truthfulness has been attacked by opinion or reputation evidence or otherwise.

(B) **Specific instances of conduct.** Specific instances of the conduct of a witness, for the purpose of attacking or supporting the witness's character for truthfulness, other than conviction of crime as provided in Evid.R. 609, may not be proved by extrinsic evidence. They may, however, in the discretion of the court, if clearly probative of truthfulness or untruthfulness, be inquired into on cross-examination of the witness (1) concerning the witness's character for truthfulness or untruthfulness, or (2) concerning the character for truthfulness or untruthfulness of another witness as to which character the witness being cross-examined has testified.

The giving of testimony by any witness, including an accused, does not operate as a waiver of the witness's privilege against self-incrimination when examined with respect to matters that relate only to the witness's character for truthfulness.

**History:** Amended, eff 7-1-92.

## RULE 609. Impeachment by Evidence of Conviction of Crime

(A) **General rule.** For the purpose of attacking the credibility of a witness:

(1) Subject to Evid. R. 403, evidence that a witness other than the accused has been convicted of a crime is admissible if the crime was punishable by death or imprisonment in excess of one year pursuant to the law under which the witness was convicted.

(2) Notwithstanding Evid. R. 403(A), but subject to Evid. R. 403(B), evidence that the accused has been convicted of a crime is admissible if the crime was punishable by death or imprisonment in excess of one year pursuant to the law under which the accused was convicted and if the court determines that the probative value of the evidence outweighs the danger of unfair prejudice, of confusion of the issues, or of misleading the jury.

(3) Notwithstanding Evid. R. 403(A), but subject to Evid. R. 403(B), evidence that any witness, including an accused, has been convicted of a crime is admissible if the crime involved dishonesty or false statement, regardless of the punishment and whether based upon state or federal statute or local ordinance.

(B) **Time limit.** Evidence of a conviction under this rule is not admissible if a period of more than ten years has elapsed since the date of the conviction or of the release of the witness from the confinement, or the termination of community control sanctions, post-release control, or probation, shock probation, parole, or shock parole imposed for that conviction, whichever is the later date, unless the court determines, in the interests of justice, that the probative value of the conviction supported by specific facts and circumstances substantially outweighs its prejudicial effect. However, evidence of a conviction more than ten years old as calculated herein, is not admissible unless the proponent gives to the adverse party sufficient advance written notice of intent to use such evidence to provide the adverse party with a fair opportunity to contest the use of such evidence.

(C) **Effect of pardon, annulment, expungement, or certificate of rehabilitation.** Evidence of a conviction is not admissible under this rule if (1) the conviction has been the subject of a pardon, annulment, expungement, certificate of rehabilitation, or other equivalent procedure based on a finding of the rehabilitation of the person convicted, and that person has not been convicted of a subsequent crime which was punishable by death or imprisonment in excess of one year, or (2) the conviction has been the subject of a pardon, annulment, expungement, or other equivalent procedure based on a finding of innocence.

(D) **Juvenile adjudication.** Evidence of juvenile adjudications is not admissible except as provided by statute enacted by the General Assembly.

(E) **Pendency of appeal.** The pendency of an appeal therefrom does not render evidence of a conviction inadmissible. Evidence of the pendency of an appeal is admissible.

(F) **Methods of proof.** When evidence of a witness's conviction of a crime is admissible under this rule, the fact of the conviction may be proved only by the testimony of the witness on direct or cross-examination, or by public record shown to the witness during his or her examination. If the witness denies that he or she is the person to whom the public record refers, the court may permit the introduction of additional evidence tending to establish that the witness is or is not the person to whom the public record refers.

**History:** Amended, eff 7-1-91; 7-1-03.

## RULE 610. Religious Beliefs or Opinions

Evidence of the beliefs or opinions of a witness on matters of religion is not admissible for the purpose of showing that by reason of their nature the witness' credibility is impaired or enhanced.

**History:** Amended, eff 7-1-07.

## RULE 611. Mode and Order of Interrogation and Presentation

(A) **Control by court.** The court shall exercise reasonable control over the mode and order of interrogating witnesses and presenting evidence so as to (1) make the interrogation and presentation effective for the ascertainment of the truth, (2) avoid needless consumption of time, and (3) protect witnesses from harassment or undue embarrassment.

(B) **Scope of cross-examination.** Cross-examination shall be permitted on all relevant matters and matters affecting credibility.

(C) **Leading questions.** Leading questions should not be used on the direct examination of a witness except as may be necessary to develop the witness' testimony. Ordinarily leading questions should be permitted on cross-examination. When a party calls a hostile witness, an adverse party, or a witness identified with an adverse party, interrogation may be by leading questions.

**History:** Amended, eff 7-1-07.

## RULE 612. Writing Used to Refresh Memory

If a witness uses a writing to refresh memory for the purpose of testifying, either: (1) while testifying; or (2) before testifying, if the court in its discretion determines it is necessary in the interests of justice, an adverse party is entitled to have the writing produced at the hearing. The adverse party is also entitled to inspect it, to cross-examine the witness thereon, and to introduce in evidence those portions which relate to the testimony of the witness. If it is claimed that the writing contains matters not related to the subject matter of the testimony the court shall examine the writing in camera, excise any portions not so related, and order delivery of the remainder to the party entitled thereto. Any portion withheld over objections shall be preserved and made available to the appellate court in the event of an appeal. If a writing is not produced or delivered pursuant to order under this rule, the court shall make any order justice requires, except that in criminal cases when the prosecution elects not to comply, the order shall be one striking the testimony or, if the court in its discretion determines that the interests of justice so require, declaring a mistrial.

**History:** Amended, eff 7-1-07; 7-1-11.

## RULE 613. Impeachment by Self-Contradiction

(A) **Examining witness concerning prior statement.** In examining a witness concerning a prior statement made by the witness, whether written or not, the statement need not be shown nor its contents disclosed to the witness at that time, but on request the same shall be shown or disclosed to opposing counsel.

(B) **Extrinsic evidence of prior inconsistent statement of witness.** Extrinsic evidence of a prior inconsistent statement by a witness is admissible if both of the following apply:

(1) If the statement is offered solely for the purpose of impeaching the witness, the witness is afforded a prior opportunity to explain or deny the statement and the

opposite party is afforded an opportunity to interrogate the witness on the statement or the interests of justice otherwise require;

(2) The subject matter of the statement is one of the following:

(a) A fact that is of consequence to the determination of the action other than the credibility of a witness;

(b) A fact that may be shown by extrinsic evidence under Evid. R. 608(A), 609, 616(A), 616(B) or 706;

(c) A fact that may be shown by extrinsic evidence under the common law of impeachment if not in conflict with the Rules of Evidence.

(C) **Prior inconsistent conduct.** During examination of a witness, conduct of the witness inconsistent with the witness's testimony may be shown to impeach. If offered for the sole purpose of impeaching the witness's testimony, extrinsic evidence of the prior inconsistent conduct is admissible under the same circumstances as provided for prior inconsistent statements by Evid. R. 613(B)(2).

**History:** Amended, eff 7-1-98.

### RULE 614. Calling and Interrogation of Witnesses by Court

(A) **Calling by court.** The court may, on its own motion or at the suggestion of a party, call witnesses, and all parties are entitled to cross-examine witnesses thus called.

(B) **Interrogation by court.** The court may interrogate witnesses, in an impartial manner, whether called by itself or by a party.

(C) **Objections.** Objections to the calling of witnesses by the court or to interrogation by it may be made at the time or at the next available opportunity when the jury is not present.

### RULE 615. Separation and Exclusion of Witnesses

(A) Except as provided in division (B) of this rule, at the request of a party the court shall order witnesses excluded so that they cannot hear the testimony of other witnesses, and it may make the order of its own motion. An order directing the 'exclusion' or 'separation' of witnesses or the like, in general terms without specification of other or additional limitations, is effective only to require the exclusion of witnesses from the hearing during the testimony of other witnesses.

(B) This rule does not authorize exclusion of any of the following persons from the hearing:

(1) a party who is a natural person;

(2) an officer or employee of a party that is not a natural person designated as its representative by its attorney;

(3) a person whose presence is shown by a party to be essential to the presentation of the party's cause;

(4) in a criminal proceeding, a victim of the charged offense to the extent that the victim's presence is authorized by statute enacted by the General Assembly. As used in this rule, "victim" has the same meaning as in the provisions of the Ohio Constitution providing rights for victims of crimes.

**History:** Amended, eff 7-1-01; 7-1-03.

### RULE 616. Methods of Impeachment

In addition to other methods, a witness may be impeached by any of the following methods:

(A) **Bias.** Bias, prejudice, interest, or any motive to misrepresent may be shown to impeach the witness either by examination of the witness or by extrinsic evidence.

(B) **Sensory or mental defect.** A defect of capacity, ability, or opportunity to observe, remember, or relate may be shown to impeach the witness either by examination of the witness or by extrinsic evidence.

(C) **Specific contradiction.** Facts contradicting a witness's testimony may be shown for the purpose of impeaching the witness's testimony. If offered for the sole purpose of impeaching a witness's testimony, extrinsic evidence of contradiction is inadmissible unless the evidence is one of the following:

(1) Permitted by Evid. R. 608(A), 609, 613, 616(A), 616(B), or 706;

(2) Permitted by the common law of impeachment and not in conflict with the Rules of Evidence.

**History:** Effective 7-1-91; amended, eff 7-1-98.

## ARTICLE VII
## OPINIONS AND EXPERT TESTIMONY

### RULE 701. Opinion Testimony by Lay Witnesses

If the witness is not testifying as an expert, the witness' testimony in the form of opinions or inferences is limited to those opinions or inferences which are (1) rationally based on the perception of the witness and (2) helpful to a clear understanding of the witness' testimony or the determination of a fact in issue.

**History:** Amended, eff 7-1-07.

### RULE 702. Testimony by Experts

A witness may testify as an expert if all of the following apply:

(A) The witness' testimony either relates to matters beyond the knowledge or experience possessed by lay persons or dispels a misconception common among lay persons;

(B) The witness is qualified as an expert by specialized knowledge, skill, experience, training, or education regarding the subject matter of the testimony;

(C) The witness' testimony is based on reliable scientific, technical, or other specialized information. To the extent that the testimony reports the result of a procedure, test, or experiment, the testimony is reliable only if all of the following apply:

(1) The theory upon which the procedure, test, or experiment is based is objectively verifiable or is validly derived from widely accepted knowledge, facts, or principles;

(2) The design of the procedure, test, or experiment reliably implements the theory;

(3) The particular procedure, test, or experiment was conducted in a way that will yield an accurate result.

**History:** Amended, eff 7-1-94.

### RULE 703. Bases of Opinion Testimony by Experts

The facts or data in the particular case upon which an expert bases an opinion or inference may be those perceived by the expert or admitted in evidence at the hearing.

**History:** Amended, eff 7-1-07.

### RULE 704. Opinion on Ultimate Issue

Testimony in the form of an opinion or inference otherwise admissible is not objectionable solely because it embraces an ultimate issue to be decided by the trier of fact.

### RULE 705. Disclosure of Facts or Data Underlying Expert Opinion

The expert may testify in terms of opinion or inference and give the expert's reasons therefor after disclosure of the underlying facts or data. The disclosure may be in response to a hypothetical question or otherwise.

**History:** Amended, eff 7-1-07.

### RULE 706. Repealed

## ARTICLE VIII HEARSAY

### RULE 801. Definitions

The following definitions apply under this article:

(A) **Statement.** A "statement" is (1) an oral or written assertion or (2) nonverbal conduct of a person, if it is intended by the person as an assertion.

(B) **Declarant.** A "declarant" is a person who makes a statement.

(C) **Hearsay.** "Hearsay" is a statement, other than one made by the declarant while testifying at the trial or hearing, offered in evidence to prove the truth of the matter asserted.

(D) **Statements which are not hearsay.** A statement is not hearsay if:

(1) **Prior statement by witness.** The declarant testifies at trial or hearing and is subject to cross-examination concerning the statement, and the statement is (a) inconsistent with declarant's testimony, and was given under oath subject to cross-examination by the party against whom the statement is offered and subject to the penalty of perjury at a trial, hearing, or other proceeding, or in a deposition, or (b) consistent with declarant's testimony and is offered to rebut an express or implied charge against declarant of recent fabrication or improper influence or motive, or (c) one of identification of a person soon after perceiving the person, if the circumstances demonstrate the reliability of the prior identification.

(2) **Admission by party-opponent.** The statement is offered against a party and is (a) the party's own statement, in either an individual or a representative capacity, or (b) a statement of which the party has manifested an adoption or belief in its truth, or (c) a statement by a person authorized by the party to make a statement concerning the subject, or (d) a statement by the party's agent or servant concerning a matter within the scope of the agency or employment, made during the existence of the relationship, or (e) a statement by a co-conspirator of a party during the course and in furtherance of the conspiracy upon independent proof of the conspiracy.

**History:** Amended, eff 7-1-07.

### RULE 802. Hearsay Rule

Hearsay is not admissible except as otherwise provided by the Constitution of the United States, by the Constitution of the State of Ohio, by statute enacted by the General Assembly not in conflict with a rule of the Supreme Court of Ohio, by these rules, or by other rules prescribed by the Supreme Court of Ohio.

### RULE 803. Hearsay Exceptions; Availability of Declarant Immaterial

The following are not excluded by the hearsay rule, even though the declarant is available as a witness:

(1) **Present sense impression.** A statement describing or explaining an event or condition made while the declarant was perceiving the event or condition, or immediately thereafter unless circumstances indicate lack of trustworthiness.

(2) **Excited utterance.** A statement relating to a startling event or condition made while the declarant was under the stress of excitement caused by the event or condition.

(3) **Then existing, mental, emotional, or physical condition.** A statement of the declarant's then existing state of mind, emotion, sensation, or physical condition (such as intent, plan, motive, design, mental feeling, pain, and bodily health), but not including a statement of memory or belief to prove the fact remembered or believed unless it relates to the execution, revocation, identification, or terms of declarant's will.

(4) **Statements for purposes of medical diagnosis or treatment.** Statements made for purposes of medical diagnosis or treatment and describing medical history, or past or present symptoms, pain, or sensations, or the inception or general character of the cause or external source thereof insofar as reasonably pertinent to diagnosis or treatment.

(5) **Recorded recollection.** A memorandum or record concerning a matter about which a witness once had knowledge but now has insufficient recollection to enable him to testify fully and accurately, shown by the testimony of the witness to have been made or adopted when the matter was fresh in his memory and to reflect that knowledge correctly. If admitted, the memorandum or record may be read into evidence but may not itself be received as an exhibit unless offered by an adverse party.

(6) **Records of regularly conducted activity.** A memorandum, report, record, or data compilation, in any form, of acts, events, or conditions, made at or near the time by, or from information transmitted by, a person with knowledge, if kept in the course of a regularly conducted business activity, and if it was the regular practice of that business activity to make the memorandum, report, record, or data compilation, all as shown by the testimony of the custodian or other qualified witness or as provided by Rule 901(B)(10), unless the source of information or the method or circumstances of preparation indicate lack of trustworthiness. The term "business" as used in this paragraph includes business, institution, association, profession, occupation, and calling of every kind, whether or not conducted for profit.

(7) **Absence of entry in record kept in accordance with the provisions of paragraph (6).** Evidence that a matter is not included in the memoranda, reports, records, or data compilations, in any form, kept in accordance with the provisions of paragraph (6), to prove the nonoccur-

rence or nonexistence of the matter, if the matter was of a kind of which a memorandum, report, record, or data compilation was regularly made and preserved, unless the sources of information or other circumstances indicate lack of trustworthiness.

(8) **Public records and reports.** Records, reports, statements, or data compilations, in any form, of public offices or agencies, setting forth (a) the activities of the office or agency, or (b) matters observed pursuant to duty imposed by law as to which matters there was a duty to report, excluding, however, in criminal cases matters observed by police officers and other law enforcement personnel, unless offered by defendant, unless the sources of information or other circumstances indicate lack of trustworthiness.

(9) **Records of vital statistics.** Records or data compilations, in any form, of births, fetal deaths, deaths, or marriages, if the report thereof was made to a public office pursuant to requirement of law.

(10) **Absence of public record or entry.** To prove the absence of a record, report, statement, or data compilation, in any form, or the nonoccurrence or nonexistence of a matter of which a record, report, statement, or data compilation, in any form, was regularly made and preserved by a public office or agency, evidence in the form of a certification in accordance with Rule 901(B)(10) or testimony, that diligent search failed to disclose the record, report, statement, or data compilation, or entry.

(11) **Records of religious organizations.** Statements of births, marriages, divorces, deaths, legitimacy, ancestry, relationship by blood or marriage, or other similar facts of personal or family history, contained in a regularly kept record of a religious organization.

(12) **Marriage, baptismal, and similar certificates.** Statements of fact contained in a certificate that the maker performed a marriage or other ceremony or administered a sacrament, made by a clergyman, public official, or other person authorized by the rules or practices of a religious organization or by law to perform the act certified, and purporting to have been issued at the time of the act or within a reasonable time thereafter.

(13) **Family Records.** Statements of fact concerning personal or family history contained in family Bibles, genealogies, charts, engravings on rings, inscriptions on family portraits, engravings on urns, crypts, or tombstones, or the like.

(14) **Records of documents affecting an interest in property.** The record of a document purporting to establish or affect an interest in property, as proof of the content of the original recorded document and its execution and delivery by each person by whom it purports to have been executed, if the record is a record of a public office and an applicable statute authorizes the recording of documents of that kind in that office.

(15) **Statements in documents affecting an interest in property.** A statement contained in a document purporting to establish or affect an interest in property if the matter stated was relevant to the purpose of the document, unless dealings with the property since the document was made have been inconsistent with the truth of the statement or the purport of the document.

(16) **Statements in ancient documents.** Statements in a document in existence twenty years or more the authenticity of which is established.

(17) **Market reports, commercial publications.** Market quotations, tabulations, lists, directories, or other published compilations, generally used and relied upon by the public or by persons in particular occupations.

(18) **Learned Treatises.** To the extent called to the attention of an expert witness upon cross-examination or relied upon by the expert witness in direct examination, statements contained in published treatises, periodicals, or pamphlets on a subject of history, medicine, or other science or art, established as a reliable authority by the testimony or admission of the witness or by other expert testimony or by judicial notice. If admitted, the statements may be read into evidence but may not be received as exhibits.

(19) **Reputation concerning personal or family history.** Reputation among members of the declarant's family by blood, adoption, or marriage or among the declarant's associates, or in the community, concerning a person's birth, adoption, marriage, divorce, death, legitimacy, relationship by blood, adoption or marriage, ancestry, or other similar fact of the declarant's personal or family history.

(20) **Reputation concerning boundaries or general history.** Reputation in a community, arising before the controversy, as to boundaries of or customs affecting lands in the community, and reputation as to events of general history important to the community or state or nation in which located.

(21) **Reputation as to character.** Reputation of a person's character among the person's associates or in the community.

(22) **Judgment of previous conviction.** Evidence of a final judgment, entered after a trial or upon a plea of guilty (but not upon a plea of no contest or the equivalent plea from another jurisdiction), adjudging a person guilty of a crime punishable by death or imprisonment in excess of one year, to prove any fact essential to sustain the judgment, but not including, when offered by the Government in a criminal prosecution for purposes other than impeachment, judgments against persons other than the accused. The pendency of an appeal may be shown but does not affect admissibility.

(23) **Judgment as to personal, family, or general history, or boundaries.** Judgments as proof of matters of personal, family or general history, or boundaries, essential to the judgment, if the same would be provable by evidence of reputation.

**History** Effective: July 1, 1980; amended effective July 1, 2006; July 1, 2007.

## RULE 804. Hearsay Exceptions; Declarant Unavailable

(A) **Definition of unavailability.** "Unavailability as a witness" includes any of the following situations in which the declarant:

(1) is exempted by ruling of the court on the ground of privilege from testifying concerning the subject matter of the declarant's statement;

(2) persists in refusing to testify concerning the subject matter of the declarant's statement despite an order of the court to do so;

(3) testifies to a lack of memory of the subject matter of the declarant's statement;

(4) is unable to be present or to testify at the hearing because of death or then-existing physical or mental illness or infirmity;

(5) is absent from the hearing and the proponent of the declarant's statement has been unable to procure the declarant's attendance (or in the case of a hearsay excep-

tion under division (B)(2), (3), or (4) of this rule, the declarant's attendance or testimony) by process or other reasonable means.

A declarant is not unavailable as a witness if the declarant's exemption, refusal, claim of lack of memory, inability, or absence is due to the procurement or wrongdoing of the proponent of the declarant's statement for the purpose of preventing the witness from attending or testifying.

(B) **Hearsay exceptions.** The following are not excluded by the hearsay rule if the declarant is unavailable as a witness:

(1) **Former testimony.** Testimony given as a witness at another hearing of the same or a different proceeding, or in a deposition taken in compliance with law in the course of the same or another proceeding, if the party against whom the testimony is now offered, or, in a civil action or proceeding, a predecessor in interest, had an opportunity and similar motive to develop the testimony by direct, cross, or redirect examination. Testimony given at a preliminary hearing must satisfy the right to confrontation and exhibit indicia of reliability.

(2) **Statement under belief of impending death.** In a prosecution for homicide or in a civil action or proceeding, a statement made by a declarant, while believing that his or her death was imminent, concerning the cause or circumstances of what the declarant believed to be his or her impending death.

(3) **Statement against interest.** A statement that was at the time of its making so far contrary to the declarant's pecuniary or proprietary interest, or so far tended to subject the declarant to civil or criminal liability, or to render invalid a claim by the declarant against another, that a reasonable person in the declarant's position would not have made the statement unless the declarant believed it to be true. A statement tending to expose the declarant to criminal liability, whether offered to exculpate or inculpate the accused, is not admissible unless corroborating circumstances clearly indicate the truthworthiness of the statement.

(4) **Statement of personal or family history.** (a) A statement concerning the declarant's own birth, adoption, marriage, divorce, legitimacy, relationship by blood, adoption, or marriage, ancestry, or other similar fact of personal or family history, even though the declarant had no means of acquiring personal knowledge of the matter stated; or (b) a statement concerning the foregoing matters, and death also, of another person, if the declarant was related to the other by blood, adoption, or marriage or was so intimately associated with the other's family as to be likely to have accurate information concerning the matter declared.

(5) **Statement by a deceased or incompetent person.** The statement was made by a decedent or a mentally incompetent person, where all of the following apply:

(a) the estate or personal representative of the decedent's estate or the guardian or trustee of the incompetent person is a party;

(b) the statement was made before the death or the development of the incompetency;

(c) the statement is offered to rebut testimony by an adverse party on a matter within the knowledge of the decedent or incompetent person.

(6) **Forfeiture by wrongdoing.** A statement offered against a party if the unavailability of the witness is due to the wrongdoing of the party for the purpose of preventing the witness from attending or testifying. However, a statement is not admissible under this rule unless the proponent has given to each adverse party advance written notice of an intention to introduce the statement sufficient to provide the adverse party a fair opportunity to contest the admissibility of the statement.

**History:** Amended, eff 7-1-81; 7-1-93; 7-1-01.

## RULE 805. Hearsay Within Hearsay

Hearsay included within hearsay is not excluded under the hearsay rule if each part of the combined statements conforms with an exception to the hearsay rule provided in these rules.

## RULE 806. Attacking and Supporting Credibility of Declarant

(A) When a hearsay statement, or a statement defined in Evid. R. 801(D)(2), (c), (d), or (e), has been admitted in evidence, the credibility of the declarant may be attacked, and if attacked may be supported, by any evidence that would be admissible for those purposes if declarant had testified as a witness.

(B) Evidence of a statement or conduct by the declarant at any time, inconsistent with the declarant's hearsay statement, is not subject to any requirement that the declarant may have been afforded an opportunity to deny or explain.

(C) Evidence of a declarant's prior conviction is not subject to any requirement that the declarant be shown a public record.

(D) If the party against whom a hearsay statement has been admitted calls the declarant as a witness, the party is entitled to examine the declarant on the statement as if under cross-examination.

**History:** Amended, eff 7-1-98.

## RULE 807. Hearsay Exceptions; Child Statements in Abuse Cases

(A) An out-of-court statement made by a child who is under twelve years of age at the time of trial or hearing describing any sexual act performed by, with, or on the child or describing any act of physical violence directed against the child is not excluded as hearsay under Evid. R. 802 if all of the following apply:

(1) The court finds that the totality of the circumstances surrounding the making of the statement provides particularized guarantees of trustworthiness that make the statement at least as reliable as statements admitted pursuant to Evid. R. 803 and 804. The circumstances must establish that the child was particularly likely to be telling the truth when the statement was made and that the test of cross-examination would add little to the reliability of the statement. In making its determination of the reliability of the statement, the court shall consider all of the circumstances surrounding the making of the statement, including but not limited to spontaneity, the internal consistency of the statement, the mental state of the child, the child's motive or lack of motive to fabricate, the child's use of terminology unexpected of a child of similar age, the means by which the statement was elicited, and the lapse of time between the act and the statement. In making this

determination, the court shall not consider whether there is independent proof of the sexual act or act of physical violence.

(2) The child's testimony is not reasonably obtainable by the proponent of the statement.

(3) There is independent proof of the sexual act or act of physical violence.

(4) At least ten days before the trial or hearing, a proponent of the statement has notified all other parties in writing of the content of the statement, the time and place at which the statement was made, the identity of the witness who is to testify about the statement, and the circumstances surrounding the statement that are claimed to indicate its trustworthiness.

(B) The child's testimony is "not reasonably obtainable by the proponent of the statement" under division (A)(2) of this rule only if one or more of the following apply:

(1) The child refuses to testify concerning the subject matter of the statement or claims a lack of memory of the subject matter of the statement after a person trusted by the child, in the presence of the court, urges the child to both describe the acts described by the statement and to testify.

(2) The court finds all of the following:

(a) The child is absent from the trial or hearing;

(b) The proponent of the statement has been unable to procure the child's attendance or testimony by process or other reasonable means despite a good faith effort to do so;

(c) It is probable that the proponent would be unable to procure the child's testimony or attendance if the trial or hearing were delayed for a reasonable time.

(3) The court finds both of the following:

(a) The child is unable to testify at the trial or hearing because of death or then existing physical or mental illness or infirmity;

(b) The illness or infirmity would not improve sufficiently to permit the child to testify if the trial or hearing were delayed for a reasonable time.

The proponent of the statement has not established that the child's testimony or attendance is not reasonably obtainable if the child's refusal, claim of lack of memory, inability, or absence is due to the procurement or wrongdoing of the proponent of the statement for the purpose of preventing the child from attending or testifying.

(C) The court shall make the findings required by this rule on the basis of a hearing conducted outside the presence of the jury and shall make findings of fact, on the record, as to the bases for its ruling.

**History:** Effective 7-1-91.

# ARTICLE IX AUTHENTICATION AND IDENTIFICATION

## RULE 901. Requirement of Authentication or Identification

(A) **General provision.** The requirement of authentication or identification as a condition precedent to admissibility is satisfied by evidence sufficient to support a finding that the matter in question is what its proponent claims.

(B) **Illustrations.** By way of illustration only, and not by way of limitation, the following are examples of authentication or identification conforming with the requirements of this rule:

(1) **Testimony of witness with knowledge.** Testimony that a matter is what it is claimed to be.

(2) **Nonexpert opinion on handwriting.** Nonexpert opinion as to the genuineness of handwriting, based upon familiarity not acquired for purposes of the litigation.

(3) **Comparison by trier or expert witness.** Comparison by the trier of fact or by expert witness with specimens which have been authenticated.

(4) **Distinctive characteristics and the like.** Appearance, contents, substance, internal patterns, or other distinctive characteristics, taken in conjunction with circumstances.

(5) **Voice identification.** Identification of a voice, whether heard firsthand or through mechanical or electronic transmission or recording, by opinion based upon hearing the voice at any time under circumstances connecting it with the alleged speaker.

(6) **Telephone conversation.** Telephone conversations, by evidence that a call was made to the number assigned at the time by the telephone company to a particular person or business, if (a) in the case of a person, circumstances, including self-identification, show the person answering to be the one called, or (b) in the case of a business, the call was made to a place of business and the conversation related to business reasonably transacted over the telephone.

(7) **Public records or reports.** Evidence that a writing authorized by law to be recorded or filed and in fact recorded or filed in a public office, or a purported public record, report, statement, or data compilation, in any form, is from the public office where items of this nature are kept.

(8) **Ancient documents or data compilation.** Evidence that a document or data compilation, in any form, (a) is in such condition as to create no suspicion concerning its authenticity, (b) was in a place where it, if authentic, would likely be, and (c) has been in existence twenty years or more at the time it is offered.

(9) **Process or system.** Evidence describing a process or system used to produce a result and showing that the process or system produces an accurate result.

(10) **Methods provided by statute or rule.** Any method of authentication or identification provided by statute enacted by the General Assembly not in conflict with a rule of the Supreme Court of Ohio or by other rules prescribed by the Supreme Court.

## RULE 902. Self-Authentication

Extrinsic evidence of authenticity as a condition precedent to admissibility is not required with respect to the following:

(1) Domestic public documents under seal. A document bearing a seal purporting to be that of the United States, or of any State, district, Commonwealth, territory, or insular possession thereof, or the Panama Canal Zone, or the Trust Territory of the Pacific Islands, or of a political subdivision, department, officer, or agency thereof, and a signature purporting to be an attestation or execution.

(2) Domestic public documents not under seal. A document purporting to bear the signature in the official capacity of an officer or employee of any entity included in paragraph (1) hereof, having no seal, if a public officer having a seal and having official duties in the district or political subdivision of the officer or employee certifies

under seal that the signer has the official capacity and that the signature is genuine.

(3) Foreign public documents. A document purporting to be executed or attested in the official capacity by a person authorized by the laws of a foreign country to make the execution or attestation, and accompanied by a final certification as to the genuineness of the signature and official position (a) of the executing or attesting person, or (b) of any foreign official whose certificate of genuineness of signature and official position relates to the execution or attestation or is in a chain of certificates of genuineness of signature and official position relating to the execution or attestation. A final certification may be made by a secretary of embassy or legation, consul general, consul, vice consul, or consular agent of the United States, or a diplomatic or consular official of the foreign country assigned or accredited to the United States. If reasonable opportunity has been given to all parties to investigate the authenticity and accuracy of official documents, the court may, for good cause shown, order that they be treated as presumptively authentic without final certification or permit them to be evidenced by an attested summary with or without final certification.

(4) Certified copies of public records. A copy of an official record or report or entry therein, or of a document authorized by law to be recorded or filed and actually recorded or filed in a public office, including data compilations in any form, certified as correct by the custodian or other person authorized to make the certification, by certificate complying with paragraph (1), (2), or (3) of this rule or complying with any law of a jurisdiction, state or federal, or rule prescribed by the Supreme Court of Ohio.

(5) Official publications. Books, pamphlets, or other publications purporting to be issued by public authority.

(6) Newspapers and periodicals. Printed materials purporting to be newspapers or periodicals, including notices and advertisements contained therein.

(7) Trade inscriptions and the like. Inscriptions, signs, tags, or labels purporting to have been affixed in the course of business and indicating ownership, control, or origin.

(8) Acknowledged documents. Documents accompanied by a certificate of acknowledgment executed in the manner provided by law by a notary public or other officer authorized by law to take acknowledgments.

(9) Commercial paper and related documents. Commercial paper, signatures thereon, and documents relating thereto to the extent provided by general commercial law.

(10) Presumptions created by law. Any signature, document, or other matter declared by any law of a jurisdiction, state or federal, to be presumptively or prima facie genuine or authentic.

**History:** Amended, eff 7-1-07.

## RULE 903. Subscribing Witness' Testimony Unnecessary

The testimony of a subscribing witness is not necessary to authenticate a writing unless required by the laws of the jurisdiction whose laws govern the validity of the writing.

# ARTICLE X
# CONTENTS OF WRITINGS, RECORDINGS AND PHOTOGRAPHS

## RULE 1001. Definitions

For purposes of this article the following definitions are applicable:

(1) **Writings and recordings.** "Writings" and "recordings" consist of letters, words, or numbers, or their equivalent, set down by handwriting, typewriting, printing, photostating, photographing, magnetic impulse, mechanical or electronic recording, or other forms of date compilation.

(2) **Photographs.** "Photographs" include still photographs, X-ray films, video tapes, and motion pictures.

(3) **Original.** An "original" of a writing or recording is the writing or recording itself or any counterpart intended to have the same effect by a person executing or issuing it. An "original" of photograph includes the negative or any print therefrom. If data are stored in a computer or similar device, any printout or other output readable by sight, shown to reflect the data accurately, is an "original."

(4) **Duplicate.** A "duplicate" is a counterpart produced by the same impression as the original, or from the same matrix, or by means of photography, including enlargements and miniatures, or by mechanical or electronic re-recording, or by chemical reproduction, or by other equivalent techniques which accurately reproduce the original.

## RULE 1002. Requirement of Original

To prove the content of a writing, recording, or photograph, the original writing, recording, or photograph is required, except as otherwise provided in these rules or by statute enacted by the General Assembly not in conflict with a rule of the Supreme Court of Ohio.

## RULE 1003. Admissibility of Duplicates

A duplicate is admissible to the same extent as an original unless (1) a genuine question is raised as to the authenticity of the original or (2) in the circumstances it would be unfair to admit the duplicate in lieu of the original.

## RULE 1004. Admissibility of Other Evidence of Contents

The original is not required, and other evidence of the contents of a writing, recording, or photograph is admissible if:

(1) **Originals lost or destroyed.** All originals are lost or have been destroyed, unless the proponent lost or destroyed them in bad faith; or

(2) **Original not obtainable.** No original can be obtained by any available judicial process or procedure; or

(3) **Original in possession of opponent.** At a time when an original was under the control of the party against

whom offered, that party was put on notice, by the pleadings or otherwise, that the contents would be subject of proof at the hearing, and that party does not produce the original at the hearing; or

(4) **Collateral matters.** The writing, recording, or photograph is not closely related to a controlling issue.

**History:** Amended, eff July 1, 2007.

### RULE 1005. Public Records

The contents of an official record, or of a document authorized to be recorded or filed and actually recorded or filed, including data compilations in any form if otherwise admissible, may be proved by copy, certified as correct in accordance with Rule 902, Civ. R. 44, Crim. R. 27 or testified to be correct by a witness who has compared it with the original. If a copy which complies with the foregoing cannot be obtained by the exercise of reasonable diligence, then other evidence of the contents may be given.

### RULE 1006. Summaries

The contents of voluminous writings, recordings, or photographs which cannot conveniently be examined in court may be presented in the form of a chart, summary, or calculation. The originals, or duplicates, shall be made available for examination or copying, or both, by other parties at a reasonable time and place. The court may order that they be produced in court.

### RULE 1007. Testimony or Written Admission of Party

Contents of writings, recordings, or photographs may be proved by the testimony or deposition of the party against whom offered or by that party's written admission, without accounting for the nonproduction of the original.

**History:** Amended, eff July 1, 2007.

### RULE 1008. Functions of Court and Jury

When the admissibility of other evidence of contents of writings, recordings, or photographs under these rules depends upon the fulfillment of a condition of fact, the question whether the condition has been fulfilled is ordinarily for the court to determine in accordance with the provisions of Rule 104. However, when an issue is raised (a) whether the asserted writing ever existed, or (b) whether another writing, recording, or photograph produced at the trial is the original, or (c) whether other evidence of contents correctly reflects the contents, the issue is for the trier of fact to determine as in the case of other issues of fact.

## ARTICLE XI
## MISCELLANEOUS RULES

### RULE 1101. [Reserved]

### RULE 1102. Effective Date

(A) **Effective date of rules.** These rules shall take effect on the first day of July, 1980. They govern all proceedings in actions brought after they first take effect and also all further proceedings in actions then pending, except to the extent that in the opinion of the court their application in a particular action pending when the rules take effect would not be feasible or would work injustice, in which event former evidentiary rules apply.

(B) **Effective date of amendments.** The amendments submitted by the Supreme Court to the General Assembly on January 14, 1981, and on April 29, 1981, shall take effect on July 1, 1981. They govern all further proceedings in actions then pending, except to the extent that their application in a particular action pending when the amendments take effect would not be feasible or would work injustice, in which event the former procedure applies.

(C) **Effective date of amendments.** The amendments submitted by the Supreme Court to the General Assembly on January 12, 1990, and further revised and submitted on April 16, 1990, shall take effect on July 1, 1990. They govern all proceedings in actions brought after they take effect and also all further proceedings in actions then pending, except to the extent that their application in a particular action pending when the amendments take effect would not be feasible or would work injustice, in which event the former procedure applies.

(D) **Effective date of amendments.** The amendments submitted by the Supreme Court to the General Assembly on January 10, 1991 and further revised and submitted on April 29, 1991, shall take effect on July 1, 1991. They govern all proceedings in actions brought after they take effect and also all further proceedings in actions then pending, except to the extent that their application in a particular action pending when the amendments take effect would not be feasible or would work injustice, in which event the former procedure applies.

(E) **Effective date of amendments.** The amendments filed by the Supreme Court with the General Assembly on January 14, 1992 and further filed on April 30, 1992, shall take effect on July 1, 1992. They govern all proceedings in actions brought after they take effect and also all further proceedings in actions then pending, except to the extent that their application in a particular action pending when the amendments take effect would not be feasible or would work injustice, in which event the former procedure applies.

(F) **Effective date of amendments.** The amendments submitted by the Supreme Court to the General Assembly on January 8, 1993 and further filed on April 30, 1993 shall take effect on July 1, 1993. They govern all proceedings in actions brought after they take effect and also all further proceedings in actions then pending, except to the extent that their application in a particular action pending when the amendments take effect would not be feasible or would work injustice, in which event the former procedure applies.

(G) **Effective date of amendments.** The amendments submitted by the Supreme Court to the General Assembly on January 14, 1994 and further filed on April 29, 1994 shall take effect on July 1, 1994. They govern all proceedings in actions brought after they take effect and also all further proceedings in actions then pending, except to the extent that their application in a particular action pending when the amendments take effect would not be feasible or would work injustice, in which event the former procedure applies.

(H) **Effective date of amendments.** The amendments to Rules 101, 102, and 403 filed by the Supreme Court with the General Assembly on January 5, 1996 and refiled on April 26, 1996 shall take effect on July 1, 1996. They govern all proceedings in actions brought after they take effect and also all further proceedings in actions then pending, except to the extent that their application in a particular action pending when the amendments take effect would not be feasible or would work injustice, in which event the former procedure applies.

(I) **Effective date of amendments.** The amendments to Rules 607, 613, 616, 706, and 806 filed by the Supreme Court with the General Assembly on January 15, 1998 and further revised and refiled on April 30, 1998 shall take effect on July 1, 1998. They govern all proceedings in actions brought after they take effect and also all further proceedings in actions then pending, except to the extent that their application in a particular action pending when the amendments take effect would not be feasible or would work injustice, in which event the former procedure applies.

(J) **Effective date of amendments.** The amendments to Rules 101 and 1102(I) filed by the Supreme Court with the General Assembly on January 13, 1999 shall take effect on July 1, 1999. They govern all proceedings in actions brought after they take effect and also all further proceedings in actions then pending, except to the extent that their application in a particular action pending when the amendments take effect would not be feasible or would work injustice, in which event the former procedure applies.

(K) **Effective date of amendments.** The amendments to Evidence Rule 407 filed by the Supreme Court with the General Assembly on January 13, 2000 and refiled on April 27, 2000 shall take effect on July 1, 2000. They govern all proceedings in actions brought after they take effect and also all further proceedings in actions then pending, except to the extent that their application in a particular action pending when the amendments take effect would not be feasible or would work injustice, in which event the former procedure applies.

(L) **Effective date of amendments.** The amendments to Evidence Rules 615 and 804 filed by the Supreme Court with the General Assembly on January 12, 2001, and refiled on April 26, 2001, shall take effect on July 1, 2001. They govern all proceedings in actions brought after they take effect and also all further proceedings in actions then pending, except to the extent that their application in a particular action pending when the amendments take effect would not be feasible or would work injustice, in which event the former procedure applies.

(M) **Effective date of amendments.** The amendments to Evidence Rules 609 and 615 filed by the Supreme Court with the General Assembly on January 9, 2003 and refiled on April 28, 2003, shall take effect on July 1, 2003. They govern all proceedings in actions brought after they take effect and also all further proceedings in actions then pending, except to the extent that their application in a particular action pending when the amendments take effect would not be feasible or would work injustice, in which event the former procedure applies.

(N) **Effective date of amendments.** The amendment to Evidence Rule 803 and the repeal of Evidence Rule 706 filed by the Supreme Court with the General Assembly on January 12, 2006 shall take effect on July 1, 2006. The amendment and repeal govern all proceedings in actions brought after they take effect and also all further proceedings in actions then pending, except to the extent that their application in a particular action pending when the amendments take effect would not be feasible or would work injustice, in which event the former procedure applies.

(O) **Effective date of amendments.** The amendments to the Rules of Evidence filed by the Supreme Court with the General Assembly on January 11, 2007 and refiled April 30, 2007 shall take effect on July 1, 2007. They govern all proceedings in actions brought after they take effect and also all further proceedings in actions then pending, except to the extent that their application in a particular action pending when the amendments take effect would not be feasible or would work injustice, in which event the former procedure applies.

(P) **Effective date of amendments.** The amendments to the Rules of Evidence filed by the Supreme Court with the General Assembly on January 5, 2011 and refiled on April 21, 2011 shall take effect on July 1, 2011. They govern all proceedings in actions brought after they take effect and also all further proceedings in actions then pending, except to the extent that their application in a particular action pending when the amendments take effect would not be feasible or would work injustice, in which event the former procedure applies.

**History:** Amended, eff 7-1-81; 7-1-90; 7-1-91; 7-1-92; 7-1-93; 7-1-94; 7-1-96; 7-1-98; 7-1-99; 7-1-00; 7-1-01; 7-1-03; 7-1-06; 7-1-07; 7-1-11.

## RULE 1103. Title

These rules shall be known as the Ohio Rules of Evidence and may be cited as "Evidence Rules" or "Evid. R."

# OHIO RULES OF JUVENILE PROCEDURE

**Complete with amendments through July 1, 2011.**



## RULE 1. Scope of rules: applicability; construction; exceptions

(A) **Applicability.** These rules prescribe the procedure to be followed in all juvenile courts of this state in all proceedings coming within the jurisdiction of such courts, with the exceptions stated in subdivision (C).

(B) **Construction.** These rules shall be liberally interpreted and construed so as to effectuate the following purposes:

(1) to effect the just determination of every juvenile court proceeding by ensuring the parties a fair hearing and the recognition and enforcement of their constitutional and other legal rights;

(2) to secure simplicity and uniformity in procedure, fairness in administration, and the elimination of unjustifiable expense and delay;

(3) to provide for the care, protection, and mental and physical development of children subject to the jurisdiction of the juvenile court, and to protect the welfare of the community; and

(4) to protect the public interest by treating children as persons in need of supervision, care and rehabilitation.

(C) **Exceptions.** These rules shall not apply to procedure (1) Upon appeal to review any judgment, order, or ruling; (2) Upon the trial of criminal actions; (3) Upon the trial of actions for divorce, annulment, legal separation, and related proceedings; (4) In proceedings to determine parent-child relationships, provided, however that appointment of counsel shall be in accordance with Rule 4(A) of the Rules of Juvenile Procedure; (5) In the commitment of the mentally ill and mentally retarded; (6) In proceedings under section 2151.85 of the Revised Code to the extent that there is a conflict between these rules and section 2151.85 of the Revised Code.

When any statute provides for procedure by general or specific reference to the statutes governing procedure in juvenile court actions, procedure shall be in accordance with these rules.

**History:** Amended, eff 7-1-91; 7-1-94; 7-1-95.

## RULE 2. Definitions

As used in these rules:

(A) "Abused child" has the same meaning as in section 2151.031 of the Revised Code.

(B) "Adjudicatory hearing" means a hearing to determine whether a child is a juvenile traffic offender, delinquent, unruly, abused, neglected, or dependent or otherwise within the jurisdiction of the court.

(C) "Agreement for temporary custody" means a voluntary agreement that is authorized by section 5103.15 of the Revised Code and transfers the temporary custody of a child to a public children services agency or a private child placing agency.

(D) "Child" has the same meaning as in sections 2151.011 and 2152.02 of the Revised Code.

(E) "Chronic truant" has the same meaning as in section 2151.011 of the Revised Code.

(F) "Complaint" means the legal document that sets forth the allegations that form the basis for juvenile court jurisdiction.

(G) "Court proceeding" means all action taken by a court from the earlier of (1) the time a complaint is filed and (2) the time a person first appears before an officer of a juvenile court until the court relinquishes jurisdiction over such child.

(H) "Custodian" means a person who has legal custody of a child or a public children's services agency or private child-placing agency that has permanent, temporary, or legal custody of a child.

(I) "Delinquent child" has the same meaning as in

section 2152.02 of the Revised Code.

(J) "Dependent child" has the same meaning as in section 2151.04 of the Revised Code.

(K) "Detention" means the temporary care of chi'ldren in restricted facilities pending court adjudication or disposition.

(L) "Detention hearing" means a hearing to determine whether a child shall be held in detention or shelter care prior to or pending execution of a final dispositional order.

(M) "Dispositional hearing" means a hearing to determine what action shall be taken concerning a child who is within the jurisdiction of the court.

(N) "Guardian" means a person, association, or corporation that is granted authority by a probate court pursuant to Chapter 2111 of the Revised Code to exercise parental rights over a child to the extent provided in the court's order and subject to the residual parental rights of the child's parents.

(O) "Guardian ad litem" means a person appointed to protect the interests of a party in a juvenile court proceeding.

(P) "Habitual truant" has the same meaning as in section 2151.011 of the Revised Code.

(Q) "Hearing" means any portion of a juvenile court proceeding before the court, whether summary in nature or by examination of witnesses.

(R) "Indigent person" means a person who, at the time need is determined, is unable by reason of lack of property or income to provide for full payment of legal counsel and all other necessary expenses of representation.

(S) "Juvenile court" means a division of the court of common pleas, or a juvenile court separately and independently created, that has jurisdiction under Chapters 2151 and 2152 of the Revised Code.

(T) "Juvenile judge" means a judge of a court having jurisdiction under Chapters 2151 and 2152 of the Revised Code.

(U) "Juvenile traffic offender" has the same meaning as in section 2151.021 of the Revised Code.

(V) "Legal custody" means a legal status that vests in the custodian the right to have physical care and control of the child and to determine where and with whom the child shall live, and the right and duty to protect, train, and discipline the child and provide the child with food, shelter, education, and medical care, all subject to any residual parental rights, privileges, and responsibilities. An individual granted legal custody shall exercise the rights and responsibilities personally unless otherwise authorized by any section of the Revised Code or by the court.

(W) "Mental examination" means an examination by a psychiatrist or psychologist.

(X) "Neglected child" has the same meaning as in section 2151.03 of the Revised Code.

(Y) "Party" means a child who is the subject of a juvenile court proceeding, the child's spouse, if any, the child's parent or parents, or if the parent of a child is a child, the parent of that parent, in appropriate cases, the child's custodian, guardian, or guardian ad litem, the state, and any other person specifically designated by the court.

(Z) "Permanent custody" means a legal status that vests in a public children's services agency or a private child-placing agency, all parental rights, duties, and obligations, including the right to consent to adoption, and divests the natural parents or adoptive parents of any and all parental rights, privileges, and obligations, including all residual rights and obligations.

(AA) "Permanent surrender" means the act of the parents or, if a child has only one parent, of the parent of a child, by a voluntary agreement authorized by section 5103.15 of the Revised Code, to transfer the permanent custody of the child to a public children's services agency or a private child-placing agency.

(BB) "Person" includes an individual, association, corporation, or partnership and the state or any of its political subdivisions, departments, or agencies.

(CC) "Physical examination" means an examination by a physician.

(DD) "Planned permanent living arrangement" means an order of a juvenile court pursuant to which both of the following apply:

(1) The court gives legal custody of a child to a public children's services agency or a private child-placing agency without the termination of parental rights;

(2) The order permits the agency to make an appropriate placement of the child and to enter into a written planned permanent living arrangement agreement with a foster care provider or with another person or agency with whom the child is placed.

(EE) "Private child-placing agency" means any association, as defined in section 5103.02 of the Revised Code that is certified pursuant to sections 5103.03 to 5103.05 of the Revised Code to accept temporary, permanent, or legal custody of children and place the children for either foster care or adoption.

(FF) "Public children's services agency" means a children's services board or a county department of human services that has assumed the administration of the children's services function prescribed by Chapter 5153 of the Revised Code.

(GG) "Removal action" means a statutory action filed by the superintendent of a school district for the removal of a child in an out-of-county foster home placement.

(HH) "Residence or legal settlement" means a location as defined by section 2151.06 of the Revised Code.

(II) "Residual parental rights, privileges, and responsibilities" means those rights, privileges, and responsibilities remaining with the natural parent after the transfer of legal custody of the child, including but not limited to the privilege of reasonable visitation, consent to adoption, the privilege to determine the child's religious affiliation, and the responsibility for support.

(JJ) "Rule of court" means a rule promulgated by the Supreme Court or a rule concerning local practice adopted by another court that is not inconsistent with the rules promulgated by the Supreme Court and that is filed with the Supreme Court.

(KK) "Serious youthful offender" means a child eligible for sentencing as described in sections 2152.11 and 2152.13 of the Revised Code.

(LL) "Serious youthful offender proceedings" means proceedings after a probable cause determination that a child is eligible for sentencing as described in sections 2152.11 and 2152.13 of the Revised Code. Serious youthful offender proceedings cease to be serious youthful offender proceedings once a child has been determined by the trier of fact not to be a serious youthful offender or the juvenile judge has determined not to impose a serious youthful offender disposition on a child eligible for discretionary serious youthful offender sentencing.

(MM) "Shelter care" means the temporary care of children in physically unrestricted facilities, pending court adjudication or disposition.

(NN) "Social history" means the personal and family history of a child or any other party to a juvenile proceeding and may include the prior record of the person with the juvenile court or any other court.

(OO) "Temporary custody" means legal custody of a child who is removed from the child's home, which custody may be terminated at any time at the discretion of the court or, if the legal custody is granted in an agreement for temporary custody, by the person or persons who executed the agreement.

(PP) "Unruly child" has the same meaning as in section 2151.022 of the Revised Code.

(QQ) "Ward of court" means a child over whom the court assumes continuing jurisdiction.

**History:** Amended, eff 7-1-94; 7-1-98; 7-1-01; 7-1-02.

## RULE 3. Waiver of rights

A child's right to be represented by counsel at a hearing conducted pursuant to Juv. R. 30 may not be waived. Other rights of a child may be waived with the permission of the court.

**History:** Amended, eff 7-1-94.

## RULE 4. Assistance of counsel; guardian *ad litem*

(A) **Assistance of counsel.** Every party shall have the right to be represented by counsel and every child, parent, custodian, or other person in loco parentis the right to appointed counsel if indigent. These rights shall arise when a person becomes a party to a juvenile court proceeding. When the complaint alleges that a child is an abused child, the court must appoint an attorney to represent the interests of the child. This rule shall not be construed to provide for a right to appointed counsel in cases in which that right is not otherwise provided for by constitution or statute.

(B) **Guardian ad litem; when appointed.** The court shall appoint a guardian ad litem to protect the interests of a child or incompetent adult in a juvenile court proceeding when:

(1) The child has no parents, guardian, or legal custodian;

(2) The interests of the child and the interests of the parent may conflict;

(3) The parent is under eighteen years of age or appears to be mentally incompetent;

(4) The court believes that the parent of the child is not capable of representing the best interest of the child.

(5) Any proceeding involves allegations of abuse or neglect, voluntary surrender of permanent custody, or termination of parental rights as soon as possible after the commencement of such proceeding.

(6) There is an agreement for the voluntary surrender of temporary custody that is made in accordance with section 5103.15 of the Revised Code, and thereafter there is a request for extension of the voluntary agreement.

(7) The proceeding is a removal action.

(8) Appointment is otherwise necessary to meet the requirements of a fair hearing.

(C) **Guardian ad litem as counsel.**

(1) When the guardian ad litem is an attorney admitted to practice in this state, the guardian may also serve as counsel to the ward providing no conflict between the roles exist[s].

(2) If a person is serving as guardian ad litem and as attorney for a ward and either that person or the court finds a conflict between the responsibilities of the role of attorney and that of guardian ad litem, the court shall appoint another person as guardian ad litem for the ward.

(3) If a court appoints a person who is not an attorney admitted to practice in this state to be a guardian ad litem, the court may appoint an attorney admitted to practice in this state to serve as attorney for the guardian ad litem.

(D) **Appearance of attorneys.** An attorney shall enter appearance by filing a written notice with the court or by appearing personally at a court hearing and informing the court of said representation.

(E) **Notice to guardian ad litem.** The guardian ad litem shall be given notice of all proceedings in the same manner as notice is given to other parties to the action.

(F) **Withdrawal of counsel or guardian ad litem.** An attorney or guardian ad litem may withdraw only with the consent of the court upon good cause shown.

(G) **Costs.** The court may fix compensation for the services of appointed counsel and guardians ad litem, tax the same as part of the costs and assess them against the child, the child's parents, custodian, or other person in loco parentis of such child.

**History:** Amended, eff 7-1-76; 7-1-94; 7-1-95; 7-1-98.

## RULE 5. [Reserved]

## RULE 6. Taking into custody

(A) **[When.]** A child may be taken into custody:

(1) pursuant to an order of the court;

(2) pursuant to the law of arrest;

(3) by a law enforcement officer or duly authorized officer of the court when any of the following conditions exist:

(a) There are reasonable grounds to believe that the child is suffering from illness or injury and is not receiving proper care, and the child's removal is necessary to prevent immediate or threatened physical or emotional harm;

(b) There are reasonable grounds to believe that the child is in immediate danger from the child's surroundings and that the child's removal is necessary to prevent immediate or threatened physical or emotional harm;

(c) There are reasonable grounds to believe that a parent, guardian, custodian, or other household member of the child has abused or neglected another child in the household, and that the child is in danger of immediate or threatened physical or emotional harm;

(d) There are reasonable grounds to believe that the child has run away from the child's parents, guardian, or other custodian;

(e) There are reasonable grounds to believe that the conduct, conditions, or surroundings of the child are endangering the health, welfare, or safety of the child;

(f) During the pendency of court proceedings, there are reasonable grounds to believe that the child may abscond or be removed from the jurisdiction of the court or will not be brought to the court;

(g) A juvenile judge or designated magistrate has found that there is probable cause to believe any of the conditions set forth in division (A)(3)(a), (b), or (c) of this rule are present, has found that reasonable efforts have been made to notify the child's parents, guardian ad litem or custodian that the child may be placed into shelter care, except where notification would jeopardize the physical or emotional safety of the child or result in the child's removal from the court's jurisdiction, and has ordered ex parte, by telephone or otherwise, the taking of the child into custody.

(4) By the judge or designated magistrate ex parte pending the outcome of the adjudicatory and dispositional hearing in an abuse, neglect, or dependency proceeding, where it appears to the court that the best interest and welfare of the child require the immediate issuance of a shelter care order.

(B) **Probable cause hearing.** When a child is taken into custody pursuant to an ex parte emergency order pursuant to division (A)(3)(g) or (A)(4) of this rule, a probable cause hearing shall be held before the end of the next business day after the day on which the order is issued but not later than seventy-two hours after the issuance of the emergency order.

**History:** Amended, eff 7-1-94; 7-1-96.

## RULE 7. Detention and shelter care

(A) **Detention: standards.** A child taken into custody shall not be placed in detention or shelter care prior to final disposition unless any of the following apply:

(1) Detention or shelter care is required:

(a) to protect the child from immediate or threatened physical or emotional harm; or

(b) to protect the person or property of others from immediate or threatened physical or emotional harm.

(2) The child may abscond or be removed from the jurisdiction of the court;

(3) The child has no parent, guardian, custodian or other person able to provide supervision and care for the child and return the child to the court when required;

(4) An order for placement of the child in detention or shelter care has been made by the court;

(5) Confinement is authorized by statute.

(B) **Priorities in placement prior to hearing.** A person taking a child into custody shall, with all reasonable speed, do either of the following:

(1) Release the child to a parent, guardian, or other custodian;

(2) Where detention or shelter care appears to be required under the standards of division (A) of this rule, bring the child to the court or deliver the child to a place of detention or shelter care designated by the court.

(C) **Initial procedure upon detention.** Any person who delivers a child to a shelter or detention facility shall give the admissions officer at the facility a signed report stating why the child was taken into custody and why the child was not released to a parent, guardian or custodian, and shall assist the admissions officer, if necessary, in notifying the parent pursuant to division (E)(3) of this rule.

(D) **Admission.** The admissions officer in a shelter or detention facility, upon receipt of a child, shall review the report submitted pursuant to division (C) of this rule, make such further investigation as is feasible and do either of the following:

(1) Release the child to the care of a parent, guardian or custodian;

(2) Where detention or shelter care is required under the standards of division (A) of this rule, admit the child to the facility or place the child in some appropriate facility.

(E) **Procedure after admission.** When a child has been admitted to detention or shelter care the admissions officer shall do all of the following:

(1) Prepare a report stating the time the child was brought to the facility and the reasons the child was admitted;

(2) Advise the child of the right to telephone parents and counsel immediately and at reasonable times thereafter and the time, place, and purpose of the detention hearing;

(3) Use reasonable diligence to contact the child's parent, guardian, or custodian and advise that person of all of the following:

(a) The place of and reasons for detention;

(b) The time the child may be visited;

(c) The time, place, and purpose of the detention hearing;

(d) The right to counsel and appointed counsel in the case of indigency.

(F) **Detention hearing.**

(1) Hearing: time; notice. When a child has been admitted to detention or shelter care, a detention hearing shall be held promptly, not later than seventy-two hours after the child is placed in detention or shelter care or the next court day, whichever is earlier, to determine whether detention or shelter care is required. Reasonable oral or written notice of the time, place, and purpose of the detention hearing shall be given to the child and to the parents, guardian, or other custodian, if that person or those persons can be found.

(2) Hearing: advisement of rights. Prior to the hearing, the court shall inform the parties of the right to counsel and to appointed counsel if indigent and the child's right to remain silent with respect to any allegation of a juvenile traffic offense, delinquency, or unruliness.

(3) Hearing procedure. The court may consider any evidence, including the reports filed by the person who brought the child to the facility and the admissions officer, without regard to formal rules of evidence. Unless it appears from the hearing that the child's detention or shelter care is required under division (A) of this rule, the court shall order the child's release to a parent, guardian, or custodian. Whenever abuse, neglect, or dependency is alleged, the court shall determine whether there are any appropriate relatives of the child who are willing to be temporary custodians and, if so, appoint an appropriate relative as the temporary custodian of the child. The court shall make a reasonable efforts determination in accordance with Juv. R. 27(B)(1).

(G) **Rehearing.** If a parent, guardian, or custodian did not receive notice of the initial hearing and did not appear or waive appearance at the hearing, the court shall rehear the matter promptly. After a child is placed in shelter care or detention care, any party and the guardian ad litem of the child may file a motion with the court requesting that the child be released from detention or shelter care. Upon the filing of the motion, the court shall hold a hearing within seventy-two hours.

(H) **Separation from adults.** No child shall be placed in or committed to any prison, jail, lockup, or any other place where the child can come in contact or communication with any adult convicted of crime, under arrest, or charged with crime.

(I) **Physical examination.** The supervisor of a shelter or detention facility may provide for a physical examination of a child placed in the shelter or facility.

(J) **Telephone and visitation rights.** A child may telephone the child's parents and attorney immediately after being admitted to a shelter or detention facility and at reasonable times thereafter.

The child may be visited at reasonable visiting hours by

the child's parents and adult members of the family, the child's pastor, and the child's teachers. The child may be visited by the child's attorney at any time.

**History:** Amended, eff 7-1-94; 7-1-01.

## RULE 8. Filing by electronic means

A court may provide, by local rules adopted pursuant to the Rules of Superintendence, for the filing of documents by electronic means. If the court adopts such local rules, they shall include all of the following:

(A) Any signature on electronically transmitted documents shall be considered that of the attorney or party it purports to be for all purposes. If it is established that the documents were transmitted without authority, the court shall order the filing stricken.

(B) A provision shall specify the days and hours during which electronically transmitted documents will be received by the court, and a provision shall specify when documents received electronically will be considered to have been filed.

(C) Any document filed electronically that requires a filing fee may be rejected by the clerk of court unless the filer has complied with the mechanism established by the court for the payment of filing fees.

**History:** Effective 7-1-94; amended, eff 7-1-96; 7-1-01.

## RULE 9. Intake

(A) **Court action to be avoided.** In all appropriate cases formal action should be avoided and other community resources utilized to ameliorate situations brought to the attention of the court.

(B) **Screening; referral.** Information that a child is within the court's jurisdiction may be informally screened prior to the filing of a complaint to determine whether the filing of a complaint is in the best interest of the child and the public.

## RULE 10. Complaint

(A) **Filing.** Any person having knowledge of a child who appears to be a juvenile traffic offender, delinquent, unruly, neglected, dependent, or abused may file a complaint with respect to the child in the juvenile court of the county in which the child has a residence or legal settlement, or in which the traffic offense, delinquency, unruliness, neglect, dependency, or abuse occurred.

Persons filing complaints that a child appears to be an unruly or delinquent child for being an habitual or chronic truant and the parent, guardian, or other person having care of the child has failed to cause the child to attend school may also file the complaint in the county in which the child is supposed to attend public school.

Any person may file a complaint to have determined the custody of a child not a ward of another court of this state, and any person entitled to the custody of a child and unlawfully deprived of such custody may file a complaint requesting a writ of habeas corpus. Complaints concerning custody shall be filed in the county where the child is found or was last known to be.

Any person with standing may file a complaint for the determination of any other matter over which the juvenile court is given jurisdiction by the Revised Code. The complaint shall be filed in the county in which the child who is the subject of the complaint is found or was last known to be. In a removal action, the complaint shall be filed in the county where the foster home is located.

When a case concerning a child is transferred or certified from another court, the certification from the transferring court shall be considered the complaint. The juvenile court may order the certification supplemented upon its own motion or that of a party.

(B) **Complaint: general form.** The complaint, which may be upon information and belief, shall satisfy all of the following requirements:

(1) State in ordinary and concise language the essential facts that bring the proceeding within the jurisdiction of the court, and in juvenile traffic offense and delinquency proceedings, shall contain the numerical designation of the statute or ordinance alleged to have been violated;

(2) Contain the name and address of the parent, guardian, or custodian of the child or state that the name or address is unknown;

(3) Be made under oath.

(C) **Complaint: juvenile traffic offense.** A Uniform Traffic ticket shall be used as a complaint in juvenile traffic offense proceedings.

(D) **Complaint: permanent custody.** A complaint seeking permanent custody of a child shall state that permanent custody is sought.

(E) **Complaint: temporary custody.** A complaint seeking temporary custody of a child shall state that temporary custody is sought.

(F) **Complaint: planned permanent living arrangement.** A complaint seeking the placement of a child into a planned permanent living arrangement shall state that placement into a planned permanent living arrangement is sought.

(G) **Complaint: habeas corpus.** Where a complaint for a writ of habeas corpus involving the custody of a child is based on the existence of a lawful court order, a certified copy of the order shall be attached to the complaint.

**History:** Amended, eff 7-1-75; 7-1-76; 7-1-94; 7-1-98; 7-1-01; 7-1-02.

## RULE 11. Transfer to another county

(A) **Residence in another county; transfer optional.** If the child resides in a county of this state and the proceeding is commenced in a court of another county, that court, on its own motion or a motion of a party, may transfer the proceeding to the county of the child's residence upon the filing of the complaint or after the adjudicatory or dispositional hearing for such further proceeding as required. The court of the child's residence shall then proceed as if the original complaint had been filed in that court. Transfer may also be made if the residence of the child changes.

(B) **Proceedings in another county; transfer required.** The proceedings, other than a removal action, shall be so transferred if other proceedings involving the child are pending in the juvenile court of the county of the child's residence.

(C) **Adjudicatory hearing in county where complaint filed.** Where either the transferring or receiving court finds that the interests of justice and the convenience of the parties so require, the adjudicatory hearing shall be held in the county wherein the complaint was filed. Thereafter the proceeding may be transferred to the county of the child's residence for disposition.

(D) **Transfer of records.** Certified copies of all legal

and social records pertaining to the proceeding shall accompany the transfer.

**History:** Amended, eff 7-1-94; 7-1-98.

## RULE 12. [Reserved]

## RULE 13. Temporary disposition; temporary orders; emergency medical and surgical treatment

(A) **Temporary disposition.** Pending hearing on a complaint, the court may make such temporary orders concerning the custody or care of a child who is the subject of the complaint as the child's interest and welfare may require.

(B) **Temporary orders.**

(1) Pending hearing on a complaint, the judge or magistrate may issue temporary orders with respect to the relations and conduct of other persons toward a child who is the subject of the complaint as the child's interest and welfare may require.

(2) Upon the filing of an abuse, neglect, or dependency complaint, any party may by motion request that the court issue any of the following temporary orders to protect the best interest of the child:

(a) An order granting temporary custody of the child to a particular party;

(b) An order for the taking of the child into custody pending the outcome of the adjudicatory and dispositional hearings;

(c) An order granting, limiting, or eliminating visitation rights with respect to the child;

(d) An order for the payment of child support and continued maintenance of any medical, surgical, or hospital policies of insurance for the child that existed at the time of the filing of the complaint, petition, writ, or other document;

(e) An order requiring a party to vacate a residence that will be lawfully occupied by the child;

(f) An order requiring a party to attend an appropriate counseling program that is reasonably available to that party;

(g) Any other order that restrains or otherwise controls the conduct of any party which conduct would not be in the best interest of the child.

(3) The orders permitted by division (B)(2) of this rule may be granted ex parte if it appears that the best interest and welfare of the child require immediate issuance. If the court issues the requested ex parte order, the court shall hold a hearing to review the order within seventy-two hours after it is issued or before the end of the next court day after the day on which it is issued, whichever occurs first. The court shall appoint a guardian ad litem for the child prior to the hearing. The court shall give written notice of the hearing by means reasonably likely to result in the party's receiving actual notice and include all of the following:

(a) The date, time, and location of the hearing;

(b) The issues to be addressed at the hearing;

(c) A statement that every party to the hearing has a right to counsel and to court appointed counsel, if the party is indigent;

(d) The name, telephone number, and address of the person requesting the order;

(e) A copy of the order, except when it is not possible to obtain it because of the exigent circumstances in the case.

(4) The court may review any order under this rule at any time upon motion of any party for good cause shown or upon the motion of the court.

(5) If the court does not grant an ex parte order, the court shall hold a shelter care hearing on the motion within ten days after the motion is filed.

(C) **Emergency medical and surgical treatment.** Upon the certification of one or more reputable practicing physicians, the court may order such emergency medical and surgical treatment as appears to be immediately necessary for any child concerning whom a complaint has been filed.

(D) **Ex parte proceedings.** In addition to the ex parte proceeding described in division (B) of this rule, the court may proceed summarily and without notice under division (A), (B), or (C) of this rule, where it appears to the court that the interest and welfare of the child require that action be taken immediately.

(E) **Hearing; notice.** In addition to the procedures specified in division (B) of this rule and wherever possible, the court shall provide an opportunity for hearing before proceeding under division (D) of this rule. Where the court has proceeded without notice under division (D) of this rule, it shall give notice of the action it has taken to the parties and any other affected person and provide them an opportunity for a hearing concerning the continuing effects of the action.

(F) **Probable cause finding.** Upon the finding of probable cause at a shelter care hearing that a child is an abused child, the court may do any of the following:

(1) Upon motion by the court or of any party, issue reasonable protective orders with respect to the interviewing or deposition of the child;

(2) Order that the child's testimony be videotaped for preservation of the testimony for possible use in any other proceedings in the case;

(3) Set any additional conditions with respect to the child or the case involving the child that are in the best interest of the child.

(G) **Payment.** The court may order the parent, guardian, or custodian, if able, to pay for any emergency medical or surgical treatment provided pursuant to division (C) of this rule. The order of payment may be enforced by judgment, upon which execution may issue, and a failure to pay as ordered may be punished as contempt of court.

**History:** Amended, eff 7-1-94; 7-1-96.

## RULE 14. Termination, extension or modification of temporary custody orders

(A) **Termination.** Any temporary custody order issued shall terminate one year after the earlier of the date on which the complaint in the case was filed or the child was first placed into shelter care. A temporary custody order shall extend beyond a year and until the court issues another dispositional order, where any public or private agency with temporary custody, not later than thirty days prior to the earlier of the date for the termination of the custody order or the date set at the dispositional hearing for the hearing to be held pursuant to Division (A) of section 2151.415 of the Revised Code, files a motion requesting that any of the following orders of disposition be issued:

(1) An order that the child be returned home with custody to the child's parents, guardian, or custodian without any restrictions;

(2) An order for protective supervision;

(3) An order that the child be placed in the legal custody of a relative or other interested individual;

(4) An order terminating parental rights;

(5) An order for long term foster care;

(6) An order for the extension of temporary custody.

(B) **Extension.** Upon the filing of an agency's motion for the extension of temporary custody, the court shall schedule a hearing and give notice to all parties in accordance with these rules. The agency shall include in the motion an explanation of the progress on the case plan and of its expectations of reunifying the child with the child's family, or placing the child in a permanent placement, within the extension period. The court may extend the temporary custody order for a period of up to six months. Prior to the end of the extension period, the agency may request one additional extension of up to six months. The court shall grant either extension upon finding that it is in the best interest of the child, that there has been significant progress on the case plan, and that there is reasonable cause to believe that the child will be reunited with one of the child's parents or otherwise permanently placed within the period of extension. Prior to the end of either extension, the agency that received the extension shall file a motion and the court shall issue one of the orders of disposition set forth in division (A) of this rule. Upon the agency's motion or upon its own motion, the court shall conduct a hearing and issue an appropriate order of disposition.

(C) **Modification.** The court, upon its own motion or that of any party, shall conduct a hearing with notice to all parties to determine whether any order issued should be modified or terminated, or whether any other dispositional order set forth in division (A) should be issued. The court shall so modify or terminate any order in accordance with the best interest of the child.

**History:** Amended, eff 7-1-94.

## RULE 15. Process: issuance, form

(A) **Summons: issuance.** After the complaint has been filed, the court shall cause the issuance of a summons directed to the child, the parents, guardian, custodian, and any other persons who appear to the court to be proper or necessary parties. The summons shall require the parties to appear before the court at the time fixed to answer the allegations of the complaint. A child alleged to be abused, neglected, or dependent shall not be summoned unless the court so directs.

A summons issued for a child under fourteen years of age alleged to be delinquent, unruly, or a juvenile traffic offender shall be made by serving either the child's parents, guardian, custodian, or other person with whom the child lives or resides. If the person who has physical custody of the child or with whom the child resides is other than the parent or guardian, then the parents and guardian also shall be summoned. A copy of the complaint shall accompany the summons.

(B) **Summons: form.** The summons shall contain:

(1) The name of the party or person with whom the child may be or, if unknown, any name or description by which the party or person can be identified with reasonable certainty.

(2) A summary statement of the complaint and in juvenile traffic offense and delinquency proceedings the numerical designation of the applicable statute or ordinance.

(3) A statement that any party is entitled to be represented by an attorney and that upon request the court will appoint an attorney for an indigent party entitled to appointed counsel under Juv. R. 4(A).

(4) An order to the party or person to appear at a stated time and place with a warning that the party or person may lose valuable rights or be subject to court sanction if the party or person fails to appear at the time and place stated in the summons.

(5) An order to the parent, guardian, or other person having care of a child alleged to be an unruly or delinquent child for being an habitual or chronic truant, to appear personally at the hearing and all proceedings, and an order directing the person having the physical custody or control of the child to bring the child to the hearing, with a warning that if the child fails to appear, the parent, guardian, or other person having care of the child may be subject to court sanction, including a finding of contempt.

(6) A statement that if a child is adjudicated abused, neglected, or dependent and the complaint seeks an order of permanent custody, an order of permanent custody would cause the parents, guardian, or legal custodian to be divested permanently of all parental rights and privileges.

(7) A statement that if a child is adjudicated abused, neglected, or dependent and the complaint seeks an order of temporary custody, an order of temporary custody will cause the removal of the child from the legal custody of the parents, guardian, or other custodian until the court terminates the order of temporary custody or permanently divests the parents of their parental rights.

(8) A statement that if the child is adjudicated abused, neglected, or dependent and the complaint seeks an order for a planned permanent living arrangement, an order for a planned permanent living arrangement will cause the removal of the child from the legal custody of the parent, guardian, or other custodian.

(9) A statement, in a removal action, of the specific disposition sought.

(10) The name and telephone number of the court employee designated by the court to arrange for the prompt appointment of counsel for indigent persons.

(C) **Summons: endorsement.** The court may endorse upon the summons an order directed to the parents, guardian, or other person with whom the child may be, to appear personally and bring the child to the hearing.

(D) **Warrant: issuance.** If it appears that the summons will be ineffectual or the welfare of the child requires that the child be brought forthwith to the court, a warrant may be issued against the child. A copy of the complaint shall accompany the warrant.

(E) **Warrant: form.** The warrant shall contain the name of the child or, if that is unknown, any name or description by which the child can be identified with reasonable certainty. It shall contain a summary statement of the complaint and in juvenile traffic offense and delinquency proceedings the numerical designation of the applicable statute or ordinance. A copy of the complaint shall be attached to the warrant. The warrant shall command that the child be taken into custody and be brought before the court that issued the warrant without unnecessary delay.

**History:** Amended, eff 7-1-94; 7-1-98; 7-1-01; 7-1-02.

## RULE 16. Process: service

(A) **Summons: service, return.** Except as otherwise provided in these rules, summons shall be served as provided in Civil Rules 4(A), (C) and (D), 4.1, 4.2, 4.3, 4.5

and 4.6. The summons shall direct the party served to appear at a stated time and place. Where service is by certified mail, the time shall not be less than seven days after the date of mailing.

Except as otherwise provided in this rule, when the residence of a party is unknown and cannot be ascertained with reasonable diligence, service shall be made by publication. Service by publication upon a non-custodial parent is not required in delinquent child or unruly child cases when the person alleged to have legal custody of the child has been served with summons pursuant to this rule, but the court may not enter any order or judgment against any person who has not been served with process or served by publication unless that person appears. Before service by publication can be made, an affidavit of a party or party's counsel shall be filed with the court. The affidavit shall aver that service of summons cannot be made because the residence of the person is unknown to the affiant and cannot be ascertained with reasonable diligence and shall set forth the last known address of the party to be served.

Service by publication shall be made by newspaper publication, by posting and mail, or by a combination of these methods. The court, by local rule, shall determine which method or methods of publication shall be used. If service by publication is made by newspaper publication, upon the filing of the affidavit, the clerk shall serve notice by publication in a newspaper of general circulation in the county in which the complaint is filed. If no newspaper is published in that county, then publication shall be in a newspaper published in an adjoining county. The publication shall contain the name and address of the court, the case number, the name of the first party on each side, and the name and last known address, if any, of the person or persons whose residence is unknown. The publication shall also contain a summary statement of the object of the complaint and shall notify the person to be served that the person is required to appear at the time and place stated. The time stated shall not be less than seven days after the date of publication. The publication shall be published once and service shall be complete on the date of publication.

After the publication, the publisher or the publisher's agent shall file with the court an affidavit showing the fact of publication together with a copy of the notice of publication. The affidavit and copy of the notice shall constitute proof of service.

If service by publication is made by posting and mail, upon the filing of the affidavit, the clerk shall cause service of notice to be made by posting in a conspicuous place in the courthouse in which the division of the common pleas court exercising jurisdiction over the complaint is located and in additional public places in the county that have been designated by local rule for the posting of notices pursuant to this rule. The number of additional public places to be designated shall be either two places or the number of state representative districts that are contained wholly or partly in the county in which the courthouse is located, whichever is greater. The notice shall contain the same information required to be contained in a newspaper publication. The notice shall be posted in the required locations for seven consecutive days. The clerk also shall cause the summons and accompanying pleadings to be mailed by ordinary mail, address correction requested, to the last known address of the party to be served. The clerk shall obtain a certificate of mailing from the United States Postal Service. If the clerk is notified of a corrected or forwarding address of the party to be served within the seven day period that notice is posted pursuant to this rule, the clerk shall cause the summons and accompanying pleadings to be mailed to the corrected or forwarding address. The clerk shall note the name, address, and date of each mailing in the docket.

After the seven days of posting, the clerk shall note on the docket where and when notice was posted. Service shall be complete upon the entry of posting.

(B) **Warrant: execution; return.**

(1) By whom. The warrant shall be executed by any officer authorized by law.

(2) Territorial limits. The warrant may be executed at any place within this state.

(3) Manner. The warrant shall be executed by taking the party against whom it is issued into custody. The officer is not required to have possession of the warrant at the time it is executed, but in such case the officer shall inform the party of the complaint made and the fact that the warrant has been issued. A copy of the warrant shall be given to the person named in the warrant as soon as possible.

(4) Return. The officer executing a warrant shall make return thereof to the issuing court. Unexecuted warrants shall upon request of the issuing court be returned to that court.

A warrant returned unexecuted and not cancelled or a copy thereof may, while the complaint is pending, be delivered by the court to an authorized officer for execution.

An officer executing a warrant shall take the person named therein without unnecessary delay before the court which issued the warrant.

**History:** Amended, eff 7-1-94; 7-1-98.

## RULE 17. Subpoena

(A) **Form; issuance.**

(1) Every subpoena shall do all of the following:

(a) State the name of the court from which it is issued, the title of the action, and the case number;

(b) Command each person to whom it is directed, at a time and place specified in the subpoena, to do one or more of the following:

(i) Attend and give testimony at a trial, hearing, proceeding, or deposition;

(ii) Produce documents or tangible things at a trial, hearing, proceeding, or deposition;

(iii) Produce and permit inspection and copying of any designated documents that are in the possession, custody, or control of the person;

(iv) Produce and permit inspection and copying, testing, or sampling of any tangible things that are in the possession, custody, or control of the person.

(c) Set forth the text of divisions (D) and (E) of this rule.

A command to produce and permit inspection may be joined with a command to attend and give testimony, or may be issued separately.

(2) The clerk shall issue a subpoena, signed but otherwise in blank, to a party requesting it, who shall complete it before service. An attorney who has filed an appearance on behalf of a party in an action also may sign and issue a subpoena on behalf of the court in which the action is pending.

(3) If the issuing attorney modifies the subpoena in any way, the issuing attorney shall give prompt notice of the

modifications to all other parties.

(B) **Parties unable to pay.** The court shall order at any time that a subpoena be issued for service on a named witness upon an ex parte application of a party and upon a satisfactory showing that the presence of the witness is necessary and that the party is financially unable to pay the witness fees required by division (C) of this rule. If the court orders the subpoena to be issued, the costs incurred by the process and the fees of the witness so subpoenaed shall be paid in the same manner that similar costs and fees are paid in case of a witness subpoenaed in behalf of the state in a criminal prosecution.

(C) **Service.** A subpoena may be served by a sheriff, bailiff, coroner, clerk of court, constable, probation officer, or a deputy of any, by an attorney or the attorney's agent, or by any person designated by order of the court who is not a party and is not less than eighteen years of age. Service of a subpoena upon a person named in the subpoena shall be made by delivering a copy of the subpoena to the person, by reading it to him or her in person, or by leaving it at the person's usual place of residence, and by tendering to the person upon demand the fees for one day's attendance and the mileage allowed by the law. The person serving the subpoena shall file a return of the subpoena with the clerk. If the witness being subpoenaed resides outside the county in which the court is located, the fees for one day's attendance and mileage shall be tendered without demand. The return may be forwarded through the postal service or otherwise.

(D) **Protection of persons subject to subpoenas.**

(1) A party or an attorney responsible for the issuance and service of a subpoena shall take reasonable steps to avoid imposing undue burden or expense on a person subject to that subpoena.

(2)(a) A person commanded to produce under division (A)(1)(b)(ii), (iii), or (iv) of this rule is not required to appear in person at the place of production or inspection unless commanded to attend and give testimony at a trial, hearing, proceeding, or deposition.

(b) Subject to division (E)(2) of this rule, a person commanded to produce under division (A)(1)(b)(ii), (iii), or (iv) of this rule may serve upon the party or attorney designated in the subpoena written objections to production. The objections must be served within fourteen days after service of the subpoena or before the time specified for compliance if that time is less than fourteen days after service. If objection is made, the party serving the subpoena shall not be entitled to production except pursuant to an order of the court that issued the subpoena. If objection has been made, the party serving the subpoena, upon notice to the person commanded to produce, may move at any time for an order to compel the production. An order to compel production shall protect any person who is not a party or an officer of a party from significant expense resulting from the production commanded.

(3) On timely motion, the court from which the subpoena was issued shall quash or modify the subpoena, or order appearance or production only under specified conditions, if the subpoena does any of the following:

(a) Fails to allow reasonable time to comply;

(b) Requires disclosure of privileged or otherwise protected matter and no exception or waiver applies;

(c) Requires disclosure of a fact known or opinion held by an expert not retained or specially employed by any party in anticipation of litigation or preparation for trial if the fact or opinion does not describe specific events or occurrences in dispute and results from study by that expert that was not made at the request of any party;

(d) Subjects a person to undue burden.

(4) Before filing a motion pursuant to division (D)(3)(d) of this rule, a person resisting discovery under this rule shall attempt to resolve any claim of undue burden through discussions with the issuing attorney. A motion filed pursuant to division (D)(3)(d) of this rule shall be supported by an affidavit of the subpoenaed person or a certificate of that person's attorney of the efforts made to resolve any claim of undue burden.

(5) If a motion is made under division (D)(3)(c) or (D)(3)(d) of this rule, the court shall quash or modify the subpoena unless the party in whose behalf the subpoena is issued shows a substantial need for the testimony or material that cannot be otherwise met without undue hardship and assures that the person to whom the subpoena is addressed will be reasonably compensated.

(E) **Duties in responding to subpoena.**

(1) A person responding to a subpoena to produce documents shall, at the person's option, produce the documents as they are kept in the usual course of business or organized and labeled to correspond with the categories in the subpoena. A person producing documents pursuant to a subpoena for them shall permit their inspection and copying by all parties present at the time and place set in the subpoena for inspection and copying.

(2) When information subject to a subpoena is withheld on a claim that it is privileged or subject to protection as trial preparation materials, the claim shall be made expressly and shall be supported by a description of the nature of the documents, communications, or things not produced that is sufficient to enable the demanding party to contest the claim.

(F) **Sanctions.** Failure by any person without adequate excuse to obey a subpoena served upon that person may be a contempt of the court from which the subpoena issued. A subpoenaed person or that person's attorney who frivolously resists discovery under this rule may be required by the court to pay the reasonable expenses, including reasonable attorney's fees, of the party seeking the discovery. The court from which a subpoena was issued may impose upon a party or attorney in breach of the duty imposed by division (D)(1) of this rule an appropriate sanction, that may include, but is not limited to, lost earnings and reasonable attorney's fees.

(G) **Privileges.** Nothing in this rule shall be construed to authorize a party to obtain information protected by any privilege recognized by law or to authorize any person to disclose such information.

(H) **Time.** Nothing in this rule shall be construed to expand any other time limits imposed by rule or statute. All issues concerning subpoenas shall be resolved prior to the time otherwise set for hearing or trial.

**History:** Amended, eff 7-1-94.

## RULE 18. Time

(A) **Time: computation.** In computing any period of time prescribed or allowed by these rules, by the local rules of any court, by order of court, or by any applicable statute, the date of the act or event from which the designated period of time begins to run shall not be included. The last day of the period so computed shall be included, unless it is a Saturday, a Sunday, or a legal holiday, in which event the period runs until the end of the next day that is not a Saturday, a Sunday or a legal holiday. Such extension of time includes, but is not limited to, probable cause, shelter care, and detention hearings.

Except in the case of probable cause, shelter care, and detention hearings when the period of time prescribed or allowed is less than seven days, intermediate Saturdays, Sundays, and legal holidays shall be excluded in computation.

(B) **Time: enlargement.** When an act is required or allowed to be performed at or within a specified time, the court for cause shown may at any time in its discretion (1) with or without motion or notice, order the period enlarged if application therefore is made before expiration of the period originally prescribed or of that period as extended by a previous order, or (2) upon motion permit the act to be done after expiration of the specified period if the failure to act on time was the result of excusable neglect or would result in injustice to a party, but the court may not extend the time for taking any action under Rule 7(F)(1), Rule 22(F), Rule 29(A) and Rule 29(F)(2)(b), except to the extent and under the conditions stated in them.

(C) **Time: unaffected by expiration of term.** The period of time provided for the doing of any act or the taking of any proceeding is not affected or limited by the expiration of a term of court. The expiration of a term of court in no way affects the power of a court to do any act in a juvenile proceeding.

(D) **Time: for motions; affidavits.** A written motion, other than one which may be heard ex parte, and notice of the hearing thereof, shall be served not later than seven days before the time specified for the hearing unless a different period is fixed by rule or order of the court. For cause shown such an order may be made on ex parte application. When a motion is supported by affidavit, the affidavit shall be served with the motion, and opposing affidavits may be served not less than one day before the hearing unless the court permits them to be served at a later time.

(E) **Time: additional time after service by mail.** Whenever a party has the right or is required to do an act within a prescribed period after the service of a notice or other paper upon the person and the notice or other paper is served upon the person by mail, three days shall be added to the prescribed period. This division does not apply to service of summons.

**History:** Amended, eff 7-1-94.

## RULE 19. Motions

An application to the court for an order shall be by motion. A motion other than one made during trial or hearing shall be in writing unless the court permits it to be made orally. It shall state with particularity the grounds upon which it is made and shall set forth the relief or order sought. It shall be supported by a memorandum containing citations of authority and may be supported by an affidavit.

To expedite its business, unless otherwise provided by statute or rule, the court may make provision by rule or order for the submission and determination of motions without oral hearing upon brief written statements of reasons in support and opposition.

**History:** Amended, eff 7-1-94.

## RULE 20. Service and filing of papers when required subsequent to filing of complaint.

(A) **Service: when required.** Written notices, requests for discovery, designation of record on appeal and written motions, other than those which are heard ex parte, and similar papers shall be served upon each of the parties.

(B) **Service: how made.** Whenever under these rules or by an order of the court service is required or permitted to be made upon a party represented by an attorney, the service shall be made upon the attorney unless service is ordered by the court upon the party. Service upon the attorney or upon the party shall be made in the manner provided in Civ. R. 5(B).

(C) **Filing.** All papers required to be served upon a party shall be filed simultaneously with or immediately after service. Papers filed with the court shall not be considered until proof of service is endorsed thereon or separately filed. The proof of service shall state the date and the manner of service and shall be signed and filed in the manner provided in Civil Rule 5(D).

**History:** Amended, eff 7-1-94.

## RULE 21. Preliminary conferences

At any time after the filing of a complaint, the court upon motion of any party or upon its own motion may order one or more conferences to consider such matters as will promote a fair and expeditious proceeding.

## RULE 22. Pleadings and motions; defenses and objections

(A) **Pleadings and motions.** Pleadings in juvenile proceedings shall be the complaint and the answer, if any, filed by a party. A party may move to dismiss the complaint or for other appropriate relief.

(B) **Amendment of pleadings.** Any pleading may be amended at any time prior to the adjudicatory hearing. After the commencement of the adjudicatory hearing, a pleading may be amended upon agreement of the parties or, if the interests of justice require, upon order of the court. A complaint charging an act of delinquency may not be amended unless agreed by the parties, if the proposed amendment would change the name or identity of the specific violation of law so that it would be considered a change of the crime charged if committed by an adult. Where requested, a court order shall grant a party reasonable time in which to respond to an amendment.

(C) **Answer.** No answer shall be necessary. A party may file an answer to the complaint, which, if filed, shall contain specific and concise admissions or denials of each material allegation of the complaint.

(D) **Prehearing motions.** Any defense, objection or request which is capable of determination without hearing on the allegations of the complaint may be raised before the adjudicatory hearing by motion. The following must be heard before the adjudicatory hearing, though not necessarily on a separate date:

(1) Defenses or objections based on defects in the institution of the proceeding;

(2) Defenses or objections based on defects in the

complaint (other than failure to show jurisdiction in the court or to charge an offense which objections shall be noticed by the court at any time during the pendency of the proceeding);

(3) Motions to suppress evidence on the ground that it was illegally obtained;

(4) Motions for discovery;

(5) Motions to determine whether the child is eligible to receive a sentence as a serious youthful offender.

(E) **Motion time.** Except for motions filed under division (D)(5) of this rule, all prehearing motions shall be filed by the earlier of:

(1) seven days prior to the hearing, or

(2) ten days after the appearance of counsel.

Rule 22(D)(5) motions shall be filed by the later of:

(1) Twenty days after the date of the child's initial appearance in juvenile court; or

(2) Twenty days after denial of a motion to transfer.

The filing of the Rule 22(D)(5) motion shall constitute notice of intent to pursue a serious youthful offender disposition.

The court in the interest of justice may extend the time for making prehearing motions.

The court for good cause shown may permit a motion to suppress evidence under division (D)(3) of this rule to be made at the time the evidence is offered.

(F) **State's right to appeal upon granting a motion to suppress.** In delinquency proceedings the state may take an appeal as of right from the granting of a motion to suppress evidence if, in addition to filing a notice of appeal, the prosecuting attorney certifies that (1) the appeal is not taken for the purpose of delay and (2) the granting of the motion has rendered proof available to the state so weak in its entirety that any reasonable possibility of proving the complaint's allegations has been destroyed.

Such appeal shall not be allowed unless the notice of appeal and the certification by the prosecuting attorney are filed with the clerk of the juvenile court within seven days after the date of the entry of the judgment or order granting the motion. Any appeal which may be taken under this rule shall be diligently prosecuted.

A child in detention or shelter care may be released pending this appeal when the state files the notice of appeal and certification.

This appeal shall take precedence over all other appeals.

**History:** Amended, eff 7-1-77; 7-1-94; 7-1-01.

## RULE 23. Continuance

Continuances shall be granted only when imperative to secure fair treatment for the parties.

## RULE 24. Discovery

(A) **Request for discovery.** Upon written request, each party of whom discovery is requested shall, to the extent not privileged, produce promptly for inspection, copying, or photographing the following information, documents, and material in that party's custody, control, or possession:

(1) The names and last known addresses of each witness to the occurrence that forms the basis of the charge or defense;

(2) Copies of any written statements made by any party or witness;

(3) Transcriptions, recordings, and summaries of any oral statements of any party or witness, except the work product of counsel;

(4) Any scientific or other reports that a party intends to introduce at the hearing or that pertain to physical evidence that a party intends to introduce;

(5) Photographs and any physical evidence which a party intends to introduce at the hearing;

(6) Except in delinquency and unruly child proceedings, other evidence favorable to the requesting party and relevant to the subject matter involved in the pending action. In delinquency and unruly child proceedings, the prosecuting attorney shall disclose to respondent's counsel all evidence, known or that may become known to the prosecuting attorney, favorable to the respondent and material either to guilt or punishment.

(B) **Order granting discovery: limitations; sanctions.** If a request for discovery is refused, application may be made to the court for a written order granting the discovery. Motions for discovery shall certify that a request for discovery has been made and refused. An order granting discovery may make such discovery reciprocal for all parties to the proceeding, including the party requesting discovery. Notwithstanding the provisions of subdivision (A), the court may deny, in whole or part, or otherwise limit or set conditions on the discovery authorized by such subdivision, upon its own motion, or upon a showing by a party upon whom a request for discovery is made that granting discovery may jeopardize the safety of a party or, witness, or confidential informant, result in the production of perjured testimony or evidence, endanger the existence of physical evidence, violate a privileged communication, or impede the criminal prosecution of a minor as an adult or of an adult charged with an offense arising from the same transaction or occurrence.

(C) **Failure to comply.** If at any time during the course of the proceedings it is brought to the attention of the court that a person has failed to comply with an order issued pursuant to this rule, the court may grant a continuance, prohibit the person from introducing in evidence the material not disclosed, or enter such other order as it deems just under the circumstances.

**History:** Amended, eff 7-1-94.

## RULE 25. Depositions

(A) Depositions in the following matters shall be governed by the Rules of Civil Procedure:

(1) Those taken in parentage actions and original actions to determine custody or the allocation of parental rights and responsibilities to which the State of Ohio is not a party;

(2) Those taken in any post-dispositional matters to which neither the State of Ohio nor any public child protective services agency is a party.

(B) Depositions shall only be taken with leave of court in delinquency, unruly, juvenile traffic offender, abuse, neglect, and dependency actions and all other juvenile court proceedings not specified in division (A). Except as provided in division (A)(2), depositions taken under this division shall only be taken to preserve testimony when it appears probable that a prospective witness will be unable to attend or will be prevented from attending a hearing, and if it further appears that the testimony is material and that it is necessary to take the deposition in order to prevent a miscarriage of justice. Depositions taken under this division shall be taken upon such terms and conditions and in such manner as the court may fix.

**History:** Amended, eff 7-1-09.

## RULE 26. [Reserved]

## RULE 27. Hearings: general

(A) **General Provisions.** Unless otherwise stated in this rule, the juvenile court may conduct its hearings in an informal manner and may adjourn its hearings from time to time.

The court may excuse the attendance of the child at the hearing in neglect, dependency, or abuse cases.

(1) Public access to hearings. In serious youthful offender proceedings, hearings shall be open to the public. In all other proceedings, the court may exclude the general public from any hearing, but may not exclude either of the following:

(a) Persons with a direct interest in the case;

(b) Persons who demonstrate, at a hearing, a countervailing right to be present.

(2) Separation of juvenile and adult cases. Cases involving children shall be heard separate and apart from the trial of cases against adults, except for cases involving chronic or habitual truancy.

(3) Jury trials. The court shall hear and determine all cases of children without a jury, except for the adjudication of a serious youthful offender complaint, indictment, or information in which trial by jury has not been waived.

(B) **Special provisions for abuse, neglect, and dependency proceedings.**

(1) In any proceeding involving abuse, neglect, or dependency at which the court removes a child from the child's home or continues the removal of a child from the child's home, or in a proceeding where the court orders detention, the court shall determine whether the person who filed the complaint in the case and removed the child from the child's home has custody of the child or will be given custody and has made reasonable efforts to do any of the following:

(a) Prevent the removal of the child from the child's home;

(b) Eliminate the continued removal of the child from the child's home;

(c) Make it possible for the child to return home.

(2) In a proceeding involving abuse, neglect, or dependency, the examination made by the court to determine whether a child is a competent witness shall comply with all of the following:

(a) Occur in an area other than a courtroom or hearing room;

(b) Be conducted in the presence of only those individuals considered necessary by the court for the conduct of the examination or the well being of the child;

(c) Be recorded in accordance with Juv. R. 37 or Juv. R. 40. The court may allow the prosecutor, guardian ad litem, or attorney for any party to submit questions for use by the court in determining whether the child is a competent witness.

(3) In a proceeding where a child is alleged to be an abused child, the court may order that the testimony of the child be taken by deposition in the presence of a judge or a magistrate. On motion of the prosecuting attorney, guardian ad litem, or a party, or in its own discretion, the court may order that the deposition be videotaped. All or part of the deposition is admissible in evidence where all of the following apply:

(a) It is filed with the clerk;

(b) Counsel for all parties had an opportunity and similar motive at the time of the taking of the deposition to develop the testimony by direct, cross, or redirect examination;

(c) The judge or magistrate determines there is reasonable cause to believe that if the child were to testify in person at the hearing, the child would experience emotional trauma as a result of the child's participation at the hearing.

**History:** Amended, eff 7-1-76; 7-1-94; 7-1-96; 7-1-01.

## RULE 28. [Reserved]

## RULE 29. Adjudicatory hearing

(A) **Scheduling the hearing.** The date for the adjudicatory hearing shall be set when the complaint is filed or as soon thereafter as is practicable. If the child is the subject of a complaint alleging a violation of a section of the Revised Code that may be violated by an adult and that does not request a serious youthful offender sentence, and if the child is in detention or shelter care, the hearing shall be held not later than fifteen days after the filing of the complaint. Upon a showing of good cause, the adjudicatory hearing may be continued and detention or shelter care extended.

The prosecuting attorney's filing of either a notice of intent to pursue or a statement of an interest in pursuing a serious youthful offender sentence shall constitute good cause for continuing the adjudicatory hearing date and extending detention or shelter care.

The hearing of a removal action shall be scheduled in accordance with Juv. R. 39(B).

If the complaint alleges abuse, neglect, or dependency, the hearing shall be held no later than thirty days after the complaint is filed. For good cause shown, the adjudicatory hearing may extend beyond thirty days either for an additional ten days to allow any party to obtain counsel or for a reasonable time beyond thirty days to obtain service on all parties or complete any necessary evaluations. However, the adjudicatory hearing shall be held no later than sixty days after the complaint is filed.

The failure of the court to hold an adjudicatory hearing within any time period set forth in this rule does not affect the ability of the court to issue any order otherwise provided for in statute or rule and does not provide any basis for contesting the jurisdiction of the court or the validity of any order of the court.

(B) **Advisement and findings at the commencement of the hearing.** At the beginning of the hearing, the court shall do all of the following:

(1) Ascertain whether notice requirements have been complied with and, if not, whether the affected parties waive compliance;

(2) Inform the parties of the substance of the complaint, the purpose of the hearing, and possible consequences of the hearing, including the possibility that the cause may be transferred to the appropriate adult court under Juv. R. 30 where the complaint alleges that a child fourteen years of age or over is delinquent by conduct that would constitute a felony if committed by an adult;

(3) Inform unrepresented parties of their right to counsel and determine if those parties are waiving their right to counsel;

(4) Appoint counsel for any unrepresented party under Juv. R. 4(A) who does not waive the right to counsel;

(5) Inform any unrepresented party who waives the right to counsel of the right: to obtain counsel at any stage of the proceedings, to remain silent, to offer evidence, to cross-examine witnesses, and, upon request, to have a record of all proceedings made, at public expense if indigent.

(C) **Entry of admission or denial.** The court shall request each party against whom allegations are being made in the complaint to admit or deny the allegations. A failure or refusal to admit the allegations shall be deemed a denial, except in cases where the court consents to entry of a plea of no contest.

(D) **Initial procedure upon entry of an admission.** The court may refuse to accept an admission and shall not accept an admission without addressing the party personally and determining both of the following:

(1) The party is making the admission voluntarily with understanding of the nature of the allegations and the consequences of the admission;

(2) The party understands that by entering an admission the party is waiving the right to challenge the witnesses and evidence against the party, to remain silent, and to introduce evidence at the adjudicatory hearing.

The court may hear testimony, review documents, or make further inquiry, as it considers appropriate, or it may proceed directly to the action required by division (F) of this rule.

(E) **Initial procedure upon entry of a denial.** If a party denies the allegations, the court shall:

(1) Direct the prosecuting attorney or another attorney-at-law to assist the court by presenting evidence in support of the allegations of a complaint;

(2) Order the separation of witnesses, upon request of any party;

(3) Take all testimony under oath or affirmation in either question-answer or narrative form; and

(4) Determine the issues by proof beyond a reasonable doubt in juvenile traffic offense, delinquency, and unruly proceedings; by clear and convincing evidence in dependency, neglect, and abuse cases, and in a removal action; and by a preponderance of the evidence in all other cases.

(F) **Procedure upon determination of the issues.** Upon the determination of the issues, the court shall do one of the following:

(1) If the allegations of the complaint, indictment, or information were not proven, dismiss the complaint;

(2) If the allegations of the complaint, indictment, or information are admitted or proven, do any one of the following, unless precluded by statute:

(a) Enter an adjudication and proceed forthwith to disposition;

(b) Enter an adjudication and continue the matter for disposition for not more than six months and may make appropriate temporary orders;

(c) Postpone entry of adjudication for not more than six months;

(d) Dismiss the complaint if dismissal is in the best interest of the child and the community.

(3) Upon request make written findings of fact and conclusions of law pursuant to Civ. R. 52.

(4) Ascertain whether the child should remain or be placed in shelter care until the dispositional hearing in an abuse, neglect, or dependency proceeding. In making a shelter care determination, the court shall make written finding of facts with respect to reasonable efforts in accordance with the provisions in Juv. R. 27(B)(1) and to relative placement in accordance with Juv. R. 7(F)(3).

**History:** Amended, eff 7-1-76; 7-1-94; 7-1-98; 7-1-01; 7-1-04.

## RULE 30. Relinquishment of jurisdiction for purposes of criminal prosecution

(A) **Preliminary hearing.** In any proceeding where the court considers the transfer of a case for criminal prosecution, the court shall hold a preliminary hearing to determine if there is probable cause to believe that the child committed the act alleged and that the act would be an offense if committed by an adult. The hearing may be upon motion of the court, the prosecuting attorney, or the child.

(B) **Mandatory transfer.** In any proceeding in which transfer of a case for criminal prosecution is required by statute upon a finding of probable cause, the order of transfer shall be entered upon a finding of probable cause.

(C) **Discretionary transfer.** In any proceeding in which transfer of a case for criminal prosecution is permitted, but not required, by statute, and in which probable cause is found at the preliminary hearing, the court shall continue the proceeding for full investigation. The investigation shall include a mental examination of the child by a public or private agency or by a person qualified to make the examination. When the investigation is completed, an amenability hearing shall be held to determine whether to transfer jurisdiction. The criteria for transfer shall be as provided by statute.

(D) **Notice.** Notice in writing of the time, place, and purpose of any hearing held pursuant to this rule shall be given to the state, the child's parents, guardian, or other custodian and the child's counsel at least three days prior to the hearing, unless written notice has been waived on the record.

(E) **Retention of jurisdiction.** If the court retains jurisdiction, it shall set the proceedings for hearing on the merits.

(F) **Waiver of mental examination.** The child may waive the mental examination required under division (C) of this rule. Refusal by the child to submit to a mental and physical examination or any part of the examination shall constitute a waiver of the examination.

(G) **Order of transfer.** The order of transfer shall state the reasons for transfer.

(H) **Release of child.** With respect to the transferred case, the juvenile court shall set the terms and conditions for release of the child in accordance with Crim. R. 46.

**History:** Amended, eff 7-1-76; 7-1-94; 7-1-97.

## RULE 31. [Reserved]

## RULE 32. Social history; physical examination; mental examination; investigation involving the allocation of parental rights and responsibilities for the care of children

(A) **Social history and physical or mental examination: availability before adjudication.** The court may order and utilize a social history or physical or mental examination at any time after the filing of a complaint under any of the following circumstances:

(1) Upon the request of the party concerning whom the history or examination is to be made;

(2) Where transfer of a child for adult prosecution is an issue in the proceeding;

(3) Where a material allegation of a neglect, dependency, or abused child complaint relates to matters that a history or examination may clarify;

(4) Where a party's legal responsibility for the party's acts or the party's competence to participate in the proceedings is an issue;

(5) Where a physical or mental examination is required to determine the need for emergency medical care under Juv. R. 13; or

(6) Where authorized under Juv. R. 7(I).

(B) **Limitations on preparation and use.** Until there has been an admission or adjudication that the child who is the subject of the proceedings is a juvenile traffic offender, delinquent, unruly, neglected, dependent, or abused, no social history, physical examination or mental examination shall be ordered except as authorized under subdivision (A) and any social history, physical examination or mental examination ordered pursuant to subdivision (A) shall be utilized only for the limited purposes therein specified. The person preparing a social history or making a physical or mental examination shall not testify about the history or examination or information received in its preparation in any juvenile traffic offender, delinquency, or unruly child adjudicatory hearing, except as may be required in a hearing to determine whether a child should be transferred to an adult court for criminal prosecution.

(C) **Availability of social history or investigation report.** A reasonable time before the dispositional hearing, or any other hearing at which a social history or physical or mental examination is to be utilized, counsel shall be permitted to inspect any social history or report of a mental or physical examination. The court may, for good cause shown, deny such inspection or limit its scope to specified portions of the history or report. The court may order that the contents of the history or report, in whole or part, not be disclosed to specified persons. If inspection or disclosure is denied or limited, the court shall state its reasons for such denial or limitation to counsel.

(D) **Investigation: allocation of parental rights and responsibilities for the care of children; habeas corpus.** On the filing of a complaint for the allocation of parental rights and responsibilities for the care of children or for a writ of habeas corpus to determine the allocation of parental rights and responsibilities for the care of a child, or on the filing of a motion for change in the allocation of parental rights and responsibilities for the care of children, the court may cause an investigation to be made as to the character, health, family relations, past conduct, present living conditions, earning ability, and financial worth of the parties to the action. The report of the investigation shall be confidential, but shall be made available to the parties or their counsel upon written request not less than three days before hearing. The court may tax as costs all or any part of the expenses of each investigation.

**History:** Amended, eff 7-1-73; 7-1-76; 7-1-91; 7-1-94.

## RULE 33. [Reserved]

## RULE 34. Dispositional hearing

(A) **Scheduling the hearing.** Where a child has been adjudicated as an abused, neglected, or dependent child, the court shall not issue a dispositional order until after it holds a separate dispositional hearing. The dispositional hearing for an adjudicated abused, neglected, or dependent child shall be held at least one day but not more than thirty days after the adjudicatory hearing is held. The dispositional hearing may be held immediately after the adjudicatory hearing if all parties were served prior to the adjudicatory hearing with all documents required for the dispositional hearing and all parties consent to the dispositional hearing being held immediately after the adjudicatory hearing. Upon the request of any party or the guardian ad litem of the child, the court may continue a dispositional hearing for a reasonable time not to exceed the time limit set forth in this division to enable a party to obtain or consult counsel. The dispositional hearing shall not be held more than ninety days after the date on which the complaint in the case was filed. If the dispositional hearing is not held within this ninety day period of time, the court, on its own motion or the motion of any party or the guardian ad litem of the child, shall dismiss the complaint without prejudice.

In all other juvenile proceedings, the dispositional hearing shall be held pursuant to Juv. R. 29(F)(2)(a) through (d) and the ninety day requirement shall not apply. Where the dispositional hearing is to be held immediately following the adjudicatory hearing, the court, upon the request of any party, shall continue the hearing for a reasonable time to enable the party to obtain or consult counsel.

(B) **Hearing procedure.** The hearing shall be conducted in the following manner:

(1) The judge or magistrate who presided at the adjudicatory hearing shall, if possible, preside;

(2) Except as provided in division (I) of this rule, the court may admit evidence that is material and relevant, including, but not limited to, hearsay, opinion, and documentary evidence;

(3) Medical examiners and each investigator who prepared a social history shall not be cross-examined, except upon consent of all parties, for good cause shown, or as the court in its discretion may direct. Any party may offer evidence supplementing, explaining, or disputing any information contained in the social history or other reports that may be used by the court in determining disposition.

(C) **Judgment.** After the conclusion of the hearing, the court shall enter an appropriate judgment within seven days. A copy of the judgment shall be given to any party requesting a copy. In all cases where a child is placed on probation, the child shall receive a written statement of the conditions of probation. If the judgment is conditional, the order shall state the conditions. If the child is not returned to the child's home, the court shall determine the school district that shall bear the cost of the child's education and may fix an amount of support to be paid by the responsible parent or from public funds.

(D) **Dispositional orders.** Where a child is adjudicated an abused, neglected, or dependent child, the court may make any of the following orders of disposition:

(1) Place the child in protective supervision;

(2) Commit the child to the temporary custody of a public or private agency, either parent, a relative residing within or outside the state, or a probation officer for placement in a certified foster home or approved foster care;

(3) Award legal custody of the child to either parent or to any other person who, prior to the dispositional hearing, files a motion requesting legal custody;

(4) Commit the child to the permanent custody of a public or private agency, if the court determines that the child cannot be placed with one of the child's parents

within a reasonable time or should not be placed with either parent and determines that the permanent commitment is in the best interest of the child;

(5) Place the child in a planned permanent living arrangement with a public or private agency if the agency requests the court for placement, if the court finds that a planned permanent living arrangement is in the best interest of the child, and if the court finds that one of the following exists:

(a) The child because of physical, mental, or psychological problems or needs is unable to function in a family-like setting;

(b) The parents of the child have significant physical, mental or psychological problems and are unable to care for the child, adoption is not in the best interest of the child and the child retains a significant and positive relationship with a parent or relative;

(c) The child is sixteen years of age or older, has been counseled, is unwilling to accept or unable to adapt to a permanent placement and is in an agency program preparing the child for independent living.

(E) **Protective supervision.** If the court issues an order for protective supervision, the court may place any reasonable restrictions upon the child, the child's parents, guardian, or any other person including, but not limited to, any of the following:

(1) Ordering a party within forty-eight hours to vacate the child's home indefinitely or for a fixed period of time;

(2) Ordering a party, parent, or custodian to prevent any particular person from having contact with the child;

(3) Issuing a restraining order to control the conduct of any party.

(F) **Case plan.** As part of its dispositional order, the court shall journalize a case plan for the child. The agency required to maintain a case plan shall file the case plan with the court prior to the child's adjudicatory hearing but not later than thirty days after the earlier of the date on which the complaint in the case was filed or the child was first placed in shelter care. The plan shall specify what additional information, if any, is necessary to complete the plan and how the information will be obtained. All parts of the case plan shall be completed by the earlier of thirty days after the adjudicatory hearing or the date of the dispositional hearing for the child. If all parties agree to the content of the case plan and the court approves it, the court shall journalize the plan as part of its dispositional order. If no agreement is reached, the court, based upon the evidence presented at the dispositional hearing and the best interest of the child, shall determine the contents of the case plan and journalize it as part of the dispositional order for the child.

(G) **Modification of temporary order.** The department of human services or any other public or private agency or any party, other than a parent whose parental rights have been terminated, may at any time file a motion requesting that the court modify or terminate any order of disposition. The court shall hold a hearing upon the motion as if the hearing were the original dispositional hearing and shall give all parties and the guardian *ad litem* notice of the hearing pursuant to these rules. The court, on its own motion and upon proper notice to all parties and any interested agency, may modify or terminate any order of disposition.

(H) **Restraining orders.** In any proceeding where a child is made a ward of the court, the court may grant a restraining order controlling the conduct of any party if the court finds that the order is necessary to control any conduct or relationship that may be detrimental or harmful to the child and tend to defeat the execution of a dispositional order.

(I) **Bifurcation; Rules of Evidence.** Hearings to determine whether temporary orders regarding custody should be modified to orders for permanent custody shall be considered dispositional hearings and need not be bifurcated. The Rules of Evidence shall apply in hearings on motions for permanent custody.

(J) **Advisement of rights after hearing.** At the conclusion of the hearing, the court shall advise the child of the child's right to record expungement and, where any part of the proceeding was contested, advise the parties of their right to appeal.

**History:** Amended, eff 7-1-94; 7-1-96; 7-1-02.

## RULE 35. Proceedings after judgment

(A) **Continuing jurisdiction; invoked by motion.** The continuing jurisdiction of the court shall be invoked by motion filed in the original proceeding, notice of which shall be served in the manner provided for the service of process.

(B) **Revocation of probation.** The court shall not revoke probation except after a hearing at which the child shall be present and apprised of the grounds on which revocation is proposed. The parties shall have the right to counsel and the right to appointed counsel where entitled pursuant to Juv. R. 4(A). Probation shall not be revoked except upon a finding that the child has violated a condition of probation of which the child had, pursuant to Juv. R. 34(C), been notified.

(C) **Detention.** During the pendency of proceedings under this rule, a child may be placed in detention in accordance with the provisions of Rule 7.

**History:** Amended, eff 7-1-94.

## RULE 36. Dispositional review

(A) **Court review.** A court that issues a dispositional order in an abuse, neglect, or dependency case may review the child's placement or custody arrangement, the case plan, and the actions of the public or private agency implementing that plan at any time. A court that issues a dispositional order shall hold a review hearing one year after the earlier of the date on which the complaint in the case was filed or the child was first placed into shelter care. The court shall schedule the review hearing at the time that it holds the dispositional hearing. The court shall hold a similar review hearing no later than every twelve months after the initial review hearing until the child is adopted, returned to the child's parents, or the court otherwise terminates the child's placement or custody arrangement. A hearing pursuant to section 2151.415 of the Revised Code shall take the place of the first review hearing. The court shall schedule each subsequent review hearing at the conclusion of the review hearing immediately preceding the review hearing to be scheduled. Review hearings may be conducted by a judge or magistrate.

(B) **Citizens' review board.** The court may appoint a citizens' review board to conduct review hearings, subject to the review and approval by the court.

(C) **Agency review.** Each agency required to prepare a case plan for a child shall complete a semiannual administrative review of the case plan no later than six months after the earlier of the date on which the complaint in the case was filed or the child was first placed in shelter care. After the first administrative review, the agency shall complete semiannual administrative reviews no later than every six months. The agency shall prepare and file a written summary of the semiannual administrative review that shall include an updated case plan. If the agency, parents, guardian, or custodian of the child and guardian ad litem stipulate to the revised case plan, the plan shall be signed by all parties and filed with the written summary of the administrative review no later than seven days after the completion of the administrative review. If the court does not object to the revised case plan, it shall journalize the case plan within fourteen days after it is filed with the court. If the court does not approve of the revised case plan or if the agency, parties, guardian ad litem, and the attorney of the child do not agree to the need for changes to the case plan and to all of the proposed changes, the agency shall file its written summary and request a hearing. The court shall schedule a review hearing to be held no later than thirty days after the filing of the case plan or written summary or both, if required. The court shall give notice of the date, time, and location of the hearing to all interested parties and the guardian ad litem of the child. The court shall take one of the following actions:

(1) Approve or modify the case plan based upon the evidence presented;

(2) Return the child home with or without protective supervision and terminate temporary custody or determine which agency shall have custody;

(3) If the child is in permanent custody determine what actions would facilitate adoption;

(4) Journalize the terms of the updated case plan.

**History:** Effective 7-1-94; amended, eff 7-1-96.

## RULE 37. Recording of proceedings

(A) **Record of proceedings.** The juvenile court shall make a record of adjudicatory and dispositional proceedings in abuse, neglect, dependent, unruly, and delinquent cases; permanent custody cases; and proceedings before magistrates. In all other proceedings governed by these rules, a record shall be made upon request of a party or upon motion of the court. The record shall be taken in shorthand, stenotype, or by any other adequate mechanical, electronic, or video recording device.

(B) **Restrictions on use of recording or transcript.** No public use shall be made by any person, including a party, of any juvenile court record, including the recording or a transcript of any juvenile court hearing, except in the course of an appeal or as authorized by order of the court or by statute.

**History:** Amended, eff 7-1-96; 7-1-01.

## RULE 38. Voluntary surrender of custody

(A) **Temporary custody.**

(1) A person with custody of a child may enter into an agreement with any public or private children services agency giving the agency temporary custody for a period of up to thirty days without the approval of the juvenile court. The agency may request the court to grant a thirty day extension of the original agreement. The court may grant the original extension if it determines the extension to be in the best interest of the child. A case plan shall be filed at the same time the request for extension is filed. At the expiration of the original thirty day extension period, the agency may request the court to grant an additional thirty day extension. The court may grant the additional extension if it determines the extension is in the child's best interest. The agency shall file an updated case plan at the same time it files the request for additional extension. At the expiration of the additional thirty day extension period, or at the expiration of the original thirty day extension period if no additional thirty day extension was requested, the agency shall either return the child to the custodian or file a complaint requesting temporary or permanent custody and a case plan.

(2) Notwithstanding division (A)(1) of this rule, the agreement may be for a period of sixty days if executed solely for the purpose of obtaining the adoption of a child less than six months of age. The agency may request the court to extend the temporary custody agreement for thirty days. A case plan shall be filed at the same time the request for extension is filed. At the expiration of the thirty day extension, the agency shall either return the child to the child's custodian or file a complaint with the court requesting temporary or permanent custody and a case plan.

(B) **Permanent custody.**

(1) A person with custody of a child may make an agreement with court approval surrendering the child into the permanent custody of a public children service agency or private child placing agency. A public children service agency shall request and a private child placing agency may request the juvenile court of the county in which the child had residence or legal settlement to approve the permanent surrender agreement. The court may approve the agreement if it determines it to be in the best interest of the child. The agency requesting the approval shall file a case plan at the same time it files its request for approval of the permanent surrender agreement.

(2) An agreement for the surrender of permanent custody of a child to a private service agency is not required to be approved by the court if the agreement is executed solely for the purpose of obtaining an adoption of a child who is less than six months of age on the date of the execution of the agreement.

One year after the agreement is entered and every subsequent twelve months after that date, the court shall schedule a review hearing if a final decree of adoption has not been entered for a child who is the subject of an agreement for the surrender of permanent custody.

**History:** Effective, 7-1-94.

## RULE 39. Out of county removal hearings

(A) **Notice of removal hearing.** Upon the filing of a removal action, the court in which the complaint is filed shall contact the court that issued the original dispositional order for information necessary for service of summons and issuance of notice of the removal hearing. The court that issued the original dispositional order shall respond within five days after receiving the request.

Summons shall issue pursuant to Juv. R. 15 and 16.

Notice of the removal hearing shall be sent by first class mail, as evidenced by a certificate of mailing filed with the clerk of court, to the following, not otherwise summoned, at least five days before the hearing:

(1) The court issuing the dispositional order;

(2) The guardian ad litem for the child;

(3) Counsel for the child;

(4) The placing entity;

(5) The custodial entity;

(6) The complainant;

(7) The guardian ad litem and counsel presently representing the child in the court that issued the original dispositional order;

(8) Any other persons the court determines to be appropriate.

(B) **Removal hearing.** The removal hearing shall be held not later than thirty days after service of summons is obtained. If, after the removal hearing, the court grants relief in favor of the complainant, the court shall send written notice of such relief to the juvenile court that issued the original dispositional order.

**History:** Effective, 7-1-98.

## RULE 40. Magistrates

(A) **Appointment.** The court may appoint one or more magistrates who shall have been engaged in the practice of law for at least four years and be in good standing with the Supreme Court of Ohio at the time of appointment. A magistrate appointed under this rule also may serve as a magistrate under Crim. R. 19. The court shall not appoint as a magistrate any person who has contemporaneous responsibility for working with, or supervising the behavior of, children who are subject to dispositional orders of the appointing court or any other juvenile court.

(B) **Compensation.** The compensation of magistrates shall be fixed by the court, and no part of the compensation shall be taxed as costs.

(C) **Authority.**

(1) **Scope.** To assist juvenile courts of record and pursuant to reference under Juv. R. 40(D)(1), magistrates are authorized, subject to the terms of the relevant reference, to do any of the following:

(a) Determine any motion in any case, except a case involving the determination of a child's status as a serious youthful offender;

(b) Conduct the trial of any case that will not be tried to a jury, except the adjudication of a case against an alleged serious youthful offender;

(c) Upon unanimous written consent of the parties, preside over the trial of any case that will be tried to a jury; except the adjudication of a case against an alleged serious youthful offender;

(d) Exercise any other authority specifically vested in magistrates by statute and consistent with this rule.

(2) **Regulation of proceedings.** In performing the responsibilities described in Juv. R. 40(C)(1), magistrates are authorized, subject to the terms of the relevant reference, to regulate all proceedings as if by the court and to do everything necessary for the efficient performance of those responsibilities, including but not limited to, the following:

(a) Issuing subpoenas for the attendance of witnesses and the production of evidence;

(b) Ruling upon the admissibility of evidence;

(c) Putting witnesses under oath and examining them;

(d) Calling the parties to the action and examining them under oath;

(e) When necessary to obtain the presence of an alleged contemnor in cases involving direct or indirect contempt of court, issuing an attachment for the alleged contemnor and setting the type, amount, and any conditions of bail pursuant to Crim. R. 46;

(f) Imposing, subject to Juv. R. 40(D)(8), appropriate sanctions for civil or criminal contempt committed in the presence of the magistrate.

(D) **Proceedings in Matters Referred to Magistrates**

(1) **Reference by court of record.**

(a) **Purpose and method.** A court may, for one or more of the purposes described in Juv. R. 40(C)(1), refer a particular case or matter or a category of cases or matters to a magistrate by a specific or general order of reference or by rule.

(b) **Limitation.** A court may limit a reference by specifying or limiting the magistrate's powers, including but not limited to, directing the magistrate to determine only particular issues, directing the magistrate to perform particular responsibilities, directing the magistrate to receive and report evidence only, fixing the time and place for beginning and closing any hearings, or fixing the time for filing any magistrate's decision on the matter or matters referred.

(2) **Magistrate's order; motion to set aside magistrate's order.**

(a) **Magistrate's order.**

(i) **Nature of order.** Subject to the terms of the relevant reference, a magistrate may enter orders without judicial approval if necessary to regulate the proceedings and if not dispositive of a claim or defense of a party.

(ii) **Form, filing, and service of magistrate's order.** A magistrate's order shall be in writing, identified as a magistrate's order in the caption, signed by the magistrate, filed with the clerk, and served on all parties or their attorneys.

(iii) **Magistrate's order include.** A magistrate's order includes any of the following:

(A) Pretrial proceedings under Civ. R. 16;

(B) Discovery proceedings under Civ. R. 26 to 37, Juv. R. 24, and Juv. R.25;

(C) Appointment of an attorney or guardian ad litem pursuant to Juv. R. 4 and Juv. R.29(B)(4);

(D) Taking a child into custody pursuant to Juv. R. 6;

(E) Detention hearings pursuant to Juv. R. 7;

(F) Temporary orders pursuant to Juv. R. 13;

(G) Extension of temporary orders pursuant to Juv. R. 14;

(H) Summons and warrants pursuant to Juv. R. 15;

(I) Preliminary conferences pursuant to Juv. R. 21;

(J) Continuances pursuant to Juv. R. 23;

(K) Deposition orders pursuant to Juv. R. 27(B)(3);

(L) Orders for social histories, physical and mental examinations pursuant to Juv. R. 32;

(M) Proceedings upon application for the issuance of a temporary protection order as authorized by law;

(N) Other orders as necessary to regulate the proceedings.

(b) **Motion to set aside magistrate's order.** Any party may file a motion with the court to set aside a magistrate's order. The motion shall state the moving party's reasons with particularity and shall be filed not later than ten days after the magistrate's order is filed. The pendency of a motion to set aside does not stay the effectiveness of the magistrate's order, though the magistrate or the court may by order stay the effectiveness of a magistrate's order.

(3) **Magistrate's decision; objections to magistrate's decision.**

(a) **Magistrate's decision.**

(i) **When required.** Subject to the terms of the relevant reference, a magistrate shall prepare a magistrate's decision respecting any matter referred under Juv. R. 40(D)(1).

(ii) **Findings of fact and conclusions of law.** Subject to the terms of the relevant reference, a magistrate's decision may be general unless findings of fact and conclusions of law are timely requested by a party or otherwise required by law. A request for findings of fact and conclusions of law shall be made before the entry of a magistrate's decision or within seven days after the filing of a magistrate's decision. If a request for findings of fact and conclusions of law is timely made, the magistrate may require any or all of the parties to submit proposed findings of fact and conclusions of law.

(iii) **Form, filing, and service of magistrate's decision.** A magistrate's decision shall be in writing, identified as a magistrate's decision in the caption, signed by the magistrate, filed with the clerk, and served on all parties or their attorneys no later than three days after the decision is filed. A magistrate's decision shall indicate conspicuously that a party shall not assign as error on appeal the court's adoption of any factual finding or legal conclusion, whether or not specifically designated as a finding of fact or conclusion of law under Juv. R. 40(D)(3)(a)(ii), unless the party timely and specifically objects to that factual finding or legal conclusion as required by Juv. R. 40(D)(3)(b).

(b) **Objections to magistrate's decision.**

(i) **Time for filing.** A party may file written objections to a magistrate's decision within fourteen days of the filing of the decision, whether or not the court has adopted the decision during that fourteen-day period as permitted by Juv. R. 40(D)(4)(e)(i). If any party timely files objections, any other party may also file objections not later than ten days after the first objections are filed. If a party makes a timely request for findings of fact and conclusions of law, the time for filing objections begins to run when the magistrate files a decision that includes findings of fact and conclusions of law.

(ii) **Specificity of objection.** An objection to a magistrate's decision shall be specific and state with particularity all grounds for objection.

(iii) **Objection to magistrate's factual finding, transcript or affidavit.** An objection to a factual finding, whether or not specifically designated as a finding of fact under Juv. R. 40(D)(3)(a)(ii), shall be supported by a transcript of all the evidence submitted to the magistrate relevant to that finding or an affidavit of that evidence if a transcript is not available. With leave of court, alternative technology or manner of reviewing the relevant evidence may be considered. The objecting party shall file the transcript or affidavit with the court within thirty days after filing objections unless the court extends the time in writing for preparation of the transcript or other good cause. If a party files timely objections prior to the date on which a transcript is prepared, the party may seek leave of court to supplement the objections.

(iv) **Waiver of right to assign adoption by court as error on appeal.** Except for a claim of plain error, a party shall not assign as error on appeal the court's adoption of any factual finding or legal conclusion, whether or not specifically designated as a finding of fact or conclusion of law under Juv. R. 40(D)(3)(a)(ii), unless the party has objected to that finding or conclusion as required by Juv. R. 40(D)(3)(b).

(4) **Action of court on magistrate's decision and on any objections to magistrate's decision; entry of judgment or interim order by court.**

(a) **Action of court required.** A magistrate's decision is not effective unless adopted by the court.

(b) **Action on magistrate's decision.** Whether or not objections are timely filed, a court may adopt or reject a magistrate's decision in whole or in part, with or without modification. A court may hear a previously-referred matter, take additional evidence, or return a matter to a magistrate.

(c) **If no objections are filed.** If no timely objections are filed, the court may adopt a magistrate's decision, unless it determines that there is an error of law or other defect evident on the face of the magistrate's decision.

(d) **Action on objections.** If one or more objections to a magistrate's decision are timely filed, the court shall rule on those objections. In ruling on objections, the court shall undertake an independent review as to the objected matters to ascertain that the magistrate has properly determined the factual issues and appropriately applied the law. Before so ruling, the court may hear additional evidence but may refuse to do so unless the objecting party demonstrates that the party could not, with reasonable diligence, have produced that evidence for consideration by the magistrate.

(e) **Entry of judgment or interim order by court.** A court that adopts, rejects, or modifies a magistrate's decision shall also enter a judgment or interim order.

(i) **Judgment.** The court may enter a judgment either during the fourteen days permitted by Juv. R. 40(D)(3)(b)(i) for the filing of objections to a magistrate's decision or after the fourteen days have expired. If the court enters a judgment during the fourteen days permitted by Juv. R. 40(D)(3)(b)(i) for the filing of objections, the timely filing of objections to the magistrate's decision shall operate as an automatic stay of execution of the judgment until the court disposes of those objections and vacates, modifies, or adheres to the judgment previously entered.

(ii) **Interim order.** The court may enter an interim order on the basis of a magistrate's decision without waiting for or ruling on timely objections by the parties where immediate relief is justified. The timely filing of objections does not stay the execution of an interim order, but an interim order shall not extend more than twenty-eight days from the date of entry, subject to extension by the court in increments of twenty-eight additional days for good cause shown.

(5) **Extension of time.** For good cause shown, the court shall allow a reasonable extension of time for a party to file a motion to set aside a magistrate's order or file objections to a magistrate's decision. "Good cause" includes, but is not limited to, a failure by the clerk to timely serve the party seeking the extension with the magistrate's order or decision.

(6) **Disqualification of a magistrate.** Disqualification of a magistrate for bias or other cause is within the discretion of the court and may be sought by motion filed with the court.

(7) **Recording of proceedings before a magistrate.** Except as otherwise provided by law, all proceedings before a magistrate shall be recorded in accordance with procedures established by the court.

(8) **Contempt in the presence of a magistrate.**

(a) **Contempt order.** Contempt sanctions under Juv. R. 40(C)(2)(f) may be imposed only by a written order that recites the facts and certifies that the magistrate saw or heard the conduct constituting contempt.

(b) **Filing and provision of copies of contempt order.** A contempt order shall be filed and copies provided forthwith by the clerk to the appropriate judge of the court and to the subject of the order.

(c) **Review of contempt order by court; bail.** The subject of a contempt order may by motion obtain immediate review by a judge. A judge or the magistrate entering the contempt order may set bail pending judicial review of the order.

**History:** Amended, eff 7-1-75; 7-1-85; 7-1-92; 7-1-95; 7-1-98; 7-1-01; 7-1-03, 7-1-06; 7-1-11.

## RULE 41. [Reserved]

## RULE 42. Consent to marry

(A) **Application where parental consent not required.** When a minor desires to contract matrimony and has no parent, guardian, or custodian whose consent to the marriage is required by law, the minor shall file an application under oath in the county where the female resides requesting that the judge of the juvenile court give consent and approbation in the probate court for such marriage.

(B) **Contents of application.** The application required by division (A) of this rule shall contain all of the following:

(1) The name and address of the person for whom consent is sought;

(2) The age of the person for whom consent is sought;

(3) The reason why consent of a parent is not required;

(4) The name and address, if known, of the parent, where the minor alleges that parental consent is unnecessary because the parent has neglected or abandoned the child for at least one year immediately preceding the application.

(C) **Application where female pregnant or delivered of child born out of wedlock.** Where a female is pregnant or delivered of a child born out of wedlock and the parents of such child seek to marry even though one or both of them is under the minimum age prescribed by law for persons who may contract marriage, such persons shall file an application under oath in the county where the female resides requesting that the judge of the juvenile court give consent in the probate court to such marriage.

(D) **Contents of application.** The application required by subdivision (C) shall contain:

(1) The name and address of the person or persons for whom consent is sought;

(2) The age of such person;

(3) An indication of whether the female is pregnant or has already been delivered;

(4) An indication of whether or not any applicant under eighteen years of age is already a ward of the court; and

(5) Any other facts which may assist the court in determining whether to consent to such marriage.

If pregnancy is asserted, a certificate from a physician verifying pregnancy shall be attached to the application. If an illegitimate child has been delivered, the birth certificate of such child shall be attached.

The consent to the granting of the application by each parent whose consent to the marriage is required by law shall be indorsed on the application.

(E) **Investigation.** Upon receipt of an application under subdivision (C), the court shall set a date and time for hearing thereon at its earliest convenience and shall direct that an inquiry be made as to the circumstances surrounding the applicants.

(F) **Notice.** If neglect or abandonment is alleged in an application under subdivision (A) and the address of the parent is known, the court shall cause notice of the date and time of hearing to be served upon such parent.

(G) **Judgment.** If the court finds that the allegations stated in the application are true, and that the granting of the application is in the best interest of the applicants, the court shall grant the consent and shall make the applicant referred to in subdivision (C) a ward of the court.

(H) **Certified copy.** A certified copy of the judgment entry shall be transmitted to the probate court.

**History:** Amended, eff 7-1-80; 7-1-94.

## RULE 43. Reference to Ohio Revised Code

A reference in these rules to a section of the Revised Code shall mean the section as amended from time to time including the enactment of additional sections, the numbers of which are subsequent to the section referred to in the rules.

**History:** Amended, eff 7-1-94.

## RULE 44. Jurisdiction unaffected

These rules shall not be construed to extend or limit the jurisdiction of the juvenile court.

**History:** Effective: July 1, 1972.

## RULE 45. Rules by juvenile courts; procedure not otherwise specified

(A) **Local rules.** The juvenile court may adopt rules concerning local practice that are not inconsistent with these rules. Local rules shall be adopted only after the court gives appropriate notice and an opportunity for comment. If the court determines that there is an immediate need for a rule, the court may adopt the rule without prior notice and opportunity for comment but promptly shall afford notice and opportunity for comment. Local rules shall be filed with the Supreme Court.

(B) **Procedure not otherwise specified.** If no procedure is specifically prescribed by these rules or local rule, the court shall proceed in any lawful manner not inconsistent with these rules or local rule.

**History:** Amended, eff 7-1-94.

## RULE 46. Forms

The forms contained in the Appendix of Forms which the Supreme Court from time to time may approve are sufficient under these rules and shall be accepted for filing by courts of this state. Forms adopted by local courts that are substantially similar to the forms in the Appendix of Forms may also be accepted for filing. The forms in the Appendix of Forms are intended to indicate the simplicity and brevity of statement which these rules contemplate.

**History:** Amended 7-1-11.

## RULE 47. Effective Date

(A) **Effective date of rules.** These rules shall take effect on first day of July, 1972. They govern all proceedings in actions brought after they take effect and also all further proceedings in actions then pending except to the extent that their application in a particular action pending when the rules take effect would not be feasible or would work injustice, in which event the former procedure applies.

(B) **Effective date of amendments.** The amendments submitted by the Supreme Court to the General Assembly on January 12, 1973, shall take effect on the first day of July, 1973. They govern all proceedings in actions brought after they take effect and also all further proceedings in actions then pending, except to the extent that their application is a particular action pending when the amendments take effect would not be feasible or would work injustice, in which event the former procedure applies.

(C) **Effective date of amendments.** The amendments submitted by the Supreme Court to the General Assembly on January 10, 1975, and on April 29, 1975, shall take effect on July 1, 1975. They govern all proceedings in actions brought after they take effect and also all further proceedings in actions then pending, except to the extent that their application in a particular action pending when the amendments take effect would not be feasible or would work injustice, in which event the former procedure applies.

(D) **Effective date of amendments.** The amendments submitted by the Supreme Court to the General Assembly on January 9, 1976 shall take effect on July 1, 1976. They govern all proceedings in actions brought after they take effect and also all further proceedings in actions then pending, except to the extent that their application in a particular action pending when the amendments take effect would not be feasible or would work injustice, in which event the former procedure applies.

(E) **Effective date of amendments.** The amendments submitted by the Supreme Court to the General Assembly on January 14, 1980, shall take effect on July 1, 1980. They govern all proceedings in actions brought after they take effect and also all further proceedings in actions then pending, except to the extent that their application in a particular action pending when the amendments take effect would not be feasible or would work injustice, in which event the former procedure applies.

(F) **Effective date of amendments.** The amendments submitted by the Supreme Court to the General Assembly on December 24, 1984 and January 8, 1985 shall take effect on July 1, 1985. They govern all proceedings in actions brought after they take effect and also all further proceedings in actions then pending, except to the extent that their application in a particular action pending when the amendments take effect would not be feasible or would work injustice, in which event the former procedure applies.

(G) **Effective date of amendments.** The amendments submitted by the Supreme Court to the General Assembly on January 10, 1991 shall take effect on July 1, 1991. They govern all proceedings in actions brought after they take effect and also all further proceedings in actions then pending, except to the extent that their application in a particular action pending when the amendments take effect would not be feasible or would work injustice, in which event the former procedure applies.

(H) **Effective date of amendments.** The amendments filed by the Supreme Court with the General Assembly on January 14, 1992 and further filed on April 30, 1992, shall take effect on July 1, 1992. They govern all proceedings in actions brought after they take effect and also all future proceedings in actions then pending, except to the extent that their application in a particular action pending when the amendments take effect would not be feasible or would work injustice, in which event the former procedure applies.

(I) **Effective date of amendments.** The amendments filed by the Supreme Court with the General Assembly on January 14, 1994 and further revised and filed on April 29, 1994 shall take effect on July 1, 1994. They govern all proceedings in actions brought after they take effect and also all future proceedings in actions then pending, except to the extent that their application in a particular action pending when the amendments take effect would not be feasible or would work injustice, in which event the former procedure applies.

(J) **Effective date of amendments.** The amendments to Rules 1, 4, and 40 filed by the Supreme Court with the General Assembly on January 11, 1995 and further revised and filed on April 25, 1995 shall take effect on July 1, 1995. They govern all proceedings in actions brought after they take effect and also all further proceedings in actions then pending, except to the extent that their application in a particular action pending when the amendments take effect would not be feasible or would work injustice, in which event the former procedure applies.

(K) **Effective date of amendments.** The amendments to Rules 6, 8, 13, 27, 34, 36, and 37 filed by the Supreme Court with the General Assembly on January 5, 1996 and refiled on April 26, 1996 shall take effect on July 1, 1996. They govern all proceedings in actions brought after they take effect and also all further proceedings in actions then pending, except to the extent that their application in a particular action pending when the amendments take effect would not be feasible or would work injustice, in which event the former procedure applies.

(L) **Effective date of amendments.** The amendments to Rule 30 filed by the Supreme Court with the General Assembly on January 10, 1997 and refiled on April 24, 1997 shall take effect on July 1, 1997. They govern all proceedings in actions brought after they take effect and also all further proceedings in actions then pending, except to the extent that their application in a particular action pending when the amendments take effect would not be feasible or would work injustice, in which event the former procedure applies.

(M) **Effective date of amendments.** The amendments to Rules 2, 4, 10, 11, 15, 16, 29, 39, and 40 filed by the Supreme Court with the General Assembly on January 15, 1998 and further revised and refiled on April 30, 1998 shall take effect on July 1, 1998. They govern all proceedings in actions brought after they take effect and also all further proceedings in actions then pending, except to the extent that their application in a particular action pending when the amendments take effect would not be feasible or would work injustice, in which event the former procedure applies.

(N) **Effective date of amendments.** The amendments to Juvenile Rules 2, 7, 8, 10, 15, 22, 27, 29, 37, and 40 filed by the Supreme Court with the General Assembly on January 12, 2001, and revised and refiled on April 26, 2001, shall take effect on July 1, 2001. They govern all proceedings in actions brought after they take effect and also all further proceedings in actions then pending, except to the extent that their application in a particular action pending when the amendments take effect would not be feasible or would work injustice, in which event the former procedure applies.

(O) **Effective date of amendments.** The amendments to Juvenile Rules 2, 10, 15, and 34 filed by the Supreme Court with the General Assembly on January 11, 2002, and refiled on April 18, 2002 shall take effect on July 1, 2002. They govern all proceedings in actions brought after they take effect and also all further proceedings in actions then pending, except to the extent that their application in a particular action pending when the amendments take effect would not be feasible or would work injustice, in which event the former procedure applies.

(P) **Effective date of amendments.** The amendments to Juvenile Rule 40 filed by the Supreme Court with the General Assembly on January 9, 2003 and refiled on April 28, 2003, shall take effect on July 1, 2003. They govern all proceedings in actions brought after they take effect and also all further proceedings in actions then pending, except to the extent that their application in a particular action pending when the amendments take effect would not be feasible or would work injustice, in which event the former procedure applies.

(Q) **Effective date of amendments.** The amendments to Juvenile Rule 29 filed by the Supreme Court with the General Assembly on January 7, 2004 and refiled on April 28, 2004 shall take effect on July 1, 2004. They govern all proceedings in actions brought after they take effect and also all further proceedings in actions then pending, except to the extent that their application in a particular action pending when the amendments take effect would not be feasible or would work injustice, in which event the former procedure applies.

(R) **Effective date of amendments.** The amendments to Juvenile Rule 40 filed by the Supreme Court with the General Assembly on January 12, 2006 shall take effect on July 1, 2006. They govern all proceedings in actions brought after they take effect and also all further proceedings in actions then pending, except to the extent that their application in a particular action pending when the amendments take effect would not be feasible or would work injustice, in which event the former procedure applies.

(S) **Effective date of amendments.** The amendments to Juvenile Rule 25 filed by the Supreme Court with the General Assembly on January 14, 2009 and revised and refiled on April 30, 2009 shall take effect on July 1, 2009. They govern all proceedings in actions brought after they take effect and also all further proceedings in actions then pending, except to the extent that their application in a particular action pending when the amendments take effect would not be feasible or would work injustice, in which event the former procedure applies.

(T) **Effective date of amendments.** The amendments to Juvenile Rules 40 and 46 filed by the Supreme Court with the General Assembly on January 5, 2011 and refiled on April 21, 2011 shall take effect on July 1, 2011. They govern all proceedings in actions brought after they take effect and also all further proceedings in actions then pending, except to the extent that their application in a particular action pending when the amendments take effect would not be feasible or would work injustice, in which event the former procedure applies.

**History:** Amended, eff 7-1-73; 7-1-75; 7-1-76; 7-1-80; 7-1-85; 7-1-91; 7-1-92; 7-1-94; 7-1-95; 7-1-96; 7-1-97; 7-1-98; 7-1-01; 7-1-02; 7-1-03; 7-1-04; 7-1-06; 7-1-09; 7-1-10; 7-1-11.

## RULE 48. Title

These rules shall be known as Ohio Rules of Juvenile Procedure and may be cited as "Juvenile Rules" or "Juv. R.____"

# OHIO TRAFFIC RULES

## Complete with amendments through July 1, 2011.



### RULE 1. Scope of rules; applicability; authority and construction

(A) **Applicability.** These rules prescribe the procedure to be followed in all courts of this state in traffic cases and supersede the "Ohio Rules of Practice and Procedure in Traffic Cases For All Courts Inferior To Common Pleas" effective January 1, 1969, and as amended on January 4, 1971, and December 7, 1972.

(B) **Authority and construction.** These rules are promulgated pursuant to authority granted the Supreme Court by R.C. § 2935.17 and § 2937.46. They shall be construed and applied to secure the fair, impartial, speedy and sure administration of justice, simplicity and uniformity in procedure, and the elimination of unjustifiable expense and delay.

**History:** Effective January 1, 1975.

### RULE 2. Definitions

As used in these rules:

(A) "Traffic case" means any proceeding, other than a proceeding resulting from a felony indictment, that involves one or more violations of a law, ordinance, or regulation governing the operation and use of vehicles, conduct of pedestrians in relation to vehicles, or weight, dimension, loads or equipment, or vehicles drawn or moved on highways and bridges. "Traffic case" does not include any proceeding that results in a felony indictment.

(B) "Traffic ticket" means the traffic complaint and summons described in Traffic Rule 3 and that appears in the Appendix of Forms.

(C) "Highway" includes a street or an alley.

(D) "Petty offense" means an offense for which the penalty prescribed by law includes confinement for six months or less.

(E) "Serious offense" means an offense for which the penalty prescribed by law includes confinement for more than six months.

(F) "Court" means a municipal court, county court, juvenile division of the court of common pleas, or mayor's court.

(G) "Judge" means judge of a municipal court, county court, or juvenile division of the court of common pleas, a magistrate of a municipal or county court, or a mayor or mayor's court magistrate presiding over a mayor's court.

(H) "Prosecuting attorney" means the attorney general of this state, the prosecuting attorney of a county, the law director, city solicitor, or other officer who prosecutes a criminal case on behalf of the state or a city, village, township, or other political subdivision, and the assistant or assistants of any of them.

(I) "State" means this state, a county, city, village, township, other political subdivision or any other entity of this state that may prosecute a criminal action.

(J) "Clerk of court" means the duly elected or appointed clerk of any court of record, or the deputy of any of them, and either the mayor of a municipal corporation having a mayor's court or any clerk appointed by the mayor.

**History:** Effective January 1, 1975; amended, eff February 1, 2002; January 1, 2006; January 1, 2010.

#### Traffic Rules Review Commission

#### Commentary (January 1, 2006 Amendment)

The amendment deleting the definition of "Review Commission" is made upon transition of the oversight of the Ohio Traffic Rules from the Review Commission to the Commission on the Rules of Practice and Procedure in Ohio Courts as adopted by the Supreme Court of Ohio effective January 1, 2006.

#### Commentary (February 1, 2002 Amendment)

The amendment to the definition of "traffic case" clarifies that the Ohio Traffic Rules do not apply in proceedings that arise from a felony indictment. In traffic cases that arise from a felony indictment, such as felony drunk driving cases, the Ohio Rules of Criminal Procedure would apply. See Rule 1(C), Ohio Rules of Criminal Procedure.

The amendment also corrects references to certain courts and makes other nonsubstantive changes.

### RULE 3. Complaint and summons; form; use

(A) **Traffic complaint and summons.** In traffic cases, the complaint and summons shall be the "Ohio Uniform Traffic Ticket" as set out in the Appendix of Forms.

(B) **Traffic complaint and summons form.** The Ohio Uniform Traffic Ticket shall consist of four sheets, padded together and bound at the top or bottom edge. Each sheet shall be four and one-fourth inches in width and nine and one-half inches in length from a perforation below the binding to the bottom edge. The first sheet shall be white and the second sheet shall be canary yellow. Where an additional copy is needed by an agency, it may be added. The first and second sheets shall be at least fifteen pound paper.

The first sheet shall be the court record.

The second sheet shall be the abstract of court record for the Bureau of Motor Vehicles as required by Section 4507.021 [4507.02.1] of the Revised Code. The second sheet may be omitted from the Ticket if the court reports violations to the Bureau by electronic or other means acceptable to the Bureau.

The third sheet shall be the defendant's copy.

The fourth sheet shall be the enforcement agency record.

A wrap-around may be added to the first sheet. The issuing authority may use the front and back of the wrap-around for any data or information it may require.

Each ticket sheet shall be perforated tab bound at the edge or end with carbon paper interleaved so that all carbon paper is securely bound to the tab and removable with it, or shall be on treated paper so that marking from the top sheet is transferred legibly to successive sheets in the group.

(C) **Use of ticket.** The Ohio Uniform Traffic Ticket shall be used in all moving traffic cases, but its use for parking and equipment violations is optional in each local jurisdiction. Any ticket properly issued by a law enforcement officer shall be accepted for filing and disposition in any court having jurisdiction over the offense alleged. An officer may include more than one alleged violation on a single ticket provided the alleged violations are numbered sequentially on the face of the ticket. An officer who completes a ticket at the scene of an alleged offense shall not be required to rewrite or type a new complaint as a condition of filing the ticket, unless the original complaint is illegible or does not state an offense. If a new complaint is executed, a copy shall be served upon defendant as soon as possible.

(D) **Issuance of tickets to enforcement agency.** The judge in a single-judge court, and the administrative judge in multi-judge courts, shall designate the issuing authority for tickets and prescribe the conditions of issuance and accountability. The issuing authority may be the clerk of the court, the violations clerk, or the enforcement agency of the municipality.

When a single enforcement agency, except the State Highway Patrol, regularly has cases in more than one court, the ticket used by the agency shall be issued through the court for adults in the most populous area in the jurisdiction of the agency. Tickets used by the State Highway Patrol shall be issued by the Superintendent of the State Highway Patrol.

(E) **Duty of law enforcement officer.**

(1) A law enforcement officer who issues a ticket shall complete and sign the ticket, serve a copy of the completed ticket on the defendant, and, without unnecessary delay, file the court copy with the court. If the issuing officer personally serves a copy of the completed ticket on the defendant, the issuing officer shall note the date of personal service on the ticket in the space provided. If the issuing officer is unable to serve a copy of the completed ticket on the defendant, the completed ticket may be served by another law enforcement officer of the law enforcement agency issuing the ticket or filed with the clerk of the court for issuance of a warrant or summons pursuant to Crim. R. 4. Tickets that solely allege one or more minor misdemeanor violations must initially be issued by summons.

(2) The officer shall notify defendant that if defendant does not appear at the time and place stated in the citation or comply with division (C) of section 2935.26 of the Revised Code, defendant's license will be cancelled, defendant will not be eligible for the reissuance of the license or the issuance of a new license for one year after cancellation, and defendant will be subject to any applicable criminal penalties.

(F) **Use of electronically produced tickets.**

(1) Local rules adopted pursuant to the Supreme Court Rules of Superintendence for the Courts of Ohio may provide for the use of a ticket that is produced by computer or other electronic means, provided that the ticket conforms in all substantive respects, including layout and content, to the "Ohio Uniform Traffic Ticket" set forth in the Appendix of Forms. The provisions of division (B) of this rule relative to the color and weight of paper and method of binding shall not be applicable to a ticket that is produced by computer or other electronic means.

(2) Local rules adopted pursuant to the Supreme Court Rules of Superintendence for the Courts of Ohio may provide for the filing of the ticket by electronic means. If a ticket is issued at the scene of an alleged offense, the local rule shall require that the issuing officer provide the defendant with a paper copy of the ticket as required by division (E) of this rule. A law enforcement officer who files a ticket electronically shall be considered to have certified the ticket and shall have the same rights, responsibilities, and liabilities as with all other tickets issued pursuant to these rules.

**History:** Effective January 1, 1975; amended, eff August 4, 1980; February 26, 1990; November 28, 1990; June 1, 1992; February 1, 2002; October 1, 2006; May 1, 2008; January 1, 2010.

### Traffic Rules Review Commission

### Commentary (October 1, 2006 Amendment)

The October 1, 2006 amendment added language to division (E)(1) to provide an alternative means of serving the defendant with a completed traffic ticket. At least one trial court and three courts of appeal have held that former Traf. R. 3(E) and the Uniform Traffic Ticket, when read together, require a law enforcement officer who issues a traffic citation to personally serve the defendant with a copy of the citation. See *Akron v. Detweiler* (1978), 54 Ohio Misc. 5, 6; *Oregon v. Fox* (Jan. 21, 1983), Lucas App. No. L-82-317; *State v. Campbell*, 150 Ohio App. 3d 90, 2002-Ohio-6064; and *Columbus v. Ford*, 2004-Ohio-5715. Although personal service is easily accomplished when a typical traffic citation is issued, compliance is difficult in "hit-skip" cases and other situations where the offender is not cited at the time of the violation or in cases where the defendant resides outside the jurisdiction in which the offense occurred.

The amendment to division (E)(1) retains the requirement that the issuing officer serve the ticket and, together with the Uniform Traffic Ticket, contemplates that service will be made personally in the majority of cases by the issuing officer. However, if the issuing officer is unable to personally serve the ticket on the defendant, service may be accomplished through issuance of a warrant or summons pursuant to Rule 4 of the Ohio Rules of Criminal Procedure.

**Commentary (February 1, 2002 Amendment)**

The February 1, 2002 amendment added division (F) to authorize the use of traffic tickets that are produced by computer or other electronic means and the adoption of local rules relative to the electronic filing of traffic tickets. The intent of division (F)(1) is to retain the uniform substance of traffic tickets produced by jurisdictions throughout Ohio from the standpoint of the layout and content of the ticket, but recognize that electronically generated tickets need not comply with certain requirements applicable to traditional printed forms of traffic tickets. In developing electronic traffic tickets, courts, clerks, and law enforcement agencies should ensure that the electronic ticket comports as closely as possible to the Uniform Traffic Ticket contained in the Appendix of Forms.

The amendment to add division (F)(2) is based on a recommendation from the Digital Signatures Committee of the Ohio Judicial Conference. The amendment authorizes the adoption of local rules, consistent with standards contained in the Rules of Superintendence, relative to the electronic filing of traffic tickets. The amendment requires that the defendant be provided a paper copy of the ticket and states the issuing officer's responsibility with respect to issuance of an electronically filed ticket.

## RULE 4. Bail and security

(A) **Posting of bail; depositing of security.** The posting of bail or the depositing of security is for the purpose of securing appearance or compliance with R.C. 2935.26(C). The forfeiture of the bail or security may be a substitute for appearance in court, compliance with R.C. 2935.26(C), and payment of penalty imposed on a finding of guilt, with consent of all parties.

(B) **Bail and security procedure.** Criminal Rule 46 governs bail in traffic cases. In addition, the provisions of R.C. 2937.221 and R.C. 2935.27 apply in traffic cases.

**History:** Effective January 1, 1975; amended, eff August 4, 1980; January 1, 2010.

## RULE 5. Joinder of offense and defendants; consolidation for trial; relief prejudicial joinder

Criminal Rules 8, 13 and 14 govern joinder of offenses and defendants, consolidation of cases for trial and relief from prejudicial joinder in traffic cases.

**History:** Effective January 1, 1975.

## RULE 6. Summons, warrants: form, service and execution

(A) **Form.** The form of summons and warrants, other than the ticket, shall be as prescribed in Criminal Rule 4.

(B) **Service and execution.** Summons, other than the ticket, and warrants shall be served and executed as prescribed by Criminal Rule 4.

**History:** Effective January 1, 1975.

## RULE 7. Procedure upon failure to appear

(A) **Issuance of summons, warrant.** When a defendant fails to appear pursuant to a ticket issued to him, the court shall issue a supplemental summons or warrant.

If a supplemental summons is not served or a warrant is not executed within twenty-eight days of receipt by the serving officer, the court may place the case in a file of cases disposed of subject to being reopened. Where bond is forfeited, the disposition shall be reported to the Registrar of Motor Vehicles. For all other purposes, including disposition reports, the cases shall be reported as disposed of, subject to being reopened, if defendant subsequently appears or is apprehended.

(B) **Issuance of notice to nonresident.** When a nonresident of this state fails to appear pursuant to a supplemental summons or a warrant issued under division (A), the court may send by ordinary mail to defendant's address as it appears on the ticket, or the summons or warrant return, a notice ordering defendant to appear at a specified time and place.

If the defendant fails to appear or answer within twenty-eight days after the date of mailing of the notice, the court shall place the case in the file of cases disposed of subject to being reopened.

The mailing of notice in parking cases is discretionary with the court.

(C) **Effect of waiting periods and bail forfeiture.** The waiting period prescribed in division (A) does not affect forfeiture of bail.

If there is a breach of a condition of bail, the court shall declare a forfeiture of bail. Forfeiture proceedings shall be promptly enforced as provided by law.

If defendant fails to appear at the time and place specified on the citation and fails to comply with division (C) of Section 2935.26 of the Revised Code, or fails to comply with or satisfy any judgment of the court within the time allowed, the court shall declare the forfeiture of defendant's license. Thirty days after the declaration, the court shall forward a copy of the declaration to the Registrar of Motor Vehicles for cancellation in accordance with division (D) of Section 2935.27 of the Revised Code. If defendant deposits a sum of money or other security with the court, the deposit immediately shall be forfeited to the court if he fails to appear or comply with division (C) of Section 2935.26 of the Revised Code.

**History:** Effective January 1, 1975; amended, eff August 4, 1980; November 28, 1990.

## RULE 8. Arraignment

(A) **Arraignment time.** Where practicable, every defendant shall be arraigned before contested matters are taken up. Trial may be conducted immediately following arraignment.

(B) **Arraignment procedure.** Arraignment shall be conducted in open court and shall consist of reading the complaint to the defendant, or stating to him the substance of the charge, and calling on him to plead thereto. The defendant shall be given a copy of the complaint, or shall acknowledge receipt thereof, before being called upon to plead and may in open court waive the reading of the complaint.

(C) **Presence of defendant.** The defendant must be present at the arraignment, but the court may allow the defendant to enter a not guilty plea at the clerk's office in person, by his attorney in person, or by his attorney by mail, within four days after receipt of the ticket by the defendant.

(D) **Explanation of rights.** Before calling upon a defendant to plead at arraignment the judge shall cause him to be informed and shall determine that defendant knows and understands:

(1) That he has a right to counsel and the right to a reasonable continuance in the proceedings to secure

counsel, and, pursuant to Criminal Rule 44, the right to have counsel assigned without cost to himself if he is unable to employ counsel;

(2) That he has a right to bail as provided in Rule 4;

(3) That he need make no statement at any point in the proceeding; but any statement made may be used against him;

(4) That he has, where such right exists, a right to jury trial and that he must, in petty offense cases, make a demand for a jury pursuant to Criminal Rule 23;

(5) That if he is convicted a record of the conviction will be sent to the Bureau of Motor Vehicles and become a part of his driving record.

(E) **Joint arraignment.** If there are multiple defendants to be arraigned, the judge may advise, or cause them to be advised, of their rights by general announcement.

**History:** Effective January 1, 1975.

## RULE 9. Jury demand

(A) **Jury demand.** Jury demands shall be made pursuant to Criminal Rule 23.

(B) **Jury demands in mayor's court.** Where, in a mayor's court, a defendant is entitled to a jury trial and a jury demand is made pursuant to Criminal Rule 23, the mayor shall transfer the case pursuant to subdivision (C).

If a jury demand is not made pursuant to Criminal Rule 23, and the defendant waives his right to a jury trial in writing, a mayor may try the case if (1) his compensation as a judge is not directly dependent upon criminal case convictions, or (2) he is not the chief executive and administrative officer of the municipality and as such responsible for the financial condition of the municipality. Guilty and no contest pleas may be taken by any mayor, including mayors whose compensation as a judge is directly dependent upon criminal case convictions and mayors who as chief executive and administrative officer of the municipality are responsible for the financial condition of the municipality.

(C) **Transfer.** Where transfer is required, the mayor's court shall make a written order directing the defendant to appear at the transferee court, continuing the same bail, if any, and making appearance before the transferee court as a condition of bail, if any. Upon transfer, the mayor's court shall transmit to the clerk of the transferee court the ticket and all other papers in the case, and any bail taken in the case.

Upon receipt of such papers the clerk of the transferee court shall set the case for trial and shall notify the defendant by ordinary mail of his trial date.

**History:** Effective January 1, 1975.

## RULE 10. Pleas; rights upon plea

(A) **Pleas.** A defendant may plead not guilty, guilty or, with the consent of the court, no contest. All pleas may be made orally. If a defendant refuses to plead, the court shall enter a plea of not guilty on behalf of the defendant.

(B) **Effect of guilty or no contest plea.** With reference to the offense or offenses to which the plea is entered:

(1) The plea of guilty is a complete admission of the defendant's guilt.

(2) The plea of no contest is not an admission of defendant's guilt, but is an admission of the truth of the facts alleged in the complaint and such plea or admission shall not be used against the defendant in any subsequent civil or criminal proceeding.

(3) When a plea of guilty or no contest is accepted pursuant to this rule, the court shall proceed with sentencing under Criminal Rule 32.

(C) **Misdemeanor cases involving serious offenses.** In misdemeanor cases involving serious offenses, the court may refuse to accept a plea of guilty or no contest and shall not accept such plea without first addressing the defendant personally and informing him of the effect of the pleas of guilty, no contest, and not guilty and determining that he is making the plea voluntarily. Where the defendant is unrepresented by counsel, the court shall not accept a plea of guilty or no contest unless the defendant, after being readvised that he has a right to be represented by retained counsel, or pursuant to Criminal Rule 44 by appointed counsel, waives this right.

(D) **Misdemeanor cases involving petty offenses.** In misdemeanor cases involving petty offenses, except those processed in a traffic violations bureau, the court may refuse to accept a plea of guilty or no contest and shall not accept such pleas without first informing the defendant of the effect of the plea of guilty, no contest, and not guilty. This information may be presented by general orientation or pronouncement.

The counsel provisions of Criminal Rule 44(B), (C) and (D) apply to this subdivision.

(E) **Refusal of court to accept plea.** If the court refuses to accept a plea of guilty or no contest, the court shall enter a plea of not guilty on behalf of the defendant. In such cases neither plea shall be admissible in evidence nor be the subject of comment by the prosecuting attorney or court.

(F) **Immediate trial.** Upon written consent of defendant and the prosecuting attorney, trial may be conducted immediately after the acceptance of a plea at arraignment. If the defendant seeks a continuance, or demands a jury trial where such right exists, the court shall cause the case to be set for trial.

**History:** Effective January 1, 1975; amended eff. January 1, 2010.

## RULE 11. Pleadings and Motions before Plea and Trial: Defenses and Objections

(A) **Pleadings and motions.** Pleadings in traffic cases shall be the complaint, the pleas of not guilty, guilty, and no contest. Defenses and objections shall be raised before plea and trial by motion to dismiss or to grant appropriate relief.

(B) **Motions before plea and trial.** Any defense, objection, or request which is capable of determination without the trial of the general issue may be raised before plea or trial by motion.

(1) The following defenses and objections must be raised before plea:

(a) Defenses and objections based on defects in the institution of the prosecution;

(b) Defenses and objections based on defects in the complaint other than failure to show jurisdiction in the court or to charge an offense, which objections shall be noticed by the court at any time during the pendency of the proceeding.

(2) The following motions and requests must be made before trial:

(a) Motions to suppress evidence, including but not

limited to identification testimony, on the ground that it was illegally obtained;

(b) Requests and motions for discovery under Criminal Rule 16;

(c) Motions for severance of charges or defendants under Criminal Rule 14.

(C) **Motion date.** Pre-plea motions shall be made before or at arraignment. All pretrial motions, except as provided in Criminal Rule 16(M), shall be made within thirty-five days after arraignment or seven days before trial, whichever is earlier. The court, in the interest of justice, may extend the time for making pre-plea or pretrial motions.

(D) **Disclosure of evidence by prosecuting attorney.** At the arraignment, or as soon thereafter as is practicable, the defendant may, in order to raise objections prior to trial under subsection (B)(2), request notice of the prosecuting attorney's intention to use evidence in chief at trial, which evidence the defendant is entitled to discover under Criminal Rule 16.

(E) **Ruling on motion.** A motion made before trial, other than a motion for change of venue, shall be timely determined before trial. Where factual issues are involved in determining a motion, the court shall state its essential findings on the record.

(F) **Effect of failure to raise defenses or objections.** Failure by the defendant to raise defenses or objections or to make motions and requests which must be made prior to plea, trial, or at the time set by the court pursuant to subdivision (C), or prior to any extension thereof made by the court, shall constitute waiver thereof, but the court for good cause shown may grant relief from the waiver.

(G) **Effect of plea of no contest.** The plea of no contest does not preclude a defendant from asserting upon appeal that the trial court prejudicially erred in ruling on a pretrial motion, including a pretrial motion to suppress evidence.

(H) **Effect of determination.** If the court grants a motion to dismiss based on a defect in the institution of the prosecution or in the complaint, the court shall dismiss the case unless the prosecuting attorney can, pursuant to Criminal Rule 7(D), amend the complaint.

(I) **State's right of appeal.** The state may take an appeal in traffic cases pursuant to Criminal Rule 12(K).

**History:** Effective January 1, 1975; amended effective February 1, 2008; July 1, 2011.

### Traffic Rules Review Commission

### Commentary (February 1, 2008 Amendment)

The February 1, 2008 amendment to division (I) corrects an inaccurate reference in the previous version of the rule to Criminal Rule 12(J). The previous division (I) expressly limited the state's right of appeal to two types of cases under Traffic Rule 13(B)(1) & (3). Such a limitation precluded the state from seeking review of adverse rulings on evidentiary matters in all first and second offense OVI cases and, arguably third OVI case in municipal court. The amendment, in applying the Criminal Rule 12(K) standard, promotes uniformity in addressing the state's right of appeal in all traffic cases.

## RULE 12. Receipt of guilty or no contest plea

The pleas of guilty and no contest shall be received only by personal appearance of the defendant in open court, except that, the plea of guilty may be received in accordance with Rule 13 at a regularly established traffic violations bureau, or by plea in absentia presented in proper written form with leave of court, and in open court with the prosecutor participating. Pleas in absentia may be taken on charges involving operation of a motor vehicle in violation of section 4511.19 of the Revised Code or any substantially similar municipal ordinance with consent of the prosecutor. The plea in absentia shall contain a rights waiver, acknowledgement of penalties, and the defendant's signature.

The receipt of a plea contrary to the provisions of these rules is forbidden.

**History:** Effective January 1, 1975; amended eff. January 1, 2010.

## RULE 13. Traffic violations bureau

(A) **Establishment and operation of traffic violations bureau.** Each court shall establish a traffic violations bureau. The juvenile division of the court of common pleas may establish a violations bureau pursuant to Traffic Rule 13.1. The court shall appoint its clerk as violations clerk. If there is no clerk, the court shall appoint any appropriate person of the municipality or county in which the court sits. The violations bureau and violations clerk shall be under the direction and control of the court. Fines and costs shall be paid to, receipted by, and accounted for by the violations clerk.

The violations bureau shall accept appearance, waiver of trial, plea of guilty, and payment of fine and costs for offenses within its authority.

(B) **Authority of violations bureau.** All traffic offenses except those listed in this division may be disposed of by a traffic violations bureau. The following traffic offenses shall not be processed by a traffic violations bureau:

(1) Indictable offenses;

(2) Operating a motor vehicle while under the influence of alcohol or any drug of abuse;

(3) Leaving the scene of an accident;

(4) Driving while under suspension or revocation of a driver's or commercial driver's license;

(5) Driving without being licensed to drive when jail is a possible penalty;

(6) A third moving traffic offense within a twelve-month period when jail is a possible penalty;

(7) Failure to stop and remain standing upon meeting or overtaking a school bus stopped on the highway for the purpose of receiving or discharging a school child;

(8) Willfully eluding or fleeing a police officer;

(9) Drag racing.

(C) **Schedule of fines.** The court shall establish and publish a schedule of fines and costs for all offenses. The schedule shall be distributed to all law enforcement agencies operating within the jurisdiction of the court and shall be prominently displayed at the place in the violations bureau where fines are paid.

(D) **Defendant's appearance, plea and waiver of trial.**

(1) At any time prior to arraignment or thereafter with leave of court, a defendant charged with an offense that can be processed by a traffic violations bureau may do either of the following:

(a) Appear in person at the traffic violations bureau, sign a plea of guilty and waiver of trial provision of the ticket, and pay the total amount of the fine and costs;

(b) Sign the guilty plea and waiver of trial provision of

the ticket and mail the ticket and a check, money order, or other approved form of payment for the total amount of the fine and costs to the traffic violations bureau;

(2) A court may establish a procedure for accepting, through its traffic violations bureau, guilty pleas, waivers of trial, and payments of fines and costs by telephone or other electronic means. The form of payment accepted by telephone or other electronic means shall be approved by the bureau.

(3) Remittance of the fine and costs to the traffic violations bureau by any means other than personal appearance by the defendant at the bureau constitutes a guilty plea and waiver of trial whether or not the guilty plea and waiver of trial provision of the ticket are signed by the defendant.

(E) **Records.** All cases processed in the violations bureau shall be numbered and recorded for identification and statistical purposes. In any statistical reports required by law, the number of cases disposed of by the violations bureau shall be listed separately from those disposed of in open court.

(F) **Hours of operation; personnel.** The court shall appoint a law enforcement officer as a deputy violations bureau clerk to act as violations clerk when the violations clerk is not on duty.

**History:** Effective January 1, 1975; amended, eff August 4, 1980; February 26, 1990; November 1, 1994; July 1, 1997; May 3, 1999; February 1, 2002; January 1, 2010; July 1, 2011.

**Traffic Rules Review Commission**

**Commentary (February 1, 2002 Amendment)**

The February 1, 2002 amendment to division (A) authorizes the establishment of a juvenile violations bureau in the court of common pleas. For additional background, see the commentary accompanying the February 1, 2002 amendment to Traffic Rule 13.1.

## RULE 13.1. Juvenile traffic violations bureau

(A) By local rule of court, the juvenile division of the court of common pleas may establish a violations bureau for juvenile traffic offenders. Except as provided in division (B) of this rule, a juvenile traffic violations bureau shall function in the same manner as a violations bureau established pursuant to Traffic Rule 13.

(B) All juvenile traffic offenses may be disposed of by a violations bureau, except as follows:

(1) An offense listed in Traffic Rule 13(B)(1) to (5) and (7) to (9);

(2) A second or subsequent moving offense;

(3) An offense that involves an accident.

**History:** Effective February 1, 2002.

**Traffic Rules Review Commission**

**Commentary (February 1, 2002 Amendment)**

In Section 7 of Amended Substitute Senate Bill 179 of the 123rd General Assembly, the General Assembly recommended that the Supreme Court authorize the juvenile division of the court of common pleas "to create violations bureaus for the payment of tickets that involve first offense minor misdemeanor traffic offenses that did not result in an accident." This rule implements this recommendation by allowing juvenile violations bureaus to be created by local rule of court. The rule provides that the procedures established for adult violations bureaus under Traffic Rule 13 apply to juvenile violations bureaus and lists offenses committed by a juvenile traffic offender that cannot be disposed of by the bureau.

## RULE 14. Magistrates

(A) A court may appoint one or more magistrates for the purpose of receiving pleas, determining guilt or innocence, receiving statements in explanation and in mitigation of sentence, and recommending penalty to be imposed. A magistrate shall have been engaged in the practice of law for at least four years and be in good standing with the Supreme Court of Ohio at the time of appointment. A magistrate shall be provided with court room accommodations resembling as nearly as possible traffic court rooms.

(B) A court may refer nonjury traffic cases to a magistrate. If the offense charged is an offense for which imprisonment is a possible penalty, the case may be referred only with the unanimous consent of the parties, in writing or on the record in open court. The consent of an alleged juvenile traffic offender or his or her parent, guardian, or custodian shall not be required.

(C) Proceedings before the magistrate shall be conducted as provided in Criminal Rule 19. A defendant's payment of a fine does not constitute a waiver of the defendant's right to file objections to the magistrate's decision.

**History:** Effective January 1, 1975; amended, eff September 1, 1996; February 1, 2002; October 1, 2006; July 1, 2011.

**Traffic Rules Review Commission**

**Commentary (October 1, 2006 Amendment)**

The October 1, 2006 amendment altered the cross-reference to Criminal Rule 19 to conform to the July 1, 2006 amendments to Criminal Rule 19.

**Commentary (February 1, 2002 Amendment)**

The February 1, 2002 amendment conforms the authority of traffic court magistrates to that of criminal magistrates contained in Criminal Rule 19, as amended effective July 1, 2000. Division (A) retains language of the rule as it existed prior to the amendment and adds that a traffic court magistrate may determine issues of guilt or innocence.

Division (B) specifies that any nonjury traffic case, including those involving an alleged juvenile traffic offender, may be referred to a magistrate, removing any references to the consent of the parties that was contained in the prior rule. In cases where imprisonment, as defined in R.C. 1.05, is a possible penalty, the case may be heard by a magistrate only with the written consent of the parties.

Reference to Civil Rule 53 has been replaced with a requirement that proceedings before a traffic magistrate will be conducted in accordance with Criminal Rule 19. The rule also states that the payment of a fine by the defendant does not constitute a waiver of the defendant's right to object to the decision of the magistrate.

## RULE 15. [Reserved]

**Traffic Rules Review Commission**

**Commentary (October 1, 2006 Amendment)**

The October 1, 2006 amendment repealed former Traf. R. 15. Division (A) of that rule authorized contempt proceedings before the Supreme Court against any judge, clerk, or other personnel who willfully failed to apply or adhere to the Ohio Traffic Rules. This provision is deemed unnecessary since a party may object to or raise on appeal a court's noncompliance with the Ohio Traffic Rules or application of local rules that are inconsistent with the Ohio Traffic Rules.

Division (B) of former Traf. R. 15 authorized the institution of criminal contempt proceedings against any person who improperly disposed of a traffic ticket. This provision is deemed unnecessary in light of the existence of statutes that would allow for the imposition of criminal penalties against a person who improperly disposes of a traffic ticket.

## RULE 16. Judicial conduct

The Code of Judicial Conduct as adopted by the Supreme Court applies to all judges and mayors.

It shall be the obligation of each mayor to conduct his court and his professional and personal relationships in accordance with the same standards as are required of judges of courts of record.

**History:** Effective January 1, 1975; amended, eff February 1, 2002.

### Traffic Rules Review Commission

### Commentary (February 1, 2002 Amendment)

The amendment conforms the rule to the Compliance Provision of the Code of Judicial Conduct, which specifies that the Code applies to any person, "* * * whether or not a lawyer, who is an officer of a judicial system performing judicial functions * * *."

## RULE 17. Traffic case scheduling

(A) **Arraignment and trial by traffic division.** Where a court sits in divisions and one division is designated as traffic court, all traffic defendants shall, where practicable, be arraigned and tried in such division.

(B) **Arraignment and trial by traffic session.** Where a court not sitting in separate divisions designates a particular session as a traffic session, traffic defendants shall, where practicable, be arraigned and tried at such session.

(C) **Single-judge courts.** In single-judge courts, traffic cases shall, where practicable, be called before nontraffic cases. Uncontested traffic cases shall be disposed of first and contested cases scheduled for later hearing.

**History:** Effective January 1, 1975; amended eff. January 1, 2010.

## RULE 18. Continuances

Continuances shall be granted only upon a written motion which states the grounds for the requested continuance.

When a court grants a continuance, it shall set a definite date for the hearing or trial.

**History:** Effective January 1, 1975.

## RULE 19. Rule of court

The expression "rule of court" as used in these rules means a rule promulgated by the Supreme Court or a rule concerning local practice adopted by another court and filed with the Supreme Court. Local rules shall be supplementary to and consistent with these rules. Each court shall publish its local rules, distribute them within its jurisdiction, and keep copies for inspection.

**History:** Effective January 1, 1975.

## RULE 20. Procedure not otherwise specified

If no procedure is specifically prescribed by these rules, the Rules of Criminal Procedure and the applicable law apply.

**History:** Effective January 1, 1975.

## RULE 21. Forms

The forms contained in the Appendix of Forms are mandatory, except that additional copies of any portions of the ticket may be made. The reverse of the enforcement agency record shall be made in the form prescribed by the issuing authority.

**History:** Effective January 1, 1975.

## RULE 22. [Reserved]

(Former Rule 22 entitled Review Commission was repealed effective January 1, 2006. The functions of the Review Commission were transferred to the Supreme Court Commission on the Rules of Practice and Procedure on that date.)

## RULE 23. Title

These rules shall be known as the Ohio Traffic Rules and may be cited as "Traffic Rules" or "Traf. R.____."

**History:** Effective January 1, 1975.

## RULE 24. Effective date

(A) **Effective date of rules.** These rules take effect on January 1, 1975. They govern all proceedings in actions brought after they take effect, and also all further proceedings in actions then pending, except to the extent that their application in a particular action pending when the rules take effect would not be feasible or would work injustice, in which event the former procedure applies.

(B) **Use of tickets conforming to prior rules.** Traffic tickets conforming to the requirements of the "Ohio Rules of Practice and Procedure in Traffic Cases For All Courts Inferior to Common Pleas" may be used after the effective date of these rules.

After the effective date of these rules, issuing authorities shall order only tickets conforming to these rules.

**History:** Effective January 1, 1975.

## RULE 25. Effective date of amendments

(A) The amendments to these rules and the Uniform Traffic Ticket adopted by the Supreme Court of Ohio on June 17, 1980 shall take effect on August 4, 1980.

(B) The amendments to the Uniform Traffic Ticket shall take effect on September 15, 1985. The amendment to Traffic Rule 22 shall take effect on July 27, 1988.

(C) The amendment to Traffic Rule 22, adopted by the Supreme Court on December 5, 1989, shall take effect on December 5, 1989.

(D) The amendments to Traffic Rules 3, 13, and 25, and the Uniform Traffic Ticket, adopted by the Supreme Court of Ohio on February 13, 1990, shall take effect on February 26, 1990.

(E) The amendments to Traffic Rules 3 and 7, adopted by the Supreme Court of Ohio on November 20, 1990, shall take effect on November 28, 1990.

(F) The amendments to Traffic Rule 3 and to the "Reverse of Defendant's Copy" of the Uniform Traffic Ticket, adopted by the Supreme Court of Ohio on March 16, 1992, shall take effect on June 1, 1992.

(G) The amendments to Traffic Rule 22, adopted by the Supreme Court of Ohio on August 17, 1994, shall take effect on September 19, 1994. The amendments to Traffic Rule 13 and to the Uniform Traffic Ticket, adopted by the Supreme Court of Ohio on August 17, 1994, shall take effect on November 1, 1994.

(H) The amendments to Traffic Rule 14, adopted by the Supreme Court of Ohio on July 10, 1996, shall take effect on September 1, 1996.

(I)(1) The amendments to Traffic Rule 13, adopted by the Supreme Court of Ohio on March 31, 1997, shall take effect on July 1, 1997.

(2) The amendments to the Uniform Traffic Ticket, adopted by the Supreme Court of Ohio on March 31, 1997, shall take effect on July 1, 1997. Through June 30, 1998, jurisdictions may use tickets printed in the format that was authorized prior to July 1, 1997. All tickets ordered for use on or after July 1, 1997 and all tickets used on or after July 1, 1998 shall conform to the format of the July 1, 1997 Uniform Traffic Ticket.

(J) The amendments to Traffic Rule 13, adopted by the Supreme Court of Ohio on March 30, 1999, shall take effect on May 3, 1999.

(K) The amendments to Traffic Rules 2, 3, 13, 13.1, 14, 16, and 25, adopted by the Supreme Court of Ohio on December 11, 2001, shall take effect on February 1, 2002.

(L) The amendments to Traffic Rules 2 and 22, adopted by the Supreme Court of Ohio on October 25, 2005, shall take effect on January 1, 2006.

(M) The amendments to Traffic Rules 3, 14, and 15, adopted by the Supreme Court of Ohio on August 8, 2006, shall take effect on October 1, 2006.

(N) The amendments to Traffic Rule 11, adopted by the Supreme Court of Ohio on December 11, 2007, shall take effect on February 1, 2008.

(O) The amendments to Traffic Rule 3, adopted by the Supreme Court of Ohio on April 22, 2008 shall take effect on May 1, 2008.

(P) The amendments to Traffic Rules 2, 3, 4, 10, 12, 13, and 17 and the Uniform Traffic Ticket adopted by the Supreme Court of Ohio on September 29, 2009 shall take effect on January 1, 2010. Through June 30, 2010, jurisdictions may use tickets printed in the format that was authorized prior to January 1, 2010. All tickets ordered for use on or after July 1, 2010 and all tickets used on or after July 1, 2010 shall conform to the format of the January 1, 2010 Uniform Traffic Ticket.

### Temporary Provision

Notwithstanding Traffic Rule 3, the Bowling Green Municipal Court is authorized to develop and use a modified version of the Uniform Traffic Ticket in all moving traffic cases. The modified version of the Uniform Traffic Ticket shall be used by the Bowling Green Municipal Court beginning on a date not later than three months from October 21, 1991 and its use shall terminate one year from the date on which it is first used. As used in the Ohio Traffic Rules and defined by Traffic Rule 2, "traffic ticket" shall include the modified version of the Uniform Traffic Ticket in all moving traffic developed and used by the Bowling Green Municipal Court pursuant to this provision.

Effective: October 21, 1991.

### Temporary Provision

Notwithstanding Traffic Rule 3, the Akron Municipal Court, Berea Municipal Court, Licking County Municipal Court, Newton Falls Municipal Court, Parma Municipal Court, Brown County Court, Broadview Heights Mayor's Court, Moraine Mayor's Court, North Royalton Mayor's Court, and the Ohio Highway Patrol are authorized to use the modified version of the Uniform Traffic Ticket approved by the Supreme Court Traffic Rules Review Commission in all moving traffic cases. The modified version of the Uniform Traffic Ticket shall be used by these courts and the Highway Patrol beginning on a date no earlier than April 1, 1996. The use of the modified Uniform Traffic Ticket shall continue for a period of six months from the date on which it is first used in the individual courts or by the Highway Patrol. As used in the Ohio Traffic Rules and defined by Traffic Rule 2, "traffic ticket" shall include the modified version of the Uniform Traffic Ticket used pursuant to this provision.

Effective: April 1, 1996.

### Temporary Provision

A law enforcement officer who issues an automated traffic ticket is considered to have signed the ticket, for purposes of Traffic Rule 3(E), if the issuing officer properly authorizes the appearance of his or her facsimile signature on the ticket.

For purposes of this Temporary Provision:

(A) "Automated traffic ticket" means the computerized traffic citation developed by the Office of Criminal Justice Services, Ohio Highway Patrol, and local law enforcement agencies and courts and being used on a pilot project basis by the Licking County Sheriff's Office, Newark Police Department, Heath Police Department, Licking County Municipal Court, Circleville Police Department, Pickaway County Sheriff's Office, Circleville Municipal Court, the Circleville Post of the Ohio Highway Patrol, the Newark Post of the Ohio Highway Patrol, and the General Headquarters of the Ohio Highway Patrol.

(B) "Properly authorizes" means the issuing officer uses a secure password, in the manner demonstrated to the Traffic Rules Review Commission at its December 18, 1998 meeting, that, when entered, allows an electronic version of the his or her signature to appear on the automated traffic ticket and on any printed version of that ticket.

Effective: January 12, 1999.

# APPENDIX OF FORMS

(Amended, eff 8-4-80; 9-15-85; 2-26-90; 6-1-92; 11-1-94; 7-1-97; 10-19-09; 1-1-10)

## MULTI-COUNT UNIFORM TRAFFIC TICKET

**Commission Commentary (January 1, 2010 Amendments).**

On December 1, 2009, the Supreme Court of Ohio adopted a correction to the Multi-Count Uniform Traffic Ticket previously published on October 19, 2009. The correction is on the reverse side of the defendant's copy. The specific language is located under the checkbox for "Waiverable through traffic violations bureau". To comply with language adopted by the Court in Traf. R. 13(D)(1), the phrase "within seven days of the day you receive the ticket" has been replaced with "at any time prior to arraignment".

The corrected ticket is effective January 1, 2010 and mandatory July 1, 2010. Through June 30, 2010, jurisdictions may use tickets printed in the format that was authorized prior to January 1, 2010. All tickets ordered for use on or after January 1, 2010 and all tickets used on or after July 1, 2010 shall conform to the format of the January 1, 2010 Uniform Traffic Ticket.

**Commission Commentary (July 1, 1997 Amendments).**

The Supreme Court Traffic Rules Review Commission has developed the following Multi-Count Uniform Traffic Ticket. This ticket will significantly change the way in which traffic offenses are processed in the State of Ohio.

The Commission's comments are intended to provide an overview of the major changes, both in information and layout, to assist in understanding the new form. The Commission has worked with the input of law enforcement, judges, the Ohio Bureau of Motor Vehicles, and court personnel to solve most of the issues raised in the devising of this type of ticket. Separate comments for each side of the Multi-Count Uniform Traffic Ticket, which will be referred to as UTT.

**Training, Implementation, and General Comment.**

Although all jurisdictions are required to use the basic UTT, some courts might not use the Face of Court Record or paper Abstract, while other might use the Face of Court Record but not the paper Abstract.

Training on the new UTT will be of great importance. Although there are a number of changes, after some relatively basic training the forms can be implemented without a significant shock in changing from the pre July 1, 1997 version of the UTT.

In the Commission's work, many issues have been raised regarding inclusion or exclusion of language, information, and what would go best in what locations. Many of the issues which may be raised as training proceeds will be primarily issues that can be resolved in training and actual use of the ticket.

**Face of Court Record.**

The new Face of Court Record provides for the ability to write up to six separate traffic citations on one traffic ticket. The Face of Court Record is identical to the face of Defendant's copy and the Enforcement Agency Record front copy.

The Driver's Identification Information is substantially similar to the previous UTT, although certain information items, such as eye glasses and driving restrictions were deleted. Boxes are printed for officer compliance with S.B. 20, to indicate whether Financial Responsibility Proof is shown at time of the traffic stop, to provide a record for the Court System on S.B. 20 compliance.

The Citation Section consists of six separate boxes, four of which identify specific types of offenses. The two remaining boxes would be for other offenses. The Statutory Code Box provides for a check-off as to whether Ordinance, State Code, or Turnpike Rule is being cited. The Speed Section includes identification for all of the various speed measurement devices currently in use in the State of Ohio. The OMVI Section would be for the writing of one of the two potential OMVI charges, with a second OMVI charge being written in one of the other offense sections. The Driver's License Section would deal with all license-related charges, whether DUS, NOL, or restriction type offenses. The Safety Belt Section would address all belt or restraint offenses.

The Weather and Pavement information is similar to current traffic ticket forms. The UTT would not be used for the citing of non-traffic criminal charges in a traffic stop, which would be written under a separate criminal citation form. The information above the Defendant's Summons would be completed to indicate whether another complaint exists, as well as the total number of offenses being cited on the ticket for the Court to match up the total number of offenses which the officer has written. The Defendant's Summons is similar to the current Defendant's Summons.

**Reverse of Court Record.**

The Reverse of Court Record is a significant departure from the current Reverse of Court Record, primarily so that up to six citations could be resolved on one document. The proposed Reverse of Court Record retains all of the necessary information from the current Reverse of Court Copy, but redesigns the layout to enable for information to be recorded efficiently.

The "Court Action: Orders" Section of the old ticket is replaced by the new section with bail and rescheduling information. The Bail Section enables the court to record the bail status of the Defendant, whether released without bail or bail being set, including the type of bond, and the Depositor's identification information. The Continuance Section enables space to be allotted for sufficient continuances of cases with new dates indicated, including check-off boxes for the various Failure to Appear Sanctions available under Traffic Rule 7, including License Forfeiture for Failure to Appear.

The Court Entry Section enables a court to take pleas on and dispose of up to six charges on one form. Defendant's pleas, findings and sentencing are handled vertically for each charge, as indicated (court will use "G, NG, NC" for plea and finding notations). The initial plea in each respective charge would be indicated by a "G/NG/NC" designation with a comparable finding code in the finding box. The fine would be noted and imposed for each particular offense in its appropriate box as would any jail days imposed. Any suspended costs, fines, or jail would be noted in the appropriate boxes.

Additional space is provided for limited sentencing parameters for certain mandatory OMVI issues. A 72-Hour Program box in noted. Sections include not only driver's license suspension information, but information regarding modified privileges when granted. The Court Section also provides the waiver approval so that waiver could be checked off and signed by the Judicial Official by checking the box and signing off.

The Clerk's Use Section includes all the appropriate financial information needed by the clerks, including the breaking out of local and state costs for accounting purposes. The Check Box Section provides check-off process for the waiver process and also appropriate S.B. 20 information as to the showing or failing to show of insurance proof.

The Commission acknowledges that on this page, and others, that space is at a premium. In the implementation of the UTT, fine point pens should almost certainly be used on all writing on the documents to enable all print to be read. Notwithstanding the limitations, sufficient space would be available for all necessary entries. The form in no way precludes the addition of any other forms or entries which a court may use in conjunction with the Reverse of Court Record, but this Reverse of Court Record provides a simple one-write system for a court to use, if desired.

**Reverse of Defendant's Copy.**

The current Reverse of Defendant's Copy has been revised to not only include currently required information, but to incorporate a new warning on S.B. 20 compliance.

The language throughout the Defendant's copy is substantially similar to current language, except syntax has been changed, now referring to multiple offenses on the citation, and to also note the changes in Traffic Rule 13(B) effective November 1, 1994. It also includes the warning of License Cancellation and Forfeiture for Failure to Appear or Pay Fines. On the bottom, the clerk's receipt signature on the waiver form was eliminated, as this would be kept on the Reverse of Court Record form with receipts being separately given to the defendant.

The center of Reverse of Defendant's Copy contains a new insurance warning to place all traffic violators on notice regarding mandatory insurance showing under S.B. 20. The sections that were block lettered were done so to identify in bolder type the sanctions and warnings, to place all defendants on notice of the requirements of S.B. 20. Although the form has a blank line for filling in information as to the courts, this information could be pre-printed in the space provided to eliminate the officer having to fill in this information.

**Abstract of Court Record.**

The Abstract of Court Record is the manual copy that is sent to the Bureau of Motor Vehicles (BMV) for the processing of necessary conviction and other information to the BMV. Many courts currently are on computer to computer information transfer to the BMV, and it may well be that all courts eventually will report electronically. This form would be used by those courts that manually report their information to the BMV.

The top two-thirds of the Abstract of Court Record is identical to the Face of Court Record with the identifying information of original charges and driver's identification information. The court code and case number identifies the court sending the Abstract. The "No FR" boxes are to identify to the BMV those situations where there has not been compliance with S.B. 20, which the clerk reports to the BMV.

The Box Section would list, vertically, for each of the offenses for which BMV requires reporting the various information items in the required BMV format, including the plea, points assessed and the BMV offense code. A Section for Reduced Offenses is also present, based upon the required reporting of reduction of OMVI and DUS offenses, regardless of disposition, to the BMV. Child Restraint convictions are included in the BMV reporting based upon current law which require escalated fines based upon prior Child Restraint convictions. The two blank boxes would be for the two charges that would come from the "other offense" boxes.

The License Information Section provides a check-off to notify the BMV of any driver's license suspension, including indication for modified driving privileges, and to indicate the charge for which the suspension was imposed. In the event of a license forfeiture, the Abstract would be accompanied by a BMV form 2528. The other information box is to provide that the clerk could send additional information. This would be dome [sic] on the reverse side of the paper Abstract by placing the information on the back side, which will be blank. The checking of this box will advise the BMV to check for additional information on the reverse side.

**Reverse of Enforcement Agency Record.**

This is the Reverse Side of the Enforcement Agency's copy of the basic ticket. This side provides an information and tracking process for the Enforcement Agency to track court action on the case and to provide the officer with space for limited notes as to the offense at the time of citation, including identification of witnesses. The bottom of the form is to provide information location to the officer for PUCO and weight citations, so that the information may be preserved.

________________ COURT ________________ COUNTY, OHIO

STATE OF OHIO ________________ TICKET # ________________

☐ City ☐ Village ☐ Township CASE # ________________

NAME ________________

STREET ________________

CITY, STATE ________________ ZIP ________

PRESENT ADDRESS

| OPERATOR LICENSE / STATE ID# ☐ None* | BIRTH DATE | ISSUE DATE | STATE |
|---|---|---|---|
| | | | |

| CLASS | EXPIRES | ENDORSEMENT(s)/RESTRICTION(s) | SS# (last 4 digits) |
|---|---|---|---|
| | | ☐CDL ☐MC ☐Other ______ | |

| SEX | HEIGHT | WEIGHT | EYES | HAIR | RACE | FINANCIAL RESPONSIBILITY PROOF? |
|---|---|---|---|---|---|---|
| | | | | | | ☐ Yes ☐ No ☐ N/A |

* If no OL/State ID, **REQUIRED** documentation attached: ☐ Yes

**TO DEFENDANT: COMPLAINT** ON __________, 20____ AT __________ AM/PM, YOU

Operated/Passenger/Parked/Walked a ☐ Passenger ☐ Motorcycle ☐ Bicycle ☐ Other ________

☐ Commercial DOT# ________ ☐ ≥26,001 lbs. ☐ <16 Pass. Bus ☐ ≥16 Pass. Bus ☐ Haz. Mat.

VEHICLE: YEAR ________ MAKE ________ MODEL ________

COLOR ________ LICENSE # ________ STATE ________

UPON A PUBLIC HIGHWAY, NAMELY ________________

AT/NEAR ________________ (M.P. ______ )

IN THE ________ OF ________ IN ________

COUNTY (NO.) ______ STATE OF OHIO AND COMMITTED THE FOLLOWING OFFENSE(S).

☐ **SPEED:** ______ MPH in ______ MPH zone ☐ ORC ☐ ORD ☐ T.P.
☐ Over limits ☐ Unsafe for conditions ☐ ACDA
☐ Radar ☐ Air ☐ VASCAR ☐ Pace ☐ Laser ☐ Stationary ☐ Moving

☐ **OVI:** ☐ Under the influence of alcohol/drug of abuse. ☐ ORC ☐ ORD ☐ T.P.
☐ Prohibited blood alcohol concentration. ______ BAC
☐ Blood ☐ Breath ☐ Urine ☐ Refused

| Prior OVIs: | # of prior OVIs | Years of prior OVIs |
|---|---|---|
| | | |

☐ **DRIVER LICENSE:** ☐ None ☐ Not on person ☐ Revoked ☐ Suspended ☐ ORC ☐ ORD ☐ T.P.
EXPIRED: ☐ <6 months ☐ >6 months ☐ Failure to Reinstate
Suspension Type: ________

☐ **SAFETY BELT:** Failure to wear ☐ ORC ☐ ORD ☐ T.P.
☐ Driver ☐ Passenger ☐ Child Restraint ☐ Booster Seat

☐ **OTHER OFFENSE:** ________________ ☐ ORC ☐ ORD ☐ T.P.

☐ **OTHER OFFENSE:** ________________ ☐ ORC ☐ ORD ☐ T.P.

SIGNATURE X

☐ DRIVER LICENSE HELD ☐ VEHICLE SEIZED ☐ JUVENILE OFFENDER

PAVEMENT: ☐ Dry ☐ Wet ☐ Snow ☐ Icy # of Lanes ____ ☐ **Construction Zone**
VISIBILITY: ☐ Clear ☐ Cloudy ☐ Dusk ☐ Night ☐ Dawn
WEATHER: ☐ Rain ☐ Snow ☐ Fog ☐ No Adverse
TRAFFIC: ☐ Heavy ☐ Moderate ☐ Light ☐ None
AREA: ☐ Business ☐ Rural ☐ Residential ☐ Industry ☐ School
CRASH: ☐ **Yes** ☐ No ☐ Almost Caused ☐ Non-Injury ☐ **Injury** ☐ **Fatal**

Crash Report Number:

REMARKS:

ACCOMPANYING CRIMINAL CHARGE ☐ Yes ☐ No TOTAL # OFFENSES ______

CO. RES. ______

**TO DEFENDANT: SUMMONS** **PERSONAL APPEARANCE REQUIRED** ☐ Yes ☐ No

You are summoned and ordered to appear on __________, 20____ at ______ AM/PM,

in ____________ Court, at ____________

**If you fail to appear at this time and place you may be arrested or your license may be cancelled.**

This summons served personally on the defendant on __________ 20____

The issuing/charging law enforcement officer states under the penalties of perjury and falsification that he/she has read the above complaint and that it is true.

PHONE ( )

| COURT CODE | UNIT | POST | DISTRICT |
|---|---|---|---|
| | | | |

________________
Charging Law Enforcement Officer

________________
Issuing Law Enforcement Officer ☐ **SAME AS ABOVE**

**Issuing Officer: Verify address. If different from license address, write present address in space provided.**

OHP0060 10-0060-00 (REVISION 12/09) **COURT RECORD** OSHP HP7 [B6305]

Docket #________ Page #________ Case #________

Defendant's Attorney ________
Name / Address / Telephone

| DATE | COURT ACTION: ORDERS |
|---|---|
| | **BAIL** |
| | ☐ **No Bail** - Defendant cited and released. |
| | ☐ **Bail** in the amount of $______ set by Judge pursuant to bail schedule. |
| BOND AMOUNT | **BOND TYPE** |
| $______ | ☐ Cash ☐ Personal ☐ 10% ☐ AAA/Insurance Bond<br>☐ Unsecured ☐ Surety ☐ O.L. Held ☐ Other ______ |

Depositor: ________
Name / Address / Telephone

☐ Defendant released upon execution of Bail as noted: ______ See Bond forms – received by ______

| CONTINUANCE Requester: | New **DATE** |
|---|---|
| CONTINUANCE Reason: | |
| ☐ Defendant Failed to Appear | |
| ☐ Order Supplemental Summons to New Date | |
| ☐ Order Operator's License Forfeiture ☐ Bond Forfeiture | |
| ☐ Order Warrant: Bond Amount $______ | |
| ☐ Summons Issued Served **DATE**: | |
| ☐ Warrant Issued Executed **DATE**: | |

________ / /
Judge/Magistrate **DATE**

**COURT ENTRY**

Defendant present with/without Counsel. All rights pursuant to Criminal Rules 10 & 11, Traffic Rules 8 & 10 explained.

| | COUNT | | | | | |
|---|---|---|---|---|---|---|
| | SPEED | OVI | LICENSE | SEATBELT | | |
| Initial Plea | | | | | | |
| Trial Date | | | | | | |
| Finding | | | | | | |
| Fine $ | | | | | | |
| Costs $ | | | | | | |
| Jailtime (Days) | | | | | | |
| | SUSPENDED | | | | | |
| Fines $ | | | | | | |
| Costs $ | | | | | | |
| Jailtime (Days) | | | | | | |

**ADDITIONAL ORDERS**

☐ **If OVI conviction:** 72 hour program permitted in lieu of jail.

☐ Defendant's License is **SUSPENDED** for ______ days / month(s) / year(s), which shall commence on ______ and end on ______

☐ Defendant is granted **Limited Driving Privileges** as follows, effective: ______

☐ Defendant to pay fines on **Payment Program** – see separate entry.

☐ If **WAIVERED**: ☐ MET Requirements of Waiver ☐ PAID Fines and Costs ☐ ACCEPTED Guilty Plea(s) ☐ MADE Guilty Finding(s). Imposed Fines and Costs noted below.

________ / /
Judge/Magistrate **DATE**

| FOR CLERK'S USE | COUNT | | | | | |
|---|---|---|---|---|---|---|
| | SPEED | OVI | LICENSE | SEATBELT | | |
| Fines $ | | | | | | |
| Costs - Local $ | | | | | | |
| Costs - State $ | | | | | | |
| **TOTAL $** | | | | | | |
| Receipt #(s) | | | | | | |

☐ If **WAIVERED**: Guilty Plea(s), Waiver(s) and Payments made: ☐ In Person ☐ By Mail
Receipt supplied to defendant: ☐ In Person ☐ Check is receipt ☐ By Mail via USPS First Class Letter Rate mail to defendant's present address.
Waiver reviewed, found to be correct and approved.

☐ Financial Responsibility PROOF SHOWN

☐ NO Financial Responsibility PROOF: Clerk to notify BMV

☐ Financial Responsibility PROOF NOT APPLICABLE

________
Clerk / Violations Clerk / Deputy Clerk

/ / ______ / / ______
**DATE** Abstract Mailed to BMV **DATE** Mayor's Court Transfer/Notice of Appeal

**COURT RECORD reverse side**

__________ COURT __________ COUNTY, OHIO

STATE OF OHIO __________ ☐ City ☐ Village ☐ Township TICKET # __________

CASE # __________

NAME __________

STREET __________

CITY, STATE __________ ZIP __________

PRESENT ADDRESS

| OPERATOR LICENSE / STATE ID# ☐ None* | BIRTH DATE | ISSUE DATE | STATE |
|---|---|---|---|
| | | | |

| CLASS | EXPIRES | ENDORSEMENT(s)/RESTRICTION(s) | SS# (last 4 digits) |
|---|---|---|---|
| | | ☐CDL ☐MC ☐Other______ | |

| SEX | HEIGHT | WEIGHT | EYES | HAIR | RACE | FINANCIAL RESPONSIBILITY PROOF? |
|---|---|---|---|---|---|---|
| | | | | | | ☐ Yes ☐ No ☐ N/A |

* If no OL/State ID, **REQUIRED** documentation attached: ☐ Yes

**TO DEFENDANT: COMPLAINT** ON __________, 20 ____ AT __________ AM/PM, YOU

Operated/Passenger/Parked/Walked a ☐ Passenger ☐ Motorcycle ☐ Bicycle ☐ Other __________

☐ Commercial DOT# __________ ☐ ≥26,001 lbs. ☐ <16 Pass. Bus ☐ ≥16 Pass. Bus ☐ Haz. Mat.

VEHICLE: YEAR __________ MAKE __________ MODEL __________

COLOR __________ LICENSE # __________ STATE __________

UPON A PUBLIC HIGHWAY, NAMELY __________

AT/NEAR __________ (M.P. ______ )

IN THE __________ OF __________ IN __________

COUNTY (NO.) __________, STATE OF OHIO AND COMMITTED THE FOLLOWING OFFENSE(S).

☐ **SPEED:** __________ MPH in __________ MPH zone — ☐ ORC ☐ ORD ☐ T.P.
☐ Over limits ☐ Unsafe for conditions ☐ ACDA
☐ Radar ☐ Air ☐ VASCAR ☐ Pace ☐ Laser ☐ Stationary ☐ Moving

☐ **OVI:** ☐ Under the influence of alcohol/drug of abuse. — ☐ ORC ☐ ORD ☐ T.P.
☐ Prohibited blood alcohol concentration. __________ BAC
☐ Blood ☐ Breath ☐ Urine ☐ Refused

| Prior OVIs: | # of prior OVIs | Years of prior OVIs | | | | | | |
|---|---|---|---|---|---|---|---|---|
| | | | | | | | | |

☐ **DRIVER LICENSE:** ☐ None ☐ Not on person ☐ Revoked ☐ Suspended — ☐ ORC ☐ ORD ☐ T.P.
EXPIRED: ☐ <6 months ☐ >6 months ☐ Failure to Reinstate
Suspension Type: __________

☐ **SAFETY BELT:** Failure to wear — ☐ ORC ☐ ORD ☐ T.P.
☐ Driver ☐ Passenger ☐ Child Restraint ☐ Booster Seat

☐ **OTHER OFFENSE:** __________ — ☐ ORC ☐ ORD ☐ T.P.

☐ **OTHER OFFENSE:** __________ — ☐ ORC ☐ ORD ☐ T.P.

☐ DRIVER LICENSE HELD ☐ VEHICLE SEIZED ☐ JUVENILE OFFENDER

SIGNATURE X

Court Case __________ COURT NAME __________

Case # __________ FR SHOWN ☐ YES ☐ NO FR SHOWN - BMV to process.

CO. RES.

| If Bond Forfeiture, | Speed | OVI | License | Child Restraint | | |
|---|---|---|---|---|---|---|
| DATE FORFEITED: | | | | | | |
| CONVICTION DATE: | | | | | | |
| MOVING VIOLATION? | YES NO | YES NO | YES NO | NO | YES NO | YES NO |
| PLEA CODE | | | | | | |
| POINTS ASSESSED | | | | | | |
| BMV OFFENSE CODE | | | | | | |
| IF AMENDED, OFFENSE CODE | | | | | | |
| FATALITY | | | | | | |

FOR BMV USE

☐ License Suspended __________ days/months/years Effective: __________ to __________
☐ Suspension Class __________
☐ MO – Limited Driving Privileges Effective: __________ to __________
(See Separate Entry) Suspension is on Count: __________ ☐ FRA SUSPENSION
☐ License Forfeiture — See separate BMV Form 2528
☐ OL Confiscated — Date sent to BMV: __________
☐ Other Information — See reverse side.

PHONE ( )

I hereby certify that the above statements are taken from the records of this Court.

__________ Authorized Signature ____ / ____ / ____ DATE

Send completed copy to: Ohio Bureau of Motor Vehicles
P.O. Box 16583
Columbus, OH 43216-6583

**ABSTRACT OF COURT RECORD**

Intentionally blank paper.

ABSTRACT OF
COURT RECORD COPY Reverse Side

______________________ COURT ______________________ COUNTY, OHIO

STATE OF OHIO ______________________ TICKET # ______________________
☐ City ☐ Village ☐ Township
CASE # ______________________

NAME ______________________

STREET ______________________

CITY, STATE ______________________ ZIP ______________________

| OPERATOR LICENSE / STATE ID# ☐ NONE* | BIRTH DATE | ISSUE DATE | STATE |
|---|---|---|---|
| | | | |

| CLASS | EXPIRES | ENDORSEMENT(s)/RESTRICTION(s) | SS# (last 4 digits) |
|---|---|---|---|
| | | ☐ CDL ☐ MC ☐ Other ______ | |

| SEX | HEIGHT | WEIGHT | EYES | HAIR | RACE | FINANCIAL RESPONSIBILITY PROOF? |
|---|---|---|---|---|---|---|
| | | | | | | ☐ Yes ☐ No ☐ N/A |

* If no OL/State ID, **REQUIRED** documentation attached: ☐ Yes

**TO DEFENDANT: COMPLAINT** ON ______________, 20 ____ AT ____________ AM/PM, YOU
Operated/Passenger/Parked/Walked a ☐ Passenger ☐ Motorcycle ☐ Bicycle ☐ Other ______
☐ Commercial DOT# ________ ☐ ≥26,001 lbs. ☐ <16 Pass. Bus ☐ ≥16 Pass. Bus ☐ Haz. Mat.
VEHICLE: YEAR ________ MAKE ________ MODEL ________
COLOR ________ LICENSE # ________ STATE ________
UPON A PUBLIC HIGHWAY, NAMELY ______________________
AT/NEAR ______________________ (M.P. ______)
IN THE ________ OF ______________ IN ______________
COUNTY (NO.) ______ STATE OF OHIO AND COMMITTED THE FOLLOWING OFFENSE(S):

☐ **SPEED:** ________ MPH in ________ MPH zone — ☐ ORC ☐ ORD ☐ T.P.
☐ Over limits ☐ Unsafe for conditions ☐ ACDA
☐ Radar ☐ Air ☐ VASCAR ☐ Pace ☐ Laser ☐ Stationary ☐ Moving

☐ **OVI:** ☐ Under the influence of alcohol/drug of abuse. — ☐ ORC ☐ ORD ☐ T.P.
☐ Prohibited blood alcohol concentration. ________ BAC
☐ Blood ☐ Breath ☐ Urine ☐ Refused
Prior OVIs: # of prior OVIs ______ Years of prior OVIs ______

☐ **DRIVER LICENSE:** ☐ None ☐ Not on person ☐ Revoked ☐ Suspended — ☐ ORC ☐ ORD ☐ T.P.
EXPIRED: ☐ <6 months ☐ >6 months ☐ Failure to Reinstate
Suspension Type: ______________

☐ **SAFETY BELT:** Failure to wear — ☐ ORC ☐ ORD ☐ T.P.
☐ Driver ☐ Passenger ☐ Child Restraint ☐ Booster Seat

☐ **OTHER OFFENSE:** ______________ — ☐ ORC ☐ ORD ☐ T.P.

☐ **OTHER OFFENSE:** ______________ — ☐ ORC ☐ ORD ☐ T.P.

☐ DRIVER LICENSE HELD ☐ VEHICLE SEIZED ☐ JUVENILE OFFENDER

PAVEMENT: ☐ Dry ☐ Wet ☐ Snow ☐ Icy # of Lanes ____ ☐ **Construction Zone**
VISIBILITY: ☐ Clear ☐ Cloudy ☐ Dusk ☐ Night ☐ Dawn
WEATHER: ☐ Rain ☐ Snow ☐ Fog ☐ No Adverse
TRAFFIC: ☐ Heavy ☐ Moderate ☐ Light ☐ None
AREA: ☐ Business ☐ Rural ☐ Residential ☐ Industry ☐ School
CRASH: ☐ **Yes** ☐ No ☐ Almost Caused ☐ Non-Injury ☐ **Injury** ☐ **Fatal**
Crash Report Number:
REMARKS:

ACCOMPANYING CRIMINAL CHARGE ☐ Yes ☐ No TOTAL # OFFENSES ______

**TO DEFENDANT: SUMMONS** **PERSONAL APPEARANCE REQUIRED** ☐ Yes ☐ No
You are summoned and ordered to appear on ______________, 20 ____ at ______ AM/PM,
in ______________ Court, at ______________
**If you fail to appear at this time and place you may be arrested or your license may be cancelled.**
This summons served personally on the defendant on ______________, 20 ____
The issuing/charging law enforcement officer states under the penalties of perjury and falsification that he/she has read the above complaint and that it is true.

| COURT CODE | UNIT | POST | DISTRICT |
|---|---|---|---|
| | | | |

______________________
Charging Law Enforcement Officer

______________________
Issuing Law Enforcement Officer ☐ **SAME AS ABOVE**

**Issuing Officer: Verify address. If different from license address, write present address in space provided.**

PRESENT ADDRESS ______________________
SIGNATURE X ______________________
CO. RES. ______________________
PHONE ( ) ______________________

OSHP HP7
OHP0060 10-0060-00 (REVISION 12/09) **DEFENDANT'S COPY BLUE** (B6305)

**TO DEFENDANT: Read this material carefully.**

☐ **Personal Appearance Required.**
If the officer marked this block on the face of the ticket, you must appear in court. Your appearance in court is required because the offenses cannot be processed by a traffic violations bureau.

**Failure to Appear and/or Pay:**

- The posting of bail or depositing your license as bond is to secure your appearance in court or the processing of the offenses through a traffic violations bureau. It is not a payment of fines or costs.
- If you do not appear at the time and place stated in the citation or if you do not timely process this citation through a traffic violations bureau, your license will be cancelled.
- Also, a warrant may be issued for your arrest and you may be subject to additional criminal penalties.

The following offenses require court appearance and may not be processed by a traffic violations bureau:

- Any indictable offense;
- Operating a vehicle under the influence of alcohol or any drug of abuse;
- Leave scene of accident;
- Driving while under suspension or revocation of driver's or commercial driver's license;
- Driving without being licensed to drive, except where the driver's or commercial driver's license has been expired for six months or less;
- A third moving traffic offense within 12 months;
- Passing a standing school bus;
- Willfully eluding or fleeing a police officer;
- Drag racing.

☐ **Waiverable through traffic violations bureau.**
If you are charged with offenses other than those listed above, you may, at any time prior to arraignment, **plead guilty** to the offenses charged and dispose of the case without court appearance by:

(1) appearing personally at the traffic violations bureau, signing the waiver printed below and paying the fines and costs or

(2) signing the waiver printed below and mailing it and a check, money order, or other approved payment for the total of the fines and costs to the traffic violations bureau at the following address:

Traffic Violations Bureau Address: ______________________

______________________

**INSURANCE WARNING**

**Under Ohio law** you are required to show proof of financial responsibility or insurance.
If you did not do so at the time of receiving this ticket, **you must submit proof** of insurance when you appear in court on these offenses.

**If you do not submit the required proof:**
- your driver's license will be suspended and
- you may be subject to additional fees and insurance sanctions

If you have any questions regarding the **proof filing**, you may call the traffic violations bureau at the telephone indicated.

For information regarding your **Duty To Appear** or the **Fines and Costs** amount(s), call:

______________________
Telephone Number(s)

**Contested Case; Court Appearance Required.**

If you desire to **contest the offenses** or if court **appearance is required**, you must appear at the time and place stated in the summons.

**Notice to Defendant under age eighteen.**

You **must appear** before the Juvenile Court at the time and place determined by that Court.
The Juvenile Court will notify you when and where to appear.
This ticket will be filed with the Juvenile Court and may be used as a juvenile complaint.

______________________
Juvenile Court Address

______________________
For information regarding your **Duty to Appear** at Juvenile Court call:

______________________
Telephone Number(s)

**Guilty Pleas, No Contest Pleas, Waiver of Trial, Payment of Fines and Costs**

I, the undersigned defendant, do hereby enter my written pleas of guilty to the offenses charged in this ticket. I realize that by signing these guilty pleas, I admit my guilt of the offenses charged and waive my right to contest the offenses in a trial before the court or jury. Further, I realize that a record of this plea will be sent to the Ohio Bureau of Motor Vehicles. I have not been convicted of, pleaded guilty to, or forfeited bond for two or more prior moving traffic offenses within the last 12 months. I plead guilty to the offense(s) charged.

FINES $ __________ X ______________________
Defendant's Signature

COSTS $ __________ ______________________
Address

TOTAL $ __________ ______________________

**DEFENDANT'S COPY Reverse Side**

__________ COURT __________ COUNTY, OHIO

STATE OF OHIO __________ TICKET # __________

☐ City ☐ Village ☐ Township

CASE # __________

NAME __________

STREET __________

CITY, STATE __________ ZIP __________

PRESENT ADDRESS

| OPERATOR LICENSE / STATE ID# ☐ None* | BIRTH DATE | ISSUE DATE | STATE |
|---|---|---|---|
| | | | |

| CLASS | EXPIRES | ENDORSEMENT(s)/RESTRICTION(s) | SS# (last 4 digits) |
|---|---|---|---|
| | | ☐CDL ☐MC ☐Other ______ | |

| SEX | HEIGHT | WEIGHT | EYES | HAIR | RACE | FINANCIAL RESPONSIBILITY PROOF? |
|---|---|---|---|---|---|---|
| | | | | | | ☐ Yes ☐ No ☐ N/A |

* If no OL/State ID, **REQUIRED** documentation attached: ☐ Yes

**TO DEFENDANT: COMPLAINT** ON ______, 20 ____ AT ______ AM/PM, YOU

Operated/Passenger/Parked/Walked a ☐ Passenger ☐ Motorcycle ☐ Bicycle ☐ Other ______

☐ Commercial DOT# ______ ☐ ≥26,001 lbs. ☐ <16 Pass. Bus ☐ ≥16 Pass. Bus ☐ Haz. Mat.

VEHICLE: YEAR ______ MAKE ______ MODEL ______

COLOR ______ LICENSE # ______ STATE ______

UPON A PUBLIC HIGHWAY, NAMELY ______

AT/NEAR ______ (M.P. ____ )

IN THE ______ OF ______ IN ______

COUNTY (NO.), ______ STATE OF OHIO AND COMMITTED THE FOLLOWING OFFENSE(S).

SIGNATURE X

☐ **SPEED:** ______ MPH in ______ MPH zone — ☐ ORC ☐ ORD ☐ T.P.

☐ Over limits ☐ Unsafe for conditions ☐ ACDA

☐ Radar ☐ Air ☐ VASCAR ☐ Pace ☐ Laser ☐ Stationary ☐ Moving

☐ **OVI:** ☐ Under the influence of alcohol/drug of abuse. — ☐ ORC ☐ ORD ☐ T.P.

☐ Prohibited blood alcohol concentration. ______ BAC

☐ Blood ☐ Breath ☐ Urine ☐ Refused

| Prior OVIs: | # of prior OVIs | Years of prior OVIs |
|---|---|---|
| | | |

☐ **DRIVER LICENSE:** ☐ None ☐ Not on person ☐ Revoked ☐ Suspended — ☐ ORC ☐ ORD ☐ T.P.

EXPIRED: ☐ <6 months ☐ >6 months ☐ Failure to Reinstate

Suspension Type: ______

☐ **SAFETY BELT:** Failure to wear — ☐ ORC ☐ ORD ☐ T.P.

☐ Driver ☐ Passenger ☐ Child Restraint ☐ Booster Seat

☐ **OTHER OFFENSE:** ______ — ☐ ORC ☐ ORD ☐ T.P.

☐ **OTHER OFFENSE:** ______ — ☐ ORC ☐ ORD ☐ T.P.

☐ DRIVER LICENSE HELD ☐ VEHICLE SEIZED ☐ JUVENILE OFFENDER

PAVEMENT: ☐ Dry ☐ Wet ☐ Snow ☐ Icy # of Lanes ____ ☐ **Construction Zone**

VISIBILITY: ☐ Clear ☐ Cloudy ☐ Dusk ☐ Night ☐ Dawn

WEATHER: ☐ Rain ☐ Snow ☐ Fog ☐ No Adverse

TRAFFIC: ☐ Heavy ☐ Moderate ☐ Light ☐ None

AREA: ☐ Business ☐ Rural ☐ Residential ☐ Industry ☐ School

CRASH: ☐ **Yes** ☐ No ☐ Almost Caused ☐ Non-Injury ☐ **Injury** ☐ **Fatal**

Crash Report Number:

REMARKS:

CO. RES.

ACCOMPANYING CRIMINAL CHARGE ☐ Yes ☐ No TOTAL # OFFENSES ______

**TO DEFENDANT: SUMMONS** **PERSONAL APPEARANCE REQUIRED** ☐ Yes ☐ No

You are summoned and ordered to appear on ______, 20 ____ at ____ AM/PM,

in ______ Court, at ______

PHONE ( )

**If you fail to appear at this time and place you may be arrested or your license may be cancelled.**

This summons served personally on the defendant on ______ 20 ____

The issuing/charging law enforcement officer states under the penalties of perjury and falsification that he/she has read the above complaint and that it is true.

| Court Code | Unit | Post | District |
|---|---|---|---|
| | | | |

______

Charging Law Enforcement Officer

______

Issuing Law Enforcement Officer ☐ SAME AS ABOVE

**Issuing Officer: Verify address. If different from license address, write present address in space provided.**

OSHP HP7

OHP0060 10-0060-00 (REVISION 12/09) **AGENCY RECORD PINK** [B6305]

## REPORT OF ACTION ON CASE

**DATE OF ARREST** ______________________ ________ AM/PM
Month / Day / Year Time

**COURT ACTION**

☐ GUILTY ☐ RELEASED TO OTHER AUTHORITY

☐ NOT GUILTY ☐ ______________________

**OFFICER'S NOTES**

A/V Record # ______________________

**WITNESSES:**

______________________
Name Address Telephone

______________________
Name Address Telephone

**ARREST NOTIFICATION**

**VIOLATION:** ______________ **R.C. SECTION** ______

**SCALE LOCATION** ______________ ☐ **PLATFORM** ______ ☐ **PORTABLE**

**AMOUNT OF OVERLOAD** ______________

**OVERLOADED ON:** ☐ Single Axle ☐ Tandem ☐ Inner Bridge

☐ Gross — Length if gross ______ Ft.

**DOT #** ______________

**PUCO #** ______________

______________________
Permit Holder or Company Name or Vehicle Owner Name

______________________
Street Address

______________________
City State Zip

**NOTIFICATION OF ARREST ONLY.**
**NO FURTHER ACTION IS NECESSARY.**

**AGENCY RECORD Reverse Side PINK**

______________________ COURT ______________________ COUNTY, OHIO

STATE OF OHIO ______________________ TICKET # ______________________
☐ City ☐ Village ☐ Township
CASE # ______________________

NAME ______________________

STREET ______________________

CITY, STATE ______________________ ZIP ______________________

| OPERATOR LICENSE / STATE ID# ☐ None* | BIRTH DATE | ISSUE DATE | STATE |
|---|---|---|---|
| | | | |

| CLASS | EXPIRES | ENDORSEMENT(s)/RESTRICTION(s) | SS# (last 4 digits) |
|---|---|---|---|
| | | ☐CDL ☐MC ☐Other______ | |

| SEX | HEIGHT | WEIGHT | EYES | HAIR | RACE | FINANCIAL RESPONSIBILITY PROOF? |
|---|---|---|---|---|---|---|
| | | | | | | ☐ Yes ☐ No ☐ N/A |

* If no OL/State ID, **REQUIRED** documentation attached: ☐ Yes

**TO DEFENDANT: COMPLAINT** ON ______________, 20______ AT ______________ AM/PM, YOU Operated/Passenger/Parked/Walked a ☐ Passenger ☐ Motorcycle ☐ Bicycle ☐ Other______________

☐ Commercial DOT# ______________ ☐ ≥26,001 lbs. ☐ <16 Pass. Bus ☐ ≥16 Pass. Bus ☐ Haz. Mat.

VEHICLE: YEAR ______________ MAKE ______________ MODEL ______________

COLOR ______________ LICENSE # ______________ STATE ______________

UPON A PUBLIC HIGHWAY, NAMELY ______________

AT/NEAR ______________ (M.P. ______ )

IN THE ______________ OF ______________ IN ______________

COUNTY (NO.) ______, STATE OF OHIO AND COMMITTED THE FOLLOWING OFFENSE(S).

☐ **SPEED:** ______________ MPH in ______________ MPH zone — ☐ ORC ☐ ORD ☐ T.P.
☐ Over limits ☐ Unsafe for conditions ☐ ACDA
☐ Radar ☐ Air ☐ VASCAR ☐ Pace ☐ Laser ☐ Stationary ☐ Moving

☐ **OVI:** ☐ Under the influence of alcohol/drug of abuse. — ☐ ORC ☐ ORD ☐ T.P.
☐ Prohibited blood alcohol concentration. ______________ BAC
☐ Blood ☐ Breath ☐ Urine ☐ Refused

| | # of prior OVIs | Years of prior OVIs | | | | | | |
|---|---|---|---|---|---|---|---|---|
| Prior OVIs: | | | | | | | | |

☐ **DRIVER LICENSE:** ☐ None ☐ Not on person ☐ Revoked ☐ Suspended — ☐ ORC ☐ ORD ☐ T.P.
EXPIRED: ☐ <6 months ☐ >6 months ☐ Failure to Reinstate
Suspension Type: ______________

☐ **SAFETY BELT:** Failure to wear — ☐ ORC ☐ ORD ☐ T.P.
☐ Driver ☐ Passenger ☐ Child Restraint ☐ Booster Seat

☐ **OTHER OFFENSE:** ______________ — ☐ ORC ☐ ORD ☐ T.P.

☐ **OTHER OFFENSE:** ______________ — ☐ ORC ☐ ORD ☐ T.P.

☐ DRIVER LICENSE HELD ☐ VEHICLE SEIZED ☐ JUVENILE OFFENDER

PAVEMENT: ☐ Dry ☐ Wet ☐ Snow ☐ Icy # of Lanes ______ ☐ **Construction Zone**
VISIBILITY: ☐ Clear ☐ Cloudy ☐ Dusk ☐ Night ☐ Dawn
WEATHER: ☐ Rain ☐ Snow ☐ Fog ☐ No Adverse
TRAFFIC: ☐ Heavy ☐ Moderate ☐ Light ☐ None
AREA: ☐ Business ☐ Rural ☐ Residential ☐ Industry ☐ School
CRASH: ☐ **Yes** ☐ No ☐ Almost Caused ☐ Non-Injury ☐ **Injury** ☐ **Fatal**

Crash Report Number:

REMARKS:

ACCOMPANYING CRIMINAL CHARGE ☐ Yes ☐ No TOTAL # OFFENSES ______________

**TO DEFENDANT: SUMMONS** **PERSONAL APPEARANCE REQUIRED** ☐ Yes ☐ No

You are summoned and ordered to appear on ______________, 20______ at ______ AM/PM,

in ______________ Court, at ______________

**If you fail to appear at this time and place you may be arrested or your license may be cancelled.**

This summons served personally on the defendant on ______________ 20______

The issuing/charging law enforcement officer states under the penalties of perjury and falsification that he/she has read the above complaint and that it is true.

| Court Code | Unit | Post | District |
|---|---|---|---|
| | | | |

______________
Charging Law Enforcement Officer

______________
Issuing Law Enforcement Officer ☐ **SAME AS ABOVE**

**Issuing Officer: Verify address. If different from license address, write present address in space provided.**

PRESENT ADDRESS ______________

SIGNATURE X ______________

CO. RES. ______________

PHONE ( ) ______________

OSHP HP7

OHP0060 10-0060-00 (REVISION 12/09) **AGENCY RECORD 2 BUFF** [B6305]

## REPORT OF ACTION ON CASE

**DATE OF ARREST** ______________________ AM/PM
Month / Day / Year Time

**COURT ACTION**

☐ GUILTY ☐ RELEASED TO OTHER AUTHORITY

☐ NOT GUILTY ☐ ____________________

**OFFICER'S NOTES**

Radar # Cal. Times

Laser # Cal. Times

A/V Record #

**If juvenile, parents names:**

**WITNESSES:**

Name Address Telephone

Name Address Telephone

**ARREST NOTIFICATION**

**VIOLATION:** ____________ **R.C. SECTION** ____________

**SCALE LOCATION** ____________ ☐ **PLATFORM** ____________ ☐ **PORTABLE**

**AMOUNT OF OVERLOAD** ____________

**OVERLOADED ON:** ☐ **Single Axle** ☐ **Tandem** ☐ **Inner Bridge**

☐ **Gross — Length if gross** ____________ **Ft.**

**DOT #**

**PUCO #**

Permit Holder or Company Name or Vehicle Owner Name

Street Address

City State Zip

**AGENCY RECORD 2 Reverse Side BUFF**

# RULES OF SUPERINTENDENCE FOR THE COURTS OF OHIO

**Complete with amendments through July 1, 2011.**



## RULE 10. Notifying Law Enforcement Agencies of Criminal or Civil Protection Orders

(A) Upon issuance of a civil or criminal protection order by a court pursuant to section 2151.34, 2903.213, 2903.214, division (E)(2) of 2919.26, or 3113.31 of the Revised Code, the court shall complete "Form 10-A." "Form 10-A" and a copy of the order shall be filed by the court with the local enforcement agency for entry in the "National Crime Information Center" database and nationwide dissemination. To accommodate local court or law enforcement procedures, the format of "Form 10-A" may be modified, provided the modification does not affect the substantive content of "Form 10-A."

(B) A court shall follow the instructions in "Form 10-B" for thorough and accurate completion of "Form 10-A" and to facilitate correct entry of criminal or civil protection orders in the "National Crime Information Center" database.

**History:** Amended, eff 3-24-98; 3-1-00; 6-1-02; 5-1-07; 7-1-10.

### COMMENTARY (MARCH 1, 2000)

This rule was amended, effective March 1, 2000 to implement R.C. 2903.213 and 2903.214.

### COMMENTARY (JULY 1, 1997)

This rule was adopted, effective July 1, 1996, and implements R.C. 2919.26 and 3113.31.

## FORM 10-A: PROTECTION ORDER NOTICE TO NCIC

**(Required fields appear in bold print)**

☐ **Initial NCIC Form**
☐ **Modification of Previous Form**
_____ of _____ Pages

**SUBJECT NAME** ______________________________
(LAST) (FIRST) (M.I.)

ADDRESS ______________________________
(STREET) (CITY) (STATE) (ZIP)

PHYSICAL DESCRIPTION: HGT ____ WGT _____ HAIR ______ EYES ______ **RACE** ______ **SEX** ______

**NUMERICAL IDENTIFIER (NOTE: Only ONE of the 4 numerical identifiers is needed.)**
1. SSN ____ / ____ / ____
2. DOB ____ / ____ / ____
3.* DRIVER'S LIC. NO. ____________ STATE ____ EXPIRATION YR. ____
4.* VEHICLE LIC. NO. ____________ STATE ____ EXPIRATION YR. ____ LIC. TYPE ____

(* If #3 or #4 is used as a numerical identifier, entire line MUST be completed.)

**BRADY DISQUALIFIERS:**
**(Pursuant to 18 U.S.C. 922(g)(8), a "yes" response to all three Brady questions disqualifies the subject from purchasing or possessing any firearms, including a rifle, pistol, revolver, or ammunition.)**

- Does Order protect an intimate partner or child(ren)? ☐ YES ☐ NO
- Did subject have opportunity to participate in hearing regarding Order? ☐ YES ☐ NO
- Does Order find subject a credible threat or explicitly prohibit physical force? ☐ YES ☐ NO

**CASE / ORDER NO.** ____________________ (15 DIGIT MAXIMUM)

**COURT ORIGINATING AGENCY IDENTIFIER** ____________ (9 DIGIT ORI ASSIGNED BY NCIC)

☐ R.C. 2903.213 ☐ R.C. 2903.214 ☐ R.C. 2151.34 NAME OF JUDGE ____________
☐ R.C. 2919.26 ☐ R.C. 3113.31

**DATE OF ORDER** ____ / ____ / ____ **EXPIRATION OF ORDER** ____ / ____ / ____
(IN R.C. 2919.26 CASES, "NONEXP" MAY BE USED)

**TERMS AND CONDITIONS OF ORDER (Mark all that are applicable):**

☐ 01 The subject is restrained from assaulting, threatening, abusing, harassing, following, interfering, or stalking the protected person and/or the child(ren) of the protected person.
☐ 02 The subject shall not threaten a member of the protected person's family or household.
☐ 03 The protected person is granted exclusive possession of the residence or household.
☐ 04 The subject is required to stay away from the residence, property, school, or place of employment of the protected person or other family or household member.
☐ 05 The subject is restrained from making any communication with the protected person, including but not limited to, personal, written, or telephone contact, or their employer, employees, or fellow workers, or others with whom the communication would be likely to cause annoyance or alarm the victim.
☐ 06 The subject has visitation or custody rights of the children named in this Order.
☐ 07 The subject is prohibited from possessing and/or purchasing a firearm or other weapon.
☐ 08 See the Miscellaneous Field for comments regarding the specific terms and conditions of this Order.
Miscellaneous comments: ______________________________

OHP DATA ONLY

☐ 09 The protected person is awarded temporary exclusive custody of the children named.

**LIST ALL PROTECTED PERSONS** (Total of 9 allowed, may attach additional forms; **SSN is NOT necessary if DOB is given**):

#EPO

**PROTECTED PERSON** ______________________________
(LAST) (FIRST) (M.I.)
**DOB** ____ / ____ / ____ SSN ____ / ____ / ____ RACE ____ SEX ____

**PROTECTED PERSON** ______________________________
(LAST) (FIRST) (M.I.)
**DOB** ____ / ____ / ____ SSN ____ / ____ / ____ RACE ____ SEX ____

MIS/

**PROTECTED PERSON** ______________________________
(LAST) (FIRST) (M.I.)
**DOB** ____ / ____ / ____ SSN ____ / ____ / ____ RACE ____ SEX ____

**Authorized by (signature):** ______________________ **Date** ________
**Judge/Magistrate (circle one)**

**FORM 10-A: PROTECTION NOTICE TO NCIC**

**Amended: July 1, 2010**
**Discard all previous versions of this form**

## FORM 10-B: HOW TO COMPLETE A PROTECTION NOTICE TO NCIC

These instructions are intended to assist the court in the proper completion of Form 10-A, Protection Notice to NCIC, in compliance with requirements of Ohio and federal law. Thorough and accurate completion of Form 10-A is critical, as this form is the sole method used to enter the terms and conditions of the protection orders issued by the court into the computerized index of criminal justice information maintained by the National Crime Information Center ("NCIC"). Inaccurate or inconsistent information in Form 10-A will result in delay in entering the protection order into the NCIC index and enforcing the order. Form 10-A must be completed each time the court approves, issues, modifies, renews, or terminates a protection order or consent agreement, regardless of whether it is an *ex parte* or full hearing order.

### ELEMENTS OF FORM 10-A

**(A)** The required fields in Form 10-A appear in **BOLD.**

**(B)** Form 10-A is the primary method used to inform law enforcement of the terms and conditions of the protection order. The court should be cautious to mark the appropriate box in the upper right corner of the form. The court must check the box next to "Initial NCIC Form" anytime the court is issuing a protection order out of the same set of facts for the first time, i.e., an *ex parte* order or a full hearing order where an *ex parte* order was not issued. The court must check the box next to "Modification of Previous NCIC" anytime the court has already issued a protection order arising out of the same facts and is now modifying or terminating the order or is making a clerical or orthographical correction to the form.

**(C)** **SUBJECT'S NAME, RACE, & SEX.** The subject's full name, including first and last name, race and sex, are mandatory identifiers that the court must provide to have the form accepted by NCIC. The other identifiers under physical description, i.e., height ("HGT"), weight ("WGT"), hair, and eyes, are not mandatory, yet they are helpful information to ensure the correct person is identified if a violation of the order occurs. Similarly, the address is not mandatory information.

**(D)** **NUMERICAL IDENTIFIER.** The FBI requires the court to provide certain numerical identifiers to properly identify the person subject to the protection order. While completion of all the numerical identifiers is very useful, the FBI mandates that only **one** of the following numerical identifiers be entered to have the form accepted by NCIC:

1. SOCIAL SECURITY NUMBER ("SSN");

2. DATE OF BIRTH ("DOB");

3. DRIVER'S LICENSE NUMBER ("DRIVER'S LIC. NO."): In the instance the driver's license number is to be provided, the state that issued the driver's license and the expiration date of the driver's license must also be included for this entry to be accepted by NCIC;

4. VEHICLE LICENSE NUMBER ("VEHICLE LIC. NO."): In the instance the vehicle's license plate is to be provided, the state that issued the license plate and the expiration date of the license plate must also be included for this entry to be accepted by NCIC.

**(E)** **BRADY DISQUALIFIERS.** Federal law makes it illegal for certain persons subject to a protection order to purchase or possess a firearm, including a rifle, pistol or revolver, or ammunition. This section guides the court in properly identifying those persons subject to a protection order that are also Brady disqualified. An affirmative response to all three questions on Form 10-A results in disqualifying the person subject to a protection order from purchasing or possessing firearms pursuant to 18 U.S.C. 922(g)(8).

Generally, a person subject to a protection order is Brady disqualified under 18 U.S.C. 922(g)(8) when the protected party is a spouse, former spouse, person living or who lived as a spouse, a child of the person subject to the protection order or a child of a spouse, former spouse, or person living or who lived as a spouse. The court must afford the person

**[Page 2 of Form 10-B]**

subject to the protection order an opportunity to be heard and, after evaluating all the evidence, find that the person subject to the order poses a credible threat of harm to the protected party.

**(F)** **CASE/ORDER NO.** The case/order number of the protection order is a required element. It is particularly relevant when the court modifies, renews, or terminates a protection order. Law enforcement and NCIC will use the case/order number to cross-reference the appropriate order. In addition, law enforcement also uses this information to verify the currency of an order.

**(G)** **COURT ORIGINATING AGENCY IDENTIFIER.** To accept a Form 10-A entry into the federal protection order database, NCIC mandates the court issuing the protection order to include its agency identifier. The agency identifier is a unique nine digit alphabetic and/or numeric series issued by the FBI that easily allows identification of the court issuing the order. Although the "Name of Judge" is not a mandatory field, it is prudent to include the name of the judicial officer issuing the protection order. Similarly, NCIC does not require a court to indicate under which Revised Code section the order is being issued. However, this information is useful for law enforcement to quickly determine the relationship between the parties and determine how to assess risk if the order is violated.

**(H)** **DATE OF ORDER AND EXPIRATION OF ORDER.** The court must note on the form the date the protection order was issued and the date when it will expire. The protection order database will automatically purge the orders on their expiration date. If a protection order is terminated before the original expiration, it is critical the court explicitly indicate on Form 10-A the new expiration date to allow proper removal of the order from the database.

**(I)** **TERMS AND CONDITIONS OF ORDER.** The court must check every box that corresponds to all provisions of the protection order as ordered by the court. Note the numbering next to each term and condition in Form 10-A does not correspond to the sequence of the remedies listed in the protection orders. However, the remedies in the protection order forms cross-reference, by number, the terms and conditions listed in Form 10-A.

The court should submit a modified Form 10-A to the appropriate law enforcement reporting agency in every instance that any court order, i.e., divorce decree or custody order, results in the modification of a term or a protected party in a protection order.

**(J)** **LIST ALL PROTECTED PERSONS.** The court must provide the full name and date of birth for all persons who are protected by the protection order. The protected person's social security number, race, and gender are not required entry in Form 10-A.

**(K)** **AUTHORIZED SIGNATURE.** The judge or magistrate who issued the protection order must sign and date Form 10-A.

**FORM 10-B: HOW TO COMPLETE A PROTECTION NOTICE TO NCIC**

**Effective Date: July 1, 2010**

## RULE 10.01. Standard Civil Protection Order Forms—Domestic Relations Division

(A) The domestic relations division of a court of common pleas shall distribute, upon request, a forms and instructions packet for use in civil protection order proceedings under section 3113.31 of the Revised Code. The packet shall include, at a minimum, forms and instructions that are substantially similar to "Forms 10.01-A through 10.01-H."

(B) An action for a civil protection order pursuant to section 3113.31 of the Revised Code shall be commenced by filing a petition form that is substantially similar to "Form 10.01-D."

(C) In every case in which the domestic relations division of a court of common pleas issues or approves an ex parte civil protection order, a full hearing civil protection order, or a consent agreement pursuant to section 3113.31 of the Revised Code, the court shall use, as applicable, forms that are substantially similar to "Forms 10.01-H through 10.01-J."

(D) Every ex parte civil protection order, full hearing civil protection order, and consent agreement that the domestic relations division of a court of common pleas issues or approves pursuant to section 3113.31 of the Revised Code shall include a cover sheet that is substantially similar to "Form 10.01-G."

(E) In every case in which the domestic relations division of a court of common pleas modifies the terms of a full hearing civil protection order or a consent agreement pursuant to section 3113.31 of the Revised Code, it shall use the applicable forms that are substantially similar to "Forms 10.01-L and 10.01-M."

(F) In every case in which the domestic relations division of a court of common pleas terminates a full hearing civil protection order or a consent agreement before its original expiration date pursuant to section 3113.31 of the Revised Code, it shall use the applicable form that is substantially similar to "Form 10.01-L."

**History:** Effective 1-1-98; amended, eff 6-1-00; 6-1-02; 7-1-10.

### COMMENTARY (JANUARY 1, 1998)

On December 9, 1994, Am.Sub.H.B. No. 335 became effective, which made significant changes to Ohio's domestic violence laws. Section 4 of Am.Sub.H.B. No. 335, states as follows:

The General Assembly hereby requests the Supreme Court, in consultation with the Department of Human Services, to prescibe a form that is to be filed by a petitioner seeking a civil protection order under section 3113.31 of the Revised Code and that makes reference to all the forms of relief that a court is authorized to grant under division (E) of section 3113.31 of the Revised Code, as amended by this act, contains space for the petitioner to request any of those forms of relief, and includes instructions for completing the form so that a petitioner may file the form without the assistance of an attorney.

The Supreme Court, in consultation with its Domestic Violence Task Force, developed Forms 10.01-C and 10.01-D in response to the General Assembly's request in Am.Sub.H.B. No. 335.

During its eighteen months of study, the Supreme Court's Domestic Violence Task Force determined that pro se victims of domestic violence often do not have access to the forms necessary to obtain a civil protection order pursuant to section 3113.31 of the Revised Code. The Task Force also found that due to the variety of protection order forms used by Ohio courts, it can be difficult for law enforcement officers to recognize valid protection orders and understand the pertinent provisions of such orders. Further, the Task Force discovered that misconceptions exist in regard to the penalties for violating protection orders. The Court developed this rule and Forms 10.01-A, 10.01-B, and 10.01-E through 10.01-J to address these concerns.

This rule applies to all courts of common pleas that have jurisdiction over civil protection orders and consent agreements pursuant to section 3113.31 of the Revised Code.

# FORM 10.01-A: GENERAL INFORMATION ABOUT DOMESTIC VIOLENCE PROTECTION ORDERS

## DEFINITIONS YOU NEED TO KNOW

**Domestic violence** is when a family or household member uses physical violence, threats, intimidation, and/or emotional, sexual, and economic abuse to maintain power and control over the other person, usually within an intimate relationship. Domestic violence is most often a combination of psychological and physical actions; the physical results are just the most visible. Domestic violence is a pattern of conduct in which one intimate partner uses force or threats of force to control the other person.

State law has determined that some forms of abuse do not constitute criminal behavior or behavior requiring the Court's intervention. For example, psychological battering, economic abuse, or verbal harassment without evidence of threats or physical harm are not recognized by Ohio law as domestic violence that allows a petitioner to obtain a protection order or request that criminal charges be filed.

When a family or household member tries to cause you bodily harm by hitting, pushing, beating, or physically hurting you, that is domestic violence. When a family or household member makes you afraid that you will be harmed, that is domestic violence. When a family or household member stalks, commits sexually oriented offenses against you, or forces sexual relations on you, that is domestic violence. When a family or household member abuses your children, that is domestic violence.

IN A **CIVIL** DOMESTIC VIOLENCE CASE:

**Petition for Domestic Violence Civil Protection Order ("CPO")** is the document a domestic violence victim, the victim's parent, or an adult household member of the victim must file with the domestic relations division of the Court to obtain a civil protection order against an alleged offender.

**Domestic Violence Civil Protection Order ("CPO")** ***Ex Parte*** is an emergency order the Court issues in response to the Petition for a Civil Protection Order after an *ex parte* hearing. The *ex parte* hearing is described in this form on page 3.

**Domestic Violence Civil Protection Order ("CPO") Full Hearing** is the final order the Court issues after a full hearing. The full hearing is described in this form on page 3. The full hearing CPO replaces the *ex parte* CPO. Sometimes the final order issued by the Court is a **Consent Agreement and Domestic Violence Civil Protection Order**, Form 10.01-J, upon terms agreed to by the parties.

**Petitioner** is the person asking or "petitioning" the Court for protection. By filing the Petition for a CPO, YOU are the Petitioner.

**Respondent** is the alleged domestic violence offender. Petitioner seeks protection from the Respondent by filing for a CPO.

IN A **CRIMINAL** DOMESTIC VIOLENCE CASE:

**Motion for a Domestic Violence Criminal Temporary Protection Order ("DVTPO")** is the document that must be filed in a criminal case if a victim of domestic violence or victim of a sexually oriented offense wishes to obtain a protection order against an alleged offender, who is a family or household member. The criminal case must allege the offender committed negligent assault, criminal damaging or endangering, criminal mischief, burglary, aggravated trespass, endangering children, any offense of violence, or any sexually oriented offense against a family or household member. The prosecutor has a form for this purpose.

**Domestic Violence Temporary Protection Order ("DVTPO")** is the order the Court issues in response to the Motion for Temporary Protection Order. The DVTPO requires the offender to stop abusing and to stay away from the victim(s) named in the Motion for Temporary Protection Order. A DVTPO expires when the alleged offender's criminal case ends or when a new CPO is issued based on the same facts.

**Alleged Victim** is the person asking the Court for protection in the Motion for a DVTPO.

**Defendant** is the person the Motion for a DVTPO is filed against. The Defendant is the person accused of the crimes of negligent assault, criminal damaging or endangering, criminal mischief, burglary, aggravated trespass, endangering children, any sexually oriented offense, or any offense of violence against a family or household member.

## FEES

UNDER FEDERAL AND STATE LAW YOU CANNOT BE CHARGED ANY COSTS OR FEES FOR OBTAINING A PROTECTION ORDER.

## CIVIL PROTECTION ORDERS

**What is a Domestic Violence Civil Protection Order ("CPO")?**

A CPO is issued by a domestic relations division of the Court to protect a victim of domestic violence. A CPO is intended to prevent further domestic violence. It orders someone who has been abusive to do or not do certain things in the future. You may want to consider getting a CPO even if you have a DVTPO from a criminal court because a CPO lasts longer and provides more benefits – such as child custody and support orders. Domestic violence includes the commission of sexually oriented offenses.

Violating a CPO is a crime. If the Respondent violates the CPO, he or she may be arrested, jailed, and fined for disobeying the CPO. A CPO can remain in effect for up to five years. If the Respondent violates the CPO, you can call the police, go back to the domestic relations division of the Court to file a contempt charge, and go to the prosecutor's office to have the Respondent charged with the crime of violating the CPO.

**Why get a Domestic Violence Civil Protection Order?**

If you are a victim of domestic violence, a CPO may help you. Once domestic violence starts, the violence often happens more often and gets increasingly severe. A CPO may stop this cycle of violence because the Court orders the Respondent to stop hurting or threatening you and your family or household members. The Court can use a CPO to order the Respondent to stay away from you for up to five years. A CPO can give you time to "sort things out" and decide what you want to do next without having to be afraid all of the time. If your children have seen domestic violence, a CPO may give all of you a chance to get some help so that you and your children are safe.

Domestic violence is a crime. A CPO tells the Respondent you and the Court are serious about requiring the Respondent to stop his or her abusive behavior and not to hurt or threaten you again.

A CPO sets some "rules" that the Respondent must obey while the CPO is in effect. These rules may require the Respondent to pay child or spousal support; give up possession of a home or car; and/or obey the Court's orders about visitation.

A CPO issued by a domestic relations division of the Court may last longer than a DVTPO issued by a criminal court and can provide more kinds of help. You should know that if you get a CPO based upon the same facts as the DVTPO, the DVTPO from the criminal court will automatically end, even if the criminal case continues.

**Who can get a Domestic Violence Civil Protection Order?**

You can apply for a CPO if you are related to the Respondent by blood or marriage AND have lived with Respondent at any time; OR you are living with or have lived with the Respondent during the past five years; OR you used to be married to the Respondent; OR you have a child with the Respondent, whether or not you ever married or lived together.

You can also get a CPO for any member of your household.

You <u>may</u> be able to get a CPO if you have been dating the Respondent; if you share family or financial responsibilities with the Respondent; AND you have an intimate relationship with the Respondent.

<u>Remember</u> that a CPO has limits. If you suspect that the Respondent will not obey the terms of a CPO, contact your local domestic violence program or the Ohio Domestic Violence Network at 800-934-9840.

[Page 3 of Form 10.01-A]

**Do I need an attorney for me to obtain a Domestic Violence Civil Protection Order?**

No, but you are often better off having legal representation in your CPO proceeding. Neither the Clerk of Court nor other Court employees can give you legal advice. Having an attorney represent you is especially helpful when your case involves contested custody and visitation and/or when an attorney represents the Respondent. If you cannot afford an attorney, contact your local legal aid office at 866-LAWOHIO (toll free), bar association, or Ohio State Legal Services (800-589-5888) for information on low cost or free legal representation.

**Must there be a court hearing for me to obtain a Domestic Violence Civil Protection Order?**

Yes. There are two hearings involved in a CPO case: the *ex parte* hearing and the full hearing.

***Ex Parte* Hearing:** At this hearing only you are present. The Respondent is not present.

An *ex parte* hearing is held the same day a Petition for Civil Protection Order is filed. If a Petition for a CPO is filed early enough in the day, an *ex parte* hearing is held that same day. At the *ex parte* hearing, you take an oath to tell the truth and a judge or magistrate hears your statement of what happened. If the judge or magistrate finds that the events you described meet the requirements of the law, the Court will issue an *Ex Parte* CPO and schedule a full hearing. If the Respondent is asked to vacate the home in which you live, there will be a full hearing within seven business days. Otherwise, a full hearing will be set within ten business days. The Court can hold a full hearing only after the Respondent has been served with the *Ex Parte* CPO. You may need to fill out forms for the Clerk of Court to cause service.

**Full Hearing:** The full hearing is the final hearing.

At this hearing, both you and the Respondent can testify. You must be present at the full hearing. You should bring any witnesses and other evidence to support your case. If the Court issues a Full Hearing CPO, it remains in force until the date indicated in the CPO, with five years being the maximum.

If the Respondent does not show up for the full hearing, you can still obtain a final CPO. However, if the Respondent is not served with the *Ex Parte* CPO before the full hearing, the Court postpones the full hearing until the Respondent is served. If the full hearing is postponed, the *Ex Parte* CPO remains in effect until the full hearing is held.

**You may bring an advocate with you to the *ex parte* and full hearings for support. Some domestic violence shelters and victim assistance programs can provide advocates to go with you to these hearings. Contact your local domestic violence program or the Ohio Domestic Violence Network, 800-934-9840, for program and shelter information.**

## DOMESTIC VIOLENCE CRIMINAL TEMPORARY PROTECTION ORDERS

Your local criminal court grants a DVTPO. You ask the Court for a DVTPO when a criminal complaint is filed alleging someone has committed domestic violence or a sexually oriented offense against you. The DVTPO orders someone who has abused you to do or stop doing certain things in the future. Violating a DVTPO is a crime. If the Defendant violates the DVTPO, the Defendant may be arrested, jailed, and fined for disobeying the DVTPO. Violating a DVTPO is also a reason for the Court to revoke the Defendant's bail. A DVTPO lasts only until the criminal case is ended or a CPO, based on the same facts, is issued by a domestic relations division of the Court.

## RESOURCES

You can find information about Domestic Violence Civil Protection Orders in R.C. 3113.31 and information about Domestic Violence Temporary Protection Orders in R.C. 2919.26.

You may be able to find additional information about domestic violence at the following Websites:

| | |
|---|---|
| Ohio Domestic Violence Network | www.odvn.org |
| Ohio State Legal Services Association's DV Resource Center | www.ohiodvresources.org |
| National Resource Center on Domestic Violence | www.nrcdv.org |

**PLEASE NOTE:** Computer use can be monitored. It is impossible to completely clear all website footprints. If you are in danger, please use a safer computer that your abuser cannot access directly or remotely. For example, computers at a public library, internet café, domestic violence shelter, or community technology center, which can be found through www.ctcnet.org, would be safer computers.

**FORM 10.01-A: GENERAL INFORMATION ABOUT DOMESTIC VIOLENCE PROTECTION ORDERS**

**Amended: July 1, 2010**
**Discard all previous versions of this form**

# FORM 10.01-B: HOW TO OBTAIN A DOMESTIC VIOLENCE CIVIL PROTECTION ORDER ("CPO")

## FORMS TO FILL OUT FOR A DOMESTIC VIOLENCE CPO

To obtain a CPO, you need the following documents. You can get all of these documents from the Clerk of Court's office:

1. Petition for Domestic Violence Civil Protection Order, Form 10.01-D.
2. Domestic Violence Civil Protection Order *Ex Parte*, Form 10.01-H.
3. If you are requesting temporary custody of a child, Information for Parenting Proceeding Affidavit, Form 10.01-F.
4. If you request financial support, you might need to fill out additional forms that the Clerk of Court's office will provide you.

Complete the Petition for a CPO form. Complete additional forms if applicable. Take these documents to the Clerk of Court's office.

## FILING THE PETITION FOR A DOMESTIC VIOLENCE CPO FORM

Present your completed forms to the filing window/counter of the Clerk of Court's office for filing. Do **NOT** file the *Ex Parte* CPO form at this time.

A Clerk of Court's office employee helps you file your documents. You should know that neither the Clerk of Court nor other Court employees can provide you with legal advice.

There is **NO FEE** for filing the Petition for a CPO form.

Ask a Clerk of Court's office employee or your local domestic violence assistance group about local Court procedures.

## VICTIM ADVOCATE

State law permits you to have a victim advocate with you at all times in court during protection order proceedings. "Victim advocate" means a person who provides support and assistance for a victim of an offense during Court proceedings. Contact your local victim assistance program, local domestic violence program, or the Ohio Domestic Violence Network, 800-934-9840, for advocate information.

## ATTENDING THE *EX PARTE* COURT HEARING

You must appear in front of a judge or magistrate for the *ex parte* hearing. The judge or magistrate listens to your testimony.

You should tell the judge or magistrate what the Respondent did to make you fear that you or a family member may be in danger. Tell the judge or magistrate if the Respondent injured you, attempted to injure you, or threatened you.

Tell the judge or magistrate what you would like the Court to do to help keep you and other family members safe and to protect the children. For example, you might ask the judge or magistrate to:

1. Order the Respondent to stay away from you;
2. Order the Respondent to be removed from your home;
3. Order the Respondent to get counseling;
4. Award you custody of any children;
5. Order the Respondent to have visitation only under conditions that will keep you and the children safe;
6. Order the Respondent to pay you child support and/or spousal support (alimony);
7. Order the Respondent to be prohibited from having any weapons;
8. Award you possession of a car for your use;
9. Award you possession of your personal property and the children's personal property.

**FORM 10.01-B: PROCEDURES FOR OBTAINING A DOMESTIC VIOLENCE CIVIL PROTECTION ORDER**

**Amended: July 1, 2010**
**Discard all previous versions of this form**

**[Page 2 of Form 10.01-B]**

If the judge or magistrate determines that you or your family or household members are in danger of domestic violence, the judge and/or magistrate signs an *Ex Parte* CPO.

The judge or magistrate then sets a second hearing (called a "full hearing") within seven to ten business days to give the Respondent a chance to be heard. You must appear at the full hearing. Some issues, such as support, may be postponed until this second hearing.

Take the signed *Ex Parte* CPO to the Clerk of Court's office and have it filed. Tell the Clerk's office where law enforcement officers can find the Respondent to serve him or her with the *Ex Parte* CPO and other necessary papers.

**YOU MUST ATTEND THE FULL HEARING**

The full hearing on the Petition for a CPO will be set within seven to ten business days after the *ex parte* hearing. You **must** attend the full hearing. You may have an attorney present with you at the full hearing.

At the full hearing you must tell what happened again. This time you tell what happened in more detail. Bring with you any witnesses and evidence you have, such as photographs, answering machine tapes, other audio and video recordings, papers such as police reports, hospital records, etc, and any other evidence that will help you prove that the Respondent committed domestic violence against you or another family or household member. Tell the judge or magistrate why you fear the Respondent. You may call the Respondent as a witness to help you prove your case. Tell the judge or magistrate again what you want the Court to do to help keep you and your family members safe.

The Respondent may have an attorney. You may want to ask for a continuance in order to get an attorney. The Respondent may also present evidence and call you as a witness. You may be asked questions by the Respondent or the Respondent's attorney.

After the hearing, if the judge or magistrate decides you are entitled to a CPO, the Court issues a new CPO called a "Domestic Violence Civil Protection Order 'CPO' Full Hearing." This CPO is usually more detailed than the *Ex Parte* CPO issued after the first hearing. The judge or magistrate could also deny your Petition for a CPO if the Court decides you are not entitled to a CPO. The law does not allow the Court to issue a protection order against you, unless the Respondent has filed a separate action against you.

At the full hearing, you and the Respondent can decide to enter into a Consent Agreement instead of having a hearing in front of the judge or magistrate. If you decide to enter into a Consent Agreement, give the judge or magistrate the Consent Agreement and Domestic Violence Civil Protection Order Form 10.01-J contained in the "How to Get a Domestic Violence Protection Order" packet. The Court should also have a Consent Agreement and Domestic Violence Civil Protection Order form available.

**ENFORCING YOUR CPO**

Your CPO remains in effect for five years, unless the Court sets a different expiration date.

**Violating a CPO is a crime**. If the Respondent violates the CPO, it is a crime. Immediately contact the police.

You may also bring a contempt action in domestic relations division of the Court for CPO violations. A contempt action is brought because the Respondent is disregarding the Court's order. You must complete and file a contempt motion with the Clerk of Court's office to begin a contempt action against the Respondent.

**CRIMINAL COURT**

In addition to the *ex parte* hearing and full hearing in domestic relations division of the Court, you should attend all meetings and hearings as requested by the prosecutor and the Court related to any criminal case filed against the Respondent.

Tell the domestic relations division of the Court about any pending criminal cases. Tell the criminal court about any pending domestic relations division of the Court cases.

Any Domestic Violence Temporary Protection Order ("DVTPO") issued by a criminal court expires as soon as the criminal case is ended. A DVTPO issued by a criminal court also expires when a CPO is issued by the domestic relations division of the Court based upon the same facts.

**FORM 10.01-B: PROCEDURES FOR OBTAINING A DOMESTIC VIOLENCE CIVIL PROTECTION ORDER**

**Amended: July 1, 2010**
**Discard all previous versions of this form**

# FORM 10.01-C: HOW TO COMPLETE A PETITION FOR A DOMESTIC VIOLENCE CIVIL PROTECTION ORDER

These instructions will help you to prepare the Petition for Domestic Violence Civil Protection Order. Only the domestic relations division of the Court in your county hears a Petition for a Domestic Violence Civil Protection Order. **Throughout the Petition, you are called *Petitioner* and the person you are filing this Petition against (the alleged domestic violence offender) is called *Respondent*.**

## SOME HINTS BEFORE YOU BEGIN

- All forms must be typed or printed.
- When you write your name on the Petition, use the same name you use when you write your signature.
- Write your name and Respondent's name the same way throughout the Petition.
- Fill out the Petition as completely and accurately as possible.
- If you have any questions about completing the Petition, ask the Clerk of Court's office for assistance or contact your local victim assistance program, domestic violence program, or the Ohio Domestic Violence Network at 800-934-9840.
- Under federal and state law you **cannot be charged any fees** to obtain a protection order.

## FILLING OUT THE PETITION: Mark each instruction below after you read and complete it

☐ **On the front page, leave the "Case No." line and "Judge" lines BLANK.** The Clerk of Court's office fills in this information.

☐ **On the top left-hand side of the front page, fill in the requested information about yourself.** If you do not want your present address to be known, write "confidential" in the space for your address. Do not write your address anywhere on the Petition if you want it to be confidential. However, you must include someone's mailing address on the Petition to allow the Court to send you legal notices concerning your case.

☐ **On the top left-hand side of the front page, fill in the requested information about Respondent as best you can.** You may use Respondent's work address if you do not know Respondent's home address. If you do not know Respondent's date of birth, leave that line blank. Do not attempt to obtain this information unless it is safe to do so.

☐ **Paragraph 1:** If you are filing the Petition to protect yourself, mark the first box and the box that describes your relationship to Respondent.

☐ **Paragraph 2:** If you are filing the Petition to protect a family or household member, mark the box and fill in their name(s) and the other information requested in the chart. You may attach additional pages if you need more room.

☐ **Paragraph 3:** State the date(s) of the incident(s) that caused you to file the Petition. Provide a brief description of what happened. You may attach additional pages if you need more room to complete your description. You may attach an affidavit instead of or in addition to the written description.

☐ **Paragraph 4:** Indicate what action you want the Court to take by marking the boxes next to the numbered paragraphs that apply to your situation.

☐ **Paragraph 4(b):** Provide the address of the residence that you want Respondent to stay away from. If you do not want your present address known, write "address confidential." Do not write your address anywhere on the Petition if you want it to be confidential.

☐ **Paragraphs 4(d) and (e):** If you want temporary custody of your minor children or want the Court to establish temporary visitation rights, list the names and birth dates of the children. If you have children whose custody or visitation will be at issue in this domestic violence case, you must also complete and file a Parenting Proceeding Affidavit, Form 10.01-F. There is a separate form and instructions for the Parenting Proceeding Affidavit, Form 10.01-E and Form 10.01-F.

☐ **Paragraph 4(i):** If you want the Court to grant you use of a motor vehicle, describe that vehicle.

☐ **Paragraph 4(j):** Write any special court orders you believe would help ensure you and your family or household members' safety and protection.

☐ **Paragraph 5:** If you need an emergency ("*ex parte*") protection order mark the box next to Paragraph 5.

☐ **Paragraph 9:** List ALL present court cases and pertinent past court cases or investigations that involve you or a household member that may be related to you, your children, your family, or household members. This list should include all civil, criminal, divorce, juvenile, custody, visitation, and bankruptcy cases. Write the case name, the court, the case number, if known, the type of case, and the result of the case. If the case is not over, write "pending." You may attach additional pages if you need more room.

**SIGNING THE PETITION:** Try to fill out the Petition before you go to the courthouse. AFTER YOU HAVE FILLED OUT THE PETITION, TAKE IT TO A NOTARY PUBLIC TO HAVE YOUR SIGNATURE NOTARIZED. ***DO NOT SIGN THE PETITION UNLESS YOU ARE IN FRONT OF A NOTARY PUBLIC.*** **An employee of the Clerk of Court's office may be available to take your oath.**

**FILING THE PETITION:** After you have your signature notarized, file your Petition at the Clerk of Court's office. The Clerk of Court's office will tell you when and where your *ex parte* hearing will take place. **There is no filing fee for a Petition for a CPO.**

**FORM 10.01-D: PETITION FOR DOMESTIC VIOLENCE CIVIL PROTECTION ORDER**

**IN THE ______________________ COURT**
**______________________ COUNTY, OHIO**

| | |
|---|---|
| ______________________ **Petitioner** : | Case No. ______________________ |
| ______________________ Address : | Judge ______________________ |
| ______________________ City, State, Zip Code : | |
| Date of Birth: ______________ : | **PETITION FOR DOMESTIC VIOLENCE CIVIL PROTECTION ORDER (R.C. 3113.31)** |
| **v.** : | |
| ______________________ **Respondent** : | **Notice to Petitioner: Throughout this form, check every ☐ that applies.** |
| ______________________ Address : | **DO NOT WRITE YOUR ADDRESS ON THIS FORM IF YOU ARE REQUESTING CONFIDENTIALITY. PLEASE PROVIDE AN ADDRESS WHERE YOU CAN RECEIVE NOTICES FROM THE COURT.** |
| ______________________ City, State, Zip Code : | |
| Date of Birth: ______________ : | |

☐ 1. Petitioner is a family or household member of Respondent and a victim of domestic violence and seeks relief on Petitioner's own behalf. The relationship of Petitioner to Respondent is that of:

- ☐ Spouse of Respondent
- ☐ Former spouse of Respondent
- ☐ The natural parent of Respondent's child
- ☐ Other relative (by blood or marriage) of Respondent/ Petitioner who has lived with Respondent at any time
- ☐ Child of Respondent
- ☐ Parent of Respondent
- ☐ Foster Parent
- ☐ Person "living as a spouse of Respondent" defined as:
  - now cohabiting;
  - or cohabited within five years before the alleged act of domestic violence

☐ 2. Petitioner seeks relief on behalf of the following family or household members:

| NAME | DATE OF BIRTH | HOW RELATED TO PETITIONER | HOW RELATED TO RESPONDENT | RESIDES WITH |
|---|---|---|---|---|
| | | | | |
| | | | | |
| | | | | |
| | | | | |
| | | | | |
| | | | | |

3. Respondent has engaged in the following act(s) of domestic violence (describe the acts as fully as possible, add additional pages if necessary): ______________________
______________________
______________________

**FORM 10.01-D: PETITION FOR DOMESTIC VIOLENCE CIVIL PROTECTION ORDER**

**Amended: July 1, 2010**
**Discard all previous versions of this form**

**[Page 2 of Form 10.01-D]**

4. Petitioner requests that the Court grant relief under R.C. 3113.31 to protect the Petitioner and or the family or household members named in this Petition from domestic violence by granting a civil protection order that:

☐ (a) Directs Respondent not to abuse Petitioner and the family or household members named in this Petition by harming, attempting to harm, threatening, following, stalking, harassing, forcing sexual relations upon them, or by committing sexually oriented offenses against them.

☐ (b) Requires Respondent to leave and not return to or interfere with the following residence and grants Petitioner exclusive possession of the residence: ______________________________
______________________________________________________________

☐ (c) Divides household and family personal property and directs Respondent not to remove, damage, hide, or dispose of any property or funds that Petitioner owns or possesses.

☐ (d) Temporarily allocates parental rights and responsibilities for the care of the following minor children and suspends Respondent's visitation rights until a full hearing is held (include names and birth dates of the minor children): ______________________________
______________________________________________________________
______________________________________________________________
______________________________________________________________

☐ (e) Establishes temporary visitation rights with the following minor children and requires visitation to be supervised or occur under such conditions that the Court determines will insure the safety of Petitioner and the minor children (include names and birth dates of the minor children): ____________
______________________________________________________________
______________________________________________________________
______________________________________________________________
______________________________________________________________
______________________________________________________________

☐ (f) Requires Respondent to provide financial support for Petitioner and the other family or household members named in this Petition.

☐ (g) Requires Respondent to complete batterer counseling, substance abuse counseling, or other counseling as determined necessary by the Court.

☐ (h) Requires Respondent to refrain from entering, approaching, or contacting (including contact by telephone, fax, e-mail, and voice mail) the residence, school, business, and place of employment of Petitioner and the family or household members named in this Petition.

☐ (i) Requires Respondent to permit Petitioner or other family or household member to have exclusive use of the following motor vehicle: ______________________________

☐ (j) Includes the following additional provisions: ______________________________
______________________________________________________________

☐ 5. Petitioner further requests that the Court issue an *ex parte* (emergency) protection order under R.C. 3113.31(D) and (E) and this Petition.

6. Petitioner further requests that the Court issue no mutual protection orders or other orders against Petitioner unless all of the conditions of R.C. 3113.31(E)(4) are met.

7. Petitioner further requests that if Petitioner has a victim advocate, the Court permit the victim advocate to accompany Petitioner at all stages of these proceedings as required by R.C. 3113.31(M).

**FORM 10.01-D: PETITION FOR DOMESTIC VIOLENCE CIVIL PROTECTION ORDER**

**Amended: July 1, 2010**
**Discard all previous versions of this form**

[Page 3 of Form 10.01-D]

8. Petitioner further requests that the Court grant such other relief as the Court considers equitable and fair.
9. Petitioner lists here all present court cases and pertinent past court cases (including civil, criminal, divorce, juvenile, custody, visitation, and bankruptcy cases) that relate to the Respondent, you, your children, your family, or your household members:

| CASE NAME | CASE NUMBER | COURT/COUNTY | TYPE OF CASE | RESULT OF CASE |
|---|---|---|---|---|
| | | | | |
| | | | | |
| | | | | |
| | | | | |

**I hereby swear or affirm that the answers above are true, complete, and accurate to the best of my knowledge. I understand that falsification of this document may result in a contempt of court finding against me which could result in a jail sentence and fine, and that falsification of this document may also subject me to criminal penalties for perjury under R.C. 2921.11.**

Sworn to and subscribed before me on this ______ day of ______________ , ______________ .

______________________________
**SIGNATURE OF PETITIONER**

**DO NOT WRITE YOUR ADDRESS BELOW IF YOU ARE REQUESTING CONFIDENTIALITY. PLEASE PROVIDE AN ADDRESS WHERE YOU CAN RECEIVE NOTICES FROM THE COURT.**

______________________________
**NOTARY PUBLIC**

______________________________

______________________________
Signature of Attorney for Petitioner (if applicable)

______________________________
Name

______________________________
Address

______________________________

______________________________
Attorney Registration Number

______________________________
Phone Number

**FORM 10.01-D: PETITION FOR DOMESTIC VIOLENCE CIVIL PROTECTION ORDER**

**Amended: July 1, 2010**
**Discard all previous versions of this form**

# FORM 10.01-E: HOW TO COMPLETE THE INFORMATION FOR PARENTING PROCEEDING AFFIDAVIT

These instructions will help you prepare the Information for Parenting Proceeding Affidavit. The Affidavit must be filed if you are requesting a parenting (custody) order in a Petition for a Domestic Violence Civil Protection Order. **IF ANOTHER COURT IS ADDRESSING OR HAS ADDRESSED CUSTODY ISSUES INVOLVING THE CHILDREN, CUSTODY ISSUES WILL BE HANDLED IN THAT CASE, NOT THE DOMESTIC VIOLENCE CASE.**

**FILLING OUT THE FORM: Check each instruction below after you read and complete it**

☐ **Print or type only.** Attach an additional page to the Affidavit for your answers if you need more room.

☐ **At the top of the front page, fill in the names.** YOU are the "Petitioner." The person you want protection from is the "Respondent." Leave the Case No. and Judge lines blank for the Clerk of Court to complete.

☐ **First Paragraph.** Fill in your legal name in the blank line.

☐ **Paragraph 1:** Check this box if you wish your current address to remain confidential.

☐ **Paragraph 2:** On the blank line fill in the number of children that are subject to this court case. For each table at the top write in the child's name, place of birth, date of birth, sex, and address unless confidential. As you write on each line going across the table start with the length of time, the address unless confidential, the adult the child lived with at that time, and the relationship of that adult to the child. There are three tables. If you have more than three children that are subject to this court case, attach additional pages containing the requested information for each of those additional children.

☐ **Paragraph 3:** Mark the box showing whether or not you have participated as party, witness, or in any capacity concerning any civil or criminal case regarding custody or visitation of any of the children that are subject to this court case. If you have been involved in such a case fill in the details requested in lines a, b, c, and d.

☐ **Paragraph 4:** Mark the box showing whether or not you have any information concerning any case that could affect the current case including any case relating to custody, domestic violence and or protection orders, dependency, neglect, or abuse allegations or adoptions other than those listed in paragraph 3. If you do have such information, fill in the details requested in lines a, b, c, and d.

☐ **Paragraph 5:** List the criminal background and history of yourself and members of your household including any convictions or guilty pleas of any offense resulting in a child being an abused or neglected child, any offense that is a violation of R.C. 2919.25, any sexually oriented offense defined by R.C. 2950.01, and any offense involving a victim who was a family or household member at the time of the offense and caused physical harm to the victim during the commission of the offense.

☐ **Paragraph 6:** Check the first box if you do not know of any person not a party to this case who has physical custody or claims to have custody or visitation rights with respect to any child subject to this case. Check the second box if you do know anyone who is not a party to this case who has physical custody or claims to have custody or visitation rights with respect to any child subject to this case. If you check the second box you will fill in the required information for each person that you know who is not a party to this case who has physical custody or claims to have custody or visitation rights with respect to any child subject to this case.

**Paragraph 7:** You have an on-going duty to notify the Court of any custody, visitation, parenting time, divorce, dissolution of marriage, separation, neglect, abuse, dependency, guardianship, parentage, termination of parental rights, or domestic violence case concerning the children that are subject to this case.

**SIGNING THE FORM:** AFTER YOU HAVE FILLED OUT THE FORM, TAKE THE FORM TO THE CLERK OF COURT'S OFFICE OR TO A NOTARY PUBLIC TO HAVE YOUR SIGNATURE NOTARIZED. ***DO NOT SIGN THE FORM UNLESS YOU ARE IN FRONT OF A NOTARY PUBLIC.***



**Amended: July 1, 2010**
**Discard all previous versions of this form**

**FORM 10.01-F: INFORMATION FOR PARENTING PROCEEDING AFFIDAVIT**

**IN THE ______________________ COURT**
**______________ COUNTY, OHIO**

______________________
**Petitioner** : **Case No.** ______________________
:
: **Judge:** ______________________
**v.**
:
: **INFORMATION FOR PARENTING PROCEEDING AFFIDAVIT (R.C. 3127.23(A))**
______________________
**Respondent** : **(Filed with Petition for Domestic Violence Civil Protection Order)**

**NOTE:** By law, an affidavit **must** be filed and served with the first pleading filed by each party in every parenting (custody/visitation) proceeding in this Court, including a Petition for a Domestic Violence Civil Protection Order. Each party has a continuing duty while this case is pending to inform the Court of any parenting proceeding concerning the child(ren) in any other court in this or any other state. **If more space is needed, attach an additional page.**

I (full legal name) ______________________, being sworn according to law, certify these cases involve the custody of a child or children and the following statements are true:

1. ☐ I am requesting the Court to not disclose my current address or that of the child(ren). My address is confidential pursuant to R.C. 3127.23(D) and should be placed under seal in that the health, safety, or liberty of myself and/or the child(ren) would be jeopardized by the disclosure of the identifying information.

2. **(Number):** __________ **Minor child(ren) are subject to this case as follows:**

(Insert the information requested below. The residence information must be given for the last FIVE years.)

| **a. Child's name** | | **Place of birth** | **Date of birth** | **Sex** |
|---|---|---|---|---|
| Period of residence | ☐ Address Confidential | Person child lived with (name & address) | Relationship | |
| to present | ☐ Address Confidential | | | |
| to | ☐ Address Confidential | | | |
| to | ☐ Address Confidential | | | |
| to | ☐ Address Confidential | | | |

**FORM 10.01-F: INFORMATION FOR PARENTING PROCEEDING AFFIDAVIT**

**Amended: July 1, 2010**
**Discard all previous versions of this form**

**[Page 2 of Form 10.01-F]**

**Case No.______________________**

| **b. Child's name** | | **Place of birth** | **Date of birth** | **Sex** |
|---|---|---|---|---|
| Period of residence | ☐ Address Confidential | Person child lived with (name & address) | Relationship | |
| to present | ☐ Address Confidential | | | |
| to | ☐ Address Confidential | | | |
| to | ☐ Address Confidential | | | |
| to | ☐ Address Confidential | | | |

| **c. Child's name** | | **Place of birth** | **Date of birth** | **Sex** |
|---|---|---|---|---|
| Period of residence | ☐ Address Confidential | Person child lived with (name & address) | Relationship | |
| to present | ☐ Address Confidential | | | |
| to | ☐ Address Confidential | | | |
| to | ☐ Address Confidential | | | |
| to | ☐ Address Confidential | | | |

e. Additional children are listed on Attachment 2(d). (Provide requested information for additional children on an attachment labeled 2d.)

3. **Participation in custody case(s): (only one)**

☐ **I HAVE NOT** participated as a party, witness, or in any capacity in any other case, in this or any other state, concerning the custody of or visitation (parenting time) with any child subject to this case.

☐ **I HAVE** participated as a party, witness, or in any capacity in any other case, in this or any other state, concerning the custody of or visitation (parenting time) with any child subject to this case. Explain:

a. Name of each child ______________________
b. Type of case ______________________
c. Court and State ______________________
d. Date and court order or judgment (if any): ______________________

**FORM 10.01-F: INFORMATION FOR PARENTING PROCEEDING AFFIDAVIT**

**Amended: July 1, 2010**
**Discard all previous versions of this form**

[Page 3 of Form 10.01-F]

Case No.________________

4. **Information about custody case(s): (only one)**

☐ **I HAVE NO INFORMATION** of any cases that could affect the current case, any cases relating to custody, domestic violence or protection orders, dependency, neglect or abuse allegations or adoptions concerning any child subject to this case.

☐ **I HAVE THE FOLLOWING INFORMATION** concerning cases that could affect the current case, including any cases relating to custody, domestic violence or protection orders, dependency, neglect or abuse allegations or adoptions concerning any child subject to this case, other than listed in Paragraph 3. Explain:

a. Name of each child ________________
b. Type of case ________________
c. Court and state ________________
d. Date of court order or judgment (if any): ________________

5. List all of the criminal convictions including guilty pleas for you and the members of your household for the following offenses: any criminal offense involving acts that resulted in a child being abused or neglected; any offense that is a violation of R.C. 2919.25; any sexually oriented offense as defined in R.C. 2950.01; and any offense involving a victim who was a family or household member at the time of the offense and caused physical harm to the victim during the commission of the offense.

| NAME | CASE NUMBER | COURT/STATE/COUNTY | CHARGE |
|---|---|---|---|
| | | | |
| | | | |
| | | | |

6. **Persons not a party to this case: (only one)**

☐ **I DO NOT KNOW OF ANY PERSON** not a party to this case who has physical custody or claims to have custody or visitation rights with respect to any child subject to this case.

☐ **I KNOW THAT THE FOLLOWING NAMED PERSON(S)** not a party to this case has/have physical custody or claim(s) to have custody or visitation rights with respect to any child subject to this case:

a. Name and address of person ________________

☐ has physical custody ☐ claims custody rights ☐ claims visitation rights

Name of each child ________________

b. Name and address of person ________________

☐ has physical custody ☐ claims custody rights ☐ claims visitation rights

Name of each child ________________

c. Name and address of person ________________

☐ has physical custody ☐ claims custody rights ☐ claims visitation rights

Name of each child ________________

**FORM 10.01-F: INFORMATION FOR PARENTING PROCEEDING AFFIDAVIT**

**Amended: July 1, 2010**
**Discard all previous versions of this form**

**[Page 4 of Form 10.01-F]**

**Case No.______________________**

7. **I understand that I have a continuing duty to advise this Court of any custody, visitation, parenting time, divorce, dissolution of marriage, separation, neglect, abuse, dependency, guardianship, parentage, termination of parental rights, or protection from domestic violence case concerning the child(ren) in this state or any other state about which information is obtained during this case.**

***OATH OF AFFIANT***

**I hereby swear or affirm that the answers above are true, complete, and accurate to the best of my knowledge. I understand that falsification of this document may result in a contempt of court finding against me which could result in a jail sentence and fine, and that falsification of this document may also subject me to criminal penalties for perjury under R.C. 2921.11.**

________________________________________
**AFFIANT**

Sworn to and subscribed before me on this ________ day of _____________, _______________

________________________________________
**NOTARY PUBLIC**

**FORM 10.01-F: INFORMATION FOR PARENTING PROCEEDING AFFIDAVIT**

**Amended: July 1, 2010**
**Discard all previous versions of this form**

## FORM 10.01-G: WARNING CONCERNING THE ATTACHED DOMESTIC VIOLENCE PROTECTION ORDER

***NOTE***: *Rules 10.01 and 10.02 of the Rules of Superintendence for the Courts of Ohio require this Warning to be attached to the FRONT of all civil and criminal domestic violence protection orders issued by the courts of the State of Ohio. TO BE USED WITH FORMS 10.01-H, 10.01-I, 10.01-J, 10.01-M, and 10.02-A.*

### WARNING TO RESPONDENT / DEFENDANT

Violating the attached Protection Order is a crime, punishable by imprisonment or fine or both, and can cause your bond to be revoked or result in a contempt of court citation against you.

This Protection Order is enforceable in all 50 states, the District of Columbia, tribal lands, and U.S. Territories pursuant to the Violence Against Women Act, 18 U.S.C. 2265. Violating this Protection Order may subject you to federal charges and punishment.

As a result of this Order or Consent Agreement, it may be unlawful for you to possess or purchase a firearm, including a rifle, pistol, or revolver, or ammunition pursuant to federal law under 18 U.S.C. 922(g)(8). If you have any questions whether these laws make it illegal for you to possess or purchase a firearm, you should consult an attorney.

Only the Court can change this Order. The Petitioner/Alleged Victim cannot give you legal permission to change this Order. If you go near the Petitioner/Alleged Victim, even with the Petitioner's/Alleged Victim's consent, you may be arrested. If you and the Petitioner/Alleged Victim want to resume your relationship you must ask the Court to modify or terminate this Protection Order. Unless the Court modifies or terminates this Order, you can be arrested for violating this Protection Order. You act at your own risk if you disregard this WARNING.

### WARNING TO PETITIONER / ALLEGED VICTIM

You **cannot** change the terms of this Order by your words or actions. Only the Court can allow the Respondent/Defendant to contact you or return to your residence. This Order **cannot** be changed by either party without obtaining a written court order.

### NOTICE TO ALL LAW ENFORCEMENT AGENCIES AND OFFICERS

The attached Protection Order is enforceable in all jurisdictions. Violation of this Protection Order, regardless of whether it is a criminal or civil Protection Order, is a crime under R.C. 2919.27. Law enforcement officers with powers to arrest under R.C. 2935.03 for violations of the Ohio Revised Code must enforce the terms of this Protection Order as required by R.C. 2919.26, 2919.27 and 3113.31. If you have reasonable grounds to believe that Respondent/Defendant has violated this Protection Order, it is the preferred course of action in Ohio under R.C. 2935.03 to arrest and detain Respondent/Defendant until a warrant can be obtained. Federal and state law prohibit charging a fee for service of this Order.

**FORM 10.01-G: WARNING CONCERNING THE ATTACHED DOMESTIC VIOLENCE CIVIL PROTECTION ORDER**

**Amended: July 1, 2010**
**Discard all previous versions of this form**

**FORM 10.01-H: DOMESTIC VIOLENCE CIVIL PROTECTION ORDER (CPO) EX PARTE**

**IN THE COURT OF COMMON PLEAS**
______________ **COUNTY, OHIO**

# Order of Protection

Per R.C. 3113.31(F)(3), this Order is indexed at

______________________
**LAW ENFORCEMENT AGENCY WHERE INDEXED**

(      )      –
**PHONE NUMBER**

Case No. [ ]

Judge ______________

County [ ] State **OHIO**

**DOMESTIC VIOLENCE CIVIL PROTECTION ORDER (CPO) *EX PARTE* (R.C. 3113.31)**

**PETITIONER:**

First Middle Last

**v.**

**PERSON(S) PROTECTED BY THIS ORDER:**

Petitioner: ______________ DOB: ______

Petitioner's Family or Household Member(s) (May attach additional forms):

______________ DOB: ______
______________ DOB: ______
______________ DOB: ______
______________ DOB: ______

**RESPONDENT:**

First Middle Last

Relationship to Petitioner: ______________

Address where Respondent can be found:

______________
______________

RESPONDENT IDENTIFIERS

| SEX | RACE | HT | WT |
|---|---|---|---|
| | | | |

| EYES | HAIR | DATE OF BIRTH |
|---|---|---|
| | | |

| DRIVER'S LIC. NO. | EXP. DATE | STATE |
|---|---|---|
| | | |

Distinguishing features: ______________

☐ **WARNING TO LAW ENFORCEMENT: RESPONDENT HAS FIREARMS ACCESS – PROCEED WITH CAUTION**

(Violence Against Women Act, 18 U.S.C. 2265, Federal Full Faith & Credit Declaration: Registration of this Order is not required for enforcement.)

**THE COURT HEREBY FINDS:**
That it has jurisdiction over the parties and subject matter, and the Respondent will be provided with reasonable notice and opportunity to be heard within the time required by Ohio law. **Additional findings of this Order are set forth below.**

**THE COURT HEREBY ORDERS:**
That the above named Respondent be restrained from committing acts of abuse or threats of abuse against the Petitioner and other protected persons named in this Order, as set forth below. Additional terms of this Order are set forth below.

The terms of this Order shall be effective until _____ / _____ / _______ **(DATE CERTAIN).**

**WARNING TO RESPONDENT: See the warning page attached to the front of this Order.**

[Page 2 of Form 10.01-H]

Case No.________________________

This proceeding came on for an *ex parte* hearing on ______________________ (Respondent not being present), upon the filing of a Petition by Petitioner for a domestic violence civil protection order (CPO) against the Respondent, pursuant to R.C. 3113.31. In accordance with R.C. 3113.31(D)(1), the Court held an *ex parte* hearing on the same day that the Petition was filed.

The Court finds that the protected persons herein are in immediate and present danger of domestic violence and for good cause shown, the following temporary orders are necessary to protect the persons named in this Order from domestic violence.

**ALL OF THE PROVISIONS CHECKED BELOW APPLY TO THE RESPONDENT**

☐ 1. **RESPONDENT SHALL NOT ABUSE** the protected persons named in this Order by harming, attempting to harm, threatening, following, stalking, harassing, forcing sexual relations upon them, or by committing sexually oriented offenses against them. [NCIC 01 and 02]

☐ 2. **RESPONDENT SHALL IMMEDIATELY VACATE** the following residence: ______________________
________________________________________________

☐ 3. **EXCLUSIVE POSSESSION OF THE RESIDENCE** located at: ______________________
is granted to: ______________________. Respondent shall not interfere with this individual's right to occupy the residence including, but not limited to canceling utilities or insurance, interrupting telephone service, mail delivery, or the delivery of any other documents or items. [NCIC 03]

☐ 4. **RESPONDENT SHALL SURRENDER** all keys and garage door openers to the above residence at the earliest possible opportunity after service of this Order to the law enforcement agency that serves Respondent with this Order or as follows: ______________________
________________________________________________
________________________________________________

☐ 5. **RESPONDENT SHALL NOT ENTER** or interfere with the residence, school, business, place of employment, day care centers, or child care providers of the protected persons named in this Order, including the buildings, grounds, and parking lots at those locations. Respondent may not violate this Order **even with the permission of a protected person**. [NCIC 04]

☐ 6. **RESPONDENT SHALL STAY AWAY FROM PETITIONER** and all other protected persons named in this Order, and not be present within 500 feet or ______________ (distance) of any protected persons wherever those protected persons may be found, or any place the Respondent knows or should know the protected persons are likely to be, **even with Petitioner's permission**. If Respondent accidentally comes in contact with protected persons in any public or private place, Respondent must depart *immediately*. This Order includes encounters on public and private roads, highways, and thoroughfares. [NCIC 04]

☐ 7. **RESPONDENT SHALL NOT INITIATE OR HAVE ANY CONTACT** with the protected persons named in this Order or their residences, businesses, places of employment, schools, day care centers, or child care providers. Contact includes, but is not limited to, telephone, fax, e-mail, voice mail, delivery service, writings, or communications by any other means in person or through another person. Respondent may not violate this Order **even with the permission of a protected person**. [NCIC 05]

☐ 8. **RESPONDENT SHALL IMMEDIATELY SURRENDER POSSESSION OF ALL KEYS TO THE FOLLOWING MOTOR VEHICLE:** ______________ to the law enforcement agency that served Respondent with the Order or as follows ______________________
and Petitioner is granted exclusive use of this motor vehicle.

**FORM 10.01-H: DOMESTIC VIOLENCE CIVIL PROTECTION ORDER (CPO) EX PARTE**

**Amended: July 1, 2010**
**Discard all previous versions of this form**

**[Page 3 of Form 10.01-H]**

**Case No.**______________________

☐ **9. RESPONDENT SHALL NOT REMOVE, DAMAGE, HIDE, OR DISPOSE OF ANY PROPERTY OR PETS** owned or possessed by the protected persons named in this Order. Personal property shall be apportioned as follows:

____________________________________________

____________________________________________

____________________________________________

☐ **10. RESPONDENT SHALL NOT CAUSE OR ENCOURAGE ANY PERSON** to do any act prohibited by this Order.

☐ **11. RESPONDENT SHALL NOT POSSESS, USE, CARRY, OR OBTAIN ANY DEADLY WEAPON.** Respondent shall turn over all deadly weapons in Respondent's possession to the law enforcement agency that serves Respondent with this Order or as follows: ____________________________

____________________________________________

____________________________________________

Any law enforcement agency is authorized to take possession of deadly weapons pursuant to this paragraph and hold them in protective custody until further Court order [NCIC 07]

☐ **12. PARENTAL RIGHTS AND RESPONSIBILITIES ARE TEMPORARILY ALLOCATED AS FOLLOWS: [NCIC 09]**

____________________________________________

____________________________________________

This Order applies to the following child(ren): ____________________________

____________________________________________

☐ **13. VISITATION ORDERS DO NOT PERMIT RESPONDENT TO VIOLATE THE TERMS OF THIS ORDER.**

☐ (A) Respondent's visitation rights are suspended; or

☐ (B) As a limited exception to paragraphs 6 and 7, temporary visitation rights are established as follows: [NCIC 06]

____________________________________________

____________________________________________

____________________________________________

____________________________________________

____________________________________________

This Order applies to the following child(ren): ____________________________

____________________________________________

☐ **14. LAW ENFORCEMENT AGENCIES**, including but not limited to, ________________________
are ordered to assist Petitioner in gaining physical custody of the child(ren) if necessary.

☐ **15. RESPONDENT SHALL SUPPORT** the protected persons named in this Order as follows: __________

____________________________________________

____________________________________________

☐ **16. RESPONDENT MAY PICK UP CLOTHING** and personal items from the above residence only in the company of a uniformed law enforcement officer within seven days of the filing of this Order. Arrangements may be made by contacting: ____________________________________

☐ **17. RESPONDENT SHALL NOT USE OR POSSESS** alcohol or illegal drugs.

**FORM 10.01-H: DOMESTIC VIOLENCE CIVIL PROTECTION ORDER (CPO) EX PARTE**

**Amended: July 1, 2010**
**Discard all previous versions of this form**

[Page 4 of Form 10.01-H]

Case No.____________________

☐ **18. IT IS FURTHER ORDERED:** [NCIC 08] ________________________________________

______________________________________________________________________

______________________________________________________________________

______________________________________________________________________

______________________________________________________________________

**19. IT IS FURTHER ORDERED** that the Clerk of Court shall cause a copy of the Petition and this Order to be delivered to the Respondent as required by law. The Clerk of Court shall also provide certified copies of the Petition and this Order to Petitioner upon request. This Order is granted without bond. Under federal and state law, the Clerk shall not charge any fees for filing, issuing, registering, or serving this protection order.

**20. ALL OF THE TERMS OF THIS ORDER SHALL REMAIN IN FULL FORCE AND EFFECT UNTIL** ____________________, __________ unless earlier modified by or dismissed by order of this Court. Except for paragraphs 12, 13, 14, and 15 above, this Order survives a divorce, dissolution of marriage, or legal separation.

**IT IS SO ORDERED.**

| ________________________ | ________________________ |
|---|---|
| **MAGISTRATE** | **JUDGE** |

**<u>NOTICE TO RESPONDENT</u>: THE PERSONS PROTECTED BY THIS ORDER CANNOT GIVE YOU LEGAL PERMISSION TO CHANGE OR VIOLATE THIS ORDER. IF YOU VIOLATE ANY TERMS OF THIS ORDER EVEN WITH THE PROTECTED PERSON'S PERMISSION, YOU MAY BE ARRESTED. ONLY THE COURT CAN CHANGE THIS ORDER. IF THERE IS ANY REASON WHY THIS ORDER SHOULD BE CHANGED, YOU MUST ASK THE COURT TO CHANGE IT. <u>YOU ACT AT YOUR OWN RISK IF YOU DISREGARD THIS WARNING.</u>**

**A FULL HEARING** on this Order, and on all other issues raised by the Petition, shall be held

before Judge ____________________

or Magistrate ____________________

on the _____ day of __________, 20 ____

at _______ a.m./p.m. at the following location:

______________________________

______________________________

**<u>TO THE CLERK</u>**

**COPIES OF THIS ORDER SHALL BE DELIVERED TO:**

☐ Petitioner
☐ Respondent (by personal service)
☐ Police Department Where Petitioner Resides:
______________________________
☐ The ______________ County Sheriff's Office
☐ Police Department Where Petitioner Works:
______________________________
☐ Other: ____________________

**FORM 10.01-H: DOMESTIC VIOLENCE CIVIL PROTECTION ORDER (CPO) EX PARTE**

**Amended: July 1, 2010**
**Discard all previous versions of this form**

**FORM 10.01-I: DOMESTIC VIOLENCE CIVIL PROTECTION ORDER (CPO) FULL HEARING**

**IN THE COURT OF COMMON PLEAS**
________________ **COUNTY, OHIO**

# Order of Protection

Per R.C. 3113.31(F)(3), this Order is indexed at

____________________
**LAW ENFORCEMENT AGENCY WHERE INDEXED**

( ) -
**PHONE NUMBER**

Case No. __________

Judge __________

County __________ State **OHIO**

**DOMESTIC VIOLENCE CIVIL PROTECTION ORDER (CPO) FULL HEARING (R.C. 3113.31)**

☐ **WITH SUPPORT ORDER**

**PETITIONER:**

First Middle Last

v.

**RESPONDENT:**

First Middle Last

Relationship to Petitioner: __________

Address where Respondent can be found:

__________

__________

**PERSON(S) PROTECTED BY THIS ORDER:**

Petitioner: __________ DOB: ______

Petitioner's Family or Household Member(s) (May attach additional form):

__________ DOB: ______

__________ DOB: ______

__________ DOB: ______

__________ DOB: ______

RESPONDENT IDENTIFIERS

| SEX | RACE | HT | WT |
|---|---|---|---|
| | | | |
| EYES | HAIR | DATE OF BIRTH | |
| | | | |

| DRIVER'S LIC. NO. | EXP. DATE | STATE |
|---|---|---|
| | | |

Distinguishing features: __________

☐ **WARNING TO LAW ENFORCEMENT: RESPONDENT HAS FIREARMS ACCESS – PROCEED WITH CAUTION**

(Violence Against Women Act, 18 U.S.C. 2265, Federal Full Faith & Credit Declaration: Registration of this Order is not required for enforcement.)

**THE COURT HEREBY FINDS:**

That it has jurisdiction over the parties and subject matter, and the Respondent was provided with reasonable notice and opportunity to be heard within the time required by Ohio law. **Additional findings of this Order are set forth below.**

**THE COURT HEREBY ORDERS:**

That the above named Respondent be restrained from committing further acts of abuse or threats of abuse against the Petitioner and other protected persons named in this Order, as set forth below. Additional terms of this Order are set forth below.

The terms of this Order shall be effective until ____ / ____ / ____ **(DATE CERTAIN – FIVE YEARS MAXIMUM)**

**WARNING TO RESPONDENT: See the warning page attached to the front of this Order.**



**Amended: July 1, 2010**
**Discard all previous versions of this form**

[Page 2 of Form 10.01-I]

Case No.____________________

This proceeding came on for a hearing on ____________________ before the Court and the *Ex Parte* Order filed on ____________________. The following individuals were present: ____________________________________________________________.

The Court hereby makes the following findings of fact: ____________________________________________________________________________________________________________________

The Court further finds by a preponderance of the evidence: 1) that the Petitioner or Petitioner's family or household member(s) are in danger of or have been a victim of domestic violence or sexually oriented offenses as defined in R.C. 3113.31(A) committed by Respondent; and 2) the following orders are equitable, fair, and necessary to protect the persons named in this Order from domestic violence.

**ALL OF THE PROVISIONS CHECKED BELOW APPLY TO THE RESPONDENT**

☐ 1. **RESPONDENT SHALL NOT ABUSE** the protected persons named in this Order by harming, attempting to harm, threatening, following, stalking, harassing, forcing sexual relations upon them, or by committing sexually oriented offenses against them. [NCIC 01 and 02]

☐ 2. **RESPONDENT SHALL IMMEDIATELY VACATE** the following residence: ________________________________________

☐ 3. **EXCLUSIVE POSSESSION OF THE RESIDENCE** located at: ____________________ is granted to: ____________________. Respondent shall not interfere with this individual's right to occupy the residence including, but not limited to canceling utilities or insurance, interrupting telephone service, mail delivery, or the delivery of any other documents or items. [NCIC 03]

☐ 4. **RESPONDENT SHALL SURRENDER** all keys and garage door openers to the above residence at the earliest possible opportunity after service of this Order to the law enforcement agency that serves Respondent with this Order or as follows: ________________________________________

☐ 5. **RESPONDENT SHALL NOT ENTER** or interfere with the residence, school, business, place of employment, day care centers, or child care providers of the protected persons named in this Order, including the buildings, grounds, and parking lots at those locations. Respondent may not violate this Order **even with the permission of a protected person**. [NCIC 04]

☐ 6. **RESPONDENT SHALL STAY AWAY FROM PETITIONER** and all other protected persons named in this Order and not be present within 500 feet or ________________ (distance) of any protected persons wherever those protected persons may be found, or any place the Respondent knows or should know the protected persons are likely to be, **even with Petitioner's permission**. If Respondent accidentally comes in contact with protected persons in any public or private place, Respondent must depart *immediately*. This Order includes encounters on public and private roads, highways, and thoroughfares. [NCIC 04]

☐ 7. **RESPONDENT SHALL NOT INITIATE OR HAVE ANY CONTACT** with the protected persons named in this Order or their residences, businesses, places of employment, schools, day care centers, or child care providers. Contact includes, but is not limited to, telephone, fax, e-mail, voice mail, delivery service, writings, or communications by any other means in person or through another person. Respondent may not violate this Order **even with the permission of protected person**. [NCIC 05]



Amended: July 1, 2010
Discard all previous versions of this form

**[Page 3 of Form 10.01-I]**

**Case No.**____________________

☐ **8. RESPONDENT SHALL IMMEDIATELY SURRENDER POSSESSION OF ALL KEYS TO THE FOLLOWING MOTOR VEHICLE,** __________________, to the law enforcement agency that served Respondent with the Order or as follows __________________________________________
and Petitioner is granted exclusive use of this motor vehicle.

☐ **9. RESPONDENT SHALL NOT REMOVE, DAMAGE, HIDE, OR DISPOSE OF ANY PROPERTY OR PETS** owned or possessed by the protected persons named in this Order. Personal property shall be apportioned as follows:
__________________________________________________________________
__________________________________________________________________

☐ **10. RESPONDENT SHALL NOT CAUSE OR ENCOURAGE ANY PERSON** to do any act prohibited by this Order.

☐ **11. RESPONDENT SHALL NOT POSSESS, USE, CARRY, OR OBTAIN ANY DEADLY WEAPON.** Respondent shall turn over all deadly weapons in Respondent's possession to the law enforcement agency that serves Respondent with this Order or as follows: ________________________________________
__________________________________________________________________
__________________________________________________________________
Any law enforcement agency is authorized to take possession of deadly weapons pursuant to this paragraph and hold them in protective custody until further Court order. [NCIC 07]

☐ **12. PARENTAL RIGHTS AND RESPONSIBILITIES ARE TEMPORARILY ALLOCATED AS FOLLOWS:** [NCIC 09]
__________________________________________________________________
__________________________________________________________________
This Order applies to the following child(ren): ____________________________________
__________________________________________________________________

☐ **13. VISITATION ORDERS DO NOT PERMIT RESPONDENT TO VIOLATE THE TERMS OF THIS ORDER.**

☐ (A) Respondent's visitation rights are suspended; or

☐ (B) As a limited exception to paragraphs 6 and 7, temporary visitation rights are established as follows: [NCIC 06]
__________________________________________________________________
__________________________________________________________________
__________________________________________________________________
__________________________________________________________________
This Order applies to the following child(ren): ____________________________________
__________________________________________________________________

☐ **14. LAW ENFORCEMENT AGENCIES** including but not limited to _______________________________
are ordered to assist Petitioner in gaining physical custody of the child(ren) if necessary.

☐ **15. RESPONDENT SHALL SUPPORT** the protected persons named in this Order as follows: ____________
__________________________________________________________________
__________________________________________________________________

☐ **16. RESPONDENT MAY PICK UP CLOTHING** and personal items from the above residence only in the company of a uniformed law enforcement officer within seven days of the filing of this Order. Arrangements may be made by contacting: ____________________________________________________

☐ **17. RESPONDENT SHALL NOT USE OR POSSESS** alcohol or illegal drugs.

**FORM 10.01-I: DOMESTIC VIOLENCE CIVIL PROTECTION ORDER (CPO) FULL HEARING**

**Amended: July 1, 2010**
**Discard all previous versions of this form**

**[Page 4 of Form 10.01- I]**

**Case No.** ____________________

☐ **18. IT IS FURTHER ORDERED:** [NCIC 08] ____________________
____________________
____________________
____________________

☐ **19. RESPONDENT SHALL COMPLETE THE FOLLOWING COUNSELING PROGRAM:** ____________________
____________________

**Respondent shall contact this program within** ______ **days after receiving this Order and immediately arrange for an initial appointment.** The counseling program is requested to provide the Court a written notice when Respondent attends the initial appointment, if the Respondent fails to attend or is discharged, and when Respondent completes the program. Respondent is required to sign all necessary waivers to allow the Court to receive information from the counseling program.

☐ **Respondent is ordered to appear before Judge** ____________ **or Magistrate** ____________ **,** **on** ____________ **at** ____________ **a.m. / p.m., to review Respondent's compliance with this counseling order. Respondent is warned: If you fail to attend the counseling program you may be held in contempt of court. If you fail to appear at this hearing, the Court may issue a warrant for your arrest.**

**20. IT IS FURTHER ORDERED** that the Clerk of Court shall cause a copy of this Order to be delivered to the Respondent as required by law. The Clerk of Court shall also provide certified copies of this Order to Petitioner upon request. This Order is granted without bond. Under federal and state law, the Clerk shall not charge any fees for filing, issuing, registering, or serving this Protection Order.

**21. ALL OF THE TERMS OF THIS ORDER SHALL REMAIN IN FULL FORCE AND EFFECT FOR A PERIOD OF FIVE YEARS FROM ISSUANCE, OR UNTIL** ____________________ unless earlier modified or terminated by order of this Court. Except for paragraphs 12, 13, 14, and 15 above, this Order survives a divorce, dissolution of marriage, or legal separation. Until this Order is delivered to Respondent, the terms of the *ex parte* CPO remain in effect.

**IT IS SO ORDERED.** **APPROVED and ADOPTED by:**

____________________ ____________________
**MAGISTRATE** **JUDGE**

**<u>NOTICE TO RESPONDENT</u>: THE PERSONS PROTECTED BY THIS ORDER CANNOT GIVE YOU LEGAL PERMISSION TO CHANGE OR VIOLATE THIS ORDER. IF YOU VIOLATE ANY TERMS OF THIS ORDER, EVEN WITH THE PROTECTED PERSON'S PERMISSION, YOU MAY BE ARRESTED. ONLY THE COURT CAN CHANGE THIS ORDER. IF THERE IS ANY REASON WHY THIS ORDER SHOULD BE CHANGED, YOU MUST ASK THE COURT TO CHANGE IT. <u>YOU ACT AT YOUR OWN RISK IF YOU DISREGARD THIS WARNING.</u>**

***<u>NOTICE OF FINAL APPEALABLE ORDER</u>***

Copies of the foregoing Order, which is a final appealable order, were mailed by ordinary U.S. mail or hand-delivered to the parties indicated on the

______ day of ____________, 20 ____.

By: ____________________
CLERK OF COURT

**<u>TO THE CLERK:</u>**
**COPIES OF THIS ORDER SHALL BE DELIVERED TO**

☐ Petitioner ☐ Attorney for Petitioner
☐ Respondent ☐ Attorney for Respondent
☐ Counseling Program: ____________
☐ The ____________ County Sheriff's Office
☐ Police Department Where Petitioner Resides:
____________________
☐ Police Department Where Petitioner Works:
____________________
☐ CSEA
☐ Other: ____________________

**FORM 10.01-I: DOMESTIC VIOLENCE CIVIL PROTECTION ORDER (CPO) FULL HEARING**

**Amended: July 1, 2010**
**Discard all previous versions of this form**

**FORM 10.01-J: CONSENT AGREEMENT AND DOMESTIC VIOLENCE CIVIL PROTECTION ORDER**

**IN THE COURT OF COMMON PLEAS**

______________________ **COUNTY, OHIO**

# Order of Protection

Per R.C. 3113.31(F)(3), this Order is indexed at

______________________
**LAW ENFORCEMENT AGENCY WHERE INDEXED**

( ) -
**PHONE NUMBER**

Case No. ______

Judge ______

County ______ State **OHIO**

**CONSENT AGREEMENT AND DOMESTIC VIOLENCE CIVIL PROTECTION ORDER (R.C. 3113.31)**

☐ **WITH SUPPORT ORDER**

**PETITIONER:**

First Middle Last

v.

**RESPONDENT:**

First Middle Last

Relationship to Petitioner: ______

Address where Respondent can be found: ______

**PERSON(S) PROTECTED BY THIS ORDER:**

Petitioner: ______ DOB ______

Petitioner's Family or Household Member(s)(May attach additional forms):

______ DOB ______
______ DOB ______
______ DOB ______
______ DOB ______

RESPONDENT IDENTIFIERS

| SEX | RACE | HT | WT |
|---|---|---|---|
| | | | |

| EYES | HAIR | DATE OF BIRTH |
|---|---|---|
| | | |

| DRIVER'S LIC. NO. | EXP. DATE | STATE |
|---|---|---|
| | | |

Distinguishing Features: ______

☐ **WARNING TO LAW ENFORCEMENT: RESPONDENT HAS FIREARMS ACCESS – PROCEED WITH CAUTION**

(Violence Against Women Act, 18 U.S.C. 2265, Federal Full Faith & Credit Declaration: Registration of this Order is not required for enforcement.)

**THE COURT HEREBY FINDS:**
That it has jurisdiction over the parties and subject matter, and the Respondent was provided with reasonable notice and opportunity to be heard within the time required by Ohio law. **Additional findings of this Order are set forth below.**

**THE COURT HEREBY ORDERS:**
That the above named Respondent be restrained from committing acts of abuse or threats of abuse against the Petitioner and other protected persons named in this Order, as set forth below. Additional terms of this Order are set forth below.

The terms of this Order shall be effective until ____ / ____ / ____ **(DATE CERTAIN – FIVE YEARS MAXIMUM)**

**WARNING TO RESPONDENT: See the warning page attached to the front of this Order.**

**FORM 10.01-J: CONSENT AGREEMENT AND DOMESTIC VIOLENCE CIVIL PROTECTION ORDER**

**Amended: July 1, 2010**
**Discard all previous versions of this form**

**[Page 2 of Form 10.01-J]**

**Case No.**____________________

This proceeding came on for a hearing on ________________ before the Court and the *Ex Parte* Order filed on ______________. The following individuals were present: __________________________________________________________________________________

The parties agree to waive their notice and hearing rights and their rights under Civ. R. 53, including the right to request findings of fact and conclusions of law and to file objections to the Magistrate's Decision in this matter.

**ALL OF THE PROVISIONS CHECKED BELOW APPLY TO THE RESPONDENT.**

☐ **1. RESPONDENT SHALL NOT ABUSE** the protected persons named in this Order by harming, attempting to harm, threatening, following, stalking, harassing, forcing sexual relations upon them, or by committing sexually oriented offenses against them. [NCIC 01 and 02]

☐ **2. RESPONDENT SHALL IMMEDIATELY VACATE** the following residence: __________________________________________________________

☐ **3. EXCLUSIVE POSSESSION OF THE RESIDENCE** located at: __________________________ is granted to: __________________________. Respondent shall not interfere with this individual's right to occupy the residence including, but not limited to canceling utilities or insurance, interrupting telephone service, mail delivery, or the delivery of any other documents or items. [NCIC 03]

☐ **4. RESPONDENT SHALL SURRENDER** all keys and garage door openers to the above residence at the earliest possible opportunity after service of this Order to the law enforcement agency that serves Respondent with this Order or as follows: ____________________________________________________

☐ **5. RESPONDENT SHALL NOT ENTER** or interfere with the residence, school, business, place of employment, day care center, or child care providers of the protected persons named in this Order, including the buildings, grounds, and parking lots at those locations. Respondent may not violate this Order **even with the permission of a protected person**. [NCIC 04]

☐ **6. RESPONDENT SHALL STAY AWAY FROM PETITIONER** and all other protected persons named in this Order and not be present within 500 feet or ________ (distance) of any protected persons, wherever those protected persons may be found, or any place the Respondent knows or should know the protected persons are likely to be, **even with Petitioner's permission**. If Respondent accidentally comes in contact with protected persons in any public or private place, Respondent must depart *immediately*. This Order includes encounters on public and private roads, highways, and thoroughfares. [NCIC 04]

☐ **7. RESPONDENT SHALL NOT INITIATE OR HAVE ANY CONTACT** with the protected persons named in this Order or their residences, businesses, places of employment, schools, day care centers, or child care providers. Contact includes, but is not limited to, telephone, fax, e-mail, voice mail, delivery service, writings, or communications by any other means in person or through another person. Respondent may not violate this Order **even with the permission of a protected person**. [NCIC 05]

☐ **8. RESPONDENT SHALL IMMEDIATELY SURRENDER POSSESSION OF ALL KEYS TO THE FOLLOWING MOTOR VEHICLE,** __________________, to the law enforcement agency that served Respondent with the Order or as follows ____________________________________________________ and Petitioner is granted exclusive use of this motor vehicle.

☐ **9. RESPONDENT SHALL NOT REMOVE, DAMAGE, HIDE, OR DISPOSE OF ANY PROPERTY OR PETS** owned or possessed by the protected persons named in this Order. Personal property shall be apportioned as follows: __________________________________________________________

☐ **10. RESPONDENT SHALL NOT CAUSE OR ENCOURAGE ANY PERSON** to do any act prohibited by this Order.

**[Page 3 of Form 10.01-J]**

**Case No.**____________________

☐ **11. RESPONDENT SHALL NOT POSSESS, USE, CARRY, OR OBTAIN ANY DEADLY WEAPON.** Respondent shall turn over all deadly weapons in Respondent's possession to the law enforcement agency that serves Respondent with this Order or as follows: ____________________________________

____________________________________________________________

Any law enforcement agency is authorized to take possession of deadly weapons pursuant to this paragraph and hold them in protective custody until further Court order. [NCIC 07]

☐ **12. PARENTAL RIGHTS AND RESPONSIBILITIES ARE TEMPORARILY ALLOCATED AS FOLLOWS: [NCIC 09]**

____________________________________________________________

____________________________________________________________

This Order applies to the following child(ren): ________________________________

____________________________________________________________

☐ **13. VISITATION ORDERS DO NOT PERMIT RESPONDENT TO VIOLATE THE TERMS OF THIS ORDER.**

☐ (A) Respondent's visitation rights are suspended; or

☐ (B) As a limited exception to paragraphs 6 and 7, temporary visitation rights are established as follows: [NCIC 06]

____________________________________________________________

____________________________________________________________

This Order applies to the following child(ren): ________________________________

____________________________________________________________

☐ **14. LAW ENFORCEMENT AGENCIES,** including, but not limited to, ____________________________ are ordered to assist Petitioner in gaining physical custody of the child(ren) if necessary.

☐ **15. RESPONDENT SHALL SUPPORT** the protected persons named in this Order as follows: ________________

____________________________________________________________

☐ **16. RESPONDENT MAY PICK UP CLOTHING** and personal items from the above residence only in the company of a uniformed law enforcement officer within seven days of the filing of this Order. Arrangements may be made by contacting: __________________________________________________

____________________________________________________________

☐ **17. RESPONDENT SHALL NOT USE OR POSSESS** alcohol or illegal drugs.

☐ **18. IT IS FURTHER ORDERED:** [NCIC 08] ____________________________________________

____________________________________________________________

____________________________________________________________

☐ **19. RESPONDENT SHALL COMPLETE THE FOLLOWING COUNSELING PROGRAM:** ______________

____________________________________________________________

**Respondent shall contact this program within ______ days after receiving this Order and immediately arrange for an initial appointment.** The counseling program is requested to provide the Court a written notice when Respondent attends the initial appointment, if the Respondent fails to attend or is discharged, and when Respondent completes the program. Respondent is required to sign all necessary waivers to allow the Court to receive information from the counseling program.

☐ **Respondent is ordered to appear before Judge** ____________________________________________

**or Magistrate** ______________________________ **on** ______________ **at** _________ **a.m. / p.m, to review Respondent's compliance with the counseling order. Respondent is warned: If you fail to attend the counseling program you may be held in contempt of court. If you fail to appear at this hearing, the Court may issue a warrant for your arrest.**

[Page 4 of Form 10.01-J]

Case No.____________________

20. **IT IS FURTHER ORDERED** that the Clerk of Court shall cause a copy of the Petition and this Order to be delivered to the Respondent as required by law. The Clerk of Court shall also provide certified copies of the Petition and this Order to Petitioner upon request. This Order is granted without bond. Under federal and state law the Clerk shall not charge any fees for filing, issuing, registering, or serving this Protection Order.

21. **ALL OF THE TERMS OF THIS ORDER REMAIN IN FULL FORCE AND EFFECT FOR A PERIOD OF FIVE YEARS FROM ISSUANCE, OR UNTIL** ____________ unless earlier modified or terminated by order of this Court. Except for paragraphs 12, 13, 14, and 15 above, this Order survives a divorce, dissolution of marriage, or legal separation. Until this Order is delivered to Respondent, the terms of the *Ex Parte* CPO remain in effect.

**IT IS SO ORDERED.**

______________________________
**MAGISTRATE**

**APPROVED and ADOPTED by:**

______________________________
**JUDGE**

**<u>NOTICE TO RESPONDENT</u>: THE PERSONS PROTECTED BY THIS ORDER CANNOT GIVE YOU LEGAL PERMISSION TO CHANGE OR VIOLATE THIS ORDER. IF YOU VIOLATE ANY TERMS OF THIS ORDER, EVEN WITH THE PROTECTED PERSON'S PERMISSION, YOU MAY BE ARRESTED. ONLY THE COURT CAN CHANGE THIS ORDER. IF THERE IS ANY REASON WHY THIS ORDER SHOULD BE CHANGED, YOU MUST ASK THE COURT TO CHANGE IT. <u>YOU ACT AT YOUR OWN RISK IF YOU DISREGARD THIS WARNING.</u>**

***I have read this Consent Agreement and Civil Protection Order and agree to its terms.***

______________________________
**SIGNATURE OF PETITIONER**

______________________________

______________________________
Address of Petitioner

______________________________
Signature of Attorney for Petitioner

______________________________

______________________________
Address of Attorney for Petitioner

***I have read this Consent Agreement and Civil Protection Order and agree to its terms.***

______________________________
**SIGNATURE OF RESPONDENT**

______________________________

______________________________
Address of Respondent

______________________________
Signature of Attorney for Respondent

______________________________

______________________________
Address of Attorney for Respondent

***<u>NOTICE OF FINAL APPEALABLE ORDER</u>***

Copies of the foregoing Order, which is a final appealable order, were mailed by ordinary U.S. mail or hand-delivered to the parties indicated on the

______ day of ______________, 20 ______

By: ______________________________
CLERK OF COURT

**<u>TO THE CLERK</u>**
**COPIES OF THIS ORDER SHALL BE DELIVERED TO:**

☐ Petitioner ☐ Attorney for Petitioner
☐ Respondent ☐ Attorney for Respondent
☐ Counseling Program: ______________________
☐ The ______________________ County Sheriff's Office
☐ Police Department Where Petitioner Resides:
______________________________
☐ Police Department Where Petitioner Works:
______________________________
☐ CSEA
☐ Other: ______________________________

FORM 10.01-J: CONSENT AGREEMENT AND DOMESTIC VIOLENCE CIVIL PROTECTION ORDER

Amended: July 1, 2010
Discard all previous versions of this form

**FORM 10.01-K: MOTION TO MODIFY OR TERMINATE DOMESTIC VIOLENCE CIVIL PROTECTION ORDER OR CONSENT AGREEMENT**

**IN THE COURT OF COMMON PLEAS**
**____________________ COUNTY, OHIO**

| | | |
|---|---|---|
| ____________________ **Petitioner** | : | Case No. ________________ |
| ____________________ Address | : | Judge ________________ |
| ____________________ City, State, Zip Code | : | |
| v. | : | **MOTION TO MODIFY OR TERMINATE DOMESTIC VIOLENCE CIVIL PROTECTION ORDER OR CONSENT AGREEMENT** |
| ____________________ **Respondent** | : | **DO NOT WRITE YOUR ADDRESS ON THIS FORM IF YOU ARE REQUESTING CONFIDENTIALITY. PLEASE PROVIDE AN ADDRESS WHERE YOU CAN RECEIVE NOTICES FROM THE COURT.** |
| ____________________ Address | : | |
| ____________________ City, State, Zip Code | : | |

Petitioner/Respondent moves this Court to modify or terminate the Domestic Violence Civil Protection Order or Consent Agreement issued on ____________________. In the original proceeding, I was the ☐ Petitioner ☐ Respondent.

The terms of the civil protection order or consent agreement to be modified or terminated are: __________
________________________________________
________________________________________
________________________________________

The reasons for the modification or termination are: ____________________
________________________________________
________________________________________
________________________________________

If you are the Petitioner, you cannot be assessed court fees or other costs for filing a Motion to Modify or Terminate Domestic Violence Civil Protection Order or Consent Agreement.

Respectfully submitted,

______________________________
**SIGNATURE OF PETITIONER/RESPONDENT**

**[Page 2 of Form 10.01-K]**

**Case No.**____________________

Address where Petitioner/Respondent can be contacted:

________________________________________

________________________________________

________________________________________

**DO NOT WRITE your address on this form if you are requesting confidentiality. Please provide an address where you can receive notices from the Court.**

________________________________________
Signature of Attorney for Petitioner/Respondent (if applicable)

________________________________________
Name

________________________________________

________________________________________

________________________________________
Address

________________________________________
Attorney Registration Number

________________________________________
Telephone Number

________________________________________
Fax Number

________________________________________
Email

## REQUEST FOR SERVICE

Please serve a copy of the foregoing Motion upon ________________________________________ by certified mail or personal service at the following address: ________________________________________

______________________________________________________________________________

**FORM 10.01-L: JUDGMENT ENTRY ON MOTION TO MODIFY/TERMINATE DOMESTIC VIOLENCE CIVIL PROTECTION ORDER OR CONSENT AGREEMENT**

**IN THE COURT OF COMMON PLEAS**
**______________________ COUNTY, OHIO**

______________________________ :
**Petitioner** : Case No. ______________________

Date of Birth: __________________ :

: Judge ______________________

: **JUDGMENT ENTRY ON MOTION TO MODIFY/TERMINATE DOMESTIC VIOLENCE CIVIL PROTECTION ORDER OR CONSENT AGREEMENT**

**v.** :

______________________________ :
**Respondent** :

Date of Birth: __________________ :

Upon the motion of ☐ Petitioner ☐ Respondent, this proceeding came on for a hearing on ______________ before the Court to modify/terminate the Domestic Violence Civil Protection Order or Consent Agreement issued on ______________________.

☐ The Petitioner was present.

☐ The Petitioner was not present, but had reasonable notice and opportunity to be heard.

☐ The Respondent was present.

☐ The Respondent was not present, but had reasonable notice and opportunity to be heard.

The Court has considered the following factors:

1. Petitioner ☐ consents ☐ does not consent to the ☐ modification ☐ termination of the Domestic Violence Civil Protection Order or Consent Agreement.

2. Petitioner ☐ continues to fear ☐ does not fear the Respondent.

3. The current nature of the relationship between the Petitioner and Respondent is as follows: ______________ ______________________________________________

4. Relative proximity of the Petitioner's and Respondent's workplaces and residences.

5. Petitioner and Respondent ☐ have ☐ do not have minor children together.

6. Respondent has ☐ complied ☐ failed to comply with the terms and conditions of the original civil protection order or consent agreement.

7. Respondent ☐ has ☐ does not have a continuing involvement with illegal drugs or alcohol.

**[Page 2 of Form 10.01-L]**

**Case No.**____________________

8. Respondent ☐ has been ☐ has not been convicted of or pleaded guilty to an offense of violence since the protection order was issued or the consent agreement was approved.

9. Other protection orders, consent agreements, restraining orders, or no contact orders ☐ have been ☐ have not been issued against the Respondent pursuant to R.C. 3113.31 or 2919.26, any other provision of state law, or the law of any other state.

10. Respondent ☐ participated ☐ has not participated in a domestic violence treatment, intervention program, or other counseling addressing domestic violence.

11. Respondent ☐ completed ☐ has not completed the domestic violence treatment, intervention program, or other counseling addressing domestic violence.

12. ________ (time) has elapsed since the protection order was issued or the consent agreement was approved.

13. The age and health of the Respondent is as follows: ______________________________

________________________________________________________

14. The last incident of abuse, threat of harm, or commission of a sexually oriented offense occurred on:

________________________________________________________

________________________________________________________

15. Other information considered concerning the safety and protection of the Petitioner or other protected parties:

________________________________________________________

________________________________________________________

Based on all relevant factors, including those set in R.C. 3113.31(E)(8), the Court finds:

☐ The terms of the original civil protection order or consent agreement are no longer appropriate. The Order shall be **modified** as follows: ______________________________

________________________________________________________

________________________________________________________

________________________________________________________

☐ The civil protection order or consent agreement is no longer needed. The Order is **terminated**.

☐ The civil protection order or consent agreement remains in full force and effect. The motion is **denied**.

**A new Protection Notice to NCIC, Form 10-A, has been prepared to show the modification or termination of the prior order. In the event of modification, a Modified Domestic Violence Civil Protection Order (Form10.01-M) has been filed with this entry.**

The costs of this action are ☐ assessed against the Respondent ☐ waived.

**IT IS SO ORDERED.** **APPROVED and ADOPTED by:**

__________________________ __________________________

**MAGISTRATE** **JUDGE**

**FORM 10.01-L: JUDGMENT ENTRY ON MOTION TO MODIFY/TERMINATE DOMESTIC VIOLENCE CIVIL PROTECTION ORDER CONSENT AGREEMENT**

**Effective Date: July 1, 2010**

**FORM 10.01-M: MODIFIED DOMESTIC VIOLENCE CIVIL PROTECTION ORDER**

**IN THE COURT OF COMMON PLEAS**
______________________ **COUNTY, OHIO**

# Order of Protection

Per section R.C. 3113.31(E)(8), this Order is indexed at

______________________
**LAW ENFORCEMENT AGENCY WHERE INDEXED**

( ) -
**PHONE NUMBER**

Case No. [ ]

Judge ______________________

County [ ] State **OHIO**

**MODIFIED DOMESTIC VIOLENCE CIVIL PROTECTION ORDER (R.C. 3113.31)**

**PETITIONER:**

[ ]

First Middle Last

**v.**

**PERSON(S) PROTECTED BY THIS ORDER:**

Petitioner: ______________________ DOB: __________

Petitioner's Family or Household Member(s)(May attach additional forms):

______________________ DOB: __________
______________________ DOB: __________
______________________ DOB: __________
______________________ DOB: __________

**RESPONDENT:**

[ ]

First Middle Last

Relationship to Petitioner: ______________________

Address where Respondent can be found:

______________________

______________________

RESPONDENT IDENTIFIERS

| SEX | RACE | HT | WT |
|---|---|---|---|
| | | | |

| EYES | HAIR | DATE OF BIRTH |
|---|---|---|
| | | |

| DRIVER'S LIC. NO | EXP. DATE | STATE |
|---|---|---|
| | | |

Distinguishing Features: ______________________

______________________

☐ **WARNING TO LAW ENFORCEMENT: RESPONDENT HAS FIREARMS ACCESS – PROCEED WITH CAUTION**

(Violence Against Women Act, 18 U.S.C. 2265, Federal Full Faith & Credit Declaration: Registration of this Order is not required for enforcement.)

**THE COURT HEREBY FINDS:**

That it has jurisdiction over the parties and subject matter, and the Petitioner and Respondent were provided with reasonable notice and opportunity to be heard within the time required by Ohio law. **Additional findings of this Order are set forth in the companion judgment entry.**

**THE COURT HEREBY ORDERS:**

That the above named Respondent be restrained from committing acts of abuse or threats of abuse against the Petitioner and other protected persons named in this Order. Additional terms of this Order are set forth below.

The terms of this Order shall be effective until ___ / ___ / ___ **(SHALL BE SAME EXPIRATION DATE AS IN CIVIL PROTECTION ORDER OR CONSENT AGREEMENT)**

**WARNING TO RESPONDENT: See the warning page attached to the front of this Order.**

[Page 2 of Form 10.01-M]

Case No. ______________________

This proceeding came on for a hearing on ____________________. Based on the evidence presented and consideration of factors set forth in R.C. 3113.31(E)(8), the Court finds that the motion to modify the prior Domestic Violence Civil Protection Order issued on ____________________ is well taken.

**ALL OF THE PROVISIONS CHECKED BELOW APPLY TO THE RESPONDENT**

☐ 1. **RESPONDENT SHALL NOT ABUSE** the protected persons named in this Order by harming, attempting to harm, threatening, following, stalking, harassing, forcing sexual relations upon them, or by committing sexually oriented offenses against them. [NCIC 01 and 02]

☐ 2. **RESPONDENT SHALL IMMEDIATELY VACATE** the following residence: ______________________________
______________________________________________________________

☐ 3. **EXCLUSIVE POSSESSION OF THE RESIDENCE** located at: ______________________________
is granted to: ____________________. Respondent shall not interfere with this individual's right to occupy the residence including, but not limited to canceling utilities or insurance, interrupting telephone service, mail delivery, or the delivery of any other documents or items. [NCIC 03]

☐ 4. **RESPONDENT SHALL SURRENDER** all keys and garage door openers to the above residence at the earliest possible opportunity after service of this Order to the law enforcement agency that serves Respondent with this Order or as follows: ______________________________
______________________________________________________________

☐ 5. **RESPONDENT SHALL NOT ENTER** or interfere with the residence, school, business, place of employment, day care centers, or child care providers of the protected persons named in this Order, including the buildings, grounds, and parking lots at those locations. Respondent may not violate this Order **even with the permission of a protected person**. [NCIC 04]

☐ 6. **RESPONDENT SHALL STAY AWAY FROM PETITIONER** and all other protected persons named in this Order, and not be present within 500 feet or ______________ (distance) of any protected persons wherever those protected persons may be found, or any place the Respondent knows or should know the protected persons are likely to be, **even with Petitioner's permission**. If Respondent accidentally comes in contact with protected persons in any public or private place, Respondent must depart *immediately*. This Order includes encounters on public and private roads, highways, and thoroughfares. [NCIC 04]

☐ 7. **RESPONDENT SHALL NOT INITIATE OR HAVE ANY CONTACT** with the protected persons named in this Order or their residences, businesses, places of employment, schools, day care centers, or child care providers. Contact includes, but is not limited to, telephone, fax, e-mail, voice mail, delivery service, writings, or communications by any other means in person or through another person. Respondent may not violate this Order **even with the permission of protected person**. [NCIC 05]

☐ 8. **RESPONDENT SHALL IMMEDIATELY SURRENDER POSSESSION OF ALL KEYS TO THE FOLLOWING MOTOR VEHICLE** ____________________ to the law enforcement agency that served Respondent with the Order or as follows ______________________________
and Petitioner is granted exclusive use of this motor vehicle.

☐ 9. **RESPONDENT SHALL NOT REMOVE, DAMAGE, HIDE, OR DISPOSE OF ANY PROPERTY OR PETS** owned or possessed by the protected persons named in this Order. Personal property shall be apportioned as follows:
______________________________________________________________
______________________________________________________________

☐ 10. **RESPONDENT SHALL NOT CAUSE OR ENCOURAGE ANY PERSON** to do any act prohibited by this Order.

**FORM 10.01-M: MODIFIED DOMESTIC VIOLENCE CIVIL PROTECTION ORDER**

**Effective Date: July 1, 2010**

**[Page 3 of Form 10.01-M]**

**Case No.** ______________________

☐ **11. RESPONDENT SHALL NOT POSSESS, USE, CARRY, OR OBTAIN ANY DEADLY WEAPON.** Respondent shall turn over all deadly weapons in Respondent's possession to the law enforcement agency that serves Respondent with this Order or as follows: ______________________

Any law enforcement agency is authorized to take possession of deadly weapons pursuant to this paragraph and hold them in protective custody until further Court order. [NCIC 07]

☐ **12. PARENTAL RIGHTS AND RESPONSIBILITIES ARE TEMPORARILY ALLOCATED AS FOLLOWS:** [NCIC 09]

______________________

This Order applies to the following child(ren): ______________________

☐ **13. VISITATION ORDERS DO NOT PERMIT RESPONDENT TO VIOLATE THE TERMS OF THIS ORDER.**

☐ (A) Respondent's visitation rights are suspended; or

☐ (B) As a limited exception to paragraphs 6 and 7, Respondent's visitation rights are established as follows: [NCIC 06]

______________________

This Order applies to the following child(ren): ______________________

☐ **14. LAW ENFORCEMENT AGENCIES** including but not limited to ______________ are ordered to assist Petitioner in gaining physical custody of the child(ren) if necessary.

☐ **15. RESPONDENT SHALL SUPPORT** the protected persons named in this Order as follows: ______________________

☐ **16. RESPONDENT MAY PICK UP CLOTHING** and personal items from the above residence only in the company of a uniformed law enforcement officer within seven days of the filing of this Order. Arrangements may be made by contacting: ______________________

☐ **17. RESPONDENT SHALL NOT USE OR POSSESS** alcohol or illegal drugs.

☐ **18. IT IS FURTHER ORDERED:** [NCIC 08] ______________________

______________________

[Page 4 of Form 10.01-M]

Case No. ____________________

☐ **19. RESPONDENT SHALL COMPLETE THE FOLLOWING COUNSELING PROGRAM:** ____________________

____________________________________________________________

**Respondent shall contact this program within ________ days after receiving this Order and immediately arrange for an initial appointment.** The counseling program is requested to provide the Court a written notice when Respondent attends the initial appointment, if the Respondent fails to attend or is discharged, and when Respondent completes the program. Respondent is required to sign all necessary waivers to allow the Court to receive information from the counseling program.

☐ **Respondent is ordered to appear before Judge ____________ or Magistrate ____________ on ____________ at ________ a.m. / p.m., to review Respondent's compliance with this counseling Order. Respondent is warned: If you fail to attend the counseling program you may be held in contempt of court. If you fail to appear at this hearing, the Court may issue a warrant for your arrest.**

20. **IT IS FURTHER ORDERED** that the Clerk of Court shall cause a copy this Order to be delivered to the Respondent as required by law. The Clerk of Court shall also provide certified copies of this Order to Petitioner upon request. This Order is granted without bond. Under federal and state law, the Clerk shall not charge any fees for filing, issuing, registering, or serving this Protection Order to the Petitioner.

21. **ALL OF THE TERMS OF THIS ORDER SHALL REMAIN IN FULL FORCE AND EFFECT FOR A PERIOD OF NOT TO EXCEED THE DATE SET IN THE PRIOR ORDER OR UNTIL ______ / ______ / ______** unless earlier modified or terminated by order of this Court. Except for paragraphs 12, 13, 14, and 15 above, this Order survives a divorce, dissolution of marriage, or legal separation. Until this Order is delivered to Respondent, the terms of the prior Domestic Violence Civil Protection Order remain in effect.

**IT IS SO ORDERED.** **APPROVED and ADOPTED by:**

______________________________ ______________________________

**MAGISTRATE** **JUDGE**

**NOTICE TO RESPONDENT: THE PERSONS PROTECTED BY THIS ORDER CANNOT GIVE YOU LEGAL PERMISSION TO CHANGE OR VIOLATE THIS ORDER. IF YOU VIOLATE ANY TERMS OF THIS ORDER, EVEN WITH THE PROTECTED PERSON'S PERMISSION, YOU MAY BE ARRESTED. ONLY THE COURT CAN CHANGE THIS ORDER. IF THERE IS ANY REASON WHY THIS ORDER SHOULD BE CHANGED, YOU MUST ASK THE COURT TO CHANGE IT. YOU ACT AT YOUR OWN RISK IF YOU DISREGARD THIS WARNING.**

***NOTICE OF FINAL APPEALABLE ORDER***

Copies of the foregoing Order, which is a final appealable order, were mailed by ordinary U.S. mail or hand-delivered to the parties indicated on the

________ day of ____________ , 20 ______ .

By: ______________________________
CLERK OF COURT

**TO THE CLERK:**
**COPIES OF THIS ORDER SHALL BE DELIVERED TO**

☐ Petitioner ☐ Attorney for Petitioner
☐ Respondent ☐ Attorney for Respondent
☐ Counseling Program: ____________________
☐ The ____________ County Sheriff's Office
☐ Police Department Where Petitioner Resides:
____________________
☐ Police Department Where Petitioner Works:
____________________
☐ CSEA
☐ Other: ____________________

FORM 10.01-M: MODIFIED DOMESTIC VIOLENCE CIVIL PROTECTION ORDER

Effective Date: July 1, 2010

# FORM 10.01-N: HOW TO COMPLETE A MOTION FOR CONTEMPT FOR VIOLATING A DOMESTIC VIOLENCE CIVIL PROTECTION ORDER

## ENFORCING YOUR CIVIL PROTECTION ORDER

Violating a Domestic Violence Civil Protection Order ("CPO") is a crime. If the Order is violated, call the police or prosecutor. You may also bring a contempt action in the Court that issued your CPO if the other party is not obeying the Order. You may hire an attorney to assist you. You must file a contempt motion with the Clerk of Court to begin a contempt action.

## SOME HINTS BEFORE YOU BEGIN

- All forms must be typed or printed.
- When you write your name on the Motion for Contempt of a Domestic Violence Civil Protection Order, use the same name that is on your CPO.
- Fill out the Motion as completely and accurately as possible.

## FORM YOU WILL NEED

You can get the Motion from the Clerk of Court. Complete the Motion as explained below:

☐ Fill in the name of the Court, the case number and the judge's last name.

☐ **If you obtained the CPO, you are the Petitioner.** Fill in your name and address. If you want your address to be confidential, do not write your address anywhere on the Motion. However, you must include someone's mailing address to allow the Court to send you legal notices about your case.

☐ **If the Court issued the CPO against you, you are the Respondent.** Fill in your name and address.

☐ Fill in the other party's name and address.

☐ Complete the first paragraph.

☐ In the numbered paragraphs, check every box that applies. There is space at the end of the Motion for any facts or explanations that you want to tell the Court. Attach additional pages, if needed.

☐ **Signing the Motion:** Try to fill out the Motion before you go to the courthouse. AFTER YOU HAVE FILLED OUT THE MOTION, TAKE IT TO A NOTARY PUBLIC TO HAVE YOUR SIGNATURE NOTARIZED. ***DO NOT SIGN THE MOTION UNLESS YOU ARE IN FRONT OF A NOTARY PUBLIC.*** **An employee of the Clerk of Court may be available to notarize your Motion.**

☐ Complete the Instructions for Service at the end of the Motion. This tells the Clerk of Court how you want the Motion delivered.

## FILING THE MOTION FOR CONTEMPT OF A DOMESTIC VIOLENCE CPO

- Present your completed Motion to the filing window/counter of the Clerk of Court's office for filing.
- A Clerk of Court's office employee helps you file the Motion.
- The Court shall not charge a fee for filing a contempt motion to you if the CPO was issued for your protection.
- Ask a Clerk of Court's office employee or your local domestic violence assistance provider about your local court procedures.

[Page 2 of Form 10.01-N]

## VICTIM ADVOCATE

State law permits you to have a victim advocate with you at all times in Court during protection order proceedings. Victim advocate means a person who provides support and assistance for a victim of an offense during Court proceedings. Contact your local victim assistance program, local domestic violence program, or the Ohio Domestic Violence Network, 800-934-9840, for advocate information.

## ATTENDING THE CONTEMPT HEARING

At the hearing, you should tell the judge or magistrate what the other party did to fail to obey the CPO. If you have any physical evidence (photographs, documents, broken property, etc), bring it to this hearing. If you have any witnesses to the violations, bring them to this hearing. If you want the Court to order any witness to appear at the hearing, you can ask the Clerk of Court to issue a subpoena. This needs to be done as far in advance of the hearing as possible.

The Court will give each party the opportunity to present evidence and witnesses.

After all the evidence is presented at the contempt hearing, the Court may find that the Respondent or Petitioner has failed to comply with the CPO. If so, the Court may order the offending party to do or stop certain acts to comply with the terms of the CPO. The Court can also order the offending party to serve time in jail, pay a fine, or both.

**FORM 10.01-O: MOTION FOR CONTEMPT OF A DOMESTIC VIOLENCE CIVIL PROTECTION ORDER**

**IN THE COURT OF COMMON PLEAS**
**____________________ COUNTY, OHIO**

| | | |
|---|---|---|
| ____________________ Petitioner | : | Case No. ________________ |
| ____________________ Address | : | Judge ________________ |
| ____________________ City, State, Zip Code | : | **MOTION FOR CONTEMPT OF A DOMESTIC VIOLENCE CIVIL PROTECTION ORDER** |
| v. | : | **Notice: Throughout this form, check every ☐ that applies** |
| ____________________ Respondent | : | **DO NOT WRITE YOUR ADDRESS ON THIS FORM IF YOU ARE REQUESTING CONFIDENTIALITY. PLEASE PROVIDE AN ADDRESS WHERE YOU CAN RECEIVE NOTICES FROM THE COURT.** |
| ____________________ Address | : | |
| ____________________ City, State, Zip Code | : | |

☐ Petitioner ☐ Respondent moves this Court to find ____________________ in contempt of this Court's Civil Protection Order dated ________________ for the reasons below.

For any item that needs additional explanation, you may use paragraph 18 and/or attach additional pages as needed.

1. ☐ Respondent violated the Civil Protection Order by engaging in one or more of the following acts against me and/or another protected person:

   ☐ Harmed or attempted to harm
   ☐ Threatened
   ☐ Followed
   ☐ Stalked
   ☐ Harassed
   ☐ Forced sexual relations upon
   ☐ Committed a sexually oriented offense
   ☐ Other ____________________________

2. ☐ Respondent failed to vacate the residence at ____________________
________________________________________

3. ☐ Respondent interfered with the exclusive possession of the residence located at ________________
________________________________________

   Furthermore, Respondent interfered with my right to occupy the residence by
   ☐ Canceling utilities
   ☐ Canceling insurance
   ☐ Interrupted telephone service
   ☐ Interrupted mail delivery
   ☐ Interrupted delivery of any other documents or items

[Page 2 of Form 10.01-O]

Case No.____________________

4. ☐ Respondent failed to surrender keys and/or garage door openers to the residence for which exclusive use was ordered in the Civil Protection Order.

5. ☐ Respondent entered or interfered with the residence, school, business, place or employment, day care center, or child care provider of the protected persons.

6. ☐ Respondent violated the stay away provision of the Civil Protection Order.

7. ☐ Respondent violated the no contact provision of the Civil Protection Order.

8. ☐ Respondent failed to surrender the keys to the motor vehicle for which exclusive use was granted to the Petitioner in the Civil Protection Order.

9. ☐ Respondent removed, damaged, hid or disposed of personal property or pets in violation of the Civil Protection Order.

10. ☐ Respondent caused or encouraged another person to do acts prohibited by the Civil Protection Order.

11. ☐ Respondent violated the Civil Protection Order by possessing, using, carrying, obtaining or failing to turn over a deadly weapon.

12. ☐ ☐ Petitioner ☐ Respondent violated the temporary allocation of parental rights and responsibilities (custody).

13. ☐ ☐ Petitioner ☐ Respondent violated the visitation order.

14. ☐ ☐ Petitioner ☐ Respondent violated the support provision of the Civil Protection Order.

15. ☐ Respondent used or possessed alcohol and/or illegal drugs in violation of the Civil Protection Order.

16. ☐ ☐ Petitioner ☐ Respondent failed to attend the ordered counseling program.

17. ☐ List other violations of the Civil Protection Order here: ____________________________________

______________________________________________________________________

18. ☐ Additional explanation here: ________________________________________________

______________________________________________________________________

**I hereby swear or affirm that the statements above are true, complete, and accurate to the best of my knowledge. I understand that falsification of this document may result in a contempt of court finding against me which could result in a jail sentence and fine, and that falsification of this document may also subject me to criminal penalties for perjury under R.C. 2921.11.**

______________________________________

**SIGNATURE OF PETITIONER/RESPONDENT**

**FORM 10.01-O: MOTION FOR CONTEMPT OF A DOMESTIC VIOLENCE CIVIL PROTECTION ORDER**

**Effective Date: July 1, 2010**

**[Page 3 of Form 10.01-O]**

**Case No.**________________

**DO NOT WRITE YOUR ADDRESS BELOW IF YOU ARE REQUESTING CONFIDENTIALITY. PLEASE PROVIDE AN ADDRESS WHERE YOU CAN RECEIVE NOTICES FROM THE COURT.**

______________________________
Address

______________________________

______________________________

______________________________
Signature of Attorney (if applicable)

______________________________
Name

______________________________
Address

______________________________

______________________________
Attorney Registration Number

______________________________
Phone Number

Sworn to and subscribed before me on this ________ day of ____________, _________.

______________________________
**NOTARY PUBLIC**

**INSTRUCTIONS FOR SERVICE**

Please serve a copy of the foregoing Motion upon __________________________________________
by ☐ personal service or ☐ certified mail, return receipt requested at the following address: ________________
______________________________________________________________________________
______________________________________________________________________________

## RULE 10.02. Standard Domestic Violence Criminal Temporary Protection Order Forms.

(A) A court that has jurisdiction to issue a temporary protection order pursuant to section 2919.26 of the Revised Code shall distribute upon request a forms and instructions packet for use in domestic violence temporary protection order proceedings. The packet shall include, at a minimum, forms and instructions that are substantially similar to Forms 10.01-A, 10.01-B, 10.01-G, 10.02-A, and the motion for temporary protection order form set forth in section 2919.26 of the Revised Code.

(B) In every case in which the court issues a temporary protection order pursuant to section 2919.26 of the Revised Code, it shall use a form that is substantially similar to Form 10.02-A.

(C) Every temporary protection order that the court issues pursuant to section 2919.26 of the Revised Code shall include a cover sheet that is substantially similar to Form 10.01-G.

**History:** Effective 1-1-98; amended, eff 6-1-02; 5-1-07; 7-1-10.

### COMMENTARY (JANUARY 1, 1998)

During its eighteen months of study, the Supreme Court's Domestic Violence Task Force determined that due to the variety of protection order forms used by Ohio courts, it can be difficult for law enforcement officers to recognize valid protection orders and understand the pertinent provisions of such orders. The Task Force also discovered that misconceptions exist in regard to the penalties for violating protection orders. Upon recommendation of the Task Force, the Court developed this rule and Forms 10.02-A and 10.01-G to address these concerns.

**FORM 10.02-A: DOMESTIC VIOLENCE TEMPORARY PROTECTION ORDER (DVTPO)**

**IN THE ______________________________ COURT**

**______________________________ COUNTY, OHIO**

# Order of Protection

Per R.C. 2919.26(G)(3), this Order is indexed at

______________________________

**LAW ENFORCEMENT AGENCY WHERE INDEXED**

( ) -

**PHONE NUMBER**

**STATE OF OHIO/CITY OF** ______________________

**v.**

______________________________

**DEFENDANT**

Case No. [ ]

Judge ______________________

County [ ] State **OHIO**

**DOMESTIC VIOLENCE TEMPORARY PROTECTION ORDER (DVTPO) (R.C. 2919.26)**

☐ New Order ☐ Modification of Previous Order

**ALLEGED VICTIM:**

First Middle Last

**PERSON(S) PROTECTED BY THIS ORDER:**

Alleged Victim ______________________ DOB: ________

Alleged Victim's Family or Household Member(s):

______________________ DOB: ________

______________________ DOB: ________

______________________ DOB: ________

______________________ DOB: ________

**DEFENDANT:**

First Middle Last

Address where Defendant can be found:

______________________________

______________________________

DEFENDANT IDENTIFIERS

| SEX | RACE | HT | WT |
|---|---|---|---|
| | | | |
| EYES | HAIR | DATE OF BIRTH | |
| | | | |

| DRIVER'S LIC. NO. | EXP. DATE | STATE |
|---|---|---|
| | | |

Distinguishing Features: ______________________

☐ **WARNING TO LAW ENFORCEMENT: RESPONDENT HAS FIREARMS ACCESS – PROCEED WITH CAUTION**

☐ ***Ex Parte* DVTPO Granted:** ______________ **(Date)**

☐ **DVTPO Granted:** ______________ **(Date)**

(Violence Against Women Act, 18 U.S.C. 2265, Federal Full Faith & Credit Declaration: Registration of this Order is not required for enforcement.)

**THE COURT HEREBY FINDS:**

That it has jurisdiction over the parties and subject matter, and the Defendant has been or will be provided with reasonable notice and opportunity to be heard within the time required by Ohio law. **Additional findings of this Order are set forth below.**

**THE COURT HEREBY ORDERS:**

That the above named Defendant be restrained from committing acts of abuse or threats of abuse against the Alleged Victim and other protected persons named in this Order, as set forth below. Additional terms of this Order are set forth below.

**WARNING TO DEFENDANT: See the warning page attached to the front of this Order.**

**FORM 10.02-A: DOMESTIC VIOLENCE TEMPORARY PROTECTION ORDER (DVTPO)**

**Amended: July 1, 2010**
**Discard all previous versions of this form**

[Page 2 of Form 10.02-A]

Case No.____________________

Upon a hearing held on ____________________ (*Ex Parte DVTPO*) OR ____________________ (DVTPO) the Court finds that the Motion for a Domestic Violence Temporary Protection Order is well taken. The Court finds that the safety and protection of protected persons named in this Order may be impaired by the continued presence of Defendant. Therefore, the following orders, which are designed to ensure the safety and protection of protected persons named in this Order, are issued to Defendant as pretrial conditions in addition to any bail set under Crim. R. 46.

**ALL OF THE PROVISIONS CHECKED BELOW APPLY TO THE DEFENDANT**

☐ 1. **DEFENDANT SHALL NOT ABUSE** protected persons named in this Order by harming, attempting to harm, threatening, following, stalking, harassing, forcing sexual relations upon them, or by committing sexually oriented offenses against them. [NCIC 01 and 02]

☐ 2. **DEFENDANT SHALL NOT ENTER** the residence, school, business, place of employment, day care centers, or child care providers of the protected persons named in this Order, including the buildings, grounds, and parking lots at those locations. Defendant may not violate this Order **even with the permission of a protected person**. [NCIC 04]

☐ 3. **DEFENDANT SHALL NOT INTERFERE** with protected persons' right to occupy any residence by canceling utilities or insurance and interrupting telephone service, mail delivery, or the delivery of any other documents or items. [NCIC 03]

☐ 4. **DEFENDANT SHALL SURRENDER** all keys and garage door openers to the following residence: ____________________

____________________ at the earliest possible opportunity after service of this Order to the law enforcement agency that serves Defendant with this Order or as follows: ____________________

____________________

☐ 5. **DEFENDANT SHALL STAY AWAY FROM PROTECTED PERSONS NAMED IN THIS ORDER**, and shall not be present within 500 feet or ____________________ (distance) of any protected persons wherever those protected persons may be found, or any place the Defendant knows or should know the protected persons are likely to be, **even with the protected persons' permission**. If Defendant accidentally comes in contact with protected persons in any public or private place, Defendant must depart *immediately*. This Order includes encounters on public and private roads, highways, and thoroughfares. [NCIC 04]

☐ 6. **DEFENDANT SHALL NOT INITIATE OR HAVE ANY CONTACT** with the protected persons named in this Order at their residences, businesses, places of employment, schools, day care centers, or child care providers. Contact includes, but is not limited to, telephone, fax, e-mail, voice mail, delivery service, writings, or communications by any other means in person or through another person. Defendant may not violate this Order **even with the permission of a protected person**. [NCIC 05]

☐ 7. **DEFENDANT SHALL NOT REMOVE, DAMAGE, HIDE, OR DISPOSE OF ANY PROPERTY OR PETS** owned or possessed by the protected persons named in this Order.

☐ 8. **DEFENDANT SHALL NOT CAUSE OR ENCOURAGE ANY OTHER PERSON** to do any act prohibited by this Order.

☐ 9. **DEFENDANT SHALL NOT POSSESS, USE, CARRY, OR OBTAIN ANY DEADLY WEAPON.** Defendant shall turn over all deadly weapons in Defendant's possession to the law enforcement agency that serves Defendant with this Order as follows: ____________________

____________________

Any law enforcement agency is authorized to take possession of deadly weapons pursuant to this paragraph and hold them in protective custody until further Court order. [NCIC 07]

☐ 10. **DEFENDANT MAY PICK UP CLOTHING** and personal items from the following residence: ____________________

____________________ only in the company of a uniformed law enforcement officer within seven days of the filing of this Order or the date of Defendant's release on bond in connection with this charge, whichever is later. Arrangements may be made by contacting: ____________________

____________________

**FORM 10.02-A: DOMESTIC VIOLENCE TEMPORARY PROTECTION ORDER (DVTPO)**

**Amended: July 1, 2010**
**Discard all previous versions of this form**

[Page 3 of Form 10.02-A]

Case No.____________________

☐ **11. DEFENDANT SHALL NOT USE OR POSSESS** alcohol or illegal drugs.

☐ **12. IT IS FURTHER ORDERED:** [NCIC 08] ________________________________________

________________________________________________________________________

________________________________________________________________________

☐ **13. DEFENDANT IS ADVISED THAT VISITATION ORDERS DO NOT PERMIT DEFENDANT TO VIOLATE ANY OF THE TERMS OF THIS ORDER.**

**14. IT IS FURTHER ORDERED** that a copy of this Order shall be delivered to Defendant on the same day that the Order is entered.

**15. THIS ORDER REMAINS IN EFFECT:** (1) until modified by this Court; or (2) until the criminal proceeding arising out of the complaint upon which these orders were issued is disposed by this Court or by the court of common pleas to which the defendant is bound over for prosecution; or (3) until a Court issues a Domestic Violence Civil Protection Order ("CPO") arising out of the same activities as those that were the basis of the complaint filed in this action.

**IT IS SO ORDERED.**

| | |
|---|---|
| ______________________________ | ______________________________ |
| **MAGISTRATE – DATE OF *EX PARTE* DVTPO** | **JUDGE – DATE OF *EX PARTE* DVTPO** |
| ______________________________ | ______________________________ |
| **MAGISTRATE – DATE OF DVTPO** | **JUDGE– DATE OF DVTPO** |

**<u>NOTICE TO DEFENDANT</u>: THE PERSONS PROTECTED BY THIS ORDER CANNOT GIVE YOU LEGAL PERMISSION TO CHANGE OR VIOLATE THIS ORDER. IF YOU VIOLATE ANY TERMS OF THIS ORDER EVEN WITH THE PROTECTED PERSON'S PERMISSION, YOU MAY BE ARRESTED. ONLY THE COURT CAN CHANGE THIS ORDER. IF THERE IS ANY REASON WHY THIS ORDER SHOULD BE CHANGED, YOU MUST ASK THE COURT TO CHANGE IT. <u>YOU ACT AT YOUR OWN RISK IF YOU DISREGARD THIS WARNING.</u>**

**A HEARING** on this Order shall be held before

Judge ________________________ or

Magistrate ________________________

on ______________ , at ________ a.m./p.m.,

(the next court day) at the following location:

____________________________________

____________________________________

**<u>TO THE CLERK:</u>**
**COPIES OF THIS ORDER SHALL BE DELIVERED TO:**

☐ Prosecutor
☐ Alleged Victim
☐ Defendant (by personal service)
☐ Attorney for Defendant
☐ Police Department Where Alleged Victim Resides:
________________________________________
☐ Police Department Where Alleged Victim Works:
________________________________________
☐ The ____________________ County Sheriff's Office
☐ Other ________________________

**Service acknowledged:** ____________________________________ ________________________
**Defendant Signature** **Date**

**<u>WAIVER OF HEARING</u>**

**I HAVE BEEN ADVISED OF MY RIGHT TO HAVE A HEARING ON THE MOTION FOR A DOMESTIC VIOLENCE TEMPORARY PROTECTION ORDER AND HEREBY KNOWINGLY AND VOLUNTARILY WAIVE THE HEARING ON THE MOTION AND AGREE TO BE BOUND BY THE TERMS OF THIS ORDER.**

**DEFENDANT:** ________________________________________ **DATE:** ________________________

**FORM 10.02-A: DOMESTIC VIOLENCE TEMPORARY PROTECTION ORDER (DVTPO)**

**Amended: July 1, 2010**
**Discard all previous versions of this form**

## RULE 10.03. Standard Criminal Protection Order Forms and Standard Civil Stalking Protection Order or Civil Sexually Oriented Offense Protection Order Forms.

(A) A court that has jurisdiction to issue a criminal protection order pursuant to section 2903.213 of the Revised Code shall distribute, upon request, a form packet for use in criminal protection order proceedings. The packet shall include, at a minimum, a form that is substantially similar to "Form10.03-A."

(B) A court that has jurisdiction to issue a civil stalking protection order or civil sexually oriented offense protection order pursuant to section 2903.214 of the Revised Code shall distribute, upon request, a forms and instructions packet for use in civil stalking protection order or civil sexually oriented offense protection order proceedings. The packet shall include, at a minimum, forms and instructions that are substantially similar to "Forms 10.03-D, 10.03-E, and 10.03-G."

(C) In every case in which a court issues a criminal protection order pursuant to section 2903.213 of the Revised Code, it shall use the applicable form that is substantially similar to "Form 10.03-B" and a cover sheet that is substantially similar to "Form 10.03-H."

(D) In every case in which a court issues a civil stalking protection order or civil sexually oriented offense protection order pursuant to section 2903.214 of the Revised Code, it shall use the applicable form that is substantially similar to "Form 10.03-E or 10.03-F" and a cover sheet that is substantially similar to "Form 10.03-H."

**History:** Effective 3-1-00; amended, eff. 6-1-02; 5-1-07; 2-1-09; 7-1-10.

### COMMENTARY (MARCH 1, 2000)

In Sub. H.B. 302, effective July 29, 1998, the General Assembly revised the law relative to issuance of stalking protection orders and the violation of those orders. Following the enactment of Sub. H.B. 302, the Supreme Court of Ohio Standard Forms Committee developed Sup. R. 10.03 and forms relative to the application for and issuance of civil and criminal stalking protection orders.

**FORM 10.03-A: MOTION FOR CRIMINAL PROTECTION ORDER (CRPO)**

**IN THE ______________________ COURT**

**______________________ COUNTY, OHIO**

**STATE OF OHIO/CITY OF** :

______________________________ : **Case No.** ______________________

:

**v.** **Judge** ______________________

:

______________________________

**DEFENDANT** : **MOTION FOR CRIMINAL PROTECTION ORDER (CRPO) (R.C. 2903.213)**

______________________ (Name of person), moves the Court to issue a protection order containing terms designed to ensure the safety and protection of the complainant or the alleged victim in the above captioned case, in relation to the named defendant, pursuant to its authority to issue a protection order under R.C. 2903.213.

A complaint, a copy of which has been attached to this motion, has been filed in this Court charging the named defendant with a violation of R.C. 2903.11 (*Felonious Assault*), 2903.12 (*Aggravated Assault*), 2903.13 (*Assault*), 2903.21 (*Aggravated Menacing*), 2903.211 (*Menacing by Stalking*), 2903.22 (*Menacing*), or 2911.211 (*Aggravated Trespass*) or a violation of a municipal ordinance substantially similar to R.C. 2903.13, 2903.21, 2903.211, 2903.22, or 2911.211, or the commission of sexually oriented offenses as defined in R.C. 2950.01.

I understand that I must appear before the Court, at a time set by the Court not later than the next day that the Court is in session after the filing of this motion, for a hearing on the motion, and that any protection order granted pursuant to this motion is a pretrial condition of release and is effective only until the disposition of the criminal proceeding arising out of the attached complaint or until the issuance under R.C. 2903.214 of a protection order arising out of the same activities as those that were the basis in the attached complaint.

______________________________

Signature of Alleged Victim

______________________________

______________________________

Address of Alleged Victim

*NOTES:* *(1) This form must be provided by the Clerk of Court, per R.C. 2903.213(B).*

*(2) By its own definitions [see R.C. 2903.213(A)], this statute does not apply to a complaint that involves a person who is a family or household member. In those cases where the Alleged Victim is a family or household member of the defendant, use Domestic Violence Temporary Protection Order (DVTPO) forms and procedures under R.C. 2919.26, and/or Civil Protection Order (CPO) forms and procedures under R.C. 3113.31.*



**Amended: July 1, 2010**
**Discard all previous versions of this form**

FORM 10.03-B: CRIMINAL PROTECTION ORDER (CRPO)

IN THE ______________________ COURT
______________________ COUNTY, OHIO

# Order of Protection

Per R.C. 2903.213(G)(2), this Order is indexed at

______________________
LAW ENFORCEMENT AGENCY WHERE INDEXED

(   )   -
PHONE NUMBER

STATE OF OHIO/CITY OF ______________

v.

______________________
DEFENDANT

Case No. [                    ]

Judge ______________________

County [          ] State **OHIO**

**CRIMINAL PROTECTION ORDER (CRPO)**
**(R.C. 2903.213)**

☐ New Order ☐ Modification of Previous Order

**ALLEGED VICTIM**

[                    ]

First Middle Last

**PERSON(S) PROTECTED BY THIS ORDER:**

Alleged Victim ______________ DOB: ________

Alleged Victim's Family or Household Member(s) (May attach additional form):

______________ DOB: ________

______________ DOB: ________

______________ DOB: ________

______________ DOB: ________

**DEFENDANT:**

[                    ]

First Middle Last

Address where Defendant can be found:

______________________

______________________

DEFENDANT IDENTIFIERS

| SEX | RACE | HT | WT |
|---|---|---|---|
| | | | |
| EYES | HAIR | DATE OF BIRTH | |
| | | | |
| DRIVER'S LIC. NO. | EXP. DATE | STATE | |
| | | | |

Distinguishing Features: ______________________

☐ **WARNING TO LAW ENFORCEMENT: DEFENDANT HAS FIREARMS ACCESS – PROCEED WITH CAUTION**

☐ ***Ex Parte* CRPO Granted:** ____________ **(Date)**

☐ **CRPO Granted:** ____________ **(Date)**

(Violence Against Women Act, 18 U.S.C. 2265, Federal Full Faith & Credit Declaration: Registration of this Order is not required for enforcement.)

**THE COURT HEREBY FINDS:**

That it has jurisdiction over the parties and subject matter, and the Defendant has been provided with reasonable notice and the opportunity to be heard within the time required by Ohio law. **Additional findings of this Order are set forth below.**

**THE COURT HEREBY ORDERS:**

That the above named Defendant be restrained from committing acts of abuse or threats of abuse against and contacting the Alleged Victim and other protected persons named in this Order, as set forth below. Additional terms of this Order are set forth below.

**WARNING TO DEFENDANT: See the warning page attached to the front of this Order.**

**FORM 10.03-B: CRIMINAL PROTECTION ORDER (CRPO)**

**Amended: July 1, 2010**
**Discard all previous versions of this form**

**[Page 2 of Form 10.03-B]**

**Case No.**____________________

This matter came before the Court on ______________________________ for hearing on Alleged Victim's Motion for Criminal Protection Order. The Court finds the Motion of the Alleged Victim for a Criminal Protection Order is well taken. The Court finds that the safety and protection of the Alleged Victim and protected persons named in this Order may be impaired unless the Court acts. The following provisions of this Order are designed to enhance the safety of those covered by its terms. They are issued to the Defendant as pretrial conditions, in addition to any bail.

**ALL OF THE PROVISIONS CHECKED BELOW APPLY TO THE DEFENDANT**

☐ **1. DEFENDANT SHALL NOT ABUSE** the protected persons named in this Order by harming, attempting to harm, threatening, following, stalking, harassing, contacting, forcing sexual relations upon them, or by committing sexually oriented offenses against them. [NCIC 01 and 02]

☐ **2. DEFENDANT SHALL NOT ENTER** the residence, school, business, place of employment, day care centers, or child care providers of the protected persons named in this Order, including the buildings, grounds, and parking lots at those locations. Defendant may not violate this Order **even with the permission of a protected person**. [NCIC 04]

☐ **3. DEFENDANT SHALL NOT INTERFERE** with protected persons' right to occupy the residence including, but not limited to canceling utilities, insurance, interrupting telephone service, mail delivery, or the delivery of any other documents or items. [NCIC 03]

☐ **4. DEFENDANT SHALL SURRENDER** all keys and garage door openers to the following residence: ____________
______________________________________________________________________
at the earliest possible opportunity after service of this Order to the law enforcement agency that serves Defendant with this Order or as follows: ______________________________
______________________________________________________________________

☐ **5. DEFENDANT SHALL STAY AWAY** from protected persons named in this Order, and shall not be present within 500 feet or ____________ (distance) of any protected persons, wherever those protected persons may be found, or any place the Defendant knows or should know the protected persons are likely to be, **even with protected persons' permission**. If Defendant accidentally comes in contact with protected persons in any public or private place, Defendant must depart *immediately*. This Order includes encounters on public and private roads, highways, and thoroughfares. [NCIC 04]

☐ **6. DEFENDANT SHALL NOT REMOVE, DAMAGE, HIDE, OR DISPOSE OF ANY PROPERTY OR PETS** owned or possessed by the protected persons named in this Order.

☐ **7. DEFENDANT SHALL NOT INITIATE OR HAVE ANY CONTACT** with the protected persons named in this Order at their residences, businesses, places of employment, schools, day care centers, or child care providers. Contact includes, but is not limited to, telephone, fax, e-mail, voice mail, delivery service, writings, or communications by any other means in person or through another person. Defendant may not violate this Order **even with the permission of a protected person**. [NCIC 05]

☐ **8. DEFENDANT SHALL NOT CAUSE OR ENCOURAGE ANY OTHER PERSON** to do any act prohibited by this Order.

☐ **9. DEFENDANT SHALL NOT POSSESS, USE, CARRY, OR OBTAIN ANY DEADLY WEAPON.** Defendant shall turn over all deadly weapons in Defendant's possession to the law enforcement agency that serves Defendant with this Order or as follows: ______________________________
______________________________________________________________________
Any law enforcement agency is authorized to take possession of deadly weapons pursuant to this paragraph and hold them in protective custody until further Court order. [NCIC 07]

☐ **10. IT IS FURTHER ORDERED:** [NCIC 08] ______________________________
______________________________________________________________________
______________________________________________________________________
______________________________________________________________________

**FORM 10.03-B: CRIMINAL PROTECTION ORDER (CRPO)**

**Amended: July 1, 2010**
**Discard all previous versions of this form**

[Page 3 of Form 10.03-B]

Case No.______________________

11. **IT IS FURTHER ORDERED** that a copy of this Order shall be delivered to Defendant on the same day that the Order is entered.

12. **THIS ORDER REMAINS IN EFFECT:** (1) until modified by this Court; or (2) until the criminal proceeding arising out of the complaint upon which these orders were issued is disposed by this Court or by the court of common pleas to which the Defendant is bound over for prosecution; or (3) until the Court issues a Civil Stalking Protection Order ("CSPO") or Civil Sexually Oriented Offense Protection Order ("CSOOPO") arising out of the same activities as those that were the basis of the complaint filed in this action.

**IT IS SO ORDERED.**

| | |
|---|---|
| ______________________ | ______________________ |
| **MAGISTRATE – DATE OF *EX PARTE* CRPO** | **JUDGE – DATE OF *EX PARTE* CRPO** |
| ______________________ | ______________________ |
| **MAGISTRATE – DATE OF CRPO** | **JUDGE– DATE OF CRPO** |

**NOTICE TO DEFENDANT: THE PERSONS PROTECTED BY THIS ORDER CANNOT GIVE YOU LEGAL PERMISSION TO CHANGE OR VIOLATE THIS ORDER. IF YOU VIOLATE ANY TERMS OF THIS ORDER, EVEN WITH THE PROTECTED PERSON'S PERMISSION, YOU MAY BE ARRESTED. ONLY THE COURT CAN CHANGE THIS ORDER. IF THERE IS ANY REASON WHY THIS ORDER SHOULD BE CHANGED, YOU MUST ASK THE COURT TO CHANGE IT. YOU ACT AT YOUR OWN RISK IF YOU DISREGARD THIS WARNING.**

*NOTES: By its own definitions [see R.C. 2903.213(A)], this statute does not apply to a complaint that involves a person who is a family or household member. In those cases where the Alleged Victim is a family or household member of the Defendant, use the Domestic Violence Temporary Protection Order ("DVTPO") forms and procedures under R.C. 2919.26, and/or Domestic Violence Civil Protection Order ("DVCPO") forms and procedures under R.C. 3113.31.*

**A HEARING** on this Order shall be held before

Judge ______________________

or Magistrate ______________________

on ________ , at ______________ a.m./p.m.

(the next court day) at the following location:

______________________

______________________

**TO THE CLERK**

**COPIES OF THIS ORDER SHALL BE DELIVERED TO:**

- ☐ Prosecutor
- ☐ Alleged Victim
- ☐ Defendant (by personal service)
- ☐ Attorney for Defendant
- ☐ Police Department Where Alleged Victim Resides: ______________________
- ☐ Police Department Where Alleged Victim Works: ______________________
- ☐ The ______________ County Sheriff's Office
- ☐ Other: ______________________

**Service acknowledged:** ______________________ ______________
**Defendant Signature** **Date**

**WAIVER OF HEARING**

**I HAVE BEEN ADVISED OF MY RIGHT TO HAVE A HEARING ON THE MOTION FOR A CRIMINAL PROTECTION ORDER AND HEREBY KNOWINGLY AND VOLUNTARILY WAIVE THE HEARING ON THE MOTION AND AGREE TO BE BOUND BY THE TERMS OF THIS ORDER.**

**DEFENDANT:** ______________________ **DATE:** ______________________

**FORM 10.03-B: CRIMINAL PROTECTION ORDER (CRPO)**

**Amended: July 1, 2010**
**Discard all previous versions of this form**

**FORM 10.03-D: PETITION FOR CIVIL STALKING PROTECTION ORDER OR CIVIL SEXUALLY ORIENTED OFFENSE PROTECTION ORDER**

**IN THE COURT OF COMMON PLEAS**

_____________________ **COUNTY, OHIO**

| | |
|---|---|
| _____________________<br>**Petitioner** | **Case No.** _____________________ |
| _____________________<br>Address | **Judge** _____________________ |
| _____________________<br>City, State, Zip Code | **PETITION FOR CIVIL STALKING PROTECTION ORDER OR CIVIL SEXUALLY ORIENTED OFFENSE PROTECTION ORDER (R.C. 2903.214)** |
| Date of Birth: _____________ | |
| **v.** | **Notice to Petitioner: Check every ☐ that applies.** |
| _____________________<br>**Respondent** | **DO NOT WRITE YOUR ADDRESS ON THIS FORM IF YOU ARE REQUESTING CONFIDENTIALITY. PLEASE PROVIDE ANOTHER ADDRESS WHERE YOU CAN RECEIVE NOTICES FROM THE COURT.** |
| _____________________<br>Address | |
| _____________________<br>City, State, Zip Code | **The Respondent does NOT have to be related to Petitioner in any way for Petitioner to be eligible for relief.** |
| Date of Birth: _____________ | |

☐ 1. Petitioner seeks relief on Petitioner's own behalf.

☐ 2. Petitioner seeks relief on behalf of the following family or household members:

| NAME | DATE OF BIRTH | HOW RELATED TO PETITIONER |
|---|---|---|
| | | |
| | | |
| | | |
| | | |
| | | |
| | | |

Ohio law defines "Menacing by Stalking" as follows:

*"No person by engaging in a pattern of conduct shall knowingly cause another person to believe that the offender will cause physical harm to the other person or cause mental distress to the other person."* R.C. 2903.211(A)(1).

*"No person, through the use of any electronic method of remotely transferring information, including, but not limited to, any computer, computer network, computer program, or computer system, shall post a message with purpose to urge or incite another to commit a violation of division (A)(1) of this section* (above)*"* R.C. 2903.211-(A)(2).

"Sexually oriented offenses" are defined in R.C. 2950.01.



**Amended: July 1, 2010**
**Discard all previous versions of this form**

**[Page 2 of 10.03-D]**

**Case No.**____________________

3. Petitioner states that Respondent has engaged in the following act(s) which create an immediate and present danger. For (a), (b), or (c) below, attach additional paper if you need more room.

☐ (a) For a civil stalking protection order due to menacing by stalking, describe the nature and extent of the pattern of conduct that causes you to believe that Respondent will cause you physical harm or causes (or has caused) mental distress. Also describe any previous convictions of Respondent for the crime of Menacing by Stalking, if known.

______________________________________________________________________________
______________________________________________________________________________
______________________________________________________________________________
______________________________________________________________________________
______________________________________________________________________________

☐ (b) For a civil sexually oriented offense protection order due to a sexually oriented offense, describe the acts of Respondent as fully as possible. You do not need to include any pattern of conduct information for a protection order due to a sexually oriented offense.

______________________________________________________________________________
______________________________________________________________________________
______________________________________________________________________________
______________________________________________________________________________
______________________________________________________________________________
______________________________________________________________________________

☐ (c) For electronic monitoring of the Respondent, describe the nature and extent of the Respondent's conduct before the filing of this Petition that puts you or your family or household members' health, welfare, or safety at risk. Also describe how the Respondent presents a continuing danger to you or your family or household members.

______________________________________________________________________________
______________________________________________________________________________
______________________________________________________________________________
______________________________________________________________________________
______________________________________________________________________________

4. Petitioner requests the Court grant relief under R.C. 2903.214 for the Petitioner and the family or household members named in this Petition by granting a Civil Stalking Protection Order or Civil Sexually Oriented Offense Protection Order that:

☐ (a) Requires Respondent not to abuse the Petitioner and the family or household members named in this Petition by harming, attempting to harm, threatening, following, stalking, harassing, contacting, forcing sexual relations upon them, or by committing sexually oriented offenses against them.

☐ (b) Requires Respondent to refrain from entering the residence, school, business, place of employment, child care providers, or day care centers of Petitioner and the family or household members named in this Petition, including the buildings, grounds, and parking lots at those locations.

☐ (c) Requires Respondent not to interfere with Petitioner's right to occupy the residence including, but not limited to canceling any utilities, insurance, interrupting phone service, mail delivery, or the delivery of any other documents or items.

**FORM 10.03-D: PETITION FOR CIVIL STALKING PROTECTION ORDER OR CIVIL SEXUALLY ORIENTED OFFENSE PROTECTION ORDER**

**Amended: July 1, 2010**
**Discard all previous versions of this form**

**[Page 3 of 10.03-D]**

**Case No.**____________________

☐ (d) Requires Respondent not to remove, damage, hide, or dispose of any property or pets owned or possessed by the Petitioner and Petitioner's family or household members named in this Petition.

☐ (e) Requires Respondent not to possess, use, carry, or obtain any deadly weapon.

☐ (f) Requires Respondent to be electronically monitored.

☐ (g) Includes the following additional provisions: ________________________________________

__________________________________________________________________________

☐ 5. Petitioner further requests that the Court issue an *ex parte* (emergency) protection order under R.C. 2903.214(D) and this Petition.

☐ 6. Petitioner further requests that the Court not issue any mutual protection orders or other orders against Petitioner unless all of the conditions of R.C. 2903.214(E)(3) are met.

☐ 7. Petitioner further requests that if Petitioner has a victim advocate, the Court permit the victim advocate to accompany Petitioner at all stages of these proceedings as required by R.C. 2903.214(L).

☐ 8. Petitioner further requests that the Court grant such other relief as the Court considers equitable and fair.

☐ 9. The following is a list of all present and past court cases involving Respondent, that Petitioner knows of:

| CASE NAME | CASE NUMBER | COURT/COUNTY | OUTCOME OF CASE |
|---|---|---|---|
| | | | |
| | | | |
| | | | |
| | | | |

**I hereby swear or affirm that the answers above are true, complete, and accurate to the best of my knowledge. I understand that falsifying this document may result in a contempt of court finding against me which could result in a jail sentence and fine, and that falsifying this document may also subject me to criminal penalties for perjury under R.C. 2921.11.**

__________________________________________
**SIGNATURE OF PETITIONER**

Sworn to and subscribed before me on this _________ day of ________________ , _________ .

__________________________________________
**NOTARY PUBLIC**

[Page 4 of 10.03-D]

Case No.____________________

**DO NOT WRITE YOUR ADDRESS BELOW IF YOU ARE REQUESTING CONFIDENTIALITY. PLEASE PROVIDE ANOTHER ADDRESS WHERE YOU CAN RECEIVE NOTICES FROM THE COURT.**

______________________________________

______________________________________

______________________________________

______________________________________
Signature of Attorney for Petitioner (if applicable)

______________________________________
Name

______________________________________
Address

______________________________________
City, State, Zip Code

______________________________________
Attorney Registration Number

______________________________________
Telephone Number

______________________________________
Fax

______________________________________
Email

FORM 10.03-E: CIVIL STALKING PROTECTION ORDER OR CIVIL SEXUALLY ORIENTED OFFENSE PROTECTION ORDER *EX PARTE*

IN THE COURT OF COMMON PLEAS
_______________ COUNTY, OHIO

# Order of Protection

Per R.C. 2903.214(F)(3), this Order is indexed at

_______________
LAW ENFORCEMENT AGENCY WHERE INDEXED

( )
PHONE NUMBER

Case No. ____________

Judge ____________

County ____________ State **OHIO**

☐ **CIVIL STALKING PROTECTION ORDER *EX PARTE* (R.C. 2903.214)**

☐ **CIVIL SEXUALLY ORIENTED OFFENSE PROTECTION ORDER *EX PARTE* (R.C. 2903.214)**

**PETITIONER:**

First Middle Last

**v.**

**PERSON(S) PROTECTED BY THIS ORDER:**

Petitioner: ____________ DOB: ____________

Petitioner's Family or Household Member(s):

____________ DOB: ____________
____________ DOB: ____________
____________ DOB: ____________
____________ DOB: ____________

**RESPONDENT:**

First Middle Last

Address where Respondent can be found:

____________
____________

RESPONDENT IDENTIFIERS

| SEX | RACE | HT | WT |
|---|---|---|---|
| | | | |

| EYES | HAIR | DATE OF BIRTH |
|---|---|---|
| | | |

| DRIVER'S LIC. NO. | EXP. DATE | STATE |
|---|---|---|
| | | |

Distinguishing Features: ____________

☐ **WARNING TO LAW ENFORCEMENT: RESPONDENT HAS FIREARMS ACCESS – PROCEED WITH CAUTION**

(Violence Against Women Act, 18 U.S.C. 2265, Federal Full Faith & Credit Declaration: Registration of this Order is not required for enforcement.)

**THE COURT HEREBY FINDS:**
That it has jurisdiction over the parties and subject matter, and the Respondent will be provided with reasonable notice and opportunity to be heard within the time required by Ohio law. **Additional findings of this Order are set forth below.**

**THE COURT HEREBY ORDERS:**
That the above named Respondent be restrained from committing acts of abuse or threats of abuse against the Petitioner and other protected persons named in this Order, as set forth below. Additional terms of this Order are set forth below.

The terms of this Order shall be effective until ____ / ____ / ____ **(DATE CERTAIN).**

**WARNING TO RESPONDENT: See the warning page attached to the front of this Order.**

FORM 10.03-E: CIVIL STALKING PROTECTION ORDER OR CIVIL SEXUALLY ORIENTED OFFENSE PROTECTION ORDER *EX PARTE*

**Amended: July 1, 2010**
**Discard all previous versions of this form**

**[Page 2 of Form 10.03-E]**

**Case No.**____________________

This proceeding came on for an *ex parte* hearing on ____________________, ________ (Respondent not being present), upon the filing of a Petition by Petitioner for a civil stalking protection order or civil sexually oriented offense protection order against the Respondent, pursuant to R.C. 2903.214. In accordance with R.C. 2903.214(D)(1), the Court held an *ex parte* hearing not later than the next day that the Court was in session after the Petition was filed.

The Court finds that the protected persons named herein are in immediate and present danger and, for good cause shown, the following temporary orders are necessary to protect the persons named in this Order.

**ALL OF THE PROVISIONS CHECKED BELOW APPLY TO THE RESPONDENT**

☐ 1. **RESPONDENT SHALL NOT ABUSE** the protected persons named in this Order by harming, attempting to harm, threatening, following, stalking, harassing, forcing sexual relations upon them, or by committing sexually oriented offenses against them. [NCIC 01 and 02]

☐ 2. **RESPONDENT SHALL NOT ENTER** the residence, school, business, place of employment, day care centers, or child care providers of the protected persons named in this Order, including the buildings, grounds and parking lots at those locations. Respondent may not violate this Order **even with the permission of a protected person**. [NCIC 04]

☐ 3. **RESPONDENT SHALL NOT INTERFERE** with protected persons' right to occupy the residence including, but not limited to canceling utilities, insurance, interrupting telephone service, mail delivery, or the delivery of any other documents or items.

☐ 4. **RESPONDENT SHALL SURRENDER** all keys and garage door openers to the following residence:

________________________________________

at the earliest possible opportunity after service of this Order to the law enforcement agency that serves Respondent with this Order or as follows: ______________________________

________________________________________

☐ 5. **RESPONDENT SHALL STAY AWAY FROM** protected persons named in this Order, and shall not be present within 500 feet or _______ (distance) of any protected persons wherever those protected persons may be found, or any place the Respondent knows or should know the protected persons are likely to be, **even with protected persons' permission**. If Respondent accidentally comes in contact with protected persons in any public or private place, Respondent must depart *immediately*. This Order includes encounters on public and private roads, highways, and thoroughfares. [NCIC 04]

☐ 6. **RESPONDENT SHALL NOT REMOVE, DAMAGE, HIDE, OR DISPOSE OF ANY PROPERTY OR PETS** owned or possessed by the protected persons named in this Order.

☐ 7. **RESPONDENT SHALL NOT INITIATE OR HAVE ANY CONTACT** with the protected persons named in this Order at their residences, businesses, places of employment, schools, day care centers, or child care providers. Contact includes, but is not limited to, telephone, fax, e-mail, voice mail, delivery service, writings, or communications by any other means in person or through another person. Respondent may not violate this Order **even with the permission of a protected person**. [NCIC 05]

☐ 8. **RESPONDENT SHALL NOT CAUSE OR ENCOURAGE ANY OTHER PERSON** to do any act prohibited by this Order.

☐ 9. **RESPONDENT SHALL NOT POSSESS, USE, CARRY, OR OBTAIN ANY DEADLY WEAPON.** Respondent shall turn over all deadly weapons in Respondent's possession to the law enforcement agency that serves Respondent with this Order or as follows: ______________________________

________________________________________

Any law enforcement agency is authorized to take possession of deadly weapons pursuant to this paragraph and hold them in protective custody until further Court order. [NCIC 07]

Case No.______________________

☐ **10. IT IS FURTHER ORDERED:** [NCIC 08] ______________________________________

________________________________________________________________________

________________________________________________________________________

________________________________________________________________________

11. **IT IS FURTHER ORDERED** that the Clerk of Court shall cause a copy of the Petition and this Order to be delivered to the Respondent as required by law. The Clerk of Court shall also provide certified copies of the Petition and this Order to Petitioner upon request. This Order is granted without bond. Under federal and state law, the Clerk shall not charge any fees for filing, issuing, registering, or serving this Protection Order.

12. **ALL OF THE TERMS OF THIS ORDER REMAIN IN FULL FORCE AND EFFECT UNTIL**

____________________, _________ .

**IT IS SO ORDERED.**

| | |
|---|---|
| ____________________________ | ____________________________ |
| **MAGISTRATE** | **JUDGE** |

**<u>NOTICE TO RESPONDENT</u>: THE PERSONS PROTECTED BY THIS ORDER CANNOT GIVE YOU LEGAL PERMISSION TO CHANGE OR VIOLATE THIS ORDER. IF YOU VIOLATE ANY TERMS OF THIS ORDER, EVEN WITH THE PROTECTED PERSON'S PERMISSION, YOU MAY BE ARRESTED. ONLY THE COURT CAN CHANGE THIS ORDER. IF THERE IS ANY REASON WHY THIS ORDER SHOULD BE CHANGED, YOU MUST ASK THE COURT TO CHANGE IT. <u>YOU ACT AT YOUR OWN RISK IF YOU DISREGARD THIS WARNING.</u>**

**A FULL HEARING** on this Order shall be held before

Judge __________________________ or

Magistrate __________________________

on ____________________, at __________ a.m./p.m.

at the following location:

__________________________________________

__________________________________________

**<u>TO THE CLERK:</u>**

**COPIES OF THIS ORDER SHALL BE DELIVERED TO:**

☐ Petitioner
☐ Respondent (by personal service)
☐ Police Department Where Petitioner Resides:
___________________________________________
☐ Police Department Where Petitioner Works:
___________________________________________
☐ The ____________________ County Sheriff's Office
☐ Other: ____________________________________

FORM 10.03-F: CIVIL STALKING PROTECTION ORDER OR CIVIL SEXUALLY ORIENTED OFFENSE PROTECTION ORDER FULL HEARING

IN THE COURT OF COMMON PLEAS
____________________ COUNTY, OHIO

# Order of Protection

Per R.C. 2903.214(F)(3), this Order is indexed at

____________________
LAW ENFORCEMENT AGENCY WHERE INDEXED

( ) -
PHONE NUMBER

Case No. __________

Judge __________

County __________ State **OHIO**

☐ **CIVIL STALKING PROTECTION ORDER FULL HEARING (R.C. 2903.214)**

☐ **CIVIL SEXUALLY ORIENTED OFFENSE PROTECTION ORDER FULL HEARING (R.C. 2903.214)**

**PETITIONER:**

First Middle Last

**v.**

**RESPONDENT:**

First Middle Last

Address where Respondent can be found:

____________________

____________________

**PERSON(S) PROTECTED BY THIS ORDER:**

Petitioner: __________ DOB: ______

Petitioner's Family or Household Member(s):

__________ DOB: ______

__________ DOB: ______

__________ DOB: ______

__________ DOB: ______

RESPONDENT IDENTIFIERS

| SEX | RACE | HT | WT |
|---|---|---|---|
| | | | |
| EYES | HAIR | DATE OF BIRTH | |
| | | | |

| DRIVER'S LIC. NO. | EXP. DATE | STATE |
|---|---|---|
| | | |

Distinguishing Features: __________

☐ **WARNING TO LAW ENFORCEMENT: RESPONDENT HAS FIREARMS ACCESS – PROCEED WITH CAUTION**

(Violence Against Women Act, 18 U.S.C. 2265, Federal Full Faith & Credit Declaration: Registration of this Order is not required for enforcement.)

**THE COURT HEREBY FINDS:**
That it has jurisdiction over the parties and subject matter, and the Respondent was provided with reasonable notice and opportunity to be heard within the time required by Ohio law. **Additional findings of this Order are set forth below.**

**THE COURT HEREBY ORDERS:**
That the above named Respondent be restrained from committing acts of abuse or threats of abuse against the Petitioner and other protected persons named in this Order, as set forth below. Additional terms of this Order are set forth below.

The terms of this Order shall be effective until _____ / _____ / _____ **(DATE CERTAIN – FIVE YEARS MAXIMUM)**.

**WARNING TO RESPONDENT: See the warning page attached to the front of this Order.**

FORM 10.03-F: CIVIL STALKING PROTECTION ORDER OR CIVIL SEXUALLY ORIENTED OFFENSE PROTECTION ORDER FULL HEARING

**Amended: July 1, 2010**
**Discard all previous versions of this form**

**[Page 2 of Form 10.03-F]**

**Case No.**____________________

This proceeding came on for a hearing on ____________________ before the Court and the Civil Stalking Protection Order *Ex Parte* or Civil Sexually Oriented Offense Protection Order *Ex Parte* filed on ____________________ all in accordance with R.C. 2903.214. The following individuals were present: ____________________

________________________________________

The Court hereby makes the following findings of fact: ____________________

________________________________________

________________________________________

________________________________________

________________________________________

________________________________________

☐ The Court finds by a preponderance of the evidence that 1) the Respondent has knowingly engaged in a pattern of conduct that caused Petitioner to believe that the Respondent will cause physical harm or cause or has caused mental distress; and 2) the following orders are equitable, fair, and necessary to protect the persons named in this Order from stalking offenses.

☐ The Court finds by a preponderance of the evidence that 1) the Petitioner or Petitioner's family or household member(s) are in danger of or have been a victim of a sexually oriented offense as defined in R.C. 2950.01, committed by Respondent; and 2) the following orders are equitable, fair, and necessary to protect the persons named in this Order from sexually oriented offenses.

☐ The Court finds by clear and convincing evidence that 1) the Petitioner or Petitioner's family or household member reasonably believed the Respondent's conduct before the filing of the Petition endangered the health, welfare, or safety of the Petitioner or Petitioner's family or household member(s); 2) the Respondent presents a continuing danger to the Petitioner or Petitioner's family or household member(s); and 3) the following orders are equitable, fair, and necessary to protect the person(s) named in this Order.

**ALL OF THE PROVISIONS CHECKED BELOW APPLY TO THE RESPONDENT**

☐ **1. RESPONDENT SHALL NOT ABUSE** the protected persons named in this Order by harming, attempting to harm, threatening, following, stalking, harassing, forcing sexual relations upon them, or by committing sexually oriented offenses against them. [NCIC 01 and 02]

☐ **2. RESPONDENT SHALL NOT ENTER** the residence, school, business, place of employment, day care centers, or child care providers of the protected persons named in this Order, including the buildings, grounds, and parking lots at those locations. Respondent may not violate this Order **even with the permission of a protected person**. [NCIC 03]

☐ **3. RESPONDENT SHALL NOT INTERFERE** with protected persons' right to occupy the residence including, but not limited to canceling utilities, insurance, interrupting telephone service, mail delivery, or the delivery of any other documents or items.

☐ **4. RESPONDENT SHALL SURRENDER** all keys and garage door openers to the following residence:

________________________________________

at the earliest possible opportunity after service of this Order to the law enforcement agency that serves Respondent with this Order or as follows: ____________________

________________________________________

☐ **5. RESPONDENT SHALL STAY AWAY** from protected persons named in this Order, and shall not be present within 500 feet or ________ (distance) of any protected persons, wherever those protected persons may be found, or any place the Respondent knows or should know the protected persons are likely to be, **even with protected persons' permission**. If Respondent accidentally comes in contact with protected persons in any public or private place, Respondent must depart *immediately*. This Order includes encounters on public and private roads, highways, and thoroughfares. [NCIC 04]

[Page 3 of Form 10.03-F]

Case No.____________________

☐ 6. **RESPONDENT SHALL NOT REMOVE, DAMAGE, HIDE, OR DISPOSE OF ANY PROPERTY OR PETS** owned or possessed by the protected persons named in this Order.

☐ 7. **RESPONDENT SHALL NOT INITIATE OR HAVE ANY CONTACT** with the protected persons named in this Order at their residences, businesses, places of employment, schools, day care centers, or child care providers. Contact includes, but is not limited to, telephone, fax, e-mail, voice mail, delivery service, writings, or communications by any other means in person or through another person. Respondent may not violate this Order **even with the permission of a protected person**. [NCIC 05]

☐ 8. **RESPONDENT SHALL NOT CAUSE OR ENCOURAGE ANY OTHER PERSON** to do any act prohibited by this Order.

☐ 9. **RESPONDENT SHALL NOT POSSESS, USE, CARRY, OR OBTAIN ANY DEADLY WEAPON.** Respondent shall turn over all deadly weapons in Respondent's possession to the law enforcement agency that serves Respondent with this Order or as follows: _____________________________________________________________________________________________________________________________________________________________________

Any law enforcement agency is authorized to take possession of deadly weapons pursuant to this paragraph and hold them in protective custody until further Court order. [NCIC 07]

☐ 10. **IT IS FURTHER ORDERED:** [NCIC 08] __________________________________________________________________________________________________________________________________________________________________________________________________________________________________________________

☐ 11. **RESPONDENT IS ORDERED TO COMPLETE** the following counseling program: ___________________________________________________________________________________________________________________________________________________________________

**Respondent shall contact this program within seven days after receiving this Order and immediately arrange for an initial appointment.** The counseling program is requested to provide the Court a written notice when Respondent attends the initial appointment, if the Respondent fails to attend or is discharged, and when Respondent completes the program. Respondent is required to sign all necessary waivers to allow the Court to receive information from the counseling program.

☐ **Respondent is ordered to appear before Judge ________________ or Magistrate ________________ on _____________________________ at ______ a.m. / p.m., to review Respondent's compliance with this Counseling Order. Respondent is warned: If you fail to attend the program you may be held in contempt of court. If you fail to appear at this hearing, the Court may issue a warrant for your arrest.**

☐ 12. **RESPONDENT SHALL NOT USE OR POSSESS** alcohol or illegal drugs.

☐ 13. **RESPONDENT SHALL BE SUBJECT TO ELECTRONIC MONITORING.** Respondent is ordered to report to ______________________________________ for the placement of a global positioning system for the purpose of electronic monitoring for the duration of this Order or until ______________________________________, whichever expires first. The Court further imposes the following terms and conditions: ________________________________________________________________________________________________________________________________

14. **IT IS FURTHER ORDERED** that the Clerk of Court shall cause a copy of the Petition and this Order to be delivered to the Respondent as required by law. The Clerk of Court shall also provide certified copies of the Petition and this Order to Petitioner upon request. This Order is granted without bond. Under federal and state law, the Clerk shall not charge any fees for filing, issuing, registering, or serving this Protection Order.

[Page 4 of Form 10.03-F]

Case No.____________________

**15. ALL OF THE TERMS OF THIS ORDER REMAIN IN FULL FORCE AND EFFECT FOR A PERIOD OF FIVE YEARS FROM ISSUANCE, OR UNTIL ________________**

**IT IS SO ORDERED.** **APPROVED and ADOPTED by:**

______________________________ ______________________________

**MAGISTRATE** **JUDGE**

**NOTICE TO RESPONDENT: THE PERSONS PROTECTED BY THIS ORDER CANNOT GIVE YOU LEGAL PERMISSION TO CHANGE OR VIOLATE THIS ORDER. IF YOU VIOLATE ANY TERMS OF THIS ORDER, EVEN WITH THE PROTECTED PERSON'S PERMISSION, YOU MAY BE ARRESTED. ONLY THE COURT CAN CHANGE THIS ORDER. IF THERE IS ANY REASON WHY THIS ORDER SHOULD BE CHANGED, YOU MUST ASK THE COURT TO CHANGE IT. YOU ACT AT YOUR OWN RISK IF YOU DISREGARD THIS WARNING.**

***NOTICE OF FINAL APPEALABLE ORDER***

Copies of the foregoing Order, which is a final appealable order, were mailed by ordinary U.S. mail or hand-delivered to the parties indicated on the following date:

____________________, __________

By: ______________________________

CLERK OF COURT

**TO THE CLERK**

**COPIES OF THIS ORDER SHALL BE DELIVERED TO:**

☐ Petitioner ☐ Attorney for Petitioner

☐ Respondent ☐ Attorney for Respondent

☐ Police Department Where Petitioner Resides:

______________________________

☐ Police Department Where Petitioner Works:

______________________________

☐ The ________________ County Sheriff's Office

☐ Other: ______________________________

**WAIVER**

I, ____________________, understand that I have the right to a full hearing on the Petition for Civil Stalking Protection Order or Civil Sexually Oriented Offense Protection Order, and acknowledge each of the following:

1. I waive the right to have a full hearing on this Protection Order;
2. I waive the right to cross-examine witnesses and review evidence submitted in support of this Protection Order;
3. I waive the right to present witnesses and evidence on my own behalf;
4. I waive the right to request specific factual findings from the Court concerning the issuance of this Protection Order.

I understand that based on the foregoing waivers a Protection Order will be entered against me.

**RESPONDENT:** ____________________ **DATE:** ____________________

# FORM 10.03-G: HOW TO OBTAIN A CIVIL STALKING PROTECTION ORDER OR CIVIL SEXUALLY ORIENTED OFFENSE PROTECTION ORDER

These instructions are intended to assist you in preparing the Petition for a Civil Stalking Protection Order or Sexually Oriented Offense Protection Order, which can only be heard by the court of common pleas in your county. **Throughout the Petition you are called *Petitioner* and the person you are filing this Petition against is called *Respondent.***

## SOME HINTS BEFORE YOU BEGIN

- All forms must be typed or printed.
- When you print your name on the Petition, use the same name you use when you write your signature.
- Write your name and Respondent's name the same way throughout the Petition.
- Fill out the Petition as completely and accurately as possible.
- If you have any questions about completing the Petition, ask the Clerk of Court's office for assistance or contact your local domestic violence program or the Ohio Domestic Violence Network at 800-934-9840.
- Under federal and state law no fees may be charged to obtain a protection order.

## FILLING OUT THE PETITION: Mark each instruction below after you read and complete it

☐ **On the front page, leave the "Case No." line and "Judge" lines blank.** The Clerk of Court's office will fill in this information.

☐ **On the top left-hand side of the front page, fill in the requested information about yourself.** If you do not want your present address to be known, write "confidential" in the space for your address, but list someone else's address where you can receive notices from the Court.

☐ **Also on the top left-hand side of the front page, fill in the requested information about Respondent as best you can**. You may use Respondent's work address if you do not know Respondent's home address. If you do not know Respondent's date of birth, leave that line blank. Do not attempt to obtain this information unless it is safe to do so.

☐ **Paragraph 1:** If you are filing the Petition on behalf of yourself, mark the first box.

☐ **Paragraph 2:** If you are filing the Petition on behalf of a family or household member, mark the box and fill in their name(s) and the other information requested in the chart. You may attach additional pages if you need more room.

☐ **Paragraph 3(a):** State the date(s) of the incident(s) that caused you to file the Petition. Exact date(s) is not necessary; approximate time frame may be sufficient. If you are requesting a civil stalking protection order due to stalking, provide a brief description of the pattern of conduct (two or more instances) that caused you to believe that the Respondent will cause physical harm or cause mental distress to you or another family member. (NOTE: Petitioner and/or Respondent need not be related in any way for Petitioner to obtain the protection order.) If you are aware of any prior convictions of the Respondent for menacing by stalking or similar offenses, or prior convictions of Respondent for any sexually oriented offenses, list what information you know about those convictions. You may attach additional pages if you need more room to complete your description.

☐ **Paragraph 3(b):** State the date(s) of the incident(s) that caused you to file the Petition. Exact date(s) is not necessary; approximate timeframe may be sufficient. If you are requesting a civil sexually oriented offense protection order due to a sexually oriented offense, you do not have to provide a description of a pattern of conduct. A brief description of what happened that caused you to request the protection order will be enough. (NOTE: Petitioner and/or Respondent need not be related in any way for Petitioner to obtain the protection order.) If you are aware of any prior convictions of the Respondent for menacing by stalking or similar offenses, or prior convictions of Respondent for any sexually oriented offenses, list what information you know about those convictions. You may attach additional pages if you need more room to complete your description.

☐ **Paragraph 3(c):** State the date(s) of the incident(s) that caused you to file the Petition and request electronic monitoring of the Respondent. Exact date(s) is not necessary; approximate timeframe may be sufficient. If you are requesting electronic monitoring of the Respondent, describe the nature and extent of the Respondent's conduct before the filing of this Petition that puts you or your family or household members' health, welfare, or safety at risk. Also describe how the Respondent presents a continuing danger to you or your family or household members.

☐ **Paragraph 4:** Indicate the action you want the Court to take by marking the boxes next to the numbered paragraphs that apply to your situation.

**FORM 10.03-G: HOW TO OBTAIN A CIVIL STALKING PROTECTION ORDER OR CIVIL SEXUALLY ORIENTED OFFENSE PROTECTION ORDER**

**Amended: July 1, 2010**
**Discard all previous versions of this form**

**[Page 2 of Form 10.03-G]**

☐ **Paragraph 4(f):** Write any special court orders you believe would help protect you and your family or household members.

☐ **Paragraph 5:** Be sure to mark the box next to Paragraph 5 if you need an emergency ("*ex parte*") protection order.

☐ **Paragraph 9:** List ALL present or past court cases or investigations that involve Respondent. This includes all criminal, divorce, custody, visitation, and any other case that may have a bearing on the safety of you or your family or household members. Write the case name, the court, the case number, and the outcome of the case, if known. You may attach additional pages if you need more room.

## SIGNING THE PETITION

Try to fill out the Petition before you go to the courthouse. AFTER YOU HAVE FILLED OUT THE PETITION, TAKE IT TO A NOTARY PUBLIC TO HAVE YOUR SIGNATURE NOTARIZED. ***DO NOT SIGN THE PETITION UNLESS YOU ARE IN FRONT OF A NOTARY PUBLIC.*** **An employee of the Clerk of Court's office may be available to take your oath.**

## FILING THE PETITION

After you have your signature notarized, file your Petition at the Clerk of Court's office. The Clerk of Court's office will tell you when and where your *ex parte* hearing will take place.

## FEES

Under federal and state law, you cannot be charged any costs or fees for filing and obtaining a protection order.

## FORM 10.03-H: WARNING CONCERNING THE ATTACHED PROTECTION ORDER

***NOTE***: *Rule 10.03 of the Rules of Superintendence for the Courts of Ohio requires this Warning to be attached to the FRONT of all protection orders issued pursuant to R.C. 2903.213 and 2903.214 by the courts of the State of Ohio. TO BE USED WITH FORMS 10.03-B, 10.03-E, and 10.03-F.*

### WARNING TO RESPONDENT/ DEFENDANT

Violating the attached Protection Order is a crime, punishable by imprisonment or fine or both, and can cause your bond to be revoked or result in a contempt of court citation against you.

This Protection Order is enforceable in all 50 states, the District of Columbia, tribal lands, and U.S. Territories pursuant to the Violence Against Women Act, 18 U.S.C. 2265. Violating this Protection Order may subject you to federal charges and punishment.

As a result of this Order, it may be unlawful for you to possess or purchase a firearm, including a rifle, pistol, or revolver, or ammunition pursuant to federal law under 18 U.S.C. 922(g)(8). If you have any questions whether these laws make it illegal for you to possess or purchase a firearm, you should consult an attorney.

Only the Court can change this Order. The Petitioner/Alleged Victim cannot give you permission to violate this order. If you go near the Petitioner or other protected persons, even with their consent, you may be arrested. You act at your own risk if you disregard this WARNING. If you want to change the Order you must ask the Court.

### WARNING TO PETITIONER / ALLEGED VICTIM

You cannot change the terms of this Order by your words or actions. This Order **cannot** be changed by either party without obtaining a written court order.

### NOTICE TO ALL LAW ENFORCEMENT AGENCIES AND OFFICERS

The attached Protection Order is enforceable in all jurisdictions. Violating this Protection Order, whether it is a criminal or civil Protection Order, is a crime under R.C. 2919.27. Law enforcement officers with powers to arrest for violations of the Ohio Revised Code must enforce the terms of this Protection Order as required by R.C. 2919.27, 2903.213, and 2903.214. If you have reasonable grounds to believe that Respondent/Defendant has violated this Protection Order, in Ohio under R.C. 2935.03, you should arrest and detain Respondent/Defendant until you can obtain a warrant. Federal and state laws prohibit charging a fee for service of this order.

**FORM 10.03-H: WARNING CONCERNING THE ATTACHED PROTECTION ORDER**

**Amended: July 1, 2010**
**Discard all previous versions of this form**

**RULE 10.04. Standard Notice Concerning Possession or Purchase of a Firearm.**

(A) A court that has jurisdiction to convict a person of a misdemeanor offense of violence against a family or household member shall provide notice to the defendant pursuant to section 2943.033 of the Revised Code.

(B) In every case prior to accepting a guilty plea or plea of no contest to an indictment, information, or complaint that charges a person with a misdemeanor offense of violence against a family or household member, the court shall use a form that is substantially similar to Form 10.04-A unless the court provides oral notice to the defendant.

**History:** Effective 2-1-09.

## FORM 10.04-A: NOTICE CONCERNING POSSESSION OR PURCHASE OF FIREARMS

***NOTE***: Rule 10.04 of the Rules of Superintendence for the Courts of Ohio requires notice of possible firearm restrictions be provided to the Defendant before entering a guilty plea or plea of no contest to a misdemeanor crime of violence against a family or household member.

Pursuant to R.C. 2943.033, you are advised that if you enter a guilty plea or plea of no contest to a misdemeanor crime involving violence where you are or were any of the following:

- A spouse, person living as a spouse, former spouse of the Alleged Victim;
- A parent or child of the Alleged Victim;
- A parent or child of a spouse, person living as a spouse, or former spouse of the Alleged Victim;
- The natural parent of any child of whom the Alleged Victim is the other natural parent or the putative natural parent

it may be unlawful for you to ship, transport, purchase, or possess a firearm or ammunition as a result of any conviction for a misdemeanor offense of violence pursuant to federal law under 18 U.S.C. 922(g)(9).

**If you have any questions whether this law makes it illegal for you to ship, transport, purchase, or possess a firearm or ammunition, you should consult an attorney.**

FORM 10.04-A: NOTICE CONCERNING THE POSSESSION OR PURCHASE OF FIREARMS

Amended: July 1, 2010
Discard all previous versions of this form

## RULE 18. Minor Misdemeanors: Violations Bureau—Municipal and County Courts

Each municipal and county court shall establish a violations bureau for minor misdemeanors utilizing the citation system and procedure set forth in Criminal Rule 4.1.

### COMMENTARY (JULY 1, 1997)

Only nonsubstantive changes were made to former M.C. Sup. R. 11 in the 1997 amendments to this rule.

A minor misdemeanor is any offense specifically classified as such or any unclassified offense for which the only penalty is a fine not exceeding one hundred dollars. R.C. 2901.02.

Crim. R. 4.1 provides that a court may establish a violations bureau for all or particular minor misdemeanors. Thus, each court, by local rule, must specify that all or particular minor misdemeanors are to be processed by violations bureau.

Crim. R. 4.1 specifies the form of citation to be used and that the citation "* * * shall inform the defendant that, in lieu of appearing at the time and place stated, he may, within that stated time, appear personally at the office of the clerk of court and upon signing a plea of guilty and a waiver of trial pay a stated fine and stated costs, if any."

Crim. R. 4.1(E) requires the court to establish a fine schedule listing the fines and court costs for each minor misdemeanor. The fine schedule is to be prominently posted at the place violation fines are paid.

## RULE 20. Appointment of Counsel for Indigent Defendants in Capital Cases

I. **Scope of rules.**

(A) Rules 20 through 20.05 of the Rules of Superintendence for the Courts of Ohio shall apply in cases where an indigent defendant has been charged with aggravated murder and the indictment includes one or more specifications of aggravating circumstances listed in division (A) of section 2929.04 of the Revised Code. These rules shall apply in cases where a juvenile defendant is indicted for a capital offense, but because of the juvenile's age, cannot be sentenced to death.

(B) The provisions for the appointment of counsel set forth in Sup. R. 20 through 20.05 apply only in cases where the defendant is indigent and counsel is not privately retained by or for the defendant.

(C) If the defendant is entitled to the appointment of counsel, the court shall appoint two attorneys certified pursuant to Sup. R. 20 through 20.05. If the defendant engages one privately retained attorney, the court shall not appoint a second attorney pursuant to this rule.

(D) The provisions of Sup. R. 20 through 20.05 apply in addition to the reporting requirements created by section 2929.021 of the Revised Code.

II. **Appointment of counsel for indigent defendants in capital cases.**

(A) **Trial counsel.** At least two attorneys shall be appointed by the court to represent an indigent defendant charged with aggravated murder and the indictment includes one or more specifications of aggravating circumstances listed in R.C. 2929.04(A). At least one of the appointed counsel shall maintain a law office in Ohio and have experience in Ohio criminal trial practice. The counsel appointed shall be designated "lead counsel" and "co-counsel" and must meet the qualifications set forth in Sup. R. 20.01.

(B) **Appellate counsel.** At least two attorneys shall be appointed by the court to appeal cases where the trial court has imposed the death penalty on an indigent defendant. At least one of the appointed counsel shall maintain a law office in Ohio. Appointed counsel shall meet the qualifications for appellate counsel set forth in Sup. R. 20.01.

(C) **Exceptional circumstances.** If an attorney does not satisfy the requirements of divisions (A) or (B) of this section, the attorney may be certified as lead counsel, co-counsel, or appellate counsel if it can be demonstrated to the satisfaction of the Committee on the Appointment of Counsel for Indigent Defendants in Capital Cases that competent representation will be provided to the defendant. In so determining, the committee may consider all of the factors in Sup. R. 20.01 and any other relevant considerations.

III. **Procedures for court appointments of counsel.**

(A) **Appointing counsel.** Only counsel who have been certified by the committee shall be appointed to represent indigent defendants charged with aggravated murder and the indictment includes one or more specifications of aggravating circumstances listed in division (A) of section 2929.04 of the Revised Code. Each court may adopt local rules establishing qualifications in addition to and not in conflict with those established by Sup. R. 20.01. Appointments of counsel for these cases should be distributed as widely as possible among the certified attorneys in the jurisdiction of the appointing court.

(B) **Workload of appointed counsel.**

(1) In appointing counsel, the court shall consider the nature and volume of the workload of the prospective counsel to ensure that counsel, if appointed, could direct sufficient attention to the defense of the case and provide competent representation to the defendant.

(2) Attorneys accepting appointments shall provide each client with competent representation in accordance with constitutional and professional standards. Appointed counsel shall not accept workloads that, by reason of their excessive size, interfere with the rendering of competent representation or lead to the breach of professional obligations.

(C) **Notice to the committee.**

(1) Within two weeks of appointment, the appointing court shall notify the committee secretary of the appointment on a form prescribed by the committee. The notice shall include all of the following:

(a) The court and the judge assigned to the case;

(b) The case name and number;

(c) A copy of the indictment;

(d) The names, business addresses, telephone numbers, and certification of all attorneys appointed;

(e) Any other information considered relevant by the committee or appointing court.

(2) Within two weeks of disposition, the trial court shall notify the committee secretary of the disposition of the case on a form prescribed by the committee. The notice shall include all of the following:

(a) The outcome of the case;

(b) The title and section of the Revised Code of any crimes to which the defendant pleaded or was found guilty;

(c) The date of dismissal, acquittal, or that sentence was imposed;

(d) The sentence, if any;

(e) A copy of the judgment entry reflecting the above;

(f) If the death penalty was imposed, the name of counsel appointed to represent the defendant on appeal;

(g) Any other information considered relevant by the Committee or trial court.

(D) **Support services.** The appointing court shall provide appointed counsel, as required by Ohio law or the federal Constitution, federal statutes, and professional standards, with the investigator, mitigation specialists, mental health professional, and other forensic experts and other support services reasonably necessary or appropriate for counsel to prepare for and present an adequate defense at every stage of the proceedings including, but not limited to, determinations relevant to competency to stand trial, a not guilty by reason of insanity plea, cross-examination of expert witnesses called by the prosecution, disposition following conviction, and preparation for and presentation of mitigating evidence in the sentencing phase of the trial. Lead counsel bears overall responsibility for the performance of the defense team and shall allocate, direct, and supervise the work in accordance with Sup. R. 20 through 20.04 and professional standards. In addition, all counsel bear a responsibility to comply with Sup. R. 20 through 20.04 and professional standards.

**History:** Amended, eff. 1-6-03; 3-7-05; 3-1-10.

**COMMENTARY (JULY 1, 1997)**

This rule is identical to former C.P. Sup. R. 65.

## RULE 20.01. Qualifications Required for Appointment as Counsel for Indigent Defendants in Capital Cases.

(A) **Generally.** Every attorney representing a capital defendant shall have all of the following:

(1) Demonstrated commitment to providing high quality legal representation in the defense of capital cases;

(2) Substantial knowledge and understanding of the relevant state, federal, and international law, both procedural and substantive, governing capital cases;

(3) Skill in the management and conduct of complex negotiations and litigation;

(4) Skill in legal research, analysis, and the drafting of litigation documents;

(5) Skill in oral advocacy;

(6) Skill in the use of expert witnesses and familiarity with common areas of forensic investigation, including fingerprints, ballistics, arson, forensic pathology, and DNA evidence;

(7) Skill in the investigation, preparation, and presentation of evidence bearing upon mental status;

(8) Skill in the investigation, preparation, and presentation of mitigating evidence;

(9) Skill in the elements of trial advocacy, such as jury selection, cross-examination of witnesses, and opening and closing statements.

(B) **Lead counsel.** Lead counsel shall satisfy all of the following:

(1) Be admitted to the practice of law in Ohio or admitted to practice *pro hac vice*;

(2) Have at least five years of civil or criminal litigation or appellate experience;

(3) Have specialized training, as approved by the committee, on subjects that will assist counsel in the defense of persons accused of capital crimes in the two-year period prior to making application;

(4) Have at least one of the following qualifications:

(a) Experience as "lead counsel" for the defense in the jury trial of at least one capital case;

(b) Experience as "co-counsel" for the defense in the jury trial of at least two capital cases.

(5) Have at least one of the following qualifications:

(a) Experience as "lead counsel" in the jury trial of at least one murder or aggravated murder case;

(b) Experience as "lead counsel" in ten or more criminal or civil jury trials, at least three of which were felony jury trials;

(c) Experience as "lead counsel" in three murder or aggravated murder jury trials; one murder or aggravated murder jury trial and three felony jury trials; or three aggravated or first- or second-degree felony jury trials in a court of common pleas in the three years prior to making application.

(C) **Co-counsel.** Co-counsel shall satisfy all of the following:

(1) Be admitted to the practice of law in Ohio or admitted to practice *pro hac vice*;

(2) Have at least three years of civil or criminal litigation or appellate experience;

(3) Have specialized training, as approved by the committee, on subjects that will assist counsel in the defense of persons accused of capital crimes in the two years prior to making application;

(4) Have at least one of the following qualifications:

(a) Experience as "co-counsel" in one murder or aggravated murder jury trial;

(b) Experience as "lead counsel" in one first-degree felony jury trial;

(c) Experience as "lead" or "co-counsel" in at least two felony jury or civil jury trials in a court of common pleas in the three years prior to making application.

(D) **Appellate counsel.** Appellate counsel shall satisfy all of the following qualifications:

(1) Be admitted to the practice of law in Ohio or admitted to practice *pro hac vice*;

(2) Have at least three years of civil or criminal litigation or appellate experience in Ohio;

(3) Have specialized training, as approved by the committee, on subjects that will assist counsel in the appeal of cases in which the death penalty was imposed in the two years prior to making application;

(4) Have experience as counsel in the appeal of at least three felony convictions in the three years prior to making application.

(E) **Definition.** As used in this rule, "trial" means a case concluded with a judgment of acquittal under Rule 29 of the Ohio Rules of Criminal Procedure or submission to the trial court or jury for decision and verdict.

**History:** Eff. 3-1-10.

## RULE 20.02. Committee on the Appointment of Counsel for Indigent Defendants in Capital Cases.

(A) **Committee creation.** There shall be a Committee on the Appointment of Counsel for Indigent Defendants in Capital Cases.

(B) **Appointment of committee members.** The committee shall be composed of five attorneys. Three members shall be appointed by a majority vote of all members of the Supreme Court of Ohio; one shall be appointed by the Ohio State Bar Association; and one shall be appointed by the Ohio Public Defender Commission.

(C) **Eligibility for appointment to the committee.** Each member of the committee shall satisfy all of the following qualifications:

(1) Be admitted to the practice of law in Ohio;

(2) Have represented criminal defendants for not less than five years;

(3) Demonstrate a knowledge of the law and practice of capital cases;

(4) Currently not serving as a prosecuting attorney, city director of law, village solicitor, or similar officer or their assistant or employee, or an employee of any court.

(D) **Overall composition.** The overall composition of the committee shall meet both of the following criteria:

(1) No more than two members shall reside in the same county;

(2) No more than one shall be a judge.

(E) **Terms; vacancies.** The term of office for each member shall be five years, each term beginning on the first day of January. Members shall be eligible for reappointment. Vacancies shall be filled in the same manner as original appointments. Any member appointed to fill a vacancy occurring prior to the expiration of a term shall hold office for the remainder of the term.

(F) **Election of chairperson.** The committee shall elect a chairperson and such other officers as are necessary. The officers shall serve for two years and may be reelected to additional terms.

(G) **Powers and duties of the committee.** The committee shall do all of the following:

(1) Prepare and notify attorneys of procedures for applying for certification to be appointed counsel for indigent defendants in capital cases;

(2) Certify attorneys as qualified to be appointed to represent defendants in capital cases;

(3) Periodically provide all common pleas and appellate court judges and the Ohio Public Defender with a list of all attorneys who are certified to be appointed counsel for indigent capital defendants;

(4) Periodically review the list of certified counsel, all court appointments given to attorneys in capital cases, and the result and status of those cases;

(5) Develop criteria and procedures for retention of certification including, but not limited to, mandatory continuing legal education on the defense and appeal of capital cases;

(6) Monitor the performance of attorneys providing representation in capital proceedings;

(7) Investigate and maintain records concerning complaints about the performance of attorneys providing representation in capital cases and take appropriate corrective action pursuant to Rule 20.03 of the Rules of Superintendence;

(8) Expand, reduce, or otherwise modify the list of certified attorneys as appropriate and necessary;

(9) Review and approve specialized training programs on subjects that will assist counsel in the defense and appeal of capital cases;

(10) Recommend to the Supreme Court of Ohio amendments to this rule or any other rule or statute relative to the defense or appeal of capital cases;

(11) Adopt best practices for representation of indigent defendants in capital cases and disseminate those best practices appropriately.

(H) **Meetings.** The committee shall meet at the call of the chairperson, at the request of a majority of the members, or at the request of the Supreme Court of Ohio. A quorum consists of three members. A majority of the committee is necessary for the committee to elect a chairperson and take any other action.

(I) **Compensation.** All members of the committee shall receive equal compensation in an amount to be established by the Supreme Court of Ohio.

**History:** Eff. 3-1-10.

## RULE 20.03. Monitoring of Counsel; Removal.

(A) **Duty of court.** The appointing court shall monitor the performance of all defense counsel to ensure that the client is receiving representation that is consistent with the American Bar Association's "Guidelines for the Appointment and Performance of Defense Counsel in Death Penalty Cases" and referred to herein as "high quality representation." The court, in addition to any other action it may take, shall report an attorney to the Committee on the Appointment of Counsel for Indigent Defendants in Capital Cases who has not provided high quality representation. Where there is a complaint from a judge that an attorney has not provided high quality representation, the committee shall investigate the complaint. The committee will not start an investigation while counsel is still appointed in the matter.

(B) **Investigation of complaint.** The chairperson shall appoint a member of the committee or appoint an attorney qualified as lead counsel under this rule, who will investigate complaints made by a judge that defense counsel appointed pursuant to this rule failed to provide high quality representation under this rule.

(1) As part of the investigation of a complaint from a judge, the attorney shall be notified and given an opportunity to respond.

(2) After an investigation and after the attorney has been given an opportunity to respond to the factual allegations, the members of the committee, excluding the investigator and chairperson, will meet and vote whether a violation of rules 20 through 20.05 has occurred and whether the violation requires removal from the list of qualified attorneys.

Before taking action making an attorney ineligible to receive additional appointments, the committee shall provide written notice that such action is being contemplated, and give the attorney an opportunity to respond. If there is no apparent merit to the allegation the complainant will be advised and the matter will be closed.

(3) If an attorney is deemed ineligible to remain on the list of attorneys qualified to accept appointments, the attorney may appeal the decision of the committee to the chairperson. Upon appeal, the chairperson will review all applicable allegations, findings, and responses and determine whether a violation has occurred and whether appropriate action was taken and issue a decision. The decision of the chairperson is final.

(C) **Revocation.** An attorney whose certification has been revoked pursuant to this rule shall be restored to the roster only in exceptional circumstances. The findings made by the committee are not related to or part of the grievance process governing all attorneys in Ohio and the findings made by the committee are only for the purpose of determining continued eligibility for appointment.

**History:** Eff. 3-1-10.

## RULE 20.04. Programs for Specialized Training.

(A) **Programs for specialized training in the defense of persons charged with a capital offense.**

(1) Attorneys seeking to qualify to receive appointments shall be required to satisfactorily complete a comprehensive training program, approved by the Committee on the Appointment of Counsel for Indigent Defendants in Capital Cases, in the defense of capital cases. To be

approved a program should include, but not be limited to, presentations and training in the following areas:

(a) Relevant state, federal, and international law;

(b) Pleading and motion practice;

(c) Pretrial investigation, preparation, and theory development regarding trial and sentencing;

(d) Jury selection;

(e) Trial preparation and presentation, including the use of experts;

(f) Ethical considerations particular to capital defense representation;

(g) Preservation of the record and of issues for post-conviction review;

(h) Counsel's relationship with the client and his family;

(i) Post-conviction litigation in state and federal courts;

(j) The presentation and rebuttal of scientific evidence, and developments in mental health fields and other relevant areas of forensic and biological science;

(k) The unique issues relating to the defense of those charged with committing capital offenses when under the age of eighteen;

(l) The best practices for representing an indigent capital defendant adopted by the committee pursuant to division (G)(11) of Rule 20.02 of the Rules of Superintendence for the Courts of Ohio;

(m) Death penalty appellate and post-conviction litigation in state and federal courts.

(B) **Programs for specialized training in the appeal of cases in which the death penalty has been imposed.**

(1) To be approved by the committee, a death penalty appeals seminar shall include instruction devoted to the appeal of a case in which the death penalty has been imposed.

(2) The curriculum for an approved death penalty appeal seminar should include, but is not limited to, specialized training in the following areas:

(a) An overview of current developments in death penalty law;

(b) Completion, correction, and supplementation of the record on appeal;

(c) Reviewing the record for unique death penalty issues;

(d) Motion practice for death penalty appeals;

(e) Preservation and presentation of constitutional issues;

(f) Preparing and presenting oral argument;

(g) Unique aspects of death penalty practice in the courts of appeals, the Supreme Court of Ohio, and the United States Supreme Court;

(h) The relationship of counsel with the appellant and the appellant's family during the course of the appeals;

(i) Procedure and practice in collateral litigation, extraordinary remedies, state post-conviction litigation, and federal habeas corpus litigation;

(j) The best practices for representing an indigent capital defendant adopted by the committee pursuant to Sup. R. 20.02(G)(11).

(C) **Application for training approval.** The sponsor of a program for specialized training under division (A) or (B) of this rule shall apply for approval from the committee at least sixty days before the date of the proposed seminar. An application for approval shall include the curriculum for the seminar and include biographical information of each member of the seminar faculty.

(D) **Verification of attendance.** The committee shall obtain a list of attendees from the Supreme Court Commission on Continuing Legal Education that shall be used to verify attendance and grant credit for each committee-approved seminar. Credit for purposes of this rule shall be granted to instructors using the same ratio provided in Rule X of the Supreme Court Rules for the Government of the Bar of Ohio.

(E) **Accreditation of other programs.** The committee may accredit programs other than those approved pursuant to divisions (A) and (B) of this rule. To receive accreditation, the program shall include instructions in all areas set forth in divisions (A) and (B) of this rule. Application for accreditation of an in-state program may be made by the program sponsor or a program attendee and shall be made prior to the program. Application for accreditation of an out-of-state program may be submitted by the program sponsor or a program attendee and may be made prior to or after completion of the program. The request for credit from a program sponsor shall include the program curriculum and individual faculty biographical information. The request for credit from a program attendee shall include all of the following:

(1) Program curriculum;

(2) Individual faculty biographical information;

(3) A written breakdown of sessions attended and credit hours received if the seminar held concurrent sessions;

(4) Proof of attendance.

(F) **Specialized Training for Sup. R. 20 certification.**

(1) To be certified as lead or co-counsel or to retain certification, an attorney shall complete at least twelve hours of committee-approved specialized training every two years. To maintain certification as lead counsel or co-counsel, the twelve hours shall be devoted to instruction in the trial of capital cases.

(2) To be certified as appellate counsel or to retain certification as appellate counsel, an attorney shall complete at least twelve hours of committee-approved training every two years. At least six of the twelve hours shall be devoted to instruction in the appeal of capital cases.

(3) On or before the last day of December, each certified counsel shall complete the applicable specialized training requirements of divisions (A) and (B) of this rule. The committee shall review the list of certified counsel for the prior two years and revoke the certification of any attorney who has not complied with the specialized training requirements of this rule. An attorney whose certification has been revoked shall not be eligible to accept future appointment as counsel for an indigent defendant charged with or convicted of an offense for which the death penalty can be or has been imposed.

(4) The committee may accredit an out-of-state program that provides specialized instruction devoted to the investigation, preparation, and presentation of a death penalty trial or specialized instruction devoted to the appeal of a case in which the defendant received the death penalty, or both. Requests for credit for an out-of-state program may be submitted by the seminar sponsor or a seminar attendee. The request for credit from a program sponsor shall include the program curriculum and individual faculty biographical information. The request for credit from a program attendee shall include all of the following:

(a) Program curriculum;

(b) Individual faculty biographical information;

(c) A written breakdown of sessions attended and credit hours received if the seminar held concurrent sessions;

(d) Proof of attendance.

(5) An attorney who has previously been certified but whose certification has been revoked for failure to comply with the specialized training requirements of this rule must, in order to regain certification, submit a new application that demonstrates that the attorney has completed twelve hours of committee approved specialized training in the two year period prior to making application for recertification.

**History:** Eff. 3-1-10.

## RULE 20.05. Effective dates.

(A) The effective date of this rule shall be October 1, 1987.

(B) The amendments to Section II(A)(5)(b), Section III(B)(2), and to the Subcommittee Comments following Section II of this Rule adopted by the Supreme Court of Ohio on June 28, 1989, shall be effective on July 1, 1989.

(C) The amendments to Sections I(A)(2), I(A)(3), I(B), and II, and the addition of Sections I(C) and IV, adopted by the Supreme Court of Ohio on December 11, 1990, shall be effective on January 1, 1991.

(D) The amendments to this rule adopted by the Supreme Court of Ohio on April 19, 1995, shall take effect on July 1, 1995.

(E) The amendment to Sup. R. 20 adopted by the Supreme Court on December 4, 2002, shall take effect on January 6, 2003.

(F) The amendment to Sup. R. 20 adopted by the Supreme Court on February 1, 2005, shall take effect on March 7, 2005.

(G) On January 12, 2010, former Rule 20 and Rule 21 of the Rules of Superintendence for the Courts of Ohio was repealed by the Supreme Court and Rules 20 through 20.05 were adopted. Rules 20 through 20.05 are effective March 1, 2010.

**History:** Eff. 3-1-10.

## RULE 21. Reserved

## RULE 22. Verification of Indigency

Where required by law to appoint counsel to represent indigent defendants in cases for which the county will apply to the Ohio Public Defender Commission for reimbursement of costs, the court shall require the applicant to complete the financial disclosure form. The court shall follow rules promulgated by the Commission pursuant to division (B)(1) of section 120.03 of the Revised Code as guidelines to determine indigency and standards of indigency.

### COMMENTARY (JULY 1, 1997)

This is a new rule added in the 1997 amendments to the Rules of Superintendence. The rule is intended to facilitate compliance with the statutes and administrative rules relative to the appointment of counsel for indigent defendants in criminal cases.

## RULE 36. Designation of Trial Attorney; Assignment System

(A) **Designation of trial attorney.** In civil cases the attorney who is to try the case shall be designated as trial attorney on all pleadings. In criminal cases, except felonies, the attorney who is to try the case, upon being retained or appointed, shall notify the court that he or she is the trial attorney by filing a written statement with the clerk of the court.

(B)(1) **Individual assignment system.** As used in these rules, "individual assignment system" means the system in which, upon the filing in or transfer to the court or a division of the court, a case immediately is assigned by lot to a judge of the division, who becomes primarily responsible for the determination of every issue and proceeding in the case until its termination. All preliminary matters, including requests for continuances, shall be submitted for disposition to the judge to whom the case has been assigned or, if the assigned judge is unavailable, to the administrative judge. The individual assignment system ensures all of the following:

(a) Judicial accountability for the processing of individual cases;

(b) Timely processing of cases through prompt judicial control over cases and the pace of litigation;

(c) Random assignment of cases to judges of the division through an objective and impartial system that ensures the equitable distribution of cases between or among the judges of the division.

(2) Each multi-judge general, domestic relations, and juvenile division of the court of common pleas shall adopt the individual assignment system for the assignment of all cases to judges of the division. Each multi-judge municipal or county court shall adopt the individual assignment system for the assignment of all cases to the judges of that court, except as otherwise provided in division (C) of this rule. Modifications to the individual assignment system may be adopted to provide for the redistribution of cases involving the same criminal defendant, parties, family members, or subject-matter. Any modifications shall satisfy divisions (B)(1)(a) to (c) of this rule and be adopted by local rule of court.

(C) **Assignment system.** In each multi-judge municipal or county court, cases may be assigned to an individual judge or to a particular session of court pursuant to the following system:

(1) **Particular session.** A particular session of court is one in which cases are assigned by subject category rather than by the individual assignment system. The following subject categories shall be disposed of by particular session:

(a) Civil cases in which a motion for default judgment is made;

(b) Criminal cases in which a plea of guilty or no contest is entered;

(c) Initial appearance in criminal cases;

(d) Preliminary hearings in criminal cases;

(e) Criminal cases in which an immediate trial is conducted upon initial appearance;

(f) Small claims cases;

(g) Forcible entry and detainer cases in which the right to trial by jury is waived or not demanded.

(h) Cases where a party has made application to, or has been accepted into, a specialized court or docket.

To guarantee a fair and equal distribution of cases, a judge who is assigned a case by subject matter pursuant to Sup. R. 36(B)(2), or by virtue of a specialized court or docket pursuant to Sup. R. 36(C)(1)(h), may request the administrative judge to reassign a similar case by lot to another judge in that multi-judge common pleas, municipal, or county court.

(2) **Assignment.** Cases not subject to assignment in a

particular session shall be assigned using the individual assignment system. Civil cases shall be assigned under division (C)(2) of this rule when an answer is filed or when a motion, other than one for default judgment, is filed. Criminal cases shall be assigned under division (C)(2) of this rule when a plea of not guilty is entered.

(3) **Duration of assignment to particular session.** The administrative judge shall equally apportion particular session assignments among all judges. A judge shall not be assigned to a particular session of court for more than two consecutive weeks.

(D) **Assignment of refiled cases.** In any instance where a previously filed and dismissed case is refiled, that case shall be reassigned to the judge originally assigned by lot to hear it unless, for good cause shown, that judge is precluded from hearing the case.

(E) **Assignment — new judicial positions.** After the date of election, but prior to the first day of the term of a new judicial position, the administrative judge of a court or division through a random selection of pending cases shall equitably reassign cases pending in the court or division between or among the judges of the court or division and shall create a docket similar to a representative docket. Reassignment shall be completed in a manner consistent with this rule and may exclude criminal cases and cases scheduled for trial. Any matters arising in cases assigned to the docket for the new judicial position prior to the date on which the judge elected to that position takes office shall be resolved by the administrative judge or assigned to another judge.

**History:** Amended, eff 11-1-06.

## COMMENTARY (November 1, 2006)

### Rule 36 (C)(1)(h)

This amendment specifies that if a judge is assigned cases as a result of a specialized docket, that judge may request that the administrative judge of the court assign similar cases to another judge in order to ensure the fair and equitable distribution of cases within a court.

## COMMENTARY (July 1, 1997)

This rule merges the provisions of former C.P. Sup. R. 4 and M.C. Sup. R. 3 into a single rule governing the assignment of cases pursuant to the individual assignment system.

### Rule 36(A) Designation of trial attorney

Rule 36(A) requires attorneys who are to serve as trial counsel in either civil or criminal cases to notify the court of that fact. Notification in civil cases is accomplished by designation of the trial attorney on all pleadings. In criminal cases, immediately upon being retained or appointed, the trial attorney is required to file a written notification of the attorney's retention or appointment with the clerk of court.

### Rule 36(B)(1) Individual assignment

The individual assignment system is defined by the rule as a system whereby, upon the filing or transfer of a civil case, or upon arraignment in a criminal case, the case is immediately assigned to a judge of the court. The rule sets forth three purposes of the individual assignment system. All multi-judge divisions of the court of common pleas and all multi-judge municipal and county courts, except as provided in division (C)(2) of the rule, are required to adopt the individual assignment system. Courts or divisions are permitted to deviate from the individual assignment system only if the modifications satisfy the three stated purposes of the system and are adopted by local rule of court pursuant to Rule 5. Permissible modifications include the assignment and consideration of cases involving the same criminal defendant, parties, family members, or subject-matter.

The distinguishing feature of the individual assignment system is that it places responsibility upon one judge for the disposition of cases. Once a case is assigned to a judge under this system, all matters pertaining to the case are to be submitted to that judge for determination. An exception is made where that judge is unavailable. In that instance, the administrative judge may act in the assigned judge's absence.

Under Rule 36(B), the administrative judge is responsible for the assignment of cases to the individual judges of the court. Assignment may be made by the administrative judge personally or by court personnel at the administrative judge's direction. All assignments of cases to individual judges must be made by lot.

The purpose of the random assignment, by lot, of cases is to avoid judge-shopping on the part of counsel and to distribute the cases equitably among the judges. "Lot" mandates an assignment arbitrated by chance; the determination must be fortuitous, wholly uncontrolled.

Assignment to the judges of the division in an established order of rotation does not comply with the rule, even if the order of rotation is altered periodically.

An acceptable method of assignment is a form of drawing from a pool of the names of the judges, using paper, balls, or other objects as lots or counter. The pea pool system or the bingo cage are examples. To be an assignment by lot, the entire base of the number of judges in the division must be utilized in each assignment.

A computer may be used for lot selection as long as random assignment is maintained.

Assignment by lot can be systematized. Judges can be identified by number. Those numbers can then be arranged in random order by chance over any given range of numbers. The greater the range, the greater the validity of the arrangement. The range of numbers might well represent the total of three years or so of filings. Slips of paper are then printed with serial control numbers on the front and a line for writing in a case number upon assignment. The judges' numbers are printed in the order of their lot determination on the back of the serially arranged slips. The slips are then padded so that the judges' numbers may not be seen. The evidence of the selection or printing list shall not be revealed. When a case is to be assigned, a slip is removed, the case number written on it, the code number of an individual judge is revealed, and a control sheet maintained.

The practice of making no assignment until "X" number of cases have accumulated when there are "X" number of judges, merely provides for assignment by lot within a very small control and the operation of chance is minimized. That method is only a modified form of rotation and is not assignment by lot.

Once a case is assigned to an individual judge, by lot, it may be reassigned or transferred to another judge by order of the administrative judge. See the Instructions for Preparation concerning the proper use and reporting of transfers.

Although many ancillary matters, and in fact the entire case, frequently may be handled by a magistrate, the assignment system mandates responsibility for every case be affixed to a judge. The assigned judge's report form will reflect action taken by the magistrate.

See Rule 43(E) and its commentary concerning how the numbering system is geared to the record keeping requirements of the individual assignment system.

### Rule 36(C) Assignment system

In multi-judge municipal and county courts, Rule 36(C) establishes a dual system for the assignment of cases. Under this system, certain types of cases are processed in a court session, designated particular session, presided over by a judge or magistrate for a specified period of time. Other types of cases are assigned to an individual judge pursuant to the individual assignment system.

### Rule 36(C)(1) and (2) Particular session; assignment

The types of cases designated in division (C)(1) for disposition in particular sessions of court are high volume cases that may be processed by a judge or magistrate at a single session. The rule does not preclude the processing of types of cases, other than those listed, that are susceptible to disposition in particular sessions.

Cases that may not be processed by particular session are civil cases where an answer is filed or a motion, other than one for default judgment, is filed and criminal cases in which a plea of not guilty is entered. These cases are to be assigned pursuant to the individual assignment system at the time the answer, motion, or plea is filed or made.

### Rule 36(C)(3) Duration of assignment to particular session

Assignments to particular session are to be equally divided among the judges of the court and are to be limited to two-week periods. The two week limitation accommodates the individual assignment system, and allows each judge adequate time to work on the cases individually assigned to the judge. Judges should not be assigned to a particular session or a series of particular sessions for more than two consecutive weeks.

### Rule 36(D) Assignment of refiled cases

To promote judicial economy and discourage judge-shopping, this division mandates that all dismissed and subsequently refiled cases be reassigned to the originally assigned judge. An exception exists for circumstances in which the original judge is barred from hearing the refiled case.

### Rule 36(E) Assignment — new judicial positions

This provision governs the reassignment of pending cases where a new judicial position is added to the court or division. Reassignment of cases must be random, equitable, and accomplished in a manner consistent with the principles set forth in division (B)(1) of the rule. In effect, a random selection system must be used, rather than culling cases from pending dockets. Certain dockets or portions of dockets may be created through the individual assignment system. This method may be particularly useful in assigning criminal cases. The process set forth in division (E) should facilitate the creation of a balanced docket with a minimum disruption of the pending caseload of the court or division.

## RULE 39. Case Time Limits

(A) **Appellate and civil case time limits.** The time limits for disposition of appellate and civil cases shall be as indicated on the Supreme Court report forms.

(B) **Criminal case time limits.**

(1) In common pleas court, all criminal cases shall be tried within six months of the date of arraignment on an indictment or information. In municipal and county court, all criminal cases shall be tried within the time provided in Chapter 2945. of the Revised Code. Whenever a hearing or trial time is extended or shortened pursuant to section 2945.72 of the Revised Code or Criminal Rule 5 or 45, the judge shall state the reason for the change in an order and journalize the order.

(2) **Grand jury proceedings.** When an accused has been bound over to a grand jury and no final action is taken by the grand jury within sixty days after the date of the bindover, the court or the administrative judge of the court shall dismiss the charge unless for good cause shown the prosecuting attorney is granted a continuance for a definite period of time.

(3) **Felony preliminary hearing.** A preliminary hearing in a felony case shall be held within one month of the date of arrest or the date of issuance of the summons.

(4) **Sentencing.** Provided the defendant in a criminal case is available, the court shall impose sentence or hold a sentencing hearing with all parties present within fifteen days of the verdict or finding of guilt or receipt of a completed pre-sentence investigation report. Any failure to meet this time standard shall be reported to the administrative judge, who shall take the necessary corrective action. In a single judge division, the failure shall be reported by the judge to the Case Management Section, which shall refer the matter to the Chief Justice of the Supreme Court for corrective action.

(5) **Post-conviction relief petitions; death penalty cases.** All post-conviction relief petitions filed in death penalty cases shall be ruled upon within one hundred eighty days of the date of filing. In any month where a post-conviction relief petition in a death penalty case is filed, pending, or terminated, the administrative judge shall submit the Post-Conviction Relief Petition Report detailing the status of the petition.

(C) **Reporting.** Any failure to comply with the time limits specified in this rule, and the reason for the failure, shall be reported immediately to the administrative judge, who shall take the necessary corrective action. In a single-judge court or division, the failure shall be reported by the judge to the Case Management Section. The Case Management Section shall report to the Chief Justice, who may take such action as may be necessary to cause the delinquent case to be tried forthwith.

**History:** Amended, eff 7-1-09.

### COMMENTARY (JULY 1, 1997)

Rule 39 consolidates the time limits contained in former C.P. Sup. R. 8 and 8.01 and M.C. Sup. R. 5. The provisions of C.P. Sup. R. 8.01(B) have been moved to Rule 42. Division (B)(5) is a new time guideline and reporting requirement.

The time limits applicable to criminal cases are for the purpose of facilitating the prompt disposition of criminal cases. These time limits in no way affect the statutorily mandated limits contained in R.C. 2945.71. However, the failure to dispose of cases within these time guidelines may result in intervention by the Chief Justice. While the administrative guidelines set out in Rule 8(B) are keyed to the date of arraignment, the requirement of R.C. 2945.71 begins to run from the date of arrest.

Although criminal cases are not reported as filed on Common Pleas Form A until the accused is arraigned on an indictment or information, the responsibility of the court of common pleas for the processing of the case beings upon receipt of the papers in the case pursuant to Crim. R. 5(B)(7). When no final action has been taken by a grand jury within sixty days after bindover, the court or administrative judge should dismiss the charge unless the prosecutor is, for good cause, granted a continuance. The key date for purposes of division (B)(2) is the date of bindover. Thus, the summoning of a grand jury under Crim. R. 8 should not be unduly delayed. Although R.C. 2945.71 does not mandate a time limit for completion of the grand jury process, the statutory time limit runs from the date of arrest, including time taken in the grand jury process.

The dismissal contemplated by division (B)(2) is not a dismissal with prejudice.

Crim. R. 5(B)(1) provides time guidelines for preliminary hearings only. Crim. R. 5(A)(2) and 5(B)(1) each contain provisions pertaining to the extension of preliminary hearing time limits. Crim. R. 45(A) explains the method to be used in computing time. Crim. R. 45(B) provides for the enlargement or reduction of time provisions.

Division (B)(1) provides for the journalization of all actions taken pursuant to section 2945.72 of the Revised Code, Crim.

R. 5(A)(2), 5(B)(1) or 45(B), which either extend or shorten the time periods provided in section 2945.71 of the Revised Code or Crim. R. 5. The journal entry must include the fact of the extension or shortening of time and a statement of the reasons therefor to provide a record should any question arise concerning compliance with section 2945.71 of the Revised Code.

### Rule 39(B)(4) Sentencing

If the defendant is available, the court must take action within fifteen days of the verdict or finding of guilty or within fifteen days of the receipt of a completed presentence investigation report. This action may be to impose sentence, to place on probation, or to hold a hearing on the report.

Although R.C. 2945.71 is satisfied if the accused is brought to trial within the appropriate period from arrest, the Form A report keys termination to the sentencing or granting of probation. Thus, the six month guidelines contained on the report form includes any period of time between the commencement of trial and the imposition of sentence.

Failure to meet the time standard of this section must be reported to the administrative judge for corrective action. In a single judge division, any failure is to be reported to the Case Management Section.

The fifteen day time limit of division (B)(4) of this rule should not be confused with the requirement of Sup. R. 7 that the journal entry be made within thirty days of the judgment.

### Rule 39(B)(5) Post-conviction relief petitions; death penalty cases

Prior to July 1997, no reporting requirements existed for post-conviction relief petitions, and these petitions were treated as motions in previously terminated cases. In view of the public policies reflected by the November 1994 constitutional amendment abolishing intermediate appeals in death penalty cases and legislation affecting post-conviction relief actions (Am. Sub. S.B. 4 of the 121st General Assembly, effective September 21, 1995), it is imperative that courts provide timely consideration of death penalty cases and ensuing post-conviction relief petitions in those cases. To assist in the management of post-conviction relief petitions in death penalty cases, division (B)(5) of this rule establishes a one hundred eighty day time guideline for the disposition of these petitions and provides for the monthly reporting of the status of the petitions. The one hundred eighty day time guideline is identical to the guideline contained in Rule 35 of the Ohio Rules of Criminal Procedure, effective July 1, 1997.

Although the assigned judge is ultimately responsible for the termination of the case and is so designated on the report form, the administrative judge is responsible for tracking and reporting the status of these petitions.

### Rule 39(C) Reporting

The time limits imposed by this rule are for administrative purposes only. Failure to comply with these time limits does not give rise to the sanctions imposed by R.C. 2945.71. However, failure to dispose of cases within these times limits may result in the intervention of the administrative judge and the Chief Justice.

The reports required by this rule should be submitted monthly to the administrative judge or the Case Management Section. A case should be listed on this report for each month during which it is delinquent.

Although no specific form is prescribed for this report, it should contain, at a minimum, the style of the case, the offense charged, the date of its filing, an explanation of the delay in disposition, and the date on which it is anticipated that the case will be completed.

Failure to meet the time standard of this section must be reported to the administrative judge for corrective action. In a single-judge division, any failure is to be reported to the Case Management Section.

# VICTIMS OF CRIME COMPENSATION PROGRAM

[For current forms relating to the *Ohio Victims of Crime Compensation Program*, see *www.ohioattorneygeneral.gov* or contact Ohio Attorney General, 30 E. Broad St., 14th Floor, Columbus, OH 43215, (800) 282-0515.]

## User's Guide to the Index

Two guidelines for using this index are:

(1) *Consult the most pertinent subject.* For example, if you were looking in an evidence book for information about depositions, you would start with DEPOSITIONS rather than broader headings like EVIDENCE, TESTIMONY or WITNESSES. The broader headings may also exist, but to find the material more quickly, look for the specific subject first.

(2) *Cross references.* Pay close attention to and make full use of the index cross references. An index cross reference directs the index user to go to another part of the index to find treatment.

The index benefits from customer suggestions. Especially helpful are popular names or legal terms specific to your area of practice. We are grateful for your assistance in the ongoing improvement of the index.

To make comments or suggestions to improve this index or for assistance in locating material within this index, please use one of the following methods:

- Toll Free Number: 1-800-897-7922.
- Email: LNG-CHO-Indexing@lexisnexis.com

For issues not directly related to the Index, such as missing pages, ordering or other customer service information, you may contact Customer Service via a toll-free number, 1-800-833-9844, or by toll-free fax at 1-800-828-8341.

# INDEX

## D

## F

## J

## N

## O

## S

## T

## U

# Notes

# Notes

# Notes

# Notes

# Notes

## Notes

## Notes

# Notes

# Notes

## Notes

# Notes

## Notes

## Notes

# Notes

# Notes

# Notes

# Notes

## FEATURES

**Hypertext Links.** Instantly move from the integrated table of contents to your desired section, from section to section, and then back to your original location. All in the blink of an eye.

**Search Engine.** Now with faster searches! Folio Views® software allows the user to search by note, by section, by words and phrases, and even allows wild card searches! Scroll through your "hit list" in seconds to find the information you need.

**Customize Electronically.** Use a bookmark to mark your favorite spots; a highlighter to mark a key word in long sections; and a notepad to jot down important notes. Save them all for future use.

**Print and Save.** Print and save blocked text, a whole section, or a series of selected records. Download the information into Word, WordPerfect, text files, and/or many other word processing formats.

**Support.** With online help, full-time technical support, an easy-to-use online user manual, and point-and-click Windows access, you can do research with the security that LexisNexis's expert staff will back you up.

**Expanded Content.** Contains all the statutes included in the book, plus additional case law annotations and historical citations to enhance your research.

## HOW TO USE IT

If you experience any problems during the installation procedure, please call Technical Support at **1-800-223-5297** for assistance.

1. Insert the CD into the CD-ROM drive; the installation should begin automatically.

   If the installation fails to launch, select **Run** from the Start menu. Type **d:\setup** and click on OK. (If the CD reader drive is not **D:**, substitute the correct letter.)
2. In the Welcome screen, click **Next**. Read and **accept** the Master Agreement. You must accept the Master Agreement to complete the installation process. (Declining will cancel installation.)
3. Your 20-digit Codeword should be hardcoded in your installation. If it is not, locate it on your packing slip, and enter it in the corresponding fields. Click **Next**.
4. Click Close in the Products & Publications screen. Select a directory and/or drive to receive the software; click **Next**.
5. Complete the installation by following the prompts.

## SYSTEM REQUIREMENTS

- Intel® Pentium®-based 133-Mhz or faster PC
- 32 MB RAM for Win 95/98/98SE; 64 MB RAM for Win ME/NT4/2000/XP
- 35 MB free hard disk space
- 8x or faster CD-ROM drive
- Microsoft Windows 95® or higher

## SUPPORT

For support call **1-800-223-5297**.

Press **3** for questions regarding installation.

Press **2** for questions related to use of the product (searching, printing, etc.).